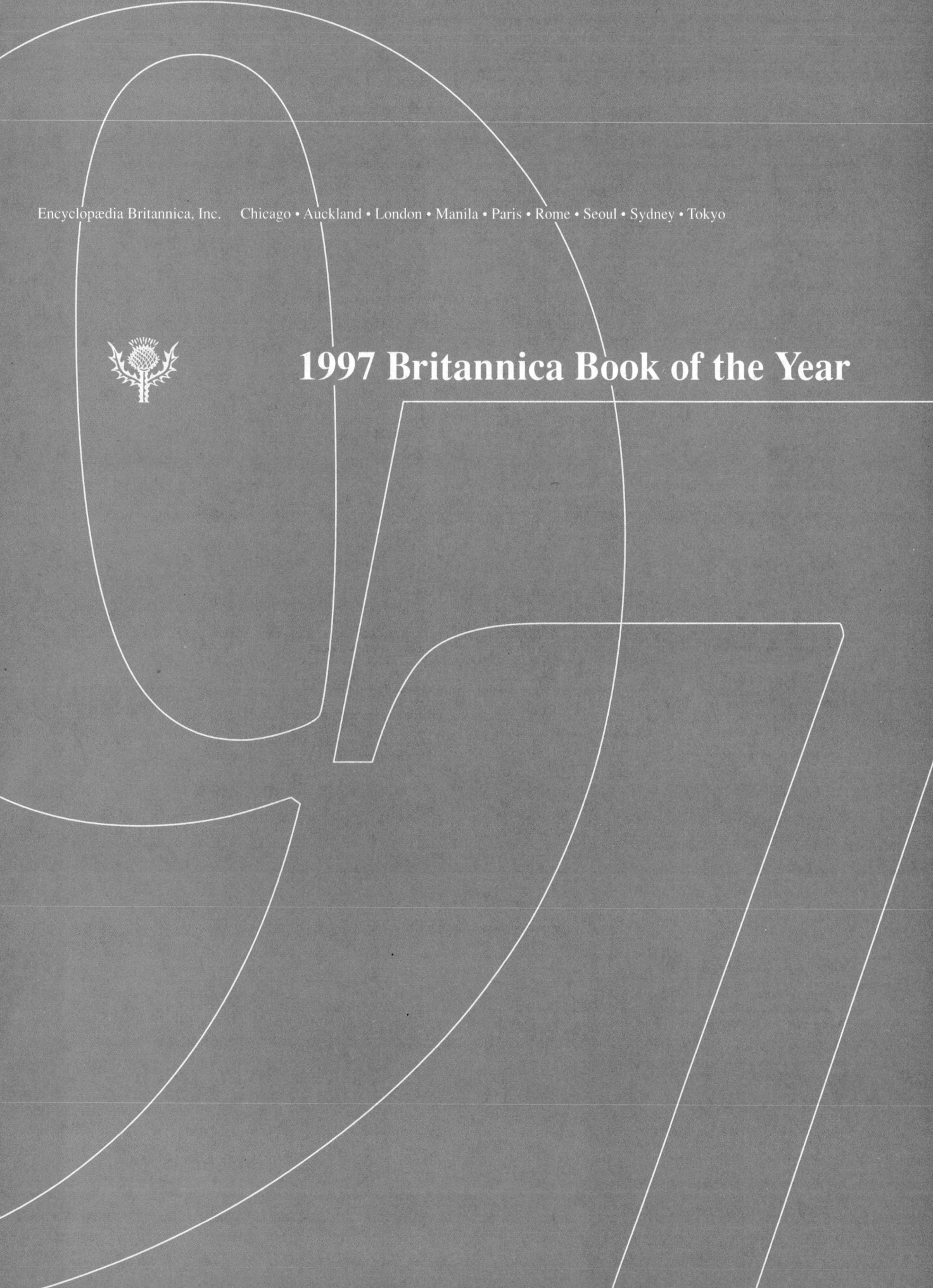

Encyclopædia Britannica, Inc.   Chicago • Auckland • London • Manila • Paris • Rome • Seoul • Sydney • Tokyo

1997 Britannica Book of the Year

On behalf of the staff of *Britannica Book of the Year,* I am proud to present our compilation of the events, developments, and trends of 1996. The year had its share of triumphs and failures, from peace after 35 years of civil war in Guatemala and improving conditions in South Africa and Bosnia and Herzegovina to turmoil and bloodshed in central Africa and Afghanistan. The Centennial Olympic Games in Atlanta encapsulated the year's contrasts, drawing a record number of national teams to a place of peaceful competition and pageantry and then suffering a terrorist bomb in a nearby public park.

Special features in the yearbook discuss many of these developments. They include the Olympics and the U.S. elections and also focus on such diverse topics as the success stories among the countries of Africa, the increasingly important role of the Japanese in South America (thrown into sharp relief by the events at the Japanese embassy in Lima), and the resurgence of ethnic and national identity in Europe.

A special report describes how computer-generated images are now the dominant form of animation in the movies, with 1995's *Toy Story* the first 100% computer-animated feature film. More than 100 million land mines buried in 68 nations stretching from Cambodia to Costa Rica are described as "mass destruction in slow motion," killing or maiming more than 20,000 people—mostly civilians—each year. The problems of detecting and removing them are discussed in the Military Affairs special report. In addition, the yearbook begins with an illuminating interview with Lee Teng-hui, recently elected president in Taiwan's first direct popular presidential poll.

Elsewhere in the book, the chronology of the year's events has been expanded to allow for increased coverage in both text and illustrations. For the first time, *Britannica Book of the Year* includes three photo essays—one depicting the plight of Europe's Gypsies (Roma), a second portraying warriors for the environment in England, and a third illustrating the problems encountered by refugees. Finally, I am glad that we will once again be able to include the results of the most recent Super Bowl, information that our previous production schedule made unavailable.

Not to be overlooked, of course, are the regular features in *Britannica Book of the Year* and the wealth of information to be found in the accompanying BRITANNICA WORLD DATA. I hope that you will find this book both informative and entertaining. If you have suggestions on how to make it better, please write and let us know.

David R. Calhoun, Editor

CONTENTS

FEATURE

6   **A Conversation with Lee Teng-hui**
    Introduction
    by Frank B. Gibney

THE YEAR IN REVIEW

10   **Chronology of 1996**
58   Disasters

PEOPLE OF 1996

62   Nobel Prizes
65   Biographies
91   Obituaries

EVENTS OF 1996

123   Agriculture and Food Supplies
133   Anthropology and Archaeology
137   Architecture and
     Civil Engineering
141   The Great Man-Made River
     by Charlotte Blum
144   Art, Antiques, and Collections
146   SPECIAL REPORT:
     Blockbuster Art Exhibitions
     by Sandra Millikin
153   Business and Industry Review
176   SPECIAL REPORT:
     Satellite TV
     by Robert Stoffels
180   Computers and
     Information Systems
182   Deep Blue
     by Steven Monti
183   Earth Sciences
188   Economic Affairs
200   Microbanking
     by John H. Mathews
203   Education
206   Environment
207   PHOTO ESSAY:
     Eco-Warriors
216   Fashions
218   Health and Disease
220   SPECIAL REPORT:
     For Nursing, New
     Responsibilities, New Respect
     by Margretta Madden Styles
223   Law, Crime, and
     Law Enforcement
230   Libraries and Museums
232   Life Sciences
240   Literature
253   Mathematics and
     Physical Sciences
255   The First Antiatoms
     by David G.C. Jones
261   Media and Publishing
263   The Boom of Science-
     Fiction TV
     by Amanda E. Fuller
269   Military Affairs
274   SPECIAL REPORT:
     Combating the Land Mine
     Scourge
     by Douglas L. Clarke
277   Performing Arts
278   Der Ring des Nibelungen
     by Robert Rauch

292   SPECIAL REPORT:
     Computer Animation
     by Bruce C. Steele
295   Population Trends
298   PHOTO ESSAY:
     Hutu Return to Rwanda
300   Religion
307   Conflict in Orthodoxy
     by Todd M. Johnson
312   Social Protection
317   Sports and Games
333   World Cup
     by Andrew Longmore
364   SPECIAL REPORT:
     The Centennial Olympic
     Games
     by Melinda C. Shepherd
372   Transportation
375   World Affairs
393   Austria Turns 1,000
     by Michael T. Calvert
400   SPOTLIGHT: The Japanese in
     Latin America
     by Sarah Cameron
416   SPOTLIGHT: Signs of Hope in
     Africa
     by Kenneth Ingham
422   SPOTLIGHT: Fourth World
     Resurgence in Europe
     *by Richard A. Griggs and
     Peter R. Hocknell*
428   PHOTO ESSAY:
     Gypsies of Eastern Europe
442   SPOTLIGHT: Democracy and
     Development in Asia
     by Ricardo Saludo
450   SPOTLIGHT: A Postnuclear Era
     in the Pacific
     by Barrie Macdonald
466   Russia's Democratic Election
     by Elizabeth Teague
468   SPOTLIGHT: Rocky Road to
     Caribbean Unity
     by David Renwick
480   SPOTLIGHT: Central Asia's
     Next "Great Game"
     by Bess Brown
492   SPECIAL REPORT:
     The U.S. Presidential Election
     by George Russell

BRITANNICA UPDATE

505   **Major New Revisions from the
     Encyclopædia Britannica**
505   English Literature:
     Literature After 1945
508   Telecommunications (in part)
514   Turkey and Ancient Anatolia
     (in part)
525   **Bibliography: Recent Books**

530   **Book of the Year
     Contributors**

535   WORLD DATA

895   INDEX

EVERETT COLLECTION

Ella Fitzgerald, page 101   Gene Kelly, page 106

Aung San Suu Kyi, page 28   Boris Yeltsin, page 34

Bill Clinton, page 492

Theodore J. Kaczynski, page 22   U.S. gymnasts at the Olympics, page 348

Rowan Atkinson as
Mr. Bean, page 67

Researchers
in Antarctica,
page 382

A

CONVERSATION

WITH

Lee

Teng-hui

Encyclopædia Britannica was honoured to have the opportunity to speak with Lee Teng-hui, who in March 1996 won a landslide victory in the first direct presidential elections in the Republic of China (Taiwan). The interview, which because of space considerations is printed here in a slightly abridged version of the written responses by President Lee, took place in Taipei on Oct. 22, 1996, and was conducted by Frank B. Gibney, president of the Pacific Basin Institute, Santa Barbara, Calif., and vice-chairman of the Encyclopædia Britannica Board of Editors.

Encyclopædia Britannica. *Taiwan (the Republic of China) captured the attention of the world with its recent democratic elections. How would you characterize democracy in Taiwan? How did it evolve?*

Pres. Lee Teng-hui. Western political theory defines democracy as a political system in which the principal policy maker is chosen by popular vote through regular, free, and open elections. Although the ROC [Republic of China] government began holding elections immediately after relocating to Taiwan in 1949, we must admit that prior to 1969 elections had been restricted to the local level. Elections were held between 1969 and 1989 to select central-level representatives, but they were limited to constituencies in the Taiwan area. The vast majority of members sitting in central parliamentary organs had been elected on the Chinese mainland and had never faced reelection. The constitutional amendments in 1990 and 1991, however, allowed for all members of these bodies to be elected directly by the people of the Taiwan area. Moreover, in 1994 the method of selecting the governor of Taiwan province and the mayors of the two special municipalities of Taipei and Kao-hsiung was changed from appointment to direct popular election. Finally, beginning this year the president of the ROC was also chosen directly by the entire electorate. In the short space of 10 years, democracy has developed in the ROC through a process that in some Western countries took centuries. This process—from restrictiveness to openness, from openness to diversity, from diversity to democracy—has infused our society with new vitality and earned us respect in the eyes of the world.

After 30 years of economic development, our people understandably felt that the political system needed to be reformed as well. The ROC government, closely following popular opinion, moved step by step toward liberalization and openness. Herein lies the greatest difference between our democratization and that in other nations: the government did not adopt a stance in opposition to the will of the people. Nor did democratization in the ROC cause the social upheavals and bloody revolutions that have occurred in so many countries on the road to democracy. The ROC's successful experience, our "Quiet Revolution," has already become a new model for democratic development.

We can proudly say that democracy has not disrupted stability. On the contrary, it has enabled us to value even more the expression of different opinions. It has implanted within us the new spirit of mutual tolerance and respect.

EB. *Many Asian economies, Taiwan included, achieved great progress under some form of authoritarian rule. Could this process be continued indefinitely, or is there a point at which a modern economy needs democratic institutions and a firm rule of law to prosper? Are there other alternative developmental models?*

President Lee. A number of factors have contributed to Taiwan's economic success, including a dynamic civil society, strong political leadership, a talented group of technocrats, and an excellent educational system. Combined with the work ethic of the people of Taiwan and government policies that ensured a stable environment for investment, these factors enabled us to lay down a solid foundation for economic growth. Of course, the booming global economy of the postwar period was also a beneficial international factor.

Some social scientists have argued that some form of authoritarianism may be a necessary condition for economic development in newly industrializing countries. They often cite Taiwan, South Korea, Brazil, and Mexico as their examples. Based on my personal experience, however, I must say that this hypothesis is not valid.

Just as economist Milton Friedman argued in his book *Capitalism and Freedom,* economic freedom leads to political freedom. Once a society steps onto the path toward economic development, no insightful political leader can impede the emergence of democratic institutions or refuse the demands of citizens for more open political participation. Continuous economic progress requires an open society built upon a political foundation of democratic institutions and the firm rule of law.

A repressive regime may be able to achieve industrialization within a short period of time, but without democratic reforms and a free market, no country can sustain economic growth. Furthermore, in fiercely competitive global markets, a country must remain creative, flexible, and dynamic in order to build its international competitiveness. Only democracy is able to provide a suitable environment in which these traits may continue to flourish.

"The President," a military aide announces in a parade-ground voice. The doors to the reception room open, and a large, rather commanding figure strides inside. He hardly needs the ringing introduction. Trim, tall (1.85 m—6 ft 1 in), and feisty at age 73, Lee Teng-hui has the kind of magnetism that makes people turn when he enters. He is enthusiastic and confident, as well he can be after some 40 years of academic lecturing, bureaucratic governance, and shrewd political management capped by his huge victory in the March 1996 presidential election. He is full of ideas. Once he is engaged in conversation, his words come rushing out—equally effective in Chinese, English, or Japanese. Lee reads widely in all three languages, and his conversation is peppered with an almost overpowering citation of statistics, as befits one of the Asia-Pacific region's leading agricultural economists.

Lee was born on Jan. 15, 1923, near Tan-shui, Taiwan. He studied at Kyoto (Japan) Imperial University and National Taiwan University, Taipei (B.A., 1948), and then pursued degrees in agricultural economics at Iowa State University (M.A., 1953) and at Cornell University, Ithaca, N.Y. (Ph.D., 1968). While teaching economics at National Taiwan and Chengchi universities from 1958 to 1978, he also served as a member of the Sino-American Joint Commission on Rural Reconstruction. He held the posts of mayor of Taipei (1978–81) and governor of Taiwan (1981–84) before serving as Pres. Chiang Ching-kuo's vice president. When Chiang died in January 1988, Lee became the first Taiwanese-born president of the Republic of China.

The 21 million people of the Republic of China—Taiwan—represent a united and prosperous democracy with a dazzling postwar economic success story. Taiwan's gross national product of $12,500 per capita is one of Asia's highest. "The Republic of China," the president has written, "is a sovereign state, with sovereign power in the hands of the people." Lee wants the world to recognize it as such, complete with restored membership in the UN, which it had to leave in 1971 when the "China seat" was given to the People's Republic of China (PRC).

Beijing, however, sees Taiwan and Lee through a different set of lenses. To the PRC leadership, Taiwan is a renegade province that must be regarded as a part of the mainland Chinese state. Beijing wants reunification sooner rather than later, suspecting that Taiwan, with U.S. assistance, is heading for total independence from the mainland.

Lee does not dispute the "one-China" policy, long regarded as an article of faith by both Beijing and Taipei. Over the past decade Taiwan's government has sanctioned the huge investments on the mainland made by its businesses, supported extensive people-to-people exchanges, and canceled the old anticommunist pronouncements of the Kuomintang (the Nationalist Party, founded by Sun Yat-sen and carried by Chiang Kai-shek to Taiwan in 1949).

Still, Lee wants to go slow on any actual reunification—particularly in view of Beijing's domestic antidemocratic stance and ominous signs of a political crackdown on Hong Kong after it reverts to Chinese sovereignty in 1997. His demands for the Republic of China's recognition as a nation and his equally forthright denunciation of Beijing's "hegemonic stance" are partly a reaction against Beijing's constant pressure to diminish Taiwan's independent standing in international organizations.

For the moment, however, neither Lee nor his countrymen seem to be pushing hard either for complete independence or for immediate reunification with the mainland.

(FRANK B. GIBNEY)

EB. *Various forms of official corruption, cronyism, and nepotism have damaged democracy in Asia and fueled political opposition to governments holding power. Taiwan, too, has had its problems here. Are these problems endemic in Asian democracy?*

President Lee: Corrupt officials cause headaches in governments throughout the world, but clearly the problem is particularly serious in Asian countries. The main factor behind this corruption is the rapid pace of economic growth in Asia and the inability of legal systems to keep up with the pace of economic and social developments. An insufficiently comprehensive legal system coupled with executive power unrestrained by appropriate standards creates opportunities for backdoor deal making and influence peddling. This eventually harms the development of democracy.

Asia's traditional cultural emphasis on personal relationships is also a major culprit. In order to foster a clean reputation for ROC officials, however, our government has adopted systematic and strict measures to prevent corruption. Laws already require that civil servants make a public declaration of their assets. We also restrict retired civil servants from assuming private-sector positions related to their previous service. We are moving to establish more detailed and comprehensive legal standards concerning matters such as legislative and administrative lobbying and civil service administrative ethics.

EB. *How do you view Taiwan's relations with Japan and Korea?*

President Lee. Since severing diplomatic relations on Sept. 29, 1972, the ROC and Japan have continued to engage in exchanges as part of their substantive relations. Over the past 20 years trade, scientific and technological cooperation, cultural exchanges, and tourism between the ROC and Japan have expanded every year. In 1995 the total value of bilateral trade between the ROC and Japan reached $43,437,000,000, up more than 25-fold from the time of the diplomatic break in 1972.

A continuously growing trade deficit, however, and several unsettled issues, such as compensation for Taiwanese "comfort women" and Taiwanese men who served in the Japanese army and the matter of sovereignty over the Tiaoyu Islands [Diao Yu or Senkaku Islands, an uninhabited group of islets northeast of Taiwan], have important implications for improving ROC-Japan relations. Other problems include the treatment accorded to ROC representatives stationed in Japan and the upgrading of official exchanges.

The ROC's trade and other substantive relations with the Republic of Korea are also very close. At present, the ROC government does not maintain formal contacts with North Korea. In the interest of safeguarding the peace and stability of the Asia-Pacific region, however, the ROC is willing to develop cooperative relations with North Korea based on the principles of reciprocity and mutual benefits.

EB. *What hope do you see for a Pacific community following the blueprints worked out in APEC, PECC, and similar organizations? What is the American role here?*

President Lee. I strongly agree with the efforts of the Asia-Pacific Economic Cooperation [APEC] and the Pacific Economic Cooperation Council [PECC] to strengthen regional trade and investment liberalization as well as economic and technological cooperation. The members of APEC and its related forums will, in accordance with the Osaka Action Agenda passed last year, formulate an action plan by the end of this year for implementation in 1997. This action plan will knit together more closely the economic development of the Asia-Pacific community. I am confident that such actions will promote a sense of community in the Asia-Pacific area.

In the long run, the APEC agenda will inevitably go beyond the limits of the current economic discussion and enter the realms of politics and regional security. The past conflict in the South China Sea, the March 1996 crisis in the Taiwan Strait, and the recent tensions over the Tiaoyu Islands all clearly demonstrated that the ROC is an indispensable link in the Asia-Pacific political security system. There is a pressing need to establish effective channels for security dialogue and maintenance in the Asia-Pacific. If certain factors have prevented existing international organizations that deal with regional security from embracing all nations in the Asia-Pacific region, then APEC should consider including these issues in its agenda and developing its functions more fully.

The U.S. position in the Pacific region has always been important. In April 1996 the U.S. and Japan reaffirmed their security accord. I believe these two nations' joint commitment is a basic guarantee of regional security and stability. In addition to this bilateral security league, I believe that the region must develop a multilateral security system that includes all Asian nations in order to consolidate the development of cooperative relations and economic prosperity.

EB. *What are the best hopes for increased cooperation with mainland China?*

President Lee. I have stressed repeatedly that the two sides should work under the principle of reciprocity and "win-win" interaction as well as the spirit of "Chinese helping Chinese." Thus, we should emphasize constructive cultural, news, scientific, technological, trade, and economic exchanges; expand trade and economic relations; help improve agriculture and the standard of living on the mainland; and promote negotiations aimed at signing agreements to ensure the peace and stability of the Taiwan Strait and enhance the peace and prosperity of the Asia-Pacific region. Through such exchanges and cooperation, we hope we can gradually create the conditions for democratic, free, and mutually prosperous reunification.

The restoration of Chinese sovereignty over Hong Kong in 1997 symbolizes the end of over 150 years of British colonial rule in Hong Kong. We cannot deny, however, Great Britain's contribution in recent decades to building Hong Kong into a free-trade port and international financial centre. The mainland authorities have promised to follow policies of "one country, two systems" and a "high level of autonomy" with regard to Hong Kong, to allow "Hong Kong people to rule Hong Kong," and to "maintain the status quo for 50 years."

I must add, however, that the Taiwan situation is completely different from that of Hong Kong. We are absolutely opposed to any attempt by the mainland authorities to apply the "one nation, two systems" formula to the Republic of China. Furthermore, we hope that Hong Kong's change of status in 1997 will not substantively affect the close relations that the ROC and Hong Kong have enjoyed for many years.

The economic integration of the Asia-Pacific nations is in line with a world economic trend. It is natural that the Taiwan area of the ROC should become economically linked with the mainland and even with Southeast Asia so as to form a link in the chain of East Asian economic integration.

It must be stressed, however, that, owing to past political antagonism between Taiwan and the mainland, the economic and trade exchanges between the people of the two sides were very limited prior to November 1987. At that time our government began allowing people in Taiwan to visit their relatives on the mainland. Subsequent to this change in policy, increased cross-strait person-to-person exchanges led to a rapid increase in economic and trade activities between the two sides. By the end of 1995, the accumulated total of cross-strait trade amounted to almost $90 billion, $22.5 billion of which was conducted last year alone. Investment in the mainland by Taiwan businesses has surpassed $10 billion. Thus, the two sides have developed very close economic and trade relations.

We cannot overlook the fact that in the past year the mainland authorities have done everything they can to suppress and threaten Taiwan politically, diplomatically, and militarily. They have ignored the ROC government's friendly appeals and adopted many unfriendly measures against Taiwan, refusing to resume cross-strait negotiations. At the same time, the mainland authorities have sought to attract and win over Taiwan enterprises with such appealing slogans as "politics should not interfere with the economy" and "the separation of politics and economics," as well as the lure of short-term economic benefits. We cannot help but raise our political vigilance toward their tactics of "pulling the Taiwan authorities over by expanding cross-strait economic exchange and cooperation." Therefore, I recently called on the ROC people and our businesspeople to remain patient and avoid impulsive responses. This was with an eye toward alerting everyone to mainland China's current strategy and calling upon them to respond with caution.

EB. *How strong is the independence movement in Taiwan? Why is Taiwan seeking United Nations membership, especially in view of the fact that mainland China wields veto power over new admissions?*

President Lee. Currently, though Taiwan and the Chinese mainland are ruled separately by two autonomous political entities, most Chinese in the Taiwan area still maintain that the two sides should expand their international space individually while adhering to the premise of one China and that eventually reunification should be achieved by gradually reducing the distance between the two sides and melding the two systems. Public opinion polls have repeatedly shown that advocates of independence for Taiwan have always been in the minority. Continued suppression of the ROC and deliberate obstruction of its international involvement by the mainland authorities will only feed this movement, however.

The Republic of China's bid to be part of the United Nations is aimed at UN General Assembly Resolution 2758, which has seriously infringed upon the basic rights of our people. The ROC has put forth a proposal requesting that the General Assembly establish an ad hoc committee to study ways of resolving the problem. Through the reexamination of Resolution 2758 and the rectification of its shortcomings, the ROC will once more be allowed to be part of the UN. This proposal need not go through the UN Security Council but can be addressed directly by the General Assembly. Though the mainland authorities will likely try their best to thwart the ROC bid, they will have no opportunity to exercise their veto power.

It should also be noted that the ROC's proposal aims only to ensure that the fundamental right to participation in world affairs of the 21.3 million people in the Taiwan area is safeguarded. We have no intention of challenging mainland China's current status in the UN. Thus, the proposal is reasonable and workable.

EB. *What are your personal hopes for the future of Taiwan, the China relationship, and the Asia-Pacific community?*

President Lee. Over the past 40-plus years, Taiwan has overcome many hardships to achieve substantial democratization and economic liberalization. Given that achievement, I have high expectations and great confidence with regard to Taiwan's future. Our efforts are aimed at setting up a more orderly and civilized society with a more generalized sense of community as well as enabling the populace to truly enjoy the pleasures of family life—thus strengthening our democratic system. We will advocate resource conservation, plan the appropriate utilization of land, and step up environmental protection education; thus, our offspring will be able to enjoy the beauties of their homeland. We will invest more manpower and material resources to raise Taiwan's science and technology up to the standard of the advanced industrialized nations. To the people on the Chinese mainland, Taiwan's experience will remain a beacon, pointing the way to development, prosperity, freedom, and democracy.

Our policy toward the Chinese mainland is carried out in accordance with the Guidelines for National Unification. It can be divided into three general phases: exchanges and reciprocity, mutual trust and cooperation, and consultation and reunification. Currently, cross-strait interaction is still in the first phase. There is no timetable, and the pace of progress depends entirely on how cross-strait relations develop.

With this in mind, I made it very clear in my inaugural address on May 20 of this year that both sides should come to terms with the fact that the two sides of the Taiwan Strait are ruled separately. The two sides need to establish a dialogue and, with the utmost sincerity and patience, resolve our differences and seek common ground. I also issued a solemn call for the two sides of the strait to deal squarely with the important issue of ending the enmity between us. Finally, I expressed my willingness to make a journey of peace to the Chinese mainland to meet and exchange views with the authorities there. It is my hope that the leaders in Peking [Beijing] will respond positively to these ideas and thus open the door to a new era of peaceful competition across the strait.

The ROC has always played an active role in economic cooperation. We hope to cooperate with other Asia-Pacific nations in jointly creating a new Asia-Pacific age—an age in which the region will be more peaceful, open, and advanced and in which all countries will strive to settle disputes peacefully, seek reasonable solutions to their problems, and avoid senseless arms races or the use of military force. Moreover, these nations can further cooperate with each other to jointly develop the ocean's resources.

When in the past I put forth the concept of collective Asia-Pacific security, it was with the hope that each country would consider Asia-Pacific security from the standpoint of the collective interest. A security dialogue could be established, with all the nations involved participating on equal footing and making a common contribution. In addition, an international cooperative enterprise could be founded to tap the resources of the South China Sea, with the profits going toward a program aimed at maintaining peace. I personally hope that the Asia-Pacific region can remain faithful to the principles of open regionalism and develop further in the direction of free trade.

> The ROC's successful experience, our "Quiet Revolution," has already become a new model for democratic development.

Chronology of 1996

1

King Fahd cedes power

Still experiencing the effects of a stroke suffered in November 1995, Saudi Arabia's King Fahd, who also held the post of prime minister, ceded temporary power to Crown Prince Abdullah, his legal successor. A spokesman said that the monarch needed time for rest and recuperation. Though no significant change was expected in Saudi Arabia's domestic or foreign policies, Abdullah had shown a greater inclination to foster ties with other Arab groups than with Western nations. His local power base was provided by the National Guard, an internal security organization, which he had commanded for more than 30 years.

•

Khun Sa surrenders

Government authorities in Myanmar (Burma) reported that Khun Sa, the world's most notorious trafficker in heroin, had surrendered at his base in Ho Mong and that his stronghold in eastern Myanmar was under the control of government troops. Khun Sa had earlier expressed a willingness to retire if his conditions for surrender were accepted by Myanmar's military rulers. For some 30 years Khun Sa had operated with virtual impunity in the so-called Golden Triangle, a region straddling the borders of Myanmar, Thailand, and Laos. Military campaigns to wipe out his operation had failed because government troops proved to be no match for the 20,000-man outlaw army that protected the mountain area that they occupied. The U.S. had reportedly offered a $2 million reward for information leading to Khun Sa's conviction in a U.S. court, but a U.S. request that Khun Sa be extradited to the U.S. was not expected to be honoured.

4

Heat sets record in 1995

The British Meteorological Office and the University of East Anglia in Norwich released preliminary figures indicating that 1995 had the highest average temperature ever recorded by meteorologists since they began compiling such statistics in 1856. They calculated that the average global temperature in 1995 was 14.84° C (58.72° F). The Goddard Institute, operated by NASA, came up with a slightly higher figure. Although certain scientists and environmentalists were quick to cite these numbers as clear evidence of global warming, others contended that no definitive conclusions could be reached about permanent changes in the Earth's climate without studying data collected over a much longer period of time.

5

Whitewater papers found

The White House released documents that federal and congressional investigators had been demanding since 1994. David Kendall, the personal attorney of Pres. Bill Clinton and his wife, Hillary Rodham Clinton, said that the long-sought records detailing Hillary Clinton's work for the Rose Law Firm in the mid-1980s had been discovered the previous day by Carolyn Huber, the first lady's personal assistant. On January 18 Huber told a Senate committee that she found the Rose billing records on a table in a small room in the White House private quarters. She further stated that the documents had not been there when she entered the room three or four days earlier. Investigators wanted to learn, among other things, whether Hillary Clinton's work for the now defunct Madison Guaranty Savings and Loan involved a conflict of interest. The question arose because its owner, James McDougal, was accused of fraud and had been a partner of the Clintons in the Whitewater Development Corp., a trouble-plagued real estate venture.

•

Haiti asks UN to stay

René Préval, scheduled to become president of Haiti on February 7, formally petitioned the United Nations to keep its 5,800-man peacekeeping force in the country for an additional six months. The UN mandate was due to expire on February 29. While expressing a willingness to continue its support for the still struggling Caribbean nation, the UN indicated that the size of its peacekeeping force would probably be drastically reduced.

7

Arzú wins in Guatemala

In a runoff election, Alvaro Arzú of the National Advancement Party (PAN) won the presidency of Guatemala by defeating Alfonso Partillo, candidate of the Guatemalan Republican Front (FRG). The results posted by the Supreme Electoral Tribunal showed that Arzú was the choice of 51.2% of those who cast ballots. Partillo's greater popularity in 18 of the country's 22 provinces was offset by Arzú's appeal to voters in Guatemala City, the nation's capital and largest city, which he had governed as mayor from 1985 to 1990. During the campaign, Arzú, a businessman, expressed support for a free-market economy. He also pledged to improve the nation's human rights record, fight rampant crime, and make a concerted effort to terminate the country's 35-year-old civil war.

Residents of Port-au-Prince flee violence. After Pres.-elect René Préval had formally requested on January 5 that the United Nations retain its peacekeeping troops in Haiti, the international body twice authorized extended stays for a smaller force.

9

Cardoso revokes decree

A 1991 presidential decree barring non-Indians from challenging land allocations made to indigenous peoples was revoked by Brazilian Pres. Fernando Cardoso. The original decree had been enacted to protect the traditional lands of Indians from encroachment by loggers, ranchers, and miners. Businessmen, however, complained that the more than 200 reservations already created—and some 300 others awaiting recognition—were a hindrance to economic growth, especially in the Amazon, where most were located.

•

Kim admits money gifts

In the course of a nationally televised address, South Korean Pres. Kim Young Sam acknowledged that he had accepted political funds, but not bribes, from businessmen before his election to the presidency. No politician, he contended, could "have avoided such wrong practices" at the time. Kim's

ties to business interests had been questioned after his predecessor, Roh Tae Woo, admitted that he had built up a secret $650 million slush fund accumulated from contributions made by the heads of dozens of business conglomerates. Kim Dae Jung, a prominent member of the political opposition, admitted that he had benefited from Roh's fund and challenged Kim to acknowledge that he too had received such money. Kim, however, did not address the issue directly, nor did he identify those who had contributed financially to his presidential campaign.

11

Hashimoto to lead Japan

Following the abrupt resignation of Prime Minister Tomiichi Murayama on January 5, both houses of Japan's Diet (parliament) approved the appointment of Ryutaro Hashimoto as the nation's new leader. He had been elected head of the Liberal-Democratic Party (LDP) in September 1995. Murayama, leader of the Social Democratic Party of Japan (SDPJ), had held office for only 18 months, but the time had come, he said, "to inject fresh blood into the leadership." As a member of Murayama's Cabinet, Hashimoto had gained international prominence as a tough negotiator during an automobile trade dispute between the U.S. and Japan. His new Cabinet included 12 members of the LDP, 6 from the SDPJ, and 2 from New Party Sakigake. One

woman joined the Cabinet as the minister of justice.

•

Peru sentences U.S. woman

Peru's Supreme Council of Military Justice convicted Lori Berenson, a 26-year-old U.S. citizen, of treason and sentenced her to life in prison. She had been arrested in late 1995 along with 22 others and accused of involvement with guerrillas of the Tupac Amaru Revolutionary Movement (MRTA), which planned to seize control of the Congress building and take legislators hostage. On January 8 Berenson had publicly defended Tupac Amaru, saying that it was not a terrorist but a revolutionary group fighting injustice and inequality. She consistently refused to distance herself from the MRTA despite entreaties to do so. During her secret trial, before judges whose identities were concealed, Berenson had not been allowed to challenge evidence, cross-examine government witnesses, or call witnesses on her own behalf.

•

Drug lord flees prison

José Santacruz Londoño, a major figure in Colombia's Cali drug cartel, escaped from a maximum security prison in the capital city of Bogotá. He had been arrested in July 1995 and was awaiting trial on a variety of charges, including murder. It was not immediately clear how he managed to escape, but officials suggested that a car used by prosecutors may

have been involved. Such vehicles were not searched when they left the facility. The only other major figure in the Cali cartel still at large was Helmer Herrera, identified as the group's military leader.

14

Portuguese elect Sampaio

The successful presidential campaign waged by Jorge Sampaio gave Portugal's Socialist Party control of both the presidency and the prime ministership for the first time in more than 20 years. Sampaio captured 53.8% of the popular vote in defeating Aníbal Cavaco Silva, a former prime minister representing the Social Democratic Party. During the campaign Sampaio had promised to use his presidential powers to stabilize the nation's economy. Cavaco Silva, however, had warned voters that a Sampaio victory would lead to a "dictatorship of the majority." Following the election there was speculation that Sampaio might invoke his powers to dissolve the unicameral legislature and call for new elections in the hope that the Socialist Party could gain an absolute majority in the Assembly of the Republic.

15

King dies in accident

Lesotho's King Moshoeshoe II and his chauffeur were killed when their car plunged over a cliff near the capital city of Maseru. The monarch was returning home early in

Prime Minister Ryutaro Hashimoto of Japan receives a bouquet at the Liberal-Democratic Party convention. Hashimoto was elected head of the party in 1995.

Supporters of Hanan Ashrawi, seated in the automobile, campaign for their candidate in the January 20 Palestinian elections, in which Yasir Arafat won the presidency of the Palestine National Authority. Ashrawi, long a spokeswoman for the Palestinians, won a seat from Jerusalem in the PNA legislative council.

the morning after inspecting his herds of cattle. He had been twice deposed but in January 1995 regained the throne from his son King Letsie III, who then became crown prince. After Moshoeshoe's death, Queen Mamohato held the post of regent until the Traditional College of Chiefs named (February 7) Crown Prince Letsie the nation's new ruler. He would again be known as King Letsie III.

•

Papandreou resigns

Acknowledging that debilitating lung and kidney infections had undermined his ability to govern Greece, Prime Minister Andreas Papandreou tendered his resignation. Three days later the ruling Panhellenic Socialist Movement (Pasok), which Papandreou continued to lead, elected Kostas Simitis prime minister. After he and his Cabinet took the oath of office on January 22, Simitis called for a restructuring of the government and improved ties with the U.S. To facilitate implementation of reforms that he was contemplating, he dismissed numerous Papandreou loyalists, many of whom had not supported his election. Theodoros Pangalos, an advocate of reform, was then named foreign minister. Vasso Papandreou, who was not related to the former prime minister, was given responsibilities that included promoting investment and overseeing privatization.

16
Strasser ousted

A group of army officers in Sierra Leone ousted Valentine Strasser from his post as chairman of the Supreme Council of State. He was allowed safe passage to neighbouring Guinea, where many of his compatriots had earlier fled to escape the perils of civil war. Strasser was replaced by Brig. Julius Maada Bio, the former vice chairman of the council and head of government. He announced that multiparty elections would be held in February as planned and said that he would attempt to persuade the Revolutionary United Front to negotiate an end to their five-year-old insurrection.

17
Abdel Rahman sentenced

Michael Mukasey, a district court judge in New York City, sentenced Sheikh Omar Abdel Rahman, a blind Egyptian cleric, to life imprisonment without parole. He and nine other Muslim militants had been convicted in October 1995 of having conspired to bomb the UN headquarters and other landmarks in New York City and of having plotted to assassinate political leaders, including Egyptian Pres. Hosni Mubarak. The heart of the government's case consisted of more than 100 hours of tape-recorded conversations secretly made by an informer. None of the defendants was sentenced to less than 25 years in prison. Before being sentenced, Abdel Rahman was allowed to address the court. He described the U.S. as an infidel country and an enemy of Islam.

•

Keating mends fences

Australian Prime Minister Paul Keating returned home after strengthening Australia's relations with Malaysia and Singapore. During talks in Kuala Lumpur, Keating and Malaysian Prime Minister Dato Seri Mahathir bin Mohamad agreed to paper over past differences and resume trade talks at the ministerial level. Keating had earlier offended Mahathir by calling him "recalcitrant" for declining to attend a 1993 Asia-Pacific Economic Cooperation meeting in the United States. Mahathir remarked that his meeting with Keating was important because the two men addressed "minor misunderstandings and lack of appreciation of each other." Singapore and Australia underscored the degree of importance they placed on good relations by issuing a joint statement. It expressed support for free trade in the area and endorsed a five-nation defense pact that also included Malaysia, New Zealand, and the United Kingdom.

•

Art thieves convicted

Four men were convicted by a court in Oslo of having

stolen and/or attempted to sell Edvard Munch's 1893 masterpiece "The Scream." Two were found guilty of having stolen the painting from the National Art Museum in Oslo in February 1994. (It was rescued undamaged the following May.) The court ordered one of the defendants to spend six years and three months in prison; the other, four years and nine months. Their two associates were convicted of having conspired to sell the painting, which had an estimated market value of $55 million. Both were also given prison terms.

20
Arafat wins presidency

Palestinian voters in the Gaza Strip and West Bank overwhelmingly supported Yasir Arafat's bid to become president of the self-ruling Palestine National Authority. Arafat's only rival, Samiha Khalil, garnered only 9.3% of the vote. Arafat hailed the election as "the foundation for our Palestinian state." Incomplete tabulation of ballots cast for legislators suggested that the Arafat-led al-Fatah faction within the Palestine Liberation Organization would occupy about 65 of the 88 seats in the legislative council. Officials estimated that 75% of eligible voters had gone to the polls, a clear rejection of the boycott called by Hamas, Islamic Jihad, and the Palestine Front for the Liberation of Palestine.

22
Galileo data analyzed

During a news conference in California, scientists at NASA's Ames Research Center reported that preliminary analyses of data transmitted from the Galileo spacecraft raised many questions and required a reevaluation of theories about the formation and evolution of the solar system. For about an hour in December 1995, when Galileo made a turbulent entry into Jupiter's atmosphere, it relayed a massive amount of data for 57 minutes before being destroyed by intense heat and pressure. The Ames researchers noted that the data received did not necessarily represent the conditions of

the entire planet because the probe had descended into one of Jupiter's less cloudy regions. Even so, the scientists were highly skeptical that life of any kind existed on the largest planet in the solar system.

23

Chun Doo Hwan indicted

Prosecutors in South Korea charged former president Chun Doo Hwan with sedition for his role in the May 1980 massacre in Kwangju of pro-democracy demonstrators. That same day Roh Tae Woo, Chun's successor, was charged with insurrection. Roh had commanded government troops in Kwangju, but he was not accused of having participated in the killings. Both men also faced charges of bribery on a massive scale. After the 1979 assassination of Pres. Park Chung Hee, Chun moved against his rivals and quickly became the de facto authority in South Korea even though Choi Kyu Hah held the post of president. In May 1980 the military declared martial law. Three months later Chun

was elected president by the nation's electoral college.

26

U.S. ratifies START II

By a vote of 87–4, the U.S. Senate ratified the second Strategic Arms Reduction Talks (START II) treaty. The accord, however, would not take effect until it had been ratified by both houses of Russia's Federal Assembly. The pact committed both nations to eliminating all of their land-based intercontinental ballistic missiles armed with multiple warheads and to drastic reductions in missile- and bomber-based warheads by the year 2003.

27

Coup succeeds in Niger

Col. Ibrahim Baré Maïnassara led a successful military coup against Mahamane Ousmane, Niger's first democratically elected president. After ordering Ousmane and Prime Minister Hama Amadou arrested, Baré declared himself chairman of a national council that would temporarily govern the country. He also outlawed political parties and suspended the constitution. The U.S. condemned the coup and automatically suspended aid to Niger because U.S. law required such action when violence was used to overthrow a government. France also condemned the coup and cut off aid to its former colony even though Niger desperately needed foreign assistance.

29

Fire guts La Fenice

One of Venice's most glorious monuments, the 204-year-old Teatro La Fenice opera house, was almost totally destroyed by a fire

that raged for nine hours before it was extinguished. Only the walls of the foyer and the marble facade remained standing amid the debris. The Italian government immediately pledged $12.5 million to help rebuild the historic structure, which Giuseppe Verdi had selected to premiere five of his operas, including *Rigoletto* (1851) and *La Traviata* (1853). Luciano Pavarotti, one of many world-renowned singers who had performed at La Fenice, announced that he would hold a fund-raising concert to help restore the opera house. Architects estimated that the total cost would be in excess of $300 million.

31

Cubans leave Guantánamo

Some 125 Cubans, the last of numerous refugees who had been housed at the U.S. Guantánamo Bay Naval Base in Cuba, were flown to Florida. The camps were then officially closed. In August 1994 U.S. President Clinton, hoping to discourage Cuban refugees from embarking on a perilous voyage to the U.S., reversed a long-standing U.S. policy by announcing that Cuban refugees would no longer be automatically admitted into the U.S. Those who were picked up at sea—many on makeshift rafts or in unseaworthy boats—were taken to Guantánamo Bay. At one point the base was home to some 29,000 Cubans and 21,000 Haitians.

Charred ruins are all that remain of Venice's historic La Fenice opera house after it was gutted by fire on January 29.

Two Cuban refugees wave plastic U.S. flags from a bus window as they and numerous others leave the U.S. naval base at Guantánamo Bay, Cuba, where they had been confined since being picked up at sea while trying to escape from Cuba. After their release on January 31, they were flown to Florida.

2
FEBRUARY

Soldiers of UNITA (the rebel National Union for the Total Independence of Angola) remain loyal to Jonas Savimbi.

2
Canada gets regional veto

Three Canadian provinces (British Columbia, Ontario, and Quebec) and two "prairie regions" were granted veto power over any changes in the constitution that were sponsored by the federal government. The bill, initially proposed by Prime Minister Jean Chrétien in November 1995, became law when it was approved by Gov.-Gen. Roméo LeBlanc. The Senate and House of Commons had already approved the legislation, which had been drafted, among other reasons, to satisfy French-speaking Quebeckers who felt that their concerns were not being adequately addressed in formulating national policies.

Bahrain arrests Shi'ites

Authorities in Bahrain announced that 41 Shi'ite Muslims had been arrested and charged with rioting and sabotage. In mid-January, when some 200 Shi'ite protesters were taken into custody, officials said that 8 would face trial as members of a "subversive organization." The Shi'ite community had long complained that the al-Khalifah family, which ruled the emirate, reserved choice positions in the government and business for fellow Sunni Muslims even though the Shi'ite population was more than twice that of the Sunni. The Shi'ite demands included the restoration of the legislature, which had been disbanded in 1975, the right to free speech, better job opportunities, and the release of political prisoners. The government had acknowledged that 600 Shi'ites were being held, but others believed the true number to be closer to 2,000.

6
Kirby joins High Court

A vacancy on Australia's High Court was filled when Michael Kirby was sworn in as the court's 40th justice since its establishment in 1903. Kirby replaced Sir William Deane, who had resigned in 1995 to become governor-general of Australia. Kirby had previously served as president of the New South Wales

Court of Appeals, deputy president of the Australian Conciliation and Arbitration Committee, and chairman of the Australian Law Reform Commission.

7
Polish leader replaced

Wlodzimierz Cimoszewicz, who had been deputy speaker of Poland's Sejm (parliament), took the oath of office as prime minister. The promotion had been approved by the former communist Democratic Left Alliance, which held a plurality of seats in the Sejm, and the leftist Polish Peasant Party, which had strong support in rural areas. Both were members of the ruling coalition. Cimoszewicz, however, had no current ties to any political party. In 1990 he had made an unsuccessful run for the presidency as an independent socialist. The prime ministership became vacant when Jozef Oleksy resigned in order to spend full time refuting charges that he had given state secrets to spies from the former Soviet Union.

8
UN to stay in Angola

The United Nations Security Council agreed to extend its peacekeeping mission in Angola an additional three months. It hoped that its rejection of the six-month extension recommended by UN Secretary-General Boutros Boutros-Ghali would pressure Jonas Savimbi, leader of the rebel National Union for the Total Independence of Angola (UNITA), to speed up the demobilization of his 62,000-man army. To date, only some 9,000 of the promised 16,500 troops had met an

agreed-upon deadline and gathered in designated areas. UNITA and the Popular Movement for the Liberation of Angola, headed by Pres. José Eduardo dos Santos, had signed a peace pact in November 1994. If implemented, it would end a civil war that had taken the lives of half a million people since the country gained independence from Portugal in 1975.

12
Bishops back condom use

The Social Commission of the Roman Catholic bishops of France issued a report that called the use of condoms a necessary means to prevent the spread of AIDS. Even though the report insisted that the use of condoms was not a proper substitute for adult sexual education, its basic statement contradicted the teaching of Pope John Paul II, who maintained that abstinence was the only morally acceptable way to avoid being infected with HIV, the virus that causes AIDS.

15
Stankevicius promoted

One week after Lithuania's Seimas (unicameral legislature) voted 94–26 in support of Pres. Algirdas Brazauskas's January 29 decree removing Prime Minister Adolfas Slezevicius from power, the legislature awarded the post to Laurynas Stankevicius, a member of the ruling Lithuanian Democratic Labour Party. Slezevicius's fate was sealed when a scandal was uncovered in the government's takeover of Lithuania's two largest privately owned banks. Senior management officers were accused of

fraud, and several were arrested. In December 1995, when authorities declared the banks insolvent, they held nearly one-quarter of the nation's bank deposits. An uproar ensued when it was learned that the prime minister had withdrawn his personal deposits shortly before the banks were shut down and their assets frozen. When Slezevicius refused to resign after admitting that he had made "a moral and political mistake," he was removed from office.

Grozny palace destroyed

One week after Russian Prime Minister Viktor Chernomyrdin was made head of a commission that was to explore ways of ending the fighting in Chechnya, Russian troops demolished the presidential palace in the

Chechen capital of Grozny. It had been the symbol of independence for Chechen separatists, who had been fighting government forces since December 1994. On February 8 Russian Pres. Boris Yeltsin had told reporters that if the fighting did not stop and Russian troops were not withdrawn, he would be wasting his time if he ran for the presidency because "people won't elect me."

•

Bangladeshi go to the polls

In parliamentary elections boycotted by the three main opposition parties, Prime Minister Khaleda Zia's Bangladesh Nationalist Party (BNP) won 205 of the 300 contested seats in the 330-member Parliament. The election was preceded by strikes, protest marches, bloody clashes, and threats of violence against anyone who went to the polls. Even though the BNP faced no significant challenge on election day, there were numerous reports of fraud in some areas. As a consequence, the ballots at more than 10% of the polling places reportedly were declared invalid.

16
Italy seeks new leader

Following the resignation of Italian Prime Minister Lamberto Dini on January 11 and the failure of Prime Minister-designate Antonio Maccanico to form a coalition government supporting constitutional reforms, Pres. Oscar Luigi Scalfaro dissolved Parliament and ordered new elections to be held on April 21. Until that time Dini would continue to head the government in the role of caretaker. The political atmosphere had changed when former prime minister Silvio Berlusconi of Forza Italia and Massimo D'Alema of the Party of the Democratic Left—both supporters of electoral reform—announced that they no longer opposed a general election.

17
Ads banned in Russia

Ignoring the protests of some businessmen, Russian Pres. Boris Yeltsin ordered a complete media ban on advertisements promoting tobacco and alcoholic products. Those who contravened the ban, he said, would be fined and the money used to promote public health education. Russia had the world's highest rate of alcohol consumption, and nearly 70% of adult Russians smoked. Health officials predictably praised the ban, saying that the health of ordinary Russians was deplorable.

18
New effort at peace

During talks at the Italian Foreign Ministry in Rome, leaders of the three warring factions in Bosnia and Herzegovina pledged to resolve the problems that had impeded implementation of the peace treaty signed in Paris in December 1995. Hard-liners on all sides had opposed elements of the treaty, which had been designed to establish a multiethnic state in Bosnia and Herzegovina, once an integral part of Yugoslavia. Among the most emotion-

Defiant Chechens demonstrate on a roadside as their native Chechnya continued its battle to secede from the Russian Federation.

FEBRUARY

Kweisi Mfume is sworn in as president and chief executive officer of the National Association for the Advancement of Colored People on February 20. His son Donald holds the Bible as son Keith looks on.

charged issues that arose during negotiations was the arrest of two Bosnian Serb military officers whom the Muslim-dominated government of Bosnia and Herzegovina had accused of war crimes. Success in resolving this and other differences rested with Pres. Alija Izetbegovic of Bosnia and Herzegovina, Croatian Pres. Franjo Tudjman, and Serbian Pres. Slobodan Milosevic.

•

IRA bombs London bus

A terrorist bomber was killed and at least eight other persons injured when a double-decker bus exploded in flames in London. The Provisional Irish Republican Army (IRA) claimed responsibility. Several days earlier the IRA had detonated a powerful bomb in central London. It killed two persons and caused extensive damage to buildings in the area. During an interview that appeared in a weekly newspaper published by Sinn Fein, the political wing of the IRA, a spokesman for the IRA declared that the cease-fire was no longer in effect. The words seemed to imply that the political status of Northern Ireland was about to trigger another round of violence.

20
Iraqi defectors murdered

After being granted amnesty by Saddam Hussein, Iraq's president and prime minister, two high-ranking military

HARRY HAMBURG—NEW YORK DAILY NEWS/KRT

officers who had defected to Jordan in August 1995 returned home. Their wives, who accompanied them when they left Iraq, were both daughters of Hussein. Lieut. Gen. Hussein Kamel Hasan al-Majid had been in charge of the nation's weapons program and Col. Saddam Kamel Hasan al-Majid head of special forces. On February 23 the Interior Ministry announced that the two men, their father, and a brother had been slain at their residence outside Baghdad by members of their own clan.

•

Mfume assumes office

During a ceremony at the Justice Department in Washington, D.C., Kweisi Mfume was sworn in as president and chief executive officer of

CRISPIN RODWELL—REUTERS

A young boy holds a paper dove during a peace rally in Belfast, N.I. The rally, a response to an Irish Republican Army bombing in London on February 9, drew thousands of demonstrators. Another IRA bombing occurred later in the month.

the National Association for the Advancement of Colored People (NAACP). He had relinquished his seat in the U.S. House of Representatives two days earlier. Mfume faced a formidable challenge as he planned strategy to rebuild the organization's financial base and overcome a crisis in leadership created by his predecessor, Benjamin Chavis, Jr., who had been fired in 1994 after revelations that he had misused NAACP funds.

21
Farrakhan ends tour

The Rev. Louis Farrakhan, leader of the Nation of Islam, returned to the U.S. after a controversial "world friendship tour," which, he said, had been undertaken to promote peace and solidarity among Muslims. Iran, Iraq, Libya, Nigeria, The Sudan, and Syria were among the nearly 20 countries that he visited. Farrakhan's critics included black activists who were dismayed that he had agreed to accept $1 billion from Libyan leader Muammar al-Qaddafi to fund political activities in the U.S. Qaddafi was quoted as saying, "Our confrontation with America used to be like confronting a fortress from the outside. Today we have found an opening to enter the fortress and to confront it from within."

22
Indian officials charged

Prosecutors in India ended another phase of their inves-

tigation into bribery with the indictment of 14 high-ranking politicians, most of whom belonged to Prime Minister P.V. Narasimha Rao's Congress (I) Party. Four of the group were top ministers who had resigned in the face of the impending indictments. Evidence of corruption came mainly from the diaries of Surendra Jain, a former industrialist who had been arrested in 1995. His diaries contained the names of more than 100 persons to whom he had given money. Under Indian law all payments made to public officials were presumed to be illegal gratifications unless proved otherwise.

•

France to cut military

In a televised address to the nation, French Pres. Jacques Chirac proposed major reductions in military spending to help reduce the budget deficit. He noted that the Cold War was over and that the U.S. and the U.K. had already reevaluated their military expenditures. Among other things, Chirac called for an end to conscription, a 30% cut in the armed forces, the development of a rapid response force, a drastic reduction in nuclear weapons, the closing of the only facility in France that produced plutonium and weapons-grade uranium, and the dismantling of France's Hades missile launches. As expected, there were voices of dissent, especially regarding the abolition of France's citizen army, which had been an uninterrupted tradition for more than 90 years.

Blacks enter white school

Following a February 16 order issued by South African Supreme Court Justice Tjibbe Spoelstra, black students, previously turned away, were admitted to a primary school in Potgietersus, a rural area about 260 km (160 mi) north of Johannesburg. Because of a parental boycott, only about 30 of the 700 white students attended school that day. The population of Potgietersus consisted of 120,000 blacks and 10,000 whites. After South Africa began integrating its schools in 1991, many black children had entered white schools without incident.

24
Cuba downs two planes

Four Cuban exiles living in Florida were killed when their two unarmed Cessna 337 planes were shot down by Cuban MiG fighter jets over the Caribbean. The aircraft belonged to an organization called Brothers to the Rescue, which operated out of Miami. The U.S. called an emergency meeting of the UN Security Council, which issued a statement "strongly deploring" the shooting down of civilian aircraft. On February 26 President Clinton suspended all charter flights between the U.S. and Cuba and said that travel to the U.S. by Cuban diplomats would be restricted. Although Cuban exiles had previously flown over Havana to drop antigovernment leaflets, the U.S. contended that in this instance the planes were over international waters. Cuba claimed otherwise.

25
Hamas bombs kill 27

An Israeli bus was ripped apart by a bomb that exploded as the vehicle neared the Central Bus Station in West Jerusalem. The terrorist died along with 24 other passengers. Less than an hour later, a much smaller bomb was detonated in the Israeli town of Ashkelon. A man disguised as an Israeli soldier detonated the device after joining a group of Israeli soldiers looking for rides back to their base. The bomber died along with a female soldier. The military

wing of Hamas claimed responsibility for both suicide attacks. Yasir Arafat, president of the Palestine National Authority, vigorously condemned the bombings, which were the deadliest to have occurred in Israel in 20 years.

Obiang's election illegal

Brig. Gen. Teodoro Obiang Nguema Mbasogo, president of Equatorial Guinea, won 99% of the vote in an election that had been called early in violation of the nation's constitution. Outside observers as well as political opponents at home characterized the election process as a charade. All five opposition candidates, who had been optimistic when they began to campaign in the country's first multiparty presidential election, later sought unsuccessfully to have their names stricken from the ballots. Some people speculated that Obiang had called for an early election in order to profit personally from revenues that were

expected to come from an oil field discovered off Biako in 1995.

28
Diana agrees to divorce

The British public was officially informed that Diana, princess of Wales, had agreed to divorce Charles, prince of Wales, her husband of nearly 15 years. Several months earlier Queen Elizabeth II had urged the estranged couple to end their relationship, which had provided the tabloids with a steady stream of scandals, real or manufactured.

Daiwa pleads guilty

Officials of Japanese-owned Daiwa Bank Ltd. pleaded guilty in a New York City court to 16 of the 20 counts listed in an indictment. The pleas included 10 counts of falsifying books and records, 2 counts of conspiracy, 2 counts of wire fraud, one count of obstructing a U.S. Federal Reserve Board ex-

amination, and one count of attempting to cover up $1.1 billion in losses from illegal bond trading at its New York City offices. The $340 million fine was the largest sum ever imposed on a financial institution.

Jim Bolger finds ally

With his National Party (NP) occupying only 43 of the 99 seats in New Zealand's House of Representatives, Prime Minister Jim Bolger strengthened his political position by forming a coalition with the United New Zealand (UNZ) party. Having been assured of a post in Bolger's Cabinet, Peter Dunne of the UNZ was destined to become the first Cabinet member in 54 years to serve in a government ruled by another party. A 1993 referendum, which guaranteed representation in Parliament to any party that received at least 5% of the popular vote, had ended political domination of the government by either the NP or the Labour Party.

ROBERTO SCHMIDT—AFP

Cuban-Americans in Miami, Fla., protest the downing on February 24 of two small planes by Cuban military aircraft off the coast of Cuba. The planes belonged to a humanitarian organization that had often flown over the Straits of Florida in an effort to aid and support Cuban refugees fleeing on rafts or in small boats.

3
MARCH

1
Bosnian Serb charged

Gen. Djordje Djukic, a Bosnian Serb, was charged with war crimes by the United Nations International War Crimes Tribunal in The Hague. He had been placed in charge of logistics for the Bosnian Serb army when civil war broke out in 1992 and became a senior aide to Gen. Ratko Mladic, commander of the army. The tribunal's chief prosecutor alleged that Djukic had co-ordinated the bombardment of civilian targets in Sarajevo during the Bosnian Serbs' assault on the capital. The tribunal was also investigating Djukic's possible role in the transportation of Muslim and Croat civilians to work camps and detention centres.

2
Labor loses in Australia

Australian Prime Minister Paul Keating's Labor Party suffered a crushing defeat at the polls when John Howard's Liberal Party–National Party coalition won 94 of the 148 seats in the House of Representatives. Analysts believed the personalities of the two men significantly affected the outcome, but the candidates also took different positions on major issues. They disagreed on such subjects as the state of the economy, the wisdom of having a national wage scale, and the possible consequences of partially privatizing the company that held a monopoly on local telephone services.

●

Caldera loses support

The government of Venezuelan Pres. Rafael Caldera lost control of both the Senate and the House of Deputies when the Movement to Socialism (MAS) party, the Social Christian Party, and the Radical Cause formed an alliance. MAS had previously allied itself with Caldera's National Convergence and the Democratic Action Party, but differences over financial policies caused it to seek new partners. Among the difficult problems Caldera faced were bank failures, serious inflation, a growing national debt, and labour unrest.

3
Turkish rivals unite

After unsuccessful attempts by various political parties to agree on terms for a coalition government, Turkey's two-month-old political crisis came to an end. Interim prime minister Tansu Ciller of the True Path Party and Mesut Yilmaz of the Motherland Party agreed that Yilmaz would head their coalition government for the rest of the year. During the following two years, Ciller would be in charge. During the two years after that, if the coalition still survived, the prime ministership would be split between Yilmaz and a member of the True Path Party. The two rivals were able to come together because both were determined to isolate the Islamic Welfare Party, which in December 1995 had won a plurality of 158 seats in the Turkish Grand National Assembly. Although the new coalition controlled only 267 seats in the Assembly—just short of an absolute majority—two leftist parties that controlled 124 seats indicated that they would allow the conservative coalition to manage the government.

6
Canada cuts social budget

A blueprint for Canada's 1996–97 fiscal year, presented to the House of Commons by Finance Minister Paul Martin, indicated that the government would continue its effort to reduce the budget by trimming funds for social programs. Pensions and retirement savings plans were specifically targeted for slower growth, but other benefits for the elderly were also likely to be affected because there appeared to be no other way to control the deficit. In the future, single persons earning more than Can$52,-000 a year (the current limit was Can$85,000) and couples earning more than Can$78,-000 (currently Can$170,000) would not qualify for Old Age Security benefits.

7
Okinawa rape trial ends

A panel of three Japanese judges in Naha, Okinawa,

A Buddhist monk takes part in a demonstration protesting the continued presence of U.S. military bases on Okinawa as discussions took place between the U.S. and Japan on the reduction of bases. Numerous anti-U.S. protests took place on Okinawa after a Japanese court on March 7 found three U.S. servicemen guilty of the 1995 rape of an Okinawan girl.

TOSHIFUMI KITAMURA—AFP

convicted three U.S. servicemen of the rape of a 12-year-old Japanese girl in Okinawa in September 1995. A marine and a navy seaman were each sentenced to seven years in prison. A second marine was sentenced to six and a half years. All three had pleaded guilty to having participated in the child's abduction, but of the two who admitted raping her, one later retracted his confession. The judges remarked that the evidence left no room for sympathy because the crime had been premeditated. Nonetheless, the sentences they handed out were less than the 10 years demanded by the prosecution.

•

Arafat convenes council

The 88-member Palestine Legislative Council, chosen in general elections in January, convened for the first time in Gaza City under the chairmanship of Yasir Arafat, president of the Palestine National Authority. During his speech Arafat hailed "the birth of a new democracy in the Middle East" while deploring recent acts of terrorism against Israel, including two bombings in February that killed 25 Israelis. Such attacks, he vowed, would not halt the peace process. Arafat's authority was further strengthened when Ahmed Qurie (Abu Ala) was elected speaker of the Council. He was among those who had signed the Palestinian peace treaty with Israel.

•

Austrian parties reunite

After months of negotiations, Austria's two largest parties agreed to reestablish the coalition that they had formed in November 1994 after both lost seats in the National Council elections. One year later the People's Party withdrew its support from the Social Democratic Party because it had failed to implement a program of greater fiscal austerity. With the Social Democrats still holding a plurality of seats in the legislature, the People's Party agreed to become part of a coalition government again if the budget deficit was reduced by billions of dollars. Chancellor Franz Vranitzky, a Social Democrat, agreed that such cuts could be made.

IAN WALDIE—REUTERS

A child lays flowers outside Dunblane Primary School in Scotland. On March 13 a gunman entered the school and killed 16 first-graders and their teacher and wounded 12 others in the class.

•

Turkey curbs free speech

Yasar Kemal, generally regarded as Turkey's foremost living author, was given a 20-month suspended prison sentence for having published several articles in which he criticized the government for placing certain restrictions on free speech. The court found Kemal guilty of having violated the country's antiterrorist law because his remarks allegedly "fomented enmity between peoples." In a separate trial three months earlier, Kemal had faced similar charges for having condemned the government's military campaign against the Kurds. In that instance he was acquitted.

•

Drug firms to merge

Sandoz AG and Ciba-Geigy AG announced that they planned to merge under the name Novartis. The two giant Swiss pharmaceutical firms would then become one of the largest drug companies in the world, with annual sales of nearly $11 billion. The market value of Novartis, which would control 4.4% of the world market, was estimated to be $62 billion. After the merger, which had to be approved by stockholders of each company and by international regulatory agencies, Ciba-Geigy's chief executive would become chairman of Novartis and the head of Sandoz's pharmaceutical division would become president.

8
Thai workers recompensed

The California Department of Industrial Relations distributed checks to Thai workers who in August 1995 had been discovered working in sweatshops. Most were illegal immigrants. Authorities had calculated that they were owed a total of $1.1 million in back wages. The checks they received ranged in size from $64 to $37,000. The seven Thai citizens who had operated the sweatshops had pleaded guilty to charges of conspiracy, harbouring illegal aliens, and slavery. They were to be sentenced later.

13
Gunman slays 16 children

In what appeared to be a totally random act of violence, a gunman shot and killed 16 small children and their teacher at the Dunblane (Scot.) Primary School. He then killed himself. The heavily armed man fired several shots in the playground before going to the gymnasium, where the children had gathered. Only one of the 29 children was unscathed. As police began their investigation, they were at a loss to explain the gunman's behaviour.

•

Liggett settles lawsuit

The largest class-action suit ever filed against the tobacco industry was partially settled when the Liggett

Group agreed to contribute 5% of its annual pretax profits, up to a maximum of $50 million each year, for a period of 25 years to programs aimed at helping people quit smoking. Individuals would receive no compensation. Liggett also negotiated a settlement with five states that had sued to recover Medicare money they had spent treating those suffering from tobacco-related illnesses. Although Liggett ranked fifth among U.S. cigarette manufacturers, its sales represented only 2% of the U.S. market. Liggett's settlements broke the unified front the tobacco companies had formed to fight a flood of lawsuits.

15
Duma revokes treaties

Russia's State Duma (parliament) voted 250–98, with numerous abstentions, to annul the 1991 treaties that dissolved the Soviet Union. The vote kindled fears that Russia might resort to force to reunite the now sovereign republics, especially if Gennady Zyuganov, the leader of the communists, defeated Boris Yeltsin in Russia's presidential election. There appeared to be little likelihood that the former Soviet republics would voluntarily relinquish their recently won independence.

•

Menem gets special powers

According to published reports, Argentina's Senate

and Chamber of Deputies had agreed to give Pres. Carlos Menem special economic powers for one year so that he could better cope with the nation's financial problems. Fearing that Argentina could not otherwise meet the 1996 fiscal targets imposed by the International Monetary Fund, the legislators granted Menem the power to increase tax rates and impose new taxes without its prior approval. There was a stipulation, however, that the president would have to present his tax proposals to a special congressional committee for screening.

17
Mugabe runs unopposed

After his two political opponents had demanded that their names be removed from the ballots, Zimbabwe's president, Robert Mugabe, was automatically elected to another six-year term. He had ruled the country continuously since 1980, the year it gained independence from Great Britain. Abel Muzorewa, a retired bishop, had withdrawn his candidacy after the Supreme Court rejected his request to have "unfair electoral rules" changed and the election postponed. Muzorewa said that Zimbabwe was now ruled "by a black minority one-party dictatorship." Mugabe's party controlled 147 of 150 seats in the legislature. The Rev. Ndabaningi Sithole had also withdrawn from the race owing to electoral policies that he alleged were unfair.

•

The Sudan holds election

Sudanese Pres. Omar Hassan Ahmad al-Bashir was assured of five more years in office after an election that lasted 12 days. The outcome of the first voting in The Sudan since 1986 was never in doubt. Political parties had been banned, and the names of the 40 or so presidential candidates who challenged Bashir meant little to a large segment of the voters. Most opposition leaders had called for a boycott of the election and requested that their names not be placed on the ballots. Observers generally viewed the election as a transparent effort by Bashir to gain some measure of legitimacy for his military regime. Since ousting The Sudan's democratically elected government in 1989, Bashir and the National Islamic Front had ruled the country with near absolute power. On March 23 Bashir declared that he would rule the country under "Islamic law and dignity" without a return of party politics.

18
Benin elects Kérékou

In a runoff election for the presidency of the small West African republic of Benin, Mathieu Kérékou defeated incumbent Pres. Nicéphore Soglo by capturing 52.5% of the vote. After leading a successful military coup in 1972, Kérékou used his position to promote Marxist policies. He stepped aside in 1990 during a period of economic and social instability. After regaining power, Kérékou promised to continue the free-market policies of his predecessor and to support democracy.

19
Sarajevo region reunited

For the first time since 1992, Sarajevo and five suburbs were united under the authority of the Muslim-dominated government of Bosnia and Herzegovina. Under terms of a 1995 peace accord, Bosnian Serb authorities were obliged to relinquish control of the five specified suburbs. The transfer of authority came amid a massive exodus of Serbs from the affected area. Of the 70,000 Serbs who had lived in the Sarajevo suburbs, only 7,000 remained. Their departure highlighted the problems authorities faced in establishing a multiethnic state in Bosnia and Herzegovina. Ethnic animosities were too intense for a speedy reconciliation.

22
Union workers end strike

With near unanimity, some 1,700 members of United Auto Workers (UAW) Local 696 voted to end their strike

Residents of Sarajevo walk past a building that was set on fire by departing Serbs. Under an accord signed in 1995, on March 19 the city and five suburbs were united under the government of Bosnia and Herzegovina.

ISSOUF SANOGO—AFP

A rally for Mathieu Kérékou takes place in Porto-Novo, Benin, before the March 18 presidential election runoff. Kérékou, who had ruled Benin from 1972 to 1990, defeated the incumbent, Nicéphore Soglo.

against the General Motors Corp. (GM). Only two brake-manufacturing plants in Dayton, Ohio, were directly affected, but GM was forced to lay off 178,000 other UAW workers when 26 of its 29 North American production plants had to be shut down for lack of parts. The strike, which was the automobile industry's largest since 1970, had cost the automaker an estimated $50 million a day in pretax earnings through lost production of 240,000 cars. The strikers' central complaint was GM's outsourcing of brake work to the U.S. unit of a German company. In-house production would have provided employment to an additional 128 union workers, but it would have made GM even less competitive against its chief U.S. rivals, the Chrysler Corp. and the Ford Motor Co. While the issue of outsourcing was not resolved, GM executives agreed to pay each UAW worker $1,700 and, among other things, to reduce the required amount of overtime from 40% to 20% of the regular workweek.

23
Lee Teng-hui reelected

In the first direct presidential election in Chinese history, Lee Teng-hui won a second five-year term as president of the Republic of China on Taiwan. He easily defeated three other candidates by capturing 54% of the vote. The election board reported that 76% of eligible voters had cast ballots. Lee was the first native-born Taiwanese to head the ruling Kuomintang (KMT; Nationalist Party). Peng Ming-min, who supported his Democratic Progressive Party's (Minchintang's) policy of independence for Taiwan, received 21% of the vote. The other candidates, both former members of the KMT, ran as independents and together won 25% of the vote. In a victory speech in Taipei, Lee remarked that the election marked a historic moment in China's history because "the door of democracy is now completely open." In a reference to China, which had tried to undermine support for Lee by firing rockets off the northern and southern coasts of the island, the president said, "In this very difficult and dangerous moment, with threats coming from outside, we have completed our mission."

26
Japan banks post losses

With the announcement that 10 more of Japan's largest banks would report losses for the 1995 fiscal year, a total of 17 of the country's leading commercial and trust banks would post a combined deficit of $33 billion. This figure reflected a decision by the directors of the banks to write off about $95 billion in bad debts. Fuji Bank Ltd. and Sakura Bank Ltd. were each expected to report losses of about $4 billion.

27
EU bans "mad cow" beef

The European Union (EU) announced a worldwide ban on the export of British beef products amid fears that bovine spongiform encephalopathy ("mad cow" disease) was linked to a similar disease that affected humans. Both diseases were fatal. Britain had reported nearly 160,000 cases of mad cow disease since it was first diagnosed in 1986. The Standing Veterinary Committee of the EU had evaluated the possible health hazards before approving the ban 14–1. British Prime Minister John Major expressed dismay at the decision, saying it could not be justified by available scientific evidence. Nonetheless, the impact of the ruling was immediate and far-reaching; the number of British cows sent to slaughter dropped by 98%.

•

Yigal Amir convicted

After a two-month trial in Tel Aviv District Court, a panel of three judges found Yigal Amir guilty of the premeditated murder of Prime Minister Yitzhak Rabin in November 1995. By law only Nazi war criminals were subject to capital punishment in Israel. Amir, therefore, received the mandatory life sentence imposed on murderers. Amir, who was smiling broadly when arrested at the scene of the crime, told the court that he had shot Rabin to halt the Israeli-Palestinian peace process. He claimed that what he had done was for God, the Torah, and the people and land of Israel. Prime Minister Shimon Peres remarked that the punishment meted out to Amir "pales in my eyes in comparison with the crime."

28
Line-item veto passed

Another item in the Republican Party's "Contract with America" was due to become U.S. law when President Clinton announced that he had decided to sign legislation granting "line-item veto" powers to the president. The new law would allow the U.S. president to veto specific parts of legislation authorizing new entitlement programs without having to reject the entire bill because he could not subscribe to all of its provisions. Congress could reinstate the deleted item, but if the president vetoed it a second time, a two-thirds majority would be needed in both houses of Congress to override the veto. The new law was opposed by those who contended that it improperly transferred legislative powers to the executive branch of government.

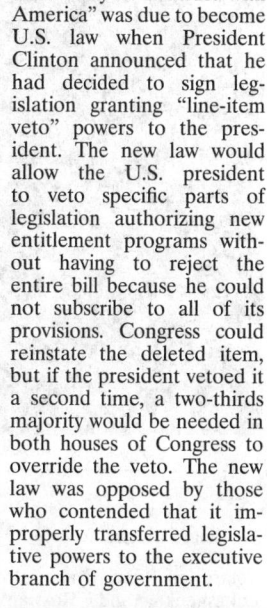

A supporter of Lee Teng-hui celebrates Lee's reelection as president of Taiwan on March 23. The first native-born Taiwanese to hold the post, Lee won 54% of the vote in the country's first direct presidential election.

APRIL

Theodore Kaczynski, who was believed to be the so-called Unabomber, is escorted to a court hearing. Federal agents arrested Kaczynski at his mountain cabin in Montana on April 3.

2

Belarus signs accord

Belarusian Pres. Alyaksandr Lukashenka and Russian Pres. Boris Yeltsin signed a treaty creating an "integrated political and economic community." Even though the two nations agreed to form the union, for the present they remained totally independent and sovereign. Nothing had been decided about merging at some future date. Belarus, Russia, Kazakstan, and Kyrgyzstan earlier had signed a pact that committed them to strengthening economic ties. Speaking mainly to those who were pondering the significance of growing cooperation between the former Soviet republics, Yeltsin remarked, "Those who do not lament the disintegration of the [Soviet] Union do not have a heart. But those who are dreaming of its restoration do not have a brain."

3

Unabomber suspect nabbed

U.S. federal agents in Montana apprehended Theodore J. Kaczynski, who they believed was the serial killer known as the "Unabomber."

On April 4 Kaczynski, a former university professor, was charged with the federal felony of possessing materials used in destructive devices. Over a period of 17 years, the Unabomber had killed 3 persons and injured 23 with explosives sent through the mail. Kaczynski was tracked down after his brother notified the FBI that in his mother's house he had come across papers suggesting that Theodore might be the long-sought terrorist.

•

Ron Brown dies in crash

U.S. Secretary of Commerce Ronald Brown died, along with 32 other Americans and 2 Croatians, when a U.S. Air Force jet crashed into a mountain in Croatia. Brown was visiting Croatia and Bosnia and Herzegovina with other U.S. government officials and businessmen. The purpose of their visit was to secure contracts to help rebuild the war-damaged nations. There were indications that human error and bad judgment had caused the accident.

•

Afrikaners go to prison

Five members of the Afrikaner Resistance Move-

ment were sentenced to 26 years in prison for killing 21 persons in three 1994 bombings. The white extremists were part of an effort by right-wing elements to disrupt South Africa's first all-race parliamentary elections. Of the 13 others who were put on trial, 4 were acquitted and 5 given prison sentences of a minimum of three years. The sentencing of four others was suspended because they had escaped.

•

U.K. to hold referendum

British Prime Minister John Major announced that his Cabinet had agreed to a national referendum to decide whether Great Britain should join the European Monetary Union and accept a common European currency. Kenneth Clarke, chancellor of the Exchequer, had threatened to resign if the Cabinet sought public approval of its policy in a referendum, the first ever sanctioned by a ruling Conservative Party government. Clarke agreed to stay on after Major assured him that he would force the resignation of any Cabinet member who publicly advocated rejection of the referendum before the voters had cast their ballots.

4

U.S. trims farm supports

President Clinton signed legislation that would eliminate or drastically reduce federal subsidies and price supports that benefited farmers. The Freedom to Farm Act, which had received strong support in both the Senate (74–26) and the House of Representatives (318–89), was expected to save the government some $2 billion over seven years. Among other things, under the new law, which took into account many different situations, subsidies that farmers had been paid not to grow crops that were in oversupply would be reduced gradually for seven years, at which time they would cease. Sugar, peanut, and tobacco farmers were among those who would not be affected by the new policy.

6

Chaos reigns in Liberia

The worst factional fighting in more than three years turned Monrovia, the capital of Liberia, into a battlefield. It also disrupted a peace plan designed to end the civil conflict. Following the declaration of a cease-fire, a six-man Council of State had been established to run the government while the warring parties disarmed and preparations were made for elections in August. The uncertain calm gave way to violence when the council ordered the arrest of faction leader D. Roosevelt Johnson on murder charges. When his followers began seizing Lebanese women and children as well as West African peacekeeping personnel, the U.S. quickly moved to evacuate hundreds of its citizens and other foreign nationals whose lives were in jeopardy. A new cease-fire was announced on April 19, but it did not solve the problems of the more than one million people—half the population—who remained homeless.

7
Korean DMZ violated

North Korean troops ended three days of military exercises in the demilitarized zone that separated North and South Korea. Because there was no sign of an impending attack against the South, political analysts speculated that the North was

merely attempting to convince UN officials that it would be in their interest to conclude a bilateral treaty with the North formally ending the Korean War. North Korea had previously stipulated that South Korea was to be excluded from the treaty negotiations.

10
Clinton veto criticized

President Clinton's veto of a bill that would have outlawed "partial-birth" abortions was denounced, as expected, by pro-life groups. The House of Representatives had approved the legislation by more than the two-thirds majority required for overriding a veto, but the Senate had not. The medical procedure, performed only after 20 weeks of a pregnancy, involved the partial removal of a fetus and the crushing of the skull or the sucking out of the brain. Sen. Bob Dole summed up his position, saying, "A partial-birth abortion blurs the line between abortion and infanticide and crosses an ethical and legal line we must never cross. President Clinton now stands on the wrong side of

JONATHAN DRAKE—REUTERS

A South Korean soldier (foreground) and his North Korean counterpart face each other across the demarcation line separating the two countries.

this line." Clinton defended his veto on the grounds that such abortions were rare and resorted to only when the mother or fetus had serious medical problems that were discovered after it was too late to perform other types of abortion.

•

China turns to Europe

China's offer to buy 30 passenger planes from Airbus Industrie, a European consortium, was formally approved by French Prime Minister Alain Juppé during a meeting in Paris with Chinese Premier Li Peng. Because the U.S.-owned Boeing Co. dominated the Chinese market, it appeared that Chinese officials were venting their displeasure with the U.S. for its criticism of China's human rights record and, among other things, its perceived reluctance to crack down on Chinese companies pirating copyrighted materials.

11
Africa bans nuclear arms

During a meeting in Cairo, representatives from virtually all of the African nations signed a treaty banning nuclear arms from the continent. The signatories pledged not to test, build, or stockpile nuclear weapons of any kind. To give added meaning to the treaty, China, France, the U.K., and the U.S. signed protocols promising not to test or use nuclear weapons in Africa or use the continent as a dumping ground for nuclear waste. Russia, the only other nation that publicly acknowledged having a nuclear capability, objected

to parts of the treaty, including a section that excluded the Indian Ocean island of Diego Garcia, where the U.S. maintained a military base.

•

Kim's party flounders

South Korean Pres. Kim Young Sam's New Korea Party lost its majority in the National Assembly, but it did not suffer the stinging defeat many had predicted before the legislative election. This was due in part, some analysts believed, to a desire on the part of many voters to support the government in the face of provocations from North Korea. Kim had cited North Korea's military exercises in the demilitarized zone as a reminder that the nation must be ever vigilant. The balance of power in the new legislature was such that Kim would be able, with expected support from independents, to continue his program of economic and political reforms without having to form a coalition government.

12
Pakistan gets U.S. arms

In a letter to Congress, U.S. Deputy Secretary of State Strobe Talbott revealed that the Clinton administration had decided to deliver $368 million worth of military equipment to Pakistan. The shipment would not include the 28 F-16 fighter jets Pakistan had already paid for. A 1985 amendment to a U.S. foreign aid bill had prohibited the sale of military items to countries thought to be developing nuclear weapons. The president, consequently, had to certify that

ROGER JOB—GAMMA LIAISON

NO PARKING

Young soldiers of one of Liberia's warring factions take to the streets of Monrovia. The fighting on April 6 was reported to be the worst in more than three years.

APRIL

Landless peasants patrol an area in the Brazilian state of Pará. On April 17 state police killed at least 19 protesters.

Pakistan was qualified to receive the shipment, which had been delayed because Pakistan had purchased from China 5,000 ring magnets that could be used to enrich uranium for nuclear weapons.

17
Brazilian police kill 19

At least 19 members of Brazil's landless peasant movement were killed when Pará state police tried to open a highway they were blocking. Police claimed that they had fired on the crowd only after peasants had fired at them. A professionally shot videotape, shown on national television, proved otherwise. On countless occasions members of the landless movement had occupied unused sections of large rural

A. ESTADO—AFP

estates to press their case for land redistribution. Many of the local police ordered to evict the trespassers were said to be paid by the estate owners. The peasants and their cause had a friend in Pres. Fernando Henrique Cardoso, who had signed

decrees expropriating rural land from large estates.

18
Israeli shells hit camp

More than 100 civilians were killed and numerous others

injured when Israeli soldiers fired artillery shells into a UN camp at Qana, Leb., that housed Lebanese refugees. For days Israeli warplane and helicopter gunships had been hitting various targets in Lebanon as part of a military operation against Hezbollah (Party of God) guerrillas who had launched rockets into northern Israel. On April 26 both Israel and Hezbollah signed a cease-fire agreement.

•

Tourists killed in Egypt

Islamic militants shot and killed 18 Greek tourists outside their hotel about 30 km (20 mi) from Cairo. There was some evidence that the terrorists had mistakenly thought that the tourists were Israelis. The attack, like others before it,

A woman grieves by the coffins of those killed in an Israeli artillery attack on southern Lebanon that on April 18 mistakenly hit a UN camp housing refugees. Israel had attacked Lebanon in retaliation for shellings of northern Israel by Hezbollah guerrillas.

was an attempt to cause turmoil in Egypt and destabilize the pro-Western government of Pres. Hosni Mubarak. The Muslim Brotherhood, tolerated but officially banned, called the murders "a disgrace to humanity." The police later rounded up 1,500 Islamic fundamentalists in a sweep through three poor areas of Cairo.

20
Bolivians end strike

A month-long strike came to an end when the Bolivian Workers' Central, which represented most of the country's public-sector workers, reached an agreement with the government. It included a 13% pay raise for teachers and a 9% increase for other workers. The state-employed teachers had walked out on

March 18 to protest their low wages and government plans to privatize some state-owned industries. The teachers were then joined by students, health care personnel, public transportation employees, and workers in the oil industry. On April 2 some 50,000 strikers had created chaos in the streets of La Paz, the capital, by looting stores and hurling sticks of dynamite at police.

21
Italy holds election

For the first time in Italian history, a leftist coalition emerged from parliamentary elections with a plurality of seats in both the Senate and the Chamber of Deputies. The victorious Olive Tree coalition, led by Romano Prodi, included the Democratic Party of the Left (PDS) and the Italian Renewal Party formed by Prime Minister Lamberto Dini. Massimo D'Alema, the popular leader of the PDS, was urged to seek the prime ministership, but he declined. He said he believed that Prodi would be a better choice and would be well received by the electorate, in part because most Italians did not associate him with a political system that they considered corrupt.

22
Eurotunnel reports loss

Sir Alastair Morton, cochairman of the Anglo-French authority that operated the Channel Tunnel (Eurotunnel), reported a loss of $1.4 billion during 1995. Morton said that the tunnel's 225 creditor banks had not yet responded to proposals for restructuring the debt, but he expressed optimism about the future because the tunnel was handling about 45% of the freight and passenger traffic moving across the English Channel.

24
PLO revokes basic policy

Fulfilling a pledge Yasir Arafat had made to Israel at the signing of a second-stage peace accord in September 1995, the Palestine National Council voted 504–54, with 14 abstentions, to rescind clauses in the Palestine Liberation Orga-

nization's (PLO's) charter that called for guerrilla warfare against Israel and the destruction of the Jewish state. Israeli Prime Minister Shimon Peres referred to Arafat, the newly elected president of the Palestine National Authority, as an integral partner in Israel's search for peace. He also characterized the modifications made in the PLO charter as the most important change in ideology in a century.

Chechen leader slain

Secessionists in Russia's autonomous republic of Chechnya confirmed reports that Pres. Dzhokhar Dudayev had been killed three days earlier when his jeep was hit by a rocket fired from a Russian plane. At the time, Dudayev was reportedly using a cellular phone to converse with a Russian negotiator. The phone signal was evidently used to target the rocket. A Russian official later took credit for the "assassination." Dudayev, a former general in the Soviet air force, had led the fight for Chechen independence after being elected president in 1991. His death, some felt, would motivate Chechens to resist the Russian army with renewed determination.

French doctors strike

Three of the four French doctors unions, upset that access to the public health system would be restricted by some of the budget-cutting reforms announced by Prime Minister Alain Juppé, called a protest strike even though they knew the ordinances would take effect after being debated in the National Assembly. When Juppé first unveiled his proposals in 1995, the social security budget deficit was projected to reach $3.3 billion. Subsequent calculations nearly doubled that figure. The government concluded that the only feasible solution was to adopt a managed-care system similar to those now widely used by U.S. health care providers. Under Juppé's plan, patients would have to consult general practitioners before visiting specialists. Records, moreover, would identify those who overused the public health system.

26
Germany cuts welfare

Faced with a budget deficit that was becoming intolerable, German Chancellor Helmut Kohl announced a series of welfare reforms and spending cuts. Earlier in the month he had failed to persuade employers and workers to back his proposals. He continued to argue, however, that Germany's generous welfare system could no longer be financed because of recent downturns in the economy. The plan he presented included a reduction in the "solidarity surcharge" earmarked for the development of former East Germany as well as cuts in such areas as state pensions, benefits accorded certain immigrants, and wages received by workers during long-term illnesses.

27
Pipeline deal sealed

Kazakstan, Oman, and Russia signed an agreement to build a 1,400-km (900-mi) oil and gas pipeline running from western Kazakstan through Russia to the Russian Black Sea port of Novorossiysk. The three nations would hold a 50% interest in the consortium. The other 50% would be owned by eight oil companies. The major participants would be Chevron Corp. with a 15% interest, the Russian oil company Lukoil with 12.5%, and Mobil Corp. with 7.5%. The project, expected to cost at least $1.2 billion, was scheduled for completion in the year 2001.

28
Gunman slays 35

In what was described as the worst massacre in Australian history, a gunman killed 35 people in Port Arthur, Tasmania. The incident occurred at an old colonial prison frequented by tourists. After killing 20 people in a small cafe, he used a semi-automatic rifle to murder 12 more people visiting the prison ruins. He then held three persons hostage in a guest cottage, which he set afire the next morning. The man was captured when he fled the burning building, but the three hostages had burned to death.

MAY 5

1
Shipbuilder goes under

Germany's largest shipbuilder, Bremer Vulkan Verbund AG, initiated bankruptcy proceedings after its creditor banks rejected proposals for restructuring the company's debt. When Bremer Vulkan announced early in the year that it had sustained some $650 million in losses, its executives acknowledged that the state funds the company had received in the early 1990s had been misused. The company's collapse was expected to be most keenly felt in the port cities of Bremen and Bremerhaven.

3
Land mines restricted

During a conference at the United Nations headquarters in Geneva, delegates from around the world debated the use of land mines but did not concur that all land mines should be eliminated immediately. While there was wide agreement that land mines were uncontrollable and inhumane, some insisted that they were still necessary for defense until new technology provided an acceptable alternative. China, India, Russia, and the U.S. were among the nations unwilling to endorse an immediate ban on all land mines.

Charging the government with human rights abuses, citizens march in Guatemala City. On May 6 the U.S. State Department released documents pertaining to alleged human rights abuses by the Guatemalan military.

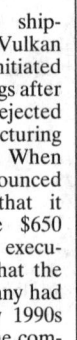
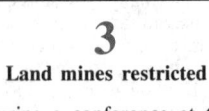

6
Report on Guatemala

The U.S. State Department made public some of its official documents on human rights abuses allegedly perpetrated by the Guatemalan military. A spokesman for the State Department used the occasion to declare that U.S. government officials in Guatemala had had "no reason not to believe" Sister Dianna Ortiz when she reported that she had been kidnapped, raped, and tortured by Guatemalan security forces in 1989. Ortiz had gone on a hunger strike to compel the government to review her case and make public its findings. The newly released documents revealed that the U.S. ambassador had cabled Washington, D.C., at the time to say that he believed that Sister Ortiz's story was a hoax concocted to persuade the U.S. to cut off aid to Guatemala.

7
Sex offenders identified

The U.S. House of Representatives supported (418–0) an amendment to a 1994 federal anticrime bill requiring state officials to notify communities when a convicted sex offender had moved into their area. Two days later the Senate approved the measure by voice vote. On May 17 President Clinton signed the bill into law. Virtually all states had already enacted legislation obliging authorities to keep track of paroled sex offenders, but few laws stipulated that the public was to be notified where such criminals were living.

8
New charter approved

By a vote of 421–2, with 10 abstentions, South Africa's Constitutional Assembly approved a new democratic constitution. Most sections of the new charter would take effect as soon as the Constitutional Court stipulated that the document embodied the principles set forth in the interim charter that had been in force since South Africa's first all-race national election in April 1994. Among many other things, the constitution established a strong presidency, a two-house national legislature, and an independent judiciary. It also guaranteed free speech (so long as it was not "hate speech") and the right to restitution for land seized by the government under apartheid.

9
Canada protects gays

Canada's House of Commons passed (153–76) an amendment to the federal Human Rights Act that prohibited discrimination against homosexuals who worked for the federal government or in institutions regulated by the government. After Prime Minister Jean Chrétien assured fellow members of the ruling Liberal Party that they were free to vote their convictions, 29 rejected the amendment. Impetus for a federal amendment came by way of the Supreme Court of Canada, which in 1995 had affirmed that the Human Rights Act implicitly protected homo-

sexuals against discrimination. The fact that 7 of Canada's 10 provinces had already passed laws forbidding discrimination on the basis of sexual orientation was further evidence that the laws had wide support throughout the country.

•

U.K. military bans gays

The British House of Commons rejected (188–120) a bill that would have revoked laws banning homosexuals from serving in the military. Two days earlier a select committee in the House of Commons had issued a statement supporting a continuation of the ban, saying, "There has to be a balance between the rights of the individual and the needs of the whole." The committee also rejected as impractical the U.S. policy of "don't ask, don't tell" and the German approach, which limited the types of assignments given to homosexuals.

10
Vietnamese refugees riot

In an effort to prevent their forcible repatriation, thousands of Vietnamese refugees in Hong Kong's Whitehead detention camp rioted. Several dozen buildings and more than 50 cars were set ablaze, and 15 or more wardens were briefly taken hostage. During the confusion about 30 detainees were able to elude the police and escaped to freedom. The Hong Kong government had set the repatriation process in motion on orders from China, which demanded that all 18,000 boat people held in Hong Kong camps be sent home before the crown colony reverted to Chinese sovereignty on July 1, 1997.

•

Australia curbs guns

Following the massacre in Tasmania of 35 people in late April, the national, state, and territorial governments of Australia agreed to outlaw the sale and possession of all automatic and semiautomatic weapons. The decision was reached during an emergency meeting called by Prime Minister John Howard, who labeled the new restrictions on guns "a signal to people all around the country that ours is not a gun culture." The opposition Labor Party also voiced its approval of the legislation, but some 70,000 disgruntled gun owners held a protest march in Melbourne on June 1.

11
Museveni wins election

Election officials in Uganda announced that Pres. Yoweri Museveni had won 74.2% of the popular vote in the no-party election held on May 9. It was the first presidential election since the country gained independence from Great Britain in 1962. Paul K. Ssemogerere, Museveni's principal opponent, denounced the election as neither free nor fair. As evidence he cited the restrictions placed on political parties. He also charged that local officials had been bribed and voters intimidated by government-instigated violence. Even though political parties as such could not raise money, hold meetings, or conduct campaigns, outside observers were generally restrained in their criticism of the government, which had fostered a free-market economy with favourable results.

15
Chirac cajoles U.K.

During an address to a joint session of the British Parliament, French Pres. Jacques Chirac encouraged the nation's leaders to be more positive in evaluating the benefits that would accrue to the nation if they gave whole-hearted support to a tightly integrated European Union (EU). Reassuring those who claimed that Britain's sovereignty had already been violated by the EU ban on exporting beef that might be contaminated by "mad cow" disease, Chirac pledged that Britain's voice would be heard loud and clear once the nation had committed itself fully to a strongly united economic and monetary union. In a private meeting, Chirac and British Prime Minister John Major discussed the Channel Tunnel's (Eurotunnel's) financial problems and a proposal to form a joint arms-purchasing agency with Germany. Several days earlier France's Matra Hachette SA and British Aerospace PLC had agreed to merge to form Europe's largest manufacturer of guided weapons.

18
Prodi assumes office

The centre-left Olive Tree coalition took over the reins of government in Italy with the swearing in of Prime Minister Romano Prodi, a member of the Popular Party. His 20-member Cabinet included 9 members of the Party of the Democratic Front (PDS), which represented the largest group within the coalition. The PDS, however, was not given several influential posts that it had hoped to fill. Two former prime ministers were awarded Cabinet portfolios: Lamberto Dini, Prodi's predecessor and a member of the Italian Renewal Party, was appointed foreign minister, and Carlo Azeglio Ciampi, an independent, was named head of the Treasury and Budget ministries.

•

Demirel escapes attack

A man identified as a Muslim extremist was tackled by bodyguards as he was about to fire a handgun at Turkish Pres. Suleyman Demirel. The incident occurred during a ceremony for the opening of a shopping mall in the town of Izmit. The gunman was apparently one of many Turkish Muslims who were incensed at the government for allowing Israeli military aircraft to conduct maneuvers in Turkish airspace. Demirel had also incurred the wrath of Muslims by refusing to transform Turkey into an Islamic state.

20
Iraq accepts oil deal

After repeatedly refusing to allow the UN to dictate the terms under which Iraq could export oil to finance the purchase of urgently needed food and medicine, Iraqi Pres. Saddam Hussein endorsed UN Security Council Resolution 986. It permitted Iraq to sell $2 billion worth of oil during an initial six-month period. During that time UN officials would carefully monitor the oil flow and verify that the food and medicine that had been purchased were reaching those most in need. One-third of the oil revenues would be deposited in an account to reimburse those who had been victimized during Iraq's invasion of Kuwait in 1990. At least $130 million worth of supplies would be earmarked for Kurds living in the northern part of the country. If the UN was satisfied with the way things were proceeding, Iraq would be allowed to sell $1 billion worth of oil during successive three-month periods.

22
Hackers worry Pentagon

Computer experts at the U.S. General Accounting Office (GAO) reported that hackers had attempted to invade computer files at the Defense Department about 250,000 times during 1995. About 65% of those attempts, principally using the Internet, had been successful. The GAO called attention to the potential for "catastrophic damage" unless the situation was seriously addressed and remedied. Jack L. Brock, Jr., who headed the investigation, warned that inadequate security opened the door for terrorists or enemy nations to wreak havoc with Pentagon communications.

23
UNHCR reports on CIS

The United Nations High Commissioner for Refugees (UNHCR) issued a report on the migration of peoples who had been Soviet citizens before the breakup of the U.S.S.R. in 1991. An estimated 50 million–60 million people suddenly found themselves living outside their native republics in newly independent nations. The UNHCR described the situation in these new countries as "the largest, most complex, and potentially most destabilizing" phenomenon in Europe since the end of World War II. This was true despite the fact that the former Soviet republics had agreed to join together in a loose association called the Commonwealth of Independent States (CIS). During a meeting in Geneva at the end of May, representatives of some 80 countries discussed problems that had been created by forced migration within the CIS. A nonbinding program was approved urging each CIS nation to grant citizenship rights to former Soviet citizens living within its borders and to take steps to protect the rights of minority peoples.

24
SLORC tightens its grip

News sources reported that Myanmar's (Burma's) ruling State Law and Order Restoration Council (SLORC) had arrested more than 250 members of the National League for Democracy (NLD) in an effort to disrupt its scheduled party conference at the home of its leader, Daw Aung San Suu Kyi. Undeterred by the fact that she had been under house arrest until July 1995, Suu Kyi began the conference on May 26, the sixth anniversary of the landmark 1990 national election. Only 18 delegates were allowed to attend the conference, but some 10,000 others gathered outside her home in a show of support. The NLD's agenda included the drafting of a new constitution, which would invalidate SLORC's seizure of power after the military declared the NLD's overwhelming election victory in 1990 null and void.

25
King visits homeland

Responding to an invitation from a group of Bulgarian intellectuals wishing to discuss the future of their country, King Simeon II visited his homeland in the company of his wife. He was welcomed in Sofia, the capital, by an estimated half a million people, even though fewer than 20% of Bulgarians said that they would like to see the monarchy restored. Simeon was six years old when he ascended the throne in 1943 upon the death of his father. He had not lived in Bulgaria since 1946, when he and his mother fled the country to escape the Soviet army. Simeon, who had never abdicated the throne, made his living in Spain as a business consultant. Bulgaria's socialist government characterized the king's visit as an attempt to revive fascism.

26
Albania holds election

In a national election held to decide representation in Albania's People's Assembly, the Democratic Party of Albania (DPA) of Pres.

Daw Aung San Suu Kyi speaks to supporters of her National League for Democracy from her home in Yangon (Rangoon), Myanmar (Burma). It was reported on May 24 that the government had arrested more than 250 members of the NLD in an effort to disrupt a party conference.

IRENE SLEAT—PANOS

Sali Berisha won 95 of the 115 seats filled by direct election. The results were generally welcomed by U.S. and Western European leaders because Pres. Berisha had enhanced stability in the Balkan region by persuading the large minority of Albanians who were living in Yugoslavia to soften their demand for autonomy. Nonetheless, the Organization for Security and Cooperation in Europe did not hesitate to confirm the truth of charges leveled by Berisha's political foes that ballots had been altered by DPA supporters and that voters had been intimidated by armed men who invaded polling places.

27
African mutiny quelled

French troops stationed in the Central African Republic were finally able to quell an uprising by mutinous soldiers. On May 18 rebellious soldiers had surrounded the presidential palace to give teeth to their demand for back pay. They also wanted to take back control of the national armoury from presidential guards who had been assigned that duty after the uprising on April 18. France helped resolve the latest crisis by providing back pay to soldiers as well as to teachers and civil servants who had gone on strike to demand their own overdue wages. In 1993 Ange-Félix Patassé had won the country's first multiparty presidential election, but many inside and outside the country considered him an incompetent and corrupt leader.

28
McDougals, Tucker guilty

James and Susan McDougal and Arkansas Gov. Jim Guy Tucker were found guilty of fraud and conspiracy by a federal jury in Little Rock, Ark. All had previously been associated with President Clinton and his wife in business deals connected with the Whitewater affair. The defendants were convicted of having arranged fraudulent loads amounting to some $3 million through Capital Management Services and Madison Guaranty Savings and Loan, a now-defunct institution in Arkansas that James Mc-

Dougal had owned. Federal insurance carried by the two institutions allowed the losses to be repaid with tax revenues. James McDougal was convicted on 18 of the 19 counts against him. Susan McDougal, his ex-wife, was convicted on four counts and Tucker on two. All convicted said they would appeal the verdicts.

•

Bulgaria gets IMF loan

After satisfying itself that Bulgaria would adhere to the terms of an agreement designed to put the country on the road to economic recovery, the International Monetary Fund (IMF) authorized a $400 million standby loan. Among other things, Prime Minister Zhan Videnov agreed to shut down 64 unprofitable state-owned enterprises and to reform the banking system, which was responsible for millions of dollars in bad loans. Videnov's Socialist Party had made only a token effort to adopt a free-market economy, but drastic changes were mandated under IMF guidelines. Tens of thousands of workers were expected to lose their jobs if broad reforms were instituted.

•

Ukraine leader replaced

Leonid Kuchma used his authority as president of Ukraine to name Pavlo Lazarenko prime minister. Before his promotion, he had been first deputy prime minister. Yevhen Marchuk had been removed as prime minister the previous day for "using all his energy to promote his own political image." Marchuk was viewed by many as a politician positioning himself for a run at the presidency in 1999.

29
Netanyahu defeats Peres

In a general election closely followed around the world, Benjamin Netanyahu, chairman of the Likud bloc, defeated Israeli Prime Minister Shimon Peres by the narrowest of margins. Official tallies showed that Netanyahu had captured 50.4% of the vote. Throughout the campaign his recurrent theme had been national security first and foremost. Analysts, accordingly, interpreted the election results as evidence that Israelis were more concerned about security than about an Arab-

Israeli peace accord. In separate balloting for the 120-seat Knesset (parliament), both the ruling Labor Party and Likud lost seats. As a consequence, small parties were expected to have a larger voice in government than their absolute numbers warranted.

30
GM chooses Thailand

After surveying various sites in Southeast Asia and evaluating the advantages that each offered, the General Motors Corp. (GM) announced that it would build a major automobile assembly plant in Thailand. Smaller GM factories were already operating in India, Indonesia, and Taiwan. The company, which was the world's largest manufacturer of cars, reportedly hoped that its new $750 million facility in Thailand would eventually help double its share of the Asian market, which currently stood at 5%. Thailand reportedly had supported its bid by offering to build a $15 million automobile training centre on the condition that employees of other automobile companies would be allowed to train there.

A French soldier patrols a street in Bangui, Central African Republic. On May 27 French troops helped put down an uprising in the country.

A supporter of Benjamin Netanyahu's candidacy for prime minister of Israel raises a campaign poster in celebration of his victory on May 29. Netanyahu, head of the Likud bloc, defeated Shimon Peres with just over 50% of the votes.

JUNE

1

Gowda to lead India

With the swearing in of H.D. Deve Gowda as prime minister, India came under the rule of a new government. The 13-party United Front coalition, which included leftist and regional parties, was able to survive a confidence vote on June 12 when the Congress (I) Party decided to support the Front without joining the coalition. Congress officials, however, had first demanded that the new government continue to pursue the free-market reforms that had been initiated by former prime minister P.V. Narasimha Rao. Gowda had no hesitation in making that pledge because he had earlier introduced similar policies in his home state of Karnataka. For the first time since India gained independence in 1947, the Cabinet was not dominated by Brahmins; most members, like Gowda himself, came from lower castes.

4

Bahrain jails suspects

The interior minister of Bahrain announced that 34 of the 44 persons arrested on June 3–4 had confessed to having conspired to overthrow the monarchy that ruled the tiny Persian Gulf emirate. On June 5 six men appeared on television and pleaded guilty to the charges against them. One said that he had worked with an Iranian official who reported directly to Ayatollah Ali Khamenei, Iran's highest authority. These statements and alleged evidence that the Bahraini suspects had received terrorist training in both Iran and at bases run by the Hezbollah Party in Lebanon prompted Bahrain to downgrade its diplomatic relations with Iran. Iran denied any involvement in the alleged plot, which was purportedly aimed at establishing a Shi'ite Muslim regime favourable to Iran.

5

Medicare facing crisis

The six trustees overseeing the U.S. Medicare Hospital Insurance Trust Fund reported that the fund would run a $53 billion deficit by the year 2001 unless changes were made in the program. Their study focused on Part A of Medicare, which relied primarily on payroll deductions to cover the cost of hospital stays. Part B, which paid for visits to doctors' offices and certain other medical expenditures, was not an immediate financial concern. Secretary of the Treasury Robert Rubin, one of the trustees, said that a short-term solution could be implemented immediately by cutting spending by $116 billion over six years. Such a step, he contended, would keep the program solvent until the year 2006. Those who reported on government affairs generally agreed that the Republican and Democratic members of Congress would resolve the problem through compromise, but not before the presidential election in November because neither party wanted to anger elderly voters by proposing cuts in their Medicare benefits.

10

Peace plan for Chechnya

A new accord aimed at ending the conflict between Chechen secessionists and the Russian government was signed by the Chechen chief of staff and the Russian nationalities minister. Under the terms of the agreement, elections in Chechnya would be postponed until September, after all Russian troops had been withdrawn from the area. The accord also called for the removal of roadblocks by July 7 and the disarmament of Chechen soldiers by August 7. Both sides also agreed that armament would not be used in battle. Previous ceasefire violations and recent skirmishes tempered expectations that the civil conflict had actually come to an end.

12

Church fires condemned

Speaking at the dedication of a new sanctuary at the Mt. Zion African Methodist Episcopal Church in Greeleyville, S.C., President Clinton condemned the recent burning of numerous churches, mostly in the South and with predominantly African-American congregations. During the previous 18 months, more than 30 churches had been destroyed or badly damaged. In most cases arson was suspected. Authorities, unaware of any evidence indicating the existence of a national or regional conspiracy, were inclined to conclude that some of the fires had been set by copycats.

•

Election in Bangladesh

In national parliamentary elections, the opposition Awami League, led by Sheikh Hasina Wazed, defeated the ruling Bangladesh Nationalist Party (BNP) by capturing 146 seats; the BNP won 116. Because its representation in Parliament was short of an absolute majority, the Awami League invited the Jatiya Party, which finished third in the election with 32 seats, to join a coalition government. Its leader, former president Hossain Mohammed Ershad, was released from prison so he could occupy the seat he had won in the election. On June 23 Sheikh Hasina, who had played a major role in toppling Ershad's military government in 1990, took the oath of office as prime minister. Her 19-member Cabinet included Abdus Samad Azad, who was given the post of foreign minister. Sheikh Hasina reserved the defense minister post for herself.

13

Racial districts voided

In two 5–4 decisions, the U.S. Supreme Court ruled that the 14th Amendment of the Constitution had been violated in the racial gerrymandering of four congressional districts. One case involved a black district in North Carolina; the other, three majority black and Hispanic districts in Texas. The court's majority ruled that race had been too dominant a factor in the drawing of the boundaries of the districts. The justices had earlier declared that the consideration of race to promote the political influence of minorities could be defended only if it passed strict judicial scrutiny, a constitutional standard that required a compelling state interest in redressing specific racial discrimination.

MUFTY MUNIR—AFP

Whitewater Committee issued two reports, one by the majority Republican membership headed by Alfonse D'Amato, the other by the Democrats. At a news conference D'Amato summed up his position, saying, "History will judge these hearings as a revealing insight into the workings of an American presidency that misused its power, circumvented the limits of authority, and attempted to manipulate the truth." The report issued by the Democrats stated in part, "The American people deserve to know, and now can take comfort in knowing, that this yearlong investigation shows no misconduct or abuse of power by their president or first lady." The purpose of the probe was to determine, if possible, the relationship that existed between Bill and Hillary Clinton and the Whitewater Development Corp., a failed real-estate venture in the 1980s.

Holed up on a ranch outside Jordan, Mont., a group calling itself Freemen held off law-enforcement officials for 81 days. The standoff ended peaceably when the last of the Freemen surrendered on June 13.

●

Last Freemen surrender

After an 81-day standoff, the last 16 members of a group known as Freemen surrendered to authorities at a farm near Jordan, Mont. The 390-ha (960-ac) farm had been owned by Richard and Emmett Clark until the government issued a foreclosure notice in 1995 for nonpayment of taxes. The Freemen were bound together by their opposition to taxation and government interference in their lives. A crisis developed when two leaders of the Freemen were arrested on March 25 and charged with fraud and intimidation. In subsequent indictments the Freemen were accused of having defrauded banks, credit-card companies, and mail-order businesses of nearly $2 million. This was done by means of false checks and money orders. Many farmers in the area who had been sympathetic to the Freemen later criticized federal agents for not having used more aggressive tactics to end the stalemate sooner.

15

German workers protest

An estimated 350,000 workers held a rally in Bonn to protest the deep budget cuts that had been announced in April by German Chancellor Helmut Kohl. The leaders of the country's largest labour unions had organized the demonstration in part because the government had announced the austerity measures without first reaching a negotiated compromise with the unions. In addition, the labour leaders contended that workers were being forced to bear the burden of the cuts while wealthy corporations were left comparatively unscathed. Kohl's plan called for a $33 billion reduction in pensions, in payments during sick leave, and in other social programs. He had made the decision to implement the changes, he said, because Germany's entry into the European Union was contingent on major reductions in the nation's deficit.

17

U.K. revamps divorce laws

The British Parliament gave overwhelming approval (427–9) to basic reforms in the nation's divorce laws. Beginning in 1999, the termination of all marriages would be so-called no-fault divorces granted solely on the grounds that the marriage had "irretrievably broken down." As a consequence, specific failings such as infidelity or alcoholism would no longer of themselves be considered justifiable grounds for granting a divorce. Moreover, divorces could not be initiated in the first year of marriage, and no divorce would be finalized until one year after the couple had separated. If children were involved, the waiting period would be 18 months or longer if suitable arrangements had not been made for their financial support.

●

ValuJet planes grounded

The U.S. Federal Aviation Administration (FAA) told ValuJet Airlines to ground its entire fleet. An intensive investigation of the low-cost airline had been ordered after one of its planes crashed in Florida in May. All 110 persons aboard were killed. At the time, David Hinson, head of the FAA, and Federico Peña, secretary of transportation, contended that ValuJet was a safe carrier. On June 19, however, Hinson acknowledged that repairs on ValuJet aircraft had not been properly done, that repairs had not been documented, that planes with maintenance safety problems had taken off, and that FAA safety directives had been disregarded.

18

Report on Whitewater

After a 13-month investigation, the special U.S. Senate

Yeltsin promotes Lebed

Two days after winning a slim plurality of votes in the first round of Russia's presidential election, Boris Yeltsin appointed retired general Aleksandr Lebed to two high-level Kremlin posts. The former paratrooper had finished third in the voting. Former Soviet president Mikhail Gorbachev received only 0.5%. On June 17 Yeltsin had delivered a televised address during which he appealed to followers of Lebed and two other defeated candidates to support him in the runoff election against Gennady Zyuganov, leader of the Communist Party, so that the nation would not "return to revolutions" but "move forward toward stability and prosperity."

Aleksandr Lebed stands ready to answer questions at a news conference after being appointed by Russian Pres. Boris Yeltsin on June 18 to be his national security adviser and secretary of the Security Council. The retired general had come in third in the first round of the Russian presidential elections.

JUNE

U.S. servicemen view the ruins of a building near Az-Zahran, Saudi Arabia—which had been used as a residence for U.S. troops—after it was bombed on June 25. The explosion, set off by terrorists, killed 19 U.S. servicemen and wounded hundreds of other people.

Ulmanis wins reelection

In secret balloting, members of Latvia's Saeima (parliament) granted Pres. Guntis Ulmanis another three-year term. Prime Minister Andris Skele and the members of several political parties had made public declarations supporting Ulmanis's reelection. Ilga Kreituse, who held the post of chairwoman of Saeima, finished second in the voting with 25 votes, less than half the number received by Ulmanis. Five parliamentarians cast votes for Alfreds Rubiks, the imprisoned candidate of the Latvian Communist Party.

21
FBI files misused

Kenneth Starr, an independent counsel investigating firings in the White House travel office, received expanded authority from a federal appeals court in Washington, D.C., to investigate the White House acquisition of hundreds of confidential files maintained by the FBI. Louis Freeh, director of the FBI, said that his agency had been victimized by the White House and that both the FBI and the White House were guilty of "egregious violations of privacy." He promised that no such thing would ever happen again while he headed the FBI. President Clinton claimed that the improper acquisition of the files was due to a bureaucratic mix-up. The initial request for the files had been made on a form letter bearing the name of Bernard Nussbaum, then White House counsel. On June 5 Nussbaum denied under oath that he had ever authorized the sending of the letter.

23
Arab League warns Israel

All 20 attending members of the Arab League—Iraq was not invited—concluded a two-day emergency meeting in Cairo with a warning to the new government in Israel that any attempt to stall or renege on agreements reached by the previous government would compel the Arab world to reevaluate the Middle East peace process. Yasir Arafat, president of the Palestine National

AFP PHOTO

Authority, also attended the meeting and played a prominent role in the discussions. Israeli Prime Minister Benjamin Netanyahu dismissed out of hand Arab demands that included, among other things, Israeli withdrawal from all occupied Arab lands and the establishment of a Palestinian state in Gaza, the West Bank, and East Jerusalem.

25
Bomb kills U.S. soldiers

A massive truck-bomb explosion killed 19 U.S. servicemen stationed near the Saudi Arabian city of Az-Zahran. Several hundred other persons were injured. The bomb, apparently detonated by terrorists, left a 10.5-m (35-ft) crater on the perimeter of the military complex, where U.S., British, French, and Saudi military personnel were housed. Night guards at the complex became suspicious when a fuel truck pulled alongside the perimeter fence, which was just 32 m (35 yd) from the eight-story building. Before they could reach the vehicle, the driver jumped into a waiting car and was spirited away. Worried that such an attack might take place, the U.S. had petitioned Saudi authorities to move the fence farther away from the men's living quarters, but the request was denied. In October 1983, 241 servicemen had been

killed in Beirut, Lebanon, by a Shi'ite Muslim suicide bomber.

26
Court rules against VMI

The U.S. Supreme Court ruled (7–1) that the Virginia Military Institute (VMI), which was funded by the state of Virginia, violated the 14th Amendment of the Constitution by refusing to accept female cadets. Unless it became private and received no funds from the state, VMI would have to end its 157-year-old tradition of training only males. The head of VMI called the ruling a "savage disappointment," especially since an alternative program had been set up for females at Mary Baldwin College, Staunton, Va. The court, however, concluded not only that the military education provided at Baldwin fell far short of that at VMI but that the state had not met the legal requirement of providing an "exceedingly persuasive justification" for excluding females.

27
Rape termed war crime

The United Nations International Criminal Tribunal in The Hague indicted eight Bosnian Serb soldiers and policemen on charges of rape. It was the first time that rape had been offi-

cially identified as a war crime. According to people in the area, thousands of rapes had taken place during the war in Bosnia and Herzegovina as part of a campaign to brutalize and terrorize the population. The cases presented to the tribunal involved 14 Muslim women who allegedly had been beaten and gang-raped by Bosnian Serbs in the town of Foca in 1992 and 1993.

Gay marriages legalized

Iceland's unicameral Althing (parliament) passed legislation legalizing civil marriages, but not church weddings, between homosexuals. The law allowed joint custody of existing children but did not permit gay couples to adopt children or attempt to have children through artificial insemination.

Klaus forms new coalition

Vaclav Klaus, prime minister of the Czech Republic and leader of the Civic Democratic Party (ODS), heeded the request of Pres. Vaclav Havel and formed a minority government. Because the coalition government he headed had failed to win a majority in the May and June parliamentary elections, Klaus sought a new partner. The Social Democratic Party (CSSD) agreed to become a junior partner in a coalition government on the condition that no further steps would be taken to privatize the energy and transportation sectors of the economy. Milos Zeman, leader of the CSSD, became leader of Parliament.

28

New Ukrainian charter

At the urging of Pres. Leonid Kuchma, Ukraine's national legislature approved a new constitution. It was the nation's first new charter since it became independent of the Soviet Union in 1991. Although strong opposition was voiced by members of the Communist Party, the largest bloc in the legislature, the vote comfortably exceeded the two-thirds majority needed for ratification. Among other things, the new constitution confirmed the right to private property and free enterprise. It also declared that Ukrainian was the nation's only official language, even though about 22% of the population con-

sidered Russian to be their first language.

29

Grímsson wins presidency

By capturing a plurality of 41% of the popular vote, Ólafur Ragnar Grímsson easily defeated Pétur Hafstein in a race for the presidency of Iceland. Grímsson replaced Vigdís Finnbogadóttir, who had been exceptionally popular during her 16 years in office. Despite his victory, Grímsson was considered by some to be a left-wing extremist because he opposed Iceland's membership in NATO and questioned the nation's close ties to the U.S. By contrast, Hafstein, a Supreme Court judge, generally supported right-wing policies.

30

Mongolia's MPRP ousted

In a dramatic reversal of the 1992 parliamentary elec-

tions, the Mongolian People's Revolutionary Party (MPRP) was soundly defeated by the Democratic Union Coalition (DUC). Official results released by the election committee gave the MPRP only 25 seats in the Great Hural, a net loss of 45. The DUC—which included the National Democratic Party, the Social Democratic Party, and two smaller parties—had called for political reforms and faster implementation of more liberal economic policies. Before the election, there was a general consensus that the coalition could claim a moral victory if it managed to win one-third of the seats, which was sufficient to veto legislation. Shortly after the election, Mendsaihan Enhsaihan was named prime minister.

•

Fernández wins election

In a runoff election for the presidency of the Dominican Republic, Leonel Fernández

Renya of the Dominican Liberation Party defeated José Francisco Peña Gómez by garnering more than 51% of the popular vote. He was scheduled to formally replace 89-year-old Joaquín Balaguer, who had served seven nonconsecutive terms beginning in 1960, on August 16. Unlike past elections, which had often been marred by flagrant fraud, this election was praised for its integrity. During the campaign Fernández had welcomed the support of the National Patriotic Front, which had been formed by Balaguer and his longtime political rival Juan Bosch to undermine support for Peña. Fernández assured the electorate that he had not compromised his integrity by making any promises in exchange for such support. Peña, who was of Haitian descent, called the alliance racist, saying that it had been formed "to stop a man because of his colour, and because he is the son of the poorest sector of the country."

ROBERTO SCHMIDT—AFP

In line behind a pole wrapped with election posters, voters wait to cast their ballots in the Dominican Republic's presidential runoff election on June 30. Leonel Fernández Reyna of the Dominican Liberation Party won just over 51% of the votes.

2

Lockheed to build X-33

U.S. Vice Pres. Al Gore announced in California that Lockheed Martin Corp. had been awarded the contract to design and build the prototype of a new-generation reusable rocket ship designated X-33. The goal of the project was to replace the NASA space shuttle with one that was privately owned and operated. NASA would then be free to concentrate on research and development. Daniel Goldin, head of NASA, explained that NASA and Lockheed would work together "to build a vehicle that takes days, not months, to turn around; dozens, not thousands, of people to operate; reliability 10 times better than anything flying today; and launch costs that are a tenth of what they are now." Before making its final decision, NASA had carefully reviewed the contract bids submitted by Rockwell International Corp. and McDonnell Douglas Corp.

3

Yeltsin wins reelection

In a runoff election for the presidency of Russia, incumbent Boris Yeltsin defeated Gennady Zyuganov, candidate of the Communist Party, by winning 53.8% of the popular vote. About 5% of the electorate cast ballots indicating that they rejected both candidates. Outside observers, who viewed the election as a critical moment in modern Russian history, declared that the process had been free and fair. They read the results as an endorsement of democratic reforms and a free-market economy and a rejection of the political philosophy preached by the communists and their political allies. On July 4 Yeltsin announced that he would renominate Viktor Chernomyrdin for the post of prime minister.

7

Bucaram defeats Nebot

Boris Yeltsin campaigns in Kazan, Tatarstan. Yeltsin won reelection as president of Russia over the Communist Party candidate, Gennady Zyuganov, in a runoff on July 3.

In Ecuador, even before the official results had been announced, Jaime Nebot Saadi, candidate of the Social Christian Party, publicly congratulated Abdalá Bucaram Ortíz of the Ecuadorian Roldosist Party on winning the country's runoff presidential election. Bucaram had finished second to Nebot in the first round of voting, but he managed to garner about 54% of the final ballots by appealing to the indigenous population and the smaller political parties that represented their interests. Nebot was generally favoured by the business community, which was concerned that Bucaram would abandon the free-market reforms begun by incumbent Pres. Sixto Durán Ballén. Bucaram, however, reassured businessmen that as president he would promote private industry and encourage foreign investment.

9

Mandela visits Europe

South African Pres. Nelson Mandela arrived in London, where he was honoured with a military parade and a state banquet for which Queen Elizabeth II served as host. Two days later he became the first foreign leader since Charles de Gaulle in 1960 to address a joint session of Parliament at Westminster Hall. He used the occasion to call for an increase in aid to the nations of Africa and an end to racism. Before departing for France, Mandela visited with Prime Minister John Major, former prime minister Margaret Thatcher, and other prominent politicians and businesspeople. He also received eight honorary degrees at a ceremony held in Buckingham Palace and traveled to Brixton, a district in London that was predominantly black, where crowds numbering in the thousands greeted him enthusiastically. In France, Mandela attended the annual Bastille Day military parade as a guest of honour of Pres. Jacques Chirac.

•

Prudential to pay fine

Insurance regulators from 30 states and the District of

Columbia concluded, after a 14-month investigation of Prudential Insurance Company of America, that senior executives had known that its agents had given clients misleading information about the cost of their insurance premiums and that they did nothing to halt the nationwide practice. The company agreed to pay $35.3 million in fines and reimbursements, the largest settlement in the industry's history, even though the regulators had no legal power to enforce their finding of guilt. Prudential executives also declared that they would seek to settle outstanding claims in states that had not been represented.

11
Poland joins OECD

The Organisation for Economic Co-operation and Development welcomed Poland as its 28th member. It was the third former communist state to join the research group, which studied economic conditions in industrialized nations. On March 29 Hungary had been admitted to the Paris-based organization, its membership having been contingent on compliance with conditions laid down by the International Monetary Fund to justify giving Hungary a standby loan of $387 million.

12
Italy to try ex-leaders

An Italian judge in Milan ruled that Silvio Berlusconi and Bettino Craxi, both former prime ministers, would have to stand trial on charges related to illegal funding of political parties. Several executives of Fininvest SpA, a media conglomerate controlled by Berlusconi, were among 10 others facing prosecution. Craxi's Socialist Party was said to have received $6.5 million in 1991 from Fininvest, which funneled the money through a company to which it was linked. In a separate trial, Berlusconi faced charges of having used Fininvest money to bribe tax officials.

•

House passes marriage law

By a vote of 342–67, the U.S. House of Representatives passed the Defense of Marriage Act, which barred federal recognition of same-sex marriages and gave each state the right not to recognize such unions, even if they were legal in another state. President Clinton had earlier declared his intention to sign such legislation if it passed both houses of Congress because he accepted the traditional view of marriage as the union of one man and one woman. Congress believed that such legislation was needed because the legalization of homosexual marriages was being debated in Hawaii and the U.S. Constitution required states to give "full faith and credit" to the public acts and records, including marriages, of other states.

16
Bosnians to get U.S. arms

Representatives of the government of Bosnia and Herzegovina, of the Muslim-Croat federation, and of the U.S. signed an agreement that allowed the joint Muslim-Croat army to receive $360 million worth of military equipment. The ordnance included tanks, helicopters, armoured personnel carriers, and radio telephones. The U.S. had offered to finance $100 million of the total cost; the rest would be covered by contributions from other countries. The purpose of the shipment was to establish a military balance between the Bosnian Serbs and the Muslim-Croat federation. The delivery of the arms, however, was contingent on the departure of all Iranian troops from the area and the maintenance of a joint Muslim-Croat army. All of the ordnance was expected to arrive in the area before the end of the year because NATO's mandate in Bosnia and Herzegovina was due to expire at that time.

•

Canberra cuts ABC funds

Australian Communications Minister Richard Alston announced that the budget of the Australian Broadcasting Corporation (ABC) would be cut 10% in the 1996–97 fiscal year. ABC, the nation's publicly funded television and radio service, would also be obliged to adhere more closely to its traditional programming, which focused on news, current affairs, and programs for children. Employees, fearing layoffs, staged a protest strike that disrupted transmission for nearly 24 hours.

17
TWA flight 800 crashes

Some 30 minutes after taking off from New York City's Kennedy International Airport, Trans World Airlines (TWA) flight 800 crashed into the Atlantic Ocean. Eyewitnesses reported seeing two explosions before the 747 jetliner plummeted in flames into the sea. All 230 persons aboard the aircraft were killed. Federal aviation officials were reportedly considering three possible

explanations for the crash: a mechanical failure, a bomb, or a surface-to-air missile. With most of the wreckage resting on the ocean floor, no one could predict how long it would take to recover the remains of the victims. It would take even longer to transport the shattered plane to the surface and reassemble it so that experts might then determine the cause of the crash.

•

500,000 Israelis strike

Responding to a call made by the leaders of Histadrut, a trade union federation, an estimated 500,000 Israeli workers took part in a 10-hour general strike to protest broad budget cuts proposed by Prime Minister Benjamin Netanyahu and his Likud-led coalition government. The strike shut down the Tel Aviv Stock Exchange, banks, factories, and public utilities. It also slowed operations at the country's airports, post offices, government agencies, and hospitals. The workers threatened further disruptions if the government carried out its plan to raise bus fares, increase the cost of health care and education, and cut back child care allowances and pensions. These and similar cuts, they contended, would place an unjustified burden on the poor and on the middle class.

18
ASEAN policy challenged

After opening its week-long annual meeting in Jakarta, Indon., the seven members of the Association of Southeast Asian Nations (ASEAN) granted Myanmar (Burma) observer status and accepted membership applications from Cambodia and Laos. During the same week, the ASEAN Regional Forum meeting was held and was attended by invited representatives from China, the European Union (EU), India, Japan, Russia, South Korea, and the U.S. Clearly upset over ASEAN's overtures to Myanmar, the EU and the U.S. especially were insistent that ASEAN put pressure on the military leaders of Myanmar to negotiate with pro-democracy leader Daw Aung San Suu Kyi and accept the fact that her National League

for Democracy had won the 1990 parliamentary election. Warren Christopher, the U.S. secretary of state, warned the delegates that Myanmar's refusal to tolerate political dissent was an open invitation to instability and bloodshed and could cause a flood of refugees.

19

Karadzic forced to quit

After several days of negotiations that involved former U.S. assistant secretary of state Richard Holbrooke and Serbian Pres. Slobodan Milosevic, Radovan Karadzic agreed in writing to resign as chairman of the Serbian Democratic Party and president of the self-styled Bosnian Serb Republic. The Bosnia and Herzegovina peace accord, signed in 1995, stipulated that Karadzic and all other indicted war criminals were to be removed from positions of power and prohibited from running for office in the general election scheduled for mid-September. Even though Karadzic had finally complied with the terms of the peace agreement, there were serious doubts that he would cease exercising de facto control over Bosnian Serb affairs.

21

Prisoners exchanged

After several months of secret negotiations, and with the apparent consent of Iran and Syria, Hezbollah (Party of God) and Israel exchanged several dozen prisoners and the remains of many others who had died in combat or in captivity. Among those not released were two high-ranking Islamic leaders held by Israel and an Israeli airman believed to be held captive by Shi'ite Muslims. The exchange, brokered by a German official, involved more individuals than any other that had taken place in Lebanon during the 13 years of conflict. Syria and Iran were involved behind the scenes because Syria had a major voice in Lebanese affairs and Iran supported the Hezbollah guerrillas.

•

Anpilov loses post

In Russia during a two-day meeting of the Communist

Workers' Party plenum, Viktor Anpilov was ousted as first secretary of the party organization in Moscow. Because he was among the party's most prominent members, he apparently felt no need to consult the membership before publicly endorsing Gennady Zyuganov's bid for the presidency. On August 7 the Communist Party of the Russian Federation and dozens of other left-wing and nationalist political parties founded a new coalition that they called the Popular-Patriotic Union of Russia. Anpilov had not been named to the organizing committee.

23

ETA leader apprehended

In an early-morning raid, French police captured Julian Achurra, one of the top leaders of Homeland and Liberty (ETA), a guerrilla organization seeking to establish an independent state for the Basque population. Achurra, who was apprehended at a farmhouse near the Spanish border, reportedly had arms and explosives in his possession; he was believed to be in charge of arms and logistics for ETA. Authorities said that 18 warrants had been issued for his arrest, all related to terrorist attacks in Spain.

24

Pravda presses silenced

One of the Greek co-owners of *Pravda,* the Russian newspaper of the Communist Party founded by V.I. Lenin in 1912, suspended publication when the owner was denied access to his *Pravda* office. At the height of its popularity, 11 million copies of *Pravda* were sold each day, but more recently circulation had dropped to about 200,-000 as the paper continued to promote a staunchly pro-communist line. The two brothers who owned the paper said that they hoped to resume publication under a new editor in chief.

25

Court upholds amnesty

South Africa's Constitutional Court ruled that the nation's Truth and Reconciliation Commission had the authority to offer amnesty to

Residents of the capital of Burundi, Bujumbura, show their support for Maj. Pierre Buyoya, who was appointed interim president after a military coup on July 25. The Tutsi-controlled army ousted the Hutu president, Sylvestre Ntibantunganya.

those who admitted that they were guilty of abuses during the period of apartheid. At the same time, the court rejected the pleas of the families of slain antiapartheid activists who were demanding that those who had committed crimes be punished. Although some of those charged with crimes pleaded not guilty in court, numerous others, both supporters and political foes of the National Party during the apartheid era, were expected to plead guilty to past human rights abuses and seek amnesty.

•

Burundi coup condemned

The Tutsi-dominated army of Burundi took over control of the country by ousting Pres. Sylvestre Ntibantunganya, a Hutu. The army then appointed Maj. Pierre Buyoya interim president, dissolved the National Assembly, outlawed political parties and demonstrations, sealed the border, and declared a curfew. The coup was vigorously denounced by the United Nations, the Organization of African Unity, the European Union, South Africa, and the United

States. After having seized power in a bloodless coup in 1987, Buyoya supported a democratic election in 1993, which he unexpectedly lost to Melchior Ndadaye, a Hutu. In Burundi, as in neighbouring Rwanda, the Tutsi constituted less than 15% of the population.

•

U.S. pressures Myanmar

Hoping to force the military regime in Myanmar (Burma) to tolerate political dissent and end its support of illegal trafficking in drugs, the U.S. Senate voted to deny visas to officials from Myanmar, except in special circumstances, and to cut back aid to the country. Sen. William Cohen had proposed an additional provision that would have forbidden all U.S. investments in Myanmar. The final version of the amendment, however, did not outlaw investments in Myanmar so long as the military government did not repress or arrest political dissidents. Cohen subsequently accused the Clinton administration of having a "blind moral spot" in its dealings with Myanmar.

Supporters of Megawati Sukarnoputri protest an army raid on her party's headquarters in Jakarta, Indon.

27
Indonesians riot

Thousands of people took to the streets in Jakarta, Indon., to protest an early-morning military raid on the headquarters of the Indonesian Democratic Party (PDI), one of two opposition parties sanctioned by the government. More than a dozen banks and government buildings were destroyed in what observers said was the most serious antigovernment protests since President Suharto seized power from President Sukarno following a bloody upheaval in 1965. At least three persons were killed, hundreds injured, and hundreds of others taken into custody. The riot was directly connected to an event in late June in which the government conspired with a rival of the PDI to oust Megawati Sukarnoputri (Sukarno's daughter) as head of the PDI. About 150 angry PDI members refused to heed an order to vacate the party's headquarters. The July 27 riot began when the military carried out a command to oust them by force.

•

Bomb mars Olympics

One person was killed and 111 injured when a pipe bomb exploded in Centennial Olympic Park during the Summer Olympic Games in Atlanta, Ga. A second person died of a heart attack while racing to the bomb scene. Police immediately began gathering evidence that might lead them to the person who had planted the knapsack that contained the bomb. Stringent security had been the order of the day at most of the Olympic sites, but an exception was made for the park so that the general public could enter the grounds free of charge to enjoy the fountain, picnic, and listen to a music concert.

29
Hashimoto visits Yasukuni

Ignoring anticipated criticism, Japanese Prime Minister Ryutaro Hashimoto paid a visit to Yasukuni Shrine, a cemetery reserved for Japanese war dead and the burial site of seven Japanese executed for war crimes. Because such a visit by the nation's highest government official was seen by many as an implicit endorsement of Japan's past militarism, no prime minister since Yasuhiro Nakasone in 1985 had visited the Shinto shrine. China's foreign minister chided Hashimoto for making a visit that "hurt the feelings of all the people from every country, including China, which suffered under the hands of Japanese militarists." Hashimoto responded to the criticism, saying, "Why should it matter any more? It's time to stop letting that sort of thing complicate our international relations."

•

Free speech on Internet

Three federal judges in New York City ruled that censorship of the Internet computer network would violate the First Amendment of the U.S. Constitution, which guaranteed free speech. The judges, in a unanimous decision, struck down the 1996 Communications Decency Act because it denied consenting adults access to "indecent materials." The intent of the act was to protect children from viewing materials that they could not legally obtain from other sources. The judges agreed with the editor of the *American Reporter* that the act, as presently phrased, was so broadly drawn that it violated constitutionally protected free speech. The judges also pointed out that there was no effective way to block out indecent material transmitted from foreign countries.

Bystanders offer help to people wounded in the explosion of a pipe bomb in Centennial Olympic Park in Atlanta, Ga., on July 27. One person was killed and 111 injured in the explosion.

AUGUST

1

Aydid dies of wounds

The leader of the most powerful clan in strife-torn Somalia, Gen. Muhammad Farah Aydid, died from wounds he had sustained on July 24 in factional fighting. A few days later Hussein Muhammad Aydid, his son, was named his successor. Aydid had been instrumental in overthrowing the president, Gen. Muhammad Siad Barre, in January 1991. When the dictator departed, he left behind a nation facing economic ruin and riven by rival clans vying for political power. In 1992 the UN authorized a humanitarian mission to alleviate mass starvation. The effort was hailed as a major success, but Aydid's forces so bedeviled the UN forces that the Security Council ordered Aydid's arrest, to no avail. In March 1995 the UN finally abandoned its goal of bringing peace to the region and establishing a functioning government.

2

Korean airspace opened

The International Air Transport Association announced that after 16 months of negotiations, North Korea had agreed to grant overflight privileges to international airlines. All parties to the agreement would benefit financially because North Korea would collect overflight dues and airlines would save substantial quantities of fuel by flying more direct routes to certain destinations. Although North and South Korea remained political enemies, South Korean aircraft would also be allowed to fly over North Korean territory after the pact went into effect in December.

4

Summer Olympics end

After 16 days of competition, closing ceremonies for the Summer Olympic Games were held in Atlanta, Ga. Some 10,000 athletes representing 197 Olympic federations had participated in the athletic events. Officials were pleased that for the first time in history, all the invited delegations had attended what was the centenary of the modern Olympic Games. Among many other memorable moments, Josia Thugwane finished just three seconds ahead of Lee Bong Ju of South Korea in the marathon. It was the closest such finish in Olympic history and the first time a black South African had won an Olympic gold medal.

6

Epidemic strikes Japan

Health authorities in Japan announced that the 9,000 cases of food poisoning reported from several regions of the country constituted an epidemic. Medical personnel then began to implement measures to protect the general public. The rare bacterium that caused the outbreak was identified as *E. coli* O157:H7. This caused concern because the infection could cause kidney failure and brain damage even though its visible symptoms (vomiting, fever, diarrhea, cramps) were generally classified as minor. Seven deaths had already been reported. Tainted radishes were thought to be the source of the problem because students in state-run schools in Sakai and residents of a retirement home in Habikino had become sick after eating the suspect radishes provided by the same supplier.

•

NASA assesses meteorite

Daniel Goldin, head of NASA, reported that scientists had made "a startling discovery that points to the possibility that a primitive form of microscopic life may have existed on Mars more than three billion years ago." He noted that the evidence, while compelling, was not conclusive. The 1.9-kg (4.2-lb) meteorite studied by the scientists was the oldest of 12 meteorites found on Earth and identified as having come from Mars. The one being analyzed had been found in Antarctica in 1984. If the meteorite did indeed provide evidence of primitive life, it would be the first direct indication that life had existed beyond Earth. William Schopf, an expert on ancient Earth bacteria, remarked during a news conference that in his opinion it was "unlikely" that the meteorite contained evidence of biological activity.

9
Burundi faces embargo

Zaire formally declared an embargo against its neighbour Burundi. Among all the nations that had committed themselves to such

action during an emergency meeting of the Organization of African Unity on July 31, Zaire was the last to make a public announcement. The aim of the sanctions was to force Maj. Pierre Buyoya, who had been named president after a successful coup on July 25, to restore democracy. Buyoya, a member of the Tutsi clan, had traveled to Uganda and Tanzania in late July to ask for understanding, but his pleas for help were ignored despite repeated assurances that he would restore democracy eventually and make no distinction in his treatment of Tutsi and the rival Hutu.

•

Tobacco firm loses case

After two days of deliberations, a six-member jury in Jacksonville, Fla., ordered Brown & Williamson Tobacco Corp. to pay $750,000 in damages to a man who had developed lung cancer after smoking the company's cigarettes for some 40 years. In only one of numerous earlier cases had a jury decided that a cigarette manufacturer was guilty of marketing a defective product and of not adequately informing the public of the danger of smoking. The jury's verdict in that case had been overturned on appeal.

16
Gorilla rescues child

An eight-year-old female gorilla called Binti Jua astonished attendants at the Brookfield Zoo near Chicago when she rescued a three-year-old boy who had fallen over the guardrail and into the gorilla pit 5 m (18 ft) below. The

gorilla gently picked up the injured boy and carried him to an entrance so that zoo personnel could easily reach him. Zookeepers speculated that Binti Jua's unusual behaviour may have been affected by the care she had received from humans after she was abandoned by her mother shortly after birth. The young ape had later been transferred from the Cincinnati (Ohio) Zoo to one in San Francisco, then to the Brookfield Zoo, where she had continued to be hand reared. Zookeepers believed that it was the rapport Binti Jua had established with humans that caused her to treat the injured boy with apparent tenderness. They also noted that the mother gorilla carried her 17-month-old daughter on her back as she moved slowly to the entrance of the pit.

19
Australians protest cuts

Hundreds of Australian students, workers, and Aborigines, some using sledgehammers and a battering ram, forced their way into the Parliament building in Canberra, the capital. Police battled the protesters for some two hours before order was restored. About 60 people were injured in the melee. The rioters had broken off from a group of 15,000 demonstrators who had taken to the streets to vent their anger over planned budget cuts that Prime Minister John Howard had said were needed to balance the federal budget by fiscal year 1998–99. Before the Liberal Party–National Party coalition government assumed power in March, Howard had pledged not to raise taxes if he was elected. Instead, he proposed to balance the budget by cutting various programs, including some that affected the sick, the elderly, students, employees, and Aborigines. The treasury minister called the cuts "balanced, strong, and fair." Others called them draconian.

20
India vetoes treaty

During a UN-sponsored conference on disarmament in Switzerland, India vetoed a draft of the Comprehensive Test Ban Treaty, which out-

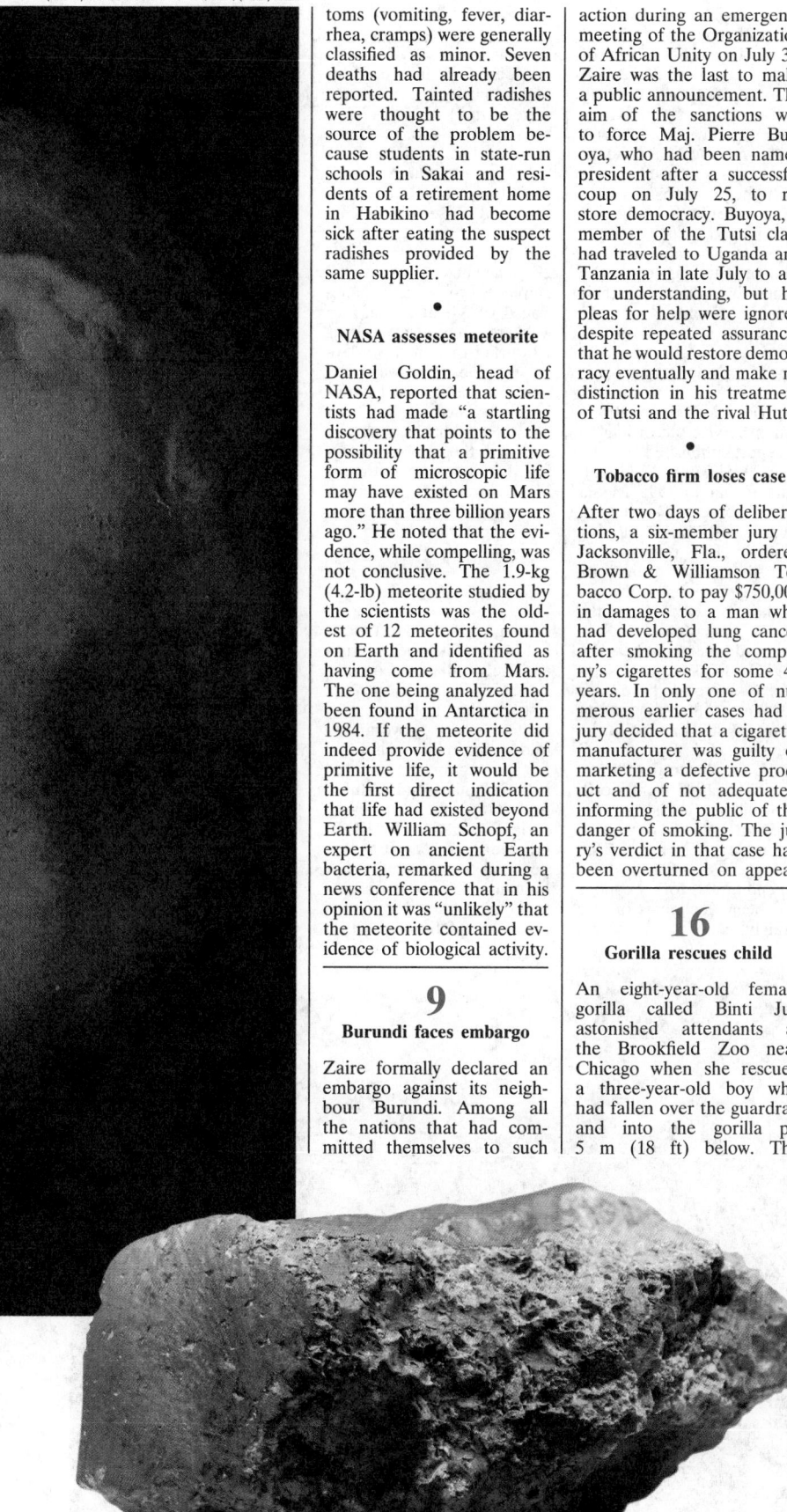

This mosaic of Mars, made up of 102 images of the planet taken by the Viking Orbiter, shows the 2,000-km (1,243-mi)-long Valles Marineris canyon system. NASA officials announced on August 6 that analysis of a meteorite (inset) discovered in Antarctica in 1984 and believed to have come from Mars showed fossil evidence of primitive life, but other scientists questioned their conclusions.

lawed all testing of nuclear weapons. China, France, the U.K., Russia, and the U.S.—the five nations that admitted possessing nuclear weapons—had already endorsed the treaty. India, however, was able to effectively kill the treaty because there was an understanding that the treaty would not take effect unless 44 specified nations (which included India) signed it. The list included Israel and Pakistan, both of which were believed capable of producing nuclear weapons. Pakistan had expressed no reservations about the treaty itself but announced that it would not be party to the arms treaty so long as India refused to add its name to the list of signatories.

Students riot in Seoul

South Korean police finally ended a violent student protest that began on August 12 at Yonsei University in Seoul, the nation's capital. After thousands of police surrounded two university buildings occupied by some 1,500 students, police in riot gear stormed one of the buildings. Students then evacuated the other building, aware that they could not resist such force. Before the confrontation ended, however, more than 1,000 students and police sustained injuries. The ultimate goal of

the students was reunification with communist North Korea. For achievement of that goal, they demanded that the U.S. withdraw all its troops from South Korea and negotiate a bilateral treaty with the North. South Korea was to have no role in the negotiations. The positions taken by the students were judged by most people to be so extreme that few thought anything could be gained by addressing their demands directly.

Russia leads arms sales

The U.S. Congressional Research Service, according to a report published in the *New York Times,* had calculated that in 1995 Russia led all other countries in arms sales to developing nations. (For purposes of the study, the term "developing nations" included all nations except Australia, Japan, New Zealand, Russia, and the members of NATO.) Russian arms sales were estimated to have been worth about $6 billion, more than 60% higher than in the previous year. By comparison, U.S. sales to developing nations in 1995 were worth $3.8 billion. Although developing nations accounted for more than half of all recent arms purchases, their expenditures for weapons had been declining for five straight years.

Minimum wage raised

President Clinton signed legislation raising the minimum wage in the U.S. to $4.75 an hour from $4.25, effective October 1, and to $5.15 on Sept. 1, 1997. On August 2 the House of Representatives had passed the bill by a vote of 354–72 and the Senate by a margin of 76–22. The new law allowed employees to pay a "training wage" of $4.25 an hour to workers under the age of 20 during their first 90 days on the job. The wage for workers who received gratuities remained at $2.13 an hour. Republicans generally opposed the new law, saying that it would ultimately result in layoffs for many minimum-wage workers.

21
De Klerk repeats apology

During lengthy testimony before South Africa's Truth and Reconciliation Commission, F.W. de Klerk, the last president to head a white-minority government under apartheid, reiterated his apology for the pain and suffering many had endured under the official policy of racial segregation. De Klerk, however, refused to accept personal responsibility for human rights abuses, saying that he had never issued an order sanctioning torture

or murder. He placed the blame on rogue security forces and on the social and political conditions of the times, which he said were conducive to violations of human rights. He claimed, moreover, that the African National Congress and other black groups were partly responsible for the hostile attitudes that then prevailed. Some days later Eugene de Kock was found guilty on 89 of 121 criminal charges, including 6 counts of murder. He had committed the crimes while serving as a high-ranking police officer during the apartheid era.

22
U.S. reforms welfare

President Clinton signed a welfare reform bill that, he contended, would "make welfare what it was meant to be: a second chance, not a way of life." At the same time, he acknowledged that the new legislation was "far from perfect." He then promised to work to have certain provisions of the law amended. On July 31 the House of Representatives had passed the measure by a vote of 328–101; the vote in the Senate the next day was 78–21. The new law, which was expected to save the federal government $55 billion over six years, replaced the Aid to Families with Dependent Children

Student protesters from Yonsei University in Seoul demanding a U.S.-negotiated reunification with North Korea battle South Korean police. On August 20 the police finally ended the confrontation, which had begun on August 12.

program with lump sum payments to the states. They would, within certain limitations, determine how their welfare programs would be designed and administered. Most families that had been on welfare for a total of five years would be denied benefits. Heads of households who failed to find jobs within two years would have their benefits reduced. Most welfare benefits would be denied to legal immigrants who were not citizens. These and other provisions of the highly complex legislation were vociferously denounced by the National Organization for Women, the Children's Defense Fund, and others.

•

Hindus die in storm

Several hundred Hindus lost their lives in the Himalayas after being trapped by a sudden snowstorm that had begun on August 22. Six days earlier the first of some 80,000 Hindus had set out on an annual pilgrimage to the Amarnath Cave to pay homage to an ice statue of Shiva, the paramount Hindu god, who is both destroyer and restorer. Because many of those making the trek were lightly clothed and walking barefoot, officials sought to call off the pilgrimage once they became aware of the magnitude of the storm, but many of the worshipers had already made their way into the mountainous state of Jammu and Kashmir.

23
Police invade church

French riot police used axes to break down the doors of a Roman Catholic church in Paris in order to remove some 300 illegal African immigrants who had taken refuge inside. Armed with tear gas and night sticks, the police entered St. Bernard de la Chapelle and forcibly evicted those who resisted. More than 200 illegal immigrants were then transported to detention centres, but those who had grown weak from a prolonged hunger strike were taken to military hospitals for treatment. A few of the aliens were immediately deported to Africa. Popular reaction to the raid was mixed. Some expressed sympathy for the immigrants, especially for those who had

lived in France for years. By August 26 most of the detainees had been released, but the government indicated that the majority would not be granted permanent residence in France.

26
Chun sentenced to death

Three judges representing the District Criminal Court in Seoul, S.Kor., sentenced former president Chun Doo Hwan to death after finding him guilty on charges related to the 1979 coup that brought him to power and to the massacres of pro-democracy demonstrators in the city of Kwangju in 1980. He was also convicted of bribery. Roh Tae Woo, who succeeded Chun, was sentenced to 22½ years in prison for having supported the coup and accepted bribes. In addition, Chun was fined the equivalent of $270 million and Roh slightly more—the amount of money each was said to have received illegally. The judges also found dozens of businessmen and military officers guilty on a wide variety of charges, some related to bribery.

•

Cuba convicts Vesco

Robert Vesco, who had been wanted by U.S. authorities for more than 20 years on charges of embezzlement, drug trafficking, and making an illegal $200,000 contribution to Richard Nixon's 1972 presidential campaign, was convicted in Havana on charges of fraud and illicit economic activity. His partner in marketing the drug Trixolane without government approval was Donald Nixon, Jr., a nephew of the former president. Nixon was arrested along with Vesco, but he was released and allowed to return to the U.S. Trixolane had been marketed as a wonder drug capable of curing a wide range of diseases, including cancer and AIDS.

27
Illegals denied aid

Implementing one provision of a referendum that had been approved by California voters in 1994, Gov. Pete Wilson signed an executive order that prohibited state agencies and state-funded

institutions of higher learning from providing benefits to illegal immigrants. Wilson had delayed action until the courts had disposed of legal challenges. Illegal aliens could attend public primary and secondary schools and receive emergency medical care, but they remained ineligible for such benefits as public housing and prenatal care. The Justice Department had not yet decided how a person's legal status would be verified. Opponents of the referendum argued that the denial of ordinary health care would force illegal aliens to flock to more expensive hospital emergency rooms.

30
Farrakhan accepts reward

The leader of the Nation of Islam, Louis Farrakhan, accepted a human rights award in Tripoli, the capital of Libya. He declined the $250,000 cash prize that accompanied the award because he had been informed by the U.S. Treasury Department that receiving such money would be a violation of U.S. law. Farrakhan vowed to take his case to the courts. After leaving Libya he visited Iran, Iraq, The Sudan, and Cuba, all of which had been classified by the U.S. government as sponsors of terrorism and put under economic sanctions. While in Cuba, Farrakhan called such punishment inhumane.

31
Peace comes to Chechnya

Using the unrestricted authority he had been granted by Russian Pres. Boris Yeltsin, Aleksandr Lebed, secretary of Russia's Security Council, reached agreement with the commander of the Chechen secessionist army to cease hostilities and terminate the 21-month-old civil conflict. Gen. Aslan Maskhadov agreed that his people would set aside their demand for independence for five years. Lebed remarked that the two sides could then sort out their relationship "with cool heads, calmly and soberly." In the interim, a joint commission would monitor the withdrawal of all Russian troops from Chechnya and work to reduce crime and acts of terrorism in the region.

Illegal immigrants from Africa take refuge in St. Bernard de la Chapelle, a church in Paris. On August 23 French police raided the church and removed some 300 of the immigrants.

3
Perry to rule Liberia

Ruth Perry, a former senator, was installed as Liberia's head of state and assigned the responsibility of running the government until democracy could be restored through a general election. Her appointment had been approved on August 17 by leaders of the Economic Community of West African States, whose members hoped that the multifactional fighting that had torn Liberia asunder since 1989 would finally cease. The new agreement was signed by the leaders of Liberia's three main factions: Charles Taylor, who headed the National Patriotic Front of Liberia; Alhaji Kromah, leader of the United Liberation Movement of Liberia for Democracy faction; and George Boley, head of the Liberian Peace Council.

4
U.S. planes attack Iraq

For the second straight day, U.S. Navy ships and Air Force planes fired cruise missiles at Iraqi military and command targets south of the 32nd parallel. The operation was launched to punish Iraq for sending troops northward across the 36th parallel (latitude 36° N) and into a Kurdish area under the protection of the United Nations. Iraqi Pres. Saddam Hussein had ordered his troops into action after the Kurdistan Democratic Party requested help in its fight with the Patriotic Union of Kurdistan, a rival Kurdish faction. On September 3 the U.S. expanded the southern no-fly zone in Iraq northward to the 33rd parallel. Iraqi aircraft could then fly only between the 33rd and 36th parallels without fear of being fired upon.

5
Jordan to try rioters

The government of Jordan announced that 145 persons would be put on trial in connection with two days of food riots in mid-August. At the time, King Hussein had declared that he would handle the situation with "an iron fist"; he suspended the National Assembly and ordered curfews in several cities. Violence had first erupted in Kerak, a city about 90 km (55 mi) from Amman, the capital, then spread to other cities. In order to meet the conditions for a loan from the International Monetary Fund, the government had cut its subsidies for certain foods, an act that more than doubled the price of bread, a staple in the diet of Jordanians. The rioting that ensued was the worst since 1989.

•

Education gap narrows

The U.S. Census Bureau released a report entitled "Educational Attainment in the United States: March 1995." The statistics indicated that, for the first time, the high-school graduation rate for black Americans was roughly equal to that for whites. The study showed

A U.S. fighter takes off from a ship in the Persian Gulf. On September 4, after cruise missiles had destroyed air-defense installations in southern Iraq in retaliation for Iraqi military operations in a Kurdish area, U.S. fighters began to patrol a newly expanded no-fly zone to secure the area from further Iraqi incursion.

GUSTAVO FERRARI—SIPA

that 86.5% of blacks 25 to 29 years old had received high-school diplomas. The figure was 81.7% in 1990 and 76.6% in 1980. Comparable figures for whites in the same age group were 87.4% in 1995, 86.3% in 1990, and 86.9% in 1980. The study further showed that Hispanic-American students lagged far behind, with only 57.1% of those in the age group receiving high-school diplomas in 1995.

•

New leader in Suriname

The United People's Assembly, which included all elected members of the National Assembly plus officials of local and regional governments, elected Jules Wijdenbosch president of Suriname. Having outpolled incumbent Pres. Ronald Venetiaan, he took the oath of office on September 14. The vote in the United People's Assembly followed an inconclusive national election on May 23 and then two rounds of voting in the 51-member National Assembly. All had failed because no party gained the two-thirds majority needed to name a president. Wijdenbosch had been an aide of Col. Dési Bouterse, who had seized power in 1980. Under intense international pressure, Bouterse had resigned in 1987, having been accused of solidifying power by murdering political enemies. Foreign observers, worried that Bouterse might still be a potent behind-the-scenes political force in Wijdenbosch's government, expressed reservations about the future of democracy in Suriname.

•

Zafy forced to resign

When the High Constitutional Court in Madagascar upheld a parliamentary vote impeaching Pres. Albert Zafy, the nation's leader agreed to resign on October 10. The court then appointed Prime Minister Norbert Ratsirahonana interim president. Zafy had assumed office in 1993, one year after leading a pro-democracy movement that ousted a military-dominated regime. He subsequently clashed repeatedly with the National Assembly for refusing to meet the conditions for financial assistance from the Interna-

tional Monetary Fund and for backing a referendum that transferred key powers from the National Assembly to the president.

9
Clinton partner jailed

Susan McDougal, already convicted and sentenced to prison for having accepted a fraudulent government-backed loan in 1986, was ordered jailed for refusing to answer questions before a grand jury in Little Rock, Ark. Speaking to reporters outside the courtroom, McDougal said that she had refused to cooperate with the prosecutors because she felt that they "always wanted something on the Clintons." McDougal had been a business partner of President Clinton and his wife, Hillary Rodham Clinton, in the Whitewater Development Corp., a failed real-estate venture.

10
Ex-generals sentenced

Six former East German generals were sentenced to prison for having sanctioned the shooting of anyone trying to escape to West Germany after the border was sealed in 1961. In the years that followed, an estimated 800 Germans lost their lives attempting to flee their communist homeland. The judge who presided over the court in Berlin sentenced Klaus-Dieter Baumgarten, a former East German deputy defense minister, to six and a half years in prison after finding him guilty on multiple charges of manslaughter and attempted manslaughter. Five other generals, who were convicted as accomplices, received sentences of at least three years.

ALBERTO PIZZOLI—SYGMA

14
Bosnians to share power

In the first national election in the Republic of Bosnia and Herzegovina, each of the three major ethnic groups elected a president to represent its interests in a collective leadership. Alija Izetbegovic was elected by the Muslims with 80% of their vote and named chairman of the three-man leadership. Momcilo Krajisnik was chosen by 68% of the Serbs and Kresimir Zubak by 88% of the Croats. A settlement resulting from negotiations held near Dayton, Ohio, in 1995 had raised hopes that the bitter and vicious four-year-old civil war had come to an end. Under terms of that agreement, formally signed in Paris on Dec. 14, 1995, the nation would be divided into two regions, one of which would be a Muslim-Croat federation and the other a Serbian entity. Despite the success in bringing the three factions together, foreboding about the future persisted in many quarters because, among other reasons, the rules of the election itself, specifically endorsed by all parties, had been blatantly violated.

15
Italians support unity

During a meeting in Venice, Umberto Bossi, who had founded the Northern League political party in 1984, announced the creation of a new "independent and sovereign federal republic." For more than a decade, he and fellow secessionists had claimed that citizens in the northern part of Italy would be more prosperous if they were no longer "overtaxed" in order to support poorer regions in the south. The proposed new nation, to be called Padania, would include such major cities as Venice, Bologna, Turin, and Milan. Polls, however, indicated that only about 7% of Italians supported Bossi's movement. Such low-level support seemed to be confirmed when only 10,000–20,000 attended the Bossi-led rally in Venice while an estimated 150,000 gathered in Milan at the same time in support of national unity.

18
South Korea hunts spies

Troops deployed by South Korea began an intense search for North Korean agents after a taxi driver spotted an abandoned North Korean submarine that had run aground off the east coast city of Kangnung. By September 26 a total of 20 North Koreans were dead, either killed by South Korean soldiers or possibly by fellow North Koreans because they were members of the submarine crew and not trained to avoid detection. One captured North Korean told interrogators that several of his companions were not accounted for and had presumably escaped. Acting

SEPTEMBER

Umberto Bossi (centre) on September 15 proclaimed an independent republic in northern Italy.

HAVIV—SABA

Serbs attend a political rally in Pale, a town near Sarajevo, before the September 14 elections in Bosnia and Herzegovina. Under terms of the 1995 Dayton accords, citizens voted for national and regional offices, including three presidents, one for each of the country's main ethnic groups—Bosnians (Slavic Muslims), Serbs, and Croats.

on that information, South Korean soldiers set out to track them down. According to South Korean officials, the grounded submarine represented the 310th known attempt by North Korea to infiltrate the South during the past 25 years.

19
Rebels sign peace pact

Government officials and representatives of the Guatemalan National Revolutionary Unity, which represented the country's major rebel forces, concluded negotiations in Mexico City that were designed to end 35 years of civil conflict. Both sides hailed the UN-mediated settlement as a momentous event. An estimated 140,000 Guatemalans had been killed since fighting began after democratically elected Pres. Jacobo Arbenz, a leftist, was overthrown in a 1954 military coup supported by the U.S.

20
Meri wins reelection

An expanded electoral college broke a political impasse by electing Estonian Pres. Lennart Meri to a second five-year term. In late August the 101-member national legislature had twice failed to support either presidential candidate with the 68 votes required for election. The stalemate ended when the electoral college was expanded to include 273 local officials. In the second round of ballots, the expanded college gave Meri 196 votes. Arnold Ruutel, who received 126 votes, had served as president when Estonia was under communist rule.

22
Socialists win in Greece

The ruling Panhellenic Socialist Movement (Pasok) party retained power in Greece by capturing 162 of the 300 seats in the Chamber of Deputies—a net loss of 8 seats. Although the New Democracy Party lost 3 seats, it still controlled 108 and would continue to be the main party in opposition. Three smaller parties won the remaining 30 seats. When Prime Minister Konstantinos Simitis called for a general election in August,

his Pasok party was expected to win handily, but the 10-month-old Democratic Social Movement gained sudden popularity that siphoned off Pasok support. The main issue in the campaign had been Greece's economic health and its participation in the European Union.

•

Patient killed legally

Under a new law that took effect in Australia's Northern Territory on July 1 and was upheld by a 2–1 vote of the territory's Supreme Court on July 24, a terminally ill cancer patient was injected with a lethal dose of barbiturates by his doctor. The law permitting euthanasia required that the patient be at least 18 years old and mentally competent. The primary physician's diagnosis of terminal illness, moreover, had to be confirmed by two other doctors, one of whom had to be a psychiatrist. The law also required a nine-day waiting period before the patient was put to death. On September 9 a bill, supported by Prime Minister John Howard and opposition leader Kim Beazley, was introduced in the federal Parliament that, if passed, would repeal the law.

•

Ter-Petrosyan reelected

In Armenia's second democratic election since independence from the Soviet Union in 1991, Pres. Levon Ter-Petrosyan retained his office by winning nearly 52% of the vote. His chief challenger was former prime minister Vazgen Manukyan, whose candidacy was supported by more than 41% of the electorate. On October 2 the Organization for Security and Cooperation in Europe reported that "very serious breaches of the election law" had marred the election. More than 22,000 ballots that had been cast were not accounted for, a larger number than Ter-Petrosyan's margin of victory.

23
IRA explosives seized

In a predawn raid on suspected Provisional Irish Republican Army (IRA) hideouts, London police seized some 10 tons of homemade explosives. The largest

cache included fertilizer (ammonium nitrate) explosives and Semtex. A high-ranking police officer reported that some explosive devices had already been assembled and were ready for use. The raids also netted guns, ammunition, detonators, and timers. During the raid one suspected IRA member was killed and five were arrested. London's police commissioner said that his officers had prevented the IRA from carrying out "significant and imminent attacks with the probability of grave loss of life [and] serious damage." In June an IRA bomb had injured more than 200 people when it was set off in Manchester.

24
Israel angers Muslims

At least 60 Palestinians and 15 Israelis were killed in violent protests that followed a decision by the Israeli government of Prime Minister Benjamin Netanyahu to open a new entrance to an archaeological tunnel near a sacred Muslim site in Jerusalem. The incident was viewed by many Palestinians as another attempt by the Israelis to stall the Middle East peace process. They noted that Netanyahu had authorized the expansion of Jewish settlements in Arab lands and had delayed the withdrawal of Israeli troops from Hebron, a city in the West Bank. Palestinians were also suffering economically because many were prevented from going to their jobs in Israel. The border had been closed after bombings by Palestinian extremists.

25
Lebed speaks out for army

During an interview Aleksandr Lebed, secretary of Russia's Security Council, criticized the government for having not paid military personnel for the previous three months. Lebed said that some soldiers were suffering from malnutrition and that others were being forced to beg or steal. Russia's official government newspaper had earlier warned that the military could take "unpredictable action" if their situation did not improve. All told, the armed forces were owed some $4.3 billion.

26
Lucid sets space records

U.S. astronaut Shannon Lucid returned to Earth aboard the space shuttle *Atlantis* after setting new space endurance records (188 days) for a woman and for a U.S. astronaut. Lucid's stay on the Russian space station *Mir* was extended six weeks beyond schedule because of problems with the *Atlantis* booster rockets. After the two space vehicles linked up, the Russian and U.S. crews spent five days transferring new supplies and equipment into *Mir* and removing other items for a return trip to Earth.

•

Howard greets Dalai Lama

Australian Prime Minister John Howard held a 35-

Palestinian youths take to the streets on September 24 after the Israeli government allowed a second entrance to an archaeological tunnel to be opened near a sacred Muslim site in Jerusalem. The protests escalated into the country's worst violence in decades.

minute private meeting in Sydney with the Dalai Lama, despite warnings from China that trade relations between the two countries would be adversely affected if such an event took place. Howard had earlier remarked that he would welcome the head of Tibetan Buddhism as a spiritual leader, not as the exiled head of the Tibetan government. Chinese troops had occupied Tibet in 1950 on the grounds that it was historically part of China. When China squelched an uprising against Chinese rule in 1959, the Dalai Lama fled to India and set up a government-in-exile.

•

ValuJet meets criteria

The U.S. Department of Transportation announced that ValuJet Airlines was "fit, willing, and able" to resume service because it now complied with all federal regulations. The airline's entire fleet had been grounded by federal authorities on June 17 for various violations, including improper maintenance procedures. An investigation of the low-fare airline had been ordered after one of its DC-9s crashed in Florida on May 11. The government had certified that ValuJet aircraft were safe to fly, but a lawyer for the Association of Flight Attendants said that his clients were not at all convinced that this was true. He would, accordingly, petition the court to keep the planes grounded.

27
Taliban capture Kabul

After two years of fighting, the Muslim fundamentalist group called the Taliban ("students") captured Kabul, the capital of Afghanistan. That same day a six-member council, headed by Mohammad Rabbani, was appointed to rule the areas under their control, which were to be governed by strict Islamic law. Before Kabul fell, Afghan Pres. Burhanuddin Rabbani, Prime Minister Gulbuddin Hekmatyar, and the defense minister escaped to the northeastern region of the country, which was still controlled by ethnic Tajiks. All had been sentenced to death by the Taliban. Two former Afghan officials, however, were captured inside a United Nations facility in Kabul and executed. They were former communist president Mohammad Najibullah, who had ruled the country from 1987 to 1992, and his brother, the former head of security.

•

Gambian leader reelected

Following an election that was widely described as a travesty, Yahya Jammeh retained his post as president of The Gambia. Weeks before the election, Jammeh had guaranteed his continued control of the West African nation by outlawing major opposition parties and forbidding his political rivals to talk with foreign diplomats. Government soldiers, moreover, disrupted rallies by opposition candidates, and security personnel intimidated voters by standing watch as they cast their ballots. The election was an apparent attempt to legitimize Jammeh's regime because he had gained power in July 1994 by staging a military coup that ousted democratically elected Pres. Dawda Jawara.

1

UN removes sanctions

The United Nations Security Council unanimously approved the lifting of the 1992 sanctions that it had imposed on the federation of Yugoslavia (which included only Serbia and Montenegro after the nation disintegrated in 1991). The goal of the sanctions was to force Serbia to end its support of ethnic Serbs who were engaged in a civil war with Croats and Muslims in Bosnia and Herzegovina. With a fragile peace settlement in place, the Security Council agreed to remove the sanctions, but it did not restore Yugoslavia's membership in the UN General Assembly or release the nation's assets that were frozen in foreign banks.

2

Gunman kills Lukanov

An unidentified gunman shot and killed former prime minister Andrey Lukanov outside his home in Sofia, the capital of Bulgaria. Following a series of strikes and protests, Lukanov had resigned in November 1990 just a few months after his Socialist (formerly Communist) Party won the parliamentary election. He remained active on the political scene, frequently serving as the voice of his party, which was often at odds with Prime Minister Zhan Videnov. The assassination did not delay the presidential election. In a runoff on November 3, Petar Stoyanov of the Union of Democratic Forces defeated Ivan Marazov by winning 59.9% of the vote.

6

Mideast leaders at impasse

After failing to make headway in their negotiations in Washington, D.C., on October 1–2, Benjamin Netanyahu, prime minister of Israel, and Yasir Arafat, head of the Palestine Liberation Organization, resumed their talks at the Israeli–Gaza Strip border. Their stated goal was to revitalize the Middle East peace process by resolving several issues, including the withdrawal of Israeli troops from the West Bank city of Hebron. Arafat accused Netanyahu of seeking to renegotiate an agreement already ratified by his nation, but Netanyahu insisted that he was merely seeking to make adjustments in the existing agreement. It was apparent to all who paid close attention to the proceedings that the road to definitive peace would be long and arduous. In an address to the Knesset (parliament) on October 7, Shimon Peres, Netanyahu's predecessor, declared that Israel had lost a lot of goodwill around the world because there had been nothing but "talk about the need to talk" during the 111 days that Netanyahu's government had been in power.

12

Peters ponders options

New Zealand's parliamentary elections ended with neither the ruling National Party of Prime Minister Jim Bolger nor the main opposition Labour Party having sufficient representation in

Latinos march in Washington, D.C., on October 12 to protest changes in U.S. laws affecting immigration and welfare benefits. Tens of thousands attended the rally.

the expanded House of Representatives to form a government. As a consequence, the balance of power devolved on the New Zealand First Party (NZFP) led by Winston Peters. Although he was in a position to negotiate with either party and bring the NZFP into a coalition government as a junior partner, neither of the two major parties was prepared to accept some of the basic policies advocated by the NZFP. Under a new electoral system, voters had cast two ballots, one for an individual and one for a political party. The purpose of the dual ballot was to ensure that any party receiving at least 5% of the vote had the right to be represented in the national unicameral legislature even if none of its candidates won a seat outright.

PAUL FUSCO—MAGNUM

•

Hispanics march in D.C.

Tens of thousands of Latinos held a rally in Washington, D.C., to emphasize their common bonds, underscore their importance as a political bloc, and protest new laws that denied benefits to legal immigrants who were not citizens. The new legislation also made it more difficult to qualify for political asylum and to prove discrimination when employers failed to hire Latinos in the belief that they had entered the country illegally. The gathering, called the Latino and Immigrants' Rights March, was organized by the director of Coordinadora 96.

14
ADM to pay huge fine

The Archer Daniels Midland Co. announced that it would plead guilty to charges of conspiracy with competitors to fix the price of lysine, a feed additive, and of citric acid, which is used in foods and beverages. The company also agreed to pay a fine of $100 million—a penalty almost seven times larger than any the U.S. Justice Department had previously imposed in a criminal price-fixing case. Evidence against the company had been secretly obtained by Mark Whitacre, who recorded incriminating conversations during hundreds of meetings that he attended as a senior executive. As part of the settlement, the Justice Department agreed not to pursue its investigation of other alleged instances of price-fixing, possible bribes, and theft of technology.

15
Christopher visits Africa

Warren Christopher ended a nine-day diplomatic journey that took him to Angola, Ethiopia, Mali, South Africa, and Tanzania. It was the first visit to Africa by a U.S. secretary of state since 1987. During his key policy address at the University of the Witwatersrand, Johannesburg, S.Af., he noted that African nations were abandoning military rule and one-party political systems and embracing democratic principles. While recognizing that many of the continent's nations had made social

and economic progress, he added that prospects for the future would be greatly improved through sound policies and international support. He promised that the U.S. would give Africa the "attention it deserves" while recalling that the U.S. had helped negotiate the peace settlement in Angola and, among other things, had undertaken humanitarian missions to relieve starvation in Africa. Christopher's call for an all-African crisis-intervention force was generally well received by leaders in the region.

•

U.S. troops reach Bosnia

A task force of some 5,000 U.S. soldiers began arriving in Bosnia and Herzegovina to protect the last 15,000 U.S. peacekeeping troops during their withdrawal from the country. They had been part of a 48,000-member international force led by NATO. Some weeks earlier, during a meeting in Norway, the NATO ministers had asked Gen. George Joulwan, NATO's supreme commander in Europe, to study the feasibility of a new peacekeeping force that would be capable of preventing another outbreak of ethnic fighting between Bosnian Serbs, Croats, and Muslims. Fears were expressed that the civil war would almost certainly erupt again unless an international force capable of enforcing the peace accord was deployed on the ground in Bosnia and Herzegovina.

16
U.S. policy draws fire

The European Union (EU) requested that the World Trade Organization decide whether the Helms–Burton act violated international trade laws. The legislation had been passed by the U.S. Senate (74–22) and by the House of Representatives (336–86) in March. One provision of the law allowed U.S. citizens to file lawsuits in U.S. courts against foreign companies that "trafficked" in property that had belonged to them before it was confiscated by the Cuban government. In effect, the U.S. law was an attempt to force other nations to observe the economic embargo that the U.S. had

imposed on Cuba. Canada, Mexico, and members of the EU challenged the right of the U.S. to dictate their policy toward Cuba, arguing that the Helms–Burton act was an illegal extraterritorial extension of U.S. law.

•

U.K. may ban handguns

In the wake of recommendations made by a panel of investigators assigned to review the random slaying in March of 16 children and a teacher in Dunblane, Scot., the British government announced that it would propose a plan to outlaw the private possession of most handguns. Although Great Britain already had some of the world's most restrictive laws on the possession of guns, Thomas Hamilton, who committed the murders, had been able to obtain his handguns legally.

17
Yeltsin fires Lebed

Using television as a forum, Russian Pres. Boris Yeltsin signed a decree dismissing Aleksandr Lebed as secretary of the nation's Security Council. On October 19 his place was taken by Ivan Rybkin, who had been speaker of the State Duma (parliament). Although Lebed, a retired general, had negotiated an end to the civil conflict in Chechnya, he had angered Yeltsin by questioning government policies and creating friction among high-ranking officials. Lebed had earlier threatened to resign when he was not named head of a commission on military appointments. After his dismissal, Lebed, who was generally considered one of the country's most popular politicians, pledged to continue speaking out on domestic and foreign affairs. He openly acknowledged that he hoped one day to be president while pledging to use only constitutional means to attain his goal.

•

Strike disrupts France

Public employees went on strike throughout France to protest the government's plan to prepare for a common European currency by cutting its deficit through reduced spending. The strike provoked bitter

OCTOBER

conflict among union members, some of whom were willing to admit that steps had to be taken to control, among other things, the social security and health insurance programs, which were billions of dollars in debt. The call to strike was issued after the government announced that it would not fill 6,000 civil service jobs when they became vacant in 1997 because workers had quit or retired. The number of civil servants, however, would still exceed five million. The strike kept about one-half of the country's teachers at home and seriously hobbled air, rail, and public transportation. The protest was joined by many doctors, who denounced Prime Minister Alain Juppé for demanding that the cost of medical treatment and drugs be lowered.

A man holds photographs of some of the victims of a sex and child-kidnapping ring that was discovered in Belgium in August. Demonstrators marched in Brussels on October 20 to protest the government's handling of this and other criminal cases.

18

DNC suspends Huang

The Democratic National Committee (DNC), under fierce attack for having accepted what were said to have been illegal contributions to President Clinton's reelection campaign, announced that it had suspended John Huang, its vice-chairman for financial operations. Huang, a Chinese-born naturalized U.S. citizen, had solicited huge sums of money from the Asian business community. The DNC had already returned one illegal gift of $250,000 from a South Korean electronics firm. Another sizable contribution had apparently been concealed by using a Buddhist temple in California as a front. Huang had also received money from the Riady family, which controlled the Lippo Group, a vast banking and real-estate empire in Indonesia. Huang had worked for the Lippo Group before becoming deputy assistant secretary for international economic policy at the U.S. Commerce Department. Huang reportedly had turned over to the DNC nearly $1 million from U.S. associates of the Riady family and from subsidiaries of the Lippo Group.

20

Japan holds election

In parliamentary elections Japanese Prime Minis-

ter Ryutaro Hashimoto's Liberal-Democratic Party (LDP) gained 28 seats in the lower house of the Diet (parliament), but its 239-seat total fell short of an absolute majority. There was little doubt, however, that Hashimoto would continue to head the government, whether or not the Social Democratic Party of Japan and New Party Sakigake continued to support the LDP as partners in a coalition government. Under a newly adopted electoral system, the number of seats in the lower house was reduced from 511 to 500—300 of which were filled from single-seat districts and 200 by proportional representation. Commentators, trying to explain the record-low 59.9% voter turnout, frequently cited public disgust with political corruption, indifference to the outcome, and skepticism that the new

electoral system would bring about any significant positive change.

•

Sex case angers Belgians

More than a quarter of a million people held a peaceful march in Brussels, the capital of Belgium, to vent their frustration over the government's perceived reluctance to investigate vigorously a pedophile and child-pornography ring that was involved in kidnapping, sexual abuse, and murder. The frustration and anger of ordinary people had reached new intensity when the nation's highest court removed the chief magistrate, Jean-Marc Connerotte, from the case because he accepted a free dinner at a fund-raiser for the parents of children still missing. Connerotte, who had been widely admired for his handling

of the case, was reportedly about to reveal the names of senior government officials who had been identified on compromising videotapes. His dismissal raised questions of a possible government cover-up.

•

Alemán defeats Ortega

In a race for the presidency of Nicaragua, Arnoldo Alemán, candidate of the Liberal Alliance party, handily defeated his main rival, former president Daniel Ortega Saavedra of the Sandinista National Liberation Front. Incomplete returns indicated that Alemán had won more than 45% of the popular vote, the minimum required for avoiding a runoff. Ortega charged that "serious irregularities" had tainted the election, but outside observers were satisfied that such problems as a shortage

of ballots in some polling stations, incomplete voter lists, and late openings of some voting precincts were the result of poor organization and did not involve fraud. Alemán was scheduled to replace Violeta Barrios de Chamorro as president on Jan. 20, 1997.

21
Chirac backs Palestinians

On the first day of a state visit to Israel, French Pres. Jacques Chirac called for the establishment of a Palestinian state as a step toward bolstering security in the Middle East. The following day Israeli Prime Minister Benjamin Netanyahu voiced his opposition to such a plan on the grounds that a Palestinian state would present a threat to Israel because it could then form an alliance with Israel's enemies. Nonetheless, Netanyahu insisted that he was eager to conclude a definitive peace agreement with the Palestinians, but not on the same terms envisioned by his predecessor, the late Yitzhak Rabin. Chirac's visit was widely viewed as an effort to restore France's historic role in the region.

23
Swiss reputation sullied

Flavio Cotti, Switzerland's foreign minister, announced that the government would immediately intensify its investigation of a scandal that had angered Jewish communities throughout the world, as well as the Swiss people and foreign governments. During research at the Swiss National Archives, Peter Hug, a historian at the University of Bern, came across documents confirming that Switzerland had secretly used dormant assets of Jewish victims of the Holocaust to compensate Swiss businessmen for losses that they had sustained through confiscation during World War II. Switzerland had entered into confidential agreements with Bulgaria, Hungary, Poland, Romania, and Yugoslavia to settle their debts through such compensation. The scandal embarrassed the Swiss government and tarnished its carefully cultivated reputation for honesty in financial dealings.

•
Brundtland resigns

After announcing that she was stepping down as prime minister of Norway, Gro Harlem Brundtland declared that she would remain a Labour Party MP and seek reelection in 1997. When she began her first term in 1981, she was the youngest person and the first woman ever to have held the post. On October 25 Thorbjørn Jagland was sworn in as prime minister by King Harald V.

•
GMC workers end strike

The Canadian Auto Workers ratified a new three-year contract with General Motors of Canada (GMC) and returned to work after a 21-day strike. The shutdown had forced GMC to lay off temporarily some 19,900 workers in the U.S. and Mexico and thousands of others who manufactured automobile parts. The strike cost the Canadian economy an estimated $750 million. Under terms of the new contract, workers would receive annual pay increases of 2% and an immediate bonus of $259. The company, moreover, would be allowed to sell two auto parts plants in Ontario so long as the benefits workers received were protected for a number of years. GMC agreed to offer those workers attractive buyout options and in its remaining plants to replace jobs that had been lost by channeling business to outside suppliers.

26
Chaos reigns in Zaire

The United Nations evacuated its personnel from Bukavu, Zaire, convinced that the escalating conflict between ethnic Tutsi and government forces created a situation that was unacceptably dangerous. The UN also acknowledged that the refugee problem had reached unmanageable proportions. Two years earlier about one million Hutu had crossed the border into Zaire and set up refugee camps to avoid the vicious Hutu-Tutsi conflict in Rwanda and Burundi. These refugees, fearing that the warring Tutsi would attack their camps to seek revenge

for the earlier murder of some 500,000 Tutsi, fled the camps in panic. Hundreds of thousands sought safety in the bush, even though they carried with them virtually no food, drinking water, or personal belongings.

28
Sant turns back on EU

A new head of government assumed power in Malta when Pres. Ugo Mifsud Bonnici administered the oath of office to Alfred Sant. The constitution required the president to appoint Sant prime minister after the Labour Party, which he led, defeated the Nationalist Party by capturing slightly more than one-half of the popular vote. During the campaign Sant pledged to abolish an unpopular value-added sales tax, a decision that effectively voided Malta's bid to join the European Union. Sant also promised to seek closer ties with Libya, which was situated just 360 km (225 mi) south of Malta, and to relinquish Malta's associate membership in NATO.

30
Wang Dan jailed again

After a four-hour closed trial, a Chinese court in Beijing convicted Wang Dan of having plotted to subvert the government and sentenced him to 11 years in prison. The court cited Wang's writing for foreign publications and his association with other dissidents. After the Tiananmen Square massacre on June 4, 1989, Wang headed the government's most-wanted list of pro-democracy dissidents. After turning himself in, he was imprisoned for nearly four years. In May 1995 he was rearrested and held incommunicado until October 7, when he was charged with the capital offense of subversion. With Wang's imprisonment, all of China's prominent dissidents were either behind bars, in labour camps, or in exile. China watchers generally agreed that Wang's sentence indicated that China's leaders no longer feared that harsh suppression of dissent would cause Western nations to be less friendly toward their country.

BOBBY YIP—REUTERS

A member of the Hong Kong legislature demonstrates outside the de facto Chinese embassy in the British crown colony to demand the release of Chinese dissident Wang Dan. On October 30 a Chinese court sentenced Wang to 11 years in prison.

BOB STRONG—SIPA

Fireworks over the Old State House in Little Rock, Ark., are set off in celebration of the reelection of Bill Clinton on November 5. Clinton became the first Democratic president since Franklin D. Roosevelt to win a second term.

5
Clinton defeats Dole

After a political campaign that many Americans considered far too long and much too expensive, Democrat Bill Clinton was reelected U.S. president with 379 electoral votes. He captured 31 states and the District of Columbia and 49% of the popular vote. He thus became the first Democratic president to win a second term since Franklin D. Roosevelt in 1936. Former senator Bob Dole, the Republican candidate, earned 159 electoral votes by capturing 19 states; his share of the popular vote was about 41%. H. Ross Perot, carrying the banner of the Reform Party, was supported by 8.5% of those who cast ballots, but he won no electoral votes. The Republicans increased their majority in the Senate (55–45) by picking up two additional seats. They also retained control of the House of Representatives by a mar-

gin of 226–207. Although party changes occurred in two gubernatorial races, the overall balance remained the same—32 Republicans and 17 Democrats. The term of the governor of Maine, an independent, was not due to expire until 1998. The overall voter turnout—less than 50%—was the lowest in modern times.

•

Yeltsin has heart surgery

An all-Russian team of 12 surgeons performed successful seven-hour multiple heart bypass surgery on Russian Pres. Boris Yeltsin at the Moscow Cardiological Centre. Six weeks earlier world-renowned U.S. heart surgeon Michael DeBakey had arrived in Moscow to act as consultant. He advised that the surgery be delayed until Yeltsin's health problems could be treated. Ailments that could complicate the surgery included anemia, high cholesterol, and intestinal bleeding. On November

NAVEED SHEIKH—AFP

Benazir Bhutto, the former prime minister of Pakistan, waves to supporters. Bhutto was dismissed on November 5 after charges of corruption were leveled at her government and at her husband.

6 Yeltsin reassumed the powers he had temporarily delegated to Prime Minister Viktor Chernomyrdin.

•

President ousts Bhutto

For the second time in her political career, Pakistani Prime Minister Benazir Bhutto was dismissed from office. Pres. Farooq Ahmed Leghari, responding to widespread charges that Bhutto's government was rife with corruption, dissolved the National Assembly and called for new elections on Feb. 3, 1997. In his decree of dismissal, Leghari remarked that "public faith in the integrity and honesty of the government has disappeared." That same day he installed Malik Meraj Khalid as interim prime minister. The antigovernment protests that began in late October had paralyzed Islamabad, the capital. Many of the charges of corruption were directed at Asif Ali Zardari, Bhutto's husband, who allegedly had taken bribes and channeled money from government contracts into private bank accounts. There was also talk about his possible involvement in the September murder of Mir Murtaza Bhutto, the prime minister's estranged brother.

7
Hashimoto reelected

With the backing of 262 of the 500 members of Japan's House of Representatives, the lower house

of the Diet (parliament), Ryutaro Hashimoto was reelected prime minister. Although his Liberal-Democratic Party (LDP) had won a plurality in the October Diet elections, he could not persuade the Social Democratic Party of Japan and the Sakigake Party to resume the roles they had played as formal partners in his previous coalition government. The new Cabinet included only members of the LDP, with each of the LDP's main factions nearly equally represented.

•

Army probes sex cases

U.S. Army officials publicly acknowledged that a wide-ranging investigation of alleged sexual assaults and harassment was under way at the Aberdeen Proving Ground in Maryland and at

CAROL GUZY—THE WASHINGTON POST

other military compounds. The charges ranged from violations of the ban on consensual sex with trainees to rape, forcible sodomy, sexual assault, threats of severe bodily harm or death, and obstruction of justice. As the investigation proceeded, thousands of additional complaints from other female recruits made it clear that the problem of abuse was far more widespread and serious than had earlier been believed. Many females reported that male military officers had simply ignored their complaints when they were reported at the time of the alleged incidents.

10

Chile is summit host

Most of Latin America's heads of state, as well as the leaders of Spain and Portugal, gathered in Viña del Mar, Chile, for the sixth annual Ibero-American Summit. During the two-day conference the main topics of discussion were drug trafficking, corruption, poverty, and the U.S. economic embargo of Cuba. The final communiqué urged Fidel Castro to begin introducing democratic reforms in Cuba. At the same time, it criticized the U.S. policy toward Cuba, especially its recent law allowing U.S. citizens to sue foreign businesses occupying property that had belonged to U.S. citizens before it was confiscated by the Cuban government.

11

Lithuania holds election

After the second round of elections to Lithuania's Seimas (parliament), the Homeland Union (HU) party under the leadership of Vytautas Landsbergis occupied 70 of the 141 seats. Having previously allied itself with the Christian Democratic Party, which controlled 16 seats, the HU was in a position to elect Landsbergis speaker of the Seimas and prime minister. During the campaign he had pledged to continue Lithuania's effort to join the European Union and NATO.

15

Hutu return to Rwanda

After more than two years in Zaire, hundreds of thousands of Hutu refugees began returning voluntarily to their homes in neighbouring Rwanda. The unexpected turn of events immediately called into question the need for a UN humanitarian mission to prevent massive starvation and the spread of life-threatening diseases, especially in the North Kivu province of Zaire. There were, however, still hundreds of thousands of refugees, many from Burundi, whose whereabouts were unknown. Their number included Hutu militants, who were the main target of Tutsi warriors bent on revenge for the earlier massacre of some 500,000 of their fellow tribesmen.

•

Texaco settles lawsuit

A financial deal amounting to $176.1 million was approved by Texaco, a major U.S. oil company, to settle a discrimination lawsuit filed in 1994 by some 1,400 of the company's black employees. The plaintiffs charged that they had been denied deserved promotions and pay

Hutu refugees carry their belongings as they make their way from Zaire back to their homes in neighbouring Rwanda. It was reported on November 15 that hundreds of thousands of Hutu refugees were voluntarily returning two years after having fled Rwanda to escape the civil war.

comparable to that of white employees. On November 4 what appeared to be damaging evidence against Texaco officials was made public. It was a low-quality audiotape recording of Texaco executives making what appeared to be disparaging racial remarks and discussing the alteration or destruction of compromising documents related to the case. As part of the settlement, which had to be approved by the U.S. District Court in White Plains, N.Y., Texaco agreed to help create a task force of outside experts, which would operate under court supervision and oversee Texaco's human resources program for a period of five years.

•

Deutch defends CIA

Hoping to dispel doubts about CIA involvement in the distribution of illegal drugs in inner-city neighbourhoods during the 1980s, CIA director John Deutch visited the Watts area of Los Angeles to answer questions posed by black leaders. In August the *San Jose* (Calif.) *Mercury News* had reported that the CIA had had connections to Nicaraguans who sold crack cocaine in U.S. inner cities. The CIA had then reportedly used some of the profits from the illegal drug sales to finance Contra rebels fighting the Sandinista government in Nicaragua. Although Deutch asserted that he had no evidence of such CIA activity, he said that he would reserve final judgment until the CIA had completed a thorough investigation.

17
Thai government falls

The Thai Nation (Chart Thai) party of Prime Minister Banharn Silpa-archa was soundly defeated in elections to the House of Representatives, losing 53 of the 91 seats it had held. The New Aspiration Party, led by Defense Minister Gen. Chavalit Yongchaiyudh, gained 68 seats for a new total of 125, a slight plurality. The Democrat Party of former prime minister Chuan Leekpai finished second with 123 seats. Under intense pressure to resign over charges of corruption and fiscal mismanagement, Banharn had finally agreed to step aside

after a 207–180 vote of no-confidence. He then reneged and called for new elections. On November 18 Chavalit announced that he had succeeded in forming a new coalition government that included four former prime ministers, all of whom were leaders of political parties.

•

Romania chooses president

Romanian voters ended Ion Iliescu's seven-year reign by electing as president Emil Constantinescu, candidate of the centre-right Democratic Convention of Romania (CDR) party. Two weeks earlier the electorate had signaled its desire for change by displacing the former communist government with a centre-right parliament. The CDR and the Social Democratic Union, which were allied, controlled 213 of the 343 seats in the Chamber of Deputies and 94 of the 143 seats in the Senate. Observers expected Romania to move more quickly toward a market economy and encourage foreign investment by easing restrictions on repatriating profits.

19
U.S. ousts Boutros-Ghali

Exercising its veto power in the UN Security Council, the U.S. formally voted against the reelection of Boutros Boutros-Ghali to a second five-year term as secretary-general of the United Nations. Madeleine Albright,

the U.S. ambassador, made it clear that the U.S. would not capitulate to pressure and join the majority of nations that favoured extending Boutros-Ghali's term. The position of the United States was based on Boutros-Ghali's perceived lack of leadership and his inability or unwillingness to carry out reforms that the U.S. viewed as vital if the UN hoped to fulfill its mission as an effective international organization.

•

Castro visits John Paul II

During a private meeting in the Vatican, Pope John Paul II accepted an invitation from Cuban Pres. Fidel Castro to pay a state visit to his country in 1997. The Roman pontiff, who was generally credited with having hastened the collapse of communism in Eastern Europe, first insisted that he be allowed to travel freely throughout the country and address gatherings without restrictions. No pope had ever visited Cuba. Before the nation's constitution was amended in 1992, Cuba was officially an atheistic country. The communist government, which had been headed by Castro for 37 years, had confiscated church property, expelled or imprisoned clergymen, and forbidden public worship. In 1996 only 250 priests were taking care of the spiritual needs of an estimated five million Roman Catholics, who constituted almost one-half of the country's population.

20
Poland reinstates abortion

Aleksander Kwasniewski, president of Poland, signed legislation that returned to women the right to terminate a pregnancy, up to the 12th week, if they chose to do so for financial or emotional reasons. The vote in the Diet had favoured abortion rights 228–198, sufficient to override a Senate veto. During communist rule the law had permitted abortion on demand, but new legislation in 1993 banned abortions, in part because the vast majority of Poles were members of the Roman Catholic Church, which condemned the practice.

•

Student scores compared

According to information released by the U.S. Department of Education, middle-school students in Singapore posted higher scores in both mathematics and science than any other group of eighth-grade students in the 41 nations that participated in the Third International Mathematics and Science Study. South Korea finished second in math, Japan third, Hong Kong fourth, and Belgium fifth. In science the Czech Republic was second and Japan third. South Korea and Bulgaria tied for fourth place. In the overall rankings, the U.S. was 28th. There was no apparent relationship between achievement and the hours of instruction. U.S. students,

Demonstrators march in Belgrade to protest the cancellation of election victories by opponents of the government of Slobodan Milosevic. Despite the protests, on November 24 a court voided further election results.

SRDJAN SUKI—EPA/AFP

A procession returning the Stone of Scone arrives in Edinburgh on November 30. The stone, which was the coronation seat of Scottish kings, had been taken to England by King Edward I.

for example, received an average of 143 hours of math instruction each year, compared with 117 hours given in Japan.

21

CIA officer called spy

A federal grand jury in Alexandria, Va., indicted Harold Nicholson on one count of conspiracy to commit espionage for Russia. He was the highest-ranking CIA official ever charged with spying. At the time of his arrest on November 16, Nicholson was preparing to board a plane to Switzerland, allegedly carrying with him a briefcase filled with classified documents. Before being named branch chief at the CIA's counterterrorism centre, Nicholson had been an instructor at the agency's training school for spies. Among the information he was said to have given the Russians were the names of spies he had trained. According to an affidavit made public on November 18, Nicholson received some $180,000 for the information.

24

Serbian elections voided

Despite public protests that began on November 19 as

a warning to Serbian Pres. Slobodan Milosevic not to repudiate the results of recent local elections, the First District Court in Belgrade voided the elections of 33 local council seats that had been won on November 17 by opposition candidates from the Zajedno coalition. Victories by other members of the opposition had earlier been negated by court rulings or official proclamations. The situation had all the elements of a pending crisis because there was growing evidence that the protesters were in no mood to capitulate.

25

APEC meets near Manila

The 18 members constituting the Asia-Pacific Economic Cooperation (APEC) forum ended their two-day annual meeting at Subic Bay, north of Manila, with a pledge to "substantially eliminate tariffs" on computers and high-tech products by the year 2000. The ministers, aware that the problems each faced were different, made allowances for "flexibility" in implementing the agreement. Issues that remained unresolved included China's tense relationship with Taiwan, the proliferation of nuclear technology, and the

linkage between trade and observance of human rights. In a major side development, President Clinton and Chinese Pres. Jiang Zemin agreed to exchange state visits in 1997.

29

French truckers end strike

A successful 12-day strike by French truck drivers ended when the trucking companies agreed, among other things, to lower the retirement age to 55 after 25 years of service, to compensate drivers for the time they waited while their cargo was loaded and unloaded, and to expand the ban on Sunday work to include foreign truckers working in France. The truckers had seriously disrupted French life by setting up some 250 road barricades that prevented the delivery of essential goods, including fuel. The strike also prevented commercial traffic across the English Channel and made it impossible for Spanish and Portuguese drivers to reach their destinations if their route took them through France.

•

Islamic parties banned

The Algerian government announced that in the na-

tional referendum held on November 28, the electorate had approved a new constitution that expanded the powers of Pres. Liamine Zeroual and severely undermined the political power of Islamic-based parties by outlawing those "founded on a religious basis." When the government canceled the second round of legislative elections in January 1992, which would almost certainly have led to the establishment of an Islamic state in Algeria, militant Muslims initiated a civil conflict that in the following five years claimed an estimated 50,000 lives.

30

Stone of Scone returned

A block of gray sandstone known as the Stone of Scone was returned to Scotland 700 years after it had been taken to England as war booty by King Edward I. The stone, which had been transported to Westminster Abbey in London, had been the coronation seat of Scottish kings and was, therefore, regarded as a symbol of Scottish nationalism. Prince Andrew, representing Queen Elizabeth II, attended the festivities that marked the return of the stone to Edinburgh Castle.

DECEMBER

KARL RONSTROM—REUTERS

Carrying the Mars Pathfinder space vehicle, a Delta rocket blasts off from Cape Canaveral, Florida, on December 4. Pathfinder, which included a rover named Sojourner, was to reach the planet on July 4, 1997.

1

Jiang visits India

Chinese Pres. Jiang Zemin ended a four-day visit to India after he and Indian Prime Minister H.D. Deve Gowda had signed a series of accords aimed at reducing tensions between their countries. Among other things, the two leaders agreed to reduce the number of troops each country had stationed along the 4,000-km (2,500-mi) common border. In 1962 fierce border skirmishes had driven the two countries farther apart, but in 1976 the two nations restored diplomatic relations. After Jiang's visit serious differences remained, including China's reported sale of armaments and nuclear technology to Pakistan, India's longtime rival. Jiang's visit had special significance because he was the first Chinese head of state to visit India since the country became independent in 1947.

Lucinschi wins election

In a runoff election for the presidency of Moldova, Petru Lucinschi, a left-of-centre independent and the speaker of Parliament, defeated incumbent Pres. Mircea Snegur by capturing 54% of the vote. Lucinschi,

54

who had been a member of the Politburo of the Communist Party of the Soviet Union before Moldova became independent, promised to promote Moldovan neutrality and to respect the powers granted to Parliament.

2
OSCE to update pact

During their fourth summit meeting in Lisbon, the 54 members of the Organization for Security and Cooperation in Europe (OSCE) began discussions on updating the Conventional Forces in Europe treaty, which had been signed by NATO and the Warsaw Pact nations in 1990. With the Warsaw Pact no longer a reality and NATO preparing to expand its membership in Central and Eastern Europe, OSCE considered it an appropriate time to reset limits on tanks, artillery, and military aircraft deployed in Europe in order to allay Russian concerns about its security.

3
Gay unions become issue

Kevin S.C. Chang, a circuit court judge in Honolulu, ruled that a state ban on same-sex marriages was unconstitutional and ordered the state to issue licenses for such unions. On the following day lawyers for the state were granted a stay pending the outcome of an appeal to the state Supreme Court. Anticipating Chang's ruling, in September the U.S. Congress had passed the Defense of Marriage Act, which denied federal recognition of same-sex marriages and federal benefits to partners in such unions.

4
U.S. launches Mars probe

The unmanned space vehicle Mars Pathfinder began a seven-month voyage to Mars that was scheduled to reach its destination on July 4, 1997. Its main science mission was to study the Martian atmosphere and investigate the geology and chemical composition of the planet's rocks and soils. When Pathfinder took off from Cape Canaveral, Florida, it carried a 10-kg (22-lb) wheeled rover device

dubbed Sojourner. The rover was designed to move slowly across the surface of Mars taking photographs, gathering other scientific data, and testing autonomous-vehicle technology on the Martian terrain.

5
Clinton fills Cabinet posts

Madeleine Albright, well known in the international community as the U.S. ambassador to the United Nations, was nominated by President Clinton to replace Warren Christopher as secretary of state. There was near unanimous agreement that her appointment would be approved after a brief pro forma hearing before the Senate. Albright, who was born in Czechoslovakia, was regarded as an expert on European affairs. She had strongly backed U.S. military intervention in Haiti, Iraq, and Bosnia and Herzegovina and had supported the establishment of war-crimes tribunals to punish those responsible for atrocities committed in Rwanda and the Balkans. Other Clinton nominations included William Cohen for the post of secretary of defense and Anthony Lake as director of central intelligence.

•
Taiwan reacts to setback

John Chang, the foreign minister of the Republic of China on Taiwan, announced that his government was recalling its ambassador to South Africa, terminating $80 million in annual aid, and suspending most of the treaties the two had signed. Officials on Taiwan felt that they had no other choice after South Africa announced on November 27 that it was severing diplomatic ties with the Republic of China at the insistence of the People's Republic of China. South Africa had been one of 30 countries that maintained a formal diplomatic relationship with the government on Taiwan.

7
Ghanaians reelect Rawlings

The people of Ghana reelected Jerry Rawlings president by giving him 57.2% of their votes. John Kufuor, his closest rival, was favoured by 39.9% of the electorate. In contests for seats in the unicameral House of Parliament, Rawlings's National Democratic Congress captured 130 of the 200 seats. The former air force pilot, after seizing power in

1981, had headed a military government until 1992. Then, after an election denounced as fraudulent by his opponents, he assumed the office of president as a civilian. International observers declared the most recent election free and fair.

9
Iraqi oil deal approved

Boutros Boutros-Ghali, secretary-general of the United Nations, gave final approval to a plan that would allow Iraq to resume its exportation of oil in order to alleviate a serious shortage of food and medicine; some money would also be used to reimburse victims of Iraq's 1990 invasion of Kuwait. A similar plan approved by the UN in May had been shelved after Iraq intervened militarily in a conflict between Kurdish factions in the northern part of the country. On December 10 Iraqi Pres. Saddam Hussein turned on a pumping station to symbolize Iraq's reentry into the world's oil markets.

10
Mandela signs new charter

South African Pres. Nelson Mandela signed a new con-

WALTER DHLADHLA—AFP

Pres. Nelson Mandela (seated) signs the new South African constitution on December 10. The ceremony took place in Sharpeville, the site of a 1960 massacre of citizens demonstrating against apartheid.

DECEMBER

stitution that completed a transition from a long period of white-minority rule to full-fledged democracy. A broad bill of rights immediately became the law of the land, but certain other provisions of the charter would take effect in stages. Following recommendations made by the Constitutional Court, the final document gave somewhat greater powers to a 60-member Council of Provinces, which replaced the 90-member Senate as the upper house of the bicameral national legislature. The signing ceremony took place at Sharpeville, a township 55 km (35 mi) from Johannesburg. That site was chosen because it had been the scene of a 1960 massacre of antiapartheid demonstrators. Mandela remarked, "Out of the many Sharpevilles which haunt our history was born the unshakeable determination that respect for human life, dignity, and well-being must be enshrined as rights beyond the power of any force to diminish."

11
Hong Kong leader chosen

A 400-member special election committee, approved by China, overwhelmingly chose Tung Chee-hwa to fill the office of chief executive of Hong Kong when the British crown colony reverted to Chinese sovereignty on July 1, 1997. Tung, who had been highly successful as head of the Orient Overseas International Ltd. shipping company founded by his father, was generally favoured by the business community, but his endorsement of China's plan to dissolve the colony's elected legislature and replace it with appointees had riled pro-democracy activists. The current governor of Hong Kong, Christopher Patten, challenged Tung to defend Hong Kong's interests after he assumed office and to insist that China honour the promises it had made to allow Hong Kong to exercise considerable autonomy after the British departed.

•

Russian miners end strike

Having received government assurances that some $470 million in back wages would be paid to striking coal miners before the end of the

year, officials of the Russian Coal Industry Workers' Union ordered its members to return to their jobs. More than 400,000 workers had walked off their jobs in protest on December 3. The delay in payments was due in part to the fact that coal customers owed the government nearly $1.5 billion in unpaid bills.

13
Annan to head UN

The UN Security Council ended a contentious debate by approving Kofi Annan of Ghana as secretary-general of the United Nations. On December 17 the UN General Assembly confirmed his appointment as successor to Boutros Boutros-Ghali as of Jan. 1, 1997. At the time of his election, Annan held the post of undersecretary-general for UN peacekeeping operations. Annan, who had earned academic degrees in both the U.S. and Switzerland, declared that he would seek to restore confidence between governments and the UN and strive to revitalize the UN's political and moral authority and its sense of common purpose in order to carry out its mission.

15
Airplane rivals to merge

The Boeing Co., which already dominated the global market for commercial aircraft, announced plans to buy the McDonnell Douglas Corp., a leading manufacturer of military aircraft. The $13.3 billion deal would make the new company the only U.S. manufacturer of commercial jets and the largest aerospace company in the world. Industry analysts viewed the planned

JON LEVY—AFP

WALTER HUPIU—AFP

merger as an ideal partnership because it brought together two complementary segments of airplane manufacturing and improved the new company's competitive position against such rivals as the formidable European consortium Airbus Industrie.

16
Chun given life sentence

An appellate court in Seoul, S.Kor., upheld the convictions of former presidents Chun Doo Hwan and Roh Tae Woo on charges that ranged from treason to corruption, but it then reduced Chun's death sentence to life imprisonment. Roh, who had been sentenced to 22½ years in prison, had his sentence reduced to 17 years.

17
Peru crisis begins

About 20 heavily armed guerrillas of the Túpac Amaru Revolutionary Movement (MRTA) invaded the Japanese embassy in Lima, Peru, and took several

hundred reception guests hostage. The dignitaries had gathered to celebrate the birthday of Japanese Emperor Akihito. The MRTA, which had maintained ties with similar Marxist groups in other Latin-American countries, demanded, among other things, the release of fellow rebels imprisoned in Peru and other countries. The organization had been considered moribund after many of its members accepted the terms of a government amnesty program and returned to society. Although the government cut off the embassy's utilities and refused to negotiate, the guerrillas released most of their hostages because the 80 or so they still held served their purpose and lessened the strain created by so many people living in cramped quarters. On December 31, with no end of the standoff in sight, a group of reporters with camera equipment evaded police barricades and entered the compound. The guerrillas welcomed the opportunity to gain wider publicity for their cause.

Women march in Lima, Peru, to show support for those taken hostage by the Túpac Amaru Revolutionary Movement on December 17. The standoff continued at year's end.

Kofi Annan of Ghana sits in front of the UN emblem during a press conference. On December 13 the UN Security Council chose him to become secretary-general, effective Jan. 1, 1997.

Red Cross workers slain

Five nurses and one construction worker, all members of the International Committee of the Red Cross, were shot and killed in a Chechen village hospital by unidentified gunmen. The killings were described as the worst premeditated atrocities against Red Cross personnel in the 133-year history of the organization. With no hard evidence to guide them, officials could only speculate that the acts of brutality were an attempt to undermine the peace settlement reached by Chechen separatists and Russia's central government. The attack had one immediate effect: the Red Cross, Doctors of the World, and the UN High Commissioner for Refugees agency all withdrew their workers from the area.

19
TV programs to be rated

Responding to a congressional mandate contained in the 1996 Telecommunications Act and to demands from the general public that television programs be rated for their violence, profanity, and sexual content, a panel of television industry personnel proposed a system keyed to the age of the viewers. After 10 months of often intense debate, the group approved six rating categories, one of which would be indicated on the television screen just before a program was aired and would be published beforehand in television guides. V-chip technology would soon be available to block out controversial programming. The first two ratings would apply to children's programming, and other programs would receive one of the four other ratings. TV-Y meant suitable for all youngsters and TV-Y7 suitable for children at least seven years old. Whereas TV-G programs would contain virtually no questionable material, TV-PG would warn that parental guidance was needed because the program contained potentially objectionable material; TV-14 would indicate a higher level of violence, sexual content, or profanity that might render them unsuitable for children under 14 years of age. TV-M programs were intended for adults only. News programs and sports events would not be rated.

26
South Koreans strike

Hundreds of thousands of South Korean union workers went on strike to protest a law that union leaders contended could lead to widespread layoffs. The legislation had been passed by the National Assembly in secret without opposition deputies present. The Federation of Democratic Unions, which had been outlawed, claimed that more than 200,000 of its workers had walked off their jobs at 172 automobile factories, shipyards, and other sites producing major exports. The following day the strike escalated when workers belonging to the government-approved Federation of Korean Trade Unions, which represented 472 unions, joined the protest. Hopes for a quick settlement of the strike began to recede when the finance and economy minister declared that the government would "not tolerate this illegal strike for any reason."

27
Lebed forms own party

Having already declared his intention to seek the presidency of Russia, Aleksandr Lebed announced that he was forming his own political party to give the voters an alternative to Pres. Boris Yeltsin or the Communist Party. Lebed, a popular retired general who had been Yeltsin's national security adviser before being summarily fired in October for causing dissension, claimed that he had the backing of bankers and financiers. He reiterated his contention that Yeltsin was in such poor health that he could not deal effectively with Russia's problems, which included unpaid government wages, delinquent tax collecting, and the formulation and financing of social programs.

29
Peace comes to Guatemala

During a ceremony that was more subdued than festive, the guerrilla leaders of the Guatemalan National Revolutionary Unity and members of the government's Peace Commission signed the Accord for a Firm and Lasting Peace, which formally ended 36 years of civil war. Many of those who watched the televised proceedings, which took place in the public square outside the National Palace in Guatemala City, had never known peace. A large number had family members or friends among the 100,000 who had died or the 40,000 who had "disappeared" during the years of conflict. Even though most Guatemalans said that they welcomed an end to the hostilities, they also expressed doubts that the peace would endure because problems rooted in poverty and injustice had never been adequately addressed.

KIMBERLY WHITE—REUTERS

Guerrilla leaders and government officials attend a ceremony in Guatemala City on December 29 for the signing of an agreement to end 36 years of civil war in Guatemala. It was estimated that the fighting had taken the lives of 100,000 people.

Disasters

The loss of life and property from disasters in 1996 included the following:

Aviation

January 8, Kinshasa, Zaire. An Antonov-32 cargo plane that apparently was overloaded failed to achieve liftoff and plowed through a bustling open market situated near the runway; an estimated 350 persons were killed as the craft ripped through vendor stalls made of corrugated iron and wood. The Russian crew members who escaped with minor injuries were taken into protective custody when an angry mob attempted to exact punishment for the crash.

January 17, Kano, Nigeria. An airplane crash reportedly claimed the lives of 14 persons, including the son of Nigeria's head of state; details were not made available.

February 4, Asunción, Paraguay. A Colombian cargo plane with a crew of three and one passenger exploded in midair after its left turbine engine erupted; 22 persons died when the craft dived into a residential area.

February 6, Off the coast of Dominican Republic. A Boeing 757 en route to Frankfurt and Berlin and carrying 189 persons, mostly German tourists, crashed and sank in shark-infested waters shortly after takeoff, apparently after the pilot gauged that he had enough speed to maintain altitude after he consulted a faulty speedometer; all aboard perished.

February 29, Near Arequipa, Peru. A Boeing 737 with 123 persons aboard slammed into a mountain and fell into a canyon while making its approach to land at an altitude below the authorized level; there were no survivors.

April 3, Near Dubrovnik, Croatia. An air force T-43A passenger jet carrying prominent U.S. officials, including Commerce Secretary Ron Brown, veered off course and crashed into a mountain during a driving rainstorm and heavy fog; all 35 persons aboard the craft were killed.

May 3, Near Khartoum, The Sudan. A Sudanese passenger plane crashed during a sandstorm when the pilot attempted to make an emergency landing in an open field because sand had covered the runways at the nearby airport; 48 passengers and 5 crew members died.

May 10, Santa María de Otáes, Mex. A plane transporting a group of miners crashed near a remote airstrip in the mountains of northwestern Mexico; 16 persons were killed, and 3 were seriously injured.

May 10, Camp Lejeune, North Carolina. Two helicopters taking part in a British-U.S. military exercise collided in the dark and plunged into a densely forested marsh; of the 16 persons aboard the two aircraft, 14 perished.

May 11, Near Miami, Fla. A DC-9 airliner crashed in the Everglades shortly after takeoff and minutes after the crew had reported smoke in the cockpit and cabin; the craft, which carried 109 persons, was mired in sticky muck; there were no survivors.

June 12, Near Townsville, Australia. Two army Blackhawk helicopters that were participating in nighttime antiterrorist maneuvers and flying with their anticollision lights turned off crashed after their rotors touched while they were landing in a training range; 18 persons were killed, and 10 were injured, 3 seriously.

July 15, Eindhoven, Neth. A Belgian military cargo plane that was carrying 41 persons, including members of a Dutch army band, crashed and burst into flames when it landed on the side of the runway; 32 persons perished, including all 4 crew members.

July 17, Off the coast of New York. A Boeing 747 jumbo jet carrying 230 persons en route to Paris exploded in midair and fell into the Atlantic Ocean; the cause of the blast, which claimed the lives of all aboard TWA flight 800, was still under investigation at year's end.

August 29, Spitsbergen, Nor. A Russian passenger plane carrying coal miners slammed into a snowcapped mountain while attempting to land in dense fog; all 141 persons aboard were killed.

October 2, Near Ancón, Peru. A Boeing 757 airliner plunged into the Pacific Ocean shortly after it took off from Lima and minutes after the pilot had radioed that his cockpit instrumentation was malfunctioning; the crash, in which all 70 persons aboard were killed, occurred after workers forgot to remove the duct tape that they had placed over key sensors while cleaning the plane.

October 22, Manta, Ecuador. A Miami-bound cargo plane exploded shortly after takeoff when it grazed a church bell tower; the plummeting aircraft ripped roofs off homes and sent a shower of fiery debris upon the densely populated neighbourhood; at least 23 persons were killed, including the 3 crew members.

October 31, São Paulo, Braz. An airliner carrying 96 persons to Rio de Janeiro failed to gain altitude after takeoff and plowed through a busy residential area; at least 104 persons were killed, including 8 on the ground who were engulfed in flames as the airliner spewed chunks of fuselage and drenched passersby with fuel.

November 7, Imota, Nigeria. A Boeing 727 airliner with 141 persons aboard went down in a swamp outside Lagos after losing radio contact midway into its flight; there were no survivors.

November 12, Near New Delhi. A midair collision between a Saudi Boeing 747 passenger plane with 312 persons aboard and a Kazak airliner carrying 37 passengers and crew claimed the lives of all 349 persons; it was the worst midair collision in aviation history.

November 19, Quincy, Ill. A runway collision between two small commuter planes and the ensuing fire claimed the lives of all 13 persons aboard the two planes.

November 22, Off the coast of Cape Mendocino, California. A military HC-130, which was conducting a training mission, crashed with 11 crew aboard, shortly after the pilot had reported a complete electrical failure; one airman survived.

November 23, Off the coast of the Comoros. A hijacked Ethiopian airliner, a Boeing 767 that

A relative stands before a funeral pyre outside a town in northern India. The dead were among the 349 people killed when a Saudi Arabian jumbo jet collided with a Kazak airliner near New Delhi on November 12 in the worst midair crash in aviation history.

had run out of fuel, bounced on the water before crash-landing nose first just short of the beach; of the 175 persons aboard, at least 120 were killed.

November 27, Central Siberia, Russia. A military cargo plane that was carrying some 30 tons of commercial goods crashed into a mountain and exploded; all 23 persons aboard were killed.

November 30, Near Medellín, Colom. A small passenger plane slammed into a hill shortly after experiencing mechanical failure moments after takeoff; of the 15 persons aboard, one survived.

December 17, Northwestern Russia. A military cargo plane with 17 persons aboard crashed during takeoff; there were no survivors.

Fires and Explosions

Early January, Shenzhen, Guangdong province, China. An early-morning fire engulfed a factory where some 1,000 workers were sleeping; 19 persons were killed as they scrambled to escape the flames, and 37 were injured in the melee.

January 18, Lübeck, Ger. A fire of an undetermined origin broke out at a four-story hostel that was sheltering asylum-seeking refugees from Syria, Lebanon, Zaire, and Togo and ethnic German emigrants from Poland; 10 persons, 4 of them children, were killed in the blaze.

Late January, Mecca, Saudi Arabia. A fire in a hospital claimed the lives of 13 persons and injured 33.

January 31, Shaoyang, Hunan province, China. A five-story apartment building was destroyed when 10 tons of dynamite stored illegally in the structure's basement exploded; at least 100 persons were killed, and the surrounding neighbourhood was demolished.

February 17, Taichung, Taiwan. A fire that erupted in a hotel and sauna killed 17 persons, who were burned beyond recognition after succumbing to smoke inhalation.

February 27, Taichung. A predawn fire that swept through an eight-story building claimed the lives of 13 persons and injured 17.

March 19, Manila. A fire in a discotheque, which was certified to hold no more than 35 persons, killed 159 of the 400 revelers packed into the funnel-shaped structure as they stampeded toward a lone exit; the blaze of unknown origin was the country's worst fire, and many victims were burned beyond recognition.

March 28, Bogor, Indon. An early-morning fire that broke out on the top floor of a three-story commercial building quickly engulfed the lower two levels; though 77 people were initially believed dead, the toll was lowered to 10 female workers when the morgue disclosed that some body bags contained charred mannequins, which had been counted among the dead.

April–early May, Mongolia. Tinder-dry forests and grasslands were engulfed in at least 72 separate fires that were spread by strong winds; 25 persons were killed and at least 60 injured as more than 24,000 persons fought the raging blazes, which had burned 106,000 sq km (41,000 sq mi) and threatened to incinerate other areas before beneficial rains helped firefighters extinguish the flames.

April 11, Düsseldorf, Ger. An unexplained fire, which presumably started in a flower shop, spread noxious fumes into elevators, ventilation ducts, and lounges in the arrivals section at the city's airport and claimed the lives of at least 15 persons.

June 6, Red Sea. A fire aboard a ship that was traveling illegally from Eritrea into Saudi Arabian waters claimed the lives of at least 72 persons.

June 11, Oscasco, Braz. A powerful explosion that ripped through a shopping mall during lunchtime, when between 1,000 and 2,000 shoppers were present, claimed the lives of more than 40 persons and injured 100; the force of the blast destroyed parts of two concrete walls and caused a corner of a second-story parking lot to collapse.

June 29, Piya, Sichuan province, China. An explosion at a fireworks factory that had reopened illegally after having been shut down two months earlier killed at least 36 persons and injured 52, some of whom were seriously burned.

July 17, Shenzhen, China. A hotel fire that started in a restaurant on the second floor swept

Rescuers remove the body of a victim of a fire that destroyed an overcrowded discotheque on March 19 in Manila, killing 159 people. Most of those killed in the fire—said to be the worst in Philippine history—were students, and many of the victims were burned beyond recognition.

through the structure and claimed the lives of 29 persons, including patrons who were suffocated by thick smoke as they slept; the cause of the fire was unknown.

August 14, Arequipa, Peru. A stray rocket hit a high-voltage cable during a fireworks display and knocked the line onto spectators; 35 persons were electrocuted, and 42 were badly burned.

October 9, Kampung Sessang, Sarawak, Malaysia. A dormitory fire at an elementary school complex claimed the lives of 11 children.

October 20, Anhui province, China. An explosion at a firecracker factory that was operating without a license and illegally using child labour killed at least 13 children and injured 19.

November 21, San Juan, P.R. A downtown six-story building exploded while employees from the gas company were investigating a possible leak; at least 29 persons lost their lives, and some 82 were injured.

November 21, Hong Kong. A raging fire on the upper floors of a 16-story office building blazed for 21 hours before it was brought under control; it claimed the lives of 39 persons, and dozens more were injured.

Marine

Mid-January, Off the coast of Sumatra, Indon. A ferry that was transporting some 210 passengers and a cargo of cement, building materials, and vehicles sank quickly after ramming into rocks during a brisk wind; at least 51 passengers were known dead, and at least 100 were missing.

January 24, Off the southeastern coast of Nigeria. A boat carrying some 260 persons to Gabon capsized after a gale-force wind suddenly pitched the vessel and threw its contents into the sea; at least 172 persons were killed, and several were missing and feared dead.

February 17, Off the northern coast of Taiwan. A Greek-registered cargo ship sank in choppy waters near the island of Peng Chia-yu; of the 30 seamen aboard the boat, 19 were missing and presumed drowned.

February 18, Off the coast of Cadiz, Negros Island, Phil. A dilapidated wooden-hulled ferry that carried more than 200 passengers, twice its capacity, and had been deemed unseaworthy earlier in the month sank as high winds buffeted it and panicked passengers rushed to one side of the vessel; at least 54 persons were killed, including 31 children, and several were missing.

February 19, Taiwan Strait. A Chinese cargo ship with 30 crewmen aboard disappeared without a trace and presumably sank; all aboard were lost at sea.

March 1, Lake Victoria, Uganda. A boat loaded with passengers capsized during inclement weather between Masolya and Bumba Island, and 66 persons drowned; two weeks earlier another boating accident at the same location, involving a collision between two vessels, had claimed the lives of 39 persons.

March 28, Caribbean Sea. An overcrowded Haitian ferry sank shortly after leaving the port of Les Irois and striking some rocks; more than 100 drowned.

May 6, Off the coast of Sierra Leone. An overloaded boat capsized during inclement weather with at least 210 persons aboard, many of them merchants who were transporting commercial goods; at least 140 persons were feared drowned.

May 21, Lake Victoria. An overcrowded ferry that was transporting 222 more passengers than its official capacity capsized and sank some 32 km (20 mi) short of its destination, the western town of Mwanza, Tanz.; 549 persons lost their lives.

May 24, Jamuna River, Bangladesh. A passenger ferry sank in choppy waters after colliding with another ferry that was carrying cars and trucks; at least 77 persons were feared drowned.

June 15, Off the coast of South Korea. A Cyprus-registered cargo ship sank some 32 km southeast of the port city of Pusan after colliding with a Greek freighter in heavy fog; all 26 seamen aboard the cargo ship drowned, but the Greek freighter remained intact.

July 27, Off the coast of the Comoros. A ferry that was traveling from Moroni began taking on water and quickly sank as it approached the island of Mwali; of the 69 persons aboard, only 5 were rescued.

September 26, Nile River, near Beni Hasan, Al-Minya governorate, Egypt. An overloaded ferry with a capacity of 50 passengers was transporting funeral mourners when it collided with a barge; 56 of the 75 persons aboard the ferry drowned.

October 14, Off the coast of Fort Pierce, Fla. A sailboat sank in rough Atlantic waters; the 16 persons aboard the craft had radioed that they were boarding a life raft, but rescuers failed to find them.

November 14, Nile River, southern Egypt. A cruise boat carrying Czech and Slovak tourists capsized during a strong wind as the captain tried to dock the vessel; 20 persons drowned.

November 14, Off the eastern coast of South Africa. A Panamanian-registered freighter sank in turbulent seas while being buffeted by high winds; all 29 crewmen aboard were lost.

December 25, Off the coast of Malta. A small ship that apparently had been stolen from Malta and was carrying illegal immigrants from India, Pakistan, and Sri Lanka to Europe sank after colliding with a larger ship that was bound for Greece, from which the immigrants had been transferred; survivors charged that some 280 of their fellow travelers drowned, but authorities were not able to locate the wreckage.

Mining and Tunneling

January–April, South Africa. A total of 178 miners were killed in accidents during the first four months of the year, and more than 2,400 were injured.

May, Hunan province, China. An explosion at the Pindingshan coal mine killed 84 miners.

May, Gansu province, China. Flooding at a lead and zinc mine in the northern part of the province killed 33 miners. As a result, the government closed the mine, the second largest complex at Lijiaguo.

June, Yunnan province, China. Two landslides in a gold mine resulted in the deaths of at least 227 miners.

November 27, Shanxi province, China. A gas explosion in an underground mine entombed some 90 miners.

November 27, Free State province, South Africa. A mud slide at a diamond mine trapped 56 miners, 22 of whom were killed.

Natural

January 7–8, Northeastern U.S. The punishing Blizzard of '96, which blanketed at least 20 states, dumped record amounts of snow in Philadelphia, which recorded more than 76 cm (30 in); forced a state of emergency to be called in all or parts of Kentucky, Pennsylvania, Virginia, West Virginia, Maryland, New York, New Jersey, Delaware, and Georgia; shut down virtually all means of transportation; closed governments, schools, and businesses; and claimed the lives of at least 100 persons, many of them victims of heart attacks.

January 20, Northeastern U.S. An unexpected thaw that melted the snowpack of the Blizzard of '96 caused massive flooding as rivers and streams burst their banks in Virginia, West Virginia, Maryland, Pennsylvania, Delaware, New Jersey, New York, and Connecticut; at least 15 deaths were attributed to the flooding.

February 2–4, U.S. Bitter cold gripped the nation from the Rocky Mountains in the West to the Atlantic coast and into the Deep South as record low temperatures were recorded in Salt Lake City, Utah, −24° C (−12° F); Huntsville, Ala., −14° C (7° F); and Tower, Minn., −60° C (−76° F), the coldest place in the U.S.

February 3, Lijiang, Yunnan province, China. A magnitude-7 earthquake demolished the town and leveled as many as 186,000 homes, killed more than 240 persons, and injured some 14,000 others, 3,800 of them seriously; survivors huddled in the open as aftershocks as strong as 6 rocked the region.

February 10, Near Sapporo, Japan. A 50,000-ton slab of rock fell on a road tunnel through which a bus and a car were traveling; 19 persons on the bus and one person in the car were crushed to death.

February 12–14, São Paulo and Rio de Janeiro states, Braz. Some of the heaviest rains in 25 years caused severe flooding, which claimed the lives of at least 50 persons and left thousands of others homeless; many of the dead were killed in mud slides, which entombed them in their hill-side shanties.

February 17, Biak Island, Indonesia. An earthquake of magnitude 7.9 followed by tidal waves as high as 4 m (13 ft) destroyed more than 5,000 homes and claimed the lives of 108 persons, most of whom were swept out to sea.

February 21, Northern Peru. A tidal wave lashed the coast following an earthquake of magnitude 6.7; 10 fishermen were killed.

March 16, Kashmir, Pak. An avalanche in the village of Kel claimed the lives of at least 32 persons.

March 18, Kashmir. The second avalanche in two days in Kashmir buried seven houses in a tiny village near Muzaffarabad; at least 40 persons were feared dead.

March 19, Xinjiang Uygur, China. An earthquake of magnitude 6.9 accompanied by aftershocks as strong as 5.1 toppled some 15,000 structures in the region and claimed the lives of at least 28 persons.

March 28, Central Ecuador. An earthquake of magnitude 5.9 struck near Cotopaxi and claimed the lives of at least 19 persons.

April, Afghanistan. Heavy rains and melting snow caused massive flooding, the worst in decades, which led to the deaths of at least 100 persons and damage to some 3,000 homes.

April 27–28, Salvador, Braz. Driving rainstorms were blamed for the deaths of at least 30 and injuries to 24.

Late April, Recife, Braz. Mud slides triggered by heavy rains swept away shanties perched on hillsides in the coastal city; as many as 32 persons were feared dead.

May 3, Inner Mongolia, China. A strong earthquake of magnitude 5.9 shook the city of Baotou and the county of Guyang; 18 persons were killed, and some 200,000 were left homeless.

May 13, Bangladesh. A tornado that rampaged through the district of Tangail and packed winds of 200 km/h (125 mph) uprooted trees, flattened some 80 villages, killed more than 440 persons, and injured some 32,000.

May 31 and June 3, Yunnan province, China. In the space of four days, relentless rains caused two landslides on Laojin Mountain, the site of the Daping gold mine; 100 persons were known dead, 138 were missing, and 77 were injured.

Mid-June, India. Two cyclones, one that battered the southeastern coast and another that lashed the west coast states of Gujarat and Maharashtra, claimed the lives of more than 260 persons; in addition, 120 fishermen were lost at sea.

Mid-June, Central Yemen. Torrential rains in Shabwa province triggered heavy flooding, which led to the deaths of at least 158 persons and the destruction of some 1,274 homes.

June 16–19, Karachi, Pak. A scorching heat wave accompanied by high humidity claimed the lives of 37 persons, including a number of homeless drug addicts who were found dead on the street.

Early July, Oklahoma and Texas. A blistering eight-day heat wave with temperatures staying near or above 38° C (100° F) was blamed for the deaths of at least 20 persons; 54 people in Dallas were treated for heat-related illnesses.

Early–mid-July, Caribbean and U.S. Hurricane Bertha, which rampaged through the Caribbean and hit Puerto Rico and the Virgin Islands before smashing into the east coast of the United States and blasting the states of Florida, North Carolina, South Carolina, Virginia, New York, and New Jersey, claimed the lives of more than 30 persons, 20 of whom drowned after the cruise ship that they were aboard capsized near St. Thomas. The storm inflicted serious property damage on St. Thomas and North Carolina.

Mid–late July, Northern Bangladesh and eastern India. Two weeks of relentless monsoon rains caused massive flooding, which claimed the lives of at least 291 persons; 2.2 million persons were left homeless as a result of the deluge.

July–August, Southern and central China. Monsoon rains swelled the Chang Jiang (Yangtze River), Huang Ho (Yellow River), and Hai He (Hai River) to dangerous levels and caused flooding of calamitous proportions in nine provinces and areas; some 2,000 persons were feared dead, and damages to property and crops were estimated at $11 billion.

July 20–21, Northeastern Quebec. Torrential rains washed out bridges and roads and caused massive flooding that destroyed or damaged between 1,500 and 2,000 homes in the Saguenay region; at least 10 lives were lost as a result of the flooding, which caused damage as high as $1.5 billion.

July 26, Near Chorwon, S.Kor. Heavy monsoon rains triggered landslides and floods that claimed the lives of more than 50 persons, including 20

soldiers who were killed when a landslide buried two barracks in which they were sleeping.

July 27–28, Colombia, Costa Rica, Nicaragua, and Mexico. Hurricane Cesar unleashed its fury on Colombia and Costa Rica before losing force and being downgraded and designated Tropical Storm Douglas as it hit Nicaragua and then menaced Mexico; at least 16 persons were known dead, and 21 were missing in Costa Rica.

July 31–August 1, Taiwan. Typhoon Herb, the country's most costly storm to date, with more than $507 million in damages to agriculture and fishery operations, brutalized the landscape with high winds and pounding rain; at least 41 persons were killed.

August 8, Northern Spain. Flash floods raced through a campground in the Pyrenees after a river burst its banks during a torrential downpour; as many as 70 persons were killed as the raging waters swept away cars, tents, and campers in a torrent of mud and debris.

August 14, Off the coast of Vietnam. A fierce storm claimed the lives of about 400 fishermen who were lost at sea when their small wooden boats were shattered.

August 17–18, Northwestern Vietnam. A fierce storm caused widespread flooding and led to the deaths of at least 53 persons.

August 29, Perak, Malaysia. Torrential rains triggered a landslide in the remote area of Kampar in Perak; 13 persons were known dead, and 37 were missing after their flimsy huts were washed into a jungle river.

Late August, Jammu and Kashmir, India. A freak snowstorm interspersed with driving rains stranded thousands of Hindu pilgrims on the slopes of the Himalayas as they were making an annual pilgrimage to the ancient Amarnath Cave to worship Shiva, the Hindu god of destruction and restoration; 239 persons were known dead, many of them from exposure, and many more were missing.

September 2, Omdurman province, The Sudan. Heavy rains caused severe flooding in the areas of Al-Jaili and Umbaddah; 15 persons lost their lives, and more than 1,000 homes were demolished.

September 5–7, North Carolina, South Carolina, Virginia, and West Virginia. Hurricane Fran churned winds of up to 195 km/h (120 mph) that toppled power lines, propelled trees into houses, and produced heavy rain, which caused extensive flooding; at least 28 deaths were attributed to the storm, 17 of them in North Carolina, where 34 counties were declared disaster areas. The states of Maryland and Pennsylvania also were soaked by the storm.

September 9, Guangdong province, China. Typhoon Sally roared into southern China with punishing winds that smashed more than 200,000 homes and interrupted electricity and water supplies; hardest hit were the cities of Zhanjian and Maoming, where at least 139 persons were killed and 110 were missing.

September 10–14, Puerto Rico and Dominican Republic. Hurricane Hortense delivered devastating damages to the Dominican Republic and Puerto Rico, where at least 22 persons lost their lives and about $100 million in crop damage was sustained, before brushing the Turks and Caicos Islands and roaring past The Bahamas on a northerly course. The storm knocked out power and lashed Nova Scotia before weakening.

October–November, Central and northern Vietnam. Monthlong flooding in the Mekong delta followed a series of storms that deluged the country, causing $400 million in damage; at least 162 persons were killed, and thousands of homes were damaged or destroyed.

Mid-October, Costa Rica, Cuba, Honduras, and Nicaragua. Hurricane Lili battered the countries with punishing torrential rain that weakened homes, destroyed crops, and killed at least 10 persons.

Mid-October, Andhra Pradesh and Tamil Nadu, India. Five days of relentless rains inundated low-lying coastal districts in both states, causing widespread flooding that killed some 350 persons, left some 100,000 homeless, and caused considerable damage to railway tracks and bridges.

AFP PHOTOS

A man fishes from the roof of a house that was all but submerged by flooding north of Hangzhou, China. Monsoon rains in July and August in nine central and southern provinces resulted in some 2,000 deaths and damage to property and crops estimated at $11 billion.

November 6, Andhra Pradesh. A cyclone that roared in from the Bay of Bengal annihilated the country's southeastern coast and killed at least 1,000 people; the fate of another 600, many of them Balusutippa fishermen, was unknown.

November 12, Southern Peru. A powerful earthquake of magnitude 6.4 shook the tourist town of Nazca, where some 40 miners were trapped in a gold mine; about 95% of the homes there, most made of adobe, were damaged.

November 17, Near Brownsville, Texas. Waves about 3 m (10 ft) high consumed a group of men, women, and children who were carrying passports from Pakistan and were apparently attempting to cross the Rio Grande into the U.S.; some 10 persons were feared drowned.

November 18–22, Northwestern U.S. Rain in Oregon and snow and ice in Washington knocked out power and unleashed mud slides in Oregon, where a huge sinkhole swallowed one tractor-trailer and damaged another; 12 deaths were attributed to the severe weather.

November 24–25, Southern Plains and Mississippi valley, U.S. Ice storms made travel treacherous and contributed to snapping power lines and trees; at least 17 persons lost their lives in traffic accidents—6 in Oklahoma, 6 in Texas, 3 in Wisconsin, and 2 in Missouri.

December 3–6, Manam Island, Papua New Guinea. A volcano unleashed a cloud of gas and volcanic ash and a torrent of lava fragments, which swept down its slopes and obliterated the village of Budua; 12 persons were known dead.

December 25, Sabah, Malaysia. Tropical Storm Greg roared through the region, leveled houses and thatched huts, and claimed the lives of more than 200 persons, many of whom were washed away in floodwaters; hardest hit was Keningau, where more than 100 corpses were found under debris or floating in rivers.

December 26–31, California, Idaho, Nevada, Oregon, and Washington. Incessant rain and snowstorms killed at least 29 persons.

Late December, Europe. A continentwide deep freeze claimed the lives of at least 150 persons during the last week of the month; in addition, as many as 300 persons in Russia were trapped in a tunnel with their vehicles when avalanches stranded them.

Railroad

February 16, Near Washington, D.C. A head-on collision between a Chicago-bound Amtrak train and a Maryland commuter train resulted in the deaths of 11 persons, all of them apparently on the commuter train; some of the more than 175 passengers and crew aboard the Amtrak train sustained minor injuries.

Early April, Near Mweka, Zaire. A train crash following a derailment left 30 dead and 30 injured.

April 7, Near Korogwe, Kenya. A freight train collided with a bus at a railroad crossing; 33 persons, mostly bus passengers, lost their lives, and 24 were injured.

April 18, Northern India. A passenger train collided with a freight train; 20 persons were known dead, and at least 100 were injured.

September 18, Japeri, Braz. An out-of-control freight train rear-ended a passenger train stopped at the station; 15 persons lost their lives.

September 26, Southern Russia. A train traveling at full speed in dense fog plowed into a school bus at a railroad crossing; at least 21 children were killed, and 20 persons, including the driver and 3 adults, were seriously injured.

Traffic

January 1, Near Sonoita, Mex. A bus inexplicably crossed into oncoming traffic and collided head-on with another bus; 27 persons were killed, and at least 25 were injured in the crash.

February 12, Northern Italy. A chain-reaction pileup involving as many as 300 vehicles occurred on a fog-shrouded highway between Vicenza and Verona; at least 11 persons were killed, and more than 100 were injured.

February 24, Pakistan. A crowded bus plunged into a canal after the driver swerved to avoid an oncoming car; at least 23 persons lost their lives as they were carried away in the swift-moving current.

February 25, Bolivia. Two buses traveling at high speed during a rainstorm collided head-on some 45 km (28 mi) outside La Paz; at least 35 persons perished, and dozens were injured.

February 28, Near Bailén, Spain. A passenger car veered across the centre line and slammed into a charter bus, which burst into flames; 29 persons were killed, and 17 were injured.

March 14, Saudi Arabia. A vehicle carrying a group of illegal immigrants, most of them from Yemen, overturned while heading toward the town of Jizan, Saudi Arabia, where the deportees were being sent; 47 persons were killed.

July 2, Dniprodzerzhynsk, Ukraine. A streetcar that was barreling down a hill at top speed derailed and slammed into a concrete wall when its brakes failed; at least 32 persons were killed, and 75 were injured.

July 15, Central Mexico. A bus plunged off a rain-slickened highway after the driver apparently lost control of the vehicle while speeding down the slippery road; 17 persons lost their lives, and 26 were injured.

September 2, Mexico. A bus en route to the town of Cuautla in the state of Morelos hit a truck and fell on its side; at least 20 persons were killed, and some 15 were injured.

September 15, Southern Bangladesh. A bus that was racing past a bus station in Comilla hit several bicycle rickshaws; 12 persons were killed, and 11 were injured.

October 5, Near Warmbaths, S.Af. A bus collided with a gasoline tanker after attempting to pass another vehicle while traveling through thick smoke emanating from a wildfire; at least 38 persons were killed in the fiery crash, and 12 were seriously injured.

October 10, Southern Turkey. A bus carrying about 30 German, Dutch, and Swiss tourists overturned and plunged into a ravine while barreling down a slick road; 11 persons were killed, and 19 were injured.

November 10, Near Tbilisi, Georgia. A bus that was traveling on the narrow mountain road between Tskhaltubo and Ambrulauri plummeted over a precipice into a river; at least 23 persons were killed.

December 25, Southern Philippines. A minibus traveling between the towns of Tipo-tipo and Maluso crashed and erupted in flames after the driver of the overloaded vehicle was unable to maneuver down a steep descent; 17 persons burned to death, and 12 were injured.

December 25, Saudi Arabia. A bus traveling from Jordan to an unknown destination in Saudi Arabia veered off the road and overturned; 17 persons were killed, and at least 40 were injured.

Miscellaneous

May 13, Nairobi, Kenya. A supermarket marquee collapsed and crushed 16 persons who had taken shelter under it during a heavy downpour.

June 12, Hyderabad, Pak. A four-story building collapsed in the early-morning hours as residents slept inside the 50-year-old structure; because suffocating summer heat had prompted many male occupants to sleep in the street, most of the 21 casualties were women and children.

June 20, Salvador, Braz. A newly built cement warehouse collapsed and trapped 25 dock workers, 14 of whom lost their lives.

July 15, Ujjain and Hardwar, India. At least 60 worshipers gathered to celebrate a new moon festival were killed, including 39 persons who were trampled in Ujjain as some 200,000 devotees rushed down marble steps to an underground temple, and 21 persons who died when a crowd stampeded across an overcrowded bridge while rushing to bathe in the Ganges River in Hardwar.

July 31, Tembisa, S.Af. A stampede at a railway station occurred when private security guards, in an attempt to ensnare fare dodgers, closed exits and began prodding commuters with batons, which some claimed were electrified; 15 persons were trampled to death in the ensuing chaos, many of them as they tried to elude the batons as the crowd surged forward. The incident provoked a rash of stoning and arson.

August 7, Bhiwandi, India. Food poisoning was blamed for the deaths of at least 52 persons who dined at a local restaurant and ate rice that was laced with datura, a poisonous weed.

September 18, Calcutta. At least 17 men who climbed up into a tree to view a concert free were killed when the branches holding them broke and spilled them onto a live electric wire; 18 persons were injured in the resulting stampede.

October 16, Guatemala City, Guat. A stampede by soccer fans entering a stadium to watch a qualifying World Cup match that had been oversold resulted in the deaths of more than 80 persons, who died after a crowd of gate-crashers raced past security guards and trampled them.

October 27, Heliopolis, Egypt. A 12-story apartment building in a suburb of Cairo collapsed and killed at least 15 occupants; 60 others were missing in the debris, which covered 5 stories.

December, Glasgow, Scot. A food-poisoning outbreak occurred after church parishioners were served tainted meat at a luncheon in November; by December, 15 of the 45 hospitalized persons suffering from the illness blamed on the *Escherichia coli* bacterium had died.

December 20, Guangdong province. A 91-m (100-yd) section of a 160-m (175-yd) bridge that was under construction and nearing completion collapsed and entombed workers under tons of debris; at least 24 workers lost their lives, and 63 were injured.

People of 1996

NOBEL PRIZES

Prize for Peace

Not inclined to shy away from international conflicts, the Norwegian Nobel Committee gave worldwide publicity to the dissident movement in East Timor by awarding the 1996 Nobel Prize for Peace to two East Timorese activists, Bishop Carlos Filipe Ximenes Belo and José Ramos-Horta. East Timor, which occupies the eastern half of the island of Timor, was a somewhat neglected colony of Portugal for most of the 20th century. An independence movement in the mid-1970s prompted Portugal to withdraw from the island in November 1975 when the leading warring faction, the leftist group Fretilin, declared independence for East Timor. This freedom, however, did not last long. Neighbouring Indonesia, with the tacit approval of Western nations concerned about the spread of communism, invaded East Timor in early December and incorporated it as a province the following year. The Indonesian government used military might to impose its will on a noncompliant population. Human rights organizations estimated that one-third of the 600,000 inhabitants lost their lives in the years that followed Indonesia's control of the territory. Although Indonesia called East Timor its 27th province, it was not recognized as such by the United Nations or any nation except Australia.

In naming the award recipients, the Nobel Committee did not mince words when it described Indonesia's 20-year rule as "systematic oppression." Indonesia expressed "regret" over the committee's choices, particularly that of the exiled activist José Ramos-Horta, a longtime proponent of independence. The 46-year-old former guerrilla was first exiled from East Timor in 1970 by the Portuguese but returned in 1972 to participate in the civil war with the Fretilin faction before leaving in 1975, only days before Indonesian troops took control. He remained in exile in Australia. Later renouncing his connections to guerrilla forces, Ramos-Horta sought international support for an ambitious peace plan for the region; he also served on the faculty of the University of New South Wales, Sydney.

Belo, a 48-year-old native Timorese, was ordained a Roman Catholic bishop in 1983. As a patriot and spiritual leader of a territory that was more than 90% Catholic, he was the foremost critic of the brutal tactics of Indonesian President Suharto, who ruled a country that was 90% Muslim. Belo's high profile and outspoken nature made him a target for at least two attempts on his life, one in 1989 and the other in 1991. His protests were most notable following the massacre of about 200 demonstrators at a cemetery in Dili, the capital, in November 1991. He personally ushered many of the wounded to safety. In an open letter written in July 1994, he outlined his concern for the East Timorese people and proposed that the Indonesian government reduce its troops, curtail repressive measures, extend freedoms to the Catholic Church, permit free speech, enter dialogue with international groups, and allow East Timor to hold a democratic referendum on self-determination or, barring that, to create legislation granting East Timor special territorial status and greater autonomy. In his speech accepting the prize in December, Belo urged a nonviolent resolution of the problem, citing the example of 1964 Nobel laureate Martin Luther King, Jr.

(TOM MICHAEL)

Prize for Economics

The awarding of a Nobel Prize comes with more than just a hefty sum of money ($1,120,000 accompanied each prize in 1996). There is also immediate international fame and sudden widespread recognition for research that previously may have gone unnoticed outside the narrow confines of academia. The recipients, who are generally notified of the award by an early-morning phone call, may awaken to media pressures to which they are unaccustomed. Such was the case with William S. Vickrey, the Canadian-born economist at Columbia University, New York City, who shared the 1996 Nobel Memorial Prize in Economic Science with Scottish-born James Alexander Mirrlees of the University of Cambridge. Vickrey, perhaps straining under a flurry of unprecedented activity and scrutiny, died three days after receiving the honour, apparently of a heart attack. Upon selection, the two economists, who did not work together, were lauded for their analytic research on economic incentives in situations with incomplete, or asymmetrical, information.

The area of microeconomics on which the pair worked is related to game theory, a branch of mathematics that examines how the players of a game affect its outcome by revealing or shielding information from one another. Vickrey and Mirrlees helped elucidate situations in which incomplete information poses unforeseen problems. For example, a government that hopes to institute a progressive income tax system that is both efficient and equitable must consider the possibility that stepped income brackets with increasing tax penalties may affect a worker's incentive to earn greater wages and, consequently, distort productivity. This "optimal income tax" problem parallels the "moral hazard" problem, which is exemplified by an insurance policy that offers such sizable coverage that a policyholder may take greater than usual risks. Classical economic models, which assume that all parties have access to the same information, tend not to incorporate incentives and similar variables into their equations.

Vickrey was born June 21, 1914, in Victoria, B.C., and was educated at Yale University (B.S., 1935) and Columbia University (M.A., 1937; Ph.D., 1947), where he taught throughout his career. Because of his interest in human welfare, he

José Ramos-Horta (left) and Bishop Carlos Ximenes Belo

James A. Mirrlees

often chose projects that had practical applications. His studies of traffic congestion concluded that pricing on commuter trains and toll roads should vary according to usage, with higher fares and tolls during peak-use periods. This time-of-day cost structure was later widely adopted by electric and telephone utilities. Although proposals of this kind gained him the audience of city planners worldwide, few of his ideas were adopted at the time. In his influential article "Counterspeculation, Auctions, and Competitive Sealed Tenders" (1961), he proposed what came to be known as the Vickrey auction, which, through sealed bidding, awards the auctioned item to the holder of the highest bid but at the sum bid by the second highest bidder. According to Vickrey, in guaranteeing the lower price, both buyers and sellers would benefit, because bidders would be more likely to bid what they believed the item to be worth, as opposed to submitting a lowball bid and risking losing the item for a sum less than the item's perceived value.

Born July 5, 1936, in Minnigaff, Scot., Mirrlees studied mathematics at the University of Edinburgh (M.A., 1957) and Trinity College, Cambridge (Ph.D., 1963). He taught at the University of Oxford (1969–95) and at Cambridge. His technically refined mathematical skills complemented Vickrey's theoretical creativity, and his groundbreaking models and equations, published in the 1970s, illustrated the "optimal income taxation" and "moral hazard" problems often treated in Vickrey's books. Mirrlees's methodology became the standard in the economics of informational asymmetries and was used by a generation of later economists in a variety of applications.

(TOM MICHAEL)

Prize for Literature

Polish poet Wisława Szymborska was little known outside her country before being chosen to receive the 1996 Nobel Prize for Literature. The reclusive poet, who had published only seven volumes of verse in Poland during the past three decades, was considered difficult to translate owing to the subtlety of her technique. Collections of her poetry did appear, however, in several languages; her English-language titles were *Sounds, Feelings, Thoughts* (1981), *People on a Bridge* (1990), and *View with a Grain of Sand* (1995). Observers such as Polish poet Czesław Miłosz, winner of the 1980 Nobel Prize for Literature, regarded the selection of Szymborska as international confirmation of the brilliance of Polish poetry in the period following World War II. Szymborska, along with fellow poets Zbigniew Herbert and Tadeusz Różewicz, held common witness to the struggles of modern Poland—World War II, the Holocaust, Soviet occupation, postwar Stalinism, martial law, and transition to democracy. She tempered this, however, with a strong humanism and a desire to deal with sophisticated philosophical issues.

Szymborska diverged from her compatriots in her universal approach to personal issues; daily occurrences were regularly reexamined in broad perspective in her verse. Her delicate style was classical in its wit, depth, and detachment yet decidedly modern with its irony and nonchalance. Her language was unpretentious, reflecting the stripped-down, straightforwardness of social realism, which held sway in Eastern European poetry in the mid-1950s. Her tone was often wry and conversational.

Her plainspoken language, however, belied a complexity of thought, in both structure and content. These hidden depths were exemplified in the poem "The Three Oddest Words" (1996):

> When I pronounce the word Future,
> the first syllable already belongs to the past.
> When I pronounce the word Silence,
> I destroy it.
> When I pronounce the word Nothing,
> I make something no nonbeing can hold.

Szymborska was born on July 2, 1923, in the town of Bnin (now part of Kornik) in western Poland, near Poznan. From 1931 she lived in Krakow, where in 1945–48, at Jagiellonian University, she studied literature and sociology. Her verse was first published in 1945, and her first two books of poetry, which she had since disclaimed

for their slavish devotion to social realism, appeared in 1952 and 1954. Her first collection published after the Soviet loosening of censorship, *Wołanie do Yeti* (1957; "Calling Out to Yeti"), commented on Stalinism through the title character, Yeti, or the Abominable Snowman. Later volumes included *Sól* (1962; "Salt") and *Sto pociech* (1967; "No End of Fun"). The title work of *Wszelki Wypadek* (1972; "Could Have") examined chance, one of her common themes. Later books included *Wielka liczba* (1977; "A Large Number"), *Ludzie na moście* (1986; "The People on the Bridge"), and *Koniec i początek* (1993; "The End and the Beginning").

From 1953 to 1981 Szymborska worked for the weekly *Zycie literackie* ("Literary Life"), contributing a column entitled *Lektury nadobowiazkowe* ("Noncompulsory Reading"); these columns were collected into bound editions in 1973, 1981, and 1992. In the 1980s she contributed to the periodicals *Arka* and *Kultura*—the latter an expatriate journal published in Paris. Symborska was also a noted translator, with a particular expertise in French poetry of the 16th and 17th centuries.

(TOM MICHAEL)

Prize for Chemistry

The 1996 Nobel Prize for Chemistry was awarded to a group of British and U.S. researchers who discovered fullerenes, a previously unrecognized form of carbon that opened a new branch of chemistry. Fullerenes are hollow, spherical clusters of carbon atoms bonded together into highly symmetrical, cagelike structures. Bonds in the prototype molecule, C_{60}, resemble the seams on a soccer ball. Geometrically, C_{60} is a polygon with 60 vertices and 32 faces, 12 of which are pentagons and 20 of which are octagons. In the 1985 paper describing their work, the discoverers chose a whimsical name for C_{60}. They called it "buckminsterfullerene" after R. Buckminster Fuller, the U.S. architect whose geodesic dome design, the best-known example of which was the U.S. pavilion for Expo 67 in Montreal in 1967, had a similar structure. Chemists began calling C_{60} "buckyball." The name and the elegant netlike structure of fullerenes galvanized public fancy in a way that few other basic advances in chemistry had.

"For chemists the proposed structure was uniquely beautiful and satisfying," the Royal Swedish Academy of Sciences said in its citation. "It corresponds to an aromatic, three-dimensional system in which single and double bonds alternated, and was thus of great theoretical significance."

The prize, worth $1,120,000, was shared by Richard E. Smalley and Robert F. Curl, Jr., of Rice University, Houston, Texas, and Sir Harold W. Kroto of the University of Sussex, Brighton, Eng. Kroto, Curl, and Smalley did their landmark experiment over a period of 11 days in 1985. The Swedish academy noted the assistance of their graduate students James R. Heath and Sean C. O'Brien, who did not share in the award.

At the time of the discovery, Kroto was using microwave spectroscopy techniques to analyze gas in carbon-rich giant stars and clouds of gas in interstellar space. He had discovered long, chainlike molecules of carbon and nitrogen in stellar atmospheres and in gas clouds. Kroto wanted to study the vaporization of carbon to find out how these carbon chains form, but he lacked the apparatus to vaporize carbon. He mentioned the problem to a friend, Curl, who worked with Smalley. Curl told Kroto that Smalley had designed and built an instrument that seemed perfect for Kroto's research. Smalley was an authority on cluster chemistry, the study of aggregates of atoms or molecules that range in size between the microscopic and the visible. Specifically, Smalley was interested in clusters of metal atoms of potential use in electronic semiconductor materials. His laboratory instrument, the laser-supersonic cluster beam apparatus, could vaporize almost any known material into a plasma of atoms and then be used to study the resulting clusters.

Kroto thus traveled to Rice University to work with Smalley and Curl on carbon vaporization and long-chained carbon molecules. The spectra from the first experiments did, indeed, have peaks that indicated the presence of those molecules. But the spectra also had peaks corresponding to a seventh and previously unrecognized form of carbon. Peaks on the spectra suggested molecules containing even numbers of carbon atoms—anywhere from 40 to more than 100. Under certain laser vaporization conditions, most of the new carbon molecules had a structure of C_{60}. Kroto arrived at Rice on Sept. 1, 1985, and dispatched a research paper announcing the discovery of the structure of C_{60} on September 12; the report was published on November 14.

Kroto was born in 1939 in Wisbech, Cambridgeshire, Eng., and received a Ph.D. from the University of Sheffield, Eng., in 1964. He joined the faculty at Sussex in 1967 and was named Royal Society research professor in 1991. Smalley was born in 1943 in Akron, Ohio, and worked as a research chemist with Shell Chemical Co. before receiving a Ph.D. from Princeton University

MICHAEL SCATES/JOHN CONNOR PRESS ASSOCIATES—SYGMA

Sir Harold W. Kroto

in 1973. He joined the Rice faculty in 1976. Curl was born in 1933 in Alice, Texas, and received a Ph.D. from the University of California, Berkeley, in 1957. He joined Rice University in 1958.

(MICHAEL WOODS)

Prize for Physics

Three U.S. scientists shared the 1996 Nobel Prize for Physics for their 1972 discovery of superfluid helium-3 (^{3}He), one of the world's most bizarre liquids. A superfluid like ^{3}He lacks the internal friction that exists in normal liquid and thus flows without resistance. Helium-3 can ooze through cracks and pores that normal liquids cannot penetrate, climb the walls of containers and spill out, and even flow uphill.

But Douglas Osheroff, David Lee, and Robert Richardson did not receive the prize, which totaled $1,120,000, because ^{3}He can perform magic tricks. Rather, ^{3}He allowed scientists to study directly in macroscopic—or visible—systems the strange quantum mechanics effects that previously could be studied only indirectly in invisible molecules, atoms, and subatomic particles. "The study of this exotic quantum liquid has led to concepts that are of general importance," the Royal Swedish Academy of Sciences said in its citation.

The research, for instance, helped scientists understand how the first structures began to form in space microseconds after the big bang, the primordial explosion that formed the universe. Helium-3 is anisotropic: it displays different properties in different directions along which the property is measured. The physical transitions from one form of ^{3}He to another have been used as a model for the cosmological phase transitions thought to have occurred a split second after the big bang, the Academy said. Experts believed that in the early universe, such transitions may have formed strange, linelike defects termed cosmic strings. These strings, in turn, may have formed the first physical structures in the universe. Cosmic strings have special properties that make them ideal candidates for giving rise to structures that evolved into the first stars and constellations. For instance, cosmic strings cannot have ends and must form closed loops. They are trillions of times thinner than an atom and yet so immensely dense that a cosmic string one meter long would weigh 1,020 kg (2,245 lb).

Helium-3 may also help in understanding and developing high-temperature superconductors, the Academy added. These ceramic materials, discovered in 1986, lose resistance to the flow of electricity at higher temperatures than did previous superconductors. Like ^{3}He, they also have different properties in different directions. Helium-3 thus might be used to model their behaviour and develop general theories about how to make materials that become superconducting closer to room temperature.

Lee and Richardson were professors at Cornell University, Ithaca, N.Y. Osheroff was a professor at Stanford University. At the time of the discovery of ^{3}He, Richardson and Lee were senior researchers at Cornell, and Osheroff was a graduate student on their research team.

Richardson, Lee, and Osheroff discovered superfluidity in ^{3}He by a fortunate accident. The group was not looking for superfluidity but was instead studying other aspects of helium-3. They were experts in low-temperature physics and had built their own cooling apparatus at Cornell. But in their initial measurements of ^{3}He, a problem occurred with their thermometer as temperatures dropped below a few thousandths of a degree of absolute zero ($-273°$ C). Therefore, they decided to monitor the internal pressure of the ^{3}He sample while applying external pressure that varied with time.

"It was the research student Osheroff who observed a change in the way the internal pressure varied with time," the Nobel citation pointed out. Even the most experienced senior researchers are tempted to dismiss such small deviations as more or less inexplicable peculiarities of the equipment, the citation explained. "He did not put the observation aside as being due to some feature of the apparatus, but instead insisted that it was a real effect."

Rolf Zinkernagel

David Lee

Lee was born in Rye, N.Y., in 1931 and received a Ph.D. from Yale University in 1959. Osheroff was born in 1945 in Aberdeen, Wash., and received a Ph.D. in 1973 from Cornell University. Richardson was born in 1937 in Washington, D.C., and received a Ph.D. in 1966 from Duke University, Durham, N.C. (MICHAEL WOODS)

Prize for Physiology or Medicine

Australia's Peter Doherty and Switzerland's Rolf Zinkernagel shared the 1996 Nobel Prize for Physiology or Medicine for their simple explanation of how the immune system distinguishes virus-infected cells from normal cells. In this key step in battling viral infections, specialized white blood cells termed cytotoxic T cells, or killer T cells, somehow recognize virus-infected cells and then eliminate them, but these T cells leave normal body cells unharmed.

Their discovery established a foundation for understanding how the immune system makes critical decisions about whether a cell is "self" or "nonself." A normally functioning immune system does not harm "self" cells that are part of the body. Yet it can recognize, and target for death, infected cells, invading microorganisms, and other foreign materials or antigens.

"The work fundamentally changed our understanding of the development of the immune response," said the Nobel Assembly at the Karolinska Institute in Stockholm, which awards the medicine prize. "Apart from vaccines, the work has guided attempts to use the immune system to hunt down and destroy microscopic cancer cells that have escaped from tumours. It has also

helped scientists as they design ways to suppress harmful immune system attacks on the body's own tissue, as seen in multiple sclerosis and diabetes."

Doherty and Zinkernagel did their landmark research on laboratory mice between 1973 and 1975 while at the John Curtin School of Medical Research in Canberra, Australia. Doherty in 1996 was chairman of the department of immunology at St. Jude Children's Research Hospital in Memphis, Tenn. He was born in 1940 in Australia and received a veterinary medicine degree in 1966 from the University of Queensland, Australia, and a Ph.D. in 1970 from the University of Edinburgh. Zinkernagel was in 1996 head of the Institute of Experimental Immunology at the University of Zürich, Switz. He was born in 1944 in Switzerland, received an M.D. in 1970 from the University of Basel, Switz., and a Ph.D. in 1975 from Australian National University, Canberra.

When Doherty and Zinkernagel began their research, they wanted to identify causes of the fatal destruction of brain cells in mice infected with lymphocytic choriomeningitis virus (LCMV). In the experiments they developed an assay to test their theory that killer T cells caused the damage while attacking virus-infected cells. They mixed T cells from sick mice with mouse cells infected with LCMV and found that the T cells did, indeed, destroy the infected cells. By lucky accident, all the mice were members of the same inbred strain. They thus were as genetically alike as identical twins and had identical major histocompatibility complex (MHC) antigens.

There was an unexpected discovery when Doherty and Zinkernagel mixed the T cells with virus-infected cells from another strain of mice. Doherty and Zinkernagel expected that the T cells, primed for attack, would strike the instant they came into contact with LCMV-infected cells. Instead, they acted as if they did not see the virus. Recognition, Doherty and Zinkernagel suspected, required the presence of some other protein on the surface of an infected cell. Further research showed that T cells must recognize two separate signals on an infected cell. One is the signal of a foreign invader, the virus inside the infected cell. The other is the "self" signal from the cell's MHC antigens. In Doherty and Zinkernagel's experiments, the T cells were looking not just for virus-infected cells but also for cells with the MHC antigens characteristic of the original strain of mice. The T cells could not recognize MHC antigens from the new strain, and no immune response occurred. This concept of simultaneous recognition of both self and foreign molecules formed the basis for a new understanding of cellular immunity, the Nobel Assembly said.

Researchers then began using cytotoxic T cells to kill viruses in bone marrow prior to bone marrow transplants. They also began developing vaccines, including those for certain forms of cancer and AIDS, that produce cytotoxic T cells.

(MICHAEL WOODS)

BIOGRAPHIES

Aikman, Troy Kenneth

U.S. professional football quarterback Troy Aikman not only led the Dallas Cowboys of the National Football League (NFL) to three Super Bowl victories (1993, 1994, 1996) but also helped restore the lustre that the squad once enjoyed as "America's Team." The Cowboys, one of the most dominant and popular teams in the 1970s, had fallen on lean times by 1989, when Jerry Jones bought the club, replacing longtime head coach Tom Landry with Jimmy Johnson and building a star-studded backfield around quarterback Aikman (drafted 1989) and running back Emmitt Smith (drafted 1991). By the mid-1990s, owing to his rugged good looks and the precision and the power of his passing game, Aikman was one of football's top celebrities. In his first seven seasons with the Cowboys, he completed nearly 63% of his passes, including 98 touchdown throws.

Aikman was born on Nov. 21, 1966, in West Covina, Calif., and raised in Cerritos, a suburb of Los Angeles, before moving to the small town of Henryetta, Okla., where he was an all-state high school standout. He was hotly recruited by coaches Barry Switzer of the University of Oklahoma and Johnson of Oklahoma State University; both later coached him as a professional. Aikman chose Switzer, who introduced the wishbone formation to the Oklahoma offense, emphasizing a running game at the expense of Aikman's strong passing skills. As a sophomore in 1985, Aikman broke his leg in the fifth game of the season and, because he was not well suited to the wishbone offense, lost his place as starting quarterback. Oklahoma went on to win the national championship, and Aikman went on to attend the University of California, Los Angeles, where, as a transfer student, he had to sit out the 1986 season. He shone in his remaining two years at UCLA, completing 65% of his passes and leading his squad to a 20–4 record, with postseason victories in the Aloha Bowl (December 1987) and the Cotton Bowl (January 1989). Named All-American in his senior year, he placed third in the polling for the Heisman Trophy, college football's most prestigious award.

In 1989 the Cowboys made Aikman their number one draft selection and the wealthiest rookie in league history, with a six-year, $11 million contract. He fared poorly in his first few seasons, throwing more interceptions than touchdown passes and missing games because of injuries. In 1992–93, however, his first season without injuries, Aikman led the team to a Super Bowl victory and was named the game's Most Valuable Player. On the way to a second Super Bowl win in 1994, he became the highest-paid player in NFL history, with an eight-year, $50 million contract. In March 1994 Johnson was replaced as head coach by Switzer, who oversaw the Cowboys' continued success—much of which was due to Aikman's heroics in postseason play, during which he held the career record for passing percentage, highest average yard gain, and longest pass completion.

(TOM MICHAEL)

Alagna, Roberto, and Gheorghiu, Angela

In 1996 French-born tenor Roberto Alagna and Romanian soprano Angela Gheorghiu created their own personal operatic libretto with a highly publicized romance that resulted in marriage in May. The pair first met in 1992 while appearing opposite each other as Rodolfo and Mimi in Giacomo Puccini's *La Bohème* with the Royal Opera, Covent Garden, London, and they fell in love two years later while Gheorghiu sang the role of Violetta in Sir Georg Solti's 1994 production of Giuseppe Verdi's *La traviata* at Covent Garden.

Alagna was born to Sicilian parents in a suburb of Paris on June 7, 1963, and was discovered while he was singing for tips in a Paris pizzeria. Although he was mostly self-taught, his first audition in 1988 resulted in the tenor lead as Alfredo in Glyndebourne's touring production of *La traviata*. Alagna went on to enter the 1988 Luciano

Christiane Amanpour

Pavarotti International Competition and won. In 1990 he reprised the role of Alfredo for La Scala in Milan. He overcame personal tragedy to sing a highly acclaimed Romeo in the Royal Opera's 1994 production of Charles Gounod's *Roméo et Juliette* only a few weeks after his wife succumbed to a brain tumour, leaving him with a four-year-old daughter.

While Alagna was considered a consummate performer, with a strong physical stage presence, some critics questioned whether he was overstraining his voice, especially since he had had no formal training. As the first genuine lyric tenor to appear in many years, however, Alagna was continually hailed as the "fourth tenor." He shrugged off all comparisons to the famed trio of Pavarotti, Placido Domingo, and José Carreras, claiming he wanted to establish his own style.

Gheorghiu, two years Alagna's junior, had a much more traditional background. She was born in Adjud, Rom., where her father worked for the railroad. Gheorghiu realized her love for singing early and was supported by her family in her desire for a career in opera. She left home at age 14 to study at the Academy of Music in Bucharest and made her debut in 1992 as Zerlina in Mozart's *Don Giovanni* at Covent Garden. Gheorghiu, an elegant and compelling artist, was praised in London as one of the great Violettas. Her performance in *La Bohème* for the New York City Metropolitan Opera in early 1996—a production that marked the U.S. debut for both her and Alagna—was described as "ideal." Like Alagna, she did not work with a teacher, subscribing to their shared philosophy of self-reliance. Gheorghiu had less pressure on her than Alagna, but she did not welcome the comparisons to Maria Callas, preferring to be recognized for her own voice.

Aggressive marketing, combined with the talented duo's fairy-tale romance, brought them increased attention. Alagna and Gheorghiu were booked jointly for the next few years with recording studios and opera houses throughout the world, and the hope—especially for Alagna—was that they would continue to plan wisely for long and rewarding careers.   (AMANDA E. FULLER)

Amanpour, Christiane

Throughout the 1990s, in war zones throughout the world, there was one constant. No matter how distant or dangerous the battlefield, viewers of the Cable News Network (CNN) could count on the reporting of Christiane Amanpour. One of a small group of female foreign correspondents, Amanpour had gained a reputation as the leading war reporter of her generation. As senior international correspondent for CNN, she cov-

ered conflicts in the Persian Gulf, Somalia, Haiti, Rwanda, and Bosnia and Herzegovina. In 1996 she signed a contract with the CBS network to appear on the prestigious "60 Minutes" as a correspondent. In an unprecedented arrangement, Amanpour would also keep her job at CNN.

Amanpour was born in London in 1958. Her father, an Iranian airline executive, moved the family to Tehran shortly after her birth. Politically connected and wealthy, the Amanpours led a privileged life in Iran. At the age of 11, Amanpour was sent back to England to attend the Holy Cross Convent School in Buckinghamshire. She stayed at Holy Cross until she was 16, when she went to the exclusive New Hall School, the oldest Roman Catholic girls' school in the U.K. In January 1979 the Islamic revolution in Iran toppled the shah, forcing many of his followers to leave the country, the Amanpour family among them. Her father lost everything he had owned in Iran. Amanpour later credited her desire to be a journalist to this firsthand experience.

Amanpour moved to the U.S. and attended the University of Rhode Island, majoring in journalism. Following her graduation, she worked at an NBC affiliate in Providence, R.I. In September 1983 she was hired at the fledgling CNN as an assistant for the international news desk. By 1986 she was working at CNN's New York bureau as a producer-correspondent. Amanpour received her big break in 1989, when she was promoted to a post in Frankfurt, Ger. She arrived there at an opportune time; the pro-democracy movement was sweeping Eastern Europe, and Amanpour quickly became CNN's reporter on the spot.

Amanpour gained distinction in Europe, but it was during the Persian Gulf War that she became a familiar face. She covered the conflict from the Iraqi invasion of Kuwait to the eventual triumph of the U.S.-led coalition. After the war she reported on the Kurdish uprising in northern Iraq. In 1992 Amanpour went to Bosnia and Herzegovina to cover the outbreak of violence that she felt would become "my generation's war." Her reporting was credited with bringing the savage nature of that conflict to the attention of the world, although some criticized her for what they felt was her tendency to editorialize rather than report, claiming that she was clearly biased against the Serbs. Amanpour responded by stating that "objectivity means giving all sides a hearing. It doesn't mean treating all sides equally."

(JOHN H. MATHEWS)

Andreessen, Marc

From recent college grad to cofounder of Netscape Communications Corp., computer programmer Marc Andreessen accomplished what many could only dream of. At age 25 he was a top officer of a software company that reported revenues totaling $55 million for the first quarter of 1996, and he graced the cover of *Time* magazine to illustrate a story on the "Golden Geeks" of the 1990s (in 1994 *Time* had named him one of the top 50 people under the age of 40). Just a few months earlier, he had been given the 1995 *Computerworld* Smithsonian Award for Leadership.

Andreessen grew up in New Lisbon, Wis. While still in grammar school he taught himself BASIC, a programming language, so that he could write his own computer games; he later attempted to design a program that would do his math homework. Andreessen planned a career in electrical engineering. That changed, however, when he entered the University of Illinois at Champaign-Urbana and landed a part-time job at the school's computer lab, the National Center for Supercomputing Applications (NCSA). There he and a handful of his peers created Mosaic, a user-friendly browser application that integrated graphics and point-and-click simplicity to make it easier for nontechnical people to navigate the World Wide Web (the graphic subsection of the Internet). It was a hit. NCSA made Mosaic available free of charge over the Internet, and more than two million copies were downloaded within a year.

After graduating in 1993 with a bachelor's degree in computer science, Andreessen headed to California's Silicon Valley to work for a small company that made security products for use in electronic commerce. Soon he was contacted by James Clark, the founder and former president of Silicon Graphics, Inc. Clark was searching for an exciting new venture, and he found it with Andreessen. With Clark's $4 million investment and Andreessen's genius, the dynamic duo founded Mosaic Communications Corp. (later rechristened Netscape Communications) in April 1994. Andreessen recruited the original masterminds behind Mosaic and set out to create the "monster" software, which they initially dubbed Mozilla (meaning Mosaic Killer). It was commercially launched as Netscape Navigator and, almost overnight, became the most popular browser used on the Web, taking over 75% of the market share by mid-1996.

Netscape's main objective was to enable individuals and companies around the globe to exchange information. And, as vice president of technology, Andreessen earned the role of setting the company's technical path as it prepared to ride the "bandwidth tidal wave," which Andreessen predicted would transform the wireless communications industry.

(MARIA OTTOLINO RENGERS)

Arkayev, Leonid Yakovlevich

At the 1996 Olympic Games in Atlanta, Ga., legendary Russian gymnastics coach Leonid Arkayev turned in a performance worthy of a 10 as he led the Russian men to yet another team gold; in Olympics in which his teams had participated, it was his fourth consecutive victory in the event. Moreover, Russia's strong gymnastic performance—eight medals, including the women's team silver—came amid the departure of former stars who had gone on to compete for their respective homelands in the wake of the Soviet Union breakup.

Born on June 3, 1940, in Moscow, Arkayev was the youngest of three children; his father died in 1943 while serving in World War II. In 1954, helped by the sister of Olympic champion Yekaterina Kalinchuk, Arkayev was admitted to the gymnastics section of the Stroyitel ("builder") sport society. He was named master of sport of the U.S.S.R. in 1958 and from 1959 to 1969 was a member of the national team. Interested in training, he became a coach for the Soviet team following its disastrous showing at the 1972 world championships in Ljubljana, Yugos. (now in Slovenia). Arkayev, who eventually became the head coach, restructured the country's gymnastic program, using Japan, then the world leader in the sport, as a model. In particular, he stressed continuity in training, allowing a gymnast's original coach to remain involved in the athlete's development after his or her selection to the national team. From 1975 the country's elite gymnasts trained at the Krugloye Ozero Sport Base, practicing two to three times a day, six days a week.

Though Arkayev never competed on the Olympic level, it was there that his athletes shone, not only dominating the sport but also providing historic performances. At the 1980 Games in Moscow, which were boycotted by the U.S. and Japan, among others, Aleksandr Dityatin became both the first athlete to win eight medals in a single Olympics and the first male gymnast to receive a perfect score of 10. Moreover, the Soviet team captured a total of nine gold medals. After boycotting the 1984 Games in Los Angeles, the Soviets competed in Seoul, S.Kor., winning 19 medals, 11 of which were gold. Following the breakup of the Soviet Union in 1991, the Unified Team was formed, consisting of the Commonwealth of Independent States and Georgia. At the 1992 Games in Barcelona, Spain, Vitaly Sherbo won six gold medals in the most successful gymnastics performance in Olympic history. In addition, the women won the team competition, their third successive victory in the event. From 1980 to 1996, Arkayev's Olympic teams won more than 65 medals, including 32 gold. Arkayev, who received his master's degree in education in 1995, proved that as a teacher he was as good as gold.

(AMY TIKKANEN)

Armbruster, Peter

On Feb. 9, 1996, German physicist Peter Armbruster and a multinational team of scientists at the Institute for Heavy Ion Research (GSI), Darmstadt, Ger., synthesized element 112, thereby attaining yet another goal in their quest to discover increasingly heavy chemical elements. Armbruster and physicist Sigurd Hofmann led the researchers who made the new element, their third such achievement in less than two years.

In 1971 Armbruster became chief scientist at GSI, where he worked for more than two decades to synthesize the superheavy elements—*i.e.,* a group of relatively stable elements with atomic numbers (numbers of nuclear protons) around 114 and mass numbers (numbers of nuclear protons and neutrons) around 298. Scientists began creating new elements with atomic numbers higher than that of uranium, element 92, in the early 1940s. As they attempted to make elements heavier than fermium, element 100, the extreme instability of those elements posed increasing challenges. In response, Armbruster and physicists at other accelerators around the world developed more sophisticated synthetic techniques. At GSI the approaches proved quite successful. In the early 1980s Armbruster and co-workers produced elements 107 through 109, and in 1994, within a two-month period, they created elements 110 and 111.

Element 112, with an atomic mass of 277, was the heaviest yet to be produced in the laboratory. It was created from the fusion of the nuclei of lead and zinc when zinc atoms were raised to high kinetic energies in a heavy-ion accelerator and aimed at a lead target. The two nuclei combined, and element 112 was born. Only one atom of the element was detected in the experiment, and in less than a thousandth of a second it decayed. In spite of its short life span, the new element was expected to provide insight into the nature of nuclear structure.

The synthesis of increasingly heavy elements allowed physicists to test predictions about the stability of atomic nuclei. Scientists had identified certain "magic" numbers of protons and neutrons that should confer particular stability to a nucleus. The stability arises because the internal nuclear structure can arrange itself such that the binding energy of the nucleus is increased. Element 112 has 161 neutrons in its nucleus, which is only one short of the predicted magic number of 162 neutrons.

Armbruster was born in Dachau, Bavaria, on July 25, 1931. He received his doctorate from the Technical University of Munich. Throughout his career he remained intrigued by the reactions between heavy nuclei and applied the results of his studies to understanding atomic and solid-state physics. As 1996 progressed, Armbruster continued his work to extend the periodic table beyond its current limits, hoping in the near future to create the superheavy element predicted to be the most stable of the group—element 114.

(MARY JANE FRIEDRICH)

Armstrong, Karen

Though once a refugee from religion, in 1996 author Karen Armstrong completed *In the Beginning: A New Interpretation of Genesis,* worked closely with a major television series on the book of Genesis: "Genesis: A Living Conversation," and completed her most ambitious project to date: *Jerusalem: One City, Three Faiths,* a history of Jerusalem from the Bronze Age to the present. Armstrong, one of the leading commentators on religion in Britain and once a practicing Roman Catholic, described herself as a "freelance monotheist."

Armstrong was born on Nov. 14, 1944, in Worcestershire, Eng. At 17 she entered a Catholic convent. Though she had "pictured the religious life as a series of philosophical conversations sandwiched between prayerful ecstasies," she was rudely awakened. She entered the convent just as the Second Vatican Council was getting under way, long before its reforms were introduced into Catholic institutions. Armstrong found herself searching for God in the midst of the severe and outdated Victorian subculture of her convent. After seven years of tortured experience, she emerged nonreligious and recounted her journey in the autobiographical *Through the Narrow Gate* (1981). She graduated from the University of Oxford with a degree in literature and then taught modern literature at the University of London before serving as the head of the English department at a girls' school. By 1982 she had become a freelance writer and broadcaster. This new vocation gradually led her back to the subject of religion. In 1983 she wrote and presented a six-part documentary TV series on the life and work of the Apostle Paul. Much of the background work for the series was done on-site in the Middle East, where Armstrong gained a fresh appreciation for Christianity, Judaism, and Islam. She then went on to other television series, including "Varieties of Religious Experience" (1984) and "Tongues of Fire" (1985). A teacher at the Leo Baeck College for the Study of Judaism and the Training of Rabbis and Teachers, she was also an honorary member of the Association of Muslim Social Scientists.

Armstrong's work *A History of God: The 4,000-Year Quest of Judaism, Christianity, and Islam* (1993) was on the *New York Times* best-seller list for more than a year. Her other works include *Beginning the World* (1983), *The Gospel According to Woman: Christianity's Creation of the Sex War in the West* (1986), *Holy War: The Crusades and Their Impact on Today's World* (rev. ed., 1991), *Muhammad* (1991), *The English Mystics of the Fourteenth Century* (1991), and *The End of Silence: Women and the Priesthood* (1993).

(TODD M. JOHNSON)

Asahina, Takashi

Octogenarian maestro Takashi Asahina, widely credited with having popularized the compositions of Beethoven, Bruckner, and Mahler in Japan, considered giving up the baton in 1996 until a word of encouragement from Emperor Akihito changed his mind. The encounter took place in 1994 when Asahina received the Order of Culture, a decoration that acknowledged outstanding achievements in the arts. As Asahina jokingly explained it in his memoirs, he interpreted the emperor's advice to "hang in there" as an "imperial edict."

Asahina was born in Tokyo on July 9, 1908. In early infancy he was adopted by his father's colleague, an engineer who specialized in the construction of railway tunnels. As a child Asahina suffered from asthma and lived for a time in a seashore area outside Tokyo. He took up soccer to strengthen his body and learned to play the violin. Asahina opted to study law at Kyoto University after failing a university entrance examination in Tokyo. He continued to play the violin in university extracurricular activities but quit soccer to make time for music.

Following graduation in 1931, Asahina took the examination required of those seeking positions in the government. To his dismay, the one topic he was certain would not be asked, and which he had not studied, was asked. He turned in a blank paper, fully aware that his plans for a career in government would never be realized.

Asahina landed a job with a private railway company that owned a chain of department stores. For two years he worked as a passenger train engineer and a department store clerk, and he then reentered the university (1933) to study philosophy. He also became seriously interested in music and studied the violin and conducting. Asahina looked up to Emmanuel Metter, a Russian who taught at Kyoto University from 1926 to 1938, as his orchestra-conducting mentor. Asahina made his professional debut as a conductor in 1939. After conducting the Shanghai Symphony Orchestra and the Harbin Symphony Orchestra in Japanese-occupied China during World War II, he estab-

Rowan Atkinson

lished the Kansai Symphony Orchestra in Osaka in 1947 and became its regular conductor, the position he retained when the Osaka Philharmonic Orchestra replaced the Kansai orchestra in 1960. Since his European debut in Helsinki in 1953, he had conducted more than 60 orchestras in 15 countries. Because he saw himself as a conductor who received no formal education at a music school, Asahina humbly declined to take protégés under his wing.   (TEIJI SHIMIZU)

Atkinson, Rowan Sebastian

It is no surprise that a painfully shy person would hide behind a mask, but it can be highly risky to borrow that mask's main features from a gargoyle. Such were the facial contortions and attributes displayed with manic genius by British comic actor Rowan Atkinson, whose alter ego, Mr. Bean, made its transatlantic jump to U.S. television in 1996. Transcending both the traditional lines drawn by "English humour" and the verbal repartee of his previous TV incarnation, Blackadder, Atkinson found millions of devotees for his gormless, all-but-silent working-class nerd.

Born to wealthy Durham farmers on Jan. 6, 1955, Atkinson grew up knowing the importance of education, hard work, and a proper career. He attended Durham Cathedral Choristers' School, where he was dubbed "Moon Man" (among other things) by his peers owing to the "idea that I was related to an alien force." At the University of Newcastle upon Tyne he studied electrical engineering, progressing to the University of Oxford for his master's degree. Taking to the stage to satisfy an inner urge, he met Richard Curtis and Howard Goodall, and together they ventured to the Edinburgh Festival. There his classic schoolmaster sketch rocketed him to fame and the distinction of being at the time the youngest person to have a one-man show in London's West End.

PHOTOGRAPH COURTESY OF AMERICAN PROGRAM SERVICE

In 1979 the satirical television show "Not the Nine O'Clock News" introduced him to millions of delighted British viewers.

In 1983 the first installment of "Blackadder," written by Atkinson and Curtis, slithered onto British TV screens, featuring the twisted relationship between four incarnations of the groveling, spineless Lord Blackadder and his foully fleshed retainer, Baldrick, as they cajoled their way through history from the Crusades to the end of World War I. The series established Atkinson as one of England's finest comic actors and led to "Mr. Bean" (1990), which won the 1990 Montreux Festival Golden Rose, a 1991 International Emmy for best popular arts program, and a 1994 American Cable Ace Award. At its peak "Mr. Bean" was British television's most popular comedy, with 18 million viewers.

Atkinson's motion picture credits included *The Witches, Four Weddings and a Funeral,* and *The Lion King,* and a film version of "Mr. Bean" was in the works. Atkinson's latest TV incarnation was Police Inspector Raymond Fowler in "The Thin Blue Line."

Despite his success, the fiercely private Atkinson insisted that he was not a funny man. "I am," he said, "essentially a rather quiet, dull person, who just happens to be a performer."
(LESLEY EDMONDSON)

Aznar López, José María

On May 4, 1996, the Spanish Cortes (parliament) approved José María Aznar López, the leader of the centre-right Popular Party (PP), as the new prime minister of Spain. A former tax inspector who was little known outside his native country, Aznar had narrowly defeated incumbent Felipe González Márquez in the general elections on March 3. Though Aznar's victory fell far short of the landslide that had been predicted, it helped bring to an end 13 years of Socialist rule in Spain and signified a major political turning point for Western Europe's youngest democracy.

Aznar was born on Feb. 25, 1953, in Madrid. Although both his father and grandfather held government jobs during the fascist regime of Gen. Francisco Franco, throughout his career Aznar advocated a much more moderate conservatism. After graduating from the University of Madrid and while working as a tax inspector during the 1970s and early '80s, Aznar became an active member of the right-wing Popular Alliance, which later became the PP. Aznar was instrumental in leading the party toward the political centre, and the PP elected him to succeed retiring party leader Manuel Fraga Iribarne in 1989.

First elected to the Cortes from Avila in 1984, Aznar later served as president of the Castile-León region (1987–89). He was elected to the Cortes from Madrid in 1989 and, as head of the PP, continued to reform the party, actively recruiting women and young people and cutting ties to the far right.

In 1995, after being slightly wounded by a car bomb that was attributed to the Basque separatist group Euskadi Ta Askatasuna, Aznar led the PP to large gains in the general elections. During his campaign to become prime minister, he focused on the numerous scandals that had plagued González's government, citing them as evidence that the Socialist regime needed to be replaced by a "clean" party. He also was able to turn his uncharismatic popular image to his advantage, stressing his "ordinariness" and his reputation for being an earnest, levelheaded leader.

In his effort to be named prime minister, Aznar was forced to seek the backing of several of Spain's small, regionally aligned political parties, since the PP had fallen short of winning a legislative majority in the March elections. Facing possible instability with a minority government, Aznar remained unperturbed. He declared that Spain had "begun a new chapter in its history" and reaffirmed his goals of liberalizing the economy, cutting the public deficit, and rooting out the rampant corruption that had plagued González's government.   (SHERMAN HOLLAR)

Bailey, Donovan

At the 1996 Olympic Games in Atlanta, Ga., Canadian sprinter Donovan Bailey won the 100-m dash in 9.84 sec to earn the appellation "the world's fastest man." Then he ran the last leg of the 4 × 100-m relay and helped the Canadian team win a gold medal in that event. These were impressive accomplishments for a man who had emerged as a factor in international track only in 1994 and did not set a world record until 1996.

Bailey was born on Dec. 16, 1967, in Manchester, Jam., and moved to Oakville, Ont., in 1981 to live with his father. He was on the track team in high school, and at age 16 he ran the 100-m dash in 10.65 sec. He did not pursue running seriously, however, because his first love was basketball. He played forward on the basketball team at Sheridan College, Oakville, where he studied economics. After receiving a diploma in business administration, Bailey started his own marketing and investment-consulting business. Sports became his hobby. He played recreational basketball and occasionally entered sprint races. In 1991 he won the 60-m dash at the Ontario indoor championships. Training only sporadically, Bailey did not make the Canadian track team for the 1991 world championships or the 1992 Olympics.

In 1993 Bailey was a member of the Canadian track team at the world championships in Stuttgart, Ger. It was there that he met coach Dan Pfaff, who invited Bailey to train with him. After Bailey began training with him in March

1994, first in Baton Rouge, La., and then at the University of Texas at Austin, Pfaff overhauled his technique and helped him polish his style. As a result, Bailey improved his starts and his ability to sustain his speed throughout the race. By the end of 1994, he was ranked eighth in the world in the 100-m dash. He ran the 100 m in less than 10 seconds for the first time in the spring of 1995. In July Bailey set a Canadian record of 9.91 sec at the Canadian track and field championships, and in August he won the 100 m at the world track and field championships in Göteborg, Swed. He set his first world record in 1996 in the 50-m dash at the Reno Air Games.

Bailey structured his 100-m run as 20 m of start, 50 m of acceleration, and 30 m of relaxation. Shortly after the Atlanta Olympics, he competed again in Europe. He won the 100-m at the Grand Prix in Monte Carlo and the IAAF Grand Prix in Cologne, Ger. Bailey, who developed an interest in the history of track and field and had great respect for those who built the sport, like Jesse Owens, received the Canadian Sport Award in March 1996.   (DIANE LOIS WAY)

Ban, Shigeru

Before a catastrophic earthquake devastated the Kobe area in Japan on Jan. 17, 1995, Shigeru Ban was recognized as a rising Japanese architect. He therefore felt he had to help the afflicted people and went to the city in February. By the end of the summer, his relief work had brought to a section of Kobe what was popularly called a paper dome to temporarily replace a ruined Roman Catholic church and paper-tube cabins to shelter some of those who had lost their homes. Ban used recycled, durable, strong, and environment-friendly paper material to construct the paper dome on the grounds where the church had stood before it was leveled by the earthquake. He had actually used paper tubes in 1985–86 in building structures, including a gallery for fashion designer Issey Miyake. He even suggested to the United Nations High Commissioner for Refugees (UN-HCR) in 1994 that shelters made of paper be constructed for Rwandan refugees.

Ban was born on Aug. 5, 1957, in Tokyo. He studied at the Southern California Institute of Architecture in 1980 and later moved to the Cooper Union School in New York City because he wanted to study under architect John Hejduk. Ban received a degree in architecture in 1984 and the following year opened his own office.

The construction of the rectangular-shaped church, featuring a rounded canvas roof, started in July and finished in September with the help of 160 volunteers, most of them architecture students. A total of 58 paper tubes, each measuring 5 m (16.4 ft) long, 33 cm (13 in) in diameter, and 15 cm (6 in) in thickness, were arranged in an oval form inside the church. Ban designed the structure so that it could be easily constructed and

(Right) Shigeru Ban and (below) paper church

dismantled, then used again, perhaps in Rwanda or some such place when its mission as a temporary facility ended. A few companies donated construction materials, but the building cost 9 million yen, some of which was contributed by the public. Ban and his student volunteers also simultaneously built 22 paper cabins for quake-stricken people during the two-month period, using beer crates containing sand bags as their foundations and coated tenting fabrics for the roofs. Ban's service was acknowledged with an award from a Japanese architecture association, which praised him for displaying an architect's sense of mission based on deeply rooted human love. He became a UNHCR consultant and a part-time professor of architecture at Yokohama National University in 1995 and a part-time professor of architecture at Nihon University in 1996.   (TEIJI SHIMIZU)

Bossi, Umberto

In the already fractious world of Italian politics, secessionist Umberto Bossi raised eyebrows in 1996 by calling for a complete break—dividing Italy into separate nations. In September Bossi, the leader of the rightist Northern League political party, declared independence for a portion of northern Italy that he dubbed the Republic of Padania. Exploiting the economic and cultural differences between north and south, he argued that wealthy northern cities were hampered by poorer, less-developed cities to the south and that the breakaway republic would hold its own as a member of the European Union. He illustrated his vision of Padania with flashy iconography that recalled the historic Lombard League, a medieval alliance between northern Italian towns that defeated the Holy Roman emperor Frederick I Barbarossa at the Battle of Legnano in 1176.

As a political reality, however, the proposed republic remained mired in mythology; very few Italians actually supported secession. In fact, on the day of Bossi's main rally in Venice, many

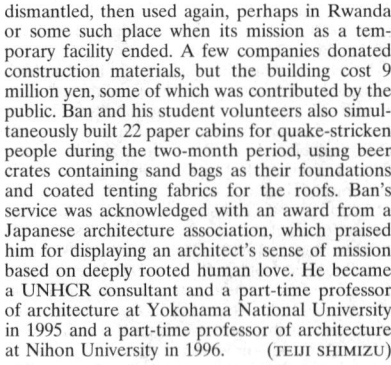

more attended a counterdemonstration in Milan held by the far-right National Alliance, led by Gianfranco Fini. Observers noted, however, that despite widespread indifference to Bossi's separatist agenda, he succeeded in garnering support for his platform of federalist reform and participation in the European Monetary System.

Bossi was born on Sept. 19, 1941, in the Varese province town of Cassano Magnago, north of Milan. He received a high-school diploma and worked as a hospital orderly in Pavia before entering politics. In 1979 he met Bruno Salvadori, a federalist reformer from the northwestern Italian region of Valle d'Aosta, who inspired him in the mid-1980s to form a regional party called the Lombard League, which captured seats in the national legislature in 1987, installing Bossi as senator. Two years later the Lombard League won representation in the European Parliament.

In 1991 Bossi refashioned the Lombard League as the Northern League, which soon proved dominant in northern Italy. The party's membership in government swelled after the elections of 1992, when Bossi was voted into the Chamber of Deputies. In 1994 the Northern League became the largest political faction in the nation on the strength of its federalist message, distance from incumbent corruption, and timely alliance with Silvio Berlusconi, who was elected prime minister that March. By December 1994, however, the Northern League had retreated from this alliance, and Bossi's threat of a no-confidence vote forced Berlusconi's resignation. In the 1996 national elections, the party won 10.1% of the vote for the Chamber of Deputies and 10.4% of the Senate vote.   (TOM MICHAEL)

Bucaram Ortíz, Abdalá

Campaigning in 1996 under the name El Loco ("The Madman"), Abdalá Bucaram Ortíz seemed an unlikely choice for president of Ecuador. The flamboyant politician traveled with a rock band, often singing "Jailhouse Rock," a song associated with Elvis Presley, before his speeches. His unconventional style, however, and his attacks on the wealthy business establishment proved popular with the country's eight million poor, who helped elect him president on July 7, 1996.

Bucaram was born on Feb. 20, 1952, in Guayaquil, Ecuador. An accomplished athlete, he was a member of Ecuador's track and field team and competed as a hurdler in the 1972 Olympic Games in Munich, Ger. He earned a law degree at the State University in Guayaquil but turned his attention to politics after his uncle became prominent in the populist movement. In 1982 Bucaram founded the leftist Ecuadorian Roldosist Party (PRE), and two years later he was elected mayor of Guayaquil, Ecuador's largest city. His two terms in office were marked by controversy. Businessmen accused him of extortion, claiming that he demanded money and harassed those who refused to pay. Bucaram called the payments donations. In 1985 his criticism of the Ecuadoran army resulted in a warrant for his arrest. Bucaram fled to Panama, where he was arrested for cocaine possession but was not convicted. He claimed that rivals had planted the drugs on him. In 1987 he was allowed to return to Ecuador, and he ran for the presidency in 1988 and 1992. Though he was unsuccessful in both bids, election returns showed that he had won a surprisingly large number of votes.

In the 1996 elections, with Rosalia Arteaga as his running mate, Bucaram focused on the gap separating the rich and the poor. He criticized the "oligarchy," which he defined as wealthy businesses and banks, and campaigned for social welfare programs and the construction of new housing. In a country where 67% of the people were poor, it was a popular platform. After the May 19 election, Bucaram and Jaime Nebot of the Social Christian Party were declared eligible for the second-round runoff. Nebot, who was supported by businesses and banks, was favoured to win. Critics cited Bucaram's vague economic policy and the fear that he would discourage investors, particularly foreigners, as major weaknesses in his campaign. His promise of change, however, galvanized much of the electorate. In

Abdalá Bucaram ("El Loco"), left

the July elections Bucaram won by a comfortable margin, capturing 54.5% of the votes.

After his victory Bucaram, a man noted for his unpredictability, moderated his populist rhetoric, leaving many to wonder if he would abandon his campaign promises. While Ecuador awaited the answer, it seemed clear that Bucaram's presidency would hold numerous surprises.

(AMY TIKKANEN)

Bustillos, Edwin
In 1996 human rights activist and environmentalist Edwin Bustillos continued his campaign to save Mexico's Sierra Madre Occidental mountain range from loggers and drug traffickers. Though his work resulted in five attempts on his life and daily death threats, Bustillos remained committed to the cause that made him as endangered as the land and people he sought to protect.

The Sierra Madre Occidental, located in northern Mexico, extends over 1,100 km (700 mi) of mountains and canyons. Considered North America's most diverse ecosystem, it is home to endangered species, such as the jaguar and Mexican gray wolf, and to the world's most varied forest of pine, oak, and cedar. In addition, four native human cultures have lived in the region for over 2,000 years. By 1996, however, loggers and drug traffickers were threatening the Sierra Madre. Lumber companies, which had begun logging in the late 1800s, had destroyed 98% of the area's original forest growth. Moreover, in recent years the area's isolation had attracted drug traffickers, who forced the Indians to grow marijuana and opium poppies; refusal often led to death or removal from the land. The region consequently became one of the largest producers of drug crops in the world.

Part Tarahumara, Bustillos was born in the Sierra Madre on May 16, 1964. It was while working for a timber company that he became aware of the problems in the region. In 1992 he founded Consejor Asesor de la Sierra Madre, A.C. (CASMAC; "Advisory Council of the Sierra Madre"), an organization that, while addressing environmental issues, concentrated on securing rights for the indigenous people. Operating with a staff of only three and on an annual budget of $80,000, Bustillos successfully lobbied for a new constitution for the state of Chihuahua that included unprecedented protection of the rights and lands of the native cultures; he also helped eradicate more than 100 ha (250 ac) of drug crops. CASMAC's goal was the creation of a two million-hectare (five million-acre) biosphere comprising community reserves, protected areas used for traditional purposes such as grazing and plant gathering.

The challenges Bustillos faced were numerous. His work angered loggers and drug traffickers, who vowed to kill him. He also had to contend with bribed officials and a Mexican government

that ignored the problem or offered ineffective solutions. The few arrests were often of Tarahumara, who cultivated drug crops, and the spraying of herbicide to destroy the illicit crops damaged plants and the water supply that the Indians relied upon for survival. In 1996 Bustillos received the Goldman Environmental Prize and the Condé Nast Environmental Award.   (AMY TIKKANEN)

Carson, David
In 1996 U.S. graphic designer David Carson consolidated his reputation with the publication of *The End of Print: The Graphic Design of David Carson,* the first comprehensive collection of his distinctive graphic imagery. Designed by Carson, with text by design writer Lewis Blackwell, the beautifully produced book surveyed Carson's career and showcased the best of his designs for the counterculture magazines *Beach Culture* and *Ray Gun,* as well as never-before-published illustrations and photos and a sampling of his print and television ad campaigns. Although some decried Carson's "fractured layouts and tortured typography," his unconventional style revolutionized visual communication in the 1990s.

Born on Sept. 8, 1955, in Corpus Christi, Texas, Carson came to the world of graphic design relatively late in life. At 26 he was a competitive surfer—eighth in the world—and was teaching in a California high school when he enrolled in a two-week commercial design class and found a new calling. After six months at a commercial art school, he worked at a small surfer magazine, *Self and Musician.* During his four years as a part-time designer for the magazine *Transworld Skateboarding,* ample space and budget permitted bold experimentation. His chaotic spreads overlapped photos and mixed, twisted, and shattered type fonts, drawing both admirers and detractors. Photographer Albert Watson, for whom Carson designed a collection of work called *Cyclops,* declared, "He uses type the way a painter uses paint, to create emotion, to express ideas."

In 1989 Carson became art director at *Beach Culture.* Although he produced only six issues before the journal folded, he collected over 150 design awards. The visual rhythms of Carson's work caught the eye of Marvin Scott Jarrett, publisher of the ultrahip alternative-music magazine *Ray Gun,* and he hired Carson in 1992. During the three years he served as its art director, *Ray Gun* tripled its circulation. Carson's ability to connect with a youthful marketing segment attracted corporations such as Nike and Levi Strauss, which commissioned him to design their print ads. Carson also branched into directing television commercials for Citibank and *TV Guide.* Meanwhile, the American Center for Design praised his designs as "the most important work" of 1994.

Fired from *Ray Gun* in November 1995, Carson found himself busier than ever before. He established David Carson Design with offices in New

York City and San Diego, Calif., and attracted such corporate clients as MCI, Nike, Kodak, Gannett Outdoor, Ray-Ban, and Jaguar. In April 1996 Carson unveiled the quarterly *Speak,* which he designed and characterized as including "design, culture, and a smattering of rock and roll." He also worked with John Kao, then at Harvard Business School, on a documentary called *Jamming: The Art and Discipline of Business Creativity.*

(ALISSA SIMON)

Choi Won Suk
From the barren Sahara to the grasslands of the North African coast, a dramatic ecological transformation was under way in the world's largest desert. South Korea's Dong Ah Construction Industrial Co., under the leadership of Choi Won Suk, was undertaking a Libyan construction project of titanic proportions, the creation of a huge waterway—"the Great Man-Made River (GMR) Project. (*See* ARCHITECTURE AND CIVIL ENGINEERING: *Sidebar.*)

Thousands of kilometres of pipeline were linked together to form a network to transport water from natural underground reservoirs deep in the Sahara Desert to densely populated coastal areas. The multibillion-dollar project was also attempting to transform the vast wasteland of the Sahara into one of the world's largest areas of fertile farmland. Libyan leader Col. Muammar al-Qaddafi likened the project to the Seven Wonders of the World.

The central figure in the waterway project was Choi, chairman of the Dong Ah company, which was composed of 16 subsidiaries primarily engaged in construction, transportation, tourism, and finance. The company successfully completed the first stage of the five-phase $27 billion project. It involved the installation of a 1,900-km (1,200-mi) waterway built with prestressed concrete cylinder pipes 4 m (13 ft) in diameter and some 7 m (23 ft) in length. After a decade of construction, the stage-one watercourse was completed at a total cost of $3.8 billion. Up to two million tons of water could flow daily through the network of pipes and ditches connected to 234 wells dug in eastern Libya. The $6.4 billion phase two involved construction of a similar watercourse in western Libya. Completion of the entire project was scheduled for 1999.

Nicknamed "Big Man" and "Thinking Bulldozer," Choi majored in economics at Hanyang University in Seoul. After his graduation in 1967, he took over Dong Ah from his father, who had started the construction business in 1945. Choi's reputation as one of South Korea's most respected businessmen was established as he successfully completed mammoth road-construction, a nuclear electric power plant, and land-reclamation projects at home and abroad over a period of three decades. He was also well respected for his leadership role with the Construction Association of Korea, Korea Federation of Construction Associations, and Korea Construction Financial Cooperation. Choi spent a sizable portion of his wealth on the promotion of Korean culture by inaugurating the Business Council for the Arts.

A setback in Choi's steady rise occurred in 1996 when he and a number of other prominent South Korean businessmen were implicated in a political scandal over corporate contributions to former president Roh Tae Woo. Although such payments were traditional and had been considered normal business practice, a court ruled that they constituted bribes. Choi was found guilty by the court in August, but his sentence was suspended. (*See* WORLD AFFAIRS: *Korea, Republic of.*)   (PARK CHANG SEOK)

Chung Mong Joon
When the Fédération Internationale de Football Association (FIFA) announced in mid-1996 that South Korea and Japan would serve as cohosts of its World Cup 2002, the South Korean people were both elated by the news and filled with admiration for National Assemblyman Chung Moon Joon, the man who made what seemed an impossible dream come true. Chung had seen South Korea transform itself from a war-ravaged country into one of the world's leading industrialized

nations. More important, he watched his father develop a small automobile repair shop into a conglomerate known as the Hyundai Group. He also took pride in the fact that his father was largely responsible for bringing the Olympic Games to Seoul in 1988.

Chung was born on Oct. 17, 1951, in Seoul. He attended the prestigious Seoul National University, where he majored in economics, and then obtained a master of business administration degree at the Massachusetts Institute of Technology and a doctorate in international relations at Johns Hopkins University, Baltimore, Md. During his youth Chung excelled in soccer, basketball, and skiing. His strong interest in sports led to his becoming president of the Korean Archery Association (1983–85), president of the Korean Football Association (from 1993), and vice president of FIFA (from 1994). With such a background he was able to persuade authorities that South Korea should be the host of World Cup 2002.

On the basis of his research and the practical experience he gained as chairman of Hyundai Heavy Industries, Chung wrote *The Government-Business Relationship of Japan.* Critics agreed that this book made a valuable contribution to an understanding of the role of the government in industrial development, not only in Japan but also in other countries, particularly those that were trying to catch up with the more advanced nations. Chung also served as chairman of the board of trustees of the University of Ulsan (from 1983) and as a board member of Johns Hopkins University (from 1995).

Chung's political career began in 1988 when he ran for the National Assembly from Ulsan, the seat of many Hyundai industries, including automobile, shipbuilding, and steel. He was reelected in 1996.

Chung's numerous honours included a National Medal of Zaire (1982), Decoration for the Hosting of the Seoul Olympics (1988), and a Silver Monument Medal for Industry (1994).

(LEE JAI SEONG)

Clark, Glen David

When British Columbia Premier Glen Clark and his socialist New Democratic Party (NDP) were returned to power with a majority government in the general election held on May 28, 1996, the victory was viewed as running counter to a recent Canadian political trend toward conservatism. Clark had been elected leader of the provincial NDP on Feb. 18, 1996, to replace Premier Mike Harcourt, who had resigned over a scandal involving the party's use of charitable funds for political purposes. When Clark assumed office as the 31st premier of British Columbia on Feb. 22, 1996, he broke with tradition by having the swearing-in ceremony in his home riding (electoral district) rather than at the legislature in Victoria.

Born on Nov. 22, 1957, in Nanaimo, B.C., Clark grew up in a working-class neighbourhood in Vancouver. He received a B.A. in history and political science from Simon Fraser University, Burnaby, B.C., and an M.A. (1985) in community and regional planning from the University of British Columbia. His thesis examined the role played by provincial government policy in the crises in British Columbia's forest industry. Clark had joined the Ironworkers' Union during a summer when he worked at a steel fabrication plant. After graduation he became a union organizer, a post that served as a training ground for politics.

Clark worked as an assistant to Canadian parliamentarian Ian Waddell before he was elected (1986) to the British Columbia legislature from the riding of Vancouver-Kingsway. There he made a name for himself as a harsh critic of the government. When the NDP came to power in November 1991, Clark was appointed government house leader and minister of finance and corporate relations. He delivered two budgets that raised taxes and the provincial debt to record levels, and in 1993 he proposed a tax on houses worth more than $500,000. Following a public outcry, Clark was moved to the Ministry of Employment and Investment. This experience taught him the necessity of discussing policies before announcing them.

As premier, Clark proposed that the government invest in education and training, resource development, and megaprojects, areas that would create jobs and secure the economic future of the fast-growing province. Thus, Clark believed it was foolish to cut funding for health care, education, and the environment at a time when demand for these services was growing. Clark, who described himself as a "B.C.-firster," was prepared to make the federal government more aware of British Columbia's importance to the country.

(DIANE LOIS WAY)

Clinton, Bill

On Nov. 5, 1996, Bill Clinton was reelected president of the U.S. over Republican nominee Bob Dole (*q.v.*). The Democratic candidate's campaign was buoyed by a strong economy and by the voters' dislike for certain Republican policies that many people, particularly women, saw as harsh. Although the president and his running mate, Vice Pres. Al Gore, won only 49% of the popular vote, they took 379 of the 538 votes in the electoral college, showing particular strength in the Northeast, the industrial Midwest, and the Far West.

Clinton's victory would have seemed impossible only two years earlier. In the 1994 elections the Republicans had won control of both the House of Representatives and the Senate, and for the first few months of 1995 they dominated U.S. politics. When, however, the president vetoed the 1996 budget, Republican leaders forced two partial government shutdowns, a tactic that angered the public. Despite a number of subsequent stopgap measures, a final budget agreement was not reached until April 1996.

The president's record with Congress on other issues in 1996 was mixed but overall seemed to redound to his benefit. In April he vetoed a ban on certain controversial late-term abortions, and in May he vetoed limits on product liability suits. In August, over the strong objections of many fellow Democrats, the president agreed to sign a welfare-reform bill that, among other things, transferred funds and responsibility to the states. The president and Congress reached agreement on minor reforms in health insurance, and Clinton won an increase in the minimum wage.

The president and his wife, Hillary Rodham Clinton, continued to be dogged by allegations of wrongdoing. The Whitewater investigation continued, with the president twice called on to give videotaped testimony and the first lady subpoenaed by a federal grand jury; in May three former Clinton business associates were found guilty of fraud and conspiracy in the affair. Questions continued about the 1993 firing of White House travel office employees and White House requests for FBI files on employees of the preceding administrations. In January an appeals court ruled that a sexual harassment suit filed earlier against the president could proceed while he was in office; in May he filed an appeal with the Supreme Court. During the Democratic convention, Clinton's chief political adviser resigned in a sex scandal; later there were revelations of questionable Democratic fund-raising practices. None of these matters seemed to be decisive for the electorate, however, and the president became the first Democrat since Franklin D. Roosevelt to win reelection.

Clinton, who was born William Jefferson Blythe IV on Aug. 19, 1946, in Hope, Ark., later took the name of his stepfather. He was educated at Georgetown University, Washington, D.C., was a Rhodes scholar at the University of Oxford, and received a law degree from Yale University. He taught, practiced law, and held elective office in Arkansas. He was elected governor of the state five times before winning the U.S. presidency in 1992.

(ROBERT RAUCH)

Coelho, Paulo

In 1995 the mystical author Paulo Coelho, one of Brazil's most successful novelists and probably its best-selling writer abroad, expanded his international popularity by penetrating the U.S. market, and sales of his lyrical fiction showed no signs of waning in 1996. Early in the year *By the*

Paulo Coelho

River Piedra I Sat Down and Wept, the English translation of his 1994 novel *Na margem do rio Piedra eu sentei e chorei* (film rights to which had been secured by the French actress Isabel Adjani), was published in the United States in an initial press run of 50,000 copies. Coelho's U.S. publisher doubtless hoped that the book would approach the popularity of *The Alchemist* (the English translation of his best-known book, *O alquimista*), which by the end of 1995 had sold some 280,000 trade paperback copies in the United States. By 1996 four of Coelho's six books had been translated into at least 26 languages and had sold more than 7.5 million copies, with more than one million copies sold in France alone.

Coelho was born in August 1947 in Rio de Janeiro. He dropped out of law school in 1970 and traveled through South America, Mexico, North Africa, and Europe. In 1972 he returned home and wrote pop music lyrics, scoring several hits with Raul Seixas, one of Brazil's best-known singers. In 1974 Coelho was briefly imprisoned for alleged subversive activities against the Brazilian government. After his release he worked for Polygram and CBS Records until 1980, when he embarked on new travels in Europe and Africa. It was during this trip that he walked the 830-km (516-mi) Road of Santiago, the ancient Spanish road used by pilgrims traveling from France to Spain. This extensive journey formed the basis of his first book, *O diário de um mago* (1987), which was published in English as *The Diary of a Magus* in 1992 and was reissued as *The Pilgrimage* in 1995.

In 1988 Coelho published *O alquimista*, a mystical account of an Andalusian shepherd boy's journey across North Africa in search of treasure. After being dropped by its first publisher, the book was reissued and subsequently became one of Brazil's all-time best-sellers, with more than two million copies sold. The novel, which was widely translated, topped the best-seller list of the French publisher's magazine *Livres Hebdo* for a record 92 weeks and sold more than 150,000 copies in Italy. His latest book, *Frases*, a collection of short excerpts from his unpublished works and best-sellers, remained at or near the top of the Brazilian nonfiction best-seller list throughout most of 1996.

Although Coelho's critical reception did not always match his popularity, as he once told a U.S. radio interviewer, "I try to share with my readers my inner quest; that's basically my spiritual quest. I don't have anything to teach . . . but actually I do have something to share. It is how I am experiencing this strange and sometimes very tricky path."

(MICHAEL T. CALVERT)

Coen, Ethan and Joel

By 1996, after having made only six motion pictures, brothers Ethan and Joel Coen had established themselves among the most versatile filmmaking talents in the U.S. Joel wrote and directed, while Ethan wrote and produced. Their clever screenplays, toying with the conventions of film genre while paying homage to them and peopled with vivid, oddball characters were acclaimed for their striking imagery. The Coens credited precise and detailed storyboards, in which every element was preplanned. In 1996 the brothers joined an elite group of repeat award winners when their latest feature, *Fargo,* a quirky tale of crime and punishment set in the snowy Midwest, captured the best director prize at the Cannes Film Festival.

Joel was born on Nov. 29, 1955, and Ethan arrived on Sept. 21, 1958; both were born in St. Louis Park, Minn. The children of university professors, the brothers showed an early interest in filmmaking, shooting home movies of their friends with a Super-8 camera.

Joel refined his craft at the New York University Film School and after graduation found work as an assistant editor on low-budget horror films. Ethan, meanwhile, studied philosophy at Princeton University. After graduation he joined his brother in New York City, and together they began writing scripts for independent producers.

The brothers riveted the attention of the film world in 1984 with *Blood Simple,* a stylish thriller that they co-wrote and financed through private investors. Although Joel took the director's credit and Ethan that of producer, they insisted that their roles were interchangeable.

The critical success of *Blood Simple* enabled the brothers to make a deal with an independent production company that granted them complete creative control. The films that followed were as different from *Blood Simple* as they were from each other. *Raising Arizona* (1987), an irreverent comedy about babies, Harley Davidsons, and high explosives, and *Miller's Crossing* (1990), a period gangster drama, firmly established the Coens' reputation as idiosyncratic talents. *Barton Fink,* about an edgy, neurotic would-be writer, claimed the best picture, best director, and best actor awards during the 1991 Cannes competition, the first such sweep in the festival's history.

The Coens turned to Hollywood to produce their fifth feature, *The Hudsucker Proxy* (1994), a fairy tale in which a small-town hayseed becomes the head of a big-time corporation. Written a decade earlier by the brothers and horror film maven Sam Raimi, the project boasted an all-star cast but was a critical and financial flop. *Fargo* marked a return to both small-budget, independent filmmaking and the brothers' Minnesota roots.   (ALISSA SIMON)

Cook, Robin Finlayson

Once a left-wing socialist who believed that Great Britain should abandon nuclear weapons and leave NATO, Robin Cook had turned by 1996 into one of the key allies of Tony Blair, the reform-minded leader of Britain's Labour Party. Not only did Cook chair Labour's Policy Forum, which oversaw the process of replacing doctrinaire socialism with more modern, market-friendly policies, he also served as foreign secretary in Labour's shadow cabinet. There was every prospect that he would head the Foreign Ministry if Labour won the general election due to be held by May 1997 and thus take charge of the United Kingdom's relations with the United States, whose military strategy he had so fiercely opposed for much of the 1970s and early '80s.

Cook was born in Belshill, Lanarkshire, near Glasgow, Scot., on Feb. 28, 1946, and was educated at Aberdeen Grammar School and the University of Edinburgh. He was a teacher for five years before entering the House of Commons in 1974, at the age of 28, as Labour MP for Edinburgh Central. Because of boundary changes, he moved to become MP for nearby Livingston in 1983.

For most of his first 10 years in Parliament, Cook was a left-wing MP. He also led the minority Labour faction that opposed his own party's plans

to create an elected assembly in Scotland. In the 1980s, however, Cook started his journey toward the political centre. In 1981 he broke with Tony Benn, the unofficial leader of Labour's left wing, because he opposed Benn's decision to seek to wrest the deputy leadership of the Labour Party from Denis Healey, the moderate incumbent. In 1983 Cook managed Neil Kinnock's successful campaign to become leader of the Labour Party; subsequently, he backed Kinnock's strategy of modernizing the party and gradually abandoning unpopular left-wing policies.

Blair's decision to appoint Cook as shadow foreign secretary in 1994, following Blair's election as leader, made Cook one of Blair's three most senior lieutenants. (The other two were deputy leader John Prescott and shadow chancellor Gordon Brown.) At first Cook appeared the most junior of the triumvirate, but he gradually gained ground by virtue of his sharp intellect and even sharper debating skills, which regularly cheered Labour MPs and depressed Conservatives. Few doubted that Cook would be a major—and formidable—member of a future Labour government.   (PETER KELLNER)

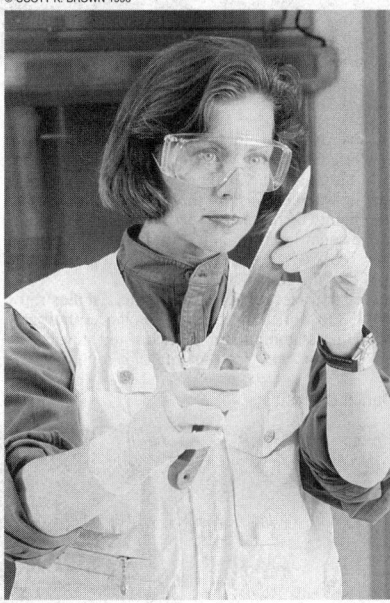

Patricia Cornwell

Cornwell, Patricia

U.S. crime novelist Patricia Cornwell signed a contract with G.P. Putnam's Sons in 1996 that would make her one of the most successful and well-paid women writers in the world. She was to receive $24 million for her next three books.

Cornwell appeared to have gravitated to the sinister crime-mystery genre because her young life was ridden with feelings of darkness and uncertainty. Born on June 9, 1956, in Miami, Fla., Cornwell was deserted at age five by her father. Several years later, while residing in Montreat, N.C., Cornwell's depressed mother attempted to give her away to neighbours, missionaries Ruth and Billy Graham. Ruth placed Cornwell with another family of missionaries while her mother recovered from a nervous breakdown apparently triggered by lack of food, fuel, money, and clothes.

These experiences left Cornwell battling for a sense of control. She attended Davidson (N.C.) College and, during her years there, fought anorexia nervosa and bulimia. She spent some time in a mental hospital that she said could have been the scene of any number of horrific novels. She graduated in 1979, married (1980) an English professor 17 years her senior, and began working at the *Charlotte* (N.C.) *Observer.*

As a police reporter at the *Observer,* Cornwell dealt firsthand with crime, and she sought out experiences that would reveal its intricacies. She

interviewed medical examiners, volunteered as a police officer, spent endless hours in the morgue's medical library, and took classes, such as forensic science, at the police academy. A job she took at the morgue allowed her to observe autopsies.

In 1983 Cornwell wrote her first book, a biography of Ruth Graham. Having developed a "healthy respect for evil" while working for the *Observer,* she wanted her second novel to focus on crime.

A self-proclaimed overachiever, Cornwell had a determination that brought her face-to-face with something worse than death: failure. She wrote three crime novels, and all were rejected. Depressed but not defeated, Cornwell solicited the advice of an editor who encouraged her to develop the character of Kay Scarpetta. Very much like Cornwell in appearance and ideology, Scarpetta had appeared in minor roles in the early, unsuccessful works. When Scarpetta took the lead role as medical examiner in *Postmortem,* Cornwell's writing career took off. Each year brought a new mystery for Scarpetta to solve, and each year fans clamoured for more.

The best-selling author of seven novels, with an eighth book and a movie deal in the works, Cornwell employed a staff of eight and occupied a suite of offices. She surrounded herself with bodyguards, rented private jets and helicopters, and erected a shrine to herself filled with Scarpetta memorabilia: T-shirts, caps, and posters.   (KATHERINE I. GORDON)

Dawkins, (Clinton) Richard

University of Oxford zoologist Richard Dawkins made a career out of trying to present science in terms that could be understood by the general public. Through television appearances, opinion articles in newspapers, five books, and a CD-ROM, Dawkins had taken up the job of breaking down the barriers between the scientific community and the rest of the world. This led to his being named in 1995 the first Charles Simonyi professor of public understanding of science at Oxford. At the same time, however, he remained controversial, not just because of his views on evolution but also because he had become one of the country's best-known atheists.

Dawkins was born March 26, 1941, in Nairobi, Kenya, where his father was stationed during World War II. The family moved back to England in 1949, and in 1959 Dawkins entered Oxford, where he studied zoology. After receiving his doctorate, he became (1967) an assistant professor of zoology at the University of California, Berkeley, and then returned to Oxford to teach two years later. In 1976 he published his first book, *The Selfish Gene,* in which he tried to set straight what he thought was a widespread misunderstanding of Darwinism. Dawkins argued that natural selection did not take place on the level of the species or the individual but rather among genes. Genes, he maintained, used the bodies of living things to further their own survival. He also introduced the concept of "memes," the cultural equivalent of genes; ideas—such as fashion, religion, or other cultural phenomena—took on a life of their own within society and, along with genes, affected the progress of human evolution. The book was notable not just because of what it espoused but also because of the way it was written—it appealed to both the general reader and the scientist. More books followed, including *The Extended Phenotype* (1982), *The Blind Watchmaker* (1986), *River Out of Eden* (1995), and *Climbing Mount Improbable* (1996). He also released an interactive CD-ROM in 1996, *The Evolution of Life,* in which users could create "biomorphs," computer-simulated examples of evolution first introduced in *The Blind Watchmaker.* In fact, it was Dawkins's fascination with computers that contributed to much of the controversy surrounding his ideas. He felt that evolution boiled down to a sort of binary information transfer between genes that could best be expressed through computer simulation.

Dawkins often appeared on talk shows and debates, defending not only his theories but also his atheism. He likened religious faith to the childish habit of needing someone to blame for anything otherwise inexplicable. He was the winner of a

"Prom Dress," a photograph by Roy DeCarava (right)

number of awards, both literary and scientific, including the Royal Society of Literature Award. His notoriety only increased with his marriage to Lalla Ward, an actress who had played an assistant to the fictitious television scientist Dr. Who.

(ANTHONY G. CRAINE)

DeCarava, Roy

In 1996 nearly 200 black-and-white photographs by the groundbreaking African-American photographer Roy DeCarava were displayed at New York City's Museum of Modern Art. The exhibition "Roy DeCarava: A Retrospective" featured a variety of subjects shot by the artist between 1949 and 1994, ranging from pictures of daily life in the Harlem section of New York City to the civil rights protests of the early 1960s to lyrical studies of nature. It also included a selection of DeCarava's remarkable jazz photographs, which captured such musical legends as Louis Armstrong, John Coltrane, Billie Holiday, and Milt Jackson at their peak form. The most comprehensive survey ever of DeCarava's work, the exhibition traveled to major museums in the United States throughout the year.

DeCarava was born on Dec. 9, 1919, in Harlem. After graduating from high school, he studied painting and printmaking at the Cooper Union School of Art, New York City, for two years. During the 1940s he continued his studies at the Harlem Community Art Center and the George Washington Carver Art School, where he created images of black life. When DeCarava switched to the medium of photography in the late 1940s, he retained his interest in depicting the concerns of his community and began photographing life in Harlem. In his Harlem series he aimed for "a creative expression, the kind of penetrating insight and understanding of Negroes which I believe only a Negro photographer can interpret." In 1952 he was awarded a Guggenheim fellowship in support of the project, the first African-American photographer to receive this prestigious grant. Of his Harlem photographs, 140 appeared in the book *The Sweet Flypaper of Life* (1955), a collaboration with poet Langston Hughes, who provided the lively fictional text. In 1955 DeCarava also opened A Photographer's Gallery in New York City, which marked an early attempt to gain recognition for photography as an art.

A dedicated amateur saxophonist, DeCarava began taking photographs of jazz artists in 1956. His photos present the performers in the act of creation, capturing the music's effect on the musicians rather than on the audience. DeCarava intended the photos for a book called *The Sound I Saw,* but it was never published. His prints,

however, were exhibited in a show with that title at Harlem's Studio Museum in 1983.

In his Guggenheim application DeCarava wrote that he wanted "to show the strength, the wisdom, the dignity of the Negro people." These qualities are evident in his photos of both labourers in New York City's garment district and participants in the civil rights protests.

DeCarava left his job as a commercial illustrator in 1958 to work full time as a freelance photographer on assignment for agencies and magazines. In 1963 he was instrumental in founding the

Daniel Dennett

Kamoinge Workshop, an association of African-American photographers based in Harlem, where he taught for three years. From 1969 to 1972 DeCarava served as adjunct instructor at the Cooper Union School of Art. In 1975 he ended his freelance career to teach photography at Hunter College.

(ALISSA SIMON)

Dennett, Daniel C.

For centuries philosophers had grappled with the problem of the nature of consciousness, and at the end of the 20th century the mind-body problem still provoked lively debate. At home in this contentious milieu was philosopher Dan Dennett, head of the Center for Cognitive Studies at Tufts University, Medford, Mass. Beginning in the 1960s Dennett argued, in an elegant and engaging style, for the materialist viewpoint—the idea that the mind can be described solely in terms of the workings of the brain. His latest book, *Kinds of Minds*, which appeared in 1996, advanced that argument yet another step.

Dennett was born March 28, 1942, in Boston. His father was a diplomat and a scholar of Islamic history; his mother, an editor and a teacher. After receiving a B.A. in philosophy from Harvard University in 1963, he moved to the University of Oxford, where he studied with the philosopher Gilbert Ryle. There, as a graduate student, Dennett became interested in the problem of consciousness and wrote his first thesis on the topic, which he later turned into his first book, *Content and Consciousness* (1969). He received a doctorate in philosophy in 1965, whereupon he returned to the U.S. to teach at the University of California, Irvine. In 1971 he moved to Tufts, eventually achieving the distinction of distinguished arts and sciences professor.

Although trained in the philosophical tradition, Dennett was conversant in the fields of artificial intelligence, neuroscience, and cognitive psychology. He educated himself in those disciplines, having become convinced that only by being informed by science could the philosophical debate about mind be productive. His somewhat unorthodox approach, which reflected his skepticism of traditional methods of philosophy, cast him as a radical among his colleagues. Nevertheless, his interdisciplinary strategy was becoming more prevalent among philosophers as scientific researchers gathered more information about the brain's mechanisms.

In 1996 Dennett was involved with a team at the Massachusetts Institute of Technology that was attempting to construct an intelligent, and perhaps even conscious, robot called Cog. He also continued to write. Throughout his career he authored a number of books that detail his theories of consciousness. Two recent efforts, *Consciousness Explained* (1991) and *Darwin's Dangerous Idea* (1995), examine how the mindless process of natural selection can account for the evolution of the brain and human consciousness. *Kinds of Minds* continued to explore and, in Dennett's view, to demystify those phenomena.

(MARY JANE FRIEDRICH)

Dole, Robert ("Bob") Joseph
In the election on Nov. 5, 1996, Bob Dole, a longtime leader in the U.S. Senate, lost his bid for the presidency. The Republican candidate was not able to exploit the vulnerabilities of his Democratic opponent, Pres. Bill Clinton (*q.v.*), and gain a significant number of votes outside the core of his own party; he showed strength only in parts of the South and in the Plains states. Dole took 41% of the total vote but received only 159 of the 538 votes in the electoral college.

Dole was born on July 22, 1923, in Russell, Kan. He was a high-school athlete and in 1941 entered the University of Kansas as a premed student. He joined the U.S. Army in 1943 and in 1945, during an assault on an enemy position, was hit by an exploding shell. His right shoulder destroyed and his body largely paralyzed from the neck down, Dole spent three years in hospitals undergoing surgery and rehabilitation. Although his right arm remained disabled, he persisted in learning to walk again and to use his damaged left arm and hand. In 1952 he received A.B. and LL.B. degrees from Washburn University, Topeka, Kan.

Beginning in 1950 Dole won a succession of elective positions, first at the state and local levels. In 1960 he was elected to the first of four terms in the U.S. House of Representatives, where he opposed the spending policies of liberal Democratic administrations. In 1968 he won the first of five terms in the Senate, eventually becoming the Republican head, as both majority (1985–86 and 1995–96) and minority (1987–94) leader. He also chaired the Republican National Committee from

1971 to 1973. Dole generally advocated conservative fiscal policies, but on other issues he took stands that ranged from right of centre to moderate. He supported civil rights and voting rights bills and food stamp programs but voted against proposals for other social programs, including the original bill establishing Medicare. Above all, he developed a reputation as a pragmatic politician and skillful legislative leader.

Dole was the vice presidential candidate in Pres. Gerald R. Ford's unsuccessful 1976 campaign. After losing his own bids for the presidential nomination in 1980 and 1988, Dole stumbled early in 1996, then quickly won a series of primary victories. Before the Republican national convention, he resigned from the Senate and chose former secretary of housing and urban development Jack Kemp (*q.v.*) as his running mate. Although the party's platform emphasized the views of Republican social conservatives, the Dole forces carefully managed the convention itself to project a more moderate image. A dramatic speech by Dole's wife, Elizabeth, who herself had held powerful positions in both the public and private sectors, was the highlight of the convention. Despite vigorous campaigning, which included the promise of a 15% tax cut and emphasized themes such as character and honesty, the Dole-Kemp ticket went down to defeat. (ROBERT RAUCH)

Elizabeth II
The 70th birthday celebration of Queen Elizabeth II in April 1996 was a muted affair. Despite her own undiminished popularity after 44 years on the throne of the United Kingdom, the queen was surrounded by family turmoil and public pressures on the British monarchy to change its ways. Two of her children—Charles, prince of Wales, the heir to the throne, and Andrew, duke of York— were in the process of getting divorced amid a welter of salacious stories about their wives, Diana, princess of Wales, and Sarah, duchess of York. (The queen's daughter, Princess Anne, had already divorced and remarried, while her youngest son, Prince Edward, remained unmarried.) The publicity surrounding the divorces provoked widespread demands that the royal family adopt a more modern and open approach to their official roles. The queen responded by agreeing, for the first time, to pay income tax on her private investments and to accept a reduction in the Civil List (payments made by the British government to the royal family for fulfilling their public functions). Doubts continued to grow, however, about the ability of the British monarchy to survive much beyond Elizabeth's reign.

Born in London on April 21, 1926, Elizabeth seemed destined to a life of relative obscurity. Her father, the duke of York (later King George VI), was the younger brother of the heir to the throne. However, her childless uncle abdicated the throne in December 1936 after 11 uneasy months as King Edward VIII, and Elizabeth became heir presumptive. When George died in 1952, Elizabeth, aged only 25 and with a Greek-born husband and two young children, became queen. She quickly established herself as a popular monarch, more devoted to public service than many of her predecessors. She also sought to tread a careful path between the maintenance of pomp and tradition and adjustment to the modern world. She never gave interviews (although she permitted her children and husband, Philip, duke of Edinburgh, to do so), yet from time to time she allowed television cameras into Buckingham Palace and her other residences to film her both at work and relaxing with her family.

Although the private life of the royal family was widely reported, Elizabeth's more formal role as head of state also provoked controversy. As a strictly constitutional monarch, she had no power to intervene in the actions of her elected government, but she made clear her devotion to social cohesion in Britain and to the cause of a multiracial Commonwealth. Thus, the readmission of South Africa to the Commonwealth in 1994 and Pres. Nelson Mandela's state visit to London in July 1996 provided bright interludes in an otherwise dismal decade for the queen.

(PETER KELLNER)

Erbakan, Necmettin
On July 8, 1996, the national legislature of Turkey confirmed a coalition government headed by Necmettin Erbakan, who, among other things, advocated strengthening ties to Islamic nations. His Welfare (Refah) Party had won the most votes in the legislative elections held in December 1995, taking 158 of the 550 seats and thereby becoming the first Islamic party ever to win a general election in Turkey. After a centre-right coalition collapsed in June, Erbakan and Tansu Ciller, a former prime minister and head of the True Path Party, formed a coalition.

Erbakan was born in Sinop, a town in northern Turkey on the Black Sea, in 1926. He was the son of one of the last Islamic judges of the Ottoman Empire, whose system of religious courts was replaced by a secular legal code after the founding of modern Turkey in 1923. The future political leader received degrees in mechanical engineering from Istanbul Technical University, where he later taught, and the Rhenish-Westphalian Technical University of Aachen, then in West Germany. Elected to the legislature as an independent in 1969, the next year he formed an Islamic party, but it was banned by the military government in 1971. He re-formed the party in 1972 and twice during the 1970s served as a deputy prime minister. In 1980 the military again banned his party and briefly put Erbakan in prison. He was prohibited from engaging in politics from 1980 to 1987. His third attempt to form a political party was more successful, and the Welfare Party became especially well organized on the local level, where it opposed what many saw as the arrogant corruption of the leaders of the established parties. In the 1995 campaign Erbakan advocated withdrawing from NATO, abrogating agreements with Israel, and developing closer ties with such Middle Eastern nations as Syria and Iran. His proposals were particularly unsettling to Western leaders, who had long depended on a friendly secular government in Turkey as a basis for their policy in the Middle East.

Early in 1996 Erbakan tried but failed to form a coalition government. A centre-right coalition of the True Path and Motherland parties then held power until internal disagreements brought it down in June. Erbakan was again asked to try to form a coalition, and this time, when Ciller agreed to join him, he succeeded. Under the agreement, Erbakan and Ciller would alternate as prime minister, with Ciller initially holding the posts of deputy prime minister and minister of foreign affairs. The various other ministries were divided between the two parties. The Welfare Party headed such departments as Finance, Labour, Justice, and Culture, which gave the Islamists considerable influence over domestic affairs. The True Path Party, however, controlled not only Foreign Affairs but also such ministries as Defense and Interior and thus strengthened its hand, and that of the military, in the conduct of foreign policy. (ROBERT RAUCH)

Evora, Cesaria
After performing for many years for little or no pay in local bars and taverns, Cape Verdean singer Cesaria Evora captured the international limelight when her album *Cesaria Evora* was nominated in 1996 for a Grammy award in the category of best world music album. With a rich, husky voice, she captivated audiences when she sang *mornas,* sorrowful folk songs passed from generation to generation of Cape Verdeans as part of their cultural heritage. The emotion-charged songs chronicled the country's long and bitter history of isolation, slave trade, and native population loss due to emigration.

Singing in Creole-Portuguese without much embellishment, Evora was accompanied by such acoustic instruments as guitar, piano, violin, accordion, clarinet, and the cavaquinho, a four-stringed instrument similar to a ukelele. The barefoot diva—she never wore shoes while performing— was often compared to singers Billie Holiday and Edith Piaf for her ability to transcend language and spellbind audiences with haunting interpretations of songs about suffering and yearning. Evora's spare, elegant style was also reminiscent

Cesaria Evora

of one of her own favourite performers—Mahalia Jackson. Though the *morna* was her specialty, she did record a few *coladeiras, mornas* with a faster tempo.

Evora was born in 1941 in Mindelo, a port city on the island of São Vicente, Cape Verde, off the west coast of Africa. She sang with her father's band before launching a solo career, and though her artistry was not monetarily rewarded, she developed a huge following. In 1988 concert promoter José da Silva took her to Paris, where she recorded *La Diva aux pieds nus,* which was followed by a steady stream of new material. It was in 1992, however, after the release of *Miss perfumado,* that Evora achieved popularity with European audiences.

Her other albums include *Mar azul, Distino di belita,* and *Saudades.* Though she maintained a Paris base while on tour, the singer continued to live in Cape Verde surrounded by her family—a daughter, a son, and two grandchildren. While commenting on her success, Evora reflected, "In all the years when I sang in bars and in front of foreigners, I sometimes had an idea that I might someday be successful outside my country. The thought never stayed with me for very long, but here I am." (AMANDA E. FULLER)

Fernández Reyna, Leonel

On Aug. 16, 1996, after a bitter campaign filled with charges of racism and personal attacks, 42-year-old Leonel Fernández Reyna of the Dominican Liberation Party (PLD) was sworn in as the Dominican Republic's president; he was the youngest person ever to be elected to the office.

Though Fernández lost in the first round of elections to former Santo Domingo mayor José Francisco Peña Gómez of the Dominican Revolutionary Party, he won the second round by a narrow margin after forming an alliance with the ruling Social Christian Reformist Party. Fernández would succeed Joaquín Balaguer, who had run the country off and on over a period of nearly 30 years. At 89 and almost blind, he was prevented from running for office again. Fernández, who represented a "generational change of command" in Dominican politics, appealed to middle-class voters weary of a fractured system. He was elected with the support of both Balaguer and

PLD founder Juan Bosch, who put aside their differences to ensure that Fernández, who was of mixed race, would win over Peña, a Haitian.

Fernández, the son of a soldier and a teacher, was born on Dec. 26, 1953, in Santo Domingo but was raised mostly in New York City. Growing up, he was an avid basketball player and fan of the New York Knicks basketball team. After his mother became concerned that he was becoming too American, he returned to the Dominican Republic in his late teens. He graduated with honours in law from the University of Santo Domingo and became a successful teacher and journalist. He practiced law privately before making the transition to politics.

Fernández vowed to end political corruption and, in one of his first moves as president, increased the salaries of various government officials, including his own, maintaining that if employees were properly paid, they would be less willing to accept bribes. Other areas that came under his scrutiny were the judiciary, police, military, and state-owned companies. He also planned to address severe economic problems, especially unemployment. The latter had prompted approximately one million Dominicans to move to the U.S., sometimes illegally, in order to find work. He also promised to strengthen manufacturing and agriculture and to improve foreign policy.

Though Fernández inherited a country rife with problems, he seemed enthusiastic and regarded the situation as a challenge. "Countries can be governed democratically," he said. "Instead of seeing this as a weak administration, we should see this as an opportunity."

(AMANDA E. FULLER)

Franz, Dennis

Playing villains and cops—and sometimes villainous cops—Dennis Franz established himself as one of the finest actors on television. In 1996 he collected his second Emmy award for his portrayal of detective Andy Sipowicz on the popular weekly dramatic series "NYPD Blue." Franz achieved stardom and critical acclaim by using his size and tough-guy Chicago accent to create a commanding on-screen presence. Though he had also appeared in a number of feature films, it was his recent TV work that attracted the attention of director Michael Corrente, who cast Franz in a starring role opposite Dustin Hoffman in the film adaptation of David Mamet's play *American Buffalo.*

Franz was born Dennis Schlachta on Oct. 28, 1944, in Maywood, Ill. He was active in drama first in high school and then at junior college and Southern Illinois University before enlistment in the army took him to Vietnam. Returning to the stage after his discharge in 1970, Franz was invited to join Chicago's Organic Theatre Company. There he appeared in *Bleacher Bums* (1978), which focused on a group of fans at a Chicago Cubs baseball game. Film director Brian De Palma watched Franz perform in an Organic production of *Cops* and invited him to appear in his film *The Fury* (1978). Other thrillers followed, including *Dressed to Kill* (1980), *Blow Out* (1981), and *Psycho II* (1983).

After portraying a police officer in a series called "Chicago Story" (1982), Franz landed a guest-starring role on the hit police drama "Hill Street Blues," playing the role of corrupt detective Sal Benedetto during the 1982–83 season. When that character was killed, Steven Bochco, creator of "Hill Street Blues," cast Franz in a new project, "Bay City Blues," a short-lived series about a minor-league baseball team. Franz returned to "Hill Street Blues" for the 1985–86 season as a regular member of the ensemble, playing Lieut. Norman Buntz.

After "Hill Street Blues" left the air, Franz was cast in similar roles in such unsuccessful series as "Beverly Hills Buntz," "Nasty Boys," and "NYPD Mounted." He had minor roles in the films *Die Hard 2* (1990) and *The Player* (1992) and appeared in several television movies before Bochco offered him a starring role in "NYPD Blue," which debuted in September 1993. The program was controversial because of its graphic depictions of violence and sex but was nonethe-

less well received by critics and viewers. The show received a record 26 Emmy award nominations in 1994, including Franz's nomination for the award for best lead actor in a dramatic series, which he won. (ANTHONY G. CRAINE)

Fu Mingxia

One month after capping her career with two gold medals at the 1996 Olympic Games in Atlanta, Ga., Chinese diver Fu Mingxia announced her retirement, explaining, "I am already too old." These might seem like hoary words for an 18-year-old, but such was the accelerated pace of an athlete who began diving (at age 7) before she knew how to swim and became the youngest diver ever to win a world championship (at 12) and an Olympic gold medal (at 13). Her retirement, however, needed the approval of the government sports commission. Throughout the 1990s Fu remained a standout on the Chinese team, which gradually eclipsed the U.S. and former-Soviet teams as the most dominant in the sport. Standing at about 1.5 m (5 ft) tall and weighing 45 kg (100 lb), the tiny veteran loomed large at the 1996 Games, where she accomplished a rare Olympic sweep of the 10-m platform event (521.58 points) and the 3-m springboard (547.68), outscoring the field by more than 42 and 35 points, respectively.

Born on Aug. 16, 1978, Fu was raised in the city of Wuhan in the central Chinese province of Hubei. At the age of nine, she was recruited by coach Yu Fen, who shepherded her into a strenuous state-sponsored diving program in the capital city of Beijing. At the national training centre, she developed technical grace and distinguished herself as a fearless and disciplined worker, regularly devoting more than 40 hours a week to the grueling regimen. She first plunged into international competition at age 11 and scored a win in the 10-m platform at the 1990 Goodwill Games in Seattle, Wash. The following year, at the world championships in Perth, Australia, she posted a score of 426.51 to capture the platform event, edging out Yelena Miroshina of the Soviet squad by just over 23 points.

Fu's victory at the world championships led to the institution of a rule requiring that competitors, at the minimum, must turn 14 years old in the year of a given international meet. Fortunately, her 14th birthday arrived shortly after the conclusion of the 1992 Olympic Games in Barcelona, Spain, where she became the second youngest gold medalist in Olympic history. Fu won the 10-m platform with a score of 461.43, drowning second-place Miroshina by nearly 50 points and executing one of the most difficult dives of the program—a 3½ back tuck. Despite growing 7.5 cm (3 in) and gaining 9 kg (20 lb) between Olympic appearances, Fu remained at the top of her field, successfully defending her title in the 10-m platform at the 1994 world championships in Rome. (TOM MICHAEL)

Galliano, John Charles

The arrival in October 1996 of maverick British fashion designer John Galliano as designer in chief at Christian Dior heralded a fresh start for the beleaguered reputation of haute couture. His appointment followed his 11-month stint at Givenchy, where he was the controversial choice to replace Hubert de Givenchy, the refined founder of the house. Galliano's first couture collection featured sumptuous bouffant ball gowns, bowed dresses, and belted suits. He confessed, however, that Dior's New Look—an ensemble that paired jackets with padded shoulders and ample, ankle-length skirts—was closer to his own aesthetic than were the conservative linear designs of Givenchy. Bernard Arnault, head of Louis Vuitton Möet Hennessy (LVMH), which owned both Givenchy and Christian Dior) hoped that the 36-year-old Galliano would attract a younger clientele, not just to couture but also to the seasonal ready-to-wear lines, produced by both houses.

Galliano, the son of a Spanish plumber, was born on Nov. 28, 1960. At the age of six he moved with his family from Gibraltar to south London, where he was educated. At age 16 he left Wilson's Grammar School for Boys, where he was known as an undistinguished student, to study textile de-

John Galliano

sign at East London College. In 1980 he entered St. Martin's School of Art, London, where he became enamoured of historical costuming. His incredible 1984 French Revolution-inspired graduate collection, Les Incroyables, was purchased straight off the college's catwalk by Joan Burstein, owner of the exclusive London fashion boutique Browns. After graduating with first-class honours, Galliano set up a studio in a condemned and deserted warehouse in London's East End and established himself as the "boy wonder" of British fashion. He was crowned British Fashion Council Designer of the Year in 1987 and 1994, and in 1991 he made his Paris catwalk debut.

Twice, however, Galliano's business went bankrupt. Then, in 1994, John A. Bult, a Swiss-born New York-based investment banker, rescued Galliano and set him up in an atelier near Place de la Bastille in Paris. Upon his appointment at Dior, LVMH bought Galliano's company from Bult. As designer in chief of two fashion houses, Galliano enjoyed an unrivaled position among British designers. In October 1995, for the third time and second consecutive year, he was named British Designer of the Year.

(BRONWYN COSGRAVE)

Gardner, David and Tom

U.S. entrepreneurs David and Tom Gardner, co-founders of the Motley Fool: The Online Investment Forum for the Individual Investor, emerged in 1996 as investment gurus of the '90s. Utilizing the power tool of the age, the Internet, the brothers Gardner built an empire on "Fool" foundations: the power of electronic communication combined with a straightforward investment formula aimed at the individual.

The creators of the Motley Fool were both successful students—in English. Older brother David was born in Washington, D.C., on May 16, 1966, and graduated from the University of North Carolina at Chapel Hill in 1988. Tom, who was born in Philadelphia on April 16, 1968, attended Brown University, Providence, R.I. (B.A., 1990), and did graduate work in linguistics and geography at the University of Montana. Although they had long been interested in money management (they began investing at age 18), they resisted the lure of Wall Street and instead became its competitors.

In 1993 David began an investment newsletter, which was largely unsuccessful until the following year, when Tom promoted it on America Online (AOL). Realizing that the Internet was a perfect forum for their product, they launched the Motley Fool site on AOL in August 1994 (they later added a World Wide Web site). They wrote essays, provided market insights, recommended how much, when, and where subscribers should invest, and suggested the kind of return they could expect on their money. David's shed—located behind the house he shared with his wife and daughter in Alexandria, Va.—became information central, or "Fool Global Headquarters."

The Gardners' personal portfolio was proof of their genius (or foolhardiness), as they consistently outperformed Standard & Poor's Market Index. In the first year they finished 40 points ahead of the market. Business quickly outgrew the shed, and they moved into office space in Alexandria and hired a staff.

The Gardners emphasized that their product was revolutionary because it created a shift in power from big-money investors and brokers to "the little guy" who had never before had convenient and affordable access to investment information. They also believed it was successful because of its simplicity. David said, "If the forward-growth rate of a company is 30% annually and the price/earnings ratio is 15, the Fool Ratio is 0.5. We like to buy stocks at that ratio."

The Gardners, also best-selling authors of *The Motley Fool Investment Guide: How the Fool Beats Wall Street's Wise Men and How You Can Too* (1996), named their service Motley Fool so that if they "totally screwed up (they) could fall back on the fact that (they're) just Fools." By late 1996 they headed the most frequently consulted financial service on AOL, and the Motley Fool, Inc., had projected annual revenues of more than $3 million. The Gardners also wrote a monthly column for the magazine *SmartMoney* and aspired to expanding their services to television and radio.

(KATHERINE I. GORDON)

Gates, Henry Louis, Jr.

A pioneering critic and scholar, Henry Louis Gates, Jr., emerged as an influential spokesman for African-American culture and almost single-handedly revitalized and redefined African-American literature and literary theory. To many his name was synonymous with African-American studies itself.

Gates was born on Sept. 16, 1950, in Keyser, W.Va. He visited Africa on a fellowship in 1970 and 1971, traveling through 15 nations. After graduating with a bachelor's degree in history from Yale University in 1973, he went on to earn master's (1974) and doctoral (1979) degrees from Clare College, Cambridge. There he worked with Nigerian writer Wole Soyinka, whose interest in Yoruba culture influenced Gates's later work. Gates taught literature at Yale (1979–85), Cornell University, Ithaca, N.Y. (1985–90), and Duke University, Durham, N.C. (1990–91) before moving to Harvard University in 1991, where he held the positions of W.E.B. Du Bois professor of the humanities, professor of English, chair of Afro-American studies, and director of the W.E.B. Du Bois Institute for Afro-American Research. At Harvard Gates began assembling a collection of prestigious African-American scholars, who were expected to influence public policy—and the wider culture—as well as scholarly discourse.

A prolific essay writer on issues as diverse as the First Amendment, anti-Semitism, ethnic identity, and rap music, Gates first gained recognition as a "literary archaeologist," bringing to light lost writings of 19th-century African-Americans, particularly slave narratives by women. He rediscovered and restored many lost works by black writers, including Harriet E. Wilson's *Our Nig; or Sketches from the Life of a Free Black* (1859), the earliest-known novel by a black American and the first by a black woman. In literary theory Gates's concept of "signifyin(g)" linked African and African-American literature as a continuous dialogue—provocative, humorous, or insulting—with what preceded it and examined works of black writers in that context. He developed his influential theory in the article "The Blackness of Blackness," which appeared in the journal *Critical Inquiry* (June 1983), *Figures in Black: Words, Signs, and the "Racial" Self* (1987), and *The Signifying Monkey: Towards a Theory of Afro-American Literary Criticism* (1988). Gates edited a number of influential critical collections, such as *Black Literature and Literary Theory* (1984), *"Race," Writing, and Difference* (1986), *Reading Black, Reading Feminist* (1990), and the April 29/May 6, 1996, issue of *The New Yorker* entitled "Black in America."

Known as "Skip," Gates frequently moved in circles outside the academy, publishing hip-hop album reviews in *Entertainment Weekly* and political commentary in *The New Yorker*. He took unconventional means to develop his department at Harvard, including inviting director Spike Lee to teach a course on contemporary black film.

(ANN M. BELASKI)

Glover, Savion

A pair of size 12½ EE feet—and the young man attached to them—made a big noise on Broadway in 1996, in *Bring in 'da Noise, Bring in 'da Funk*. Savion Glover, the show's choreographer-star, employed the rhythms of hip-hop music and his unique pounding style of tap dancing, called "hitting," in a series of vignettes illustrating the history of African-Americans and the part tap dancing played in keeping rhythm in their lives. *Noise* had moved to Broadway in April after playing to full houses Off-Broadway for three months beginning in late 1995. Its popularity continued, and it went on to garner nine Tony award nominations—including two for Glover, for choreography and for leading actor in a musical—and win four, a best choreographer award for Glover among them.

Glover was born Nov. 19, 1973, in Newark, N.J. Even as a two-year-old, he showed an affinity for rhythms, beating them out on everything he touched around the house. He began drumming lessons at age four, but the teacher deemed him too advanced for the class, so he was enrolled at the Newark Community School of the Arts. By the time he was five, he had become the youngest student ever to receive that institution's scholarship. He began tap lessons at age seven and, after seeing an exhibition of rhythm tap, decided

Savion Glover

that was what he wanted to do. From then on he tapped wherever he went.

Glover's Broadway debut came in 1984 when he took over the lead role in *The Tap Dance Kid* after having served as understudy. He returned to Broadway in 1989 in the revue *Black and Blue* and was nominated for a Tony, one of the youngest people ever to be so honoured. A role in the motion picture *Tap* (1989) followed. Glover, who had long made a point of learning as much as he could from the old tap masters, soon began teaching tap classes. He also developed his own tap style, which he christened "free-form hard core," while working with such dancers as Gregory Hines, Henry Le Tang, and Sammy Davis, Jr. He created his first choreography in 1990, for a festival at New York City's Apollo Theatre, and in 1992 he became the youngest-ever recipient of a National Endowment for the Arts grant, for choreography. *Jelly's Last Jam* took him to Los Angeles in 1991 before opening on Broadway the following year and touring to 65 cities in 1994; he taught tap classes in each of those cities. Among his other appearances were his regular role on the Public Broadcasting Service's children's television show "Sesame Street" and his tribute to Gene Kelly (*see* OBITUARIES) on the 1996 Academy Awards telecast, and in April 1996 he added another "youngest-ever" honour to his list of accomplishments—a Dance Magazine Award. According to the highly regarded tap veteran Hines, Glover was "possibly the best tap dancer that ever lived."   (BARBARA WHITNEY)

Harnoy, Ofra

On March 26, 1996, Canadian cellist Ofra Harnoy, who had already established a reputation as an internationally acclaimed virtuoso of classical music, stood poised to achieve pop success with the release of *Imagine*, a crossover recording featuring 22 of the Beatles' greatest hits. As one of the leading solo cellists of her generation, she had recorded 36 albums and won 5 Juno Awards in Canada for the best classical soloist.

Born on Jan. 31, 1965, in Hadera, Israel, Harnoy moved to Toronto with her family in the early 1970s. At the age of six she began to study the cello with her father, an amateur violinist, before receiving formal training from Vladimir Orloff in Toronto and William Pleeth in London. She had master classes with Pierre Fournier, Jacqueline du Pre, and Mstislav Rostropovich. Harnoy made her professional debut at age 10 as a soloist with the Boyd Neel Orchestra in Toronto and thereafter won every competition she entered: the 1978 Montreal Symphony Competition, the 1979 Canadian Music Competition, and the 1982 New York Concert Artists Guild Competition. She was the youngest winner in the history of the latter

competition, an honour that resulted in her making her debut at Carnegie Hall at 17, two years after she made her London bow at the Royal Festival Hall.

Harnoy, who designed the gowns she wore at solo recitals and as a soloist with orchestras performing on all continents, captivated audiences with her showmanship and artistry. In 1983 she was the soloist for the world premiere performance and recording of Jacques Offenbach's Cello Concerto with the Cincinnati (Ohio) Symphony Orchestra, and she gave the North American premiere of Sir Arthur Bliss's Cello Concerto in Santa Barbara, Calif. In 1993 she performed in world premiere recordings of two works: a cello concerto by Giovanni Battista Viotti and a cello concerto by Josef Myslivecek.

She was the first Canadian artist since Glenn Gould to be signed to an exclusive worldwide contract with a major recording company (RCA), and her recordings won numerous awards, including 1987, 1989, 1991, 1992, and 1993 Juno Awards and the Grand Prix du Disque (1988). Her recording of two Haydn concerti won praise from Haydn scholar H.C. Robbins Landon, and her recording of Vivaldi cello concerti was one of the world's best-selling classical albums in 1990. It also won *Gramophone*'s award for the best album of the year. Harnoy was perhaps best identified, however, with Pablo Casals's *Song of the Birds*, which she often performed.

Harnoy, who was the subject of the 1985 documentary *Ofra Harnoy: The Music Inside*, performed on a 100-year-old cello that was crafted by Neapolitan maker Vincenzo Postigliani. She had chosen this instrument when she was 13 for its warm sound and responsiveness to a variety of touches. With it, she felt she could communicate her emotions without barriers.

(DIANE LOIS WAY)

Harrell, Tom

Tall, lean Tom Harrell stands hunched forward on the bandstand, head bowed, a private man seemingly lost in a world of his own. Until, that is, he raises his trumpet to his lips—and then the lines of bright, sophisticated melody pour out with full confidence. The 1996 album *Labyrinth*, his first for a major label (RCA Victor), featured his compositions for quintet and nonet. There were songs with the standard chord changes as well as "Cheetah," a free jazz experiment with a spontaneous harmonic structure and shifting tempi. Through it all, there was Harrell's vibratoless, uninflected trumpet improvisation, a wholly lyrical art accomplished with warmth and sweetness. The collection also included a one-man duet, "Darn

That Dream," with Harrell's flügelhorn solo accompanied by himself on piano. Altogether the album was among his most varied and musically successful.

Harrell's victory as top trumpet player in the 1996 Down Beat critics poll was especially satisfying for three reasons. First, it came as a surprise after more than a decade of well-publicized trumpet wars between Wynton Marsalis, the preeminent jazz conservative, and the influential innovator Lester Bowie. (Harrell, unusually, was a success on jazz's right and left wings as well as in the wide area between.) Second, it climaxed Harrell's daring decision in 1989, after a comfortable career as a well-traveled sideman, to lead his own groups and play his own compositions. Third, it validated the personal bravery of an artist who had refused to succumb to profound emotional illness.

Born June 16, 1946, in Urbana, Ill., Harrell spent most of his youth in the San Francisco Bay area, where he began playing in jazz groups when he was 13. He graduated from Stanford University in 1969 with a major in composition and also studied with alto saxophonist Lee Konitz. His highly varied résumé included tours with big bands, including Stan Kenton's (1969) and Woody Herman's (1970–71), and work with pianist Bill Evans (1979) and in Konitz's latter-day cool-jazz nonet (1979–81). It was as a trumpet soloist in "hot" hard-bop combos led by Horace Silver (1973–77) and Phil Woods (1983–89), however, that he attracted most attention. All the while, Harrell was composing prolifically and leading his own recordings by the time he left Woods to go out on his own. While leading groups in the 1990s, he also toured the U.S. and Europe as a freelance sideman, most notably with Charlie Haden's Liberation Music Orchestra.

As a young man Harrell was diagnosed as having borderline schizophrenia, and later assessments suggested more serious emotional illness. His problems were manifested as debilitating depression, and he had also suffered from lung problems. Most people who suffered from such illness would be condemned to a marginal existence, but music provided Harrell with a way out. He in turn provided listeners with an example of courage and grace as well as uncommon musical creativity.   (JOHN LITWEILER)

Hashimoto, Ryutaro

Before he was elected prime minister of Japan in January 1996, Ryutaro Hashimoto was a veteran politician highly respected for his knowledge of domestic affairs. He thus surprised his political friends and foes alike when he moved into foreign policy, announcing, days before U.S. Pres. Bill Clinton made a state visit to Tokyo in April 1996, that the U.S. had agreed to return the Marine Corps Air Station Futenma on Okinawa to Japan in five to seven years.

Hashimoto was born on July 29, 1937, and graduated from Keio University, Tokyo, in 1960. He briefly worked at Toyobo Co., a spinning firm, until his father's untimely death. He then became a second-generation politician, campaigning from his father's constituency in Okayama prefecture. At the age of 26, he was elected to the House of Representatives. Always part of the Liberal Democratic Party's (LDP's) mainstream, Hashimoto was named health and welfare minister in 1978 and subsequently held the portfolios of transport, finance, and international trade and industry.

He faced a serious political crisis in 1991 when it was revealed that a major securities company had secretly compensated for losses incurred by its principal customers and that his own private secretary was involved in a bank loan scandal. He promptly resigned as finance minister in the Cabinet of Prime Minister Toshiki Kaifu.

Hashimoto also was partly blamed for the failure of seven housing loan companies known as *jusen*. In 1990, in an attempt to control land prices that had soared during Japan's bubble economy in the late 1980s, the Finance Ministry, which Hashimoto headed, imposed a ceiling on bank lending for real-estate projects. Because the *jusen* companies were excluded from the restrictions, the possibility of imprudent loans was ever present.

Hashimoto was known outside Japan as a tough negotiator, but at home he was rated both high and low by those who knew him well. He was regarded as a man who looked after people who were junior to him, but he was also described as a loner who was arrogant, short-tempered, and politically hawkish. He was head of the Japan Association of War-Bereaved Families until he was named president of the LDP on Sept. 22, 1995. Perhaps because of this association, Hashimoto visited Yasukuni Shrine on July 29, 1996, his birthday. He did so, knowing that the visit would anger a segment of the population. Yasukuni was the burial site not only of the war dead but also of executed war criminals.

Hashimoto dissolved the lower house of the Diet (parliament) on Sept. 27, 1996, after settling the Okinawa bases issue with the U.S. and the governor of the prefecture and committing 685 billion yen of taxpayers' money to liquidating moribund housing loans made by *jusen* firms.

(TEIJI SHIMIZU)

Hasina Wazed, Sheikh
Following two years of political tumult, Sheikh Hasina Wazed, president of the Awami League, was elected prime minister of Bangladesh on June 12, 1996. Her government was expected to bring political stability and renewed economic vitality to the 25-year-old country.

Hasina was born on Sept. 28, 1947, in the village of Tungipara. She was the daughter of Sheikh Mujibur Rahman, who led Bangladesh to independence from Pakistan in 1971 and instilled in his daughter a loyalty to her country and a dedication to improving Bangladeshi quality of life.

Hasina was married in 1968 to M.A. Wazed Miah, an eminent Bangladeshi scientist. While at the University of Dhaka in the late 1960s, she was active in politics and served as her father's political liaison while he was imprisoned by Pakistani rulers. Hasina and other members of her family were also forced into captivity briefly in 1971 after they participated in an uprising during the liberation war.

On Aug. 15, 1975, following Bangladesh's freedom from Pakistani leadership, Hasina's father, mother, and three brothers were assassinated in their home by Bangladeshi military officers. Hasina, who was out of the country at the time, spent six years in exile. During this time she was elected to the leadership of the Awami League, the largest political organization in Bangladesh.

On her return home in 1981, Hasina immersed herself in the fight for democracy, an activity that resulted in her being placed under numerous house arrests. She ultimately secured a seat as leader of the opposition in Parliament, where

Sheikh Hasina Wazed

MILADINOVIC—SYGMA

she opposed the violence of military rule and initiated measures to increase basic human rights. In December 1990 the last military leader of Bangladesh, Lieut. Gen. Hossain Mohammad Ershad, resigned in disgrace following an ultimatum that was issued by Hasina and supported by the Bangladeshi people.

The first free general election in Bangladesh in 16 years was held in 1991. Hasina failed to obtain a majority in Parliament, and governing power was granted to her opponent Khaleda Zia, leader of the Bangladesh Nationalist Party (BNP). The Awami League challenged the BNP with accusations of dishonesty, and they, along with other opposition parties, boycotted Parliament, again causing violent demonstrations and political chaos. The Awami League demanded the institution of a permanent, democratic election system free from corruption. Although the BNP government denied allegations of vote fraud, Zia succumbed to demands that she relinquish her office to a nonparty caretaker government that would oversee a new election. Hasina, who insisted on being addressed as "sir," was then elected to replace Prime Minister Zia.

(KATHERINE I. GORDON)

Hirst, Damien
On Nov. 28, 1995, Damien Hirst was awarded the Turner Prize, Great Britain's most prestigious award for contemporary art. Whether Hirst's work indicated a new direction in British art was an open question, however, for while other avant-garde artists continued to work with traditional materials, Hirst's chosen means of expression for his best-known works was animals—dead or alive. In an exhibit at the Tate Gallery following his short-listing for the 1995 Turner (he was also short-listed in 1992), Hirst presented some of his classic pieces, including "Mother and Child Divided," a work consisting of four glass-and-steel tanks containing the severed halves of a cow and calf preserved in formalin, an aqueous formaldehyde solution. Some critics loved his work, while others accused him of striving only for shock value. Regardless of critical opinion, the Turner Prize established Hirst as one of Britain's most important new talents.

Hirst was born in Bristol in 1965 and grew up in Leeds. In the early 1980s he moved to London, where he worked in the building trades before studying art at Goldsmiths College. His early work included a series of dot paintings, as well as mixed-media sculpture. His career received a boost in 1988 when British advertising mogul Charles Saatchi attended an influential student show curated by Hirst. Saatchi subsequently became the leading collector of Hirst's work, purchasing a number of pieces, including "A Thousand Years," which consisted of a large tank containing a box of maggots, an electronic bug zapper, and a rotting cow's head on which the surviving flies laid more eggs.

In 1994 Hirst organized a show for young artists at the Serpentine Gallery in London, "Some Went Mad, Some Ran Away...." His contributions included "The Physical Impossibility of Death in the Mind of Someone Living," which consisted of a glass tank containing a 4.3-m (14-ft) tiger shark pickled in formaldehyde, and "Away from the Flock," a lamb suspended in a similar tank. The show was a resounding success and garnered enormous publicity for Hirst, particularly when another artist poured ink into "Away from the Flock" and renamed it "Black Sheep."

Hirst attempted to stage a major exhibition in New York City in September 1995, but his plan for the centrepiece of the show—a display of dead cows that had not been preserved—was forbidden by the New York Health Department. He returned to New York in 1996 with a new exhibit at the Gagosian Gallery. Entitled "No Sense of Absolute Corruption," this show presented some of Hirst's classic dead animals, as well as his newer work, including a series of large paintings done by pouring paint on a round canvas and then mechanically spinning it at a high rate of speed. Hirst also directed several short videos, notably a music video for the British rock group Blur.

(JOHN H. MATHEWS)

Howard, John Winston
Prime Minister John Howard welcomed U.S. Pres. Bill Clinton to Australia in November 1996 with a heavy heart. Under considerable pressure from unexpectedly hostile public opinion, kept in the dark by the Australian army about potential radioactive debris from a Russian satellite that could crash in the outback, worried about his wife (who was recovering from a dangerous illness), and having just had his most recent flight to Tasmania aborted after his aircraft was struck by lightning, Howard was at a low ebb.

The year had started well; Howard won a landslide election victory in March and began his term in office by stressing that the Australian people had voted his centre-right Liberal-National coalition into office with full knowledge that the conservatives were going to make changes to the industrial relations scene. One of the biggest debates was over the sale of one-third of Telstra, the state-owned telecommunications company. After months of wrangling, the deal was approved by the Senate in early December.

Howard's initial battles over industrial reform were overshadowed, however, by an unforeseen debate over immigration levels and race relations in Australia. This was generated in September by the maiden speech of an independent MP, Pauline Hanson, in which she was critical of special programs for Aboriginal citizens, the rate of Asian immigration, and multiculturalism. Howard agreed that some of the comments by the outspoken MP were an accurate reflection of what people felt, and this response angered migrant, refugee, and Aboriginal groups, which accused him of turning a blind eye to racism.

His critics concluded that Howard's refusal to confront racist observations from independent MPs was a sign that he was unwilling or unable to silence the rebels. "Howard's shameful silence" was how the *Australian Financial Review* saw it. Whether he was weak, misguided, or secretly sympathetic, his refusal to condemn the new right-wing racism undermined his early strong showing as a forceful and dominating leader, qualities displayed in his handling of the tragic massacre of 35 people by a lone gunman at Port Arthur, Tas., in April.

Howard was born July 26, 1939, and studied law at the University of Sydney. After being admitted as a solicitor to the Supreme Court of New South Wales in 1962, he took up a political career and was first elected to the parliament for Bennelong in 1974. His long political service included periods focused on industrial relations, manpower, trade negotiations, business, and consumer affairs. His chief accomplishment was as treasurer (1977–83) under Prime Minister Malcolm Fraser. In September 1985 Howard, then deputy head of the Liberal Party, became leader of the official opposition when he was unexpectedly chosen to replace the party's embattled leader, Andrew Peacock.

(A.R.G. GRIFFITHS)

Huppert, Isabelle Anne
When asked why she chose a career in acting, Isabelle Huppert responded that performing allowed her to be silent. This seemingly contradictory answer underscored the enigma of this French actress, whose reverence for quiet was evidenced in both her desire for anonymity offscreen and her understated performances onscreen. Her portrayals, noted for their subtle gestures and restrained emotions, won critical praise and established Huppert as one of the premier actresses in Europe. Although best known for her cinematic work, she also performed on the stage. In 1996 she made her London stage debut, playing the title role in Friedrich von Schiller's *Mary Stuart* at the National Theatre.

Huppert, the youngest of five daughters, was born on March 16, 1955, in Paris. She developed an interest in acting as a teenager and entered the Versailles Conservatory in 1968. Three years later, at the age of 16, she made her film debut in *Faustine et le bel été* (1971; *Faustine and the Beautiful Summer*). Though cast in a bit part, she attracted notice and began working steadily; by the mid-1970s she had made more than 15 films. It was not until 1977, however, that she

Isabelle Huppert

received international acclaim. In *La Dentellière* (*The Lacemaker*) her portrayal of Pomme, a young woman who suffers a nervous breakdown after being abandoned by her lover, earned Huppert the British Academy of Film and Television Arts award as most promising newcomer. The following year she won best actress at the Cannes Film Festival for her performance as a woman who casually murders her father (*Violette Nozière; 1978*).

Although she was a versatile actress, adept in both comedic and serious roles, Huppert's forte was playing antiheroines with questionable morals. In the film adaptation of Gustave Flaubert's *Madame Bovary* (1991), she played the tragic Emma Bovary, an unhappy middle-class wife whose adulterous affair eventually leads to her suicide. For her performance Huppert received some of the most notable reviews of her career. Later roles included a nun turned pornographer (*Amateur*, 1994) and a town gossip-murderess (*La Cérémonie,* 1995), for which she received a best actress award at the Venice Film Festival.

Arguably, the only disappointment in Huppert's career was her lack of success in the United States. She made her U.S. debut in *Heaven's Gate* (1980), a movie panned by critics and ignored by audiences. Subsequent U.S. movies also met with little success. (AMY TIKKANEN)

Jackson, Philip Douglas

Although the media delighted in calling attention to his fascination with Eastern philosophy and Native American culture, Phil Jackson, head coach of the National Basketball Association's (NBA's) Chicago Bulls, stressed the basics: teamwork and defense. Skillfully managing the talents and egos of a squad that included the great Michael Jordan, all-star Scottie Pippen, former European standout Toni Kukoc, and the irrepressible Dennis Rodman (*q.v.*), Jackson earned NBA Coach of the Year honours in 1996 as his team won a league-record 72 games during the regular season and its fourth NBA title in six years.

Jackson was born in Deer Lodge, Mont., on Sept. 17, 1945. His father was a Pentecostal minister, his mother an evangelist. While television, rock and roll, and other such pursuits of youth were prohibited in the Jackson home, Phil did engage in sports and earned a basketball scholarship at the University of North Dakota. Drafted by the New York Knicks in 1967, he played 13 seasons in the NBA, 11 of them with New York, which won championships in 1970 and 1973. A low-scoring forward, he relished his role as a defender and rebounder. Jackson's book *Maverick* (1975) raised eyebrows with candid descriptions of his drug experimentation and sexual promiscuity. His reputation initially alienated him from the NBA's establishment. Eventually, Jackson's unconventional philosophy, which he articulated to the public in his second book, *Sacred Hoops: Spiritual Lessons of a Hardwood Warrior* (1995), came to be a celebrated aspect of his approach to coaching.

Jackson's coaching career began when he was traded to the New Jersey Nets in 1978 and became a player-assistant coach. His playing career ended in 1980. He took a job coaching the Albany Patroons of the Continental Basketball Association in 1982 and won the CBA title in 1984. Jackson landed a job as an assistant coach with the Bulls in 1987 and then gained the head coaching position in 1989. The Bulls had the league's best player in Jordan but had never won a championship. Jackson implemented a new scheme, which called for Jordan's teammates to play a larger role in handling the ball; it made Jordan much more potent, as opponents were forced to defend all five Bulls players. Championships followed in 1991, 1992, 1993, and 1996. Jackson became the ninth man to win titles as both a player and a coach, and he reached 200 victories faster than any other coach in NBA history. After the 1995–96 season he held a .721 winning percentage in the regular season and an all-time-high .723 winning percentage in the play-offs. (ANTHONY G. CRAINE)

Karadzic, Radovan

On July 19, 1996, it was announced that Radovan Karadzic would step down as president of the self-proclaimed Republika Srpska and as head of the Serbian Democratic Party of Bosnia and Herzegovina. A year earlier, on July 25, and again on Nov. 16, 1995, the UN International Criminal Tribunal for the Former Yugoslavia, held in The Hague, had indicted him for crimes that included genocide, murder, rape, and other mistreatment of civilians. As the leader of the Bosnian Serbs, Karadzic was held to be responsible for the "ethnic cleansing" of Serb-held areas of Bosnia, during which tens of thousands of Muslims and other non-Serbs had been killed and driven from their homes.

Karadzic was born on June 19, 1945, in a mountain village in the Yugoslav republic of Montenegro. His father was a member of the Chetniks, the Serbs who fought both the Nazis (along with their Croatian collaborators) and the Partisans, the communist guerrillas led by Josip Broz Tito. In 1960, at age 15, Karadzic moved to Sarajevo, where he later studied medicine. A physician and psychiatrist, he also published poetry and books for children.

In 1985 Karadzic was imprisoned for 11 months for fraud involving the use of state funds. In 1990 he helped found the Serbian Democratic Party and became its president. Two years later, when the Bosnian Serbs declared an independent state allied with Yugoslavia, Karadzic became its president. With the support of Slobodan Milosevic, president of Serbia, and with Gen. Ratko Mladic, the Bosnian Serb military leader who was also indicted for war crimes, Karadzic began a campaign to take control of parts of the country and to purge the areas of non-Serb peoples. Throughout the period from 1992 to 1995, he alternately pursued ruthless military actions and expressed interest in peace efforts advanced by Western leaders.

At the end of 1995, after Milosevic had closed the borders with Bosnia and apparently withdrawn support from the Bosnian Serbs, Karadzic was pressured into signing accords reached in talks near Dayton, Ohio, that provided for a division of the country into Bosnian-Croat and Serb sections but with a unified presidency.

The Dayton Accords specified that no one indicted for war crimes could participate in the elections scheduled for Sept. 14, 1996; thus, Karadzic was required to relinquish his government and party positions. He was replaced in both by deputies who shared his political views, and although he was prohibited from making appearances in public or by media, it was by no means certain that he would not continue to influence events. NATO troops, charged with enforcing the Dayton Accords, had the authority to arrest him, but they did not take such action against him, and Karadzic continued to live in Pale, the Bosnian Serb headquarters. (ROBERT RAUCH)

Karelin, Aleksandr

Sometimes referred to as the World's Meanest Man, Aleksandr Karelin, Russia's superman of Greco-Roman superheavyweight wrestling, continued his decade-long winning streak by gaining his third Olympic gold medal on July 23, 1996. His final match of the Games in Atlanta, Ga., was against longtime adversary Matt Ghaffari of the U.S., who had dedicated his career to conquering Karelin. Despite a painful recovery from shoulder surgery, Karelin dominated Ghaffari, crushing his apparently impossible dream.

Karelin was born in 1968 in Novosibirsk, Siberia. He weighed 6.8 kg (15 lb) at birth and grew to 1.95 m (6 ft 3 in) and 132 kg (290 lb). He began his wrestling career at the age of 13 and, until beginning his partnership with coach Viktor Kuznetsov two years later, had only his impressive size in his wrestling favour.

The year Karelin turned 18 he beat all but one of the wrestlers he opposed. The following year he was named world junior champion and became a member of the U.S.S.R. national team. When he perfected the reverse body lift, a move common in lighter-weight wrestling classes but never before used in heavyweight competition, Karelin became unbeatable. The maneuver would begin with Karelin on his knees facing the hips and feet of his prone opponent. He would join his hands around the opponent's hips and lift as he rose to his feet. Then, with his opponent against his body in a crosslike hold, Karelin would arch and throw his heavy burden. For the grand finale he would slam his body into the body of his unfortunate, perhaps unconscious, foe. The result was undoubtedly several points for Karelin but often serious bodily injury to his opponent. The reverse body lift became Karelin's ferocious trademark, and no opponent escaped it; in fact, most allowed themselves to be pinned rather than be victimized by the lift.

Karelin was selected a member of the 1988 Olympic team and went to Seoul, S.Kor., to win his well-anticipated gold medal. He gained his second gold medal at the Olympics in Barcelona, Spain (1992), and won his seventh world championship at Prague in 1995. He had never been pinned in international competition.

The Russian hero with the vicious reputation compared his wrestling style to poetry. The descendant of intellectuals exiled to Siberia, Karelin was a student of literature, poetry, opera, and ballet. (KATHERINE I. GORDON)

Kemp, Jack French

U.S. veteran politician Jack Kemp stepped into the limelight on Aug. 10, 1996, when Republican presidential candidate Bob Dole (*q.v.*) announced that Kemp would be his running mate. Kemp had squared off against Dole in the 1988 presidential primaries, and they were known to be adversaries on several issues. Nonetheless, the two set aside differences and focused on like goals under the motto "Unity does not require unanimity."

Kemp was born on July 13, 1935, in Los Angeles. His father owned a small trucking company, and his mother was a schoolteacher and social worker. He attended Occidental College, Los Angeles, where he majored in physical education, played quarterback for the football team, and courted a cheerleader, who became his wife.

When Kemp graduated in 1957, he was drafted by the Detroit Lions professional football team, but he was released during the preseason. After five unremarkable years playing with various teams, Kemp was sent to the Buffalo Bills. There he learned that his real talent was his ability to lead and inspire other players. He used those skills to steer the Bills to their first winning season (1963) and to American Football League (AFL) championships in 1964 and 1965. He earned the AFL's Player of the Year Award in 1965 and was named Most Valuable Player of that year's championship game.

Kemp's football career caused him to become a public figure in Buffalo and, therefore, a popular Republican choice for a seat in Congress. He won the election in 1970 and represented suburban Buffalo for nine terms, during which he became known for his defense of the Vietnam War, enthusiastic support of supply-side economics, and promotion of civil rights initiatives. While in Congress he was a member of the Budget Committee and served as chair of the Republican House Conference.

After an unsuccessful attempt to gain the Republican nomination for president in 1988, Kemp was named head of the Department of Housing and Urban Development by Pres. George Bush. That Cabinet position had been tainted by scandal and fraud, and Kemp acted speedily to restore the integrity and productivity of the office while furthering the affirmative action agenda for which he had become known.

During the past few years, Kemp had strongly advocated programs that benefited minorities and the downtrodden and thus had become increasingly known as a political centrist. His ability to garner the minority vote made him an attractive addition to the 1996 Republican ticket.

(KATHERINE I. GORDON)

Khan, Nusrat Fateh Ali

Nusrat Fateh Ali Khan, considered the greatest living singer of *qawwali*, a Sufi Muslim devotional music, found himself at centre stage in the U.S. entertainment business in 1996. He recorded songs for movie soundtracks (most notably a duet with Eddie Vedder of Pearl Jam for the film *Dead Man Walking*), appeared on MTV, and recorded secular songs that appealed specifically to Western audiences. All this might have seemed like a betrayal of the spiritual heritage that gave rise to the music and of the admiring millions in his native Pakistan, but Khan maintained that he had given up nothing and was only exploring the depths of his voice. He had been eager to share his talent and musical heritage with broader audiences, yet he had also been careful to move slowly and not compromise his beliefs.

Khan was born Oct. 13, 1948, in Lyallpur (now Faisalabad), Pak. His father, Ustad Fateh Ali Khan, and two of his uncles were *qawwals* who sang in the classical form. Nusrat received music lessons from his father but did not devote himself to the *qawwali* tradition until he sang at his father's funeral in 1964. Two years later he gave his first public performance, singing with his uncles. By the early 1970s he had established himself throughout Pakistan as the outstanding *qawwal* of his time. After he sang in 1985 at a world music concert in the U.K., word of his talent began to spread, and he was soon performing regularly throughout Europe. He first toured the U.S. in 1989 and in 1992 spent a year as artist in residence at the University of Washington.

Qawwali music began in Persia in the 12th century. It is characterized by simple melodies, forceful rhythms, and wild improvisations intended to stir the audience into a euphoric state. The music is based upon medieval Sufi poems that often express deep religious faith through images of romantic love. The *qawwal* memorizes these poems, and he (*qawwals* are traditionally male) then uses phrases and passages from different poems to create a new expression or idea. The performances, traditionally held in shrines, are marked by passionate shouting and dancing. As in American gospel music, *qawwali* uses repetition and a series of emotional peaks and rests to intoxicate the audience.

Usually accompanied by tabla (small hand drums), harmoniums, and backing vocals, Khan sang in a very high register (a family trademark) and had a powerful and highly expressive voice. Perhaps his most exceptional qualities were his melodic creativity and legendary stamina. He had been known to perform for 10 hours, though by 1996 diabetes and age had drained some of his energy. Despite his success in the West, Khan continued to live in Lahore, Pak., and to perform regularly in his homeland.   (JAMES HENNELLY)

Kiarostami, Abbas

When *Badkonake sefid* (1995; "The White Balloon"), a deceptively simple look at life in Tehran through the eyes of a seven-year-old girl, won the Camera d'Or for best first film at the 1995 Cannes International Film Festival (the first Iranian film to be so honoured), distributors from around the world hurried to buy it. Critical acclaim, coupled with the attendant publicity as the film opened internationally, brought the name of its screenwriter, Abbas Kiarostami, to prominence in 1996. Kiarostami, a director-writer-producer-editor active in the Iranian film industry since 1969, had long been recognized by cineasts as one of the world's great filmmakers. Known for experimenting with the boundaries between reality and fiction, and for creating a unique brand of neorealist cinematic humanism, Kiarostami had directed 9 features and 16 short films to date and won awards for them at a multitude of international film festivals.

Kiarostami was born in Tehran in 1940 and studied painting and graphic arts at the University of Tehran. After a period spent designing posters, illustrating children's books, and directing advertisements and film credit sequences, he was hired in 1969 by the Institute for the Intellectual Development of Children and Young Adults to establish its film division. The institute produced his first film as a director, the lyrical short *Nan va kucheh* (1970; "Bread and Alley"). It featured elements that would define his later work: improvised performances, documentary textures, real-life rhythms, and social-realist subject matter—all fashioned with an artist's eye. His first feature, *Mosafer* (1974; "The Traveller"), about a rebellious village boy determined to go to Tehran and watch a soccer match, is an indelible portrait of a troubled adolescent. Kiarostami's documentaries *Avaliha* (1985; "First Graders") and *Mashq-e shab* (1989; "Homework") offer fascinating insights into the problems faced by Iranian schoolchildren.

Kiarostami's favourite film was *Namay-e nazdik* (1990; "Close-Up"), a complex re-creation of the bizarre circumstances surrounding the case of a frustrated film buff who swindles a Tehran family while impersonating Iranian director Mohsen Makhmalbaf. A documentary, it explores the subjective nature of filmed truth and the overlap between film and reality. Kiarostami further expanded the boundaries between documentary and fiction in a loose trilogy: *Khaneh-ye dust kojast?* (1987; "Where Is the Friend's Home?"), *Va zendegi edameh darad* (1992; "And Life Goes On . . .,") and *Zir-e darakhtan-e zeyton* (1994; "Through the Olive Trees"). In 1996 he was completing a new feature about a middle-aged intellectual who had lost his will to live.

(ALISSA SIMON)

Kiraly, Karch

Already considered by many to be the greatest volleyball player in history, U.S. athlete Charles ("Karch") Kiraly further solidified his presence in the sport's annals by winning a gold medal with partner Kent Steffes at the 1996 Olympic Games. Having already won gold medals in 1984 and 1988 in the indoor game, Kiraly became the first volleyball player to triumph three times in Olympic competition, competing in 1996 in beach volleyball, which made its debut as a medal sport at the Games in Atlanta, Ga. With the conquest, Kiraly's career had come full circle; he had learned to play volleyball from his father on the beaches of California and had since gone on to play the indoor game as well as anyone ever had.

Kiraly was born Nov. 3, 1960, in Jackson, Mich., and his family moved to Santa Barbara, Calif., when Karch was four years old. His father, Laszlo Kiraly, had played on the national volleyball team in his native Hungary. Karch was introduced to the game at the age of six, and by the time he was 11, he had entered his first beach tournament with his father. With a vertical leap of 104 cm (41 in), Kiraly was a standout at Santa Barbara High School and was named the best player in the state his senior year. He attended the University of California, Los Angeles, where he was a four-time All-American and led his squad to three national titles in four years. He joined the U.S. national team in 1981. With Kiraly on board as an outside hitter, Team USA won gold medals at the Olympic Games in 1984 in Los Angeles and 1988 in Seoul, S.Kor. (where he was named the tournament's Most Valuable Player). The team also struck gold at the world championships in 1982 and 1986 (when he was named best player in the world, an honour repeated in 1988), and at the 1987 Pan American games.

© JACK VARTOOGIAN

Nusrat Fateh Ali Khan

In 1989 the 1.88-m (6-ft 2-in), 97.5-kg (215-lb) Kiraly left the U.S. national team to play with Il Messaggero of Ravenna, Italy, where he was named Most Valuable Player when the team won the world club championship in 1991. He then concentrated on the financially lucrative beach game that earned him the Association of Volleyball Professionals' Most Valuable Player title five times (1990 and 1992–95). By January 1996 his career earnings had exceeded $2 million.

(ANTHONY G. CRAINE)

Lebed, Aleksandr Ivanovich
On June, 18, 1996, after Aleksandr Lebed had run a strong third in the first round of the Russian presidential elections, Pres. Boris Yeltsin appointed him to be secretary of the Security Council and national security adviser. Lebed appeared to strengthen his position in the government when he later negotiated a cease-fire in Chechnya. By year's end the ambitious retired general, who espoused popular themes such as Russian nationalism and law and order but was politically naive and showed a penchant for trenchant speech and public faux pas, was being seen by some observers as Yeltsin's heir apparent.

Lebed was born April 20, 1950, in Novocherkassk, in the Don Cossack region of southwestern Russia, U.S.S.R. Both his grandfather and his father, who was a metalworker, had fought in the Red Army in World War II. A boxer early in his life, Lebed graduated from an academy for airborne troops in 1973, and in 1981–82 he commanded a paratroop battalion in Afghanistan, for which he was decorated as a Hero of the Soviet Union. He later became a critic of the Afghan war. He graduated from the Frunze (now Bishkek, Kyrgyzstan) Military Academy in 1985, and in 1991, somewhat serendipitously, he headed the successful defense of the Moscow White House in the attempted coup against Soviet Pres. Mikhail Gorbachev. In 1992 he was made commander of the Russian 14th Army, stationed in the Transdniester area of Moldova. In 1995, after he had denounced Defense Minister Pavel Grachev's policies, including attempts to impose control over Chechyna, he was forced to resign from the army.

Lebed won a seat in the Russian parliament in the December 1995 elections. In 1996 he campaigned for the presidency, advocating policies that included postponing democracy until such time as the people might be prepared for it. His authoritarian, sometimes anti-West rhetoric appealed to many Russians, and he won almost 15% of the votes in the first round. By appointing him to the government and thus co-opting his support, Yeltsin was able to win the second round of presidential voting against the Communist candidate, Gennady Zyuganov (*q.v.*). A number of top-ranking military and defense officials (including Grachev) were fired, and in August Lebed was handed responsibility for dealing with the situation in Chechnya. He immediately made trips to the breakaway republic to meet with both the Chechen separatists and the Russian military commanders, and by the end of the month he had negotiated a cease-fire that included the agreement to defer a decision on Chechen independence for five years. On October 17 Yeltsin dismissed Lebed as security chief, saying that he was not a team player and was too obvious about his presidential aspirations. In late December Lebed introduced his newly formed Russian Popular Republican Party, announced his intention to continue to campaign for the presidency, and urged Yeltsin to resign because of his poor health.

(ROBERT RAUCH)

Lee Kun Hee
For South Korean businessman Lee Kun Hee, 1996 was a year of noteworthy events—both good and bad. As chairman of the Samsung Group of South Korea, he had left management to a corporate staff since taking over control of the conglomerate in 1987 from his late father, Lee Byung Chull, who founded Samsung in 1938. In June 1993, however, Lee Kun Hee launched a dramatic revolution from the top to make his 28 companies—the largest Asian conglomerate out-

side Japan—internationally competitive. Declaring that Samsung was "second rate" by global standards, he called on each employee "to change everything but your family." Lee attributed the shortcomings of Samsung to basic weaknesses in Korean society, including an educational system that stressed learning by rote and an authoritarian style of leadership. He ordered radical reforms. Under what Lee termed a "new management" concept, Samsung insisted that subordinates point out errors to their bosses. It also stressed quality of products over quantity, promoted women to the ranks of senior executives, and discouraged bureaucratic practices. By 1996 Samsung Electronics ranked as the world's leading exporter of memory chips, and the entire group's revenues in 1995 totaled $87 billion, equivalent to about 19% of South Korea's gross domestic product.

Lee was born on Jan. 9, 1942, in the town of Uiryung, Kyongnam province, Korea. He majored in economics at Waseda University, Tokyo, and earned a master of business administration degree at George Washington University, Washington, D.C. Lee joined Samsung in 1968 as the quiet understudy of his father, who exercised absolute control over his conglomerate and decided against making two older sons his successors. The youngest Lee thus inherited control of a huge enterprise engaged in electronics, machinery, chemicals, and financial services.

Lee Kun Hee

Having emerged from a shy figurehead to an assertive chief executive, Lee pushed Samsung into many new activities, such as automobile manufacturing. Bolstered by a surge of investment, he aimed to make 20% of Samsung's products outside South Korea by the year 2000. Consequently, he built an electronics manufacturing complex in Wynyard, Eng., and semiconductor plants in both Austin, Texas, and Suzhou, China. He also acquired such companies as the U.S. computer maker AST Research, Rollei Camera in Germany, and Lux, a Japanese manufacturer of audio products.

An active sportsman, Lee spent his leisure time riding horses, racing sports cars on a private track, and raising dogs. In addition, he was president of the Korean Amateur Wrestling Association and was involved with a professional baseball team and amateur athletics. In July 1996 he was elected a member of the International Olympic Committee.

Lee was among 11 prominent South Korean businessmen drawn into a political scandal over corporate contributions to former president Roh Tae Woo. A court ruled that such payments—though customary in South Korea—were bribes. In August 1996 Lee was sentenced to two years in prison, but the punishment was suspended for three years. (*See* WORLD AFFAIRS: *Korea, Republic of.*)

(LOUIS KRAAR)

PHOTOGRAPH, EDWARD KIM, COURTESY OF SAMSUNG

Lovett, Lyle Pierce

Boasting what may have been the biggest hair and the largest band in alternative country music, Lyle Lovett released his sixth album, *The Road to Ensenada* (1996), to the praise of what had become an almost cult following. Lovett's witty lyrics, innovative musical style, and songs, including such gems as "She's No Lady, She's My Wife," delighted fans across a broad spectrum. Lovett consistently pushed the envelope by refusing to write music that could be categorized. He had established a solid country following with his first album, *Lyle Lovett* (1986), and continued to acquire new fans with his many genre-bending deviations from traditional country themes and instrumentation. With his most recent album, which was marketed to country, easy-listening, and alternative-rock radio stations, he successfully returned to his earliest Texas roots while maintaining his complex musical style.

Born on Nov. 1, 1957, in Klein, Texas, Lovett spent his early years listening primarily to country music and the blues. He was inspired by Hank Williams, Willie Nelson, Nat King Cole, and Ray Charles and contended that the structure of his backup group was based on "the idea of using the big band more as punctuation than as an overall ambitious arrangement (as Ray Charles did)." After earning degrees in journalism and German from Texas A&M University (1982), Lovett spent a few years abroad. During a concert in Luxembourg, he met the band that became the nucleus of his Large Band, and in 1984 they made a demo album that led to his first big record contract. The albums that followed—*Lyle Lovett, Pontiac* (1988), *Lyle Lovett and His Large Band* (1989), *Joshua Judges Ruth* (1992), *I Love Everybody* (1994), and *The Road to Ensenada*—collectively displayed a range of emotions and an intellectual depth not usually encountered in the music industry. Lovett also appeared in such films as *The Player* (1992), *Short Cuts* (1993), *Ready to Wear* (1994), and *Bastard out of Carolina,* which was premiered on cable television in December 1996.

Shy and unassuming by nature, Lovett was thrown into the media spotlight in 1993 when he married actress Julia Roberts after only a one-month courtship. After the couple split amicably in 1995, Lovett maintained that the relationship had positively influenced his music and resulted in two of his most expressive and popular albums.

(SARA BRANT)

McKay, David Stewart

In 1996, a year in which extraterrestrials were the focus of movies, television shows, and books, David McKay proved that the real drama was taking place in a science laboratory. On August 7 McKay, leader of a NASA research team, announced that a 1.9-kg (4.2-lb) meteorite from Mars had yielded evidence indicating that primitive life may have existed on the planet. The news came only weeks after the 20th anniversary of the first Viking landing on Mars, which had concluded that the planet was sterile.

McKay was born on Sept. 25, 1936, in Titusville, Pa. He earned a master's degree in geochemistry from the University of California, Berkeley, in 1960 and four years later received a Ph.D. in geology from Rice University, Houston, Texas. In 1965 he began working at the Manned Spacecraft Center (later Johnson Space Center), where he instructed Apollo astronauts in geology and analyzed soil samples they retrieved from the Moon. McKay worked on a variety of projects, including the development of a method for extracting oxygen and water from lunar materials that would enable people to live on the Moon. It was his work on ALH84001, the meteorite originally discovered in Antarctica in 1984, however, that placed the mild-mannered scientist in the spotlight.

The meteorite, believed to be about 4.5 billion years old, had initially been classified as a diogenite, a common type of rock. It was not until 1994 that it was determined to be Martian. One of only 12 such known meteorites, the rock quickly attracted special interest. A research team was assembled with McKay as its leader. The study, which took more than two years, revealed several peculiarities. First was the pres-

Terry McMillan

ence of polycyclic aromatic hydrocarbons (PAHs). While these organic compounds are commonplace, found throughout the solar system, the PAHs in the meteorite were unusual in appearance, resembling the type that result from the decay of organic matter. The presence of the molecules within the rock and their absence on its surface ruled out Earth contamination. The team also discovered carbonate globules, which are closely associated with bacteria found on Earth. Moreover, iron sulfides and magnetite were present. These compounds, which are so small that one billion of them can fit on the head of a pin, do not usually coexist. Certain bacteria, however, synthesize them simultaneously.

These discoveries, published by McKay and his co-workers in the journal *Science,* indicated the possibility of ancient life on Mars. While the news generated a flurry of debate, McKay stressed that the findings were not definitive proof and that further research was planned.   (AMY TIKKANEN)

McMillan, Terry

In late 1995 pop-fiction author Terry McMillan delighted in watching her third book, *Waiting to Exhale,* make the transition to the silver screen. The story of four middle-class black women and their relationships with men struck a familiar chord among women, especially African-Americans, who flocked to see the film. By mid-1996 it had grossed nearly $70 million at the box office. On the heels of the film's success, McMillan reportedly received $6 million for her fourth novel, *How Stella Got Her Groove Back,* which received an initial printing of 800,000 copies, arrived in bookstores in the spring of 1996, and was sold for a film adaptation.

McMillan was born on Oct. 18, 1951, in Port Huron, Mich., the eldest of five children. Her parents divorced when she was 13, and at age 16 she began shelving books at the local public library to help out with household expenses. It was there that she was drawn to books and began fantasizing about life outside Michigan. At 17 she moved to California, where she worked and attended school, receiving her B.A. in journalism from the University of California, Berkeley. She then studied film at Columbia University, New

York City. While she was there, her first novel, the largely autobiographical *Mama,* evolved from what originally had been a short story. To ensure its success, McMillan took an active role in promoting the book, garnering the attention of bookstores and colleges and scheduling her own book tour. After its publication in 1987, she moved to Wyoming to accept a teaching position, leaving behind a failed relationship with Leonard Welch, the father of her son.

In 1989 McMillan's second novel, *Disappearing Acts,* was published. Although the book was only loosely based on her liaison with Welch, he found it a bit too autobiographical and in 1990 sued McMillan, unsuccessfully, for defamation of character. The book went on to sell several hundred thousand copies and established McMillan's voice in the African-American community.

By 1989 she had moved to Arizona to accept another teaching position. It was there that *Waiting to Exhale* (1992) took shape, mainly fueled by her own experiences with relationships. Following its publication, hardback and paperback sales reached nearly four million copies. As with *Disappearing Acts,* controversy accompanied *Exhale.* In answer to accusations of "male bashing," McMillan stated that the male characters were not intended to be representative of all men but were an integral part of the story. It remained on the best-seller list for 38 weeks and by its third week of release was already in its 10th printing.

It was in this same semiautobiographical vein that *Stella* was written. The book told the story of Stella Payne, a 42-year-old woman who travels to Jamaica and falls in love with a man half her age. The story line mirrored McMillan's trip to Jamaica and her romance with Jonathan Plummer, who was in his 20s.   (ANTHONY L. GREEN)

Mahathir bin Mohamad, Datuk Seri

When the United Malays National Organization (UMNO), Malaysia's dominant political party, held its triennial elections in October, Datuk Seri Mahathir bin Mohamad was reelected party president without opposition. The victory guaranteed that Mahathir would extend his record 15 years as prime minister through 1999. As a vocal critic of the West, Mahathir promoted an Asian and Malaysian agenda with slogans such as "look East" and "buy British last" in an effort to make Malaysia an industrialized nation by the year 2020. However, because Mahathir was 70 years old and had undergone heart bypass surgery in 1989, some party members wondered whether the time was approaching when he should step aside and make way for a successor, perhaps Deputy Prime Minister Anwar Ibrahim.

Mahathir was born on Dec. 20, 1925, in Alor Setar, Kedah state, and received a medical degree in 1953 from the University of Malaya in Singapore. He became active in politics in the mid-1940s, joining UMNO in 1946. He was expelled from the party in 1969 for opposing the policies of party president Tunku Abdul Rahman, but he was readmitted in 1972. After holding several governmental posts, Mahathir succeeded Hussein bin Onn as prime minister in July 1981.

Outspoken when it came to having Malaysia's voice heard internationally, Mahathir had accused Western media and even the Internet of spreading what he called "smut and violence." He also remarked: "Not only are distorted pictures of our countries being broadcast but our own capacity to understand what is happening is being undermined. In the past, Western missionaries spread the gospel. Today the media has taken over and all our cherished values and diverse cultures are being destroyed." While some members of his government winced at such statements, the general consensus was that such comments had a positive effect on the country. Even as he scolded the West, Mahathir welcomed foreign investment on his own terms. As a result, Malays as well as other ethnic groups were enjoying one of their greatest periods of prosperity.

In November 1995 UMNO's general assembly all but guaranteed Mahathir's reelection by passing a resolution stipulating that the top two party posts would go uncontested in 1996. The only serious challenge to Mahathir's prime ministership had come in 1987, when he narrowly defeated Tengku Razaleigh Hamzah, a former ally. Then in 1988 Mahathir announced the formation of UMNO Baru (New UMNO), from which Razaleigh and his supporters were to be excluded. Razaleigh registered a new splinter party called Semangat '46 in 1989, but it was dissolved in October 1996 because it had failed to attract adequate support. When Razaleigh reconciled with Mahathir and rejoined UMNO, he fueled speculation that he might seek Mahathir's job when the time was ripe.   (ANTHONY L. GREEN)

Maïnassara, Ibrahim Baré

On Jan. 27, 1996, Col. Ibrahim Baré Maïnassara led a successful military coup against the democratically elected (1993) Nigerois government of Pres. Mahamane Ousmane, which had been locked in an internal power struggle since 1995.

Though many thought that democratic institutions were well established and that Niger had made a successful transition to the multiparty system, Baré attacked the politicians, calling them "greedy, badly prepared, and incapable of adapting to the demands of democratic power."

Following the coup, Baré placed Mahamane under house arrest, banned all political parties, and suspended the constitution. International reaction was swift. The United States withdrew all economic and military aid, France suspended all monetary support, and South Africa and Germany vocally condemned the action.

Baré, saying he had no wish to remain in power, stated he would draw up a timetable for a return to civilian rule. He called for elections on July 7 and 8, in which he ran as an independent candidate. Baré insisted upon those dates, causing rumours to circulate that he had consulted practitioners of traditional magic who deemed the dates auspicious. After the first round of elections, the polls were closed early amid confusion, and Baré had his opponents placed under house arrest. He then disbanded the CENI (Independent National Electoral Commission) and set up his own National Election Commission, and on July 21 the Supreme Court validated the commission's declaration that Baré had won the election with 52.2% of the vote.

AFP PHOTOS

Ibrahim Baré Maïnassara

Baré was born in 1949 in Maradi, Niger. A professional soldier, he enlisted in 1970 and became Pres. Seyni Kountché's aide-de-camp in 1974. Under Kountché's rule, Baré was appointed commander of the Presidential Guard and subsequently headed the parachute division. He held a series of overseas posts, including military attaché to the Nigerois embassy in Paris, before serving as health minister from 1987 to 1988, ambassador to Paris (1988–90), and ambassador to Algeria (1990–92). He then returned to Niger to become defense adviser to Cheiffou Amadou, the transitional prime minister. In 1993 Mahamane appointed Baré his chief of staff, and in 1995 Prime Minister Hama Amadou named him army chief.
(AMANDA E. FULLER)

Malouf, David George Joseph

In May 1996, after a meeting that lasted five days, Australia's David Malouf beat 125 nominees from 50 countries and a final shortlist of six other major authors—V.S. Naipaul, José Saramago, Jane Urquhart, Connie Palmen, Cees Nooteboom, and John Banville—to win the inaugural International IMPAC Dublin Literary Award for his sixth novel, *Remembering Babylon* (1993). The prize money of £Ir 100,000 (about $160,000) was greater than that offered by the Nobel Prize for Literature, the Miles Franklin Award, and the Booker Prize.

Remembering Babylon is the story of a British-born young man in the 1840s who is cast away off Queensland as a boy and rescued by Aborigines, only to find himself trapped between two cultures when he returns to life among white colonials. The book had already won the New South Wales (NSW) Premier's Literary Award and been shortlisted for the 1994 Booker. Malouf continued to explore the challenges of multicultural Australia and the spiritual power of the outback in his acclaimed 1996 novel, *The Conversations at Curlow Creek*. Set in 1827, this work examines the growing bond between a condemned Irish convict and the immigrant Irish bush ranger sent to hang him.

Malouf could draw on a long personal history both for his understanding of multiculturalism and for his poetic style. The son of a Lebanese Christian father and a British-born Portuguese Jewish mother, he was born March 20, 1934, and educated at the University of Queensland. He worked as a university lecturer in Sydney (1968–77), but he spent many years living off and on in Europe, particularly in Italy.

In 1970 Malouf published *Bicycle and Other Poems*, the first of 11 volumes of poetry, for which he won such awards as the Australian Literature Society Gold Medal. His career as a prizewinning novelist began in earnest with the NSW Premier's award for his second novel, *An Imaginary Life* (1978). His other popular and successful works of fiction include *Johnno* (1975), *Fly Away Peter* (1982), *Harland's Half Acre* (1984), and *The Great World* (1990). Additional literary prizes included the Miles Franklin Award, the Adelaide Festival Award, the Commonwealth Writers Prize, and the French Prix Fémina Étranger. He also wrote short stories, plays, three opera librettos, and an autobiography, *12 Edmonstone Street* (1985).
(A.R.G. GRIFFITHS)

Menken, Alan

The prolific composer Alan Menken, whose captivating scores helped invigorate the recent animated feature films of Walt Disney Pictures, collected his seventh and eighth Academy Awards in 1996. He won Oscars for his work in Disney's *Pocahontas* in the categories of best musical or comedy score and best original song ("Colors of the Wind"). Menken was born on July 22, 1949, in New Rochelle, N.Y. He initially enrolled in a premedical program at New York University but graduated with a degree in music. He then performed in clubs, composed advertising jingles, and provided accompaniment for ballerinas at practice. One such ballerina would later accompany him in life; he married a professional dancer. A career break came when playwright and lyricist Howard Ashman picked Menken to collaborate with him on the 1979 play *God Bless You, Mr. Rosewater*. Although they attained mild success with that production, it was not until 1982 that they achieved significant critical and commercial acclaim with the off-Broadway production of *Little Shop of Horrors*. The duo subsequently adapted their score for the 1986 film.

In the late 1980s Jeffrey Katzenberg, at the time chairman of Walt Disney Pictures, offered the team a list of projects. Menken and Ashman chose to tackle an animated musical version of the Hans Christian Andersen story "The Little Mermaid," which was released in 1989. The resulting collaboration earned Menken two Academy Awards, two Grammy awards, and two Golden Globe awards, among other accolades. The team's next Disney project, *Beauty and the Beast* (1991), in addition to being nominated for best picture and winning Menken another two Oscars, went on to become a successful Broadway production. Ashman died in 1991 after having begun work with Menken on what would become another Disney success, *Aladdin* (1992), and Menken teamed up with lyricist Tim Rice. *Aladdin* became Disney's biggest animated hit to that time. For his next two Disney films, Menken collaborated with lyricist Stephen Schwartz on *Pocahontas* and *The Hunchback of Notre Dame* (1996).

Although Menken's association with Disney identified him with children's projects, he saw his work as the natural evolution of the theatrical musical. Menken said, "I write for the broadest possible audience . . . and sometimes they call it kid stuff, and I admit it pains me." As 1996 drew to a close, Menken was working with lyricist David Zippel on *Hercules*, Disney's 35th full-length animated musical.   (ANTHONY L. GREEN)

Merchant, Ismail, and Ivory, James

The film producer-director team of Merchant and Ivory celebrated their 35th anniversary as creative partners in 1996 and, along with screenwriter Ruth Prawer Jhabvala (who wrote the majority of their films), were identified by the *Guinness Book of World Records* as cinema's longest-running partnership. The two had produced an unequaled string of impressive low-budget adaptations of complex novels by such authors as Henry James, E.M. Forster, and Kazuo Ishiguro and were known for their richly textured cinematography and ability to evoke brilliant performances from some of the world's finest actors.

Born on Dec. 25, 1936, in Bombay, India, Ismail Noormohamed Merchant immigrated to the U.S. in 1958 and soon began producing films. His first feature-length motion picture, *The Householder* (1963), was an adaptation of one of Jhabvala's early novels and marked the beginning of Merchant's collaboration with both Jhabvala and Ivory. James Francis Ivory, born on June 7, 1928, in Berkeley, Calif., had already graduated with an M.A. in cinema from the University of Southern California and had directed two films by the time he met Merchant. Recognizing early that they possessed a mutual respect for one another's work and common creative sensibilities, the pair wasted no time and produced seven films in the first 10 years of their partnership, including *Shakespeare Wallah* (1965) and *Bombay Talkie* (1970).

Fueled by Jhabvala's sensual screenplays, Merchant and Ivory then embarked on a pair of James adaptations, *The Europeans* (1979) and *The*

Bostonians (1984), which were followed by three Forster adaptations: *Maurice* (1987), *A Room with a View* (1986), and *Howards End* (1992)—all of which won awards. For the latter two films, Ivory received Academy Award nominations for best director. By the time *The Remains of the Day* was released in 1993, the filmmaking team was well established, and Ivory was nominated a third time for best director by the academy. Their 1996 film, *Surviving Picasso*, continued their preoccupation with sensuality by recounting a 10-year tryst between the flamboyant painter and one of his many mistresses.

The revolutionary filmmakers were heralded by literary and film enthusiasts as the team that both revitalized film adaptations and introduced more sensitive and thoughtful character portrayals. When Ivory was chosen in 1994 to be the 25th recipient of the coveted Director's Guild D.W. Griffith Award for distinguished lifetime achievement, he said of his longtime friend Merchant, "It all works because he is there and it wouldn't work otherwise."   (SARA BRANT)

Morissette, Alanis

Canadian singer-songwriter Alanis Morissette shocked the recording world and the listening public in 1995 with the raw tone and explicit lyrics of her explosive debut single "You Oughta Know," a searing fantasy of revenge against an unfaithful lover. The song and such singles as "You Learn" and "Ironic" appeared on Morissette's debut album, *Jagged Little Pill* (1995), which sold over 14 million copies and remained atop the international billboard charts throughout 1995 and 1996. As a result, Morissette became firmly entrenched—not without controversy—as alternative rock's foremost female vocalist. In 1996 the star won Grammy awards for album of the year and best rock album for *Jagged Little Pill*. She also collected Grammys for best rock song (songwriter) and best female rock vocal performance for "You Oughta Know." Morissette was hailed by critics as "raw" and "passionate" and "authentic," and her strong, pliable voice, confessional lyrics, and technically explosive performance gained her worldwide critical and popular acclaim.

Born June 1, 1974, in Ottawa, Morissette began studying piano at six and composing at seven; she

Alanis Morissette

wrote her first songs at nine. By 10 she was acting in Nickelodeon's kids' series "You Can't Do That on Television." She used her earnings from that show to cut her first single. At age 14 she signed a song-publishing deal that led to two dance-pop albums, *Alanis* (1991), which sold 100,000 copies and earned her Canada's Juno award, and *Now Is the Time* (1992), which sold more than 50,000 copies. Escaping from the pressures of her then-fizzling teen career, Morissette left home after high school to create a more satisfying and authentic style. After two years she found her place in Los Angeles and her muse in Glen Ballard, a veteran songwriter-producer. Together the two wrote and recorded *Jagged Little Pill* in record speed and at negligible cost. She signed with Madonna's label, Maverick, and shed her dance-queen image with the release of her first album. The 12 jarringly honest and frequently provocative songs rang true with admiring listeners, and the album was an unqualified success. Morissette considered it to be her real debut, for with it she switched from "entertaining people . . . to sharing revelations." Accused of being a poseur because of her quick rise to fame, her association with Ballard and Madonna, and her dance-queen past, Morissette countered claims of inauthenticity, saying, "Most people's growth is done in private. . . . An artist's growth is done in public."

Following her climb to the top, the singer toured to ever-increasing audiences and fielded offers for tours, movies, and sound tracks. Morissette planned to record another album with Ballard in late 1996.   (ANN M. BELASKI)

Netanyahu, Benjamin

In May 1996 Israeli voters went to the polls to elect a new prime minister. For many, the choice they faced was couched in deceptively simple terms—peace versus security. Shimon Peres, the incumbent prime minister and leader of the Labor Party, pledged to carry on the legacy of the late Yitzhak Rabin, whose efforts at establishing a lasting peace between Israel and the Palestine Liberation Organization (PLO) had earned him both the Nobel Peace Prize and an assassin's bullet. The candidate of the Likud bloc, Benjamin Netanyahu, had a different message—peace with security—which struck a chord with Israeli voters. Netanyahu won the election with the slimmest of margins.

Netanyahu was born in Tel Aviv, Israel, on Oct. 21, 1949. His father, a prominent right-wing Zionist and historian, moved the family to the United States when Netanyahu was a teenager. The young Netanyahu attended high school in Philadelphia, returning to Israel to join the army, where he served in the elite Sayeret Matkal commando unit and rose to the rank of captain.

Netanyahu returned to the United States and attended Harvard University and the Massachusetts Institute of Technology. He caught the eye of Israeli Ambassador Moshe Arens, who brought Netanyahu to the embassy in Washington. He then moved on to become the Israeli ambassador to the UN. In 1988 he was elected to the Knesset (parliament) as a member of Likud and quickly established himself as an adept politician. Capitalizing on the national and international exposure he had gained during the Persian Gulf War as one of the leading Israeli spokesmen, he became leader of Likud in 1993.

Netanyahu's election bid was seen by many as Israel's first "American-style" campaign. Handsome, charismatic, and glib, he used the media to his advantage, appearing at the scenes of terrorist bombings to speak out against the establishment of a Palestinian state, against further concessions to the PLO, and in favour of the continued settlement of Jews in disputed areas. Twice-divorced, Netanyahu was married to Sara Ben-Artzi, a child psychologist.

The first native-born prime minister in Israel's history, "Bibi" (as he was called in Israel) Netanyahu took office at a critical time. His narrow victory in the election demonstrated the deep political divisions that existed in Israeli society, while his hard-line stance on security issues made negotiations with the Arab world difficult. By year's end, however, he had backed down from some

of his more hawkish pronouncements and even entered into dialogue with Syria. In his campaign Netanyahu had promised peace with security, a promise that Israel fervently hoped he could keep.
              (JOHN H. MATHEWS)

Pérec, Marie-José

Sprinter Michael Johnson of the U.S. was not the only Olympic athlete to claim the rare double victory in the long sprints, the 200-m and 400-m races, at the 1996 Games in Atlanta, Ga.; he was not even the first. On August 1, minutes before Johnson raced, French speedster Marie-José Pérec accomplished the feat first, outkicking Merlene Ottey of Jamaica in the last 10 m of the 200-m dash to win in 22.12 sec. Three days earlier Pérec had set an Olympic record with the third fastest 400-m race ever run by a woman (48.25 sec), surging past Cathy Freeman of Australia in the homestretch to successfully defend her 1992 Olympic title and become the first athlete ever to log consecutive 400-m Olympic wins.

Pérec was born on May 9, 1968, on the West Indian island of Basse-Terre in Guadeloupe, an overseas administrative district of France. In 1984 she was recruited by a visiting French coach, who took her to the mainland, where she placed second in the 200-m dash at the French junior championships. In 1988, at 20 years of age, she set her first national record in the 400 m (51.35 sec) and made her Olympic debut in Seoul, S.Kor., advancing to the quarterfinals of the 200 m. In 1991 Pérec broke 11 seconds in the 100 m and 50 seconds in the 400 m, initiating a legacy of dominance in the latter event with victories at the world championships (1991, 1995) and the Olympic Games (1992, 1996).

Marie-José Pérec

Called "La Gazelle" by the French media, the lithe and leggy sprinter stood 180 cm (5 ft 10 in) tall, weighed 60 kg (130 lb), and had a stride covering 2.5 m (8.2 ft). Since 1992 she had been the highest-ranked 400-m runner in the world, except in 1993, when, over the objections of her coach, Jacques Piasenta, she focused instead on the 200 m, clocking a personal best of 21.99 sec. The following spring, in part to avoid the pressures of her celebrity in France, she left Piasenta to train in California under U.S. coach John Smith, enlarging her repertoire with the 400-m hurdles. In that event she beat world-record holder Kim Batten of the U.S. in all three of their competitions in 1995. (TOM MICHAEL)

Prusiner, Stanley

In San Francisco in the early 1970s, a young neurology resident named Stanley Prusiner was in charge of a patient who died of a rare fatal degenerative disorder of the brain called Creutzfeldt-Jakob disease. At the time little was known about this class of neurodegenerative disorders—the spongiform encephalopathies—that caused progressive dementia and death in humans and animals. Prusiner decided to remedy this lack of information. In 1974 he set up a laboratory to study scrapie, a related disorder of sheep, and in 1982 he claimed to have isolated the scrapie-causing agent. Prusiner claimed that this pathogenic agent, which he named "prion," was unlike any other known pathogen, such as a virus or bacterium, because it consisted only of protein and lacked the genetic material contained within all life-forms that is necessary for replication. When first published, the prion theory met with much criticism, probably as much for Prusiner's brash style as for the idea itself. In the years since then, the evidence for the theory had increased, and, although some scientists remained skeptical, Prusiner's views became widely accepted. In 1996, when a new variant of Creutzfeldt-Jakob disease emerged in the U.K., Prusiner's research was the focus of national attention.

Fears abounded that the new variant of Creutzfeldt-Jakob disease might be linked to "mad cow" disease, a brain disorder that appeared in British cattle in the mid-1980s. Some evidence suggested that the mad cow prion may have jumped species, infecting humans who consumed beef contaminated with the infectious agent. Because mad cow disease was believed to have been caused when the agent that causes scrapie in sheep was transmitted to cattle in feed, there was precedent for species-jumping events to occur. Whether this was the route of transmission, however, remained for Prusiner and other researchers in the field to determine. Prusiner's research also could have significant implications for such disorders as Alzheimer's disease and Parkinson's disease, which seemed to share certain characteristics with the diseases caused by prions.

Prusiner was born in Des Moines, Iowa, on May 28, 1942, and grew up in Cincinnati, Ohio. He began his scientific career at the University of Pennsylvania, where he earned an A.B. in 1964 and an M.D. in 1968. After spending four years in biochemical research, he became (1972) a resident in neurology at the University of California, San Francisco, School of Medicine. He joined the faculty there in 1974 and became a professor of neurology and biochemistry. A member of the National Academy of Sciences, he received numerous honours, including the prestigious Albert Lasker Basic Medical Research Award in 1994.

(MARY JANE FRIEDRICH)

Redgrave, Steven Geoffrey

In Atlanta, Ga., on July 27, 1996, British oarsman Steve Redgrave joined an exclusive club; he had won a gold medal in four consecutive Olympic Games. Only the Hungarian fencer Aladar Gerevich, the U.S. shot-putter Al Oerter, the Danish yachtsman Paul Elvstrom, and the U.S. track star Carl Lewis had equaled or surpassed Redgrave's Olympic record, which included one gold in the coxed fours at the Los Angeles Olympics in 1984 and three in the coxless pairs, with Andy Holmes in 1988 and Matthew Pinsent in 1992 and 1996. Others may have won more medals, but few could sustain Redgrave's level of intensity over such a long period, his burning commitment to victory, or his psychological dominance over his opponents.

Redgrave was born close to the River Thames in Marlow, Eng., on March 23, 1962, and took up rowing at the age of 16 at his school, Marlow Comprehensive. The first outlines of a sporting legend were drawn in a school race when one of the crew missed his stroke and got the oar caught behind his back. The rest of the crew gave up the race until Redgrave roared at them to keep rowing. They won. He first represented Great Britain in the junior world championships in 1979 and moved to the senior team two years later, narrowly missing selection for the Moscow Olympics in 1980. It was not until after he had stroked the British four to a memorable victory over the U.S. in Los Angeles and flirted with both single sculls and bobsled that Redgrave settled on rowing pairs as his best discipline. Though never a classical rower, he generated enormous power from his 1.96-m (6-ft 5-in), 102-kg (225-lb) frame and developed into a clever tactician on the water, knowing instinctively when to dominate other crews and when to hold back. His first partnership with Holmes broke up amid some acrimony, but in the Oxford-educated Pinsent, eight years Redgrave's junior, he found someone who shared his lust for competition and perfection.

In addition to his four Olympic golds (the last won by less than a second over the Australian crew), Redgrave collected six world championship golds and two silvers, three Commonwealth golds, and an Olympic bronze in Seoul, S.Kor., in 1988, when he and Holmes narrowly failed to complete a unique double of coxed and coxless pairs. He was made MBE in 1987 (raised to CBE after his triumph in Atlanta) and published a book, *Steven Redgrave's Complete Book of Rowing*, in 1992. After his return from Atlanta, Redgrave announced his retirement from international rowing. He was reportedly considering a coaching job in Australia, but the lure of a fifth successive Olympic gold proved to be too much, and in November Redgrave proclaimed that he and Pinsent would be wearing the British vest once again at the Sydney Games in the year 2000, probably in the coxless fours. (ANDREW LONGMORE)

Redwood, John Alan

As the Conservative government of British Prime Minister John Major stumbled from one crisis to the next, a young politician who had served briefly as a junior member of Major's Cabinet emerged as the leader of the Conservative Party's right wing. In any debate about the future of the free market, the European Union (EU), or the U.K.'s constitution, John Redwood was sure to be in the thick of the action—writing newspaper articles, appearing in television debates, and delivering thought-provoking speeches.

Redwood was born in Dover, Kent, on June 15, 1951. A ferociously bright student, he was awarded one of the highly prized fellowships of All Souls College, Oxford, when he was only 21. For some years he combined academic study of philosophy with more pragmatic work in the form of a job with a leading London merchant bank, Robert Fleming & Co. As one of the young intellectuals on the Conservative right wing, he was well placed to capitalize on Margaret Thatcher's election as prime minister in 1979. Thatcher in 1983 appointed Redwood the head of her office's Policy Unit, where he became one of the driving forces behind the government's policy of privatizing state-owned industries.

Elected as an MP for the safe Conservative seat of Wokingham, Berkshire, in 1987, Redwood had to wait only two years before becoming a junior minister at the Department of Trade and Industry and just six years before reaching the Cabinet; Major appointed him secretary of state for Wales in 1993. Two years later came the event that catapulted Redwood into the spotlight. Major, exasperated by divisions within the party, resigned as leader and challenged his critics to fight him for his post. Redwood resigned from the Cabinet and stood as standard-bearer for those right-wing MPs who wanted the government to reduce both taxes and public spending and to adopt more critical policies toward the EU.

Although Redwood lost, he surprised many people with the vigour of his campaign and the strength of his support: 89 MPs, compared with the 218 who backed Major. Redwood had managed to build himself a base within an important section of the party and had started to dispel his reputation as a remote, passionless politician. It seemed certain that Redwood would be a strong contender for the leadership of his party, whenever Major decided to stand down.

(PETER KELLNER)

Richardson, Dorothy

As a little girl, U.S. softball player Dot Richardson dreamed of standing on the highest tier of the Olympic podium, bowing her head to receive a gold medal. Amid proud tears, her dream came true in July 1996 at the Olympic Games in Atlanta, Ga., as the U.S. team steamrollered into first place with a record of 8–1 in the debut of Olympic softball competition. The 34-year-old team captain blasted three home runs, batted in seven runs, and made only one error at shortstop while her squad's crack pitching staff held opponents to an average of one run a game. The U.S. team had long dominated the sport internationally and in the 10 years preceding the Olympics had posted only one loss in 111 games. Richardson was no small part of that legacy.

The hardworking veteran, who had been an international champion since winning a gold medal at the 1979 Pan American Games in Puerto Rico, seemed to reach the zenith of her softball playing just as she was staking out a career as an orthopedic surgeon. Boundless energy and frenetic scheduling allowed her to juggle her medical studies and softball training, for which she even built a batting cage in her bedroom. After graduating from the University of Louisville (Ky.) Medical School, she began her residency at the University of Southern California, from which she took a one-year leave of absence in preparation for the 1996 Olympics.

Richardson was born on Sept. 22, 1961. Because her father was an air force mechanic, she spent her early years on various military bases in the U.S. and abroad. She first entered softball competition in Orlando, Fla., at the age of 10 and became, at age 13, the youngest player in the Women's Major Fast Pitch League. In 1980 she received collegiate All-American honours at Western Illinois University, where her .480 batting average was the nation's highest. She earned the honour three more times while attending (1981–83) the University of California, Los Angeles, where she led the team in hitting all three years. While being feted by the National Collegiate Athletic Association as Player of the Decade in the 1980s, she helped the U.S. softball team gain international prestige by participating in several Pan American Games and International Softball Federation women's world championships. At the national level, in the Amateur Softball Association, Richardson was named All-American 14 times, best defensive player 7 times, and most valuable player of the championship series 3 times; she also competed in 11 U.S. Olympic Festivals.

(TOM MICHAEL)

Rodman, Dennis Keith

After being eliminated from the National Basketball Association (NBA) play-offs in 1995, the Chicago Bulls took a chance and traded for the flamboyant Dennis Rodman, a 2.03-m (6-ft 8-in) forward considered one of the best rebounders and defenders in the game. In theory, a player with Rodman's skills was the final piece in Chicago's championship puzzle. Players and fans alike, however, were skeptical; Rodman sported provocative body tattoos, an ever-changing rainbow of hair colours, a rough, confrontational style of play developed during his years with the Detroit Pistons (the self-proclaimed "bad boys" of basketball who had won NBA championships in 1989 and 1990), and a history of disruptive behaviour and off-court antics that included dating the pop music star Madonna and posing nude for a magazine pictorial.

Rodman was born on May 13, 1961, in Trenton, N.J., and grew up in Dallas, Texas. His two sisters were talented basketball players—both college All-Americans—but Rodman did not play in high school, when he stood only 1.80 m (5 ft 11 in). After graduation, however, the boy known to his friends as the Worm (because of his squirming style of pinball playing) grew 20 cm (8 in). He played basketball at Southeastern Oklahoma State University, averaging 25.7 points and 15.7 rebounds in a 96-game career, and was selected by Detroit in the second round of the 1986 NBA draft. Originally known as a hard-working, by-the-book player, Rodman grew restless after the 1992 departure from Detroit of coach Chuck Daly, whom he admired. As time passed, his off-court high jinks began to be scrutinized as closely as his on-court performance.

In 1993 Rodman was traded to San Antonio, where he often clashed with the Spurs' coaches and management. Although he tied a league mark by winning his fourth consecutive rebounding title in 1994–95, the Spurs were anxious to ship him elsewhere. Under the guidance of the Bulls' unconventional head coach, Phil Jackson (q.v.), however, Rodman's season with Chicago was both colourful and successful. He won another rebounding crown and was named to the NBA All-Defensive team for the sixth time, while his high-energy, antagonistic style of play was credited with

Dennis Rodman

JOHN W. MCDONOUGH

helping the Bulls to a league-record 72 regular-season victories and their fourth league title.

In early 1996 Rodman released an autobiographical book, *Bad as I Wanna Be,* and, with his usual flair for the dramatic, arrived at a book signing in a formal dress and full makeup. The book was a best-seller. After the season he negotiated deals for a series of cable-television shows, a costarring role in an action feature film, and a substantial pay increase for his upcoming second season with the Bulls.   (ANTHONY G. CRAINE)

Rybakov, Anatoly

In 1996 Russian novelist Anatoly Rybakov's gripping epic of life in the Soviet Union during the rule of Joseph Stalin came to a close with the publication of *Prakh i pepel* (*Dust and Ashes*). Concluding the story that began with *Deti Arbata* (1987; *Children of the Arbat,* 1988) and continued in *Strakh* (1990; *Fear,* 1992), *Dust and Ashes* cemented Rybakov's place among the top rank of contemporary Russian novelists. The trilogy follows a group of young Muscovites, once childhood friends from the upper-class Arbat neighbourhood, through the turmoil of the Soviet Union in the 1930s. The first novel describes the growing disillusionment among the young during the early stages of Stalin's rule. *Fear* offers a chilling description of the interrogation methods of the NKVD, the Soviet secret police. The third volume follows the characters through World War II. Throughout the trilogy Rybakov juxtaposes the lives of the young people against an intimate psychological portrait of Stalin, frankly depicting the ruler's cruelty and inhumanity.

Rybakov wrote *Children of the Arbat* in the 1960s, but it was suppressed by Soviet authorities. Although he could have published the novel abroad, he declined, believing that the story had special meaning to his people and that to publish it first in another country would be a betrayal of his duty as a writer. As the Soviet government eased its repressive policies in the 1980s, the novel was finally released to the public. Though the trilogy's discussion of Stalin's brutality did not surprise Western audiences, it stirred controversy in Russia.

Rybakov was born Jan. 1 (Jan. 14, New Style), 1911, in Chernigov, Ukraine, Russian Empire. Like the hero of his trilogy, Aleksandr Pankratov, he grew up in Arbat. He graduated from the Moscow Institute of Transport Engineering in 1934 but soon after was exiled for three years to Siberia for making "subversive" statements. He later worked as an engineer for transport companies throughout the Soviet Union. During World War II, Rybakov cleared his record by serving as a tank commander in the Soviet army.

After the war Rybakov took up writing. His early works include *Kortik* (1948; *The Dirk,* 1954), a children's novel, and *Voditeli* (1950; "The Drivers"), an adult novel that earned him a Soviet state prize. He also wrote for television, film, and theatre. Rybakov gained international attention in 1979 with the publication of *Tyazhely pesok* (*Heavy Sand,* 1981). The novel follows a family of Russian Jews from the beginning of the 20th century through the horrors of World War II and the Nazi occupation.   (JAMES HENNELLY)

Samper Pizano, Ernesto

Even when judged by the rough-and-tumble standards of Colombian politics, Pres. Ernesto Samper Pizano's political career was unusually turbulent. In 1989, as he stood talking to José Antequera, a member of the left-wing Patriotic Union, an assassin opened fire, killing Antequera and putting four bullets into Samper. He recovered to become leader of the Liberal Party and to win the presidential election in 1994. Samper then encountered new troubles, however, as rumours of the Liberal Party's involvement with the Cali drug cartel were supported by the release of tape recordings of telephone conversations between the cartel's leaders, in which they discussed campaign contributions to the Liberal Party and meetings with Santiago Medina, the campaign's treasurer.

In 1995 Colombia's attorney general, Alfonso Valdivieso, announced that his office was beginning a large-scale investigation of the ties between

the cartel and the government. By the end of 1995, a number of party officials had been indicted, including Medina and Defense Minister Fernando Botero Zea, who had also served as Samper's campaign manager. In 1996, as more evidence of collaboration between the drug lords and the politicians surfaced, calls arose for Samper's resignation.

Samper refused to step down, however, and continued to deny personal knowledge of the financial contributions from the cartel. In May he received a boost when a special congressional committee recommended to Congress that charges not be brought against him. The committee, however, was dominated by members of the Liberal Party, and Congress decided to pursue the investigation. In June the members of the Chamber of Deputies voted to clear Samper of the charge of knowingly receiving funds from drug traffickers. This decision ensured that he could not be reinvestigated and would not be impeached.

Samper was born in Bogotá on Aug. 3, 1950. He graduated from Javeriana University, Bogotá, in 1972 with a degree in economics and earned his law degree from the same university the next year. In 1974 he joined the faculty of his alma mater, serving as a professor in the School of Law and Economics. Samper started out in politics as a Bogotá councillor and later moved to the national Senate. He served as campaign treasurer and coordinator during the unsuccessful presidential run of Alfonso López Michelsen in 1982.

Opposition parties labeled Samper's acquittal as "the farce of the century" and pledged strikes and other protests in response. Ironically, Samper had proved popular with the public for what was perceived as a legitimate effort to step up the war on the drug lords. Cynics pointed out that this effort probably resulted more from the threats of political and economic sanctions by the United States than from any deeply held convictions on Samper's part.   (JOHN H. MATHEWS)

Sarandon, Susan

After four nominations for the best actress Academy Award but no wins, Susan Sarandon finally was honoured with an Oscar in 1996 for her portrayal of Sister Helen Prejean, the Louisiana nun whose memoirs of her experiences as the spiritual adviser for two death-row inmate formed the basis of *Dead Man Walking,* a moving argument against capital punishment. An actress with tremendous range who began her career with ingenue and character roles, Sarandon blossomed into one of Hollywood's most celebrated leading ladies as she entered her 40s, redefining the onscreen possibilities for mature actresses as she imbued her typically strong-willed, intelligent characters with a sensuality routinely denied to actresses over 40.

Born in New York City on Oct. 4, 1946, Susan Abigail Tomalin, the oldest of nine children in a family of Welsh-Italian descent, was raised in New Jersey. She graduated in drama from Catholic University of America (B.A., 1968), Washington, D.C., where she met and married actor Christopher Sarandon (they divorced in 1979). With no intention of pursuing an acting career, she read with her husband at one of his auditions and soon found herself a female lead in the film *Joe* (1970). Small film roles and television work (notably in "A World Apart") followed until 1975, when Sarandon shone as the naive ingenue in *The Rocky Horror Picture Show* and starred opposite Robert Redford in *The Great Waldo Pepper.* Two films directed by Louis Malle (with whom she was romantically involved) brought her even greater attention: *Pretty Baby* (1978) and *Atlantic City* (1981). As a love interest of Burt Lancaster's aging mob henchman in the latter, Sarandon earned her first Oscar nomination. She also won praise for her work onstage in *A Coupla White Chicks Sitting Around Talking* and *Extremities* and in the films *Tempest* (1982), *The Hunger* (1983), and *Compromising Positions* (1985).

Sarandon's role as the sultry literature instructor and molder of men in the romantic comedy *Bull Durham* (1988) began both a string of unforgettable performances and her relationship with costar Tim Robbins, an actor-writer-director who shared Sarandon's longstanding commitment to political activism (together they interrupted their presentation of an Oscar at the 1993 Academy Awards to draw attention to the plight of HIV-positive Haitian refugees). Prominent among Sarandon's recent film appearances were her Oscar-nominated performances as the worldly waitress turned outlaw in *Thelma and Louise* (1991), the indefatigable mother searching for a cure for her son's disease in *Lorenzo's Oil* (1992), and the compassionate lawyer who protects a young murder witness in *The Client* (1994).

(JEFF WALLENFELDT)

Schulte, Dieter
During 1996 German postal and public-sector workers held a series of "warning" strikes and protests opposing Chancellor Helmut Kohl's plans to cut social benefits and slash public spending. The largest protest rally, held in Bonn on June 15, was organized by the 10-million-strong German Trade Union Federation (DGB), headed by Dieter Schulte. He brought 350,000 demonstrators together, including union activists, church group representatives, students, and government opposition leaders. The participation equaled that of another massive demonstration, the 1982 anti-NATO protest.

Schulte, who was born in the North Rhine Hanseatic city of Duisburg in 1940, worked as an apprentice bricklayer and laid furnace bricks for Thyssen, the steel giant, before beginning his labour career at the age of 25. In the late 1970s he helped IG Metall, Germany's largest trade union, in its major industrial dispute with Thyssen. He was elected to IG Metall's board in 1991. After the death of DGB leader Heinz-Werner Meyer in 1994, Schulte was drafted for the job because of his impressive credentials.

As leader of the DGB, Schulte oversaw the needs of 15 major trade unions and coped with opposition from the government, employers, and even employees, who had begun to negotiate directly with employers without the help of the unions. While some members pledged limited allegiance to the union, younger workers were reluctant to join because they did not see their support as beneficial, especially since the high unemployment rate remained unchanged. Schulte claimed, however, that a recent decline in union membership had not drastically affected his still powerful organization. He promised, "If government and management are looking for conflict, then they will meet with our clenched fist."

(LEE ANNE WIGGINS)

Shepard, Sam
It took some 30 years, but Sam Shepard, one of the leading U.S. playwrights, finally made it to Broadway in 1996 when his 1979 Pulitzer Prize-winning play *Buried Child* received a celebrated revival. This recognition came after Shepard already was renowned for his work as an actor, notably in the film *The Right Stuff* (1983), for which he received an Academy Award nomination as best supporting actor.

The son of a career army officer, Samuel Shepard Rogers was born on Nov. 5, 1943, in Fort Sheridan, Ill. He grew up on military bases and on an avocado ranch in California. After one year of junior college, he joined a touring repertory group, and in 1963 he arrived in New York City to pursue an acting career. It was as the writer of experimental one-act plays in Off-Off Broadway theatre in the mid-1960s, however, that Shepard first made his mark. His early plays, memorably *Cowboy Mouth* (written with poet-singer Patti Smith), were characterized by striking language and imagery, violence and fantasy, and an innovative structure based on psychological reality. Shepard also played the drums with the rock band the Holy Modal Rounders, which fostered a rock-and-roll sensibility that informed his plays. Particularly notable was *The Tooth of Crime*, written in London, where Shepard and his wife, actress O-Lan Johnson (they later divorced), lived from 1971 to 1974.

Returning to the U.S., Shepard won growing praise and became the resident playwright at San Francisco's Magic Theatre. In the mid-1970s his plays became increasingly realistic and linear in structure, though they continued to be concerned with myth, especially that of the American West. With *Curse of the Starving Class* (1976), *Buried Child* (1978), and *True West* (1980), Shepard also began to focus on families haunted by dark secrets and ones grappling with sexual taboos and rivalry. He began his film career in *Days of Heaven* (1978), establishing a rough-hewn image reminiscent of Gary Cooper. In *Frances* (1982), *Country* (1984), and *Crimes of the Heart* (1986), he costarred with Jessica Lange, with whom he had a long relationship and two children. Shepard's filmography also includes his lead role in *Fool for Love* (1985, adapted from his 1983 play) and the screenplay for Wim Wenders's *Paris, Texas* (1984), loosely based on Shepard's book *Motel Chronicles* (1982). His prose writing includes the collections *Hawk Moon* (1973) and *Cruising Paradise* (1996) and his firsthand account of Bob Dylan's 1975 tour of New England, *Rolling Thunder Logbook* (1977). Later, Shepard's dramatic output slowed. His most recent works include *A Lie of the Mind* (1985), the less-well-received *States of Shock* (1988), and *Simpatico* (1994). He also wrote and directed the films *Far North* (1988) and *Silent Tongue* (1994).   (JEFF WALLENFELDT)

Queen Silvia
On Aug. 27, 1996, Queen Silvia of Sweden welcomed representatives from over 100 countries to Stockholm for the first World Congress Against Commercial Sexual Exploitation of Children. Ironically, hers was one of several countries in which possession of child pornography was not a crime.

In July, during a rare television interview, the queen sparked controversy when she denounced Sweden's weak child pornography laws and called on the Riksdag (parliament) to take action. While the publication and distribution of child pornography were made illegal in Sweden in 1980, possession of such materials was protected under a constitutional law that guaranteed freedom of speech. The queen went so far as to propose that politicians be made to watch a film containing child pornography, suggesting that this would compel them to amend the law more quickly. Having viewed such material herself, she said, "It was the worst thing I have seen. It shows torture

Queen Silvia

LEBRUN—PHOTO NEWS/GAMMA LIAISON

of the worst kind." As a result of constitutional changes made in the 1970s, the Swedish royalty served primarily as figureheads, with no executive power. Many Swedes, even those who agreed with her motivation, questioned whether it was appropriate for the queen to speak out.

Queen Silvia was born Silvia Renate Sommerlath on Dec. 23, 1943, in Heidelberg, Ger., to a Brazilian mother and German father. When she was three years old, her family moved to São Paulo, Brazil, where she spent much of her childhood. After they returned to West Germany in 1957, Silvia completed her schooling. She received a degree in Spanish in 1969 from the Munich School of Interpreting. Following her graduation she worked at the Argentine consulate in Munich and served as hostess at the 1972 Olympic Games, where she met her future husband, King Carl XVI Gustaf. The then crown prince, reported to have been somewhat shy, was immediately smitten with the gregarious and strikingly beautiful Silvia. After a courtship spanning some four years, they were married on June 19, 1976.

As queen, Silvia directed much of her energy toward organizations serving the needs of children. While some might not have agreed with her decision to add her voice publicly to the fight against child pornography, it appeared that her efforts might prove fruitful. In the autumn of 1996, a parliamentary commission set up to review proposed constitutional changes that would ban possession of child pornography announced plans to make Sweden's laws some of the world's most stringent.   (SANDRA LANGENECKERT)

Simitis, Konstantinos
Following months of political paralysis in Greece caused by the failing health of Prime Minister Andreas Papandreou, Konstantinos Simitis was selected on Jan. 18, 1996, by Panhellenic Socialist Movement (Pasok) parliamentary deputies to succeed the ailing leader. During his first months in office, Simitis's aim was to move Greece's socialist government into the European mainstream. He advocated a moderate foreign policy, gradual privatization, and a plan for economic stability that would help Greece follow European Union (EU) policies in preparation for an EU single currency. In August Simitis, confident that Pasok had grown in popularity during his brief tenure, called for an early election. Initial statistics showed Simitis's approval rating at about 70%, but the race between him and conservative New Democracy candidate Miltiades Evert took on a competitive edge when, in the first weeks of the campaign, the polls showed the candidates running neck and neck. Simitis pulled steadily ahead, however, and was elected on Sept. 22, 1996, to serve four years in office.

Born on June 23, 1936, in Athens, "Kostas" was the son of George Simitis, an attorney and prominent leftist politician. Like his father, Simitis pursued a career in law and government, receiving both a bachelor's and a J.D. degree (1959) from the University of Marburg, Ger. He did postgraduate studies at the London School of Economics (1961–63). Simitis practiced law and in 1971 worked as a lecturer at the University of Konstanz, Ger. By the end of that year, he had become a full professor of commercial and civil law at Justus Liebig University of Giessen, Ger. Simitis also participated in clandestine political activities against the 1967–74 ruling dictatorship. For five years (1969–74) he was exiled in Germany, where he continued to be active in Greek liberation politics, arranging public meetings, producing radio broadcasts, lecturing, and writing articles for publications that opposed the junta.

After the junta collapsed in 1974, Simitis returned to Greece and assisted in the formation of Pasok. From 1977 to 1981 he was a professor of commercial law at the Pantion University of Political Sciences, Athens. In the years after 1981, when Pasok first became the ruling party in Greece, Simitis served as a member of parliament for the district of Piraeus and held such portfolios as agriculture (1981–85), national economy (1985–87), education (1989), and industry, energy, technology and commerce (1993–95).

(KATHERINE I. GORDON)

Michelle Smith

Smith, Michelle

Prior to 1996, Ireland had won only five Olympic gold medals, and no medal (gold, silver, or bronze) had been won by Irish women. In one memorable week in July, Michelle Smith single-handedly changed all that at the Centennial Olympic Games in Atlanta, Ga. The 26-year-old swimmer from Rathcoole won the gold in three events—the 200-m individual medley, the 400-m individual medley, and the 400-m freestyle—and captured the bronze medal in the 200-m butterfly. She became a national hero and Ireland's most successful Olympian ever, a remarkable achievement in a nation that did not even have an Olympic-size pool for training. Her triumph, however, was somewhat tarnished by unsubstantiated rumours that she had used performance-enhancing drugs. Some observers questioned her dramatic improvements in time and pointed to her marriage to a Dutch discus thrower who had been suspended from international competition for steroid use. Smith passed all the pre- and post-Olympic drug tests, however, and no other evidence emerged of any illegal or unsportsmanlike activity.

Smith was born in 1970 in Rathcoole, a village south of Dublin. She began swimming competitively at the age of 13, waking up at 5 AM to practice before school. Though she developed into one of Ireland's premier junior swimmers, Smith realized that without more advanced facilities and training techniques, she would never be able to compete at the international level. She went to the United States to attend school and swim at the University of Houston, Texas, where she graduated with a degree in communications. Her times steadily improved, and she made the Irish Olympic teams in 1988 and 1992. At both of those Games, however, she was eliminated in the preliminary rounds.

In 1994 Smith moved to The Netherlands with her coach and future husband, Erik de Bruin, to prepare for the Atlanta Games. The next year she emerged as an elite athlete, winning the 200-m butterfly and the 200-m individual medley at the European championships. She continued to improve in 1996, taking 19 seconds off her best time in the 400-m freestyle. In response to questions about her sudden turnaround, Smith credited more sophisticated training techniques and a single-minded focus on swimming. She also pointed out that she was probably the most tested athlete in Irish history and that she had never tested positive for banned substances.

An estimated one-half of Ireland's 3.6 million people stayed up past midnight to watch Smith's races on television. Following her Olympic tri- umph, she returned home to a hero's welcome at the Dublin airport, where thousands, including Irish Pres. Mary Robinson, waited in the rain to greet her.

(JOHN H. MATHEWS)

Son, Masayoshi

Before traveling to the United States to study in 1973, Masayoshi Son repeatedly tried to meet Den Fujita, president of McDonald's Corp. (Japan), Ltd., to seek his advice. When they finally met, Son was told to study computer science. Nearly 20 years later the two met again. Son had become a leading distributor of computer software and related publications in Japan and was president of Softbank Corp. Fujita was deeply moved when Son thanked him for the advice he had given years earlier.

Son was born in Saga prefecture, Japan, on Aug. 31, 1957; he was a third-generation Korean with Japanese citizenship. Son graduated from the University of California, Berkeley, in 1980 with a major in computer science. While in school, he and a group of other students developed a sound-translation device capable of converting Japanese into English and German. He sold the technology to Sharp Corp. and used the proceeds to establish the predecessor to Softbank after his return to Japan in 1981.

Son's spectacular success often invited comparisons to Bill Gates, cofounder of Microsoft Corp.; Akio Morita, longtime head of Sony Corp.; and Soichiro Honda, founder of the automobile- and motorcycle-manufacturing company that bore his name. Son, however, differed from the others because he alone expanded his business by using aggressive merger-and-acquisition tactics. Since he first offered Softbank shares on the over-the-counter market in July 1994 to obtain capital, Son was said to have invested between $3 billion and $5 billion on mergers and acquisitions. These included the purchase of Phoenix Publishing Systems Inc., Ziff-Davis Communications Co.'s convention operations and publishing division; the rights to host Comdex, the computer industry's largest trade show from the Interface Group; and a majority share in Kingston Technology Corp., a U.S. memory-card maker. In 1996 Softbank joined News Corp. of Australia, which was run by media tycoon Rupert Murdoch, in the purchase of a 21% share of Asahi National Broadcasting Co., a major Japanese commercial television station. A segment of the media called the announcement an unexpected foreign capital invasion of the Japanese broadcasting world. Softbank's sales in the fiscal year that ended March 31, 1996, were reported to have amounted to some $1.4 billion, its assets $3.8 billion, and borrowings $230 million.

Son financed mergers and acquisitions by issuing corporate bonds rather than obtaining loans from banks. That was perhaps one reason why his company took great care of the stock market and its shareholders. Son defined his merger-and-acquisition tactics as "diplomatic warfare" in which both Softbank and the firm it sought to acquire gained something without having engaged in an all-or-nothing confrontation.

(TEIJI SHIMIZU)

Spelling, Aaron

On Jan. 21, 1996, with the premier of "Savannah," a southern drama that earned channel WB its highest ratings, Aaron Spelling once again proved he was the most successful independent producer in television history. The show was his latest in a string of hits that included "Beverly Hills 90210," which began in 1992 as a high-school drama and costarred his daughter, Tori, and "Melrose Place," a prime-time soap opera popular with those in their 20s. While critics had long dismissed his shows as "cotton candy for the mind," Spelling, who had produced more than 45 programs, again found a recipe for success as millions of viewers continued to tune in.

Spelling was born on April 22, 1923, in Dallas, Texas. He was the son of a Russian-Jewish immigrant tailor and grew up in a poor working-class neighbourhood. He attended Southern Methodist University (B.A., 1950), Dallas, where he began writing dramas and in 1947 and 1948 received the Eugene O'Neill Award for original one-act plays. Following graduation he directed in regional theatres before settling in Los Angeles. There he acted in bit parts on television and wrote in his spare time. In 1956 he sold his first script to "Dick Powell's Zane Grey Theater," and in 1960 he was named the show's producer. Two years later he created and produced his first series, "The Lloyd Bridges Show," which lasted only one season. In 1963, however, he had his first hit with "Burke's Law" (1963–66), a popular detective series featuring plush settings, beautiful women, and guest appearances by Hollywood stars, elements that became Spelling's trademark. In 1967 he formed a production company with actor Danny Thomas, and the following year "Mod Squad" (1968–73), a police drama that appealed to youths, debuted and was a huge success.

Spelling became partners with Leonard Goldberg in 1972, and the duo had a parade of hits, most notably "Charlie's Angels" (1976–81), a crime series that centred on three attractive female private detectives. Though critics charged that it was exploitive, the show was popular with viewers—in the mid-1990s it could still be found in syndication. The pair also created "Family" (1976–80), which was a departure from the action-packed and sometimes violent plots that characterized many of Spelling's earlier shows. The domestic drama, noted for its realism, won four Emmy awards. In 1977 Aaron Spelling Productions (later Spelling Entertainment Group) was formed. The company's first show, "The Love Boat" (1977–86), became one of the longest-running prime-time network series. Other Spelling programs included "Starsky and Hutch" (1975–79), "Fantasy Island" (1978–84), and "Dynasty" (1981–89). Spelling, whose estimated wealth was over $250 million, also produced numerous motion pictures and made-for-television movies.

(AMY TIKKANEN)

Stott Despoja, Natasha

Though young members of Parliament were rare in Australia and young women members were even rarer, in 1996 Natasha Stott Despoja became the youngest woman ever elected to sit in the Senate. The 27-year-old Democrat, who represented South Australia, served as a role model and torchbearer for a generation that usually lacked political representation.

She entered Parliament by filling a vacancy in November 1995 and was elected to office in her own right on March 2, 1996, to a term due to expire in June 2002. Her party responsibilities were to oversee employment and training, higher education, youth affairs, immigration and multicultural affairs, and science and technology. This daunting task reflected the party's small size rather than her experience, which had been limited to working as a shop assistant, student association president, and a researcher for Australian Democrat party leaders.

Stott Despoja aimed to change not only the average age in Parliament (which was nearly 50) but its gender. "It's a men's club," she quipped. "I always joke about the fact that the Parliament House flagpole is the largest in the southern hemisphere, so size does matter in Parliament."

A proud representative of Generation X, Stott Despoja sported Doc Marten shoes and bemoaned the fact that the chief preoccupation of the press was her footwear—not her ideas. By the end of her term in office, she wanted to see more of her generation involved in politics. Indeed, following her appointment, membership in her party rose sharply in the 18–24 age group. "We want a new generation of Democrats and Democrat politicians," said Stott Despoja, but she was also prepared to face difficulties in persuading the young and disillusioned to take an interest in the political process.

Stott Despoja was born on Sept. 9, 1969, in Adelaide, S.Aus. She attended Canberra Boys Grammar School in a failed coeducational experiment and graduated (1991) with a B.A. degree from the University of Adelaide, where she majored in politics and history. Her mother, a former literary editor, was Stott Despoja's enduring role model, and she gave her daughter insight into the many problems that single mothers had in the Australian community.   (A.R.G. GRIFFITHS)

Street, Picabo
Carving a name for herself on the international slopes of professional skiing, a 25-year-old American with the singular moniker Picabo Street entered the 1996–97 World Cup season as the two-time defending champion of the downhill event. Noted for her natural talent and easygoing charm, Street became one of the leading figures of the sport, both in the U.S. and abroad. She first skied to stardom with silver medals in the combined event (slalom and downhill) at the 1993 world Alpine ski championships in Morioka-Shizukuishi, Japan, and in the downhill at the 1994 Winter Olympic Games in Lillehammer, Norway. During an extraordinary 1994–95 season, Street captured six downhill victories in nine races on the World Cup circuit to become the first non-European ever to win the downhill title. She repeated as the World Cup downhill champion in 1995–96, adding three more circuit victories, as well as first- (downhill) and third-place (supergiant slalom) finishes at the world Alpine ski championships in Sierra Nevada, Spain. She capped the season in March with two gold medals (downhill and supergiant slalom) at the U.S. Alpine ski championships in Sugarloaf, Maine. In December, however, she suffered a knee injury that required surgery and put her out of competition for the remainder of the 1996–97 season.

Street was born on April 3, 1971, in Triumph, a small town in Blaine county, Idaho. The sole girl among eight children, she was called Baby Girl for three years by her counterculture parents before they settled on Picabo (pronounced "peek-a-boo"), naming her after a nearby town known by the American Indian word for "shining waters." Also in the county was Sun Valley, the ski resort where Street at age six first began racing. She developed into a junior champion at the regional and then national level, making the world junior championship team twice, in 1989 and 1990.

Taking herself to the next level of competition proved to be an uphill battle for the downhill speedster. She was asked to leave the U.S. ski team during the summer of 1990 for poor conditioning and attitude. Committing herself anew, she rejoined the national squad on the B-team and in 1993 posted several high finishes in World Cup races, captured a silver medal at the world Alpine ski championships, and placed first (supergiant slalom), second (combined), and third (downhill) at the U.S. Alpine ski championships. For her efforts she was rewarded with a position

on the U.S. A-team and was named *Ski Racing* U.S. Alpine Skier of the Year—an honour she revisited in 1995 and 1996; in 1995 she also won *Ski Racing* International Alpine Skier of the Year.
    (TOM MICHAEL)

Tan, Lucio
In 1996 reclusive Philippine businessman Lucio Tan found himself all but untouched by an ongoing government probe into the legitimacy of his operations. Tan, who was accused of tax evasion and other unsavoury business practices that dated back to his association with Pres. Ferdinand Marcos during the 1960s and '70s, avoided conviction on any of the charges. As owner of the formerly state-owned Philippine Airlines Inc. (PAL) and with an estimated net worth between $1 billion and $8 billion, Tan was considered the richest man in the Philippines. The government, however, wanted to know just how much of his wealth had been obtained legally, although disclosure seemed unlikely at year's end.

Tan was born Tan Eng Tsai on July 17, 1933, in Amoy, Fujian province, China, the oldest of eight children. He earned a degree in chemical engineering from Far Eastern University, Manila. In one of his early jobs, he worked as a janitor in a cigarette factory before his promotion to tobacco "cook," regulating the product mix. In 1966 Tan started his own tobacco company, which by 1996 commanded nearly 75% of the Philippine market.

Tan and Marcos reportedly met in the early 1960s when Marcos was a senator. By 1972 their friendship had strengthened, and Marcos had already served seven years as president when he declared martial law and served as the catalyst for what would become three of the country's largest businesses. When Tan's Fortune Tobacco Corp. allegedly received tax breaks, it was able to beat its rivals. In 1977 Tan acquired the insolvent General Bank and Trust (later renamed Allied Banking Corp.) for a pittance, and three years later he launched Asia Brewery Inc. when Marcos rescinded a measure prohibiting the establishment of new beer companies. After the fall of Marcos, the administrations of Corazon Aquino and Fidel Ramos tried to prove that Tan's companies had been secretly owned by Marcos and therefore should be confiscated. In addition, it was alleged that Tan had not been duly assessed his fair share of taxes on his holdings. In August 1996, however, a Supreme Court ruling stated in essence that the tax bureau had prosecuted the matter in an improper manner.

In 1992, unbeknownst to the Aquino government, Tan had secretly financed the winning bid that secured the purchase of the newly privatized PAL. In January 1995 he became chairman of the airline, and in September 1996 he won a lengthy battle with PAL's corporate structure to take ruling control of the carrier. Two days later the House of Representatives approved a bill that favoured tax breaks for his beer and cigarette concerns. At year's end it appeared that Tan would move forward unscathed and could spend time grooming his three sons for business.
    (ANTHONY L. GREEN)

Tendulkar, Sachin Ramesh
India was long known for its habit of producing young cricket players who rose fast and faded with equal speed. It was a measure of the talent of Sachin Tendulkar, who was made captain of his country's team at the age of just 23 in August 1996, that when he first burst onto the cricket scene, no one had any doubt he was the genuine article: a batsman of good temperament, sound technique, and true elegance. In size, if not quite build, the 1.68-m (5-ft 6-in) Tendulkar was a natural successor to the great Sunil Gavaskar, the diminutive opener whose courage and powers of concentration made him the most prolific run-scorer in Indian and, for a time, all Test (competition involving teams that represent countries) history. In 1996 Tendulkar already had 10 centuries to his name, and his average of 54.92 put him in the very highest class of Test batsmen.

Sachin Tendulkar

Like Gavaskar, Tendulkar came from Bombay (Mumbai), where he was born on April 24, 1973, the youngest of four children. His father was a teacher of Marathi (his native tongue), and his mother worked for a life insurance firm. He was given his first bat when he was 11 and as a 14-year-old used it to score 329 out of a world-record stand of 664 in a school match. A year later he scored a century on his first-class debut for Bombay, and at 16 years 205 days, he became India's youngest Test cricketer, making his debut against Pakistan in Karachi in November 1989.

Tendulkar quickly established himself as the darling of Indian cricket. In 1995 he signed a contract with a satellite television company for a reputed $7.5 million over five years, an enormous sum for a cricketer. In early 1996 Star TV wanted to televise his marriage to an Anglo-Indian doctor, but the couple rejected the offer and barred all photographers until the reception the following day, a measure of Tendulkar's lack of ease when in the public eye.

Although he shied away from extravagant comparisons, Tendulkar was often likened to Sir Don Bradman of Australia, the greatest batsman of all, in his single-minded dedication to scoring runs and the certainty of his strokeplay off both front and back foot. In Australia, when he was 18, Tendulkar scored two centuries (148 in Sydney and 114 in Perth), both in losing causes. In Nagpur, India, in 1994, he scored 179 against the West Indies, hitting bowler Courtney Walsh for six to bring up his hundred.

Despite Tendulkar's own efforts (top run scorer, with 523 runs) in the 1996 World Cup, India was headed for defeat when it defaulted to Sri Lanka in the semifinal. The Indian side's loss hastened his almost inevitable elevation to the captaincy. Tendulkar's ultimate aim was to score 40 Test centuries and 15,000 Test runs. Few doubted that he had the ability to achieve both and finally eclipse Gavaskar.   (ANDREW LONGMORE)

Vasella, Daniel Lucius
Early in 1996 Daniel Vasella, chief executive officer (CEO) of Sandoz Pharma Ltd., was named president of the newly formed Swiss pharmaceutical giant Novartis, which was established as a result of the largest merger ever in the pharmaceutical industry. The combined company would unite industry giants Sandoz Ltd. and Ciba-Geigy Ltd., two Swiss-based health care groups, in a $29 billion merger that would make Novartis a titan second in size and influence only to Britain's Glaxo Wellcome, the world's largest pharmaceutical concern. Vasella predicted that the merger "will considerably strengthen our competitiveness while freeing up resources for further growth." He would assume a joint leadership role with Novartis chairman Alex Krauer, who had served as chairman of Ciba-Geigy. The two would be

responsible for overseeing the company's overall development and direction, and Vasella would also serve as head of the company's executive committee.

Vasella was born in 1953 and received a M.D. in 1980 from the University of Bern, Switz. For the next four years, he held residencies at various hospitals in Bern and Zürich before serving (1984–88) as the attendant physician at C.L. Lory Haus at the University Hospital in Bern. He left medicine in 1988 and joined the marketing department of Sandoz Pharmaceuticals Corp. in New Jersey, the U.S.-based division of Sandoz Pharma. Vasella moved up quickly in the marketing and sales department to become department head of special product marketing. He was appointed assistant vice president in 1992 and became head of the corporate marketing department the following year. In 1994 Vasella returned to Switzerland and accepted the position of head of the worldwide development office at Sandoz's headquarters in Basel. He was named CEO of Sandoz the following year. As president of Novartis, which concentrated on research and development in the three main areas of health care, agriculture, and nutrition, Vasella would also be responsible for coordinating the integration of the Sandoz and Ciba-Geigy product lines.

Vasella, who was awaiting final U.S. Federal Trade Commission approval for completion of the merger, was nonetheless optimistic about Novartis's future, saying, "We will now move forward to build our company based on a common spirit of entrepreneurial energy, teamwork, and enthusiasms for our new future."

(AMANDA E. FULLER)

Wallace, David Foster
Heralded by many critics as a literary virtuoso at the age of 34, David Foster Wallace published (1996) his second novel—the 1,079-page Lannan Prize winner *Infinite Jest*—to extraordinary fanfare and exceptional sales. In one of the most multilayered plots since Thomas Pynchon's *Gravity's Rainbow,* Wallace introduced an unforgettable cast of postmodern characters that included recovering alcoholics, foreign statesmen, residents of a halfway house, and high-school tennis stars. Presenting a futuristic vision of a world in which advertising had become omnipresent, *Infinite Jest* takes place during calendar years that have been named by companies that purchased the rights to promote their products, most notably the Year of Dairy Products from the American Heartland and the Year of the Depend Adult Undergarment. With his witty writing style and uniquely poetic grace, Wallace won over many readers who delighted in his accurate satirizations of current popular culture.

Born on Feb. 21, 1962, in Ithaca, N.Y., Wallace, the son of a philosophy professor and an English teacher, received a B.A. from Amherst (Mass.) College. He was completing a master's degree in creative writing at the University of Arizona when his highly regarded debut novel, *The Broom of the System* (1987), was published. His first collection of short stories, *Girl with Curious Hair* (1989), was said to display a full range of his talents as he "renders the incredible comprehensible, the bizarre normal, the absurd hilarious, the familiar strange." In 1990 he published the nonfiction work *Signifying Rappers: Rap and Race in the Urban Present.* A professor at Illinois State University, Wallace, who was hired to teach creative writing, said he preferred teaching freshman literature because he was able to show students who did not like to read that "reading literary stuff is sometimes hard work, but it's sometimes worth it and . . . can give you things that you can't get otherwise."

Often compared to such postmodernist writers as William S. Burroughs, Don DeLillo, and John Barth, Wallace was the neophyte in a tradition that had produced some of the U.S.'s most bizarre and outspoken literary voices. Though the author admitted that he was unable to do much reading during the four years he spent researching and writing the originally 1,700-page *Infinite Jest,* he proclaimed himself to be "severely overeducated" and inspired by such writers as John Donne, Cormac McCarthy, Cynthia Ozick, and Tobias Wolff.

Wallace was one writer who was true to his philosophy, proving time and again that readers could be challenged and enlightened—but most of all entertained.

(SARA BRANT)

Weah, George Oppong
The gulf between working as a telephone technician in poverty-stricken Liberia and the luxurious lifestyle of an Italian association football (soccer) star is enormous, but striker George Weah of AC Milan appeared to have bridged it quite successfully. In 1995–96 he achieved the triple honour of being elected European, African, and World Footballer of the Year, the first player ever to achieve such a treble. In October 1996 he was named Commonwealth Sportsman of the Year. Two months later he received a six-game ban for head butting an opponent, an unusual event for a player known for his good conduct on the field.

Weah was born in Monrovia on Oct. 1, 1966, and left school at age 15 to work as a phone technician. He played for several minor teams in Liberia before joining the country's most popular team, Invincible Eleven, in 1986. There he established himself as a centre-forward with goal-scoring ability and not a little technique and was noted for his clever footwork. Standing 1.84 m (6 ft) and weighing 76 kg (168 lb), Weah was the ideal build for a central spearhead. After a spell with Africa Sports Abidjan in Côte d'Ivoire, the Cameroon club Tonnerre Yaoundé signed him to a three-year contract.

Within six months AS Monaco made a tempting offer, and Weah signed with that French League team for five years. In four seasons he scored 47 goals, winning a French Cup medal in 1991 and European Cup-Winners' Cup runners-up honours in 1992. Weah was then transferred to Paris St. Germain for £3 million. During his second season with it, the club won the French championship. Sections of the club's supporters, however, were critical of him; there were racist chants directed his way; and he had differences with the coaching staff. In the summer of 1995, AC Milan paid £6.5 million for Weah, and in his first season there, it won the Italian League championship. At the time of his triple award, he had scored 131 goals in 310 competitive games in France and Italy.

Although Liberia did manage to reach the final stages of the African Nations Cup in 1996, it was not a success for Weah, who was accused of being more interested in meeting South African Pres. Nelson Mandela than in playing for his country.

Weah, a deeply religious Muslim, was generous with his money back home. He personally paid the £5,000 debts owed by the Liberia Football Association to both the African Confederation and the world governing body. He also negotiated a special sponsorship deal for the Lone Stars (Liberia's national team) and financed a junior team. A national hero at home, he had four postage stamps issued in tribute to him.

(JACK ROLLIN)

Weston, Randy
At 205 cm (6 ft 8 in) tall, with hands so big that they covered an octave and a half on the piano, Randy Weston was a hard man to overlook. Even more imposing was his body of work—compositions and recordings as bandleader as well as soloist—in a career that spanned nearly half a century. Nevertheless, during the 1950s and '60s the waves of fashion had bypassed maverick pianists like Weston. With the popularity of "world music," especially African popular music, however, Weston arrived at the height of his career.

"African Rhythms" was what Randy Weston called the music he played: "This music that you call jazz, or blues or spirituals all comes out of African civilization. We have a tree, at the root of which is African music with its infinite variety, and we have our masters—Art Tatum, Duke Ellington, Charlie Parker, John Coltrane—and from this trunk we spread out into branches." While Weston was unmistakably a jazz pianist, African scenes and themes inspired many of the pieces he composed. Characteristically, in his 1996 compact disc (CD) *Saga,* one of his finest, the throb of African percussion alternately provided musical interplay and undercurrent.

Africa, in fact, had engrossed Weston for most of his life. Randolph Edward Weston was born April 6, 1926, in Brooklyn, N.Y., where he grew up; his father, of Jamaican ancestry, read books on African culture and took Randy to hear not only the jazz greats but also West Indian popular music. Weston studied piano, but he was in such awe of those musical masters that he did not begin his professional career until he was 23, a relatively advanced age for a jazz artist. His best-known compositions, "Hi-Fly" and "Little Niles," first appeared on his handful of recordings from the 1950s. The opportunity of a lifetime came in 1961: to play at a festival in Nigeria. After two more African journeys, Weston settled in Tangier, Mor., where he owned a nightclub in 1968–72.

An outstanding concert of unaccompanied Weston piano solos at the 1974 Montreux (Switz.) Jazz Festival began his latter-day climb to fame. He returned to the solo piano medium for some of his finest work, including interpretations of Thelonious Monk, Ellington, and his own songs on three 1989 CDs. Both in solo and with his bands, he advanced Monk's and especially Ellington's concepts of freely spaced phrasing, dynamics, spontaneous arranging, and incorporation of African-derived rhythms. The result was a vividly original music rich in harmonic flavour, rhythmic subtlety, and drama. "From Duke I learned commitment, from Monk perseverance," said Weston.

(JOHN LITWEILER)

Wilson, Robert
In one sense the opening in June 1996 of Robert Wilson's *Time Rocker* in the Thalia Theatre in Hamburg, Ger., marked the culmination of the controversial theatre director's enormously successful career in Europe. In another sense, however, it marked his growing acclaim in his homeland. For more than two decades, Wilson had been one of the most original and sought-after artists in Europe, but he was little known in his native United States.

The 1995 premiere of his *Hamlet: A Monologue* at the Alley Theatre in Houston, Texas, was a major homecoming event for Wilson. Working as writer, director, designer, and solo performer, he presented Hamlet at the moment of his death flashing backward through 15 of the original's scenes. He danced awkwardly, threw childish tantrums, growled, and was haunted by props that eerily evoked absent characters. Wilson followed the success of Hamlet with a production of *Snow on the Mesa,* a dance work that paid tribute to Martha Graham at the Kennedy Center in Washington, D.C., and a staging of Gertrude Stein and Virgil Thomson's 1934 opera *Four Saints in Three Acts* for the Houston Grand Opera.

Back in Europe *Time Rocker* was the final production in a trio of works for the Thalia company that began with *The Black Rider* (1990) and continued with *Alice* (1992), a retelling of the Lewis Carroll books, both with music by Tom Waits. Like most of his recent works, *Time Rocker* had much to do with Wilson's minimalist decor and lighting and less to do with music (by Lou Reed) or dialogue (by Darryl Pinckney). The Hamburg trilogy, dubbed "art musicals," offered an alternative experience to the typical Broadway production, which Wilson believed was becoming more and more like television, with a programmed audience reaction every few seconds.

Wilson was born Oct. 4, 1941, in Waco, Texas. He studied business administration at the University of Texas at Austin, but he dropped out in 1962 to move to New York City to pursue his interest in the arts. After earning a degree in interior design from the Pratt Institute in Brooklyn in 1966, he started his own experimental theatre group, the Byrd Hoffman School of Byrds, which operated out of his loft in the SoHo neighbourhood of Manhattan. Wilson quickly gained recognition among New York's art elites. His productions were praised for their innovative use of lighting, space, and sound and their provocative contradictions of time and place. By the early 1970s he was staging works throughout Europe.

Wilson's range was vast; he produced Japanese No plays, standard operas such as *The Magic Flute* and *Salome,* and 12-hour-long theatre pieces.

Robert Wilson

Among his best-known works were *The Life and Times of Joseph Stalin* (1974), *Einstein on the Beach* (1976), on which he collaborated with composer Philip Glass, *Death, Destruction, and Detroit* (1979), and *The Civil Wars* (1983). Wilson also received critical attention as an installation artist and as a furniture designer. (JAMES HENNELLY)

Yang Lan

In 1996 one of China's top television journalists, Yang Lan returned to her country after a two-year absence, during which she pursued graduate studies at Columbia University, New York City. Prior to her departure, Yang was cohost of the weekly show "Zheng Da Variety Show," having been chosen from among 1,000 applicants. This was China's top-rated talk show from 1990 to 1993. Yang focused attention on such issues as the economic tensions among families in China's growing middle class, avoiding the sensationalism and steamy revelations that she said characterized U.S. talk shows. She did not seem to chafe under the programmatic control of her government employers, Chinese state television, and she told *Newsweek* magazine, "In my personal view, certain censorship is important, since nations have different social and cultural backgrounds. I certainly have enough room to move around in my programs." In 1993 she was awarded China's Golden Microphone Award for television hosts.

The daughter of two professors, Yang was born on March 31, 1968, in Beijing. In 1990 she received her bachelor's degree in English language from Beijing Foreign Studies University. That same year she won the open audition at China Central Television—China's only nationwide television network—and with it her position with the "Zheng Da Variety Show." Her efforts landed her a place among the country's most popular celebrities, and she served as master of ceremonies on many occasions, including the opening ceremony of the United Nations Fourth World Conference on Women in Beijing in 1995. In 1996 Yang was awarded a master's degree in international affairs from Columbia University. She had attracted so little attention to herself that her classmates had no idea of her high profile in the Chinese media.

Upon her return to China, Yang launched a new documentary show called "Yang Lan's Horizon." It examined the cultural ties between the U.S. and China, exploring topics such as the parallels between Broadway musicals and Peking opera. Her new program already had approximately 200 million viewers. Yang was concerned with the need to improve Chinese television by having it develop more of its own shows and rely less on imports from the U.S. While she believed Chinese television could produce good shows to replace the American ones, however, her hope was to "promote the bond between the two countries, instead of breaking them up." (AMANDA E. FULLER)

Zeroual, Liamine

As the violent struggle between Islamic fundamentalists and Algeria's military-dominated government continued in 1996, Pres. Liamine Zeroual unveiled proposals for constitutional reforms aimed at resolving his country's severe domestic crisis. The proposed reforms, which Zeroual outlined publicly in May, included prohibiting displays of militancy by Algeria's political parties, establishing a senate and supreme court, and promoting a free-market economy. The proposals marked the culmination of months of effort by Zeroual to lay the groundwork for an end to the Islamic insurgency, in which more than 40,000 Algerians had died since 1992.

Zeroual was born on July 3, 1941, in the military quarter of Batna, Alg. He joined the Algerian army at the age of 16 and fought against France during Algeria's war of independence. In 1965 Zeroual went to the U.S.S.R. for military training, after which he was posted to Sidi bel Abbes, Alg., to head an artillery unit. During the 1970s and '80s, he rose steadily through the army's ranks, commanding three of Algeria's key military regions before being named (1989) land forces chief.

That same year Zeroual resigned from the army after a dispute with Pres. Chadli Bendjedid. He later served (1990–91) as ambassador to Romania, and he was named Algeria's defense minister in 1993. Following his appointment as president by the High Security Council in January 1994, Zeroual attempted on two occasions to broker peace negotiations with the Islamic Salvation Front (FIS), Algeria's main opposition party. Although both attempts ended in failure, Zeroual continued to express an openness to future negotiations on the condition that the FIS would renounce the use of violence.

With his easy victory in Algeria's first multicandidate presidential elections on Nov. 16, 1995, Zeroual legitimized his status as Algeria's head of state. Stressing peace and reconciliation as the twin themes of his presidency, he declared as his goal a broad-based government in which both secular and Islamic parties would work together toward implementing democracy. Although the FIS rejected Zeroual's blueprint for constitutional reform, most of Algeria's legal opposition parties voted in favour of the reforms at a national conference held in September 1996. The new constitution was approved by referendum in November. As part of a pact aimed at ending Algeria's crisis and bloodshed, Zeroual also promised legislative elections in 1997. (SHERMAN HOLLAR)

Zyuganov, Gennady Andreyevich

Of the independent nations that emerged after the dissolution of the Soviet Union, Russia had appeared to be among the most eager to embrace the free market. For many, however, the promises of a capitalist society never materialized. Economic power remained concentrated in the hands of a few, violent crime increased, and ethnic groups throughout Russia embarked on campaigns, sometimes violent, to win autonomy or independence. Many in Russia longed for a return to the days of communism, when a strong central regime guaranteed personal and economic security. In the 1995 parliamentary elections, the newly revitalized Communist Party of the Russian Federation made a strong showing, and its leader, Gennady Zyuganov, emerged as a serious challenger to Pres. Boris Yeltsin.

Zyuganov was born on June 26, 1944, in Mymrino, a farming village in Oryol oblast, south of Moscow. His parents were schoolteachers, and Zyuganov followed in their footsteps after graduating from the state teacher-training school. He joined the Communist Party of the Soviet Union (CPSU) in the early 1960s while stationed in East Germany with the army. He rose through the ranks of the CPSU in Oryol oblast, becoming the head of the Komsomol and the regional chief for ideology and propaganda. In 1983 he was given a high-level position in Moscow in the CPSU propaganda department, a hotbed of opposition to reform. He emerged as a leading critic of Mikhail Gorbachev's efforts at reform and wrote several influential papers in the early 1990s attacking Gorbachev and calling for a return to the authoritarian ways of the preglasnost era.

Zyuganov entered the 1996 presidential election as the standard-bearer of the Russian Communist Party. He attacked the infiltration of Western ideals into Russian society and portrayed Russia as a natural empire that had been dismantled from within by traitors and from without by capitalists who sought the dissolution of Russia's authority in order to exploit its resources. These themes were central to his book *Derzhava* (1994; "Great Power").

In the election on June 16, Zyuganov finished second, with 32% of the vote, trailing only Yeltsin, who captured 35%. Zyuganov prepared for the July 3 runoff election with confidence. He ran a campaign focusing on the president's ill health and pledged to return Russia to its days of glory. Yeltsin, however, gained most from the elimination of the many smaller parties and the support of Aleksandr Lebed (*q.v.*) and won the two-man showdown comfortably. Political observers suggested that Zyuganov was still a force to be reckoned with in Russian politics and that his next task would be to remake the communists into a strong opposition. (JOHN H. MATHEWS)

Gennady Zyuganov

OBITUARIES

Abu Seif, Salah, Egyptian filmmaker whose movies, noted for their realism and progressive political messages, drew criticism from Muslim religious leaders and the Egyptian government; several of his films were banned (b. May 10, 1915—d. June 23, 1996).

Agnew, Spiro Theodore, U.S. politician (b. Nov. 9, 1918, Baltimore, Md.—d. Sept. 17, 1996, Berlin, Md.), served as vice president (1969–73) under Pres. Richard Nixon until a tax-evasion scandal forced his resignation. After earning a law degree from the University of Baltimore, Agnew practiced until he was elected to public office in 1962. He served as executive of Baltimore county before becoming governor of Maryland in 1967. Agnew gained Nixon's attention when he chastised African-American leaders during riots in Baltimore following the assassination of the Rev. Martin Luther King, Jr., accusing them of remaining silent while militants stirred up the crowds. Although he was virtually unknown to the public when Nixon chose him as his running mate in the 1968 election campaign, Agnew's colourful attacks on the media ("nattering nabobs of negativism") and antiwar demonstrators ("pusillanimous pussyfooters") won him national recognition. Shortly after he took office for his second term as vice president, however, a Baltimore grand jury investigated him (1973) on charges of extortion, bribery, and income-tax violations dating back to his tenure as governor. He resigned from office—only the second U.S. vice president to do so and the first because of legal difficulties—and pleaded nolo contendere to one count of income-tax evasion. He was fined and sentenced to unsupervised probation. After being disbarred (1974) by the state of Maryland, he turned to private business and became a consultant to foreign business concerns.

Ai Qing (JIANG HAICHENG), Chinese poet (b. March 27, 1910, Jinhua, Zhejiang province, China—d. May 5, 1996, Beijing, China), created works that at their best were simple and powerful while at their worst were marred by propagandistic intent. The son of a wealthy landowner, Jiang lived the first five years of his life with an impoverished wet nurse. From 1928 to 1932 he studied in Paris, where he gained an appreciation for Western literature. Upon his return to China, he was imprisoned for his radical political associations, and while in jail he wrote a poem about his wet nurse that established his popularity. After his release some three years later, he joined Mao Zedong and dedicated his poetry to the communist cause. He published more than 30 volumes of chiefly nationalistic, folk-oriented verse and served in many cultural offices, but in 1957 he was officially censured. He remained silent for 21

Ai Qing

Spiro Agnew

years, interned in labour camps in Heilongjiang and Xinjiang provinces. *Selected Poems of Ai Qing* was published in 1982.

Ake, Claude, Nigerian political scientist and activist who was an expert on African politics and economics, founded and directed the Centre for Advanced Social Science, Port Harcourt, and served as a visiting professor at Yale University; in 1995 he resigned from a Shell Oil commission to protest the execution of activist Ken Saro-Wiwa and eight others (b. Feb. 18, 1939—d. Nov. 7, 1996).

Albrecht (PRINCE ALBERT LUITPOLD FERDINAND MICHAEL), DUKE OF BAVARIA, German head of the more than 800-year-old House of Wittelsbach and pretender to the Bavarian throne; he survived the Nazi concentration camps of World War II and went on to become an internationally known forestry expert (b. May 3, 1905—d. July 8, 1996).

Albright, Josephine Patterson, U.S. journalist who belonged to one of the most prominent American journalism families yet worked for a rival newspaper in Chicago, where she interviewed murderers and covered criminal court proceedings; she also bred horses, ran a dairy and pig farm, and piloted planes that flew the mail (b. Dec. 2, 1913—d. Jan. 15, 1996).

Alea, Tomás Gutiérrez ("TITÓN"), Cuban filmmaker (b. Dec. 11, 1928, Havana, Cuba—d. April 16, 1996, Havana), worked within the stringencies of revolutionary Cuba to satirize bureaucracy. Regarded as the nation's finest director, he stimulated the Cuban film industry as one of the leaders of the Instituto Cubano del Arte e Industria Cinematográficos, which was founded in 1959 when Cuba adopted socialism. His masterwork, *Memorias del subdesarrollo* (1968; *Memories of Underdevelopment*), is a sophisticated study of an intellectual who is searching for his place in revolutionary Cuba. His most popular piece—*Fresa y chocolate* (1993; *Strawberry and Chocolate*)—about a homosexual man living in a macho society, was feted at international film festivals and became the first Cuban motion picture to be nominated for an Academy Award. Alea graduated with a degree in law from the University of Havana before studying (1951–53) at the Centro Sperimentale film school in Rome, which at the time was awash in the Neorealist influences of Roberto Rossellini and Luis Buñuel. In his first full-length feature, *Historias de la revolución* (1960; *Stories of the Revolution*), Alea was in-

fluenced by Rossellini. Later he borrowed from Buñuel in such films as *La última cena* (1976; *The Last Supper*) and *Los sobrevivientes* (1978; *The Survivors*). These and other pieces—such as *La muerte de un burócrata* (1966; *Death of a Bureaucrat*)—made sharp use of humour to probe the prevailing bourgeois mentality. With cancer encroaching, he invited Juan Carlos Tabío to co-direct his last two films—*Fresa y chocolate* and *Guantanamera* (1995).

Allen, Mel (MELVIN ALLEN ISRAEL), U.S. sports broadcaster who charmed baseball audiences with his congeniality and catchphrase "How about that!" as head announcer for the New York Yankees professional baseball team (1940–64) and the television program *This Week in Baseball* (1977–95). He was elected to the Baseball Hall of Fame in 1978 (b. Feb. 14, 1913—d. June 16, 1996).

Alton, John (ALDAN JACKO), Hungarian-born U.S. cinematographer who helped create the stark, shadowy look of film noir in the 1940s. He also fostered the development of the Argentine film industry in the 1930s, wrote the esteemed primer *Painting with Light* (1949), and won an Academy Award for shooting the colourful ballet sequence that closes Vincente Minnelli's 1951 musical *An American in Paris* (b. Oct. 5, 1901—d. June 2, 1996).

Ambartsumian, Viktor Amazaspovich, Armenian astrophysicist (b. Sept. 18, 1908, Tbilisi, Georgia, Russian Empire—d. Aug. 12, 1996, Yerevan, Armenia), studied the origin and evolution of stellar systems and the processes that contribute to stellar evolution. In 1947 he discovered a new type of star system that surrounds galaxies; it is characterized by loose clusters of young stars that are constantly forming, and he named it a stellar association. He also studied radio signals that originate outside the Milky Way Galaxy and demonstrated that, contrary to accepted theories, the signals are not generated by the collision of star systems but are the result of enormous explosions in the dense centres of galaxies. Ambartsumian showed an early aptitude for mathematics and physics. When he graduated in 1928 from the University of Leningrad (St. Petersburg), he already had 10 published scientific papers to his name. After receiving a doctorate (1931) in astrophysics from Pulkovo Observatory near Leningrad, he served as professor of astrophysics at his alma mater until 1943. During this time he developed various theories concerning the processes of stars, and in 1939 he published an influential work that was translated into English as *Theoretical Astrophysics* in 1958. He moved to Yerevan State University, where he oversaw the construction of the Byurakan Astronomical Observatory on Mt. Aragats and served as its director from 1944 to 1988. Through Ambartsumian's efforts the observatory became an international centre of astronomy. He served as president of the Armenian Academy of Sciences (1947–93), the International Astronomical Union (1961–64), and the International Council of Scientific Unions (1968–72). In 1953 he was elected a full member of the Academy of Sciences of the U.S.S.R. Among the numerous awards he received were two Stalin Prizes and five Orders of Lenin.

Amin, Mohamed, Kenyan news photographer and cameraman whose television reports of the 1984 famine in Ethiopia attracted worldwide attention and prompted a massive outpouring of relief, including the Live Aid concert; his more than 30-year career was ended by the crash of a hijacked Ethiopian airliner off the Comoros (b. Aug. 29, 1943—d. Nov. 23, 1996).

Amsterdam, Morey, U.S. comedian and master of the one-liner who performed in vaudeville and on radio before moving to television, where he portrayed the wisecracking Buddy on "The Dick Van Dyke Show," 1961–66 (b. Dec. 14, 1912?—d. Oct. 28, 1996).

Asaf Ali, Aruna Ganguli, Indian political activist who became prominent during Mohandas Gandhi's Quit India movement against British rule when she managed to sneak past police, hoist the Indian flag publicly in Bombay, and then evade arrest; she went on to become important in the underground and after independence moved between the Congress, Socialist, and Communist parties before returning to the Congress Party and being elected mayor of Delhi. She also published a newspaper, *Patriot,* and a magazine, *Link* (b. July 16, 1909?—d. July 29, 1996).

Atsumi, Kiyoshi (TADOKORO YASUO), Japanese comic actor (b. March 10, 1928, Tokyo, Japan—d. Aug. 4, 1996, Tokyo), portrayed the character Tora-san—the beloved bumbling hero of the 48-episode film series *Otoko wa tsurai yo* (1969–96; "It's Tough Being a Man"), the longest-running cinema series ever. Tora-san (Kuruma Torajiro) is a middle-aged peddler in a frumpy beige suit and hat who, in a typical story line, sells trinkets to passersby; visits his half sister, a candy shop owner in old Tokyo; tours a picturesque provincial town; and, most centrally, unsuccessfully courts a pretty woman. Atsumi infused the role with witty wordplay and a folksy sincerity that struck a chord of nostalgia among moviegoers who remembered a simpler, gentler era. Atsumi grew up in a run-down neighbourhood of Tokyo. While still a child, he left school to work in factories during World War II and then took odd jobs in the theatre. He later established a reputation as a comedian in the city's Asakusa entertainment district. Atsumi first played the role of Tora-san on television in 1968 and made his film debut the following year. Despite their formulaic sentimentality and lack of international appeal, the films were box-office hits in Japan, grossing an average of $10 million each. Until 1988 Tora-san installments were released biannually, in the summer and on New Year's Day. Atsumi made few other films and rarely appeared in public, but when he did, he generally wore his character's trademark garb. In 1980 the Japan Academy Awards honoured Atsumi for his portrayal of the lovable loser.

Aydid, Gen. Muhammad Farah (MUHAMMAD FARAH HASSAN), Somali faction leader (b. c. 1930, Beledweyne, Italian Somaliland—d. Aug. 1, 1996, Mogadishu, Somalia), was the most dominant of the clan leaders at the centre of the civil war that had raged in Somalia since 1991 in spite of UN intervention. In 1995, though his forces controlled only about half of the country, his supporters elected him president of all of Somalia. He remained, however, on the front lines in command of his troops. Aydid adopted an "official"

birthday of Dec. 15, 1934. He was given military training in Italy, and after Somalia became independent (1960), he was promoted to captain. He received further training in the U.S.S.R., and his career advanced. When Muhammad Siad Barre seized power in 1969, Aydid was made chief of staff. Barre mistrusted him, however, and imprisoned him for six years, until 1975. Two years later Aydid's military skills were needed, so he was promoted to brigadier general and given an advisory role in Somalia's war with Ethiopia (1977–78). He continued as a military adviser until Barre, still feeling threatened, sent him to India as ambassador for five years (1984–89). Aydid then went to Italy and led one of the dissident groups plotting the overthrow of Barre. He returned to Somalia in 1991 after Barre had been forced from Mogadishu, the capital, but Ali Mahdi Muhammad, another factional leader, was named interim president. Warfare continued, first against Barre's forces and then between clans struggling for dominance. UN and U.S. troops were dispatched in 1992 to attempt to negotiate a peace agreement and facilitate the distribution of food, but in 1993, after his forces ambushed Pakistani UN troops and killed a number of them, Aydid was declared an outlaw. The attempt to capture him led to many more deaths, and—following publicity that included films of the mutilated bodies of U.S. soldiers being dragged through the streets—troops were withdrawn. Aydid then intensified his campaign against Ali Mahdi. He reportedly died of a heart attack a week after having been wounded in battle.

Ayres, Lew (LEWIS AYER), U.S. actor who memorably portrayed a disillusioned German soldier in the 1930 film *All Quiet on the Western Front* before he was blacklisted for declaring himself a conscientious objector during World War II; he voluntarily served, however, as a medic and chaplain's aide and won three silver stars for gallantry, an action that helped relaunch his career, notably as Dr. Kildare in eight films, 1939–42 (b. Dec. 28, 1908—d. Dec. 30, 1996).

Azikiwe, Nnamdi (BENJAMIN AZIKIWE; "ZIK"), Nigerian political leader (b. Nov. 16, 1904, Zungeru, Nigeria—d. May 11, 1996, Enugu, Nigeria), was a longtime champion of African nationalism and became Nigeria's first president when the country became a republic in 1963. Although he was in office only until 1966, when he was ousted in a coup, he came to be regarded as Nigeria's elder statesman. Azikiwe was educated in the U.S. and taught at Lincoln (Pa.) University before returning to Africa in 1934, first to the Gold Coast (now Ghana), where he worked as a newspaper editor, and then in 1937 to Nigeria. There he founded a chain of newspapers and became active in politics. He wrote columns promoting nationalism, joined the Nigerian Youth Movement, and was (1944) one of the founders of the National Council of Nigeria and the Cameroons. In 1948 Azikiwe became a member of the Nigerian Legislative Council, in 1952 he became a member of the Western House of Assembly, and from 1954 to 1959 he served as premier of the Eastern Region. He became governor-general of the newly independent Nigeria in 1960 and served in that post until he became president. In 1967 when his fellow Igbo (Ibo) attempted to form the independent Republic of Biafra, Azikiwe at first supported them and tried to gain the recognition and help of other countries. By 1969, however, he had concluded that the cause was lost, and he shifted his allegiance to the federal government. Although he was denounced for this move and kept a low profile for a time, he became a leader of the new Nigerian People's Party and ran unsuccessfully for president in 1979 and 1983.

Babu, Abdul Rahman Mohammed, Tanzanian politician who, as left-wing champion of the anticolonial Pan-African movement of the mid-20th century, laid the ideological groundwork for the Zanzibar revolution of January 1964, which led, three months later, to Tanganyika's uniting with Zanzibar to form Tanzania (b. Sept. 22, 1924—d. Aug. 5, 1996).

Badr, Muhammad al-, Yemeni king and imam who came to power in 1962 but was almost immediately overthrown during an Egyptian-backed coup; after his numerous attempts to restore the monarchy failed, he went into exile in the U.K. (b. Feb. 25, 1929—d. Aug. 6, 1996).

Bainbridge, Kenneth, U.S. physicist and director of the Trinity test, the first test explosion of the atomic bomb, which took place in the remote Jornado del Muerto desert in central New Mexico on July 16, 1945; he later served as chairman of the physics department at Harvard University and opposed nuclear weapons testing (b. July 27, 1904—d. July 14, 1996).

Balsam, Martin, U.S. character actor who provided durable support in a wide variety of roles onstage and in such films as *Twelve Angry Men, Psycho, Breakfast at Tiffany's,* and *A Thousand Clowns,* for which he won an Academy Award for best supporting actor (b. Nov. 4, 1919—d. Feb. 13, 1996).

Baltzell, E(dward) Digby, U.S. sociologist who popularized the term *WASP,* an acronym for "white Anglo-Saxon Protestant"; though the term reportedly originated in 1957, not until 1964, when Baltzell used it in the highly influential *The Protestant Establishment: Aristocracy & Caste in America,* did it achieve widespread usage (b. Nov. 14, 1915—d. Aug. 17, 1996).

Bass, Saul, U.S. graphic designer who created a number of corporate logos and won an Academy Award for the documentary short subject *Why Man Creates* but was best known for introducing a new art form with his opening credit sequences for such films as *The Man with the Golden Arm, Anatomy of a Murder, West Side Story,* and *Psycho* (b. May 8, 1921—d. April 25, 1996).

Bazin, Hervé (JEAN-PIERRE-MARIE HERVÉ-BAZIN), French writer (b. April 17, 1911, Angers, France—d. Feb. 17, 1996, near Angers), scandalized the French public with his denunciation of motherhood, the family, and the Roman Catholic Church in his first novel, *Vipère au poing* (1948; *Viper in the Fist,* 1951; U.K. trans., *Grasping the Viper,* 1950). Born into a wealthy bourgeois family, Bazin was consigned to the care of a grandmother, who died when he was 11. He was a difficult child, and when his mother took up her parental duties, neither was happy. Expelled from several schools, Bazin disregarded his parents' expectations and determined to be a writer, eventually taking a degree in literature from the Sorbonne. He had published some slight poetry while in his 20s, but not until the publication of the autobiographical *Vipère au poing*—with its trenchant portrayal of a monstrous woman, based on his own mother—did his name become a household word. He followed this first novel of the Rezeau family with *La Mort du petit cheval* (1950; "The Death of the Little Horse") and *Le Cri de la chouette* (1972; "Screech of the Barn Owl"). His acerbic perceptions also surfaced in *Le Tête contre les murs* (1949; *Head Against the Wall,* 1952), a novel about mental institutions, and in such works as *Qui j'ose aimer* (1956; *A Tribe of Women,* 1958) and *Le Matrimoine* (1967; "The Matrimonk"). For roughly the last two decades, he was president of the Académie Goncourt.

Bell, Quentin Claudian Stephen, British artist, critic, university professor, and writer who chronicled the Bloomsbury group, which was founded by his parents, Clive and Vanessa Bell, and wrote an authoritative two-volume biography of his mother's sister, the novelist Virginia Woolf (b. Aug. 19, 1910—d. Dec. 16, 1996).

Belli, Melvin Mouron, U.S. lawyer (b. July 29, 1907, Sonora, Calif.—d. July 9, 1996, San Francisco, Calif.), was renowned for his flamboyant presentations in court and was dubbed the "King of Torts" because of the large awards he gained for clients involved in personal-injury cases. Belli was educated at the University of California, Berkeley, and at that university's law school,

Boalt Hall, from which he graduated in 1933. He first gained attention in the early 1940s with a number of high-profile cases, including one in which a young woman's leg had been severed by a San Francisco trolley. When the trolley company appealed the original award, Belli made a dramatic presentation to the jury—a package that contained her artificial leg. He won her an award that was even larger than the first judgment and much higher than was customary for a severed limb. Later victories included a $19 million settlement for families of U.S. servicemen killed in a plane crash in Newfoundland and a $32 million judgment against California crematoriums that mishandled human remains; by 1987, Belli estimated, he had won over $350 million for his clients, most of whom were "ordinary" people. He also represented the famous, including Errol Flynn, Mae West, Lana Turner, and Lenny Bruce; in the case that made Belli a celebrity, he defended Jack Ruby after Ruby killed Lee Harvey Oswald (accused of assassinating U.S. Pres. John F. Kennedy). In 1995, however, Belli had to file for bankruptcy when he had difficulties collecting money due from the Dow Corning breast-implant case. Belli was the author or coauthor of dozens of books, some of which were used as textbooks.

Beltrán, Lola (MARÍA LUCIA BELTRÁN ALCAYAGA), Mexican singer (b. 1931?, Sinaloa, Mexico—d. March 24, 1996, Mexico City, Mexico), infused mariachi ballads with such drama, emotion, and style that she came to be known as Lola la Grande, the queen of mariachi. Her regal bearing was enhanced by extravagant costuming and ornate jewels and by the drama with which she clutched her trademark shawl. Beltrán began singing when she was a young child, and in 1953 she moved with her mother to Mexico City in hopes of breaking into show business. While working as a secretary at a radio station, she performed on one of its weekly talent shows. Within a year she was starring in her own show. For more than 40 years, her popularity did not wane. Besides performing for a number of Mexico's presidents and other world leaders, she toured extensively. Beltrán was featured in some 50 musical motion pictures and recorded scores of albums. In many songs, including her signature "Cucurrucucu paloma," which became a classic, her heartfelt expressions of the melancholy despair of love and betrayal left her listeners inspired and moved. Her "Soy infeliz" was the opening theme for Pedro Almodóvar's hit motion picture *Women on the Verge of a Nervous Breakdown* (1988).

Benhadugah, 'Abd al-Hamid, Algerian writer who was considered the father of modern Arabic literature in Algeria; among the concerns he addressed in such novels as *Rih al-janub* (1971; "The Wind from the South") were the limitations that societal tradition imposes on young people as they strive for progress and the struggle of women for emancipation (b. Jan. 9, 1925—d. Oct. 20/21, 1996).

Bentine, Michael, British comedian who was a founding member of "The Goon Show" on BBC radio and went on to such television programs as the children's shows "The Bumblies" and "The Potties" as well as the outrageous "It's a Square World"; he was appointed CBE in 1995 (b. Jan. 26, 1922—d. Nov. 26, 1996).

Berghaus, Ruth, German director and choreographer (b. July 2, 1927, Dresden, Ger.—d. Jan. 25, 1996, Zeuthen, Ger.), developed techniques of body language and movement that she taught and incorporated into her direction of opera and theatre productions for over three decades. Her personal, radical approach inspired both controversy and admiration throughout her career. Berghaus studied dance and choreography in Dresden and in 1951, impressed by a Berliner Ensemble production of Bertolt Brecht's *Mutter Courage und ihre Kinder,* moved to East Berlin. She continued her studies, first with Wolfgang Langhoff and then at the Berliner Ensemble, where she met the composer Paul Dessau, with whom she collaborated until his death in 1979. They were married in 1954. Berghaus gained international attention with her battle scene choreography for the Berliner Ensemble's production of *Coriolanus* (1964), combining acting and dancing in a radical new way. She became head of the company in 1971 and served until 1977. After that, most of her work was in opera direction, regularly with the Deutsche Staatsoper but also for other companies internationally. Her production of Richard Wagner's *The Ring of the Nibelung* tetralogy in Frankfurt in the mid-1980s was a cult event, and the last performance of the series, *Götterdämmerung* (1987), was given a 75-minute standing ovation. Among the last works that Berghaus directed were Rolf Liebermann's *Freedom for Medea* in Hamburg and Johann Strauss's *Die Fledermaus* in Leipzig, both in 1995.

Berman, Pandro Samuel, U.S. motion picture producer whose memorable works included seven of the Fred Astaire–Ginger Rogers musicals, *The Blackboard Jungle,* and such Elizabeth Taylor films as *National Velvet, Father of the Bride,* and *Butterfield 8* (b. March 28, 1905—d. July 13, 1996).

Bernard, Jessie Shirley, U.S. sociologist (b. June 8, 1903, Minneapolis, Minn.—d. Oct. 6, 1996, Washington, D.C.), conducted meticulous research and wrote numerous books that provided insights into women, sex, marriage, and family-community interaction. She was called a founding mother of sociology, and her work was considered to have provided a scholarly foundation for modern feminism. Following her education at the University of Minnesota (B.A., 1923; M.A., 1924), Bernard accompanied her husband, sociologist Luther Lee Bernard, who had been one of her professors, to his various academic posts over the next several years. She received a Ph.D. from Washington University, St. Louis, Mo., in 1935, worked as a social science analyst for the U.S. Bureau of Labor Statistics, and in 1940, at Lindenwood College for Women, St. Charles, Mo., began her teaching career. From 1947 to 1964 she was professor of sociology at Pennsylvania State University. Her early books included *American Family Behavior* (1942), *American Community Behavior* (1949), and *Academic Women* (1964). Following her retirement from Penn State, she

moved to Washington, D.C., and served in such capacities as scholar in residence for the U.S. Commission on Civil Rights—studying sex discrimination—and founding board member of the Center for Women in Policy Studies. Bernard had her first child when she was 39 and her last when she was 47; her husband died six months later. She thus was able to bring the perspective of both wife and single mother to her writings, and she came to realize that she had long been a feminist. Bernard's later works, such as *The Sex Game* (1968), *Women and the Public Interest* (1971), *The Future of Marriage* (1972), *The Future of Motherhood* (1974), and *The Female World* (1981), established the importance of her scholarship to the women's movement.

Bernardin, Joseph Louis Cardinal, U.S. Roman Catholic prelate (b. April 2, 1928, Columbia, S.C.—d. Nov. 14, 1996, Chicago, Ill.), was the highest-ranking figure in the Roman Catholic Church in the U.S. and for some three decades was at the centre of most of its important developments. A moderate and a consensus builder, he was considered a possible successor to Pope John Paul II. Bernardin earned a B.A. (1948) from St. Mary's Seminary, Baltimore, Md., and an M.A. (1952) from the Catholic University of America, Washington, D.C. He was ordained a priest in 1952 and he spent 14 years in Charleston, S.C. He became the youngest bishop in the U.S. when he was appointed auxiliary bishop of Atlanta, Ga., in 1966. Bernardin served (1968–72) as general secretary of the National Conference of Catholic Bishops, guiding the reorganization of the U.S. church following the second Vatican Council, and for the next 10 years was archbishop of Cincinnati, Ohio. In addition, he was president of the national conference from 1974 to 1977. In 1982 Bernardin was named archbishop of Chicago, and he was elevated to cardinal the following year. In 1983 the publication of a U.S. bishops' pastoral letter on nuclear war, "The Challenge of Peace," brought Bernardin to public notice. His guidance as chair of the committee that produced the antinuclear document was illustrative of his ability to find a common ground. In 1987 he guided the formulation of a policy of tolerance concerning educational programs advocating the

Joseph Cardinal Bernardin

use of condoms in AIDS-prevention efforts, and in 1991, after the church had been shaken by scandals involving priests' sexual abuse of minors, he established procedures for investigating and dealing with these incidents. Two years later Bernardin was accused of having sexually abused a young man in the 1970s. He strongly denied the charges, and his accuser recanted four months later. Shortly before his accuser died from AIDS in late 1994, Bernardin met and prayed with him. In June 1995 Bernardin was diagnosed with pancreatic cancer, and though he went into remission after surgery and chemotherapy and radiation treatment, the cancer recurred. Facing death with dignity and serenity, Bernardin extended his ministry to large numbers of cancer patients and the dying. A week before his death, in a letter to the U.S. Supreme Court, he urged that the right to physician-assisted suicide not be recognized. In September 1996 Bernardin was awarded the Presidential Medal of Freedom.

Bernstein, Edward Morris, U.S. economist who, at the Bretton Woods Conference (1944), where a global post-World War II financial strategy was drafted, played an influential role in convincing British economist John Maynard Keynes and others that the U.S. would not enter a postwar depression (b. Dec. 16?, 1904—d. June 9, 1996).

Bhutto, Murtaza, Pakistani political activist who was the rival of his sister, Benazir Bhutto, for the mantle of their father, Zulfikar Ali Bhutto, who was deposed as prime minister in 1977 and executed in 1979 (b. Sept. 18, 1954—d. Sept. 20, 1996).

Blackwell, Ewell ("THE WHIP"), U.S. sidearm fastball pitcher for the Cincinnati Reds baseball team during the 1940s and '50s whose whiplike delivery intimidated batters; he compiled a career record of 82 wins and 78 losses, with a 3.30 earned run average (b. Oct. 23, 1922—d. Oct. 29, 1996).

Bleustein-Blanchet, Marcel, French advertising magnate and entrepreneur who founded France's first advertising agency, Publicis, where he created a number of unforgettable advertising slogans and pioneered the use of radio for publicity purposes; he also founded Le Drugstore, a chain of 24-hour emporiums (b. Aug. 21, 1906—d. April 11, 1996).

Bokassa, Jean-Bédel, African military officer and political leader (b. Feb. 22, 1921, Bobangui, Oubangui-Chari, French Equatorial Africa [now in Central African Republic]—d. Nov. 3, 1996, Bangui, Central African Republic), was president of the Central African Republic (1966–77) and self-styled emperor of the Central African Em-

pire (1977–79). His rule was characterized by brutality and greed. After the assassination of his father, a village chief, and the suicide of his mother, Bokassa was raised by missionaries. In 1939 he joined the French army, and his bravery during the conflict in Indochina led to numerous honours, including the Croix de Guerre and admittance into the Legion of Honour. Bokassa achieved the rank of captain, and in 1961 he left the French armed forces to command the army of the newly independent Central African Republic. In 1966 he overthrew Pres. David Dacko and seized control of the republic. During Bokassa's rule political opponents were often tortured and executed. Moreover, the country's economy, one of the poorest in the world, suffered further strain as Bokassa plundered the uranium and diamond industries to finance his lavish lifestyle. In 1977 he proclaimed himself Emperor Bokassa I in an opulent ceremony modeled upon the coronation of Napoleon I and rumoured to cost $200 million. His reign over the country, renamed the Central African Empire, was short-lived, however. In 1979 his participation in the massacre of 100 schoolchildren who had protested mandatory school uniforms led to a French military coup that reestablished the republic; Dacko was reinstated, and Bokassa was forced into exile. After his return home in 1986, Bokassa was tried and found guilty of murder (he was acquitted on charges of cannibalism). His death sentence, however, was commuted, and Bokassa was released from prison in 1993.

Bombeck, Erma Louise, U.S. humorist (b. Feb. 21, 1927, Dayton, Ohio—d. April 22, 1996, San Francisco, Calif.), turned her views of daily life in the suburbs into satirical newspaper columns and such best-selling books as *I Lost Everything in the Post-Natal Depression* (1973); *The Grass Is Always Greener over the Septic Tank* (1976), which was adapted (1978) into a television film; and *If Life Is a Bowl of Cherries, What Am I Doing in the Pits?* (1978). The self-deprecating humour she employed in accounts of everyday crises of home and family struck a chord of familiarity among readers, who saw their lives mirrored in the situations she described. Bombeck began writing columns when she was in junior high school. She worked at the *Dayton Journal Herald* while she was in school and after graduation (1949) from the University of Dayton. She left the paper in 1953 to start a family, but later, with three children in school, she felt "too old for a paper route, too young for Social Security and too tired for an affair." She persuaded the editor of a suburban weekly to let her produce a column. The success of "At Wit's End" drew the attention of the *Journal Herald*'s editor, who hired her to

Erma Bombeck

write three columns a week. A short time later her columns were syndicated and eventually appeared in more than 900 newspapers. Bombeck also was a contributor to a number of magazines, including *Good Housekeeping, Redbook,* and *McCall's;* created, wrote, and produced a television series, "Maggie" (1981); and appeared (1975–86) on the "Good Morning America" television program. She underwent a mastectomy in 1992, and shortly afterward her kidneys began to fail. She underwent dialysis and was placed on waiting lists for a transplant, but though a donor match was found, she died of complications after the surgery.

Boorda, Jeremy Michael ("MIKE"), U.S. naval commander (b. Nov. 26, 1938, South Bend, Ind.—d. May 16, 1996, Washington, D.C.), joined the military as an enlisted sailor and rose through the ranks to become a four-star admiral (1987) and chief of naval operations (1994–96)—the navy's senior military officer and commander of all its active-duty and reserve personnel. In 1956 Boorda fled his unhappy childhood home by dropping out of high school and falsifying his age in order to enlist. He was educated at Officer Candidate School, Newport, R.I. (1962), and at the University of Rhode Island (B.A., 1971), and he undertook postgraduate study at the Naval War College, Newport. During the Vietnam War he was promoted from ensign to lieutenant to commander, although he did not engage in combat there. From 1991 to 1994 he was based in Naples, where he was in charge of NATO forces in southern Europe. He became involved in the war in Bosnia and Herzegovina and became a proponent of U.S. intervention there. In 1994 he led NATO forces in attacks against Bosnian-Serb fighter planes violating a UN "no-fly" zone and in support of air strikes on Gorazde—the first time in NATO history that its forces had been used in an offensive mission. As chief of naval operations, it fell to him to face the political fallout from several high-profile misconduct scandals, including the 1991 sexual assault incident known as the Tailhook affair. Boorda committed suicide hours after reporters had inquired about two combat-related medals that he had worn until 1995. Following his death, high-ranking navy officials disagreed over whether Boorda, who during the Vietnam War had served aboard a ship traveling in a combat zone, had a right to wear the medals.

Bourassa, Robert, Canadian politician (b. July 14, 1933, Montreal, Que.—d. Oct. 2, 1996, Montreal), as premier of Quebec (1970–76, 1985–93) during a period of escalating tensions between federalists

Jean-Bédel Bokassa

and Quebec separatists, attempted to preserve the province's French culture while maintaining unity with Canada. After earning a law degree from the University of Montreal, Bourassa studied at Harvard University and the University of Oxford. In 1966 he won a seat in Quebec's National Assembly. Although inexperienced and relatively unknown, he was elected leader of the Quebec Liberal Party, led it to victory in the April 1970 elections, and was named premier. In October 1970 a radical Quebec separatist group murdered a Cabinet member and kidnapped the British trade commissioner. Bourassa was harshly criticized for his handling of the crisis; the federal government intervened, suspending civil liberties and sending armed troops to Montreal. Bourassa's economic policy, however, which focused on large-scale development, notably the James Bay hydroelectric project, was popular, and he won reelection in 1973. The following year he signed Bill 22, which made French the official language of the province and limited the use of English. The bill, which increased tensions between federalists and Quebec nationalists, contributed to his defeat in the 1976 elections. Bourassa withdrew from politics. In 1980 his tireless campaigning against a referendum on Quebec independence won favour with the Liberal Party, and in 1983 he was reelected its leader. With the Liberals' victory in 1985, Bourassa was again named premier; he was reelected in 1989. In 1990 a dispute over land claims led to a standoff with Mohawk Indians. Bourassa, who had been diagnosed with skin cancer, delayed medical treatment during the 78-day crisis, which ended peacefully. His health, however, deteriorated, and in 1993 he resigned.

Bourdet, Claude, French human rights activist and journalist who led the French Resistance during World War II and was a prominent figure in the Parisian leftist intelligentsia as cofounder and editor of the political weekly *France-Observateur* (b. Oct. 28, 1909—d. March 20, 1996).

Brancker, Sir John Eustace Theodore, Barbadian politician and lawyer who fought for black rights, particularly suffrage, while a member of the Barbados parliament, 1937–76 (b. Feb. 9, 1909—d. April 25, 1996).

Broccoli, Albert Romolo ("CUBBY"), U.S. film producer (b. April 5, 1909, New York, N.Y.—d. June 27, 1996, Beverly Hills, Calif.), popularized the fictional character James Bond, the charismatic British hero of Ian Fleming's spy novels, by producing 17 internationally successful motion pictures. Broccoli, the son of Italian immigrants, worked for relatives first in the vegetable business and later at a coffin company before moving to California, where he held a succession of odd jobs. He landed an entry-level position at the Hollywood film studio Twentieth Century Fox and worked his way up to the post of assistant director on the film *The Outlaw* (1943). After serving in the U.S. Navy during World War II and working as a Hollywood talent agent, he launched his career as an independent producer in Great Britain in the early 1950s, making a string of money-making adventure films with U.S. émigré Irving Allen. In 1962 he paired with Canadian producer Harry Saltzman to create the first James Bond film, *Dr. No,* for the United Artists studio. The movie, starring Sean Connery, was a box-office hit and prompted Broccoli and Saltzman to produce eight more films together until Saltzman sold out to United Artists. Broccoli, who retained rights to the series, continued to make James Bond films, drafting his daughter and stepson to produce the most recent film, *GoldenEye* (1995).

Brodkey, Harold (AARON ROY WEINTRAUB), U.S. short-story writer and novelist (b. Oct. 25, 1930, Staunton, Ill.—d. Jan. 26, 1996, New York, N.Y.), was a staff writer for *The New Yorker* magazine for 30 years before publishing the novel he had been working on for most of his adult life. His inability to produce the promised novel, coupled with his sinuous, self-reflective style, unabashedly autobiographical oeuvre, and high self-regard, made him a controversial figure in the lit-

erary world. Having lost his mother at 17 months, Brodkey was adopted by cousins whose name he took. His adoptive parents, too, died while he was a boy, events that both traumatized him and informed his art. Brodkey attended Harvard University and soon began publishing short stories. His first collection, *First Love and Other Sorrows* (1957), contained stories of youthful romance and marriage for which he used incidents from his own life. He then began writing the autobiographical novel that occupied him for most of the next 30 years. Titled *The Runaway Soul,* it was finally published in 1991 to mixed reviews. Excerpts from it were published earlier as *Women and Angels* (1985). Wiley Silenowicz, the protagonist of *The Runaway Soul,* is also featured in 12 of the 18 tales in *Stories in an Almost Classical Mode* (1988). Brodkey in 1994 published another novel—*Profane Friendship,* about a homosexual affair in Venice—shortly after his dramatic announcement in the pages of *The New Yorker* that he had AIDS.

Brodsky, Joseph (IOSIP ALEKSANDROVICH BRODSKY), Russian-born U.S. poet and essayist (b. May 24, 1940, Leningrad, U.S.S.R.—d. Jan. 28, 1996, New York, N.Y.), produced powerful, meditative poetry that treats language, exile, and the universal concerns of life, death, and the meaning of existence. He was a leading dissident writer of his generation and was awarded the Nobel Prize for Literature in 1987 for his lyric and elegiac verse. Brodsky quit school at the age of 15, taking a series of menial jobs, reading voraciously, and developing his art. His early poetry had begun to earn him a reputation among the writers of Leningrad when he was arrested in 1964 and sentenced to five years of hard labour for "social parasitism." Under international and domestic pressure, Soviet authorities commuted his sentence after 18 months, but in 1972 he was forcibly exiled from the Soviet Union. He lived thereafter in the U.S., eventually becoming a citizen, and worked as a poet-in-residence and visiting professor at several universities. Brodsky's earlier works include *Stikhotvoreniya i poemy* (1965; "Verses and Poems") and *Ostanovka v pustyne* (1970; "A Halt in the Wasteland"); these and other poems were translated by George L. Kline in *Selected Poems* (1973). His important later works include the poetry collections *A Part of Speech* (1980), *History of the Twentieth Century* (1987), and *To Urania* (1988) and the prose collections *Less than One* (1986) and *On Grief and Reason* (1995). Notable, too, is *Fondamenta degli Incurabili* (1991; *Watermark,* 1991), a quietly intense prose reflection on his relationship with the city of Venice.

Bronfman, Peter Frederick, Canadian business tycoon who, with his brother, Edward, built the country's largest corporate empire after the two were forced by their Montreal-based cousins to sell their blocks of shares in Seagram Co. Ltd.; they also owned (1971–78) the Montreal Canadiens ice hockey team, but in later years Peter focused on community service activities. He died one day before he was to have been presented with the Order of Canada (b. Oct. 2, 1929—d. Nov. 30, 1996).

Brother Adam (KARL KEHRLE), German-born Benedictine monk and bee breeder (b. Aug. 3, 1898, Mittlebiberach, Ger.—d. Sept. 1, 1996, Buckfast, South Devon, Eng.), was regarded as an authority on bees for his revolutionary work, most notably the development of the Buckfast bee, a breed that was considered one of the hardiest and most prolific producers of honey ever bred. At the age of 11 he was sent from his home in Germany to England, where he joined the order of Benedictine monks at St. Mary's Abbey in Buckfast. He began working in the abbey's apiaries in 1915. During World War I Britain was beset by the Isle of Wight epidemic that destroyed nearly every bee colony in the country. Brother Adam began crossbreeding different strains of the insect, attempting to create a breed that was both an abundant producer of honey and resistant to acarine, the disease largely responsible for the devastation. His work led to the creation of the

Buckfast bee. Brother Adam continued to develop different varieties of bees, traveling around the world in search of native strains; at the age of 89 he was carried up Mt. Kilimanjaro in search of an elusive bee. His crossbreeds were so prized that thieves stole two queens from the abbey's apiaries in 1982. He wrote several books on beekeeping that were considered classics in the field and in 1974 was made an OBE. In 1992, much to the outrage of bee breeders worldwide, the monastery's new abbot forced Brother Adam to abandon his research.

Brown, Edmund Gerald ("PAT"), U.S. politician who instituted civil rights laws, public works programs, and consumer-protection measures while serving (1959–67) as two-term governor of California; his son, Jerry, was also a politician (b. April 21, 1905—d. Feb. 16, 1996).

Brown, George Mackay, Scottish writer (b. Oct. 17, 1921, Stromness, Orkney Islands, Scot.—d. April 13, 1996, Kirkwall, Orkney Islands), celebrated Orkneyan life and its ancient rhythms in verse, short stories, and novels. Brown, the son of a Gaelic-speaking Highlander and an Orkney postman, studied at Newbattle Abbey College, near Edinburgh, where Orkney poet Edwin Muir encouraged him to develop his craft. Muir published Brown's first collection of poetry, *The Storm,* in 1954. After graduating from the University of Edinburgh, Brown returned to Stromness, his beloved fishing village. From that vantage point he captured the struggles and simple pleasure of island life and its mythic origins. His collections of poetry include *Loaves and Fishes* (1959) and *The Year of the Whale* (1965). His well-regarded short stories are collected in such volumes as *A Calendar of Love* (1967) and *A Time to Keep* (1969). His novel *Beside the Ocean of Time* (1994) was short-listed for the Booker Prize. He also collaborated with the composer Peter Maxwell Davies on a number of musical works.

Brown, Ronald Harmon, U.S. politician (b. Aug. 1, 1941, Washington, D.C.—d. April 3, 1996, near Dubrovnik, Croatia), was regarded as an adroit deal maker and political strategist who helped resuscitate both the Democratic Party as its national chairman (1989–93) and the U.S. Department of Commerce as its secretary (1993–96). A prominent member of Pres. Bill Clinton's Cabinet, he wielded heavy influence in international trade but was criticized for alleged misdealings in his personal finances. Born into a successful African-American family, Brown was raised in Harlem, New York City, where his father managed the Hotel Theresa, which catered to the black elite. Educated at exclusive preparatory schools, he attended Middlebury (Vt.) College (B.A., 1962) and then served (1963–67) in the army. He returned to New York City, became involved in the civil rights movement, and studied law at St. John's University (J.D., 1970) under Mario M. Cuomo, later governor of New York. Brown worked for the National Urban League (1968–79) before moving to Washington, D.C., where he helped manage the presidential campaigns of Edward Kennedy in 1980 and Jesse Jackson in 1984 and 1988. In 1981 he joined the law firm Patton, Boggs & Blow and the Democratic National Committee. He worked to unite the Democratic Party at its 1988 and 1992 national conventions. As secretary of commerce, Brown traveled widely, securing trading partners in emerging nations. He was on such a trip, to war-torn Croatia, when he was killed in a plane crash along with a score of U.S. corporate executives.

Bufalino, Gesualdo, Italian novelist (b. Nov. 15, 1920, Comiso, Sicily, Italy—d. June 14, 1996, Vittoria, Sicily), saw his literary career blossom after his retirement from teaching in 1976. Bufalino, a talented stylist who wrote rich, sensuous prose, created highly imaginative works that were tinged with bitter realism. He attended Catania and Palermo universities, but service during World War II took him away from Sicily in 1942. Bufalino fought with the partisans in northern Italy and was captured by the Germans. Although he managed to escape, he contracted tuberculosis while in hiding and was sent to a sanatorium after the war. In 1947 Bufalino returned to his beloved native island. There he taught humanities at a teacher-training school in Vittoria, where he also wrote prose and translated French poetry. In 1981, with the aid of novelist Leonardo Sciascia, Bufalino published his first novel, *Diceria dell'untore* (*The Plague Sower*, 1988), which he had started writing in the 1950s. Based upon his experiences in the sanatorium, it was awarded the Campiello Prize. *Museo d'ombre* (1982), a collection of prose pieces, and the novel *Argo il cieco* (1984; *Blind Argus*, 1989) both reflected on life in Sicily. Bufalino displayed the depth of his craftsmanship in *L'uomo invaso* (1986; *The Keeper of Ruins*, 1994), a collection of short stories. His third novel, *Le menzogne della notte* (1988; *Night's Lies*, 1990, reissued as *Lies of the Night*, 1991), related tales exchanged by four prisoners on the eve of their execution and was heralded for its intellectual inventiveness. It won the Strega Prize in 1988. Other novels include a thriller, *Qui pro quo* (1991), and *Calende greche* (1990). He also wrote a play, verse, and essays and translated the works of Charles Baudelaire, Paul-Jean Toulet, and Jean Giraudoux.

Bundy, McGeorge, U.S. government official (b. March 30, 1919, Boston, Mass.—d. Sept. 16, 1996, Boston), as national security adviser (1961–66) to Presidents John F. Kennedy and Lyndon B. Johnson, was one of the principal architects of U.S. foreign policy. He played a major role in the Bay of Pigs invasion, the Cuban missile crisis, the escalation of the Vietnam War, and the intervention in the revolution in the Dominican Republic. Bundy graduated (1940) from Yale University and became (1941) a junior fellow at Harvard University. Because he was very nearsighted, he memorized the eye-test chart so that he could serve in the army during World War II. After the war Bundy collaborated with former secretary of war Henry L. Stimson on the latter's memoirs, worked with Thomas E. Dewey on the 1948 presidential campaign, and in 1949 joined the department of government at Harvard. He became dean of arts and sciences in 1953 and remained in that post until he joined the Kennedy administration. Bundy helped formulate the strategy for escalating the Vietnam War, and even after leaving (1966) government service and becoming president of the Ford Foundation, he continued to support the war. By 1968, however, he had come to believe that the war could not be won.

George Burns

Bundy remained at the Ford Foundation until 1979 and then served (1979–89) as professor of history at New York University. In 1990 he went to the Carnegie Corporation of New York, where he chaired the committee on reducing the danger of nuclear war and, at the time of his death, was scholar-in-residence. Bundy's books include *The Strength of Government* (1968) and *Danger and Survival: Choices About the Bomb in the First Fifty Years* (1988).

Burke, Arleigh Albert, admiral (ret.), U.S. Navy (b. Oct. 19, 1901, near Boulder, Colo.—d. Jan. 1, 1996, Bethesda, Md.), distinguished himself as one of the finest naval commanders in World War II and reinvigorated the U.S. Navy during the Cold War as chief of naval operations (1955–61). In 1923 he graduated from the U.S. Naval Academy, Annapolis, Md., where he pursued postgraduate work in ordnance explosives; he earned a master's degree in chemical engineering from the University of Michigan in 1931. In January 1943 he entered World War II as the commander of a squadron of destroyers in the Solomon Islands. Proving himself to be an able strategist, he led more than 20 military engagements against the Japanese from November 1943 to February 1944, with much success. After the war he helped guide naval policy and, despite briefly falling from political favour in 1949, was elevated to rear admiral in 1950. Rewarded for his skills in leadership and strategic planning, Burke was promoted over 92 more senior admirals to chief of naval operations, serving an unprecedented three terms under Pres. Dwight D. Eisenhower. In this post Burke modernized the navy, adapting it for the Cold War by giving it the versatility to handle smaller, limited missions and by adopting new technology, such as arming nuclear-powered submarines with Polaris missiles. For his efforts, remembered long after his retirement in 1961, he was awarded the National Medal of Freedom in 1977, and in 1991 the navy launched the USS *Arleigh Burke,* a state-of-the-art destroyer named in his honour.

Burns, George (Nathan Birnbaum), U.S. comedian and actor (b. Jan. 20, 1896, New York, N.Y.—d. March 9, 1996, Beverly Hills, Calif.), enjoyed a career in show business that lasted 93 years and encompassed vaudeville, radio, television, nightclubs, and motion pictures. With his gravely voice—between puffs on his ever-present cigar—he delivered wryly humorous comments or launched into old vaudeville ditties. Burns's stage name was the last of those he had used dur-

ing his early performing years, which began in neighbourhood saloons and on the Staten Island ferry when he was seven. He went on to perform on the vaudeville circuit, improvising with whatever type of act booking agents were looking for. In the early 1920s Burns met Gracie Allen and persuaded her to team up with him in a comedy act. At first Burns delivered the gags to Allen's straight lines, but he soon realized that she elicited the laughs and reversed their roles. He also recognized that she was the love of his life, and they married in 1926. They worked their way to top-billing status in vaudeville and in 1929 first performed on radio. "The George Burns and Gracie Allen Show" began in 1932 and ran until 1950, when it moved to television. At the end of each show, Burns said, "Say good night, Gracie," with which Allen would happily comply: "Good night, Gracie." Burns and Allen also appeared in films, notably *The Big Broadcast* films of 1932, 1936, and 1937 and *A Damsel in Distress* (1937). When ill health forced Allen to retire (1958), Burns soloed on the television show for another season before making nightclub and occasional television appearances. After Allen's death (1964), however, his career faltered until he was called upon to replace the late Jack Benny in the motion picture *The Sunshine Boys* (1975); he won the Academy Award for best supporting actor. His later films included *Oh, God!* (1977) and two sequels, *Oh, God! Book II* (1980) and *Oh, God! You Devil* (1984), *Going in Style* (1979), and *Eighteen Again* (1988). Burns also was coauthor of such books as *Gracie: A Love Story* (1988) and *All My Best Friends* (1989). He received a Kennedy Center award for lifetime achievement in 1988. Burns continued making stage appearances and had made plans for several 100th birthday shows, but failing health following a fall in 1994 forced him to cancel.

Burton, Beryl, British cyclist (b. May 12, 1937, Leeds, Eng.—d. May 5, 1996, Yorkshire, Eng.), dominated British women's cycling from the late 1950s to the early '80s. She won more than 100 titles, including several in which she competed against men. She became interested in cycling at the age of 15 after meeting Charlie Burton, an amateur cyclist who became her husband in 1955. She first attracted attention in 1957 when she placed second in the British 100-mi championship. (One mile = 1.61 km.) Later she won the national 25-, 50-, and 100-mi titles, which earned her the British Best All-Rounder (1959), an award for the fastest woman in the three distances. She held that title for 25 years. Burton set numerous national records, including several that still stood in 1996. Though she rarely competed in international races, she won seven world titles—two in the road race and five in the 3,000-m pursuit. At her peak she regularly defeated male competitors, most notably at the 12-hour time trial in 1967. Burton's winning distance of 277.75 mi was 5.75 mi farther than the men's record. She won her last title in 1986 and was riding her bicycle in a training session for an upcoming championship when she died. In 1986 her autobiography, *Personal Best,* was published. Burton was made an MBE in 1964 and an OBE in 1968.

Caesar, Irving, U.S. lyricist for such U.S. standards as "Swanee" and "Tea for Two," one of the most frequently sung and recorded tunes ever written (b. July 4, 1895—d. Dec. 17, 1996).

Cao Yu (Wan Jiabao), Chinese playwright who was the first in his country to incorporate Western dramatic conventions; he created such works as *Leiyu* (1934; *Thunderstorm*), *Richu* (1936; *Sunrise*), and *Yuanye* (1937; *Wilderness*), which formed a loose trilogy and poignantly explored pressing social issues in Shanghai. He also served as director of the People's Theater and was a longtime member of the Communist Party (b. 1910—d. Dec. 13, 1996).

Carné, Marcel (Albert Cranche), French film director (b. Aug. 18, 1906, Paris, Fr.—d. Oct. 31, 1996, Clamart, near Paris), created—with screenwriter Jacques Prévert—a group of motion pic-

tures that exemplified a golden age of French cinema. His *Les Enfants du paradis* (1945; *Children of Paradise*), filmed under dangerous circumstances during the German occupation and at the time the most expensive French film ever made, came to be regarded as a masterpiece of world cinema. Carné developed a love for motion pictures when he was a young child and became a film critic in his 20s. He also became an assistant to the director Jacques Feyder on such films as *Les Nouveaux Messieurs* (1928), *Le Grand Jeu* (1934), and *La Kermesse héroïque* (1935; *Carnival in Flanders*) and to the director René Clair on *Sous les toits de Paris* (1930). In 1929 Carné made his first film, the documentary *Nogent, Eldorado du dimanche* (*Nogent, Sunday's Eldorado*), and in 1936 he directed his first feature, *Jenny*. That film also marked the beginning of his collaboration with Prévert. The two created a number of works—among them, *Quai des brumes* (1938; *Port of Shadows*) and *Le Jour se lève* (1939; *Daybreak*)—that were characterized as "poetic realism," reflecting the fatalistic mood of the country as it drifted toward World War II. During the war Carné and Prévert also made the period melodrama *Les Visiteurs du soir* (1942; *The Devil's Envoys*). Their last real collaboration, *Les Portes de la nuit* (*Gates of Night*), took place in 1946. Of Carné's later works, *Les Tricheurs* (1958; *The Cheaters*) was the most successful. Carné was elected to membership in the French Academy in 1980, and in 1984 the Cannes Film Festival was dedicated to him.

Carter, Wilfred Arthur Charles, ("WIF"; "MONTANA SLIM"), Canadian country music singer whose down-home, simple songs about fur trappers, cowboy life, and other homegrown subjects made him one of the country's most popular attractions during a more than 60-year career (b. Dec. 18, 1904—d. Dec. 5, 1996).

Casarès, Maria-Victoria, Spanish-born French tragedienne who brought her regal bearing, deep voice, and expressive eyes to such classic stage roles as Phaedra and Medea during her half-century career; she also appeared in such films as *Les Enfants du paradis* and *Orphée* and even portrayed King Lear (b. Nov. 21, 1922—d. Nov. 22, 1996).

Ceausescu, Nicu, Romanian public figure and playboy who was the youngest son of dictator Nicolae Ceausescu; he had a long history of dissolute behaviour and had been imprisoned for his part in the deaths of scores of demonstrators during the 1989 revolution that toppled his parents and led to their execution (b. Sept. 1, 1951—d. Sept. 26, 1996).

Celibidache, Sergiu, Romanian-born German conductor noted for both his perfectionism, which occasioned numerous rehearsals, and his opposition to recording music; from 1979 he was the director of the Munich Philharmonic (b. June 28, 1912—d. Aug. 14, 1996).

Chancellor, John William, U.S. television journalist (b. July 14, 1927, Chicago, Ill.—d. July 12, 1996, Princeton, N.J.), spent more than 40 years as a broadcaster for NBC, where he established a reputation for professionalism, thoughtfulness, and intelligence. He reported from over 50 countries and interviewed every U.S. president since Harry Truman, British prime minister since Clement Attlee, and Israeli prime minister since Golda Meir. Chancellor's appetite for the news business was whetted by an after-school job as a copy boy at the *Chicago Daily News* when he was 14. After dropping out of Chicago's Navy Pier campus of the University of Illinois, he became (1947) a copy boy at the *Chicago Sun-Times* and worked his way up to feature writer before leaving to join Chicago's NBC affiliate, first on radio and then on television. Chancellor gained national attention for his coverage of the 1957 school integration crisis in Little Rock, Ark. He then was posted to Vienna (1958), London (1959–60), and Moscow (1960–61); served (1961–62) as host of the *Today* show; and covered (1962–63) the Com-

mon Market meetings in Brussels. One of Chancellor's most memorable broadcasts was aired in 1964 when he was covering the Republican Party's national convention. Arrested for blocking an aisle while conducting an interview, he signed off by saying, "This is John Chancellor, somewhere in custody." Chancellor spent two years (1965–67) as director of the Voice of America but then returned to NBC as a national correspondent. From 1970 to 1982 he served as anchorman of the "NBC Nightly News," a post that made him a celebrity but left him unsatisfied, and in 1982 he became a senior commentator. After having delivered an estimated 1,500 commentaries, he retired from NBC in 1993. In 1994 Chancellor was narrator of Ken Burns's "Baseball," a nine-part Public Broadcasting Service documentary.

Chapman, Douglas George, Canadian-born U.S. mathematical statistician who during the 1960s proposed to the International Whaling Commission annual fin whale catch quotas that would permit the depleted populations of this species to recover (b. March 20, 1920—d. July 9, 1996).

Cheek, John, Falkland Islands advocate and businessman who served on the Legislative Council and, while in London in 1982 when Argentina invaded the Falkland Islands/Islas Malvinas, became known worldwide for supporting the islanders' cause (b. Nov. 18, 1939—d. Sept. 3, 1996).

Chermayeff, Serge (SERGEY IVANOVITCH ISSAKOVITCH), Russian-born U.S. architect noted for designing modernistic buildings during the 1930s, particularly the De La Warr Pavilion at the coastal resort town of Bexhill, Eng. (b. Oct. 8, 1900—d. May 8, 1996).

Chiriaeff, Ludmilla Otzup, Canadian dancer, choreographer, and director (b. Jan. 10, 1924, Riga, Latvia—d. Sept. 22, 1996, Montreal, Que.), was the founder of the company that became Les Grands Ballets Canadiens. Chiriaeff grew up in Berlin and had begun her ballet career there when Nazi doctors decided that her body measurements indicated that she was Jewish, though she was not, and sent her to a labour camp. Following World War II she danced and choreographed in Switzerland, opened a school, and formed a company, Ballets des Arts, before moving (1952) to Montreal. Chiriaeff developed a troupe there and presented her dancers on the newly formed French television service, calling them Les Ballets Chiriaeff and creating more than 300 short ballets. The group began stage performances in 1955 and in 1957 was renamed Les Grands Ballets Canadiens. It began touring in 1959, and in the

1960s Chiriaeff brought in Anton Dolin as artistic adviser and hired such choreographers as Brian Macdonald and Fernand Nault. The first European tour took place in 1969, and Nault's ballet of the rock opera *Tommy* (1970), with music by The Who, was especially popular on tour. Chiriaeff ceased directing the company in 1974 and concentrated on educational activities, including the company's school, until ill health forced her retirement in 1992. She was named a Companion of the Order of Canada in 1984, and in 1993 she was one of six Canadians honoured with the Governor-General's Award for the Performing Arts.

Chukovskaya, Lidiya Korneyevna, Russian writer who courageously opposed the Soviet government's persecution of dissidents and was a staunch champion of human rights (b. March 24, 1907—d. Feb. 7, 1996).

Clark, Raymond ("OSSIE"), British fashion designer whose whimsical and romantic creations of the mid-1960s to early '70s epitomized that free-spirited era; his designs, often worn by musicians and actors, were noted for their excellent cut (b. June 9, 1942—d. Aug. 6, 1996).

Clément, René, French motion picture director who was best known for his disturbing 1952 film, *Les Jeux interdits* ("Forbidden Games"), which won an Academy Award for best foreign film (b. March 18, 1913—d. March 17, 1996).

Colbert, Claudette (LILY CLAUDETTE CHAUCHOIN), U.S. actress (b. Sept. 13, 1903, Paris, Fr.—d. July 30, 1996, Cobblers Cove, Barbados), enjoyed a more than 60-year career, performing in over 60 films as well as on stage and television. It was in her chic, sophisticated screwball comedy roles that she especially caught the public's fancy, and she was forever identified as the runaway heiress in *It Happened One Night* (1934), for which she won a best actress Academy Award. Colbert moved to the U.S. with her family when she was a young child. While studying fashion design, she landed a small role in the Broadway play *The Wild Wescotts* (1923) after meeting the playwright at a party. Other Broadway and touring productions followed, and in 1927 she made her film debut in *For the Love of Mike*. Colbert's role in *The Sign of the Cross* (1932) provided one of her most memorable scenes, a bath in what was said to be asses' milk. She was for many years one of the highest-paid film stars. Among her comedies were *Bluebeard's Eighth Wife* (1938), *Midnight* (1939), and *The Palm Beach Story* (1942), and she had notable dramatic roles in such films as *I Cover the Waterfront* (1933), *Cleopatra* (1934), *Imitation*

ARCHIVE PHOTOS

Marcel Carné

Claudette Colbert

of Life (1934), *Since You Went Away* (1944), and *Three Came Home* (1950). Her last film was *Parrish* (1961). Colbert returned to the stage in 1951 in Westport, Conn., with Noël Coward's *Island Fling* and to the Broadway stage in 1956 with *Janus*. Other stage appearances included *The Marriage-Go-Round* (1958), *The Irregular Verb to Love* (1963), *The Kingfisher* (1978), and *Aren't We All?* (1985). Colbert appeared on television from the 1950s in such productions as *Blithe Spirit* (1956), with Coward, and the miniseries "The Two Mrs. Grenvilles" (1987), her last major project. In 1989 she was honoured with a Kennedy Center award for lifetime achievement.

Colby, William Egan, U.S. government official (b. Jan. 4, 1920, St. Paul, Minn.—d. April 27, 1996, Rock Point, Md.), pursued a policy of openness during his turbulent tenure (1973–76) as director of the CIA. He showed unusual candour while testifying before Congress in 1975 in the wake of various leaks about CIA covert operations, such as spying on U.S. citizens, plotting coups and assassinations abroad, conducting controversial experiments without the knowledge of the subjects, and involving itself in the Vietnam War and the Watergate scandal. His candidness, championed by some as having resuscitated CIA credibility during its most troubled period, led to his premature resignation and ultimately brought the agency under congressional oversight. After graduating with honours from Princeton Univer-

sity (B.A., 1940), Colby joined the U.S. Army. He served with distinction in World War II as a paratrooper for the Office of Strategic Services, the forerunner of the CIA. After the war he earned a law degree from Columbia University, New York City (1947), and practiced law until 1950, when he joined the CIA, serving first in Stockholm (1951–53) and then in Rome (1953–58). As chief of CIA operations in Saigon, South Vietnam (1959–62), and then in all of Asia (1962–67), he orchestrated CIA activities during the Vietnam War. In 1971 he returned to the agency's headquarters in Washington, D.C., where he pursued the directorship. After he was forced into retirement by Pres. Gerald Ford, Colby resumed his law practice and became an advocate for the reduction of nuclear arms. His memoirs were entitled *Honorable Men* (1978) and *Lost Victory* (1989).

Colley, Russell, U.S. designer who created pressurized suits for barnstorming aviators, the space suit worn by astronaut Alan B. Shepard, Jr., and a multitude of devices, including a rubberized pneumatic deicer used to clear airplane wings and a Riv-nut that allowed a single worker to affix rivets to airplane wings (b. 1899—d. Feb. 4, 1996).

Combs, Lewis B., U.S. Navy admiral (ret.) who established (1942) the Seabees, the naval construction battalions that speedily built docks, housing, and airstrips in combat zones during World War II (b. April 7, 1895—d. May 20, 1996).

Condon, Richard Thomas, U.S. novelist who wrote such thrillers as *The Manchurian Candidate* and *Winter Kills,* both concerning political assassination, and *Prizzi's Honor,* about a family of mobsters (b. March 18, 1915—d. April 9, 1996).

Conover, Willis, U.S. radio broadcaster and jazz promoter (b. Dec. 18, 1920, Buffalo, N.Y.—d. May 17, 1996, Alexandria, Va.), was the longtime host of the "Music USA" program on the Voice of America (VOA). His voice was perhaps the best known overseas of any American of his era. After winning a talent contest while a university student, Conover became a jazz disc jockey in Washington, D.C., during World War II. He was invited to work for the VOA in 1955, during the Cold War, and his nightly programs, which featured a mix of jazz styles—from Dixieland through bebop to the avant-garde—immediately found enormous success, especially in Eastern Europe, the U.S.S.R., and Asia. He scrupulously averted any attempts to politicize his show, and he never held a staff position with the U.S. government radio station, preferring to work on a freelance basis for more than 40 years. Still,

Conover viewed jazz as a lever to promote racial equality and harmony in the United States and abroad, and early in his career as a concert promoter he was instrumental in helping desegregate Washington nightclubs. Later, through interviews and airplay, he promoted such talented young musicians as Polish pianist Adam Makowicz and South African singer Miriam Makeba. Despite the ravages of cancer, Conover was at the microphone until a few weeks before his death. Because of a government regulation stipulating that VOA programs could not be broadcast to the U.S., he was little known in his own country. Nonetheless, he received a commendation from the House of Representatives in June 1993 for his role in foreign policy and was the recipient of *Down Beat* magazine's 1995 Lifetime Achievement Award.

Cowie, Mervyn Hugh, British wildlife conservationist who was the founder and, for 20 years, director of Kenya's Royal National Parks; he also assisted in the development of parks and tourism throughout East Africa and was appointed CBE in 1960 (b. April 13, 1909—d. July 19, 1996).

Cray, Seymour R., U.S. electronics engineer and computer designer (b. Sept. 28, 1925, Chippewa Falls, Wis.—d. Oct. 5, 1996, Colorado Springs, Colo.), led the design of the world's first transistor-based computer and was recognized as the father of the supercomputer industry. After graduating (1950) from the University of Minnesota, Cray went to work for Engineering Research Associates (ERA), a leading digital computer company. In 1957, when ERA was taken over in a series of corporate mergers, Cray left to help found Control Data Corp., which became a major computer manufacturer. At Control Data he led the design of the CDC 1604, the first commercial computer to replace vacuum tubes with smaller transistors. Cray had purchased the transistors at a local electronics store. Eager to pursue his vision of building the fastest computers in the world, Cray left Control Data in 1972 and founded Cray Research, Inc. His company's first supercomputer, the Cray-1, which came out in 1976, was 10 times faster than any other computer on the market. Ever-faster and more powerful designs followed, including the Cray-2 (1985) and the Cray Y-MP (1988). In 1989 Cray established Cray Computer Corp., which was eventually forced to file for bankruptcy (1995) as advances in technology made it possible for smaller computers to reach the processing speeds of much larger supercomputers. Undaunted, however, Cray opened another company, SRC Computer Inc., in August 1996, only two months before his death as a result of injuries sustained in a car crash.

Seymour Cray

Crépin, Jean-Albert-Emile, French military officer and industrialist who helped liberate Paris during World War II and who commanded French forces in the Algerian War of Independence before rising to the rank of five-star general; he later oversaw the development of the country's strategic missiles, including the Exocet (b. Sept. 1, 1908—d. May 4, 1996).

Crowther, Leslie Douglas Sargent, British television personality who enjoyed a more than 30-year career highlighted by a long run on the children's program "Crackerjack" in the 1960s and a stint as host of the '80s game show "The Price Is Right" (b. Feb. 6, 1933—d. Sept. 28, 1996).

Culhane, James, ("SHAMUS"), U.S. pioneering animator who gave life to the characters in *Snow White and the Seven Dwarfs,* Walt Disney's first feature-length cartoon (b. Nov. 12, 1908—d. Feb. 2, 1996).

Dairo I(saiah) K(ehinde), Nigerian musician and composer who—as leader from 1957 of the 10-piece Morning Star Orchestra (later renamed the Blue Spots)—brought new life and international popularity to Yoruban juju music by introducing a broad range of rhythms, such instruments as the electric guitar and the accordion, and other innovative elements; in 1963 he was the first African musician to be created MBE (b. 1930—d. Feb. 7, 1996).

Daniel, Frank, Czechoslovak-born filmmaker who, faced with Soviet persecution, fled to the U.S. after producing the 1965 movie *The Shop on Main Street,* which won an Academy Award for best foreign film; in the U.S. he headed several film schools (b. April 14, 1926—d. Feb. 29, 1996).

Danzig, Sarah Palfrey, U.S. tennis champion who combined grace and skill at the net to capture 18 Grand Slam titles, 16 of them collected in doubles and mixed doubles competition (b. Sept. 18, 1912—d. Feb. 27, 1996).

Daume, Willi, German sports administrator who, as president of the West German Olympic Committee, played a key role in returning the Olympic Games to Germany after an interval of 36 years; those Games, however, which were held in Munich in 1972, were marred by the murder of 11 Israeli athletes by Arab terrorists (b. May 24, 1913—d. May 20, 1996).

Davenport, Marcia Gluck, U.S. writer who was best known for her biography *Mozart* and the bestseller *The Valley of Decision* (b. June 9, 1903—d. Jan. 16, 1996).

Dearmer, Geoffrey, British poet who wrote verse based on his experiences as a soldier during World War I; his poetry was largely forgotten for 70 years until the 1993 publication of the collection titled *A Pilgrim's Song* (b. March 21, 1893—d. Aug. 18, 1996).

Debré, Michel-Jean-Pierre, French politician (b. Jan. 15, 1912, Paris, Fr.—d. Aug. 2, 1996, Montlouis-sur-Loire, Fr.), during his career in public service was closely associated with Charles de Gaulle. Debré was the primary author of the constitution of the Fifth Republic and served (1959–62) as its first premier. After graduating from the University of Paris law school, Debré entered the civil service as an aide to Paul Reynaud, the finance minister. He joined the army at the beginning of World War II, was captured by the Germans in 1940, and in 1941 escaped and went to Morocco. There he joined the Resistance and then returned to work in the underground in German-occupied France. After Allied troops liberated France (1944), Debré became commissioner for the Angers region, and in 1945 he joined the provisional government headed by de Gaulle. By creating the National School of Administration, he brought about a new efficiency in the civil service. Debré served in the Senate from 1948 to 1958. When de Gaulle became premier in 1958, Debré was appointed minister of justice and helped fashion a new constitution. When de Gaulle assumed the presidency early the next year, he named Debré premier. Though Debré strongly favoured the French presence in Algeria, he supported de Gaulle's disengagement policy. Nevertheless, he left office in 1962 following the French withdrawal from Algeria. Debré was a member of the National Assembly from 1963 until 1986 and served in the posts of minister of economics and finance (1966–68), foreign minister (1968–69), and minister of defense (1969–73). In 1981 he was a Gaullist candidate for the presidency, but he won less than 2% of the vote. Debré wrote a number of political works, including three volumes of memoirs, and in 1988 was elected to the French Academy.

Dominguín (LUIS MIGUEL GONZÁLEZ LUCAS), Spanish bullfighter whose intense rivalry with his brother-in-law was the inspiration for the Ernest Hemingway novel *The Dangerous Summer* (b. Dec. 9, 1926—d. May 8, 1996).

Donoso, José, Chilean novelist and short-story writer (b. Oct. 5, 1924, Santiago, Chile—d. Dec. 7, 1996, Santiago), was the country's best-known writer and one of the major figures of the 1960s and '70s Latin-American literary boom. In his more than 20 novels and short-story collections, he employed nightmarish surrealism, black comedy, and social satire to explore the fears, frustrations, dreams, and obsessions of his characters. Donoso studied at the Pedagogical Institute of Santiago for three years and then went on scholarship to Princeton University, where he received (1951) a B.A. degree. Stories he wrote at Princeton—in English—were among the first works he published. Following his return to Chile, Donoso taught, worked as a journalist, and in 1955 published the short-story collection *Veraneo y otros cuentos* at his own expense. He established his reputation with his first novel, *Coronación* (1957; *Coronation,* 1965), for which he was awarded the William Faulkner Foundation Prize in 1962. Donoso moved to Mexico in 1963 and later traveled to the U.S. and lectured (1965–67) at the University of Iowa. From there he moved to Spain. In 1970 he published what was said to be his masterpiece, *El obsceno pajaro de la noche* (*The Obscene Bird of Night,* 1973), which gained him worldwide fame. Donoso, however, considered his best work to have been *Casa de campo* (1978; *A House in the Country,* 1984). In the early 1980s he returned to Chile, wrote some antigovernment articles, and in 1985 was briefly detained after he protested the dismissal of some dissident writers from their teaching positions. Later works include *La desesperanza* (1986; *Curfew,* 1988) and *Donde van a morir los elefantes* (1995). *El mocho* was completed shortly before his death.

Donovan, Terence Daniel, British photographer who in the 1960s helped revolutionize fashion photography and redefine the relationship between photographer and model; he also directed more than 3,000 rock videos and television commercials (b. Sept. 14, 1936—d. Nov. 22, 1996).

Dove, Ulysses, U.S. dancer and choreographer who created dances for many of the leading U.S. and European companies and for the Philip Glass opera *The Civil Wars* (b. Jan. 17, 1947—d. June 11, 1996).

Draper, Paul, U.S. 1930s and '40s dance star who performed to classical music in concert halls, using a combination of tap and ballet; his partnership with harmonica player Larry Adler ended when both were blacklisted during the early 1950s (b. Oct. 25, 1909—d. Sept. 20, 1996).

Drew, Dame Jane Beverly, British architect (b. March 24, 1911, Thornton Heath, Surrey, Eng.—d. July 27, 1996, Cotherstone, Durham, Eng.), paid lavish attention to the harmony of design with the environment, a characteristic that made her one of Great Britain's best-loved architects. Especially during her partnership with her second husband, Maxwell Fry, she specialized in providing innovative large-scale town planning for tropical countries. Drew studied at the Architectural Association School, London, and became a member of the Modern Architectural Research Group. It was through that group that she met Fry. They were married in 1942, and their partnership lasted until his death in 1987. Among their many global projects were schools, universities, and hospitals in West Africa, notably the University of Ibadan, Nigeria. Their best-known work was the design for Chandigarh, the new capital of Punjab, India, on which Drew persuaded the Swiss architect Le Corbusier to collaborate. Drew's other projects included the Institute of Contemporary Arts, London; the School for the Deaf, Herne Hill, London; and the Open University, Milton Keynes, Eng. She wrote such books as *Architecture for Children* (1944; with Fry), *Village Housing in the Tropics* (1947; with Fry and Harry L. Ford), and *Tropical Architecture in the Humid Zone* (1956; with Fry) and contributed articles to architectural journals. Drew was the first woman to serve on the Council of the Royal Institute of British Architects and was a lifelong fellow. She was created DBE in 1996.

Dru, Joanne (JOANNE LACOCK), U.S. film actress and captivating leading lady in the Westerns *Red River, She Wore a Yellow Ribbon,* and *Wagonmaster* (b. Jan. 31, 1923—d. Sept. 10, 1996).

Druckman, Jacob Raphael, U.S. composer, teacher, and conductor who was influential in promoting contemporary music and won a Pulitzer Prize in 1972 for his orchestral work *Windows* (b. June 26, 1928—d. May 24, 1996).

Duby, Georges Michel Claude, French medieval scholar, lecturer, and member of the French Academy who taught the history of Western medieval societies at the Collège de France (1970–92) and wrote more than two dozen books on the social history of the European Middle Ages (b. Oct. 7, 1919—d. Dec. 3, 1996).

Dudayev, Dzhokhar, Chechen separatist leader and former Soviet military officer whose declaration of Chechen independence, made after his victory in Chechnya's 1991 presidential election, resulted in prolonged fighting with Russia, which refused to allow the secession; he was killed during a missile attack (b. April 15, 1944—d. April 21, 1996).

Dulles, Eleanor Lansing, U.S. career diplomat and prominent economic specialist for the U.S. State Department in Austria and West Germany, where she was hailed as "the Mother of Berlin" for helping to revitalize the economy and culture of the warworn city during the 1950s; she was also the sister of high-ranking government officials John Foster Dulles and Allen Welsh Dulles (b. June 1, 1895—d. Oct. 30, 1996).

Duras, Marguerite (MARGUERITE DONNADIEU), French writer (b. April 4, 1914, Gia Dinh, near Saigon, French Indochina [now Vietnam]—d. March 3, 1996, Paris, Fr.), was one of the leading figures of the French postwar literary scene; her chief themes were obsession and impossible love. She was best known as the author of the screenplay for Alain Resnais's classic film *Hiroshima mon amour* (1959) and for her novel *L'Amant* (1984; *The Lover,* 1984), which won the Prix Goncourt and was made into a popular motion picture in 1992. Duras also directed a number of films, notably *India Song* (1975). Reared in Indochina, Duras moved to Paris as a teenager to study at the Sorbonne. Although she published her first novel in 1943, she first tasted success with the semiautobiographical *Un Barrage contre le Pacifique* (1950; *The Sea Wall,* 1967), which portrayed a woman's attempt to keep the sea from swallowing her land. This she followed with two intricate and lyrical works, *Le Marin de Gibraltar* (1952; *The Sailor from Gibraltar,* 1967) and *Moderato cantabile* (1958; Eng. trans. 1960), both of which revealed her ear for dialogue. After working with Resnais, she wrote several more screenplays, some of them adaptations of her own work. Her novels grew increasingly spare and abstract, characteristics that caused some to associate her with the *nouveau roman* ("new novel") movement. Duras restored her literary reputation with the publication of *L'Amant,* reaching a new generation of readers with her evocative story of an adolescent French girl in Indochina and her forbidden affair with a wealthy young Chinese man. In 1990 Duras's last, brief novel, *La Pluie d'été* (*Summer Rain,* 1992), was published.

Duval, Sir Gaetan, Mauritian politician noted for his flamboyant style and a penchant for making unpredictable swings toward the left or right; he served in the Legislative Assembly and held numerous cabinet posts (b. Oct. 9, 1930—d. May 5, 1996).

Edwards, Vince, U.S. television and film actor who was best known for his 1961–66 stint as the handsome but surly, no-nonsense neurosurgeon Ben Casey on the television show of the same name (b. July 9, 1928—d. March 11, 1996).

Einem, Gottfried von, Austrian composer (b. Jan. 24, 1918, Bern, Switz.—d. July 12, 1996, Oberndürnbach, Austria), created operas and orchestral works that combined the influence of the Romantic composers with the more contemporary styles of jazz and atonality. His best-known works were operas that reflected the dark atmospheres of the stories that inspired them. Einem was educated in Germany and England and in 1938 became a coach at the Berlin State Opera and the Bayreuth (Ger.) Festival. He studied (1941–43) with the composer Boris Blacher, who later wrote the librettos for four of Einem's works. In 1944 Einem enjoyed success with his first stage work, the ballet *Prinzessin Turandot,* which established his musical credentials and resulted in his appointment as resident composer and music adviser for the Dresden State Opera. Einem's international reputation was assured after the premiere of his first opera, *Dantons Tod* (*Danton's Death*), at the Salzburg (Austria) Festival in 1947. Another opera, *Der Prozess* (*The Trial*), also premiered (1953) at Salzburg. Based on the Franz Kafka novel, it recalled Einem's experiences with the Nazis when he helped a number of people escape from Germany and was arrested and interrogated by the Gestapo. One of his later operas, *Der Besuch der alten Dame* (*The Visit of the Old Woman*), first performed in 1971, was considered by many to be his greatest operatic success. It was based on the Friedrich Dürrenmatt play, and Dürrenmatt wrote the libretto. The 1980 premiere of Einem's opera *Jesu Hochzeit* caused a scandal with its erotic encounter between Jesus and a female representing Death. Over the years Einem also served in administrative positions for the Salzburg and Vienna festivals and taught composition at the Vienna Academy of Music.

Elder, Lonne, III, U.S. playwright whose critically acclaimed masterwork, *Ceremonies in Dark Old Men* (1965; revised, 1969), depicted the frustrations of a disenfranchised African-American family living in the Harlem neighbourhood of New York City in the 1950s (b. Dec. 26, 1931—d. June 11, 1996).

Elytis, Odysseus (ODYSSEUS ALEPOUDHELIS), Greek poet (b. Nov. 2, 1911, Iraklion, Crete [now part of Greece]—d. March 18, 1996, Athens, Greece), was the winner of the Nobel Prize for Literature in 1979. Born into a wealthy Cretan family, he passed his boyhood in Athens. As a young man he appreciated the antirational poetry of the French Surrealists, and he began to publish his own poetry in the avant-garde Greek periodical *Nea grammata.* Soon he abandoned his law studies and devoted himself to poetry. He adopted the pen name Elytis to disassociate his writing from the family soap business. His first two volumes of verse—*Prosanatolismoi* (1940; *Orientations,* 1974) and *Elios o protos* (1943; "Sun the First")—reveal his love of the sunny Greek landscape and the sparkling Aegean Sea. During World War II Elytis served as an officer on the Albanian front, an experience he wrote about in his long poem *Asma heroiko kai penthimo gia ton chameno anthy-*

polochago tes Alvanias (1945; *Heroic and Elegiac Song for the Lost Second Lieutenant of the Albanian Campaign,* 1965). He did not publish again until 1959, when one of his most complex and best-known works, *To Axion Esti* ("Worthy It Is"; *The Axion Esti,* 1967), was published. Elytis often traveled abroad, and he lived in Paris for about four years after the Greek military coup of 1967. His later works include *Ho Helios ho heliatoras* (1971; *The Sovereign Sun,* 1974), *Ta heterothale* (1974; "The Stepchildren"), *Maria Nephele* (1978; Eng. trans. 1981), *Ho mikros nautilos* (1986; *The Little Mariner,* 1988), and *Ta elegeia tes oxopetras* (1991; "The Oxopetra Elegies").

Enders, Thomas, U.S. diplomat who played a leading role in the secret bombing of Cambodia during the Vietnam War, dealt with the aftermath of the first OPEC oil crisis, and guided U.S. policy in Central America during the administration of U.S. Pres. Ronald Reagan (b. Nov. 28, 1931—d. March 17, 1996).

Endo, Shusaku, Japanese novelist (b. March 27, 1923, Tokyo, Japan—d. Sept. 29, 1996, Tokyo), brought a Roman Catholic perspective to examinations of the differences between Eastern and Western cultures, questions of faith, and the conflicts between modern and traditional beliefs and values. He was so highly regarded as to be considered a likely contender for the Nobel Prize, and his work was translated into at least 25 languages. Endo was brought up in China but returned to Japan with his mother when his parents divorced. They lived with a Roman Catholic aunt, and after Endo's mother converted to Christianity, the two persuaded Endo to be baptized. He graduated (1949) from Keio University, Tokyo, and then studied (1950–53) French literature at the University of Lyon, Fr. His first novel, *Shiroi hito* ("White Man"), appeared in 1955 and was awarded the prestigious Akutagawa Prize. Three years later the controversial *Umi to dokuyaku* (*The Sea and Poison,* 1972), about Japanese doctors performing vivisection on a downed U.S. pilot during World War II, firmly established his reputation. Other works considered to be among Endo's finest were the powerful *Chimmoku* (1966; *Silence,* 1969), about Portuguese priests in Japan and their converts' martyrdom; *Iesu no shogai* (1973; *A Life of Jesus,* 1978), which won the Dag Hammarskjöld Prize; and *Samurai* (1980; *The Samurai,* 1982), which won the Noma Prize for Literature. Endo also wrote comic novels, short stories, dramas, essays, and a biography and was president of the Japanese branch of the international literary guild PEN.

Erdos, Paul, Hungarian mathematician (b. March 26, 1913, Budapest, Hung.—d. Sept. 20, 1996, Warsaw, Pol.), pioneered the fields of number theory and combinatorics and was regarded as one of the century's greatest mathematicians. At the age of 20 he discovered a proof for a classic theorem of number theory that states that there is always at least one prime number between any positive integer and its double. After receiving (1934) a Ph.D. from the University of Budapest, Erdos was awarded a postdoctoral fellowship at the University of Manchester, Eng. In 1938 he immigrated to the U.S. On fellowship at the Institute for Advanced Study in Princeton, N.J., Erdos founded the study of probabilistic number theory with Aurel Wintner and Mark Kac and proved important results in approximation theory with Paul Turan. Erdos and Atle Selberg astounded the mathematics community in 1949 by giving an elementary proof of the prime number theorem—for more than 50 years it had been assumed that no elementary proof could be given. After spending much of the 1950s in Israel, Erdos traveled almost constantly, earning a reputation as a restless "wandering scholar" who collaborated with hundreds of mathematicians on a variety of problems. "Another roof, another proof," was his legendary motto. In later years Erdos worked primarily in the field of combinatorics, an area of mathematics fundamental to computer science. When he won the Wolf Foundation Prize in 1983, he gave fellow mathematicians most of the

prize money he received. He also received many honorary degrees and was a member of the Hungarian Academy of Sciences (1956), and he was a foreign associate of the academies of the U.S. (1979), India (1988), and the U.K. (1989). At the time of his death, Erdos had published more than 1,500 mathematical papers.

Ewell, Norwood H. ("BARNEY"), U.S. sprinter who, at the age of 30, won one gold medal and two silver medals in the 1948 Olympics; the winning 400-m relay team initially was disqualified on a ruling about Ewell's passing of the baton to a teammate, but the decision was reversed three days later (b. Feb. 25, 1918—d. April 4, 1996).

AP/WIDE WORLD

Norwood Ewell

Eyre de Lanux, Elizabeth, U.S. artist, writer, and Art Deco designer who created lacquered furniture and geometric patterned rugs in Paris during the 1920s; she later wrote short stories about her European travel and illustrated a number of children's books (b. March 1894—d. Sept. 8, 1996).

Factor, Max, Jr. (FRANCIS FACTOR), U.S. cosmetician who, with his father, developed Pan-Cake makeup so actors would not appear green in colour motion pictures and, when it began to be worn offscreen as well, mass-produced it and built their company into an international cosmetics empire (b. Aug. 18, 1904—d. June 7, 1996).

Ferreira, Vergílio, Portuguese novelist and essayist (b. Jan. 28, 1916, Melo, Port.—d. March 1, 1996, Sintra, Port.), was a leading literary figure who created extremely sympathetic and eloquent characters—often old men looking back on their lives—who sought the ultimate meaning of human existence. Contrary to the wishes of his family, Ferreira abandoned his religious training for a degree in classics from the University of Coimbra. Thereafter, living under the Fascist-friendly prime ministership of António de Oliveira Salazar, Ferreira taught school. During this period he also wrote several neorealist novels of muted protest against authoritarianism in all its forms. Works of his early phase include *Onde tudo foi morrendo* (1944), *Vagão "J"* (1946), and *Manhã submersa* (1954). Beginning with *Mudança* (1949)—generally considered Portugal's first existentialist novel—Ferreira's work took on an increasingly introspective and psychological tone. He was much influenced by the work of the French existentialists, especially Jean-Paul Sartre, of whom he wrote an incisive study. Among Ferreira's notable later works are *Aparição* (1959), *Estrela polar* (1961), *Alegria breve* (1965), and *Até ao fim* (1987), each of which won a national literary prize. Beginning in 1980, his diary was published in series as *Conta corrente.*

Fini, Léonor, Argentine-born Surrealist artist who created erotically tinged paintings, posters, and sets and was internationally known for designing the sets and costumes for such venues as the Paris Opéra, the Comédie-Française, and Milan's La Scala (b. Aug. 30, 1908—d. Jan. 18, 1996).

Finley, Charles Oscar ("CHARLIE"), U.S. sports executive (b. Feb. 22, 1918, Ensley, near Birmingham, Ala.—d. Feb. 19, 1996, Chicago, Ill.), introduced innovations to major league baseball as the unconventional and successful owner of the Athletics in Kansas City (1960–67) and Oakland (1968–80); he shepherded his ball club to three consecutive World Series titles in 1972–74. Challenging baseball traditions, he promoted the adoption of the designated hitter, team mascots, colourful player uniforms, and night and weekend World Series games. He was also known for ideas that did not catch on, such as orange baseballs, a walk awarded on three instead of four balls, the designated runner, and a closer right-field fence. Earlier, Finley worked in a steel mill in Gary, Ind., and in an ordnance plant during World War II. While recovering from tuberculosis in a sanitarium in 1946–48, he originated a plan to sell group insurance to physicians, which became a lucrative venture with the formation of his own company in 1954. As owner of the Athletics for two decades, he was regarded as a micromanager with a confrontational style; he hired a total of 18 managers, some of them twice. Known as a tough contract negotiator, he unwittingly introduced (1974) free agency to baseball when his failure to adhere to the contract terms of his star pitcher, Catfish Hunter, resulted in arbitration that ended with Hunter's being allowed to deal with any team. In 1976 Finley's attempt to sell the rights to three of his top players—Rollie Fingers, Vida Blue, and Joe Rudi—before he lost them to free agency was blocked by the baseball commissioner, Bowie Kuhn. With the decline of the team's financial and athletic fortunes, he sold the franchise in 1980.

Fish, Hamilton, Jr., U.S. politician who was the fourth Hamilton Fish to serve in the U.S. Congress; a moderate Republican from New York, he supported civil rights and gun control and figured in the passage of such laws as the Americans with Disabilities Act (b. June 3, 1926—d. July 23, 1996).

Fitzgerald, Ella, U.S. singer (b. April 25, 1917, Newport News, Va.—d. June 15, 1996, Beverly Hills, Calif.), possessed a sweet, clear voice that propelled her to the status of international legend during a career that spanned some six decades. Employing her enormous vocal range and stylish inventive interpretations, in both ballads and jazz improvisations known as "scat," she sold more than 40 million records. As a child, Fitzgerald wanted to be a dancer, but when she panicked at an amateur contest in 1934 at New York City's Apollo Theatre and sang instead, she won first prize. She soon was singing with the Chick Webb orchestra. She made her first recording, "Love and Kisses," in 1935, and her first hit, "A-Tisket, A-Tasket"—fashioned from the children's song—followed in 1938. After Webb died (1939), Fitzgerald led the band until it broke up in 1942. She then soloed in cabarets and theatres, toured internationally with such pop and jazz stars as Benny Goodman, Louis Armstrong, Duke Ellington, the Mills Brothers, the Ink Spots, and Dizzy Gillespie, and recorded prolifically. In the mid-1950s the jazz impresario Norman Granz became Fitzgerald's manager, and from 1956 to 1967 he produced the "songbook" albums that defined her legacy. In that 19-volume series, she sang some 250 songs—a blend of the well-known and the little-known—by such composers as George Gershwin, Cole Porter, Jerome Kern, Richard Rodgers, and Irving Berlin. Fitzgerald also appeared in films, notably *Pete Kelly's Blues* (1955), on television, and in concerts with symphony orchestras, and she recorded a number of live concert albums. Health problems that began in the 1970s slowed her down, but even after heart surgery (1986) she continued performing.

In 1993, however, her career was curtailed following complications stemming from diabetes, which resulted in the amputation of both of her legs below the knees. Fitzgerald won numerous Grammy awards, was a 1979 recipient of the Kennedy Center Honors for lifetime achievement, and in 1987 was awarded the National Medal of Arts.

Flavin, Dan, U.S. sculptor whose works featuring fluorescent lighting tubes made him one of the leading exponents of minimalist art and importantly influenced the direction of international contemporary art (b. April 1, 1933—d. Nov. 30, 1996).

Fox, Harold, U.S. clothier who claimed to have created and named the zoot suit—a wide-shouldered jacket with high-waisted pants, often offset by a long-chained watch—favoured by fops of the 1940s (b. July 9, 1910—d. July 28, 1996).

Franey, Pierre, French chef (b. Jan. 13, 1921, Saint-Vinnemer, Fr.—d. Oct. 15, 1996, Southampton, Eng.), as the masterful head chef (1945–60) at the legendary Le Pavillon restaurant in New York City, used his culinary expertise to elevate the establishment to the rank of the country's first world-class French restaurant; he

Ella Fitzgerald

METRONOME/ARCHIVE PHOTOS

later won fame as a cookbook author and *New York Times* food columnist. After an apprenticeship at Drouant, one of Paris's most famous restaurants, Franey accepted a job as a cook in the French pavilion at the 1939 New York World's Fair. Beginning in 1976, he teamed with *New York Times* food critic Craig Claiborne to write "The 60-Minute Gourmet" column, which featured Franey's recipes for simplified French cooking. He also collaborated with Claiborne on five well-received cookbooks and published an autobiography, *A Chef's Tale* (1994). In the 1990s Franey starred as a television chef and toured as a cooking instructor; he died three days after suffering a stroke aboard the *Queen Elizabeth 2,* where he had given a cooking demonstration.

Fujiko, Fujio F. (HIROSHI FUJIMOTO), Japanese cartoonist who, with his childhood friend Motoo Abiko, created the character Doraemon, a robot cat that appeared in books, magazines, and animated films and television shows and gained worldwide popularity (b. Dec. 12, 1933—d. Sept. 23, 1996).

Fuller, Ray W., U.S. biochemist who, as a pharmacological researcher at Eli Lilly & Co. from 1963, helped to create fluoxetine—the popular antidepressant drug known by the trademark Prozac. The drug, which combated depression by slowing the reabsorption of serotonin in the brain, was synthesized in 1972 and marketed in 1987 (b. Dec. 16, 1935—d. Aug. 11, 1996).

Gad al-Haq Ali Gad al-Haq, Egyptian religious leader who, as grand sheikh of al-Azhar, the Muslim world's highest religious body, issued rulings based on strict Islamic orthodoxy, including support for female circumcision and harsh punishment for those breaking the fast during Ramadan (b. April 5, 1917—d. March 15, 1996).

Galindo, Gabriel Lewis, Panamanian businessman, foreign-policy expert, and diplomat who, as Panama's ambassador to the U.S. during the late 1970s, was instrumental in helping the U.S. government reach agreement on and ratify treaties providing for the transfer of sovereignty of the Panama Canal to Panama in the year 2000 (b. Feb. 24, 1929—d. Dec. 19, 1996).

Galland, Adolf Joseph Ferdinand, German aviator (b. March 19, 1912, Westerholt, Ger.—d. Feb. 9, 1996, Oberwinter, Ger.), was one of the country's most famous World War II fighter pilots, shooting down more than 100 Allied planes. Nonetheless, as a result of his arrangements for procuring a replacement artificial leg for a captured Royal Air Force flyer, he gained the respect of his British enemies. Galland became a glider pilot when he was in his teens and began working for the civilian airliner Lufthansa in 1932. When the Luftwaffe was formed—secretly, because the Treaty of Versailles, signed at the end of World War I, did not allow Germany to have a military air force—Galland transferred to it. He flew several missions with the Condor Legion during the Spanish Civil War (1937–38) and, after providing ground support during the invasion of Poland (1939) that began World War II, returned to air combat. His first kills came in May 1940 over Belgium, and in July he entered the Battle of Britain as commander of a fighter squadron. In November 1941 Galland became inspector of fighters, and the next year he was promoted to major general, becoming at age 30 the youngest general in the German armed forces. Because he was critical of many of the tactics devised by Nazi leaders, Galland gradually lost favour despite his able leadership, and in January 1945 he was relieved of his command and returned to active duty. He formed a jet-fighter unit and in May was shot down and captured. Following his release (1947) from a prisoner-of-war camp, he served for six years in Argentina as a technical adviser to the air force and then returned (1955) to West Germany, where he worked as an aviation consultant.

Games, Abram, British graphic designer best known for the World War II posters he created while serving as official war poster designer for England; his works were noted for their vividness and clarity and bore the influences of Futurism, Abstraction, and Surrealism (b. July 29, 1914—d. Aug. 27, 1996).

Garson, Greer, Irish-born actress (b. Sept. 29, 1903?, County Down, Ire.—d. April 6, 1996, Dallas, Texas), represented an ideal of courage with her portrayal of a British wartime housewife in *Mrs. Miniver* (1942). She received an Academy Award for her performance and was nominated for an Oscar a total of seven times throughout her career. Garson received a scholarship from the University of London and worked for Encyclopædia Britannica and a market research firm before turning to acting. Her stage debut in 1932 was highly praised. Film mogul Louis B. Mayer saw her in London in the late 1930s and signed her to a one-year contract with MGM. Garson was cast as the young wife who died in *Goodbye, Mr. Chips* (1939) and received her first Oscar nomination. Her next film was *Remember?* (1939), and she was subsequently cast opposite Laurence Olivier in *Pride and Prejudice* (1940) and Ronald Coleman in *Random Harvest* (1942). She received Oscar nominations for *Blossoms in*

Greer Garson

the Dust (1941), *Madame Curie* (1943), *Mrs. Parkington* (1944), and *The Valley of Decision* (1945). Her image was one of elegance, poise, and virtue, and her roles seldom varied from that type. Her career lost ground after World War II and did not recover. She starred with Clark Gable in *Adventure* (1946) and appeared in *Desire Me* (1947), but neither film was successful. *That Forsyte Woman* (1949) did appeal to the public, but *The Miniver Story* (1950), a sequel to her earlier film, failed to lure audiences into the theatre. In 1949 Garson married Texas oil millionaire E.E. ("Buddy") Fogelson. The couple maintained residences in Dallas and Los Angeles and a ranch near Santa Fe, N.M., where Garson turned her attention to philanthropic work in the performing arts. She continued to work sporadically, and her later efforts included a lively performance as Auntie Mame on Broadway in 1958. She garnered another Oscar nomination for her portrayal of Eleanor Roosevelt in *Sunrise at Campobello* (1960).

Gavazzeni, Gianandrea, Italian composer and conductor who was best known for his nearly 50 years of conducting opera at La Scala in Milan (b. July 25, 1909—d. Feb. 5, 1996).

Geisel, Ernesto, Brazilian army general and politician (b. Aug. 3, 1908, Bento Gonçalves, Brazil—d. Sept. 12, 1996, Rio de Janeiro, Brazil), was president of Brazil from 1974 to 1979, the fourth of the five generals who ruled the country from 1964 to 1985. Although he had participated in the coup that installed the military dictatorship, he was instrumental in readying the country for the return to democracy. Geisel was a career army officer and had a part in both the 1930 military coup that installed the dictatorship of Getúlio Vargas and the overthrow of Vargas's government 15 years later. He then held a number of important offices and, following the 1964 coup, served the first three military presidents in several capacities. In 1969 Geisel became president of Petrobrás, Brazil's national oil corporation. He modernized the company, increasing its production and leading it into an international role. After assuming the presidency of Brazil, Geisel began liberalizing the government. He permitted

open legislative elections in 1974, relaxed censorship and repression, and brought some civilians into his administration. Though the "Brazilian miracle" of economic growth that had been taking place was fading, Geisel worked to develop domestic industry and lessen the country's dependence on trade with Europe and the U.S.

Ghiz, Joseph A., Canadian premier (1986–92) of Prince Edward Island and eloquent advocate for the failed Meech Lake and Charlottetown accords, which would have granted special powers to Quebec in an attempt to quell the separatist movement (b. Jan. 27, 1945—d. Nov. 9, 1996).

Giacosa, Dante, Italian auto designer for Fiat whose small, economical cars, particularly the popular Fiat 500, helped motorize Italy in the 1950s (b. Jan. 3, 1905—d. March 31, 1996).

Gladwyn, Hubert Miles Gladwyn Jebb, BARON, British diplomat (b. April 25, 1900, Firbeck Hall, Yorkshire, Eng.—d. Oct. 24, 1996, Halesworth, Suffolk, Eng.), helped draft the Charter of the United Nations and in 1950 became Great Britain's first permanent UN representative. Educated at Eton College and Magdalen College, Oxford, Gladwyn entered the British diplomatic service in 1924. Recognized early for his efficiency and organizational skills, he advanced steadily, and in 1942 he was named head of the new reconstruction department of the Foreign Office, which was responsible for developing Britain's post-World War II policy. In 1943 Gladwyn prepared early plans for the proposed United Nations; the first draft of the UN Charter was also prepared under his direction. After serving as acting secretary-general of the UN (1946) and as Britain's first permanent UN representative (1950–54), Gladwyn served as Britain's ambassador to France (1954–60). In 1960 he was given a hereditary peerage in the House of Lords, and from 1965 to 1988 he served as deputy leader of the Liberal Party. A gifted speaker and writer, Gladwyn contributed to parliamentary debates and to many journalistic publications. *The Memoirs of Lord Gladwyn* appeared in 1972.

Goldschmidt, Berthold, German-born British composer (b. Jan. 18, 1903, Hamburg, Ger.—d. Oct. 17, 1996, London, Eng.), was among Germany's most promising composers when the Nazi Party came to power in 1933. After his work was banned, Goldschmidt fled to England in 1935; following decades of obscurity, however, his lyrical music enjoyed a triumphant renaissance in the 1980s and '90s. Goldschmidt, who was influenced by the music of Ferruccio Busoni and Gustav Mahler, was an assistant conductor (1926) at the Berlin State Opera before moving (1927) to the Darmstadt Opera, where in 1929 he became the company's composer in residence. During the early '30s he was an adviser to the Berlin Municipal Opera. Goldschmidt's first opera, *Der gewaltige Hahnrei*, premiered in Mannheim in 1932 and was the last opera by a Jewish composer to premiere in Germany before the Nazis took power. He became a British citizen in 1947, thereafter eking out a living as a teacher, singing coach, and occasional conductor while composing a number of works that were largely ignored. An unexpected commission in 1982 for his Clarinet Quartet began an extraordinary revival of interest in Goldschmidt's music. The first complete performance of his 1951 opera *Beatrice Cenci* was given in London in 1988. Goldschmidt's works were also featured at the 1987 and 1994 Berlin Festivals. In 1995, at age 92, Goldschmidt conducted the Birmingham Symphony Orchestra in recordings of his 1925 overture, *The Comedy of Errors,* and a new rondeau he had composed for violin and orchestra. A cycle of French songs for baritone and orchestra, *Les Petits Adieux,* was completed in 1994.

Goldsmith, Myron, U.S. architect who was internationally known for sleek, sculptural projects, notably the McMath-Pierce Solar Telescope Facility at the Kitt Peak (Arizona) National Observatory (b. Sept. 15, 1918—d. July 15, 1996).

Gordon, Irving, U.S. songwriter who won a Grammy award in 1992 for "Unforgettable" after Nat King Cole's daughter Natalie recorded a new version of the song, a digital duet with her late father; he was the lyricist for "Prelude to a Kiss," the composer of such songs as "Me, Myself and I" and "What Will I Tell My Heart?," and the writer of the classic Abbott and Costello comedy routine "Who's on First?" (b. Feb. 14, 1915—d. Dec. 1, 1996).

Gould, Morton, U.S. composer, conductor, and pianist (b. Dec. 10, 1913, Richmond Hill, N.Y.—d. Feb. 21, 1996, Orlando, Fla.), was noted for compositions that bridged the gap between classical and popular music. He combined jazz, folk, and pop elements in music for Broadway shows, ballets, motion pictures, and television, as well as the concert stage. Gould's musical talent became apparent when he was a young child. At age four he was able to improvise on the piano; he composed a waltz at six; and at eight he received a scholarship to the New York Institute of Musical Art (later the Juilliard School). While in his teens Gould gave piano recitals that featured improvisations on themes suggested by audience members. He went on to act as composer, arranger, and conductor on radio programs, first (1935–42) for a weekly show on the Mutual Network station WOR and then (1942–45) for sponsored broadcasts. Among his works during that period were *American Concertette* for piano and orchestra, which Jerome Robbins choreographed as *Interplay, Latin-American Symphonette,* and *Lincoln Legend.* Another notable composition was for Agnes de Mille's ballet *Fall River Legend* (1947), based on the Lizzie Borden murder case. Gould wrote the scores for two Broadway musicals, *Billion Dollar Baby* (1945) and *Arms and the Girl* (1950), motion pictures, such as *Windjammer* (1958), and the television miniseries "Holocaust" (1978). In 1966 he won a Grammy award for a recording of Charles Ives's music made with the Chicago Symphony Orchestra. Beginning in 1959 he was on the board of the American Society of Composers, Authors, and Publishers, and he served as its president from 1986 to 1994. Gould received a Kennedy Center award in 1994 and the following year won a Pulitzer Prize for the composition *Stringmusic.*

Green, Joseph (JOSEPH GREENBERG), Polish-born film director whose four Yiddish-language films, notably *Yidl Mitn Fidl* (1936; *Yiddle with His Fiddle*), represent the height of Yiddish filmmaking (b. April 23, 1900—d. June 20, 1996).

Grosz, Karoly, Hungarian communist politician (b. Aug. 1, 1930, Miskolc, Hung.—d. Jan. 7, 1996, Godollo, Hung.), as prime minister (1987–88), initiated economic reforms that led to his party's collapse. Despite his loyalty to the Hungarian Socialist Workers' Party (HSWP), his program of austerity steered the government away from communism, prompting more radical politicians to replace him in order to accelerate the transition to a market economy. Grosz joined the Communist Party at age 15, embarking on a career in the propaganda department. His successful political career experienced a momentary setback in 1979 when he was banished to a party position in his hometown of Miskolc but rebounded in the mid-1980s when he was recalled to Budapest and shortly thereafter joined the Politburo. Janos Kadar, longtime leader of Hungary, grappling with a stagnant economy and his own flagging popularity, appointed the reform-minded Grosz prime minister in June 1987; less than a year later, Grosz took over Kadar's post as general secretary of the HSWP. His economic reforms, which included the institution of income taxes and value-added taxes, were accompanied by a rise in unemployment, inflation, and the cost of living. After resisting social reform, he was pressured to step down as head of the government in November 1988. Although he was part of a quadrumvirate that ruled briefly in 1989, he opposed the transformation of the HSWP into the Hungarian Socialist Party, and his hard-core splinter group was soundly defeated in the elections of 1990.

Morton Gould

Guevara Arze, Walter, Bolivian politician who in 1941 helped form the Nationalist Revolutionary Movement and led it to power 10 years later. He figured prominently in national politics, serving an 85-day tenure as president in 1979 (b. March 11, 1912—d. June 20, 1996).

Gullikson, Timothy Edward ("TIM"), U.S. tennis player and coach who had a successful career in doubles with his identical twin, Tom, but was better known for guiding the careers of other players, including Mary Joe Fernandez, Martina Navratilova, and, especially, Pete Sampras (b. Sept. 8, 1951—d. May 3, 1996).

Habibi, Emile, Israeli Arab writer (b. Aug. 29, 1922, Haifa, Palestine [now in Israel]—d. May 2, 1996, Nazareth, Israel), became one of the most popular authors in the Middle East as a result of works depicting the conflicts in loyalties experienced by Palestinians living as an Arab minority in the Jewish state of Israel. In such works as *Strange Events in the Disappearance of Said Abu al-Nahs al-Mutashael* (1974), the most notable of his seven novels, he explored the duality of those Arabs who, like himself, did not leave their homeland during the 1948–49 Arab-Israeli war; in his will he asked that his tombstone include the phrase "remained in Haifa." Habibi became a communist in the early 1940s and helped found the Communist Party of Israel. He served (1952–72) as a Communist member of the Knesset (parliament) and for over 30 years as editor of the party's newspaper, but he left the party in 1991 after his fellow members would not accept Soviet Pres. Mikhail Gorbachev's liberal ideas. Habibi began writing fiction in the 1970s and created plays and short stories in addition to his novels. He was committed to nonviolence and peaceful coexistence between Arabs and Jews. In 1990 the Palestine Liberation Organization presented Habibi with the Jerusalem Medal, its highest literary prize. Two years later when he became the first Arab to win Israel's top cultural award, the Israel Prize, Habibi was criticized by some Arab intellectuals, but he was convinced the award could help promote peace.

Haidari, Buland al-, Kurdish Iraqi poet who was a pioneer of free verse in the 1950s. His realistic verse, which helped modernize Arabic poetry, often ran afoul of the Iraqi government, and he spent much of his adult life in exile. Haidari's last anthology was published just days before his death (b. Sept. 26, 1926—d. Aug. 6, 1996).

Hamilton, Charles, Jr., U.S. handwriting expert who unmasked the so-called Hitler diaries as "patent and obvious forgeries" and created the term *philography* to describe his craft (b. 1914?—d. Dec. 11, 1996).

Hanson, Duane Elwood, U.S. sculptor whose life-size, very lifelike figures made of cast fibreglass and polyester resin and dressed in real clothes often fooled the public into believing that they were viewing real people (b. Jan. 17, 1925—d. Jan. 6, 1996).

Harris, Eddie, U.S. jazz musician who played tenor saxophone with a high, pure sound, as exemplified in his 1961 hit recording of the theme from the film *Exodus.* He also experimented with electronic saxophone attachments, altered saxophones (using brass mouthpieces), and fusion music. Harris composed the jazz standard "Freedom Jazz Dance" and became most popular on the pop-soul-funk fringes of jazz, though he often returned to straightforward, melodic bop improvisation, of which he was a master (b. Oct. 20, 1934—d. Nov. 5, 1996).

Heissenbüttel, Helmut, German avant-garde novelist and poet whose works, notably *D'Alemberts Ende,* reflected his belief that the only real subject of literature was language itself (b. June 21, 1921—d. Sept. 19, 1996).

Helm, Brigitte (GISELE EVE SCHITTENHELM), German actress who starred in silent movies and early talkies and was best remembered for her dual performance as the innocent Maria and her counterpart, a hypersexed robot, in Fritz Lang's 1926 futuristic cult classic *Metropolis* (b. March 17, 1906—d. June 11, 1996).

Hemingway, Margot ("MARGAUX"), U.S. model and actress—and the granddaughter of Ernest Hemingway—who was paid $1 million as the spokesperson for the Fabergé fragrance Babe and made her film debut in 1976 in *Lipstick* (b. Feb. 1, 1955—found dead July 1, 1996).

Hersant, Robert Joseph Émile, French publisher and politician who, as founder of France's largest media empire, was accused of controlling the press, particularly to advance his political career while a member of the French Parliament, 1956–78 (b. Jan. 31, 1920—d. April 21, 1996).

Hill, Julian Werner, U.S. research chemist whose discoveries led to the creation of nylon (b. Sept. 4, 1904—d. Jan. 28, 1996).

Hiss, Alger, U.S. government official (b. Nov. 11, 1904, Baltimore, Md.—d. Nov. 15, 1996, New York, N.Y.), was a central figure in an espionage case that ushered in the anticommunist McCarthy era and brought Richard M. Nixon to national attention as one of the most prominent congressional investigators in the case. Hiss received a bachelor's degree (1926) from Johns Hopkins

Alger Hiss

University, Baltimore, and a degree (1929) from Harvard Law School before serving (1929–30) as law clerk to Supreme Court Justice Oliver Wendell Holmes, Jr. He entered (1933) government service during the Franklin D. Roosevelt administration and by 1936 was working at the State Department. At the 1945 Yalta Conference, Hiss was an adviser to Roosevelt, and at the conference in San Francisco that created the UN, he served as temporary secretary-general. After the FBI had been alerted to the possibility that Hiss was a Soviet agent, it was arranged for him to become (1946) the president of the Carnegie Endowment for International Peace, a largely ceremonial position that he held until 1949. In 1948, in hearings before the House Un-American Activities Committee, former Soviet agent Whittaker Chambers accused Hiss of having been a member of a communist espionage ring in the 1930s. Hiss denied the charges and, when Chambers repeated them publicly, sued him for slander. Chambers then produced material that he claimed Hiss had given him to pass along to the Soviets. Both men testified before a federal grand jury, which believed Chambers. As the statute of limitations on espionage had run out, Hiss was indicted on two charges of perjury. A first trial ended in a hung jury, but he was convicted (1950) after a second trial and subsequently served more than three

years of a five-year prison sentence, all the while continuing to maintain his innocence. In 1992, after the Cold War had ended, Hiss thought he finally had been vindicated when a Russian general in charge of military and KGB intelligence archives announced that he had found no evidence that Hiss had been a spy. The general later recanted, however, and in 1996 the U.S. National Security Agency released documents suggesting that Hiss could have been the Soviet agent known as "Ales."

Hojo, Hideji, Japanese playwright (b. 1902, Osaka, Japan—d. May 19, 1996, Kamakura, Japan), was the author of more than 200 plays and the leader of commercial theatre in Japan after World War II. His psychological dramas about average citizens appealed to mainstream audiences. Hojo studied Japanese literature at Kansai University, Osaka, supplementing the proceeds from his writing career by working for an electric company and, later, an electric railroad. In the 1930s he apprenticed under noted dramatist Okamoto Kido, developing a modern style known as *shimpa* ("new school"), by loosening traditional kabuki forms and broadening the roles of female characters. By 1940 he was a fulltime playwright, scoring his first great success with *Kakka* (1940; "Her Highness"). His popularity grew along with his critical status, and soon his plays were being performed by the stars of Japanese theatre. He found an outlet for his progressive style in the Shinkokugeki ("New National Theatre"), which was founded in 1917 but did not flourish until after World War II. His masterwork, *Osho* (1947, "Chess Master"), based on the true story of a chess grandmaster, was made into an acclaimed film. His last drama, *Shinano no Issa* (1993), was a poignant biography of the 18th–19th-century haiku poet Kobayashi Issa.

Holmboe, Vagn, Danish composer of more than 350 works, most notably string quartets, and developer of the "metamorphosis" technique, whereby a motif evolves, by means of constant transformation, into a complete composition (b. Dec. 20, 1909—d. Sept. 1, 1996).

Huncke, Herbert, U.S. writer who gave the Beat Generation its name; a drug addict, thief, and prostitute who spent much of the 1950s in prison, he was muse to such writers as Jack Kerouac and William Burroughs, and he often appeared in their novels (b. Dec. 9, 1915—d. Aug. 8, 1996).

Hunter, Ross (MARTIN FUSS), U.S. motion picture producer who became one of the most successful Hollywood filmmakers ever by aiming to satisfy popular taste with such opulent films as *Magnificent Obsession, Pillow Talk, Imitation of Life,* and *Airport* (b. May 6, 1926—d. March 10, 1996).

Iharos, Sandor, Hungarian middle-distance runner who during 14 months in 1955–56 set world records for seven distances (b. March 10, 1930—d. Jan. 24, 1996).

Jacobs, Bernard B., U.S. theatrical producer who wielded immense power and influenced the opening and closing of shows for 24 years as joint president of the Shubert Organization, which owned 17 of Broadway's 32 commercial theatres (b. 1916—d. Aug. 27, 1996).

Jay of Battersea, Douglas Patrick Thomas Jay, BARON, British Labour Party politician and economist whose vehement opposition to the U.K.'s membership in the European Economic Community led to his dismissal as the president of the Board of Trade in 1967, though he retained his seat in Parliament until 1983 (b. March 23, 1907—d. March 6, 1996).

Jayewardene, J(unius) R(ichard), Sri Lankan lawyer and politician (b. Sept. 17, 1906, Colombo, Ceylon [now Sri Lanka]—d. Nov. 1, 1996, Colombo), served as prime minister (1977–78) and president (1978–89) of Sri Lanka. He was praised for modernizing the country's economic system, but his inability to ease ethnic tensions

ultimately led to his resignation. Jayewardene, the son of a Supreme Court judge, graduated (1932) from Ceylon Law College in Colombo, but his interest soon turned to politics. In 1943 he was elected to the State Council, and four years later he entered Parliament. After Ceylon achieved independence from Great Britain in 1948, Jayewardene was named minister of finance. He joined the moderate United National Party (UNP) and in 1973 became its leader. In 1977 he led the UNP to a landslide victory and was named prime minister. Once in office he instituted a constitutional amendment that created an executive presidency; in 1978 he was sworn in as the country's first elected president. As president he dismantled Sri Lanka's socialist economic system, encouraging foreign investment and privatization. He also established a free-trade zone north of Colombo. In 1982 he was elected to a second six-year term. The following year the long-standing hostilities between the country's Sinhalese Buddhist majority and its Hindu Tamil minority erupted in violence. Tamil guerrillas began an insurgency in an attempt to create a separate Tamil state. Jayewardene's attempts to end the uprising were unsuccessful, and in 1987 he allowed Indian troops to enter the country to disarm the rebels. Faced with the unpopularity of that decision and the continued fighting, which had claimed thousands of lives, Jayewardene retired in 1989.

Jellicoe, Sir Geoffrey Alan, British landscape architect (b. Oct. 8, 1900, London, Eng.—d. July 17, 1996, Seaton, Devon, Eng.), considered landscape design the "mother of all arts" and for seven decades was one of its greatest practitioners. Such projects as the grounds of the Royal Lodge at Windsor, the Kennedy Memorial at Runnymede, and Sutton Place, near Guildford, Surrey, all of which featured a sensitivity to purpose and environment, illustrated why he was considered as important to the 20th century as Capability Brown was to the 18th. Jellicoe attended Cheltenham College and then studied architecture at the Architectural Association School of Architecture, London. His appetite for landscape design was whetted by a tour of Italy that he and fellow student J.C. Shepherd took (1924) to study the gardens there. Their book about the trip, *Italian Gardens of the Renaissance* (1925), became a standard textbook. Though Jellicoe helped found (1929) the Institute of Landscape Architects and later the International Federation of Landscape Architects (of which he served as honorary life president), he at first set up an architectural practice rather than concentrating on the design of landscapes. The Caveman Restaurant at Cheddar Gorge (1934), designed to blend gracefully with its surroundings, was the first of his works to gain attention. Jellicoe did pursue his interest in landscape architecture, however, with such commissions as the garden at James Gibbs's mansion at Ditchley Park, Oxfordshire, and the Earle's Cement Works in Derbyshire, and by the 1960s most of his attention was devoted to landscapes. One of his most important books, *The Landscape of Man* (1975; co-written with his wife, Susan), reflects his interest in Carl Jung's writings about the subconscious. That book inspired the work that was the culmination of Jellicoe's career, the Moody Historical Gardens in Galveston, Texas. He began the project in the mid-1980s, and, when finished, it was intended to present a landscape history of civilization. Jellicoe was appointed CBE in 1961 and knighted in 1979.

Jeppesen, Elrey B., U.S. mail pilot, barnstormer with a flying circus, and expert navigator who used his detailed terrain notes to chart the skies and create a multimillion-dollar business that published air-navigation charts and other flying aides (b. 1907?—d. Nov. 26, 1996).

Johnson, (Francis) Benjamin ("BEN"), U.S. motion picture actor who worked as a horse wrangler and stuntman before appearing in supporting roles in such films as *Shane, One-Eyed Jacks, The Wild Bunch,* and *The Last Picture Show,* for which he won an Academy Award (b. June 13, 1918—d. April 8, 1996).

Johnson, Harald Norlin, U.S. microbiologist and international specialist on such arthropod-borne viral diseases as rabies and encephalitis; while working, 1938–72, for the Rockefeller Foundation, he developed the strain of the rabies virus used in the 1960s vaccine that helped control the disease among dogs in the U.S. (b. March 31, 1907—d. Aug. 28, 1996).

Jordan, Barbara Charline, U.S. lawyer, politician, and teacher (b. Feb. 21, 1936, Houston, Texas—d. Jan. 17, 1996, Austin, Texas), was the first African-American woman to serve in the Texas legislature, the first Southern black woman elected to Congress, and one of the two first Southern blacks elected to Congress since Reconstruction. During the Watergate impeachment hearings (1974), however, she became best known for the power and authority of her voice when she delivered a stirring proclamation of her faith in the Constitution. Other memorable speeches included the keynote addresses at the Democratic national conventions in 1976 and 1992. Jordan graduated magna cum laude from the all-black Texas Southern University and earned (1959) a law degree from Boston University. She practiced law from her parents' dining room in Houston and became a volunteer during the 1960 presidential campaign, first licking envelopes for Lyndon B. Johnson's bid for the nomination and then directing a voter drive. Jordan made two unsuccessful runs (1962 and 1964) for the Texas House of Representatives before winning (1966) a seat in the Texas Senate, and in 1972 she won election to the U.S. House of Representatives. With the help of her mentor, Johnson, she won a seat on the House Judiciary Committee. She was considered a possible vice presidential candidate for the 1976 election. After three terms in the House, however, she returned to her home state and became a political ethics professor at the Lyndon B. Johnson School of Public Affairs at the University of Texas, Austin. Jordan chaired the U.S. Commission on Immigration Reform, and in late 1995 her eloquence was heard once more when she spoke out in Congress in opposition to a proposal to deny citizenship to children born in the U.S. to illegal immigrants.

Kabua, Amata, Marshallese politician who founded the Political Movement for the Marshall Islands Separation from Micronesia (1972) and served as president of the Marshall Islands from 1979 when the republic gained independence; he was elected to his fifth term of office in 1995 (b. Nov. 17, 1928—d. Dec. 19, 1996).

Kades, Charles Louis, U.S. lawyer who, as a lieutenant colonel under Gen. Douglas MacArthur during World War II, oversaw the drafting of Japan's postwar constitution (adopted May 3, 1947), in which the quasi-divine emperor was replaced with a constitutional monarchy and the nation made a formal renunciation of war (b. March 12, 1906—d. June 18, 1996).

Kallai, Gyula, Hungarian politician who helped restore communist rule in Hungary after the 1956 pro-democracy uprising and later held numerous government positions, including that of prime minister, 1965–67 (b. June 1, 1910—March 12, 1996).

Kanemaru, Shin, Japanese politician (b. Sept. 17, 1914, Suwa village, Yamanashi prefecture, Japan—d. March 28, 1996, Yamanashi), served in three Cabinet posts and as deputy prime minister (1986–87), but his real power was exercised behind the scenes, where he was the kingmaker who handpicked at least four prime ministers. He was known as Japan's "godfather" for decades until a bribery and tax-evasion scandal ended his career and the long reign of the Liberal Democratic Party (LDP). Kanemaru was educated at the Tokyo University of Agriculture. He became involved in politics when he was elected (1958) to the Diet (parliament) as an LDP representative for Yamanashi prefecture. A firm supporter of most U.S. policies, Kanemaru in 1960 carried the speaker of Japan's House of Representatives to

Barbara Jordan

his seat when opponents of a security treaty with the U.S. blocked the entrance to the chamber. He worked closely with Prime Ministers Kakuei Tanaka and Noboru Takeshita, both members of what later was the party's most powerful faction. He also became very successful at holding the LDP's various factions together and was skilled at procuring government projects and aid for his district. Kanemaru's power was strongest in the 1980s, but in 1992 he had to resign from the Diet and relinquish his post as party vice president when it was revealed that he had accepted over $4 million in bribes. A raid on his home and office uncovered a huge stash of securities, cash, and gold bars. He was indicted on tax-evasion charges the following year, but his health was broken, and his trial was suspended shortly before his death.

Kardar, Abdul Hafeez, Indian-born Pakistani cricketer and politician who played three Test matches for India and led Pakistan in 23 Tests after partition (1947); he retired from the game in 1957 with a first-class career total of 6,814 runs (including eight centuries), then served on the Pakistani national cricket board and held office as a member of the Punjab Provincial Assembly, a federal government minister, and ambassador to Switzerland (b. Jan. 17, 1925—d. April 21, 1996).

Karmal, Babrak, Afghan politician (b. Jan. 6, 1929, near Kabul, Afg.—d. Dec. 3, 1996, Moscow, Russia), was the U.S.S.R.-backed president of Afghanistan from 1979, when the Soviet Union invaded the country, until 1986, when the Soviet government decided that fighting there was no longer in Moscow's interest. Karmal became involved in Marxist political activities while a student at Kabul University and was imprisoned. Upon his release, he served in the army and returned to the university for a law degree. Karmal was a founding member of the People's Demo-

cratic Party of Afghanistan (PDPA) and from 1965 to 1973 served in the National Assembly. When the party split (1967) into the Khalq ("People's") and the Parcham ("Banner") parties, he became leader of the more moderate, pro-Soviet Parcham. The Khalq and the Parcham reunited in 1977, and in 1978—with Soviet help—the PDPA seized the government. Karmal became deputy prime minister, but rivalries within the government soon resulted in his being sent as ambassador to Prague. The PDPA was attempting to modernize the country drastically along Marxist lines, but there were major rebellions in the countryside, and in December 1979, Soviet troops invaded Afghanistan and called Karmal back to be president. The rebels persisted with aid from the West, and the area became a Cold War battleground. Moscow came to consider Karmal a burden and publicly blamed him for the country's problems, and in November 1986 he resigned from office, claiming poor health. Shortly thereafter Karmal moved to Moscow, where he spent most of his remaining years.

Keane, Molly (MARY NESTA SKRINE; "M.J. FARRELL"), Anglo-Irish writer (b. July 4, 1904, Ballyrankin, County Kildare, Ire.—d. April 22, 1996, Ardmore, County Waterford, Ire.), enjoyed two distinct literary careers. Born into the Anglo-Irish gentry, Keane began to publish while in her early 20s. Writing as M.J. Farrell—she said, "Young men would have been afraid of you if they thought you could read, let alone write"— Keane used her sharp eye and mischievous wit to satirize the personal intrigues and pursuits of the leisure class, to which she herself belonged. She especially delighted in describing its passionate obsession with horses and fox hunting. Her first novel, *The Knight of Cheerful Countenance* (1928), was followed by several others of the same tenor. The success of her comedy *Spring Meeting* (1938, written with John Perry) led Keane to branch out into playwriting as well. Her insights into the genteel occupations of the rural gentry, however, fell out of step with the literary output of the times, and this, coupled with the untimely death of her husband, kept her silent for about three decades. In 1981 Keane returned to the subject she knew best with the acclaimed novel *Good Behaviour.* She went on to write two more novels, *Time After Time* (1983) and *Loving and Giving* (1988; U.S. title, *Queen Lear,* 1989).

Kelly, Eugene Curran ("GENE"), U.S. dancer, actor, choreographer, and director (b. Aug. 23, 1912, Pittsburgh, Pa.—d. Feb. 2, 1996, Beverly Hills, Calif.), revolutionized the motion picture musicals of the 1940s and '50s by taking his dance numbers off Hollywood sound stages and out onto the streets in scenes that featured athleticism in contrast to the aristocratic elegance of Fred Astaire. Kelly blended the techniques of ballet, tap, and jazz in choreography that reflected his own robust, acrobatic style and created innovative scenarios in which, for example, he danced with an "alter ego" image of himself, in *Cover Girl* (1944), and with a cartoon mouse, in *Anchors Aweigh* (1945). Kelly studied dance as a child, and after graduating (1933) from the University of Pittsburgh with a degree in economics, he taught dance, danced in vaudeville with his brother, and directed local plays. He debuted on Broadway in 1938—as a chorus boy in *Leave It to Me*—and the next year was featured in *The Time of Your Life.* The title role in *Pal Joey* followed in 1940 and led to a Hollywood contract. In 1942 Kelly starred in his first motion picture, *For Me and My Gal.* For MGM he made such films as *Anchors Aweigh, The Pirate* (1948), and *An American in Paris* (1951). The latter, which ended with a nearly 20-minute ballet, won the Academy Award for best picture, and Kelly was given a special Oscar for his contributions to film musicals. It was while on loan to Columbia for *Cover Girl,* however, that he first collaborated with director Stanley Donen and began the experimentation that changed the face of movie musicals, creating dance numbers that utilized motion picture techniques and that advanced the plot rather than serving merely as entertainment. In 1949 Kelly and Donen co-directed *On the Town,* about three sailors on leave in New York City, which broke film musical tradition by being shot entirely on location. Their next effort was *Singin' in the Rain* (1952), which many consider the finest of all screen musicals. Among the films that he directed but did not appear in were *Hello, Dolly!* (1969) and *The Cheyenne Social Club* (1970). Kelly was the recipient of the Lifetime Achievement Award from the American Film Institute (1985) and the National Medal of the Arts (1994).

Kerr, Walter Francis, U.S. drama critic and playwright (b. July 8, 1913, Evanston, Ill.—d. Oct. 9, 1996, Dobbs Ferry, N.Y.), served for more than 30 years as one of the most influential theatre critics in the country. In 1978 he was awarded a Pulitzer Prize for criticism for "the whole body of his critical work." Kerr's reviewing career began when he was 13, critiquing films for the *Evanston Review.* After his education in drama at Northwestern University, Evanston, he joined the drama department at Catholic University of America, Washington, D.C., and began directing, writing, and adapting plays. After the musical comedy *Count Me In,* on which Kerr had collaborated, had a short run on Broadway in 1942, he was encouraged to continue writing. Several other modest hits followed, some co-written with his wife, Jean. He also directed on Broadway. Kerr had become the critic for *Commonweal* in 1949 and in 1951 moved to the *New York Herald Tribune.* When that paper closed (1966), he went to the *New York Times,* where he remained until his retirement in 1983. Kerr continued to write occasional pieces for the *Times* and was the author of 10 books. In 1990 the restored Ritz Theatre was renamed the Walter Kerr Theatre in his honour, and on the evening after his death was announced, lights on Broadway were dimmed briefly in tribute.

Khariton, Yuly Borisovich, Russian physicist who figured prominently in the development of nuclear physics research in the Soviet Union in the 1930s and '40s and, as director of the nuclear research centre Arzamas-16, oversaw the construction of the first Soviet nuclear bomb, which was built according to plutonium bomb designs stolen from the U.S. and was detonated in August 1949 (b. Feb. 27, 1904—d. Dec. 19, 1996).

Kieslowski, Krzysztof, Polish film director (b. June 27, 1941, Warsaw, Pol.—d. March 13, 1996, Warsaw), crafted psychological dramas that examined moral issues with intellect and passion and was regarded as one of the finest filmmakers in Europe. He was known internationally for his final work, the trilogy *Trois Couleurs* (*Three Colors*). It comprises *Bleu* (1993; *Blue*), the story of a Frenchwoman who tries to escape her shattered past; *Blanc* (1993; *White*), a black comedy about a Polish man who plots revenge on his French former wife; and *Rouge* (1994; *Red*), about the relationship between a misanthropic retired judge and a caring young woman model in Switzerland. After training at the School of Cinema and Theatre in Łodz, Kieslowski began his screen career shooting documentaries about communist Poland. He first earned critical acclaim with the feature films *Amator* (1979; "The Camera Buff"), *Przypadek* (1981; "Blind Chance"), and *Bez konca* (1984; "No End"), which was coauthored by Krzysztof Piesiewicz, a lawyer who helped write the remainder of Kieslowski's films. *Dekalog* (1988; "Decalogue"), often considered his masterwork, is a collection of 10 short films based on ethical dilemmas posed by the Ten Commandments. Two of them were expanded into feature-length motion pictures—*Krotki film o zabijaniu* ("A Short Film About Killing") and *Krotki film o miłosci* ("A Short Film About Love"). With *La Double Vie de Véronique* (1991), he began shooting outside Poland, mainly in collaboration with French studios. He retired from filmmaking in 1994.

Gene Kelly

Kirstein, Lincoln Edward, U.S. arts patron (b. May 4, 1907, Rochester, N.Y.—d. Jan. 5, 1996, New York, N.Y.), was a dance authority and cofounder and general director (1948–89) of the New York City Ballet. Together with choreographer George Balanchine, he changed the course of dance in the U.S. Their collaboration lasted until Balanchine's death in 1983. Kirstein was ambitious, financially independent, and keenly interested in high culture. While at Harvard University, he founded and edited (1927–34) the literary magazine *Hound & Horn.* Having developed a passion for classical ballet, he recruited the young Balanchine to help him establish an American ballet company. They opened the School of American Ballet (now the affiliated school of the New York City Ballet) in 1934. The next year the American Ballet dance company was inaugurated. The company disbanded during the early 1940s, and Kirstein joined the army. In 1946, again with Balanchine, Kirstein founded Ballet Society, another dance troupe. Two years later this troupe danced the premiere of Igor Stravinsky's *Orpheus,* a performance that was considered a landmark of modern dance. That same year the corps became the resident company of the City Center of Music and Drama, and Kirstein and Balanchine continued to transform it into one of the world's leading ballet companies, moving with it in 1964 to its present home in the Lincoln Center for the Performing Arts. Kirstein's literary output was eclectic and prolific. He wrote about dance in such works as *Dance: A Short History of Classic Theatrical Dancing* (1935), *Ballet Alphabet* (1939), *Movement & Metaphor* (1970), *The New York City Ballet* (1973), and *Nijinsky Dancing* (1975). His poetry is published in such volumes as *Rhymes and More Rhymes of a Pfc* (1966), first published in 1964 under the title *Rhymes for a Pfc,* and *The Poems of Lincoln Kirstein* (1987). He produced a series of monographs on visual artists, including *Elie Nadelman* (1973), *Paul Cadmus* (1984), and *Tchelitchev* (1994). In the last decade of his

life, Kirstein wrote a number of memoirs, notably *Quarry* (1986), *By With To & From* (1991), and the slightly scandalous *Mosaic* (1994), in which he reported a number of heterosexual and homosexual affairs.

Kngwarreye, Emily Kame, Australian artist (b. *c.* 1910, Utopia, Soakage Bore, N.Terr., Australia—d. Sept. 2, 1996, Alice Springs, N.Terr.), took Aboriginal art to a new audience internationally. Although she was in her 70s before she began painting, she was considered one of the country's greatest artists. Kngwarreye grew up in an extremely remote area and was nine years old before she saw a white person. When she was a young woman, she worked as a stockhand at a cattle station on tribal lands. She also was educated in the sacred tribal traditions and became a tribal elder. In the mid-1970s a batik-making program for a local women's group became Kngwarreye's introduction to art, and her talent became apparent in the adaptations of traditional body markings she transferred to silk. When the group began (1988–89) working with acrylics on canvas, she found that a more suitable medium for the bold colour and vigour with which she painted visions of her country, traditions, and myths. Kngwarreye had two one-woman shows in 1990, received a government fellowship in 1992, and had displayed her art in more than 50 exhibitions throughout the world by 1993. Her style shifted over the years, from colourful dots over linear patterns in her early work to bold stripes, often on dark grounds, by the mid-1990s. Her works were eagerly sought by both galleries and private collectors, and she earned a great deal of money, but Kngwarreye continued to live a traditional Aboriginal life and shared her wealth with her kinspeople.

Kobayashi, Koji, Japanese visionary industrialist who guided the NEC Corp. as president (1964–76) and then chairman (until 1988) toward computers and other high-tech products; he registered more than 100 patents and in 1977 coined NEC's watchword, "C and C," a prediction that computers and communications would merge into a single information infrastructure (b. 1907—d. Nov. 30, 1996).

Kobayashi, Masaki, Japanese film director (b. Feb. 14, 1916, Otaru, Hokkaido, Japan—d. Oct. 4, 1996, Tokyo, Japan), created exquisitely stylized motion pictures known for their harsh critiques of Japanese society and portrayals of dissident individuals. Though he was opposed to Japan's involvement in World War II, Kobayashi was drafted into the military in 1942 and spent the last year of the war as a prisoner on Okinawa. Released in 1946, he returned to Tokyo and served as an apprentice director with the Shochiku Motion Picture Co. He made his directorial debut in 1952 with *Musuko no seishun* (1952; *My Son's Youth*), followed by *Kabe atsuki heya* (1953; *The Thick-Walled Room*) and *Anata kaimasu* (1956; *I'll Buy You*). Kobayashi's epic trilogy, *Ningen no joken* (1959–61; *The Human Condition*), was the best example of his cinema of social concern and a powerful indictment of the brutality inherent in a militaristic society. The trilogy established Kobayashi's reputation as a major director. He attracted wider admiration with *Seppuku* (1962; *Harakiri*), which attacked the moral code of the samurai, and *Kaidan* (1964; *Kwaidan*), a quartet of fantastic ghost stories; each movie won the Special Jury Prize at the Cannes Film Festival. Later films include *Kaseki* (1974; *Fossil*), *Tokyo saiban* (1983; *The Tokyo Trials*), and *Shokutaku no nai ie* (1985; *The Empty Table*).

Koc, Vehbi, Turkish businessman and philanthropist who built his business into the country's largest conglomerate—comprising over 80 companies and employing over 40,000 people—and one of the world's top 100 companies (b. July 20?, 1901—d. Feb. 25, 1996).

Kokkonen, Joonas, Finnish composer who was the country's most important since Jean Sibelius; his some 50 works include four symphonies and other orchestral pieces, several choral works, a number of chamber pieces, and only one opera, *Viimeiset kiusaukset* (*The Last Temptations*), which nevertheless was his best-known creation (b. Nov. 13, 1921—d. Oct. 2, 1996).

Komar, Chris, U.S. dancer who, as a member of the Merce Cunningham Dance Company, created roles in over 45 of the choreographer's works and in 1992 became assistant artistic director of the troupe (b. Oct. 30, 1947—d. July 17, 1996).

Kosterlitz, Hans Walter, German-born British pharmacologist who had already retired from the University of Aberdeen, Scot., when he discovered (1975), with John Hughes, enkephalins, two potent naturally occurring opiates in the brain (b. April 27, 1903—d. Oct. 26, 1996).

Krol, John Joseph Cardinal, U.S. Roman Catholic prelate (b. Oct. 26, 1910, Cleveland, Ohio—d. March 3, 1996, Philadelphia, Pa.), was archbishop of Philadelphia from 1961 to 1988. During his 27-year tenure he demonstrated administrative skills and espoused traditionalist views. As a leader of the church's conservative wing in the U.S., he opposed the relaxation of authority and discipline that followed the Second Vatican Council (1962–65). Krol was ordained a priest in 1937, served a parish in Cleveland for a year, and, after earning (1942) a doctorate in canon law at the Catholic University of America, Washington, D.C., taught canon law at a seminary in Cleveland. He became auxiliary bishop of Cleveland in 1953 and archbishop of Philadelphia in 1961. After serving the Second Vatican Council as an undersecretary, working on scheduling and organization, Krol was elevated to cardinal in 1967. He was president of the National Conference of Catholic Bishops from 1971 to 1974. Krol was influential in the election (1978) of Pope John Paul II, and the pope placed him on the committee that oversaw the Vatican's financial operations. His managerial skills and knowledge of real estate and finance proved valuable, especially in the wake of the Italian banking scandal in the late 1980s. He was also active in relief activities after Poland's military cracked down (1981) on the efforts of the Solidarity trade union. Krol retired in 1988.

Kubelik, Rafael Jeronym, Bohemian-born Swiss conductor and composer (b. June 29, 1914, Bychory, Bohemia, Austria-Hungary [now in Czech Republic]—d. Aug. 11, 1996, Lucerne, Switz.), was known for his powerful and invigorating interpretations, especially of the music of composers from his homeland. He made frequent guest appearances with major orchestras throughout the world and held a number of important directorship posts. Kubelik, a son of the violinist Jan Kubelik, attended the Prague Conservatory, made his debut with the Czech Philharmonic Orchestra in 1934, and became that orchestra's conductor in 1936. He served as director of the Brno Opera from 1939 to 1941 and then returned to the Czech Philharmonic. In 1948, when the communists took over, Kubelik left the country, vowing not to return as long as they were in power; he settled first in England and later in Switzerland, where he became (1967) a citizen. He served a tempestuous three seasons (1950–53) with the Chicago Symphony and in 1955 was appointed music director at London's Covent Garden. His stint there was also controversial, in part because of his policy of having the operas performed in English, and he left in 1958. Kubelik was guest conductor with the Vienna Philharmonic and the Israel Philharmonic, principal conductor of the Bavarian Radio Symphony (1961–79), and music director of the Metropolitan Opera, New York City (1973–74). In 1990, after the fall of communism, he returned to Prague and conducted the Czech Philharmonic in three performances of Bedrich Smetana's *Ma vlast* (*My Country*). Kubelik counted operas, requiems, symphonies, and concerti among his compositions, and a number of his notable recordings were reissued many times.

Kuhn, Thomas S., U.S. philosopher of science (b. July 18, 1922, Cincinnati, Ohio—d. June 17, 1996, Cambridge, Mass.), was the author of *The Structure of Scientific Revolutions* (1962), one of the most widely read and influential books in 20th-century social sciences, humanities, and philosophy. Kuhn studied physics at Harvard University, where he earned (1949) a Ph.D. in physics. He remained there as a junior fellow, then taught at the University of California, Berkeley, Princeton University, and the Massachusetts Institute of Technology. His first book, *The Copernican Revolution* (1957), was a study of the development of Renaissance heliocentrism. His second book, *The Structure of Scientific Revolutions,* argued that scientific work and thought are defined by "paradigms" consisting of formal theories, classic experiments, and trusted methods. Scientists use the resources of paradigms to refine theories, explain puzzling data, and establish increasingly precise measures of standards and phenomena. Confidence in paradigms, however, can be eroded by unresolvable theoretical problems or experimental anomalies, and the accumulation of such difficulties eventually creates a crisis that can be resolved only by revolutions in which new paradigms are formulated to replace the old. The overthrow of Ptolemaic cosmology by Copernican heliocentrism and Newtonian mechanics by quantum physics and general relativity are both examples of fundamental paradigm shifts. The book received polite but not extravagant reviews and significant criticism when it first appeared. By the mid-1960s, however, it had clearly become one of the most influential works in post-World War II scholarship. It revolutionized the history and philosophy of science by inspiring accounts that gave increased weight to external social and cultural factors in shaping scientific work and thought and made the term "paradigm" part of common English. Kuhn's collection of essays, *The Essential Tension* (1977), was followed by his last book, *Black-Body Theory and the Quantum Discontinuity* (1978), a highly technical study that some considered an implicit rejection of his earlier work.

Kumar, Raaj (KULBHUSHAN NATH PANDIT), Indian motion picture actor whose elegant delivery of dialogue graced more than 60 films in some 40 years and helped make him a cult figure among college youths (b. Oct. 8, 1927?—d. July 3, 1996).

Lacoste, (Jean-)René, French tennis player and sportswear manufacturer (b. July 2, 1904, Paris, Fr.—d. Oct. 12, 1996, Saint-Jean-de-Luz, Fr.), was a leading competitor during the 1920s and later transformed his nickname, "Le Crocodile," into a popular emblem on polo shirts around the world. Lacoste was the last survivor of the legendary Four Musketeers of French tennis (the others were Jean Borotra, Jacques Brugnon, and Henri Cochet); among them, the four won all six Wimbledon singles titles from 1924 to 1929. A methodical player who was recognized as perhaps tennis's greatest groundstroker and one of its most astute tacticians, Lacoste won the Wimbledon singles in 1925 and 1928, won the French Open singles in 1925, 1927, and 1929, and became the first foreigner to win the U.S. Open singles championship twice (1926-27). He also helped France win its first Davis Cup in 1927 by defeating U.S. tennis great Bill Tilden. By that time sportswriters had begun calling Lacoste "Le Crocodile" to describe his tenacious playing style on the court. Following his retirement from tennis in 1929, Lacoste started a sportswear company, La Société Chemise Lacoste; decades later, after Lacoste's son had expanded the business into a global operation, polo shirts embroidered with Lacoste's "crocodile" emblem (somehow it was changed into an alligator) became famous as status symbols worldwide. Lacoste also designed tennis rackets and golf clubs and wrote a book, *Lacoste on Tennis* (1928). He and his fellow Musketeers were elected to the International Tennis Hall of Fame in 1976.

Lalic, Ivan V., Serb poet who considered himself steeped in the Mediterranean tradition rather than belonging to a specific ethnic group; he imbued his poems with the importance of memories, both personal and cultural (b. June 8, 1931—d. July 27, 1996).

Lamour, Dorothy (MARY LETA DOROTHY SLATON), U.S. actress (b. Dec. 10, 1914, New Orleans, La.—d. Sept. 22, 1996, Los Angeles, Calif.), was best remembered by filmgoers as the sarong-clad object of Bob Hope's and Bing Crosby's attention in a series of "Road" pictures. She was a favourite pinup of troops in World War II, frequently visited the Hollywood Canteen to dance and talk with GIs, and was a dedicated promoter of U.S. war bonds. After winning the 1931 Miss New Orleans contest, Lamour began her performing career as a singer in nightclubs and on the radio, first in Chicago and then in New York City. She made her motion picture debut—and her first appearance in a sarong—in *The Jungle Princess* (1936). *The Hurricane* (1937) and *Her Jungle Love* (1938) followed. She then changed pace for the gangster melodrama *Johnny Apollo* (1940). The first "Road" picture, *Road to Singapore* (1940), was such a success that four more were made in the 1940s, another in 1953, and the last in 1962. Lamour was also in such films as the wartime musical *The Fleet's In* (1942), *The Greatest Show on Earth* (1952), and *Donovan's Reef* (1963). She had roles in some 60 films in all, made guest appearances in television series, and also toured in stage shows such as *Hello, Dolly!* and a one-woman show comprising songs, reminiscences, and a question-and-answer session. Lamour's autobiography, *My Side of the Road,* appeared in 1980.

Lanusse, Alejandro Agustín, Argentine general and politician (b. Aug. 28, 1918, Buenos Aires, Arg.—d. Aug. 26, 1996, Buenos Aires), as president of Argentina from 1971 to 1973, attempted to restore democracy to the country. Born into an upper-middle-class family, Lanusse graduated from military college in 1938 and joined the cavalry. In 1951 he was sentenced to life in prison for his participation in a failed attempt to oust Pres. Juan Perón. When Perón was deposed in 1955, Lanusse was released and promoted to lieutenant colonel. He became part of the army's high command and aligned himself with Gen. Juan Carlos Onganía, who became president in 1966. Lanusse was named commander in chief of the army in 1968 and in March 1971 led a coup that brought him to power. Peronists and student militants, among others, protested Lanusse's regime, and the army employed violent tactics to silence the dissenters. With escalating unrest, Lanusse attempted to achieve stability by calling for free elections. He scheduled Argentina's first democratic polls in more than 20 years and reestablished political parties. The Peronists won the 1973 elections, and by year's end Perón was president. In the mid-1970s army hard-liners came to power and unleashed a "dirty war," in which as many as 30,000 people were killed or "disappeared." Lanusse denounced the violence and in 1985 testified against the deposed military rulers during their trial for human rights violations. In a three-volume autobiography, Lanusse cited mistakes made during military rule but continued to support the army. A committed anti-Peronist, he served 10 days of house arrest in 1994 for his criticism of Peronist Pres. Carlos Menem.

Larson, Jonathan, U.S. composer and author of the Tony award-winning pop-rock musical *Rent,* which he based on Giacomo Puccini's tragic opera *La Bohème* and for which he was awarded posthumously the Pulitzer Prize for Drama (b. Feb. 4, 1960—d. Jan. 25, 1996).

LaRue, Albert ("LASH"), U.S. film actor who was best remembered for his portrayal of the black-clad hero who wielded a 4.5-m (15-ft) bullwhip in a series of B westerns in the 1940s (b. June 15, 1917—d. May 21, 1996).

Lavin, Mary, U.S.-born Irish writer who was best known for her short stories that revealed the complexities and remarkableness of seemingly ordinary small-town Irish life (b. June 11, 1912—d. March 25, 1996).

Lawton, Thomas ("TOMMY"), British association football (soccer) player who was a commanding

EVERETT COLLECTION

Dorothy Lamour

centre forward just before and after World War II, scoring 231 goals in 390 League matches and 22 goals in 23 appearances for England (as well as 25 goals in 23 wartime international games). Lawton switched teams several times for then-record transfer fees and tried his hand as a manager in the 1950s and '60s; from 1984 he wrote a newspaper column for the *Nottingham Evening Post* (b. Oct. 6, 1919—d. Nov. 6, 1996).

Laye, Evelyn (ELSIE EVELYN LAY), British actress and singer who had a nearly 80-year career and between the two world wars was London's most successful star of stage musicals and operettas (b. July 10, 1900—d. Feb. 17, 1996).

Le Mai, Vietnamese politician who held numerous diplomatic posts, including deputy foreign minister, and was instrumental in improving relations with the U.S. following the Vietnam War (b. 1940—d. June 12, 1996).

Leakey, Mary Douglas, British-born archaeologist and paleoanthropologist (b. Feb. 6, 1913, London, Eng.—d. Dec. 9, 1996, Nairobi, Kenya), made a number of significant finds of prehuman

Mary Leakey

UPI/CORBIS-BETTMANN

fossils in East Africa, discoveries that helped to supplant the formerly held notion that the human species evolved in Asia. Through her work as an excavator and an illustrator of tools found at various archaeological sites in England, she met archaeologist Louis Leakey; they were married in 1936 and shortly thereafter left for an expedition to East Africa, an area that became the central location of their work. Her skill at the painstaking work of excavation surpassed her husband's, whose brilliance lay in interpreting and publicizing the fossils that she uncovered. Her first important find was made in 1948 on Rusinga Island in Lake Victoria, Kenya. There she unearthed the skull of *Proconsul africanus,* an 18 million-year-old apelike creature. Her next major discovery was made on July 17, 1959, at Olduvai Gorge, the now-famous ravine in the Great Rift Valley of Tanzania. The jaw of the early hominid *Zinjanthropus* (now *Australopithecus) boisei* that she teased from its 1,750,000-year-old resting place brought worldwide recognition to the couple, although the claim that this was the "missing link" between primitive ape-men and early humans was later disproved. Not long after this find, the Leakey team discovered in a nearby spot in Olduvai Gorge skull fragments more similar to a modern human's, designated *Homo habilis.* After her husband's death in 1972, Leakey continued her work in Africa. In 1978 at Laetoli, a site about 48 km (30 mi) south of Olduvai Gorge, she made what she believed was her most important find, a trail of several sets of hominid footprints preserved in volcanic ash that were approximately 3.5 million years old. These prints provided evidence that hominids walked in an upright position at a much earlier date than had previously been thought. Leakey retired from fieldwork in 1983 and in 1984 published an autobiography, *Disclosing the Past.*

Lear, Frances, U.S. feminist activist and founder of the magazine *Lear's,* a publication for women who "weren't born yesterday"; she financed the venture with $25 million from a more than $100 million divorce settlement received from television producer Norman Lear, who reportedly modeled the title character of "Maude" after her (b. July 14, 1923—d. Sept. 30, 1996).

Leary, Timothy, U.S. educator turned drug-culture guru (b. Oct. 22, 1920, Springfield, Mass.—d. May 31, 1996, Beverly Hills, Calif.), was considered the "messiah of LSD" and other hallucinogenic drugs in the 1960s. Urging people to "turn on, tune in, drop out," he spread a message promoting social rebellion and the psychedelic experience. Leary dropped out of both the College of the Holy Cross, Worcester, Mass., and the United States Military Academy, West Point, N.Y., but by 1950 he had earned a bachelor's degree from the University of Alabama, a master's from Washington State University, and a Ph.D. from the University of California, Berkeley. He taught at Berkeley from 1950 to 1955, was director of psychological research at the Kaiser Foundation Hospital, Oakland, Calif., from 1955 to 1958, and in 1959 became a lecturer at Harvard University. Leary's first drug experience came in 1960 in Mexico when he ate some hallucinogenic mushrooms. Back at Harvard he began experimenting with mind-altering drugs, but he was dismissed in 1963 when it was revealed that he had given drugs to students. Leary and a colleague then took over a mansion in Millbrook, N.Y., where they continued to engage in counterculture activities. Problems with the law began in the mid-1960s, and in 1970 Leary was imprisoned in California. The revolutionary group known as the Weather Underground aided him in a spectacular escape, and he fled first to Algeria and eventually to Afghanistan, where he was captured in 1973 and returned to a California prison. He was released in 1976. Leary spent the next few years on the lecture circuit, at times participating in debates with a onetime adversary, Watergate figure G. Gordon Liddy. He also became a computer aficionado, and his home page on the Internet chronicled his death from prostate cancer. Leary's last wish was to have his remains launched into space.

Lelyveld, Arthur, U.S. rabbi and Reform Judaism leader whose social activism embraced support for recognition of Israel two years before that country's birth, the fostering of closer relations between Jews and African-Americans, and civil rights work that included the registration of black voters in the South in the early 1960s (b. Feb. 6, 1913—d. April 15, 1996).

Lennep, Emile van, Dutch public official who was secretary-general of the Organisation for Economic Co-operation and Development, 1969–84, and helped build its effectiveness as a forum for international cooperation (b. Jan. 20, 1915—d. Oct. 3, 1996).

Lewis, Henry Jay, U.S. orchestra conductor who was the first African-American conductor and music director of a major American orchestra and the first black to conduct at the Metropolitan Opera in New York City (b. Oct. 16, 1932—d. Jan. 26, 1996).

Libuda, Reinhard, German association football (soccer) right winger who played with Schalke 04, Borussia Dortmund, and the West German national team in the 1960s and early '70s. His tremendous skill as a dribbler was a major factor in Dortmund's 1966 European Cup-Winners' Cup championship and West Germany's hard-fought-for trip to—and third-place finish in—the 1970 World Cup finals (b. 1942—d. Aug. 25, 1996).

Lindwall, Raymond Russell, Australian cricketer (b. Oct. 3, 1921, Mascot, N.S.W., Australia—d. June 23, 1996, Brisbane, Australia), was one of the most admired fast bowlers of the post-World War II era; between 1946 and 1962 he took 794 first-class wickets (average 21.36), including 228 in 61 Test matches (average 23.03). An effective batsman, he also made 5,042 runs, including 1,502 in Tests (average 21.15), and five centuries, two in Tests. Lindwall showed great athletic ability as a boy and played for the St. George Cricket Club in

Timothy Leary

Sydney at age 16. While fulfilling his wartime service with the Australian army in the South Pacific, he perfected his bowling technique on the beach in his free time. Lindwall joined the Australian Services postwar tour of England in 1945 and returned home with an arsenal of balls employing speed, pace, and versatility. He was selected for the 1946–47 Test series against England, in which he batted his first century at Melbourne and took 7 for 63 at Sydney. He played professionally for New South Wales until 1955, when he transferred to Queensland. He retired as a player in 1962 and was made MBE in 1965.

Lipson, Paul, U.S. actor who performed the role of Tevye in *Fiddler on the Roof* more times (over 2,000) than any other actor (b. Dec. 23, 1913—d. Jan. 3, 1996).

Livesay, Dorothy Kathleen May, Canadian feminist and poet whose sensitive and reflective verse spanned six decades and dealt with women's and political issues; she won Governor General's awards for *Day and Night* (1944) and *Poems for People* (1947) and was made an Officer of the Order of Canada in 1987 (b. Oct. 12, 1909—d. Dec. 29, 1996).

Lloyd, Seton Howard Frederick, British archaeologist who led a number of digs in Iraq and Turkey and was the first director of the British Institute of Archaeology at Ankara, Turkey (b. May 30, 1902—d. Jan. 7, 1996).

Lorengar, Pilar (PILAR LORENZA GARCÍA), Spanish opera singer who was an internationally acclaimed soprano best known for her interpretations of Mozart heroines (b. Jan. 16, 1928—d. June 2, 1996).

Ludwig, Peter, German chocolatier and art collector who amassed one of the world's largest private art collections and helped found a number of art museums, to which he donated or lent pieces from his collection (b. July 9, 1925—d. July 22, 1996).

Luening, Otto Clarence, U.S. composer, conductor, and flutist (b. June 15, 1900, Milwaukee, Wis.—d. Sept. 2, 1996, New York, N.Y.), created more than 300 musical pieces in a wide variety of styles but was perhaps best remembered for his innovations in electronic music. His experimental collaborations with Russian-born composer Vladimir Ussachevsky, including *Rhapsodic Variations for Tape Recorder and Orchestra* (1953), won him widespread praise. Luening was active in the music industry, helping to found the American Composers Alliance, the American Music Center, and the record label Composers Recordings Inc. His father, an immigrant German pianist and conductor, moved the family in 1912 from Milwaukee to Munich, Ger., and then, in 1917, to Zürich, Switz., where Luening studied under the Italian-born composer Ferruccio Busoni. After returning to the U.S. in 1920, he launched a teaching career that took him to successive posts at the Eastman School of Music, Rochester, N.Y., the University of Arizona, Bennington (Vt.) College, Barnard College, Columbia University, and Juilliard School, the latter three all in New York City. At Columbia he was co-director of the Columbia-Princeton Electronic Music Center (1959–80). He began experimenting with the magnetic tape recorder in *Fantasy in Space* (1952), in which he played flute to a recorded accompaniment. Among his major nonelectronic works were *Symphonic Fantasia No. 1* (1922–24), *Louisville Concerto* (1951), and *A Wisconsin Symphony* (1975). His autobiography, *The Odyssey of an American Composer,* appeared in 1980.

Lukanov, Andrey, Bulgarian politician (b. Sept. 26, 1938, Moscow, U.S.S.R.—d. Oct. 2, 1996, Sofia, Bulg.), was prime minister (1990) during the first stage of Bulgaria's transition from communism to democracy and later became a powerful critic of the government. Educated in the Soviet Union, Lukanov entered the Bulgarian foreign service in 1963, the same year that he became a member of the Bulgarian Communist Party. He held a series of senior posts during the communist regime, including minister of foreign economic relations (1987–89), before helping to orchestrate the overthrow of longtime dictator Todor Zhivkov in November 1989. Lukanov served as prime minister from February to November 1990, when he resigned owing to Bulgaria's rapid economic deterioration. In 1992, during the rule of Prime Minister Filip Dimitrov, Lukanov was held in custody for six months during a period when he was investigated for allegedly having enriched (1980s) his purse from the public coffers. Lukanov was never brought to trial, however, and he subsequently was appointed chairman (1995) of the Bulgarian-Russian gas company Topenergy. When Bulgaria's socialist government came to power in January 1995, his sharp criticism and vociferous support for democratic reform attracted publicity. In an apparent move to improve relations with the new Bulgarian government, Topenergy removed Lukanov from his post in July 1996. Lukanov was shot and killed by unknown assailants as he left his downtown apartment building in Sofia.

Lyubarsky, Kronid Arkadyevich, Russian human rights activist whose work led to his arrest and emigration in the 1970s; following the 1991 breakup of the U.S.S.R., he returned to Russia, where he served as chairman of the human rights monitoring group Moscow Helsinki Watch and as editor of *Novoye Vremya,* a pro-democracy magazine (b. April 1935—d. May 23, 1996).

MacCaig, Norman Alexander, Scottish poet (b. Nov. 14, 1910, Edinburgh, Scot.—d. Jan. 23, 1996, Edinburgh), was one of the most important Scottish men of letters of the 20th century. After graduating from the University of Edinburgh, MacCaig held various teaching positions, mostly in Edinburgh. His early published works, which he later disavowed, were *Far Cry* (1943) and *The Inward Eye* (1946). With the publication of *Riding Lights* in 1955, his characteristic poetic voice—recalling the polished, metaphysical elegance of John Donne—was first revealed. Many of his images were taken from the natural world, and his poetry was noted for its wit, humour, apt observation, and command of metaphor, though he claimed, as he got older, to have grown to hate metaphors. He considered life on a small scale and, having found his voice, produced a number of volumes of verse, including *The Sinai Sort* (1957), *A Common Grace* (1960), *A Round of Applause* (1962), *Measures* (1965), *Rings on a Tree* (1968), *A Man in My Position* (1969), and several later volumes of selected poems. A volume of his collected poems was published in 1985.

McCampbell, David, U.S. naval pilot and World War II captain who commanded the fearsome Air Group 15 in the Philippines in 1944 and personally destroyed 34 enemy Japanese planes—shooting down 9 in a span of 95 minutes—for which he was awarded the Medal of Honor (b. Jan. 16, 1910—d. June 30, 1996).

McGeown, Patrick, Irish political figure who in 1981 barely survived a 42-day hunger strike while he was serving a prison term for his part in an Irish Republican Army bombing in Belfast, N.Ire.; he later became a leader of Sinn Fein, the IRA's political wing (b. Sept. 3, 1956—found dead Oct. 1, 1996).

McGhee, Walter Brown ("BROWNIE"), U.S. blues musician (b. Nov. 30, 1915, Knoxville, Tenn.—d. Feb. 16, 1996, Oakland, Calif.), brought the lively finger-picking style of blues that originated in the rural Piedmont region of the Carolinas to a young, largely white, urban audience, particularly in his longtime partnership with the blind harmonica player Sonny Terry. McGhee learned guitar as a boy from his musician father and traveled through the South as an itinerant bluesman or with gospel shows and carnivals. In the early 1940s he settled in New York City, where he and Terry performed with other bluesmen, notably Leadbelly (Huddie Ledbetter), and with folk singers, including Woody Guthrie and Pete Seeger. By the 1960s McGhee and Terry were among the most popular folk-blues acts. Separately and together, they toured extensively, recorded numerous albums, and appeared on Broadway in Tennessee Williams's *Cat on a Hot Tin Roof* (1955–57) and Langston Hughes's *Simply Heaven* (1957). McGhee also owned and operated the Home of the Blues Music School in Harlem in the 1940s and recorded several motion picture sound tracks. The partnership gradually crumbled in the late 1970s, and McGhee retired after Terry's death in 1986.

McIntire, Ray, U.S. chemical engineer who inadvertently created what became known as Styrofoam while working for the Dow Chemical Co., where he was attempting to develop a rubberlike polymer to be used as a flexible insulator (b. Aug. 24, 1918—d. Feb. 2, 1996).

Maclean, Sorley (SOMHAIRLE MACGILL-EAIN), Scottish poet who was regarded as the 20th century's greatest Gaelic poet; with such works as the collection *Dain Do Eimhir* (1943; *Poems to Eimhir,* 1971), he brought new attention and respect to the language (b. Oct. 26, 1911—d. Nov. 24, 1996).

McNeill, Don, U.S. radio personality who served as the genial host of the "Don McNeill's Breakfast Club" variety show, which ran for more than 35 years and was broadcast on as many as 300 stations in the 1940s (b. Dec. 23, 1907—d. May 7, 1996).

Madison, Guy (ROBERT OZELL MOSELEY), U.S. film and television actor who starred as television's Wild Bill Hickok (1951–58) and in some 85 motion pictures, mostly westerns (b. Jan. 19, 1922—d. Feb. 6, 1996).

Mandino, Augustine A., U.S. author of some 19 books, notably the 1968 best-seller *The Greatest Salesman in the World,* which sold some 16 million copies and launched his career as a sought-after motivational speaker (b. Dec. 12, 1923—d. Sept. 3, 1996).

Manning, Ernest Charles, Canadian politician (b. Sept. 20, 1908, Carnduff, Sask.—d. Feb. 19, 1996, Calgary, Alta.), served (1943–68) as the dynamic and decisive premier of Alberta while concurrently enjoying a career as an evangelist on radio, where he was heard weekly on the North American broadcast of "Back to the Bible Hour." During his political career he was credited with guiding the province through the Great Depression and shaping it into a model of economic prosperity, in part owing to the discovery of a major oil field at Leduc in 1947 and his innovative rules concerning the proper management of petroleum reserves. As a young man he studied under the charismatic evangelist William Aberhart, the founder of the populist Social Credit political movement. After Aberhart's Social Credit Party captured 56 of 63 seats in the 1935 election, Aberhart became premier and Manning joined the Cabinet as provincial secretary. When Aberhart died in 1943, Manning was elected party leader and premier. Manning, who was reelected seven times, was also the father of Preston, later the leader of the Reform Party.

Maruyama, Masao, Japanese political scientist, writer, and educator (b. March 22, 1914, Osaka, Japan—d. Aug. 15, 1996, Tokyo, Japan), as one of Japan's leading political thinkers, helped shape Japanese politics and thought following World War II. Maruyama, the son of a political journalist, graduated from the Tokyo Imperial University in 1937 and became a faculty member there. In 1944 he was drafted into the army, and at the war's conclusion he returned to the university. In 1950 he was made full professor, a position he held until his retirement in 1971. In his writings and teachings, Maruyama analyzed the social aspects and ideology of Japan and examined their impact on the country's political system. An outspoken critic of the Establishment, he wrote extensively on the Japanese government, arguing that the country's postwar democracy was actually fascism in disguise. In his seminal work, *Chokokka shugi no ronri to shinri* (1946; "The Logic and Psychology of Ultranationalism"), Maruyama examined the psychological underpinnings of Japan's antidemocratic organizations and sparked controversy with his criticism of a system that had an emperor as head of state. Maruyama was praised for his ability to apply abstract concepts to actual events, and his writings, noted for their eloquence and clarity, were required reading for students of Japan's modernization. His work inspired the student antigovernment demonstrations in the 1960s, though Maruyama denounced the violence of the protests, claiming that his ideas had been misinterpreted. In 1982 he was made a member of the Japan Academy.

Mastroianni, Marcello, Italian actor (b. Sept. 28, 1924, Fontana Liri, Italy—d. Dec. 19, 1996, Paris, Fr.), was a handsome, charming, and internationally renowned leading man whose roles in more than 120 films established his screen image as the quintessential modern European male. Throughout his career on stage and screen, he portrayed

Marcello Mastroianni

an array of characters in both dramatic and comic works. The son of a poor cabinetmaker, Mastroianni trained as a surveyor. During World War II he drew maps in Italy and spent a brief stint in a labour camp, from which he escaped to Venice. After the war he embarked on an acting career, making his film debut in the film *I miserabili* (1947), an Italian version of *Les Misérables.* In 1948 he joined an innovative theatrical group headed by Luchino Visconti and performed in a variety of plays. By the early 1950s he was a well-known actor in Italy, but it was not until his work in the film *Le notti bianche* (1957), for which he won the 1958 Italian Film Critics' Silver Ribbon, that his career took off. His performance in Federico Fellini's film *La dolce vita* (1960) established his international reputation. He gained accolades for his portrayal of a bored Sicilian baron eager to dispose of his wife in *Divorce—Italian Style* (1961) and for his work in another Fellini film, *8½* (1963). His screen partnership with Sophia

Loren was extremely successful, and the two were paired in a number of films, notably the comedy *Yesterday, Today and Tomorrow* (1963). In films such as *A Special Day* (1977), in which he played a homosexual, Mastroianni defied his stereotypical image of the romantic leading man. His later works include *Dark Eyes* (1987), *I Don't Want to Talk About It* (1993), and *Three Lives and Only One Death* (1996), in which he appeared with his daughter Chiara.

Mauriac, Claude, French critic and novelist (b. April 25, 1914, Paris, Fr.—d. March 22, 1996, Paris), was best known for his innovative multivolume, nonchronological diary, *Le Temps immobile* (1974–88), a reflection of his literary and political life. Mauriac was the son of Nobel Prize-winning novelist François Mauriac. The relationship gave him some of the material for his biographies of such figures as Jean Cocteau and André Malraux as well as for his journals. He served as a private secretary to Charles de Gaulle (1944–49) and worked as a film and literary critic for the newspaper *Le Figaro* (1945–77). In 1957 he published the first of several novels, *Toutes les femmes sont fatales* (*All Women Are Fatal*, 1964). It revealed his interest in the stylistic conceits of the *nouveau roman* ("new novel"). Like the series of novels it initiated—all five known under the general title of *Le Dialogue intérieur*—it was essentially formless, concentrating on states of mind and shifting perceptions of reality rather than on the more standard elements of plot, character, and theme. Although he also wrote several plays, he was probably best remembered as a memoirist and critic.

Mazia, Daniel, U.S. cell biologist (b. Dec. 18, 1912, Scranton, Pa.—d. June 9, 1996, Monterey, Calif.), studied the structure, division, and regulation of cells and was best known for having isolated the cellular structures involved in mitosis (the process by which chromosomes within the nucleus of a cell double and divide), research that he carried out in 1951 with Japanese biologist Katsuma Dan. Mazia, who was interested in all aspects of cell reproduction, focused on a variety of other issues in cellular biology, such as the role of DNA in chromosomes and the function of the centrosome, an organizing structure of the cell. He carried his enthusiasm into the classroom, where he was a stimulating and inspiring lecturer. Mazia was raised in Philadelphia and studied zoology at the University of Pennsylvania (A.B., 1933; Ph.D., 1937). After graduation he was a National Research Council fellow at Princeton University and at the Marine Biological Laboratories in Woods Hole, Mass. Between 1938 and 1950 he taught at the University of Missouri, taking time out to serve in World War II. Mazia joined the faculty of the University of California, Berkeley, where he was professor of zoology until his retirement in 1979. He then moved to Stanford University and was professor emeritus of biological sciences at the Hopkins Marine Station in Pacific Grove, Calif. Mazia was a member of the National Academy of Sciences and the American Academy of Arts and Sciences, and he served one term as president of the International Cell Research Organization of UNESCO.

Meadows, Audrey, U.S. Emmy award-winning actress who portrayed Alice, a strong-minded yet tenderhearted housewife whose verbal bantering with her husband, Ralph (Jackie Gleason), defined television's classic comedy "The Honeymooners" (b. Feb. 8, 1926—d. Feb. 3, 1996).

Méndez Montenegro, Julio César, Guatemalan politician who served as president from 1966 to 1970 but was a puppet of the military, which launched a campaign of repression that saw 10,000 civilians assassinated during Méndez's presidency (b. Nov. 23, 1915—d. April 28, 1996).

Merino Castro, José Toribio, Chilean admiral who, along with Gen. Augusto Pinochet, led the 1973 coup that ousted Pres. Salvador Allende; Merino was an integral member of the military junta that ruled until 1990 (b. Dec. 14, 1915—d. Aug. 31, 1996).

Michener, Percy Zell, U.S. civil engineer who supervised the construction, completed in 1964, of the 28-km (17½-mi) Chesapeake Bay Bridge-Tunnel across the mouth of the Chesapeake Bay in eastern Virginia, considered a marvel of modern engineering and one of the most impressive transportation facilities in the world (b. Jan. 22, 1904—d. Feb. 2, 1996).

Miller, Delvin Glenn ("DEL"), U.S. Hall of Fame harness-racing driver who, in a career of some 60 years, logged nearly 2,500 official victories and won more than $11 million in purses; he also bred some of the finest Standardbred horses of the mid-20th century (b. July 5, 1913—d. Aug. 19, 1996).

Milne, Christopher Robin, British author and bookseller whose childhood was the inspiration for the popular *Winnie-the-Pooh* children's books written by his father, A.A. Milne (b. Aug. 21, 1920—d. April 20, 1996).

Minnesota Fats (RUDOLF WALTER WANDERONE, JR.), U.S. billiards player (b. Jan. 19, 1913?, New York, N.Y.—d. Jan. 18, 1996, Nashville, Tenn.), popularized American billiards in the late 20th century as the prototypical smooth-talking pool hustler. His larger-than-life personality matched his corpulent frame (1.78 m and as heavy as 136 kg [5 ft 10 in; 300 lb]) and his penchant for telling tall tales about himself. By age 10 he was playing adults for money in poolrooms in New York City. In his prime as a player, from the 1930s through the 1960s, he made his living by wagering on private games in pool halls throughout the United States, which contributed to his legendary standing as one of the best players in the nation. Initially known by the moniker "New York Fats," he adopted the identity "Minnesota Fats" after Jackie Gleason played a pool shark by that name in the 1961 film *The Hustler*. He came into wide celebrity in the 1960s as a competitor in promotional tournaments and as host of television shows on billiards. He became the leading ambassador of the game in the U.S. and held an executive position at a billiards equipment manufacturer. In a series of televised tournaments in the late 1970s, he charmed audiences with his constant tableside banter despite being bested by challenger Willie Mosconi. In 1984 Minnesota Fats was elected to the Hall of Fame of the Billiard Congress of America for "meritorious service" to the game.

Miron, Gaston, French-Canadian award-winning poet whose erotic verse rhapsodized Quebec's landscape, culture, language, and customs; his measured poetry was published in *L'Homme rapaillé*, 1970, and *Courtepointes,* 1975 (b. Jan. 8, 1928—d. Dec. 14, 1996).

Mitchell, Joseph, U.S. writer and journalist (b. July 27, 1908, Fairmont, N.C.—d. May 24, 1996, New York, N.Y.), chronicled the lives of New York City's Fulton Fish Market vendors, Mohawk Indian construction workers, and eccentric denizens of Lower Manhattan saloons. His vignettes, which appeared mostly in *The New Yorker* magazine from the late 1930s through the early '60s, were viewed as stylistic precursors to the subjective "new journalism" later identified with Tom Wolfe and Norman Mailer. After attending the University of North Carolina, Mitchell took up residence in New York City, where he remained for the rest of his life. Before joining *The New Yorker* staff in 1938, he wrote (1929–38) for the *New York Herald Tribune,* the *Morning World,* and the *World-Telegram.* Mitchell was perhaps best remembered for the depictions of the patrons of McSorley's Saloon, a tavern located off Manhattan's Cooper Square. There such characters as Joseph Ferdinand Gould, who claimed to be writing a multimillion-word "Oral History of Our Times," and Commodore Dutch, who threw an annual charity benefit for himself, spent their days. A collection of sketches of McSorley's patrons was published under the title *McSorley's Wonderful Saloon* (1943). In 1992 four of Mitchell's books were published in an omnibus edition under the title *Up in the Old Hotel.*

Mitchell, Maurice B., U.S. business executive and educator who served in such positions as president of Encyclopædia Britannica Films, president of Encyclopædia Britannica, Inc., chancellor of the University of Denver, Colo., president of the Center for the Study of Democratic Institutions, chairman of National Public Radio, and chairman of the Pacific Basin Institute (b. Feb. 9, 1915—d. Nov. 30, 1996).

Mitford, Jessica Lucy, British-born U.S. writer and journalist (b. Sept. 11, 1917, Gloucester, Eng.—d. July 23, 1996, Oakland, Calif.), was known as "queen of the muckrakers" for her investigative works on such aspects of U.S. life as the funeral industry, the prison system, and the medical profession. Mitford, known as "Decca" to friends and family, was one of seven children in an eccentric aristocratic family; her sister Unity was an ardent follower of Adolf Hitler, her sister Diana married British fascist leader Oswald Mosley, and her parents and brother were also fascist sympathizers. Another sister, Nancy, was a famous novelist. Mitford eloped (1937) with a distant cousin, Es-

JAMES D. WILSON—GAMMA LIAISON

Jessica Mitford

mond Romilly, Winston Churchill's nephew, and went to Spain to fight for the communists in the Spanish Civil War. They were married shortly thereafter and in 1939 moved to the U.S. Romilly, who had joined the Royal Canadian Air Force, was killed in action (1941) in World War II, and in 1943 Mitford married lawyer Robert Treuhaft. She became a U.S. citizen the following year. The couple were members of the American Communist Party until 1958, and Mitford was active in the civil rights movement. As a result, she was considered a subversive and was summoned to testify before the House Un-American Activities Committee. Mitford began her writing career with the self-published pamphlet *Lifeitselfmanship* (1956). Her first book, the autobiographical *Daughters and Rebels* (1960), was followed by the one that established her reputation. *The American Way of Death* (1963), a caustic exposé of unscrupulous practices in the funeral industry, was a best-seller and led to a Federal Trade Commission investigation. Other books included *The Trial of Dr. Spock* (1969), about the trial of the pediatrician and four others on conspiracy charges resulting from anti-Vietnam War activities; *Kind and Usual Punishment: The Prison Business* (1973), a study condemning the U.S. prison system; *A Fine Old Conflict* (1977), an autobiographical account of her time as a communist; and *The American Way of Birth* (1992), a criticism of U.S. obstetric care. She also exposed the Famous Writers School as a fraud. Shortly before her death, Mitford prepared a revised edition of *The American Way of Death,* to be published in 1997.

Mitterrand, François-Maurice-Marie, French statesman (b. Oct. 26, 1916, Jarnac, Fr.—d. Jan. 8, 1996, Paris, Fr.), served two terms (1982–95) as president of France, during which his top priority became the promotion of a united Europe, with close French and German cooperation at its core. He saw his goal realized when agreement was reached on the Maastricht Treaty on European economic and political union in December 1991. He also left as his legacy the abolition of the death penalty, decentralization of the government, and construction of a number of public works. Mitterrand earned a degree in law and political science at the University of Paris and, after the outbreak of World War II, served in the army. He was wounded and captured (1940) by the Germans but escaped after 18 months and returned to France. Mitterrand then served as an official in the collaborationist Vichy government—a fact he kept secret until 1994—but in 1943 he joined the Resistance. Following the liberation of Paris (August 1944), he was a member of Charles de Gaulle's provisional government, and in 1946 he was elected to the National Assembly. The next year he took the first of the numerous Cabinet posts he held in 11 short-lived Fourth Republic governments. With the foundation of the Fifth Republic and de Gaulle's assumption of the leadership of the government in 1958, Mitterrand began forging a union of the opposition. He won enough votes in the 1965 election to force de Gaulle into a runoff for the presidency and—after having become (1971) leader of the Socialist Party (PS)—ran again in 1974. He was once again defeated by a narrow margin, but in 1981 he was elected. As president he instituted a number of economic reforms, but these led to such problems as increases in inflation and unemployment and a soaring trade deficit, and the PS abandoned socialist economic policies in favour of free-market liberalism. After his party lost the 1986 general elections, Mitterrand had to share power with a prime minister from the right wing, Jacques Chirac, in a unique arrangement known as "cohabitation." This lasted until 1988, when Chirac challenged Mitterrand for the presidency and lost. Continuing domestic economic difficulties and some unfortunate political decisions caused the Socialists', and thus Mitterrand's, popularity to slump, and a 1992 referendum on the Maastricht Treaty only narrowly passed. A number of scandals involving Socialist leaders tainted the party even further, and the 1993 elections resulted in a rout and made a new cohabitation necessary. In 1995 Mitterrand, seriously ill with prostate cancer, retired at the end of his term. He had served longer than any other French president.

Monroe, William Smith ("BILL"), U.S. musician (b. Sept. 13, 1911, Rosine, Ky.—d. Sept. 9, 1996, Springfield, Tenn.), originated the bluegrass style of popular music in the mid-1940s with his wailing tenor voice and frenetic mandolin playing. Identified by his white ten-gallon hat and bushy sideburns, he was a practitioner of traditional bluegrass, which features a driving syncopated rhythm and tight, complex harmonies. Monroe grew up in poverty in Kentucky and Indiana. His early musical influences included his uncle Pen Vandiver, a fiddler, and a local blues guitarist named Arnold Schultz. In 1927 Monroe began playing the mandolin professionally with his older brothers in a band that appeared on local radio stations; they later toured with a barn-dance show and, from 1936, recorded songs. In 1938 he formed his own band, the Blue Grass Boys, which had an impressive debut the following year during a radio audition for the Grand Ole Opry in Nashville, Tenn., where Monroe later became a regular performer. By the mid-1940s he had perfected the classic bluegrass sound, with a lineup that included singer-guitarist Lester Flatt, banjoist Earl Scruggs, fiddler Chubby Wise, and bassist Howard Watts. Although Flatt and Scruggs left in 1948 to form their own band (much to the consternation of Monroe), he continued to work with premier musicians. During the 1950s country and western and rock and roll overshadowed bluegrass, but the music enjoyed a revival during the '60s, especially at annual festivals, such as the one founded by Monroe in 1967 at Bean Blossom, Ind. Late in his career he was honoured with the election (1970) to the Country Music Hall of Fame, a 1989 Grammy award, and a 1993 lifetime achievement award from the National Academy of Recording Arts and Sciences. In 1994 a retrospective, *The Music of Bill Monroe: From 1936 to 1994,* was released on compact disc.

Montana, Patsy (RUBYE BLEVINS), U.S. singer who was identified by her yodeling-cowgirl songs, especially "I Want to Be a Cowboy's Sweetheart," with which she became the first woman to have a million-selling country music hit song (b. Oct. 30, 1914—d. May 3, 1996).

Moshoeshoe II (CONSTANTINE BERENG SEEISO), king of Lesotho (b. May 2, 1938, Thabang, Basutoland [now Lesotho]—d. Jan. 15, 1996, in the Maloti Mountains, Lesotho), struggled to define the role of the monarchy and was twice sent into exile and once deposed. He was educated locally at Roma College, Maseru, and in Great Britain both at Ampleforth College and at Corpus Christi College, Oxford. As descendant and namesake of Moshoeshoe (Mshweshwe)—who founded the Sotho kingdom, Basutoland, in the 19th century—he claimed his royal birthright by succeeding his father, Seeiso Griffith, as paramount chief of the country in 1960. When the U.K. granted independence to Basutoland in 1966, he became Moshoeshoe II, the first king of Lesotho. Despite his national popularity and his efforts to become more than just a figurehead, he faced political opposition in his own country and in neighbouring South Africa, which surrounds Lesotho. Concerned with Moshoeshoe's involvement in politics, Prime Minister Leabua Jonathan placed him under house arrest, first in 1966 and again in 1970, forcing Moshoeshoe into exile in The Netherlands for eight months while his wife, Queen Mamohato, functioned as regent. He was restored to the throne on the condition that he abstain from political activities. In 1986 Jonathan was toppled in a military coup by Maj. Gen. Justin Lekhanya, who subsequently suspended Moshoeshoe's executive powers and forced him into exile in England. While in exile the king attempted to initiate democratic elections and, as a result, was deposed and replaced by his eldest son, Crown Prince Letsie III. Moshoeshoe remained popular with the people of Lesotho, however, and, in 1991, when the government was seized by another military figure, Maj. Gen. Elias Ramaema, plans were laid for Moshoeshoe's eventual return in 1992. In 1993 Lesotho held free elections, and with the assistance of Letsie III and Nelson Mandela of South Africa, Moshoeshoe was reinstated as king of Lesotho on Jan. 25, 1995.

Mott, Sir Nevill Francis, British physicist (b. Sept. 30, 1905, Leeds, Eng.—d. Aug. 8, 1996, Milton Keynes, Eng.), shared the 1977 Nobel Prize for Physics with Philip Anderson and John Van Vleck for research into the electronic properties of noncrystalline, or amorphous, solids. This work showed that amorphous materials, which are easier and less expensive to manufacture than crystalline substances, could be used in such electronic tools as computers, pocket calculators, and transistor radios. Although originally interested in the theoretical aspects of quantum mechanics, Mott focused on the practical applications of this knowledge. His interest in science was inspired by his parents, who studied at Cavendish Laboratory with J.J. Thomson, the discoverer of the electron. After receiving a master's degree in 1930 from the University of Cambridge, Mott became a fellow and lecturer at Gonville and Caius College, Cambridge, serving there later (1959–66) as master. In 1933 he moved to the University of Bristol as a professor of theoretical physics, and in 1948 he became director of the physics laboratories there. He then was appointed Cavendish professor of physics at Cambridge, a position he held from 1954 until he retired in 1971. During his tenures at Bristol and Cambridge, Mott staffed his laboratories with world-class scientists, who made significant contributions to solid state physics. Mott also published such influential books as *The Theory of Atomic Collisions* (1933; with H.S.W. Massey) and *Electronic Processes in Ionic Crystals* (1940; with R.W. Gurney). He was elected a fellow of the Royal Society of London in 1936 and knighted in 1962.

Mourão-Ferreira, David, Portuguese writer whose passionate works, including fiction, poetry, and essays, won numerous prizes and established him as one of the country's leading literary figures (b. February 1927—d. June 16, 1996).

Mulligan, Gerald Joseph ("GERRY"), U.S. jazz musician and arranger (b. April 6, 1927, New York, N.Y.—d. Jan. 20, 1996, Darien, Conn.), was an outstanding baritone saxophonist, a founder of

François Mitterrand

the 1950s cool jazz idiom, and one of that era's standout stars. The quartet he formed in 1952 lacked the conventional piano to provide harmonic support; in its place Mulligan soloed with only bass and drums backing him, then created countermelodies to accompany the delicate solos of trumpeter Chet Baker. The group's unique sound and horn interplay won it almost immediate fame, and successive Mulligan quartets, featuring trumpeter Art Farmer and trombonist Bob Brookmeyer, offered a similar melody-oriented music. Mulligan's collaborations included recordings with alto saxophonists Lee Konitz and Paul Desmond. After growing up in Philadelphia, Mulligan moved to New York City in 1946 and became a cool jazz arranger and player in Miles Davis's pioneering 1948–50 Birth of the Cool nonet. He also composed big band arrangements for Stan Kenton, Elliot Lawrence, and, most notably, Gene Krupa ("Disc Jockey Jump"). His most original arrangements were adaptations of cool jazz for the short-lived big bands that he formed later in his career, most prominently the pianoless early-'60s Concert Jazz Band. Most of his later career was as a soloist, including the years 1968–72, when he performed in a quartet with pianist Dave Brubeck. His highly distinctive style fused swing era tenor saxophonist Lester Young's phrasing with bebop harmonies. Mulligan played his weighty instrument with a light sound and frequently interjected whimsical humour ("Blight of the Fumble Bee"). His solos grew in richness and authority over time.

Muskie, Edmund Sixtus, U.S. politician (b. March 28, 1914, Rumford, Maine—d. March 26, 1996, Washington, D.C.), served as governor, senator, and U.S. secretary of state during a long career and was the Democratic Party's vice presidential candidate in 1968, but he was perhaps better remembered for his failure to win the presidential nomination in 1972. While campaigning in New Hampshire and angrily denouncing *Manchester Union Leader* attacks on his wife, he seemed to some to be crying. Though he said that what appeared to be tears on his face was really melting snow, Muskie could not shake an image of weakness. After graduating cum laude from Bates College, Lewiston, Maine, in 1936 and from Cornell Law School, Ithaca, N.Y., in 1939, Muskie began practicing law in Waterville, Maine. He served in the navy during World War II and then returned to his practice in Waterville. His political career began in the state legislature, and in 1954 he became the first Democrat in 20 years to be elected Maine's governor. In that post Muskie stressed environmental concerns, supporting clean air and water legislation. His continued support of environmental issues during his years in the U.S. Senate (1959–80) earned him the nickname "Mr. Clean." Laws regarding water quality, regional clean air standards, and a model cities program were among his successes. Muskie first gained nationwide public recognition when Hubert Humphrey selected him as his running mate in the 1968 presidential election campaign. In a close contest, the Democrats lost to the Richard Nixon–Spiro Agnew ticket. In 1980 Muskie left the Senate to serve as secretary of state during the last months of Jimmy Carter's administration. After Carter left office in 1981, Muskie returned to law. He was a senior partner in the Washington, D.C., office of a New York law firm at the time of his death.

Najibullah, Maj. Gen. Mohammad, Afghan politician (b. 1947, Gardez, Paktia province, Afg.—d. Sept. 27, 1996, Kabul, Afg.), was the president of Afghanistan for six years after being installed by the Soviet Union in 1986. He managed to hang on to power for nearly three years after Soviet troops pulled out in 1989 but was ousted in 1992 and afterward lived in refuge in a UN compound. Najibullah began studying medicine at Kabul University in 1964 and received his medical degree in 1975, but he never practiced medicine. He had joined the Parcham ("Banner") faction of the communist People's Democratic Party of Afghanistan (PDPA) in 1965, and he was twice imprisoned for political activities. The PDPA

Mohammad Najibullah

staged a successful coup in 1978, but the Khalq ("People's") faction soon gained supremacy, and Najibullah briefly served as ambassador to Iran and then went into exile in Eastern Europe until the U.S.S.R. intervened (1979) and supported a Parcham-dominated government. Najibullah was made head of the secret police and became known for his brutality and ruthlessness. His methods proved invaluable to the regime in view of escalating Islamic guerrilla warfare, but as the war grew in intensity, the Soviet Union withdrew. As president, Najibullah attempted to gain support by relaxing his strict control, but he was widely despised and was finally forced from office by the Islamic rebels. Factional fighting continued, and when the Taliban militia took over the capital, Kabul, they executed Najibullah.

Nannen, Henri, German journalist who was one of the founders of the general-interest weekly magazine *Stern,* served as its editor, 1948–80, and was acting as its publisher when, in 1983, the magazine published what it believed to be Adolf Hitler's diaries; the scandal that resulted when the diaries were revealed to be a hoax forced Nannen to resign (b. Dec. 25, 1913—d. Oct. 13, 1996).

Nasr, Sheikh Muhammad Hamid Abu an-, Egyptian religious leader who from 1986 was the supreme guide of the country's largest Islamic fundamentalist group, the Muslim Brotherhood, as it grew in power and influence (b. Jan. 20, 1913—d. Jan. 20, 1996).

Nelson, Gene (EUGENE LEANDER BERG), U.S. actor-dancer best remembered for his role as Will Parker in the motion picture musical *Oklahoma!* (b. March 24, 1920—d. Sept. 16, 1996).

Ngor, Haing S., Cambodian physician and actor (b. 1950?, Cambodia—d. Feb. 25, 1996, Los Angeles, Calif.), won the Academy Award for best supporting actor for his performance in *The Killing Fields* (1984). In his portrayal of Dith Pran—who acted as assistant to *New York Times* correspondent Sydney Schanberg in Cambodia and risked his life to save journalists' lives when the Khmer Rouge seized power in 1975 but was left behind, taken prisoner, and tortured before escaping—he relived his own ordeal. When the Khmer Rouge arrested and tortured Ngor, he pretended to be a taxi driver because intellectuals were being executed; he had to hide the fact that he was a physician even when his wife was dying in child-

birth. After the Vietnamese invasion of Cambodia (1979), he escaped to Thailand and worked in the refugee camps before moving (1980) to the U.S. He was working as a job counselor for refugees in Los Angeles when he was chosen for the role in *The Killing Fields.* Ngor appeared in a few other films, most notably *Heaven and Earth* (1993), and became active in the campaign to bring those who conducted the massacres to justice. He lectured widely and helped form two organizations that aided Cambodian refugees still in camps. Ngor was shot to death while being robbed outside his home.

Nguyen Huu Tho, Vietnamese political leader (b. July 10, 1910, Cho Lon, near Saigon [now Ho Chi Minh City], Vietnam—d. Dec. 24, 1996, Ho Chi Minh City), was the leader of the communists' political efforts in South Vietnam during the Vietnam War and following the war served in the government of the reunified country. Tho studied law in Paris in the 1930s and returned to Saigon to practice. He was imprisoned (1954) for activities opposing the French colonial rule of Vietnam and the U.S. patrolling of the southern Vietnamese coast and, except for a brief period in 1958, remained in detention until he escaped in 1961. In 1962 Tho became chairman of the National Liberation Front (NLF), the organization formed in South Vietnam in 1960 to aid the communist North Vietnamese in the struggle to overthrow the U.S.-backed South Vietnamese government. In addition, when the NLF established (1969) a Provisional Revolutionary Government, he was made chairman of its advisory council. When the war ended (1975) and Vietnam reunified, Tho became (1976) one of the country's two vice presidents. He served as acting president in 1980–81 and as vice president of the Council of State from 1981 to 1984. Although Tho was thought to have retired from political life in 1994, in July 1996 a radio broadcast in Vietnam identified him as a member of the Communist Party's newly elected Central Committee.

Niarchos, Stavros Spyros, Greek shipping magnate (b. July 3, 1909, Athens, Greece—d. April 15, 1996, Zürich, Switz.), fulfilled the promise of his surname, which means "master of ships," as one of the world's most successful shipping magnates. He founded Niarchos, Ltd., an international shipping company that at one time operated more than 80 tankers worldwide. Niarchos's parents were naturalized U.S. citizens who made their fortune in Buffalo, N.Y. He grew up in the port city of Piraeus, Greece, and earned a law degree from the University of Athens. Family reversals forced him to join a flour-milling operation owned by his uncles. In an effort to cut costs, Niarchos persuaded his uncles to purchase several freighters to transport their grain from Argentina. The venture was a success, and he was able to widen operations to include London and New York. At the start of World War II, he leased his fleet to the Allies and joined the Royal Navy. Most of his fleet was lost, but Niarchos collected $2 million in insurance and proceeded to build an empire. He had a lifelong rivalry with Aristotle Onassis, a struggle that dominated the business world and extended to their personal affairs. Niarchos was married five times, including a union with a former wife of Onassis. Besides controlling the shipping trade, Niarchos invested in stocks, real estate, and race horses and owned an impressive collection of fine art, including the 1585 *Pietà* by El Greco. He kept residences throughout the world and had his own private island.

Okello, Gen. Tito, Ugandan military officer who helped oust Idi Amin in 1979 and who briefly ruled Uganda following the 1985 military coup that overthrew Pres. Milton Obote (b. 1914—d. June 3, 1996).

Opperman, Sir Hubert Ferdinand ("OPPY"), Australian cyclist and politician (b. May 29, 1904, Rochester, Victoria, Australia—d. April 18, 1996, Melbourne, Australia), dominated long-distance cycling in the 1920s and '30s before serving in the Australian Parliament. He began biking while a messenger boy, and after winning several local competitions he traveled to France, the centre of road racing. His legend was established while he competed in the 1928 Bol d'Or, a race in which the participants pedaled as far as possible in 24 hours. After two of Opperman's bicycles broke, a result, he claimed, of sabotage, he was forced to ride his translator's bike until the necessary repairs were made. His come-from-behind victory made headlines in Europe, and the French voted him Athlete of the Year. In 1931 he won the Paris–Brest–Paris event, a nonstop 1,160-km (720-mi) race. During his cycling career, he set over 100 world records, some of which remained unbroken. After his retirement from competitive cycling in 1943, the Australian Liberal Party persuaded him to enter politics, and he was elected to Parliament in 1949. Opperman held several appointments, and as minister for immigration (1963–1966) he was instrumental in ending the country's immigration policy that discriminated against nonwhites. In 1967 he left Parliament to serve as Australia's first high commissioner to Malta, and the following year he was knighted. His autobiography, *Pedals, Politics, and People,* was published in 1977. Opperman, who continued to cycle after his retirement, died while on his exercise bike.

Packard, David, U.S. entrepreneur and electrical engineer (b. Sept. 7, 1912, Pueblo, Colo.—d. March 26, 1996, Stanford, Calif.), was a co-founder of the Hewlett-Packard Co., a leading manufacturer of electronic measurement equipment, computers, and computer printers. Packard studied electrical engineering at Stanford University (B.A., 1934), where he met William Hewlett, and returned there for graduate study in 1938 after working for General Electric. With a loan of $538, Hewlett and Packard launched their company in 1939 in a rented garage in Palo Alto, Calif. The site became an official state landmark and "the birthplace of Silicon Valley." Packard handled business and administrative matters, and Hewlett was responsible for product design and manufacturing. The company's growth paralleled the booming electronics sector of the U.S. defense industry and was fueled by the move from the manufacture of electronic instruments to the production of calculators, computers, and computer printers. The firm eventually employed over 100,-000 workers and produced revenues of $31 billion in 1995. Packard's renowned management philosophy, the "HP Way," emphasized the creation of an organizational environment in which workers could show initiative and creativity. He also advocated that executives employ "management by walking around" shop floors and office corridors. Packard headed the company as president, chief executive officer, or chairman of the board from its incorporation in 1947 until 1993. Although semiretired during the 1980s, he returned in 1991 to steer the company through a financial slump. He also left the company (1969–71) to serve as deputy secretary of defense in the administration of Pres. Richard Nixon. Throughout the 1970s and '80s, he was a prominent adviser to Republican administrations on defense procurement and management. He was also a major contributor to conservative institutions and causes. Packard received numerous awards, including the Presidential Medal of Freedom.

Packard, Vance Oakley, U.S. social critic and author of the 1957 best-selling book *The Hidden Persuaders,* in which he deplored manipulative advertising techniques that used subliminal images and symbols to stimulate consumer sales (b. May 22, 1914—d. Dec. 12, 1996).

Paisley, Robert ("Bob"), British association football (soccer) player and manager who, at the time of his retirement in 1983, was the most successful team manager in the history of English soccer; between 1974, when he took command of the Liverpool Football Club, and 1983 he steered Liverpool to six League titles, three League Cups, three European Cups, one UEFA Cup, and the 1977 European Super Cup (b. Jan. 23, 1919—d. Feb. 14, 1996).

Panozzo, John, U.S. drummer who was a co-founder of the rock group Styx, which enjoyed its greatest popularity in the late 1970s and early '80s with such hits as "Come Sail Away," "Renegade," and "Babe" (b. Sept. 20, 1947—d. July 16, 1996).

Papandreou, Andreas Georgios, Greek politician and educator (b. Feb. 5, 1919, Chios, Greece—d. June 23, 1996, Ekáli, near Athens, Greece), served (1981–89 and 1993–96) as the first socialist prime minister of Greece. His fiery speeches and nationalistic rhetoric made him a popular leader at home, though he often inspired bewilderment and irritation abroad. The son of politician Georgios Papandreou, Andreas, a Trotskyite, was imprisoned in 1939 for his work in a resistance group. Upon his release the following year, he immigrated to the U.S., where he earned a Ph.D. (1943) in economics from Harvard University and became a U.S. citizen (1944). He taught at several universities, including Harvard and the University of California, Berkeley, until 1963, when his father was named prime minister. Andreas renounced his U.S citizenship and returned home, where he campaigned with his father's party, the Centre Union, and won a seat in Parliament. In 1965, however, King Constantine, distrustful of both Papandreous, dismissed the government. Andreas's continued rise within the left wing of the Centre Union fueled speculation that he would become the real power in the government if his father was swept back into office in the 1967 elections. As a result, a military junta seized power, Andreas was arrested and later forced into exile, and his father was put under house arrest and died shortly thereafter. When the military dictatorship collapsed in 1974, Papandreou returned to Greece and established the Panhellenic Socialist Movement (Pasok). His anti-Western, anti-American views struck a national chord. Pasok won the 1981 elections, and Papandreou was named prime minister. Once he was in office, his foreign policies proved moderate; though he opened an embassy in Cuba, he renewed U.S. leases on military bases and never followed through on his threats to withdraw from NATO. Domestically, he introduced generous social-welfare programs, abolished censorship, and promoted women's rights. In the 1985 elections Pasok again won a majority, and Papandreou remained prime minister. His second term, however, was marked by scandal. Papandreou and three Cabinet members were charged with bribery and embezzlement. In addition, his extramarital affair with a younger woman was highly publicized. These scandals, combined with an ailing economy—Greece was the poorest country in the European Community—led to Pasok's defeat in 1989 and Papandreou's resignation as prime minister. After his 1992 acquittal, he continued as leader of Pasok, and with the party's victory in the 1993 elections, he began his third term as prime minister. His health, however, deteriorated, and in January 1996 he was forced to retire.

Pearl, Minnie (Sarah Ophelia Colley Cannon), U.S. entertainer (b. Oct. 25, 1912, Centerville, Tenn.—d. March 4, 1996, Nashville, Tenn.), performed at Nashville's Grand Ole Opry for more than 50 years and on the television show "Hee Haw" for 20 years. Announcing her presence with a signature "How-dee! I'm just so proud to be here!" and sporting a trademark flowered hat with a $1.98 price tag dangling from it, she regaled audiences with tales of her search for a "feller." Pearl's character was a composite of a number of people she had known in the early days of her career. She had planned to be an actress and dancer and, following graduation from what was later Belmont University, Nashville, taught dance before traveling to small southern towns with a theatrical company based in Atlanta, Ga. Pearl's character developed as she appeared before local groups to publicize the shows, and in 1940 she auditioned for "The Grand Ole Opry" radio show. Her popularity grew rapidly, and she became a permanent member of the company that same year. Pearl recorded a number of albums, but only one of her records, the single "Giddyup—Go Answer" (1966), became a top-

10 country hit. She was elected to the Country Music Hall of Fame in 1975. A bout with cancer led Pearl to do volunteer work with the American Cancer Society, and in 1987 she was presented with the society's courage award. In 1992 she received a National Medal of Art, but a stroke she had suffered the previous year—which ended her career at the Opry—kept her from attending the White House ceremony.

Pearsall, Phyllis Isobel Gross, British artist, writer, and publisher who created the popular *London A–Z* maps, exhaustive guides to the city's 23,000 streets, after having walked over 4,800 km (3,000 mi) researching the maps; the business later expanded to produce maps for other cities (b. Sept. 25, 1906—d. Aug. 28, 1996).

Pertwee, John Devon Roland ("Jon"), British actor who performed on the stage, screen, and radio but was best known for his television portrayals of the time-traveling Dr. Who and the talking scarecrow Worzel Gummidge (b. July 7, 1919—d. May 20, 1996).

Peterson, Roger Tory, U.S. ornithologist, author, conservationist, and wildlife artist (b. Aug. 28, 1908, Jamestown, N.Y.—d. July 28, 1996, Old Lyme, Conn.), wrote the pocket-size field guides that were instrumental in stimulating U.S. and European interest in the study of birds. His illustrations emphasized the features that would aid in identification of each species and used arrows to indicate key characteristics; he grouped birds on the basis of their resemblance to one another instead of by species; and he included descriptions that were short and to the point. Peterson became interested in nature, and especially birds, when he was a young boy. His seventh-grade science teacher encouraged him to apply his meticulous attention to detail to the drawing of birds. Peterson studied in New York City at the Art Students League (1927–29) and the National Academy of Design (1929–31). He then taught (1931–34) at the Rivers School, Brookline, Mass., and worked (1934–43) for the National Audubon Society. A fellow birder, impressed with Peterson's knowledge, had suggested that he produce a guide, and in 1934 *A Field Guide to the Birds* was published—after having been rejected by at least four publishers. The initial print run of 2,000 sold out within two weeks. Many other books followed, some in the field guide series and others of a more general nature, among them *A Field Guide to Western Birds* (1941), *Birds over America* (1948), *A Field Guide to the Birds of Britain and Europe* (1954; coauthored with Guy Mountfort and P.A.D. Hollom), and *Wild America* (1955). Peterson's books sold in the millions and were translated into at least a dozen languages. His awards included the New York Zoological Society Gold Medal (1961), the World Wildlife Fund Gold Medal (1972), and the Presidential Medal of Freedom (1980). He was twice nominated for the Nobel Peace Prize. In 1986 the Roger Tory Peterson Institute of Natural History was founded in Jamestown, N.Y.

Poher, Alain-Émile-Louis-Marie, French politician who, as president of the French Senate (1968–92), was twice called upon to serve as short-term interim president of France—in 1969 and again in 1974. He was also president (1966–69) of the European Parliament (b. April 17, 1909—d. Dec. 9, 1996).

Post, Sir Laurens Jan van der, South African-born writer whose novels and autobiographical reminiscences explored mysticism, spirituality, the Jungian concept of the collective unconscious, and the evils of South African racial policies, as well as his own experiences as a prisoner of the Japanese during World War II (b. Dec. 13, 1906—d. Dec. 15, 1996).

Poulin, A(lfred A., Jr.), U.S. poet who from 1971 taught at the State University of New York College at Brockport, where in 1976 he founded BOA Editions, one of the top independent U.S. publishers of contemporary poetry and often credited with advancing the careers of lesser-known poets (b. March 14, 1938—d. June 5, 1996).

Proops, (Rebecca) Marjorie Israel, British journalist who was best known for the advice she dispensed as "Dear Marje," the *Daily Mirror*'s "agony aunt"; she was appointed OBE in 1969 (b. 1911?—d. Nov. 10, 1996).

Prowse, Juliet, British actress and tall, leggy dancer who captured the spotlight when Soviet leader Nikita Khrushchev visited the set of the film *Can-Can* and proclaimed her dancing "immoral"; her romances with Frank Sinatra and Elvis Presley preceded a long stage and television career (b. Sept. 25, 1936—d. Sept. 14, 1996).

Quinlan, Joseph, U.S. "right-to-die" advocate who spearheaded the movement that tackled the ethical, legal, theological, and medical issues in prolonging the lives of the terminally ill after his

daughter Karen Ann slipped into a coma in 1975; his daughter, who was removed from a respirator in 1976 after a landmark New Jersey Supreme Court ruling, died of pneumonia in 1985 (b. April 2, 1925—d. Dec. 7, 1996).

Rahi, Sultan (MUHAMMAD SULTAN), Pakistani actor whose film *Maula Jat* broke box-office records and established Punjabi as the major language of Pakistani cinema (b. 1938—d. Jan. 9, 1996).

Rama Rao, N(andamuri) T(araka) ("NTR"), Indian motion picture actor and politician (b. May 28, 1923, Nimmakuru, India—d. Jan. 18, 1996, Hyderabad, India), starred in over 300 Telugu-language films between 1948 and 1982 and, taking advantage of his popularity and cult-figure status, was elected chief minister of Andhra Pradesh state three times. Onscreen he often portrayed a Hindu god, particularly the warrior god Krishna,

Roger Tory Peterson

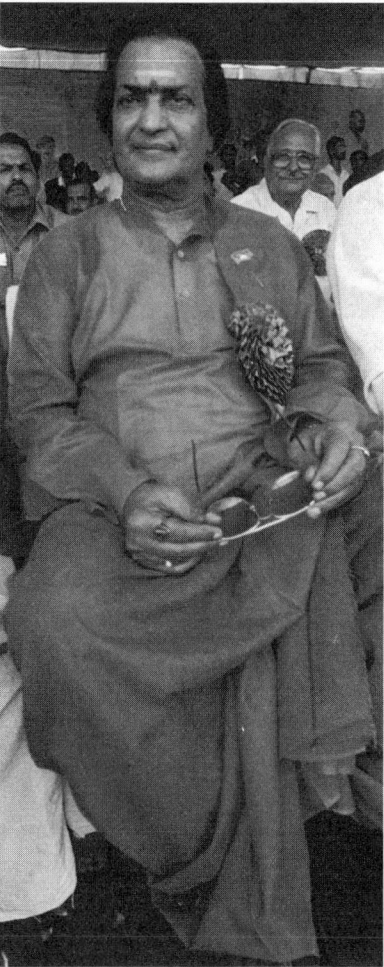

N.T. Rama Rao

and his adoption of the white or saffron robes of his costumes as his everyday dress reinforced that image. Rama Rao formed the Telugu Desam Party in 1982 in protest against the Congress Party's control of the state and the next year was elected chief minister. After being dismissed because of party factionalism, he was reelected in 1985 and served until 1989, when he was defeated as a result of corruption and mismanagement charges. After Rama Rao, a widower, took (1992) as his second wife a woman over 30 years his junior, he ran for office again (1994) and was victorious. Other members of his family, also party officials, became increasingly unhappy with his wife's growing role in the government. A party revolt ensued (1995), and Rama Rao was ousted. At the time of his death, he was making preparations for another comeback.

Rand, Paul, U.S. graphic designer (b. Aug. 15, 1914, New York, N.Y.—d. Nov. 26, 1996, Norwalk, Conn.), was one of the most innovative and influential graphic designers of the 20th century. Employing the simplicity of modernism, with its clean geometric type and use of white space, he created some of the most recognizable corporate logos in the U.S.—among them, those for IBM, Westinghouse, United Parcel Service, and ABC—as well as textiles, posters, packages, and illustrations for children's books. Rand began his art studies by attending night school at the Pratt Institute, New York City, when he was in high school. Studies at the Parsons School of Design and the Art Students League followed, but he also gleaned valuable information from foreign design magazines. Rand first worked for the George Switzer Agency, but by 1935 he had opened his own studio in New York City. He became art

Paul Rand

director of Esquire-Coronet the next year, and in 1941, when a partner at the company started an advertising agency, Rand became its art director. He was a professor of graphic design at Yale University from 1956 until he became professor emeritus in 1993, and from 1977 he taught at Yale's summer program in Brissago, Switz. Thereafter he continued his prolific design career and also served as guest professor at a number of U.S. schools. Rand was the author of such books as *Thoughts on Design* (1947) and the memoirs *Paul Rand: A Designer's Art* (1985), *Design, Form, and Chaos* (1993), and *From Lascaux to Brooklyn* (1996).

Rankin, (James) Lee, U.S. lawyer who successfully argued before the U.S. Supreme Court in *Brown* v. *Board of Education of Topeka* (1954), overturning the "separate but equal" doctrine of racial segregation in public schools. He also served as U.S. solicitor general (1956–61) and was appointed counsel to the Warren Commission (1963–64), which investigated the assassination of Pres. John F. Kennedy (b. July 8, 1907—d. June 26, 1996).

Red Thunder Cloud (CARLOS WESTEZ), U.S. Native American storyteller who was believed to have been the last speaker of the Catawba language, which was not his mother tongue. He made several recordings of the language and many others of songs (b. 1919—d. Jan. 8, 1996).

Reddy, Neelam Sanjiva, Indian politician who was the sixth president of India (1977–82) and a member of the Janata Party; he was first nominated for the presidency in 1969 by the Congress Party, but, in a divisive move, Prime Minister Indira Gandhi supported V.V. Giri, who won (b. May 19, 1913—d. June 1, 1996).

Reese, (John) Terence, British bridge authority who was one of the game's best players ever and was considered its most outstanding and prolific writer (b. Aug. 28, 1913—d. Jan. 29, 1996).

Reichstein, Tadeus, Polish-born Swiss chemist (b. July 20, 1897, Wloclawek, Pol.—d. Aug. 1, 1996, Basel, Switz.), identified the steroid hormones of the adrenal cortex and studied their structure and biological effects. For his role in this discovery, he shared the Nobel Prize for Physiology or Medicine in 1950 with Philip S. Hench and Edward C. Kendall, who carried out independent research on steroids. Reichstein showed that the adrenal cortex, the outer portion of the adrenal glands located at the upper ends of the kidneys, produces many hormones. He and his colleagues isolated and examined about 29 of them, including cortisone, which was discovered to be an anti-inflammatory agent useful in the treatment of arthritis. Reichstein graduated (1920) with a degree in chemical engineering from the Federal Institute of Technology, Zürich, where he obtained a Ph.D. two years later. In 1930 he became an instructor there, and he had risen to the level of associate professor by the time he left in 1937. His early research with Nobel Prize-winning chemist Hermann Staudinger included identifying the chemicals in coffee that impart flavour and aroma, work that provided the basis for the development of powdered coffee. He also devised a method for synthesizing (1933) vitamin C in the laboratory, a procedure that remained widely in use in commercial production of the vitamin. In 1938 Reichstein moved to the University of Basel and was appointed director of the Pharmaceutical Institute; in 1946 he became head of the newly created Institute of Organic Chemistry. There he studied plant-derived glycosides, chemicals that have a wide range of biological effects, to determine their usefulness as pharmaceuticals. This work also was important in plant classification. Although he retired in 1967, Reichstein conducted significant research into his 90s.

Reid, Beryl Elizabeth, British character actress known for her versatility and best remembered for her roles as the lesbian radio soap opera actress in the stage and motion picture versions of *The Killing of Sister George* and the seductive landlady in the stage and film versions of *Entertaining Mr. Sloane;* she was appointed OBE in 1986 (b. June 17, 1920—d. Oct. 13, 1996).

Reinhold, Robert, U.S. journalist at the *New York Times* (1964–94) and the *Los Angeles Times* (1994–96) who set a standard for precise reporting as a science writer, national correspondent, and editorialist (b. Dec. 18, 1941—d. Aug. 28, 1996).

Revueltas, Rosaura, Mexican actress (b. 1910?, Durango, Mex.—d. April 30, 1996, Cuernavaca, Mex.), gave a vibrant performance in the controversial film *Salt of the Earth* (1954), which was based on a violent mining strike in Silver City, N.M. She portrayed Esperanza Quintero, who was caught up in the struggle for workers' and women's rights. The film was denounced by the House Un-American Activities Committee, and many of the cast and crew were blacklisted. Revueltas was arrested by U.S. immigration agents, charged with illegal entry, and faced deportation to Mexico. Ultimately, the miners union headquarters in Silver City was burned, and the film was officially banned. The illegal-entry case against Revueltas was dropped, and she left the U.S. voluntarily but never acted again. She first studied dancing and acting in Mexico City and in 1946 made her theatrical debut in *La deconocida de arras.* Revueltas also appeared in a handful of films including *Islas Marias* and *Muchachas de uniforme,* both released in 1950. Two years later she had a minor role in the U.S. film *Sombrero.* After she was blacklisted, Revueltas worked with Bertolt Brecht's Berliner Ensemble from 1957 to 1960.

Rey, Margret Elisabeth, German-born U.S. writer and illustrator who (with her husband, H.A. Rey, and later with Allan J. Shalleck) created the widely popular children's books about Curious George, an irrepressible monkey; the adventure books sold more than 20 million copies in 12 languages (b. May 1906—d. Dec. 21, 1996).

Robinette, John Josiah, Canadian trial lawyer who was lauded as the country's most eloquent and finest courtroom counsel; he argued more cases before the Supreme Court than any other lawyer during a 62-year career in which he defended common criminals and represented high-profile businesses and clients (b. Nov. 20, 1906—d. Nov. 18, 1996).

Rollins, Howard, U.S. actor best remembered for his role as chief of detectives in the television series "In the Heat of the Night" before he was dropped from the cast after the 1992–93 season owing to drug abuse; he also was nominated for a 1981 Academy Award for his role in the film *Ragtime* (b. Oct. 17, 1950—d. Dec. 8, 1996).

Romero, Celedonio, Spanish musician and composer (b. March 2, 1918, Málaga, Spain—d. May 8, 1996, San Diego, Calif.), was an internationally acclaimed classical guitarist who performed as a soloist and as a member of Los Romeros, a quartet he formed with his three sons. Romero first performed in public at the age of 10, and he made his formal debut when he was 22. He toured throughout Spain but had difficulty accepting foreign engagements because of the oppressive government of Francisco Franco. In 1958 he immigrated to the United States with his family, and two years later he formed Los Romeros with sons Celin, Pepe, and Angel. After touring the U.S. in 1961, the group obtained a recording contract and soon became known as the "royal family of the guitar." They performed overseas and with nearly every major U.S. orchestra and gave special performances, including an appearance at the Vatican for Pope John Paul II. Owing to the lack of repertory for guitar quartet, Romero transcribed chamber works and commissioned pieces from such composers as Joaquín Rodrigo. As a soloist, Romero was praised for the warmth of his tone and his rhythmic flexibility. In addition, he wrote music for solo guitar, including suites, studies, and character pieces.

Ross, (James) Sinclair, Canadian writer of works that were exquisitely crafted and portrayed the bleakness found on the Canadian prairie; his most acclaimed book, *As for Me and My House,* poignantly described a desolate Depression-era existence in Horizon, Sask. (b. Jan. 22, 1908—d. Feb. 29, 1996).

Rouse, James Wilson, U.S. real-estate developer (b. April 26, 1914, Easton, Md.—d. April 9, 1996, Columbia, Md.), altered the U.S. landscape during the second half of the 20th century with a series of innovative projects. He pioneered the enclosed suburban shopping mall in the 1950s, created the planned community of Columbia in the '60s, revitalized inner-city districts with retail-and-office complexes called festival marketplaces in the '70s and '80s, and financed low-income housing in the '80s and '90s. Known as a visionary with a social conscience, he was better regarded for his success as a social engineer than for the architecture of his buildings. Rouse attended the Universities of Virginia and Maryland, began a career as a mortgage banker, and served in World War II. In 1939 he cofounded what would later be known as the Rouse Co. The town of Columbia, which was designed as an alternative to suburban sprawl, was fashioned around multiple small-scale community centres. The racially integrated town had affordable housing and featured lakes and greenways. Rouse later lived there himself. In the 1970s he turned his attention to large cities, renovating old buildings to transform decaying urban centres into modern town squares, such as Faneuil Hall Marketplace in Boston, South Street Seaport in New York City, and Harborplace in Baltimore. He helped make the Rouse Co. one of the largest real-estate developers in the country. After his retirement in 1979, Rouse established the Enterprise Foundation, a nonprofit organization that worked with community groups to provide homes for the urban poor. He was awarded the Presidential Medal of Freedom in 1995.

Royster, Vermont Connecticut, U.S. journalist (b. April 30, 1914, Raleigh, N.C.—d. July 22, 1996, Raleigh), had a long and distinguished career with *The Wall Street Journal,* rising from reporter to editor of the newspaper and serving as president (1960–71) of its publishing company, Dow Jones & Co. He guided the paper through spectacular growth and helped shape it into a top business daily. Royster, whose family had a tradition of naming children after states, graduated from the University of North Carolina at Chapel Hill in 1935. The following year he became a reporter

on the staff of the New York City News Bureau. He moved to the *Journal* later in 1936 and was assigned to the Washington, D.C., bureau. After service in the navy during World War II, Royster returned to the *Journal.* He was associate editor (1948–51), senior associate editor (1951–58), editor (1958–71), and senior vice president (1960–71) before retiring in 1971. From 1971 to 1986 he was a contributing editor, columnist of the weekly "Thinking Things Over," and William Rand Kenan professor of journalism and public affairs at his alma mater. Royster was awarded two Pulitzer Prizes. He received his first (1953) for editorial writing in recognition of the consistent excellence of his work. His second, for distinguished commentary, came in 1984. In 1986 Royster was honoured with the Presidential Medal of Freedom.

Rozelle, Alvin Ray ("PETE"), U.S. sports executive (b. March 1, 1926, South Gate, Calif.—d. Dec. 6, 1996, Rancho Santa Fe, Calif.), as commissioner of the National Football League (NFL) for nearly 30 years, instituted a number of changes that made professional football the most widely followed sport in the United States. He oversaw more than a doubling of the number of teams in the league, negotiated the most lucrative television sports contract, introduced Monday night football on TV, and—most notably—created the Super Bowl. Rozelle graduated (1950) from the University of San Francisco, stayed there two more years to be assistant athletic director, and then served as publicity director for the Los Angeles Rams (1952–55), a partner in a San Francisco public relations firm (1955–57), and general manager of the Rams (1957–60). In 1960 he became the compromise choice for NFL commissioner on the 23rd ballot after the team owners deadlocked. Rozelle thereupon moved NFL headquarters to New York City and set about to improve the relationship between football and television. He convinced team owners that they would benefit from collective negotiation of TV rights and equal sharing of revenue and led the lobbying effort that persuaded Congress to exempt this action from

antitrust restrictions. After the rival American Football League flourished, Rozelle arranged a game between the league champions that became the Super Bowl. He then negotiated a merger of the two leagues, effective in 1970. Rozelle also set up a program of fines and suspensions for gambling violations, and he aided the effort to combat alcohol and drug abuse. Rozelle was elected to the Pro Football Hall of Fame in 1985 and retired as commissioner in 1989.

Ruiz Soler, Antonio ("ANTONIO"; "EL BAILARÍN"), Spanish flamenco dancer and choreographer who was known for his artistry, showmanship, and technique and who brought the male back to prominence in Spanish dance (b. Nov. 4, 1921—d. Feb. 5, 1996).

Ruppe, Loret Miller, U.S. government official who as director, 1981–89, of the Peace Corps reversed its decade-long decline by reinstituting programs abroad and strengthening its core of volunteers; she then served as ambassador to Norway from 1989 to 1993 (b. Jan. 3, 1936—d. Aug. 6, 1996).

Rushton, William George ("WILLIE"), British actor, comedian, cartoonist, and writer best known for his contributions to the satirical magazine *Private Eye* (which he cofounded) and his appearances on radio and television programs, including "That Was the Week That Was" (b. Aug. 18, 1937—d. Dec. 11, 1996).

Sabia, Laura Villela, Canadian feminist leader who rallied more than 30 women's lobbying groups that pressured Canada into establishing the Royal Commission on the Status of Women, which resulted in the founding in 1972 of the National Action Committee on the Status of Women; Sabia was also a successful broadcast journalist and columnist whose outspoken views often sparked controversy (b. Sept. 18, 1916—d. Oct. 17, 1996).

Sagan, Carl Edward, U.S. astronomer and exobiologist (b. Nov. 9, 1934, New York, N.Y.—d. Dec. 20, 1996, Seattle, Wash.), studied such diverse aspects of the solar system as the conditions of planetary surfaces and atmospheres and the possibility of extraterrestrial life; he stimulated popular interest in these subjects through his enthusiastic writings, lectures, and televised presentations. An avid reader of science fiction as a boy, Sagan developed an interest in astronomy early in life. He studied at the University of Chicago, where he earned four degrees (A.B., 1954; B.S., 1955; M.S., physics, 1956; and Ph.D., astronomy and astrophysics, 1960). After graduation he lectured at the University of California, Berkeley, and at Harvard University before moving to Cornell University, Ithaca, N.Y., in 1968. There he became director of the Laboratory for Planetary Studies and (1970) professor (from 1976 David Duncan professor) of astronomy and space sciences. Some of Sagan's earliest theories about planetary conditions concerned Mars and Venus, predictions that were confirmed by unmanned space probes during the late 1960s and '70s. Sagan was involved in designing experiments to be carried out on a number of these planetary missions. Intrigued since his graduate-school days by the question of the way that life on Earth originated, Sagan conducted experiments showing how various organic molecules could be produced from a simulated gaseous atmosphere of primitive Earth. Sagan's willingness to speculate about the possibility of life elsewhere in the universe helped to gain credibility for the search for extraterrestrial life. He also perceived the threat that the nuclear arms race posed to humanity, and in 1983 he coauthored an article warning about the possible consequences of a nuclear exchange. Although scenarios, such as an atmospheric cooling dubbed "nuclear winter," predicted by the authors were shown to be unlikely, the article spurred discussion of this serious topic. Sagan was a prolific writer of popular science and won a Pulitzer Prize in 1978 for *The Dragons of Eden: Speculations on the Evolution of Human Intelligence.* His passion for science was contagious, and his ability to in-

Pete Rozelle

Carl Sagan

spire others to share that interest became evident when the TV series "Cosmos," a program he narrated and helped to write, began airing in 1980 and became an immediate success.

Salam, Abdus, Pakistani physicist (b. Jan. 29, 1926, Jhang Maghiana, Punjab, India [now Pakistan]—d. Nov. 21, 1996, Oxford, Eng.), shared the 1979 Nobel Prize for Physics with Steven Weinberg and Sheldon Lee Glashow. Each had

Abdus Salam

independently formulated a theory explaining the underlying unity of the weak nuclear force and the electromagnetic force, two of the four basic forces of nature. This so-called electroweak theory showed that the two forces are actually manifestations of a single fundamental force and laid the groundwork for the development of an as-yet-unachieved unified field theory, in which all four forces of nature (including the strong nuclear force and gravity) are described in terms of a single framework. Salam was the first person from an Islamic country to win a Nobel Prize. He received the highest scores ever recorded on an entrance examination to the Punjab University system and entered Government College at Lahore to study mathematics (M.A., 1946). Salam won a scholarship to the University of Cambridge, where he took highest honours in mathematics and physics (B.A., 1949) and received a doctorate in theoretical physics (1952). He went on to teach in Pakistan (1951–54), but frustration at the dearth of research opportunities in his native land prompted him to return to Cambridge. In 1957 he became professor of theoretical physics at the Imperial College of Science, Technology, and Medicine, University of London, and carried out research there until his death. Salam, who was interested in the education and professional development of scientists in Third World countries, helped found the International Centre for Theoretical Physics in Trieste, Italy, a research institute set up to train young scientists from less-developed countries. He served as director of the institute (1964–93) and president (1994–96) and was involved in a number of international and national committees, such as the United Nations Advisory Committee on Science and Technology (1964–75) and Pakistan's Atomic Energy Commission (1958–74). He was elected a fellow of the Royal Society in 1959 and was the recipient of many awards, including the Copley Medal (1990).

San Yu, U, Myanmar (Burmese) politician who headed a repressive military government while serving as president from 1981 to 1988 (b. 1919—d. Jan. 28, 1996).

Savio, Mario, U.S. protest leader who gave rise to the campus sit-in as the fiery speaker of the Free Speech Movement at the University of California, Berkeley, during the 1960s (b. Dec. 8, 1942—d. Nov. 6, 1996).

Schapiro, Meyer, U.S. art historian, teacher, and critic (b. Sept. 23, 1904, Siauliai, Lithuania—d. March 3, 1996, New York, N.Y.), was an important figure in New York intellectual circles for over 50 years. Although he gained his reputation in the field of art history, he was determined

to discover the relationships between all schools of knowledge, and he shared his insights and enthusiasm in lectures and books, aided by his remarkable photographic memory of both books he had read and works of art he had seen. When Schapiro was a schoolchild, his parents encouraged the free reign of his curiosity, and he explored a number of diverse activities; among them was an evening art class, at which he was the only child. He graduated from high school at 16 and entered Columbia University, New York City, with the aid of two scholarships. He received a bachelor's degree in 1924 and went on to earn a Ph.D. in art history in 1929. Schapiro had taught himself German and read the work of the scholars Wilhelm Vöge and Alois Riegl, and it was those writings that led him to the subject of his doctoral dissertation: the cloister and portal of a French abbey, Moissac, known for its Romanesque sculptures. His five years of research revealed that the sculptures were not merely antiquarian religious artifacts, as had been thought, but in addition had been created for aesthetic reasons, as expressions of beauty that captivated observers across the centuries. When part of the dissertation was published in *The Art Bulletin* in 1931, Schapiro gained wide recognition. Appointed lecturer at Columbia in 1928, he spent most of his teaching career there, advancing through the ranks to university professor in 1965 and professor emeritus in 1973. He also lectured at New York University (1932–36) and the New School for Social Research (1936–52) and was Charles Eliot Norton lecturer at Harvard University (1966–67) and Slade professor of art at the University of Oxford (1968). Among his notable books are a four-volume series of essays and lectures: *Romanesque Art* (1977), *Modern Art: 19th & 20th Centuries* (1978), *Late Antique, Early Christian and Mediaeval Art* (1979), and *Theory and Philosophy of Art: Style, Artist, and Society* (1994).

Schine, G. David, U.S. political figure and businessman who gained notoriety as a member of Sen. Joseph McCarthy's staff, which was attempting to expose corrupt and communist influences in U.S. government; Schine unintentionally figured in the senator's public downfall in 1954, during widely televised congressional hearings to determine whether McCarthy and his staff had secured Schine preferential treatment when he was a private in the U.S. Army (b. Sept. 11, 1927—d. June 19, 1996).

Schön, Helmut, German association football (soccer) player and coach who, during 14 years, 1964–78, as coach of the West German national team, guided West Germany to the World Cup final twice (losing in 1966 and coming back to win in 1974) and to the European championship twice (winning in 1972 and losing on a penalty shootout in 1976); he retired with a career record of 87 wins, 31 draws, and 21 losses (b. Sept. 15, 1915—d. Feb. 22, 1996).

Scott, Ronald ("RONNIE"), British jazz entrepreneur and musician whose London nightclub, Ronnie Scott's, presented many of the outstanding U.S. and European jazz musicians and became one of the world's most famed jazz venues; a gifted bop tenor saxophonist, Scott also led small combos and played (1962–73) in the Kenny Clarke-Francy Boland big band (b. Jan. 28, 1927—d. Dec. 23, 1996).

Shakur, Tupac, U.S. rap singer and actor whose violent and sexually explicit lyrics mirrored his own tumultuous life, which was marked by frequent run-ins with the authorities, including arrests for assault and battery and a 1994 conviction for sex abuse, a verdict that his lawyers were appealing when he was murdered in a drive-by shooting (b. June 16, 1971—d. Sept. 13, 1996).

Shenandoah, Leon, U.S. Native American leader of the Onondaga Indians and, from 1969, Tadadaho—chief of chiefs, the spiritual and political spokesman—of the Six Nations of the Iroquois Confederacy (b. May 18, 1915—d. July 22, 1996).

Shostak, Marjorie, U.S. writer who conducted pathbreaking anthropological studies on tribal women while living among the !Kung San tribe in Africa's Kalahari Desert from 1968 to 1971; Shostak learned their difficult clicking language (! represents the click sound) and documented her findings in *Nisa: The Life and Words of a !Kung Woman*, 1981 (b. May 11, 1945—d. Oct. 6, 1996).

Shulman, Alexander, Canadian-born surgeon who in the 1950s discovered the efficacy of using ice water to treat burns; he also helped to introduce improvements in the treatment of various other conditions, including the use of a minimally invasive procedure for hernia repair and the prescription of the blood-thinning drug heparin for patients at risk for heart attacks (b. June 22, 1915—d. July 7, 1996).

Siegel, Jerry, U.S. cocreator of Superman and comic book writer who, with his artist partner, Joe Shuster, sold the rights to the "Man of Steel" in 1938 for $130; in 1978 their byline was restored and they were awarded an annual stipend (b. Oct. 17, 1914—d. Jan. 28, 1996).

Siles Zuazo, Hernán, Bolivian politician (b. March 21, 1914, La Paz, Bol.—d. Aug. 6, 1996, Montevideo, Uruguay), played a key role in the Bolivian National Revolution in 1952 and helped enact social reforms that modernized the country before serving two terms as president (1956–60, 1982–85). Siles Zuazo, nicknamed *"el conejo"* ("the rabbit"), was the son of Hernando Siles Reyes, president of Bolivia from 1926 to 1930. Trained as a lawyer, Siles Zuazo cofounded (1942) the Nationalist Revolutionary Movement (MNR). In 1952 he was coleader of an uprising that became one of Latin America's most important social revolutions. The military junta was overthrown, and the MNR came to power with Siles Zuazo as vice president. The revolutionary government nationalized the country's tin mines, granted universal suffrage, and briefly abolished the army. In 1953 a landmark decree was enacted that granted land to indigenous peoples. When Siles Zuazo was elected president in 1956, he faced an economic crisis after the price of tin, upon which Bolivia depended, plummeted. He implemented the International Monetary Fund's austerity program, which alienated the labour movement. He also rebuilt the army. Though he introduced educational and agrarian reforms, his policies were largely unpopular, and he was defeated in the 1960 elections. After the military's return to power in 1964, Siles Zuazo was forced into exile. He returned to Bolivia in 1978 and was elected president two years later. The army, however, barred him from office, and it was not until 1982 that Siles Zuazo was sworn in, ending 18 years of military rule. In his second term he again faced economic turmoil. The country was virtually bankrupt and had a $4 billion foreign debt as the world price of tin reached an all-time low. Labour strikes paralyzed the country, and severe flooding in 1983 destroyed much of the crops. Siles Zuazo refused to implement the IMF's strict financial plan, and Bolivia officially defaulted on its loan. By the mid-1980s the annual rate of inflation was over 20,000%. In 1985 the country's bishops, in what became known as the "church coup," proposed that the general elections be moved up one year, which effectively ended Siles Zuazo's term. He acquiesced and went into self-imposed exile in Uruguay.

Silliphant, Stirling Dale, U.S. television and film writer whose screenplays were used on the TV shows "Alfred Hitchcock Presents," "Route 66," and "The Naked City" and whose films included *In the Heat of the Night,* for which he won an Academy Award, and *Charly* as well as the high-budget disaster films *The Poseidon Adventure* and *The Towering Inferno* (b. Jan. 16, 1918—d. April 26, 1996).

Sleet, Moneta J., Jr., U.S. *Ebony* magazine photographer who captured many of the defining images of the U.S. civil rights struggle and won a Pulitzer Prize for his poignant photograph of Coretta Scott King at the funeral of her husband, the Rev. Martin Luther King, Jr. (b. Feb. 14, 1926—d. Sept. 30, 1996).

Smythe, Pat (PATRICIA ROSEMARY KOECHLIN-SMYTHE), British equestrian who was the four-time European ladies champion and the first woman to win a medal (bronze) in the hitherto men-only show-jumping event at the 1956 Olympic Games; she also wrote two autobiographies and several popular children's books (b. Nov. 22, 1928—d. Feb. 27, 1996).

Snell, George Davis, U.S. immunogeneticist (b. Dec. 19, 1903, Bradford, Mass.—d. June 6, 1996, Bar Harbor, Maine), was a winner (with Baruj Benacerraf and Jean Dausset) of the 1980 Nobel Prize for Physiology or Medicine for research into the genes that determine proteins located on the surface of cells that control the body's immune response to foreign tissue grafts. This work enabled transplant surgeons to make better matches between organ and tissue donors and the intended recipients and thereby reduce the threat of graft rejection. Snell conducted his experiments at the Jackson Laboratory in Bar Harbor, where he spent most of his professional career studying mammalian genetics. He was educated at Dartmouth College, Hanover, N.H. (B.S., 1926), and Harvard University (Sc.D., 1930). After graduating he received a National Research Council fellowship to work at the University of Texas at Austin with the future Nobelist Hermann J. Muller, who was using X-rays to produce mutations in the chromosomes of fruit flies. In 1935 Snell moved to the Jackson Laboratory and studied X-ray-induced mutations in mice. In the 1940s he changed his focus to the genetics of organ and tissue transplantation, collaborating with British geneticist Peter Gorer. In experiments carried out in mice, the two scientists identified the chromosomal location of genetic factors responsible for tissue rejection. The group of proteins that these genes encode, called the major histocompatibility complex, is found in all higher vertebrates, where it plays an extremely important role in the rejection of not only foreign tissue grafts but also many other foreign substances. Snell was credited with coining the term *histocompatibility* (*histo,* from the Greek word meaning "web," denotes tissue). He was elected to the American Academy of Arts and Sciences in 1952 and to the National Academy of Sciences in 1970.

Snyder, James G. ("JIMMY THE GREEK"; DIMETRIOS GEORGOS SYNODINOS), U.S. gambling oddsmaker and television personality whose success as a betting analyst won him an $800,000-a-year stint on the CBS sports show "NFL Today" that ended in 1988 because he made an ethnic slur (b. 1918—d. April 21, 1996).

Spínola, António Sebastião Ribeiro de, Portuguese military officer who briefly served as his country's president following the military coup that toppled dictator Marcelo Caetano and set Portugal on the road to democracy (b. April 11, 1910—d. Aug. 13, 1996).

Stokes, Carl Burton, U.S. politician who was the first African-American mayor of a major U.S. city (Cleveland, Ohio, 1967–71), New York City's first black television news anchorman, a municipal judge, and an ambassador to Seychelles (b. June 21, 1927—d. April 4, 1996).

Stryjkowski, Julian (JULIAN STARK), Polish writer acclaimed for novels that described Jewish life in Poland, particularly a trilogy that chronicled the decay of Orthodox villages due to outside pressures (b. April 27, 1905—d. Aug. 8, 1996).

Sudoplatov, Pavel Anatolyevich, Soviet security and intelligence agent who was responsible for political assassinations, including that of Leon Trotsky; Sudoplatov was imprisoned for 15 years and made the claim in his autobiography that the Soviet Union obtained atomic secrets with the aid of Manhattan Project scientists (b. 1907—d. Sept. 24, 1996).

Suenens, Léon Joseph Cardinal, Belgian prelate who, as a moderator of the Second Vatican Council (1962–65), was instrumental in effecting liberal change within the Roman Catholic Church, though many of his later proposals, including the acceptance of birth control, were rejected (b. July 16, 1904—d. May 6, 1996).

Suharto, Siti Hartinah ("IBU TIEN"), Javanese-born wife of Indonesian President Suharto who was his trusted confident and, though never overtly involved in politics, was instrumental in the introduction of legal limitations on traditional Islamic polygamy in Indonesia, the world's most populous Muslim nation (b. Aug. 23, 1924?—d. April 28, 1996).

Sullivan, Walter Seager, Jr., U.S. journalist whose career as science reporter, editor, and correspondent for the *New York Times* spanned a half century, took him all over the world, and won him nearly every science journalism prize (b. Jan. 12, 1918—d. March 19, 1996).

Sutherland, Efua Theodora, Ghanaian playwright, poet, and children's author (b. June 27, 1924, Cape Coast, Gold Coast [now in Ghana]—d. Jan. 22, 1996), founded the Drama Studio in Accra (now the Writers' Workshop in the Institute of African Studies at the University of Ghana at Legon). She was one of Africa's best-known women writers. After teachers training in her native land, Sutherland studied at Homerton College, Cambridge, and at the University of London's School of Oriental and African Studies. When she returned to Accra, she helped establish the literary magazine *Okyeame* and the Drama Studio, which began as a workshop for writers of children's literature. Her own best-known plays were produced in 1962, notably *Edufa* (published in 1967), based on Euripides's *Alcestis,* and *Foriwa* (1967), a play that stresses the importance of melding new ways with tradition. *The Marriage of Anansewa: A Storytelling Drama* (1975) was often considered Sutherland's most valuable work. Her writings for children included the pictorial essays *Playtime in Africa* (1960) and *The Roadmakers* (1961) and the plays *Vulture! Vulture!* and *Tahinta* (both 1968). One of her later plays, *Nyamekye,* a version of *Alice in Wonderland,* shows the influence of the folk-opera tradition. Sutherland's book of fairy tales and folklore of Ghana, *The Voice in the Forest,* was published in 1983.

Takemitsu, Toru, Japanese composer (b. Oct. 8, 1930, Tokyo, Japan—d. Feb. 20, 1996, Tokyo), achieved worldwide renown for works that combined the tradition of Western classical music and the sounds of traditional Eastern instruments, especially the *biwa* (a short-necked lute) and the *shakuhachi* (a bamboo flute), in addition to serial music and *musique concrète.* His compositions also used percussion in unusual ways, electronic alteration of orchestral sounds, and even silence to return to music the sensuality he thought it had lost. In addition to concert works, he composed more than 90 film scores, including *Woman in the Dunes* (1964) and *Ran* (1985). Takemitsu was, for the most part, self-taught, though he did study intermittently with the composer Yasuji Kiyose. He first performed in public in 1950 and the following year helped found a new group, the Experimental Workshop. Takemitsu's first composition to attract international attention was *Requiem for Strings* (1957), which became one of his most popular works. Igor Stravinsky and Aaron Copland promoted his music, and it began to be performed abroad. Major orchestras also began to commission and perform his compositions, among them what was possibly his best-known work, *November Steps* (1967). Takemitsu's later music reflected the influence of Claude Debussy, George Gershwin, and Olivier Messiaen and incorporated elements of tonal harmony along with those of serial music. He also claimed that the Japanese formal garden inspired the structure of his music, as illustrated by such works as *A Flock Descends into the Pentagonal Garden* (1978) and *Tree Line* (1988). Takemitsu was active in festivals of modern music and was director of the Space

Theatre at Expo '70 in Osaka, Japan. Among his awards were the Gravemeyer Award (1994) and the Glenn Gould Prize (1996). Takemitsu's last work was a piece for the flute, and he was working on his first opera at the time of his death.

Tesich, Steve (STOYAN TESICH), U.S. screenwriter and playwright who won an Academy Award for *Breaking Away* and also scripted such films as *Eyewitness* and *The World According to Garp* (b. Sept. 29, 1942—d. July 1, 1996).

Thomas, Richard Clement Charles ("CLEM"), Welsh Rugby Union player and journalist who excelled as an aggressive back row forward in a 10-year career, 1949–59, that included 26 appearances for Wales—9 as captain—and a prominent place in the British Lions 1955 tour of South Africa; after retiring from the game in 1959, he was rugby correspondent for *The Observer* and, from 1994, for the *Independent on Sunday* (b. Jan. 28, 1929—d. Sept. 5, 1996).

Tiny Tim (HERBERT KHAURY), U.S. ukelele-strumming, straggly-haired singer whose reputation rested largely on his 1968 falsetto rendition of "Tip-Toe thru' the Tulips with Me"; his 1969 televised wedding to a 17-year-old fan, "Miss Vicki" Budinger, attracted some 40 million household viewers to "The Tonight Show," one of the program's largest audiences ever (b. April 12, 1930?—d. Nov. 30, 1996).

Toumanova, Tamara Vladimirovna, Russian-born U.S. ballerina and actress (b. March 2, 1919, near Tyumen, Siberia—d. May 29, 1996, Santa Monica, Calif.), was the most glamorous of the "baby ballerinas," three young teenage stars of Les Ballets Russes de Monte-Carlo in the 1930s. She was dubbed the "black pearl of the Russian ballet" because of her beautiful black hair, large brown eyes, and almond skin and her dazzling technique. Toumanova was born in a boxcar of a train headed for Shanghai as her parents fled Russia after the Revolution of 1917. The family later settled in Paris, where she studied ballet with Olga Preobrajenska, a former prima ballerina. Toumanova had already danced at the Paris Opéra, in a student performance of *L'Éventail de Jeanne,* when George Balanchine recruited her for Les Ballets Russes in 1932 and created roles for her in *Cotillon* and *La Concurrence.* She accompanied him when he left to form Les Ballets 1933, and when it disbanded she returned to Les Ballets Russes. Among her notable roles over the next four years were the Ballerina in *Petrushka,* Aurora in *Aurora's Wedding,* and the title character in *The Firebird.* When the company divided (1938), Toumanova went with Léonide Massine's new Ballet Russe de Monte Carlo and added such ballets as *Giselle* and *Le Spectre de la rose* to her repertoire. She starred in the Broadway musical *Stars in Your Eyes* in 1939 and later appeared with both Ballet Russe companies as well as a number of U.S. and European companies, among them Ballet Theatre (now American Ballet Theatre), London Festival Ballet, and the Paris Opéra Ballet. At the latter the title role in *Phèdre* was created for her in 1950. Toumanova made her motion picture debut in *Days of Glory* (1944) and appeared in such other films as *Invitation to the Dance* (1956), *Torn Curtain* (1966), and *The Private Life of Sherlock Holmes* (1970).

Touvier, Paul, French war criminal who ordered the execution of seven Jews in 1944 and, after evading capture for over 40 years, became in 1994 the only Frenchman ever convicted of crimes against humanity; he died in a prison hospital (b. April 3, 1915—d. July 17, 1996).

Tran Van Tra, Vietnamese general (b. 1918 Quang Ngai province, Vietnam, 1918—d. April 20, 1996, Ho Chi Minh City, Vietnam), proved to be an able commander in the Vietnam War by leading communist raids on Saigon both during the Tet offensive of 1968 and during the city's capture in 1975. Raised in southern Vietnam, he began his military career in the late 1930s fighting against the French in the Viet Minh resis-

Tamara Toumanova

tance movement. Following the Geneva Accords of 1954 that partitioned the country, he assumed various posts in the North Vietnamese army. In 1963 he was sent back to the south, where he led Viet Cong guerrillas against U.S. and South Vietnamese forces. Although he scored many battlefield victories and was appointed military head of the underground communist government in South Vietnam, he often clashed with party leaders over wartime strategy. He returned briefly to Hanoi in the mid-1970s to help plan the final assault on Saigon, in which he was the frontline commander. Dismayed at the lack of official credit he and other generals from South Vietnam received following the war, he wrote a personal account of the conflict, which was censored upon its publication in 1982. Despite falling from favour in Hanoi, Tra retained his influence among former army officials, with whom in 1987 he organized a war veterans association. The group was vocal in its opposition to government policies and was banned in 1990.

Travers, P(amela) L(yndon) (HELEN LYNDON GOFF), Australian-born British writer (b. Aug. 9, 1899, Maryborough, Queensland, Australia—d. April 23, 1996, London, Eng.), created the popular character Mary Poppins and wrote a series of children's books that were translated into more than 20 languages. In her late teens Travers moved to England, where she worked as an actress, dancer, and journalist. During that period she became acquainted with the poets William Butler Yeats and George William Russell (known as AE), with whom she shared a deep interest in myth. Through Russell, who became her mentor, she was introduced to London literary society. Her first book, *Mary Poppins* (1934), featuring a magical, no-nonsense, but endearing nanny, was

an immense success. Her first sequel in 1935 helped her to decide on a career as a writer. Traveling throughout the U.S. and Europe, she lectured, wrote, and served as writer-in-residence at several colleges. Her later works include several travel books and a collection of essays on myth published in 1989.

Trilling, Diana Rubin, U.S. writer (b. July 21, 1905, New York, N.Y.—d. Oct. 23, 1996, New York), was one of the last members of the circle of writers and critics in the 1930s through the '50s that was known as the New York intellectuals. Her social and literary criticism was published in many of the most highly respected magazines, including *The New Yorker, Harper's, The Nation,* and *The Partisan Review.* Educated in fine arts at Radcliffe College, Cambridge, Mass., and having married (1929) the critic Lionel Trilling, she began (1941) her writing career after she overheard her husband in a telephone conversation with the literary editor of *The Nation,* who was seeking someone to write the literary notes column; she suggested herself. For much of the following decade, she read a book and a half a day—some of the most important new works—and produced trenchant reviews. Trilling's political essays reflected the liberal anticommunism she espoused after having been a member of a number of communist front organizations in the 1930s. After her husband died (1975), Trilling edited a 12-volume uniform edition of his work. Her own writings were collected in such volumes as *Claremont Essays* (1964), *We Must March My Darlings* (1977), and *Reviewing the Forties* (1978). Trilling achieved more widespread renown in 1981 with the publication of *Mrs. Harris: The Death of the Scarsdale Diet Doctor,* a report of the trial of Jean Harris for the murder of her lover. That was followed by

Diana Trilling

The Beginning of the Journey (1993), an account of her married life. Shortly before her death, Trilling finished *A Visit to Camelot,* recounting an evening the Trillings spent at the White House during John F. Kennedy's presidency.

Tudor, David Eugene, U.S. avant-garde composer and pianist who gained prominence after 1950 as an interpreter of the works of such composers as Pierre Boulez, Karlheinz Stockhausen, and, most notably, John Cage, with whom he collaborated often and whom he succeeded in 1992 as music director of the Merce Cunningham Dance Company at Black Mountain (N.C.) College (b. Jan. 20, 1926—d. Aug. 13, 1996).

Tuttle, Elbert Parr, U.S. lawyer and judge who supported the civil rights movement in the South while serving on the U.S. Court of Appeals for the 5th Circuit (1954–81) and presiding there as chief judge (1961–67). He enforced racial integration of public schools, including the University of Georgia in 1961, and was awarded the Presidential Medal of Freedom in 1981 (b. July 17, 1897—d. June 23, 1996).

Uno, Chiyo, Japanese writer (b. Nov. 28, 1897, Iwakuni, Yamaguchi prefecture, Japan—d. June 10, 1996, Tokyo, Japan), deliberately flouted conservative Japanese mores by having numerous affairs and by wearing Western clothing, but by the 1970s she had gained respectability as a grande dame of Japanese letters. She also became a celebrated designer and fashion magazine publisher, and in 1990 the Japanese emperor named her a "person of cultural merit." Uno was raised in southwestern Japan, graduated from high school, and became a schoolteacher. She promptly scandalized her co-workers by wearing makeup and having an affair with a male colleague. After her first marriage failed (she married and divorced three times), Uno moved to Tokyo to develop her career as a writer. In 1921 she received her first literary recognition when she won a newspaper contest with her short story "Shifun no kao" ("A Face with Makeup"). During the 1920s and '30s, Uno had affairs with various members of Tokyo's bohemian literati and continued to defy conventional social and moral codes. In 1930 she met and began a notorious relationship with Togo Seiji, a painter famous for a failed suicide pact with his previous lover. Her first novel, *Irozange* (1935; *Confessions of Love,* 1989), was based on their five-year affair. In 1936 Uno founded *Sutairu* ("Style"), Japan's first Western-style fashion magazine, which was published—except for a break during World War II—until 1959. During this period she also began designing kimonos, and she continued to operate a successful boutique until

her death. Her best-known and most critically acclaimed novel, *Ohan,* was published in 1957. A memoir, *Ikite yuku watakushi* (1983; "I Will Go On Living"), became a best-seller and was made into a serialized television movie.

Uys, Jamie, South African filmmaker whose biggest comedic success, *The Gods Must Be Crazy,* was an international hit (b. May 30, 1921—d. Jan. 29, 1996).

Valverde, José María, Spanish poet and scholar (b. Jan. 26, 1926, Valencia de Alcántara, Spain—d. June 6, 1996, Barcelona, Spain), was one of the leading voices of Spanish literature. His contemplative poetry explores the human condition in a religious or existential context. Valverde began writing verse at the age of 13 and published *Hombre de Dios* (1945) while a student at the University of Madrid. During that time he met the poets Leopoldo Panero, Luis Felipe Vivanco, and Luis Rosales. They shared Valverde's Christian faith and became important influences on his work, which showed his leanings toward liberation theology. Valverde's second book of poetry, *La espera* (1949), won the José Antonio Primo de Rivera National Prize for Literature in 1949. While teaching at the University of Barcelona, Valverde supported several colleagues who were dismissed for having participated in a student protest. As a result, he resigned and went into voluntary exile in 1967. While teaching abroad, Valverde published *El profesor de español* (1971) and *Enseñanzas de la edad: poesía 1945–1970* (1971), which included most of his early work and a new collection entitled "Años inciertos." In 1977 he returned to Barcelona. Valverde's writings also extended to philosophy and social commentary. He translated into Spanish works by James Joyce, Herman Melville, William Shakespeare, Johann Wolfgang von Goethe, Rainer Maria Rilke, and, most notably, the Catalan poet Joan Maragall. His greatest scholarly contribution was the 10-volume *Historia de la literatura universal* (1957), on which he collaborated with Martín de Riquer.

Van Fleet, Jo, U.S. actress who played bold, matronly women on stage and screen, notably in Elia Kazan films, beginning with her role as the mother of James Dean's character in *East of Eden* (1955), for which she won an Academy Award (b. Dec. 30, 1919—d. June 10, 1996).

Vassall, (William) John, British junior civil servant who succumbed to blackmail in regard to his homosexuality (which was then illegal) and spied for the KGB during his posting at the British embassy in Moscow in the mid 1950s and after his return to London. His arrest in 1962 and sub-

sequent imprisonment (he was released in 1972) provoked a political scandal that brought disgrace on the government of Prime Minister Harold Macmillan and triggered a public investigation of the British security services (b. Sept. 20, 1924—d. Nov. 18, 1996).

Versalle, Richard, U.S. opera singer and tenor with the New York City Metropolitan Opera since 1978; he died onstage after having sung the line "Too bad you can only live so long" before falling from a ladder (b. March 12, 1932—d. Jan. 5, 1996).

Vickrey, William S., Canadian-born U.S. economist and co-winner of the 1996 Nobel Memorial Prize in Economic Science just three days before his death from an apparent heart attack (b. June 21, 1914—d. Oct. 11, 1996). (*See* NOBEL PRIZES.)

Vinay, Ramón, Chilean opera singer (b. Aug. 31, 1912, Chillán, Chile—d. Jan. 4, 1996, Puebla, Mexico), achieved his greatest recognition as a heroic tenor, most notably in the title role in Giuseppe Verdi's *Otello.* He performed at New York City's Metropolitan Opera for 16 seasons (1946–61), at the summer Richard Wagner festival at Bayreuth, Germany, for 6 seasons (1952–57), and throughout Europe and South America, and his 1947 broadcast of *Otello,* with Arturo Toscanini conducting the NBC Orchestra, was recorded by RCA and became one of the most famous operatic recordings. Vinay, whose father was French and mother Italian, was educated in France and then worked in Mexico. He also began voice lessons, and in 1931 in Mexico City he made his stage debut in a baritone role, Alphonse in Gaetano Donizetti's *La favorite.* Vinay continued in baritone roles for several years but, after having resumed study when he found that his voice was changing, made his debut as a tenor in 1943. He sang his first Otello at the Mexico City Opera in 1944. Vinay made his New York debut in 1945 in the role of Don José in *Carmen* for the New York City Opera, and a few months later came his Metropolitan Opera bow, also as Don José. Among his other roles at the Met, in addition to Otello, were Canio in Ruggero Leoncavallo's *Pagliacci,* Samson in Camille Saint-Saëns's *Samson et Dalila,* and Radames in Verdi's *Aida.* His roles during his six seasons at Bayreuth included Siegmund in *Die Walküre,* Tristan in *Tristan und Isolde,* and the title roles in *Parsifal* and *Tannhäuser,* and in 1962 he returned to that festival, having resumed singing baritone roles, as Telramund in *Lohengrin.* Another of Vinay's baritone roles was Iago, which he sang in a production of *Otello* that he directed in Santiago, Chile. On Sept. 22, 1969, however, in the last act of the performance that was his farewell to the stage, he returned one last time to the role of Otello.

Vouyouklaki, Aliki, Greek actress who had a more than 40-year career primarily in motion pictures but also onstage and was known as "the National Star" (b. July 20, 1933—d. July 23, 1996).

Wallenda, Angel (ELIZABETH PINTYE WALLENDA; b. March 20, 1968—d. May 3, 1996, Sayre, Pa.), **Gunther** (b. 1927—d. March 16, 1996, Sarasota, Fla.), and **Helen Kreis** (b. Dec. 11, 1910, Germany—d. May 9, 1996, Sarasota), U.S.- and German-born U.S. high-wire performers, were members of the Great Wallendas, an internationally known daredevil circus act famous for performing death-defying stunts without a safety net. Helen, the last member of the original troupe, joined the Wallendas when she was 16. The act toured Europe before moving to the U.S. in 1928, when it began an association with the Ringling Brothers and Barnum & Bailey Circus that continued intermittently through 1946. Helen and Karl Wallenda, the founder of the group, were married in 1935. Until she retired in 1956, she was balanced at the peak of the seven-person pyramid, a formation that was the most famous and the most dangerous of the Wallendas' acts. Gunther, Karl's nephew, began training on the wire at age five, though he was already part of the act. In 1944, in what became the worst circus tragedy ever, a fire broke out in a circus tent in Hartford, Conn., midway through the Wallendas' act; Gunther helped rescue a number of the spectators. In 1962 in Detroit the pyramid fell, and two members were killed and one left paralyzed. Gunther was the only one left standing and was able to help rescue three who were clinging to the wire. He quit the act suddenly in 1969 following an accident during a rehearsal. He graduated from high school, got a university degree, and became a history and geography teacher, though he continued to train high-wire performers. Angel married into the family in 1985, when she was 17, and began training on the wire. Soon, however, she became ill with cancer. In 1987 her right leg had to be amputated, and in 1988 parts of both lungs were removed. Nonetheless, later that year she returned to the act, becoming the only person with an artificial leg ever to walk a high wire. The cancer recurred, though, and she gave her final performance in 1990.

Waller, Calvin Agustine Hoffman, lieutenant general (ret.), U.S. Army, who was one of the highest-ranking African-Americans in the army and during the Persian Gulf War served under Gen. Norman Schwarzkopf as deputy commander of U.S. forces (b. Dec. 17, 1937—d. May 9, 1996).

Wang Li, Chinese revolutionary and ardent supporter of Chairman Mao Zedong and his Cultural Revolution of the late 1960s who nonetheless was imprisoned, 1967–82, on Mao's orders after he incited the Red Guards to seize the Foreign Ministry (b. 1921—d. Oct. 21, 1996).

Watson, Johnny ("GUITAR"), U.S. rhythm and blues singer and guitarist who during a 40-year career influenced such musicians as Jimi Hendrix, Eric Clapton, and Frank Zappa (b. Feb. 3, 1935—d. May 17, 1996).

Welitsch, Ljuba, Bulgarian-born Austrian opera singer whose international career in the 1940s and '50s was highlighted by her interpretation of the title role in Richard Strauss's *Salome* (b. July 10, 1913—d. Sept. 2, 1996).

Weston, Jack (JACK WEINSTEIN), U.S. stage, motion picture, and television actor who for four decades proved adept at portraying characters that ranged from menacing, in *Wait Until Dark,* to comic, in *The Ritz* and *The Four Seasons* (b. Aug. 21, 1924?—d. May 3, 1996).

Whittle, Sir Frank, British aviation engineer (b. June 1, 1907, Coventry, Warwickshire, Eng.—d. Aug. 8, 1996, Columbia, Md.), was a pioneer in the field of jet propulsion, which he used to develop aircraft that could fly at faster speeds and higher altitudes than airplanes of the 1920s. Whittle patented the turbojet engine in 1930 and in 1936 formed the company Power Jets to build and test his invention. The engine was tested on the ground in 1937 and made its maiden flight in the Gloster E.28/39 aircraft on May 15, 1941. Whittle's was not the first jet-propelled aircraft to lift off, however. The German engineer Hans Pabst von Ohain, who had independently conceived of the jet engine, had flown the first jet-propelled aircraft on Aug. 27, 1939. After the start of World War II, the British Air Ministry contracted Whittle's company to produce aircraft for the Royal Air Force (RAF), although up to that time the British government had shown little interest in Whittle's invention. Growing up, Whittle was influenced by his father, a mechanic known for his inventiveness. Whittle joined the RAF as an apprentice at the age of 16 and soon entered RAF College, Cranwell, as a cadet. He wrote a thesis on *Future Developments in Aircraft Design* and graduated in 1928. He then served as a flying instructor and a test pilot and continued his studies at the RAF engineering school and the University of Cambridge, where he delved into mechanical sciences. He was promoted to air commodore near the end of the war and retired from the RAF in 1948, the same year he was knighted. He subsequently acted as a consultant for various organizations, including the British Overseas Airways Corporation and Bristol-Siddeley Engines. He moved to the U.S. in 1976 and the following year began work as a research professor at the U.S. Naval Academy at Annapolis, Md.

Wiegand, Clyde E., U.S. physicist who worked on the Manhattan Project, which produced the atomic bomb, and later, in the 1950s, was part of a team that discovered the antiproton, using the bevatron particle accelerator at Lawrence Berkeley National Laboratory, Berkeley, Calif. Although his contribution was considered crucial, Wiegand was excluded when two other members of the research team (Owen Chamberlain and Emilio Segrè) were awarded the 1959 Nobel Prize for Physics for this work (b. May 23, 1915—d. July 5, 1996).

Wilkinson, Sir Geoffrey, British chemist (b. July 14, 1921, Todmorden, Yorkshire, Eng.—d. Sept. 26, 1996, London, Eng.), was the corecipient, with Ernst Fischer, of the 1973 Nobel Prize for Chemistry for work in organometallic chemistry in which the "sandwich" structure and properties of molecules known as metallocenes—with a metal atom between two flat hydrocarbon rings—was identified. Their explanation of this previously unknown manner in which metals and organic substances could merge opened up new areas of research. Wilkinson was studying for his Ph.D. at the Imperial College of Science and Technology, University of London, when he was recruited (1943) to work with the Atomic Energy Project in Canada. After teaching at the University of California, Berkeley (1946–50), the Massachusetts Institute of Technology (1950–51), and Harvard University (1951–55), he returned (1956) to Imperial College, where he served as professor (Sir Edward Frankland professor from 1978) of inorganic chemistry until becoming professor emeritus in 1988. He continued with his research until his death. Wilkinson's work on organometallic compounds led to discoveries having significant industrial applications—among them, catalysts used in producing low-lead fuels and the compound known as Wilkinson's catalyst, which aided in the development of methods for synthesizing pharmaceutical chemicals. With F.A. Cotton, Wilkinson published a textbook, *Advanced Inorganic Chemistry* (1962), that became a standard and changed the approach to the teaching of the subject. He completed his work on its sixth edition the week before he died. Wilkinson was elected a fellow of the Royal Society in 1965 and was knighted in 1976.

Williams, Garth, U.S. book illustrator whose cherished and heartwarming drawings appeared in such children's classics as *Stuart Little* and *Charlotte's Web* (b. April 16, 1912—d. May 8, 1996).

Wolf, Daniel, U.S. journalist who was one of the founders of the *Village Voice* weekly newspaper and served as its first editor, 1955–70 (b. May 25, 1915—d. April 11, 1996).

Worlock, Derek John Harford, British Roman Catholic priest for 52 years who was archbishop of Liverpool, 1976–96, and was highly respected for his support of ecumenism and for his leadership in solving the social problems of his diocese (b. Feb. 4, 1920—d. Feb. 8, 1996).

Sir Frank Whittle

Events of 1996

Agriculture and Food Supplies

A world food crisis was averted in 1996 by the recovery of grain production. Grain stocks were expected to increase from the record-low levels recorded at the end of the 1995–96 marketing year. Increased stocks would provide added security against any crop failure in 1997. The increase in grain production was widespread among less-developed countries (LDCs). As a result, food-aid needs were expected to drop in late 1996 and into 1997 as the larger crop was harvested and prices declined. Also noteworthy in 1996 were the World Food Summit, where nations committed themselves to efforts to reduce the number of undernourished people by half by 2015, and bovine spongiform encephalopathy (BSE)—"mad cow" disease—which shocked beef producers and consumers in the United Kingdom. The shock (but not the disease) was felt throughout the European Union (EU) and beyond.

World agriculture in 1996 was also affected by longer-term forces. World markets for food and feed gradually had become more integrated. Nations continued to reform their domestic agricultural policies and reduce trade barriers. Part of the reform was needed to meet commitments

to the Uruguay round trade agreement. One important example was new agricultural legislation in the United States. As a result of recent reforms, producers and consumers in many nations were responding more quickly to world market forces. This was demonstrated by the many farmers who shifted large areas of cropland from other uses to grain production in 1996. Many barriers to integrated world markets still remained, however.

A second force was the rapidly increasing income of people in many LDCs. With more income they demanded more food—especially meat and fresh fruits and vegetables. In China, for example, the rapidly growing demand for meat was felt around the world in the form of expanded demand for feed grains and oilseed meal. In addition, the higher incomes of people in LDCs enabled them to gain better access to food. A survey by the Food and Agriculture Organization (FAO) of the United Nations showed that in the early 1990s there were about 850 million people with inadequate access to food—down from 900 million 20 years earlier—even though the population of LDCs had increased by 1.5 billion over that period.

A third force was the decline in food production and consumption throughout the 1990s in the countries of Eastern Europe and the former Soviet Union. By 1996 there was evidence that this was halting in some countries, but the overall decline continued.

INTERNATIONAL ISSUES

Food-Aid Needs. The FAO and other international aid organizations have stressed that two kinds of food-related assistance are usually needed. There is the short-run need for donors to provide food to meet emergencies caused by natural and man-made disasters. There also is the longer-run need to assist countries in improving their agricultural sectors. In the mid-1990s some LDCs—for example, Sierra Leone and Rwanda—emerged from prolonged civil strife and were facing the possibility of peace and increased stability. These countries would be especially suitable targets for longer-term assistance. A healthy agricultural sector would not only provide more food but also improve the incomes and access to food of the large proportion of the population that lived in rural areas.

In 1996–97 the short-term food prospects improved in many low-income food-deficit countries (LIFDCs). Although food-aid needs declined worldwide, shortages persisted in many countries owing to crop failures, natural disasters, and continuing civil strife. According to the results of an annual analysis by the Economic Research Service of the U.S. Department of Agriculture (USDA), LDCs would need about 9 million to 11 million tons of food aid in the form of cereals during the 1996–97 crop year. Food-aid needs were concentrated in sub-Saharan Africa, Bangladesh,

---

Table I. Selected Indexes of World Agricultural and Food Production
(1989–91 = 100)

Region or country	Total agricultural production					Total food production					Per capita food production				
	1992	1993	1994	1995	1996	1992	1993	1994	1995	1996	1992	1993	1994	1995	1996
Developed countries	99	95	97	95	98	99	96	97	96	98	98	94	95	93	95
Canada	101	103	108	112	113	102	103	107	111	113	99	99	102	105	105
Europe	98	96	94	94	95	98	96	94	94	95	97	96	93	93	93
Japan	101	94	99	96	95	101	95	100	96	95	100	94	98	95	94
Russia	83	85	74	75	74	83	85	74	75	74	82	85	74	75	74
South Africa	85	96	99	85	98	85	97	101	87	100	81	91	93	78	87
United States	110	100	116	109	116	110	100	116	109	116	108	97	111	104	109
Less-developed countries	107	111	116	122	125	107	112	118	124	127	103	106	109	113	114
Argentina	105	102	109	113	118	107	103	111	114	119	104	100	106	107	111
Bangladesh	104	104	100	104	105	104	104	100	104	105	99	97	92	94	93
Brazil	106	109	115	117	119	107	110	116	120	121	103	105	109	110	109
China	110	119	130	141	147	111	121	133	145	152	108	117	127	137	142
Egypt	111	115	113	118	118	111	114	114	119	119	106	106	105	107	104
Ethiopia	...	107	107	114	114	...	108	108	114	115	...	99	95	99	...
India	106	108	112	115	116	106	108	112	115	116	102	101	104	105	104
Indonesia	109	110	109	113	115	109	110	109	114	116	106	105	102	105	105
Malaysia	106	113	114	115	117	109	120	120	122	125	104	111	109	109	108
Mexico	102	108	111	118	122	104	110	113	119	122	99	103	104	108	108
Nigeria	118	125	127	132	134	118	125	128	132	134	111	115	113	114	113
Philippines	103	109	112	114	117	102	109	114	116	119	98	103	105	104	105
Turkey	103	104	103	105	108	103	104	105	105	109	99	98	97	95	97
Venezuela	108	107	117	118	113	109	108	118	119	114	103	101	108	106	99
Vietnam	111	116	120	126	132	111	115	119	124	130	106	108	109	111	114
Zaire	107	108	102	101	101	107	110	102	101	101	100	100	90	86	84
World	103	104	107	110	113	103	104	108	111	114	100	99	101	102	104

Sources: Food and Agriculture Organization of the United Nations, *FAO Quarterly Bulletin of Statistics* (Nov. 7, 1996); World Wide Web site for the FAO: http://apps.fao.org (Dec. 31, 1996).

North Koreans receive rice from the World Food Programme. The widespread flooding in North Korea in 1995 contributed to the country's severe shortage of food.

Afghanistan, and North Korea. The 1996–97 estimate was down from the previous year's estimated needs as a result of improved harvests and increased commercial imports at lower prices in countries receiving aid. Donor nations, however, were expected to supply only 7.5 million tons of cereal aid. (*See* TABLE II.)

The USDA estimate of food-aid needs was obtained by examination of the requirements of 65 LDCs. "Aid needs" for each country were defined as the difference between a target level of food consumption and what could be grown and commercially imported. The target was the average level of food consumption per capita over the previous five years. The 9 million to 11 million tons needed to meet this target in 1996–97 would still fall far short of supplying minimum nutritional standards.

The FAO estimated that 40% of the population of Africa had been undernourished in recent years. In addition, civil strife in various parts of Africa had caused greatly diminished local food production and created several million refugees who needed emergency food aid. A year after the UN forces left Somalia, clan-based fighting continued, and the food emergency worsened in 1996. Cereal harvests also were much below normal. The fighting also disrupted emergency food aid to Somalia by international organizations. Poor cereal harvests and fighting created a food emergency in the capital, Mogadishu. The Sudan suffered from severe floods, pest infestation, and civil war that reduced cereal production

and disrupted emergency food assistance. Continuing strife in Liberia also led to a sharp decline in food production in 1996 and disrupted food assistance. Much of the Liberian population took refuge in neighbouring states. By the end of the year, however, there was evidence that a peace agreement might enable relief supplies to move and allow farmers to return to their fields and tend the crops.

In the Great Lakes region of Africa (Burundi, Rwanda, Tanzania, and Zaire), masses of refugees moved between countries to escape civil strife. Local food production was devastated. The food situation in these countries in 1996 was precarious, and emergency food was urgently needed. Thousands of refugees returned to their farms and homes in Rwanda in 1996 as some stability returned to the country. As a result, there was some recovery of food production.

Owing to strong economic growth and above-average 'cereal harvests, food-aid needs were down in most of the LDCs in Latin America and Asia in 1996. In Afghanistan and Iraq, however, production was down, and food-aid needs increased.

Table II. Shipment of Food Aid in Cereals

In 000-metric ton grain equivalent

Region and country	Average 1991–92 to 1993–94	1994–95	1995–96	1996–97[1]
Australia	262	258	236	240
Canada	805	595	457	500
European Union[2]	3,995	3,451	2,449	2,650
By members	1,164	1,017	869	...
By organizations	2,831	2,434	1,580	...
Japan	373	419	761	770
Norway	53	33	15	20
Switzerland	54	55	45	50
United States	7,791	4,304	2,910	3,000
Others	544	231	290	270
Total	13,877	9,346	7,163	7,500
To LIFDC[3]	9,842	7,866	5,660	5,900
Sub-Saharan Africa	4,744	3,296	2,276	...
To other countries	4,035	1,480	1,503	1,600

[1] Estimated, partly on the basis of minimum commitments under the Food Aid Convention of 1995.
[2] Shows contribution of 15 member countries for all years.
[3] Low-income food-deficit countries with per capita incomes under U.S. $1,395 in 1994.
Source: FAO, November 1996.

Table III. World Cereal Supply and Distribution

In 000,000 metric tons

	1993–94	1994–95	1995–96[1]	1996–97[2]
Production				
Wheat	559	525	537	580
Coarse grains	790	869	796	885
Rice, milled	353	365	371	377
Total	1,702	1,759	1,703	1,842
Utilization				
Wheat	562	549	552	571
Coarse grains	838	858	839	861
Rice, milled	358	367	370	376
Total	1,758	1,774	1,760	1,808
Food use		852	858	883
Feed use		673	644	665
Other uses		249	258	260
Exports				
Wheat	118	111	108	104
Coarse grains	99	104	105	97
Rice, milled	16	22	20	19
Total	233	237	233	220
Ending stocks[3]				
Wheat	142	118	103	112
Coarse grains	123	134	91	115
Rice, milled	51	50	50	51
Total	316	302	244	278
Stocks as % of utilization				
Wheat	25	21	19	20
Coarse grains	15	16	11	14
Rice, milled	14	14	14	13
Total	18	17	14	15
Stocks held by U.S. in %				
Wheat	11	12	10	11
Coarse grains	22	34	16	30
Stocks held by EU in %				
Wheat	12	10	10	14
Coarse grains	15	10	10	12

[1] Estimated. [2] Forecast. [3] Data not available for all countries.
Source: USDA, December 1996.

Food shortages also persisted in North Korea and Laos owing to extensive flooding. The countries of the former Soviet Union generally experienced increased cereal production and some expansion of commercial trade, which thus reduced their need for food aid. In Tajikistan and Turkmenistan, however, food shortages persisted.

Food-Aid Supplies. Wealthy countries provided food aid to other countries in two ways: as a direct aid shipment and as a concessional sale at a reduced price or with a low-interest loan. Because of the world cereal shortage in 1995–96, cereal prices were at record highs. As a result, aid shipments were down, and concessional sales were nearly eliminated. The FAO estimated that LIFDCs increased their expenditures on cereal imports by 35% from the previous year, even though they imported less.

Total cereal-aid shipments (mostly wheat) in 1995–96 were estimated by the FAO to have been 7.2 million tons, with 5.7 million tons having gone to LIFDCs and the remaining 1.5 million tons to other countries. The record-low aid to LIFDCs was down nearly 30% from the previous year and down nearly 40% from the average of the previous four years. Much of the decline in shipments was to sub-Saharan Africa, but aid shipments to Latin-American and Caribbean countries also declined

sharply. Considerably more food aid was sent to North Korea. Food-aid shipments to countries in Eastern Europe and the former Soviet Union (non-LIFDCs) were down 30% from 1994–95. Among donor nations most of the decline was due to reduced shipments by the U.S. and the EU, which combined still accounted for 75% of the cereal food aid. Japan increased its aid shipments. In 1994–95, 30% of food-aid shipments went through multilateral channels such as the World Food Programme.

In November 1996 the FAO estimated 1996–97 food-aid shipments at 7.5 million tons, an increase of 4% over the previous year. Most of the increase was expected to come from the EU and go to the LIFDCs in Africa and Asia.

World Food Summit. The World Food Summit, held Nov. 13–17, 1996, at the Rome headquarters of the FAO, brought together world leaders to discuss global food security. At a similar conference in 1974, leaders had pledged a goal of eradicating hunger within a decade. It did not happen. The FAO estimated that in 1996 about 14% of the world's population suffered from chronic undernutrition. The FAO had classified more than 80 nations as LIFDCs—half in sub-Saharan Africa. The world's population, expected to increase 50% by 2030, faced a declining per-person

supply of tillable land and fresh water. These basic facts provided the background for the 1996 summit. The record-low cereal stocks and sharp increases in cereal prices on world markets in 1995 and 1996 added to the urgency of the summit.

The summit produced a "Declaration on World Food Security" that identified the causes of food insecurity and the actions pledged by governments to correct the problem. According to this declaration, food security is attained "when all people, at all times, have physical and economic access to sufficient, safe, and nutritious food to meet their dietary needs and food preferences for an active and healthy life." The summit's goal was "reducing the number of undernourished people to half their present level no later than 2015.

The summit declaration recognized that the primary cause of food insecurity was poverty, not a global shortage of food. Poverty eradication would require a peaceful and stable community where job opportunities existed and skills could be improved. It was ironic that the majority of the world's hungry lived in rural areas. The declaration called for more investment in agriculture in LDCs to reduce rural poverty as well as to increase food supplies. The declaration also emphasized the need for the world to be better prepared to deal with food-aid needs caused by natural and man-made disasters. Over the last half-century, world cereals markets had had to deal with surpluses most years. Although reducing poverty was a major focus of the declaration, the future need for stable and expanding food supplies and effective emergency food assistance was also highlighted.

A plan of action was adopted by the summit to achieve its objectives. No new international bureaucracies were established, and nations were not asked to make specific pledges of support. Individual nations, international organizations, and nongovernmental organizations were expected to decide their individual courses of action in fulfilling the plan. The FAO Committee on World Food Security would have responsibility for monitoring progress.

New U.S. Farm Legislation. Big changes were made in U.S. farm and food policy with the passage of the seven-year Federal Agricultural Improvement and Reform (FAIR) Act of 1996. In keeping with the liberalization of farm policy that had been taking place in other countries, the FAIR Act shifted to farmers much of the government's control of production of grains and cotton. Less-dramatic changes were made in government programs for dairy, sugar, and peanuts. In addition to reducing government intervention in production, the act would reduce government costs, increase agricultural exports, promote conservation, continue food aid, and stay within the limits on agricultural-production subsidies and export subsidies specified by the World Trade Organization.

The act terminated farm-deficiency payments on grains and cotton. Deficiency payments increased when farm prices fell. They were replaced with annual payments to farmers that were fixed by formula for each farm throughout the seven-year life of the program. The total cost of these payments would be 7% less than the cost of deficiency payments over the seven years prior to 1996. In addition, farmers would

Table IV. World Production of Major Oilseeds and Products

In 000,000 metric tons

	1994–95	1995–96[1]	1996–97[2]
Total production of oilseeds	**260.7**	**255.4**	**256.3**
Soybeans	**137.8**	**124.3**	**133.7**
U.S.	68.5	59.2	63.8
China	16.0	13.5	13.3
Argentina	12.6	12.6	13.5
Brazil	25.9	23.2	26.0
Cottonseed	**32.9**	**35.2**	**33.4**
U.S.	6.9	6.2	6.5
Former Soviet republics	3.7	3.3	3.2
China	7.7	8.4	6.6
Peanuts	**26.3**	**25.9**	**26.4**
U.S.	1.9	1.6	1.6
China	9.7	10.2	9.8
India	8.4	7.4	8.2
Sunflower seed	**23.4**	**25.8**	**23.8**
U.S.	2.2	1.8	1.5
Former Soviet republics	4.4	7.4	5.3
Argentina	5.6	5.6	5.0
European Union	4.1	3.2	3.8
Rapeseed	**30.3**	**34.5**	**29.8**
Canada	7.2	6.4	5.0
China	7.5	9.7	9.0
European Union	7.3	8.3	6.9
India	5.5	6.2	6.0
Copra	**5.5**	**5.0**	**5.1**
Palm kernel	**4.5**	**4.8**	**5.0**
Oilseeds crushed	**207.2**	**215.7**	**213.5**
Soybeans	109.9	111.6	113.0
Oilseed ending stocks	**26.9**	**22.3**	**21.3**
Soybeans	23.5	17.2	18.0
World production[3]			
Total fats and oils	**82.0**	**85.2**	**86.5**
Edible vegetable oils	67.5	70.4	71.9
Soybean oil	19.7	20.1	20.4
Palm oil	14.8	15.6	16.4
Animal fats	13.0	13.4	13.4
Marine oils	1.5	1.4	1.2
High-protein meals[4]	**136.0**	**139.3**	**138.4**
Soybean meal	87.2	88.6	89.1
Fish meal	10.3	9.8	9.2

[1] Preliminary. [2] Forecast. [3] Processing potential from crops in year indicated. [4] Converted, on the basis of product's protein content, to weight equivalent of soybeans of 44% protein content.
Source: USDA, November 1996.

receive some protection against unusually low market prices for grains, cotton, and oilseeds. As a trade-off for reduced income protection, grain and cotton farmers would no longer be required to reduce their planted area in order to receive payments. The government would, however, continue to offer multiyear contracts to pay farmers for retiring fragile land from production and switching it to conservation uses.

Changes in the act essentially removed the U.S. government as the buyer of last resort in order to support market prices. In addition, subsidies provided to farmers for storing grain were eliminated. Stockholding of agricultural commodities would be left to the private sector. For its contribution to global food security, however, the U.S. government would continue to provide a four million-ton grain reserve.

Programs to expand U.S. agricultural exports were continued with some modification. Export credit guarantees, export market promotion, and export subsidies—the Export Enhancement Program—were extended, but the level of funding was reduced.

Domestic and foreign food-aid programs were continued. The Food Stamp Program, by far the largest domestic food program, would continue to assist low-income households with food purchases, but it was authorized for only an additional two years. When the FAIR Act was passed, Congress expected to incorporate food stamps into a new and reformed total welfare program. Other food programs continued by the FAIR Act provided for the purchase and distribution of food for food banks and soup kitchens and for other special needs. These programs were authorized for seven years. Funding was also continued for overseas food aid and for low-cost long-term credit for food purchases by LDCs.

"Mad Cow" Disease. In March the U.K. announced a possible link between BSE, or "mad cow" disease, which was primarily found in the U.K., and Creutzfeldt-Jakob disease, a rare but fatal condition in humans. Though the announcement stressed that the evidence for this connection was weak, consumers in the EU immediately cut back on beef purchases. Beef prices in stores and cattle prices in the country sharply declined. In response to the crisis, the European Commission and the British government took action to ban all exports of cattle, beef, or beef products from the U.K. and to ban the consumption of milk from infected cattle. In addition, the U.K. began a plan to destroy hundreds of thousands of infected cattle over a five-to-seven-year period. A similar plan was later announced by Switzerland, the second most infected country. As a result of the health scare, beef consumption in the EU was expected to be down in 1996.

Scientists believed that BSE was transmitted through infected feedstuffs. The infected feed contained meat and bone meal improperly rendered from carcasses of sheep infected with scrapie disease. BSE, which primarily affected cattle, was fatal, and there was no treatment, but it did not spread from animal to animal. Control of the disease was complicated because signs of the illness did not appear for three to five years after infection. Nearly all cases of BSE were in the U.K., but a few were reported in other European countries.

Table V. Livestock Inventories and Meat Production in Major Producing Countries

In 000,000 head and 000,000 metric tons (carcass weight)

Region and country	1995[1]	1996[2]	1995	1996[1]
	Cattle and buffalo		Beef and veal	
World total	...	...	55.37	56.5
Canada	13	13	0.9	1.0
United States	104	102	11.6	11.8
Mexico	28	27	1.9	1.8
Argentina	54	52	2.6	2.6
Brazil	152	153	4.7	5.0
Uruguay	10	11	0.3	0.4
European Union	83	83	7.8	7.3
Eastern Europe[4]	13	13	1.0	1.0
Kazakstan	7	5	0.5	0.5
Russia	40	37	2.8	2.6
Ukraine	18	16	1.2	1.0
Australia	27	27	1.7	1.8
India	276	277	1.2	1.3
China	124	128	4.2	4.4
	Hogs[3]		Pork	
World total	...	...	81.8	83.9
Canada	12	12	1.3	1.2
United States	58	57	8.1	7.8
Mexico	11	10	1.0	1.0
European Union	114	114	15.4	15.2
Eastern Europe[5]	39	37	3.3	3.6
Russia	23	21	1.9	1.7
Ukraine	13	13	0.8	0.8
Japan	10	10	1.3	1.3
China	441	409	36.5	36.4
Taiwan	10	11	1.2	1.3
			Poultry meat	
World total[4]	...	...	53.9	56.5
United States	...	...	13.8	14.6
Mexico	...	...	1.1	1.1
Brazil	...	...	4.1	4.1
European Union	...	...	7.7	7.9
Eastern Europe[6]	...	...	0.9	0.9
Russia	...	...	0.9	0.8
Ukraine	...	...	0.2	0.2
Japan	...	...	1.3	1.3
China	...	...	9.3	11.0
			Sheep, goat meat	
World total	...	...	10.3	10.6
			All meat	
Total[4]	...	...	205.0	211.4

[1] Preliminary.   [2] Forecast.   [3] Livestock members at year's end.   [4] Bulgaria, Czech Republic, Poland, and Romania.
[5] Bulgaria, Czech Republic, Hungary, Poland, and Romania.   [6] Hungary, Poland, and Romania.
Source: Country data: USDA, October 1996.   World totals: FAO, May–June 1996.

A man harvests sugarcane in Holguín province in Cuba. Sugar was the country's single most important export, and as the world consumption of sugar rose, production in Cuba continued its upward trend and set a new record.

Table VI. World Production of Milk[1]

In 000,000 metric tons

Region and country	1994	1995[2]	1996[3]
Developed countries	**349**	**347**	**347**
United States	70	71	70
Canada	8	8	8
Europe	158	160	159
European Union	124	126	125
France	26	26	26
Germany	28	29	29
Italy	12	12	12
Netherlands	11	11	11
United Kingdom	15	15	15
Eastern Europe			
Poland	12	12	11
Romania	4	4	4
Former Soviet republics			
Russia	43	39	35
Ukraine	18	17	17
Australia/New Zealand[4]	18	18	19
Japan	8	8	9
Less-developed countries	**184**	**189**	**192**
Latin America	49	50	51
Brazil	17	18	19
Africa	19	20	20
Asia	116	119	122
China	8	8	8
India	63	64	67
World total	**532**	**536**	**539**

[1] Includes milk from cattle, buffalo, camels, sheep, and goats. [2] Preliminary. [3] Forecast.
[4] Year ended June 30 for Australia and May 31 for New Zealand.
Source: FAO, December 1996.

Table VII. World Production of Centrifugal
(Freed from Liquid) Sugar
In 000,000 metric tons raw value

Region and country	1994–95	1995–96	1996–97[1]
North America	**11.9**	**11.5**	**11.2**
United States	7.2	6.7	6.5
Mexico	4.6	4.7	4.6
Caribbean	**4.2**	**5.5**	**5.7**
Cuba	3.3	4.4	4.6
Central America	**2.7**	**2.8**	**3.0**
Guatemala	1.3	1.3	1.4
South America	**18.4**	**20.0**	**20.7**
Argentina	1.2	1.6	1.3
Brazil	12.5	13.7	14.5
Colombia	2.1	2.0	2.0
Europe	**19.6**	**20.4**	**21.5**
Western Europe	16.6	17.1	17.4
European Union	16.5	17.0	17.2
France	4.4	4.6	4.4
Germany	4.0	4.2	4.6
Eastern Europe	3.0	3.3	4.1
Poland	1.5	1.7	2.2
Former Soviet republics[2]	**5.7**	**6.4**	**5.4**
Russia	1.7	2.1	1.9
Ukraine	3.6	3.8	3.0
Africa and Middle East	**10.2**	**10.1**	**11.5**
South Africa	1.8	1.8	2.5
Turkey	1.7	1.4	2.0
Asia	**37.3**	**40.1**	**39.9**
China	5.9	6.8	7.0
India	16.4	18.3	17.0
Indonesia	2.4	2.1	2.4
Pakistan	3.2	2.6	2.8
Philippines	1.6	1.8	1.8
Thailand	5.4	6.3	6.5
Oceania	**5.8**	**5.6**	**6.1**
Australia	5.2	5.1	5.6
Totals			
Beginning stocks	18.6	20.8	24.7
As % of consumption	16.4	17.7	20.3
Production	115.8	122.5	125.0
Consumption	113.6	118.6	122.9
Exports	30.5	35.1	35.5

[1] Preliminary. [2] Includes Estonia, Latvia, and Lithuania.
Source: USDA, November 1996.

The disease was first diagnosed in the U.K. in 1986. The number of confirmed infections in cattle peaked in 1992 and then rapidly declined. By 1996 about 150,-000 cases had been confirmed among the U.K.'s 11 million dairy and beef cattle. The disease was expected to be eradicated in about five years by eliminating the infected feedstuffs and by destroying infected cattle. In an effort to offset some of the loss of income of cattle farmers, the EU instituted programs of direct income support to affected producers and increased government procurement of beef.

AGRICULTURAL COMMODITIES

Grains. Early in 1996 the world faced a shortage of grain. (*See* TABLE III.) This was the culmination of forces that had been at work over several years. The rapidly growing world demand for grain appeared to have caught up with forces that were limiting world grain production. More grain had been needed in recent years to feed livestock to meet the rapidly expanding demand for meat in China and other LDCs; therefore, grain used for livestock feed competed with grain used for direct human consumption. Supplies had been abundant and world market prices depressed mainly owing to subsidized grain exports and the release of government-controlled stocks by the U.S. and the EU. Consequently, there had been no growth in total world grain production since 1990.

The possibility of a world grain shortage emerged in late 1995, when it became clear that the 1995 crop, plus available stocks carried forward from 1994, would fall short of expected world use. Although the world wheat and rice crops in 1995 were larger than in the previous year, coarse grain production was down more than 8%, mainly owing to a poor harvest in the U.S. and in the countries of the former Soviet Union. Production of all types of grain was down only 3%, but there were very few available grain stocks carried over from the previous year to make up the shortage. As a result, grain prices rapidly increased.

More danger signs appeared in early 1996 as weather in the U.S. caused major delays in corn (maize) planting. Concerns of a potential crisis pushed grain prices to record-high levels. By May corn prices on the commodities market in Chicago had doubled from a year earlier. As the season progressed, however, crop conditions improved in the U.S. and in much of the world. Several months later it was becoming apparent that farmers around the world had responded to higher prices by planting more grain—reversing a downward trend since 1981 in area planted. By November the FAO and USDA expected a record-high yield per hectare and a record grain harvest that would be 8% larger than the previous year's crop. A crop that large was expected to meet the growth in world demand and allow some rebuilding of stocks. The crisis passed, and grain prices declined.

Large increases in grain production were expected in 1996 in the major grain-exporting countries. Farmers in the U.S. and the EU planted a larger area to grain in 1996 and obtained above-average yields. As a result, grain production was up 19% over 1995 in the U.S. and up 16% in the EU. Farmers in Africa increased grain production nearly 11% and those in Asia 3%. The only major grain-growing areas of the world to show a decline in production were the countries of the former Soviet Union and Eastern Europe, where production by 1996 was down a third from 1990.

As a result of grain shortages and high prices, world grain consumption during the 1995–96 crop year declined for the first time in years. In the competition between humans and animals for the reduced supply of grain, animals lost. Slightly more grain was consumed as human food and used for industrial purposes, but less was consumed by livestock. Both feed and food consumption were expected to be up 3% in 1996–97 as a result of the larger supply.

The volume of world grain trade had changed little over the past 10 years. Trade volume in 1996–97, however, was expected to decline 6% owing to above-average grain harvests in importing countries.

In mid-1996, at the end of the 1995–96 crop year, world stocks of all grains had dropped to 244 million tons. The stocks-to-use ratio was under 14%—the lowest on record. Virtually none of these stocks were available for export. The FAO in late 1995 estimated that world grain production would have to increase at least 4% in 1996 in order to provide a minimum level of food security. As of December 1996, the crop was estimated to have increased by 8%. The added production was expected to permit more stocks to be available at the end of the crop year in 1997. They would provide some increased security against crop failures in that year, but even so the world stock-to-consumption ratio—15%—would be the second lowest on record.

World coarse grain production in 1996–97 was expected to increase 11% over the poor harvest of 1995–96 and to slightly exceed the old production record set in 1992–93. Area harvested increased 2%, and average yield was up nearly 9% to set a new record. World wheat production was expected to increase 8% and rice 2% over 1995–96.

Oilseeds. World production of oilseeds in 1996–97 was expected to slightly exceed the previous year's production but to fall short of the record set in 1994–95. (*See* TABLE IV.) Farmers around the world reduced their area planted to oilseeds in 1996–97 in order to expand what was expected to be more profitable grain production. Higher yields, especially for soybeans in the U.S., offset the drop in area harvested. A larger world soybean harvest compensated for reduced production of cottonseed, sunflower seed, and rapeseed. Increased production of soybeans in the U.S. (up 8%) and Brazil (up 12%) accounted for most of the world's expected increase in soybean production.

Sunflower-seed production in the republics of the former Soviet Union and rapeseed production in Canada, Europe, and China declined because farmers shifted land into wheat and corn. Likewise, cottonseed production dropped in China and India because land was transferred from cotton, which was expected to be less profitable, to grains and other oilseeds.

The demand for vegetable oil and meal (a livestock feed) from crushed oilseeds continued to grow in 1996–97. But owing to the very low level of world stocks at the end of the 1995–96 crop year and virtually no expansion in production in 1996–

Table VIII. World Green Coffee Production
In 000,000 60-kg bags

Region and country	1994–95	1995–96[1]	1996–97[2]
North America	**17.2**	**18.2**	**18.5**
Costa Rica	2.5	2.6	2.6
El Salvador	2.3	2.3	2.4
Guatemala	3.5	3.5	3.5
Honduras	2.3	2.3	2.5
Mexico	4.0	4.5	4.7
South America	**46.1**	**34.6**	**45.5**
Brazil	28.0	16.8	27.5
Colombia	13.0	12.5	13.0
Ecuador	2.6	2.2	2.2
Peru	1.5	1.8	1.4
Africa	**18.2**	**17.6**	**18.2**
Cameroon	1.0	1.2	1.0
Côte d'Ivoire	3.7	2.8	3.2
Ethiopia	3.8	3.8	3.9
Kenya	1.6	1.6	1.7
Uganda	3.1	3.4	3.2
Zaire	1.3	1.0	1.2
Asia and Oceania	**16.3**	**16.4**	**16.8**
India	3.1	3.5	3.2
Indonesia	6.0	5.8	6.5
Thailand	1.4	1.3	1.3
Vietnam	3.5	3.4	3.5
Total production	**97.7**	**86.8**	**99.1**
Exportable	75.1	63.7	74.8
Beginning stocks	30.8	36.8	29.2
Exports[3]	69.7	71.6	76.8

[1] Preliminary.   [2] Forecast.   [3] By exporting countries.   Source: USDA, June 1996.

Table IX. World Cocoa Bean Production
In 000 metric tons

Region and country	1994–95	1995–96	1996–97[1]
North and Central America	**114**	**118**	**119**
South America	**395**	**394**	**368**
Brazil	228	225	198
Africa	**1,450**	**1,914**	**1,724**
Cameroon	107	130	110
Côte d'Ivoire[2]	873	1,200	1,050
Ghana	315	420	390
Nigeria[3]	130	140	150
Asia and Oceania	**439**	**450**	**450**
Indonesia	255	275	280
Malaysia	134	125	120
Total production	**2,398**	**2,876**	**2,660**
Net production	2,374	2,847	2,633
Cocoa grindings	2,544	2,697	2,775
Change in stocks	−170	+150	−142

[1] Forecast.   [2] Includes some cocoa marketed between Ghana and Côte d'Ivoire.   [3] Includes cocoa marketed through Benin.   Source: USDA, October 1996.

Table X. World Cotton Production and Consumption
In 000,000 480-lb bales

Region and country	1994–95	1995–96[1]	1996–97[2]
Production	**85.5**	**91.5**	**87.0**
Western Hemisphere	25.6	23.8	24.5
United States	19.7	17.9	18.6
Brazil	2.5	1.8	1.6
Europe	2.0	2.3	2.1
Former Soviet republics	8.8	8.3	7.4
Uzbekistan	5.8	5.7	5.1
Africa	5.6	6.6	7.2
Asia and Oceania	43.6	50.5	45.7
China	19.9	21.9	17.5
India	10.8	12.3	12.2
Pakistan	6.2	8.2	7.1
Consumption	**84.7**	**84.6**	**85.7**
United States	11.2	10.6	11.0
China	20.2	19.8	19.8
India	10.5	11.4	11.8
Pakistan	6.8	7.0	6.7
European Union	5.4	5.1	5.1
Southeast Asia	4.6	4.5	4.5
Russia	1.3	1.2	1.0

[1] Estimated.   [2] Forecast.   Source: USDA, October and November 1996.

97, world markets for oilseeds, meal, and oil were expected to be tight. No buildups of year-end stocks were expected.

China's large and rapidly expanding meat industry needed more meal in 1996–97, and the growing population needed more oil. The USDA expected China to use over 30% more soybean meal in 1996–97 than in 1994–95, but its oilseed crop was expected to be smaller. Consequently, China likely would increase imports of oilseeds and their products in 1996–97. Similar circumstances existed in the oilseed markets of other major Asian importing countries. In India, however, imports were expected to decline because of increased domestic production and abundant stocks at the beginning of the year.

Livestock and Meat. The FAO forecast a 3% increase in world meat production in 1996, consisting of a 5.5% increase in LDCs and a very small increase in the rest of the world. The increased output in LDCs amounted to a 3% increase per capita. These July 1996 forecasts by the FAO, however, were high relative to later forecasts by the USDA for major producing countries. (*See* Table V.) World meat production continued a slow but steady shift toward poultry meat and pork and away from other meats, especially in LDCs.

World poultry production in 1996 was expected to increase 5% over the previous year. Production in the U.S., the leader, was up 6%, and in China, the second largest producer, up 18% because of strong domestic and foreign demand. Even though poultry meat prices were up owing to higher feed costs, world exports of poultry meat were expected to increase 5% over 1995 and 28% over 1994. Major importers were China, Japan, and Mexico.

Pork production worldwide was forecast by the FAO to increase 3% in 1996, while the USDA expected no change from 1995. The swine industry in China, which produced over 40% of the world's pork, had difficulties in 1996. In response to favourable economic conditions in 1995, swine farmers in China significantly enlarged their herds. Going into 1996, the herd was overexpanded, pork prices were down, and feed prices were up. As a result, the herd was reduced, and feeding was cut back. Pork production in China was expected to remain about the same as in 1995 as more breeding stock and fewer fat pigs were slaughtered. In the EU the BSE outbreak led to a shift in meat demand to pork and poultry. Pork prices rose, but production expansion was limited. Environmental controls on manure production had, in effect, placed an upper limit on the swine industry in the EU. Pork production in the U.S. slightly declined in 1996 owing to high feed prices.

The FAO expected world beef and veal production to increase 3% over 1995 (the USDA expected no increase). A small rise was expected in North America. More production in Brazil was expected owing to a strong domestic demand. The cattle industry in Poland and Romania also continued to rebound in 1996, but beef production in Kazakstan, Russia, and Ukraine continued its postreform decline because of inefficient production, high grain prices, and low beef prices. The BSE scare led to a reduction of 24% in the U.K.'s beef production in 1996. Diseased cattle were destroyed, and other cattle, suspected of

A worker prepares to shovel grain at an elevator in Corson, S.D. Although there were record-low levels of grain stocks at the end of the 1995–96 marketing year and a world shortage seemed possible, a widespread recovery in grain production in 1996 helped avert a crisis.

being diseased, were withheld from slaughter. As a result, beef production for the 15 countries of the EU was forecast to be down 6% in 1996.

Mainly as a result of herd expansion in China, India, and Australia, sheep meat production was expected to increase 3% in 1996 (the USDA forecast no change). The downward trend in herd size continued in the EU, South America, the U.S., and Eastern Europe. There was a substantial reduction in sheep meat production in the countries of the former Soviet Union.

Dairy. The FAO forecast that world milk production would increase slightly in 1995 and 1996 (*see* Table VI), reversing a gradual decline in production since 1990. Small increases in many countries offset lower output in the republics of the former Soviet Union. Milk production in the EU was limited by production quotas. Over-quota production by any country would be subject to a large penalty. The British dairy herd was reduced because of BSE, but production was expected to be near the quota. Milk production in Australia and New Zealand was expected to be up more than 5%, setting records in both countries; both were forecast to sharply increase their exports of dairy products in 1996. On the other hand, exports of dairy products by the U.S. and the EU were expected to be down. Relatively high domestic prices for milk products and reduced export subsidies discouraged U.S. and EU exports. Subsidy reductions were in line with levels agreed upon under the Uruguay round trade agreement.

In the republics of the former Soviet Union, milk production continued its post-1990 decline. Cow numbers were down. In addition, milk yield per cow decreased owing to poor-quality feed. Large state and collective farms continued to produce most of the milk. High-cost production plus an inefficient processing and marketing system

resulted in high-priced milk at retail outlets. Demand for dairy products also was down because prices increased more rapidly than did personal income. Similar conditions existed in most Eastern European countries.

Sugar. In 1996 about 70% of the world's sugar supply came from cane and the remainder from beets. World production of sugar from both sources in 1996–97 was forecast to increase 2% over the previous year's record harvest. (*See* Table VII.) Favourable weather was the main reason for increased output in Brazil (up 6%), Eastern Europe (up 24%), Africa and the Middle East (up 14%), and Australia (up 10%). Sugar production was down 16% from the previous year in the former Soviet republics owing to poor weather and down 7% in India owing to reduced plantings.

World sugar consumption was expected to continue its upward trend in 1996–97. Most of the growth continued to be in the less-developed world. This was especially true in Asian countries that had low per capita sugar consumption and rapidly increasing incomes. Brazil, the world's largest sugar producer and consumer, also processed cane for fuel. Consumer preferences for sugar substitutes in developed countries continued to depress their demand for sugar. World sugar trade was expected to increase slightly in 1996–97, led by expected import expansion by Russia, China, and the U.S.

World sugar carryover stocks, as a percentage of consumption, were at a record low of 16% at the beginning of the 1994–95 crop year. Each year thereafter production exceeded consumption, and stocks accumulated. At the beginning of 1996–97, stocks reached 20% of consumption. Carryover stocks were expected to increase to 22% by the end of 1996–97, with over one-fourth in India.

Coffee. The 1996–97 world green coffee

A farmer tends to ostriches on a ranch in Arizona. Touted as a healthy alternative to beef, ostrich meat was especially popular in parts of the growing Asian market, and it was predicted that within a few years ostriches would replace beef as the major meat consumed in China.

crop was forecast to be 14% larger than the relatively small crop harvested in 1995–96. (*See* TABLE VIII.) Most of the rise was due to large increases in production in Brazil, Indonesia, Colombia, and Côte d'Ivoire. Production in Brazil, which accounted for a quarter of the world's green coffee output, was down 40% in 1995–96 owing to severe frost damage. Production was expected to almost fully recover in 1996–97.

Because of the poor coffee harvest in 1995–96, world end-of-year coffee stocks were drawn down 30%. The effect of the 1994 frost in Brazil was still being felt in world coffee markets in late 1996. Retail coffee prices in the U.S. were down somewhat from 1995, but they still were 40% above prices prior to the frost.

Cocoa. In 1996 the USDA sharply increased its earlier estimate of 1995–96 world cocoa production as its record-breaking size became evident. For 1996–97, however, world cocoa output was forecast to fall by 8% to 2,660,000 tons. (*See* TABLE IX.) Production in 1996–97 in Côte d'Ivoire and Ghana was forecast to decline from the previous year by 12% and 7%, respectively, owing to poor weather conditions and normal cyclical declines that tend to occur after a record harvest. Brazil's crop was forecast to be down 12% because of poor weather and disease problems. World consumption was expected to exceed production, and carryover stocks were expected to be drawn down by 142,000 tons by the end of the 1996–97 crop year.

Cotton. World cotton production in 1995–96 was the second largest on record. The USDA forecast that the 1996–97 crop would be down about 5%. (*See* TABLE X.) Farmers in many countries shifted land from cotton to grain in 1996. Output in the U.S., the largest producer, was expected to increase 4% in 1996–97, and African countries were expected to increase produc-

tion 9%. Output was forecast to be down 20% in China, the second largest producer of cotton. Cotton production in the former Soviet republics was expected to continue its downward trend, declining 11% from 1995–96 and more than 40% from the 1980s. In response to high prices, farmers in the U.S. in 1995 increased the area planted to cotton by 23%, but an unusually poor growing season caused production actually to decline. Because of prospects for higher profits from growing grain and the added planting flexibility provided by the new government farm program, U.S. farmers in 1996 reduced the area planted to cotton by 16%. Near-record yields, however, boosted production over the previous year.

A very small increase in world cotton consumption was forecast for 1996–97, reversing the downward trend of recent years. Small growth in consumption in India and the U.S. accounted for most of the global increase. World cotton trade was expected to continue its decline in 1996–97. With production expected to exceed world consumption again in 1996–97, cotton stocks at the end of 1996–97 were forecast to grow 3–4% over the level at the beginning of the crop year. China held more than 40% of the world's stocks, but virtually all the growth was expected to be by the U.S.

(JERRY A. SHARPLES)

See also Business and Industry Review: *Textiles;* The Environment: *Gardening.*

This article updates the *Macropædia* article The History of AGRICULTURE.

FISHERIES

According to the latest figures released by the UN Food and Agriculture Organization (FAO), 1994 produced the highest-ever world fish catch, a 7.3 million-metric-ton increase over the 1993 total, to reach a staggering 109.6 million metric tons. Fish

for human consumption rose from 72.9 million metric tons in 1993 to 74.8 million in 1994 and for nonhuman consumption increased from 29.3 million metric tons in 1993 to 34.7 million in 1994.

The South Americans were taking advantage of the bumper numbers of anchoveta available while they could, since these stocks can fluctuate widely depending on the prevailing conditions caused by El Niño. With the anchoveta catch reaching 11.9 million metric tons, it came close to approaching the record haul of 13 million metric tons caught during 1970. Alaska pollock finished second again, but third-place Chilean jack mackerel recorded its highest catch ever, with 4.3 million metric tons.

The most interesting aspect of these catch statistics was the precautionary note sounded by the FAO, which reiterated its previous warnings that despite the increases shown, the majority of the species that were subject to fishing were either fully or overly exploited. The FAO also commented that the potential for additional increases in the catch yields in the long term was extremely limited; indeed, preliminary figures for 1995 revealed that the catch had already taken a downward turn.

With a record total of 20,720,000 metric tons, China in 1994 again topped the list of fish-producing nations. Increases in the production of farmed fish (aquaculture), especially varieties of carp, accounted for most of the 3.2 million-metric ton gain over 1993. China also increased its catch of such wild species as largehead hairtails, scad, and filefishes.

Along with the larger catch of anchoveta, Peru increased its catch of South American pilchard by 450,000 metric tons, while Chile's catch of Chilean horse mackerel rose by 810,000 metric tons.

Two major fishing nations again recorded declines in catch during 1994. While remaining the world's largest tuna-catching nation by landing 710,000 metric tons of tuna during 1994, Japan suffered a reduction of 770,000 metric tons in its total catch, mainly owing to reduced landings of Japanese pilchard and skipjack tuna. Russia also recorded a decline in catch from 4.5 million metric tons in 1993 to 3.8 million metric tons in 1994. More than half of the decrease was due to reductions in the catch of Alaska pollock.

Another large step forward in obtaining consensus in the utilization of the world's fisheries was completed in October 1995 with the final agreement and adoption of a Code of Conduct for Responsible Fisheries. The code, which was voluntary, established 10 main objectives, the first and foremost of which was to establish princi-

Top 10 Species Landed, 1994	
In order of tonnage	
Species	**Metric tons**
Anchoveta	11,896,808
Alaska pollock	4,298,619
Chilean jack mackerel	4,254,629
Silver carp	2,233,669
Atlantic herring	1,886,105
Grass carp	1,821,606
South American pilchard	1,793,425
Common carp	1,627,198
Chubb mackerel	1,507,497
Skipjack tuna	1,462,637

ples, in accordance with the relevant rules of international law, for responsible fishing and fisheries activities, taking into account all relevant biological, technical, economic, social, environmental, and commercial aspects. Prevention of overfishing by the implementation of sound management strategies was emphasized.

A significant area of concern during the year was bycatch and the implementation of selective and environmentally safe fishing gear and practices. Bycatch are fish caught unintentionally during fishing operations. This was a particular problem with trawling, especially shrimp trawling; large-scale gillnetting; and some purse seine and longline fisheries.

Most commercial fishing operations were governed by some form of quota system that allowed fishing vessels to catch and, more important, to land a certain amount of a particular species that were above a certain agreed-upon minimum size. If fish were caught for which a vessel did not have a license or that might be under the minimum size, this bycatch was traditionally dumped back into the sea. Recent studies of bycatch published by the FAO found that up to 27 million metric tons of fish might be destroyed in this way every year. This was more than a quarter of the world's total marine catch.

If serious efforts were made to control the dumping of fish at sea and to utilize the bycatch for human consumption, potentially significant increases in the availability of fish for human consumption could be made without any additional pressure on fish stocks.

Several countries, including Canada, Mexico, and Norway, implemented policies

ROBERT VISSER—GREENPEACE/UPI

Greenpeace activists in the Bering Sea call for the banning of factory trawlers, which environmentalists said overfished for pollock. According to the UN Food and Agriculture Organization, Alaska pollock was one of the world's top 10 species landed.

to promote the use of fishing methods that would reduce the amount of bycatch. One method that was gaining in popularity was the use of escape panels and grates incorporated into trawl nets just ahead of the

cod end of the net; these allowed the escape of undersized fish and/or nontargeted species. An example of this type of device was the Nordmore grate, which was used off eastern Canada and in Norway to reduce groundfish (such as cod, flounder, and haddock) bycatch in fisheries that used small mesh trawls; these included fisheries for shrimp and silver hake. Studies revealed that bycatch could be reduced to 1–2% of the catch with the use of such devices.

Since 1992 fishermen in Newfoundland had faced a moratorium on the catching of cod and other groundfish species for either commercial or recreational purposes. The devastation of the Grand Banks cod had been caused by a combination of environmental changes and years of overfishing by Canadian and foreign fleets, and it had a profoundly depressing effect on fishing communities in Newfoundland and Nova Scotia. During September, however, the Canadian government felt confident enough to open the cod fishery for a brief experimental period during two weekends for food fishers only. The results of this short reopening plus indications that the cod stocks were beginning to recover brought hope that the reopening of the cod fishery on a larger but tightly regulated scale might at least be within the foreseeable future.

(MARTIN J. GILL)

This article updates the *Macropædia* article Commercial FISHING.

FOOD PROCESSING

Consumers in the developed countries became increasingly willing in 1996 to take ethical and environmental issues into account when purchasing food, placing a greater emphasis on health. Such considerations and the scare over bovine spongiform encephalopathy (BSE, or "mad cow" dis-

World Fisheries, 1994[1]				
	Catch in metric tons		Trade in $000	
Country	Total	Inland	Imports	Exports
China	20,718,903	9,040,158	855,705	2,320,125
Peru	11,587,339	41,600	2,201	979,502
Chile	7,811,031	26,206	27,574	1,303,974
Japan	7,363,314	168,599	16,140,465	742,972
United States	5,940,737	303,677	7,043,431	3,229,685
India	4,540,180	2,028,508	6,618	1,125,440
Indonesia	3,954,228	983,007	120,674	1,503,416
Russia	3,780,638	293,004	61,225	1,191,192
Thailand	3,432,000	292,000	816,616	4,190,036
South Korea	2,700,037	30,900	718,451	1,411,052
Norway	2,551,478	432	322,087	2,718,132
Philippines	2,276,197	587,139	108,193	533,087
Denmark	1,886,851	38,368	1,415,239	2,359,034
North Korea	1,800,000	112,800	—	—
Iceland	1,560,184	1,110	25,209	1,264,615
Spain	1,380,000	32,750	2,638,697	1,021,015
Mexico	1,280,015	175,202	158,627	480,872
Other Asia	1,248,895	188,214	560,799	2,213,259
Malaysia	1,173,480	24,501	304,260	326,187
Vietnam	1,150,000	287,500	—	—
Bangladesh	1,090,596	811,054	—	—
Canada	1,010,582	36,476	913,404	2,182,078
United Kingdom	953,946	18,121	1,880,350	1,180,158
Argentina	949,344	12,720	66,805	728,091
France	838,332	58,890	2,706,710	704
Myanmar (Burma)	824,468	224,385	—	—
Brazil	820,000	220,000	261,453	178,548
Morocco	750,088	1,850	7,044	620,451
Turkey	604,104	52,766	38,149	70,705
Pakistan	551,899	133,325	152	153,265
World Total	109,585,200	19,173,600	51,548,000	47,014,000

[1]Excludes aquatic mammals, crocodiles and alligators, pearls, corals, sponges, and aquatic plants.
Source: United Nations Food and Agriculture Organization, *Yearbook of Fishery Statistics*, vol. 78 and 79.

ease) and its possible link to human disease generated a swing to meat substitutes and vegetarian foods, although the number of true vegetarians rose very little. Processed ready-to-eat meals and convenience foods experienced accelerated growth. Consumption of bread and canned foods continued to decline, while that of breakfast cereals, bakery products other than bread, soft drinks, snack foods, and frozen, chilled, and fresh products increased.

Dietary fibre was back in favour. Interest grew, particularly in Japan, in "functional foods," said to offer protection against chronic degenerative diseases. Examples included cherry juice that enhances the growth of beneficial digestive bacteria and a nonfat milk containing oat flour that may lower cholesterol levels in many people. Additional scientific evidence of the health benefits of fish oils was presented.

Some two-thirds of shoppers looked for the date of expiration mark on food packages, whenever it was available, and about half scanned the lists of ingredients. Senior citizens placed greater importance on food-safety advice and manufacturers' instructions; teenagers and young adults were six times more likely to suffer food poisoning than were the elderly.

Food poisoning did not abate; major outbreaks in Australia originating from contaminated peanut butter and meat products damaged public confidence. Apple juice, salami, and cheese were implicated in outbreaks in the U.K., where more than 30% of poultry was estimated to carry salmonella, the most common food-poisoning organism. In Scotland's worst-ever outbreak, *E. coli*-contaminated cooked meat killed 15. Radish sprouts were suspected at least in part as the cause of an outbreak in Japan that killed 11 and sickened some 9,000. Despite worldwide concern about BSE, in the U.K., where the problem originated, very few deaths were attributed to consumption of a BSE-contaminated meat product.

Supermarket chains in Europe and the U.S. experienced a spate of product tampering. Manufacturers responded by increasing the production of tamper-proof packaging.

Business Trends. Though industrial growth in the U.S. continued to be slow, the number of food and beverage plants increased to an estimated 15,000, substantially up from the estimated 13,000 of the previous year; however, the number of dairy plants declined. Profit margins increased. U.S. food investments in overseas countries again exceeded foreign investments in the U.S. Sales by U.S.-owned overseas food plants were forecast to exceed $100 billion, compared with some $50 billion for foreign firms manufacturing in the U.S.

Counterfeiting of branded products in the U.S. reached crisis level. The Food and Drug Administration (FDA) discovered large-scale illegal manufacturing. Large quantities of recalled and time-expired products were illicitly relabeled and sold to unwitting supermarkets and grocery stores.

World sales of frozen foods climbed to an estimated $75 billion, of which 28% were in the U.S. The success in the U.S. of frozen yogurt, now estimated to have 10% of the ice cream market there, was not matched in Europe except in The Netherlands, where it gained 6% of the ice cream market.

In the U.K. about 10,000 food workers were affected by the BSE crisis; 2,500

slaughterhouse workers out of 7,000 were laid off. Demand increased for products that would be alternatives to beef. U.K. exports of manufactured products containing beef declined sharply, but total British food exports increased to an estimated $15 billion, 13% higher than in 1995.

By the spring of 1996, U.K. sales of alcoholic soft drinks, or "alcopops," had grown to about $200 million in less than a year from their launch in June 1995; there was a concurrent decline in the sales of cider. The drinks were condemned by consumer groups for encouraging underage drinking.

Company Developments. Nestlé SA of Switzerland retained its position as the world's largest food producer, its sales increasing by 3.4% in the 12-month period ended Dec. 31, 1995. Nestlé sold Wine World Estates, which owned 2,630 ha (6,500 ac) of vineyards in California, to a newly formed U.S. consortium comprising Silverado Partners and Texas Pacific Group. Nestlé sold twice the amount of soft drinks in Europe as PepsiCo, and Italy's San Benedetto overtook Cadbury Schweppes PLC of the U.K., but Coca-Cola Co. outsold all four put together.

Cadbury Schweppes sold its beverage plants in the U.K. to Coca-Cola Enterprises, a subsidiary of the U.S. company, for about $930 million. The company also sold its 51% stake in Coca-Cola & Schweppes Beverages to Coca-Cola but bought Neilson Cadbury from George Weston Ltd. for about $165 million.

McDonald's, Pizza Hut, and Burger King of the U.S., in that order, retained their dominance of the fast-food market in Europe. H.J. Heinz Co. of the U.S., whose sales in the European food-service trade had increased 75% since it entered that market in 1994, acquired Britwest Ltd., a food-service supplier in the U.K. and France. United Biscuits Holdings PLC of the U.K. sold its U.S. cookie and cracker business for $487.5 million to Inflo Holdings Corp.

New Products and Ingredients. Ethnic dishes, especially Mexican-style foods, became more popular around the world.

Products containing the fat replacer Omega-3 were launched in Ireland, the U.K., and Denmark. A margarine containing plant sterols said to reduce blood cholesterol levels dramatically appeared in Finland under the name Benecol.

Technology. A microwave process for pasteurizing raw eggs without breaking the shells, developed at Purdue University, West Lafayette, Ind., was commercialized. A pilot plant using a cold sterile bottling process for noncarbonated soft drinks, developed jointly by the German equipment maker Krones AG and the Coca-Cola Co., was established at Radeberg, near Dresden, Ger. Research in Sweden showed that the replacement of fat in hard cheese with gelatin improved taste, texture, and yield.

The trend toward solving equipment-malfunction problems on-site by using modem communication and computer diagnostics increased. Via modem the equipment manufacturer was able to see what the food manufacturer saw on its computer screen and could then fix the problem.

Packaging. After a seven-year development program, Carnaud Metalbox SA of France launched a new material consisting of aluminum coated with polyethylene

terephthalate (PET) plastic. The plastic provided better protection for the aluminum than did lacquer. The material was used initially for ends of beverage cans. The Swiss company Aisa introduced tubes made of a laminate of PET and polypropylene from which alternatives to glass jars could be made.

Bonar Teich Flexibles of Germany introduced a polyolefin material called Microx for packaging microwavable snack foods. Its ability to absorb moisture without becoming heated during microwaving allowed microwaved chips (french fries) and other foods to be eaten straight from the bag.

S&A Foods of the U.K., working with Rexam Foil & Paper Ltd., introduced a cardboard cooking dish for its Balti refrigerated and frozen meals. It incorporated a special device highly reactive to microwave energy so as to make the microwaved dishes sizzle when served. A plastic laminate over the device prevented the food from catching fire.

Government Action. Olestra, a fat substitute under development by Procter & Gamble Co. for 25 years, received FDA approval in the U.S. for use in certain snack foods. The company launched it commercially in June under the brand name Olean and used it for a fat-free variety of its main snack brand, Pringles; Frito-Lay and Nabisco also marketed olestra-based snacks. Procter & Gamble claimed to have solved certain side-effect problems associated with olestra, but the FDA stipulated that these be highlighted on the package labels.

The U.S. Congress announced radical legislative proposals that would repeal the Delaney clause, which prohibited any trace in food of materials causing cancer in laboratory animals. The proposals would also require government regulators to prove food to be unsafe before it could be banned, which thus would reverse the present law requiring processors to prove their products were safe and also would open U.S. markets to products made in countries where regulations were less stringent.

In the European Union (EU), restrictions were placed on the use of many commonly used food colours. Regulations were drafted listing approved flavourings and their conditions of use. Brand protection enforceable across the EU was allowed. Antidumping duties on imports of aspartame sweetener from the U.S. and Japan, imposed in 1991, were lifted. Following the British government's disclosure in March that there might be a link between BSE and its human counterpart, Creutzfeldt-Jakob disease, the European Commission imposed a global ban on exports of U.K. beef and beef products. (See *International Issues,* above.)

The Canadian government introduced subsidies on pasta exports and restricted imports, virtually halting imports from Italy (which had more than doubled in two years). China required all imported food products to carry complete Chinese labeling as of August 31; those not in compliance would be refused entry.

(ANTHONY WOOLLEN)

See also Business and Industry Review: *Beverages; Tobacco;* The Environment; Health and Disease.

This article updates the *Macropædia* article FOOD PROCESSING.

Anthropology and Archaeology

ANTHROPOLOGY

Physical Anthropology. Another specimen of the Western Hemisphere primate *Branisella* dating from the late Oligocene or early Miocene Epoch, about 23.7 million years ago, was found in 1996. It was an important discovery because fossils of New World primates are rare and because analysis revealed that it is probably ancestral to the callitrichines (marmosets) but not to all the platyrrhines. The latter group, which includes the marmosets and comprises the diverse majority of the Central and South American monkeys today, must have undergone an explosive radiation during the early to middle Oligocene, presumably on their arrival from Africa.

A new anthropoid fossil, *Eosimias,* dated at about 40 million years ago, was found during the year in China. It could provide evidence that the very early evolution of the higher primates occurred in Asia as well as in Africa. Another new fossil discovery shed some light on the time that apes stopped walking about like monkeys. A *Dryopithecus* from the Miocene in Spain, it consists of both cranial and postcranial bones, which indicate that by at least 9.5 million years ago these apes were not generalized quadrupeds but were moving about in a manner similar to the modern orangutan. Also, in central Turkey a find of an almost complete face of a 10 million-year-old ape, *Ankarapithecus meteai,* was found. Because of its unique features, it is not considered to be ancestral to any apes or humans and is another example of the Miocene radiation of the apes during the period from 18 million to 9 million years ago.

Workers search the Atapuerca site, near Burgos, Spain, for fossils. Human fossils found there were dated to at least 780,000 years ago, among the oldest in Europe.

Fossilized bones that South African scientists found in caves at the country's Sterkfontein site in 1996 indicate that humans were present in Africa more than three million years ago.

Also uncovered during the year was new evidence about the nonlinear evolution of bipedalism. At Sterkfontein, S.Af., researchers found the most complete australopithecine fossil skeleton since "Lucy"—that of an individual with a humanlike pelvis but with limb proportions similar to those of a modern chimpanzee. Thus, it may have spent time both walking on the ground and climbing in the trees. It was identified as an *Australopithecus africanus* by Phillip Tobias of the University of the

Witwatersrand, Johannesburg, S.Af. Also, an australopithecine fossil was discovered outside the Rift Valley system in Chad, some 2,400 km (1,500 mi) to the west. The site was dated at 3 million–3.5 million years, and the fossil resembles *A. afarensis.*

The "savanna hypothesis"—that bipedalism evolved when the tropical forest became replaced by open grassland—may be too simplistic. Paleoclimatologists agree that there was a major climatic change about 2.8 million years ago that resulted in more open land and less tropical forest. This, however, is considerably later than the appearance of the first bipeds, though it may coincide with the origin of the genus *Homo.*

In November a team of Canadian, Ethiopian, Israeli, and U.S. scientists announced the discovery in northern Ethiopia of an upper jaw described as the oldest and most convincing definitively dated fossil of the genus *Homo.* The jaw, dated at 2,330,000 years, was 400,000 years older than any previously found *Homo* fossil.

Longgupo Cave in Sichuan province, China, yielded evidence of hominids that existed from 1.7 million to 1.9 million years ago. The fossils may be those of *Homo habilis,* which raises the possibility that it was this form of early human that migrated out of Africa and then gave rise to *H. erectus* in Asia as well as Africa. Possibly equally early finds of not yet fully described hominids from Atapuerca, Spain, may indicate that these "pre-erectus" forms migrated to the west out of Africa, possibly by way of the Middle East.

New Neanderthal remains were found at Arcy-sur-Cure, Fr. There, a temporal bone with the distinctive anatomy of the Neanderthal inner ear was discovered in the archaeological context of the early Upper Paleolithic Châtelperronian industry; the bone was dated at 34,000 years ago. This provided further evidence for the long coexistence and possible cultural interactions of the Neanderthals and modern humans. Yet coexistence probably did not result in similarity in lifestyles or exploitation of the environment. According to Erik Trinkhaus of the University of New Mexico and Christopher Ruff of Johns Hopkins University, Baltimore, Md., in Israel, where there was a long coexistence, the Neanderthals are anatomically different enough to indicate adaptations to the environment that differed from those of their modern human counterparts, even if they were using some of the same tools.

Theories about the peopling of the Western Hemisphere have depended heavily on the analysis of linguistic, archaeological, and genetic evidence. The main questions continued to be the time and numbers of migrations. A site in Brazil indicated occupation by forest-living foragers 11,000 years ago, which would make them contemporary but culturally different from the Clovis culture mammoth hunters 8,000 km (5,000 mi) to the north. Also, analyses of new DNA and mitochondrial DNA data suggest that the genetic variation in the geographically widespread groups of native Americans is compatible with one, or possibly two, Asian migrations. Current studies of the noncoding part of the Y chromosome (the equivalent of mtDNA for inheritance in the male line) may reveal more on the relationships between the native people in the Americas.

(HERMANN K. BLEIBTREU)

Cultural. Cultural anthropology continued to be a discipline in the throes of change in 1996. Although the developed nations of the West remained the primary centres of professional training, employment, and theoretical development, anthropologists from nations in Africa, Asia, and the former Soviet bloc exerted increasing influence. No longer content to work in the West or restrict research to societies within national borders, non-Western ethnologists, such as Komei Sasaki, who had conducted fieldwork in Nepal, China, and India as well as in his native Japan, worked to expand ethnographic horizons. At the same time, growing numbers of Western ethnographers increasingly focused their attention upon their own societies. Whatever their nationality or wherever they worked, anthropologists throughout the world continued to redefine their discipline, reassess their roles, and reconsider the subjects and locations of their ethnographic studies.

In a front-page article in the December 1996 issue of *Anthropology Newsletter,* published by the American Anthropological Association, University of Chicago anthropologist Richard Shweder contrasted competing views of cultural anthropology as a platform for moral and political activism; as a nonmoral, value-free objective science; and as a forum for postmodern critics challenging the existence of objective knowledge. Recognizing that knowledge of the world is incomplete when regarded from one point of view and incoherent when seen from all points at once, Shweder championed a pluralistic anthropology. Such an approach would examine "multiple cultural realities" from "manywheres" rather than from such particular "places" as the individual ethnocentric view or the objective "view from 'nowhere in particular' " and rather than giving no view at all, as favoured by postmodern critics.

Scholars continued with considerable warmth to conduct the debate as to whether anthropology is a science. Representing scientific anthropology at a symposium convened in 1995 by the New York Academy of Sciences entitled "The Flight from Science and Reason," anthropologist Robin Fox of Rutgers University, New Brunswick, N.J., addressed assertions claiming that science was invalid because its findings could be wrong, trivial, biased, or used for evil purposes. Noting that science by its very nature was designed to deal with error, triviality, and experimenter bias, Fox urged colleagues to distinguish between the use and abuse of the enterprise and not give up on the search for scientific truth in the service of humanistic goals and understanding.

Anthropologists debating the role of science in their discipline were part of the wider international dialogue assessing the role of evolution and the relative impacts of biology and culture on human behaviour. Responding to critics who censured science as merely another belief system and evolution as simply an erroneous belief, personalities as varied as the pope and a historian of science rallied to the support of the scientific perspective. In a pronouncement made at the 1996 annual meeting of the Pontifical Academy of Sciences, Pope John Paul II stated that the theory of evolution was more than a hypothesis and that its teaching was not incompatible with Roman Catholic doctrine. In a highly publicized

and potentially influential study entitled *Born to Rebel: Birth Order, Family Dynamics, and Creative Lives,* Massachusetts Institute of Technology (MIT) visiting scholar Frank J. Sulloway used the example of Darwin's formulation of the theory of evolution and the Darwinian evolutionary perspective to show how competition for parental attention within families between firstborns and those born later affected personality development and, by extension, larger cultural events. Sulloway demonstrated that firstborns, firmly established in secure familial niches, tended to support the status quo, while children born later, forced to compete for parental favour, tended to develop more rebellious personalities. Statistically analyzing more than 20,000 biographies written during the past 500 years, Sulloway found that those born later played major roles in revolutionary movements. He proposed that competition between individuals within families rather than community competition between kin groups exerted the most profound influence upon culture and history.

Science and scientists themselves increasingly became subjects of anthropological inquiry in 1996. In *Making PCR: A Story of Biotechnology,* University of California, Berkeley, anthropologist Paul Rabinow described the intensely complex commercial technological environment within which the polymerase chain reaction essential to genetic engineering was invented and developed. In *Nuclear Rites: A Weapons Laboratory at the End of the Cold War,* MIT anthropologist Hugh Gusterson contrasted the perspectives of Lawrence Livermore National Laboratory (Livermore, Calif.) weapons scientists who believed in the deterrent effect of nuclear weapons with antinuclear activists concerned by the threat of nuclear war. He found "each side holding tenaciously to their corner of a larger truth"—that people need "to rethink our relationship with nuclear weapons and our use of science."

Anthropologists working among the more than 12 million native people in the Western Hemisphere continued to be involved in those peoples' ongoing struggles over land, sovereignty, and fishing, hunting, and water rights. Many supported the findings of a major report released by the Canadian government in 1996 that showed that self-governing tribes fared much better than did those subjected to governmental supervision.

(ROBERT S. GRUMET)

ARCHAEOLOGY

Eastern Hemisphere. As had been the case increasingly in recent years, archaeological field activity in the Eastern Hemisphere faced political problems in 1996. Much of southwestern Asia was not a comfortable or even safe region in which to undertake excavation. In Iraq, where foreigners had not been permitted to excavate for some years, looters were active, and material from the national museums was also said to be available for sale. Much the same situation existed in Afghanistan.

In Israel, for religious reasons, it was no longer permissible to export excavated artifacts for study abroad, and human burials that archaeologists encountered were to be immediately reburied by religious officials. A political crisis in Jerusalem during the year centred on Israeli-Arab concerns over

JIM LO SCALZO—U.S. NEWS & WORLD REPORT

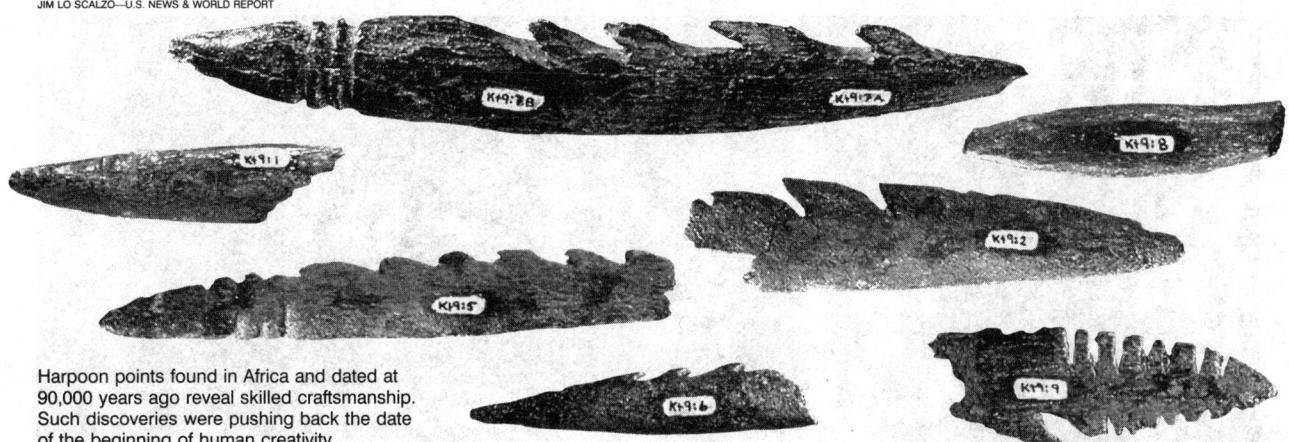

Harpoon points found in Africa and dated at 90,000 years ago reveal skilled craftsmanship. Such discoveries were pushing back the date of the beginning of human creativity.

the so-called archaeological tunnel that runs under two of Islam's most sacred mosques, the Dome of the Rock and al-Aqsa, in central Jerusalem. The region is considered sacred by the Jews and the Muslims, and allowing people to tour through it is believed to be unsacred.

The most surprising new evidence of Pleistocene prehistoric times consisted of claims that cave art in northwestern Australia with datings apparently reaching back toward 75,000 years ago had been found. The art is simple, mainly small circles engraved by hand into rock faces. Traces of red ochre also appeared along with stone tools. The findings suggested that new considerations could be necessary concerning early Pacific geography and the eastward spread of early humans.

Among other discoveries from prehistoric times, "harpoon points" of a type familiar in Europe about 40,000 years ago were found in Zaire dating to about 90,000 years ago. In southern France a stone slab structure within a cave, undoubtedly built by Neanderthals, was dated to about 47,-000 years ago. Impressions of woven cloth were detected on fired clay recovered some years earlier in a Czechoslovak site of about 27,000 years ago. In Siberia 10,000-year-old flint arrowheads of a type characteristic of the early American Clovis points suggested the region from which very early peoples moved to the New World.

UNIVERSITY OF PENNSYLVANIA MUSEUM

A 7,000-year-old jar from Iran was analyzed in 1996 and shown to have held wine, which indicated that people were drinking wine 2,000 years earlier than had been thought.

During 1996 studies increased speculation that Tutankhamen may have been murdered. Several years earlier a British specialist had made X-rays of the young king's skull (in his tomb in Egypt's Valley of the Kings) and suggested that his death may have been due to a blow to the back of his head. Also in Egypt the assistant field director of the Oriental Institute in Chicago at its Luxor excavation undertook a study on artistic change as seen in the reliefs and statuary of King Amenhotep III. At the University of Cambridge, a beer residue found in Egyptian pottery was analyzed, and a British brewery copied it.

For ancient southwestern Asia not beer but wine gained attention; residue in a 7,000-year-old jar recovered some years earlier at the Hajji Firuz Tepe site in northwestern Iran was proved during the year to have been of wine made of wild grapes. Also in southwestern Asia a five-roomed tomb built of limestone slabs, with gold beads of the type seen in ancient Troy, was cleared near Dayr az-Zawr, Syria. In northeastern Syria a University of California, Los Angeles, team finished eight years of work and identified their site as the ancient Hurrian city of Urkesh. In Israel a joint U.S.–Israeli team established that Tel Miqne, southwest of Jerusalem, held the remains of the Philistine city Ekron. It appeared that the site would yield useful information on the Philistines.

From the regions of ancient Greece and Rome, a study of very early farming procedures and yields in Crete was under way. Also, a U.S.-owned firm in Rio Nareca in southern Spain began mining substantial beds of gold once worked by the Romans.

A conference covering recent finds in western China took place in April at the University of Pennsylvania. Many of the finds were naturally mummified human corpses buried in the clothes they had worn; these were people who had lived in the Tarim Basin area from about 4,000 to 2,000 years ago. The features of the corpses were unmistakably Caucasian, and the weaving of the material for their clothes, including plaids, also appeared to be European. Thus, early Indo-Europeans appeared to have spread farther east than had been previously imagined.

In China the government refused to allow large-scale archaeological efforts to save sites and artifacts in the vast Chiang Jiang's (Yangtze River's) Three Gorges area, which would be flooded upon the completion

of an enormous new dam currently under construction. The Chinese government engineers would not yield to an appeal by hundreds of China's historians, archaeologists, and other scholars to save the many cultural remains that the flooding would destroy.

In northeastern Thailand flooding damaged the foundations of the spectacular Wat Chai Wattanaram temple complex. Thirteen birch-bark scrolls from eastern Asia were studied in the U.K. and reported to be of the 1st or 2nd century AD and thus the oldest known Buddhist writings.

(ROBERT J. BRAIDWOOD)

Western Hemisphere. Archaeologists had often assumed that the first Americans were big-game hunters, preying on such animals as the mammoth and the mastodon. The big-game stereotype was based on Clovis culture kill sites on the North American plains dating to about 9500 BC. Archaeologist Anna Roosevelt of the Field Museum of Natural History in Chicago recently debunked this myth with her excavations in Caverna da Pedra Pintada in dense rain forest on the Amazon River in Brazil. Roosevelt found that the cave had been occupied more or less continuously from about 9200 BC until about 400 years ago, when Europeans first invaded the Amazon. The earliest inhabitants were contemporary with the Clovis people of North America. They foraged for plant foods and small game near the cave and also took fish from the Amazon. The walls of the cave are covered with red and yellow handprints and paintings of humans, animals, and geometric designs that were claimed to be the earliest in the Western Hemisphere. The Pedra Pintada finds showed that, contrary to popular belief, the first Americans adapted to diverse environments, including tropical rain forest, soon after their arrival.

While the Pedra Pintada discovery was dated to Clovis times, another early site in the Saltville Valley in far southwestern Virginia, found by Jerry MacDonald of the Smithsonian Institution, Washington, D.C., was radiocarbon-dated to about 12,-000 BC. At Saltville MacDonald discovered that early Americans skinned and cut up a mammoth carcass.

Further evidence of skilled environmental exploitation in later times by native Americans came from a Genesee culture site of five or six houses on the banks of the Niagara River at the eastern end of Lake Erie dating to about AD 675. Waterfowl

Paintings decorate the wall of a cave on the Amazon River in Brazil. Archaeologists reporting on the excavation of the cave said that it also showed other evidence of human habitation, including spear points and the remains of plants and animals, dating to more than 11,000 years ago.

and fish abounded at this location, which may have served as a regional gathering place for groups living a considerable distance away.

Many archaeological finds were now coming from museum collections rather than new excavations. Archaeologists at the Nevada State Museum recently restudied a human mummy excavated from Spirit Cave in eastern Nevada in 1940. The male mummy, believed to be 2,000 years old, was found lying on its side, wrapped in a skin robe. He was about 1.57 m (5 ft 2 in) tall and suffered from a fractured skull and severe teeth abscesses. He wore moccasins and was wrapped in shrouds woven from marsh plants. Ervin Taylor of the University of California, Riverside, radiocarbon-dated the body to about 7400 BC, a time when western North America was becoming much drier. The textiles found with the corpse were very sophisticated, revealing the antiquity of this craft in native American culture.

Archaeologists digging Maya cities were working in close collaboration with epigraphists (those who study ancient inscriptions) and as a result could sometimes establish why individual buildings were erected and by whom. They also found the burials of some of the people who commissioned pyramids and lesser ceremonial structures. At La Milpa in Belize, a site with pyramids surrounding a central plaza, Boston University archaeologist Norman Hammond unearthed the tomb of a ruler of about AD 450 named Bird Jaguar. Hammond uncovered layers of limestone and flint chips filling a shaft that led to an underground burial chamber carved out of solid rock about 3 m (10 ft) below the surface. Bird Jaguar died when he was between 35 and 50 years old, somewhat young for a Mayan lord. He wore a jade necklace of coloured and matched apple-green jade. A pendant in the form of a vulture head, a symbol of kingship, hung from the

necklace. The jade in the tomb came from sources more than 400 km (250 mi) away in Guatemala.

A spectacular archaeological discovery resulted from a volcanic eruption at 6,400 m (20,700 ft) above sea level in the Andes Mountains in Peru. Falling volcanic ash melted the ice and snow on the summit of a peak named Nevado Ampato. The Inca considered Ampato a sacred mountain, home of a deity who brought rain and plentiful harvests. Anthropologist Johan Reinhard and his climbing partner Miguel Zárate were close to the summit when Zárate spotted a small fan of red feathers protruding from a slope. The feathers were part of the headdress of one of three Inca gold, silver, and seashell statues, each with a feather headdress, that they found there; the statues had once stood on a now-collapsed ceremonial platform. Reinhard and Zárate tracked the collapse 60 m (200 ft) downslope, where they spotted a mummy bundle of a young girl that had once lain in a grave above. She was a deep-frozen Inca sacrificial victim of 500 years ago.

Inside her outer garments, the girl was wrapped in a dress encircled with a belt. She wore a shawl fastened with a silver pin. Her head was bare, but she wore leather slippers. On the basis of a headdress found with a second mummy at a lower altitude, it was thought that she may have once worn a plumed fan that arched over a feather-wrapped cap. Her hair was in a pigtail and was tied to her waistband by a thread of black alpaca, which suggested that other people helped dress her, either before or after her death. Her silver shawl pins were hung with miniature wood carvings, including a wooden box and two drinking vessels. Subsequently, two Inca children, perhaps a boy and an eight-year-old girl, were recovered in sacrificial graves at a somewhat lower altitude, 5,855 m (19,200 ft). Reinhard believed they may have been sacrificed together in a symbolic marriage, a custom

recorded by early Spanish chroniclers. The girl wore a reddish-brown feathered headdress, made of tropical macaw feathers. Her grave contained clay vessels, wooden ceremonial drinking spoons, weaving tools, and offering bundles.

The Ampato mummies promised a rich fund of medical information, which could reveal how the victims died. The textiles alone revolutionized knowledge of Inca weaving. One statue wore some of the finest Andean cloth known, a miniature vicuña garment with a weave count (number of strands per unit area) as high as that of modern machine-made clothing.

Marine archaeologist Barto Arnold of the Texas Historical Commission located the wreck of the French ship *Belle*, a vessel used by French explorer René-Robert Cavelier, Sieur de La Salle on his ill-fated expedition in search of the mouth of the Mississippi River in 1684. The *Belle* was the smallest ship of the four on the expedition and sank off the eastern Texas coast in 1686. The wreck lay in 3.6 m (12 ft) of water off the present shoreline and was identified by means of a 1.8-m (6-ft)-long bronze cannon bearing the distinctive crest of Louis XIV, king of France. Other finds included pewter plates, lead shot, a stoneware pitcher, a sword hilt, glass trade beads, and an iron pike with part of its wooden handle. Only one of La Salle's ships returned to France. Another was captured by the Spanish, and the third was wrecked while entering Matagorda Bay. The Texas Historical Commission was searching for that wreck. La Salle himself was murdered by his crew when they mutinied during an attempt to reach the Mississippi on foot. All but 12 of the 180 crew members and colonists subsequently perished from disease or Indian attacks.   (BRIAN FAGAN)

This article updates the *Macropædia* articles Human EVOLUTION; The Study of HISTORY: *Archaeology;* THE SOCIAL SCIENCES: *Cultural Anthropology.*

Architecture and Civil Engineering

ARCHITECTURE

Two architects, one Spanish and the other American, dominated much of the world's architectural news in 1996. Each won a prestigious award. José Rafael Moneo received the $100,000 Pritzker Architecture Prize, the world's most prestigious architecture honour, and in late 1996 it was announced that Richard Meier would receive the 1997 Gold Medal of the American Institute of Architects (AIA). Both prizes were for career achievement rather than for any one building.

Moneo received his Pritzker at a ceremony in Los Angeles in June, the same month in which he was chosen to design a new $50 million Roman Catholic cathedral for that city, intended to replace the structure damaged in a 1994 earthquake. The proposed demolition of the old cathedral was stopped by court order, however, after a protest by historic preservation groups, and at year's end the outcome was not clear. Other Moneo buildings under construction in 1996 included a major addition to the Museum of Fine Arts, Houston, Texas, and museums of art and architecture in Stockholm. Among the architect's completed works, the best known was the National Museum of Roman Art in Mérida, Spain, completed in 1986 and regarded as a masterpiece.

Richard Meier's gold medal was announced during a year in which the first section opened of his enormous Getty Center, an institution for the study and conservation of art, the construction cost of which was expected to reach some $1 billion. Dramatically sited on a ridge overlooking the Pacific Ocean in Los Angeles, the Getty was scheduled to be completed in 1997. Like Moneo, Meier had designed buildings in many parts of the world; these included the Museum of Contemporary Art in Barcelona, Spain, the Museum of Television and Radio in Beverly Hills, Calif., and a federal courthouse in Islip, N.Y.

The opening of a branch of the Guggenheim Museum in Bilbao, Spain, designed by Pritzker Prize winner Frank Gehry of the U.S., scheduled for 1997, was much anticipated. A pile of sharply twisting, curving shapes, surfaced in titanium and rising to a height of 30 m (100 ft), it might signal the beginning of a new free-form kind of architecture that had become possible because of computers, without which Gehry's complex forms could not have been designed, engineered, or constructed.

Awards. It was announced that the Phillips Exeter Academy Library in Exeter, N.H., by Louis I. Kahn, would receive the 1997 "Twenty-Five Year Award" from the AIA. This prize was given each year to an American building that had proved its merit during at least a quarter of a century. The library, a simple, monumental cube of brick, was one of the early successes of Kahn, whom many regard as the most influential architect of his generation. The AIA also named 10 winners of its 1997 Honor Awards for the best designs of the year. Among the more prominent were the

The new European home of the Guggenheim Foundation stands on a bank of the Nervíon River in Bilbao, in the Basque Country of northern Spain. The building, designed by Frank Gehry as a response to features of the city and surrounding area, was to open in 1997.

renovation of the New Victory Theater in New York City's Times Square by Hardy Holzman Pfeiffer and the Tokyo International Forum by the Uruguayan-born U.S. architect Rafael Viñoly.

Earlier in the year the AIA had announced its Honor Awards for 1996, which included Gehry's Center for the Visual Arts in Toledo, Ohio; the Munich (Ger.) Order Center by Murphy/Jahn of Chicago; and the urban design of the Cleveland (Ohio) Gateway district by Sasaki Associates. The Aga Khan Award for Architecture, given every three years to promote good architecture and urban design in the Islamic world, announced 12 winners, which included a plan for the restoration of some 500 buildings in Bukhara, Uzbekistan, and the IBM tower in Kuala Lumpur, Malaysia, that was cited as an example of high-rise architecture responsive to a tropical climate.

Civic Buildings. A design was announced for what had been described as the most important overseas American building of the century—a new embassy in Berlin. It was to be constructed at a corner of the city's main civic square, the Pariser Platz, next to the landmark Brandenburg Gate. Six architects were asked to submit designs for the embassy. The designs were then evaluated by a jury of architects and public officials. The winner was the Los Angeles firm of Moore Ruble Yudell, with Gruen Associates, which proposed a building that included many echoes of traditional architecture. One such echo was a "lodge" in an interior courtyard, intended as a social gathering place for the embassy staff that would evoke memories of both a U.S. suburban house and the visitors' lodges of the national parks.

A new Main Public Library in San Francisco was designed by James Ingo Freed of the firm Pei Cobb Freed & Partners, the architect of the famed Holocaust Memorial Museum in Washington, D.C. Freed dealt with the problem of inserting an up-to-date library in the city's historic Civic Center by using such modern materials as stainless steel to re-create traditional motifs such as

classical columns. A huge free-form skylit atrium dominated the interior.

The 1996 Olympic Games in Atlanta, Ga., failed to produce significant architecture, a disappointment after the spectacular Olympics of other years. Unlike Games in other parts of the world, Atlanta's were privately financed, and the buildings were routine and inexpensive. An attempt was made, however, to spin off some long-term benefits for the city, including a new downtown park and new trees and artworks intended to provide a better environment for pedestrians.

In Leipzig, Ger., a huge new convention centre, the Neue Messe Leipzig, featured a spectacular vaulted glass hall. Potential heat and glare in the space were controlled by external sprinklers, which sprayed the glass, and by computer-controlled ventilation systems. The building was seen as a symbol of the resurgence of the former East Germany. In Japan the Tokyo International Forum, a vast complex containing four large theatres and a convention centre, was scheduled to open officially in early 1997.

Cultural Buildings. The Aronoff Center for Design and Art opened at the University of Cincinnati, Ohio. It was designed by the experimental U.S. architect Peter Eisenman. Like Gehry's Guggenheim in Bilbao, it was regarded as the harbinger of a new generation of free-form computer-generated designs—although Eisenman's irregular shapes tended to be angular rather than curved. The construction drawings for the building were not conventionally dimensioned in feet or metres. Instead, 8,000 key points were plotted in three dimensions by computer and then located on the building site by an engineer using a laser transit. Eisenman argued that this process allowed him to create a building "so fractured that the space is no longer contained by form—it's rattled loose."

In Chicago an almost equally controversial but very different building for the arts was the new Museum of Contemporary Art. It was designed by the German architect Josef Paul Kleihues in a sober, symmetrical, neo-classical style. One architectural magazine said that "it seems to summarize a composure and restraint that has blessedly come to us after an era in which the over-the-top, program-be-damned hedonism of museums like Peter Eisenman's Wexner Center [in Ohio] and Gehry's Vitra Museum [in Germany] has been celebrated." Kleihues used local Indiana limestone at the base of his building and then switched to panels made of aluminum sandblasted with iron filings at the upper levels, a material expected to age and weather well in the Chicago climate.

Another large cultural project was the Skirball Cultural Center in Los Angeles by Moshe Safdie, a museum of Jewish life not far from Meier's Getty Center. Like the Getty, the Skirball was a cluster of buildings sited on a hill, visible from a distance on the freeways.

At Harvard University, Philadelphia architects Venturi, Scott Brown and Associates restored the university's largest building, the Victorian-style Memorial Hall, into an up-to-date dining hall with a basement of student fast-food counters and study nooks. In Mexico City Ricardo Legoretta and other architects created a new National Center for the Arts.

Commercial Buildings. Probably the most discussed and written-about commercial venture of 1996 was the opening of the new town of Celebration outside Orlando, Fla., created by the Walt Disney Co. Many prominent architects, including Jaquelin Robertson, Robert A.M. Stern, Cesar Pelli, Michael Graves, Charles Moore, Philip Johnson, Aldo Rossi, William Rawn, and the firm of Venturi, Scott Brown, collaborated in the planning of the town and the design of its buildings. Unlike less-wealthy developers, Disney was able to begin the project by building the town's downtown, in which shops, restaurants, and entertain-

ment facilities faced an artificial lake, even before there was a resident population. Celebration was intended to be a normal community, not an exclusive gated enclave, and was expected to reach a population of approximately 20,000. Exteriors but not interiors of the houses had to conform to an elaborate set of guidelines intended to re-create the atmosphere of the small-town America of the pre-World War II era. Of the buildings completed by the year's end, a movie complex in Art Deco style by Pelli, a cylindrical post office by Graves, and two office buildings by Rossi were among the more notable.

Celebration was regarded as the most visible example of the increasingly influential movement known as New Urbanism, which could be summarized as an attempt to return to the pedestrian-friendly, compactly built town of the past, as opposed to what the New Urbanists described as the car-dominated suburban sprawl of freeways, malls, and widely dispersed single-family houses. Admired by many, Celebration and other examples of New Urbanism were criticized by others as a retreat to a dreamworld of the American past, one that would appeal to only a small slice of the current population.

Also during the year, in Britain, another New Urbanist town opened its first 250 homes. This was Poundbury, sponsored by Prince Charles, designed by the Luxembourg architect Leon Krier, and intended, like Celebration, to re-create the values of the past.

Also for Disney—now regarded as the world's leading private patron of architecture—was an office building in Anaheim, Calif., by Gehry, much of it covered in iridescent quilted sheet-metal panels that to passing motorists appeared to be changing colour. Gehry's competition-winning Disney Concert Hall for downtown Los An-

geles, however, remained mired in political and budgetary problems and seemed likely never to be built.

Competitions. A national competition was under way in the United States to design a memorial to veterans of World War II on a prominent site near the Washington Monument on the Mall in Washington, D.C. It drew more than 400 entries, from which 6 finalists were chosen. No announcement of a winner had been made by the year's end.

A design by Berlin-based architect Daniel Libeskind, featuring irregular, heaped-up, angular shapes, was chosen from more than 100 proposals for a new wing for the Victoria and Albert Museum in London. Pritzker Prize winner Christian de Portzamparc won a competition to plan the Massena neighbourhood of Paris.

Controversies and News Events. The proliferation of memorials in Washington, D.C., led critics to complain that the Mall was in danger of turning into a world's fair. Partly in response, a new plan for the civic core of Washington—in which future monuments would be dispersed along North, South, and East Capitol streets, which radiate from the U.S. Capitol—was proposed by the National Capital Planning Commission. The intention was to return to the original planning concept of Washington as created by Pierre L'Enfant. Meanwhile, in addition to the World War II memorial, a U.S. Air Force memorial design by Freed in the shape of the air force insignia's five-pointed star was approved for a site across the Potomac River from the Lincoln Memorial.

The question of how to make government buildings secure from such threats as the bombing of an Oklahoma City, Okla., office structure in 1995 came to a head during the year in Washington as the National Park Service published five proposals

A long underground concourse is the most visually striking feature of the Aronoff Center for Design and Art on the campus of the University of Cincinnati, Ohio. The concourse connects the parts of the four schools housed in the building, which was designed by Peter Eisenman.

TIMOTHY HURSLEY

The new air traffic control tower at Los Angeles International Airport rises above an adjoining five-story office building. Architect Kate Diamond drew on elements from aviation and space technology to design structures that flaunted rather than concealed their high-tech features.

for the future of the area around the White House. After the Oklahoma City bombing, the White House and the section of Pennsylvania Avenue in front of it were closed to vehicular traffic. The plan preferred by the Park Service would reopen the avenue for service vehicles and special events only. Critics feared that the new emphasis on security might have a dampening effect on the street life of cities. Similarly, a new U.S. embassy in Peru, by the Miami, Fla., firm Arquitectonica, was described in a U.S. architecture magazine this way: "Forget architecture as goodwill ambassador. The message here is, 'Keep out!'" The Berlin embassy, however, following German preference, was to be built to the edge of the sidewalk, with normal-sized windows and without visible barriers or setbacks.

The battle for the title of world's tallest building continued in East Asia. The Petronas Towers in Kuala Lumpur, designed by Cesar Pelli, captured the title in April at 452 m, topping the Sears Tower in Chicago (1 m = 3.28 ft). But foundation work was under way in Shanghai for the 460-m Shanghai World Financial Center, and in Hong Kong approval was expected for the 468-m Nina Tower. New engineering techniques, often using high-strength concrete frames in addition to steel, were employed in all the towers.

(ROBERT CAMPBELL)

See also Business and Industry Review: *Building and Construction*.

This article updates the *Macropædia* article The History of Western ARCHITECTURE.

BRIDGES

The spectacular recent triumph of the cable-stayed bridge was overshadowed in 1996 by the resurgence of the suspension bridge. Several record-breaking examples of the latter were either completed or were close to it.

Suspension bridges—those with a curved, usually steel, cable slung between two towers and anchored back behind them—traditionally produce the longest spans. They support the deck from vertical hanger cables off the main cable. The cable-stay, where the cables radiate out in straight lines directly from the tower to the deck, had begun to challenge the suspension design for medium-length bridges. The main span lengths of cable-stays had now reached once unbelievable 856 m (1 m = 3.28 ft).

Suspension bridges such as the Tsing Ma in Hong Kong, the Great Belt's (Storebælt's) East Bridge in Denmark, and Akashi Kaikyo in Japan, all currently taking final shape, were, however, even longer. Tsing Ma, which, when completed in 1997 would connect Hong Kong with its new airport on Lantau Island, was 1,377 m long and carried a dual three-lane highway as well as the new airport railway on a lower deck.

The Great Belt, which would help link Copenhagen, on the island of Zealand, to mainland Europe, was even longer at 1,624 m. Cables for this bridge were finished in November, in record time, through the use of a new computer-controlled "spinning" system that promised to halve the cost of fabricating suspension cable. The Great Belt would be the longest in the world when it opened in 1998.

Almost immediately, however, an even longer bridge, Japan's Akashi, would take the record with a stunning 1,991-m-long central span. By late 1996 cables and decks had been completed, and the 10-year-long construction program was scheduled to finish in 1998.

Bridge building action was becoming increasingly significant in the Pacific area. Apart from Japan, China was coming to the fore. A 990-m dual two-lane road bridge was completed across the Chang Jiang (Yangtze River) at Sandouping between Yichang and Chongqing. The bridge linked the two sides of the huge Three Gorges Dam project, which was well under way just upstream. Construction began on an even bigger Yangtze bridge, the Jiangyin. With a 1,385-m span, it would be the fourth largest in the world when completed in 1999. It would not use spinning construction, where the wires are laid one by one in the air, but would employ a preformed-cables method favoured by the Japanese.

Also nearing completion in China was the Humen Bridge, an 888-m-long suspension bridge across the Pearl River at the so-called Tiger's Mouth (Boca Tigris) downstream from Guangzhou (Canton). It was not only one of the country's first suspension bridges but also part of a longer link across the river estuary that included several kilometres of viaduct and a 260-m concrete box span, also a record length.

The Severn II, with a span of 456 m (1,496 ft), was the U.K.'s longest road bridge. The cable-stayed structure, which opened in mid-1996, was built to relieve congestion by providing a second bridge connection between England and Wales over the Severn Estuary.
GRANT SMITH

Increasingly, the main bridge was merely part of a very long link. Akashi, for example, was part of three very long links to Shikoku Island from Japan's "mainland" island, Honshu. The Great Belt's suspension bridge was part of an overall viaduct, concrete bridge, and tunnel link. In Scandinavia work was also well under way for the long Øresund connection between Copenhagen and western Sweden, which again included tunnels, as well as a concrete viaduct totaling 12 km (7.5 mi). Included was an artificial island and a cable-stayed bridge. In the U.K. the 5.2-km (3.2-mi) second crossing of the Severn Estuary with a 456-m-long central span became part of the country's longest connection in the summer.

(ADRIAN LEE GREEMAN)

BUILDINGS

Major developments during 1996 included the topping out of the Petronas Towers in Kuala Lumpur, Malaysia. At 452 m (1 m = 3.28 ft), the twin towers were, at least temporarily, the tallest buildings in the world. Construction also began on other buildings that would be more than 375 m in height. The 420-m-high Jin Mao development in Shanghai was under construction, and plans were under way for Millennium towers in Tokyo and London, at 840 m and 385 m, respectively. The former would be a quantum leap in building heights if it was built.

Construction was under way near Paris for the 80,000-seat Stade de France for the 1998 World Cup. Of particular interest was the flat annular disklike roof to be suspended 45 m above ground level from 18 slender steel pylons. The pylons were situated behind the upper tier of seats and projected through holes in the steel-framed roof, which was supported from the pylons by sloping steel cables. The roof would extend as far as 69 m inward from the pylons and 25 m on the outside. The inner part of the disk would be clad with translucent glass to avoid light contrast between sky and roof.

At Alexandria, Egypt, a monumental (design life of 200 years) library was being built. This area was known for its difficult ground conditions, both for construction and for the design of foundations. Consequently, the building design featured four levels below ground level and up to six floors above. The high water table in the porous strata on which the building was situated made exclusion of water during construction difficult, and the completed structure had to be designed against flotation. The basement wall took the form of a reinforced-concrete diaphragm wall, extending down 35 m and built by placing the concrete in a trench excavated in the ground and filled with bentonite mud. In order to support the building and prevent flotation, some 700 reinforced-concrete piles up to 1.5 m in diameter were bored down to a depth of 37 m. Owing to the corrosive nature of the groundwater, all construction in contact with the ground had to be carefully designed and built to ensure the intended design life.

PETER REINA

Work proceeded on a complex of offices and housing at Berlin's Potsdamer Platz, which had been destroyed in World War II. The designation of Berlin as the new capital of Germany and anticipation of an increased demand for business and residential space prompted the redevelopment.

The superstructure of the glass hall at the Tokyo International Forum was lens-shaped in plan, about 207 m long by 32 m wide at the centre and nearly 60 m high. While the structure was of large scale, the engineers sought to keep individual components small in order to produce a delicate total building. The roof was carried on two columns situated 124 m apart on the long axis. The upper side was nominally flat and glass-clad, and the structure supporting it was made up of steel ribs up to 12.5 m deep, much like the hull of a ship. Within this were compression and tension members providing strength both for carrying the weight and for the lateral wind load from the walls. The glass-clad walls were carried on vertical mullions 10.5 m apart that took the form of light trusses spanning vertically up to 32.5 m to carry the wind loads on the walls.

An interesting new concept of grid shells for lightweight roofs was developed in Germany. Spherical and irregular doubly curved surfaces are impossible to modularize totally. Through the use of a quadrangular mesh with members of equal length, how-ever, these shapes can be formed, provided that the panel shapes are allowed to vary from square to diamond-shaped. The system provides for the panel side members to be joined at the ends to allow in-plane rotation and, at the same time, enable clamping of continuous bracing cables on the diagonals, which are necessary to maintain the geometry. Glass-clad roofs with spans as large as 33 m were constructed in this way, using members one metre in length.

(GEOFFREY M. PINFOLD)

DAMS

More than 1,100 dams were under construction throughout the world during 1996. The leading countries were China (270), Turkey (173), Japan (134), South Korea (134), India (77), Spain (50), Italy (46), the U.S. (37), Romania (36), and Iran (27).

Privatization of power generation and its impact on dam building was under way in many countries. Zimbabwe was inviting private investment to start the Batokan Gorge Dam, which was to supply 600 MW on the Zambezi River. Mexico was looking for private capital to develop its two Temascal dams, which would add 200 MW to the nation's system.

In Turkey construction began on the Ermenek Dam, designed to be 190 m high and generate 1,022 GW-hr. Turkey and Syria were having a dispute over the allocation of the waters of the Euphrates River. Syria demanded that Turkey halt work on the Birecik Dam. The dispute was intensified because of the reduction of river flow by Turkey to allow repairs at Ataturk Dam, with its 24,000 MW plant.

Syria was also pursuing an aggressive dam-building program. Just completed was the Thawrah Dam on the Snobar River, with a reservoir that would hold 98 million cu m and irrigate 9,600 ha. Syria was also nearing completion of the Khahour Dam, which would irrigate 55,000 ha and store 600 million cu m of water. (1 ha = 2.47 ac; 1 cu m = 35.3 cu ft.)

Iran completed its largest-volume dam, the Karkheh on the river of the same name. The 127-m-high dam would supply irrigation water to 220,000 ha and produce 400 MW of power.

The Great Man-Made River

One of the largest water-transmission projects in the world, the Great Man-Made River (GMR) in Libya was aimed at bringing high-quality sweet water from underground aquifers deep in the Sahara to the populated areas along the Libyan coast for drinking water and irrigation. The project had several arms, some of which would be under construction until about 2007.

Water was first discovered in the Al-Kufrah area in Libya's southeastern desert in the 1970s during exploration drilling for oil. Initially, the government planned to set up a large-scale agricultural project in the desert where the water was found, but plans were changed in the early 1980s, and designs were prepared for a massive pipeline to the coast. In 1983 the South Korean company Dong Ah was awarded a contract for the construction, and in 1991 the first arm of the pipeline, known as GMR1, was completed. Hundreds of water wells were drilled at two fields, Tazirbu and Sarir, where water was pumped up from an underground reservoir at a depth of between 80 and 400 m (260 and 1,300 ft). The water, which did not need purification, was then transported by gravity through a 1,900-km (1,200-mi) pipeline to a holding reservoir at Ajdabiya and to the coastal cities of Surt and Banghazi.

The pipeline itself was the largest in the world with a diameter of 4 m (13 ft). It was being manufactured on-site in Libya at a factory that had been built especially for the purpose. The pipe, manufactured in 7-m (23-ft) sections, was made up of layers of concrete and steel plates, and the sections were laid by specially made cranes, which were capable of lifting as much as 200 metric tons. Some 13,000 people were working in Libya on the project at any one time, 2,500 of them in the pipeline-construc-tion plant. GMR1 was capable of transporting 2 million cu m (70.6 million cu ft) of water per day. In 1996 only a quarter of the capacity was used, but volumes were expected to increase with the completion of an ongoing program to drill more water wells.

A second pipeline, GMR2 in western Libya, was completed in September 1996 and started supplying Libya's capital, Tripoli, with drinking water from three well fields in the Jabal Nafusah mountain region. Additional well drilling and reservoir construction was scheduled to be completed in 1999. The pipeline's capacity was to be 2.5 million cu m (88.3 million cu ft) of water a day, but only some 600,000–1 million cu m (21 million–35 million cu ft) would be needed for drinking water in Tripoli. The additional capacity in GMR1 and 2 was to be used for agriculture. For this purpose the GMR project included large-scale investments in irrigation infrastructure, which had yet to be started at the year's end.

(CHARLOTTE BLUM)

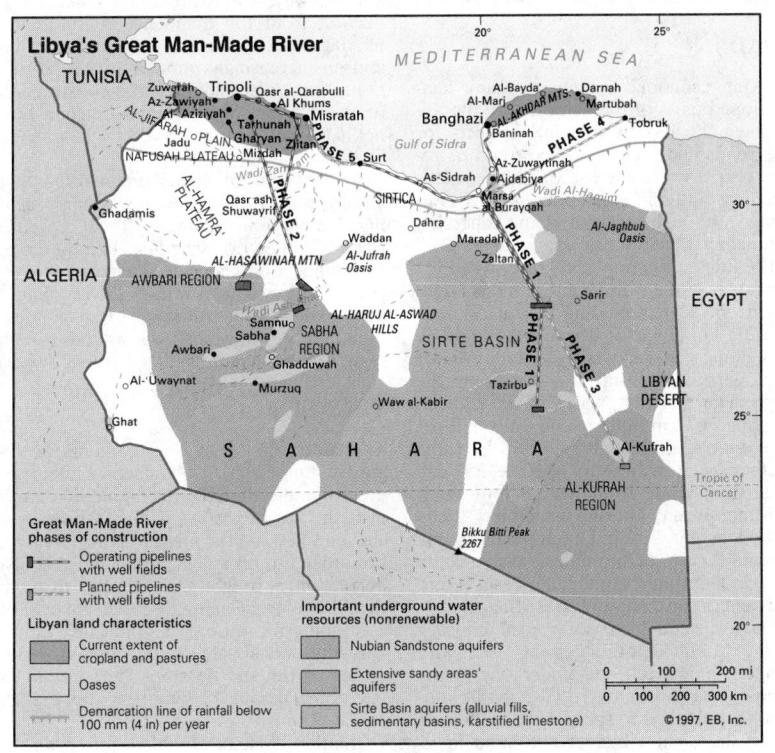

Libya's Great Man-Made River

Great Man-Made River phases of construction
- Operating pipelines with well fields
- Planned pipelines with well fields

Libyan land characteristics
- Current extent of cropland and pastures
- Oases
- Demarcation line of rainfall below 100 mm (4 in) per year

Important underground water resources (nonrenewable)
- Nubian Sandstone aquifers
- Extensive sandy areas' aquifers
- Sirte Basin aquifers (alluvial fills, sedimentary basins, karstified limestone)

©1997, EB, Inc.

In India construction was continuing on the Sardar Sarovar Dam despite protests regarding the resettlement of people from the reservoir area. The government considered the need of water for irrigation to be paramount.

Of China's 270 large dams under construction, 15 were designed to be more than 100 m high. The huge Three Gorges project on the Chang Jiang (Yangtze River) was running ahead of schedule. The Chinese claimed that all the environmental objections to the dam were being satisfied and that the benefits would be much greater than originally envisioned by the planners. The river diversion was expected to take place in October 1997, a year earlier than planned, and the entire project was scheduled to be completed by the year 2009. By the end of 1996, China had more than 20,-000 large dams in operation.

In Malaysia the long-awaited Bakun Dam was started during the year by the award of the construction contract. The dam was to be 205 m high and would produce 2,400 MW of power. It was scheduled to be completed in 2002.

In Portugal the Algueva Dam on the Guadiana River would provide 240 MW and was to impound what would be Europe's largest reservoir. Financial and environmental problems cast doubt, however, as to whether the construction would proceed on schedule.

In Nigeria the Kafin Zaki Dam was under construction. It was to have a reservoir capacity of 2,500 cu m.

In the United States 37 dams were under construction, and 9 new hydroelectric plants were placed in operation, the largest of which was Rocky Mountain, with an installed capacity of 848 MW at a cost in excess of $1 billion. As compared with the 1960s, when 1,675 dams were built, only 63 had been constructed in the 1990s as of the end of 1996.   (T.W. MERMEL)

ROADS

Growing economic activity in many less-developed parts of the world led to the announcement in 1996 of many projects for new roads and highways. The trend of recent years toward the use of private-sector financing and the collection of tolls continued, although automated toll-collection systems remained unproven.

The longest highway-construction project under way in the world was the Indus Highway in Pakistan. Covering a total distance of 1,200 km (1 km = 0.6 mi), the highway runs along the valley of the Indus River from Kotri in the south to Peshawar in the north. The first two phases of the project, covering 767 km and costing $220 million, were to be completed by 1997. In India another large project to upgrade 330 km of existing roads from two to four lanes was announced. The largest project to be funded by the Asian Development Bank, it would cost $220 million and include work in five states: Andhra Pradesh, Bihar, Haryana, Rajasthan, and West Bengal.

The expected increase in road building in the Middle East began in 1996, with projects announced and under way in the United Arab Emirates. In Dubayy the municipality planned to spend $260 million on roads, the highest budget allocation in its history. Abu Dhabi began work on a $272 million project to upgrade the road link to Dubayy to an international standard divided highway.

The Silk Road, which was established about 2,000 years ago to connect the ancient civilizations of Rome and China, could once again become an international highway. Under a program promoted by the International Road Federation (IRF) and reflecting the growing importance of trade in the Caucasus region, the plan would involve a regionwide improvement in road connections in Turkmenistan, Uzbekistan, Kazakstan, and neighbouring countries.

Other countries in the former Soviet Union were developing their road networks. In Russia plans were under way to upgrade the road linking the two main cities, Moscow and St. Petersburg, to be financed by tolls. Both Ukraine and Belarus were building new expressway connections to their western borders with Poland.

In Eastern Europe the aftermath of war in former Yugoslavia had left a legacy of damaged roads. Studies were under way in Croatia to develop its road network to reflect its new independent status. Bosnia and Herzegovina estimated that it required $3 billion for major infrastructure repairs and was hoping to attract international aid and private finance; 1,000 km of its roads, along with 70 bridges and 20 tunnels, were destroyed in the civil war.

The development of a true highway network in Western Europe took a step closer to reality with the launch of a continent-wide program called "Eurovia." Promoted by the IRF, it intended to reflect the growing international trade in the region and the importance of integration with other transport modes instead of the country-by-country development that had occurred previously.

The world's most northerly road project was under way in Norway. This 28.5-km highway would provide a direct connection from the mainland to the island of Magerøya, Europe's northernmost point and an increasingly popular tourist attraction. The project involved the construction of the world's longest undersea road tunnel, 6.8 km long, and would be completed in 1998.

At the end of 1996, the world's first all-electronic toll highway was approaching completion. Highway 407 in Toronto was built ahead of schedule, but the commissioning of its advanced electronic toll-collection system, in which drivers would pay for road use through transponders mounted on the windshield instead of with cash, was proving difficult.   (RUSS SWAN)

TUNNELS

The most significant developments in regard to tunnels in 1996 concerned their operation rather than their construction. Faith in tunnels as important public facilities was shaken when, on the night of November 18, fire broke out on a heavy truck being transported on a freight train shuttle through the 50-km-long Channel Tunnel. Instead of continuing the journey to the U.K. terminal—the official safety procedure—the operator of the shuttle stopped the train in the tunnel about 13 km from the French portal. The fire, exacerbated by the forced ventilation system, disabled the train by burning through the overhead power supply and caused extensive damage to the concrete lining of the tunnel and its services and track. The 31 passengers and 3 shuttle crew evacuated to safety into the central service tunnel, and firefighting crews from both France and the U.K. had the fire extinguished by the following morning.

Eurotunnel, the company that built and operated the Channel Tunnel, had been successfully increasing its market share of the cross-Channel transport business before the incident. Limited services continued through the undamaged north tunnel, but the loss of business during the busy end-of-year holidays shook Eurotunnel's already fragile financial situation. It was expected to take several weeks or months to repair the damaged tunnel and resume normal operations.

Activity during 1996 centred mainly on the continuation of projects already in progress, including subway (metro) projects in many cities throughout the world, the undersea Trans-Tokyo Bay highway project in Japan, and the regular requirement for water supply, sewerage, and utility tunnels in urban areas. The concentration of tunneling activity during 1996 remained in the Far East.

Tunneling on the Los Angeles subway project remained embroiled in controversy and scandal. As work was beginning to return to normal after the sacking of the contractor associated with the Hollywood Boulevard tunnel collapse in June 1995, the new senior management of the reorganized Metropolitan Transportation Authority was accused of corruption in the evaluation and award of the $65 million contract to manage construction of the new $670 million Eastside extension.

Other major tunneling jobs that encountered trouble during the year included the Athens subway. There tunneling was suspended for investigation into why the tunnel-boring machines engaged on the project were inducing excessive settlement or failing to reach optimum progress rates in the prevailing ground conditions.

On the brighter side, tunneling gained a high profile on some exciting new projects. More than 22 km of single- and twin-tube tunneling under the streets of London as well as through the chalk hills of the Kent countryside were included on the 110-km Channel Tunnel railway link, the construction and operation of which was awarded to a privately financed consortium in early 1996. With the Ted Williams Tunnel under Boston Harbor completed in 1995, work continued on Boston's $10 billion project, in which 13 km (8 mi) of tunnels and roads were being built through the heart of the city.

The trend toward more and more tunneling in cities around the world to utilize the environmental, social, and technical advantages of underground space was confirmed in 1996. To illustrate the trend, London Electricity had completed its first man-entry electricity cable tunnel beneath the streets of London in 1990. By the end of 1996, it had committed to more than 30 km of these cost-effective, safe, easily operated, and efficient alternatives to the open-trench burial of electricity cables.

(SHANI WALLIS)

This article updates the *Macropædia* articles BUILDING CONSTRUCTION; PUBLIC WORKS.

Notable Civil Engineering Projects (in work or completed, 1996)

Name	Location	Year of completion	Notes
Airports		**Area (ha)**	
Chek Lap Kok	ex-Chek Lap Kok Island, Hong Kong	1,248	1997	Artificial island, terminal, bridge, tunnel links
Sepang International Airport	near Kuala Lumpur, Malaysia	100	1998	Project includes high-speed rail link to Kuala Lumpur
Aqueducts		**Length (m)**	
Great Man-Made River (Phase 2)	Sarir/Tazirbu wellfields, Libya	1,670,000	1998	Phase 2: Delivered first water to Tripoli
Lesotho Highlands Water Project	Maluti Mountains, Lesotho-South Africa	82,000	2020	Breakthrough (Phase 1) March 3, six dams
Bridges		**Length (main span; m)**	
Akashi Kaikyo	Kobe, Japan	1,991	1998	World record (suspension) upon completion
Great Belt (Storebælt) East	Halsskov-Knudshoved, Denmark	1,624	1998	World record (suspension) if completed before Akashi Kaikyo
Jiangyin Yangtze	Jiangsu province, China	1,385	1999	Fourth longest in world (suspension) upon completion
Tsing Ma	Tsing Yi-Ma Wan Isls., Hong Kong	1,377	1997	Cable-spinning finished 1995
High Coast	Västernorrland, Sweden	1,210	1997	Begun 1993, elevation above water 40 m
Xiling Yangtze	Three Gorges Dam, China	900	1996	Part of Three Gorges project
Tatara (Great)	Japan	890	1999	World record (cable-stayed) upon completion
Humen	Humen, China	888	1996	Completed July 10, 1996
Trans-Tokyo Bay Highway	Kisarazu, Japan	590	1997	Includes 10-km tunnel to Kawasaki
Kobbholet	Mager Island, Norway	520	1998	Part of 28.5-km bridge-tunnel link to Norwegian mainland
Øresund	Flinterenden, Denmark-Sweden	492	2000	18-km road/rail tunnel/bridge link
Severn II (Second Severn Crossing)	Severn Estuary, U.K.	456	1996	Opened June 5; U.K. record (cable-stayed)
Tagus II	Lisbon, Portugal	420	1997	Total length 18 km
Glebe Island	Sydney, Australia	345	1996	Australian record (cable-stayed), opened December 2
Confederation (Northumberland Strait)	New Brunswick-Prince Edward Island, Canada	250	1997	250-m single spans, 12.9 km total length
Kimpo Grand	Seoul, South Korea	100	1997	Links Seoul to Kimp'o Int'l Airport
Buildings		**Height (m)**	
Chongqing Tower	Chongqing, China	457	1997	World record upon completion
Petronas I and II	Kuala Lumpur, Malaysia	452	1996	Twin towers, world record
Jin Mao	Shanghai, China	420	1998	Part of Pudong area development
Shun Hing Square	Shenzhen SEZ, China	325	1996	Asian record, January 1996 completion
Tokyo Opera City	Tokyo, Japan	235	1996	Third tallest building in Tokyo
City		**Area (ha)**	
Putrajaya	near Kuala Lumpur, Malaysia	4,400	1998	Planned national capital; government transfer 2000
Dams		**Crest length (m)**	
Yacyretá-Apipé	Paraná River, Argentina-Paraguay	69,600	1998	Hydroelectric power, navigation, irrigation
Three Gorges	Chang Jiang (Yangtze River), China	1,983	2009	Stage 1: 1993–97; 2: 1998–2003; 3: 2004–09
Bakun	Balui, Bakun Rapids, Malaysia	900	2002	Adverse court decision June 19, 1996
Longtan	Hongshui River, China	800		Pumped storage power facility
Ertan	Yalong River, China	763	1998	Second largest hydroelectric power project in China
Katse	Malibamatso, Lesotho	700	1996	Part of Lesotho Highlands Water Project; see above
Tehri	Bhagirathi River, India	575	1997	World's sixth highest upon completion
Xiaolangdi	Huang Ho (Yellow River), China		2001	Flood, ice, silt control, irrigation, power
Highway		**Length (km)**	
Indus	Kotri-Peshawar, Pakistan	1,200	1998	Phases 1 & 2 scheduled to be completed by 1997
Railways		**Length (km)**	
Beijing–Kowloon	Beijing–Kowloon, China	2,553	1996	Inaugurated Aug. 31, 1996, 150 tunnels, 1,110 bridges
South Xinjiang	Kashi–Korla, China	975	2000	Completes 1,470-km Turpan–Kashi Railway
Nanning–Kunming Electric Railway	Nanning–Kunming, China	898.7	1997	258 tunnels, 447 bridges
Seoul–Pusan	Seoul–Pusan, South Korea	426.2	2002	High-speed; controversy over Kyongju segment
Subways		**Length (m)**	
Seoul Metro (extensions)	Seoul, South Korea	61,500	1997	Lines 6, 7, 8
Bangkok: MRTA Red Line (BERTS)	Bangkok, Thailand	60,000	1998	Bangkok Elevated Road and Train System
Pusan Metro (Line 2 extension)	Pusan, South Korea	39,100	1996	Phase 1: 22.4 km, phase 2: 16.7 km
Taegu Metro (Line 1)	Taegu, South Korea	27,600	1997	Phase 1 (of 6): 29 stations
Guangzhou (Canton) Subway: Line 1	Guangzhou, China	18,200	1997	Line 1 (of 3): 16 stations
London Metro (Jubilee Extension)	London, England	15,600	1998	Twin tunnels
Chongqing Metro: Line 1	Chongqing, China	15,000	1998	Line 2 planned 1996–2000
Taipei Mucha (Brown)	Taipei, Taiwan	10,800	1996	Phase 1 opened March 28, 1996
Towers		**Height (m)**	
Kuala Lumpur Tower (Telekom Malays)	Kuala Lumpur, Malaysia	421	1996	Opened Oct. 1, 1996
Stratosphere (Vegas World) Tower	Las Vegas, Nev., U.S.	350	1996	Hotel and tower opened April 30, 1996
Tunnels		**Length (m)**	
Pinglin Highway	near Taipei, Taiwan	12,900	1999	Twin 11.8-m tunnels under Sheuhshan range
Trans-Tokyo Bay I & II	Tokyo, Japan	9,300	1997	Twin tunnels
FATIMA (Magerøy)	Norway	6,820	1998	World's longest subsea road tunnel
Øresund	Copenhagen–Malmö, Denmark-Sweden	3,750	2000	Twin tunnels: world-record immersed tube
Huangpu	Shanghai, China	2,207	1996	Opened Nov. 30, 1996
Cumberland Mountain	Cumberland Gap, U.S.	1,402	1996	Underground parking garages preserve environment
Central Artery/Tunnel	Boston, Mass., U.S.	330	2004	"One of the most complex construction challenges of this century"
Urban Development			
Potsdamer Platz	Berlin, Germany		2000	19 buildings

1 m = 3.28 ft; 1 km = 0.62 mi; 1 ha = 2.47 ac

Art, Antiques, and Collections

The art market in 1996 continued to rebound from the 1990 crash as auction sales remained buoyant. The major auction houses Christie's and Sotheby's had the most success for good paintings in the middle market range ($300,000–$2 million), but the sky-high prices seen in the late 1980s showed no sign of reappearing. Asian art, which experienced a boom, was showcased in March at the second International Asian Art Fair in New York City. The major exhibition "Splendors of Imperial China" made a limited tour of the U.S., while Taiwanese protesters argued that many of their treasures were too fragile to tour. The Hermitage Museum in St. Petersburg announced the discovery and exhibition of still more artworks that had been removed from Germany during World War II. The important cache of prints and drawings included one of Vincent van Gogh's most famous images, "Boats at Saintes-Maries." The issue of repatriating the artworks was left unresolved.

In London scandal tainted the work of British painter Ben Nicholson. No buyers could be found for any of his paintings at the spring modern art sales in London after word leaked out that a ring of forgers had doctored records pertaining to his work. The media circus surrounding the Jacqueline Kennedy Onassis estate sale aroused the general public's interest in art, antiques, and collectibles. Such "Camelot" mementos as faux pearls and rocking chairs brought prices usually associated with Old Master paintings.

The international auction market received a proposal for French auction reform (to take effect in 1998) that would end the monopoly French auction houses had held on French sales for more than 400 years. The reform would allow foreign auction houses such as Christie's and Sotheby's to hold sales on French soil. As a result, important property from French estates would not necessarily be auctioned abroad and would therefore be more likely to remain in French hands.

Two major British museums, London's Tate Gallery and the National Gallery, orchestrated a grand art exchange in order to enhance their respective collections; 52 works of 19th-century art would leave the Tate for the National Gallery, which would send the Tate 14 of its 20th-century paintings, including Claude Monet's monumental "Water Lilies" (after 1916).

The end of the art year coincided with the closing of an exhibit at the American Museum of Natural History, New York City, of the *Codex Leicester,* a notebook of brilliant scientific musings by Renaissance master Leonardo da Vinci.

(REBECCA KNAPP)

ART EXHIBITIONS

Several art exhibitions were mounted at the 1996 Olympic Games in Atlanta, Ga., as part of the Olympic Arts Festival, which took the unifying spirit of the Olympic movement as its theme. Organizers were faced with the formidable task of harmonizing cultural events with athletic competition.

The "blockbuster" show of the Games was "Rings: Five Passions in World Art," which was on view during the summer at Atlanta's High Museum and was named for the five Olympic rings. The exhibit was the centrepiece of the Olympic Arts Festival, and it marked the 100th anniversary of the modern Olympic Games. Designed to attract a broad audience, it featured over 125 works of art and represented 7,500 years of civilization. Included were Greek antiquities, African sculptures, paintings by Monet, Pablo Picasso, and European Old Masters as well as works by Auguste Rodin, Edvard Munch, Thomas Eakins, and Tony Cragg.

"Mysteries of Ancient China," which represented artifacts dating from 4500 BC to AD 220, was seen at the British Museum in the autumn and was expected to attract more than 150,000 visitors during its four-month stay in London. The exhibit, on loan from China, was the first showing of the remarkable discoveries made during excavations of Chinese tombs since the death of Mao Zedong in 1976. The show was scheduled to travel extensively after it closed in London in January 1997.

"Mysteries" featured some of the most spectacular finds of the past 20 years. The discoveries provided new evidence of a previously unknown civilization that dated from about 3000 BC. Aside from the fascination of their archaeological significance, the objects themselves were breathtaking in their diversity and artistic merit, showing great sophistication and virtuosity of technique. Media included bronze, jade, lacquerwork, and silk. One magnificent exhibit was a jade burial suit belonging to Prince Liu Sheng, king of Zhongshan from 154 until 113 BC. It comprised 2,498 separate plaques knotted together with 1,100 g of gold wire and was one of the most extraordinary archaeological finds of the 20th century.

"Imperial Tombs of China" comprised about 250 funerary objects made for seven dynasties of Chinese royalty between 475 BC and AD 1912. The standouts at the show were life-size terra-cotta warriors from the tomb "army" of the First Emperor. It was the largest exhibition of its kind ever seen in the U.S. and attracted considerable interest. The show, seen first in the summer of 1996 at the Oregon Art Museum in Portland, would later travel to the Museum of Natural History in Denver, Colo., and the Orlando (Fla.) Museum of Art.

Other shows devoted to Asian art included "New Art In China, Post-1989," which focused on 84 works created by 30

In "The Portable War Memorial," an assemblage created in 1968 by U.S. artist Edward Kienholz, the raising of the U.S. flag on Iwo Jima is re-created on a picnic table, and a woman in an upside-down trash can sings "God Bless America" in Kate Smith's voice. Kienholz, who died in 1994, was honoured during 1996 with a retrospective of 90 of his works at the Whitney Museum of American Art in New York City.

young Chinese artists since the Tiananmen Square student massacre in 1989. The exhibit opened in 1996 at the Fort Wayne (Ind.) Museum of Art before moving to Kansas City, Mo. It would travel to Chicago and San Jose, Calif., in 1997.

A major international exhibition, "Contemporary Art in Asia," included 65 works by 28 Indian, Indonesian, Philippine, Thai, and Korean artists. It was organized by the Asia Society Galleries, opened in late 1996 at three venues in New York City, and would be mounted in Canada, India, Singapore, South Korea, and Japan.

The Greek Ministry of Culture organized "The Macedonians: The Northern Greeks and the Era of Alexander the Great." It was a companion show to "Alexander the Great," which was organized by the Fondazione Memmo in Rome. The two shows presented over 500 objects, including sculptures, mosaics, manuscripts, paintings, and precious objects. The exhibit opened in Rome and later traveled to the Florida International Museum in St. Petersburg, where it would stay until the spring of 1997.

Japan's Agency for Cultural Affairs mounted "Japan's Golden Age: Momoyama," an exhibition devoted to the years in the Azuchi-Momoyama period, between 1574 and 1600. On view in the autumn of 1996, only at the Dallas (Texas) Museum of Art, it included paintings, armour, textiles, and ceramics. Of some 160 objects showcased, more than one-third were registered with the Japanese government as cultural properties and national treasures.

The blockbuster "Splendors of Imperial China: Treasures from the National Palace Museum, Taipei" contained about 450 objects from one of the world's greatest collections of Chinese art and was the most comprehensive such show ever mounted in the U.S. Featured were 120 paintings and works of calligraphy as well as jades, bronzes, ceramics, and decorative pieces. The exhibit was organized by the museum in Taipei and the Metropolitan Museum of Art in New York City. After its New York stay in the spring, the show traveled to the Art Institute of Chicago, the Asian Art Museum in San Francisco, and the National Gallery of Art in Washington, D.C.

"The American Discovery of Ancient Egypt," which opened in late 1995 at the Los Angeles County Museum of Art and later traveled to St. Louis, Mo., and Indianapolis, Ind., showcased more than 200 artifacts found by U.S. archaeologists in Egypt.

A number of notable exhibitions either were devoted to women in art or concentrated on works by female artists. "Women in Ancient Egypt" belonged to the former and was on view at the Cincinnati (Ohio) Art Museum in late 1996 and scheduled to travel to the Brooklyn (N.Y.) Museum in early 1997. The show "Mistress of the House, Mistress of Heaven: Women in Ancient Egypt" featured more than 200 objects that illustrated the roles of women in ancient Egypt, ranging from working women to royalty and goddesses.

An exhibition of plaster models and stone sculptures of ancient Egypt was mounted by the Metropolitan Museum of Art in New York City in late 1996 and celebrated the opening of a new gallery devoted to the Amarna period in Egypt. The featured works in "Queen Nefertiti and the Royal

Women" were portrait sculptures from the workshop of master sculptor Thutmose.

Greek women were the subject of "Pandora's Box: Women in Classical Greece," organized by the Walters Art Gallery in Baltimore, Md., and seen there in late 1995 and early 1996 before moving to Dallas and Basel, Switz. The show comprised around 140 works portraying women in Greece in the 5th century BC. Notable were a kore, or standing female figure, from the Acropolis in Athens and diverse items of marble, pottery, bronze, and terra-cotta.

One of the most famous examples of feminist art, "The Dinner Party" by artist Judy Chicago, was a vast sculptural installation that made its California debut in the spring at the UCLA Armand Hammer Museum of Art and Cultural Center in Los Angeles.

The controversial British sculptor Rachel Whitehead—perhaps best known for "House," a concrete cast of a condemned East London home that was destroyed after its showing—had the first full-scale survey of her work in autumn at the Tate Gallery in Liverpool. The show included sculptures cast in a variety of media, including resin, plaster, and rubber. British sculptor Damien Hirst, winner of the 1995 Turner Prize, had a new show at the Gagosian Gallery in New York City. (*See* BIOGRAPHIES.)

At the Whitney Museum of American Art in New York City, works by another controversial artist, Edward Kienholz, were on view. The retrospective included 90 of his works, which served as powerful and sometimes harsh indictments of American society. Especially notable were such assemblages as the antimilitarist piece "The Portable War Memorial" (1968), the sexually provocative "Back Seat Dodge '38" (1961), and the disconcerting "Sollie 17" (1980), featuring the bleak existence of an old man living in a fleabag hotel.

In London an exhibition of some 170 works by Paul Cézanne arrived at the Tate Gallery after having attracted about 6,000 visitors a day in Paris. The National Gallery mounted the summer blockbuster "Degas: Beyond Impressionism." It was much smaller than the Cézanne exhibit at the Tate and displayed the artist's technical expertise with pastels and the manner in which he used wax sculptures as models for drawings and paintings. The show of nearly 100 paintings, drawings, pastels, and sculptures covered the last 30 years of the artist's career, ranging from the last Impressionist exhibition of 1886 to his death in 1917. The blockbuster's only showing in the U.S. was at the Art Institute of Chicago in the autumn.

The National Gallery's companion exhibition, "Degas as a Collector," comprised works that belonged to the artist during

his lifetime. Shortly after his death, Degas's collection of about 500 paintings and drawings and more than 5,000 prints was sold at auction. It included works by such contemporaries as Paul Gauguin, Cézanne, Édouard Manet, and van Gogh as well as works by such influential artists of the previous generation as Eugène Delacroix and Jean-Auguste-Dominique Ingres. Included were "Woman with a Mango" by Gauguin, lent by the Baltimore Museum of Art, and 11 works that the National Gallery had purchased.

After the Cézanne show moved on to the Philadelphia Museum of Art, the big autumn exhibition at the Tate was "Grand Tour: The Lure of Italy in the 18th-

(continued on page 148)

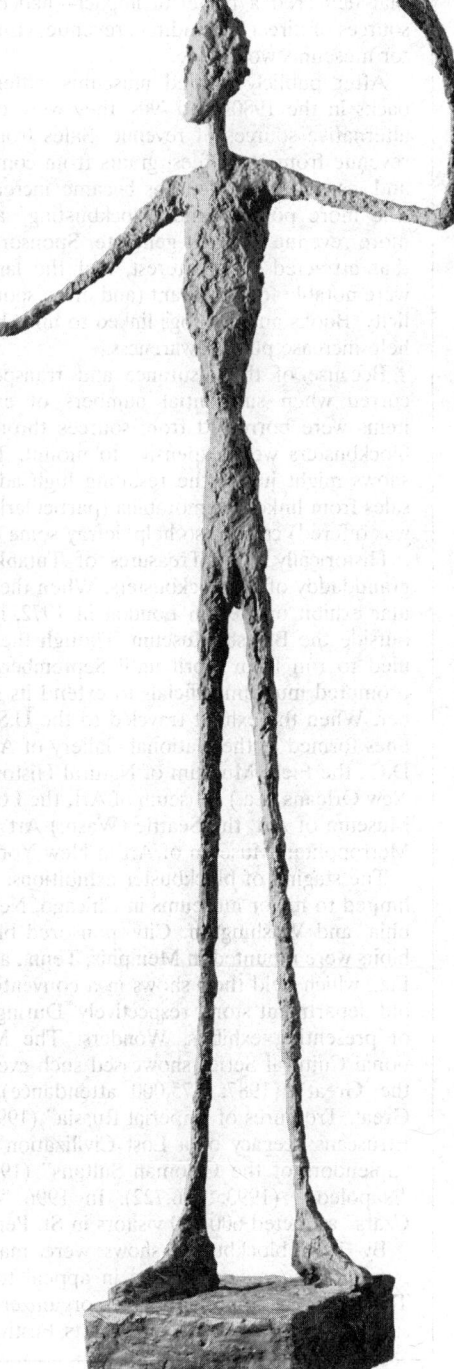

"L'Homme au doigt," created in 1947 by Swiss sculptor Alberto Giacometti, was among the artist's distinctive elongated figures displayed during the year at a retrospective shown in Vienna, Edinburgh, and London.

Blockbuster Art Exhibitions

BY SANDRA MILLIKIN

Blockbuster, a highly explosive word not usually associated with art, has now entered the lexicon as a term applied to art exhibitions. By 1996 so-called blockbuster exhibitions—big, popular, moneymaking showcases that delivered a powerful impact—had become important sources of direct and indirect revenue, visibility, and prestige for museums worldwide.

After publicly funded museums suffered financial cutbacks in the 1980s and '90s, they were compelled to seek alternative sources of revenue. Sales from museum shops, revenue from entry fees, grants from commercial sponsors, and, especially, exhibitions became increasingly important. The more popular and "blockbusting" an exhibition, the more revenue it might generate. Sponsors preferred shows that attracted wide interest, and the largest blockbusters were notable for attendant (and often sponsor-funded) publicity. Books and catalogs linked to an exhibition could also help increase public awareness.

Because of the insurance and transportation costs incurred when substantial numbers of extremely valuable items were borrowed from sources throughout the world, blockbusters were expensive to mount. The most popular shows might justify the resulting high admission fees, and sales from linked memorabilia (particularly when exclusivity was offered) could also help defray some of the cost.

Historically, the "Treasures of Tutankhamen" was the granddaddy of all blockbusters. When the enormously popular exhibit opened in London in 1972, huge lines formed outside the British Museum. Though the show was scheduled to run from April until September, popular interest prompted museum officials to extend its stay until December. When the exhibit traveled to the U.S. in 1976, endless lines formed at the National Gallery of Art in Washington, D.C., the Field Museum of Natural History in Chicago, the New Orleans (La.) Museum of Art, the Los Angeles County Museum of Art, the Seattle (Wash.) Art Museum, and the Metropolitan Museum of Art in New York City.

The staging of blockbuster exhibitions, however, was not limited to major museums in Chicago, New York, Philadelphia, and Washington. City-sponsored blockbuster art exhibits were mounted in Memphis, Tenn., and St. Petersburg, Fla., which held their shows in a convention centre and an old department store, respectively. During a 10-year period of presenting exhibits, Wonders: The Memphis International Cultural Series showcased such events as "Ramesses the Great" (1987; 675,000 attendance), "Catherine the Great: Treasures of Imperial Russia" (1991; 605,000), "The Etruscans: Legacy of a Lost Civilization" (1992; 119,771), "Splendors of the Ottoman Sultans" (1992; 212,089), and "Napoleon" (1993; 416,722). In 1996 "Treasures of the Czars" attracted 600,000 visitors in St. Petersburg.

By 1996 blockbuster shows were mainstream cultural events by no means limited in appeal to art cognoscenti. That the 1996 Olympic Games organizers in Atlanta, Ga., saw fit to include an Olympic Arts Festival, featuring such an ambitious show as "Rings: Five Passions in World Art," was testimony to the manner in which art exhibitions had taken centre stage in the entertainment world. The concept of art sharing time and space with sporting events might have seemed unthinkable 20 years earlier.

During 1995–96 there were several notable blockbusters, many of them devoted to the 19th century, particularly the Impressionists and Postimpressionists. The public gravitated to these shows with often well-known and usually stunningly beautiful objects; some 965,000 attended the massive 1995 Claude Monet retrospective at the Art Institute of Chicago. It was surprising, therefore, that in 1996 one of the best-attended and most sought-after shows was devoted to the 17th-century Dutch painter Johannes Vermeer, whose extant pictures of domestic interiors numbered only about 35. The exhibit of 22 of his paintings was the first ever devoted solely to his works. Organized by the National Gallery in Washington and the Royal Cabinet of Paintings, Mauritshuis, The Hague, it was seen in Washington in the winter of 1995–96 and in The Hague in the spring of 1996. In Washington, where the viewing days were shortened by a government budget crisis and exceptionally severe winter weather, the show became a "pilgrimage site," attracting 327,551 visitors. The exhibition was small, intimate, and select, with an inward focus offering a vastly different experience from the usual blockbuster. There were no drawings or preparatory works—none exist—and no "school of . . ." pictures. The canvases were simply hung in plain interiors, offering an unprecedented opportunity to compare the masterpieces of this artist, whose works, though limited in subject matter, were vast in emotional impact.

The blockbuster Postimpressionist show of the year displayed the work of Paul Cézanne. After opening at the Grand Palais in Paris in 1995, it was mounted by the Tate Gallery in London in the spring and later moved to its only U.S. venue, the Philadelphia Museum of Art.

Blockbuster exhibitions even influenced permanent museum installations. Following the success of the 1995 show at the Hermitage in St. Petersburg, "Hidden Treasures Revealed," featuring 74 masterpieces of Impressionist and Postimpressionist paintings from German private collections thought to have been lost in World War II, the museum rehung 57 of the 74 paintings in a separate gallery.

Blockbusters were not limited to shows displaying paintings. An exhibition devoted to the work of Scottish architect, designer, and painter Charles Rennie Mackintosh attracted thousands of visitors at its first venue in Glasgow. It was on view at the McLellan galleries throughout the summer. Mackintosh's best-known works were in Glasgow, particularly a series of tearooms designed in the late 19th and early 20th centuries, replete with Mackintosh chairs, light fittings, and teacups. The show, which featured some 250 objects ranging from architectural drawings and models to furniture, landscape paintings, and watercolours, traveled in late 1996 to the Metropolitan Museum of Art, the site of the first retrospective of the artist's work in the U.S. Later showings were scheduled for 1997 at the Art Institute of Chicago and the Los Angeles County Museum of Art. Other notable blockbuster exhibitions included "Mysteries of Ancient China" and shows devoted to Pablo Picasso, Edgar Degas, and Jean-Baptist-Camille Corot.

While blockbusters provided advantages for many art institutions and businesses, their popularity became a mixed blessing to some art lovers, who frequently coped with long lines, crowds, and high costs as the price of seeing much-loved art works.

Sandra Millikin is an art historian.

Featured at major blockbuster art exhibitions in 1996 were a clock made by turn-of-the-century Scottish architect, designer, and painter Charles Rennie Mackintosh and "Lady Writing a Letter with Her Maid" by 17th-century Dutch painter Johannes Vermeer. The Mackintosh show opened in Glasgow and later traveled to New York City, Chicago, and Los Angeles, while the Vermeer exhibit of 22 paintings was shown in Washington, D.C., and The Hague. The Vermeer collection represented two-thirds of the artist's surviving output and was the most extensive gathering of the artist's work since his lifetime. The exhibit attracted large crowds. Mackintosh became noted for creating almost all-white interiors characterized by tall, attenuated chairs and cabinets that were inlaid with beaten silver and stained glass. He also designed and furnished a number of tearooms in Glasgow, one of which was re-created for the exhibition.

(continued from page 145)
Century" and included paintings, drawings, and sculptures. The show illustrated the magnetic attraction of 18th-century British travelers to the Italian cities of Venice, Florence, Rome, and Naples.

A show dedicated to the work of Peter Paul Rubens was staged at the National Gallery in London in the autumn and was the first such show to focus on his abilities as a landscape painter. Featured as the exhibit's centrepiece was the panoramic "Landscape with Het Steen."

The retrospective "Alberto Giacometti 1901–1966," devoted to the work of the Swiss sculptor, was mounted at the Scottish National Gallery of Modern Art in Edinburgh in the summer after having opened at the Kunsthalle in Vienna in February. It was the first important exhibition of his work to be seen in Britain since the 1965 retrospective at the Tate the year before his death. The show comprised 80 sculptures, 30 paintings, and a selection of drawings that included his well-known series of elongated standing male figures. The comprehensive survey of his works moved in the autumn to the Royal Academy in London.

On April 16 the Pushkin Museum of Fine Arts in Moscow unveiled 259 priceless items that constituted "Gold of Troy," an exhibit that was on view for the first time since 1941. The objects were secured in 19 bulletproof cases and included pins, pendants, earrings, bracelets, chokers, and beads. The items, dating to the Bronze Age, were unearthed in 1873 in Turkey by Heinrich Schliemann and had formerly been part of the Berlin Museum's collection. During World War II the collection had been housed in bunkers near the Berlin Zoo, but in 1945 Soviet occupation forces removed it to the U.S.S.R. under cloudy circumstances. In 1993 the Pushkin Museum acknowledged its possession of the Schliemann collection—some 8,000 objets d'art and 60,000 documents. Both Germany and Turkey promptly filed claims for it.

"Corot 1796–1875" was a huge French-organized bicentenary retrospective that marked the 200th anniversary of Jean-Baptiste-Camille Corot's birth. It was shown in Paris at the Grand Palais in the spring, at the National Gallery of Canada in Ottawa in the summer, and at the Metropolitan Museum of Art in New York City in the

A two-handled gold vessel is one of the items on display at the Pushkin Museum in Moscow. Among the artifacts unearthed by Heinrich Schliemann in the 19th century at the site of ancient Troy and given to the German government at his death, the items were being seen in public for the first time since they had been taken from Berlin by the Soviet Army in 1945.

autumn. The exhibition represented a wide range of work from early oil landscape studies that he painted in Rome when he was in his late 20s and early 30s to large landscapes for exhibition at the Salon. It demonstrated the degree to which Corot linked the past and the future, from the classical tradition of 17th-century French painting to the freedom of Impressionism, with elements of Realism, Symbolism, and Romanticism. Figure studies for portraits revealed his interest in costume and character. The huge show was the first full-scale European retrospective of Corot's work in 60 years and the first U.S. retrospective in 35 years devoted to his work.

A summer exhibition at the National Gallery in Washington, "In the Light of Italy: Corot and Early Open-Air Painting," focused on artists working in Rome and southern Italy at the end of the 18th century and the early part of the 19th century. On view were about 130 paintings, including a selection of 20 of the best Italian sketches and small landscapes by Corot. The show would also travel to the Brooklyn Museum and the St. Louis Art Museum.

A major Picasso exhibition was organized by the Museum of Modern Art (MOMA) in

New York City with the Musée Picasso in Paris. A large show, "Picasso and Portraiture: Representation and Transformation," was seen in New York in the summer, while a smaller representation of works traveled to the Grand Palais in the autumn. The show concentrated on the artist's work as a portraitist, showing in detail via drawings and paintings the artist's relations with those important in his life: family, friends, and lovers. Included were about 100 paintings and 50 works on paper. Masterpieces and lesser-known works were juxtaposed, which created a visual biography of the artist's life as his style changed along with his relationships. The final drawing was the searching crayon self-portrait of 1972, created a few months before his death.

Venice was the first venue for a major retrospective devoted to the artist Giovanni Battista Tiepolo and organized to commemorate the 300th anniversary of his birth. The show included paintings, drawings, and prints and was on view in the latter half of 1996 at the Ca' Rezzonico. It would later travel to the Metropolitan Museum of Art. In Venice some frescoes not normally shown to the public were unveiled as part of a walking tour linked to the show.

A detail from "Dwelling in the Fu-ch'un Mountains," painted by Huang Kung-wang in 1350, was included in the "Splendors of Imperial China," a collection of about 450 objects exhibited in New York City, Washington, D.C., Chicago, and San Francisco.

"Volterra, the Citadel" was among the works of Camille Corot on exhibit at the Bibliothéque Nationale and Grand Palais in Paris. The show, which marked the 200th year of Corot's birth, moved to the National Gallery of Canada in Ottawa and the Metropolitan Museum of Art in New York City.

The largest Winslow Homer show in over 30 years was seen in late 1995 at the National Gallery in Washington, before moving in 1996 to the Museum of Fine Arts in Boston and the Metropolitan Museum of Art. Included was a selection of about 75 paintings and 95 watercolours representing the artist's career. A separate section of the show demonstrated the working methods he employed.

"By the Light of the Crescent Moon: The Near East in Nineteenth-Century Danish Art and Literature" was devoted to perceptions and depictions of Middle Eastern themes by 19th-century Danish artists and included drawings and travel journals by Hans Christian Andersen. The show was staged at the David Collection in Copenhagen in the summer.

A summer exhibition at the National Gallery of Victoria in Melbourne, Australia, was devoted to the work of English landscape painter Joseph Mallord William Turner (1775–1851). It included about 60 paintings and watercolours lent by private and public collections in Europe and the U.S. The Art Gallery of South Australia in Adelaide showed the "William Paley Collection of Post-Impressionism and Early Modernism," a display of works that illustrated the transition from late Impressionism to Modernism, with works by Cézanne, Pierre Bonnard, Manet, and Picasso. The exhibit was on loan from the MOMA.

(SANDRA MILLIKIN)

PHOTOGRAPHY

In 1996 the long-predicted age of the electronic image established itself on a much broader base than ever before. Increasing numbers of archives, museums, libraries, picture agencies, publishers, and galleries digitized their visual images for storage and access. Linked to these sources by an explosively growing Internet, millions could bring incredible riches of photography to their computer screens—e.g., classic Civil War scenes from the U.S. Library of Congress, historically organized selections from *Life* magazine's archives, spectacular views of space from NASA, and a growing number of smaller, specialized collections from such sources as galleries and auction houses.

Major exhibitions included large retrospectives by two of the U.S.'s most distinguished living photographers: Roy DeCarava (*see* BIOGRAPHIES), 77, and Harry Callahan, 83. New York City's Museum of Modern Art displayed nearly 200 black-and-white prints encompassing DeCarava's notable career from the 1940s to the present, during which he recorded Harlem street life, civil rights protests, and famous jazz musicians. His ability to recognize and capture peak, densely packed fragments of time produced a memorable, moving visual record. The National Gallery in Washington, D.C., honoured Callahan with a comprehensive overview of his long, influential career. Best known as a formalist and an advocate of straight photography and much admired for the elegance and clarity of his style, Callahan also experimented with high-contrast printing, colour, multiple exposures, montages, and collages.

Other retrospectives were "Julia Margaret Cameron: The Creative Process" at the J. Paul Getty Museum, Malibu, Calif., and Nan Goldin's "I'll Be Your Mirror" at the Whitney Museum of Art, New York City. The Cameron show included 38 prints by this impassioned Victorian Englishwoman, who took up photography as an amateur in midlife and, with her tightly cropped portraits of famous contemporaries and sentimental Pre-Raphaelite compositions, became one of the medium's first stylists. In striking contrast to Victorian sensibilities, the Whitney show was a retrospective of work by photographer-diarist Nan Goldin, whose book *The Ballad of Sexual Dependency* and slide show had provoked considerable attention 10 years earlier. Her gritty, unsparing images documented urban life on the margin with portraits of friends, lovers, prostitutes, drug addicts, dying victims of AIDS, and herself as a battered woman. Also at the Whitney, a historical group exhibition, "Perpetual Mirage: Photographic Narratives of the Desert West," explored the camera's crucial role during more than 150 years in shaping varied perceptions of the Great American Desert, especially through photographic books. The images ranged from the grandiloquent to the starkly minimal, and the photographers from 19th-century Timothy O'Sullivan and Carleton Watkins to contemporary Robert Adams and Richard Misrach.

For photojournalists and documentary photographers, 1996 was a year of decreasing markets and shrinking space for their work. The eighth International Festival of Photojournalism in Perpignan, Fr., founded by Jean-François Leroy as an alternative to the long-established Arles festival of photography, provided a forum for discussion among photographers, picture agents, and editors on the topic and an opportunity to display serious photo reportage neglected by mainstream media. "In Times of War and Peace" at the International Center of Photography Midtown, New York City, was an overwhelming retrospective of photojournalism by twins David and Peter Turnley.

Paul Outerbridge, Jr., emerged as an auction superstar. During his lifetime he had achieved considerable fame for the precise, cubist geometry of the colour still lifes that he created in both commercial and personal work. Although his reputation waned after

"Nan and Brian in Bed, NYC" is among the many images, often bleak and gritty, that reveal urban life in the late 20th century as experienced by photographer Nan Goldin. A retrospective of her works, "I'll Be Your Mirror," was mounted during the year at the Whitney Museum of American Art in New York City.

his death in 1958, it had recently revived, and at a 1996 Christie's photographic auction, Outerbridge prints dramatically soared in value. A 1922 "Saltine Box," originally estimated at $60,000 to $80,000, sold for $200,500, more than double his previous auction record, while the total for 36 Outerbridge prints came to about $1 million.

The 1996 Pulitzer Prize for spot news photography was awarded to freelancer Charles Porter IV for his picture of a rescue worker holding a fatally injured baby after the Oklahoma City, Okla., bombing. The Pulitzer for feature photography went to freelancer Stephanie Welsh for a picture story on a female circumcision rite in Kenya (*see page 316*). At the 53rd Annual Pictures of the Year Competition, sponsored by the National Press Photographers Association and the University of Missouri-Columbia School of Journalism, freelancer Eugene Richards took the title of Magazine Photographer of the Year and Torsten Kjellstrand of the *Jasper* (Ind.) *Herald* was named Newspaper Photographer of the Year. At the 39th Annual World Press Photo Contest, the World Press Photo of the Year award went to Lucian Perkins of the *Washington* (D.C.) *Post*. The primary W. Eugene Smith Grant in Humanistic Photography was awarded to South African photographer Gideon Mendel for continuing documentation of the spread of AIDS in Africa. A secondary award went to Dutch photographer Ad van Dendeven for photo reportage on the rising power of Eastern Jews in Israel. The first Howard Chapnick Grant for Leadership in Photojournalism was given to freelance picture editor Colin Jacobson for research into sources for photojournalism outside publications.

(ARTHUR GOLDSMITH)

ART AUCTIONS AND SALES

In 1996 bullish activity and exceedingly high asking prices for works of art concealed the complexities of a market shrouded in crises and transition. The impact of dwindling supplies became apparent as the price of high-quality items soared, leaving behind a trail of unsold works too expensive for most buyers.

As a result, several trends emerged, notably a massive transfer of interest. Collectors who had favoured Impressionists shifted to later schools or to Old Masters. In July Dutch master Willem van de Velde the Younger's painting of two boats at anchor brought $2.1 million, exceeding Sotheby's estimate by about 250%. Attention was also lavished on so-called minor masters. In Baden-Baden, Ger., two still lifes painted in the 1760s by Catharina Treu, who was virtually unknown outside her native Germany, commanded £516,000.

The success of new auction venues raised speculation that activity at major auction houses might erode. The offerings at both the first Asia Arts Fair in New York City in May and the annual art fair in Maastricht, Neth., were reportedly, for the most part, better than those at the major auction houses.

Asian arts also gained in popularity. At Christie's sale of the Junkunc collection, a small bronze T'ang dynasty rhinoceros brought $178,500. Sotheby's best lot, though not the top sale, was a T'ang figure of a "masked foreigner," which commanded $112,500, more than three times the presale estimate.

The aggressive activity that characterized the year was most evident at Sotheby's April sale of the estate of Jacqueline Kennedy Onassis. The four-day televised event, which experts predicted would gross $5 million, brought $34.5 million as buyers paid $343,500 for John Wooten's oil "Lord Bateman's Arabian," $167,500 for Martin Drölling's "Portrait of Barthelemy Charles Comte de Dreux Nancré," and $118,000 for Charles-François Daubigny's *plenair* landscape "Les Bords de l'Oise."

The contemporary art market, driven by U.S. buyers, fueled sales at the major auction houses. Christie's New York held its most successful sale since 1993, setting the ceiling for the market with "Mailbox," Willem de Kooning's 1948 canvas, which made $3.7 million. "Something of the Past," Jackson Pollock's 1946 colourful nondrip canvas, went for $2.4 million. Sotheby's also held its highest-grossing contemporary sale in six years. Jean Dubuffet's oil, sand, and putty work "Hommes et arbres somnambuliques," *c.* 1946, fetched $1.3 million. Andy Warhol's portrait icon "Mao," painted in 1972 and estimated to sell for $154,000–$231,000, became the object of a bidding war before it was claimed for $1 million. Americans unable to acquire name U.S. artists for less than $700,000 looked to underappreciated artists who usually were collected only by Europeans. Paintings by Lucian Freud, Lucio Fontana, and Yves Klein led this mid-priced market.

Impressionist and modern art sales reached their highest level since 1990, thanks in large part to the return of Asian buyers. Christie's scored the season's coup when it sold van Gogh's "Interieur d'un restaurant" for $10.3 million, though Paul Gauguin's "Nature morte a l'esperance" failed to sell at $5 million. In May Sotheby's sold Monet's "Les Meules, Giverny, effect du matin" for $7.2 million and Cezanne's "Gran arbres au Jas De Bouffan" for $7.9 million. Other encouragement came from the strength of works in the $300,000–$800,000 range. Picasso's 1912 newspaper collage "Bouteille et guitare sur une table" fetched $574,500.

Sales of U.S. paintings were buoyant. U.S. Impressionists remained the liveliest segment of the market, with works by Childe Hassam and Mary Cassatt fetching prices from $800,000 to $4 million. "In the Box" by Cassatt set an auction record for an oil painting by the artist, commanding $4 million. John LaFarge's "Paradise Valley" sold for a record $2.2 million. John Singer Sargent's "Capri Girl" made $4.8 million, and Maxfield Parrish's "Daybreak" sold for $4.3 million. At regional auction houses, works by Southern painters continued to rise in value, with Alexander Drysdale and Alice R.H. Smith leading the way.

While Old Masters did not elicit much excitement, "The Fall of Man" by Hendrick Goltzius made $1.5 million, and Canaletto's "A View of the Rialto Bridge" sold for $2 million. Among 19th-century art, Jean-François Millet's "La Cardeuse" fetched $3.1 million, and James Tissot's "Preparing for the Gala" brought $1.8 million.

Latin-American art sales were lacklustre owing to the dearth of important work and a buyer's market. Frida Kahlo's "Los cuatro habitantes de México," 1937, was a hard sell at $882,500. Rufino Tamayo's "Pájaros" went for $288,500, but the best Tamayo on the market, "Danza de la alegriá," failed to sell.

Sales of British paintings pointed to signs of a recovery tempered with continuing selectivity. Christie's single-owner collection of the Marquess of Bute marked the summer's high; the sale totaled £10.7 million. At Sotheby's, William Hogarth's "The Jones Family Conversation Piece" was spared the hammer in a private treaty sale to the National Museums and Galleries of Wales for the greatly reduced sum of £425,000.

Fine prints saw an active upturn, but prices did not rise across the board, and

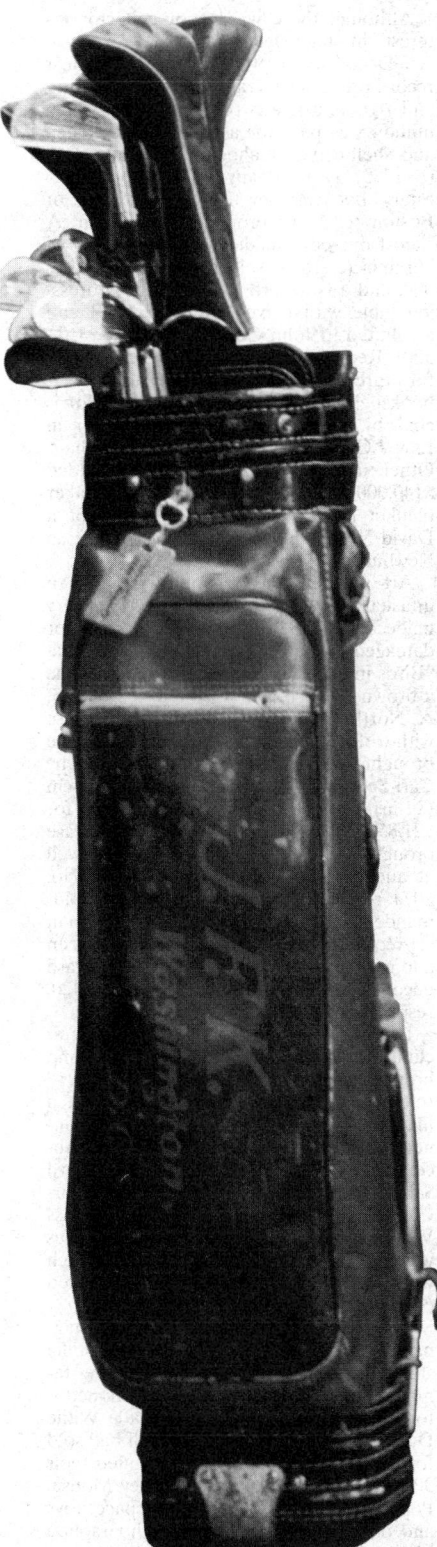

A set of John F. Kennedy's MacGregor wood golf clubs in a bag inscribed "J.F.K. Washington, D.C." was auctioned for $772,500 as part of the April sale of the estate of Jacqueline Kennedy Onassis.
R. MAIMAN—SYGMA

20th-century travel albums earned $23,000, more than four times the estimate. Sotheby's played to the high end of the market with a whole-plate daguerreotype portrait of a Boston surgeon, which made $96,000. Christie's sale of André Kertesz's "Fork" brought $90,500.

For the first six months of the year, Sotheby's reported earnings of $786 million, and Christie's reported $739 million.

(REGINA GALGANO KOLBE)

ANTIQUARIAN BOOKS

Interest in books and manuscripts remained strong in 1996, with private collectors constituting the majority of the buyers and thereby ensuring continuous recirculation of rare and valuable goods. At Christie's, *German Florilegium of the 17th Century,* a manuscript depicting 398 flowers, was sold for its high estimate of $229,000. Leonhard Baldner's *Rechts natürliche Beschreibung und Abmahlung der Wasservögel, Fischen, Vierfissign Thier, Inseckten und Gerwin . . .* (1666–67), depicting the natural history of the Strasbourg region, commanded $137,200. *Biblia Pauperum,* a rediscovered block book forgotten since 1897, sold for £240,000, while a previously unrecorded fragment of an aria by Mozart brought $120,200. A *Louisiana Purchase Proclamation* from the library of Mrs. Charles W. Englehard sold for $772,000 in a postauction private sale.

At Sotheby's the 12-volume *Le Grande Atlas* of 1667 by Willem and Jan Blaeu of the Netherlands commanded $255,000. The Pierre Joseph Redouté "triplets"—*Lilacées,* 1802–16; *Roses,* 1817–24; and *Choix des plus belle fleurs,* 1827–33—fetched $585,000. The Jacqueline Kennedy Onassis estate sale contained 3,000 volumes. The most expensive book, John F. Kennedy's copy of a U.S. Government Printing Office printing of *Inaugural Addresses of the Presidents of the United States,* featuring Kennedy's handwritten notations to his own speech, sold for $134,500. Kennedy's copy of the 1961 *Encyclopædia Britannica World Atlas* with presentation leaf from publisher William Benton, estimated at $400–$600, brought $40,250. Albert Einstein's 1912 autograph manuscript on his theory of relativity, estimated at $4 million to $6 million, sold privately for substantially more than the low estimate.

California Book Auctions sold the 1901 first issue of Beatrix Potter's *The Tale of Peter Rabbit* for $42,000. At Pacific Book Auction Galleries, George Catlin's *American Indian Portfolio, Hunting Scenes and Amusements of the Rocky Mountains and Prairies* fetched $88,000. Felix Paul Wierzbicki's *California as It Is, and as It May Be; or A Guide to the Gold Region* (1849), the first book in English printed in California, commanded $60,500—more than double its presale estimate.

At F. Drölling in Hamburg, Ger., the highest price was reached for the collection of views by Luca Carlevaris, *Le fabriche,*

et vedute di Venezia (1703), which went for $23,300. Among atlases, *Neuer Weltatlas* (Nürnberg, 1712) sold for $22,000.

(REGINA GALGANO KOLBE)

PHILATELY

During 1996 stamp collectors and enthusiasts were offered several chances to view outstanding displays of philatelic items. Collectors attending the Olympic Games in Atlanta, Ga., were treated to a free exhibit, OLYMPHILEX '96, which showcased more than 17,000 pages of Olympic and sports stamps offered since 1896. The event, also known as the World Olympic and Sports Stamp Exhibition, was held July 19–August 3. Britain's Queen Elizabeth II gave permission for selections of the Royal Philatelic Collection—which was started by King George V and remained the personal property of the monarchy—to be shown in public other than at major international philatelic exhibitions. In addition to the customary display at the first meeting of the Royal Philatelic Society, London, over 100 pages of the 1837 Treasury Essays were seen at the autumn STAMPEX in London. A major portion of the Mauritius issues in the Royal Collection from the major 1847 "Post Office" rarities were on view at London's National Postal Museum.

Active buying by senior collectors ensured a healthy market for rare stamps and postal history items. A Hawaii 1852 13-cent blue on cover sold for $286,000, while a Portugal 1853 100-reis lilac, mint pair commanded $235,580. A France 1869 five-franc gray-violet "Laureated," mint block of 30 fetched $118,500, and British stamps, overprinted with a swastika and the date "1940" but not issued by German occupation forces in Jersey, Channel Islands, made £19,900 for a set of 15 different values. The high point of the year came in November with the sale of the Treskilling Yellow. The tiny Swedish stamp, originally issued in the 1850s, sold at auction in Zürich for Sw F 2.9 million ($2.3 million). It was the most ever paid for a stamp and was $1 million more than its previous sale price, in 1990.

The Marshall Islands offered a set of stamps to mark the 50th anniversary of U.S. atomic weapons testing on Bikini atoll. The U.S. Postal Service introduced a number of souvenir stamps to commemorate the Centennial Olympic Games. Also issued in the U.S. were commemorative stamps honouring the Smithsonian Institution's 150th anniversary, Utah's 100-year statehood, and Hollywood legend James Dean. Some 32-cent memorial stamps featuring Pres. Richard Nixon were found inverted; the first one auctioned went for $16,675.

Philatelic history was made in June when the 127-year-old Royal Philatelic Society elected Jane Moubray its first woman president.

(KENNETH F. CHAPMAN)

NUMISMATICS

On March 25, 1996, the U.S. Federal Reserve System began issuing series 1996 100-dollar notes that featured the most sweeping design changes in U.S. paper money since 1929. Among other distinctions, each new note included a watermark, colour-shifting ink, and an enlarged, off-centre portrait, elements expected to make greenbacks more difficult to counterfeit. Although U.S. Trea-

bargains were still to be found. Cassatt's "Woman Bathing" was the season's star, making $321,500. Among Modernists, Marc Chagall's "Four Tales from the Arabian Nights" brought $376,500. Contemporary prints struggled on, with Jasper John's "Flags1" peaking at $57,000.

Swan's in New York reported its strongest photography sale in its history. Two early-

sury officials made reassurances that older 100-dollar notes would not be demonetized, fears of a recall were widespread in Russia, where some traders charged extra to handle them. Federal Reserve notes were the world's best-known currency, with up to $140 billion circulating inside the U.S. and about $250 billion abroad.

The Swiss National Bank unveiled a 20-franc note, the second denomination in a series of high-tech designs. The ultramodern note carried more than 20 security features and had an embossed square at one end to aid the blind.

The coin-auction market set records in 1996 as some of the world's greatest rarities were sold. In May a Kansas City, Mo., dealer paid $1,485,000 for a 1913 Liberty nickel—one of five known—the highest price ever realized for a U.S. coin at public auction. The sale also included a unique 1873 Carson City, Nev., silver dime without arrows at the date, which brought $550,000, a record for a U.S. dime, and a 1796 "no pole" half cent for $506,000, a record for a U.S. copper coin.

In other sales at auction, a 1943 Lincoln cent made in Denver, Colo., on a bronze planchet brought $82,500 in May, a record for a U.S. Lincoln cent, and an ancient Roman coin—a gold aureus of Saturninus—brought £264,000 in a July London sale, possibly a record for a coin of ancient Rome. Meanwhile, the city of Omaha, Neb., sold part of its Byron Reed collection for $6.1 million in October. The proceeds would be used to renovate the museum that housed the remainder of the collection. At year's end a 1907 U.S. Saint-Gaudens 20-dollar piece—with Roman numerals and ultrahigh relief—sold for $825,000, a record auction price for a gold coin.

The U.S. economy generated heavy demand for hard money, and 1996 coin production was expected to exceed the record 19.8 billion pieces made in 1995. Experts predicted that the Bureau of Engraving and Printing would create about 10 billion Federal Reserve notes during the year, a total that included the first two-dollar bills printed since the late 1970s. Among other items, the U.S. Mint sold to collectors 16 coin types commemorating the 1996 Atlanta Centennial Olympic Games and gold and silver pieces honouring the 150th anniversary of the Smithsonian Institution. The U.S. Congress approved legislation that would replace the Washington quarter with 50 circulating commemorative coins, one for each state. The treasury secretary had to conduct a feasibility study and approve the program before coins could be made.

In February Canada began replacing its two-dollar note with a bimetallic coin made with a core of aluminum and bronze and an outer ring of nickel. The Royal Canadian Mint received reports that the core had fallen out of several coins, but mint officials reported that the separated coins they examined had been mutilated. Canada expected to save Can$250 million in production costs over 20 years because coins would last much longer in circulation than bills. The U.K. issued a five-pound coin commemorating the 70th birthday of Queen Elizabeth II on April 21. Australia circulated a 100-dollar note made of plastic, completing a series of five plastic notes that were more durable and harder to counterfeit than paper money.   (ROGER BOYE)

This article updates the *Macropædia* article COINS AND COINAGE.

COLLECTIBLES

The Jacqueline Kennedy Onassis sale was the antiques and collectibles media event of the year. Costume jewelry worn by Onassis sold for 80–90 times the presale estimates. A faux diamond and coloured-stone necklace and earrings estimated at $1,000–$1,500 brought $90,500. Her signature faux pearls sold for $211,500, while her sterling silver Tiffany tape measure fetched $48,875. The golf clubs and bag belonging to her first husband, Pres. John F. Kennedy, brought $772,500. Other presidential memorabilia sold at high, but not unexpected, prices. The desk used when the Nuclear Test-Ban Treaty was signed realized $1.4 million. The president's two oak rocking chairs brought $442,500 and $453,500. (See *Art Auctions and Sales,* above.) These prices fell in the same range as presidential items sold at other auctions during the year. Pres. George Washington's upholstered walnut chair from Mt. Vernon sold for $341,000, and his cut velvet jacket and vest coat brought $577,500.

Trade cards (advertising cards) from the 19th and early 20th centuries continued to rise in price, many selling for over $50 each. Designer-made furniture from the 1960s and '70s sold well in the U.S. and Europe, and American "fantasy" silver continued to sell at higher-than-expected prices.

Although there was major collector interest in high-style Victorian, Western, Art Deco, and 1950s-style furniture, most record prices were realized for 18th-century and Arts and Crafts pieces. A record $3.6 million was paid for a Queen Anne block and shell-carved mahogany kneehole desk (c. 1780). A mahogany bonnet-topped secretary bookcase by Edward Jackson of Boston (c. 1740) brought $1.4 million. A slant-front desk made by John Shearer of Virginia (c. 1816) sold for a record $110,000, and a Newport, R.I., mahogany dressing table with carved shell (c. 1750) and attributed to John Goddard brought $310,500. Records were set for 20th-century furniture, including $9,350 for a Roycroft bookshelf, $12,100 for a flat-armed Morris chair by Gustav Stickley, and $8,625 for an L. & J.G. Stickley paddle-arm Morris chair. Other important furniture sales included $140,000 for a red-orange painted Shaker blanket box (c. 1848) and $96,800 for a David Wood Federal shelf clock made in Newburyport, Mass.

Art pottery sales remained strong. An unusual collection of Van Briggle pottery made before 1920 brought high prices for damaged as well as perfect pieces. A blue "Birds in Flight" vase sold for $4,070, while a brown "Two Bears" vase realized $4,675. A North Dakota School of Mines vase with a decoration of tepees in a landscape brought $3,080. A Rockwood iris vase by Carl Schmidt fetched $41,800, and a 69-cm (27-in) Weller glossy Hudson vase sold for $21,850. A rare 12-cm (5-in) Losanti vase brought $12,100. Mettlach steins sold well at auction; No. 2494 brought $3,630, No. 2074 realized $3,080, and No. 2824 commanded $7,150. Several pieces of Nippon set records, notably a 47-cm (18½-in) green and gold urn and a cobalt and gold tankard decorated with roses at $7,700 and $2,420, respectively.

Lamps with glass shades continued to climb in value. A Handel Poppy lamp brought $55,000. Three Pairpoint "puffies" sold well: a begonia lamp for $35,200, a lilac tree lamp for $55,000, and a rose bonnet lamp for $44,000. Prices for rare 19th-century bottles remained high; a record $40,250 was paid for a sapphire blue Taylor-Cornstalk portrait flask by Baltimore Glass Works. One of the high-priced metal pieces was a Dirk Van Erp red warty vase, which went for $9,350, while a Roycroft hammered copper cylindrical vase brought $2,310.

The baseball card market remained stagnant, but old or rare cards and memorabilia still sold. A postal worker won the famous Honus Wagner card and auctioned it for a record $640,500. A U.S.-made Willie Dunn's Stars and Stripes gutty golf ball sold for $28,600. Toys and dolls continued their 30-year escalation in price. Mickey Mouse, Popeye, celebrity-related, and space toys and dolls all sold well. A tin lithographed Mickey Mouse mechanical bank set a record at $36,850. A 1930s Shirley Temple doll in a Texas Ranger costume, made by Ideal Toy, fetched $5,880, and a plastic Madame Alexander 1957 Infant of Prague doll sold for $56,100. The Calamity iron mechanical bank showing three football players brought $44,000.   (RALPH AND TERRY KOVEL)

This article updates the *Macropædia* articles COINS AND COINAGE; The History of Western PAINTING; PHOTOGRAPHY; The History of Western SCULPTURE.

The new 100-dollar bill issued by the U.S. Federal Reserve System in 1996 includes a watermark, colour-shifting ink, and an enlarged off-centre portrait of Benjamin Franklin in order to make the bills more difficult to counterfeit. These were the most significant design changes in U.S. paper money in nearly 70 years. The U.S. was expected to introduce redesigned 50-dollar bills in 1997 and other denominations in later years.

U.S. TREASURY, BUREAU OF ENGRAVING AND PRINTING

Business and Industry Review

As became clear in 1996, the previous year had been a disappointment in business and industry. Particularly in the industrialized countries, the acceleration of 1994 had faded away as fast as it had appeared. Even then the slowdown that took place in industrial production in 1995 was not fast enough, for demand fell even more rapidly and inventories built up that in many countries continued to act as a drag on output into 1996. Nowhere was this more evident than in the main European economies, where industrial production, having grown about 50% more rapidly than total output in 1994, slowed to a snail's pace in the course of 1995 and early 1996.

Manufacturing production increased by 3.1% in 1995, a sharp deceleration from the 4.7% growth of 1994. The slowdown was more pronounced in the industrialized countries, where it fell from 4.6% to 2.7%. The less-industrialized economies, by contrast, managed to repeat their 5.1% growth of 1994. Even so, there were some spectacular failures, notably Mexico, where output tumbled in 1995 as the cumulative effects of the previous year's currency crisis took hold.

Across the main industrial countries, while the deceleration in activity was common to all, performance varied markedly. The U.S., which might have been expected to show signs of flagging, since it was into its fifth year of recovery, was a surprise on the upside. The growth of industrial production slowed from a near 6% rate in 1994 to a little over 3% in 1995, but, helped by a boom in industrial investment and a resilient consumer, the inventory problem proved short-lived.

The U.S. also benefited from a weak currency, which helped exports outpace im-

Table I. Annual Average Rates of Growth of Manufacturing Output, 1980–95
Percent

Area	1980–86	1987–91	1992	1993	1994	1995
World[1]	2.0	1.7	−0.2	0.2	4.7	3.1
Industrial countries	1.7	1.3	−1.0	−0.5	4.6	2.7
Less industrialized countries	4.3	3.8	3.6	4.3	5.1	5.1

[1] For definition, see Table IV.
Source: UN, *Monthly Bulletin of Statistics*.

Table II. Manufacturing Production in Eastern Europe[1]
1990 = 100

Country	1991	1992	1993	1994	1995	%[2]
Bulgaria[3]	78	65	64	67	68	1
Hungary	75	62	64	70	74	6
Poland	90	94	104	118	136	15
Romania	76	54	54	56	63	13

[1] Former Czechoslovakia and former Soviet Union not available.
[2] % change, latest year shown from previous year.
[3] All industries.
Source: UN, *Monthly Bulletin of Statistics*.

Table III. Pattern of Output, 1992–95
Percent change from previous year

	World[1]				Developed countries				Less-developed countries			
	1992	1993	1994	1995	1992	1993	1994	1995	1992	1993	1994	1995
All manufacturing	0	0	5	3	−1	−1	5	3	4	4	5	5
Heavy industries	−1	0	6	4	−2	−1	6	4	4	6	6	6
Base metals	−3	1	5	3	−3	−1	4	2	2	8	4	5
Metal products	−2	0	6	5	−2	−1	6	5	3	6	7	7
Building materials, etc.	−1	0	4	2	−2	−2	3	1	4	5	6	5
Chemicals	3	1	5	3	2	0	5	3	6	4	5	5
Light industries	1	1	3	1	0	0	2	0	3	3	4	4
Food, drink, tobacco	1	1	3	3	1	1	2	1	4	3	6	6
Textiles	−1	−2	1	−1	−2	−3	0	−3	1	1	3	1
Clothing, footwear	−3	−2	0	−2	−4	−2	0	−3	0	1	1	2
Wood products	1	1	4	0	1	1	4	0	3	2	4	0
Paper, printing	1	2	3	1	1	2	3	1	4	6	3	4

[1] Excluding Albania, China, North Korea, Vietnam, former Czechoslovakia, former Soviet Union, and former Yugoslavia.
Source: UN, *Monthly Bulletin of Statistics*.

Table IV. Index Numbers of Production, Employment, and Productivity in Manufacturing Industries
1990 = 100

Area	Production 1994	Production 1995	Employment 1994	Employment 1995	Productivity[2] 1994	Productivity[2] 1995	Area	Production 1994	Production 1995	Employment 1994	Employment 1995	Productivity[2] 1994	Productivity[2] 1995
World[2]	104	107	...	...	...	...	Denmark	111	116	...	...	...	...
Industrial countries	101	104	...	...	...	...	Finland	108	117	76	81	142	144
Less-industrialized countries	118	122	...	...	...	...	France	99	101	...	...	...	...
North America[3]	115	120	...	...	...	...	Germany (1991 = 100)	94	95	...	...	...	...
Canada	106	110	...	89	...	123	Greece	96	98	...	...	...	...
United States	113	117	96	97	118	121	Ireland	135	162	104	110	130	147
Latin America[4]	111	112	...	...	...	...	Netherlands	101	104	...	...	...	...
Brazil	109	111	...	...	...	...	Norway	109	111	...	...	...	...
Mexico	110	103	...	...	...	...	Portugal	93	96	...	...	...	...
Asia[5]	105	111	...	...	...	...	Sweden	105	115	...	...	...	...
India	113	131	...	...	...	...	Switzerland	107	113	...	...	...	...
Japan	92	95	103	100	90	95	United Kingdom	99	102	...	...	...	...
South Korea	134	151	97	98	138	153	Rest of the world[7]	...	...	...	...	...	...
Europe[6]	94	95	...	...	...	...	Oceania	114	118	...	...	...	...
Austria	104	111	86	...	121	...	South Africa	96	103	96	97	100	106
Belgium	100	104	...	...	...	...							

[1] This is 100 times the production index divided by the employment index, giving a rough indication of changes in output per person employed.
[2] Excluding Albania, China, North Korea, Vietnam, former Czechoslovakia, former Soviet Union, and former Yugoslavia.
[3] Canada and the United States.
[4] South and Central America (including Mexico) and the Caribbean islands.
[5] Asian Middle East and East and Southeast Asia, including Japan, Israel, and Turkey.
[6] Excluding Albania, former Czechoslovakia, former Yugoslavia, and European countries of the former Soviet Union.
[7] Africa and Oceania.
Sources: UN, *Monthly Bulletin of Statistics*; ILO, *Yearbook of Labour Statistics*.

ports. It was the opposite in Japan, which suffered a surge in the value of the yen in the first half of 1995. Added to this were the Kobe earthquake, the weakness of consumer spending, and the import penetration that market liberalization, given extra impetus by a strong yen, provided.

The situation was similar in Europe, where the main economies, which had benefited from strong export-led growth in 1994, were taken by surprise by the slowdown in demand. Throughout Europe inventories built up and held back output, not just in 1995 but also into the first half of 1996. For the main economies of continental Europe, an additional factor was the preparation of the economic and monetary union for convergence of the members' currencies. The need to reduce budget deficits to below 3% of gross domestic product made fiscal deflation the order of the day and held back domestic demand. Given the interdependence of the economies of the European Union (EU), where demand in one country resulted in exports from another, the slowdown in domestic demand was reinforced by a weaker trade performance.

Another factor holding back the EU economies was the drift of new production to the low-cost economies of Eastern Europe, especially those farthest down the road toward economic reform. The Czech Republic and Poland, and to a lesser extent Hungary, were the main beneficiaries of investment from the EU, the effect of which was beginning to be demonstrated by a rapid growth in industrial production in their economies. Even Romania recorded strong growth in 1995.

Elsewhere in the industrializing world, the Asian economies continued to grow rapidly as the search for lower-cost locations moved away from the Pacific Rim into northeastern and southern Asia. While some of the original so-called tiger economies showed signs of their age—manufacturing output had been flat in Hong Kong for a number of years, and South Korea was experiencing the problem of a widening trade gap—the baton had been taken up by China, the biggest of them all. There industrial production rose by more than 20% in 1993 and again in 1994, though it slowed to a more sedate 16% in 1995. Chinese exports rose more than 50% in 1994–95 combined.

As shown by Table IV, since 1990, the base year for the indexes, U.S. industry had raised its output by 17%. The contrast with the other G-7 (Group of Seven major industrial countries) economies was stark. In Japan and Germany industrial output was languishing some 5% below its 1990 levels, while in France, the U.K., and Italy it had barely changed in the five-year period. Only Canada, where output was up 10%, came anywhere close to matching the U.S. performance and that presumably because of the close trading relationship between the two economies.

(GEOFFREY R. DICKS)

ADVERTISING

Bolstered by the traditionally heavy spending associated with both an Olympic Games and a U.S. presidential election year, spending on advertising increased significantly in 1996, with those two events alone pumping as much as $1 billion into the media marketplace.

Total U.S. advertising spending in 1996 was expected to climb 7.4%, to $172.8 billion, from $160.9 billion in 1995, according to forecaster Robert J. Coen of McCann-Erickson Worldwide. He estimated that national advertising spending would rise 7.9%, to $101.7 billion, led by strong growth in television and magazines. Local advertising was expected to increase 6.8%, to $71.1 billion.

Political advertising had the greatest impact on local television stations in the U.S. in 1996, while the Olympic Games boosted spending nationally. NBC, a unit of General Electric, sold a record $675 million in advertising for the Olympics, with the average spot airing in prime time costing advertisers $550,000. Many advertisers bought package deals for $3 million to $20 million. Worldwide, advertisers spent an estimated $5 billion on Olympics-related campaigns, promotions, and events, a total that moved the trade publication *Advertising Age* to declare the 1996 Summer Games "the marketing event of the century."

For 1996 ad spending outside the U.S., Coen predicted a total of $213.1 billion, up 7% from $199.2 billion in 1995. In all, worldwide advertising in all media, including Yellow Pages and direct mail, was expected to climb 7.2%, to $385.9 billion. Much of the increase was attributed to significant growth in spending in countries like China and Mexico.

Signs that 1996 would be a robust year in the U.S. became clear in June when advertisers began buying time for the 1996–97 broadcast television season. Even as its audience was eroding, broadcast TV remained the ad industry's dominant force, with more than $5.6 billion of advertising time sold in what is known as the up-front market. According to Nielsen Media Research, the total share of audience commanded by the six broadcast networks declined from 78% to 74% during the 1995–96 season. The chief reason cited for the decline was that viewers were being attracted to a growing list of alternative programs on cable television.

Still, "Seinfeld" and "ER," both airing on NBC, became the first regularly scheduled network TV series to break the $1 million-per-commercial-minute barrier. "Seinfeld" commanded $550,000 per 30-second spot, while "ER" fetched $500,000 for 30 seconds of commercial time.

Advertisers continued flocking to the World Wide Web, the Internet's most user-friendly area, with scores of start-up companies creating Web advertising for firms like Levi Strauss, Saturn, and Colgate-Palmolive. Web-based advertising came in two forms: a company could set up its own Web site or buy an ad on someone else's site. Web expenditures were still tiny compared with the advertising dollars spent on newspapers, magazines, and TV. Only $37 million was spent on Web advertising in all of 1995, although the figure jumped to $66.7 million in the first half of 1996, according to Jupiter Communications. Long-term growth, however, might be stalled until the ad industry agreed on a way to measure the number of Web users who saw ads and the impression they made.

Another controversy over audience measurement methods erupted when Advance Publication's Condé Nast division publicly dismissed Mediamark Research after complaining that the firm's audience surveys

were outmoded and unwieldy. An industry task force convened by the Magazine Publishers of America joined with advertisers and media research companies to find ways to make the data more stable.

Seagram officially ended the liquor industry's almost five-decade-old self-imposed practice of not advertising on television by airing a series of 30-second commercials for Chivas Regal and Crown Royal Canadian whiskeys on stations in Boston and Corpus Christi, Texas. The company's stance was that it was seeking to level the playing field with beer and wine, which advertised freely on television. There never had been a federal prohibition of advertising distilled spirits on television.

One of the year's largest advertising campaigns came from McDonald's, which in May launched a $75 million introduction of the Arch Deluxe, the signature sandwich of a new line. The so-called deluxe sandwiches were aimed at increasing the chain's adult patronage.

Tough new restrictions on the advertising of tobacco, proposed by U.S. Pres. Bill Clinton, would ban all imagery on outdoor advertising, in most magazine ads, and at points of sale. Tobacco companies would be barred from giving away brand name merchandise and from using brand names in sponsoring events or sports teams. Advertising trade groups claimed that the restrictions, which would become effective in 1997, would have an impact of $1,140,000,000 annually in spending on tobacco marketing, and they opposed the ban on the basis that it would restrict the advertising of what were legal products in the U.S.

Consolidation among ad agencies continued in 1996. Paris-based Publicis acquired a controlling interest in BCP, the seventh largest ad agency in Canada, and also bought 51% of Romero y Asociados, in Mexico City, and 60% of Norton Publicidade, based in Brazil. D'Arcy Masius Benton & Bowles, meanwhile, agreed to buy N.W. Ayer & Partners, which was the oldest U.S. advertising agency, founded in 1869 in Philadelphia. Omnicom Group acquired Ketchum Communications, a specialty business marketing firm.

Despite some progress, women remained unhappy with the way they were depicted in

Most Valuable Brands Worldwide		
1995 rank (1994 rank)	Brand name	Brand value
1 (2)	Marlboro	$44,614,000,000
2 (1)	Coca-Cola	$43,427,000,000
3 (—)	McDonald's	$18,920,000,000
4 (3)	IBM	$18,491,000,000
5 (—)	Disney	$15,358,000,000
6 (7)	Kodak	$13,267,000,000
7 (9)	Kellogg's	$11,409,000,000
8 (8)	Budweiser	$11,026,000,000
9 (10)	Nescafé	$10,527,000,000
10 (11)	Intel	$10,499,000,000
11 (12)	Gillette	$10,292,000,000
12 (4)	Motorola	$ 9,624,000,000
13 (14)	GE	$ 9,304,000,000
14 (13)	Pepsi	$ 8,895,000,000
15 (—)	Sony	$ 8,800,000,000
16 (5)	Hewlett-Packard	$ 8,111,000,000
17 (16)	Frito-Lay	$ 7,786,000,000
18 (15)	Levi's	$ 7,376,000,000
19 (—)	Nike	$ 7,267,000,000
20 (19)	Campbell's	$ 6,464,000,000

Source: *Financial World*, July 8, 1996.

advertising, according to a survey by Saatchi & Saatchi Advertising, a unit of Cordiant. The ads that appealed to the women polled reflected values they considered important, such as the ability to be both caring and competent. This suggested that if advertisers created messages celebrating these values and accurately conveying women's changing roles, they were more likely to succeed.   (LAURIE FREEMAN)

AEROSPACE

The economic health of airlines generally continued to rise throughout 1996. Predictions were that profits for the U.S. industry would break all records, despite a substantial rise in spot fuel prices as a result of Middle East tensions and the failure of Iraqi oil to come on-line. Improvements were attributed to severe cost containment, closer control between traffic and capacity, more stable fares, and the pruning of unprofitable operations. British Airways, which maintained its standing as one of the world's most efficient operators, said that it would cut 5,000 jobs (10% of its workforce) and reduce cabin staff wages by 40%.

Because airline revenues had improved, there came a surge of orders for new aircraft as well. By August backlogs stood at 1,114 for Boeing, 211 for McDonnell Douglas, and 651 for the European consortium Airbus Industrie. Boeing announced plans to take on an additional 10,000 workers by year's end, although hiring was difficult as workers began to rebel at the continuous stop-and-go pattern of employment characteristic of the aerospace industry.

The two principal commercial transport builders, Boeing and Airbus, began positioning themselves for the next round of orders. Boeing's major new project was the 500-seat 747-500/600, to succeed the 747-400, with the company projecting sales of some 350 aircraft through the year 2014. Also a priority was the Boeing 777-100X very-long-range twin-engined transport. Boeing hoped to launch both types by the end of the year. Airbus was looking for international partners—perhaps a consortium of South Korea, Taiwan, and Singapore—to launch the 540-seat, double-deck A3XX long-range, wide-body transport during 1997–98, at an estimated cost of $8 billion. Russia was viewed as another potential A3XX partner, with perhaps a 20–25% stake. Meanwhile, to broaden its product base, McDonnell Douglas was studying the MD-20, a project midway between its 300-seat MD-11 trijet and the 150-seat MD-90 "twin."

To power the new U.S. and European four-engined transports, the two U.S. big-engine companies, Pratt & Whitney and General Electric, agreed to pool their resources to produce a more efficient engine of approximately 76,000 lb of thrust. Given the huge cost of developing the new high-bypass power plants, they felt that the big-engine market was not adequate to support three companies (the third being Great Britain's Rolls-Royce).

The industry's most spectacular news—the $13 billion acquisition of McDonnell Douglas by Boeing—was announced in mid-December. Moving quickly after McDonnell Douglas had been eliminated from the bidding on the Pentagon's huge Joint Strike Fighter project, Boeing concluded

Mechanics work on a jet engine at a maintenance centre of EVA Air in Taipei. The airline, which was founded in 1989 by the Evergreen Group of Taiwan and offered both passenger and cargo service, owed its spectacular success in part to high maintenance standards.

the largest aerospace merger in history and created a behemoth of a company with 200,000 employees and $48 billion in estimated revenues for 1997.

The European regional aircraft business consolidated when British Aerospace joined with ATR (itself a consortium of France's Aerospatiale and Italy's Alenia) to form Aero International Regional, a marketing company, for their range of such aircraft.

In January Germany's Daimler-Benz AG group abandoned its historic but ailing Dutch subsidiary, aircraft builder Fokker. The Dutch government gave the company short-term funding to continue work on its backlog of regional transport aircraft while potential purchasers were sought; the manufacturer, however, declared bankruptcy in March. By year's end hopes had fizzled that the Korean Samsung group might buy in. Daimler-Benz also disposed of Dornier, another historic name, to a holding company with an 80% share held by Fairchild of the U.S.

The French industry also continued in crisis, and the government requested that Aerospatiale and Dassault merge to form a single, national airframe group, with a view toward privatization. Thomson SA would become the core of the national defense and electronics group.

The Arab and Pacific Rim countries continued to expand their aerospace visibility by means of the burgeoning number of international air shows in Dubai, Malaysia, Singapore, Indonesia, South Korea, and China. Berlin and Farnborough, Eng., constituted Europe's shows.

Farnborough was notable for the first appearance of the experimental Russian Sukhoi Su-37 long-range fighter. It demonstrated an amazing tumble maneuver that

in combat would enable its weapon sensors to lock on to an adversary regardless of its position relative to the enemy fighter. Also at Farnborough, Britain signed up to launch production of the Eurofighter 2000—Europe's biggest military aircraft program—and waited for partners Italy, Germany, and Spain to do likewise. The Northrop B-2 stealth bomber flew direct to Farnborough from the U.S. on the first day, circled the show but did not land, and returned to its base. It represented the kind of strategic, long-range operation that U.S. Air Force B-52s had achieved earlier in the summer, operating against Iraq from a U.K. airfield in the Indian Ocean because no other country would base them.

The most famous name in U.S. airline history came to the fore again in 1996 when, during September, a revived Pan Am (the original had gone bankrupt in 1991) began scheduled services with three aircraft. The new company, however, intended to operate only an internal, long-haul U.S. route network, a far cry from the international visibility of the famed flag carrier of earlier times.   (MICHAEL WILSON)

APPAREL

Clothing. Allegations of widespread sweatshop and labour abuses, both in the U.S. and elsewhere, plagued the apparel-manufacturing industry in 1996. The discovery of an apparel factory in El Monte, Calif., where undocumented Thai immigrants were being forced to work off the cost of their passage to the U.S. galvanized government and union activists. The issue exploded into the public consciousness when television talk show host Kathie Lee Gifford was accused of using sweatshops in Honduras and New York City in the manufacture of women's apparel bearing her name. Gifford made tearful protestations of innocence and indignation. Such celebrities as Michael Jordan, Jaclyn Smith, and Kathy Ireland were also accused of using sweatshops in the manufacture of their apparel and footwear lines.

The U.S. apparel-manufacturing industry struggled to adapt to increased foreign competition brought about by the North American Free Trade Agreement and by the gradual elimination of trade barriers under the World Trade Organization. Apparel manufacturing in the U.S. continued its employment decline, dropping to 833,-000 workers by September 1996. Increasing competition from low-wage countries caused more U.S. companies to consolidate their domestic operations and, in some cases, to move production facilities offshore to Mexico and Central America.

U.S. consumers again split their apparel dollars equally between U.S.-manufactured and imported clothing. The source of imported apparel continued its shift from traditional suppliers in East Asia (China, South Korea, Taiwan, and Hong Kong) to Mexico and Central America. The adoption of "quick-response" manufacturing practices by U.S. companies, in answer to retailers' demands for short-cycle production and just-in-time inventory, prompted greater U.S. investment in manufacturing facilities in the Western Hemisphere. The recurring spectre of a trade war with China, reinforced by a proposed U.S. government sanction list of apparel and textiles from that country, also caused many U.S. importers to look for more reliable sources of apparel products.

Price deflation made consumer apparel one of the best values for disposable income in 1996, yet spending did not increase demonstrably. Among the bright spots were garments appropriate for casual office wear, a category that appeared to confuse many consumers and that prompted huge retail promotions. A survey conducted by Levi Strauss & Co. indicated that as many as 90% of all U.S. workplaces had adopted a casual policy, with more and more companies, such as IBM and the Ford Motor Co., switching to a full-time casual policy. Another interesting shift in apparel consumption was an apparent shift to "investment" purchases; consumers during the 1995 holiday shopping season seemed to buy a few comparatively expensive luxury items, rather than ordinary apparel.

(ALLISON WHEELER WOLF)

Footwear. Faced with a dwindling number of merchants and dramatic decreases in same-store sales in the fourth quarter of 1995, many shoe companies were faced in 1996 with the strategy of wooing retailers and sacrificing margins. Such name brands as Converse, L.A. Gear, K-Swiss, and Stride Rite's Keds division recorded losses. While third-quarter profits sank for Reebok International, which sold its Avia brand, growth was seen by fashion brands Nine West Group and Wolverine World Wide—maker of Hush Puppies, Caterpillar, and Wolverine Wilderness—which posted soaring third-quarter results. Timberland, after suffering losses in the second quarter, reported that third-quarter earnings more than doubled. Giants Nike and Fila Holding had record-shattering sales.

The Olympic Games, held in Atlanta, Ga., marked one of the biggest promotional blitzes ever put forth by athletic footwear companies, with Nike, Reebok, Adidas America, and Fila spending more than $100 million on advertising. Nike spent a record $35 million, and Reebok spent about $30 million plus the $20 million it laid out as the official footwear supplier.

Footwear stocks were dragged down by disastrous performances by companies such as Edison Brothers Stores, operator of Bakers and the Wild Pair stores, which was in bankruptcy proceedings. Woolworth received a shareholder proposal to spin off its athletic footwear chains, including Foot Locker. Melville spun off its footwear operations to shareholders, creating an entity named Footstar that would include FootAction USA and Meldisco's leased shoe departments in Kmart stores. In addition, Melville disclosed plans to close down its remaining Thom McAn stores by mid-1997.

May Department Stores decided to spin off its Payless ShoeSource operation. As part of the deal, Payless closed or relocated about 450 stores in the second quarter of 1996. Herman's Sporting Goods liquidated, but Finish Line reported that it planned to open 75 stores in two years, and Melville said that it would convert up to 100 of its former Thom McAn sites to FootAction stores. Sports Authority said that it also planned to add 55 to 60 locations within a year.

(BONNIE BABER)

Furs. Retail sales of fur apparel bounced back strongly in the frigid early months of 1996 as one of the harshest winters on record boosted fur sales by 10–20% over the previous year's sales of $1.2 billion and brought industry inventories to their lowest levels in years. Animal rights organizations had claimed credit for having put a damper on U.S. fur sales, which had peaked at $1.9 billion in 1987 before falling to half that amount and then rising steadily.

Furriers witnessed the sharpest increases in skin prices in memory. World production of both ranched and wild furs had dropped precipitously since 1987, when the market collapsed because of oversupply and a decline in demand as a result of worldwide economic recession and a series of mild winters. Not only were there fewer pelts to supply the traditional markets, but there was also a tremendous increase in demand from Russia and China, two large fur consumers that had historically relied on their own domestic supplies. Sudden economic growth in those countries was accompanied by a major upswing in consumer demand for luxury items. The two countries became new competitors for the world's fur supplies, joining South Korea, which had entered the market a few years earlier.

Another positive factor was the increased use and promotion of furs by major international fashion designers, many of whom had never used furs before and were now using them as trimmings on their textile and leather outerwear and for such accessories as hats—in such countries as Russia and China. At the same time, there was an increase in favourable media coverage, which featured furs in fashions and downplayed coverage of antifur demonstrations.

Members of the Animal Liberation Front raided 22 mink farms, liberating animals and causing millions of dollars in damage. An agreement was reached in December that would enable Canada and Russia to continue to ship furs into the European Union (EU), which had legislated a ban on such items from countries that had not outlawed the use of steel-jawed leghold traps. The U.S., the world's largest fur source, was still balking at year's end and faced the prospect of having its goods alone banned from EU countries. (SANDY PARKER)

AUTOMOBILES

The year 1996 represented a milestone for U.S. automakers and their suppliers. The U.S. industry celebrated its 100th anniversary, tracing its roots to the 13 cars built by the Duryea brothers in 1896 rather than to any of the single vehicles that had preceded the series they produced. Yet while the industry trumpeted its centennial with a number of celebrations, it did not burden itself with sentimentality. General Motors abandoned its longtime headquarters in midtown Detroit, which had been built by its first chairman, William Durant, and which had been the largest office building in the world when it was completed in 1920. Ironically, GM moved into the glass towers of the Renaissance Center in downtown Detroit, which had been built by Henry Ford II, and quickly notified the Ford Motor Co. that it would not renew Ford's leases in the office complex.

From a more immediate standpoint, 1996 marked the greatest period of prosperity the U.S. auto industry had enjoyed in 30 years. Not since the 1960s had there been such ongoing strength in the market. The industry entered its fourth straight year of solid sales, strong employment, and robust earnings, largely thanks to the resilience of the U.S. economy and the continuing boom in the truck segment, which continued to be dominated by the Big Three.

Sales of new vehicles in Japan, however, were up only 1.5%, and they still had not recovered their levels of the late 1980s. In Europe sales were slightly stronger, but they were well below the record set in 1992. Several less-developed markets such as China and Argentina struggled through rough economic conditions. The Mexican market, while showing great percentage gains, continued to run far below the sales levels it had enjoyed just a few years earlier.

The length of the U.S. automotive recovery prompted many analysts to wonder how long it could last. The growth of gross domestic product came under increasing scrutiny, since the U.S. consistently devoted about 4.5% of its GDP to the purchase of new vehicles. As long as the U.S. economy continued to grow, analysts reasoned, the automotive market would too. During the year the economy continued to post ongoing, albeit modest, growth, with low levels of inflation, interest rates, and unemployment. These conditions led economists at the Big Three to conclude that the strong auto market would continue well into 1997, and they forecast a sales rate of slightly over 15 million units, compared with about 15.3 million units in 1996.

While some industry observers also began wondering how long the truck segment could continue to grow, it showed no signs of abating. Whereas the total U.S. market grew more than 3% in 1996, truck sales jumped more than 8%. Passenger car sales were essentially flat. The truck segment accounted for 43% of the total market, and there were few analysts who doubted that by the end of the decade trucks would account for one of every two vehicles sold. (Of course, the fact that vans and sport utility vehicles, not just pickups, were classified as trucks affected these numbers.)

The domestic U.S. automakers benefited tremendously from their dominance in the truck segment, which stood at an impressive 86% share. Not only was the segment growing strongly, but it also generated a disproportionate amount of U.S. automakers' profits. On some top-of-the-line vehicles, such as the Ford Expedition, Chevrolet Suburban, and Jeep Grand Cherokee, financial analysts estimated that each automaker was earning as much as $10,000 in variable profits.

General Motors, Ford, and Chrysler each offered a mix of truck products that greatly appealed to customers, but they also continued to benefit from U.S. gasoline prices, which by world standards were extremely low. Gasoline prices in Europe and Japan were two to three times more than they were in the U.S. The low price of fuel in the U.S., about $1.30 per gallon, continued to encourage buyers to opt for full-size trucks, vans, and sport utility vehicles with large V-6 and V-8 engines. Since there were few other markets in the world where such vehicles were competitive, few foreign automakers were willing to make the huge investment needed to develop these types of trucks and engines. Those foreign automakers who chose to sell pickups in the U.S. also had to make them in the U.S. or pay a 25% import duty. In late 1995 Japan's largest and richest automaker, Toyota, announced that it would build a new plant in Princeton, Ind., to make 100,000 full-size pickup trucks annually. No other foreign automaker revealed plans to do the same, however.

That did not stop Japanese automakers from trying to find their own niche in the truck segment, with smaller sport utility vehicles priced under the more popular U.S. models. Toyota began importing the RAV4 to the U.S. market, and its immediate sales success prompted Honda to announce that it would import the CR-V. Subaru also announced that it would bring in the Streega from Japan. The South Korean automaker Kia also introduced the Sportage, which was priced below the Japanese entries. The Sportage also pioneered the first application of a knee air bag. The air bag deployed quickly just below the steering column and pushed the driver's knees back, thus straightening the torso and putting the driver in a better position for the chest air bag, which deployed a fraction of a second later.

Upscale sport utility vehicles were not the only products to attract affluent buyers. Most European luxury cars enjoyed a double-digit sales growth in 1996, while their U.S. and Japanese counterparts floundered. BMW, Mercedes-Benz, Audi, Porsche, and Jaguar all benefited from new models, most of them aggressively priced, that stole sales away from the Japanese luxury brands. Volkswagen, too, enjoyed a healthy sales surge. Yet despite their recent success, the European brands were just starting to get back to the sales levels they had enjoyed in the mid- to late 1980s.

The year was also marked by strikes and labour negotiations. In March the United Automobile Workers struck two General Motors plants in Dayton, Ohio, that made brake parts. The union objected to GM's buying antilock brakes from Robert Bosch GmbH, an outside supplier, instead of building them in-house. The practice of buying parts that formerly had been made in-house, commonly called outsourcing, was a particularly contentious issue between manufacturers and labour unions. The shortage of brake parts from the idled Dayton plants quickly forced most other GM plants to close as well. The strike lasted only 17 days, but before it was over, GM had lost 96,000 vehicles, and the company blamed a $900 million loss in the second quarter on the lost production. Most analysts felt, however, that General Motors had showed a new resolve in taking on the union, something it had been reluctant to do earlier, when its balance sheet was weak and it was losing money in North America.

Later, in the fall, each of the Big Three and many of their suppliers had to negotiate a new three-year labour contract with both the UAW and the Canadian Automobile Workers. Ford and Chrysler breezed through their negotiations with virtually no disruptions, but GM ran into difficulties, especially with the CAW. Once again the issue centred on outsourcing and job security, and once again the company lost significant amounts of production. GM's troubles with its unions stemmed from the fact that it needed to negotiate a contract that would allow it to shed a staggering 50,000 to 60,000 workers in order to match the productivity levels that Ford and Chrysler had achieved. The difficulty was compounded by the fact that Ford and Chrysler had completed most of their outsourcing during the severe automotive recession of the early 1980s, while General Motors was trying to reduce its workforce drastically during a prosperous period, something the unions resisted.

Designers work on a prototype of the Smart, an automobile that was being developed by Mercedes-Benz and the watchmaker Swatch. The so-called microcar, just 2.3 m (7.5 ft) long, was to be sold in Europe beginning in 1998 and marketed to city dwellers as a second vehicle.

At first blush the contracts settled with each of the unions seemed to be decidedly pro-labour. They guaranteed that each automaker would retain 95% of its workforce during the length of the contract. Every hourly employee was given a $2,000 signing bonus, and over the life of the contract each employee would earn an additional $10,000 in wages and benefits. Each automaker also committed itself to looking for opportunities to bring more work in-house to preserve jobs.

As more details of the contracts began to leak out, however, it became apparent that the automakers had negotiated enough loopholes to allow them to achieve ongoing reductions in the cost of labour. It was learned, for example, that the 95% job guarantee applied only to outsourcing. Any plant that was able to reduce its workforce by means of productivity improvements would not be held to the 95% level. Nor did the guarantee apply to contract workers or to plants that were sold, and it would not apply during an economic downturn. Moreover, any new workers hired to make automotive parts, as opposed to those involved in vehicle or power train assembly, could be paid a substantially lower wage.

The Office for the Study of Automotive Transportation (OSAT), affiliated with the University of Michigan, released a study showing that over 30% of the automotive workforce was already more than 50 years old. The study predicted that more than 40% of this hourly and salaried workforce, representing several hundred thousand people, would retire by 2003.

As automakers continued to outsource more work to supplier companies, those companies in turn experienced a great increase in their business. The larger supplier companies embarked on a major buying spree during the year, trying to acquire smaller companies. They did so for several reasons. First, they were trying to broaden their technical capabilities and product lines. Second, they were essentially buying new customers by acquiring firms that did business with other automakers or even other suppliers. Third, they were trying to expand their presence in overseas markets. A report from Morgan Stanley showed that during the period from February 1995 through February 1996, there were 75 acquisitions of publicly traded supplier companies, nearly two a week, representing $17 billion in transactions.

Some of the more notable mergers and acquisitions during the year included the giant German supplier Robert Bosch, which paid $1.5 billion in cash for the brake business of AlliedSignal (the company that had long been known as Bendix). Hayes Wheels International and the Motor Wheel Corp. merged in a $1.1 billion deal. Lucas Industries and the Varity Corp. merged to form a $6.7 billion company.

The giant seating supplier Lear bought Automotive Industries and Masland. Lear's formidable competitor Johnson Controls purchased the Prince Corp. for $1,350,-000,000. Tenneco bought Clevite for $300 million, snatching it away from Mayflower at the last moment. Sweden's Autoliv acquired the auto-safety division of the U.S.-based Morton for $750 million to form a giant air-bag supplier. Finally, Textron bought Germany's Kautex Group for more than $300 million.

All of this activity led several executives at Chrysler and Ford to denounce it as "merger mania." They warned suppliers that it was not necessary to own other companies and that they could get the same benefits by cooperating with them instead of buying them. The automakers worried about supplier executives being distracted by their acquisition activity. They also openly wondered how suppliers would manage their debt loads during the next economic downturn.

For their part, however, many supplier executives suspected that the automakers simply did not like the fact that supplier companies were becoming so big and powerful. They assumed that the automakers opposed their growth because suppliers would be in a better position to resist pressures to cut prices. Besides, they argued, mergers and acquisitions enabled them to achieve better value for their stockholders. The facts seemed to bear them out. The stock of the publicly traded automotive supplier companies actually outperformed the Standard & Poor's 500 index, including the stock performance of the automakers themselves.

Elsewhere in the supply business, General Motors and Ford studied the possibility of selling parts to each other as they tried to increase their presence in the Southeast Asian market. Rather than have each company build components for itself in this part of the world, GM's Delphi and Ford's Automotive Parts Operations discussed how they could coordinate their activities to prevent any overlap. They were especially interested in not duplicating factories that required heavy capital investment. The companies also studied how they might locate their supplier plants close to one another's assembly plants. Japanese automakers already did much the same thing in some Asian countries. Toyota, for example, made engine cylinder blocks for Nissan and Isuzu in Thailand. Nissan, in turn, made engine cylinder heads for the others, while Isuzu made connecting rods and camshafts.

Toyota and Honda also introduced cars designed specifically for the Southeast Asian market that were not just stripped-down versions of existing cars. Toyota's car, called the Affordable Family Car, or AFC, was derived from the company's four-door Tercel. To hold prices to affordable levels ($12,000 to $16,000), Toyota dropped certain equipment such as antipollution devices, a heater, and some safety beams. Nonetheless, it offered air-conditioning, a modern design, and the possibility of optional air bags on higher-priced models. Honda introduced the City, a four-door subcompact that was developed exclusively for the region and was powered by a 1.3-litre engine.

Ford increased its equity in its Japanese partner, Mazda, to 33.4% from 24.5%, effectively taking legal control of the company. Ford also named Henry Wallace president of Mazda, the first time in history that a non-Japanese executive had run a Japanese auto company. The need for Ford's financial involvement was clear. Mazda's debt had swelled to $7 billion, and it had lost money. Ford also pulled several product-development programs out of the U.S. and Europe in favour of Mazda. Specifically, it yanked development of a new engine family (known as the I-4/I-5

program) out of Europe and gave it to the Japanese company. It also killed a small sport utility vehicle being developed in the U.S. in favour of a joint Ford-Mazda program that was already under way. This undoubtedly helped Mazda, but several European and U.S. supplier companies that had invested in the projects were angry at being left out.

General Motors became the first major automaker in the modern era to offer a mass-produced electric-powered vehicle. Called the EV1, it became available for lease at Saturn dealerships in Los Angeles and San Diego, Calif., and in Phoenix and Tucson, Ariz. The move was part of a deal that automakers had reached with the California Air Resources Board. The CARB agreed to drop its 1998 mandate that 2% of automakers' sales in California had to be electric vehicles, provided that automakers agreed to introduce electric vehicles. The CARB did not, however, rescind its mandate that 10% of all vehicles sold in 2003 had to be electrics. Toyota and Honda quickly announced their own plans to make electric-powered vehicles available in 1997. Other automakers were also expected to announce similar plans.

Air bags came under scrutiny in 1996 when they were identified as potentially lethal devices for children and for short drivers, especially small women. To protect unbelted occupants in a car, as required by law, air bags needed to deploy very quickly. Because they deployed at nearly 325 km/h (200 mph), they were dangerous for anyone who was too close to them and potentially lethal for anyone small enough to be flung back by them. Air bags were identified as the cause of death for a small number of children and adults involved in minor accidents and as the cause of abrasions, bruises, and broken ribs for some adults.

Safety advocates called for the introduction of so-called smart bags that would sense how quickly or powerfully they had to deploy, depending on the size and position of the occupant. Automakers countered that the technology for smart bags was not yet reliable. They argued instead in favour of air bags that would not deploy as quickly yet would protect passengers who wore seat belts. Both sides urged parents to keep their children belted in the backseat. The National Highway Traffic Safety Administration contemplated issuing a regulation mandating a more stringent warning label in cars. At the end of the year, however, the issue had not been resolved.

(JOHN MCELROY)

BEVERAGES

Beer. The largest U.S. brewers were determined to be as many things to as many people as possible in 1996 in an effort to generate more than marginal growth. Anheuser-Busch, Miller Brewing, and Adolph Coors all made no secret of their desire to cut in on the booming craft beer market, and, just as they had in 1994 and 1995, all three indulged in an upscale, low-volume strategy, trying to pluck off microbrewing's relatively few but valuable consumers.

More important, however, the large brewers paid close attention to their mainstream marketing efforts. Reasoning that the premium segment was the biggest of all, Coors relaunched its Original Coors brand as "the last real beer." Similarly, Miller lent its trademark to a new label simply called Miller Beer. Each was trying to siphon off shares from Anheuser-Busch's Budweiser, the sales leader.

Anheuser-Busch, the world's largest brewer, took shots at its much-smaller competitors in 1996. The company introduced dating to remind drinkers that Budweiser was fresh, not "skunked" (stale), as some imports tended to be. When Budweiser radio ads lambasted a competitor for not being what it said it was, the competitor was not Miller or Coors. It was instead the comparatively small Boston Beer, the marketer of the leading microbrew, Samuel Adams, which Anheuser-Busch criticized for not brewing in Boston. By year's end Anheuser-Busch had come up with Pacific Ridge Pale Ale, just for California.

As for the craft-style beers that had led the revolution in taste, they continued to increase their sales in double-digit percentages in 1996 while at the same time proliferating in numbers. It was estimated that by year's end there were 4,400 brands of beer available in North America, most of them created by small brewpubs (restaurants that made their own beer) for limited clientele. Still, the many beers available continued to affect tastes, whether they appealed to the traditional consumer or to those willing to experiment, even with fruit flavours. So-called alcopops, like an alcoholic lemonade, became popular in Australia and the U.K., and several companies were exploring their possibilities in the U.S.

Spirits. The marketing development of 1996 involved advertising practice in the U.S. After 60 years of voluntarily avoiding the airwaves, the sellers of distilled spirits in the U.S. declared that they would change their policy. Liquor, like beer and wine, would seek customers through radio and television advertising, a common practice elsewhere in the world.

The spirits industry called it a matter of equity. Beer companies called this a specious argument (given the difference in the alcoholic content of a glass of spirits and a mug of beer) and did not care to be lumped with the so-called hard liquor industry. Would-be guardians of morals, from Pres. Bill Clinton on down, fretted that whiskey commercials would be bad for children. The chairman of the Federal Communications Commission, Reed Hundt, talked about new regulations; others planned to turn to Congress for a solution. The major broadcast networks declared that they did not want to run such ads anyway, but local stations and cable operators did not seem to mind. One thing was apparent. By running almost no advertising but merely talking about it, the spirits industry had probably gained more publicity than at any time since the repeal of Prohibition in 1933. Ironically, the talk of instituting new advertising regulations for alcoholic beverages came at a time when there was relatively little pressure to enact prohibitionist legislation. Drunk-driving figures had steadily declined over the previous decade, and some watchdog groups had come to recognize that alcohol marketers were taking a substantial measure of responsibility for the use of their goods.

The sales of spirits continued to lag. Demographers pointed to an aging population that was not as interested as its parents were in traditional bar drinks. The industry responded in 1996 by unleashing wave after wave of unique products. Among the spirits introduced were Teton Glacier Potato Vodka; Rain Vodka, the first American vodka to be distilled from organically grown ingredients; a zesty line of liqueurs from Belgium called Smeets FruitJenever; and, in a nod to craft brewers, Jacob's Well, billed as "the world's first micro-bourbon." The most unusual package was for Rohol, a German whiskey drink that came in a miniature crude-oil can. (GREG W. PRINCE)

Wine. Vintage 1996 provided the usual roller-coaster ride of good and bad results. In California and Oregon the vintage was generally fairly good, continuing a trend of the entire decade of the 1990s. The real problem there was of supply and demand. As more Americans consumed a more varied selection of wines, the demand for premium-quality wines drove prices generally higher if suitable grapes could be found at all. This was exemplified by merlot, whose prices soared as supplies dwindled.

In Europe the outlook was generally optimistic. French growers had to deal with rains just prior to harvest, but these were not a great problem except for the "right bank" wines of Pomerol and Saint Emilion in Bordeaux and in the wines of the southern Rhone Valley.

Medoc was promising a good vintage; Burgundy growers were enthusiastic, especially about their whites; Alsace should prove an exceptional vintage; and the northern Rhone Valley should produce some fine wines. Champagne producers were expected to declare a vintage and were excited about the quality of the grapes. In Italy Tuscan producers promised a good vintage, while their colleagues in the Piedmont were happy with the results of the harvest.

Southern Hemisphere producers continued to improve the quality of their wines. Australia was plagued by drought, and so the crops were small. The increased demand for wine in Australia, therefore, led to less wine being available for export. South American wines continue to become more available and were of improved quality. South African wines gained in availability and popularity.

Sales continued strong, with a more international flavour to consumption. Increasing numbers of producers on both sides of the Atlantic were sending their products overseas, giving consumers a more varied selection. (HOWARD HERING)

Soft Drinks. People could not miss Coca-Cola in 1996 if they watched the Olympic Games, held in the carbonation giant's headquarter city, Atlanta, Ga. The company invested an estimated $500 million to plaster its name all over the world's most watched event. Later in the year Coca-Cola swooped into Venezuela, one of the few markets where it was outsold by Pepsi-Cola, and reversed the situation by signing with Pepsi's powerful bottler, the Cisneros Group. Pepsi struck back in November by signing a deal with Polar, the Venezuelan brewer and packager, to bottle and distribute its goods.

As U.S. soft drink consumption continued to increase at a better than 3% annual clip, both Pepsi and Coke managed to enjoy good fortunes at home. Pepsi inaugurated "Pepsi Stuff," a promotion that allowed consumers to save "points" from packages and receive apparel and sporting goods with the Pepsi logo. Outside the U.S., the company began Project Blue, which included a newly designed blue can.

While colas remained king throughout the world, there was no shortage of contenders for "next big thing" in 1996. At a time when Snapple and AriZona iced tea sales were lagging, a vacuum was waiting to be filled. There were soft drinks with names like Black Lemonade and exotic ingredients like ma huang and ginkgo biloba. Energy drinks included Guts, made with guarana, a South American extract said to offer beneficial effects. Even cola was not safe from spice, whether it be sodas spiked with coffee (including one marketed by Pepsi) or the U.S. debut of the British sensation Virgin Cola. In December Coca-Cola introduced Surge, a high-calorie and high-caffeine citrus drink targeted at Pepsico's Mountain Dew market.

Clearly Canadian grabbed a wave of publicity in 1996 by floating gelatinous spheres in a juice drink and calling it Orbitz. Yet for all the effort that many entrepreneurial companies invested into gaining the spotlight, the most publicity went to a simple

**Leading Spirits-Consuming Countries in 1995
(in litres of pure alcohol per capita)**

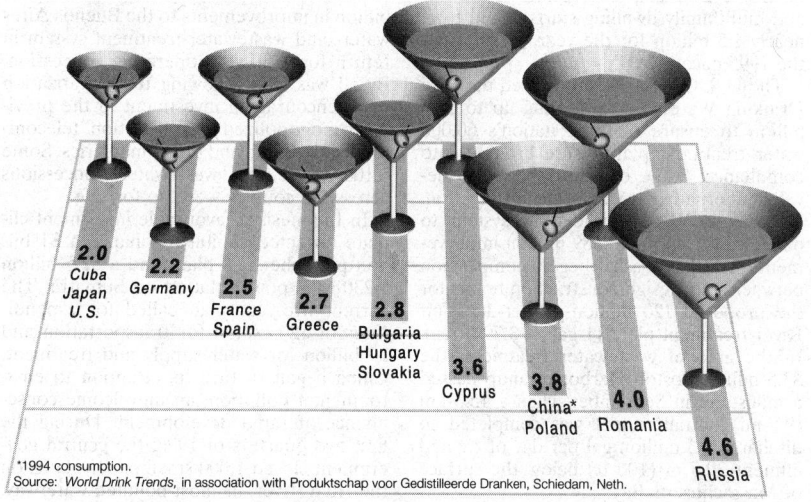

2.0 Cuba Japan U.S.
2.2 Germany
2.5 France Spain
2.7 Greece
2.8 Bulgaria Hungary Slovakia
3.6 Cyprus
3.8 China* Poland
4.0 Romania
4.6 Russia

*1994 consumption.
Source: *World Drink Trends*, in association with Produktschap voor Gedistilleerde Dranken, Schiedam, Neth.

A man on a camel passes a Pepsi billboard in the Egyptian desert. There was no letup in the battle between Coca-Cola and Pepsi-Cola in 1996, with Coke challenging Pepsi in the Venezuelan market and Pepsi launching an international marketing campaign that included a new blue can.

product: bottled water. The hottest new product of the year, much imitated in North America, was Water Joe, uncarbonated water with caffeine.   (GREG W. PRINCE)

BUILDING AND CONSTRUCTION

The pace of new construction eased slightly in mid-1996 in the U.S., but it rebounded strongly in September. Total new construction spending rose in September to a record annual rate of $573.4 billion, according to U.S. Department of Commerce figures. Strong third-quarter support came from nonresidential building. The major stimulus was government spending, with gains in highways, schools, urban public housing and redevelopment, hospitals, and water-treatment plants. By contrast, housing starts declined after a brisk pace in the first quarter. According to the National Association of Home Builders, new residential single- and multifamily dwelling starts would total nearly 1.5 billion for the year, 7.7% above the 1995 pace.

The U.S. Congress reauthorized the Safe Drinking Water Act, allocating up to $9.6 billion to ensure that the nation's 60,000 water treatment plants were brought into compliance. Some operators began to develop alternatives to chlorine disinfection. Milwaukee, Wis., upgraded its system to ozone disinfection, an $89 million improvement. Seattle, Wash., began competition between four design-construction teams for the proposed 120 million-gal-per-day Tolt River treatment plant (1 gal = 3.79 litres). In the area of wastewater treatment, the $3.5 billion Boston Harbor cleanup passed a milestone in September when a 15.3-km (9.5-mi) outfall tunnel was completed to discharge 1.3 million gal per day of treated effluent 30.5 m (100 ft) below the surface of Massachusetts Bay.

Canadian nonresidential construction fell 8.6% during the first quarter of 1996, but residential construction surged as monthly housing starts for the period averaged 113,000 units, a pace that would mark a 4.2% increase for the year. Contractors made significant progress on the $500 million Northumberland Strait Crossing, which would connect Prince Edward Island and New Brunswick.

Construction in Mexico rebounded in the second quarter of 1996, advancing 7.8%, after having slumped 23% in 1995. Traditional construction remained weak overall, but the telecommunications sector continued to attract infrastructure investment from carriers preparing to compete for long-distance customers in January 1997.

Like many other less-developed nations, Argentina was raising capital for infrastructure by privatizing government businesses. A French-led consortium was investing $4 billion in improvements to the Buenos Aires water- and wastewater-treatment system in return for a 30-year operating concession. Brazil was also following the privatization path, encouraging investment in the previously monopolized transportation, telecommunications, oil, and utility industries. Some 1,100 water and wastewater concessions across the country were up for sale.

In Indonesia a favourable investment climate attracted capital to finance a $1 billion petrochemical plant and a $2.5 billion 1,230-MW power station on Sumatra. The current five-year plan called for expenditures of $20 billion for transportation and $9 billion for water supply and treatment. China began to turn its attention to environmental pollution, an unwelcome consequence of rapid development. During the first two quarters of 1996, the central government closed 1,000 small paper plants on the Huai River, its most polluted waterway.

The country was seeking to increase the budget for environmental protection above the current level of 0.7% of gross domestic product. Disastrous floods during the summer gave impetus to the massive Three Gorges Dam project, a $25 billion flood-control and hydropower project that would displace well over a million people.

(ANDREW G. WRIGHT)

CHEMICALS

The high production and plant-operating rates seen in 1995 continued to mark most of the world's chemical industry in 1996. The high and rising sales levels reflected the generally healthy economies of countries around the globe. The high volume of products sold, however, did not always translate into record profits, particularly for the makers of big-volume petrochemicals. While employment rose in the chemical industry in the U.S., added personnel was not as visible in industrialized countries as was higher productivity—fewer workers turning out more products.

Countries in Asia, South America, and the Middle East continued to strengthen their roles in chemical production, and as the economies of many of the nations of Eastern Europe continued to improve—notably Poland, the Czech Republic, and Hungary—they were beginning to surpass the production marks set before the breakup of the Soviet bloc. The few records from Russia itself gave little evidence of recovery.

There was concern, however, as to whether some of the capital expansion projects slated for the latter half of the 1990s—many to come into operation beginning in 1997 and 1998—might be ill-timed. This was particularly the case with crackers for the production of ethylene, propylene, and butadiene and for facilities making pure terephthalic acid, used in polyester fibres, film, and bottles. It was being asked if the industry had once more been overly ambitious. The new plants could lead to even more serious market competition that would shrink profit margins.

It was competition and the search for higher profits that kept up pressures for mergers and the reshuffling of business units at major companies around the world. The big three German firms, for example—BASF, Bayer, and Hoechst—were reevaluating their operations and selling some business units and merging others. These developments also were seen among other companies in Europe and in the U.S. Even in Japan, where the merger pace remained slower, two chemical units of the Mitsui group announced plans to combine in 1997.

The strong performance that developed in the chemical industry in 1996 came from a powerful 1995 base, the last year for which figures were available. The dollar value of world chemical shipments reached an estimated $1,545,000,000,000 in 1995, up 12.2% from 1994. Production indexes, however, were not as impressive. U.S. production rose by just 1% in 1995 after having gained 5% in 1994. The U.S. chemical industry remained the largest in the world, turning out 23.8% of the world's production in 1995, but its dominance was slipping, for in 1985 it had held a 28.4% share.

Western Europe's production increased 2.5% in 1995, but performance varied greatly among countries. Germany's production index, for example, was 102.7, compared with its 1994 mark of 105.2. Germany remained Europe's largest producer, with 8.1% of the world's sales in 1995, worth $125.4 billion. France raised its chemical sales to $85.3 billion, up 8% in 1995, and its production index was at 119.2, up from 117, almost 1.8%. France had about a 5.5% share of the world's chemical business. The U.K., with a 4% share, saw its sales volume rise to $61.6 billion, up 10%, and its production rise to 3.6%.

Italy showed a striking growth in sales, to $50.9 billion, up 15%. Its production rose about 3%. It had 3.3% of world production. Belgium, Spain, and The Netherlands all registered sales above $30 billion in 1995.

Large increases were seen in Poland, Turkey, and Hungary in 1995. Poland's sales rose to $6.7 billion, up more than 45%, and production increased 12%. Turkey had sales of $6 billion, an even more impressive jump of 76.4%. Hungary, still well below its production level of 1991 and not growing as fast as it did in 1994, nonetheless raised its production by 1.6% and hiked sales to $3.3 billion, a gain of 50%.

Although South America's chemical industry experienced good growth in the 1990s, only Brazil had a domestic sales volume that put it in the ranks of the large European countries. In 1995, for example, the latest year for which figures were available, its total sales volume was $39,390,000,000. Next largest in South America was Argentina, with sales of $13,110,000,000. Mexico's sales totaled $19.7 billion, only slightly less than Canada's, at $23,520,000,000.

The picture in Asia continued to change with remarkable speed. Japan, with an output valued at $255.1 billion in 1995, had 16.5% of the world's chemical business. Chemical production was up 7%. Because Japan's plants were generally too small for serious competition in the export field and had high costs (Japan had to import naphtha as raw material for most key petrochemicals), the country's large chemical producers were increasing investments elsewhere in Asia, including Taiwan, South Korea, and China.

Taiwan, which was relatively early to draw Japanese investors, had a 1995 sales volume of $28,570,000,000, which put it in the ranks of major European countries. Although dwarfed by Japan, South Korea's chemical industry, with domestic sales of $43,120,000,000 in 1995, was behind only four countries in Europe. The chemical enterprises of China, with domestic sales at $84,550,000,000 in 1995, exceeded those of all but one nation of Europe, Germany. China's expansion in chemicals continued at about 10% per year.

International chemical trade in 1995 was valued at $437 billion, some 15% above the 1994 mark. The falloff in trade that was seen in the latter part of 1995, however, carried into 1996.

Many of the leading exporters continued to be strong importers. Countries of the European Union, for example, exported $158 billion in chemicals, up 12%, in 1995 and imported $132 billion, up 14%. Germany retained its position as the world's export leader, shipping goods valued at $70.5 billion, up 6%, and importing chemicals valued at $43 billion, up 11%. Italy made the biggest gains, raising exports 29%, to $20 billion, and increasing imports 23%, to $28 billion.

The U.S. in 1995 shipped out chemical goods valued at $62 billion, up 20%, and increased imports to $40 billion, a 19% change over 1994. Japan had a 19% export gain, to $30 billion, and imported 16% more than in 1994, or $25 billion.

Stimulated by the need to exploit new technology effectively, a number of business alliances were announced in 1996. These included links between Germany's BASF and E.I. Du Pont de Nemours & Co. (Du Pont) of the U.S., which would work on a venture in China to capitalize on a new way to make key raw materials for the two most common types of nylon (nylon 6 and nylon 6/6).

In the U.S., Exxon Chemical Co. and Union Carbide Co. combined their skills to cooperate on the commercial development of the new metallocenes, or single-site catalysts, which produced superior-quality polyolefins. Exxon also joined Netherlands-based DSM in exploiting metallocene technologies for types of specialty rubber made primarily of ethylene and propylene.

Dow Chemical Co. and Du Pont set up Du Pont Dow Elastomers, with Dow's expertise on metallocenes a central factor. Similarly, Dow and Montell Polyolefins, the European polypropylene giant created in 1994 by the combined interests of the Dutch and British conglomerate Royal Dutch/Shell and Montedison of Italy, joined forces. Dow also formed links with the U.K.-based BP Chemicals, a subsidiary of the British Petroleum Company PLC, in polyethylene process cross-licensing.

Less-spectacular technological advances continued to come as part of the chemical industry's efforts to minimize pollution, to find processes that employed less-hazardous intermediates, to emphasize recycling, and to find ways to clean up water and soil that had been contaminated. Much of the environmental research had been entered into reluctantly to meet regulations that the industry felt were not justifiable. Having gained greater plant efficiencies, in part as a result of research done to meet stricter laws, however, the industry appeared willing to live with many of the regulations that had brought environmental improvements.

(J. ROBERT WARREN)

ELECTRICAL

Global demand for the products of the electrical manufacturing industry were at an all-time high throughout 1995, but by August 1996 a perceptible slowdown had been detected. This was especially the case in Western Europe and particularly in Germany, where the strong Deutsche Mark and high wage settlements dampened the economy. Little change was expected in Europe in 1997, because of pressures on national economies to meet the stiff monetary convergence requirements of the move to a common currency in 1999. In North America the market was affected by uncertainty about deregulation of the electric power industry, which delayed equipment orders.

These minor market losses were largely balanced, however, by increased business in East Asia. Expansion of the Asian Pacific economies continued apace, led by a small number of giant corporations that manufactured a vast range of goods, from cars and electrical power products to cameras.

Although multinational companies in the developed countries continued to specialize, acquiring complementary specialist firms and divesting uneconomical or disparate subsidiaries, the top priority was shifting to the redistribution, or globalization, of their manufacturing bases. The electrical equipment manufacturing industry was leading the way in this development. For example, the head of the German electrical multinational Siemens pointed out that nearly 60% of its business was with customers outside Germany, while most production took place inside, an imbalance the company was working to change.

Although globalization would help cut production costs, constant innovation also was vital for success in the electrical and electronic engineering industry. Organizational changes in electrical companies had been aimed primarily at ensuring that innovations in basic technologies were applied across the complete product range.

ABB Asea Brown Boveri (ABB), which ran a close second to Siemens, the world's largest electrical equipment manufacturer, was even farther down the road toward globalization. Nearly 17% of its total sales were in the Asia-Pacific area, compared with less than 10% at Siemens. ABB had manufacturing bases in 46 countries. Partly as a result of the company's globalization (employment had increased by 7,000 in Asia and declined by 4,000 in Europe), its personnel costs, for the first time, fell below 30% of adjusted revenues. Personnel cost reduction had been a main contributor to improvement in the company's operating margin.

Globalization was also being taken seriously at General Electric (GE). The U.S. company said that it was accelerating its globalization by approaching joint-venture partners, including sovereign states,

An operator tends the Genting San Yen power plant, Malaysia's largest facility for producing electricity. Despite improvements to and expansion of its electrical production and distribution systems after a 1992 outage, the Malay Peninsula suffered another power failure on Aug. 3–4, 1996.

as multibusiness teams, sharing knowledge among countries, and assembling supportive financing packages from its subsidiary GE Capital. Global revenues over the previous 10 years had increased from 20% to 38% by 1995, and in the next four or five years the majority of GE revenue was expected from outside the U.S.

Unlike Siemens and ABB, however, GE continued to be a multibusiness company. Only 39% of its total revenue in 1995 came from electrical equipment manufacturing; most of the remainder was from broadcasting, plastics, and aircraft engines. GE thus dismissed one of the hottest trends in business—breaking up multibusiness companies and spinning off the components because of the idea that size and diversity inhibited competitiveness.

One multibusiness company that had been undergoing a breakup for several years was AEG, the once huge German conglomerate. The company was now owned by Daimler-Benz, but its domestic appliance business had gone to Electrolux, GE had taken over its low-voltage business, and much of its automation business was now in French hands. The latest move was the sale of the company's electric power transmission and distribution business to GEC Alsthom in September 1996. GEC Alsthom, an Anglo-French manufacturer of power equipment, was fourth in revenue in the electrical industry. Its policy of globalization had resulted in sales in Asia reaching 26% of the total, with 11% in the Americas.

In November Westinghouse announced that it would divide its multibusiness company into two parts. One company would take the industrial businesses, including power generation; the second, CBS and the other broadcasting businesses.

After 30 years of meetings and debate, the International Electrotechnical Commission was expected in 1997 to finalize a standard design of a 230-v plug-and-socket system for domestic and commercial application. The publication of the standard would have wide implications. As well as the whole of Europe, much of East Asia and Africa were expected to adopt the new standard.   (T.C.J. COGLE)

ENERGY

Petroleum. The price of crude oil rose strongly in 1996 as the generally buoyant world economy underpinned energy demand. The price of Brent Blend, the U.K.'s North Sea crude oil that serves as a global price benchmark, surged to a post–Persian Gulf War high of more than $25 per barrel in mid-October. The average for the year was expected to be about $20, an increase of about $3 per barrel over 1995.

The strong performance of oil prices came in two waves. In April the demand for crude oil surged as refiners in the U.S. were caught short of supplies during a late cold snap. That caused the administration of Pres. Bill Clinton to release stocks from the Strategic Petroleum Reserve as a move to stem a sharp rise in the politically sensitive retail price of gasoline. Crude oil prices then retreated during the summer before rising strongly again starting in late August.

The second and strongest buying wave was triggered in part by the suspension in September of the United Nations oil-for-food plan with Iraq, under which the Iraqi government was to be allowed to export

$2 billion worth of oil every six months to cover the cost of buying food, medicine, and other essential items for civilians. Events occurring in the Kurdish areas of northern Iraq caused the UN to suspend the program, however, shortly before it was due to begin.

The suspension of the agreement with Iraq came at a time when global oil demand was particularly buoyant. It also coincided with delays in production at some of the new fields in the North Sea. During the autumn there was also very strong demand for heating oil in the U.S. and in Western Europe during the period before winter, a factor that underpinned the particularly sharp rise in crude oil prices in October.

The volatility of crude and refined product prices during the year also was exacerbated by changes in oil company policies on inventory management. In the past refiners had tended to maintain large stocks of crude oil. The relatively low profit margins in recent years in the refining industry, however, had caused oil companies to seek substantial reductions in their operating costs, and reducing inventories proved to be one of the quickest ways for companies to make savings. In the U.S., where oil companies had made the deepest cuts, crude oil stocks fell dramatically. In September 1994, for example, storage tanks at U.S. refineries held 330 million bbl of crude oil. The figure fell to 303 million bbl by September 1996, however, as just-in-time techniques of inventory management took hold.

The impact of such changes was to increase price volatility. Any sudden surge in oil demand or unforeseen interruption in supplies tended to cause refiners to enter the market en masse in 1996. The fact that they all were scrambling to secure additional stocks at the same time pushed prices up sharply. The same volatility could be seen at times of price weakness. In those circumstances refiners tended to put off building up their stocks until as late as possible in the hope that prices would fall even farther.

The poor commercial performance of much of the West's refining industry in recent years caused several of the largest oil companies to announce partial mergers during 1996. British Petroleum and Mobil of the U.S. announced that they would combine their refining and marketing operations in Europe, while Shell Oil, the U.S. division of the Anglo-Dutch oil group, Texaco of the U.S., and the Star joint venture between Texaco and Saudi Arabia announced plans to merge their refining operations in the U.S. Higher oil prices, however, provided a financial bonanza to members of OPEC, which accounted for about 25 million of the nearly 72 million bbl of oil consumed across the world each day.

The OPEC basket price, an average of seven international crude oils, was comfortably above the group's target price of $21 per barrel for much of the second half of the year. The average for the full year was expected to be just shy of the target, at around $20.30 per barrel.

By November OPEC members were reported to be producing more than one million barrels a day over their self-imposed production ceiling of 24,520,000 bbl a day. Strong demand, especially in fast-growing economies in Asia and Latin America, however, caused the overproduction to have little impact on prices. Strong demand and the high price of oil also helped to paper over political cracks in the organization.

A number of OPEC states persistently cheated on their production quotas. This was done much to the annoyance of Saudi Arabia, the group's dominant producer, which had kept its output steady at eight million barrels per day in recent years, even though it had idle capacity capable of producing an additional two million barrels per day. Saudi Arabia and other large Persian Gulf producers, such as the United Arab Emirates and Kuwait, were increasingly worried that other OPEC members were following production policies that undermined the group's efforts to support prices.

Venezuela, the only Latin-American member of OPEC, came under strong criticism for overproducing in 1996. Its output of 3 million bbl per day toward the end of the year was well in excess of its OPEC quota of 2.3 million bbl per day. A series of policy initiatives by the Venezuelan government in 1996 to open its oil industry to large-scale foreign investment as part of an ambitious plan to increase oil production to six million barrels per day by 2005 triggered market speculation that the country might eventually leave OPEC. The Venezuelan government, however, denied such suggestions. At its November meeting OPEC voted to maintain a production ceiling of 25,030,000 bbl a day until June 1997.

Other issues confronting OPEC during the year included the strengthening of the unilateral U.S. sanctions against Iran and Libya, both members of the organization. Moves by the U.S. government to limit individual foreign investments in Iran's oil industry to $40 million were widely criticized, particularly in Europe. The Iranian government had opened its offshore oil sector in the Persian Gulf to foreign investment, although only one project, organized by Total of France, was under way by the end of the year.

Because of strong demand the eventual return of Iraqi oil to world markets in December under a revitalized oil-for-food program had little negative impact on prices. Nor did Iraq have any difficulty in securing buyers for its crude oil. The long-term status of Iraq as a leading oil exporter remained in doubt, however.

The full removal of the UN oil embargo on Iraq was expected to trigger massive investment in the country from Western oil companies, many of which were struggling to replace reserves. UN arms inspectors, however, said that the Iraqi government was still some way from meeting the demands that it cooperate fully on the dismantling of its ability to manufacture weapons of mass destruction.

Advances in technology continued to drive down the costs of oil production during the year and to make previously uneconomic small fields commercially viable. Schlumberger, a French-U.S. group that was one of the world's largest oil service companies, predicted that average worldwide recovery rates could be boosted from 35% to 50% within 10 years because of steady technological progress.

One of the most vivid examples of how technology had revolutionized the oil industry was the continuing rise in output from deepwater areas of the U.S. sector of the Gulf of Mexico. Ten years earlier few in the industry believed that oil could be recovered from water depths approaching 1,525 m (5,000 ft). By the end of 1996, however, there were 39 confirmed discoveries in the deep water of the Gulf of Mexico, with 11 fields producing and another 10 under development. Individual wells were drilled in water depths approaching 2,440 m (8,000 ft), and engineers were studying how to produce oil and gas in depths as great as 3,050 m (10,000 ft).

Natural Gas. The popularity of natural gas grew in 1996 because of its environmental advantages and the new uses found for it. Exxon, for example, announced progress in converting natural gas into middle distillates, a group of fuels that included diesel and kerosene.

There was progress in 1996 in liberalizing natural gas markets in various countries. Plans to allow Great Britain's 19 million residential consumers a choice of supplier advanced with the successful start of a test among 500,000 households. Full competition was due to begin in 1998. In the U.S. nearly 12 million natural gas users, or about a quarter of all households connected to gas networks, would be able to select their supplier by the year 2000.

Progress was also made during the year in liberalizing continental European natural gas markets. In December the energy ministers of the European Union set the summer of 1997 as a target for reaching agreement on allowing large consumers of gas to shop around for their supplies. EU states remained divided, however, between those, such as Britain and Germany, that wanted a rapid opening of the market and those, such as France, that favoured a more gradual approach.   (ROBERT CORZINE)

Coal. World hard coal production in 1996 was estimated to be about 3.7 billion metric tons, only 60 million metric tons more than in 1995. In the U.S., however, coal production increased by more than 2%, to some 1,055,000,000 short tons (1 short ton = 0.9 metric ton) owing to strong demand for steam coal. U.S. coal exports increased to 88 million short tons (of which 40% was steam coal and 60% coking coal).

China and India remained large coal producers (about 1.3 billion and 240 million metric tons, respectively) although not important exporters. Australia remained the number one coal exporter. South African coal production was estimated to have risen less than 1% in 1996, but exports were expected to be 62 million metric tons. Coal production in the European Union was expected to fall to 128.4 million metric tons. In Russia and Poland production in 1996 was similar to that of the previous year.

Environmental legislation continued to have a strong impact on new coal facilities, making the cost of coal-fired power plants more expensive and making natural gas and other fuels more attractive. It did not appear, however, that stricter legislative requirements were imposing insurmountable obstacles to new coal power plants and mines.   (ROBERT J.M. WYLLIE)

Nuclear. Statistical data for 1995, released by the International Atomic Energy Agency early in 1996, indicated that there were a total of 437 units operating in nuclear power stations in 31 countries at the beginning of the year, with a total capacity of 343,792 MW. This compared with 432 units with a total capacity of 340,347 MW one year earlier. There were 39 units under construction in 14 countries, and 4 of these were connected to the grid for the first time during the year. Four new reactor construction starts were scheduled for 1996. Worldwide during 1995 nuclear power units delivered a total of 2,223.56 TWh (terawatt-hours; 1 terawatt-hour = 1 billion kilowatt-hours). Countries with the largest proportion of national electricity production from nuclear power were Lithuania (76.4%), France (75.3%), Belgium (55.8%), and Sweden (51.1%). The total number of commercial power reactors shut down throughout the world reached 71.

Engineers continued to concentrate on extending the working life of nuclear units. Total lifetimes of up to 60 years were being considered for a typical plant after a thorough refurbishment. Calder Hall, the world's first commercial nuclear power station in Great Britain, which celebrated the 40th anniversary of its opening in October, was authorized to continue operating for another 10 years. After a study of its 54 pressurized-water reactor (PWR) units, EdF, the French national utility, concluded that its reactors could achieve 40- or possibly 50-year lives.

Privatization of the U.K. electricity industry was completed with the sale of British Energy, previously Nuclear Electric, together with the country's fleet of advanced gas-cooled reactors and the new Sizewell B PWR. British Energy announced before the sale that it had no plans for further nuclear units. The company intended, however, to maintain its export collaboration in the nuclear power area with Westinghouse. Meanwhile, in Canada plans to privatize Ontario Hydro excluded the utility's 19 nuclear units, which would be run by four subentities on a competitive basis while being held in public ownership.

Public opinion continued to run strongly against new nuclear projects. In the first local referendum to be held on the construction of a new unit in Japan, residents of the town of Maki rejected a proposed station. There also was continuing lack of progress on plans for the disposal of radioactive materials in the U.S. A bill to require the Department of Energy to move irradiated fuel stored at power plants to an aboveground storage facility in Nevada failed to move through Congress. A U.S. Court of Appeals, however, ruled that the Department of Energy had to take possession of the spent fuel by the end of January 1998.

General Electric won a $1.8 billion order from Taiwan Power for the two reactors at Lung-men. They were to be GE's advanced boiling-water reactor (BWR) design. Lung-men would be Taiwan's seventh and eighth nuclear units.

The China National Corporation awarded a contract to Atomic Energy of Canada Ltd. for two CANDU 6 pressurized heavy-water reactors to be built on the same site as the Chinese-constructed Qinshan PWR power station. TDA new nuclear power nation, Romania, started up its first Canadian-designed CANDU-type pressurized heavy-water reactor at Cernavoda after a troubled history that had led to the delay of the first unit, construction of which started in 1981. This marked the first CANDU-type reactor to go into operation in Europe.

International pressure to find a solution to the problems of cleaning up the Chernobyl site in Ukraine continued during the year. The work included the decommissioning of blocks 1, 2, and 3; waste management on-site and in the exclusion zone; the storage of spent fuel and high-level waste; and the enclosure of the destroyed unit 4. A group of international companies led by SGN of France were discussing the problem with institutions that might finance the project. It was agreed that unit 1 would be shut down at the end of November, ready for decommissioning and dismantling over the next five to six years. Ukrainian authorities complained, however, that none of the $2.3 billion of Western aid, promised in return for the government's commitment to closing Chernobyl completely by 2000, had been received.   (RICHARD A. KNOX)

Alternative Energy. A study published in 1996 by the International Energy Agency (IEA), the Paris-based group that monitors energy developments on behalf of the Western industrialized countries, concluded that the demand for alternative energy sources would grow strongly in the coming years. Even so, these sources would account for only a small portion of the world's energy mix by 2010. The IEA estimated that fossil-based fuels would account for almost 90% of total demand in 2010. Nonhydroelectric renewable sources, such as biomass, wind, wave, solar, and geothermal power, however, were expected to register the highest growth rate. The IEA predicted that renewable sources would account for only about 1% of the total supply by 2010, compared with almost 3% for hydropower.

The World Energy Council, a nongovernmental international group that promotes sustainable energy policies, estimated that renewable sources could provide 5–8% of the world's power requirements by 2020 but only with additional spending on research and development. The current levels of government support for alternative energy sources had resulted in steadily declining costs. The cost of photovoltaic cells, for example, had fallen from tens of thousands of dollars per watt in the 1960s to about $6. The world market for solar power remained small, however. (ROBERT CORZINE)

See also Architecture and Civil Engineering; Transportation.

This article updates the *Macropædia* articles ENERGY CONVERSION; FOSSIL FUELS.

GAMES AND TOYS

The 1996 holiday season in the U.S., like those in previous years, saw the frenzy caused by shoppers' desperate search for a "must-have" toy. The "hot" commodity in 1996 was Tyco Toys Inc.'s Tickle Me Elmo, a Sesame Street character that wiggled, giggled, and talked when tickled. It retailed at about $30. Even after about one million of the toys had been shipped, stores sold out of them in minutes and could not keep them in stock. A number of people who had earlier managed to purchase Elmo attempted to take advantage of the situation, and offers to sell at highly inflated prices—sometimes to the highest bidder—began appearing in newspapers and even on the World Wide Web.

A new version of an old favourite also made news late in the year. Cabbage Patch Kids Snacktime Kids dolls—about 700,000 of which had been distributed by Mattel Inc., the toy's manufacturer, since its introduction in August—had battery-powered movable jaws designed to "eat" plastic carrots and french fries. After Christmas, however, reports began to emerge that the doll was chewing on children's hair—sometimes down to the scalp—and fingers. At the end of the year, Mattel advised the removal of the batteries and announced that future dolls would carry warning labels, but it was likely that the company would soon take the toy off the market.

Mattel and Tyco had both been in the news earlier in the year. In January Mattel disclosed that it had been holding merger talks with another toy manufacturer, Hasbro Inc., since the preceding April. Mattel had offered $5.2 billion in stock in a deal that would have joined the two largest toy makers in the U.S.—and brought together such classic products as Scrabble, Monopoly, Mr. Potato Head, Barbie dolls, and G.I. Joe—but Hasbro rejected the offer, fearing antitrust difficulties. Mattel, which had hoped that Hasbro's stockholders would pressure the board into negotiating, withdrew its offer in February, citing Hasbro's "unbending stance" against the merger.

In November Mattel made another surprise announcement—that it would buy Tyco, the third largest toy company in the U.S. and the maker of the miniature Matchbox cars. Holders of Tyco stock would be given Mattel stock worth $12.50 for each Tyco share in the $737 million deal, which was to be finalized in 1997. The acquisition would give Mattel worldwide sales of $4.3 billion and solidify its number one position.

Another merger that made headlines was the purchase of Baby Superstore by Toys "Я" Us, the world's largest toy retailer, in hopes of improving both the stock price and

the Babies "Я" Us unit's growth. The company had been seeking opportunities for growth since its previous fiscal year's 72% earnings nosedive. It also had been hit with accusations of having used its influence to prevent discount stores from obtaining certain popular toys from manufacturers. Toys "Я" Us's business expansion would include putting Babies "Я" Us into Baby Superstore spaces and constructing superstores that would combine various businesses under one roof.

In addition, in March it was announced that the Melville Corp. would sell the Kay-Bee Toys chain, the second largest U.S. toy retailer, to the Consolidated Stores Corp. for $315 million. This move was expected to lower prices, attract more shoppers to Kay-Bee's more than 1,000 stores, and make Consolidated, a seller of closeout merchandise at a discount, one of the largest small-toy retailers.

Electronic games continued to be important both as toys and as educational tools, and some 2,000 programs were available. The speed, diversity, and interest level of computer games were increasing, and studies were showing that these games had a positive effect on children's mental and neurological development. Many games could be played on the Internet. A network version of Parker Brothers' Monopoly allowed competition between players in different countries, and subscribers to the San Francisco-based Total Entertainment Network's Web site could choose among a number of games to play against each other. FormGen Inc.'s Duke Nukem 3D and id Software Inc.'s Quake were also extremely popular.

The number of console video game users was diminishing, but sales remained high, and the major game makers—Nintendo, Sega, and Sony—still produced fast, entertaining games. The Nintendo Co.'s new Ultra 64, with three-dimensional images and the power to handle 64 bits of information at a time, was especially successful. Expectations were that 1996 sales of the unit would reach one million, largely on the strength of what was considered the company's best game ever, Super Mario 64. Sales of Sony Corp.'s PlayStation reached 10 million units by year's end; popular games included Sony's Crash Bandicoot and Eidos Interactive's Tomb Raider, with its gun-toting heroine Lara Croft. Sega, bundling three games with its Saturn unit, expected to reach one million in sales during the year.

The perennial favourite Barbie, which in Japan had always been greatly outsold by a doll named Licca, designed to look younger than the teenager Barbie, finally began to catch on there. Mattel's softened look for that market's doll, as well as Japanese girls' changing tastes, was responsible for the inroads Barbie was making.

(BARBARA WHITNEY)

GEMSTONES

During 1996 the recession that had lasted for several years in the jewelry business, traditionally one of the last to recover from slowdowns, began to lift. In Western countries sales began to rise, and among European countries the U.K. had a reasonably confident jewelry and gemstone trade once more. The high end of the gemstone and jewelry market had stood up well to long-persisting trade conditions.

In the salesroom demand for the finest gemstones was never higher, and the increased size of London salesroom jewelry catalogs was perhaps the clearest sign of recovery in this area. Demand from Asia for the finest stones continued to rise, and Middle Eastern buyers were still prominent, though perhaps to a slightly less extent.

For gemologists the problem of treated stones had still not been resolved. While evidence of treatment (for example, the use of glass and plastic infillings in rubies and diamonds and the oiling of emeralds) was becoming more widely recognized, the question of disclosure had not been settled. More serious was the gradual spread of synthetic gem-quality diamonds; at least one stone, on reaching a laboratory for grading, turned out to be a completely unsuspected synthetic. The San Francisco firm of Chatham, long celebrated for its synthetic emeralds, was negotiating with Russia for the establishment of a synthetic-diamond-making plant. Russia continued to produce good-quality synthetic alexandrite, emeralds, and red spinel.

Newly located deposits of gemstones include a site in Mali, from which attractive yellow-green garnets came on the market. An orange-red garnet was reported from Kashmir. The supply of fine gemstones from the countries of the former Soviet Union appeared less plentiful than in previous years, but Vietnam was providing good-quality red spinel and blue sapphire. Madagascar was producing gemstones again, with blue sapphires of reasonable quality, as well as emeralds, coming on the market. There were reports of Canadian diamonds' achieving commercial gemstone status, but exploration was still in progress.

De Beers apparently achieved a working agreement with Russian diamond producers but announced that it wanted a signature on the contract from either Pres. Boris Yeltsin or Prime Minister Viktor Chernomyrdin. The Western Australian Argyle diamond producers broke away from De Beers late in the year and began selling stones directly. (MICHAEL O'DONOGHUE)

HOME FURNISHINGS

Furniture. In a survey conducted by Brian Carrol and published in *Furniture/Today,* the number of furniture sites on the World Wide Web skyrocketed in 1996. In April, Carrol found 98 entries; three months later the number was 242. It was not clear if this was simply a fad or if those who were first in the electronic marketplace would earn a great deal of money from it. The National Home Furnishings Association, the national organization for furniture retailers, also went on-line in 1996.

In manufacturing the three leaders for 1995 were, according to surveys by *Furniture/Today,* Masco ($2,014,000,000 in revenues, up 6.8%), Furniture Brands International ($1,073,900,000), and La-Z-Boy ($914.9 million). The first and third rankings were the same as in 1995, but this apparent stability was misleading. By August 1996 Masco Home Furnishings had become a new company, Lifestyle Furnishings International, in a $1,050,000,000 deal, and La-Z-Boy changed its name to the La-Z-Boy Companies. Furniture Brands International, which formerly was Interco, acquired Thomasville late in 1995. According to the American Furniture Manufacturers Association, factory shipments for 1996 were expected to reach $20.1 billion, a growth rate of 5.9%.

In retailing Levitz ($1,008,400,000 in revenues), Heilig-Meyers ($844.2 million), and Pier 1 Imports ($459.2 million) held the same top three positions as a year earlier, but by October 1996 the picture was changing. Heilig-Meyers had taken over the fourth-ranked company, Rhodes, to increase its number of stores to some 1,000, and Levitz, having suffered a $7.2 million loss in September, was struggling with a reorganization.

Retailers' earnings had nose-dived in 1995, and, consequently, 1996 was a year of "no" promotions (no down payments, no monthly payments, no interest). The focus on price was the antithesis of the approach advocated by many, particularly the Home Furnishings Council, an umbrella organization.

Unlike years past, when the market had a dominant theme—French, say, or country casual—the trend in style in 1996 was to diversity. Overall, designs were formal, with a hint of classical elements. The style to watch seemed to be the Latin look, a rustic version of the Mediterranean style. This coincided with the introduction of Market-Place Mexico, a cooperative exhibit of 14 producers, at the Furniture Exposition in High Point, N.C.

Leather continued to garner attention, while fabric upholstery featured combinations of materials and textures on a single piece. Improved designs of futons made them more appealing. Home offices and ready-to-assemble categories were hot, but home theatres were not.

The American Society of Furniture Designers presented the first-ever Pinnacle awards to nine designers, with Berry & Clark Design Associates being named Designers of the Year and Ethan Allen receiving special recognition. Four people were inducted at the eighth annual Furniture Hall of Fame banquet: Hollis Siebe Baker of Baker Furniture, Mary McKenzie Henkel of Henkel-Harris, J. Wade Kincaid of Kincaid Furniture, and Joseph E. Richardson II of Richardson Brothers.

(ABBY CHAPPLE)

Housewares. During 1995 U.S. consumers spent nearly $58 billion on items included in the general category of housewares, a 6.3% increase over 1994. The average U.S. household paid $567 for such items as tabletop appliances, health and beauty aids, cleaning equipment, and plates and dining utensils. That figure was nearly as much as the amount paid for medical services and more than was spent on education or on fruits and vegetables.

Small appliances, floor-cleaning tools, sewing machines, electric kitchen devices, portable heating and cooling equipment, and microwave ovens represented more than 9% of the housewares market. During the year sewing machine sales dropped a dramatic 50%, while microwave purchases shot up 18% and cookware sales fell by 26%. The trend for ease made store-bought items more attractive to consumers and overrode a strong movement toward a "simpler" life—making instead of purchasing goods. The "back to nature" boom, however, resulted in dozens of new gardening publications and a 65% increase in sales of lawn and garden equipment.

Television shopping networks reached more than 50 million households; 13% of purchasers bought small kitchen appliances. Though retailing via the Internet was beginning to take hold, concerns about electronic security, dull Web sites, and unreliable technologies were holding back sales in this medium. (KIRA GOULD)

INSURANCE

World insurance news in 1996 was again highlighted by losses from catastrophes. The crash off Long Island of TWA Flight 800, which caused 230 deaths, had $600 million of potential liability. By 1996 the insurance payouts for weather-related disasters for the 1990s had reached $48 billion, compared with $16 billion for all of the 1980s. Hurricane Fran topped U.S. losses in 1996 as it slammed into the North Carolina coast to cause an estimated $1.6 billion in insured damages. A spectacular $300 million fire in Paris devastated a Crédit Lyonnais bank.

Deregulation, privatization, and liberalization of international insurance markets provided new marketing opportunities. A 10% growth rate in Asia outpaced the global average of 4%. In the U.K. the Lutine bell at Lloyd's of London was rung an unprecedented three times on the news of government approval of a $5 billion recovery plan that ended lengthy litigation. After five years of losses totaling more than $12 billion, Lloyd's reported earnings of about $2 billion for 1993. Canadian insurers encountered hardening markets, with problems plaguing Ontario's auto insurance, and they also saw banks entering the life insurance business, as well as rising costs for new technology. Global reinsurance rates were generally continuing a decline that had begun two years earlier.

In the U.S. property insurers hoped that gains on automobile insurance and workers' compensation would offset windstorm losses. Sales of ordinary life insurance were again disappointing, having remained flat for the past 10 years at approximately $10 billion of new annualized premiums and $1 trillion of face amount. Life insurers posted a 4.7% gain in total surpluses for the first six months of 1996. Individual annuities recovered from the decline in 1995, following an average growth rate of 15% in each of the preceding 10 years. In comparison with first-half results in 1995, variable annuity sales were up a sharp 62%.

The role of technology had escalated rapidly in insurance. For example, brokers and companies formed new electronic exchanges for global communication and price information through the Internet and other networks. Sparked by rising claims for sexual harassment and wrongful termination, interest grew in employer liability insurance with high limits and large deductibles. Wal-Mart spurred sales of a new product called corporate-owned life insurance by purchasing $20 billion payable to itself on 325,000 employees.

Integrated financial planning had become the driving force for many changes in personal insurance sales. New U.S. Supreme Court rulings allowed more banks into insurance. At midyear one large stockbroker began direct life insurance sales. Managed-care plans, which restricted patient and doctor choices, slowed the escalation of health insurance and workers' compensation costs.

Consolidations of insurers continued at a rapid pace in 1996, following 1995's record $27 billion of assets in merged firms. In the U.S., after having sold its property and casualty unit to the Travelers Insurance Group for $4 billion in 1995, Aetna Life and Casualty announced plans to purchase U.S. Healthcare for almost $9 billion. General Electric acquired First Colony. In the competitive reinsurance field, two giants became even larger. Munich Reinsurance (Re) Co. bought American Re for $3.3 billion, and Swiss Re agreed to purchase Mercantile & General Re for $2.7 billion. Allstate Re sold its U.S. business to Skor-Paris, and General Re acquired National Re. The multibillion-dollar merger of Royal Insurance Holdings and the Sun Alliance Group formed the largest composite insurance company in the U.K. In Mexico, Seguros Comercial America (Group Pulsar) acquired the government-owned Aseguradora Mexicana.

Sales of insurance company stock more than doubled—to $4.6 billion—from 1995. American Mutual Life Insurance became the first mutual life company under a new Iowa law to convert to a stock company while creating its own parent holding company. In a controversial trend, Cigna received regulatory approval for dividing its subsidiary Insurance Company of North America into two corporations in order to alleviate pending asbestos and other liability claims.

With the encouragement of state regulators, U.S. insurers phased in expanded underwriting guidelines for property and liability insurance in urban areas. In contrast, some insurers announced plans to curtail sales in coastal areas. A new earthquake insurance program was approved in California in order to make such protection more widely available. The potential liability of businesses and insurers for the cleanup of 1,300 hazardous-waste sites identified by the Superfund was estimated to include $41 billion of unfunded costs. A federal appeals court approved an asbestos claims payment plan that could total $3.3 billion. In the wake of several large fines for misleading sales practices, including fines against Prudential, a compliance program supported by the industry for self-regulation began. Model sales illustration and disclosure laws in many states were to go into effect early in 1997. Federal antitrust and price-fixing agencies showed increasing interest in the large number of mergers by health maintenance organizations and other insurers in the health care field.

(DAVID L. BICKELHAUPT)

MACHINERY AND MACHINE TOOLS

The worldwide production of machine tools in 1995 was valued at $36.5 billion, considerably above the 1994 total of $28.2 billion. In both years the countries that were the top five producers were, in order: Japan, Germany, United States, Italy, and Switzerland. The 1995 and 1994 production totals for the five countries were, respectively: Japan, $9.1 billion and $6.7 billion; Germany, $7.6 billion and $5.3 billion; the U.S., $4.9 billion and $3.8 billion; Italy, $3 billion and $2.3 billion; and Switzerland, $2.2 billion and $1.7 billion. As can be seen, these countries significantly increased their 1995

production over that of 1994. This occurred in response to increased worldwide demand for such equipment. The four additional countries that had 1995 machine-tool production in excess of $1 billion were Taiwan and China, each with $1.6 billion; South Korea, with $1.2 billion; and the United Kingdom, with $1 billion.

Worldwide in 1995 metal-cutting machines accounted for $26 billion of the $36.5 billion total. Metal-forming machines accounted for the balance.

Countries having a trade surplus in machine tools in 1995 included Germany, Italy, Japan, Switzerland, and Taiwan. Japan exported machine tools valued at $6.2 billion, while its imports totaled $530 million. Germany's exports were valued at $5.4 billion and its imports at $1.7 billion.

The U.S. was the leading installer of machine tools in 1995, with consumption valued at $7.1 billion. Germany ranked second with $3.9 billion. Japan and China each had consumption levels of approximately $3.5 billion. The other countries with levels over $1 billion were: Italy, $2.4 billion; South Korea, $2.3 billion; France, $1.3 billion; Taiwan, $1.2 billion; and Canada and the United Kingdom, each with approximately $1.1 billion.   (JOHN B. DEAM)

MATERIALS AND METALS

Glass. Glassmakers around the world experienced mixed fortunes in 1995, the last year for which figures were available. Although not considered a bad year, with a slight but steady increase in the volume of production, it was not as good as 1994 for some sectors, especially flat glass. Container glass fared satisfactorily in 1995, while special glass was influenced by the worsening of general industrial demand later in the year.

On the other hand, the fibreglass sector continued to grow, reaching record production and shipment figures. Demand for reinforced fibreglass continued to soar during 1995, a boom that started in 1994 and was felt throughout the world, even leading to temporary shortages. The demand for optical fibre also continued to increase. The global market for optical fibre and cable expanded by 20% per year between 1990 and 1995, and the production of reinforced fibres went up by more than 25% in the countries of the European Union (EU), from 370,000 metric tons in 1994 to more than 460,000 metric tons in 1995.

The EU produced almost 25.7 million metric tons of glass in 1995, an increase of 2.7% over the previous year. Of this figure, the glass container industry produced 16.4 million metric tons, showing only a 3.5% growth for 1995, down from 6% in 1994. Production of flat glass in the EU remained stable at 6.2 million metric tons. No increase in sales was expected for 1996 for this sector, and growth estimates for the following years were low, at about 1% per year.

In the U.S. demand for window and windshield glass for cars and trucks continued to increase, totaling about seven million metric tons in 1995. Container glass production in 1995 totaled about 20 million metric tons in the U.S. and in Canada was about one million metric tons.

An international survey of almost 1,000 primary glass manufacturing companies found that two-thirds of the respondents

were considering the implementation of new technology to meet environmental requirements. Use of oxygen-based fuel, which had been widely discussed and promoted in the industry for several years, was the technology most likely to be implemented by those companies seeking to reduce air pollution.

Sales of machine-made and hand-gathered glassware were recovering well after a poor performance during the previous two years. With a trend toward informal dining, machine-gathered glass had gained ground. New lightweight designs were leading crystal manufacturers to adapt themselves to catering to more casual dining. This sector was expected to grow about 2% annually until the year 2000.

The long-established growth trend in European glass recycling was sustained in 1995. A new all-time high was reached, with 7,487,000 metric tons being collected.

(THERESA GREEN)

Ceramics. Business activity in the ceramics industry mirrored the performance of national economies in 1996. New processes and technologies continued to have an impact on all segments of the industry, and environmental and energy issues influenced operational strategies.

The growth in construction and high automobile sales were strong motivators for the production of flat glass in 1996. Evolving technologies continued to reduce the cost of the float process, and surface-coating technologies that controlled ultraviolet, visible, and infrared transmission and reflection were key factors affecting competition in the industry. Electrochromic (undergoing a change in colour upon the passage of an electric current) research made significant advances, and small components such as rearview mirrors were already in production. The glass container market continued to slide in 1996, although specialty markets in pharmaceuticals and cosmetics and in some beverage segments grew. Technologies focusing on weight reduction, surface treatments for durability and strength, and bulk and ion-exchange strengthening processes held the potential for improved market penetration against polymers.

Advanced ceramics had grown to more than $20 billion in sales by 1996. Electronic materials continued to dominate the category (75%), and the high growth rate of computers and communications equipment made electronic ceramics the fastest-growing major product sector. Multilayer ceramic capacitors gained market share by improving their cost-effectiveness through a reduction in thickness, which increased the efficiency of the material to sustain a steady electric field and serve as an insulator. Multilayer, multicomponent (MLMC) electronic packages were also beginning to enter the market. The technology, which significantly reduced the cost of complex devices, permitted several electronic components, such as capacitors and inductors, to be built into a multilayer ceramic package, thereby producing circuits for use in the large-volume consumer market. Fuzzy-logic circuits, for example, which were already in use in military equipment, emerged in consumer products such as camcorders. Because of competition from improvements in the heat-removal capabilities of polymer packages, there was a sharp decrease in the production of conventional ceramic packages for integrated circuits.

Advanced structural and composite ceramics, historically limited to aerospace and military applications, continued a slow but steady market penetration in the industrial sector because of lower costs and higher reliability. Demand was particularly evident for heat- and wear-resistant structural ceramics for industrial equipment and engines. Biologically compatible materials continued to gain market share as a result of advances in biocompatible surface technologies, such as those based on hydroxyapatite and derivative compounds. Orthopedic and dental implants were a majority of this segment.

The newest and fastest-growing group of high-technology materials was optical and electro-optical glass and ceramic materials, particularly active devices that enabled optical switching and logic structures. These materials, which included optical fibres, sensors, and planar structures, were in high demand for electronic applications.

Whiteware ceramics, principally floor and wall tile, dinnerware, sanitaryware, and artware, continued to show steady growth over the long term. There was substantial growth in areas such as the Pacific Rim. Fast firing, a standard part of tile processing, was overcoming technical hurdles in the sanitaryware and dinnerware processes and was contributing to higher productivity. Raw-material quality, availability, and costs continued as a concern for all segments. A principal concern among whiteware manufacturers during 1996 was the conversion to lead-free glazes and decorations to reduce workplace risks and to skirt marketplace regulations in some states. Continued strong development and implementation of pressure casting continued in whiteware production as a result of improvements in equipment and successes of plant trials.

Environmental issues continued to be a strong factor in all segments of the industry. Of particular note were product regulations and recycling policies that motivated the development of disassembly, material recovery, and recycling processes, particularly for ceramics containing hazardous elements such as lead and cadmium. Cathode-ray tubes and lead and cadmium compounds in contact with food were two examples. The enormous amounts of glass obtained from municipal recycling programs continued to motivate research on the potentially high value in reusing ceramic products.

(RICHARD L. LEHMAN)

Rubber. The labour side of the rubber industry took centre stage in 1996 as one of the longest strikes in U.S. history came to an end and plant closings announced in Austria and Greece provoked violent reactions. In the U.S. the 27-month contract dispute with Bridgestone/Firestone ended when a tentative pact was achieved in November. The workers voted in December to ratify the proposal. The strike was begun by the United Rubber Workers of America and settled by the United Steelworkers of America, which absorbed the URW during the strike. It was a bitter dispute that saw the union take its case to Bridgestone's Japanese headquarters and file numerous charges of unfair labour practices.

In Traiskirchen, Austria, Continental's plans to cut production at its Semperit tire-manufacturing facility met with strong opposition from both the workforce and government leaders. A boycott of Continental products was called for by the union and the Austrian chamber of commerce after the company announced plans to move production machinery to another subsidiary plant in the Czech Republic. A compromise kept 1,200 of the 2,300-person workforce and halved tire production to two million units per year. The company left capacity available to increase production if warranted.

The announced closing by Goodyear of the last tire-manufacturing facility in Greece caused employees to occupy the site for a time. Some of the 350-person workforce threatened to stop the movement of equipment out of the plant in Thessaloníki. Goodyear was moving the production to other European facilities.

Changes in plants and equipment to increase efficiency and, therefore, profitability were taking place throughout the world. Toyo Tire announced that it was transferring tire production from its facility in Itami, Japan, to a newer plant in Kuwana. Pirelli SpA closed its tire plant in Nashville, Tenn., and Mark IV Industries announced that it was closing down five plants—four in Europe and its Dayco hose and belt plant in North Carolina. Continental closed its tire facility in Dublin and laid off 500 workers at its tire plant in Mayfield, Ky. Two condom manufacturers closed U.S. plants; Carter-Wallace shut down its facility in Trenton, N.J., and London International Group announced plans to close its plant in Anderson, S.C.

Major acquisitions that took place in 1996 included the Michelin purchase of majority control of Taurus Rubber from Hungary's state privatization agency. Taurus had two tire and three industrial rubber products plants. Michelin later sold the industrial plants to Germany's Phoenix. Other acquisitions included the purchase by Tomkins of Great Britain of U.S.-based Gates Rubber, which was purchasing Nationwide Rubber Enterprises of Australia. Norton Performance Plastics bought two silicone product manufacturers in France and two in Germany. Sweden's Trelleborg was buying rubber product manufacturer Horda and its five Swedish plants, and Trelleborg also purchased Michelin's hose and rubber sheeting business in France. Goodyear bought the assets of Sime Darby in the Philippines, which included a shut-down tire plant. Mark IV bought hose maker Imperial Eastman, and Tenneco bought Clevite Elastomer, a maker of automotive suspension parts.

Asia was the primary location for many of the expansion projects announced in 1996. Among the major announcements was a Chinese tire plant with an annual capacity of 1.6 million tires in Hainan province. South Korea's Kumho announced that it would build a three million-per-year tire facility in India. Hankook Tire of South Korea opened its Kumsan plant and announced that it would be part of a tire and tube plant to open in China in 1998. India's MRF planned to have a radial tire plant in operation in 1997 in Pondicherry, and Yokohama Rubber said that it intended to have a Philippine passenger tire facility operating by 1998 near Manila. Outside Asia, Michelin began construction on a passenger tire facility near Göteborg, Swed. Dunlop India, with technical support from Pirelli, was involved in a project to construct the first tire-manufacturing facility in the Middle East, to be located in the United Arab

Emirates. Titan Tire was building an off-the-road tire facility in Texas, and Bridgestone/Firestone was expanding its Joliette, Que., plant by almost 30%.

Rubber industry suppliers made plans to add capacity in Asia to keep pace with demand. Bayer announced plans to build two polybutadiene (BR) and styrene butadiene (SBR) rubber facilities with capacities of between 100,000 and 120,000 tons annually. China and India were the likely locations. Hyundai Petrochemical opened a SBR-BR-nitrile facility in Daesan, S.Kor. Synthetics & Chemicals increased the SBR capacity at its India facility. A plant that would produce 100,000 tons of SBR per year was planned for Thailand by Bangkok Synthetics, and a similar plant was scheduled for Nantong province in China.

The International Natural Rubber Agreement was ratified by China and the U.S., the last two signatories. The agreement would attempt to stabilize prices and supplies. In India the government said that it would keep import controls on natural rubber to help protect local growers. Many manufacturers complained of shortages.

(DONALD SMITH)

Plastics. The plastics industry, relatively immune to the business recession of the early 1990s, continued its healthy growth during 1996. In terms of production, the major plastic materials in 1995, the last year for which figures were available, were low-density polyethylene (with the largest use being packaging film), polyvinyl chloride (pipe), high-density polyethylene (bottles), polypropylene (fibres), and polystyrene (food-packaging containers). Overall, more than 40% of the markets and products for plastics were in packaging and in building and construction, but they were also used widely in a variety of other products, including motor vehicles, aircraft, household appliances, and furniture. The projected growth rate worldwide to the year 2000 was 3.8% per year.

Plastics continued to replace conventional materials because they were easier to manufacture, were tougher, and provided thermal and electrical insulation. Other attractive characteristics included their wide range of rigidity/flexibility, adhesion/self-lubrication/nonstick behaviour; their transparency/opacity and colour possibilities; and their resistance to water, rust, and rot.

Improvements in materials were led by the development of metallocene catalysts for the production of polyethylene and polypropylene, which provided improvements in rigidity and flexibility, toughness, scuff and heat resistance, and clarity. New grades of polystyrene demonstrated improved performance, which made them competitive with expensive specialty plastics. New polyethylene naphthalate was superior to conventional polyester for such products as fibres, bottles, and films. Deposition of a thin inorganic silica surface on plastic films produced transparent packaging film with barrier properties that made it competitive with aluminum foil.

Improvements in machinery and processes continued in many areas. Polyethylene polymerization by new vapour-phase technology resulted in major increases in productivity at British Petroleum, Exxon, Shell, and Union Carbide. The coextrusion of multilayer film, of up to eight different layers, was facilitated by the design of stackable dies for blown-film extrusion, combining the best qualities of all the layers.

New products made from plastics included body panels, grilles, and under-the-hood parts in autos; disposable medical products for diagnostic and treatment kits; high-barrier and selectively permeable containers and films for food packaging; suspension bridge cables that were superior to steel; bicycle wheels; outdoor lumber more durable than wood; and auto fenders that would not dent or rust. Plastic products that continued to show rapid growth included kitchen, bath, and commercial interiors (25% per year); house siding (20%); polyethylene pipe for natural gas transmission and other fluids (8.5%); reinforced polypropylene for washing machines, dishwashers, ovens, and refrigerators; replacement for glass in appliances; molded interconnects for electronics, compact discs, and CD-ROMs; and wood-grain-vinyl structural foam that would outlast natural wood.

Recycling technology continued to improve, but the economics of recycling were limited by the reliance on voluntary manual collection and sorting. In the U.S., plastic bottle recycling reached 22% of new production, plastic packaging 7%, and total plastics 2%, and it was growing at a rate of 21% per year. European Union targets were considerably higher. While thermoset plastic scrap was usually considered unrecyclable, the conversion of flexible polyurethane foam into rug underlays was a dramatic example of successful recycling.

(RUDOLPH D. DEANIN)

Advanced Composites. During 1996 the market for composite materials continued to increase. It was estimated that shipments of composites of all types reached 1.5 million metric tons, an increase of about 3% above the level of 1995. It was the fifth consecutive year that shipments of composites had increased. The 1996 increases were consistent across all markets except for the aircraft-aerospace-defense sector, which had remained fairly constant.

The market for advanced polymeric composites, primarily composites reinforced with carbon fibres, had stabilized since the early 1990s, a period characterized by a reduced military market after the end of the Cold War and a worldwide recession. After 1993 the recovery of the commercial aircraft market and the increased use of composite materials in the sporting goods and industrial equipment sectors helped the industry make a transition from defense to higher-volume, lower-cost applications. This transition led the industry to emphasize the development of cost-effective materials and manufacturing processes. For example, processes that produced low-cost carbon fibres in bundles with an increasing number of filaments were finding applications in high-volume markets. In addition, innovative automated processing methods—such as pultrusion, robotic tow placement, and resin transfer molding—were successfully demonstrated and beginning to find wider acceptance.

The industry was attempting to make greater penetration into two potentially large markets that would make use of lower-cost materials and processing methods—construction and automobiles. The application of advanced composite technology in construction and infrastructure renewal continued to show promise. Examples of

technologies that were being evaluated included composite bars for reinforcing concrete, fibre-reinforced composite civil engineering structures, composite reinforcement and overwrap for seismic and structural upgrades and repairs, and composite reinforced wood laminates for beam structures.

Composites in the form of sheet molding compounds (SMC) were becoming especially important in the production of automobiles. The amount of SMC used by the automotive industry had increased more than 70% since 1990. The application of high-performance composites in automobiles was inhibited, however, by improvements in the strength and toughness of metals (including aluminum, magnesium, and steel alloys), the relatively high cost of composite materials and manufacturing processes, and the difficulty of recycling advanced composites.   (THOMAS E. MUNNS; ROBERT E. SCHAFRIK)

Iron and Steel. The iron and steel industry had a good year in 1995, the last year for which complete figures were available, although there were considerable regional variations. The North American steel market remained strong, with a buoyant automotive industry and a strong residential sector, and the European market rose to a peak in the first half of the year, led by the automotive industry and by machinery and equipment. Elsewhere conditions were quieter. China's demand was subdued after the import binge of 1993 and 1994, and the recovery in Japanese steel consumption was hesitant. The decline in consumption in the countries of the former Soviet Union continued but at a much more moderate rate than in previous years.

World crude steel output rose by more than 3%, to 753.4 million metric tons. Japan remained the leading producer, with 101.6 million metric tons. Reflecting the strong domestic market and the installation of new capacity, the U.S. returned to second place, with 95.2 million metric tons, ahead of China, where production stagnated at just under 93 million metric tons.

The underlying rate of steel consumption remained firm throughout 1996, but excess inventories that had built up in Europe and Japan in 1995 caused a slowdown in deliveries to those markets. Reflecting this, crude steel production in the European Union in the first nine months of 1996 was 7.7% below that in the same months of 1995, while in Japan the decline was 5%. Reduced export potential affected the output of the Central European steel producers (down 11.5%) and, compounded by declining domestic demand, that of the countries of the former U.S.S.R. (down 2.2%).

Steel producers in other regions fared better. Despite some technical problems in the United States steel industry, continuing growth in capacity (especially from casting technology that permitted the production of flat goods, using the electric arc furnace) allowed crude steel output to grow by 1.3% in the first nine months of 1996 compared with 1995, while production growth resumed in China (5% in the first nine months). Despite slowing domestic demand, production also increased during this period in Taiwan (11.1%) and South Korea (7.1%). World output, however, was down 1.4%.

Toward the end of 1996, there was optimism that the excess inventories in Europe and Japan had been reabsorbed and that,

despite stagnation in the former Soviet countries and in Japan, global steel consumption would resume its growth in 1997.

(ANTHONY TRICKETT)

Light Metals. The production of aluminum in 1996 was 16 million metric tons. The industry was not able to sustain the price recovery that took place in 1995. A generally flat product market and an increase in the London Metal Exchange inventory contributed to the lower prices. With the expiration in 1996 of the two-year memorandum of understanding signed by major producers in 1994, some capacity was restarted. Nonetheless, much production capacity remained idle.

Cans for the beverage industry remained the largest single product market for aluminum, consuming 2.1 million tons of metal in the U.S. alone. During 1996, however, the market remained static, the first time in its 35-year history that it had not exhibited growth. Several production facilities in the U.S. were closed, and some European lines switched from aluminum to steel can production. Growth potential still existed in the Middle Eastern, Asian, and South American areas, however, where new plants were being built.

Transportation continued to be the second largest aluminum market. During 1996 the use of aluminum in new U.S. motor vehicles increased 4%, to an average of 94 kg (203 lb).

Magnesium production in 1996 totaled 310,000 metric tons. During 1996 a new plant in Israel began production, with an annual capacity of 27,000 metric tons. The price of magnesium was lower than in 1995, but it varied widely, depending on the source and purity of the metal.

The titanium industry appeared to be continuing a difficult but successful transition from a market dominated by military aerospace to a more balanced one that included such consumer products as golf clubs and tennis rackets. There also were increasing applications in the commercial aircraft market, especially as in the Boeing 777. Total world production figures remained elusive in 1996 because many suppliers declined to report data that they considered confidential. The U.S. titanium industry, which produced 20,000 metric tons and was effectively sold out for 1996, announced capacity expansions.

Beryllium production remained in the range of 650 to 700 metric tons in 1996. Its use continued to be limited by the relatively high price, which confined it to niche markets in nuclear reactors, aerospace items, copper alloys, and specialty electronic components.

Lithium continued to emerge as an addition to aluminum alloys for use in space programs. Its relatively high price could be justified by use in a space vehicle or station, where the reduction of payload was critical.   (GEORGE J. BINCZEWSKI)

Metalworking. After double-digit annual growth during the first half of the 1990s, there was stagnation in the shipment of metal parts in 1996. Sales of ferrous castings dropped by an estimated 4%, to 16.5 million tons, owing primarily to slowing machinery sales, while aluminum and magnesium castings showed slight gains. Shipments of powder metal parts were up only 2.6%, to 375,000 tons, after early 1996 losses caused by strikes at General Motors.

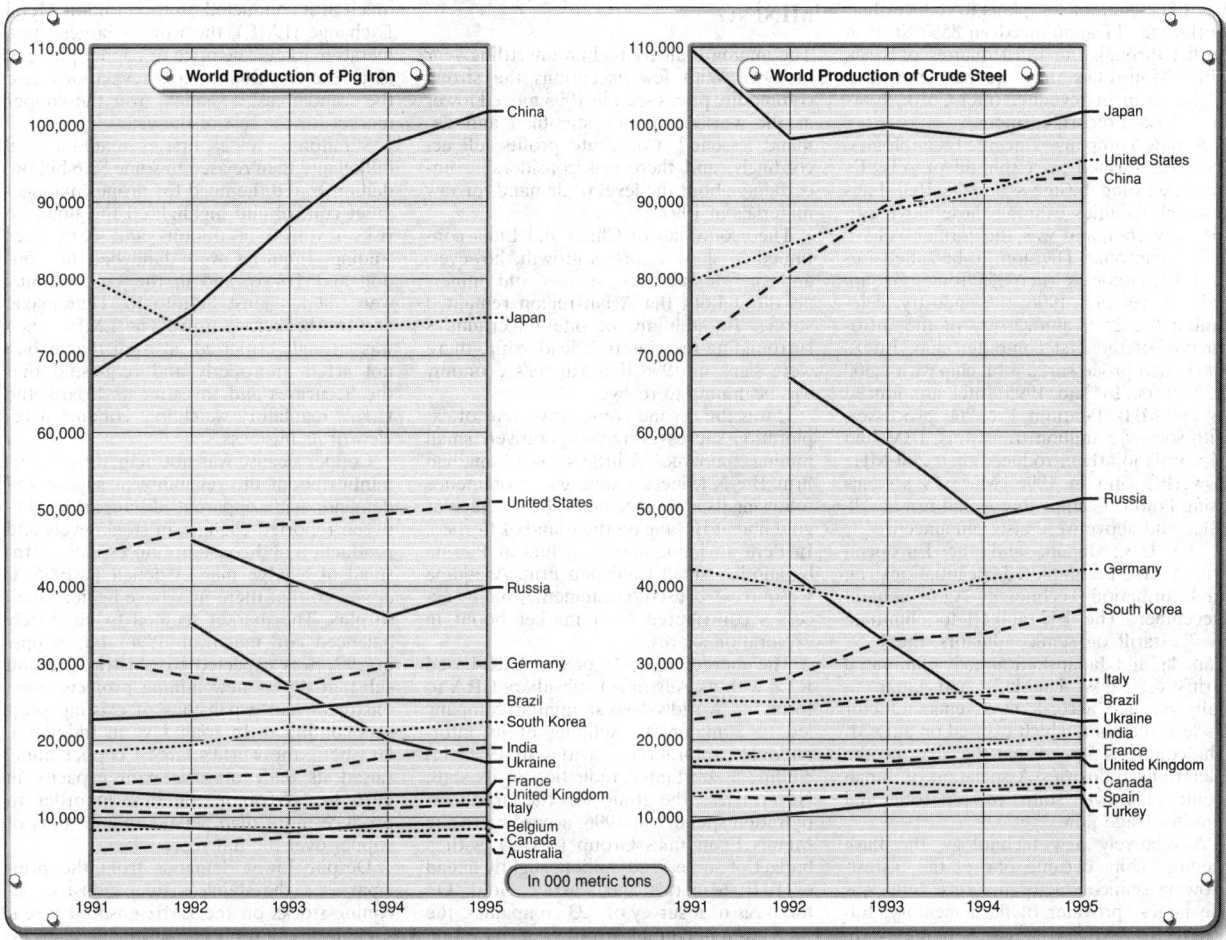

World Production of Pig Iron

World Production of Crude Steel

In 000 metric tons

Source: *International Iron and Steel Institute.*

Forging sales continued to increase, but at a reduced rate of 7.5%, to a total of 1.6 million tons. Shipments of extruded aluminum shapes dropped slightly, to 1.7 million tons, owing primarily to increased competition from plastics and roll-formed steel sheet in construction products. Copper and copper alloy extrusions, meanwhile, maintained hefty growth because of strength in electrical and welding products.

In general, the markets for metal parts were expected to rebound to a growth rate of 3–5% in 1997. Powder-forged connecting rods were now being used in 13 different engines of the Big Three U.S. automakers and could capture 50% of the market by the year 2000. The metal injection moulding sector of the powder metallurgy industry was increasing at a 25% rate, with market expansion from medical, firearm, business, automotive, cutting tool, and eyeglass applications. Growth in domestic forging shipments was expected as the improved competitive posture of U.S. forge shops helped attract orders for automotive parts that were currently being imported.

While the projected continuation of a weak U.S. dollar would allow increased sales of metal parts to foreign markets, a greater influence on growth would be the revived global competitiveness of U.S. manufacturers and the adoption of new technologies. In response to inroads from plastics and composites, new alloys with higher strength, resulting in metal parts with reduced weight, were being brought to market. As an example, General Motors developed a new

generation of zinc alloys for die casting. In addition to higher strength, the aluminum-copper-zinc alloys had greater resistance to creep (slow deformation) and wear than traditional zinc alloys. Additional levels of competitiveness resulted from the expanded use of computer-aided engineering tools. Progressive foundries and die casters, for example, integrated solid modeling, process simulation, and rapid prototyping to speed up product delivery and improve quality. The overall health of the $31 billion North American metalworking market was best indicated by the record number of attendees and exhibitors at metalworking equipment and process trade shows in 1996.

(HOWARD A. KUHN)

MICROELECTRONICS

Projected worldwide sales of semiconductors in 1996 fell by 10.5% to $129.2 billion, according to the Semiconductor Industry Association (SIA). This was the first time in 11 years that the industry had experienced negative growth. As telecommunications and consumer products made greater use of semiconductor products, the SIA expected a growth rate of 7.4% in 1997, 17.1% in 1998, and 21.6% in 1999 (to $197.6 billion).

Although the Americas (North and South) experienced an 11.1% decline in 1996 to $41.7 billion, that market was expected to retain its lead in the world chip markets into the year 2000. The Americas market represented about one-third of the world market. The Japanese supplied

another 26.1%, down 14.8% from 1995 to $39.6 billion. The Asia-Pacific market, including South Korea, Taiwan, China, and Singapore, despite a 9.2% decline to $26.8 billion, continued to be the fastest-growing market. The European market declined only 4.8% in 1996 to $26.8 billion but should reach $40.2 billion in 1999, retaining approximately 20% of the world chip market.

In spite of the decline, several manufacturers were planning to construct new facilities. Motorola, Inc., announced plans to build a $40 million corporate campus for its Messaging Information and Media Sector in Elgin, Ill. National Semiconductor proposed to spend up to $270 million to upgrade its plant in Greenock, Scot. Taiwanese semiconductor maker Mosel-Vitelic and Siemens AG of Germany planned a $1.7 billion manufacturing plant in Taiwan.

Motorola, attempting to increase demand for its PowerPC chip, and Apple Computer, Inc., announced a licensing agreement in February whereby Motorola could sublicense the Macintosh operating system (Mac OS) to other manufacturers that bought Motorola motherboards as well as allow Motorola to market the OS under its own name. Hyundai Electronics Industries Co., and Fujitsu Microelectronics, Inc., announced a joint venture involving co-development and technology licensing.

The downturn in the semiconductor industry resulted in a number of companies, including Motorola, Advanced Micro Devices, Inc. (AMD), and Texas Instruments,

Inc. (TI), announcing plans to reduce their workforce. TI announced an 85% drop in profits through the third quarter of 1996, while Motorola's third quarter showed a 58.5% drop in revenue. Intel Corp., however, posted record earnings.

A new company, Lucent Technologies, Inc., was formed by a spin-off of AT&T's manufacturing business and its Bell Labs research facilities. Among those moving to the new company was the former AT&T Microelectronics Division, to be called Lucent Technologies Microelectronics Group.

In November 1996 the industry celebrated the 25th anniversary of the introduction of the first computer chip, Intel's 4004 microprocessor, a 4-bit chip with 2,300 transistors. In late 1995 Intel announced its 200-MHz Pentium Pro 200 processor, with some 5.5 million transistors. IBM and Motorola jointly introduced their 200-MHz PowerPC chip in 1996. Mac OS systems using PowerPC chips that would run at 225 MHz and above were also announced.

The U.S., Japan, and the European Union (EU) completed negotiations on an Information Technology Agreement in December. The EU agreed to eliminate its 7% tariff on semiconductors; the U.S., Canada, and Japan had already eliminated tariffs on chips. The U.S. and Japan finally reached accord on a semiconductor trade agreement, which expired on July 31. The countries agreed that the SIA and the Electronic Industries Association of Japan would take over statistical reporting and monitor trade flow.

A relatively new technology, the flash memory chip, became one of the fastest-growing semiconductor markets. Intel was the largest provider of flash memory, followed by AMD. The cards, which were about the size of a book of matches, were available in capacities of up to 64 megabytes and could be used to store images or data in digital cameras, digital wireless messaging, audio voice recorders, personal digital assistants, and solid-state hard drives.

Another new technology, "smart cards" (credit-card-sized cards with embedded memory), was being driven by the credit-card, airline, and travel and leisure industries as an alternative to cash. Motorola became the first company to manufacture the required microchip in the U.S. The cards were already popular in Europe, where applications included fingerprint identification cards and health care cards.

New applications for digital signal processing chips, which were widely used in image and sound compression, included drive positioning, error correction, and tracking accuracy for portable CD-ROM drives, supporting V.34 digital simultaneous voice data modems and full duplex speaker phones, and providing the functions of a base transceiver station in cellular networks.

Owing to the popularity of the Internet and World Wide Web, faster modems were required for downloading the larger amount of image and graphic data. New modems with speeds of 56,000 bits per second were being developed by a number of vendors to work over analog phone lines. The first such modem was announced by U.S. Robotics Corp. of Skokie, Ill. New cellular chip technology was expected to provide for the new personal communications service and other digital cellular applications.

(THOMAS E. KROLL)

MINING

The mining industry had an unsettling year in 1996. With few exceptions the strong commodity prices seen in 1995 moved lower as the world economy stumbled and demand lessened. Corporate profits fell accordingly, and there was considerable uncertainty about the level of demand for raw materials in 1997.

The economies of China and India continued to show vigorous growth, however, and the demand for metals and minerals throughout the Asian region remained strong. In addition, despite uncertainties surrounding the country's leadership, there were signs in 1996 that Russia's economy was beginning to recover.

It was the second consecutive year of exploration successes by comparatively small mining companies. A little-known Canadian firm, Bre-X Minerals, sprang to prominence following its announcement of a spectacular gold find at Busang on the island of Borneo. In Peru an impressive gold find at Pierina by another small Canadian firm, Arequipa Resources, caused excitement. Such successes contributed to a market boom in exploration shares.

The merger in 1995 of the U.K.-based RTZ with its Australian subsidiary CRA to form the world's largest mining company led to a major streamlining of its international exploration activities in 1996, including a substantial reduction in its staff. Nevertheless, the group was the largest exploration spender in 1996, according to the Metals Economics Group (MEG), with a budget of some $280 million, slightly ahead of BHP Minerals and Barrick Gold. On the basis of a survey of 223 companies, the MEG estimated that worldwide exploration spending for nonferrous metals in 1996 rose by 30%, to some $4.6 billion. South America attracted most attention, followed by Australia and Canada. In the diamond sector a feature of exploration activity was the interest in marine deposits off the coast of Namibia and South Africa.

In those countries with state-controlled mining organizations, privatization continued to be seen as an effective means of increasing efficiency and raising fresh capital. In 1996 privatization went ahead in Peru, and in Poland the government prepared to sell off KGHM Polska Miedz, Europe's biggest copper producer. In Brazil the government's advisers prepared a lengthy document for the proposed privatization of Companhia Vale do Rio Doce, one of the world's largest and most successful mining and industrial conglomerates.

Plans to privatize the Zambian copper mining industry were deferred until after the November general elections. In Zaire political uncertainties and economic malaise limited the private sector's interest in that country's copper mining industry. The privatization of Ghana's Ashanti Goldfields was an undoubted success, however. The company subsequently acquired two additional gold mining companies and maintained an active exploration program in several other African countries.

The base metals markets were dominated by the Sumitomo affair. In June the Japanese company revealed that it had incurred huge losses over a 10-year period as a result of unauthorized futures trading by its then chief copper trader, Yasuo Hamanaka,

much of it conducted on the London Metal Exchange (LME), the world's largest base metals market. The price of copper plunged as a result of Sumitomo's revelations, and the scandal cast a shadow over the copper market for the rest of the year.

Sumitomo's losses, first estimated at $1.8 billion and then revised to some $2.6 billion, demonstrated the need for proper management control and highlighted the financial risks involved in options and derivatives trading. Inquiries were launched in London and Tokyo, and in the U.S. lawsuits were filed against Sumitomo, Hamanaka, and two brokerage firms. The LME, which was strongly criticized, insisted that it had not acted improperly and requested that the Securities and Investments Board, the U.K.'s regulatory watchdog, conduct a review of its business.

Copper's cause was not helped by uncertainties about the reliability of supply and demand, with apparent discrepancies between reported changes in stock levels and production and consumption estimates. Instead of a large market deficit in 1995, it appeared that there may have been a small surplus. The market seemed to be closely balanced for much of 1996, but supply in 1997 was expected to outstrip demand substantially as new mining projects came onstream and expansions of existing projects continued. In Irian Jaya in Indonesia, Grasberg, the world's largest copper mine, raised its daily ore-treatment capacity in 1996 to 125,000 metric tons in order to produce more than 500,000 metric tons of copper over the full year.

Despite lower demands from the principal user, the stainless steel industry, declining stocks on the LME ensured a reasonable price level for nickel in 1996, and the market was able to absorb the continuing high level of exports from Norilsk in Russia, the world's largest producer. Nickel prices weakened significantly at the year's end, however, as consumers used up their excess stocks.

There was a battle for the control of the giant Voisey's Bay nickel-copper-cobalt deposit in Labrador, which had been discovered in 1994 by the small Canadian firm Diamond Fields Resources. There were numerous suitors, but the contest eventually narrowed down to a fight for control between Canada's two major nickel producers, Falconbridge and Inco. Falconbridge made a Can$4 billion bid in February, but Inco eventually emerged as the winner after a complex counterbid in March worth Can$4.3 billion.

Low stocks helped to buoy prices for lead despite a big increase in exports by China, and in late March the metal was trading at its highest price in more than five years. A steady fall in stocks helped support the zinc market, and although prices showed no major improvement, producers were optimistic about prospects for 1997. Aluminum consumption fell by 4% in the first half of 1996, and, while demand subsequently began to improve, the price fell steadily, to the puzzlement of many producers.

Gold supply and demand remained tightly balanced in 1996; speculators showed little interest, and by the end of 1996 the price of gold had dipped to a two-year low. In South Africa, the world's dominant producer, productivity continued to be impaired by unrest at the mines as the workforce pressed for better pay and conditions. Since South Africa's political transformation, the number of public holidays had been increased, which also affected productivity. Nevertheless, the production decline of about 5% in 1996 was not as severe as the 10% fall in 1995. Offsetting the decline in South Africa were increases in the U.S., Australia, and Canada. Anglo American Corp. of South Africa made progress in 1996 in developing a large new open-pit mine at Sadiola in Mali, and Randgold Resources acquired control of the Syama mine in Mali from the Australian firm BHP.

Platinum-group metals enjoyed another good year in 1996, with industrial demand the driving force. The supply of platinum-group metals was more than sufficient to meet the demand, and market prices remained steady. South Africa was the dominant producer, but Russian exports of both platinum and palladium continued to be maintained at levels believed to be far in excess of the country's production capability, which implied that much of its sales was from stocks. The size of Russia's stockpile was a closely guarded secret.

The commissioning of Hartley, a new platinum mine in Zimbabwe, began in April, and the Australian owners of the $264 million project, BHP and Delta Gold, expected that production would start in mid-1997. At full production the mine would produce some 4,245,000 g (150,000 oz) of platinum per year.

Also in April the European Commission announced that it was blocking the planned merger of the platinum mining interests of U.K.-based Lonrho and the South African company Gencor. The commission said that the merger would have been against European Union interests, since it would have established a duopoly in the platinum market between Lonrho-Gencor and Anglo American. Together the two groups would have had a 63% share of the platinum market and control of about 90% of the world's platinum reserves. In October, Anglo American became the main shareholder in Lonrho, whose assets included South African platinum mines. The move triggered another anticompetition investigation by the commission.

The De Beers Consolidated Mines monopoly in rough (uncut) diamonds came under pressure during 1996. In February a memorandum of understanding was reached with Russia concerning an extension to the marketing agreement that had expired in 1995, but there was dissatisfaction in Moscow about some of the proposals. No formal agreement was finalized, and substantial quantities of Russian diamonds were reported to be "leaking" onto the market. Russia accounted for 26% by value of the world's supply.

A clear challenge to the De Beers single marketing channel, its Central Selling Organisation (CSO), arose in midyear when the Argyle joint-venture partners in Australia announced that they would not renew the marketing agreement with the CSO and would sell their diamonds independently. Although the Argyle mine was the largest diamond producer by volume, accounting for almost 40% of the world's supply, it contributed only 6% of the CSO's intake by value.

Iron ore producers secured significant price increases for the second successive year in 1996, and there were expectations that production would exceed the record one billion metric tons achieved in 1995. China had become the world's biggest producer, with annual production of approximately 250 million metric tons, but its ore was generally of low grade. Brazil and Australia continued to dominate world trade in iron ore.

For several years uranium producers had suffered from low prices, with annual mine production no more than 33,000 metric tons. Despite the supply shortage, prices remained low because of the abundance of uranium held in inventories. With these stocks being depleted, however, the price revived during the year. By mid-May the spot price was double the 1991 low, which encouraged producers.

An aerial view of Grasberg, the world's largest copper mine, in Irian Jaya, in Indonesia, reveals extensive open-pit operations. Irian Jaya's abundant natural resources, ranging from extensive rain forests to rich mineral deposits, remained vital to the Indonesian government, but a strong separatist organization there was fighting what tribal groups felt was the spoliation of their lands by mining.

GEORGE STEINMETZ

In the U.S. low-cost projects involving in situ leaching of uranium were being reconsidered. The method, used widely in the uranium-producing republics of the former Soviet Union, involves sinking wells and injecting acid solutions to dissolve the uranium, which is then pumped to the surface. In Canada, which accounted for 30% of global uranium output, innovative technology was being tested at the high-grade underground deposit at Cigar Lake. High-pressure water was injected into frozen ground to reach the ore, which was then pumped to the surface in a slurry; human contact was thereby eliminated.

The new government in Australia indicated that it would end that country's long-held three-mine uranium policy. This gave rise to expectations that in the Northern Territory one of the world's largest deposits, Jabiluka, would at last be developed. Uncertainty remained about the uranium-production capabilities in the republics of the former Soviet Union and about how much of the uranium that they previously used for military purposes could be converted to civilian use.

Despite concerns that carbon dioxide produced by coal burned in power stations was contributing to the greenhouse effect and thus contributing to climate change, the demand for coal to generate power continued to increase. The opportunities offered by the Asian market encouraged producers in Australia and Indonesia to expand production, and efforts to raise output were also being made in such countries as Colombia and Venezuela.

In the U.S. environmental regulations, including the country's 1990 Clean Air Act, had served to increase the attractiveness of the low-sulfur-coal deposits of the Powder River Basin of Wyoming and Montana.

Wyoming had become the leading U.S. coal producer, with its mines producing in excess of 240 million metric tons annually, equivalent to more than one-quarter of the total U.S. output.

Perhaps the most significant environmental incident in 1996 took place on Marinduque Island in the Philippines. Marcopper Mining suspended operations in March after material that eventually totaled approximately four million metric tons was released into the local river system when a concrete plug failed in a drainage tunnel leading from a mined-out open pit used to store tailings. No human life was lost, but three senior mine officials were charged with criminal offenses, and a public outcry led the Philippine government to review the environmental provisions of its new mining law.

The global interdependence of mining and its implications for employment were demonstrated during 1996 by the Century zinc saga. RTZ-CRA, which had discovered a major zinc deposit in Queensland, Australia, was frustrated in its attempt to develop the Century mine there because of an impasse in negotiations with local Aboriginal groups. The Australian government sought to intervene in a bid to expedite the project.

Meanwhile, in The Netherlands the government was worried about environmental problems at the Budel zinc smelter, which would be forced to close unless it could be fed with zinc concentrates low in iron content. Century could provide such feed, but there were doubts as to whether the mine could be developed in time.

(ROGER ELLIS)

See also Earth Sciences.

This article updates the *Macropædia* article Extraction and Processing INDUSTRIES.

PAINTS AND VARNISHES

The U.S. paint industry did well in 1996. The volume of paint shipments jumped by 12.5% during the first half of the year, following record sales during 1994 and 1995. European demand was flat and in some countries even receded. Japan failed to return to its output peak of the late 1980s. The Asian Pacific paint industries, particularly China, remained the star performers, however.

Acquisitions in 1996 included Imperial Chemical Industries's (ICI's) $390 million purchase of Bunge Paints of South America and Valspar's $125 million gain of the Coates can coatings business from the French company Total SA. The Bunge holdings raised ICI's share of the South American market from 2.5% to 15% and confirmed ICI as the world leader in paint. Valspar's acquisition of Coates gave it 40 sites worldwide, including entry into Europe.

Sherwin-Williams, ICI's rival for Grow Group in 1995, also turned its attention to South America, buying a string of companies there, among them Productos Quimicos y Pinturas in Mexico and its licensee Sherwin-Williams in Argentina, followed by Elgin, Lazzuril, and Globo, all in Brazil, and the Stierling Group in Chile.

In Europe, PPG Industries acquired the German Schwaab, a producer of commercial transport coatings, while Du Pont bought its U.K. licensee Carr Paints. Akzo Nobel purchased paintmaker Nobiles of Poland. In the Asian Pacific region, China continued to act as a magnet for Western technology and investment. PPG opened its first manufacturing facility at Tientsin, while BASF of Germany and Kansai and Nippon of Japan were among the companies embarking on joint ventures there.

Environmental considerations continued to be the major driving force behind technical innovation, typified by the search for technically viable coatings with little or no solvent content. The battle among the alternatives was being fought in the automotive original equipment market. U.S. paint manufacturers were pushing for powder coatings, European for water-based paints. Herberts, the market leader in the field, had begun to supply Opel's plant at Eisenach, Ger., with a complete water-based range, from primer to top coat. Market victory, however, was far from assured.

Environmental regulation continued in 1996, though at a somewhat gentler pace. The Environmental Protection Agency issued rules for architectural and maintenance coatings in the U.S., and the shelved solvent directive in the European Union was revived. (HELMA JOTISCHKY)

PHARMACEUTICALS

The U.S. pharmaceutical industry failed to benefit from a more conservative Congress in 1996. The industry's long-sought reform of the Food and Drug Administration was not enacted. After the U.S. elections in November, it seemed clear that any future reform legislation would be moderate.

The industry in the United States received an unexpected boost from managed health care. To compete for patients, some managed-care organizations (MCOs) added drug coverage. This raised the consump-

Indexes of Production, Mining and Mineral Commodities

(1980 = 100)

	1991	1992	1993	1994	1995	1996 1st qtr.	1996 2nd qtr.
Mining (total)							
World[1]	97.7	101.3	103.2	106.7	116.2	116.7	...
Developed market economies[2]	107.0	107.9	108.7	113.6	115.8	121.7	116.4
North America[3]	94.6	94.3	93.8	96.4	97.8	98.1	99.3
European Economic Community[4]	91.8	91.7	93.2	100.3	102.4	117.9	102.3
Less-developed market economies[5]	91.3	96.9	99.4	102.1	116.4	113.2	...
Coal							
World[1]	98.6	96.0	91.4	90.7	91.3	93.1	...
Developed market economies[2]	92.7	88.7	82.6	81.4	80.3	78.9	77.8
North America[3]	123.5	121.8	116.9	127.5	128.4	126.2	129.8
European Economic Community[4]	72.3	67.0	58.7	51.2	48.4	46.2	44.0
Less-developed market economies[5]	203.1	226.0	246.9	255.7	285.9	344.9	...
Petroleum and natural gas							
World[1]	90.8	95.8	99.6	104.0	115.7	116.2	...
Developed market economies[2]	103.5	106.9	112.5	122.7	126.3	139.5	128.3
North America[3]	81.3	80.6	81.5	82.9	83.1	83.6	85.1
European Economic Community[4]	108.5	114.0	125.8	147.2	153.2	192.3	151.7
Less-developed market economies[5]	85.8	91.4	94.5	96.6	111.5	107.1	...
Metals							
World[1]	137.3	138.4	134.6	132.9	137.0	137.5	...
Developed market economies[2]	148.6	149.4	145.8	141.2	144.5	144.2	140.7
North America[3]	143.1	145.8	138.6	135.5	143.7	142.9	139.2
European Economic Community[4]	69.5	64.9	49.3	47.3	54.7	43.1	65.1
Less-developed market economies[5]	117.5	119.3	115.1	118.5	124.0	125.8	...
Manufacturing (total)	125.2	124.9	125.2	131.1	135.6	135.7	...

[1] Excluding Albania, China, former Czechoslovakia, North Korea, former U.S.S.R., Vietnam, and former Yugoslavia.
[2] Includes North America (Canada and the United States), Europe (excluding former Czechoslovakia and the European countries of the former U.S.S.R.), Australia, Israel, Japan, New Zealand, and South Africa.
[3] Canada and the United States.
[4] Now European Union; includes Belgium, Denmark, France, Germany, Greece, Ireland, Italy, Luxembourg, The Netherlands, Portugal, Spain, and the United Kingdom.
[5] Includes Caribbean nations, Central and South America, Africa (excluding South Africa), Asia (excluding China, North Korea, Israel, Japan, Vietnam, and Asian countries of the former U.S.S.R.), and Oceania (excluding Australia and New Zealand).

tion of, if not the profit margins on, many pharmaceuticals. A shift of Medicare patients into managed care further expanded volume. Results from large companies with a majority of their business in managed care reflected the trend. For the first three quarters of the year, Merck gained a 16% rise in net income, Schering-Plough 45%, and Johnson & Johnson 20%. Pfizer and SmithKline Beecham achieved double-digit growth, partly based on new products.

MCOs also demonstrated more acceptance of new, innovative medicines at premium prices and of partnerships with pharmaceutical companies. Pharmacia & Upjohn's Greenstone unit formed an alliance in disease management with Cigna's Lovelace Healthcare Innovations. Still unknown, however, was the ultimate effect of a large settlement between a number of drug companies and a coalition of retail pharmacists. It was thought that the deal, which could allow many retailers to obtain the same discounts as large health maintenance organizations, might suppress company earnings.

Perhaps the year's biggest scientific surprise was the good news concerning the treatment of AIDS. It was found that cocktails of new protease inhibitors and older antivirals could reduce HIV in patients' blood to undetectable levels, and new studies indicated similar results in other tissues. Problems with manufacturing, distribution, pricing, and reimbursement plagued the newer medicines, however. Merck, maker of the leading protease inhibitor, Crixivan, struggled to keep pace with exploding demand worldwide.

The European Agency for the Evaluation of Medicinal Products claimed a successful year, evaluating dozens of new products. Europe continued a sobering debate about pharmaceutical prices, however.

In Japan government ministers and industry officials reeled from a scandal that involved some 2,000 hemophiliacs infected by HIV-tainted blood transfusions. Meanwhile, liberalization of government pricing controls developed slowly. Global flight was the industry response to the tightly controlled domestic market. Lesser-known companies such as Eisai, the developer of a new Alzheimer's medicine, joined better-known firms such as Fujisawa Pharmaceutical and Takeda Chemical Industries in developing a business presence in the U.S. and Europe.

Worldwide, many companies entered a period of postmerger restructuring and strategy. Some recent mergers, like Pharmacia & Upjohn, lost profits to greater-than-expected restructuring costs. Nonetheless, merger fever continued unabated, with the behemoth in 1996 being Novartis under president Daniel Vasella (see BIOGRAPHIES), a merger of the Swiss giants Sandoz and Ciba-Geigy, which became the second largest company in the industry worldwide after gaining approval from the U.S. in December. (WAYNE KOBERSTEIN)

PHOTOGRAPHY

In 1996 the photographic industry ushered in two major developments, the Advanced Photo System (APS) and digital cameras designed and priced for the mass market. Developed as a joint effort by Kodak, Fuji, Canon, Nikon, and Minolta, APS was an ambitious, totally new system of photography integrating a 24-mm film format, cameras, and photofinishing equipment. APS film, provided in a leaderless cassette about 60% the size of a 35-mm cassette, allowed APS cameras to be made smaller or include more features in the same space. The cassette provided virtually foolproof drop-in loading and unloading, during which the user never touched the film. Three print formats—standard, moderate wide-angle, and panoramic—could be interchangeably selected on the same roll of film, which also magnetically recorded data designed to aid photofinishing and imprinting picture time and date. After processing by an APS-equipped photofinisher, prints were returned with the uncut roll of negatives in the original cassette and a colour index print (similar to a proof sheet) for reference and reordering.

APS got off to an uncoordinated start with ineffective advertising, shortages of film and cameras, and a lack of properly equipped photofinishers. As the year continued, however, Kodak, Fuji, Nikon, Minolta, Agfa, Olympus, Samsung, and others introduced a wide array of APS products, including many point-and-shoot cameras and a few single-lens-reflex (SLR) models. Canon's innovative ELPH 490Z was an ultracompact, aluminum-clad point-and-shoot APS camera that included a 4-to-1 zoom 22.5–90-mm lens, a novel clamshell lens cover that swung up to position a flash head, and a hybrid active-passive autofocus (AF) system. Elegantly styled and finished in stainless steel, Canon's EOS IX SLR combined APS features with a comprehensive array of advanced technology including three AF and 13 metering modes.

Digital cameras that captured images electronically rather than on film broke into the mass consumer market with many new models priced to compete with conventional cameras. The newcomers, whose image resolution was low compared with the multimillion-pixel (picture element) capability of costly digital cameras designed for photojournalism and industrial photography, were targeted mainly at the burgeoning population of computer fans who wanted to send personal pictures over the Internet. An economy-level entry into the field was the Kodak DC20, which had a resolution of about 146,000 pixels and provided simple programs for adding pictures to greeting cards, stretching or squeezing images, and designing and sending Internet postcards. Sony's DSC-F1 was claimed to be the first digital camera with a built-in infrared transceiver for transferring images directly from its four-megabyte memory to a nearby computer or printer without intermediate cables or disks. More than a digital camera, Nikon's CoolPix 300 was a three-way multimedia device that recorded images, written text, and as much as 17 minutes of sound.

Nikon added the F5 as its new top-of-the-line 35-mm SLR for professionals. The camera's dazzling array of features included a maximum eight-frames-per-second film advance, versatile five-sensor autofocusing, a new type of metering system using a 1,005-pixel colour-identifying charge-coupled diode (CCD), and 24 customizing function settings. Fuji introduced the GA645, the first medium-format camera with autofocus. The camera's relatively light, compact design provided the image quality of 120- or 220-size roll film with point-and-shoot convenience. Its 60-mm f/4 Super EBC Funinon lens switched automatically from passive AF for distant subjects to active infrared AF for nearby ones. (ARTHUR GOLDSMITH)

PRINTING

The printing industry continued to expand during 1996, aided in large part by the easing of paper shortages and the growth in print advertising, publications, and packaging on a worldwide basis. Technology had an impact on every aspect of print production, with major advances occurring in prepress document control for output to virtually any device for monochrome or colour preparation or reproduction.

The introduction of Acrobat version 3.0 from Adobe Systems (U.S.) created a portable document format (PDF) that provided an intermediate file between layout programs and the raster image processors that are used to drive film, plate, printer, and direct-to-press printout. The PDF allowed viewing on computer monitors or digital distribution over the World Wide Web or via new digital video discs. PDF publishing allowed one file format to serve most requirements for information dissemination in print or electronic publishing form. It also provided a standard mechanism for allowing advertisements to be incorporated into publications electronically for digital reproduction.

Digital printing advanced as the Scitex Spontane (Israel), Xerox DocuColor 40 (U.S.), and Canon CLC 1000 (Japan) brought colour printing to a price and performance point half that of Indigo (The Netherlands) and Xeikon (Belgium), the latter of which had improved quality and reduced costs in order to be more competitive with lithographic printing. Hybrid presses that integrated platemaking on press by applying Presstek (U.S.) technology and marketed by Heidelberg (Germany) and Omni-Adast (Czech Republic) sold record numbers of systems as printers worldwide moved aggressively into totally digital work flows that eliminated graphic arts film, manual stripping, and other labour-intensive processes.

Ink jet and dye sublimation colour proofing systems became able to support computer-to-plate approaches from Gerber Scientific Products (U.S.), Creo (Canada), and other suppliers. Digital plates, led by the Eastman Kodak (U.S.) thermal and Agfa (Germany) silver halide plates, achieved high levels of acceptance. The result for printers was the ability to reduce production times and handle an increasing number of short-run jobs (under 5,000 copies) to meet customer requirements for on-demand, just-in-time delivery.

Acquisitions continued in 1996. Heidelberger Druckmaschinen acquired Linotype-Hell (Germany), and the Agfa division of Bayer acquired the Hoechst (Germany) Enco plate division. (FRANK J. ROMANO)

RETAILING

It was survival of the fittest for retailers in 1996, a year marked by mergers, takeovers, and cutthroat competition. Big companies got bigger by gobbling up ri-

A Pakistani child stitches soccer balls. The use of poorly paid Third World children to produce goods endorsed by Western entertainers and athletes received a flurry of publicity in 1996.

vals, opening new stores, and expanding into international markets. Smaller chains scrambled to boost sales by offering new products and services. Companies that did not adapt quickly enough went out of business, victims of a crowded marketplace and tightfisted consumers.

Exemplifying the atmosphere, Petsmart, the largest pet food and supply retailer in the U.S., bought the U.K.'s Pet City Holdings for $239.1 million in stock. Petsmart, whose stores carried products ranging from gerbil food to dog sweaters, was looking for additional acquisitions.

Staples, the second largest U.S. office products chain, proposed to acquire number one Office Depot for $3.5 billion in stock. The combined business would have more than 1,000 stores and sales of about $10 billion. The proposed deal raised antitrust concerns.

Rite Aid, the biggest U.S. drugstore operator, agreed to buy Thrifty PayLess Holdings, the leading chain on the West Coast, for $2.3 billion in stock and assumed debt. Rite Aid had withdrawn a $1.8 billion takeover bid for Revco D.S. after the Federal Trade Commission (FTC) said that a combination of the two largest drug chains would drive up prices. J.C. Penney, meanwhile, said that it would buy Eckerd for $3.3 billion in cash, stock, and assumed debt, which would put Penney's Thrift Drug business into the number two spot.

Toys "Я" Us agreed to buy competitor Baby Superstore for $376 million. Toys "Я" Us had opened a handful of stores geared to infants and toddlers, and the acquisition of Baby Superstore gave it a major presence in the market.

Meanwhile, Toys "Я" Us faced charges from the FTC that it used its buying power to keep hot-selling toys out of competitors' stores. The FTC accused Toys "Я" Us of refusing to stock certain toys carried by discount-oriented warehouse clubs and thereby pressuring manufacturers to stop selling to the clubs or lose Toys "Я" Us as a customer. Toys "Я" Us, which controlled an estimated 20% to 30% of the U.S. market, acknowledged that it did not sell toys available in warehouse clubs but said that the practice was not illegal.

Consumer spending remained under pressure in many parts of the world. In Germany and Japan retail sales through the first half of 1996 were flat compared with the same period in 1995. Sales rose, however, in the U.S., Great Britain, and, to a lesser extent, Canada. Canadian consumers, despite the lowest interest rates in decades, were reluctant to spend because of worries about layoffs and weak economic growth. The dearth of consumer spending was a key factor in the bankruptcy of one of the country's biggest retail chains, Consumers Distributing. Christmas sales in the U.S. were generally disappointing.

Not all retailers were struggling. U.S. gourmet coffee purveyor Starbucks said that it planned to open more than 300 stores in the fiscal year that began in September, which would bring its total outlets to 1,000. Blockbuster Video, the fast-growing U.S. chain of rental stores, broke into the Scandinavian market by acquiring Christianshavn Video of Denmark.

Wal-Mart Stores, the world's largest retailer, opened its first discount stores in China and Indonesia. It had previously expanded into Mexico, Puerto Rico, Canada, Argentina, and Brazil. It was not immune to the difficulties affecting other retailers, however. The company reported a drop in profit for the quarter that ended January 31, the first time since becoming a publicly traded company in 1970 that profits had not increased. Kmart, the number two U.S. discounter, secured about $4.7 billion in new financing, which restored stability at the company after a difficult 1995.

As competition intensified, retailers searched for novel ways to win customers. In the U.K., supermarket operator J. Sainsbury joined with the Bank of Scotland to provide deposit, lending, and other banking services beginning in 1997. U.K supermarkets had sought other means of generating business, including selling gasoline. In the U.S., Wal-Mart, in an alliance with Microsoft, was one of many retailers to begin selling products over the World Wide Web. Outdoor clothing retailer Eddie Bauer, a unit of Spiegel, began offering tours to Peru, Nepal, and other exotic destinations. The tours, with activities that included archaeological digs and white-water rafting, were priced from $1,975 to $4,995.

One type of retailing establishment, the cigar store, had no trouble ringing up sales. Many retailers faced shortages of premium cigars, thanks to the newfound popularity of stogies, which were glorified in glossy magazines. The Cigar Association of America said that sales of premium cigars were set to double in 1996, to 257 million units.

(JOHN HEINZL)

SHIPBUILDING

Figures produced by Lloyd's Register of Shipping for the June quarter of 1996 showed little change in the leading shipbuilding countries. Shipbuilding continued, in terms of tonnage, to be dominated by Japan and South Korea, which had 30.2% and 28.2%, respectively, of the world order book. If China, Taiwan, and Singapore were included, the East Asian shipbuilders had 66.5% of the world order book. The order book, in millions of gross tons (gt), for the principal shipbuilding areas of the world was as follows: Japan, 13,594; South Korea, 12,668; Western Europe, 7,892; Eastern Europe, 5,835; rest of world, 5,018.

In addition to gross tons, Lloyd's Register now included the unit compensated gross tonnage. This unit reflected not only the size of the ship but also the complexity of the work involved in building a sophisticated and high-value vessel such as a liquefied-gas carrier as compared with, for example, a bulk carrier. For any ship type the coefficient decreased with increasing ship size—the larger the ship, the smaller the man-hour requirements per gross tonnage. Thus, when the order book figures were calculated in compensated gross tonnage, a different picture emerged: Western Europe, 8,404; Japan, 8,229; South Korea, 6,494; Eastern Europe, 4,903; rest of world, 4,016. These figures confirmed that European builders were concentrating on sophisticated high-value tonnage and leaving tankers and bulk carriers to the assembly lines of East Asia.

This was not to say that there was no European interest at all in very large crude carrier/ultralarge crude carrier (VLCC/ULCC) tonnage. The E3 tanker design, a collaborative venture by Fincantieri, Bremer Vulkan Verbund, HDW, AESA, and Chantiers de l'Atlantique, was intended to return VLCC/ULCC building to Europe. AESA obtained an order for one vessel from the Spanish owner Navierra Tapias, with an option for another.

During 1995 there was a generally strong freight market in shipping, which led to a high level of ordering (25.5 million gt). This equaled the level of ordering in 1994 and was double the orders reported a decade earlier, in 1985. Ore and bulk carriers represented 10.2 million gt of the orders, general cargo and containerships 8.1 million gt, and tankers 3.3 million gt.

By June 1996 there were 2,589 ships of 45 million gt in the world order book (ships under construction plus confirmed orders placed but not started). The cargo-carrying component of the order book was 2,012 ships of 44.5 million gt (62.9 million deadweight tons) and of these the principal ship types, in millions of gross tons, were dry-bulk carriers, 15; containerships, 9.2; oil tankers, 8.8; general cargo ships, 2.4; lique-fied-gas ships, 2; passenger ships, 1.7; and chemical carriers, 1.7.

The cruise ship market remained buoyant with the delivery of several new vessels, including the largest ever, Carnival Cruise Lines' 101,353-gt *Destiny* from Italy's Monfalcone yard. In some quarters there were fears that berth capacity could exceed demand. In 1990 there were 93,452 international cruise ship lower berths available. By 1996 there were 147,484, and it was estimated that by 1999 there would be 185,632.

In East Asia, Japan moved to a partial deregulation of its building facilities. All of the main Japanese yards had suffered from the strong yen, which made them less competitive. The situation began to improve, however. At 80 yen to the dollar Japanese yards could not compete, but at 105–110 yen they could just about manage.

South Korea brought more of its shipbuilding capacity on stream. Yard capacity in South Korea had been built on the assumption of cheap and abundant labour. This situation, however, was replaced with a high-wage economy and strikes by workers. The remedy was productivity increases and cuts in costs.   (EDWARD CROWLEY)

TELECOMMUNICATIONS

In February 1996 the U.S. Congress passed and Pres. Bill Clinton signed a bill designed to deregulate the telecommunications industry. The act would eventually allow long-distance and regional phone companies and cable companies to offer any service provided by the others. One stipulation in the bill was that no company currently providing local service could carry long-distance services until it had met a checklist of 14 conditions, including full interconnection with its competitors and telephone number portability when a customer changed carriers. In addition, the bill would deregulate rates for all cable TV customers by March 31, 1999. In November the U.S. Supreme Court upheld an appeals court ruling in favour of the local carriers, freezing the rules of the Federal Communications Commission (FCC) that were being used to implement the act at least until January 1997. The rules addressed interconnections, universal service, and access charges.

As a result of the telecommunications act, a number of industry mergers were announced. In February the former Bell company US West bought the third largest cable operator in the U.S., Continental Cablevision, for $10.8 billion. Continental provided service to more than four million subscribers in key markets in Florida,

Georgia, Michigan, Ohio, and the Chicago area. US West planned to upgrade the cable facilities to provide two-way telephone service by the year 2000.

In April SBC Communications (formerly Southwestern Bell) purchased Pacific Telesis (formerly Pacific Bell) in a deal worth more than $16 billion. The merger created the second largest phone company, after AT&T. The new company planned to retain the name SBC Communications. Later in April, NYNEX and Bell Atlantic announced a merger valued at more than $20.5 billion. In June the terms of the merger were changed so that Bell Atlantic would purchase NYNEX. The combined company, to be known as Bell Atlantic, would service the East Coast from Maine through Virginia.

In August a new company, MFS WorldCom, was proposed from the purchase of MFS Communications by LDDS WorldCom, the number four long-distance provider. Worth $12.4 billion, the new company would provide local and long-distance services and Internet access via high-speed fibre-optic networks to business customers in major metropolitan areas. Before its merger with WorldCom, MFS had completed a $2 billion purchase of Internet provider UUNET Technologies.

The second largest long-distance provider, MCI Communications, shocked the industry on November 3 when it agreed to be bought by British Telecommunications for about $21 billion. It would be the largest takeover ever of a U.S. corporation by a foreign firm. The new company, to be called Concert Global Communications, would require the approval of regulators in the U.S., the U.K., and the rest of Europe.

(continued on page 177)

Workers continue on the job at the Bremer Vulkan shipyards after the firm went into bankruptcy proceedings in May. The company, Germany's largest shipbuilder, blamed its losses on the misuse of state funds that had been intended to modernize yards in the eastern part of the country.

HARALD SCHMITT—STERN/BLACK STAR

Satellite TV

BY ROBERT STOFFELS

By the end of 1996, several thousand artificial satellites were circling the Earth. About 1,000 of them were in a geosynchronous orbit—that is, they were located over the Equator—at an altitude of 35,900 km (22,300 mi). At that distance they circled the Earth once every 24 hours, and since the Earth rotates on its axis once each 24 hours, the satellites appear to be stationary.

A primary function of many of these satellites is to provide television service. Programs are transmitted up to a satellite (the uplink), where they are received, modified, and retransmitted to the Earth (the downlink). Because the majority of such systems operate at low power, the dish-shaped receiving antenna must be large, 3 or more metres (10 or more feet) in diameter. By 1992, however, improved technology allowed smaller antennas to be used. These systems were called VSATs (very small aperture terminals), and the dishes were only 1.2 m (4 ft) in diameter.

Although most of the downlinks are terminated at a commercial cable TV company's facility, it is possible for individuals to subscribe directly to TV service by capturing a signal from one of the downlinks. This, however, requires the purchase and installation of an antenna. Most people consequently choose the commercial cable TV companies. These organizations receive signals from the downlink and distribute them to subscribers via a coaxial cable network.

Some 64% of the households in the United States subscribed to such television service in 1996, and most found it satisfactory. However, many potential customers lived far

A communications satellite, measuring 26 m (86 ft) from wing tip to wing tip, is one of three in geosynchronous orbit used by DirecTV to deliver programming to subscribers. The broadcasting of television signals by satellite continued to grow in 1996.

COURTESY DIRECTV® INC.

away from a coaxial cable and therefore could not take advantage of the service. For these people there is now an alternative, direct-broadcast satellite television (DBS).

The first U.S. high-powered DBS satellite was made by Hughes Aircraft Co. and owned by Hughes Electronic Corp.'s DirecTV and Hubbard Broadcasting's United States Satellite Broadcasting (USSB). Providing 150 television channels, it was launched on Dec. 17, 1993, from Kourou, French Guiana. Some months earlier, on July 22, 1993,

Spain launched DBS Hispasat 1B into a geosynchronous orbit. The power of DBS permits receivers to use an antenna that is only 46 cm (18 in) in diameter. Such an antenna can be clamped to a windowsill or mounted on the roof or on a pedestal outside the house. It is easier to mount than previous antennas and is also more secure—and much less expensive. A June 1996 promotional campaign by one company offered antennas for $199. By 1996, according to the National Cable Television Association, DBS subscribership was doubling each year. Satellites continue to be launched, and improvements in technology allow increasingly larger numbers of TV channels to be downlinked. The orbital slots available over the Equator are carefully controlled by the International Telecommunications Union (ITU), however. The ITU requires each nation to coordinate its satellite slots with its neighbours'. The last available slot for DBS satellites that could reach all of the U.S. was sold in January 1996 to MCI Communications Corp. for $682.5 million.

DBS systems were expanding rapidly not only in the U.S. but also in many other countries. Among the systems in operation, or slated for operation, were: British Sky Broadcasting (BSkyB), Galaxy Latin America, Japan Sky Broadcasting, the News Corp./TCI Latin America, the News Corp./TCI Australia, Star TV (Asia and Japan), and China Aerospace Corp.

Significant advantages of DBS are the high quality of its signals, its capacity to handle 120 or more channels, and the access it provides to programming regardless of a customer's location. Supporters of DBS continue to insist that it is indeed the wave of the future and will compete success-

fully with cable TV. Detractors, on the other hand, suggest that its sudden upsurge is nothing more than the embracing of a new technology by "early adopters." They also note that DBS provides little local programming; legal restraints prevent DBS from delivering local broadcast signals.

One other disadvantage to DBS—one that seems likely to become increasingly significant—is its lack of interactivity. DBS has, as its middle name, "broadcast." That means that communication is essentially one way—the same set of signals is sent to all potential receivers, and the channel selection is made at the receiver. But how does one send information from the receiver to the broadcaster? In a cable TV system such a channel can be installed (though at a high price), but with DBS it becomes necessary to use the telephone to send information to the originator.

Robert E. Stoffels, formerly editor of Telephone Engineer & Management *magazine, is a telecommunications consultant.*

(continued from page 175)
It would have more than 43 million customers in over 70 countries.

While many telecommunications companies were in the process of merging during 1996, AT&T was in the process of completing the divestiture of its equipment-manufacturing business, renamed Lucent Technologies, and its computer division, renamed NCR (its name before it was bought by AT&T in 1990). In April an initial public offering of Lucent stock on the New York Stock Exchange resulted in the largest number of shares ever traded on a corporation's first day. The spin-off of Lucent was completed on October 1, and the divestiture of NCR was completed at the end of 1996.

AT&T Wireless introduced ground-to-air calling on a number of domestic and international airlines. Motorola and others began providing their mobile-phone customers with E-mail and text-based Internet access. In addition to using the Internet to place phone calls, several companies were providing facsimile capabilities, eliminating the costly telephone charges associated with international faxes. Two major outages on on-line services occurred in 1996. On August 7 America Online, the largest provider, went off-line for 19 hours, stranding its six million users. On November 7 AT&T WorldNet, the number two Internet provider, was unable to deliver E-mail to many of its customers.

In May the FCC completed its auction of personal communications services licenses on the 30-MHz broadband spectrum for $10.2 billion. The 500 licenses were aimed at small businesses in basic trading areas.

New products introduced in 1996 included a compact 249-g (8.7-oz) digital, portable handset that integrated cellular calling, two-way radio, and alphanumeric paging into a single device. New 56-Kbit/sec modems were announced in October. Meant to work over voice-grade lines, the modems operated at almost twice the speed of previous models. Global Village Communication introduced its NewsCatcher, a wireless device that used radio transmission to provide information via on-line resources and news and sports wires.

(THOMAS E. KROLL)

TEXTILES

The textile industry in 1996 was coming out of a depressed market. Asia was the only area where markets had not experienced a slump, and they continued to grow.

Individual companies were entering into joint ventures in various countries to gain better market positions. Egypt's cotton and textile industry, for example, was initiating joint ventures with companies such as Benetton and Wrangler. Japanese firms were starting to produce acrylic, nylon, and polyester fibres and yarns and to do dyeing and printing operations in China. Japanese spinning operations and woolen fabric production were also being moved there, and the Taiwanese and U.S. industries were developing cooperative efforts with Chinese companies.

The textile chemicals business was also experiencing this shift in focus. Amoco was developing joint ventures in various countries. Ciba-Geigy's joint venture with Atul of India was producing polyurethanes, and Atul entered into an agreement with BASF to export vat dyes. Mitsui Sekka of Japan was joining with Amoco in Indonesia to produce terephthalic acid. In the dye industry Ciba-Geigy merged with Sandoz to form Novartis. The dyestuffs businesses of Bayer and Hoechst Celanese merged.

Biotechnology continued to exert its influence on the textile industry. Monsanto, Du Pont, and Bayer were among the companies working on genetically altered cotton, with improved fibre performance and properties as well as resistance to pesticides and disease.

Man-Made Fibres. The capacity for production of man-made cellulosic filament fibres worldwide was 953,000 metric tons in 1996. The capacity for man-made cellulosic staple and tow fibres was 2,450,000 metric tons, for acrylic and modacrylic fibres 3,191,000 metric tons, for nylon and aramid fibres 5,427,000 metric tons, and for polyester fibres 15,387,000 metric tons. The total noncellulosic man-made fibre production capacity, excepting olefins, was at a level of 24,309 metric tons. It was reported that olefins (polypropylene) were produced at a level of 18,386,000 metric tons, an increase over 1995.

The U.S. Federal Trade Commission received four applications for generic fibre types in 1996. Teijin of Japan received a classification for a fibre named Rexe with stretch properties similar to spandex but composed of polyester and polyether segments. Courtaulds applied for a classification for its lyocell fibre trademarked Tencel, a highly crystalline microfibre with high wet and dry strength. Du Pont applied for a classification for its polytetrafluoroethylene fibre, which had low friction and abrasion-resistance properties. BASF received a temporary classification for its Basofil, a fibre with high flame- and heat-resistance properties useful in protective clothing and textiles. Japan's Asahi Chemical Industry and Toray Industries produced fibres that absorbed some of the odours in cigarette smoke. Asahi's product was named Smoklin and Toray's product Cinagon. Kanebo's Bellfresh deodorant fibre decomposed odours of the kitchen and bathroom.

(DENNIS LOY)

Wool. The world wool clip in 1996–97 was estimated at 1,437,000 metric tons clean, down from 1,454,000 metric tons in 1995–96. Raw wool prices continued to drift lower. Australia remained the dominant producer, with 445,000 metric tons clean, essentially the same as in 1995–96. New Zealand's clip was 195,000 metric tons clean, down 2%. Both Australia and New Zealand had an approximate 16% reduction in raw wool exports during 1996, with the major reductions being to Japan, by 43%, and to the major countries of Western Europe, by 15.4%. Factors contributing to the decline included high unemployment and extraordinarily mild weather from September to November in Western Europe and bargain buying by consumers. Demand for wool worldwide amounted to 8.64% of the total natural fibre and 4.27% of the total fibre. Purchases of wool apparel grew by 1% in Western Europe, 2% in North America, Japan, and China, and 8% in South Korea and Taiwan.

New technology made spun lamb's and soft Shetland wool available for licensing by Woolmark spinners in 1996. Enzymes were being used to improve the appearance and feel of wool fabrics, and there were technological advances in the dyeing of wool. One process used a chemical that allowed wool to be dyed either below the boiling point of water or at the boiling point for less time. Among new sportswear products was Sportwool, a double-faced knitted fabric with wool on the inside and polyester on the outside.

Cotton. Worldwide cotton production reached 19.3 million metric tons in 1996. The four major producers were the U.S., China, India, and Pakistan. Only the U.S. showed an increase over 1995. Production in China, India, and Pakistan was lower because of insect infestation and leaf virus and a decrease in planted area.

World consumption of raw cotton was 18.6 million metric tons, up 1.1% from 1995. Consumption increased in the four major cotton-producing countries. In the U.S., cotton had 67% of the apparel market; worldwide, cotton claimed 45.1% of the total textile fibre market. Demand for casual wear, denim, and specialty fabrics was the primary reason for increased use.

The U.S. continued to dominate the export markets. In 1996 the U.S. exported 1,437,000 metric tons of cotton, primarily to Mexico, Japan, South Korea, and Indonesia. The amount was down from 1.7 million metric tons in 1995. The three other major cotton exporters were Uzbekistan, French Africa, and Australia.

For the first time, commercial cotton growers in Australia and the United States planted genetically engineered cotton, developed by Monsanto. The cotton contained the Bollgard gene derived from *Bacillus thuringiensis*, a soilborne bacterium that was toxic to heliothis caterpillars. A new genetically altered cotton that was resistant to Buctril herbicide was available in 1996.

(EVERETT E. BACKE)

Silk. In 1996 worldwide demand for silk declined, and prices eased slightly. As a result, there was a 40% reduction in the spring crop of high-quality cocoons in China. Because the stock of silk was already small, industry observers feared that only a slight upturn in demand would cause it to disappear and thus lead to a rapid increase in prices. Some mulberry trees in the more developed provinces were dug up or neglected.

China made an effort to regularize the export prices of raw materials, including silk, through a system of export licenses. This slowed trade, but whether it helped regulate prices was debatable.

Meanwhile, business in Europe was stagnant. Demand for silk neckties was good, but silk was not in fashion for women's wear—with the exception of fabrics with a surface sheen. Arrangements for licensing the import of silk garments from China seemed to be effective, but some of the quotas established by the European Union were not entirely filled.

Silk noils were also out of fashion, and as a result, the supply was plentiful. Spun silk showed signs of revival with a slight increase in prices.

In 1995 China produced 76,400 metric tons of raw silk. India's production was estimated at 15,045 metric tons and Japan's at 3,228. Total world production was approximately 99,000 metric tons.

(ANTHONY H. GADDUM)

A Kentucky tobacco farmer works in his field. U.S. growers, already competing with cheaper tobacco from elsewhere, felt more pressure in 1996 from the antismoking movement and from steps by the federal government to regulate tobacco as a drug and so prohibit sales to minors.

TOBACCO

The production and consumption of tobacco did not in 1996 respond to the ever more intense antismoking movement. Manufacturers produced some 5,569,000,000,-000 cigarettes in 1996, close to a record, with consumption edging up in some key markets, including the United States. In much of the less-developed world, smoking increased wherever economic well-being improved and tobacco taxes were comparatively low.

The world production of raw tobacco, at approximately 6,330,000 metric tons, was the largest since 1993, with China, the U.S., India, and Brazil the top producers. The consumption of raw materials by the makers of cigarettes, cigars, and other tobacco products was likewise high, with manufacturers running down carryover stocks from previous harvests. World stocks continued to be down heavily, partly because manufacturers refined "just-in-time" production methods.

On August 23, U.S. Pres. Bill Clinton approved regulations declaring nicotine an addictive drug and giving the Food and Drug Administration the authority to regulate the marketing and sale of tobacco products to young people. The FDA's reg-

ulations were being challenged in court, however, which delayed their implementation. Other U.S. antitobacco activity, which inspired like movements elsewhere, focused increasingly on seeking legal redress from cigarette manufacturers. There was only limited and mixed success, however, for claimants in U.S. courts in 1996.

In East Asia, where almost half the world's cigarettes were smoked, the World Health Organization admitted that its objective of making the region smoke-free by the year 2000 was unattainable. WHO intensified its efforts to eliminate tobacco advertising there by 2000 by trying to persuade governments to ban promotionals.

(MICHAEL F. BARFORD)

TOURISM

As 1996 began, contradictory trends influenced international tourism. On the one hand, the stronger dollar and the Wall Street boom favoured outbound travel from North America. On the other, the continuing recession in European Union nations such as France and Germany and Japan's hesitant economic recovery made consumers there unusually cautious. Countries with strong currencies or those beset by political uncertainty tended to suffer.

Tourists pet a gray whale off the Mexican coast. Some observers said that "ecotourism," meant to combine sight-seeing with preservation of the environment, was actually causing harm.

Under the circumstances, Africa fared quite well. Morocco's tourism increased 11%, while 6% more Europeans visited Tunisia. South of the Sahara, Malawi's move to democracy spurred plans for a tourist revival based on park lodges and Lake Malawi. Tourism was also profitable for Africa's island destinations, where Mauritius welcomed 11% more visits. During October, at a conference held in the Comoros, Indian Ocean nations such as Mauritius, Seychelles, and Madagascar agreed to joint marketing. While Tanzania expected 326,-000 visitors in 1996, Kenya, where tourism fell back to 690,500 arrivals, moved to rehabilitate infrastructure and promote safaris through a new Kenya Tourist Board.

With some exceptions the countries of the Americas recorded a good tourist season in 1996. Foreign tourism accounted for 10% of all jobs in the U.S., and tourism earnings, growing at 4% per annum, contributed $80 billion to the economy. While the weak Canadian dollar slowed cross-border travel in North America, the strong growth of U.S.-bound tourism from such Pacific Rim countries as South Korea compensated. In The Bahamas tourism grew by 5%, in Canada by 4%, in Ecuador by 9%, in Jamaica by 16%, in Mexico by 14%, and in Nicaragua by 13%. Tourism, however, marked time in some Caribbean destinations, such as Antigua and St. Martin.

The Asian-Pacific region continued to be the powerhouse of international tourism in 1996, accounting for 15% of world arrivals and 20% of receipts. Leading destinations were Singapore, with a 36% growth in arrivals, China with 17%, Hong Kong with 16%, Japan with 15%, and Australia with 14%. Thailand's international tourist nights grew by 15%, and the country welcomed many new visitors from Eastern Europe.

Tourism along the Silk Road was promoted by fairs and forums held in China, Uzbekistan, and Turkmenistan. The Japanese government granted a credit of $140 million to modernize airports at Samarkand, Uzbekistan, and elsewhere along this fabled tourist route. In South Asia tourism moved ahead in India (11%)

Leading International Tourist Destinations
Number of tourist arrivals from abroad

Destination	1994	1995
France	60,840,000	60,000,000
United States	45,504,000	45,504,000[1]
Spain	43,232,000	44,886,000
Italy	27,480,000	29,953,000
United Kingdom	20,855,000	23,746,000
China	21,070,000	21,070,000[1]
Hungary	21,425,000	20,700,000
Poland	18,800,000	19,200,000
Austria	17,894,000	17,894,000[1]
Mexico	17,182,000	17,182,000[1]
Czech Republic	17,000,000	15,500,000
Canada	15,971,000	15,971,000[1]
Germany	14,494,000	14,847,000
Switzerland	12,200,000	11,500,000
Greece	10,072,000	10,130,000
Portugal	9,132,000	9,706,000
Hong Kong	9,331,000	9,331,000[1]
Malaysia	7,197,000	7,197,000[1]
Turkey	...	7,083,000
Netherlands, The	6,178,000	6,574,000

[1]1994 figure.
Source: World Tourism Organization, *Tourism Market Trends*, 1996.

and the Maldives (6%), but political events in Pakistan and Sri Lanka overshadowed foreign travel, which decreased 8% and 20%, respectively.

Europe presented a mixed picture in 1996. Arrivals continued to decline in established destinations with strong currencies, as in Austria (− 1%), France (− 3%), and Switzerland (− 9%). Holiday travel sales in Germany, the key European outbound market, stagnated as the German government proposed welfare cuts and adopted a tight budget. Tourism prospered in other European countries, however, including Poland (5%), Spain (10%), Turkey (12%), and the U.K. (11%). There was also a spectacular recovery in tourism to Croatia, formerly part of Yugoslavia, as a result of the regional peace accord. The Euro '96 football (soccer) championships attracted an extra 100,000 travelers to Great Britain during June, while the country's fashion and heritage attractions drew a record three million tourists during August. In September at Thessaloníki, Greece, Hyatt International opened Europe's largest casino. The peak season was too much for Italy's heritage city of Florence, however, which moved to control a rising tide of tourists by limiting to 225 the daily number of touring buses admitted and introducing reservations procedures at the legendary Uffizi Gallery. Portugal's tour operators opted to diversify their products, emphasizing golf and sailing holidays and introducing wine tours of the Douro Valley.

Pressure on margins led to mergers and acquisitions—among others, the purchase by Granada of the multinational hotelier Forte in the U.K. In the U.S., AAA (American Automobile Association) and Thomas Cook, two of the most recognized names in the industry, announced plans to form the world's largest leisure travel alliance, with nearly 3,000 retail outlets. Doubletree acquired the Renaissance Hotel Group.

Middle Eastern tourism continued to reap a peace dividend in 1996. In Egypt arrivals soared 25% and receipts 24%. Jordan (6%) and Syria (9%) also experienced a boom. In Israel tourism grew by 4% but was not without setbacks, one being an Arab-Israeli dispute during September over a new entrance to a tourist tunnel on Jerusalem's Temple Mount.

(PETER SHACKLEFORD)

WOOD PRODUCTS

Wood. The year 1996 was one of contrasts for the wood products market. While traditional sources of timber continued to experience heavy pressure, there was also a drop in prices for many forest products, especially pulp, panels, and nonstructural lumber. The contrast was a result of increasing long-term demand from a growing world population and a scarcity of raw materials coupled with short-term oversupply as technology improved the efficiency of manufacturing processes.

Scarce raw materials spurred technology to make better use of both traditional and alternative sources of fibre. Such products as laminated veneer lumber, oriented strand board, and medium-density fibreboard, which used smaller trees and wood waste, enjoyed gains in consumer acceptance and manufacturing capacity. In North America alone, new capacity in oriented

strand board in the first quarter of 1996 exceeded the first-quarter levels of 1995 by five times.

Constraints on federal timber harvests continued to pummel U.S. lumber manufacturers, although 1996 brought some relief. A strong economy led to a 14% increase in housing starts in the first half of 1996, pushing Western lumber demand up 2.1% over 1995. The closing of mills in the West, less timber from federal forests, and near-capacity production in the South, however, limited the ability of producers to increase output significantly. The forecast for 1996 was a modest increase in lumber production, to 76,690,000 cu m (1 cu m = 423.8 bd-ft). The balance would be imported, mainly from Canada.

Tropical timber producers, particularly in Asia, suffered shortages of raw materials, low prices, and increased international competition in 1996. Indonesia, the world's largest tropical plywood producer, expected production to fall 7%, to nine million cubic metres, and exports to fall 8%, to eight million cubic metres, by 1996. Malaysia, in line with an international agreement among tropical producers to reduce harvests to sustainable levels, announced that it would cut annual harvests 19%, to 30 million cu m, by 2000.

Japan's economic recovery strengthened the demand for wood products, but there was also a shift in consumer preferences. Japanese imports of hardwood logs from Southeast Asia shifted to imports of softwood logs from Russia, and imports of tropical plywood were being replaced with softwood plywood. Japan also expected to see a doubling of imported housing from the U.S., Europe, and Australia, to 11,325 units, in 1996.

Owing to slow economic growth, European imports of wood products were weak in 1996. Oversupply was also a factor, as high-producing nations in Scandinavia joined the European Union, which made it easier for those countries to supply continental Europe. The U.K. was increasing production from forests planted in the north after World War II.

The U.S. and Canadian governments reached agreement on a quota system to limit Canadian imports of lumber into the U.S. In 1996 Canadian lumber imports were expected to reach 39,640,000 cu m, marginally below the level reached in 1995. Late in the year U.S. home builders experienced sharply rising prices for lumber, which they blamed partly on import quotas for spruce from Canada.

Russia, with about 57% of the world's softwood reserves, had seen lumber output fall drastically since 1989, from 80 million cu m to 22.3 million cu m in 1996. Although the allowable cut for 1995 was 490 million cu m, only about 120 million of this was achieved. Poor infrastructure continued to make access to Russian forests difficult, and political instability made large capital investments unfavourable. Some stabilization in Russia's lumber production, which was forecast to fall only 1.1 million cu m short of 1995 production levels, was expected in 1996, however.

(WORLD FOREST INSTITUTE)

Paper and Pulp. Trends in 1996 showed that output would grow only marginally and that the year might see the end of the record set in 1995, the 13th year in a row

that world pulp, paper, and board output had increased. World production in 1995, the last year for which figures were available, rose to 277.8 million metric tons, an increase of 3.4% over 1994.

The U.S. industry was set for a robust 2.5% growth rate each year for the foreseeable future. Growth would come from heavy investments in productivity improvements, rather than in new machines, setting the stage for enhanced competitiveness. China, however, remained the world's fastest growing country, and there were other rapidly expanding capacities on the Pacific Rim. Pulp production in Indonesia, for example, rose to more than two million metric tons, and it was estimated that Indonesia might be one of the top 10 pulp and paper producers in the world by 2005. The U.S. remained the largest producer and consumer per capita, making 29.1% of the world's output.

Eastern Europe, especially Russia, made a noteworthy comeback. Paper and board output increased by more than one million metric tons, and pulp production grew even faster, up 1.4 million metric tons, or 22.5%, mostly in Russia. Elsewhere in Europe growth was modest. The industry in Germany was profitable in 1995, but it was adversely affected by vast increases in pulp and wastepaper prices in the second half of the year. In Canada operating rates declined in 1996, but producers had returned to profitability in 1995 after cumulative losses of Can$5.1 billion between 1991 and 1994. At the end of 1995, the Canadian pulp and paper industry completed a significant investment program to comply with environmental regulations. Newsprint production declined, while manufacturers were shifting toward printing and writing papers.

For the past three years, pulp prices had been on a roller-coaster ride. Aggressive pricing by pulp producers was the result of a bid to maintain market share in East Asia in the face of new low-cost competition from Indonesia and substantial U.S. expansion in the deinked market. In 1995 recycled paper prices topped in June at approximately $200 per ton but were down to $25 per ton in December.

Because the world had shrunk, and pulp, paper, and board had become truly global commodities, it was expected that there would be even greater consolidation between competitive companies, a process already clearly under way. Such a development could improve environmental standards around the world as the best practices were transferred between paper industry supergroups. From an environmental perspective, North American mills would have to minimize the waste generated through the life cycle of paper to remain competitive during the next 5 to 10 years.

(H.-CLAUDE LAVALLÉE)

This article updates the *Macropædia* articles BEVERAGE PRODUCTION; BUILDING CONSTRUCTION; DRESS AND ADORNMENT; ELECTRONICS; ENERGY CONVERSION; FORESTRY AND WOOD PRODUCTION; INDUSTRIAL GLASS AND CERAMICS; Chemical Process INDUSTRIES; Extraction and Processing INDUSTRIES; Manufacturing INDUSTRIES; Textile INDUSTRIES; INSURANCE; MARKETING AND MERCHANDISING; PHOTOGRAPHY; PRINTING, TYPOGRAPHY, AND PHOTOENGRAVING; TELECOMMUNICATIONS SYSTEMS; TOOLS.

Computers and Information Systems

The Internet. It was the year of the Internet's World Wide Web, which by the end of 1996 had so permeated the public's consciousness that even nontechnical adults were likely to speak of the "Net" and the "Web." Companies large and small began including a Web-site address in their print advertising and television commercials. Big telecommunications firms such as AT&T and MCI Communications Corp. began offering their customers Internet access services, competing with America Online, Inc., CompuServe Inc., and hundreds of smaller firms that already did so. Meanwhile, Internet access was no longer limited to computers. New smart telephones were able to send Internet E-mail messages, and televisions equipped with special set-top boxes were able to provide access to the Web.

As a result, some Internet-related companies had a big year in the stock market. Yahoo! Inc., an Internet search engine company that held its initial public stock offering in April, watched its stock rise from the offering price of $13 a share to $33 a share at the close of the next day's trading. It was the most closely watched high-tech public offering since the explosive 1995 debut of Netscape Communications Corp., the Web

Protesters in San Francisco demonstrated against proposals to restrict content on the Internet. Governments in a number of countries, including the U.S. and Germany, attempted in 1996 to ban pornographic and other kinds of on-line material or to restrict access to it.

browser company founded by entrepreneur James Clark and software developer Mark Andreessen. (*See* BIOGRAPHIES.)

Profitability, however, eluded most companies doing business on the Internet. While Web-site advertising grew by 83% in the first half of 1996, few commercial business operations on the Internet made money. In fact, most of the advertisers were high-tech companies buying advertising on each other's Web sites. Consumer product

companies continued to be cautious about Internet advertising.

Most advertisers tried to capitalize on the Internet's strength—reaching narrowly defined audience groups. For example, the Discovery Channel Online—the Internet cousin of the cable TV Discovery channel—sought to provide information on the Web that would appeal to the same demographic segment as its TV audience, mainly well-educated, upscale men aged 25 to 54.

This graphic depicts the so-called browser wars taking place between Netscape and Microsoft. Netscape, a small company that had 80% of the Internet browser market with its Navigator software, was facing an all-out challenge from Microsoft's new Internet Explorer.

DAVE EMBER

There was great interest in extending the Internet to more people. In March U.S. Pres. Bill Clinton participated in a new California school event that spawned subsequent efforts across the country. Called NetDay96, it was a grassroots volunteer campaign to wire schools for Internet access at little cost to the public. By the year's end other states were promoting similar efforts, but the Internet revolution still had not reached many public libraries and schools that could most benefit from easy access to a world of information. An amendment to the Telecommunications Act of 1996 authorized subsidies for information technology to libraries and schools, but late in the year the federal government was just receiving recommendations on how to make that happen.

Some studies suggested the Internet might facilitate learning. The Center for Applied Special Technology, based in Washington, D.C., reported that a study of urban school districts showed that elementary school students with access to the Internet had an advantage in learning over those without access. The study concentrated on 500 fourth- and sixth-grade students in Chicago, Ill.; Dayton, Ohio; Detroit, Mich.; Memphis, Tenn.; Miami, Fla.; Oakland, Calif.; and Washington, D.C. Its results showed that students who used the Internet scored higher on nine learning criteria, which included greater insight into a topic and accuracy in handling information.

Meanwhile, the major telephone and cable television companies tried to participate in the Internet boom by offering Net access services at previously unheard-of speeds. A new high-speed cable modem that would allow a personal computer (PC) to access the Internet through the same fibre-optic cables that transmitted cable TV programs was introduced in selected cities. It offered access speeds more than 300 times faster than those of most consumer computer modems. Telephone companies spent the closing months of 1996 preparing to introduce "xDSL" transmission technologies, which would allow telephone lines to access the Internet more than 50 times faster than present modems. As the year ended, there were questions about how soon either telephone companies or cable TV companies could introduce the new services to the general population, since in many areas the transmission lines would need to be upgraded before consumers could take advantage of the new services.

Telecommunications reform became more controversial than ever before when the U.S. Congress early in 1996 approved a bill containing the hotly debated Communications Decency Act. The act provided for fines and jail sentences for Internet content providers who distributed "indecent materials" to minors. In June a three-judge federal panel ruled that the Communications Decency Act was unconstitutional. As part of the opinion, one judge wrote, "As the most participatory form of mass speech yet developed, the Internet deserves the highest protection from governmental intrusion."

That ruling faced federal court appeals, however, and, in the meantime, some states began passing their own restrictive laws governing on-line content. Connecticut, Maryland, New York, and Oklahoma passed laws that restricted the transmission of on-line material. This raised the possibility of widely varied regulations based on geographic boundaries.

Moral questions dogged other media as well. To deal with concerns about the content of television programs, work continued on technology that would allow in-home blocking of certain programs based on a system of ratings. Necessary for such blocking was computer circuitry called the V-chip, which would be built into TV sets.

Computer Consumer Technologies. Digital video (or versatile) disc (DVD) was one of the most talked-about consumer computer technologies in 1996, even though most consumers had not yet seen it. A DVD player would read a shiny disc similar in appearance to a computer CD-ROM but able to hold about 4.7 billion bytes of data, compared with 650 million bytes on a CD-ROM. (Future DVD discs were expected to hold more than eight billion bytes.) The increased DVD storage capacity also would make possible higher-quality video and sound than could be obtained with a videocassette recorder tape and would make it feasible for a moviemaker to sell a single DVD containing several different endings to the same film or multiple versions of the same movie, each in a different language. The first consumer DVD players were expected to debut in the U.S. in early 1997.

Digital photography, a marriage of computer chips and traditional cameras that could capture photos in electronic form, began to trickle into the U.S. market during 1996. These electronic cameras had previously cost from $1,500 to $30,000, but prices had dropped dramatically. Proponents hoped digital cameras costing less than $1,000 would compete for part of the $13 billion that U.S. consumers were expected to spend in 1996 on conventional cameras, photographic accessories, and film processing, while camera manufacturers and computer makers hoped that consumers would be interested in taking digital photos that could be edited on PC screens.

Industry Developments. The computer industry's Internet obsession also fueled competition. The biggest rivalry in 1996 may well have been the one between software giant Microsoft Corp. and Netscape. In a battle for "mind share" in the Internet market, each company pitted its free Internet browser software against the other's. The war between Netscape Navigator and Microsoft Internet Explorer was fought mainly in the reviewers' columns of computer trade journals, and for most consumers choosing a winner was largely subjective. The contest was important to Netscape, which was trying to maintain its lead as the most innovative Internet communications firm as well as its 80% market share, and to Microsoft, which was trying to prove that it had abandoned its reluctance to develop for the on-line world.

The battle became a legal one as well. In August Netscape sent a letter to the U.S. Justice Department accusing Microsoft of deliberately preventing companies such as Netscape from running some types of Internet server software on Microsoft's Windows NT 4.0 Workstation system software. Microsoft responded that the NT Workstation software was not appropriate for the use Netscape intended.

One of the major new markets for the computer industry in 1996 was the Intranet, an internal company version of the Internet. Intranets allowed workers with PCs to access information from company computers via the same user-friendly browsing software used on the Internet. Corporations that adopted this approach said Intranets simplified employees' work and thus led to higher worker productivity and lower frustration levels.

Computer-security experts continued to worry about on-line hackers who attacked corporate computers. One of the newest trends was the "denial-of-service" attack, in which a series of phony messages were sent to the target computer via the Internet. This kept the computer so busy that legitimate users could not gain access to it. The potential for such attacks was intensified by the ease with which hackers could learn to become attackers. Anyone could learn denial-of-service techniques simply by visiting Web sites that published information of interest to hackers.

Hackers also broke into U.S. government-related computer systems and altered official Web sites operated by the Justice Department (in August), the CIA (in October), and the air force (in December). Although no serious damage was done, it was increasingly apparent that improved security measures would be crucial on the expanding Internet.

One of the most talked-about new computer products of 1996 was the "network computer," a stripped-down machine intended to replace the limited-function computer terminals used by corporate workers such as bank tellers, retail clerks, and airline ticketing agents. Priced in the range of $700 without a computer screen, the network computer was designed for users who did not need the complexity of a PC and its software. IBM's first such machine, the Network Station, was to use only browsing software for accessing the Internet or an Intranet. Other companies—notably Sun Microsystems, Inc., and Oracle Corp.—quickly announced their own network computers. To some extent, the network computer threatened to undermine the PC market by providing a lower-cost alternative for some types of work.

Intel Corp., which manufactured the microprocessor chips that controlled most PCs, launched a counterattack by declaring that it would make PCs more affordable by lowering the costs of using them in computer networks. For instance, it said it would offer products that made it easier to diagnose PC problems remotely over a network. The aim was to make PCs more competitive with network computers, which were relatively low-maintenance devices.

Windows 95, which was heavily promoted by Microsoft during the summer of 1995, sold 40 million copies in its first 12 months, which made it a success by any standard. Some software companies that wrote programs for Windows 95 had expected even greater sales of the upgraded operating system (OS), however, and were disappointed. Sales were slowest among corporations, which typically were reluctant to replace the previous version of Windows, which seemed to be working well. Most Windows 95 sales were made through the sale of new PCs that came equipped with the software. Another Microsoft product, the Windows NT OS, continued to sell briskly, and analysts estimated that by year's end it would outsell all types of the Unix operating software.

Meanwhile, the PC increased in power in 1996 to 200–225 MHz, nearly twice the speed of the fastest consumer computer a year earlier. At the same time, next-generation PCs were being developed that would raise performance to the range of entry-level supercomputers, the high-performance machines used in science and industry. Exponential Technology, Inc., demonstrated a 500-MHz microprocessor chip, while Intel planned its model P7 chip, which would process instructions 64 bits at a time rather than 32 bits at a time, as did the microprocessors used in 1996 PCs.

No matter how powerful computers became, the human mind could still withstand their challenge. In February 1996 Russian chess champion Garry Kasparov defeated Deep Blue, an IBM machine touted as the world's best chess computer. (*See* SIDEBAR.)

Some traditional computer suppliers suffered in 1996. The year ended with the future of PC industry pioneer Apple Computer, Inc., still in doubt. While the company reported a $25 million profit in the last quarter of its 1996 fiscal year, which ended in late September, its sales declined by almost $700 million compared with the same period a year earlier. In addition, Apple lost more than $800 million during its fiscal year. Gilbert F. Amelio, Apple's chairman since early 1996, was engaged in what was expected to be a three-year corporate turnaround.

The direction of that turnaround took on a new dimension at year's end when Apple, which had been negotiating with Be, Inc., for the use of its Be OS, unexpectedly announced the acquisition of NeXT Software, Inc., for $400 million. The deal also signaled the return to Apple of its cofounder, Steven Jobs, who formed NeXT after being ousted from Apple by the board of directors in a 1985 power struggle. It was uncertain how NeXT's highly regarded but little-used NeXTSTEP OS would be incorporated into a new, more advanced replacement for the aging Macintosh operating system (Mac OS). Jobs would reportedly be a part-time adviser at Apple while continuing in his role as the chief executive at Pixar Animation Studios, which took the world by storm in 1996 with its full-length computer-animated film, *Toy Story.* (*See* PERFORMING ARTS: *Motion Pictures:* Special Report.)

Apple also hoped to get a boost from the decision of Motorola, Inc., which manufactured the PowerPC microprocessor chips used in recent Macintosh computers, to begin making "clones," PCs that would run the Mac OS. Although Apple had previously been reluctant to license the Mac OS, in 1996 licensed clone makers included Power Computing Corp., DayStar Digital, Inc., and the Taiwanese manufacturer Umax Data Systems, Inc.

Digital Equipment Corp. also continued to be troubled, losing $433 million in the fiscal year ended in mid-1996 and announcing it would eliminate 7,000 jobs. In its following quarter DEC lost another $66 million, disappointing Wall Street with a decline that was far larger than expected.

It also was a year for consolidation in the PC industry. In June U.S. PC manufacturer Packard Bell said it would merge with the PC operations of Japanese computer manufacturer NEC. The $300 million deal would create the largest PC firm in the U.S., which would be headed by Packard Bell management. NEC previously had been a major shareholder in Packard Bell.

During 1996 government agencies and corporations appeared to be taking a more serious look at the computer problems posed by the approaching end of the century. Because of a flaw in the way some computer programs handled calendar dates, many programs would cease functioning or give wrong answers in the year 2000. For more than 30 years, most computer programmers had been abbreviating calendar-date years as the last two digits—a shortcut that originally served the purpose of saving expensive computer memory capacity but continued as common practice long after computer memory had become relatively cheap. As a result, while all computer programs could recognize that "96" meant 1996, most either could not make sense of the year 2000 abbreviated as "00" or else concluded that it meant 1900. The problem was complicated by the ingenuity of the original computer programmers, who hid date calculations inside programs in clever and unexpected ways and thus made it difficult for modern programmers to locate and change all two-digit dates to four-digit ones. Some analysts calculated that the cost of finding and fixing all "year 2000 problem" flaws would be between $300 billion and $600 billion worldwide by the end of the decade.

In a sense, the year 2000 problem had already arrived by 1996, because forward-looking business programs, such as those that calculated home mortgages or interest or that did sales forecasting, already had bumped up against the year 2000 in their daily tasks. As a result, a mini-industry of year 2000 consulting and programming services was growing up to help corporate and government computer users solve their problems.

The computer industry lost a major talent when computer pioneer Seymour Cray (*see* OBITUARIES) died of injuries suffered in an automobile accident in October.

(STEVE ALEXANDER)

This article updates the *Macropædia* articles COMPUTERS; INFORMATION PROCESSING AND INFORMATION SYSTEMS.

Deep Blue

In February 1996 Garry Kasparov, the world's best chess-playing human, sat down against Deep Blue, the world's best chess-playing computer, for the start of a six-game match. When Deep Blue defeated Kasparov in the first game, the shock was felt around the world. Had machines finally reached the same level of intelligence as humans?

The interest in having computers play chess began in about 1950. The first step was the development of an algorithm for constructing chess programs. Programmers "told" the computer certain rules it should follow (*e.g.*, develop its pieces toward the centre of the board, get its king into safety, and attack its opponents' king). Further enhancements came with the ability of the computer to analyze numerous positions quickly.

By the mid-1980s a computer called Hitech was strong enough to be rated in the lower ranks of the world's grand masters. In 1988 Deep Thought, the predecessor of Deep Blue, became the first computer to defeat a grand master. Deep Thought was soon capable of searching 750,000 positions per second (compared with one or two positions for humans). In 1989 Kasparov, world champion at that time, played Deep Thought in a two-game match and won both games.

That same year a new project began at IBM, headed by Chung-Jen Tan. He was assisted by Feng-Hsiung Hsu, Murray Campbell, A. Joseph Hoane, and Gershon Brody. (Hsu and Campbell had worked on Deep Thought.) The result was Deep Blue, a 32-node IBM PowerParallel SP2 high-performance computer with 256 microprocessors working in tandem. The team improved the calculating speed so that Deep Blue could look at more than one billion positions per second. It also had a massive opening database based on one million games from the past 100 years and an endgame database (which was activated when only five chess pieces remained) holding billions of scenarios.

In 1995 a match between Deep Blue and Kasparov was negotiated. Each participant would have two hours to make the first 40 moves, a common rate of play in human competition, and the winner would receive $400,000 out of a $500,000 purse. Experts were astounded when the computer beat back a dubious attack by Kasparov and made him resign on the 37th move in the first game. At first Kasparov was demoralized by the defeat, but, as he admitted later, it was the best thing that could have happened, because it forced him to treat Deep Blue as an opponent instead of just a machine.

As the match progressed, Kasparov changed his strategy. He played sound chess and avoided weaknesses in his position, limiting Deep Blue's potential to attack his king. He aimed for positions that would cause the computer to have trouble in analyzing the position and make it unable to come up with a plan. Consequently, it made weak moves. Kasparov then built up a superior position that enabled him to win. After the initial loss, Kasparov won three and drew two for a 4–2 victory.

Kasparov and the programmers for Deep Blue agreed to a rematch and scheduled it for May 1997. The programmers planned to upgrade the machine's sense of positional strategy so that Deep Blue could better analyze positions and be more flexible, but they admitted it would be a painstaking process.

In the end, Kasparov demonstrated the flexibility and adaptability of human reasoning. Whether Deep Blue, or any machine, would ever be able to match that, only time would tell.

(STEVEN MONTI)

Earth Sciences

GEOLOGY AND GEOCHEMISTRY

More than 5,000 geologists attended the 30th International Geological Congress in Beijing during August 1996. Song Ruixiang, president of the congress, outlined the role of geology in China's five-year plan, emphasizing the search for minerals and petroleum with a view to protection of the environment. Increasing recognition of the fact that environmental protection is one aspect of resource exploitation was also apparent at the 1996 annual meeting of the Geological Society of America in Denver, Colo., during October. Of some 200 technical sessions, 25% addressed the ways that Earth science is relevant to environmental problems, ranging from groundwater contamination to the cleanup of radioactive waste. At the General Assembly of the International Council of Scientific Unions in Washington, D.C., in September, much attention was paid to the "sustainable development" of society through the next century. The problems and progress were presented in a booklet, *Understanding Planet Earth,* which described processes occurring in the outer layers of the Earth during the fairly recent past as a basis for predicting future changes.

The Earth may be in transition from an ice age to a global greenhouse, with the rate of change probably being enhanced by society's contributions of greenhouse gases such as carbon dioxide to the atmosphere from the combustion of fossil fuels. A recent report by Robert Gastaldo of Auburn (Ala.) University and two colleagues analyzed the changes in vegetation worldwide during the two icehouse-greenhouse transitions that occurred in the late Paleozoic (about 300 million and 275 million years ago). Plant life changed during the geologically short time interval of 1,000 to 10,000 years; the primeval forests were replaced by vegetation dominated by seed plants. Recognizing such patterns of change would, the geologists believed, help them make predictions about future changes.

Geologists everywhere were concerned that although the need for interdisciplinary science for environmental management is recognized, the central role of geology in both resource acquisition and environmental problems was not appreciated by policy makers and the public in general. There was a scarcity of geologists among scientific advisers to government at all levels. Consequently, many efforts were under way to educate the public and policy makers about the reciprocal relationship between geology and society and the ways in which the world's aggressive agricultural and industrial activities are changing the biosphere and the geologic cycles.

The geochemical activities of the biosphere (the outer shell of the world where life exists) may help compensate for the degradation of the environment by human activities. For example, J. Craig Venter of the Institute for Genomic Research in Rockville, Md., and his team reported the complete genetic identification of a tiny, single-celled organism collected in 1983 from a hot submarine hydrothermal vent in the Pacific Ocean, 1,600 km (995 mi)

from Baja California. Since the DNA and genes of the organism differ from those of organisms in the two major groups of living things, the prokaryotes and eukaryotes, it had been assigned to a third branch of life called archaea. It was proposed that up to 20% of the Earth's biomass may be inhabited by this organism and its relatives, associated with the hot vents of the deep oceans. The ability of the organism to recycle methane and digest heavy metals, converting them into other compounds, might one day be exploited by humans.

Another discovery of previously unknown organisms, reported in August, generated much excitement and debate. David S. McKay (*see* BIOGRAPHIES) of NASA's Johnson Space Center, with eight coauthors, reported evidence for the occurrence of bacterial microfossils in a 4.5 billion-year-old meteorite from Mars that reached Earth about 13,000 years ago. The meteorite contains cracks filled with carbonate material, presumably deposited by solution at a time when Mars still supported free water. The carbonates contain organic material and structures resembling microfossils, along with iron sulfide and magnetite minerals similar to those produced by bacteria on the Earth. Some scientists believed that inorganic processes could yield the same products. A later investigation by Colin Pillinger and colleagues at the Open University, Milton Keynes, Eng., found carbon isotope ratios in the sample consistent with those formed by microscopic life forms on Earth. Pillinger also reported similar findings for a second meteorite from Mars that was only 600,000 years old.

The process of evolution—the history of the biosphere—is recorded both in rocks

and in the genes of animals. Recent advances in molecular biology were revealing molecular evidence of evolution that had yet to be reconciled with the fossil evidence. Gregory Wray, Jeffrey Levinton, and Leo Shapiro at the State University of New York at Stony Brook studied the genes of more than 200 species of 16 animal groups. They reported that the huge genetic differences they discovered between the groups, which they calibrated against changes in dated fossils of the many species, indicated that the animals last shared a common ancestor as long ago as 1.2 billion years. In contrast, the evidence from the fossil record was that nearly all known groups of animals appeared during a few million years in the early Cambrian Period, about 540 million years ago.

There was little evidence to show how life evolved before the Cambrian Period until one of the greatest discoveries about evolution in many years was reported by John Grotzinger at the Massachusetts Institute of Technology and three colleagues at the end of 1995. They explored rocks of Cambrian and older ages in Namibia and found a large selection of fossils in rocks of Vendian age, older by tens of millions of years than the Cambrian. The time interval just before the Cambrian Period was suddenly filled with a great variety of previously unknown, complex life forms.

Paleontology and evolutionary biology were both challenged by this discovery. The Cambrian fossils were preserved because they contained shells or skeletons. One possibility was that the animals had existed and evolved as soft-bodied creatures through perhaps 500 million years until predators evolved, which led to the development of

On the basis of recent research, geologists now believe that the Earth's solid inner core consists of a complex alignment of iron crystals that move about in response to the rise of hotter iron toward the surface of the core. Previously, many geophysicists had believed that the inner core was a perfectly aligned mass of iron crystals.

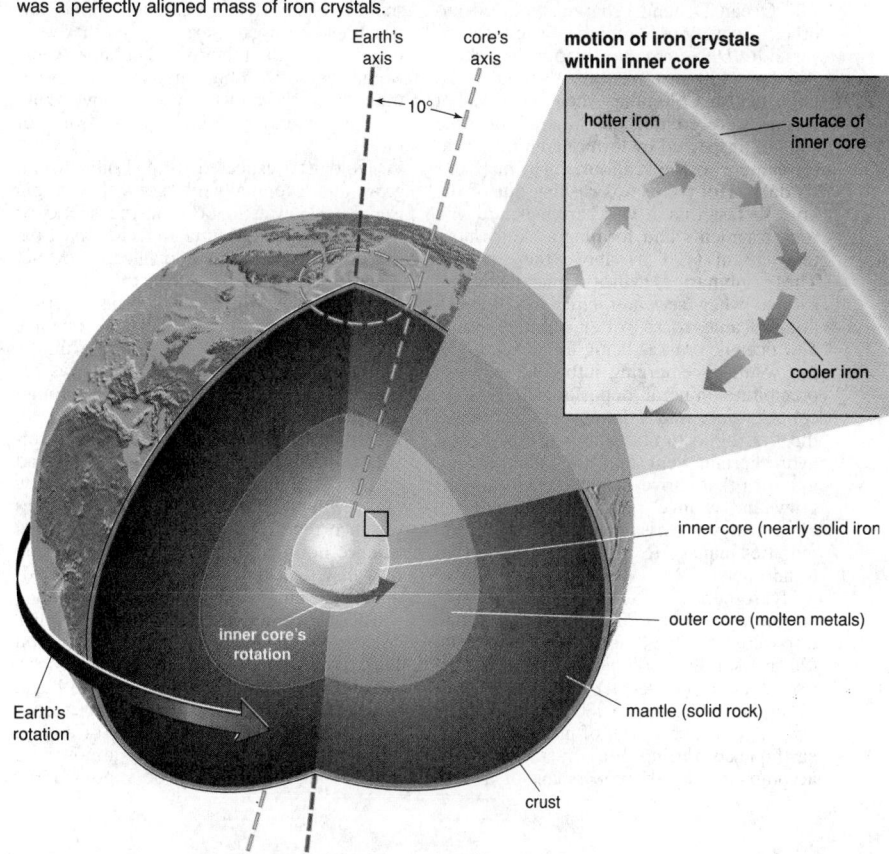

A cloud of smoke and ash rises 10 km (6 mi) above Mt. Ruapehu, which is located in a skiing area on New Zealand's North Island. Although the eruption of the volcano on June 17 was spectacular to see, the damage was relatively minor in the lightly populated area.

hard body parts as protection. Further geologic studies in selected older rocks and better precision for the molecular clock were required.

Many geologic and geochemical processes are intimately involved with the biosphere. The Ocean Drilling Program reported another discovery in September. The research vessel *JOIDES Resolution* was drilling about 240 km (150 mi) west of Vancouver Island, British Columbia, when two new hot springs were created on the seafloor. One site was inspected by lowering an underwater camera to the seafloor, 2,448 m (8,031 ft) deep. Hot water was rushing out of the hole so fast that it was carrying mud and rock fragments and forming a cloud more than 30 m (100 ft) above the seafloor. These submarine hydrothermal vents are formed when seawater circulates through hot volcanic rocks, often located where new oceanic crust is being formed, and the hot solutions emerging into cold seawater precipitate mineral deposits rich in iron, copper, zinc, and other metals. This was the first opportunity to watch how a new hydrothermal vent and the animal communities that thrive in those environments grow and change with time. One of the biggest mysteries is how the animal communities manage to migrate from one vent to another.

Hydrothermal vents also occur on submarine volcanoes. Loihi, a growing volcano discovered in 1954 approximately 30 km (20 mi) southeast of the island of Hawaii, rises 3,500 m (11,480 ft) from the seafloor to about 1,000 m (3,280 ft) below sea level. An intense swarm of more than 4,000 earthquakes during July and August was accompanied by the conversion of a cone

called Pele's Vents into a crater 260 m (850 ft) wide and 300 m (985 ft) deep, now called Pele's Pit. Alexander Malahoff of the Hawaii Undersea Research Laboratory organized an expedition with a research ship and a submarine to map and sample the reshaped volcano. The researchers found new fractures and hydrothermal vents that were more active than before. The new vents were covered with huge mats of chemosynthetic bacteria, and the water above Loihi was turbid and teeming with a "soup of life."

Geologists expected that Loihi would grow and eventually merge with the big island of Hawaii to become the successor to the volcanoes Mauna Kea, Mauna Loa, and Kilauea, which would become extinct as they were carried across the plume of hot rock rising from the Earth's interior. Details of the growth of those massive volcanoes, and of the deep mantle plume from which the lavas were derived, was being determined from deep drilling through the flanks of Mauna Loa and Mauna Kea. The drilling yielded information unavailable from surface reconstructions and had already established that the previous view of growth stages of Hawaiian volcanoes was incorrect. During the year the National Science Foundation recommended funding of a new drill hole to a depth of approximately 4.5 km.

The gases emerging from volcanoes play a crucial role on the Earth. The global carbon cycle, connecting the biosphere with rocks, air, and water, may be considered to begin in volcanic gases. Occasional massive eruptions pump such large quantities of carbon dioxide and acid gases into the atmosphere that global climate may be modified for

years. It was reported by Peter Francis and colleagues at the Open University that they were able to measure the concentrations of several components of volcanic gases from a distance by using Fourier-transform infrared spectroscopy.   (PETER J. WYLLIE)

GEOPHYSICS

Seismic activity was high during recent months. One of the largest earthquakes occurred on Oct. 9, 1995, near the coast of Jalisco, Mex., and left 19 persons dead, more than 100 injured, and at least 1,000 homeless, mostly in Colima. The quake was felt in Mexico City and by persons in highrise buildings as far away as Houston and Dallas, Texas, and in Oklahoma City, Okla. A tsunami estimated to have reached a maximum height of 5 m (17 ft) was generated. It was registered throughout the Pacific Basin, in the Marquesas Islands, the Hawaiian Islands, French Polynesia, Western Samoa, and even Southport, Australia, where its peak-to-trough amplitude was four centimetres.

Five shocks occurred with magnitudes of 7.9: on Dec. 3, 1995, in the Kuril Islands; on Feb. 17, 1996, in Indonesia; on June 10 in the Andreanof Islands off the coast of Alaska; on June 11 near the Philippine island of Samar; and on June 17 in the Flores Sea near Indonesia. Although the quake in the Andreanofs caused a tsunami that was registered in Hawaii, Crescent City, Calif., and Port Angeles, Wash., only the earthquake of February 17 caused fatalities and appreciable damage. It left 108 dead, 423 injured, and 58 missing and destroyed or seriously damaged more than 5,000 homes, some owing to a tsunami.

A survivor of an earthquake on February 3 in southwestern China's Yunnan province surveys the damage. Although the quake was not the strongest of the year, it was the most devastating, killing some 250 people, injuring 4,000, and leaving an estimated 1 million homeless.

It is not always the most powerful earthquakes that are the most destructive. The most devastating earthquake of 1996 occurred on February 3, in Yunnan province, China, where at least 251 people were killed and more than 4,000 were injured. It was estimated that 329,000 homes were destroyed throughout northwestern Yunnan and that one million people were left homeless. The magnitude of the shock was 6.6. Another shock on Oct. 6, 1995, in southern Sumatra, magnitude 6.7, killed 84, injured more than 1,800, damaged more than 17,000 homes, and left 65,000 homeless.

Two smaller earthquakes, of magnitude 5.9 each, caused fatalities. The first, on March 28 in Ecuador, killed at least 19 and injured 58; the second occurred on May 3 in western Neimenggu, China, and left 18 dead and 300 injured. A total of 15 earthquakes of magnitude 7.0 or greater occurred. February was exceptionally active, experiencing eight shocks with magnitudes between 6.0 and 6.9 and four of magnitude 7.0 or higher.

The most notable volcanic activity was the continuing series of eruptions of the Soufrière Hills volcano on Montserrat in the West Indies, which began on July 18, 1995. It was the first volcanic activity that was recorded on the island since it was visited by Columbus in 1493. The volcano began by producing clouds of ash that slowly increased in duration. New vents opened on July 18 and July 30. Low-level activity continued until an ash explosion formed a third vent on August 20, when some 5,000 people were evacuated. On August 27 there was a magma eruption, producing a lava flow and an ash cloud that coated the nearby city of Plymouth and blotted out

the light for 25 minutes. On the next day ejecta were hurled as far as three kilometres (two miles) from the summit. This time 6,000 residents took refuge at the northern end of this the island, which is only 13 km (8 mi) in length. Twice afterward the situation became ominous to the degree that three other evacuations took place, in November 1995, April 1996, and September 1996.

While seismic activity and other indicators have been effective in predicting eruptions in many instances, additional methods are needed. During the year a geochemist, Tobias Fischer, at Arizona State University found one that appeared to have great promise. Volcanologists had determined that the mechanics of volcanism result in a predictable chain of events. The molten magma gives off a volatile mix of gases, containing carbon, hydrochloric acid, and sulfur dioxide. These escape under great pressure, forcing out rainwater in the form of steam. When the tubes or fissures become clogged owing to the accretion of minerals or by cooling of the surface rock, pressure builds within them until it is released with explosive force. In June 1992 Fischer began monitoring the content of the gases escaping from the active Galeras volcano in Colombia. He found definite changes in gas temperature and the percentages of the various chemicals before an eruption. In the week prior to the latest large event, the temperature of the surface rock dropped from 750° to just over 400° C, and the amount of the very soluble hydrogen chloride dropped to one-thirtieth of the mixture, while that of the insoluble carbon dioxide remained unchanged.

Fischer reasoned that water was not ex-

pelled because the channels were blocked and the water consequently seeped into the rocks, dissolving the salt. This increase in salt indicated blocked tubes, which in turn indicated a pressure buildup and an imminent eruption.

According to the long-accepted theory of isostasy, mountains float on the denser mantle, similar to icebergs in the ocean. The mass of the mountain below the surface of the ground, extending downward as much as 60 km (37 mi), is greater than that of the visible portion. This is apparently not so for the Sierra Nevada mountains, however, according to Stephen Parks and his team, who began working on the Southern Sierra Continental Dynamics project in 1992. Using extensive seismic refraction surveys, they determined the thickness to the mantle beneath the mountains to be only about five kilometres (three miles). Furthermore, electrical resistivity surveys showed that there were areas of partially molten rock beneath the crust. This indicated to the investigators that the mountain roots were being melted and were less than half the size they had been 15 million–20 million years ago. Thus, in theory, the Sierra Nevada chain, which contains Mt. Whitney, the highest peak in the contiguous U.S., should be sinking rather than rising. Further research efforts would be designed to map the magma, date deep cores, and attempt to determine whether the Sierras were higher in the past.

Another study of geodynamics produced rather startling results. The most widely accepted theory of plate tectonics supposes that the plates float on the mantle or at least move independently of it. Recently, however, researchers from the Carnegie Institution of Washington, D.C., and the University of São Paulo, Brazil, found a fossil plume buried deep in the mantle beneath Paraná flood basalt that has remained stationary with respect to the South American plate, which thus demonstrates that a portion of the mantle is moving with the plate and that the mantle and the continent have been coupled since the opening of the South Atlantic Ocean about 130 million years ago.   (RUTLAGE J. BRAZEE)

METEOROLOGY AND CLIMATE

Aided by advanced numerical models, the scientific understanding of the atmosphere—and of the interactions between the ocean and atmosphere—and the ability to forecast large- and small-scale meteorologic and hydrologic phenomena on a variety of time scales have increased dramatically during the past two decades. Rapid technological advances have also increased the capability to collect and process vast amounts of atmospheric data. This knowledge and technology provide meteorologists and hydrologists with many research opportunities that are expected to lead to improved forecasts.

Long-term outlooks for periods of as much as a year into the future are now possible. While such long-range predictions do not have the precision of tomorrow's forecast, they can provide useful planning information for such industries as utilities, agriculture, and water-supply management. One basis of seasonal prediction is the

GILLES PERES—MAGNUM

A courier tries to cycle down the middle of a street in New York City after a January storm dropped more than 50 cm (20 in) of snow, the most to fall on the city since 1947. Some scientists speculated that this and other severe storms were further evidence of global warming.

ocean-atmospheric interaction in the South Pacific Ocean. The research on this interaction has enabled the prediction of tropical sea-surface temperature variations for as long as a year. With this knowledge forecasters have been able to predict seasonal temperature and rainfall variations over North America. Increasingly sophisticated regional models of the atmosphere are be-

ing developed to bring these forecasts down to the regional scale.

Global-scale climate changes based upon the possible consequences of increases in "greenhouse" gases in the atmosphere are being studied. These gases, which include carbon dioxide, can affect climate and weather by modifying the radiative characteristics of the atmosphere.

NASA GODDARD SPACE FLIGHT CENTER—LABORATORY FOR ATMOSPHERES

The eye of Hurricane Fran is clearly visible in this satellite image as the storm traveled westward toward the coast of Florida. Fran affected parts of the East Coast of the U.S. during September and was among the most damaging of an unusually large number of hurricanes during 1996.

As the accuracy of models of large-scale changes in the atmosphere increases and as computers become faster, research efforts will continue to improve medium-range (three-to-five-day) forecasts. That these efforts have paid dividends was demonstrated when the forecast models developed by the National Weather Service accurately predicted the superstorm of March 1993 five days in advance. Five-day forecasts in 1996 were as good as three-day forecasts were 15 years ago.

Considerable research was also taking place in regard to short-term forecasts. Improved models of the atmosphere have resulted from the incorporation of sophisticated representations of physical processes, such as the effects of ocean temperature and topographic variation at the Earth's surface. Such research has led to rapid progress in "mesoscale" meteorology—the meteorology of severe local storms.

Because short-term and long-term meteorology is global in scope, it has historically fostered international cooperation. Efforts were expected to continue in such areas as the exchange of real-time data, scientific collaboration, and technology transfer. One example was in the area of river forecasting and water management. The performance of recently implemented forecast systems (using U.S. river-forecasting techniques) during the extensive flooding in the summer of 1996 in China was widely praised.

In spite of these improvements in forecasting, some of the most deadly meteorological menaces, such as tornadoes, lightning, and flash floods, still could not be forecast with total precision. In an effort to improve such forecasts, the U.S. deployed advanced observing instruments, such as Doppler radar, satellites, and telemetering observation systems, to provide real-time data in order to mitigate the loss of life from rapidly evolving small-scale meteorological events. Doppler radars can detect the speed and direction of wind as well as precipitation within developing storms. This allowed early detection of severe thunderstorms and tornadoes and also provided precipitation estimates important to forecasting of flooding. Geostationary satellites provided images of storm systems as frequently as every six minutes during severe weather situations. Automated surface-observing systems provided a significant increase in the number of observing sites, including many airports.

New forecast capabilities could also benefit the economy. A new field of meteorological application was unfolding as industry learned to apply the improved weather products and services to the benefit of their companies. The future of meteorology thus seemed certain to be an expanding collaborative endeavour between federal and state governments, academia, and the private sector.   (ELBERT W. FRIDAY, JR.)

OCEANOGRAPHY

Two distinctive features of research in oceanography during 1996 were the importance of new technology in carrying out observations and the evident necessity of observational programs extending over many years, not only for long-term monitoring but also for developing a conceptual background that would help researchers formulate new scientific questions.

The Ocean Drilling Program (ODP) had its inception in an attempt, in 1961, to drill through the ocean floor to the Mohorovicic discontinuity separating the Earth's crust from the mantle beneath. This effort became the Deep Sea Drilling Program in 1968 and was transformed into the present ODP in 1984, when the drilling ship JOIDES Resolution was commissioned. When drilling was begun, the ideas of plate tectonics were in their infancy, and scientists' view of the events that shape the seafloor emphasized processes that occur over geologic time scales. But during the lifetime of the drilling programs, even more evidence has been found supporting the importance of sudden events. Several of these were observed in 1996. The ability to detect them and to put observers above them at sea while they were occurring was possible only because of advances in ocean technology during the past decade.

In late February the U.S. Navy's Sound Surveillance System (SOSUS) detected seismic events near the northern Gorda Ridge about 350 km west of the coast of northern California (1 km = 0.62 mi). By early March scientists were at sea in the region sampling the water column—a plume of heated water 10 km across that rose 1,500 m off the seafloor (1 m = 3.28 ft). Further studies in April and June found microorganisms that demonstrated the ability to grow at temperatures as high as 90° C (194° F) but could not grow at normal ocean temperatures.

Loihi Seamount is an underwater volcano about 30 km southeast of the island of Hawaii. A hydrothermal vent system at a depth of about 1,000 m previously capped the summit. Seismicity was intense there for a month beginning in mid-July. Again, scientists were able to take field observations during the event. The newly changed seafloor was mapped acoustically; volcanic glass fragments were recovered, using submersible vehicles; and plumes of hydrothermally altered water were observed. At the conclusion the summit vent system had collapsed into a broadened summit crater whose floor was 1,350 m deep. Continued volcanism at Loihi over thousands of years would ultimately build the summit upward to the ocean surface.

In September, while the JOIDES Resolution was drilling into metal-rich deposits formed by an old and inactive hydrothermal vent system about 240 km west of Vancouver Island (British Columbia) and just a few kilometres from an active vent, two new vents were created. Repeated visits to this site were expected to provide a unique opportunity for scientists to learn how the particular collection of organisms that flourish only in the extreme conditions near the vent colonize a new site.

The World Ocean Circulation Experiment (WOCE) began a global survey of the circulation of the world ocean in 1990. In the Atlantic, WOCE data based on analyses of the distribution of tritium in the water were beginning to give a consistent picture of the "age" of subsurface waters (the time elapsed since those waters participated in exchanges across the air-sea interface), a picture that would be important in refining estimates of such quantities as oxygen consumption by living organisms at different depths. Tritium is primarily a product of atmospheric nuclear weapons testing, and its distribution thus provides information about water motions since the 1960s.

Chlorofluorocarbons have entered the oceans as by-products of industrial activity, primarily refrigeration and air-conditioning. The WOCE measurements of the chlorofluorocarbon distribution in the Pacific were completed in 1996; levels of those compounds were below detectability in the deep waters of the northern Pacific but were well above detectability in the deep waters of the southern Pacific and in deep northward-flowing Pacific currents.

Most of the WOCE fieldwork was scheduled to be finished by the end of 1997. The project largely attained its goal of providing a basic global picture of the circulation of the ocean over a period of several years. An important part of that picture is the global pattern of heat transport and of water exchange between the air and the sea. One of the most important practical applications for this knowledge is climate prediction. Planning began for a global study of the coupled atmosphere-ocean climate system and its predictability on time scales of seasons to years. This Climate Variability and Predictability Program was scheduled to begin in 1998 and was to last for 15 years so that year-to-year variability could be understood adequately.

The complexity and variability of seafloor and fluid environments greatly complicates efforts to understand the abundance and variability of marine populations. Even so, during 1996 technological developments originating in physical oceanography made possible an open ocean test of the hypothesis that in regions of the ocean where nutrients and light are available in abundance yet phytoplankton populations are lower than expected, it is a lack of iron that is the limiting factor. In work carried out in 1995 and reported in 1996, an area about 30 km on a side in the equatorial eastern Pacific was initially surveyed to check that temperature and salinity, as well as biological and chemical conditions, were uniform, so that the sinking of cold or salty water relative to adjacent cold or relatively fresh water would be minimal. A small part of this region, about eight kilometres on a side, was then seeded with iron (as acidic iron sulfate) mixed with the inert tracer sulfur hexafluoride previously used to study vertical diffusion rates in California coastal waters and in the central Atlantic. A freely drifting buoy that constantly radioed its satellite-derived geographic position to the ship was used to mark the centre of the seeded patch. The ship carried out continuous surveys through the seeded patch around the buoy, measuring dissolved iron, sulfur hexafluoride, nitrate, and chlorophyll over a 19-day period. Chlorophyll levels increased by as much as 27 times several days after the last addition of iron, which indicated phytoplankton growth, and nitrate levels were correspondingly depleted.

(MYRL C. HENDERSHOTT)

See also Business and Industry Review: Energy; Mining; Chronicle: Disasters; The Environment; Life Sciences.

This article updates the Macropædia articles ATMOSPHERE; CLIMATE AND WEATHER; DINOSAURS; The EARTH; The EARTH SCIENCES; EARTHQUAKES; GEOCHRONOLOGY; The HYDROSPHERE; OCEANS; PLATE TECTONICS; RIVERS; VOLCANISM.

Economic Affairs

World economic and financial conditions charted a favourable course during 1996, and growth became more widespread, particularly in the less-developed countries (LDCs). According to International Monetary Fund (IMF) and World Bank estimates, global economic output expanded close to 3.8%, a little faster than the year before, despite a disappointing economic performance in many Western European countries.

The rate of economic growth in the developed economies as a whole picked up a little to an estimated 2.3%, compared with 2.1% in 1995. (*See* Table I.) The effect of the midcycle dip, much in evidence in 1995, still influenced many countries. Lower interest rates, introduced in 1995 to counter faltering growth, together with steady exchange rates (particularly in Japan and Germany) should have stimulated economic activity in the developed countries more strongly than they actually did. In some Western European countries, however, this easier monetary stance was countered by tighter budgetary policies in preparation for economic and monetary union (EMU). Thus, economic growth in the European Union (EU) drifted down to an estimated 1.6% from the 1995 level of 2.5%. With the exception of the U.K., where growth remained steady, the slowdown in countries such as France, Germany, and Italy was seen as an unfavourable development, as the recovery from the 1992–93 recession was still incomplete, with unemployment at relatively high levels. By contrast, economic activity rebounded in the U.S. and Japan, partly in response to the relaxed monetary conditions. The Japanese economy registered the strongest growth for 20 years in the opening quarter but lost momentum as the effect of the 1995 measures to stimulate the economy wore off. Even so, gross domestic product (GDP) in Japan expanded by around 3.75%. There was a similar upsurge in the U.S. during the second quarter, but more moderate growth conditions returned in the second half. Thus, for the first time in many years, growth in the world's two largest economies was more synchronized. Despite close links with the U.S. economy, output continued to decline in Canada in response to tight policies. Benefiting from relatively buoyant conditions in the Pacific region, Australia and, to a lesser extent, New Zealand experienced an upturn.

Relatively strong economic growth—at around 6%—was maintained in the LDCs

during 1996. (*See* Table IV.) In many countries investment and exports were the main sources of growth. The expansion in exports from the LDCs, both to the developed countries and to each other, partly offset economic weakness in industrialized countries and enabled the LDCs to sustain above-average growth rates.

As in previous years, this overall high growth rate concealed many regional and national differences. Despite a slowdown, growth in South and East Asia remained close to 8%, the highest rate within the less-developed regions. While rapid growth in some of the "Tiger Economies" (Singapore, Hong Kong, Taiwan, South Korea, and Thailand) cooled as a result of tighter monetary policies, rapid growth was maintained in China. Vietnam, benefiting from strong foreign investment, registered the fastest growth rate in the region, nearly 10%.

Growth accelerated in Africa from around 3% in 1995 to an estimated 5%. As this was ahead of population growth for the first time since the mid-1980s, per capita income registered significant growth. Favourable weather conditions and supportive economic policies were the main reasons for the upturn. Despite this economic recovery, most African countries re-

mained among the poorest in the world. Latin America emerged from the 1995 recession, which was induced by the financial crisis in Mexico. Growth remained patchy in the region, however, as a number of large countries, including Brazil, Chile, and Colombia, experienced a slowdown.

As inflationary pressures remained subdued and public-sector deficits contracted, policy makers in the developed countries were concerned with nurturing noninflationary growth. This led to a modest easing of monetary policy during 1996, particularly in Europe. In the U.S. the Federal Reserve Board (Fed) refrained from further interest-rate cuts in 1996 as the economy responded to the previous year's relaxation of policy. In Japan interest rates were held steady to sustain economic recovery. In Europe, against a background of sluggish economic activity and low inflation rates, monetary policy was eased further, particularly in Germany, France, and other countries where the monetary policy shadowed that of Germany. A similar trend was in evidence in the U.K., where base rates were reduced in three steps despite reservations by the Bank of England. Then in November the chancellor of the Exchequer, Kenneth Clarke, unexpectedly raised short-term interest rates by 0.25%, signaling a turning point in the interest-rate cycle.

Public-sector deficits continued to shrink in 1996 as policy makers in most countries kept fiscal policy on a tight rein. In the U.S., as budget deficits continued to fall, fiscal policy remained largely neutral ahead of the November presidential elections. The deadlock relating to the budget negotiations for the fiscal year ending September 1996 dragged on until April 1996. Even so, there was no firm agreement on how to balance the budget in the long term. The Japanese authorities adopted a "wait-and-see" policy as they judged that the economy did not require further economic-stimulation packages. It was argued that what the Japanese economy required was a speeding

Table II. Consumer Prices in OECD Countries
% change from preceding year

Country	1992	1993	1994	1995	1996[1]
United States	3.0	3.0	2.6	2.8	3.0
Japan	1.7	1.3	0.7	−0.1	0
Germany	5.1	4.5	2.7	1.8	1.5
France	2.4	2.1	1.7	1.7	1.8
United Kingdom	3.7	1.6	2.5	3.4	3.2
Canada	1.5	1.8	0.2	2.2	1.5
Italy	5.3	4.2	3.9	5.4	3.4
Austria	4.0	3.6	3.0	2.2	1.9
Belgium	2.4	2.8	2.4	1.5	2.0
Denmark	2.1	1.3	2.0	2.1	2.3
Finland	2.9	2.2	1.1	1.0	1.1
Greece	15.9	14.4	10.9	9.3	8.5
Iceland	4.0	4.0	1.6	1.7	1.5
Ireland	3.1	1.4	2.3	2.5	1.9
Luxembourg	3.2	3.6	2.2	1.9	1.5
Netherlands	3.2	2.6	2.8	1.9	2.4
Norway	2.3	2.3	1.4	2.5	1.1
Portugal	8.9	6.5	5.2	4.1	4.9
Spain	5.9	4.6	4.7	4.7	3.6
Sweden	2.6	4.7	2.4	2.9	0.2
Switzerland	4.0	3.3	0.9	1.8	0.8
Turkey	70.1	66.1	105.1	89.1	79.6
Australia	1.0	1.8	1.9	4.6	2.1
New Zealand	1.0	1.3	1.8	3.8	2.4
OECD Total	4.8	4.3	4.4	5.5	4.9

[1]Twelve-month rate of change in October 1996.
Sources: OECD, *The Economist*.

Table I. Real Gross Domestic Products of Selected OECD Countries
% annual change

Country	1992	1993	1994	1995	1996[1]
United States	2.7	2.2	3.5	2.0	2.3
Japan	1.1	0.1	0.5	0.9	3.5
Germany[2]	2.2	−1.2	2.9	1.9	1.5
France	1.2	−1.3	2.8	2.2	1.1
United Kingdom	−0.5	2.3	3.8	2.4	2.3
Canada	0.8	2.2	4.6	2.2	1.6
Italy	0.7	−1.2	2.2	3.0	0.9
All developed countries	1.8	1.0	2.7	1.9	2.2
Seven major countries above	1.8	1.0	2.8	1.9	2.0
European Union	1.0	−0.6	2.7	2.5	

[1]Estimated.   [2]From 1992, figures include former East Germany.
Sources: OECD, *The Economist*.

up of the deregulation and liberalization moves already under way. The thrust of fiscal policy in Europe remained tight during 1996, as many countries were concerned with reducing their public-sector deficits in order to meet the criteria for the EMU under the Maastricht Treaty on European Union, due to start in 1999. Budget deficit reduction measures were adopted in Germany, France, Belgium, Italy, and other EU countries. Many of these measures were not as severe as some official commentators made out, as "creative-accounting" techniques, particularly in France, were utilized to reduce the deficits without deep cuts. There were extensive protests from workers in France and Germany on proposed cutbacks on social benefits, and doubts were expressed by economists as to whether France and Germany would succeed in reducing their public deficits to 3% of GDP by 1997. The British public-sector deficit proved to be more stubborn than expected. The 1996–97 outturn, at £26.5 billion, while lower than the previous year's £32 billion, was double the target set in 1993.

With the exception of the U.S. and the U.K., employment growth experienced another disappointing year. There was no perceptible improvement in the unemployment rate in the developed countries belonging to the Organisation for Economic Co-operation and Development (OECD), where unemployment remained at around 7.3%. This excluded those who had retired early (often involuntarily) or who for various reasons were discouraged from joining the ranks of job seekers. (*See* Table III.)

The U.S. economy had been most successful in creating new jobs. During 1996 the number of people in work increased by nearly two million. Even though the labour force grew by around 800,000 people, largely as a result of legal immigrants (an estimated 300,000 illegal immigrants were excluded from labour force data), unemployment at year's end stood at 5.3%, compared with 5.5% a year earlier. Similarly, in the U.K. the number of those out of work and claiming unemployment ben-

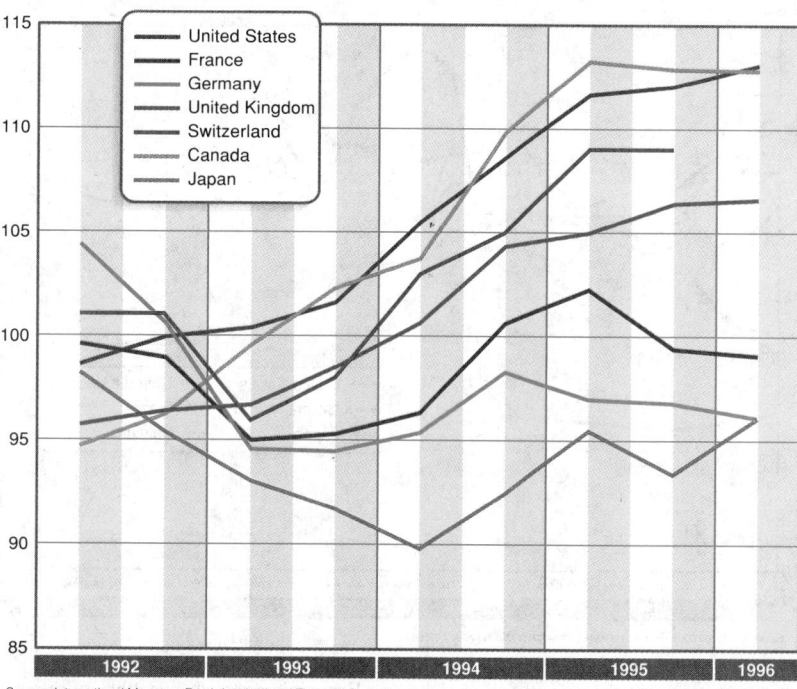

Industrial Production
semiannual averages: 1990 = 100

- United States
- France
- Germany
- United Kingdom
- Switzerland
- Canada
- Japan

1992 1993 1994 1995 1996

Source: International Monetary Fund, *International Financial Statistics.*

efits steadily fell during the year and in November stood at 2,030,000, which gave an unemployment rate of 7.2% (down from 8.1% the year before). In France and Germany sluggish economic growth and rigid employment markets led to higher unemployment rates. There was a small rise in unemployment in Japan as the hesitant economic recovery failed to create sufficient new job opportunities to absorb a rise in the labour force. This trend hit hardest the young and led to a youth unemployment rate of double the national average. The IMF and similar organizations, citing the examples of relatively more flexible

labour markets in the U.S., the U.K., and New Zealand and their success in reducing structural unemployment, urged other developed countries to speed up the reform of their labour markets.

As a result of sluggish growth in the developed countries, the volume of world trade expanded at an estimated 6.4%, compared with nearly 9% the year before. Not surprisingly, little progress was made in eliminating the large regional deficits. The U.S. trade balance grew, as stronger domestic demand sucked in higher imports, and was heading for a $175 billion deficit, a deterioration of 60%. Weaker export markets, combined with a depreciating currency, led to a 25% reduction in the Japanese trade surplus as measured in U.S. dollars.

The IMF projections pointed to continued easing of the debt problems of the LDCs. This was partly attributed to a larger part of the capital inflows being non-debt-bearing. The growing volume of exports further eased the problem of servicing existing debts.

NATIONAL ECONOMIC POLICIES

United States. Having achieved a soft landing in 1995, the U.S. economy avoided slipping into a recession in 1996. Partly as a result of the easing of monetary conditions that began in mid-1995, economic activity picked up in 1996 and reached 4.7% in the second quarter. A slowdown in the summer put the economy on course for a sustainable growth rate and led to GDP growth for the year of 2.3%—a little ahead of 1995.

Economic growth was sustained by a recovery in domestic demand, in particular personal consumption. During the first half of the year, consumers spent freely with the aid of easily available credit. Having grown at a fast rate of 4%, consumer

Inflation Rate
Percentage change from December to December

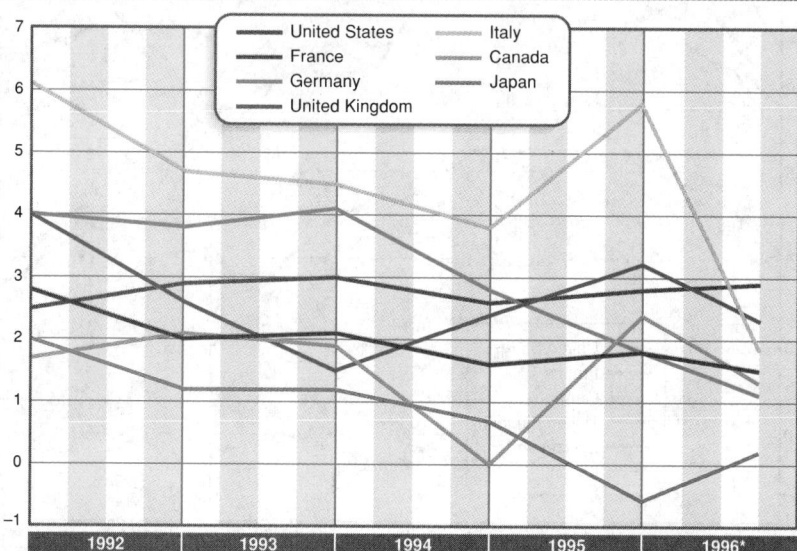

- United States
- France
- Germany
- United Kingdom
- Italy
- Canada
- Japan

1992 1993 1994 1995 1996*

*Percentage change from October 1995 to October 1996.
Source: International Monetary Fund, *International Financial Statistics.*

Interest Rates: Short-term
three-month money market rates

Percent

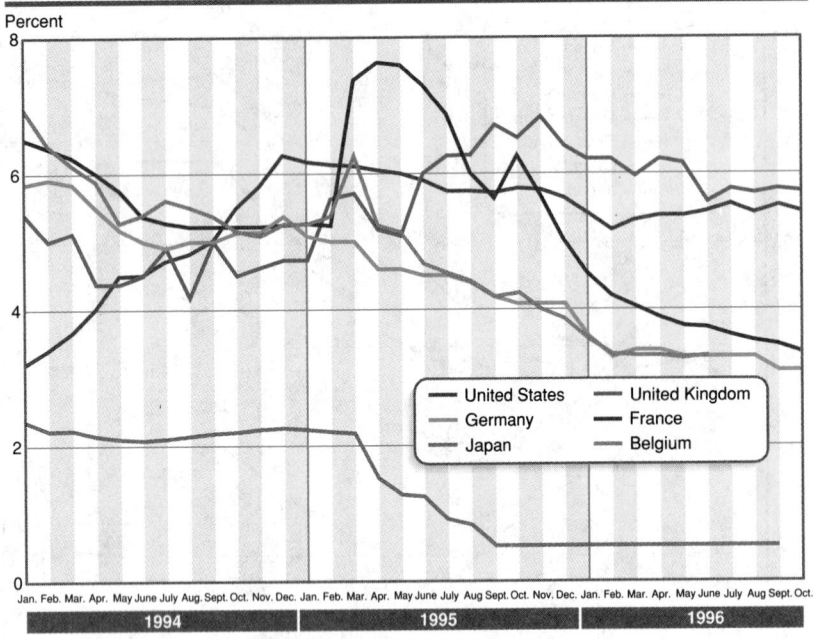

Source: International Monetary Fund, *International Financial Statistics*.

spending cooled in the second half as debt levels rose to record levels and fears of higher interest rates resurfaced. In contrast, government spending remained flat. Investment, both business and housing, staged a recovery and grew by around 6%. Business investment reflected the ending of the inventory overhang and an improvement in manufacturing output. Capacity utilization rose to 83%, close to its post-World War II average. As long-term interest rates rose in the autumn, there was some evidence of a slowdown in both industrial output and the rate of business investment.

Continuing economic growth enabled further gains to be made in reducing unemployment. In November the U.S. jobless rate stood at 5.3%, compared with 5.5% a year earlier. The December rate remained unchanged. Since 1992, 10 million jobs had been created, more than Pres. Bill Clinton promised during his campaign that year. Four million of these jobs had been created since the beginning of 1995, and, unlike in previous years, two-thirds were in sectors paying above-average wages. Despite full employment, inflation remained subdued. In November the core inflation rate, excluding food and energy, was running at 2.7%, compared with 3% a year earlier. Economic observers were surprised by the lack of upward pressures on prices despite the jobless rate's falling well below 6% (often regarded as the threshold for accelerating inflation). Structural changes in the labour market and stagnation in real wages were seen as possible reasons.

The combination of robust domestic demand with a stronger dollar halted the improvement in the trade balance. On the basis of incomplete data, the trade balance was heading for a $175 billion deficit— much higher than the previous year's deficit of $108 billion. The current account was likely to remain largely unchanged as a result of higher capital inflows into the U.S. and a smaller deficit on investment income.

Economic policy during 1996, both monetary and fiscal, remained largely neutral. While it did not provide any stimulus to the economy, the primary goal of economic policy makers remained one of ensuring that the noninflationary growth was sustained. As the economy responded to lower interest rates—introduced between

July 1995 and February 1996—and activity rates picked up, the monetary authorities kept the base rates under review. In the wake of the 4.7% GDP growth in the second quarter and continued growth in employment, independent observers started worrying that interest rates might have to be raised soon to counter the threat of future higher inflation. The Fed took the view that there was no need for higher interest rates, as economic growth would be moderating spontaneously, the inflation risk remained low, and lower levels of unemployment were sustainable without triggering higher wage rates. The economic indicators available at the close of the year pointed to this judgment's being accurate. Fiscal policy, having achieved a reduction in the U.S. budget deficit in the last three years, was largely neutral in 1996. Clinton's proposals for fiscal 1997 (beginning Oct. 1, 1996) allowed for only a slight growth in spending on many programs, with the exception of health care and similar mandatory programs.

Japan. The long-awaited economic recovery in Japan ran out of steam after an exceptionally strong performance in the first quarter. The recovery that got under way in the second half of 1995 accelerated in the winter, leading to a 3% growth over the previous quarter (an annualized growth of 12.7%)—the strongest growth in more than 20 years. While the surge in activity was boosted by exceptional factors, there was no denying the strength of the underlying trend. This led to an upward revision of economic forecasts to 4.25%, putting Japan at the top of the economic growth league among major economies. In the event, economic activity lost momentum

Interest Rates: Long-term

Percent

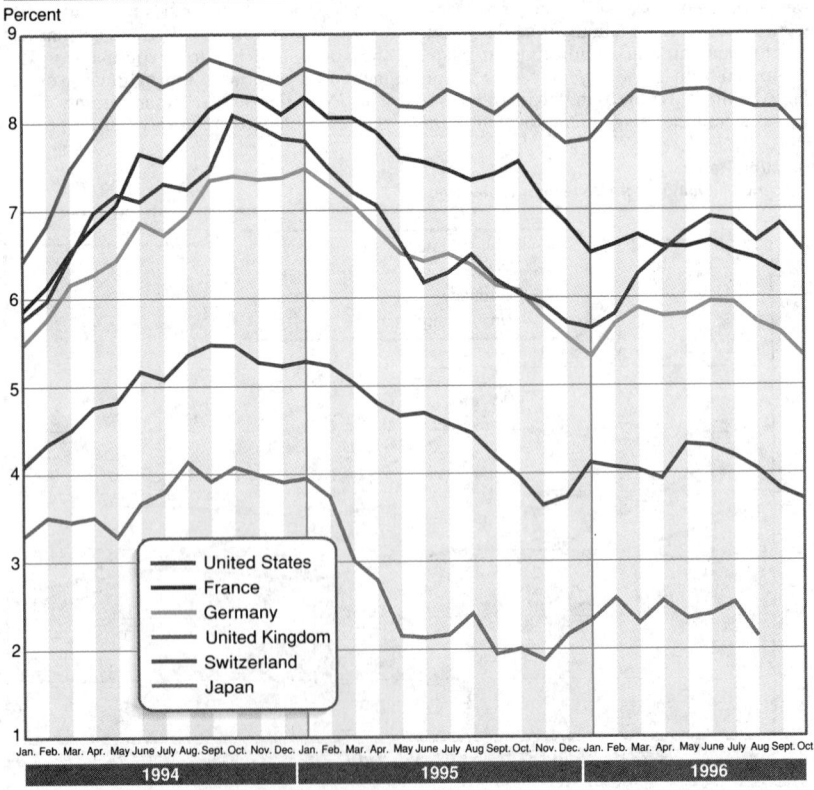

Source: International Monetary Fund, *International Financial Statistics*.

and the next quarter registered a decline, followed by a minuscule rise in the third quarter. Despite this uneven performance, GDP in Japan was estimated to have grown by about 3.7% during 1996 as a whole—the best performance in five years.

The strong recovery early in the year reflected the large stimulus provided by the lower interest rates and public-investment programs announced in April and September 1995. The subsequent slowdown was attributable to the effect of these measures fading away. Domestic demand was the main driving force supported by strong growth in investment. Consumer spending, which was boosted by gains in disposable income, lost momentum in the second half of the year. Sales of automobiles, personal computers, and such high-tech equipment as mobile phones, car navigation systems, and digital cameras registered good gains. Sales in supermarkets and some department stores remained relatively weaker.

Housing investment grew robustly, stimulated by prospects of higher interest rates later in the year and the planned rise in the consumption tax in April 1997. The commercial construction industry benefited from the huge injections of public-works investment in the economy and the reconstruction of Kobe after the 1995 earthquake. Spending on plant and equipment strengthened during the year, reflecting improved business confidence and record-low interest rates. Although business investment grew by 5% over the year, compared with 10% for private housing, as the year drew to a close, the trend of the former was pointing upward while the latter was decidedly downward.

Against the background of a recovery in economic activity, fiscal policy remained largely neutral and monetary policy was accommodating. There were no pump-priming emergency packages that had been repeatedly used in past years to stimulate the economy. On the contrary, policy makers began anticipating a tightening in 1997 on the assumption of sustained recovery. In June the Cabinet approved a rise in the consumption tax from 3% to 5%, effective from April 1997.

Interest rates remained at a record low but would have risen before the year-end had rapid economic growth been sustained. Maintaining interest rates at low levels was deemed by the authorities to be beneficial to the banking system, which had not recovered from the problems caused by "nonperforming" loans. Several bills were passed to bolster the role of regulatory and supervisory bodies to forestall future collapse of financial institutions, but these could not prevent further bankruptcies among financial institutions. The $9 billion bankruptcy of Nichiei Finance in late October marked the largest collapse in Japan's corporate history. This would have resulted in further claims on the deposit insurance scheme and added to the government's already large deficit, which had risen to 5% of GDP—an unsustainable level against the low-inflation and low-growth economic backdrop.

As unemployment is usually a lagging indicator, the uneven recovery did not halt the inexorable rise in Japanese unemployment. The unemployment rate reached a new peak of 3.5% in May, its highest since 1953, and fell to 3.4% in November. This looked low in comparison with rates in the U.S. and Europe, but it was significantly understated because of the way Japanese statistics were calculated. Despite the rise in unemployment, wages rose in 1996. The spring *shunto* round of wage negotiations resulted in a weighted average pay raise of 2.86%. Although the nominal gains were low in both 1995 and 1996, the minimal increase in the consumer price index resulted in a good real rise.

Despite the currency value's weakening from 80 yen to the dollar in April 1995 to 113 to the dollar in autumn 1996, there was little evidence that inflation was picking up. Following a 0.3% fall in the first quarter, the subsequent rise resulted in a 0.2% increase overall. Given the sharp rise in import prices in yen terms, inflation was expected to upturn significantly in 1997.

The slowdown in domestic demand, coupled with the decline in the value of the yen, resulted in a slowdown in the growth of imports. Compared with a 16% overall rise in 1995, imports toward the end of 1996 were 3% up on the year before (both in yen terms). Exports rose by 3%, but export growth was held back by sluggish growth in many OECD countries. Because of the depreciating yen, Japan's trade surplus and the current-account balance declined in dollar terms. The trade surplus was heading for $100 billion ($135 billion in 1995), compared with a $75 billion current-account surplus ($111 billion in 1995).

United Kingdom. Economic growth in the U.K. gained momentum during the year, reversing the previous year's second-half downturn. Stronger consumer spending and a small pickup in key European export markets were the main influences behind the upturn. These stronger-than-expected developments enabled GDP to grow by 2.5%—a similar pace to that of the year before.

Consumer spending was driven higher by incomes from employment growing almost 2% above the inflation rate, a slight easing in the tax burden, and lower interest rates on home mortgages. Consumer confidence was also boosted by a gradual recovery in the housing market. After many years of decline, house prices rose by an average of 6%. The improvement in the housing market spilled into related sectors of consumer spending, such as furniture, carpets, and do-it-yourself products. Consumer spending as a whole expanded by almost 4%, the fastest rate since 1989.

Although investment charted an erratic course during 1996, assisted by lower interest rates and a rebound in housing investment, it expanded by an average of 3% and contributed to domestic demand. Investment by industry lagged behind, reflecting weak manufacturing output, which was held back as industrialists tried to clear excess inventories that had built up. In the fourth quarter of 1996, factory production finally rebounded, despite export orders' remaining flat.

Against a background of higher economic activity rates, unemployment continued to fall and reached the lowest rate since 1991. At the year's end the total number of unemployed stood at around two million, or 7.2% of the workforce, compared with 8.1% a year earlier. The fall in unemployment was probably exaggerated by a large number of people's leaving the workforce, as well as by a change in the benefits system that tightened conditions for eligibility. While the ruling Conservative Party tried to make political capital from the continuing decline in unemployment ahead of the 1997 general election, financial markets were unsettled by fears that it could be fueling inflationary pressures and bringing forward the need for another interest-rate rise. These worries were heightened by a gradual acceleration in the inflation rate, particularly the underlying rate, which excluded mortgage interest rates. Having remained at around 3% for most of the year, in the autumn the underlying rate moved up to 3.3%, well above the government's medium-term target of 2.5%. Even so, it remained low by historical standards.

Economic policy was aimed at nurturing economic growth and consumer confidence in the hope that this would translate to electorate support for the Conservatives. During the first half of 1996, interest rates were trimmed back by 0.75% in three steps, despite reservations voiced by the governor of the Bank of England. Chancellor Clarke was influenced by the stagnation in manufacturing output and wanted to ensure that the slowdown in economic growth did not turn into a recession. Taking a chance that cost pressures on industry would remain constrained, in June he unexpectedly cut interest rates to 5.75%. This surprising move was followed by an equally unexpected rise back to 6% in November.

Compared with the relative freedom the chancellor enjoyed in framing monetary policy, the scope for tax cuts in his last budget before the election was severely limited. The main constraint was the stubbornly high public-sector borrowing requirement (PSBR). Revised summer forecasts pointed to a £25 billion PSBR, below the 1995 level of £32.2 billion but double the original £12 billion target. As in 1995, Clarke found room to cut personal taxes by £2.2 billion but recouped most of it through a £1.5 billion rise in indirect taxes. Similarly, a large increase in key areas such as education, health, and law and order was offset by a £1.9 billion planned reduction in overall public spending.

Germany. The economic decline that took place in the last quarter of 1995 and early in 1996 came to an end, and the economy rebounded. Since the recovery was not strong enough to fully offset the earlier weakness, GDP for the year as a whole expanded by an estimated 1.5%, compared with 1.9% in 1995 and 2.9% in 1994. The recovery was partly due to a rebound of activity from the exceptionally severe 1995–96 winter. An improvement in competitiveness, following the reversal of 1995's currency appreciation, and the priority given to cost reductions were also strong contributory factors.

Although the second-half recovery was partly investment-led, export growth was relatively strong. Consumer spending was also strong, despite sluggish growth in real incomes and rising unemployment levels. Business investment strengthened throughout the year as confidence improved, reflecting stronger export demand and lower interest rates. While most of the investment was intended to improve efficiency, about a third of it was for expanding capacity. In contrast to the manufacturing sector, investment in construction fell during 1996 as a whole. This reflected the severe recession

Table III. Standardized Unemployment Rates in Selected Developed Countries

% of total labour force

Country	1992	1993	1994	1995	1996[1]
United States	7.3	6.9	6.1	5.6	5.2
Japan	2.2	2.5	2.9	3.1	3.4
Germany	4.6	7.9	8.4	8.2	10.7[2]
France	10.5	11.7	12.3	11.6	12.6
United Kingdom	10.1	10.5	9.6	8.8	7.2
Canada	11.3	11.2	10.4	9.5	10.0
Italy	10.5	10.3	11.4	11.9	12.2[3]
All developed countries	7.4	7.8	7.7	7.3	7.3
Seven major countries above	7.0	7.2	7.1	6.8	6.9
European Union	9.5	10.6	11.5	11.4	11.7

[1]October, national definitions.   [2]July.   [3]Not seasonally adjusted.
Sources: OECD, The Economist.

sweeping through the construction sector following the ending of the postunification boom.

Consumer spending charted an uneven course. Early in the year it was up 0.75%, encouraged by income tax reductions for people on low incomes and termination of an 8.5% annual levy on electricity bills. Although spending in the shops remained positive in the second half of the year, as job insecurity and low wage settlements held back consumer spending, its overall rate of growth was weaker than in 1995.

Industrial production picked up in the spring and registered a 3% increase for the year as a whole. This was accompanied by an improvement in the overall business climate following the deterioration in 1995. Exports rose by nearly 6%, helped by the weakening of the Deutsche Mark and the efforts of German companies to reduce costs by restructuring and rationalization of production. More encouraging was the fact that foreign orders were running considerably higher toward the end of the year. As a result of sluggish import growth coupled with stronger export performance, the trade surplus improved in Deutsche Mark terms, but the gain was much smaller when measured in U.S. dollars.

While inflation remained low, averaging 1.5%, with no upward pressure from producer prices, the unemployment position continued to deteriorate. The upward trend that started in mid-1994 continued until the spring. The jobless total (excluding disguised unemployment) peaked at 3,993,000 (seasonally adjusted) and then fell back slightly in the summer. The unemployment rate toward the year's end stood at 10.1%, compared with 9.2% a year earlier. This high unemployment prompted the German government to introduce a "Program for Growth and Jobs." The main elements of this included reducing government expenditure as a proportion of GDP back to preunification levels, lowering social security insurance contributions, and introducing measures to make the labour market more flexible and to reduce nonwage labour costs. Many independent observers thought the aim of halving the unemployment rate by the year 2000 had little chance of being realized.

Despite the fiscal-consolidation measures in place, the sluggishness of the German economy resulted in a smaller-than-expected reduction in the budget deficit during 1995. As a result, a tough action plan was introduced in 1996, which aimed at achieving budget savings of DM 70 billion from 1997 onward. The savings were a mixture of cuts in the federal budget, state and local authority spending, and social security spending. Despite opposition from the Bundesrat (the upper house), the government was able to pass most of its austerity budget. As in France, however, doubts remained whether Germany would be able to meet the Maastricht Treaty requirement for a budget deficit/GDP ratio of 3%.

Monetary policy was further eased during 1996 against the background of low inflation and sluggish economic activity. The Bundesbank cut its discount rate and Lombard rates in April. The securities repurchase rate (Repo rate), which influences money market rates, remained unchanged between February and August. It was then cut by a larger-than-expected rate, signaling a further loosening of monetary policy.

France. Continuing the weakness experienced during the latter part of 1995, the French economy remained sluggish during 1996, despite a large rebound in the opening quarter. Reflecting the underlying weakness, GDP as a whole grew by around 1% during 1996, compared with 2.2% the year before.

In the early part of the year, economic activity was sustained by buoyant consumer consumption, which was up 2% during the first half of the year. The upturn was partly due to a reduction in interest rates and a package introduced in January to encourage personal consumption and home buying. As the year progressed, however, household consumption weakened, which reflected the cumulative effect of a 2% rise in value-added-tax rates in August 1995, a social-debt levy of 0.5% effective from February 1996, and a wage freeze applying to civil servants.

As a consequence of weakening demand, the trend of industrial production remained downward, capacity utilization remained flat, and new investment by manufacturing companies grew modestly. In the absence of need for new capacity, new investment was undertaken mostly for modernization purposes. Export activity gathered pace during the year and made a positive contribution to growth as a result of sustained growth in Japan, the U.S., and the U.K., the leading importers of French goods. A 2.5% total increase in the volume of French exports of good and services was matched by a similar rise in imports. Nevertheless, the trade balance remained in healthy surplus, as did the current-account balance.

Because of the slow economic growth, the unemployment position continued to worsen in France. By October unemployment as a proportion of the labour force had reached 12.6%. At this level it was one percentage point higher than a year earlier. The young as well as those in the older age groups were most affected. Consumer price inflation, having edged up since late 1995, peaked at an annual rate of 2.4% in the summer. Following a subsequent moderation, the average increase for the year was expected to be 2%, compared with 1.7% in 1995.

The economic policy continued to be framed to enable France to meet the conditions for joining the EMU in 1999. Hence, increased fiscal stringency was heaped on top of the previous year's austerity measures. Some progress was made in reducing the budget deficit in France in 1995, and the goal of the government was to reduce the public deficit to 3.6% of GDP in 1996 and to 3% in 1997—the level required by the Maastricht Treaty. The draft budget announced in September 1996 aimed to keep overall public expenditure at the same level as in the previous year. Given an inflation rate of 2%, this meant a decline in the volume of central government expenditure. Cuts in welfare spending, a reduction in the number of civil servants, virtual standstill on education spending, higher gasoline taxes, and a freeze on family allowances were the main measures introduced to reduce the deficit.

As in 1995, cutbacks in social and welfare spending led to large-scale protests and strikes, although those in 1996 were not as widespread or prolonged. The need for larger public-sector spending cuts, which would have triggered more widespread social disturbances, was avoided by some creative accounting, including a F 37.5 billion pension-fund transfer from France Telecom to reduce the budget deficit. Among other sweeteners, the outlines of a tax-reform program were announced. This included a proposed reduction in some income taxes over a five-year period from 1997. While the stance of fiscal policy remained restrictive, as in previous years, the Bank of France continued to reduce short-term interest rates in small increments shadowing cuts by the Bundesbank in Germany. Thus, after a series of cuts, the French central bank's intervention rate fell to 3.5% in the autumn—the lowest level in 20 years. The business community remained unimpressed, however, believing that commercial bank base rates were still too high, given the low level of inflation.

Table IV. Changes in Output in Less-Developed Countries

% annual change in real gross domestic product

Area	1992	1993	1994	1995	1996[1]
All less-developed countries	6.4	6.3	6.6	5.9	6.3
Africa	0.8	0.9	2.9	3.0	5.0
Asia	8.8	8.7	9.1	8.6	8.0
Middle East and Europe	6.2	4.2	0.5	3.6	3.9
Western Hemisphere	2.8	3.2	4.7	0.9	3.0

[1]Estimated.
Sources: International Monetary Fund, World Economic Outlook, October 1996.

The Former Centrally Planned Economies. In 1996, following five consecutive years of decline, economic output in these nations was expected to increase by a modest half a percentage point. In 1995 the decline had moderated sharply to 1.3% after four years in which economic output had fallen by between 8.5% and 15%. The prospects for 1997 were for growth of around 4%. While progress was being made, however, real levels of GDP remained well below 1989 levels for nearly all countries, according to European Bank for Reconstruction and Development estimates. In 1996 only Poland, which had been quick to implement market reforms, had surpassed its 1989 output. In several countries, including Azerbaijan, Georgia, Moldova, and Lithuania, GDP was less than 40% of its value in 1989.

Performance throughout the region was, as in previous years, not uniform. In Central and Eastern Europe, growth was 1.6%, compared with 1.2% in 1995. If Belarus and Ukraine were excluded, the expansion was 4.2%, reflecting a slowdown from the year before (4.9%) but nevertheless making it the third year of strong growth. The rest of the Central and Eastern European countries—except Bulgaria, which was expected to register negative growth—saw progress. A few Eastern European countries (including Poland, Romania, and Slovakia) experienced a slowdown in expansion, partly because of weaker demand in Western Europe. In Ukraine output fell by 8%, more slowly than in the previous four years. In Russia, which had a fall of only around 1%, the decline in output appeared to be coming to a halt. Both of these countries were expected to see a rise in production in 1997.

In the Transcaucasus and Central Asia, the decline in output was halted for the first time in five years, and output was expected to rise by a symbolic 0.6%. Many of the nine countries in the region were at an intermediate stage of transition. Armenia, for the third year running, achieved growth of 5–7%, but this apparent progress followed several years of sharp contraction. Production rose by 8% in Georgia and by 6.2% in Turkmenistan. Only Azerbaijan, Tajikistan, and Uzbekistan were still registering drops in output, but the rate of decline for all three continued to fall sharply.

Inflationary pressures eased, with consumer prices rising on average by around 40%, compared with 128% in 1995. There was no longer any sign of the hyperinflation that had been running at four and five figures in the 1992–94 period, when price liberalization first started to take place. Nevertheless, many countries remained vulnerable as governments reduced subsidies and took measures to restructure their economies.

In Central and Eastern Europe (including Belarus and Ukraine), consumer price rises were expected to fall from 26% to 21% per annum. In Bulgaria inflation accelerated to over 70% as a result of a drop in the exchange rate that followed a collapse of confidence in the financial system. In Albania the rate rose from 8% to 12%. In the Transcaucasus and Central Asia, all countries registered sharp falls in the inflation rate, mainly from three to two digits. The average rate, which fell from 259% to 69%, was being held up by the continuing hyperinflation in Tajikistan and Turkmenistan, where the rates declined only slightly, to 633% and 904%, respectively. An IMF-supported stabilization program had been adopted in Tajikistan and was expected to bring the rate down during 1997 and 1998.

Financial-sector reforms proceeded only slowly in 1996. The degree to which securities and nonbank financial institutions developed in 1995 and 1996 depended largely on the method of privatization and financial requirements of governments. There was an urgent need for improvements to banking systems, in particular, across the region. In most countries governments and central banks failed to provide adequate regulation, and the role of banks as providers of investment finance remained modest.

Privatization continued to be an important element in the region's progress. Several of the countries that had reached advanced stages of transition to market-orientated economies—including the Czech Republic, Estonia, Hungary, Poland, and Slovenia—had privatized most of their industrial firms and were concentrating their efforts on the financial sector and those areas that had not been privatized earlier because they were perceived to be of strategic importance to the state. In Estonia and Hungary the focus in 1996 was on privatization of utilities and transport, with Estonia's national airline and Hungarian power companies among the enterprises coming under foreign control. In Slovenia mass privatization proceeded slowly, but by the end of 1996 three-quarters of the 1,549 companies that had completed their plans for privatization had been given approval to go ahead.

In countries at the intermediate stage of transition, such as Albania, Bulgaria, and Romania, mass voucher-based privatization programs moved ahead in 1996. In Russia, however, the pace slowed because of political uncertainties, and in July 1996 a new privatization program was adopted by the government. Among other things, it withdrew the privileged access to ownership share previously extended to collectives and enabled regional authorities to initiate privatization.

While considerable progress had been made in 1996, many problems associated with restructuring remained to be solved.

Unemployment was an inevitable consequence of dismantling inefficient and over-manned enterprises and of improved productivity. Social protection systems in most countries were both inadequate and too expensive, needing urgent reform. It became increasingly apparent that if maximum benefits were to be derived from foreign investment, it was important that earnings be able to be repatriated and foreign investors be given sufficient legal protection in, for example, property rights.

Less-Developed Countries. Thanks to a recovery in Latin America and strengthening of growth in Africa, real economic growth in the LDCs as a whole averaged 6.5%, a little higher than the previous year. Economic activity in the LDCs was underpinned by the relatively strong domestic situation and continued large foreign inward investment flows. Despite a slowdown in some Asian economies, including China and Thailand, this region grew by nearly 8%, marginally below the 1995 level. China, Malaysia, Vietnam, and Thailand produced GDP growth of 8% per annum or more. Latin America bounced back as the effects of the Mexican financial crisis faded further. Chile was the most successful economy in this region, followed by Brazil.

Inflation remained under control despite continued rapid economic growth. The IMF expected the median inflation rate in 1996 to fall to 7% from the previous year's 10%. Latin America was no longer the region with the highest inflation rate. Persistently high inflation in some Middle Eastern countries pushed this region to the top of the inflation league.

Rapid export growth in recent years had been one of the remarkable features of these countries. Since 1994 export volume of this group had expanded by more than 10% per annum, much faster than imports. Even so, there was a slight rise in the balance of payments deficits of LDCs, but the debt burden of most countries remained stable.

INTERNATIONAL TRADE AND PAYMENTS

In 1996 the improvement in world growth was reflected in continued buoyant trade in goods and services, which the IMF projected to have risen by 6.7% over the previous year. This compared with a better-than-expected rise of 8.9% in 1995. In value terms the rise was 5.7% above 1995 at a projected $6.6 billion, with just over half being accounted for by the industrial countries. Once again the momentum in the market came from the LDCs, which provided the strongest growth markets for world exports. In value terms their imports rose by a projected 11.3%, while those of the industrialized countries increased by only 5.3%. There was a similar picture on the supply side, with exports from LDCs up 10.3% in 1995 and from the industrial countries by 4.3% (7.3% in 1995). Trade volumes in the "countries in transition" were maintained at close to the high levels of 1995, when exports rose by 12.2% (10.7% projected for 1996).

At the first ministerial meeting of the World Trade Organization, held in Singapore in December, agreement was reached on the elimination of tariffs on information technology products and on the need

Table V. Changes in Consumer Prices in Less-Developed Countries					
	% change from preceding year				
Area	1992	1993	1994	1995	1996[1]
All less-developed countries	35.7	42.7	46.8	19.8	13.3
Africa	31.7	29.5	36.8	32.1	21.3
Asia	6.9	9.6	13.4	10.9	7.9
Middle East and Europe	25.9	24.0	31.5	32.5	25.6
Western Hemisphere	151.5	209.5	210.9	35.6	20.4

[1]Estimated.
Sources: International Monetary Fund, *World Economic Outlook*, October 1996.

to ease restrictions on the importation of textiles from LDCs.

The shifting balance of trade toward the LDCs continued in 1996, and a value rise in exports (excluding services) of 11.2% followed a 20% rise in 1995. Goods exported from the LDCs, together with four of the Tigers—Hong Kong, South Korea, Singapore, and Taiwan—were projected at $2 billion, around 38% of all goods exported. The share had been rising steadily; in 1990 it was 32%. At the same time, however, far-reaching structural reforms, particularly trade liberalization and the removal of domestic product and financial distortions, had led to an expansion of the manufacturing sector and export capabilities in many of the LDCs. In Africa, for example, exports were expected to increase by 13% in volume (7% in value), with exports from sub-Saharan Africa rising 7.9% (5.1% in value). LDC trade continued to be dominated by Asia, with two-thirds of the LDC exports in 1996.

Among the industrial countries, it was the seven major economies (the U.S., Japan, Germany, France, Italy, the U.K., and Canada) that saw the greatest overall deterioration, with export growth declining from 7.7% in 1995 to 3.9% in 1996. This compared with a fall from 7.3% to 4.3% for all industrialized countries. Japan saw the increase in volume of its exports tumble from 5% to less than 1%, and Germany's rate was down from 5.9% to 3.3%. Italy and Canada experienced sharp declines from the 12% growth each achieved in 1995 to around 4%. Most buoyant were the U.S. and U.K. exporters, whose sales were expected to be over 6% above the year before. Export growth of industrial countries outside the major seven grew by 5.2% overall, one percentage point less than in 1995 but substantially below the 8.7% increase in 1994. The import picture was similar for most industrialized countries, with growth dropping from 7.8% in 1995 to 5.3% in 1996. Only Japan maintained its high level; its imports were expected to increase by nearly 13%, similar to the rise in 1995.

There was an improvement in the current-account position of many of the industrial countries, although cumulatively there was expected to be a fall in the 1995 surplus to $2.5 billion. This was because Japan's large surplus, which had for many years been a cause of controversy with its trading partners, was falling sharply. In the few years to 1995, the surplus had been in the range of $110 billion to $132 billion. From September 1995, however, it had been on a monthly year-on-year decline and was expected to end 1996 at around $6.5 billion. Elsewhere, in North America the Canadian deficit of $8 billion in 1995 was expected to give way to a small surplus. In the U.S. the current-account deficit of $150 billion was expected to have eased slightly.

The current-account surplus of the 15 EU countries was expected to increase from $54 billion to $74 billion, with most EU countries improving their positions. Of the major countries, Germany's deficit fell slightly to around $18 billion, and in the U.K. the deficit was expected to fall from $9 billion to around $3.5 billion. France and Italy were expected to increase their surpluses to $22.5 billion and $22.8 billion, respectively. Outside Europe, Australia's deficit fell by around $2 billion to $16 bil-

lion, while New Zealand's increased to $3.1 billion from $2.5 billion in 1995.

In the countries in transition, the trade performance was comparable to that of the LDCs. Imports rose by 12.3%, just one percentage point less than in 1995, while exports rose by 10.7% (12.2% in 1995). The continued buoyancy of trade was an important factor in attracting foreign investment and, therefore, in helping the process of restructuring.

Direct foreign investment continued to be concentrated in Hungary and the Czech Republic, which in the period 1989–95 reached $11.5 billion and $5.5 billion, respectively. Other countries where the cumulative flow reached over $1 billion included Poland, Russia, and Kazakstan. On a per capita measure, Slovenia and Estonia ranked among the top four, along with Hungary and the Czech Republic. Social and economic stability in these countries meant, as was also the case in Poland, that the investors' perception of the relative risk was low. In Hungary and Estonia another factor affecting investors was the deliberate focus of their governments on attracting foreign investors to their privatization programs.

In the LDCs the trade performance remained impressive compared with that of the industrialized countries. Exports increased by a projected 11.2%, with imports rising faster at 12.5%. This was, however, in marked contrast to 1995, when the increases were 19.9% and 20.3%, respectively. The slowdown in demand from the industrialized countries was partly responsible for the deceleration. A key factor was the sluggish performance of exports of electronic products from Asia, which was by far the largest trading region in the less-developed world. A 7% fall in sales of semiconductors—mainly used by the computer industry—hit the Tigers, especially South Korea, from which semiconductor exports rose 21% (year-on-year) in the first quarter, after which the rate of increase fell sharply and actually turned into a decline in the third quarter. While this problem may have been short-term—it was caused to some extent by the overstocking of semiconductors in the U.S.—the international price of memory chips had fallen sharply, and it was questionable whether it could recover fully given the overcapacity of the market. Overall export performance in Africa reflected the progress that had been made in restructuring and the increasing role of the private sector in the economy. Rising commodity prices in 1995 had led to a 14% increase in the value of exports, but the falling back in prices meant exports rose only 7.1% in 1996.

In the LDCs the 1995 deterioration in the current-account deficit from $90 billion to $112 billion was due to the growing deficit in Asia, where some of the economies were overheating. The rapid growth in the value of exports was more than matched by import demand, which created a trade deficit of $54 billion. By the end of 1996, there were signs of greater stability in some of the economies, notably those of Thailand and Malaysia.

Export values were up by around 10% in the Middle East, being boosted by higher oil prices. In Latin America lower commodity prices meant that in overall terms the value of exports rose much more slowly—

under 10%, compared with over 20% in 1995. Venezuela benefited from higher oil prices, and Mexico's general economic recovery was export-led.   (IEIS)

This article updates the *Macropædia* articles ECONOMIC GROWTH AND PLANNING; GOVERNMENT FINANCE; INTERNATIONAL TRADE.

STOCK EXCHANGES

In 1996 the world's stock exchanges continued the bull run that got under way during the previous year and registered a 12% gain in dollar terms (15% in local currency), as measured by the *Financial Times*/Standard & Poor's (FT/S&P) World Index. Sustained economic growth (or recovery) and continuing low or falling interest and inflation rates, coupled with higher corporate profitability, were the main factors that drove up the world markets. Successive record-breaking performances of the Dow Jones industrial average (DJIA) also acted as a locomotive for the world bourses. Starting from a lower base and recovering from the past year's disappointing performance, Europe rose by 19%, while the Pacific markets, including Japan, lagged behind with a 3% gain (both in local currency). (*See* Table VI.)

These broad gains would have been higher had it not been for a sharp correction in early December following remarks by Alan Greenspan, the Fed chairman, about "irrational exuberance" in asset markets. While most markets subsequently recovered a large part of the 2–3% fall suffered on that "Frantic Friday," they remained volatile during the closing weeks of the year. The markets interpreted Greenspan's comments as a veiled signal that the Fed would, sooner rather than later, have to raise interest rates to cool off potentially inflationary pressures. There was a similar midsummer setback on Wall Street and in other equity markets when it looked as if the U.S. interest rates were about to rise. As the Fed left the U.S. interest rates unchanged, share prices recovered and then reached record levels in many countries.

Given Wall Street's runaway form, it was not surprising that some of the features seen in the 1980s staged a comeback. Salaries on Wall Street and to a lesser extent in London broke records, with massive bonuses for high-flying investment bankers and equity dealers. Many investment houses on both sides of the Atlantic poached each other's best staff with massive pay offers.

The main stimulus for the U.S. market was continuing low interest rates, which made deposit accounts unattractive to investors and in turn encouraged high levels of money to flow into mutual funds. Productivity improvements leading to robust earnings growth, stock repurchase by corporations, and considerable merger-and-acquisition activity were the other main factors behind the exceptional performance of Wall Street. In Europe the rises seen during the first half of the year mirrored declining short-term interest rates in Germany and other European countries with currencies that shadowed the Deutsche Mark in the foreign exchange markets. The Japanese market was driven up early in the year by the dual stimulus to the economy of the decline in the value of the yen against the U.S. dollar and the cumulative effect of the

Effective Exchange Rates*
average rates, 1990 = 100

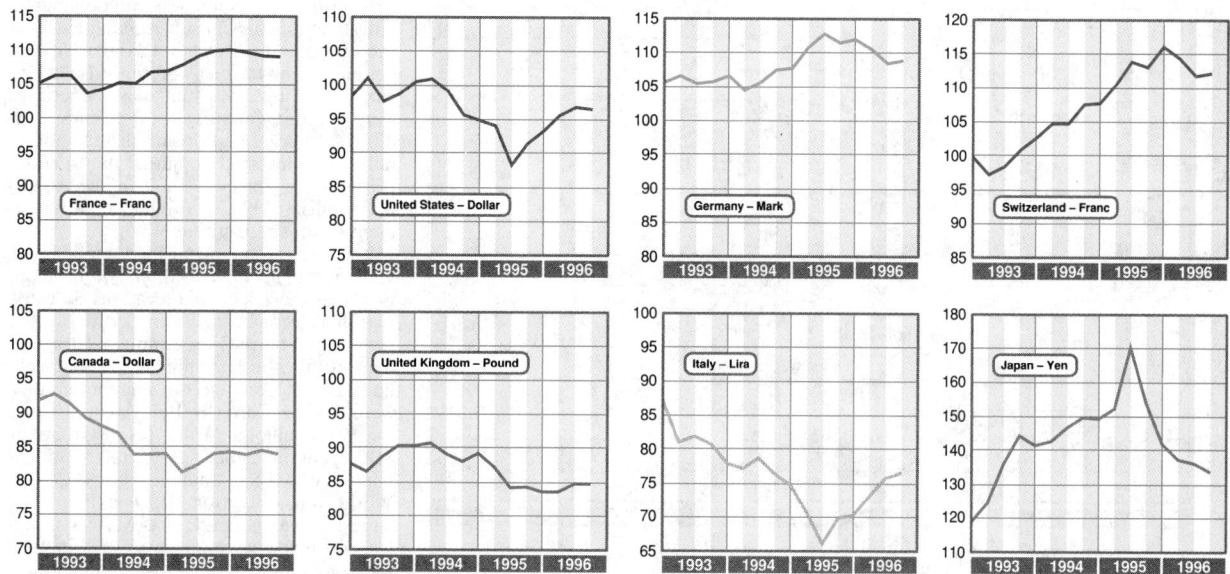

*Measure of a currency's value relative to a weighted average of the values of the currencies of the country's principal trading partners.

Source: International Monetary Fund, *International Financial Statistics.*

fiscal packages introduced the year before. Foreign investors' enthusiasm for Japanese equities also propelled the Japanese market. The Japanese market came under pressure in early autumn and could not hold on to its earlier gains.

The mixture of continued low inflation and gently declining long-term interest rates against a background of higher economic activity turned out to be a favourable backdrop to government bonds. A major beneficiary of this trend was the European Bond markets, in particular German and French bonds. (IEIS)

United States. The U.S. stock market maintained a strong bullish trend in 1996 as investors, hungry for stock to buy, invested more than $104.5 billion through November, exceeding the full-year record total of $102.3 billion set in 1993, according to the Securities Data Corp. A record number of new issues, rising corporate earnings, low inflation, privatizations of overseas government entities, continued restructuring of U.S. corporations, and a strong demand for stock mutual funds combined to propel the market to record levels. Most analysts were surprised by the performance of the stock market in 1996 after the 1995 bull market, when the DJIA rose by 30%; a lacklustre 1996 had been expected. Instead, the index of leading indicators rose month by month, the value of stocks relative to GDP was at record levels, and all of the major stock indexes achieved new highs. (*See* Table VII.)

The DJIA began the year at 5200, rose to 5600 in February, climbed irregularly to 5800 in May, leveled off in June, and then dropped from 5600 to 5400 in July. It rose sharply from 5400 at the beginning of August to 6000 by the end of October, followed by a steep rise after the general election to close November above 6500. Extreme volatility reigned in December as the postelection rally vied with investor concerns over the economy. The DJIA fell almost 100 points to 6300 on December 12.

One week later, on December 19, it climbed nearly 127 points. The Dow reached an all-time high of 6560.91 on December 27 but dropped more than 101 points on the final day of trading to end the year at 6448.27. (*See* Table VIII.)

The Dow was up 26% for the year. At year's end the Dow transportation index was up 14%, the utilities were up 4%, and the composite was ahead 20%. The average price-earnings ratio on the DJIA ranged from a low of 15.8 in January to 18.3 in

New York Stock Exchange Composite Index, 1996
Stock prices (Dec. 31, 1965 = 50)

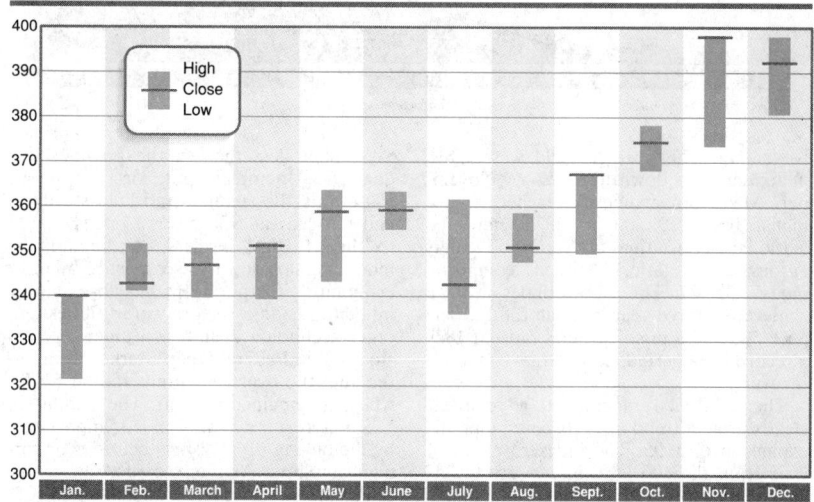

Average daily share volume
In thousands of shares

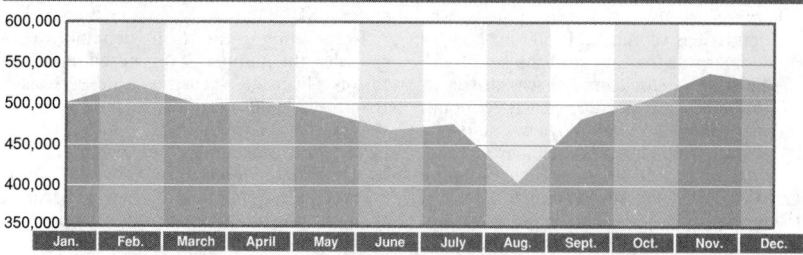

Sources: *Barron's National Business and Financial Weekly; The Wall Street Journal.*

New York Stock Exchange Common Stock Index Closing Prices
Stock prices (Dec. 31, 1965 = 50)

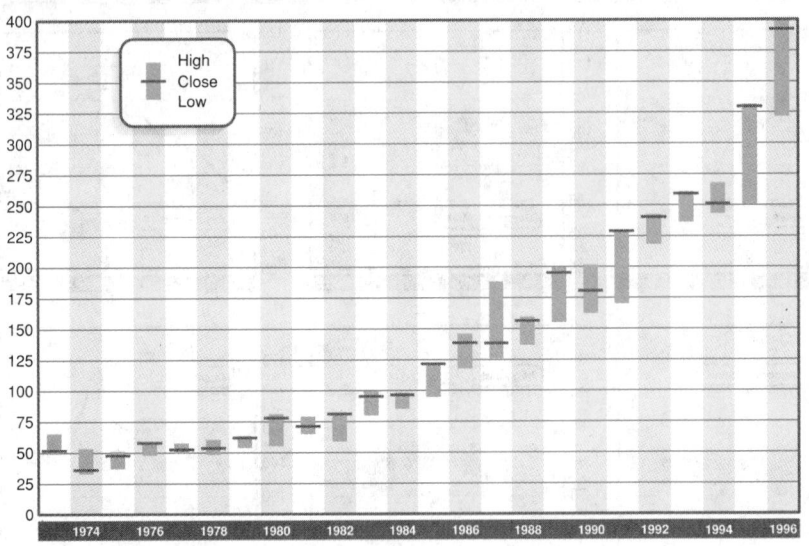

Number of shares sold
In billions of shares

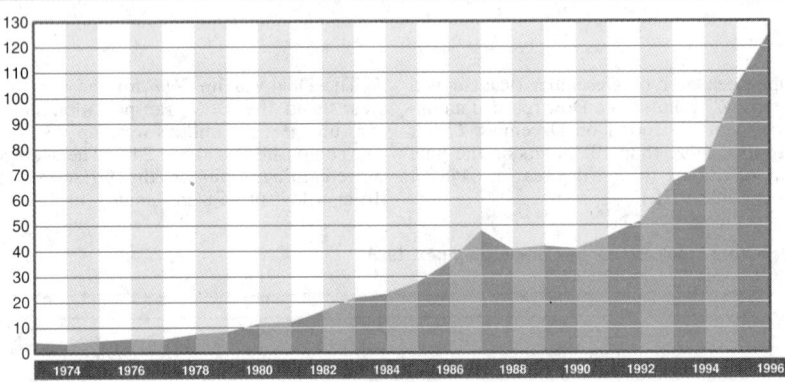

Sources: *Barron's National Business and Financial Weekly; The Wall Street Journal.*

November. The average yield was 2.28% in January and down to 2.07% by November. Many other indexes reached record highs. The S&P 500 hit 757.03 and the National Association of Security Dealers automated quotation (Nasdaq) composite index 1,316.27. The Dow utilities average achieved a three-year high at 238.12. The S&P 500 had a price-earnings ratio of 18.9, a record for a period of moderate economic recovery.

The S&P 500 maintained a relatively steady growth trend in 1996, continuing the expansion of 1995. The index rose irregularly from the 600 level in January to 757 by the end of November before a year-end pullback to 740.74, up 20% for the year. There was a 50-point plunge in July, the worst retreat since the 1990 recession, but otherwise no untoward development. The dividend yield of the S&P 500 at 2.1% in September was the lowest of the century.

The soaring stock market was driven by a confluence of positive macroeconomic factors—like low unemployment and stable interest-rate and inflation environments. Growth slowed from its breakneck speed early in 1996, and there were no signs of rising wage pressures. The employment cost index, published by the Labor Department, increased only 0.6% between June and

September, less than in the previous two quarters. Unemployment was just above 5% during the summer and held steady to end the year at 5.3%. Bond prices soared to their highest levels in six months. A moderate slowdown was expected by most economists. Corporate profits rose sharply in 1996. Leading sectors were utilities, energy, technology, and consumer cyclical stocks. The Federal Open Market Committee kept the overnight funds rate at 5¼%, where it remained all year. The stability in U.S. interest rates was aided importantly by the buying of Treasury securities by foreign investors. At the end of August, this figure passed the $1 trillion mark, or 30% of all Treasuries outstanding. For the 1996 fiscal year, the federal budget deficit was $107 billion, lower than in any other year since 1981.

Responding to the strong demand for retail sales, the number of registered representatives—licensed securities salespersons—rose to 527,000, the most in the history of the market. The Internet, which brought buyers and sellers together, was perceived as a threat to brokers. By providing information and a market, it was performing many of the functions normally performed by brokers—information, advice, and execution. A popular example of this trend

was the Motley Fool World Wide Web site run by David and Tom Gardner. (*See* BIOGRAPHIES.)

Investor sentiment was predominantly bullish in 1996. Consumer confidence in the economy held steady through November, according to the Conference Board Index, which indicated that most Americans were optimistic about current business conditions. Nearly one-third of all U.S. households were invested in mutual funds, either privately or through their office 401(k) plans, during 1996, according to the Investment Company Institute.

The merger-and-acquisition market was very strong in 1996, with major developments in the telecommunications industry. British Telecom, which owned 20% of MCI Communications Corp., announced a tender offer for the remaining 80% for $22 billion. The biggest telecom mergers in 1996 were: Nynex Corp. by Bell Atlantic Corp. for $21.3 billion; Pacific TelesisGroup by SBC Communications, Inc., for $16.5 billion; and MFS Communications Co. by WorldCom, Inc., for $13.4 billion. The largest previous merger was McCaw Cellular, which was acquired by AT&T in 1993 for $15.7 billion. The British Telecom deal brought the total volume of mergers in the first 10 months of 1996 to $537 billion, up from $518 billion for all of 1995 and well ahead of the $341.9 billion in all of 1994. The trend continued in December with the much-publicized $14 billion merger of Boeing Co. and McDonnell Douglas Corp.

The Securities and Exchange Commission (SEC) was considering a review of its net capital rules owing to the widespread use of derivatives. Net capital rules were becoming increasingly important as securities firms delved deeper in the trading of exotic securities that often required hefty capital levels. Because of the net capital rules, this business was moving overseas. The SEC began legal action to control stock promotion on the Internet. Many stock promoters were reaching unwary browsers on the net with less than the required disclosures. The SEC had about a dozen investigations pending to see if mutual funds and investment advisers improperly pocketed rebates from handling their trades. At issue were so-called soft-dollar arrangements between mutual funds and brokers who handled the lucrative business of trading for the funds. Competition for the mutual fund trading business was intense. The SEC required the mutual funds to disclose such arrangements to their shareholders in order to lessen the apparent conflict of interest. The National Securities Markets Improvement Act of 1996, a significant overhaul of the securities regulatory structure, provided for SEC oversight of investment advisers and offered consumers access to records of disciplinary action against them. The SEC changed the rules to curtail abuses of "offshore" offerings. Under Regulation S, corporations could make placements offshore without registration in the U.S. Frequently, this led to abuse as unregistered securities placed offshore went back into the U.S. market without the usual disclosures. Under the new rule, such offerings would have to be disclosed to U.S. investors. Corporations were required to detail the price, amount, and date of sale for the offering and give a general description of the purchasers.

Securities firms had the most profitable

Table VI. Selected Major World Stock Market Indexes[1]

Country and index	1996 range[2] High	Low	Year-end close	Percent change from 12/31/95
Australia, Sydney All Ordinaries	2425	2096	2425	10
Austria, Credit Aktien	395	349	382	11
Belgium, Brussels BEL20	1897	1575	1895	22
Canada, Toronto Composite	6019	4740	5927	26
Denmark, Copenhagen Stock Exchange	472	368	472	29
Finland, HEX General	2496	1652	2496	46
France, Paris CAC 40	2349	1898	2316	24
Germany, Frankfurt FAZ Aktien	1006	819	992	22
Hong Kong, Hang Seng	13,531	10,205	13,451	34
Ireland, ISEQ Overall	2726	2235	2726	22
Italy, Milan Banca Comm. Ital.	674	572	666	13
Japan, Nikkei Average	22,667	19,162	19,361	−3
Mexico, IPC	3434	2736	3347	20
Netherlands, The, CBS All Share	437	432	437	36
Norway, Oslo Stock Exchange	1644	1260	1644	30
Philippines, Manila Composite	3374	2579	3171	22
Singapore, SES All-Singapore	610	504	536	−3
South Africa, Johannesburg Industrials	8739	7569	7922	−1
Spain, Madrid Stock Exchange	445	324	445	39
Sweden, Affarsvarlden General	2403	1707	2403	38
Switzerland, SBC General	1323	1114	1321	17
Taiwan, Weighted Price	6983	4690	6934	34
Thailand, Bangkok SET	1415	817	832	−35
Turkey, Istanbul Composite	97,589	38,779	97,589	144
United Kingdom, FT-SE 100	4119	3632	4119	12
United States, Dow Jones Industrials	6561	5033	6448	26
World, MS Capital International	837	726	826	33

[1] Index numbers are rounded.   [2] Based on daily closing price.
Source: *Financial Times.*

year ever in 1996. For the first nine months, total profits before tax were $9.2 billion, more than for all of 1995. The 603 initial public offerings (IPOs) through September surpassed the record set in 1993 by 5%. At that rate IPOs for 1996 hit $46.9 billion, or 13% more than the record achieved in 1993. The total value of merger-and-acquisitions activity was on a pace to hit $496 billion in 1996. The leading underwriters in the IPO market were: Goldman Sachs & Co., Morgan Stanley, Merrill Lynch, Smith Barney, and Alex Brown & Sons for the 12 months ended Oct. 30, 1996. Through November, Bloomberg Financial Markets counted 863 IPOs, which raised a total of $57 billion. For all of 1995 there were 666 deals, with $37 billion raised.

The yield on 30-year Treasury bonds fell from 8.16% in 1995 to 6.64% in 1996. The proportion of Treasury securities held by foreign governments, individuals, and institutional investors climbed to 30%, largely because of favourable comparative yields vis-á-vis foreign government bonds. As of October 31, long-term corporate bond yields were at 7.43%. The prime rate in the U.S. held steady at 8.25%.

Trading volume on the New York Stock Exchange (NYSE) was a record 104.6 billion shares, up from 87.9 billion in 1995. Average daily share volume on the Big Board was a record 412 million, with July 16 (680.9 million) and December 20 (654.1 million) being the two busiest days ever recorded. Advances exceeded declines 2,498 to 1,256, with 141 issues unchanged. Micron Technology and Iomega Corp. topped the active list, with each trading more than 1.4 billion shares.

The NYSE reported that a seat had sold for $1,160,000 in August, down $287,500 from the previous sale of a seat on May 7. By December 30 the price had risen to

$1,285,000. To curb some perceived abuses, the NYSE governing board took positions opposed to "preferencing dealers," where dealer orders were favoured over public orders, and payment for order flow because customers were not aware that they were getting less than the best prices.

Volume on the American Stock Exchange (Amex) in the first 11 months of 1996 was 5,201,917,000 shares traded, up from 4,656,800,000 in the corresponding period of 1995. In a drive for increasing membership, 55 companies were persuaded to list their stocks on the Amex by the end of September, 35% more than in the comparable period of 1995. Stocks that moved from Nasdaq to the Amex showed a big decline in volatility, as measured by intraday deviations in price, from typical trading. The specialist system was credited with reduction of volatility. It was used on the Big Board and the Amex but not on Nasdaq. The Emerging Company Market,

which was established in 1992 to attract fledgling companies to the exchange, was abandoned in 1996 because of adverse publicity. The Amex differed from the NYSE in two important ways; the Amex permitted the issuer to choose the specialist firm that would trade its stock, and, unlike the Big Board, it had no rule preventing companies from leaving its market at will.

Through November volume on Nasdaq was 126,431,543,000 shares traded, up from 90,236,881,000 in 1995. At year's end 2,676 issues had advanced, 1,967 had declined, and 79 were unchanged. Once again, the microprocessor company Intel Corp. was by far the most active issue, trading nearly 2,339,000 shares. Nasdaq decided to impose tougher listing standards for companies trading on the lower-tier Nasdaq SmallCap market. The lower tier housed some 2,000 of the more than 6,000 issues. Such companies would be required to obtain shareholder permission for any significant change in the company's capitalization. They would also require at least two outside directors and an audit committee including such outside directors. Both the U.S. Department of Justice and the SEC investigations found that spreads between bid and asked prices on Nasdaq and dealer manipulation commonly found in that market were harmful to investors.

Stock and bond mutual funds numbered more than 7,000 in 1996, representing some $3 trillion in individual and institutional accounts. There were also more than 1,000 money market funds. Equity funds had assets totaling $1,250,000,000,000 in 1996. Through September investors flooded stock funds with $179 billion, compared with $88 billion through September 1995. The average management fee climbed to 1.4% of assets, versus 1.2% in 1995. The average stock fund was up 14.06% through October 1996, while bond funds were up 3.5%. The top sector was financial services, up 19.94%. There were also more than 22,000 investment clubs and more than 4,700 hedge funds in operation during the year.

Trading in stock options in 1996 hit a record high. The Options Industry Council said that through November, 180,693,189 options contracts had been traded on U.S. exchanges. With a month of trading left in the year, the total topped the annual record of 174,380,236 contracts set in 1995. The Chicago Mercantile Exchange (Merc) established links to exchanges in London and Paris to boost business in the increasingly

Table VII. Selected U.S. Stock Market Indexes[1]

	1996 range[2] High	Low	Year-end close	Percent change from 12/31/95
Dow Jones Averages				
30 Industrials	6561	5033	6448	26
20 Transportation	2315	1883	2256	14
15 Utilities	238	205	233	4
65 Composite	2059	1656	2026	20
Standard & Poor's				
500 Index	757	598	741	20
Industrials	888	702	870	21
Utilities	214	185	199	−2
Others				
NYSE Composite	399	321	392	19
Nasdaq Composite	1316	989	1291	23
Amex Market Value	615	526	583	6
Russell 2000	365	302	363	15

[1] Index numbers are rounded.   [2] Based on daily closing price.
Sources: *Financial Times, Chicago Tribune, Globe and Mail.*

competitive and global futures industry. In the U.S., financial futures such as short-term and long-term interest rates increased in volume to more than 600 million contracts in 1996.

The Commodity Futures Trading Commission filed complaints against several grain-elevator operators that marketed "hedge-to-arrive" contracts, grain-trading instruments that generated losses of hundreds of millions of dollars across America's Farm Belt in 1996. Hedge-to-arrive contracts were designed to help farmers manage price risk. Financial disaster was caused in the summer when corn prices soared to record highs and farmers used loopholes to defer delivery under lower-priced grain-supply contracts with elevators. The rally increased the cost to elevators of maintaining their own hedges in the futures markets. Margin requirements could not be met. Some of the contracts were illegal because they were essentially off-exchange futures contracts.

Canada. With interest rates at 40-year lows, the Canadian stock exchanges did a booming business in 1996. In the third quarter the Canadian economy had its best spurt of growth in more than two years. GDP was at an annual rate of 3.3%, up from 1.1% and 1.2%, respectively, in the first two quarters. Exports climbed, and corporate profits were favourable. The government's drive for fiscal stringency resulted in a decline in the federal national debt, while the current-account deficit was replaced by a surplus. Canadian fundamentals included moderate growth, a 1.25% inflation rate, falling interest rates, and a rising Canadian dollar. The Bank of Canada cut interest rates continually, citing the rising Canadian dollar as the reason. It reduced rates for the 20th time in 18 months, cutting the bank rate to 3.5%, the lowest level in more than 30 years, at the end of October and dropping the prime rate to 4.75%, the lowest since 1956. The country's unemployment rate remained high, near 10%.

The Toronto Stock Exchange index of 300 stocks (TSE 300) hit 6018.65 by the end of November. The Montreal index peaked at 3030.98, and the Vancouver Stock Exchange index rose to 1472.55. The TSE 300 ended the year up 25.7% at 5927.03, Montreal was up 27.4%, and Vancouver rose 49.6%. Average daily volume for the first 11 months was 94.7 million shares. The financial sector performed best (up 50%), along with real estate (39.4%) and oil and

gas (36.6%). Forest products (up 7.5%) and the metals sector (6.8%) performed poorly. Gold issues were down 4% year-to-date in November but recovered enough to manage a small gain.

Some 15%, or 189, of the 1,260 issues listed on the TSE also were listed on a U.S. exchange. In 1995 the Toronto market handled more than 60% of the volume in Canadian listed stocks. In 1996 the NYSE share rose to 10% from 9%, and the Nasdaq stock market's share increased to 11% from 9%. It was expected that trading volume would increase, offsetting the loss in spreads in Canada. The Vancouver Stock Exchange (VSE) had corporate financings of Can$1.4 billion in its 1996 fiscal year, about one-eighth the size of the TSE. The number of listings on the VSE was 1,477 as of March 31, down from 1,527 a year earlier. The VSE embarked on a major marketing campaign focusing on its upgraded standards.

The four Canadian stock exchanges switched from pricing stocks in eighths (like the U.S. markets) to the decimal system followed by European and Asian markets. The Canadians would quote prices in dollars and cents, with stocks priced at less than Can$5 a share priced in one-cent increments and stocks above Can$5 priced in five-cent increments. Decimalization was a popular move among investors, especially institutional investors, but some brokers were not pleased with the switch, since they feared it might cut into their trading desk revenue.

During August the Canadian government issued inflation-adjusted bonds. Known as Canada Real Return bonds, they had interest rates adjustable semiannually for inflation. In November the Canadian government sold, at an average yield of 5.273%, a total of Can$2.7 billion 7% bonds maturing Sept. 1, 2001. Canadian bonds were up 14.2% in November compared with the same period of 1995. Investor sentiment was strongly bullish throughout most of 1996.   (IRVING PFEFFER)

Western Europe. Most European stock exchanges performed strongly during 1996 and provided a good rate of return for investors who were not deterred by the previous year's lacklustre performance. Encouraged by prospects of further cuts in short-term interest rates, economic recovery, and improved corporate profitability, as well as higher performance in London and on Wall Street, continental bourses started the new

year in good form. By the summer, average gains of 10% had been achieved on the back of a series of small cuts in interest rates. A summer consolidation and a Wall Street-induced setback were followed by a recovery and rise to higher levels. Notwithstanding Frantic Friday, the FT/S&P Euro Index of 720 leading shares was 18% up on the year. The best gains in Europe were seen in markets in Spain, The Netherlands, France, and Germany, all with at least a 20% rise in local currency since the beginning of the year. London, having strongly outperformed continental bourses in 1995, lagged behind in 1996, but a strong rise in the external value of sterling offset the relative weakness of London to the foreign investors.

Although the *Financial Times* Stock Exchange 100 (FT–SE 100) in London reached a new all-time high of 4,118.5 at year-end, its overall gain lagged behind most of its European counterparts. As British interest rates were reduced by 0.5% point in two steps in the spring in response to a sluggish economy, the FT–SE 100 rose by over 150 points to a spring peak of 3,860. Corporate earnings growing in line with expectations and prospects of economic recovery, as well as buoyancy in stock markets elsewhere, were the main factors behind the rise. As evidence of faster economic activity on both sides of the Atlantic emerged in the summer, rekindling fears that higher interest rates were on the way, the market came under pressure. In the event, base rates were unexpectedly cut by 0.25% in the summer, and, contrary to expectations, interest rates remained unchanged in the U.S. Continuing good earnings figures, coupled with a strong upturn in the DJIA, resulted in a record-breaking late summer rally by the FT–SE 100. Many institutions, with strong cash positions, thanks to special dividends and share buybacks, bought back into the market, which sent it higher. The soaring London Stock Exchange was upset and the FT–SE 100 fell well below the psychologically important 4000 level when the base rates were unexpectedly raised by 0.25% in early November. Although the actual increase was small and merely restored the base rate to its June level, it signaled a turning point in the interest-rate cycle. Following a prudent budget and the continuing bull run on Wall Street, the London market rose above the 4000 territory again. Then came the sudden drop on Frantic Friday. While this turned out to be a short-lived upset, it confirmed earlier fears that the market was looking expensive at this stage in the economic cycle. Political uncertainties and the approaching general elections in 1997 also added to market uncertainty, but the FT-SE 100 recovered at year's end and eked out a rise to record territory on December 31 to finish the year with a gain of 11.6%.

The Paris Bourse performed in line with continental Europe and rose by almost 25% during 1996. Lower interest rates offset the sluggish economy and improved corporate profitability. The CAC 40 Index benefited from Wall Street's buoyancy and followed the broad pattern set by the DJIA. A spring rally, which took the index 10% higher, was followed by a summer correction. As interest rates fell to their lowest level in 30 years in August, and inflationary pressures receded, the Paris market staged a pow-

Table VIII. Monthly Dow Jones Industrial Average							
	Average mean close[1]		% Change[2]		Average P/E[3]		Average yield[4]	
	1995	1996	1995	1996	1995	1996	1995	1996
January	3872.46	5179.37	+0.24	+5.43	17.0	15.8	2.76	2.28
February	4011.05	5518.73	+4.34	+1.67	15.7	17.3	2.71	2.15
March	4062.78	5612.24	+3.65	+3.31	15.9	17.6	2.68	2.15
April	4230.66	5579.86	+3.93	−0.32	15.8	17.9	2.58	2.15
May	4391.57	5616.71	+3.32	+1.33	15.1	18.1	2.51	2.18
June	4510.75	5671.51	+2.03	+0.20	15.6	18.2	2.46	2.18
July	4684.76	5496.26	+3.34	−0.02	15.3	17.6	2.40	2.26
August	4639.27	5685.50	−2.07	+1.57	14.4	17.7	2.46	2.22
September	4746.76	5804.01	+3.87	+4.73	14.7	18.0	2.45	2.18
October	4760.46	5996.21	−0.70	+2.50	14.7	18.3	2.43	2.15
November	4935.81		+6.70		15.0		2.37	
December	5136.10		+0.84		15.6		2.29	

[1]Based upon the closing average for each day during the month.   [2]The difference between the recent month's close and the previous month's close.   [3]Rates of share price to company earnings.   [4]Dividend yield.
Source: *Barron's.*

Financial Times Industrial Ordinary Share Index
Annual averages, 1973–96

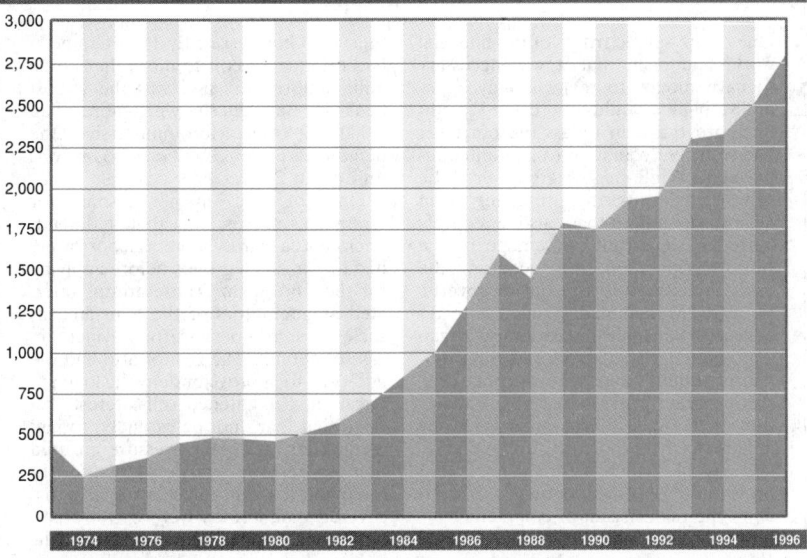

Source: *Financial Times.*

erful rally. In the autumn it was hit by a combination of events, including two weeks of chaos caused by the truckers strike and blockade and the abandonment of plans to privatize Thomson, the electronics and defense group. Even before Frantic Friday, sentiment was adversely affected by calls from former president Valéry Giscard d'Estaing for a devaluation of European currencies—and of the French franc, unilaterally if necessary—against the dollar.

The Dax Index of 30 stocks in Germany performed similarly, recording a 22% gain. Compared with Paris, Frankfurt was less volatile, and during the summer it consolidated the spring gains before rising to an all-time high of 2909.91 in early December. The German market got over the slack summer period encouraged by a weaker Deutsche Mark against the U.S. dollar and indicators of faster economic activity. Sentiment also improved when the Bundesbank further eased monetary policy in August. The approval of the government's austerity budget also gave a boost to the German market. In The Netherlands, where the economy was closely linked to Germany's, the stock market was among the best European performers, with a nearly 30% rise. The presence of many international companies, in particular oil companies, which benefited from higher oil prices, pushed the Dutch market to uncharted territory in 1996.

Some of the other bigger gains in Europe were made at the fringes of the continent. Countries such as Spain and Italy were perceived to be a net beneficiary of the moves toward the EMU. As was the case with sterling, the strength of the lira provided a better return to overseas investors. Apart from lower interest rates and economic recovery, factors common to other European countries, the Spanish market was also stimulated by the spring general election victory of the centre-right party, as well as privatization issues. Likewise, the Nordic bloc outperformed, with Sweden showing a 38% gain. Switzerland, having risen by some 23% in 1995, staged another good performance in 1996. After the weakness of the Swiss

currency was taken into account, however, the 17% gain deteriorated to a 5% gain in dollar terms. The decline in value of the Swiss currency was largely attributable to record-low interest rates of 1%.

Other Countries. Asian stock markets, having recovered strongly in 1995, made little progress in 1996. The disappointing performance of the Tokyo stock market and economic slowdown in the smaller export-driven "Tiger Economies" resulted in significant underperformance against U.S. and European markets. Apart from the relative strength of the dollar (many of the Tigers fixed their exchange rates against the U.S. currency), sluggish European and Japanese export markets adversely affected these countries. Better returns available in the major markets discouraged investors from allocating additional funds to Asian shares. The FT/S&P Pacific Index, which included Japan, increased by only 3% in local currency terms. Excluding Japan, the region's performance was up 16%, largely because of Hong Kong and Malaysia.

The Japanese market performed well until the middle of the summer, with the Nikkei 225 Index rising 12% to 22,666.8. The market was positively influenced by the weakness of the yen against the dollar, the economic upturn, and foreign investor enthusiasm for Japanese shares. After July the market came under pressure from the economy's running out of momentum, a glut of new issues, paralysis of government policy in the run-up to the October general election, and profit taking.

Despite more cheerful news on the economy and corporate profitability in the autumn, the recovery in the market was patchy, and the Nikkei made up for only 50% of the summer losses. Even before Frantic Friday, the Nikkei was struggling to stay above the 21,000 level. Greenspan's comments led to near panic selling in Japan, with the index down by 667 points, the biggest single-day loss of the year. Despite a subsequent bounce back, the Japanese market ended the year showing a 3% overall loss.

Of the other larger markets in the region, Hong Kong, up more than 33%, was the

star performer. Hong Kong benefited from the rising confidence about the territory's prospects after the handover to China in 1997 and a boost to the property sector from low interest rates. Hong Kong's performance was all the more impressive in view of the fact that during the first six months of the year, the stock market was in a subdued mood. Malaysia, with a gain of 23%, also went against the regional trend. Unlike Hong Kong, Malaysia was particularly strong in the first half of the year, thanks to the improved economic outlook and strong liquidity.

Singapore disappointed investors by declining 3.5%. Although the Singapore Straits Index rose strongly during the first half, it fell back, undermined by the economy's heavy dependence on the electronics industry, where exports collapsed. Taiwan produced the best performance among the smaller markets, with a rise of 34%. Against the backdrop of confrontation with China early in the year and uncertainty during the run-up to the presidential elections, this was an impressive achievement. Indonesia and the Philippines produced reasonable gains in the region of 20%, while Thailand and South Korea declined. Thailand produced the worst performance, down by 35%, as a result of weak government and a severe recession in the property sector. The South Korean market was another poor performer, down 19%.

Australia produced a modest gain of 10% despite a favourable response by investors on economic liberalization measures and lower interest rates. Weaker commodity prices, however, were a bearish factor. New Zealand, by comparison, performed better, with a 19% gain, on the back of economic recovery and hopes of lower interest and inflation rates.

Commodity Prices. Commodity prices declined during 1996, largely in response to relatively weak demand and low global interest and inflation rates. In early December *The Economist* Commodities Price Index was 6.5% below the level at the beginning of the year in dollar terms (13% in Sterling terms).

The price of crude oil, which was not included in the *The Economist* Index, rose by 34% during 1996. From the second quarter, oil prices were on a steep upward trend and rose by 40%. In December the North Sea Brent, which serves as a global price benchmark, traded at $24 a barrel, the highest level since the Persian Gulf War. At one stage it was over $25 a barrel, but with the resumption of limited oil sales by Iraq in mid-December, oil prices moderated. Strong demand for refined products, such as heating oil, pushed up prices during 1996, as did the fact that stocks held by the oil companies were low.

The two main components of *The Economist* Index, food and industrials, showed a similar overall decline of 6% in dollar terms. Bumper cereal crops, including wheat and barley, led to a steep fall in cereal prices. Sugar prices fell less sharply (15%, compared with 45%). Coffee prices also slumped as a result of overproduction and excess stock overhang. Tea prices declined but not as much. *The Economist* nonfood agricultural products index was largely unchanged. Performances of the main commodities differed widely. While rubber, cotton, and wool fell by 20%, 8%, and 2%, respectively, hides and timber rose by 23% and 50%. Rubber prices were hit by weak demand and excess stocks; timber prices reflected restricted shipments from Canada. Prices for hides rose partly because of the "mad cow" crisis in the U.K., which reduced supplies. Higher prices by U.S. packers also increased hide prices.

The gold price disappointed again in 1996. Having risen by 7% to $415 per troy ounce in February, it fell back steeply. Toward the year-end it was trading at $367, 5% below that prevailing at the beginning of the year.   (IEIS)

This article updates the *Macropædia* article MARKETS.

BANKING

International. The banking industry was rocked by accusations that banks in Switzerland had concealed extensive World War II gold trading with Nazi Germany and that Swiss banks had deliberately hidden the deposits of Holocaust victims (mainly Jews). Jewish groups claimed that the banks held billions of dollars in assets, which they had prevented Holocaust survivors and their heirs from collecting, often by demanding unobtainable proofs and official documents, including original bank books and death certificates for those killed in the concentration camps. Swiss officials argued that no more than a few thousand dollars had been identified, but, under pressure from U.S. Sen. Alfonse D'Amato, the Swiss Bankers Association agreed to join with Jewish organizations to investigate the claims. A seven-member commission, headed by former U.S. Federal Reserve Board (Fed) chairman Paul Volcker, was expected to make its report in 1998.

Many Eastern European countries suffered banking crises in 1996, notably the Czech Republic, where the Czech National Bank stepped in to take over Agrobanka Praha (the nation's largest privately owned bank and the fifth largest overall) in September. More than two dozen people were charged with fraud, including five top financial officials charged in connection with the failure in August of Kreditni Banka Plzen (the country's sixth largest), with losses of close to $500 million. Twelve smaller banks had also been liquidated or placed under forced administration during the past three years (six in 1996 alone) because of fraud or excessive loan losses. On August 1 a new regulation come into force, aimed at improving bank security. In October the Prague government announced plans to reorganize the largely state-owned industry and privatize the four largest banks. In the first half of 1996 alone, 145 Russian banks had their licenses withdrawn, while new regulations were also introduced in Romania, Bulgaria, Lithuania, and Latvia.

In Japan, after 15 bank failures in a two-year period, the government allowed Hanwa Bank Ltd. to close. This was generally perceived as an indication that the government was at last dealing with the industry's underlying problems of bad loans and over-valued land assets. Meanwhile, Japanese banks remained atop the list of the world's largest, led by Tokyo-Mitsubishi Bank, a $738 billion financial institution formed by the merger in April of Mitsubishi Bank and Bank of Tokyo.

At the other end of the spectrum "micro-

Microbanking

One of the simple truths of the financial world had been that it was necessary to have money to make money. Generally, banks would not extend credit or approve a loan unless the borrower had sufficient collateral to guarantee repayment. While this system ensured the solvency of banks by protecting them against default, it had also effectively barred a significant percentage of the world's population from acquiring the capital necessary to rise out of poverty. In 1976 Muhammad Yunus, a U.S.-educated Bangladeshi economist, began a program designed to address this problem. Commonly known as microbanking, this program operated on the assumption that small loans, guaranteed by members of the borrower's community and payable within a short time, could provide the poor with enough capital to enter the mainstream of commerce.

As a testing ground for his theory, Yunus picked his native Bangladesh, one of the world's poorest nations. Yunus founded Grameen Bank, an institution designed to serve those whom traditional banks ignored. Grameen's clients were the poorest of the poor, many of whom had never possessed any money and relied on a barter economy to meet their daily needs. Through loans of as little as $1, Grameen provided these people with the means to rise above their hand-to-mouth existence. Some were able to purchase livestock or start their own businesses. By 1996 Grameen had extended credit to more than three million borrowers and was the largest bank in Bangladesh, with more than 1,000 branches. More impressive, the default rate on Grameen's loans was only about 2%.

One of the main reasons for Grameen's success was that it did not operate as a charity. Potential borrowers had to join small groups before applying for their first loan. These groups operated as guarantors of the loan and, as such, were responsible for payment in case of default. The groups also had the authority to approve or deny the loan application. Enlightened self-interest dictated that loans not be extended to bad credit risks, and peer pressure ensured that the borrowers made every effort to repay the loans in full. Having also discovered that women were better credit risks than men, Grameen organized its lending policies accordingly. With rare exceptions it extended credit only to women.

The success of microbanking in Bangladesh led to similar programs in other less-developed nations, including Bolivia and Indonesia. Even wealthy nations benefited from microbanking, as was evidenced by programs in the United States aimed at extending credit to those in poverty-stricken city neighbourhoods and on Indian reservations.

(JOHN H. MATHEWS)

---

banking," which sought to help poor borrowers by providing loans of very small amounts, had become extremely successful in Bangladesh and elsewhere. (*See* Sidebar.) In Canada Native Indians and Inuits were expected to gain from the creation of the First Nations Bank of Canada, a joint partnership between Toronto Dominion Bank and a federation of Saskatchewan native chiefs.

Major privatizations continued in several countries, including Australia, Brazil, Venezuela (which offered stakes in the country's two largest banks), and Austria (which finally accepted bids on Creditanstalt Bankverein, more than six years after announcing its privatization plans).

The British banking industry was shaken in July by the apparent suicide of Amschel Rothschild, chief executive of asset management and investment for the London branch of the Rothschild dynasty and heir apparent to the family's global banking operations. In December Michael Bruno, a chief economist with the World Bank in Washington, D.C., and the former hyper-inflation-fighting governor of the Bank of Israel, died.   (MELINDA C. SHEPHERD)

United States. Wearing flowered, open-necked shirts and sipping colourful cocktails, bankers attending the 1996 gathering of the American Bankers Association in Honolulu toasted a year of record profits. Back on the mainland, their stockholders were also celebrating. U.S. banks earned more than $50 billion in 1996, a new record, and their stock prices soared. Money-centre banks led the way, with the value of their

shares increasing by nearly 50% for the year, more than twice the increase in the Standard & Poor's 500. Just eight years earlier the U.S. had been on the brink of a recession, the savings-and-loan crisis was becoming a scandal, and the banks' sizable commercial loan portfolios were falling apart. What changed? First and foremost, the economy. Low interest rates meant strong profit margins on loans and healthy returns on government bonds, both key sources of bank earnings. Commercial loan volume soared, fueled by an explosion in merger-and-acquisition activity. Syndicated loans—big multibank loans to companies—topped $1 trillion in 1996, a new record.

U.S. banks continued to become increasingly shareholder-oriented and to focus their attention on the bottom line, boosting investments in back-office technology while encouraging consumers to bank by telephone and automated teller. Efficiency ratios, which measure how much a bank spends for every dollar of additional revenue it brings in, improved to their lowest level since the 1950s.

Many banks used excess cash to launch major stock buybacks, which in turn helped boost their share prices. New York City-based Chase Manhattan Corp., the country's biggest bank, and San Francisco-based BankAmerica Corp., the third biggest, offered multiyear options packages to all full-time and most part-time bank employees, joining a small but growing cadre of companies in other industries that used stock options as performance incentives.

Although consolidation in the industry,

which set a record in 1995, eased a bit, two of the biggest deals in banking history happened in 1996. In January San Francisco-based Wells Fargo successfully completed its $11.6 billion hostile acquisition of in-state rival First Interstate, the largest bank merger ever. In late August Charlotte, N.C.-based NationsBank Corp. stunned rivals with an $8.7 billion acquisition of St. Louis, Mo.-based Boatmen's Bancshares, the third largest bank deal on record.

In December Citicorp engaged in unsuccessful talks to acquire American Express, a transaction that, if completed, would have been the largest merger in U.S. history, worth more than $25 billion. The deal would have had the potential to reshape the financial services landscape, uniting the nation's leading provider of revolving credit (Citicorp) with the leading provider of nonrevolving credit (American Express) and creating an international investment-management powerhouse, with operations in well over 100 countries.

Banks did face several obstacles in 1996, including worrisome losses in their credit card portfolios. Credit card delinquency rates, which measure the percentage of payments more than 30 days late, hit 3.66% at midyear—a new record—before tapering off slightly. Meanwhile, personal bankruptcies topped the one million mark for the first time. Even as they were writing off credit card loans worth tens of billions of dollars, however, banks were pocketing hefty earnings on those same portfolios, collecting record spreads between their cost of funds and what they charged consumers in credit card interest. Nevertheless, credit cards were the number one item on analysts' worry lists for 1997, with some predicting dire consequences in the event of a national recession.

Bankers also failed to persuade Congress to repeal the Glass-Steagall Act, the Depression-era law separating commercial and investment banking. In 1987 the Fed began granting some banks the power to underwrite stocks and corporate bonds—taking advantage of a loophole in the 1933 law—but it had imposed severe constraints on how significant their involvement in those activities could be. As 1996 drew to a close, the Fed responded to Congress's inaction by dramatically raising the cap on investment-banking activity. Bankers hailed the move but vowed to continue their legislative battle in 1997.   (STEPHEN E. FRANK)

This article updates the *Macropædia* article BANKS AND BANKING.

LABOUR-MANAGEMENT RELATIONS

Europe. In Europe a generally high level of unemployment continued throughout 1996. In January the president of the European Commission, Jacques Santer, proposed a "confidence pact for employment," which, while emphasizing the need for sound economic policies, also stressed the value of the European Union's single market and infrastructure policies and modernization of the labour market.

In addition to unemployment, there were other important issues engaging governments and labour and management organizations in several countries. One not confined to Europe was concern about the heavy costs of the social security arrangements developed over the years, particularly pensions, health care, and unemployment benefits, with labour unions striving to prevent cutbacks proposed by governments. A second problem arose from the plan for economic and monetary union (EMU) in 1999. After this had been decided in the Maastricht Treaty, there was doubt as to the desire of various member countries to join and their ability to satisfy the stringent criteria laid down for entry relating, notably, to public deficits, price stability, long-term interest rates, exchange-rate stability, and independent central banks. By 1996, however, it had become apparent that a substantial number of member governments had decided in favour of entry and that several of them would have to follow tough economic and expenditure policies to satisfy the entry criteria. In some of the countries, the proposed policies provoked union-led demonstrations during the year.

Though no major initiatives concerning labour relations were launched by the European Commission, the year was not uneventful. For example, using the special procedure agreed upon at Maastricht, European employer organizations and unions reached an agreement concerning parental leave and asked the Commission to propose it as a directive, which was duly effected. And the European Works Council Directive, requiring many multinational companies (except most of the British ones, on account of Great Britain's opting out of the Maastricht social policy) to set up consultative bodies for their workers in member countries, became effective in September.

Two noteworthy disputes in Britain were mainly in the form of repeated short stoppages of work. One, involving London Underground train drivers, concerned wages and working hours and was settled by an agreement to reduce the workweek to 35 hours by 1998, with pay increases over the intervening period at less than the rate of inflation. The other was in the Post Office's Royal Mail service and concerned flexible working practices and pay structure. Both disputes caused some irritation to the public and led the government to announce that it was considering legislation that would cause unions striking in "essential" public services to lose their immunity from legal action for damages, even if a pre-strike ballot had been in favour of a strike. It was recognized that it would be difficult to produce workable legislation to this effect. One question that particularly exercised the British labour movement during the year was the desirability of a national minimum wage. Though the government and employers generally saw no virtue in this, both the unions and the Labour Party were committed supporters. The party's intention was to set up a commission that, when the party came to power, could make recommendations concerning the amount of such a minimum. The unions, however, generally supported a target figure of half the median male earnings (at present £4.26 an hour). The two views clashed at the Trades Union Congress (TUC) conference in September when, eager to avoid disharmony that might hurt the Labour Party's chances in the upcoming general election, the TUC insisted on maintaining the union viewpoint but also supported the establishment of a commission on minimum wage, which would name a figure.

In January the German government, unions, and employers agreed on a program for the economy aimed at increasing investment and jobs. It envisioned substantial reductions in public expenditure and changes in social security contributions and arrangements for early retirement. Implementation was going to be difficult, but with future entry into the EMU in mind, as well as Germany's weakened competitiveness, the government decided to press on with its proposed reforms, which also included pay freezes for government workers and for unemployment benefits, together with other measures to reduce public expenditure. A sticking point in the negotiations was the unions' unwillingness to accept cutbacks in Germany's generous sick-pay scheme, from 100% to 80% of wages. In the metals industry, the union argued that the industry's

A worker assembles a steering column at a General Motors parts plant in Saginaw, Mich. After GM threatened to sell the plant, owing to its high labour costs and poor productivity, and outsource the work, an increasingly common practice in many U.S. businesses and industries, plant managers and union workers agreed to production changes that kept their operation going.

PETER YATES—SABA

sick-pay arrangements were contractual and could not be broken because of a change in government policy. The chancellor then made it known that in his view contractual arrangements did indeed have precedence in this case, and the metal employers agreed to deal with the matter in their forthcoming round of negotiation. In December negotiators agreed to keep workers in Lower Saxony on full pay during sick leave for five years.

In Belgium tripartite talks aimed at reducing unemployment, improving competitiveness, and moving to meet the criteria for entry into the EMU resulted in an agreement in April, which one of the two major union confederations—the socialist-inclined Fédération Générale du Travail de Belgique (FGTB)—did not ratify. The government then decided to legislate, again in consultation with the unions and employers organizations. Again the FGTB disassociated itself from the proposals, but the legislation was approved by Parliament on July 26. Its most unusual feature was a reform of the wage-determination system, requiring that the maximum annual wage increase not be more than the average increases in the neighbouring countries of France, Germany, and The Netherlands. The minimum level of increase would be indexed to the Belgian rate of inflation, and agreements would run for two years. A procedure was laid down for negotiation, with the government mediating a decision if the parties could not agree. The central deal would be followed by industry-sector and company-level negotiations within the framework established. Subsequent negotiations proved difficult.

On January 25 the Spanish employers organizations and the main trade union centres finalized an agreement providing for compulsory mediation of several types of labour disputes. The mediator was to be chosen from a list maintained by the parties and would be given a maximum of 10 days to propose a solution. While the parties would be free to reject the mediator's proposal, they might then call in an independent arbitrator, who would make a binding decision. A new health and safety law came into force in February. It gave workers the right to stop work if they believed there to be a serious and imminent risk to their health or safety.

In Portugal a central agreement for 1996 was made in January by the government, employers organizations, and the trade union confederation. It provided a general increase in wages, contractual annual bonus payments, increased government help for the unemployed, and a phased reduction of the normal working week to 40 hours.

North America. On August 20 U.S. Pres. Bill Clinton signed a bill raising the U.S. federal minimum wage to $4.75 an hour, effective October 1, the first increase since 1991. A further increase to $5.15 an hour was scheduled for Sept. 1, 1997. The Teamwork for Employees and Managers Act, which would have effectively repealed section 8(a)2 of the National Labor Relations Act (1935), which forbade the establishment of employee groupings that were dominated by the employer, was vetoed by President Clinton on July 30. There were not enough votes in favour of the bill in Congress to override the veto.

The most important collective bargaining

of the year took place in the automobile industry. The United Automobile Workers (UAW) union first focused on the Ford Motor Co., where it secured a range of improvements including a strong job guarantee (guaranteed minimum employment floor of 95% of current covered jobs) and an up-front lump-sum payment of $2,000. An agreement with Chrysler Corp. containing similar job-security provisions followed. Finally the union turned to the General Motors Corp. (GM), which was the most difficultly placed of the "big three" in that it believed it needed to eliminate a considerable number of jobs. Agreement was reached on November 2, however, and it also included a measure of employment protection. The negotiations were concluded without any full-scale strikes (though two GM plants went on strike in the late stage of the GM-UAW negotiations). Canada, on the other hand, experienced a three-week strike in its GM factories—which also caused layoffs in some U.S. plants—before all of the companies and the union reached agreement.

Australia. For more than 90 years, Australian labour relations centred on a system of federal and state tribunals to which unions and employers took their claims and responses. From 1983 to 1996 the system also depended heavily on the series of "accords" made between the Labor Party government and the Australian Council of Trade Unions (ACTU). An era ended when a Liberal-National Party coalition came to power in March. The new government lost no time in presenting its Workplace Relations and Other Legislation Amendment Bill. It proposed a system of Australian Workplace Agreements in which employees could appoint a bargaining agent (which might, but need not, be a trade union) to negotiate on their behalf, or they could also negotiate individually. A new public official, the employment advocate, would be available to advise employees and employers. Limitations were proposed on the right to strike. The powers of the federal tribunal, the Industrial Relations Commission, would be reduced, though it retained many of its functions and was expected to provide a safety net of minimum conditions. The government gave a guarantee that workers would not be worse off as a result of the legislation.

The bill was strongly opposed by the unions, the Labor Party, and the Australian Democrats in the Senate, who were in a position, together with the Labor senators, to block it. In an agreement between the government and the Senate Democrats made in October, however, the government made sufficient concessions to permit the bill to become law without further opposition by the Democrats.   (R.O. CLARKE)

See also Business and Industry Review.

This article updates the *Macropædia* article WORK AND EMPLOYMENT.

CONSUMER AFFAIRS

In November 1996 governments and nongovernmental organizations from around the world gathered in Rome for the United Nations Food and Agriculture Organization's (FAO's) World Food Summit. The conference identified policies needed at the national, regional, and international levels to alleviate global hunger and malnutrition.

Its aim was to motivate government departments to tackle major global problems related to nutrition and the sustainability of the food supply.

As part of World Consumer Rights Day 1996, on March 15, Consumers International, a federation of 215 consumer organizations in more than 90 countries, issued a booklet, entitled *Safe Food for All,* that discussed crucial food concerns throughout the world, including agricultural trade policies, advertising, and issues of scarcity. The UN Environment Programme used the booklet as part of its global campaign to educate consumers on various aspects of food production and consumption and their impact on the environment.

Concerns about food safety became headline news in 1996 as consumers across England and much of Europe stopped buying English beef because of fear of bovine spongiform encephalopathy (BSE), or "mad cow" disease. An international furor occurred after several young people died of a new strain of Creutzfeldt-Jakob disease, which was thought to be related to BSE, and consumer groups demanded that governments make more rigorous efforts to eliminate BSE from the food chain.

The genetic manipulation (or modification or engineering) of food was another major food issue of 1996. Generally, this aspect of biotechnology refers to such processes as transferring genes from one organism to another—for example, from bacteria to plants or from humans to cows. One important application is the creation of pest-resistant crops. The genetic manipulation of everyday foods became an issue of increasing concern by consumers during the year as, for the first time, supermarkets in many countries stocked genetically engineered tomato paste and cheese. Genetically modified soybeans were expected to enter the European market by the beginning of 1997.

Consumer organizations were insisting that products created by genetic manipulation be rigorously monitored and properly labeled and that consumers understand the pros and cons of food that had undergone such processes. Few regulations requiring labeling of most genetically engineered food currently existed on national or regional levels. In October the World Health Organization and the FAO held an expert consultation on food safety and biotechnology in an effort to determine basic policies on both of these issues.

Western European consumer groups heavily lobbied the European Commission to pass strict laws on the labeling of genetically modified foods. The Commission was expected to pass regulations by the end of 1996.

In Central and Eastern Europe, as well as in the countries of the former Soviet Union, the dumping of poor-quality and mislabeled food from other countries was the major consumer concern in 1996. At the same time, however, many consumers in those regions believed that foreign food was better than the domestic offerings, which thereby undermined the local producers. A similar problem in the region existed in regard to pharmaceuticals. Medicine was commonly available on the black market, and people thus were able to prescribe for themselves. Aggressive marketing heavily influenced citizens, who, less aware of the influence of advertising than their Western counterparts, tended to believe advertisers' promises.

Consumer groups were tackling these issues in a variety of innovative ways. In Poland, for example, a consumer group issued an information packet that looked identical to a box of aspirin. Entitled "Med-Sense," it contained leaflets on common medications and ways in which consumers could assert their rights.

In Latin America and the Caribbean, consumer organizations focused on obtaining access to basic goods and services for vulnerable consumers as well as on ensuring that consumers played an active and critical role in decision-making and legislative processes. A major area of concern during the year was consumer input into the operation of newly privatized public utilities. The British Overseas Development Administration in 1995 began funding a two-year organizing, training, advocacy project in Argentina, Brazil, Chile, Colombia, Mexico, and Uruguay to empower Latin-American consumer organizations to represent the consumer on matters related to public utilities.

Many countries in Asia and the Pacific deregulated and liberalized trade and services to meet the challenges of the global market. But increased choices for consumers did not come in tandem with adequate market rules and controls. In many countries policies governing quality and safety were nonexistent or not enforced. Fast-track development such as indiscriminate logging and unplanned housing and road construction caused serious environmental problems. In the South Pacific consumers grappled with the problems of toxic-waste dumping and the poor quality of foodstuffs, pharmaceuticals, and other products.

In response to such problems, the consumer movement continued to flourish. Consumers International's Asia office held the first-ever joint meeting with the China Consumer Association on the subject of consumer complaints and law. Considerable growth occurred in India, where more than 700 consumer organizations were operating. Western Samoa passed its first consumer protection legislation.

The Model Consumer Protection Law for Africa was launched in 1996. The law marked a milestone in the development of the consumer movement on a continent where only two countries (Zimbabwe and South Africa) had small claims courts and only a handful had adopted legislation conforming to the 1985 UN Guidelines for Consumer Protection. (ALINA TUGEND)

In February the U.S. Congress passed and Pres. Bill Clinton signed into law the most wide-ranging reform of the nation's telecommunications laws since 1934, promising consumers a new level of price competition and a wider array of services through the telephone, television, and computer. Amid many complicated provisions, a basic goal of the reforms was to dismantle regulations that gave the seven regional Bell phone companies monopoly control over their respective local service areas. Although consumers had been able to choose from various long-distance companies since the partial breakup of the phone monopoly in 1984, such competition was not allowed for local phone service (except for relatively

expensive cellular offerings). Meanwhile, the Bells were not allowed to compete in the long-distance or the cable television markets, so additional competition and innovation were quelled there. The new Telecommunications Act freed the Bells to offer long-distance service to their customers, providing they opened their local markets to competitors such as the long-distance carriers and cable companies. The main issues remaining were how quickly anticipated consumer benefits would accrue and who would be left behind.

Health care as a consumer issue continued to provoke legislative attention in the U.S., at both the federal and state level. Federal mandates for minimum maternity stays in hospitals were signed into law. Concerns about access to health insurance prompted federal reforms that guaranteed "portability." For example, people who had insurance at a previous job were promptly eligible for coverage at their next job, regardless of preexisting medical conditions. Health insurance consumers were also offered a new tax incentive to facilitate their financial control over health care in a pilot program that allowed them to buy less-expensive, high-deductible insurance policies and keep the tax-free savings in so-called medical savings accounts for their future medical spending. At the state level campaigns by provider and consumer groups focused attention on the growing managed-care insurance industry. Some 33 states enacted laws regulating managed-care plans, largely aimed at practices designed to limit patient care. These included laws prohibiting or restricting contractual "gag clauses," which limited what physicians could tell patients about treatment options under their plans; laws guaranteeing access to specialists; and reform of methods for reviewing doctors' practice patterns.

Twenty-four states' attorneys general asked the U.S. Supreme Court to uphold the states' powers to limit the late fees that credit-card companies charge consumers. The court ruled in early June, however, that national credit-card companies can charge the maximum allowable fees applicable within the state where each credit-card company is based and thus were not subject to rate restrictions in other states. Some consumer groups argued that banks would begin charging consumers higher rates. Industry observers noted, however, that vigorous competition kept such fees to a minimum, regardless of the court's sanction.

The U.S. Food and Drug Administration approved olestra, the first calorie-free fat substitute. The approval limited its use to potato chips and other salty snacks, but the manufacturer of olestra, Procter & Gamble, wanted approval eventually for a wider range of foods. Some medical experts, including five members of the Food and Drug Administration's advisory panel that recommended approval, raised concerns about olestra's side effects, especially possible detrimental nutrient loss, particularly in children. Procter & Gamble's safety studies were criticized as too limited in scope.

Gasoline prices temporarily rose to the highest levels since the Persian Gulf War in 1991, which prompted several consumer groups and politicians to call for a federal investigation of the pricing practices of oil companies. This overlooked the fact, re-

ported in April by the American Petroleum Institute, that gas prices were about half what they had been when government price controls were first lifted in 1981. As a result of deaths and injuries to children and frail adults caused by air bags, the National Highway Traffic Safety Administration proposed in December that car makers be authorized to reduce the air bag inflation power by 20–35%. (PETER L. SPENCER)

See also Business and Industry Review: *Advertising; Retailing;* The Environment.

Education

Noteworthy educational news in 1996 concerned literacy efforts, the renovation of educational systems in Eastern Europe, the preparation of students for changing labour markets, the operation of schools by religious organizations, ways to improve students' welfare, university enrollment changes, improved opportunities for women, and corruption in higher education. Among the persistent issues in the United States were: academic deficiencies of students in comparison with those from other industrialized nations; government support for parents to select their children's schools; increasing costs of higher education; the need to connect schools to the information superhighway; drug abuse and violence in schools; and the need for training programs for unemployed and underemployed adults whose skills had become obsolete or dated.

Primary and Secondary Education. The importance of literacy education was emphasized in a study of social and economic conditions in 162 countries. The report concluded that industrialized nations should redirect aid for less-developed countries into literacy programs. According to the study's authors, the reduction of illiteracy could empower underprivileged nations to become partners of wealthy countries and reduce the gap between rich and poor societies.

Innovative methods for promoting literacy were being adopted in various parts of the world. Following its success in Australia, a literacy project for less-privileged children, entitled First Step, was introduced for experimental use in the United Kingdom. Another approach to literacy training imported from Australia appeared in the British Link-into-Learning centres, which were designed to provide adults with sufficient reading and writing skills to obtain work and help their children with school tasks. In Uganda a program named REFLECT, which engaged learners in creating their own written materials, was credited with enabling 60% to 70% of the course participants to become literate; previous programs had achieved only 12% success. A Finger Phonics scheme that associated letter sounds with finger movements gained popularity in Canada and the U.K.

Within Russia debates ensued over the role that minority-group languages should assume in schools that had used Russian as the primary medium of instruction for more than five decades. Ever since the republics at the end of the 1980s won the right to direct their own educational systems, advocates of using local languages in schools had vied against proponents of maintaining Russian as the dominant national tongue.

Provincial leaders argued that their languages would be lost if not given a key role in the curriculum.

Throughout Eastern Europe increasing numbers of youths were attending bilingual schools that offered an opportunity to study foreign languages that had been forbidden under communist regimes prior to 1989. English had become the most popular language to learn.

In his state of the union message to Congress on Jan. 23, 1996, U.S. Pres. Bill Clinton urged an educational technology initiative to improve education, proposing that every U.S. classroom be equipped with computers and connected to the Internet by the year 2000. The president also recommended that states and local districts adopt national standards to assess students' academic progress, supported the right of parents to choose the public school of their choice, encouraged organization of charter schools, and emphasized the need for values and character education.

Although there were proposals in the U.S. Congress to reduce federal spending for education by 17%, the reductions in the bill that passed Congress totaled 9%. The 1996 bill allocated $400 million for the AmeriCorps national service program, $69.5 million less than fiscal 1995 and $417 million less than the president requested. It granted $350 million for Goals 2000 education initiatives, $22 million less than 1995 funding, and allocated $3,570,000,000 for Head Start funding, $36 million more than in 1995. Spending for programs assisting public-school children was set at $7.2 billion, $1 billion more than Republicans had sought. The total allocation for education was $25,323,000,000, compared with $26.8 billion in fiscal 1995.

A National Educational Summit, the second such conference held in the U.S., met on March 26–27, 1996, in Palisades, N.Y. Like the earlier conference in 1989, the 1996 meeting—attended by leaders in business, government, and education—focused on U.S. students' academic deficiencies, particularly in mathematics and science, in comparison with students from other industrialized countries. Calling for improved academic achievement, the summit recommended that state and local districts establish specific standards for basic academic subjects, especially in English, science, and mathematics. Addressing the summit, President Clinton called for assessment of academic competency through standardized state competency testing in basic academic subjects. Critics of the summit, deciding its focus was too narrow, contended it should have considered broader issues, including school choice. Critics also alleged that comparisons of U.S. students' academic achievement with those of other countries rested on invalid criteria.

In the 1996 election campaign, the Republican and Democratic platforms and positions differed on educational policy. The Republicans promised abolition of the Department of Education and an end to federal funding of the National Endowment for the Arts, the National Endowment for the Humanities, and the Corporation for Public Broadcasting.

The two major parties continued to differ on "school choice" and using vouchers to provide parents with public funds for their children to attend their school of choice.

While Republicans supported vouchers for both public and private schools, Democrats opposed them for private schools.

The charter school movement in the U.S. experienced continued growth in 1996, attracting support in 25 states of the U.S. as an alternative form of school organization. Though public schools, charter schools provided an alternative to those conventionally established and maintained by a local district. Charter schools exhibited the following characteristics: (1) the state authorized organizations to establish and operate charter schools and issued a waiver freeing them from many regulations governing public schools; (2) the school was "public"—that is, nonsectarian and supported by public funds; (3) the school, through its charter, was responsible for students' academic progress; (4) the school was one of choice for educators and parents; the choice, however, was within the public, not the private, sector.

While the charter school movement gained momentum, the trend to privatize public-school operations and services experienced setbacks in 1996. The board of education of Hartford, Conn., for example, canceled its contract with Educational Alternatives, which had previously operated the district's schools.

With regard to curriculum and instruction, constructivism continued to be popular, especially in elementary schools. Constructivism emphasized learning by problem-solving rather than by receiving information. Students constructed their own knowledge base from direct interaction with sources in the environment. Through social interaction, they actively created meaning out of their individual and group constructions of reality.

The 28th Phi Delta Kappa/Gallup Poll for 1996 revealed public attitudes toward public schools in the U.S. According to the poll, 43% of the respondents gave their local public schools high marks, an A or B, for overall educational performance. This ranking remained consistent with previous polls in that respondents rated the performances of their local public schools higher than those of public schools nationally. In rank order, the major problems facing public schools were identified as drug abuse, lack of discipline, violence and gangs, and lack of adequate financial support.

Concern about the quality of mathematics instruction was voiced in the U.K. after tests of 13-year-olds in nine nations showed that pupils in England correctly answered only 53% of math problems, compared with 79% by pupils in Singapore. Youngsters in Taiwan and South Korea also earned high scores. The author of the study, David Reynolds of the University of Newcastle, suggested that the dominant method of teaching mathematics in England since the 1960s concentrated on the brightest pupils and neglected the others, which thereby produced overall low test results. He advocated changing to the "whole-class" teaching system used in the East Asian countries, Germany, and Switzerland, a system that challenged all pupils to reach a minimum standard of attainment.

Observers of Great Britain's programs for training non-university-bound adolescents charged that the nation lacked adequate provisions for vocational training, so many young people seeking jobs were unable to

carry out such simple tasks as basic mathematical calculations. As a result, according to critics, the economy was locked into a low-quality, low-pay production system. Advisers proposed restructuring the government's Youth Training Scheme to emphasize communication and number skills, information technology, and other general abilities required by industry.

Computer-literacy instruction advanced in China, where urban schools were increasingly providing such training. The number of Chinese families owning personal computers rose in 1996 to more than one million, a figure expected to reach five million by the year 2000. At the same time, schools emphasized training children in the use of the abacus, the traditional method of calculating sums by moving wooden beads along wires set in a wooden frame. Proponents of the abacus asserted that in contrast to computer instruction, abacus training equipped children to visualize calculations and thereby fostered speed and accuracy in mental arithmetic.

The operation of schools by religious groups gained attention in Canada and China. Legislators in Canada's Newfoundland province voted to eliminate from the provincial constitution its unique system of providing public funds to pay the costs of schools operated by seven Christian denominations. Critics of the vote feared that it might encourage legislatures in Alberta, Ontario, Quebec, and Saskatchewan to remove the constitutional protection for the public funding of Roman Catholic schools in those provinces. In December the Supreme Court of Canada ruled that Ontario did not have to finance non-Catholic religious schools even though it had paid for Catholic schools for more than a century.

In China local communist officials introduced a policy of permitting Christian churches to operate primary schools in regions too poor to finance children's education. To pay the cost of erecting the first of such schools in Guangdong province, Christians in the village of Baiwan solicited the aid of Hong Kong's Christian Council to raise the $150,000 needed to build a modern four-story concrete school, furnish it, and pay teachers' salaries. The Baiwan school offered a secular curriculum, was tuition-free, and was managed by a board composed of local Christians and non-Christians.

Following the reunification of Germany in 1990, officials in the five eastern German states sought to devise a satisfactory means of implementing the central government's West German mandate that religious education be provided as a regular school subject. The solution in four of the states (Saxony, Saxony-Anhalt, Thuringia, and Mecklenburg-West Pomerania) was to offer students a choice between traditional religious instruction (Lutheranism or Roman Catholicism) as in western Germany or a nonreligious ethics course. The fifth state, Brandenburg, in 1996 created an integrated course entitled "Lifestyle, Ethics, and Religion," focusing on the comparative study of religions and philosophies rather than indoctrination in a single faith.

Steps intended to enhance students' welfare were adopted in Japan and Israel. Japanese authorities focused attention on the issue of students' being terrorized by classmates. Although reported incidents of

Chinese children work at computers in a private school in Guangzhou. As the number of Chinese homes with computers increased, and much larger numbers were predicted, urban schools were introducing children to computers early; at the same time, though, they continued to train them to use the traditional abacus.

bullying had declined to 7,000 by 1996, compared with 22,000 several years earlier, officials still considered pupil harassment a serious problem that called for heightened teacher vigilance and prompt disciplinary action.

In past years critics had claimed that Israel's tradition of including eight subject fields in national diploma examinations placed too great a burden on the high-school juniors and seniors who needed to pass the tests in order to gain admission to a university. To reduce the emotional pressure on students, Israeli Education Minister Amnon Rubinstein in 1996 established a system by which an annual lottery would be held to determine which five subjects the year's examinations would comprise and which three would be exempt. In the 1996 lottery the exempt fields were Bible, Jewish history, and mathematics. An objection to the plan was voiced by the country's new prime minister, Benjamin Netanyahu, who contended that failing to test students' command of Bible and Jewish history would be ignoring Israel's cultural roots. In response, defenders of the plan asserted that students' high-school grades in the exempt subjects would be sufficient evidence of their knowledge in those fields.

Higher Education. In Eastern Europe the renovation of the region's postsecondary institutions continued in the aftermath of the fall of communist governments. Since 1990 most of eastern Germany's 60 higher-learning institutions had been reformed to fit western Germany's pattern of higher education. Staffs in the eastern sector were reduced to 60% of their former size, and 20,000 academics were left without jobs. In early 1996 the total enrollment in the 60 institutions reached 198,000 students, which indicated rapid progress toward the 10-year goal of doubling the 1989 total of 134,000 students. Within the next five years, officials expected to provide enough places to accommodate approximately 35% of the college-age population, the same proportion as in western Germany.

Throughout Romania during the early 1990s, hundreds of private institutions sprang up to serve students not accommodated in public universities. In 1996, however, serious doubts were voiced about the quality of education provided by private colleges. Only 73 private institutions had earned state accreditation, and no more than 5% of their graduates had passed government-administered examinations.

Although the four universities in Bosnia and Herzegovina had remained open during that country's civil war, not until the signing of a peace accord at the end of 1995 were officials able to start repairing the wartime damage. In 1996 what was described as a "stampede" of new and returning students descended on the institutions, located in Sarajevo, Mostar, Banja Luka, and Tuzla. Before the war the University of Sarajevo had enrolled 30,000 students, a number that dropped to 7,000 by late 1995 but then rebounded to 15,000 in the fall term of 1996. The shelling of Sarajevo during the war seriously damaged all 26 of the university's schools, which placed officials in the difficult position of providing classrooms and offices with limited aid from Western nations. The institutions in Mostar and Tuzla were endeavouring to repair similar damage. Although the World Bank agreed to finance elementary- and secondary-education programs in Bosnia, it did not support higher education.

In contrast to the liberalization of education in Eastern Europe, the Chinese government increased efforts to strengthen communist ideology on campuses by establishing a China Foundation for Marxism Studies, designed to support the teachings of Marxism and Leninism and the philosophy of Mao Zedong. This plan to counter the declining popularity of communist theory in postsecondary institutions included new rules giving each university's Communist Party control over instructional matters, a reversal of liberal policies in the 1980s that accorded university presidents ultimate responsibility for their institutions' affairs.

The heads of five of Hong Kong's seven universities were appointed to the 150-member committee charged with directing the 1997 transfer of the British colony to Chinese sovereignty. Observers speculated that the composition of the preparatory committee, with its 94 delegates from Hong Kong and 56 from China, reflected the intent of the Chinese government to permit Hong Kong's business and educational communities the freedom to operate as they had under British rule.

The South African government sought to improve the nation's higher education by spending $231 million on universities and high-level technical institutions in 1996. The amount surpassed the 1995 allotment by 21% for universities and 31% for technical schools. At the same time, the nation struggled to overhaul its traditional dual-track higher-education system, which under apartheid had maintained one track for whites and the other for the black and Coloured population.

France's minister of education, François Bayrou, spent the early months of 1996 meeting with university representatives to find solutions to the problems underlying the student strike over university funding that shut down half of the nation's 90 universities in late 1995. Statistics compiled by the Organisation for Economic Co-operation and Development indicated that France spent less per student on its universities than did any of the OECD's other 25 members except Italy. Bayrou charged that the OECD figures were faulty but admitted that many politicians, including some Cabinet members, believed the country's universities were failing in their mission and perhaps could not be satisfactorily reformed.

Many educational systems continued to cope with the task of producing graduates who could find appropriate employment in a changing job market. The recent economic boom in India had resulted in a severe shortage of experts in such fields as business management, computer software, financial services, telecommunications engineering, and television programming. The greatest need was for graduates skilled in the use of computers. To meet the demand for such specialists, enterprising educators opened a host of private colleges, and policy makers called on established higher-education institutions to update their curricula, reduce the number of students in general courses, and increase the number of students in technical fields.

A Russian survey revealed a marked rise in graduates choosing careers in economics, computers, law, finance, and the humanities as the nation's economy began to demand more workers schooled in such specialties. The popularity of careers in engineering and teaching declined because of lower wages in those occupations.

Proposals by Greece's education minister, George Papandreou, to modernize Greece's antiquated higher-education system set off student riots that extended from late 1995 into 1996 and resulted in $20 million in damage to institutions in Athens alone. For years critics had charged that Greek universities were woefully behind the times, still operating like the 19th-century French and German institutions on which they were modeled. Since the 1930s Greek institutions had provided free tuition and textbooks, had not required students to attend class, and had virtually guaranteed a degree to applicants who scored high on entrance examinations. The riots stemmed from students' fear that the reforms would require them to help pay for their education and would alter their study habits and fields of study. In the 1990s many university graduates proved ill-equipped to fill the needs of the nation's economy, a situation Papandreou's plans were designed to remedy. His proposed changes were also stimulated by the fact that other members of the European Union were refusing to recognize Greek diplomas until proper reforms had been instituted.

The status of women in higher education continued to improve. Konai Helu Thaman, a Tongan specialist on Pacific Islands education and culture, became the first woman appointed to a professorial chair at the University of the South Pacific, the institution that provided higher education for a number of Pacific Island nations. Women assumed the three most visible leadership posts in Australian higher education when Amanda Vanstone was appointed minister of education, empowered to negotiate educational issues with Fay Gale, president of the Australian Vice-Chancellors' Committee, and with Carolyn Allport, head of the academics' National Tertiary Education Union. The U.S. Supreme Court ruled the Virginia Military Institute's all-male enrollment policy unconstitutional. Following this decision the Citadel, Charleston, S.C., announced that it would admit female cadets. This ended the all-male policy at the last two public institutions of higher education in the U.S. that had practiced this form of discrimination. In Canada the University of Montreal established a fellowship program enabling women who took maternity leave from doctoral programs to return later and complete their studies. Prospects for the education of women in Afghanistan dimmed in late 1996, however, as Taliban military forces captured the capital city of Kabul and imposed strict Islamic rule that included closing girls' schools and confining women to their homes.

University enrollment trends became a concern in a variety of countries. Following steady growth since the 1970s, the enrollment in Canadian universities in 1996 declined by 0.4% to 574,300 students. Analysts speculated that the decrease was caused by a combination of higher student fees, reduced government grants, and uncertain job prospects following graduation. The drop in applicants motivated higher-education officials to devise innovative student-loan programs, refine student services, and focus on attracting the students most likely to succeed in university studies.

Australian university officials predicted that by the year 2010 the number of fee-paying foreign students in Australian institutions would have increased fivefold over current figures. The anticipated number should reach 200,000 and account for 26% of all students on Australian campuses, compared with 10.6% in 1993. The countries expected to send the most students in the future were China, India, Indonesia, and Iran, displacing the recent leaders—Malaysia, Hong Kong, and Singapore. Forecasters focusing on future worldwide university enrollments estimated that over the next 15 years, the number of students studying outside their own countries would increase more than 130% to 2.8 million, with more than half of the total coming from Asia.

Evidence of corruption in academia surfaced in Italy and Kenya. The Italian case concerned appointments to university professorships on the basis of political favouritism rather than professional competence. Although medical faculties were cited as particularly affected by this practice, observers contended that nepotism and cronyism were widespread in the assignment of candidates to tenured posts in other disciplines as well. As one effort to correct abuses, an administrative tribunal in Rome nullified 45 appointments to senior tenured positions in medical schools in the wake of a suit brought by four professors who had been turned down for chairs in general surgery.

Political analysts accused Kenya's president, Daniel arap Moi, of having destroyed the nation's higher-education system by preventing freedom of inquiry and expression. Moi maintained executive control over the country's five public universities by appointing each institution's vice-chancellor, who in turn controlled the appointment and dismissal of all university personnel. To eliminate potential opposition, Moi's government arrested dissidents and outlawed faculty associations and student unions. Despite a $55 million World Bank investment in Kenya, such basic educational supplies as chalk and paper were seldom available to the schools, library holdings were outdated, and subscriptions to scholarly journals had lapsed.

In the U.S., President Clinton called for expanding work-study programs, providing $1,000 merit scholarships for the top 5% of high-school graduates, and making $10,000 a year of college tuition tax-deductible. He reiterated the need to develop retraining programs for unemployed and underemployed persons through vouchers to community colleges.

The Republican platform in the election campaign attributed rising tuition costs in higher education to the colleges and universities themselves. Robert Dole, the Republican presidential nominee, would have allowed low- and middle-income families to invest up to $500 per year in a savings account and earn tax-free interest to help pay for a child's college expenses.

The Democratic Party platform emphasized education as a key issue. Clinton, the Democratic nominee, proposed creating a $1,500 tax credit and a $10,000 tax deduction for a family's expenditures for higher education. He also proposed devoting $1 billion over a five-year period for the AmeriCorps national-service program. The Democratic platform also endorsed, in contrast to the Republican, continued federal funding for the arts and the humanities.

In the U.S. the "cultural wars," the decade-long debates over multiculturalism in the curriculum, continued. The debates focused on whether the curriculum should promote a common cultural core and if that core should remain centred in Western history and culture.

(GERALD LEE GUTEK; ROBERT MURRAY THOMAS)

See also Libraries and Museums.

This article updates the *Macropædia* articles History of EDUCATION; TEACHING.

The Environment

INTERNATIONAL ACTIVITIES

International Cooperation. Controversy arose in 1996 over the wording of one chapter in *Climate Change 1995,* the latest report of the Intergovernmental Panel on Climate Change (IPCC). The Global Climate Coalition (GCC), an umbrella group of some 60 industrial concerns, claimed the part of the main text dealing with human influences on climate had been substantially rewritten after it had passed peer review and been approved. The IPCC mounted a robust defense of the published version, but the argument continued most of the year.

On September 19 Canadian Foreign Affairs Minister Lloyd Axworthy presided at the signing ceremony in Ottawa of an agreement to create a joint Arctic Council, with the aim of protecting the environment while encouraging long-term development in the region. The eight signatory nations were Canada, Denmark (on behalf of Greenland), Finland, Iceland, Norway, Russia, Sweden, and the U.S.

United States. On the evening of January 19, the *North Cape,* a 104-m (340-ft) barge, ran aground near Block Island, Rhode Island, a wildlife refuge, ruptured 9 of its 14 compartments, and eventually spilled more than 828,000 gal of heating oil from its cargo of 4 million gal (1 gal = 3.79 litres). The accident occurred after the tugboat towing the barge caught fire in a storm. About 600,000 gal of the oil were believed to have evaporated or dissipated in the water, but the remainder caused a 19-km (12-mi) slick, most of which was driven out to sea by the wind. Eklof Marine, which owned both the tugboat and the barge, accepted responsibility and hired workers and vessels to help with the cleanup and to pump the remaining oil into another barge. On January 21–22, 1.8 million gal of oil were removed, which left 1.4 million gal on board in undamaged compartments. Some of this was pumped out later.

In December 1995 it was reported that Rep. Jim Saxton had drafted a bill to create a National Institute for the Environment, to be funded by combining environmental research programs from several federal agencies so that it would require no new financing. The idea was pursued by the Committee on Environment and Natural Resources (CENR) of the National Science and Technology Council. In May 1996 the CENR was said to be exploring ways of merging all federal environmental programs into a single network responsible for ecological research and monitoring and reportedly had identified about 30 suitable programs.

The House of Representatives passed a bill in October approving a $21.5 billion budget for research by the major civil agencies in 1996. This was $3 billion less than the 1995 budget and $3.6 billion less than the budget requested by Pres. Bill Clinton. A large proportion of the 22% cut in the research and development budget of the Environmental Protection Agency (EPA) would be taken from research into global warming. The National Oceanic and Atmospheric Administration budget would be cut by 19%.

In August U.S. District Judge Joseph Anderson rejected a request from South Carolina for an emergency injunction to prevent the shipment of spent fuel rods containing highly enriched uranium from Europe and South America to storage pools at the Department of Energy's Savannah River site. On September 23 the first cargo of 280 rods from Germany, Switzerland, Sweden, Colombia, and Chile arrived under Coast Guard escort at the Naval Weapons Station in North Charleston, S.C. The program to recover spent fuel aimed to prevent the proliferation of nuclear weapons and involved 41 countries.

Western Europe. The U.K. suffered its worst oil spill since the *Torrey Canyon* incident when the Liberian-registered single-hull tanker *Sea Empress* ran aground on Feb. 15, 1996, near the entrance to Milford Haven harbour in Dyfed, Wales, and eventually spilled about 70,000 metric tons of oil. The 147,000-metric ton ship was carrying approximately 130,000 metric tons of light crude from the North Sea Forties field to the Texaco refinery through one of the most ecologically sensitive areas in Britain. According to an interim bulletin from the Marine Accident Investigation Branch, published on March 7, those in charge of the ship failed to anticipate a changing tidal stream across the harbour entrance. The ship went out of control and slewed onto rocks, spilling some 6,000 metric tons of oil. The harbour master, local pilots, and the local countryside authorities asked that the ship be towed out to sea where it would be safe from the tides and spilled oil could be dealt with before it reached the coast, but their proposal was overruled by the government's Joint Response Centre and the salvagers.

The Countryside Council for Wales would not permit the ship to be towed into port immediately. Instead, it was decided to detain it in the shipping channel outside the harbour while the cargo was transferred, but the available tugs were unable to hold the ship in heavy seas and 8-m (26-ft) tides. The tanker grounded again at low tide on a rock pinnacle and remained fast despite efforts by eight tugs to free it. By that time much of the neighbouring Welsh coast had been contaminated, and there was a 13-km (8-mi)-long slick offshore; this eventually reached 19 km (12 mi). At 6 PM on February 21, an hour before high tide, the tanker was finally freed by 12 tugs; it was towed into Milford Haven, where what remained of the cargo was transferred to smaller tankers. By mid-March oil from the *Sea Empress* had contaminated more than 95 km (about 60 mi) of coastline in County Wexford, Ireland, but most of the sandy beaches had been cleaned by April.

The European Commission on May 14 published a report on bathing-water quality on beaches. It found that 20% of Portuguese beaches, 11% of British beaches, 6.2% of French beaches, and 1.6% of Greek beaches failed to meet minimum standards. Sweden had the cleanest beaches, followed by Ireland. In all, 3,000 beaches failed to meet standards laid down in the 1986 European Union (EU) directive.

On June 19 the European Commission proposed a directive aimed at reducing levels of vehicle emissions by 70% over 10 years. Tighter emission standards for passenger vehicles and higher-quality standards for diesel fuel and gasoline would be introduced by 2000. Further improvements would be introduced from 2005 according to evidence available by the end of 1998. By 2010, emissions of carbon monoxide would be reduced by 70% and of nitrogen oxides by 65%. The proposed directive drew criticism from environmental lobbyists, who said the proposed controls on the contents of diesel fuel and gasoline were lower than the existing EU average and one-third higher than those already enforced in some Scandinavian countries and the U.S., which raised the possibility of conflict with those member nations planning stricter controls.

In Britain the Environment Agency began work on April 1, when it took over responsibilities formerly exercised by the National Rivers Authority, the Inspectorate of Pollution, and local authority waste inspectors. It had an annual income of £550 million, one-third as government grant and the remainder from fees and charges. The new agency promised to pressure industry to invest in environmental protection, conduct a major public education campaign, and publish regular "state of the environment" reports on the Internet.

On October 1 the Landfill Tax came into force in Britain, imposing a charge of £7 per ton for domestic rubbish dumped in landfill sites and £2 per ton for inert material such as builders' waste. The tax was intended to encourage additional recycling to meet the government target of 25% of domestic waste by 2000. The Association of Metropolitan Authorities said the tax would add a net £90 million to council tax bills, amounting to an average tax increase of £5 a year per household.

On May 8 the first of 110 shipments of radioactive waste from the French reprocessing plant at Cap De La Hague, Normandy, arrived at Dannenberg, Ger., where some 35 metric tons of waste were transferred to a low-loader truck for the final stage of its journey to storage at Gorleben.

German police use a water cannon to try to disperse a large crowd of demonstrators protesting the shipment of nuclear waste to a storage facility in Gorleben, near Hannover, in May. Although the waste was shipped from a French reprocessing plant, it had been produced by a German reactor and was the first of more than 100 shipments scheduled to be stored at Gorleben.

Protesters blocked railway lines, erected burning barricades, and fought police with stones, firecrackers, and flares. The Hamburg-to-Hannover railway line was closed for a time because of a bomb threat; a fake bomb was found. Pitched battles, in which the police used water cannons, tear gas, and baton charges, continued for several days and involved 15,000 police. At least 30 people were injured.

Asia and the Pacific. It was reported in August that the Hong Kong University of Science and Technology was developing a project to map and model the environment of the South China Sea, with support from Chinese and Vietnamese officials. Called Econet, the model would take 15 years to establish and cost $150 million.

In June there were reports that the Australian mining company BHP had agreed to pay at least $A 550 million in an out-of-court settlement to villagers in Papua New Guinea affected by pollution from mining operations. Every year since 1984, when seismic activity and torrential rains caused a dam to collapse, about 60 million metric tons of rocky slurry had poured from the Ok Tedi gold and copper mine. Contaminated with copper and cadmium, the waste flowed into the Ok Tedi and Fly rivers. People from surrounding villages claimed wildlife was killed, parts of the river became too shallow for navigation, and the local way of life was destroyed. BHP agreed to pay for the relocation of 10 villages, establish a trust fund to compensate landowners and villagers, and pay the landowners' legal costs. BHP was also investigating alternative ways to clean up the area.

ENVIRONMENTAL ISSUES

Climate Change. In July delegates met in Geneva for the second meeting of signatories to the UN Framework Convention on Climate Change. The U.S. and the EU won
(continued on page 210)

PHOTO ESSAY

Eco-Warriors

During early 1996, as the construction of the Newbury Bypass in England routinely made the headlines, self-proclaimed "eco-warriors" began to take up residence in trees that were threatened with demolition for the bypass construction. They made treehouses ranging in size from a mere platform to multitree units containing separate cooking and sleeping areas. Protesters used precarious rope walkways to make their way from tree to tree.

The Newbury Bypass was to be the last segment of a four-lane highway linking the south of France with Scotland via the Channel Tunnel (Eurotunnel). Those arguing for the bypass stated that it would relieve congestion and shorten the trip around Newbury. This convenience, however, involved cutting a large swath though one of England's few remaining areas of outstanding natural beauty, threatening wildlife habitats.

The photographs below by Anthony Almos illustrate the daring tactics and determination of these "eco-warriors." Even though surrounded by police and security guards, the protesters clung to the trees while contractors chopped away branch by branch, eventually trapping them. By the year's end, after more than 900 arrests, this peaceful demonstration had succeeded in delaying the construction.

(continued from page 207)

agreement to their proposal requiring Organisation for Economic Co-operation and Development (OECD) member states to adopt legally binding limits to greenhouse gas emissions, with targets and timetables for their reduction, from 2000. Australia, Russia, and members of OPEC opposed the proposal, and less-developed countries (LDCs) were concerned about the effect of mandatory reductions on their emerging economies; the convention required only developed countries to reduce emissions to 1990 levels by 2000.

Climate Change 1995, the IPCC report published in June, claimed that global warming had been detected. After allowing for the cooling effects of aerosols, IPPC Working Group I predicted a temperature rise of 1°–3.5° C (1.8°–6.3° F) by 2100 and a sea-level rise of 15–95 cm (6–37 in). Working Group II, addressing the possible consequences of climate change, said warming at the higher end of this range would shift climatic zones poleward by about 550 km (340 mi). Some tree species might not survive, and in places hardwood forest might give way to grassland and scrub. Tropical diseases might extend into higher latitudes, which would lead to 50 million to 80 million additional cases of malaria annually (10–15% increase) by late in the 21st century and an increased incidence of dengue, yellow fever, and viral encephalitis. The report was criticized by the GCC for having had chapter 8 reedited before publication, after it had been peer-reviewed and approved. This chapter dealt with potential human influence on climate change, and John Shlaes, GCC executive director, said the substantial deletions and significant changes to the approved version made the chapter unbalanced. The charge was vigorously rebuffed by the IPCC.

The World Energy Council reported in July that global carbon dioxide emissions from burning fossil fuels rose 12% between 1990 and 1995, the increase from LDCs being three times that from industrialized countries. Most OECD members increased emissions 4%; those in the Asia-Pacific region (except Australia, New Zealand, and Japan) registered a 30% increase. Those in the Middle East rose 35%, in Africa 12.5%, and in Latin America 8%. Apart from France, Germany, and Great Britain, industrialized countries were unlikely to meet their target of returning emissions to 1990 levels by 2000. In Central and Eastern Europe, 1995 emissions were 75% above 1990 levels (70% in the former U.S.S.R.).

It was reported in August that Norway was about to start burying one million metric tons of carbon dioxide a year in rocks one kilometre (0.62 mi) below the seafloor in the North Sea. The carbon dioxide was a waste product from natural gas from the Sleipner West field. If released into the air, it would increase Norwegian emissions 3% and cost Statoil, the Norwegian state oil and gas company, about $54 million a year because of the country's carbon tax. The plan was to pass the gas through an amine solvent in an absorption tower, release it from the solvent by heating, compress it into a supercritical fluid, and pump it into pores in sandstone from which gas had been extracted in the past. The gas might react with water or with the rocks themselves, locking it away permanently.

Ozone Layer. Signatories to the Montreal Protocol met in Vienna and in December 1995 agreed on new limits on ozone-depleting substances. Industrial countries agreed to phase out methyl bromide by 2010, and LDCs planned to stabilize its use at average 1995–98 levels by 2002.

A report in May found that tropospheric concentrations of chlorine attributable to halocarbons released by human activities peaked near the beginning of 1994 and by mid-1995 were decreasing at a rate of 20–30 parts per trillion per year. Bromine concentrations were still increasing, but the combined effect of all halogens was a decrease. The study calculated that stratospheric concentrations of chlorine and bromine would reach a maximum between 1997 and 1999 and decrease thereafter, assuming the adjusted and amended limits set by the Montreal Protocol on Substances That Deplete the Ozone Layer were not exceeded.

At a conference on climate and ozone arranged by the European Commission environmental research program and held in Brussels in May, Paul Crutzen (a Dutch scientist with the Max Planck Institute for Chemistry, Mainz, Ger., who shared the 1995 Nobel Prize for Chemistry for his research into the decomposition of ozone) said ozone smogs over rural Brazil, central Africa, and the island of Borneo were often worse than those in European cities and that during the dry season carbon dioxide emissions were greater in the Southern than in the Northern Hemisphere. The reason, he said, was mainly biomass burning by farmers, including forest fires, savannah grassland burning, burning farm wastes, and slash-and-burn cultivation. Together, these released between 1.8 billion and 4.7 billion metric tons of carbon a year as carbon monoxide, methane, and carbon dioxide, as well as nitrogen oxides, with ozone as a by-product. Crutzen urged that more resources be devoted to long-term atmospheric research in the tropics.

Air Pollution. On February 12 the World Health Organization (WHO) reported in Geneva that a study had shown that smog claimed 350 lives a year in Paris and that pollution, mainly from vehicle exhausts, made it 10 to 100 times more dangerous to live in a city than inside a nuclear power plant. Air pollution, according to the study, causes cancer and lung diseases and might be reducing male potency.

Concern grew over PM10, a category of airborne particles less than 10 micrometres (millionths of a metre) in size. In October 1995 WHO reported that there was no safe level for exposure to PM10 and calculated that in a city of one million people, a three-day episode of PM10 at 50 micrograms per cubic metre would produce 1,000 additional asthma attacks and four deaths. In Britain the Expert Panel on Air Quality Standards published a review in November 1995 in which it found that PM10 caused 2,000–10,000 British deaths a year. A second report, from the Committee on the Medical Effects of Air Pollutants, published on the same day, warned that although there was little evidence that particulate matter caused cancer, the particles contained substances that might do so. The chief medical officer, Kenneth Calman, announced a new maximum limit of 50 micrograms of particulates per cubic metre of air averaged over 24 hours. According to *Airborne*

Particulate Matter in the United Kingdom, a report from the Quality of Urban Air Review Group published in May 1996, that level was exceeded in London on 139 days during 1992–94, about 86% of the PM10 being from road traffic, while in Oxford levels had been found five times higher than the limit. At the same time, a report by the Natural Resources Defense Council on 239 U.S. cities estimated that about 64,000 U.S. deaths annually from cardiopulmonary causes could be attributable to particulate air pollution.

On September 25 the British company PowerGen announced that it was to close its Ince power station, near Chester, for commercial reasons. Ince was the only British power station burning Orimulsion, a mixture of bitumen and water that had been described as "the world's dirtiest fuel." PowerGen said it would not be using Orimulsion again in the foreseeable future.

Acid Rain. It was reported in September that 22 studies in 12 countries published by the European Forest Institute showed that tree growth in Europe had increased over the past few decades. Although the studies found no clear growth trend for trees in far northern Europe, there was a positive trend in most of central Europe and some of southern Europe. Faster growth might be due to increased soil nitrogen, carbon dioxide from car exhausts, local climate changes, or the fact that many of the forests studied were relatively young. Heinrich Spiecker, a coeditor of the report, said he expected no catastrophic loss of forest in the near future. Others disagreed. Hubert Weinzierl, of the German conservation group BUND, suggested that increased tree growth might be a response to damage. This view was supported by the Forest Ecosystems Research Center at the University of Göttingen, whose scientific secretary said increased tree growth is associated with chronic shock and weakness. The forestry department of the German Ministry of Food, Agriculture and Forestry found that 60% of trees on the 5,000 sites under observation were losing leaves or needles and therefore were damaged. The European Commission published a survey of forest conditions in the EU that discovered 20% of all trees at specified sites showing clear signs of leaf or needle damage. Damage was most extensive in central Europe.

Studies of the Hubbard Brook Experimental Forest in New Hampshire, conducted over 30 years and published in April, found that although sulfur dioxide emissions had fallen in the U.S., Canada, and the countries of the EU, the acidity of surface waters had not declined as expected. Scientists found that the acid waters had leached base mineral ions from the soil and thus reduced buffering.

In a letter to the International Maritime Organization in June, Jan Thompson of the executive body overseeing the Convention on Long-Range Transboundary Air Pollution warned that sulfur pollution from ships was increasing so rapidly it might soon negate improvements made by reducing emissions from power stations. Thompson said that by 2010 total emissions from merchant fleets could more than double and that in some sensitive areas ships could be one of the main contributors to sulfur deposition, or even the primary source.

Fresh Water. The Xinhua news agency in China announced on October 1 that all paper mills on the upper reaches of the Chang Jiang (Yangtze River) were to be closed in order to reduce pollution and minimize the effects of the Three Gorges Dam project. A budget of about 90 million yuan had been allocated for an environmental monitoring network.

In its biannual report, published in July, the International Joint Commission for the Great Lakes recommended that the U.S. and Canadian governments impose a total ban on persistent organic pollutants. These reached the Great Lakes from the air, often traveling great distances. Some had been identified as coming from as far away as California and Florida.

It was reported in January that a pipeline spill of some 31,000 gal of oil in the southern Urals had polluted drinking water in several villages in the Bashkortostan republic, 965 km (600 mi) from Moscow, and had threatened to contaminate the Kama River.

Dioxin. In December 1995 the U.S. House Committee on Science heard arguments concerning the toxicity of low levels of exposure to dioxin. A report from the EPA said that even at the background levels present in most human bodies, dioxin can cause cancer and infertility and interfere with fetal development. Critics of the report, who maintained that dioxin is harmless at low exposure levels, were said by environmentalists to be representing the interests of industries producing dioxin.

Coalite Products of Bolsover, Derbyshire, Eng., was fined £150,000 and ordered to pay court costs in Leicester Crown Court on February 21 in a case brought by the Inspectorate of Pollution. When it burned large amounts of chemical waste at low temperature, in breach of its own guidelines, for four days in 1990 and again in June and August 1991, Coalite had failed to prevent potentially harmful dioxin emissions from its waste-incineration plant. It was believed that human health had not been harmed.

In July an internal report by the Japanese Ministry of Health and Welfare proposed bringing down Japanese limits for dioxin exposure. Japanese limits, of 100 picograms per kilogram body weight per day, were 10 times higher than the maximum level recommended by WHO, but the ministry had no immediate plans to reduce them.

Toxic Waste. The U.S. Department of the Interior called in February for a further study of proposals to dump low-level radioactive waste at a site in Ward Valley, California. The four-to-six-month study, to be conducted by the Lawrence Livermore National Laboratory, Livermore, Calif., would monitor the movement of radioisotopes deposited by weapons fallout, to make sure that waste leachates would not contaminate groundwater or the Colorado River. The proposals had already been argued back and forth for nearly 10 years.

It was reported in August that the Chinese authorities had refused entry to a shipment of 200 metric tons of plastic waste from the U.S. intended for recycling. The waste was returned to the trader in Hong Kong who had negotiated the deal, but the Hong Kong authorities also refused to accept it, saying it should be returned to the U.S. The situation arose because China was faster than both Hong Kong and the U.S. in incorporating into its law the Basel Convention on the Control of Transboundary Movements of Hazardous Wastes and Their Disposal, signed in 1989, which required all exported waste to have an export permit as well as import approval from the destination country. Chinese authorities said nine cargoes of scrap metal were also being held prior to their rejection because they were contaminated with rubbish, including medical waste.

Lead. In March a report from a University of Michigan team said most children in African cities had blood-lead levels high enough to cause neurological damage and in some cities more than 90% of children suffered from lead poisoning. Africa accounted for 20% of the global emission of atmospheric lead, the relatively high figure being due partly to severe reductions elsewhere.

In September a study by the Warentest Foundation of 9,000 samples of drinking water collected throughout Germany since 1994 reported that those from areas throughout the former East Germany and also from around Hamburg contained lead at concentrations up to 10 times the German legal limit.

Dirty air lies over Mexico City, where winter thermal inversions have trapped pollutants from large numbers of automobiles and industries. A World Health Organization report in 1996 claimed that air pollution made living in a city more dangerous than living in a nuclear power plant.

Animal bones lie on a dry stretch of Lake Nakuru's bed in Kenya. The lake, part of a national park and once a major site for wildlife that included flocks of migrating flamingos, was mysteriously shrinking and becoming polluted as a result of tourism and the growth of a nearby industrial town.

The U.S. Consumer Product Safety Commission announced on October 1 that despite an 18-year ban on lead-based paints, playgrounds across the country had dangerously high levels of lead from paint. A study of 26 playgrounds in 13 cities found unacceptably high levels of lead from paint in 16 playgrounds in 11 cities. In addition to its test results, the commission said it had received reports of lead paint in 125 playgrounds in 11 cities. Most of the paint remained from before the 1978 ban, and in some cases paint had been used that was intended for industrial purposes.

Environmental Estrogens. Concern grew during the year that chemicals released into the environment might mimic estrogens in their physiological effects, reducing male fertility in a range of species. Results of research published in June indicated that although individually the estrogenic substances were much less potent than estrogens occurring naturally, when two or more of them were tested in combination, they were 10 to 1,600 times more potent. It was reported in September that British industrial discharges of two groups of estrogenic compounds, phthalates and nonylphenols, possibly exceeded proposed new safety limits. Scientists from the British and Scottish environmental agencies said discharges of these compounds from textile and electronics factories might be high enough to cause sex changes in fish.

Asbestos. In July the French government banned almost all production and use of asbestos from January 1997 after INSERM, the national medical research agency, reported that at least 1,950 people would die in 1996, about 750 from mesothelioma and 1,200 from lung cancer, all as a result of past exposure and nearly all work-related. On July 14 Pres. Jacques Chirac announced

that about 38,000 students and 10,000 staff were to be moved out of the Jussieu campus of Paris VI and Paris VII universities by the end of 1997 because the 26 high-rise blocks forming the campus were contaminated by asbestos. A few days later François Bayrou, the education minister, refuted the president's statement, saying there would be no relocation of staff or students and no limit to the state's financial commitment for removing the asbestos. The cost was estimated at $176 million to $200 million.

Chernobyl. "Health Consequences of the Chernobyl and Other Radiological Accidents," a conference held in Geneva in November 1995 and attended by about 600 scientists, public health specialists, and policy makers from 59 countries, discussed studies of the health effects of the 1986 accident. These revealed three main areas of concern: the increase in psychological disorders, especially among workers dealing with the accident and people living in highly contaminated areas; thyroid cancer among children; and illnesses that were expected to emerge in the future, including leukemia, breast cancer, bladder cancer, and kidney diseases. The accident had caused severe radiation sickness in 134 people and 30 deaths and had exposed about 5 million people to significant radiation. Dillwyn Williams, professor of histopathology at the University of Cambridge, warned that the 680 cases of thyroid cancer detected in children since 1986 in Belarus, Ukraine, and Russia might increase and that up to 40% of the children exposed to the highest levels of fallout when they were under a year old could develop thyroid cancer as adults. He said babies were 30 times more likely to contract the disease than children 10 years old at the time. Most of the 680 thyroid cancer cases in children

had been treated successfully, but figures presented at a meeting in Vienna on April 8 showed this illness increasing, especially among children, in areas of Ukraine, Belarus, and Russia close to the reactor site. In 1995, 133 cases were reported in Belarus and Ukraine in children under 15, compared with 121 in 1994 and an average of 5 cases a year prior to the accident.

At a Moscow meeting of 45 nongovernmental organizations in April, Aleksey Yablokov, head of the Centre for Russian Environmental Policy, said the medical consequences of the accident had been seriously underestimated; data gathered by scientists from the former Soviet Union showed biological alterations at many levels in exposed populations and an increased incidence of many ailments. Western scientists were cautious because of the lack of controls and uncertainties about diagnoses. It was reported in April that genetic mutations had been detected in people and in two species of vole exposed to radiation after the accident.   (MICHAEL ALLABY)

WILDLIFE CONSERVATION

In 1996 as part of a last-ditch attempt to increase the size of the western flock of Siberian cranes (*Grus leucogeranus*), two captive-raised adult males from the U.S. were released in Iran to join the small flock (8–11 birds) that wintered in the Caspian lowlands. If they paired with wild females and flew north, transmitters attached to the birds would enable the unknown breeding grounds in Russia to be located. The only other flock of the western population, which wintered at Keoladeo National Park in India, had been feared extinct when the birds did not appear for two consecutive winters in 1993–94 and 1994–95, but four birds arrived in the winter of 1995–96. Six captive-raised California condors (*Gymnogyps californianus*) were released in Arizona north of the Grand Canyon in early December.

In February scientists in Chile located what might be the last remaining viable wild population of the liana *Berberidopsis corallina,* which grew only in Chile and was essential to rural basket weavers. Its survival in the wild had been jeopardized by clearance of lowland forest, and seed was collected as a first step to restoring the species.

A network of sites to protect some 60 species of birds that migrate from the Arctic down eastern Asia to Australia was launched in March at a meeting of the 92 signatories to the Ramsar Convention (on Wetlands of International Importance). Australia, China, Hong Kong, Japan, New Zealand, and the Philippines were expected to nominate sites for the scheme, which would be known as the East Asian–Australasian Shorebird Reserve Network.

In the spring Russia established a new 4,200-sq km (1,620-sq mi) nature reserve in the Severnaya Zemlya archipelago, including Domashniy Island, home to the world's largest colony of ivory gulls (*Pagophila eburnea*). Wapusk in northern Manitoba became Canada's 37th national park. It contained one of the world's largest known polar bear (*Ursus maritimus*) denning sites and provided shelter for thousands of migratory waterfowl and shorebirds. New Zealand established the Kahurangi National Park in northwestern Nelson; it contained some of the country's rarest birds and 100 plant species seen nowhere else.

In May the Congo bay owl (*Phodilus prigoginei*) was seen for the first time since 1951 in the Itombwe forest in eastern Zaire. The forest was considered to be the most important area for bird conservation in Africa, but it was unprotected and was threatened by logging, hunting, and agriculture. Other rediscoveries reported in 1996 included the lesser masked owl (*Tyto sororcula;* not recorded since 1922) in the Tanimbar archipelago of Indonesia and Edwards's pheasant (*Lophura edwardsi;* not seen since 1928) in Bach Ma National Park in cen-

tral Vietnam. In October 1995 the Tibetan red deer (a subspecies of *Cervus elaphus*), which had been thought to be extinct, was discovered in southeastern Tibet. Most of the deer were in scattered remnant herds, but one viable population was discovered in hills where there were good prospects for its conservation, and moves were made to establish a reserve for the animal in cooperation with local residents.

The future of the endangered Madagascar tortoise, or angonoka (*Geochelone yniphora*), was threatened by the theft of two breeding females and 73 young from the world's only captive-breeding centre for the species, 145 km (90 mi) from Baly Bay, Madagascar, the only place in the world where the species occurred in the wild. On May 31 Malaysia and the Philippines established the world's first conservation area for marine turtles to cross international borders. The Turtle Islands Heritage Protected Area included nine islands that housed the largest green turtle (*Chelonia mydas*) nesting population in Southeast Asia and an important hawksbill turtle (*Eretmochelys imbricata*) nesting ground.

Long-term turtle-protection efforts appeared to have paid off in Mexico, where there was evidence of rising populations of olive ridleys (*Lepidochelys olivacea*) in Oaxaca and of Kemp's ridleys (*L. kempii*) at Rancho Nuevo, Tamaulipas. The first documented case of a sea turtle species' returning to nest at a site where it had been experimentally imprinted was recorded. Two Kemp's ridleys, which had been hatched from eggs laid at Rancho Nuevo and reared, tagged, and released in the 1980s at Padre Island, Texas, returned to nest at the release beach.

News of the leatherback (*Dermochelys coriacea*) was not so good; numbers crashed in Mexico, where half the world's leatherbacks nest. Only 500 turtles nested in the 1995–96 season, compared with 6,500 in 1984. Numbers of this species had been falling steadily worldwide, and it was possible that the population had reached a critical level.

In June it was reported that 20,000 Swainson's hawks (*Buteo swainsoni*) had died after feeding on grasshoppers at their

winter feeding grounds in the La Pampa region of Argentina. Organophosphate pesticides used in intensive crop cultivation were thought to be to blame. In July U.S. scientists announced that the cause of an epidemic that killed 158 of the 2,600 manatees (*Trichechus manatus*) in Florida in March and April was a toxin produced by the red tide that had been affecting Florida's west coast.

Two new species of mammals were reported in August; a new species of bushy-tailed cloud rat, *Crateromys heaneyi,* from Panay Island in the Philippines brought the total number of known bushy-tailed cloud rats to four, all from the Philippines, and a new marmoset in the southern Amazon, between the Tapajós and Madeira rivers in Brazil, had been named *Callithrix sateri* after the Sateri people, on whose land it was discovered.

Rhino horns weighing a total of 240 kg (530 lb) and worth almost £3 million were seized by police in London in September. The horns, the largest seizure ever recorded, were believed to be destined for Taiwanese, Hong Kong, and Chinese communities in the U.K. and were probably from private collections gathered from animals shot earlier in the century.

During the year new categories and criteria developed by IUCN-the World Conservation Union were used to evaluate the status of the world's wild animal species. The results were published in the IUCN Red List of Threatened Animals in October at the World Conservation Congress in Montreal.   (JACQUI M. MORRIS)

ZOOS

The cause of the tragic fire at the Philadelphia Zoo on Christmas Eve 1995, the worst zoo fire in U.S. history, was identified as a malfunction in an electrical heat trace cable used to prevent pipes from freezing. The fire destroyed the World of Primates building and 23 of its inhabitants, including the longest-established gorilla family in the United States, which died from smoke inhalation. The zoo immediately began fundraising efforts to build a new primate house, estimated to cost about $21 million. Donations poured in so quickly that officials planned to begin construction early in 1997 and open the new facility in spring 1999.

Other primate exhibits around the world made headlines in 1996. On August 16 at the Brookfield Zoo near Chicago, Binti Jua, a female West African gorilla, rescued a three-year-old boy who had slipped and fallen into the primate pavilion. Before anyone could reach the child, the gorilla scooped him up into her arms. She cradled and protected the boy from the other gorillas as she carried him to the entrance of the enclosure and deposited him at the feet of astounded zoo personnel. At the Copenhagen Zoo, space was made in the primate house for a unique display: two *Homo sapiens.* A Danish couple moved into temporary living quarters at the zoo with the intention of reminding visitors of their close kinship to the apes.

Two giant pandas arrived from China in September to reside at the San Diego (Calif.) Zoo for the next 12 years. The pandas, the first to be allowed into the United States since 1993, were on loan as part of the American Zoo and Aquarium Associ-

The Madagascar tortoise (*Geochelone yniphora*), one of the world's most endangered species, with only a few hundred thought to remain, does not reach sexual maturity until age 20. Seventy-five Madagascar tortoises—2 adult females and 73 hatchlings—were stolen in 1996 from Ampijoroa in Madagascar, the only place where they had been successfully bred in captivity, probably to be sold to collectors of rare reptiles.

DON REID—WILDLIFE PRESERVATION TRUST INTERNATIONAL

Binti Jua, an eight-year-old gorilla raised mostly by humans in San Francisco and on loan to Chicago's Brookfield Zoo, prepares to pick up a three-year-old boy after he had fallen into her enclosure. In a remarkable show of interspecies goodwill, the gorilla, with her infant daughter clinging to her side, then carried the boy to the door so that zoo attendants could retrieve him.

ation Giant Panda Species Survival Plan, a program dedicated to conservation, education, research, and captive breeding. In return, the San Diego Zoo was to donate $1 million annually to habitat-preservation projects in China. Six California condors bred at the Los Angeles Zoo and at the Peregrine Fund World Center for Birds of Prey in Boise, Idaho, were released into northern Arizona by the U.S. Fish and Wildlife Service in December. About four hectares (ten acres) of federal land around the site were closed temporarily to protect the birds until they dispersed.

In efforts to enhance contributions to wildlife conservation, research, and education and to provide more realistic environmental settings for their animals, many zoos continued to create exhibits that represented major ecosystems. In exhibits such as the RainForest at the Cleveland (Ohio) Metroparks Zoo, which opened in 1992, complex relationships between plants, animals, and environment were explored. To celebrate its centennial the Denver (Colo.) Zoological Gardens opened Primate Panorama, a new naturalistic wildlife habitat, in 1996.

Unfortunately, a number of zoos remained financially strapped and unable to make necessary improvements. One such was the zoo in Santiago, Chile, built in 1920, never renovated, and considered one of the worst facilities in Latin America by many veterinarians and animal rights activists. The zoo received national attention in 1996 when a pair of lions twice escaped from their cages.   (MARY JANE FRIEDRICH)

BOTANICAL GARDENS

The development of international policies to harmonize the responses to the Convention on Biological Diversity (CBD) domi-

nated the international activities concerning botanical gardens during 1996. At the third meeting of the Conference of Parties to the CBD, held in Buenos Aires, Arg., an international working group was established.

A conference for botanical gardens in Latin America and the Caribbean was held in Caxias do Sul, Brazil. The program included courses on collection maintenance and botanical illustration. Also in that region, about 80% of the collections of the 100-year-old Cienfuegos Botanic Garden in Cuba was badly damaged or destroyed by a hurricane in October. The garden then launched an international appeal for funds for restoration. In Paraná, Arg., a workshop was held at the National University of Entre Ríos to plan the development of its new botanical garden.

Work was completed by Botanic Gardens Conservation International (BGCI) on a new version of the International Transfer Format for botanic garden living plant records. This international standard was used to help facilitate the transfer of electronic data between botanic gardens.

Meetings of a European joint advisory group to BGCI and the International Association of Botanic Gardens were held in Pisa, Italy, and Córdoba, Spain, to strengthen links between European botanical gardens and between the gardens and the European Union. Representatives from the major botanical gardens of the EU nations were included. Also during the year in Europe, the Dutch Botanic Gardens Foundation produced a catalogue of the 7,000 conifer trees in cultivation in Dutch botanic gardens. The Lyon (France) Botanic Garden celebrated its 200th anniversary by serving as host of a congress of the French botanical gardens association.

A project in the U.K. to establish a national botanic garden in Wales received

funding from the U.K. national lottery. A new greenhouse display on plant evolution was opened at the Royal Botanic Gardens, Kew, near London. The Cambridge University Botanic Garden celebrated its 150th anniversary. A new plant-collections network for Britain and Ireland, PlantNet, was launched at a conference held at the Oxford University Botanic Garden, which also celebrated its 375th anniversary during the year.

The Australian Network for Plant Conservation produced new guidelines for germ plasm (the bearers of heredity) conservation in Australia. Workshops on the development of computer databases for botanical garden collections in Indonesia were held at two gardens, in Java and Bali. An international workshop on biodiversity conservation and evaluation took place at the Tropical Botanic Garden and Research Institute, Trivandrum, India.

The Center for Plant Conservation (CPC), headquartered in St. Louis, Mo., developed an emergency plan to prevent the genetic loss of 110 of Hawaii's most critically endangered species. The CPC linked 28 U.S. botanical gardens and arboretums to maintain a collection of 500 of the nation's rarest plants.

Great Britain's Darwin Initiative for the Survival of Species funded BGCI for a three-year project to prepare computer software for Russian botanical gardens and to hold a series of training workshops. A workshop on "Institutional Management for Botanic Gardens in the Former Soviet Union" was held at the Central Siberian Botanic Garden in Novosibirsk.

(PETER S. WYSE JACKSON)

GARDENING

In nonindustrialized parts of Asia, flower gardens were proliferating in concert with the opening of the economy to private enterprise and the increased availability and affordability of food. In China a large flower market opened near the Temple of Heaven in Beijing, and an even larger one was planned in a southeastern suburb that had traditionally housed those who for centuries had provided the flowers used in the Imperial Palace.

The growth in floral popularity, partly fueled by young Chinese suitors who began observing Valentine's Day, prompted peasants in rural areas to turn over garden space to flowers that would be sold in Beijing. The rise of a significant middle class in India affected gardening there as well. With sufficient income to add fresh vegetables to their diet on a regular basis, Indian consumers were driving the creation of a produce packing and shipping industry resembling that of the United States. The use of hybrid vegetable seed by growers in India, as in the U.S., swelled from 25% to about 45% of the market.

India's middle class was also increasing its purchases of ornamental plants, especially foliage plants, which were easier to maintain in India's diverse but almost entirely hot climates. A whole industry of small nursery operators sprouted to provide these plants. In addition, landscape contractors were hired to create private gardens and yard landscapes, an activity that was previously restricted, for the most part, to public institutions.

The 1995–96 winter in Europe was very hard, with cold temperatures, little snow cover, and a late spring all the way from the Baltic region to Hungary and Romania. As a result, many perennials died back, production was reduced for many nurseries, and consumer sales were delayed until late in the season. Among Central and Eastern European suppliers, however, sales were robust, owing primarily to the rise of a middle class with money to spend and an interest in improving their lives and property.

Four gold medals were awarded in 1996 by Fleuroselect, the European-based international seed-testing organization. A hybrid, *Delphinium* Centurion Sky Blue, was the first of its kind to receive this prestigious award. It was taller, 90–120 cm (35–47 in), than many of the newly introduced delphiniums, and it bloomed the first year from seed. The flowers were a clear, light blue with a white centre, or "eye."

Celosia argentea cristata Bombay Purple was slightly taller and was bred primarily for professional growers of cut flowers. The plant was extremely uniform in habit, and the blooms, which were triangular, 15 cm (6 in) on a side, were borne singly on erect stems.

The sun-loving hybrid *Gazania splendens* Daybreak Bright Orange was a bedding plant. This low-growing South African native, the second of the Daybreak series to win a Fleuroselect gold medal, reached only 23 cm (9 in) but had a spread of almost 30 cm (12 in). The flowers were bright orange, with a narrow brown ring around the ochre centre, and were about 8 cm (3 in) in diameter.

Myosotis sylvatica Rosylva was a biennial. The small, 6–8-mm (0.2–0.3-in), flowers were borne in unusually tight florets, appeared earlier and lasted longer than other forget-me-nots, and were pink rather than blue. The plants grew to about 20 cm (8 in) tall and had a spread of 25 cm (10 in).

The winter was also very harsh in the eastern U.S., where gardens got off to their slowest start in decades. The cold affected many producers and marketers of garden seeds and plants, though once the weather warmed up late in the season, sales returned to near normal levels. Consolidation in the seed industry continued at a rapid pace.

All-America Selections (AAS) awarded medals to three vegetable entries, two flower entries, and one bedding plant entry, *Zinnia angustifolia* Crystal White. The small-flowered, heat-tolerant, long-blooming relative to the common *Zinnia elegans* had a high tolerance to most common zinnia diseases and grew only to about 25 cm tall. Of the flower winners, Prestige Scarlet *Celosia* was one of a new type called "multiflora" celosia, which provided more and smaller blooms than older types. Prestige Scarlet's deep-coloured blooms, about 90–100 mm (3.5–3.9 in) in diameter, were borne on plants 40–50 cm (16–20 in) tall and were useful for both fresh and dried bouquets.

Gypsy baby's breath, *Gypsophila muralis,* was a dwarf that grew to only 25–40 cm (10–16 in) instead of the 75–100 cm (29–39 in) more common for the perennial form *G. paniculata* yet was more substantial than the annual form *G. elegans*. The 0.6-cm (0.25-in) stellarlike pink blooms were borne on bushy plants with finely textured foliage ideal for containers.

AAS awards for vegetables in the 1997 season went to Dynamo hybrid cabbage, a green variety that matured in about 70 days and was resistant to Fusarium wilt (yellows) and stressful growing conditions. Okra Cajun Delight was a new okra hybrid suitable even for northern gardens. The pods were ready to harvest at the 7–10-cm (3–4-in) stage only 55 days after being transplanted into fully warmed soil.

An herb, Siam Queen Thai basil, an improved form of the standard Licorice basil, captured the final AAS award. Plants were stocky, reaching a mature height of 60–91 cm (24–36 in) and spread of about 60 cm, with dense, dark violet flowers. First harvest could occur only 45–50 days after transplantation into thoroughly warm soil.

(SHEPHERD OGDEN)

See also Agriculture and Food Supplies; Business and Industry Review: *Energy;* Life Sciences.

This article updates the *Macropædia* articles CONSERVATION OF NATURAL RESOURCES; GARDENING AND HORTICULTURE.

Old roses, with their distinctive fragrances and flower forms, were becoming popular again among gardeners. Some growers even searched old gardens, cemeteries, and ruins to find the flowers, prized for their differences from modern hybrids.

Fashions

The spring-summer 1996 international
women's ready-to-wear collections were
marked by the absence of a singular definitive look. Designers in London, Paris, Milan, and New York presented a number
of options, including bright colours, particularly orange and lime green, and bold-
patterned clothes. Designer Tom Ford produced what was christened "hippie chic" for
the Italian fashion house Gucci. The style
featured lace and velvet caftans and was
reportedly inspired by the 1960s socialite
Talitha Getty. Most talked-about were two
wardrobe alternatives: a casual, wearable
style that the press called "no-fuss chic"
and a more frivolous look that came to be
known as "good taste/bad taste."

No-fuss chic took a simple approach to
dressing. It was based on a wardrobe of
neat, interchangeable separates: a pair of
tailored trousers shown with or without a
matching jacket, a crisp white shirt, or a
sleek sweater cut close to the body, and
stylish yet sensible shoes—either flats or
footwear with "block" heels. Karl Lagerfeld at Chanel showed the look best, sending models onto the runway in a casual
mix-and-match ensemble: loosely cut pastel
tweed Chanel jackets, cotton piqué shirts,
and chinos.

Meanwhile, good taste/bad taste featured
the mixing of fashion elements. Sharply tailored items like skirts and trousers were
cut from cheap functional fabrics such as
polyester, and textiles were printed with
odd, clashing patterns in off colours—bile
green, purple, brown, and cream. Such
clothes were shown mostly by such young
designers as Jean Colonna, Anna Sui, and
Gianni Versace's sister Donatella. Miuccia
Prada, the foremost purveyor of the style,
produced a collection of "geek" prints that
fell flat and confused usually complimen-
tary critics. Her new designs were in sharp
contrast to those of previous seasons: subtle, tailored clothes often cut from couture
fabrics.

At the international men's collection, the
spring-summer styles were decidedly toned
down following a year of hit-and-miss flam-
boyance. Men adopted styles to suit their
own lives and occupations, which made the
designer-dictated wardrobe obsolete.

For the night of the Academy Award
presentations, U.S. actress Sharon Stone,
a symbol of Hollywood glamour followed
the men's lead. She rejected ensembles of-

Psychedelic dress by Jean-Paul
Gaultier
PIERRE VAUTHEY—SYGMA

fered to her by Valentino and Vera Wang,
two prominent fashion designers. Instead,
Stone opted for a mix of her own clothes:
a Gap black turtleneck, a floor-length Ar-
mani evening coat, and a pair of diamond
earrings. Meanwhile, 21-year old model-
actress Chloe Sevigny, the star of Larry
Clark's *Kids* and the model for Prada's

diffusion line Miu Miu, explained the hip
ideal for young people to London's *Evening
Standard* newspaper. "Just day to day," she
said, "I'm trying to be antifashionable."

Fashion, it seemed, was out of fashion.
After years of offering a form of mass entertainment, the industry suffered from a
wave of negative publicity. Clothes shopping was no longer a diversion in the U.S.,
where corporate downsizing coupled with
a loss of interest in fashion among baby
boomers depressed the apparel industry.

Other sectors of the industry were
plagued by a series of setbacks and scandals. Terrorist bombings in Paris and the
necessary security checks at the spring-
summer pret-a-porter collections caused a

general feeling of unease among those in
attendance. Then, in early winter, a series
of general strikes hit France, threatening
to delay production involved in the spring-
summer couture collections that were presented in January.

In New York City in January, Barneys,
the high-fashion chain of stores run by the
Pressman family, sought protection from
creditors under Chapter 11 of the U.S.
Bankruptcy Code. Barneys had been a fashion leader in the U.S. during the 1980s,
with an innovative approach to advertising,
merchandising, and the creation of stylish
shop interiors. Problems also beset the New
York-based Council of Fashion Designers
of America, which had organized the stag-

ing of fashion collections held biannually at tent shows in Manhattan's Bryant Park. A few weeks before the autumn-winter collections were set to debut, Ralph Lauren and Donna Karan backed out without notice or much explanation, announcing that they would show their work in more "intimate" venues. Such high-profile designers as Joan Vass, Badgely Mischka, Todd Oldham, and Ghost followed them. Some claimed that the cost of producing a tent-sized show was too high (an estimated $100,000 for an hour-long presentation) and that the presence of lower-priced apparel lines diminished the feeling of exclusivity. The general consensus was that the circuslike atmosphere created by staging fashion shows in large venues such as tents and even in the Carrousel du Louvre, a Paris structure that was expressly built for that purpose but was rejected by most French designers for their autumn-winter shows and couture collections, no longer suited the more minimal, less overtly glamorous spirit of fashion.

In the spring the fashion media were involved in two scandals. Supermodel Naomi Campbell was reportedly "highly insulted" and unhappy with the representation given black models after the editor of American *Vogue,* Anna Wintour, relocated Campbell's cover photo to the inside fold and featured white model Nikki Taylor on the cover instead. In its assessment of the situation, *The Times* (London) reported that sales figures had been known to drop when a black model was featured on the cover of a women's fashion magazine.

In London controversy erupted after pictures of the very thin, partially exposed form of model Trish Goff appeared in the June issue of British *Vogue.* In response the Omega Watch Corp., a major source of *Vogue*'s advertising revenues, announced that it would stop placing ads in the magazine, claiming that officials were angered by the "anorexic proportions" of the "skeletal models" featured in the magazine. Though Omega retreated from its stance one week after the scandal went public, the incident highlighted the emaciated images that were often presented to the public.

"No-fuss chic" by Chanel

PHOTOGRAPHS, DAN LECCA

The womanly proportions of the '80s supermodel had by 1996 disappeared from fashion's spotlight. In September German model Claudia Schiffer announced her retirement. Now popular on the autumn-winter runways were models the *New York Times* summed up as "skinny, white, young, and devoid of personality." They suited "heroin chic," the glamorous junkie look that proved popular with stylists and makeup artists who put together the autumn-winter shows for Vivienne Westwood, Helmut Lang, and Ann Demeulemeester, among others. Reportedly inspired by the drug culture, on view in the film *Trainspotting* and the Broadway musical *Rent,* this style raised questions about drug habits among models and further highlighted the turbulence within the industry.

Innovation was hard to find at the autumn-winter ready-to-wear and couture collections. Karl Lagerfeld had revived black lycra leggings, a fashion element that most critics had hoped women left behind with the '80s. Meanwhile, the dominant trend

"Heroin chic" by Helmut Lang

among most designers of ready-to-wear was a '70s style: a long lean silhouette, featuring maxicoats, long skirts, knee-high boots, and a slimmer variation of bell bottoms, known now as boot-cut trousers. Rich colours such as plum, chocolate, and navy replaced basic black. Also shown were military looks, ranging from drab olive green trousers and sophisticated tailored jackets featuring epaulets and gold accessories to androgynous tailored trouser suits, styles that belonged to previous seasons.

The '70s also became a dominant theme in autumn-winter men's collections, as symbolized by such sartorial statements as fur- and faux fur-trimmed coats, jackets with sharply emphasized shoulders or those with wide lapels, and boot-cut trousers. More important was a distinct move away from loose, unconstructed clothes. Tailoring made a return, and tapering, which made garments and suiting slimmer fitting, was introduced. Particularly influential on the men's front

Design by Alexander McQueen

was the U.S. designer Ralph Lauren, whose two lines—Purple Label and Blue Label—featured tailored one-button and double-breasted suits worn with solid-coloured ties and white shirts.

Midyear, fashion mourned the loss of two trendsetters. The U.S.-born, Paris-based model Wallis Franken, the muse and wife of French fashion designer Claude Montana, was found dead outside her Paris apartment, apparently a suicide. In August British designer Ossie Clark (*see* OBITUARIES) was found murdered in his apartment in London. His lover, Diego Cogolato, was later arrested and charged with murder. Though living close to the poverty line at the time of his death, Clark had been one of the most influential British designers of the late '60s. He had dressed Mick and Bianca Jagger and designed the clothes for the film *Bonnie and Clyde,* among other projects.

Despite the bleak outlook, there was reason to celebrate. The year 1996 marked both the 50th anniversary of the introduction of Louis Reard's bikini and the 30th anniversary of Yves Saint Laurent's "le smoking," a classic tailored tuxedo pantsuit for women.

British fashion scored a triple coup. The London-educated designer John Galliano (*see* BIOGRAPHIES) assumed the role of designer in chief at the French fashion house Givenchy in January before replacing Gianfranco Ferre as designer in chief of couture and ready-to-wear at Christian Dior in October. (Both fashion houses were owned by the French company Louis Vuitton Moët Hennessy.) Meanwhile, the London-based avant-garde designer Alexander McQueen replaced Galliano at Givenchy and was later named British Fashion Designer of the Year. His "bumsters," trousers that revealed the top half of the buttocks, helped revive the long, lean silhouette that proved successful for many designers. British model Stella Tennant became "the official face of Chanel." (BRONWYN COSGRAVE)

See also Business and Industry Review: *Apparel.*

This article updates the *Macropædia* article DRESS AND ADORNMENT.

Health and Disease

Health issues played a prominent role in politics around the world in 1996. In the United States, Pres. Bill Clinton made the prevention of tobacco use by children a campaign issue. His Republican opponent, Bob Dole, citing statistics showing a resurgence in teenage drug use, charged the Clinton administration with failure to combat drug abuse among American youth. While Dole opposed abortion, Clinton championed abortion rights and vetoed a controversial bill banning late-term "partial birth" abortions. There was bipartisan support, however, for legislation to make health insurance "portable" when workers change or lose jobs.

Amid new revelations about exposure of U.S. troops to chemical weapons in the 1991 Persian Gulf War, Congress and a White House commission investigated critics' charges that the Pentagon had failed to respond adequately to Gulf veterans' health

GARY CLARK

An *Aedes aegypti* mosquito feeds on human blood. This species carries infectious diseases, including dengue and yellow fever, outbreaks of which were increasing.

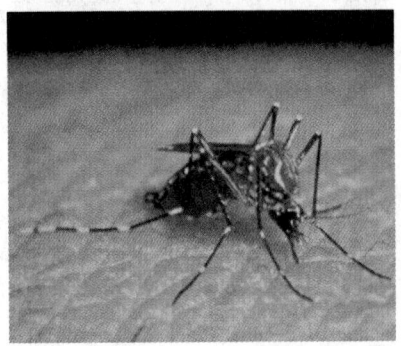

problems. Great Britain, the Czech Republic, and Slovakia also announced that they would broaden investigations of their Gulf troops' health complaints.

In November Russian Pres. Boris Yeltsin underwent coronary artery bypass surgery to treat the severe heart disease that had threatened his personal and political health throughout the year. In Great Britain the government of Prime Minister John Major faced a crisis in consumer confidence as evidence mounted of a link between "mad cow" disease and a new form of a fatal human brain disorder; fears about the safety of the food supply led many European countries to ban the import of British beef. Another controversy erupted in July when fertility clinics in England were required to discard thousands of unclaimed frozen human embryos that had been stored for five years, the maximum time allowed by law.

Genetics. The pace of the Human Genome Project accelerated in 1996. In October scientists from the U.S., Canada, Europe, and Japan published the most complete map to date, detailing the sequence and location of more than 16,000 of the estimated 50,000–100,000 human genes. The new map, available on the Internet through the U.S. National Library of Medicine (http://www.ncbi.nlm.nih.gov/science96/), was expected to be a valuable tool in the search for genes that predispose individuals to disease.

Progress continued to be made in locating specific disease-related genes. Scientists in Seattle, Wash., identified the gene for Werner's syndrome, a rare inherited disease marked by premature aging. Affected individuals usually die in their 40s of heart attacks or cancer. Further study of the gene, located on chromosome 8, was expected to yield clues to the normal aging process.

After a four-year search U.S., Australian, and Swedish researchers cloned a tumour suppressor gene that, when mutated, was believed to be responsible for basal-cell skin cancers. A research team in Philadel-

phia identified a gene that may be involved in esophageal, stomach, and colon cancers, and U.S. and Swedish scientists announced the discovery of a gene believed to predispose men to cancer of the prostate. U.S. and Italian researchers identified a site on chromosome 4 that is linked to some cases of Parkinson's disease, a common neurodegenerative disorder.

A collaborative study by researchers in several countries revealed the gene responsible for Friedreich's ataxia, a disorder that affects gait and strength in the legs and confines most victims to a wheelchair by their late 20s.

The prospect of a simple, noninvasive prenatal test based on the isolation of fetal cells from the mother's blood was advanced by scientists at the University of California, San Francisco, who used the technique to diagnose inherited blood disorders in two fetuses. As genetic testing became more feasible, its potential pitfalls became more apparent. A study of individuals with a family history of breast or ovarian cancer found that fewer than half wanted to undergo an experimental test for genetic susceptibility. Many declined because of concerns about job and insurance discrimination if they tested positive. Another study of 332 individuals in families with genetic disorders found that one-fourth believed they had been discriminated against in terms of obtaining life insurance; one-fourth reported discrimination in obtaining health insurance, and 13% reported discrimination in employment.

Cardiovascular Disease. Two studies sponsored by the U.S. National Institutes of Health (NIH) found that dietary changes and weight loss can prevent and control high blood pressure (hypertension). A multicentre investigation involving more than 450 adults with and without hypertension, found that reducing overall fat intake and eating more fruits and vegetables (9 to 10 servings a day) and low-fat dairy products (3 servings a day) were as effective as drugs

Outbreaks: Emerging and Reemerging Infectious Diseases, 1995–96

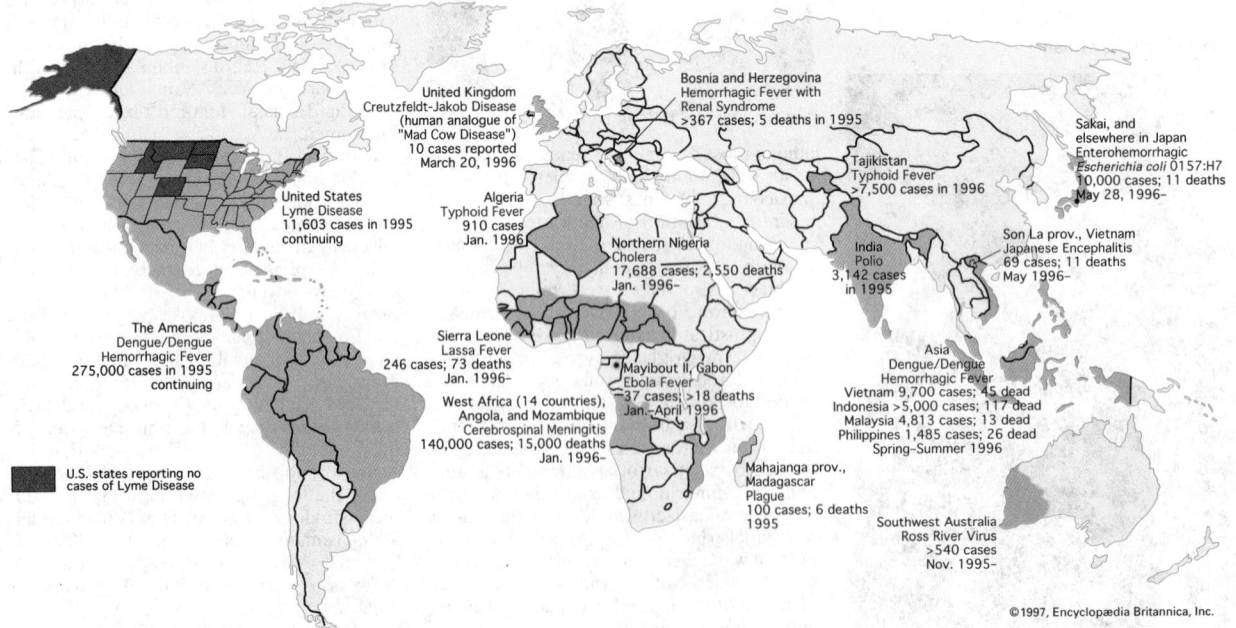

United Kingdom
Creutzfeldt-Jakob Disease
(human analogue of
"Mad Cow Disease")
10 cases reported
March 20, 1996

Bosnia and Herzegovina
Hemorrhagic Fever with
Renal Syndrome
>367 cases; 5 deaths in 1995

Sakai, and
elsewhere in Japan
Enterohemorrhagic
Escherichia coli 0157:H7
10,000 cases; 11 deaths
May 28, 1996–

United States
Lyme Disease
11,603 cases in 1995
continuing

Algeria
Typhoid Fever
910 cases
Jan. 1996

Tajikistan
Typhoid Fever
>7,500 cases in 1996

Northern Nigeria
Cholera
17,688 cases; 2,550 deaths
Jan. 1996–

India
Polio
3,142 cases
in 1995

Son La prov., Vietnam
Japanese Encephalitis
69 cases; 11 deaths
May 1996–

The Americas
Dengue/Dengue
Hemorrhagic Fever
275,000 cases in 1995
continuing

Sierra Leone
Lassa Fever
246 cases; 73 deaths
Jan. 1996–

Mayibout II, Gabon
Ebola Fever
37 cases; >18 deaths
Jan.–April 1996

Asia
Dengue/Dengue
Hemorrhagic Fever
Vietnam 9,700 cases; 45 dead
Indonesia >5,000 cases; 117 dead
Malaysia 4,813 cases; 13 dead
Philippines 1,485 cases; 26 dead
Spring–Summer 1996

West Africa (14 countries),
Angola, and Mozambique
Cerebrospinal Meningitis
140,000 cases; 15,000 deaths
Jan. 1996–

Mahajanga prov.,
Madagascar
Plague
100 cases; 6 deaths
1995

Southwest Australia
Ross River Virus
>540 cases
Nov. 1995–

U.S. states reporting no
cases of Lyme Disease

©1997, Encyclopædia Britannica, Inc.

in lowering blood pressure. A study of more than 900 people aged 60 to 80 found that blood pressure control could be safely maintained in many subjects by means of weight loss and reduced salt intake without the use of antihypertensive drugs.

The debate over the contribution of dietary sodium (salt) to hypertension continued. A meta-analysis of 56 trials of salt restriction published in May found that older people with high blood pressure benefited, but younger individuals with normal blood pressure did not. The Canadian authors concluded that current recommendations calling for universal dietary sodium restriction are unnecessary. They were challenged, however, by scientists from the Intersalt study, an investigation of the relationship between salt and blood pressure in more than 10,000 people in 32 countries. An update of the 1988 Intersalt data, also published in May, reaffirmed the importance of salt restriction in the control of blood pressure.

Researchers at Tufts University, Medford, Mass., found that high levels of a "bad" form of cholesterol, known as lipoprotein (a), can double a man's risk of premature heart attack. New research showed that the fatty substances known as triglycerides can thicken the blood and increase the risk of heart attacks at lower levels than previously thought. A large study of an experimental blood-thinning drug called clopidogrel found it to be more effective and safer than aspirin in preventing heart attacks, while a separate study showed that an experimental clot-inhibitor, integrelin, works better than aspirin in patients suffering from reduced blood flow to the heart.

There was further evidence of the life-saving potential of thrombolytic, or clot-dissolving, drugs for treatment of acute heart attack. Research at Erasmus University, Rotterdam, Neth., highlighted the importance of administering the drugs as soon as possible after the attack. This conclusion was supported by work in Scotland that showed that in patients receiving thrombolytic drugs two or more hours after the onset of symptoms, every hour's delay in the administration of the drugs had an appreciable effect on long-term survival.

A Dutch study published in January found that laser surgery to open blocked arteries—laser angioplasty—is no more effective than balloon angioplasty, a procedure in which a balloon threaded into a blocked vessel is inflated at the site of the blockage. Not all physicians who perform balloon angioplasty have sufficient experience with the procedure, however. According to a report presented at the annual meeting of the American Heart Association in November, patients whose doctors performed an annual average of only 30 balloon angioplasties had higher death rates and required additional surgery more often than those whose clinicians performed 50 or more procedures.

An analysis of 300 men and women with coronary heart disease in Belgium reawakened interest in personality as a factor that—along with cholesterol, blood pressure, and other variables—can affect prognosis. It showed that those with so-called type-D personality—characterized by depression, social alienation, and the suppression of feelings—had significantly higher death rates than those with other personal-

ity types. A Harvard Medical School study of 1,305 veterans found that the grumpiest old men—those who reported episodes of extreme anger—were at three times greater risk than their more placid counterparts.

Cancer. More than three decades after the first U.S. surgeon general's report on smoking and lung cancer, scientists finally uncovered a distinct biological mechanism by which tobacco use can cause lung tumours. Researchers demonstrated that benzo[a]pyrene, a component of tobacco smoke, damages specific regions of the key tumour suppressor gene $p53$. These same regions are commonly found to be mutated in human lung cancer patients.

The National Cancer Institute (NCI) reported in November that U.S. cancer death rates had decreased in the 1990s—the first such drop recorded in the 20th century. Experts attributed the reduction of nearly 3% between 1991 and 1995 to inroads against smoking, earlier diagnosis, and better treatments. The decline in cancer deaths was greater in men than in women. This disparity was attributed to the drop in deaths from lung, colorectal, and prostate cancers. The smaller reduction observed among women reflected declining death rates from breast, colorectal, and gynecologic cancers. Lung cancer deaths in women had continued to rise, however. Moreover, despite lower mortality rates, U.S. cancer incidence—the number of new cases reported—had increased during the 1990s.

Researchers at the Harvard School of Public Health announced that the vast majority of cancer deaths resulted from unhealthy lifestyles. Their report, published in the journal *Cancer Causes and Control*, concluded that only 2% of cancer mortality was attributable to environmental exposures and only 10% to genetics.

A study by the NCI found that black men have higher overall rates of new cancers and of cancer deaths than whites, largely because they have a disproportionate incidence of prostate and lung cancers. An expert panel convened by the NIH called for

broader screening for cervical cancer, noting that regular use of the Pap test could virtually eradicate the disease.

Infectious Diseases. The 11th International Conference on AIDS, held in July in Vancouver, B.C., was marked by unprecedented optimism. Most encouraging was the news that for many people with AIDS, proper treatment may prolong life indefinitely. Several studies found that combination therapy—the concurrent use of two or more anti-HIV drugs—reduces the amount of virus circulating in the blood, delays the progression of HIV infection to AIDS, and improves patient survival. By the year's end U.S. physicians had access to nine different anti-HIV drugs for use alone or in combination. In much of the world, however, the cost of such therapies put them out of reach of most HIV-infected individuals.

The year was also marked by significant advances in the understanding of how HIV infects cells and why some people who are exposed to the virus do not become infected. First, two coreceptors for HIV were identified. Coreceptors are molecules on a cell's surface that, together with other molecules, mediate the entry of substances into the cell. A single HIV receptor, CD4, had long been recognized, but the existence of others was suspected. In 1996 scientists identified two of these, which they named fusin and CKR-5 (also called CCR-5). It was subsequently discovered that people who possess two mutated copies of the gene that codes for CKR-5 are virtually immune to the most common strains of HIV. Moreover, infected persons who have one mutated gene for the receptor are slower than others to progress to AIDS.

Nearly every continent was affected by outbreaks of infectious disease in 1996. Dengue, a mosquitoborne viral infection, was responsible for at least 8,000 cases of illness in the Mekong delta of Vietnam, while the even more deadly variant known as dengue hemorrhagic fever killed some 300 people and made thousands more ill

(continued on page 221)

A Japanese laboratory technician checks culture samples of a virulent strain of the *Escherichia coli* bacterium that some health officials believed to be increasing worldwide. In the summer thousands of Japanese were victims of an outbreak of food poisoning caused by the bacterium.

JUNJI KUROKAWA—AFP

For Nursing, New Responsibilities, New Respect

BY MARGRETTA MADDEN STYLES

In remote villages around the world—whether in southern Africa, Latin America, or southwestern Asia—the community's mobilizer for health, sanitation, and housing services may well be a nurse. In the rural or inner-city U.S., a clinic serving the entire community may well be run solely by nurses.

The head of a national family-planning program may be a nurse. The chief executive officer of a hospital or health care system may be a nurse with additional training in economics or business administration. The attorney representing a client in high-stakes health care litigation may be a nurse with training in the law.

In fact, all of the above-mentioned positions are presently or have been held by nurses. Adapting to current social, economic, and health-care trends, nurses today are attaining higher levels of education than in the past and are applying their newly acquired knowledge, skill, and confidence to expanded roles and in novel settings.

Worldwide, the nursing profession is responding to myriad health care needs and challenges. These include the escalation of health care costs, the fragmentation of care resulting from growing specialization, the rampant spread of AIDS, malaria, cholera, and tuberculosis, and other infectious diseases, and the worldwide increase in the number of elderly persons, with its corresponding increase in aging-associated health problems.

Nurses have been called upon to meet these diverse challenges for a number of reasons. First and foremost, in most countries nurses constitute the largest group of health care providers. Because nursing is defined variably around the globe, it is difficult to arrive at exact figures, but, as just one example of their significant numbers, there are more than 2.2 million registered nurses in the United States alone. Nurses are geographically more evenly distributed than other health care providers, and more of them serve in rural, remote, and poor areas.

Changes at the grassroots of nursing have been stimulated and assisted by both governmental and nongovernmental organizations (NGOs) on all levels. The governmental system includes, in ascending order, local, state, and federal departments or ministries of health and, internationally, the World Health Organization (WHO), with its six geographic regions. The International Labour Organisation (ILO), a UN agency, specifically addresses economic and general welfare issues for workers in all occupations, including nursing. Principal among the NGOs advocating for nursing are the 114 national nurses associations constituting the International Council of Nurses (ICN). Conveniently, the ICN, WHO, and the ILO are all headquartered in Geneva, where their close proximity permits intensive communication and cooperation.

Nursing education has had to change dramatically to prepare nurses for their expanded roles. Traditional hospital-based nursing schools do not provide community nursing experience, nor can they offer the liberal arts curriculum of the university. Moreover, traditional nursing schools have isolated students from the mainstream of higher education. To remedy this situation, nursing education is now occurring increasingly in academic rather than clinical settings. In fact, in some countries the training of nurses has moved exclusively into the universities. Despite the extension and reform of nursing education, the costs of educating a nurse remain only a fraction of those required for educating a physician.

As nurses have become better educated and their roles have been enlarged, the legal scope of their practice has been extended accordingly. In recent years, largely through the combined efforts of the ICN and WHO, there has been an accelerated movement to expand the practice boundaries of the profession. In some countries nurses are now authorized to make diagnoses, to prescribe medication, and even to admit patients to hospitals under their care.

The government or private, so-called third-party, health insurers pay for some or all of health care in most countries. When nurses provide "expanded" services, the health care system must provide for their reimbursement, just as it does for physician-rendered services. In nations with centralized, single-payer health care systems, such adjustments have been easily accommodated. In the United States, ongoing negotiations with the federal government, state agencies, and private insurance companies have inched forward to gain authorization for reimbursement of advanced nursing services.

Incentives have been a major enabling factor in the advanced-practice movement. Nurses are encouraged to seek additional education and to assume roles of greater scope and responsibility when patients recognize their expertise and seek out their care and when they are appropriately compensated by employers. The profession long suffered from the "a-nurse-is-a-nurse" complex, and little motivation was provided for nurses to better themselves. Although inequities in salaries and practice privileges persist, progress has been made in establishing career ladders and salary structures that appropriately distinguish those individuals who have attained higher qualifications and assumed greater responsibilities.

Historically a female profession, nursing has long been a natural standard-bearer for the economic and social rights of women. Battles continue to be waged on many fronts and at many levels, with nurses and nursing organizations often leading the fray. As just one example, many nurses were at the negotiating tables of the UN Fourth World Conference on Women in September 1995 in Beijing, where they spoke persuasively for the educational, economic, and health rights of women around the world.

The emerging new roles and responsibilities of nurses have already had a dramatic impact on health care. Studies show that the expanded services provided by well-qualified nurses are different in nature from those provided by physicians. For example, nurses spend more time with patients; the treatments they provide are often more conservative and less intrusive. Most telling, so-called outcomes—cure and survival rates, cost savings—are as good or better. As sweeping changes occur in health care technology and in the structure and priorities of health care delivery systems, nurses will continue to be at the patient's side, assuring quality care, providing expertise, and offering comfort.

Margretta Madden Styles is president of the International Council of Nurses and the American Nurses Credentialing Center.

(continued from page 219)
in New Delhi. Public health officials in South America worked to contain an epidemic of another mosquitoborne viral infection, Venezuelan equine encephalitis, a disease that affects both horses and humans. Meningitis killed more than 4,500 in western Africa, and the rare but extremely lethal Ebola virus, which had surfaced in Zaire in 1995, claimed 10 lives in Gabon.

Foodborne diseases captured the headlines in developed countries. A deadly strain of the bacterium *Escherichia coli,* earlier blamed for the deaths of U.S. youngsters who ate undercooked hamburgers, affected about 9,500 people in Japan between May and November. In the U.S. a small outbreak of *E. coli* infection was traced to unpasteurized apple juice. Individuals in 11 states and Canada fell victim to a gastrointestinal disorder attributed to a little known organism, *Cyclospora cayetanensis;* investigators traced the infection to raspberries grown in Guatemala, but the source of the contamination remained undetermined.

Lifestyle, Habits, and Health. Blindness was added to the long list of adverse consequences of smoking. Two Boston studies found that pack-a-day male and female smokers were more than twice as likely as nonsmokers to develop age-related macular degeneration, the leading cause of blindness in elderly Americans. A study of deaths among Minnesota alcoholics found that one-half had died of smoking-related causes, including heart disease and cancer, while only about one-third succumbed to alcohol-related disorders.

Research conducted in Sydney, Australia, and London added to the rapidly accumulating evidence that passive smoking is a substantial cause of heart disease. The investigation focused on the capacity of the arteries to dilate in response to bodily demands for increased blood supply. Impairment of this capacity had been implicated in the onset of atherosclerosis (narrowing of the arteries due to buildup of fatty deposits) and had been demonstrated in young cigarette smokers. The new research showed that the capacity of the arteries to dilate is also significantly reduced in young adults who have never smoked but have been exposed to tobacco smoke for at least one hour daily for three or more years.

Two studies, however, found intriguing evidence of tobacco's positive effect on the brain. Neuroscientists at Baylor College of Medicine, Houston, Texas, described how low concentrations of nicotine in the blood help to improve memory by triggering communication between nerve cells, while scientists at Case Western Reserve University, Cleveland, Ohio, found that nicotine may help prevent or delay the formation of neural plaques, brain lesions characteristic of Alzheimer's disease.

The Centers for Disease Control and Prevention (CDC) reported that about 90% of tobacco use was initiated among youngsters aged 18 and under and that tobacco use among teens was continuing to rise. Concern about this problem propelled the U.S. Food and Drug Administration (FDA) to declare tobacco an addictive drug. The agency also finalized new regulations that required store clerks to ask for verification of age before selling tobacco products to young people. (Minimum age for purchase was 18.) Restrictions on tobacco advertis-

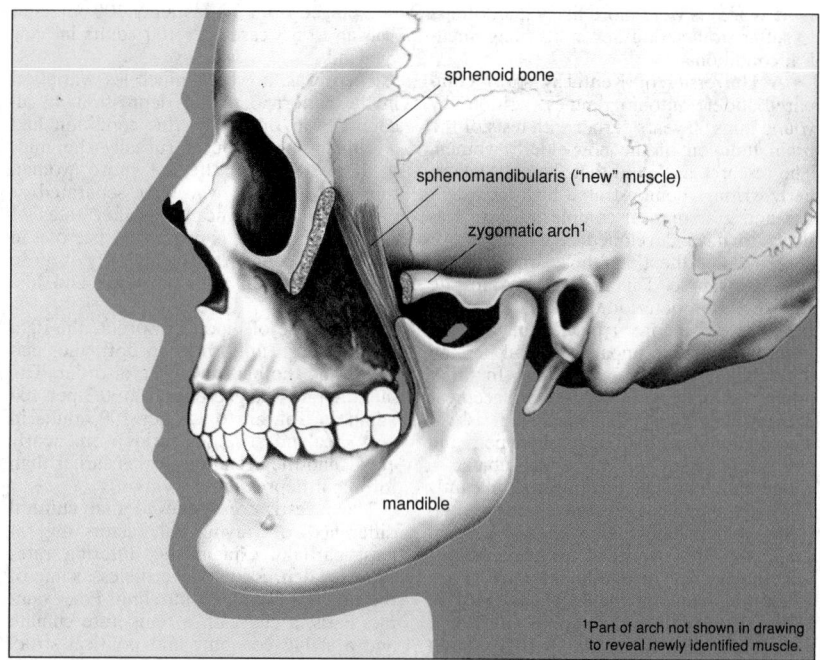

sphenoid bone

sphenomandibularis ("new" muscle)

zygomatic arch[1]

mandible

[1]Part of arch not shown in drawing to reveal newly identified muscle.

The sphenomandibularis extends from behind the eye socket to the lower jaw. Anatomists had previously thought that this muscle was an extension of the temporalis muscle, but in 1996 researchers discovered that it actually is independent, with its own blood and nerve supply.

ing and promotion were also made more stringent.

The federal government reported that alcohol-related driving deaths rose by 4% in 1995, the first such increase in a decade. About 4 out of 10 traffic fatalities involved alcohol.

A 17-year follow-up survey of 11,000 vegetarians and "health-conscious" people in the U.K. showed that those who ate fresh fruit each day had a 24% lower risk of dying from coronary heart disease and a 32% lower risk of dying as a result of a stroke. The overall death rate in this group was also 21% lower than that of a control group of individuals who did not eat fruit regularly. In addition to reduced mortality from heart disease and stroke, the decline in deaths overall was largely attributable to a decreased rate of deaths from lung cancer and respiratory conditions, which may have reflected the low proportion of smokers (11%) in the sample.

In April the FDA approved the first antiobesity drug in 23 years, a chemical called dexfenfluramine, which helps dieters eat less by reducing the craving for food. The drug was already available in Europe. Dexfenfluramine and related medications were not without risk, however. A European study found a slight increase in primary pulmonary hypertension (elevated pressure in vessels carrying blood to the lungs), a potentially fatal condition, in patients taking these drugs.

The first U.S. surgeon general's report on physical activity and health, released in July, concluded that any activity that burns at least 150 calories per day can help reduce the risk of such chronic ailments as heart disease, diabetes, and depression. Such activity can include swimming laps (20 minutes), gardening (30–45 minutes), and washing and waxing a car (45–60 minutes). The report noted, however, that more than 60% of U.S. adults are not physically active

on a regular basis, and of these, 25% do not get any exercise at all.

Other Developments. An extensive investigation into sudden infant death syndrome (SIDS, or cot death) in the U.K. demonstrated that infants were at heightened risk if the mother had smoked during pregnancy. Household exposure to tobacco smoke had an additional, independent effect in increasing the likelihood of SIDS. Clinicians in New Zealand reported that there was an appreciably lower risk of SIDS among infants who slept in the same room—but *not* those who slept in the same bed—as their parents.

An analysis conducted at the Stanford University School of Medicine clarified the benefits to be obtained by screening healthy individuals for the ulcer-causing bacterium *Helicobacter pylori* and treating those who are infected with antibiotic drugs. When present in the stomach, *H. pylori* is an important risk factor for gastric cancer, the second leading cause of death from cancer worldwide. Although the bacterium occurs in 30–40% of the U.S. population, fewer than 1% of these people develop cancer. The Stanford study showed, however, that screening and treatment are potentially cost-effective in preventing gastric cancer, especially in high-risk populations like that of Japan and other Asian countries. In the U.S. a breath test for detecting the bacterium was licensed for use by health care professionals.

Still other newsworthy developments of 1996 included the following:

• The Pentagon announced that it was stepping up efforts to investigate possible causes of Persian Gulf War veterans' health complaints. Although two reports published during the year showed that U.S. troops who served in the Gulf did not have higher death or hospitalization rates than other military personnel, preliminary findings from two other studies indicated that

Gulf War vets were more likely than others to suffer from serious, even disabling, medical conditions.

● A University of Kentucky study compared brief autobiographies written by young nuns 60 years earlier with tests of the brain function of the now-elderly women. The researchers found that the nuns whose early writings demonstrated high idea density and grammatical complexity were less likely to have developed Alzheimer's disease in later life than those whose prose style was simple. This finding may indicate that the brain deterioration of Alzheimer's begins long before typical signs of the disease—cognitive impairment and personality changes—become apparent. In other Alzheimer's research, estrogen replacement therapy was shown to reduce the risk of the disease in postmenopausal women, and one small study—of only 12 subjects—found that estrogen treatment significantly improved memory and concentration in elderly women diagnosed with Alzheimer's.

● The United Network for Organ Sharing, the agency responsible for allocating all donor organs in the U.S., changed the national liver transplantation guidelines, giving top priority on the waiting list to critically ill individuals with sudden onset of a liver disorder, who had the best survival chances. Previously, priority had been given to those suffering from chronic liver disease, who, because of their long-term illness, were less likely to make a successful recovery.

● The CDC formally endorsed a change in the schedule of routine childhood immunizations, recommending that all U.S. children receive two injections of inactivated polio vaccine (IPV), followed by two doses of oral polio vaccine (OPV). Previously, the schedule had called for four doses of OPV. The change was made because the oral vaccine, which uses live virus, was occasionally known to cause the disease. IPV was already being used for routine immunization in Scandinavia, France, The Netherlands, and Canada.

● U.S. automotive safety experts issued new warnings that air bags, intended to save lives during a car crash, may pose a significant risk of death to children under 12 and to some small adults sitting in the front passenger seat. They advised drivers to keep younger children belted in the back seat.

(BERNARD DIXON; CRISTINE RUSSELL)

MENTAL HEALTH

In 1996, for the first time, a multinational study was able to demonstrate clear similarities and differences in the rates of specific mental illnesses in several countries throughout the world. Unlike previous investigations, in which different methods were employed in different countries, the new survey was based on a uniform methodology. Its purpose was to assess the pattern and extent of two conditions, major depression and bipolar disorder, in Canada, France, the former West Germany, Italy, South Korea, Lebanon, New Zealand, Puerto Rico, Taiwan, and the U.S.

One principal finding was that major depression varied considerably in incidence. The lifetime rate ranged from 1.5 cases per 100 adults in Taiwan to 19 cases per 100 adults in Lebanon. Similarly, the annual rate ranged from 0.8 cases per 100 adults in Taiwan to 5.8 cases per 100 adults in New Zealand.

There was, however, much less variation in the pattern of major depression. In all countries in the study, this condition had a similar age of onset (usually the mid- to late 20s) and affected more women than men. Persons who were separated or divorced had significantly higher rates of major depression than married persons in most of the countries. The majority of those affected reported both insomnia and loss of energy.

In the case of bipolar disorder, the data showed more uniformity in both the incidence and the pattern of the disorder. The lifetime rates ranged only from 0.3 per 100 adults in Taiwan to 1.5 per 100 adults in New Zealand. The sex ratios were nearly equal, and the age at onset was earlier than for major depression.

The investigators believed that cultural differences or varying risk factors may at least partially explain the differing rates of major depression. Nevertheless, some of the findings remained puzzling. For example, Paris, a city with a temperate climate and a stable economy and political structure, had a rate of major depression almost as high as that of Beirut, Leb., which was ravaged by war for some 15 years.

Psychiatrists in London reported that black Caribbean and African patients suffering from certain psychotic illnesses differed from whites in the likelihood of involuntary hospitalization. The subjects were individuals from two areas in the south of the city; they had conditions such as schizophrenia and psychotic affective disorder. The higher rate of compulsory detention for blacks was independent of psychiatric diagnosis and was irrespective of other factors such as employment and marital status. The reasons for the disparity were unclear. The authors of the report speculated, however, that black people may perceive mental health services as "untherapeutic." They thus delay seeking help and thereby increase the chances that they will be hospitalized involuntarily.

A major problem in treating psychotic patients was that up to 80% of them failed to take their medication as directed. Given the efficacy of modern antipsychotic drugs and the potentially serious consequences of relapse, ensuring compliance became a major goal of mental health researchers. One group in London showed that an approach known as "compliance therapy" could significantly improve patients' reliability in taking their drugs. It also produced long-lasting results.

The therapy aimed to help people to change their behaviour by means of interviews intended to provide motivation but to avoid the confrontation and stalemate that often impair the relationship between patient and psychiatrist. In the London experiment, those receiving the new therapy were five times more likely to attain an acceptable level of compliance than patients simply given their medication and instructed to take it regularly but provided with no further encouragement or support.

Researchers in Valencia, Spain, reported progress in helping patients with severe depression resistant to all drugs normally used to treat this condition. The new technique involved placing an electrical coil on the patient's scalp and creating a rapidly changing magnetic field, which reached the brain structures beneath, specifically a region known to be linked with depression. When 17 patients with intractable depression were treated in this way, 11 experienced a pronounced improvement that lasted for about two weeks. With further refinement of the therapy, more permanent results should be possible.

An English trial of estrogen therapy for severe postnatal depression reported encouraging results. The subjects were 61 women who within three months of childbirth had developed major depression, which had then persisted for up to 18 months. During their three months of treatment with estrogen delivered by means of a skin patch, the women receiving treatment found that their depression waned rapidly. Although those receiving a placebo also felt slightly better, improvement in the estrogen-treated women was much more dramatic.   (BERNARD DIXON)

This article updates the *Macropædia* article MENTAL DISORDERS and Their Treatment.

VETERINARY MEDICINE

Ramifications of the fatal cattle disease bovine spongiform encephalopathy (BSE), also known as "mad cow" disease, dominated the veterinary news in much of the Western world in 1996. The disease, found mainly in the U.K., was attributed to the practice of feeding dairy cows manufactured feeds containing protein material from sheep infected with scrapie, a similar disease. It takes some years for signs of BSE to appear in infected animals, the main manifestation being erratic behaviour and increasing difficulty in moving.

First identified in England in 1986, BSE had been the subject of an ongoing eradication process based on the slaughter of affected animals. This process had been proceeding more or less according to plan; the numbers of new cases of BSE had declined sharply from a peak in 1993, and it was predicted that the disease would be eliminated from herds in the U.K. soon after the year 2000.

In 1996, however, scientists announced a possible link between consumption of beef from BSE-infected cows and several cases of a new form of Creutzfeldt-Jakob disease, a fatal neurodegenerative disorder. Further, contrary to earlier predictions, preliminary results of long-term studies in the U.K. suggested that BSE might be transmissible from cow to calf. As a result, the European Commission prohibited the U.K. from exporting beef and beef products and cattle, and beef sales dropped sharply throughout Europe.

The new findings prompted demands from the Commission for more urgent measures to eradicate the disease before the export ban could be lifted. These included the establishment of rigid precautions in slaughterhouses, as well as the destruction of hundreds of thousands of cattle born before 1993. The proposals for mass slaughter, which meant that many healthy cattle would have to be killed, caused an outcry from veterinarians, farmers, and animal welfare activists in the U.K. Many argued that the program already in place would have eradicated the disease just as quickly as the new plan.

A British farmer ponders the fate of his cattle. Researchers continued to investigate the possibility of a link between some cases of Creutzfeldt-Jakob disease in humans and bovine spongiform encephalopathy, or "mad cow" disease, which broke out in Great Britain in the mid-1980s.

A report from the World Health Organization (WHO) on the progress of the European campaign to control—and, it was hoped, eradicate—rabies by laying vaccine-impregnated baits for foxes, the main carrier of the disease, found that rabies prevalence had been reduced to 20% of its former level. The success rates in the 14 participating countries differed considerably, however, and the cost—$83 million in total to date—was causing support to wane in some areas. The authors of the WHO report called for a review of the campaign to identify problems responsible for the variable success rate and to draw up guidelines for the future.

The physical attributes of different breeds of dog are well-defined, but the temperamental characteristics, although of equal importance to a potential owner, are much less so. J.W.S. Bradshaw and colleagues at the University of Southampton, Eng., surveyed veterinarians and animal-care professionals to establish an objective assessment of behavioral traits such as excitability, watchdog behaviour, and aggression toward other dogs in 50 popular breeds. They also asked whether males or females were more likely to exhibit a particular behaviour. The results broadly confirmed existing anecdotal opinion. They showed that females were, in general, easier to train, more demanding of affection, and more mature than males. The most aggressive breeds were rottweilers, German shepherds, Doberman pinschers, and bull terriers; the least aggressive included the spaniels, setters, and sheepdogs.   (EDWARD BODEN)

See also Life Sciences: *Molecular Biology.*
This article updates the *Macropædia* articles DIAGNOSIS AND THERAPEUTICS; DISEASE; INFECTIOUS DISEASES; MEDICINE.

Law, Crime, and Law Enforcement

LAW

As the sovereignty of nation-states was increasingly diluted by their inability to act on international issues without taking into account the views and possible reactions of the world and regional communities, international law continued to reflect this change. The emphasis on the judicialization of interstate relations and the structural politicization of those relations within regional and global organizations was a clear feature of international law in 1996 as it slowly took on a strong resemblance to constitutional law.

International Adjudication. The success of the International Court of Justice in attracting a wider clientele raised the question of how it would cope with the increased caseload. This issue was discussed at a seminar arranged by the British Institute of International and Comparative Law (BIICL) in February, attended by the court's president, its vice president, and several of its judges. The discussion, based on a report of the BIICL on the weaknesses in the court's procedure, revealed the court's unpreparedness and, indeed, its unwillingness to change from a highly academic and high-quality but leisurely solver of diplomatic disputes into a more practical workaday tribunal with a clientele extending beyond the chanceries and foreign ministries of the nations.

Two elements in particular were potentially fatal to the court's acceptance of a wider role, whether as a supervisory "supreme court" overseeing the newly proliferating international tribunals or in handling a wider variety of legal issues. These elements were: (1) the pitifully small size of the court's secretariat (and budget), which was already overstretched, and (2) the psychology of the judges in refusing to accept the idea that they should aim to produce more than about two final judgments per year. The caseload of about a dozen at the end of 1996 was, therefore, a cause for concern rather than for satisfaction.

On a request by the UN General Assembly, the court delivered an advisory opinion on July 8 in which it held, by the casting vote of the president, that while in principle the use or threat of nuclear weapons would be contrary to the laws of war, in the present state of international law the court could not definitively hold that such use in the extreme circumstance of self-defense would be illegal. On the same day, the court refused to answer a second request, this time from the World Health Organization (WHO), for an advisory opinion on the legality of the use of nuclear weapons on the ground that the subject matter of the request did not fall within the competence of WHO, which was concerned only with the effects on health and not with the legality of the acts that produced those effects. During these proceedings argument was heard from 43 nations in writing and 22 at the oral hearings.

On July 11 the court delivered a judgment rejecting Yugoslavia's preliminary objections to the court's jurisdiction in the genocide case *Bosnia & Herzegovina* v. *Yugoslavia* and gave Yugoslavia 12 months in which to file its response to the decision. Disposal in February of the action concerning the Aerial Incident of July 3, 1988, *Iran* v. *USA,* illustrated a new interconnectedness between proceedings in different international tribunals. The incident, the shooting down by the U.S. of an Iranian civil airliner, led to claims by Iran before both the court and (as regards certain banking matters) the Iran-United States Claims Tribunal. The U.S. disputed the jurisdiction of the court, but before pleadings had been completed on that preliminary objection, the two parties began negotiations that resulted in a settlement whereby, basically, the U.S. would pay compensation to all victims of the incident. Thereupon, the actions before the court and before the tribunal were withdrawn on the same day. In March the court ordered provisional measures regarding the land-boundary dispute *Cameroon* v. *Nigeria,* and in September it held hearings in the oil platforms case *Iran* v. *USA.* In May Botswana and Namibia submitted their boundary dispute to the court under a Special Agreement of the previous February.

Two important new international tribunals began operations in 1996. The World Trade Organizations's (WTO's) Appellate Body, appointed to hear appeals against WTO panel reports, adopted its rules of procedure in February and delivered its first judgment in April. In *Venezuela and Brazil* v. *USA (Standards for Reformulated and Conventional Gasoline),* the tribunal found that there were errors of law in the report but that, nonetheless, the U.S. had infringed Article XX of the General Agreement on Tariffs and Trade (GATT). The Appellate Body's second judgment was delivered in November; in *EC, Canada & USA* v. *Japan (Taxes on Alcoholic Beverages),* it upheld the panel's findings that Japan had infringed Article III of GATT. The 21 judges of the International Tribunal for the Law of the Sea were appointed in August, and the tribunal held its inaugural meeting in Hamburg, Ger., in October.

The Iran-United States Claims Tribunal, having resolved nearly all the claims before it except for several by the Iranian government, was reaching the end of its life. Its last surviving original member, Judge George H. Aldridge, analyzed its accomplishments in *The Jurisprudence of the Iran-United States Claims Tribunal,* published in October.

The International Criminal Tribunal (ICT) for former Yugoslavia acquired a new set of rules of procedure in April in the form of a consolidation in Revision 8. This included a new Rule 40*bis* that instituted a system of provisional detention of suspects in the tribunal's detention unit. The tribunal's special prosecutor, Richard Goldstone, retired from the post (to take up a seat on the South African Constitutional Court) and was replaced on October 1 by Louise Arbour (formerly judge of the Court of Appeal of Ontario). The tribunal's first actual trial began in May.

The ICT for Rwanda, also with Arbour as special prosecutor as of October 1, was to have begun its first trial (of Jean-Paul Akayesu) in Tanzania in September, but after arraignment of the accused the trial was reluctantly postponed at the insistence of the prosecutor and the defense and had not begun by the year's end. On the other hand, the first of a series of Rwandan genocide tribunals began the trial of Deo Bizimana and Egide Gatanazi on December 27 at Kibungu. Two more genocide trials began at a second tribunal at Kigali on December 30.

The UN Preparatory Committee on the Establishment of an International Criminal Court, set up pursuant to a General Assembly resolution of December 1995, continued preparing a workable text for a statute for the court, aiming to have it ready by April 1998. At its second session the committee recommended the convening of a diplomatic conference to adopt a convention on the court in late 1998.

The long-established European courts also experienced winds of change. The procedures of the European Court of Justice (ECJ), which in spite of a number of earlier reforms was still finding it difficult to cope with a rising caseload and an output of some 200 cases each year, were the subject of an in-depth analysis by the BIICL, which, however, made only minor recommendations for change. At the same time, the ECJ came under sustained attack by a group of British nationalist members of Parliament, an attack that was adopted (in milder form) by the British government in its proposals for reform of the court presented to the intergovernmental conference (IGC) on reform of the European Union (EU). Opinion 2/94 by the ECJ concluded that the Maastricht Treaty did not give the EU the power to adhere to the European Convention on Human Rights.

A positive development for the European courts was the appearance of two major books at the year's end. One was an exhaustive practitioner treatise on the procedures of the ECJ, the Court of First Instance, and the European Free Trade Association Court (*European Courts: Practice and Precedents* by Richard Plender), and the other was a descriptive analysis of those courts plus the European Commission and Court of Human Rights as working institutions (*The European Courts* by Neville March Hunnings).

International Organizations. New regional organizations included the Arctic Council, which was inaugurated in September and comprised Canada, Denmark, Finland, Iceland, Norway, Sweden, Russia, and the U.S.; the Inuit Circumpolar Conference, the Saami Council, and the Russian Association of Indigenous Minorities of the North, Siberia, and the Far East were named as "permanent participants." The council planned to meet biennially at the ministerial level to oversee such matters as environmental protection of the region, economic and social development, improved health conditions, and cultural well-being. It was especially significant because of the special status accorded to nonstate nations, a phenomenon that was also to be found in a diluted form in the EU's Committee of the Regions and that foreshadowed an important likely development of classical international law away from its exclusive concern with nation-states. (*See* Spotlight: *Fourth World: Resurgent Nations in the New Europe.*)

Portugal and six of its former colonies (Angola, Brazil, Cape Verde, Guinea-Bissau, Mozambique, and São Tomé and Príncipe) formed the Community of Portuguese-Speaking Countries in June, modeled after the Commonwealth of Nations and La Francophonie (association of French-speaking nations). Chile and Canada signed a free-trade agreement in November that was to enter into force in July 1997 and prepare the way for Chile to join the North American Free Trade Agreement; Chile had already signed a similar agreement with Mexico. In June the three Baltic states (Estonia, Latvia, and Lithuania) signed a free-trade agreement for agricultural goods. The South Pacific Forum, which expelled France in 1995 following the latter's nuclear tests in the Pacific, readmitted it in September. The heads of state and government of the Andean Pact countries in March decided to convert the pact into an Andean Community along the lines of the EU.

The Arab League summit meeting in Cairo in June resolved to establish a Code of Conduct for Arab Security and Cooperation and to set up the Mechanism for the Prevention, Management, and Resolution of Conflicts Among Arab States and also to request the league to establish a Greater Arab Free Trade Area. The WTO began a series of interorganization linkups by signing a cooperation agreement with the International Monetary Fund in December and discussing the forms of future cooperation with the UN Conference on Trade and Development. It also held its first general meeting, in Singapore in December, with ministerial delegations from 128 countries in attendance.

(NEVILLE MARCH HUNNINGS)

Court Decisions. During 1996 a number of important decisions concerning human rights were handed down by courts throughout the world. These cases may be classified in two major categories: (1) age, race, and sex discrimination; and (2) other civil rights.

In *United States* v. *Virginia* the Supreme Court of the United States held that the admission policy of Virginia Military Institute (VMI) violated the equal protection clause of the U.S. Constitution. VMI, a state-supported college, was founded and operated as an all-male institution with a mission of producing citizen-soldiers who were prepared for leadership in civilian and military life. Its educational program placed emphasis on physical rigour, absence of privacy, mental stress, and close regulation of personal behaviour. On the assumption that this program was incompatible with the abilities and special needs of women, VMI refused to matriculate females. The court ruled that no state-supported institution could discriminate in this way, and it held that Virginia's proposed remedy of establishing a separate women's institution to be run on parallel lines to that of VMI did not cure the constitutional violation.

In Italy the Constitutional Court ruled unconstitutional the electoral laws that established quotas for candidates based on sex. In those laws a percentage of candidate places were reserved for women only. The court said that such reservations were contrary to notions of equality and that sex must be treated as irrelevant when selecting candidates for election.

In 1992 Colorado adopted a constitutional amendment prohibiting the state from enacting or enforcing any statute whereby homosexual orientation could entitle any person to quota preference or claim to minority or protected status. In 1996, however, the U.S. Supreme Court in *Romer* v. *Evans* held that this amendment violated the equal protection clause of the federal constitution. The court maintained that the Colorado amendment put homosexuals in a solitary class and denied them, and only them, specific legal protection.

The Italian Constitutional Court struck down as unconstitutional a provision in the Criminal Code providing for a compulsory postponement of the incarceration of any person affected by HIV, the virus associated with AIDS. The code rule was based on the idea that jail detention of individuals having AIDS was incompatible with that person's health and, perhaps more important, with the safety of other prisoners. The court said that though these concerns had merit, the judge should not be barred from imposing a prison sentence in all cases involving persons with HIV but should be free to consider each case on its merits.

In the U.S. the 435 seats in the House of Representatives are allocated among the states in accordance with population, and, therefore, the census taken every 10 years is a matter of major importance to the body politic. When a state's population becomes relatively greater or smaller, it will gain or lose a seat or seats in the House, and this calls for it to reapportion its congressional districts. Two major cases involving these phenomena as a result of the 1990 census came before the U.S. Supreme Court in 1996. *Wisconsin* v. *City of New York* involved the charge that the 1990 census had undercounted the population of the state of New York by not including some individuals, essentially members of certain minority groups. This undercount, it was alleged, benefited the state of Wisconsin. The U.S. secretary of commerce, to whom matters involving the census have been delegated, refused to employ any method of statistical adjustment to change the count. The Supreme Court sustained his decision, stating that it was consonant with the text and history of the federal constitution.

Because of the 1990 census, North Carolina was required to reapportion its congressional districts. In doing so, it established a district in which the majority of residents were African-Americans. This district, highly irregular in shape and geographically noncompact, was designed to give African-Americans voting strength and possibly assure them a "safe" seat in the House of Representatives. In *Shaw* v. *Hunt* the Supreme Court declared that the redistricting plan violated the equal protection clause of the U.S. Constitution. In *Bush* v. *Vera* a similar fate befell the state of Texas in its efforts to give African-Americans and Hispanics assured voting strength.

Several cases in 1996 involved the death penalty. In *Reckley* v. *Minister of Public Safety,* the Privy Council held that under the constitution of The Bahamas the exercise of the prerogative of mercy could not be challenged legally. The person sentenced to death has no voice in determining whether the minister of public safety will invoke, or not invoke, his discretion as to whether the death sentence should be carried out.

In the U.S. a federal appellate court held in *Fierro* v. *Gomez* that the use of cyanide gas to carry out a death sentence imposes cruel and unusual punishment on the prisoner in violation of the Eighth Amendment to the federal constitution. In this connection the court found that the pain caused by cyanide gas is intense and continues for several minutes.

The U.S. Supreme Court in *Loving* v. *The United States* sustained the power of the president to prescribe the factors to be taken into account for a court-martial to sentence a member of the armed forces to death. The contention, which the court rejected, was that only Congress had that authority.

Many countries had by 1996 enacted forfeiture laws, largely to deter the smuggling of drugs and to make that business less profitable. Under these laws the vehicle used for the illegal activity could be seized and forfeited to the state. Legal questions arising from the use of these laws usually involved a determination of the property that could be seized and the rights of innocent co-owners of that property. These questions arose in two cases during the year. The first, from Canada, *Joys* v. *Minister of National Revenue,* concerned the seizure and forfeiture of a fishing boat that had been used to smuggle narcotics and of the fishing license required for using the vessel to fish. The court held that the boat could be legally seized and forfeited but that the fishing license could not. The court opined that the license was necessary to fish but not to smuggle and that it, therefore, had an insufficient relationship to that activity to permit forfeiture. The second case, from the U.S., *Bennis* v. *Michigan,* did not involve drugs but concerned the forfeiture as a public nuisance of an automobile used by its co-owner as the site of assignation with a prostitute. The wife of the guilty party was the co-owner of the automobile and asserted that her interest in the car should not be seized because of her lack of knowledge that her husband would use it to violate the state's indecency laws. In spite of this assertion, the Michigan court held that her interest could be seized legally without compensation. The U.S. Supreme Court, in a sharply divided opinion, affirmed this ruling.

Conceptually, a state's taking of property as a direct or indirect result of legislation or administrative regulation is a form of forfeiture, but in many countries it requires the state to compensate the owner for any loss. This matter arose in France during the year. An appropriate administrator refused to allow the owner of a van Gogh painting to remove it from France for the purpose of selling it abroad. The ruling was predicated on the ground that the painting was a historic monument, which the owner denied. The Cour de Cassation ruled the administrator had the authority to prohibit the exportation of the painting but decreed that the owner was to be compensated for his loss. The loss, in this regard, was the difference between the price he could obtain in France and the price he could reasonably expect to receive on the international market.

In *Goodwin* v. *United Kingdom* the European Court of Human Rights handed down an important decision under Article 10(1) of the European Convention for the Protection of Human Rights, which guarantees freedom of expression. The case involved a British journalist, William Goodwin, who was called by an informant and given unsolicited information about the finances of a certain company. Goodwin proposed to publish the information and called the company in question, asking it to verify the correctness of his proposed draft and to offer comments about it. The company immediately sought and obtained an injunction prohibiting the publication of the draft and a ruling requiring Goodwin to reveal his sources. Pursuant to the injunction, Goodwin did not publish the article, but he refused to reveal the source of his information and was fined £5,000 for contempt. He then filed a complaint with the European Commission of Human Rights on the grounds that his freedom of expression guaranteed by Article 10 had been abridged. The Court of Human Rights agreed in part. It ruled that the injunction against publication was properly within the discretion of the English court but that its additional disclosure order went too far.

The U.S. Supreme Court held in *Jaffee* v. *Redmond* that confidential communications between a patient and a psychotherapist, including a licensed social worker, in the course of psychotherapy were privileged and could not be required to be disclosed. In a dissent Justice Antonin Scalia pointed out that the majority of the court had concentrated only on the benefit that would be achieved by the creation of the evidentiary privilege, namely the encouragement of psychotherapeutic counseling. "It has not mentioned the purchase price: occasional injustice. That is the cost of every rule which excludes reliable and probative evidence."

The Supreme Court of Canada, in *R.* v. *O'Connor,* seemed to take the same position as Justice Scalia, at least in a criminal case. The case involved the effort of a person charged with sexual assault to obtain the medical and psychological records of the victim. In a 5–4 decision the majority held that it was necessary for the accused to have these records in order to ensure a fair trial. The minority expressed concerns about the privacy of the victim. Almost echoing Justice Scalia, the majority said those concerns were too great a price to pay when the criminal liability of the accused was at stake. Priority must be given to the right of the accused to a fair trial.

The Federal Court of Canada ruled that certain applications of the Canadian Immigration Act violated freedom of association guaranteed by section 2 of the Canadian Charter of Rights. The case, *Yamani* v. *Canada,* involved an effort to exclude a Palestinian, Yamani, because of his membership in the Popular Front for the Liberation of Palestine (PFLP), an association that engaged in both violent and nonviolent activities. There was no evidence that Yamani was personally involved in the functions of the PFLP or was a danger to the lives or safety of persons in Canada. Under these circumstances, an order excluding him violated his right to freedom of association.   (WILLIAM D. HAWKLAND)

See also World Affairs: *Multinational and Regional Organizations; United Nations.*

This article updates the *Macropædia* articles CONSTITUTIONAL LAW; INTERNATIONAL LAW.

CRIME

Terrorism. On July 27, 1996, the detonation of a single homemade pipe bomb reverberated around the world as the scourge of terrorism struck the Centennial Olympic Games in Atlanta, Ga. The crude device, left in a knapsack in a park near the main Olympic sites, exploded amid tens of thousands of people. One person was killed by the blast, and a photojournalist died of a heart attack while running to cover it; 111 were injured. The bombing was the first such attack against the Olympics since the 1972 Games in Munich, Ger., when Palestinian terrorists killed 11 Israeli team members.

The attack in Atlanta occurred despite the mounting of the most extensive peacetime security operation in U.S. history to protect the world's premier sporting event, and it took place only days after Americans had been stunned by the loss of a Trans World Airlines (TWA) jumbo jet, which was at first widely presumed to have been destroyed by a terrorist bomb or missile. On July 17 TWA Flight 800, en route to Paris from New York City, crashed into the sea following a fiery midair explosion shortly after takeoff. All 230 persons aboard the 747 aircraft perished.

Law-enforcement officials investigating the Atlanta attack pinpointed U.S. citizens rather than international terrorist groups as the most likely suspects, with initial suspicion falling on a security guard, Richard Jewell, who had originally alerted police to the presence of the knapsack containing the bomb. In late October Jewell was officially exonerated of any involvement in the bombing. A multiagency task force, headed by the FBI, continued to investigate the attack.

A massive investigation involving the National Transportation Safety Board, the FBI, and other agencies also continued into the causes of the TWA crash. With more than 90% of the plane recovered from the ocean and after extensive scientific testing of the wreckage, it seemed likely that the jet plunged into the Atlantic Ocean as a result of a mechanical malfunction.

In September U.S. Pres. Bill Clinton said he would request $1 billion from Congress to place bomb-detection devices in airports and to bolster FBI efforts to fight terrorism. Earlier, Clinton had sought greater cooperation from the world's major powers to carry out new international agreements on more effective ways of preventing, investigating, and prosecuting terrorism. In June at the annual meeting in Lyons, Fr., of the leaders of the Group of Seven—the world's seven richest industrial democracies—Clinton advanced a 40-point list of recommendations to combat terrorism, including the imposition of sanctions on Iran, Libya, and other countries the U.S. accused of backing terrorist attacks.

On December 17 about 20 members of Peru's left-wing Tupac Amaru Revolutionary Movement seized the residence of the Japanese ambassador in Lima during a party attended by nearly 500 guests, including many high officials. They held the guests hostage, demanding that their jailed comrades be freed before any hostages would be released. Pres. Alberto Fujimori of Peru refused to accept their demands, and a standoff resulted. By the year's end the

A Palestinian woman, sitting outside her West Bank home, holds a photograph of her grandson, who died in a suicide bomb attack against the Israelis. The large number of bombings in Middle Eastern countries in 1996 increased instability in the area.

rebels had released many of the hostages but continued to hold 83.

The U.S. State Department's 1996 report *Patterns of Global Terrorism* said that Iran remained the "premier state sponsor of international terrorism and is deeply involved in the planning and execution of terrorist acts." The report also noted that in 1995 the level of international terrorism in most countries continued a downward trend of recent years, with the number of fatalities worldwide declining from 314 in 1994 to 165 in 1995 but the number of persons injured increasing substantially.

In the Middle East a series of murderous attacks by extremist groups in Israel, Egypt, and Saudi Arabia took a heavy toll in human life. The radical Islamic resistance movement Hamas claimed responsibility for four suicide bombings in Israel that killed 60 people, including the terrorists, during nine days in February and March. The bombings were said to be in revenge for the assassination of a Hamas bomb maker, Yahya Ayyash, who was killed

by a remote-controlled booby-trapped cellular telephone in Gaza on January 5. Israeli secret service agents were believed responsible for Ayyash's death.

On June 25 a powerful truck bomb exploded outside a military dormitory at King Abdul Aziz Air Base near the eastern Saudi Arabian Gulf city of Dhahran. The blast, which killed 19 U.S. servicemen and wounded hundreds of other people, followed the public beheading on May 31 of four Islamic militants who were convicted in the car bombing of a U.S. military installation in Riyadh in November 1995. In September an official U.S. inquiry into the Dhahran bombing blamed the U.S. Defense Department and the field commander in the Gulf for having placed U.S. troops at risk in the dormitory despite clear warnings about their vulnerability to terrorist attack. In October it was disclosed that Saudi authorities had arrested six persons suspected of having carried out the bombing.

A 17-month cease-fire in the long-standing conflict in Northern Ireland was shattered on February 9 in London's Canary Wharf in the Docklands area by a huge bomb explosion that killed 2 people, injured more than 100, and caused up to $250 million in property damage. The Irish Republican Army (IRA) claimed responsibility for this and several more bomb blasts during the year, including an October 7 attack on the British army's headquarters near Belfast, N.Ire., that left one soldier dead and 30 people injured.

War Crimes. In July the UN war crimes tribunal for former Yugoslavia issued international arrest warrants against the Bosnian Serb political leader, Radovan Karadzic (*see* BIOGRAPHIES), and his military commander, Gen. Ratko Mladic. The two men were accused of responsibility for genocide and war crimes during the 43-month Balkan conflict, including the siege of Sarajevo, where more than 12,000 civilians died, and the attack on the "UN safe area" of Srebrenica, where more than 6,000 Muslims disappeared after a Bosnian Serb assault. Meanwhile, an ethnic Croat soldier, Drazen Erdemovic, became the first person convicted by the tribunal following his confession in June of having participated in the murder of at least 1,200 Muslim civilians after the fall of Srebrenica in July 1995. He was sentenced to 10 years in prison.

Drug Trafficking. Drug law-enforcement officials expressed concern about the resurgence of drug trafficking into the U.S. and other countries via Caribbean routes. Drugs were often brought into the islands by planes or ships that dropped their cargo in the sea, where it was picked up by small high-speed boats and taken to safe houses. The drugs were then delivered to Puerto Rico, which officials said was becoming the centre for the Caribbean flow of drugs to the U.S. mainland, Canada, and Europe. Puerto Rico was also said to be an island under siege by the problems of drug trafficking, including being afflicted by the highest per capita murder rate in the U.S. In 1995 more than 65% of the 850 murders in Puerto Rico were drug related.

Mexico also continued to be a major conduit for drugs entering the U.S., as well as a centre for money laundering for the drug trade. Pres. Ernesto Zedillo Ponce de León of Mexico labeled drug smuggling as the biggest threat to the country's national security, citing drug-related killings across the nation, including the assassination of seven federal prosecutors in Tijuana, allegedly by members of the local drug cartel. The president said some successes had been achieved in arresting major drug dealers. These included Juan García Abrego, a fugitive on the FBI's 10-most-wanted list, who was captured by Mexican drug agents in January in northern Mexico and immediately deported to the U.S. to face a 20-count indictment on charges including drug trafficking, money laundering, and murder. Abrego, the head of the Gulf drug cartel based in the border city of Matamoros, was believed to have been responsible for the shipment of perhaps a third of the cocaine consumed in the U.S. during the past decade.

Murder and Other Violence. The crime rate in the U.S. fell in 1995 to its lowest level in a decade, according to the FBI's annual survey of law-enforcement agencies, with the violent crime rate in 1995 drop-

L. VAN DER STOCKT—GAMMA LIAISON

Investigators examine a mass grave in Bosnia and Herzegovina. Although Radovan Karadzic, the Bosnian Serb political leader, and his military commander, Gen. Ratko Mladic, were indicted by a UN tribunal in 1996 for genocide and other war crimes, neither was arrested.

ping 4% from the previous year. The survey showed that every region of the U.S., with the exception of the West, had lower levels of crime. The reduction in violent crime was marked by an 8% decrease from the previous year in the rate of murders, 21,-597 of which were reported to the police nationwide during 1995. Smaller reductions were recorded in robberies and aggravated assaults. Criminologists suggested that the continuing drop in crime could be the result of a number of factors, including the aging of the population, with baby boomers reaching middle age and now well beyond their most crime-prone years; more aggressive and imaginative police tactics; a tripling of the nation's prison population over the past 15 years; new gun-control laws; and the increasing use of new crime-prevention measures with young people. Experts also cautioned that the figures might still mask a continuing rise in violent crime among young people and that a rapid future escalation might occur in crime rates because the number of teenagers in the population was expected to grow by 20% during the next decade.

Community concerns about crime, and especially violent crime, were not limited to the U.S. In Japan polls suggested that many Japanese no longer felt safe, at least partly because they had been exposed to massive media publicity about criminal cases like the nerve-gas attack launched on the Tokyo subway in 1995. Despite these fears, the statistics showed that the risks of becoming the victim of a violent crime in Japan were still extremely low. In 1995, for example, there were 32 gun murders in all of Japan, compared with more than 15,000 in the U.S., although the population of the U.S. is only a little over twice that of Japan. Most of those slain with guns in Japan were gangsters shot by other gangsters. Public anxiety about these gun-related murders was suffi-

cient to lead the Japanese government to further tighten restrictions on gun ownership, which were already among the most stringent in the world.

Gun control dominated community debate about crime in the United Kingdom and Australia during 1996 following two horrific mass killings. On March 13 Thomas Hamilton, a social misfit with a passion for guns, walked into a primary school in the Scottish town of Dunblane. Armed with four legally possessed handguns and more than 700 rounds of ammunition, he opened fire with a 9-mm Browning semiautomatic pistol, killing a teacher and 16 children and wounding another 12 pupils and two teachers before taking his own life. The killings sparked national outrage and a call for much tougher gun laws. In October, after receiving the report of an official inquiry into the incident, the British government proposed outlawing almost all private possession of handguns.

On April 28 a lone gunman, armed with military-style semiautomatic weapons, went on a shooting spree at the quiet tourist resort of Port Arthur in the Australian island state of Tasmania. Before being captured alive by police after a 16-hour siege, the alleged gunman, Martin Bryant, a psychologically disturbed and unemployed Tasmanian resident, killed 35 people and wounded another 19. The shooting, the worst peacetime massacre by a single gunman in recent history, shocked Australians and resulted in almost immediate bipartisan political support for the introduction of new national gun-control laws designed to outlaw most semiautomatic weapons and to put in place uniform requirements for the possession, registration, sale, and security of all firearms.

The first World Congress Against Commercial Sexual Exploitation of Children met in Stockholm in August. The head

Haitian police recruits watch a demonstration as part of their training. After U.S. troops departed Haiti early in 1996 and the UN peacekeepers left late in the year, the difficult task of maintaining civil order there fell largely to a newly formed police force.

of UNICEF told the delegates from 126 countries that sexual exploitation of children had become a global multi-billion-dollar industry and that no part of the world could claim to be immune.

White Collar Crime and Theft. In June the giant Japanese company Sumitomo revealed that its chief copper trader, Yasuo Hamanaka, had caused losses of $1.8 billion accumulated over a 10-year period of unauthorized transactions. This disclosure of one of the world's largest financial trading losses rocked the London Metal Exchange, the dominant international copper market, and prompted an immediate investigation into the scandal by Britain's Serious Fraud Office. Sumitomo fired Hamanaka after announcing the losses, and Japanese prosecutors ordered a special task force to examine whether to file criminal breach-of-trust charges against the trader. The Sumitomo case was the third in 16 months in which the actions of individual traders like Hamanaka had created enormous financial losses for multinational corporations and came only eight months after another Japanese giant, the Daiwa Bank, had admitted that a senior trader in its New York City office had caused $1.1 billion in losses over an 11-year period through unauthorized trades on the bond markets. Both the Sumitomo and Daiwa cases raised critical questions about the adequacy of the internal and external controls maintained over Japanese corporations.

Two U.S. government officials were arrested late in the year and charged with espionage. Harold Nicholson of the CIA was accused in November of having spied for Russia from 1994 to 1996, for which, prosecutors said, he was paid $180,000. In December Earl Pitts, an FBI supervisor, was accused of having sold classified information to Moscow in return for payments of $224,000. The FBI was most concerned about 1987–89, when Pitts was assigned to sensitive counterintelligence operations.

LAW ENFORCEMENT

The FBI revealed plans in 1996 to double its presence in other nations by opening new offices in 23 cities outside the U.S. The expansion was intended to cope with the increasing demands of investigating international terrorism, organized crime, and drug trafficking affecting U.S. citizens. Some critics suggested that it might detract from the FBI's main role as a domestic federal law-enforcement agency and could lead to duplication of the work already being carried out by the CIA and the Drug Enforcement Administration (DEA). Congress, however, remained sympathetic to the proposal and approved the opening of the first of the new offices in Beijing, Cairo, Islamabad, Pak., and Tel Aviv, Israel.

An accelerated use of electronic surveillance was reported by U.S. federal law-enforcement agencies in 1996. This surveillance was said to be a particularly effective tool in pursuing drug dealers. In one recent case, code named Zorro II, investigators set up more than 90 separate wiretaps in a number of major U.S. cities as they built up evidence against 130 suspected cocaine importers, shippers, and distributors. The entire drug network was subsequently destroyed as a result of the accumulated wiretap information made available. Electronic surveillance remained, however, an expensive and labour-intensive investigative technique, but the DEA was reported to be carrying out a $33 million program to replace single-line wiretapping equipment with new technology that could monitor 40 wires simultaneously and process the intercepts by computer.

An 18-year search by the FBI for the so-called Unabomber, the person responsible for a mail-bomb terror campaign that left 3 people dead and 23 injured, ended in April with the arrest of a suspect, Theodore Kaczynski. The likely bomber was identified to the FBI by his brother, David, who made a connection between published Unabomber documents and Kaczynski's writings. Kaczynski, a recluse who formerly had been a university mathematics professor, was captured in a remote cabin in Montana, where he had lived for 25 years.

The dramatic capture in May of one of the most powerful and ruthless Mafia bosses, Giovanni Brusca, gave fresh hope and impetus to the bitter struggle by Italian law-enforcement authorities to curb the power of organized crime in that country. As many as 400 police were involved in the operation that led to Brusca's arrest at a house in Cannatello, near Agrigento on Sicily's southern coast. Brusca was believed responsible for the assassination in May 1992 of Giovanni Falcone, Italy's main prosecutor of the Mafia, as well as for leading the group that planted car bombs in 1993 that did great damage to the world-famous Uffizi Gallery in Florence and to other historic buildings in Rome and Milan. Prosecutors said these bombings were in retaliation for the arrest of Salvatore Riina, the Mafia's "boss of bosses" and as a response to the pope's denunciation that year of the Cosa Nostra.

After a 19-month trial in Pretoria, S.Af., a former police colonel, Eugene de Kock, was convicted in August on 89 charges including 6 relating to murders he committed during South Africa's apartheid era. De Kock, who once called himself the nation's most efficient assassin, was commander of a police unit based at a farm outside Pretoria where apartheid activists were alleged to have been tortured and killed. In a presentence hearing De Kock made a number of dramatic allegations about the complicity of senior leaders of the former apartheid regime, including former president Pieter W. Botha. De Kock also claimed that a South African police spy, Craig Williamson, had been involved in the assassination in 1986 of Swedish Prime Minister Olof Palme. The assassination, which until now had remained one of Europe's most perplexing unsolved murder cases, was said to have been part of Operation Long Reach, a secret program carried out by the apartheid government to harass or silence its opponents overseas. Palme was a committed foe of apartheid and had close ties to African National Congress leader Nelson Mandela. De Kock's allegations were later denied by Williamson, who said he would soon be testifying about his involvement in Operation Long Reach before South Africa's Truth and Reconciliation Commission, which began a series of hearings in April. De Kock was also expected to testify before the commission.   (DUNCAN CHAPPELL)

PRISONS AND PENOLOGY

With a few notable exceptions, the trend toward a tougher criminal policy throughout the world resulted in an increased reliance upon imprisonment in 1996. Prison conditions in many countries deteriorated; almost invariably, untried persons were held under the worst circumstances. Prisoners in Russia, for example, suffered high mortality rates and a prevalence of tuberculosis that was 40 times higher than in the general population. The Russian prison population grew, on average, by 3,500–4,000 per month, reaching an incarceration rate of 570 prisoners per 100,000 inhabitants. This rate was similar to those of some other former Soviet republics, such as Kazakstan and Belarus. Such was the pressure of numbers in Turkmenistan that several people suffocated in overcrowded cells.

Russia and the United States were among the countries with the highest proportions of their inhabitants in prison. In the U.S., where in 1996 more than 1.5 million were held in federal, state, and local facilities, the indications were that recent "three strikes and you're out" measures of mandatory prison sentences enacted by several states and the federal government would lead to further huge increases. The National Council on Crime and Delinquency, an independent agency, estimated that the nation's total prison population could rise to as high as 7.5 million if legislative and other proposals were acted upon.

Concerns increasingly were being raised that some European countries were on track to follow the U.S. example. In Italy, for example, the prison population doubled between 1990 and 1995, with 52,000 people held in 33,000 places. The prison population in England and Wales increased by 40% between 1992 and 1996, and was

MALCOLM LINTON—BLACK STAR

Several women, most of them sentenced for having brewed alcohol, share a cell in a prison in The Sudan. The use and abuse of imprisonment continued to increase in much of the world.

forecast to grow at an even faster rate if the government's mandatory minimum sentencing proposals were put into effect.

Appalling prison conditions were reported in many other parts of the world. In Nigeria an average of 10 people each week died, many of malnutrition, in two of the main prisons in Lagos. A total of 35,000 prisoners were awaiting trial, some after as long as 10 years. In Kenya, where the prison population increased from 13,000 to 40,000 between 1963 and 1995, more than 800 prisoners died during 1995, mostly as a result of the spread of malaria, dysentery, tuberculosis, and AIDS. Elsewhere in Africa the situation was even more grim. In Rwanda severe overcrowding resulted in prisoners' being held in food warehouses and in tents. The situation in some parts of Latin America also worsened. El Salvador's 16 prisons operated at three times their capacity. Space was at such a premium that prisoners were forced to sleep in a sitting position. Overcrowding was also considered a factor in the deaths of 25 inmates in a Caracas, Venez., prison during a fire.

High levels of crowding and declining conditions were associated with serious riots in several prisons. In April a riot at the prison near Goiania, Brazil (where 5,000 prisoners shared 100 cells), was followed by the escape of 30 prisoners. In the Dominican Republic six prisoners were killed at San Cristobel prison in May during rioting that was touched off by crowded conditions. Riots also occurred in 20 prisons in Argentina in April amid concerns about the length of time people were held before trial. Serious rioting took place in March 1996 at five Greek prisons, and in July 12 prisoners in Turkey died during a hunger strike.

A few countries took steps intended to reduce the use of imprisonment. The new Czech penal code took effect in January, enabling the courts to make use of community service as an alternative to prison sentences of five years or less. In the Canadian province of Quebec, the Ministry of Public Security declared that in contrast to the trend sweeping across North America, "Quebec has decided to turn its back on the repressive model" and adopt a system

based on "prevention, resolution of conflict and the use of incarceration only for individuals who pose a threat to the population's security." By contrast, the Dutch government announced measures aimed at ensuring tougher sentences for drug traffickers. By 1996 two U.S. states—Florida and Arizona—were using chain gangs. Alabama, however, discontinued their use.

Death Penalty. In March 1996 Amnesty International reported that in regard to the death penalty, 100 of the world's nations could be described as abolitionist either in law or in practice and that 94 retained it. During 1995 South Africa, Moldova, and Mauritius were added to the list of countries that had abolished the death penalty. Although regarded as an underestimate by Amnesty International, there were 2,931 persons known to have been executed during 1995 in 41 countries. Of this total, 2,190 were carried out in China, 192 in Saudi Arabia, and more than 100 in Nigeria. Large numbers of executions also occurred in Iraq, but exact figures were not available. In Russia there were 710 persons on death row, and at least 16 were executed (although Amnesty International independently confirmed that 28 executions took place). At least 30 persons were executed in Kyrgyzstan and at least 63 in Kazakstan. In the U.S. in 1996 (where 39 states had restored the death penalty since 1976), 45 executions took place, and more than 3,150 persons were held on death row, including 47 juveniles. Federal funding was removed from the legal aid centres that represented defendants and appellants in capital cases, and in Texas it was decreed that family members of the victim were to be invited to view the execution. Although there were no executions in Ghana, some prisoners in that nation had been on death row for up to 13 years in conditions described by a human rights group as "excruciating."

(ANDREW RUTHERFORD)

See also World Affairs: *Multinational and Regional Organizations; United Nations.*

This article updates the *Macropædia* articles CONSTITUTIONAL LAW; CRIME AND PUNISHMENT; INTERNATIONAL LAW; POLICE.

Libraries and Museums

LIBRARIES

In 1996 libraries around the world were both shaping their collections and being shaped by the continued spectacular growth of the Internet, a worldwide network of computers. The role of libraries as disseminators and providers of some of the most valued information available on the Internet was a heartening development for a profession that had historically experienced limited visibility, respect, and prestige. Equally important to librarians, however, was the growing promise of the Internet to mitigate some of their most pressing problems: static or shrinking resources and ever-growing demands for information and services. Affordable technologies allowed libraries to retrieve text, images, and sound rapidly from remote locations around the globe. In April the New York Public Library, as part of its centennial celebration, served as host of a summit attended by leaders from 50 of the world's main libraries to discuss the "Global Library Strategies for the 21st Century."

Although the Internet is too diffuse and volatile to categorize easily, most of the host computers and users were located in North America, Australia, Europe, and Asia. The relative dearth of development in Africa and Latin America added credence to librarians' concerns for the "info-poor." Indeed, while thousands of libraries logged onto the Internet in 1996, a donkey-powered bookmobile plied the countryside in Zimbabwe.

In many parts of the world, national libraries and governments played a leading role in developing new facilities and resources. Turkey appointed a librarian to develop a national network of university libraries, while the government in Singapore announced plans to spend S$1 billion to enhance and expand library services with a goal of making Singapore a "Renaissance City of the New Asia." The initiative would also provide librarians with high-tech training, regular salary reviews, and career structures to transform them into "cybarians" and "knowledge navigators."

Spectacular and expensive national library buildings neared completion in England, France, and Denmark. Other libraries continued to digitize catalogs, collections, and other data to enable 24-hour-a-day access from anywhere in the world. The British Library, for example, introduced GABRIEL (Gateway and Bridge to Europe's National Libraries), an on-line multilingual directory that offered a single point of access to a number of national libraries in Europe.

In Egypt the Library of Alexandria neared completion, while the Shanghai Library, China's second largest facility, planned to enhance its collection and on-line services by moving into a new 830,000-sq m (8,934,000-sq ft) facility, also home to that city's Institute of Scientific and Technical Information. Increased access to the contents of the Internet, particularly World Wide Web sites, produced a number of concerns. While the Chinese government announced plans to limit and/or screen out some electronic information, public libraries worried about children accessing some very adult images and text. In the U.S. the American Library Association was the lead plaintiff in a suit challenging the Communications Decency Act, which sought to ban as "indecent" a broad category of electronic information. In June, however, a federal district court ruled the act unconstitutional. Copyright infringement was another complex problem exacerbated by a wired world.

Attempts to restore the collections and bibliographic records of the war-ravaged National Library of Bosnia continued with assistance from UNESCO and OCLC (the Online Library Computer Center of Dublin, Ohio). No decision had been made, however, about the fate of the ornate Euro-arabesque building, though proposals were made to either leave the structure unrestored as a memorial or restore it to its original function as Sarajevo's city hall. Restoration of the Accademia dei Georgofili, the museum library of Florence's Uffizi Gallery, also continued. The Uffizi had been damaged in 1993 by a bomb blast that Italian police blamed on the Mafia.

In the U.S., San Francisco opened the most technically advanced library in the world. The seven-story New Main facility occupied 35,000 sq m (376,000 sq ft) and boasted 11 special-interest centres and 400 computer workstations, 100 of them with Internet access. Some denounced the discarding of about 200,000 books and a decision, later rescinded, to dispose of the card catalog. The New York Public Library opened a new $100 million Science, Industry, and Business Library for use by the general public and small businesses.

Microsoft chairman Bill Gates announced a $10.5 million program called Libraries Online!, which would help 41 libraries in North America expand their electronic services. A survey conducted by the National Commission on Libraries and Information Science showed that 45% of public libraries in the U.S. were connected to the Internet.

The International Federation of Library Associations and Institutions (IFLA) held its annual meeting in Beijing in August. IFLA also launched its own World Wide Web site, IFLANET, which could be accessed by association members in 70 nations.

(GORDON FLAGG; THOMAS GAUGHAN)

This article updates the *Macropædia* article LIBRARIES AND LIBRARY SCIENCE.

MUSEUMS

The year 1996 was marked by anniversaries, new beginnings, and the continuation of powerful trends in museums throughout the world. In November the International Council of Museums (ICOM) celebrated its 50th anniversary. Founded by Chauncey Hamlin of the U.S. soon after the end of World War II, ICOM was conceived in the shadow of the United Nations as an organization that would unite museums across the globe to promote cultural understanding and world peace. By 1996 it had some 13,000 members in 145 countries. The anniversary celebrations took place at the Louvre in Paris, the location of ICOM's founding.

In May museums throughout the Arab world convened in Egypt for the first meeting of ICOM's Regional Organization for Arab Countries. The group planned to develop a handbook in order to standardize the compilation of inventories (an important tool in fighting theft and illicit trafficking of cultural objects) and also to set up a system for exchanging information within the region.

A patterned skylight and gate are features of the James C. Hormel Gay and Lesbian Center, part of the San Francisco Main Public Library. Completed during the year, the seven-story New Main was made of granite and stainless steel and occupied 35,000 sq m (376,000 sq ft). It included 11 special-interest centres and 400 computer workstations, 100 of them with access to the Internet. Library officials had originally decided to dispose of the old library's card catalog before moving into the new structure, but after many protests they changed their minds.

TIMOTHY HURSLEY

The first world meeting of representatives from science centres and science museums took place in June in Vantaa, Fin. Jointly organized by the Association of Science-Technology Centers in the U.S. and the European Collaborative for Science, Industry and Technology Exhibitions, the theme for this gathering was "Learning for Tomorrow" and focused on the important role these institutions played in science education and new technologies.

Blockbuster exhibitions were mounted throughout the world in 1996. Most notably, an exhibition of paintings by Jan Vermeer drew record crowds at the National Gallery of Art in Washington, D.C. (*See* ART, ANTIQUES, AND COLLECTIONS: *Art Exhibitions*.)

Several museums opened during the year. Among them was the Jean Tinguely Museum in Basel, Switz., in a building designed by Swiss architect Mario Botta. The museum contained 30% of Tinguely's surviving work. Japan began work on the nation's first museum commemorating World War II amid protests by many Japanese, who claimed that the museum, whose mission was to focus on the suffering of Japanese families and soldiers, offered a one-sided view of history. During the summer, on the anniversary of the inaugural flight of the first zeppelin in 1900, the Zeppelin Museum was opened in Friedrichshafen, Ger., the town where Count Ferdinand von Zeppelin began his enterprise. A new museum opened in Shanghai in October and quickly gained acclaim for its outstanding collection of ancient Chinese art.

Museums in many parts of the world continued to suffer from damage caused by armed conflict as well as by natural disasters. In Sarajevo, Bosnia and Herzegovina, collections were being stored in the basements of museum buildings battered by four years of war. Museums in Grozny, Chechnya, were also badly damaged by the conflict of that republic with Russia.

New efforts were made during the year to combat the effects of these disasters. To provide a quick response in cases of emergency, the International Committee of the Blue Shield (ICBS) was created through the cooperation of ICOM, the International Council on Monuments and Sites, the International Council on Archives, and the International Federation of Library Associations and Institutions. The ICBS aimed to provide advice in cases of natural disaster or armed conflict, to facilitate international response, to encourage respect for cultural property, and to promote higher standards of risk preparedness.

Ivories of a river goddess (left) and a lion hunt (below) from Bagram, the summer capital of the Kushan empire in the 1st century AD, were among the most treasured works of art stolen from the National Museum near Kabul, Afg. Over years of war between the Soviet Union and Afghanistan and ongoing civil war, the museum was looted of about 70% of its possessions, many of which were for sale on the international art market.

Museums continued to grapple with new technologies during the year; an increasing number were developing sites on the Internet and using multimedia within their exhibits. Issues of copyright were being hotly debated as museums and artists fought to retain their rights to images while also realizing the benefit of making those images accessible through digitalization.

(HELEN J. WECHSLER)

U.S. museums faced dizzying changes during 1996. Dealing with the challenges of new technology, a downsizing federal government, and increasing competition, they were forced to present themselves as innovative, self-sufficient, and, above all, relevant to issues ranging from economic development to educational reform.

Perhaps the most exciting developments involved the new technologies as hundreds of institutions loaded the Internet with information on collections and programs. The most sophisticated experimented with revolutionary programming such as the on-line exhibition. Combining visual presentation of artifacts, essays, bibliographies, and outreach materials for teachers and schools, these shows gathered all of the elements of the traditional exhibition into a single "virtual" venue. Some institutions also began to digitize collections with the help of a new federal program that funded community-wide information infrastructure projects.

Museums strengthened their role in formal education during the year. Taking advantage of new legislation at the state level, two children's museums, one history-technology museum, and one natural history museum established semi-independent "charter" schools, joining the many museums that had cooperative programs with local public schools. All used museum collections for multidisciplinary instruction, modeling new ways to teach and learn,

The Museum of Contemporary Art in Chicago was completed in 1996. Designed by German architect Josef Paul Kleihues, it provided the largest exhibition space for contemporary art in the U.S., 14,000 sq m (151,000 sq ft). Its galleries were kept bright by a computerized system that filtered daylight and fluorescent light through frosted-glass barrel vaults.

while the best also served as resources for other educators in their regions.

(ANDREW FINCH)

See also Art, Antiques, and Collections. This article updates the Macropædia article MUSEUMS.

Life Sciences

ZOOLOGY

Zoological research during the past year contributed to an improved understanding of the relationships between genetics and the aging process, further explored some of the intricacies of internal physiology, and uncovered the first known example of eusociality in a marine organism. A new species of mammal was discovered in the rain forests of the Philippines, and studies of turtles and lizards provided insight into current conservation issues. Molecular techniques established that the guinea pig is not a rodent, as had been thought.

Bernard Lakowski and Siegfried Hekimi of McGill University, Quebec, presented

evidence that four genes, named the Clock genes, interact to determine the life span of the nematode Caenorhabditis elegans, a microscopic, wormlike soil animal used extensively in genetic studies. The Clock genes appear to extend life span by a mechanism distinct from that of other Caenorhabditis genes, the dauer genes, that previously had been found to affect life span. Nematodes containing mutations in both a Clock gene and a dauer gene lived nearly five times longer than normal wild-type nematodes— the greatest increase in life span over the species average that had been achieved by any means in any organism. The Clock genes also were found to affect other timed processes, including the length of development and the cell cycle. The study showed that Clock-gene mutations affect the rate of development and adult life span in a similar manner, which suggests that the long life of the mutant nematodes may be a consequence of a "slower rate of living," possibly due to a slower rate of metabolism. The Clock genes may be regulatory genes that control metabolic rates and influence a general physiological clock in nematodes.

Lawrence C. Rome and Stephen M.

Baylor of the University of Pennsylvania and colleagues investigated the physiological mechanisms that allow muscle fibres involved in sound production in vertebrates to have contraction cycles 10–20 times faster than most vertebrate locomotory muscles. The tail muscles causing the rattling of western diamondback rattlesnakes (Crotalus atrox) contract repeatedly at about 90 hertz (Hz; cycles per second), whereas muscles that surround the swim bladders of the oyster toadfish (Opsanus tau) and are used in creating a mating call contract at about 200 Hz, the fastest known rate for any vertebrate. The investigators found in both instances that calcium, the trigger for muscle contraction, cycles in a manner that allows the muscle fibres to activate and relax at a rapid rate. Movement of calcium through toadfish bladder muscle is as much as 50 times faster than through most muscles used for locomotion. In addition, the myosin-filament cross bridges, whose repeated binding to actin filaments and subsequent release generate the force in muscle contraction, attach and detach about 50 times faster as well. One significant revelation of the study was that the physiological traits necessary to permit muscle fibres to move rapidly evolved independently in the rattlesnake and toadfish.

A study of the rubber boa (Charina bottae), a nocturnally active snake, by Michael E. Dorcas and Charles R. Peterson of Idaho State University revealed that the internal temperature of the animal's head is significantly warmer than either its internal body temperature or cool nighttime air temperatures. Precise regulation of temperature in the head region of an organism is presumed to be advantageous in optimizing functions of the central nervous system. Although differential temperatures in parts of a reptile body had been reported for other species, the findings in the rubber boa represented the first instance of the phenomenon in a reptile active at night. The study suggested that some reptiles may have greater versatility in regulating temperatures in different bodily regions than formerly suspected.

Social insects, such as ants, honeybees, and termites, and the naked mole rat, a mammal, are considered eusocial, with reproduction often being limited to a single female, or queen, within a colony. Additional characteristics of eusociality are cooperative care of the young and division of labour among nonreproductive members of the colony. The discovery by J. Emmett Duffy of the Virginia Institute of Marine Science, Gloucester Point, Va., of eusociality in a coral-reef shrimp (Synalpheus regalis) was the first such report in a marine organism or a crustacean. S. regalis lives in the internal canals of sponges. Duffy dissected more than 30 sponges from the coast of Belize, each of which housed a shrimp colony with a single reproductive female and usually with multiple generations of her offspring. Examination of the shrimp colonies supported previous hypotheses that altruistic behaviour among nonbreeding members of a colony can be favoured as a result of kin selection in species living in enclosed habitats that provide protection against predators and an adequate food supply.

In the area of conservation ecology, investigators found evidence that the use of turtle excluder devices (TEDs) by shrimp trawlers indeed did result in reduction of the numbers of sea turtles killed in trawling operations. TEDs are grid attachments within trawl nets that retain shrimp but allow most turtles to escape. Without TEDs, shrimpers can unintentionally drown turtles in their nets. Larry B. Crowder and J. Andrew Royle of North Carolina State University and Sally R. Hopkins-Murphy of the South Carolina Department of Natural Resources completed a statistical analysis of the numbers of dead loggerhead sea turtles washed ashore in South Carolina in a 15-year period. In years when shrimping was under way, 44% fewer dead turtles turned up on shore when TEDs were in use than when they were not. TED use also reduced the rate of decline in the population of nesting females along South Carolina beaches and, according to the investigators, had the potential for allowing the loggerhead population to expand by a factor of 10 by the year 2055.

In a continuation of a long-term study on islands in The Bahamas, Thomas W. Schoener and David A. Spiller of the University of California, Davis, experimentally demonstrated the way in which introduction of a predator (an anole lizard) into a system can have devastating effects on the diversity and abundance of prey species (web spiders). The investigators ran a seven-year experiment in which they selected four groups of three islands each, one inhabited by lizards and two without lizards; all of the islands were inhabited by spider species. In each trio of islands, lizards were introduced onto one of the two lizard-free islands. Within two years the islands onto which lizards had been introduced were almost identical in spider diversity and abundance to those with natural lizard populations.

A frog found in Minnesota has an extra leg. Many frogs with similar deformities were found in parts of the U.S. and Canada. Possible causes of the deformities included exposure to pesticides, toxic metals, acid rain, and increased ultraviolet light.

The proportion of spider species becoming extinct on islands with introduced lizards was 12.6 times higher than on islands with no lizards, and most rare species disappeared. The study underscored the impact that predator introductions can have in some situations by severely threatening species composition and integrity of natural systems.

The order Rodentia traditionally has been divided on the basis of morphology into several suborders, one of which, Caviomorpha, includes such animals as chinchillas, degus, agoutis, porcupines, capybaras, and guinea pigs. On sequencing the complete genome, or genetic endowment, of the mitochondrion (a DNA-containing cell organelle) of the guinea pig (*Cavia porcellus*) and using three distinct analytic methods, Anna Maria D'Erchia and Cecilia Saccone of the University of Bari, Italy, and colleagues provided evidence supporting an earlier contention that guinea pigs are in a separate phylogenetic line from the rodents. They concluded that guinea pigs should be placed in a new order of mammals distinct from Rodentia.

A new mammalian species from the Philippine rain forest was reported by Robert Kennedy of the Cincinnati (Ohio) Museum of Natural History & Planetarium and Pedro Gonzales of the National Museum of the Philippines. Named the Panay cloudrunner (*Crateromys heaneyi*), the tree-dwelling, squirrellike rodent has soft brown fur, small ears and eyes, and a long black tail and weighs about 4.5 kg (10 lb).

(J. WHITFIELD GIBBONS)

Entomology. Anne-Geneviève Bagnères of the Laboratory for Neurobiology-Chemical Communication, Marseille, France, and colleagues reported on the way in which one species of paper wasp, *Polistes atrimandibularis*, which is incapable of building a nest or producing a worker caste, persists as an obligatory social parasite on a related host species, *P. biglumis bimaculatus*. Social insects characteristically produce chemical signatures that enable colony members to recognize each another. Annually in late June a fertile parasitic *P. atrimandibularis*

The Panay cloudrunner, a squirrellike nocturnal species of mammal previously unknown to science, was discovered during the year by residents of the Philippine island of Panay in the treetops of the rain forest. Weighing about 4.5 kg (10 lb) and measuring 28 cm (11 in) long, it feeds on fruit and leaves.

queen searches for the nest of her host species. At that time the chemical signatures of the two species differ, with the cuticle of the parasite producing a family of hydrocarbons distinct from the composition of hydrocarbons produced by the host. On colonizing the nest, however, the parasite ceases producing the distinguishing hydrocarbons, and a month later her signature, based on gas chromatography and mass spectrometry, is indistinguishable from that of the host queen. For the remainder of the colonial cycle before the emergence of adult wasps and mating in late summer, *P. biglumis bimaculatus* workers feed and care for parasite offspring as they do the offspring of their own species. The study demonstrated the versatility of the parasite in adjusting its chemical signature at a critical time in its colonial cycle and supported the idea that, in addition to a simple role as an enclosure and a barrier, the cuticle of insects functions as a true gland.

Researchers used training techniques to explore the ability of honeybees to distinguish between symmetry and asymmetry, a critical skill for pollinators in that the symmetry of a flower may indicate its quality. Martin Giurfa, Birgit Eichmann, and Randolf Menzel of the Free University of Berlin presented bees with different stimuli designed to be distinguishable only on the basis of their bilateral symmetry or asymmetry. One group of bees was rewarded for selecting symmetrical patterns, the other for selecting asymmetrical ones. Afterward, both were presented with either symmetrical or asymmetrical patterns that they had not seen before. Individual performance was measured by means of a microphone apparatus, adjusted to detect the bee's flight noise. The investigators recorded how often a bee chose the novel symmetrical or asymmetrical patterns, how close the bee went, and how long it hovered. The results indicated that bees could easily be taught to favour either symmetrical or asymmetrical patterns and could transfer that learning to patterns not seen before. Although bees could be trained to prefer symmetrical or asymmetrical patterns, they showed a predisposition for symmetrical ones. Previous studies had shown that bees are attracted to symmetrical shapes, but the new study demonstrated that they recognize symmetry as a property and respond to it on the basis of their experience.

Mary E.A. Whitehouse and Klaus Jaffe of Simón Bolívar University, Caracas, Venez., studied leaf-cutting ants of the species *Atta laevigata* to investigate two laws of combat strategy. The linear law proposes that a few good fighters are a better strategy than many poor fighters in a series of one-on-one conflicts. The square law holds that if all individuals are equally susceptible to attack, many poor fighters are better than a few good ones. During manipulative field experiments the investigators staged battles between ants from one colony and those of another or against vertebrate predators. The ants responded to vertebrate threats according to the linear law, by recruiting specialized soldier ants from their colony. On the other hand, their response to threats from other ant colonies followed the square law; they recruited large numbers of smaller individuals. Thus, leaf-cutting ants alter their mode of fighting according to the threat and follow the combat strat-

egy law most effective for the situation.
(ANNE R. GIBBONS)

This article updates the *Macropædia* article INSECTS.

Ornithology. Scientists regarded birds' use of tools as mostly stereotyped and their manufacture of tools as involving only limited modification of material objects. In 1996 Gavin R. Hunt of Massey University, Palmerston North, N.Z., reported that to assist in capturing insect prey, New Caledonian crows make and use two different types of hook tools from twigs and one kind of stepped-cut tool from the barbed leaf of the pandanus tree. According to Hunt, these instances of tool manufacture by a bird species had three features new to tool use in nonhuman animals: a high degree of standardization, distinctly discrete tool types with a definite imposition of form in the shaping of the tool, and the use of hooks. During the course of human evolution, such features first appeared in stone and bone tool-using cultures only after the Lower Paleolithic Period (about 2.5 million to 200,000 years ago).

The foraging success and habits of pelagic (open-ocean) seabirds were largely unknown. Using satellite transmitters attached to the birds in conjunction with recorders for measuring feeding times and the weight of ingested food, researchers found that wandering albatrosses on foraging trips from the nest encountered prey on average every 4.4 hours and consumed 2.1 kg (4.6 lb) of food daily. Birds traveled as far as 3,600 km (2,200 mi) from the nest in search of scarce prey, mostly pelagic squid.

Ornithologists had long hypothesized that seagoing birds such as petrels use their sense of smell to find food in the open ocean. Research in the past year showed that petrels indeed can sniff out minute amounts of a telltale chemical released by plankton. Gabrielle Nevitt of the University of California, Davis, and Richard Veit and Peter Kareiva of the University of Washington staged a number of experiments in the waters around the sub-Antarctic island of South Georgia. They created small "slicks" of vegetable oil laced with small amounts of the compound dimethyl sulfide (DMS). Microscopic plants in plankton release DMS when consumed by small animals such as krill. Because petrels and their relatives eat such animals, the researchers reasoned that the birds might be able to detect DMS. In fact, DMS turned out to be highly attractive to several seabird species, including Wilson's storm petrels, black-bellied storm petrels, and prions. As storm petrels and their allies often hunt by night, they would gain from their sensitivity to DMS. Furthermore, some areas of the open ocean, where plankton thrive, tend to have higher concentrations of DMS than others. Birds may be able to detect these chemical patterns and use them to help navigate over the otherwise featureless oceans.

Two fossil discoveries prompted paleontologists to rethink theories about the diversity of bird life in the age of the dinosaurs. The beautifully preserved bones of *Vorona berivotrensis*, a new, very primitive bird species unearthed in Madagascar, was the first specimen from the Mesozoic Era (245 million to 66 million years ago) to be found in a large portion of the ancient continent of Gondwana (mainly present-day South America, Africa, India, Australia,

and Antarctica). It was also the first pre-Holocene bird (older than 10,000 years) found in Madagascar. The lower limb of the crow-sized fossil indicated a close relationship to the extinct Enantiornithes, the most common group of birds contemporary with the dinosaurs.

The second fossil, *Eoalulavis hoyasi*, from Spain, showed that birds had evolved their efficient, modern style of flight as early as 115 million years ago. According to Luis Chiappe of the American Museum of Natural History, New York City, who helped describe the Madagascan and Spanish fossils, "The diversity of early birds was much larger than we thought five years ago." *E. hoyasi* was about the size of a goldfinch. Its remains included a well-preserved wing with many feathers in their original positions and showed a crucial stage in the evolution of flight. It lived only about 30 million years after the first bird, *Archaeopteryx*, but already possessed the alula, or bastard wing, that allows modern birds to maneuver among trees. (JEFFERY BOSWALL)

This article updates the *Macropædia* article BIRDS.

MARINE BIOLOGY

The discovery of a species of marine animal that appeared to constitute an entirely new phylum was reported in the science journal *Nature* as the "zoological highlight of the decade." Two Danish investigators proposed that their newfound invertebrate species, *Symbion pandora*, be attributed to a new phylum, Cycliophora, related to the phyla Ectoprocta (Bryozoa) and Entoprocta. *Symbion* is an acoelomate metazoan—*i.e.*, a multicellular animal lacking an internal fluid-filled body cavity. Its sessile stages were found abundantly on the mouthparts of the Norway lobster

Symbion pandora, a tiny marine invertebrate that lives on the mouthparts of the Norway lobster, was discovered by two Danish scientists and classified in a new phylum, Cycliophora.

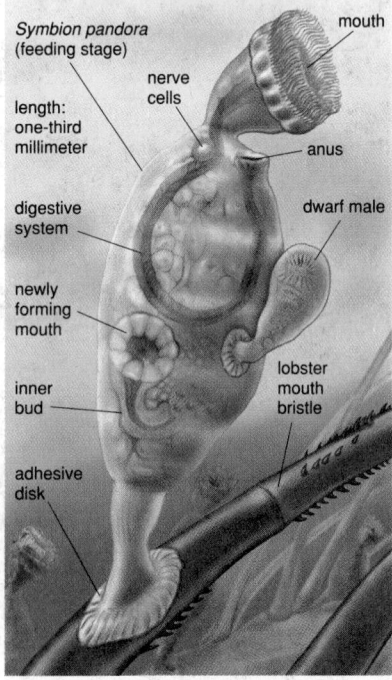

Symbion pandora (feeding stage)

length: one-third millimeter

nerve cells

digestive system

newly forming mouth

inner bud

adhesive disk

mouth

anus

dwarf male

lobster mouth bristle

(*Nephrops norvegicus*), where they capture food being ingested by their host.

Vertical migration rhythms in plankton living in the open sea typically show a daily pattern. However, a U.K. study of newly hatched larvae of the shore crab *Carcinus maenas* demonstrated endogenous rhythms geared to the tides. Upward swimming during ebb tides evidently disperses the larvae offshore and thus prevents their premature stranding onshore in the intertidal area. In a Polish study two species of mid-water lantern fish from the Atlantic, *Hygophum macrochir* and *H. taaningi*, were shown to avoid vertical migration at night during the new moon lunar phase. The fish stayed in cold water below 400 m (1,300 ft) at new moon and did not, as during other lunar phases, rise to warmer surface waters at night. The lunar variations of vertical migration were found to be recorded in the animals' otoliths, so-called ear stones used in maintaining balance. The microstructure of the otolith shows a pattern of daily growth rings, which varies according to the sea temperatures experienced by the fish. A similar record of carbon isotope ratios was detected in baleen plates taken from stranded southern right whales from South Africa. Changes of isotope ratios along the length of the plates provided the first direct evidence of seasonal migrations of the whales north and south of the Subtropical Convergence.

French and German researchers fitted five albatross of the species *Diomedea exulans* with miniature sea-temperature recorders and satellite transmitters and released the birds to forage over the Southern Ocean. During frequent pauses on the sea surface, the birds transmitted, via satellite to a tracking station, the sea-surface temperature where they rested. The technique could be useful for verifying the accuracy of satellite-measurement data and for obtaining data from remote areas when cloud cover precluded direct satellite measurement. *Caulerpa taxifolia*, a green alga with a circumpolar distribution, was observed for the first time in the Mediterranean Sea in 1984. During 1996 the alga was reported to occur in the Mediterranean over an area of 1,000–2,000 ha (2,500–5,000 ac) and to be spreading annually by a factor of 2–10.

The marine coccolithophore *Emiliana huxleyi* is a single-celled alga that undergoes massive blooms, or rapid population increases, worldwide. Researchers estimated that once the algal masses die off and sink, they transport 800 million tons of carbon as calcite (a form of calcium carbonate) and 500 million tons of carbon as organic compounds to the seabed each year, which confirms the major role of the blooms in regulating global ocean carbon flux. The blooms also emit into the atmosphere dimethyl sulfide, a greenhouse gas, which was shown by European researchers to derive from death of the algal cells following viral infection, which contributes to the termination of the blooms.

A laboratory study carried out in the U.S. showed that the tropical flatfish *Bothus ocellatus* can adjust its pigment patterns for camouflage purposes with surprising fidelity in two to eight seconds to blend with different backgrounds. It even was able to adapt to a black-and-white checkerboard pattern put into the laboratory tank. U.S. and Australian investigators marked coral-

reef damselfish (*Pomacentrus* species) with fluorescent dyes and tiny, implanted, code-carrying tags, which for the first time allowed long-term recognition of individual reef fish in studies of immigration and emigration. Related studies around Apo Island in the central Philippines provided evidence of the emigration of adult fish from protected reserves to fished areas, justifying the establishment of reserves.

Larvae of vestimentiferans, gutless worms that live around deep-sea hydrothermal vents and cold seeps, were cultured and described for the first time. The larvae resemble trochophores, the free-swimming larvae characteristic of polychaete annelid worms, which places the vestimentiferans phylogenetically closer to that group than hitherto recognized. An investigator reported the first known case of eusociality in a marine invertebrate, analogous to the social behaviour of bees and termites. A sponge-dwelling shrimp, *Synalpheus regalis*, was found to live in colonies of more than 300 individuals. A single reproductive animal functions as a queen, while other members serve to protect the colony against intruders. (See *Zoology*, above.) Living specimens of the sea anemone *Gerardia*, obtained from a depth of 620 m (2,034 ft) off The Bahamas, were revealed by means of carbon-dating techniques to have been alive for 1,500–2,100 years.   (ERNEST NAYLOR)

This article updates the *Macropædia* articles CRUSTACEANS; FISHES; MOLLUSKS; etc.

BOTANY

The remarkable similarities between plants and animals became more evident in 1996 as scientists unraveled details of the hormonal communication system used by plants to regulate their physiological activities. The natural organic compounds known as steroids play major roles as hormones in animals, but their functions in plants have been much less clear. During the year researchers in California discovered that a plant steroid called brassinolide, which in

its molecular structure closely resembles the human male androgen sex hormone, is used by plants as a hormone, although not for sex. Joanne Chory and her team at the Salk Institute, La Jolla, Calif., examined a stunted form of thale cress (*Arabidopsis thaliana*), a small, fast-growing plant often used for genetics experiments. The stunting was caused by the plant's failure to respond to light, and the problem was traced to a defective gene involved in making brassinolide.

Animals use another hormonal communication system based on fairly large, complex molecules called peptides, which are short chains of linked amino acids, the building blocks of proteins. Plant researchers from The Netherlands and Germany, led by Karin van de Sande, reported their discovery that a peptide in legume plants carries signals involved in building special nodules on the plants' roots, where symbiotic nitrogen-fixing bacteria live. Communication in plants previously had been thought to be the work of small molecules, but if peptide signaling turns out to be widespread, it would challenge scientists' current view of the sophistication of plant physiology. (See *Molecular Biology*, below.)

Genetic research revealed some startling insights into plant development. Two separate discoveries showed that a simple genetic switch is all that is needed to transform ordinary green shoots into flowers. Working with *A. thaliana*, Detlef Weigel and Ove Nilsson of the Salk Institute demonstrated that by jamming into the "on" position the "master switch" gene that controls the other genes involved in flowering, they could not only turn side shoots into flowers but also make the plant flower much sooner than normal. In subsequent experiments they switched on the flowering genes of aspen trees and thereby cut the time to flowering from years to months. Similar results, although by means of a different gene, were achieved by Alejandra Mandel of the University of Arizona and Martin Yanofsky of the University of California, San Diego. A third gene was revealed by biologists at the

Monique Simmonds and Paul Green, scientists at Kew Gardens near London, view part of Kew's collection of *Calceolaria*. After British researchers isolated from *Calceolaria andina* two naphthoquinones, compounds that showed promise as insecticides, scientists at Kew began to survey related species for similar chemicals.

ROYAL BOTANIC GARDENS, KEW

Featuring a spike almost two meters (six feet) tall, a titan arum (*Amorphophallus titanum*) blooms at Kew Gardens. Such plants rarely flower, and the blooms last only a few days. When it first opens, the flower smells like rotting meat in order to attract flies to pollinate it. A few gardeners working near the plant were overcome by its odour.

and colleagues at the University of Chile, Santiago, collected some 400 plant species. Among them was the yellow-flowered *Calceolaria andina,* from the foothills of the Chilean Andes, which was found to contain two powerful insecticides. These so-called napthoquinones selectively target a range of highly damaging sap-sucking insects, including a virulent strain of the tobacco whitefly, a serious global agricultural pest that was resistant to many current commercial sprays.   (PAUL SIMONS)

MOLECULAR BIOLOGY

Self-Defense in Plants. Rooted to the ground and thus unable to flee, plants need defenses against a variety of predators and disease-causing microorganisms. While obvious structural features such as thorns can deter large animal predators, more covert defenses are required against plant-eating insects and microorganisms. When organic chemists first began analyzing the chemical composition of plants, they found a bewildering array of compounds whose functions were totally unknown. The compounds were collectively termed secondary metabolites, which seemed to imply that they were not of great importance. Since the early 1990s it has become increasingly clear that most of these compounds function as part of a remarkably sophisticated passive-aggressive defense system, which ongoing work in 1996 continued to explore.

The interaction of the disease-causing fungus *Phytophthora* with a tomato or tobacco plant can serve as an example of the way that part of the defense system was found to work. In the immediate vicinity of contact with the fungus, the plant dramatically changes its metabolism so as to prevent the growth of the fungus. It increases its local production of certain highly reactive, oxygen-derived chemical species—namely, hydrogen peroxide and groups of atoms called free radicals. It also steps up local production of toxic compounds called phytoalexins. The oxygen-derived species and phytoalexins cause local cell death. This activity leads to a spot of dead tissue on the leaf, but it also impedes the spread of the fungus. Concomitant with the local reaction, the plant produces chemical signals that circulate systemwide throughout the plant and induce changes leading to general resistance.

As *Phytophthora* attempts to infect the plant, it secretes small proteins, called elicitins, that ultimately serve a structural role for the fungus. It is the elicitins that turn on the defensive responses of the plant. In fact, it was shown experimentally that a light touch of a dilute solution of pure elicitins induces both the local acute response and the systemic response. The signal within the plant that mediates the systemic changes leading to resistance is carried by salicylic acid, which is made in response to elicitins. This simple compound serves several kinds of signaling roles in plants and is more familiar to people in the form of a chemical derivative, aspirin.

Recent research also revealed that plants mount other types of defenses to ward off plant-eating insects like caterpillars and beetles. The response may involve the production and release of compounds distasteful or toxic to the insect. In some cases the plant releases volatile compounds that

John Innes Centre, Norwich, Eng., to direct the location at which plant flowers sprout. Normally the gene stops the main stems of snapdragons from producing flowers at their tips, but by interfering with the gene they made each plant bloom only at the tip of its stem.

Genetic engineering of plants continued to make progress. Tobacco plants, normally killed by salty water, were given a gene that allowed them to survive brackish waters. This achievement helped to open the way for the development of new crop plants that can grow in arid, salty areas of the world. Potatoes were programmed to commit suicide if they became afflicted with an infectious disease; the intent was to limit disease spread, which in turn would reduce pesticide use. On the other hand, fears for the safety of genetically engineered plants found some support. Danish scientists conducting field trials on oilseed rape (*Brassica napus*) discovered that a gene inserted into the crop spread alarmingly fast to a wild relative, *B. campestris*. This raised concern that weeds could accidentally be genetically modified.

Paradoxically, while scientists engineered new varieties of crops, the natural genetic diversity of the world's crop plants was rapidly vanishing, leaving the remaining varieties prone to pests and plague. In June

150 government representatives meeting in Leipzig, Ger., pledged to halt the decline in crop varieties, many of which dated back thousands of years. The statistics were alarming; for instance, since 1900 the U.S. had lost most of its 20,000 varieties of agricultural plants. Governments were responding with an international network of gene banks that made use of refrigerated seed-storage facilities and farms to conserve threatened varieties. One big step in plant conservation was the announcement by Kew Gardens, near London, that it would build the world's largest seed bank for wild plants. It would cost $32 million and eventually could be expanded to house as much as 10% of the world's wild plant species, many of which were on the verge of extinction.

One of the great attractions of conservation was the potential for finding new drugs and other useful compounds in plants. Scientists studying watercress, for example, discovered compounds that counter the cancer-causing effects of nicotine. Other researchers discovered a protein in snowdrop (*Galanthus nivalis*) that reduces appetite in sap-sucking pests; the gene that codes for the protein was being introduced into potato and tobacco plants to combat aphids. In a search for new biologically active substances, Hermann Niemeyer

attract predators or parasites of the insect. In addition, the mechanical injury caused by the insect sets off a signaling cascade that induces the entire plant to adapt to the attack. The first element in the cascade is a short chain of amino acids, or oligopeptide, called systemin, which is produced in response to the mechanical damage. Systemin activates the production of jasmonic acid, which in turn signals the entire plant to prepare for attack. This systemic call to arms includes the production of lignin and a protease inhibitor. Lignin is a woody polymer that caterpillars and beetles find indigestible. The protease inhibitor prevents digestive enzymes called proteases from breaking down proteins in foods and thus keeps insects from benefiting from the plant protein that they ingest. Protease inhibitors, which are proteins themselves, are abundant in such seeds as soybeans as a defense against seed eaters. Humans circumvent natural protease inhibitors in foods by cooking, which inactivates them and renders the food digestible.

The recent discoveries about plant defense systems uncovered parallels between them and the defensive responses and signaling reactions of mammals. For example, the phagocytic white blood cells of the human body respond to invading organisms by producing hydrogen peroxide and a free radical called superoxide, similar to the response of plants. Furthermore, the human body produces signaling molecules, called prostaglandins, made from the polyunsaturated fatty acid arachidonic acid; plants produce jasmonic acid from a similar fatty acid, linolenic acid.

The existence of chemical defenses in plants is a powerful argument for the maintenance of maximum biological diversity. Scientists have only begun to explore the compounds involved in these systems, and the same can be said for the defense systems of insects, amphibians, and many other organisms. Unraveling these secrets may provide as great a benefit to human beings as have the discoveries of the major antibiotics, like penicillin and streptomycin, which are defensive antimicrobial compounds made by molds and bacteria.

Lou Gehrig's Disease. Advances continued in the past year in the understanding of the molecular and genetic basis of amyotrophic lateral sclerosis (ALS), or Lou Gehrig's disease. ALS is a degenerative disease of the motor neurons—the nerve cells that control muscular movements. The inexorably progressive paralysis that results usually begins during the third or fourth decade of life, and victims of ALS usually die within a few years after the appearance of symptoms. ALS occurs in two forms, one familial (FALS) and the other sporadic (SALS). Except for the heritable character of FALS, the two forms are symptomatically indistinguishable.

The search for a genetic defect involved in the cause of FALS led first to chromosome 21 and then, in the early 1990s, to a gene called *SOD1*. The gene was found to encode—*i.e.*, to carry the genetic code for making—an enzyme called superoxide dismutase. The enzyme protects the body's cells against the destructive effects of accumulating superoxide radicals by catalyzing their conversion into molecular oxygen and hydrogen peroxide.

FALS is genetically dominant, which means that one copy of the defective gene is sufficient to cause the disease. The corollary is that one copy of the normal gene cannot prevent the disease. In theory, mutations in the *SOD1* gene could cause FALS by specifying a superoxide dismutase product that has modestly decreased activity or, alternately, by giving the enzyme a novel deleterious activity. The latter mechanism recently was shown to be the case in experiments that involved mice genetically engineered to carry a normal or defective human form of the *SOD1* gene in addition to the natural mouse form of the gene. When the normal human *SOD1* gene was expressed in mice, they did not develop paralysis. On the other hand, when genes coding for FALS-associated mutant forms of *SOD1* were expressed, the mice did become paralyzed. Since the transferred human genes were expressed against a background of normal mouse *SOD1* genes and the mice did indeed show normal levels, or even somewhat greater-than-usual levels, of superoxide dismutase, their paralysis could not have been due to a lack of the enzyme.

What toxic property of mutant superoxide dismutase could cause degeneration of motor neurons? As of 1996 two possibilities had been put forward, with data supporting each. One is that the mutant enzyme catalyzes novel oxidation reactions that ultimately destroy the motor neurons. The other is that it catalyzes the addition of nitrate groups to tyrosine, one of the amino-acid building blocks of proteins. In fact, tests devised specifically to detect the nitrated tyrosine product found it in the spinal cords of ALS patients but not in those of persons free of the disease.

Although many aspects of ALS remained mysterious, given the impressive gains in understanding in the past few years, investigators looked forward to a time in the near future when they would be able to predict, prevent, or at least slow the progress of the disease. Of course, the sporadic form of ALS does not involve mutations in the *SOD1* gene. Nevertheless, because its symptoms are so similar to those of FALS, there is likely some similarity in causation.

(IRWIN FRIDOVICH)

DNA Vaccines. If treating a disease is good, preventing it is better. For the past several generations, through the widespread practice of vaccination, that concept has been realized for a growing number of serious and often fatal infections. Indeed, organized vaccinations of children worldwide against smallpox led to the eradication of the known natural reservoirs of its causative virus in the 1970s.

While the concept of vaccination—exposing an individual to some modified form of a disease-causing microorganism in order to generate an immune response—has been around for many years, vaccines themselves have undergone a stepwise evolution toward greater safety. Thus, vaccination has progressed from infection with a related but less virulent microorganism (*e.g.*, cowpox virus in place of smallpox virus) to exposure to a live but attenuated (partially crippled) or heat-killed form of the virulent organism to injection with benign preparations of immunity-triggering proteins derived from the organism (*e.g.*, the modern three-part vaccine against the hepatitis B virus). Along the way, vaccines against polio, tetanus, diphtheria, mumps, measles, rubella, and other devastating diseases have saved the lives and preserved the health of innumerable children and adults.

Two fundamental and interconnected problems have remained, however. The first is that not all disease organisms have proved susceptible to control by conventional vaccines. Some viruses and other infectious agents possess the ability to mutate, or alter their surface proteins over time, such that antibodies generated by exposure to the surface proteins of one variety or strain become useless against future infections.

The second problem is that the safer heat-killed or protein-based vaccines can be less effective at stimulating immunity than their more dangerous predecessors. In brief, this loss of efficacy reflects the fact that a human body exposed solely to a foreign protein will generate antibodies against that protein, whereas a human body whose cells are infected by a live virus—and thus tricked into making that same foreign protein as part of the process of viral replication—will generate both antibodies and killer cells (a type of white blood cell) that recognize the protein. As their name implies, killer cells retain the ability to target and kill any virally infected cells that make the foreign protein. A combined immune response of antibodies and killer cells not only offers a surer defense against infection but also allows the body to develop immunity against both the surface proteins of an infectious organism and its normally hidden internal proteins, which become visible to the body's immune system after the organism infects the cell. This point is a key one, because many disease agents are able to change their surface proteins, but few, if any, can change their internal proteins as well.

In recent years a number of research groups, notably Margaret Liu and her colleagues of Merck Research Laboratories, West Point, Pa., and Stephen Johnston and his colleagues of the University of Texas Southwestern Medical Center at Dallas have developed an alternative approach to vaccines that may provide the best of both worlds—safety and long-lasting immunity against, at least in theory, almost any disease agent.

The new vaccines are actually preparations of DNA, not protein, designed to be taken up by the cells of the recipient. The DNA consists of nonreplicating plasmids, or DNA loops, that correspond to either specifically chosen or random fragments of the DNA of the disease organism. The fragments are flanked by additional regulatory DNA sequences intended to encourage the host cells to make the proteins or protein fragments encoded by the foreign DNA. As the cells synthesize these foreign proteins, parts of them make their way to the cell surface and thereby attract the attention of that part of the immune system responsible for generating killer cells. Because each plasmid carries only a small fraction of the total DNA of the disease organism, there is essentially no risk of infection. Furthermore, because the plasmids carry DNA for both internal and surface proteins of the disease organism, immunity can be elicited even against those organisms that have learned to change their surface proteins.

As of 1996, tests of the new vaccines in animals had produced results better than anticipated. In addition, studies designed to test for potential risks associated with the new vaccines, such as permanent integration of the plasmids into the DNA of the host cell or complications arising from an immune response against the introduced DNA, detected no evidence of such events. Clinical trials in humans were under way.

Yeast Genome Project. Much of what is known about living systems and the way that they function has been learned not from the study of humans but from the study of so-called model organisms, including bacteria, yeast, flies, worms, and mice. Indeed, the founders of the Human Genome Project so valued these other organisms and their contributions to biomedical science that obtaining the whole genome of each—*i.e.,* establishing the exact sequence of DNA for the organism's entire genetic blueprint— was established as an important goal in addition to obtaining the whole genome of humans. The past year witnessed the completion of the first of these whole-genome sequencing efforts for a eukaryote—*i.e.,* for a cellular organism whose cells contain a distinct nucleus. The target was the genome of the yeast *Saccharomyces cerevisiae,* strains of which are the familiar baker's, brewer's, and vintner's yeasts.

The yeast genome project was initiated in 1989 by the European community of yeast researchers, but the effort soon expanded into a global collaboration involving laboratories in the U.K., continental Europe, the U.S., Canada, and Japan. Their combined efforts enabled the complete sequence of the *S. cerevisiae* genome to be published in April as a database on the Internet's World Wide Web (http://genome-www.stanford.edu).

Both the short- and the long-term benefits of the *Saccharomyces* genome database (SGD) promised to be enormous. For example, in terms of genome anatomy, data from the SGD revealed that the yeast genome is highly compact, with its genes tending to be much smaller and much less dispersed than those of the human genome. The data also predict that about 70% of the yeast genome encodes various protein molecules, specifically about 6,000 different proteins. Of this number, only about 40% had been identified previously in genetic studies. Of the remaining 60% (roughly 3,700 proteins), more than half bear no significant sequence similarity to any previously identified sequences for proteins of known function from any other organism. The sheer numbers of these "orphan" proteins stood as humbling testimony to how little scientists yet knew about so "simple" an organism as yeast.

Perhaps the most obvious benefit of biomedical relevance to emerge from the availability of the SGD is the ability to quickly find yeast counterparts, or homologues, of genes in humans that are associated with specific diseases. In recent years researchers have made significant advances in identifying those genes that, when either absent or present in defective form, are responsible for a number of hereditary human diseases—for example, Huntington's disease, Batten disease, and fragile X syndrome. Although the identification of a disease gene can offer powerful new tools to aid in diagnosis, appropriate treatment requires at least some fundamental understanding of the normal function of the gene and the protein product that it encodes.

Unfortunately, knowledge of the sequence of a given gene may offer little insight into its function, especially if no similar sequences of known function have been found, as is the case for many human disease genes. It is in such cases that a yeast homologue can provide a major benefit, since the ease with which yeast can be genetically and biochemically manipulated allows studies of gene function to be conducted more quickly in yeast than in human or other mammalian cells. The insights gained in studying the yeast homologue of a gene may then be transferred back, either wholly or partly, to the corresponding human disease gene. Indeed, oftentimes the functions of homologous human and yeast genes are so similar that a human sequence can be substituted successfully for a missing homologous sequence in yeast and thus enable direct studies of both normal and defective forms of the human sequence in a genetically and biochemically amenable yeast model system.

(JUDITH L. FRIDOVICH-KEIL)

PALEONTOLOGY

In 1996 students of fossils continued to provide new insights about past life that resulted in new philosophical challenges. A major event was the sixth North American Paleontological Convention (NAPC), held in June in Washington, D.C., and attended by 650 paleontologists, about 120 from outside North America. The meeting opened with discussions by J. William Schopf and Bruce Runnegar of the University of California, Los Angeles, about Precambrian life (before about 545 million years ago) and the oldest known fossils on Earth—3.5 billion-year-old bacterial filaments.

Two months later David McKay (*see* BIOGRAPHIES) of NASA and colleagues announced the finding of organic residue and bacteria-like structures about 3.6 billion years old in a meteorite thought to be from the planet Mars. The findings may be the first indications of life on another planet and the first real data available to the science of exobiology. Debate over the interpretation of the findings was just beginning. For example, Schopf (an expert in very ancient microfossils) reckoned, "I think it's very unlikely they [McKay and colleagues] have remnants of biological activity."

Another notable event at the NAPC was the firm placement of conodont animals among jawless vertebrates and closer to lampreys than to amphioxus. Conodonts are known mostly from abundant disarticulate toothlike microfossils. The most recent work meant that conodonts finally yielded the title "fossils of unknown affinities." They had eyes, an asymmetrical ray-supported tail fin, and a notochord (the

Three clustered flowers, from a plant in the oak and beech family some 90 million years old, were found preserved in amber in central New Jersey. Dating from the age of the dinosaurs, they were the oldest intact flowers found in amber to date and were providing scientists with important information about evolution in flowering plants.

Holding a human skull for comparison, U.S. paleontologist Paul Sereno stretches out next to the 1.63-m (5-ft 4-in)-long skull of *Carcharodontosaurus*, a carnivorous dinosaur found by Sereno and his research team in Morocco.

forerunner of the spinal column of higher vertebrates), as reported by M.A. Purnell of the University of Leicester, Eng., and I.J. Sansom and M.P. Smith of the University of Birmingham, Eng., and colleagues. Twenty-nine researchers from around the world devoted a full day to the origin and evolution of whales. Eocene fossils (about 50 million years ago) provide the missing links documenting the transition of land mammals to amphibious whales that lived along rivers to marine whales, as reported by J.G.M. Thewissen of Northeastern Ohio Universities College of Medicine and colleagues.

Other advances in the study of vertebrates included new information on dinosaurs. Gregory M. Erickson of the University of California, Berkeley, and colleagues reported that according to the results of their experiments, *Tyrannosaurus rex* had very strong, impact-resistant teeth that could withstand the stresses associated with struggles during prey capture. Their data did not resolve the debate as to whether *T. rex* was a hunter or a carrion feeder; they did show that *T. rex* was not mechanically limited by its dentition to scavenging carrion. John A. Ruben of Oregon State University and colleagues reported that their analyses of the nasal regions of four dinosaur species indicated that dinosaurs had metabolic rates significantly lower than those in modern warm-blooded animals. Their data were derived from the study of the cross-sectional area of the nasal passages and the presence or absence of nasal turbinate bones, which in warm-blooded animals are involved in warming and cooling the blood during respiration. As the *Washington Post* noted in its Sept. 2, 1996, issue: "Paleontology: Cold-Blooded Idea Ahead by Nose." Paul Sereno of the University of Chicago and colleagues announced the discovery of two large car-

nivorous dinosaurs from Cretaceous rocks (about 90 million years ago) of Morocco. The larger dinosaur, *Carcharodontosaurus saharicus,* had a skull measuring 1.63 m (64 in), which may be larger than that of the largest known *T. rex.* The other dinosaur, *Deltadromeus agilis,* had long, slender limbs, which suggested agility and speediness.

Paleobotanists held their twice-a-decade international meeting in Santa Barbara, Calif. A major theme was early land plants and the environments of early terrestrial ecosystems. C.L. Hotton and F.M. Hueber of the Smithsonian Institution, Washington, D.C., discussed evidence for environmental partitioning among Lower Devonian (about 400 million years ago) plants with embryos in the rocks of Gaspé, Que. T.N. Taylor of the University of Kansas and colleagues reported that in the Lower Devonian rocks of Scotland, fungi functioned as saprophytes (living on decayed material), parasites, and various types of mutualists (two organisms living together for the benefit of both). Lichen terrestrial mutualism is also present in these rocks. William Shear of Hampden-Sydney (Va.) College and Paul Seldon of the University of Manchester, Eng., noted that terrestrial arthropods are known to occur with vascular and nonvascular land plants in rocks ranging in age from Late Silurian to Late Devonian (about 410 million to 360 million years ago) in both North America and Europe. Shear and Seldon indicated that none of the arthropods known to date are herbivores but rather are detritus feeders or predators. Thus, in early terrestrial ecosystems, plants and animals were decoupled in the food chain, and primary productivity flowed through detritivores. At the NAPC, C.C. Labandeira of the Smithsonian presented data showing that by Late Pennsylvanian time (about 295

million years ago) insect herbivores were partitioning food use of plant tissues in major and essentially modern ways.

David A. Grimaldi of the American Museum of Natural History, New York City, was directing the collecting of rich deposits of amber-preserved fossils in the Cretaceous rocks of New Jersey; the amber is about 90 million to 94 million years old. To date, about 100 previously unknown species of insects and plants were identified. Included in this amber treasure trove were a mushroom, a bee, a mosquito, a moth, a blackfly, flowers, and a feather.

The year was one of festivals celebrating fossils. In addition to the standard professional and amateur gatherings, Dinofest International was held in April at Arizona State University, Tempe, and Fossilfest at the Museum of Natural History and Science in Cincinnati, Ohio. In November the Florida Museum of Natural History, Gainesville, served as host for Paleofest 96. In part, all three festivals were sponsored by the Paleontological Society. They were designed to increase the public's knowledge about fossils and to give hands-on experience with collecting and identifying fossils. The three festivals attracted at least 250,000 people. (JOHN POJETA, JR.)

See also Anthropology; Earth Sciences; The Environment.

This article updates the *Macropædia* articles Animal BEHAVIOUR; BIOCHEMICAL COMPONENTS OF ORGANISMS; The BIOLOGICAL SCIENCES; BIOSPHERE; CELLS; CONSERVATION OF NATURAL RESOURCES; DISEASE; The Theory of EVOLUTION; The Principles of GENETICS AND HEREDITY; GEOCHRONOLOGY; INFECTIOUS DISEASES; MAMMALS; MUSCLES AND MUSCLE SYSTEMS; PLANTS; REPRODUCTION AND REPRODUCTIVE SYSTEMS.

Literature

In many ways 1996 was a dispiriting year for literature. While more books were published than ever before, the rift between serious literary writing and the vast majority of titles grew wider. This was the result, particularly in the "first world," of four converging trends: the continuing absorption of independent publishing houses; the focus on cultural studies that dominated literary theory; the growth of the Internet; and the rise of the superstore.

As the number of publishing venues continued to shrink, greater emphasis was being placed on books that would be profitable for their publishers. Editors, consequently, were becoming considerably less willing to risk enthusiasm on a work they were not sure would find a large audience.

The virtual coup that contemporary literary theory staged in colleges and universities had by 1996 made its way into publishing as well, as numbers of recent English majors had entered the business as editors or marketers. This had a chilling effect on the purchase of literary fiction in general and resulted in a boom for books that answered the criteria of social usefulness or cultural diversity.

Interest in the Internet and its on-line magazines such as *Slate* and *Salon* continued to increase as greater numbers of people seemed to be doing their reading in front of computer terminals; simultaneously, the explosion of the World Wide Web, with its "home pages" and "conversation sites," made everyone a virtual author. Finally, the rise of the superstore—where one could buy not only books but audiotapes, compact discs, videotapes, magazines, newspapers, and cappuccino—caused trouble for many independent bookstores and resulted in a 6% decline in their number in 1996.

Highlights of the year included a Turkish translation of James Joyce's *Ulysses* and well-regarded new English translations of the *Odyssey* and *Genesis,* as well as new work from such internationally known authors as J.M. Coetzee, Jacques Derrida, Colleen McCullough, Breyten Breytenbach, Tomas Tranströmer, Christa Wolf, Gabriel García Márquez, Carlos Fuentes, Margaret Atwood, Peter Hoeg, Jostein Gaarder, Joyce Carol Oates, Naguib Mahfouz, Wole Soyinka, and David Malouf. (*See* BIOGRAPHIES.) A poet relatively little known in the West, Wisława Szymborska, won the Nobel Prize; it was the first time the prize had been awarded to a Slavic woman. (*See* NOBEL PRIZES.)

Internationally, perhaps three trends might be highlighted. As the century drew to a close, more and more writers from around the world were meditating on the century's earlier events, particularly World War II. As well, novels were again addressing political issues as the century's obsession with issues of form—postmodernism, minimalism—began to wane. In many countries—especially France, Turkey, Poland, and Japan—women writers dominated the publishing scene. Though fundamentalist and authoritarian regimes continued to persecute writers, three Iranian women, two of them living in exile in Sweden, enjoyed literary success.

(STEPHEN BAUER)

Richard Ford

BRUCE DAVIDSON—MAGNUM

ENGLISH

United States. One might ask how many years a reviewer could continue to employ Dickens's line about the age simultaneously being the best of times and the worst of times. With regard to the American publishing industry, the reviewer might say that it would be applicable as long as the slow burn of the current crisis continued. The anything-for-profit ethic of most editorial houses seemed to have proliferated in 1996, adding to the amount of swill that came out between hard covers and less than gently nudging more good work in the direction of smaller, independent houses outside New York City, toward hibernation, or, alas, toward oblivion altogether. With this said, however, there remained a great deal to celebrate in terms of new work by serious U.S. writers, a few of them with large followings, most of them with small but solid reputations, and some newcomers to the scene.

The opening line "We were the Mulvaneys, remember us?" of Joyce Carol Oates's engrossing new novel, *We Were the Mulvaneys,* asked a question easily answered by any serious reader who finished the marvelously rendered story of an upstate New York farm torn apart by a sexual assault on the daughter of the household. The Mulvaneys are storybook people living in a storybook house, but their story is adult, deeply humane, heartrending, and beautiful. Anyone who read about them would remember them, and reviewers were nearly unanimous in their praise of the novel.

Not so fortunate either in its execution or its reception was a new novel, her first in a dozen years, by the well-regarded writer Joan Didion. *The Last Thing He Wanted,* an opaque rendering of intrigue in the U.S. espionage community and its effect on the daughter of a retired spy, did little for Didion's reputation. Previously lauded novelist Jay McInerney did not do much better with his new novel, *The Last of the Savages,* which seemed to disappear from view almost immediately upon publication. Mona Simpson's novel *A Regular Guy* received a mixed response.

Veteran novelist George Garrett published *The King of Babylon Shall Not Come Against You,* an interesting and effective story that yoked crimes in a small Florida town some decades ago with the contemporary American soul. Richard Bausch brought out the evocatively titled *Good Evening Mr. and Mrs. America, and All the Ships at Sea,* a touching coming-of-age novel set in the 1960s. Vicki Covington published *The Last Hotel for Women,* a beautifully wrought novel about Birmingham, Ala., in the midst of the first freedom rides. *The Here and Now* by Robert Cohen was set in New York City and successfully illuminated the crisis in the soul of a depressed magazine editor in love with the wife of an Orthodox Jew. Certainly the most successful experimental novel of the year was David Markson's *Reader's Block,* a tour de force about an aging writer contemplating the composition of a new book even as he plots his own suicide.

In *The Visiting Physician,* Susan Richards Shreve portrayed a small Midwestern town in the midst of a social crisis. Prolific young novelist Madison Smartt Bell's *Ten Indians* went to the heart of inner-city affairs.

Supporting the Sky by Patricia Browning Griffith successfully took on the subject of middle-class life in Washington, D.C. In *Going to the Sun,* James McManus created an appealing narrator—a diabetic female graduate student from Chicago—who took readers on a bicycle trip along the northern rim of the U.S. David Madden carried readers back to East Tennessee and to Civil War battlefields in other areas in his episodic historical fiction *Sharpshooter.* Much farther afield was *Manchu Palaces,* Jeanne Larsen's third novelistic excursion into the history of China.

Among the nominees for the National Book Award for Fiction were both good works and bad—specifically, Ron Hansen's flawed novel *Atticus,* set in southern Mexico, and Elizabeth McCracken's charming *The Giant's House,* which told the tale of an affair between a 26-year-old Cape Cod librarian and an appealing adolescent with a growth problem. Absent from the list of nominees, and stirring up some dust because of it, was the huge, sprawling experimental novel *Infinite Jest* by David Foster Wallace (*see* BIOGRAPHIES), a book tedious in the extreme but with a small cult following.

In his moving first novel, *Mason's Retreat,* the acclaimed storywriter Christopher Tilghman took the estuaries and inlets of the eastern shore of Maryland as his setting, the years just before World War II as his time, and an Anglo-American family in turmoil as his subject. In her steamy first novel, *Suspicious River,* acclaimed poet Laura Kasischke followed the misfortunes of a promiscuous young woman in a northern Michigan town in the doldrums. Story writer Marly Swick transported readers back to the 1960s and into the midst of a Midwestern family in crisis in her fine first novel, *Paper Wings.*

Among short-story collections published in 1996 was an auspicious first book by the Dominican-American writer Junot Díaz, whose *Drown* included 10 clearly articulated coming-of-age tales set in the Dominican Republic and in northern New Jersey. There also was a wonderful last book, Ralph Ellison's *Flying Home,* posthumously published short fiction by one of the greatest novelists of the post–World War II period. The book was edited by the scholar John F. Callahan, who was preparing for publication the manuscript of Ellison's fabled second novel, which had remained unpublished, and possibly unfinished, at Ellison's death. Two highly regarded storywriters were represented by new collections—Andre Dubus with *Dancing After Hours* and Tobias Wolff with *The Night in Question.* Fantasy writer Ray Bradbury showed off his powers in *Quicker than the Eye.* Richard Bausch received a rare honour for a living American writer, seeing his *Selected Stories* appear in a Modern Library edition.

Poet Gary Snyder made an already strong year for poetry a memorable one by offering *Mountains and Rivers Without End,* his cycle some 30 years in the writing. U.S. Poet Laureate Robert Hass produced a new book of lyric poems, *Sun Under Wood,* including the beautifully luminous "Dragonflies Mating," with its images of "steam rising from the pond the color of smoky topaz" and "a pair of delicate, copper-red, needle-fine insects" mating "in the unopened crown of a Shasta daisy." *The Old Life*—four short poems,

three elegies, and a long poem—came from Donald Hall, and Maxine Kumin published *Connecting the Dots.* At the age of 83, the California poet Virginia Hamilton Adair made a much-publicized debut with *Ants on the Melon.*

C.K. Williams's *The Vigil* was a striking new collection of his cerebral, long-line story poems. The 1993 Pulitzer Prize winner Louise Glück made her presence felt with *Meadowlands,* as did Henry Taylor with his new volume, *Understanding Fiction: Poems 1986–1996.* Robert Pinsky, whose translation of Dante's *Inferno* had won him much praise in 1995, showed 30 years of his own work in *The Figured Wheel: New and Collected Poems, 1966–1996.* *The World at Large: New and Selected Poems, 1971–1996,* by James McMichael also appeared. In the area of translation was Princeton classicist Robert Fagles's new version of the *Odyssey.*

No single work of nonfiction stood out above the rest in a field of interesting and well-made books in 1996, though some of the subjects may have been more interesting than others to various readers and some higher in literary value. For example, among travel books there was William Langewiesche's engaging *Sahara Unveiled.* In *Great Books* readers heard how David Denby had gone back to his alma mater, Columbia University, and read his way through the core humanities course. Paul Hendrickson returned to the Vietnam War era in his biographical study *The Living and the Dead: Robert McNamara and Five Lives of a Lost War.* James Howard Kunstler, author of the highly praised *Geography of Nowhere* (1993), continued his argument about planning for a livable American landscape in *Home from Nowhere.* Attorney and novelist Richard Dooling took an entertaining polemical stance in *Blue Streak: Swearing, Free Speech, and Sexual Harassment.*

The year 1996 marked the death of the flamboyant and controversial fiction writer Harold Brodkey (*see* OBITUARIES) and the publication of *This Wild Darkness,* the journal he had kept to record the progress of his decline from AIDS. Among the living, the highly regarded essayist and fic-

tion writer William Kittredge contributed a book-length essay titled *Who Owns the West?* Native American writer Leslie Marmon Silko came out with a collection of disparate pieces—*Yellow Woman and a Beauty of the Spirit*—that ranged from the practical and biographical ("On Nonfiction Prose") to the lyrical ("An Essay on Rocks"). Phillip Lopate published a book of occasional essays titled *Portrait of My Body.* Less successful was California novelist William T. Vollmann's *The Atlas,* a series of multiple short takes on political upheaval, travel, sex, and art.

Lynne Sharon Schwartz wrote about her experiences in *Ruined by Reading.* National Public Radio news show host Noah Adams described his quest to master a musical instrument in midlife in *Piano Lessons.* Classical pianist Russell Sherman wrote splendidly about musical matters in *Piano Pieces.* David Quammen did the same for biology and ecology in his essays on island species, *The Song of the Dodo. A Queer Geography: Journey Toward a Sexual Self* was Frank Browning's intelligent assay of homosexual mores around the West.

Among autobiographical volumes Alfred Kazin's *A Lifetime Burning in Every Moment* stood out for its literary and historical interest. Author bell hooks took time out from the analysis of race and gender to write *Bone Black,* a memoir of a country childhood. Walter Bernstein looked back to a bad time in *Inside Out,* his memoir of the blacklist of the 1950s.

Literary biographies flourished, with no set pattern to be discerned among them. Ralph Freedman completed *Life of a Poet,* his biography of Rainer Maria Rilke, which had been long in the making. Melville scholar Hershel Parker published the first volume of a new biography, *Herman Melville. Melville and His Circle* was the title of a book by William B. Dillingham about the author's reading in his last years. Brenda Wineapple wrote a dual biography in *Sister Brother: Gertrude and Leo Stein,* as did Joan Mellen in *Hellman and Hammett.* Sheldon M. Novick challenged some of the views of biographer Leon Edel in *Henry*

Joyce Carol Oates

KARL GEHRING—GAMMA LIAISON

Junot Díaz

James: The Young Master. Jeffrey Meyers attacked the conventional wisdom about the U.S.'s greatest 20th-century poet in *Robert Frost.* Closer to contemporary times were James Park Sloan's *Jerzy Kosinski* and Jackson Benson's *Wallace Stegner: His Life and Work.*

While good literary biographies came off the presses in 1996, it was not a great year for literary criticism. Here and there the reader could find clear and useful insights, but these usually appeared in essay form rather than in book-length works. William H. Gass, for example, came out with *Finding a Form,* a collection of interesting and readable essays, including the brilliant "A Failing Grade for the Present Tense."

Two editions of correspondence offered insight into the work of important 20th-century fiction writers—Matthew Bruccoli's *The Only Thing That Counts: The Ernest Hemingway–Maxwell Perkins Correspondence, 1925–1947,* and Michael Steinman's *The Happiness of Getting It Down Right: Letters of Frank O'Connor and William Maxwell, 1945–1966.* Novelists Nicholas Delbanco and Alan Cheuse coedited the unpublished essays and notes of the late Bernard Malamud in *Talking Horse: Bernard Malamud on Life and Work.* Toni Morrison edited *Deep Sightings and Rescue Missions,* a posthumous collection of stories and essays by Toni Cade Bambara.

Dan Hofstadter's interesting study *The Love Affair as a Work of Art* fell more into the category of belles lettres than criticism. Roger Shattuck's *Forbidden Knowledge* was intellectual history, but Harold Bloom's *Omens of Millennium: The Gnosis of Angels, Dreams, and Resurrection* stood in a class by itself, part literary criticism, part theology, part polemic.

The most controversial work of history during 1996 was Daniel Jonah Goldhagen's *Hitler's Willing Executioners: Ordinary Germans and the Holocaust,* which continued to cause a stir in Europe. Political biographies included Cary Reich's first volume of *The Life of Nelson A. Rockefeller: Worlds to Conquer, 1908–1958.*

Richard Ford won both the Pulitzer Prize

for Fiction and the PEN/Faulkner Award for Fiction with his novel *Independence Day.* Jorie Graham won the Pulitzer Prize for Poetry for her collection *The Dream of the Unified Field.* Andrea Barrett won the National Book Award for fiction with her story collection *Ship Fever,* and Hayden Carruth took the prize in poetry for his collection *Scrambled Eggs and Whiskey: Poems 1991–1995.* Novelist Howard Norman was among those awarded a Lannan prize for 1996.

(ALAN CHEUSE)

Canada. One of literature's enduring metaphors was that of the journey, and there were many journeys undertaken in collections of Canadian poetry in 1996. Some were symbolic, as in Janis Rapoport's *After Paradise,* in which the intrepid explorer encountered the physical and spiritual in all their splendid confusion, and others actual, as in Stephen Scobie's *Taking the Gate: A Journey Through Scotland.* More familiar departures from reality were exemplified in *The Cheat of Words* by Steve McCaffery, who exposed the truth of politics through the lies politicians tell. In *Nightwatch: New and Selected Poems, 1968–1996,* while scanning the sidereal skies for invisible allies, Dennis Lee suggested that one must stand guard and be ever-vigilant. *Exiles Among You* was the title of Kristjana Gunnars's dark but lively meditations. In *Search Procedures* Erin Mouré investigated the investigators, while the crisscross contradictions of the different ways people take formed the texture of Marilyn Bowering's autobiography.

Weather was used as an extended metaphor in both Crispin Elsted's *Climate and the Affections: Poems: 1970–1995* and Charles Lillard's *Shadow Weather: Poems Selected and New,* while Al Purdy, in *Rooms for Rent in the Outer Planets: Selected Poems 1962–1994,* created his own strangely homely atmosphere.

A different kind of domestic note was struck by Kaushalya Bannerji in *The Faces of Five O'Clock,* which echoed across the wild terrains of war, politics, and love. In her first collection of poetry, *A Really Good Brown Girl,* Marilyn Dumont brought the past into the present, playing one against the other to the elucidation of both.

Katherine Govier

The past was the destination of many Canadian prose writers in 1996, as in *The Ancestral Suitcase* by Sylvia Fraser, in which a backward traveler through time stumbled across an ancient murder mystery while uncovering answers to questions she had yet to ask. Murder was also the focus of *Alias Grace,* Margaret Atwood's trenchant retelling of the story of an infamous 19th-century murderer, Grace Marks, a servant girl clever enough to outwit her doctor. Death by natural causes and the resurrection of both body and spirit enlivened *Last Seen,* Matt Cohen's deftly comic dissection of despair and grief.

It seemed that the past most frequented by novelists in 1996 was World War II and its era, and a wide variety of characters were to be encountered there. They ranged from the octogenarian photographer in Katherine Govier's *Angel Walk,* flipping through the pictures that informed her life, and the 15-year-old girl in *The Cure for Death by Lightning* by Gail Anderson-Dargatz, living on a farm in the British Columbia hinterland and facing the sometimes brutal realities of her personal situation amid the chaos of global confrontations, to the Holocaust survivor, and the son of other survivors who studied his life, in *Fugitive Pieces* by Anne Michaels. Not all of the action took place abroad. In *You Went Away,* Timothy Findley explored the intricacies of love and deception on the home front, and the fate of displaced people in Canada after the war formed a large part of Janice Kulyk Keefer's *The Green Library.*

Later history was rewritten by West Coast writer Des Kennedy in *The Garden Club and the Kumquat Campaign: A Novel,* which spoofed the struggle over logging in Clayoquot Sound. In poet Dionne Brand's first novel, *In Another Place, Not Here,* two women from the Caribbean encountered Toronto in the 1970s and '80s. Guy Vanderhaeghe's *The Englishman's Boy* juxtaposed 1920s Hollywood and a 19th-century massacre in the Cypress Hills, and Shauna Singh Baldwin's *English Lessons and Other Stories* began in 1919 but swept forward to the present. Lessons in art and love were taught and received by both apprentice and master in Ann Ireland's *The Instructor.* Cordelia Strube traced the spiraling path of dementia through the bleak streets of modern urban existence in *Teaching Pigs to Sing,* while Elisabeth Harvor's collection of short stories *Let Me Be the One* grappled with existence in a myriad of forms.

(ELIZABETH WOODS)

United Kingdom. Retrospection was a dominant theme of all aspects of British literature in 1996 and most notably in the novel. Ian Jack, editor of *Granta* magazine, observed at the year's end, "As one of the judges of the 1996 Booker Prize, I was struck by how many new English novels were preoccupied with the past. . . . This is the Literature of Farewell." He was arguing that Britain as a cohesive concept was no more, that the country had divided itself into its constituent parts (England, Scotland, Wales, and Northern Ireland), and that a fin de siècle trend of looking backward, often without nostalgia or romance, to the vanished days of empire and influence had taken over cultural life in general and works of literature in particular. The best of the latter he described as "valedictory realism."

All six finalists for the Booker Prize tackled historical times in their works. Beryl Bainbridge's *Every Man for Himself* recreated the doomed maiden voyage of the *Titanic* with a cast of characters from above and below deck. Margaret Atwood's *Alias Grace* was based on the true 19th-century story of a 16-year-old ax-murdering servant. Shena Mackay's *The Orchard on Fire* depicted the rural England of the 1950s, and Rohinton Mistry's *A Fine Balance* was set in the 1970s in India. The judges were divided, however, between Ulster poet Seamus Deane's first novel, *Reading in the Dark,* a semiautobiographical story set in Derry in mid-century, and Graham Swift's reflective *Last Orders,* about four Londoners traveling to the south coast of England to scatter a friend's ashes into the sea. The shortlist, which the *Sunday Times* applauded as "strikingly successful," was less controversial than in past years, as was the October 29 announcement of the winner, *Last Orders,* which defeated Deane's work by three votes to two. *Last Orders,* of which only three copies had been sold in the U.K. the week before, leaped to number five on the best-seller list soon afterward. The book, written in a demotic London English, was, according to the *Times Literary Supplement,* "emotionally charged and technically superb" in its tackling of "how we live and how we die and our struggle to make abiding connections between the two."

The other major literary award, the Whitbread, aroused more controversy. Kate Atkinson's first novel, *Behind the Scenes at the Museum,* was named Book of the Year, beating Salman Rushdie's *The Moor's Last Sigh* and Roy Jenkins's biography *Gladstone.* Atkinson, a single mother of two, had once called the family a pernicious and tyrannical institution, and her book, charting three generations of a Yorkshire family, underscored this outlook. The *Daily Mail* called the decision "a victory for political correctness," and Julian Critchley, one of the judges, said that the women on the panel had voted for Atkinson out of a sense of "sisterhood."

A new fiction award, the Orange Prize, offering £30,000 for the best English-language novel of the year written by a woman (£10,000 more than the Booker and £9,000 more than the Whitbread), was launched in January to a mixed reception. A.S. Byatt, the Booker Prize-winning author of *Possession,* was among the skeptical. "I am against anything which ghettoizes women," she told *The Independent.* "My opinion is for the last 10 years or so it is observable that there have not been as many good women writers as men." The first awardee, announced in May, was Helen Dunmore, a lyrical writer whose novel *A Spell in Winter* had won high praise.

Other notable fiction published during the year included Julian Barnes's *Cross Channel,* a collection of stories about France and the English people's relation to it. The *Literary Review* acclaimed the book for its central story, "Evermore," about a sister's annual pilgrimage to the grave of her brother, killed 50 years earlier in France in World War I. *The Lady and the Laptop* by Clive Sinclair was admired for its whimsical stories. Among the many new offerings from established authors were Doris Lessing's *Love, Again,* Margaret Drabble's *The Witch of Exmoor,* Ben Okri's *Danger-*

ous Love, Roddy Doyle's *The Woman Who Walked into Doors,* and John le Carré's *The Tailor of Panama.* The latter, a spy story about a half-Jewish, half-Irish tailor, Harry Pendel, who is recruited as a British agent, caused irritation among Panamanians whom le Carré had befriended while collecting material for the work. Patrick O'Brian, at age 82, published *The Yellow Admiral,* his 18th novel in the Aubrey-Maturin seafaring series set during the Napoleonic Wars. The *Financial Times* declared it one of the finest, despite its lack of a major naval battle.

Edwina Curry, in an attempt to replicate the huge commercial success of that other politician-turned-novelist, Jeffrey Archer, brought out a second novel, *A Woman's Place,* about the escapades of a woman junior minister. The book was, however, received without enthusiasm.

Scotland drew attention for its production of new and exciting fiction, much of it not in the retrospective tone of the literature south of the border. Many books were written in local dialect, such as James Kelman's *How Late It Was, How Late* and Irvine Welsh's *Ecstasy.* Janice Galloway's story collection *Where You Find It* contained a wry tale entitled "Tourists from the South Arrive in the Independent State" that spoke to the mood of cultural autonomy.

Rushdie entered his eighth year of living under an Iranian death threat, and negotiations between the European Union and the Iranian government to have the edict rescinded came to nought. The author, however, made several public appearances, most strikingly as an honoured guest at the British Book Awards dinner in March, where he received an Author of the Year award. The Committee for the Defense of Salman Rushdie continued to lobby on his behalf, while Rushdie himself declared that he wished to resume as normal a life as possible.

The year was extraordinarily rich in biography. The long-awaited authorized biography of Samuel Beckett by James Knowlson was a much-praised work that combined biography with literary criticism and featured a hitherto unknown but extensive correspondence between Beckett and an American woman with whom he had had an affair in the 1950s. Carl Rollyson's *Rebecca West: A Saga of the Century* was declared "excellent" by the *Literary Review,* and Margaret Drabble's *Angus Wilson: A Biography* was similarly praised by the *Sunday Times* as "a beautiful picture of mid-century English society." Michael Billington's *Harold Pinter* drew interesting links between the playwright's often obscure texts and his life. A more mixed reception attended Ben Pimlott's biography *The Queen,* a 651-page supposedly "serious" biography of Queen Elizabeth II undertaken, however, without the aid of interviews with its subject.

Another book that sparked intense controversy was *Before the Dawn,* Sinn Fein leader Gerry Adams's autobiography. A scheduled book launch in the House of Commons was canceled because of the author's political affiliations. Appearing at a time when the peace process had become mired down and the cease-fire had been violated, the book was, nonetheless, for most a valuable insight into the continuing conflict in Ulster. Although a *Times* editorial found it disingenuous, Lord Merlyn Rees in *The Guardian* declared the book

"compulsory reading," and *Time* magazine praised Adams's style as "graceful." The book enjoyed less commercial success in Britain than in Ireland, where it was a best-seller for months.

Another political biography was Robert Shepherd's on Enoch Powell, an idiosyncratic conservative whose intolerant views on immigration and race relations had contributed to his dismissal from the front bench in the late 1960s but had also won him a popular following.

Eminent literary figures of the Victorian age continued to attract biographers. Rosemary Ashton's *George Eliot: A Life* was deemed by *The Guardian* somewhat insubstantial in its literary criticism but valuable in that it "irradiates the fiction with a new luminosity of context." Lewis Carroll attracted two new biographies that laid varying degrees of stress on the author's habit of photographing naked young girls and of constructing elaborate mathematical problems during insomniac nights. Nicholas Murray's *A Life of Matthew Arnold* was an accessible study of a poet and essayist who in his day could attract an audience of more than a thousand to his lectures.

Poets from Ireland remained prominent in 1996. Seamus Heaney's *The Spirit Level,* his first poetry collection since winning the Nobel Prize in 1995, drew accolades from most commentators. Another Irish poet, Bernard O'Donoghue, now living in England, won the poetry section of the Whitbread awards. The author's *Gunpowder* collection was strongly rooted in his memory of an Irish childhood. A new translation of Charles Baudelaire's *Les Fleurs du mal,* published under the title *Poems of the Damned* by Irishman Ulick O'Connor, successfully preserved much of the rhyming and cadence of the originals.

A collection of never-before-published poems by T.S. Eliot, which he had requested never see the light of day, provoked intense debate. They appeared under the title *Inventions of the March Hare: Poems 1909–1917,* edited by Christopher Ricks. The *Guardian* critic Eric Griffiths hailed them as "a long lost map to a treasure trove" where readers would find that "the iron filings of Eliot's imagination lie all around in heaps but without the magnet needed to spring into pattern." Others saw a racist and an anti-Semitic sensibility in them, as in the poem describing a ribald encounter between Christopher Columbus and King Bolo, a black monarch. Eliot, who observed that "while the mind of man has altered, verse has stood still," came across as a poet trying, as Griffiths put it, "to jog the lyrical needle out of the groove."

David Jones, a contemporary of Eliot's, enjoyed a renaissance during the year. A war poet, painter, and polymath, Jones was the subject of two exhibitions, a series of conferences, and two books. *A Fusilier at the Front,* edited by Anthony Hyne, brought together his pencil drawings and verse, and *The Maker Unmade* by Jonathan Miles and Derek Shiel was a highly regarded illustrated biography.

The long-awaited, exhaustively researched *The Dictionary of Art* was published by Macmillan to warm notices. Twenty years in the making, the book retailed at £4,900, and the *Times Literary Supplement* hailed it as a reference work that would soon prove indispensable. Another reference work, *The*

New Fowler's Modern English Usage, edited by R.W. Burchfield, was criticized by *The Observer* for being no true successor to Fowler's tradition of prescriptive advice to writers. The writer and politician Roy Hattersley, however, praised it for making the "crucial point that what is important in writing is respecting not arbitrary rules but the resonance of the English language."

Sir Laurens Jan van der Post (*see* OBITUARIES), author of *The Heart of the Hunter* and *A Mantris Carol* and more than a dozen other titles, died at age 90. He was known for his books and films on the people of the Kalahari and was an outspoken critic of apartheid. At the year's end, Frederick Forsyth, author of *The Day of the Jackal,* and Kenneth Rose, a *Daily Telegraph* diarist and biographer of George V, were made CBE. (SIOBHAN DOWD)

Other Literature in English. Established as well as emerging writers from Australia, New Zealand, and sub-Saharan Africa provided noteworthy works in 1996. In Australia author Colleen McCullough brought out *Caesar's Women,* the fourth installment in her epic Masters of Rome series. Morris West released his 26th novel, *Vanishing Point,* simultaneously in the U.S., the U.K., and Australia. The novel created a compelling story of one man's willful disappearance and another's reluctant pursuit. Rod Jones issued the strikingly original *Billy Sunday,* set in the American frontier and working as both murder mystery and historical fiction.

David Malouf (*see* BIOGRAPHIES), who published his novel *The Conversations at*

Akosua Busia

B. KING—SYGMA

Curlow Creek, also won the inaugural International IMPAC Dublin Literary Award, at $160,000 the world's richest literary prize for a work of fiction. He was nominated for *Remembering Babylon* (1993), the story of a white man who returned to a pioneer community after living for 16 years among Aborigines. Titles by other important Australian writers included Janette Turner Hospital's novel *Oyster,* Barry Humphries's autobiographical novel *Women in the Background,* and Les Murray's verse collection *Subhuman Redneck Poems.*

New Zealand poet Allen Curnow published *New and Collected Poems 1941–1995,* and Maurice Gee released his latest verse collection, *Loving Ways.* The poet, short-story writer, novelist, and scriptwriter Stephanie Johnson brought out *The Heart's Wild Surf,* a novel set in Fiji after World War I, and 26-year-old Emily Perkins caused much excitement with her collection *Not Her Real Name: And Other Stories,* which won the Montana New Zealand Book Award for a first work of fiction.

South Africa produced two important and provocative essay collections, J.M. Coetzee's *Giving Offense: Essays on Censorship* and Breyten Breytenbach's *The Memory of Birds in Times of Revolution.* André Brink published the novel *Imaginings of Sand.* David Lambkin's thriller *The Hanging Tree* became a best-seller in South Africa before its release in the U.S., and new fiction from Christopher Hope (*Darkest England*) and Steve Jacobs (*The Enemy Within*) also attracted attention. In nonfiction Mike Nicol examined the events leading up to the election of Nelson Mandela in *The Waiting Country: A South African Witness.*

There was a spate of Nigerian fiction dealing with issues of individual, social, and national identity, including Festus Iyayi's *Awaiting Court Martial,* Femi Olugbile's *Batolica!,* and Chukwuemeka Ike's *To My Husband from Iowa.* The problems experienced by Nobel laureate Wole Soyinka, who issued his personal examination of the Nigerian crisis, *The Open Sore of a Continent,* continued when a production of his play *The Trials of Brother Jero* was suspended in February.

Tanzanian author Abdulrazak Gurnah published his fifth book, *Admiring Silence,* which portrayed the despair of being torn from one's roots. Ghanaian-born actress Akosua Busia welcomed the publication of her first novel, *The Seasons of Beento Blackbird,* to much fanfare in the U.S. The equally precocious J. Nozipo Maraire, a multilingual author, neurosurgeon, and art gallery owner born and raised in Zimbabwe, made her own literary debut with *Zenzele: A Letter for My Daughter,* in which a cultural, maternal legacy was passed on to a woman's daughter as the latter entered a new world in leaving Zimbabwe to study in the U.S. at Harvard University.

Ngugi wa Thiong'o of Kenya received the 1996 Fonlon-Nichols Award, given annually to honour excellence in African creative writing and contributions to the struggle for human rights and freedom of expression.

(DAVID D. CLARK)

GERMANIC

German. Controversy continued to mark the German literary landscape during the past year. Karl Corino, a literary editor at

Hessischer Rundfunk, published an article in the newspaper *Die Zeit* in October in which he questioned the authenticity of Stephan Hermlin's autobiography. Hermlin, a prominent figure in the literature and politics of the former German Democratic Republic (GDR), had achieved mythic status as an antifascist freedom fighter. The article served as a prelude to Corino's book about Hermlin.

The charged atmosphere of mistrust and betrayal involved in the revelations about the involvement of writers such as Christa Wolf, Heiner Müller, and Sascha Anderson in the Stasi (the East German state security police) had abated by 1996. Nonetheless, the relationship between writers and the Stasi was the focus of Joachim Walther's *Sicherungsbereich Literatur.* The work provided an overview of the cultural and political function of the Stasi, its structure and history, the methods deployed, the role of collaborators, and other matters. Walther's contribution to the debate lent insight into the role of culture and its producers in the paranoid security system of the former GDR.

Heiner Müller's *Germania 3: Gespenster am Toten Mann* was published and performed posthumously. It completed the playwright's *Germania Tod in Berlin* (1956–71) with the death of the GDR in a demonstration of the ways in which German history was haunted by the likes of Adolf Hitler and Joseph Stalin. Müller's piece showcased the role played by Bertolt Brecht, the three mourning women involved with him, and the directors of the Berliner Ensemble in the management of East German cultural history.

In *Medea: Stimmen,* a novel about the relationship between a woman, the reigning powers, and society, Christa Wolf returned to Greek mythology to make allegorical points about the German present. Much as she had in *Kassandra,* Wolf imagined an alternative history, a specifically female version of events that had shaped Western thought.

Klaus Schlesinger, in his well-received novel *Die Sache mit Randow,* narrated the events of one day on a particular street six years after the end of World War II. From the perspective of the post-1989 period, the narrator Thomale looked back on the efforts of the young criminal Randow (Ambach), known as the Al Capone of Berlin, to escape. In an effort to repress his own complicity in Randow's fate, the narrator revisited the lives of his friends and neighbours in Dunckerstrasse. In Schlesinger's colloquial, readable prose, the novel masterfully evoked an identity specific to a given street in everyday East Berlin before the building of the Berlin Wall.

The Berlin Wall also played a role in Monika Maron's *Animal triste,* a novel about an East Berlin woman's obsessive love, memory, and forgetting. The narrator, a paleontologist, recounted through repressed and replayed memories her affair with a West German researcher and its tragic end. The differences between East and West informed the couple's relationship, and the narrator looked back with bitter amazement at the wall that sealed her off. In precise and unflinching prose, Maron created a heroine whose life revolved around a love so passionate that it consumed her completely.

Peter Härtling produced the compelling *Künstlerroman, Schumanns Schatten,* which narrated the final two years of the composer's syphilitic sufferings in chapters alternating with formative events from his youth, his passion for literature and music, and his love for Clara. Härtling relies on many sources, including the diary of a doctor who treated Schumann and kept a record of his behaviour during the composer's physical and mental deterioration.

Among publications in poetry was Sarah Kirsch's *Bodenlos.* The winner of the Büchner-Preis, Kirsch treated the familiar theme of the relationship between nature and the poet in an unornamented language of uncanny precision, concision, and longing. Bert Papenfuss-Gorek let his highly political poems unfold in the volume *Berliner Zapfenstreich: Schnelle Eingreifsgesänge.* His virtuosity included diction ranging from the colloquial to the mildly obscene, all signed with his critical rage and wit.

The publication of *Irgendwo: noch einmal möcht ich sehn,* edited by Ines Geipel, marked the first substantial volume dedicated to the work of Inge Müller. The book collected her poetry, prose, and diary entries and included commentary about the work. Wolfgang Koeppen died in 1996. He was among the first to portray in modernist prose the sinister continuities between the fascist past and the "democratic" postwar present of the Federal Republic of Germany.   (PATRICIA A. SIMPSON)

Netherlandic. In *Kijken is bekeken worden,* the leading Dutch poet Gerrit Komrij made a significant comment on modern literature in general and Dutch publications of 1996 in particular when he wondered aloud why modern literature had never enjoyed the success of modern art. Komrij indirectly answered his own question by pointing out that although lines and colours could have a meaning of their own, words, if too disconnected, did not communicate. Readers liked to read stories.

A bridge between the abstract school of the 1950s and the reemergence—be it in different form—of the traditional narrative was the highly productive author A.F.Th. van der Heijden. His unfinished supernovel, *De tandeloze tijd,* begun when he was just 16, comprised more than 3,000 pages in four volumes. The series would probably never be finished, for van der Heijden, like his older fellow writer Gerard Reve, with his *Het boek van violet en dood,* was trying to write "the complete book." Reve's strongly narrative and autobiographical novel also did not turn out to be the book "that made all other books, except the Bible and the telephone directory, redundant," in spite of the author's undertaking begun three decades earlier.

The autobiographical element, manifestly present in most contemporary Dutch novels, took an extreme form in some works. Prominent among them was Harry Mulisch's *Bij gelegenheid,* a collection of thought-provoking essays.

F.B. Hotz, who made his debut in 1976, claimed in *De vertegenwoordigers* that the ability to tell a fascinating story does not alone make a great writer. The story also has to be told with precision and in a personal style. The books of seasoned authors Ward Ruyslinck, in *Het geboortehuis,* Jef Geeraerts, in *Goud,* and J.J. Voskuil, in *Het bureau,* as well as the younger writers

Koos van Zomeren, in *Meisje in het veen,* and the Moroccan-born Hafid Bouazza, in *De voeten van Abdullah,* all proved to meet these conditions.   (MARTINUS A. BAKKER)

Danish. Among Danish publications of international interest in 1996 were Karen Blixen's letters, *Karen Blixen i Danmark: Breve 1931–62,* which provided insight into the difficulties the writer (who published under the name Isak Dinesen) had in accommodating herself to Denmark after returning from Africa. Hans Edvard Nørregård-Nielsen wrote an outstanding biography in his three-volume study of the great painter Christen Købke.

Among the nation's thriller writers, not the least was Leif Davidsen. His *Den serbiske dansker,* about a mission to execute a *fatwa* in Denmark on a visiting author who was welcomed by PEN but cold-shouldered by politicians, had clear overtones of the Salman Rushdie affair. Peter Høeg moved into a fantasy world with *Kvinden og aben,* about an ape, loose in London, learning to speak and having an affair. There was fantasy, too, in the shape of a maritime ghost, in Hanne Marie Svendsen's *Rejsen med Emma,* about a woman writer who sailed to the Pacific to put her life in order. Dorrit Willumsen, internationally known for her novel *Marie,* again turned to the 19th century with *Bang,* a novel about the author Herman Bang, while, in *Tavshed i oktober,* Jens Christian Grøndahl portrayed a man of 44 looking back on his life to discover why his wife had left him after 18 years of marriage.

In *Det skabtes vaklen: Arabesker,* Søren Ulrik Thomsen again showed himself to be a philosophical poet continuing a well-established Danish tradition, rooted in the intellectual stylists of the 18th and 19th centuries. In *Tabernakel,* Niels Frank produced a series of philosophical and well-wrought poems in a rather more subdued style than his earlier collections. The young poet Naja Marie Aidt produced another volume of poems, *Huset overfor,* and the productive veteran Klaus Rifbjerg added to his work with *Leksikon.* Per Højholt completed his *Praksis* series, which was sometimes prose, sometimes poetry, with *Anekdoter,* a sequence of eight varied and sophisticated prose pieces.

Henrik Nordbrandt was awarded the Danish booksellers' distinguished Golden Laurels, the first poet in 20 years to win the prize. The Critics' Prize also went to a poet, this time to Per Højholt.
   (W. GLYN JONES)

Norwegian. The most charming contribution to Norwegian literature in 1996 was Jostein Gaarder's *Hallo?—er det noen her?,* which presented cosmological issues from a child's perspective with intelligence and humour. Promiscuity blossomed in Ketil Bjørnstad's novel *Drift,* a portrait of Norway around 1970. The life of the main character in *Drift* during subsequent years was presented in the sequel, *Drømmen om havet.* Erotic tensions between two married couples were analyzed against a Spanish backdrop in Knut Faldbakken's *Når jeg ser deg.* Sex and drugs emerged in Anders W. Cappelen's novel *Meska.* In *Erobreren,* Jan Kjærstad returned to his television personality Jonas Wergeland from the 1993 novel *Forføreren,* providing a heady mixture of sex and social satire. Peter Serck's short stories in *Ansiktene* spoke eloquently of the

irredeemable loneliness of the soul, not the least during sexual encounters.

Finn Carling presented a synthesis of the world's many trouble spots in *En annen vei,* in which a doctor taken hostage reflects on the mad world surrounding him. Sissel Lange-Nielsen's semidocumentary historical novel *Den norske løve* brought to life the hardships and instabilities inflicted on the united kingdom of Denmark-Norway by the Napoleonic Wars during the years leading up to 1814. Bergljot Hobæk Haff's elegantly written novel *Skammen* was a family saga rooted in 20th-century Norway. Stylish playfulness characterized Ernst Orvil's collected short stories, *Samlede noveller.* The collected poems of Inger Hagerup, Gunvor Hofmo, and Sigmund Mjelve were published in 1996. Rolf Jacobsen's verse was analyzed by Erling Aadland in *Poetisk tenkning i Rolf Jacobsens lyrikk.*

Torill Steinfeld's *Den unge Camilla Collett* offered a rich portrait of the 19th-century feminist. Irene Engelstad, Liv Køltzow, and Gunnar Staalesen provided a portrait of another feminist in *Amalie Skrams verden.* Øystein Rottem published his three-volume *Etterkrigslitteraturen. Knut Hamsuns brev 1908–1914,* edited and annotated by Harald S. Næss, was notable for 130 passionate letters to Hamsun's second wife, Marie. Rottem's *Hamsuns liv i bilder* was a survey of Hamsun's life in words and pictures.   (TORBJØRN STØVERUD)

Swedish. The year 1996 saw a number of new works by established Swedish authors. Kerstin Ekman's *Gör mig levande igen* chronicled life in present-day Sweden and the collapse of established values in conjunction with the impact of the war in former Yugoslavia. Sara Lidman's novel *Lifsens rot* continued the narrative of her pentalogy (1977–85) with the introduction of a female character who sealed the fate of a rural community. Birgitta Trotzig's prose poems in *Sammanhang* emphasized similar values within the framework of an investigation of language and being. Göran Tunström's *Skimmer* was a novel about desire, hatred, and love in which the relationship between a father, a son, and a mother assumed mythical resonances.

Important books of poetry included Tomas Tranströmer's *Sorgegondolen,* in which the metaphoric use of details helped counteract a sense of isolation, and Göran Sonnevi's *Mozarts tredje hjärna,* which explored the role of change as a basis of awareness. The poems in Lars Gustafsson's *Variationer över ett tema av Silfverstolpe* drew on music to investigate the concept of time, while Gunnar D. Hansson's *AB Neanderthal* was a metapoetical work that explored artistic intuition. Jesper Svenbro's poems in *Vid budet att Santo Bambino di Aracœli slutligen stulits av maffian* combined Swedish and classical landscapes to paint fragile idylls, while those in Lukas Moodysson's *Souvenir* conveyed a fragmented world.

Ulf Eriksson's *Paradis* was a collection of short stories in which the elliptical style offered scant shelter against ennui and loneliness. While the short stories in Inger Frimansson's *Där inne vilar ögat* focused on relationships, those in Maria Larsson's *Mimers brunn* ventured into the world of science fiction. Identity was a central theme in both Bodil Malmsten's novel *Nästa som rör mig* and Steve Sem-Sandberg's *Theres,* while Elsie Johansson's *Glasfåglarna* re-

Sara Lidman

volved around a working-class childhood and Åke Smedberg's *Strålande stjärna* investigated the generation gap. Carina Burman's novel *Den tionde sånggudinnan* and Jacques Werup's *Den ofullbordade himlen* both explored the situation of women in the early decades of the 20th century, and Märta Tikkanen's *Personliga angelägenheter* combined tales of loneliness and desire.

(EDITORS)

FRENCH

France. With some 500 novels published in France in the autumn alone, 1996 was marked by a proliferation of fiction. Confronted with this abundance, many readers had recourse to the familiar, such as Patrick Modiano, who reprised his customary themes in *Du plus loin de l'oubli,* in which a man reminisces over inexplicable chance encounters that have shaped his life. Pierre Michon wrote two short novels also revolving around formative chance encounters, this time with women. In *La Grande Beune* a young schoolteacher, assigned to a tiny rural town, comes to desire local women, whose bodies poetically coalesce with the countryside to form a geography of desire, while in *Le Roi du bois,* a peasant's life is forever changed when he sees a noblewoman in a compromising position and then develops the desire to become a prince himself in order to win her.

Besides these literary veterans, several newcomers also made their mark. They included 27-year-old Marie Darrieussecq, whose first novel, *Truismes,* the story of a woman transformed into a sow strangely purer than swinish modern society, was one of the year's two literary sensations. The other was *Lila dit ça,* written by Chimo, an obvious pseudonym for an author whose true identity sparked wild speculation in light of the book's feigned literary naïveté. The novel was the story of a powerful but doomed teenage love between a French Arab and a blond girl, set against the despair of ghetto life. In 23-year-old Mehdi Belhaj Kecem's *Vies et morts d'Irène Lepic,* the voice of youth is expressed by the virulent protest of a young woman, isolated by her own intelligence, against the cattle-like conformity of society in general and of her nonconformist group of friends in particular.

Protest was transformed into political parody in Jean Jouet's *La Montagne R.,* in which bureaucratic clichés abound in the absurdity of a corrupt government project to combat unemployment and unrest by mobilizing the workforce to build a useless mountain. In Claude Pujade-Renaud's *La Nuit la neige,* a political occurrence—the dismissal in 1714 of a longtime favourite, 72-year-old Marie-Anne de la Trémoille, princesse des Ursins, from the court of Spain's King Philip V by the king's new

young wife—offered the chance to examine years of political intrigue through a polyphony of women's voices, from the most humble to the most illustrious. Politics mixed with metaphysics in Bernard Noël's *Le Roman d'Adam et Eve,* an examination of how easily the desire to return to original perfection can enslave man, here through Joseph Stalin's attempt to re-create a Soviet Garden of Eden.

The metaphysical was expressed as a journey in Sylvie Germain's *Éclats de sel,* in which metaphors of salt surround a Czech returning home to overcome the "flavourlessness" of his spiritual bankruptcy through the learnings of a 16th-century rabbi. The fantastic completely took over the everyday life of an abandoned housewife in Marie Ndayic's *La Sorcière;* the familial traditions of the witch, passed on from mother to daughter through the centuries, prove too weak to combat the 20th-century disintegration of the family.

In poetry simplicity was a major theme. Joël Vernet's *Totems de sable* celebrated the simplicity of gardens and childhood, and Dominique Pagnier's *La Faveur de l'obscurité,* that of the country's humble nobility. In *Éboulements et Taillis,* Bertrand Degott used old forms, such as the poem of circumstance, complete with verse and rhyme, to describe small, everyday occurrences. The novelist Michel Butor also published a collection of poems, *A la frontière,* an examination of spatiality and geography, not only of the world but also of the beholder's view, in which the mixture of poetic prose and prose poetry itself raised the question of literary frontiers.

In the realm of essays, Jacques Derrida published *Apories,* in which, from his deconstructionist point of view, he argued that in the questions that are concerned with time and death a person must maintain the aporia (a logical problem with no solution). In *La Haine de la musique,* Pascal Quignard, best known for his novel celebrating music, *All the Mornings of the World,* wrote of his newfound hatred of music and of the invasive, noisy suffering it causes in the hearer who seeks only silence and solitude. Christian Prigent wrote *Une Erreur de la nature,* a defense of "unreadable" or difficult writers, such as himself, who maintain the ungraspable chaos of reality in their works rather than falsely reassuring readers with illusions of a stable, understandable universe.

The Prix Femina was awarded to Geneviève Brisac for her *Week-end de chasse à la mère,* the story of a single mother whose son has become her last source of stability and joy in the world. The Prix Médicis went to two authors: Jacqueline Harpman for her psychoanalytic tale of androgyny, *Orlanda,* in which a woman possesses the mind and body of a man; and Jean Rolin for his *L'Organisation,* the fictionalized autobiography of his misadventures in the Maoist revolutionary movement of 1968 France. The Prix Renaudot also went to a fictionalized autobiography, Boris Schreiber's *Un Silence d'environ une demi-heure,* the story of the flight of the author's family across Europe to escape the Nazis. The Prix Goncourt was awarded to Pascale Roze's first novel, *Le Chasseur Zéro,* which recounted a woman's obsession for her long-dead father and the Japanese kamikaze pilot who killed him in World War II. (VINCENT AURORA)

Canada. The old dominated, and the new struggled to break through in 1996 in French-Canadian literature. Marie-Claire Blais, whose high-angst Gothic style had shaped a generation of writers, won the country's top fiction prize, the Governor General's Literary Award, for her 1995 novel *Soifs.* Meanwhile, younger writers like Louis Hamelin tried to break through. His adventure novel *Le Soleil des gouffres* was set in Quebec and Mexico and featured the evildoings of a cult.

Old political issues were among the dominant themes of the year. After the 1995 referendum on independence, Quebeckers had a choice among a host of analyses, some discussing why both sides lost. Josée Legault continued to be the main spokeswoman for Quebec nationalists with her collection *Les Nouveaux Démons: chroniques et analyses politiques,* while historian Jacques Lacoursière's *Historie populaire du Québec* gave French Canadians an accessible window to their past.

Fiction from immigrant writers continued to supply the most startling energy on the Quebec literary scene. Dany Laferrière, in his novel *Pays sans chapeau,* described the difficult journey back to his native Haiti. Brazilian-born Sergio Kokis, in *Errances,* combined political intrigue, male adventure, and meditations on the state and the artist and showed in the process how a skilled immigrant writer can bypass the shopworn theme of "coming to the new land." Nancy Huston, who was born in Calgary, Alta., and in 1996 lived in Paris, had a literary and popular success with her novel *Instruments des ténèbres.* Her book combined a tale set in pre-Revolutionary France with the story of a modern woman's exploration in America. Other French-Canadian writers scored popular hits with largely female audiences: Marie Laberge with *Annabelle* and Chrystine Brouillet with *C'est pour mieux t'aimer, mon enfant.*

Poets can sometimes face a thankless task when it comes to reaching an audience, though José Acquelin with his *Traversée du désert* managed to create a readership. At the end of 1996, French-Canadian letters lost Gaston Miron—poet, cultural agitator, and harmonica player. (*See* OBITUARIES.)

(DAVID HOMEL)

ITALIAN

If literature reflects the society and culture in which it is produced, the least one could say was that Italians were deeply dissatisfied with themselves in 1996. Following the ever-increasing and much-lamented popularity of violent themes in motion pictures and on television, the wave of new pulpfiction writers indulged in the not entirely parodic representation of mindless homespun violence. The few novels that seriously addressed contemporary topics were critical of Italian society and pessimistic about its future. The main culprit was seen to be the national obsession with money.

Nowhere was this theme more evident than in Ferdinando Camon's short novel *La terra e di tutti,* in which the northeastern part of Italy was depicted as being poisoned by its wealth. Camon's characters, like the Lombard ones of Aldo Busi's *Suicidi dovuti,* were a frightening mixture of ignorance and power, their only saving feature being the likelihood, suggested between the lines,

that their excesses might be a biological compensation for the extremes of deprivation suffered by their ancestors. Roberto Pazzi's intense psychological novel *Incerti di viaggio* did not offer much comfort either; his cultured middle-aged, middle-class childless couple, traveling by night train from Naples to the north, experienced their enforced proximity as a prison from which neither could escape.

Most novels, however, were set either in the past or far away from Italy or both. In *Le stagioni di Giacomo,* the writer Mario Rigoni Stern evoked the life of his native Alpine community between the two world wars, while in *Esilio* Enzo Bettiza, inspired by the tragic wars unfolding in his native Dalmatia, told the saga of his family through the past two centuries and of his own exile from his homeland since 1945. The best-seller of the year was the short and captivating, though rather insubstantial, *Seta* by the young writer Alessandro Baricco. It was the somewhat Calvinian story of a 19th-century Frenchman who, year after year, traveled to Japan and back, ostensibly to acquire precious silkworms but actually in search of an indefinite and ever-elusive object of desire. Equally exotic with its exquisite Asia Minor settings, though more ambitious in conception and richer in style, was *Giocando a dama con la luna* by Giuliana Morandini, in which the myth of classical Greece, as lived by the 19th-century German archaeologist Karl Humann, was shown to harbour the sickness that took over and ultimately destroyed Germany. The Nazi occupation of Austria provided a dark background to Paolo Maurensig's second novel, *Canone inverso,* the story of a bewitched and bewitching violin and of the double personality of its bizarre Hungarian player. The notion that goodness is not normal was central to Anna Maria Ortese's *Alonso e i visionari,* the strange story of a little puma that, taken to Italy from Arizona, causes passions and hatred to burn intensely and dark fantasies to conquer reality.

Readers could hardly find respite from the general gloom. Even a senseless sequence of events stunningly narrated in *Fontano da casa* by Franco Ferrucci coalesced into a destiny only because of an individual act of violence that returned an Italian emigrant who thought he had found happiness in 1920s America to the anonymity of Genoa. The violent intolerance of Turinese bourgeois in the 1920s was the setting of *Il bacio della Medusa,* Melania Mazzucco's impressive first novel about the passionate love that drew together two women of disparate social backgrounds. Stefano Benni's satirical *Elianto* provided a measure of comic relief, even if at the expense of a country transparently named Tristalia. One of the most compelling books of the year was Fausta Garavini's *Diletta Costanza,* a lucid, intelligent, and compassionate half-fictional and half-historical reconstruction of the life and times of the remarkable Costanza Monti, daughter of Vincenzo Monti, a major Italian poet in the Napoleonic era.

A telling sign of the times was the appearance of the periodical *Il semplice,* a "prose almanac" edited by a group of young writers around Gianni Celati and Ermanno Cavazzoni. It was devoted to the publication of ordinary or artfully "underwritten"

narratives, an attempt to denounce the meretricious use of literature.

A major event in poetry was the centenary of the birth of the Nobel laureate Eugenio Montale, who died in 1981. His *Diario postumo: 66 poesie e altre,* a collection of new or little known poems, appeared during the year. Montale's acknowledged successor, Andrea Zanzotto, published *Meteo,* 20 compositions focusing on an "ecosystem" ambiguously poised between life and death but ultimately threatened more than ever before by contamination and violence.

Gesualdo Bufalino (*see* OBITUARIES), the Sicilian novelist and author of many works much acclaimed by critics and the public alike, died in 1996, as did Amelia Rosselli, a distinguished voice among contemporary Italian poets.   (LINO PERTILE)

SPANISH

Spain. Arturo Pérez-Reverte's gripping tale of ecclesiastical intrigue, *La piel del tambor* (published in 1995), set in contemporary Seville and full of charmingly improbable characters and labyrinthine plot twists, was the blockbuster novel of 1996. Manuel Vázquez Montalbán, winner of the National Letters Prize, produced three works. *Un polaco en la corte del Rey Juan Carlos* offered a semifictionalized collage of interviews conducted with 30 prominent figures shortly before the national elections in March. In *Recetas inmorales* the author, an acknowledged expert on Spanish gastronomy, spiced 62 of his favourite recipes with delicious commentaries on their erotic properties, and in a thinly veiled roman à clef entitled *El premio,* his detective hero, Pepe Carvalho, cracked a new case, this time involving the murder of a suspiciously influential publishing mogul whose final act was to serve as host of the year's most lavish literary award banquet. Fernando Schwartz accepted the Planeta Prize for *El desencuentro,* a suspense-filled, bittersweet reflection, in the form of contrasting diaries, on opportunity lost and love squandered. The highest honour in Hispanic letters, the Cervantes Prize, went to the Spanish poet José García Nieto.

Terenci Moix, who won the newly established Fernando Lara Prize, returned to the Egyptian setting of his earlier fiction in *El amargo don de la belleza,* a stylized, pseudohistorical narration immersed in the convulsive reign of the pharaoh Akhenaton. José María Merino's evocation of the persecuted 16th-century visionary Lucrecia de León in *Las visiones de Lucrecia* was more rigorously faithful to the historical record. Néstor Luján's *La cruz en la espada,* which explored an obscure episode in the life of the classical poet Francisco de Quevedo y Villegas, appeared shortly after the author's death at age 73.

Carmen Martín Gaite published her 14th novel, *Lo raro es vivir,* a compelling first-person narration of a week in the life of a woman forced to reassess her existence upon the death of her illustrious mother. Javier Marías offered 12 superb short stories in a widely praised collection entitled *Cuando fui mortal.* Critics were also impressed by the short fiction in *El silencio del patinador* by the promising young writer Juan Manuel de Prada.

Two well-known essayists attracted many readers. Vicente Verdú inveighed against the globalization of American culture in *El planeta americano,* and Eduardo Haro Tecglen's memoir, *Un niño republicano,* gave a moving account of his boyhood during the Second Republic. (ROGER L. UTT)

Latin America. Andrés Rivera's *El farmer* was a best-seller in 1996. The novel concerned the declining years of the legendary 19th-century Argentine dictator Juan Manuel de Rosas. The work was centred on a winter's night of recollections, with Rosas's rambling monologue bringing back to life for him the glories of his reign and the perfidy of his enemies. In the process he articulated fragments of a modern ideology of authoritarian control.

Tununa Mercado's *La madriguera* focused on the author's childhood. The work was not autobiographical in any common sense of the word, however, but rather involved a feminist theory of memory.

Jorge Salessi's *Médicos maleantes y maricas: higiene, criminología y homosexualidad en la construcción de la nación Argentina (Buenos Aires, 1871–1914)* exemplified the work being done to provide an adequate social history for Latin America, which often meant dealing with topics that official scholars had avoided. Salessi's work was concerned with the public discourse regarding sexual deviance and the police and with medical responses to it.

Reina Roffé's *El cielo dividido* interwove the stories of seven Argentine women. The account of their lives, in addition to being an impressive attempt to record a mosaic of women's history in Argentine society, connected their personal narratives with national political discourse. In the process Roffé provided a lucid explanation of the way in which history in Argentina has referred only to the lives of men or to women only as figures in the lives of men.

Gabriel García Márquez's *Noticia de un secuestro* was published simultaneously in numerous Latin-American centres, a growing practice with authors of his stature. Continuing his interest in violence and codes of masculinity, García Márquez explored the kidnapping of a prominent woman ordered by the drug czar Pablo Escobar. The author combined documentary sources and narrative re-creations to fashion a testimonial on the social contradictions of Colombia.

Fernando Vallejo's *Chapolas negras* was a biography of a short-lived 19th-century Colombian poet, José Asunción Silva. The poet was associated with the beginnings of a decadent, bohemian cultural tradition in Latin America, and Vallejo's interest in him continued the series of explicitly homosexual novels he had published.

First published in Spain in 1995, Reinaldo Arenas's posthumous *Adiós a Mamá* was published in the U.S. in 1996. A few of the stories were written in Cuba before Arenas's escape with the Marielitos, but most were written during the 10 years he resided in the U.S. These bitter stories, which reflected Arenas's interest in his later works with exile and with the lives of homosexuals, had to do with individuals who were unable to identify with the dominant social structures and felt a sense of alienation.

Rafael Loret de Mola's potboiler *Alcobas de palacio* was one of the fiction hits of the year in Mexico. The author's trashy novel exemplified one more element of U.S. influence: the luridly sexual as an index for political corruption.

Elena Garro continued as the reigning matriarch of feminist writing in Mexico. Her *Busca mi esquela & Primer amor* consisted of two short novels. The first related an erotic relationship between a young woman and an older man, a theme that Garro treated with her customary acerbic view of the limits of human aspirations. The second had a post–World War II setting in a summer vacation retreat in France at which the ugly history of the war could not be kept at bay by a newfound hedonism.

In late 1995 Carlos Fuentes published *La frontera de cristal.* Fuentes had in his fiction established a vast mosaic of contemporary Mexico, and he examined various social and political issues via stories and novels that continued to bear his customary

Gabriel García Márquez

mark of sharp insight and fluid storytelling. The stories of the collection dealt with migration, the issue that continued to sour relations between Mexico and the U.S. The ways in which Mexicans viewed U.S. border policy—as racism, economic exploitation, and linguistic and cultural jingoism—were represented. Magali García Ramis's *Las noches del Riel de Oro* was a collection of short stories that developed the author's interest in the cultural and social contradictions of Puerto Rico's divided identity as a Latin-American country that was also a political unit of the U.S. García Ramis emphasized women's lives.

Mayra Santos Febres's *Pez de vidrio* was a fine collection of short stories describing the experiences of women in San Juan, the capital of Puerto Rico. There had been a considerable amount of women's writing in recent years in Puerto Rico, and this collection confirmed the interest of those authors in turning away from the representation of women in traditional women's spaces (the home, the church, the school, the convent) and placing them instead not only in strategic positions in public life but also in urban life, where so many changes in women's lives in recent decades had taken place.

(DAVID WILLIAM FOSTER)

PORTUGUESE

Portugal. Portuguese fiction had a vintage year in 1996. The number of novels published was not higher than in previous years, but the quality of work produced by well-known authors was outstanding. Alexandre Pinheiro Torres, a distinguished academic, completed a remarkable fresco of Portuguese society under the Salazar regime with the publication of *A quarta invasão Francesa,* a fascinating tale of intrigue that ends in a political assassination. The project started in 1977 with *A nau de Quixibá* and developed into five novels depicting 50 years of contemporary Portuguese life.

The Association of Portuguese Authors awarded the Great Prize for Fiction to Teolinda Gersão for her novel *A casa da cabeça de cavalo,* a subtle tale of women's feelings as seen through three generations. In a remote and provincial town, where the presence of an outsider upsets the stability of daily life, women nurture their passions in silence, imposed by a patriarchal society that resists change. A clandestine language is invented between two lovers who have been tricked by paternal authority. Conventions are slowly eroded, and when freedom dawns on the people, they are emotional cripples.

José Saramago published his long-awaited novel *Ensaio sobre a cegueira,* a hallucinatory tale that was also a dramatic warning on the ills of contemporary society. His characters and the place of action are nameless. Characters are known for the functions they perform, and the events described may have taken place anywhere and nowhere. A strange epidemic of blindness gradually strikes a whole community, sparing only the woman who witnesses it all. To avoid the spreading of the disease, the government sends soldiers to contain the blind in a ghetto. A group of bullies takes over and rules in an orgy of brutality and rape that tests human emotions beyond endurance. As inexplicably as the blindness had started, people begin to recover their eyesight, while the woman fears the moment when the disease might start again, making her one of its victims. It is a philosophical tale of feverish dramatic intensity on the moral blindness of humans and the perversities of their behaviour that seem to be leading to self-destruction.

(L.S. REBELO)

Brazil. Among the works of fiction that received widespread attention in 1996 was Marcelo Rubens Paiva's *Não és tu, Brasil,* a narration of the guerrilla movements of the late 1960s and early 1970s in Brazil and written as a catharsis for the suffering of the author's father during the rule of the military regime. New fiction by Silviano Santiago, Fausto Wolff, and José Sarney also appeared.

Rubem Fonseca published a new collection of short stories, *O buraco na parede,* which returned to the theme of gratuitous violence in everyday life in Rio de Janeiro. A collection of heretofore unknown detective stories written by Pagu (Patrícia Galvão), the muse of Brazilian modernism, in the 1940s under the pseudonym King Shelter was published as *Safra macabra.* The last book of poems of Carlos Drummond de Andrade appeared under the title *Farewell.* Many of them suggested the anguish of his last years and his desire for death.

In drama Antunes Filho characterized his *Drácula e outros vampiros* as *fonemonol,* reflecting his new interest in discovering the musicality of the Portuguese language. Mauro Rasi once again turned to autobiographical themes in his new play *As tias de Mauro Rasi.* Clara Góes's *Gregório* dealt with the life of the Pernambucan communist activist Gregório Bezerra. George Moura published *Paulo Francis: o soldado fanfarrão,* a much-debated study of the role of Paulo Francis in the Brazilian theatre of the 1950s and early 1960s.

New biographies of João Cabral de Melo Neto, by José Castello, and of João do Rio, by João Carlos Rodrigues, appeared during the year. Luiz Carlos Maciel's memoirs, *Geração em transe: memórias do tempo do Tropicalismo,* highlighted the vanguard movement that began in the late 1960s. Of note also was the new contribution by Paulo Coelho (*see* BIOGRAPHIES) to the self-help theme, *O monte cinco,* in which biblical angels appear, mentioned in the same breath as the Internet.

Giovanni Pontiero, the highly regarded translator into English of Brazilian poets and Portuguese writers, died in February.

(IRWIN STERN)

RUSSIAN

The death of Joseph Brodsky (*see* OBITUARIES) on Jan. 28, 1996, signaled the end not only of an important literary career but also of an era in Russian poetry. Although Brodsky had lived in the U.S. since 1972, his death provoked a stream of critical commentary, memoirs, and reflections that filled Russia's newspapers and literary journals.

The battle of literary schools and generations, pitting realism against postmodernism and the old against the new (or young), continued in 1996. The realist tendency in Russian literature was represented by such works as Viktor Astafyev's post-Soviet, fiercely honest *Tak khochetsya zhit* ("A Thirst for Life"), Andrey Dmitriyev's *Povorot reki* ("A Bend in the River"), Petr Aleshkovsky's 19th-century-styled *Vladimir Chigrintsev,* and Andrey Sergeyev's *Albom dlya marok* ("A Stamp Album"), the last of which won the 1996 Russian Booker Prize. Other prominent writers trying in their own way to tell the "truth" about Russia included Boris Yekimov, Gennady Golovin, Viktoriya Tokareva, and Aleksandr Solzhenitsyn. In December 1995 Aleksey Varlamov was awarded an "anti-Booker Prize" by the literary weekly *The Independent* in protest against the Booker awarded to Georgy Vladimov.

Postmodern works included Viktor Pelevin's *Chapayev i pustota* ("Chapayev and Emptiness"), a highly controversial book that not only satirized a classic of Soviet lit-

erature but also, in the author's own words, was the first Russian Buddhist novel. Aleksandr Borodynya's *Tsepnoy shchenok* ("The Guard Dog") depicted incestuous love between a mother and son set against the backdrop of civil war in the Abkhazian region of Georgia. There also were new works from Aleksandr Vernikov, Nina Sadur, and Valeriya Narbikova.

One of the most important books was Dmitry Bakin's collection of stories *Strana proiskhozhdeniya* ("Country of Origin"),

Joseph Brodsky

which fell somewhere between the realist and postmodern camps. Bakin, who had been compared to Camus and Sartre, depicted an existential world of consciousness-burdened individuals wandering through time. Other noted works of prose included pieces by Vladimir Sharov and novellas by Lyudmila Ulitskaya and Mikhail Kurayev.

Russian poets continued to produce an ample and impressive stream of verse in 1996. From the older generation came works from Bella Akhmadulina, Andrey Voznesensky, Vladimir Sokolov, and Yevgeny Yevtushenko, who followed up his 1995 1,053-page anthology of 20th-century Russian poetry with a long poem entitled "Trinadtsat" ("The Thirteen"), an obvious allusion to, and attempted outdoing of, Aleksandr Blok's *Dvenadtsat* (*The Twelve*), a reflection on the Revolution of 1917.

Neomodern and postmodern approaches to poetic form and language were represented in new works from Sergey Biryukov, Genrikh Sapgir, Arkady Dragomoshchenko, Aleksey Parshchikov, Dmitry Prigov, and Lev Rubinshtein. More traditional voices could be heard in works from Oleg Chukhontsev, Sergey Gandlevsky, Yelena Kabysh, Vladimir Gandelsman, Svetlana Kekova, and Ilya Kutik. Two of the more important poets to publish new volumes were Yelena Shvarts, perhaps the strongest of the post-Symbolist Russian voices, and Aleksandr Kushner, who was named a laureate of the Russian state for his quieter, more classical verse.

Most Russian literary criticism remained highly ideological, whether pro- (Andrey Nemzer, Pavel Basinsky) or anti- (Vyacheslav Kuritsyn) realism. Lev Annensky and Alla Latynina showed themselves to be more objective and conscientious. On a higher level, Boris Paramonov, Georgy Gachev, Mikhail Epshtein, and Boris Grois continued to contribute to both Russian and Western criticism. Two titles were especially notable: Aleksandr Etkind's *Sodom i Psikheya* ("Sodom and Psyche"), a continuation of his ongoing psychological analysis of Russian culture, and Aleksandr Genis and Petr Vail's *60-iye* ("The '60s"), their study of *Homo sovieticus*.

The business of Russian literature remained rocky. While publishers specializing in detective, fantasy, erotic, and romance novels thrived, scholarly publishing remained largely moribund because of the withdrawal of government subsidies. Serious literature approximated more to the Western model, with relatively high prices and small pressruns. After a makeover of the magazine market, three journals in particular came of age in 1996: *Znamya* ("Banner"), a formerly Soviet "thick journal" (*i.e.,* a monthly magazine of several hundred pages devoted to literature and culture), which succeeded in attracting readers by presenting a somewhat eclectic but high-quality mix of the important writers of the day; *Kommentarii* ("Commentaries"), which emerged as the most sophisticated of the elite little magazines; and *Novoe literaturnoe obozrenie* ("The New Literary Review"), which presented professional literary criticism and philology. (THOMAS EPSTEIN)

EASTERN EUROPEAN

Overall, literary developments in Eastern Europe were quite eventful in 1996. It was a memorable year for Polish literature in particular. For the first time, the Nobel Prize was awarded to a Slavic woman poet, Wisława Szymborska. (*See* NOBEL PRIZES.) A volume of Stanisław Czycz's best-known short stories, revised just before his death in 1996 and entitled *Ajol i Laor* ("Ajol and Laor"), was published. It concluded with a lengthy interview of the author by Krzysztof Lisowski. A selection of Czesław Miłosz's wartime essays, *Legendy nowoczesności* ("Legends of Modernity"), in which he questioned certain modernist ideals and values, appeared. The second part of the volume consisted of his correspondence with Jerzy Andrzejewski from the same period. Miłosz also published a biographical work of his late friend the poet Anna Swirszczyńska, *Cóż to za gościa mieliśmy* ("What a Guest We Had"). The growing presence of women's voices was exemplified by Urszula Kozioł's volume of poetry *Wielka pauza* ("The Great Pause"). In it Kozioł employed her traditional poetic devices, such as the use of dialogue and digressions, yet added new elements such as poems related to her journeys or based on classical myths and motifs. Anna Burzyńska's novel *Fabulant: Powiastka intertekstualna* ("The Fabulist: An Intertextual Tale"), filled with quotations and parodies borrowed from classical or fashionable literary works, was considered one of the most interesting debuts of the year.

In the South Slavic region, literature continued to be at the centre of cultural life. The NIN award, the most prestigious of Serbian literary awards, was given to Svetlana Velmar-Janković for her novel *Bezdno* ("Bottomless"). Velmar-Janković, who belonged to the generation of writers born before World War II, was considered the most powerful woman writer of Serbian literature. Her new novel was a historical work set in the second half of the 19th century in Serbia. Among her characters were members of the Obrenović dynasty. The most important literary event of the year, however, was the publication of the late Borislav Pekić's essays *Radjanje Atlantide* ("The Birth of Atlantis"). Selected from his diaries after his death in 1992, they dealt partly with an account of the writing of his popular novel *Atlantis*. Another important collection of essays, *Virtuelna Kabala* ("The Virtual Kabbalah"), established Svetislav Basara as Serbia's foremost analyst of literary, historical, and cultural issues.

The English translation by Bogdan Rakić and Stephen Dickey of Meša Selimović's *Death and the Dervish* filled an important gap in the literature of Bosnia and Herzegovina. Although Selimović's first-person narrative took place in the 18th century in Turkish-occupied Sarajevo, it conveyed a universal truth about the dilemma of humankind during times of crisis. The Dominik Tatarek Literary Award for the best book of the year went to Ivan Kadlečik for *Hlavolamy* ("Brain Twisters"). Kadlečik was a prose writer, essayist, and former dissident who in the 1970s had been banned from publishing in his country. His new book consisted of monologues, aphorisms, and tales that interwove lofty ideas with banal concerns.

The literary scene in the Czech Republic remained as vigorous in 1996 as in previous years. One of the most popular contemporary Czech fiction writers, Michal Viewegh, published the novel *Účastníci zájezdu* ("The Excursion Participants"). It was a grotesque description of participants attending a convention and was filled with tragicomic effects. In poetry Petr Borkovec, representative of the younger generation of Czech poets, published his fourth volume of poetry, *Mezi oknem, stolem a pos-*

Wisława Szymborska

telí ("Between the Window, the Table, and the Bed").

Since 1989 a free press and the abolition of censorship had created a new period in the literary life of Romania. The most flourishing genre was nonfiction. Memoirs, diaries, and journals covering the period 1947–89 gave voice to the diverse experiences of a nation oppressed by the former communist regime. The trend was best epitomized by Mircea Zaiciu's *Journal,* an exceptionally vivid document whose third volume was published in 1996. Written from a personal point of view, it represented the tragedy of Romanian intellectuals silenced during the Nicolae Ceauşescu regime. The unprecedented growth and interest in the political essay was another literary phenomenon. Horia-Roman Patapievici's book of essays *Cerul vazut prin lentila* ("The Sky Seen Through a Lens") best represented the genre. In it the author questioned the previously idealized Romanian identity shaken by the 1990 miners' "revolt." In May 1996 Patapievici received an award from the Writers Union (Premiile Uniunii Scriitorilor) for the best book written by a beginner. The Writers Union awards, covering 10 different categories, and the annual book fair in Bucharest, were the main events in 1996. The book fair not only served as a showcase of literary talent but also was an event in which the entire literary establishment participated.

(BOŻENA SHALLCROSS)

JEWISH

Hebrew. The main issue of Hebrew fiction since its revival in the 19th century, that of identity, was reflected in 1996 in novels dealing with the early days of Tel Aviv. They included Nathan Shaham's *Lev Tel Aviv* ("The Heart of Tel Aviv") and the new edition of Dan Tsalka's *Filip Arbes.* The same topic was explored on the one hand in a novel that went back to the Holocaust—Ori Dromer's *O'ri* ("My Skin")—and on the other in novels that examined Israelis in the United States, including Dorit Abush's *Ha-Yored* ("The Deserter") and Sam Bacharach's *Shnei darkonim* ("Two Passports"). The veteran writer Yehudit Hendel published the collection of stories *Arukhat boker tmima* ("An Innocent Breakfast"), and Gabriel Moked collected a number of his existential tales. Yossel Birstein penned the disappointing novel *Al tikra li Iyov* ("Don't Call Me Job"), and Aharon Megged examined again the inequities of the literary world in his novel *Avel* ("Iniquity").

The most interesting novel published by the younger generation in 1996 was Lea Aini's *Mishehi tzrikha liheyot kan* ("Someone Must Be Here"). First novels included Marit Benisrael's *Asur lashevet al tzamot* ("Let Down Your Braids") and Eli Gdor's *Biktzei ha-mahane* ("At the Settlement's Edge"). First collections of short stories were represented by Shoham Smith's postmodernist-oriented *Libi omer li ki zikhroni boged bi* ("Things That My Heart Fails to Tell") and Yaron Avitov's *Adon slihot* ("Master of Forgiveness").

The main event in poetry in 1996 was the publication of Nathan Zach's *Mikhevan she'ani baSviva* ("Because I'm Around"). Other significant books included Ory Bernstein's *Zman shel aherim* ("Temps des autres"), Avner Treinin's *Ma'alot Ahaz* ("The Dial of Ahaz"), and Roni Somek's *Gan eden le-orez* ("Rice Paradise").

Important critical studies included Avner Holtzman's work on the formative years of M.J. Berdyczewski and Shmuel Werses's book on Yiddish-Hebrew writers and the transformations of their works from one language to the other. The Palestinian writer Emile Habibi (*see* OBITUARIES) and the poet David Avidan died in 1996.

(AVRAHAM BALABAN)

Yiddish. A sad note that coloured 1996 was the announcement by editor Avrom Sutskever that *Di goldene keyt* ("The Golden Chain"), the Yiddish world's premier literary journal, would cease publication. Historian David Fishman's engrossing *Shaytlekh aroysgerisn fun fayer* ("Pieces of Wood Pulled out of the Fire") brightened the scene, however, with its analysis of the priceless Yiddish volumes of every genre that had been discovered and preserved in Vilnius, Lithuania.

Yoysef Bar-El penned an appreciative analysis of the writing of an important scholar, *Di shire fun Yankev Fridman* ("The Poetry of Yankev Fridman"). Yankl Nirenberg compiled a well-researched and documented memoir about the underground activities of the Jewish Bund in Poland's Lodz ghetto during World War II, *Zikhroynes fun Lodzsher geto* ("Memoirs of the Lodz Ghetto"). Elisheve Koyen-Tsedik's novel *Farges-mikh-nisht* ("Forget-me-not") presented an epic narrative describing a generation of Jewish idealists in the Soviet Union.

Three well-crafted collections of short stories were published. Sixty tales in Tsvi Ayznman's *Bleter fun a farsmalyetn pinkes* ("Pages from a Charred Notebook") proved him once again to be the current master of the short story in Yiddish letters. Tsvi Kanar wrote affecting observations of the Holocaust in *Opgegebn broyt* ("Returned Bread"). *Shlof nisht, Mameshi* ("Don't Sleep, Mama Dear") included eight fascinating stories by one of Israel's most distinguished authors, Mordkhe Tsanin.

The richest segment of Yiddish publishing continued to be poetry. Volumes appeared in France, Israel, and Ukraine. From Israel came Hadasa Rubin's delicate tapestry of lyrics, *Rays nisht op di blum* ("Don't Tear Up the Flower"). The father-and-son team of Yoysef Kerler and Boris Karlov published *Shpigl-ksav* ("Mirror-writing"). Infused with sly humour and thoughtful reflections, Yitskhak Niborski's *Vi fun a pustn fas* ("As Though out of an Empty Barrel") consisted of a medley of lyrics. The prolific Yankev Tsvi Shargel contributed poems and translations in *Tsum eygenem shtern* ("To My Own Star").

(THOMAS E. BIRD)

TURKISH

Turkish literature had a lively and controversial year in 1996. Yashar Kemal dominated the news when a court sentenced him to a deferred 20-month jail term for alleged seditious statements. He received numerous international awards.

Orhan Pamuk published several essays in Turkey and elsewhere. He received the literary award of Le Comité Franco-Turque for the French translation of his novel *Kara kitap* ("The Black Book").

The most impressive achievement in poetry came from Hilmi Yavuz, who celebrated his 60th birthday with a collection entitled *Çöl* ("Desert"), a culmination of his synthesis of traditional, mainly Ottoman, sensibilities and modern culture.

In fiction Ahmet Altan's *Tehlikeli masallar* ("Dangerous Tales") was a runaway best-seller. Singer, columnist, and politician Zülfü Livaneli published *Engererin gözündeki kamaşma* ("The Viper's Eye Dazzled"), a striking novel dealing with Ottoman history. Critics praised Ahmet Ümit's *Sis ve gece* ("Fog and Night") as the first Turkish detective novel of distinctive literary merit. The complete short stories of Orhan Duru became available during the year.

Two major prizes went to women, Erendiz Atasü (novel) and Ayşe Kulin (short stories). TÜYAP (the Istanbul Book Fair) honoured woman novelist Peride Celal, whose literary career had started in 1936. Ayla Kutlu published a remarkable new novel about women's plight in rural society.

Translation activity was brisk as usual. The translation event of the year was Nevzat Erkmen's courageous undertaking of a Turkish version of James Joyce's *Ulysses.*

The poet Cahit Külebi received the President's Award, and the Turkish Language Association's prize for fiction went to the novelist Erhan Bener.

(TALAT S. HALMAN)

PERSIAN

In Afghanistan, Tajikistan, and Iran, the environment for literary creativity deteriorated considerably in 1996. As the number and quality of works published locally dwindled, publishing in exile increased.

In March 'Abbas Ma'rufi, an Iranian novelist, was forced to leave the country. In September bands of Hezbollah vigilantes raided several gatherings of writers, and in November Faraj Sarkuhi, a magazine editor, was arrested in Tehran. Partly as a result of such developments, the trend toward publishing politically safe books accelerated. After a hiatus of two decades *The Persian Encyclopedia,* known by the name of its originator as *The Mosahab Encyclopedia,* was completed. The third volume of Yahya Arianpur's *Az Saba ta Nima* ("From Saba to Nima") was published posthumously under the title *Az Nima ta ruzegar-e ma* ("From Nima to Our Time"). Also notable was Tajik scholar Rowshan Rahman's *Afsanehha-ye Dari* ("Dari Legends"). State-sponsored works, primarily serving as propaganda, appeared in abundance but met with limited popular acceptance.

Women continued to rise in prominence. Fattaneh Hajseyyedjavadi's *Bamdad-e khomar* ("Morning Hangover"), a novel published late in 1995, had a total run of over 70,000 copies, only the second fictional work by an Iranian woman to have reached that level. Two other women residing outside Iran, both in Sweden, published noteworthy works. Shahrnush Parsipur's *Khaterat-e zendan* ("Prison Memoirs") became the first major prison narrative of the 20th century written by a woman, and Jila Mosa'ed's *Pari-zadegan* ("Born of the Fairies") became the author's first major work published in exile. The year marked the death of the novelist and short-story writer Ghazaleh 'Alizadeh.

(AHMAD KARIMI-HAKKAK)

ARABIC

Two years after the attack on his life by Islamic fundamentalists, the Egyptian Nobel laureate Naguib Mahfouz published *Aṣdā as-sīrah ad-dhātiyyah* ("Echoes of the Autobiography") in 1996. Other Egyptian novels included ʿAlāʾ ad-Dībʾs *Qamar ʿalā al-mustanqaʾ* ("A Moon on the Quagmire"), with insight into the Arab condition, and Ibrāhīm ʿAbd al-Majīdʾs *Lā aḥad yanām fi al-Iskandariyyah* ("No One Sleeps in Alexandria"), a fascinating narrative with a historical dimension. Two first novels appeared: Muntaṣir al-Qaffāshʾs *Taṣrīḥ bi-ʾl-ghiyāb* ("Permission for Absence") and Said Noohʾs *Kulamā raʾayt bintā ḥulwah aqūl yā Suʿād* ("Whenever I See a Beautiful Girl, I Cry Suad!").

The yearʾs most fascinating novel from Lebanon was Iskandar Najjārʾs *Durūb al-hijrah* ("Ways of Migration"), which recorded the tribulations of the countryʾs European minority. Ḥasan Dāwūdʾs *Sanat al-utūmātīk* ("The Automated Year") and Muḥammad Abi-Samraʾs *Al-Rajul as-sābiq* ("The Previous Man") were noted especially for their precision, narrative structure, and exploration of new experience. *Bāṣ al-awādim* ("The Folkʾs Bus") was written jointly by Najwā Barakāt, a Lebanese woman novelist, and Nāṣir Khumair, a Tunisian filmmaker.

Morocco produced a number of novels rich in symbolism and experimental narrative, the most noted among them being *Samāsirat as-sarāb* ("The Middlemen of Mirage") by Sālim Ḥumaysh, *Janūb ar-rūḥ* ("South of the Soul") by Muhammad al-Ashʿari, and *Rāʾiḥat al-Jannah* ("The Smell of Paradise") by Shuʿayb Ḥalīfī. Morocco also produced one of the yearʾs most fascinating collections of short stories, *Mashārif at-tīh* ("Overlooking the Maze") by the talented woman writer Rabʿa Rayhḥān. The best short-story collection of the year was, without doubt, *Sāʿat maghrib* ("Time of Sunset") by the distinguished Egyptian writer Muhammad al-Bisāṭi, marked by poetic language and an apt perception of the contemporary condition. Sulaymān Fayyāḍʾs *Nubalāʾ wa-awbāsh* ("Noblemen and Riffraff") was a successful satire of the literary world.

Noted collections of Arabic poetry in 1996 included those by Muḥammad Ṣāliḥ, Rifʿat Sallām, Imād Abū-Ṣāliḥ, and Muḥammad Mutawalli, along with the poets of the avant-garde journal *Locusts* (Egypt); Yahyā Jābir, ʿAbduh Wāzin, and Bassām Ḥajjār (Lebanon); Nūri al-Jarrāḥ (Syria); and ʿAbd al-Laṭīf Luʿabi, Muḥammad Binnīs, M. Bin Talḥah, Mahdi Khuraif, and Tiraibaq Aḥmad (Morocco). For the first time since being banned in 1926, the unabridged *Fī ash-Shiʿr al-Jāhilī* ("On Pre-Islamic Poetry") by Ṭāhā Ḥusayn was republished.

A number of Arabic writers died in 1996. They included the eminent Egyptian critic Fuʾād Duwwārah, who left his mark on the field of dramatic criticism in particular; the Israeli Arab writer Emile Habibi (*see* OBITUARIES); the Egyptian writer Ṣāliḥ Mursī, father of the Arabic novel of political espionage; the critic and journalist Aḥmad Bahāʾ ad-Dīn; Laṭīfah az-Zayyāt, the pioneer of women writers in Egypt; and ʿAbd al-Hamid Benhadugah (*see* OBITUARIES), the father of modern Arabic literature in Algeria. (SABRY HAFEZ)

CHINESE

Chinese literature had an active year in 1996. This was particularly true of the novel, where, for example, the number of published works rose to between 800 and 900. First-rate works, however, were rare.

The Nanjing author Zhou Meiseng published *Renjian zhengdao* ("The Way of Living in the World"), a work highly varied in its artistic techniques and dynamic descriptions. Some critics believed that Han Shaogongʾs novel *Ma Qiao cidian* ("Ma Qiao Dictionary") indicated the maturing of a new consciousness in Chinese literature; others thought that Han had created a new literary style. One critic later pointed out that the novel was an imitation of the Serbian writer Milerad Paviʾs *Khazar Dictionary*.

The number of experimental novels, appreciated by only a minority of readers, decreased in 1996. Writers were thus being forced into other directions, emphasizing story line, plot structure, and character development. Overall, however, the fevered atmosphere in novel writing, which was related to government interest and lucrative prize moneys, continued.

It was not a good year for short stories, however. Some critics claimed that the short story had become the forgotten corner of the Chinese literary world or had sunk into a state of hibernation. Awards promoting the genre had little monetary value, and writers were thus often not interested.

In poetry only a few good works were published in 1996. One was Wang Huairangʾs long poem *Zhongguoren: buguide ren* ("Chinese: A People Not on Its Knees"). Important journalistic literature included *Zhangjiagang ren* ("People of Zhangjiagang") and *Chizi qinghuai* ("Loyalty").
(QIAN ZHONGWEN)

In Taiwan the literary market continued to be dominated by popular literature, both locally produced and in translation. Literary competitions remained active, with enthusiastic participation by both seasoned and new writers. In addition, journalistic literature had a significant year. (EDITORS)

JAPANESE

The Japanese economy had remained at a low ebb for several years, and the economic syndrome seemed to be infectious in 1996 even in the literary domain. Some of the countryʾs important literary magazines disappeared, and the jury for the Junʾichirō Tanizaki Award announced that there would be no winner.

One of the remarkable best-sellers of the year was the memoir *Otōto* ("My Brother") by Shintarō Ishihara, who had made his brilliant literary debut when he was in his early 20s and had later become a conservative politician. Ishiharaʾs memoir was a spontaneous and readable account of his brother Yujirō, who had died of cancer several years earlier. There was, however, an irony in its commercial success, with the dead Yujirō turning out to be more appealing than the author.

It might seem that the literary vitality of contemporary Japan was being maintained mainly by female authors. One of the most impressive short works of 1996 was *Otto no shimatsu* ("How to Manage My Husband") by Sumie Tanaka, the octogenarian novelist

Otohiko Kaga

who was the winner of the Women Writersʾ Prize of the year. The work was an outspoken autobiography, but it was very readable and humorous. The authorʾs husband happened to be a well-known dramatist, but he had a limited income. Tanaka, therefore, had worked hard as a screenwriter for movies and the radio while caring for both her son and her daughter, who suffered from serious diseases. A devout Catholic, she remained an active and lively person, and her outspokenness was effective, even infectious. The work was a tour de force.

Another strong contender for the Women Writersʾ Prize was Yōko Tawada, who published *Gottoharuto tetsudō* ("St. Godhard Railway and Other Stories"). The stories were impressive, with evocative prose and fantastic settings suggestive of Kafka. Tawada lived in Germany and published her stories in both Japanese and German, unusual for a Japanese author.

There were two remarkable novels by male authors in 1996. Otohiko Kagaʾs *Ento* ("Burnt Metropolis") was a voluminous chronicle of wartime Tokyo, and Tsujii Takashiʾs *Owarinaki shukusai* ("Endless Fiesta") was a nostalgic evocation of the complicated emotional and sexual relations of a prewar group of pioneering Japanese feminists.

The Sakutarō Hagiwara Prize in Poetry for 1996 was awarded to Masao Tsuji for *Haikai Tsuji shū* ("Poems of Haikai Tsuji"), a collection that was colloquial and humorous, a happy fusion of traditional haiku and modernism. Saiichi Maruyaʾs *Hihyōshū* ("Collection of Critical Essays") in six volumes was both stimulating and readable. Inuhiko Yomotaʾs *Kishu to tensei—Nakagami Kenji* ("Kenji Nakagami—Noble Descent and Metamorphosis") was an ambitious reassessment of the late novelist, comparing Nakagami with Yukio Mishima in a historical and Pan-Asiatic perspective. Shun Akiyamaʾs *Nobunaga,* a lively reinterpretation of the eccentric samurai hero of the 16th century, was rich in fresh critical insight. (SHOICHI SAEKI)

Mathematics and Physical Sciences

MATHEMATICS

The year 1996 was notable for the successful application of recent advances in mathematics to such practical concerns as the coiling of wire and the manipulation of digital images. In one instance a team at the Spring Research and Manufacturers' Association in Sheffield, Eng., employed methods of data analysis derived from chaos theory, which studies apparently random or unpredictable behaviour in physical systems governed by deterministic laws, to develop a novel quality-control test for wire used in spring manufacture. For decades the spring industry had faced the problem of predicting whether a given sample of wire had good or bad coilability. The new test was carried out in a few minutes by a machine called a FRACMAT, which coils a long test spring, measures the spacing of successive coils with a laser micrometer, and analyzes the resulting numbers, using methods originally developed to find chaotic attractors—geometric descriptions of the behaviour of chaotic systems—in the behaviour of fluid flow.

Other novel applications were based on a mathematical technique called wavelet analysis. The technique was introduced in the early 1980s and was established firmly in 1987 by Ingrid Daubechies, then at AT&T Bell Laboratories, Murray Hill, N.J. Wavelet analysis represents data in terms of localized bliplike waveforms called wavelets. The resultant, often greatly simplified representation of the original data is called a wavelet transform. Perhaps the best-known application of wavelet analysis to date derived from the U.S. FBI's decision in 1993 to use a wavelet transform for encoding digitized fingerprint records. A wavelet transform occupies less computer memory than conventional methods for image storage, and its use was predicted to reduce the amount of computer memory needed for fingerprint records by 93%.

Some of the most recent applications of wavelets involved medical imaging. In the past two decades, medical centres had come to employ various kinds of scanner-based imaging systems, such as computed tomography and magnetic resonance imaging, that use computers to assemble the digitized data collected by the scanner into two- or three-dimensional pictures of the body's internal structures. Dennis Healy and his team at Dartmouth College, Hanover, N.H., demonstrated that a poor digitized image can be smoothed and cleaned up by taking a wavelet transform of it, removing unwanted components, and "detransforming" the wavelet representation to yield an image again. The method reduced the time of the patient's exposure to the radiation involved in the scanning process and thus made the imaging technique cheaper, quicker, and safer. His team also used wavelets to improve the strategies by which the scanners acquired their data at the start. Other researchers were applying the data-enhancement capabilities of wavelets to such tasks as improving the ability of military radar systems to distinguish objects

and cleaning up noise from sound recordings. (IAN STEWART)

This article updates the *Macropædia* articles ANALYSIS; INFORMATION PROCESSING AND INFORMATION SYSTEMS.

CHEMISTRY

Nuclear Chemistry. In 1996 scientists at Germany's Institute for Heavy Ion Research (GSI) in Darmstadt added a new entry to the periodic table with the creation of element 112. The element, so far unnamed, was synthesized by a multinational team headed by Peter Armbruster (*see* BIOGRAPHIES) and Sigurd Hofmann. The researchers first accelerated a beam of zinc ions to high energies in GSI's heavy-ion accelerator UNILAC. They then shot the ions into a lead target, whereupon the zinc and lead nuclei fused. The team detected a single nucleus of the new element consisting of 112 protons and 165 neutrons, which gives it an atomic mass of 277. It was thus the heaviest nucleus ever created in the laboratory. GSI teams previously had discovered several other new chemical elements, including two—elements 110 and 111—in 1994 alone.

Like other superheavy elements created in the past, element 112 decays in a small fraction of a second, but its discovery provided encouragement that scientists would soon succeed in efforts to create element 114. Theoretical studies predicted that beginning at element 114, the periodic table contains an "island of stability"—a region of comparatively long-lived superheavy elements that would be easier for scientists to use in their studies of the composition and properties of matter.

Francium is a short-lived radioactive element created naturally in trace amounts in uranium deposits; its longest-lived isotope, francium-223, has a half-life of 21 minutes. Francium's fleeting existence has made it difficult for scientists to study its properties. Luis A. Orozco, Gene D. Sprouse, and associates at the State University of New York at Stony Brook developed a way to create francium atoms and trap them in a glass bulb. They bombarded a gold target with oxygen-18 atoms, creating atoms of francium-210, which then were moved into a glass bulb having a reflective coating that kept the atoms from escaping. Fortified with laser beams and a magnetic field, the bulb held the francium atoms for only about 20 seconds before they decayed or escaped, but new atoms were continuously produced, so about 1,000 were constantly present inside. The apparatus set the stage for the first detailed studies of francium's atomic characteristics.

Organic Chemistry. The buckminsterfullerene molecule, nicknamed buckyball and symbolized C_{60}, consists of 60 carbon atoms bound together into a three-dimensional spherical cage with a bonding structure that looks like the seams on a soccer ball. Named for its resemblance to the geodesic domes created by the late U.S. engineer and architect R. Buckminster Fuller, the molecule has fascinated scientists and the public since the 1980s, when it was first discovered. C_{60} recently was proclaimed "The Most Beautiful Molecule" in a popular book of that title, yet by the mid-1990s no major commercial or industrial application for the material had emerged.

During the year Ben Z. Tang and Nai-Ten Yu of the Hong Kong University of Science and Technology, Kowloon, reported what they hailed as the first such application. They discovered that C_{60} has novel optical properties that allow it to block light of specific wavelengths over most of the ultraviolet and visible spectrum. Tang and Yu developed transparent materials incorporating C_{60} that filter out harmful ultraviolet wavelengths and block or limit transmission of other undesirable wavelengths. Traditional techniques for manufacturing glass and plastic light-filtering materials were complex and costly; making coloured glass filters, for instance, involved high-temperature processes that required multiple steps and consumed large amounts of energy. By contrast, the process for making filter materials with C_{60} was gel-based and was carried out at room temperature. Furthermore, changing the optical properties of the filter required adjusting only one variable, the quantity of C_{60} itself.

Chemists long have recognized that the internal cavity of the buckminsterfullerene cage, which measures seven angstroms (Å) in diameter, could act as a container for atoms. (An angstrom is a ten-billionth of a metre.) The cavity is large enough to hold an atom of any element in the periodic table and thus could serve as the basis for the synthesis of a range of commercially valuable endohedral (inside-the-cage) chemical species. Among the most alluring were metal-atom-containing C_{60} complexes, or endohedral metallofullerenes, which could, for example, provide a new and useful family of superconductors. Getting large metal atoms inside the cavity by opening holes in the cage, however, was proving difficult. Yves Rubin and co-workers at the University of California, Los Angeles, reported their creation of the largest hole yet opened in buckminsterfullerene. Moreover, they succeeded in attaching a cobalt atom over the hole with a bridge of carbon atoms, although the hole was not large enough for the metal atom to slip inside. (*See* Figure on p. 254.) Rubin's group speculated that it might be possible to move the cobalt atom inside, a process they termed "stuffing the turkey," by thermally exciting the complex to stretch the hole.

Researchers at Purdue University, West Lafayette, Ind., reported the first direct method for alkynylation of carbon-hydrogen bonds, an advance that other chemists described as "unique" and "unprecedented." The technique allowed chemists to attach alkyne groups to hydrocarbons, ethers, and other commercially important organic molecules faster, easier, and in higher yields than previously possible. Alkynes are hydrocarbons like acetylene (ethyne; $HC{\equiv}CH$) that contain a carbon-carbon triple bond. Traditional alkynylation techniques were inefficient and difficult and involved multiple reactions. The single-step technique was discovered serendipitously by Philip L. Fuchs and Jianchun Gong.

Inorganic and Physical Chemistry. Ever since 1778, when the Swedish scientist Carl Wilhelm Scheele discovered molybdenum blue, chemists have been mystified about the structural features that give this material its unusual properties. The chemical is familiar to chemistry students studying qualitative analysis, who try to identify the chemical composition of unknown materi-

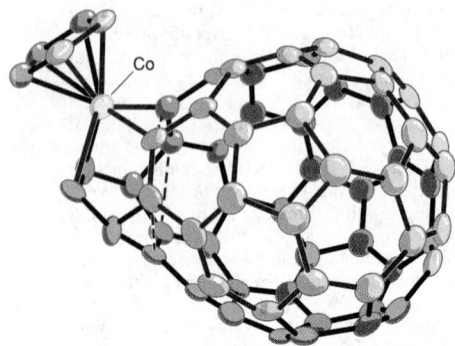

Chemists succeeded in opening a large hole in the buckminsterfullerene molecule and bracing a cobalt atom (Co) just outside. Their next task was to move the metal atom through the hole.

als. If a reducing agent is added to a solution under analysis and causes a characteristic colour change due to the formation of molybdenum blue, the result confirms the presence of the molybdate ion. However, chemists have not been able to determine whether molybdenum blue is an amorphous or crystalline material, a colloid or a solution, or a distinct compound or a mixture.

Achim Müller and co-workers at the University of Bielefeld, Ger., proposed a structure for molybdenum blue that explains some of its features. The structure suggests that molybdenum blue is the ammonium salt of a large doughnut-shaped anion (negatively charged ion) comprising a cluster of MoO_3 units combined with hydroxyl (OH) groups and water molecules. Molybdenum blue's apparent amorphous nature may result from the large size of the anionic cluster, which would not fit easily into a crystalline structure. The water molecules and other hydrophilic (water-seeking) surface components of the cluster would explain the substance's high solubility in water, alcohol, and certain other solvents.

Chemists at Pennsylvania State University reported synthesis of a compound of potassium and nickel that may open a new area of high-pressure chemistry. Because of differences in the electronic structures and sizes of their atoms, potassium, which is an alkali metal, and nickel, which is a transition element, normally do not combine. John V. Badding and co-workers found that potassium develops characteristics of a transition element when subjected to pressures of about 31 gigapascals, 310,000 times greater than normal atmospheric pressure. It then forms chemical bonds with nickel. Badding's group reported that other alkali metals, including rubidium and cesium, also assume traits of transition elements at high pressures. They used a diamond anvil cell and infrared laser heating to form the new compound. Evidence that potassium binds to nickel under pressure supported a theory that radioactive potassium exists in the Earth's core, perhaps bound to iron. The researchers planned to test that theory as they worked to make other exotic compounds from atoms that will not bond at milder pressures.

The hydroxyl radical is the most important free radical in the lower atmosphere. It plays a major role in the photochemical reactions that remove the greenhouse gas methane and other natural and human-made atmospheric emissions. This scav-

enger has only a fleeting existence, and measuring hydroxyl levels has been difficult, requiring elaborate ground-based instruments that project a laser beam through many kilometres of air. Hans-Peter Dorn and co-workers at the Jülich (Ger.) Research Centre's Institute for Atmospheric Chemistry reported making accurate OH measurements with more compact instruments that can fit in aircraft and ships. The technique, called laser-induced fluorescence spectroscopy, bounces a laser beam between two sets of mirrors only 38.5 m (126 ft) apart. It could permit the first routine measurements of OH, including point measurements of OH at specific locations.

In 1993 W. Ronald Gentry and associates at the University of Minnesota at Minneapolis reported detecting the first helium dimers, two-atom molecules of helium, at conditions of extremely low temperature. They concluded from theoretical calculations that the bond between the helium atoms in the dimer is the longest and weakest chemical bond in any molecule. They estimated that the bond is 55 Å long, a far cry from the 1–2 Å that separate atoms bonded together in most other molecules. During 1996 the group reported experimental verification of the dimer's record status. They measured the bond length at 62 Å with a possible error of ± 10 Å. Gentry said that helium dimers promised to be of considerable value in helping scientists understand the forces that operate among atoms bonded together into molecules. One, the Casmir force, comes into play when the distance between two atoms is very large, as it is in the helium dimer.

Hydrogen bonding is one of the fundamental ways in which atoms link together. It is the attraction between a positively charged hydrogen atom in one molecule and a negatively charged atom or group in another molecule. Hydrogen bonding between molecules of water (H_2O), where oxygen serves as the negatively charged atom, accounts for the unexpectedly high melting and boiling points of the compound. Robert Crabtree of Yale University and co-workers discovered a new kind of hydrogen bond that they termed the dihydrogen bond. Crabtree detected the bond between molecules of a compound with one hydrogen atom that is negatively charged and another that is positively charged. The positively charged hydrogen on one molecule attracts the negatively charged hydrogen on a second molecule. According to Crabtree, the strong dihydrogen bond explained the properties of some compounds. For example, dihydrogen bonding occurs in H_3BNH_3, which melts at 104° C (220° F). By contrast, the similar compound H_3CCH_3 does not exhibit dihydrogen bonding and melts at −181° C (−294° F).

Applied Chemistry and Materials. Zeolites are compounds of aluminum, silicon, and alkali and alkaline-earth metals like sodium and calcium. Their crystal structures are riddled with millions of tiny pores and channels that can absorb a variety of atoms and molecules. The pore walls of the aluminosilicate zeolites are strongly acidic, which gives them a catalytic effect widely exploited by the petroleum industry and elsewhere. Zeolites have other industrial applications, including use as molecular sieves for absorbing and separating materials. All known natural and synthetic zeolites con-

tain pores that are ringed by no more than 12 aluminum or silicon atoms (each bonded to four oxygen atoms in an elegant tetrahedral arrangement). C.C. Freyhardt of the California Institute of Technology and co-workers reported making the first aluminosilicate zeolites with pores ringed by 14 atoms. The larger rings mean larger pores, which range from 7.5 to 10 Å. Freyhardt noted that large-pore zeolites were much in demand for containing and catalyzing reactions involving larger organic molecules. Although other researchers previously had synthesized large-pore zeolites, the materials had drawbacks that seriously limited practical applications.

Ceramics are of major commercial interest for components of engines, tools, electrical devices, and other products that demand hardness, stiffness, and high-temperature stability. Two of the most appealing ceramics were those based on silicon nitride and silicon carbide. Silicon nitride, however, begins to decompose at about 1,400° C (2,550° F) and has an ultimate thermal stability limit of 1,500° C (2,730° F), which has limited its use in extremely hot environments such as engines and turbines.

Ralf Riedel of the Technical University of Darmstadt, Ger., and co-workers reported synthesis of a new composite ceramic based on silicon nitride and silicon carbide that is stable to 2,000° C (3,630° F). The material, silicoboron carbonitride, can be processed into bulk ceramic materials or coatings or into spun fibres suitable for use as composite reinforcing material. The researchers did not yet understand the basis for silicoboron carbonitride's enhanced thermal stability. Riedel predicted that the new ceramic would have considerable potential in technologies such as energy-efficient power generation and mechanical and chemical engineering projects.   (MICHAEL WOODS)

This article updates the *Macropædia* articles CHEMICAL BONDING; CHEMICAL COMPOUNDS; CHEMICAL ELEMENTS; CHEMICAL REACTIONS; INDUSTRIAL GLASS AND CERAMICS; Chemical Process INDUSTRIES; The PHYSICAL SCIENCES: *Chemistry.*

PHYSICS

In 1996 scientists produced the first atoms of antimatter—specifically, antihydrogen atoms—in a long-awaited confirmation of fundamental theory. (*See* Sidebar.) At the other end of the periodic table, an atom of element 112, heavier than any other known element, was synthesized for the first time. (*See Chemistry,* above.) Experiments involving the trapping and observation of single atoms furthered investigations into the strange properties of the quantum world, while several results in particle-physics research raised questions about possible flaws in the standard model. In the continuing debate over the age of the universe, astrophysicists appeared to be converging on an agreed value, although one that posed considerable problems for theorists.

Advances in ultrahigh-vacuum techniques coupled with high-precision laser spectroscopy allowed physicists to carry out some of the most fascinating experiments of the year. Single atoms and ions could be trapped and held for hours, even weeks, and their interactions with electromagnetic fields explored in minute detail with high-precision lasers. One of the greatest subjects of contention in the past few decades has been the precise nature of the electromagnetic field, which is most familiar as the propagating electromagnetic radiation called light. Since the invention of the laser, the concept of the photon as a fundamental "particle of light," or quantized packet of electromagnetic energy, has had to be rediscussed and refined. Strangely, although the quantum nature of light was postulated by Albert Einstein in 1905, not until quite recently did unambiguous evidence of this quantization exist. During the year two groups of researchers, using single atoms, carried out work that demonstrated the nature of these quantum effects and even pointed the way forward toward the possibility of quantum computers.

An experiment conducted by David Wineland and colleagues of the National Institute of Standards and Technology, Boulder, Colo., made use of a single beryllium ion. The ion was held at ultrahigh vacuum in an ion-confinement device called a Paul trap by a radio-frequency field, cooled until nearly motionless, and observed as it executed simple harmonic oscillation in the field. At the extremely low energies involved, the oscillatory motion was quantized. The ion could possess only one particular energy out of a "staircase" of energies, for which the energy difference between two stairs was a quantized packet of oscillatory energy called a phonon. Energy is gained or lost by the absorption or emission of a phonon.

The situation was identical to that of a single vibrational mode of an electromagnetic field, with the difference being that for the field, the energy steps are photons and the total field energy is defined by the total number of photons in the mode. The electromagnetic field may exist in different "states," which can be defined only by measuring the probability of detecting a number of photons. This probability distribution is different, depending on whether the source of light is a laser or a conventional light source. In the ion-oscillation experiment, similar probability distributions of phonons could be produced, and the oscillation could be stimulated in classical and quantum states. Among other experiments, the group claimed to have prepared a beryllium ion in "Schrödinger's cat" states—states that are a superposition of two different possible results of a measurement. In the 1930s quantum theory pioneer Erwin Schrödinger proposed his famous thought experiment, in which a cat in a closed box appears to be both alive and dead at the same time until someone observes it, as a demonstration of the philosophical paradoxes involved in quantum theory. The possibility of the experiment's actually being done could have far-reaching effects on the heated philosophical debate about the meaning of quantum theory. On the practical side, atoms held in two different superposed quantum states could serve as logic elements in quantum computers, which might be able to make use of the superpositions to carry out many calculations simultaneously.

In an experiment almost the reverse of the one discussed above, Serge Haroche and co-workers of the École Normale Supérieure, Paris, isolated and counted a small number of photons in the microwave region of the electromagnetic spectrum. Their "photon trap" was a cavity 3 cm (1.2 in) in length, bounded by two curved superconducting mirrors. To detect the trapped photons, the experimenters projected atoms of rubidium through the cavity, one at a time. Each atom had been carefully prepared in a single excited state that survived long enough to cross the cavity. As the atom crossed, it exchanged energy with the electromagnetic field inside. Counting the number of atoms that arrived in an excited or de-excited state gave the experimenters a direct picture of the interactions in the field. The picture confirmed directly that the energy states of the field in the cavity were quantized.

In elementary-particle physics, confirmation of the existence of the top quark in 1995 appeared to complete the experimental evidence for the standard model, which describes all matter in terms of the interactions between six leptons (particles like the electron and its neutrino) and six quarks (which make up particles like protons and neutrons). On the other hand, the team at the Fermi National Accelerator Laboratory (Fermilab) near Chicago that discovered the top quark also found evidence suggesting that quarks may themselves consist of something even smaller. The evidence came from the results of extremely high-energy collisions between protons and antiprotons. Observations of particle jets produced by such collisions showed that, for jet energies above 350 GeV (billion electron volts), the experimental results appeared to diverge dramatically from those predicted by quantum chromodynamics, that part of the standard model that describes the interaction of quarks via the strong nuclear force.

A theory of elementary particles that goes beyond the standard model is that of supersymmetry. The theory predicts that every known fundamental particle has a supersymmetric partner. If the particle is a carrier of one of the fundamental forces, like the photon (which carries the electromagnetic force) or the gluon (which carries the strong force), the partner is of the non-force-carrying kind, like quarks or leptons. Likewise, non-force-carrying particles have their force-carrying supersymmetric partners. Researchers working with the Karlsruhe Rutherford Medium Energy Neutrino (KARMEN) experiment at the Rutherford Appleton Laboratory, Chilton, Eng., claimed to have observed results that suggest the existence of a photino, the supersymmetric partner of the photon. Similarly, researchers at Fermilab identified particle-collision events that suggested the creation of selectrons, the supersymmetric partners of electrons. Other explanations, however, were possible for both results.

Data from the Liquid Scintillator Neutrino Detector at the Los Alamos (N.M.) National Laboratory added to evidence, first reported from that facility in 1995, that

---

The First Antiatoms

It has been known for decades that each fundamental particle in nature has its antiparticle. The first antiparticle to be discovered, in 1932, was the positron, identical to the negatively charged electron but having a positive electric charge. The negatively charged antiproton, the antiparticle of the positively charged proton, was first produced in 1955. The existence of a whole set of antiparticles argues for the possibility of antiatoms and bulk antimatter, identical to atoms and "normal" matter except for the reversal of electric charge and certain other quantum properties of its constituent particles. On the other hand, it is a fact that the collision of a particle and its antiparticle results in the immediate annihilation of both particles. Thus, although it may be easy to envisage an atom of the simplest element, hydrogen (made up of one proton and one electron), matched by an atom of antihydrogen (made up of an antiproton and a positron), the antiatom would survive only as long as it did not meet a normal atom.

The apparent symmetry between normal matter and antimatter, juxtaposed with the observation that the universe appears to consist exclusively of normal matter, has long been a puzzle to physicists and cosmologists. Recent developments in experimental technique have made it possible to test this symmetry to very high precision, which makes the goal of producing antihydrogen in the laboratory of major importance to the continued study of both matter and antimatter.

In early 1996 a team of physicists reported achieving that goal, although fleetingly, in the Low Energy Antiproton Ring (LEAR) storage facility at CERN (European Laboratory for Particle Physics) near Geneva. The team, led by Walter Oelert of the Institute for Nuclear Physics Research, Jülich, Ger., began with a stored beam of antiprotons circulating in the ring and squirted a jet of xenon atoms across its path. Interaction between the xenon and the antiprotons sometimes produced pairs of electrons and positrons, and very occasionally one of the positrons teamed up with an antiproton, forming an atom of antihydrogen. Once made, the neutral antiatoms left the magnetic confinement of the storage ring and were detected. Over the course of three weeks, the experimenters reported the detection of nine such antiatoms, which existed for an average of 40 billionths of a second before they annihilated with normal matter.

If scientists can create, trap, and then isolate antihydrogen atoms for times on the order of thousandths of a second or longer, they can make extremely precise comparisons of the properties of atoms and antiatoms, including the way that gravity affects them, and so carry out a very searching test of matter-antimatter symmetry. Such work was being planned both at CERN and at the Fermi National Accelerator Laboratory near Chicago. The results in turn could provide clues as to why normal matter seems to dominate the universe.

(DAVID G.C. JONES)

neutrinos—the most elusive of common elementary particles—may have a small mass. Very difficult to detect because of their weak interaction with other particles of matter, neutrinos had been thought for decades to be entirely massless. Should they prove to have even a tiny mass, they could offer one possible solution to the problem of the "missing mass" of the universe— the idea, based on cosmological theory and observations of the gravitational behaviour of galaxies, that the universe contains much more mass than can be accounted for by adding up the masses of all of the observable objects.

The ongoing debate over the age of the universe appeared to be approaching a consensus. The vital parameter defining the age is Hubble's constant (H_0), which expresses the rate at which the universe is expanding. A high value for H_0 implies a young universe, and vice versa. Wendy Freedman of the Carnegie Observatories, Pasadena, Calif., used the Earth-orbiting Hubble Space Telescope to observe the apparent brightness of pulsating stars known as Cepheid variables in distant galaxies. Her result for H_0 of 73 ± 11 km per second per megaparsec implied an age of about 11 billion years. On the other hand, Allan Sandage of the same institution, studying the apparent brightness of supernovas in distant galaxies, reported a value of 57 ± 4 km per second per megaparsec, which suggested an age of about 14 billion years. Although the two values nearly overlapped at the extremes of their error ranges, the age range that they encompassed presented difficulties. First, the oldest globular star clusters in the Milky Way Galaxy appeared to be at least 12 billion years old and could be several billion years older. Second, galaxies with an apparent age almost as great as that of the universe were observed in 1996 by several groups. The presence of "old" stars and galaxies in a relatively "young" universe made it difficult for theorists to find the time needed for the universe to have formed galaxies and stars and for some of those objects to have become as old as they appeared to be.

One eagerly anticipated experiment did not take place. The European Space Agency's Cluster mission, in which four artificial satellites were to be placed in stationary orbits relative to one another to give a three-dimensional picture of the solar wind and its effect on Earth, was destroyed by the explosion of its Ariane 5 launch vehicle.

(DAVID G.C. JONES)

This article updates the *Macropædia* articles The COSMOS; ELECTROMAGNETIC RADIATION; MECHANICS: *Quantum Mechanics;* Principles of PHYSICAL SCIENCE; The PHYSICAL SCIENCES: *Physics;* SUBATOMIC PARTICLES.

ASTRONOMY

For astronomy, 1996 would probably be remembered as the year in which scientists announced evidence for ancient life in a meteorite thought to have originated on Mars. It was also a year in which astronomers discovered a host of extrasolar planets, some perhaps with the physical and chemical conditions necessary to harbour life as it is known on Earth. Amateur astronomers and the public alike delighted in Comet Hyakutake, the most spectacular

comet seen in two decades. Orbiting Earth, the Hubble Space Telescope produced a remarkable image of the most ancient galaxies in the universe found to date.

Solar System. The most exciting astronomical discovery of the year was made without the aid of telescopes, radio antennas, or spacecraft, the main tools of modern astronomical exploration. In August a team headed by David McKay (*see* BIOGRAPHIES) of NASA's Johnson Space Center, Houston, Texas, and Richard Zare of Stanford University announced that it had found strongly suggestive evidence for Martian life's having existed more than 3.6 billion years ago. The claim was based on a wide variety of studies of a meteorite called ALH84001. This particular meteorite was found in 1984 in the Allan Hills ice field of Antarctica. It was recognized to be of possible Martian origin only in 1994 and was one of only about a dozen meteorites found to date on Earth whose chemistry matches the unique Martian chemistry found by the Viking spacecraft that landed on Mars in 1976.

The softball-sized igneous rock weighs about 1.9 kg (4.2 lb) and has a complex history. Its origin was dated to about 4.5 billion years ago, when Mars and the other planets formed. It was thought to have originally formed beneath the Martian surface and then been fractured by a meteorite impact some 3.6 billion years ago. Penetrated by water and minerals, it then encapsulated and fossilized whatever matter was present at the time. The meteorite appeared to have been ejected from Mars about 16 million years ago following a large asteroid impact with the planet and subsequently to have reached Earth about 13,000 years ago.

Using high-resolution scanning electron microscopy and laser mass spectrometry to study ALH84001, the NASA-funded research team reported finding the first organic molecules of Martian origin, several mineral features characteristic of biological activity, and what the team suggested were microscopic fossils of primitive, bacteria-like organisms. The organic molecules, called polycyclic aromatic hydrocarbons, are characteristic of the residue found after terrestrial microorganisms die and their initially more complex organic molecules subsequently degrade. Possibly the most suggestive evidence comprised tubular and egg-shaped structures that resembled, though on a much smaller scale, the fossils of ancient single-celled bacteria found on Earth. Many scientists commented that although the evidence from ALH84001 was compelling, it was not conclusive proof for the presence of ancient life on Mars. At year's end an independent group of British scientists reported evidence for ancient life in another presumed Martian meteorite, designated EETA79001, which formed only about 175 million–180 million years ago and was ejected from Mars only about 600,000 years ago. Although NASA was already involved with several missions to study Mars in the near future, the meteorite discoveries prompted an increased commitment to the search for extraterrestrial life with a series of unmanned Martian observers, explorers, and, ultimately, a mission to return rock samples to Earth. (See *Space Exploration,* below.)

On Dec. 7, 1995, the Galileo spacecraft reached the giant planet Jupiter after a six-

year, 3.7 billion-km (2.3 billion-mi) journey. Galileo consisted of two parts: a small probe designed to plunge into the Jovian atmosphere and a larger orbiter whose mission was to survey Jupiter and its four major (Galilean) moons over a two-year period by taking pictures and making magnetic, thermal, and other measurements of their properties. On the day that Galileo arrived, its probe descended into Jupiter's thick atmosphere, surviving a mere 57 minutes while it radioed its measurements back to the orbiter. Among the surprises that emerged in subsequent weeks as astronomers analyzed the probe's data were the discoveries that Jupiter's atmosphere contains less water than had been thought, that its outer atmosphere is 100 times denser and hotter than previously predicted, and that its atmospheric winds, with speeds up to 530 km (330 mi) per hour, are faster than had been suspected.

Data collected by the orbiter over the ensuing year showed that Jupiter's moon Io, the first satellite in the solar system known to have active volcanoes, has a dense inner core, likely made of iron, and possibly its own magnetic field. Another moon, Ganymede, was found to be covered by grooves, faults, and fractures suggesting that it was considerably hotter and more active in the past than planetary scientists had thought. Perhaps most exciting of all were the images of the moon Europa suggesting that it may have had, and might still have, a watery interior. Some scientists proposed that because of tidal heating of the satellite by the strong gravitational pull of Jupiter, Europa's warm interior sea of water could have the conditions to harbour life.

Comets and asteroids also made news in 1996. Comet Hyakutake, discovered in January by Japanese amateur astronomer Yuji Hyakutake, streaked across the sky in March, April, and May, the brightest comet visible from Earth since Comet West in 1976. Sky watchers all over the world

Earth Perihelion and Aphelion, 1997	
Jan. 2	Perihelion, 147,094,700 km (91,400,238 mi) from the Sun
July 4	Aphelion, 152,103,870 km (94,512,783 mi) from the Sun

Equinoxes and Solstices, 1997	
March 20	Vernal equinox, 13:55[1]
June 21	Summer solstice, 08:20[1]
Sept. 22	Autumnal equinox, 23:56[1]
Dec. 21	Winter solstice, 20:07[1]

Eclipses, 1997	
March 8–9	Sun, total (begins 23:17[1]), the beginning visible in southeastern and eastern Asia; the end visible in eastern Siberia and Alaska.
March 24	Moon, partial (begins 01:40[1]), visible throughout North and South America except for Alaska and northwestern Canada, throughout Europe, Africa, and extreme western Asia.
Sept. 1–2	Sun, partial (begins 21:44[1]), the beginning visible in Australia and New Zealand; the end visible in the far southern Pacific Ocean near Antarctica.
Sept. 16	Moon, total (begins 16:11[1]), the beginning visible in eastern Europe, eastern Africa, Asia, and the Indian Ocean; the end visible in extreme eastern South America, Europe, and eastern Greenland.

[1]Universal time.
Source: *The Astronomical Almanac for the Year 1997* (1996).

A Deep Field image of a tiny area of the sky taken by the Hubble Space Telescope over a 10-day period shows space filled with hundreds of differently shaped galaxies, some thought to date from the early universe. To a ground-based telescope, the area would have appeared empty.

were delighted by its long feathery tail and high brightness, which made it visible even against bright city lights. Professional astronomers found the comet to be a source of new insights into the nature of these icy wanderers of the solar system. A team of NASA scientists using the NASA Infrared Telescope Facility in Hawaii detected ethane and methane in the tail of Hyakutake, the first time those molecules had been seen in a comet. Because as much as 2% of the frozen gases of Hyakutake appeared to consist of ethane and methane, scientists speculated that the comet had a very different history from many other well-studied comets. Perhaps even more startling was the discovery by the Earth-orbiting German-U.S.-British ROSAT satellite that X-rays were coming from Hyakutake, the first time such high-energy radiation had been detected from any comet.

Two puzzling solar system objects were discovered in late 1996. The first, designated Asteroid 1996 PW, has the photographic appearance of an ordinary asteroid, most of which were thought to be made of rocky material. But while most asteroids orbit the Sun in a region called the asteroid belt, which lies between the orbits of Mars and Jupiter, Asteroid 1996 PW moves in a highly elliptical orbit, traveling from the outer solar system toward the Sun in a path that resembles those of most comets. The second object, Comet 1996 N2, has the photographic appearance of a comet with a well-developed tail but moves in a circular orbit entirely within the asteroid belt. Taken together, the two objects left scientists with a new set of puzzles about the origin and evolution of comets and asteroids and the distinction between them.

Stars. The discovery of the first planet orbiting a Sun-like star, 51 Pegasi, was announced in late 1995. However, with a mass about half that of Jupiter and a surface temperature of 1,000° C (1,832° F), the planet appeared unlikely to harbour life as scien-

tists understood it. Early in 1996 Geoffrey Marcy of San Francisco State University and Paul Butler of the University of California, Berkeley, announced the detection of the first extrasolar planets whose surface temperatures would allow the presence of surface or atmospheric water, considered to be a necessary prerequisite for life. So began a remarkable year in the ongoing search for planets outside the solar system.

Since extrasolar planets are themselves too dim to photograph in the glare of their parent stars, their presence is detected by the effect they have on the observed motion of their stars. To find such planets,

astronomers usually look either for small periodic wobbling motions of the star's position in space or for changes in the star's velocity as indicated by studies of its spectral lines. By late 1995 Marcy and Butler had been monitoring the spectra of 120 stars for eight years, using a spectrograph attached to the 3-m (120-in) telescope at Lick Observatory on Mt. Hamilton, California. Detailed analysis of the spectra of two of the stars indicated that they oscillate back and forth along the line of sight to Earth. The unseen body orbiting the star 47 Ursae Majoris, in the constellation Ursa Major (the Big Dipper), was determined

Comet Hyakutake displays its impressive head and tail. Hyakutake was clearly visible beginning in March as it came within 15 million km (9.3 million mi) of Earth.

to have a mass about three times that of Jupiter. It revolves around the star at about twice the Earth–Sun distance in roughly three years, and although its surface temperature was determined to be only about −90° C (−130° F), its atmosphere is warm enough to contain liquid water. A second star that they studied, 70 Virginis, in the constellation Virgo, is orbited by a planet several times the mass of Jupiter with a moderate surface temperature of about 84° C (183° F), which would allow any water present to exist as a liquid.

The fourth closest star to Earth, Lalande 21185, which lies about eight light-years away, was also reported to have a planet. George Gatewood of the Allegheny Observatory, Pittsburgh, Pa., observed periodic changes in the angular position of the star suggesting the presence of a planet with a mass $^9/_{10}$ that of Jupiter orbiting the star every 5.8 years—and possibly a second planet with an orbital period of about 30 years. Report of yet another large planet by Christopher Burrows of the Space Telescope Science Institute (STScI), Baltimore, Md., was based on entirely different types of observations of the star Beta Pictoris. Its surrounding dusty disk has long been thought to be a nursery for planetary formation. The newly observed warping of the disk seemed to indicate the presence of a Jupiter-sized planet that is perturbing the disk. Although a truly Earth-like planet orbiting a Sun-like star remained to be found, by year's end at least nine planets revolving around relatively nearby normal stars had been reported. Within the space of one year, astronomers had begun to suspect that the existence of planets around other stars is the rule rather than the exception.

Galaxies and Cosmology. Ever since its launch, the Hubble Space Telescope (HST) had been pointed at specific visible objects to help uncover their secrets. In an exciting reversal of that approach, Robert Williams, director of the STScI, decided to use his director's discretionary time on the HST to do the opposite—to stare at a region of the sky not known to contain any bright objects. The instrument was trained on a small area, only about $^1/_{30}$ the diameter of the Moon, in a dark region of Ursa Major. Almost 350 separate images were taken over a 10-day period, building up a mosaic of the region that was the deepest-seeing astronomical photograph ever taken. Lying within this Hubble Deep Field, as the image was called, are at least 1,500 galaxies, among which are the faintest and therefore probably the most distant galaxies ever seen. Scientists began to study the galaxies by combining data from the image with data gathered from Earth-based telescopes. One early finding was that many of the galaxies are irregular or distorted in appearance. Furthermore, the galaxies were formed when the universe was no more than a billion years old, less than 10% of its present age and much sooner after the initial big bang explosion than had been expected. The Deep Field image also revealed that the universe contains 50% more galaxies than had been previously estimated. (See *Physics*, above.)

(KENNETH BRECHER)

This article updates the *Macropædia* articles THE COSMOS; GALAXIES; THE PHYSICAL SCIENCES: *Astronomy;* THE SOLAR SYSTEM; STARS AND STAR CLUSTERS.

SPACE EXPLORATION

The world's space agencies moved closer in 1996 to realizing two major dreams: the assembly of an International Space Station (ISS) and the discovery of life elsewhere in the solar system. The United States and Russia continued to field joint missions to Russia's operating space station, *Mir,* and to develop hardware for the international station, scheduled to begin assembly in space in late 1997.

Manned Spaceflight. During the year NASA launched seven space shuttle missions, which included two that docked with *Mir.* In January the shuttle *Endeavour* retrieved two satellites, Japan's Space Flyer Unit (SFU) and the OAST-Flyer developed by NASA. The SFU had been launched in March 1995 to test new technologies in orbit. The OAST-Flyer, on a similar mission, was put into space on the January *Endeavour* flight and retrieved two days later. Launched in late February, *Columbia* took back into space the Tethered Satellite System, which had jammed on its first flight in 1992. This time deployment went smoothly until 19.6 km (12.2 mi) of tether had been unwound, whereupon the line broke and the satellite package sailed away into its own orbit. Investigators later determined that small amounts of dust had collected on the tether during processing in the clean room. The dust caused a static electric charge to build up and then burn through the Kevlar tether. The satellite eventually entered Earth's atmosphere and burned up.

The Life and Microgravity Spacelab mission was flown aboard *Columbia* in June and July. The science crew conducted a series of experiments on the way in which plants, humans, and nonhuman animals adapt to the weightlessness of space. Other microgravity experiments were conducted in May aboard *Endeavour,* which carried the Spacehab laboratory module and which also deployed the first inflatable antenna, a demonstration of technologies that could allow large structures to be built in orbit via the inflation of specially designed balloons.

Two missions flown by *Atlantis* in March and September took astronauts and cargo to and from *Mir.* U.S. astronaut Shannon W. Lucid arrived on *Mir* in March for what was to have been a 115-day stay in space. It stretched to 188 days, however—a record for women and for Americans—when her ride home was delayed three times by a booster problem discovered during *Columbia's* July launch and by two hurricanes that swept the launch pad. Lucid was finally replaced by astronaut John E. Blaha in September.

The year's shuttle missions ended in November with *Columbia* flying the Wake Shield Facility (WSF) a third time. Despite operating problems on two previous flights, the WSF functioned as planned, successfully growing semiconductor crystals in the ultrahard vacuum that was created on the lee side of the facility as it temporarily orbited separately from the shuttle. A stuck hatch on *Columbia* forced cancellation of two planned space walks, while bad weather extended the mission to a record length for a shuttle flight of 17 days 15 hours 53 minutes.

Among shuttle missions planned for 1997 was one in December to contribute to the initial assembly of the ISS. Shuttle astronauts were to attach the first of two U.S.-built nodes, which served as assembly points for the station, to the FGB (functional block) module that would have been launched by Russia the previous month. Additional modules were to be added in 1998 and beyond. To support the ISS program, NASA planned improvements to the shuttle system that would add 7,816 kg (17,231 lb) of payload to its lifting capability.

Manned operations involving Russian and non-Russian crew members continued aboard *Mir.* Russia launched two replacement crews to the station on Soyuz TM-23 in February and TM-24 in August. In addition, Russia launched the Priroda science module in April to round out *Mir's* laboratory capabilities. On May 24 cosmonauts Yury Onufriyenko and Yury Usachev conducted a space walk to install solar panels

U.S. astronaut Shannon W. Lucid and Russian cosmonaut Aleksandr Y. Kaleri prepare to move her space suit from the *Mir* space station to the space shuttle *Atlantis.* Lucid had been aboard the Russian space station for 188 days, setting a record for women and for a U.S. astronaut.

NASA

that would boost the electrical power to *Mir*. The panels, delivered by space shuttle in November 1995, were built by Lockheed Martin Corp. and used the same basic designs as those planned for ISS.

Space Probes. Arguably the greatest excitement in planetary exploration came not from a probe but from an Antarctic meteorite, believed to be from Mars, that was reported to contain organic material and microfossil-like structures suggestive of primitive life. (See *Astronomy,* above; EARTH SCIENCES: *Geology and Geochemistry;* LIFE SCIENCES: *Paleontology.*) Exploration of Mars already had been revitalized by the planned launches of three missions in late 1996. Although the Mars rock announcement came too late to affect the year's launches, space scientists were rethinking strategies for later missions.

The U.S. Mars Global Surveyor was the first mission to Mars since 1993, when the ill-fated Mars Observer lost contact with Earth just before it was to go into Mars orbit. Mars Global Surveyor carried instruments built from Mars Observer's spare parts. Launched on November 7, it was to arrive at Mars in September 1997. After establishing a circular orbit, the spacecraft would conduct a full Martian year (687 days) of observations starting January 1998. Instruments included a camera, a laser altimeter, and plasma and electric field sensors.

The U.S. Mars Pathfinder, launched December 4, was the first landing attempt since the two Viking spacecraft in 1976. After descending to the Martian surface in July 1997 with the aid of parachutes, rockets, and air bags, the tetrahedral craft would deploy instruments to study Mars and a small, six-wheeled "microrover," dubbed Sojourner, to explore as far as 500 m (1,640 ft) from the lander.

Mars 96 was Russia's first exploratory mission to Mars since the breakup of the U.S.S.R. Comprising a large orbiter with two 50-kg (110-lb) small landers and two 65-kg (145-lb) surface penetrators, it was launched November 16 and put into Earth orbit. However, its fourth-stage engine, which was to have been directed it toward Mars, failed, which allowed the spacecraft to slip back into the atmosphere and then fall to Earth.

NASA's Near Earth Asteroid Rendezvous (NEAR) spacecraft, the first designed to orbit an asteroid, was launched February 17 toward a June 1997 flyby of asteroid Mathilde and then a flyby of Earth in 1998 to boost its speed. In 1999 NEAR was to enter a loose orbit of asteroid Eros. Eventually the orbit would be tightened to 15 km (9 mi) above the surface as NEAR took pictures and measured the surface profile of Eros.

The Galileo spacecraft, in orbit around Jupiter since December 1995, offered a separate set of hints that life might be found elsewhere in the solar system. Galileo continued to take pictures and make measurements of Jupiter and its moons, while its orbit was tweaked every few days or weeks to allow flybys as close as 250 km (155 mi) of Ganymede, Callisto, Europa, and Io on a grand tour of this miniature planetary system. Returned images showed that ice covering some areas of Europa has been cracked into large chunks and shifted by tidal effects of Jupiter's powerful gravita-

JPL/NASA

Sojourner is an instrumented, solar-powered "microrover" launched December 4 on Mars Pathfinder, the second of a series of low-cost U.S. planetary missions. The vehicle was expected to begin explorations of the surface of Mars after Pathfinder's touchdown on July 4, 1997.

tional pull. Planetary scientists interpreted this and other signs of activity as evidence that tidally heated "warm ice" or even liquid water might exist below the surface, harbouring conditions that could conceivably support life. (See *Astronomy,* above.)

Unmanned Satellites. Several satellites were launched to help provide an improved understanding of global environmental changes on Earth. Sent aloft August 17, Japan's Midori (originally, Advanced Earth Observation Satellite) carried several instruments to measure changes in the global environment, including a total-ozone mapping spectrometer and radar scatter-

ometer from NASA and a greenhouse-gas monitor from Japan. By September the ozone spectrometer had produced the first global image of ozone in the upper atmosphere. Other launches of Earth-observing satellites included India's IRS-P3 on March 21, on an Indian rocket, and NASA's Total Ozone Mapping Spectrometer–Earth Probe on July 2.

The astronomer's range of tools was expanded during the year with the U.S. X-Ray Timing Explorer, launched Dec. 30, 1995, and Italy's small X-ray Astronomy Satellite (SAX), launched April 30. One of the oldest space telescopes, the Interna-

Manned Spaceflights, 1996

Flight	Date	Crew*	Mission
STS-72, *Endeavour*	January 11–20	Brian Duffy, Brent W. Jett, Jr., Winston E. Scott, Leroy Chiao, Daniel T. Barry, Koichi Wakata	Deploy and retrieve OAST-Flyer; retrieve Space Flyer Unit; practice space walks for International Space Station
Soyuz TM-23	February 21	Yury Onufriyenko, Yury Usachev	Deliver crew to *Mir;* return crew to Earth (September 2)
STS-75, *Columbia*	February 22–March 9	Andrew M. Allen, Scott J. Horowitz, Franklin R. Chang-Díaz, Umberto Guidoni, Jeffrey A. Hoffman, Maurizio Cheli, Claude Nicollier	Refly Tethered Satellite System; conduct microgravity materials experiments
Soyuz TM-22 (return)	February 29	Yury Gidzenko, Sergey Avdeyev, Thomas Reiter	Return *Mir* crew to Earth
STS-76, *Atlantis*	March 22–31	Kevin Chilton, Richard Searfoss, Ronald M. Sega, Linda Godwin, M. Richard Clifford, Shannon W. Lucid	Deliver Lucid and supplies to *Mir;* space walk for International Space Station
STS-77, *Endeavour*	May 19–29	John H. Casper, Curtis L. Brown, Jr., Andrew S.W. Thomas, Daniel W. Bursch, Mario Runco, Jr., Marc Garneau	Launch PAMS/STU stabilization-technology satellite; deploy and retrieve Inflatable Antenna Experiment; conduct materials experiments in Spacehab
STS-78, *Columbia*	June 20–July 7	Terence T. Henricks, Kevin R. Kregel, Susan J. Helms, Richard M. Linnehan, Charles E. Brady, Jr., Jean-Jacques Favier, Robert Brent Thirsk	Conduct Life and Microgravity Spacelab mission to study biological effects of space travel
Soyuz TM-24	August 17	Valery Korzun, Aleksandr Kalery, Claudie Andre-Deshays	Deliver crew to *Mir;* return crew to Earth (1997)
STS-79, *Atlantis*	September 16–26	William F. Readdy, Thomas D. Akers, Terrence W. Wilcutt, John E. Blaha (stays on *Mir*), Jay Apt, Carl E. Walz, Shannon W. Lucid (returns to Earth)	Conduct experiments in Spacehab Double Module; dock with *Mir;* exchange Lucid with Blaha
STS-80, *Columbia*	November 19–December 7 (longest shuttle mission to date)	Kenneth D. Cockrell, Kent V. Rominger, Tamara E. Jernigan, Thomas D. Jones, F. Story Musgrave	Deploy and retrieve ORFEUS-SPAS II astrophysics satellite and Wake Shield Facility; conduct space walks to test new tools and techniques

*Commander listed first.

A computer-generated image shows the configuration of the Lockheed Martin VentureStar, selected by NASA in July as the X-33 half-scale demonstrator for the Reusable Launch Vehicle. As a successor to the space shuttle, the full-size craft would be ready to launch early in the 21st century.

tional Ultraviolet Explorer, was turned off September 30. It was launched in January 1978 on what was to have been a three-year mission to observe the stars in ultraviolet light. NASA started preliminary design of a Next Generation Space Telescope designed to deploy an 8-m (26-ft) primary mirror for observations in the infrared spectrum to look deeper into the recesses and the past of the universe. Launch was planned for 2005.

The addition of three new geophysics satellites to the International Solar Terrestrial Physics program was muted by the loss of the European Space Agency's Cluster mission, a set of four satellites that were destroyed during launch when their Ariane 5 rocket failed. (See *Launch Vehicles*, below.) On February 24 the U.S. launched Polar, which carried visible-light and ultraviolet cameras to take pictures of the dayside and nightside auroras, and on August 21 it launched the Fast Auroral Snapshot Explorer (FAST), which had instruments to make high-time-resolution "snapshots" of electric fields, magnetic fields, and energetic electron and ion distributions at altitudes of 1,920–4,160 km (1,190–2,580 mi) near the Earth's magnetic poles. On August 29 Russia launched the Interbol-2 spacecraft, which released its complementary Czech-built Magion-5 subsatellite.

Launch Vehicles. Two unique launch-vehicle concepts, the Reusable Launch Ve-hicle (RLV) and Sea Launch, moved ahead. NASA selected Lockheed Martin Corp. to develop the company's wedge-shaped VentureStar concept, which would first be built as the X-33 RLV demonstrator. Like the current space shuttle, the RLV would launch vertically and land horizontally. Unlike the shuttle, it would be unmanned and would not drop boosters and fuel tanks; rather, it would use the single-stage-to-orbit (SSTO) concept, which promised to reduce the cost of launching satellites and probes. The RLV also would use a more robust metal heat shield in place of the shuttle's silica tiles. The X-33 was intended to demonstrate the feasibility of RLV technology in suborbital flights as fast as Mach 15 (15 times the speed of sound). Test flights were planned to start in early 1999 and last into 2000. Flight tests with the DC-XA, an advanced version of the DC-X vertical takeoff and landing rocket and a precursor to the X-33 project, ended on July 31 when a landing leg failed to extend, which caused the craft to topple on its side at the end of a test flight. Earlier flights, on May 18 and June 7, had been successful.

In a more conventional vein, Sea Launch Co., LDC, a Boeing Co. multinational venture, began converting an offshore oil-drilling platform to serve as a launch pad that could be towed to the Equator (where the Earth's rotation gives a rocket the greatest running start). Sea Launch would use Zenit 3SL rockets, developed by the former U.S.S.R. and currently marketed by companies based in Russia and Ukraine. The launch platform and its assembly-and-control ship would operate out of Long Beach, Calif., and launch south of Hawaii.

The debut of Europe's Ariane 5 rocket turned to disaster on June 4 when the vehicle veered off its course and was destroyed along with its payload of satellites. An investigation revealed that the guidance system, successfully used in the Ariane 4 series of rockets, had not been properly modified to account for subtle differences between the performances of the Ariane 4 and Ariane 5 models.

The launch industry was surprised in August when the Boeing Co. announced that it would purchase the aerospace and defense sectors of Rockwell International. The purchase included Rockwell's Space Division, which built and maintained the space shuttle orbiters, and Rocketdyne, which built the shuttle main engines. The transaction put Boeing in a strong position as it bid for the U.S. Air Force's Evolved Expendable Launch Vehicle program.

(DAVE DOOLING)

See also Business and Industry Review: *Telecommunications;* Media and Publishing: *Television.*

This article updates the *Macropædia* articles EXPLORATION: *Space Exploration;* TELESCOPES.

Media and Publishing

TELEVISION

The television industry focused its plans for expansion on digital pay television in 1996. Old players and relative newcomers formed partnerships that were ostensibly aimed at sharing digital-TV development costs. In the U.S., cable TV stocks foundered despite a marked increase in subscribers to basic cable.

Organization. Europe's biggest pay-TV operators—France's Canal Plus SA, British Sky Broadcasting (BSkyB) Group PLC, and Germany's Bertelsmann AG—aligned forces. BSkyB later withdrew and joined Germany's Kirch Group. Canal Plus acquired Nethold NV, a pay-TV venture in The Netherlands, to create one of the largest television companies, serving 8.5 million subscribers in France, Italy, Spain, Scandinavia, the Benelux countries, and Germany. Nethold's parent companies, Richemont SA of Switzerland and MIH Holdings Ltd. of South Africa, acquired 6.1 million shares of Canal Plus and $45 million. MIH retained former Nethold operations in South Africa, the Middle East, Greece, and Cyprus.

Canal Plus and Nethold signed an agreement with DirecTV, a subsidiary of General Motors Corp.'s Hughes Electronics Group, and with Grupo Prisa (Spain) and Cisneros Group (Venezuela) to offer digital TV to Spain and Venezuela. Galaxy Latin America was launched in both Brazil and Mexico.

Nethold NV's Benelux unit merged with TeleSelect, a joint pay-TV venture of two leading operators of cable television networks, Philips Electronics NV and Royal PTT Nederland NV. Together the alliance claimed a near monopoly of pay-TV in The Netherlands. PTT Nederland, the parent company of Casema BV, was the largest cable-TV operator, with access to 60% of Dutch households. Philips Electronics, together with United International Holdings Inc. of Denver, Colo., owned UPC, the Amsterdam-based cable operator in The Netherlands, Austria, Belgium, France, Germany, and Israel.

Bertelsmann and Deutsche Telekom AG pulled out of Multimedia Betriebs GmbH digital pay-TV consortium. Other members were Canal Plus, German commercial broadcaster RTL, and public broadcasters ARD and ZDF. The rival Kirch Group began broadcasting digital pay-TV by satellite in July. Deutsche Telekom, a state-run telephone utility with a monopoly of the cable TV infrastructure, emerged as Europe's single largest broadcaster by becoming an independent distributor of digital-TV programs.

Bertelsmann remained Europe's largest free-TV broadcaster by merging with Compagnie Luxembourgeoise pour la Télédiffusion SA (CLT). The German Federal Cartel Office referred the Bertelsmann-CLT pact to the European Commission, which had blocked other mergers—among them, the CLT, Endemol Entertainment BV, and VNU NV (a Dutch publisher) merger; the merger between Deutsche Telekom AG, Kirch Group, and Bertelsmann to provide cable TV in Germany; and the Nordic Satellite Distribution alliance. CLT later pulled out of its plans with Bertelsmann to develop the German Club RTL channel into a digital pay-TV channel, deciding to focus instead on Premiere, another pay-TV venture.

Former Italian prime minister Silvio Berlusconi was tried for corruption on January 17 in Milan. The owner of Fininvest (which included three TV networks and several publications), Berlusconi was accused of having bribed members of the Italian financial police in order to avoid tax inspection.

Hungary's media law, passed in December 1995 after four years of political dispute, paved the way for the privatization of two national TV stations. According to the regulatory body, Orszagos Radio es Televizio Testulet (ORTT), only consortia were to bid, no single company would be allowed more than a 49% stake, and Hungarians would hold a minimum of 26%. Luxembourg's CLT expressed interest in the prospective acquisition, having already started TV stations in Poland and Finland.

Malaysia's Measat Broadcast Network Systems began operating 22 TV channels and 8 radio channels that could be received via a 60-cm (2-ft)-diameter satellite dish. The Broadcasting Act of 1988 needed an amendment to exempt the Measat satellite dishes from the general ban on such dishes. On July 26 three-year-old Indovision pay-TV began operating under StarTV management following an agreement between Rupert Murdoch and Indovision-owner Peter Gontha in 1995 to launch 15 channels, including several in the Bahasa Indonesian language. Early in 1996 Sir Run Run Shaw, China's most famous filmmaker, sold 6.9% of Hong Kong Television Broadcasts (TVB) Ltd. to British Pearson PLC for $1,290,000,000.

On February 8 U.S. Pres. Bill Clinton

Kimberly Williams and David Conrad take the roles of lovers in the new ABC series "Relativity." Some called the popular show a 20-something *Romeo and Juliet.*

EVERETT COLLECTION

signed into law the 1996 Telecommunications Act. The first major rewrite of communications law since 1934, the law would permit, among other things, cable TV companies and local telephone companies to compete with one another in offering services. The president and the congressional authors of the measure promised that such competition would yield lower prices, innovative services, and thousands of new high-paying jobs.

At the year's end, the promises accompanying the act had not been fulfilled. Telephone and cable companies, which had claimed to be eager to explore new frontiers, discovered significant technological, regulatory, and financial obstacles. Rather than explore possibilities in the telecommunications industry, cable companies spent much of the year looking over their shoulders at direct broadcast satellite (DBS) companies. In May Denver-based EchoStar Communications Corp. joined DirecTV and United States Satellite Broadcasting in offering satellite-to-home TV, an alternative to cable that required a 46-cm (18-in) "dish" antenna and satellite receiver. EchoStar entered the market as a low-cost option, offering dishes for $199 (plus installation) and $19.95 a month for the basic programming package.

Rupert Murdoch's News Corp. and long-distance giant MCI forged yet another DBS venture. ASkyB, as they dubbed their service, would be available in the late 1990s. To make the service more attractive, ASkyB planned to offer not only the usual lineup of cable programming but also local broadcast signals.

Partly because of the DBS competition, cable had a miserable year on the stock market. A $100 investment in leading cable stocks on January 1 was worth just $100.89 on November 1, according to the Bloomberg Cable Index. To resuscitate the stocks, cable executives gave assurances that they would follow through with promises to introduce digital-TV technology and high-speed data modems with many of their systems. Digital TV would close the gap with DBS by making room for additional channels and improving the quality of their pictures. With computer owners demanding faster access to the Internet, the modems had the potential to be the lucrative new business cable companies had long sought.

There were also during the year an increase in the number of basic cable subscribers, a loosening of federal rate regulations, and increased advertising revenue in the cable industry. According to the Nielsen ratings, cable subscribership rose 2.7% between January and November, topping off at 67 million homes—69% of all TV homes. The growth occurred despite an estimated 7% increase in cable rates. The additional subscribers and higher rates combined to drive up cable subscription revenue nearly 9% to $23.7 billion. The Cabletelevision Advertising Bureau gave cable investors hope by projecting that cable advertising sales would top $6 billion for 1996, up 13% from the previous year's $5.3 billion.

Broadcast TV had a solid year as revenue totaled nearly $35 billion, up 8% over 1995. Taking advantage of relaxed ownership limits in the Telecommunications Act, Murdoch's Fox Broadcasting cut the year's biggest station deal when it purchased the New World Communications Group, Inc.,

Actor George Clooney shares a laugh with Rosie O'Donnell, host of a syndicated daytime talk show. The new program, which booked show business celebrities as guests and forsook trash TV for a light, pleasant approach, turned out to be a big hit with audiences.

for $2.5 billion. With New World's 10 stations, Fox's portfolio increased to 20 stations and its reach to more than 40% of all homes with TVs, an industry high. Reaching 32% of all TV homes, Westinghouse/CBS was the second largest station group.

Complaints about TV programming prompted the federal government to regulate on-screen violence and to mandate educational programs for children. Congressional Democrats inserted a provision in the 1996 Telecommunications Act that required inclusion of so-called V-chip technology in all TV sets within three years. The V-chip would enable parents to adjust their TV sets to black out particular programming. In December the networks announced a rating system—similar to the one used for movies—that they planned to start using early in 1997. The ratings were: TV-Y, suitable for all children; TV-Y7, designed for children 7 and above; TV-G, for general audience; TV-PG, parental guidance suggested; TV-14, parents strongly cautioned; and TV-M, mature audience only.

The Clinton administration played a key role in ensuring adoption of Federal Communications Commission rules requiring that TV stations each air at least three hours of educational programming for children every week. Reed Hundt, the Clinton-appointed chairman of the FCC, pressed hard for the rules but was blocked by other commissioners sympathetic to broadcasters' complaints that the rules violated their First Amendment rights. Clinton, who favoured the rules, called for a second summit on children's TV in late July. By the time the second conference was set to begin, however, broadcasters had withdrawn their opposition, and the FCC adopted the proposal within a month.

Programming. NBC won the 1995–96 prime-time ratings war on the strength of its powerful Thursday night lineup, which included the season's four top-rated shows ("ER," "Seinfeld," "Friends," and "Caroline in the City"). Rounding out the 10 top-rated

shows were "NFL Monday Night Football" (ABC), "Single Guy" (NBC), "Home Improvement" (ABC), "Boston Common" (NBC), "60 Minutes" (CBS), and "NYPD Blue" (ABC).

For the season NBC posted a 11.7 rating and 19 share. ABC finished second at 10.6/18, CBS was a disappointing third (9.6/16), and Fox was fourth (7.3/12). Significantly, Fox beat CBS among the 18–49-year-olds, a key demographic group for advertisers.

NBC also scored big during TV's usually lacklustre summer with marathon coverage of the Olympic Games in Atlanta, Ga. The games attracted record audiences, which probably justified the $456 million the network paid for the TV rights.

The 1996–97 TV season started off in mid-September just where the 1995–96 season had ended—with NBC leading the ratings race. Through October NBC retained its prime-time lead, posting a 10.9 rating and 18 share. Although Fox continued in fourth place for the season, it boasted its first weekly win. With the help of an exciting World Series—the New York Yankees came from behind to beat the Atlanta Braves—and the debut of its much-hyped science-fiction series, "Millennium" to accompany its popular "X-Files" (see Sidebar), Fox was the number one network for the week of October 21 (15.8/26).

The erosion of the broadcast audience that began in the late 1970s continued at the start of the 1996–97 season. According to the Nielsen ratings, the 41 top cable networks' share of the prime-time audience during broadcasting's premiere week increased from 32 to 35. The broadcast networks posted a commensurate decline, 77 to 74.

Cable TV's strength in the ratings was underscored at the 48th annual Emmy awards in September, where it picked up an unprecedented 26 statuettes. With 14 awards HBO was the top cable winner and the second largest overall. Only prime-time champ NBC garnered more, with 20 overall. ABC

won 12 Emmys and CBS 11. Award winners from NBC included Helen Hunt from "Mad About You" (best actress, comedy) and John Lithgow from "3rd Rock from the Sun" (best actor, comedy). Dennis Franz (see BIOGRAPHIES), from ABC's "NYPD Blue," won for best actor in a drama; and Kathy Baker, of CBS's "Picket Fences," won for best dramatic actress. Ironically, Baker's award came after CBS had canceled the show.

MSNBC, a joint venture between NBC and computer software powerhouse Microsoft, launched a cable news show in July in hopes of rivaling CNN. It was followed in October by Fox Cable News, an all-news entry from Rupert Murdoch.

Broadcasters and manufacturers of TV sets had hoped the FCC would set a new technical standard for digital TV based on the so-called Grand Alliance system that they had jointly developed and presented to the agency in late 1995. The standard would permit stations to broadcast high-definition television (HDTV)—crystal-clear, wide-screen pictures with high-fidelity stereo sound—and air several additional channels with pictures similar to those achieved with current technology. In late December the industry's detailed proposal was granted FCC approval.

The news was good for broadcasters in their efforts to secure a second channel for digital TV. Each TV station needed a second channel so that it could simultaneously air both the new digital signal and the conventional TV signal. (Not airing the conventional signals would render obsolete every TV set currently in use in the U.S.) The new Telecommunications Act required the FCC to assign each station the second channel. Some officials hoped to reverse the policy in 1997 so that broadcasters would have to pay for their extra channels.

Sydney, Australia-based but Hong Kong-controlled Television Shopping Network (TVSN) was beamed to Japan, North and South Korea, Taiwan, Hong Kong, and the Philippines around the clock. TVSN would eventually extend from the Mediterranean to Hawaii and from northern Japan to New Zealand.

Wharf Cable Ltd. opened a 24-hour shopping channel in Hong Kong in late 1996 even as it challenged Hongkong Telecom's new interactive video-on-demand (VOD) service, which included a teleshopping component. Hong Kong's Office of Telecommunications Authority (OFTA) decided that VOD—the practice of providing movies and programming to homes through telephone lines and charging a fee—would not be considered pay-TV.

It was discovered during the year that a 1989 interview of lawyer Tsutsumi Sakamoto—in which he criticized the Aum Shinrikyo cult—was allegedly shown in 1996 by Tokyo Broadcasting System (TBS) to members of the cult responsible for the 1995 gas attack on Tokyo's subways. The lawyer, his wife, and his infant son were found dead several months after the attack.

The Roman Catholic Church activated its own cable TV channel, Faith Asian Network (FAN), on Thai Sky satellite August 15. Beamed to Southeast Asia, South Korea, Japan, China, and India, FAN began with broadcasts in the Thai language but planned to eventually broadcast multiple

(continued on page 264)

The Boom of Science-Fiction TV

"Star Trek," the show whose mission was "to boldly go where no man has gone before," celebrated its 30th anniversary in 1996. First televised in 1966, the series ran for only three seasons before it was canceled, yet it generated an unprecedented cult following. Revived in syndication in the late 1970s, "Star Trek" saw its legacy continued in three spin-off shows ("Star Trek: The Next Generation," "Star Trek: Deep Space Nine," and "Star Trek: Voyager") and eight movies. "Star Trek" began what became a minor television revolution—there were more than a dozen science-fiction series on network television during the 1996 season, as well as a Sci-Fi cable channel, which celebrated its fourth anniversary during the year.

Part of the reason for the increased popularity of science fiction was the wide range of content of the programs. Audiences were reminded that science fiction is not limited to gadgetry and special effects; programs also explored the less-definable aspects of the genre, such as fantasy and the paranormal.

Science fiction came to television during the late 1950s and early '60s with such shows as "Captain Video," "Flash Gordon," "The Twilight Zone," and "The Outer Limits." "Dr. Who" was first televised in Great Britain in 1963, and "Lost in Space" appeared in the U.S. two years later. Many of these early shows struggled in an industry that paid them scant attention, and the result was weak casts and wooden special effects. In addition, many shows lacked a strong conceptual base. "Star Trek" maintained a strong focus by using the consistent mission to explore new worlds as a way to examine the human condition.

A large part of science fiction's appeal lies in its ability to convince the audience of the believability of the world it portrays. "Star Trek" was created with a certain philosophical concept in mind, and the writers developed a history for the universe they created. Individual episodes, while mostly self-contained, were supported by the overall concept of the series.

Continuing the tradition begun by "Star Trek" was "Babylon 5," first televised in 1994. Based on a proposed five-year story line, the program played out an epic struggle between good and evil that involved humans and aliens. Like "Star Trek," individual episodes worked within a framework of an established focus and utilized various aspects of the science-fiction genre. While maintaining a strong plot, "Babylon 5" also concentrated on affordable special effects. Most of the show's action took place within an 8-km (5-mi)-long multilevel space station, and many of the most exciting scenes, such as the battle sequences, were created on Macintosh computers. Because computer-generated special effects were comparatively inexpensive to produce, networks began to embrace science fiction.

In the hit series "The X-Files," which began its fourth season in 1996, the show's creators relied less on computer-generated graphics and focused more on the atmosphere created by the actors, sets, and plot. "The X-Files" was a dark, brooding show that spun a tale of government conspiracy, extraterrestrials, and paranormal activity. FBI agents Fox Mulder and Dana Scully filled the respective roles of believer and skeptic regarding the possible paranormal explanations for their cases. The eerie nature of the show was reminiscent of "The Twilight Zone" and played as large a role in its success as any other element. "The X-Files" inspired several other series, including "Dark Skies" and "Millennium," which both debuted in 1996.

These and other shows like them helped to give science fiction a firm and permanent foothold in television—one that reflected the scientific possibilities of the rapidly advancing technological world. Science-fiction writer Ray Bradbury commented that we were now "a science fiction generation." Perhaps the explanation of its popularity lay in our ability to see ourselves in the various universes laid out before us, reminding us that our own world was as large as we cared to make it.

(AMANDA E. FULLER)

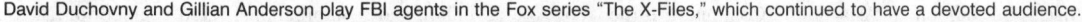

David Duchovny and Gillian Anderson play FBI agents in the Fox series "The X-Files," which continued to have a devoted audience.

TWENTIETH CENTURY FOX/SHOOTING STAR INTERNATIONAL

Singer Brandy Norwood (left) played the title role and Sheryl Lee Ralph her stepmother in "Moesha." The UPN comedy series centred on a teenage girl's life with her family.

(continued from page 262)
audio channels that would provide the information in other languages.

A 10-year contract between the U.S.-based satellite operator PanAmSat Corp. and China Central Television (CCTV), the country's main broadcaster, was scheduled to provide six digital channels of programming to be broadcast to Europe, the Middle East, and Africa, in addition to Asia and North America.

In Jakarta, Indon., a proposed law would allow private TV networks to broadcast news subject to government censorship. The proposal also would require all TV stations to slash imported program content to 20% of total airtime. The government advocated a large dose of local programs to prevent TV stations from becoming "trumpets of foreign interests." The imam (high priest) of the Grand Mosque of Mecca, Sheikh 'Abd ar-Rahman as-Sudeiss, marked the end of the annual Muslim pilgrimage with a veiled criticism of "the cultural, intellectual and moral invasion" by Western culture via satellite TV received in Islamic countries.

In Mexico, Televisa's telenovelas, tearjerkers that were dubbed and sold to 100 countries, accounted for 6% of the company's total revenues ($1,380,000,000). The most popular telenovela in Asia was "Marimar," led by actress-singer Thalía (Ariadna Sodi Miranda) and Eduardo Capetillo. The show's popularity, along with its female lead's star power, was displayed in a concert on September 21 in Manila.

The Cartoon Network and Children's Television Workshop developed "Big Bag," a weekly preschool program without commercial interruption that aired first in the Philippines on September 7. The Philippines' Department of Education, Culture, and Sports (DECS) encouraged both city and municipal mayors in the national capital region to install TV monitors in public elementary-school classrooms to propagate TV-assisted instruction. TV sets were do-

nated by ABS-CBN, producers of some of the children's programs that had been made mandatory viewing.

County Cork, Ireland's premiere recording studio, invested in state-of-the-art technology for dubbing programs to provide materials to the new Irish-language TV station, Teilifís na Gaeilge. Sulan Studios was the first studio in Ireland to provide systems that allowed music and dialogue to be mixed, matched, and blended.

Carlton Communications, Great Britain's largest commercial TV company, had new stations in France, India, and Singapore and gained entry into British cable TV during 1996. Carlton and Pearson PLC were partners in a new Indian satellite-TV venture. Granada Group PLC teamed up with BSkyB to launch eight new satellite channels, including Granada Gold Plus, which offered such vintage shows as "Coronation Street," a 35-year-old soap opera that pulled top ratings. Bloomberg International Television introduced a French-language version on September 11.

ESPN debuted a 24-hour sports news network, and BSkyB added to its two existing sports channels with a third. Digitales Fernsehen 1 (DF1), a satellite company jointly owned by Kirch and BSkyB, won the rights to broadcast Formula One automobile racing.

Italy's Telepiu launched digital satellite TV in February and offered viewers live matches between top teams in the Italian soccer leagues. Early in July Kirch Group spent $2.2 billion for the world's most prized soccer broadcasting rights: the World Cup finals in 2002 and 2006. The only stipulation was that the games were to be aired on "free" TV.

Similarly, the International Olympic Committee turned down a $2 billion bid from Murdoch's News Corporation for European broadcasting rights to the Olympic Games between 2000 and 2008 in favour

Mexican singer and actress Thalía (Ariadna Sodi Miranda) performs in Manila. She was the star of the Televisa telenovela "Marimar," said to be the most popular program in Asia.

of a lower bid from a group of public broadcasters.

Technology. Toshiba Corp.'s new wide-screen TV sets and tuners were formatted to be compatible with Japan's interactive broadcasting system. Mitsubishi Electric Corp. introduced 71-cm (28-in) Diamond Web Internet TVs at $2,500 each.

Compaq Computer Corp. and Thomson Consumer Electronics, a unit of Thomson SA (France), decided to develop jointly a combination PC/TV that would be completed during the first half of 1997. Also anticipated for 1997 were Philips Electronics NV's flat-screened TVs, which could be hung from a wall like a painting.

Europe's biggest digital-TV companies agreed before the European Commission to integrate their decoder technologies so that subscribers could receive programs broadcast by rival companies. The Commission had the power to make a common interface mandatory under a European Union directive.

RADIO

Irish tycoon Tony O'Reilly, chairman of H.J. Heinz Co., bought 41 of New Zealand's commercial radio stations during 1996 for New Zealand Radio Network, a consortium dominated by his business interests. The Maori Council claimed ownership of the stations, however, on the basis of the country's founding Treaty of Waitangi, signed in 1840. The High Court rejected an injunction to halt the sale, but the council would have the opportunity to appeal.

Philippine broadcast network GMA posted a record when its flagship AM radio station, DZBB Radyo Bisig Bayan, became a finalist in the New York Festival's 1996 international radio competition. A total of 1,398 entries from 31 countries participated. DZBB's coverage of the 10th anniversary of the People Power Revolution, titled "Salubungan Meeting," was named a finalist for best ongoing news story.

Hutchison Telecom, British telecommunications arm of Hutchison Whampoa, sought to heighten the company's profile—especially for its fast-growing Orange mobile phone network—by spending £3 million in a sponsorship deal over the next three years with Virgin Radio, the national network owned by British entrepreneur Richard Branson. BBC World Service, which had an audience of 140 million listeners a week (twice that of its nearest competitor, Voice of America), had its capital budget chopped by the British Foreign Office. John Birt, director-general of the BBC, announced the reorganization of World Service, with its news-gathering operations integrated into the rest of the BBC.

By significantly relaxing radio ownership restrictions in the U.S., the 1996 Telecommunications Act touched off a frenzy of buying and selling as a handful of publicly traded companies competed to outbid one another for prime radio stations. The biggest deal of the year was Westinghouse/CBS's $4.9 billion bid for New York-based Infinity Broadcasting. Counting the Infinity stations, Westinghouse/CBS gained ownership of 83 stations in 15 markets. Other aggressively acquisitive companies included Clear Channel Communications, Jacor Communications, American Radio Systems, and Evergreen Media. Overall, the more than 10,200 commercial radio stations reaped nearly $12 billion in revenues in 1996, up 6% from 1995.

The market for radio stations began to cool in the fall, owing mostly to a vigilant U.S. Department of Justice. Cheered on by advertisers and small radio groups, the department imposed its own local ownership cap. In examining proposed radio markets, the department made clear that no company could control more than 50% of the radio advertising revenue in a given market, regardless of how many stations the law said it could own.

The FCC reprimanded Howard Stern, fining a radio station in Richmond, Va., $10,000 for airing his nationally syndicated morning show. The agency found Stern's explicit sex talk "patently offensive." Infinity Broadcasting, the show's owner, had claimed that Stern was "cleaning up his act" when it agreed to pay the government $1.7 million in 1995 to settle indecency fines, levied when FCC Chairman Alfred Sikes led a crackdown on indecent radio.

Country music was again the most ubiquitous radio format. According to the *Wall Street Journal*'s October 1996 count, 2,525 commercial stations claimed country as their primary format. Adult contemporary was the second most popular (1,572 stations), with news/talk a close third (1,272). Other established formats splintered as stations searched desperately for niche markets. Evergreen Media's WKTU dominated the FM band in New York with a disco format that traced its ancestry to the 1970s.

(RAMONA MONETTE S. FLORES; HARRY A. JESSEL; LAWRENCE B. TAISHOFF)

Amateur Radio. Starting in July, thousands of applications poured into the FCC to request new "vanity" calls—the alphanumerics that ham operators use to identify themselves on air. For the first time, ham operators could pick and choose their calls the same way drivers could choose their license plates. Permitted to apply first were those operators who were requesting calls that they or members of their family had previously held.

The American Radio Relay League (ARRL), based in Newington, Conn., encouraged hams to flood the FCC with letters protesting another grab for their radio frequencies. The threat came from applicants for a new class of low-orbiting satellites. ARRL officials also voiced concern about federal legislation that would permit the FCC to auction off a small piece of the amateur spectrum in 1997.

The FCC estimated that in 1996 there were more than two million hams worldwide, with 708,000 licensed operators in the U.S. Hams in New York and New Jersey helped in the recovery efforts following the crash of TWA Flight 800 off the coast of Long Island in July. The ARRL reported that some 125 operators contributed 2,500 hours. President Clinton recognized amateur radio in a letter written for the annual simulated emergency tests in October. Wrote the president, "Ham radio operators have helped to make our world a true global village." (HARRY A. JESSEL; LAWRENCE B. TAISHOFF)

See also Business and Industry Review: *Advertising; Telecommunications;* Performing Arts: *Motion Pictures; Music.*

This article updates the *Macropædia* article BROADCASTING.

SUNDAY INDEPENDENT

Journalist Veronica Guerin enjoys a moment with her husband and child not long before she became the victim of a contract killing on June 26. Guerin, an award-winning investigative reporter with Dublin's *Sunday Independent,* had written extensively on organized crime in Ireland.

NEWSPAPERS

There were many issues affecting international print media, including newspapers, in 1996. One issue in Asia was the matter of creating a new centre for printing. The Subic Bay Freeport Zone in the Philippines was slated to become an Asian centre. The location was seen as a good one because of the well-developed infrastructure, low labour costs, strategic location, and availability of skilled English-speaking workers. The *Asian Wall Street Journal,* being printed in Kuala Lumpur, claimed to be the first regional newspaper to print in Malaysia. A new English-language business daily, *Asia Times,* produced by Sondhi Limthongkul, the Thai chairman of Manager Media Group, competed regionally with the *Asian Wall Street Journal.*

Competition also spawned collaboration between media. In Japan the newspaper *Sankei Shimbun* and the Fuji Television Network launched an electronic news service. The Dutch newspapers *De Telegraaf* and *De Volkskrant* joined *NRC Handelsblad* on the Internet. In the U.K. the Reed Elsevier Group created an interactive multimedia television listings guide, *TV Times,* which included preview clips from major broadcast and satellite channels.

Electronic projects included AOL Europa, a joint venture between Bertelsmann and America Online to provide newspapers and magazines to European customers. Included were the *Daily Mirror* and *Sunday Mirror, The Sporting Life, The Independent* and the *Independent on Sunday,* as well as the magazines *GQ* and *Vogue.* German AOL subscribers also received the magazines *Stern* and *Geo,* while French subscribers received *La Tribune Desfossés* and the magazines *Le Nouvel Observateur* and *Mieux Vivre Votre Argent.* The U.K. service was launched with Mirror Group Newspapers, Newspaper Publishing, and Condé Nast Publications.

In South Africa new print products were being launched, existing titles upgraded, and cover prices raised. Independent News-

papers of Ireland acquired 58% of Argus Newspapers, the biggest publisher of English-language daily newspapers in South Africa.

The international media continued to compete with domestic media. The shift to pan-European newspapers, such as the *International Herald Tribune, The Wall Street Journal Europe,* and the *European,* which targeted an upscale business elite, might not be as thorough in some respects as the domestic media, but they did provide a global environment for international advertisers. France, which advocated a stronger domestic market, complained about the expansion of international media empires. The opposite was true for Australia, however, where conservatives wanted to liberalize laws barring TV owners from holding more than 15% of a newspaper. Such a relaxation of cross-media and foreign-ownership rules would result in new companies entering the Australian market, where foreign stakes in newspapers had earlier been assessed on a case-by-case basis.

In Hungary a new law provided for partial privatization, and the state-owned national newspaper, *Magyar Nemzet,* was put up for sale. Changes in the law in Greece would force the media to publish rate cards, including discount combinations and commissions, which would encourage foreign competition. In Germany laws governing competition were challenged by Burda and Springer.

Price cutting, the rising cost of newsprint, fear of inflation, and high unemployment reduced the print market in Italy. In the U.K. these same factors closed Rupert Murdoch's *Today,* and in France *Le Nouveau Dimanche* suspended publication. *Pravda,* which had reflected communist and Soviet thought since 1912, ceased publication in July. Two Chinese-language dailies, the *Express* and the *United Daily News,* closed.

Sweden announced plans to launch a newspaper in Poland, to be called *Pulse,* a variation of the parent newspaper, *Dagens Industri.* An English-language daily, the *Peninsula,* was being launched in Qatar by Da ash-Sharq, which also published an Arabic daily, *ash-Sharq.* The *Peninsula* would have a home-delivery system, a first for Qatar. (LEARA D. RHODES)

After a pummeling in 1995, the U.S. newspaper industry improved in 1996. There were no major newspaper closings during the year, and much of the underlying economic news was good. The bitter 17-month strike at Knight-Ridder's *Detroit* (Mich.) *Free Press* and Gannett's *Detroit News* continued in 1996, however. Both companies, which published the two papers through a joint operating agreement, had prepared well for the strike and held their hard line with the unions, even though circulation dropped. The Thomson Corp. sold more of its U.S. newspaper holdings.

According to the Newspaper Association of America, total advertising expenditures for the first three quarters of 1996 grew by 6.2% over the same period in 1995, and total advertising revenue grew by $2 billion, to $27 billion, in the same period. The price of newsprint, which had risen to a high of $750 per metric ton at the beginning of the year, was under $500 toward the end of 1996. In a major legislative victory, U.S. Pres. Bill Clinton in August signed a bill that would allow newspapers to treat most of their carriers and distributors as contractors, not employees, and thus save millions of dollars in taxes and benefits. Rising stock prices reflected these developments, although the prices represented other communications ventures as well, since most U.S. companies dominated by newspapers had been diversifying into television, radio, and other media.

Despite their image as communications-age dinosaurs, newspapers moved to the forefront of experimentation with new modes of delivering their content. By the end of 1996, the number of U.S. newspapers delivered on-line had tripled, to nearly 175. Many of these simply repackaged their contents in an on-line format, but others added new content. Media companies also began forming a complex set of partnerships with firms like Microsoft in order to enhance their on-line packages and increase their modes of delivery.

Meanwhile, journalists at some newspapers had become expert at adding to their print editorial product. A series in the *Philadelphia Inquirer* on the fate of the U.S. middle class, for example, was enhanced with additional information as well as games and quizzes related to the articles. Other journalists produced controversial investigative series. A series in the *San Jose* (Calif.) *Mercury News,* for example, claimed a connection between the rise of crack cocaine in California in the 1980s and dealers linked to the Contra rebels who, supervised by the CIA, had fought the leftist government of Nicaragua during that period. The claim was later attacked in major articles in the *Los Angeles Times, Washington Post,* and *New York Times.*

Another newspaper development that continued to spread in 1996 was the movement known as civic, or public, journalism. Its underlying argument was that civic life in the U.S. had deteriorated and that if citizens were no longer connected to civic life, they could not feel any connection to news. Thus, civic journalists aimed to reconnect readers to the public discussion of issues and problems. Critics, however, argued that in the attempt to solve problems, civic journalists were making news rather than merely covering it. One advocate of civic journalism, Cole Campbell, assumed a major position in 1996 when he became editor of the *St. Louis* (Mo.) *Post-Dispatch.*

USA Today, the national Gannett daily that had often been criticized for substituting simpleminded happy talk for more sophisticated coverage, indicated that it might be taking another direction. In 1996 it formed two in-depth reporting teams and produced notable and hard-hitting journalism, particularly in a series that analyzed the rise of arson at African-American churches in the South, a complicated story that much of the rest of the press had oversimplified. The paper's management conceded that it had come to realize that the newspaper could attract occasional buyers with bright but weak journalism but that repeat readers—the ones advertisers liked—tended to want substance. Readers seemed to agree, for, according to figures released by the Audit Bureau of Circulations near the end of the year, *USA Today* had posted the largest gain of any U.S. newspaper.

The 1996 Pulitzer Prize for public service went to the *Raleigh* (N.C.) *News and Observer* for a series on the environmental effects of corporate farming. Robert D. McFadden of the *New York Times* won the award for spot news reporting. The prize for investigative reporting went to the *Orange County* (Calif.) *Register* for a series on fraud in a local fertility clinic. Robert B. Semple, Jr., of the *New York Times* won the prize for editorial writing, and Bob Keeler of *Newsday* the prize for beat reporting for a series on a church on Long Island. Alix M. Freedman of *The Wall Street Journal* won the award for national reporting for articles on the U.S. tobacco industry, and David Rohde of *The Christian Science Monitor* the award for international reporting for his discovery of Muslim mass graves in Srebrenica, Bosnia and Herzegovina. Rick Bragg of the *New York Times* received the prize for feature writing for a series of articles on the contemporary U.S. Laurie Garrett of *Newsday* achieved the honour for explanatory journalism for her reporting on the outbreak of the Ebola virus in Zaire. The award for commentary went to E.R. Shipp of the *New York Daily News* for her columns on racial and social issues, and the award for criticism to Robert Campbell, a writer on architecture at the *Boston Globe.* Jim Morin of the *Miami* (Fla.) *Herald* won the prize for editorial cartooning. Herb Caen, a columnist at the *San Francisco Chronicle,* was given a special award for his many years of writing on the city.

(MIKE HOYT)

MAGAZINES

Many established magazines moved into alternate language markets during 1996. In Latin America cross-border publications in Spanish included the business magazine *Summa,* which reprinted business news from such magazines as *Forbes* and *The Economist. Newsweek* launched a Spanish-language edition in Latin America. Dow Jones & Co. published the business magazine *América Economia* in Spanish and launched a Portuguese-language edition for Brazil with local publisher Editoria Meio & Mensagem.

U.S. publications seeking international markets included *Ebony* and *Elle.* Condé Nast Publications launched *Vogue* in South Korea, where Hachette Filipacchi also launched its movie magazine, *Premiere.* A *Reader's Digest* edition was produced for Thailand, and *Architectural Digest* was launched in Italy.

The Russian newsweekly *Ponyedelnik* closed in 1996 owing to cash-flow problems. A new Russian-language newsweekly, *Itogi* ("Summing Up"), was subsequently launched. *Itogi,* which was similar to *Newsweek,* was produced by Newsweek, Inc., and Russia's Most Group to be distributed in Moscow and St. Petersburg.

In the Czech Republic a thriving new trade press launched more than 20 titles, ranging from *Logistika* ("Logistics"), a trucking and warehousing magazine, to

Union members rally in support of striking workers at the *Detroit* (Mich.) *Free Press* and *Detroit News.* The two newspapers, published through a joint operating agreement by owners Knight-Ridder and Gannett, respectively, continued in operation despite the 17-month-long strike.

JIM WEST—IMPACT VISUALS

In Lucian Perkins's photograph "Looking Back on Chechnya," a boy peers out the window of a bus leaving the country's war zone. Perkins, who had done work in Russia and in Bosnia and Herzegovina, as well as in other parts of the world, won first prize in the 1996 World Press Photo contest.

Zdravotnicke noviny, a magazine for health care workers, to *Vy* ("You"), which was aimed at Czech women aged 20–35.

Some new publications in Germany included *Alina,* a weekly magazine targeted at women between the ages of 30 and 60, *Elter Family,* designed for parents with children between the ages of 3 and 15, and *Men's Health,* a collaboration between Motorpresse in Stuttgart and Rodale Press of the U.S. In Belgium *Sport* magazine was relaunched, and the news magazine *Tempo* returned to Indonesia after having been banned in 1994.   (LEARA D. RHODES)

The electronic revolution continued to change magazine publishing during 1996, with an estimated 4,000–5,000 full-text magazines on-line by the year's end. The best-publicized on-line title in 1996 was Microsoft's *Slate*—edited by Michael Kinsley, the former editor of *The New Republic.* The political and cultural magazine was aimed primarily at Internet users; however, there was also a 30-page paper edition. Many libraries mounted projects to provide more popular titles on-line, including the University of California libraries, whose venture, SCAN, succeeded in increasing the number of scholarly journals available through the Internet.

Publishers on the World Wide Web faced numerous problems, particularly user hostility to subscription fees. Since many magazines were still available free of charge, only a few with special appeal succeeded in charging a user fee. There were almost as many economic casualties as new sites. *Web Review,* one of the best-known Internet magazines, suspended publication in May

owing to a lack of financial support, but it returned in September.

The proliferation of nonsensical articles in U.S. scholarly journals was emphasized by a parody that a University of Minnesota professor published as a genuine contribution to social-scientific thought in the summer issue of *Social Text.* The impenetrable hodgepodge of jargon passed the magazine's editorial board. Explaining the purpose of the hoax in the June issue of *Lingua Franca,* the author asked, "Why should self-indulgent nonsense . . . be lauded as the height of scholarly achievement?"

The value of market research for magazine editors was highlighted in the weekly publication *The Spectator.* A market survey showed that 24% of the magazine's readership felt that there was too much of a focus on sports in the publication. At the time of the study, there was no sports coverage in the periodical whatsoever.

With the advent of desktop publishing technology, many new low-budget magazines were launched. The scores of new 1996 titles included *Go,* a minipostcard-size magazine with short articles on fashion, film, and music; *Biblio,* an overview of books and manuscripts for collectors; *Searcher,* a magazine for database professionals; *Double Take,* an impressive literary review; and *George,* a general-interest title for young professionals. A May *New York Times* survey indicated that *Reader's Digest* was consistently among the world's top three magazines.

The winners of the year's National Magazine Award included *Business Week* for general excellence and *The New Yorker* for

reporting and essays. For the second consecutive year, *GQ* won the feature-writing medal, and a newcomer, *Saveur*—a food magazine—gathered two awards, one for photography and the other for special-interest articles. *Harper's* won the fiction award.

Marketing magazine subscriptions by means of sweepstakes in the mail did not fare as well in 1996 as it had in previous years. Publisher's Clearing House reported that new subscribers brought in by their mailings declined by an estimated 20–30%. Marketing experts believed this falloff was due to a rise in legalized gambling and general consumer boredom with sweepstakes.

(WILLIAM A. KATZ)

BOOK PUBLISHING

While the Net Book Agreement (NBA) all but completely collapsed in the U.K., during 1996—in part because of the threat posed by a flood of cheap U.S. titles coming from The Netherlands—Belgium, Greece, Italy, and Portugal all either strengthened existing restrictions on discounted books or considered introducing such books to their marketplaces for the first time. The Netherlands extended its temporary system for fixing prices for another 10 years. A final verdict on the status of the NBA would not be decided by the Restrictive Practices Court until January 1997.

In the U.K. the discounting of non-Net books was more sporadic than expected, and supermarkets did not make much effort to increase market shares. As a result, few independent bookstores were forced to shut down, though publishers' profits continued to be reduced by rising paper costs, higher authors' royalties, and lower wholesale prices. Hodder Headline, for example, issued a warning about reduced profits in May, which caused its stock price to fall to just over half its value in 1995.

Considerable restructuring took place in the U.K. during the year. In December 1995 Microsoft Corp. sold its 18% stake in Dorling Kindersley after the latter's stock value had risen nearly eightfold since 1991. In February 1996 Pearson agreed to pay $580 million for the educational publishing interests of Rupert Murdoch's HarperCollins publishing group, and in May Reader's Digest put Davis & Charles up for sale. In June CINVen, a venture capital company, acquired Routledge from the Thomson Corp. for $42 million, and Macmillan bought media tie-in publisher Boxtree. Alison and Busby was acquired by the Spanish newspaper group Editorial Prensa Iberica during July. Reed Elsevier in August expanded its legal-publishing business with the $150 million purchase of Tolley from United News and Media. Reed took its Consumer Books division off the market in March 1996, however, after failing to obtain a satisfactory price in light of the collapse of the NBA. Elsewhere in Europe, Piper Verlag of Germany acquired Malik Verlag, and Hachette of France bought Hatier, the third largest educational publisher, for an estimated 500 million francs. As a result, Hachette and Groupe de la Cité controlled 85% of the French educational book market.

Companies such as Penguin Books built up their stock of titles converted from print to CD-ROM but found it difficult to add sufficient value to the product in order to justify a price of about $75 (with the book itself generally a free bonus). They accordingly put their multimedia activity on hold in July, only two years after the project began—as had HarperCollins in June and Reed International in October 1995. Publishers Burda of Germany and Pearson also encountered problems with electronic publishing when Europe Online filed for bankruptcy in August 1996.

Scandal broke out in the anthropology community after Cambridge University Press decided not to publish an already accepted text on Macedonian history, fearing for the safety of its staff members in Greece. Along with three academic advisers, many writers chose to boycott the press for being too reactionary and denying the author of the manuscript the right to free speech.   (PETER J. CURWEN)

It was not surprising that in 1996, an election year, two books of a political nature took centre stage in the United States. *Primary Colors* (Random House), a novel whose characters were thinly disguised caricatures of Pres. Bill Clinton and first lady Hillary Rodham Clinton, made a rapid climb up the *New York Times* best-seller list. Its long run on the list, however, was due mainly to the mystery surrounding the unknown author. Because of the amount of insider information contained in the book, the author was rumoured to be a top government official. Magazines and newspapers devoted columns to analyzing the writing patterns and use of imagery, and many hazarded guesses as to the author's true identity. *New York* magazine speculated that it was Joe Klein, *Newsweek*'s political columnist, which prompted Klein

Joe Klein admits at a news conference that he is Anonymous, author of the best-selling novel *Primary Colors*, which featured characters remarkably like U.S. Pres. Bill Clinton and Hillary Rodham Clinton. The *Newsweek* columnist was criticized for having earlier denied authorship.

to write a column denying the accusation. When a *Washington Post* reporter obtained a copy of the original manuscript, the newspaper had the handwriting analyzed and confirmed that the author was, indeed, Klein. The discovery set off a storm of criticism targeted at Klein, who many said had breached journalistic ethics by lying about his true identity in print.

Hillary Clinton had her say with the January publication of her book, *It Takes a Village: And Other Lessons Children Teach Us* (Simon & Schuster). Taking as its premise the African proverb "It takes a village to raise a child," Clinton discussed family issues and social policies. The book reached the number 1 spot on the *New York Times* nonfiction best-seller list in its first week of publication. All profits from the book were donated to children's hospitals.

Actress and novelist Joan Collins also set the publishing industry abuzz about her legal battle with Random House. The former star of television's "Dynasty" had previously published two novels with Simon & Schuster before being lured to Random House by a $4 million deal for two novels. The company had paid Collins a reported $1.3 million when she submitted her first manuscript, but it then deemed the work unpublishable and sued to recover the money. Collins countersued, demanding the full $4 million. A jury concluded that she had met the terms of her agreement by delivering the first manuscript. The decision was seen as a major victory for writers. Random House announced that it would appeal the decision.

The U.S. Federal Trade Commission (FTC) ended a 17-year investigation into publishers' pricing and promotional practices. Begun in 1979, the probe received new energy in 1982 when the American Booksellers Association (ABA) and 20 regional associations sent resolutions to Congress asking for the funding for further investigation. In 1988 six major publishers—Random House, Simon & Schuster, Macmillan, Hearst, Harper & Row, and Putnam

Berkley—were charged with illegal pricing practices that favoured bookstore chains over independent bookstores. In 1992, although the six cited publishers agreed to modify some pricing practices, the agreements were not ratified by the full FTC. The FTC dismissed the pricing cases in September 1996 without reaching a decision about whether any of the publishers had engaged in illegal activity. The commission stated that further investigation "would not be a prudent use of scarce public resources."

The 1996 Pulitzer Prize for Fiction was awarded to Richard Ford, author of *Independence Day* (Alfred A. Knopf). Tina Rosenberg won in the general nonfiction category for *The Haunted Land: Facing Europe's Ghosts After Communism* (Random House). Fiction best-sellers for 1995, as reported by *Publishers Weekly*, were *The Rainmaker* by John Grisham (2,375,000 copies), *The Lost World* by Michael Crichton (1,730,691), and *Five Days in Paris* by Danielle Steel (1,550,000). Nonfiction best-sellers were *Men Are from Mars, Women Are from Venus* by John Gray (2,196,935), *My American Journey* by Colin Powell with Joseph Persico (1,538,469), and *Miss America* by Howard Stern (1,398,880). Total book sales in the U.S. rose 5% in 1995 to $19.8 billion. The National Book Award for fiction went to Andrea Barrett for her collection of tales *Ship Fever and Other Stories*, for nonfiction to James Carroll for *An American Requiem: God, My Father, and the War That Came Between Us*, and for poetry to Hayden Carruth for *Scrambled Eggs and Whiskey: Poems 1991–1995*, and the newly created prize for young people's literature went to Victor Martinez for *Parrot in the Oven: Mi Vida*. Toni Morrison, winner of the 1993 Nobel Prize for Literature, received the 1996 National Book Foundation Medal for Distinguished Contribution to American Letters.

(BETH S. LEVINE)

See also Literature.
This article updates the *Macropædia* article PUBLISHING.

Military Affairs

Fifty-one years into the atomic era, the five acknowledged nuclear-weapons powers agreed in 1996 to ban nuclear explosions permanently, while the actions of one suspected nuclear-weapons state—India—complicated the long-term prospects for the Comprehensive Test Ban Treaty (CTBT). For the first time in many years, the guns were largely silent in former Yugoslavia as the NATO-led Implementation Force (IFOR) in Bosnia and Herzegovina enforced the peace accords negotiated in Dayton, Ohio, in November 1995 and signed in Paris the following month. As the year ended, however—and with it IFOR's mandate—the countries involved pondered their next move to preserve the shaky peace. The bitter war in the Russian republic of Chechnya continued to demoralize a Russian military already battered by several years of inadequate funding. Russian political and military leaders continued to warn NATO that its expansion into Central and Eastern Europe would endanger European security and most of the nuclear and conventional arms control agreements of recent decades. Two of the world's traditional flash points—the Middle East and the Korean peninsula—were once again the sites of dangerous military confrontations, and bloody civil wars continued in Central and South Asia.

Arms Control and Disarmament. When India vetoed the draft CTBT at the UN Conference on Disarmament (CD) in August because it did not commit the five acknowledged nuclear powers—the United States, Russia, China, France, and the United Kingdom—to a timetable for complete nuclear disarmament, it looked as if the 40-year effort to ban all nuclear explosions had failed again. The treaty was submitted directly to the UN General Assembly, however, where the CD's consensus requirement did not apply, and it was approved on September 10. The CTBT was opened for signature on September 24, with U.S. Pres. Bill Clinton the first to sign. Before it could enter into force, the treaty had to be signed by the 44 states that had either nuclear power or research reactors. By the end of the year, 131 nations had signed, including 41 of the required 44. India led the holdouts, joined by another "threshold" nuclear power, Pakistan, which said it would not sign unless India did. In July the International Court of Justice gave an ambiguous and nonbinding ruling that the use or threat of nuclear weapons in war should be outlawed but that their use in self-defense would not violate international law. The five nuclear weapons powers signed the South Pacific Nuclear Free Zone Treaty, but the U.S. said it was unable to support a similar zone in Southeast Asia because it believed that the treaty would inhibit freedom of the seas. Of the 53 African nations, 45 signed the Pelindaba Treaty establishing an African Nuclear Weapons Free Zone, as did all the nuclear powers.

The U.S. Senate passed a resolution of ratification of the Strategic Arms Reduction Talks II (START-II) treaty in January, but the Russian Federal Assembly (parliament) refused to take it up, with many legislators

A member of the NATO-led force charged with implementing the Dayton peace accords in Bosnia and Herzegovina patrols Grbavica, a suburb of Sarajevo. In December countries that were providing troops for the force agreed to continue with smaller deployments for another year.

expressing the opinion that in 1993 Russia had been too hasty in signing what they considered to be a disadvantageous agreement. Both countries continued to cut their strategic nuclear forces in conformity with the earlier START-I treaty. All former Soviet nuclear weapons were repatriated from Ukraine by June 1, but Belarus continued to balk at allowing the last 18 SS-25 mobile intercontinental ballistic missiles to leave the country despite an earlier pledge that they would be out by the end of the year.

The number of states ratifying the Chemical Weapons Convention reached 65; as a result, the treaty would enter into force in April 1997. While neither of the countries admitting to having the largest stockpiles of chemical weapons—Russia and the U.S.—had ratified the treaty, as signatories they would be required to abide by its provisions.

Conventional weapons were in the arms control spotlight much of the year, and while the first review conference of the 1980 Inhumane Weapons Convention failed to ban antipersonnel land mines, the antimine movement gained momentum. (*See* Special Report.) Negotiators at the review conference of the Conventional Forces in Europe (CFE) treaty agreed to relax temporarily some of the limits placed on the numbers of weapons Russia could deploy in northwest Russia and in its troubled Caucasus region.

United States. Legislation covering defense spending in two fiscal years was passed by the Congress in 1996: a revised defense authorization bill for fiscal year 1996 to replace the one vetoed by President Clinton in December 1995 and the authorization and appropriations bills for fiscal year 1997. In both cases the Republican-controlled Congress gave the military more than Clinton had requested. The revised fiscal year 1996 bill set defense spending at $265 billion, $7 billion more than the president had wanted, but it dropped the requirement to deploy a national antiballistic missile system by 2003 that had prompted Clinton's veto of the original bill. The fiscal year 1997 defense authorization bill, which Clinton signed in September, provided $265.6

billion, $11.5 billion more than the administration had requested. While some in the Congress wanted to reopen the B-2 stealth bomber production line, President Clinton directed that B-2 procurement funds added to the fiscal year 1996 budget by Congress be used to modernize the current fleet and bring the operational fleet to 21 aircraft by upgrading the B-2 test-flight vehicle.

In its second and third trials, the army's Theater High-Altitude Area Defense system failed to intercept another missile. The program was cut back by the Pentagon in a move that drew the ire of a number of Republicans in Congress. During the year the navy christened its first Seawolf submarine and the last of the Los Angeles-class attack submarines that preceded it, as well as the 18th and last Trident ballistic missile submarine.

Tragedy involving military forces overseas struck twice during the year. On April 3 an air force transport jet carrying Commerce Secretary Ron Brown (*see* OBITUARIES) and 34 other people crashed while attempting to land near Dubrovnik, Croatia. In the subsequent investigation, 2 generals and 14 other officers were censured. A terrorist bomb exploded on June 25 outside a barracks housing air force personnel in Dhahran, Saudi Arabia, killing 19 and injuring hundreds. An inquiry faulted the local U.S. commander as well as his superiors. Revelations that as many as 20,000 U.S. military personnel might have been exposed to nerve gas when an Iraqi weapons dump was blown up during the 1991 Persian Gulf War prompted renewed investigations into the Gulf War syndrome, a puzzling set of health complaints by some veterans of that action.

The chief of naval operations, Adm. Jeremy Boorda (*see* OBITUARIES), took his own life on May 16 after allegations that he had worn unearned attachments for valour on two Vietnam War ribbons. He was succeeded by Adm. Jay Johnson. Carol Mutter was promoted to lieutenant general in the Marine Corps in March, the first woman to achieve three-star rank.

Adm. J. Paul Reason, who took command of the Atlantic Fleet in May, became the navy's first African-American four-star admiral. William Perry announced that he would step down as secretary of defense; William Cohen, a former Republican senator, was named as his replacement. The army began a service-wide investigation of sexual harassment after revelations that instructors at two training centres, the Aberdeen Proving Ground in Maryland and Ft. Leonard Wood, Missouri, had fraternized with, raped, and sexually abused female recruits.

An army medic was dismissed from the service after a court-martial convicted him of disobeying a lawful order when he refused to wear a UN beret while serving on a peacekeeping mission in former Yugoslavia. Two marines and an air force sergeant were also court-martialed when they refused to have their blood screened for a military DNA bank, a program established to make it easier to identify future battlefield casualties. Federal courts in California, Washington, and the District of Columbia ruled in favour of the government in three cases in which servicemen who admitted they were gay had been discharged for violating the military's "Don't Ask, Don't Tell" policy on homosexuals. One case was appealed to the U.S. Supreme Court, which refused to hear it.

NATO. Operation Joint Endeavor, the NATO-led operation in Bosnia and Herzegovina that began in December 1995, marked its first ground force operation, its first deployment "out of area" (*i.e.,* not on the territory of one of its members), and its first joint operation with its "Partnership for Peace" (PfP) allies and other non-NATO countries.

NATO put off any announcement as to which countries would be invited to join the alliance until a summit meeting tentatively scheduled for mid-1997 was held. Russians across the political spectrum continued to be strongly opposed to the alliance's expanding into Central and Eastern Europe, while NATO leaders went out of their way to try to build stronger ties with Russia. NATO and Russian officials discussed the possibility of a formal charter between the two parties to regulate their consultations and joint actions, while NATO military leaders talked of enhancing the PfP into a "PfP Plus," creating a more meaningful military relationship with Russia in the process. With Europe's other traditionally neutral states—Austria, Finland, and Sweden—already members of the PfP, the Swiss government announced in September that it had agreed in principle to join.

The Netherlands ended conscription in August. Both Spain and France, whose military forces were not part of NATO's integrated military structure, indicated that they were considering changing that policy. France received a setback when the U.S. balked at a French proposal that a European officer head NATO's Southern Command, a post that had traditionally been filled by a U.S. admiral.

The Canadian military continued to be buffeted by the fallout from the scandal over an alleged coverup of the incidents of brutality against civilians by Canadian peacekeepers in Somalia in 1992 and 1993, a process exacerbated by allegations of similar misconduct by Canadian soldiers serving in Bosnia and Herzegovina. The minister of defense and the chief of defense staff both resigned in October. NATO allies Greece and Turkey had a serious military confrontation in January over a disputed island in the Aegean Sea.

United Kingdom. Gen. Sir Charles Guthrie, the head of the British army, was named the new chief of defense staff. In August the defense minister announced that a new Joint Rapid Deployment Force would be formed that could quickly deploy as many as 8,000 troops anywhere in the world. The last Polaris ballistic missile submarine, HMS *Repulse,* was decommissioned in August, cutting the U.K.'s operational strategic nuclear submarine fleet to two Trident submarines.

With surveys showing that four-fifths of military personnel approved of the ban on homosexuals' serving in the armed forces, the government announced in March that it had decided after a review that the ban would remain in effect. Parliament in May voted down legislation that would have overturned it. After a two-year investigation of the elite Household Cavalry Regiment, the Commission for Racial Equality charged that the military had been slow in developing and implementing plans to stop racial discrimination.

France. Pres. Jacques Chirac announced revolutionary changes in France's military posture: ending the draft, doing away with all land-based nuclear missiles, and embarking on a five-year program to transform the current 500,000-strong military into an all-

A man walks through the shadow of a gun along the remains of the principal commercial street in Kabul, the capital of Afghanistan. Much of Kabul was almost totally destroyed in the country's civil war, and it was claimed that the city had one of the world's highest concentrations of land mines.

volunteer force numbering some 350,000. Included would be a 50,000-strong rapid reaction force capable of fighting "one and a half wars" at the same time. Conscription was to end in January 1997, to be replaced with a week of civic education that would be mandatory for all men turning 18; beginning in 2002 it would be mandatory for women as well. In July Defense Minister Charles Millon announced that 38 army regiments would be disbanded and one of the navy's two aircraft carriers would be retired.

France conducted its last nuclear test in January and then began dismantling its test site at Mururoa and Fangatuafa atolls in French Polynesia. The last 15 remaining Mirage IVP nuclear bombers were retired in July, and the land-based component of the French strategic nuclear triad was abandoned in September when the 18 S3D intermediate-range ballistic missiles based in silos on the Plateau d'Albion were decommissioned. President Chirac also announced that France would stop producing fissile nuclear material and dismantle its Hades short-range nuclear missiles.

Germany. Finally ending its postwar reluctance to send its armed forces outside the country, Germany sent 4,000 troops to Croatia and contributed electronic warfare, reconnaissance, and transport aircraft as well as medical, transportation, army helicopter, and logistic units to IFOR in Bosnia and Herzegovina. In September plans for a 1,000-strong elite special combat unit patterned after the British Special Air Service (SAS) were announced to give Germany a rapid-response capability. Defense Secretary Volker Rühe also said that the military would be reduced from 370,000 to 338,000 and one of the army's eight divisions would be eliminated.

Turkey. The continuing armed confrontation with the militants of the Kurdish Workers' Party (PKK) and the rise to power of a fundamentalist Muslim party served to dampen Turkey's relations with its NATO allies. In May Turkish troops forayed into northern Iraq in pursuit of PKK guerrillas, while in September and November the government launched major offensives against the PKK in eastern Turkey. In October the government announced an ambitious 30-year plan to spend some $150 billion to modernize its armed forces.

The Rest of Europe. By mid-February the initial deployment of the NATO-led IFOR into Bosnia and Herzegovina had been completed. Thirty-two nations had been part of the deployment, with nearly 50,000 troops provided by all NATO nations with armed forces and approximately 10,000 from the 18 non-NATO contributors to the overall effort. IFOR was given the responsibility for monitoring and enforcing compliance with the military aspects of the peace agreement. These included monitoring the withdrawal of the forces of the former combatants to their respective territories, establishing zones of separation, and controlling the airspace over Bosnia and Herzegovina as well as military traffic over key ground routes. Operation Sharp Guard, the naval embargo enforcement effort jointly carried out by NATO and the Western European Union (WEU), was terminated on October 1, when the UN lifted the economic sanctions against former Yugoslavia. On June 14 the warring factions in Bosnia signed a "subregional" arms control agreement patterned after the CFE treaty, agreeing to limit their holdings in the CFE's five categories of offensive weapons while destroying the excess over a 16-month period. NATO intelligence officers expressed concern in October that the Bosnian Serbs had far more heavy weapons than they had declared. The U.S. funded a program to train and equip the army of the Bosnian Muslim-Croat Federation to make it more militarily viable once the IFOR had withdrawn.

Bosnian Serb military chief Gen. Ratko Mladic, an indicted war criminal, was fired in November. He refused to step down and instead established an alternate military headquarters with staff officers loyal to him. In December the countries providing troops to IFOR agreed to provide a smaller force totaling 30,000 for another 18 months. Some of these units would be earmarked for use in Bosnia if needed but would be stationed in adjacent areas.

Switzerland revealed in May that it had maintained a secret nuclear weapons program for 43 years, with plans to build 400 nuclear warheads. The program was abandoned in 1989. While declining an invitation to provide a military contingent for IFOR, the Swiss sent 80 logistics troops to Bosnia under the auspices of the Organization for Security and Cooperation in Europe (OSCE). The U.S. and the U.K. disclosed that they had both hidden stockpiles of arms in Austria during the early years of the Cold War. The weapons would have been used by Austrian anticommunist guerrillas in the event of a Soviet invasion. On September 9 Hungary and Romania signed a treaty providing for advance notification of troop movement within 80 km (50 mi) of their common border.

Commonwealth of Independent States (CIS). The war in the breakaway republic of Chechnya continued to top the list of Russian security concerns. A group of Chechen separatists in January attacked Russian soldiers in the town of Kyzlar in the neighbouring republic of Dagestan and holed up in a hospital with nearly 2,000 hostages. Although they were promised free passage back to Chechnya in return for the release of most of the hostages, their convoy was attacked and encircled by Russian forces in the village of Pervomayskoye, Dagestan. The Russians bombarded the village for four days and nights. In the end most of the Chechen fighters escaped. The incident exposed further shortcomings within the demoralized Russian military and other security forces. In late February the federal forces began a new phase of the war by concentrating on routing armed Chechen self-defense units from rural towns and villages, often with considerable loss of civilian lives. In response, the Chechen separatists in early March conducted a successful foray into the Russian-held Chechen capital of Grozny, briefly holding one-third of the city. On March 31 Russian Pres. Boris Yeltsin announced a peace plan that included an immediate halt to most military operations. The armed forces, however, intensified their offensive operations in western and eastern Chechnya. On April 22 Chechen president Dzhokhar Dudayev (see OBITUARIES) was killed by a missile launched from a Russian helicopter while he was making a satellite telephone call. Largely as the result of OSCE mediation, a preliminary cease-fire document was initialed in the Kremlin by Russian and Chechen leaders, and detailed armistice protocols were signed June 10. The Russians agreed to withdraw the troops not permanently assigned to the North Caucasus Military District by the end of August.

Yeltsin was reelected president in July, with Aleksandr Lebed (see BIOGRAPHIES), the former commander of the 14th Army in Moldova, finishing a strong third. Yeltsin named Lebed secretary of the Security Council and fired Defense Minister Pavel Grachev while purging many generals in the armed forces. Grachev was succeeded by Col. Gen. Igor Rodionov, best known in the West for the bloody suppression of civilians in Tbilisi, Georgia, in 1989 by troops under his command. Federal forces in Chechnya had resumed offensive operations following the presidential elections.

On August 6 the Chechen separatists stunned the federal forces by retaking most of Grozny. This prompted Yeltsin to name Lebed as his plenipotentiary envoy to Chechnya. On August 22 Lebed signed a cease-fire agreement with Chechen chief of staff Aslan Maskhadov. On August 31 the two signed a landmark accord in Khasavyurt, Dagestan, to end the war and demilitarize Chechnya. Although nationalists branded the accord a sellout, some federal military commanders threatened to sabotage it, and Yeltsin was slow to endorse it, the agreement held for the rest of the year. Often publicly at odds with many of his colleagues in the government, Lebed was fired by Yeltsin on October 17.

During his reelection campaign Yeltsin had issued a decree calling for the military to do away with conscription by the turn of the century. It was clearly a step the military could not afford, and Rodionov finally said as much, noting that it would be at least 2005 before an all-volunteer force would be economically possible. Indeed, government support for the military was so meagre that morale was low, and there were reports of suicides among the officers.

After an October meeting in Moscow between Ukrainian Pres. Leonid Kuchma and the ailing Yeltsin, it looked as if the two countries had finally resolved the problem of dividing the former Soviet Black Sea Fleet, but such hopes remained illusory. While the division of the ships, airplanes, and most shore facilities had been agreed upon long ago, the two remained at odds over the fate of the Crimean port of Sevastopol, where the Russians insisted that only its fleet must have its headquarters.

Civil war threatened to break out again in Tajikistan, where tribal and ethnic loyalties took precedence over national ones. Early in the year the elite 1st Motorized-Rifle Brigade briefly mutinied. Rather than extending the UN-moderated cease-fire when it expired in late May, government troops began an offensive against the opposition forces. Moscow helped to reconvene on July 8 the UN-mediated inter-Tajik negotiations in Ashgabat, Turkmenistan, which produced an armistice agreement on July 19 between the Moscow-backed government and the armed opposition. Government troops immediately violated the armistice, however, by launching a successful operation to seize the town of Tavildara. In mid-September the opposition routed superior but clearly unmotivated government forces in Garm, the narrow "waist" section of Tajikistan connecting the western and eastern parts of the country. This prompted the Russian commander in Tajikistan to seek the aid of the Afghan government in sealing off the border to United Tajik Opposition infiltrators who regularly operated out of Afghanistan. This aid was short-lived, as the Afghan government became preoccupied with its struggle with the Taliban militia.

Georgian Pres. Eduard Shevardnadze withheld consent to the renewal of the Russian "peacekeeping" forces' existing mandate, which expired on July 19. He indicated Georgia would not ratify the treaty allowing the Russians to maintain three military bases in Georgia unless Russia helped end the Abkhazian independence effort.

Middle East. According to U.S. intelligence estimates, by early 1996 Iraqi Pres. Saddam Hussein had rebuilt his armed forces into a smaller but more capable force than he possessed before his ill-fated invasion of Kuwait in 1990. Rolf Ekeus, the chief UN weapons inspector in the country, said that Iraq could have as many as 16 mobile missiles armed with biological warheads and that his inspectors had been barred from several sites. Still not convinced that Iraq had complied with all its resolutions, the UN Security Council refused to lift the economic embargo on the nation. On August 31 an Iraqi force estimated at as large as 40,000 troops pushed into the northern exclusion zone that had been established by the U.S., Great Britain, and France to protect the Kurds living in that region. Hussein was responding to an appeal from the Kurdistan Democratic Party (KDP) led by Massoud Barzani to counter what Barzani claimed was support of another Kurdish faction, the Patriotic Union of Kurdistan (PUK), by Iran. President Clinton responded by ordering U.S. navy and air force units to fire 34 cruise missiles at Iraqi air defense installations in

Approximate Strengths of Selected Regular Armed Forces of the World

Country	Military personnel in 000s				Warships				Combat aircraft[1]			Tanks[3]	Defense expenditure as % of 1995 GDP
	Total	Army	Navy	Air Force[2]	Submarines		Aircraft Carriers/ Cruisers	Destroyers/ Frigates	Bombers and fighter-ground attack	Fighters	Recon-nais-sance		
					Nuclear	Diesel							
I. NATO													
Belgium	46.3[4]	30.1	2.6	12.3	—	—	—	2	132	—	—	334	1.7
Canada	70.5[4]	21.5	9.5	16.4	—	3	—	20	123	—	18	114	1.6
Denmark	32.9	19.0	6.0	7.9	—	5	—	3	66	—	—	353	1.8
France	398.9[4]	236.6	63.3[5]	88.6	11	6	3	40	424	126	66	766	3.1
Germany	358.4[4]	252.8	28.5	77.1	—	17	—	14	484	241	29	2,988	2.0
Greece	168.3	122.0	19.5	26.8	—	8	—	14	214	154	24	1,735	4.6
Italy	325.1[4]	167.2	44.0	68.0	—	8	2	30	227	92	18	1,164	1.8
Netherlands, The	63.1[4]	32.4	14.0	12.4	—	4	—	16	108	—	13	734	2.2
Norway	30.0[4]	14.7	6.4	7.9	—	12	—	4	59	15	6	170	2.6
Portugal	54.2[4]	29.7	12.5	7.3	—	3	—	11	84	—	6	186	2.9
Spain	206.8	142.2	36.1[5]	28.5	—	8	1	17	49	137	21	698	1.5
Turkey	639.0	525.0	51.0[5]	63.0	—	15	—	21	284	110	40	4,280	3.6
United Kingdom	226.0	113.0	48.0[5]	65.0	14	—	3	35	393	122	23	462	3.1
United States	1,483.8	495.0	600.6[5]	388.2	95	—	43	101	3,420	869	243	10,900	3.8
II. NON-NATO EUROPE													
Albania	54.0	45.0	2.5	6.5	—	2	—	—	47	51	—	721	2.8
Armenia	57.4[4]	56.6	—	—	—	—	—	—	5	1	—	102	4.4
Austria	55.8	51.5	—	4.3	—	—	—	—	53	—	—	170	1.0
Azerbaijan	70.7	57.3	2.2	11.2	—	—	—	2	16	30	—	300	5.0
Belarus	85.5[4]	50.5	—	25.7[2]	—	—	—	—	141	166	42	2,320	3.3
Bosnia and Herzegovina	92.0	92.0	—	—	—	—	—	—	—	—	—	75	18.8
Bulgaria	103.5[4]	51.6	6.1	20.1	—	2	—	1	167	84	21	1,550	3.3
Croatia	64.7	63.0	1.1	0.6	—	2	—	—	25	—	—	250	12.6
Czech Republic	70.0[4]	28.0	—	16.0[2]	—	—	—	—	60	66	—	953	2.8
Finland	32.5	26.0	2.5	4.0	—	—	—	—	—	118	—	232	2.0
Hungary	64.3	48.0	—	16.3	—	—	—	—	—	115	12	835	1.4
Poland	248.5	178.7	17.8	52.2[2]	—	3	—	2	115	329	23	1,721	2.5
Romania	228.4[4]	129.8	18.5[5]	47.6	—	1	—	6	88	256	24	1,375	3.1
Slovakia	42.6[4]	25.0	—	12.2	—	—	—	—	33	84	8	478	2.8
Sweden	62.6	43.1	10.0	9.5	—	14	—	—	177	185	51	664	2.9
Ukraine	400.8[4]	187.8	16.0[5]	124.0[2]	—	3	—	4	404	457	112	4,026	3.0
Yugoslavia	113.9	90.0	7.2	16.7	—	4	—	4	94	78	32	1,360	22.1
III. RUSSIA													
Russia	1,270.0[4]	460.0	190.0	420.0[6]	102	31	25	141	1,517	1,560	225	17,650	7.4
IV. MIDDLE EAST AND NORTH AFRICA; SUB-SAHARAN AFRICA; LATIN AMERICA													
Algeria	123.7	107.0	6.7	10.0	—	2	—	3	55	116	9	960	2.5
Egypt	440.0	310.0	20.0	110.0[2]	—	8	—	7	176	371	20	3,650	4.3
Iran	513.0[4]	345.0	18.0[5]	30.0	—	2	—	5	170	125	14	1,440	3.9
Iraq	382.5	350.0	2.5	30.0	—	—	—	1	136	180	—	2,700	14.8
Israel	175.0	134.0	9.0	32.0	—	2	—	—	222	205	22	4,300	9.2
Jordan	98.6	90.0	0.6	8.0	—	—	—	—	67	30	—	1,051	6.7
Lebanon	48.9	47.5	0.6	0.8	—	—	—	—	—	3	—	300	5.3
Libya	65.0	35.0	8.0	22.0	—	4	—	2	200	209	11	2,210	5.5
Morocco	194.0	175.0	6.0	13.0	—	—	—	1	97	15	—	224	4.3
Saudi Arabia	105.5	70.0	13.5[5]	22.0[2]	—	—	—	8	167	124	10	1,055	10.6
Sudan, The	89.0	85.0	1.0	3.0	—	—	—	—	50	10	—	280	4.3
Syria	421.0	315.0	6.0	100.0	—	3	—	2	240	325	14	4,600	6.8
Tunisia	35.0	27.0	4.5	3.5	—	—	—	—	44	—	—	84	2.0
United Arab Emirates	64.5	59.0	1.5	4.0	—	—	—	1	65	26	8	201	4.8
Yemen	42.0	37.0	1.5	3.5	—	—	—	—	33	32	—	1,125	3.9
Angola	97.0	90.0	1.5	5.5	—	—	—	—	26	10	—	400	4.8
Burundi	22.0[4]	18.5	—	—	—	—	—	—	7	—	—	—	5.3
Cameroon	22.1[4]	11.5	1.3	0.3	—	—	—	—	9	—	—	—	1.8

the southern exclusion zone. After driving the PUK out of Erbil, the Iraqi forces retired. Subsequently, the PUK retook much of the territory it had lost to the Iraqi-assisted KDP, which raised concerns that Hussein might again intervene.

In March Libyan leader Col. Muammar al-Qaddafi said that Arabs had a right to possess chemical and biological weapons to compensate for Israeli nuclear weapons. CIA sources had reported that Libya was building the world's largest underground chemical weapons plant near Tarhunah.

Israel signed two military cooperation agreements with Turkey, one of which allowed Israeli air force jets to use Turkish bases and airspace for training. Both countries were concerned about Syria, which had moved troops toward the Turkish border in June. Israeli media reports disclosed that in August Syria had tested a long-range Scud-C missile that had the ability to reach all of Israel's major cities. The following month Israel's Arrow 2 antimissile missile passed its first test under combat conditions when it successfully intercepted a missile at high altitude. The Israeli-Palestinian peace process slowed under the government of Prime Minister Benjamin Netanyahu and took an ugly turn in September when Israeli troops and Palestinian police exchanged gunfire as Palestinians rioted in the Gaza Strip and on the West Bank.

South and Central Asia. Although repulsed by government forces when they attacked Kabul in May, the Taliban Islamic militia swept into the Afghan capital in September and looked as if they would soon overrun the entire country. When they tried to push on to the north to the strategic Panshir Valley and Salang Tunnel, however, they were stopped by the combined forces of Gen. 'Abd ar-Rashid Dostam and Ahmad Shah Masoud, the military adviser of deposed president Burhanuddin Rabbani. At the year's end the Taliban seemed firmly in control of Kabul.

(Continued on page 276)

Approximate Strengths of Selected Regular Armed Forces of the World (continued)

| Country | Military personnel in 000s | | | | Warships | | | | Combat aircraft[1] | | | Tanks[3] | Defense expenditure as % of 1995 GDP |
| | Total | Army | Navy | Air Force[2] | Submarines | | Aircraft Carriers/ Cruisers | Destroyers/ Frigates | Bombers and fighter-ground attack | Fighters | Recon-nais-sance | | |
					Nuclear	Diesel							
Chad	30.3[4]	25.0	—	0.3	—	—	—	—	—	—	—	—	25.4
Kenya	24.2	20.5	1.2	2.5	—	—	—	—	30	—	—	76	2.3
Mozambique	34.8	30.0	0.8	4.0	—	—	—	—	43	—	—	80	3.7
Nigeria	77.1	62.0	5.6	9.5	—	—	—	1	92	—	—	200	2.9
South Africa	137.9[4]	118.0	5.5	9.0	—	3	—	—	234	—	8	250	2.9
Tanzania	34.6	30.0	1.0	3.6	—	—	—	—	—	24	—	65	2.7
Uganda	50.0	48.8	0.4[5]	0.8	—	—	—	—	9	—	—	20	2.6
Zaire	49.1[4]	25.0	1.3[5]	1.8	—	—	—	—	22	—	—	60	2.0
Zimbabwe	43.0	39.0	—	4.0	—	—	—	—	44	14	15	40	4.2
Argentina	72.5	36.0	24.5[5]	12.0	—	3	—	13	225	—	8	296	1.7
Bolivia	33.5	25.0	4.5	4.0	—	—	—	—	38	10	—	—	2.6
Brazil	295.0	195.0	50.0[5]	50.0	—	5	1	18	259	16	5	61	1.7
Chile	89.7	51.7	24.0[5]	14.0	—	4	—	9	91	15	20	119	3.8
Colombia	146.3	121.0	18.0[5]	7.3	—	2	—	4	74	—	—	—	2.0
Cuba	100.0	85.0	5.0[5]	10.0	—	2	—	2	14	116	—	1,500	2.8
Dominican Republic	24.5	15.0	4.0[5]	5.5	—	—	—	—	10	—	—	—	1.3
Ecuador	57.1	50.0	4.1[5]	3.0	—	2	—	2	38	14	—	—	3.4
Guatemala	44.2	42.0	1.5[5]	0.7	—	—	—	—	14	—	—	—	1.3
Mexico	175.0	130.0	37.0[5]	8.0	—	—	—	7	87	10	9	—	0.9
Peru	125.0	85.0	25.0[5]	15.0	—	8	2	5	66	23	7	300	1.6
Uruguay	25.6	17.6	5.0[5]	3.0	—	—	—	3	36	—	1	—	2.6
Venezuela	79.0[4]	34.0	15.0[5]	7.0	—	2	—	6	104	—	4	70	1.1
V. SOUTH AND CENTRAL ASIA; EAST ASIA AND OCEANIA													
Australia	57.8	26.0	14.7	17.1	—	4	—	11	103	—	23	71	2.5
Bangladesh	117.5	101.0	10.0	6.5	—	—	—	4	57	—	—	140	1.8
Cambodia	87.7[4]	36.0	1.2	0.5	—	—	—	—	6	19	—	100	4.7
China	2,935.0	2,200.0	265.0[5]	470.0	6	57	—	54	1,006	4,411	298	8,000	5.7
India	1,145.0	980.0	55.0[5]	110.0	—	19	2	24	413	379	54	3,500	2.5
Indonesia	299.2	235.2	43.0[5]	21.0	—	2	—	17	65	12	25	—	1.6
Japan	235.5[4]	148.0	43.0	44.5	—	17	—	60	110	249	130	1,130	1.1
Kazakstan	40.0	25.0	—	15.0	—	—	—	—	69	77	27	630	3.0
Korea, North	1,054.0	923.0	46.0	85.0	—	25	—	3	611	—	—	3,400	25.2
Korea, South	660.0	548.0	60.0[5]	52.0	—	4	—	40	303	130	51	2,050	3.4
Laos	37.0	33.0	0.5	3.5	—	—	—	—	31	—	—	30	4.2
Malaysia	114.5	90.0	12.0	12.5	—	—	—	6	39	33	7	—	4.5
Mongolia	21.1[4]	15.5	—	2.0	—	—	—	—	13	—	—	650	2.8
Myanmar (Burma)	321.0	300.0	12.0[5]	9.0	—	—	—	—	55	36	—	106	6.2
Pakistan	587.0	520.0	22.0[5]	45.0	—	9	—	11	168	243	16	2,050	6.5
Philippines	107.5	68.0	23.0[5]	16.5	—	—	—	1	36	7	8	—	1.6
Singapore	53.9	45.0	2.9	6.0	—	—	—	—	93	38	6	60	5.9
Sri Lanka	115.3	95.0	10.3	10.0	—	—	—	—	24	—	—	25	4.9
Taiwan	376.0	240.0	68.0[5]	68.0	—	4	—	36	386	—	37	630	5.0
Thailand	254.0	150.0	64.0[5]	43.0	—	—	—	12	192	51	30	253	2.5
Uzbekistan	30.0[4]	25.0	—	4.0	—	—	—	—	52	64	10	404	3.6
Vietnam	572.0	500.0	42.0[5]	30.0[2]	—	—	—	8	71	125	4	1,300	4.3

Note: Data exclude most paramilitary, security, and irregular forces. Naval data exclude vessels of less than 100 tons standard displacement. Figures are for June 1996. Because of substantive changes in national forces and reassessments of evidence, data may not be comparable with previous editions.
[1]Includes combat aircraft from all services, including naval and air defense. Light strike/counterinsurgency aircraft are included in bomber/fighter-ground-attack category. Reconnaissance includes maritime reconnaissance and antisubmarine warfare aircraft.
[2]Includes air defense troops.
[3]Main battle tanks (MBT), weighing at least 16.5 metric tons with gun of at least 75-mm calibre.
[4]Some countries have staffs, centrally controlled units, support services, military police, regular armed forces not responsible to the Ministry of Defense, and the like, which means total armed forces are greater than the sum of the three armed forces.
[5]Includes marines or naval infantry.
[6]Includes strategic missile forces.
Source: International Institute for Strategic Studies, 23 Tavistock Street, London, *The Military Balance 1996–1997*.

Combating the Land Mine Scourge

BY DOUGLAS L. CLARKE

U.S. Secretary of State Warren Christopher has called them "weapons of mass destruction in slow motion"—the 110 million land mines buried in 68 countries stretching from Cambodia to Costa Rica. The United Nations has estimated that they kill or maim roughly 20,000 people each year. Most of the casualties are innocent civilians, many of them children, because practically all of the mines in place today have no self-destruction or neutralization features. They remain deadly hazards long after a conflict has ended or the lines of confrontation have moved. With some 23 million land mines buried in its sands, Egypt has more unexploded mines than any other country. Many of these date from World War II, and the others are from the 1948, 1956, 1967, and 1973 Arab-Israeli wars. The most densely mined country is Bosnia and Herzegovina, where there are an average of 152 mines per square mile. As international publicity and abhorrence to these indiscriminate killers have grown, so have the public and private efforts to remove the mines already planted and to ban or at least severely restrict their use in the future.

Land mines fall into two broad categories: those that target tanks, trucks, and heavy vehicles and those designed to kill or injure people. Antimine efforts have focused on this latter group, commonly known as antipersonnel mines. Compared with the magnitude of the task, these efforts have been almost insignificant. Twenty times as many new mines are laid each year as are cleared. Many of the countries that are the most heavily mined—Afghanistan, Angola, Cambodia, Mozambique—are also among the poorest in the world, and the social and economic price they pay is enormous. Afghanistan is thought to have 10 million unexploded mines, one for every two members of the population. Some 15 million mines are scattered throughout Angola, a country with 70,000 amputees from land mine explosions and where much of the agricultural land is unusable because of mines.

Opponents of land mines placed high hopes that the first review conference of the 1980 Geneva Convention on Inhumane Weapons would result in an outright ban on antipersonnel land mines, but they were quickly disappointed. The conference met three times in late 1995 and early 1996, but it was obvious from the beginning that too few parties supported an outright ban. In the end the conference did agree on some important changes. The rewritten convention, which deals with antipersonnel mines, will apply in civil as well as international conflicts. The delegates mandated a transition from "dumb" to "smart" antipersonnel mines; except for those planted in mapped and guarded areas, mines must be equipped with devices that will render them permanently harmless after 120 days. As some existing mines are made out of plastic or wood and can be detected only by slow and dangerous probing by hand, the conference also directed that future mines have a metal mass of at least eight grams. Parties to the convention were given nine years to bring their stockpiles up to these standards.

Disappointed that antipersonnel mines were not outlawed entirely by the review conference, its critics also complained that the delegates failed to approve a verification or enforcement regime for the convention and had failed to effectively block the trade in land mines. Critics also argued that the fuzzy definition of antipersonnel mines agreed upon by the conference opened the door for the use of antitank mines against personnel as technological advances blur the distinctions between the two types of mines. The convention had made no stipulations with regard to antitank mines. UN Secretary-General Boutros Boutros-Ghali told the delegates they had ignored the "groundswell in public opinion" against mines and warned them that by the time of the next review conference, in 2001, "an additional 50,000 human beings will have been killed and a further 80,000 injured by land mines." Canada served as host for a conference in October on antipersonnel mines attended by 50 countries. It adopted a declaration calling for the earliest-possible agreement on a global ban, but many crucial nations, including Russia and most Middle Eastern countries, did not sign it, and China did not even attend.

Land mine opponents hoped that unilateral and regional actions by governments might be more successful in the long run than the global approach exemplified by the Convention on Inhumane Weapons. In March 1995 Belgium became the first country to enact a law completely banning the manufacture, trade, use, and stockpiling of antiper-

Douglas L. Clarke, a retired captain in the U.S. Navy, is a military analyst and author of The Missing Man: Politics and the MJA.

Landmines in the World

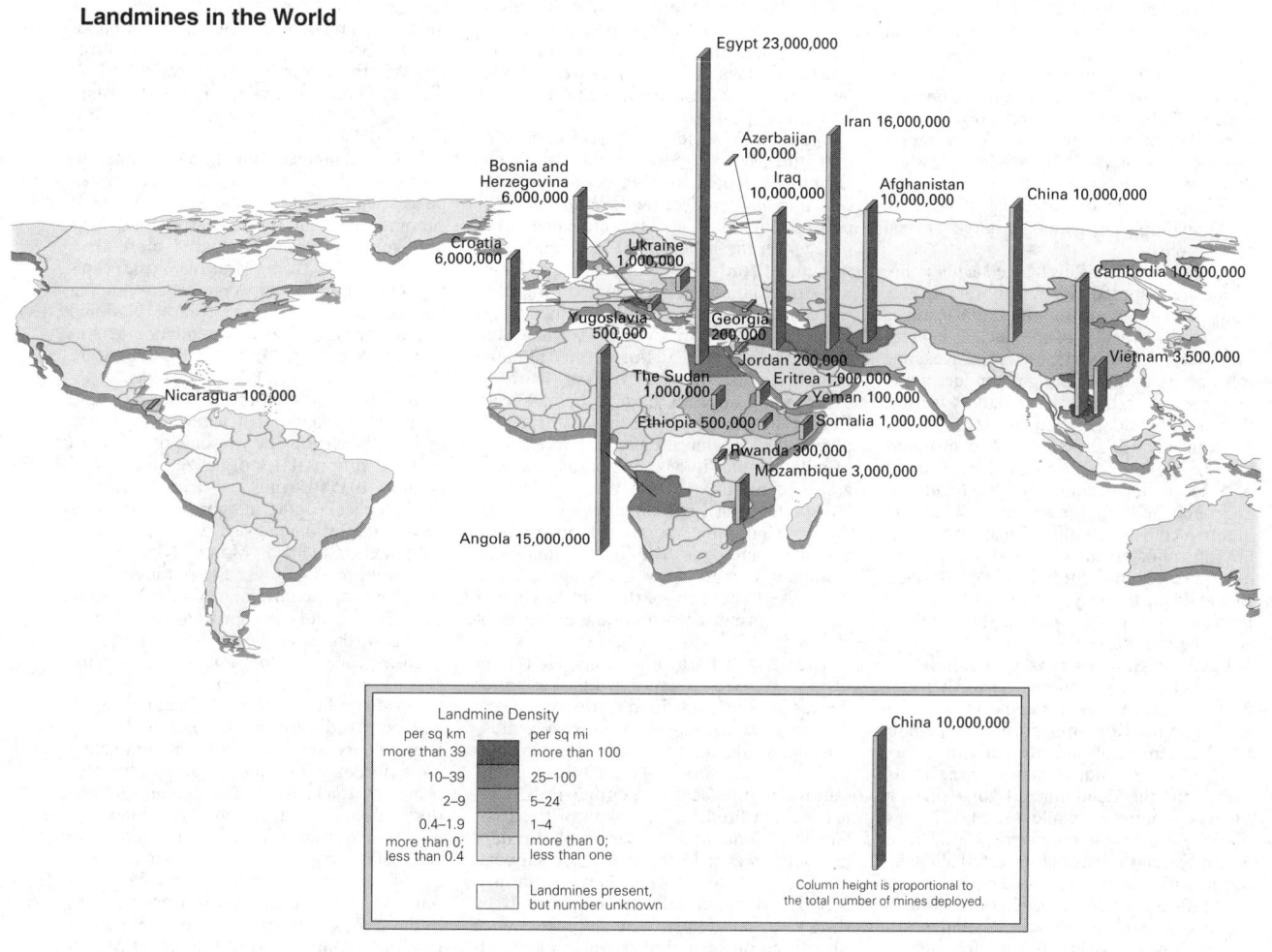

Egypt 23,000,000
Iran 16,000,000
Azerbaijan 100,000
Iraq 10,000,000
Afghanistan 10,000,000
China 10,000,000
Bosnia and Herzegovina 6,000,000
Croatia 6,000,000
Ukraine 1,000,000
Cambodia 10,000,000
Yugoslavia 500,000
Georgia 200,000
Jordan 200,000
Vietnam 3,500,000
The Sudan 1,000,000
Eritrea 1,000,000
Yemen 100,000
Nicaragua 100,000
Ethiopia 500,000
Somalia 1,000,000
Rwanda 300,000
Mozambique 3,000,000
Angola 15,000,000

Landmine Density

per sq km	per sq mi
more than 39	more than 100
10–39	25–100
2–9	5–24
0.4–1.9	1–4
more than 0; less than 0.4	more than 0; less than one

Landmines present, but number unknown

China 10,000,000

Column height is proportional to the total number of mines deployed.

sonnel mines. That same year South Africa announced a permanent ban on the export of antipersonnel mines, while France established a moratorium on their production. In April 1996 Germany renounced the use of antipersonnel mines by its armed forces and said that it planned to destroy the remaining mines of that kind. In September Italy, one of the largest producers of land mines, pledged to renounce the production and export of these weapons and thus became the 33rd nation with a moratorium on the export of antipersonnel mines.

In his 1994 UN General Assembly address, U.S. Pres. Bill Clinton called for the eventual elimination of antipersonnel land mines, an appeal he repeated at the UN in September 1996. In March 1996 the U.S. announced a unilateral ban on the use of "dumb" antipersonnel mines and pledged to destroy its stockpile of such weapons by the end of 1999. It made a significant exception to this new policy, however; it would not apply in Korea, where such "dumb" mines would be used to "defend the United States and its allies from armed aggression across the Korean Demilitarized Zone." Many military authorities questioned the military utility of mines, but this U.S. policy strongly implied otherwise. Other countries saw a useful role for these weapons. Both China and Finland advocated "reasonable limits" rather than an outright ban and pointed to the defensive nature of mines along a border. Chile employed mines to combat drug merchants crossing the mountains.

Whatever the prospects are for restricting or banning the manufacture and use of land mines, the herculean task of removing the millions of mines already in place remains. It took Germany three years and $175 million to clear the last 1,100 mines along the old border between the former East and West Germanys, a remnant of the more than 1.5 million mines once planted there. Furthermore, most of the countries plagued by mines are at the other end of the economic and technological spectrum from Germany, and they need international help. The UN and its agencies are operating demining programs in Afghanistan, Angola, Bosnia and Herzegovina, Cambodia, Croatia, El Salvador, Mozambique, Nicaragua, and Somalia. The Organization of American States is seeking to clear all land mines from Central America by 2000 (there are an estimated 170,000 mines in Nicaragua, Honduras, Guatemala, and Costa Rica) and in May announced an initiative that could lead to the world's first land-mine-free zone.

New technologies are being sought to make demining quicker and safer. Sniffer dogs are being used by some countries to detect the vapours given off by the mines' explosives. Lasers, infrared sensors, and ground-penetrating radars are also being used to locate mines. Superman has even been called in to help the effort in Bosnia; in a comic book in Serbo-Croatian, distributed by the U.S. government, the superhero teaches children about the dangers of land mines.

(continued from page 273)

In a major offensive in April, Sri Lankan armed forces took control of the entire northern Jaffna peninsula, the heartland of the Liberation Tigers of Tamil Eelam separatists. Three months later, however, the Tamil Tigers dealt the Sri Lankan army its worst defeat of the 13-year-old war when they overran a government base on the mainland, killing or capturing more than 1,000 soldiers and gaining a large arsenal of weapons.

Pakistan and India exchanged artillery fire along the disputed Kashmir border in late January. That same month India tested a longer-range version of the nuclear-capable Prithvi surface-to-surface missile. Reacting to rumours that India might conduct a second nuclear test, Pakistani leaders warned that they would respond in kind. Despite concerns about Pakistan's nuclear program, the U.S. government approved the transfer of $368 million in military equipment that had been held up for six years. The shipments included three P-3C maritime patrol aircraft, antiship missiles, and artillery but not the 28 F-16 fighters Pakistan had paid for. Instead, the U.S. government sought a foreign buyer for the jets so that Pakistan could be reimbursed.

East and Southeast Asia, Oceania. Several military provocations by North Korea against South Korea created a tense atmosphere on the Korean peninsula throughout the year. In April and May heavily armed North Korean soldiers staged three incursions into the demilitarized zone dividing the two countries, while on May 22 five North Korean gunboats were chased from South Korean territorial waters. That same day a North Korean air force pilot defected to South Korea in his MiG-19 fighter. At a press conference he warned that North Korea was preparing for an invasion of the South. In the most serious incident, a North Korean minisubmarine was found beached on South Korea's eastern coast in September. Of the estimated 26 North Koreans who came ashore from the submarine, 1 was captured, 13 were killed by South Korean troops, and 11 others were found dead in what seemed to be a case of murder-suicide. The episode prompted South Korean Pres. Kim Young Sam to replace his defense minister and fire two army commanders.

Early in the year China mobilized as many as 400,000 troops along its eastern coast in what was seen as an attempt to intimidate Taiwan during its presidential election campaign. In March China carried out a series of ballistic missile tests just off the coast of Taiwan, which led President Clinton to order a second carrier battle group to the region. In response, China canceled a planned visit to Washington by its defense minister. Chinese-U.S. relations were also strained by allegations that China had supplied missile technology to Pakistan.

Anti-American feelings remained high in Japan after the conviction in March of three U.S. servicemen for the rape of an Okinawan girl in 1995. The U.S. government agreed to return some of the land it used for bases on the island. President Clinton and Japanese Prime Minister Ryutaro Hashimoto issued a joint declaration on security in April that pledged to keep 100,000 U.S. troops in the Asia-Pacific region and not cut U.S. forces in Japan.

Caribbean and Latin America. In February Cuban jets shot down two small civilian aircraft from the U.S. over international waters off Havana. The planes were piloted by members of a group opposed to Cuban Pres. Fidel Castro.

Faced with widespread police corruption, the Mexican government transferred an unprecedented number of military officers into law enforcement. While the Zapatista rebels in Chiapas were negotiating peace with the government, a second rebel movement, the leftist Popular Revolutionary Army, launched coordinated attacks in three states in August. Leftist rebels were also active in Colombia, where the Revolutionary Armed Forces of Colombia in late August won its greatest victory in overrunning an army base at Las Delicias. Earlier in the year, the government had placed five provinces under a limited form of military rule. In March Colombia signed a five-year military cooperation pact with Russia, the first Latin-American country to do so. That same month the government of Guatemala and the rebel Guatemala National Revolutionary Unity agreed to a cease-fire. The two parties in December signed a formal accord ending 36 years of civil war.

The head of Paraguay's army, Gen. Lino Oviedo, refused to step down in April after he was fired by Pres. Juan Carlos Wasmosy. The impasse was broken when Wasmosy said he would name Oviedo defense minister, a pledge he broke following public outrage at the deal. Argentine Pres. Carlos Menem fired the chairman of the Joint Chiefs of Staff and the heads of the navy and air force in October for not supporting his military reforms. Peruvian armed forces had apparently been infiltrated by drug smugglers, as cocaine shipments were uncovered on several naval vessels and military aircraft. Peru and Ecuador agreed to begin direct talks to resolve their longstanding border dispute, which had led to armed clashes in 1995. Nicaragua built up its naval presence in the Caribbean as a result of territorial disputes with Colombia and Honduras.

The U.S. was embarrassed by revelations that in the 1980s training manuals at the School of the Americas in Ft. Benning, Georgia, a military school for Latin-American officers, had included suggestions that torture and other human rights violations were acceptable tactics in counterinsurgency operations.

Africa South of the Sahara. Ethnic animosity between the Tutsi and Hutu continued to spark violence in Burundi, Rwanda, and Zaire and threatened to degenerate into a three-way regional war. The Tutsi-controlled army in Burundi was engaged in a virtual civil war with the Hutu majority population before seizing control of the government in July. In Zaire government soldiers attacked camps housing refugees from Rwanda, and there were several border clashes between the two countries. Rwandan army units crossed into Zaire to aid Tutsi rebels in seizing the cities of Bukavu and Goma. A Canadian-led international military force was sent to eastern Zaire in November to ensure the safety of the estimated 750,000 refugees there. Major contributions to the force were made by the U.S., Great Britain, and France. The military under Gen. Ibrahim Baré Mainassara (*see* BIOGRAPHIES) also seized power in Niger, and it took the intervention of 1,700 French troops to put down an army revolt in the Central African Republic. Soldiers in Guinea mutinied in early February over pay, shelling and destroying the presidential palace.

Liberia remained in a state of virtual anarchy, with the 8,600-strong West African peacekeeping force unable to halt the long-running civil war. During April and May U.S. military forces evacuated more than 2,300 persons from Monrovia, the capital. The cease-fire in Angola between the government and the opposition National Union for the Total Independence of Angola movement held, but both sides were slow in implementing the 1994 peace accord. The UN announced that it would keep to its schedule of withdrawing some of its 7,000 troops by the end of the year. A U.S. proposal to organize, train, and equip a 10,000-strong all-African force for future peacekeeping missions on the continent made little headway.

In February and March Nigeria and Cameroon clashed over the potentially oil-rich Bakassi peninsula, claimed by both. The dispute between Eritrea and Yemen over two islands in the Red Sea moved toward a peaceful resolution. In late August Eritrea announced it would withdraw its troops from Lesser Hamish Island, which it had occupied early in the month. In May Ethiopia accused The Sudan of conducting cross-border operations in preparation for a major attack, while The Sudan charged that Ethiopian artillery fire in support of rebels in southern Sudan had killed more than 800 people. In September Uganda threatened to retaliate against what it reported was an attack on an army barracks in the northern town of Moyo by Sudanese jets. Each country accused the other of harbouring and aiding rebel groups.

With the UN forces gone from Somalia, the various factions resumed their internecine fighting. A brief cease-fire in Mogadishu followed the August 1 death of faction leader Muhamad Farah Aydid. (*See* OBITUARIES.) He was succeeded by his son, Hussein, who had served with the U.S. Marine Corps in Somalia. In October Kenya brokered a short-lived cease-fire agreement between the leaders of the three main factions.

South Africa continued to form its new, integrated South African National Defense Force. Budgetary constraints forced the government in March to cancel many planned major weapons acquisition programs. Parliament in May adopted a new defense policy that banned discrimination against women and gays in the armed forces. In October Gen. Magnus Malan, a former South African defense minister, was acquitted of murder and conspiracy charges in connection with a 1987 massacre of 13 African National Congress supporters.

New Technology. A scaled-down prototype of the U.S. X-36 tailless jet fighter was unveiled in February. The aircraft used split ailerons to provide directional control. In a joint U.S.-Israeli test, a ground-based laser downed an unguided rocket of the type typically used in modern multiple-launch rocket systems.

(DOUGLAS L. CLARKE)

This article updates the *Macropædia* article The Technology of WAR.

C. MAC BURNIE

In Lowell Liebermann's *The Picture of Dorian Gray,* the title character, sung by tenor Jeffrey Lentz, kneels beside his portrait. Written in a neo-Romantic style with a libretto drawn from Oscar Wilde's novel, the work had its premiere at the Opéra de Monte-Carlo in May.

Performing Arts

MUSIC

Classical. Amid the usual parade of festivals, celebrations, premieres, and commemorations, the world of classical music in 1996 endured forces of change, tribulation, and even crisis, plagued by sobering new economic realities and labour difficulties that were becoming increasingly common in an era of reduced public and private support for the arts. Performers and executives alike were held to stringent new standards of economic accountability, forced to reevaluate their positions and to offer unprecedented justifications for the financial support they had traditionally received.

In the U.S. the trend toward increased privatization and decentralization of arts funding continued, with budgets of government agencies such as the National Endowment for the Arts suffering cuts by as much as 40%. Two of the so-called Big Five U.S. orchestras, those in Philadelphia and Cleveland, Ohio, suffered contract disputes between musicians and management, and

performances were canceled. Construction of a new concert hall for the Los Angeles Philharmonic had to be suspended when $150 million in funding was suddenly withdrawn. Even Europe, traditionally a model of government arts sponsorship, was not immune from the new austerity. Some funding for musical organizations in Great Britain was restored only after a wave of indignant protests; prominent organizations, including the Royal Opera House, found themselves in serious financial trouble. Members of the London Philharmonic waived their fees for one concert, using the money instead to support protest efforts against budget cutbacks. The venerable D'Oyly Carte Opera Company was forced by budget problems to postpone its autumn tour. In Paris the bicentennial celebration of the Conservatoire was tainted by threatened reductions in government support, and a huge tax hike in Germany created new economic burdens on foreign musicians, making it harder for German groups to attract prominent soloists and conductors.

Of course, there were causes for celebration that stood above the fray. Birthday anniversaries were marked by composer Gian Carlo Menotti (85), composer Henri

Dutilleux (80), violinist-conductor Yehudi Menuhin (80), and composer Hans Werner Henze (70). While the Edinburgh Festival enjoyed its 50th year, a festival of new music was born in Israel, and in New York City the first Lincoln Center Festival offered an eclectic array of premieres, rarities, and music in and out of the mainstream. There were also important discoveries in 1996: a major collection of Handel letters was revealed in England; a trove of classic Italian violins, including some crafted by Amati and Guadagnini, was unveiled, also in England; and a well-preserved, historically significant collection of instruments and music was brought out from its hiding place in a Welsh castle.

The phenomenon of the "Three Tenors" felt no economic pain; José Carreras, Plácido Domingo, and Luciano Pavarotti played to rock-concert-like crowds in arenas in Tokyo, London, Munich, Ger., Vancouver, B.C., Vienna, and New York City. Tours with somewhat lower profiles were undertaken by the Pittsburgh (Pa.) Symphony, celebrating its 100th year with concerts in Europe and Israel; by the Czech Philharmonic, touring England to celebrate its 100th anniversary; and by the Cleveland Orchestra, also touring major concert halls in Europe. Important new orchestral positions were announced for Herbert Blomstedt, named to succeed Kurt Masur as the music director of the Leipzig (Ger.) Gewandhaus Orchestra in 1998, and for Charles Mackerras, who agreed to lead the Czech Philharmonic for three years as its principal guest conductor, temporarily filling a post left vacant when Gerd Albrecht resigned amid claims of political persecution. David Zinman was named to replace Lawrence Foster as music director of the Aspen (Colo.) Music Festival. The news from Vienna was the end of a tradition: Agnes Grossman became the first woman to lead the Vienna Boys Choir. Many hoped that Grossman's appointment would inspire Vienna's premiere orchestra to end the long-lived exclusionary trend of its own, but the Vienna Philharmonic remained a solitary male bastion.

George Walker became the first African-American to be awarded the Pulitzer Prize in music (Scott Joplin was cited posthumously in 1976), for his *Lilacs.* The Grawemeyer Award for Music Composition was given to Ivan Tcherepnin, son of Alexander Tcherepnin, for his *Double Concerto for Violin, Cello, and Orchestra.* Musicians who died in 1996 included composers Jacob Druckman, Gottfried von Einem, Morton Gould, Otto Luening, and Toru Takemitsu; conductors Sergiu Celibidache, Rafael Kubelik, and Henry Lewis; and pianist David Tudor. (*See* OBITUARIES.) Composers Miriam Gideon, Joonas Kokkonen, Vaclav Nelhybel, and Louise Talma, conductors Spiros Argiris and Enrique Jorda, pianists Rebecca LaBrecque and Peter Stadlen, musicologists Joseph Braunstein and Judith Kaplan Eisenstein, and critic Howard Taubman also died during the year.

In the world of opera in 1996, artists and audiences welcomed plans for newly renovated performing spaces in several locales. Officials in Venice announced their ambitions to rebuild the historic opera house La Fenice after a fire, though work was not set to begin until the cause of the tragedy had been fully investigated. The San Francisco Opera performed in other venues while that city's War Memorial Opera House underwent a full-scale renovation and earthquake proofing. In Paris the Palais Garnier reopened after a yearlong restoration.

A number of new operas were premiered in 1996. Surely the oddest, and one that stretched conventional artistic and categorical boundaries, was Tod Machover's *Brain Opera,* a computer-based interactive experience performed at the Lincoln Center Festival and also accessible on the Internet. Another was Luciano Berio's *Outis,* premiered at La Scala in Milan, which cast an eclectic and decidedly personal perspective on modern society, borrowing themes from Homer's *Odyssey.* Hans-Jürgen von Bose found surprisingly effective operatic possibilities in Kurt Vonnegut's *Slaughterhouse Five* (Munich Opera Festival), using stylistic variety to help depict the main character's temporal dislocations. Notable literary inspirations were also evident in the new operas *Emmeline,* which was Tobias Picker's treatment of the Oedipal myth as told in the Judith Rossner novel of the same name (Santa Fe, N.M.), in John Metcalf and Mark Morris's *Kafka's Chimp,* inspired by Franz Kafka's *A Report to an Academy* (Banff, Alta.), and in Lowell Liebermann's *The Picture of Dorian Gray* (Opéra de Monte-Carlo), from the Oscar Wilde novel. Other noteworthy operatic premieres included Georges Aperghis's *De la nature de la gravité,* sung in Latin, French, and an invented language (Banff), Michael Torke's *King of Hearts,* a new operatic version of a work originally composed as a radio opera for the BBC (Aspen, Colo.), Marcel Landowski's *Galina,* inspired by the autobiography of the Russian soprano Galina Vishnevskaya (Opéra de Lyon, Fr.), Paul Stuart's *Kill Bear Comes Home,* based on

Michael Tilson Thomas turns to lead the audience in the national anthem at the opening of the 1996–97 season of the San Francisco Symphony. Tilson Thomas, in his second season with the orchestra, took it on a U.S. tour and led it in well-received recordings.

Der Ring des Nibelungen

As the climax to its 41st season, in March 1996 the Lyric Opera of Chicago presented its first-ever production of Richard Wagner's four-part music drama *Der Ring des Nibelungen.* Staging *The Ring* cycle, with a total performance time of more than 15 hours, is a monumental task and one that tests the mettle of any opera company. But the sheer power and overwhelming popularity of *The Ring* make it an essential part of any opera repertory. The sold-out Lyric performances, which drew an audience from throughout the U.S. and from a number of other countries, received kudos from both opera lovers and critics.

The Lyric's *Ring* cycle actually began in the 1992–93 season with the staging of the first of the works, *Das Rheingold,* which was followed, one per year, by *Die Walküre, Siegfried,* and *Götterdämmerung.* After the close of the regular 1995–96 season, the company then gave three performances of the complete cycle in three consecutive weeks. The Lyric production, which was directed by August Everding, used clean, stylized but highly expressive sets that featured, among other things, neon lighting in

various shapes and colours. The swimming Rhinemaidens were represented by jumpers on bungee cords, the galloping Valkyrie by acrobats on trampolines, and the giants by huge robotlike figures. Overall, the production focused on the mythic elements in Wagner's drama of gods, dwarfs, giants, and humans—of heroes and villains engaged in struggles for wealth and power and motivated by greed and love.

Six months later, in September, the Royal Opera presented a controversial new *Ring* at Covent Garden in London that eschewed magic and fantasy in favour of the 20th-century Theatre of the Absurd. Indeed, director Richard Jones said, "There is a duty not to present the Ring in a romantic context, so that it can be honoured as the warning it is." The Royal Opera offered the Rhinemaidens in rubbery body suits that made them appear plumply, grotesquely naked and introduced automobiles, a cluttered urban landscape, and a bearded goddess Fricka onstage.

Der Ring des Nibelungen was an enormous challenge from its inception. Wagner laboured on the tetralogy for more than 25 years, starting in 1848 when he

began the verse on which he based the librettos for his epic story derived from Germanic myth. The music for *Götterdämmerung* was finished in 1874, and the complete cycle was mounted for the first time two years later at the composer's purpose-built theatre in Bayreuth, Ger. The first U.S. production was in 1889 at New York City's Metropolitan Opera (the Met). By the 1990s most of the world's major opera companies had accepted *The Ring* as the ultimate test of commitment and endurance. Many Wagnerian fans experienced the tetralogy dozens of times with almost cultlike devotion: some were known to travel thousands of kilometres to see a new production.

In more than a century of *Ring* performances, the varied interpretations included classical, modern dress, Freudian, neofascist, Marxist, and even science fiction. In the 1990s they ranged from the relatively traditional naturalism of the Met (in a production first staged in 1988–89 and scheduled to be revived in 1996–97) to the stark, witty modernism of the Lyric to the philosophically bleak avant-garde reinterpretation at Covent Garden.   (ROBERT RAUCH)

a Native American legend (Opera Theatre of Rochester, N.Y.), Harold Blumenfeld's *Seasons in Hell* (University of Cincinnati [Ohio] College–Conservatory of Music), James MacMillan's *Inés de Castro* (Scottish Opera, at the Edinburgh Festival), and Peter Maxwell Davies's *The Doctor of Myddfai* (Welsh National Opera).

The year in opera also included important new productions and discoveries. The Dresden (Ger.) Festival featured the first performance of Viktor Ullmann's *Der zerbrochene Krug,* a musical comedy that was the last work he completed before his death in the Theresienstadt (Terezín) concentration camp in 1944. In New York City the American Chamber Opera presented the stage premiere of *The Garden of Mystery,* an opera written by Charles Wakefield Cadman in 1922 and loosely based on "Rappaccini's Daughter," one of Nathaniel Hawthorne's *Twice-Told Tales.* The Lyric Opera of Chicago staged its first complete Ring Cycle. (*See* Sidebar.) At England's Glyndebourne Festival, Peter Sellars presented a critically acclaimed staging of *Theodora,* one of Handel's last oratorios.

Orchestras continued to program new works in 1996, usually as brief side trips from tours through the musical museums of standards and warhorses. One premiere was actually a rediscovery; Michael Tilson Thomas led a performance of Henry Cowell's 1919 ballet *Atlantis* at the Festival of American Music in San Francisco. Harrison Birtwistle unveiled his *Slow Frieze* (London Sinfonietta), Hans Werner Henze his *Three Pieces for Orchestra* (BBC Philharmonic), and Peter Maxwell Davies his Symphony No. 6 (Royal Philharmonic). New concertos were premiered by William Bolcom (for piano left hand, Baltimore [Md.] Symphony), Philip Glass (saxophone quartet, Royal Philharmonic), Lorin Maazel (cello, Pittsburgh Symphony), James MacMillan (cello, London Symphony), and David Stock (violin, Pittsburgh Symphony). Also premiered were concertos for orchestra by Robin Holloway (London Symphony) and Gerard Schurmann (Pittsburgh Symphony), Ellen Taaffe Zwilich's Triple Concerto (Minnesota Orchestra), David Diamond's Concerto for String Quartet (Juilliard Orchestra), John Tavener's *Feast of Feasts* (Royal Kirov Philharmonic/Russian State Academic Choir), Giya Kancheli's *Trauerfarbenes Land* (Chicago Symphony), Christopher Rouse's *Envoi* (Atlanta [Ga.] Symphony), and Kaija Saariaho's *Château de l'âme* (Philharmonia Orchestra, at the Salzburg Festival [Austria]). Important new works for smaller ensembles included Milton Babbitt's Clarinet Quintet, Lee Hoiby's *Creatures of the Rain Forest,* and Lee Hyla's *Trans.*

The recording industry was heartened by an important agreement between Bridge Records and the U.S. Library of Congress to release recordings from the Library Music Division's concert archive. The series would feature never-before-released recordings from more than 60 years of concerts by artists such as Rudolf Serkin, Claudio Arrau, Leontyne Price, Jan DeGaetani, and the Budapest and Juilliard string quartets. Meanwhile, the first releases began to appear from Revelation, a new Russian label drawing from the archives of the Russian state television and radio company Gostelradio. Also in 1996, a new compact disc

(CD) by guitarist Eliot Fisk presented the first performances of previously unheard works of Andrés Segovia (MusicMasters). In honour of Yehudi Menuhin's 80th birthday, there were new releases of some of the violinist's performances from the 1920s and '30s (Biddulph) and a set of recordings of Menuhin conducting all of the Beethoven symphonies (IMG/Carlton). Violinist Gyorgy Pauk celebrated his 60th birthday with a new disc of Bela Bartok sonatas (Naxos). The revival of zarzuela, the Spanish equivalent of operetta, was heralded by a series of new recordings (Auvidis Valois) celebrating that genre. To commemorate the poet Robert Burns on the bicentennial of his death, a new CD brought together 14 settings of Burns's poetry that an Edinburgh publisher had commissioned by great composers of his day, including Haydn and Beethoven (BE Records, Dundee, Scot.). A CD of Pierre Boulez and the Cleveland Orchestra performing music of Claude Debussy (Deutsche Grammophon) was honoured with Grammy awards for best classical album and best orchestral performance. The *Gramophone* magazine Record of the Year was Hyperion's recording of concertos by Emil von Sauer and Xaver Scharwenka, performed by pianist Stephan Hough and the City of Birmingham (Eng.) Symphony Orchestra, conducted by Lawrence Foster.

Among the year's noteworthy new books were Paul Roberts's *Images: The Piano Music of Claude Debussy* and a collection of correspondence between Kurt Weill and Lotte Lenya entitled *Speak Low (When You Speak Love).* Richard Taruskin came out with books reflecting two of his passions: a collection of essays on musical performance and authenticity entitled *Text and Act: Essays on Music and Performance* and a monumental two-volume study of Igor Stravinsky and his heritage, *Stravinsky and the Russian Traditions.* Publishers responded to a surge of interest in the life and music of the U.S. composer Charles Ives, manifested in a proliferation of performances, festivals, and recordings, by releasing four new books on the subject, most notably Jan Swafford's *Charles Ives: A Life with Music,* the first true biography of the composer. Perhaps the most timely, and sobering, new book was Norman Lebrecht's *When the Music Stops . . . : Managers, Maestros and the Corporate Murder of Classical Music.*

(PHILIP LAMBERT)

Jazz. In another year when no trends dominated in jazz, the remarkable reissue in 1996 of *Lennie Tristano–Warne Marsh* (Blue Note) spotlighted one of the sources of the cool jazz sensibility—pianist Tristano's 1948–49 sextet, including two of his notable students, saxophonists Marsh and Lee Konitz. Tristano's ideals included pure melody and total spontaneity in improvising, achieved with pure, uninflected instrumental sounds. While these players' refinement of emotion and sound had long been unfashionable, it continued to result in fine jazz in 1996. Altoist Konitz's *Rhapsody II* (Evidence) was notable for the leader's melodic creativity, gentle humour, and urge for adventure that led him from unaccompanied swing duets (with Gerry Mulligan) to experiments in free jazz. A happy further blossoming of the Tristano legacy was the work of the Australian Bernie McGann, an alto saxophonist who advanced the Marsh

style, at times to harmonically liberated extremes, in a rare visit to North America (at the Vancouver [B.C.] Jazz Festival) and on the album *McGann* (Rufus and Reckless). A problematic extension of Konitz was the alto playing of Argentine-born Guillermo Gregorio amid his post-Webern settings on *Approximately* (hatART).

Some questioned whether this was jazz. The same question could also be raised about *Et on ne parle pas du temps* (FMP) by clarinetist Louis Sclavis and cellist Ernst Reijseger, *Tao-Njia* (Tzadik) by trumpetercomposer Wadada Leo Smith, or the virtuoso playing of bassist Joëlle Léandre's Canvas Trio, with accordionist-clarinetist Rüdiger Carl and expressive violinist Carlos Zingaro. The antecedents for their music were clearly in the classical tradition, yet much of their music was improvised, with a freedom of form and feeling and a recurring, irreverent wit characteristic of jazz. Moreover, these musicians attracted the largely young audience that attended underground jazz events. Several of them were Europeans whose work was not widely known in the United States, partly because it was U.S. policy to subject concert promoters to a maze of red tape should they attempt to import the musicians.

Canada had no such restrictions, with the result that the annual festivals in Victoriaville, Que., and in Vancouver were once again among the world's major venues for new music in 1996. In eight cities, from Montreal to Victoria, B.C., jazz festivals lasting a week or more were held across Canada between June 21 and July 7, with the timing easing the problems of travel arrangements and allowing some bands to appear at several festivals. In the U.S. the JVC Jazz Festival in New York City had serious competition across town. The What Is Jazz? Festival, held in Manhattan and Brooklyn, featured 200 concerts by the kind of mainstream musicians and young lions who played the JVC festival, sharing stages with free jazz artists who had seldom or never played the JVC event. The festival was initiated by the Knitting Factory nightclub, the noted avant-garde venue that also booked stages at three European festivals, operated a record company, and planned to present live jazz on the Internet.

A possible sign of an improved U.S. economy was the jazz museum projects that were announced in 1996. Since 1952 the Down Beat Jazz Hall of Fame had existed only on paper, with musicians chosen in annual readers and critics polls in *Down Beat* magazine. The hall of fame was to become incarnate in 1998 as part of an entertainment complex next to Universal Studios Florida in Orlando. In New York City the Louis Armstrong archives were to be housed in a museum in the great trumpeter's three-story former home in Corona, Queens. In Chicago the Jazz Unites organization planned to build a jazz museum, while the Blues Heaven Foundation, headed by the widow of blues songwriter Willie Dixon, planned to house a blues museum in the former Chess Records studios, the source of many valuable blues and jazz recordings. A group of jazz notables including alto saxophonist Jackie McLean, composer Gunther Schuller, and author Albert Murray constituted the board of directors of a planned jazz museum in Kansas City, Mo. Meanwhile, in Robinsonville, Miss., the

Jazz pianist Randy Weston was influenced by Thelonious Monk and Duke Ellington, as well as by a time spent living in Africa. Weston's *Saga* was one of a number of new jazz recordings that received critical acclaim during the year.

Horseshoe Casino and Hotel, which had brought a measure of prosperity to Tunica county, until recently one of the most impoverished counties in the U.S., announced a $60 million expansion that would include a blues museum and hall of fame.

A major disappointment for filmgoers and music lovers alike was Robert Altman's *Kansas City,* in which the much-vaunted jazz proved to be bits and pieces played over a rhythm section that had difficulty swinging in two-beat metre. On the other hand, there were fine recordings, ranging from the African-influenced concepts of pianist Randy Weston (*see* BIOGRAPHIES) on *Saga* (Verve) to the hard bop and modal musings of pianist Mal Waldron on *My Dear Family* (Evidence) and the unclassifiable lyric trumpet of Tom Harrell (*see* BIOGRAPHIES) on *Labyrinth* (RCA Victor). *Sonny Rollins + 3* (Milestone) was one of the few of the great tenor saxophonist's many post-1960s albums to capture his imagination and authority. Alto saxophone great Ornette Coleman abandoned his unique jazz-rock idiom to invent two *Sound Museum* CDs, *Three Women* and *Hidden Man* (Harmolodic/Verve), with a fiery jazz quartet; the CDs had alternate versions of 13 Coleman songs.

The Galaxy label, while releasing a series of Art Pepper rediscoveries, presented the altoist with pianist Duke Jordan in the exceptional *In Copenhagen 1981.* Delmark Records climaxed a highly active year by reissuing *Sound* by the Roscoe Mitchell Sextet, a landmark in the evolution of free jazz. A major reissue in boxed sets was *The Complete Columbia Studio Recordings* of Miles Davis and Gil Evans (6 CDs from Columbia; 11 LPs from Mosaic). The year's largest reissue box had 20 Frank Sinatra CDs from 1960–88, *The Complete Reprise Studio Recordings,* by the label that he founded. Sue Mingus, angry at bootleg reissues of the music of her late husband, Charles Mingus, formed her own Revenge recordings label to release the music legally.

Nearly 30 years after the death of Billy Strayhorn, David Hadju's biography *Lush Life* shed new light on the composer's life

and prolific career. *Chris McGregor and the Brotherhood of Breath* by his widow, Maxine McGregor, was a biography of the South African bandleader. As it was published, the Ogun label issued *The Blue Notes Legacy* by the outlawed pioneering sextet from a 1964 concert in Durban and reissued the band's successor in exile, *Chris McGregor's Brotherhood of Breath Live at Willisau,* from 1973. Other notable books included *Stan Getz: A Life in Jazz* by Donald L. Maggin and *Hot Jazz & Jazz Dance* by critic-historian Roger Pryor Dodge. The year's deaths included singer Ella Fitzgerald, saxophonist Gerry Mulligan, bluesman Brownie McGhee, and longtime Voice of America jazz disc jockey Willis Conover. (*See* OBITUARIES.) Bandleader Mercer Ellington, drummer Alan Dawson, clarinetist Herb Hall, and saxophonist Eddie Harris also died during the year.   (JOHN LITWEILER)

Popular. In Great Britain popular music in 1996 was dominated by Oasis, a five-piece guitar band from Manchester that became a national obsession, acquiring a following that rivaled even that enjoyed by their own heroes, the Beatles, in the 1960s. In August 1996 the group performed in front of a quarter of a million fans at Knebworth, outside London—the largest paying British audience for a single band in the history of British pop music. Five percent of the nation's population applied for tickets.

The songs of Oasis, a mixture of old-fashioned 1960s-influenced melodies and 1990s anguish and aggression, appealed to a wide age group, and even the most conservative and serious newspapers gave them extensive coverage. In return, Oasis provided the press with a news story almost every day throughout the summer, involving, for the most part, the feuding between the band's songwriter, Noel Gallagher, and his younger brother, singer Liam. Soon after the Knebworth triumph, Liam failed to appear onstage for an important concert to be recorded by the television music channel MTV, choosing instead to watch the show from the audience. He then failed to join the rest of the band for the opening dates of a U.S. tour, and when he did finally

arrive in the U.S., he caused controversy with his antics at the MTV video awards. A week later, the tour was abandoned, this time because Noel decided that he had had enough. He flew back to Britain, leaving fans and press alike speculating wildly as to the band's future. Their record company insisted that this was not the end—Oasis was still together, though the group wouldn't be touring "in the foreseeable future." U.S. fans—who had never been as impressed as their British counterparts—were left wondering what all the fuss had been about.

The other celebrities of the continuing "Britpop" revival were the Sheffield band Pulp, which won the year's Mercury Music Prize for its album *Different Class.* Singer and songwriter Jarvis Cocker succeeded with witty, self-deprecating, bravely honest songs that dealt, for the most part, with sex and the pains of growing up. On a more experimental level, the Bristol-based producer and performer Tricky was greeted as "the black David Bowie" (and praised by Bowie himself) for his "trip hop" style, mixing snatches of hip-hop, blues, and anything else that took his fancy into drifting, unpredictable songs. Not one to follow conventional pop strategies, he followed up the much-praised *Maxinquaye* with *Nearly God,* an atmospheric set that he recorded in just two weeks, with guest vocalists ranging from Terry Hall to the quirky Icelandic star Björk.

It was a good year too for Norma Waterson, best known for her interpretation of traditional songs, first as a member of the Watersons and then in Waterson: Carthy. At the age of 57 the veteran folksinger finally got around to recording her first-ever solo album, and she was runner-up for the Mercury Prize for her direct, personal treatment of songs by the likes of Jerry Garcia, Elvis Costello, and Richard Thompson. The backing band included her husband, the guitarist Martin Carthy, and their daughter, singer and fiddle player Eliza Carthy, who emerged as the most promising young folk newcomer of the year with her album *Heat Light & Sound.*

Among the more established performers, Mark Knopfler finally embarked on a full-scale solo career away from the band Dire Straits. His album *Golden Heart,* which made use of musicians from Ireland, Louisiana, and Nashville, Tenn., showed his continued interest in anything from traditional Celtic styles to Cajun and country. From the 1960s era Pete Townshend of The Who found himself back in fashion, with highly successful stage productions of his rock opera *Tommy* running in New York City and London. He also revived another such opera, *Quadrophenia,* which received its first-ever live performance 23 years after being released as a record. The Who were reunited for the event, a fund-raising concert in a London park for a trust set up by Prince Charles to help young people.

British royalty, including Queen Elizabeth II, were also present at another exceptional London pop concert, held to celebrate a visit by Pres. Nelson Mandela of South Africa. British performers included Phil Collins, who was backed for the first time by his new jazz-influenced big band, but the stars of the evening were South African musicians, including veterans Ladysmith Black Mambazo and Hugh Masekela and newcomers Bayete, who skillfully mixed town-

The British band Oasis performs at one of its sold-out concerts. Oasis, which combined 1990s sentiments with 1960s Beatle-like melodies, continued to be one of the Great Britain's most popular groups, but their U.S. tour was cut short when members quarreled among themselves.

Fugees included Haitian-born guitarist and rapper Wyclef Jean; his cousin Prakazrel Michel, whose parents had also emigrated from Haiti to the U.S.; and singer and rapper Lauryn Hill, who had grown up in East Orange, N.J., and met her partners in high school. The group joined Busta Rhymes, A Tribe Called Quest, Cypress Hill, Spearhead, and Ziggy Marley on the Smokin' Grooves Tour, one of the year's most successful concert draws.

Rock acts Metallica, Soundgarden, the Ramones, Rancid, Screaming Trees, and Psychotica made up the sixth Lollapalooza festival of rock and alternative music, while acts popular in the 1970s such as Kiss, REO Speedwagon, Styx, the Sex Pistols, the Isley Brothers, and George Clinton's P-Funk All-Stars also mounted tours. Cable channel VH1 fueled the nostalgia for older acts by broadcasting vintage TV programs, movies, and archival concert footage from the 1970s. David Bowie, radio personality Tom Donahue, Jefferson Airplane, Little Willie John, Gladys Knight and the Pips, Pink Floyd, Pete Seeger, the Shirelles, and the Velvet Underground were enshrined in the Rock and Roll Hall of Fame.

Heroin use continued to be a serious problem for rock bands. The Stone Temple Pilots halted a tour when a judge ordered front man Scott Weiland to a drug-treatment facility, and Jonathan Melvoin, a touring keyboardist with Smashing Pumpkins, died of a heroin overdose, which prompted the band to replace drummer Jimmy Chamberlin, who police said was using drugs with Melvoin at the time of his death. Writer, singer, and actor Tupac Shakur died in Las Vegas, Nev., of gunshot wounds received in a drive-by shooting following a boxing match. (*See* OBITUARIES.) Shakur's *All Eyez on Me,* the first double album in rap

ship styles with soul and West African influences. Other strong African albums came from the Paris-based Ugandan singer Geoffrey Oryema, mixing African, French, and Cajun themes on his album *Night to Night,* and from Malian performer Oumou Sangare. Arguably the finest and most versatile female performer in West Africa, she was joined by James Brown's celebrated horn player Pee Wee Ellis on *Worotan,* an album that mixed traditional styles with echoes of Western funk. Also enjoying considerable popularity was Cape Verdean folksinger Cesaria Evora. (*See* BIOGRAPHIES.)

As 1996 drew to a close, many U.S. record company ledgers reflected disappointing sales for the second year in a row. Introduction of the compact disc in the early 1980s had created a business boom, but sales later slowed as consumers finished converting collections from vinyl records to CDs and began investing in computer-related software and services. According to the Recording Industry Association of America, annual revenue growth dropped from 20% in 1994 to 2% in 1995, with no signs of major recovery in 1996. Some business executives also blamed lagging sales on a lacklustre crop of new releases that failed to capture the imagination of the record-buying public.

Some artists clearly had the touch, however. *Jagged Little Pill,* the album released in 1995 by the Canadian rock singer Alanis Morissette (*see* BIOGRAPHIES), had sold more than 14 million copies by year's end and was threatening to overtake *Boston,* by the rock group of the same name, with sales of some 15 million copies, as the top-selling debut album of all time. Morissette won four trophies at the 38th annual Grammy awards, including two—album of the year and best rock album—for *Jagged Little Pill* and two—best rock song and best female rock vocal—for the kiss-off rant "You Oughta Know."

"Macarena," recorded by Los Del Rio—Spanish guitarists Antonio Romero and Rafael Ruiz—became a big dance hit, rising to number one on the *Billboard* pop chart, where it stayed for 14 weeks. First released

in Spain in April 1993, the song caught on in the U.S. in a version remixed by Miami's Bayside Boys. An up-tempo rhythm-driven song with a contagious chorus, "Macarena" and its accompanying dance were performed everywhere.

The Fugees managed to appeal to both urban and suburban audiences on their second album, *The Score.* Blending hip-hop, reggae, funk, and pop, the collection had sold more than five million copies by year's end and yielded the breakthrough hit "Killing Me Softly," a remake of Roberta Flack's chart-topping 1973 release. The

The Fugees, or Refugee Camp, a trio of two Haitian immigrants to the U.S. and a New Jersey-born rapper, blended hip-hop, reggae, funk, and pop. Their best-selling album *The Score* included a version of "Killing Me Softly," a 1970s hit of singer Roberta Flack.

Patti Smith performs on her first tour as a headliner since 1979. Her album *Gone Again,* which included tributes to her late husband, Fred ("Sonic") Smith, and to a number of friends who had died, was released in 1996.

history, sold more than six million copies from the time of its release in February to the end of the year, and his *The Don Killuminati: The 7 Day Theory,* released posthumously under the pseudonym Makaveli, debuted at number one on the *Billboard* album chart.

Country music singer Garth Brooks set ticket-sales records in concert halls throughout the United States in 1996, but sales of *Fresh Horses,* his late-1995 album release, totaled only four million, disappointing by Brooks's standards. Shania Twain's *The Woman in Me* surpassed the eight million mark in sales and became the best-selling album of all time for a female country singer.

Newcomer LeAnn Rimes, a 13-year-old Texan, shook up the country music world with "Blue," a single featuring a vintage musical arrangement and a Patsy Cline-like vocal. Her album of the same name kept the young star at the top of *Billboard*'s country album chart for nearly 20 weeks. Brooks & Dunn became the first duo ever to be named Entertainer of the Year by the Country Music Association.

Deaths in 1996 included Bill Monroe, the father of bluegrass music and a member of the Grand Ole Opry cast and the Country Music Hall of Fame; beloved comedienne Minnie Pearl, who also was a member of the Opry and the Hall of Fame; and Patsy Montana, known for her 1935 hit "I Want to Be a Cowboy's Sweetheart." (*See* OBITUARIES.) Montana, Buck Owens, and Ray Price were inducted into the Country Music Hall of Fame.   (ROBIN DENSELOW; JAY ORR)

This article updates the *Macropædia* article The History of Western MUSIC.

DANCE

North America. Lincoln Kirstein (*see* OBITUARIES), one of the few supermen behind the establishment of ballet in the U.S. and whose death darkened the beginning of 1996, might have been amused by the frequency with which the word *ballet,* if not always the expected product, was heard during the year. In and around New York City, audiences saw companies from around the world, all promising ballet. Les Ballets Africains, one of those groups that did not deliver ballet as people had come to expect it, offered instead a heady and thrilling dose of music and dance from Guinea. In a similar vein, Companie Azanie, an African-based troupe from Lyon, France, showed a slightly more intimate but equally impressive kind of performance. The flamenco-based National Ballet of Spain, from Madrid, and the expressionist-dance-theatre-based Le Ballet C de la B, from Belgium, included few of the accoutrements normally associated with ballet.

No single company performed with standard-setting consistency in 1996. The major U.S. troupes, New York City Ballet (NYCB) and American Ballet Theatre (ABT), each had runs more dutiful than inspired. Male dancers tended to dominate the productions. Both NYCB and ABT featured George Balanchine's *Apollo,* a 20th-century classic famous for its central male role. At ABT, Vladimir Malakhov, Julio Bocca, Guillaume Graffin, and José Manuel Carreño all danced the title role; at NYCB, Ethan Steifel, Peter Boal, Nilas Martins, and Igor Zelensky each performed. None of NYCB's new ballets did more than pass their time in the repertoire they hoped to enrich; ABT's new production of Ben Stevenson's evening-long *Cinderella* proved thin on actual dancing. One gratifying exception to the undistinguished new ballet roster came from ABT with Twyla Tharp's *The Elements,* a wildly wonderful suite of numbers electrifyingly danced to an old French master, Jean-Féry Rebel. By year's end the protean Tharp was off on her own with a nationally touring triple bill simply called *Tharp!* and filled with often effortless virtuosities. An exhibit called "Classic Black" at the New York Public Library for the Performing Arts documented the history of African-Americans in U.S. ballet.

In the area of ballerina talent, ABT continued to claim its radiant Julie Kent and its irrepressible Paloma Herrera. At NYCB, where such ballerina talent had lately been lacking, the company showcased the impressive gifts of 20-year-old Maria Kowroski, while the up-and-coming Miranda Weese continued to grow and blossom. With strongly danced weeklong seasons at the John F. Kennedy Center for the Performing Arts in Washington, D.C., and at New York's City Center, Pacific Northwest Ballet (PNB) proved to be a troupe unusually strong on expert female dancers. Led by a knife-sharp Patricia Barker, a lithe, willowy Louise Nadeau, and a young comer named Carrie Imler, PNB's season left strong and winning impressions. Dance Theatre of Harlem offered an extensive repertoire at the Kennedy Center, including a chicly postmodernist premiere from Alonzo King called *Ground.* Miami (Fla.) City Ballet's strengths were revealed in a special Balanchine/Stravinsky program the company took

to the Jacob's Pillow Dance Festival near Lee, Mass. NYCB dancer and promising novice choreographer Christopher Wheeldon gave the annual performances of the School of American Ballet a charming new ballet called *Danses Bohémiennes.*

Departures and transitions at the level of artistic director were experienced by a number of U.S. and Canadian companies in 1996. William Whitener settled in at the State Ballet of Missouri, while Peter Anastos left the Cincinnati (Ohio) Ballet. Patricia Wilde announced her departure from Pittsburgh (Pa.) Ballet Theatre, and Terry Orr was hired as her replacement. Boston Ballet announced the appointment of gifted former Royal Danish Ballet dancer Sorella Englund as company ballet mistress. Sonia Arova and Thor Sutowski of Alabama's Ballet South did a farewell tour by taking their moderately ambitious production of *Swan Lake* to Brooklyn (N.Y.) College. Soon thereafter it was announced that ABT's gifted Wes Chapman would take over at Ballet South. Kirk Peterson of the Hartford Ballet continued to advance his Connecticut troupe with an award-winning performance by Carlos Molina in the New York International Ballet Competition and with a half-million-dollar grant to create a Native American *Nutcracker* in 1997. The San Francisco Ballet, on a vagabond 18-month circuit owing to the renovation of its home theatre, toured widely and successfully, even if it hardly had time to introduce substantial new repertoire. The Joffrey Ballet of Chicago toured as well, including a dutiful run at the Kennedy Center and much-maligned appearances in London. Feld Ballets/NY continued and expanded its popular "Kids Dance" programs, showcasing pupils of the Feld school.

Elsewhere, silver anniversaries were a trend. The Trisha Brown Dance Company celebrated its 25th year at the Brooklyn Academy of Music's "Next Wave Festival" (NWF). Both the innovative and ever-youthful Pilobolus and the ever-disjointed and eccentric Garth Fagan Dance celebrated turning 25, as did the Hartford Ballet. Ten-year milestones came for Ohio's Tom Evert Dance Company and for New York's Stephen Petronio Dance Company.

Some of the year's most beautiful and mesmerizing dancing came from the four-legged stars of Bartabas's Zingaro Equestrian Theater. Offering *Chimère* at the NWF, the one-ring wonder of appearing and disappearing dancing horses and elegant riders created a spectacle, tinged with Indian music, that was unforgettable. Other less-spectacular foreign visitors included the shiningly clean Paris Opéra Ballet, a cosmetically good-looking Les Ballets de Monte Carlo, a sweetly youthful Ballet Ullate, a bland Rambert Dance Company, a fulsome Joaquín Cortés (*Pasión Gitana*), a thunderingly percussive "Riverdance," and two nicely schooled troupes from Italy—MaggioDanza di Firenze, directed by American punkstress Karole Armitage, and Aterballeto. Two companies with Bolshoi monikers proved mildly controversial. One, called "Stars of the Bolshoi Ballet," met legal problems because its dancers were actually only former Bolshoi dancers; the other, the Bolshoi Ballet itself, charged wildly high ticket prices ($300 top) for appearances in Las Vegas, Nev., and Los Angeles. The legendary Bolshoi ballerina Maya Pliset-

JOHAN ELBERS

Dancers in Twyla Tharp's company perform one of her new works, part of a triple bill called *Tharp!* The program, which featured virtuosic dancing, went on a national tour of the U.S. in 1996, and another of Tharp's new works was performed by American Ballet Theatre.

skaya performed in New York City amid a gala program of star-turn ballet numbers. A thrilling Argentine *Tango × 2* dazzled with its switchblade legwork and intense

A rider and his horse strike a pose during a performance of *Chimère,* an innovative dance by Bartabas's Zingaro Equestrian Theater. The company appeared in the 1996 Next Wave Festival at the Brooklyn (N.Y.) Academy of Music.

JOHAN ELBERS

partnering. Kazuo Ohno, Japan's grand old man of buto, was celebrated with a performance and film series at the Japan Society. In *Bring in 'da Noise, Bring in 'da Funk,* dancer-choreographer Savion Glover (*see* BIOGRAPHIES) impressed Broadway with his unique style of tap dancing, called "hitting."

Except for the Alvin Ailey American Dance Theater, which became a kind of centrepiece to the inaugural Lincoln Center Festival (LCF) with a gaudy world premiere by Judith Jamison to a specially commissioned Wynton Marsalis score, most of the so-called moderns had a lower profile in 1996. Neither the Paul Taylor Dance Company nor the Merce Cunningham Dance Company (MCDC) had full-scale New York seasons. MCDC did have prominence at the LCF with the East Coast premiere of *Ocean.* Taylor produced a wonderful video recording of three of his pop music dances, slyly called *The Wrecker's Ball.* The affecting Isadora Duncan Repertory Ensemble opened the Kennedy Center's two-year celebration of American dance. Mark Morris's dance company offered New York City his lovely childlike staging of *Orfeo ed Euridice.* The Dayton (Ohio) Contemporary Dance Company made an impressive New York appearance, largely because of its sterling dancers. To cap the NWF, Donald Byrd performed his urban Christmas dance, called *The Harlem Nutcracker.*

The National Ballet of Canada (NBC) went through a changing of the guard in 1996. Newly appointed director James Kudelka took over as Karen Kain announced a year of farewell dancing and Gizella Witkowsky gave a farewell perfor-

mance. NBC's history was documented in *Power to Rise,* a scrupulously researched account of the company by James Neufeld. A grossly uneven three-part historical video series called *Footnotes,* narrated by former NBC dancer Frank Augustyn, brought less honour to Canadian ballet. The Royal Winnipeg Ballet's year included performing Rudi van Dantzig's own *Romeo and Juliet,* one of the ballet's lesser-known versions. Les Grands Ballets Canadiens included in its year a company premiere of Antony Tudor's elegiac *The Leaves Are Fading.*

Videos of interest included five additional releases of *The Balanchine Library* from Nonesuch Records and a five-part compilation called *The World of Alwin Nikolais.* The New York Film Festival included a penetrating documentary by Anne Belle and Deborah Dickson, *Suzanne Farrell: Elusive Muse.* Among the books published in 1996 were *No Intermissions: The Life of Agnes de Mille* by Carol Easton, *Alvin Ailey: A Life in Dance* by Jennifer Dunning, *The Joffrey Ballet: Robert Joffrey and the Making of an American Dance Company* by Sasha Anawalt, and *Nijinsky's Crime Against Grace: Reconstruction Score of the Original Choreography for Le Sacre du Printemps* by Millicent Hodson.

Besides Kirstein's, the year's deaths included Gene Kelly, Ulysses Dove, Chris Komar, Paul Draper, Ludmilla Chiriaeff, and Juliet Prowse. (*See* OBITUARIES.) Larry Grenier, William Douglas, Dale Harris, Bert Terborgh, Calvin Shawn Landers, Miguel Godreau, Robert Ellis Dunn, and Philip Jerry also died during 1996.

(ROBERT GRESKOVIC)

Vladimir Malakhov rehearses in a studio. A principal male dancer at American Ballet Theatre and considered by many critics to be the best male dancer in the world, Malakhov was born in the Ukrainian S.S.R., now Ukraine, and began ballet lessons at the age of four.

Europe. Copenhagen, designated as the cultural capital of Europe for 1996, presented a number of well-known ballet companies in its spring festival, and the city was also in the news with the announcement that Maina Gielgud would become artistic director of the Royal Danish Ballet in March 1997. Not only was she the deposed director of the Australian Ballet, but she also was a woman breaking into the male hierarchy of one of Europe's oldest and most distinguished companies.

The English-born Gielgud, with two decades behind her as a leading European dancer, had directed the Australian company for 14 years until the board decided that it was time for change and chose not to renew her contract. Others regarded this as a harsh reward for her work in stabilizing the company, developing a repertoire of classical and modern ballets, and encouraging Australian creativity. Because of the Royal Danish Ballet's historic importance, Gielgud's new job would present rigorous challenges. These would range from maintaining the classics, especially the 19th-century August Bournonville works that were crucial to the company's standing, to discovering choreographers who would shape ballet's future.

Two choreographers whose works created an impact during the year turned postmodern eyes toward ballet classics and tradition. Matthew Bourne's *Swan Lake,* choreographed in 1995 for his British company Adventures in Motion Pictures (with men supplanting women as the swans and in the transformation becoming wilder creatures) made further history in 1996 with a four-month season in London's West End. The transfer made the production accessible to a wider public, and such was this *Swan Lake*'s success that it was filmed by BBC television.

For the Hamburg (Ger.) Ballet, choreographer Mats Ek turned to another Tchaikovsky masterpiece, *The Sleeping Beauty,* and gave the fairy tale an anarchic updating, setting it in the rock and roll era and including scenes of heroin addiction. The Swedish Ek was internationally acclaimed for his reinterpretation of 19th-century classics, and in 1997 his new *Sleeping Beauty* would also be presented by the Cullberg Ballet, the Stockholm company founded by his mother, where most of his work had been created.

Elsewhere in Germany there were stormy debates about closings and cuts in funding, especially in Bremen, Leipzig, and Frankfurt, with suggestions that a nationwide arts policy would help dance's plight. The most public arguments were in Berlin, where, after the heady freedom of unification, dance was said to have reached a period of stagnation and decline. In particular, there was controversy over the future of the city's three large ensembles, and the new artistic director of Berlin's Deutsche Oper Ballet, Richard Cragun, found himself quickly caught in the cross fire.

The Stuttgart (Ger.) Ballet, where Cragun had once been part of a celebrated dancing partnership with Marcia Haydée, concluded an era with Haydée's departure as director following a period of bitter wrangling. Her successor was Reid Anderson, who himself had been a Stuttgart dancer before taking over at the head of the National Ballet of Canada. Birgit Keil, yet another star of Stuttgart's golden era in the 1970s, founded the Tanzstiftung Birgit Keil to foster creative development in young professional dancers. In France Charles Jude, celebrated dancer with the Paris Opéra Ballet, accepted the directorship of the Ballet-Théâtre de Bordeaux.

In the independent sector there was no shortage of small-scale experimental work. Financial constrictions tended to dictate the number of dancers an independent choreographer could work with, which was perhaps a factor behind seasons in Vienna and London that featured solo dancers, with results pointing to radically different conceptualizations of dance. *Enter Achilles,* a work by Lloyd Newson and his British company DV8 that mixed dance with social realism, was transferred from the stage to the screen to win the year's Special Prize in the television music and arts category of the Prix Italia.

European historians were increasingly concerned with reconstructing lost seminal works and were attracting critical debate about changing values. For the Ballet of the Zürich (Switz.) Opera, the British-based dance and art historians Millicent Hodson and Kenneth Archer reconstructed *Skating*

A dancer of Matthew Bourne's Adventures in Motion Pictures portrays a male swan in Bourne's version of *Swan Lake.* The widely acclaimed ballet, which opened in 1995, moved to London's West End in 1996.

Rink, a 1922 ballet choreographed by Jean Börlin for Les Ballets Suédois, with music by Arthur Honegger and Cubist designs by Fernand Léger. The setting was a 1920s roller-skating arena frequented by Paris's working classes, and the critical response was favourable.

The Edinburgh International Festival celebrated its 50th anniversary in 1996 with a strong dance program that looked across modernism's past. The return of the Martha Graham Dance Company, in its first British season in 17 years, included reconstructions of several of Graham's early works and occasioned widespread interest. Mark Morris, Jiri Kylian, and Pina Bausch displayed their companies in early works, and both Morris and Bausch presented full-length operas to illustrate the power of movement to expand the meaning of the word.

In France the Montpellier Festival likewise turned to remembrance as a theme and included revivals of early Postmodernist pieces that had originated at New York City's Judson Church and of works by the choreographer Dominique Bagouet, who died in 1992. Other festivals focused on social critiques. The Internationales Sommertheater Festival in Hamburg, for example, examined alienation by looking at cross-cultural dance.

There was change at two landmark theatres in 1996. In France the dancers of the Paris Opéra Ballet returned to the Garnier Opera House after an 18-month closing, during which time the Ministry of Culture had funded a major program of restoration and modernization. In Britain the Sadler's Wells Theatre, home in the formative period of what became the Royal Ballet and later an international showcase for dance, was demolished in preparation for a two-year rebuilding program, financed in large part by the national lottery. The Wells's management team moved to another London theatre, the Royalty (renamed the Peacock), to ensure continuity of presentation.

Another person who broke through the bastion of traditionalism was Deborah Bull, a principal dancer with Britain's Royal Ballet. She opposed the Oxford Union's motion that "this house believes the arts in this country are elitist" and helped win the debate for her team, an achievement that attracted major press coverage. Bull also played a part in launching a new book published by the Calouste Gulbenkian Foundation in London. Called *Fit to Dance? The Report of the National Inquiry into Dancers' Health and Injury* and edited by Peter Brinson and Fiona Dick, it was the fruit of years of research and revealed that, contrary to popular opinion, dancers needed to take urgent steps to improve their fitness and prevent injury.

Deaths during the year included Antonio Ruiz Soler, the most celebrated Spanish dancer of his day, and Tamara Toumanova, renowned in the 1930s as a "baby ballerina" with Les Ballets Russes de Monte-Carlo and creator of many roles, including Balanchine's *Cotillon.* (*See* OBITUARIES.) Nicholas Beriozoff, the Lithuanian-born dancer, choreographer, and ballet master; Joy Newton, a founding dancer with the Vic-Wells Ballet, director at the Turkish Ballet School, and teacher at the Royal Ballet School; and Paula Hinton, British ballerina, also died during the year.

(ANN NUGENT)

ALASTAIR MUIR

Diana Rigg plays Martha and David Suchet her husband, George, in Howard Davies's production of Edward Albee's *Who's Afraid of Virginia Woolf?,* which ran at the Almeida and Aldwych theatres. Both won rave notices, with Rigg being named best actress by the *Evening Standard.*

THEATRE

Great Britain and Ireland. The Royal National Theatre (RNT), both in London and on tour, continued to rule the roost in 1996, while the Royal Shakespeare Company (RSC), in London and Stratford-upon-Avon, showed signs of wear and tear. Arts Council of Great Britain annual grants and subsidies were frozen, for the fourth year in a row, at £186 million. While national lottery money went to maintain old buildings and supply new facilities, Arts Council funds for companies, actors, writers, and directors were, in real terms, diminishing.

Trevor Nunn, former director of the RSC and the man responsible for staging *Cats, Les Misérables, Starlight Express,* and *Sunset Boulevard,* was named as Richard Eyre's successor at the RNT. His appointment at the age of 56, which was to take effect in September 1997, surprised most observers, who were expecting to hear the names of younger men such as Stephen Daldry (of the Royal Court Theatre) or Sam Mendes (Donmar Warehouse). Daldry, meanwhile, masterminded the exit of the Royal Court from its Sloane Square home to the West End. While the Royal Court was being refurbished and rebuilt, thanks to £16 million of lottery money, its program of new plays was to be spread over two West End houses, the Duke of York's and the Ambassadors, itself temporarily divided into two small venues. The Royal Court continued to discover gifted new dramatists, and Eyre alleged that the new writing talent in the British theatre was now greater than at any other time since the Arts Council was formed in 1947, which included the Royal Court's golden era in the 1950s.

One impressive debut in 1996 was that made by 26-year-old Martin McDonagh, whose *The Beauty Queen of Leenane* arrived at the Royal Court from the Druid Theatre Company in Galway, Ire., going from there to the Duke of York's, after a long Irish tour and winning for McDonagh the award for the most promising playwright from the *Evening Standard* (ES) en route. McDonagh appeared to have taken John Millington Synge's *The Playboy of the Western World* as his model in his vengeful comedy of a suppressed spinster and her cantankerous mother in a remote Connemara kitchen. There were also themes of emigration and escape and of sexual longing and cultural identity wrapped up in ferociously good dialogue and faultless plotting.

Another notable Royal Court discovery was Mark Ravenhill, whose controversially titled drama contained scenes of explicit sex but also a terrifying authenticity in its study of a lost generation pumped up on drugs, fast food, and false dreams. The work played in tandem at the Ambassadors with Harold Pinter's *Ashes to Ashes,* a short but poignant mysterious two-person contemporary drama of unspoken violence and terror in the shadow of Auschwitz. Lindsay Duncan and Stephen Rea played their roles to perfection.

There were two other Holocaust plays in the West End, both already seen in the U.S., Diane Samuels's *Kindertransport* and Jon Marans's *Old Wicked Songs.* Both boiled down to sentimental, not very memorable encounters between, respectively, a mother and daughter and a Viennese music professor and his pupil. Neither had the public impact of *Art* (ES best comedy), translated from the French of Yasmina Reza by Christopher Hampton and played to wildly enthusiastic audiences at the Wyndham's by Albert Finney, Tom Courtenay, and Ken Stott. *Art* portrayed male friendships torn apart by arguments over the merits of a large white blank canvas. Much of the comedy pandered to an audience only too prepared to scoff at the very notion of modern art, and the play might have benefited from proposing a more ambiguously interesting painting. One great moment occurred as Finney advanced on the derided exhibit in order to deface it, and the audience, which shared his contempt, suddenly stopped laughing and drew in its breath at the possibility of brutal vandalism.

Two fine plays by Stephen Poliakoff were presented during the year. In *Sweet Panic,* at the Hampstead Theatre, a child psychiatrist is stalked through a hot London summer by the mother of a young patient; the piece was expertly performed by Harriet Walter and Saskia Reeves. In *Blinded by the Sun,* at the RNT, Frances de la Tour and Douglas Hodge played science researchers at a provincial university threatened with financial cuts to its research programs.

Two other new plays stood out at the RNT. Pam Gems's *Stanley* (ES best play) starred Antony Sher as the mystical, screwed-up, sexually insatiable British painter Stanley Spencer, torn between his wife and his mistress, and it had fine performances by Deborah Findlay and Anna Chancellor. John Caird's production transformed the Cottesloe auditorium into a Spencerian wraparound mural of bulky artisans in tweed suits and cloth caps. In Wallace Shawn's *The Designated Mourner,* the U.S. director Mike Nichols appeared alongside David de Keyser and Miranda Richardson in a stunning but static production by David Hare that dolefully reported the end of civilization as we know it: the barbarians were through the gates, literary society was destroyed, and everyone on Earth who could read John Donne was now dead.

Richardson was one of the year's outstanding performers. After the Shawn play she went to the Edinburgh International Festival and gave a brilliant solo performance in Virginia Woolf's *Orlando,* ingeniously adapted by the U.S. poet Darryl

DONALD COOPER—PHOTOSTAGE

In Henrik Ibsen's *John Gabriel Borkman,* Paul Scofield plays the title character and Vanessa Redgrave plays Ella, his wife's sister and the woman he once loved. The production was staged by Richard Eyre, who was to retire as director of the Royal National Theatre in 1997.

Pinkney and directed by Robert Wilson. (*See* BIOGRAPHIES.) Another star turn was made by Janet McTeer as Nora in Henrik Ibsen's *A Doll's House.* It was a definitive performance, directed by Anthony Page at the Playhouse in Charing Cross, full of pent-up justification from the start for her shattering exit. For once, the viewer believed in the sexuality of Nora's marriage to Torvald, who was well played by Owen Teale, and when the hapless husband innocently protested that no man had ever sacrificed his independence for his marriage, the air crackled as McTeer wheeled savagely around with "Thousands of women have!"

Diana Rigg continued her astonishing late flourish in roles once thought beyond her range as the alcoholic earth mother Martha in Edward Albee's *Who's Afraid of Virginia Woolf?* (ES best actress) at the Almeida in Islington. Howard Davies's production, in which David Suchet was equally good as George, then transferred to the Aldwych. The restored version of Shakespeare's Globe opened on the South Bank in August with a modern-dress production of *The Two Gentlemen of Verona.* The arena was exciting and its potential clear, and after more work on the relationship between the stage and the audience, the venue was expected to reopen for an extended summer season in 1997.

The Donmar Warehouse in Covent Garden scored with Katie Mitchell's revival of Samuel Beckett's *Endgame.* The two touring companies, Mike Alfreds's Method and Madness and Stephen Unwin's English Touring Theatre, made an impact, the latter with a wonderful *Hedda Gabler* (the year's second great Ibsen performance, this time from Alexandra Gilbreath in the title role) and a lucid, enjoyable account of Shakespeare's *Henry IV, Parts One and Two,* in which a real-life father and son, Timothy and Samuel West, played Falstaff and Prince Hal.

The French film star Isabelle Huppert was a welcome visitor to London in the RNT's *Mary Stuart* by Friedrich von Schiller, directed by Davies, and Sir Peter Hall returned to the South Bank to direct Sophocles's two Oedipus plays. Eyre produced a stunning *John Gabriel Borkman* in which Paul Scofield (ES best actor) gave his best stage performance in 30 years as Ibsen's disgraced financier waiting for the world to welcome him home. On a snowbound hillside, Scofield's battered, dying, and remorseful hero sang a croaking lament to his life and to the loves of two sisters, played by Vanessa Redgrave and Eileen Atkins. It was one of the greatest of all RNT productions.

The RSC found its best voice on smaller stages; the Stratford-upon-Avon season was illuminated by Katie Mitchell's (ES best director) whirling and inspirational revival of Euripides's forgotten *Phoenician Women* and by a truly magical new version of *The Comedy of Errors,* directed by Tim Supple in the Other Place. The latter venue also provided Peter Whelan's riveting new play about Shakespeare's second daughter, *The Herbal Bed,* and an eye-opening version of the medieval morality play *Everyman,* directed by Kathryn Hunter and Marcello Magni of Theatre de Complicité. The main Stratford stage offered an enjoyable *Troilus and Cressida,* with Joseph Fiennes—Ralph's younger brother—and Victoria Hamilton, and a decent *As You Like It.*

The Stratford season would now run from November to August, as RSC head Adrian Noble was rejuggling the scheduling in the Barbican, the company's London home, and on tour. In London the company failed badly with a stage version of the film *Les Enfants du paradis.* Its productions seemed random and rudderless, although the company received a shot in the arm with a rare revival of Shakespeare's *Henry VIII* in the Stratford Swan that combined the values of pageant and power politics to an exhilarating degree.

The postmodernist tendency of British culture to look to the past was reflected in a disappointing West End season that included the courtroom classic *Twelve Angry Men,* admittedly given an electrifying production by Pinter, the old thriller *Dial M for Murder,* and the rather sad sight of Tony Randall and Jack Klugman reheating their TV performances in Neil Simon's *The Odd Couple.* When Jason Donovan stepped up in Emlyn Williams's creaky thriller *Night Must Fall,* the outcry was deafening and the show was removed almost immediately. Simon was also represented by an undistinguished revival of *Chapter Two,* starring Tom Conti and Sharon Gless, and a distinctly below-average London premiere of his Sid Caesar tribute, *Laughter on the 23rd Floor,* in which Gene Wilder was misleadingly winsome and sedated as the tyrannical comic surrounded by gag writers.

Lynn Redgrave drew rave reviews but sparse audiences—London had forgotten about the peerless actress during her U.S. sojourn—in her *Shakespeare for My Father.* Middle-aged, middle-class Londoners tapped their toes in nostalgia to Ned Sherrin's affectionate revival of *Salad Days,* the 1954 nostalgic musical revue, and to the pleasantly diverting *By Jeeves,* Sir Andrew Lloyd Webber and Alan Ayckbourn's improved version of their 1975 flop *Jeeves.*

The big musical hope of producer Cameron Mackintosh, *Martin Guerre,* by the authors of *Les Misérables* and *Miss Saigon,* opened to indifferent reviews in July, was withdrawn and rewritten in the autumn, and reopened to a better reception in November. It still seemed unlikely, however, that an interesting attempt to rework the story best known from films starring Gérard Depardieu and Richard Gere would become the talk of the town. Director Declan Donnellan and designer Nick Ormerod eventually came up with a lucid, tough, and often moving production, with wonderful stomping choreography for the peasant community by Broadway veteran Bob Avian, but it seemed that it may have been too little too late.

Stephen Sondheim's *Passion* (ES best musical) struggled at the box office, but it impressed audiences with its emotional fervour, the knockout performances of Maria Friedman and Michael Ball, the ingenious intricacy of the music, and the sense of satirical homage to 19th-century opera. Those Sondheim admirers who lamented the absence of jokes preferred Sam Mendes's blistering revival of Sondheim's earlier *Company,* which transferred intact to the West End but failed commercially.

Sir Henry Irving's "temple of the drama," the Lyceum Theatre in Covent Garden, reopened as a theatre on a permanent basis for the first time since 1939. The event was triumphantly marked by a sensational production, by Gale Edwards, of Lloyd Webber and Tim Rice's first commercial blockbuster, *Jesus Christ Superstar.* Zubin Varla was an evil, troubled, Iago-like Judas Iscariot. John Napier's design placed some of the audience on the stage as spectators in a Colosseum-like arena that spilled out toward the audience in walkways along the side boxes and climaxed in a Golgotha-like rubble mountain behind the action.

The international theatre impinged to good effect on the British repertoire. The Québécois auteur Robert Lepage brought his final seven-hour version of *The Seven Streams of the River Ota* to the RNT, but he failed to deliver *Elsinore,* his one-man show based on *Hamlet,* to the Edinburgh Festival when a rivet on the complicated design proved impossible to fix. *Elsinore* later returned to some acclaim on a British tour starting at the Nottingham Playhouse.

The Romanian director Silviu Purcarete brought his French-financed restoration of a lost Aeschylean trilogy, *The Danaïds,* to the International Conference Centre in Birmingham, courtesy of the Birmingham Rep. The tale of 50 brides for 50 brothers and of the birth of the Greek nation was a fine example of spectacular theatre of minimal means: brandished torches for the brutal invaders, white suitcases for the emigrant women. The scene of mass murderous betrayal on the wedding night was brilliantly done under the cover of simple white tents, the wedding sheets then doubling as body bags.

The best new Irish play was Marina Carr's *Portia Coughlan* at the Abbey Theatre in Dublin, in which Derbhle Crotty played an incestuous sister troubled by her twin's death by drowning. The form of the piece, using flashbacks and memorial confessional speeches, was unusual and daring. The production visited the Royal Court.

Regional theatres battled on in an atmosphere of deepening crisis. The Glasgow Citizens' Theatre made the most impact on its smaller stages with revealing excursions into the forgotten territory of leading U.S. dramatists Tennessee Williams and Albee. The former's *In the Bar of a Tokyo Hotel* was amazingly restored by director Philip Prowse, while the latter's *Seascape* was a genuinely funny echo of *Who's Afraid of Virginia Woolf?*

The West Yorkshire Playhouse continued to be lively, and the Nottingham Playhouse put on Ben Elton's *Popcorn,* a Shavian discussion play, to continue the debate on violence in movies. The Birmingham Rep tried hard to hang on to dwindling audiences with a topical play about the monarchy, Whelan's *Divine Right,* and an excellent rewrite by David Edgar of his own *Dr. Jekyll and Mr. Hyde.*

Much-loved actors who died in 1996 included Beryl Reid (*see* OBITUARIES), Margaret Courtenay, and Simon Cadell. Veteran musical star Vivian Ellis also died. Shaftesbury Avenue dimmed its lights in honour of Jack Tinker, the effervescent 58-year-old critic on the *Daily Mail* for a quarter of a century, whose death was all the more shocking for its unexpectedness. Tinker was probably the last great critic in the tabloid and middle-brow press, someone who performed in print vividly and relentlessly, night after night, often surprising himself as much as his readers with the vehemence of his recommendations for the untried and unexpected. Theatre coverage in Britain, and theatre itself, was incalculably diminished by his departure.

(MICHAEL COVENEY)

U.S. and Canada. In 1996 sleaze died on New York City's 42nd Street. The redevelopment of the Broadway theatre district—in the works for the better part of a decade—took a giant leap forward as the Walt Disney Co. began a $34 million restoration of the historic 1,800-seat New Amsterdam Theater, once home to the Ziegfeld Follies, and opened an expansive retail store a few doors down at the corner of 42nd Street and 7th Avenue. Disney's heightened presence (the stage version of its animated musical *Beauty and the Beast* had been running since April 1994) galvanized efforts to close Times Square pornography shops, clean up street crime, and transform the district's rough-and-tumble atmosphere into that of a safe, spiffy, neon-lit theme park—as the press would have it, the Disneyfication of Broadway.

Disney was not the only entertainment corporation staking its claim on Broadway in 1996. Warner Bros. Studios signed a long-term lease for One Times Square, the building from which the ball drops on New Year's Eve. Commercial theatre observers believed the neighbourhood's shiny new image would translate into healthier ticket sales and increased family audiences, but some worried that there would be a homogenizing effect on the kinds of shows that were produced. A live version of another animated hit, *The Lion King,* and a musical rendition of the biblical tale of King David were among Disney's announced stage projects.

The U.S. theatrical season's most notable success, on Broadway and beyond, was, however, a far cry from squeaky-clean Disney fare. *Rent,* a high-decibel pop-rock musical that updated Puccini's *La Bohème* to New York City's grimy East Village of the '90s, deals with such unsavoury issues as homelessness, drug addiction, AIDS, and dog-eat-dog capitalism—though it infuses these darker realities of contemporary life with a lyrical, wide-eyed optimism. A media sensation attended the show's February opening at off-Broadway's New York Theatre Workshop after its 35-year-old composer and librettist, Jonathan Larson, died suddenly of an aortic aneurysm on the night

As the scheming slave Pseudolus, Nathan Lane mugs in the revival of *A Funny Thing Happened on the Way to the Forum,* his first major starring role on Broadway.

JOAN MARCUS

of the final dress rehearsal in late January.

Larson's propulsive, grunge-influenced score, sung by a youthful, exuberant cast—including Adam Pascal and Daphne Rubin-Vega as the doomed lovers Roger and Mimi, struggling against the ticking of their HIV-positive clocks—helped *Rent* capture the zeitgeist and the attention of the entertainment industry's rich and powerful (mogul David Geffen produced the cast recording and held an option to film the play). At the year's end director Michael Greif's original production was housed in Broadway's Nederlander Theater, a U.S. tour was under way, and international productions were in rehearsal. *Rent* won the 1996 Pulitzer Prize for Drama and the Tony for best musical as well as Obie, Drama Desk, and other awards.

Rent was, in fact, the centrepiece of an exceptional year for the American musical. Critical adulation and jubilant audience response also greeted the innovative *Bring in 'da Noise, Bring in 'da Funk*, which used tap dancing as a lens through which to explore the African-American experience in the U.S. A collaborative creation of the prodigious young dancer Savion Glover (*see* BIOGRAPHIES), director George C. Wolfe, and the poet Reg E. Gaines, *Noise/Funk* brought the energy, anger, and virtuosity of street dancing to the Broadway stage. It originated at the Public Theater/New York Shakespeare Festival.

A pair of highly original chamber musicals—Adam Guettel's fierce and melancholic *Floyd Collins,* based on the true story of a Kentucky spelunker fatally trapped in a cave, and Polly Pen's delicately modulated *Bed and Sofa,* which musicalizes a Russian silent film about a ménage à trois—debuted at Philadelphia's American Music Theater Festival and New York's Vineyard Theatre, respectively.

Among the most produced plays of the regional theatre season were David Ives's sextet of comic vignettes *All in the Timing,* Edward Albee's potent memory play *Three Tall Women,* and Wendy Wasserstein's barbed comedy *The Sisters Rosensweig.* New plays earning critical approbation included

Terrence McNally's Tony-winning *Master Class,* in which an aging Maria Callas intimidates and inspires young singers; and *One Flea Spare,* Naomi Wallace's harsh drama about London's Great Plague of 1665, which debuted at Actors Theatre of Louisville, Ky., and won the Susan Smith Blackburn Prize.

Shakespeare had a heady year in film, and his plays remained a staple of the American stage as well, with Tony Taccone's high-octane *Coriolanus* at the Oregon Shakespeare Festival, Rene Buch's unadorned *Romeo and Juliet* at the same theatre, and two strong-minded reenvisionings of the plot-heavy early histories *Henry VI: Parts 1, 2, and 3* (Michael Kahn's Bard-meets-Mel Gibson version at Washington, D.C.'s Shakespeare Theatre, and experimentalist Karin Coonrod's darker, more cerebral reading at New York's Public Theater with a cast of only 10 playing four times that many roles). Vanessa Redgrave and her Moving Theatre company from Great Britain took up residence at the Alley Theatre in Houston, Texas, where the actress directed and acted in a controversial *Antony and Cleopatra;* by year's end she was in New York City refining her vision of the play for a new production at the Public.

Redgrave was but one of a virtual pantheon of British actors working in the U.S. On Broadway, Michael Gambon portrayed the unhappy, blustering antihero of David Hare's *Skylight* with precision; the luminous Fiona Shaw managed to encapsulate the sorrows of a century in her staged recitation of T.S. Eliot's *The Waste Land;* Roger Rees and David Threlfall, indelibly teamed in the Royal Shakespeare Company's *Nicholas Nickleby* a decade earlier, were reunited in a less-than-sturdy rendering of Jean Anouilh's *The Rehearsal* at the Roundabout Theatre Company; and Daniel Massey earned kudos for his bravura turn as conductor and accused Nazi sympathizer Wilhelm Furtwängler in *Taking Sides.*

The year's landmarks included the launch of a major international theatre festival at Lincoln Center, where the complete works of Samuel Beckett were showcased in a visit

from Dublin's Gate Theatre; the October closing, after a six-month run, of *Big,* a $10 million-plus megamusical that could prove one of the most costly failures in Broadway history; the dissolution of Circle Repertory Company, the groundbreaking playwrights' theatre, after several years of financial struggle; and the passing of such notable theatrical figures as Bernard B. Jacobs, the influential president of the Shubert Organization, author and former *New York Times* critic Walter Kerr (*see* OBITUARIES), the director Norman Rene, and the playwright Steve Tesich.

In Canada headlines went to the development and debut of a pair of ambitious musicals based on rather unlikely literary sources. Lynn Ahrens and Stephen Flaherty's Broadway-bound adaptation of E.L. Doctorow's *Ragtime* was produced by the Livent company. Toronto critics heartily approved of the *Once on This Island* team's musicalization of Doctorow's popular fact-meets-fiction novel, though visiting New York critics had some reservations. A $10 million touring production was scheduled to open in Los Angeles in mid-1997, prior to the Toronto original's later move to New York. The second adaptation—an almost through-sung $4.5 million version of *Jane Eyre* penned by Paul Gordon and John Caird and produced by Mirvish Productions—opened simultaneously in Toronto, to less-approving response.

One of the most interesting new plays in Canada was *2 Pianos, 4 Hands,* which follows the lives of two pianists-in-training as they pursue careers in classical music. Ted Dykstra and Richard Greenblatt's funny and perceptive play debuted in the spring at Toronto's Tarragon Theatre, winning the 1996 Dora Mavor Moore award for outstanding midsize production. *High Life,* a first-time play by Lee MacDougall that premiered at Toronto's Du Maurier World Stage Festival, makes energetic comedy out of the adventures of four morphine addicts who pull a bank job to support their habit.

(JIM O'QUINN)

This article updates the *Macropædia* article The History of Western THEATRE.

CAROL ROSEGG/JOAN MARCUS

The vital but struggling young people of the off-Broadway musical *Rent* are late-20th-century updates of the suffering artists of Giacomo Puccini's opera *La Bohème,* which debuted a century earlier. A hit with audiences, *Rent* won a Pulitzer Prize in 1996 and then moved to Broadway.

A building explodes in the science-fiction film *Independence Day,* which opened in previews on July 2 and immediately set new records for earnings. The account of an invasion of the U.S. by aliens from outer space, the film included a number of spectacular special effects.

MOTION PICTURES

The celebration of the centenary of the cinema, which had begun in 1995, continued throughout 1996. A number of major cities presented exhibitions, either to commemorate the past century or to predict the next one. One film made in 1995 to mark the occasion, *Lumière et Cie (Lumière and Company),* was shown during the year. In the work 39 contemporary filmmakers—including such diverse directors as Spike Lee, the producer-director team of Ismail Merchant and James Ivory (*see* BIOGRAPHIES), and Zhang Yimou—agreed to make a short film under the conditions in which the Lumière cameramen had worked—using a restored Cinématographe camera and with film prepared according to the original Lumière formula. Each director was limited to one 15-m (50-ft) length (about 50 seconds) made without artificial lighting or editing. Those who saw the result found it fascinating.

Cinema in English-Speaking Countries. Hollywood's runaway box-office hit of the year was Roland Emmerich's *Independence Day,* which brought the full armory of special effects, spectacle, vast crowd scenes, and formula characters to the well-worn doomsday formula of invasion from outer space. Other box-office winners of the year also relied on spectacular or violent action and special effects: *Twister,* directed by Jan de Bont from a story by Michael Crichton about people battling a tornado; Brian de Palma's espionage thriller *Mission: Impossible;* and *The Rock,* Michael Bay's outrageously improbable drama about crazed militarists taking over Alcatraz. *Star Trek: First Contact,* the eighth film in the series, was the first without any of the original cast.

Other top-earning dramatic films included *A Time to Kill,* a courtroom drama about racial tensions in the Deep South, directed by Joel Schumacher and based on a John Grisham best-seller; and *Ransom,* Ron Howard's remake of a 1956 thriller about a businessman (Mel Gibson) who defies the police and the FBI in order to rescue his kidnapped son. In Milos Forman's *The People vs. Larry Flynt,* Woody Harrelson played the role of the man who started *Hustler* magazine.

Comedy, too, figured among the year's most popular films. Mike Nichols (as director) and Elaine May (as writer), former partners in stand-up comedy, collaborated for the first time on a film with *The Birdcage,* reworking the French stage and screen warhorse *La Cage aux folles.* Eddie Murphy starred in a remake of Jerry Lewis's *The Nutty Professor.* Hugh Wilson's *The First Wives Club* triumphantly teamed three distinctive female stars—Bette Midler, Diane Keaton, and Goldie Hawn—as former college friends bent on revenge upon their ex-husbands. In Jon Turteltaub's sentimental *Phenomenon,* John Travolta starred as a young man who suddenly receives marvelous abilities. Tom Cruise played a losing sports agent in Cameron Crowe's *Jerry Maguire.*

The Walt Disney Co. had huge box-office successes with a live-action remake of the 1961 cartoon feature, *101 Dalmatians* directed by Stephen Herek and starring Glenn Close as the wicked Cruella De Vil, and with an animated version of *The Hunchback of Notre Dame,* directed by Gary Trousdale and Kirk Wise. (*See* Special Report).

Several established directors appeared in outstanding form during the year. In *Everyone Says I Love You,* Woody Allen used the formulas of 1930s romantic musicals to tell a story of modern neuroses. Spike Lee followed *Girl 6,* a low-key portrait of a young black actress working as a phone sex operator, with a return to low-budget production and one of his most satisfying films, *Get on the Bus.* In the latter he transformed an anecdote about a score of Los Angeles men on a cross-country bus trip to join the "Million Man March" into a microcosm of black American life at the end of the century. John Sayles's *Lone Star* was a polished drama that showed a small Texas border town disrupted by the (literal) unearthing of a buried skeleton. Robert Altman called his music-filled *Kansas City* "a jazz memory"—the re-creation of his remembered 1930s childhood in a story of crime and politics at election time.

With *Fargo* the Coen brothers (Ethan as producer, Joel as director; both as co-writers—*see* BIOGRAPHIES) made one of their best films to date. They used intrigue and irony in manipulating genre conventions to tell a story they said was based on the real case of a businessman who disastrously plotted to have his own wife kidnapped so that he might share the ransom money paid by his father-in-law.

British directors were in evidence in Hollywood. Alan Parker captured the musical quality and textures of Sir Andrew Lloyd Webber's musical *Evita,* with Madonna cast as the charismatic one-time first lady of Argentina. Nicholas Hytner followed his debut success with *The Madness of King George* with a handsome but more conventional adaptation of Arthur Miller's play about the Salem witch trials, *The Crucible.* Anthony Minghella's *The English Patient* adapted Michael Ondaatje's novel set in pre-World War II North Africa and postconflict Italy.

Younger independent directors seemed increasingly drawn to gentler styles in social comedy, exemplified by Stanley Tucci and Campbell Scott's *Big Night,* about immigrant Italian restaurateurs, or Greg Mottola's *The Daytrippers,* describing the ructions in a bourgeois family when their son-in-law is suspected of infidelity. Edward Burns's *She's the One* related the contrasting romantic affairs of two Irish-American brothers. Actor Steve Buscemi returned to his own youthful memories in Long Island for *Trees Lounge,* a story of bored deadbeats who hang about a neighbourhood bar.

Todd Solondz's *Welcome to the Dollhouse,* winner of the main prize at the Sundance

A rural police chief (Frances McDormand) investigates the murder of a state trooper in *Fargo*. The film was the latest offering from Joel and Ethan Coen, who also collaborated on the screenplay.

Festival, related the misery of a confused 11-year-old who was bullied at school and upstaged by a smarter, younger sister.

Outstanding debuts in independent films were Scott Silver's *Johns,* a study of male friendship in the dismal world of prostitution in Los Angeles, and Jim McKay's *Girls Town,* an acute observation of the lives and preoccupation of young working-class women. Curiosity about the 1960s invested Mary Harron's re-creation of Valerie Solanas's assassination attempt in *I Shot Andy Warhol.*

The year witnessed one of the biggest international box-office successes in British film history, Danny Boyle's *Trainspotting,* based on Irvine Welsh's cult novel and set in Edinburgh. Boyle brought visual flair and invention to the film's ribald, affectionate, nonjudgmental portrait of a group of young Thatcher-era outsiders caught in a drug culture.

Among longer-established British directors, Mike Leigh made the excellent *Secrets & Lies,* an exploration of the emotional recesses of ordinary lives, specifically the story of a lonely, feckless white working-woman who is sought out by the illegitimate daughter, now an attractive black adult, whom she put up for adoption years before. In *Carla's Song* Ken Loach told the story of a Scottish bus driver who finds himself in Nicaragua alongside the rebels. Peter Greenaway directed one of his most esoteric and erotic works, *The Pillow Book,* based on a 10th-century Japanese work and exploring the subtle seductions of creating fine calligraphy on the loved one's body.

Two prominent Hollywood actors made creditable debuts as directors. Tom Hanks's *That Thing You Do!* was a warm and likeable anecdote of the rapid rise and fall of a small-town rock band in the 1960s. Al Pacino made a sympathetic documentary, *Looking for Richard,* in which, while describing the process of setting up, casting, and rehearsing a production of *Richard III,* he presented a personal, idiosyncratic, and intelligent analysis of the play.

Richard Loncraine intelligently adapted to the screen Ian McKellen and Richard Eyre's National Theatre production of *Richard III,* convincingly set in an imaginary 1930s totalitarian state, and Baz Luhrmann, the Australian director of *Strictly Ballroom,* created a boldly modernized version of *William Shakespeare's Romeo & Juliet.* At about four hours, Kenneth Branagh's ambitious *Hamlet,* using the complete unedited original text, was the second longest major English-language film of all time. The director-star's own indeterminate performance and the distractions of spotting the all-star walk-ons made for a demanding but finally unsatisfying experience. Other directors went for the Bard's comedies—Trevor Nunn with a well-dressed but pedestrian *Twelfth Night* and Adrian Noble with *A Midsummer Night's Dream* based on the Royal Shakespeare Company's stage production, in which the play was swamped by settings.

Other literary adaptations included New Zealander Jane Campion's adaptation of Henry James's *The Portrait of a Lady*—tasteful and painstakingly wrought but cold and uninvolving despite some fine performances—and Douglas McGrath's playful and witty adaptation of Jane Austen's *Emma.* With *Jude* Michael Winterbottom made a bold attempt at Thomas Hardy's lengthy novel *Jude the Obscure,* underplaying the period decoration and modernizing the sentiments. Anthony Hopkins made his directorial debut with *August,* a decent if uninspired adaptation of Anton Chekhov's *Uncle Vanya.*

British directors continued to be drawn to unconventionally troubled relationships. Angela Pope's *Hollow Reed* was a tough and well-played story about a child-custody battle between a father in a gay relationship and a mother whose sadistic lover abuses the child. Hettie MacDonald's *Beautiful Thing* was a modest but touching adaptation of Jonathan Harvey's play about a shy love affair between two working-class teenage boys. Richard Spence's *Different for Girls* depicted with honesty and sincerity a relationship between a shy transsexual and a macho biker.

Two films stood out for the novelty of their themes. Terence Ryan's *The Brylcreem Boys* set its wartime adventure in an Irish internment camp where British and German prisoners of war are held side by side. Mark Herman's *Brassed Off,* set in a north-of-England mining town that boasts a brass band but is fighting coal pit closures, ably managed an ensemble character cast and nicely balanced character comedy and social concern.

A distinctive Irish cinema was increasingly in evidence. Hollywood-financed Neil Jordan's study of the legendary Irish patriot *Michael Collins* seemed often to have more about it of gangster movie than of political drama. More engaging, both politically and emotionally, was *Some Mother's Son,* Terry George's first feature as director after writing 1993's *In the Name of the Father.* This film re-created a more modern episode in the history of Anglo-Irish relations—the deaths of hunger strikers in 1981 thanks to the British government's refusal to grant political status to Irish Republican Army prisoners.

Australia's outstanding success of the year was Scott Hicks's *Shine,* a somewhat fictionalized film biography of David Helfgott, the gifted Australian pianist whose career was interrupted by periods of mental instability. Rolf de Heer followed his horror-comic *Bad Boy Bubby* with *The Quiet Room,* a delicate portrayal of a seven-year-old girl who reacts to her parents' marital problems by ceasing to speak. Several of the year's best Australian films were directed by women. Monica Pellizzari's debut feature *Fistful of Flies* was a humorous and forthright story of a young girl of the far outback discovering her sexuality. Clara Law's *Floating Life* feelingly recorded the experiences of a Hong Kong family immigrating to suburban Australia. A triumph of no-budget production, student filmmaker Emma-Kate Croghan's wittily observed, Melbourne-based college comedy *Love and Other Catastrophes* proved an international commercial success. Shirley Barrett's *Love Serenade* shrewdly observed the disruption in the humdrum life of two sisters produced by the arrival of a sleazy new local disc jockey in their small outback town.

The most notorious Canadian production of the year was David Cronenberg's intelligent adaptation of J.G. Ballard's novel *Crash,* whose theme of sexual excitement achieved through crashing cars attracted worldwide controversy. From the French-Canadian cinema came the second film of the distinguished theatre director Robert Lepage; *Le Polygraphe* was a complex mystery story about the theatrical re-creation of a real-life murder case that leads the main actress to identify perilously with the original victim.

Continental Europe. The French cinema's most substantial work of the year was Bertrand Tavernier's reflective *Capitaine Conan,* set in a bizarre, forgotten corner of World War I, when French forces in the Balkans fought on for months after the armistice. World War II was the starting point for Jacques Audiard's *Un Héros très discret (A Self-Made Hero),* the tale of a nonentity who compensates for his distinctly unheroic war record by successfully creating a false history as a Resistance hero.

Period films were represented by Édouard Molinaro's decorative and delicate biography of the 18th-century playwright and playboy in *Beaumarchais l'insolent* and by Patrice Leconte's scabrous comedy of wit and intrigue at the court of Louis XVI, *Ridicule.*

Other directors reassuringly maintained their distinctive preoccupations. In *Level 5* Chris Marker pursued his career-long experiments in visual communication, with a philosophical essay and indictment of the process of war. Eric Rohmer's *Conte d'été (A Summer's Tale)* brought a light touch to the amorous entanglements of a boy and three girls at a summer resort. Bertrand Blier, always delighting to shock, wrote and directed *Mon homme,* about a pleasant prostitute who promotes a grubby but appealing bum to be her pimp.

Étienne Chatilliez, delighting in teasing the bourgeoisie, contributed a sharp comedy, *Le Bonheur est dans le pré,* about a man who ingeniously changes his life and wife. The Georgian émigré Otar Iosseliani offered a sardonically comic allegory of social organization, *Brigands,* showing the same group of petty thieves and rascals coming to the top in various historical periods, from medieval times to contemporary ethnic wars. Another émigré, the Chilean Raúl Ruíz, gave Marcello Mastroianni (*see* OBITUARIES) four different roles for his last film appearance in the engaging puzzle film *Three Lives and Only One Death.*

The Belgian director Jaco Van Dormael followed his notable debut film, *Toto le héros,* with *Le Huitième Jour (The Eighth Day),* about the mutually enriching friendship of an emotionally starved businessman and a young man with Down syndrome.

The few Italian productions that captured international attention during 1996 were mostly the work of established directors. The brothers Paolo and Vittorio Taviani made a handsome but academic adaptation of Goethe's *The Elective Affinities,* with French stars Isabelle Huppert (*see* BIOGRAPHIES) and Jean-Hugues Anglade as the aristocratic couple whose marriage is undone when each falls in love with an outsider. Bernardo Bertolucci worked in his native Italy for the first time in 15 years to make *Stealing Beauty,* about a young American girl on a visit to an English community in Tuscany, where she probes the secrets of her parents' generation. One of the most intriguing Italian productions of the year was *Celluloide,* a dramatic re-creation of the making of Roberto Rossellini's postwar classic *Rome, Open City,* conceived and directed by a witness to those times, veteran filmmaker Carlo Lizzani.

Germany was still experiencing the cinematic doldrums, from which few films attracted international notice. Among the rare exceptions was Heiner Stadler's *Warshots,* which looked at the moral challenges facing a reporter and a press photographer working in a country in the grip of civil war. The veteran gay filmmaker Rosa von Praunheim made a comic, caustic tribute to himself at 50, *Neurosia: Fünfzig Jahre Pervers.*

While Spain's commercial cinema was flourishing, with a predictable variety of popular fare, Pilar Miró brought vibrant life to a Spanish classic, Lope de Vega's court intrigue *El perro del hortelano (Dog in the Manger).* Carlos Saura's *Taxi* related the growing horror of a young woman as she discovers the involvement of her father and her lover in neofascist street terrorism. In *Libertarias* Vicente Aranda looked at the hitherto-neglected role of women in the Spanish Civil War. Portugal meanwhile enjoyed the biggest national box-office success in the country's film history with a contemporary erotic comedy, Joaquim Leitao's *Adão e Eva (Adam and Eve).*

Scandinavian cinema boasted one of the year's outstanding international successes, both critically and commercially—Lars von Trier's *Breaking the Waves,* a Franco-Danish co-production, shot in English in Scotland. The story tells how a simple young Scottish girl, cowed and confused by her upbringing in a fiercely austere religious atmosphere, marries an oil-rig worker. When her husband is paralyzed in an accident, she loyally and lovingly fulfills his erotic yearning that she have sex with other men and relate the experiences to him.

The biggest Swedish production of the year, simultaneously shaped as a TV miniseries, was Bille August's handsome, dutiful, and uninspiring adaptation of the classic Selma Lagerlöf saga *Jerusalem,* about immigrants in Palestine early in the century. A Norwegian production by the Swedish director Jan Troell, *Hamsun,* investigates the story of Knut Hamsun (notably played by Max von Sydow), revered in the 1920s as Norway's greatest writer but later bitterly reviled for his wartime adherence to the Nazis. From Norway, Anja Breien's *Wives III* took up the story of the lives and relationships of three women that she had begun 21 years before in the original *Wives.* In Finland, Aki Kaurismäki was at the top of his form with *Drifting Clouds,* a painful and funny account of the suffering and strains of a not-so-young couple suddenly finding themselves out of work.

Sergey Bodrov's *Prisoner of the Mountains,* the Russian cinema's first statement (continued on page 295)

A junkie lies on the tracks in *Trainspotting.* The Scottish film, which was directed by Danny Boyle and depicted a group of young Edinburgh heroin users and their friends with realism and humour, was a surprise hit in both Great Britain and the U.S.

Computer Animation

BY BRUCE C. STEELE

"*Jurassic Park* will turn me into a dinosaur!" predicted one 3-D animator upon seeing the computer-generated lizards in Steven Spielberg's 1993 summer blockbuster. Indeed, some two years later, that forecast may have been fulfilled. In the world of feature filmmaking, CGI (computer-generated images) have crushed the demand for the kind of 3-D, or "stop-motion," animation of scale model puppets that had held sway in Hollywood since even before the original *King Kong* (1933). The victorious CGI troop was not a herd of velociraptors but a menagerie of playthings in what reviewer Jack Mathews in 1996 quickly dubbed the "irrepressible, magical, 100 percent computer-animated" feature film *Toy Story*.

Released by the Walt Disney Co., in November 1995, *Toy Story* drew audiences steadily into the early months of 1996, earned its computer-generated heroes a featured bit on the Academy Awards telecast in March, with a special Oscar for director John Lasseter, and may eventually earn more than half a billion dollars in theatres and on video in the United States alone. Bearing out every 3-D animator's worst fear, *Toy Story*'s returns were 10 times that of Disney's April 1996 partly animated, partly stop-motion animated release *James and the Giant Peach* (based on Roald Dahl's 1961 children's book). Even the studio's traditional "cell-animated" (hand-drawn, or 2-D) *The Hunchback of Notre Dame,* released in June, and Warner Brothers' splashy, heavily promoted *Space Jam* (combining 2-D and CGI animation with live action), though hugely successful by most measures, could not compare.

The first feature-length effort produced at the northern California company Pixar Animation Studios, *Toy Story* set the standard in a year that saw hit after hit build its success upon the magic of CGI, from top-grossing *Independence Day* and *Twister* to Disney's own year-end smash, the live-action remake of *101 Dalmatians* (with computer-duplicated puppies). Animation expert Edwin Catmoll, in the industry magazine *Millimeter,* predicted before *Toy Story*'s release that "like *Snow White* and *Star Wars,* it is going to affect

the entire film industry." So it did. As studio after studio expanded its feature animation division—including Disney, Warner Brothers, Twentieth Century-Fox, Universal Pictures, and Spielberg's two-year-old DreamWorks SKG— many 3-D animators left their poseable puppets in favour of well-paid CGI jobs. All 27 computer animators on *Toy Story,* Disney reported, had backgrounds in stop-motion, cell, or clay animation.

With the potential for hundreds of millions of dollars in revenues, the art of film animation in 1996 often stood in the shadow of the huge business of financing these projects. Some industry observers estimated the studio's expenses on *Space Jam,* for example, at more than $100 million (a figure Warner Brothers said was inflated). Marketing tie-ins became vital to offset the high production price tags. For *Toy Story* alone, Disney relied on an estimated $125 million worth of promotions through "advertising partners" such as Frito Lay, Minute Maid, and Burger King, the last of which also signed up for the *Hunchback* launch and the year's video rerelease of Disney's 1988 cartoon feature *Oliver & Company.* This figure did not include the studio's additional earnings from the sales of related toys, collectibles, and clothing.

It was somehow appropriate, then, that *Space Jam*—

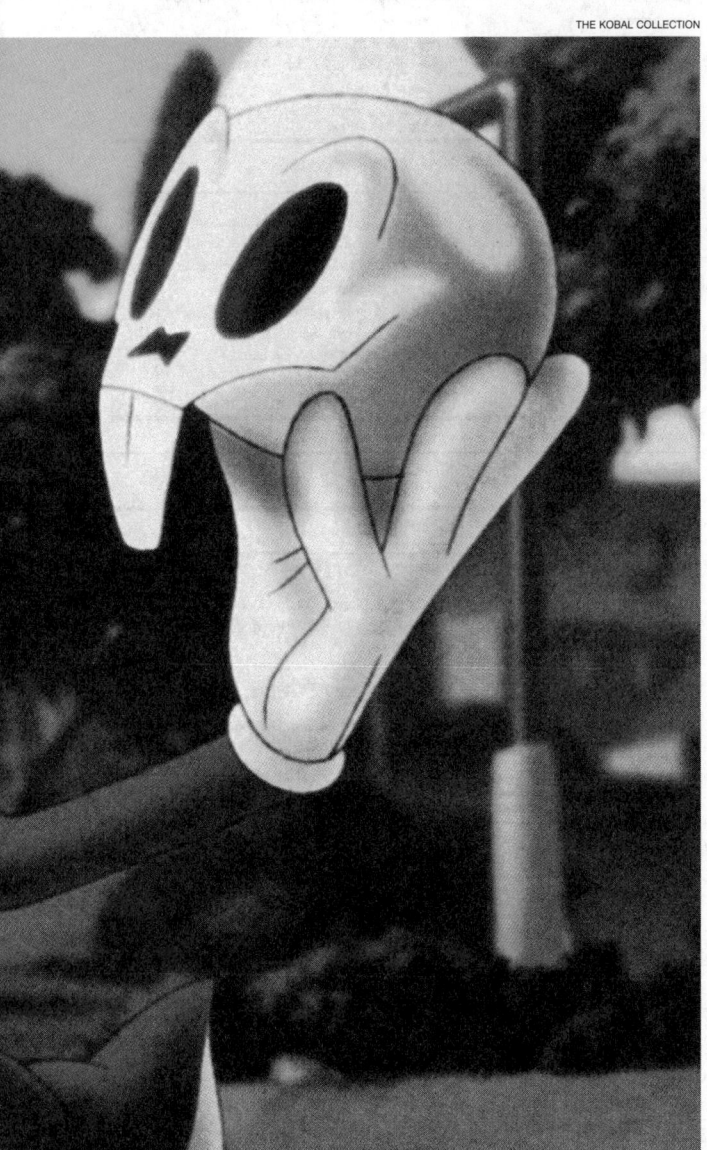

THE KOBAL COLLECTION

in which basketball star Michael Jordan teamed up with the studio's classic Looney Tunes characters, such as Bugs Bunny and Daffy Duck—was inspired in part by a 1992 Nike footwear TV commercial pairing Jordan and Bugs. The director of that ad, Joe Pytka, also directed the Warner Brothers feature. Wall Street firm Smith Barney dubbed *Space Jam* a "totally integrated consumer product event."

The fact that stop-motion could not compete in this new game was driven home during the production of another Warner Brothers release, director Tim Burton's *Mars Attacks!,* a live-action film with animated Martians. English stop-motion animator Barry Purvis and a crew of 70 worked for eight months posing puppets, one frame at a time, in the fashion of *James and the Giant Peach* and the popular *The Nightmare Before Christmas* (1993), both of which Burton had produced. With little warning, however, the studio shut down Purvis's *Mars Attacks!* unit. Their work was discarded and replaced by CGI.

The only bright spot of the year for stop-motion's success in movie theatres came from the clay man-and-dog duo Wallace and Gromit, created by British animator Nick Park. A feature-length omnibus including the latest half-hour Wallace and Gromit adventure, *A Close Shave,* which won Park his third Oscar in March, was an art house hit and a favourite holiday gift on video. Park, however, works in short forms and relies on work in television commercials for income. Wallace and Gromit are not movie stars.

The CGI revolution in feature animation, for all its sweeping implications, did not originate with brazen young independent filmmakers. It came from within the industry establishment itself. Lasseter and *Peach* director Henry Selick both studied animation (along with Burton) at the Disney-founded California Institute of the Arts in the late 1970s, and both were Disney staff animators on 2-D projects such as *The Fox and the Hound* (1981) before turning to CGI and stop-motion. In truth, *Toy Story*'s success owed as much to its adherence to movie traditions as to the novelty of its images. Early features with CGI such as *Tron* (1982) and *The Last Starfighter* (1984) hooked their effects to the popularity at the time of video arcade games. *Toy Story* tapped a richer vein by building its story around a classic "buddy picture" premise—rival toys Woody the pull-string cowboy and flashy plastic Buzz Lightyear must join forces to survive a difficult journey.

In fact, Disney had been traveling quietly down the CGI highway for many years. In 1992 the studio shared with Pixar a special Oscar for development of a computer animation process called CAPS, used in Disney's 2-D feature *Beauty and the Beast* (1991). The most famous CAPS shot is part of that film's ballroom sequence, when the camera seems to fly in a circle from the ceiling to a close-up of the waltzing couple—a shot parodied by the antiheroes of the 1996 feature animation release by Paramount Pictures, *Beavis and Butt-head Do America.* The homage makes an unintended point: as divergent as each animated film may be, the winners inevitably return to the lessons of previous successes. Except for the word "computers," Lasseter's comments in the *Toy Story* production notes could easily have come from Walt Disney himself: "We're storytellers who happen to use computers. Story and character come first and that is what drives everything else. You can dazzle an audience with brand-new technology but in the end people walk away from a movie remembering the characters."

Bruce C. Steele is the executive editor of Out *magazine.*

Basketball star Michael Jordan and cartoon classic Bugs Bunny team up in *Space Jam.* The film combined computer-generated imagery and traditional animation techniques with live-action footage.

International Film Awards 1996

Golden Globes, awarded in Beverly Hills, Calif., in January 1996

Best motion picture drama	*Sense and Sensibility* (U.S.; director, Ang Lee)
Best musical or comedy	*Babe* (Australia; director, Chris Noonan)
Best director	Mel Gibson (*Braveheart*, U.S.)
Best actress, drama	Sharon Stone (*Casino*, U.S.)
Best actor, drama	Nicolas Cage (*Leaving Las Vegas*, U.S.)
Best actress, musical or comedy	Nicole Kidman (*To Die For*, U.S.)
Best actor, musical or comedy	John Travolta (*Get Shorty*, U.S.)
Best foreign-language film	*Les Misérables* (France; director, Claude Lelouch)

Sundance Film Festival, awarded in Park City, Utah, in January 1996

Grand Jury Prize, dramatic film	*Welcome to the Dollhouse* (U.S.; director, Todd Solondz)
Grand Jury Prize, documentary	*Troublesome Creek: A Midwestern* (U.S.; directors, Jeanne Jordan, Steven Ascher)
Audience Award, dramatic film	*Care of the Spitfire Grill* (U.S.; director, Lee David Zlotoff)
Audience Award, documentary	*Troublesome Creek: A Midwestern* (U.S.; directors, Jeanne Jordan, Steven Ascher)

Berlin International Film Festival, awarded in February 1996

Golden Berlin Bear	*Sense and Sensibility* (U.S.; director, Ang Lee)
Special Jury Prize	*All Things Fair* (Sweden/Denmark; director, Bo Widerberg)
Best director	Yim Ho (*The Sun Has Ears*, China) Richard Loncraine (*Richard III*, U.K.)
Best actress	Anouk Grinberg (*Mon homme*, France)
Best actor	Sean Penn (*Dead Man Walking*, U.S.)

Césars (France), awarded in March 1996

Best French film	*La Haine* (director, Mathieu Kassovitz)
Best director	Claude Sautet (*Nelly et M. Arnaud*)
Best actress	Isabelle Huppert (*La Cérémonie*)
Best actor	Michel Serrault (*Nelly et M. Arnaud*)
Best first film	*Les Trois Frères* (directors, Didier Bourdon, Bernard Campan)

Academy of Motion Picture Arts and Sciences (Oscars, U.S.), awarded in Los Angeles in March 1996

Best film	*Braveheart* (U.S.; director, Mel Gibson)
Best director	Mel Gibson (*Braveheart*, U.S.)
Best actress	Susan Sarandon (*Dead Man Walking*, U.S.)
Best actor	Nicolas Cage (*Leaving Las Vegas*, U.S.)
Best supporting actress	Mira Sorvino (*Mighty Aphrodite*, U.S.)
Best supporting actor	Kevin Spacey (*The Usual Suspects*, U.S.)
Best foreign-language film	*Antonia's Line* (The Netherlands; director, Marleen Gorris)

British Academy of Film and Television Arts, awarded in London in April 1996

Best film	*Sense and Sensibility* (U.S.; director, Ang Lee)
Outstanding British film	*The Madness of King George* (director, Nicholas Hytner)
Best director	Michael Radford (*Il postino*, Italy)
Best actress	Emma Thompson (*Sense and Sensibility*, U.S.)
Best actor	Nigel Hawthorne (*The Madness of King George*, U.K.)
Best supporting actress	Kate Winslet (*Sense and Sensibility*, U.S.)
Best supporting actor	Tim Roth (*Rob Roy*, U.S.)
Best foreign-language film	*Il postino* (Italy; director, Michael Radford)

Cannes International Film Festival, France, awarded in May 1996

Palme d'Or	*Secrets & Lies* (U.K./France; director, Mike Leigh)
Grand Jury Prize	*Breaking the Waves* (Denmark/France; director, Lars von Trier)
Special Jury Prize	*Crash* (Canada; director, David Cronenberg)
Best director	Joel Coen (*Fargo*, U.S.)
Best actress	Brenda Blethyn (*Secrets & Lies*, U.K./France)
Best actor	Daniel Auteuil and Pascal Duquenne (*Le Huitième Jour*, Belgium)
Caméra d'Or	*Love Serenade* (Australia; director, Shirley Barrett)
International Critics' Prize	*Prisoner of the Mountains* (Russia; Sergey Bodrov)

Montreal World Film Festival, awarded in August–September 1996

Best film (Grand Prix of the Americas)	*Different for Girls* (U.K.; director, Richard Spence)

Best actress	Laura Dern (*Citizen Ruth*, U.S.)
Best actor	Rupert Graves (*Intimate Relations*, U.K.)
Best director	Olivier Schatzky (*L'Élève*, France)
Special Grand Prix of the Jury	*Un Air de famille* (France; director, Cédric Klapisch) *Sleeping Man* (Japan; director, Kohei Oguri)
Best screenplay	*Adosados* (Spain; director, Mario Camus)

Toronto International Film Festival, awarded in September 1996

Best Canadian Feature Film	*Long Day's Journey Into Night* (David Wellington)
Special Jury Citation	*Kissed* (Lynne Stopkewich)
Best Canadian Short Film	*Letters from Home* (Mike Hoolboom)
Special Jury Citations	*Sin Cycle* (Ben Famiglietti, Jack Cocker) *Lodela* (Philipe Baylaucq)
Metro Media Award	*Shine* (Australia; director, Scott Hicks)
International Film Critics' Award	*Life* (Australia; director, Lawrence Johnston)
People's Choice Award	*Shine* (Australia; director, Scott Hicks)

Venice Film Festival, Italy, awarded in August–September 1996

Golden Lion	*Michael Collins* (U.S./U.K.; director, Neil Jordan)
Special Jury Prize	*Brigands* (France/Georgia; director, Otar Iosseliani)
Volpi Cup, best actress	Victoire Thivisol (*Ponette*, France)
Volpi Cup, best actor	Liam Neeson (*Michael Collins*, U.S./U.K.)

Chicago International Film Festival, awarded in October 1996

Best feature film	*Ridicule* (France; director, Patrice Leconte)
Special Jury Prize	*Sling Blade* (U.S.; director, Billy Bob Thornton)
Best actress	Shabana Azmi (*Fire*, Canada)
Best actor	Christopher Eccleston (*Jude*, U.K.)
Best first feature	*La seconda volta* (Italy; director, Mimmo Calopresti)
Best screenplay	*Adosados* (Spain)
Getz World Peace Medal	*To Speak the Unspeakable* (Hungary/France; director, Judit Elek)

San Sebastián International Film Festival, Spain, awarded in September 1996

Best film	*Bwana* (Spain; director, Imanol Uribe) *Trojan Eddie* (Ireland; director, Gillies MacKinnon)
Best director	Francisco Lombardi (*Under the Skin*, Peru)
Best actress	Norma Aleandro (*Autumn Sun*, Argentina)
Best actor	Michael Caine (*Blood and Wine*, U.S.)
Special Jury Prize	*Engelchen* (Germany; director, Helke Misselwitz)
Euskal Media Prize	*Johns* (U.S.; director, Scott Silver)
International Critics Award	*Capitaine Conan* (France; director, Bertrand Tavernier) *The Emperor's Shadow* (China; director, Zhou Xiaowen)

Tokyo International Film Festival, awarded in October 1996

Grand Prix	*Kolya* (Czech Republic; director, Jan Sverak)
Special Jury Prize	*Cwal* (Poland; director, Krzysztof Zanussi)

Vancouver International Film Festival, Canada, awarded in October 1996

Air Canada Award	*Breaking the Waves* (Denmark/France; director, Lars von Trier)
Federal Express Award	*Fire* (Canada; director, Deepa Mehta)
City TV Award for Best Canadian Film	*Hard Core Logo* (director, Bruce McDonald)
Rogers Award	Noel S. Baker (*Hard Core Logo*)
NFB Award	*Predictions of Fire* (U.S./Slovenia; director, Michael Benson)
Dragons and Tigers Award for Young Cinema	*The Day a Pig Fell into the Well* (South Korea; director, Hong Sang) *Rainclouds over Wushan* (China; director, Zhang Ming)

European Film Awards (Felix), awarded in Berlin in December 1996

Best European film of the year	*Breaking the Waves* (Denmark/France; director, Lars von Trier)
Best young European film of the year	*Some Mother's Son* (Ireland; director, Terry George)
Best European actress	Emily Watson (*Breaking the Waves*, Denmark/France)
Best European actor	Ian McKellan (*Richard III*, U.K.)

(continued from page 291)
on the conflict in Chechnya, reduced the senseless war to its tragic human terms. The best Hungarian films of the year were Judit Elek's fine documentary *To Speak the Unspeakable,* which looked at the Holocaust through the experiences of one celebrated survivor, Elie Wiesel, and Ibolya Fekete's *Bolshe Vita,* a dark comedy about the experiences of Russian migrants in Budapest in the first heady days after the fall of communism. In Poland several veterans made notable historical films. Andrzej Wajda's low-key but accomplished *Holy Week* was a grim drama about a Jewish woman hidden in a Warsaw apartment block in 1943. Barbara Sass's *Temptation* was a tough drama about the pressures brought upon a young nun in the oppressive socialist 1950s.

The outstanding Czech film of the year, Jan Sverak's enchanting *Kolya,* achieved instant worldwide success with its comic and touching story of the reluctant alliance between a politically outcast musician in latter-day socialist Czechoslovakia and a small but characterful Russian boy. Petr Vaclav's *Marian* used boys from orphanages and public institutions to re-create the story of a well-intentioned Roma (Gypsy) lad hardened into a criminal by the repressive social policies of the 1970s.

Latin America. Vital if sporadic film activity was evident in many parts of Latin America. The veteran Brazilian director Carlos Diegues's *Tieta di Agreste* was a variant on Friedrich Dürrenmatt's *The Visit,* relating the return to her native village, from which she had once been ignominiously expelled, of a fabulously rich lady. From Peru, Francisco Lombardi's *Bajo la piel (Under the Skin)* was a horror story about events in a small town when sacrificial rites of the ancient Moche culture are mysteriously revived. The Mexican Arturo Ripstein's *Profundo Carmesi (Deep Crimson)* was the story of a sinister liaison between two middle-aged people, a lonely and disappointed woman and a professional philanderer. Argentina replied to *Evita* with its own biography *Eva Perón,* most remarkable for the fine central performance by Esther Goris.

North Africa and the Middle East. The Tunisian Férid Boughédir's *Un Été à la Goulette* was a rich human portrait of the community of a seaside resort in the 1960s, nostalgically recalling former times of happy coexistence between Muslim, Jew, and Christian. Iran sustained its recent record of high-quality production with Mohsen Makhmalbaf's *Gabbeh,* a lyrical study of the life and myth of nomadic tribes in southeastern Iran. Women directors were rare in Iran, but the actress Jasmine Malex directed herself in the role of a neurotic woman writer in a well-characterized chamber film, *The Common Plight.*

Asia. The most attractive films to emerge from Japan were Kohei Oguri's *Sleeping Man,* which portrayed relationships in a village where people still feel close to older traditions governing the approach to nature, life, and death, and Higashi Yoichi's *Village of Dreams,* a magical evocation of the world of childhood. Adapted from the nostalgic memoirs of the artist Tashima Seizo, he and his twin brother were played by the enchanting Matsuyama twins. Ryosuke Hashiguchi's *Like Grains of Sand* was a delicate study of school life, centring on

an adolescent's homosexual passion for his fellow student.

China's cultural repression seemed virtually to have silenced domestic filmmakers, though some Chinese artists were working abroad. In Hong Kong, for instance, Chen Kaige made the melodramatic *Temptress Moon,* about the disintegration of a rich family undone by opium and sexual excess in the 1920s.

From South Korea, Lee Min-Yong's *A Hot Roof* offered an effective comic parable on emerging feminist consciousness with the story of a group of women who withstand a rooftop siege after dealing out justice to a wife beater. Park Kwang-su's *A Single Spark* explored the nature of political activism in a story about a committed contemporary journalist who sets out to investigate the life and death of a real-life labour activist of the 1970s.

Indian directors boldly tackled previously taboo subjects, as in Deepa Mehta's *Fire* (a lesbian love affair) and Amol Palekar's *The Square Circle* (transvestites). The innovative Palekar also completed the powerful *The Village Has No Walls,* about the economic disintegration of a rural community. In *Naseem,* portraying a delicate relationship between a young girl and her bedridden grandfather, Saeed Akhtar Mirza viewed the tragedy of Hindu-Muslim tensions from the viewpoint of ordinary individuals. Biblap Ray Chaudhuri's *The Hustings* offered an unsparing, ironic anecdote about a group of indigent villagers who struggle to keep a dying pauper alive long enough to collect his election bribe. Adoor Gopalakrishnan's *Kathapurushan* was a story of the triumph over disadvantage and defeat of a humble man with a stammer who becomes a militant political ideologue.

Africa. A few notable African films reached the international festival circuit during the year. Most notable among them was *Clando,* the first feature by Cameroonian director Jean-Marie Teno, the story of a young opponent of the repressive government who becomes an illegal immigrant in Germany. From Zaire, José Laplaine's *Macadam Tribu* offered a lively portrait of an urban neighbourhood community. Madagascar legends figured in the French-produced *When the Stars Meet the Sea,* directed by Raymond Rajaonarivelo, which made effective use of dramatic locations to tell the story of a young man weighed down by the belief that he was born with supernatural powers. (DAVID ROBINSON)

Nontheatrical Films. The Swedish company Dockhouse scored an unusual victory in 1996, taking the grand prize at the U.S. International Film and Video Festival in Chicago for the second year with another Volvo promotional film, *Beams and Dreams,* along with 14 additional awards. The American documentary *Looking into the Face of Evil* by Sam Nahem, which graphically depicted the horror of the Holocaust, won a prestigious CINE Golden Eagle and several other top awards.

An animated Czech film, *Repete,* by Michaela Pavlatova took the grand prize at Japan's Hiroshima '96 Festival. The film followed three couples determined to break from the mechanical routine that determined their lives.

The most successful film from Florida State University, which had moved into the

top ranks of cinema schools, was *Paul McCall,* the story of a shy second-grader who outwitted class bullies. A student film by Benjamin Hershleder, it was screened at 38 festivals and won eight awards. *Short Order* by Marc Marriott of the University of California, Los Angeles, took the Canal+ award at France's Henri Langlois Festival. The film featured a businessman whose work as a short-order cook transformed him.

The *Water Carrier* by Patricia Cardoso won the Academy and Directors Guild student awards and screenings at 25 festivals. Set in 1926, the film showed a blind man in Colombia who had to decide whether to go through with an eye operation.

(THOMAS W. HOPE)

See also Art, Antiques, and Collections: *Photography;* Media and Publishing: *Radio; Television.*

This article updates the *Macropædia* article MOTION PICTURES.

Population Trends

DEMOGRAPHY

At midyear 1996 world population stood at 5,771,000,000, according to estimates prepared by the Population Reference Bureau. The figure is almost 800 million higher than in 1987, when world population first reached 5 billion. The 1996 total represented an increase of about 88 million over the previous year. The annual rate of increase declined to about 1.52% in 1996 from 1.54% in 1995, a result of birthrate declines in both less-developed and industrialized nations. If the 1996 growth rate were to continue, the world's population would double in 46 years.

In 1996, 140 million babies were born, 126 million (90%) in less-developed countries (LDCs). Each day world population increased by 240,000, the result of 383,000 births and 143,000 deaths. New data from censuses in the following countries were reported to the United Nations in 1996. (*See* WORLD DATA: *Area and population.*)

Worldwide, 57% of married couples in 1996 used one or more methods of contraception. Exactly half of all couples were using a "modern" method such as clinically supplied contraceptive devices or sterilization. In the less-developed countries, 54% were practicing some form of family planning and 48% were using a modern one. This proportion, however, dropped sharply for LDCs other than China, where a vigorous family-planning program raised usage to high levels. Excluding China, only 35% of couples in the LDCs were using a modern method of family planning. This dropped to a low of 11% in sub-Saharan Africa and reached a high in Latin America and the Caribbean, at 53%.

Worldwide, 32% of the population was below the age of 15 in 1996, but that figure was 38% in LDCs outside China. In the more developed countries (MDCs), 20% were below age 15, and that dropped as low as 15% in Italy and 16% in Germany and Japan. The continued high percentage of young people in the LDCs would result in a large number of youth entering the childbearing ages in the near future and, consequently, considerable potential for population growth. This situation remained unchanged in 1996. Only 5% of the population in the LDCs was over the age of 65, compared with 14% in the MDCs. Sweden, with 17%, remained the country with the highest percentage above age 65.

Nearly half, 43%, of the world population in 1995 lived in urban areas. In the LDCs 35% was classified as urban, compared with 75% in the MDCs. Among the world's least urbanized countries was Rwanda, with only 5% living in urban centres.

Throughout the world life expectancy at birth was 64 years for males and 68 for females. In the MDCs the same figures were 70 and 78 and in the LDCs, 62 and 65, respectively. The 1996 world infant mortality rate stood at 62 infant deaths per 1,000 live births. For the first time, infant mortality in the MDCs fell to single digits, nine infant deaths per 1,000 live births, but it remained at a high level of 68 in the LDCs.

Less-Developed Countries. In 1996 the population of the LDCs grew at 1.9% per year; for the LDCs other than China, the rate was 2.2%. The growth rate of the latter countries, should it continue, would cause their population to double in only 32 years. Of the 88 million people added to the world population during the year, 98% were living in LDCs. At the 1996 pace of childbearing, the total fertility rate, the average number of children a woman would bear during her lifetime at the current rate, was 3.4 in the LDCs, slightly down from the 3.5 figure in 1995. In the LDCs, excluding the large statistical effect of China's 1.2 billion population, women averaged four children each, unchanged from a year earlier. This remained far from the "two-child family" essential to slowing population growth to zero and stabilizing world population size.

During 1996 Africa remained the region with the highest fertility, an average of 5.7 children per woman, 6.1 in populous sub-Saharan Africa. Debate concerning future population growth in Africa increased in 1996 for two reasons. First, while there were indications that the birthrate in Africa may have begun a slow decline, the speed of the decline was in doubt. Second, the effect of AIDS in Africa made news in 1996, particularly with new U.S. Census Bureau studies of the prevalence of the disease. These studies now pointed to higher death rates in at least 20 countries. Nonetheless, in the long term, even severe effects of AIDS would likely result in a reduction of sub-Saharan Africa's population by only about 100 million, or less than 10% of the total, by 2025.

In 1996 life expectancy in Africa, at 53 years for males and 56 for females, was the world's lowest. But with the world's highest birthrate, the continent had the world's fastest population growth, at 2.8% annually. Overall, Africa's population was 732 million, up from 720 million in 1995.

In 1996 Latin America's population totaled 486 million, and the annual growth rate was 1.9%, the same as in 1995. The total fertility rate (TFR) remained at 3.1, ranging from 5.2 in Honduras to 1.5 in Cuba, the latter being the lowest level of fertility ever recorded in the region. Life expectancy remained at 66 years for males and 72 for females.

Asia's population was 3.5 billion in 1996, by far the largest of the world's continents. The growth rate fell slightly to 1.6%, but if China was excluded, it remained at a high 1.9%. With a very low TFR of 1.8, China, as was the case in the industrialized countries, was facing some of the problems associated with aging. Speculation centred on possible future increases in China's birthrate, which might reverse the downward trend in the world population growth rate. In India prospects for continued decline in the birthrate were of major interest. Data released in 1996 revealed that in the country's most populous state, Uttar Pradesh, the total fertility rate was 4.5, well above the national average of 3.4. The future trend of fertility in this and other states with high fertility and illiteracy would play a significant role in the growth of India's population, which stood at 950 million in 1996.

More Developed Countries. During 1996 Europe continued to report a negative rate of natural increase (birthrate minus the death rate) of −0.1%. This was primarily due to the collapse of the birthrate in the European republics of the former Soviet Union and to continued low fertility in Western Europe. In 1996 Latvia set a record for natural decrease at −0.7%. No fewer than 13 countries of Europe experienced more annual deaths than births: Belarus, Bulgaria, Croatia, the Czech Republic, Estonia, Germany, Hungary, Italy, Latvia, Lithuania, Romania, Russia, and Ukraine. The total fertility rate dropped to the 1.3–1.5 range in Belarus, Estonia, Latvia, Russia, and Ukraine. For many of the countries of the former Soviet Union, life expectancy fell even farther than in previous years. In Russia male life expectancy dropped to only 57 years, nearly as low as in many industrialized countries at the beginning of the 20th century. The highest life expectancy was in Japan, 83 for females, while males in Iceland enjoyed a life expectancy of 77. Japan also recorded the lowest rate of infant mortality in the world, 4.2 infant deaths per 1,000 live births.

The population of the U.S. was 265,575,000 in September 1996, up from 263,211,000 a year earlier. This represented an increase of 2,364,000, or 0.9%. The National Center for Health Statistics (NCHS) reported that during the 12 months ended in February 1996, natural increase amounted to 1,563,000, the net result of 3,877,000 births and 2,314,000 deaths. During that period the birthrate dropped to 14.7 births per 1,000 population, compared with 15.2 in the 12 months ended in February 1995. The U.S. total fertility rate declined to 1.97, the first time since 1989 that it had been below two children per woman. Natural increase through February 1996 was 110,000 less than in the previous 12-month period, which signaled a reversal of the rising trend that had begun in the late 1980s.

The age-adjusted death rate in the U.S. for the 12-month period ended in January 1996 was 501.6 per 100,000 population, a

World's 25 Most Populous Urban Areas[1]

Rank	City and country	City proper Population	Year	Metropolitan area Population	Year
1	Tokyo, Japan	7,836,665	1995 est.	27,856,000	1995 est.
2	São Paulo, Brazil	9,842,059	1993 est.	16,417,000	1995 est.
3	New York City, U.S.	7,333,253	1994 est.	16,329,000	1995 est.
4	Mexico City, Mex.	9,815,795	1990 cen.	15,643,000	1995 est.
5	Bombay (Mumbai), India	9,925,891	1991 cen.	15,093,000	1995 est.
6	Shanghai, China	8,930,000	1993 est.	15,082,000	1995 est.
7	Los Angeles, U.S.	3,448,613	1994 est.	12,410,000	1995 est.
8	Beijing, China	6,690,000	1993 est.	12,362,000	1995 est.
9	Calcutta, India	4,399,819	1991 cen.	11,673,000	1995 est.
10	Seoul, S.Kor.	10,873,055	1991 cen.	11,641,000	1995 est.
11	Jakarta, Indon.	8,259,266	1990 cen.	11,500,000	1995 est.
12	Buenos Aires, Arg.	2,960,976	1991 cen.	10,990,000	1995 est.
13	Tianjin, China	5,000,000	1993 est.	10,687,000	1995 est.
14	Osaka, Japan	2,478,628	1995 est.	10,601,000	1995 est.
15	Lagos, Nigeria	1,347,000	1992 est.	10,287,000	1995 est.
16	Rio de Janeiro, Brazil	5,547,033	1993 est.	9,888,000	1995 est.
17	Delhi, India	7,206,704	1991 cen.	9,882,000	1995 est.
18	Karachi, Pak.	5,208,132	1981 cen.	9,863,000	1995 est.
19	Cairo, Egypt	6,849,000	1994 est.	9,656,000	1995 est.
20	Paris, France	2,156,766	1991 cen.	9,469,000	1995 est.
21	Manila, Phil.	1,894,667	1991 cen.	9,280,000	1995 est.
22	Moscow, Russia	8,570,200	1994 est.	9,233,000	1995 est.
23	Dhaka, Bangladesh	3,397,187	1991 cen.	7,832,000	1995 est.
24	Istanbul, Tur.	7,331,927	1993 est.	7,817,000	1995 est.
25	Lima, Peru	[2]	[2]	7,452,000	1995 est.

[1]Ranked by population of metropolitan area.
[2]Administrative unit within which a separate city proper is not distinguished.

Causes of death in the United States

(year ended January)

Rank in 1996	Rate per 100,000 population 1995	1996
1. Diseases of the heart	278.5	278.4
2. Malignant neoplasms	207.4	203.6
3. Cerebrovascular diseases	58.9	59.6
4. Chronic obstructive pulmonary diseases	38.4	39.4
5. Accidents and adverse effects	34.1	34.1
6. Pneumonia and influenza	30.1	31.0
7. Diabetes mellitus	21.2	22.2
8. HIV infection	15.8	16.0
9. Suicide	11.8	11.3
10. Nephritis, nephrotic symptoms, and nephrosis	9.5	9.8
11. Chronic liver disease and cirrhosis	9.9	9.5
12. Homicide and legal intervention	9.2	8.5
13. Septicemia	7.6	8.1
14. Atherosclerosis	6.5	6.2
15. Certain conditions of the perinatal period	5.5	5.1

decline of 1.2% from the same period of the previous year. The infant mortality rate for the period ended in February 1996—7.5 infant deaths per 1,000 live births, compared with 7.9 a year earlier—continued the sharp decline of the previous few years. The NCHS reported that during 1994 life expectancy at birth rose again after having declined slightly in the previous year. At 75.7 years in 1994, it nearly equaled the all-time high of 75.8, set in 1992. Female life expectancy was 79, while that of males rose to 72.4. African-American men had the lowest life expectancy in 1994, 64.9 years, but the gain over 1993's 64.7 years reversed a one-year downward trend.

(CARL V. HAUB)

See also World Data.

REFUGEES AND INTERNATIONAL MIGRATION

In the absence of massive new refugee influxes on the scale experienced in recent years, the world's refugee population decreased from 14.5 million to 13.2 million in 1996. More than one million refugees returned to their country of origin, which reflected the increasing focus on repatriation as a solution for many of the world's displaced people. Similarly, the overall population of concern to the Office of the United Nations High Commissioner for Refugees (UNHCR) fell to some 26.1 million, of whom 3.4 million were returnees, 4.6 million were internally displaced persons (persons who were in a refugee-like situation but had not crossed an international border), and 4.8 million were others of humanitarian concern, for the most part victims of conflict. UNHCR continued to implement its distinctive international protection mandate in respect to those persons, which involved promoting, safeguarding, and developing principles of refugee protection; strengthening international commitments; and promoting durable solutions, be they in the form of voluntary repatriation, local integration, or resettlement.

For the most part of 1996, there was little change in the humanitarian crisis affecting the African Great Lakes region, where more than two million Rwandans and Burundians had fled their countries in 1994. Large-scale return movements from Zaire, where many had settled, to Rwanda began in December 1996 as conflict engulfed eastern Zaire. At one time, in mid-December, the number of persons crossing the border between Zaire and Tanzania was estimated at as many as 15,000 each hour. Following this development, the government of Tanzania, having determined that the conditions in Rwanda allowed people to return in safety, took steps to begin the repatriation of the approximately 535,000 Rwandan refugees on its territory.

In southern Africa operations for the voluntary repatriation of some 1.7 million refugees from Mozambique concluded after 17 years of conflict and devastation. In contrast, in West Africa renewed violence in Liberia postponed efforts to repatriate some 750,000 Liberian refugees. In nearby Mali, however, political stability allowed for the repatriation of more than 100,-000 Malian refugees from Algeria, Burkina Faso, Mauritania, and Niger. The Horn of Africa and East Africa, emerging from years of prolonged conflict, saw the return of some 27,000 Ethiopian and 25,000 Eritrean refugees from The Sudan. An estimated 500,000 Somali refugees had returned to Somalia from Kenya and Ethiopia during the past few years.

In former Yugoslavia, as a result of the cessation of hostilities in Bosnia and Herzegovina, an estimated 250,000 people—mostly internally displaced persons—had, by the end of 1996, settled or resettled in areas where their ethnic group was in the majority. Reconstruction activities, such as UNHCR's shelter project, which repaired some 20,000 homes, were gathering momentum and helping to create conditions favourable for the return of refugees and displaced persons. Many of those who returned, however, especially the Bosnian Serbs, continued to face many political, psychological, and practical obstacles.

In the Caucasus, where some 1.1 million refugees and displaced persons fled as a result of the conflict between Armenia and Azerbaijan over the region of Nagorno Karabakh, UNHCR continued to promote and facilitate local solutions, pending the result of ongoing peace negotiations. In the Commonwealth of Independent States (CIS), the far-reaching geopolitical changes following the breakup of the former Soviet Union had resulted in an estimated nine million people moving within or between countries of the CIS. Of these, some 2.3 million internally displaced persons and approximately 70,000 refugees were victims of conflicts. Recognizing the scale and complexity of these movements, UNHCR, together with the International Organization for Migration (IOM) and the Organization for Security and Cooperation in Europe, held a regional conference in Geneva on May 30–31. A "Program of Action," a comprehensive framework for managing migratory flows as well as for developing institutional capacity to prevent mass displacement, was drawn up. While implementation of the program essentially rested with the CIS countries, UNHCR and the IOM began developing a three-to-four-year joint strategy to guide their activities in the region.

In Western Europe the number of people seeking asylum continued to decline, partly as a result of visa requirements, reinforced border controls, and restricted social benefits in some countries. The rate of recognition of those applying for refugee status had dropped from 42% in 1984 to some 10% by the mid-1990s.

Afghan refugees, who began streaming out of their country after its invasion by Soviet forces in 1979, continued to constitute the largest refugee caseload of concern to UNHCR, with 1.4 million persons in Iran and 820,000 in Pakistan. Despite the continuing civil war in Afghanistan, however, approximately 130,000 refugees returned to Afghanistan from Pakistan and Iran in 1996, which brought the total number of returnees to some 3,890,000. As of September, Kabul, along with Jalalabad and the remainder of the eastern areas of Afghanistan, had come under control of the Taliban forces, who quickly enforced strict Islamic rules. This violent and sudden change in the control of these important population centres resulted in large-scale internal displacements and renewed refugee outflows into Pakistan. Many of those who fled included women, to whom the Taliban denied access to education and the freedom to work outside their homes. Efforts to engage the parties in a negotiation process continued, as did rehabilitation projects to encourage returns and reintegration in peaceful areas of the country.

In Iraq armed conflict in August 1996 between two opposing Kurdish factions resulted in significant population displacements, both within Iraq and into Iran. The majority of those persons, however, returned to Iraq after October. In Yemen the influx of new arrivals from Somalia increased during the first quarter of 1996, mainly as a result of security problems and renewed fighting in Somalia. Most asylum seekers traveled by boat to Yemen from Boosaaso, in northeastern Somalia, in dangerous conditions caused by the prevailing monsoon season.

In Southeast Asia the successful conclusion of the Comprehensive Plan of Action (CPA) for Indochinese refugees ended more than 20 years of international humanitarian efforts to resolve the aftermath of the conflict in that region. Since 1975 some 1,075,000 Vietnamese and Laotian refugees had fled their homelands, and the majority had resettled in other countries. By the end of 1996, Vietnam had received back almost 100,000 Vietnamese since the implementation of the CPA in 1989; just over 6,000 Vietnamese remained in camps in Hong Kong. UNHCR continued to advocate the voluntary return of some 40,000 Muslim refugees from Myanmar (Burma), who were in Bangladesh, and for solutions for the approximately 85,000 Bhutanese stranded in southeastern Nepal, two situations intimately linked to the political will of the governments concerned.

In the Americas and the Caribbean at the beginning of 1996, there were more than 1.5 million refugees and returnees of concern to UNHCR. Of this total, however, only some 82,300 continued to be in need of material support from UNHCR. This stood in sharp contrast to the situation that had prevailed in the region less than a decade earlier, prior to the 1989 International Conference on Central American Refugees and the profound political changes that had taken place in large parts of Latin America. The only major refugee situation that required sustained attention was that of the Guatemalan refugees, some 38,000 of whom remained in camps and settlements in Mexico. Reconciliation in Guatemala, however, ending 36 years of civil conflict, was expected to help to resolve the situation, as was the recent agreement of the Mexican government to allow those not wishing to return to settle in Mexico.

In North America, despite the tendency toward further immigration restrictions, the United States and Canada increased their efforts to address the issues of asylum requests resulting from sexual violence and discrimination based on gender. The U.S. Congress in September approved a bill that would make it more difficult for illegal aliens to cross the nation's borders, speeded the deportation of criminal aliens, and restricted some public benefits to legal immigrants; such immigrants could be deported if they received public benefits, including child care, for more than 12 months.

(UNHCR)

This article updates the *Macropædia* article POPULATION.

PHOTO ESSAY

Hutu Return to Rwanda

Life in Rwanda has long been dominated by conflicts between the Hutu and the Tutsi. When the Tutsi seized control of the government in 1994, more than one million Hutu fled across the border to eastern Zaire, where they lived in refugee camps.

Zaire, facing its own political problems and eager to maintain control over its mineral-rich eastern regions, tried to persuade the Hutu to return to Rwanda in 1996, but without much success. Later in the year, however, native Tutsi in Zaire took up arms against the refugees and drove many of them back to Rwanda, accomplishing what the government could not do.

Carol Guzy shot these photographs on both sides of the Rwanda-Zaire border. She captured the masses of people moving on foot and by motor vehicle to escape the crowding, violence, and sickness of the camps. For some the journey ended in a welcome home by friends and relatives.

Religion

During 1996 religious groups were pitted against governments on issues ranging from freedom of belief and practice to public policy matters such as abortion. In some cases faith groups found themselves in disagreement with one another on such subjects as evangelism and the significance of the Holocaust. Christians found themselves debating some core beliefs, including the identity of Jesus and the existence of hell.

Leaders of more than 40 Christian organizations met in Washington, D.C., in January to draw attention to the plight of persecuted Christians and to urge the U.S. Congress to take up their cause. They reported that in places such as China, Vietnam, Cuba, the Middle East, and northern Africa, Christians faced arrest, torture, imprisonment, and extrajudicial executions for practicing their faith. The House of Representatives and Senate adopted resolutions deploring such persecution in September, with the Senate calling for "a thorough examination of all United States policies that affect persecuted Christians" and for the appointment of a special presidential adviser on religious persecution.

Two of the high-profile cases that involved persecution of Christians during the year were the abduction and murder of seven Trappist monks in Algeria by terrorists who called themselves the Armed Islamic Group and the conviction of Robert Hussein Qambar, a Muslim convert to Christianity, on a charge of apostasy by an Islamic court in Kuwait in May. Hussein left the country in August rather than face an appeals hearing in September.

France in 1996 had 172 groups classified as religious sects, according to a report released by the nation's Parliament in June. The government subsequently organized a watchdog group to recommend police investigations of the sects whenever it found them warranted. The parliaments of Belgium and Switzerland launched similar investigations. In Germany the ruling Christian Democratic Union (CDU) called for a ban on members of the Church of Scientology working in government jobs and asked for a government investigation of the group in October. Such a ban had already been initiated by the state of Bavaria. The youth branch of the CDU urged a boycott of the film *Mission: Impossible* because its star and director, Tom Cruise, was a Scientologist. While German officials called the church a threat to democracy, leaders of the church said Germany was using fascist tactics against it.

Roman Catholic Archbishop Norberto Rivera Carrera drew fire from Mexican officials in October when he said that if the government "openly denies fundamental human rights, then one has to deny it obedience." It was unclear to what he was referring, but Armando López Campa, director of religious affairs at the Interior Secretariat, said the remarks may have violated a legal ban on using pulpits to preach against the laws of the country.

On the first day of the year, the Israeli Supreme Court disbanded government religious councils in Jerusalem and the town of Kiryat Tivon because they excluded Reform and Conservative Jews; the court also ordered a Conservative and a Reform representative appointed to the religious council in Haifa. In July a Reform leader accused Sephardic Chief Rabbi Eliahu Bakshi-Doron of sanctioning the murder of Reform Jews; in a radio broadcast the rabbi said the biblical figure Phinehas had committed a "pure act" when he killed another Jew for having an intimate relationship with a Gentile woman. During the broadcast the rabbi described the victim as "the first Reform Jew."

In Sweden the government took the first steps to distance itself from the state Lutheran church by revoking the law requiring that children born to at least one Lutheran parent automatically become members of the church. After 2000 the church rather than the state would appoint its own bishops.

During Russia's presidential campaign all the major candidates, including Communist Gennady Zyuganov, actively sought support from the Orthodox Church. Zyuganov visited monasteries and dropped atheism from his party's platform. Ultranationalist Vladimir Zhirinovsky declared himself a believer and renewed his marriage vows in a widely publicized church ceremony. Pres. Boris Yeltsin appeared as often as possible in public with Patriarch Aleksey II, who all but officially endorsed his reelection. Although only about 10% of Russians attended services regularly, opinion polls found that they rated the Orthodox Church as the institution they most respected.

In the United States, Pres. Bill Clinton was denounced by leaders of several religious groups for his veto of a bill banning a late-term abortion procedure. Top leaders of the U.S. Roman Catholic Church said the veto was "beyond comprehension for those who hold human life sacred," and leaders of Clinton's own denomination, the Southern Baptist Convention, urged him to repent and "express publicly your personal regret" for the veto. On the other side, 36 religious leaders in the Religious Coalition for Reproductive Choice said they supported the president's action. Where religious people had differences on such matters, they said, "the government must not legislate, and thus impose, one religious view on all our citizens."

The Southern Baptist Convention unleashed a firestorm by adopting a resolution at its annual meeting in June in New Orleans calling for increased efforts to bear witness to Jewish people and appointing a new home missionary seeking to evangelize Jews in the U.S. The action was widely denounced as insensitive by mainstream Jewish organizations.

Holocaust survivor Elie Wiesel in July described the presence of crosses at the site of the Nazi Birkenau concentration camp in Poland as an "insult" and a "blasphemy" and urged their removal, thereby drawing criticism from Poland's Roman Catholic bishops. The Polish church's Commission for Dialogue with Judaism said the cross was regarded by Jews as a "sign of fear and hatred," while Poles considered it a symbol of "liberation from occupying powers."

The National Institute for Healthcare Research and the John Templeton Foundation of Philadelphia awarded grants to 11 medical schools to help teach future physicians to consider the spiritual as well as physical condition of patients. And the National Institutes of Health financed a $28,797 study at the University of New Mexico on the effect of prayer on alcoholics and drug abusers. In a book titled *Timeless Healing: The Power and Biology of Belief,* Herbert Benson, president of the Mind/Body Medical Institute of Boston's Deaconess Hospital, wrote that "our genetic blueprint has made believing in an Infinite Absolute part of our nature."

Other research focused on the success of church attendance and religious-based programs on preventing or reducing crime and substance abuse. A study by Harvard University economist Richard Freeman found regular church attendance to be a better predictor than family structure or income of the likelihood that urban youth would turn to drugs or crime, and another survey found more than 30 studies that showed a correlation between religious participation and avoidance of such behaviour. Such studies bolstered a provision of the new law overhauling the U.S. welfare system that enabled the federal government for the first time to be able to give money to churches and other religious groups in order to provide services to the poor.

On the other side of the coin, a federal judge in St. Paul, Minn., struck down Medicare and Medicaid payments to Christian Science healers on the ground that they violated the constitutional separation of church and state. Earlier the U.S. Supreme Court had upheld a $1.5 million award against four Christian Scientists in the case of an 11-year-old Minnesota boy who had died in 1989 after being treated with prayer rather than medical care.

The Religious Freedom Restoration Act, passed in 1993 to tighten conditions under which government in the U.S. could restrict religious practice, was interpreted in different ways during 1996. In May an appeals court in St. Louis, Mo., said it enabled a church in New Hope, Minn., to keep money tithed by a couple in the year before they filed for bankruptcy. But in a June ruling involving a dispute over whether a church in Cumberland, Md., could raze property that the city wanted preserved, a Baltimore judge said the law was unconstitutional because it "usurped the Supreme Court's authority to determine the scope and meaning of the First Amendment." In October the U.S. Supreme Court agreed to review the law in a case that involved its use by the archdiocese of San Antonio, Texas, against an ordinance in Boerne, Texas, that prevented a church in the city's historic district from building an addition. Congress passed a law in 1996 establishing a $10 million fund to provide loans and grants to rebuild churches that were destroyed by arson; a number of African-American churches in the southern U.S. were destroyed by fire during the year.

In their issues dated April 8, the day after Easter, the three major U.S. weekly newsmagazines all featured cover stories on new scholarly theories about the historical Jesus, many of which cast doubt on the literal nature of his resurrection. Many reflected the work of the controversial Jesus Seminar, which itself was criticized by former Roman Catholic priest Luke Timothy Johnson in a volume titled *The Real Jesus: The Misguided Quest for the Historical Jesus and the Truth of the Traditional Gospels.* A survey conducted in March by the Barna

Research Group found that 30% of "born-again" Christians did not believe that Jesus "came back to physical life after he was crucified."

Traditional concepts of the nature of hell were debated in January when the doctrine commission of the Church of England issued a report suggesting that it might more accurately be thought of as annihilation for nonbelievers rather than as a place of eternal torment. The Barna survey found that 31% of Americans saw hell as a place of physical torment while 37% said it represented a "state of permanent separation from the presence of God."

Ordination of homosexuals to the ministry and gay marriages drew varying responses from religious groups in 1996. The United Methodist Church voted at its quadrennial General Conference in Denver, Colo., in April to retain its position that the practice of homosexuality is incompatible with Christian teaching despite a petition from 15 bishops urging the church to ordain homosexuals. In a May ruling in Wilmington, Del., an Episcopal Church court dismissed heresy charges against retired bishop Walter Righter for having ordained a gay man as a deacon, ruling that a 1979 resolution by bishops against ordaining practicing homosexuals does not have the force of canon law. The General Assembly of the Presbyterian Church (U.S.A.), meeting in Albuquerque, N.M., in July, sent to presbyteries for a vote a measure that would require fidelity in marriage and chastity while single for all church officers and thus bar practicing homosexuals from ordination. Earlier, the Judicial Commission of the denomination's Cincinnati (Ohio) Presbytery had nullified the ordination of an allegedly gay man. In November a church in Toledo, Ohio, that belonged to the Universal Fellowship of Metropolitan Community Churches ordained a lesbian.

In March the Central Conference of American Rabbis, a Reform Jewish group, endorsed same-sex marriage as a civil right but stopped short of recommending that rabbis perform such ceremonies. In June the Unitarian-Universalist Association endorsed the legalization of such unions and voted to "proclaim the worth of marriage between any two committed persons."

Architect Philip Johnson celebrated his 90th birthday July 8 by unveiling a model for a $20 million cathedral in Dallas, Texas, for the Universal Fellowship of Metropolitan Community Churches, a 3,000-member congregation composed primarily of homosexuals. He described the structure, which would be taller than Notre Dame Cathedral, as "the most important job of my life."

While some Christians debated doctrinal points, a major rift in the ranks of Orthodox Christianity threatened to explode over the affiliation of the Estonian Orthodox Church. The church was forced under the jurisdiction of the Russian Orthodox Church by the Soviet Union in 1945. When Ecumenical Patriarch Bartholomew I approved its return to the jurisdiction of the patriarchate in Constantinople in February, Russian Orthodox Patriarch Aleksey II refused to recognize the change. The dispute was settled in May when Moscow and Constantinople agreed to allow parishes and priests in the Estonian church to decide their individual affiliations. (See *Orthodox Church:* Sidebar, below.) Meanwhile, Or-

thodox, Roman Catholic, and Protestant groups agreed to form a Christian Interconfessional Consultative Committee to promote cooperation and mutual understanding in the Commonwealth of Independent States and the Baltic countries.

A survey reported that church attendance in the U.S. was at the lowest level in two decades, with attendance dropping especially among seniors and baby boomers. Noting that these trends went against traditional patterns for people in their mid-40s to mid-60s, pollster George Barna cited the failure of churches to be relevant and turbulence within families as factors.

The $1 million Templeton Prize for Progress in Religion was awarded to Bill Bright, a Presbyterian layman who founded the Campus Crusade for Christ in 1951. The evangelical ministry, represented in 165 countries, was best known for its pamphlet *The Four Spiritual Laws* and a film on the life of Jesus that had been translated into more than 350 languages and shown in more than 200 countries. The 74-year-old Bright said he would use the money to establish a program to educate church leaders worldwide on fasting and prayer.

(DARRELL J. TURNER)

PROTESTANT CHURCHES

Anglican Communion. A church court dismissed heresy charges in May against the retired Episcopal bishop of Iowa, Walter C. Righter. In early 1995 Righter had been charged by 10 bishops under church canons for "teaching publicly and advisedly that a practicing homosexual may properly be ordained" and for violating his ordination vows. The court, however, held that neither the doctrine nor discipline of the Episcopal Church prohibited the ordination of a noncelibate homosexual person. The bishops who filed the charges said at a May news conference that they would not appeal the ruling. They did, however, plan to present a canonical change at the next general convention that would obligate all members of the clergy to "abstain from sexual relations outside Holy Matrimony."

Ellen F. Cooke, the former national church treasurer who admitted to embezzling $2.2 million in church funds, was sentenced to a five-year prison term by a U.S. District Court judge in Newark, N.J., in July. She began her sentence at a federal prison in Alderson, W.V., on August 26.

Bishop Winston Ndungane was installed in September as the successor to Desmond Tutu as archbishop of Cape Town, the highest office of the Anglican Church in southern Africa. Formerly bishop of Kimberley and Kuruman in the Northern Cape, Bishop Ndungane served a three-year prison term from 1963 to 1966 for his anti-apartheid activities as a student. In the Philippines, Bishop Idnacio Capuyan Soliba of the diocese of Northern Luzon was chosen the prime bishop of the Episcopal Church in the Philippines at the church's June synod.

In late 1995 the Church in the Province of the West Indies became the 15th Anglican province to vote in favour of ordaining women to the priesthood. Others included the Anglican churches in Australia, Brazil, Burundi, Canada, England, Hong Kong and Macao, Ireland, Kenya, New Zealand, the Philippines, southern Africa, Uganda, the United States, and West Africa. Meanwhile, the General Synod of Japan's Anglican church, Nippon Sei Ko Kai, rejected a proposal to ordain women priests after the bishops voted against it. Clergy and lay delegates at the synod had voted by a two-thirds majority in favour of ordination.

The assistant bishop of the Kirinyaga diocese in Kenya, Andrew Adano Tuye, was killed on July 27. Bishop Tuye died with senior government officials when the police helicopter they were traveling in crashed just outside Marsabit.

In February the Rev. Barbara Brown Taylor, rector of Grace-Calvary Church in Clarkesville, Ga., was named one of the 12 most effective preachers in the English-speaking world. The selections were made by researchers at Baylor University, Waco, Texas, in a poll of 1,500 other preachers and seminary professors. Taylor was the only woman and only Episcopalian on the list.

(DAVID E. SUMNER)

DANA LIXENBERG

The Rev. Barry Stopfel (right), standing beside his companion, the Rev. Will Leckie, was ordained in 1990 as an Episcopal deacon by Bishop Walter Righter, who knew that Stopfel was a noncelibate homosexual. Charged with heresy for this action, Righter was later cleared.

The Rev. Levi Pickens stands in front of the charred remains of the Mount Zion Baptist Church in Boligee, Ala., one of many African-American churches that burned during the year.

Baptist Churches. During 1996 some prominent African-American church leaders in the United States joined with secular business interests to boost black spending power. Among those denominations urging their parishioners to buy the products of the Revelation Corp. of America were the National Baptist Convention, U.S.A., Inc. (7.5 million members), National Baptist Convention of America, Inc. (3 million), and the Progressive National Baptist Convention, Inc. (2.7 million). According to the plan, if substantial numbers of parishioners cooperated, a portion of the corporation's profits would be funneled to local churches. The Revelation Corp. of America was a for-profit merchandising creation of John Lowery, a Memphis, Tenn., developer.

The Southern Baptist Convention (SBC), the largest Protestant denomination in the U.S., with 15,614,060 members, passed resolutions in its June meeting to boycott Disney enterprises because the Walt Disney Co. was providing health care benefits to companions of gay employees. The SBC also objected to Disney's "hosting of homosexual theme nights at its parks."

At the same meeting, the SBC resolved to evangelize the Jews. The resolution criticized "an organized effort on the part of some either to deny that Jewish people need to come to their Messiah, Jesus, to be saved; or to claim, for whatever reason, that Christians have neither right nor obligation to proclaim the gospel to the Jewish people."

The president of the National Baptist Convention of America, Inc., the second largest African-American Baptist denomination, rejected the SBC's recent apology for racism. Pres. E. Edward Jones told the 4,000 delegates at the denomination's annual meeting in Dallas, Texas, "The civil rights struggle is still going on and we need more than an apology."

American Baptist Churches USA issued a call to prayer and concern for the churches being burned in the southern U.S. Grants and building loans were offered by the American Baptist Office of World Relief and the National Ministries' Office of National Disaster Response.

At a recent gathering in Toulouse, France, the Baptist World Alliance was told that the organization was developing strategies to increase its membership significantly in predominantly Roman Catholic countries in Europe. Some 186 Baptist bodies worldwide were related to the Baptist World Alliance. Nilson Fanini, president of the Alliance, said, "Given our doctrinal differences, there will always be a need for Baptists to plant churches, even where there are many Catholic congregations." But Fanini cautioned that Baptists needed to exercise "courtesy and fellowship with those who have ploughed the ground before us and who believe in many Christian doctrines precious to Baptists."

(NORMAN R. DE PUY)

Christian Church (Disciples of Christ). Actions taken during summer meetings of racial and ethnic constituencies, along with a churchwide response to help rebuild burned African-American churches, highlighted much of 1996 for the Christian Church (Disciples of Christ). The North American denomination, based in Indianapolis, Ind., gave more than $60,000 to a special fund established by the National Council of Churches. In other action July assemblies of African-American and Hispanic Disciples released statements condemning the racism behind the arson fires. The fires were a sobering testimony "that racism continues to plague our land," said the Disciples' general minister and president, Richard L. Hamm, in a July pastoral letter. He also announced that the 1997 General Assembly would examine racism in North America.

The assembly of Hispanic Disciples also criticized U.S. immigration laws, which it termed discriminatory. A first-time gathering of Asian-American Disciples and United Church of Christ members called for the removal of U.S. bases and personnel from Okinawa.

Other highlights included national television appearances by two Disciples of Christ congregations; The Easter program, "Resurrecting Hope," featured the 8,000-member Mississippi Boulevard Christian Church in Memphis, Tenn., and renowned Disciples preacher Fred Craddock spoke from historic Beargrass Christian Church in Louisville, Ky., for a Christmas special, "Awakening the Quest."

(CLIFFORD L. WILLIS)

Churches of Christ. A growing emphasis on benevolence, especially among the urban poor, characterized the Churches of Christ in 1996. The Prestoncrest Church of Christ topped the list of 18 large metropolitan churches in Dallas, Texas, in the total amount of help given to the disadvantaged, in both time and money; Prestoncrest earmarked 31% of its budget of $1.6 million for this purpose.

Healing Hands International sent 23 shipments of medical aid, valued at $4 million, to 13 countries, including the Republic of Georgia, Guatemala, and Nigeria. Church of Christ Disaster Relief of Nashville, Tenn., and White's Ferry Road Relief Ministry of Louisiana coordinated relief in the wake of Hurricane Fran in September.

E-mail and the Internet were used worldwide to contact mission points and develop teaching programs. National television ministries expanded, including Herald of Truth and "Key to the Kingdom." World Bible School correspondence courses, including a new edition in Arabic for the Muslim world, were used to convert thousands. Sunset International Bible Institute in Lubbock, Texas, conducted a seminar to consider ways to reach the Islamic world for Christ.

Let's Start Talking, a student evangelistic ministry of English-language instruction using the Bible as text, marked its 15th year with 45 teams in 24 countries. The Russian Children's Bible was published by Eastern European Mission. Children and youth camps were held in Ukraine and Russia.

Paid positions of ministry for women increased during the year. WINGS, a network ministry for women in need, using E-mail and telephone, was begun by the department of marriage and family therapy at Harding University, Searcy, Ark. A "Methusalah" conference for seniors emphasized their growing numbers and needs.

(M. NORVEL YOUNG)

Church of Christ, Scientist. At its 101st annual meeting the church's first Latin-American president, Juan Carlos Lavigne, sounded the theme of reaching out to address today's growing demand for spirituality: "To the degree that God's love becomes closer and more real to us, our capacity to love expands. It overflows the limits of individual affection, and we embrace our community and the world. . . . We begin to pray for others." Lavigne, a Christian Science practitioner and teacher from Argentina, conducted the June 3, 1996, meeting in Boston.

About 3,000 members listened to officers' reports describing how the church was endeavouring to fulfill its mission as stated by founder Mary Baker Eddy—"to commemorate the word and works of our Master, which should reinstate primitive Christianity and its lost element of healing." In line with this, the church's clerk reported "encouraging signs of our membership renewing their healing careers" and the increasing involvement of young people in Sunday school and in Wednesday testimony meetings. New members were welcomed from 42 countries, and a Christian Science church was established in Russia for the first time in almost 70 years.

Among the year's other noteworthy developments, Eddy's primary work, *Science and Health with Key to the Scriptures,* was being sold in bookstores throughout the United States, Canada, Australia, and the United Kingdom, and Eddy was inducted into the (U.S.) National Women's Hall of Fame. *The Christian Science Monitor* received its sixth Pulitzer Prize, and an unusually large number of church members from around the world contributed articles to the denomination's religious magazines for the first time. In Boston the restoration of the Mother Church buildings reached the halfway point. Also during the year, the church launched three sites on the Internet: its own official home page, an electronic version of the *Monitor,* and a nondenominational Religious Freedom home page.

(M. VICTOR WESTBERG)

Church of Jesus Christ of Latter-day Saints. The seventh largest church in the United States, the Church of Jesus Christ of Latter-day Saints (LDS) in 1996 crossed a demographic Rubicon: for the first time,

it had more members living outside than inside the U.S. By the year's end the church had 10 million members in 156 nations and territories. The 50,000 full-time missionaries were recruiting approximately 300,000 new members per year. In addition to 4.8 million members in the U.S., there were 800,000 in Mexico, 600,000 in Brazil, 400,000 in Chile, 400,000 in the Philippines, 300,000 in Asia, and sizable numbers in Europe, Canada, and the South Pacific. An attempt was being made to universalize the LDS message and to draw attention to the Christian dimension of its theology.

Rex E. Lee, who had served for seven years as president of Brigham Young University, Provo, Utah, resigned for reasons of health (he died shortly thereafter) and was replaced in January 1996 by Merrill J. Bateman, formerly dean of business administration and management at the university and presiding bishop of the church. Simultaneously, Bateman was appointed a member of the First Council of Seventy, which marked the first time that a general authority of the church had served as president of the church university.

Despite his age—he was 86 in 1996—the church president, Gordon B. Hinckley, visited large congregations in many countries throughout the world. He dedicated new temples in San Diego, Calif.; Hong Kong; and American Fork, Utah. By the end of 1996 there were 49 working temples throughout the world, 6 under construction, and plans announced for 6 more. The First Presidency also announced its intention to build a new meeting hall north of Temple Square in downtown Salt Lake City, Utah, that would seat 25,000 people.

(LEONARD J. ARRINGTON)

Jehovah's Witnesses. During an age when families were disintegrating, a journalist described Jehovah's Witnesses as persons who "live by Scriptures" and "stress family togetherness." To help persons live by the Bible, the Witnesses arranged a series of worldwide conventions beginning in 1996. During hundreds of seminars held in dozens of cities, the 192-page book *The Secret of Family Happiness* was released to the

millions who attended. In less than a year, more than 14 million copies of this book, which explains how applying Bible principles can build strong families, had been published in 85 languages.

The emphasis on living by the Bible contributed to the 170% increase in the number of Witnesses since 1986. As of 1996 they numbered 5,199,895 in 232 countries. During 1995 the Witnesses spent more than one billion hours obeying Jesus's command to spread his teachings to "people of all the nations." They distributed Bibles and Bible aids throughout the world and translated them into 303 languages. In 1995 the 32-page brochure *Enjoy Life on Earth Forever* was translated into 18 additional languages; this brought the total to 237 and made it the most widely translated publication of the Witnesses. During 1995 and 1996 their modern-language *New World Translation of the Holy Scriptures* was completed in Finnish and in Norwegian, and the New Testament of the Bible was translated into Chinese and four African languages, which brought the total to 29 languages. Thus, it was available in languages spoken by over 50% of the world's population.

(MILTON HENSCHEL)

Lutheran Communion. The Council of the Lutheran World Federation (LWF), meeting in Geneva in September 1996, heard reports from its president, Gottfried Brakemeier of Brazil, and its general secretary, Ishmael Noko of Zimbabwe, on the present state of this international body of 122 member church organizations. A major item on the agenda was the ninth assembly of the LWF, to meet in July 1997 in Hong Kong, soon after control of that city reverted to China. After some earlier difficulties with the Chinese government, it seemed clear that the LWF would celebrate its 50th anniversary with its first assembly in Asia. Resolutions adopted by the council included approval of sanctions against Iraq and affirmation of the human rights of children. The council approved a process to further develop a joint declaration between the member churches of the LWF and the Roman Catholic Church on the doctrine

W. Grant McMurray, shown in the group's temple in Independence, Mo., was elected president of the Reorganized Church of Jesus Christ of Latter-day Saints in April. He was the first person to be chosen to head the church who was not a descendant of Mormonism's founder, Joseph Smith.

of justification. One result of this declaration, to be considered for final official approval in 1998, would be the recognition that certain condemnations that were made in the 16th century between Lutherans and Roman Catholics would now be regarded as invalid.

In the Lutheran churches of Norway and Finland, the number of baptisms and confirmations increased. The constitutional separation of the Church of Sweden and the Swedish government continued; it was to be completed in 2000. Ecumenical progress between several Nordic and Baltic Lutheran churches and a number of Anglican churches in the U.K. moved forward.

Lutherans held international dialogues with the Orthodox churches and the Roman Catholic Church and a theological consultation with the Seventh-day Adventist Church. Regional dialogues between Lutherans and Mennonites in Germany and between Lutherans and Moravians in the U.S. took place. In India, Hong Kong, and Switzerland, women were selected for major leadership positions. Lutheran churches in Germany, Finland, and the U.S. discussed human sexuality as a potential church-dividing issue. In Germany Lutherans marked the 450th anniversary of the death of Martin Luther. In the U.S. bishops of the Evangelical Lutheran Church in America (ELCA) and of the Episcopal Church in the USA held their first joint meeting. The ELCA was considering entering into full communion with the Episcopal Church and three Reformed churches in 1997, as well as accepting the "Joint Declaration on the Doctrine of Justification" with the Roman Catholic Church.   (WILLIAM G. RUSCH)

Methodist Churches. The quadrennial General Conference of the United Methodist Church was held in Denver, Colo., in April 1996. Delegates voted to retain the United Methodist Church's Book of Discipline's prohibition of the ordination of "self-avowed practicing homosexuals." The conference approved the establishing of a commission to create a plan for the possible union of four Methodist churches: the United Methodist, the African Methodist Episcopal, the African Methodist Episcopal Zion, and the Christian Methodist Episcopal Churches. The conference also voted to become part of the Consultation on Church Union covenanting community, which aimed to promote spiritual rather than structural unity.

The 17th World Methodist Conference took place in Rio de Janeiro in August. Some 2,700 delegates assembled from Methodist churches throughout the world. Under the broad theme "Holy Spirit: Giver of Life," the conference explored the nature and gifts of the Holy Spirit in the life of the church. During the conference the World Methodist Council, consisting of 500 elected representatives from the 71 member church organizations, held meetings. The council welcomed into membership the Church of South India and the Methodist Church of Paraguay, adopted a statement on "Wesleyan Essentials of Christian Faith," approved Methodist participation in ecumenical planning for the celebration of the 2,000th anniversary of the birth of Jesus Christ, received the report "The Word of Life: A Statement on Revelation and Faith" from the Joint Commission of the Roman Catholic Church and the World Methodist

Conference, authorized the establishment, in cooperation with His Holiness the Ecumenical Patriarch, of an international dialogue with the Orthodox churches, and adopted a report of the Anglican-Methodist International Commission.

Other resolutions included a call to daily prayer at noon, whenever possible, asking for the guidance of the Holy Spirit in transforming the world away from violence and injustice, and a call to the International Monetary Fund and the World Bank to celebrate the millennium by canceling the debt of the less-developed countries. The council also adopted resolutions instructing the officers and the executive committee to review the structure and role of the council and its relation to the conference.

The 1996 World Methodist Peace Award was given to Bishop Stanley Mogoba, the presiding bishop of the Methodist Church of Southern Africa, for "his consistency in never advocating violence . . . in the struggle against apartheid; his courage in seeking reconciliation."   (JOHN C.A. BARRETT)

Pentecostal Churches. During 1996 a revival at the Brownsville Assembly of God church in Pensacola, Fla., attracted news and visitors on a scale experienced only by the "Toronto Blessing" in 1995. By August the number of visitors totaled more than 700,000, while the "professions of faith" totaled 25,000 persons. By the end of the year, the Brownsville meetings were spawning similar revivals in other churches throughout the U.S.

In April the International Church of the Foursquare Gospel (founded by Aimee Semple McPherson) reelected John R. Holland to a third four-year term as president. The Church of God (Cleveland, Tenn.) in August elected Paul Walker as general overseer. For decades Walker had served as pastor of the largest congregation in the denomination, the Mount Paran Church of God in Atlanta, Ga. In July Pentecostals in the U.S. mourned the passing of C.M. Ward, the longtime ABC network radio preacher on the Assemblies of God national broadcast known as "Revivaltime." The new Pentecostal/Charismatic Churches of North America met in September in Memphis, Tenn., to "revisit" the "Miracle of Memphis," which brought black and white Pentecostals together in 1994.

There was discord between Pentecostals and Roman Catholics in Brazil in January, when the 3.5 million-member Universal Church of the Kingdom of God, led 200,000 members into the streets to protest verbal attacks by the government and a Catholic-owned television station. On the other hand, healing and harmony made news in April when 60,000 Italian Catholic charismatics met in Rimini, Italy, and pledged cooperation with the many Protestants, pentecostals, and charismatic observers in the sessions. (VINSON SYNAN)

Reformed, Presbyterian, and Congregational Churches. Western theology is no longer the universal form for understanding the Christian gospel, according to the international consultation on gospel and cultures organized by the World Alliance of Reformed Churches (WARC) in Indonesia in February 1996. The sense that a fundamental theological shift had taken place pervaded the consultation as it recognized that many issues look quite different from the perspectives of different cultures.

Another kind of universality came under attack in the WARC consultation on Reformed faith and economic justice, held in Geneva in May, when it protested against the exclusion of millions of people from a world economy that was supposed to meet their needs. The two consultations were part of an intense process of preparation for the 23rd WARC General Council, scheduled to take place in Debrecen, Hung., in August 1997. Its theme was to be "Break the Chains of Injustice."

Meeting in Detmold, Ger., in August, the WARC executive committee agreed on new guidelines for international dialogue. A first round of international Reformed-Pentecostal dialogue took place in Torre Pellice, Italy, in May.

At the Reformed Ecumenical Council (REC) meeting in Grand Rapids, Mich., in August, delegates from churches in Asia and Africa challenged the council to accept the implications of the gospel of Jesus Christ in a world of poverty and pain, where ecological crises, military dictatorships, proliferation of arms, and crushing international debts impoverish peoples' lives. REC had been founded in opposition to WARC in 1946, but by 1996 the two organizations had moved closer together. The REC General Assembly reaffirmed its desire to establish a joint committee with WARC, with a view to promoting better understanding and fostering areas of cooperation.

Nine churches were admitted to WARC membership in 1996: the Congregational Federation of Australia, the Isua Krista Kohhran and the Reformed Presbyterian Church (Northeast India), the Gereja Toraja Mamasa (Indonesia), the Iglesia Presbiteriana Asociada Reformada (Mexico), the Ekalesia Kelisiano Tuvalu and the Ekalesia Niue (Pacific), the Reformed Presbyterian Church in Uganda, and the Korean Presbyterian Church in America (U.S.). By late 1996 WARC linked more than 70 million Christians in 208 churches in 102 countries.   (PÁRAIC RÉAMONN)

The Religious Society of Friends. After Quaker women from the economically deprived part of the world returned from the UN Fourth World Conference on Women in Beijing in 1995, they urged Quakers throughout the world and in their home communities to make positive changes in the cultural attitudes and customs that continued to keep women second-class citizens in many countries. They reminded their audience that Friends' Christian testimony on equality needed to be lived at home by means of participatory decision making.

The Friends World Committee for Consultation Asia/West Pacific Section held its triennial representatives meeting in July 1996 at Darwin, Australia. Delegates from the region were excited to see the variety of work and witness of Friends in this large section, particularly in Vietnam, Cambodia, and India.

In late August 57 leaders and pastors representing 19 African Quaker groups and 12 Mission and Service agencies working in Africa met to worship and to listen and learn from one another. They sought to further develop their strengths, one of which was a growing convergence between Mission and Service through a better recognition of their underlying unity. In focusing on the horrifying situation in Rwanda and Burundi, the group was moved by the presence of Friends from those countries, most of them now refugees. They told of the fear and hatred around them but also of the sheltering of God's love in desperate circumstances. Some had lost close family members, others their homes. Although some church buildings had been destroyed, no one as of late 1996 had been killed in a Friends church. The meeting concluded with a call for better communication and united positive action, including the gathering and sharing of information on the growing arms trade within Africa.

(THOMAS F. TAYLOR)

Salvation Army. During 1996 the Salvation Army invested in its future strength and growth. The first meeting of the International Spiritual Life Commission took place in July. It reviewed methods by which Salvationists could further develop and maintain spiritual life. The International Forum on Youth was scheduled for 1997. Entitled "Breakthrough Generation," it was planned by Gen. Paul A. Rader to focus the energy, passion, and commitment of Salvation Army youth on the continuation of their mission.

Touring South Korea, Pakistan, India, Australia, and the U.S., General Rader strengthened the Army's worldwide presence and forged new spiritual links. Setting an example of altruism, retired general Eva Burrows received the 1996 Living Legacy Award from the Woman's International Center, San Diego, Calif.

Humanitarian care and uniting to overcome disaster remained vital to the Army's concept of "active" Christianity. The murders of a teacher and pupils at Dunblane (Scot.) Primary School and of 35 people in Port Arthur, Tas., shocked the world. Salvationists joined other denominations in comforting and later helping to rebuild those communities. Salvation Army emergency relief teams provided assistance following an explosion in London's Docklands, and after an earthquake in Yunnan province, China, the Army provided aid.

Royal Navy Lieut. Tony Brooks embarked on a 19,300-km (12,000-mi) charity bicycle ride from London to the Bering Straits, Siberia. His aim was to raise funds for a Salvation Army detoxification and rehabilitation unit. Epitomizing Salvationist philosophy, the journey was unofficially dubbed "Life Cycle."

(CHARMAINE FLETCHER)

Seventh-day Adventist Church. Meeting in Costa Rica, the Annual Council of the church's executive committee voted in 1996 to restructure the Asia-Pacific division of the world church. Instead of one administrative unit stretching from Korea to Indonesia, the region would have two units, a northern one with headquarters near Seoul, S.Kor., and a southern one with headquarters near Manila. The restructuring reflected the growth of the church in the region, particularly in China. With these changes the worldwide Seventh-day Adventist Church comprised 12 divisions, with a membership (as of Dec. 31, 1995) of 8,812,555 from 208 countries.

Plans were laid for a four-year emphasis on the message and mission of the church among Adventists worldwide. For 1997 the theme would be "Experience the Joy of Salvation in Christ."

The year also was marked by the largest evangelistic outreach in the church's history.

A five-week program of meetings originating in Orlando, Fla., was transmitted via satellite to about 3,000 sites in North America, Central America, South America, and Europe. The meetings were made available in 12 languages to a combined audience of approximately 250,000.

Humanitarian services continued to be provided by ADRA, the Adventist Development and Relief Agency, which worked in 143 countries. The Annual Council in Costa Rica gave particular attention to the challenge presented by AIDS, stressing the need for education as well as help to victims.

A second round of consultations with representatives of the Lutheran World Federation was held near Toronto. Discussions focused on justification by faith, law, and the Sabbath. The church also engaged in official dialogue with the Worldwide Church of God. (WILLIAM G. JOHNSSON)

Unitarian (Universalist) Churches. Vitality and growth continued to characterize North America's Unitarian Universalist movement in 1996. Local church budgets climbed 63% from 1993 to 1996, membership was increasing at an annual rate of 4%, and the denomination's presence on college campuses had quintupled since 1994.

The annual General Assembly of the Unitarian Universalist Association of Congregations, June 20–26, 1996, drew more than 3,100 registrants to Indianapolis, Ind. Dedicated to the theme "The Future Is Now" and emphasizing youth issues, it attracted the largest gathering of young people in the denomination's history.

Resolutions for study or final acceptance dealt with problems of economic injustices, environment, energy conservation, and racial and cultural diversity. Overwhelming support greeted resolutions in support of same-sex marriages and those expressing outrage over the violence inflicted upon African-American churches.

The Canadian Unitarian Council, concerned about the loss of the nation's social safety net, passed a resolution on economic justice in a time of financial uncertainty. Its professionally produced video, "Sharing Our Vision," was shown on the Vision TV network nationally and was being used by congregations.

The (U.K.) General Assembly of the Unitarian and Free Christian Churches held its 1996 meetings in Glasgow, Scot. Resolutions on social issues included calling on the government to introduce tighter control over handguns by requiring their owners to submit to an annual test of psychological fitness, and to reform the national lottery in order to alleviate its perceived worst effects on society.

Around the world, Unitarian congregations were formed as far apart as Russia (Moscow, St. Petersburg) and Ushuaia, Arg., near the southern tip of South America. The 200th anniversary of the Unitarian Christian Church of Madras, India, was observed in 1995. (JOHN NICHOLLS BOOTH)

The United Church of Canada. The United Church's December 1995 pastoral letter on the economy continued to draw considerable response in 1996. Media interest in the letter generated both criticism and support for the church's call to its members to find ways "to stop a growing war against the poor." Shifting spending priorities, the impact of costs related to the relocation of the national offices in

1995, and lower-than-anticipated revenues combined to result in organizational restructuring and staff layoffs in 1996. The total amount of money raised for all purposes in United Church congregations was Can$311,855,276. Of this, Can$30,291,561, less than 10%, was directed to the national funds of the church. The United Church remained Canada's largest Protestant denomination, with some three million known members and adherents in 1996.

Like other institutions within Canadian society, the United Church continued to deal with sensitive legal issues, including those related to claims by former residents of a now-closed Indian residential school. Clergy employment disputes and claims of sexual harassment were the predominant cases that came before both the church and civil courts in 1996. For the first time in many years, the church had a surplus of clergy. Unfortunately, this was happening at a time when the financial viability of some congregations to support full-time or multiple ministry was in question and when the number of congregations was in gradual decline. A churchwide study was beginning to assess this development.

The denomination's new hymnal, *Voices United,* was published in April to widespread acclaim. Also during the year, the Ethnic Ministries Council met for the first time and began its program of supporting ethnic ministries throughout the church.

(DOUGLAS L. FLANDERS)

United Church of Christ. In 1996 the United Church of Christ celebrated the 150th anniversary of the American Missionary Association, a historic church mission agency that engaged in prophetic service and action with African-Americans, Puerto Ricans, Native Americans, Appalachian whites, and people moving to the United States from many nations and cultures. The AMA founded churches, schools, and hospitals and was involved in community development and publishing.

Work to reshape the structure of the church in the U.S. intensified during the year. This new structure, to be implemented in 1999, was to include three ministry units—Local Church, Justice and Witness, and Wider Church—along with an Office of General Minister and President. This would be the first comprehensive national reshaping since the formation of the 1.5 million-member church in 1957.

Critical theological deliberation continued within the church, sparked to a significant degree by the ongoing Seasons of Theological Reflection and the introduction in 1995 of *The New Century Hymnal.* The editors of the hymnal stated that "one of the great gifts to our time is the spirit . . . calling us to affirm the fullness of God, the goodness of creation, and the value of every person. The search for language and metaphor to express that breadth and richness marks this book." Spirited deliberations about the theological appropriateness of the language and metaphors used in the hymnal were ongoing.

The church strengthened its efforts to implement its commitment to be "a multiracial, multicultural church," remained active in the public realm primarily through support of poor and exploited people throughout the world, and furthered its involvement in a number of ecumenical relationships. Continued attention was given to evangelism and stewardship concerns in light of continued membership losses and reduced financial support.

(PAUL H. SHERRY)

ROMAN CATHOLIC CHURCH

Violence against Roman Catholic clergy was particularly evident in 1996. The Chinese government agitated against memorial services for Bishop Peter Joseph Fan Xueyan, a leader of the underground, pro-Vatican Chinese church that could number as many as 10 million members; the bishop had died in 1992. Political intimidation turned into outright violence as the government sought to weaken the underground church while promoting the so-called Patriotic Church, the government-sanctioned Catholic Church. In Nicaragua Sandinistas and their sympathizers carried out raids against clergy and churches to protest the papal visit in February. In Ghana Christian-Muslim strife had cost some 2,000 lives in 1995, and struggles continued well into the new year. Muslim extremists in Algeria murdered seven aged Trappist monks in May and then killed Bishop Pierre Lu-

cien Claverie in August. In Rwanda and Burundi antagonism between warring Hutu and Tutsi did not spare clergymen. In September Archbishop Joachim Ruhuna of Burundi, a Tutsi, was ambushed and killed, presumably by Hutu. Earlier, Bishop Simon Ntamwana, a Hutu, was threatened but proclaimed his intention to stay.

Throughout the world various bodies of Catholic clergy carried on struggles with the secular culture. In South Africa bishops opposed a gay rights initiative. The bishops of Argentina and of the Philippines complained about birth control campaigns launched by the governments of those countries. The Chilean bishops attacked efforts to loosen divorce laws, while the bishops of former East Germany objected to government efforts to minimize religious instruction in public schools. In the United States, Bishop Fabian Bruskewitz of Lincoln, Neb., announced that persons belonging to organizations that opposed official church teachings would be automatically excommunicated. He had in mind Catholic reform groups such as Call to Action as well as organizations that had no official connection with the church.

Catholics in Hong Kong were attempting to take a more vigorous role in political life and to gain representation in the eventual provincial legislature. In South Korea 61 Catholics were elected to the 299-member legislature. Alterations in ecclesiastical administration paralleled these more evidently secular trends. New dioceses were created, or boundaries were substantially altered, in Kenya, Nigeria, Ethiopia, Uganda, and Brazil. The church's awareness of its growing presence in Africa and Asia was reflected in its decision to beatify two missionaries, one to Africa and one to China, and to canonize a missionary to China.

As the church continued to struggle against the secularism of many modern cultures, it also faced dissent within its own rank. In 1995 some 500,000 Catholics in Austria had signed petitions calling for the ordination of women, an end to obligatory priestly celibacy, the election of bishops by laypeople, a "more humane church," and "acceptance of the value of sexual relationships." These petitions were consistent with a survey of U.S. Catholics that found 69% favouring married clergy, 65% supporting local election of bishops, and 78% insisting on more voice for ordinary believers. Joseph Cardinal Bernardin of Chicago (*see* OBITUARIES) issued a document entitled "Called to Be Catholic" that spoke of "a time of peril" for the American church and instituted a committee to discuss the painful issues dividing Catholics in the U.S. Cardinal Bernardin was forced to retreat when some of his brother bishops, especially Bernard Cardinal Law of Boston and James Cardinal Hickey of Washington, said that there was no room for dissent from "revealed truth" and that dissident Catholics should be encouraged to abandon their opposition to official teachings.

In Rome the existence of this contention was acknowledged in a number of subtle ways. Whereas 1995 was a year of extraordinary activity, with encyclicals and pastoral letters being issued almost every month, there were few major pronouncements in 1996. In the apostolic constitution *Universi Dominici Gregis* (February 23) the pope made technical adjustments in the procedures for electing a pope but basically affirmed the existing system. The Vatican in March issued an "apostolic exhortation" entitled *Vita Consecrata* that commented in detail on the history, importance, and duties of the consecrated religious life. In October the pope issued a formal statement in which he said, "Fresh knowledge leads to recognition of the theory of evolution as more than just a hypothesis."

If these major documents responded only obliquely to challenges faced by the church, other means were used to respond more directly. The pope employed many of his Sunday Angelus messages to affirm traditional Catholic education and to stress the role of the parents as the primary educators of the young. In his addresses to bishops' delegations in Rome for their required periodic visits, the pope repeatedly emphasized the need for bishops to hand on church teachings unchanged and unblemished and to preserve traditional moral norms. An unsigned essay in *Osservatore Romano* (Feb. 7, 1996) criticized a collection of essays published in Germany and critical of the 1993 encyclical *Veritatis Splendor*. The tenor of the essay was that truth must never

PEDRO UGARTE—AFP PHOTO

A man raises a cross and a Vatican flag in a crowd who came to hear Pope John Paul II celebrate mass in Managua, Nicaragua, in February. It was the pope's second visit to Nicaragua, part of a four-country tour of Latin America.

Conflict in Orthodoxy

The most serious threat of schism in centuries occurred in Eastern Orthodoxy in February 1996 when Bartholomew I, ecumenical patriarch of Constantinople, decreed that the Estonian Orthodox Apostolic Church was autonomous under his authority rather than under the authority of the Russian Orthodox Church. Aleksey II, patriarch of Russia, responded by formally "suspending communion" between the Russian church and Constantinople. The conflict arose in the wake of two years of failed negotiations regarding the patriarchate to which the Estonian church was subject. The church was under the Moscow patriarchate until 1923, when Soviet interests in Estonia threatened it and a special diocese was created by Constantinople to offer spiritual protection to its members. In 1945, soon after Estonia was annexed by the Soviet Union again, all Orthodox communities in Estonia were reconstituted as a diocese under the Moscow Patriarchate. In 1947 Estonian Orthodox Christians in exile in Stockholm successfully sought the official protection of Constantinople.

At stake in Estonia was jurisdiction over 54 clerics and 60,000 members of the Orthodox Church. Some estimated that as much as 5% of Estonian land was Orthodox Church property. Most of the prominent Orthodox leaders throughout the world publicly took sides in the conflict. The Estonian government and the Orthodox Church in Finland supported Bartholomew. Dissident and controversial leaders in Ukraine and Russia, such as the disputed head of the Ukrainian Orthodox Church, supported him as well.

Aleksey's position appeared to be in the best interests of the Russian government and the Russian church. He was supported by leaders of the Orthodox churches in Antioch, Jerusalem, Serbia, Bulgaria, and Poland. Nevertheless, his aggressive defense of ethnic Russians and historic Russian interests in surrounding countries caused concern that a traditionalist, nationalist Slavic orthodoxy might become dominant.

In May the ecumenical patriarchate announced that in order to maintain Orthodox unity, each Estonian Ortho-

dox parish would be allowed to choose to which ecclesiastical head it would relate. The Moscow patriarchate responded by restoring full communion with the ecumenical patriarchate. This solution, however, was likely to repeat the pattern of conflict in Orthodoxy in the U.S., where individual congregations had battled over preferred patriarchates, creating many congregations with ties to various overseas bodies.

Globally, the potential schism marked an increasing uneasiness over the role of Constantinople in guiding Eastern Orthodoxy's 250 million members worldwide. Though Bartholomew was considered "first among equals" among Orthodox patriarchs, there was growing concern over Constantinople's intervention in Estonia, Ukraine, and Japan, as well as the patriarch's training under the Pontifical Oriental Institute in Rome and his strong opposition to SCOBA, the pan-Orthodox synod of bishops in North America. Also at stake were the emerging dialogues with the Roman Catholic, Oriental Orthodox, and other Christian bodies.   (TODD M. JOHNSON)

Humility and patience are preached at Easter night services in a Russian Orthodox church at the Sagorsk monastery in Moscow.

be regarded as contingent or relative. It seemed clear that Rome had decided on a widespread effort to insist that much of the struggle in the contemporary Catholic Church was attributable to poor education and weak leadership.

Despite constant press reports about his allegedly poor health, the pope maintained a vigorous schedule of routine activities in Rome and of travels outside Italy. The year found the pope in Central America in February, in Tunisia in April, in Slovenia in May, in Germany in June, and in France in September. The latter visit occasioned some controversy because some of the sites selected for visitation were meant to recall the 1,500th anniversary of the baptism of Clovis, whom some regarded the first king of France. The point of the commemoration was to highlight the deep roots of French Catholicism. In October the pope had his appendix removed; his physicians announced that no new or serious illness was discovered during the surgery.

See WORLD AFFAIRS: *Vatican City State.*
(THOMAS F.X. NOBLE)

THE ORTHODOX CHURCH

Late in 1995 the Estonian government recognized as the only Orthodox church in the nation the Estonian Orthodox Apostolic Church, formerly in exile in Sweden. This created serious ethnic, legal, and property issues for the Russian Orthodox Church in Estonia. (*See* Sidebar.)

In Bulgaria the rivalry continued between Patriarch Maxim, who was recognized as the canonical head of the Bulgarian Orthodox Church by other Orthodox churches but whom the government had refused to recognize in 1992, and Pimen, elected as patriarch by a state-supported synod of bishops. Pimen's group acted in June to establish itself as a second Orthodox church in Bulgaria, intending to seek state recognition.

In Russia the Orthodox Church proclaimed a policy of noninvolvement in the July 3 elections for president of the nation, but unofficially it opposed former communist Gennady Zyuganov. In reaction to the moral decay in Russian society associated with capitalism, however, numerous clergy and laity supported Zyuganov.

In Albania Archbishop Anastasios reported in March that during the five years of his regime, 47 new churches had been built, 50 had been restored, and 30 churches, monasteries, and ecclesiastical buildings were currently being renovated. In August the Albanian government refused to accept three Greek nationals who were appointed by the ecumenical patriarchate as bishops of the dioceses of Korçë, Vlorë, and Gjirokastër. Archbishop Anastasios supported the government's action. Late in August police apprehended three teenagers who attended Iranian-taught Islamic fundamentalist classes, accusing them of having desecrated 18 300-year-old frescoes at the St. Michael Church in Voskopojë (Moschopolis). The head of the Muslims in Albania denounced the desecration as an act of intolerance.

At a synod on July 30, the ecumenical patriarchate elected U.S.-born Archbishop Spyridon of Italy archbishop of the Greek Orthodox Archdiocese of America. He succeeded Archbishop Iakovos, who had retired the previous day after 37 years in the position. Archbishop Spyridon was installed on September 21 in New York City. The synod concurrently established three new jurisdictions: the metropolitanates of Canada, Central America, and South America; their parishes were formerly under the authority of Archbishop Iakovos.
(STANLEY S. HARAKAS)

ORIENTAL ORTHODOX CHURCHES

The Coptic Orthodox Church in Egypt during 1996 began circumventing government policies designed to frustrate its need to repair old churches and construct new church buildings by purchasing closed and abandoned Eastern Orthodox and Roman Catholic churches. These closings had resulted from the policies of former presidents Gamal Abdel Nasser and Anwar as-Sadat against non-Egyptian Christians in Egypt. Approximately 50 church buildings were purchased at reasonable prices because their owners preferred that they be used as Christian churches rather than for secular purposes.

On May 8, 1996, Karekin I, the catholicos of the Armenian Apostolic Church based in Echmiadzin, Armenia, conducted an official visit at the headquarters of the Eastern Orthodox Patriarchate of Constantinople (Istanbul). He met with Ecumenical Patriarch Bartholomew, saying that he was committed to promoting Orthodox unity. Satisfaction was expressed regarding the elimination of doctrinal differences between the two traditions as a result of theological dialogue.

The leader of the Armenian Orthodox jurisdiction headquartered in Beirut, Lebanon, Catholicos Aram I, conducted a 21-day visit to California beginning June 20. His branch of the Armenian Church was working for closer cooperation with other branches.
(STANLEY S. HARAKAS)

JUDAISM

Of 120 Knesset (parliament) members elected in Israel on May 29, 1996, 23 belonged to the three religious parties, compared with 16 in the previous Knesset. This increase could be seen in the context of changes in the electoral system that favoured the small parties.

Israel's newly elected prime minister, Benjamin Netanyahu (*see* BIOGRAPHIES), included the three religious parties in his governing coalition. Guidelines issued by his bureau stated that "the Government will act to bring the religious and secular closer through mutual understanding and respect. The Government will retain the status quo on religious matters."

Aryeh Deri, leader of Shas, the largest religious party, insisted that the religious parties should not use their voting power to bargain for religious legislation. Despite this declaration, in August, in the wake of a Supreme Court ruling that Bar-Ilan Street in Jerusalem should remain open on the Sabbath, Orthodox members of the Knesset threatened to bring down the government unless it supported legislation to change the way in which Supreme Court justices were chosen; they were, however, heavily outvoted.

In reaction to rising tensions between religious and secular Jews and between the religious groups, several Jewish bodies as well as prominent leaders called for communal unity and mutual understanding. The Conference of European Rabbis, meeting in London in April, adopted 13 resolutions, mostly aimed at strengthening Orthodox leadership, education, and observance but also including calls for better relations between religious and secular Jews and for tolerance and the cessation of violence.

In July, nevertheless, considerable resentment was aroused in the United States

Rabbi Isaac Levi, the last Jew in Afghanistan, examines the holy Torah in his synagogue in Kabul. More than 10,000 Jews once lived in Afghanistan, but they fled because of persecution during the communist rule of the country.

by a sermon given in Jerusalem by Israel's Sephardic Chief Rabbi Eliahu Bakshi Doron, in which he compared Reform Jews to the biblical character Zimri, the adulterous Israelite prince rightfully slain by Phinehas. Reform Jews accused Bakshi Doron of incitement to violence, a charge he vigorously denied.

Various Jewish religious groups from Reform to Hasidic continued to attract adherents in Russia and other parts of the former Soviet Union. At the Centre for Jewish Studies at Moscow State University, Russian students graduated for the first time with a state-recognized degree in Jewish studies, and several of them attended a conference on the Teaching of Jewish Civilization at the Russian Academy of Sciences.

In Britain, Clause 9 of the Divorce Bill, which passed through Parliament and awaited royal assent, authorizes a court to decline to make a divorce absolute if one of the parties claims that the marriage has not been properly dissolved according to religious law. If the bill was enacted, it would ease the plight of Jewish women whose husbands would otherwise be unwilling to initiate a *get,* or religious divorce. Meanwhile, the prenuptial agreement recommended by the chief rabbi and Beth Din (Jewish religious court) was signed by almost half of the couples to whom it had been offered; in its weaker version it commits couples to consult the Beth Din in case of marriage breakdown, and in the stronger version it authorizes the Beth Din to act as arbitrators.

In August *Commentary,* the monthly journal of the American Jewish Committee, published a symposium, "What Do American Jews Believe?" The 47 respondents, not typical of the general U.S. Jewish population, because they were "prominent rabbis and thinkers across the denominational spectrum," appeared to support the contention that "among affiliated Jews in general, religion is back, and it is fueled by traditionalism," a finding greatly at variance with the results of a similar survey in 1966 but not out of keeping with trends in the U.S. generally.

On June 9 in Teaneck, N.J., the Metivta, the rabbinical seminary of the Union for Traditional Judaism, conferred ordination on its first four graduates. The Union was the most recently formed Jewish denomination and was expected to appeal to the nonfundamentalist but tradition-oriented Jew.

Among major international interfaith events during the year was a Jewish-Christian Symposium on the Jubilee, convened by the World Council of Churches and the Ecumenical Institute at Bossey, Switz., in May. Jews and Christians worked together for four days on the task of applying scripture to the modern world, with special reference to environmental issues and the problem of international debt.

(NORMAN SOLOMON)

BUDDHISM

A Nepali-led international archaeological team announced in February 1996 the discovery in 1995 of a stone they believed was laid by Emperor Ashoka of India in the 3rd century BC to mark the Buddha's birthplace in Lumbini, Nepal. The announcement followed an October 1995 UNESCO mission that recommended that Lumbini be placed on the World Heritage List. The birthplace claim, however, remained highly contested. In June 1996 the British Library announced that birch-bark scrolls acquired in 1994 may be the earliest extant Buddhist manuscripts, dating from the end of the 1st century AD or the beginning of the 2nd century.

China celebrated the 11th Panchen Lama's June 1996 initiation into Buddhist monkhood with festivals including the presentation to the Panchen Lama's Tashilhunpo Monastery of a golden board bearing Chinese Pres. Jiang Zemin's inscription, "Safeguarding the Motherland and Working in Interests of the People." In January the six-year-old initiate, whose December 1995 enthronement by the Chinese as the 10th Panchen Lama's reincarnation was contested by the Dalai Lama, had affirmed his loyalty to Jiang. Amnesty International expressed concern in January for the Dalai Lama's candidate, missing since his May 1995 selection; in February the Dalai Lama speculated that the boy had been executed. During May, Chinese forces injured or arrested scores of Tibetan Buddhists, killing at least two monks who were protesting a new Chinese ban on possessing pictures of the Dalai Lama and wearing Buddhist protective cords. In June, at the Tibetan Freedom Concert sponsored by rock stars in San Francisco, there were demonstrations against U.S. Pres. Bill Clinton's renewal of China's most-favoured-nation status.

Throughout the year leaders in Myanmar (Burma) negotiated with China to bring the Buddha's left tooth relic to their country in late 1996 for public display in Yangon (Rangoon) and Mandalay. In May the Myanmar government prevented Nobel Peace Prize winner Daw Aung San Suu Kyi and her National League for Democracy from performing the customary Buddhist New Year fish-releasing ceremony.

In January Cambodian First Prime Minister Norodom Ranariddh retired to a Buddhist monastery following disagreements with his father, King Norodom Sihanouk, who in July affirmed his own "Buddhist tolerance" while pardoning a newspaper editor accused of defamation. Later in July Sihanouk assured minorities that the campaign for national unity would not require them to become Buddhist. In November security forces in Vietnam arrested several Buddhist monks and seized a pagoda in Hue that the government said was a centre of anticommunist activities.

Throughout the year Buddhist monks protested the Sri Lankan government's peace proposal extended to the Tamil insurgents, fearing Buddhist political power would be compromised. In February police warned of rebel Tamil Tigers posing as monks; later that month they arrested the reputed chief of Tiger operations in Colombo at his rented room in a Buddhist monastery. In July police discovered a time

Fragments of birch-bark scrolls found in Afghanistan and dating from the 1st or 2nd century AD were thought to be the oldest Buddhist manuscripts in existence.

PA NEWS

bomb amid flowers offered to a Buddhist temple in northern Sri Lanka.

A U.S. cosmetics firm apologized to the Thai government in January for disrespectful use of a Buddha image in its advertising. During the spring Chinese courts settled lawsuits against a sausage producer who used vegetarian monks in advertisements and a brewery producing "Buddha" beer.

(JONATHAN S. WALTERS)

HINDUISM

In India the installation on May 16, 1996, of a new central government led by the Hindu nationalist Bharatiya Janata Party (BJP) raised fears that the country would be thrown into grave communal conflicts between Hindus and religious minorities. The new prime minister, Atal Behari Vajpayee, however, quickly assured Muslims and other religious minorities that India would remain a constitutionally secular state and that the BJP's ideal of "Hindutva" meant only Indian cultural identity and not a Hindu nation. Unable to gain sufficient support in Parliament, the governing coalition put together by the BJP lasted only two weeks and was replaced on June 1 by a coalition of parties representing the poor, minorities, and Hindu lower castes. To some observers the new government underscored the increase in political power of the lower castes and regional parties, as well as the failure of the once dominant Congress Party to achieve the kind of society, free of caste hierarchy and discrimination, envisioned by Mohandas Gandhi and Jawaharlal Nehru.

In March conservation work was completed on the 12th-century temple of Jagannatha ("Lord of the World") in Puri, one of the greatest temples in India. The Archaeological Survey of India (ASI) undertook the conservation in 1975 when stones forming the building's exterior began falling because of the weight and the excessive salinity of layers of lime that had been applied as a preservative on the walls and domes during the past 300 years. The restoration revealed the splendid original temple carvings.

Two sets of calamities befell Hindu worshipers in the summer. On July 15, during the festival of Somavati Amavasya, sacred to devotees of Shiva, stampedes at two of the seven holiest sites in India left at least 60 dead and dozens more seriously injured. At Hardwar, where 1.5 million pilgrims had gone to bathe in the sacred Ganges River to celebrate the festival and pray for monsoon rains, 21 were killed in a stampede on a narrow bridge. Another 39 died when worshipers fell on top of one another on a slippery stairway leading to an underground shrine of the Mahakaleshwar temple at Ujjain, where some 200,000 had gathered for the festival. In late August the bodies of more than 120 pilgrims were recovered from along a mountain path leading to the Amarnath cave in Kashmir, where it is believed Shiva imparted the secret of immortality and where the god is worshiped in the phallic form of a stalagmite of ice. More than 110,000 pilgrims, the largest number in years, had registered for an annual pilgrimage to the sacred cave, and about 50,000 of them were caught in a blizzard at 4,575 m (15,000 ft) with virtually no shelter, food, or water. Many died from exposure, while others fell into ravines hundreds of metres below the narrow trail.

July 11 marked the 30th anniversary of the founding in New York City of the International Society for Krishna Consciousness (ISKCON), popularly known as the Hare Krishnas. Its founder, A.C. Bhaktivedanta Swami Prabhupada, brought from India a form of Hinduism that arose in the 16th century and directed devotion to Hare ("Lord") Krishna through ecstatic dancing and chanting. It quickly won converts among thousands of Americans, mostly young people. By 1980, three years after Prabhupada's death, the movement had established temples in about 40 U.S. cities, with 5,000 resident devotees, opened a chain of vegetarian restaurants, founded a publishing house, and instituted inner-city and international relief programs.

The Hindu belief that deity can assume any number of forms underlay the erection throughout Andhra Pradesh of shrines dedicated to the popular film star N.T. Rama Rao following his death on January 18 at the age of 72. (*See* OBITUARIES.)

(H. PATRICK SULLIVAN)

ISLAM

Muslims in most places in the world continued in 1996 to be subject to outbursts of violence, military operations by government and insurgent forces, and disappointed economic and social expectations. Various groups and leaders continued to call for Islamist action—that is, for Islamic solutions that emphasized the implementation of traditional behaviour and the Islamic Shari'ah law code. These calls were often labeled as fundamentalist; that term, however, continued to become less useful and accurate, because various Islamist groups generally had their own agendas that were based on a common theme of Islamic social justice but could be nuanced in a number of ways. The more specific religious concerns remained inextricably blended with political, and often nationalistic and cultural, concerns. At the same time, in Europe and North America, Islamic influences continued to expand.

Violence continued in many places: Algeria, Egypt, Pakistan and India, Afghanistan, Tajikistan, The Sudan, China, and Israel and the West Bank and Jerusalem. The disorders were often a continuation of the patterns of recent years: disaffected groups and their leaders called for reforms based on Islamic principles; there were attacks against governmental authority, sometimes obliquely in the form of terrorist attacks on tourists (Egypt in April); and those attacks were generally met by swift government reprisals. Leaders of the disaffected groups and their followers tended to be economically insecure or unemployed, disgusted by the social and cultural milieu about them, unhappy at the rapid changes and alien values they perceived as overwhelming their society, and longing for now disintegrated traditional values. Many of these disaffected persons were relatively well educated and members of the middle class. The solutions they proffered for ending the ills were couched in the language, symbols, and systematic exposition of Islam.

Events in Algeria, Egypt, The Sudan, Tajikistan, India and Pakistan, and China were confined to outbreaks of violence in specific areas and were dealt with swiftly. Other areas faced outright civil war. In Afghanistan the Taliban Islamists, after occupying the southern half of that country for about two years, began to expand northward, taking the capital Kabul in September. In the name of Islam, they announced a strict code of behaviour that included limitations on women's activities, such as clos-ing girls' schools and ordering women to remain at home in seclusion. The Shari'ah was to be the enforced law. In Iraq the national forces supported a move by one Kurdish group in the north against its rival Kurdish group, an action that brought a reprisal strike in southern Iraq by the U.S. in September.

In Turkey the Islamic Welfare (Refah) Party, which won a plurality in elections at the end of 1995, was finally able in June to form a coalition government under Prime Minister Necmettin Erbakan. (*See* BIOGRAPHIES.) It was the first time since the early 1920s that an Islamic religious party had held parliamentary power in Turkey. In the Philippines, after many years of rebellion in the southern island of Mindanao, Islamic guerrilla forces and the government signed a truce early in September, which signified a new era of shared power; the agreement was objected to by some Christian and other groups. In Bosnia and Herzegovina the truce seemed to be holding, and elections supervised by the Organization for Security and Cooperation in Europe were held in September.

The situation in the West Bank and Israel worsened considerably during the year as the government of Prime Minister Benjamin Netanyahu, which came to power as the result of Israel's May election, appeared to have a different timetable for the implementation of the agreements of 1993 between Israel and the Palestine Liberation Organization. Outbreaks of violence occurred throughout the year, but the situation became especially severe in September and October over the Temple Mount area in Jerusalem, the location of the al-Aqsa Mosque, the third holiest Islamic shrine. (*See* ISRAEL.)

In the U.S. the Islamic presence continued to grow and be recognized. One estimate numbered mosques there at more than 1,200. In late spring a national meeting of Muslims attracted thousands of attendees; in May an international women's conference was held in Washington, D.C., to discuss issues of interest to Muslim women throughout the world. Louis Farrakhan, leader of the organization the Nation of Islam, visited a number of Islamic countries early in the year, including Iran and Libya, with which the U.S. did not have regular diplomatic relations. As a result, and because of remarks Farrakhan made, the trip caused controversy. The Nation of Islam continued its efforts to reach out to inmates in U.S. prisons and also its controversial patrol service of inner-city housing complexes suffering high crime rates. Discrimination and isolated incidents of harassment and attacks on U.S. Muslims were reported.

In July Citibank opened a bank in Bahrain that followed Islamic legal rules for banking practices, the first such Western bank in the Persian Gulf. Citibank's decision could be understood in light of the fact that Islamic banks now managed funds valued in the $50 billion–$100 billion range.

(REUBEN W. SMITH)

This article updates the *Macropædia* articles The Buddha and BUDDHISM; CHRISTIANITY; EASTERN ORTHODOXY; HINDUISM; Muhammad and the Religion of ISLAM; JUDAISM; PROTESTANTISM; The Study and Classification of RELIGIONS; ROMAN CATHOLICISM; and *Micropædia* entries on the various denominations.

Students in Turkey study the Qur'an, an academic pursuit that had received increased emphasis since an Islamic political party gained a role in the nation's government and its leader, Necmettin Erbakan, became Turkey's prime minister.

Worldwide Adherents of All Religions by Six Continental Areas, Mid-1996

	Africa	Asia	Europe	Latin America	Northern America	Oceania	World	%	Number of countries
Christians	360,874,000	303,127,000	555,614,000	455,819,000	255,542,000	24,253,000	**1,955,229,000**	33.7	260
Roman Catholics	125,376,000	94,250,000	269,021,000	408,968,000	75,398,000	8,452,000	**981,465,000**	16.9	249
Protestants	114,726,000	45,326,000	79,534,000	34,816,000	121,361,000	8,257,000	**404,020,000**	7.0	236
Orthodox	25,215,000	13,970,000	171,665,000	460,000	6,390,000	650,000	**218,350,000**	3.8	105
Anglicans	27,200,000	650,000	28,357,000	1,089,000	6,300,000	5,540,000	**69,136,000**	1.2	158
Other Christians	68,357,000	148,931,000	7,037,000	10,486,000	46,093,000	1,354,000	**282,258,000**	4.9	118
unaffiliated Christians	60,234,000	11,561,000	29,376,000	12,164,000	54,148,000	4,937,000	**172,420,000**	3.0	215
affiliated Christians	300,640,000	291,566,000	526,238,000	443,655,000	201,394,000	19,316,000	**1,782,809,000**	30.7	260
Atheists	440,000	175,450,000	40,845,000	3,010,000	1,850,000	600,000	**222,195,000**	3.8	139
Baha'is	1,923,000	3,230,000	95,000	722,000	357,000	77,000	**6,404,000**	0.1	210
Buddhists	38,000	321,985,000	1,563,000	569,000	920,000	200,000	**325,275,000**	5.6	92
Chinese folk religionists	13,000	220,653,000	120,000	68,000	100,000	17,000	**220,971,000**	3.8	60
Confucians	1,000	5,050,000	4,500	2,500	27,000	1,000	**5,086,000**	0.1	12
Ethnic religionists	70,250,000	30,350,000	1,150,000	1,042,000	45,000	108,000	**102,945,000**	1.8	104
Hindus	1,986,000	786,991,000	1,650,000	760,000	1,365,000	323,000	**793,075,000**	13.7	94
Jains	59,000	4,835,000	16,000	4,500	4,500	1,000	**4,920,000**	0.1	11
Jews	165,000	4,257,000	2,432,000	1,084,000	5,836,000	92,000	**13,866,000**	0.2	134
Mandeans	0	45,000	0	0	0	0	**45,000**	0.0	2
Muslims	308,660,000	778,362,000	32,032,000	1,356,000	5,530,000	385,000	**1,126,325,000**	19.4	184
New-Religionists	21,000	103,361,000	803,000	919,000	900,000	11,000	**106,015,000**	1.8	27
Nonreligious	3,567,000	752,759,000	90,389,500	16,053,000	21,315,000	2,845,000	**886,928,500**	15.3	226
Parsees	1,500	185,000	1,000	1,000	1,000	1,000	**190,500**	0.0	10
Sikhs	37,000	18,465,000	494,000	9,000	496,000	7,000	**19,508,000**	0.3	21
Shintoists	0	2,893,000	1,000	1,000	1,500	1,000	**2,897,500**	0.0	12
Spiritists	4,500	1,120,000	18,000	8,834,000	315,000	1,000	**10,292,500**	0.2	30
Other religionists	90,000	100,000	450,000	190,000	1,072,000	50,000	**1,952,000**	0.0	182
Non-Christians	**387,256,000**	**3,210,091,000**	**172,064,000**	**34,625,000**	**40,135,000**	**4,720,000**	**3,848,891,000**	**66.3**	**262**
Total population	**748,130,000**	**3,513,218,000**	**727,678,000**	**490,444,000**	**295,677,000**	**28,973,000**	**5,804,120,000**	**100.0**	**262**

Continents. These follow current UN demographic terminology. UN practice began by dividing the world into 5 continents in 1949, then into 18 regions (1954), then into 8 major continental areas (called macro regions in 1987) and 24 regions (1963), then into 7 major areas and 22 regions (1988), and most recently into the 6 major areas shown above and 21 regions (1994). *See* United Nations, *World Population Prospects: The 1994 Revision* (New York: UN, 1995), with populations of all continents, regions, and countries covering the period 1950–2025. The table above therefore combines its former columns "East Asia" and "South Asia" into one single continental area, "Asia," which also now includes the former Soviet Central Asian states. Note also that "Europe" now extends eastward to Vladivostok, the Sea of Japan, and the Bering Strait.
Countries. The last column enumerates sovereign and nonsovereign countries in which each religion or religious grouping has a numerically significant following.
Rows. The list of non-Christian religions is arranged in alphabetical order.
Adherents. As defined and enumerated for each of the world's countries in *World Christian Encyclopedia* (1982), projected to mid-1996, adjusted for recent data.
Christians. Followers of Jesus Christ affiliated with churches (church members, including children: 1,782,809,000) plus persons professing in censuses or polls though not so affiliated.
Other Christians. Denotes Catholics (non-Roman), marginal Protestants, crypto-Christians, and adherents of African, Asian, Black, and Latin-American indigenous churches.
Atheists. Persons professing atheism, skepticism, disbelief, or irreligion, including antireligious (opposed to all religion).
Buddhists. 56% Mahayana, 38% Theravada (Hinayana), 6% Tantrayana (Lamaism).
Chinese folk religionists. Followers of the traditional Chinese religion (local deities, ancestor veneration, Confucian ethics, Taoism, universism, divination, some Buddhist elements).
Confucians. Non-Chinese followers of Confucius and Confucianism, mostly Koreans in Korea.
Hindus. 70% Vaishnavites, 25% Shaivites, 2% neo-Hindus and reform Hindus.
Jews. Adherents of Judaism. For detailed data on "core" Jewish population, *see* the annual "World Jewish Populations" article in the American Jewish Committee's *American Jewish Year Book.*
Muslims. 83% Sunnites, 16% Shi'ites, 1% other schools. Up to 1990 the ethnic Muslims in the former U.S.S.R. who had embraced communism were not included as Muslims in this table. After the collapse of communism in 1990–91, these ethnic Muslims were once again enumerated as Muslims if they had returned to Islamic profession and practice.
New-Religionists. Followers of Asian 20th-century New Religions, New Religious movements, radical new crisis religions, and non-Christian syncretistic mass religions.
Nonreligious. Persons professing no religion, nonbelievers, agnostics, freethinkers, dereligionized secularists indifferent to all religion.
Other religionists. Including 70 minor world religions and a large number of spiritist religions, New Age religions, quasi religions, pseudo religions, parareligions, religious or mystic systems, religious and semireligious brotherhoods of numerous varieties.
Total population. UN medium variant figures for mid-1996, as given in *World Population Prospects: The 1994 Revision* (New York: UN, 1995).

Religious Adherents in the United States of America, AD 1900–2000

Adherents	Year 1900	%	mid-1970	%	mid-1990	%	Annual change, 1990–95: Natural	Conversion	Total	Rate (%)	1995	%	2000	%
Christians	**73,270,000**	**96.4**	**186,121,000**	**90.8**	**213,924,000**	**85.6**	**2,281,400**	**−39,200**	**2,242,200**	**1.03**	**225,135,000**	**85.5**	**234,875,000**	**85.4**
Professing Christians	73,270,000	96.4	186,121,000	90.8	213,924,000	85.6	2,281,400	−39,200	2,242,200	1.03	225,135,000	85.5	234,875,000	85.4
Unaffiliated Christians	18,845,000	24.8	32,920,000	16.1	28,373,000	11.4	302,600	−117,400	185,200	0.64	29,299,000	11.1	29,785,000	10.8
Affiliated Christians	54,425,000	71.6	153,201,000	74.7	185,551,000	74.2	1,978,800	78,200	2,057,000	1.08	195,836,000	74.4	205,090,000	74.5
Roman Catholics	10,775,000	14.2	48,391,000	23.6	56,665,000	22.7	604,300	−47,300	557,000	0.96	59,450,000	22.6	61,800,000	22.5
Protestants	35,000,000	46.1	70,653,000	34.5	82,072,000	32.8	875,300	−189,700	685,600	0.82	85,500,000	32.5	88,800,000	32.3
Evangelicals	26,598,000	35.0	50,689,000	24.7	67,743,000	27.1	722,500	244,900	967,400	1.39	72,580,000	27.6	76,815,000	27.9
Anglicans	1,600,000	2.1	3,234,000	1.6	2,480,000	1.0	26,400	−52,400	−26,000	−1.07	2,350,000	0.9	2,203,000	0.8
Orthodox	400,000	0.5	4,387,000	2.1	4,250,000	1.7	45,300	230,900	276,200	5.79	5,631,000	2.1	6,260,000	2.3
Black Christians	5,750,000	7.6	19,679,000	9.6	32,598,000	13.0	347,700	92,700	440,400	1.32	34,800,000	13.2	37,200,000	13.5
Black Evangelicals	5,320,000	7.0	13,551,000	6.6	17,248,000	6.9	183,900	50,500	234,400	1.32	18,420,000	7.0	19,548,000	7.1
Catholics (non-Roman)	100,000	0.1	473,000	0.2	646,000	0.3	6,900	5,900	12,800	1.91	710,000	0.3	800,000	0.3
Other Christians	800,000	1.1	6,384,000	3.1	9,680,000	3.9	103,200	100,800	204,000	2.02	10,700,000	4.1	12,100,000	4.4
Doubly-affiliated Christians	0	0.0	0	0.0	−2,840,000	−1.1	−30,300	−62,700	−93,000	3.08	−3,305,000	−1.3	−4,073,000	−1.5
Non-Christians	**2,725,000**	**3.6**	**18,928,000**	**9.2**	**35,997,000**	**14.4**	**383,700**	**39,500**	**423,200**	**1.15**	**38,113,000**	**14.5**	**40,244,000**	**14.6**
Atheists	1,000	0.0	200,000	0.1	770,000	0.3	8,200	12,600	20,800	2.57	874,000	0.3	925,000	0.3
Baha'is	3,000	0.0	138,000	0.1	600,000	0.2	6,400	10,200	16,600	2.63	683,000	0.3	750,000	0.3
Buddhists	30,000	0.0	200,000	0.1	1,680,000	0.7	17,900	18,900	36,800	2.10	1,864,000	0.7	2,000,000	0.7
Chinese folk religionists	70,000	0.1	90,000	0.0	76,000	0.0	800	−1,200	−400	−0.53	74,000	0.0	70,000	0.0
Hindus	1,000	0.0	100,000	0.0	650,000	0.3	6,900	22,100	29,000	4.11	795,000	0.3	950,000	0.3
Jews	1,500,000	2.0	6,700,000	3.3	5,535,000	2.2	59,000	−62,400	−3,400	−0.06	5,518,000	2.1	5,500,000	2.0
Muslims	10,000	0.0	800,000	0.4	3,600,000	1.4	38,400	−5,000	33,400	0.91	3,767,000	1.4	3,950,000	1.4
Black Muslims	0	0.0	200,000	0.1	1,250,000	0.5	13,300	16,700	30,000	2.29	1,400,000	0.5	1,650,000	0.6
New-Religionists	0	0.0	110,000	0.1	575,000	0.2	6,100	−500	5,600	0.96	603,000	0.2	675,000	0.2
Nonreligious	1,000,000	1.3	10,069,000	4.9	21,364,000	8.5	227,800	35,400	263,200	1.20	22,680,000	8.6	24,034,000	8.7
Sikhs	0	0.0	1,000	0.0	160,000	0.1	1,700	4,300	6,000	3.50	190,000	0.1	220,000	0.1
Tribal religionists	100,000	0.1	70,000	0.1	280,000	0.1	3,000	2,000	5,000	1.73	305,000	0.1	350,000	0.1
Other religionists	10,000	0.0	450,000	0.2	707,000	0.3	7,500	3,100	10,600	1.46	760,000	0.3	820,000	0.3
Total population	**75,995,000**	**100.0**	**205,049,000**	**100.0**	**249,921,000**	**100.0**	**2,665,100**	**0**	**2,665,400**	**1.04**	**263,248,000**	**100.0**	**275,119,000**	**100.0**

Methodology. This table extracts a microcosm of the world table above. It depicts the United States, the country with the largest number of adherents of Christianity, the world's largest religion. Statistics for five points in time across the 20th century are presented. Also analyzed is each religion's *Annual change* by: *Natural* increase (births minus deaths, plus immigrants minus emigrants) per year and *Conversion* (new converts minus new defectors per year, which together constitute the *Total* increase per year. *Rate* is then computed as percentage per year.
Christians. Professing Christians are all persons who profess publicly (in censuses or polls) to follow Jesus Christ as Lord and Saviour. This category is subdivided into **affiliated Christians** (church members) and **unaffiliated** (nominal) **Christians** (professing Christians not affiliated with any church).
Evangelicals. Churches, agencies, and individuals that call themselves by this term usually emphasize five or more fundamental doctrines (salvation by faith, personal acceptance, verbal inspiration of Scripture, depravity of man, Virgin Birth, miracles of Christ, atonement, evangelism, Second Advent).
Black Christians. Members of denominations initiated by African-Americans.
Other Christians. This term denotes members of denominations and churches that regard themselves as outside mainline Protestant/Catholic/Orthodox Christianity.
Doubly-affiliated Christians. Members of more than one denomination.
Non-Christians. Followers of non-Christian religions or of no religion; the 12 largest such varieties are listed.
Jews. Core Jewish population relating to Judaism, excluding Jewish persons professing a different religion but including immigrants from the former U.S.S.R., Eastern Europe, Israel, and other areas.
Other categories. Definitions as given above under the Worldwide Adherents table.

(DAVID B. BARRETT; TODD M. JOHNSON)

Social Protection

A prevailing concern among countries in 1996 was the financial stability of their social protection programs. The U.S. overhauled its welfare system, and Canada dealt with the repercussions following a substantial cut in benefits in 1995. In Western Europe a variety of austerity measures were either taken or heatedly debated, while countries in Central and Eastern Europe experimented with ways to ensure that large segments of the population would not fall below the poverty line. In industrialized Asia and the Pacific, an effort was made to increase support to families. Some emerging and less-developed countries introduced reforms, but inadequate social security coverage and financial imbalances persisted for many of them.

North America. The United States entered a new era in social policy in 1996 by enacting historic legislation that changed the philosophy as well as the structure of protection for the needy. After 61 years under a welfare system in which the federal government had guaranteed cash assistance to the poor for an indefinite period, welfare policy was revised to put new emphasis and reliance on the states while stressing individual self-sufficiency and the initiation or resumption of work among beneficiaries. The Personal Responsibility and Work Opportunity Reconciliation Act, the official name of welfare reform, was passed by Congress in August. Pres. Bill Clinton, who twice before had vetoed Republican-sponsored reform bills, signed the measure despite deep divisions within his administration. The president called the act "far from perfect" but pointed out that it ended "welfare as we know it."

The new law, which took effect on Oct. 1, 1996, gave states broad authority over the core federal cash-assistance program—Aid to Families with Dependent Children (AFDC)—and also over food stamps and

Supplemental Security Income (SSI) for the elderly and disadvantaged poor. The federal government would end entitlement programs that guaranteed welfare checks to all eligible low-income mothers and children, a practice that was established during the New Deal presidency of Franklin D. Roosevelt. Instead, Washington would send states predetermined lump sums or block grants, based mainly on each state's welfare expenditures between 1992 and 1994.

While states would assume near-total control over establishing rules for eligibility and benefits, they were instructed to work within the new federal guidelines that required able-bodied welfare recipients to find work within two years after the state program took effect in order to prevent a loss of benefits and that limited recipients to five years of benefits over their lifetime. About one-half of all AFDC recipients received benefits for five years or longer. States could, however, exempt up to 20% of their caseloads from the five-year time limit for reasons of hardship. The law also created a comprehensive child-support system, required unmarried teenage parents on welfare to live at home and stay in school, and provided an additional $4 billion in child-care funds for welfare parents who were required to work.

Other provisions of the bill stipulated that:

● Cash aid and food stamps would be denied to anyone convicted of felony drug charges, although that person's family could still receive benefits.

● Adults between the ages of 18 and 50 who did not have children would be limited to receiving three months of food stamps over three years unless they were working. If they were laid off, they would be eligible for an additional three-month supply.

● Food stamps, SSI, and a variety of other low-income federal social services would be denied to legal immigrants who were not citizens.

● Single mothers on welfare who refused to cooperate in identifying the fathers of

their children could lose at least one-fourth of their benefits. Improvements would be made in tracking and prosecuting parents who did not pay court-ordered child support.

The new approach would save an estimated $55 billion over the next six years, mostly by reducing food-stamp payments and cutting benefits to legal immigrants. Advocates for the poor, who maintained that the changes would dramatically hurt states, localities, and the poor, were planning to mount legal challenges to state programs. The Urban Institute estimated that nearly 4.9 million children would be dropped from welfare rolls under the law by the year 2005 and 1.1 million would be pushed into poverty.

At the end of 1995, 12.8 million persons received AFDC benefits, two-thirds of them children. The number was down 1.3 million, or 9%, from the total in January 1993; 42 states showed declines in welfare rolls over that period. Food stamps were issued to 26 million persons, while SSI was given to 6.5 million others.

One-half of the children on the welfare rolls were born out of wedlock, including 20% born to mothers under 21. Of the recipients, 38% were white, 37% African-American, 19% Hispanic, and 5% non-citizens. The federal share of AFDC benefits in 1995 was $22 billion.

States had until July 1, 1997, to submit their plans for administering welfare. More than 40 states had been experimenting with welfare ideas under waivers granted by the federal government. Some of the state programs rejected entitlements in favour of work and job training; others required teenage mothers on welfare to live at home and stay in school or reduced assistance for mothers who had additional out-of-wedlock births while on welfare. Most of these experiments would continue regardless of the new federal law.

While most legal immigrants would lose food stamps and a variety of other federal assistance under the welfare bill, regulations that would have limited their access to public schools and federally funded HIV and AIDS treatment were dropped from an immigration bill passed in 1996. Instead, that measure concentrated on increasing the Border Patrol and other enforcement efforts to prevent illegal immigrants from entering the U.S.

Also abandoned in the face of strong Democratic opposition and a veto threat by Clinton was a Republican-backed overhaul of Medicaid, the federal-state health insurance program for the poor. That legislation would have put Medicaid on the same path as welfare by ending the federal guarantee of coverage and turning control of Medicaid over to the states.

The welfare-reform legislation did, however, make some changes in Medicaid. States were permitted to deny Medicaid to adults who were dropped from welfare rolls because they did not meet work requirements, and states could decide whether to deny Medicaid coverage to legal immigrants.

In another area of health care, Congress passed the Health Insurance Portability and Accountability Act. Described as the most significant expansion of health care access in more than 30 years, the law guaranteed continued health insurance coverage for 25

A mother holds her young son as she fills out an application at a job fair in Detroit. Congress enacted changes to the U.S. welfare system in 1996 that, among other provisions, required most recipients to find work within two years or lose their benefits.

JIM WEST—IMPACT VISUALS

million workers if they lost or left their jobs. Previously, workers lost coverage if they left their jobs.

After a lengthy debate Congress also passed the first minimum-wage-increase legislation since 1989. The minimum rose from $4.25 to $4.75 on Oct. 1, 1996, and was scheduled to increase an additional 40 cents on Sept. 1, 1997.

The hike came as the inflation-adjusted value of the minimum wage approached a 40-year low. Supporters complained that the increase was only a partial step in making up lost ground, while opponents contended that the raise would destroy thousands of low-wage jobs and thus hurt the people it was intending to help.

About 10 million workers, 5.3% of the total workforce, received the minimum wage, down from an all-time high of over 15% in the early 1980s. Of the 10 million, 46% were over 25 years old, and most of the rest were single and under 25.

Persons on Social Security also would receive more money. Congress voted to increase the earnings limit—the amount that beneficiaries aged 65–69 who held jobs could earn without losing any of their benefits. Earnings had been capped at $11,520 (indexed for inflation); for every $3 earned above that, a recipient lost $1 of benefits. Under the changes the threshold would increase gradually to $30,000 over seven years. This would affect about 800,000 beneficiaries, according to the Social Security administration, and cost an estimated $5.6 billion over seven years.

The 44 million retirees who received Social Security would receive a 2.9% cost-of-living raise, effective January 1997, the largest since 1992. The increase would boost the average retirement check from $724 to $745 a month. The maximum earnings from which Social Security tax was deducted would rise from $62,700 to $65,400 in 1997. The tax was 12.4%, split equally between employees and employers. An additional 2.9% Medicare tax, also split evenly, was levied on all wages.

The Census Bureau reported in September that in 1995, for the first time in six years, household income had risen and that the number of Americans living below the poverty line had fallen for the second year in a row. The median household income increased to $34,076, up 2.7% from 1994 after adjusting for inflation. The number of people living in poverty declined to 36.4 million, or 13.8% of the population—down from 38 million and 14.5% in 1994.

The poverty rate for African-Americans (30.3%) was the lowest since the Census Bureau began collecting data in 1966. The number of children living in poverty fell from 15.3 million to 14.7 million, but they remained the age group most likely to be poor.

Two factors were generally credited for the rise in incomes—more household members working more hours and increases in other kinds of income such as Social Security, pensions, interest, and dividends. In Canada the province of British Columbia reinstated a controversial residency requirement for welfare recipients, and Ontario boasted about reducing its welfare rolls to 1.2 million after implementing (October 1995) a 21.6% cut in social-assistance benefits for all but the elderly and permanently disabled. As a result, community workers

and food banks reported dire conditions for those who received cuts in aid and could no longer afford food or shelter.

Western Europe. Measures especially targeted at health care were taken to improve the financial stability of various social security programs. A number of governments introduced austerity programs, elements of which were met with open hostility.

In the United Kingdom the government launched a major campaign aimed at preventing social security fraud as a means of ensuring the viability of the welfare program. France embarked on major health care reform and introduced new regulations for social security financing to deal with a deficit that was judged unacceptable. To control health expenditures, the reform limited patients' freedom to bypass general practitioners and consult directly with specialists or receive diagnostic tests. Patients received a health-record booklet that was to be presented upon treatment. Pressure was put on doctors to cut back both on the amounts of medications that they prescribed and on the use of the more expensive types. The hospitalization system was also revised to strengthen coordination between public- and private-sector facilities. Several short-term emergency financial measures were taken to reduce the deficit, including the introduction of a special tax levied on employer contributions for coordinating benefits and the creation of a special body to manage the refinancing of the social security debt.

The German government introduced reform legislation in its "Program for Increased Growth and Employment," which was heatedly debated throughout the country in the fall of 1996. Two proposals were particularly controversial. Sick-leave pay would be reduced from 100% to 80% of regular wages during the first six weeks of a worker's absence, and after six weeks the benefit paid would be reduced by 10%. Protests by workers caused many German employers to continue to pay 100%. The second measure dealt with a sooner-than-

expected increase in the retirement age needed for both men and women to be eligible for social security. Both would be required to work until age 65, men starting in 2002 instead of 2007 and women beginning in 2005 rather than 2017.

Austria's main political parties agreed on an austerity package to raise taxes, cut spending on civil services, and lower welfare benefits for students, the unemployed, and people in need of permanent care. To deal with increasing health-insurance deficits, reductions in sick-leave pay were discussed.

The Netherlands privatized most benefits regarding sickness, making employers responsible for continued wage payments, including 70% of a sick worker's wages, which would be payable for a period of up to 52 weeks. The Netherlands also replaced their survivors' benefits program with a new scheme that required tighter eligibility rules and an income threshold. Various proposals were made throughout the year to improve the financial equilibrium of the public old-age pension program, including substantially higher contributions and contributions based on occupation.

In Sweden changes in social security health insurance were proposed for January 1997. Among other measures, the government proposed to limit the amount of sick-leave pay that employers could recover from the government.

In Finland agreement was reached in April on reforming unemployment benefits. The government estimated that reform was necessary to eliminate those structures of the unemployment system that undermined the will to work. Savings were to be achieved by eliminating automatic cost-of-living increases in 1997–99 and by altering the qualifying conditions for the receipt of benefits. In January the mandatory employers' earnings-related pension plan underwent changes that encouraged employees to remain working until age 65.

Social security was also a major topic in Swiss public debate throughout 1996. Strong controversy arose in relation to old-age

An old-age pensioner lives in poverty in her house in Siberia. Russia was among a number of former Soviet countries that, despite economic problems, were attempting to improve their social security programs, including support for the elderly.

pensions. There was debate over whether the country should move from a system of universal social insurance to means testing and private provision.

Central and Eastern Europe. As countries continued to face economic problems, they reformed their social security systems and experimented with various ways of maintaining minimum standards of living. Old-age pensions and unemployment benefits were the most pressing problems.

Despite the political will to introduce private pensions, the Russian government experienced difficulties in its efforts to promote occupational pensions, mainly owing to lack of public trust in the viability of the existing private funds, the absence of a formal law regulating private pensions, and resistance by older workers who strongly favoured a state system.

Members of the Polish Sejm (parliament) reached agreement on social security reform but debated the extent to which old-age pensions should be privatized. In July in Slovakia it became possible to establish supplementary pension funds through collective agreements. Provision was made for employee and employer contributions, and a minimum membership of 100,000 was fixed for a fund to be registered.

New arrangements were made for compulsory unemployment insurance in Latvia. An independent Employment Fund to manage unemployment insurance was formed. Benefit levels were established on the basis of previous salary and length of service.

Industrialized Asia and the Pacific. Support to families was high on the agenda in 1996. In February a new maternity allowance was introduced in Australia to assist families with the extra costs incurred at the time of birth. The allowance, in the form of a lump-sum payment, was designed to replace income lost when a mother left the workforce. Australia also implemented changes that gave caregivers better access to financial support.

In Japan new legislation was implemented that made it mandatory for employers to grant a maximum family-care leave of three consecutive months to male and female employees. Employers were also prohibited from dismissing employees who took such leave. New Zealand introduced administrative changes, altering the timetable when benefits were paid to better serve beneficiaries and make welfare payments less visible to recipients' neighbours and friends. With only voluntary employer-sponsored retirement plans, the government in Hong Kong proposed the introduction of a compulsory retirement benefit system that would have far-reaching initial and long-term costs for employers.

Emerging and Less-Developed Countries. As many nations faced inadequate social security coverage and financial imbalances, a number of reforms were implemented.

Mexico and Uruguay followed the path taken in recent years by other Latin-American countries, where social security pensions were totally or partially privatized. In April Uruguay implemented a system whereby residents under age 40 with an income exceeding a specified amount would be required to put one-half of their social security pension contribution into a personal account. The accounts would be managed by six private-sector funds. In Mexico the Chamber of Deputies approved the es-

tablishment of individual worker pension accounts that would be managed by private-sector administrators.

Argentina reformed its industrial accident system. Starting in March, employers were required to either take out an industrial accident insurance policy for employees or provide them with company-sponsored insurance.

Social security reform in Brazil was stalled owing to a legal dispute over a vote in the legislature on reform legislation. Discussions, however, continued throughout the year.

An important development in Africa was the creation in July of the Inter-African Conference of Social Welfare Institutions, a monitoring and technical-support organization with authority over countries that use the CFA franc as their currency. South Africa introduced legislation to improve the accountability of managed pension funds and launched welfare programs targeting particularly vulnerable groups, such as unemployed women with young children.

In Tunisia the amalgamation of two separate social security schemes for those self-employed in agriculture and industry was used to introduce new regulations that increased the number of people covered. In addition, a provision providing compensation for damages resulting from work injury and occupational diseases was extended to include employees in the public sector.

The central government of China organized a national audit of pension and unemployment funds and continued to work on the legal framework for social insurance that would cover all urban employees by the year 2000.

(CHRISTIANE KUPTSCH; DAVID M. MAZIE)

HUMAN RIGHTS

Major human rights issues that emerged during 1996 included growing concerns over the status and rights of minority groups; self-determination and autonomy in such regions as Rwanda and Burundi, China (Tibet), Turkey (the Kurds), and the republics of the former Soviet Union; problems as-

sociated with forced migration; the status and treatment of an ever-increasing number of refugees; the status and treatment of women; economic and social rights; and the rights of development. Problems of special significance were also reported in Burundi, China, Turkey, Nigeria, and Chechnya.

Ethnic Conflict in Burundi. Escalating ethnic conflicts between the minority Tutsi and majority Hutu populations in Burundi mirrored similar difficulties in Rwanda and threatened to result in comparable horrendous practices. The UN Special Rapporteur for Burundi reported that 800 civilians and 900 soldiers were being killed each month, with many thousands more forced to flee their communities as refugees or internally displaced persons. Many executions took place in reprisal for massacres of the Tutsi during a 1994 Hutu uprising. These problems were compounded by the continuing presence in Burundi of large numbers of Hutu refugees, who were fleeing ethnic strife in Rwanda. The international community responded with a series of monitoring and diplomatic missions and threatened to extend to Burundi the mandate of the International Criminal Tribunal for Rwanda. By year's end the Hutu refugee camps in Burundi had been closed.

Human Rights Violations in China. China became the focus of considerable international attention following the UN Fourth World Conference on Women, held in Beijing in September 1995. Activities associated with the planning and convening of the conference highlighted continuing major human rights violations involving repression of dissidents and autocratic control and occupation of Tibet.

Shortly after the conference, Human Rights Watch revealed that many government-operated orphanages treated children cruelly and denied them proper medical care, which resulted in death rates of more than 25% in many facilities.

These problems were among those cited by the U.S. and other Western nations in 1996 as a basis for seeking a resolution from the UN Commission on Human Rights condemning the Chinese government's hu-

An infant lies in a crib in a Shanghai orphanage. China continued to be criticized for human rights violations, including charges that government-run orphanages mistreated children and denied them medical care, which resulted in death rates of more than 25% at some facilities.

The rubble of war-torn Peace Street in Grozny, Chechnya, lies behind a boy orphaned by the fighting there. Civilians' rights under international law were repeatedly violated during the year by both Chechen forces and the Russian army.

man rights record. For the second straight year the resolution failed to pass by a narrow margin.

The U.S. government also failed in its attempt to link China's human rights performance to the granting of most-favoured-nation (MFN) status. Although the administration initially sought to obtain human rights concessions from China before renewing MFN status, the bulk of these demands were dropped when faced with Chinese intransigence and economic pressures. This dramatized the difficulty of applying human rights standards in situations of apparent conflict with other political, economic, and security considerations.

Throughout the year the Chinese government continued its crackdown on dissidents, arresting prominent leaders and threatening others with criminal prosecution. In October Wang Dan, student leader of the 1989 Tiananmen Square democracy movement, was charged with a capital offense and sentenced to 11 years in prison, while Liu Xiaobo was sentenced without trial to three years in a labour camp.

China's scheduled assumption in July 1997 of jurisdiction over Hong Kong also raised concerns. The Chinese government established its own ruling body to replace Hong Kong's elected Legislative Council, threatened to establish an appellate body to review judicial decisions, and opted to resurrect a number of repressive laws used by the British during colonial times.

Persecution of the Kurds in Turkey. The treatment of the Kurdish community by the government of Turkey remained one of the most significant violations of human rights

receiving international attention. Facing terrorism and armed rebellion by one of the Kurdish factions, Turkish forces destroyed Kurdish towns and persecuted Kurdish political parties and leaders. Among those affected were elected members of the parliament representing Kurdish areas, scholars whose works promoted Kurdish national identity, medical personnel providing care to Kurdish victims of torture, and members of human rights groups publicizing the atrocities.

In reaction to these policies, the European Tariff Union delayed approval of Turkey's entry into the union. Complaints were filed before the European Human Rights Commission and Court, and U.S. organizations questioned the desirability of selling U.S. military equipment that would be used to bomb Kurdish villages.

Executions in Nigeria. The military government in Nigeria continued to violate human rights on a major scale, particularly in the Ogoniland region. Following the 1995 execution of Ken Saro-Wiwa and eight other leaders of the Movement for the Survival of the Ogoni People on charges of treason, other leaders and sympathizers of the group were arrested and detained after demonstrations in January 1996 and again in March and April.

Threats to Civilians in Chechnya. In Chechnya the rights and safety of civilians under the Geneva Conventions and international humanitarian law were violated on numerous occasions by both Russian military and rebel secessionist forces. In January Chechen rebels took 2,000 civilians hostage in neighbouring Dagestan and an-

other 1,000 from a hospital in Kizlyar. The Russian army repeatedly bombarded civilian targets with massive and indiscriminate aerial and artillery attacks. The situation in Chechnya, along with similar atrocities committed in Bosnia and Herzegovina and Turkey, demonstrated an increasing threat to civilians.

Prosecuting War Crimes and Other Major Human Rights Violations. International criminal tribunals were established by the UN in 1994 to prosecute war crimes and crimes against humanity resulting from ethnic conflicts in Bosnia and Herzegovina and Rwanda. A total of 52 criminal indictments were handed down for Bosnia, while 21 were prepared for Rwanda. The trial of Dusan Tadic, accused of having murdered Bosnian Muslim civilians, was begun, while the trial of Jean-Paul Akayesu, the former mayor of Taba, Rwanda, accused of having abetted the massacre of some 2,000 Tutsi in his village, was rescheduled in November for Jan. 9, 1997. At the end of his term in office, Richard Goldstone, chief prosecutor of the tribunals, noted that political pressures associated with the Dayton (Ohio) peace accords made it difficult to extend the court's jurisdiction to some of the most prominent war criminals. Bosnian Serb Pres. Radovan Karadzic and Gen. Ratko Mladic had not been arrested or prosecuted for fear of jeopardizing the delicate political balance created by the peace settlement. Both the Bosnian and Rwandan tribunals also had to struggle with inadequate budgetary support from the UN.

One approach that gained support was the establishment of a permanent international criminal tribunal that would be vested with ongoing authority and financial support and have jurisdiction over a wider range of violations of international law.

Refugees and Forced Migrations. Problems associated with forced migrations and the treatment of refugees increased dramatically. Massive numbers of refugees were forced from their homelands as a result of armed conflicts and very real threats of ethnic slaughter. The office of the UN High Commissioner for Refugees estimated that there were approximately 14.5 million refugees and 30 million internally displaced persons as of November 1995, some 15 times the number in 1975.

War-ravaged Bosnia and Herzegovina, Rwanda, and Burundi were prime examples of this phenomenon. During 1996 major migrations caused by ethnic conflicts took place in Burundi and Iraq, spilling over into neighbouring nations, such as Zaire, where large numbers of refugees were temporarily maintained. In addition, problems bred from past mass migrations caused new difficulties in Hong Kong, where thousands of Vietnamese were forced to return home in anticipation of the July 1, 1997, takeover of Hong Kong by China and China's announced refusal to maintain the long-standing refugee camps there. The repatriation occurred after China ordered Hong Kong to return them before the takeover.

The rights and treatment of ethnic mi-norities were closely related to the burgeoning refugee problem, since mass migration often followed ethnic conflict and failed attempts at self-determination. A major future concern for the international human rights community would be protecting minority interests while maintaining the sovereign rights of existing states. Several new human rights treaties under consideration would expand recognition of the rights of minority communities. (*See also* WORLD AFFAIRS: *Spotlight: Fourth World: Resurgent Nations in the New Europe.*)

"Truth Commissions." Increasing use was made of "truth commissions" as a method for identifying and documenting human rights violations and helping to bring perpetrators of abuses to justice. Although these fact-finding bodies had no authority to prosecute crimes, they were designed to obtain and publicize information about past atrocities as a first step toward acknowledging responsibility and promoting reconciliation.

Haiti's truth commission produced a lengthy report, *If I Don't Cry Out,* which identified 8,652 specific cases of human rights violations committed under the highly repressive military dictatorships that ruled prior to 1994. The documentation of these cases remained secret, and individual violators, for the most part, were not being prosecuted.

In South Africa amnesty was granted to those who admitted human rights violations during the years of apartheid. As a result, few criminal prosecutions took place. Former defense minister Magnus Malan, who had been charged, along with three generals and other security officials, in connection with the creation, training, and supervision of secret "hit squads" that murdered antiapartheid advocates, was acquitted in October. Col. Eugene de Kock, however, was convicted on similar charges and subsequently admitted having played a key role in a long series of murders and assaults. The peace agreement that was signed on December 29 in Guatemala also took the approach of granting broad amnesty for past violations.

Women's Rights. One issue of paramount concern to women was female genital mutilation (FGM), also referred to as female circumcision. The procedure, usually performed before the onset of puberty, could involve cutting away the tip of the clitoris or removing all exterior genitalia. Some 85 million to 115 million women worldwide—primarily in Africa and Asia—had undergone this right-of-passage ritual, which was performed without anesthetic and often with unsterilized instruments. The ancient practice was most prevalent among women in Mali (93%), The Sudan (89%), and Egypt (70–90%), the latter of which reported at least two deaths even though the country's health minister banned FGM.

A new report was issued documenting the seriousness of the problem and urging concerted international action to outlaw this practice. The matter was brought to international attention after Fauziya Kasinga of Togo claimed refugee status in the U.S., fearing persecution through forced administration of FGM in her own country. Initially, the U.S. government rejected her request for asylum, indicating that fear of FGM did not come within any of the five recognized grounds for protection set out in the Convention on the Status of Refugees. U.S. courts eventually rejected this argument and accepted Kasinga's position that sexual abuse was a justified basis for fear of persecution.

Women's rights took on special significance in Afghanistan as a result of the takeover of the government by the Taliban militia in September 1996. They imposed harsh restrictions on the employment, education, and social rights of women, in accordance with that fundamentalist group's strict interpretation of Islamic doctrines. Attention was also focused on the special problems women faced in situations of war and armed conflict where rape and forced impregnation occur. The UN in June cited rape in this context as a war crime.

Rights Related to Development and Basic Economic and Social Needs. In June Habitat II, a UN conference dealing with housing needs, was held in Istanbul. This was followed in November by a World Food Summit in Rome, sponsored by the UN Food and Agriculture Organization. The purpose of the latter conference was to encourage action to eliminate hunger and malnutrition. The year was also designated the International Year for the Eradication of Poverty.   (MORTON SKLAR)

See also Business and Industry Review: *Insurance;* Education; Health and Disease.

This article updates the *Macropædia* article SOCIAL WELFARE.

A young African woman examines her wounds after being circumcised. A number of human rights and women's groups continued their attempts to curb the custom of female circumcision, still practiced in many parts of Africa and in other areas of the world.

Sports and Games

In 1996 the Centennial Olympic Games in Atlanta, Ga. (*see* Special Report), overshadowed most professional sports, but for some it was a banner year. U.S. major league baseball players and owners finally ended a four-year feud and approved a five-year, no-strike labour contract that promised, among other things, experimental interleague play in 1997. It remained to be seen whether the deal would bring back fan support lost during and after the prolonged 1994 strike. In the cricket World Cup, Sri Lanka, which was prevented from sharing duties as host with India and Pakistan when Australia and West Indies refused to play games scheduled there, redeemed itself and the quadrennial one-day tournament with a seven-wicket victory over Australia. (*See* Sidebar.)

The much-anticipated return of professional association football (soccer) to the U.S. arrived with major league soccer (MLS). Most of the 10 MLS teams attracted fairly good crowds, and the first-ever final was an exciting match that ended with the Washington, D.C., United defeating the Los Angeles Galaxy 3–2 in overtime. Women's professional basketball also debuted in the U.S. with the creation of the American Basketball League, which began playing in October, and the Women's National Basketball Association, scheduled to start in June 1997.

In Canada the 20-event Women's Curling Tour opened in late 1996 in preparation for the 1997 qualification bonspiel for the 1998 Winter Olympic Games. Although the tour would consist only of preexisting spiels at first, it was expected to provide a framework for future growth in the sport.

In several sports 1996 was the year of the rookie, as young, newly professional athletes came to the fore. Chief among these was Eldrick ("Tiger") Woods, the 20-year-old U.S. golf phenomenon who turned pro after winning his third U.S. Amateur title and then won 2 of the 11 tournaments in which he played. At age 21, rookie pro golfer Karrie Webb of Australia won four events (having captured the 1995 Women's British Open as an amateur) and ended the season as the first woman golfer to earn over $1 million in a single season. Czech-born Martina Hingis (age 16), representing Switzerland on the professional tennis circuit, achieved two singles victories, the women's doubles title at Wimbledon, and a fourth-place ranking in the world. In basketball two 18-year-olds—Kobe Bryant of the Los Angeles Lakers and Jermaine O'Neal of the Portland Trail Blazers—were drafted into the National Basketball Association out of high school.

(MELINDA C. SHEPHERD)

ARCHERY

With a score of 251 out of a possible 270, the United States men's team of Richard Johnson, Justin Huish, and Rod White won the gold medal in the 1996 Olympic Games. No country had been a clear favourite. In women's competition South Korea, with Kim Jo Sun, Kim Kyung Wook, and Yoon Hye Young, won its third consecutive Olympic gold, as expected, with a final-

FITA Outdoor World Target Archery Championships				
Year	Men's individual		Men's team	
	Winner	Points	Winner	Points
1987	V. Esheyev (U.S.S.R.)	329	West Germany	891
1989	S. Zabrodsky (U.S.S.R.)	332	U.S.S.R.	985
1991	S. Fairweather (Austl.)	334	South Korea	998
1993	Park Kyung Mo (S.Kor.)	113	France	249
1995	Lee Kyung Chul (S.Kor.)	109	South Korea	255
Year	Women's individual		Women's team	
	Winner	Points	Winner	Points
1987	Ma Xiangjun (China)	330	U.S.S.R.	884
1989	Kim Soo Nyung (S.Kor.)	338	South Korea	995
1991	Kim Soo Nyung (S.Kor.)	333	South Korea	1,030
1993	Kim Hyo Jung (S.Kor.)	104	South Korea	236
1995	N. Valeyeva (Moldova)	113	South Korea	247

NATHAN BILOW—ALLSPORT

(From left) Justin Huish, Rod White, and Richard Johnson of the U.S. take aim during the finals of the men's archery team event at the Olympic Games in Atlanta, Ga. The U.S. team won the gold medal, and Huish also won the gold medal in the men's individual event.

round victory of 245–235 over Germany. Large scoreboards, both men and women shooting from 70 m, judges in concealed bunkers in front of the target, and instant posting of scores were new features of the competition that won approval from daily crowds of more than 5,000.

The men's silver medal was taken by South Korea, which lost to the U.S. by only two points in a contest that required close examination of several arrows. The bronze went to Italy, which posted 247 to Australia's 244. Poland upset Turkey 244–239 to win the women's bronze medal.

In the individual competition the women's gold medalist was Kim Kyung Wook with a 113–107 win (120 perfect) over He Ying of China. Olena Sadovnycha of Ukraine won the bronze medal by defeating Elif Altinkaynak of Turkey.

The men's gold went to Huish, who defeated Magnus Petersson of Sweden in the 12-arrow final 112–107 (120 perfect). Oh Kyo Moon of South Korea scored a record-high 115 to defeat Paul Vermeiren of Belgium for the bronze.

In the U.S. the National Field Archery Association indoor winners in the unlimited professional division were Terry Ragsdale and Nancy Zorn. The limited professional

winners were Carolyn Elder and William Boyd. In the outdoor competition the unlimited pro champions were Doug Williams, Jr., and Inga Low, and the limited pro winners were Lori Draeving and Steve Gibbs.

(LARRY WISE)

AUTOMOBILE RACING

Grand Prix Racing. Formula One automobile racing gained added interest in 1996 because 1995 world champion Michael Schumacher of Germany transferred from the Williams-Renault team to Ferrari, whose cars became effective only when the season of 16 races was nearly over. Damon Hill, a British driver who was following the great career of his father, Graham, was the most obvious challenger to Schumacher. Jacques Villeneuve, a French-Canadian on the Williams team, proved another factor in the final outcome, however, almost winning the first round at Melbourne, Australia, before giving way to Hill because of engine problems.

It became clear from the outset that the World Drivers' Championship was likely to be a bitter battle between Hill and Schumacher, and indeed it was not settled until the final race in Japan. Hill drove a marvelous race to win the second round, the Brazilian Grand Prix at São Paulo, in almost impossible conditions of torrential rain and near-impossible visibility; Villeneuve slid off the track under the difficult racing conditions. The scene then moved to Argentina, where at Buenos Aires Hill won an exciting race from Villeneuve by 12 seconds, proving again the superiority of the Renault-engined Williams cars, which were as far ahead of the opposition as they had been in 1995.

The next race was the Grand Prix of Europe at Nürburgring, Ger., where the promise of the newcomer Villeneuve was demonstrated over a difficult course. He gained his first Formula One victory and proved well able to hold off Schumacher's Ferrari. At the San Marino Grand Prix, Hill won his fourth race.

The Monaco Grand Prix, the only true road race, with all its traditional hazards,

Formula One Grand Prix Race Results, 1996			
Race	Driver	Average speed (km/h)	Fastest lap
Australian GP	D. Hill	198.736	J. Villeneuve, 204.313
Brazilian GP	D. Hill	167.673	D. Hill, 190.932
Argentine GP	D. Hill	160.013	J. Alesi, 171.478
European GP	J. Villeneuve	196.006	D. Hill, 201.585
San Marino GP	D. Hill	193.761	D. Hill, 198.032
Monaco GP	O. Panis	124.014	J. Alesi, 140.611
Spanish GP	M. Schumacher	153.785	J. Alesi, 161.274
Canadian GP	D. Hill	190.541	J. Villeneuve, 194.291
French GP	D. Hill	190.183	J. Villeneuve, 194.631
British GP	J. Villeneuve	199.576	J. Villeneuve, 204.497
German GP	D. Hill	225.410	D. Hill, 230.628
Hungarian GP	J. Villeneuve	172.372	D. Hill, 178.352
Belgian GP	M. Schumacher	208.442	G. Berger, 221.857
Italian GP	M. Schumacher	236.034	M. Schumacher, 241.226
Portuguese GP	J. Villeneuve	182.423	J. Villeneuve, 189.398
Japanese GP	D. Hill	197.520	J. Villeneuve, 202.900

WORLD DRIVERS' CHAMPIONSHIP: Hill 97 points, Villeneuve 78 points, Schumacher 59 points.
MANUFACTURERS' WORLD CHAMPIONSHIP: Williams-Renault 175 points, Ferrari 70 points, Benetton-Renault 68 points.

JOHN PRYKE—REUTERS

International Cup for Formula One Manufacturers			
Year	Car	Year	Car
1991	McLaren/Honda	1994	Williams/Renault
1992	Williams/Renault	1995	Benetton/Renault
1993	Williams/Renault	**1996**	**Williams/Renault**

World Championship of Drivers		
Year	Winner	Car
1992	N. Mansell (U.K.)	Williams/Renault
1993	A. Prost (Fr.)	Williams/Renault
1994	M. Schumacher (Ger.)	Benetton/Ford
1995	M. Schumacher (Ger.)	Benetton/Renault
1996	**D. Hill (U.K.)**	**Williams/Renault**

Le Mans 24-Hour Grand Prix d'Endurance		
Year	Car	Drivers
1992	Peugeot	Y. Dalmas, M. Blundell, D. Warwick
1993	Peugeot	G. Brabham, C. Bouchut, E. Helary
1994	Dauer Porsche	Y. Dalmas, H. Haywood, M. Baldi
1995	McLaren	Y. Dalmas, J.J. Lehto, M. Sekiya
1996	**TWR Porsche**	**M. Reuter, D. Jones, A. Wurz**

Damon Hill of the U.K. waves from his Williams-Renault after winning the Japanese Grand Prix, held at Suzuka on October 13. With his narrow victory over Germany's Michael Schumacher, Hill clinched the 1996 World Drivers' Championship, which Schumacher had won in 1994 and 1995.

Monte-Carlo Rally		
Year	Car	Driver, codriver
1992	Lancia Delta Integrale	Auriol, Occelli
1993	Toyota Celica	Auriol, Occelli
1994	Ford Escort	Delecour, Grataloup
1995	Subaru Impreza	Sainz, Moya
1996	**Ford Escort**	**Bernardini**

was a disaster for Hill, whose Williams-Renault was in the lead when the engine blew up. Villeneuve also failed to finish, and the winner was Olivier Panis of France in a Ligier-Mugen-Honda, the first Grand Prix victory for that car since 1981. By this time the Ferraris were beginning to improve, and Schumacher gave a perfect exhibition of car control at great speeds in the rain in the Spanish Grand Prix at Barcelona, for his first victory of the season.

The racing went next to Montreal for the Canadian Grand Prix. Villeneuve's supporters were out in force to see the local boy win, but he was unable to match the experience of Hill, who triumphed once again. In the French Grand Prix at Magny-Cours, the Williams-Renaults again proved to be superior as Hill led from start to finish, followed by Villeneuve. At Silverstone, where a vast crowd of hopeful Britishers willed Hill to win, he made one of his hopeless starts and later retired with brake problems. Villeneuve took Hill's place and thereby

ensured victory at least for a British-based car in this British Grand Prix. In the German Grand Prix at Hockenheim, it was looking as if Ferrari might finally triumph, but then the engine of Austrian driver Gerhard Berger failed near the end of the race, and Hill was able to score another win. In the Hungarian Grand Prix at Budapest, Hill made up for a muffed start and almost overtook his teammate, but Villeneuve was the winner by a small margin.

Next was the tricky Spa circuit in Belgium, where both the Williams-Renaults had unexpected problems, which allowed Schumacher to win for Ferrari. In the Italian Grand Prix at Monza, Schumacher delighted the furiously supportive Ferrari crowd with a victory. Hill eliminated himself by colliding with tire markers erected at the turns to indicate the high curbs, which the drivers themselves had approved of in practice. Schumacher also hit this obstacle, but less hard, and his Ferrari continued on to victory.

At the Portuguese Grand Prix at Estoril, it was Villeneuve's day. He outpaced Hill, in spite of the latter's fine start, and made the overtaking maneuver of the year when he passed Schumacher's Ferrari around the outside at a corner.

This left everything to drive for at Suzuka in Japan, where the championship would be clinched. Before a delirious British contingent, Hill won by a narrow margin from Schumacher's Ferrari. Prior to Hill's magnificent year for Williams, however, had come the announcement that Frank Williams had dispensed with Hill's place on the Williams team for 1997.   (WILLIAM C. BODDY)

U.S. Auto Racing. The Indianapolis 500-mi classic, now a part of Indianapolis Motor Speedway owner Tony George's Indy

Racing League (IRL) schedule, faced its first competition ever. Championship Auto Racing Teams (CART), an organization of the car owners, defected and staged its own 500-mi race on the same day at the Michigan International Speedway. This intensified a battle for supremacy between the two organizations, which developed quickly into a struggle for racing venues and corporate backers. Mercedes-Benz, Honda, Ford, and Toyota built engines for CART, and Oldsmobile and Nissan did the same for

Indy Car Champions	
Year	Driver
1991	Mi. Andretti
1992	B. Rahal
1993	N. Mansell
1994	A. Unser, Jr.
1995	J. Villeneuve
1996	**J. Vasser**

Indianapolis 500		
Year	Winner	Avg. speed in mph
1992	A. Unser, Jr.	134.479
1993	E. Fittipaldi	157.207
1994	A. Unser, Jr.	160.872
1995	J. Villeneuve	153.616
1996	**B. Lazier**	**147.956**

National Association for Stock Car Auto Racing (NASCAR) Winston Cup Champions	
Year	Winner
1991	D. Earnhardt
1992	A. Kulwicki
1993	D. Earnhardt
1994	D. Earnhardt
1995	J. Gordon
1996	**T. Labonte**

(Above) Buddy Lazier (91) passes Davy Jones to win the Indianapolis 500 on May 26. Driving a Reynard-Ford, Lazier won the race by less than a second. (Left) Jimmy Vasser displays the Vanderbilt Cup he won at the first U.S. 500, held as an alternative to the Indianapolis 500 on the same day in Brooklyn, Mich., and organized by Championship Auto Racing Teams (CART). Vasser, who drove a Reynard-Honda, also won the CART season championship in 1996.

the new IRL race cars that were to debut in 1997.

At the Indianapolis 500, Buddy Lazier of Hemelgarn Racing, driving a Reynard-Ford with a special seat to allay pain from a crash nine weeks earlier that broke his back in 16 places, won $1,370,000 of a record $8.1 million purse, finishing less than one second ahead of Davy Jones in a Lola-Mercedes. Lazier's average speed was 147.956 mph. Richie Hearn (Reynard-Ford) was third. The inaugural IRL season also included races at Phoenix, Ariz.; Orlando, Fla.; Las Vegas, Nev., and Loudon, N.H.

After a 12-car crash just before the start sent most of the field into backup cars, only two drivers finished all 250 laps in the competing CART race. Jimmy Vasser in a Reynard-Honda bested Mauricio Gugelmin (Reynard-Ford) by 10.995 sec., averaging 156.403 mph. Vasser, driving for Chip Ganassi, won the CART season championship, which included competitions in Brazil, Australia, and Canada.

The National Association for Stock Car Auto Racing (NASCAR) enjoyed a banner year. The Winston Cup, its premier series, went down to the finale of a 31-race season before Terry Labonte dethroned his Rick Hendricks Chevrolet teammate Jeff Gordon 4,657 points to 4,620. Dale Jarrett in a Ford Thunderbird finished third, 52 points behind Gordon. Labonte, who had been

World Badminton Championships

Year	Men's singles	Women's singles	Men's doubles	Women's doubles
1987	Yang Yang (China)	Han Aiping (China)	Li Yongbo, Tian Bingyi (China)	Lin Ying, Guan Weizhen (China)
1989	Yang Yang (China)	Li Lingwei (China)	Li Yongbo, Tian Bingyi (China)	Lin Ying, Guan Weizhen (China)
1991	Zhao Jianhua (China)	Tang Jiuhong (China)	Park Joo Bong, Kim Moon Soo (S.Kor.)	Guan Weizhen, Nong Qunhua (China)
1993	J. Suprianto (Indon.)	S. Susanti (Indon.)	R. Subagja, R. Gunawan (Indon.)	Nong Qunhua, Zhou Lei (China)
1995	H. Arbi (Indon.)	Ye Zhaoying (China)	R. Subagja, R. Mainaky (Indon.)	Gil Young Ah, Jang Hye Ock (S.Kor.)

All-England Championships—Singles

Year	Men	Women
1992	Liu Jun (China)	Tang Jiuhong (China)
1993	H. Arbi (Indon.)	S. Susanti (Indon.)
1994	H. Arbi (Indon.)	S. Susanti (Indon.)
1995	P.-E. Hoyer-Larsen (Den.)	Lim Xiao Qing (Swed.)
1996	P.-E. Hoyer-Larsen (Den.)	Bang Soo Hyun (S.Kor.)

Uber Cup (women)

Year	Winner	Runner-up
1987–88	China	S.Korea
1989–90	China	S.Korea
1991–92	China	S.Korea
1993–94	Indonesia	China
1995–96	Indonesia	China

Thomas Cup (men)

Year	Winner	Runner-up
1987–88	China	Malaysia
1989–90	China	Malaysia
1991–92	Malaysia	Indonesia
1993–94	Indonesia	Malaysia
1995–96	Indonesia	Denmark

champion in 1984, won only twice to Gordon's 10 times, but he was more consistent.

Jarrett included the Daytona 500, the Charlotte Coca Cola 600, and the Indianapolis Brickyard 400—NASCAR's three richest events—among his four victories. At Daytona he edged seven-time Winston champion Dale Earnhardt by 0.12 seconds. At Indianapolis he defeated Ernie Ervan, and at Charlotte he beat Earnhardt by 11.982 seconds. Randy LaJoie won the NASCAR Busch series crown over David Green, and in the Craftsman Truck Series Ron Hornaday, Jr., won over Jack Sprague. All drove Chevrolet-powered vehicles.

The International Motor Sports Association (IMSA) staged a nine-race series in its World Sports Car category. Cars with Oldsmobile and Ford engines challenged Ferrari 333 SPs in the competition, which included the 24 Hours of Daytona and the 12 Hours of Sebring. Driving a Doyle racing car with an Oldsmobile engine, Wayne Taylor won both the Daytona and the Sebring events and also gained the drivers' championship. Oldsmobile later announced that it was curtailing its IMSA program to concentrate on IRL engine development. In the Sports Car Club of America Trans-Am series, Tom Kendall edged Dorsey Schroeder. Both were driving Ford Mustangs.　(ROBERT J. FENDELL)

BADMINTON

Poul-Erik Hoyer-Larsen, known as the "Great Dane," laid claim to badminton's two most important titles in 1996, a gold medal in men's singles at the Olympic Games in Atlanta, Ga., and a second consecutive men's singles All-England championship in March in Birmingham, Eng. He won in a sport almost completely dominated by Asia. At the Olympics he was the only European to place first, second, or third in any badminton event; Indonesia, China, South Korea, and Malaysia took 14 out of a possible 15 medals.

The 1996 Olympic Games would likely be the last for two of badminton's legendary players. Indonesia's "Queen of Badminton," Susi Susanti, surrendered her Olympic crown to South Korea's Bang Soo Hyun and was expected to leave the game soon after her marriage in February 1997 to teammate and fellow 1992 gold medalist Alan Budi Kusuma. Also stepping down was South Korea's 1992 Olympic doubles gold medalist Park Joo Bong, whose comeback in mixed doubles fell a bit short when he and partner Ra Kyung Min succumbed

in 1996 to Kim Dong Moon and Gil Young Ah of South Korea in the Olympic gold medal match. Gil's gold in mixed doubles was her second of the 1996 Olympic competition, as she also took silver in women's doubles. This marked the first time in badminton history that an athlete had won two medals in a single Olympic competition.

Indonesia won both the men's Thomas Cup and the women's Uber Cup world team championships in May in Hong Kong. The Indonesian men's 5–0 victory over Denmark was their 10th Thomas Cup championship, a title that had been won by only three countries (Indonesia, China, and Malaysia) since its inception in 1948. Indonesia's 4–1 Uber Cup victory over China marked its third such title.　(PAUL PAWLACZYK)

BASEBALL

In 1996 major league baseball produced its first full season since 1993. In 1994 a players' strike had occurred in mid-August, and failed negotiations on a new collective bargaining agreement had caused cancellation of the World Series. In 1995 there was still no contract, and the regular schedule was cut to 144 games after a court order effected a belated start. On Nov. 26, 1996, the major league owners voted 26–4 to ratify a collective bargaining agreement. Soon afterward the union ratified the agreement, which provided, among other things, for limited interleague play in 1997 and 1998.

World Series. With a stirring comeback, the New York Yankees won their 23rd World Series, the most of any franchise in either league, by defeating the Atlanta Braves four games to two in the best-of-seven series. The title was the Yankees' first since 1978, and it did not come easily.

In the opener, delayed one day by rain, the defending champion Braves routed the Yankees 12–1 at New York on October 20. The Braves' attack was paced by Andruw Jones, a 19-year-old rookie from the Caribbean island of Curaçao. When Jones hit a two-run homer in the second inning, he became the youngest player to have done so in World Series history. In the next inning, Jones hit a three-run homer, more than enough support for John Smoltz, who pitched six innings in Atlanta's triumph.

In the second game at Yankee Stadium October 21, Greg Maddux pitched eight brilliant innings for the Braves, who eased to a 4–0 conquest. Fred McGriff batted in three runs for the defending champions, who assumed a seemingly insurmountable 2–0 lead in the series.

On October 22 at Atlanta-Fulton County Stadium, however, veteran David Cone pitched six strong innings for the Yankees, who prevailed 5–2. New York broke open a tight game on a two-run home run by Bernie Williams in the eighth inning. Cone's effort was particularly noteworthy because he had missed much of the regular season with an aneurysm in his right arm.

On October 23 the resilient Yankees shocked the Braves and their fans by rallying for an 8–6 triumph in 10 innings to tie the series 2–2. The Braves had surged to a 6–0 lead by the fifth inning, but the Yankees halved the deficit in the sixth. Then in the eighth, Jim Leyritz hit a three-run homer for a 6–6 deadlock.

In the 10th inning Manager Bobby Cox issued orders to load the bases by having Williams walked intentionally. The strategy backfired when pitcher Steve Avery then walked Wade Boggs to force in a run. The Yankees scored again and then fended off the Braves in the bottom of the inning to secure a landmark victory in the longest World Series game ever, 4 hours and 17 minutes.

In game five on October 24, the Yankees still faced the formidable task of beating Smoltz, who led both leagues in victories. New York's Andy Pettitte, however, with whom Atlanta had had no problems in the opener, stifled the Braves through 8⅓ innings. He was succeeded by John Wetteland, who recorded the final two outs in a tense 1–0 New York victory. The only Yankee run was scored in the fourth inning, with the help of a two-base error by Marquis Grissom, the Braves' normally dependable centre fielder.

Before an emotional crowd of 56,375 at Yankee Stadium on October 26, the Yankees earned their crown by beating the Braves 3–2. The Yankees scored three runs in the third inning off Maddux, winner of four consecutive Cy Young Awards and considered among the greatest pitchers ever. Jimmy Key earned the victory, but he needed relief from four pitchers, including Wetteland, who saved all four Yankee triumphs and thus was voted Most Valuable Player of the series.

The Yankees batted only .216 as a team in the series, but they played with a resourcefulness and efficiency that typified their season under Joe Torre, their first-year manager. Although there was precedent for a team winning a World Series after losing its first two home games, no previous team had lost its first two home games and then swept the next four.

Play-offs. The Yankees on October 9 began their postseason quest also by losing their first home game—6–2 in a best-of-five division series to the Texas Rangers. But the Yankees rallied to win the second game 5–4 in 12 innings and then took two straight in Arlington, Texas, by scores of 3–2 and 6–4. The Baltimore Orioles, meanwhile, advanced by defeating the defending American League champion Cleveland Indians in their division series three games to one.

In the opener of the American League Championship Series against Baltimore, the Yankees came back to win 5–4 in 11 innings. They were helped by a controversial ruling from Rich Garcia, the right-field umpire, on a fly ball by Derek Jeter. The ball appeared to be within the confines of Yankee Stadium, but a 12-year-old fan reached over the barrier to catch the ball, and Garcia called it a home run.

The angry and shaken Orioles won the following day 5–3. When the series moved to Baltimore, however, the Yankees swept the Orioles by scores of 5–2, 8–4, and 6–4 to claim their first pennant since 1981. The Yankees thus won all of the eight postseason games that they played away from home.

The Braves had to stage a comeback of their own after sweeping the Los Angeles Dodgers in the division series by 2–1, 3–2, and 5–2. Atlanta's next foe was the St. Louis Cardinals, who advanced by sweeping the San Diego Padres. After beating the Cardinals at Atlanta 4–2 in the opener of the National League Championship Series on October 9, the Braves lost the next three by scores of 8–3, 3–2, and 4–3.

The Braves then asserted themselves, however; they routed the Cardinals 14–0 in game five at St. Louis, returned home to tie the series with a 3–1 decision, and amassed six runs in the first inning of the seventh game before vanquishing St. Louis 15–0 for their fourth National League pennant in five seasons.

Regular Season. The Yankees had built a 12-game lead in the American League East by late July, only to see it dwindle to 2½ over the hard-charging Orioles. The Yankees prevailed with a 92–70 record, four games better than Baltimore, who earned the wild-card berth by posting the best record of any of the three second-place teams in the American League.

The Indians, with a 99–62 record, won the American League Central by 14½ games over the Chicago White Sox. Texas won the American League West by 4½ games over the Seattle Mariners.

The Braves, with a record of 96–66, won the National League East by eight games over the Montreal Expos. St. Louis took the National League Central by six games over the Houston Astros. The San Diego Padres swept the last three games from Los Angeles during the regular season to win the National League West by one game over the Dodgers, who earned the wild-card spot.

Individual Accomplishments. Alex Rodriguez of Seattle led all major leaguers with a .358 batting average. Tony Gwynn of San Diego paced National League hitters with a .353 mark.

Mark McGwire of the Oakland A's clubbed 52 home runs to lead the American League. Andres Galarraga of the Colorado

Final Major League Standings, 1996

AMERICAN LEAGUE

East Division				Central Division				West Division			
Club	W.	L.	G.B.	Club	W.	L.	G.B.	Club	W.	L.	G.B.
New York	92	70	–	Cleveland	99	62	–	Texas	90	72	–
Baltimore	88	74	4	Chicago	85	77	14½	Seattle	85	76	4½
Boston	85	77	7	Milwaukee	80	82	19½	Oakland	78	84	12
Toronto	74	88	18	Minnesota	78	84	21½	California	70	91	19½
Detroit	53	109	39	Kansas City	75	86	24				

NATIONAL LEAGUE

East Division				Central Division				West Division			
Club	W.	L.	G.B.	Club	W.	L.	G.B.	Club	W.	L.	G.B.
Atlanta	96	66	–	St. Louis	88	74	–	San Diego	91	71	–
Montreal	88	74	8	Houston	82	80	6	Los Angeles	90	72	1
Florida	80	82	16	Cincinnati	81	81	7	Colorado	83	79	8
New York	71	91	25	Chicago	76	86	12	San Francisco	68	94	23
Philadelphia	67	95	29	Pittsburgh	73	89	15				

World Series*

Year	Winning team	Losing team	Results
1992	Toronto Blue Jays (AL)	Atlanta Braves (NL)	4–2
1993	Toronto Blue Jays (AL)	Philadelphia Phillies (NL)	4–2
1994	not held		
1995	Atlanta Braves (NL)	Cleveland Indians (AL)	4–2
1996	**New York Yankees (AL)**	**Atlanta Braves (NL)**	**4–2**

*AL—American League; NL—National League.

Joe Girardi of the New York Yankees hits a triple against the defending champions, the Atlanta Braves, in the third inning of game six of the World Series. The three runs scored by the Yankees in the inning proved to be enough to win the game and the series, their first since 1978.

DOUG PENSINGER—ALLSPORT

Eddie Murray of the Baltimore Orioles acknowledges cheers after his 500th home run. He was the 15th player to hit 500 homers.

Rockies led the National League with 47. Galarraga also batted in 150 runs to set the pace in that category over Cleveland's Albert Belle, who had 148. Lance Johnson of the New York Mets had the most hits, 227, and Kenny Lofton of the Indians stole the most bases, 75.

During a season of robust hitting, Smoltz was clearly the best pitcher. He posted a 24–8 record, though Kevin Brown of the Florida Marlins managed the lowest earned run average, 1.89 per nine innings. Pettitte led the American League with 21 victories. Jeff Brantley of the Cincinnati Reds and Todd Worrell of the Dodgers tied for the most saves, 44.

Paul Molitor of the Minnesota Twins became the 21st player in baseball history to reach the 3,000-hit plateau. Eddie Murray became just the third player to collect 3,000 hits and 500 home runs, helping his Baltimore Orioles break the major league record for most home runs by a team in one season.

Smoltz was voted the Cy Young Award winner as outstanding pitcher in the National League, and Pat Hentgen of the Toronto Blue Jays earned the corresponding honour in the American League. Ivan Rodriguez of Texas was named Most Valuable Player in the American League, and San Diego's Ken Caminiti won the award in the National League. Rookies of the Year were Jeter in the American League and Todd Hollandsworth of Los Angeles in the National. The award for Manager of the Year in the American League was shared by Torre and Johnny Oates of Texas, and Bruce Bochy of San Diego won the honour in the National.

In November club president Tony Tavares announced that the California Angels were now named the Anaheim Angels. The team had played in a stadium in Anaheim for 30 years. (ROBERT WILLIAM VERDI)

Latin America. The 1996 Caribbean Series was held in Santo Domingo, Dom. Rep., February 3–8. Culiacan, representing Mexico, defeated a heavily favoured Dominican team, which included many major league stars. Mexico finished with a record of 5–1, while Puerto Rico (Arecibo) was 4–2, the Dominican Republic (Aguilas) was 2–4, and Venezuela (Magallanes) was 1–5. Culiacan, with no big-name players, was one of the most surprising champions in series history. The 1997 Caribbean Series was scheduled to be held in Hermosillo in the Mexican state of Sonora.

Cuba was undefeated at the 1996 Olympic Games, defeating Japan 13–9 for the gold medal. Cuban third baseman Omar Linares hit three home runs in the championship game. Nicaragua lost the game for third place to the United States 10–3.

During the summer the Monterrey Sultans finished the regular season with a 82–33 record, the best winning percentage in league history, and defeated the Mexico City Red Devils four games to one to win their second consecutive Mexican League championship. In August the San Diego Padres won two of three games from the New York Mets in Monterrey. The games, played there because of the Republican national convention in San Diego, were the first regular-season major league contests outside the U.S. and Canada. The series was seen as a first step toward the possibility of eventually expanding major league baseball to Mexico. (MILTON JAMAIL)

Japan. The Orix BlueWave of the Pacific League defeated the Yomiuri Giants of the Central League four games to one in the 1996 Japan Series and thus became the champions of Japanese baseball. This was the first time that the BlueWave, formerly the Hankyu Braves based in Nishinomiya, had won the Japan Series since the club moved to its new franchise in Kobe in 1988. After the BlueWave won the first two games against the Giants at their home field in Tokyo, they took the third and fifth games in Kobe. For BlueWave manager Akira Ogi, it was the first series victory in three attempts.

The 1996 Japanese season was marked by a changing of the guard, symbolized by the fact that the most valuable players of both leagues, chosen by votes of sports writers, were 22-year-old batters: Ichiro Suzuki of the BlueWave and Hideki Matsui, a Giant. Suzuki had the league's highest batting average for the third year in a row. Matsui hit 38 home runs and batted in 99 runs for the Central League champions.

Another new development during the year was that, apparently because of the two successful seasons of Hideo Nomo as a pitcher for the Los Angeles Dodgers, many players, mostly pitchers, were beginning to consider careers in the United States. For them, postseason exhibition games against the major league all-stars, which began on November 1, were opportunities to test and show off their abilities.

(TOSHIHIKO SUZUKI)

Twenty-two-year-old star hitter Ichiro Suzuki of the Orix BlueWave watches his home run leave the ballpark in the 10th inning of game one of the Japan Series against the Yomiuri Giants. The BlueWave won the first game on Suzuki's home run, and they won the series four games to one.

Japan Series*			
Year	Winning team	Losing team	Results
1992	Seibu Lions (PL)	Yakult Swallows (CL)	4–3
1993	Yakult Swallows (CL)	Seibu Lions (PL)	4–3
1994	Yomiuri Giants (CL)	Seibu Lions (PL)	4–2
1995	Yakult Swallows (CL)	Orix BlueWave (PL)	4–1
1996	**Orix BlueWave (PL)**	**Yomiuri Giants (CL)**	**4–1**

*CL—Central League; PL—Pacific League.

BASKETBALL

United States. In professional basketball, the Chicago Bulls soared even higher than superstar Michael Jordan in an astonishing 1995–96 season. They set an all-time league record by winning 72 regular-season games while losing only 10 and then went on to win their fourth National Basketball Association (NBA) championship in six years.

The Bulls did fall short of their quest to chalk up another record for play-off dominance, having to settle for an overall 15–3 postseason record. The Seattle SuperSonics staved off the threat of being shut out in the best-of-seven finals by winning twice on their home floor.

But even that worked out well, because it enabled the Bulls to win the title on their home court, where an adoring audience watched them put away the Sonics 87–75 in game 6. Their slight fade in the final series also added fuel to the debate over whether these Bulls, rather than the 69–13 Los Angeles Lakers of 1971–72, the 1966–67 Philadelphia 76ers (68–13), or the 1985–86 Boston Celtics (67–15) actually deserved to be recognized as the all-time greatest NBA team.

There was little, if any, argument, however, about the greatest player of them all. Jordan, shining even brighter than before in his first full year back from a brief retirement, was the unstoppable force in Chicago's success. At 33, he did not hang in the air en route to one of his crowd-arousing slam dunks quite as long as he used to. But his unmatched skills, instinct for the game, and, above all, his burning desire to win were undimmed by time.

Jordan proved it over and over in 1995–96, gaining both the regular-season and play-off Most Valuable Player awards. It was the fourth time he had earned each of those accolades, and he also added his league-record eighth NBA scoring title to break Wilt Chamberlain's record.

Nevertheless, Jordan had an outstanding supporting cast, with two more superstars, Scottie Pippen and Dennis Rodman (*see* BIOGRAPHIES), in the mix. His rebounding prowess, multihued hair, and bizarre off-court antics made Rodman a Chicago favourite in his first year with the Bulls.

With contemplative Coach Phil Jackson (*see* BIOGRAPHIES) using the right bench psychology, the Bulls were virtually unbeatable. They hoped to keep it going, at least for one more year, by signing Jordan for $30 million, Rodman for $7 million, and Jackson for $1.5 million.

The Kentucky Wildcats and their charismatic coach, Rick Pitino, dominated college basketball throughout the 1995–96 season.

Michael Jordan of the Chicago Bulls soars to the basket over the outstretched arm of Sam Perkins of the Seattle SuperSonics in the first game of the NBA championship finals. Jordan was named the league's Most Valuable Player for both the regular season and the play-offs.

Pitino finally won the National Collegiate Athletic Association (NCAA) tournament championship that had eluded him since 1989 at Kentucky and at Providence in a 1987 Final Four appearance.

But this was to be Kentucky's—and Pitino's—year. The Wildcats shook off an early-season loss to Massachusetts and took over the number one spot in the weekly Top 25 polls by consistently blowing away Southeastern Conference (SEC) opponents. With just one more regular-season loss, Kentucky stormed into the NCAA tournament as the odds-on favourite.

Because Kentucky had not won the tournament since 1978 and had suffered a traumatic last-second loss to Duke in the 1992 NCAA East Regional final, a heavy burden accompanied the Wildcats when they arrived in the New Jersey Meadowlands on March 30 to take on the Minutemen of Massachusetts in the semifinal game. This time the Wildcats were able to avenge their early-season loss, ousting the Minutemen 81–74. It was Kentucky's first victory margin of less than 20 points in the tournament.

The final game of the tournament pitted Kentucky against Syracuse, a Cinderella

National Basketball Association (NBA) Championship

Season	Winner	Runner-up	Results
1991–92	Chicago Bulls	Portland Trail Blazers	4–2
1992–93	Chicago Bulls	Phoenix Suns	4–2
1993–94	Houston Rockets	New York Knicks	4–3
1994–95	Houston Rockets	Orlando Magic	4–0
1995–96	**Chicago Bulls**	**Seattle SuperSonics**	**4–2**

NBA Final Standings, 1995–96

EASTERN CONFERENCE							WESTERN CONFERENCE					
Team	Won	Lost	Team	Won	Lost		Team	Won	Lost	Team	Won	Lost
Atlantic Division			**Central Division**				**Midwest Division**			**Pacific Division**		
*Orlando	60	22	*Chicago	72	10		*San Antonio	59	23	*Seattle	64	18
*New York	47	35	*Indiana	52	30		*Utah	55	27	*L.A. Lakers	53	29
*Miami	42	40	*Cleveland	47	35		*Houston	48	34	*Portland	44	38
*Washington	39	43	*Atlanta	46	36		Denver	35	47	*Phoenix	41	41
Boston	33	49	*Detroit	46	36		Dallas	26	56	*Sacramento	39	43
New Jersey	30	52	Charlotte	41	41		Minnesota	26	56	Golden State	36	46
Philadelphia	18	64	Milwaukee	25	57		Vancouver	15	67	L.A. Clippers	29	53
			Toronto	21	61							

*Gained play-off berth.

Kentucky guard Tony Delk jumps to receive a pass in the NCAA championship game. With a record-tying seven three-point shots, Delk led Kentucky to a 76–67 victory over Syracuse.

Saudia Roundtree of Georgia, voted Naismith Player of the Year, goes up for a jump shot over Latina Davis of Tennessee in the final game of the NCAA women's tournament. Freshman Chamique Holdsclaw, with 16 points and 14 rebounds, led Tennessee to an 83–65 victory.

team that had surprised everybody, including its own fans, by last defeating Mississippi State 77–69 in the other semifinal. Along the way, Syracuse Coach Jim Boeheim emerged as a hero of sorts, shedding the reputation he had acquired, perhaps unfairly, of being unable to win the big games. In reaching the finals, Syracuse increased its NCAA tourney victory total over the years to 35—the most ever won by a team that did not win the title.

In the final Kentucky had more than the sticky Syracuse zone defense to overcome before nailing down an emotional 76–67 victory to end its 18-year drought between NCAA championships. Tense and erratic, as though they were overwhelmed by all the expectations on their shoulders, the Wildcats almost blew a 13-point lead in the second half, allowing Syracuse to cut the gap to 64–62 with just 4 minutes and 46 seconds left.

It was then that Kentucky's best player, Tony Delk, rallied his squad with emotional fervour during a time-out. Wildcat

fans in the throng of 19,229 nervously pondered the probabilities of another collapse, but their fears were soon dispelled. When Delk missed a three-point shot, Walter McCarty denied Syracuse a chance to go for the tying points by tipping in the rebound, and Derek Anderson, a transfer from Ohio State, nailed a three-pointer for the biggest

basket of the game. Kentucky then pulled ahead to win by a final score of 76–67.

Overall, it was Delk's marksmanship that made the difference. The sharpshooting guard contributed seven of the winners' dozen three-point baskets, tying the individual record for an NCAA championship game that had been set by Indiana's Steve

Division I National Collegiate Athletic Association (NCAA) Championship—Men			
Year	Winner	Runner-up	Score
1992	Duke	Michigan	71–51
1993	North Carolina	Michigan	77–71
1994	Arkansas	Duke	76–72
1995	UCLA	Arkansas	89–78
1996	Kentucky	Syracuse	76–67

Division I National Collegiate Athletic Association (NCAA) Championship—Women			
Year	Winner	Runner-up	Score
1992	Stanford	Western Kentucky	78–62
1993	Texas Tech	Ohio State	84–82
1994	North Carolina	Louisiana Tech	60–59
1995	Connecticut	Tennessee	70–64
1996	Tennessee	Georgia	83–65

National Invitation Tournament (NIT) Championship			
Year	Winner	Runner-up	Score
1992	Virginia	Notre Dame	81–76
1993	Minnesota	Georgetown	62–61
1994	Villanova	Vanderbilt	80–73
1995	Virginia Tech	Marquette	65–64
1996	Nebraska	St. Joseph's	60–56

Alford in 1987 and Oklahoma's David Sieger in 1988.

Nebraska, better known as a football power, pulled off a surprise by winning the National Invitation Tournament with a 60–56 decision over St. Joseph's of Philadelphia. It took the Cornhuskers 100 years—spent mostly in obscurity on the court—to emerge, but they rode the clutch free throws of Erick Strickland, named the tourney's Most Valuable Player, to victory in the final.

In women's basketball, Tennessee trounced Georgia 83–65 on March 31 in Charlotte, N.C., to capture its fourth NCAA tournament championship. When Kentucky took the men's title a day later, the SEC became the first conference to have won both NCAA basketball tournaments in the same season. (ROBERT G. LOGAN)

International. The Olympic Games in Atlanta, Ga., was the major event of 1996 in international basketball. The U.S. team was the overwhelming favourite to win the gold medal in men's competition and fulfilled expectations by defeating Yugoslavia 95–69 in the final. Lithuania finished third. In the women's tournament the United States completed a host-country sweep by defeating Brazil 111–87 in the final. Australia was third.

In Europe a major concern was the effect of the Bosman ruling on the sport. In 1995 soccer player Jean-Marc Bosman had taken his contractual dispute to the European courts, and his success there led to basketball's playing boundaries' being thrown wide open. Players at the end of their contracts could now move freely throughout the European Union member countries and would no longer be considered "foreign" players.

The Fédération Internationale de Basketball, the world governing body for basketball, during the year launched a new competition for the top clubs in Europe to replace the European championship. The EuroLeague began for men on September 18 and for women on October 2. The guaranteed number of games and television and marketing contracts were designed to provide a guaranteed income for the clubs, which was crucial to their future.

In Africa the 18th championship for men was won by Angola, which defeated Senegal 68–55 in the final. The European champions at Junior (under 18) level were Croatia in men's competition and Russia in the women's tournament. Runners-up were France and Slovakia, respectively.

World Amateur Basketball Championship—Men

Year	Winner	Runner-up
1988	U.S.S.R.	Yugoslavia
1990	Yugoslavia	U.S.S.R.
1992	United States	Croatia
1994	United States	Russia
1996	United States	Yugoslavia

World Amateur Basketball Championship—Women

Year	Winner	Runner-up
1988	United States	Yugoslavia
1990	United States	Yugoslavia
1992	Unified Team	China
1994	Brazil	China
1996	United States	Brazil

The major club competition during the 1995–96 European season, the European Championship for Men's Clubs, was won by Panathinaikos (Greece), which defeated Barcelona (Spain) 67–66 in Paris. In other European competitions Taugres (Spain) took the European Cup by beating PAOK Salonika (Greece); Efes Pilsen Istanbul (Turkey) defeated Stefanel Milan of Italy to win the European Korac Cup; BTU Wuppertal (Germany) gained the women's European Champions Cup with a victory over defending champions SFT Como (Italy); and the Ronchetti Cup stayed in France as Tarbes defeated S.C. Alcamo (Italy).

In South America the Basketball Club League for Men was won by Olimp Venado Tuerto of Argentina. Leites Nestle of Brazil won the 11th South American Championship for Women's Champion Clubs.

(MARK HANNEN)

BILLIARD GAMES

Carom Billiards. In recent years the world's top three-cushion billiard players had steadily and relentlessly pushed the scoring averages upward. In 1986 the record high average points-per-inning (PPI) for a tournament stood at 1.3, the mark set in 1950 by Willie Hoppe of the U.S. Since then the world's top players, led initially by Raymond Ceulemans of Belgium and later by Torbjörn Blomdahl of Sweden, had set new records in almost each major tournament.

It was no different at 1995's fourth and final Billiard World Cup Association (BWA) professional tour event in Istanbul, where Blomdahl matched his own existing record of 2.3 PPI for the tournament and also set a new high minimum game PPI standard of 2.1. Blomdahl also held the world 50-point and 60-point game PPI average marks of 3.8 and 3.3, respectively. His victory over Ceulemans in the championship match in Istanbul, along with an earlier tour victory in Halle, Ger., clinched his second consecutive and fifth overall BWA title since the BWA World Cup series began in 1986.

The United States Billiard Association (USBA) national tournament was held in Simi Valley, Calif., with the winner to represent the U.S. at the Union Mondiale de Billiard world championships in Viersen, Ger., in 1997. Sang Chun Lee of New York City, USBA champion for the previous seven years, prevailed again with a 50–42 play-off victory over Detroit's Mazin Shooni after the two had tied for best record in the round-robin competition.

Pocket Billiards. The three-year joint agreement signed in December 1992 by the American Poolplayers Association (APA), consisting of more than 100,000 amateur players, and the Men's Professional Billiards Association (MPBA)/Professional Billiards Tour (PBT) groups of professional players ended in October 1995. The APA declined to give the PBT control of the Camel Pro Exhibition Tour (an APA-developed concept) as the PBT had demanded, and the agreement was terminated.

Unrest in the men's professional ranks did not stop there. The MPBA and the PBT battle over control of the professional men's tour was punctuated by five resignations from the MPBA board of directors in mid-November 1995. The five, all touring pro players, left the organization to protest "a lack of fiscal accountability and the ex-

ceeding of proper authority" by the PBT commissioner. Just prior to the year's final PBT Tour event in December, the PBT terminated the Tour-playing memberships of the five, along with those of three others who were rumoured to be planning to bolt the Tour. The players obtained a restraining order, the PBT retained a lawyer, and on the day before the start of the PBT world championship in Winston-Salem, N.C., a local court ruled that the players had the right to play in the Tour finale.

In early 1996 the former Tour players did in fact spearhead the establishment of an organization to compete with the PBT, the Professional Cuesports Association (PCA). It proposed to engage in "direct promotions, sponsorship of charitable events, setting of stringent standards in the selection of sponsors and phased-in player drug testing." The PCA's first tournament was held in April in Dallas, Texas, and featured a special $1 million prize to any player who could run off a string of 10 consecutive game wins during the event. Though the odds against doing so were calculated to be as much as 7.8 million to 1, on the first night of the event, Earl Strickland of Greensboro, N.C., promptly stunned the billiard world by running a string of 11 straight games.

The World Pool-Billiard Association held its 1996 nine-ball championships in Borlänge, Swed. Ralf Souquet of Germany was the men's champion, and Allison Fisher of the U.K. won for the women.

The ongoing quest for pool and billiards to achieve Olympic sport status took a small but potentially important step forward when the General Association of International Sports Federations (GAISF) granted provisional membership to the World Confederation of Billiard Sports. WCBS membership in GAISF allowed organizers of the 1997 World Games in Finland to consider including some form of pool or billiards as a "festival" (or nonmedal) sport. Positive reaction to a cue sport in such a tournament would greatly enhance the likelihood of eventual recognition and inclusion in the Olympics.

The Billiard Congress of America inducted Dallas West of Rockford, Ill., as the 35th member of its Hall of Fame. Still active on a world-class level, West won the 1975 U.S. Open 14.1 crown and the 1983 World Series of Tavern Pool, finished second in two world open nine-ball tourna-

World Three-Cushion Championship

Year	Winner
1992	T. Blomdahl (Swed.)
1993	T. Blomdahl (Swed.)
1994	Sang Lee (U.S.)
1995	T. Blomdahl (Swed.)
1996	T. Blomdahl (Swed.)

WPA World Nine-Ball Championships

Year	Men's champion
1993	Chao Feng-pang (Taiwan)
1994	T. Okumura (Japan)
1995	O. Ortmann (Ger.)
1996	R. Souquet (Ger.)

Year	Women's champion
1993	L.J. Jones (U.S.)
1994	E. Mataya-Laurance (U.S.)
1995	G. Hofstatter (Austria)
1996	A. Fisher (U.K.)

ments in 1995, and won countless state and regional titles throughout his more than 40 years of competition. Straight pool (14.1 Continuous) was his strongest game (high run of 425), but he also played world-class carom billiards as well.

The 1995 men's and women's Player of the Year awards were won by Efren Reyes and Loree Jon Jones, respectively. It was the first such honour for Reyes, though he had long been widely considered one of the sport's finest all-around players. For Jones, it was her fifth Player of the Year prize in a 15-year span during which she had won 30 professional titles. (BRUCE H. VENZKE)

Snooker. No obvious challenger to Stephen Hendry's position as the world's number one snooker player emerged in 1996, either before or after the remorseless Scot won his sixth world professional title at Sheffield, Eng., in May. The much-criticized ranking system would have put Hendry's compatriot John Higgins in front had he qualified for the final of the Grand Prix tournament at Bournemouth, Eng., in October, but his chance disappeared in the third round when he lost 5–3 to Tony Jones

ANTON WANT—ALLSPORT

Stephen Hendry of Scotland kisses the world professional snooker championship trophy. He won it for the sixth time by defeating Peter Ebdon of England 18–12.

of England. Hendry himself stumbled in the first round of the tournament.

Peter Ebdon of England lost his chance to overhaul Hendry by losing 5–3 to Mark Bennett of Wales in the first round at Bournemouth. The event was won by Mark Williams of Wales, who was elevated to fourth position in the provisional world rankings after his 9–5 victory over Euan Henderson of Scotland. Earlier, Ebdon had won the Regal Masters tournament at Motherwell, Scot. In November Hendry, Higgins, and Alan McManus won the World Cup for Scotland with a final-round victory of 10–7 over Ireland. (SYDNEY RISKIN)

BOWLING

World Tenpins. The fully packed year in international bowling started in 1996 in Helsinki, Fin., with national teams competing for the Cup of Europe. The tournament was first scheduled to be bowled in Israel, but because of uncertainty regarding the safety of the participants, the European federations voted in favour of moving the event to Helsinki. There, 22 men's and 18 women's teams gathered in late May. In both divisions the teams played one-game matches in a round-robin format.

In the women's tournament, Finland lost only two matches to win the championship. Norway and Sweden finished second and third, respectively. In the men's competition Sweden and Finland tied in match points, but Sweden's quintet finished first because it had knocked down more pins. Norway won the bronze medal. Individually, Finland's Pauliina Aalto paced both the men and the women with a 218.29 average. Kai Virtanen of Finland led the men with 217.33.

Early in August young players were invited to Hong Kong for the fourth world youth championships. Bowlers from 31 countries accepted the invitation. For the girls and boys, the events were singles, doubles, teams (4 players), all events (18 games), and masters (round-robin for 16 top players of all events). By the conclusion of the championship, 11 countries had shared the medals. Taiwan performed capably, capturing for the island four gold medals and one bronze. Japan and Venezuela were successful, winning two titles apiece. The remaining golds were won by Colombia and South Korea.

In September in Calgary, Alta., 16 nations bowled for the second World Tenpin Team Cup. During the tournament all teams bowled three round-robin matches, with the three best teams proceeding to the

final round. In the men's division Scandinavia dominated, with Finland placing first, Sweden second, and Denmark third. In the women's final the U.S. and Finland bowled to a tie. In the following two-frame roll-off, Finland won 56–40. Malaysia finished third.

In the AMF World Cup tournament in Belfast, N.Ire., in November Paeng Nepomuceno of the Philippines won the men's competition, defeating Drew Hylen of the United States 243–172 in the final. Cara Honeychurch of Australia was the women's champion. (YRJÖ SARAHETE)

U.S. Tenpins. The popularity of "arena" settings for the final rounds of Professional Bowlers Association (PBA) tournaments continued to grow in 1996. Under this format the tournament was moved from the bowling centre used for the qualifying round to a nearby site, often a college gymnasium, that would accommodate about 4,000 persons seated on three sides of specially installed lanes. Most bowling centres had space for only a few hundred spectators. The first three arena-style PBA tournaments were held in 1994. There were 9 in 1995, including a meet in Detroit's Joe Louis Arena that attracted 7,212 fans, and 12 in 1996. "Only the cost of installing lanes for one day's use will limit the increase in arena finals," according to PBA Commissioner Mark Gerberich. "We must find ways to assist the local proprietor with this expense."

In an arena meet at the Erie (Pa.) Civic Center—the PBA's Flagship Open on April 6—Bob Learn, Jr., an Erie resident, bowled a 300 game against Johnny Petraglia of Manalapan, N.J. (279), and received a $100,000 bonus. Learn then defeated John Mazza of Shelby township, Mich., 270–268; Parker Bohn III of Jackson, N.J., 280–279; and Randy Pedersen of Hollywood, Fla., 279–257 to capture his third championship and an additional $30,000. Learn's 1,129 for four games was a PBA record.

With a handful of tournaments remaining, Walter Ray Williams, Jr., of Stockton, Calif., with three championships in 1996, seemed the most likely to succeed Mike Aulby of Indianapolis, Ind., as PBA Player of the Year. Williams earned the honour in 1986 and 1993. Aulby was one of several bowlers with one title in 1996.

World Professional Snooker Championship			
Year	Winner	Year	Winner
1991	J. Parrott	1994	S. Hendry
1992	S. Hendry	1995	S. Hendry
1993	S. Hendry	**1996**	**S. Hendry**

Professional Bowlers Association (PBA) Tournament of Champions			
Year	Champion	Year	Champion
1991	D. Ozio	1994	N. Duke
1992	M. McDowell	1995	M. Aulby
1993	G. Branham	**1996**	**D. D'Entremont**

ABC Bowling Championships—Regular Division				
Year	Singles	Score	All-events	Score
1992	G. Blatchford, B. Youker (tie)	801	M. Tucker	2,158
1993	D. Bock	798	J. Nimke	2,254
1994	J. Weltzien	810	T. Holt	2,190
1995	M. Surina	826	J. Kwiatkowski	2,191
1996	**D. Scudder, Jr.**	**823**	**S. Kurtz**	**2,224**

WIBC Bowling Championships—Open Division				
Year	Singles	Score	All-events	Score
1992	P. Ann	680	M. Tokimoto	1,928
1993	K. Collura, K. Murph (tie)	747	A.M. Duggan	1,990
1994	V. Fifield	716	W. Macpherson-Papanos	1,940
1995	B. Owen	749	B. Owen	1,983
1996	**C. Berlanga**	**723**	**L. Nichols**	**1,985**

FIQ World Bowling Championships—Men				
Year	Singles	Pairs	Triples	Team (fives)
1983	T. Cariello (U.S.)	Australia	Sweden	Finland
1987	P. Rolland (Fr.)	Sweden	United States	Sweden
1991	Ying Chieh Ma (Taiwan)	United States	United States	Taiwan
1995	M. Doi (Can.)	Sweden	Netherlands	Netherlands

FIQ World Bowling Championships—Women				
Year	Singles	Pairs	Triples	Team (fives)
1983	L. Sulkanen (Swed.)	Denmark	West Germany	Sweden
1987	E. Piccini (Mex.)	United States	United States	United States
1991	M. Beckel (Ger.)	Japan	Canada	South Korea
1995	D. Ship (Can.)	Thailand	Australia	Finland

The increasing interest in mixed leagues—those that include both men and women—was reflected in a record entry of 1,933 four-person teams in the sixth annual mixed championships at the National Bowling Stadium in Reno, Nev. Easy Rollers #3 of Houston, Texas, won the team event and $10,000 with a score of 2,825, including a 304-pin handicap.   (JOHN J. ARCHIBALD)

BOXING

Included among the biggest upsets in world heavyweight boxing since the introduction of the Marquess of Queensberry rules more than 100 years ago was the overwhelming defeat of Mike Tyson (U.S.) in 11 rounds by Evander Holyfield (U.S.) at Las Vegas, Nev., in November. The victory gained for Holyfield the World Boxing Association (WBA) crown. In winning the heavyweight championship for the third time, he equaled a record previously held only by Muhammad Ali (U.S.). Holyfield had first become champion in 1990 by knocking out James ("Buster") Douglas (U.S.), at the time the only pugilist to have defeated Tyson, but after losing to Michael Moorer (U.S.) in 1994 and again to Riddick Bowe (U.S.) a year later, Holyfield was considered to be in the twilight of his career. It was a remarkable feat to come back and destroy Tyson in his 36th contest, especially given

the fact that at one time it was feared that Holyfield would be forced to retire because of a suspected heart condition, which, however, a thorough cardiac examination later ruled out.

Tyson had begun his comeback late in 1995 after serving three years in prison for rape. In March he regained the World Boxing Council (WBC) title by destroying Frank Bruno (Eng.) in three rounds. He then chose to take on Bruce Seldon (U.S.) and won the WBA crown, disposing of his opponent in the first round. He gave up the WBC crown to fight Holyfield. Bookmakers in Las Vegas made him a 22–1 favourite to annihilate Holyfield, but the latter's skill and courage won the battle.

Nearly 10 years earlier Tyson had eliminated the ridiculous number of heavyweight champions created by the various self-

World Light Heavyweight Champions
Top Weight 175 Pounds

WBA	
Virgil Hill (U.S.; 9/5/87)	
Thomas Hearns (U.S.; 6/3/91)	
Iran Barkley (U.S.; 3/21/92) gave up title in 1992	
Virgil Hill (U.S.; 9/92)	
WBC	
Dennis Andries (U.K.; 7/28/90)	
Jeff Harding (Austl.; 9/11/91)	
Mike McCallum (Jam.; 7/23/94)	
Fabrice Tiozzo (Fr.; 6/16/95)	
Roy Jones, Jr. (U.S.; 11/23/96)	
IBF	
Bobby Czyz (U.S.; 9/6/86)	
Charles Williams (U.S.; 10/29/87)	
Henry Maske (Ger.; 3/20/93)	
Virgil Hill (U.S.; 11/23/96)	

World Junior Middleweight Champions
Top Weight 154 Pounds
(also called super welterweight)

WBA	
Pernell Whitaker (U.S.; 3/4/95) gave up title in 1995	
Carl Daniels (U.S.; 6/16/95)	
Julio César Vásquez (Arg.; 12/16/95)	
Laurent Boudouani (Fr.; 8/21/96)	
WBC	
Terry Norris (U.S.; 3/31/90)	
Simon Brown (U.S.; 12/18/93)	
Terry Norris (U.S.; 5/7/94)	
Luis Santana (Dom.Rep.; 11/12/94)	
Terry Norris (U.S.; 8/19/95)	
IBF	
Darrin Van Horn (U.S.; 2/4/89)	
Gianfranco Rosi (Italy; 7/16/89)	
Vincent Pettway (U.S.; 9/17/94)	
Paul Vaden (U.S.; 8/12/95)	
Terry Norris (U.S.; 12/16/95)	

World Heavyweight Champions
No Weight Limit

WBA	
Evander Holyfield (U.S.; 11/6/93)	
Michael Moorer (U.S.; 4/22/94)	
George Foreman (U.S.; 11/5/94) stripped of title in 1995	
Bruce Seldon (U.S.; 4/8/95)	
Mike Tyson (U.S.; 9/7/96)	
Evander Holyfield (U.S.; 11/9/96)	
WBC	
Oliver McCall (U.S.; 9/24/94)	
Frank Bruno (U.K.; 9/2/95)	
Mike Tyson (U.S.; 3/16/96) gave up title in 1996	
IBF	
Evander Holyfield (U.S.; 11/6/93)	
Michael Moorer (U.S.; 4/22/94)	
George Foreman (U.S.; 11/5/94) gave up title in 1995	
Frans Botha (S.Af.; 12/9/95) stripped of title in 1996	
Michael Moorer (U.S.; 6/22/96)	

World Super Middleweight Champions
Top Weight 168 Pounds

WBA	
Christophe Tiozzo (Fr.; 3/30/90)	
Victor Cordoba (Pan.; 4/5/91)	
Michael Nunn (U.S.; 9/12/92)	
Steve Little (U.S.; 2/26/94)	
Frank Liles (U.S.; 8/12/94)	
WBC	
Mauro Galvano (Italy; 12/15/90)	
Nigel Benn (U.K.; 10/3/92)	
Thulane Malinga (S.Af.; 3/2/96)	
Vincenzo Nardiello (Italy; 7/6/96)	
Robin Reid (U.K.; 10/12/96)	
IBF	
Lindell Holmes (U.S.; 1/27/90)	
Darrin Van Horn (U.S.; 5/18/91)	
Iran Barkley (U.S.; 1/10/92)	
James Toney (U.S.; 2/13/93)	
Roy Jones (U.S.; 11/18/94)	

World Welterweight Champions
Top Weight 147 Pounds

WBA	
Mark Breland (U.S.; 2/4/89)	
Aaron Davis (U.S.; 7/8/90)	
Meldrick Taylor (U.S.; 1/19/91)	
Crisanto España (Venez.; 10/31/92)	
Ike Quartey (Ghana; 6/4/94)	
WBC	
Marlon Starling (U.S.; 2/4/89)	
Maurice Blocker (U.S.; 8/19/90)	
Simon Brown (Jam.; 3/18/91)	
James McGirt (U.S.; 11/29/91)	
Pernell Whitaker (U.S.; 3/6/93)	
IBF	
Simon Brown (Jam.; 4/23/88) gave up title in 1991	
Maurice Blocker (U.S.; 10/4/91)	
Felix Trinidad (P.R.; 6/19/93)	

World Cruiserweight Champions
Top Weight 195 Pounds

WBA	
Bobby Czyz (U.S.; 3/8/91) vacant	
Orlin Norris (U.S.; 11/6/93)	
Nate Miller (U.S.; 7/22/95)	
WBC	
Evander Holyfield (U.S.; 4/9/88) gave up title in 1988	
Carlos de Léon (P.R.; 5/17/89)	
Massimiliano Duran (Italy; 7/27/90)	
Anaclet Wamba (Fr.; 7/20/91)	
Marcelo Dominguez (Arg.; 4/19/96)	
IBF	
Jeff Lampkin (U.S.; 3/22/90) gave up title in 1991	
James Warring (U.S.; 9/7/91)	
Alfred Cole (U.S.; 7/30/92) **gave up title in 1996**	
Adolpho Washington (U.S.; 8/31/96)	

World Middleweight Champions
Top Weight 160 Pounds

WBA	
John David Jackson (U.S.; 10/2/93) stripped of title in 1994	
Jorge Castro (Arg.; 8/12/94)	
Shinji Takehara (Japan; 12/19/95)	
William Joppy (U.S.; 6/24/96)	
WBC	
Gerald McClellan (U.S.; 5/8/93) vacant	
Julian Jackson (U.S.; 3/17/95)	
Quincy Taylor (U.S.; 8/19/95)	
Keith Holmes (U.S.; 3/16/96)	
IBF	
James Toney (U.S.; 5/10/91) gave up title in 1993	
Roy Jones (U.S.; 5/22/93) gave up title in 1994	
Bernard Hopkins (U.S.; 4/29/95)	

World Junior Welterweight Champions
Top Weight 140 Pounds
(also called super lightweight)

WBA	
Akinobu Hiranaka (Japan; 4/10/92)	
Morris East (Phil.; 9/9/92)	
Juan Martin Coggi (Arg.; 1/12/93)	
Frankie Randall (U.S.; 9/17/94)	
Juan Martin Coggi (Arg.; 1/13/96)	
Frankie Randall (U.S.; 8/16/96)	
WBC	
Julio César Chávez (Mex.; 5/13/89)	
Frankie Randall (U.S.; 1/29/94)	
Julio César Chávez (Mex.; 5/7/94)	
Oscar de la Hoya (U.S.; 6/7/96)	
IBF	
Pernell Whitaker (U.S.; 7/18/92) gave up title in 1993	
Charles Murray (U.S.; 5/15/93)	
Jake Rodriguez (P.R.; 2/13/94)	
Kostya Tszyu (Austl.; 1/28/95)	

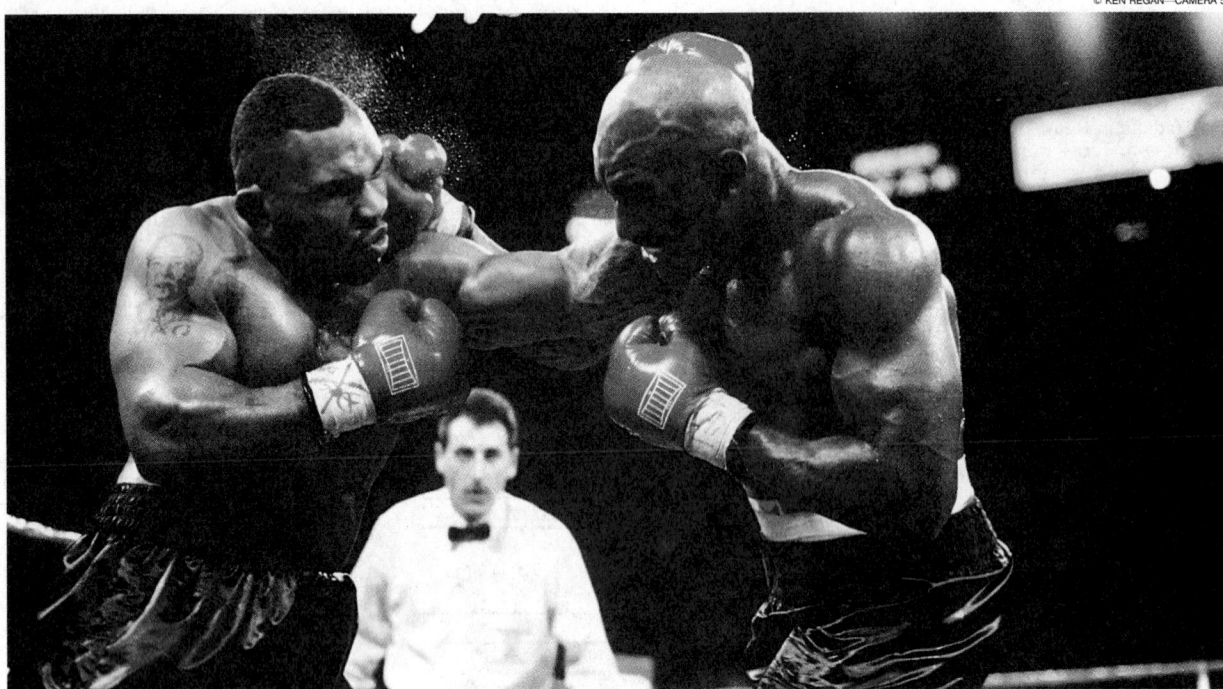

Mike Tyson (left) takes a right hook from Evander Holyfield during the fight for the WBA heavyweight crown at Las Vegas, Nev., in November. Although he was a 22–1 underdog, Holyfield surprised the boxing world by defeating Tyson decisively in 11 rounds.

World Lightweight Champions
Top Weight 135 Pounds

WBA

Pernell Whitaker (U.S.; 8/11/90)
  gave up title in 1992
Joey Gamache (U.S.; 6/13/92)
Tony Lopez (U.S.; 10/24/92)
Dingaan Thobela (S.Af.; 6/26/93)
Olzubek Nazarov (Russia; 10/30/93)

WBC

Pernell Whitaker (U.S.; 8/20/89)
  gave up title in 1992
Miguel González (Mex.; 8/24/92)
  gave up title in 1996
Jean-Baptiste Mendy (Fr.; 4/20/96)

IBF

Fred Pendleton (U.S.; 1/10/93)
Rafael Ruelas (U.S.; 2/19/94)
Oscar De La Hoya (U.S.; 5/6/95)
  gave up title in 1995
Philip Holiday (S.Af.; 8/19/95)

World Junior Lightweight Champions
Top Weight 130 Pounds

(also called super featherweight)

WBA

Joey Gamache (U.S.; 6/28/91)
  gave up title in 1991
Genaro Hernandez (U.S.; 11/22/91)
  gave up title in 1995
Choi Yong Soo (S.Kor.; 10/21/95)

WBC

Azumah Nelson (Ghana; 2/29/88)
Jesse James Leija (U.S.; 5/7/94)
Gabriel Ruelas (U.S.; 9/17/94)
Azumah Nelson (Ghana; 12/1/95)

IBF

Juan Molina (P.R.; 2/22/92)
  vacant
Eddie Hopson (U.S.; 4/22/95)
Tracy Patterson (U.S.; 7/9/95)
Arturo Gatti (U.S.; 12/15/95)

World Featherweight Champions
Top Weight 126 Pounds

WBA

Steve Cruz (U.S.; 6/23/86)
Antonio Esparragoza (Venez.; 3/6/87)
Park Yung Kyun (S.Kor.; 3/30/91)
Eloy Rojas (Venez.; 12/4/93)
Wilfredo Vasquez (P.R.; 5/18/96)

WBC

Paul Hodkinson (U.K.; 11/13/91)
Gregorio Vargas (Mex.; 4/28/93)
Kevin Kelley (U.S.; 12/4/93)
Alejandro González (Mex.; 1/7/95)
Manuel Medina (Mex.; 9/23/95)
Luisito Espinosa (Phil.; 12/11/95)

IBF

Jorge Paez (Mex.; 8/4/88)
  gave up title in 1991
Troy Dorsey (U.S.; 6/3/91)
Manuel Medina (Mex.; 8/12/91)
Tom Johnson (U.S.; 2/26/93)

World Junior Featherweight Champions
Top Weight 122 Pounds

(also called super bantamweight)

WBA

Luis Mendoza (Colom.; 9/11/90)
Raul Pérez (Mex.; 10/7/91)
Wilfredo Vásquez (P.R.; 3/27/92)
Antonio Cermeno (Venez.; 5/13/95)

WBC

Daniel Zaragoza (Mex.; 6/14/91)
Thierry Jacob (Fr.; 3/20/92)
Tracy Patterson (U.S.; 6/23/92)
Hector Acero-Sánchez (U.S.; 8/26/94)
Daniel Zaragoza (Mex.; 11/6/95)

IBF

José Sanabria (Venez.; 5/21/88)
Fabrice Benichou (Fr.; 3/10/89)
Welcome Ncita (S.Af.; 3/10/90)
Kennedy McKinney (U.S.; 12/2/92)
Vuyani Bungu (S.Af.; 8/20/94)

World Bantamweight Champions
Top Weight 118 Pounds

WBA

John Michael Johnson (U.S.; 4/22/94)
Daorung Chuvatana (Thai.; 7/16/94)
Veeraphol Sahaprom (Thai.; 9/17/95)
Nana Konadu (Ghana; 1/28/96)
Daorung Chuvatana Siriwat (Thai.; 10/26/96)

WBC

Joichiro Tatsuyoshi (Japan; 9/19/91)
  vacant
Victor Rabañales (Mex.; 3/30/92)
Byun Jong-Il (S.Kor.; 3/28/93)
Yasuei Yakushiji (Japan; 12/22/93)
Wayne McCullough (N.Ire.; 7/30/95)

IBF

Kelvin Seabrooks (U.S.; 5/16/87)
Orlando Canizales (U.S.; 7/9/88)
  gave up title in 1994
Harold Mestre (Colom.; 1/21/95)
Mbulelo Botile (S.Af.; 4/29/95)

World Junior Bantamweight Champions
Top Weight 115 Pounds

(also called super flyweight)

WBA

Khaosai Galaxy (Thai.; 11/21/84)
  gave up title in 1991
Katsuya Onizuka (Japan; 4/10/92)
Lee Hyung Chul (S.Kor.; 9/18/94)
Alima Goitia (Venez.; 7/22/95)
Yokthai Sithoar (Thai.; 8/24/96)

WBC

Nana Konadu (Ghana; 11/7/89)
Moon Sung Kil (S.Kor.; 1/20/90)
José Luis Bueno (Mex.; 11/13/93)
Hiroshi Kawashima (Japan; 5/4/94)

IBF

Julio Borboa (Mex.; 1/16/93)
Harold Grey (Colom.; 8/29/94)
Carlos Salazar (Arg.; 10/7/95)
Harold Grey (Colom.; 4/27/96)
Danny Romero (U.S.; 8/24/96)

appointed controlling bodies. He defeated the WBC, WBA, and International Boxing Federation (IBF) titleholders to prove himself undisputed champion. Internal disputes, battles for power, and legal threats, however, continued to leave the heavyweight and other weight divisions in chaos, with many mediocre champions.

On the same bill as the Tyson and Holyfield promotion were two other "world" heavyweight championship fights. Michael Moorer retained the IBF version, stopping Frans Botha (S.Af.) in 12 rounds. The South African had won the IBF crown by defeating Axel Schulz (Ger.) but lost it in a courtroom after testing positive for steroids. The World Boxing Organization (WBO) champion, Henry Akinwande (Eng.), also kept his title by battering Aleksandr Zolkin (Russia) in 10 rounds.

Apart from the heavyweights, two outstanding champions in lower weight divisions became top-class attractions. Roy Jones (U.S.), the IBF super middleweight champion, when defending the title in June against Eric Lucas (Can.), showed arrogance by taking part in a professional basketball match in the afternoon before climbing into the ring to retain his title

in 11 laborious rounds at Jacksonville, Fla. He later regained lost popularity by knocking out the top-ranked challenger, Bryant Brannon (U.S.), in two rounds in New York City. He donated his purse (apart from promotional expenses) to various charities and also contributed to medical expenses to assist Gerald McClellan (U.S.), who had received permanent injury during a challenge match with Nigel Benn (Eng.).

The other outstanding boxer was Oscar de la Hoya (U.S.), the WBC lightweight champion, who moved up to light welter-

weight and inflicted a four-round hammering on the legendary champion Julio César Chávez (Mex.). Chávez had taken part in 34 title bouts during a career approaching 100 contests. Though Chávez was obviously past his glory days, the ease with which de la Hoya handled him surprised many. Chávez, who earned $9 million against de la Hoya, hoped for a return match, and in October he crushed Joey Gamache (U.S.) in eight rounds. His $1.5 million purse was, however, paid directly to Mexican authorities for back taxes.

R. MARSH STARKS—REUTERS

JOHN GICHIGI—ALLSPORT

(Left) Oscar de la Hoya rides on the shoulders of one of his trainers after defeating Julio César Chávez in four rounds at Las Vegas, Nev., in June for the WBC light welterweight championship. (Right) Naseem Hamed of the U.K., right, knocks out Remigio Molina of Argentina in the second round at Manchester, Eng., in November to retain his WBO featherweight crown.

World Flyweight Champions Top Weight 112 Pounds
WBA
Elvis Alvarez (Colom.; 3/14/91)
Kim Yong Kang (S.Kor.; 6/1/91)
Aquiles Guzmán (Venez.; 9/26/92)
David Griman (Venez.; 12/92)
San Sow Ploenchit (Thai.; 2/13/94)
WBC
Kim Young Kang (S.Kor.; 7/24/88)
Sot Chitalada (Thai.; 6/3/89)
Muangchai Kittlkasem (Thai.; 2/15/91)
Yury Arbachakov (Russia; 6/23/92)
IBF
Phichit Sithbangprachan (Thai.; 11/29/92) vacant
Francisco Tejedor (Colom.; 2/95)
Danny Romero (U.S.; 4/22/95) **gave up title in 1996**
Mark Johnson (U.S.; 5/4/96)

World Junior Flyweight Champions Top Weight 108 Pounds
WBA
Yuh Myung Woo (S.Kor.; 11/18/92) gave up title in 1993
Leo Gamez (Venez.; 10/21/93)
Choi Hi Yong (S.Kor.; 2/4/95)
Carlos Murillo (Pan.; 1/13/96)
Keiji Yamaguchi (Japan; 5/21/96)
Pichitnoi Siriwat (Thai.; 12/3/96)
WBC
Humberto González (Mex.; 6/4/91)
Michael Carbajal (U.S.; 3/13/93)
Chiquita Gonzalez (Mex.; 2/19/94)
Saman Sorjaturong (Thai.; 7/15/95)
IBF
Michael Carbajal (U.S.; 7/29/90)
Chiquita Gonzalez (Mex.; 2/19/94)
Saman Sorjaturong (Thai.; 7/15/95) vacant
Michael Carbajal (U.S.; 3/16/96)

World Mini-flyweight Champions Top Weight 105 Pounds
(also called strawweight)
WBA
Kim Bong Jun (S.Kor.; 4/16/89)
Choi Hi Yong (S.Kor.; 2/2/91)
Ohashi Hideyuki (Japan; 10/14/92)
Chana Porpaoin (Thai.; 2/10/93)
Rosendo Alvarez (Nic.; 12/2/95)
WBC
Napa Kiatwanchai (Thai.; 11/13/88)
Choi Jum Hwan (S.Kor.; 11/12/89)
Ohashi Hideyuki (Japan; 2/7/90)
Ricardo López (Mex.; 10/25/90)
IBF
Falan Lookmingkwan (Thai.; 2/21/90)
Manny Melchor (Phil.; 9/6/92)
Ratanapol Vorapin (Thai.; 12/10/92) **stripped of title in 1996**
Ratanapol Vorapin (Thai.; 5/16/96)

Another remarkable veteran, Azumah Nelson (Ghana), retained the super featherweight crown at the age of 37, triumphing over Jesse James Leija (U.S.) in six rounds. Leija had previously drawn with and outpointed Nelson, but the Ghanaian proved himself to be one of Africa's best-ever champions.

Steve Collins (Ire.) retained the WBO super middleweight title with victories against Chris Eubank (Eng.) and Benn. Both British fighters announced their retirement, but Eubank later made a comeback as a fighter and at the same time also became a promoter, staging the first professional tournament in Egypt. There his low-rated Argentine opponent, Luis Barrerar, was easily disposed of in five rounds.

The outstanding British fighter Naseem Hamed continued his winning ways, retaining the WBO featherweight crown with a two-round win over Remigio Molina of Argentina. Hamed hoped to meet IBF featherweight champion Tom Johnson (U.S.) in 1997.

The British Medical Association continued its antiboxing campaign with a series of 60-second advertisements to be shown in 100 British movie theatres, but with television offering Holyfield and Tyson millions of dollars to meet again, the chances that professional boxing would be outlawed appeared slim, if not nonexistent.

(FRANK BUTLER)

CHESS

The world ruling body of chess, the Fédération Internationale des Échecs (FIDE), finally managed in 1996 to arrange the overdue world title match between the defending champion, Anatoly Karpov of Russia, and his challenger, Gata Kamsky of the United States. Earlier FIDE had accepted an offer from Saddam Hussein in Iraq to be organizer of the match. Angry reaction from much of the world forced cancellation of that bid. Before the cancellation the U.S. Treasury Department advised Kamsky of the huge fine and possible imprisonment that he would face if he took part in a chess match in Baghdad.

The match was finally played at Elista, Kalmykia, Russia, from June 6 to July 11. It ended in a convincing 10.5–7.5 victory for Karpov in the 18th game of the scheduled 20. Karpov won six games, drew nine, and lost three. A new feature for FIDE title matches was the absence of the right to take any rest or illness days.

The women's world championship was played in January and February at Jaén, Spain, and was enlivened by a threat from the organizer, Luis Rentero, to impose a $25,000 fine for any perceived lack of competitive spirit in the early games. Zsuzsa Polgar of Hungary, oldest of the three famous chess-playing sisters, defeated defending champion Xie Jun of China 8.5–4.5.

The World Chess Olympiad, contested from September 16 to October 2 at Yerevan, Armenia, again confirmed the strength of the former Soviet republics. Russia won the 14-round contest in a convincing manner. Top scores in the competition for 114 countries were: (1) Russia 38.5 game points; (2) Ukraine 35; (3) the U.S. on tiebreaker with (4) the U.K., each scoring 34; (5–7) Armenia, Spain, and Bosnia and Herzegovina 33.5; (8–12) Georgia, Bulgaria, Germany, Sweden, and Iceland 33; and (13–15) China, The Netherlands, and Argentina 32.5. Georgia won the women's competition, followed in order by China, Russia, Ukraine, and Hungary.

Among the strongest tournaments of the year, the 10th VSB event at Amsterdam ended in a tie for first between Veselin Topalov of Bulgaria and Garry Kasparov of Russia, with 6.5 points out of 9. At Dos Hermanas, Spain, Vladimir Kramnik and Topalov scored 6 out of 9 to lead Viswanathan Anand of India and Kasparov by a half point.

Aleksey Suetin of Moscow won the world senior championship in November on a tiebreak from Anatoly Lein of the U.S., a former Soviet grandmaster, and Janis Klovans, a Latvian international master. The world junior championship, played at the same time in Medellín, Colom., was won by Emil Sutovskij of Israel.

The year ended with the Las Palmas tournament in Spain's Canary Islands, a double rounder for six players, which gained the participation of both Kasparov and Karpov

ЧЕМПИОНАТ МИРА
ПО ШАХМАТАМ
Республика Калмыкия
ЭЛИСТА '96

Г. КАМСКИЙ   А. КАРПОВ

In the match to determine the Fédération Internationale des Échecs championship, Anatoly Karpov of Russia (right) retained his world chess title by defeating challenger Gata Kamsky of the U.S. by a score of 10.5–7.5. Karpov won six games, drew nine, and lost three.

Olympiad—Women

Year	Winner	Runner-up
1988	Hungary	U.S.S.R.
1992	Georgia	Ukraine
1986	U.S.S.R.	Hungary
1994	Georgia	Hungary
1996	**Georgia**	**China**

Olympiad—Men

Year	Winner	Runner-up
1989	U.S.S.R.	Yugoslavia
1992	Russia	Uzbekistan
1994	Russia	Bosnia
1996	**Russia**	**Ukraine**

Caro-Kann Defense

	White: Gata Kamsky		Black: Anatoly Karpov
White	Black	White	Black
1 e4	c6	24 Rd2	Bg7
2 d4	d5	25 h4	Rfe8
3 ed	cd	26 Qg3	Rc8
4 c4	Nf6	27 Nd7	Qc6
5 Nc3	e6	28 Nc5	b6
6 Nf3	Bb4	29 Nd3	Qd7
7 cd	Nd5	30 a5	Re4
8 Bd2	Nc6	31 Nf4	b5
9 Bd3	0-0	32 Rdd1	Bc4
10 0-0	Be7	33 Rac1*	h6
11 Qe2	Nf6	34 Rc3	b4
12 Ne4	Qb6	35 Rc2	Rc6
13 a3	Bd7	36 Rdc1	Bb5
14 Rfd1	Rad8	37 Kh2	Kh7
15 Nf6	Bf6	38 Rc6	Bc6
16 Qe4	g6	39 Rc4	Bf8
17 Be3	Ne7	40 Nd3	Qe6
18 Ne5	Nf5	41 d5	Bd5
19 Nc4	Qa6	42 Re4	Be4
20 a4	Bc6	43 Ba7	Bd6
21 Qf4	Bd5	44 Nf4	Qe5
22 Ne5	Qb6	45 Nh3	Qe7
23 Bf5	ef	resigns	

World Chess Championship—Men

Year	Winner	Runner-up
1987	G. Kasparov (U.S.S.R.)	A. Karpov (U.S.S.R.)
1990	G. Kasparov (U.S.S.R.)	A. Karpov (U.S.S.R.)
1993	A. Karpov (Russia)	J. Timman (Neth.)
1996	**A. Karpov (Russia)**	**G. Kamsky (U.S.)**

World Chess Championship—Women

Year	Winner	Runner-up
1988	M. Chiburdanidze (U.S.S.R.)	N. Ioseliani (U.S.S.R.)
1991	Xie Jun (China)	M. Chiburdanidze (U.S.S.R.)
1993	Xie Jun (China)	N. Ioseliani (Georgia)
1996	**Z. Polgar (Hung.)**	**Xie Jun (China)**

for the first time in nearly three years. It ended with a victory for Kasparov, who scored 6.5 points out of a possible 10. Anand finished second with 5.5, followed by Kramnik and Topalov with 5 each. Tied for last with 4 points were Karpov and Vassily Ivanchuk of Ukraine. Las Palmas hoped to be the host for the projected world "reunification" match in 1997.

In other developments FIDE and its president, Kirsan Ilyumzhinov, encountered opposition from the European chess federations, the U.S., and Canada. They were so incensed by what they considered irregularities by FIDE that they held a special meeting in Utrecht, Neth., on April 27–28. The meeting called for equal treatment for Kamsky and Karpov, the restoration of the traditional FIDE cycle of qualifying contests leading to the world title match, and a shake-up in FIDE.

To reinforce this reformation the Utrecht partners supported a candidate to challenge Ilyumzhinov at the FIDE Congress that took place alongside the World Chess Olympiad. The candidate was Jaime Sunye Neto, a grandmaster from Brazil. Ilyumzhinov was successful in mustering support from the Third World and from Russia, which won him the election 87–46.

The financial position of FIDE was not good. There was no restoration of the traditional qualifying cycle, and Ilyumzhinov's own preference for a $5 million knockout contest for the world's top 100 players was deferred from December 1996 until December 1997 with no definite sponsor announced. The Professional Chess Association, Kasparov's organization, was also restricting its activities after it lost its sponsorship from Intel Corp. when Kasparov decided to play an exhibition match in February of six games against Intel's rival IBM, using IBM's new program Deep Blue. After his loss in the first round provoked great interest, especially on the Internet, Kasparov won the match. The final score was 4–2, with a replay scheduled against a new program in 1997. (*See* COMPUTERS AND INFORMATION SCIENCES: Sidebar.)

(BERNARD CAFFERTY)

CONTRACT BRIDGE

The major event of 1996 in contract bridge was the World Team Olympiad. It was held on the Greek island of Rhodes from October 19 to November 2, and any member country of the World Bridge Federation was permitted to enter two teams, one in the Open Series and one in the Women's. Of some 100 member countries of the WBF, 72 sent teams: 71 for the Open event and 43 for the Women's. (Jamaica sent only a women's team.)

The Open title was retained by France, which beat Indonesia 358–269 in the final. Third was Denmark, which lost in overtime against Indonesia in the semifinal. The winning team comprised Alain Lévy, Hervé Mouiel, Christian Mari, Frank Multon, Henri Szwarc, and Marc Bompis, with Jean-Louis Stoppa as the nonplaying captain. Playing in its first world final, Indonesia was represented by Henky Lasut, Eddy Manoppo, Denny Sacul, Franky Karwur, Giovanni Watulingas, and Sance Panelewen.

The Women's title was won convincingly by the United States, which defeated

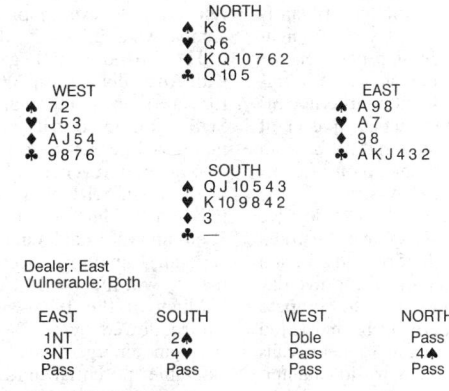

The best-played deal of the year, in the opinion of the International Bridge Press Association, was declared by Wubbo de Boer of The Netherlands, who won the Bermuda Bowl in 1993. He was competing in the Generali Individual in Paris.

```
                           NORTH
                           ♠ K 6
                           ♥ Q 6
                           ♦ K Q 10 7 6 2
                           ♣ Q 10 5
         WEST                                   EAST
         ♠ 7 2                                  ♠ A 9 8
         ♥ J 5 3                                ♥ A 7
         ♦ A J 5 4                              ♦ 9 8
         ♣ 9 8 7 6                              ♣ A K J 4 3 2
                           SOUTH
                           ♠ Q J 10 5 4 3
                           ♥ K 10 9 8 4 2
                           ♦ 3
                           ♣ —
```

Dealer: East
Vulnerable: Both

EAST	SOUTH	WEST	NORTH
1NT	2♠	Dble	Pass
3NT	4♥	Pass	4♠
Pass	Pass	Pass	Pass

Opening lead: ♣9.

The Greek player, Evangelos Nartis, opened with a slightly off-centre strong one no-trump. De Boer made a natural overcall. Paul Chemla of France made a negative double, which expressed the desire to compete for the part score. De Boer was not willing to defend against three no-trump.

Against four spades, West led a club, which declarer ruffed. This posed a problem for South. If he led a heart to the queen, East would win with the ace and play ace and another trump. Declarer would lose one spade, two hearts, and one diamond and, consequently, the contract.

De Boer crossed this hurdle by running the ♥10 to East's ace. East accurately played a top club, forcing declarer down to four trumps.

If South played on trumps, East would win the second round and play another club. With the hearts still blocked, South would not have enough trumps. And if South cashed the ♥Q first, East would put partner in with his ♦A and receive a heart ruff.

De Boer found the answer: He cashed the ♥K, crushing dummy's queen. He ruffed a low heart with dummy's ♠K, and played dummy's last trump. A moment later de Boer was able to draw trumps and run the hearts.

China 268–198. Canada finished third. The U.S. team comprised Juanita Chambers, Lynn Deas, Irina Levitina, Jill Blanchard, Gail Greenberg (Blanchard's mother), and Shawn Quinn, with Eddie Wold as the nonplaying captain. It was the first time a mother-and-daughter combination had ever won a world title. The Chinese team consisted of Gu Ling, Zhang Ya Lan, Sun Ming, Wang Hong Li, Wang Wen Fei, and Zhang Yu, with Zhang Wei Li as the nonplaying captain.

The first-ever world mixed-teams championship was also contested at Rhodes. It was the first world championship in which players representing different countries were allowed to play as pairs and/or teammates. The winners were Heather Dhondy and Liz McGowan of the U.K. and Jon Baldursson, Björn Eysteinsson, and Adalsteinn Jorgensen of Iceland. Ragnar Hermansson of Iceland was also on the team but did not play in the knockout stage. In the final they defeated Mark Feldman, Rozanne and Bill Pollack, and Sharon Osberg of the U.S. 66–55.

Geir Helgemo of Norway further solidified his reputation as the rising star of contract bridge by winning the Generali Individual competition in Paris in May ahead of 51 of the world's greatest players. The women's event was won by Elizabeth Delor of France.

Junior bridge continued to develop strongly in Europe, as demonstrated by the high standard of play at the European Junior (under 25) and Schools (under 20) championships held in Cardiff, Wales, in July. In the first event Norway triumphed, ahead of Russia, Denmark, and 23 other countries. The younger competition was won easily by Germany, in front of Israel, the U.K., and 11 other nations.

The biggest contest from the point of view of the number of competitors—more than 80,000—was the Alcatel Worldwide Pairs. It was held in two sessions in many places throughout the world on June 7–8, and the highest score of 81.4% was achieved by Wang Weidon and He Weidong of Beijing.

Terence Reese died on January 29 at the age of 82. Arguably the greatest-ever player and writer, he was on the only British team to win the Bermuda Bowl world team championship, in 1955.

(PHILLIP ALDER)

Bermuda Bowl		
Year	Winner	Runner-up
1989	Brazil	United States
1991	Iceland	Poland
1993	Netherlands	Norway
1995	United States	Canada

World Contract Bridge Pair Championship			
Year	Open winners	Women's winners	Mixed winners
1990	Marcelo Branco, Gabriel Chagas (Braz.)	Kerri Shuman, Karen McCallum (U.S.)	Peter Weichsel, Juanita Chambers (U.S.)
1994	Marcin Lesniewski, Marek Szymanowski (Pol.)	Carla Arnolds, Bep Vriend (Neth.)	Danuta Hocheker, Apolinare Kowalski (Pol.)

World Team Olympiad			
Year	Open winner	Open runner-up	Women's winner	Women's runner-up
1988	United States	Austria	Denmark	United Kingdom
1992	France	United States	Austria	United Kingdom
1996	**France**	**Indonesia**	**United States**	**China**

CRICKET

The victory of Sri Lanka in the 1996 World Cup (*see* Sidebar), though brilliantly achieved and thoroughly deserved, highlighted the increasing division between the one-day and the five-day game in terms of popularity, standards, and marketing. Sri Lanka showed itself the tactical master of one-day cricket and could rightly bask in the glow of being world champion after its seven-wicket victory over Australia in the World Cup final on March 17, but decisive defeats in all three Tests against Australia demonstrated how far the Sri Lankan team was from being a champion of the five-day game. Aware of cricket's need to compete with other, more aggressively marketed sports, its authorities began to heed calls for the establishment of a world championship of Test cricket.

"Any team claiming to be world champions can only be considered unofficial champions," Clive Lloyd, the former West Indies captain, said. "But why 'unofficial'? We are not playing unofficial Tests. Some structure should be set up where you play for the championship of the world." While tacitly agreeing that the calendar of Test cricket was coherent, with each nation deciding who it played and when, the International Cricket Council, the ruling body, indicated that in practice it would be difficult to impose a fixture list on the nine Test-playing nations because of financial considerations and a reluctance to cede power to a central body. An unofficial table, based on matches played during the previous four years and compiled by the English magazine *Wisden Cricket Monthly,* put South Africa on top, narrowly ahead of Australia and West In-

dies, jointly in second place, and India and Pakistan tied for fourth. Embarrassingly, though doubtless accurately, England was relegated to seventh place, ahead of only Zimbabwe and New Zealand.

The World Cup began in controversy, with Australia and the West Indies refusing to play their group matches in Colombo, Sri Lanka, on security grounds, and ended in a fairy-tale victory for the 66–1 outsiders, who gained revenge by beating Australia in the final. Sri Lanka's cricket was inventive and thrilling, and in the portly Arjuna Ranatunga Sri Lanka had a calm and astute captain. Ranatunga became only the fifth man to win the World Cup trophy.

Much of the 1995–96 Test cricket was overshadowed by the World Cup, though Pakistan emerged as a Test side of considerable potential under the leadership of Wasim Akram. Having collapsed disappointingly against Australia, for whom spin bowler S.K. Warne was again dominant, Pakistan went to England in the summer and outplayed the home team, winning 2–0. Akram and Waqar Younis proved again that they were the most deadly opening bowling combination in Test cricket, taking 27 wickets between them in the three-Test series, and Mushtaq Ahmed took 17 wickets at an average of 26.29 with his leg-spin. Ijaz Ahmed, who had scored 137 in the third Test against Australia, scored 344 runs at an average of 68.8 to confirm his promise as one of the classiest young stroke makers in the game. Pakistan's pool of young talent knew no bounds, it seemed. Hassan Raza was thought to be the youngest cricketer in Test history when he made his debut against Zimbabwe late in the year at the advertised age of 14 years 227 days. It was

later suggested that Raza actually might have been 15, just as Shahid Afridi—who less than two months earlier had hit the record fastest international one-day century, off 37 balls against Sri Lanka—turned out to be 19 and not 16 as first claimed.

Not all was lost for England, which had beaten India in the first series of the summer, its first series win in two years, and discovered in N.V. Knight and N. Hussain batsmen of solid technique and good temperament. With D.G. Cork not showing the spark that marked his first year in international cricket, the bowling was more of a problem. Knight scored 113 in the second Test against Pakistan and followed up with consecutive centuries in the two one-day internationals. Despite its defeat, India, too, produced another young player of quality in S. Ganguly, a left-handed batsman who found Test cricket an easy game, scoring a century on his Test debut at Lord's and another in his second Test at Nottingham. In August 23-year-old S.R Tendulkar (*see* BIOGRAPHIES), who had made his Test debut at age 16, was named India's captain.

For sheer determination and application, the innings of M.A. Atherton in the second Test against South Africa deserved better reward than a mere draw. Left to bat out a total of 165 overs with no chance of victory, the England captain made 185 not out in 645 minutes (10¾ hours) to steer his side to safety. R.C. Russell, who had earlier become the first wicketkeeper to take 11 dismissals in a match, batted for 276 minutes and 75 overs to score 29 not out. After rain had spoiled the first and third Tests in England's first series in South Africa since 1964–65, the outcome was decided in the fifth and final Test, which South Africa

Test Series Results, September 1995–September 1996

Test	Host country	Ground	Date	Scores	Result
1st	India	Bangalore	Oct. 18–20	New Zealand 145 and 233; India 228 and 151 for 2	India won by 8 wickets
2nd	India	Madras	Oct. 25–29	India 144 for 2	Match drawn (rain)
3rd	India	Cuttack	Nov. 8–12	India 296 for 8 dec; New Zealand 175 for 8	Match drawn (rain)
1st	Zimbabwe	Harare	Oct. 13–16	Zimbabwe 170 and 283; South Africa 346 and 108 for 3	South Africa won by 7 wkt
1st	Australia	Brisbane	Nov. 9–13	Australia 463; Pakistan 97 and 240	Australia won by an innings and 126 runs
2nd	Australia	Hobart	Nov. 17–20	Australia 267 and 306; Pakistan 198 and 220	Australia won by 155 runs
3rd	Australia	Sydney	Nov. 30–Dec. 4	Pakistan 299 and 204; Australia 257 and 172	Pakistan won by 74 runs
1st	South Africa	Pretoria	Nov. 16–20	England 381 for 9 dec	Match drawn (rain)
2nd	South Africa	Johannesburg	Nov. 30–Dec. 4	South Africa 332 and 346 for 9 dec; England 200 and 351 for 5	Match drawn
3rd	South Africa	Durban	Dec. 14–18	South Africa 225; England 152 for 5	Match drawn (rain)
4th	South Africa	Port Elizabeth	Dec. 26–30	South Africa 428 and 162 for 9 dec; England 263 and 189 for 3	Match drawn
5th	South Africa	Cape Town	Jan. 2–4	England 153 and 157; South Africa 244 and 70 for 0	South Africa won by 10 wkt
1st	Australia	Perth	Dec. 8–11	Sri Lanka 251 and 330; Australia 617 for 5 dec	Australia won by an innings and 36 runs
2nd	Australia	Melbourne	Dec. 26–30	Australia 500 for 6 dec and 41 for 0; Sri Lanka 233 and 307	Australia won by 10 wkt
3rd	Australia	Adelaide	Jan. 25–29	Australia 502 for 9 dec and 215 for 6 dec; Sri Lanka 317 and 252	Australia won by 148 runs
1st	New Zealand	Christchurch	Dec. 8–12	Pakistan 208 and 434; New Zealand 286 and 195	Pakistan won by 161 runs
1st	New Zealand	Hamilton	Jan. 13–17	N.Z. 230 for 8 dec and 222 for 5 dec; Zimbabwe 196 and 208 for 6	Match drawn
2nd	New Zealand	Auckland	Jan. 20–24	New Zealand 251 and 441 for 5 dec; Zimbabwe 326 and 246 for 4	Match drawn
1st	West Indies	Bridgetown	April 19–23	New Zealand 195 and 305; West Indies 472 and 29 for 0	West Indies won by 10 wkt
2nd	West Indies	St. John's	April 27–May 2	West Indies 548 and 184; New Zealand 437 and 130 for 5	Match drawn
1st	England	Birmingham	June 6–10	India 214 and 219; England 313 and 121 for 2	England won by 8 wkt
2nd	England	London (Lord's)	June 20–24	England 344 and 278 for 9 dec; India 429	Match drawn
3rd	England	Nottingham	July 4–9	India 521 and 211; England 564	Match drawn
1st	England	London (Lord's)	July 25–29	Pakistan 340 and 352 for 5 dec; England 285 and 243	Pakistan won by 164 runs
2nd	England	Leeds	Aug. 8–12	Pakistan 448 and 242 for 7 dec; England 501	Match drawn
3rd	England	London (Oval)	Aug. 22–26	England 326 and 242; Pakistan 521 and 48 for 1	Pakistan won by 9 wkt
1st	Sri Lanka	Colombo	Sept. 11–14	Sri Lanka 349; Zimbabwe 145 and 127	Sri Lanka won by an innings and 77 runs
2nd	Sri Lanka	Colombo	Sept. 18–21	Zimbabwe 141 and 235; Sri Lanka 350 and 30 for 0	Sri Lanka won by 10 wkt

won comfortably by 10 wickets. S.M. Pollock, son of the former Test fast bowler P.M. Pollock and nephew of the great left-hander R.G. Pollock, made an impressive debut in the series, taking 16 wickets at an average of 23.56. A.A. Donald of South Africa and England's Cork both took 19.

Among the most noteworthy aspects of the series was the debut of P.R. Adams, a left-arm wrist spinner whose contortionist's action caused almost as much comment as the colour of his skin. Adams was the first Cape Coloured to have broken into the Test side since the end of apartheid and, at 18, was South Africa's youngest Test cricketer.

In domestic cricket Leicestershire, led by J. Whitaker, emerged as the surprise winner of the county championship in England. Lancashire won both of the one-day knock-out trophies, and Surrey won the Sunday league. South Australia won the Sheffield Shield, that nation's premier domestic trophy, for the first time in 14 years. Auckland claimed New Zealand's Shell Trophy, Leeward Islands won the Red Stripe Cup in the West Indies, and Western Province took the Castle Cup in South Africa.

(ANDREW LONGMORE)

All-Time First-Class Test Cricket Standings (as of Sept. 30, 1996)

	England Wins	Draws	Losses	Australia W	D	L	South Africa W	D	L	West Indies W	D	L	New Zealand W	D	L
England v.				90	81	108	47	43	20	27	40	48	34	37	4
Australia v.	108	81	90				31	15	13	32	22*	27	13	11	7
South Africa v.	20	43	47	13	15	31				0	0	1	22	6	3
West Indies v.	48	40	27	27	22*	32	1	0	0				10	14	4
New Zealand v.	4	37	34	7	11	13	3	6	22	4	13	9			
India v.	14	38	31	8	18*	24	0	3	1	7	31	27	13	16	6
Pakistan v.	9	32	14	11	15	14	0	0	1	7	12	12	17	16	4
Sri Lanka v.	1	1	3	0	3	7	0	2	1	0	1	0	2	7	4
Zimbabwe v.	†			†			0	0	1	†			0	3	1

	India W	D	L	Pakistan W	D	L	Sri Lanka W	D	L	Zimbabwe W	D	L
England v.	31	38	14	14	32	9	3	1	1	†		
Australia v.	24	18*	8	14	15	11	7	3	0	†		
South Africa v.	1	3	0	1	0	0	1	2	0	1	0	0
West Indies v.	27	31	7	12	12	7	0	1	0	†		
New Zealand v.	6	16	13	4	16	17	4	7	2	1	3	0
India v.				4	33	7	8	4	1	1	1	0
Pakistan v.	7	33	4				9	5	3	4	1	1
Sri Lanka v.	1	4	8	3	5	9				2	3	0
Zimbabwe v.	0	1	1	1	1	4	0	3	2			

*Including one tie. †No matches.

Cricket World Cup

Year	Result			
1979	West Indies	286–9	England	194
1983	India	183	West Indies	140
1987	Australia	253–5	England	246–8
1992	Pakistan	249–6	England	227
1996	Sri Lanka	245–3	Australia	241

World Cup

Twenty-one years after its introduction to international cricket, Sri Lanka dominated the sixth World Cup to become the world champion of one-day cricket. To cap a remarkable tournament for the 66–1 outsiders, Sri Lanka beat the favourite, Australia, by seven wickets in a final held exactly a month after the Australian team had refused to play its group match against Sri Lanka in Colombo because of fears for the security of the team in the wake of a terrorist bomb that exploded in the Sri Lankan capital just 15 days before the start of the tournament. The West Indies team also forfeited its group match rather than play in Sri Lanka.

In terms of organization and structure, the World Cup, held in Pakistan, India, and Sri Lanka, bore out many of the fears expressed before the start. The tournament was too unwieldy, too long, and too commercialized. Teams spent nearly three weeks and played five group matches just to eliminate four teams—Zimbabwe, Kenya, The Netherlands, and the United Arab Emirates—from the field of 12. England, for example, lost three of its group matches yet still qualified for the quarterfinals. While most other nations played to the traditional patterns of one-day cricket, building an innings slowly and relying on medium-pace bowling to contain runs, Sri Lanka took advantage of the rules that allowed only two fielders to be set deep in the first 15 overs of a match to score heavily in the opening overs and used four spinners. S.T. Jayasuriya, usually a big-hitting lower-order batsman, was promoted to open the innings, a move so novel that cricket had to borrow from baseball the term *pinch hitter* to describe him.

The group matches were largely unmemorable, apart from Kenya's defeat of the West Indies by 73 runs. Typically, the West Indies beat Australia in its next group match, but a defeat by the same team in the semifinals when the West Indies lost 8 wickets for 37 runs to lose by 5 runs brought to an unhappy end the international career of R.B. Richardson, the captain, who had already announced his retirement from international cricket at the end of the tournament. Sri Lanka beat England comfortably in the quarterfinals and was leading India in the semifinals when a riot broke out in the crowd of 110,000 in Calcutta. After a 20-minute delay, the referee, former West Indies captain Clive Lloyd, was unable to restart play and awarded the win to Sri Lanka. In the final P.A. De Silva (107 not out) and A. Ranatunga (47 not out), the captain of Sri Lanka, put on 97 for the fourth wicket to guide Sri Lanka to 245 for 3 past the Australian total of 241 for 7. De Silva and Ranatunga topped the tournament batting averages, while S.R. Tendulkar (*see* BIOGRAPHIES), who succeeded Mohammed Azharuddin as captain of India later in the year, was the highest run scorer, with 523.

(ANDREW LONGMORE)

GRAHAM CHADWICK—ALLSPORT

Asanka Gurusinha of Sri Lanka bats against Australia at the one-day cricket championships in Lahore, Pak., on March 17. Underdog Sri Lanka beat Australia, which had cited security concerns in refusing to play its group match in Colombo, Sri Lanka, a month earlier.

CURLING

At the 1996 world curling championships in Hamilton, Ont., Canadian rinks won both the men's and women's crowns. Skipped by Jeff Stoughton, Canada, represented by Winnipeg, Man., beat Scotland, skipped by Warwick Smith and represented by Perth, 6–2. Rounding out the top 10, in order, were Switzerland, Norway, Sweden, England, the United States, Italy, Germany, and Australia. In the women's competition Marilyn Bodogh skipped Canada, represented by St. Catharines, Ont., to a 5–2 victory over the U.S., skipped by Lisa Schoeneberg and represented by Madison, Wis. The remaining top 10 finishes in order were Norway, Germany, Scotland, Japan, Denmark, Sweden, Switzerland, and Finland.

The U.S. Curling Association in October announced its annual awards. Schoeneberg was named Female Athlete of the Year, and Travis Way of Seattle, Wash., who led his team to the junior men's national championship, was the men's winner. Steve Brown of Madison was named Coach of the Year; his women's team, skipped by Schoeneberg, had won three U.S. championships.

(JAMES MORRIS)

World Curling Championship—Men		
Year	Winner	Runner-up
1992	Switzerland	Scotland
1993	Canada	Scotland
1994	Canada	Sweden
1995	Canada	Scotland
1996	**Canada**	**Scotland**

World Curling Championship—Women		
Year	Winner	Runner-up
1992	Sweden	United States
1993	Canada	Germany
1994	Canada	Scotland
1995	Sweden	Canada
1996	**Canada**	**United States**

CYCLING

Changes in bicycle design and equipment led to cycling's governing body, the Union Cycliste Internationale (UCI), taking action to restore the emphasis to the performance of the rider. Meeting on the eve of the 1996 world road championships in Lugano, Switz., the management committee of the UCI ruled that from Jan. 1, 1997, handlebars could not extend more than 15 cm (5.9 in) beyond the hub of the front wheel, and the distance from the bottom bracket on the bicycle frame to the front hub should not exceed 75 cm (29.5 in).

The move effectively outlawed the extended straight-arm position introduced in 1995 by British rider Graeme Obree and used widely in track racing during 1996 to establish world records in the men's individual and team pursuits, women's individual pursuit, and men's one-hour race. Expressing a wish to protect the aesthetic image of cycling by halting developments that put technology and machines above riders, the UCI stated that further measures were anticipated for 1997 to achieve the ultimate aims of reducing technical emphasis to a minimum and restoring the universal nature of the sport by keeping costs within the reach of all nations.

The aerodynamic value of the extended-arm style, dubbed the "Superman position," helped Italian riders Andrea Collinelli and Antonella Bellutti win Olympic pursuit titles in Atlanta, Ga.

During the world track championships in Manchester, Eng., the British rider Chris

Cycling World Track Championships—Men			
Year	Sprint (amateur)	Pursuit (amateur)	Motor-paced (amateur)
1993*	G. Niewand (Austl.)	G. Obree (U.K.)	J. Veggerby (Den.)
1994	M. Nothstein (U.S.)	C. Boardman (U.K.)	C. Podlesch (Ger.)
1995	D. Hill (Austl.)	G. Obree (U.K.)	not held
1996	**F. Rousseau (Fr.)**	**C. Boardman (U.K.)**	**not held**

*From 1993 professionals and amateurs competed in the same event.

Tour de France		
Year	Winner	Kilometres
1992	M. Indurain (Spain)	3,983
1993	M. Indurain (Spain)	3,700
1994	M. Indurain (Spain)	3,978
1995	M. Indurain (Spain)	3,635
1996	**B. Riis (Den.)**	**3,764**

Cycling World Track Championships—Women		
Year	Sprint	3-km pursuit
1992	E. Salumae (Est.)	P. Rossner (Ger.)
1993	T. Dubnicoff (Can.)	R. Twigg (U.S.)
1994	G. Yenyukhina (Russia)	M. Clignet (Fr.)
1995	F. Ballanger (Fr.)	R. Twigg (U.S.)
1996	**F. Ballanger (Fr.)**	**M. Clignet (Fr.)**

Cycling World Road-Racing Championships			
Year	Men (amateur)	Men (professional)	Women (amateur)
1992	F. Casartelli (Italy)	G. Bugno (Italy)	K. Watt (Austl.)
1993	J. Ullrich (Ger.)	L. Armstrong (U.S.)	L. van Moorsel (Neth.)
1994	A. Pedersen (Den.)	L. Leblanc (Fr.)	M. Valvik (Nor.)
1995	D. Nelissen (Neth.)	A. Olano (Spain)	J. Longo (Fr.)
1996*		**J. Museeuw (Belg.)**	**B. Heeb (Switz.)**

*From 1996 professionals and amateurs competed in the same event.

AFP PHOTO

Bjarne Riis (foreground) passes the Arc de Triomphe in Paris on his way to winning the 83rd Tour de France, which covered 3,764 km (2,337 mi). Riis became the first Danish cyclist to win the event, denying Spain's Miguel Indurain an unprecedented sixth consecutive championship.

Boardman adopted the extended straight-arm position to break the men's 4,000-m-pursuit record by more than eight seconds for a time of 4 min 11.114 sec. Also using the straight-arm position, Italy set a world record of 4 min 0.958 sec for the 4,000-m men's team pursuit, and the world record for the women's 3,000-m pursuit was lowered four times until it finally was established by Marion Clignet of France at 3 min 30.974 sec. Boardman returned to the Manchester track five days after the championships and covered a world-record distance of 56.357 km (1 km = 0.62 mi) in one hour, breaking the 1994 mark of 55.291 km set by Tony Rominger.

The highlight of the world road championships at Lugano was the contest in the men's road race. In a two-man battle over the 252-km (157-mi) course, Johan Museeuw of Belgium defeated Switzerland's Mauro Gianetti by one second.

As a result of the move to open competition, professionals were admitted to the Olympic Games for the first time. Also, a full world championship program was held in 1996, as opposed to previous Olympiad years, when only non-Olympic disciplines were contested.

Cycling's premier road event, the Tour de France, was won by Bjarne Riis, the first Dane to win the three-week, 3,764-km event. Miguel Indurain of Spain was unsuccessful in his bid to score an unprecedented sixth successive tour victory, finishing in 11th place more than 14 minutes behind Riis. Riis took the overall lead after winning the ninth stage to Sestriere, Italy, which was reduced from 189.5 km to 46 km because of snow at the start at Val-d'Isère and on the Col du Galibier climb.

(JOHN R. WILKINSON)

EQUESTRIAN SPORTS

Thoroughbred Racing. Cigar, the horse that dominated U.S. competition for two seasons, was retired to stud at the conclusion of the 1996 campaign, during which he raced eight times at seven tracks in three countries, equaled the longest winning streak in thoroughbred racing history, and became the leading money-winning thoroughbred of all time. In spite of losing three of his last four starts, including a third-place finish in the $4 million Breeders' Cup Classic in his final appearance, the six-year-old son of Palace Music was certain to be voted Horse of the Year, an honour he won in 1995 after being undefeated in 10 starts.

Cigar's greatest achievement came on March 27, when he scored a thrilling victory in the inaugural running of the $4 million Dubayy World Cup at Nad as-Sheba racetrack in Dubayy, United Arab Emirates. It was only his second start of the year, and the performance came a month after his training was disrupted because of a hoof problem. He tied Citation's 20th-century record for consecutive victories by a thoroughbred when he notched his 16th straight triumph on July 13 in the Arlington Citation Challenge at Arlington International Racecourse near Chicago. Cigar was thwarted in his bid to break the record when he finished second in his next start, the $1 million Pacific Classic.

Trained by Bill Mott and bred and owned by Allen Paulson, Cigar completed his brilliant career with earnings of $9,999,813. He retired with 19 victories, 4 seconds, and 5 thirds in 33 starts. Following farewell appearances before 16,000 admirers at the National Horse Show in New York City's Madison Square Garden on November 2 and before a crowd of 12,443 at Churchill Downs in Louisville, Ky., on November 9, Cigar was formally retired to Ashford Stud after one of the most expensive syndication deals ever put together in the U.S.

For the first time in its 13-year history, the Breeders' Cup was held outside the United States. The 1996 host track was Woodbine Race Course in Toronto. Seven championship stakes worth $11 million were held there on October 26.

Alphabet Soup, a five-year-old making his first venture out of the state of California in seven 1996 starts, won the Breeders' Cup Classic by a nose over the tenacious three-year-old Louis Quatorze. Cigar was another head back in third in the 1¼-mi event.

Alphabet Soup was timed in a track record 2 min 1 sec. He earned $2,080,000 for his fourth win of the campaign.

Irish-bred Pilsudski, British owned and trained, and ridden by Walter Swinburn, won the $2 million Breeders' Cup Turf. Da Hoss, whose questionable conformation had allowed his owners to purchase him for just $6,000 as a yearling, increased his career bankroll to $1,394,458 with his victory in the $1 million Breeders' Cup Mile. He had finished last in the 1995 Breeders' Cup Sprint.

Jockey Corey Nakatani's first of two Breeders' Cup Day winners came in the $1 million Breeders' Cup Sprint. Lit de Justice, which trailed the field of 13 early in the six-furlongs race, rallied strongly to prevail by 1¼ lengths in 1 min 8⅗ sec, tying the track record. The winner was trained by Jenine Sahadi, the first woman to saddle a Breeders' Cup winner. Nakatani recorded his second Breeders' Cup victory in the $1

Cycling Champions, 1996					
Event	**Winner**	**Country**	**Event**	**Winner**	**Country**
WORLD CHAMPIONS—TRACK			**WORLD CHAMPIONS—MOUNTAIN BIKES**		
Men			**Men**		
Sprint	F. Rousseau	France	Individual cross-country	J. Chiotti	France
Individual pursuit	C. Boardman	Britain	Individual downhill	N. Vouilloz	France
Kilometre time trial	S. Kelly	Australia	**Women**		
40-km points	R. Llaneras	Spain	Individual cross-country	A. Sydor	Canada
Team pursuit	A. Capelli, C. Citton, A. Collinelli, M. Trenkini	Italy	Individual downhill	A.-C. Chausson	France
Keirin	M. Nothstein	U.S.			
Olympic sprint	D. Hill, S. Kelly, G. Neiwand	Australia	**MAJOR PROFESSIONAL ROAD-RACE WINNERS**		
50-km Madison	S. Martinello, M. Villa	Italy	Tour de France	B. Riis	Denmark
Women			Tour of Italy	P. Tonkov	Russia
Sprint	F. Ballanger	France	Tour of Spain	A. Zülle	Switzerland
Individual pursuit	M. Clignet	France	Milan–San Remo	G. Colombo	Italy
500-m time trial	F. Ballanger	France	Tour of Flanders	M. Bartoli	Italy
25-km points	S. Samokhvalova	Russia	Paris–Roubaix	J. Museeuw	Belgium
			Liège–Bastogne–Liège	P. Richard	Switzerland
			Amstel Gold	S. Zanini	Italy
WORLD CHAMPIONS—ROAD			San Sebastian Classic	U. Bolts	Germany
Men			Leeds Classic	A. Ferrigato	Italy
Individual road race	J. Museeuw	Belgium	Championship of Zürich	A. Ferrigato	Italy
Individual time trial	A. Zülle	Switzerland	Paris–Tours	N. Minali	Italy
Women			Paris–Nice	L. Jalabert	France
Individual road race	B. Heeb	Switzerland	Ghent–Wevelgem	T. Steels	Belgium
Individual time trial	J. Longo	France	Flèche Wallonne	L. Armstrong	U.S.
			Tour of Romandie	A. Olano	Spain
			Dauphiné Libéré	M. Indurain	Spain
WORLD CHAMPION—CYCLO-CROSS			Midi-Libre	L. Jalabert	France
	A. van der Poel	Netherlands	Dunkirk 4-Day	P. Gaumont	France
			Grand Prix of Frankfurt	B. Zberg	Switzerland
			Tour DuPont	L. Armstrong	U.S.

The Kentucky Derby		
Year	Horse	Jockey
1992	Lil E. Tee	P. Day
1993	Sea Hero	J. Bailey
1994	Go For Gin	C. McCarron
1995	Thunder Gulch	G. Stevens
1996	**Grindstone**	**J. Bailey**

The Preakness Stakes		
Year	Horse	Jockey
1992	Pine Bluff	C. McCarron
1993	Prairie Bayou	M. Smith
1994	Tabasco Cat	P. Day
1995	Timber Country	P. Day
1996	**Louis Quatorze**	**P. Day**

The Belmont Stakes		
Year	Horse	Jockey
1992	A.P. Indy	E. Delahoussaye
1993	Colonial Affair	J. Krone
1994	Tabasco Cat	P. Day
1995	Thunder Gulch	G. Stevens
1996	**Editor's Note**	**R. Douglas**

Triple Crown Champions—U.S.	
Year	Horse
1946	Assault
1948	Citation
1973	Secretariat
1977	Seattle Slew
1978	Affirmed

million Distaff with Jewel Princess. Jewel Princess won the Eclipse Award as champion older filly or mare of 1996.

D. Wayne Lukas, who had won more Breeders' Cup races than any other trainer, gained his 13th victory when Boston Harbor won the $1 million Breeders' Cup Juvenile

by a neck, his sixth win in seven starts. Storm Song won the $1 million Breeders' Cup Juvenile Fillies and thereby clinched championship honours in her division.

In addition to Cigar, another champion was retired at the conclusion of the 1996 racing season. The Lukas-trained Serena's

Song completed an eventful career ranked as the leading money-winning female thoroughbred of all time, with earnings of $3,283,388.

The 122nd running of the Kentucky Derby at Churchill Downs on May 4 was captured by Grindstone by a nose over Cavonnier and gave trainer Lukas an unprecedented sixth straight victory in a Triple Crown race. Grindstone never raced again. Five days after the win, a bone chip was discovered in the colt's right front knee, and he was retired.

Grindstone raced in 15th place in the field of 19 three-year-olds for the first half-mile and was still 14th with half a mile left to race in the 1¼-mi classic. He was the first Kentucky Derby winner for his 78-year-old owner, William T. Young.

Jockey Pat Day accounted for his fifth victory in the Preakness Stakes in Baltimore, Md., the second jewel in the U.S.'s Triple Crown for three-year-olds, when he won the May 18 running of the 1³⁄₁₆-mi event with Louis Quatorze. The winner was trained by Nick Zito, who snapped Lukas's

Major Thoroughbred Race Winners, 1996					
Race	Won by	Jockey	Race	Won by	Jockey
United States			**England**		
Acorn	Star de Lady Ann	M. Smith	Two Thousand Guineas	Mark of Esteem	L. Dettori
Arlington Million	Mecke	R. Davis	One Thousand Guineas	Bosra Sham	Pat Eddery
Beldame	Yanks Music	J. Velazquez	Derby	Shaamit	M. Hills
Belmont	Editor's Note	R. Douglas	Oaks	Lady Carla	Pat Eddery
Breeders' Cup Juvenile	Boston Harbor	J. Bailey	St. Leger	Shantou	L. Dettori
Breeders' Cup Juvenile Fillies	Storm Song	C. Perret	Coronation Cup	Swain	L. Dettori
Breeders' Cup Sprint	Lit de Justice	C. Nakatani	Ascot Gold Cup	Classic Cliche	M. Kinane
Breeders' Cup Mile	Da Hoss	G. Stevens	Eclipse Stakes	Halling	J. Reid
Breeders' Cup Distaff	Jewel Princess	C. Nakatani	King George VI and Queen Elizabeth Diamond Stakes	Pentire	M. Hills
Breeders' Cup Turf	Pilsudski	W. Swinburn	Sussex Stakes	First Island	M. Hills
Breeders' Cup Classic	Alphabet Soup	C. McCarron	International Stakes	Halling	L. Dettori
Champagne	Ordway	J. Velazquez	Dubayy Champion Stakes	Bosra Sham	Pat Eddery
Charles H. Strub Stakes	Helmsman	C. McCarron	**France**		
Coaching Club American Oaks	My Flag	J. Bailey	Poule d'Essai des Poulains	Ashkalani	G. Mosse
Donn Handicap	Cigar	J. Bailey	Poule d'Essai des Pouliches	Ta Rib	W. Carson
Florida Derby	Unbridled's Song	M. Smith	Prix du Jockey-Club	Ragmar	G. Mosse
Futurity	Traitor	J. Velazquez	Prix de Diane	Sil Sila	C. Asmussen
Gulfstream Park Handicap	Wekiva Springs	J. Bailey	Prix Ganay	Valanour	G. Mosse
Haskell Invitational	Skip Away	J. Santos	Prix Lupin	Helissio	D. Boeuf
Hollywood Derby	Marlin	J. Velazquez	Grand Prix de Paris	Grape Tree Road	T. Jarnet
Hollywood Futurity	Swiss Yodeler	A. Solis	Grand Prix de Saint-Cloud	Helissio	O. Peslier
Hollywood Gold Cup	Siphon	D. Flores	Prix Vermeille	My Emma	C. Asmussen
Hollywood Turf Cup	Running Flame	C. McCarron	Prix de l'Arc de Triomphe	Helissio	O. Peslier
Hollywood Turf Handicap	Sandpit	C. Nakatani	Grand Critérium	Revoque	J. Reid
International	Sandpit	C. Nakatani	**Ireland**		
Jockey Club Gold Cup	Skip Away	S. Sellers	Irish Two Thousand Guineas	Spinning World	C. Asmussen
Kentucky Derby	Grindstone	J. Bailey	Irish One Thousand Guineas	Matiya	W. Carson
Kentucky Oaks	Pike Place Dancer	C. Nakatani	Irish Derby	Zagreb	P. Shanahan
Man o' War	Diplomatic Jet	J. Chavez	Irish Oaks	Dance Design	M. Kinane
Meadowlands Cup	Dramatic Gold	K. Desormeaux	Irish St. Leger	Oscar Schindler	S. Craine
Metropolitan	Honour and Glory	J. Velazquez	Irish Champion Stakes	Timarida	J. Murtagh
Mother Goose	Yanks Music	J. Velazquez	**Italy**		
Oaklawn Handicap	Geri	J. Bailey	Derby Italiano	Bahamian Knight	R. Hughes
Pacific Classic	Dare and Go	A. Solis	Gran Premio del Jockey-Club	Shantou	L. Dettori
Philip H. Iselin	Smart Strike	C. Perret	**Germany**		
Pimlico Special	Star Standard	P. Day	Deutsches Derby	Lavirco	T. Mundry
Preakness	Louis Quatorze	P. Day	Grosser Preis von Baden	Pilsudski	W.R. Swinburn
Santa Anita Derby	Cavonnier	C. McCarron	Europa-Preis	Lavirco	T. Mundry
Santa Anita Handicap	Mr Purple	E. Delahoussaye	**Australia**		
Spinster	Different	C. McCarron	Melbourne Cup	Saintly	D. Beadman
Suburban	Wekiva Springs	M. Smith	**Dubayy**		
Super Derby	Editor's Note	G. Stevens	Dubayy World Cup	Cigar	J. Bailey
Travers	Will's Way	J. Chavez	**Japan**		
Turf Classic	Diplomatic Jet	J. Chavez	Japan Cup	Singspiel	L. Dettori
Whitney	Mahogany Hall	J. Santos			
Woodward	Cigar	J. Bailey			

Cigar pulls ahead to win the Arlington Citation Challenge, the horse's 16th straight win, which tied the record set by Citation for consecutive victories by a thoroughbred. In his next race, the Pacific Classic, Cigar finished second, however, and thus failed to break Citation's record.

streak of Triple Crown race victories. It was Day's third straight Preakness triumph.

The 1½-mi Belmont Stakes on June 8 at Belmont Park near New York City went to Editor's Note and gave trainer Lukas and owner Young their second Triple Crown race victory of the year. It was Lukas's third straight Belmont Stakes triumph.

One of the most consistent three-year-olds of 1996 was Skip Away, which defeated Cigar in the $1 million Jockey Club Gold Cup at Belmont Park on October 5. Skip Away won 6 of 12 starts and $2,699,280 in purses in 1996.   (JOHN G. BROKOPP)

Helissio, beaten only once in seven appearances in France, left no doubt that he was the thoroughbred champion of Europe in 1996, climaxing the season by winning the Prix de l'Arc de Triomphe by five lengths. Pilsudski, which finished second, had previously won the Grosser Preis von Baden and later triumphed in the Breeders' Cup Turf, while Oscar Schindler, which was third, had previously gained an easy success in the Irish St. Leger.

Helissio's only failure was in the Prix du Jockey-Club (French Derby), in which he finished fifth behind Ragmar. Dominique Boeuf was then replaced as his jockey by Olivier Peslier, who rode him to victory over the Coronation Cup winner, Swain, in the Grand Prix de Saint-Cloud. Peslier also rode Helissio to his triumphs in the Prix Niel and the Prix de l'Arc de Triomphe and for the first time ended the year as France's champion jockey.

Though they did not succeed in their efforts to purchase Helissio from his Spanish owner, Enrique Sarasola, Japanese breeders did buy many other leading racehorses and stallions, most notably the unbeaten Lammtarra, winner of the Derby, King George VI & Queen Elizabeth Diamond Stakes, and Prix de l'Arc de Triomphe in his only three appearances in 1995. Pentire, which was beaten by a neck by Lammtarra in the 1995 King George but made up by winning the 1996 edition, was also sold to a Japanese owner. At the Japan Cup in Tokyo

on November 24, however, the winner was Singspiel, owned by Sheikh Muhammad al-Maktoum. Helissio tied for third.

The sale of Lammtarra for $30 million, after just one season at stud in England, shocked the industry. The size of the offer was a surprise, and so was the fact that Europe's richest owner, Sheikh Muhammad, was willing to accept it. The sheikh had been rapidly expanding his Godolphin stable by buying horses that had shown ability for other owners, such as Classic Cliche, and then by taking over horses that had begun their careers in the sheikh's name but with other trainers. Said ibn Suroor was appointed trainer in 1995, but the sheikh

retained tight control over every aspect of the operation.

In addition to Classic Cliche, the sheikh's stars in 1996 were Mark of Esteem, winner of the Two Thousand Guineas and the Queen Elizabeth II Stakes, and Halling, victorious in the Prix d'Ispahan and the Eclipse and International stakes. Mark of Esteem and Halling were expected to take the place of Lammtarra at stud in 1997. Suroor won the trainers' championship from Henry Cecil, the original trainer of Classic Cliche and Mark of Esteem.

When Mark of Esteem won the Queen Elizabeth II at Ascot on September 28, he was the third winner in three races that day for jockey Frankie Dettori, who then went on to win the remaining four contests on one of the most competitive racing days of the year. His father was 13 times champion jockey in Italy, but Dettori had spent nearly all his racing life in England. He lost his chance for a third consecutive British rider's championship when he broke his elbow in a prerace fall in June.

European racing enjoyed a revival of confidence in 1996. Demand was strong at the yearling sales, and aggregate, median, and average prices all reached record levels. The covering fees of many stallions were immediately increased.

The first running of the $4 million Dubayy World Cup on March 27 proved a benefit for the three challengers from the U.S., which took the first three places. Cigar had to battle Soul of the Matter to win by half a length and claim the richest first prize in the world, $2.4 million.

In Australia Octagonal beat Saintly in a series of stakes early in the year, including the AJC Australian Derby, and was voted Horse of the Year. But he struggled in the second half of 1996, while Saintly progressed to win both the richest weight-for-age event in the Southern Hemisphere, the Cox Plate, and its most celebrated, the Melbourne Cup.   (ROBERT W. CARTER)

Helissio, ridden by Olivier Peslier, finishes with an astonishing five-length lead to win the Prix de l'Arc de Triomphe, Europe's premier race, and confirm the colt's position as the year's middle-distance champion. He won six of seven races in France in 1996.

2,000 Guineas

Year	Horse	Jockey
1992	Rodrigo de Triano	L. Piggott
1993	Zafonic	P. Eddery
1994	Mister Baileys	J. Weaver
1995	Pennekamp	T. Jarnet
1996	**Mark of Esteem**	**F. Dettori**

The Derby

Year	Horse	Jockey
1992	Dr Devious	J. Reid
1993	Commander in chief	M. Kinane
1994	Erhaab	W. Carson
1995	Lammtarra	W.R. Swinburn
1996	**Shaamit**	**M. Hills**

The St. Leger

Year	Horse	Jockey
1992	User Friendly	G. Duffield
1993	Bob's Return	P. Robinson
1994	Moonax	P. Eddery
1995	Classic Cliche	L. Dettori
1996	**Shantou**	**F. Dettori**

Triple Crown Champions—British

Year	Winner
1915	Pommern
1917	Gay Crusader
1918	Gainsborough
1935	Bahram
1970	Nijinsky

Melbourne Cup

Year	Horse	Jockey
1992	Subzero	G. Hall
1993	Vintage Crop	M. Kinane
1994	Jeune	W. Harris
1995	Doriemus	D. Oliver
1996	**Saintly**	**D. Beadman**

Harness Racing. A historic development within the harness racing world during 1996 was the approval by the sport's administrators in the U.S., Canada, Australia, and New Zealand of the use of frozen semen for breeding. No doubt inspired by outstanding reductions in race times accomplished in North America during the year by representatives of the most fashionable pacing and trotting sire lines, breeders convinced their respective authorities that it was necessary to tap directly into such blood. By the end of the year, the semen of some of the most acclaimed U.S. standardbred stallions was being advertised and booked by brood mare owners around the world.

The Hambletonian, harness racing's most prestigious and lucrative event, and its filly counterpart, the Hambletonian Oaks, were also moving with the times and from 1997 would have an entirely new look. No longer would they be raced in the heats that for more than a century had been the norm in North American Grand Circuit competi-

The Hambletonian Trot

Year	Horse	Driver
1992	Alf Palema	M. McNicholl
1993	American Winner	R. Pierce
1994	Victory Dream	M. Lachance
1995	Tagliabue	J. Campbell
1996	**Continentalvictory**	**M. Lachance**

tion. They would each become a one-mile dash for the cash, preceded a week earlier by eliminations for the final race.

In the 1996 Hambletonian in early August, Continentalvictory, a daughter of siring sensation Valley Victory, overpowered favoured Lindy Lane to win the $1.2 million final. Driver Mike Lachance guided the black filly to a 1-min 52.1-sec victory in her elimination heat and then to a 1-min 52.4-sec clocking in the final to establish a world record time for two heats. Continentalvictory later won the World Trotting Derby at Du Quoin, Ill., and the Yonkers (N.Y.) Trot, and at the year's end she was voted the harness Horse of the Year.

Jeremy's Gambit, a two-year-old son of No Nukes, won the $800,000 Woodrow Wilson Stakes for pacers at the Meadowlands in New Jersey in August. His trainer, Brett Pelling of New Zealand, in September also won the sport's blue-ribbon classic for three-year-old pacers, the $542,220 Little Brown Jug at Delaware, Ohio, with Armbro Operative.

At the 1996 Jug meet, Jenna's Beach Boy continued his assault on world records. The four-year-old earlier in the year at the Meadowlands had paced 1 min 47.6 sec, the fastest mile ever on a one-mile (1.61-km) track and then won at Rosecroft Raceway in Maryland in 1 min 49.4 sec, the fastest race mile ever on a ⅝-mi track). In the $41,500 Senior Jug, he won by 5½ lengths in 1 min 49.6 sec, a world best on a ½-mi oval. Before the Jug racing week was ended, however, Stand Forever, four-year-old son of Dragon's Lair, had gone a notch better, winning a $40,000 invitational in 1 min 49.4 sec.

At the Solvalla track at Stockholm in May, the six-year-old French trotter Cocktail Jet outclassed seven rivals for a runaway win in the 3 million-krona Elitlopp. Driven by Jean-Étienne Dubios, Cocktail Jet scored comfortably in 1 min 54.9 sec.

At Perth's Gloucester Park in Western Australia in March, Young Mister Charles won the $A400,000 Inter-Dominion Championship Pacing Grand Final. Injured two weeks before the Grand Final, he came within an ace of being scratched from the series when his near foreleg blew up to almost twice its normal size. An intensive course of swimming allowed him to stage his remarkable comeback.

At Addington Raceway in Christchurch, N.Z., in November, five-year-old pacing stallion Il Vicolo came off a handicap of 10 m (32.8 ft) to win the $NZ350,000 New Zealand Cup. Trained and driven by Mark Purdon, Il Vicolo paced the 3,200 m (3,500 yd) in 4 min 2.3 sec.

(RONALD W. BISMAN)

Steeplechasing. Imperial Call became the first Irish-trained winner of the Cheltenham Gold Cup in 10 years, and Rough Quest, which he beat by four lengths, went on to be the first winning favourite in the Grand National since 1982. Arenice, third in France's principal jumping event two years earlier, won the Grand Steeplechase de Paris.

Show Jumping and Dressage. The 1996 Olympic Games in Atlanta, Ga., dominated most of a year in which the results of Europe's premier show, at Aachen, Ger., in late June, proved an accurate forecast for the Olympics. The German team of Ludger Beerbaum (on Ratina Z), Ulrich Kirchhoff (Jus de Pommes), Lars Nieberg (For Plea-

sure), and Franke Sloothaak (Joly) won the Nations Cup as a prelude to their Olympic gold medal on the same four horses.

In the individual competition Beerbaum triumphed at Aachen, and Kirchhoff won the Olympic gold medal. Victory in the most valuable post-Olympic event, the Hickstead Derby, went to the Belgian-based Brazilian Nelson Pessoa on Loro Piana Vivaldi. Hugo Simon of Austria on ET won the Volvo World Cup at Geneva in April.

Isabell Werth and Gigolo, who were to progress to gold medal glory in the dressage at Atlanta four weeks later, were another combination that also prepared with a victory at Aachen. In the Grand Prix, Gigolo beat Durgo and Goldstern, and all three were members of the winning German team both there and in Atlanta.

(ROBERT W. CARTER)

Polo. For the first time in history, two teams that included seven members of the same family clashed in Argentina to decide the three most important high-handicap tournaments. At the Palermo fields Indios Chapaleufú II, with three Heguy brothers (Alberto, Ignacio, and Eduardo) and Alejandro Díaz Alberdi, downed Indios Chapaleufú (four Heguy brothers: Bautista, Gonzalo, Horacio, Jr., and Marcos) 17–16 to win the Argentine Open. At the other two tournaments, the Hurlingham and Los Indios-Tortugas opens, the four-brother team won 17–15 and 12–10, respectively.

Memo Gracida led his Outback team to the championship in the U.S. Open; Outback defeated Casa Manila in the final to give Gracida his 14th Open title. The tournament was held at the Palm Beach

World Fencing Championships—Men

Year	Individual			Team		
	Foil	Épée	Sabre	Foil	Épée	Sabre
1990	P. Omnès (Fr.)	T. Gerull (W.Ger.)	G. Nebald (Hung.)	Italy	Italy	U.S.S.R.
1991	I. Weissenborn (Ger.)	A. Shuvalov (U.S.S.R.)	G. Kirienko (U.S.S.R.)	Cuba	U.S.S.R.	Hungary
1992	P. Omnès (Fr.)	E. Srecki (Fr.)	B. Szabo (Hung.)	Germany	Germany	Unified Team
1993	A. Koch (Ger.)	P. Kolobkov (Russia)	G. Kirienko (Russia)	Germany	Italy	Hungary
1994	R. Tucker (Cuba)	P. Kolobkov (Russia)	F. Becker (Ger.)	Germany	France	Russia
1995	D. Chevtchenko (Russia)	E. Srecki (Fr.)	G. Kirienko (Russia)	Cuba	Germany	Italy
1996	A. Puccini (Italy)	A. Beketov (Russia)	S. Pozdnyakov (Russia)	Russia	Italy	Russia

World Fencing Championships—Women

Year	Individual foil	Team foil	Individual épée	Team épée
1991	G. Trillini (Italy)	Italy	M. Horvath (Hung.)	Hungary
1992	G. Trillini (Italy)	Italy	M. Horvath (Hung.)	Hungary
1993	F. Bortolozzi (Italy)	Germany	O. Jermakova (Est.)	Hungary
1994	B. Szabo (Rom.)	Romania	L. Chiesa (Italy)	Spain
1995	L. Badea (Rom.)	Italy	J. Jakimiuk (Pol.)	Hungary
1996	L. Badea (Rom.)	Italy	L. Flessel (Fr.)	France

(Fla.) Polo Club, with 11 teams taking part. Outback, however, could not repeat its earlier triumphs against Isla Carroll and Bud Light, which overcame Gracida and his teammates in the final matches of the Gold Cup of Americas (14–10) and Challenge Cup (12–11), respectively. Bautista and Gonzalo Heguy were the playmakers of their quartet, Pony Express, when it defeated Isla Carroll 15–14 in overtime to win the Sterling Cup.

In Sotogrande, Spain, Scapa of Scotland, with three players from Argentina, outclassed Santa Maria 10–9 in the final to win a major tournament. In Deauville, Fr., Labegorce won the Gold Cup for the first time.

In the English high-handicap season, Ellerston White, led by Gonzalo Pieres, won the Queen's Cup; Eduardo and Ignacio Heguy's C.S. Brooks team triumphed in the Gold Cup and then defeated Ellerston White for the Prince Philip Trophy. England downed Brazil 8–4 to recover the Coronation Cup it had lost in 1995 to Argentina.   (JORGE ADRIÁN ANDRADES)

FENCING

The election for president of the Fédération Internationale d'Escrime (FIE, the governing body of fencing) held centre stage during the 1995–96 season. Voting took place at the FIE congress prior to the opening of the Olympic Games in Atlanta, Ga. Incumbent president René Roch of France held on by one vote over Jeno Kamuti of Hungary and thus could expect the support of the FIE for the next phase of his development proposals. These included increasing participation and media coverage in areas of the world where the sport is less developed.

In the Olympics the format was new. The seeding round, in the past time-consuming and uninteresting for spectators, was abolished, and direct elimination began in the first round. Also noteworthy at the Olympics were the successful debut of women's épée and the new relay format for team events. Russia was most successful in the competition, winning individual gold medals in men's épée and sabre and team golds in sabre and men's foil. No country had more than one winner in the World Cup competition. The Olympics took the place of the world championships.

(GRAHAM MORRISON)

Laura Flessel (right) makes a strike on Valerie Barlois in the women's individual épée at the Olympic Games. Flessel and Barlois, both of France, took the gold and silver, respectively.

JED JACOBSOHN—ALLSPORT

FIELD HOCKEY

One of the most sweeping changes in field hockey came into effect on Aug. 4, 1996, when, as an experimental measure, the offside rule was abandoned. The purpose of the experiment was to diminish dependence on the set pieces and encourage more goals from open play, which would thereby make the game more attractive to spectators.

Results in the Olympic Games at Atlanta, Ga., in July and August revealed a predominance of goals from corners, particularly in the later rounds of the men's event. Olympic supremacy remained in Europe, with The Netherlands displacing Germany as champion and Spain taking second place. Australia earned the bronze medal after besting Germany in the play-off. India and Pakistan had used an ineffective corner drill, which accounted for the failure of an Asian team to qualify for the semifinals. This had happened only once before in the Olympics, at Seoul, S.Kor., in 1988.

New Zealand, the Olympic champion in 1976, took an important step toward qualifying for the next World Cup tournament in 1998 at Utrecht, Neth., by winning a 12-nation tournament at Cagliari, Sardinia, Italy, in October. Pakistan was to defend the World Cup at Utrecht against 11 teams.

In women's competition Australia and South Korea proved vastly superior to the six other nations in winning the Olympic gold and silver medals, respectively, at Atlanta. The Netherlands prevailed over Great Britain in a penalty shoot-out for the bronze medal after neither team had scored at the end of regulation time.

Under a new rule applicable to men and women, the holders of the World Cup would not qualify automatically for the Olympic Games at Sydney, Australia, in 2000. The privilege of doing so was now restricted to the host country and the previous Olympic champion.   (SYDNEY E. FRISKIN)

World Cup Field Hockey Championship—Men

Year	Winner	Runner-up
1986	Australia	England
1990	The Netherlands	Pakistan
1994	Pakistan	The Netherlands

World Cup Field Hockey Championship—Women

Year	Winner	Runner-up
1986	The Netherlands	West Germany
1990	The Netherlands	Australia
1994	Australia	Argentina

Association Football National Champions

Nation	League winners	Cup winners	Nation	League winners	Cup winners
Albania	SK Tirana	SK Tirana	Israel	Maccabi Tel Aviv	Maccabi Tel Aviv
Argentina	Velez Sarsfield		Italy	AC Milan	Fiorentina
Armenia	Pyunik	Pyunik	Japan	Yokohama Marinos	Grampus Eight
Austria	Rapid Vienna	Sturm Graz	Latvia	Skonto Riga	Skonto Riga
Belarus	Dynamo Minsk	MPKC	Lithuania	Inkaras	Kareda
Belgium	FC Brugge	FC Brugge	Luxembourg	Jeunesse Esch	Union
Bolivia	San Jose		Malta	Sliema Wanderers	Valletta
Brazil	Botafogo	Cruzeiro	Mexico	Necaxa	
Bulgaria	Slavia Sofia	Slavia Sofia	Moldova	Zimbru Chisinau	Constructorul
Chile	Univ de Chile		Netherlands, The	Ajax Amsterdam	PSV Eindhoven
Colombia	Deportivo Cali		Northern Ireland	Portadown	Glentoran
Costa Rica	Alajuelense		Norway	Rosenborg	Rosenborg
Croatia	Croatia Zagreb	Croatia Zagreb	Paraguay	Olimpia	
Cyprus	Apoel Nicosia	Apoel Nicosia	Peru	Sporting Cristal	
Czech Republic	Slavia Prague	Sparta Prague	Poland	Widzew Lodz	Ruch Chorzow
Denmark	Brondby	Aarhus	Portugal	FC Porto	Benfica
Ecuador	Barcelona		Romania	Steaua Bucharest	Steaua Bucharest
El Salvador	FAS		Russia	Vladikavkaz	Lokomotiv Moscow
England	Manchester United	Manchester United	San Marino	Libertas	
Estonia	Lantana	Sadam Tallinn	Scotland	Rangers	Rangers
Faroe Islands	GI Gotu	HB Torshavn	Slovakia	Slovan Bratislava	Humenne
Finland	Haka	MyPa	Slovenia	Gorica	Olimpija
France	Auxerre	Auxerre	Spain	Atletico Madrid	Atletico Madrid
Georgia	Dynamo Tbilisi	Dynamo Tbilisi	Sweden	IFK Göteborg	AIK Stockholm
Germany	Borussia Dortmund	Kaiserslautern	Switzerland	Grasshoppers	Sion
Greece	Panathinaikos	AEK Athens	Turkey	Fenerbahce	Galatasaray
Guatemala	Comunicaciones		Ukraine	Dynamo Kiev	Dynamo Kiev
Honduras	Olimpia		Uruguay	Penarol	
Hungary	Ferencvaros	Kispest Honved	Venezuela	Minerven	
Iceland	IA Akranes	KR Reykjavik	Wales	Barry Town	Llansantffraid
Ireland	St. Patrick's Athletic	Shelbourne	Yugoslavia (Serbia and Montenegro)	Partizan Belgrade	Red Star Belgrade

European Cup-Winners' Cup

Season	Result			
1991–92	Werder Bremen (Ger.)	2	AS Monaco	0
1992–93	Parma (Italy)	3	Royal Antwerp	1
1993–94	Arsenal (Eng.)	1	Parma (Italy)	0
1994–95	Real Zaragosa (Spain)	2	Arsenal (Eng.)	1
1995–96	**Paris-St. Germain**	**1**	**Rapid Vienna**	**0**

European Cup of Champion Clubs

Season	Result			
1991–92	Barcelona	1	Sampdoria (Italy)	0
1992–93	Olympique Marseille	1	AC Milan	0
1993–94	AC Milan	4	Barcelona	0
1994–95	Ajax Amsterdam	1	AC Milan	0
1995–96	**Juventus (Italy)***	**1**	**Ajax Amsterdam**	**1**

*Won on penalty kicks.

FIFA World Cup

Year	Result			
1986	Argentina	3	West Germany	2
1990	West Germany	1	Argentina	0
1994	Brazil*	0	Italy	0

*Won on penalty kicks.

FOOTBALL

Association Football (Soccer). In June 1996 the final game of the European championships in England almost produced a repeat of 1976, when West Germany lost to Czechoslovakia in a penalty shoot-out. This time the tables were turned, however, as Germany beat the Czech Republic with a controversial goal in sudden-death overtime. The Germans had slightly more scoring opportunities in the first half but then lost Dieter Eilts to injury just before the interval. He was replaced by Marco Bode, with Christian Ziege switching from the left side to a more pivotal midfield position. The first goal was scored as a result of a disputed penalty in the 59th minute, when German sweeper Matthias Sammer brought down Karel Poborsky. On the ensuing Czech penalty kick, Patrik Berger scored with a shot under the diving body of goalkeeper Andreas Kopke. Ten minutes later German coach Berti Vogts made a second substitution that proved to be an inspired move, bringing in striker Oliver Bierhoff for the tiring midfield player Mehmet Scholl. From a 30-m (100-ft) free kick taken by

Ziege, Bierhoff headed the ball in to tie the score. As overtime approached, Czech coach Dusan Uhrin substituted Vladimir Smicer for Poborsky. The replacement almost scored with a fiercely driven shot, but it was tipped around the far post by Kopke. The extra period was just five minutes old when referee Pierluigi Pairetto and linesman Donato Nicoletti's flag indicating offside against Stefan Kuntz. The ball was struck by Bierhoff, was deflected by Michel Hornak's foot, spun away out of the hands of goalkeeper Petr Kouba, and landed inside the goalkeeper's left-hand post.

The competition as a whole lacked standout individual performances, and many teams that were expected to dominate disappointed their followers, especially disjointed Italy. Portugal and defending champion Denmark had fleeting success; France deteriorated; and the Dutch had problems off the field. Croatia had moments of enterprise and Spain improved noticeably, but it was the dogged, disciplined Germans who reached the final along with the determined and skillful Czechs. The latter did far better than had been expected, though the one red and 18 yellow cards against them amounted to the worst penalty count in the series. England, the most spirited in years, won the Fair Play Award. Goal scoring was at the modest level of 2.07 per game. A total of 1,268,201 watched the 31 matches.

In the European Cup of Champion Clubs

final at Rome on May 22, Juventus of Italy beat Ajax Amsterdam 4–2 on penalties after the game had ended 1–1 in overtime. Though a shoot-out was required for determining the winner, the Italian team deserved victory for the superior tactics it employed, pressuring Ajax at the back of the defense, where the Dutch traditionally began their attack. The Italians took the lead in the 12th minute after a mixup in the Dutch defense. Frank de Boer and goalkeeper Edwin Van der Sar left the clearance to each other, which allowed Fabrizio Ravanelli to intercept and slide the ball in from an acute angle. Ajax tied the score with a free kick after 41 minutes; De Boer drove the ball through the defensive wall of players, goalkeeper Angelo Peruzzi was able only to push it out, and Jari Litmanen reacted quickly to tie the game. The penalty shoot-out began badly for Ajax, as Edgar Davids had his shot saved; Sonny Silooy had his shot blocked as well.

In the Cup-Winners' Cup final at Brussels on May 8, Paris St. Germain won its first European honour. It defeated Rapid Vienna, which had recently won its 30th League title. St. Germain was wasteful with attempts on goal, being restricted to just one score, when Bruno N'Gotty's shot in the 29th minute was deflected low past goalkeeper Michal Konsel's right hand. The more skillful French team continued to outplay its more defensive-minded and less ambitious opponent, and the 1–0 result did not accurately reflect the one-sided nature of the game.

Bayern Munich joined Barcelona, Ajax, and Juventus as the only clubs to have won all three major European competitions when it defeated Bordeaux 5–1 on aggregate scores in the UEFA Cup. In the first leg at Munich, Ger., on May 1, captain Lothar Matthaus took a 34th-minute corner kick, and Thomas Helmer rose to head the goal. Scholl drove in the second goal after 60 minutes to give Bayern a 2–0 lead. In the return at Bordeaux, Fr., on May 15, the French, who had played a marathon 20 matches in reaching the final, attempted to take the game to the Germans but were vulnerable to the counterattack. Scholl scored after 53 minutes, and Emil Kostadinov made it 2–0 12 minutes later. A free kick by Daniel Dutuel reduced the difference to 2–1 in the 75th minute, but Jurgen Klinsmann diverted a Thomas Strunz shot with his knee to restore Bayern's two-goal advantage three minutes later.

A record 170 of the International Federation of Association Football's total of 198 nations entered the 1998 World Cup, the finals of which were to be held in France. The first of an expected 639 matches was played in the spring. For the first time, there would be 32 finalists. Unfortunately, a tragedy occurred in Zambia on June 16 during a qualifying match at Lusaka; 9 people were trampled to death and 50 others injured near the end of Zambia's match with The Sudan.

Nigeria became the first African country to win gold in soccer at the Olympics, defeating Argentina 3–2 in the final. Brazil took the bronze by defeating Portugal 5–0. In the women's final the U.S. achieved gold with a 2–1 victory over China before a crowd of 76,489, a world record for a women's match. Norway defeated Brazil 2–0 for the bronze. Aggregate attendance for the two competitions was 1,364,250.

Despite the judgment that allowed players out of contract to move freely from one country to another in Europe, the transfer record was twice broken in the summer. First, Barcelona paid the Dutch club PSV Eindhoven £13,250,000 for Brazilian striker Luiz Ronaldo, and then, in the English premier league, Newcastle United bought striker Alan Shearer from Blackburn Rovers for £15 million. Yet Gianluca Vialli, who was once transferred for £12 million, went on a free transfer from Juventus to Chelsea (England).

In September, for the first time in the 125-year history of the FA Cup in England, the world's oldest competition, a father and son played on opposing teams. Nicky Scaife, aged 21, of Bishop Auckland met his father Bobby, 41, of Pickering. Bishop Auckland won this first qualifying round 3–1. Another relatively unusual event had taken place in April when Iceland's Arnor Gudjohnson, 35, was substituted against Estonia in the 62nd minute by his son Eidur-Smari, 17. Also during the year George Weah, who played for Liberia and AC Milan, became the first person ever to be elected African, European, and World Footballer of the Year. (See BIOGRAPHIES.) Arguably the world's most successful coaches at club and international level died within a few days of each other in February—Bob Paisley of Liverpool and Helmut Schön of West Ger-

Oliver Bierhoff (right) kicks the winning goal as Germany defeats the Czech Republic 2–1 in sudden-death overtime at the finals of the European association football (soccer) championships in London in June.

many, respectively; also dying during the year was West German international Reinhard Libuda. (See OBITUARIES.)

(JACK ROLLIN)

Argentina was favoured to win the soccer championship at the Centennial Olympic Games in 1996 but lost in the final contest to Nigeria (3–2) in the last minute. Otherwise, the most important international events for South American teams during the year were the World Cup qualifying matches. In these, for the first time, nine Latin-American countries were scheduled to play one another at home and away, with the top four qualifying for the 1998 finals in France. At the end of 1996, with this qualifying tournament almost at the halfway stage, Colombia remained the only unbeaten team and led in the standings by six points. Traditional South American powerhouses Argentina and Uruguay were finding the going difficult in their efforts to qualify.

Brazil, as defending World Cup champion, was not required to qualify for the finals. It could have continued its international winning streak—which stood at 35 at the end of 1995—but instead sent its Olympic under-23 team to the CONCACAF Gold Cup (played in the U.S.) and lost 2–0 to Mexico in the final to end the streak at 39.

In Argentina Vélez Sarsfield won the 1995–96 season-closing championship to add to its opening title. After that, River Plate became Latin America's club of the year by winning the Libertadores de América Cup (South America's club championship) with a 2–1 aggregate victory over Colombia's América. The Argentines lost, however, 1–0 to Italy's Juventus in the finals of the Intercontinental Cup (world club title) in Tokyo. Argentina swept all three continental club cups as Vélez Sarsfield won the Super Cup (for Libertadores Cup winners) and Lanús the CONMEBOL Cup for other leading teams.

In Brazil Grêmio (Pôrto Alegre) won the national title and Cruzeiro (Belo Horizonte) the KO Cup. Deportivo Cali ran away with the 1995–96 title in Colombia, and its Cali neighbour, América, was doing the same at the end of 1996. Colo Colo made it a league and cup double in Chile. Paraguay's

Libertadores de América Cup			
Year	Winner (country)	Runner-up (country)	Scores
1992	São Paulo (Braz.)	Newell's Old Boys (Arg.)	0–1, 1–0, 3–2*
1993	São Paulo (Braz.)	Universidad Catolica (Chile)	5–1, 0–2
1994	Vélez Sarsfield (Arg.)	São Paulo (Braz.)	1–0, 0–1, 5–3*
1995	Grêmio (Braz.)	Atletico Nacional (Colom.)	3–1, 1–1
1996	River Plate (Arg.)	América (Colom.)	0–1, 2–0

*Winner determined in penalty shootout after tiebreaking game.

Florida wide receiver Ike Hilliard (left) leaps high to catch a pass in the end zone and score a touchdown as Florida trounced Florida State 52–20 in the Sugar Bowl at New Orleans. Florida's victory made it the top-ranked team in the U.S.

two top clubs, Olímpia and Cerro Porteno, won the 1995 and 1996 titles for the 34th and 24th time, respectively. In Uruguay Penarol retained the title in 1996 after a play-off with the country's other big club, Nacional, with which it shared the opening and closing championships.

In Peru Sporting Cristal won the championship for the third consecutive year in 1996, while Minerven won it for the first time in Venezuela's 1995–96 season. In Ecuador it was Barcelona in 1995 and Nacional in 1996, while San José and Bolívar won the respective Bolivian titles. In Mexico Necaxa retained the first division title in the 1995–96 season, and, under a changed format, newcomers Santos Laguna took the

winter title corresponding to the first part of the 1996–97 season.

In its first season major league soccer crowned Washington, D.C., United as its champion. United staged a final-period comeback to defeat the Los Angeles Galaxy 3–2 in sudden-death overtime on October 20 in Foxboro, Mass. Ten days later United also won the U.S. Open Cup by defeating the Rochester Rhinos 3–0 in Washington, D.C.   (ERIC WEIL)

U.S. Football. The University of Florida won its first national championship of college football by defeating Florida State University 52–20 in the Sugar Bowl at New Orleans, La., on Jan. 2, 1997. Southeastern Conference (SEC) champion Florida,

with a won-lost record of 12–1 after losing a game on November 30 to Florida State, was elected champion in both major polls.

Atlantic Coast Conference champion Florida State and Pacific Ten Conference champion Arizona State finished the regu-

U.S. College Football National Champions	
Season	Champion
1991–92	Miami (Fla.)*/Washington*
1992–93	Alabama
1993–94	Florida St.
1994–95	Nebraska
1995–96	Nebraska
1996–97	Florida

*Tied.

Rose Bowl				
Season	Result			
1991–92	Washington	34	Michigan	14
1992–93	Michigan	38	Washington	31
1993–94	Wisconsin	21	UCLA	16
1994–95	Penn State	38	Oregon	20
1995–96	Southern California	41	Northwestern	32
1996–97	Ohio State	20	Arizona State	17

Sugar Bowl				
Season	Result			
1991–92	Notre Dame	39	Florida	28
1992–93	Alabama	34	Miami (Fla.)	13
1993–94	Florida	41	West Virginia	7
1994–95	Florida State	23	Florida	17
1995–96	Virginia Tech	28	Texas	10
1996–97	Florida	52	Florida State	20

Orange Bowl				
Season	Result			
1991–92	Miami (Fla.)	22	Nebraska	0
1992–93	Florida St.	27	Nebraska	14
1993–94	Florida St.	18	Nebraska	16
1994–95	Nebraska	24	Miami	17
1995–96	Florida St.	31	Notre Dame	26
1996–97	Nebraska	41	Virginia Tech	21

Cotton Bowl				
Season	Result			
1991–92	Florida State	10	Texas A&M	2
1992–93	Notre Dame	28	Texas A&M	3
1993–94	Notre Dame	24	Texas A&M	21
1994–95	Southern California	55	Texas Tech	14
1995–96	Colorado	38	Oregon	6
1996–97	Brigham Young	19	Kansas State	15

lar season with the only undefeated records in Division I-A of the National Collegiate Athletic Association (NCAA), but their bowl defeats dropped them to 11–1. They could not meet in a bowl game because the Pac Ten champion was committed to play in the Rose Bowl, where fourth-ranked Arizona State lost 20–17 to second-ranked Ohio State, the 11–1 Big Ten champion. The other Division I-A team with only one defeat was fifth-ranked Brigham Young (14–1), the Western Athletic Conference (WAC) champion. Florida State ranked third in the coaches' and writers' polls, which agreed on the top 10.

Ranked 6th through 10th were Nebraska and Penn State, at 11–2, and three 10–2 teams: Colorado, Tennessee, and North Carolina. The other major bowl game outcomes were Penn State's 38–15 victory over Big Eight champion Texas (8–5) in the Fiesta, Nebraska's 41–21 victory over Big East champion Virginia Tech (10–2) in the Orange, and Brigham Young's 19–15 win over Kansas State in the Cotton.

The trend toward large conferences in Division I continued after the Southwest Conference disbanded. The Big Eight became the Big Twelve, the WAC grew to 16 teams, and both conferences followed the lead of the SEC by pitting the winners of separate divisions in a conference championship game, which enabled Texas to upset Nebraska 37–27 for the Big Twelve championship. Nebraska's bid for a third consecutive undefeated season and national championship ended in a September loss to Arizona State, whose Bruce Snyder won the Paul "Bear" Bryant Award as Coach of the Year. Florida defeated Tennessee, and Brigham Young defeated Wyoming in the SEC and WAC championship games.

Arizona State remained undefeated by winning a mid-season game in overtime, which Division I-A used for the first time to break ties in 25 games. In an overtime period, each team took possession at the opponent's 25-yd line. Teams played as many periods as were necessary to break the tie.

Other conference winners in Division I-A were Houston (7–5) and Southern Mississippi (8–3) in Conference USA, Nevada (9–3) in the Big West, and Ball State (8–4) in the Mid-American. Northwestern (9–3) tied Ohio State in the Big Ten; Miami (Fla.) and Syracuse (both 9–3) tied Virginia Tech in the Big East.

The surprising teams of the year were Army and Navy, which both went into their annual game with winning records for the first time since 1963. Army overcame an 18-point deficit to win 28–24 and take a series lead of 47–43–7. Army (10–2) led Division I with 346.5 yd rushing per game, and coach Bob Sutton won the Bobby Dodd National Coach of the Year Award.

Florida senior quarterback Danny Wuerffel won the Heisman Trophy and the Maxwell Award, both honouring the best player in Division I-A, and also the Davey O'Brien and Johnny Unitas Golden Arm awards for the top quarterback. He had the second best passer rating and was the leader, with 39 touchdown passes and 10.1 yd per pass attempt, in the regular season. Steve Sarkisian of Brigham Young was the passing leader, with 173.6 rating points, and had the best completion percentage, .688.

Florida led Division I-A with 46.6 points per game and ranked second to Nevada's

DAVID AKE—REUTERS

Green Bay Packer running back Dorsey Levens follows a block by teammate Earl Dotson for a big gain in the NFC championship game at Green Bay, Wis., on Jan. 12, 1997. Green Bay defeated Carolina 30–13 to qualify for the Super Bowl.

527.3 total yards per game. Nevada was runner-up to both Florida in scoring and Wyoming's 359.2 yd per game in passing. Wyoming's Marcus Harris won the Fred Biletnikoff Award for wide receivers with a leading 1,650 yd on 109 catches, which ranked second to Damond Wilkins's 114 for Nevada. Wyoming quarterback Josh Wallwork was the passing yardage leader with 4,090.

Ohio State junior offensive tackle Orlando Pace's fourth-place finish in the Heis-

man voting was the best in 16 years for someone who did not play an offensive ball-handling position. He won the Outland Trophy and became the first two-time winner of the Vince Lombardi Award, both recognizing the outstanding lineman.

Troy Davis of Iowa State became the first NCAA player to run for more than 2,000 yd in two consecutive seasons when he gained 2,185, and he also led Division I-A with 2,364 all-purpose yards, including receptions and returns. But the Doak

Super Bowl

	Season	Result			
XXVII	1992–93	Dallas Cowboys (NFC)	52	Buffalo Bills (AFC)	17
XXVIII	1993–94	Dallas Cowboys (NFC)	30	Buffalo Bills (AFC)	13
XXIX	1994–95	San Francisco 49ers (NFC)	49	San Diego Chargers (AFC)	26
XXX	1995–96	Dallas Cowboys (NFC)	27	Pittsburgh Steelers (AFC)	17
XXXI	**1996–97**	**Green Bay Packers (NFC)**	**35**	**New England Patriots (AFC)**	**21**

NFL Final Standings, 1996

AMERICAN CONFERENCE

Eastern Division	W	L	T	Central Division	W	L	T	Western Division	W	L	T
*New England	11	5	0	*Pittsburgh	10	6	0	*Denver	13	3	0
*Buffalo	10	6	0	*Jacksonville	9	7	0	Kansas City	9	7	0
*Indianapolis	9	7	0	Cincinnati	8	8	0	San Diego	8	8	0
Miami	8	8	0	Houston	8	8	0	Oakland	7	9	0
New York Jets	1	15	0	Baltimore	4	12	0	Seattle	7	9	0

NATIONAL CONFERENCE

Eastern Division	W	L	T	Central Division	W	L	T	Western Division	W	L	T
*Dallas	10	6	0	*Green Bay	13	3	0	*Carolina	12	4	0
*Philadelphia	10	6	0	*Minnesota	9	7	0	*San Francisco	12	4	0
Washington	9	7	0	Chicago	7	9	0	St. Louis	6	10	0
Arizona	7	9	0	Tampa Bay	6	10	0	Atlanta	3	13	0
New York Giants	6	10	0	Detroit	5	11	0	New Orleans	3	13	0

*Qualified for play-offs.

Walker Award for running backs went to rushing runner-up Byron Hanspard, who gained 2,084 yd for Texas Tech. Washington halfback Corey Dillon was the touchdown leader with 23.

Northwestern linebacker Pat Fitzgerald won his second consecutive Chuck Bednarik Award as the top defensive player and finished second to Matt Russell of Colorado for the linebackers' Dick Butkus Award. Lawrence Wright of Florida won the defensive backs' Jim Thorpe Award, and Dre' Bly of North Carolina was the interception leader with 11.

The Green Bay Packers won the 1996 championship of the National Football League by defeating the New England Patriots 35–21 in Super Bowl XXXI at New Orleans, La., on Jan. 26, 1997. Kick receiver Desmond Howard of the Packers set a Super Bowl record with a 99-yd kickoff return for a touchdown and was voted the game's Most Valuable Player, the first time that a special teams member had won the award. An 81-yd touchdown on a pass from Packer quarterback Brett Favre to wide receiver Antonio Freeman also set a Super Bowl record.

The Dallas Cowboys defended their 1995 National Football League (NFL) championship by winning a league-high fifth consecutive division title, but their 1996 regular-season record was their worst in six years, and they failed to qualify for a first-round bye in the play-offs for the first time in five years. The Cowboys, led by quarterback Troy Aikman (see BIOGRAPHIES), had won the 1995 championship on Jan. 28, 1996, by beating the Pittsburgh Steelers 27–17 in Super Bowl XXX at Tempe, Ariz., becoming the first team ever to win three Super Bowls in four years.

The Packers and the Carolina Panthers earned 1996 play-off byes in the National Football Conference (NFC) by winning their divisions with the two best records. Carolina made the play-offs in only its second season of existence, as did the Jacksonville Jaguars by earning a wild-card berth with one of the three best runner-up records in the American Football Conference (AFC).

Green Bay became the first team since the undefeated Miami Dolphins of 1972 to lead the NFL in most points scored and fewest points allowed. The Packers averaged 28.5 a game and gave up 13.1. Their 19 touchdowns allowed were the fewest in the NFL's 17 seasons of 16-game schedules, and their defense also led the NFL by allowing 259.8 total yards, 171.3 passing yards, and 15.5 first downs per game. The Packers' offense led the league in touchdowns with 56 total, 39 on passes and 8 on returns. Quarterback Favre threw for all 39 touchdowns, led the NFC with 3,899 yd passing, and won his second consecutive Most Valuable Player award.

Carolina's strength was a defense that ranked second in points allowed and first with a 32.4% third-down efficiency and 60 sacks. Coach Dom Capers confused opponents with a defense that used zone coverage instead of man-to-man on blitzes. Kevin Greene's 14.5 sacks led the league, and Lamar Lathon's 13.5 tied for second with AFC leader Bruce Smith of Buffalo, who was Defensive Player of the Year. Kicker John Kasay led the NFL with 145 points and a league-record 37 field goals.

Denver led the NFL's offenses with averages of 361.9 total yards per game and 147.6 rushing yards per game. The Broncos' John Elway had the AFC's best passer rating and Terrell Davis the most rushing yards, just 15 behind NFL leader Barry Sanders's 1,553 for Detroit. Davis, the Offensive Player of the Year, also led the league with 108 first downs. Sanders led the NFL with 2,028 total yards from scrimmage and, with Thurman Thomas of Buffalo, became the first players with 1,000 yd rushing in eight consecutive seasons.

San Francisco quarterback Steve Young won his fifth NFL passing championship in six years, with a 97.2 rating, and also led the league with a .677 completion percentage and a mere 1.9 interception percentage, throwing only six. Teammate Jerry Rice led the league with 108 catches and established NFL milestones with 100 catches in three consecutive seasons and 1,000 catches for his career. Jacksonville had the NFL's most passing yards behind Mark Brunell, the league leader with 4,367 yd passing and AFC leader with a .634 completion percentage.

Terry Allen led the NFL with 21 touchdown runs, while his Washington team had a league-high 27. The leaders in touchdown catches were Tony Martin of San Diego and Michael Jackson of the Baltimore Ravens. Marcus Allen of Kansas City set NFL career records with 112 rushing touchdowns and 576 games by a running back. Brian Mitchell of Washington led the league for the third straight time with 1,995 combined yards rushing and returning. Chris Boniol tied a record with seven field goals in a game for Dallas.   (KEVIN M. LAMB)

Canadian Football. The Toronto Argonauts defeated the Edmonton Eskimos 43–37 to win the Grey Cup championship of the Canadian Football League (CFL) at Hamilton, Ont., on November 24. The game's Most Valuable Player was Toronto quarterback Doug Flutie, who also won his fifth CFL Most Outstanding Player award and led league passers with 5,720 yd, 29 touchdowns, and a .641 completion percentage. Toronto won the league's Eastern Division with a 15–3 record and an offense that led the CFL with 426 total yards and 320 passing yards per game. Robert Drummond's 17 touchdowns led the league, and centre Mike Kiselak was voted the league's Most Outstanding Offensive Lineman.

Edmonton (11–7) led the league's defenses by allowing 19.7 points, 280 total yards, and 226 passing yards per game and defeated the Western Division champion Calgary Stampeders (13–5) to reach the championship game. Edmonton's defense featured linebacker Willie Pless, the league's Most Outstanding Defensive Player, and end Leroy Blugh, the Most Outstanding Canadian.

After three years with teams in the United States, the CFL consolidated to nine Canadian teams after the NFL's move to Baltimore forced the defending CFL champion Baltimore Stallions to move to Montreal. Four other U.S. teams disbanded.
(KEVIN M. LAMB)

Australian Football. The Australian Football League (AFL) celebrated its 100th season in 1996, and North Melbourne FC emerged as the league's premier club, defeating Sydney before a crowd of 93,102 at the Melbourne Cricket Ground. It was North Melbourne's third title—and first since 1977—since entering the competition in 1925 and Sydney's first grand final appearance since it was known as South Melbourne in 1945.

The first-round series of the season consisted of each of the 16 clubs playing 22 matches, and by September eight clubs had qualified for the finals. The 176 first-round games produced a total attendance of 5,216,148 (an average of 30,000 a game), and the eight finals drew 478,812 for a grand total of 5,694,960.

After the completion of the finals, the top five clubs, in order, were North Melbourne, Sydney, Brisbane, Essendon, and West Coast. During the year Fitzroy and Brisbane merged; in 1997 the club would be known as the Brisbane Lions. A new club, from Port Adelaide, was to also enter the AFL in 1997.

Major award winners in 1996 were: Brownlow Medal (best and fairest player in the competition), tie between James Hird of Essendon and Michael Voss of Brisbane; Norm Smith Medal (best player in the grand final), Glen Archer of North Melbourne; Coleman Medal (leading goal-kicker in the home and away rounds), Tony Lockett of Sydney.   (GREG HOBBS)

Rugby Football. No other single thing dominated Rugby Union in 1996 as much as money. A game fiercely amateur for two centuries tried—and failed in many instances—to embrace professionalism. The new professional era allowed Rugby Union to welcome back a host of players who had moved to professional Rugby League.

Political infighting scarred the year as England was first expelled from and then welcomed back into Rugby Union's oldest championship, the Five Nations. With a new stadium to pay for and mounting salaries to fund, England was forced into

AFL Final Standings, 1996
(League ladder after round 22)

Team*	W	L	D	Points
Sydney	16	5	1	66
North Melbourne	16	6	0	64
Brisbane	15	6	1	62
West Coast	15	7	0	60
Carlton	15	7	0	60
Essendon	14	7	1	58
Geelong	13	8	1	54
Hawthorn	11	10	1	46

*Teams that qualified for play-offs.

Grey Cup

Year	Result			
1991	Toronto Argonauts (EFC)	36	Calgary Stampeders (WFC)	21
1992	Calgary Stampeders (WFC)	24	Winnipeg Blue Bombers (EFC)	10
1993	Edmonton Eskimos (WFC)	33	Winnipeg Blue Bombers (EFC)	23
1994	British Columbia Lions (WFC)	26	Baltimore Stallions (EFC)	23
1995	Baltimore Stallions (SD)	37	Calgary Stampeders (ND)	20
1996	**Toronto Argonauts (EFC)**	**43**	**Edmonton Eskimos (WFC)**	**37**

negotiating its own five-year $120 million, television deal for the tournament. This naturally brought it more money than Scotland, Ireland, Wales, or France, and when it refused a five-way split, it was thrown out. Prolonged negotiations allowed it back in, but from 1998 all of England's matches at Twickenham, regarded as the home of world rugby, would be shown on satellite TV. On the field England won its second consecutive Five Nations trophy after losing to France but then beating Ireland in the decisive last match after France lost to Wales.

The domestic season in Britain also started under a cloud, with the clubs withdrawing their players from England training sessions as part of their power struggle with the governing body. Another phenomenon reached the English game with big-money owners investing tens of millions of pounds in new stadiums, transfer fees, and salaries. Their money ensured that François Pienaar, South Africa's World Cup-winning captain, signed to play for the Saracens in England after being dropped from the South African national team. He was joined in the British Isles by Joel Stransky, who had secured South Africa's victory in the 1995 World Cup final.

While the Northern Hemisphere countries struggled to cope with professionalism, those in the Southern Hemisphere stole a march, playing some of their best rugby ever. The new Super-12, which comprised 12 top teams from Australia, New Zealand, and South Africa, produced some dazzling rugby, with an average of over six tries in a match. It was won by Auckland (N.Z.), which beat Natal (S.Af.) 45–21 in the final on May 25.

At the first Tri-Nations tournament be-

REBECCA NADEN—PA NEWS

Will Carling (centre), England's captain, breaks through Ireland's defenders Jeremy Davidson (left) and David Humphreys during England's 28–15 triumph. Winning the match gained for England the Five Nations Championship of Rugby Union.

tween the same three nations, the New Zealand All Blacks produced superb form and clinched the cup with a 32–25 victory over Australia in the final in Brisbane. The sweetest victory came when the All Blacks gained revenge for their 1995 World Cup final defeat by beating South Africa 15–11.

Rugby League in England became a summer game in 1996 with the emergence of the new Super League, which allowed some of the better league players to compete in both union and league and therefore play for almost 12 months of the year.

(PAUL MORGAN)

Record of International Test Matches 1871 to Aug. 31, 1996

	England Wins	Draws	Losses	Scotland Wins	Draws	Losses	Ireland Wins	Draws	Losses	Wales Wins	Draws	Losses	British Isles* Wins	Draws	Losses
England v.				57	17	39	63	8	38	42	12	48			
Scotland v.	39	17	57				57	1	45	44	2	54			
Ireland v.	38	8	63	45	1	57				36	6	58			
Wales v.	48	12	42	54	2	44	58	6	36						
British Isles* v.															
South Africa v.	8	1	4	6	0	3	8	1	1	8	1	0	20	6	14
New Zealand v.	14	0	4	18	2	0	12	1	0	13	0	3	24	3	5
Australia v.	12	0	7	7	0	8	11	0	6	11	0	8	3	0	14
France v.	26	7	39	33	2	32	40	5	25	29	3	38			

	South Africa Wins	Draws	Losses	New Zealand Wins	Draws	Losses	Australia Wins	Draws	Losses	France Wins	Draws	Losses
England v.	4	1	8	4	0	14	7	0	12	39	7	26
Scotland v.	3	0	6	0	2	18	8	0	7	32	2	33
Ireland v.	1	1	8	0	1	12	6	0	11	25	5	40
Wales v.	0	1	8	3	0	13	8	0	11	38	3	29
British Isles* v.	14	6	20	5	3	24	14	0	3			
South Africa v.				22	3	22	24	0	11	16	5	5
New Zealand v.	22	3	22				72	5	27	24	0	8
Australia v.	11	0	24	27	5	72				10	2	13
France v.	5	5	16	8	0	24	13	2	10			

*The British Isles ("British Lions") is a combined team from the four "Home Unions" (England, Ireland, Scotland, and Wales).

Five Nations Championship

Year	Result
1992	England*
1993	France
1994	Wales
1995	England*
1996	**England**

*Grand Slam winner.

Rugby Union World Cup

Year	Result			
1987	New Zealand	29	France	9
1991	Australia	12	England	6
1995	South Africa	15	New Zealand	12

Rugby League World Cup

Year	Result			
1975*	Australia†			
1977*	Australia	13	Great Britain	12
1988	Australia	25	New Zealand	12
1992	Australia	10	Great Britain	6
1995	Australia	16	England	8

*Called International Championship from 1975 to 1977.
†Championships played without a grand final match; England was the runner-up.

© 1996 KEIICHI SATO

Eldrick ("Tiger") Woods takes a swing at the U.S. Professional Golfers' Association tour championship. Woods, who at age 18 had become the youngest golfer to win the U.S. Amateur and in 1996 became the first to win it for three consecutive years, turned professional in August.

GOLF

For much of 1996 the world of golf was seeking a new star and wondering if technological advances in club and ball manufacture were making the search more difficult. Jack Nicklaus looked back on the 35 years he had played professionally and concluded that the biggest single change he had seen was in equipment. "I think it is great for the average golfer because it can improve his game and he can get more enjoyment out of it," he said. "But for the pros I think it has had an adverse effect. You used to be able to separate yourself from most of the players by your shot-making ability, or if you were long or had a certain skill more developed than the other player. Not any more."

South African Gary Player, another of the four players in history to have won all four major championships (the Masters, United States Open, the British Open, and the U.S. Professional Golfers' Association of America (PGA) championship), added, "It's not even nearly the same game. I think golf equipment has done immeasurable harm at the professional level." The fact that the first 42 tournaments on the U.S. PGA tour produced 33 different champions, 13 of them winning for the first time, added weight to the argument.

By the end of the year, however, there was one young golfer who appeared to have the ability to stand out from the pack and the potential to lead the sport into the next millennium. Californian Eldrick ("Tiger") Woods, who in 1994 at age 18 had become the youngest-ever winner of the U.S. Amateur championship, became the first player to win it for three successive years, recovering in the final from five down to beat Steve Scott at the second extra hole at Pumpkin Ridge Golf Club in Cornelius, Ore.

In June Woods briefly led the U.S. Open on the opening day at Oakland Hills Country Club near Bloomfield Hills, Mich., and then equaled the lowest-ever total by an amateur in finishing tied for 22nd in the British Open at Royal Lytham and St. Annes in Lancashire, Eng.

It was no surprise when Woods after his third U.S. Amateur victory abandoned his Stanford University studies and turned professional. His performance in his first few weeks as a professional was remarkable. After finishing in a tie for 60th in the Greater Milwaukee Open, the 20-year-old finished 11th in the Bell Canadian Open, tied for fifth in the Quad City Classic, tied for third in the B.C. Open, and finished first in the Las Vegas Invitational after a play-off against Davis Love III. Two weeks later he triumphed again in the Walt Disney World/Oldsmobile Classic at Lake Buena Vista, Fla., though in controversial fashion when Taylor Smith, having matched Woods's 21-under-par total of 267, was disqualified for using a long putter with a grip that did not conform to the rules. In November Woods finished fifth to Greg Norman in the Australian Open.

In only eight weeks as a professional, Woods had risen into the top 40 of the Sony world rankings, and he was to finish in 24th place on the U.S. money list, with earnings of $790,594. Yet that was only the tip of a financial iceberg. The moment he left the amateur ranks, Woods became one of the hottest properties in sport. A clothing deal worth a reported $40 million over five years was signed with Nike, and another contract with Titleist to use its clubs totaled a reported $20 million over five years.

In the competition for the four major championships, the most dramatic was unquestionably in the Masters, where Greg

British Open Tournament (men)	
Year	Winner
1992	N. Faldo (U.K.)
1993	G. Norman (Austl.)
1994	N. Price (Zimb.)
1995	J. Daly (U.S.)
1996	**T. Lehman (U.S.)**

United States Open Championship (men)	
Year	Winner
1992	T. Kite (U.S.)
1993	L. Janzen (U.S.)
1994	E. Els (S.Af.)
1995	C. Pavin (U.S.)
1996	**S. Jones (U.S.)**

Masters Tournament	
Year	Winner
1992	F. Couples (U.S.)
1993	B. Langer (Ger.)
1994	J. Olazábal (Spain)
1995	B. Crenshaw (U.S.)
1996	**N. Faldo (U.K.)**

U.S. Professional Golfers' Association (PGA) Championship	
Year	Winner
1992	N. Price (Zimb.)
1993	P. Azinger (U.S.)
1994	N. Price (Zimb.)
1995	S. Elkington (Austl.)
1996	**M. Brooks (U.S.)**

British Amateur Championship (men)	
Year	Winner
1992	S. Dundas (U.K.)
1993	I. Pyman (U.K.)
1994	L. James (U.K.)
1995	G. Sherry (U.K.)
1996	**W. Bladon (U.K.)**

United States Amateur Championship (men)	
Year	Winner
1992	J. Leonard (U.S.)
1993	J. Harris (U.S.)
1994	T. Woods (U.S.)
1995	T. Woods (U.S.)
1996	**T. Woods (U.S.)**

Women's British Open Championship	
Year	Winner
1992	P. Sheehan (U.S.)
1993	K. Lunn (Austl.)
1994	L. Neumann (Swed.)
1995	K. Webb (Austl.)
1996	**E. Klein (U.S.)**

Ladies' British Amateur Championship	
Year	Winner
1992	P. Pedersen (Den.)
1993	C. Lambert (U.K.)
1994	E. Duggleby (U.K.)
1995	J. Hall (U.K.)
1996	**K. Kuehne (U.S.)**

United States Women's Open Championship	
Year	Winner
1992	P. Sheehan (U.S.)
1993	L. Merten (U.S.)
1994	P. Sheehan (U.S.)
1995	A. Sorenstam (Swed.)
1996	**A. Sorenstam (Swed.)**

United States Women's Amateur Championship	
Year	Winner
1992	V. Goetze (U.S.)
1993	J. McGill (U.S.)
1994	W. Ward (U.S.)
1995	K. Kuehne (U.S.)
1996	**K. Kuehne (U.S.)**

Ladies' Professional Golf Association (LPGA) Championship	
Year	Winner
1992	B. King (U.S.)
1993	P. Sheehan (U.S.)
1994	L. Davies (U.K.)
1995	K. Robbins (U.S.)
1996	**L. Davies (U.K.)**

Walker Cup (men; amateur)	
Year	Result
1987	United States 16½, Britain and Ireland 7½
1989	Britain and Ireland 12½, United States 11½
1991	United States 14, Britain and Ireland 10
1993	United States 19, Britain and Ireland 5
1995	Britain and Ireland 14, United States 10

Curtis Cup (women; amateur)	
Year	Result
1988	Britain and Ireland 11, United States 7
1990	United States 14, Britain and Ireland 4
1992	Britain and Ireland 10, United States 8
1994	Britain and Ireland 9, United States 9
1996	**Britain and Ireland 11½, United States 6½**

World Cup (men; professional)	
Year	Winner
1992	United States (F. Couples and D. Love III)
1993	United States (F. Couples and D. Love III)
1994	United States (F. Couples and D. Love III)
1995	United States (F. Couples and D. Love III)
1996	**South Africa (E. Els and W. Westner)**

Ryder Cup (men; professional)	
Year	Result
1987	Europe 15, United States 13
1989	Europe 14, United States 14
1991	United States 14½, Europe 13½
1993	United States 15, Europe 13
1995	Europe 14½, United States 13½

Norman of Australia, ranked first in the world throughout the season, tied the Augusta (Ga.) National course record of 63 on the first day and with a round to play was six strokes in the lead. After a string of near misses in the U.S. major tournaments, it seemed that Norman finally was to win this title. On the final afternoon, however, he collapsed to a 78 and in the end only just held on to second place, five strokes behind Nick Faldo of the U.K., whose closing 67 (for a 12-under-par aggregate of 276) gave him a third Masters victory and a sixth major in nine years.

In the U.S. Open, Davis Love, Tom Lehman, and Steve Jones all stood on the final tee at two under par. Then Love three-putted and Lehman drove into a bunker, and so Jones's par four made him the surprising champion. It was his first U.S. tour victory in 7 years, 2½ of them spent out of the game after a dirt-bike accident, and just to play in the Open he had to survive a play-off in the qualifying competition.

While Love continued to wait for a victory in a major tournament, Lehman was celebrating his own first success five weeks later in the British Open. A third-round 64 put him six shots in the lead, and with closest challenger Faldo failing to apply the pressure he had in the Masters, Lehman could afford a 73 in the final round and still beat fellow American Mark McCumber and South Africa's Ernie Els by two strokes.

The PGA championship, at the Valhalla Golf Club in Louisville, Ky., produced a play-off between two more Americans, Mark Brooks and Kenny Perry. Both were seeking their first major victory, and it was Brooks who prevailed. Perry had been two strokes ahead standing on the final tee, but bogeyed the par five and then watched Brooks birdie it to force a tie. Unfortunately for Perry, the first hole of sudden death was the same 18th, and he could not recover from driving into trouble again.

The U.S. PGA tour money list title also went to Lehman, whose six-shot victory in the season-ending tour championship at Southern Hills Country Club in Tulsa, Okla., put him ahead of Phil Mickelson with a record total of $1,780,159. Mickelson had the most wins (four) and also teamed up with Mark O'Meara and Steve Stricker to give the United States victory in the Alfred Dunhill Cup at St. Andrews in Fife, Scot. The U.S. also scored a success in the second President's Cup match against the International Team (the rest of the world minus Europe). In an exciting finish at the

Robert Trent Jones Golf Club in Lake Manassas, Va., Fred Couples sank a 10-m (33-ft) birdie putt at the second-to-last hole of the decisive singles match against Vijay Singh of Fiji for a 16½–15½ victory.

On the PGA European tour, the player with the most victories—Ian Woosnam of Wales, with four—did not win the Order of Merit. That went for a record-equaling fourth successive time to Scotland's Colin Montgomerie, who, besides winning three tournaments, had eight other top-10 finishes and earned £875,146. He remained the dominant personality on a circuit deprived in 1996 of José María Olazábal of Spain, who did not play during the year because of rheumatoid arthritis in both his feet.

Els won the Toyota World Match Play championship at Wentworth, Surrey, Eng., for an unprecedented third year in a row. He then teamed with Wayne Westner to take South Africa to a massive 18-stroke victory in the World Cup of Golf at Cape Town, S.Af.

In the U.S. Women's Open, Sweden's

Annika Sorenstam not only became just the sixth player to have made a successful defense of the title but did so by a commanding six-stroke margin at Pine Needles Lodge & Golf Club in North Carolina. In 1995 Sorenstam had become the first player, male or female, to win the most money in both the U.S. and Europe. That feat was nearly achieved again in 1996 by Laura Davies of the U.K. In the U.S. she fought a thrilling yearlong battle with Australian rookie Karrie Webb, her four victories including the McDonald's LPGA championship and the du Maurier Classic, and she also enjoyed three victories in Europe and two in Japan, the last of them by a 15-stroke margin. Webb climaxed her year with a victory in the inaugural LPGA tour championship, her fourth tournament win of the year. She also became the first LPGA player and the first rookie in golf to win more than $1 million in a single season and was named Rookie of the Year.

If the top U.S. women golfers were overshadowed at home, then they truly asserted themselves overseas. After leading by two points going into the 12 concluding singles of the Solheim Cup at the St. Pierre Country Club in Chepstow, Wales, Europe slumped to a 17–11 defeat. The U.S. retained the trophy despite omitting Emilee Klein, a seven-stroke winner of the Weetabix Women's British Open at the Woburn Golf and Country Club in Milton Keynes, Eng.

The U.S. did suffer defeat in the Curtis Cup, Britain and Ireland's women amateurs winning 11½–6½ at the Killarney Golf & Fishing Club in Ireland to maintain a remarkable record of only one loss in the last six matches. The following week, however, Kelli Kuehne of the U.S. won the Ladies' British amateur championship at Hoylake near Liverpool, Eng.; she then retained her U.S. Women's amateur title at Firethorn

Tom Lehman propels the ball out of a bunker at the British Open at Royal Lytham and St. Annes in Lancashire, Eng., where he won his first major championship. The 37-year-old Lehman became the first U.S. golfer to win a British Open since Bobby Jones, playing as an amateur, won in 1926.

DAVID CANNON—ALLSPORT

(TOP) JEFF VINNICK—REUTERS; (BOTTOM) YOSHIKAZU TSUNO—AFP

U.S. athletes (above) celebrate their gold medal in team gymnastics at the Olympic Games, the first time ever that U.S. women had won the event. Aleksey Nemov (left) of Russia, who also won a silver and three bronze medals in the Olympics, vaults for a gold medal in the men's gymnastics competition.

final rotation, when 18-year-old Kerri Strug fell on her first vault and then nailed her second (and final) attempt despite a badly sprained ankle. Her effort clinched the gold for the U.S. team and created a popular ideal of the selfless Olympic athlete that clung to Strug long after the Games were over. Liliya Podkopayeva of Ukraine was the all-around Olympic champion and added the gold medal for the floor exercise.

Among the men, Li Xiaoshuang of China added the Olympic all-around crown to his collection. Russia won the team all-around title by a narrow margin over China. In the last three Olympics, in the men's competitions, the Soviet Union and its successor countries had won 17 gold medals, followed by China with 3 and the U.S. with 1. Among the women, the Soviet Union and its successor nations had captured 9 gold medals, Romania 6, the U.S. 2, and China 1.

At the 1992 Olympics the Unified Team of Soviet gymnasts, men and women, had accounted for nine gold, five silver, and four bronze medals. At Atlanta, however, gymnasts from former Soviet republics were not as successful. The women accounted for three gold and two silver medals, and the men gained three golds, one silver, and seven bronzes. Best of the Russians individually was Aleksey Nemov, who won gold in the vault and also a silver and three bronzes. Vitaly Sherbo, winner of six gold medals at the 1992 Olympics in Barcelona, Spain, won a gold medal in the floor exercise at the 1996 world championships, but he was held to four bronze medals in Atlanta.

Spain was the surprising gold medalist in the group event in the expanded rhythmic gymnastics program, slipping past Bulgaria by less than 0.1 point. Ukraine placed first and third in the individual rhythmic event, won by Yekaterina Serebryanskaya. Yanina Batyrchina of Russia was the silver medalist.   (CHARLES ROBERT PAUL, JR.)

August. There was no team or individual all-around competition at the tournament, and so the full focus on those events was aimed at Atlanta, where the U.S. women won their first-ever team all-around Olympic gold medal. The U.S. went into the optional events closely trailing Russia. It remained a close competition until the

World Gymnastics Championships—Men

Year	All-around Team	All-around Individual	Horizontal bar	Parallel bars
1993	not held	V. Sherbo (Bela.)	S. Charkov (Russia)	V. Sherbo (Bela.)
1994	China	I. Ivankov (Bela.)	V. Sherbo (Bela.)	Liping Huang (China)
1995	China	Li Xiaoshuang (China)	A. Wecker (Ger.)	V. Sherbo (Bela.)
1996	**not held**	**not held**	**J. Carballo (Spain)**	**R. Charipov (Ukr.)**

Year	Pommel horse	Rings	Vault	Floor exercise
1993	Pae Gil Su (N.Kor.)	Y. Chechi (Italy)	V. Sherbo (Bela.)	G. Misutin (Ukr.)
1994	M. Urzica (Rom.)	Y. Chechi (Italy)	V. Sherbo (Bela.)	V. Sherbo (Bela.)
1995	Li Donghua (Switz.)	Y. Chechi (Italy)	A. Nemov (Russia)* G. Misutin (Ukr.)*	V. Sherbo (Bela.)
1996	**Pae Gil Su (N.Kor.)**	**Y. Chechi (Italy)**	**A. Nemov (Russia)**	**V. Sherbo (Bela.)**

*Tied.

World Gymnastics Championships—Women

Year	All-around Team	All-around Individual	Balance beam
1993	not held	S. Miller (U.S.)	L. Milosovici (Rom.)
1994	Romania	S. Miller (U.S.)	S. Miller (U.S.)
1995	Romania	L. Podkopayeva (Ukr.)	Mo Huilan (China)
1996	**not held**	**not held**	**D. Kochetkova (Russia)**

Year	Uneven parallel bars	Vault	Floor exercise
1993	S. Miller (U.S.)	Y. Piskun (Bela.)	S. Miller (U.S.)
1994	Li Luo (China)	G. Gogean (Rom.)	D. Kochetkova (Russia)
1995	S. Chorkina (Russia)	S. Amanar (Rom.)* L. Podkopayeva (Ukr.)*	G. Gogean (Rom.)
1996	**S. Chorkina (Russia)* Ye. Piskun (Bela.)***	**G. Gogean (Rom.)**	**G. Gogean (Rom.)* Kui Yuanyuan (China)***

*Tied.

Golf Club in Lincoln, Neb. Victory in the women's world amateur team championship in the Philippines went, for the first time, to South Korea. Australia won the men's title.

Prize money on the U.S. Seniors tour reached a staggering $37 million, with Jim Colbert, who regained his number one position by finishing third in the final event, and Hale Irwin each winning in excess of $1.6 million. Nine players earned more than $1 million—the same number as on the main circuit.   (MARK GARROD)

GYMNASTICS

The world championships of artistic gymnastics, held in Puerto Rico on April 15–21, 1996, garnered relatively little attention in its role as a lead-in to the Centennial Olympic Games in Atlanta, Ga., in July–

ICE HOCKEY

North America. When the team was the Quebec Nordiques, its prospects were good on the ice, but the financial problems that resulted from playing in one of the National Hockey League's (NHL's) smallest cities became overwhelming. Therefore, before the 1995–96 season the team was sold and moved to Denver, where it became known as the Colorado Avalanche. The payoff was immediate, a championship in the Stanley Cup play-offs.

The NHL's 26 teams each played 82 games from October 1995 to April 1996. The dominant team, by far, was the Detroit Red Wings. Under Coach Scotty Bowman they won 62 games, the most ever by an NHL team, against 13 losses and 7 ties. They lost only 3 of 41 games at home and only 3 of 28 against division rivals. Though best known for offense, they allowed the fewest goals in the league, an average of 2.2 a game.

The division winners were Detroit with 131 points, Colorado (104), the Philadelphia Flyers (103), and the Pittsburgh Penguins (102). They led 16 teams into the play-offs, including the Montreal Canadiens but not the defending champion New Jersey Devils. Montreal, after missing the play-offs the previous year for the first time since 1970, lost the first five games of the season. General manager Serge Savard and Coach Jacques Demers were fired and replaced by Rejean Houle as general manager and Mario Tremblay as coach. The Canadiens improved enough to make the play-offs but lost in the first round to the New York Rangers. New Jersey won only 37 games and became the first cup champion since the 1969–70 Canadiens to miss the next year's play-offs.

In the Western Conference play-offs, Colorado eliminated the Vancouver Canucks, the Chicago Blackhawks, and Detroit, all by four games to two. In the East the Florida Panthers, a third-year expansion team, defeated the Boston Bruins (4–1), Philadelphia (4–2), and Pittsburgh (4–3).

Colorado, coached by Marc Crawford, was favoured in the finals. It had big, strong defensemen, and it had a play-off-hardened goalie in Patrick Roy, who had forced a December trade from Montreal. Florida, in its first play-offs, was coached by Doug MacLean, in his first NHL head coach position. His team played a disciplined, tight-checking game and had a strong goalie in John Vanbiesbrouck.

The four-of-seven-game finals lasted only from June 4 through 11 as Colorado won in a four-game sweep by scores of 3–1, 8–1, 3–2, and 1–0. The last game went to triple overtime before Uwe Krupp, a Colorado defenseman from Germany, scored on a slap shot from just inside the blue line. Centre Joe Sakic, the Colorado captain, won the Conn Smythe Trophy as the series' most valuable player.

Mario Lemieux, the Pittsburgh centre, returned after a year off following back surgery and radiation treatment for Hodgkin's disease. Although he missed 12 games, he led the league in scoring (161 points), goals (69), assists (92), power-play goals (31), and shorthanded goals (8). For the third time, he won the Hart Trophy as the regular season's most valuable player.

Chris Chelios of Chicago won his third Norris Trophy as the outstanding defenseman. Jim Carey of the Washington Capitals won the Vezina Trophy for goaltending, Sergey Fedorov of Detroit the Selke Trophy as best defensive forward, winger Paul Kariya of the Anaheim Mighty Ducks the Lady Byng Trophy for gentlemanly play, winger Daniel Alfredsson of the Ottawa Senators the Calder Trophy as best rookie, and Bowman the Jack Adams Award as coach of the year.

Defenseman Ray Bourque of Boston was voted to the first-string all-star team for the 12th time, tying Gordie Howe's record. The others on the team were Carey in goal, Chelios on defense, Lemieux at centre, and Jaromir Jagr of Pittsburgh and Kariya on wing.

The Americanization of this Canadian sport continued when the Winnipeg Jets were sold and moved after the season to Phoenix, Ariz. They were renamed the Coyotes.

The NHL estimated its revenue for the 1995–96 season at $920 million, up from $562 million in 1994-95. There were increases in the number of national sponsors and in the volume of national marketing. Nevertheless, although 1995–96 attendance reached a record high of 17,041,614, one-third of the teams experienced attendance problems.

The NHL Players Association reported that the average salary climbed to $892,-000, up from $733,000 the previous season and $562,000 the season before that. For some teams new arenas made profits possible. For example, after 72 years and 3,229 games at the 18,000-seat Montreal Forum, the Canadiens moved in March into the new Centre Molson, with 21,500 seats and 135 executive suites.   (FRANK LITSKY)

International. A record-equaling 39 nations, divided into four pools, contested the 60th world ice hockey championships at Vienna in May. The winner, for the first time since the breakup of the old Czechoslovakia, was the Czech Republic, which defeated Canada 4–2 in a nail-biting final.

Patrick Roy (33), goalkeeper of the Colorado Avalanche, makes a save against the Florida Panthers in the Stanley Cup finals. The Avalanche took the National Hockey League series in four straight games, becoming the first professional sports team in Denver ever to win a championship.

NHL Final Standings, 1996

EASTERN CONFERENCE					WESTERN CONFERENCE				
	Won	Lost	Tied	Points		Won	Lost	Tied	Points
Atlantic Division					**Central Division**				
*Philadelphia	45	24	13	103	*Detroit	62	13	7	131
*New York Rangers	41	27	14	96	*Chicago	40	28	14	94
*Florida	41	31	10	92	*Toronto	34	36	12	80
*Washington	39	32	11	89	*St. Louis	32	34	16	80
*Tampa Bay	38	32	12	88	*Winnipeg	36	40	6	78
New Jersey	37	33	12	86	Dallas	26	42	14	66
New York Islanders	22	50	10	54					
Northeast Division					**Pacific Division**				
*Pittsburgh	49	29	4	102	*Colorado	47	25	10	104
*Boston	40	31	11	91	*Calgary	34	37	11	79
*Montreal	40	32	10	90	*Vancouver	32	35	15	79
Hartford	34	39	9	77	Anaheim	35	39	8	78
Buffalo	33	42	7	73	Edmonton	30	44	8	68
Ottawa	18	59	5	41	Los Angeles	24	40	18	66
					San Jose	20	55	7	47

*Qualified for play-offs.

The Stanley Cup

Season	Winner	Runner-up	Games
1991–92	Pittsburgh Penguins	Chicago Blackhawks	4–0
1992–93	Montreal Canadiens	Los Angeles Kings	4–1
1993–94	New York Rangers	Vancouver Canucks	4–3
1994–95	New Jersey Devils	Detroit Red Wings	4–0
1995–96	Colorado Avalanche	Florida Panthers	4–0

World Hockey Championship

Year	Winner
1992	Sweden
1993	Russia
1994	Canada
1995	Finland
1996	Czech Republic

Relying heavily on National Hockey League players not engaged in the Stanley Cup play-offs, Canada gained an early lead in the final with a goal by Steve Thomas of the New Jersey Devils. Robert Lang, a player for the Los Angeles Kings, then scored for the Czechs in the eighth minute of the game. In the second period Lang put the Czechs ahead, but Thomas's second goal quickly tied the score. Thanks to sterling net minding by Curtis Joseph for Canada and Roman Turek for the Czechs, there were no additional goals until, with 19 seconds left and overtime looming, Martin Prochaska caught the Canadian defense napping. Jiri Kucera then added an empty-net power-play goal.

The Czechs had a more comfortable passage in the semifinals, defeating the U.S. 5–0, while Canada overcame Russia 3–2 on penalty shots following a fruitless overtime. Within three minutes of the start of the first semifinal, the Americans were humiliated by yielding two goals to the Czechs, who had one player in the penalty box. The Czechs added a power-play goal in the 14th minute and scored twice more at even strength in the final period.

The second semifinal was a classic confrontation. At the end of the first period, Russia led 2–0. Canada then gained control to tie the score in the second period. Joseph needed to be at his brilliant best in a goalless third period and in the 10-minute "sudden death" overtime that followed. In the tense penalty shoot-out, Sergey Berezin put Russia ahead. Ray Ferraro then scored for Canada, but Berezin buried his second shot before Paul Kariya and Yanic Perreault came to Canada's rescue in a 3–2 triumph.

Overtime was also required in the play-off for third place. Brian Rolston of the New Jersey Devils scored the last goal to gain a 4–3 victory for the U.S. against Russia, which earned the Americans their first medal of any colour since 1962. Next best

of the 12-nation elite Pool A teams were Sweden, Italy, Finland, Germany, Norway, and Slovakia, with France beating Austria in the relegation play-off.

Heading the tournament scorers was Perreault, with six goals and three assists, followed by Lang and two Russians, Berezin and Aleksey Yashin. The selected all-star team comprised four Czechs—Turek, defender Michal Sykora, and forwards Robert Reichel and Otakar Vejvoda—plus the Russian defender Aleksey Zhitnik and the Canadian forward Kariya.

Replacing the demoted Austria in Pool A was Latvia, which won the eight-team Pool B tournament at Eindhoven, Neth., by edging Switzerland in the final. Belarus finished one point ahead of the fourth-place U.K. Poland placed fifth, and the bottom three finished even on points and needed to be separated by the results of the games between them, leaving Denmark and The Netherlands as survivors and Japan relegated to Pool C. Kazakstan, winner of the eight-nation Pool C, moved up to Pool B. Croatia finished last in Pool C and exchanged places with Lithuania, the host-nation winner of Pool D, which also contained eight teams after three others had failed to qualify.

Jokerit Helsinki of Finland retained its title in the 19th European Cup, open to national club champions, beating Cologne of Germany in the final by penalty shots after a scoreless overtime. HV-71 from Jönköping, Swed., took the bronze medal.

The expansion of the International Ice Hockey Federation continued with the approval of Singapore as its 52nd member. The IIHF announced an ambitious new European League to begin in the 1996–97 season, contested by 20 clubs from 12 nations. A new English rink at Manchester, with a national record crowd capacity of 17,000, enabled the nomination of its local team, Manchester Storm, to represent the U.K.

(HOWARD BASS)

ICE SKATING

Figure Skating. In 1996 international figure skating introduced some notable changes. Contested during the year was the first Champions Series, which consisted of five prestigious competitions and a final tournament in Paris. This, as well as the world and European championships, for the first time offered the considerable added incentive of lucrative prize money.

The world championships alone awarded 144 skaters $937,500. The prizes went to the top 24 finishers in each event, ranging from $50,000 for the men's and women's winners and $75,000 for the leading pair and the leading ice dance couple to $2,500 for the 24th-place singles skaters and $3,750 for the 24th-place partnerships.

Held in Edmonton, Alta., the world championships provided a worthy climax to a momentous winter. The men's competition, arguably the best ever, ended with an absorbing duel between Todd Eldredge of the U.S., the runner-up in 1995, and Ilya Kulik of Russia, the 1995 champion of Europe; each landed eight triple jumps. The nine judges split six-three in Eldredge's favour. The fast-rising U.S. skater Rudy Galindo finished third, just ahead of the defending champion, Elvis Stojko of Canada. Stojko thrilled the crowd with an awesome, still-rare quadruple toe-loop jump that he might not have risked had victory not already been out of reach.

Michelle Kwan gave the U.S. a second gold medal, gaining two sixes and seven 5.9s to edge the defending champion, Chen Lu of China. Irina Slutskaya of Russia finished third. Kwan, at 15, became the third youngest champion, behind Norway's Sonja Henie (14; 1927) and Oksana Baiul of Ukraine (15; 1993).

As in the men's competition, the crowd

World Figure Skating Champions—Men

Year	Winner
1992	V. Petrenko (UT)
1993	K. Browning (Can.)
1994	E. Stojko (Can.)
1995	E. Stojko (Can.)
1996	T. Eldredge (U.S.)

World Figure Skating Champions—Women

Year	Winner
1992	K. Yamaguchi (U.S.)
1993	O. Baiul (Ukr.)
1994	Y. Sato (Japan)
1995	Chen Lu (China)
1996	M. Kwan (U.S.)

World Figure Skating Champions—Pairs

Year	Winners
1992	N. Mishkutenok, A. Dmitriyev (UT)
1993	I. Brasseur, L. Eisler (Can.)
1994	Ye. Shishkova, V. Naumov (Russia)
1995	R. Kovarikova, R. Novotny (Cz.Rep.)
1996	M. Yeltsova, A. Bushkov (Russia)

World Ice Dancing Champions

Year	Winners
1992	M. Klimova, S. Ponomarenko (UT)
1993	M. Usova, A. Zhulin (Russia)
1994	O. Grichuk, Ye. Platov (Russia)
1995	O. Grichuk, Ye. Platov (Russia)
1996	O. Grichuk, Ye. Platov (Russia)

Fifteen-year-old Michelle Kwan (below) of the U.S. shows the form that helped her win the women's world figure skating championship in March in Edmonton, Alta. U.S. skater Todd Eldredge (right), who won the men's title, executes a jump in his program. It was the first time since 1986 that the U.S. had gained both the men's and the women's singles titles.

PHOTOGRAPHS, JAMIE SQUIRE—ALLSPORT

The pairs title was captured by Marina Yeltsova and Andrey Bushkov of Russia, who had placed third in 1994. They defeated the 1995 European champions from Germany, Mandy Wötzel and Ingo Steuer, who had led after the initial round. The Russian duo of Oksana Grichuk and Yevgeny Platov scored their third straight ice dance victory, while another Russian entry, Anjelika Krylova and Oleg Ovsiannikov, finished second.

The inaugural Champions Series confirmed the season's overall women's supremacy of Kwan, with Slutskaya placing second. Winter-long consistency was also shown by Grichuk and Platov in the ice dance as they again thwarted runners-up Krylova and Ovsiannikov. Aleksey Urmanov of Russia outpointed Stojko to win the men's title. The pairs championship went to Yevgeniya Shishkova and Vadim Naumov, ahead of their fellow Russians Yeltsova and Bushkov.

Speed Skating. The season was as revolutionary for speed skaters as for their figure counterparts. Increased amounts of prize money were introduced at all major contests. In the world championships cash was earned by the top 12 men and women, ranging from $25,000 for each all-around champion (over four distances) to $1,000 for those in 12th place.

A new event was successfully launched at Hamar, Nor.—world single-distance championships with separate titles for the winners over five men's and five women's distances, as in the Olympic Games. The men's champions were Hiroyasu Shimizu of Japan (500 m), Sergey Klevchenya of Russia (1,000 m), and three Dutch racers, Ids Postma (5,000 m), Jeroen Straathof (1,500 m), and Gianni Romme (10,000 m). The most successful woman was Annamarie Thomas of The Netherlands (1,000 m and 1,500 m), the other victors being Svetlana Zhurova of Russia (500 m) and two Germans, Gunda Niemann (3,000 m) and Claudia Pechstein (5,000 m).

The aforementioned tournament supplemented the long-established world championships held in 1996 at Inzell, Ger. Rintje Ritsma of The Netherlands and Niemann

witnessed another tense rivalry, the Kwan-Chen duel also dividing the judges by a vote of six to three, with perhaps Kwan's seven triple jumps to Chen's six deciding the issue. For the first time in a women's championship, both winner and runner-up received two maximum scores of six for presentation.

World Ice Speed-Skating Records Set in 1996 on Major Tracks

Event	Name	Country	Time
MEN			
500 m	Hiroyasu Shimizu	Japan	35.39 sec
1,000 m	Manabu Horii	Japan	1 min 11.67 sec
1,500 m	Hiroyuki Noake	Japan	1 min 50.61 sec
3,000 m	Bob de Jong	Neth.	3 min 53.06 sec

World Ice Speed-Skating Records Set in 1996 on Short Tracks

Event	Name	Country	Time
MEN			
500 m	Mirko Vuillermin	Italy	42.69 sec
1,500 m	Marc Gagnon	Canada	2 min 18.16 sec
5,000-m relay	Frédéric Blackburn, Derick Campbell, Marc Gagnon, Sylvain Gagnon	Canada	7 min 02.48 sec
WOMEN			
500 m	Isabelle Charest	Canada	45.25 sec
1,500 m	Kim Yun Mi	S. Korea	2 min 25.17 sec
3,000-m relay	Marinella Canclini, Katia Colturi, Mara Urbani, Barbara Baldissera	Italy	4 min 21.50 sec

World All-Around Speed-Skating Champions—Men

Year	Winner
1992	R. Sighel (Italy)
1993	F. Zandstra (Neth.)
1994	J.O. Koss (Nor.)
1995	R. Ritsma (Neth.)
1996	**R. Ritsma (Neth.)**

World All-Around Speed-Skating Champions—Women

Year	Winner
1992	G. Niemann (Ger.)
1993	G. Niemann (Ger.)
1994	E. Hunyady (Austria)
1995	G. Niemann (Ger.)
1996	**G. Niemann (Ger.)**

World Speed-Skating Sprint Championships

Year	Men	Women
1992	I. Zhelezovsky (UT)	Ye Qiaobo (China)
1993	I. Zhelezovsky (Bela.)	Ye Qiaobo (China)
1994	D. Jansen (U.S.)	B. Blair (U.S.)
1995	Kim Yoon Man (S.Kor.)	B. Blair (U.S.)
1996	**S. Klevchenya (Russia)**	**C. Witty (U.S.)**

World Short-Track Speed-Skating Championships—Overall Winners

Year	Men	Women
1992	Ki Hoon Kim (S.Kor.)	So He Kim (S.Kor.)
1993	M. Gagnon (Can.)	N. Lambert (Can.)
1994	M. Gagnon (Can.)	N. Lambert (Can.)
1995	Chae Ji Hoon (S.Kor.)	Chun Lee Kyung (S.Kor.)
1996	**M. Gagnon (Can.)**	**Chun Lee Kyung (S.Kor.)**

retained their men's and women's crowns. Also, Canada's former Olympic rink at Calgary, Alta., was confirmed as the world's fastest when four new world men's records were set there by three Japanese and one Dutch skater (*see* Table).

In the separate world sprint championships at Heerenveen, Neth., Klevchenya gained his first men's triumph, and Christine Witty of the U.S. took the women's prize won the previous two years by her celebrated compatriot Bonnie Blair. In the world short-track championships at The Hague, Marc Gagnon of Canada recaptured the men's title, his third in four years, and Chun Lee Kyung of South Korea retained the women's crown. (HOWARD BASS)

JUDO

During the Olympic Games in Atlanta, Ga., in July 1996, David Douillet (France) won the over-95-kg championship and Djamel Bouras (France) the 78-kg title (1 kg = 2.2 lb). Kenzo Nakamura (Japan) captured gold in the 71-kg competition, and Tadahiro Nomura (Japan) finished first in the 60-kg class. Other gold medals were awarded to Pawel Nastula of Poland (95-kg), Jeon Ki Young of South Korea (86-kg), and Udo Quellmalz of Germany (65-kg). In the women's competition, gold medals were won by Sun Fuming of China (over-72-kg), Ulla Werbrouck of Belgium (72-kg), Cho Min Sun of South Korea (66-kg), Yuko Emoto of Japan (61-kg), Driulis González of Cuba (56-kg), Marie-Claire Restoux of France (52-kg), and Kye Sun Hi of North Korea (48-kg).

Japanese *judoka* dominated the Jigoro Kano Cup tournament in Tokyo in November. Winners included Yoshiharu Makishi (over-95-kg), Yoshio Nakamura (95-kg), Kazunori Kubota (78-kg), Yukimasa Nakamura (65-kg), Tadahiro Nomura (60-kg), and Shinichi Shinohara (open-weight). Kim Dae Wook of South Korea won the 71-kg competition and Vincenzo Carabetta of

(Top) In men's judo at the Olympic Games in Atlanta, Ga., in July, Kenzo Nakamura of Japan defeats Kwak Dae Sung of South Korea to win the gold in the 71-kg (156-lb) class.

(Bottom) In the women's events, Sun Fuming of China overpowers Estela Rodríguez of Cuba to take the gold medal in the over-72-kg class.

France was victorious in the 86-kg final.

During the international women's championships in December, Ryoko Tamura (Japan) won the 48-kg title for the seventh consecutive time. Olympic champions Sun, Werbrouck, and Cho were also victorious. Other winners included Yuan Hua of China (over-72-kg), and two Japanese: Eiko Sugimura (56 kg) and Kazue Nagai (52 kg).

(ANDY ADAMS)

LAWN BOWLS

The World Bowls Board, representing the interests of 35 countries, joined with the World Indoor Bowls Council and the newly formed Professional Bowls Association to launch the World Bowls Tour on Jan. 1, 1997. Its goal was to secure increased television coverage and sponsorship in order to produce more benefits for the game.

In 1996 the world championships—contested every four years—were held. The men's events took place at Adelaide, Australia, in March, and the women's were held at Leamington Spa, Eng., in August. England's Tony Allcock retained his 1992 world singles title, defeating Jeff Rabkin (Israel) 25–15. The other men's gold medals were won by Ireland in the pairs, Scotland in the triples and England in the fours. Scotland won the team title.

South Seas (Norfolk Island) competitor Carmen Anderson captured the women's singles, trouncing England's Wendy Line 25–9. The pairs was won by Ireland's Phillis Nolan and Margaret Johnston for a record third successive time. South Africa beat Australia in the triples, but this result was reversed in the fours.

Scottish dominance was apparent at the world indoor championships at Preston, Eng., in February as David Gourlay, Jr., overcame fellow Scot Hugh Duff in the final. The pairs title went to Kelvin Kerkow and Ian Schuback of Australia, who defeated England's Gary Smith and Andy Thomson in a thrilling five-set encounter. (DONALD J. NEWBY)

RODEO

Bull riding competitions continued to have a huge impact on rodeo in 1996. Professional Bull Riders, an organization based in Colorado Springs, Colo., held its finals at the MGM Grand Hotel in Las Vegas, Nev., October 11–13, with a prize purse of $1 million. The winner was Ronny Kitchens of Kemp, Texas. The PBR's rival organization, Bull Riders Only, also planned to put on a $1 million finals event, in April 1997, slated to be televised live on the Fox television network.

At the Professional Rodeo Cowboys Association's (PRCA's) season-ending National Finals Rodeo (NFR), held Dec. 6–15, 1996, in Las Vegas, Joe Beaver of

World Lawn Bowls Championships		
Year	Singles	Pairs
1988	D. Bryant (Eng.)	New Zealand
1992	T. Allcock (Eng.)	Scotland
1996	T. Allcock (Eng.)	Ireland
Year	Triples	Fours	Team
1988	New Zealand	Ireland	England
1992	Israel	Scotland	Scotland
1996	Scotland	England	Scotland

World Judo Championships—Men				
Year	Open weights	60 kg	65 kg	71 kg
1987	N. Ogawa (Japan)	Kim Jae Yup (S.Kor.)	Y. Yamamoto (Japan)	M. Swain (U.S.)
1989	N. Ogawa (Japan)	A. Totikashvili (U.S.S.R.)	D. Becanovic (Yugos.)	T. Koga (Japan)
1991	N. Ogawa (Japan)	T. Koshino (Japan)	G. Quellmalz (Ger.)	T. Koga (Japan)
1993	R. Kubacki (Poland)	R. Sonada (Japan)	Y. Nakamura (Japan)	Yung Chung Hoon (S.Kor.)
1995	D. Douillet (Fr.)	N. Ojeguine (Russia)	U. Quellmalz (Ger.)	D. Hideshima (Japan)
Year	78 kg	86 kg	95 kg	+ 95 kg
1987	H. Okada (Japan)	F. Canu (Fr.)	H. Sugai (Japan)	G. Verichev (U.S.S.R.)
1989	Kim Bying Ju (S.Kor.)	F. Canu (Fr.)	K. Kurtanidze (U.S.S.R.)	N. Ogawa (Japan)
1991	D. Lascau (Ger.)	H. Okada (Japan)	S. Traineau (Fr.)	S. Kosorotov (U.S.S.R.)
1993	Chun Ki Young (S.Kor.)	Y. Nakamura (Japan)	A. Kovacs (Hung.)	D. Douillet (Fr.)
1995	T. Koga (Japan)	Chun Ki Young (S.Kor.)	P. Nastula (Pol.)	D. Douillet (Fr.)

World Judo Championships—Women				
Year	Open weights	48 kg	52 kg	56 kg
1987	Fengliang Gao (China)	Zhang Yun Li (China)	S. Rendle (U.K.)	C. Arnaud (Fr.)
1989	E. Rodríguez (Cuba)	K. Briggs (U.K.)	S. Rendle (U.K.)	C. Arnaud (Fr.)
1991	Zhuang Xiaoyan (China)	C. Nowak (Fr.)	A. Giungi (Italy)	M. Blasco (Spain)
1993	B. Maksymow (Poland)	R. Tamura (Japan)	R. Verdecia (Cuba)	N. Fairbrother (U.K.)
1995	M. van der Lee (Neth.)	R. Tamura (Japan)	M.-C. Restoux (Fr.)	D. González (Cuba)
Year	61 kg	66 kg	72 kg	+72 kg
1987	D. Bell (U.K.)	A. Schreiber (W.Ger.)	I. de Kok (Neth.)	Fengliang Gao (China)
1989	C. Fleury (Fr.)	E. Pierantozzi (Italy)	I. Berghmans (Belg.)	Fengliang Gao (China)
1991	F. Eickoff (Ger.)	E. Pierantozzi (Italy)	Kim Mi Jong (S.Kor.)	Moon Ji Yoon (S.Kor.)
1993	G. van de Cavaye (Belg.)	Cho Min Sun (S.Kor.)	Leng Chin Hui (China)	J. Hagn (Ger.)
1995	Jung Sung Sook (S.Kor.)	Cho Min Sun (S.Kor.)	C. Luna (Cuba)	A. Seriese (Neth.)

Men's World All-Around Rodeo Championship			
Year	Winner	Year	Winner
1991	T. Murray	1994	T. Murray
1992	T. Murray	1995	J. Beaver
1993	T. Murray	**1996**	**J. Beaver**

Huntsville, Texas, successfully defended his world champion all-around-cowboy title, earning a combined $166,103 in team roping and calf roping during the 1995–96 season. (World titles in rodeo are determined by season earnings.)

Bareback rider Mark Garrett of Spearfish, S.D., scored an upset in the final round of the NFR when three riders (including his brother, four-time world champion Marvin Garrett) failed to qualify their last rides. He earned an NFR record of 786 points on 10 broncs to win the competition. Garrett also gained the world championship with $139,868 in season earnings, including $78,517 at the NFR.

In steer wrestling, Chad Bedell of Jensen, Utah, captured his first world championship, earning $40,727 at the NFR to finish the season with $120,784. Billy Etbauer of Edmond, Okla., one of three saddle bronc riding brothers competing at the NFR, captured his second world title in his specialty event with $190,257. At the NFR he placed first overall, riding 10 broncs for a combined 805 points. His earnings at the rodeo were $66,304.

Calf roper Fred Whitfield of Hockley, Texas, maintained his late-season lead in the world standings through the NFR to capture his third world championship. The defending titleholder going into the 10-round competition, Whitfield won two early rounds to ensure his championship victory. His total earnings for the year were $155,336.

Bull rider Terry West of Henryetta, Okla., became the first world champion in two professional rodeo associations. The former two-time International Professional Rodeo Association Bull Rider of the Year claimed his first championship in the larger PRCA. West rose from 10th place in the world standings going into the NFR to first place on the strength of $70,807 won in Las Vegas. His season earnings were $125,425.

Other world champions for 1996 were: Kristie Peterson, Elbert, Colo., barrel racing, $170,083; Steve Purcella, Hereford, Texas, and Steve Northcott, Odessa, Texas, team roping, $91,069 each; and Mike Matt, Billings, Mont., wrangler bullfighting, $46,018. (GAVIN FORBES EHRINGER)

ROWING

Rowing underwent a significant change in 1996, with alterations in the 14 events contested in the Olympic Games. Three of the heavyweight events that had been a traditional part of the Olympics for the previous 20 years—the men's coxed pairs and coxed fours and the women's fours—were replaced by lightweight classes, and for the first time all entrants had to qualify for

The British team (rear) of Matthew Pinsent (left) and Steven Redgrave row to victory in the men's coxless pairs at the Olympic Games. Redgrave became the first rower to win four Olympic gold medals and only the fifth athlete ever to have won gold medals at four consecutive Olympics.

The Diamond Challenge Sculls		
Year	Winner	Min:s
1992	R. Henderson (Leander R.C.)	7:44
1993	T. Lange (Ger.)	7:39
1994	X. Muller (Grasshopper, Switz.)	7:35
1995	J. Jaanson (Parnu, Est.)	7:24
1996	**M.L.O. Vervoorn (Delft, Neth.)**	**7:42**

Grand Challenge Cup		
Year	Winner	Min:s
1992	University of London	6:04
1993	Dortmund, Ger.	6:11
1994	Charles River and San Diego	6:13
1995	San Diego Training Center	5:59
1996	**Imperial College and Queens Tower**	**6:11**

World Rowing Championships—Men

Year	Single sculls	Min:s	Double sculls	Min:s	Coxed pairs	Min:s
1992	T. Lange (Ger.)	6:51.40	S. Hawkins, P. Antonie (Austl.)	6:17.32	J. Searle, G. Searle (U.K.)	6:49.83
1993	D. Porter (Can.)	6:59.03	Y. Lamarque, S. Barathay (Fr.)	6:24.69	J. Searle, G. Searle (U.K.)	7:01.50
1994	A. Willims (Ger.)	6:46.33	R. Thorsen, L. Bjoenness (Nor.)	6:08.33	T. Frankovic, I. Boraska (Croatia)	6:42.16
1995	I. Cop (Slov.)	6:52.93	L. Christensen, M. Haldbo-Hansen (Den.)	6:17.01	L. Sartori, G. DeStabile (Italy)	7:35.11
1996	X. Müller (Switz.)	6:44.85	D. Tizzano, A. Abbagnale (Italy)	6:16.90	Y. Schulte, L. Prevot (Fr.)	7:18.26

Year	Coxless pairs	Min:s	Coxed fours	Min:s	Coxless fours	Min:s	Eights	Min:s
1992	S. Redgrave, M. Pinsent (U.K.)	6:27.72	Romania	5:59.37	Australia	5:55.04	Canada	5:29.53
1993	S. Redgrave, M. Pinsent (U.K.)	6:37.11	Romania	6:14.64	France	6:04.54	Germany	5:37.08
1994	S. Redgrave, M. Pinsent (U.K.)	6:18.65	Romania	6:06.69	Italy	5:48.44	United States	5:24.50
1995	S. Redgrave, M. Pinsent (U.K.)	6:28.11	United States	6:37.50	Italy	5:58.28	Germany	5:53.40
1996	S. Redgrave, M. Pinsent (U.K.)	6:20.09	Romania	6:25.74	Australia	6:06.37	Netherlands	5:42.74

World Rowing Championships—Women

Year	Single sculls	Min:s	Double sculls	Min:s	Quadruple sculls	Min:s
1992	E. Lipa (Rom.)	7:25.54	K. Boron, K. Köppen (Ger.)	6:49.00	Germany	6:20.18
1993	J. Thieme (Ger.)	7:26.00	P. Baker, B. Lawson (N.Z.)	7:03.42	China	6:21.07
1994	T. Hansen (Den.)	7:23.96	P. Baker, B. Lawson (N.Z.)	6:45.30	Germany	6:11.73
1995	M. Brandin (Swe.)	7:26.00	M. McBean, K. Heddle (Can.)	6:55.76	Germany	6:40.80
1996	Ye. Khodotovich (Bel.)	7:32.21	M. McBean, K. Heddle (Can.)	6:56.84	Germany	6:27.44

Year	Coxless pairs	Min:s	Coxless fours	Min:s	Eights	Min:s
1992	M. McBean, K. Heddle (Can.)	7:06.22	Canada	6:30.85	Canada	6:02.62
1993	C. Gosse, H. Cortin (Fr.)	7:24.74	China	6:42.06	Romania	6:18.88
1994	C. Gosse, H. Cortin (Fr.)	7:01.77	Netherlands	6:30.76	Germany	6:07.42
1995	M. Still, K. Slatter (Austl.)	7:12.70	United States	7:03.53	United States	6:50.73
1996	M. Still, K. Slatter (Austl.)	7:01.39	United States	6:49.48	Romania	6:19.73

America's Cup

Year	Winning yacht	Owner	Skipper	Losing Yacht	Owner
1983	*Australia II* (Australia)	A. Bond and syndicate	J. Bertrand	*Liberty* (U.S.)	Maritime College at Fort Schuyler Foundation, Inc.
1987	*Stars & Stripes* (U.S.)	Sail America syndicate	D. Conner	*Kookaburra III* (Australia)	K. Parry and syndicate
1988	*Stars & Stripes* (U.S.)	Sail America syndicate	D. Conner	*New Zealand* (New Zealand)	M. Fay
1992	*America³* (U.S.)	America³ Foundation	B. Koch	*Il Moro di Venezia* (Italy)	Compagnia della Vela di Venezia
1995	*Black Magic* (N.Z.)	P. Blake and Team New Zealand	R. Coutts	*Young America*	Pact 95 syndicate

Bermuda Race

Year	Winning yacht	Owner
1988	*Congere*	B. Koeppel
1990	*Denali*	L. Huntington
1992	*Constellation* ·	U.S. Naval Academy
1994	*Gaylark*	K. Smith
1996	*Boomerang*	**G. Coumantaros**

Transpacific Race

Year	Winning yacht	Owner
1987	*Merlin*	D. Campion
1989	*Silver Bullet*	J. DeLaura
1991	*Chance*	R. McNulty
1993	*Silver Bullet*	J. DeLaura
1995	*Merlin*	D. Sinclair

Admiral's Cup

Year	Winning team
1987	New Zealand
1989	United Kingdom
1991	France
1993	Germany
1995	Italy

the right to compete. The 10 non-Olympic events were included in the subsequent world championships in Strathclyde, Scot., where the International Rowing Federation announced plans to reduce the number of events in future championships by five. As a result, sculling events would outnumber rowing events 12–7.

Ten nations shared the honours in the Olympic competition at Lake Lanier in Georgia. All but 2 of the 14 finals were won by less than three seconds. Australia (men's coxless fours), Germany (men's and women's quadruple sculls), and the United Kingdom (men's coxless pairs) retained their 1992 Olympic gold medals. In one of the closest races Australia won in coxless fours by 0.66 sec. Xeno Müller triumphed by only 0.45 sec to become the first men's single sculls winner from Switzerland.

The British coxless pair led from the start to retain their title by 0.93 sec; the bowman, Steven Redgrave (*see* BIOGRAPHIES), thereby became the first oarsman to win four Olympic gold medals. The Netherlands won the eights for the first time, and Italy accomplished the same feat in double sculls. In the new lightweight classes, Denmark won the coxless fours by 0.55 sec, while Switzerland gained a second success in the double sculls.

In the women's events Australia had the closest win, the coxless pairs by 0.39 sec. Romania gained gold medals in eights and the new lightweight double sculls, while Canada (double sculls) and Belarus (single sculls) won the other classes.

In the world championships the three discarded Olympic classes and the seven remaining lightweight events were won by seven nations. Denmark, Romania, and the United States each won twice, while the remaining titles were taken by China, France, Germany, and Italy.

In the world junior championships, also contested at Strathclyde, Germany won three titles; Australia, Romania, and Slovenia took two each; and Canada, Denmark, The Netherlands, Poland, and Russia each won one.

At the Henley Royal Regatta in England, there were nine overseas winners. In eights, trophies went to the Neptune Rowing Club, Ireland (Thames Cup), Yale University (Temple Cup), and Brentwood College, Canada (Princess Elizabeth Cup). A second U.S. winner was the Potomac Boat Club (Double Sculls Cup), and Germany also won twice with the Berliner Rowing Club in coxed fours (Prince Philip Cup)

and the Mainzer & Neusser Rowing Club in quadruple sculls (Queen Mother Cup). Wiking of Austria triumphed in coxless pairs (Silver Goblets), while The Netherlands was also a double winner with W.S.R. Argo in coxless fours (Visitor's Cup) and M.L.O. Vervoorn capturing the Diamond Challenge Sculls. In the 142nd University Boat Race, Cambridge won by 2¾ lengths to increase its lead over Oxford to 73–68 in the series.   (K.L. OSBORNE)

SAILING (YACHTING)

As 1995 drew to a close, the classic Australian Sydney–Hobart ocean race ended. The winning boat was the ILC 41 *Terra Firma,* designed by Iain Murray and Associates and owned by Scott Carlile and Dean Wilson; they were also top scorers in the Southern Cross Cup series. Second place went to the Nelson/Marek 43 *Quest,* skippered by Bob Steel, and third was taken by *Stewart Toyota,* a Bashford/Howison 41 owned by Ray Roberts and Ian Bashford. The Southern Cross team series was won by the Australian yachts *Ragamuffin, Sycorax,* and *AMP Wild Oats.*

The death of Bashford of Australia at the age of 37 was a loss to the yacht-racing world. He had gained considerable success in many different classes on the water and

World Class Boat Champions, 1996

Class	Winner	Country
Etchells	Adam Gosling	U.K.
Flying Dutchman	Ulf Lehmann	Germany
Finn	Philippe Presti	France
Fireball	Colin Goodman	U.K.
470 (men)	Benny Kouwenhoven	Netherlands
470 (women)	Theresa Zabell	Spain
505	Paul Towers	U.K.
Hobie 16 (men)	Claudio Cardoso	Brazil
International MOTH	Nick Spence	U.K.
J/24	Chris Larson	U.S.
Laser	Robert Scheidt	Brazil
Enterprise	Mike McNamara	U.K.
Hobie 16 (women)	Kerry Ireland	Australia
OK Dinghy	Christian Carlsson	Sweden
Soling	George Shaiduoko	Russia
Solo	Jamie Lea	U.K.
Star	Enrico Chieffi	Italy
Topper	Neil Marsden	U.K.
Tornado	Roland Gaebler	Germany

also ran one of Australia's most successful yacht-building yards, exporting his products to many parts of the world.

The Europe 1 STAR single-handed race across the Atlantic was marked by both disasters and records. The victory went to Loick Peyron of France in his 18.3-m (60-ft)

Lee Lai Shan of Hong Kong competes in the Mistral class (boardsailing) yachting event at the Olympic Games, held off the coast of Georgia. The 1994 world champion took first place in the competition, becoming the first athlete from Hong Kong ever to win an Olympic gold medal.

PASCAL GUYOT—AFP

MIKE POWELL—ALLSPORT

Atle Skaardal of Norway expresses his excitement at having won the men's supergiant slalom in the world Alpine championships, held in Sierra Nevada, Spain, in February. Although the 29-year-old had been a well-known skier for more than a decade, the win was his first world title.

trimaran *Fujicolor* in a time of 10 days 10 hr 5 min. Earlier, however, the two leading trimarans had capsized as their crews strove to break the eight-year-old race record. Francis Joyon in *Banque Populaire* capsized almost in sight of the finish; if he had finished, he would have set a new record. He had said earlier, "The slightest error can prove fatal in such a race," and a moment of inattention was enough. Peter Crowther, competing for his fifth time in this event, had to take to his life raft when his yacht sank. He had just enough time to send out a Mayday call to alert the emergency services. A Royal Air Force aircraft spotted him in his raft and coordinated his rescue by bulk carrier, which picked him up and took him to Halifax, N.S. Other outstanding performances were by Gerry Roufs in his 18.3-m (60-ft) monohull *Groupe LG2*, who finished only 26 hours after the last 18.3-m trimaran, and Giovanni Soldini in his 15.2-m (50 ft) monohull *Telecom Italia*, who finished 3½ hours after Roufs to set a new Class II record by 39 hr 22 min.

Sailors at the Olympic Games, contested off the coast of Georgia, experienced much of the unpredictable weather that many had forecast as difficult light winds were intermingled with tropical storms of intense ferocity. For the most part, however, the medals were won by the prerace favourites, with the exception of the U.S. competitors, who were expected to be medal contenders in most classes but managed only two bronze medals. One of the most outstanding winners was Lee Lai Shan, who competed in the women's Mistral class and won Hong Kong's first sailing Olympic medal.

(ADRIAN JARDINE)

SKIING

Alpine Skiing. The world championships, postponed for the first time the previous year because of a lack of snow at Sierra Nevada, Spain, were successfully held at the same place in February 1996. After a decade of trying, Alberto Tomba of Italy won gold medals in both the slalom and giant slalom,

Alpine World Cup		
Year	Men	Women
1992	P. Accola (Switz.)	P. Kronberger (Austria)
1993	M. Girardelli (Lux.)	A. Wachter (Austria)
1994	K.A. Aamodt (Nor.)	V. Schneider (Switz.)
1995	A. Tomba (Italy)	V. Schneider (Switz.)
1996	L. Kjus (Nor.)	K. Seizinger (Ger.)

World Alpine Skiing Championships—Slalom						
Year	Men's slalom	Men's giant slalom	Men's supergiant	Women's slalom	Women's giant slalom	Women's supergiant
1992	F.C. Jagge (Nor.)	A. Tomba (Italy)	K.A. Aamodt (Nor.)	P. Kronberger (Austria)	P. Wiberg (Swed.)	D. Compagnoni (Italy)
1993	K.A. Aamodt (Nor.)	K.A. Aamodt (Nor.)	not held	K. Buder (Austria)	C. Merle (Fr.)	K. Seizinger (Ger.)
1994	T. Stangassinger (Austria)	M. Wasmeier (Ger.)	M. Wasmeier (Ger.)	V. Schneider (Switz.)	D. Compagnoni (Italy)	D. Roffe-Steinrotter (U.S.)
1995	not held					
1996	A. Tomba (Italy)	A. Tomba (Italy)	A. Skaardal (Nor.)	P. Wiberg (Swed.)	D. Compagnoni (Italy)	I. Kostner (Italy)

World Alpine Skiing Championships—Downhill		
Year	Men	Women
1992	P. Ortlieb (Austria)	K. Lee-Gartner (Can.)
1993	U. Lehmann (Switz.)	K. Pace (Can.)
1994	T. Moe (U.S.)	K. Seizinger (Ger.)
1995	not held	
1996	P. Ortlieb (Austria)	P. Street (U.S.)

World Alpine Skiing Championships—Combined		
Year	Men	Women
1992	J. Polig (Italy)	P. Kronberger (Austria)
1993	L. Kjus (Nor.)	M. Vogt (Ger.)
1994	L. Kjus (Nor.)	P. Wiberg (Swed.)
1995	not held	
1996	M. Girardelli (Lux.)	P. Wiberg (Swed.)

World Nordic Skiing Championships—Men

Year	10-km	15-km	30-km	50-km	Relay
1992	V. Ulvang (Nor.)	B. Daehlie (Nor.)	V. Ulvang (Nor.)	B. Daehlie (Nor.)	Norway
1993	S. Sivertsen (Nor.)	B. Daehlie (Nor.)	B. Daehlie (Nor.)	T. Mogren (Swed.)	Norway
1994	B. Daehlie (Nor.)	B. Daehlie (Nor.)	T. Alsgaard (Nor.)	V. Smirnov (Kazak.)	Italy
1995	V. Smirnov (Kazak.)	V. Smirnov (Kazak.)	V. Smirnov (Kazak.)	S. Fauner (Italy)	Norway
1996	**not held**				

World Nordic Skiing Championships—Women

Year	5-km	10-km	15-km	30-km	Relay
1992	M. Lukkarinen (Fin.)	L. Yegorova (UT)	L. Yegorova (UT)	S. Belmondo (Italy)	Unified Team
1993	L. Lazhutina (Russia)	S. Belmondo (Italy)	Ye. Vyalbe (Russia)	S. Belmondo (Italy)	Russia
1994	L. Yegorova (Russia)	L. Yegorova (Russia)	M. Di Centa (Italy)	M. Di Centa (Italy)	Russia
1995	L. Lazhutina (Russia)	L. Lazhutina (Russia)	L. Lazhutina (Russia)	Ye. Vyalbe (Russia)	Russia
1996	**not held**				

World Nordic Skiing Championships—Ski Jump

Year	90-m hill	120-m hill	Team jump	Combined	Team combined
1992	E. Vettori (Austria)	T. Nieminen (Fin.)	Finland	F. Guy (Fr.)	Japan
1993	M. Harada (Japan)	E. Bredeson (Nor.)	Norway	K. Ogiwara (Japan)	Japan
1994	E. Bredesen (Nor.)	J. Weissflog (Ger.)	Germany	F.-B. Lundberg (Nor.)	Japan
1995	T. Okabe (Japan)	T. Ingebrigtsen (Nor.)	Finland	F.-B. Lundberg (Nor.)	Japan
1996	**not held**				

Nordic World Cup

Year	Men	Women
1992	B. Daehlie (Nor.)	Ye. Vyalbe (Russia)
1993	B. Daehlie (Nor.)	L. Yegorova (Russia)
1994	V. Smirnov (Kazakh.)	M. Di Centa (Italy)
1995	B. Daehlie (Nor.)	Ye. Vyalbe (Russia)
1996	**B. Daehlie (Nor.)**	**M. Di Centa (Italy)**

Alberto Tomba (top) flies down the slopes in the world Alpine championships at Sierra Nevada, Spain. The Italian skier dominated the men's competition by taking both the slalom and the giant slalom. Pernilla Wiberg (bottom) of Sweden won both the women's slalom and the women's combined.

duplicating his double at the 1988 Winter Olympics in Calgary, Alta. Marc Girardelli of Luxembourg added yet another triumph to his impressive list of career successes by clinching his third combined title. Winner of a record five World Cups and at least one medal in every world championship since 1985, Girardelli achieved a remarkable triumph of nerve and determination in an injury-ridden career that included 13 knee operations.

Atle Skaardal, a prominent Norwegian skier for more than a decade without winning a world title, finally succeeded in the supergiant slalom (super G) just four days short of his 30th birthday. Patrick Ortlieb of Austria won a disappointing downhill that favoured the first dozen to descend, after which the course became so slushy that the later starters had no chance.

Sharing Tomba's dominance was Sweden's Pernilla Wiberg, affirming her status as the leading women's all-rounder by adding the slalom title to that of the combined event. Deborah Compagnoni, despite only six weeks of preparation following a knee operation, claimed another title for Italy in the women's giant slalom. When Isolde Kostner triumphed in the super G, Italians had won 4 of the tournament's 10 titles. Kostner's and Compagnoni's victories were the first for Italian women since 1932. Picabo Street (*see* BIOGRAPHIES) became the first U.S. skier to win the downhill.

The 30th Alpine World Cup series thrived in more plentiful snow conditions than in the previous season. Tomba, the 1995 victor, made it clear early that he had no intention of trying to do so again, switching his priority to the world championships. Lasse Kjus of Norway and Germany's Katja Seizinger won the men's and women's overall titles, respectively, each for the first time.

Hard-pressed all the way by the Austrian runner-up, Günther Mader, Kjus won races in three disciplines but did not achieve the top ranking in any. Michael von Grünigen of Switzerland headed the giant slalom list and Skaardal the super G, with Luc Alphand of France winning the downhill and his compatriot Sébastien Amiez the slalom. In the women's disciplines Seizinger was the highest scorer in the super G, Street in the downhill, Elfi Eder of Austria in the slalom, and Martina Ertl of Germany in the giant slalom.

Nordic Skiing. Unlike the Alpine competitors, the Nordic skiers did not have a world championship tournament in 1996 and thus were able to focus fully on the 17th Nordic World Cup. In that competition Bjørn Dæhlie of Norway and Vladimir Smirnov of Kazakstan continued their supremacy. Dæhlie retained the overall title, his fourth in five years, with runner-up Smirnov denied a chance to clinch a third success in six seasons because of illness before the final 50 km. Each won 6 of the season's 15 events.

Manuela Di Centa of Italy overcame ill health to recapture the women's trophy she had won in 1994, narrowly preventing the Russian defending champion, Yelena Vyalbe, from gaining a fourth victory in six years. The separate Combined World Cup prize was won by Knut Apeland of Norway and the Jumping World Cup resulted in a third consecutive victory for Andreas Goldberger of Austria.

Freestyle Skiing. In the 17th Freestyle World Cup series, Jon Moseley of the U.S. successfully defended the men's title in only his second full season, comfortably outpointing runner-up David Belhumeur of Canada. The women's trophy was retaken by Katherina Kubenk of Canada, with Donna Weinbrecht of the U.S. second.

(HOWARD BASS)

SQUASH

During 1996 the World Squash Federation and its 111 member nations saw their hopes that squash would be included in the Olympics Games in 2000 die. Expectations were high when Australia, a powerful squash nation, had won the right to serve as the host of the Games, but, despite its having fulfilled all the requirements of the International Olympic Committee, the sport was unable to gain a place.

England's men's team caused an upset in November 1995 by winning the men's world team championships in Cairo. In July 1996 an English men's team won the world junior men's title, also held in Cairo, beating host team Egypt two matches to one in the final.

In October the women's World Open and team championships were staged in Petaling Jaya, Malaysia. Michelle Martin (Australia) failed to gain her fourth consecutive World Open championship when she unexpectedly lost to fellow Australian Liz Irving three games to one in the quarterfinal round. Irving then was defeated three games to two in the semifinals by Cassie Jackman of England. Sarah Fitz-Gerald of Australia defeated Jackman three games to none in the final to win her first World Open championship. She became the first woman to win both the world junior and senior crowns.

In the team event, the Australian trio of Fitz-Gerald, Martin, and Irving combined to beat England two matches to one in the final and thus win the title for the third time in a row, despite Martin's again losing her match—this time to Jackman.

The competitive year concluded with the men's World Open in Karachi, Pak. Jansher Khan of Pakistan won the tournament

World Open Championship—Men	
Year	Winner
1992	Jan. Khan (Pak.)
1993	Jan. Khan (Pak.)
1994	Jan. Khan (Pak.)
1995	Jan. Khan (Pak.)
1996	Jan. Khan (Pak.)

World Open Championship—Women	
Year	Winner
1992	S. Devoy (N.Z.)
1993	M. Martin (Austl.)
1994	M. Martin (Austl.)
1995	M. Martin (Austl.)
1996	S. Fitz-Gerald (Austl.)

British Open Championship—Men	
Year	Winner
1991–92	Jan. Khan (Pak.)
1992–93	Jan. Khan (Pak.)
1993–94	Jan. Khan (Pak.)
1994–95	Jan. Khan (Pak.)
1995–96	Jan. Khan (Pak.)

British Open Championship—Women	
Year	Winner
1991–92	S. Devoy (N.Z.)
1992–93	M. Martin (Austl.)
1993–94	M. Martin (Austl.)
1994–95	M. Martin (Austl.)
1995–96	M. Martin (Austl.)

again to bring his record-breaking World Open tally to eight. In the final he defeated his primary recent challenger, Rodney Eyles of Australia, three games to one.

(ANDREW SHELLEY)

SWIMMING

For the first time in an Olympic year, no world records preceding the 1996 Olympic Games in Atlanta, Ga., were set by men in 50-m pools. One world mark was set in the women's 100-m breaststroke when Penelope Heyns of South Africa at Durban, S.Af., on March 4 bettered by 0.23 sec the previous world record of 1 min 7.69

sec set by Samantha Riley of Australia in Rome on Sept. 9, 1994. On July 21 at the Olympics, Heyns in the 100-m breaststroke preliminary further lowered her record to 1 min 7.02 sec.

The Olympics broke all records in numbers of competitors at the Georgia Tech Aquatic Center as 793 swimmers from 120 countries took part; 19 nations won medals, with 10 nations striking gold. In the total medal count the U.S. won 26 (13 gold, 11 silver, and 2 bronze), Russia 8 (4 gold, 2 silver, and 2 bronze), Hungary 6 (3 gold, 1 silver, and 2 bronze), Ireland 4 (3 gold and 1 bronze), Australia 12 (2 gold, 4 silver, and 6 bronze), and Germany 12 (5 silver and 7 bronze).

On July 20 Frederik Deburghgraeve of Belgium gained his country's first swimming Olympic gold, winning the 100-m breaststroke in 1 min 0.65 sec after setting a world record of 1 min 0.60 sec in the morning preliminaries. The previous world record was 1 min 0.95 sec by Karoly Guttler of Hungary on Aug. 3, 1993. On July 24 Denis Pankratov of Russia was timed at 52.27 sec in the 100-m butterfly to better by 0.05 sec his world record of 52.32 sec set in Vienna on Aug. 23, 1995. Pankratov's technique was noteworthy; he took an insurmountable lead of almost a body length after he kicked underwater to the 35-m mark.

On July 26 the U.S. men's 4 × 100-m medley relay team provided the U.S. with its only world-record victory. The team of Jeff Rouse of Fredericksburg, Va., Jeremy Linn of Harrisburg, Pa., Mark Henderson of Fort Washington, Md., and Gary Hall, Jr., of Paradise Valley, Ariz., was timed at 3 min 34.84 sec to better by 2.09 sec the previous mark, which was set at the 1988 Olympics and tied at the 1992 Games.

The outstanding U.S. woman swimmer was Amy Van Dyken of Englewood, Colo. She won gold medals in the 50-m freestyle and the 100-m butterfly and on two winning relays. Van Dyken's efforts helped the U.S. women win seven gold medals.

Michelle Smith (see BIOGRAPHIES) became the first woman to win an Olympic swimming medal for Ireland. Smith won golds in the 400-m freestyle and the 200-m and 400-m individual medleys and took

Penelope Heyns of South Africa swims to a new world record of 1 min 7.02 sec in the women's 100-m breaststroke in a preliminary heat at the Olympic Games. It was the second record Heyns had set in the event in 1996 and the first gold medal for a South African swimmer since 1952.

CHRIS COLE—DUOMO

World Swimming Records Set in 1996 in 50-m Pools

Event	Name	Country	Time
MEN			
100-m breaststroke	Frederik Deburghgraeve	Belgium	1 min 00.60 sec
100-m butterfly	Denis Pankratov	Russia	52.27 sec
4 × 100-m medley relay	U.S. national team (Jeff Rouse, Jeremy Linn, Mark Henderson, Gary Hall, Jr.)	U.S.	3 min 34.84 sec
WOMEN			
100-m breaststroke	Penelope Heyns	South Africa	1 min 07.46 sec
100-m breaststroke	Penelope Heyns	South Africa	1 min 07.02 sec

World Swimming Records Set in 1996 in 25-m Pools

Event	Name	Country	Time
MEN			
100-m breaststroke	Frederik Deburghgraeve	Belgium	59.02 sec
100-m individual medley	Jan Sievinen	Finland	53.10 sec
400-m individual medley	Jan Sievinen	Finland	4 min 06.03 sec
WOMEN			
50-m breaststroke	Han Xue	China	31.11 sec
50-m breaststroke	Han Xue	China	30.98 sec

Dmitry Sautin (top) performs a dive in the men's 10-m platform at the Olympic Games. He was the first Russian to win a gold medal in the event. Fu Mingxia (centre) waves as she receives her gold medal for the women's 3-m springboard competition. U.S. team members (bottom) celebrate their world-record victory in the 4 × 100-m medley.

a bronze in the 200-m butterfly. Athletes winning their countries' first-ever Olympic swimming gold medals were, in addition to Deburghgraeve (Belgium), Claudia Poll of Costa Rica in the 200-m freestyle and Danyon Loader of New Zealand in the 200-m and 400-m freestyle. Krisztina Egerszegi of Hungary became the most decorated female swimmer in Olympic history by earning seven individual medals, of which five were gold, and by winning the 200-m backstroke in three successive Olympic Games starting in 1988. The 1996 victory equaled the feat of Dawn Fraser of Australia, who was the first to win the same event in three successive Games (100-m freestyle, 1956–64).

Aleksandr Popov of Russia successfully defended his 50-m and 100-m freestyle Olympic titles. On his return to Moscow in September, Popov was stabbed in the abdomen during a street brawl. He recovered, however, and planned to train for the 2000 Olympic Games.

World records in 25-m pools were achieved on five occasions. On January 7 in Hong Kong, Han Xue of China lowered the record in the 50-m breaststroke with a time of 31.11 sec. On January 11 in Beijing, she further lowered her world mark to 30.98 sec. On February 17 in Bostogne, Belg., Deburghgraeve was timed at 59.02 sec, lowering by 0.05 sec the 100-m breaststroke record set by Philip Rogers of Australia on Aug. 27, 1993. A world record of 23.45 sec for the 50-m butterfly set at Sheffield by Mark Foster of the U.K. on Dec. 15, 1995, was finally ratified by FINA (Fédération Internationale de Natation Amateur) on March 12. On January 30 Jan Sievinen of Finland was timed at 53.10 sec for the 100-m individual medley, erasing his previous world record of 53.78 sec set in Espoo, Fin., on Nov. 21, 1992. Also during the year Sievinen was timed at 4 min 6.03 sec, lowering by 1.07 sec his previous world record in the 400-m individual medley, set at Malmö, Swed., on Feb. 9, 1992.

Diving. At the Olympics 121 divers from 40 countries, the largest entry ever, competed in four events. For the first time in 84 years, the U.S. failed to win at least one gold medal. The Chinese won 3 of the 4 golds

World Swimming and Diving Championships—Men

Freestyle

Year	50 m	100 m	200 m	400 m	1,500 m
1982		J. Woithe (E.Ger.)	M. Gross (W.Ger.)	V. Salnikov (U.S.S.R.)	V. Salnikov (U.S.S.R.)
1986	T. Jager (U.S.)	M. Biondi (U.S.)	M. Gross (W.Ger.)	R. Henkel (W.Ger.)	R. Henkel (W.Ger.)
1991	T. Jager (U.S.)	M. Biondi (U.S.)	G. Lamberti (Italy)	J. Hoffmann (Ger.)	J. Hoffmann (Ger.)
1994	A. Popov (Russia)	A. Popov (Russia)	A. Kasvio (Fin.)	K. Perkins (Austl.)	K. Perkins (Austl.)

Backstroke / Breaststroke / Butterfly

Year	Backstroke 100 m	Backstroke 200 m	Breaststroke 100 m	Breaststroke 200 m	Butterfly 100 m	Butterfly 200 m
1982	D. Richter (E.Ger.)	R. Carey (U.S.)	S. Lundquist (U.S.)	V. Davis (Can.)	M. Gribble (U.S.)	M. Gross (W.Ger.)
1986	I. Polyansky (U.S.S.R.)	I. Polyansky (U.S.S.R.)	V. Davis (Can.)	J. Szabo (Hung.)	P. Morales (U.S.)	M. Gross (W.Ger.)
1991	J. Rouse (U.S.)	M. López Zubero (Spain)	N. Rozsa (Hung.)	M. Barrowman (U.S.)	A. Nesty (Suriname)	M. Stewart (U.S.)
1994	M. López Zubero (Spain)	V. Selkov (Russia)	N. Rozsa (Hung.)	N. Rozsa (Hung.)	R. Szukala (Pol.)	D. Pankratov (Russia)

Individual medley / Team relays

Year	IM 200 m	IM 400 m	4 × 100-m freestyle	4 × 200-m freestyle	4 × 100-m medley
1982	A. Sidorenko (U.S.S.R.)	R. Prado (Braz.)	United States	United States	United States
1986	T. Darnyi (Hung.)	T. Darnyi (Hung.)	United States	East Germany	United States
1991	T. Darnyi (Hung.)	T. Darnyi (Hung.)	United States	Germany	United States
1994	J. Sievinen (Fin.)	T. Dolan (U.S.)	United States	Sweden	United States

Diving

Year	1-m springboard	3-m springboard	Platform
1982		G. Louganis (U.S.)	G. Louganis (U.S.)
1986		G. Louganis (U.S.)	G. Louganis (U.S.)
1991	E. Jongejans (Neth.)	K. Ferguson (U.S.)	Sun Shuwei (China)
1994	E. Stewart (Zimb.)	Yu Zhuocheng (China)	D. Saoutine (Russia)

World Swimming and Diving Championships—Women

Freestyle

Year	50 m	100 m	200 m	400 m	800 m
1982		B. Meineke (E.Ger.)	A. Verstappen (Neth.)	C. Schmidt (E.Ger.)	K. Linehan (U.S.)
1986	T. Costache (Rom.)	K. Otto (E.Ger.)	H. Friedrich (E.Ger.)	H. Friedrich (E.Ger.)	A. Strauss (E.Ger.)
1991	Zhuang Yong (China)	N. Haislett (U.S.)	H. Lewis (Austl.)	J. Evans (U.S.)	J. Evans (U.S.)
1994	Le Jingyi (China)	Le Jingyi (China)	F. van Almsick (Ger.)	Yang Aihua (China)	J. Evans (U.S.)

Backstroke / Breaststroke / Butterfly

Year	Backstroke 100 m	Backstroke 200 m	Breaststroke 100 m	Breaststroke 200 m	Butterfly 100 m	Butterfly 200 m
1982	K. Otto (E.Ger.)	C. Sirch (E.Ger.)	U. Geweniger (E.Ger.)	S. Varganova (U.S.S.R.)	M.T. Meagher (U.S.)	I. Geissler (E.Ger.)
1986	B. Mitchell (U.S.)	C. Sirch (E.Ger.)	S. Gerasch (E.Ger.)	S. Hörner (E.Ger.)	K. Gressler (E.Ger.)	M. Meagher (U.S.)
1991	K. Egerszegi (Hung.)	K. Egerszegi (Hung.)	L. Frame (Austl.)	E. Volkova (U.S.S.R.)	Qian Hong (China)	S. Sanders (U.S.)
1994	He Cihong (China)	He Cihong (China)	S. Riley (Austl.)	S. Riley (Austl.)	Liu Limin (China)	Liu Limin (China)

Individual medley / Team relays

Year	IM 200 m	IM 400 m	4 × 100-m freestyle	4 × 200-m freestyle	4 × 100-m medley
1982	P. Schneider (E.Ger.)	P. Schneider (E.Ger.)	East Germany		East Germany
1986	K. Otto (E.Ger.)	K. Nord (E.Ger.)	East Germany	East Germany	East Germany
1991	Lin Li (China)	Lin Li (China)	United States	Germany	United States
1994	Lu Bin (China)	Dai Guohong (China)	China	China	China

Diving

Year	1-m springboard	3-m springboard	platform
1982		M. Neyer (U.S.)	W. Wyland (U.S.)
1986		Gao Min (China)	Chen Lin (China)
1991	Gao Min (China)	Gao Min (China)	Fu Mingxia (China)
1994	Chen Lixia (China)	Tan Shuping (China)	Fu Mingxia (China)

and 5 of the 12 total medals. Their domination was the result of a national diving program that taught fundamentals to young children and then provided expert coaching and proper technique to bring the talented ones to the fore at a very early age. On July 27 in the women's 10-m platform, Fu Mingxia of China (see BIOGRAPHIES) began her quest to win both the platform and the springboard events, a feat last achieved in 1960. Fu flawlessly executed the most difficult dives from the 10-m platform, scoring 521.58 points to win the gold by more than 42 points over Annika Walter of Germany, the silver medalist. Mary Ellen Clark of the U.S. finished third.

Four days later Fu completed the sweep, winning the 3-m springboard with 547.68 points, more than 35 points over second-place Irina Lashko of Russia. Annie Pelletier of Canada won the bronze.

On July 29 in the men's 3-m springboard, Chinese divers won the gold and silver medals. Xiong Ni on his final dive, an inward 3½ somersault tuck, earned marks of 8.5 and 9 to win his first gold medal, scoring 701.46 to overtake Yu Zhuocheng with 690.93. It was the first time China had won an Olympic gold medal in men's springboard. Zhuocheng needed his final dive to squeeze past Mark Lenzi of the U.S. On August 2 Dmitry Sautin became the first Russian to win the men's 10-m platform. Trailing after the semifinal, Sautin hit his final six dives, scoring 692.34 points. His final dive, a back 1½ somersault with 3½ twists in the free position, earned marks of 10 and 9, or 9.5, the highest in the competition. Jan Hempel of Germany won the silver medal with 663.27 points, edging Xiao Hailiang of China with 658.20.

Synchronized Swimming. FINA omitted the solo and duet events, substituting team competition for the 1996 Olympics. In 1995 eight countries qualified for the Games. Each team of eight was required to perform the technical routines, which scored 35% of the total points, and a free routine, which scored 65%. In an almost perfect technical routine, the U.S. scored 99.200 points, a margin of almost 2 points over Canada. The U.S. free-routine performance then scored 9 out of a possible 10 perfect marks. The 99.720 points clinched the gold by 1.353 points over second-place Canada. Japan won the bronze with a score of 97.753.

(ALBERT SCHOENFIELD)

1996 Table Tennis World Rankings

Men	Women
1. Kong Linghui (China)	1. Deng Yaping (China)
2. Wang Tao (China)	2. Qiao Hong (China)
3. Saive, Jean-Michel (Belgium)	3. Chen Jing (Taiwan)
4. Waldner, Jan-Ove (Sweden)	4. Liu Wei (China)
5. Rosskopf, Joerg (Germany)	5. Wang Chen (China)

World Table Tennis Championships—Mixed

Year	Heydusek Prize
1987	Hui Jun, Geng Lijuan (China)
1989	Yoo Nam Kyu, Hyung Jung Hwa (S.Kor.)
1991	Wang Tao, Liu Wei (China)
1993	Wang Tao, Liu Wei (China)
1995	Wang Tao, Liu Wei (China)

Table Tennis World Cup

Year	Men
1992	Ma Wenge (China)
1993	Z. Primorac (Croatia)
1994	J.-P. Gatien (Fr.)
1995	Kong Linghui (China)
1996	Liu Guoliang (China)

Year	Women
1996	Deng Yaping (China)

World Table Tennis Championships—Men

Year	St. Bride's Vase (singles)	Iran Cup (doubles)	Swaythling Cup (team)
1989	J.-O. Waldner (Swed.)	J. Rosskopf, S. Fetzner (W.Ger.)	Sweden
1991	J. Persson (Swed.)	P. Karlsson, T. Von Scheele (Swed.)	Sweden
1993	J.-P. Gatien (Fr.)	Wang Tao, Lu Lin (China)	Sweden
1995	Kong Linghui (China)	Wang Tao, Lu Lin (China)	China

World Table Tennis Championships—Women

Year	G. Geist Prize (singles)	W.J. Pope Trophy (doubles)	Corbillon Cup (team)
1989	Qiao Hong (China)	Qiao Hong, Deng Yaping (China)	China
1991	Deng Yaping (China)	Gao Jun, Chen Zihe (China)	Korea
1993	Hyun Jung Hwa (S.Kor.)	Liu Wei, Qiao Yunping (China)	China
1995	Deng Yaping (China)	Deng Yaping, Qiao Hong (China)	China

TABLE TENNIS

The Chinese continued their domination of table tennis in 1996, collecting all the gold medals at the 1996 Olympic Games. Liu Guoliang, the men's singles runner-up in 1995, won men's singles by besting Wang Tao of China. Deng Yaping, the women's world singles champion in 1991 and 1995, successfully defended her 1992 Olympic singles title by beating Chen Jing of Chinese Taipei (Taiwan). Liu joined the 1995 world men's singles champion, Kong Linghui, to win the men's doubles, while Deng and 1993 world champion Qiao Hong retained their 1992 Olympic doubles title.

According to the International Table Tennis Federation world rankings that immediately preceded the Olympics, 18 of the top 19 women players playing in the federation's newly formed "Pro Tour" were Asian. The sole exception was the European and German national champion, Nicole Struse. Though the European men were not as outclassed, defending Olympic, 1989 world, and current European men's singles champion Jan-Ove Waldner of Sweden was upset in the Olympics by Johnny Huang of Canada, the 1996 North American champion. Sweden's 1991 world champion, Jorgen Persson, and France's 1993 world champion, Jean-Philippe Gatien, did not qualify for the round of 16 at the Olympics, while the top European seed, Jean-Michel Saive of Belgium, was ousted in the quarterfinals. None of the U.S. men and women made it through the preliminary rounds.

(TIM BOGGAN)

TENNIS

Celebrating a season of intrigue and fluctuating fortunes, Pete Sampras and Steffi Graf were the sport's preeminent players in 1996, each for the fourth consecutive year. Sampras sealed his bid for continued supremacy with a triumph at the United States Open, while Graf replicated her astounding 1995 feat of sweeping the French, Wimbledon, and U.S. Open singles titles.

Two men won their first Grand Slam tournaments; Richard Krajicek of The Netherlands and Yevgeny Kafelnikov of Russia finished first at Wimbledon and the French Open, respectively. Monica Seles, meanwhile, garnered her first major crown in three years when she opened her campaign by capturing the Australian Open, and the men's victor at Melbourne alongside Seles was Boris Becker, with his first Grand Slam triumph in five years.

Australian Open. Most knowledgeable observers had concluded that Becker's days of winning the biggest tournaments were well behind him, but he emphatically demonstrated his enduring talent and unwavering confidence by convincingly taking the first Grand Slam event of 1996. In January at Melbourne the 28-year-old German—fresh from an encouraging run in 1995 that included a final-round appearance at Wimbledon and an unexpected triumph at the ATP (Association of Tennis Professionals) Tour world championship in Frankfurt, Ger.—decisively defeated Michael Chang of the U.S. in the final 6–2, 6–4, 2–6, 6–2.

The defending champion, Andre Agassi, approaching the event in questionable condition after having missed most of the previous four months with a chest muscle injury, was ousted in a straight-set semifinal by Chang. The 1994 champion Sampras, seeking a third consecutive Grand Slam singles title, was ushered out of the tournament in startling fashion by Mark Philippoussis of Australia 6–4, 7–6, 7–6 in the third round.

Seles confronted a number of nagging injuries during the tournament, most significantly a tear in her left shoulder, but still managed to take the women's title as an injured Graf skipped the event. In the final Seles held back eighth-seeded Anke Huber of Germany 6–4, 6–1. Seles had not appeared in Melbourne since she won her third straight Australian Open in 1993.

French Open. Nearly everyone expected Thomas Muster to defend successfully the title he had so deservedly won on the clay courts in Paris the previous year, but the 28-year-old Austrian suffered a stunning fourth-round loss to Germany's Michael Stich. To place this defeat in perspective, Muster had been beaten only five times in 116 clay court matches in 1995–96. In addition, he had won five championships on that surface on his way to the French Open in 1996, including his second consecutive Italian Open title.

Richard Krajicek of The Netherlands lunges for the ball in the finals of the men's singles at Wimbledon against MaliVai Washington of the U.S. In the first Wimbledon finals ever played between two unseeded players, Krajicek defeated Washington 6–3, 6–4, 6–3 to take the title.

© RON ANGLE

Muster's departure turned the tournament upside down and gave much greater hope to many of the leading contenders. In the end, Kafelnikov took the top honour, his first major title. He toppled Stich in the final, winning 7–6, 7–5, 7–6, coming from 2–5 down in the second set and 2–4 in the third. Kafelnikov also captured the doubles alongside Daniel Vacek of the Czech Republic and thus became the first man since Ken Rosewall in 1968 to score triumphs in the singles and doubles on the red clay of Roland Garros in the same year.

The women produced one of their most compelling finals in this tournament. Ultimately, Graf rescued herself from the brink of defeat and subdued two-time former titlist Arantxa Sánchez Vicario 6–3, 6–7, 10–8 to collect a fifth French crown. In an even more suspenseful duel than the stirring Wimbledon final of 1995—won by Graf 4–6, 6–1, 7–5—the two gritty competitors pushed each other to their absolute limits. Sánchez Vicario served for the match twice in the third set, but Graf reached back with all of her remarkable resources and found a way to prevail.

Meanwhile, the tournament was a triumph on another level for Sampras. His coach and close friend Tim Gullikson had died of brain cancer three weeks before the event began, and so the 24-year-old American was still mourning and was poorly prepared. But driving himself to his physical and emotional limits, Sampras made it through to the semifinal round, in which he was halted by Kafelnikov in straight sets. The fact remained, though, that Sampras had claimed a semifinal slot for the first time at the world's most prestigious clay court tournament.

Wimbledon. After three years in a row of nearly perfect weather, the players and spectators were forced to endure countless

SHAUN BOTTERILL—ALLSPORT

Switzerland's Martina Hingis prepares a return in the semifinal against Germany's Steffi Graf at the U.S. Open. Graf won 7–5, 6–3, but Hingis had defeated her at the Italian Open.

rain delays at the Wimbledon tournament in London as inclement conditions persisted throughout the second week of the tournament. In the end, however, Krajicek did not allow anything to dampen his spirits or break his stride.

The 24-year-old, ranked number 13 in the world at the time but overlooked originally by the seeding committee because he had lost in the first round the previous two years at the All-England Club, defeated

1991 champion Stich in the round of 16 to set up a quarterfinal match with the top-seeded Sampras, who was in pursuit of a fourth consecutive championship on Centre Court. Krajicek was devastatingly potent in a 7–5, 7–6, 6–4 dismantling of Sampras, rising to the occasion with 28 aces, connecting with better backhand returns of serve and passing shots than his struggling opponent.

Krajicek had too much firepower in his game for the 27-year-old unseeded American MaliVai Washington in the final. The first African-American man to reach the title match since Arthur Ashe in 1975, Washington was taken apart 6–3, 6–4, 6–3 by a bigger and decidedly bolder player.

Graf won her seventh Wimbledon singles title with relative ease, defeating Sánchez Vicario 6–3, 7–5 in the final. Although the 24-year-old Spaniard rallied from 0–4 to 5–5 in the second set, she could not contain Graf from the backcourt.

All in all, Wimbledon was a bizarre event for many of the favourites. The 1992 champion, Agassi, his confidence already shaken by a second-round loss at the French Open, was knocked out in the opening round by Doug Flach of the U.S., who was ranked number 281 in the world. Becker, seeded second and seeking a fourth title, was engaged in a first-set tiebreaker with qualifier Neville Godwin in the third round when he injured his wrist while making an awkward forehand return of serve. He had to concede the match and was out of tournament tennis altogether for 10 weeks, missing the U.S. Open. Seles was expected to meet Graf in the final, but she bowed out in the second round against Katarina Studenikova of Slovakia, who was ranked number 59 in the world.

U.S. Open. Having garnered two Grand Slam singles titles a year for the previous three seasons (1993–95)—a feat last real-

Australian Open Tennis Championships—Singles

Year	Men	Women
1992	J. Courier (U.S.)	M. Seles (Yugos.)
1993	J. Courier (U.S.)	M. Seles (Yugos.)
1994	P. Sampras (U.S.)	S. Graf (Ger.)
1995	A. Agassi (U.S.)	M. Pierce (Fr.)
1996	**B. Becker (Ger.)**	**M. Seles (U.S.)**

Australian Open Tennis Championships—Doubles

Year	Men	Women
1992	T. Woodbridge, M. Woodforde	A. Sánchez Vicario, H. Sukova
1993	D. Visser, L. Warder	G. Fernandez, N. Zvereva
1994	P. Haarhuis, J. Eltingh	G. Fernandez, N. Zvereva
1995	J. Palmer, R. Reneberg	A. Sánchez Vicario, J. Novotna
1996	**S. Edberg, P. Korda**	**A. Sánchez Vicario, C. Rubin**

French Open Tennis Championships—Singles

Year	Men	Women
1992	J. Courier (U.S.)	M. Seles (Yugos.)
1993	S. Bruguera (Spain)	S. Graf (Ger.)
1994	S. Bruguera (Spain)	A. Sánchez Vicario (Spain)
1995	T. Muster (Austria)	S. Graf (Ger.)
1996	**Ye. Kafelnikov (Russia)**	**S. Graf (Ger.)**

French Open Tennis Championships—Doubles

Year	Men	Women
1992	J. Hlasek, M. Rosset	G. Fernandez, N. Zvereva
1993	L. Jensen, M. Jensen	G. Fernandez, N. Zvereva
1994	B. Black, J. Stark	G. Fernandez, N. Zvereva
1995	P. Haarhuis, J. Eltingh	G. Fernandez, N. Zvereva
1996	**Ye. Kafelnikov, D. Vacek**	**L. Davenport, M.J. Fernandez**

All-England (Wimbledon) Tennis Championships—Singles

Year	Men	Women
1992	A. Agassi (U.S.)	S. Graf (Ger.)
1993	P. Sampras (U.S.)	S. Graf (Ger.)
1994	P. Sampras (U.S.)	C. Martínez (Spain)
1995	P. Sampras (U.S.)	S. Graf (Ger.)
1996	**R. Krajicek (Neth.)**	**S. Graf (Ger.)**

All-England (Wimbledon) Tennis Championships—Doubles

Year	Men	Women
1992	J. McEnroe, M. Stich	G. Fernandez, N. Zvereva
1993	T. Woodbridge, M. Woodforde	G. Fernandez, N. Zvereva
1994	T. Woodbridge, M. Woodforde	G. Fernandez, N. Zvereva
1995	T. Woodbridge, M. Woodforde	A. Sánchez Vicario, J. Novotna
1996	**T. Woodbridge, M. Woodforde**	**H. Sukova, M. Hingis**

United States Open Tennis Championships—Singles

Year	Men	Women
1992	S. Edberg (Swed.)	M. Seles (Yugos.)
1993	P. Sampras (U.S.)	S. Graf (Ger.)
1994	A. Agassi (U.S.)	A. Sánchez Vicario (Spain)
1995	P. Sampras (U.S.)	S. Graf (Ger.)
1996	**P. Sampras (U.S.)**	**S. Graf (Ger.)**

United States Open Tennis Championships—Doubles

Year	Men	Women
1992	J. Grabb, R. Reneberg	G. Fernandez, N. Zvereva
1993	K. Flach, R. Leach	A. Sánchez Vicario, H. Sukova
1994	P. Haarhuis, J. Eltingh	A. Sánchez Vicario, J. Novotna
1995	T. Woodbridge, M. Woodforde	G. Fernandez, N. Zvereva
1996	**T. Woodbridge, M. Woodforde**	**G. Fernandez, N. Zvereva**

Davis Cup (men)			
Year	Winner	Runner-up	Results
1992	United States	Switzerland	3–1
1993	Germany	Australia	4–1
1994	Sweden	Russia	4–1
1995	United States	Russia	3–2
1996	**France**	**Sweden**	**3–2**

Fed Cup (women)			
Year	Winner	Runner-up	Results
1992	Germany	Spain	2–1
1993	Spain	Australia	3–0
1994	Spain	United States	3–0
1995	Spain	United States	3–2
1996	**United States**	**Spain**	**5–0**

ized by Björn Borg from 1978 to 1980 in the men's game—Sampras was single-minded in his determination to win the championship of his country for the fourth time and thus salvage his last chance for a major title in 1996. After surviving the most memorable struggle of the decade at Flushing Meadows, a four-hour nine-minute marathon against Spain's Alex Corretja in the quarterfinals, Sampras made good on his mission and confirmed his status as the best player in the world.

The defending champion and top seed in the tournament defeated Chang 6–1, 6–4, 7–6 in a dazzling final-round display, out-classing the number 2 seed with his shot-making virtuosity in general and his prodigious serving under pressure in particular. Sampras charged to a 5–0 first-set lead and coasted through the set from there. He swept three games in a row from 3–4 down to take the second set and saved a set point at 5–6 in the third, dominating the tiebreaker 7–3.

Graf was invincible again, defeating Seles in their first meeting since the 1995 U.S. Open final and completing another stellar performance only moments before heavy rains swept through the stadium. Losing her serve only once, delivering no fewer than 10 aces, and covering the court with alacrity, Graf prevailed 7–5, 6–4 over a spirited but overwhelmed Seles. The triumph was Graf's 21st in a Grand Slam event and moved her to within three of the all-time singles leader, Margaret Court of Australia.

Nevertheless, while Graf at 27 was still going strong, an heir apparent was making substantial strides. At the U.S. Open 15-year-old Martina Hingis of Switzerland cut down seventh-seeded Jana Novotna in a stirring quarterfinal. Then she gave Graf some anxious moments in a 7–5, 6–3 semifinal loss. Earlier in the year, Hingis had ousted Graf at the Italian Open; at the end of the year, she pushed Graf to five sets in the final of a tournament in New York's Madison Square Garden.

Other Events. In a dramatic Davis Cup final in December, France defeated Sweden 3–2 at Malmö, Swed. In the decisive fifth match, Frenchman Arnaud Boetsch came from triple match point down to stop Nicklas Kulti 7–6, 2–6, 4–6, 7–6, 10–8. In late September, with Seles leading the way, the U.S. beat Spain in Atlantic City, N.J., 5–0 to win the Fed Cup (formerly the Federation Cup). And in August in Atlanta, Ga., Americans Agassi and Lindsay Davenport won gold medals by taking the singles titles. The U.S. partnership of Mary Joe Fernandez and Gigi Fernandez won a gold medal

in the women's doubles, and Australians Mark Woodforde and Todd Woodbridge won the gold in the men's doubles.

(STEVE FLINK)

TRACK AND FIELD SPORTS (ATHLETICS)

As the year of the Centennial Olympic Games, 1996 featured fierce track and field competition both at the Games in Atlanta, Ga., and in invitational meetings before and after the quadrennial championships event.

Olympic Games. Despite the scheduling of biennial world championships, the Olympics retained their lustre for track and field athletes, and the Atlanta Olympics yielded performances of the highest calibre. The highlights included two sprint world records and new Olympic records in 17 events. Donovan Bailey of Canada (*see* BIOGRAPHIES), the reigning world champion in the 100 m, won the gold medal in his event with a 9.84-sec performance that cut 0.01 sec from Leroy Burrell's two-year-old world record.

With his record run, Bailey defeated a powerful field that included Linford Christie of the U.K. and Michael Marsh of the U.S., the 1992 Olympic 100-m and 200-m champions, respectively. Neither Christie nor Marsh earned a medal, however, as Frank Fredericks of Namibia (9.89 sec) and Ato Boldon of Trinidad and Tobago (9.90 sec) claimed silver and bronze.

The 36-year-old Christie reaped disappointment and stirred controversy in what he claimed would be his final Olympic 100-m race. Christie was called for false starts twice. After the disqualifying second call, he delayed the competition for several minutes as he argued in vain with the starter over his ejection.

Michael Johnson of the U.S. set the second world record of the Games, racing a stunning 19.32 sec in the 200 m as he became the first man to win both the 200 m and the 400 m at the same Olympics. In the span of six days, Johnson ran eight races, including an Olympic-record 43.49-sec clocking in the 400-m final that was

the fourth fastest time in history. Although Johnson had run a 19.66-sec 200 m at the U.S. Olympic trials in June for the first individual outdoor world record of his career, his Olympic final record far exceeded anyone's expectations. Fredericks raced 19.68, the third fastest time in history, yet lost by nearly five metres. Repeating the silver and bronze medal ordering of the 100 m, Boldon (19.80 sec) placed third.

Johnson was not alone as a two-event gold medalist. Marie-José Pérec of France (*see* BIOGRAPHIES) became the first athlete in Olympic history to win back-to-back Olympic 400-m titles and then followed up with a victory in the 200 m. She took the longer race in an Olympic-record 48.25 sec, the sixth fastest woman's time in history. In the 200 m Pérec surged from fifth place at the halfway mark to take the gold in 22.12 sec. In both the 800 m and 1,500 m, Svetlana Masterkova of Russia won with unanswerable bursts of speed in the final homestretch.

Merlene Ottey of Jamaica, the 200-m silver medalist in 22.24 sec, also made history, as the first woman to reach the final of any event in five Olympics. The 36-year-old Ottey remained unrewarded in her quest for an Olympic gold medal, although she earned two silvers plus a bronze in the 4 × 100-m relay to match the career record total of seven track and field medals attained in previous Games by Shirley de la Hunty and Irena Szewinska.

In the 100 m Ottey came agonizingly closer to a gold than ever before, achieving the same time as defending champion Gail Devers (10.94 sec) but placing second. Jamaican officials appealed the race's result, but reexamination of the finish photo upheld Devers's status as the second woman to repeat as Olympic 100-m champion.

Perhaps the preeminent feat of Olympic longevity, however, was that of Carl Lewis of the U.S., who won a fourth consecutive long-jump title to join discus thrower Al Oerter as a four-time gold medalist in a single event. Unlike his previous Olympic long-jump wins, in which he never trailed (continued on page 368)

Donovan Bailey of Canada races across the finish line to win the gold medal in the men's 100 m at the Olympic Games in Atlanta, Ga. Bailey, who was the reigning champion in the 100 m, set a new world record of 9.84 sec, cutting 0.01 sec off the existing time.

CHRIS COLE—DUOMO

1996 World Outdoor Records—Men

Event	Competitor and country	Performance
100 m	Donovan Bailey (Canada)	9.84 sec
200 m	Michael Johnson (U.S.)	19.66 sec
	Michael Johnson (U.S.)	19.32 sec
3,000 m	Daniel Komen (Kenya)	7 min 20.67 sec
2 mi*	Daniel Komen (Kenya)	8 min 3.54 sec
10,000 m	Salah Hissou (Morocco)	26 min 38.08 sec
50-km walk (track)	Thierry Toutain (France)	3 hr 40 min 57.9 sec
Javelin throw	Jan Zelezny (Czech Rep.)	98.48 m (323 ft 1 in)

*Not an officially ratified event; best performance on record.

1996 World Outdoor Records—Women

Event	Competitor and country	Performance
1,000 m	Svetlana Masterkova (Russia)	2 min 28.98 sec
1 mi	Svetlana Masterkova (Russia)	4 min 12.56 sec
5,000-m walk	Kerry Saxby-Junna (Australia)	20 min 3 sec
10,000-m walk (road)	Yelena Nikolayeva (Russia)	41 min 4 sec
Pole vault	Emma George (Australia)	4.30 m (14 ft 1¼ in)
	Emma George (Australia)	4.41 m (14 ft 5½ in)
	Emma George (Australia)	4.42 m (14 ft 6 in)
	Emma George (Australia)	4.45 m (14 ft 7¼ in)
Hammer throw	Mihaela Melinte (Romania)	69.42 m (227 ft 9 in)

1996 World Indoor Records—Women

Event	Competitor and country	Performance
1,000 m	Maria Mutola (Mozambique)	2 min 31.23 sec
Pole vault	Sun Caiyun (China)	4.22 m (13 ft 10 in)
	Daniela Bártová (Czech Republic)	4.22 m (13 ft 10 in)
	Sun Caiyun (China)	4.27 m (14 ft 0 in)
	Sun Caiyun (China)	4.28 m (14 ft ½ in)
	Emma George (Australia)	4.30 m (14 ft 1¼ in)
	Emma George (Australia)	4.40 m (14 ft 5¼ in)

World Track and Field Championships—Men

Event	1993	1995
100 m	L. Christie (U.K.)	D. Bailey (Can.)
200 m	F. Fredericks (Namib.)	M. Johnson (U.S.)
400 m	M. Johnson (U.S.)	M. Johnson (U.S.)
800 m	P. Ruto (Kenya)	W. Kipketer (Den.)
1,500 m	N. Morceli (Alg.)	N. Morceli (Alg.)
5,000 m	I. Kirui (Kenya)	I. Kirui (Kenya)
10,000 m	H. Gebrselassie (Eth.)	H. Gebrselassie (Eth.)
steeplechase	M. Kiptanui (Kenya)	M. Kiptanui (Kenya)
110-m hurdles	C. Jackson (U.K.)	A. Johnson (U.S.)
400-m hurdles	K. Young (U.S.)	D. Adkins (U.S.)
marathon	M. Plaatjes (U.S.)	M. Fiz (Spain)
20-km walk	V. Massana (Spain)	M. Didoni (Italy)
50-km walk	J.A. Garcia (Spain)	V. Kononen (Fin.)
4 × 100-m relay	United States (J. Drummond, A. Cason, K. Mitchell, L. Burrell)	Canada (R. Esmie, G. Gilbert, B. Surin, D. Bailey)
4 × 400-m relay	United States (A. Valmon, Q. Watts, B. Reynolds, M. Johnson)	United States (M. Ramsey, D. Mills, B. Reynolds, M. Johnson)
high jump	J. Sotomayor (Cuba)	T. Kemp (Bahamas)
pole vault	S. Bubka (Ukr.)	S. Bubka (Ukr.)
long jump	M. Powell (U.S.)	I. Pedroso (Cuba)
triple jump	M. Conley (U.S.)	J. Edwards (U.K.)
shot put	W. Günthör (Switz.)	J. Godina (U.S.)
discus throw	L. Riedel (Ger.)	L. Riedel (Ger.)
hammer throw	A. Abduvaliyev (Tajik.)	A. Abduvaliyev (Tajik.)
javelin throw	J. Zelezny (Cz.Rep.)	J. Zelezny (Cz. Rep.)
decathlon	D. O'Brien (U.S.)	D. O'Brien (U.S.)

World Track and Field Championships—Women

Event	1993	1995
100 m	G. Devers (U.S.)	G. Torrence (U.S.)
200 m	M. Ottey (Jam.)	M. Ottey (Jam.)
400 m	J. Miles (U.S.)	M.-J. Pérec (Fr.)
800 m	M. Mutola (Mozam.)	A. Quirot (Cuba)
1,500 m	Liu Dong (China)	H. Boulmerka (Alg.)
3,000 m*	Qu Yunxia (China)	S. O'Sullivan (Ire.)
10,000 m	Wang Junxia (China)	F. Ribeiro (Port.)
100-m hurdles	G. Devers (U.S.)	G. Devers (U.S.)
400-m hurdles	S. Gunnell (U.K.)	K. Batten (U.S.)
marathon	Asari Junko (Japan)	M. Machado (Port.)
10-km walk	S. Essayeh (Fin.)	I. Stankina (Rus.)
4 × 100-m relay	Russia (O. Bogoslovskaya, G. Malchugina, N. Voronova, I. Privalova)	United States (C. Mondie-Milner, C. Guidry, C. Gaines, G. Torrence)
4 × 400-m relay	United States (G. Torrence, M. Malone, N. Kaiser-Brown, J. Miles)	United States (K. Graham, R. Stevens, C. Jones, J. Miles)
high jump	I. Quintero (Cuba)	S. Kostadinova (Bul.)
long jump	H. Drechsler (Ger.)	F. May (Italy)
triple jump		I. Kravets (Ukr.)
shot put	Huang Zhihong (China)	A. Kumbernuss (Ger.)
discus throw	O. Burova (Russia)	E. Zvereva (Bel.)
javelin throw	T. Hattestad (Nor.)	N. Shikolenko (Bel.)
heptathlon	J. Joyner-Kersee (U.S.)	G. Shouaa (Syria)

*5,000 m in 1995.

IAAF World Cup—Men

	100 metre	200 metre	400 metre	800 metre	1,500 metre
1989	L. Christie (Gr.Brit.)	R. Caetano da Silva (Amer.)	R. Hernandez (Amer.)	T. McKean (Gr.Brit.)	A. Bile (Africa)
1992	L. Christie (Gr.Brit.)	R. Caetano da Silva (Amer.)	S. Bada (Africa)	D. Sharpe (U.K.)	M. Suleiman (Asia)
1994	L. Christie (Gr.Brit.)	J. Regis (Gr.Brit.)	A. Pettigrew (U.S.)	M. Everett (U.S.)	N. Morceli (Africa)

	5,000 metre	10,000 metre	Steeplechase	110-m hurdles	400-m hurdles
1989	S. Aouita (Africa)	S. Antibo (Europe)	J. Kariuki (Africa)	R. Kingdom (U.S.)	D. Patrick (U.S.)
1992	F. Bayesa (Africa)	A. Abebe (Africa)	P. Barkutwo (Africa)	C. Jackson (U.K.)	S. Matete (Africa)
1994	B. Lahlafi (Africa)	K. Skah (Africa)	M. Kiptanui (Africa)	T. Jarrett (Gr.Brit.)	S. Matete (Africa)

	4 × 100-m relays	4 × 400-m relays	Triple jump	High jump	Pole vault
1989	United States	Americas	M. Conley (U.S.)	P. Sjoberg (Europe)	P. Collet (Europe)
1992	United States	Africa	J. Edwards (U.K.)	Y. Sergeyenko (UT)	I. Potapovich (UT)
1994	Great Britain	Great Britain	Y. Quesada (Amer.)	J. Sotomayor (Amer.)	O. Brits (Africa)

	Long jump	Shot put	Discus throw	Hammer throw	Javelin throw
1989	L. Myricks (U.S.)	U. Timmermann (E.Ger.)	J. Schult (E.Ger.)	H. Weis (Europe)	S. Backley (Gr.Brit.)
1992	I. Pedroso (Amer.)	M. Stulce (U.S.)	T. Washington (U.S.)	T. Gécsek (Europe)	J. Zelezny (Europe)
1994	F. Salle (Gr.Brit.)	C.J. Hunter (U.S.)	V. Dubrovshchik (Europe)	A. Abduvaliyev (Asia)	S. Backley (Gr.Brit.)

	Team
1989	United States
1992	Africa
1994	Africa

The Centennial Olympic Games

BY MELINDA C. SHEPHERD

From July 19 to Aug. 4, 1996, the city of Atlanta, Ga., welcomed the world to join it in celebrating the XXVI Olympiad, 100 years after the first modern Olympic Games in Athens in 1896. For the first time every invited National Olympic Committee (a total of 197) sent a team, including each of the former Soviet republics, Burundi, North Korea, Palestine, and Hong Kong, which won its first (and last) gold medal before its reunification with China in 1997. More than 10,700 accredited athletes (about one-third women) competed in 271 medal events (163 for men, 97 for women, and 11 mixed), and a record 79 teams won at least one medal, with 53 of them taking at least one gold (5

for the first time). New sports added to the schedule in Atlanta included women's association football (soccer), beach volleyball, lightweight rowing events, women's softball, and cross country cycling (mountain biking).

As the first city to act as host of the Olympic Games without government financial backing, Atlanta faced special challenges. The Atlanta Committee for the Olympic Games (ACOG) was roundly criticized for the Games' problems, notably the inadequate transportation system, delays due to the tight security precautions, and computer glitches in the electronic transmission of scores. There were also questions about excessive commercialization and "chauvinism" among the U.S. spectators and the U.S. network television coverage. Although Billy Payne, head of ACOG and the chief force behind the city's successful bid, declared that the Games would break even or make a small profit, the experiment of a privately funded Olympics was unlikely to be repeated.

These problems failed to dampen the city's Southern hospitality, however, or ruin more than one million visitors' fun. The revelry was temporarily halted on July 27, however, when an unknown person set off a pipe bomb in Centennial Olympic Park. (*See* LAW, CRIME, AND LAW ENFORCEMENT: *Crime*.) One bystander was killed in the explosion, and a photojournalist died of heart failure in the ensuing rush,

but within days the park reopened in a memorial service attended by hundreds.

Among the outstanding athletes at the Games were several former gold medal winners, notably Carl Lewis of the U.S., who won his ninth gold in track; British rower Steven Redgrave (*see* BIOGRAPHIES), who took his fourth gold in four consecutive Olympics; and 17-year-old Fu Mingxia (*see* BIOGRAPHIES) of China, winner of the platform diving competition in 1992 and both the platform and the springboard events in 1996. Although U.S. sprinter Michael Johnson's gold running shoes and bravura victories in the 200 m and 400 m captured the world's attention, his golden double was matched by two women runners, Marie-José Perec (*see* BIOGRAPHIES) of France in the 200 m and 400 m and Svetlana Masterkova of Russia in the 800 m and 1,500 m. The highest individual medal total in Atlanta (6) went to Russian gymnast Aleksey Nemov. The focus poolside was mainly on Michelle Smith (*see* BIOGRAPHIES) of Ireland, who won three golds and a bronze in swimming, despite being compelled to leave Ireland to find adequate training facilities, questions over entry procedures, and strain caused by unsubstantiated rumours of illegal drug use.

Melinda C. Shepherd is associate editor of Encyclopædia Britannica Yearbooks.

Dancers create silhouettes representing athletes of the ancient Olympic Games at the opening ceremony of the XXVI Olympiad, held in Atlanta, Ga., in July and August. The opening lasted nearly five hours.

Olympic Champions, 1996 Summer Games, Atlanta

Archery

	Men	Women
Individual	J. Huish (U.S.)	Kim Kyung Wook (S.Kor.)
Team	United States	South Korea

Badminton

Men's singles	P.-E. Hoyer-Larsen (Den.)
Men's doubles	R. Subagja and R. Mainaky (Indon.)
Women's singles	Bang Soo Hyun (S.Kor.)
Women's doubles	Gu Jun and Ge Fei (China)
Mixed doubles	Gil Young Ah and Kim Dong Moon (S.Kor.)

Baseball

Winning team	Cuba

Basketball

Men	United States	Women	United States

Boxing

48-kg class	D. Bojilov (Bulg.)	67-kg class	O. Saitov (Russia)
51-kg class	M. Romero (Cuba)	71-kg class	D. Reid (U.S.)
54-kg class	I. Kovacs (Hung.)	75-kg class	A. Hernandez (Cuba)
57-kg class	S. Kamsing (Thai.)	81-kg class	V. Jirov (Kazak.)
60-kg class	H. Soltani (Alg.)	91-kg class	F. Savon (Cuba)
63.5-kg class	H. Vinent (Cuba)	91-kg+ class	V. Klichko (Ukr.)

Canoeing

Men

500-m kayak singles	A. Rossi (Italy)	1 min 37.423 sec
1,000-m kayak singles	K. Holmann (Nor.)	3 min 25.785 sec
500-m kayak pairs	K. Bluhm/T. Gutsche (Ger.)	1 min 28.697 sec
1,000-m kayak pairs	A. Rossi/D. Scarpa (Italy)	3 min 9.190 sec
1,000-m kayak fours	Germany	2 min 51.528 sec
Slalom kayak singles	O. Fix (Ger.)	141.22 pt
500-m Canadian singles	M. Doktor (Cz.Rep.)	1 min 49.934 sec
1,000-m Canadian singles	M. Doktor (Cz.Rep.)	3 min 54.418 sec
500-m Canadian pairs	C. Horvath/G. Kolonics (Hung.)	1 min 40.420 sec
1,000-m Canadian pairs	A. Dittmer/G. Kirchbach (Ger.)	3 min 31.870 sec
Slalom Canadian singles	M. Martikan (Slvk.)	151.03 pt
Slalom Canadian pairs	F. Adisson/W. Forgues (Fr.)	158.82 pt

Women

500-m kayak singles	R. Koban (Hung.)	1 min 47.655 sec
500-m kayak pairs	A. Andersson/S. Gunnarsson (Swed.)	1 min 39.329 sec
500-m kayak fours	Germany	1 min 31.077 sec
Slalom kayak singles	S. Hilgertova (Cz.Rep.)	169.49 pt

Cycling

Men

Road race	P. Richard (Switz.)	4 hr 53 min 56 sec
Indiv. time trial	M. Indurain (Spain)	1 hr 4 min 5 sec
1-km time trial	F. Rousseau (Fr.)	1 min 2.712 sec[1]
Indiv. pursuit	A. Collinelli (Italy)	4 min 20.893 sec
Team pursuit	France	4 min 5.930 sec[1]
Sprint	J. Fiedler (Ger.)	
Points race	S. Martinello (Italy)	
Cross country	B.J. Brentjens (Neth.)	2 hr 17 min 38 sec

Women

Road race	J. Longo-Ciprelli (Fr.)	2 hr 36 min 13 sec
Indiv. time trial	Z. Zabirova (Russia)	36 min 40 sec
Indiv. pursuit	A. Bellutti (Italy)	3 min 33.595 sec
Sprint	F. Ballanger (Fr.)	
Points race	N. Lancien (Fr.)	
Cross country	P. Pezzo (Italy)	1 hr 50 min 51 sec

Diving

	Men		Women	
Springboard	Xiong Ni (China)	701.46 pt	Fu Mingxia (China)	547.68 pt
Platform	D. Sautin (Russia)	692.34 pt	Fu Mingxia (China)	521.58 pt

Equestrian

	Individual	Team
3-day event	B. Tait (N.Z.)	Australia
Dressage	I. Werth (Ger.)	Germany
Jumping	U. Kirchhoff (Ger.)	Germany

Fencing

	Men		Women
Indiv. foil	A. Puccini (Italy)		L. Badea (Rom.)
Team foil	Russia		Italy
Indiv. épée	A. Beketov (Russia)		L. Flessel (Fr.)
Team épée	Italy		France
Indiv. sabre	S. Pozdnyakov (Russia)		
Team sabre	Russia		

Field Hockey

Men	Netherlands	Women	Australia

Gymnastics

Men

Team	Russia	576.778 pt
All-around	Li Xiaoshuang (China)	58.423 pt
Floor exercise	I. Melissanidis (Greece)	9.850 pt
Vault	A. Nemov (Russia)	9.787 pt
Pommel horse	Li Donghua (Switz.)	9.875 pt
Rings	Y. Chechi (Italy)	9.887 pt
Parallel bars	R. Sharipov (Ukr.)	9.837 pt
Horizontal bar	A. Wecker (Ger.)	9.850 pt

Women

Team	United States	389.225 pt
All-around	L. Podkopayeva (Ukr.)	39.255 pt
Floor exercise	L. Podkopayeva (Ukr.)	9.887 pt
Vault	S. Amanar (Rom.)	9.825 pt
Uneven bars	S. Chorkina (Russia)	9.850 pt
Balance beam	S. Miller (U.S.)	9.862 pt
Indiv. rhythmic	Ye. Serebryanskaya (Ukr.)	39.683 pt
Team rhythmic	Spain	38.933

Handball

Men	Croatia	Women	Denmark

Judo

	Men		Women
60-kg class	T. Nomura (Japan)	48-kg class	Kye Sun Hi (N.Kor.)
65-kg class	U. Quellmalz (Ger.)	52-kg class	M.-C. Restoux (Fr.)
71-kg class	K. Nakamura (Japan)	56-kg class	D. González (Cuba)
78-kg class	D. Bouras (Fr.)	61-kg class	Y. Emoto (Japan)
86-kg class	Jeon Ki Young (S.Kor.)	66-kg class	Cho Min Sun (S.Kor.)
95-kg class	P. Nastula (Pol.)	72-kg class	U. Werbrouck (Belg.)
95-kg + class	D. Douillet (Fr.)	72-kg + class	Sun Fuming (China)

Modern Pentathlon

Individual	A. Parygin (Kazak.)	5,551 pt

Rowing

Men

Single sculls	X. Mueller (Switz.)	6 min 44.85 sec
Double sculls	A. Abbagnale/D. Tizzano (Italy)	6 min 16.98 sec
Quadruple sculls	Germany	5 min 56.93 sec
Coxless pairs	S. Redgrave/M. Pinsent (U.K.)	6 min 20.09 sec
Coxless fours	Australia	6 min 6.37 sec
Eights	Netherlands	5 min 42.74 sec
Lightweight double sculls	Markus Gier/Michael Gier (Switz.)	6 min 23.47 sec
Lightweight fours	Denmark	6 min 9.58 sec

Women

Single sculls	Ye. Khodotovich (Bela.)	7 min 32.21 sec
Double sculls	K. Heddle/M. McBean (Can.)	6 min 56.84 sec
Quadruple sculls	Germany	6 min 27.44 sec
Coxless pairs	K. Slatter/M. Still (Austl.)	7 min 1.39 sec
Eights	Romania	6 min 19.73 sec
Lightweight double sculls	C. Burcica/C. Macoviciuc (Rom.)	7 min 12.78 sec

Shooting

Men

Rapid-fire pistol	R. Schumann (Ger.)	698.0 pt[1]
Free pistol	B. Kokorev (Russia)	666.4 pt
Air pistol	R. di Donna (Italy)	684.2 pt
Running game target	Yang Ling (China)	685.8 pt[1]
Small-bore rifle, 3 pos.	J.-P. Amat (Fr.)	1,273.9 pt[1]
Small-bore rifle, prone	C. Klees (Ger.)	704.8 pt[2]
Air rifle	A. Khadzhibekov (Russia)	695.7 pt[1]
Trap	M. Diamond (Austl.)	149 pt[1]
Double trap	R. Mark (Austl.)	189 pt[1]
Skeet	E. Falco (Italy)	149 pt

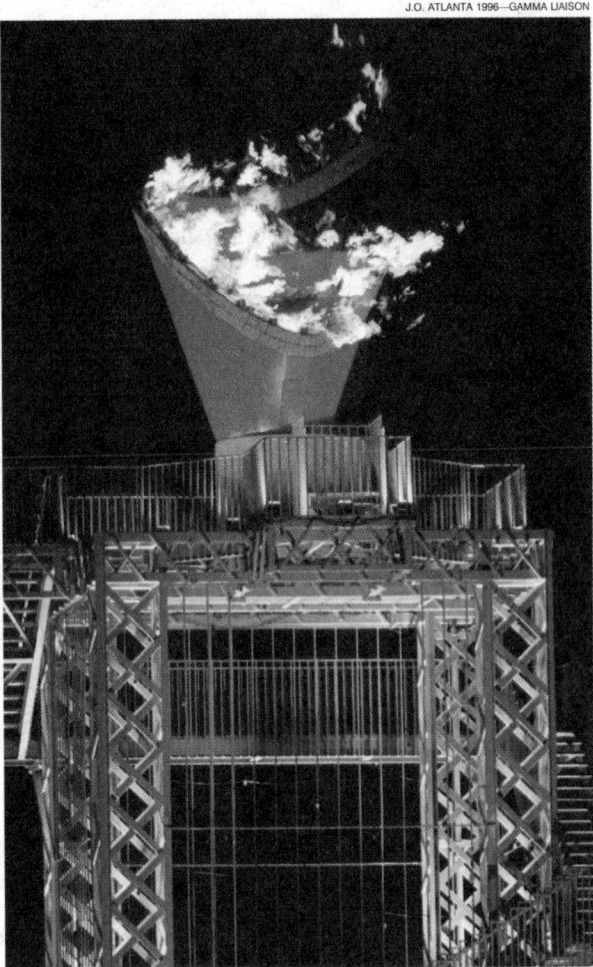

The Olympic flame burns in a cauldron atop a tower in Olympic Stadium. The torch used to light the cauldron was carried 24,150 km (15,000 mi) in an 84-day relay across the U.S.

Shooting

Women

Pistol	Li Duihong (China)	687.9 pt[1]
Air pistol	O. Klochneva (Russia)	490.1 pt[1]
Small-bore rifle, 3 pos.	A. Ivosev (Yugos.)	686.1 pt[1]
Air rifle	R. Mauer (Pol.)	497.6 pt
Double trap	K. Rhode (U.S.)	141 pt[1]

Soccer

Men	Nigeria	Women	United States

Softball

Winning team	United States

Swimming

Men

50-m freestyle	A. Popov (Russia)	22.13 sec
100-m freestyle	A. Popov (Russia)	48.74 sec
200-m freestyle	D. Loader (N.Z.)	1 min 47.63 sec
400-m freestyle	D. Loader (N.Z.)	3 min 47.97 sec
1,500-m freestyle	K. Perkins (Austl.)	14 min 56.40 sec
100-m backstroke	J. Rouse (U.S.)	54.10 sec
200-m backstroke	B. Bridgewater (U.S.)	1 min 58.54 sec
100-m breaststroke	F. Deburghgraeve (Belg.)	1 min 0.65 sec
200-m breaststroke	N. Rozsa (Hung.)	2 min 12.57 sec
100-m butterfly	D. Pankratov (Russia)	52.27 sec[2]
200-m butterfly	D. Pankratov (Russia)	1 min 56.51 sec
200-m individual medley	A. Czene (Hung.)	1 min 59.91 sec[1]
400-m individual medley	T. Dolan (U.S.)	4 min 14.90 sec
4 × 100-m freestyle relay	United States	3 min 15.41 sec[1]
4 × 200-m freestyle relay	United States	7 min 14.84 sec
4 × 100-m medley relay	United States	3 min 34.84 sec[2]

Swimming

Women

50-m freestyle	A. Van Dyken (U.S.)	24.87 sec
100-m freestyle	Le Jingyi (China)	54.50 sec[1]
200-m freestyle	C. Poll (C.Rica)	1 min 58.16 sec
400-m freestyle	M. Smith (Ire.)	4 min 7.25 sec
800-m freestyle	B. Bennett (U.S.)	8 min 27.89 sec
100-m backstroke	B. Botsford (U.S.)	1 min 1.19 sec
200-m backstroke	K. Egerszegi (Hung.)	2 min 7.83 sec
100-m breaststroke	P. Heyns (S.Af.)	1 min 7.73 sec
200-m breaststroke	P. Heyns (S.Af.)	2 min 25.41 sec[1]
100-m butterfly	A. Van Dyken (U.S.)	59.13 sec
200-m butterfly	S. O'Neill (Austl.)	2 min 7.76 sec
200-m individual medley	M. Smith (Ire.)	2 min 13.93 sec
400-m individual medley	M. Smith (Ire.)	4 min 39.18 sec
4 × 100-m freestyle relay	United States	3 min 39.29 sec[1]
4 × 200-m freestyle relay	United States	7 min 59.87 sec[1]
4 × 100-m medley relay	United States	4 min 2.88 sec
Synchronized swimming (team)	United States	99.72 pt

Table Tennis

Men's singles	Liu Guoliang (China)
Men's doubles	Liu Guoliang and Kong Linghui (China)
Women's singles	Deng Yaping (China)
Women's doubles	Deng Yaping and Qiao Hong (China)

Tennis

Men's singles	A. Agassi (U.S.)
Men's doubles	T. Woodbridge and M. Woodforde (Austl.)
Women's singles	L. Davenport (U.S.)
Women's doubles	G. Fernandez and M.J. Fernandez (U.S.)

Track and Field

Men

100 m	D. Bailey (Can.)	9.84 sec[2]
200 m	M. Johnson (U.S.)	19.32 sec[2]
400 m	M. Johnson (U.S.)	43.49 sec[1]
4 × 100-m relay	Canada	37.69 sec
4 × 400-m relay	United States	2 min 55.99 sec
800 m	V. Rodal (Nor.)	1 min 42.58 sec[1]
1,500 m	N. Morceli (Alg.)	3 min 35.78 sec
5,000 m	V. Niyongabo (Burundi)	13 min 7.96 sec
10,000 m	H. Gebrselassie (Eth.)	27 min 7.34 sec[1]
Marathon	J. Thugwane (S.Af.)	2 hr 12 min 36 sec
110-m hurdles	A. Johnson (U.S.)	12.95 sec[1]
400-m hurdles	D. Adkins (U.S.)	47.54 sec
Steeplechase	J. Keter (Kenya)	8 min 7.12 sec
20-km walk	J. Pérez (Ecua.)	1 hr 20 min 7 sec
50-km walk	R. Korzeniowski (Pol.)	3 hr 43 min 30 sec
High jump	C. Austin (U.S.)	2.39 m[1]
Long jump	C. Lewis (U.S.)	8.50 m
Triple jump	K. Harrison (U.S.)	18.09 m
Pole vault	J. Galfione (Fr.)	5.92 m[1]
Shot put	R. Barnes (U.S.)	21.62 m
Discus throw	L. Riedel (Ger.)	69.40 m[1]
Javelin throw	J. Zelezny (Cz.Rep.)	88.16 m
Hammer throw	B. Kiss (Hung.)	81.24 m
Decathlon	D. O'Brien (U.S.)	8,824 pt

Women

100 m	G. Devers (U.S.)	10.94 sec
200 m	M.-J. Pérec (Fr.)	22.12 sec
400 m	M.-J. Pérec (Fr.)	48.25 sec[1]
4 × 100-m relay	United States	41.95 sec
4 × 400-m relay	United States	3 min 20.91 sec
800 m	S. Masterkova (Russia)	1 min 57.73 sec
1,500 m	S. Masterkova (Russia)	4 min 0.83 sec
5,000 m	Wang Junxia (China)	14 min 59.88 sec[1]
10,000 m	F. Ribeiro (Port.)	31 min 1.63 sec[1]
Marathon	F. Roba (Eth.)	2 hr 26 min 5 sec
100-m hurdles	L. Engquist (Swed.)	12.58 sec
400-m hurdles	D. Hemmings (Jam.)	52.82 sec[1]
10-km walk	Ye. Nikolayeva (Russia)	41 min 49 sec
High jump	S. Kostadinova (Bulg.)	2.05 m[1]
Long jump	C. Ajunwa (Nigeria)	7.12 m
Triple jump	I. Kravets (Ukr.)	15.33 m[1]
Shot put	A. Kumbernuss (Ger.)	20.56 m
Discus throw	I. Wyludda (Ger.)	69.66 m
Javelin throw	H. Rantanen (Fin.)	67.94 m
Heptathlon	G. Shouaa (Syria)	6,780 pt

Volleyball

	Men	Women
Beach	K. Kiraly and K. Steffes (U.S.)	J. Silva and S. Pires (Braz.)
Indoor	Netherlands	Cuba

Water Polo

Winning team	Spain

Weight lifting[3]

54-kg class	H. Mutlu (Tur.)	287.5 kg[1]
59-kg class	Tang Ningsheng (China)	307.5 kg[2]
64-kg class	N. Suleymanoglu (Tur.)	335.0 kg[2]
70-kg class	Zhan Xugang (China)	357.5 kg[2]
76-kg class	P. Lara (Cuba)	367.5 kg
83-kg class	P. Dimas (Greece)	392.5 kg[2]
91-kg class	A. Petrov (Russia)	402.5 kg
99-kg class	A. Kakiasvilis (Greece)	420.0 kg[2]
108-kg class	T. Taimazov (Ukr.)	430.0 kg
108-kg+ class	A. Chemerkin (Russia)	457.5 kg

Wrestling

	Freestyle	Greco-Roman
48-kg class	Kim Il (N.Kor.)	Sim Kwon Ho (S.Kor.)
52-kg class	V. Jordanov (Bulg.)	A. Nazaryan (Arm.)
57-kg class	K. Cross (U.S.)	Yu. Melnichenko (Kazak.)
62-kg class	T. Brands (U.S.)	W. Zawadzki (Pol.)
68-kg class	V. Bogiyev (Russia)	R. Wolny (Pol.)
74-kg class	B. Saytyev (Russia)	F. Ascuy Aguilera (Cuba)
82-kg class	Kh. Magomedov (Russia)	H. Yerlikaya (Tur.)
90-kg class	R. Khadem Azghadi (Iran)	V. Oleynyk (Ukr.)
100-kg class	K. Angle (U.S.)	A. Wronski (Pol.)
130-kg class	M. Demir (Tur.)	A. Karelin (Russia)

Yachting

Men's 470 class	Ukraine	Women's Europe	K. Roug (Den.)
Women's 470 class	Spain	Laser (open)	R. Scheidt (Braz.)
Men's mistral	N. Kaklamanakis (Greece)	Star (open)	Brazil
Women's mistral	Lee Lai Shan (Hong Kong)	Tornado (open)	Spain
Men's Finn	M. Kusznierewicz (Pol.)	Soling (open)	Germany

[1]Olympic record. [2]World record. [3]New weight categories introduced in 1996.

ELIOT J. SCHECTER—FORT LAUDERDALE SUN SENTINEL

Boxing legend Muhammad Ali prepares to light the Olympic flame at the opening ceremony. Ali won a gold medal in the 1960 Olympics.

IAAF World Cup—Women

	100 metre	200 metre	400 metre	800 metre	1,500 metre
1989	S. Echols (U.S.)	S. Moller (E.Ger.)	A. Quirot (Amer.)	A. Quirot (Amer.)	P. Ivan (Europe)
1992	N. Voronova (UT)	M.-J. Pérec (Europe)	J. Miles (U.S.)	M. Mutola (Africa)	Y. Podkopayeva (UT)
1994	I. Privalova (Europe)	M. Ottey (Amer.)	I. Privalova (Europe)	M. Mutola (Africa)	H. Boulmerka (Africa)

	3,000 metre	10,000 metre	100-m hurdles	400-m hurdles	4 × 100-m relays
1989	Y. Murray (Europe)	K. Ullrich (E.Ger.)	C. Oschkenat (E.Ger.)	S. Farmer-Patrick (U.S.)	East Germany
1992	D. Tulu (Africa)	D. Tulu (Africa)	A. López (Amer.)	S. Farmer-Patrick (U.S.)	Asia
1994	Y. Murray (Gr.Brit.)	E. Meyer (Africa)	A. López (Amer.)	S. Gunnell (Gr.Brit.)	Africa

	4 × 400-m relays	Triple Jump	High jump	Long jump	Shot put
1989	Americas		S. Costa (Amer.)	G. Chistyakova (U.S.S.R.)	Zhihong Huang (Asia)
1992	Americas		I. Quintero (Amer.)	H. Drechsler (Ger.)	B. Laza (Amer.)
1994	Great Britain	A. Biryukova (Europe)	B. Bilac (Europe)	I. Kravets (Europe)	Zhihong Huang (Asia)

	Discus throw	Javelin throw	Team
1989	I. Wyludda (E.Ger.)	P. Felke (E.Ger.)	East Germany
1992	M. Marten (Amer.)	T. Sanderson (U.K.)	Unified Team
1994	I. Wyludda (Europe)	T. Hattestad (Europe)	Europe

(continued from page 362)

after the first round of the final, Lewis had to battle throughout the Atlanta event. The 35-year-old star did not reach the final until his third and last qualifying-round jump of 8.29 m (27 ft 2½ in), and in the final, Lewis did not hit his winning leap of 8.50 m (27 ft 10¾ in) until the third of six rounds.

Basking in golden glory, Lewis announced that he would be available if called upon to run on the U.S. 4 × 100-m relay team. His selection for the relay would have allowed Lewis a shot at a record 10th gold. Lewis, however, had placed eighth and last in the U.S. Olympic trials in the 100 m. Ultimately, he was not selected for the relay, and Canada, anchored by Bailey, won easily in 37.69 sec.

Besides Lewis, Devers, and Pérec, javelin thrower Jan Zelezny of the Czech Republic successfully defended his Olympic title with an 88.16-m (289-ft 3-in) throw in the third round. Two U.S. relay teams, in the men's 4 × 400 m (2 min 55.99 sec) and women's 4 × 100 m (41.95 sec), won gold for the fourth consecutive Olympics.

For track and field, Atlanta was the most international modern Olympics yet, with a record 45 nations sharing in the medals. Typical of this expanding globalization were Jefferson Pérez of Ecuador, who won the 20-km-walk gold, his nation's first Olympic medal in any sport, and Vénuste Niyongabo, who inaugurated Burundi's Olympic participation with a win in the 5,000 m.

African male distance runners strength-

ened their already formidable reputations in the long-distance runs. On a warm, humid evening on a hard Atlanta track designed for sprinters, Haile Gebrselassie of Ethiopia set an Olympic record in the 10,-000 m (27 min 7.34 sec). In a stirring battle with Paul Tergat of Kenya (27 min 8.17 sec) and Salah Hissou of Morocco (27 min 24.67 sec), Gebrselassie covered the race's second half in 13 min 11.4 sec, faster than the winning time in every previous Olympic 5,000-m race except Said Aouita's 1984 victory. The top eight places in the race were filled by Africans. After the Games, Hissou exacted some measure of revenge by breaking Gebrselassie's 14-month-old 10,000-m world record with a 26-min 38.08-sec clocking in a meet in Brussels.

Michael Johnson (centre) breaks into the lead at the Olympic Games in the men's 200 m, which he won with a world-record time of 19.32 sec. The U.S. runner also won the 400 m, the first man to take both events at the same Olympics, setting a record Olympic time of 43.49 sec.

Svetlana Masterkova of Russia finishes the mile at Zürich, Switz., with a world record time of 4 min 12.56 sec. She also set a record of 2 min 28.98 sec in the 1,000 m.

In the Olympic marathons Africans made history as well. Unheralded Fatuma Roba of Ethiopia became the first African woman to win a major championships marathon, charging into the lead one hour into the race to win in 2 hr 26 min 5 sec from the 1992 Olympic gold and silver medalists, Valentina Yegorova of Russia and Yuko Arimori of Japan. In the men's marathon Josia Thugwane earned South Africa its first track and field gold medal with a 2-hr 12-min 36-sec win.

Jan Zelezny of the Czech Republic defended his Olympic title with a javelin throw of 88.16 m (289 ft 3 in). Other track and field athletes who retained Olympic titles were Carl Lewis of the U.S. (long jump), Gail Devers of the U.S. (100 m), Marie-José Pérec of France (400 m), and the U.S. men's 4 × 400-m and women's 4 × 100-m relay teams.

Two women's events, the 5,000 m and triple jump, debuted on the Olympic program, with the gold medals going to holders of world records. Wang Junxia of China, bearer of the world standards for 3,000 m and 10,000 m, won the Olympic 5,000-m title in 14 min 59.88 sec. She later lost the 10,000 m when world champion Fernanda Ribeiro of Portugal passed her in the final stretch to take gold. Triple-jump record holder Inessa Kravets of Ukraine hopped, skipped, and jumped a season-leading 15.33 m (50 ft 3½ in) to win her event.

Men's International Competition. The Olympic season brought out extraordinary efforts in pre- and post-Games competition from those who triumphed in Atlanta, as when Zelezny launched his javelin to a world-record 98.48 m (323 ft 1 in) in May. There were, however, unprecedented achievements by athletes who had been denied Olympic participation. Chief among them was 20-year-old Daniel Komen of Kenya, a distance runner who placed fourth in his nation's Olympic trials in the 5,000 m and thus failed to qualify for Atlanta. Disappointed but not defeated by his misfortune, Komen raced to a record in the infrequently contested 2-mi run with an 8-min 3.54-sec clocking in Lappeenranta, Fin., in July. After the Olympics he was unbeatable, missing Noureddine Morceli's 3,000-m world record by only 0.05 sec in Monaco on August 10 and by 0.76 sec in Brussels on August 23. On September 1 in Rieti, Italy, Komen again attacked the 3,000-m standard, this time successfully setting a new mark of 7 min 20.67 sec. His 4.44-sec reduction of the record was the largest since Kip Keino chopped 6.4 sec from it in 1965.

Wilson Kipketer, a Kenyan immigrant to Denmark, missed the Olympics because he lacked the requisite Danish citizenship. An 800-m runner, Kipketer asserted his dominance in other meets. He raced 1 min 41.83 sec, the third fastest time in history and the swiftest clocking since 1984, won all his races, and dipped under 1 min 43 sec a record seven times during the season.

Although he placed second to a pair of world-record setters in Atlanta, sprinter Fredericks defeated Michael Johnson twice during the year and surpassed significant barriers in both the 100 m and 200 m more times in one season than any other man in history. He ran three sub-9.90-sec 100-m races and nine sub-20-sec 200-m clockings.

Women's International Competition. In the immediate aftermath of the Olympics, two women, Masterkova and Pérec, appeared equally poised to claim the 1996 season as hers. Masterkova, however, settled the issue when she posted world records at the mile (4 min 12.56 sec) and 1,000-m (2-min 28.98-sec) distances. Masterkova was pushed to the 1,000-m standard by the record's former owner, Maria Mutola of Mozambique. Mutola stayed less than 0.10 sec behind Masterkova after 800 m but succumbed in the final half lap to

World Cross Country Championships— Men (12,000 m)		
Year	Individual	Team
1992	J. Ngugi (Kenya)	Kenya
1993	W. Sigei (Kenya)	Kenya
1994	W. Sigei (Kenya)	Kenya
1995	P. Tergat (Kenya)	Kenya
1996	**P. Tergat (Kenya)**	**Kenya**

World Cross Country Championships— Women (5,000 m)		
Year	Individual	Team
1992	L. Jennings (U.S.)	Kenya
1993	A. Dias (Port.)	Kenya
1994	H. Chepngeno (Kenya)	Portugal
1995	D. Tulu (Eth.)	Kenya
1996	**G. Wami (Eth.)**	**Kenya**

World Marathon Cup		
Year	Men	Women
1987	A. Salah (Djib.)	Z. Ivanova (U.S.S.R.)
1989	K. Metaferia (Eth.)	S. Marchiano (U.S.)
1991	Y. Tolstikov (U.S.S.R.)	R. Mota (Port.)
1993	R. Nerurkar (U.K.)	Wang Junxia (China)
1995	D. Wakiihuri (Kenya)	A. Catuna (Rom.)

Boston Marathon		
Year	Men	h:min:s
1992	I. Hussein (Kenya)	2:08:14
1993	C. N'Deti (Kenya)	2:09:33
1994	C. N'Deti (Kenya)	2:07:15
1995	C. N'Deti (Kenya)	2:09:22
1996	**M. Tanui (Kenya)**	**2:09:16**
Year	Women	h:min:s
1992	O. Markova (Russia)	2:23:43
1993	O. Markova (Russia)	2:25:27
1994	U. Pippig (Ger.)	2:21:45
1995	U. Pippig (Ger.)	2:25:11
1996	**U. Pippig (Ger.)**	**2:27:12**

New York City Marathon		
Year	Men	h:min:s
1992	W. Mtolo (S.Afr.)	2:09:29
1993	A. Espinosa (Mex.)	2:10:04
1994	G. Silva (Mex.)	2:11:21
1995	G. Silva (Mex.)	2:11:00
1996	**G. Leone (Italy)**	**2:09:54**
Year	Women	h:min:s
1992	L. Ondieki (Austl.)	2:24:40
1993	U. Pippig (Ger.)	2:26:24
1994	T. Loroupe (Kenya)	2:27:37
1995	T. Loroupe (Kenya)	2:28:06
1996	**A. Catuna (Rom.)**	**2:28:18**

finish second in 2 min 29.66 sec, the third fastest time in history.

Ludmila Engquist, the Olympic 100-m hurdles champion, won $250,000 as overall Grand Prix points leader. The Russian-born Engquist obtained Swedish citizenship as the season began, and her Olympic win was that nation's first by a woman track and field athlete. Olympic shot-put champion Astrid Kumbernuss of Germany finished the year with 30 wins in 30 meets. Kumbernuss, in fact, had not lost since February 1995.

Cross Country and Marathon Running. Kenya's Paul Tergat won the men's individual title at the world cross country championships in Stellenbosch, S.Af., in March, while Ethiopia's Gete Wami took the women's crown. As in 1995, Kenya won all four team championships (seniors and juniors for both men and women). The African nation thus stretched its number of consecutive senior men's team crowns to 11 and its string of junior men's crowns to 9.

In the Olympic Games at Atlanta, Ga., Josia Thugwane of South Africa won the men's marathon in 2 hr 12 min 36 sec. The women's gold medal went to Fatuma Roba of Ethiopia in 2 hr 26 min 5 sec.

The world half-marathon championship was won by Stefano Baldini of Italy, who raced the 21.1-km (13.1-mi) road course in Palma de Mallorca, Spain, in 1 hr 1 min 17 sec. Italy won the team title. Ren Xiujuan of China took the women's championship in 1 hr 10 min 39 sec as Romania won its fourth consecutive team crown.

The men's and women's winners of other major marathons in 1996 were: Osaka women's, Katrin Dörre-Heinig (Germany) 2 hr 26 min 4 sec; Tokyo men's, Vanderlei de Lima (Brazil) 2 hr 8 min 38 sec; Boston, Moses Tanui (Kenya) 2 hr 9 min 16 sec and Uta Pippig (Germany) 2 hr 27 min 12 sec, for her third consecutive victory; Rotterdam, Belayneh Dinsamo (Ethiopia) 2 hr 10 min 30 sec and Lieve Slegers (Belgium) 2 hr 28 min 6 sec; London, Dionicio Cerón (Mexico) 2 hr 10 min 0 sec and Liz McColgan (U.K.) 2 hr 27 min 54 sec; Berlin, Abel Antón (Spain) 2 hr 9 min 15 sec and Colleen de Reuck (South Africa) 2 hr 26 min 35 sec; New York City, Giacomo Leone (Italy) 2 hr 9 min 54 sec and Anuta Catuna (Romania) 2 hr 28 min 18 sec; Tokyo women's, Nobuko Fujimura (Japan) 2 hr 28 min 58 sec; and Fukuoka men's, Lee Bong Ju (South Korea) 2 hr 10 min 48 sec.   (SIEG LINDSTROM)

VOLLEYBALL

Cuba in 1996 captured its second consecutive Olympic gold medal in women's volleyball at the Centennial Games in Atlanta, Ga., and The Netherlands improved upon its runner-up finish at the 1992 Olympics to claim its first Olympic men's volleyball gold medal. Both U.S. indoor teams were disappointing after having posted impressive performances in 1995. Considered one of the gold medal favourites, along with Cuba and China, the U.S. women lost to the eventual champions in the quarterfinals and placed seventh overall. They improved somewhat later in 1996, with a fifth-place finish at the $1.5 million World Grand Prix. Brazil upset Cuba to capture the Grand Prix crown. The U.S. men placed ninth in the 12-team field, its worst Olympic finish since failing to qualify at the 1976 Games.

World Volleyball Championships		
Year	Men	Women
1988	United States	U.S.S.R.
1990	Italy	U.S.S.R.
1992	Brazil	Cuba
1994	Italy	Cuba
1996	Netherlands	Cuba

In the Olympic debut of beach volleyball, Karch Kiraly (see BIOGRAPHIES) and Kent Steffes defeated fellow Americans Mike Dodd and Mike Whitmarsh. As a result, Kiraly became the first Olympic volleyball player to capture three Olympic gold medals (1984 and 1988 indoors). Jackie Silva and Sandra Pires defeated Monica Rodrigues and Adriana Samuel Ramos in the all-Brazil women's beach volleyball gold medal match.

In the college competition UCLA won the 1996 NCAA men's volleyball championships, and Stanford made it a California sweep by collecting the national collegiate women's title.   (RICHARD S. WANNINGER)

WEIGHT LIFTING

Because of revisions of weight classifications instituted by the International Weightlifting Federation in 1992, all total lift performances for the winning lifters were Olympic records in the 1996 Olympic Games at Atlanta, Ga. Though Bulgaria and the republics of the former Soviet Union had dominated the previous Olympics, China, Turkey, Russia, and Greece each won two gold medals in 1996. Greece also added three silver medals, and China gained one silver and one bronze; Russia won one silver medal.

The most prominent Olympic champion in 1996 was Naim Suleymanoglu of Turkey. He won his third Olympic gold to go with his seven world titles. Kilogram for kilogram, the 64-kg (141-lb) class champion was regarded by many as the finest lifter in the sport's history.

Although there was no Olympic competition for women, a separate world championship was held in Warsaw in May. The Chinese women dominated the competition, winning all nine of the weight classes.

In the 83-kg class, Wei Xiangying set a new world record of 242.5 kg for the combination of snatch and clean and jerk.

(CHARLES ROBERT PAUL, JR.)

WRESTLING

Freestyle and Greco-Roman. At the Centennial Olympic Games July 30–August 2 in Atlanta, Ga., the U.S. captured the most freestyle medals (five), followed by Russia with four. Iran and South Korea each earned three. No team scoring is kept in the Olympics, but the Russians unofficially finished first with 66 points to 63 for the U.S. By winning a bronze medal, heavyweight Bruce Baumgartner of the U.S. made Olympic history, becoming the first freestyle wrestler from any country to medal in four Olympic Games.

In the European championships at Budapest, Russia won in the 62-kg and 74-kg weight classes. Ukraine triumphed in the 52-kg class, and winners in the 90-kg and 130-kg competitions were from Georgia and Turkey, respectively.

Poland was the big winner in the Greco-Roman competition at the Olympics, picking up three gold medals and five overall to lead all nations in both categories. Poland and Russia tied for the unofficial team scoring title with 50 points each. The Americans captured three silver medals. Russian superheavyweight Aleksandr Karelin (see BIOGRAPHIES) became the first Greco-Roman wrestler to win three Olympic gold medals.

Russia dominated the European Greco-Roman championships at Budapest with victories in the 62-kg, 90-kg, and 130-kg competitions. Ukraine won the 52-kg class, and Turkey was victorious at 74 kg.

The 66th U.S. collegiate championships were held in Minneapolis, Minn., on March 21–23. Defending champion University of Iowa won its 16th title with 122.5 points over runner-up Iowa State University at 78.5 points. Ranked 17th in the *Amateur Wrestling News* pretournament poll, California State University at Bakersfield stunned the experts with a third-place showing, edging fourth-place Penn State 66–65. Oregon State's two-time champion, 80-kg (177-lb) Les Gutches, was named the meet's outstanding competitor.   (JOHN HOKE)

World Weight Lifting Champions, 1996		
MEN		
Weight	Winner and country	Performance
54 kg (119 lb)	Halil Mutlu, Turkey	287.5 kg (634 lb)
59 kg (130 lb)	Tang Ningsheng, China	307.5 kg (678 lb)
64 kg (141 lb)	Naim Suleymanoglu, Turkey	335 kg (738.5 lb)
70 kg (154.5 lb)	Zhan Xugang, China	357.5 kg (788 lb)
76 kg (167.5 lb)	Pablo Lara, Cuba	367.5 kg (810 lb)
83 kg (183 lb)	Pyrros Dimas, Greece	392.5 kg (865 lb)
91 kg (200.5 lb)	Aleksey Petrov, Russia	402.5 kg (887 lb)
99 kg (218 lb)	Akakide Kakhiashvili, Greece	420 kg (926 lb)
108 kg (238 lb)	Timur Taimazov, Ukraine	430 kg (948 lb)
+108 kg (+238 lb)	Andrey Chemerkin, Russia	457.5 kg (1,008.5 lb)
WOMEN		
46 kg (101 lb)	Guan Hong, China	172.5 kg (380 lb)
50 kg (110 lb)	Liu Xiuhua, China	185 kg (408 lb)
54 kg (119 lb)	Zhang Xixiang, China	197.5 kg (435.5 lb)
59 kg (130 lb)	Chen Xiaomin, China	207.5 kg (457.5 lb)
64 kg (141 lb)	Li Hongyun, China	225 kg (496 lb)
70 kg (154 lb)	Tang Weifang, China	222.5 kg (490.5 lb)
76 kg (167.5 lb)	Li Yan, China	225 kg (496 lb)
83 kg (183 lb)	Wei Xiangying, China	242.5 kg (534.5 lb)
+83 kg (+183 lb)	Wan Ni, China	240 kg 529 lb)

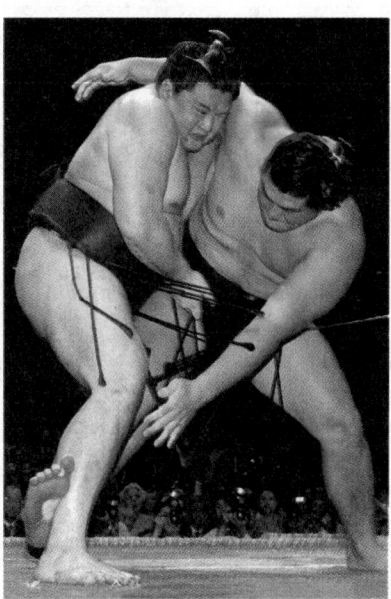

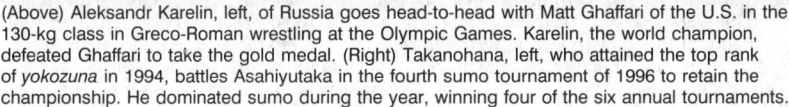

(Above) Aleksandr Karelin, left, of Russia goes head-to-head with Matt Ghaffari of the U.S. in the 130-kg class in Greco-Roman wrestling at the Olympic Games. Karelin, the world champion, defeated Ghaffari to take the gold medal. (Right) Takanohana, left, who attained the top rank of *yokozuna* in 1994, battles Asahiyutaka in the fourth sumo tournament of 1996 to retain the championship. He dominated sumo during the year, winning four of the six annual tournaments.

Sumo. *Yokozuna* (grand champion) Takanohana dominated sumo wrestling in 1996, winning four of the six annual tournaments and finishing as runner-up in a fifth, but he was sidelined in the final tourney in November by an intestinal infection and a torn muscle. The Hatsu *basho* (New Year's tournament) in Tokyo was won by *ozeki* Takanonami in a play-off with his stablemate Takanohana after both finished with 14–1 records. Takanohana won the Haru *basho* (spring tournament) in Osaka with a 14–1 mark and then triumphed with a 14–1 performance in the Natsu *basho* (summer tournament). Then in the Nagoya *basho* in July, Takanohana emerged vic-torious again with a 13–2 record for his third straight victory. In September at the Aki *basho* (autumn tournament) in Tokyo, the 24-year-old *yokozuna* had a perfect 15–0 triumph—his fourth consecutive championship and his 14th overall *yusho* (title).

With Takanohana sidelined in the year's final *basho* in November at Fukuoka, a play-off developed between five contenders with 11–4 records. *Ozeki* Musashimaru eventually won the *yusho,* his second championship. (ANDY ADAMS)

1996 Sumo Tournament Champions

Tournament	Location	Winner	Winner's record
Hatsu *basho* (New Year's tournament)	Tokyo	Takanonami	14–1
Haru *basho* (spring tournament)	Osaka	Takanohana	14–1
Natsu *basho* (summer tournament)	Tokyo	Takanohana	14–1
Nagoya *basho* (Nagoya tournament)	Nagoya	Takanohana	13–2
Aki *basho* (autumn tournament)	Tokyo	Takanohana	15–0
Kyushu *basho* (Kyushu tournament)	Fukuoka	Musashimaru	11–4

World Wrestling Championships—Freestyle

Year	48 kg	52 kg	57 kg	62 kg	68 kg
1991	V. Orudzhev (U.S.S.R.)	Z. Jones (U.S.)	S. Smal (U.S.S.R.)	J. Smith (U.S.)	A. Fadzaev (U.S.S.R.)
1992	Park Il (N.Kor.)	Li Hak (N.Kor.)	A. Puerto (Cuba)	J. Smith (U.S.)	A. Fadzaev (UT)
1993	A. Vila (Cuba)	V. Jordanov (Bulg.)	Terry Brands (U.S.)	Tom Brands (U.S.)	A.A. Fallah (Iran)
1994	A. Vila (Cuba)	V. Jordanov (Bulg.)	A. Puerto (Cuba)	M. Azizov (Russia)	A. Leipold (Ger.)
1995	V. Orudzhev (Russia)	V. Jordanov (Bulg.)	Terry Brands (U.S.)	E. Tedeev (Ukr.)	A. Gevorkian (Arm.)
1996	**Kim Il (N.Kor.)**	**V. Jordanov (Bulg.)**	**K. Cross (U.S.)**	**Tom Brands (U.S.)**	**V. Bogiyev (Russia)**

Year	74 kg	82 kg	90 kg	100 kg	130 kg
1991	A. Khadem (Iran)	K. Jackson (U.S.)	M. Khadartsev (U.S.S.R.)	L. Khabelov (U.S.S.R.)	A. Schroder (Ger.)
1992	Park Jang (S.Kor.)	K. Jackson (U.S.)	M. Khadartsev (UT)	L. Khabelov (UT)	B. Baumgartner (U.S.)
1993	Park Jang (S.Kor.)	S. Ozturk (Tur.)	A. Jadidi (Iran)	L. Khabelov (Russia)	B. Baumgartner (U.S.)
1994	T. Ceylan (Tur.)	L. Jabrailov (Moldova)	R. Khadem (Iran)	A. Sabejey (Ger.)	M. Demir (Tur.)
1995	B. Saytyev (Russia)	K. Jackson (U.S.)	R. Khadem (Iran)	K. Angle (U.S.)	B. Baumgartner (U.S.)
1996	**B. Saytyev (Russia)**	**Kh. Magomedov (Russia)**	**R. Khadem (Iran)**	**K. Angle (U.S.)**	**M. Demir (Tur.)**

World Wrestling Championships—Greco-Roman Style

Year	48 kg	52 kg	57 kg	62 kg	68 kg
1991	Duk Yong Gooun (S.Kor.)	R. Martínez (Cuba)	R. Yildiz (Ger.)	S. Martynov (U.S.S.R.)	I. Duguchiyev (U.S.S.R.)
1992	O. Kucherenko (UT)	J. Ronningen (Nor.)	An Han Bong (S.Kor.)	A. Pirim (Tur.)	A. Repka (Hung.)
1993	W. Sánchez (Cuba)	R. Martínez (Cuba)	A. Manukjan (Arm.)	S. Martynov (Russia)	I. Duguchiyev (Russia)
1994	W. Sánchez (Cuba)	A. Mkrtchyan (Ger.)	J. Melnichenko (Kazak.)	S. Martynov (Russia)	I. Duguchiyev (Russia)
1995	Sim Kwon Ho (S.Kor.)	S. Danielane (Russia)	D. Hall (U.S.)	S. Martynov (Russia)	R. Adzhy (Ukr.)
1996	**Sim Kwon Ho (S.Kor.)**	**A. Nazaryan (Arm.)**	**Y. Melnichenko (Kazak.)**	**W. Zawadzki (Pol.)**	**R. Wolny (Pol.)**

Year	74 kg	82 kg	90 kg	100 kg	130 kg
1991	M. Iskandarian (U.S.S.R.)	P. Farcas (Hung.)	M. Bullmann (Ger.)	H. Milian (Cuba)	A. Karelin (U.S.S.R.)
1992	M. Iskandarian (UT)	P. Farcas (Hung.)	M. Bullmann (Ger.)	H. Milian (Cuba)	A. Karelin (UT)
1993	N. Alamanza (Cuba)	M. Yerlikaya (Tur.)	G. Koguchavili (Russia)	M. Ljungberg (Swed.)	A. Karelin (Russia)
1994	M. Iskandarian (Russia)	T. Zander (Ger.)	G. Koguchavili (Russia)	A. Wronski (Pol.)	A. Karelin (Russia)
1995	Y. Riemer (Fr.)	H. Yerlikaya (Tur.)	H. Baser (Tur.)	M. Ljungberg (Swed.)	A. Karelin (Russia)
1996	**F. Ascuy (Cuba)**	**H. Yerlikaya (Tur.)**	**V. Oleynyk (Ukr.)**	**A. Wronski (Pol.)**	**A. Karelin (Russia)**

Transportation

In the wake of the continued but slow recovery in world trade, governments were cautious in committing themselves to increased investments in the improvement of transportation facilities. Faced with serious budget difficulties, governments were regarding privatization augmented by deregulation and/or contracting out as important ways of providing both infrastructure and services.

Against this background, technical innovations were seen as the best avenues for offering improved service without reducing safety standards. Automakers were looking to technology to develop automated vehicles or "smart" buses that could use "intelligent" highways, while expressway administrators continued to search for ways of introducing and extending politically acceptable mechanisms for collecting tolls. One common theme for those planning transportation facilities was the need to improve the quality of life in urban areas by adopting and conforming to better environmental standards.   (JOHN H. EARP)

AVIATION

The economic recovery of the world airline industry from its worst-ever period of losses continued, with the 250-member International Air Transport Association (IATA),

the airlines' trade organization, reporting a record net profit for 1995 of $5.2 billion, 4% of revenue, and forecasting a repeat performance for 1996. IATA airlines carried 1,107,000,000 passengers on scheduled services in 1995, up 3.8%, and 20.2 million metric tons of freight, up 6.7%. For 1996, increases of 7% and 5.9%, respectively, were predicted. The International Civil Aviation Organization (ICAO), the UN aviation body, forecast a 6% growth in passenger numbers for 1996, 7% in 1997, and 6.5% in 1998, with airlines in the Asia-Pacific region continuing to have the highest rate of expansion.

While the overall situation for civil aviation appeared to be positive, several factors continued to cast a cloud over the industry. Pierre Jeanniot, the director general of IATA, agreed that a third year of net profits would allow many airlines to expand their markets, issue stock, and borrow on favourable terms, but he warned that the profitability of the industry was not broadly based and that for many members it remained only "fragile."

"Government policies toward our industry, which supports in all its facets at least 24 million jobs in the world economy, remain ambiguous as ever," Jeanniot said. "Desired for its wealth generation, but frequently discriminated against in the fields of taxation, user charges, environmental policy, and commercial regulation, the industry is becoming accustomed to fighting for every dollar of net revenue."

Many governments were using the industry's partial recovery as an excuse for the continued imposition of "discriminatory, unjustified, and excessive" taxes on airlines. "Of all the problems facing the industry, unjustified taxation is the least likely to go away," Jeanniot stated.

Airlines also worried about the rising cost of airport landing and parking charges, estimated at $6,120,000,000 for 1995, and air navigation charges, at $4.9 billion. These two together represented over 9% of the industry's total operating costs. Some carriers believed that in the rush to modernize, there was an overexpansion of expensive aviation infrastructure facilities—16 airport-development projects were under way in the Asia-Pacific region.

Fuel charges, which in 1995 represented 10.9% of the industry's operating costs and which had remained relatively low since the aftermath of the Persian Gulf War, underwent a steady rise in 1996, reaching their highest levels in five years as 1996 ended. The causes were a stronger oil market and low levels of reserve stocks, and the result was that airlines had to raise fares.

There were 19 total losses of Western-built jet airliners in 1995, with the deaths of 383 passengers and 39 crew. The loss rate had remained steady for 10 years, but the industry's safety record received a severe jolt in 1996, when there were three major crashes—to a Turkish-registered aircraft carrying German passengers, to Valu-Jet, and to Trans World. (See DISASTERS.)

A salvage crew raises a section of the Boeing 747 that crashed off the coast of Long Island, N.Y., on July 17. Although most of the aircraft had been recovered by the end of the year, investigators were still uncertain whether mechanical failure or sabotage caused the crash.

A general tightening of airline safety and security measures took place in the U.S. and in Europe. The U.S. Federal Aviation Administration (FAA) rated seven countries in the Latin-American/Caribbean region Category 3, which meant that their carriers were banned from serving the U.S. In December the major U.S. airlines voluntarily agreed to install fire detectors in cargo compartments of airplanes that did not already have them. The ValuJet accident caused the FAA to focus on its regulation of the operating procedures of the new low-fare, no-frills airlines.

During the year there were moves toward redrafting the industry's passenger injury liability system. This was based on the Warsaw Convention, signed in 1929, and limited compensation to an unrealistic $25,000. Led by IATA, many of the major airlines agreed to abolish liability limits altogether.

The introduction of navigation via satellite in the Asia-Pacific region continued to help the industry make more efficient use of airspace, but in Europe a 7% increase in traffic put air traffic controllers under increasing strain, and an increase in flight delays caused concern. In Europe, also, EU airlines prepared for the final stage of liberalization, scheduled for spring 1997. With the former Aeroflot now split into more than 150 airlines, civil aviation in the former Soviet Union continued to experience severe problems, including unpaid bills, aging fleets, and lack of investment.

A trend toward alliances between airlines accelerated, but governments became increasingly concerned about the monopolies that might result from such accords and about whether consumers were fully informed about the details, including which carrier actually operated a given flight and which was responsible in case of problems.

(ARTHUR REED)

SHIPPING AND PORTS

According to figures released by Lloyd's Register of Shipping, the world fleet in 1995 increased by 14.8 million gt (gross tons) to a new high of 490.7 million gt. The bulk carrier fleet increased by 6.4 million gt to 145.5 million gt, the largest increase in 10 years. The general cargo and container fleet expanded by 4.9 million gt to 123.8 million gt, mainly owing to completions of large containerships. In the tanker fleet, however, for the first time since 1987, there was a decrease of one million to 143.5 million gt.

The high level of vessel usage in some sectors during the year affected the level of scrapping, which decreased for all types of ships by 28% to 7.5 million gt. Vessels in layup continued to decrease, by 7% in number and 15% in tonnage.

In regard to maritime trade, the Baltic Freight Index at the end of September 1996 fell below 1,000 for the first time in nine years. The first significant victim of the falling market was Maritime and Trading Asia, which went out of business at the end of May. By the end of October, however, the index had recovered to 1,311.

The 1989 International Convention on Salvage came into force on July 14. The new convention provided for an enhanced salvage award, taking into account the skill and efforts of the salvors in preventing or minimizing damage to the environment.

ANURUDDHA LOKUHAPUARACHCHI—REUTERS

Cargo lines the port of Colombo, Sri Lanka, one of the principal transshipment points in South Asia. Plans were under way to expand the port's activities by negotiating a joint venture with a foreign partner.

It further introduced a "special compensation" to be paid to salvors who had failed to earn a reward in the normal way (that is, by salvaging the ship and cargo).

On July 27 the International Transport Workers' Federation (ITF) celebrated 100 years of effort to improve the working conditions of transport workers worldwide. The most important maritime issue for the ITF, however, continued to be its campaign against flags of convenience, the practice of registering merchant ships under a foreign flag in order to profit from less-restrictive regulations.

In the continuing drive to outlaw substandard ships, the U.S. Coast Guard added Algerian and Kuwaiti vessels to a blacklist of 24 countries that it believed did not meet international standards.

Among important port initiatives, 17 Japanese companies expressed interest in developing the Russian Pacific port of Zarubino to establish a foothold for trade between Japan and Central Asian countries. The European Union (EU) planned to help Panama develop areas of the former Canal Zone when it reverted to Panamanian control. The EU was to take part in the conference on the future of the canal in 1997 and would draft a study on the environmental impact of widening it.

In April 1996 Greek shipping mogul Stavros Niarchos, a pioneer of the supertanker, died at age 86. (*See* OBITUARIES.)

(EDWARD CROWLEY)

FREIGHT AND PIPELINES

Sea freight, as reflected by container movements, continued in 1996 to have the greatest activity in the Far East Pacific region. Hong Kong, with an estimated 13.2 million TEU (20-ft equivalent units) throughput for 1996, and Singapore remained the dominant ports, though both were experiencing a slowdown in growth. Hong Kong was linking itself to China's Pearl River delta ports, in readiness for the 1997 handover to China, while Singapore was planning to privatize much of its operations. Kaohsiung, Taiwan, with 5 million TEU, was poised to become a transshipment centre for China, and other ports were expanding to accommodate trade in the Indonesia-Malaysia-Thailand growth triangle.

In Europe increased oil and TEU transshipments were taking place between Rotterdam, Neth., and Antwerp, Belg., Europe's largest "dry port" for containers. Barcelona, Spain, continued to press its claim as an intermodal port (involving more than one form of carrier).

South America was seeking to develop its container ports, with the Caribbean ports expecting to attract transshipment business. The year saw the introduction of a 6,000-TEU container vessel. Further U.S. expansion of the automatic vehicle identification (AVI) tags on intermodal freight trucks was a notable trend.

Although total worldwide construction of pipelines declined slightly in 1996, at less than 22,550 km (14,000 mi), global prospects remained buoyant. Regulatory challenges in the U.S. accounted for the reduced activity. Canada planned to expand its Northern Border Pipeline to boost gas exports to the U.S.

Privatization of energy industries was stimulating development in Argentina, Chile, Brazil, Peru, Colombia, and Venezuela. Colombia's Ocensa $240 million crude-oil line from the Cusiana and Cupiagua fields and the 1,200-km (750-mi) gas line from Argentina to Chile were typical examples. The Far East—notably Malaysia's Phase II gas field—ranked among the leading construction areas. The 918-km (570-mi), $400 million Gas Pipeline in Australia, 350 mm (14 in) in diameter, was completed during the year.

India planned a national liquids grid costing $925 million over 10 years, while two projects in Russia—a 1,900-km (1,200-mi) gas line from Lake Tengiz to Grozny and a 32,000-km (20,000-mi) line from Yamburg to Kiev—were on the drawing board. In Europe the focus was on Spain and Portugal, with a further extension of the Maghreb-Europe gas line, and on the North Sea 854-km (534-mi) gas line from the 16/11 platform to Dunkirk.

ROADS AND TRAFFIC

Global concerns for roads and traffic were focused on two areas in 1996: providing key network links and managing traffic congestion, particularly in urban areas. Constraints on government spending emphasized the need for funds from the private sector. From the U.S. to China, governments were seeking solutions to this problem, ranging from "innovative financing" to a build, own/operate, transfer framework aimed at attracting foreign investors.

The 1.9-km (1 km = 0.62 mi) Piet Hein tunnel in Amsterdam and the 2-km Western Harbour Crossing in Hong Kong were completed. The latter was one of 10 interlinked projects including the Tsing Ma Bridge. A 2.3-km underwater tunnel linking Preveza-Aktio and the building of the Rio-Antirio Bridge across the Gulf of Corinth were notable projects in Greece. Slovenia completed 66 km of expressways, and Hungary opened a 43-km section of its east-west highway. Both contributed to the Trans European Road Network, which also included the planning for two new Danube River bridges in Bulgaria. In Japan the main highway connecting Kobe and Osaka was reopened in September, 20 months after an elevated portion in Kobe was destroyed by an earthquake.

Latin America was undergoing a collective drive toward improving its highway infrastructure. The first phase of a $3 billion 2,100-km link from São Paulo, Brazil, to Buenos Aires included the Argentine-Uruguay Bridge across the Río de la Plata. A highway linking Santos, Brazil, to Arica, Chile, was also being planned. A private enterprise planned to invest $717 million into the 407-km Presidente Dutra highway in Brazil, and other major projects included $90 million to refurbish 9,900 km of dirt roads in Peru, $130 million for building more than 300 km of trunk road in Mexico, and the first stage of a $214 million Caracas-La Guaira highway in Venezuela.

A worldwide increase in charging tolls on highways took place during the year, some of it linked to efforts to combat urban pollution. Tunneling was assisting this process of improving the quality of urban life, and The Netherlands introduced a park-and-ride scheme alongside the A2 national highway at Sittard to induce car passengers to switch to intercity rail services to Utrecht and The Hague.

INTERCITY RAIL

With investment in new facilities not increasing, intercity rail faced three issues in 1996: expansion of networks, increased use of high-speed trains, and private funding of these developments. Privatization schemes were progressing in many parts of the world. Although Germany and Japan were having second thoughts about it, the majority of nations were actively promoting privatization. They included Argentina, Australia, Brazil, Canada, Chile, Ecuador, Estonia, India, Malawi, Mexico, Pakistan, Sweden, and Switzerland. In Pakistan privatization included freight services, while in Chile it was seen as an aid to lowering pollution levels in Santiago.

Europe, which pioneered high-speed rail, witnessed the construction of new 300-km/h (185-mph) lines in Germany, while Belgium also introduced new 300-km/h services between Brussels and Paris. In Asia Japanese high-speed rolling stock was to be sold to China, and South Korea was building a 425-km (265-mi) line.

Major network expansions were reported in China, the most impressive being the Jing-Jiu Railway, which provided a link to Hong Kong. In South America a new line between São Paulo, Brazil, and Chile was being supported by Inter-American Devel-

DYLAN MARTINEZ—REUTERS/ARCHIVE

A train barely clears buildings and pedestrians as it passes through a narrow street in Hanoi. Late in the year Vietnamese authorities initiated a program to improve safety by moving houses that were too close to railroad tracks.

opment Bank funding, while the Scandinavian countries were planning a new triangle service linking Malmö, Swed., Oslo, and Stockholm. Bangladesh planned to improve its rail services with a link using the newly opened bridge across the Jamuna (Brahmaputra) River. Colombia was to build a coal line linking isolated provinces to Lake Maracaibo, while Panama was considering an extension of its line outward from Panama City. Nicaragua was planning a 370-km (230-mi) train service that would connect deep seaports at Monkey Point to the Pacific Ocean.

Notable technical developments included the introduction of tilting trains, which provide enhanced performance, in Switzerland and Italy and double-decker coaches and new high-speed trains in Germany. Efforts to reduce the cost of coach construction to 50% of existing levels were the focus of research of a European Union committee. In the U.S., research was continuing to develop a maglev (magnetically levitated) train that would not be too expensive to operate and maintain.

On the environmental front both Swiss and Japanese railways took steps to reduce the impact of trackside noise levels. Safety issues were being scrutinized following a serious undersea fire in November in the Channel Tunnel (Eurotunnel) that interrupted passenger service for 16 days.

URBAN MASS TRANSIT

Almost without exception in 1996, in both developed and less-developed countries, city governments were pinning their hopes on public transportation as the backbone of urban regeneration, solving congestion problems and addressing issues of environmental degradation. Privatization was becoming increasingly important in this effort. In France 70% of all urban transit networks had private participation. Italy was supporting a similar extensive program, and

European Union funds were helping Lisbon and Oporto, Port. In the U.S., federal funding was recognized as a vital element for new systems.

During 1996 new subway lines and systems were opened in Bilbao, Spain; Madras, India; Naples; Oslo; Taipei, Taiwan; and Tokyo. Extensions to existing lines were introduced in Atlanta, Ga.; Berlin; Cairo; Lyon, Fr.; Madrid; San Diego, Calif.; San Francisco; and Los Angeles.

Agreements on construction of new subways were reported from Prague; Surabaya, Indon.; Shanghai; and Istanbul, while projects to expand existing networks were taking shape in Hong Kong, Boston, Singapore, and New York City. Amsterdam sought public approval by referendum for its subway extension, following in the footsteps of Zürich, Switz., the European city most oriented toward public transportation.

A similar buoyant situation existed for light rail and streetcar systems. New systems opened in Oberhausen, Ger.; Calgary, Alta.; Cleveland, Ohio; Dallas, Texas; and Lucerne, Switz. An automated system was developed in Kuala Lumpur, Malaysia. Construction was under way in an equally impressive list of cities, including Karachi, Pak., and Singapore. Links to airports were being made in Hong Kong, Manila, New York City, and Sydney, Australia.

Technological developments included driverless subway systems (in France), smart cards for fare collection, and passenger advisory systems in stations. People-mover systems were being used as feeder links in Singapore and Kuala Lumpur, and Moscow was examining a monorail system to augment the services of its subway lines.

(JOHN H. EARP)

See also Architecture and Civil Engineering; Business and Industry Review: *Aerospace; Automobiles; Energy;* The Environment.

This article updates the *Macropædia* article TRANSPORTATION.

World Affairs

The most striking, and potentially the most dangerous, development during 1996 was the resurgence of tensions and armed conflicts in the Middle East that had been believed contained, though not solved. While these conflicts remained localized, there was always the danger that regional disputes of this kind could develop into full-scale international wars. In the United States the administration of Pres. George Bush was belatedly criticized for not having pursued the Persian Gulf War, against Iraqi Pres. Saddam Hussein, to the end. Hussein continued to challenge the terms of the armistice, particularly with regard to inspection and disarmament. He had support from nations—including Russia, Japan, and some European countries—that wanted to gain reentrance to the Iraqi market. Hussein also flaunted the U.S.-controlled no-fly zone established to protect Kurdish refugees. On two occasions U.S. forces bombed Iraqi military installations. These strikes were largely symbolic, however, and did not do significant harm or deter Hussein from further military action, as was demonstrated by Iraq's intervention in the struggle between rival Kurdish groups when fighting in the Kurdistan region again flared up during the summer. With the help of Iraqi army units, forces of the Kurdistan Democratic Party took the offensive and seized Sulaymania, the second largest city of the area. In October units of the Patriotic Union of Kurdistan), which were supported by Iran and, apparently, by Iranian troops, started a counteroffensive and retook Sulaymania. Fighting continued, but during September—following U.S. mediation—peace talks began.

There was the danger that Turkey, which had experienced a Kurdish insurrection in the eastern part of the country, would intervene on a massive scale. Thus, Kurdistan presented a prime example of how a minor regional conflict contained the seeds of a bigger conflict. While neither Turkey, Iran, nor Iraq had the desire to become too deeply involved in the struggle for Kurdistan, there was the danger that events would get out of hand.

Turkey, a member of NATO for decades, distanced itself from its traditional Western partners during the year and followed a pro-Islamic foreign policy under Prime Minister Necmettin Erbakan. (*See* BIOGRAPHIES.) Erbakan's attempts to establish closer ties with Islamic nations were, however, only partly successful.

The other major Middle Eastern conflict to resurface was that between Israel and the Palestinian Arabs. The murder of Prime Minister Yitzhak Rabin by a Jewish nationalist fanatic in October 1995 was followed in February and March 1996 by a series of suicide bomb attacks carried out by members of the Palestinian terrorist group Hamas. This in turn contributed to the defeat of the Labor Party under Rabin's successor, Shimon Peres, and the victory of the right-wing Likud headed by Benjamin Netanyahu. (*See* BIOGRAPHIES.) The Likud coalition was opposed to the peace process as outlined in the Oslo agreements; negotiations with Syria came to a standstill, and no significant progress was achieved in the talks with the Palestinians beyond what had already been agreed upon by the previous government. Following the opening of a tunnel in the Old City of Jerusalem, there were bloody clashes between Palestinian protesters and Israeli security forces. This caused a further deterioration in the relations between Israel and its Arab neighbours. Militant Islamism played a central role in other world conflicts. In the civil war in Afghanistan, the Taliban, a fundamentalist group supported by Pakistan, controlled more than half of the country, including the capital, Kabul, by the end of the year.

Islamism (and local nationalism) played an important role in the conflict with Chechnya that had bedeviled Russian politics for years. Dzhokhar Dudayev, the leader of the Chechens, was killed in fighting in April. (*See* OBITUARIES.) Later in the year Gen. Aleksandr Lebed (*see* BIOGRAPHIES), Russian Pres. Boris Yeltsin's special adviser on security affairs, worked out an armistice with the new Chechen leaders. But in October Lebed was purged by Yeltsin (or by aides acting on behalf of the ailing Russian leader), and the future of Chechnya was again uncertain.

Conflicts between nationalities persisted during the year, and the Balkans and the Middle East were turned into what they had once been—permanent zones of conflict. The bloodiest conflicts, however, surfaced in regions considered by most observers as backwaters of global politics, particularly in Africa (the war between the Hutu and the Tutsi in Rwanda and Burundi and a conflict between Rwanda and Zaire).

Even the bones of contention between China and its neighbours were of little consequence in a wider perspective. A more aggressive Chinese policy brought about a confrontation with Taiwan when Beijing tried to prevent the Taiwanese elections from taking place. The conflict with Japan was about the ownership of Diaoyu Dai/

A Japanese coast guard patrol watches protesters plant the flag of Taiwan on one of the Senkaku (in Chinese, Diaoyu) islets. Japan's claim to the rocky, uninhabited islets, which lay in an area of possible oil reserves in the East China Sea, was contested by China, Hong Kong, and Taiwan.

AFP PHOTO

Senkaku, a group of tiny unpopulated islands in the China Sea of which only a few geographers had been previously aware. Such were (and are) latent nationalist passions in this and many other parts of the world, however, that a greater conflagration could not be ruled out, however intrinsically unimportant the issue at stake.

Europe was preoccupied chiefly with internal economic and social problems, above all competitiveness, unemployment, and rising social costs. There was social unrest such as had not been witnessed for years, leading, in the case of France, for example, to mass strikes and demonstrations. Certain foreign political issues did, however, continue to occupy European policy makers. Among these was the slow movement toward greater economic integration following the ratification of the Maastricht Treaty in 1993. While opposition to a common currency became even more outspoken, the idea of achieving this goal by 2002 was not given up. At the same time, relations with the U.S. became more acrimonious in view of differences of opinion regarding armaments. By and large, the European countries were less concerned than the U.S. about the proliferation of the means of mass destruction. Nor was there full agreement about the future character of NATO. In June the foreign ministries of the NATO countries agreed in Berlin on the reform of the alliance and a closer relationship with the Western European Union (WEU); in practical terms this meant the return of France to NATO under conditions yet to be discussed in detail.

As in past years, it was next to impossible to point to a clear trend in world politics to either the left or the right. Thus, to give but two examples, the right-of-centre Italian government was defeated in April 1996 by a left-of-centre coalition, whereas in Spain the Socialist Worker's Party, which had been in power for 14 years, lost in the general elections in March to the conservative Popular Party. In the April and May elections in India, the ruling Congress (I) Party was further weakened, and the Hindu nationalist Bharatiya Janata Party emerged as the strongest single party. Perhaps the most important elections were those in Russia in June and July, which Boris Yeltsin won by a fairly narrow victory over his neocommunist rival Gennady Zyuganov. (See BIOGRAPHIES.) During the past two years, Russia had grown less friendly toward the outside world, even though there were no open confrontations.

Another issue that preoccupied governments was the problem of international terrorism. While terrorist activities were not on a significantly greater scale in 1996, there was a growing awareness that with each year terrorists would have easier and wider access to weapons of mass destruction and that in the future terrorist attacks could have far more devastating effects than in the past.   (WALTER LAQUEUR)

This article updates the *Macropædia* article 20th-Century INTERNATIONAL RELATIONS.

UNITED NATIONS

For friends and employees of the United Nations as well as for beneficiaries of its programs, 1996 was a depressing year. An intense battle, provoked by the United States, ensued over the choice of a secretary-general to succeed Boutros Boutros-Ghali on Jan. 1, 1997; the organization was technically bankrupt; many UN activities failed to yield the positive results that had inspired them; and the UN was uncertain about its future role.

Organizational Matters. Throughout the year the U.S. opposed a second term for the secretary-general, arguing that his organizational reforms were inadequate. Other nations thought the U.S. position unseemly because the U.S. was about $1.5 billion behind in its dues payments. (The UN operating budget was depleted by the end of April, with members' unpaid assessments totaling $2.8 billion.) UN officials defended the organization's record. In April and during the summer, Joseph E. Connor, undersecretary-general for administration and management, publicized the secretary-general's plans to cut $250 million from UN operating expenses by the end of 1997; to eliminate 800 professional jobs and trim the Secretariat from 10,000 to 9,000 positions; to scale down the number and quantity of reports, publications, and policy analyses; and to reduce construction and repair costs. He also pointed out that the secretary-general for the first time in UN history had presented a no-growth balanced budget. Connor complained, however, that budgetary restrictions prevented the UN from making needed repairs to its New York City building beyond those required to bring it up to local safety standards.

Pamela Johnson, executive director of the UN efficiency board, reported that the group had collected 300 cost-saving ideas from UN departments and had put some staff members on call with beepers rather than have them report for standby work on weekends. Other changes required action by member governments, whose decisions often caused additional expenses.

The U.S. was supposed to contribute 25% of all UN funds, but on February 6 the secretary-general proposed reducing that percentage to 15% or 20% in order to diminish the UN's heavy dependence on Washington and to "better reflect the fact that this organization is indeed the instrument of all nations." The U.S. reportedly would accept the 20% figure but would not like its share to fall below 15% lest its influence decline proportionately. Its diminishing influence was illustrated when on November 8 the General Assembly for the first time denied it a seat on an important administrative and budgetary committee.

Reduced U.S. financial support affected the work of UN-connected agencies and programs, such as the UN Population Fund, which in 1996 could spend only 14% of the budget available for fiscal 1995. Nafis Sadik, the fund's executive director, said in February, "The way U.S. funding is going, 17 to 18 million unwanted pregnancies [and] . . . a couple of million abortions will take place, and . . . 60,000 to 80,000 women are going to die because of those abortions . . . all because the money has been reduced overnight."

On November 19 the United States vetoed a second term for Boutros-Ghali, as it had previously threatened to do, and on December 13 the Security Council named the undersecretary-general for peacekeeping, Kofi Annan of Ghana, to succeed Boutros-Ghali. The General Assembly formally elected Annan on December 17.

Arms Control. The first review conference of the 1980 Geneva Convention on Inhumane Weapons agreed on May 3 that signatories should curtail the use of land mines over the next decade and, eventually, make them easily detectable or self-deactivating. The conference estimated that 110 million mines were scattered around the world and killed as many as 10,000 people annually. Critics called the conference a "deplorable failure" for not completely banning the mines. (*See* MILITARY AFFAIRS: Special Report.)

On July 8 the International Court of Justice voted 7–7, on whether to adopt an advisory opinion that the General Assembly had asked for in 1994 about the legality of nuclear weapons; the court president then cast the deciding vote, in favour of the opinion. The court stated that the weapons themselves did not violate international law but warned that nations might use them lawfully only in self-defense if they were threatened with extinction.

On September 24 U.S. Pres. Bill Clinton became the first leader to sign the Comprehensive Test Ban Treaty, which aimed at banning all nuclear testing. Earlier, on August 20, India announced that it would not sign the treaty because the document lacked a timetable for eliminating existing nuclear weapons. The 61-nation standing Conference on Disarmament, a UN body, had worked on the treaty for two years. Another product of the conference, a Chemical Weapons Convention, which prohibits nations from developing, producing, stockpiling, or using these arms and calls on them to destroy existing stocks, received the 65 ratifications needed to go into effect in the spring of 1997.

Human Rights. In January the UN arranged to send human rights monitors to Burundi to check on ethnic friction there, financing the operation with a $500,000 donation from the European Union. The UN wanted to send 35 monitors for a year but could not find funds to pay the $6.6 million cost.

On January 31 the Security Council demanded by a vote of 13–0 (China and Russia abstaining) that The Sudan extradite to Ethiopia before May 10 the three people suspected of having tried to kill Egyptian Pres. Hosni Mubarak on June 26, 1995. On April 3 the U.S. ambassador to the UN, Madeleine Albright, presented evidence intended to prove that The Sudan was a "viper's nest of terrorism." When The Sudan failed to extradite the three men, the Security Council put into effect travel and diplomatic sanctions it had approved on April 26, and on August 16 it imposed an embargo on air traffic to The Sudan.

On February 19 the UN International Criminal Tribunal for Rwanda indicted on charges of genocide two Rwandans who were in jail in Zambia. If the men came to trial, it would be the first judicial proceeding to have stemmed from the 1994 massacres in Rwanda, in which an estimated half million people died. The tribunal had indicted eight former Rwandan officials in December 1995, but at the end of 1996 none had been brought to trial.

The UN Commission on Human Rights, meeting in Geneva from March 18 to April 26, was unable to adopt a resolution authorizing an investigation of human rights violations in China because China marshaled Third World nations into a bloc against the West and its allies. The vote was widely interpreted as a body blow to the commission. In other actions the commission criticized Cuba and, over the solitary opposition of the U.S., joined the Security Council in condemning Israel for military attacks in Lebanon without mentioning the activities of Hezbollah or other anti-Israeli militants.

On July 26 the UN Human Rights Committee, composed of independent experts from around the world, accused Nigeria of violating most of the provisions of the 1976 International Covenant on Civil and Political Rights by engaging in extrajudicial and summary executions, by allowing prisoners to "disappear," and by practicing torture. On October 7 the secretary-general advised Afghanistan's new Islamic rulers that the UN objected to their extreme discrimination against women and warned of "serious repercussions for the foreign-aid programs there" (at least 10 major UN agencies or offices were operating in Afghanistan in 1996). On December 11 the UN resumed aid to Afghanistan after its Taliban rulers freed four aid workers they had arrested.

Although results of UN actions were not always obvious, UN observers in Guatemala received a highly positive tribute from Rodrigo Asturias, commander of a rebel faction in the country. In an interview published in March, he said, "Three years ago, human rights was a subversive topic [in Guatemala]—you could be killed for mentioning it. The UN turned it into a priority topic on the national agenda." Moreover, the UN was influential in promoting a peace treaty, which was signed on December 29.

Former Yugoslavia. On June 18, after the Balkan states signed an arms control agreement, the Security Council ended its embargo of heavy weapons against the former Yugoslav republics. Then, on October 1, the Council voted unanimously to end embargoes on trade, travel, and transport against Serbia and Montenegro as a reward for Serbian Pres. Slobodan Milosevic's assistance in bringing peace to Bosnia and Herzegovina.

UN members continued pressing former Yugoslavia to cooperate with the UN International Criminal Tribunal in The Hague and to settle claims and other issues with its neighbours. The unwillingness of the Yugoslav states to cooperate in punishing war criminals and the reluctance of the NATO forces to apprehend alleged criminals badly hampered the tribunal. The tribunal's frustration became manifest in late July when its president, Antonio Cassese, maintained that "military leaders and all dictators" would conclude that they were free to commit acts of genocide if the Bosnian Serb leaders indicted for atrocities were not brought to justice. Even worse, he concluded, the credibility of the UN and other international institutions would be damaged. The tribunal was especially eager to get custody of the Bosnian Serb leader, Radovan Karadzic (*see* BIOGRAPHIES), who, though forced to resign formally from Serbian political life on July 19, eluded arrest largely because NATO refused to assist the tribunal. Late in the year only 7 of 75 indicted suspects were in the tribunal's custody, and on October 30 the tribunal called for the arrest of four more suspects who were believed to be working as policemen

in northwestern Bosnia. Meanwhile, UN investigators continued collecting evidence of genocide allegedly committed by Bosnian Serbs against Muslims in 1995, and the tribunal handed down its first verdict on November 29, sentencing a former Bosnian Serb soldier to 10 years in prison for having assisted in the massacre of Muslim civilians near Srebrenica in 1995.

Iraq. On June 11 and 12, citing "national security considerations," Iraq barred UN weapons inspectors from examining three of eight industrial and military installations 24 km (15 mi) west of Baghdad. UN inspectors were also denied an opportunity to en-

PERRIN PERRIN—SYGMA

When the U.S. cast a veto against him, Boutros Boutros-Ghali lost his bid for a second term as secretary-general of the United Nations. On December 17 the General Assembly elected Kofi Annan of Ghana as his successor.

ter a base of Iraq's elite Republican Guard in Baghdad. Rolf Ekeus, the UN's chief weapons inspector, went to Iraq a week later backed by Security Council demands that Iraq give full access to its inspectors. On June 24 he and Tariq Aziz, Iraq's deputy prime minister, signed an agreement to speed the process of eliminating all of Iraq's weapons of mass destruction and to allow UN inspectors "immediate, unconditional, and unrestricted access" to all suspect sites. Iraq renewed its pledges on August 28. Ekeus warned, however, that Iraq continued to conceal "some important components of weapons and telltale documents." His caution was borne out when on July 18 and August 17 Iraq again delayed UN teams from inspecting suspicious areas, and he told the Security Council on December 18 that he believed Baghdad was hiding more operational missiles than inspectors had suspected. On December 30 the Security Council condemned Iraq for its failure to cooperate with the UN.

Meanwhile, the UN announced on June 20 that it had destroyed a plant in Iraq that manufactured botulism, anthrax, and other germ-warfare agents. Demolition work took four weeks and was carried out by Iraqi workers monitored by UN observers. Iraq originally contended that the factory produced animal feed but under UN pressure

admitted in 1995 that the plant had a more sinister purpose.

After intermittent negotiations that began in February, Iraq and the UN signed an agreement on May 20 allowing the Iraqis to sell oil for the first time since they invaded Kuwait in 1990. The proceeds ($2 billion every six months) were to be used only for humanitarian needs of the civilian population, and the sales were to take place under UN supervision. One-third of the money was to go to a compensation fund for victims of the Iraqi invasion, and $130 million–$150 million of the relief goods would be reserved for Kurds in northern Iraq. Operational details remained to be worked out, but Iraq's incursion into Kurdish territory in late August and its intermittent interference with the work of UN inspectors led the secretary-general to postpone the oil-for-food plan until December 9.

Sahara. At the end of May, the UN suspended the work of its monitors in the Western Sahara who were identifying persons eligible to participate in a referendum to determine the status of the territory. Their efforts had been at an impasse since December 1995 because Morocco and the Polisario Front independence movement found it impossible to agree to give the vote to certain tribal groups. The Polisario Front insisted that those groups had no relationship to the Sahara and accused Morocco of infiltrating them into the Sahara to influence the vote.

Haiti. All 2,000 U.S. troops in a UN force of nearly 6,000 had been withdrawn from Haiti by mid-April, but the government of Haiti and UN officials were eager to retain a small peacekeeping force in the country to promote national stability. China, seeking to punish Haiti for its ties to Taiwan, did its best to frustrate the plan to retain the force, but a last-minute offer by Canada to pay for 600–700 troops beyond the authorized number ended the opposition, and on February 29 the Security Council authorized the force (1,200 troops and 300 international civilian police officers under a Canadian command) to continue its work. On December 5 the Security Council extended the mission until May 31, 1997.

On December 15 seven UN members (Austria, Canada, Denmark, The Netherlands, Norway, Poland, and Sweden) agreed to establish the Standby Forces High Readiness Brigade, which the UN could deploy to crisis spots.   (RICHARD N. SWIFT)

This article updates the *Macropædia* article UNITED NATIONS.

COMMONWEALTH OF NATIONS

Politically, the Commonwealth continued to focus in 1996 on improving the quality of democracy, governance, and human rights in its member countries. Recently suspended Nigeria remained central to its concerns, and a group of eight foreign ministers known as the Commonwealth Ministerial Action Group (CMAG) planned to visit Nigeria on a fact-finding mission in January.

Nigeria strongly objected to the plan and refused access to the CMAG. Its military regime embarked on an aggressive worldwide campaign to convince governments that criticisms of Nigeria were unjustified and that it was intent on achieving civilian rule by 1998. The CMAG threatened sanctions if its mission continued to be blocked but then accepted a Nigerian offer to send a diplomatic team to London for talks. The Nigerians left London without giving any promises, maintaining that the Commonwealth visit was not to be a fact-finding one, as it had already allowed the UN to carry out such a mission. They would give no assurances that the visitors could see any political prisoners. After more meetings in London and New York City, the CMAG agreed to visit Nigeria without any written assurances about access.

Differences of opinion on the Commonwealth approach to Nigeria ranged from the strong view of Canada, whose new foreign minister, Lloyd Axworthy, said after the June meeting that his country would impose sanctions against Nigeria unilaterally, to that of Malaysia, which opposed a strong involvement in a member country's internal affairs. The U.K., conscious of its huge financial stake in Nigeria, would not go beyond the European Union sanctions and strongly opposed an oil embargo. Ghana—whose president, Jerry Rawlings, was a military-turned-civilian leader—and South Africa began to take a more conciliatory line.

The CMAG, whose mission was to monitor governance and democracy in all member countries, found most of its attention in 1996 focused on the military regimes in West Africa. The Commonwealth played an important role in securing a peaceful handover to civilian rule in Sierra Leone, providing legal, technical, electoral, and constitutional help and sending an observer group to the February 26–27 parliamentary elections. Their report on the conduct of the elections was positive.

The Gambia was a less happy story. When the military regime there banned the main political parties, the CMAG declared the election process "obviously flawed" and said it could "lead to consolidation of military rule in another form." Because of

this, the Commonwealth did not send an observer team. It did send a team to Bangladesh—its 18th such operation since 1990—and declared the election there on June 12 credible and trouble-free.

In March a report entitled *The Future Role of the Commonwealth* was published by the British House of Commons Foreign Affairs Committee. It said: "The Commonwealth is acquiring a new significance in a rapidly transforming world and . . . United Kingdom policy-makers should bring this major change to the forefront of their thinking." It rebuked the British government for not paying enough attention to the Commonwealth in recent years and pointed to the growing opportunities for the U.K. arising from intra-Commonwealth trade. The committee's report was followed by indications of a foreign policy tilt in the direction of the Commonwealth by both the government of John Major and the opposition Labour Party.   (DEREK INGRAM)

EUROPEAN UNION

The drive to achieve economic and monetary union by 1999 and preparations for the enlargement of the European Union during the coming decade dominated the EU's political agenda during 1996. The debate about economic and monetary union (EMU) and the introduction of a single European currency were overshadowed for much of the year by the effects of recession and high unemployment and doubts as to whether EU countries would be in an economic position to meet such major challenges.

At the start of 1996, there were fears that even those EU member states that were most enthusiastic about monetary union would have great difficulty in meeting the conditions for taking part in the planned move to a single currency in January 1999. The tough qualification criteria—including limits on government budget deficits and government debt levels—as well as the 1999 monetary union timetable had been set out in the Maastricht Treaty on European Union in 1991.

The attitude of the financial markets in early 1996 was equally skeptical. There were concerns that because of the serious problems facing the French economy, the French franc might be forced to devalue against the Deutsche Mark and thus break a key condition for monetary union.

The mood began to change after a meeting of the finance ministers of the EU governments in Verona, Italy, in April. There it became clear that all member nations were determined to make the goal of EMU their overriding economic and political priority. They also agreed on the outline of a strategy to underpin EMU with a pact that would commit all of the participants in the single currency to maintain long-term policies that would be oriented toward achieving stable economies. At a meeting in June in Florence, the EU heads of government supported this approach. It thus became clear that the political will existed to achieve a single currency, even at the expense of domestic political difficulties for the governments concerned.

The extent of those difficulties became clear during the summer and fall, when one EU government after another announced strong austerity measures designed to re-

duce their budget deficits and meet the EMU criteria. During the summer, mass trade-union demonstrations took place in France against planned reforms to the social security system, and discontentment with the government's economic strategy continued to the end of the year as economic recovery brought little or no reduction in the numbers of the unemployed.

There were similar protests through the year in other countries, as anger about persistent unemployment led to questions about the wisdom of the EU governments' policies to prepare for monetary union. In Germany the unions organized strikes and demonstrations against planned cuts in welfare benefits, and there were also militant protests in Belgium and Spain. In Italy it was primarily the middle classes who objected to the government's proposals to meet the Maastricht Treaty deficit rules with new taxes and spending cuts.

In spite of these problems, the EU appeared by the end of the year to be significantly closer to the goal of a single currency. During the fall and winter, the Irish government, which occupied the rotating presidency of the EU, obtained agreements from the members on the details of the ways in which the new EMU system would operate. A formal agreement on a stability pact, on the legal status of the proposed new single currency (the Euro), and on the operation of a reformed European exchange-rate system (to link the Euro with those EU currencies outside monetary union) was finalized at a summit meeting in Dublin in December.

Reflecting this remarkable political determination to achieve the single currency, the European financial markets gradually became less skeptical about the prospects for accomplishing it. This was reflected in a remarkable narrowing of interest rates between the key EU economies—notably France and Germany.

In November the European Monetary Institute warned that in spite of the progress that had been made, governments needed to act further to ensure economic convergence, without which monetary union could fail. Simultaneously, however, the European Commission, the executive body of the EU, published forecasts of improved economic growth in 1997, which was to be the base year for judging the economic performance of countries to determine whether they could join the single currency. The Commission predicted that as many as 12 or 13 of the 15 EU member nations might expect to qualify for the EMU. Of these, however, two—Denmark and the United Kingdom—while expected to qualify economically, had already negotiated a political right to opt out of the single-currency project. Most reaction, however, focused on the Commission's belief that even relatively less-prosperous countries such as Portugal and Spain might also join the move to a single currency, and even Italy was close to qualification.

For all the growing optimism about monetary union, the German government and especially the powerful German central bank, the Bundesbank, expressed concern that the rigour of the EMU conditions might be in danger of being diluted. In the closing months of the year, debate focused on issues such as the scale of penalties a government might face if—after joining

EMU—it began breaking the rules governing budget limits, debt, and inflation.

In spite of evidence that the worst of the European recession had passed in the early months of 1996, with the EU economies expecting a recovery in growth, concern remained about unemployment. In October the Commission warned that the economic upturn risked becoming a jobless recovery. In the closing months of the year, there was a growing debate about whether the answer to unemployment depended on radical restructuring of the European labour markets and the virtual abandonment of the European system of social security. The Commission, the European Parliament, and some EU governments insisted that the European welfare model had to be reformed and adapted but not scrapped.

The other major institutional issue dominating EU politics in 1996 was the intergovernmental conference (IGC) to review the 1991 Maastricht Treaty. That agreement involved measures to strengthen the supranational decision-making authority of the EU institutions—including the Council of Ministers, the Commission, and the European Parliament. It not only set out the goal of monetary union but also envisioned further steps to full political union, including a common European foreign, security, and (eventually) defense policy.

In February the Commission president, Jacques Santer, told the European Parliament that unless radical institutional reforms were agreed upon to improve the effectiveness and accountability of the EU, it would be in no position to open its doors to new members. This was no abstract issue, as the number of applicants for EU membership continued to grow through 1995 and 1996. In April Slovenia became the 12th European nation to apply formally for membership. The EU promised to begin negotiations with at least some of the would-be new members six months after the completion of the IGC. As the discussions in the IGC dragged on through the summer and fall, however, with little concrete agreement on the key issues, doubts were raised about the likely date of any new treaty.

The Irish EU presidency said at the end of November that significant progress had already been made in reducing areas of disagreement between most countries on such sensitive questions as voting in the Council of Ministers, a reduction in the national right of veto on decisions, extensions of the role of the European Parliament, a stronger common foreign and security policy, and a bigger role for the EU in such issues as immigration and political asylum. Ireland was succeeded in the EU presidency by The Netherlands at the end of the year. Earlier, in October, the Dutch prime minister, Wim Kok, said he hoped that the 15 EU governments would be able to agree on a new treaty at the heads-of-government summit to be held in Amsterdam in June 1997.

The major difficulty facing the IGC negotiations during 1996 was the increasingly obdurate opposition of the British Conservative Party government to any further strengthening of the EU or any new move to what London described as "a federal super state." British Prime Minister John Major reiterated at the Florence summit in June and again at a special heads-of-government meeting in Dublin in Septem-

Workers in Bordeaux, Fr., burn Prime Minister Alain Juppé in effigy as part of a one-day strike to protest austerity measures proposed by the government. Like other European Union members, France was taking steps to meet the EU's criteria for full monetary union in 1999.

ber that he would veto any further extension of majority voting or any weakening of the national veto in EU matters.

Great Britain's isolation among its EU partners over institutional reform was further deepened during the summer as a result of a confrontation between the U.K. and the rest of the EU over bovine spongiform encephalopathy (BSE, or "mad cow" disease), which was thought to be linked with the human condition of Creutzfeldt-Jakob disease. Following the outbreak of BSE in Britain, the EU imposed a ban on exports of British beef and beef products. The Florence summit agreed that this ban could be lifted only when scientific experts had advised that it was safe to do so and when measures promised by the U.K. to eliminate the disease among British cattle were seen to have been enforced.

Prior to this agreement, the U.K. conducted a campaign of "noncooperation" with its EU partners, refusing to approve even broadly agreed-upon decisions and seeking to block EU business wherever possible. This campaign signally failed to persuade the EU to relax the beef ban in advance of evidence that the British authorities were taking action—including the slaughter of cattle herds at risk—to tackle the crisis. Relations between Great Britain and the other European nations worsened in November when Major demanded that the IGC effectively reverse a decision of the European Court obliging the U.K. to introduce a 48-hour limit for the workweek.

Bosnia and Herzegovina, the Middle East, and Central Africa were the main issues facing the EU in its attempt to develop a common foreign policy. Although NATO military action was required for at least a temporary peace to finally be produced in Bosnia and Herzegovina, the EU took the lead in the international economic reconstruction of the war-torn region.

Tensions between the EU and the United States over policy in former Yugoslavia arose periodically during the year. There were also sharp differences of approach to the peace process in the Middle East. In September the EU condemned the actions of the Israeli government, which it blamed as primarily responsible for the flare-up in fighting with the Palestinians. The EU also insisted on appointing its own special representative to the peace process, a move that was warmly welcomed by the Palestinian authorities and by Arab governments but was received with less enthusiasm by the U.S. and Israel.   (JOHN PALMER)

COMMONWEALTH OF INDEPENDENT STATES

There were few dramatic developments in the Commonwealth of Independent States (CIS) in 1996 as most member states focused attention on pressing domestic concerns. In January Russia's foreign counterintelligence chief Yevgeny Primakov replaced Andrey Kozyrev, a Western-oriented diplomat, as minister of foreign affairs. Primakov ushered in a certain reorientation of priorities away from the West and toward a fortification of Moscow's relations with, and influence over, the CIS states, under the banner of "reintegrating" the former Soviet republics. This approach reflected Moscow's growing dissatisfaction with the five-year-old Commonwealth structure and its ability to safeguard Russia's strategic interests.

The Russian State Duma, at Communist Party urging, expressed its disaffection in more extreme form when it passed a resolution in March renouncing the agreements of December 1991 that dissolved the U.S.S.R. and established the CIS. Although Russian Pres. Boris Yeltsin (as well as most CIS member states, the Baltic republics, and Western leaders) decried the resolution, which had no legal force, many non-Communist policy makers voiced support for the Commonwealth's transformation into a close-knit "confederation" centred in Moscow as a means to restore Russia's global authority.

The much-ballyhooed economic union of the CIS states foreseen in the treaty signed in Moscow on March 29 by the leaders of

Russia, Belarus, Kazakstan, and Kyrgyzstan remained largely on paper, but Russia succeeded in bolstering its presence outside its own territory by establishing joint border patrols along much of the southern flank of the former U.S.S.R., from Armenia to China. A CIS peacekeeping force of about 1,500 Russian troops continued its presence in the Abkhazia region of Georgia.

On April 2 Yeltsin, facing a viable challenge for the presidency from Communist candidate Gennady Zyuganov, signed a bilateral confederation agreement with Belarus. Democratic forces in both countries condemned the move, citing Belarus's negative human rights record under the Soviet-style authoritarianism of Pres. Alyaksandr Lukashenka. There were protest demonstrations in Minsk, the Belarusian capital, and other cities. A CIS summit meeting in Moscow in May expressed support for democratic reforms in Russia and for Yeltsin's reelection bid.

The violent takeover of Afghanistan by the Islamist Taliban faction perplexed the states of the CIS. At their October summit in Almaty, Kazakstan, CIS officials warned of Central Asia's potential destabilization with the Taliban in power across the border, and Russian defense authorities characterized the Afghan situation as second only to NATO expansion as a paramount national security concern. Recurring differences between Russia and Ukraine, one of the more reluctant members of the Commonwealth, over the disposition of the Black Sea Fleet delayed signing of a long-awaited friendship treaty. (KATHLEEN MIHALISKO)

MULTINATIONAL AND REGIONAL ORGANIZATIONS

On June 22 the Association of Southeast Asian Nations (ASEAN) admitted Myanmar (Burma), Cambodia, and Laos as observers of its meetings. The new status of these countries was a first step toward their full membership in the seven-member (Brunei, Indonesia, Malaysia, the Philippines, Singapore, Thailand, and Vietnam) regional organization. The invitation to Myanmar, a military regime with a poor human rights record, assumed that a closer association of Myanmar with ASEAN would avoid isolating the country and help keep it from falling into the Chinese sphere of influence. ASEAN officials contended that their policy of "constructive engagement" with Myanmar would lead to peaceful reconciliation between the Myanmar military government and the National League for Democracy (NLD), led by Nobel Peace Prize laureate Daw Aung San Suu Kyi, who insisted that the ASEAN policy had "failed miserably." Opposition to the policy came also from Australia, Canada, the European Union, the United States, and Western human rights advocates, who feared that it would strengthen the influence of the armed forces in Myanmar and who supported the right of the NLD to participate in Myanmar's political life. ASEAN members firmly rejected a Western proposal on July 24 to establish a UN "contact group" that would try to hasten political reform in Myanmar, condemning the proposal as unwarranted intervention into the affairs of a sovereign state. In November ASEAN delayed acting on Myanmar's application for membership because of the government's failure to moderate its oppressive domestic policies.

An ASEAN Internet forum in Singapore agreed on September 4 to block off sites carrying material deemed counter to Asian values. Their chief concern was "smut" in cyberspace and information that might increase religious and racial tensions in the member countries.

The ASEAN Regional Forum (ASEAN members and 14 other nations with security interests in the Asia-Pacific region) met in Jakarta, Indon., on July 23 to discuss creating a Southeast Asia Nuclear Weapon-Free Zone. Within the zone weapons would be barred not only on land but on the continental shelves and exclusive economic zones, reaching out 200 nautical miles into the sea. Both China and the U.S. objected to extending the zone seaward on the grounds that it would restrict freedom of movement on the high seas and would violate other principles set out in the UN Convention on the Law of the Sea. ASEAN, on the other hand, was eager to bar China from deploying nuclear weapons in and around disputed reefs and the Paracel and Spratly Islands in the South China Sea. To this end the ASEAN countries made it clear on July 24 that they opposed China's action in May aimed at extending its jurisdiction in the sea.

The heads of state of the governments in the European Union and 10 Asian countries (Brunei, China, Japan, Indonesia, Malaysia, the Philippines, Singapore, South Korea, Thailand, and Vietnam) met in early March in Bangkok for the first-ever Euro-Asian summit, which sought to stimulate commercial relations and policies between all those nations that attended. The conferees pledged themselves to work together to reform the UN, to oppose nuclear proliferation, to strengthen controls over conventional arms, to fight against drugs, and to develop economic relations (especially investment) between all of those in attendance. Leaders of the Asia-Pacific Economic Cooperation group, including U.S. Pres. Bill Clinton, met in Manila and on November 25 endorsed efforts to "substantially eliminate" tariffs on computers and other information technologies by the year 2000.

The Andean Group renamed itself the Andean Community when the heads of states of the member nations (Bolivia, Colombia, Ecuador, Peru, and Venezuela) met for their eighth presidential summit in March in Trujillo, Peru. The change was embodied in a modified protocol to the 1969 Cartagena Agreement that established the original Andean group. The similarity of the community's name to the European Union (formerly the European Communities) was meant to imply the Andean powers' intent to follow a similar path to integration. In addition, the members of the community agreed to create a High-Level Operation Group to take charge of the antidrug war in the five countries.

At a meeting of the Organization of American States (OAS) in Panama on June 4, member nations criticized the United States for having extended its embargo against Cuba (in the Helms-Burton law) as a probable violation of international law. The U.S. cast the sole dissenting vote in what observers regarded as a stunning defeat for U.S. policy. (RICHARD N. SWIFT)

DEPENDENT STATES

Europe and the Atlantic. On May 16, 1996, legislative elections in Gibraltar signaled a new direction for the British colony. After eight years in office the chief minister, Joe Bossano, a former trade unionist and leader of the Socialist Labour Party, was replaced by Peter Caruana, whose pro-business Social Democrats won 53% of the vote (in a 90% turnout) and 8 of the 15 elected seats in the House of Assembly. Caruana promised to be tougher on drug smuggling in the region and to establish Gibraltar as an offshore banking centre. He also sought to improve the colony's relations with both Spain and the U.K. and to renegotiate a controversial 1987 agreement on the dual use of the colony's airport, an agreement that Bossano had blocked. Despite his more conciliatory style, however, Caruana agreed that the issue of Gibraltar's sovereignty was not negotiable. Later in the year, NATO announced plans to close its regional command centre in Gibraltar.

On Jan. 8, 1996, Richard Ralph was sworn in as the new governor of the Falkland Islands/Islas Malvinas. In April the government published the results of the latest five-year census. The population of the Falklands increased slightly from 2,210 in 1991 to 2,221 in 1996, while the population of Stanley, the capital, rose from 1,557 to 1,638. Despite improved Anglo-Argentine trade and diplomatic relations, sovereignty over the Falklands remained a thorny issue. Argentina filed a complaint in March after British fishing authorities demanded a $110,000 licensing fee (later refunded) from an Argentine-registered boat fishing in the waters around South Georgia Island. In October an Argentine oil company, in partnership with British Gas, applied for a joint offshore drilling license. At year's end Argentine Pres. Carlos Menem's offer of joint sovereignty over the islands was abruptly dismissed by British Defence Minister Michael Portillo.

Offshore oil was also in the news in the Danish dependencies of Greenland and the Faroe Islands in 1996. The Faroese government announced in November that it was satisfied with the results of test drilling

---

Dependent States[1]

Australia	**Portugal**
Christmas Island	Macau
Cocos (Keeling) Islands	**United Kingdom**
Norfolk Island	Anguilla
Denmark	Bermuda
Faroe Islands	British Virgin Islands
Greenland	Cayman Islands
France	Falkland Islands
French Guiana	Gibraltar
French Polynesia	Guernsey
Guadeloupe	Hong Kong
Martinique	Isle of Man
Mayotte	Jersey
New Caledonia	Montserrat
Réunion	Pitcairn Island
Saint Pierre and Miquelon	Saint Helena and
Wallis and Futuna	Dependencies
Netherlands, The	Turks and Caicos Islands
Aruba	**United States**
Netherlands Antilles	American Samoa
New Zealand	Guam
Cook Islands	Northern Mariana Islands
Niue	Puerto Rico
Tokelau	Virgin Islands (of the U.S.)
Norway	
Jan Mayen	
Svalbard	

[1]Excludes territories (1) to which Antarctic Treaty is applicable in whole or in part, (2) without permanent civilian population, (3) without internationally recognized civilian government (Western Sahara, Gaza Strip), or (4) representing unadjudicated unilateral or multilateral territorial claims.

and would soon open the bidding for the first real drilling rights. It was expected to take about one year to issue the first licenses. The next month Greenland signed an oil-exploration agreement that would give four companies, including the government-backed Nunaoil, Inc., the concession to explore and extract oil from the Fylles Bank 150 km (90 mi) west of Nuuk.

Caribbean and Bermuda. The Chances Peak volcano in Montserrat continued to dominate life on the island throughout 1996. The volcano did not actually erupt but spewed ash and pebbles, causing the authorities to order at least three evacuations from the south of the island to the north during the year. The volcano had been behaving this way since July 1995, and the long-running uncertainty was having a debilitating effect on the economy. In the November election to the Legislative Council, the Movement for National Reconstruction (NRC), the People's Progressive Alliance (each with two of the seven elected seats), and one nonpartisan member formed a coalition government, with Bertrand Osborne of the NRC the new chief minister.

Both the government and opposition parties in the Turks and Caicos Islands spent most of the year trying to persuade Great Britain to remove the colonial governor, Martin Bourke, but London rejected a petition for his recall, signed by both sides. The hostility to Bourke was based on his alleged "abuse of power" and "lack of respect" for the islanders. His term of office was due to expire normally at year's end.

Vigorous opposition continued to the decision of the U.S. Congress to phase out section 936 tax privileges to U.S. firms in Puerto Rico, the principal fiscal instrument behind the island's development. Various substitutes were proposed, including a wage-credit scheme. Hurricane Hortense in September caused the deaths of 24 people in Puerto Rico and inflicted damage estimated at $175 million.

Two ministers resigned from the Netherlands Antilles government during the year—Labour Minister Jeffrey Corion, over problems related to the government's structural adjustment program, and Health Minister Stanley Inderson, following the deaths of nine patients at the dialysis centre in the hospital in Curaçao.

The Cayman Islands anti-money-laundering regime was adjudged "well regulated and supervised to a high standard" by the Caribbean Financial Action Task Force in September. Cayman became the first territory in the region to receive the organization's endorsement.

In June Bermuda's House of Assembly passed a motion of censure against Prime Minister David Saul, accusing him of having contravened a Bermuda Monetary Authority 1995 circular by authorizing a McDonald's hamburger facility owned by his predecessor, Sir John Swan. Frederick Wade, leader of the opposition Progressive Labour Party, died in August.

Pacific. In 1996 France, which terminated its final nuclear testing in French Polynesia, was readmitted as a dialogue partner by the South Pacific Forum and signed the protocols to the South Pacific Nuclear Free Zone Treaty. The dismantling of the test facility at Mururoa commenced under the supervision of the International Atomic Energy Agency. France agreed to provide $200 million per annum for 10 years as compensation for the loss of revenue previously accruing from testing and the associated military presence. In May Paris approved a new statute of internal autonomy that gave French Polynesia more control over immigration, marine resources, and relations with other Pacific nations. Following New Caledonia's territorial elections in October, the balance of power was held by a new, centrist political grouping (A New Caledonia for All), which aligned itself with the independence parties. Francis Sanford, independence campaigner and founder of the Ai'a Api ("New Land") Party, died in December.

American Samoa continued to have difficulty in balancing its budget and paying for government services. Samoa received approximately half of its revenue from U.S. congressional allocations and federal grants. In the November elections, Samoan Gov. A.P. Lutali lost his bid for a third term. Tiny, unpopulated Palmyra Island, one of the northern Line Islands, attracted international attention when a commercial venture to establish a storage dump for nuclear materials from Russia was announced. Guam landowners, in a dispute with the government over former military land, asked for Guam to be included on the UN list of non-self-governing territories.

The Cook Islands faced economic crisis, with a deficit in excess of $NZ 150 million and the government near bankruptcy. These problems followed a financial scandal in 1995 and difficulties with New Zealand over allegations of tax avoidance by means of Cook Islands financial institutions. Under pressure from aid donors, and with the assistance of the Asian Development Bank, the Cook Islands government agreed to halve the public sector, cut salaries and expenses, and privatize some government services. Prime Minister Sir Geoffrey Henry resisted calls for his resignation.

Following Niue's elections in February, Frank Lui secured a second term as premier. The main election issues were the measures that had been taken by the outgoing government to reduce the size of the public sector and to privatize services. In Tokelau revised constitutional arrangements brought increased responsibility for elected leaders and devolution of representative institutions, in keeping with Tokelauan traditions.

East Asia. The men and women who were to lead Hong Kong as control of the territory changed hands from Britain to China at midnight on June 30, 1997, were selected at the end of 1996. At the same time, details of the handover ceremony itself, which had been the subject of considerable debate between China and Britain, were hammered out. Tung Chee Hwa, a Shanghai-born, British-educated shipping magnate, was elected the new chief executive by a Beijing-backed 400-person committee.

Hong Kongers protested vociferously over what country held sovereignty over a small group of islands between Japan and China north of Taiwan. Tokyo, Beijing, and Taipei all claimed the islands—called Diaoyu by China and Senkaku by Japan. The protests served as a patriotic rallying point for Hong Kong Chinese. In September Hong Kong activist David Chan led a flotilla of boats from Hong Kong

A young Hong Kong man acknowledges the British colony's reversion to Chinese control, scheduled to take effect on July 1, 1997. Preparations for the change in administration continued throughout the year.

and Taiwan to the islands, but he accidentally drowned while trying to swim past a Japanese blockade. Three days later 40,000 people attended a candlelight memorial in Chan's honour.

The entire issue of whether politically motivated protest in Hong Kong would be permitted by Chinese authorities after the handover simmered throughout the year. A top Chinese official made a point of saying that Beijing would not tolerate advocacy in Hong Kong of independence for Tibet or Taiwan. Political liberals in Hong Kong decried what they saw as Beijing's interference in Hong Kong's freedoms of speech, press, and assembly.

In June a trade dispute with the U.S. erupted in which American trade officials complained that the colony was putting "Made in Hong Kong" labels on textiles actually sewn in southern China. The U.S. adopted new trade rules, which prompted angry denunciations in Hong Kong of U.S. interference and reinforced already tight business relations between Hong Kong and the mainland. Economic growth for the year hovered near 5%. In the ocean off Savannah, Ga., windsurfer Lee Lai Shan easily won the territory's first-ever Olympic gold medal and was besieged by corporations and government officials hoping to use her image on their behalf.

In Macau the last democratic elections before the Portuguese colony was handed over to China at the end of 1999 produced a surprising victory for pro-business political groups over others seen as pro-Beijing. With a depressed property market plagued by oversupply and unemployment at about 5%, Macau voters seemed determined to focus on the territory's economy. Unlike in Hong Kong, the legislature in Macau was on a "through train" and was expected to survive the handover.

(TIM HEALY; BARRIE MACDONALD; DAVID RENWICK; MELINDA C. SHEPHERD)

This article updates the *Macropædia* articles HONG KONG; PACIFIC ISLANDS; The WEST INDIES.

ANTARCTICA

Antarctica, as defined by the 42-nation Antarctic Treaty that entered into effect in 1961, comprises all lands and waters south of latitude 60° S. The land area is about 14.2 million sq km (5.3 million sq mi), principally the Antarctic continent itself and adjoining islands. Ice averaging 2,160 m (7,085 ft) in thickness covers 98% of the continent. There is no capital or permanent human habitation; scientific and support personnel, housed in some 40 year-round scientific stations, number about 4,100 in summer and about 1,000 in winter. Antarctica is effectively internationalized by the Antarctic Treaty, which places the territorial claims of seven countries (Argentina, Australia, Chile, France, New Zealand, Norway, and the United Kingdom) in abeyance for the duration of the treaty. The treaty also provides managerial mechanisms for regulating international affairs, scientific activity, environmental protection, and formal inspections to verify compliance.

Meteorites collected in Antarctica and studied separately by two research teams yielded evidence that primitive life may once have existed on Mars. U.S. investigators announced their findings in August and based them on the study of a meteorite found in 1984 in the Allan Hills area of Antarctica. The meteorite had formed on Mars approximately 4.5 billion years ago, and an impact 16 million years ago knocked it into space, where it wandered until it crashed into the Antarctic ice sheet 13,000 years ago. In October a U.K. team that had used different study methods and another Mars meteorite—found in 1979 in the Elephant Moraine region of Antarctica—announced additional evidence that pointed to the possibility of primitive life's having existed on ancient Mars. The Elephant Moraine rock, which formed an estimated 175 million–180 million years ago and was blasted off Mars some 600,000 years ago, is much younger than the ore found in the Allan Hills. If these findings were confirmed, they would mean that life could have existed on Mars as recently as 600,000 years ago. "Geologically speaking, this is sufficiently recent for there to be a good chance that life might still exist in protected areas on our planetary neighbour," the U.K. team concluded.

These two 1996 reports highlighted the value of the study of meteorites in enabling scientists to learn about the solar system. Half the world's known meteorites had been found in the past 25 years through systematic searches on Antarctic ice fields. Six of the world's 12 meteorites known to have come from Mars and 10 of the 12 meteorites from the Moon were collected in Antarctica.

Antarctica's ozone hole appeared headed for another record season; in November it was nearly as big as the U.S. and Canada put together. Of greater import, however, assessments published in 1996 showed that the hole would soon cease to exist because controls had been imposed on industrial production and the use of chemicals that destroy stratospheric ozone. The atmospheric abundance of one of those chemicals, chlorine, peaked in 1994 and was still on the way down in 1996, and a computer model showed that the ozone layer could begin recovering by the end of the 1990s. According to Charles Jackman of the NASA Goddard Space Flight Center, ozone should begin recovering by 2000 and return to 1979 levels—the year the Antarctic ozone hole became obvious—by about 2050. This prediction would hold, however, only if the chlorine controls were maintained.

Research in 1996 continued to point to Antarctica's complex involvement in global climate change. Confirmation by several research teams of ancient sea-level fluctuations led to increased attention to ice sheets, the only mechanism researchers believed could have caused the biggest of the swings. Though such sheets seemed unlikely to have existed in the warm climate that prevailed before about 50 million years ago, Princeton University scientists examined deep-sea sediment records and concluded that there may have been an Antarctic ice sheet despite overall climatic warmth. In addition, California Institute of Technology investigators working with scientists from Taiwan showed that high dust concentrations in ice cores from Greenland and Antarctica during the last glacial maximum (18,000 years ago) indicate that the tropics could have been much cooler than other data suggest, also supporting the existence of polar ice sheets. British Antarctic Survey scientists concluded that the large-scale retreat of Antarctic Peninsula ice shelves during the past 50 years was a sensitive indicator of climate change, but they said that the retreat may have resulted from only regional, rather than global, warming and that larger ice shelves farther south were not immediately threatened.

In mid-January a brief near-freezing rain broke a 24-year drought at McMurdo, a U.S. research station in Antarctica, one of the world's driest regions. Meteorologists theorized that a patch of calm air over McMurdo Sound warmed snow that blew in from the ocean, turning it to rain. Temperatures at McMurdo, 1,350 km (840 mi) from the South Pole, can reach above freezing in January, the height of summer.

Tourism increased again in the 1995–96 Antarctic summer, continuing a trend that began in 1990. Shipborne tourists numbered an estimated 9,212. Perhaps 100 tourists landed by airplane, and additional sightseers were aboard commercial flights that did not land in Antarctica. Of the shipborne tourists, 37% were from the United States. Germany, the U.K., Japan, and Australia also contributed significant numbers.

Fisheries in Antarctic waters during the 1995–96 reporting year (July 1 to June 30) landed 104,498 metric tons, of which 91% was krill (*Euphausia superba*). Of the 10 nations that participated, Japan led with more than half the catch; the other substantial fishers were Poland and Ukraine. This catch continued the modest annual increases since 1993, but it was well below the haul for the years up through 1990–91, when the breakup of the Soviet Union

Researchers using specially designed equipment explore Antarctica's winter sea ice, which forms each year. The role of the ice in the food chain of the oceans and its effect on the Earth's weather patterns were among issues of particular interest to scientists.

resulted in the disbanding of its subsidized long-distance fleet.

Bill Green, a geochemist at Miami University, Oxford, Ohio, won the John Burroughs Medal for his book *Water, Ice, & Stone: Science and Memory on the Antarctic Lakes*. Three European scientists—Willi Dansgaard of the University of Copenhagen, Claude Lorius of the French Institute of Polar Research, and Hans Oeschger of the University of Bern, Switz.—won 1996's prestigious Tyler Prize for Environmental Achievement for their pioneering analyses of climate change recorded in the ice sheets of Greenland and Antarctica.

The U.S. National Science and Technology Council, chaired by Pres. Bill Clinton, determined in an April report that the nation should continue its "active and influential presence in Antarctica, including year-round operation of South Pole Station." The report responded to a congressional request for a review of the cost and benefit of the U.S. Antarctic Research Program (administered by the National Science Foundation) and of post-Cold War Antarctic policy. In another decision, President Clinton in October signed into law the Antarctic Science, Tourism, and Conservation Act of 1996, which authorized the U.S. to ratify the 1991 Protocol on Environmental Protection to the Antarctic Treaty.

(GUY G. GUTHRIDGE)

This article updates the *Macropædia* article ANTARCTICA.

ARCTIC REGIONS

The Arctic regions may be defined in physical terms (astronomical [north of the Arctic Circle, latitude 66° 30' N], climatic [above the 10° C (50° F) July isotherm], or vegetational [above the northern limit of the tree line]) or human (the territory inhabited by the circumpolar cultures—Inuit, or Eskimo, and Aleut in North America; Saami, or Lapp, in northern Scandinavia; and, west to east, Uralic, Paleosiberian, Middle Asian, and Arctic peoples in northern Russia). No single national sovereignty or treaty regime governs the region, which includes portions of seven countries: Canada, the United States, Russia, Finland, Sweden, Norway, and Greenland (part of Denmark). The Arctic Ocean, 14,090,000 sq km (5,440,000 sq mi) in area, constitutes about two-thirds of the region, the remaining land area consisting of permanent ice cap, tundra, or taiga. Population (1996 est.) of peoples belonging to the circumpolar cultures, 1,280,000. International organizations concerned with the Arctic include: the Arctic Environmental Protection Strategy, the Council of the Euro-Arctic Region, the International Arctic Committee, the International Arctic Science Committee, the Inuit Circumpolar Conference, and (from 1996) the Arctic Council.

In October 1996 ARCO Alaska Inc. announced plans to develop the Colville River Delta, a large new 300 million-bbl oil field west of Prudhoe Bay. Work at the site was expected to begin in about one year, with oil flowing to market at a rate of 60,000 bbl a day by the year 2001. The project could bring an estimated $1 billion in royalties and taxes to the state government, which depended upon oil revenues for some 80%

of its funding. Although far smaller than the Prudhoe Bay field, the find was the first significant discovery for ARCO in Alaska since 1988 and the first field discovered on land partially owned by a native corporation; the Arctic Slope Regional Corp. would also receive a share of the royalties. The estimated $800 million development of the field would include a pipeline that eventually would be tied into the trans-Alaska oil pipeline.

In April, after four years of frenzied exploration activity, BHP announced that it was almost ready to proceed with development at Lac de Gras, the site of North America's first commercial diamond mine. It was located approximately 300 km (185 mi) northeast of Yellowknife in Canada's Northwest Territories (NWT). The $1.2 billion project was expected to last 25 years and generate $500 million a year in revenues. The mine initially would provide 1,000 construction jobs and, when operational, 650 permanent positions. Environmentalists were concerned about the mine's impact on the 350,000 caribou in the Bathurst herd and the five lakes that would be drained to remove the precious stones. Local communities and native organizations feared that aboriginal land claims would be ignored and that new wealth would result in increased crime and other social problems. These and other concerns were addressed by a federal government review panel charged with evaluating both the environmental and the social impact. In June, after nearly two years of studies and public hearings, the panel gave conditional approval for the project and made 29 recommendations on a broad range of issues. By the end of the year the federal government had accepted the panel's recommendations and approved the project. The government agreed to establish an independent monitoring agency and required that substantial progress on legally binding impact and benefit agreements with aboriginal groups affected by the project be completed before final approval was given. BHP also had begun reaching agreements with the four main native groups affected by the project. These agreements included a promise that up to two-thirds of its workforce would be hired from northern and aboriginal communities.

In October a constitutional plan was proposed that would protect native interests in the western section of the NWT once the new territory of Nunavut was carved out of the eastern section of the NWT in 1999. Under the proposal, aboriginal groups would be guaranteed at least one-third of the proposed legislative seats, and a two-thirds majority vote would be required for passing legislation.

After voting overwhelmingly against Quebec sovereignty in the 1995 provincewide referendum, the Inuit and Cree of northern Quebec considered ways in which to maintain their place in Canada as uncertainty over the future of Quebec remained. At an annual general meeting of Inuit in March, they discussed ways of sharing Inuit land-claim benefits, especially hunting and fishing rights, with Inuit in Labrador and the NWT and the possibility of establishing closer political links with Nunavut to the north and the Cree to the south.

Late in the year Canadian Prime Minister Jean Chrétien announced that the gov-

ernment had set aside land for two new national parks in the NWT. The proposed parks—Wager Bay on the western coast of Roes Welcome Sound and Bathurst Island near the magnetic North Pole—would be protected from staking for minerals or any other development until the government had secured land-claim agreements with aboriginal communities and the NWT government. In June the heritage minister announced the establishment of a new 16,340-sq km (6,310-sq mi) national park, Tuktut Nogait, on the edge of the Arctic Ocean.

In May new evidence released by Ohio State University's Byrd Polar Research Center suggested that Richard E. Byrd, the famed U.S. polar explorer who claimed to have been the first person to fly over the North Pole—on May 9, 1926—might actually have turned back 240 km (150 mi) short of his goal. The clues were found in Byrd's long-lost diary, which the centre had discovered in a mislabeled box of expedition memorabilia. Confirmation would mean that Norwegian explorer Roald Amundsen would claim title to the feat.

Studies by Canadian and Norwegian scientists over the past decade confirmed that the Arctic had become a major dumping ground for highly toxic chemicals and pesticides, including substances long banned in North America such as DDT, lead, mercury, and radioactive waste. One unexpected discovery was that the Arctic acts as a final destination and a cold trap for vaporized pollutants from the temperate climates of the world.

In March the World Meteorological Organization announced that the ozone layer had been depleted at various times during the 1995–96 winter by a record 45% over a zone stretching from Greenland to Scandinavia and western Siberia. Combined world Arctic and mid-latitude readings were reported to be about 10% below the 1957–79 mean. Although the decline did not create an ozone hole, as over Antarctica, the organization warned of even greater depletion in the future over the subarctic if cold high-altitude temperatures were combined with increasing concentrations of such ozone-depleting chemicals as the chlorine and bromine used in refrigeration, air-conditioning, and dry-cleaning activities.

After nearly 25 years of studies at eight far-northern sites in Canada, a research team from the University of Colorado reported in July that the Arctic tundra might in the near future be forested with spruce trees as a result of decades of global warming. Because of the Arctic tree line's sensitivity to climatic change, it was expected to be one of the first major vegetation boundaries to reflect greenhouse warming.

In September the eight countries (Canada, Denmark, Finland, Iceland, Norway, Russia, Sweden, and the U.S.) with Arctic territory created a new international agency, the Arctic Council, to coordinate environmental efforts in the Far North and to deal with common aboriginal issues. Permanent representation at meetings was given to three aboriginal organizations—the Inuit Circumpolar Conference, the Saami Council, and the Russian Association of Indigenous Minorities of the North, Siberia, and the Far East.

(KENNETH DE LA BARRE)

This article updates the *Macropædia* article The ARCTIC.

POLITICAL PARTIES

The following table is a guide to the principal political parties and coalitions of the world. All countries that were independent on Dec. 31, 1996, are included, except the Vatican City State. In most instances parties are included only if represented in elected parliaments (in the lower house in bicameral legislatures). (Party names may be condensed or omitted for reasons of space or to more clearly indicate party groupings.) The first column under "Parliamentary representation" indicates the number of seats obtained in the most recent general election and excludes nonelective seats and seats still undecided. If only a portion of the seats were at stake, the figure given indicates the total number of seats held by each party after the election. The second column (in parentheses) represents the number of seats in the penultimate election and may include different coalitions. The date of the most recent election follows the name of the country.

The capital letters in the column "Affiliation" show the relative positions of the parties within the political spectrum of each country. The key chosen is as follows: F-fascist; ER-extreme right; R-right; CR-centre right; C-centre; CL-centre left; SD-social democratic; S-socialist; L-non-Marxist left; K-Communist; and EL-extreme left. In addition, within some countries there are political organizations that exist chiefly to advance a special interest as distinct from a political orientation. These are represented by lowercase letters as follows: x-parties that have repudiated former Communist affiliation; e-parties based on distinct regional, ethnic, or linguistic identity; r-parties based on religion, usually fundamentalist; g-environmental, or Green; and p-parties based largely on personalities.

The numbers in the column "Voting strength" indicate proportions of the valid votes cast for the respective parties. (STEPHEN NEHER; MELINDA C. SHEPHERD)

Political Parties

Country Name of party	Affiliation	Voting strength (%)	Parliamentary representation	
Afghanistan				
Multifactional warfare from January 1993	—	—	—	
Albania (May–June 1996)				
Democratic Party	CR	55.5	122	(92)
Albanian Republican Party	CR	5.7	3	(1)
Socialist Party	x	20.4	10	(38)
Greek minority party	e	4.0	3	(2)
Others	—	14.4	2	(7)
Algeria				
Interim government since January 1992	—	—	—	
Andorra (December 1993)				
National Democratic Grouping and allies	CL	...	15	
Others and independents	—	...	13	
Angola (September 1992)				
Popular Liberation Movement of Angola–Labour Party (MPLA–PT)	x	53.7	129	(203)
National Union for the Total Independence of Angola (UNITA)	—	34.1	70	—
Others	—	12.2	21	—
Antigua and Barbuda (March 1994)				
Antigua Labour Party	C	54.4	11	(15)
United Progressive Party	C	43.7	5	(1)
Barbuda People's Movement	e	1.4	1	(1)
Argentina (May 1995)				
Justicialist National Movement (Peronist)	CR–CL	43.1	136	(125)
Radical Civic Union	C	21.7	69	(83)
Front for a Country in Solidarity (Frepaso coalition)	CL	21.0	26	(13)
Others	—	14.2	26	(36)
Armenia (July 1995)				
Armenian National Movement and allies	—	42.7	119	
Women's organization	—	16.9	8	
Democratic Party	x	12.1	7	
Others and independents	—	28.3	56	
Australia (March 1996)				
National Party of Australia	R	8.2	18	(16)
Liberal Party of Australia	C	38.7	76	(49)
Australian Labor Party	L	38.7	49	(80)
Others and independents	—	14.4	5	(2)
Austria (December 1995)				
Austrian Freedom Party	R	21.9	40	(42)
Liberal Forum	—	5.5	10	(11)
Austrian People's Party	C	28.3	53	(52)
Austrian Social Democratic Party	SD	38.1	71	(65)
The Green Alternative	Lg	4.8	9	(13)
Azerbaijan (November 1995–February 1996)				
New Azerbaijan Party	p	...	67	
Others	—	...	12	
Independents	—	...	46	
Bahamas, The (August 1992)				
Progressive Liberal Party	C	44.7	15	(31)
Free National Movement	C	55.0	34	(16)
Others	—	0.3	0	(2)
Bahrain				
Consultative Council (advisory body)	—	—	—	
Bangladesh (June–September 1996)				
Bangladesh Nationalist Party	CR	...	113	(212)
National Party (coalition)	—	...	33	*
Awami League	SD	...	176	*
Islamic Assembly	r	...	3	*
Others	—	...	5	(2)
Barbados (September 1994)				
Democratic Labour Party	C	38.8	8	(18)
National Democratic Party	—	12.1	1	(0)
Barbados Labour Party	SD	48.8	19	(10)
Belarus				
Constitutional parliament abolished November 1996				
Belgium (May 1995)				
National Front (French)	ERe	2.3	2	(1)
Vlaams Blok (Flemish)	ERe	7.8	11	(12)
Volksunie (Flemish)	Re	4.7	5	(10)
Liberals { Flemish	CR	13.1	21	(26)
Liberals { French	CR	10.3	18	(20)
Social Christians { Flemish	C	17.2	29	(39)
Social Christians { French	C	7.7	12	(18)
Socialists { Flemish	SD	12.6	20	(28)
Socialists { French	SD	11.9	21	(35)
Greens { Flemish	g	4.4	5	(7)
Greens { French	g	4.0	6	(10)
Others	—	4.0	0	(6)
Belize (June 1993)				
United Democratic Party	R	48.8	16	(13)
People's United Party	C	51.2	13	(15)
Benin (March–May 1995)				
Government party and allies	—	...	32	
Opposition parties	—	...	50	
Bhutan				
National Assembly, non-party	—	—	105	
Bolivia (June 1993)				
Civic Solidarity Union	R	13.3	19	—
Nationalist Revolutionary Movement	CR	35.1	51	(40)
Patriotic Accord (coalition)	—	21.2	36	(71)
Conscience of the Fatherland	CL	12.5	13	(9)
Free Bolivia Movement	L	5.3	7	—
Others	—	12.6	4	(10)
Bosnia and Herzegovina (September 1996)				
Muslim-nationalist party	er	37.8	19	
Serb-nationalist party	er	24.0	9	
Croat-nationalist party	er	14.0	8	
Pro multi-ethnic parties	—	11.3	4	
Others	—	12.9	2	
Botswana (October 1994)				
Botswana Democratic Party	C	54.4	27	(31)
Botswana National Front	CL	37.1	13	(3)
Brazil (October 1994)				
Progressive Renewal Party	CR	...	52	(22)
Social Democrats and allies	C	...	192	(177)
Brazilian Democratic Movement	CL	...	107	(109)
Workers' Party and ally	L	...	66	(46)
Democratic Labour Party	L	...	34	(46)
Others	—	...	62	(103)
Brunei				
Legislative Council (nonelected)	—	—	—	
Bulgaria (December 1994)				
Bulgarian Business Bloc	R	4.7	13	(0)
People's Union	CR	6.5	18	—
Union of Democratic Forces	—	24.2	69	(110)
Bulgarian Socialist Party	x	43.5	125	(106)
Movement for Rights and Freedoms (Turkish)	e	5.4	15	(24)
Burkina Faso (May 1992)				
Government coalition	...	...	84	
Opposition parties	...	...	23	
Burundi (June 1993)				
Burundi Democratic Front	—	72.6	65	
Unity for National Progress	—	21.9	16	
Cambodia (May 1993)				
Funcinpec	CR	45.5	58	
Buddhist Liberal Democrats	L	3.8	10	
Cambodian People's Party	x	38.2	51	
Others	—	12.5	1	
Cameroon (March 1992)				
People's Democratic Movement and allied party	—	...	94	(180)
Opposition parties	—	...	86	—
Canada (October 1993)				
Reform	R	18.1	52	—
Progressive Conservative	CR	16.1	2	(170)
Liberal	C	41.6	177	(82)
New Democratic	SD	6.6	9	(43)
Bloc Québécois	e	13.9	54	—
Others and independents	—	3.7	1	(0)
Cape Verde (December 1995)				
Movement for Democracy	—	61.3	50	(56)
African Party for the Independence of Cape Verde	—	29.8	21	(23)
Democratic Convergence Party	—	6.7	1	—
Central African Republic (August–September 1993)				
Central African People's Liberation Movement	—	...	34	
Others	—	...	51	
Chad				
Transitional legislature from April 1993	—	—	—	
Chile (December 1993)				
Independent Democratic Union	ER	...	15	(11)
National Renovation and allied party	R	...	31	(29)
Centre-right independents	CR	...	4	(8)
Christian Democratic Party	C	...	37	(38)
Leftist parties and independent	CL–L	...	33	(34)
China (September 1992–March 1993)				
National People's Congress	K	...	2,978	
Colombia (March 1994)				
Social Conservative Party	R	...	56	(15)
Other rightist parties	R	...	2	(24)
Liberal Party	C	...	89	(86)
Democratic Alliance–April 19 Movement	L	...	2	(15)
Others	—	...	14	(21)
Comoros (December 1996)				
Government party	p	...	36	(24)
Opposition coalition	—	...	*	(18)
National Front for Justice	r	...	3	—
Independents	—	...	4	—
Congo (May 1993–April 1995)				
Presidential Tendency	—	...	66	(69)
Opposition Coalition	—	...	57	(49)
Others	—	...	0	(7)
Costa Rica (February 1994)				
Social Christian Unity Party	CR	40.4	25	(29)
National Liberation Party	CL	44.6	28	(25)
Others	—	15.0	4	(3)
Côte d'Ivoire (December 1996)				
Democratic Party of Côte d'Ivoire	—	...	149	(147)
Rally of Republicans	C	...	13	(14)
Ivorian Popular Front	SD	...	13	(10)
Croatia (October 1995)				
Croatian Party of Rights	ERe	5.0	4	(5)
Croatian Democratic Union	Re	45.2	75	(85)
Moderate opposition coalition	R–C	18.3	20	(6)
Croatian Social-Liberal Party	CL	11.6	11	(14)
Social Democratic Party	x	8.9	9	(11)
Others and independents	—	11.0	8	(17)
Cuba (February 1993)				
Government (single) party	K	...	589	(499)
Cyprus				
Greek Zone (May 1996)				
Democratic Rally/Liberals	R	34.5	20	(20)
Democratic Party	CR	16.4	10	(11)
EDEK–SK (Socialists)	CL	8.1	5	(7)
Free Democrats Movement	CL	3.7	2	—
Progressive Party of the Working People	L	33.0	19	(18)
Turkish Zone (December 1993)				
National Unity Party	CR	29.9	17	
Democrat Party	—	29.2	15	
Communal Liberation Party	CL	13.3	5	
Republican Turkish Party	S	24.2	13	
Czech Republic (May–June 1996)				
Association for the Republic–Czech Republican Party	ER	8.0	18	(14)
Governing coalition	R–CR	44.1	99	(105)
Czech Social Democratic Party	SD	26.4	61	(16)
Liberal Social Union (coalition)	Lg	—	—	(16)
Communist (reformed) party	x	10.3	22 }	(35)
Left Bloc	K	1.8	0 }	
Others	—	9.4	0	(14)
Denmark (September 1994)				
Progress	ER	6.4	11	(12)
Liberal	R	23.3	42	(29)
Conservative People's	R	15.0	27	(30)
Christian People's	CR	1.8	0	(4)
Centre Democrats	C	2.8	5	(9)
Radical Liberal	C	4.6	8	(7)
Social Democrats	CL	34.6	62	(69)
Socialist People's	L	7.3	13	(15)
Red-Green Unity List	Lg	3.1	6	(0)
Faroe Islands and Greenland	—	—	4	(4)
Independents	—	1.0	1	(0)
Djibouti (December 1992)				
Popular Rally for Progress	—	74.6	65	(65)
New Democratic Party	—	25.4	0	—
Dominica (June 1995)				
Dominica Freedom Party	CR	35.8	5	(11)
Dominica United Workers' Party	CL	34.4	11	(6)
Labour Party	L	29.6	5	(4)
Independents/others	—	0.2	0	(1)
Dominican Republic (May 1994)				
Social Christian Reformist Party	CR	39.7	50	(40)
Dominican Revolutionary Party and allies	L	42.7	57	(36)
Dominican Liberation Party	L	16.1	13	(44)

Political Parties

Country Name of party	Affili- ation	Voting strength (%)	Parlia- mentary represen- tation	
Ecuador (May 1996)				
Social Christian Party	CR	30.7	27	(26)
Popular Democracy	C	10.4	12	(4)
Roldosist Party	C	19.9	19	(11)
Democratic Left	SD	6.3	4	(8)
Alfarist Radical Front	L	6.8	3	(2)
Democratic Popular Movement	EL	4.4	2	(8)
New Country–Pachakutik Movement (indigenous interests)	e	10.9	8	—
Others	—	10.6	7	(18)
Egypt (November–December 1995)				
New Wafd Party	R	...	6	—
National Democratic Party	CR	...	317	(348)
National Progressive Unionist	L	...	5	(6)
Other parties	—	...	3	—
Independents	—	...	113	(83)
El Salvador (March 1994)				
Nationalist Republican Alliance (Arena)	R	45	39	(39)
National Conciliation Party	R	...	4	(9)
Christian Democratic Party	CR	16	18	(26)
Democratic Convergence	L	...	1	(8)
Farabundo Martí National Liberation Front	L	29	21	—
Others	—	...	1	(2)
Equatorial Guinea (November 1993)				
Democratic Party	—	...	68	(41)
Principal opposition parties	—	—	*	—
Others	—	...	12	—
Eritrea				
Transitional government from May 1993	—	—	—	
Estonia (March 1995)				
Republican and Conservative People's Party	R	5.0	5	—
Pro Patria ("Fatherland") Coalition	CR	7.9	8	(29)
Estonian Reform Party	CR	16.2	19	—
Estonian Centre Party	CL	14.2	16	—
Coalition and Rural People's Union	CL/x	32.2	41	(17)
Moderates	SD	6.0	6	(12)
Our Home is Estonia (pro-Russian alliance)	e	5.9	6	—
Others	—	12.6	0	(43)
Ethiopia (May–June 1995)				
Ethiopian People's Revolutionary Democratic Front	...	...	493	
Major opposition parties	—	—	*	
Others and independents	—	...	54	
Fiji (February 1994)				
Ethnic Fijian seats	e	...	37	(37)
Ethnic Indian seats	e	...	27	(27)
Chinese/European seats	e	...	4	(4)
Multiracial seat	e	...	1	(1)
Rotuma Island	e	...	1	(1)
Finland (March 1995)				
Finnish Christian Union	R	3.0	7	(8)
National Coalition	CR	17.9	39	(40)
Swedish People's Party	e	5.1	12	(12)
Finnish Centre	C	19.9	44	(55)
Social Democratic Party	S	28.3	63	(48)
Left-Wing Alliance	L–K	11.2	22	(19)
Green Union	g	6.5	9	(10)
Others	—	8.1	4	(8)
France (March 1993; 1st round %s)				
National Front	ER	12.4	0	(1)
Rally for the Republic (RPR)	R	20.4	247	(127)
Other right-wing parties	R	4.7	24	(16)
Union for French Democracy (UDF)	CR	19.1	213	(129)
Socialist Party	S	17.6	54	(260)
Other left-wing parties	L	4.5	16	(16)
Communist Party	K	9.2	23	(27)
Others	—	12.1	0	(1)
Gabon (December 1996)				
Gabonese Democratic Party	—	...	76	(66)
National Rally of Woodcutters	e	...	12	(17)
Gabonese Progress Party	—	...	6	(19)
Others and independents	—	...	18	(18)
Gambia, The				
House of Representatives dissolved July 1994	—	—	—	
Georgia (November–December 1995)				
All Georgian Union of Revival	CR	6.8	32	—
National Democratic Party	CR	8.0	34	(12)
Citizens of Georgia Union	—	23.7	106	—
Others and independents	—	61.5	63	(228)
Germany (October 1994)				
Christian Social Union	R	7.3	50	(51)
Christian Democratic Union	CR	34.2	244	(268)
Free Democratic Party	C	6.9	47	(79)
Social Democratic Party	SD	36.4	252	(239)
Party of Democratic Socialism	x	4.4	30	(17)
Greens/Alliance '90	g	7.3	49	(8)
Others	—	3.5	0	(0)
Ghana (December 1996)				
National Democratic Congress	p	...	133	(189)
New Patriotic Party	—	...	60	(0)
Others	—	...	6	(11)
Greece (September 1996)				
Political Spring	CR	2.9	0	(10)
New Democracy	CR	38.1	108	(111)
Panhellenic Socialist Movement (Pasok)	S	41.5	162	(170)
Democratic Renewal Movement	L	4.4	9	
Progressive Left Coalition	L–K	5.1	10	(0)
Communist Party	K–EL	5.6	11	(9)
Grenada (June 1995)				
Grenada United Labour Party	R	26.8	2	(4)
National Democratic Congress	C	31.1	5	(7)
New National Party	C	32.7	8	(2)
Others	—	9.4	0	(2)
Guatemala (November 1995)				
National Advancement Party	Rp	34.7	43	(24)
Guatemalan Republican Front	Rp	19.5	21	(32)
Other rightist parties	R	8.7	3	(3)
National Alliance	C	13.0	7	(21)
New Guatemala Democratic Front	CL	8.5	6	—
Guinea (June 1995)				
Presidential party and allies	—	...	76	
Opposition parties	—	...	38	
Guinea-Bissau (July 1994)				
African Party for the Independence of Guinea and Cape Verde	L	46.0	62	(150)
Guinea-Bissau Resistance	—	19.2	19	—
Other opposition parties	—	34.8	19	—
Guyana (October 1992)				
United Force	CR	1.2	1	(2)
People's National Congress	Se	43.6	31	(42)
People's Progressive Party	Se	52.3	32	(8)
Working People's Alliance	L	1.7	1	(1)
Haiti (June–September 1995)				
Lavalas movement	C–L	...	68	
Others and independents	—	...	15	
Honduras (November 1993)				
National Party	R	43.0	55	(71)
Liberal Party	CR	53.0	71	(55)
Others	—	4.0	2	(2)
Hungary (May 1994)				
Independent Smallholders	R	8.8	26	(43)
Hungarian Democratic Forum	CR	11.7	37	(165)
Christian Democratic People's Party	CR	7.1	22	(21)
Alliance of Free Democrats	CL	19.8	70	(92)
Federation of Young Democrats	L	7.0	20	(21)
Hungarian Socialist Party	x	33.0	209	(33)
Others and independents	—	12.6	2	(11)
Iceland (April 1995)				
Independence Party	R	37.1	25	(26)
Progressive Party	C	23.3	15	(13)
Women's Alliance	CL	4.9	3	(5)
People's Movement	CL	7.2	4	(10)
Social Democratic Party	SD	11.4	7	
People's Alliance	L	14.3	9	(9)
India (April–May 1996)				
Bharatiya Janata Party	Rr	23.5	161	(119)
Allied parties	Rr	...	34	(4)
Congress (I)	C	29.8	136	(226)
Allied parties	C	...	5	(17)
Janata Dal and leftist allies	CL–K	...	112	(115)
Allied regional parties	e	...	58	(16)
Others (includes vacant seats)	—	...	37	(46)
Indonesia (June 1992)				
Golkar (Functional Groups)	—	68	281	(299)
United Development Party	r	17	63	(61)
Indonesian Democratic Party	—	15	56	(40)
Iran (March–April 1996)				
Society of Combatant Clergy "group"	ERr	...	110	(155†)
Servants of Iran's Construction "group"	Rr	...	80	(115†)
Others	—	...	58	
Iraq (March 1996)				
Ba'th Party	—	...	160	(250)
Allied independents	—	...	60	
Ireland (November 1992)				
Progressive Democrats	R	4.7	10	(5)
Fianna Fail (Republican)	C	39.1	68	(77)
Fine Gael (United Ireland)	C	24.5	45	(55)
Labour Party	SD	19.3	33	(16)
Democratic Left	S	2.8	4	(7)
Green Alliance	g	1.4	1	(1)
Others	—	8.2	5	(5)
Israel (May 1996)				
Moledet	ER	...	2	(3)
United Torah Judaism (orthodox)	r	3.3	4	(4)
Shas (orthodox)	r	8.6	10	(6)
National Religious Party	r	7.8	9	(6)
Likud and allies	R	24.8	32	(40)
Israel for Immigration (Russian)	Ce	5.8	7	—
The Third Way	C	...	4	—
Israel Labor Party	SD	26.6	34	(44)
Meretz	CL	7.3	9	(12)
United Arab List	e	...	4	(2)
Hadash	L	4.4	5	(3)
Italy (April 1996)				
Northern League	Re	10.1	59	(366)
Right-wing alliance	R	44.0	246	
National Alliance	R	15.7	...	(109)
Forza Italia	R	20.6	...	(112)
Centrist parties	C	43.4	319	(46)
Left-wing pact/alliance	L			(213)
Democratic Party of the Left	SD	21.1	...	(114)
Green List	g	2.5	...	(11)
Communist Refoundation Party	K	8.6	...	(41)
Others	—	2.5	6	(5)
Jamaica (March 1993)				
Jamaica Labour Party	CL	39	8	(15)
People's National Party	L	61	52	(45)
Japan (October 1996)				
Liberal-Democratic Party	R	...	239	(223)
Democratic Party	—	...	52	—
New Frontier Party (Shinshinto)	R–SD	...	156	(160)
Social Democratic Party	SD	...	15	(70)
Japan Communist Party	L	...	26	(15)
Others and independents	—	...	12	(43)
Jordan (November 1993)				
Islamic Action Front	r	...	16	(20)
Independent Islamic fundamentalists	r	...	5	(12)
Tribal/traditional candidates	C	...	49	(17)
Independent centrists	C	...	3	
Leftists	L	...	7	(11)
Kazakstan (December 1995–February 1996)				
Pro-presidential parties	—	...	53	
Opposition independents	—	...	14	
Kenya (December 1992)				
Kenya African National Union	—	...	100	(188)
Forum for Restoration of Democracy (2 wings)	—	...	62	—
Democratic Party	—	...	23	—
Others	—	...	3	—
Kiribati (July 1994)				
Christian Democratic Party	p	...	13	
Gilbertese National Progressive Party	p	...	7	
Independents	—	...	19	
Korea, North (April 1990)				
Korean Workers' Party	K	99.8	687	
Korea, South (April 1996)				
United Liberal Democrats	R	16.2	50	—
New Korea Party (former Liberal Democrats)	CR	34.5	139	(149)
Democratic Party	CL	11.2	15	(97)
National Congress for New Politics	CL	25.3	79	—
Others and independents	—	12.8	16	(53)
Kuwait (October 1996)				
Islamic fundamentalists	r	...	16	(19)
Government supporters	—	...	30	(15)
Liberal opposition	—	...	4	(6)
Kyrgyzstan (February–April 1995)				
Pro-government independents	—	...	90	
Others	—	...	15	
Laos (December 1992)				
Government (single) party	K	...	85	(79)
Latvia (October 1995)				
People's Movement for Latvia	ERp	15.1	16	—
Fatherland and Freedom	ERe	11.6	14	(6)
National Conservative Party	Re	6.2	8	(15)
Farmer's Union and allies	CR	6.1	8	(18)
Latvia's Way	C	14.7	17	(36)
Saimnieks ("In Charge")	CL	15.3	18	—
National Harmony Party (pro-Russian)	CL	5.6	6	(13)
Unity Party	K	7.2	8	—
Others	—	5.7	5	(12)
Lebanon (August–September 1996)				
Christian	—	—	64	
Maronite	—	—	34	
Greek Orthodox	—	—	14	
Greek Catholic	—	—	8	
Armenian Orthodox	—	—	5	
Others	—	—	3	
Muslim/Druze	—	—	64	
Sunnite	—	—	27	
Shi'ite	—	—	27	
Druze	—	—	8	
'Alawite	—	—	2	
Lesotho (March 1993)				
Basotho Congress Party	—	74.8	65	
Basotho National Party	—	22.7	0	
Liberia				
Transitional government from September 1995	—	—	—	
Libya				
General People's Congress	—	—	750	
Liechtenstein (October 1993)				
Progressive Citizens' Party	CR	41.3	11	(12)
Fatherland Union	C	50.1	13	(11)
The Free List	g	8.5	1	(2)

Political Parties

Country / Name of party	Affiliation	Voting strength (%)	Parliamentary representation
Lithuania (October–November 1996)			
Christian Democrats	CR	12.2	16 (13)
Homeland Union	CR	29.8	70 —
Reform Movement (Sajudis)	CR	—	— (29)
Centre Union		8.2	13 —
Social Democratic Party	SD	6.6	12 (8)
Democratic Labour Party	x	9.5	12 (74)
Others and independents	—	33.7	18 (17)
Luxembourg (June 1994)			
Christian Social People's Party	CR	29.3	21 (22)
Democratic Party	C	11.6	12 (11)
Socialist Workers' Party	S	33.5	17 (18)
Communist Party	K	2.8	0 (1)
Action Committee for Democracy and Justice		7.1	5 (4)
Green Alternative	g	10.2	5 (4)
Macedonia (October–November 1994)			
Alliance of Macedonia	x	...	95
Pro-government Albanian party	e	...	10
Anti-government Albanian party	e	...	4
Other opposition	—	...	11
Madagascar (June 1993)			
Living Forces coalition		...	75
Others		...	59
Malawi (May 1994)			
United Democratic Front	—	46.4	84 —
Malawi Congress Party	—	33.6	55 (136)
Alliance for Democracy	—	18.9	36 —
Malaysia (April 1995)			
Islamic parties	CR	17.4	13 (15)
National Front coalition	e	64.0	162 (127)
Democratic Action Party	SD	12.1	9 (20)
Others and independents		6.5	8 (18)
Maldives (December 1994)			
People's Council, non-party	—		40
Mali (February–March 1992)			
Alliance for Democracy in Mali		48.4	76
Others	—	51.6	40
Malta (October 1996)			
Nationalist Party	R	47.8	34 (34)
Malta Labour Party	SD	50.7	35 (31)
Marshall Islands (November 1995)			
House of Representatives, non-party	—		33
Mauritania (October 1996)			
Government party	R		70 (67)
Principal opposition parties	...	...	1 (*)
Others and independents	—	...	8 (12)
Mauritius (December 1995)			
Mauritian Socialist Movement and allied parties		19.7	0 } (59)
Mauritian Militant Movement }			
Mauritian Labour Party and } allied parties		65.2	62
			(3)
Others	—	15.1	0 —
Mexico (August 1994)			
National Action Party (PAN)	CR	25.9	119 (89)
Institutional Revolutionary Party (PRI)	C	48.7	300 (320)
Democratic Revolutionary Party	CL	16.6	71 (41)
Labour Party	L	2.7	10 (0)
Others	—	6.1	0 (50)
Micronesia (March 1995)			
Congress, non-party	—	...	14
Moldova (February 1994)			
Popular Front alliance	Re	7.5	9
Peasants/Intellectuals bloc	Ce	9.2	11
Agrarian Democratic Party	C–x	43.2	56
Socialist/Unity bloc (Russian)	xe	22.0	28
Others	—	18.1	0
Monaco (January 1993)			
Campora list	p	...	15
Others	p	...	3
Mongolia (June 1996)			
Democratic Union coalition	C–SD	47.0	50 (5)
United Heritage Party	—	1.6	1 —
People's Revolutionary Party	x	40.5	25 (71)
Morocco (June–September 1993)			
Constitutional Union	CR	...	54 (83)
National Democratic Party	CR	...	24 (24)
Berber parties	CRe	...	76 (47)
National Assembly of Independents	C	...	41 (61)
Democratic Bloc	CL–EL	...	120 (85)
Others and independents	—	...	18 (6)
Mozambique (October 1994)			
Mozambique Liberation Front (Frelimo)	x	44.3	129 (250)
Mozambique National Resistance (Renamo)	—	37.8	112
Democratic Union	—	5.2	9
Myanmar			
Military government since September 1988			
Namibia (December 1994)			
Democratic Turnhalle Alliance	C	20.8	15 (21)
South West Africa People's Organization (SWAPO)	L	73.9	53 (41)
Others	—	5.3	4 (10)
Nauru (November 1995)			
Parliament, non-party	p	—	18 (18)
Nepal (November 1994)			
National Democratic Party	R	17.9	20 (4)
Nepali Congress Party	C	33.4	83 (110)
Communist Party	K	30.9	88 (82)
Others and independents	—	17.8	14 (9)
Netherlands, The (May 1994)			
Christian Democratic Appeal	CR	22.2	34 (54)
People's Party for Freedom and Democracy	CR	19.9	31 (22)
Democrats 66	CL	15.5	24 (12)
Labour Party	SD	24.0	37 (49)
Green Left	Lg	3.5	5 (6)
General Union of the Elderly		4.5	6 —
Others	—	10.4	13 (7)
New Zealand (October 1996)			
ACT New Zealand	CR	6.2	8 —
National Party	CR	34.1	44 (50)
United New Zealand	C	0.9	1 —
New Zealand First	C	13.1	17 (2)
Labour Party	CL	28.3	37 (45)
The Alliance (coalition)	L	10.1	13 (2)
Nicaragua (October 1996)			
National Opposition Union	—	—	— (51)
Liberal Alliance coalition	R–C	46.0	42 —
Sandinista National Liberation Front	CL–EL	36.5	37 (39)
Others	—	17.5	14 (2)
Niger (November 1996)			
Government party	—	...	58 —
Allied parties	—	...	11 } (83)
Others and independents	—	...	14 }
Nigeria			
Military government since 1993			
Norway (September 1993)			
Progress Party	R	6.3	10 (22)
Conservative Party	R	16.9	28 (37)
Christian People's Party	CR	7.9	13 (14)
Centre Party	CR	16.8	32 (11)
Labour Party	SD	37.0	67 (63)
Socialist Left	S	7.9	13 (17)
Others	—	7.2	2 (1)
Oman			
Consultative Council (advisory body)	—		—
Pakistan (October 1993)			
Religious parties	Rr	...	10 (6)
Pakistan Muslim League (Nawaz)	—	41.0	73 } (105)
Pakistan Muslim League (Junejo)	—		6 }
Pakistan People's Party	CL	38.0	86 (45)
Mohajir Qaumi Movement	e	...	* (15)
Others and independents	—	...	26 (30)
Palau (November 1996)			
House of Delegates, non-party	—		16
Panama (May 1994)			
Democratic Revolutionary Party and allies	—	...	31 (12)
Others	—	...	41 (55)
Papua New Guinea (June 1992)			
United Party (Pangu Pati)	p	...	22 (26)
People's Democratic Movement	p	...	15 (18)
Others	p	...	40 (41)
Independents	—	...	31 (21)
Paraguay (May 1993)			
Colorado Party	R	43.0	38 (48)
Authentic Radical Liberal Party	CL	35.1	33 (19)
National Encounter coalition	—	17.1	9 —
Others	—	4.8	0 (5)
Peru (April 1995)			
Popular Christian Party	R	3.1	3 (8)
Popular Action	CR	3.3	4 —
Change 90-New Majority (coalition of independents)	p	52.1	67 (44)
Union for Peru		14.0	17 —
Independent Moralizing Front	p	4.9	6 (7)
American Popular Revolutionary Alliance	CL	6.5	8 —
Others	—	16.1	15 (21)
Philippines (May 1995)			
National People's Coalition	R	...	28 (48)
Centrist parties	C	...	13 (15)
People Power–National Union of Christian Democrats	p	...	126 (51)
Democratic Filipino Struggle	—	...	28 (87)
Others and independents	—	...	9 (0)
Poland (September 1993)			
Confederation for an Independent Poland	R	5.8	22 (46)
Non-Party Bloc to Support Reform	R	5.4	16 —
Democratic Union	CL	10.6	74 (62)
Labour Union	L	7.3	41 (4)
Democratic Left Alliance	x	20.4	171 (60)
Polish Peasant Party	x	15.4	132 (48)
German minority organizations	e	0.5	4 (7)
Others	—	34.6	0 (233)
Portugal (October 1995)			
Popular Party	R	9.1	15 (5)
Social Democratic Party	CR	34.0	88 (135)
Socialist Party	CL	43.9	112 (72)
Unified Democratic Coalition	L–K	8.6	15 (17)
Others	—	4.4	0 (1)
Qatar			
Consultative Council (advisory body)	—		—
Romania (November 1996)			
Romanian National Unity Party	Re	4.4	18 (30)
Greater Romania Party	Re	4.5	19 (16)
Democratic Convention of Romania	CR	30.2	122 (82)
Social Democratic Union	SD	12.9	53 (43)
Social Democracy Party	x	21.5	91 (117)
Hungarian Democratic Union	e	6.6	25 (27)
Others	—	19.9	0 (13)
Russia (December 1995)			
Liberal Democratic Party	ERe	11.2	51 (64)
Congress of Russian Communities	R/CLe	4.3	5 —
Our Home is Russia	CR	10.1	55 —
Forward Russia!	C	4.0	1 —
Russia's Democratic Choice	CL	3.9	9 (76)
Yabloko (Bloc of Three)	CL	6.9	45 (28)
Women of Russia	CL	4.6	3 (24)
Communist Party	L	22.3	157 (45)
Agrarian Party	L	3.8	20 (55)
Power to the People	Le	1.6	9 —
Workers' Russia	EL	4.5	1 (0)
Other parties	—	...	17 (137)
Independents	—	...	77 (21)
Rwanda			
Transitional government from July 1994	—		—
Saint Kitts and Nevis (July 1995)			
People's Action Movement	CL	...	1 (4)
St. Kitts-Nevis Labour Party	L	...	7 (4)
Concerned Citizens' Movement	e	...	2 (2)
Nevis Reformation Party (pro-secessionist)	e	...	1 (1)
Saint Lucia (April 1992)			
United Workers' Party	C	54.9	11 (9)
St. Lucia Labour Party	CL	41.9	6 (8)
Saint Vincent and the Grenadines (February 1994)			
New Democratic Party	C	54.6	12 (15)
St. Vincent Labour Party	SD	26.0	2 (0)
Movement for National Unity	L	17.3	1 (0)
San Marino (May 1993)			
Christian Democrats	CR	41.4	26 (27)
Socialist Party	S	23.7	14 (7)
Progressive Democratic Party	x	18.6	11 (18)
Popular Democratic Alliance	—	7.7	4 —
Other parties	—	8.6	5 (8)
São Tomé and Príncipe (October 1994)			
Party of Democratic Convergence	C	17	14 (33)
Movement for the Liberation of São Tomé and Príncipe	L	43	27 (21)
Independent Democratic Action	—	26	14 —
Others	—	4	0 (1)
Saudi Arabia			
Consultative Council (advisory body)	—		—
Senegal (May 1993)			
Socialist Party	SD	56.6	84 (103)
Senegalese Democratic Party	—	30.2	27 (17)
Let Us Unite Senegal	EL	4.9	3 —
Other parties	—	8.3	6 —
Seychelles (July 1993)			
People's Progressive Front	L	57.5	28 (23)
Others	—	42.5	5 —
Sierra Leone (February 1996)			
Sierra Leone People's Party	pe	36.1	27
United National People's Party	pe	21.6	17
Four other regional parties	pe	31.1	24
Paramount chiefs (non-party)	—	—	12
Singapore (August 1991)			
People's Action Party	CR	61	77 (80)
Democratic Party	CL	12	3 (1)
Workers' Party	L	14	1 (0)
Slovakia (September–October 1994)			
Slovak National Party	Re	5.4	9 (15)
Movement for a Democratic Slovakia	CR	35.0	61 (74)
Democratic Union	C	8.6	15 —
Christian Democratic Movement	CL	10.1	17 (18)
Common Choice coalition	CL–x	10.4	18 (29)
Hungarian minority coalition	e	10.2	17 (14)
Others	—	20.3	13 (0)
Slovenia (November 1996)			
Slovenian National Party	ER	3.2	4 (12)
Slovenian People's Party	R	19.4	19 (10)
Slovenian Christian Democrats	CR	9.6	10 (15)
Social Democratic Party	C–SD	16.1	16 (4)

Political Parties

Country / Name of party	Affiliation	Voting strength (%)	Parliamentary representation
Liberal Democracy of Slovenia	CL	27.0	25	—
Centre-left parties	CL	—	—	(33)
United List of Social Democrats	x	9.0	9 }	
Pensioner's party	—	4.3	5 }	(14)
Hungarian/Italian minorities	e	—	2	(2)
Solomon Islands (May 1993)				
Government Alliance	p	...	24	
Opposition party	p	...	23	
Somalia				
No government since 1991	—	—	—	
South Africa (April 1994)				
Freedom Front	ER	2.2	9	
National Party	CR	20.4	82	
Inkatha Freedom Party	e	10.5	43	
Democratic Party	C	1.7	7	
African National Congress	CL	62.7	252	
Pan-Africanist Congress	EL	1.2	5	
Others	—	1.3	2	
Spain (March 1996)				
Popular Party	CR	38.9	156	(141)
Basque Nationalist Party	Ce	1.3	5	(5)
Canarian coalition	Ce	0.9	4	(4)
Convergence and Union (Catalan)	CLe	4.6	16	(17)
Spanish Socialist Workers' Party	SD	37.5	141	(159)
United Left	L–K	10.6	21	(18)
Galician Nationalist Bloc	Le	0.9	2	(0)
Herri Batasuna (Basque radicals)	ELe	0.7	2	(2)
Other regional parties	e	1.6	3	(4)
Sri Lanka (August 1994)				
United National Party	CR	44.0	94	(125)
People's Alliance	CL	48.9	105 }	
Others and independents	—	3.6	14 }	(86)
Sri Lanka Muslim Congress	r	1.8	7	(4)
Tamil United Liberation Front	e	1.7	5	(10)
Sudan, The (March 1996)				
Government supporters	—	...	264	
Principal opposition forces	—	—	*	
Suriname (May 1996)				
National Democratic Party	p	25.6	16	(12)
Democratic Alternative '91	SD	12.4	4 }	
Pendana Lima (Javan party)	e	10.0	4 }	(9)
New Front coalition	CLe	41.4	24	(30)
Alliance		9.3	3	
Swaziland (September–October 1993)				
House of Assembly, non-party	—	—	55	
Sweden (September 1994)				
New Democracy	R	1.2	0	(24)
Christian Democrats	R	4.1	15	(27)
Moderate Coalition Party	CR	22.4	80	(80)
Centre Party	CR	7.7	27	(31)
Liberal People's Party	C	7.2	26	(33)
Social Democrats	S	45.3	161	(138)
Left Party	x	6.2	22	(16)
Greens	g	5.0	18	(0)
Switzerland (October 1995)				
Freedom Party	R	4.0	7	(8)
Swiss People's Party	R	14.9	29	(25)
Christian Democrats	CR	17.0	34	(36)
Liberal Party	CR	2.7	7	(10)
Radical Democrats	C	20.2	45	(44)
Social Democrats	SD	21.8	54	(42)
Green Party	g	5.0	9	(14)
Others	—	14.4	15	(21)
Syria (August 1994)				
Ba'th Party and allies	—	...	167	(166)
Independents	—	...	83	(84)
Taiwan (December 1995)				
New Party (pro-unification)	R	12.9	21	—
Nationalist (Kuomintang)	—	46.1	85	(96)
Democratic Progressive Party (pro-independence)	—	33.2	54	(50)
Others and independents	—	7.8	4	(15)
Tajikistan (February–March 1995)				
Communist Party	K	...	60	
Others and independents	—	...	119	
Western/Islamic parties			‡	
Tanzania (October–November 1995)				
NCCR–Maguezi	C	...	16	—
Government party	S	...	186	(216)
Civic United Front (pro-Zanzibar autonomy)	e	...	24	—
Others	—	...	6	—
Thailand (November 1996)				
Thai Nation	R	...	39	(92)
Thai Citizens	Rp	...	18	(18)
National Development Party	Rp	...	52	(53)
Social Action Party	CR	...	20	(22)
New Aspiration Party	p	...	125	(57)
Democrat Party	C	...	123	(86)
Others	—	...	16	(63)
Togo (February 1994–August 1996)				
Rally of the Togolese People	p	...	40	
Allied party and independents	—	...	3	
Action Committee for Renewal	—	...	33	
Union for Democracy	—	...	5	
Tonga (January 1996)				
Noble representatives	—	...	9	(9)
People's Party (pro-democracy commoners)	—	...	6	(6)
Other commoners	—	...	3	(3)
Trinidad and Tobago (November 1995)				
People's National Movement	C	48.8	17	(21)
National Alliance for Reconstruction	C	4.8	2	(2)
United National Congress	SD	45.7	17	(13)
Tunisia (March 1994)				
Government party	CL	97.7	144	(141)
Opposition parties	—	2.3	19	(0)
Turkey (December 1995)				
Nationalist Action Party	ER	8.2	0 }	
Welfare (Refah) Party	Rr	21.4	158 }	(62)
True Path Party	CR	19.3	135	(178)
Motherland Party	CR	19.8	132	(115)
Democratic Left Party	CL	14.7	75	(7)
Republican People's Party	CL	10.8	50	—
Other leftist	CL–L	...	0	(88)
Turkmenistan (December 1994)				
Government (single) party	x	...	50	
Tuvalu (November 1993)				
Parliament, non-party	—	—	12	
Uganda (June 1996)				
National Assembly, non-party	—	'...	276	
Ukraine (March 1994–February 1996)				
Extreme nationalist parties	ERe	...	5	
Less extreme nationalist parties	CRe	...	15	
Ukrainian Popular Movement (Rukh)	Ce	...	21	
Centrist parties	C	...	17	
Communist Party and allies	K–EL	...	132	
Independents	—	...	230	
United Arab Emirates				
Federal National Council (advisory body)	—	—	—	
United Kingdom (April 1992)				
Democratic Unionists	Re	0.3	3	(3)
Conservative Party	CR	41.9	336	(375)
Liberal Democrats	CL	17.9	20	(22)
Labour Party	L	34.4	271	(229)
Scottish National Party	e	1.9	3	(3)
Plaid Cymru (Welsh Nationalists)	e	0.5	4	(3)
Ulster Unionists	—	0.8	9	(9)
Social Democratic and Labour Party (Northern Ireland)	CLe	0.6	4	(3)
Sinn Fein (Northern Ireland)	ELe	0.2	0	(1)
Other	—	1.5	1	(2)
United States (November 1996)				
Republican	R–CR	...	227	(175)
Democratic	C–L	...	207	(259)
Other	L	...	1	(1)
Uruguay (November 1994)				
National (Blanco) Party	C	31.4	31	(39)
Colorado Party	C	32.5	32	(30)
New Space	CL	5.1	5	(9)
Progressive Encounter	L	30.8	31	
Broad Front	L	—	—	(21)
Uzbekistan (December 1994–January 1995)				
People's Democratic Party and allies	x	100.0	250	
Opposition parties			‡	
Vanuatu (November 1995)				
Union of Moderate Parties	CR	...	17	(19)
Vanuatu National United Party	CR	...	9	(10)
Unity Front coalition	—	...	20	(16)
Others and independents	—	...	4	(1)
Venezuela (December 1993)				
COPEI (Social Christians)	CR–CL	22.8	54	(67)
Democratic Action	SD	23.9	55	(97)
National Convergence }				
Movement to Socialism }	L	24.4	50	(18)
The Radical Cause	EL	21.1	40	(3)
Others	—	7.8	0	(16)
Vietnam (July 1992)				
Government (single) party	—	...	395	
Western Samoa (April 1996)				
Human Rights Protection Party	—	43.5	24	(30)
National Development Party	—	26.1	11	(14)
Independents and other	—	30.4	14	(3)
Yemen (April 1993)				
Yemeni Alliance for Reform	Rr	...	62	
General People's Congress	—	...	123	
Yemeni Socialist Party	K	...	56	
Others and independents	—	...	60	
Yugoslavia (November 1996)				
Serbian Radical Party	ERe	18.5	16	(34)
Zajedno (Together) (four-party coalition)	CR–CLe	23.9	22 }	
Serbian Democratic Movement	Ce			(20)
Democratic Party	C			(5)
Socialist Party of Serbia and allies	xe	48.1	64	(47)
Democratic Party of Socialists of Montenegro	xe	...	20	(17)
People's Party (Montenegrin pro-Serbian)	e	...	8	(4)
Others	—	...	8	(11)
Zaire				
Transitional government from April 1994	—	—	—	
Zambia (November 1996)				
Movement for Multiparty Democracy	—	60.8	127	(125)
Others and independents	—	39.2	20	(25)
Zimbabwe (April 1995)				
Zimbabwe African National Union-Patriotic Front	—	82.3	118	(117)
Others and independents	—	17.7	2	(3)

*Boycotted. †Approximate. ‡Banned.

Changes to Flags of the World

Eritrea   Ethiopia   Seychelles

AFGHANISTAN

Afghanistan is a landlocked Islamic state in central Asia. Area: 652,225 sq km (251,825 sq mi). Pop. (1996 est.): 22,664,000 (including Afghan refugees estimated to number about 1.6 million in Pakistan and about 1.4 million in Iran). Cap.: Kabul. Monetary unit: afghani, with (Oct. 11, 1996) a free rate of 4,750 afghanis to U.S. $1 (7,483 afghanis = £1 sterling). President in 1996, Burhanuddin Rabbani; prime minister, Gulbuddin Hekmatyar.

In September 1996 the long power struggle between Afghanistan's armed factions appeared to have taken a decisive turn when Taliban militias captured Kabul. Despite the fundamentalist nature of the Taliban movement, many hoped that it might mean an end to the deadly rivalry between Afghan factions, which had killed 25,000–45,000 Afghans, mostly civilians, since the collapse of Afghanistan's communist government in April 1992.

The Taliban (Persian for "students") emerged at the end of 1994, soon taking control of Afghanistan's southern city of Kandahar and neighbouring areas. The "students" were recruited from schools set up among Afghan refugees in Pakistan during the years following the Soviet invasion of Afghanistan. From the time of the first Taliban successes, Pakistan denied any official support, but most observers discounted such denials, noting the modern logistic support and sophisticated communications equipment at the disposal of the "students." With a reputation more for zeal than for experience, they offered to rid the country of the corruption and lawlessness that had flourished during the years of Soviet occupation and that had continued after the Soviet withdrawal left Afghanistan divided among warring factions and local warlords. Within a year they had overrun Herat and western Afghanistan. For most of the next year, they remained outside Kabul, launching frequent rocket attacks on the city.

In June Gulbuddin Hekmatyar, whose Hezb-i-Islami forces had bombarded the government in Kabul until driven from their positions by the Taliban, returned to rejoin the government as prime minister. He immediately attempted to open contacts with northern Afghanistan's powerful warlord, Gen. 'Abd ar-Rashid Dostam. From his power base in Mazar-e Sharif, Dostam continued to control a virtually independent northern Afghanistan.

After a rapid offensive in September, Taliban forces captured the eastern Afghan city of Jalalabad, together with important areas in Nangarhar and Laghman provinces. With these territorial advances most of Afghanistan's traditionally Pashtun homelands were united under Taliban control. The gains included Kabul's main road to Pakistan and sealed the fate of Rabbani's mostly Tajik government. On September 27, Taliban forces entered Kabul, where they met little resistance from government forces. Their first act was to execute Afghanistan's last communist president, Mohammad Najibullah (see OBITUARIES), who had been living inside the UN compound in Kabul since 1992. President Rabbani and other members of his government retreated north of Kabul. Government forces under Ahmad Shah Masoud withdrew to the Panjshir valley. In October Masoud and other former government forces formed a military alliance with General Dostam. At year's end it was reported that Taliban forces had captured an opposition air base north of Kabul.

Since their first appearance, the Taliban had been supported by many ordinary Afghans, who welcomed their promise to restore normal life after years of destructive war. Popular enthusiasm was soon diluted, however, when the Taliban turned their captured rockets against civilians, especially in Kabul. In all areas under their control, the Taliban enforced a rigorous Islamic social order, insisting that all men grow beards and forbidding women to work outside their homes. Schools for girls were closed, and Islamic law was enforced by amputations and public executions. Restrictions on women provoked international criticism.

(STEVEN SEGO)

ALBANIA

A republic in the western Balkan Peninsula of southeastern Europe, Albania is situated on the Adriatic Sea. Area: 28,748 sq km (11,100 sq mi). Pop. (1996 est.): 3,249,000. Cap.: Tiranë. Monetary unit: lek, with (Oct. 11, 1996) a free rate of 108.10 leks to U.S. $1 (170.29 leks = £1 sterling). President in 1996, Sali Berisha; prime minister, Aleksander Meksi.

The third postcommunist parliamentary elections, held on May 26, 1996, plunged Albania into its deepest political crisis since the demise of communist rule in 1991. The opposition, led by the Socialist Party (the former Communist Party), charged that Pres. Sali Berisha's Democratic Party of Albania (DPA) used intimidation and fraud to capture a large election majority. Riot police violently broke up a protest rally, and the opposition parties boycotted all further activities related to the national elections, giving the DPA de facto control over the People's Assembly, the executive, and the judiciary.

On July 11 a new Cabinet was formed comprising 16 ministries (1 without portfolio), 7 state secretaries, and 1 Cabinet secretary-general. The enlarged new executive body had four female members, the widest female representation in the history of the country.

Gross domestic product (GDP) grew by an estimated 8%, while inflation rose by about 4–5%, mainly owing to the introduction of a value-added tax. Unemployment dropped to a total of 170,000, or about 13%. The agricultural and especially the construction and private-service sectors continued to register robust two-digit growth. The Albanian economy nevertheless remained unproductive, since GDP was primarily attributable to the growth of small businesses and not to industry. Remittances from Albanian émigrés in Greece, Italy, Germany, and the U.S. still accounted for an estimated 20% of GDP. Early in the year Albania received an aid package from the U.S. worth $100 million.

JAMES NACHTWEY—MAGNUM

At a cemetery in Kabul, an Afghan woman mourns her brother, who was killed in a rocket attack during the ongoing civil war that began with the fall of Afghanistan's communist government in 1992.

The nation's relationship with Greece was improved when a high-ranking Greek official visited Albania, and a number of important cooperation agreement were signed. The impasse between Tiranë and Belgrade continued, although ethnic Albanians from Kosovo were allowed to travel to Albania. Tiranë dispatched a 33-man peacekeeping force to the German contingent of IFOR (the NATO-led Implementation Force) in Croatia, the first time in the country's history that Albanian troops had been stationed abroad. (LOUIS ZANGA)

This article updates the *Macropædia* article BALKAN STATES: *Albania*.

ALGERIA

Algeria is a republic of North Africa on the Mediterranean Sea. Area: 2,381,741 sq km (919,595 sq mi). Pop. (1996 est.): 28,566,000. Cap.: Algiers. Monetary unit: Algerian dinar, with (Oct. 11, 1996) a controlled rate of 55.83 dinars to U.S. $1 (87.95 dinars = £1 sterling). President in 1996, Liamine Zeroual; prime minister, Ahmed Ouyahia.

In the wake of his success in the presidential elections in November 1995, Liamine Zeroual (*see* BIOGRAPHIES) initiated in April 1996 a series of discussions with political leaders to plan a new course for Algeria. In a press conference on May 5, his first since the election, the president announced a three-stage program that included a national conference in mid-1996, a referendum on proposed constitutional reform, and legislative elections by mid-1997. The constitutional reforms were to consist of a new electoral law banning political parties based on language or religion and requiring all parties to have nationwide support, a limitation on the presidency to two five-year terms for any person, and the establishment of a new bicameral legislature with the lower house elected by proportional representation and the upper house chosen by appointment.

The political parties were cautious in their response. The National Liberation Front, which had elected a new leader, Boualem Benhamouda, in January, supported the presidential proposal and became a close supporter of the regime. The Hamas Party (unrelated to the Palestinian organization called Hamas) was lukewarm, while others rejected the proposals. Chief among the opponents was the Islamic Salvation Front, which, in any case, had not been invited to participate in the consultative process. Despite the opposition, the proposals were endorsed by the promised national conference in September. The new constitution was overwhelmingly approved in a national referendum in November, but critics charged that the vote was rigged.

One obvious casualty of the president's proposals was any hope of a negotiated solution to the Algerian crisis. Violence escalated throughout the year, with the Armed Islamic Group (GIA) in particular taking an ever-more-radical stand. In March the GIA kidnapped seven Trappist monks from their monastery at Tibehirine, near Medea. Two months later, on May 21, the monks were killed, and on August 1 the French bishop of Oran, Pierre Claverie, was killed by a car bomb outside his residence, just after meeting the French foreign minister, Hervé

de Charette, on a visit to Algiers. Security improved in Algiers throughout the year, but outside the capital conditions seemed to have degenerated, with widespread car bombings, attacks on railways, and repeated massacres.

Algeria's economic situation improved. Approval by the International Monetary Fund and the World Bank led to the release of $400 million in loans in March and a new $252 million loan in June.

(GEORGE JOFFÉ)

This article updates the *Macropædia* article NORTH AFRICA: *Algeria*.

ANDORRA

A landlocked parliamentary co-principality of Europe, Andorra is in the Pyrenees Mountains between Spain and France. Area: 468 sq km (181 sq mi). Pop. (1996 est.): 64,100. Cap.: Andorra la Vella. Monetary units: French franc and Spanish peseta. Co-princes: the president of France and the bishop of Urgell, Spain; head of the government in 1996, Marc Forné Molné.

Andorra took significant steps toward increased involvement in world affairs in 1996. Juli Minoves-Triquell was named the first-ever permanent representative of Andorra to the United Nations as ambassador extraordinary and plentipotentiary. He also presented his credentials to U.S. Pres. Bill Clinton as the country's ambassador to the United States. Although tourism was a major component of the Andorran economy and 70% of first-time visitors returned, few of the visitors were from the U.S. Increasing those numbers was one objective of the Andorran Mission.

Andorra also celebrated the opening of its first university. A branch of the European University, the school offered business management programs for bachelor's and master's degrees. (ANNE ROBY)

This article updates the *Micropædia* article ANDORRA.

ANGOLA

A republic, Angola is located on the Atlantic coast in southwestern Africa. The small exclave of Cabinda is separated from Angola by a strip of Zaire. Area: 1,246,700 sq km (481,354 sq mi). Pop. (1996 est.): 11,904,000. Cap.: Luanda. Monetary unit: readjusted kwanza, with (Oct. 11, 1996) an official rate of 201,994 readjusted kwanzas to U.S. $1 (318,201 readjusted kwanzas = £1 sterling). President in 1996, José Eduardo dos Santos; prime ministers, Marcolino José Carlos Moco and, from June 3, Fernando José França Van Dúnem.

In spite of the offer by donor countries of $1 billion in aid in late 1995 and also of the repeated assurances by Jonas Savimbi, leader of the opposition National Union for the Total Independence of Angola (UNITA), that his party was wholeheartedly committed to the long-drawn-out peace process, Angola's prospects for 1996 did not look good. The value of the currency had fallen by 1,823% in 1995, and the readjusted kwanza, which stood at 25,-000 kwanzas to one U.S. dollar on Jan. 1, 1996, fell throughout the year. Particularly

A man carries land mines as part of a team that was attempting to clear Angola of an estimated 26 million mines that had been laid during the long civil war.

affected by the rampant inflation were the prices of food, furniture, household appliances, clothing, and medical care.

Hopes of recovery were further diminished by the tardy efforts of UNITA to demobilize its troops in fulfillment of the Lusaka peace accord of 1994. The process began in November 1995 but was halted in December because, UNITA maintained, the government had launched a military offensive in violation of the accord. Although UNITA's claim was later proved to have been exaggerated, the result was that the demobilization of UNITA troops fell seriously behind schedule.

As a small contribution toward improving the country's financial position, the secretary of state for coffee announced plans on January 5 for the privatization of the coffee industry, which in 1995 had achieved export earnings of $6 million. On the same day, and in an attempt to allay UNITA's concerns, the government reported that it had canceled its contract with Executive Outcomes under the terms of which the South African company had provided what were described as "military advisers." These men had been widely regarded as mercenaries directly involved in military operations.

Because UNITA failed to meet the target promised by Savimbi of quartering 16,-500 troops by February 8, the UN Security Council decided to extend by only three months instead of six the period during which the UN peacekeeping force should be retained in Angola. Nevertheless, both Savimbi and Pres. José Eduardo dos Santos emerged from a meeting in Gabon on March 1 confident about the future. Savimbi had accepted the office of vice president in a government of national unity, which, he said, would be established by July. Talks between representatives of the two sides reached agreement on ministerial posts for UNITA members and UNITA's participation in a national army to be created by July.

Within a month Savimbi said he would not become vice president after all, because the office had no executive functions, a claim that was later denied by the government. Disputes also arose over the important diamond-producing provinces in eastern Angola, over which UNITA was reluctant to relinquish control.

UNITA was not the only obstacle to progress. The government itself showed little aptitude for solving the country's problems. On June 3 dos Santos dismissed his Cabinet, together with the governor of the National Bank of Angola. His new government was announced on June 7 and sworn in the following day. Its main objectives, dos Santos said, had to include the payment of arrears of salary in the public sector, the provision of adequate food for the whole population, and the achievement of at least the minimum funding needed for essential services such as defense, social assistance, health, and education. (KENNETH INGHAM)

This article updates the *Macropædia* article SOUTHERN AFRICA: *Angola.*

ANTIGUA AND BARBUDA

A constitutional monarchy and member of the Commonwealth, Antigua and Barbuda comprises the islands of Antigua, Barbuda, and Redonda in the eastern Caribbean Sea. Area: 442 sq km (171 sq mi). Pop. (1996 est.): 64,400. Cap.: Saint John's. Monetary unit: Eastern Caribbean dollar, with (Oct. 11, 1996) a par value of EC$2.70 to U.S. $1 (free rate of EC$4.25 = £1 sterling). Queen, Elizabeth II; governor-general in 1996, James Carlisle; prime minister, Lester Bird.

The damage inflicted by hurricanes on the Antigua and Barbuda economy in 1995 caused the government to tighten spending in 1996. An austerity program set to begin in April included a two-year pay freeze for civil servants and a 10% pay cut for government ministers. No new government employees were to be recruited in the foreseeable future, and official borrowing from commercial banks would be undertaken only for self-liquidating projects. Savings of EC$20 million a year were expected from these measures. "Selected government holdings" were to be privatized to meet financial commitments.

In May, Prime Minister Lester Bird reshuffled his Cabinet, causing raised eyebrows by naming his brother, Vere, to a government advisory job. In 1990 an inquiry commission headed by Louis Blom-Cooper had declared Vere unfit to hold public office. (DAVID RENWICK)

This article updates the *Macropædia* article The WEST INDIES: *Antigua and Barbuda.*

ARGENTINA

The federal republic of Argentina occupies the eastern section of the Southern Cone of South America, along the Atlantic Ocean. Area: 2,780,400 sq km (1,073,518 sq mi). Pop. (1996 est.): 34,995,000. Cap.: Buenos Aires. Monetary unit: peso, with (Oct. 11, 1996) an official (pegged) rate of A1 to U.S. $1 (A1.58 = £1 sterling). President in 1996, Carlos Saúl Menem; ministerial coordinators, Eduardo Bauzá and, from March 28, Jorge Rodríguez.

Differences within Argentina's ruling Justicialist National Movement (Peronist; PJ) became increasingly evident in early January 1996. Former minister of the interior Gustavo Béliz resigned from the party and set up the Nueva Dirigencia ("new leadership") with a view to his running for mayor of Buenos Aires at the end of June.

Jockeying for position was also evident among other political groups. In February, Sen. José Octavio Bordón—a rival of Pres. Carlos Menem who had left the PJ in 1994 to run in 1995 as the presidential candidate of the Frepaso grouping—resigned his Senate seat and left Frepaso. He appeared set to join Béliz and others in a new grouping that might seek to contest the 1999 elections.

At the end of February the government succeeded in winning congressional approval for the "special powers" bill, which conferred upon the executive the ability to raise revenues by increasing specific taxes. At the end of March, Eduardo Bauzá, who held the new post of ministerial coordinator created by the 1994 constitution, resigned for health reasons and was replaced by Education Minister Jorge Rodríguez, a moderate. In May, Defense Minister Oscar Camilión was alleged to have approved illicit arms sales by the state weapons manufacturer to Ecuador in 1995 (at the time of its border conflict with Peru) and Croatia between 1991 and 1995. Although Camilión survived a congressional move to impeach him, the controversy led to his resignation in July. At that time Minister of Justice Rodolfo Barra also stepped down following allegations that he had been involved in anti-Jewish activities while a student.

The Peronists suffered a major defeat in the Buenos Aires mayoral election at the end of June when Fernando de la Rúa of the Radical Civic Union won by a wide margin. Frepaso candidate Norberto La Porta finished in second place, and the Peronist incumbent, Jorge Domínguez (appointed by Menem), was third; Domínguez suffered from the candidacy of ex-Peronist Béliz, who finished fourth.

In late July Menem acted to replace Domingo Cavallo, who had served in the Cabinet since the start of Menem's first term in July 1989. Minister of economy and public works and services since 1991, Cavallo was the architect of the "convertibility plan," which transformed Argentina from a hyperinflationary economy with a weak currency to one in which annual inflation was very low. The former president of the central bank, Roque Fernández, replaced Cavallo.

Cavallo's departure came as no surprise, as Menem's efforts to create a new image for his second term were frustrated by the failure of the economy to rebound strongly enough from the slowdown (a 4.4% decline in gross domestic product in 1995) that began after Mexico's financial crisis in early 1995. By mid-1996 it seemed that Cavallo's forecast of 5% growth for the year was unlikely to be met (with 2.5–3% seeming more probable), and unemployment continued in the 16–17% range. On July 12 Cavallo announced cuts in social security benefits and other allowances and attempted to further tighten the rules against tax evasion. This drew criticism from political opponents as well as the announcement of a one-day general strike for August 8 by the nation's main

labour confederation (which was carried out despite Cavallo's departure). Another more wide-ranging fiscal-adjustment package was launched by Fernández on August 12, soon after he took office. The core proposals involved increasing taxes on diesel fuel and gasoline and some rises in income taxes. These again proved controversial, but the main measures were approved by the Chamber of Deputies on September 18 and subsequently approved by the Senate.

(SUSAN M. CUNNINGHAM)

ARMENIA

A landlocked republic of Transcaucasia, Armenia borders Georgia to the north, Azerbaijan to the east, Iran to the south, the Azerbaijani exclave of Nakhichevan to the southwest, and Turkey to the west. Area: 29,800 sq km (11,500 sq mi). Pop. (1996 est.) 3,765,000. Cap.: Yerevan. Armenia claims the predominantly Armenian-populated Nagorno-Karabakh region, which has been part of Azerbaijan since 1923. Monetary unit: dram, with (Oct. 11, 1996) a free rate of 412.32 drams = U.S. $1 (649.53 drams = £1 sterling). President in 1996, Levon Ter-Petrosyan; prime ministers, Hrant Bagratyan and, from November 6, Armen Sarkisyan.

The presidential election scheduled for Sept. 22, 1996, overshadowed other political developments throughout the year. Eager to avoid either jeopardizing the tenuous economic upswing that began in 1994 or exacerbating tensions within his party, the Pan-Armenian National Movement, incumbent Pres. Levon Ter-Petrosyan refused in late January to accept the resignation of Prime Minister Hrant Bagratyan. Of the seven presidential candidates formally registered in August, three withdrew in mid-September and pledged their support for the leading opposition challenger to Ter-Petrosyan, former prime minister Vazgen Manukyan. International monitors registered serious violations during the poll and vote count and queried the legality of the official results that gave Ter-Petrosyan 51.75% and Manukyan 41.29% of the vote. Manukyan's supporters launched mass demonstrations in Yerevan to protest alleged falsification of the vote and on September 25 attacked the parliament building. Fifty people were injured in ensuing clashes with government troops.

On November 4 Bagratyan resigned, as did Foreign Minister Vahan Papazyan and powerful Interior Minister Vano Siradeghyan, who was subsequently appointed mayor of Yerevan. Armen Sarkisyan, former ambassador to the U.K., was named prime minister, and Alexander Arzumanyan, former ambassador to the UN, was appointed foreign minister. (ELIZABETH FULLER)

This article updates the *Macropædia* article TRANSCAUCASIA: *Armenia.*

AUSTRALIA

A federal parliamentary state (formally a constitutional monarchy) and member of the Commonwealth, Australia occupies the smallest continent and includes the island state of Tasmania. Area: 7,682,300 sq km (2,966,200 sq mi). Pop. (1996 est.): 18,287,000. Cap.: Canberra. Monetary unit: Australian dollar, with (Oct. 11,

A security-firm supervisor in Melbourne holds a gun similar to the one used to kill 35 vacationers in Port Arthur, Tas., in April. He stands on a pile of guns turned in for scrap when Australia in May banned automatic and semiautomatic rifles and pump-action shotguns.

1996) a free rate of $A 1.26 to U.S. $1 ($A 1.99 = £1 sterling). Queen, Elizabeth II; governors-general in 1996, Bill Hayden and, from February 16, Sir William Deane; prime ministers, Paul Keating and, from March 11, John Howard.

Domestic Affairs. For the first time in more than a decade, Australian voters chose a conservative administration to run the nation. At the general election on March 2, 1996, the Australian Labor Party (ALP), which had held office continuously since 1983, was swept away. Prime Minister Paul Keating and his policies were overwhelmingly rejected by the electorate, who chose the centre-right coalition under Liberal Party leader John Howard (*see* BIOGRAPHIES) and his National Party lieutenant, Tim Fischer, to lead the nation. This followed a bitter contest distinguished by the way in which both Keating and Howard scrupulously avoided direct contact with the average voter. Instead, both party leaders preferred to maintain a disciplined campaign, during which they spoke almost exclusively to handpicked groups of their own supporters, in carefully orchestrated set pieces designed to maximize their television impact.

As the incumbent, Keating faced an electorate weary of broken promises and disillusioned with the ALP's numerous policy changes. When the vote was counted, the unexpected size of Howard's majority was so great as to leave him unchallenged and facing a routed and humiliated ALP opposition. (For detailed election results, see *Political Parties,* above.)

Howard's three key Cabinet colleagues in the new administration were as foreseen; Peter Costello became treasurer, former opposition leader Alexander Downer was appointed foreign minister, and Fischer took up the post of deputy prime minister. Within days, Keating stepped down as leader of the ALP and was replaced by Kim Beazley, whose job of rebuilding the party was made all the more difficult after the defection of Queensland ALP Sen. Malcolm Colston to sit as an independent.

During 1996, public opinion in Australia was preoccupied with other issues besides the general election, notably the impending budget cuts, the shooting massacre in April of vacationers at Port Arthur in Tasmania, and Australia's prowess as a sporting nation as Sydney prepared to serve as host of the Olympic Games in the year 2000.

The Port Arthur massacre, during which 35 people were killed, deeply disturbed Australia in that it showed that nowhere was safe from random catastrophic events. Port Arthur had transformed itself from a gruesome role in Australian history as a place of convict transportation in a savage penal colony into an idyllic tourist destination, traditionally chosen by Australians wishing to make a lifestyle change and get away from big-city crime, unemployment, and social evils. The Port Arthur shootings gave Howard overwhelming popular support for his policy of an end to the right to own semiautomatic firearms.

Unprecedented interest was shown by Australians in the Centennial Olympic Games in Atlanta, Ga. Since Sydney had been chosen to be the host of the 2000 Olympics, sports administrators and political leaders flew to the U.S. with the Australian athletes. Australian Olympic organizers watched with keen attention for ways in which to improve on the Atlanta Olympics. They took home some sobering lessons about the difficulties in staging such a huge event and intensified their planning, especially in regard to areas of special vulnerability, such as security and urban transport. The athletes themselves were almost lost sight of in the focus on the year 2000, but after a shaky start, Australia's Olympians produced 41 medals, which ensured a warm welcome on their return home.

Legal issues in several states had national repercussions during the year. Despite the High Court's 1995 ruling in favour of the Native Title Act, Western Australian Premier Richard Court and others continued to protest the way in which Aboriginal land claims were being handled by the Native Title Tribunal. In a Queensland case in December, the High Court ruled that pastoral leases do not necessarily extinguish native titles to traditional lands. Controversy intensified as the world's first voluntary euthanasia law took effect on July 1 in the Northern Territory. The first legal assisted suicide took place in September after challenges failed in the territory's high court. In October the federal Parliament, by referring the issue to a parliamentary committee, ended debate on moves to overturn the law.

The Economy. As part of its election campaign, the conservative Coalition had promised to sell off one-third of the telecommunications monopoly Telstra to private investors (to which the Senate gave its support in December) and thereby raise funds to retire public debt and to spend on environmental projects. Accordingly, the Howard government went into office with a new broom, cutting away fat in institutions that the Cabinet considered had become established gravy trains under a decade of ALP rule: the Australian Broadcasting Corporation, the state-run universities, the Aboriginal and Torres Strait Islander Commission (ATSIC), and the overseas foreign aid budget, known as the Development Import Finance Facility (DIFF) scheme. The government gave priority to building a close relationship with the Reserve Bank of Australia on the understanding that the bank would concentrate its efforts on containing inflation. The governor of the Reserve Bank, Bernie Fraser, had announced that he would retire as soon as the Keating government was defeated. He was replaced by his long-serving deputy, Ian Macfarlane. The secretary of the Australian Council of Trade Unions (ACTU), Bill Kelty, also resigned from the board. His seat was taken by Hugh Morgan, the chief executive officer of the Western Mining Corp.

Costello delivered his first budget on August 20, aiming to cut government spending. As the first conservative treasurer in 14 years, Costello blamed the need to slash government expenditure on his ALP predecessors. Conjuring up a frightening picture of a financial disaster hidden from the electorate by the Keating government, the conservatives concentrated on what they called "Beazley's Black Hole"—an $A 8 billion deficit that was not out in the open before the election.

In a break with tradition, the administration decided to release the bad news before the budget, although admittedly its hand had been forced by the leakage from government departments of some of the bad news coming up. A week before the budget announcement, the minister for Aboriginal affairs, Sen. John Herron, said that ATSIC was to have its budget of about $A 1 billion cut by $A 380 million over four years. ATSIC chairwoman Lois O'Donoghue labeled the cuts a blow to self-determination and warned that ATSIC would be forced to cut programs aimed at reducing the number of deaths of prisoners in custody. Herron replied to criticism by observing that resources had to be targeted to areas of greatest need so that health and education would be guaranteed. Aborigines protested that legal services, arts, and culture (including radio and television stations in the Northern Territory) would be destroyed.

Meanwhile, the federal government announced its intention to cut $A 1.8 billion from the funding of higher education. The minister in charge, Amanda Vanstone, was burned in effigy after she defended the decision to force students—some of whom she described as "stuck pigs"—to repay their debt for the cost of their higher education faster than under the previous ALP government and at substantially lower income levels. The Higher Education Contribution Scheme (HECS) repayment threshold was lowered from $A 28,495 to $A 20,701. Vanstone also announced a three-tier HECS system for new students from 1997 under which courses that would enable graduates to earn higher salaries would cost more. *The Advertiser,* Adelaide's daily newspaper, explained the Vanstone agenda under the headline "Buy your way into uni," a reference to the decision to allow students who had not achieved academic entry requirements to get into the degree program of their choice by enrolling as a full-fee student. A leading opponent of the changes was the Australian Democrats' spokeswoman for education and youth affairs, 27-year-old Sen. Natasha Stott Despoja, the youngest woman ever to serve in the federal Parliament. (*See* BIOGRAPHIES.)

Although the government claimed that its election victory gave it a mandate for industrial relations reform, there was an unprecedented violent response to the new economic policies. In August, during a protest rally of some 15,000 people, including trade union groups, Aborigines, and students outside Parliament House, about 1,000 people marched to the front doors to deliver their protest inside the building. An angry riot developed that left injuries on both sides and a damage bill running to about $A 75,000. Because Beazley had earlier addressed the rally, before it got out of control, the ALP lost considerable public support. More serious to the trade union cause were the attacks on ACTU Pres. Jennie George, who declined to accept responsibility for the riot, leaving it to Gareth Evans, ALP front bench MP, to sum up the damage as having been done by "crazy self-indulgent bastards."

The budget received popular support from the country electorates, as the government decided not to go ahead with the policy of ending the diesel fuel rebate, under which miners and farmers in Australia's outback were shielded from paying the same price as city dwellers for their energy costs.

Foreign Affairs. The conduct of foreign affairs in the new Howard administration was divided between Howard, Downer, and Minister for Defence Ian McLachlan. Relations with the U.S. were good; Howard strongly supported the renewed action against Saddam Hussein, including U.S. missile attacks against Iraq.

Conservative polling found that the Liberal Party's supporters were against foreign aid, and so Downer stopped concessional loans under the DIFF scheme to Australian companies engaged in projects in Indonesia, China, India, and the Philippines. The ALP spokesman, Peter Cook, described Downer's action as rude and high-handed, saying that it seriously damaged international relations by stopping worthwhile endeavours on such projects as electricity supply and special education for handicapped children.

Downer traveled to Indonesia for a series of diplomatic meetings at the gathering of regional ministers from the Association of Southeast Asian Nations. In Jakarta he took the opportunity to meet Myanmar (Burma) Foreign Minister U Ohn Gyaw and expressed concern about the continued detention of political prisoners in Myanmar as well as that nation's refusal to negotiate with Daw Aung San Suu Kyi, the leader of the National League for Democracy. Downer also called for an inquiry into the suspicious death in a Myanmar jail of a European honorary consul, James Nichols.

Relations with China remained complex in 1996. Australia's sizable trade deficits with China in 1994 and 1995 moved to a surplus of $A 32.7 million in the first three months of 1996. The new conservative administration of Australian foreign affairs and trade policy did not impress the Chinese, however. Chinese Premier Li Peng was particularly scathing about a trip to Taiwan by John Anderson, the Australian energy minister, and the visit of the spiritual leader of Tibet, the Dalai Lama, to Canberra. Downer made it clear to China that he would meet the exiled Buddhist leader and asked for mutual respect and understanding. Nor was China happy to see Australia renew its security agreement with the U.S.; the Chinese *People's Daily* called the agreement the product of an outdated Cold War mind-set and part of a pincer-like strategy of containment. In response, McLachlan said that the new strident line adopted by China over Taiwan and Beijing's unilateral extension of territorial sea limits in the South China Sea were sources of concern for Australia's regional strategy outlook. There was no doubt, said McLachlan, that China had been much more assertive since the end of the Cold War. McLachlan's solution was to try to build greater trust with China on regional security issues by establishing annual high-level military talks.

An important fresh start was made to Australian-Malaysian relations when Howard met with Prime Minister Datuk Seri Mahathir bin Mohamad. The conservatives avoided raising prickly issues and concentrated on building up bilateral trade. Relations with Malaysia were further improved when Downer made an official visit to Malaysia in August, in a relaxed and friendly atmosphere that was in sharp contrast to the Keating era, which never recovered from Keating's description of Mahathir as "recalcitrant."

(A.R.G. GRIFFITHS)

See also *Dependent States.*

AUSTRIA

The federal republic of Austria is a landlocked state of central Europe. Area: 83,858 sq km (32,378 sq mi). Pop. (1996 est.): 8,102,000. Cap.: Vienna. Monetary unit: Austrian Schilling, with (Oct. 11, 1996) a free rate of 10.77 Schillings to U.S. $1 (16.97 Schillings = £1 sterling). President in 1996, Thomas Klestil; chancellor, Franz Vranitzky.

Austria celebrated its 1,000-year history in 1996, commemorating the first documentary record in AD 996 of a territory called Ostarrîchi. (*See* SIDEBAR.) For all the millennium celebrations, however, 1996 was a difficult year. Twelve months into its membership in the European Union (EU), Austria began the year with no government, a slow-growing economy, and an electorate increasingly dissatisfied with EU membership. By the second half of 1996, the political scene was even more clouded. The extreme nationalist party, Die Freiheitlichen (the Freedom Alliance, or Freedom Movement), formerly the Freedom Party (FPÖ), was enjoying a resurgence in popularity under its outspoken leader, Jörg Haider; bomb threats had been directed at Chancellor Franz Vranitzky by a neo-Nazi group, the Bajuvarian Liberation Army; and Pres. Thomas Klestil was seriously ill with pneumonia.

The country lacked a government at the beginning of the year because an early election had been called in December 1995 when the two ruling parties, the Austrian Social Democratic Party (SPÖ) and the right-of-centre Austrian People's Party (ÖVP), had been unable to agree on the details of an austere 1996 federal budget. The SPÖ and ÖVP won the election but avoided forming an official government until a new budget that would meet the EU's strict criteria was agreed to in March. Meanwhile, the day-to-day duties of government continued uninterrupted.

A tough two-year budget was announced when the government was formed on March 12. Austerity measures included an increase in the personal tax burden, cuts in cash benefits to families (such as child allowance), and a freeze on the recruitment of civil servants. Because the economy was not growing strongly, the government largely avoided cuts or tax increases that might have damaged businesses.

Unemployment rose in the first half of the year, and more than 1,600 companies went bankrupt in the first nine months of 1996. Although EU membership did not directly cause the slowdown, increased competitive pressure on the Austrian economy after it joined the organization made many associate the EU with the country's economic woes. Some large, well-known Austrian companies were taken over by foreign buyers in 1996, which made Austrians nervous about foreign influences. This in turn led to delays in privatizing state-owned companies and to a renewed and heated debate about Austria's neutrality. The government also ran into trouble with the EU over highway tolls, which the European Commission found to be against EU rules.

A key by-product of the electorate's general dissatisfaction with EU membership was a resurgence of the far-right and vehemently "Euroskeptic" Freedom Alliance. In June the party gained a foothold in provincial government for the first time when it won seats in the government of Burgenland, supposedly a pro-EU province. On October 13 the Freedom Alliance matched the SPÖ's performance in the country's first European Parliament elections, with six seats each. The ÖVP finished just ahead, with seven seats. In provincial elections on the same day in Vienna, traditionally a socialist stronghold, the SPÖ lost 10 seats and its absolute majority, the ÖVP lost 2 seats, and the Freedom Alliance gained 7.

(FIONA MULLEN)

Austria Turns 1,000

In 1996 Austrians marked the 1,000th anniversary of a name—the name Österreich (Austria) itself. On Nov. 1, 996, the Holy Roman Emperor Otto III granted the Bavarian bishopric of Freising 30 "royal hides," or about 800 ha (2,000 ac), of land in Neuhofen an der Ybbs in what is now Niederösterreich (Lower Austria). The deed was the first recorded use of the name Ostarrîchi (which literally translates as "Eastern Realm"), from which the name Austria is derived. This area evidently had been known as Ostarrîchi for some time, and the emperor's land grant was part of an effort to consolidate control over what was then an insecure eastern borderland of the Holy Roman Empire, subject to periodic raids by warlike Magyar tribes.

The millennium celebration was partly an attempt by Austrians to salvage a coherent national identity from a turbulent past. The territory of present-day Austria has known many rulers, including the Romans, various Teutonic tribes, Asiatic Avars, the Frankish king Charlemagne, and the Magyars, who were driven out by Otto the Great in 955 at the battle of Augsburg in Bavaria. From 976 to 1246 the Babenberg dynasty ruled. They were followed by the Habsburgs, during whose regime Vienna would become the centre of the mighty Austro-Hungarian Empire.

Following the collapse of the Habsburg dynasty in 1918, an area roughly synonymous with present-day Austria enjoyed a brief existence as a federal republic before being annexed by Nazi Germany in 1938. Germany's defeat in 1945 was followed by 10 years of Allied occupation; not until 1955 did modern Austria gain full sovereignty as a nation. The anniversary of the Ostarrîchi document was first formally noted in 1946 as the newly liberated nation sought to consolidate its national identity.

Though Austria's territorial boundaries and political sovereignty may have been problematic often in the past, there is little dispute that Austria, in particular Vienna, has been home to some of the most remarkable achievements of European culture. It was chiefly this rich cultural heritage that the Austrian millennium celebrated in 1996. In Vienna a musical retrospective featuring performances of Mozart, Johann Strauss, Beethoven, Haydn, and Schubert ran from early February through late June. The principal historical exhibition was "The Danube: The Course of a Life," which took place in the huge underground vaults of the ancient Schotten Monastery in Vienna from May through September and chronicled the history of the great European river. In Lower Austria the exhibit "Ostarrîchi-Österreich: People, Myths, and Landmarks" was on view in Neuhofen an der Ybbs from May until November. This exhibit included a facsimile of the Ostarrîchi document. Dozens of art galleries, museums, monasteries, and restaurants throughout the country also sponsored special events in recognition of the 1,000th anniversary of the Ostarrîchi document. (MICHAEL T. CALVERT)

AZERBAIJAN

A republic of Transcaucasia, Azerbaijan borders Russia on the north, the Caspian Sea on the east, Iran on the south, Armenia on the west, and Georgia on the northwest. The 5,500-sq km exclave of Nakhichevan to the southwest is separated from Azerbaijan proper by a strip of Armenia. Area (including Nakhichevan): 86,600 sq km (33,400 sq mi). Pop. (1996 est.): 7,570,000. Cap.: Baku (Azerbaijani: Bakı). Monetary unit: manat, with (Oct. 11, 1996) an official rate of 4,304 manat to U.S. $1 (6,780 manat = £1 sterling). President in 1996, Heydar Aliyev; prime ministers, Fuad Kuliyev until July 19, Artur Rasizade (acting) from July 20, and, from November 26, Rasizade.

Pres. Heydar Aliyev's authoritarian rule showed no signs of weakening in 1996. Proposed tactical alliances between small opposition parties and a failed attempt in February by the parliamentary opposition to force a vote of no confidence in the government had no impact on policy. Delegates to a People's Convention held in April to assess the political aftereffects of the March 1995 insurrection by Deputy Interior Minister Rovshan Javadov castigated the opposition as a threat to the country's sovereignty, which thereby intensified the climate of oppression.

Political trials of persons accused of trying to overthrow or assassinate President Aliyev continued. Three senior government officials were sentenced to death in February and March for their roles in an alleged coup attempt in October 1994. Also in March, 26 former police officers were sentenced in connection with the March 1995 insurrection, and the trial of 37 more on similar charges began in October. Twenty-one people, including three former army generals, went on trial in October on charges of planning to assassinate Aliyev in July 1995.

In July Prime Minister Fuad Kuliyev stepped down, ostensibly for health reasons, and several other ministers—with responsibility for economic affairs, privatization, and transport—were fired or cautioned for inefficiency. Artur Rasizade, named acting prime minister, was confirmed in that post in November. Parliament Speaker Rasul Guliyev resigned in September after his criticism of the government's economic policy incurred harsh censure from the parliament; an elderly academic, Murtuz Alesqerov, was chosen as his successor.

Despite several rounds of negotiations mediated by Russia and the Organization for Security and Cooperation in Europe, no progress was made toward a settlement of the conflict with Armenia over the region of Nagorno-Karabakh. The selection in November of Robert Kocharyan as president of the self-proclaimed Republic of Nagorno-Karabakh was condemned as potentially destabilizing by both the Azerbaijani leadership and the international community. The Lezgins, an ethnic minority whose traditional homeland straddles the Russian-Azerbaijani frontier, continued to agitate for an independent state.

Russia's ongoing refusal to open its frontiers with Azerbaijan (closed in December 1994 when Russian troops invaded Chechnya) soured bilateral relations and con-

RICHARD WAYMAN

This oil field in Azerbaijan is located near Baku on the Caspian Sea. The oldest known oil-producing region in the world, Azerbaijan had suffered a decline in production in recent years because of a lack of funds to purchase equipment.

tributed to economic stagnation. Relations with Iran were clouded by the arrest in April–May of five leading members of the pro-Iranian Islamic Party of Azerbaijan. In June Azerbaijan and Turkey signed a bilateral agreement on military cooperation.

(ELIZABETH FULLER)

This article updates the *Macropædia* article TRANSCAUCASIA: *Azerbaijan.*

BAHAMAS, THE

A constitutional monarchy and member of the Commonwealth, The Bahamas comprises an archipelago of about 700 islands in the North Atlantic Ocean just southeast of the United States. Area: 13,939 sq km (5,382 sq mi). Pop. (1996 est.): 280,000. Cap.: Nassau. Monetary unit: Bahamian dollar, with (Oct. 11, 1996) a par value of B$1 to U.S. $1 (free rate of B$1.58 = £1 sterling). Queen, Elizabeth II; governor-general in 1996, Orville Turnquest; prime minister, Hubert Ingraham.

A solution to the Cuban refugee problem seemed in sight in January 1996, when The Bahamas signed an accord with Cuba providing for the repatriation of Cubans living in Bahamian detention camps. A similar agreement had been made with Haiti in 1995. Some 250 Cubans living in the camps plus 70 or more living illegally with sympathizers were returned home during the year. The Bahamas extracted a promise from Cuba to treat returnees "fairly," but the refugees themselves were not convinced and staged hunger strikes.

Bahamasair, the national airline, was much in the news during the year. In June the Supreme Court quashed the 1995 finding of a commission of inquiry that former Bahamasair chairmen Philip Bethel and

Darrell Rolle had taken bribes to agree to purchase aircraft. The court said they had not been given an opportunity to respond. In July the government extended the life of the inquiry by six months.

(DAVID RENWICK)

This article updates the *Macropædia* article The WEST INDIES: *The Bahamas.*

BAHRAIN

The monarchy (emirate) of Bahrain consists of a group of islands in the Persian Gulf between the peninsula of Qatar and Saudi Arabia. Area: 694 sq km (268 sq mi). Pop. (1996 est.): 598,000. Cap.: Manama. Monetary unit: Bahrain dinar, with (Oct. 11, 1996) an official rate of 0.38 dinar to U.S. $1 (0.59 dinar = £1 sterling). Emir in 1996, Isa ibn Sulman al-Khalifah; prime minister, Khalifah ibn Sulman al-Khalifah.

Antigovernment violence and civil unrest by Shi'ite Muslims continued to ravage Bahrain in 1996. The Shi'ites were seeking restoration of the legislature, dissolved in 1975, and jobs for their unemployed. Shi'ites comprised about 70% of Bahrain's population, while the ruling al-Khalifah family belonged to the Sunnite sect.

Relations between Bahrain and the neighbouring country of Qatar were strained because of a dispute over ownership of the Hawar Islands, presumed to have gas reserves. Although the dispute was taken to the International Court of Justice, Bahrain indicated that it might refuse a solution by the court. Instead, it favoured mediation by friendly Gulf countries, primarily Saudi Arabia.

(LOUAY BAHRY)

This article updates the *Macropædia* article ARABIA: *Bahrain.*

BANGLADESH

A republic and member of the Commonwealth, Bangladesh is situated in the northeastern part of the Indian subcontinent, on the Bay of Bengal. Area: 147,570 sq km (56,977 sq mi). Pop. (1996 est.): 123,063,000. Cap.: Dhaka. Monetary unit: taka, with (Oct. 11, 1996) an official rate of Tk 42.10 to U.S. $1 (Tk 66.32 = £1 sterling). Presidents in 1996, Abdur Rahman Biswas and, from July 23, Shahabuddin Ahmed; prime ministers, Khaleda Zia until March 30, Mohammad Habibur Rahman until June 23, and, from June 23, Sheikh Hasina Wazed.

Prime Minister Khaleda Zia decided to hold parliamentary elections on Feb. 15, 1996, despite the threat by the Awami League (AL), the main opposition party, to boycott the polls unless she stepped down and allowed a caretaker government to take power before the voting. Before the election at least 13 people were killed and hundreds wounded in clashes between the opposition and government security forces. The AL's call for a boycott was heeded, and fewer than 10% of eligible voters turned out for the polls. About a dozen people were killed during the election. The electoral commission invalidated the results for 100 of the 300 contested seats because of fraud.

Following opposition-led paralysis of the Bangladeshi economy and fearing possible military intervention, Zia offered to step down in favour of a "nonparty" government that would conduct new elections. Sheikh Hasina Wazed (*see* BIOGRAPHIES), the AL leader, rejected the offer and demanded instead that the Zia administration be replaced by a caretaker government.

Protesters demanding a caretaker government for Bangladesh prior to parliamentary elections set a police car on fire in February. During clashes with security forces, 13 protesters were killed and more than 400 were injured.

On March 26 Parliament passed a law allowing the formation of a caretaker government, and former chief justice Mohammad Habibur Rahman was chosen to head it. New elections were set for June 12. Surprisingly, this election campaign was not marred by widespread violence. Voter turnout was as high as 73%, and, according to international observers, the elections were conducted fairly. Nevertheless, Zia's Bangladesh Nationalist Party (BNP) claimed that there had been fraud and demanded new elections in 100 constituencies.

Having won a plurality, with 146 seats out of a possible 300 (to the BNP's 116 seats), Sheikh Hasina was asked to form the new government. In an ironic twist of history, however, the AL had to rely on the support of Hossain Mohammad Ershad's Jatiya Party for its parliamentary survival. The AL had been instrumental in forcing Ershad out of the presidency in 1990. Moreover, Ershad, who had been serving a prison sentence for corruption and abuse of power, had been accused by Zia of complicity in the overthrow and subsequent assassination of her late husband, Gen. Zia ur-Rahman, in 1981. In her first Cabinet, Sheikh Hasina included Anwar Hossain Manju, the secretary-general of the Jatiya Party.

In December Bangladesh and India signed a 30-year treaty to share water from the Ganges River, a sign of improving relations between the two countries.

(CLAUDE RAKISITS)

BARBADOS

The constitutional monarchy of Barbados, a member of the Commonwealth, occupies the most easterly island in the southern Caribbean Sea. Area: 430 sq km (166 sq mi). Pop. (1996 est.): 265,000. Cap.: Bridgetown. Monetary unit: Barbados dollar, with (Oct. 11, 1996) a par value of BDS$2 to U.S. $1 (free rate of BDS$3.17 = £1 sterling). Queen, Elizabeth II; governor-general in 1996, Sir Denys Williams (acting) and, from June 1, Sir Clifford Husbands; prime minister, Owen Arthur.

The House of Assembly voted in February 1996 to allow the Barbados Labour Party (BLP) government to legislate pay for government workers for a two-year period, starting April 1, 1996. This followed the failure of negotiations on proposed increases with the National Union of Public Workers, which represented one-third of government employees. The irony of this was not lost on the workers concerned, since it was the BLP that had castigated the former Democratic Labour Party administration for using wage cuts as an instrument of fiscal policy and had actually amended the law after its return to office in 1994 to prohibit such action in the future. Thus, the government could now regulate only increases in public workers' pay.

In May Barbados signed a two-year offshore oil-exploration agreement with Conoco of the U.S. in an effort to extend oil production to the marine areas.

(DAVID RENWICK)

This article updates the *Macropædia* article The WEST INDIES: *Barbados*.

BELARUS

A landlocked republic of Eastern Europe, Belarus borders Latvia on the north, Russia on the north and east, Ukraine on the south, Poland on the west, and Lithuania on the northwest. Area: 207,595 sq km (80,153 sq mi). Pop. (1996 est.): 10,322,000. Cap.: Minsk. Monetary unit: Belarusian rubel, with (Oct. 11, 1996) an official rate of 19,165 rubli = U.S. $1 (30,191 rubli = £1 sterling). President in 1996, Alyaksandr Lukashenka; prime minister, Mikhail Chyhir.

Belarus in 1996 was a country that experienced high political tension instigated mainly by an authoritarian leader's attempt to increase his powers. One observer termed Belarus "the black sheep of Europe" because it continued to cling to its Soviet past, rejecting market reforms and clamping down on opposition to the president. Thus, the power struggle persisted between Pres. Alyaksandr Lukashenka and the Supreme Soviet (parliament), backed by the Constitutional Court, which continued to overrule presidential decrees.

On April 2 Belarus signed an agreement with Russia that formed an "integrated political and economic community" with a joint legislature and a common foreign policy and economic space. By the end of 1997, it was projected, the two countries would jointly conduct investment, customs, and taxation policies. Both sides hoped other former Soviet states would adhere to the union.

Antigovernment (or anti-Lukashenka) demonstrations had taken place in Minsk, however. The first incident was on March 24 after it was announced that the agreement would be signed; riot police dispersed a crowd of about 30,000 protesters. A further 20,000 took to the streets on the day of the signing. The culmination came on April 26, however, when an estimated 50,000 congregated in the capital city to commemorate the 10th anniversary of the Chernobyl disaster. Though the demonstration began peacefully, it turned violent. Over 200 were arrested, including several prominent mem-

Prosya Tsubatova (foreground) returned to her village in Belarus 10 years after it was evacuated because of the explosion at the Chernobyl nuclear power plant.

bers of the Belarusian Popular Front (BPF) and 17 members of the Ukrainian Rukh and paramilitary UNA-UNSO parties. In September BPF leaders Zyanon Paznyak and Syarhei Naumchyk were granted political asylum in the U.S.

On November 24 Lukashenka won a heavily manipulated referendum that allowed him to introduce a new constitution, extending the presidential term of office from four to six years, creating an upper assembly (one-third of whose members he would appoint), reducing the parliament to 110 seats, and creating a new Constitutional Court, 50% of whose members would be presidential appointees. In effect, a presidential dictatorship was created in Belarus. Even the national holiday was changed from July 27 (independence day) to July 3 (the day the capital city of Minsk was liberated from German occupation in 1944).

The economy was strained: more than 70% of the population was declared to be living below the poverty line; the Belarusian rubel began to drop sharply against the U.S. dollar by the summer; and inflation was held in check only by the withholding of wages from many workers.

(DAVID R. MARPLES)

BELGIUM

A federal constitutional monarchy, Belgium is situated on the North Sea coast of northwestern Europe. Area: 30,528 sq km (11,787 sq mi). Pop. (1996 est.): 10,185,000. Cap.: Brussels. Monetary unit: Belgian franc, with (Oct. 11, 1996) a free rate of BF 31.55 to U.S. $1 (BF 49.70 = £1 sterling). King, Albert II; prime minister in 1996, Jean-Luc Dehaene.

Belgium was rocked during 1996 by a child-sex scandal that raised fundamental questions about the country's police, judicial,

and political systems. Marc Dutroux, who had been released on parole in 1992 after serving just 3 years of a 13-year prison sentence for the abduction and rape of underage girls, was arrested in mid-August—more than a year after two eight-year-old girls were kidnapped near Liège. In the following weeks, the bodies of both as well as those of two girls aged 17 and 19 were discovered on property owned by Dutroux. Two other girls Dutroux had admitted kidnapping—one 14 and the other 12—were found alive by police.

Investigations into the Dutroux case, which revealed incompetence, rivalry, and patronage on the part of the authorities, gave renewed energy to the stalled five-year inquiry into the murder in Liège in 1991 of André Cools, former deputy prime minister and leader of the French-speaking Socialist Party (PS). The latter led to a new wave of arrests, including those of three suspects who had been questioned and then freed in 1993. Among those charged was former PS regional and federal minister Alain Van der Biest.

Flower-bedecked cars move through the streets of Liège, Belg., en route to the funeral of two of four young girls murdered by previously convicted child rapist Marc Dutroux.

The two investigations revealed rivalry between local and national police forces and between differing legal courts and jurisdictions. The degree of public concern prompted King Albert II to make a rare departure from royal protocol in early September and demand a full investigation into the Dutroux case. He made it clear that he also expected the fullest possible light to be shed on the search for the killer of Cools. The outcry over the girls' abduction and murder prompted immediate calls in autumn for the return of the death penalty, which Belgium had formally abolished just weeks earlier.

Other scandals dogged the PS during the year. Guy Coëme, a former PS vice president and defense minister, became the first Belgian since 1865 to be convicted of having committed an offense while serving as a government minister. He and seven other prominent PS members were found guilty of fraud, embezzlement, and corruption. The court ruled that a research firm, Inusop, had used the income from overpriced opinion polls for government departments to make illegal electoral and other payments to PS branches and members. Coëme was given a two-year suspended prison sentence, fined BF 60,000 and ordered to repay some BF 500,000.

Jean-Luc Dehaene's coalition government adopted an austerity package of BF 82 billion for its 1997 budget. Taxes were to be raised and social security benefits cut. The budget was designed to reduce the total public deficit, which stood at 4.5% of gross domestic product in 1995, from 3% in 1996 to 2.9% in 1997.

Dehaene's hand was considerably strengthened in July when Parliament gave his government the power to change budget and social security measures by decree. The government had successfully argued that it needed to be able to raise taxes or cut spending without seeking parliamentary approval if the country was to meet the qualifying criteria for participating in the single European currency, the euro.

(RORY WATSON)

BELIZE

A constitutional monarchy and member of the Commonwealth, Belize is on the Caribbean coast of Central America. Area: 22,965 sq km (8,867 sq mi). Pop. (1996 est.): 219,000. Cap.: Belmopan. Monetary unit: Belize dollar, with (Oct. 11, 1996) a par value of BZ$2 to U.S. $1 (free rate of BZ$3.15 = £1 sterling). Queen, Elizabeth II; governor-general in 1996, Colville Young; prime minister, Manuel Esquivel.

In his 1996 New Year's Day speech, Prime Minister Manuel Esquivel unveiled his plan to contain expenditures and restructure the government to be more efficient. The new fiscal year started on April 1 with the introduction of a 15% value-added tax (VAT) on businesses that grossed BZ$100,-000 or more. The VAT would replace a number of other taxes and import-export duties. Esquivel's 1996–97 budget forecast was BZ$266,800,000. In foreign affairs Belize opened a consulate in the Dominican Republic and signed a cooperative agreement with Cuba in an effort to curb drug trafficking.

Archaeologists made a significant discov-ery beneath the ancient Mayan city of La Milpa. A Mayan king was found entombed and adorned with elaborate jade jewelry. Pottery in the tomb dated his rule at approximately AD 450.   (INES PARKER)

This article updates the *Macropædia* article CENTRAL AMERICA: *Belize*.

BENIN

The republic of Benin is on the southern coast of West Africa, on the Gulf of Guinea. Area: 112,680 sq km (43,500 sq mi). Pop. (1996 est.): 5,574,000. Cap.: Porto-Novo (executive offices remain in Cotonou). Monetary unit: CFA franc, with a par value of CFAF 100 to the French franc and (as of Oct. 11, 1996) a free rate of CFAF 518.24 to U.S. $1 (CFAF 816.38 = £1 sterling). Presidents in 1996, Nicéphore Soglo, and from April 4, Mathieu Kérékou.

In a stunning rebuff to Nicéphore Soglo, the man who led Benin's transition to multiparty democracy, voters in Benin on March 18, 1996, elected the former head of the Marxist regime (1972–90), Mathieu Kérékou, as the country's new president. Although Soglo had a slight lead in the first round of the elections held two weeks earlier, Kérékou won 52.5% of the tally in the runoff.

The Constitutional Court, which had declared 23% of the ballots cast in the first round invalid, rejected Soglo's charges of vote fraud and confirmed the results of the vote on March 24. Kérékou formed a government of national unity and appointed Adrien Houngbédji, leader of the majority Party of Democratic Renewal (PRD), prime minister. The new Cabinet was drawn from eight political groups.

The economy remained extremely weak, with few prospects for sustained growth. In April the World Bank, indicating that Benin had made little progress toward economic reform, refused to renegotiate a proposed $98 million credit agreement that had been rejected by the National Assembly at the end of 1995.   (NANCY ELLEN LAWLER)

This article updates the *Macropædia* article WESTERN AFRICA: *Benin*.

BHUTAN

The monarchy of Bhutan is a landlocked state situated in the eastern Himalayas between China and India. Area: 47,000 sq km (18,150 sq mi). Pop. (1996 est.): 842,-000 (excluding Nepalese residents declared stateless by the Bhutanese government in late 1990, nearly 100,000 of whom are now refugees in Nepal). Cap.: Thimphu. Monetary unit: ngultrum, at par with the Indian rupee (which is also in use), with (Oct. 11, 1996) a free rate of 35.65 ngultrums to U.S. $1 (56.16 ngultrums = £1 sterling). Druk gyalpo (king) in 1996, Jigme Singye Wangchuk.

In April 1996 Bhutan and Nepal held their seventh round of ministerial talks on the repatriation of nearly 100,000 Bhutanese refugees of Nepalese origin who had taken shelter in eight UN-monitored refugee camps in eastern Nepal. As with the previous talks, the participants failed to reach an agreement, particularly on the criteria for determining Bhutanese citizenship. The refugee problem developed after Bhutan launched in 1988 a national policy demanding that everyone adhere completely to Bhutanese Buddhist traditions. Bhutanese of Nepalese origin claimed that this policy was an attempt to suppress Nepalese culture, and, accordingly, thousands fled to Nepal.   (CLAUDE RAKISITS)

BOLIVIA

Bolivia is a landlocked republic in central South America. Area: 1,098,581 sq km (424,164 sq mi). Pop. (1996 est.): 7,593,-000. Administrative cap., La Paz; judicial cap., Sucre. Monetary unit: boliviano, with (Oct. 11, 1996) a free rate of Bs5.17 to U.S. $1 (Bs8.14 = £1 sterling). President in 1996, Gonzalo Sánchez de Lozada Bustamente.

The municipal elections of December 1995 shifted the balance of support from the ruling Nationalist Revolutionary Movement (MNR) to its coalition partners, Civic Solidarity Union (UCS) and Free Bolivia Movement (MBL). The MNR won 21% of the

A Bolivian farmer in the Chaparé region stands next to coca plants that he continued to grow in spite of tough antidrug policies that were enacted by the government during the year.

GREGORY BULL

vote, while the UCS won 17% and the MBL 13%. The opposition party Conscience of the Fatherland won 15%. Pres. Gonzalo Sánchez de Lozada Bustamente extended his term of office by one year until August 1998, although a public opinion survey showed little support for the government.

The social unrest of 1995 continued in 1996. A four-week general strike, including a 46-day hunger strike, was called off by the Bolivian Worker's Central (COB) at the end of April. Called in protest against the government's economic policies, including the privatization program, the strike failed as unions became more divided. The COB refused to take part in negotiations between the oil workers union and the government over the government's plan to sell the oil company Yacimientos Petroliferos Fiscales Bolivianos. The strike ended with a clear defeat for the unions: a 9% wage increase for all public-sector workers compared with the 12% they had demanded. A minimum wage of $45 per week was agreed upon for all public- and private-sector workers.

Opposition to the government's sale of the oil company resulted in the resignation in mid-April of Irving Alcaráz del Castillo, minister for social communication, who was blamed for failure to stem the opposition. In mid-March another Cabinet minister, Alfonso Revollo, was accused by jailed banker Jorge Cordova of having demanded a $50,000 election contribution to secure the merger of two leading banks. The secretary-general of the opposition Movement of the Revolutionary Left, Oscar Eid Franco, was jailed on charges of maintaining links with drug lords.   (ALAN MURPHY)

BOSNIA AND HERZEGOVINA

A federal republic of the western Balkans, Bosnia and Herzegovina borders Croatia on the north, southwest, and south, the Adriatic Sea on the south (via a narrow extension), and Yugoslavia on the east. Area: 51,129 sq km (19,741 sq mi). Pop. (1996 est.): 3.2 million (excluding about 1.3 million refugees in adjacent countries and Western Europe). Cap.: Sarajevo. Monetary unit: Bosnia & Herzegovina dinar, with (Oct. 15, 1996) a par value of 100 dinars to DM 1 (free rates of 153.78 dinars = U.S. $1 and 243.48 dinars = £1 sterling). Head of the three-member presidency in 1996, Alija Izetbegovic.

After three and a half years of bloodshed, the Republic of Bosnia and Herzegovina entered 1996 in relative peace. By the year's end, however, it appeared to be on the verge of regional violence involving the repatriation of refugees. Major developments of the year included general elections, the enforcement of the internationally brokered peace accords (negotiated in Dayton, Ohio, and signed in Paris on Dec. 14, 1995), and the beginning of the reconstruction of the war-ravaged republic. At the end of the year, the process of restoring the rule of law and of achieving economic and social rehabilitation was further complicated by continued divisions between the republic's three main ethnic groups—Serbs, Croats, and Bosnians (Slavic Muslims).

The military aspects of the Dayton accords were implemented at the beginning of 1996 without major problems. Observing the civilian provisions proved, however, to

RON HAVIV—SABA

Bosnian Muslims attend a preelection rally in Tuzla. In the election the vote split along ethnic lines. The Muslims' support for their presidential candidate, Alija Izetbegovic, was strong enough to elect him the first head of the nation's collective presidency.

be another matter altogether. The relative peace secured by the presence of some 60,000 troops of the NATO-led Implementation Force was plagued by differences in goals and strategies. For the most part, military muscle was not used to enforce the civilian provisions of the treaty. As a result, the parties to the Dayton accords (the Republic of Bosnia and Herzegovina and its two constituent entities—the Federation of Bosnia and Herzegovina and Republika Srpska) had not created the conditions for establishing a democratic country with free elections. A politically neutral environment was absent, and the nationalists on all three sides were well on their way to setting up separate, ethnically "pure" states.

Under such handicaps the elections on September 14 were bound to confirm the de facto division of the country along ethnic lines. As in 1990, when the people of Bosnia and Herzegovina had last voted in multiparty elections, the three nationalist parties swept the board. In the key battle for the triumvirate presidency of the nation of Bosnia and Herzegovina, which according to the constitution had to consist

of one Bosnian (Muslim), one Croat, and one Serb, the Bosnian Alija Izetbegovic of the Muslim Party of Democratic Action (SDA), the Croat Kresimir Zubak of the Croatian Democratic Union (HDZ), and the Serb Momcilo Krajisnik of the Serbian Democratic Party (SDS) in Republika Srpska were elected. Izetbegovic polled 724,-733 votes, Krajisnik 698,891, and Zubak 297,976. Izetbegovic thus became head of the federation until the next elections, in 1998. In the House of Representatives of Bosnia and Herzegovina the SDA became the largest party, with 19 of the 42 seats. Late in December the Serb leaders said they would not take part in the new government.

Reports by international monitoring groups revealed a highly imperfect vote, which provided ample reasons for concern about Bosnia's troubled future. President Izetbegovic later warned the UN General Assembly that the conflict could resume in Bosnia and Herzegovina if the Dayton accords were not enforced, adding that the continuation of an international military presence past the initial departure date on December 20 was necessary. Af-

Bushmen in Botswana's Central Kalahari Game Reserve flank the entrance of their thatched hut. Despite this primitive existence, the Bushmen were resisting efforts by the government to move them off the reserve, which they regarded as their ancestral land.

ter conferring with NATO allies, U.S. Pres. Bill Clinton announced in mid-November that the deployment of U.S. and NATO troops would continue well into 1998. The announcement came at a time of renewed violence over the resettlement of refugees in certain regions of Bosnia.

Bosnia and Herzegovina established bilateral relations with Yugoslavia on October 3. Though establishing relations with Belgrade may have signaled some breakthrough on the diplomatic front between the two countries, questions remained as to whether outstanding bilateral and regional problems could be resolved soon.

(MILAN ANDREJEVICH)

This article updates the *Macropædia* article BALKAN STATES: *Bosnia and Herzegovina.*

BOTSWANA

A landlocked republic of southern Africa, Botswana is a member of the Commonwealth. Area: 581,730 sq km (224,607 sq mi). Pop. (1996 est.): 1,478,000. Cap.: Gaborone. Monetary unit: pula, with (Oct. 11, 1996) a free rate of 3.51 pula to U.S. $1 (5.58 pula = £1 sterling). President in 1996, Sir Ketumile Masire.

On Feb. 12, 1996, Vice Pres. and Minister of Finance and Development Planning Festus Mogae presented Botswana's 1996–97 budget. Revenue totaled 5,421,000,000 pula and expenditures 6,057,000,000 pula. The resulting deficit of 636 million pula

was to be made up from government cash balances. Exchange controls were relaxed to promote diversification away from diamonds and to remove any limit (after tax) of remittances by temporary residents. An old-age pension of 100 pula a month was introduced for everyone over 65.

Botswana and Russia agreed to regular exchanges of information to harmonize their methods of selling diamonds and to ensure that they obtained equitable shares of the market. Botswana was the largest diamond producer after Russia.

(GUY ARNOLD)

This article updates the *Macropædia* article SOUTHERN AFRICA: *Botswana.*

BRAZIL

Brazil is a federal republic situated in eastern South America on the Atlantic Ocean. Area: 8,547,404 sq km (3,300,171 sq mi). Pop. (1996 est.): 157,872,000. Cap.: Brasília. Monetary unit: reais, with (Oct. 11, 1996) a controlled rate of 1.03 real to U.S. $1 (1.62 reais = £1 sterling). President in 1996, Fernando Henrique Cardoso.

Domestic Affairs. Contrary to the climate of optimism prevailing when Pres. Fernando Cardoso began his term a year earlier, the start of 1996 was overshadowed by political controversies that had erupted in late 1995: the award of a contract for a surveillance project in the Amazon region to the U.S. firm Raytheon, and the so-

called pink file concerning political campaign donations made by the failed Banco Economico. In addition, the government's plans to win approval for a series of constitutional reforms in the spheres of social security, administration, and taxation were running behind schedule. Despite special sessions of the National Congress during January and February, little was achieved in this regard, although the extension to mid-1997 of the emergency financial fund, formerly known as the emergency social tax, was approved. In large measure members of Congress were anticipating municipal elections scheduled for October, in which about 25% of the members of the Chamber of Deputies would run.

A further setback for the reform agenda occurred when the Senate voted in March to set up a parliamentary inquiry into the banking sector following irregularities discovered at another bank, the Banco Nacional. The inquiry was later shelved, which allowed limited headway on reforms.

In late April the Cabinet was reshuffled, partly in order to reinforce congressional backing for the reforms, with the timing being linked to the departure of Agriculture Minister José Eduardo Vieira. Vieira's post went to another member of the Brazilian Labour Party, Sen. Arlindo Porto. But the more important move was to bring into the Cabinet a member of the Brazilian Progressive Party (PPB) to help firm up votes of PPB legislators for the government. Accordingly, Francisco Dornelles, a former fi-

(continued on page 401)

SPOTLIGHT

THE JAPANESE IN LATIN AMERICA

by Sarah Cameron

illustration by Igor Kopelnitsky

Beginning in the late 1880s, millions of immigrants went to Latin America seeking freedom, land, and economic opportunities. Most were from southern Europe, fleeing persecution or poverty and taking with them their Roman Catholic, family-oriented values. About a quarter of a million arrivals in Brazil in the first half of the 1900s came from Japan, however, encouraged and supervised by their government. The first 830 Japanese immigrants arrived in 1908 in the port of Santos, Brazil, from which they were sent under contract on to the coffee plantations in the south. They were valued for their agricultural skills and contributed to developing marginal land in São Paulo and frontier regions in Paraná and Amazônia. Very few returned to their native land when their contracts expired, preferring instead to assimilate themselves into the racial melting pot of their adopted country.

By 1996 there were some one million Japanese-descended Brazilians, noted for their market gardening and still active in growing coffee, cotton, and tea but also concentrated in the major urban centres of São Paulo, Brasília, and Rio de Janeiro. In São Paulo there is a large Japanese community in an area known as Liberdade, where the streets are crammed with Japanese restaurants and shops selling Japanese goods and clothes. There are Japanese food markets and a museum of Japanese immigration with displays on the contribution of the Japanese immigrants since the first years on the coffee plantations. West of São Paulo there are also notable clusters of Japanese in Londrina and Maringá, 20th-century towns founded by immigrants. In the northeast their presence is also felt; for example, Belém has several excellent Japanese restaurants, partly as a result of a Japanese colony founded in the interior in the 1940s.

Some cultural traditions have been retained, but these are being gradually eroded by the influence of television, radio, and the educational system. There is now a division between those Japanese who have been born in the country and those who have been assigned there temporarily by their employer. Japanese-Brazilians are totally integrated into Brazilian culture; they go to Brazilian schools, and Portuguese is their first language. Some do not even speak Japanese and rarely associate with those who are temporary residents. The Japanese who go to work in Brazil for four to five years number about 5,000 at any one time, and their children go to Japanese schools.

After Brazil, Peru has the largest Japanese immigrant community, totaling up to 100,000 people. The colony is notable for having produced the first president of Japanese descent anywhere in the world outside Japan. Pres. Alberto Fujimori's parents emigrated from Japan, and he was born in Peru in 1938. This was a difficult time for the Japanese community. After Japan bombed Pearl Harbor in 1941, fears of a Japanese espionage operation in Peru led to a series of roundups of the Japanese communities along the Pacific coast, as a result of which about 1,000 inhabitants of Japanese descent were deported to concentration camps in the U.S. Many had their businesses confiscated, while others avoided deportation or arrest by bribing the police. The atomic bombs dropped on Hiroshima and Nagasaki in 1945 further alienated the community. They kept a low profile, gaining a reputation as honest, hard-working businessmen rather than as politicians, and became fully integrated into Peruvian society. When campaigning in rural areas, Fujimori makes a point of donning an Indian poncho and hat. Since his victory in the elections in 1990, which earned him the nickname "tsunami" ("tidal wave" in Japanese), several Japanese-Peruvians have gained prominent government positions: in Congress, in the Cabinet, on privatization committees, in regional government, and in government-operated companies.

Links with Japan and the rest of Asia have been promoted in the 1990s, with Peru building on its geographical position as a gateway between Latin America and Asia. It is on the waiting list to join the Asia Pacific Economic Cooperation Forum. Asian immigration is actively encouraged, with Peruvian citizenship for sale at $25,000. All those of East Asian origin, whether Japanese, Chinese, Korean, or others, are known as "chinos" in Peru. Opinion polls consistently show that Japan is the country Peruvians most trust and admire. Fujimori has made several trips to Japan since his election, and Japan has played a leading role in the "support group" of nations helping with Peru's balance of payments problems. Donations have flowed and credits have been signed, but Japanese companies have proved cautious, and there has been only a trickle of direct foreign investment.

The 10-day tour of Mexico, Chile, Peru, Brazil, and Costa Rica in 1996 by Japanese Prime Minister Ryutaro Hashimoto (*see* BIOGRAPHIES) was the first Japanese state visit to Latin America in seven years.

Late in December 1996 the presence of Japanese in Peru became known throughout the world when members of Peru's Túpac Amaru guerrilla group invaded the Japanese embassy in Lima during a large party and took those in the embassy hostage. The guerrillas demanded the release of Túpac Amaru members imprisoned in Peru. (*See* WORLD AFFAIRS: *Peru*).

Sarah Cameron is a freelance writer and editor of Footprint Handbooks.

(continued from page 399)

nance minister, was given the industry and commerce post, replacing Dorothea Werneck. Two new extraordinary ministerial posts were created: one, for land reform, went to Raúl Jungman, whose initial task was to improve confidence following a police massacre of peasants from the landless movement; the other, for congressional coordination, went to Luiz Carlos Santos of the Party of the Brazilian Democratic Movement, who had been the government leader in the Chamber of Deputies. Santos was replaced in the legislature by Benito Gama of the Liberal Front Party (PFL), Cardoso's core alliance partner. An additional change followed the departure of Planning Minister José Serra in late May to become the mayoral candidate in São Paulo on behalf of Cardoso's Party of Brazilian Social Democracy. Serra's replacement was Antônio Kandir, who in 1990–91 was economic policy secretary in the administration of Fernando Collor de Mello.

From about midyear politics was dominated by campaigning for the municipal elections. A special session of Congress was convened during the July recess to further the reform process but, again, with only limited results. A diluted version of the social security reform was, however, approved by the Chamber of Deputies and forwarded to the Senate. Obstacles to the privatization of the state mining concern Vale do Rio Doce were also overcome, with a view to a sale date in February 1997. In September the goods-circulation tax for most commodity exports and semiprocessed materials was eliminated, and a financial-transactions tax to raise funds for the health budget was approved.

The first round of the municipal elections was held on October 3. By October 9 the final tally of party results in the more than 5,000 municipalities remained to be finalized, although it appeared that the main pro-government parties had increased their showing over 1992. Immediately after the first round, the government embarked on a vigorous campaign to muster support for a constitutional amendment to permit the reelection of the president for a second term, with this possibly to be extended to other elected executive posts (state governors and mayors). The second round of elections on November 15 resulted in defeats for Cardoso's candidates in the "big three" cities of São Paulo, Rio de Janeiro, and Belo Horizonte. The most significant victory was by Celso Pitta of the right-wing Brazilian Progressive Party, an opponent of Cardoso who won 57% of the vote in São Paulo.

The Economy. On the economic front, during 1996 the Cardoso administration succeeded in maintaining the stability engendered by the Real Plan, which had been launched early in 1994. By the end of September, the annual rate of inflation was less than 14%. Under the constraint of continuing tight monetary and credit policy (despite a gradual reduction of interest rates and a modest relaxation of some credit rules), economic activity increased only marginally in the first half of 1996, with a 0.27% growth in gross domestic product (GDP). Signs of an improvement were evident in the second quarter, however, when GDP rose 2.3% above that of the same period in 1995. In August the authorities indicated that the growth forecast

for the year was being revised downward to less than 3%. This was reversed by early October, when IPEA, the research institute linked to the Planning Ministry, predicted a 3% growth rate for the year.

In the absence of fiscal reform, the public sector deficit was not brought under control. It was, however, expected to be reduced significantly—to about 3.5% of GDP in 1996 from almost 5% in 1995.

Brazil's balance of trade improved over 1995, when there was an annual deficit of $3,150,000,000. The government expected that there would be a deficit of about $2.5 billion by the end of the year. The current-account deficit was to be kept under 3% of GDP and was expected to be substantially less than the $17.6 billion deficit of 1995.

(SUSAN M. CUNNINGHAM)

BRUNEI

The sultanate of Brunei is located on the northern coast of the island of Borneo, on the South China Sea. Area: 5,765 sq km (2,226 sq mi). Pop. (1996 est.): 300,000. Cap.: Bandar Seri Begawan. Monetary unit: Brunei dollar, with (Oct. 11, 1996) a par value of B$1 to Singapore dollar (free rates of B$1.41 to U.S. $1 and B$2.22 = £1 sterling). Sultan and prime minister in 1996, Sir Muda Hassanal Bolkiah Mu'izzadin Waddaulah.

Even as Brunei planned for a time when its oil and natural gas no longer bought the tiny nation prestige beyond its size, there were unmistakable signs in 1996 that, at least so far, its stature remained undiminished. A stream of high-level visitors illustrated Brunei's importance. Malaysian Prime Minister Datuk Seri Mahathir bin Mohamad arrived in April, following earlier visits by Prime Ministers Banharn Silpa-archa of Thailand and Benazir Bhutto of Pakistan. Singaporean Prime Minister Goh Chok Tong paid an informal working visit in May, and Prince Hitachi of Japan arrived in August.

Business also went to Brunei in 1996. Malaysia made Brunei the first foreign market for its Kancil automobile. The sultan continued to support the idea that Brunei should attract Southeast Asian business by

becoming the region's hub for business services.   (TIM HEALY)

This article updates the *Macropædia* article SOUTHEAST ASIA: *Brunei.*

BULGARIA

The republic of Bulgaria is situated on the eastern Balkan Peninsula of southeastern Europe, along the Black Sea. Area: 110,-994 sq km (42,855 sq mi). Pop. (1996 est.): 8,366,000. Cap.: Sofia. Monetary unit: lev, with (Oct. 11, 1996) a free rate of 216.95 leva to U.S. $1 (341.76 leva = £1 sterling). President in 1996, Zhelyu Zhelev; prime minister, Zhan Videnov.

Petar Stoyanov, candidate of the united opposition, was elected president of Bulgaria on Nov. 3, 1996, easily defeating Ivan Mazarov of the ruling Bulgarian Socialist Party (BSP) by winning 59.96% of the vote in a runoff election.

By mid-July the Bulgarian lev, which stood at 71 to the U.S. dollar in December 1995, had fallen to 181 to the dollar. Because of a general weakness in the banking sector, the Bulgarian National Bank, facing imminent foreign payments, had insufficient reserves to defend the currency. On May 22 Pres. Zhelyu Zhelev declared that the country was on the verge of collapse.

The International Monetary Fund (IMF) demanded action as well as promises of structural reform. Prime Minister Zhan Videnov therefore announced that he would close 64 unprofitable state enterprises and restrict credit for a further 70. Other measures to decrease the budget deficit included the raising of the value-added tax from 18% to 22%, a 5% import levy, hikes in excises on alcohol and tobacco, and huge increases in fuel and public utility costs. In the third quarter the IMF was still not convinced and refused to sanction the second installment of a $580 million standby loan.

The crisis had serious consequences. Inflation rose rapidly; there were public protests that brought an estimated million people onto the streets on June 7; and in August there were rumours of an imminent military coup. Relations between Zhelev and the BSP deteriorated further, there

Simeon II, the former king of Bulgaria, is welcomed by a large crowd in Sofia in May. It was the first time that Simeon had returned to Bulgaria since 1946, when the monarchy was voted out of existence and he went into exile.

IVAN GRIGOROW—STAFF

having been disagreements already over Bulgaria's relationship to NATO, a new law on electronic media, and the state emblem.

On May 25 King Simeon II, who had left Bulgaria in 1946, returned for the first time to visit his native land. A more ominous shadow of Bulgaria's past was cast on October 2 when former prime minister Andrey Lukanov was murdered in Sofia.

(RICHARD J. CRAMPTON)

This article updates the *Macropædia* article BALKAN STATES: *Bulgaria.*

BURKINA FASO

Burkina Faso is a landlocked country of West Africa. Area: 274,400 sq km (105,946 sq mi). Pop. (1996 est.): 10,615,000. Cap.: Ouagadougou. Monetary unit: CFA franc, with a par value of CFAF 100 to the French franc and (as of Oct. 11, 1996) a free rate of CFAF 518.24 to U.S. $1 (CFAF 816.38 = £1 sterling). President (chairman) of the Popular Front in 1996, Capt. Blaise Compaoré; prime ministers, Marc Christian Roch Kaboré and, from February 9, Kadré Désiré Ouédraogo.

At the end of 1995 the new, second chamber in the National Assembly, the House of Representatives, was inaugurated. Of its 178 members, 114 (including 10 chiefs) were chosen by Burkina Faso's traditional and religious authorities. The remainder were appointed by the government. In February Prime Minister Marc Christian Roch Kaboré and his Cabinet resigned, and Kadré Désiré Ouédraogo, also of the ruling Popular Front, formed a new government. In anticipation of the 1997 legislative elections,

a complete realignment of existing political parties took place in March. New coalitions were formed; of the more than 60 separate parties that had contested seats a few years earlier, only 4 remained.

The economy continued to improve, with a 5% growth rate projected for 1996. On June 14 the International Monetary Fund approved a new three-year $57 million loan for the Structural Adjustment Program.

(NANCY ELLEN LAWLER)

This article updates the *Macropædia* article WESTERN AFRICA: *Burkina Faso.*

BURUNDI

Burundi is a landlocked republic of central Africa. Area: 27,816 sq km (10,740 sq mi). Pop. (1996 est.): 5,943,000. Cap.: Bujumbura. Monetary unit: Burundi franc, with (Oct. 11, 1996) a free rate of FBu 220.46 to U.S. $1 (FBu 347.29 = £1 sterling). Presidents in 1996, Sylvestre Ntibantunganya and, from July 25, Pierre Buyoya; prime ministers, Antoine Nduwayo and, from July 31, Pascal-Firmin Ndimira.

During the last months of 1995, increasing numbers of signs were pointing to a new wave of ethnic violence in Burundi. In his review of 1995, Pres. Sylvestre Ntibantunganya warned that the fanaticism of both Hutu and Tutsi could lead to the disintegration of the nation. In February 1996 the UN reported that civil war was taking place in many parts of Burundi and recommended that the world take action rather than wait for genocide to occur. Prime Minister Antoine Nduwayo, however, rejected suggestions for intervention. In April both

the United States and the European Union suspended their aid to Burundi on reports that the government lacked the will to end the violence.

On April 26, after an estimated 500 people had already been killed during the month, 235 villagers were killed in Buhoro in clashes between government forces and rebel Hutu. Fears of massacres on the same scale as earlier had been seen in Rwanda grew through May, and at the end of the month, France suspended military cooperation with the government. On June 25 a regional summit was held at Arusha, Tanz., between Burundi and Ethiopia, Kenya, Rwanda, Tanzania, and Uganda to discuss the deteriorating situation, and Burundi reluctantly accepted the principle of intervention. Subsequently, however, Nduwayo's Unity for National Progress party condemned the agreement as a betrayal, and both the president and prime minister were accused of treason. In July the prime minister reversed his earlier stand and said he was opposed to an international peacekeeping force.

A massacre of more than 300 Tutsi by militant Hutu at Bugendena in mid-July provided the spark that led to a coup. When the president arrived at a memorial service for the victims, angry demonstrators forced him to withdraw (he took refuge in the U.S. embassy), and on July 25 the military seized power and installed Pierre Buyoya as president. Buyoya said, "We have done this [the coup] to avoid genocide. We want to restore peace and protect the population." He ruled out intervention from outside. Reacting to the coup, the leaders of Kenya, Rwanda, Tanzania, Uganda, Ethiopia, and

Tutsi victims of a massacre by militant Hutu at Bugendena, Burundi, are buried. The massacre on July 20 was among the causes of a coup by the Tutsi-dominated army that toppled the government on July 25.

HENRY HURTAK—SYGMA

Zaire imposed sanctions on Burundi. By mid-September the Hutu rebels were claiming that 10,000 people had been killed by the army since the coup, and they called upon the country's neighbours to maintain their embargo.   (GUY ARNOLD)

This article updates the *Macropædia* article CENTRAL AFRICA: *Burundi.*

CAMBODIA

A constitutional monarchy of Southeast Asia, Cambodia occupies the southwestern part of the Indochinese Peninsula, on the Gulf of Thailand. Area: 181,916 sq km (70,238 sq mi). Pop. (1996 est.): 10,081,000. Cap.: Phnom Penh. Monetary unit: riel, with (Oct. 11, 1996) an official rate of CR 2,300 to U.S. $1 (CR 3,623 = £1 sterling). King, Norodom Sihanouk; first prime minister in 1996, Norodom Ranariddh, and second prime minister, Hun Sen.

A dry season offensive in early 1996 against Khmer Rouge bases at Phnom Malai and Pailin in western Batdambang province proved ineffective. The bases fell into government hands later in the year, however, without a single shot being fired. In June rumours surfaced that Khmer Rouge leader Pol Pot had died of malaria. The reports were later denied by the government. In August the government dropped a bombshell: it had been negotiating for three months with top Khmer Rouge official Ieng Sary and the commanders of rebel divisions defending the two Batdambang strongholds. All three, with more than 1,000 rebel troops, later broke away from the hard-line Khmer Rouge and began open peace talks with the government.

The fate of Ieng Sary became a thorny issue. There was initial hesitation about what to do with the guerrilla leader, who had been sentenced to death in 1979 for complicity in the horrors of the 1975–79 Khmer Rouge regime. In February a U.S.-sponsored inquiry, based on testimonies and the number of mass graves uncovered in 1995 and early 1996, suggested that as many as two million had died during those years, many more than had been thought. Despite Ieng Sary's perceived role in the killings, King Norodom Sihanouk pardoned him on September 14 at the request of the two prime ministers, Prince Norodom Ranariddh and Hun Sen.

The amnesty was a rare show of unity for the two leaders, who spent most of the year in an unquiet peace. At the centre of the tension was the domination of the administration by Hun Sen's Cambodian People's Party (CPP), despite the victory by Ranariddh's royalist Funcinpec in the 1993 elections. In February a court sentenced former Funcinpec secretary-general Prince Norodom Sirivudh in absentia to 10 years in prison for conspiring to kill Hun Sen during the previous year. At a Funcinpec congress the following month, Ranariddh complained that the CPP had not sufficiently shared power and threatened to take his party out of the coalition. Hun Sen answered in April by warning Sihanouk, Ranariddh, and Sirivudh, who were all in France, that if the royal family destroyed the constitution by trying to dissolve the government, he would use force to take over.

A soldier from the rebel Khmer Rouge faction stands guard under the Cambodian flag on a square in the former Khmer Rouge stronghold of Pailin in October. At the time, the leader of the faction was meeting with Cambodia's second prime minister.

The opposition fared poorly in 1996. A gray area in legislation left the status of the Khmer Nation Party, founded in November 1995 by former finance minister Sam Rainsy, in question. The KNP thus came under both political and police pressure. In July expelled member Nguon Seour formed a new party out of a breakaway KNP faction.

Foreign affairs were characterized by dispute and compromise. In January Ranariddh accused Vietnam of moving border markers some 300 m (1,000 ft) into Cambodian territory, which prompted Vietnamese Prime Minister Vo Van Kiet to visit Phnom Penh for talks. In late February the U.S. put Cambodia on a list of drug-producing or drug-transit nations.

At their July meeting in Tokyo, Cambodia's donors voiced concern about the nation's unsettled political situation. Cambodia had asked for an additional $940 million in aid on top of the $2.3 billion granted at three previous gatherings. The country was able to secure $518 million in pledges. During the year Japan also resumed yen loans to Cambodia after a hiatus of 28 years, while the European Union extended its rehabilitation assistance.

(JOSÉ MANUEL TESORO)

This article updates the *Macropædia* article SOUTHEAST ASIA: *Cambodia.*

CAMEROON

A republic of western central Africa and member of the Commonwealth, Cameroon lies on the Gulf of Guinea. Area: 475,442 sq km (183,569 sq mi). Pop. (1996 est.): 13,609,000. Cap.: Yaoundé. Monetary unit: CFA franc, with a par value of CFAF 100 to the French franc and (as of Oct. 11, 1996) a free rate of CFAF 518.24 to U.S. $1 (CFAF 816.38 = £1 sterling). President in 1996, Paul Biya; prime ministers, Simon Achidi Achu and, from September 19, Peter Mafany Musonge.

Results of the municipal elections held on Jan. 21, 1996, consolidated Pres. Paul Biya's power as the ruling Cameroon People's Democratic Movement (RDPC) took control of 218 of the 336 communes. John Fru Ndi's Social Democratic Front (SDF) finished second, winning 62 communes. Biya quickly moved to replace elected mayors with government appointees, which triggered widespread protests. In Limbe 5 demonstrators were killed and 15 injured, and security forces were brought in to restore order. On September 19 Biya reshuffled his Cabinet, appointing Peter Mafany Musonge as prime minister.

A general strike began on May 6. The government banned the press from making any mention of it. The success of the strike was disputed, but it appeared that the protest generally failed in most urban areas. University students went on strike independently, demanding better working conditions and an end to newly imposed fees, and so prompted security forces to invade the student residential quarters in mid-June. At least 200 students were arrested.

New clashes in the decade-long territorial conflict between Nigeria and Cameroon over the oil-rich Bakassi peninsula erupted in early February. Although a truce agreement, brokered by Pres. Gnassingbé Eyadéma of Togo, was signed on February 17, sporadic fighting continued for much of the year.

The economy was weak, growing at only half its expected rate. Inflation remained high.   (NANCY ELLEN LAWLER)

This article updates the *Macropædia* article WESTERN AFRICA: *Cameroon.*

CANADA

Canada is a federal parliamentary state and member of the Commonwealth covering North America north of conterminous United States and east of Alaska. Area: 9,970,610 sq km (3,849,674 sq mi). Pop. (1996 est.): 29,784,000. Cap.: Ottawa.

Monetary unit: Canadian dollar, with (Oct. 11, 1996) a free rate of Can$1.35 to U.S. $1 (Can$2.13 = £1 sterling). Queen, Elizabeth II; governor-general in 1996, Roméo LeBlanc; prime minister, Jean Chrétien.

Domestic Affairs. The threat of the separation of Quebec receded in 1996 as Lucien Bouchard, the leader of the secessionist forces and now installed as premier of Quebec, made it clear that his first priority was the strengthening of Quebec's economy. Another referendum on Quebec's future would be delayed until after the next provincial election, not expected before 1998 or 1999. The federal government in Ottawa, led by Prime Minister Jean Chrétien, was still recovering from the shock of the near victory of secession in the 1995 referendum and moved cautiously to counter the independence movement among French-speaking Quebeckers.

Bouchard left the Bloc Québécois, the party he had founded to promote secession in the federal arena, to become premier of Quebec on January 29. He replaced Jacques Parizeau, who had resigned after the defeat of the sovereignty option in the referendum. Under Bouchard, Quebec embarked on a program of austerity in public expenditures. Estimates for 1996–97 revealed projected cuts of Can$1,170,000,000, the first real reduction in Quebec's spending in 25 years. Expenditures on education would be reduced, and hospitals and health care would face a large decline in public grants. The provincial budget, announced on May 9, placed the province on a course to eliminate its deficit by 1999–2000. In so doing, Quebec was following other provinces that had taken similar action. The budget failed to mention the prospect of secession, in contrast to statements made by the previous Parizeau government. Its message was directed to business interests, which were urged to show confidence in the province through investment and job creation.

Bouchard trod carefully around the sensitive issue of language, a symbol of identity for the 80% of Quebec's 7.3 million people for whom French is the mother tongue. Resisting calls from militant separatists to toughen Quebec's language laws, he proposed no change in the regulations governing bilingual commercial signs, a stand that added fuel to the debate between nationalists demanding the supremacy of French and anglophones convinced that the observance of bilingualism was essential to their work and survival.

Chrétien's strategy to counter secession took two forms, labeled Plan A and Plan B. Plan A represented a soft approach: to appease nationalism in Quebec through transferring more powers to the provinces. A looser Canadian federation would prove more attractive to Quebec. Plan B was a firmer stance: to challenge the legality of moves that Quebec might make toward independence and to lay down terms acceptable to Ottawa and the rest of Canada should Quebec decide on secession.

Devolution, a process that the Chrétien government called "rebalancing" the federation, was discussed at a meeting of first ministers (provincial premiers) held in Ottawa on June 20–21. To the surprise of many, Premier Bouchard attended and took part in the discussions. The federal government announced that it was prepared

to transfer responsibility for labour-market training, mining, forestry, tourism, recreation, and social housing to the provinces. The withdrawal from job training, a concession long demanded by Quebec, would take place over the next three years and would be accompanied by a grant of $2 billion to the provinces to support their efforts. Although the Chrétien government regarded devolution of authority as a major thrust, it emphasized that it was not prepared to give up its responsibility to manage social programs such as universal medical care. Seen as vital to the quality of life in Canada, single-payer medical insurance was regarded by most Canadians as a defining quality marking the difference between their society and that of the United States.

Chrétien brought two new recruits into his Cabinet to shore up its Quebec wing. Stéphane Dion was a Montreal academic, a well-known spokesman for federalism in Quebec. He assumed the critical post of minister for intergovernmental affairs. Pierre Pettigrew, an experienced political adviser from Quebec, received the minor post of minister for international cooperation in the Cabinet shuffle on January 25. On October 4 he was promoted to the more important portfolio of human resources, with responsibility for managing federal health and welfare policies. The new ministers gained seats in Parliament in by-elections arranged for March 25. Four other new members were also elected on that day. The results left party standings in the House of Commons as follows: Liberals 177; Bloc Québécois (the official opposition) 53; Reform Party 52; New Democratic Party 9; Progressive Conservatives 2; independents 2; total 295.

Plan B was unveiled by Chrétien's minister of justice, Allan Rock, on September 27. It did not question the right of Quebeckers to vote for separation but challenged the Quebec government's claim that it could unilaterally declare independence. The federal government insisted that in any future referendum the question asked be explicit. Sovereignty would have to be plainly defined as independence. There could be no implication that it would automatically involve a partnership with the rest of Canada, as had been held out in the 1995 referendum. Quebeckers had to be made aware that the consequences of secession—sharing the national debt, an acceptable system of currency, the use of passports, the question of borders, the fate of the province's aboriginal population—would have to be negotiated with the federal government and the provinces before separation could occur. In a future referendum campaign, all Canadians would have to be free to participate. The issue of secession was not one to be decided solely by Quebec.

As a preliminary to the consideration of the terms of divorce, Rock stated that the federal government proposed to ask the Supreme Court of Canada, the country's highest court, to pronounce on the legality of secession. The court would be asked to decide on three questions: Since Canada's constitution contains no provision for separation, is it legal for Quebec to declare its independence unilaterally? Does self-determination, affirmed by Quebec as a basis in international law for independence, give the province the right to secede? If domestic and international law were in conflict

over Quebec's secession, which should take precedence?

The referral to the Supreme Court was considered politically risky since it might alienate moderates in Quebec. Daniel Johnson, the leader of the provincial Liberal Party, and Jean Charest, leader of the Progressive Conservative Party and a strong Quebec federalist, each held back from endorsing it. They preferred Plan A, reforming the existing federal system, as a more constructive alternative. Bouchard's Parti Québécois government denounced the reference to the Supreme Court, saying it would not participate in the hearing and would ignore any ruling made by the court. Rock's intention appeared to be to deter a majority of Quebeckers, moderate in their views on secession, from endorsing a course of action that the Supreme Court might decide was illegal. Quebec's chances of winning international recognition for its new status would also be jeopardized by an adverse ruling on secession from the court.

A final consideration was the future of Quebec's Indian and Inuit population. They did not want to become part of an independent Quebec. A Supreme Court ruling questioning the province's claim to secession would strengthen their case to remain part of Canada. It was expected that a court ruling would not be delivered for at least a year.

The Economy. Although the economy grew in 1996, the high unemployment rate continued to discourage consumer confidence. Exports mounted to record levels, especially automotive products and lumber to the U.S. Gross domestic product (GDP), seasonally adjusted at market prices, was estimated at midyear to be Can$789.5 billion. Interest rates fell, the Bank of Canada prime rate reaching 4.75% in November, the lowest level since 1956. The Canadian dollar strengthened against the U.S. currency, and inflation continued at a low level. In August the consumer price index stood at 1.4%, well within the Bank of Canada's target of 1% to 3%. Unemployment, which had remained at more than 9% of the labour force for six years, continued to be a major drag on the economy. In October it rose to 10%, erasing a slight decline earlier.

Finance Minister Paul Martin's third budget, delivered on March 6, showed steady progress in reducing Canada's deficit on government operations. Martin had set himself the goal of reducing the deficit in 1996–97 to Can$24.3 billion, or 3% of GDP, when he took over the finance portfolio in 1993. He was on course to realize this goal and predicted a further decrease of the deficit, to $17 billion, or 2% of GDP, for 1997–98. In a statement issued on October 9, Martin promised further progress. By 1998–99 the deficit should fall to $9 billion (1% of GDP), at which time the government would no longer have to use financial markets to borrow new money. Borrowing could instead be handled by rolling over the existing debt. Martin's task of deficit reduction had been made easier by the fall in interest rates, which reduced the cost of borrowing.

The budget, taking note of a general election likely to be held within about a year, contained a minimum of tax increases and few large cuts in government expenditures. It did, however, announce the end of Canada's universal old-age security pro-

Students at the University of British Columbia march on February 7 to protest the federal government's proposal to cut support for education. Although the overall Canadian economy was healthy in 1996, the government took a number of steps to reduce the budget deficit.

gram by 2001. In that year wealthier senior citizens would see their government pensions (since 1951 paid to every resident regardless of income) reduced or eliminated. Single taxpayers would lose their state pensions at an income of Can$52,000; for couples a combined income of Can$78,-000 would mean the loss of the pension. For seniors with middle-range incomes, the pension would be proportionately reduced. Lower-income seniors would receive additional support through a new Seniors Benefit to replace their old-age security and guaranteed income supplement. It was estimated that about 75% of retirees would receive the same or higher benefits. Seniors 60 years of age or older at the end of 1995 would not be affected by the changes, but those younger, the so-called baby boomers, would be directly affected.

Foreign Affairs. Canada maintained two sizable peacekeeping forces abroad in 1996. One was in Bosnia and Herzegovina, where 1,000 Canadian troops were sent early in the year to assist the NATO forces in their task of implementing the peace accord. Their tour of duty, originally intended to last one year, was expected to be lengthened into 1997 as instability persisted in the Balkan region. The second peacekeeping mission was in Haiti, from which U.S. forces were anxious to withdraw. Canada agreed to replace the United States in the UN support mission to the island. In February Canada also promised to provide an additional 750 peacekeepers to Haiti and offered to shoulder their costs. A Canadian general was selected to lead the UN mission. Canada also sent 100 members of the Royal Canadian Mounted Police to work with the Haitian police in an effort to bring law and order to the country.

Canada's new minister for foreign affairs, Lloyd Axworthy, named to the post in January, spoke out sharply against the repressive military regime in Nigeria when Commonwealth foreign ministers met in London in late April. He could not, however, persuade the 53-member Commonwealth to adopt comprehensive economic sanctions against Nigeria. Canada, which had little trade with the African country, suspended sales of equipment that could be used by the Nigerian military and cut off development aid. Nigeria was later suspended from the Commonwealth.

Trade disputes were a feature of the Canada-United States relationship in 1996. Canada took strong exception to a U.S. bill that penalized foreign companies that used expropriated Cuban property to undertake business in Cuba. Signed by U.S. Pres. Bill Clinton on July 16, the president waived for six months a provision allowing U.S. corporations to sue in U.S. courts foreign companies active in Cuba. Canada's objection to the legislation was twofold; it did not believe the bill would do anything to improve human rights in Cuba, and it could not countenance the U.S. attempt to change Canada's trade policy. Canada had traded with Cuba ever since the revolution led by Fidel Castro, and exports were now valued at about Can$274 million a year. Twenty-five Canadian companies operated within Cuba, while others, such as banks, telephone companies, and airlines, maintained less-direct links. Canada believed that the opening of the Cuban economy through trade and investment was the only long-term policy likely to promote democratic change in Cuba.

Canada also objected to the Iran and Libya Sanctions Act, signed by Clinton on August 5. This bill, by penalizing countries that invested in the two nations, struck at terrorist activity sponsored by them.

Canada's military forces found themselves deeply mired in controversy in 1996. The troubles stemmed from the misconduct of Canadian peacekeepers in Somalia in 1992–93. Two Somalis were killed around Canadian bases, and there was disturbing evidence of racist sentiment in the Airborne Regiment, one of the units sent to Somalia. The regiment was disbanded in 1995 as courts-martial found a number of its members guilty of dishonourable conduct. The Chrétien government set up a civilian board of inquiry to look into the command and operation of the Somalia mission. It discovered that documents and computer records relating to the mission were missing or had been destroyed. The conduct of the military leadership as it testified before the commission was disquieting. Canada's top soldier, Gen. Jean Boyle, in nine days of testimony before the commission in late August, acknowledged that he had violated the "spirit," if not the letter, of the federal access-to-information act in dealing with journalists' questions. General Boyle's attempt to shift the blame for the cover-up to his subordinates and his refusal to accept personal responsibility aroused widespread criticism of his leadership.

He was, however, loyally supported by the minister of national defense, David Collenette, who had appointed Boyle in January and who publicly praised his conduct, even before the inquiry had reached its conclusions. The matter was terminated unexpectedly when, on October 4, Collenette was obliged to resign his portfolio over an unrelated incident involving a breach of the ethical guidelines applying to Cabinet ministers. Collenette was found to have written to the Immigration and Refugee Board, a quasi-judicial agency, on behalf of a constituent. Five days later Boyle also resigned, stating that the Canadian forces deserved leadership that was not burdened by critical attention and controversy. Chrétien appointed a new defense minister, Douglas Young of New Brunswick, who was shifted from another portfolio. Young's first task was to find a new chief of defense who could restore confidence in the country's military command.

Canada in October sent troops to Zaire to help rescue Rwandan Hutu refugees from starvation. (D.M.L. FARR)

CAPE VERDE

The republic of Cape Verde occupies an island group in the Atlantic Ocean about 620 km (385 mi) off the west coast of Africa. Area: 4,033 sq km (1,557 sq mi). Pop. (1996 est.): 403,000. Cap.: Praia. Monetary unit: Cape Verde escudo, with (Oct. 11, 1996) a free rate of 82.97 escudos to U.S. $1 (130.70 escudos = £1 sterling). President in 1996, Antonio Mascarenhas Monteiro; prime minister, Carlos Veiga.

In the December 1995 elections for the National Assembly, the ruling Movement for Democracy (MPD) won an absolute majority, gaining 50 of the 72 seats. Although the African Party for the Independence of Cape Verde (PAICV), which had been the sole ruling party until 1991, accepted defeat, it claimed that the MPD had used its monopoly control of communications to flood the country with its propaganda; it also accused the MPD of buying votes. The PAICV obtained 21 seats and the Democratic Convergence Party the remaining seat.

In the presidential elections on February 18, Antonio Mascarenhas Monteiro of the MPD was reelected president—no other party put up a candidate—but there was

a 60% rate of abstention. In March Prime Minister Carlos Veiga carried out a major Cabinet reshuffle and brought five new ministers into his team. (GUY ARNOLD)

This article updates the *Macropædia* article WESTERN AFRICA: *Cape Verde.*

CENTRAL AFRICAN REPUBLIC

The Central African Republic is a landlocked state in central Africa. Area: 622,436 sq km (240,324 sq mi). Pop. (1996 est.): 3,274,000. Cap.: Bangui. Monetary unit: CFA franc, with (Oct. 11, 1996) a par value of CFAF 100 to the French franc and a free rate of CFAF 518.24 to U.S. $1 (CFAF 816.38 = £1 sterling). President in 1996, Ange-Félix Patassé; prime ministers, Gabriel Koyambounou and, from June 6, Jean-Paul Ngoupande.

Despite signs of improvement in the previous year, the economic situation worsened in 1996, and the country was threatened with bankruptcy. Payments to virtually all pensioners, teachers, civil servants, and soldiers were several months in arrears. In what the government described as an attempted coup, a large group of soldiers demanding their wages mutinied on April 18 at Kasai camp. The tense situation eased after blocked aid funds were released to enable salary payments to be made. One month later, however, on May 18, military units seized Kasai's armoury and took to the streets. Within hours a full-scale insurrection broke out, and clashes spread to the provinces. France sent in reinforcements to quell the rioting and looting in Bangui. At least 40 people died and more than 200 were injured during the rioting. By May 27 calm had returned, but on November 16 fighting again broke out. Foreign mediators worked to end the crisis.

Pres. Ange-Félix Patassé announced a new government of national unity. On June 6 he appointed as prime minister Jean-Paul Ngoupande, former ambassador to France. (NANCY ELLEN LAWLER)

JEAN-MICHEL TURPIN—GAMMA LIAISON

Soldiers gather in Bangui, capital of the Central African Republic, after agreeing in May to end a mutiny. The soldiers had a number of grievances, including not being paid.

This article updates the *Macropædia* article CENTRAL AFRICA: *Central African Republic.*

CHAD

Chad is a landlocked republic of central Africa. Area: 1,284,000 sq km (495,755 sq mi). Pop. (1996 est.): 6,543,000. Cap.: N'Djamena. Monetary unit: CFA franc, with a par value of CFAF 100 to the French franc and (as of Oct. 11, 1996) a free rate of CFAF 518.24 to U.S. $1 (CFAF 816.38 = £1 sterling). President in 1996, Lieut. Gen. Idriss Déby; prime minister, Djimasta Koibla.

In a referendum held at the end of March 1996, 63.5% of voters in Chad approved

AFP PHOTO

Voters in Chad line up in June at the town of Moussoro for the first round of the nation's first free presidential election since it achieved independence from France in 1960.

a new constitution for the country. Multiparty presidential elections, provided for by the constitution, were held on June 2, and there was enthusiastic participation in the first round with its field of candidates. By the end of the month, however, the opposition groups were calling for a boycott of the second round, scheduled for July 3, on the grounds of massive electoral fraud. The official results of the first round gave Pres. Idriss Déby 43.9% of the vote and his nearest rival, Gen. Abdelkader Wadal Kamougue of the Union for Renewal and Democracy, 12.39%. In the second round Déby received 69.09%, against 30.91% for Kamougue.

It was a year of reconciliation. In January the government signed a peace agreement with the Action for Unity and Development, which was legalized as a political party after it abandoned the armed struggle. At a meeting in Franceville, Gabon, in March, 13 rebel groups signed peace agreements with the government. In August an agreement with the southern-based Armed Forces for a Federal Republic was reached, and all military action was brought to an end. (GUY ARNOLD)

This article updates the *Macropædia* article WESTERN AFRICA: *Chad.*

CHILE

The republic of Chile extends along the Pacific coast of the Southern Cone of South America. Area: 756,626 sq km (292,135 sq mi), not including Chile's Antarctic claim. Pop. (1996 est.): 14,375,-000. Cap.: Santiago (national); Valparaíso (legislative). Monetary unit: Chilean peso, with (Oct. 11, 1996) a free rate of 413.55 pesos to U.S. $1 (651.47 pesos = £1 sterling). President in 1996, Eduardo Frei.

In August 1996 the U.S. ambassador, Gabriel Guerra-Mondragón, angered Chilean leaders by defending the U.S. ban on the export of advanced weapons to Chile, in force since the dictatorship of Augusto Pinochet Ugarte (1973–90). Chile's 1980 constitution, the ambassador maintained, prevents the president from removing the military commanders in chief and thus does not allow full civilian control of the Chilean armed forces. The right-wing parties accused Guerra-Mondragón of interference; the left considered that the ambassador had merely spoken the obvious. This episode and the government's low-key reaction highlighted the extent to which relations with the armed forces and the legacy of the dictatorship continued to cause problems for the government of Pres. Eduardo Frei. These were intensified by the negotiations under way with the armed forces over the succession to Pinochet, who planned to step down as commander in chief of the army in March 1998.

In August 1995 President Frei proposed reforming the 1980 constitution. He advocated a compromise on the sensitive issue of human rights violations committed under the fileatorship, accepting the 1980 amnesty law but allowing the courts to investigate "individual truths" (*i.e.,* the courts would be able to identify guilt but not sentence the guilty). Frei also proposed ending the system by which 9 of the 47 senators were appointed, 8 of them by Pinochet, rather than elected. This provision had enabled

CRIS BOURONCLE—AFP PHOTO

A contract maintenance worker polishes metal in a refinery at the Chuquicamata copper-mining complex in Chile during a 10-day strike for higher wages by more than 7,000 miners. The open-pit mine at Chuquicamata was the world's largest.

the right-wing opposition to block reforms since the return to civilian rule in 1990. Despite a deal with the main opposition party, National Renovation (RN), the reform was rejected by the Senate when 7 RN senators joined 14 others in voting against it.

In June Chile reached important trading agreements with the Southern Cone Common Market (Mercosur) and the European Union after the U.S. Congress rebuffed its attempt to join the North American Free Trade Agreement. In November, however, Chile and Canada signed a free-trade agreement. At San Luis, Arg., Frei signed a deal that made Chile an associate member of Mercosur. Tariffs on 90% of goods traded between Chile and the Mercosur countries (Argentina, Brazil, Paraguay, and Uruguay) were to be phased out over eight years. The transitional period on the other 10% was to be 10–15 years, except for wheat (18 years). The main opposition in Chile had come from farmers, who feared competition from the large-scale Mercosur producers.

Export earnings declined because of a fall in copper prices, and a deficit of $550 million in the trade balance was projected for 1996. An increase of 6.6% in gross domestic product was estimated for 1996, down from 8.5% in 1995. A decline in consumer spending became apparent from July onward. Unemployment was estimated at 7% at the end of the year. (CHARLIE NURSE)

CHINA

The People's Republic of China is situated in eastern Asia, with coastlines on the Yellow Sea and the East and South China seas. Area: 9,572,900 sq km (3,696,100 sq mi), including Tibet and excluding Taiwan. (See *Taiwan,* below.) Pop. (1996 est., excluding Taiwan): 1,218,700,000. Cap.: Beijing. Monetary unit: renminbi yuan, with (Oct. 11, 1996) a free rate of 8.30 yuan to U.S. $1 (13.07 yuan = £1 sterling). President in 1996, Jiang Zemin; premier, Li Peng.

An upsurge of popular nationalism, tinged with antiforeign sentiments, swept China in 1996. As Beijing prepared for the peaceful takeover of Hong Kong on July 1, 1997, Chinese leaders used a display of military force to warn Taiwan against drifting toward formal independence. Deng Xiaoping, frail and ailing, turned 92 in August, but the once paramount leader was no longer a player in the political game. It seemed unlikely that he would be able to visit Hong Kong in 1997 to celebrate the end of British rule, which he had successfully negotiated in 1984. As Chinese leaders continued to jockey for position in the post-Deng era, they had to contend with the economic, social, and political consequences of Deng's reforms. Meanwhile, China's economy continued to hum along at a 10% growth rate. Inflation, moreover, was finally brought under control. The tension in Sino-U.S. relations eased somewhat in the second half of the year as Beijing directed its anger at Japan, which it accused of harbouring ambitions of regional domination. Chinese leaders traded on their country's growing global economic strength to enhance their leverage on issues that they considered vital to Chinese security, particularly in respect to Taiwan and Tibet.

Domestic Affairs. Pres. Jiang Zemin dominated the Chinese political stage in 1996 in his triple capacity as general secretary of the Communist Party of China (CPC), head of state, and chairman of the CPC's Central Military Commission. A cautious centrist rather than a bold innovator, Jiang continued to rule by consensus, undertaking no policy initiatives that might cause his colleagues to unite against him. There were no significant changes in the top leadership in 1996. Major Gen. Ba Zhongtan, head of the People's Armed Police, resigned following the murder in February of Li Peiyao, vice-chairman of the National People's Congress, during a bungled burglary. Beijing Mayor Li Qiyan, who had been implicated in the 1995 scandal that led to the purge of Political Bureau member Chen Xitong, was demoted to secretary of the CPC's Committee of the Ministry of Labour. Wang Li, one of the last of the Cultural Revolution radicals, died at age 75.

Police in Beijing in June detain a group of citizens charged with criminal activity. It was estimated that as part of a drive to reduce the country's high rate of violent crime, the Chinese government executed more than a thousand people and imprisoned tens of thousands more.

A popular best-seller, *The China That Can Say No,* authored by Song Qiang and two other youthful writers, angrily denounced the U.S. for subverting the national aspirations of the Chinese and poisoning the wellsprings of their culture with Hollywood films and Western fast food. Popular nationalism complemented official nationalism but also challenged it to be more active in defending Chinese interests. Jiang wrapped himself tightly in the banner of Chinese nationalism while promoting the rather amorphous concept of socialist spiritual civilization. This was the main theme of his address to the October plenum of the CPC Central Committee. The communiqué affirmed economic reform as the central task of the CPC but stressed that the party had yet to solve the problem of promoting ideological, educational, ethical, and cultural progress. Energetic campaigns were launched to curb such national bad habits as spitting, littering, smoking, and cursing in public. Otherwise, socialist spiritual civilization seemed to be a euphemism for domestic law-and-order policies and the maintenance of tight controls over culture, literature, and the arts. For example, Wang Shuo, the popular novelist who chronicled Beijing lowlife, was criticized for decadence. The CPC deferred any serious initiatives to grapple with major economic and social issues at least to its 15th Congress, which would convene in late 1997 in the afterglow of the recovery of Hong Kong.

Lacking a distinctive vision for the future, the CPC reveled in its revolutionary past, glorifying the heroism of the famous Long March, the 60th anniversary of which was widely celebrated on stage and screen and in song. Jiang used the occasion to reemphasize a favourite theme, the loyalty of the People's Liberation Army to the CPC. Jiang's neoconservative nationalism presented the CPC as indispensable in holding Chinese society together and guiding China toward prosperity and greatness.

The CPC stepped up its campaign against rampant corruption, criticizing cadres (government and party officials) for wasting public funds by such means as extravagant banquets and unessential travel. In October Chinese prosecutors filed criminal charges against Zhou Beifang and 29 others, including two ex-Beijing officials. Zhou, who reportedly paid millions in bribes to corrupt officials in return for favours, was the son of the former chairman of Capital Iron and Steel Corp. and a confidant of Deng. The Central Committee for Discipline Inspection called for harsher punishment of corrupt officials while declaring that ethical and cultural progress should not be sacrificed in the name of economic development. This was one of several implicit criticisms of Deng's reforms. A thorough critique of the reforms was contained in the unpublished but widely circulated "Ten Thousand Character Essay," attributed to the conservative ideologue Deng Liqun. The tract, which warned that the CPC's hold on power was seriously threatened by the rise of a new Chinese bourgeoisie, revived the old Maoist emphasis on class struggle. This viewpoint was challenged by Cao Siyuan, a leading reformer who had been purged in 1989. In an article published in an obscure provincial economics journal, he argued that reform was the only way the CPC could retain power, but it would do so only if it stopped meddling in all aspects of social life. Authorities forbade republication of the article.

In April Beijing launched a new and well-publicized campaign called *yanda* ("strike hard") against violent crime, which shot up 13% in 1995. Within the first two months, according to estimates by Amnesty International, 100,000 illegal firearms were seized nationwide, tens of thousands of alleged criminals arrested, and 1,000 executed. On the information front Chinese leaders ordered stepped-up monitoring of computer bulletin boards and blocked access to numerous sites on the World Wide Web. These included those operated by foreign newspapers, human rights groups, overseas dissidents, and the Voice of America.

Chinese leaders were equally determined to root out the vestiges of domestic dissent. They brushed aside international criticism of the 14-year prison term imposed in 1995 on Wei Jingsheng, who received the European Union's prestigious Andrey Sakharov Prize for Human Rights. In October Wang Dan, a student leader of the 1989 democracy movement, was sentenced to 11 years in prison on charges of conspiring to overthrow the government. The specific charges included publishing critical articles in foreign newspapers, raising money abroad for needy dissidents, and accepting a scholarship from the University of California. Another Chinese democrat, Liu Xiaobo, was sentenced to three years in a labour camp. Along with Wang Xizhe, he had drafted a letter critical of Jiang and called on the CPC to honour political and human rights. Wang Xizhe managed to escape from China and was granted political asylum in the U.S. After his release from prison in May, Bao Tong was kept in seclusion outside Beijing. He had been the top aide to Zhao Ziyang, the CPC chief purged in 1989. As a small gesture on the U.S. on the eve of Secretary of State Warren Christopher's November visit to Beijing, China released dissident Chen Ziming, who was suffering from cancer. Chinese leaders also put Hong Kong on notice that freedom of the press, as well as free speech and assembly, would be curtailed after 1997, solemn promises to the contrary notwithstanding. Hong Kong papers, for example, would be forbidden to advocate independence for Taiwan or to engage in political advocacy.

In January, Human Rights Watch/Asia, a U.S. organization, using information supplied by a former staff physician at Shanghai's largest orphanage, charged officials there with deliberately starving unwanted orphans to death. China acknowledged an unusually high infant mortality rate at the orphanage but angrily denied the allegations, branding them part of an ongoing effort to besmirch China's international reputation.

Trouble again flared in Tibet. In May monks at the Ganden monastery attacked Chinese police and officials after the imposition of a ban on photographs of the Dalai Lama. The police stormed the monastery, shot 2 monks, and arrested 100 others. Beijing threatened economic reprisals against such countries as Australia, whose leaders disregarded Chinese warnings by meeting with the Dalai Lama. The *Tibet Daily,* the CPC's mouthpiece in the region, urged Tibetans to embrace atheism in order to counter the influence of the Dalai Lama. This was tantamount to asking Tibetans to renounce their cultural identities. In September Premier Li Peng reminded restive Muslims in the Xinjiang Uygur autonomous region that they had to obey the law and support socialism. Violent clashes erupted between Muslim separatists and Chinese authorities, and in May China tightened border controls to curb arms smuggling from Central Asia.

The Economy. The Chinese economy performed well in 1996, although massive socioeconomic problems remained unsolved. Gross domestic product grew by about 10%, while the inflation rate dropped to just 6%, four points below the government's target. Industrial output increased 13.2% in the first six months, paced by small and medium township and village enterprises. The easing of inflation was mostly due to the drop in exports, which at $90.6 billion during the January–August period were down 4% from 1995. Exports picked up in the second half of the year, however, and the overall trade surplus for the year was expected to be $6 billion. Foreign investment, the engine of economic growth, grew 20% in the first half of 1996. With the economy having made a soft landing after several years of dizzying growth, the government slightly eased lending rates while keeping a tight hand on the growth of the money supply. The steady march toward convertibility of China's currency, the renminbi yuan, continued as foreign companies operating in China were given permission to convert the yuan freely into dollars or Japanese yen.

After a record grain harvest of 466 million metric tons in 1995, another record crop of 475 million metric tons was expected in 1996. This yield was anticipated despite torrential summer rains throughout China that flooded 3,250,000 ha (8 million ac) of cropland, caused thousands of deaths, left millions homeless, and cost billions of yuan in damage. The Yellow River crested at its highest recorded level, inspiring fears of a catastrophic dike breach. Nevertheless, over the past 50 years, natural disasters on average had reduced China's harvests by just 1% annually. Work proceeded on the world's largest flood-control and hydroelectric project, the controversial Three Gorges Dam on the Chang Jiang (Yangtze River) above Yichang. Chinese planners were considering huge water-diversification projects to channel excess water from the Chang Jiang to arid northern regions.

Compared with the early 1990s, the CPC was now promoting slower growth, reasserting strong central control over the economy, and trying to redirect investments from the prosperous coastal provinces to the more slowly developing interior, especially the mountainous western provinces, where most of China's hard-core poor lived. China estimated that 65 million people, or just over 5% of the population, fell below a poverty line defined as an income of 5 yuan (60 cents) per day. The World Bank, using 8 yuan (96 cents) per day as the poverty line, estimated that 350 million (well over one-quarter of the Chinese population) fell below this line. Recalculating China's per capita income, the World Bank estimated China's 1992 per capita income at $1,800, compared with $1,210 for India, $2,970 for Indonesia, and $5,250 for Brazil. The calculations took into account the prices of goods on the various domestic markets.

Unemployment, real and prospective, cast a huge shadow over the Chinese economy. The Ministry of Labour forecast that the number of rural jobless would rise to 140 million by the year 2000 because the economy was expected to generate only 70 million new jobs for the 210 million rural workers who would be seeking employment at that time. Large state-owned enterprises continued to struggle under mountains of debt. After years of decline these firms, employing some 115 million persons (70% of the industrial workforce) accounted for

only one-third of China's industrial output and generated only 1% of industrial profits while absorbing three-quarters of industrial investments. The medium-sized and small state firms were experimenting with various ways to increase their profitability and orient themselves to a market economy, but no solutions were in sight for the industrial dinosaurs of the old state socialist economy. Many workers in state-run enterprises were given extended vacations, furloughed, simply not paid, or paid months in arrears.

The Bank of China was admitted to the Swiss-based Bank for International Settlements (the so-called bankers' bank), in recognition of China's growing international importance. China's admission to the World Trade Organization was still blocked, however, by foreign, particularly U.S., insistence on various market-opening and statistical conditions that China still had not met. This increased Chinese resentment against the U.S.

Foreign Affairs. Beijing's concern that Taiwan was drifting toward independence was heightened by Taiwan Pres. Lee Teng-hui's private visit to the U.S. in June 1995. In February–March 1996 Chinese leaders stepped up their campaign of psychological warfare vis-à-vis Taiwan that had begun in July 1995 with large-scale military exercises and missile firings into international waters near Taiwan. As the Republic of China prepared for its first direct presidential elections in March, the People's Liberation Army practiced amphibious landings and fired nine missiles off Taiwan's northern and southern coasts in an attempt to intimidate voters on the island. Beijing's belligerence boosted Lee's popularity and triggered the dispatch of two U.S. aircraft carrier groups to international waters off Taiwan, an unmistakable signal of U.S. commitment to Taiwan's security. After its strategy of intimidation backfired, Beijing refused to resume talks with Taipei, but it invited Taiwan to establish direct air and shipping links with the mainland in order to facilitate further integration of the island's economy with that of mainland China.

China's relations with Japan became strained over control of a group of five uninhabited islets and three barren rocks off Taiwan's northeast coast that the Chinese call Diaoyu and the Japanese call Senkaku. When right-wing Japanese nationalists erected a flimsy aluminum lighthouse on the main islet, nationalist outrage erupted in China, Taiwan, and even Hong Kong. A flotilla of eight small boats from Hong Kong and Taiwan carried patriotic Chinese toward the Diaoyu islands in vain attempts to wrest sovereignty from Japan, but its coast guard repelled the miniarmada. While tongue-lashing Japan, Beijing banned anti-Japanese protests by campus nationalists, perhaps fearing that hotheads might turn their anger against cautious CPC leaders who had no desire to rupture relations with Japan, one of China's major economic partners. Jiang ordered students to calm down, reassuring them that the matter would be solved through diplomacy. The waters surrounding the islands were believed to overlie extensive oil and natural gas deposits. The U.S. and several Southeast Asian states quietly informed Beijing that they would not respect China's unilateral May 1996 declaration extending its territorial waters by some 2.5 million sq km

(965,000 sq mi) in the South China Sea. Indonesia planned to conduct its largest-ever war games to warn China away from its Natuna Islands oil project.

In late July China conducted the second of two nuclear explosions, then declared a moratorium on further testing and supported the worldwide Comprehensive Test Ban Treaty. Its implementation could depend on India, which had thus far refused to sign the agreement. According to authoritative sources, China's defense expenditures, an estimated $32 billion, were second in Asia only to Japan's. China continued to investigate overseas markets for advanced weapons system, possibly including an aircraft carrier. It concluded an agreement with Russia, its main overseas arms supplier, to purchase 72 SU-27 fighter jets and to build additional jets in China under a licensing agreement. According to defense experts, such acquisitions would not alter the regional balance of power.

Sino-American relations, badly strained over Taiwan, marginally improved in the second half of the year. A last-minute agreement over the protection of intellectual property rights averted a threatened trade war between the two nations. The U.S. Congress again voted not to link unrelated issues with the granting of most-favoured-nation trade status to China. In the summer of 1996, China overtook Japan as the country with the largest surplus in trade with the U.S. Shortly after Pres. Bill Clinton's reelection, retiring secretary of state Warren Christopher visited Beijing to set up a 1997 summit meeting between Clinton and Jiang, and in December China's defense minister visited the U.S.

Chinese leaders continued their globe-trotting to countries near and far. When Jiang toured Africa in May, he dispensed aid to needy governments, and in November he became the first Chinese head of state to visit India. Li Peng visited Paris, where he awarded a large commercial airliner contract to the European Airbus consortium; in November he traveled to Brazil. The usual steady stream of major and minor state dignitaries, headed by Russian Pres. Boris Yeltsin, visited Beijing. Swedish Prime Minister Goran Persson was one of the few who raised the sensitive issue of human rights in China, such as the case of dissident Wang Dan.   (STEVEN I. LEVINE)

COLOMBIA

A republic in northwestern South America, Colombia has coastlines on the Caribbean Sea and the Pacific Ocean. Area: 1,141,568 sq km (440,762 sq mi). Pop. (1996 est.): 35,652,000. Cap.: Santafé de Bogotá, D.C. Monetary unit: Colombian peso, with (Oct. 11, 1996) a free rate of 1,015 pesos to U.S. $1 (1,599 pesos = £1 sterling). President in 1996, Ernesto Samper Pizano.

The struggle of Pres. Ernesto Samper Pizano (see BIOGRAPHIES) to survive the many calls for his resignation dominated politics in Colombia in 1996. At the end of 1995 a congressional committee dropped a charge of drug corruption against him for lack of evidence, but public opinion continued to insist that he knowingly accepted up to $6 million from the Cali drug cartel during his election campaign in 1994. Samper's campaign treasurer, Santiago Medina, supported by Fernando Botero Zea, Samper's former defense minister and campaign manager, stated that Samper was specifically aware of the drug connection. President Samper refuted these statements, questioning the motives of his accusers and insisting that his conscience was clear. Nevertheless, several of his ministers resigned, and many professional groups joined in the call for his resignation. In February Congress responded and reconvened the committee, which led to a congressional vote in June of 111–43 in favour of dropping the matter. Observers believed that many members of both Samper's party and the opposition conservatives felt their own interests would be threatened by a process leading to a Senate trial and impeachment of the president.

This did not, however, settle the matter. In March Colombia was removed from the list of countries the U.S. believed were making progress against illegal traffickers. This made the country ineligible for assistance from the U.S. Export-Import Bank. The initial reaction to the U.S. move was a wave of nationalist support for Samper, which was further increased when the U.S. canceled his visa. The U.S. insisted on harsher sentences for drug convictions (the Ochoa brothers were released in July after just less than 5½ years in jail) and the extradition to the U.S. of named international criminals.

Efforts to combat the drug cartels started badly in January when José Santacruz Londoño escaped from jail, probably with the connivance of his guards. He was, however, found and killed by police in March. The one remaining Cali cartel leader still at large, Helmer Herrera, surrendered in September; he was one of those the U.S. wished to extradite for trial. The campaign to eradicate drug crops in the southeast of the country continued, but no effective plan had emerged to compensate the local growers for loss of their livelihood. This led to significant uprisings in Putumayo and Caquetá departments, supported by the armed left-wing groups the Colombia Revolutionary Armed Forces and the National Liberation Army; they resulted in considerable loss of life. Damage by guerrillas to oil pipelines was extensive in 1996, particularly on the lines to Coveñas on the Caribbean coast.

An alliance between the guerrillas and the drug cartels to destabilize the country was a major fear of the Samper government. This was a factor restraining his agreement to extradite criminals to the U.S.; extradition had provoked the "drug wars" during 1986–90.

The economy also suffered in 1996. Inflation was expected to exceed 20% (compared with more than 18% in 1995), and gross domestic product growth was forecast at 4%, well below that of 1995. Unemployment was estimated at 12.4–18.6% in December, the highest in eight years. Not all the news was gloomy. There were significant oil and gas finds in 1996, some of excellent quality, and oil exports were expected to bring in a record $1.3 billion of revenue during the year. (PETER POLLARD)

COMOROS

The Islamic republic of the Comoros is an island state in the Indian Ocean off the east coast of Africa. Area: 1,862 sq km (719 sq mi), excluding the island of Mayotte, which continued to be a de facto dependency of France. Pop. (1996 est.; excluding Mayotte): 562,000. Cap.: Moroni. Monetary unit: Comorian franc, with a par value of CF 75 to the French franc and (as of Oct. 11, 1996) a free rate of CF 388.59 to U.S. $1 (CF 612.15 = £1 sterling). Presidents in 1996, Caabi el Yachourtu Mohamed and, from March 25, Mohamed Taki Abdoulkarim; prime ministers, Caabi el Yachourtu Mohamed and, from March 27, Tadjidine Ben Said Massounde.

At the end of 1995, a political crisis arose when Pres. Said Mohamed Djohar went to Réunion for medical treatment and Prime Minister Caabi el Yachourtu Mohamed assumed the title of interim president. Prime Minister Yachourtu called presidential elections for January 28. After two days of talks between Djohar and representatives of Yachourtu in Madagascar under the auspices of the Organization of African Unity, it was agreed that Djohar could return to Comoros to a "symbolic" role; a new electoral code laid down that the age range for presidential candidates should be between 40 and 70 (Djohar was around 80).

In the first round of the presidential elections, which had been postponed to March 6, Mohamed Taki Abdoulkarim and his National Union for Democracy in the Comoros (UNDC) won with 21% of the votes. In the second round the UNDC won with 64% of the total. Following his election Taki said he wished French troops to remain in Comoros and France to undertake the external defense of the country. He was sworn in on March 25. In April he dissolved the National Assembly and scheduled new elections to the Assembly for October 6. In the election, boycotted by the opposition coalition, the UNDC won 36 of the 43 seats.   (GUY ARNOLD)

This article updates the *Micropædia* article COMOROS.

CONGO

A republic, Congo is in central Africa on the Atlantic Ocean. Area: 342,000 sq km (132,047 sq mi). Pop. (1996 est.): 2,665,000. Cap.: Brazzaville. Monetary unit: CFA franc, with (Oct. 11, 1996) a par value of CFAF 100 to the French franc and a free rate of CFAF 518.24 to U.S. $1 (CFAF 816.38 = £1 sterling). President in 1996, Pascal Lissouba; prime ministers, Jacques Yhombi-Opango and, from September 2, David Charles Ganao.

The year 1995 closed with the signing of another pact designed to end the continuing crisis over the disarmament of urban militiamen allied to Pres. Pascal Lissouba and their integration into the Congolese army. The program nearly collapsed when around 100 former militiamen, with the support of new recruits, mutinied in mid-February. Following the March 2 call of André Milongo, president of the National Assembly, for the government to restore order in the armed services, opposition members joined with the government to establish a peace committee. It met on March 19 and agreed to the integration of additional militiamen into the army. Also, a military tribunal was set up to investigate the cause of the February revolt. Despite these moves toward peace, about 200 armed men of former president Denis Sassou-Nguesso's private militia occupied the northern town of Mossaka for a week in late July.

(NANCY ELLEN LAWLER)

This article updates the *Macropædia* article CENTRAL AFRICA: *Congo*.

COSTA RICA

The Central American republic of Costa Rica has coastlines on the Caribbean Sea and the Pacific Ocean. Area: 51,100 sq km (19,730 sq mi). Pop. (1996 est.): 3.4 million. Cap.: San José. Monetary unit: Costa Rican colón, with (Oct. 11, 1996) a free rate of ₡214.48 to U.S. $1 (₡337.86 = £1 sterling). President in 1996, José María Figueres Olsen.

In June 1996 the ruling National Liberation Party maintained its pact with the opposition Social Christian Unity Party to approve the Economic Guarantees bill. Among other measures, the bill restricted the government deficit to 1% of gross domestic product unless two-thirds of the congressional deputies agreed to a higher limit. The legislation would not be implemented until after the 1997 elections.

In late July Hurricane Cesar struck Costa Rica, causing widespread damage, especially in the south. More than 30 people died, many communities were isolated, and parts of the Pan-American Highway were destroyed. Pres. José María Figueres Olsen estimated the cost of repairs at $100 million.

The tourist industry, the country's main foreign exchange earner, was badly affected by the kidnapping of a German and a Swiss visitor in the first 2½ months of 1996. Although both were released unharmed, many overseas operators canceled tours.

(BEN BOX)

This article updates the *Macropædia* article CENTRAL AMERICA: *Costa Rica*.

CÔTE D'IVOIRE

A republic of West Africa, Côte d'Ivoire lies on the Gulf of Guinea. Area: 322,463 sq km (124,504 sq mi). Pop. (1996 est.): 14,733,000. Cap.: Abidjan; capital designate, Yamoussoukro. Monetary unit: CFA franc, with (Oct. 11, 1996) a par value of CFAF 100 to the French franc and a free rate of CFAF 518.24 to U.S. $1 (CFAF 816.38 = £1 sterling). President in 1996, Henri Konan Bédié; prime minister, Daniel Kablan Duncan.

Prime Minister Daniel Kablan Duncan formed a new 31-member Cabinet on Jan. 26, 1996. Despite expectations of a major reshuffle, 25 of the ministers were retained from the previous government. The ruling Democratic Party of the Côte d'Ivoire won control of 158 of the country's 196 communes when four million voters turned out for the municipal elections on February 11.

The presence of 300,000 Liberian refugees in the country was the cause of continuing tension. On June 7, Liberian rebels killed 15 people in an attack on Basobli, 600 km (370 mi) west of Abidjan. In July the government set up a new military zone along its entire border with Liberia.

The economy demonstrated signs of sustained vigour and was expected to grow by

6.5% in 1996. A 5% pay raise for civil servants was announced in May.

(NANCY ELLEN LAWLER)

This article updates the *Macropædia* article WESTERN AFRICA: *Côte d'Ivoire.*

CROATIA

A republic lying at the southeastern end of central Europe, Croatia is an elongated crescent-shaped country to the north, west, and southwest of Bosnia and Herzegovina. In the north it borders on Hungary and in the northwest on Slovenia. Its extensive Adriatic coastal region on the southwest includes nearly 1,200 islands and islets. Area: 56,610 sq km (21,857 sq mi). Pop. (1996 est.): 4,775,000. Cap.: Zagreb. Monetary unit: kuna, with (Oct. 11, 1996) a free rate of 5.45 kune to U.S. $1 (8.58 kune = £1 sterling). President in 1996, Franjo Tudjman; prime minister, Zlatko Matesa.

In 1996 Croatia achieved key diplomatic breakthroughs that promised a peaceful resolution of the Serb-Croat conflict that lay at the core of the violent breakup of former Yugoslavia. On January 15 the UN Security Council passed Resolution 1037, outlining the peaceful integration of eastern Slavonia, the last area under rebel Croatian Serb occupation, back to Croatian authority. The UN initiative came on the heels of the Erdut Agreement, signed at the end of 1995 by the government of Croatia and Serbian officials, in which Serbian Pres. Slobodan Milosevic agreed to give up territorial claims on eastern Slavonia. A newly created UN Transitional Authority for Eastern Slavonia, Baranja and Western Sirmium (UNTAES) was given the task of implementing both military and civilian provisions of the agreement. By June 27 all Yugoslav troops and heavy weapons had been removed, which thus completed the demilitarization of the territory. Full diplomatic relations between Croatia and Yugoslavia were established on August 23. Repatriation remained the principal domestic challenge for Croatia, especially the contentious return of some 120,000 Croats expelled from eastern Slavonia and 150,000 Serbs who fled Croatia.

As fears of renewed conflict with Serbia subsided, domestic support for the ruling Croatian Democratic Union (HDZ) waned. Public impatience with government corruption and authoritarian behaviour could no longer be mollified by popular support for Pres. Franjo Tudjman. The HDZ prevented the opposition coalition from assuming the mayorship of Zagreb, the largest city, following the previous year's loss at the polls, relying on a constitutional technicality that allowed the president to reject any candidate for mayor of the capital for "national security" reasons. About 100,000 people rallied on the main square in Zagreb in November to protest the government's efforts to close down a popular independent radio station. Concerns about the government's commitment to democratization delayed Croatia's becoming a member of the Council of Europe, though it finally did so on November 6.

Croatia's economy showed remarkable resilience. The tourism sector saw more than a million European vacationers return to the Adriatic coastline. An explosion of small and medium-sized businesses helped soak up the ranks of the unemployed. The pharmaceutical company Pliva offered its shares on the London Stock Exchange, the first industrial company from Eastern-Central Europe to do so. Inflation remained one of the lowest in Europe, and foreign exchange reserves grew.

Croatia's ambivalent relations with Western Europe contrasted with strengthening diplomatic and business ties with the U.S. Retired U.S. general Jacques Klein was chosen to command the UNTAES operation. Pres. Bill Clinton and three Cabinet members visited during the year.

(MAX PRIMORAC)

This article updates the *Macropædia* article BALKAN STATES: *Croatia.*

CUBA

The socialist republic of Cuba comprises the island of Cuba and more than 1,600 smaller islands and cays in the Caribbean Sea. Area: 110,861 sq km (42,804 sq mi). Pop. (1996 est.): 11,117,000. Cap.: Havana. Monetary unit: Cuban peso, with an official rate of 1 CUP to U.S. $1 (1.58 CUP = £1 sterling); a truer value of the peso was the authorized exchange house rate, where about 21 CUP = U.S. $1 (about 33 CUP = £1 sterling). President of the Councils of State and Ministers in 1996, Fidel Castro Ruz.

Any softening of relations between Cuba and the United States in 1995 was reversed in 1996 following an incident in February in which two aircraft piloted by Cuban exiles living in Miami, Fla., were shot down in the Caribbean Sea off the northern coast of Cuba, killing four men, after they had declared their intention of flying over Cuba. Cuba had previously issued warnings of its intention to prevent unauthorized flights into its airspace, but they had been ignored by the group of exiles known as Brothers to the Rescue. The U.S., which maintained that the planes had been shot down over international waters, reacted strongly to the incident. U.S. Pres. Bill Clinton reversed his previous opposition to key sections of the Helms-Burton bill (also known as the Cuban Liberty and Democratic Solidarity Act), which was designed to further isolate Cuba, strengthen the trade embargo against it, and extend U.S. legislation to foreign companies investing in both the U.S. and Cuba.

Despite vigorous opposition from the main trading partners of the U.S., including the European Union, Canada, and Mexico, the Helms-Burton Act was signed in the U.S. on March 12. The new law extended sanctions to non-U.S. companies that did business in Cuba and allowed U.S. citizens (including naturalized Cuban exiles) to sue foreign companies for trafficking in confiscated American property in Cuba, although President Clinton suspended authorization for lawsuits for six months. A Canadian, a Mexican, and an Italian firm each received letters warning that entry into the U.S. by their executives would be denied because of their activities in Cuba in nickel mining and telecommunications using previously U.S.-owned property. The new legislation did not deter foreign companies from entering into joint ventures with Cuban state companies, and during the year many new agreements were signed.

The Cuban economic recovery continued in the first half of 1996 with a growth of 9.6% in gross domestic product (GDP) compared with the same period in 1995. Productivity was reported to have risen by 8% and the average wage by 2.5%, while prices remained stable. The budget deficit

CHRISTOPHER MORRIS—TIME/BLACK STAR

U.S. Secretary of Commerce Ron Brown and 32 other Americans were killed on April 3 when their modified Boeing 737 military aircraft crashed near Dubrovnik. Brown had led a U.S. delegation to Croatia to discuss economic ties between the two nations.

A fruit bar in Havana is one of Cuba's recently opened "free markets," in which vendors, farmers for the most part, were allowed to keep most of the profits. The Cuban government, however, charged such vendors daily, monthly, and yearly fees.

for the year was forecast to fall to 3% of GDP. Though nickel production rose by 31%, cement by 23%, tobacco by 27%, and vegetables by 25% during the first six months of 1996, the economy continued to suffer from a shortage of hard currency, which made meeting international obligations difficult.

Economic reform and modernization progressed slowly but steadily. Banks were permitted to offer wider services. A new bank, Banco Metropolitano, began offering low-interest checking and deposit accounts as part of the aim to offer the same range of banking services as in other countries. An investment bank and an agro-industrial and commercial bank were also planned, while the Banco Popular de Ahorro, a savings bank, expanded its services to include personal and business loans. Decree-Law No. 165, published in June, governed the operation of free-trade zones in Cuba. The first zones were to include three in Havana and one in Cienfuegos on the southern coast. Those holding licenses to operate in the zones were granted exemption from customs duties and taxes on profits and were allowed free repatriation of profits and access to the domestic market, depending on the local value added.

The tourism industry continued to show rapid growth, with Canadian companies joining the leading Spanish investors in building hotels throughout the country. Canada also agreed to finance construction by Canadian companies of a third terminal at Havana's international airport.

Hurricane Lili swept through 8 of the island's 14 provinces in October, causing destruction to housing and agriculture. The storm damaged some 78,000 homes, 5,640 of which were destroyed.

(SARAH CAMERON)

This article updates the *Macropædia* article The WEST INDIES: *Cuba*.

CYPRUS

An island republic and member of the Commonwealth, Cyprus is in the eastern Mediterranean Sea. Island area: 9,251 sq km (3,572 sq mi). Island pop. (1996 est.): 767,000. Area of the Turkish Republic of Northern Cyprus (TRNC), proclaimed unilaterally (1983) in the occupied northern third of the island (controlled by Turkish Cypriots since 1974): 3,355 sq km (1,295 sq mi); pop. (1996 est.): 110,000. Cap.: Nicosia. Monetary unit: Cyprus pound, with (Oct. 11, 1996) a free rate of £C 0.47 to U.S. $1 (£C 0.73 = £1 sterling). President in 1996, Glafcos Clerides. President of the TRNC in 1996, Rauf Denktash.

Although the impasse over Cyprus continued, the events of 1996 held the potential for significant change. One impetus for change was accession to the European Union, forecast for as early as the year 2000. Although the island's partition per se would not preclude joining the European organization, accession would certainly be smoother if the partition was eliminated.

During the year the U.K. and the U.S. appointed envoys to deal with Cyprus. Despite initial hopes, their efforts did not break the deadlock. International and intra-Cypriot negotiations continued throughout 1996. Significantly, in December the European Court of Human Rights ruled that Turkey had violated the rights of a Greek Cypriot by seizing her property in the 1974 invasion of northern Cyprus.

Frustration with the status quo manifested itself in several ways. In Greek Cyprus the communist Progressive Party of the Working People won one-third of the votes in the May elections, leaving Pres. Glafcos Clerides's Democratic Rally party only marginally in the lead. Discontent be-

came violent in August as Greek Cypriots demonstrated in the UN-patrolled buffer zone. Two Greek Cypriots were killed and scores injured.

Despite these problems, the economy continued to boom, with a 5.5% growth in gross domestic product. Offshore investments totaled over $300 million, and a fifth of the world's ships flew the Cyprus flag. The Turkish sector did not share in the island's prosperity, however. Its per capita income was about a fourth of the $13,000 enjoyed by the Greek Cypriots.

(GEORGE H. KELLING)

CZECH REPUBLIC

The Czech Republic is a landlocked state of central Europe. Area: 78,864 sq km (30,450 sq mi). Pop. (1996 est.): 10,316,-000. Cap.: Prague. Monetary unit: koruna, with (Oct. 11, 1996) a free rate of 27.18 koruny to U.S. $1 (42.81 koruny = £1 sterling). President in 1996, Vaclav Havel; prime minister, Vaclav Klaus.

The top political story of 1996 was the general election of May 31–June 1, the first in the Czech Republic since the breakup of Czechoslovakia in 1993. The ruling centre-right coalition, led by Prime Minister Vaclav Klaus and his Civic Democratic Party, was expected to win an easy victory derived from a strong and well-managed economy and the government's generally popular push to integrate the country politically and economically with the rest of Europe. In the event, however, Klaus's coalition lost a total of 13 seats in the Chamber of Deputies (parliament) and lacked a majority by two seats. The big winner was the Czech Social Democratic Party (CSSD), with its program of free-market economic reforms and concern for social and environmental issues. (For a detailed breakdown, see *Political Parties,* above.)

Pres. Vaclav Havel asked Klaus to form a minority government from the three coalition parties. By agreeing to have CSSD leader Milos Zeman elected parliament chairman, Klaus gained the support of the Social Democrats, and his new government was approved in the Chamber of Deputies on July 25 by a vote of 98–40. Klaus's party fared much better in the November elections to the Senate—a new body with very little power that was being created largely because it was called for in the constitution rather than for any clear political or legislative need. Of the 81 Senate seats, the ODS won 32 and the CSSD took 25.

Stanislav Devaty, the head of the secret service, resigned in November after being accused by Deputy Prime Minister Jozef Lux of spying on officials of the government. Incidents of anti-Roma (anti-Gypsy) feelings were reported, notably a savagely racist outbreak in the parliament by Miroslav Sladek, a Republican Party deputy, in July. In November the Czech Ministry of Defense announced that it had ordered an investigation to determine if Czech troops in the 1991 Persian Gulf War had been provided adequate protection against chemical weapons and to examine their health claims.

A milestone in the postcommunist economic development of Central Europe was passed on July 1, 1996, with the closing of the Czech Privatization Ministry, its work virtually complete. Working mainly through a system of coupons, some 4,700 large state enterprises were privatized during the five-year life of the program. By 1996 an estimated 70% of the gross national product of the Czech Republic was produced by private enterprises. A crisis emerged in the heavily state-controlled banking industry, however, with the collapse in August of Kreditni Banka Plzen (the sixth largest bank in the country) and the subsequent arrest on fraud charges of five top financial officials followed by the government takeover of Agrobanka Praha (the largest privately owned bank and fifth largest overall) in September. (*See* ECONOMIC AFFAIRS: *Banking*.)

The most important foreign policy accomplishment during the year was the signing, late in December, of a document of reconciliation in which Germany expressed regret for the deeds of the Nazi regime, while the Czech Republic expressed regret for the expulsion by the former Czechoslovak state of some three million ethnic Germans from the Sudeten region of Czechoslovakia after World War II.

President Havel underwent surgery to remove a malignant tumour in his lung in early December; recuperation was complicated first by breathing problems requiring an emergency tracheotomy and later by pneumonia.   (EDITORS)

This article updates the *Macropædia* article CZECH AND SLOVAK REPUBLICS: *Czech Republic*.

DENMARK

A constitutional monarchy of north-central Europe, Denmark lies between the North and Baltic seas. Area: 43,094 sq km (16,639 sq mi), excluding the Faroe Islands and Greenland. Pop. (1996 est.): 5,244,000. Cap.: Copenhagen. Monetary unit: Danish krone (crown), with (Oct. 11, 1996) a free rate of 5.87 kroner to U.S. $1 (9.25 kroner = £1 sterling). Queen, Margrethe II; prime minister in 1996, Poul Nyrup Rasmussen.

Denmark's domestic peace was shattered in 1996 by an escalating conflict involving rival motorcycle gangs, which prompted Prime Minister Poul Nyrup Rasmussen to launch a major offensive against the feuding bikers. In a speech to the Folketing (national legislature) in October, he declared war on the Hell's Angels and the rival Bandidos gang and presented emergency legislation barring gang members from setting up bases in residential areas. The bill gave police the power to forbid members or associates of a particular group to occupy or visit a designated property "where there is an estimated risk that it will be attacked, placing in danger persons living or passing through the vicinity." The bill's sweeping powers stirred strong criticism among jurists in a country in which the freedom and rights of the individual were near-sacrosanct. The legislation was enacted after Copenhagen residents staged protests demanding the eviction of Hell's Angels in the wake of a spate of bomb, grenade, gun, and antitank missile attacks on biker clubhouses that often adjoined family homes in heavily populated urban districts.

Otherwise, Rasmussen's speech pledged improved womb-to-tomb health and welfare services, a reduction in the size of the government, a more just society, better schools, and more parish priests for the government-financed Lutheran Church. In regard to the economy, Denmark seemed poised for an upturn after a period of relative stagnation, with low inflation, the lowest central bank discount rate in 60 years, current-account and foreign-trade surpluses, growing investment and private consumption, and reduced unemployment.

Concerning foreign relations, Denmark remained a lukewarm European Union (EU) member, with polls revealing a majority of Danes opposed to joining the European economic and monetary union (EMU). Danes had voted in a 1993 referendum to endorse the Maastricht Treaty on the condition that Denmark would not participate in the EMU. Opposition to the treaty continued, however, as 11 Danish citizens won a Supreme Court ruling allowing them to mount a high court challenge to its constitutional legality in Denmark. Most analysts believed it was inconceivable for the government to lose the case, but some legal experts feared that if the 11 won, it could at worst eventually mean Denmark's exit from the EU and at best complicate the country's ratification of any revisions to the Maastricht Treaty emerging in 1997 from the EU's intergovernmental conference.

A major dispute over fishing rights in the Denmark Strait between Iceland and Greenland intensified during the year, with little sign of any compromise between Denmark and Iceland in sight. On the cultural front Copenhagen basked in the limelight throughout the year as European "capital of culture," the 12th host for an impressive 13-month arts festival involving 50,000 participants and attended by more than five million visitors.   (CHRISTOPHER FOLLETT)

DJIBOUTI

The republic of Djibouti is in the Horn of northeastern Africa on the Gulf of Aden. Area: 23,200 sq km (8,950 sq mi). Pop. (1996 est.): 604,000. Cap.: Djibouti. Monetary unit: Djibouti franc, with (Oct. 11, 1996) a par value of DF 177.72 to U.S. $1 (free rate of DF 279.96 = £1 sterling). President in 1996, Hassan Gouled Aptidon; prime minister, Barkat Gourad Hamadou.

On March 27 Pres. Hassan Gouled Aptidon dismissed Ahmed Boulaleh Barreh and Moumin Bahdon Farah, ministers, respectively, of defense and of justice, Islamic affairs and prisons. Their departure was likely to strengthen the positions of Prime Minister Barkat Gourad Hamadou and the *chef de cabinet*, Ismael Omar Guelleh, both of whom were lining up to succeed the president who had just spent three months in a French hospital.

The International Monetary Fund (IMF) agreed to a standby credit of SDR 4.6 million ($6.7 million) for 14 months to support the government's reform program. This was the first time Djibouti had used the IMF, which it joined in 1977. After having been imprisoned for a month, five deputies, including Farah, who had announced the formation of a new political party in April, went on a hunger strike in August in protest against their detention; they were accused of insulting Aptidon.   (GUY ARNOLD)

This article updates the *Macropædia* article EASTERN AFRICA: *Djibouti*.

DOMINICA

An island republic within the Commonwealth, Dominica is in the eastern Caribbean Sea. Area: 750 sq km (290 sq mi). Pop. (1996 est.): 73,800. Cap.: Roseau. Monetary unit: Eastern Caribbean dollar, with (Oct. 11, 1996) a par value of EC$2.70 to U.S. $1 (free rate of EC$4.25 = £1 sterling). President in 1996, Crispin Anselm Sorhaindo; prime minister, Edison James.

The governing United Workers' Party began putting its financial house in order in 1996 by announcing the sale of four state-owned entities—Dominica Electricity Services Ltd., the Agricultural, Industrial and Development Bank, the Dominica Export-Import Agency, and certain facilities at the port of Roseau, the capital. The government's external debt burden in January was EC$320 million and its internal debt EC$80 million.

In May, after a visit to Dominica by Cuba's foreign minister, Roberto Robaina, the two governments decided to establish diplomatic relations.   (DAVID RENWICK)

This article updates the *Macropædia* article The WEST INDIES: *Dominica*.

DOMINICAN REPUBLIC

The Dominican Republic covers the eastern two-thirds of the Caribbean island of Hispaniola, which it shares with Haiti. Area: 48,671 sq km (18,792 sq mi). Pop. (1996 est.): 7,502,000. Cap.: Santo Domingo. Monetary unit: Dominican peso, with (Oct. 11, 1996) a free rate of RD$13.78 to U.S. $1 (RD$21.71 = £1 sterling). Presidents in 1996, Joaquín Balaguer and, from August 16, Leonel Fernández Reyna.

Elections for the president of the Dominican Republic were held in two rounds, on May 16 and June 30, 1996. After the first round José Francisco Peña Gómez of the Dominican Revolutionary Party (PRD) led with 48.75% of the vote. In the second round Leonel Fernández Reyna of the Dominican Liberation Party (PLD) formed an alliance with the governing Social Christian Reformist Party (PRSC). This coalition, which was supported by smaller right-wing groups, enabled Fernández to gain 51.25% of the second vote, and he was sworn in as president on August 16.

The elections were called early because of allegations of fraud in the 1994 elections. Pres. Joaquín Balaguer, who was 89 on Sept. 1, 1996, was barred from running again.

Having achieved its aims in the elections, the PRSC changed allegiances again. On August 8 it signed an agreement with the PRD allowing the PRSC to have control over the Senate and the PRD the presidency of the Chamber of Deputies. The PLD was in a minority in both houses, which was expected to hinder President Fernández's plans to combat corruption and reform the inefficient state sector.

(SARAH CAMERON)

This article updates the *Macropædia* article The WEST INDIES: *Dominican Republic*.

ECUADOR

The republic of Ecuador is in western South America, on the Pacific Ocean. Area: 272,045 sq km (105,037 sq mi), including the Galápagos Islands. Pop. (1996 est.): 11,698,000. Cap.: Quito. Monetary unit: sucre, with (Oct. 11, 1996) a free rate of 3,309 sucres to U.S. $1 (5,213 sucres = £1 sterling). Presidents in 1996, Sixto Durán Ballén and, from August 10, Abdalá Bucaram Ortíz.

The second round of the presidential elections was won in July 1996 by Abdalá Bucaram Ortíz (*see* BIOGRAPHIES) of the centre-left Ecuadorian Roldosist Party (PRE), who took 54.5% of the vote. It was the third time that Bucaram had run for president, and much of his support came from the nation's poor, who had rejected the austerity measures imposed by the previous government.

The first round of the elections had been narrowly won by Jaime Nebot Saadi of the centre-right Social Christian Party. He had waged a strong negative media campaign against the PRE but failed to counteract the widespread resentment against the austerity program.

A scandal in late 1995 involved former vice president Alberto Dahik Garzozi, who fled the country after an order was given for his arrest on corruption charges. He was granted political asylum by Costa Rica just before being found guilty of embezzlement and illicit enrichment.

The central bank was expected to run a deficit in 1996; the new government inherited several outstanding debts from the previous administration, amounting to a to-tal of 3% of gross domestic product. Estimated real GDP growth in the first half of 1996 was 2.8%. The oil sector continued to lead the growth, expanding by 3.5% owing to rising world prices. From February inflation remained above the 1995 levels. Official estimates for inflation for the year were revised from 17–19% to 25%.

(ALAN MURPHY)

EGYPT

A republic of North Africa, Egypt has coastlines on the Mediterranean and Red seas. Area: 997,739 sq km (385,229 sq mi). Pop. (1996 est.): 60,896,000. Cap.: Cairo. Monetary unit: Egyptian pound, with (Oct. 11, 1996) a free rate of LE 3.40 to U.S. $1 (LE 5.36 = £1 sterling). President in 1996, Hosni Mubarak; prime ministers, Atef Sedki and, from January 3, Kamal al-Janzuri.

Four major developments took place in Egypt during 1996. First was the active role that Pres. Hosni Mubarak played in the peace process for the resolution of the Arab-Israeli conflict. Second was Egypt's continuing role in the Arab world as a regional power of moderation and stability. Third was the status of the major opposition political parties and their discontent with the Egyptian government's unwillingness to move forward in the democratization process as manifested in the seriously flawed legislative elections of 1995. Fourth was the Egyptian government's continuing struggle against domestic and regional terrorism.

The year began with the formation on January 3 of a new Egyptian Cabinet of 32 members, headed by the new prime minis-ter, Kamal al-Janzuri. In foreign affairs the new Cabinet emphasized Egypt's leading role in the Arab world as an advocate of peace and stability in the Middle East.

The continued support of the peace process was a major concern of President Mubarak. On March 13 he served as host of the "Summit of Peacemakers" in Sharm ash-Shaykh in response to terrorist operations by the Palestinian organization Hamas in Israel on February 25 and March 3–4. Mubarak also was host of an unprecedented Arab summit in Cairo on June 22–23. It was attended by all Arab League members except Iraq, with the leaders of 12 nations attending in person to evaluate the peace process in the aftermath of the election victory of Benjamin Netanyahu (*see* BIOGRAPHIES) over Shimon Peres in Israel. Although it was an Arab summit primarily concerned with the peace process, it clearly projected Egypt as the leader of the Arab world. Mubarak emerged from the conference a strong advocate of reconciliation and moderation with strong ties to the West and in particular to the U.S. His role in reviving the peace process was manifested when he was host to Netanyahu in July.

Hamid Abu an-Nasr, the leader of Egypt's largest Islamic fundamentalist group, the Muslim Brotherhood, died on January 20. Mustafa Mashhur, his first deputy, was chosen unanimously to succeed him. In his youth Mashhur had been an active member of the underground secret apparatus (al-Jihaz al-Sirri) of the Muslim Brotherhood, and he had spent a total of 16 years in prison. His election as the new leader of the Muslim Brotherhood did not improve the latter's image in the eyes of the Egyptian government. There were two trends in the Brotherhood. The first, the hard-line, was represented by Mashhur, who Egyptian authorities believed could lead his organization to violence and underground activity. The Egyptian interior minister, Hasan al-Alfi, in a speech in January did not mince his words when he talked about the Muslim Brotherhood: "We will continue to lie in wait for this organization and monitor its maneuvers and vile attempts at infiltration. We will monitor the steps it takes and confront it when the time is right." Thus, it was not surprising that the offices of the Brotherhood in Cairo, Al-Jizah, and Al-Fayyum were raided by the security forces of the Ministry of Interior on February 20, which led to the arrest of 46 members and the confiscation of "a very large number of inflammatory leaflets containing extremist [Muslim] Brotherhood ideas."

The second, more flexible trend was represented by a relatively younger generation of leaders. In January some prominent members of this group attempted to join some prominent Christian Copts in the formation of a party called the Centre (al-Wasat). The objective of the Muslim Brothers who formed this party was to demonstrate that they were not sectarian and to circumvent the law that banned parties that were established on a religious basis. The Coptic participation was a reaction to the ruling National Democratic Party's failure to nominate any Copts among its 439 candidates in the November–December 1995 legislative elections despite the fact that the Christian Coptic community constituted some 10% of the Egyptian population.

The major opposition party, the New

This mother and child were among some eight million people in Ecuador considered to be poor. Support from this majority of the population was largely responsible for the victory of Abdalá Bucaram Ortíz in the nation's presidential election.

GREGORY BULL

Wafd Party, held elections on June 16 to choose 40 members of the Wafdist High Command; 20 additional members were selected by the leader of the party, Fuad Saraj ad-Din.

Egyptian authorities continued to face violent actions by the Islamic Group and al-Jihad organizations. Eighteen Greek tourists, who presumably were mistaken for Israelis, were killed and 21 wounded by the Islamic Group on April 18. Terrorist operations against civilians and security forces continued throughout Egypt but mostly in Al-Minya and Asyut provinces in Upper Egypt. During the first six months of the year, 45 Islamic militants were killed and 6 were wounded, while 34 civilians were killed and 21 wounded. For the security forces 17 were killed and 20 were wounded. During the same sixth months, 2,004 Islamic militants were imprisoned.

In August an Egyptian court upheld a judge's ruling that a married man must divorce his wife because his writings insulted Islam. The man, who was a university professor of Arabic, had appealed the original ruling, which was praised by Egypt's Islamic militants. He and his wife, who was also a professor, had fled to The Netherlands after the initial ruling in order to remain together and to teach there. In September a judge ordered a stay of the August decision, and in December the stay was upheld by the Giza Emergency Appeals Court; the original ruling was suspended indefinitely.

Egypt was instrumental in the UN Security Council vote on January 31 to call upon The Sudan to extradite three suspects, members of the Islamic Group, in the assassination attempt on President Mubarak on June 26, 1995, in Ethiopia.

(MARIUS K. DEEB)

EL SALVADOR

The republic of El Salvador is situated on the Pacific coast of Central America. Area: 21,041 sq km (8,124 sq mi). Pop. (1996 est.): 5,897,000. Cap.: San Salvador. Monetary unit: Salvadoran colón, with (Oct. 11, 1996) a free rate of ₡8.75 to U.S. $1 (₡13.79 = £1 sterling). President in 1996, Armando Calderón Sol.

Inmates of the Santa Ana prison west of San Salvador began a hunger strike in July 1996 to protest overcrowding in jails. Prisoners sewed up their mouths and threatened to draw lots to determine who would be executed. The government ended the dispute when it pledged to introduce legislation within 40 days to reduce sentences. A new prison was to be constructed to relieve overcrowding, and former coffee warehouses were used temporarily.

The Democratic Party (PD) pulled out of its pact with the governing party, ARENA (the National Republican Alliance Party), in May, leaving the government without a majority in the Legislative Assembly. The split was in protest against unfulfilled government promises, as well as a political move by the PD to distance itself from ARENA before the elections for the legislature in March 1997.

Despite worsening poverty and social conditions, El Salvador became the first Central American country in several decades to be awarded a credit rating by Standard & Poor's. The nation was granted a BB rating on its long-term debt because of the political stability it had achieved and its prudent fiscal policies. (SARAH CAMERON)

This article updates the *Macropædia* article CENTRAL AMERICA: *El Salvador.*

EQUATORIAL GUINEA

The republic of Equatorial Guinea consists of Río Muni, on the Atlantic coast of West Africa, and the offshore islands of Bioko and Annobon. Area: 28,051 sq km (10,831 sq mi). Pop. (1996 est.): 406,000. Cap.: Malabo. Monetary unit: CFA franc, with a par value of CFAF 100 to the French franc and (as of Oct. 11, 1996) a free rate of CFAF 518.24 to U.S. $1 (CFAF 816.38 = £1 sterling). President in 1996, Brig. Gen. Teodoro Obiang Nguema Mbasogo; prime ministers, Silvestre Siale Bileka and, from March 29, Angel Serafin Seriche Dougan.

In the February 1996 presidential elections, Pres. Teodoro Obiang Nguema Mbasogo claimed 99% of the vote, but observers and opposition groups described the elections as a farce and made numerous accusations of fraud and malpractices. Obiang had violated the constitution by calling the elections early in the hope of catching the opposition unprepared. The so-called independent electoral commission was headed by the interior minister, Julio Ndong Ela Mangue, who spent the election campaigning for the president, while the voters roll, which had been drawn up by the UN for the September 1995 municipal elections, was replaced by a government list that excluded blocks of votes from areas where the opposition had done well the previous September. Voting had to be done in public, in front of officials.

Under those conditions the opposition candidates called upon their supporters to boycott the elections. On March 19 Amancio Nse, one of the opposition presidential candidates, was arrested after he had called on the president to form a government of national unity. (GUY ARNOLD)

This article updates the *Macropædia* article WESTERN AFRICA: *Equatorial Guinea.*

ERITREA

Eritrea is in the Horn of Africa, on the Red Sea. Area: 121,144 sq km (46,774 sq mi). Pop. (1996 est.): 3,627,000 (including about 300,000 refugees in The Sudan). Cap.: Asmara. Provisional monetary unit: Ethiopian birr, with (March 31, 1996) a preferential rate of 7.13 birr to U.S. $1 (10.88 birr = £1 sterling). President in 1996, Isaias Afwerki.

Slow progress was made toward introducing Eritrea's new constitution, and discussions of the official draft were held throughout the nation in 1996. Pres. Isaias Afwerki made it clear that while not opposed in principle to a multiparty system, the government would not permit opposition parties to reopen the ethnic and religious divisions that had previously existed in the country. Other sensitive issues in the discussions included language policy, with minority language groups voicing concern over the adoption of any official language.

Though close relations were maintained with Ethiopia, Eritrea experienced difficul-

Former soldiers and retired railroad men in Eritrea work to rebuild a 118-km (73-mi) railroad linking the Red Sea port city of Massawa with the capital, Asmara.

ties with all of its other neighbours. In mid-December 1995 a brief but sharp military conflict broke out with Yemen over the Hanish Islands, a group of islands in the Red Sea between the two countries, ownership of which had attracted little previous attention. Concerned about a Yemeni plan to build tourist facilities on the islands, the Eritreans attacked them, capturing the largest, Greater Hanish, after three days of fighting. In May, after French mediation, the two countries agreed on arbitration of the dispute.

A month earlier Djibouti had formally requested Eritrea to withdraw a new official map, which allegedly incorporated Djiboutian territory into Eritrea. Djibouti also accused Eritrean forces of opening fire on its territory. Relations with The Sudan were especially bad; each country accused the other of a military buildup on the frontier, and in January Eritrea served as host for a meeting of the Sudanese National Democratic Alliance (comprising the main groups in opposition to the government). No agreement was possible concerning repatriation of the large Eritrean refugee population in The Sudan. (CHRISTOPHER S. CLAPHAM)

This article updates the *Micropædia* article ERITREA.

SIGNS OF HOPE IN AFRICA

by Kenneth Ingham

illustration by Igor Kopelnitsky

In November 1996 the Mozambican government withdrew a draft law on defense and the armed forces from the business of the current session of the national assembly because the elected opposition had described it as unconstitutional. This apparently unremarkable act was not without significance in its African context. It would undoubtedly have met with the approval of the International Monetary Fund and other Western donors, which, for some time, have tried to make the grant of aid to African countries conditional not only upon stricter control of the economy but also upon the introduction of Western-style, multiparty democracy.

The action of Mozambique, one of the poorest countries in the world, is significant because it is not wholly typical of events in other African countries, though this is not necessarily due to a lack of effort on their part. Several countries have tried to respond to the donors' demands, but with varying degrees of success. The case of Zambia offers a partial but important explanation. After free elections on a multiparty basis in 1991, the United National Independence Party, which had held office for many years, was defeated. It was then suggested that since the victorious Movement for Multiparty Democracy embraced a number of parties representing a wide spectrum of interests, any opposition party was unnecessary. One should hasten to say that no action was taken to pursue that idea. Three years later a government established with high hopes found itself accused by the opposition of corruption and inefficiency, faults that it tried to remedy with commendable speed but with uneven success.

The task of reconciling Western-style democracy and strict control of the economy with the situation in Africa is a complex one. In the first place, Western-educated Africans have learned about multiparty democracy but have had little practical experience of it, either in colonial times or since independence. For the majority of Africans, brought up on the basis of consensus within smaller social groups, the concept of a formal opposition is still an alien one.

Given the limited economic resources of most African countries, any prospect of wielding power, exercising patronage, or acquiring wealth other than through membership of the party in office is virtually inconceivable. In these circumstances governments are unlikely to cherish opposition parties that are capable of replacing them. In addition, with the disappearance of Marxism-Leninism and African socialism as ideological forces, any idea of alternative governments in waiting, anxious to promote different political philosophies, has evaporated.

To these factors must be added a fourth. The relative, and in some cases acute, poverty of most African countries means that if members and supporters of the government acquire more than their fair share of wealth, others will suffer. Given the importance of the extended family in African culture, the benefits and disadvantages of this inequality will probably be determined by ethnic considerations. In this situation anyone wishing to challenge the government will be tempted to play upon tribal loyalties and rivalries to win support. Therefore, if not always justifiably, accusations are leveled against tribalism as the source of Africa's problems. The exception to this rule occurs when control of the armed forces lies outside the government. In those cases the temptation to intervene in the political morass and to enjoy the benefits of political power can prove irresistible, as many senior officers have discovered in various parts of the continent.

Should the West then not press quite so urgently for the introduction of Western concepts into Africa? Should Africa be allowed to move at a more leisured pace? Signs of hope in a number of countries suggest that this might be the strategy to adopt. (*See* Map.)

While both Tanzania and Senegal have opposition parties, neither can as yet be said to enjoy full, Western-style democracy, and neither has overcome its economic problems. In more than 40 years since independence, however, neither has had a military government, and, with the exception of a brief skirmish with a mutinous army soon after Tanzania became independent, both countries have been at peace. In each nation the same party remained in office, winning regular elections with widespread popular support, but the personnel of government changed, not only with the

A tire factory in Tanzania reflects that nation's efforts to diversify its economy so that it will no longer be so dependent on agriculture.

Mozambique's important harbour at Beira is the ocean terminus for railways from South Africa, Zimbabwe, Zambia, Zaire, and Malawi. It also serves as the main port for Zimbabwe and Malawi.

African Political Systems

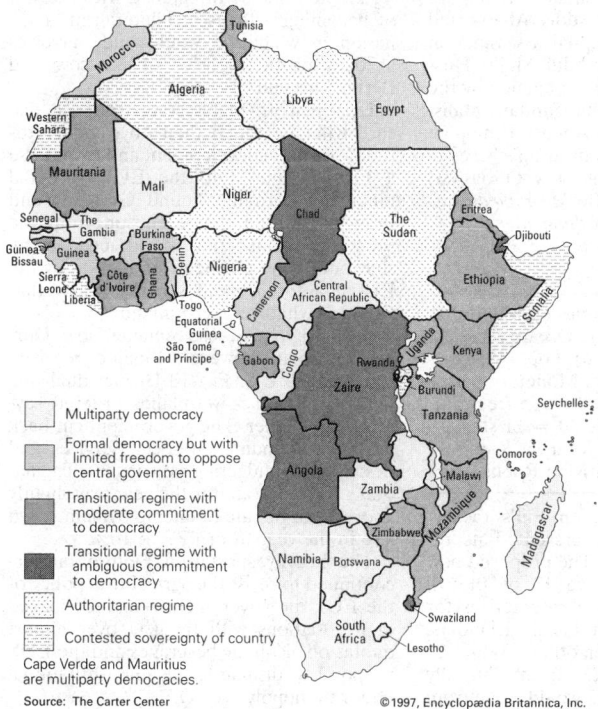

Multiparty democracy

Formal democracy but with limited freedom to oppose central government

Transitional regime with moderate commitment to democracy

Transitional regime with ambiguous commitment to democracy

Authoritarian regime

Contested sovereignty of country

Cape Verde and Mauritius are multiparty democracies.

Source: The Carter Center

©1997, Encyclopædia Britannica, Inc.

changing generations but also in response to the demands of a free electorate. Moreover, both countries survived the resignation of a charismatic leader, who guided them to independence and provided the unifying factor needed to triumph over the pitfalls of ethnic diversity. Each, it is true, had its "offshore problem"—in Tanzania's case, literally, the islands of Zanzibar and Pemba, and in the case of Senegal the secessionist movement in the southern, virtually isolated, province of Casamance. In both instances the problem was genuinely one of physical as well as of historical and cultural separation rather than of the failure of contemporary government. In neither country had this problem weakened the cohesion of the "mainland" or delayed its slow but steady response to outside pressures for economic growth, tempered by local needs.

Zimbabwe, too, after a traumatic civil war between blacks and whites, achieved a measure of stability in spite of searing drought and repeated threats by Pres. Robert Mugabe to seize white-owned land to distribute among the black population. Once again a single party has dominated the political scene after several elections, yet the Marxist-Leninist hankering of the president has been quietly curbed, and a gradual move is taking place in the direction of a market economy.

Events in South Africa since 1990 have shed new light on the possibilities of change on the African continent, but South Africa is not truly representative of the rest of Africa. Like Tanzania, Senegal, and Zimbabwe, its politics are effectively dominated by a single party with widespread support. Unlike the other countries, it has considerable wealth and powerful economic pressure groups that are not wholly controlled by the government. Consequently, the prospect of South Africa's approximating to the pattern of Western political and economic systems is far greater than in other parts of the continent.

It is a little early to assess the prospects for success in Eritrea, which emerged from a 30-year struggle for independence only in 1993. The alacrity with which the victorious Eritrean People's Liberation Front (EPLF) converted itself into the People's Front for Democracy and Justice and set up a commission to draft a new constitution by June 1996 was an indicator of good intentions, even though the transitional government, which is to remain in office for four years, is still the EPLF in civilian guise. The willingness of the transitional government to contemplate multiparty democracy, coupled with its wariness of political parties based solely upon ethnic or religious affiliations, also augurs well for a balanced society. Revitalization of the economy is desperately needed after such a lengthy period of conflict, but the foundations must be secure in the economic as well as in the political sphere.

In a region that has had more than its share of civil wars and military dictatorships there are, nevertheless, other areas—Kenya and Côte d'Ivoire among them—that fit neither the blueprint that donor countries would like to see nor yet the patterns created by Tanzania, Senegal, Zimbabwe, and South Africa. But they have achieved a measure of stability accompanied by the prospect, however distant, of economic growth. In each of these countries, innovations have been introduced as modifications of a traditional pattern, and, if economic growth is slow, it proceeds at a pace with which the people can keep in step. Moreover, where nepotism remains a problem, it is at least one that the people understand, even if those who lose out do not approve.

Kenneth Ingham is professor emeritus of history at the University of Bristol, Eng., and the author of *Politics in Modern Africa: The Uneven Tribal Dimensions.*

ESTONIA

A republic of northern Europe, Estonia borders the Baltic Sea on the west and north. Area: 45,227 sq km (17,462 sq mi). Pop. (1996 est.): 1,478,000. Cap.: Tallinn. Monetary unit: kroon, with (Oct. 11, 1996) a par value of EEK 8 to DM 1 (free rates of EEK 12.24 = U.S. $1 and EEK 19.29 = £1 sterling). President in 1996, Lennart Meri; prime minister, Tiit Vähi.

The year 1995 ended with the forced resignation of the commander of defense forces, Lieut. Gen. Aleksander Einseln, a retired U.S. army colonel, following his public clash with the minister of defense. Also, the headquarters staff became embroiled in a scandal over the illegal sale of firearms.

Prime Minister Tiit Vähi's governing coalition survived sharp infighting over economic, social, and foreign policy. In August Parliament failed to choose a president, and the decision thus fell to a specially convened electoral body, which included representatives of local government. This body endorsed the incumbent, Lennart Meri, a strong exponent of closer integration with the rest of Europe, who swore the oath of office on October 7 for a second term. Late in November the coalition government collapsed when the smaller partner, the Estonian Reform Party, withdrew because the Coalition and Rural People's Union, the larger partner, had signed a cooperation pact with the Estonian Centre Party without telling the Reform leaders that it was doing so. Prime Minister Vähi began seeking members for a new Cabinet.

(TÖNU PARMING)

This article updates the *Macropædia* article BALTIC STATES: *Estonia*.

ETHIOPIA

The landlocked republic of Ethiopia is situated in the Horn of northeastern Africa. Area: 1,133,882 sq km (437,794 sq mi). Pop. (1996 est.): 56,713,000. Cap.: Addis Ababa. Monetary unit: birr, with (Oct. 11, 1995) a free rate of 6.00 birr to U.S. $1 (9.45 birr = £1 sterling). President in 1996, Negasso Gidada; prime minister, Meles Zenawi.

Domestically, 1996 was a year of consolidation following the creation of the Federal Democratic Republic of Ethiopia in 1995. Prime Minister Meles Zenawi remained in office, with former prime minister Tamirat Layne serving as deputy prime minister and minister of defense. The coalition of regional ethnic parties, the Ethiopian People's Revolutionary Democratic Front, continued to monopolize power at both the central and regional levels, and a number of human rights violations were reported, both by external monitoring agencies and by the Ethiopian Human Rights Council (EHRCO). Many of those concerned suspected members of the Oromo Liberation Front in western Ethiopia, who were reported to have disappeared or died in custody. EHRCO reported in July that more than 100 people had "disappeared," a figure denied by the government. A number of journalists were imprisoned for publishing "mendacious reports."

Trials of some 70 leading members of the regime ousted in 1991 (many of them

in absentia) resumed in late September after a two-month recess. Evidence was given regarding the murder of former emperor Haile Selassie in 1975, the summary execution of 60 leading figures of his government in November 1974, and the torture and execution of numerous dissidents and opponents of the regime. Former leader Mengistu Haile Mariam remained in Zimbabwe, where an Ethiopian whose family had suffered under his rule attempted to assassinate him; the cost of maintaining Mengistu was reported to be causing concern to the Zimbabwean government. Meanwhile, some 1,700 junior former officials of his regime remained in prison without charge or trial.

The economy continued to be buoyant, with a 6% rise in the gross national product reported for 1995 following an excellent harvest. The resulting fall in food prices was the main factor in a 5.7% decline in retail price levels. The main rains for 1996 were exceptionally heavy over most of the country and raised expectations that Ethiopia might at last achieve its long-sought self-sufficiency in basic foodstuffs. The World Bank announced the cancellation of $250 million of Ethiopia's $270 million debt to the organization; however, total debts of about $4 billion remained outstanding, 10% of this being commercial debt and the remainder evenly divided between debts to individual countries and debts to international agencies.

Relations with Eritrea remained good, but relations with The Sudan deteriorated. Three Egyptians found guilty of having attempted to assassinate Egyptian Pres. Hosni Mubarak in Addis Ababa with Sudanese connivance in June 1995 were sentenced to death, and Ethiopia pressed for more stringent UN sanctions against The Sudan as a supporter of international terrorism. Ethiopia asserted its right to utilize Nile River waters originating in its territory, in disregard of an agreement on their use between Egypt and The Sudan. A number of bomb explosions in Addis Ababa and elsewhere and the attempted assassination of Transport Minister Abdul Mejid Hussein (an ethnic Somali) were blamed by the government on an Islamic fundamentalist Somali organization. In August Ethiopian aircraft attacked the organization's bases in Somalia. (CHRISTOPHER S. CLAPHAM)

This article updates the *Macropædia* article EASTERN AFRICA: *Ethiopia*.

FIJI

The republic of Fiji occupies an island group in the South Pacific Ocean. Area: 18,272 sq km (7,055 sq mi). Pop. (1996 est.): 802,000. Cap.: Suva. Monetary unit: Fiji dollar, with (Oct. 11, 1996) a free rate of F$1.40 to U.S. $1 (F$2.20 = £1 sterling). President in 1996, Ratu Sir Kamisese Mara; prime minister, Sitiveni Rabuka.

The review commission on Fiji's racially prescriptive constitution presented its report in September 1996. The proposed new constitution would reserve 12 of the 70 seats in the House of Representatives for ethnic Fijians and other Pacific Islanders, 10 for Indians, and 3 for others. While 25 members would be elected from ethnically defined constituencies, 45 would come from multiracial and multimember constituen-

cies. The prime minister would no longer have to be an ethnic Fijian.

The economy grew 2.9% in 1995, despite a 12% drop in sugar receipts. Inflation was projected at 2% for 1996. For 1997 the government projected expenditures of F$893 million and revenue of F$737 million, leaving a net deficit after aid and borrowing of F$92.2 million (3.6% of gross domestic product). (BARRIE MACDONALD)

This article updates the *Macropædia* article PACIFIC ISLANDS: *Fiji*.

FINLAND

The republic of Finland is situated in northern Europe, on the Gulf of Bothnia and the Gulf of Finland. Area: 338,145 sq km (130,559 sq mi). Pop. (1996 est.): 5,132,000. Cap.: Helsinki. Monetary unit: Finnish markka, with (Oct. 11, 1996) a free rate of 4.58 markkaa to U.S. $1 (7.21 markkaa = £1 sterling). President in 1996, Martti Ahtisaari; prime minister, Paavo Lipponen.

Despite efforts by nearby former socialist countries in Eastern Europe to join NATO, Finland would in "the current circumstances" remain militarily unaligned, Pres. Martti Ahtisaari said repeatedly in 1996. He and Prime Minister Paavo Lipponen reiterated that Finland would be among the first countries of the European Union (EU) to join its economic and monetary union (EMU), which was scheduled to go into operation in 1999.

Speaking in October, Lipponen said that Finland was joining the EMU to reduce the risk of again finding itself exposed and alone if Europe should once more divide into East and West. "Finland's interests cannot be pursued effectively with one foot inside the EU and one outside," he told a public seminar arranged by the country's biggest newspaper, *Helsingin Sanomat*. "In the EU and the European transformation we are continually threatened with the risk of becoming a focus of bilateralism, a situation in which we would find ourselves a focus of the policies of Moscow and Berlin," he said.

Lipponen urged his compatriots to discard what he called their "bystander attitude" on union development and to endorse a Finnish entry into the EU's potential inner ring forming around Germany and France. He said that exclusion from the prospective inner ring would mean being shut out of the planned formulation by the EU of a foreign and security policy that would inevitably affect Finland.

Spending on defense remained low. During the year, however, Finland received some of the U.S. F/A-18 Hornet dual-role fighter and attack warplanes ordered several years earlier. The government cut back its heavy spending on social services and described its budgeting as stringent. The nation's inflation rate for the year was slightly above zero. Its rate of unemployment eased late in the year from 17% to 16%.

The heavily subsidized Finnish farmers continued to resist the agricultural policy of the EU. The government remained locked in negotiations with the EU over import quotas on alcoholic beverages and the EU's proposal to dismantle the Finnish national liquor monopoly ALKO.

(EDWARD M. SUMMERHILL)

FRANCE

A republic of western Europe, France includes the island of Corsica in the Mediterranean Sea and has coastlines on the English Channel, the Mediterranean, and the Atlantic Ocean. Area: 543,965 sq km (210,026 sq mi). Pop. (1996 est.): 58,392,000. Cap.: Paris. Monetary unit: franc, with (Oct. 11, 1996) a free rate of F 5.18 to U.S. $1 (F 8.16 = £1 sterling). President in 1996, Jacques Chirac; prime minister, Alain Juppé.

The year 1996 proved to be a generally unrewarding time of transition for France and its new leaders. Many of the hopes raised by the election of Gaullist Pres. Jacques Chirac the previous May remained unfulfilled. Prime Minister Alain Juppé modified his welfare and public-sector reforms that had triggered widespread strikes and chaos in late 1995 but was forced to continue the policy of budget austerity in order to try to qualify France for the European Union's (EU's) monetary union in 1997. In a historic reversal of Gen. Charles de Gaulle's withdrawal in 1966 from NATO's military command, France announced in December 1995 its intention to reintegrate itself in a reformed Atlantic alliance. In late 1996, however, Paris was still negotiating the practical details of that reintegration.

Chirac made relatively more progress in foreign affairs and defense. He moved to phase out the century-old tradition of military conscription and to phase in a fully professional army. He mended diplomatic fences with a number of countries by putting an end to French nuclear testing in the South Pacific and gave fresh impetus to France's policies in the EU and the Middle East.

By contrast, Juppé found his prime responsibility for domestic policy heavier going. The economy recovered in the spring but fell back in the summer. Despite declining interest rates, consumption by households and investment by companies remained slack and complicated the government's goal of making further reductions in the budget deficit. The prime minister found his policies still contested by many of his parliamentary backbenchers as well as in the opinion polls.

With the far-right National Front appearing to gain support, immigration again became an issue. Corruption scandals touched some heads of public and private companies. Terrorism by nationalists increased in Corsica and moved spectacularly to the mainland in the autumn.

Domestic Affairs. The start of the year was clouded by the death on January 8 of former president François Mitterrand. (*See* OBITUARIES.) He was the only man under the Fifth Republic to serve two full seven-year presidential terms, and his chief legacies were judged to be the creation of the modern Socialist Party in France and the forging of a strong alliance with Germany. Mitterrand's death came after a prolonged struggle with prostate cancer. Just how long a struggle became clear with the sensational revelation in a book by his personal physician, Claude Gubler, that the cancer had been discovered just after Mitterrand entered office in 1981 but was hushed up until the president underwent a first operation in 1992. Gubler claimed that the

president had in fact been unfit to govern the country from the autumn of 1994 on. The Mitterrand family persuaded the government to ban the Gubler book, but not before many copies were sold and the text was put on the Internet.

Gaining in stature from the sympathetic and statesmanlike way in which he addressed the nation on the death of his old Socialist political opponent, Chirac went on to make his mark with another television address, this time on his sweeping defense reforms. He announced the progressive replacement of France's part-conscript armed forces of more than 500,000 with a fully professional force of 350,000 by the year 2002. He also set defense spending at a maximum of F185 billion a year over the same period. This constituted a sizable reduction from the previously planned total, with most of the savings to be achieved on equipment produced by a restructured defense industry.

This restructuring was to centre on the privatization of the state-owned Thomson electronics group and the merger of France's two aircraft companies, the state-owned Aerospatiale and the privately controlled Dassault. This merger had long been resisted by Serge Dassault, who held nearly 50% of the public company's shares, but his ability to continue running an independent aviation group was undermined by the international arrest warrant issued against him in May by a Belgian judge investigating alleged bribes paid by Dassault in that country. Dassault had also balked at negotiating with Louis Gallois, the head of Aerospatiale. In July the government moved Gallois on to run the SNCF railroad company in place of Loik Le Floch-Prigent, who was jailed while magistrates investigated charges that in his earlier position at the Elf-Aquitaine oil company, he had improperly used company funds in return for favours.

Juppé's "favourable" rating in the opinion polls remained below 40% throughout the year and sometimes dipped below 30%. His main preoccupation was to cut the deficits in the central government budget and the welfare system. He achieved one structural reform early in the year with a change to the constitution that would allow Parliament some supervision of the social security system, which had historically been managed (or mismanaged) by the trade unions in conjunction with employers.

Juppé's ability to handle the coalition of his own neo-Gaullist Rally for the Republic with that of the centre-right Union for French Democracy (UDF) was made no easier when a national convention of the UDF on March 31 elected François Léotard to replace former president Valéry Giscard d'Estaing as party leader. During the 1995 presidential election campaign, Léotard had been one of the strongest supporters of Prime Minister Édouard Balladur against Chirac, who had the backing of Giscard.

Juppé also found himself faced with a growing number of National Assembly backbenchers, and they pressed him to adopt more popular policies, such as faster tax cuts. On October 2 Juppé opened the autumn session by calling for a motion of confidence in the government and so daring his internal critics to vote against him. He won the motion by 464 votes to 100, but the result reflected more the size of

the centre-right's majority than a change of heart toward the prime minister.

Immigration flared up again as an issue on August 23 when police stormed a Paris church sheltering some 300 "illegal" immigrants, mainly African, 10 of whom had been on a protest hunger strike for 50 days. Some of those arrested were then deported back to Africa. The government pledged to toughen the law against illegal immigration. It also moved to strengthen France's anti-racist laws in the wake of public remarks by National Front leader Jean-Marie Le Pen about "the inequality of the races."

The government was also confronted with rising terrorist activity by Corsican nationalists, most of whom were seeking increased autonomy for the island rather than its outright independence. On the eve of a visit to Corsica by Jean-Louis Debré, the interior minister, the "historic wing" of the Corsican National Liberation Front (FLNC–Canal Historique) staged a spectacular press conference on the night of January 12 in the hills, attended by 600 masked and armed men. It offered a truce to the government. The latter ignored Corsica's demands for more political autonomy but planned to revive the island's economy with increased tax breaks. Bombings of government property and shootings—often between the FLNC and other nationalist groups—continued, and the "truce" was only nominal by the time the FLNC formally ended it in August. Violence spread to the mainland with the September 29 bombing of the main court building in Aix-en-Provence and the bombing of the town hall in Bordeaux on October 5. A bomb exploded in a Paris train station in December, killing two.

The Economy. The year was one of low growth (1.2%) sandwiched between an increase in real gross domestic product (GDP) of 2.2% in 1995 and a predicted rate of expansion of 2.3% in 1997. After the autumn 1995 strikes, output rose by 1.1% in January–March only to fall back by 0.2% in the second quarter. Lower interest rates and artificially strong automobile sales (related to the ending in September of a subsidy for car buyers) helped GDP bounce back in the third quarter by 0.9%, and growth was forecast to continue more modestly at 0.4% in the final three months of 1996. The main strength came from household spending and, to a lesser extent, from export demand, but investment remained weak.

Economic policy was dominated by government efforts to reduce the country's overall deficit from the equivalent of 5% of GDP in 1995 to 4% in 1996, with the aim of reaching 3% in 1997 and so qualifying France for the EU monetary union. Mainly through tax increases, the government had less difficulty in cutting the budget deficit to F288 billion than it did with cutting the welfare deficit. The social security system ended the year around F50 billion in the red, compared with the government target of F17 billion.

Foreign Affairs. After France set off a sixth nuclear device in the South Pacific on January 27, Chirac announced that a final two tests would not be held and that the government would close forever the test sites on the atolls of Mururoa and Fangataufa in French Polynesia. This decision created an improvement in relations with Pacific countries, which Chirac built on at the spring summit in Bangkok of leaders

A car bomb exploded in the Corsican city of Bastia on July 1, killing a Corsican nationalist leader and wounding 16 other people. Bombings continued on the island throughout the year as nationalists sought to gain increased autonomy from France.

of the EU and the Association of Southeast Asian Nations (ASEAN). In his speech there Chirac called for closer EU-ASEAN ties, approved ASEAN's plan for a nuclear-free zone, and backed Japan's case for a seat on the UN Security Council. In April Chirac played host to Chinese Premier Li Peng. Despite his rebuff of French concerns about human rights abuses in China, Li signed a $1.5 billion order for Airbus Industrie, which marked the first big entry by the French-based European aircraft consortium into a Chinese market previously dominated by U.S. aircraft companies.

In relations with his Western partners, Chirac's two main goals were to press ahead with "Europeanizing" NATO and to give a push to the intergovernmental conference negotiations inside the EU. As a prelude to the first task, he visited Washington and, in a February 1 speech to the U.S. Congress, said France was ready to assume its full role in an Atlantic alliance re-formed to give Europeans more responsibility. Chirac also chided Congress for its cuts in U.S. development aid, a theme to which he returned when he chaired the Group of Seven industrial summit in Lyon on June 27–29. NATO defense ministers agreed in Berlin on June 3 that Europeans should have "political control and strategic direction" of any NATO-financed military missions that they ran.

France worked to improve its bilateral military cooperation with Germany in the face of cuts in forces and arms programs on both sides of the Rhine, including a reduction in the number of French troops in Germany from 20,000 to 3,000 by 1999. Within the EU Chirac also sought to keep up the momentum of the country's close partnership with Germany and made a May 14–17 state visit to the U.K.

During the year France maintained its interest in Africa and in the Balkans. On October 3 Chirac presided over a meeting between the presidents of Yugoslavia and Bosnia and Herzegovina, at which the latter agreed to establish full diplomatic relations. The main diplomatic innovation, however, was France's return to the Middle East. In April Chirac visited Lebanon and Egypt, outlining France's "new Arab policy." Later in April, Foreign Minister Hervé de Charette helped broker a cease-fire between Israel and Lebanon. In mid-October Chirac visited Israel and several Arab countries to underscore the point that France wanted to play a political role commensurate with the economic aid it provided to the region.   (DAVID BUCHAN)

See also *Dependent States.*

GABON

Gabon is a republic of central Africa, situated on the Atlantic Ocean. Area: 267,667 sq km (103,347 sq mi). Pop.: (1996 est.): 1,173,000. Cap.: Libreville. Monetary unit: CFA franc, with (Oct. 11, 1996) a par value of CFAF 100 to the French franc and a free rate of CFAF 518.24 to U.S. $1 (CFAF 816.38 = £1 sterling). President in 1996, Omar Bongo; prime minister, Paulin Obame-Nguema.

In May 1996 opposition parties and the government finally reached agreement over the long-disputed timing of municipal and legislative elections. This followed a ruling by the Constitutional Court upholding the opposition's position that local elections should precede those for the National Assembly, as stated in the constitution.

Initially scheduled for September 22, the local elections were postponed until October 20 following protests that more time was needed to prepare fully for the campaign. The government also conceded that the revised electoral rolls were not yet complete.

In the first round of the elections for the National Assembly on December 15, Pres. Omar Bongo's Gabonese Democratic Party won 47 of the 55 seats. Opposition parties criticized the government for delays in issuing voter cards and displaying electoral lists.   (NANCY ELLEN LAWLER)

This article updates the *Macropædia* article CENTRAL AFRICA: *Gabon.*

GAMBIA, THE

A republic and member of the Commonwealth, The Gambia extends from the Atlantic Ocean along the lower Gambia River in West Africa; it is surrounded by Senegal. Area: 10,689 sq km (4,127 sq mi). Pop. (1996 est.): 1,148,000. Cap.: Banjul. Monetary unit: dalasi, with (Oct. 11, 1996) a free rate of 9.85 dalasis to U.S. $1 (15.51 dalasis = £1 sterling). Chairman of the Armed Forces Provisional Ruling Council in 1996 and, from September 26, president, Capt. Yahya Jammeh.

Capt. Yahya Jammeh, head of the government in The Gambia, announced early in 1996 that presidential and legislative elections would be held in June. This electoral process would return The Gambia to constitutional rule. Delays then occurred, and no June elections took place.

A referendum was set for August 7 on a new constitution, and Jammeh described it as a first step toward the restoration of normal political life. Over 80% of the eligible voters went to the polls, and more than 70% of them voted in favour of the new constitution. Presidential and legislative elections were then promised; September 26 was set for the presidential elections, and the ban on political activity was lifted. The three political parties active during the regime of Pres. Sir Dawda Jawara and anyone who had held ministerial posts during the previous 30 years were, however, barred from taking part in the campaign and from subsequently holding office. Jammeh accepted an invitation by "leaders of thought and opinion" to run as a civilian for president. In the election he defeated three rivals by a 2–1 margin to become The Gambia's second elected president.   (GUY ARNOLD)

This article updates the *Macropædia* article WESTERN AFRICA: *The Gambia.*

GEORGIA

A republic of Transcaucasia, Georgia borders Russia on the north and northeast, Azerbaijan on the southeast, Armenia and Turkey on the south, and the Black Sea on the west. Area: 69,492 sq km (26,831 sq mi). Pop. (1996 est.): 5,361,000. Cap.: T'bilisi. Monetary unit: lari, with (Oct. 14, 1996) an official rate of 1.27 lari = U.S. $1 (2.01 lari = £1 sterling). President in 1996, Eduard A. Shevardnadze; secretary of state, Niko Lekishvili.

The parliamentary and presidential elections in November 1995, which consolidated the position of Pres. Eduard Shevardnadze, and the ensuing arrest of Dzhaba Ioseliani and members of his Mkhedrioni criminal/paramilitary force ushered in a new phase of political and economic stability in Georgia. The new Parliament functioned cohesively and productively to enact crucial legislation to underpin the foundations of economic reform. During the year there were no violent terrorist incidents or political assassinations such as were regular occurrences in 1993 to mid-1995, and crime abated. In October former defense minister Tengiz Kitovani was sentenced to eight years in prison for having attempted in January 1995 to organize a march on the rebellious region of Abkhazia. In November Loti Kobalia, commander of the military units that were loyal to former president Zviad Gamsakhurdia, was sentenced to death and three of his subordinates to terms of up to 15 years on charges of treason and murder.

The economic upswing that began in 1995 continued in 1996. During the first half of the year, gross domestic product grew by 8% and industrial output by 10%; inflation fell to an annual rate of about 30%, and the lari maintained its value against the dollar. Up to 20% of the workforce remained unemployed, however.

In early spring Parliament amended the annual budget and enacted laws on land ownership and taxation to meet conditions set by the International Monetary Fund for a $246 million loan to support economic reform in 1996–98. The World Bank allocated $34 million to reform the transport sector and health service. In March Shevardnadze and Azerbaijan's Pres. Heydar Aliyev signed an agreement on construction of a major pipeline to export Azerbaijani oil via Georgia.

Relations with Russia, in particular Moscow's perceived failure to comply with the 1995 bilateral agreement permitting Russia to maintain four military bases in Georgia in return for assistance in reestablishing Georgia's control over the breakaway regions of Abkhazia and South Ossetia, continued to dominate foreign policy. The Commonwealth of Independent States summit in Moscow in January imposed an economic blockade on Abkhazia. The mandate of the CIS peacekeepers deployed in Abkhazia was extended several times, but Shevardnadze's request that they be given police powers to protect ethnic Georgians wishing to return to their homes in Abkhazia—while agreed to by Abkhazia—was rejected by the commander of the forces. Relations with Russia cooled markedly in October after the Georgian Parliament voted to reassess Georgia's policy toward Russia, including the issue of Russian military bases.

Shevardnadze and South Ossetia's parliament chairman Lyudvig Chibirov signed an agreement in May rejecting the use of force and in August reaffirmed their commitment to resolving peacefully the issue of South Ossetia's future status within Georgia. In November Chibirov was elected president of South Ossetia in elections not recognized as valid by either Georgia or the international community.　(ELIZABETH FULLER)

This article updates the *Macropædia* article TRANSCAUCASIA: *Georgia*.

GERMANY

Germany is in central Europe, on the North and Baltic seas. Area: 356,974 sq km (137,828 sq mi). Pop. (1996 est.): 81,891,000. Cap. designate, Berlin; seat of government, Bonn. Monetary unit: Deutsche Mark, with (Oct. 11, 1996) a free rate of DM 1.53 to U.S. $1 (DM 2.41 = £1 sterling). President in 1996, Roman Herzog; chancellor, Helmut Kohl.

The year 1996 in Germany was a time of agonizing reappraisal of past, present, and future. It marked approximately five years

after unification, the time set as a test period for most of the prophecies and projections made when East Germans declared themselves "one people" with West Germans and ended almost half a century of enforced separation. It also marked three years after an equally important event, the lowering of customs barriers between the member nations of the European Community by common consent, which allowed unrestricted movement to the classic elements of a market economy—persons, capital, effects, and performance—throughout Western Europe, with the sole exception of Switzerland. The throwing open of the entire area of the Common Market (*i.e.,* the European Union) suddenly revealed the German labour force for what it was— the most coddled and costly in the world. The corollary of this revelation was that Germany as an industrial location, by dint of its advanced social welfare policies and labour legislation, had effectively priced itself out of international competition.

The Economy. The simple facts were that it cost considerably more to "buy German" than it did to buy goods elsewhere in the world (as Germany was one of the world's largest industrial export nations, its competition was necessarily global) and that the difference in quality that a "made in Germany" label implied was no longer considerable. The conjunction of events—unification, consolidation of the Common Market, and liberation of Eastern Europe—augured ill for Germany. It was not only that the Germans were obliged to finance the integration of an economically devastated East Germany (the total amount of financial aid to East Germany from 1991 to 1995 was DM 615 billion); they were also obliged to make economic allowance for the ravished countries of Eastern Europe in a "German Marshall Plan" for the East. This added to the flow of German investment capital out of Germany itself, particularly to the Russian Federation. Worse still, the opening to the East undermined the German labour market even more than the opening to the West within the Common Market had done. The Czechs, Hungarians, and Poles, each with a highly qualified labour force, were willing to work for a fraction of the German standard wage (*i.e.,* a third in the Czech Republic and a half in France).

As a result of all these factors, the number of bankruptcies in Germany rose sharply: 12,893 from January to May 1996— an increase of 11% over the same period of the previous year. Worst of all, however, was the number of *Schwartzarbeiter*—illegal immigrants working at low wages in construction. In the centre of Berlin, at the Potsdamer Platz construction site, where most of the building was being done by subcontractors, only every fifth worker was German; the rest were typically English, Spanish, Italian, and Portuguese, all legally employed but at lower than standard German wages. (An ironic note: in the theatre, including television, western Germans were underbid by German colleagues from the east willing to work at one-third of the going wage in one of the few nonunion trades in Germany.)

The most alarming result of this combination of crises was the abrupt rise in unemployment, 10.6% nationally and as high as 16% or more in the eastern German *Länder* (states). This was accompanied by

a drop in production figures from a 2.15% annual increase in 1992 to a 1.2% decrease in 1993 and, after an interim rise, to no more than an 0.08% increase in 1996.

Another result of the German dilemma was a whopping national debt of DM 870 billion, the accumulation of decades of deficit spending. The alarm had sounded five years earlier, but in 1996, when 11.8% of the budget had to be allotted to interest payments on the debt, the folly of deficit spending became the subject of every substantial political discussion. With it came the realization that Germans could no longer keep themselves in the style to which they had become accustomed.

It was generally agreed that budgetary expenditure would have to be cut, but there immediately arose a hue and cry against any tampering with the elaborate network of social welfare provisions painstakingly developed during the post-World War II period. It was precisely there, however, that cuts would have to be made. Because of the many "incidental costs" accruing through labour legislation and collective bargaining, the cost to the employer of each employee was more than 1.8 times the base pay. The main areas of government support included health care, unemployment insurance, full payment for sick leave, up to 30 vacation days per annum, early retirement, and the four-week *Kur* ("cure"), a treatment available once every three years for a chronic condition and usually given in a sanatorium, where "patients" sweated through morning calisthenics and mud baths only to repair to high-calorie meals later.

In mid-June, when the German government announced its package of economic measures containing 50 items of government outlay to be more or less radically cut, the German Trade Union Federation, under Dieter Schulte (*see* BIOGRAPHIES), cried havoc and took to the streets in a mass rally in Bonn. The Social Democratic Party (SPD) and the Greens denounced most of the package, and the Bundesrat (the country's second legislative chamber), where Social Democrats were in the majority, proclaimed its opposition in advance. On September 13, however, the Bundestag (federal parliament) brought the full weight of its four-vote majority to bear and passed the three articles that fell under constitutional exemption from the consent of the Bundesrat. These included a measure to gradually raise the retirement age for women from 60 to 65 years, beginning in the year 2000, and a measure to reduce the length of a *Kur* from four to three weeks and increase the period between "cures" from three to four years. The measure that caused an immediate uproar was that to reduce the amount payable on sick leave to 80% of the employee's regular income (employees could avoid the reduction in payments by relinquishing their vacation rights at a ratio of one day of vacation to five days of sick leave).

This law was immediately seized upon by a number of the largest German firms and industry federations. The employers announced that they would cut sick-pay benefits accordingly when the law went into effect on October 1. The reaction of the trade unions was likewise immediate. There were massive strikes, demonstrations, and threats of more to come. The sum targeted

(continued on page 424)

FOURTH WORLD RESURGENCE IN EUROPE

by Richard A. Griggs and Peter R. Hocknell

illustration by Igor Kopelnitsky

Throughout the world in 1996, there were some 6,000 to 9,000 Fourth World "nations," territorial and political units that lacked recognition by the United Nations but endured as distinct political cultures within the boundaries of 191 states (the internationally recognized countries). Fourth World nations persisted despite incorporation within states, finding unity in historical, cultural, and territorial ties.

The geography and geopolitics of this "Fourth World" (those nations that do not enjoy sovereign statehood) hold significant implications everywhere, including Europe, where approximately 110 of these submerged nations are located. Often these nations occupy a recognized region within a larger state—*e.g.,* Wales, Tuscany, or Valencia. In the past they have been the building blocks of such European states as Italy and Germany, and today they define some of the political fault lines along which states break apart (Czechoslovakia and Yugoslavia). By 1996 many of these Fourth World nations were organizing for a new dispensation based not on sovereign statehood but in the context of a federal "Europe of Regions."

The Geography of Europe's Fourth World Nations. Around 15% of Europe's distinct nations would be shown on a standard political map (more than most major world regions). Andorra, Hungary, Iceland, Ireland, Liechtenstein, Luxembourg, Malta, Monaco, Poland, and San Marino are long-accepted examples of internationally recognized states composed of only one nation. The addition of Belarus, Macedonia, Bosnia and Herzegovina, Slovenia, Slovakia, Lithuania, Latvia, and Estonia during the 1990s nearly doubled the number of internationally recognized nations. Distributed within or across about 25 multinational states are another 100 Fourth World nations. These figures are partly dependent on one's definition of Europe (this article includes the newly independent Baltic states and Ukraine as the eastern boundary of Europe but excludes Russia and Turkey).

Excluding the dominant nation cores of states (for example, Svealand dominates Sweden and Castile dominates Spain) and those nations with very weak political movements (such as Pomerania), Fourth World nations can claim at least one-third of Europe's land area. They dominate more than half of Europe's coastline and form a concentrated core of smaller nations in the rugged heartland of the Alps.

The Fourth World nations can be classified as follows:

• Recognized Nations: those that have resisted long-standing attempts by states to assimilate them culturally and have achieved independence. In most cases statehood was gained by decolonization rather than expansion.

• Autonomous Nations: those that have resisted long-standing attempts by states to assimilate them culturally and have achieved a considerable measure of autonomy.

• City-States: city regions that have achieved autonomy or independence.

• Enduring Nations: those that have employed strong political movements to counter long-standing attempts to assimilate them culturally. Most have achieved a partial or limited autonomy.

• Renascent Nations: historic nations that have undergone a cultural renaissance since 1945, resulting in emboldened movements for greater political recognition.

• Remnant Nations: dormant nations with weak or incipient national movements. Most have expanding memberships and remain a geopolitical force by means of organized activity.

• Nation Cores of States: most regions within states that become both the centres of expansion and the dominant cultures of the states.

• Irredenta Nations: peoples separated by an interstate boundary because of a treaty or war.

These categories are not stagnant. Nations can move from autonomy to recognition or from remnant to renascent at different stages of their development. It is also important to understand that identity is layered and neither temporally nor spatially fixed. City-states and regions, though not specifically nationalistic, can also be part of broader movements for self-determination.

A Europe of Regions. Those who assumed that European unity would eliminate nationalist forces may be surprised at what is actually happening. The specific strategy of most Fourth World nations is aimed not at creating new independent states but at enhancing their legitimacy and strengthening confederational organizations. They seek representation in European Union institutions and domestic autonomy consistent with EU aims.

These developments synchronize two geopolitical forces and result in a squeeze on the state as the dominant form of political organization. On one side the proponents of a federal Europe argue that the individual state can no longer meet the problems posed by such continental and global problems as drugs, economic competition, and pollution. On the other side are old nations, regions, and city-states seeking more appropriate and less centralized solutions for their particularly local problems. In this scenario the EU would be large enough to wrestle with the big problems, while the region or nation could deal with the smaller ones. Middle-scale problems would be handled by EU commissions acting as facilitators between the affected nations, regions, or cities. Thus, the region rather than the traditional

Resurgent Nations in the New Europe

1 Isle of Man
2 Brussels
3 Bremen
4 Hamburg
5 Wallonia
6 Rhineland
7 Thuringia
8 Brandenburg
9 Salzburg
10 Tirolia
11 Trentino
12 Friulia
13 Montenegro

TYPES OF NATIONS

Recognized
Autonomous
City-States
Enduring
Renascent
Remnant
Nation Cores of States

Irredenta (people of one nation living within boundaries of another state) are not shown.

Data source: Richard A. Griggs, University of Cape Town, S.Af.
© 1997, Encyclopædia Britannica, Inc.

state becomes the significant subdivision of a united Europe.

Most important treaties on Europe have in one way or another facilitated the Europe of Regions. The 1987 Single European Act established the European Regional Development Fund, which was designed to equalize widespread disparities in wealth and development on a regional basis. The 1993 Treaty on European Union set up the Consultative Committee of the Regions, marking the first time that Fourth World nations, city-states, and regions had been recognized as partners in building a new Europe. Thus, those seeking to empower the European Union have often encouraged regionalism as enthusiastically as have proponents of the regions themselves.

Europe's Fourth World enjoys popular support as well. A 1992 study carried out by the European Commission found that 87% of the Europeans surveyed simultaneously in 12 states felt either strongly or fairly strongly attached to their regions. A Europe of Regions also wins the support of international capital, which is increasingly less concerned with state boundaries. Regions are aware that businesses frequently base their investment decisions on the attributes of regions rather than states—for example, Flanders rather than Belgium or Catalonia rather than Spain.

The Geopolitical Challenge Ahead. Amazingly, Europe has returned to a period of geopolitical decentralization after more than two centuries of state building. This came about because, more often than not, attempts to foster state consciousness within a state's entire populace backfired. The trauma of colonization, forced removals, and ethnic violence and genocide resides in the cultural memory of surviving peoples. Sheer persistence on the part of these vital political communities coupled with a European unity movement that tends to reduce the significance of organization by states could signal a major geopolitical reorganization of Europe.

Richard A. Griggs, formerly a political geographer at the University of Cape Town, is now head of research, Independent Projects Trust, Durban, S.Af., and author of *The Role of Fourth World Nations and Synchronous Geopolitical Factors in the Breakdown of States* (1996); Peter R. Hocknell is a research officer with the International Boundaries Research Unit, University of Durham, Eng.

(continued from page 421)
for reduction—six weeks of fully paid sick leave a year—was a sacred cow, hallowed and untouchable. It had been set in 1957 by a collective bargaining agreement, after unions staged a general strike that lasted 16 weeks.

In this new struggle, however, the employers were not united. A number of Germany's largest firms, such as Volkswagen AG and Bayerische Motoren Werke (BMW) AG, refused to apply the law because it violated standing agreements with the trade unions. As the employers saw it, the law was meant to provide a guideline for future negotiations with the unions. Many employers who had chosen to apply the law without further ado saw themselves obliged to desist. "First the government passes a law," fumed Dieter Hundt, the president of the federal Union of German Employer Groups, "and then certain members of the government admonish us not to apply the law." On October 8 employers in the metal industry began negotiations with the IG Metall union. Others announced they would apply the law. Meanwhile, the unions themselves were losing membership at an alarming rate—typically, the civil service union had lost some 25% of its clientele over the past five years.

It was, according to the German press, a confrontation that could be settled peaceably only by the Federal Constitutional Court. Unfortunately, the capacity of the court was vastly overburdened by a constant flood of constitutional complaints.

For the future the big problem was the pension fund, projected to double within the next 40 years. Trends in German actuarial tables pointed to an increase in the ratio of people aged 65 and older to the remainder of the adult population (aged 15–64) from about 22% to 55% by the year 2035. It was a matter, then, of trying to avoid passing the buck to future generations for bills the present generation could not or would not pay.

The interlocking nature of the problems made matters worse. The plethora of taxes in Germany strongly discouraged investment and consequently hampered employment. From 1990 to September 1995 foreigners invested only DM 18 billion in Germany, while the Germans invested DM 196 billion in foreign countries. Indeed, in 1990, 1991, 1993, and 1994, Americans liquidated many of their investments in Germany rather than adding to them. For example, Adam Opel AG, a branch of General Motors Corp. that manufactured cars in Germany, broke ground in Poland in October for a factory with a 10-year tax-exemption guarantee. In addition to rampant German taxation, there were other deterrents, such as compulsory "contributions" to social programs and the host of incidental expenses attendant to a bureaucracy.

Tax reform was thus Germany's cardinal problem. In the "tax haven" of eastern Germany, for example, only 20% of the auditing offices were staffed by fully trained professionals. For that matter, fewer than half of the auditing offices were staffed at all. Indeed, throughout Germany hardly more than half the auditors required were affordable in the budgetary alteration of a fiscal policy that could not be changed—except for the worse—in the prevailing atmosphere of austerity. Because the lack of funding kept auditing offices from being staffed properly, Germany sustained an estimated annual loss of DM 30 billion in unrecovered taxes. On the other hand, an investigation in early 1996 revealed that the main item of official travel expenses—itself the largest category in the sum total of expenses—was that of tax inspectors.

On April 26 Chancellor Helmut Kohl (who in October became the longest-ruling German leader since Bismarck) announced the "tax reform of the century," in which direct returns would be reduced by an estimated 23% and the procedure of filing returns simplified. There would be fewer exceptions and exemptions. The minimum level of taxable income would be raised from DM 12,000 to DM 24,000 per annum. This reform would go into effect on Jan. 1, 1999.

Foreign Affairs. This was also a year of reckoning, both geopolitically and culturally. U.S. Secretary of State Warren Christopher made a point of visiting Stuttgart on September 6 to commemorate the 50th anniversary of the speech delivered by his predecessor James F. Byrnes that signaled the about-face in U.S. policy toward Germany from the punitive Morgenthau Plan to the outright endowment of the Marshall Plan. This marked the beginning of German-American friendship and the resultant "economic miracle."

But was this not, asked some Germans in 1996, the beginning of Germany's political wardship to the United States? Was not Germany a vassal state of the American superpower? German foreign policy was always U.S. foreign policy—even after unification. When the Americans bombarded Iraq with cruise missiles in mid-1996 to rap the knuckles of a recalcitrant Saddam Hussein, did not the Germans stand to in unquestioning loyalty—as sharply distinct from most of the other members of the NATO alliance? Other Germans, however, regarded such a show of solidarity as strictly in keeping with Germany's position as most important U.S. ally on the Continent.

Culturally the German-American relationship was more problematic. Had not Germany been "coca-colonized" by American pop culture? The fact was that American television programs made up the bulk of Germany's TV entertainment programs (American television productions constituted some 80% of all European television fare, while European TV productions made up less than 8% of American television fare). German youth ran about in the T-shirts of American basketball stars.

The other side of the story was that in 1996 there were 132 full-repertory opera houses in Germany and well over 100 symphony orchestras—the largest and richest musical establishment in the world. One-third of the opera singers in Germany were Americans. The remaining two-thirds were equally divided between native Germans and all other foreigners. (*See also* Biographies: *Wilson, Robert.*) Most of the opera houses doubled as theatres in accordance with the traditional German formula for edifying entertainment based on the tripod of music, legitimate stage, and ballet. German theatre had always been heavily if not totally subsidized, however. With unification and the end of the Cold War, subsidies largely ceased—to be replaced by closings, fusions, and mergers—and the number of theatres and opera houses dwindled.

Party Politics. "The social state," ran the Bonn pronouncement after the passage of the economic measures package, "is being reduced in order to preserve its budgetary viability." The failure of even the social democratic model of the welfare state (beginning with Sweden) on the heels of the Soviet disaster wreaked electoral havoc with the German Social Democratic Party. In the Baden-Württemberg parliamentary elections in March, the SPD polled 25.1% of the vote, the worst showing in that state in the party's history. In Berlin the SPD's election results had dwindled steadily over

Trade union members rally in Stuttgart in September to protest the German government's economic austerity proposals. Despite strong union opposition, some of the measures were approved, even though employers were not united in implementing them.

WOLF-DIETRICH WEISSBAACH—AFP

the postwar period from 61% to 23% of the vote.

The fact that the causes of the virtual bankruptcy of federal, *Land,* and city governments had little to do with the political party in power merely made matters worse for the Social Democrats. The SPD had staked its claim that a political approach to economics was a guarantee of social justice. This placed before the SPD an awesome assignment: inventing a new and cogent sociopolitical philosophy. It was a challenge that made the triumvirate of the SPD leadership—Oskar Lafontaine of the Saarland, Gerhard Schröder of Lower Saxony, and Rudolf Scharping, head of the party's parliamentary group—look considerably less adept than they actually were, frequently at odds among themselves, and with no chance of taking advantage of the government's continuing discomfiture.

In Bremen, Hessen, North Rhine–Westphalia, and Lower Saxony, the SPD had entered ruling coalitions with the Greens as pilot models for a national government. The Greens were younger and more fervent and tended to split over issues of foreign policy, but in Joschka Fischer they had a prominent leader and one of the best speakers in Parliament. As for the coalition's junior partner, the Free Democrats had just managed to clear the 5% barrier (the minimum percentage of the vote required for qualifying for representation) and remain in the national government.

The Refugee Problem. It was close attention to economic issues that made Germany unprecedentedly prosperous and a magnet to the have-not countries of Eastern Europe and to Africa and the Middle East as well. In the Federal Republic, however, there were other motives for the formation of policy or, more often, the triggering of ad hoc political action. Germany remained bedeviled by its past, with the deep-seated urge to make compensation for the abomination of the Third Reich. This led to extremely loose immigration and refugee-accommodation laws, which led in turn to an influx of some 300,000 refugees from former Yugoslavia (more than the number accepted by all other European nations put together) and more than 100,000 Kurdish refugees.

The sum of such experience provided the insight that the way to keep refugees out of Germany was to participate in international police action at the geographic source of the refugees. Even the SPD and the Greens saw the light. Germany had in 1995 abandoned its long-standing noncombatant role in foreign military engagements and thus finally became a NATO member in the full sense of the term.

The repatriation of Kurdish, "Yugoslav," African, and Arab refugees was and would remain a thankless task with moral recriminations from all sides. Surely it would be better to order such matters in concert. A united Europe would be in a far better position to solve the problem than would Germany alone, but here too was a crucial complication in the form of the Maastricht Treaty and its stipulation of a maximum of deficit spending (3.5% of gross domestic product) as the basic qualification in the impending economic and monetary union (EMU). The Organisation for Economic Co-operation and Development lost no time in informing the German government

that its package of economic measures was nothing more than "a modest step in the right direction." The passage would prove to be the most difficult of all diplomatic feats—that of reversing a precedent, of undoing what had already been done, of taking away what had already been given. The EMU was the key to European unification, and European unification was Germany's highest goal, indeed its key to salvation.

(GEORGE BAILEY)

GHANA

A republic of West Africa and member of the Commonwealth, Ghana lies on the Gulf of Guinea. Area: 238,533 sq km (92,098 sq mi). Pop. (1996 est.): 16,904,000. Cap.: Accra. Monetary unit: cedi, with (Oct. 11, 1996) a free rate of 1,703 cedis to U.S. $1 (2,683 cedis = £1 sterling). Chairman of the Provisional National Defense Council and president in 1996, Jerry John Rawlings.

Political concern throughout 1996 in Ghana focused on the presidential and parliamentary elections scheduled for December. The main opposition parties worked to create a united front. In June the New Patriotic Party (NPP) and the People's Convention Party (PCP) met to iron out their differences in order to achieve a merger. After lengthy negotiations the NPP and PCP agreed to contest the December elections on a common platform. They also agreed that NPP leader John Kufuor should be the alliance's presidential candidate and PCP leader K.N. Arkaah his running mate. The ruling National Democratic Congress nominated Jerry Rawlings as its candidate. To the surprise of many who expected a close contest, Rawlings won with 57.2% of the vote.   (GUY ARNOLD)

This article updates the *Macropædia* article WESTERN AFRICA: *Ghana.*

GREECE

The republic of Greece occupies the southern part of the Balkan Peninsula and several adjoining island groups in southeastern Europe, in and between the Ionian and Aegean seas. Area: 131,957 sq km (50,949 sq mi). Pop. (1996 est.): 10,493,000. Cap.: Athens. Monetary unit: drachma, with (Oct. 11, 1996) a free rate of 239.98 drachmas to U.S. $1 (378.04 drachmas = £1 sterling). President in 1996, Konstantinos Stephanopoulos; prime ministers, Andreas Papandreou and, from January 22, Konstantinos Simitis.

Greece began 1996 with a changing of the political guard—the transition from Andreas Papandreou (*see* OBITUARIES) to Konstantinos ("Kostas") Simitis (*see* BIOGRAPHIES) as the country's prime minister. While the nation's economy improved during the year, foreign policy problems remained unresolved.

Papandreou, whose health had been precarious for several years, was rushed to the hospital in November 1995 and put on life support. On Jan. 15, 1996, he yielded to mounting pressure from leading members of his Panhellenic Socialist Movement (Pasok) and resigned as prime minister. Three days later Pasok's parliamentary deputies chose as the new prime minister Simitis, who for-

merly had held the portfolios of agriculture, economics, education, and industry. Simitis, a pragmatic reformist in the Western European social democratic tradition who had repeatedly criticized Papandreou's populist politics, defeated Interior Minister Apostolos ("Akis") Tsochatzopoulos and Defense Minister Gerasimos Arsenis.

Simitis's new Cabinet included many changes from the previous government. Most notably, Theodoros Pangalos took over as foreign minister from Karolos Papoulias, while Vasiliki ("Vasso") Papandreou (no relation) was appointed head of the newly created Development Ministry (comprising industry, energy, technology, trade, and tourism).

On June 23, days before the opening of Pasok's regular congress, Papandreou died. On June 30 Simitis was elected Pasok chairman, narrowly defeating Tsochatzopoulos. The elections of many reformists to the party's central committee further strengthened Simitis's position.

Simitis, who wanted to implement necessary economic measures and structural reforms and to strengthen his position within Pasok, called parliamentary elections for September 22, one year ahead of schedule. In the elections, Pasok lost about 5% of its previous support, but with 41.49% of the vote and an electoral law favouring the biggest party at the expense of the second largest, it won 162 of 300 seats. The conservative New Democracy fell slightly to 38.12% of the vote (108 seats). The Communist Party gained slightly and won 5.61% (11 seats), while the Progressive Left Coalition won considerably more votes than in previous elections and returned to Parliament with 5.12% (10 seats). The newly formed Democratic Social Movement of Papandreou's former finance minister, Dimitris Tsovolas, won 4.43% and 9 deputies. The nationalist Political Spring party failed to clear the 3% barrier, with 2.94%.

After the elections Simitis formed a government. He removed many longtime government ministers and reassigned others. Among the most notable changes, Ioannis Papantoniou took over the finance portfolio in addition to economics, Alexandros Papadopoulos was moved from finance to the Interior Ministry, Tsochatzopoulos was moved to defense, and Arsenis was put in charge of education.

On election night, New Democracy leader Miltiades Evert resigned, but within a week he announced that he would seek reelection, plunging the party into its deepest crisis since its founding in 1974. On October 4 Evert was reelected over Georgios Souflias. The basic problem of the party—the struggle between "traditional" rightists and centre-right liberals—remained unresolved, and another leadership change at the next party congress in the spring of 1997 could not be ruled out.

In late January a conflict between Greece and Turkey over the uninhabited Aegean islet of Imia/Kardak bore the immediate risk of an armed confrontation as military vessels from both sides gathered around the islet in a show of strength. The crisis was defused by U.S. pressure on both sides. Greek-Turkish relations hit another low in August when two Greek Cypriots were killed as demonstrators tried to cross the Green Line dividing Cyprus. On October 1–2 Simitis visited Cyprus and pledged continuing military support. Simitis and Cypriot Pres. Glafcos Clerides said that any further advance of Turkey in the island would be a cause of war.

Greece's cooperation with its European Union (EU) partners improved in 1996, as did relations with the U.S., which Simitis visited in April. Pres. Konstantinos ("Kostis") Stephanopoulos visited Tiranë, Alb., in March, and a friendship and cooperation treaty was signed. Greek schools and consulates in southern Albania opened in August, and the government pledged to legalize the status of part of the approximately 300,000 Albanians living and working in Greece illegally. The unresolved name issue prevented a further breakthrough in relations with Macedonia, but the situation had nevertheless improved since the signing of the interim accord in 1995, with persons and goods crossing the border without major problems.

To implement the EU's economic policy, the government switched to a tight fiscal policy. Inflation remained in the single-digit range throughout the year and stood at 8.5% in August. Growth in gross domestic product was estimated to be 2.6%, while the budget deficit was expected to fall to a still-high 7.6% of GDP. Unemployment stood at about 10%, while the trade deficit and public debt remained alarmingly high. In December the legislature passed an austerity budget aimed at cutting the deficit to 4.2% of GDP.   (STEFAN KRAUSE)

GRENADA

A constitutional monarchy within the Commonwealth, Grenada (with its dependency, the Southern Grenadines) is situated in the eastern Caribbean Sea. Area: 344 sq km (133 sq mi). Pop. (1996 est.): 97,900. Cap.: Saint George's. Monetary unit: Eastern Caribbean dollar, with (Oct. 11, 1996) a par value of EC$2.70 to U.S. $1 (free rate of EC$4.25 = £1 sterling). Queen, Elizabeth II; governors-general in 1996, Reginald Palmer and, from August 8, Daniel Williams; prime minister, Keith Mitchell.

The commission of inquiry into the previous government's privatization of the Grenada Electricity Co. (Grenlec) began work in January 1996. The present New National Party government alleged "misuse of funds" in the privatization process.

In February it was announced that earnings from the cocoa crop would decline by EC$1.7 million to EC$7.8 million in 1996 because of the decision by a major U.S. buyer to stop importing Grenada cocoa. The 1996 crop was estimated at 1,588 metric tons.

In May the government signed two treaties with the U.S. covering mutual legal assistance and extradition. The treaties formed part of the campaign against drug trafficking in the region. (DAVID RENWICK)
    This article updates the *Macropædia* article The WEST INDIES: *Grenada.*

GUATEMALA

A republic of Central America, Guatemala has coastlines on the Caribbean Sea and the Pacific Ocean. Area: 108,889 sq km (42,042 sq mi). Pop. (1996 est.): 10,928,-000. Cap.: Guatemala City. Monetary unit:

quetzal, with (Oct. 11, 1996) a free rate of 6.07 quetzales to U.S. $1 (9.56 quetzales = £1 sterling). Presidents in 1996, Ramiro de León Carpio and, from January 14, Alvaro Arzú Irigoyen.

During the first round of voting for the Guatemalan presidency in November 1995, Alvaro Arzú Irigoyen of the conservative National Advancement Party gained insufficient votes to win outright. A runoff election was therefore held on Jan. 7, 1996, and Arzú defeated Alfonso Portillo of the right-wing Guatemalan Republican Front by a narrow margin. Arzú's support came mainly from Guatemala City and, in particular, the urban middle class.

Arzú began his presidency by announcing a 180-day crackdown on violent crime. Human rights groups, including the United Nations mission in Guatemala, stated that military, or former military, personnel were involved in many illegal activities, especially lucrative kidnappings.

The president, backed by his military ally, Gen. Otto Pérez Molina, continued to negotiate with the left-wing guerrillas of the Guatemalan National Revolutionary Unity to end the 35-year civil war, in which an estimated 100,000 people had died. On September 19 the efforts of both sides were rewarded with the signing of a military agreement halting all hostilities. It followed a cease-fire in March, a breakthrough agreement on social reform in May, and ratification of an international convention on the rights of indigenous peoples in June. On December 4 government and rebel leaders signed a pact calling for a permanent cease-fire to end Latin America's longest war.

On October 16 more than 80 spectators were killed and about 150 injured in a stampede of fans trying to squeeze into a soccer match in Guatemala City. (*See* DISASTERS.)   (BEN BOX)
    This article updates the *Macropædia* article CENTRAL AMERICA: *Guatemala.*

GUINEA

The republic of Guinea is located in West Africa, on the Atlantic Ocean. Area: 245,-857 sq km (94,926 sq mi). Pop. (1996 est.): 6,903,000 (excluding more than 400,000 refugees from Liberia). Cap.: Conakry. Monetary unit: Guinean franc, with (Oct. 11, 1996) a free rate of GF 997 to U.S. $1 (GF 1,571 = £1 sterling). President in 1996, Gen. Lansana Conté; prime minister from July 9, Sidya Touré.

On Feb. 2, 1996, some 2,000 soldiers, incensed by refusals to grant pay increases to the army, were involved in a mutiny that quickly escalated into an attempt to overthrow the government. The rebels closed the airport and headed into Conakry. They launched an artillery attack on the presidential palace, looted the city centre, and took Defense Minister Abdourahmane Diallo hostage. Pres. Lansana Conté, from his underground refuge, promised to reconsider the salary increases. The siege ended on February 4 after loyal troops from the provinces moved into the capital and defeated the rebels. At least 50 people died, and more than 300 were injured during the two days. Arrests of some 50 officers, including many senior commanders, swiftly followed. In late March new protests

erupted following the sentencing of eight officers convicted of having led the revolt. The arrest of another 15 officers in June contributed to mounting tension; many of those originally seized in February were released in August.

On July 9 President Conté appointed economist Sidya Touré his first prime minister. Several ministers thought to have been close to the president were ousted in a major Cabinet reshuffle. Touré announced that his top priority would be to restart the country's economy, which was still mired in recession.   (NANCY ELLEN LAWLER)
    This article updates the *Macropædia* article WESTERN AFRICA: *Guinea.*

GUINEA-BISSAU

A republic of West Africa, Guinea-Bissau lies on the Atlantic Ocean. Area: 36,125 sq km (13,948 sq mi). Pop. (1996 est.): 1,096,-000. Cap.: Bissau. Monetary unit: Guinea-Bissau peso, with (Oct. 11, 1996) a free rate of 18,036 pesos to U.S. $1 (28,412 pesos = £1 sterling). President in 1996, João Bernardo Vieira; prime minister, Manuel Saturnino da Costa.

A major government reshuffle was carried out in mid-January 1996 by Prime Minister Manuel Saturnino da Costa, who was responding to the president's request for greater government efficiency. In August demonstrations against the government took place in Bissau following a government decision to accept 44 illegal immigrants from a number of African countries after they had been expelled from Spain. The Guinea-Bissau Human Rights League protested that the government had accepted money from Spain as the price of its action.

At the end of 1995, Guinea-Bissau ratified a 1993 agreement with its neighbour Senegal. It defined their maritime border and provided for the joint exploration of that area, which was believed to be rich in oil.   (GUY ARNOLD)
    This article updates the *Macropædia* article WESTERN AFRICA: *Guinea-Bissau.*

GUYANA

A republic and member of the Commonwealth, Guyana is situated in northeastern South America, on the Atlantic Ocean. Area: 215,083 sq km (83,044 sq mi). Pop. (1996 est.): 712,000. Cap.: Georgetown. Monetary unit: Guyana dollar, with (Oct. 11, 1996) an official rate of G$138.90 to U.S. $1 (G$218.81 = £1 sterling). President in 1996, Cheddi Jagan; prime minister, Sam Hinds.

The National Assembly authorized the reopening of the Omai gold mine, Guyana's largest, in February 1996, after it had been closed for almost seven months. The mine, a major earner of foreign exchange, was ordered shut in 1995 when a storage pond retaining wall collapsed, allowing 3.2 million cu m (4.2 million cu yd) of cyanide waste to contaminate the Essequibo River.

Guyana obtained substantial financial relief in May when the Paris Club of creditor nations wrote off U.S. $500 million of the nation's foreign debt. In July the country suffered severe flooding, which caused millions of dollars' worth of damage.

          (DAVID RENWICK)

HAITI

The republic of Haiti occupies the western one-third of the Caribbean island of Hispaniola, which it shares with the Dominican Republic. Area: 27,700 sq km (10,695 sq mi). Pop. (1996 est.): 6,732,000. Cap.: Port-au-Prince. Monetary unit: gourde, with (Oct. 11, 1996) a free rate of 15.10 gourdes to U.S. $1 (23.79 gourdes = £1 sterling). Presidents in 1996, Jean-Bertrand Aristide and, from February 7, René Préval; prime ministers, Claudette Werleigh and, from March 6, Rony Smarth.

René Préval, a former prime minister and close aide of the outgoing president, Jean-Bertrand Aristide, won 87% of the vote in the December 1995 presidential elections, but his victory was marred by an exceptionally low turnout of only 25% of the electorate. Nevertheless, international observers reported that the vote was fair, and the new president was inaugurated on February 7. After extensive negotiations, the legislature finally approved the president's nominee for prime minister, Rony Smarth, an agronomist, whose main task was to complete negotiations with the International Monetary Fund (IMF) over economic reforms, including privatization, which would enable the release of additional foreign aid.

The new president visited the U.S. and Canada in March, which improved relations but failed to achieve the release of frozen U.S. aid. He also visited the Dominican Republic, the first time since 1935 that a Haitian president had visited this neighbouring nation. The two presidents announced that a bilateral commission would be set up to promote trade and cooperate in immigration and the fight against drug trafficking and money laundering.

President-elect Préval on January 5 asked the UN peacekeeping force to remain in Haiti for an additional six months because of acts of violence and disputes over the new police force, which was believed to be rife with corruption and intrigue. There was disagreement within the UN Security Council over the size of the force and the length of time it should stay in Haiti. U.S. troops left in April, although 230 U.S. military personnel, such as engineers, remained to build roads, clinics, and schools. The rest of the 2,200-strong force was to leave at the end of June, but the inability of the police force to guarantee a stable and secure environment led to calls for the mandate to be extended. It was eventually agreed that a force of 600 UN soldiers plus 700 others would remain for five months from July, with the cost of the 700 to be shared by the U.S. and Canada. Canada would continue to supply about half the troops, with the rest provided by Pakistan and Bangladesh. The number of police monitors was raised from 250 to 300, to be involved in training the Haitian police force in the capital. In December the mandate was again extended for another six to eight months.

Violence continued unabated throughout the year, with murders and kidnappings, as the young and poorly trained new police force coped badly with the crime wave. Rumours of a coup circulated in Port-au-Prince in July following the murder of a former soldier who had warned of a plot to assassinate the president. Disgruntled for-

CAROL GUZY—THE WASHINGTON POST

After a funeral for a mob leader, another man, also reportedly a mob member (centre), is killed in the streets of Haiti as people pass by or look on. As Haitians' confidence in their law-enforcement and justice systems weakened, criminals and vigilantes often took control of the streets.

mer soldiers, claiming unfair dismissal and demanding unpaid severance pay and pensions, caused disruption. In August gunmen attacked the police headquarters and then the building housing the national legislature. On September 30 police foiled a plot by former soldiers to assassinate government officials.

Having collected over 5,000 testimonies of crimes committed by the former military regime, the Truth and Justice Commission handed in its report on February 5. The commission pressed for trials and reforms.

Agreement was reached with the IMF in May for a structural adjustment program that would release about $1 billion in aid. The government agreed to cut spending, reform the fiscal accounts, and sell or lease state enterprises.   (SARAH CAMERON)

This article updates the *Macropædia* article The WEST INDIES: *Haiti.*

HONDURAS

A republic of Central America, Honduras has coastlines on the Caribbean Sea and the Pacific Ocean. Area: 112,492 sq km (43,433 sq mi). Pop. (1996 est.): 5,666,000. Cap.: Tegucigalpa. Monetary unit: lempira, with (Oct. 11, 1996) a free rate of 12.07 lempiras to U.S. $1 (19.01 lempiras = £1 sterling). President in 1996, Carlos Roberto Reina.

A 25% rise in Honduras's minimum wage at the beginning of 1996 was soon eroded by a 30% increase in the cost of basic goods. Strikes in support of higher wages spread throughout the public sector, together with demands that they not be financed by job cuts. The government offered a package worth 135 million lempiras, but the unions held out for their demands to be met in full. The government was hampered by its agreement with the International Monetary Fund involving stringent spending cuts.

The government was unpopular with other sectors of the population as well. Indigenous groups demonstrated against the failure to fulfill aid commitments. The armed forces were dissatisfied with reforms reducing their power. The abolition of compulsory military service had drastically cut the size of the forces, and the police force and the profitable telephone company were being turned over to civilian control. Bomb attacks on the presidential residence in March and during a presidential address in June were suspected of being warnings by the military, despite emphatic denials by the chief of the armed forces, Gen. Mario Raúl Hung Pacheco. In July Hung Pacheco reportedly foiled an attempted rebellion against him by disgruntled officers.

(SARAH CAMERON)

This article updates the *Macropædia* article CENTRAL AMERICA: *Honduras.*

HUNGARY

A republic, Hungary is a landlocked state in central Europe. Area: 93,030 sq km (35,919 sq mi). Pop. (1996 est.): 10,-201,000. Cap.: Budapest. Monetary unit: forint, with (Oct. 11, 1996) a free rate of 155.50 forints to U.S. $1 (244.95 forints = £1 sterling). President in 1996, Arpad Goncz; prime minister, Gyula Horn.

The economy continued to preempt other domestic concerns in Hungary in 1996, and scandals and turmoil surrounding government economic agencies, exacerbated by infighting and squabbles among the parties of the ruling coalition, dominated the headlines. Finance Minister Lajos Bokros resigned on February 18 after a stormy tenure. In March 1995 he had introduced an austerity package designed to trim the bloated government budget and bring on the kind of fiscal responsibility demanded

(continued on page 430)

Gypsies of Eastern Europe

Despised by many throughout the world, the Roma, more commonly known as Gypsies, are now one of Europe's largest minorities. In recent years crimes against the Gypsies of Eastern Europe and crimes committed by the Gypsies have soared. They often suffer assaults and are threatened economically. In an Eastern Europe no longer propped up by the Soviet economy, their low-level jobs were the first to disappear. In 1996 unemployment among them in some areas of Eastern Europe hovered around 95%.

Originally from India, Gypsies began migrating throughout the world as early as the 11th century. By 1996 the Gypsies of Eastern Europe were mostly settled in mud huts on the outskirts of villages, where they lived isolated lives.

With hate crimes against them mounting, combined with chronic unemployment and an endangered way of life, organization and ethnic unity have become increasingly urgent concerns of the Gypsies. Judit Horvath and György Stalter have spent years photographing the Gypsies of Hungary and Romania. Their pictorial account follows.

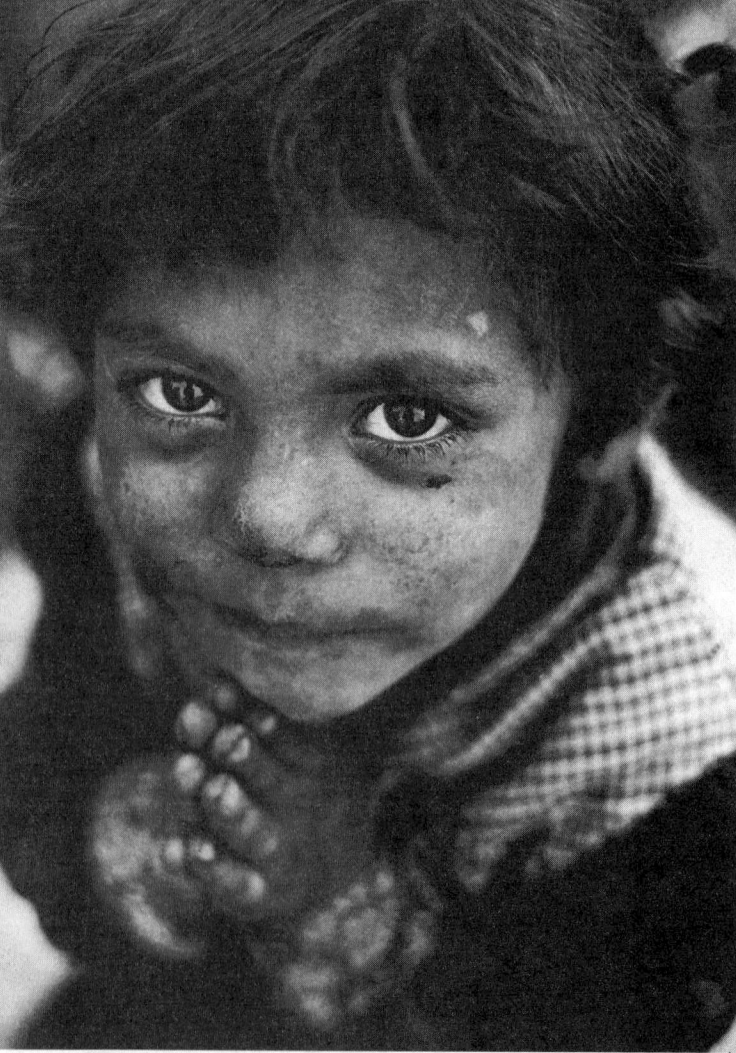

(continued from page 427)
by international lending organizations. The "Bokros package" had caused consternation in government circles, precipitated the resignation of several Cabinet ministers, and attracted public opposition. The proximate cause of his departure from office was a disagreement with Prime Minister Gyula Horn over Bokros's proposal to cut the social security deficit. Peter Medgyessy, head of the Hungarian Bank for Investment and Development, was given the finance portfolio and pledged to continue the austerity program, but he made little progress, and the economy stagnated further.

Imre Dunai, minister of industry and trade, resigned on August 15. A few weeks later a parliamentary commission endorsed accusations, first voiced in late 1995, that Dunai and his predecessor, Laszlo Pal, had been involved in a tangled influence-peddling scheme related to the repayment, partially in petroleum, of Russia's $850 million debt to Hungary. Dunai was replaced by Tamas Suchman, whose other responsibilities included overseeing privatization.

On October 6 Suchman too was sacked for his alleged mismanagement of the State Privatization and Holding Company, known as APV. During 1995 APV was responsible for bringing in over $3 billion in revenues to the state, largely from the sale of state-owned utilities. In May 1996 the company sold a majority share of a state-owned oil-drilling company under circumstances that were questionable enough to cause the dismissal of a top APV official, Attila Lascsik.

APV hired a consultant, Marta Tocsik, to negotiate with local governments on behalf of the company. The proper procedures were not followed when she was hired, however, and no formal contract was signed. Tocsik was reportedly paid $5.1 million for her services, a sum that many Hungarians, notably the Alliance of Free Democrats, the junior coalition partner, found excessive. In the event, Horn dismissed the entire APV board, along with Suchman.

Hungary's foreign policy initiatives in 1996 continued to focus on integrating the country with the rest of Europe and aggressively championing the rights of ethnic Magyars (Hungarians) in the diaspora. Hungary was admitted to the Organisation for Economic Co-operation and Development on March 29, and there was some progress toward the country's joining both the European Union and NATO.

An agreement with Slovakia, ratified by both governments by May 1996, fixed the common border and made provision for the protection of ethnic minorities in the two countries. Whatever good neighbourly relationship this may have engendered, however, threatened to be undone by the protocols of a June conference of Hungarian minorities abroad held in Budapest. The conference document mentioned "autonomy" of the Magyar minorities, a position that neither Slovakia nor Romania, which also had a large Magyar minority, was prepared to accept. Finally, in September and under some scrutiny from the Council of Europe, Horn and Romanian Prime Minister Nicolae Vacaroiu signed a document similar to the Hungarian-Slovak agreement.

Karoly Grosz, the last general secretary of the Hungarian Socialist Workers' Party and former prime minister, died in January. (*See* OBITUARIES.)   (EDITORS)

ICELAND

Iceland is an island republic in the North Atlantic Ocean, near the Arctic Circle. Area: 102,819 sq km (39,699 sq mi). Pop. (1996 est.): 270,000. Cap.: Reykjavík. Monetary unit: Icelandic króna, with (Oct. 11, 1996) a free rate of 67.12 krónur to U.S. $1 (105.73 krónur = £1 sterling). Presidents in 1996, Vigdís Finnbogadóttir and, from August 1, Ólafur Ragnar Grímsson; prime minister, Davíd Oddsson.

Iceland elected a new president on June 29, 1996. The winner was Ólafur Ragnar Grímsson, a member of the Althing (national legislature) and formerly professor of government at the University of Iceland and minister of finance and chairman of the left-wing People's Alliance. Grímsson won 41% of the vote in a four-way race.

The nation's economy in 1996 bounced back vigorously from its eight-year slump, which had been caused by limited fish catches, partly for conservation reasons. It was estimated that gross domestic product would increase 5½% in 1996 from the previous year, and in 1997 it was expected to rise another 2–3%. The upswing in growth was led by strong consumer and investment demand along with a considerable increase in exports. Iceland's unemployment fell and was expected to be about 4% in 1997. Inflation was forecast to remain in the 2–3% range.

Iceland was beginning to reap the dividends from its marine resource conservation policy of the past several years. There were signs of increased stocks of cod in the ocean, which permitted a relaxation of the previously stringent catch limits. The cod catch quota for the fishing year that began in September 1996 was increased from 155,-000 tons to 186,000 tons, and quotas for several other species were also increased.

The Swiss company Alusuisse-Lonza concluded an agreement with the Icelandic government to expand its aluminum plant from an annual production capacity of 100,-000 tons to 162,000 tons. This represented a $220 million investment and was expected to begin operation late in 1997.

Iceland engaged in three fishing disputes with other nations during the year. Icelandic vessels continued to fish in a disputed zone between the mainland of Norway and Svalbard archipelago, much to the annoyance of Norway and Russia. Iceland had a dispute with Norway, the Faroe Islands, and Russia over the herring catch in the area between Iceland and Norway. The third dispute concerned the shrimp catch off the coast of Canada in an area known as the Flemish Cap.

On November 5 massive flooding, caused by a volcanic eruption in October and subsequent glacial melting, destroyed roads and bridges and knocked out power and telephone lines. Damages were estimated at about $35 million.

                              (BJÖRN MATTHÍASSON)

INDIA

A federal republic of southern Asia and member of the Commonwealth, India is situated on a peninsula extending into the Indian Ocean, with the Arabian Sea to the west and the Bay of Bengal to the east. Area: 3,165,596 sq km (1,222,243 sq mi), including the Indian-administered portion of Jammu and Kashmir. Pop. (1996 est): 953 million, including Indian-administered Jammu and Kashmir. Cap.: New Delhi. Monetary unit: Indian rupee, with (Oct. 11, 1996) a free rate of Rs 35.65 to U.S. $1 (Rs 56.16 = £1 sterling). President in 1996, Shankar Dayal Sharma; prime ministers, P.V. Narasimha Rao until May 10, Atal Behari Vajpayee from May 16 until May 28, and, from June 1, H.D. Deve Gowda.

Domestic Affairs. An eventful but disappointing year, 1996 was marked by elections to the Lok Sabha (House of the People) and several state assemblies. They resulted in political confusion, the growth of fundamentalist religious and caste-based political parties, the arraignments of leaders of several political parties for corruption, and the prosecution of former prime minister P.V. Narasimha Rao for cheating and bribery. The only consolations were that economic liberalization made some progress, secessionist terrorism declined in Punjab and Jammu and Kashmir, and elections could be held in Jammu and Kashmir after six years of central rule.

The 11th general election to the 543-member Lok Sabha was held in April and May. Of the 592.6 million eligible voters, 57.94% went to the polls. No party secured a clear majority. The Congress (I) government led by Rao was voted out of office, with its strength falling from 260 to 140 seats and its share of the vote down from 36.6% to 29.77%. The right-wing Hindu fundamentalist Bharatiya Janata Party (BJP) won 161 seats (23.5% of the vote), up from 113, and its allies, Shiv Sena, Samata Party, and the Haryana Vikas Party, picked up another 26. The tally of the other prominent parties was: Janata Dal (JD) 46, Communist Party of India (Marxist) (CPI-M) 32, Tamil Maanila Congress (TMC) 20, Dravida Munnetra Kazhagam (DMK) 17, Samajwadi Party (SP) 17, Telugu Desam (TDP) 16, Communist Party of India (CPI) 12, Bahujan Samaj Party 11, Akali Dal 8, and Asom Gana Parishad (AGP) 5.

By virtue of heading the largest party, Atal Behari Vajpayee of the BJP was sworn in as prime minister on May 16, along with 10 other ministers. He resigned on May 28, unsure of winning a vote of confidence in the Lok Sabha; all other parties were attacking the Hindu fundamentalist policies of the BJP and its allies, holding them responsible for the destruction of a historical Muslim mosque in Ayodhya in 1992.

A hastily cobbled coalition of 13 moderate-to-left regional and caste-based parties, termed the United Front (UF), which included the JD, CPI-M, TMC, DMK, SP, TDP, CPI, and AGP, formed a new government on June 1. With the intention of keeping the BJP and its allies away from power, Congress (I) promised to support the UF government from outside in exchange for continuation of most of its policies, especially those concerning the economy.

The Janata Dal's H.D. Deve Gowda, until then chief minister of Karnataka, was sworn in as the new prime minister. The key portfolios of home, finance, defense, and external affairs went, respectively, to the CPI's Indrajit Gupta, the TMC's Palaniappan Chidambaram, the SP's Mulayam Singh

Yadav, and the JD's Inder Kumar Gujral. The UF announced a "Common Minimum Programme" emphasizing its commitment to secularism and promising the continuation of economic reforms that were initiated by Congress (I), as well as greater autonomy for states, increased assistance to farmers and lower-class workers, and reserved seats in legislatures for women.

The UF government held elections to the Jammu and Kashmir assembly in September–October. The election was seen as a rebuff to Kashmir secessionists. The National Conference won 57 out of 87 seats, and Farooq Abdullah became chief minister. He announced that the National Conference would join the UF.

Prime Minister Gowda promised a separate state of Uttarakhand to be formed with the sub-Himalayan districts of Uttar Pradesh. The UF government introduced a bill to amend the constitution to reserve one-third of the seats in the Lok Sabha and the state assemblies for women, another bill to appoint a *Lok Pal* (ombudsman) to investigate charges of corruption against government ministers (including former prime minister Rao), a commercial arbitration and conciliation bill in accordance with commitments made to the UN Commission on International Trade Law, and a bill to establish an independent Telecom Regulatory Authority.

Corruption was among the nation's principal concerns. Several ministers of the Rao government, as well as leaders of other parties and some state governors, were named by a businessman, S.K. Jain, as having received large sums of money from him.

A London-based, Indian-born businessman, Lakhubhai Pathak, claimed that he had paid $100,000 in 1983 to an influential sadhu (Hindu ascetic), Chandraswami (said to be Rao's religious mentor), as consideration to obtain an export order after Rao had promised Pathak that "your work will be done." The Central Bureau of Investigation (CBI) arrested Chandraswami and cited Rao as coaccused. The CBI also accused Rao, along with Chandraswami and five others, of having conspired in 1989 to embarrass Vishwanath Pratap Singh (who later became prime minister) by forging documents to indicate that Singh's son had an illegal bank account in St. Kitts. The CBI further accused Rao of having given a bribe of Rs 40 million to four members of Parliament belonging to the Jharkand Mukti Morcha for voting with his government on a no-confidence motion in 1993. The CBI accused Rao's son, Prabhakar Rao, of being part of a fraudulent deal worth Rs 1,330,-000,000 with a Turkish company, Karsan, for a supply of urea. The former prime minister gave up his presidency of Congress (I) in September and was succeeded by Sitaram Kesri, its treasurer. Rao resigned from his last party post in December.

In August a Delhi judge sentenced 89 persons to five years in prison and 2 to life imprisonment for their part in the anti-Sikh riots in Delhi in 1984 following the assassination of former prime minister Indira Gandhi by her Sikh bodyguards. A former Congress (I) minister, H.K.L. Bhagat, was being tried for having instigated the anti-Sikh rioters.

Following the change of name of Bombay to Mumbai in 1995, the name of Madras was changed to Chennai. In a midair collision on November 12 between Saudi Arabian and Kazakstan airliners, 351 people were killed, of whom 231 were Indians. In the first week of November, a cyclone ravaged the east coast of Andhra Pradesh, killing more than 1,000 people, damaging 400,000 houses, and causing losses estimated at Rs 50 billion. At year's end a bomb derailed a New Delhi-bound express train in Assam. As many as 300 people were feared killed.

The Economy. Because of the approaching general elections, the Rao government presented only an interim budget in February. The regular budget was presented on July 22 by P. Chidambaram of the UF government. Among its main features were decreases in income taxes and in the surcharge on companies, reductions in customs and excise duties, increases in subsidies for food and fertilizers, and additions to the list of industries eligible for automatic approval of foreign equity up to 51%.

Gross domestic product grew 7% in 1995–96, with industrial output increasing 11.7%. Exports increased by 20.8% and im-

A pipeline carrying water to wealthy neighbourhoods of Bombay (Mumbai) runs through one of the city's shantytowns. Bombay continued to attract people from throughout India in search of a better life, even though about one-half of its population lived in slums.

ports by 24.5%. Foreign exchange reserves were $17.9 billion in August. The inflation rate, which had dipped to a 10-year low of 4.2% in April, rose to 6.25% at the end of September.

Foreign Affairs. India opposed the draft of the UN Comprehensive Test Ban Treaty on the grounds that it contained no timetable for the elimination of nuclear stockpiles, did not prevent nonexplosive testing, and did not take care of India's security concerns and that the provisions with regard to inspection violated accepted norms of sovereignty. When the UN General Assembly adopted the treaty in September, India voted against the motion.

The victory of the Taliban forces in Afghanistan was viewed with reservation because of the possible repercussions on the improving situation in Kashmir. India also deplored the Pakistani prime minister's allegation that the elections in Jammu and Kashmir had been stage-managed.

Pres. Jiang Zemin of China visited India in November. An agreement was signed providing for mutual reductions of arms and troops along the India-China border.

(H.Y. SHARADA PRASAD)

INDONESIA

A republic of Southeast Asia, Indonesia consists of the major islands of Sumatra, Java, Kalimantan (Indonesian Borneo), Celebes (Indonesian: Sulawesi), and Irian Jaya (West New Guinea) and more than 13,000 smaller islands and islets. Area: 1,919,317 sq km (741,052 sq mi). Pop. (1996 est.): 198,189,000. Cap.: Jakarta. Monetary unit: rupiah, with (Oct. 11, 1996) a free rate of 2,321 rupiah to U.S. $1 (3,656 rupiah = £1 sterling). President in 1996, Suharto.

During 1996, for the first time, Indonesians began to question whether President Suharto's grip on power was finally slipping after 30 years of near-absolute rule. Riots in Jakarta in late July shook the country. According to an independent human rights commission, five people were killed and some 150 wounded. A prominent independent labour leader, Muchtar Pakpahan, and nine others were charged with subversion in December. The street violence was just one indication of growing uncertainty on several fronts. In October and again in December Muslim rioters burned Christian churches, as well as hotels, banks, automobiles, and shops owned by members of the ethnic Chinese minority, many of them Christian.

There was increasing concern over the 75-year-old president's health, especially when he made a trip to Germany in July for a medical checkup. Should Suharto not nominate himself for president again when his term ended in 1998, there was no obvious successor. Moreover, rifts were evident in the military, the main pillar of power in the country. In addition, a Roman Catholic bishop in East Timor and an activist living in exile in Australia were awarded the Nobel Prize for Peace in October for striving to end violence in the former Portuguese colony that Indonesia invaded and annexed in the 1970s. The Nobel Committee condemned the Indonesian government for "systematically oppressing the people" of East Timor. (*See* NOBEL PRIZES.)

Elsewhere in the vast archipelago, activist groups grew bolder in their criticism of Indonesia's closed political system and uneven development. The government permitted only two opposition political parties, which had no hope of voting Suharto out of office. Of some 2.3 million workers entering the job market each year, only about 300,000 could find full-time employment. Resentment over corruption and the ever-expanding business empires of Suharto's family and cronies continued to deepen.

The July riots were sparked by a police-backed raid on the headquarters of the Indonesian Democratic Party in Jakarta. Supporters of Megawati Sukarnoputri—daughter of Sukarno, Indonesia's still-popular first president—were occupying the building to protest the government's role in her ouster as party head in June. In regard to Megawati's dismissal, the court ruled that it had no jurisdiction over an internal party matter.

With parliamentary elections scheduled for June 1997, many activists believed it was time to push for change. They demanded more representative government, a retreat by the military from its central position in politics, a limit of two presidential terms, and even Suharto's departure. In early July some 20,000 striking factory labourers in Surabaya marched to protest low wages and unhealthy working conditions.

Suharto apparently worried that activists could upset political stability. On September 14 he scolded 300 of the country's business elite for neglecting the poor. He warned the assembled tycoons that if they did not "voluntarily" contribute 2% of their companies' after-tax profits to the poor, they could face the taxman's scrutiny.

Complaints in corporate boardrooms grew louder over such government actions as the exceptional tax breaks given to Suharto's son Hutomo Mandala Putra to build Indonesia's own national automobile. Suharto also seemed less capable of controlling his top military officers.

Despite political uncertainties, the economy continued to boom at a 7.5% growth rate in 1996. Inflation dropped to 7.4% in August from a peak of over 10% in January. Indonesia's trade surplus narrowed during 1996, however, and some predicted the country could be running monthly trade deficits by the end of the year. Indonesia was hard hit by slumps in key export sectors, such as plywood and textiles. The current-account deficit was expected to be 4% of gross domestic product.

The value of approved foreign investment in Indonesia was expected to fall to $27 billion, about 30% below the previous year, although the number of projects was expected to increase. The investment minister blamed the drop in value on the fact that approved foreign investments in 1995 included eight large projects, mainly in the petrochemicals sector.   (SUSAN BERFIELD)

IRAN

The Islamic Republic of Iran is situated in southwestern Asia on the Caspian and Arabian seas and the Persian Gulf. Area: 1,648,000 sq km (636,296 sq mi). Pop. (est., excluding about 1.4 million Afghan refugees and 600,000 Iraqi refugees): 62,231,000. Cap.: Tehran. Monetary unit: Iranian rial, with (Oct. 11, 1996) a fixed rate of 3,000 rials to U.S. $1 (4,726 rials = £1 sterling). *Rahbar* (spiritual leader) in 1996, Ayatollah Sayyed Ali Khamenei; president, Hojatolislam Ali Akbar Hashemi Rafsanjani.

The division between the progressive and the Islamic hard-line groups within the government of Iran grew steadily during 1996. The rift was heightened by a personal clash that adversely affected relations between the nation's spiritual leader, Ayatollah Sayyed Ali Khamenei, and the president, Hojatolislam Ali Akbar Hashemi Rafsanjani. In January a war of words erupted in which the president, backed by 14 members of the Cabinet, the mayor of Tehran, and the central bank governor, called for the modernization of Iran and greater prosperity. Followers of Khamenei in response demanded a rejection of material gain and a greater adherence to Islamic ideals.

At the political level the same theme was pursued in the election campaign for the national legislature, the first round of which took place on March 8. The election ended the previous Islamic consensus between moderates and the right wing and caused the emergence of two quite distinct sets of policies and approved candidates. Results of the first round, during which more than 70% of the voters went to the polls, were inconclusive, with only 139 of the 270 seats decided. The results of a second round on April 19 seemed to diminish the power of the right wing and offer opportunity for a small independent secular faction to have a voice in the government.

On June 2 an important vote in the legislature for the appointment of speaker brought victory to Ali Akbar Nateq-Nuri, leader of the right-wing Jame-e Rohaniyat-e Mobarez (JRM). The moderates were thus defeated in the legislature and then lost the initiative in national politics. Islamic extremist groups became increasingly active, notably Ansar-e Hizbollah, dedicated to the eradication of non-Islamic elements in society. A major campaign against proponents of secular and intellectual reforms was launched, supported by Khamenei and the JRM. Meanwhile, Rafsanjani's political future became uncertain when proposals for constitutional change to permit him to run for a third term in the July 1997 presidential elections were rejected; this further weakened the position of the moderates.

In July the U.S. introduced new sanctions against Iran to deter its alleged participation in international terrorism. The sanctions provided that third-party states, companies, and individuals must neither contribute to Iran's chemical, biological, or nuclear weapons capacity nor aid in the development of Iran's oil industry. Investment in Iran in those areas must not exceed $40 million either singly or in aggregate during any 12-month period. Those breaking U.S. sanctions may be punished by export and import embargoes, the withholding of U.S. loans, and the exclusion from financial dealings in the U.S. The sanctions, despite meeting formidable international opposition, further institutionalized Iran's position as a pariah state.

Iran's relations with its neighbours were unsettled and erratic. In April four Turkish diplomats were expelled, but in August Iran came to an agreement with Turkey for construction of a $23 billion pipeline to

Kurdish refugees hold photographs of family members killed in the fighting in Iraq. In August, at the invitation of one Kurdish faction, Iraqi Pres. Saddam Hussein intervened against its rival, effectively nullifying the U.S. policy of protecting the Kurds from attacks by the Iraqi army.

September 3 announced a northward extension of the southern no-fly zone over Iraq from latitude 32° N to latitutde 33° N. This act further weakened Iraq's sovereignty in its southern region. Hussein denounced this move and rejected the no-fly zones. The U.S. then launched cruise missiles on military targets in the new no-fly zone, and Iraq fired missiles on what it claimed were U.S. planes patrolling the extended zone. On September 13 Iraq reversed its position, announcing that it would temporarily suspend attacks on U.S. or coalition aircraft in the zone, and the crisis died down.

This conflict led to the postponement of UN resolution 986 ("oil for food"), which Iraq had previously accepted on May 20 after numerous earlier rejections. This resolution, finally implemented in December 1996, permitted a partial lifting of the UN-imposed oil embargo by allowing Iraq to sell $2 billion in oil every six months to buy food and medicine for the Iraqi people, under strict control of the UN. Oil began to be pumped in December, but full sanctions remained in effect.   (LOUAY BAHRY)

IRELAND

The republic of Ireland, separated from Great Britain by the North Channel, the Irish Sea, and St. George's Channel, shares its island with Northern Ireland to the northeast. Area: 70,285 sq km (27,137 sq mi). Pop. (1996 est.): 3,599,000. Cap.: Dublin. Monetary unit: Irish pound (punt), with (Oct. 11, 1996) a free rate of £Ir 0.62 to U.S. $1 (£Ir 0.98 = £1 sterling). President in 1996, Mary Robinson; prime minister, John Bruton.

Political life in Ireland was dominated throughout 1996 by efforts to sustain the faltering peace process in Northern Ireland. The progress made during the previous year was abruptly terminated in February by the ending of the Provisional Irish Republican Army (IRA) cease-fire and by the detonation of a bomb at Canary Wharf in London's Docklands. In a struggle to reinstate the process, both Irish Prime Minister John Bruton's government and the British under Prime Minister John Major tried to set dates for all-party talks. The majority Unionist parties (which favoured the continued unification of Northern Ireland and Great Britain) objected to the talks, however, and interminable meetings failed to break a deadlock, principally over the decommissioning of arms by the IRA and other paramilitary organizations. Further violence followed in Manchester, Eng., and in County Limerick, with the promise of more violence implicit in the discovery of a bomb factory in County Laoighis. In October an IRA bomb attack on the British army base in Lisburn, N. Ire., restored the full cycle of violence.

This left the Irish government with their overall peace strategy in ruins. There was all-party consent in the republic that Sinn Fein, the political wing of the IRA, would be excluded from talks while IRA violence continued. Despite a working agreement on talks between the Ulster Unionists and Northern Ireland's Social Democratic and Labour Party (which sought reunification with Ireland), all political parties in the republic remained convinced that talks without Sinn Fein, the political party allied with

supply natural gas. New agreements signed in December were expected to double trade between Iran and Turkey. Iran was accused in June of backing a plot by Shi'ite Muslims to overthrow the government of Bahrain, a charge that it denied. Similarly, allegations were made in March by U.S. Secretary of State Warren Christopher that Iran actively supported Hamas and Hezbollah terrorism against Israel. Iranian-backed Patriotic Union of Kurdistan (PUK) forces in Iraq were driven toward the Iranian border by the Kurdistan Democratic Party with armoured support from the Iraqi army in late August. The PUK was severely mauled, and Iran had to cope with a new surge of Kurdish refugees into its territory. Iran nonetheless condemned foreign intervention in Iraq and sought to minimize its involvement in the conflict between the U.S. and Iraq.   (KEITH S. MCLACHLAN)

IRAQ

A republic of southwestern Asia, Iraq has a short coastline on the Persian Gulf. Area: 435,052 sq km (167,975 sq mi). Pop. (1996 est.): 21,422,000. Cap.: Baghdad. Monetary unit: Iraqi dinar, with (Oct. 11, 1996) an exchange bureau rate of 1,000 dinars to U.S. $1 (1,575 dinars = £1 sterling). President and prime minister in 1996, Saddam Hussein.

On Feb. 20, 1996, two sons-in-law of Pres. Saddam Hussein, who had been living in Jordan since their defection in August 1995, returned to Baghdad after an official offer of pardon. Three days later the official Iraqi media announced their deaths in a shootout with members of their extended family. The perpetrators stated they were avenging the dishonour brought on their clan by the defectors. On December 12 Hussein's son Uday was wounded in an assassination attempt in Baghdad.

On March 24 the country held elections for 220 seats in the National Assembly. The Assembly had little real power, however, as effective control remained in the hands of Hussein and the Revolutionary Command Council (RCC). The election resulted in the Ba'thists' gaining 160 seats; the remainder went to "independent" candidates.

The Kurdistan Democratic Party (KDP), led by Mas'ud al-Barzani, and the Patriotic Union of Kurdistan (PUK), headed by Jalal at-Talabani, continued their feud that had begun in 1994. During the year Turkish and Iranian forces penetrated several times into the Iraqi Kurdish area to pursue Turkish and Iranian Kurdish rebels who staged hit-and-run operations against Turkey and Iran, respectively, from bases inside Iraq.

Events in northern Iraq took a dramatic turn for the worse on August 22. The KDP, fearing an accord between Iran and the PUK, formed an alliance with Hussein. On August 31, apparently responding to an appeal from Barzani, the Iraqi government seized the Kurdish city of Irbil. After a short but bloody purge of Hussein's enemies in Irbil, Iraq withdrew its forces from the city, leaving its administration to its new ally, Barzani. On September 9 Barzani pushed his Kurdish troops farther south and without much bloodshed occupied the city of As-Sulaymaniyah, a stronghold of Talabani and the rival PUK. Hussein then lifted a trade and travel ban that had separated the north from the rest of the country. On October 23 efforts sponsored by the U.S. to mediate the conflict between the KDP and the PUK achieved a shaky cease-fire.

The events of August through October, together with the entente between Barzani and Hussein, opened the door to the penetration of the Iraqi government forces into the northern Kurdish areas and put an end to the presence in the north of the Iraqi National Council, an umbrella opposition group composed of Sunni and Shi'ite Muslims and Kurds.

The capture of Irbil by Iraqi forces triggered a strong response from the United States, which saw the move as a violation of the cease-fire accord signed after the 1991 Persian Gulf War. The U.S. government on

the IRA, would make only limited progress and that the only route forward depended on a permanent IRA cease-fire.

The Irish economy performed well during the year, with an unprecedented boom in consumer spending and confident predictions that disposable incomes would continue to rise, boosted by declining tax rates and low inflation, which was expected to remain below 2%. Despite substantial economic growth and impressive job creation, unemployment remained stubbornly high, at an estimated 12.25%. The agricultural sector was severely affected by the discovery of bovine spongiform encephalopathy ("mad cow" disease), with both home and export markets, especially to the Middle East and Russia, badly affected. Taxpayers were faced with a penalty of £Ir 50 million from the European Commission for infringement of rules governing the beef trade.

The activities of organized gangs of criminals who were making large sums of money from illicit drug dealing caused much public concern. This culminated in June with the contract killing of Veronica Guerin, an investigative journalist who had achieved a high profile with her courageous probings into the activities of major criminals. Public outrage and condemnation of the murder led the government to introduce a £Ir 53.9 million anticrime package in July. A proposal to tighten up the bail laws was decisively approved in a referendum in November.

During Ireland's six-month presidency of the European Union, which began in July, Bruton highlighted the two major planks in his program: an international campaign against drugs and crime, and procedures to reduce the number of long-term unemployed.

The minister for health established a judicial tribunal in November to investigate the political, administrative, and medical circumstances surrounding the contamination of blood and blood products in the Irish Blood Transfusion Service. This resulted from the tragic circumstances in which 1,600 women contracted the hepatitis C virus from contaminated immunoglobulin. It was widely regarded as the most serious scandal ever to have hit the health service.

One of the republic's most celebrated citizens during the year was Michelle Smith from Rathcoole, who won three gold medals and one bronze medal in swimming at the Olympic Games in Atlanta, Ga., which ensured her place in the history books and in the hearts of the Irish people. (*See* BIOGRAPHIES.)   (MAVIS ARNOLD)

See also *United Kingdom.*

ISRAEL

A republic of southwestern Asia, Israel is situated on the Mediterranean Sea. Area: 20,320 sq km (7,846 sq mi), not including territory occupied in the June 1967 war. Pop. (1996 est.): 5,481,000. Cap.: Jerusalem (but *see* Israel table in *World Data* section). Monetary unit: New (Israeli) sheqel, with (Oct. 11, 1996) a free rate of 3.19 sheqalim to U.S. $1 (5.03 sheqalim = £1 sterling). President in 1996, Ezer Weizman; prime ministers, Shimon Peres (acting) and, from June 18, Benjamin Netanyahu.

In 1996 Israel experienced a change of government and a change of policy that threatened to unhinge the already shaky Middle East peace process. Elected prime minister in late May, the right-wing Likud leader Benjamin Netanyahu (*see* BIOGRAPHIES) insisted on renegotiating an agreement for the redeployment of Israeli forces in the West Bank town of Hebron, lifted the freeze on building by Jewish settlers, and declared that his government was no longer bound by the principle of "land for peace" that had been a basis of Middle East peacemaking. Netanyahu's new policies exacerbated relations with the Palestinians, but at the year's end it appeared that he had reached an agreement with Palestine Liberation Organization leader Yasir Arafat for a withdrawal of Israeli troops from most of Hebron.

In their first democratic elections, over 750,000 Palestinians in the West Bank and Gaza voted on January 20 to elect an 88-member Legislative Council and a president. The outcome was an overwhelming victory for Arafat, who was elected president with 88.1% of the popular vote and whose Fatah supporters won more than 60 seats on the Council. His close confidant, Ahmed Qurie (Abu Ala), one of the main Palestinian negotiators of the Oslo peace deal with Israel, was elected speaker.

Almost immediately after the election, things started to go wrong for the Palestinians, the peace process, and the incumbent Labor Party government in Israel. In early January Israeli agents had assassinated Yahya Ayyash, the fundamentalist Palestinian leader known as "the engineer" for his bomb-making expertise. Retaliation by the Hamas and Islamic Jihad fundamentalists was devastating. A spate of suicide bombings in late February and early March left more than 50 Israelis dead and led many to question the rationale behind the peacemaking with the Palestinians. Overnight, Netanyahu gained some 20% in the race against acting prime minister Shimon Peres.

In the wake of the bombings, Israel launched a determined crackdown against the fundamentalists, sealing off the Palestinian areas from Israel proper and imposing an internal closure on 465 Palestinian communities as Israeli security forces conducted house-to-house searches. Warned by the Israelis that continued violence could subvert the entire peace process, Arafat also clamped down on the fundamentalists.

Israel, Egypt, and the U.S. took the lead in coordinating international efforts to curb the terror and save the peace process. On March 13 an international antiterrorism conference, held at the Egyptian resort town of Sharm el-Sheikh, was attended by world leaders, including 14 Arab delegations, who lined up in unprecedented solidarity with Israel and against terrorism. Of the Arab states invited, only Syria and Lebanon stayed away. U.S. Pres. Bill Clinton went on to Israel and pledged a $100 million antiterrorist package, including new state-of-the-art explosive detectors.

Many observers saw the conference and the Clinton visit as thinly veiled attempts to boost Peres's reelection prospects. The impact of the bombings and a lacklustre campaign by Labor paved the way for a stunning upset at the polls on May 29. On election day, blanket support for Netanyahu from religious Jews opposed to Labor's

perceived secularism and Peres's perceived readiness to contemplate a Palestinian state that would include part of the "Holy Land" of Israel finally turned the tables, and in Israel's first-ever direct election of the prime minister, Netanyahu edged Peres by less than 1% of the popular vote.

The fierce ideological debates and growing fragmentation of Israeli society highlighted in November 1995 by the assassination of Prime Minister Yitzhak Rabin, were reflected in the strong election showing by small ideological and ethnic parties in the new 120-member Knesset (parliament). (For detailed election results, see *Political Parties,* above.)

Netanyahu's central election slogan had been "peace with security," with the emphasis on security. The consternation his promise of a tougher line caused on the Palestinian side was compounded by his initial refusal to meet Arafat face to face and by the severe economic hardship caused by the ongoing internal closure, which had prevented thousands of Palestinians from going to their jobs in Israel.

When in late September Netanyahu unilaterally opened the entrance to a 2,000-year-old tunnel that passed near the al-Aqsa Mosque and led to a Muslim quarter in East Jerusalem, the simmering unrest erupted into full-scale violence. In the ultimate malfunction of the Oslo process, Palestinian police and Israeli soldiers, who only days before had been conducting joint patrols, fired at each other. Fifteen soldiers and more than 60 Palestinians died before calm was restored.

To stop the process from breaking down altogether, Clinton summoned Netanyahu, Arafat, and Jordan's King Hussein to Washington. At the early October summit, Netanyahu warmly shook Arafat's hand and reaffirmed Israel's commitment to the peace process.

The government acted against Jewish extremists it believed were planning to provoke the Palestinians or to assassinate leading members of the right-wing government they had helped to elect and whom they were now accusing of betrayal. On March 27 Yigal Amir, the right-wing religious zealot who had gunned down Rabin, had been sentenced to life imprisonment for the assassination and an additional six years for wounding one of Rabin's bodyguards.

Relations between Israel and Syria deteriorated rapidly after the Netanyahu victory, and there was tension with Jordan and Egypt. Less than a week after Netanyahu established his new right-wing government in mid-June, the Arabs held an emergency summit in Cairo and demanded reaffirmation of the principle of "land for peace."

In late August Syrian troop movements in Lebanon caused alarm in Israel, and by October Israeli intelligence officials were, for the first time in years, speaking openly of the possibility of war. Despite a general mood of budgetary austerity, the army demanded and got special allocations to meet the new threat.

The year in regard to relations with Syria had begun very differently, with Peres pushing hard for an early peace deal. He had become prime minister in the wake of the Rabin assassination, and, although urged by close advisers to call an immediate election, he hoped first to consolidate his leadership position through a major breakthrough

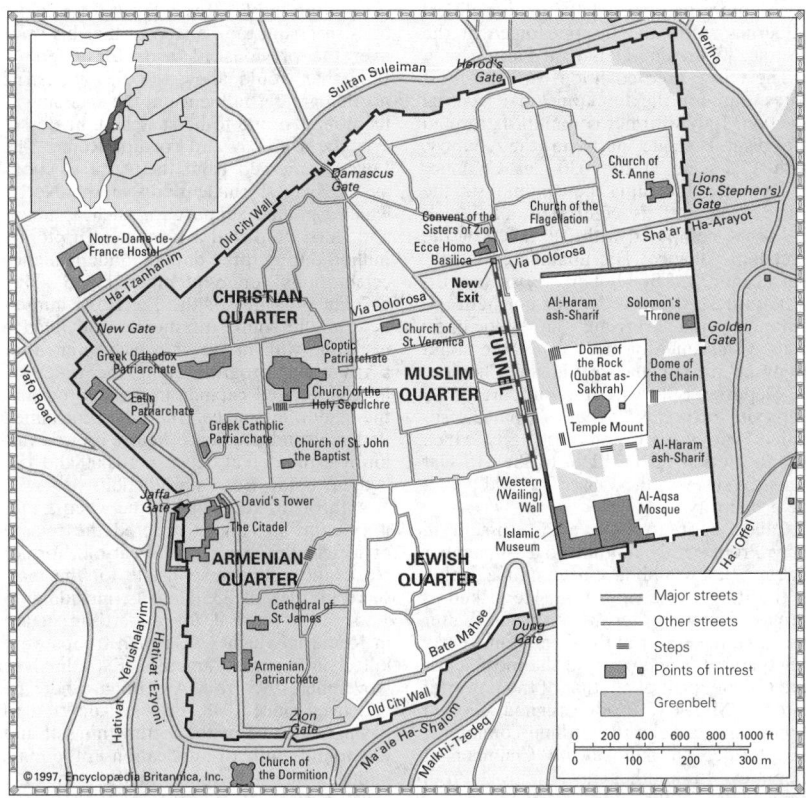

Peres responded by unleashing a major military action. For 17 days Israeli air force and artillery units pounded Hezbollah positions and Lebanese strategic installations. There was an international outcry when Israeli gunners inadvertently hit a UN post at Qana, Leb., killing some 100 Shi'ite refugees who had taken shelter there.

After nearly three weeks of fighting, U.S. Secretary of State Warren Christopher brokered a new cease-fire agreement, which prohibited attacks on civilians as well as strikes across the border into Israel. It differed only marginally from the agreement brokered by the U.S. after Israel's almost identical operation in July 1993 and did not put a stop to the low-level ongoing fighting in southern Lebanon.

Major developments in Israeli relations with Turkey in 1996 also affected Israeli-Syrian relations. In February Israel and Turkey concluded a secret agreement on military cooperation, which included Israeli air force training flights over Turkish territory close to the Syrian and Iraqi borders. In March Turkish Pres. Suleyman Demirel underlined the burgeoning relationship by visiting Israel. Syrian fears were largely allayed when the veteran Islamist leader Necmettin Erbakan (*see* BIOGRAPHIES) took over as prime minister of Turkey in late June and put ties with Israel on the back burner.

The slowdown in the peace process had an adverse effect on foreign investment. It was mostly the economy's structural problems, however, that led to a dramatic drop in economic growth, down from 7% in 1995 to 4%, with the 1997 forecast only 2%. Netanyahu's panacea was privatization, but he was slow in getting it started. He also faced strong internal opposition to plans for essential budget cuts. Inflation was held

with Syria. In February, when Syrian Pres. Hafez al-Assad indicated he would meet the Israeli leader only *after* a peace deal had been struck, Peres called an early election for May.

In early April Syrian and Iranian-backed Hezbollah fighters fired Katyusha rockets at Israeli border towns and villages. Accused of weakness in fighting terror (and in the midst of a tough election campaign),

Mourners light candles in memory of 18 people killed in the terrorist bombing of a commuter bus in Jerusalem on March 3. Several terrorist attacks in Israel early in the year were considered partly responsible for the defeat of the Labor Party and Shimon Peres in the May 29 elections.

in check at about 10% by soaring interest rates, which kept the sheqel artificially high against the dollar and hurt exports, which grew by under 4%, compared with 8.5% in 1995.

In 1996 the influx of foreign workers into Israel to take over jobs from Palestinians prevented from working by the closures took on mammoth proportions. By the year's end, estimates ranged from 200,000 to 250,000 such workers, over half of whom were in the country illegally. Government efforts to expel them were ineffectual, and a major social problem loomed.

(LESLIE D. SUSSER)

ITALY

A republic of southern Europe, Italy occupies the Apennine Peninsula and extends northward into the Alps; it also includes Sicily, Sardinia, and a number of smaller islands in the Mediterranean Sea. Area: 301,323 sq km (116,341 sq mi). Pop. (1996 est.): 57.5 million. Cap.: Rome. Monetary unit: Italian lira, with (Oct. 11, 1996) a free rate of 1,523 lire to U.S. $1 (2,399 lire = £1 sterling). President in 1996, Oscar Luigi Scalfaro; prime ministers, Lamberto Dini until January 11 and, from May 16, Romano Prodi.

Italy in 1996 was ruled by a government dominated by the left wing for the first time since the June 1946 proclamation of the Italian Republic. Other significant events during the year included the trial of a former Nazi officer accused of war crimes and the capture of a major Mafia boss.

Two events led to the new government's emergence following elections in April. The first was the resignation in January of a one-year-old, intentionally stopgap Cabinet of nonpoliticians under Lamberto Dini, a former executive at the Bank of Italy. Second was the failure the next month of a designated successor, Antonio Maccanico, to garner political support for a new team that would have tackled constitutional reform as a prelude to new elections.

Pres. Oscar Luigi Scalfaro thus dissolved the national legislature in February, kicking off a lengthy election campaign that was contested, essentially, by large centre-left and right-wing coalitions. On the right was the so-called Alliance for Freedom, led by business tycoon and media magnate Silvio Berlusconi, resounding winner of elections in 1994. The Alliance included Berlusconi's own Forza Italia ("Go Italy") movement, largely run by his business underlings, and the National Alliance (AN) of Gianfranco Fini, described by its enemies as neofascist. The rival camp, which called itself the "Olive Tree" ("L'Ulivo"), was dominated by Italy's former communists in the Democratic Party of the Left (PDS), though it included small centre parties and was led by a noncommunist, Romano Prodi, a centrist economics professor from the University of Bologna who had once headed the Institute for Industrial Reconstruction, a large state holding company.

Though Berlusconi's side claimed that it stood for a reduced presence of government in Italians' lives and the Olive Tree pledged both to retain social services and to curb the country's enormous national debt, both formations were out to capture voters in the centre of the political spectrum.

Such voters had been left in the political wilderness after the disappearance of the disgraced Christian Democrat Party.

The Olive Tree coalition won the most votes, and for the first time in a general election, Italy's former communists formed the biggest single party in the country, with 172 seats in the 630-seat Chamber of Deputies. Including the communists, the Olive Tree and its centre-left allies won 284 seats, compared with 246 taken by the Freedom Alliance. The unaffiliated Northern League, led by Umberto Bossi (see BIOGRAPHIES), which called for northern autonomy, won a surprisingly large bloc of 59 seats. Consequently, the Olive Tree could enjoy an overall majority in the Chamber of Deputies only with the support of 35 old-style "orthodox" deputies from the so-called Refounded Communist Party, which was to the left of the PDS. In the 315-seat Senate, however, the Olive Tree did gain a clear majority.

Called upon to form a government in May, Prodi swiftly announced a 20-member Cabinet that would have been unimaginable in the Italy of the Cold War. He picked as deputy prime minister, for instance, Walter Veltroni, the editor of the Communist Party newspaper *L'Unità*. And to the most sensitive Cabinet post of all, that of the powerful Interior Ministry, Prodi assigned Giorgio Napolitano, a veteran hardline communist and former speaker of the Chamber of Deputies. In another novel move, Prodi handed the Public Works Ministry to Antonio Di Pietro, the combative magistrate who had spear-headed in Milan the so-called Clean Hands anticorruption drive launched in 1992 that brought down Italy's old regime. Di Pietro took up his post after clearing himself of nine charges of extortion and "abuse of office" leveled against him by rival magistrates, but in November he resigned because he had become the target of a bribe inquiry.

At the end of May, Prodi's government, with the help of the Refounded Communist Party, won a vote of confidence in the Chamber of Deputies with 322 votes in its favour and 299 against. "We must learn to do obvious things," Prodi told the House, "such as making sure the civil service works and that the post arrives in time."

In regional elections in Sicily in June, held under the proportional system, the PDS and "Refoundation" lost to the Freedom Alliance, but its Forza Italia component lost half of the support it had won in 1994, dropping its share of the vote from 33% to 17%. The AN picked up 14%.

Subjected to filibustering in the legislature by Berlusconi's Alliance, and at times held to ransom by the Refounded Communists, Prodi's government fought above all to enable Italy, through severe spending cuts and economic rigour, to qualify for membership in the European Monetary Union, which was scheduled to come into existence in 1999. In November Prodi announced that Italy was seeking approval from European officials for the lira to reenter the European exchange rate mechanism. What best qualified for political originality during the year, however, was a scheme to have one part of Italy break away from the rest. Its author was the unpredictable, gravel-voiced Bossi, who announced on September 15 a proclamation of independence from Italy of "Padania," a big, ill-defined new state

centred on the Po River. His call for Padania's secession took a step farther his drive over the previous 12 years for a federal Italy that would allow the rich industrial north a greater influence in the spending of its money, prone to be snatched, in Bossi's eyes, by a greedy and corrupt Rome. The League emerged from the April elections as the biggest single party in the North, which signified support for such a stance, and Bossi predicted a turnout of up to 1.5 million during three days of "independence celebrations" on September 13–15 along 652 km (404 mi) of the Po. Bossi himself flew to the source of the Po and filled a test tube with its water, which later, after a triumphal progress along the waterway in a motorized catamaran, he poured into the lagoon in Venice. There he proclaimed Padania's independence before crowds variously estimated at between 10,000 and 18,000, far below Bossi's prediction.

A furor broke out in Rome when a military court in August ordered the release of Erich Priebke, an 83-year-old former Nazi officer held responsible for the massacre in 1944 of 335 Italians, including 75 Jews, as a reprisal for a partisan action in Rome in which 33 German troops were killed in a street ambush. Extradited in November 1995 from Argentina, where he had lived since 1948, Priebke admitted to having shot two of the victims himself and was found guilty of implication in the mass killing, which took place in the Ardeatine caves outside Rome; the court, however, recognized extenuating circumstances, finding that he had not acted with cruelty and premeditation. Under Italian military law, crimes committed more than 30 years earlier could not be punished in the absence of cruelty and premeditation.

Priebke, however, was not set free; distraught relatives of the victims besieged the court all night, trapping Priebke and his three judges inside as prisoners. The mayor of Rome turned off the city's lights in protest, and President Scalfaro said, "The verdict contradicts history." Priebke was then rearrested after midnight because of a request for his extradition from Germany. In October the Italian Supreme Court, responding to further appeals, ordered a retrial. It ruled all the findings of the military court null and void because the presiding judge, Agostino Quistelli, had said before the trial that he anticipated an acquittal.

Two other trials during the year concerned 77-year-old Giulio Andreotti, seven times Italy's prime minister. In Palermo he continued to be tried for criminal association with the Mafia, scornfully rejecting the accusation that for 24 years he had helped the Mafia in return for votes. Andreotti was also put in the dock in the city of Perugia, where in a second, separate trial in April, he was accused of having been instrumental in the murder of Mino Pecorelli, an investigative journalist gunned down in Rome in March 1979, allegedly by two Mafia gunmen. Pecorelli, argued the prosecution, was a persistent, "inconvenient" scoop seeker with a deep insider's knowledge of the Italian political establishment; his "inconvenience" became unacceptable when he threatened to reveal an alleged role by Andreotti in the kidnapping and murder in 1978 of former Italian prime minister Aldo Moro by Red Brigade terrorists. Andreotti brushed off the story as absurd, claiming

Supporters hold aloft the symbol of the "L'Ulivo" ("Olive Tree") coalition, dominated by communists from the Democratic Party of the Left but also including other leftist and centrist members. The coalition won control of the government of Italy in the April 21 elections.

the Mafia had concocted it in revenge for anti-Mafia legislation he had enacted.

In its conflict with the Mafia, the government scored a striking success with the capture in May of Giovanni Brusca, heir to the jailed Mafia "boss of the bosses," Toto Riina, and, according to police, the man who had pressed the remote-control button that blew up the road under the speeding car of Giovanni Falcone near Palermo in 1992, killing Italy's leading anti-Mafia judge, his wife, and their three-man escort. Brusca was arrested, together with his wanted brother, Enzo.

In January fire gutted the famous La Fenice ("The Phoenix") opera house in Venice. The theatre, first opened in 1792 and called by Italian film director Franco Zeffirelli "the most beautiful theatre in the world," was closed for restoration with the sprinkler system allegedly turned off when fire broke out at night, destroying all but the facade and outer walls. Magistrates opened an inquiry and said they could not rule out arson. Artists and theatres around Italy and the world pledged to help reconstruction, which the city elders promised would be finished by March 1999.

In a poll to mark the Italian republic's 50th birthday, 84% of Italians said they were republicans. Only 8% wanted a return of the monarchy. (DEREK WILSON)

JAMAICA

A constitutional monarchy within the Commonwealth, Jamaica occupies an island in the Caribbean Sea. Area: 10,991 sq km (4,244 sq mi). Pop. (1996 est.): 2,505,000. Cap.: Kingston. Monetary unit: Jamaica dollar, with (Oct. 11, 1996) a free rate of J$34 to U.S. $1 (J$53.56 = £1 sterling). Queen, Elizabeth II; governor-general in 1996, Sir Howard Cooke; prime minister, Percival J. Patterson.

Jamaica's "Cuban problem" continued to occupy the attention of the authorities in 1996. Following an announcement that 57

Cuban refugees would be repatriated, 43 disappeared, some reportedly making their way to Puerto Rico. Of the rest, 13 were subsequently deported, Cuba having assured the Jamaican authorities that it would not punish them.

Jamaica's crime problem continued during the year, and the government was obliged to appoint a committee representing political parties, churches, and community groups to try to find a way to end the violence. The perceived failure of police commissioner Col. Trevor Macmillan to stem the crime wave led to his departure in September after he engaged in an acrimonious exchange with the prime minister. (DAVID RENWICK)

This article updates the Macropædia article The WEST INDIES: Jamaica.

JAPAN

A constitutional monarchy in the northwestern Pacific Ocean, Japan comprises an archipelago with four main islands (Hokkaido, Honshu, Kyushu, and Shikoku), the Ryukyus (including Okinawa), and lesser adjacent islands. Area: 377,819 sq km (145,877 sq mi). Pop. (1996 est.): 125,612,000. Cap.: Tokyo. Monetary unit: yen, with (Oct. 11, 1996) a free rate of 111.64 yen to U.S. $1 (175.86 yen = £1 sterling). Emperor, Akihito; prime ministers in 1996, Tomiichi Murayama and, from January 11, Ryutaro Hashimoto.

During 1996 Japan's nagging recession continued for the fifth year. Fiscal stimulation simply added to the nation's outstanding debt, predicted to reach $2.4 trillion by April 1997. A rapidly aging population created problems for individuals and the government alike. All citizens bore the burden of liquidating the bad bank loans inherited from the "bubble economy" of the 1980s. The government also had to recompense victims of a food-poisoning epidemic and those affected by HIV-contaminated blood.

Domestic Affairs. On January 5 Tomiichi

Murayama, Japan's first Socialist prime minister in five decades, resigned. Six days later both houses of the Diet (parliament) designated Ryutaro Hashimoto (see BIOGRAPHIES), president of the Liberal-Democratic Party (LDP), prime minister. Although his party had dominated Japanese politics from 1955 to 1993, it no longer commanded a majority in the Diet. Hashimoto, therefore, sought and obtained support from the same parties that had supported Murayama. His Cabinet reflected the fluid nature of the coalition. LDP members received 11 portfolios, including that of foreign minister and chief Cabinet secretary. Social Democratic Party (SDP) members were given six Cabinet positions, including the important position of finance minister. The smallest coalition partner, the New Harbinger Party (Sakigake), took two posts.

The political opposition was represented by the New Frontier Party (Shinshinto). It was led by Ichiro Ozawa, Hashimoto's rival when both were in the LDP.

When the new Diet convened, the LDP occupied 206 seats in the House of Representatives, the SDP 63, and Sakigake, 23, which gave the coalition a total of 292 of the 511 seats. In the House of Councillors the coalition commanded 140 of the 252 seats.

In his policy speech to the Diet on January 22, Hashimoto called 1996 "the first year of structural reform." He emphasized the need for a "high-transparency financial system," the importance of building a society founded on "advanced information and telecommunications," and the need to provide health and comfort to Japan's aging population. Looking abroad, the prime minister called the Japan-U.S. security pact "our most important bilateral relationship" while urging a "realignment, consolidation, and reduction" of U.S. military bases on Okinawa.

The coalition government faced a five-month deadlock in the Diet, wrangling with the opposition over bills to liquidate housing loan firms (jusen) that had failed since the 1980s. When the government announced on March 5 that taxpayers would bear the burden of $6.8 billion in losses (plus half the "secondary" debts), the Shinshinto boycotted the budget committee for three weeks. On May 10 the Diet passed a $750 billion budget for fiscal year 1996. Finally, on June 18, one day before the session's close, the House of Councillors approved six jusen liquidation bills.

Maneuvers within factions and across party lines pointed to an election showdown. As early as February, junior LDP members had formed what they called the "New Century" group. Coalition representatives from Sakigake and the SDP acted as observers.

On August 27 Yukio Hatoyama resigned as secretary-general of Sakigake and made plans for a "neoconservative party," which was expected to support deregulation, decentralization, and small government. Two days later Hatoyama unveiled a revolutionary proposal calling for the direct election of the prime minister. On September 28 the new Democratic Party (Minshuto) was formally organized, with 37 incumbent Diet members on its rolls. The opposition also experienced the impact of change. On August 8 Shinshinto leader Ozawa reshuffled the party's leadership by appointing Takeo

Managers threatened with layoffs participate in a protest in Tokyo. Many of Japan's economic problems remained unsolved in 1996, and people who for many decades had had no experience of unemployment increasingly faced the possibility of losing their jobs.

Nishioka secretary-general. The goal was to "do well" in the next election and "to assume power." This move, and the changes that had been made in other parties, reflected a generational shift in politics.

On September 27 Hashimoto dissolved the House of Representatives. The general election that followed on October 20 was the first under a new law, which allotted 300 seats to single constituencies and reserved 200 seats for proportional representation. In a record low turnout (below 60%), the LDP improved its position by taking 239 seats. Hashimoto marshaled 262 votes to win reelection, but no party agreed to join the LDP in a coalition. Shinshinto (156 seats) remained a formidable opponent, while the Democratic Party (52) seemed to hold the balance of power. The Social Democrats (15) and Sakigake (2) were almost eliminated from the political scene. In November Hashimoto appointed a new 21-member Cabinet, all from the LDP.

Two developments on the home front originated in the realm of public health, but they profoundly affected the world of politics. In March, after a seven-year legal battle, five pharmaceutical firms apologized for having distributed HIV-contaminated drug products to hemophiliacs. They agreed to a district court settlement that awarded $430,000 to each of some 400 plaintiffs, as well as $1,500 per month to those who contracted AIDS. Health and Welfare Minister Naoto Kan frankly admitted public responsibility for what happened and agreed that the government would bear 44% of the financial burden, while the pharmaceutical firms would pay the remaining 56%.

On August 16 in Sakai, near Osaka, a 12-year-old girl died after being infected by the O157-H7 strain of *E. coli* bacteria. White radish sprouts continued to be the target of investigation. Later, domestic beef also became suspect. The health and welfare ministry called the outbreak an epidemic, the first such official declaration in two decades. Eventually, the illness affected some 9,800 patients and caused 11 deaths.

A third problem was inherited from 1995. On April 24 Shoko Asahara, founder of the Aum Shinrikyo religious cult, went on trial in the Tokyo District Court. After 17 criminal charges were read, he refused to enter a plea. Asahara and the sect had been implicated in several crimes in 1994 and 1995, including the spread of the nerve gas sarin in Tokyo subways.

The Economy. A gradual recovery continued as corporate performance in fiscal 1995 (ended March 1996) showed a double-digit growth in profits. As a result of the yen's rise, however, Japan's cost of living index was among the world's highest. (Late in 1995 the ratio of Tokyo prices to those in New York City was 1.59 to 1.) In their end-of-May reports, banks reported combined losses of 1,750,000,000,000 yen, mainly the result of failed *jusen* loans.

Japan's official discount rate was kept at a historic low of 0.5% in the hope that it could stimulate domestic demand. For senior Japanese it was a disaster. Characteristically they had saved money, but interest on their accounts, which was needed to supplement limited pensions, proved to be inadequate.

After dropping for two months, the unemployment rate reached 3.4% in April and a record high of 3.5% in May. The number of jobless had risen to over 3 million (with 63 million employed). This trend prevailed despite an increase of 3% in gross domestic product (GDP) for the last quarter (January–March) of fiscal 1995, ending a three-year period of no growth. The annualized real-term value of GDP was $4,750.000,-000,000, which included a strong growth in domestic demand. On June 25 the Cabinet authorized an increase in the national consumption tax from 3% to 5% (effective April 1, 1997).

The world's largest bank began operations April 1 after a merger of the Bank of Tokyo and Mitsubishi Bank. Their combined assets totaled $738 billion and included 756 service bases in Japan and 438 overseas.

Foreign Affairs. In 1995, for the fifth year in a row, Japan led the world in net overseas assets (ODA: government and business holdings abroad, minus debts). An increase of 13% over 1994 brought the total to $770 billion, fueled by a 10% rise in private direct investments. The Foreign Ministry announced that the ODA totaled $14.7 billion (up 9.3% over 1994).

These figures, however, were not matched in the area of Japan's merchandise trade surplus, which had produced worldwide friction in recent years. In April the surplus plunged 65% from the year before. Although exports were up (17%), the increase was half that of imports (36%), which were led by purchases of autos and parts, office equipment, electronic devices, and meat. In July the customs-cleared surplus fell 38% from the year before, the 20th straight month of decline.

In the critical realm of trade with the U.S., the April surplus dropped 56% from a year earlier to $1.6 billion, the 14th consecutive monthly decline. As a result, for the first time in years, trade friction did not dominate relations between Washington and Tokyo. Indeed, the Japan Automobile Manufacturers Association announced that in fiscal 1995, 11 firms had purchased a total of more than $21 billion in U.S. auto parts. In August trade negotiators hailed an agreement that committed Japanese companies to continuing "voluntary" imports.

In late 1995 foreign semiconductors in Japan's market exceeded 30% for the first time. The Ministry of International Trade and Industry declared that an earlier U.S.-Japan chip accord "had fully achieved its objectives" and should expire. On August 2 in Vancouver, B.C., negotiators reached an agreement regarded by the Japanese as a "symbolic event." They abandoned numerical targets as "managed trade" and embraced a global model for settling disputes.

One remaining issue involved air rights between the two nations. On May 30 U.S. Transportation Secretary Frederico Pena urged approval of six new routes for Federal Express Corp. Tokyo responded that the U.S. should reopen talks on passenger routes, specifically regarding "beyond rights"—permission to continue flights to destinations outside Japan and the U.S.

During the year negotiations also centred on security issues, specifically the status of U.S. military bases on Okinawa. The smallest of the main islands, Okinawa (with only 1% of Japan's land area), under the U.S.-Japan security treaty, was the home base of 75% of some 47,000 U.S. troops stationed on Japanese soil.

In a brief meeting with U.S. Pres. Bill Clinton on February 23 in California, Hashimoto agreed to put off discussion of vital issues until their formal summit was held in Tokyo in April. He did, however, request cooperation on the problem of Okinawa.

In September 1995 three off-duty U.S. servicemen had been charged with the rape of a 12-year-old schoolgirl in Okinawa. On March 7 a district court judge in the prefectural capital of Naha sentenced two of the men to seven years in prison and the other to six and a half years for the "brutal, arrogant act."

On the eve of the April summit, a most significant change in the U.S.-Japan security arrangement was approved during Cabinet-level negotiations. The Acquisition and Cross Servicing Agreement provided for an exchange of matériel (including weapons), a reversal of a decade-old Japanese policy banning such exports. Japan's promise to cooperate if a military threat arose in the "Far East" made the security pact "more symmetrical."

The alteration followed an April joint statement promising that the U.S. would relinquish 20% of the land occupied by U.S. forces on Okinawa. Two days later Clinton and Hashimoto hailed the security treaty as "an alliance for the 21st century."

The campaign to reduce U.S. bases continued under Okinawa Gov. Masahide Ota. His local SDP, with Japan Communist Party support, commanded 25 of the 48 seats in the prefectural assembly. Despite suits filed by the central government and rejection of Ota's appeal by the Supreme Court on August 28, he initiated a nonbinding referendum in the prefecture. The poll, held on September 8, supported Ota by a 10–1 ratio. The turnout, however, was low (below 60%), and on September 13 the governor gave up the legal fight and agreed to the renewal of the base leases.

Other islands also influenced Japan's relations with its neighbours. Hashimoto, the first Japanese prime minister to visit Moscow since 1985, met with Russian Pres. Boris Yeltsin on April 19 in an effort to revitalize talks leading to a peace treaty. A pact had been stalled by what Japanese called the "Northern Territories" issue, involving Russian occupation since 1945 of four tiny islands in the southern Kurils. Yeltsin agreed to honour the 1993 Tokyo Declaration, which formally recognized the territorial dispute. Hashimoto, however, later declined to attend Yeltsin's inaugural on August 9.

On February 20 the Hashimoto Cabinet approved a 200-nautical-mile exclusive economic zone, under a UN sea convention. The decision promptly produced friction between Japan, South Korea, and China. At issue were rocky islets in the Sea of Japan known to Koreans as Tok-do and to Japanese as Takeshima, which were under Seoul's control. Hashimoto urged calm negotiations, particularly on fishing rights, until the dispute could be settled. Indeed, on June 23 the prime minister met with South Korean Pres. Kim Young Sam on Cheju Island. They agreed to explore four-power talks between the two Koreas, China, and the U.S. to promote stability on the peninsula. The two leaders also pledged coordination in the joint staging of the World Cup soccer finals in 2002.

Japan's proposed sea zone also embraced the uninhabited Senkaku Islands (known to China as the Diaoyu chain and claimed by Beijing), now under Tokyo's control. Chinese on Taiwan also laid claim to these islets. There were numerous reports of offshore oil reserves.

During the year the largest and most important island to figure in Japanese diplomacy was Taiwan. Seat of the Republic of China, it was regarded by the People's Republic on the mainland as a renegade province. In March, during the campaign preceding the first direct presidential election on Taiwan—easily won by incumbent Lee Teng-hui—China mounted military maneuvers in the Taiwan Strait. The moves were designed to intimidate the islanders,

who, Beijing charged, were in the process of moving to separation and independence.

Japan and the U.S. had both normalized relations with Beijing, but both continued a lively trade with Taiwan. On March 31 in Tokyo, Foreign Minister Ikeda informed his Chinese counterpart that Japan could not tolerate the use of force to settle the Taiwan issue. Foreign Minister Qian Qichen firmly responded that Taiwan was a domestic Chinese issue.

Hashimoto was even less patient with a nuclear test carried out by China in July. It came on the eve of negotiations in Geneva to conclude the Comprehensive Test Ban Treaty, which Japan strongly supported. Because of China's military operations near Taiwan and its successive nuclear experiments, Tokyo continued to hold up pledged grants-in-aid, which it had suspended after China's nuclear test in May 1995.

In December members of the Peruvian guerrilla group Túpac Amaru stormed the Japanese embassy in Lima during a party. They took hostages and demanded the release of Túpac Amaru in Peruvian prisons as a condition for releasing the hostages. (*See Peru*, below.)

Meanwhile, Japan continued to make personnel contributions to global peace-keeping operations. In August a Foreign Ministry official traveled to Kabul, Afg., to support UN efforts to end fighting between warring Islamic factions. With such actions, Japan hoped to enhance its bid for a permanent seat on the UN Security Council.

(ARDATH W. BURKS)

JORDAN

A constitutional monarchy, Jordan is located in southwestern Asia and has a short coastline on the Gulf of Aqaba. Area: 89,326 sq km (34,489 sq mi). Pop. (1996 est.): 4,333,000 (including Palestinian refugees estimated to number nearly 1.3 million). Cap.: Amman. Monetary unit: Jordan dinar, with (Oct. 11, 1996) an official rate of 0.71 dinar to U.S. $1 (1.12 dinars = £1 sterling). King, Hussein I; prime ministers in 1996, Sharif Zaid ibn Shaker and, from February 4, 'Abd al-Karim Kabariti.

In early February 1996, Foreign Minister 'Abd al-Karim Kabariti formed a 31-member Cabinet, including 22 members of the National Assembly, and pledged to continue reconciliation with the Arab Gulf states and to further the normalization of relations with Israel, yet those relations were in jeopardy by October. Jordan moved squarely into the anti-Saddam Hussein camp during the year by allowing U.S. forces to use an air base on its territory to monitor the no-fly zone in southern Iraq. In April the U.S. began operating three dozen F-15s and F-16s, along with 1,500 airmen, out of the Azraq air base. On July 29 Jordan signed a $220 million deal with the U.S. to lease 16 F-16s. Jordan was also to receive 50 M60 A3 tanks and a C-130 cargo plane.

Iraq was also angered because Jordan allowed an Iraqi opposition group, the Iraq National Accord, to operate a radio station that blanketed Iraq with propaganda and to encourage the defection of high-ranking army officers, including Lieut. Gen. Nazar Khazraji. The government's policies toward Iraq were not popular with the Jordanian

business community. Jordan depended on Iraq for oil imports, averaging 75,000 bbl a day, which it purchased below market. Nearly 40% of Jordan's manufactured exports went to Iraq. Iraq had, however, accumulated a debt of $1.2 billion with Jordan, and so Jordan announced a 50% cut in its exports to Iraq according to a protocol signed in April.

On August 13 the government began to implement plans to phase out bread subsidies in an effort to reduce the government deficit. The action met with strong criticism in the National Assembly and led to riots in the town of Kerak. Two Iraqi diplomats were expelled from Jordan that month on charges of having instigated the riots.

Relations with Israel began to sour after the Israeli government under Shimon Peres launched a campaign to punish Hezbollah guerrilla forces in Lebanon, which resulted in carnage when Israel bombed a UN base in Qana, killing more than 100 civilians. Following the election of Benjamin Netanyahu, King Hussein attended the Arab summit in Cairo in June to map strategy toward Israel, at which time a reconciliation between him and Pres. Hafez al-Assad of Syria took place. In late September the opening of an archaeological tunnel under the Aqsa Mosque in Jerusalem sparked clashes between Israelis and Palestinians in which more than 70 people died. King Hussein, Yasir Arafat, and Netanyahu met in Washington at the beginning of October at the urging of U.S. Pres. Bill Clinton to resolve the issue, but nothing concrete was achieved. King Hussein warned that Israel's peace treaties with Jordan and Egypt were at risk unless Israel fulfilled its obligations to the Palestinians as agreed upon in Oslo in 1993.   (JENAB TUTUNJI)

KAZAKSTAN

A republic of Central Asia, Kazakstan borders Russia on the west and north, China on the east, Kyrgyzstan on the southeast, Uzbekistan and the Aral Sea on the south, and Turkmenistan and the Caspian Sea on the southwest. Area: 2,724,900 sq km (1,052,090 sq mi). Pop. (1996 est.): 16,677,000. Cap.: Almaty (formerly Alma-Ata); capital-designate: Aqmola (formerly Tselinograd). Monetary unit: tenge, with (Oct. 11, 1996) a free rate of 69.87 tenge = U.S. $1 (110.07 tenge = £1 sterling). President in 1996, Nursultan Nazarbayev; prime minister, Akezhan Kazhegeldin.

Throughout 1996, Western-style democracy made few gains in Kazakstan as the country floundered both politically and economically. The World Bank censured Kazakstan's failure to fully utilize the Bank's loans and warned that its level of assistance might be revised downward. Many foreign businessmen, disappointed by their investments in Kazakstan, turned to neighbouring Uzbekistan as a more promising partner.

At the opening of the new bicameral legislature's first session at the end of January, Pres. Nursultan Nazarbayev called on the deputies to support his vision of economic reform, as their predecessors had failed to do, and warned that he would dissolve the body if it attempted to exceed its authority. Despite the president's efforts to convince the parliament that it was supposed to approve his and the government's actions automatically, the Majlis (lower house of the legislature) indicated that it retained at least some of the concern for the social effects of economic reform that had brought its predecessor into conflict with Nazarbayev. In early summer the Majlis rejected a government proposal for pension reform, on the grounds that it would be too hard on the elderly. After Nazarbayev appeared on Kazak television with a plea for standardized pension benefits and for raising the legal retirement age, the Majlis passed a vote of confidence in the government.

In March leaders of Kazakstan, Kyrgyzstan, Belarus, and the Russian Federation officially inaugurated a customs union that was intended to create a common market in goods, capital, and labour; to integrate transportation networks, electric power grids, and information systems; and to ensure minimum standards of social welfare. Kazakstan's leadership, however, decisively rejected proposals for the resurrection of the U.S.S.R. that emerged during the presidential election campaign in the Russian Federation.

Relations with China, one of Kazakstan's major foreign policy concerns, were put on a new footing with the signing in April of an agreement resolving disputes over state borders and providing for the partial demilitarization of border areas.

(BESS BROWN)

This article updates the *Macropædia* article CENTRAL ASIA: *Kazakhstan.*

KENYA

A republic and member of the Commonwealth, Kenya is in eastern Africa, on the Indian Ocean. Area: 582,646 sq km (224,961 sq mi). Pop. (1996 est.): 29,137,-000. Cap.: Nairobi. Monetary unit: Kenya shilling, with (Oct. 11, 1996) a free rate of 55.98 shillings to U.S. $1 (88.19 shillings = £1 sterling). President in 1996, Daniel arap Moi.

The mutual mistrust between Pres. Daniel arap Moi and Pres. Yoweri Museveni of Uganda, which had held back progress toward East African cooperation, was set aside when they and Pres. Benjamin Mkapa of Tanzania met in Uganda in January 1996 and agreed to press ahead with joint action on both economic and social fronts.

The appointment of Robert Breneissen, a respected businessman, as chairman of the Kenya Ports Authority after the managing director and 17 senior civil servants had been placed on leave pending investigations into the disappearance of 1,200 vehicles worth £85.5 million indicated that Kenya was making an attempt to satisfy the requirement of the International Monetary Fund (IMF) that the government commit itself to reform. Before the end of January, President Moi also shelved two bills that would have severely restricted the press.

Early in February the government published a minibudget aimed at cutting the 1995–96 deficit to 1.9% of gross domestic product. Proposals included increasing customs duties on petroleum products and strengthening the operations of the country's revenue authority. It was hoped that these measures would restrain the resurgence of inflationary pressures and help to improve the nation's balance of payments. The operations and financial control of the

privatized Kenya Airways continued to improve, which induced KLM Royal Dutch Airlines to purchase a 26% stake in the company in January.

The first sign of a change in the attitude of donor institutions toward Kenya came early in February, when the World Bank approved a loan of $115 million that would be used to help rehabilitate the country's roads. A decision by the British government in March to release £5 million in aid encouraged other countries to follow suit, and a few days later they pledged an additional £500 million. But it was not until late in April that the IMF agreed to release a loan of $216 million that had been blocked since 1994.

Though a number of donors privately doubted that the government's reforms were anything more than token gestures, the government considered that with elections scheduled for 1997, it was important to encourage stability in Kenya. Whatever doubts may have been felt about President Moi's government, prospects for a viable alternative were not immediately obvious. Competition between rival leaders resulted in the breakup, barely two months after its formation, of the alliance between leading opposition parties created at the end of November 1995. One of those parties, the Forum for the Restoration of Democracy-Kenya, itself split in April, while the chairman of another party, Kenneth Matiba of the Forum for the Restoration of Democracy-Asili, alienated foreign donors by his virulent verbal attacks on the Asian community.

Moi himself continued to stress Kenya's sovereign status by holding talks in May with Pres. Jiang Zemin of China, which resulted in an agreement on economic and technical cooperation between the two countries. Similarly, in September a visit to Nairobi by Pres. Hojatolislam Ali Akbar Hashemi Rafsanjani of Iran was followed by offers of assistance by Iran for Kenya's energy, industry, and farming sectors.

(KENNETH INGHAM)

This article updates the *Macropædia* article EASTERN AFRICA: *Kenya.*

KIRIBATI

A republic in the western Pacific Ocean and member of the Commonwealth, Kiribati comprises the Gilbert Islands, Banaba (Ocean Island), the Line Islands, and the Phoenix Islands. Area: 811 sq km (313 sq mi). Pop. (1996 est.): 81,800. Cap.: Bairiki, on Tarawa. Monetary unit: Australian dollar, with (Oct. 11, 1996) a free rate of $A 1.26 to U.S. $1 ($A 1.99 = £1 sterling). President (*beretitenti*) in 1996, Teburoro Tito.

Kiribati attracted international attention in 1996 over an earlier decision that established a single time zone for the country by, in effect, extending the International Date Line east of the Line Islands. The legislation sparked a Pacificwide debate over which country would first "see the Sun" in the new millennium—an event of significance for tourism.

Kiribati projected a balanced budget in 1996 with expenditures at $A 51.5 million (an increase of 1.7%). A total of $A 13.6 million would be drawn from the Revenue Equalization Reserve Fund—a reserve es-

tablished with phosphate royalties before the exhaustion of deposits at Banaba.

(BARRIE MACDONALD)

This article updates the *Macropædia* article PACIFIC ISLANDS: *Kiribati.*

KOREA, DEMOCRATIC PEOPLE'S REPUBLIC OF

A socialist republic of northeastern Asia on the northern half of the peninsula of Korea, the Democratic People's Republic of Korea (North Korea) borders the Sea of Japan, the Yellow Sea, and the Republic of Korea at roughly the 38th parallel. Area: 122,762 sq km (47,399 sq mi). Pop. (1996 est.): 23,904,000. Cap.: Pyongyang. Monetary unit: won, with (Oct. 11, 1996) a transfer rate of 2.15 won to U.S. $1 (3.39 won = £1 sterling); a truer value of the won was on the black market where at the beginning of the year 45 won = U.S. $1 (70 won = £1 sterling). President in 1996, Kim Jong Il (designated); chairman of the Council of Ministers (premier), Kang Song San.

The food shortages in North Korea that were evident in 1995 worsened in 1996. In some areas of the country they approached famine proportions, with frequent reports of peasants being reduced to eating bark off of trees. With no credit to buy food on the open market, North Korea was dependent on charity.

Yet North Korea did not behave like a supplicant. Instead, the year was marked by some of the most bellicose provocations experienced on the Korean peninsula for years. In April several hundred North Korean soldiers entered the demilitarized zone and unloaded their mortars, recoilless rifles, and machine guns on their side of the joint security area—all in flagrant violation of the 43-year-old armistice agreement that forbids any but side arms in the DMZ. They repeated the demonstration during the following two days. The most likely explanation was that it represented an escalation of North Korea's campaign to dismantle the armistice machinery and replace it with a separate peace treaty with the parties to the 1950–53 Korean War.

Then in September came another curious event. A small North Korean submarine ran aground off South Korea's northeastern coastline. It was reportedly carrying about two dozen commandos, most of whom were killed, either by their comrades or by South Korean troops during a massive manhunt. North Korea said that the sub had strayed off course because of engine trouble, but the South Korean Defense Ministry, relying on the interrogation of one captured commando, said that it had been on a reconnaissance mission. Late in December North Korea expressed "deep regret" for the episode.

In April U.S. Pres. Bill Clinton met with South Korea's Pres. Kim Young Sam on the southern resort island of Cheju. A proposal was made that there be four-party talks between the belligerents of the Korean War—North and South Korea, China, and the U.S.—that would lead to the signing of a formal peace treaty. One purpose was to send a signal to North Korea that it should not expect to be able to hold out for separate talks with the U.S. In accepting the proposal, South Korea relaxed its insis-

North Koreans participate in a retreat on Mount Paektu, a place with sacred and patriotic connections. Despite North Korea's economic problems, which were reported to include widespread malnutrition and even famine, the government continued to maintain a bellicose attitude during 1996.

tence that any peace treaty be negotiated only between the two Koreas. The North neither agreed to nor rejected the proposal outright.   (GEORGE T. CROWELL)

This article updates the *Macropædia* article KOREA: *North Korea*.

KOREA, REPUBLIC OF

A republic of northeastern Asia on the southern half of the peninsula of Korea, the Republic of Korea (South Korea) borders the Sea of Japan, the Korea Strait, the Yellow Sea, and the Democratic People's Republic of Korea at roughly the 38th parallel. Area: 99,394 sq km (38,376 sq mi). Pop. (1996 est.): 45,232,000. Cap.: Seoul. Monetary unit: won, with (Oct. 11, 1996) a free rate of 829 won to U.S. $1 (1,306 won = £1 sterling). President in 1996, Kim Young Sam; prime minister, Lee Soo Sung.

South Korea came to a virtual halt on Aug. 26, 1996, as Kim Young Il, chief of a three-member judicial tribunal, delivered guilty verdicts against two of its former presidents, Chun Doo Hwan, and his successor, Roh Tae Woo. The sentences were then pronounced: death for Chun; 22½ years' imprisonment for Roh. The two were convicted of having plotted the 1979 coup, now officially called a "mutiny," that followed the assassination of longtime strongman Park Chung Hee. They were also found guilty of treason in connection with the May 1980 massacres of hundreds of people in the southern city of Kwangju, where protests had erupted soon after Chun extended martial law to the whole country. Roh was fined $350 million and Chun $270 million, the amount of the bribes each had

received while in office. At the year's end their sentences were under appeal.

Also convicted were the bosses of some of South Korea's largest business conglomerates, or *chaebol*. In all, nine executives were declared guilty of having bribed Chun and Roh in return for government favours. The most prominent were Kim Woo Choong, chairman of the Daewoo Group, who received two years in jail; Choi Won Suk (*see* BIOGRAPHIES), chairman of the Dong Ah Group, 2½ years; and Lee Kun Hee (*see* BIOGRAPHIES), chairman of the Samsung Group, two years, suspended. They were free on bail pending appeal, and none of the companies said that their businesses would be seriously affected by the verdicts. The business leaders maintained that they had been forced to make contributions or lose business opportunities.

This historic reckoning had begun to unfold on Oct. 27, 1995, when Roh went on television and tearfully confessed that he had amassed a $650 million political slush fund. Most South Koreans had realistically assumed that political donations were a fact of life, but they were shocked at the sheer size of the fund. They were even more astounded when Roh admitted keeping about $200 million for himself. He denied that the money was taken in exchange for favours. The sentence passed on Roh was less severe than many had expected. The tribunal took into account his democratic reforms, which allowed him to pass power on to a civilian successor, the incumbent president, Kim Young Sam.

Veteran pro-democracy activist Kim Dae Jung, who had been himself sentenced to death for allegedly having incited the Kwangju uprising, said that the verdicts failed to close the books on what many Ko-

reans considered the most traumatic event in their recent history. Although the court found Chun guilty of complicity in the bloody crackdown, it did not specifically blame anyone for it.

Student radicalism had been relatively quiescent in South Korea since democracy was restored in 1987. Students occasionally battled with riot police on the streets of Seoul, but this had become something of a fringe event. The year saw the most violent student clashes in the capital in recent times, however, during nine days in mid-August. On August 20 the unrest finally ended when riot police backed by helicopters fired tear gas and battled their way past improvised (continued on page 443)

Roh Tae Woo (left) and Chun Doo Hwan appear in court. The two former South Korean presidents were found guilty of charges that included plotting the 1979 coup.

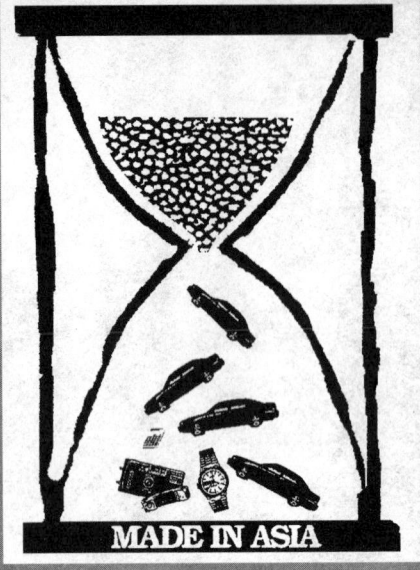

MADE IN ASIA

DEMOCRACY AND DEVELOPMENT IN ASIA

by Ricardo Saludo

illustration by Igor Kopelnitsky

In October 1996, 15 months after lifting the house arrest of Nobel Peace Prize winner Daw Aung San Suu Kyi, Myanmar's (Burma's) ruling junta, the State Law and Order Restoration Council (SLORC), cracked down on dissidents, barricading Suu Kyi's house and arresting hundreds of her supporters. The SLORC's action galvanized advocates of Myanmar democracy abroad, particularly in the U.S., and put the Association of Southeast Asian Nations (ASEAN) on the spot. ASEAN had gained some credit for Suu Kyi's release in July 1995, but the SLORC's iron fist gave ammunition to critics of the organization's policy of coaxing Myanmar toward change by quiet persuasion and cordial dialogue rather than by sanctions and confrontation.

ASEAN's Myanmar quandary again threw into sharp focus the intertwined and entrenched issues in Asian democracy and development: Can economic pressure prod despots to liberalize? Should prosperity come before political rights? The remarkable success of the East Asian economies has occurred in countries under one-person or one-party rule, including Japan, governed almost continuously by the Liberal-Democratic Party for 41 years. Rather than immediately working to establish democracy, the region's winning formula has called for economic acceleration with one person in the driver's seat. Indeed, in the 1960s and 1970s, after a decade or so of trying to stay on the democratic path set by their former foreign colonial rulers, one Asian nation after another became autocratic.

The East Asian Miracle, a much-quoted World Bank report on Japan and the newly industrialized economies, acknowledged the key role played by powerful governments whose technocrats forged sound economic and social policies—free enterprise, mass education, fiscal and monetary prudence, and business incentives—with a minimum of lobbying for special favours from politicians and interest groups. Rather than embracing the whole of Western democracy, East Asia absorbed mainly the capitalist elements. Thus, Lee Kuan Yew in Singapore, Chiang Kai-shek on Taiwan, and Park Chung Hee in South Korea sternly presided over years of relative political and social stability and spectacular business growth. Hong Kong prospered under a laissez-faire regime run by competent, unelected bureaucrats. In its reforms China has also kept draconian political control while encouraging economic free enterprise. By contrast, India adopted democracy's political processes but rejected its market economics.

If East Asia put economics first, politics eventually followed, largely as a result of social changes brought on by prosperity. The rise of a confident, affluent, and ed-

ucated middle class, the expansion of schools and mass media, the growing assertiveness of young people and women, and the increased exposure to Western culture made more and more Asians less willing to follow their leaders without question. To these social pressures for greater freedom, economics added a further impetus. Stanford University economist Paul Krugman caused a stir in late 1994 by predicting a long-term East Asian economic slowdown unless the region improved total factor productivity (TFP), the output produced per unit of input. He maintained that innovation in the workplace was needed for improvement of TFP. Lee Kuan Yew agreed, stating that new industries require work units with freedom to plan. Quite naturally, Lee concluded, such liberties could lead to demands for similar prerogatives in the political sphere, including the right to elect leaders.

Some of that is already happening in China. In a presentation for the U.S. National Endowment for Democracy, Minxin Pei, an assistant professor of politics at Princeton University, spoke of "the liberalizing effects of market forces." He notes the decreasing state control over people's economic decisions, the formation of thousands of business and professional groups, the widespread election of village councils, and even the expansion of a nongovernment press. Speaking in Shanghai in November, U.S. Secretary of State Warren Christopher acknowledged China's efforts to invest authority in its people through legal and administrative reforms and village elections. Henry Rowen, a senior fellow at the Hoover Institution, reported that the government media in China had only a third of the market in 1988, down from 95% in 1979. He predicted that if China's economy continued to grow at the present rate, its per capita gross domestic product would be $7,000 in 2015, the level at which democracy elsewhere has become stabilized.

What role, if any, have economic sanctions and international pressure played in democracy's new march across Asia and, indeed, the world? Not much. Eastern Europe and Latin America broke their chains with hardly any threats from Western nations. In Asia six nations made great strides in democracy over the past decade: Bangladesh, Pakistan, the Philippines, South Korea, Taiwan, and Thailand. None of them ever faced sanctions, most being U.S. allies. Rowen counseled patience in dealing with China and an end to "making economic relations hostage to political disputes." If anything, it appears that commerce with the rest of the world has been the best catalyst for both economic development and democratic change in Asia.

Ricardo Saludo is assistant managing editor of *Asiaweek.*

(continued from page 441)
barricades to occupy the campus of Yonsei University in Seoul, which had been taken over by several thousand pro-North Korean student demonstrators. The Hanchongnyon (Korean Federation of University Student Councils), a leftist student organization often at the centre of student agitation, had invited student counterparts from North Korea to attend a "Unification Festival" on the campus. The government warned the students that such activities would violate the strict National Security Law, which prohibits any kind of pro-North Korean demonstration. The students, however, decided to ignore the warning and sent representatives to Pyongyang, while those at the university set up barricades and prepared to battle with riot police. Ultimately, 5,500 students were arrested. More than 1,000 police and students were injured.

Pres. Kim Young Sam's police were able to crack down because, unlike in the late 1980s, when the middle classes rallied behind them, the student radicals had little broad support. Although many people may have supported their call for the withdrawal of U.S. troops and the abolition of the National Security Law, many more felt that they were naive in their undisguised support of the North Korean regime. Late in December some 350,000 workers went on strike in protest against new labour laws that gave greater freedom to businesses to lay off workers and delayed by three years the authorization of labour unions. It was the nation's largest strike ever.

Kim's ruling New Korea Party (it changed its name from the Democratic Liberal Party in December 1995) pulled victory out of what was almost certain defeat in the midterm parliamentary elections that were held on April 11. His party won 139 seats of the 299 in the National Assembly. Though short of a majority, it was considerably more than the 100 seats that the most optimistic supporters had been forecasting. Electoral disaster had been predicted since the June 1995 local elections, in which the government party candidates were soundly defeated throughout the country.

Help for President Kim's followers came from an unexpected quarter—North Korea. In the days before the voting, Pyongyang sent troops into the demilitarized zone for three consecutive days. The administration, no doubt supported by media hype over fears of a projected northern invasion, exploited the North Korean sabre rattling to good effect, especially in Seoul, particularly sensitive to such threats because of its close proximity to the border. Seoul had been a bastion of support for veteran opposition leader Kim Dae Jung, but it was the New Korea Party of President Kim that took the largest number of seats. Kim Dae Jung's party, the National Congress for New Politics, won just 79 seats, and many commentators believed that the poor showing might finally finish the veteran leader as a viable candidate for president in the 1997 election.

Foreign Affairs. In foreign affairs the most significant events were two summit meetings, one with U.S. Pres. Bill Clinton and the other with Japanese Prime Minister Ryutaro Hashimoto, both held on the southern resort island of Cheju. In the meeting with Clinton, South Korea set aside some of its suspicions and agreed to a proposal that there be a four-power

conference between the belligerents of the 1950–53 Korean War to decide upon a final peace treaty. South Korea–Japan relations, always sensitive, and soured by a flare-up over disputed islets in the Sea of Japan, were improved during the year by a friendly meeting with Hashimoto. Another chance to develop friendlier ties was the decision to serve as cohost with Japan for the 2002 World Cup in soccer.

(GEORGE T. CROWELL)

This article updates the *Macropædia* article KOREA: *South Korea.*

KUWAIT

A constitutional monarchy (emirate), Kuwait is situated in the northeastern Arabian Peninsula, on the Persian Gulf. Area: 17,818 sq km (6,880 sq mi). Pop. (1996 est.): 2,070,000. Cap.: Kuwait City. Monetary unit: Kuwaiti dinar, with (Oct. 11, 1996) a controlled rate of 0.30 dinar to U.S. $1 (0.47 dinar = £1 sterling). Emir, Sheikh Jabir al-Ahmad al-Jabir as-Sabah; prime minister in 1996, Crown Prince Sheikh Saad al-Abdullah as-Salim as-Sabah.

The major event of 1996 in Kuwait was the election of a new National Assembly on October 7. Government supporters won 30 of the 50 elective seats in the Assembly, while Islamic fundamentalists and their allies accounted for the remainder.

Among the Assembly's most controversial actions in 1996 was the passage of a law mandating gender segregation at Kuwait University. Only one member voted against the final bill, a testament to members' perceptions of Islamist strength in the electorate. The gender-segregation law touched off a firestorm of protest that coincided with the election campaign. A number of candidates running for reelection found that their support of the Islamists on the segregation issue confirmed constituents' perceptions that they had abandoned principles for politics, and several failed to win reelection. The election revealed other shifts in the domestic political scene, including the defeat of two tribally backed incumbents and the election of a Shi'ite cleric trained in Iran who advocated a shift in Kuwait's foreign policy away from dependence on the United States.

Kuwait's economy expanded throughout 1996, thanks to rising oil prices and new investments in the oil and construction industries. The stock market remained strong well into the autumn, with trading volumes running between $150 million and $200 million per day. (MARY ANN TÉTREAULT)

This article updates the *Macropædia* article ARABIA: *Kuwait.*

KYRGYZSTAN

A landlocked republic of Central Asia, Kyrgyzstan borders Kazakstan to the north, China to the southeast, Tajikistan to the south and west, and Uzbekistan to the west. Area: 198,500 sq km (76,600 sq mi). Pop. (1996 est.): 4,521,000. Cap.: Bishkek. Monetary unit: som, with (Oct. 11, 1996) a free rate of 13.4 som = U.S. $1 (21.1 som = £1 sterling). President in 1996, Askar Akayev; prime minister, Apas Jumagulov.

In February 1996 Kyrgyzstan's voters overwhelmingly approved changes to the constitution giving greater powers to Pres. Askar Akayev. Once considered the most democratically minded leader in Central Asia, Akayev issued a decree in March allowing regional governors appointed by himself to suspend the decisions of local authorities and enterprises if these contradicted decisions of the central authorities. The following month the president fired the chief editors of two of the country's most important newspapers.

After Kyrgyzstan entered a customs union with Kazakstan, Belarus, and the Russian Federation in March, Russia's state-owned energy firm offered Kyrgyzstan help in developing desperately needed hydroelectric facilities that had been started prior to the dissolution of the U.S.S.R.

Kyrgyzstan joined Kazakstan and Uzbekistan in setting up a peacekeeping force under UN auspices. The new regional force, the first of its kind in Central Asia, was to be trained under the NATO Partnership for Peace program. (BESS BROWN)

This article updates the *Macropædia* article CENTRAL ASIA: *Kyrgyzstan.*

LAOS

A landlocked republic, Laos is in the northern part of the Indochinese Peninsula. Area: 236,800 sq km (91,429 sq mi). Pop. (1996 est.): 5,023,000. Cap.: Vientiane (Viangchan). Monetary unit: kip, with (Oct. 11, 1996) a controlled rate of 920 kip to U.S. $1 (1,449 kip = £1 sterling). President in 1996, Nouhak Phoumsavan; prime minister, Gen. Khamtai Siphandon.

The sixth congress of the Lao People's Revolutionary Party, which took place in late March 1996, was the setting for a long-expected showdown between proponents of reform and the communist old guard. In the end the hard-liners triumphed, though not without having to make concessions. Nouhak Phoumsavan, a hard-liner, was retained as president but dropped from the Politburo. A new post of vice president was created, and it was filled by Agriculture Minister Sisavat Keobounphan. The standard-bearer of the reform group, Deputy Prime Minister Khamphoui Keoboualapha, who had supervised the free-market reforms of recent years, was ousted from both the Politburo and the party's Central Committee, though he retained his ministerial rank. Khamphoui's chief rival, Lieut. Gen. Choummali Saignason, enhanced his position as minister of defense in a reshuffled Politburo, of whom two-thirds were in the military. Prime Minister Khamtai Siphandon reaffirmed one-party rule but called for more economic deregulation, efficiency, and growth.

In late October President Nouhak welcomed Wang Zhaoguo, vice-chairman of the National Committee of the Chinese People's Political Consultative Conference, and called for a strengthening of ties between the two socialist nations. It was, however, amicable relations with capitalist Thailand that provided more concrete gains. The neighbours planned to begin demarcation of their disputed boundary in December. Thailand promised to address what the culturally and linguistically related

U.S. bomb casings serve as a fence in a Laotian village. Farmers found a number of innovative uses for such leftovers from the Vietnam War. Unlike most of its Southeast Asian neighbours, Laos continued in 1996 to only slowly accept change.

Laotians perceived as its condescension toward them but was thanked by Laos for refusing requests by the United States to allow broadcasts from its territory by the anticommunist Radio Free Asia. Alarmed by a likely exodus following Thailand's relaxation of restrictions against foreign labour, Laos prohibited workers from seeking jobs in labour-starved factories across the border.   (ROBERT WOODROW)

This article updates the *Macropædia* article SOUTHEAST ASIA: *Laos.*

LATVIA

A republic of northern Europe, Latvia is located on the eastern shore of the Baltic Sea. Area: 64,610 sq km (24,946 sq mi). Pop. (1996 est.): 2,490,000. Cap.: Riga. Monetary unit: lats, with (Oct. 11, 1996) a free rate of 0.55 lats to U.S. $1 (0.87 lats = £1 sterling). President in 1996, Guntis Ulmanis; prime minister, Andris Skele.

After the turmoil of the previous year, when the country was shaken by a severe banking crisis and by the indecisive results of the parliamentary elections, 1996 was a year of consolidation for Latvia. The new governing coalition, comprising six parties and headed by Prime Minister Andris Skele, grew in strength during the year but generally avoided dealing with controversial matters. On June 18 the Saeima (parliament) reelected Guntis Ulmanis as Latvia's president. The Constitutional Court held its first session in December.

Relations with Russia improved slightly. Russian officials complained less frequently concerning the alleged mistreatment of the Russians in Latvia. Toward the end of the year, the Latvian government hinted that it would drop its insistence that Russia recognize the validity of the Treaty of Riga signed in 1920. The Latvian demand was the main obstacle to the signing of a treaty establishing the border between the two countries.

With active Swedish assistance, Latvia settled a long-standing dispute with Estonia over fishing rights and signed a treaty demarcating the sea border between the two nations on July 12. Relations with Lithuania deteriorated because of a dispute concerning the sea border and oil-drilling rights in the Baltic Sea.   (SAULIUS A. GIRNIUS)

This article updates the *Macropædia* article BALTIC STATES: *Latvia.*

LEBANON

A republic of southwestern Asia, Lebanon is situated on the Mediterranean Sea. Area: 10,230 sq km (3,950 sq mi). Pop. (1996 est.): 3,776,000 (including Palestinian refugees estimated to number nearly

A woman who lost her home in southern Lebanon to war sits on a couch in the damaged Beirut apartment where she and her family took up temporary lodging. Many such squatters were evicted to make way for extensive reconstruction projects planned for the Lebanese capital.

350,000). Cap.: Beirut. Monetary unit: Lebanese pound, with (Oct. 11, 1996) a free rate of LL 1,558 to U.S. $1 (LL 2,454 = £1 sterling). President in 1996, Elias Hrawi; prime minister, Rafiq al-Hariri.

Attacks from southern Lebanon into northern Israel by pro-Iranian Hezbollah forces in April, in retaliation for the death of a Lebanese youth, injured some 30 people. Israel struck back, bombing Hezbollah targets in Beirut. On April 18 Israeli gunners shelled a UN camp at Qana, where more than 100 people were killed. Preliminary UN reports stated that Hezbollah fighters had taken refuge in the camp and that Israeli troops deliberately shelled it. The Israelis claimed that the camp was not intended to be a target and that mapping errors resulted in miscalculations. Despite meetings between U.S. Secretary of State Warren Christopher and Pres. Hafez al-Assad of Syria and between Christopher and Prime Minister Shimon Peres of Israel, aimed at ending the targeting of civilians, violence on both sides continued through May. As U.S., French, Syrian, Israeli, and Lebanese diplomats tried to work out a cease-fire, the Hezbollah bombed Israeli soldiers and Israel retaliated by shelling targets in eastern Lebanon. An April cease-fire banned attacks against civilian targets, but military and guerrilla forces on both sides continued to fire at each other.

Though disputed and called anticonstitutional by legal experts, elections for the 128-member National Assembly began on August 18 and lasted until mid-September. The winners were the pro-government candidates, who withstood competition from the Hezbollah and from Christians lukewarm to the Syrian presence. Organized in five rounds of voting on consecutive Sundays on the basis of geographic area, the elections began in the predominantly Christian area of Mt. Lebanon, where voters went to the polls in six newly created districts to elect 35 representatives. The pro-government candidates supporting the Syrian-backed Cabinet of Prime Minister Rafiq al-Hariri defeated the antigovernment nominees, who included Hezbollah representatives advocating the removal of the Israeli presence in southern Lebanon. An alliance that the Hezbollah forged during the summer with Druze leader Walid Jumblatt, who won a seat in the election, collapsed in part as a result of pressure from pro-Syrian Shi'ite Amal leader Nabih Berri, who at one point was also aligned with the Hezbollah. Elie Hobeika, a former Maronite militia leader, won on a pro-government ticket against Hezbollah-supported Christians. In Greater Beirut, Prime Minister Hariri's list of Sunni establishment candidates won handily. The Hezbollah lost seats in Beirut but retained them in southern Lebanon and the Al-Biqa region of central Lebanon.

In April French Pres. Jacques Chirac visited Lebanon. The first visit to Lebanon by a non-Arab head of state since the civil war (1975–76), the meeting resulted in an aid package for Lebanese reconstruction.

(REEVA S. SIMON)

LESOTHO

A constitutional monarchy of southern Africa and member of the Commonwealth, Lesotho forms a landlocked

CORINNE DUFKA—REUTERS

More than 2,000 Liberians fleeing the violence in Monrovia boarded the *Bulk Challenge,* a poorly equipped cargo ship. Nine days later, and only after international pressure, the ship was finally permitted to dock at Ghana's Takoradi Harbour.

enclave surrounded by South Africa. Area: 30,355 sq km (11,720 sq mi). Pop. (1996 est.): 1,971,000. Cap.: Maseru. Monetary unit: loti (plural: maloti), at par with the South African rand, with (Oct. 11, 1996) a free rate of 4.54 maloti to U.S. $1 (7.16 maloti = £1 sterling). Kings in 1996, Moshoeshoe II and, from February 7, Letsie III; prime minister, Ntsu Mokhehle.

On Jan. 15, 1996, King Moshoeshoe II was killed in a car crash on a mountain road. (*See* OBITUARIES.) He was the grandson of Moshoeshoe I, the "father" of the Basotho nation. His death came just a year after he had been restored to the throne. His son had been installed as King Letsie III by the military, which had dethroned his father, and had reigned from November 1990 to January 1995. He had abdicated voluntarily in January 1995 in favour of his father. On February 7 Letsie III was crowned again.

Four prominent Basotho were charged with treason on March 20, accused of having attempted to stage a coup by radio on February 29 and having conspired to overthrow the government between September 1995 and February 1996. The four were Makara Sekautu, president of the opposition United Party; Matsoso Bolofo, a former member of the National Security Service; and Lepoko Molapo and David Jonathan, both former members of the Royal Lesotho Defence Force. (GUY ARNOLD)

This article updates the *Macropædia* article SOUTHERN AFRICA: *Lesotho.*

LIBERIA

The republic of Liberia is located in West Africa, on the Atlantic Ocean. Area: 99,067 sq km (38,250 sq mi). Pop. (1996 est.): 2,110,000 (excluding Liberian refugees temporarily residing in surrounding countries estimated to number more than 750,000). Cap.: Monrovia. Monetary unit:

Liberian dollar, with (Oct. 11, 1996) an (inactive) official par value of L$1 to U.S. $1 and (Jan. 1, 1996) free/black market rate of L$38 = U.S. $1 (L$59 = £1 sterling). Chairmen of the Council of State in 1996, Wilton Sankawulo and, from September 3, Ruth Perry.

The precarious truce achieved between Liberia's warring factions in 1995 collapsed in April 1996 when Monrovia was convulsed by renewed fighting; many thousands fled the city. The fighting began when forces belonging to Charles Taylor's National Patriotic Front of Liberia and Gen. Alhaji G.V. Kromah of the United Liberation Movement of Liberia for Democracy (Ulimo-K) stormed the home of the dissident Gen. D. Roosevelt Johnson of Ulimo-J. Although the home was soon taken, Krahn tribesmen who supported Johnson resisted fiercely throughout the city. The Johnson forces took several hundred hostages. A new cease-fire went into effect on April 19, and Johnson released some hostages.

In August the main faction leaders agreed to another truce. Côte d'Ivoire, Burkina Faso, Mali, The Gambia, Niger, and Togo promised to supply troops for the West African peacekeeping force, and the U.S. agreed to provide $30 million. In November the peacekeeping force began disarming the rival factions. (GUY ARNOLD)

This article updates the *Macropædia* article WESTERN AFRICA: *Liberia.*

LIBYA

A socialist country of North Africa, Libya lies on the Mediterranean Sea. Area: 1,757,000 sq km (678,400 sq mi). Pop. (1996 est.): 5,446,000. Cap.: Tripoli (policy-making body meets in Surt). Monetary unit: Libyan dinar, with (Oct. 11, 1996) an official rate of 0.36 dinar to U.S. $1 (0.56 dinar = £1 sterling). De facto chief of state in 1996, Col. Muammar al-Qaddafi; secretary of the General People's Congress (nominal chief of state), Zanati Muhammad az-Zanati; secretary of the General People's Committee (premier), 'Abd al-Majid al-Qa'ud.

Libya's refusal to hand over two men accused of involvement in the bombing of a U.S. airliner over Scotland in 1988 continued to isolate the nation in 1996. The U.S.-led and UN-endorsed trade and air-traffic embargo again severely impaired the performance of the Libyan economy.

The opening of the western section of the Great Man-Made River was a major stage in Libya's massive water engineering project. Started in the early 1980s, this project would, when completed, secure fresh water supplies from the southern desert regions for Libya's heavily concentrated population on the Mediterranean coast. (*See* ARCHITECTURE AND CIVIL ENGINEERING: *Sidebar*.)

The Libyan economy benefited from the increase in oil prices during the second half of the year. Spot prices rose almost 40%. Thus, the national economy, though severely stretched by the heavy investment in the Great Man-Made River, was strengthened.

A visit by the prime minister of Turkey, Necmettin Erbakan, in October for the purpose of improving relations between the two Islamic countries backfired. At a meeting with Erbakan and in front of 50 accompanying Turkish journalists, Libya's chief of state, Col. Muammar al-Qaddafi, criticized Turkey for its suppression of Kurdish separatists and also for providing the U.S. with air bases from which attacks on Arab countries had been made.

During a football (soccer) match in Tripoli on July 9, a number of armed guards protecting a relative of Colonel Qaddafi opened fire on fans shouting protests against a call the referee had made in favour of a team controlled by Qaddafi's sons. A stampede ensued, and there were a number of deaths. Only a week earlier a riot in one of the nation's prisons had resulted in the deaths of more than 1,000 prisoners.

The nation's experiment with liberalization of retailing was given a severe jolt in mid-August when Qaddafi ordered the arrest of 1,500 businessmen and traders on charges of corruption and trade in foreign goods. He stated that he was anxious about the direction the domestic economy was taking.   (J.A. ALLAN)

This article updates the *Macropædia* article NORTH AFRICA: *Libya*.

LIECHTENSTEIN

A landlocked constitutional monarchy of central Europe, Liechtenstein is united with Switzerland by a customs and monetary union. Area: 160 sq km (62 sq mi). Pop. (1996 est.): 31,400. Cap.: Vaduz. Monetary unit: Swiss franc, with (Oct. 11, 1996) a free rate of Sw F 1.25 to U.S. $1 (Sw F 1.97 = £1 sterling). Sovereign prince, Hans Adam II; head of government in 1996, Mario Frick.

In 1996 a long-standing dispute between Liechtenstein and Russia was settled when Prince Hans Adam II negotiated the return of the royal family's archives from Russia, which had held the documents since they were seized by Soviet troops at the end of World War II. The matter was resolved when the prince, who had bought at auction the Sokolov Archive (which documents the executions of Russian Tsar Nicholas II and his family by Bolsheviks in 1918), offered an exchange. On September 4 Russian Foreign Minister Yevgeny Primakov agreed to the trade. A similar dispute with the Czech Republic over Czechoslovakia's 1945 confiscation of Prince Hans Adam's ancestral home and estates remained unresolved.

(ANNE ROBY)

This article updates the *Micropædia* article LIECHTENSTEIN.

LITHUANIA

A republic of northern Europe, Lithuania is on the southeastern shore of the Baltic Sea. Area: 65,301 sq km (25,213 sq mi). Pop. (1996 est.): 3,707,000. Monetary unit: litas, with (Oct. 11, 1996) a par value of 4 litai to U.S. $1 (6.30 litai = £1 sterling). President in 1996, Algirdas Brazauskas; prime ministers, Adolfas Slezevicius until February 8, Mindaugas Stankevicius from February 15, and, from December 10, Gediminas Vagnorius.

The decisive victory of the Homeland Union (Conservatives of Lithuania) (TS-LK) in the fall parliamentary elections ended four years of rule by the postcommunist Lithuanian Democratic Labour Party (LDDP). Together with its Christian Democratic allies, the TS-LK captured 86 of 137 seats, while the LDDP won only 12 and was unlikely to play a major role in Lithuania's political life in the future. Conservative leaders Vytautas Landsbergis and Gediminas Vagnorius regained the posts of parliament chairman and prime minister that they held in 1992.

The LDDP's loss was primarily due to its inability to improve the nation's economic situation and halt the continued growth of crime and corruption. The party chairman, Prime Minister Adolfas Slezevicius, was dismissed in February after the disclosure that he had used insider knowledge to remove his personal savings from a commercial bank whose activity was about to be sus-

A woman looks over election posters in Vilnius. In the Lithuanian elections, the Reform Movement of Vytautas Landsbergis regained power from the former communists.

JANEK SKARZYNKI—EPA/AFP

pended. The caretaker government, headed by Prime Minister Mindaugas Stankevicius, reduced the annual rate of inflation from 35% to 14%. Lithuania's economy showed modest growth of about 3%.

(SAULIUS A. GIRNIUS)

This article updates the *Macropædia* article BALTIC STATES: *Lithuania*.

LUXEMBOURG

Luxembourg is a landlocked constitutional monarchy in western Europe. Area: 2,586 sq km (999 sq mi). Pop. (1996 est.): 415,-000. Cap.: Luxembourg. Monetary unit: Luxembourg franc, at par with the Belgian franc, with (Oct. 11, 1996) a free rate of Lux F 31.55 to U.S. $1 (Lux F 49.70 = £1 sterling). Grand duke, Jean; prime minister in 1996, Jean-Claude Juncker.

Luxembourg's pioneering efforts in building broadcasting networks, satellite systems, and on-line services were met with increased competition in 1996, notably from Rupert Murdoch's News International, which owned 40% of British Sky Broadcasting. Compagnie Luxembourgeoise de Télédiffusion was one of Europe's biggest media companies, with interests in 10 television networks and 13 radio stations in eight countries. Luxembourg was also home to the world's second largest satellite company, Société Européenne des Satellites.

In May the European Union announced that only Luxembourg and France were likely to meet the conditions required for adopting the EU single currency, scheduled for introduction in 1999.   (ANNE ROBY)

MACEDONIA

A landlocked republic of the central Balkans, Macedonia borders Yugoslavia to the north, Bulgaria to the east, Greece to the south, and Albania to the west. Area: 25,713 sq km (9,928 sq mi). Pop. (1996 est.): 1,968,000. Cap.: Skopje. Monetary unit: denar, with (Oct. 11, 1996) a free rate of 40.60 denars to U.S. $1 (63.96 denars = £1 sterling). President in 1996, Kiro Gligorov; prime minister, Branko Crvenkovski.

In early February 1996 a crisis involving the two biggest parties in the ruling coalition, the Social Democratic Union of Macedonia and the Liberal Party, resulted in the coalition's breakup despite Pres. Kiro Gligorov's appeals for unity. Differences between the coalition partners centred on privatization, with the Liberals being accused of profiting from the sale of Macedonia's most attractive and lucrative enterprises. On February 10 Prime Minister Branko Crvenkovski dismissed the four Liberal ministers and extensively reshuffled his Cabinet. The Social Democrats emerged as the strongest party from the first postindependence local elections on November 17 and December 1, but the nationalist opposition made gains, winning, among others, the Skopje mayoralty. Ethnic Albanian parties also fared well.

Friction continued over the independent Albanian-language university in Tetovo, which the government regarded as illegal. In July demonstrations against the jailing of the university's dean, Fadil Sulejmani, and other Albanian activists resulted in clashes with the police.

Shepherds tend flocks of sheep in the mountains of western Macedonia. After trade embargoes were lifted, farmers began to export large amounts of lamb and mutton, although an outbreak of foot-and-mouth disease in the middle of the year required the killing of several thousand animals.

In the economy high unemployment remained a problem, and foreign trade declined. An epidemic of foot-and-mouth disease forced the authorities to order the slaughter of several thousand animals.

Macedonia's international position improved significantly with the signing with Yugoslavia on April 8 of an agreement establishing diplomatic relations. On October 7 the two countries abolished custom fees of up to 7.5%. Despite several rounds of talks, there was no breakthrough with Greece on the question of Macedonia's name, but liaison offices were opened in January, and visa fees were cut significantly in February. Relations with Albania worsened, however, mostly over the Tetovo University crisis. In September, German Pres. Roman Herzog became the first head of state of a European Union member country to visit Macedonia.   (STEFAN KRAUSE)

This article updates the *Macropædia* article BALKAN STATES: *Macedonia*.

MADAGASCAR

The republic of Madagascar occupies the island of the same name and minor adjacent islands in the Indian Ocean off the southeastern coast of Africa. Area: 587,041 sq km (226,658 sq mi). Pop. (1996 est.): 13,671,000. Cap.: Antananarivo. Monetary unit: Malagasy franc, with (Oct. 11, 1996) a free rate of FMG 3,950 to U.S. $1 (FMG 6,222 = £1 sterling). Presidents in 1996, Albert Zafy and, from September 5 (acting), Norbert Ratsirahonana; prime ministers, Emmanuel Rakotovahiny and, from May 28, Norbert Ratsirahonana.

On May 20, 1996, Prime Minister Emmanuel Rakotovahiny resigned following a motion of censure in the National Assembly. The motion appeared to be a consequence of comments made by International

Monetary Fund (IMF) managing director Michel Camdessus while visiting Madagascar; he said the IMF would not reach an agreement with the existing government, which, he claimed, lacked cohesion and would not be fully committed to implementing an IMF program. Pres. Albert Zafy then appointed Norbert Ratsirahonana, the president of the Constitutional High Court, prime minister.

In late July the National Assembly voted to begin impeachment proceedings against President Zafy, whom it accused of violating the constitution. Zafy announced that he would step down on September 5, although he insisted he had done nothing wrong. After two rounds of elections for a

new president, Didier Ratsiraka, a former military ruler, held a narrow lead.
                           (GUY ARNOLD)

MALAWI

A republic and member of the Commonwealth, Malawi is a landlocked state in eastern Africa. Area: 118,484 sq km (45,747 sq mi). Pop. (1996 est.): 9,453,000. A capital is not designated in the 1994 constitution. Current government operations are divided between Lilongwe (ministerial and financial), Blantyre (executive and judicial), and Zomba (legislative). Monetary unit: Malawi kwacha, with (Oct. 11, 1996) a free rate of 15.31 kwacha to U.S. $1

Students take notes in a primary school near Lilongwe, Malawi. The school was one of a number that received meals under a World Food Programme plan to improve students' health and thus their attendance and ability to concentrate.

Petronas Towers, owned by Malaysia's national oil company, rise to a height of 452 m (1,483 ft) in Kuala Lumpur. Officially declared the world's tallest buildings in 1996, the structures were part of a development of office, retail, hotel, and residential space in the Malaysian capital.

(24.11 kwacha = £1 sterling). President in 1996, Bakili Muluzi.

Following his acquittal on Dec. 23, 1995, on a charge of murdering four opposition politicians in 1983, former president Hastings Banda apologized in January to the people of Malawi for any suffering they might have experienced under his regime. He disclaimed any personal responsibility, however, attributing the misdeeds to selfish individuals in the government.

On May 2 Pres. Bakili Muluzi took the opportunity provided by the resignation of his second vice president, Chakunfwa Chihana, to reshuffle his Cabinet. He did not immediately fill the post vacated by Chihana but appointed 10 new members of the Cabinet and switched 9 other portfolios, leaving only 6 posts unchanged.

In January Malawi entered an agreement with the 11 other members of the Southern African Development Community to work toward the creation of a free-trade area and to encourage foreign private investors. In line with this pledge, the minister of finance, economic planning and development announced that all laws that discriminated against non-Malawians who were involved in business ventures in rural areas would be repealed.   (KENNETH INGHAM)

This article updates the *Macropædia* article SOUTHERN AFRICA: *Malawi.*

MALAYSIA

A federal constitutional monarchy of Southeast Asia and member of the Commonwealth, Malaysia consists of the former Federation of Malaya at the southern end of the Malay Peninsula (excluding Singapore) and Sabah and Sarawak on the northern part of the island of Borneo. Area: 330,442 sq km (127,584 sq mi). Pop. (1996 est.): 20,359,000. Cap.: Kuala Lumpur. Monetary unit: ringgit, with (Oct. 11, 1996) a free rate of 2.51 ringgit to U.S. $1 (3.95 ringgit = £1 sterling). Paramount ruler in 1996, with the title of *yang di-pertuan agong,* Tuanku Ja'afar ibni al-Marhum Tuanku Abdul Rahman; prime minister, Dato Seri Mahathir bin Mohamad.

Prime Minister Dato Seri Mahathir bin Mohamad experienced triumphs in 1996, reasserting his pre-eminence as leader of the United Malays National Organization (UMNO), the dominant party in the ruling National Front coalition. Though Mahathir and Deputy Prime Minister Dato Seri Anwar bin Ibrahim apparently worked harmoniously together, there were reports at the start of 1996 that Anwar might have enough momentum to challenge Mahathir for the party presidency, which carries with it the national prime ministership. But on May 4, UMNO's powerful policy-making Supreme Council ruled that no nominations would be accepted for the top two posts other than for Mahathir as party president and Anwar as deputy president, which effectively thwarted the possibility of a leadership challenge.

In October Mahathir's allies scored impressive victories at triennial party elections by winning most of the Supreme Council seats. More important, Foreign Affairs Minister Abdullah Badawi defeated Anwar loyalist Muhyiddin Yassin for one of the three vice presidential positions. The other two vice presidential slots were held by incumbents Najib Tun Razak, the popular education minister, and Selangor Chief Minister Muhammad Taib. Anwar supporters did, however, enjoy two electoral triumphs. In a surprising defeat Mahathir stalwart Rafidah Aziz, the international trade and industry minister, lost her post as head of the UMNO women's wing to Siti Zaharah Sulaiman. Rahim Tamby Chik, the UMNO youth leader, was replaced by Zahid Hamidi. Both Rafidah and Rahim had been dogged by allegations of impropriety.

Perhaps of longer-term significance was the return to UMNO of Tengku Razaleigh Hamzah. He had been a bitter foe of the government since trying unsuccessfully to displace Mahathir as party leader in 1987. Razaleigh subsequently quit UMNO and in 1989 founded an opposition party. One of the first public signs that the former allies would reconcile occurred when on May 11 Razaleigh attended celebrations for UMNO's 50th anniversary.

The government continued to promote large-scale infrastructure designed to lure international investors and to modernize the nation by the year 2020. It put new impetus into a plan to make Kuala Lumpur an international centre for advanced information technology. Referred to as the Multimedia Super Corridor, the project was to stretch from the new international airport under construction at Sepang near the Negri Sembilan state border to central Kuala Lumpur's 452-m (1,483-ft) Petronas Towers. The twin towers became the world's tallest buildings when they were completed in February.

The economy continued to perform well. Economists believed that the slowdown in growth from 9.5% to the 8–8.5% range would take some pressure off wages and inflation. There were new worries about the $7.2 billion current-account deficit, which was exacerbated by a slump in the global electronics market; electronics constituted 30.5% of the nation's exports.

(STEVEN FRANK)

This article updates the *Macropædia* article SOUTHEAST ASIA: *Malaysia.*

MALDIVES

A republic and member of the Commonwealth in the Indian Ocean, Maldives consists of about 1,200 small islands southwest of the southern tip of India. Area: 298 sq km (115 sq mi). Pop. (1996

Muslim men from rural Mali leave their shoes aside as they line up for afternoon prayers. As in some other African countries, Islam was the predominant religion of Mali, although animism was practiced by the Voltaic, Malinke, and Bambara peoples and Christianity by a very small number.

est.): 266,000. Cap.: Male. Monetary unit: rufiyaa, with (Oct. 11, 1996) a free rate of 11.77 rufiyaa to U.S. $1 (18.54 rufiyaa = £1 sterling). President in 1996, Maumoon Abdul Gayoom.

On Dec. 25, 1995, the Citizens' Majlis approved a balanced budget for 1996–97, with total revenues (and grants) estimated at 1,960,000,000 rufiyaa. A tiny economy dependent upon fishing, tourism, and a few manufactures, Maldives nonetheless had achieved steady growth over a number of years, with gross domestic product increasing in both 1994 and 1995. In recent years the government had emphasized opening up the economy to the private sector and encouraging foreign capital inflows; consequently, industrial production rose 10%, accompanied by comparable increases in exports of manufactured and processed goods. Since 1992 the increase in world commodity prices had added to the value of the nation's exports by 31–43%.

(GUY ARNOLD)

This article updates the *Micropædia* article MALDIVES.

MALI

Mali is a landlocked republic of West Africa. Area: 1,248,574 sq km (482,077 sq mi). Pop. (1996 est.): 9,204,000. Cap.: Bamako. Monetary unit: CFA franc, with (Oct. 11, 1996) a par value of CFAF 100 to the French franc and a free rate of CFAF 518.24 to U.S. $1 (CFAF 816.38 = £1 sterling). President in 1996, Alpha Oumar Konaré; prime minister, Ibrahima Boubacar Keita.

Demobilization and integration into the regular army of more than 2,700 former fighters of various Tuareg liberation movements picked up speed at the beginning

of 1996. On March 27 operation "Flame of Peace" marked the end of the five-year conflict that took thousands of lives and resulted in 120,000 refugees. An agreement signed with Niger and the UN High Commissioner for Refugees in November provided for the repatriation of 25,000 Malian Tuareg refugees living in Niger.

University students continued their strike. Although 60 students arrested in early January were released, many of their leaders remained in prison. Reacting to the educational crisis, opposition parties in the National Assembly submitted a motion for a vote of no confidence in the government, the first such motion in the country's history. In early February the motion was defeated following a 14-hour debate.

(NANCY ELLEN LAWLER)

This article updates the *Macropædia* article WESTERN AFRICA: *Mali.*

MALTA

The republic of Malta, a member of the Commonwealth, comprises the islands of Malta, Gozo, and Comino in the Mediterranean Sea between Sicily and Tunisia. Area: 316 sq km (122 sq mi). Pop. (1996 est.): 373,000. Cap.: Valletta. Monetary unit: Maltese lira, with (Oct. 11, 1996) a free rate of 0.36 lira to U.S. $1 (0.57 lira = £1 sterling). President in 1996, Ugo Mifsud Bonnici; prime ministers, Eddie Fenech Adami and, from October 28, Alfred Sant.

In May 1996 the secretary-general of the Arab League, Ahmad Esmat 'Abd al-Meguid, paid an official visit to Malta. He declared that he supported and would promote the Maltese and French proposal for a stability pact for the Mediterranean region made at the Euro-Mediterranean Conference in Barcelona, Spain.

In August the nation's drug squad made its largest drug haul ever. Approximately 7½ tons of marijuana were discovered in a container that arrived from Singapore destined for Romania via Yugoslavia.

In elections in October the Malta Labour Party won 50.7% of the vote. The Nationalist Party took 47.8%. (ALBERT GANADO)

MARSHALL ISLANDS

A republic in the central Pacific Ocean, the Marshall Islands comprises two 1,300-km (800-mi)-long parallel chains of coral atolls. Area: 181 sq km (70 sq mi). Pop. (1996 est.): 58,500. Cap.: Majuro. Monetary unit: U.S. dollar, with (Oct. 11, 1996) a free rate of U.S. $1.58 to £1 sterling. Presidents in 1996, Amata Kabua and, from December 19 (acting), Kunio Lemari.

In local and national government elections in November 1995, there were 100 candidates for 33 Nitijela (national legislature) seats and 1,000 candidates for local government councils. Issues of kinship and personality remained more important than party or policy in an election that saw Pres. Amata Kabua and all except two of his Cabinet ministers returned to office. On Dec. 19, 1996, Kabua, the nation's first and only president, died. (*See* OBITUARIES.) The government then named Kunio Lemari, minister of transport and communications, as acting president.

Nuclear-testing issues remained the focus of international attention in 1996. The government was widely criticized for its contemplation of establishing a nuclear-waste dump for the storage of contaminated material from nuclear tests conducted between 1946 and 1958. (BARRIE MACDONALD)

This article updates the *Macropædia* article PACIFIC ISLANDS: *Marshall Islands.*

A POSTNUCLEAR ERA IN THE PACIFIC

by Barrie Macdonald

illustration by Igor Kopelnitsky

France's announcement in January 1996 that it would end nuclear testing in the Pacific Islands brought the era to a close. For more than 30 years, France had conducted tests at the atolls of Mururoa and Fangataufa in French Polynesia. The last series of tests, which began in September 1995, triggered riots and civil disorder in the streets of the Polynesian capital, Papeete. It also caused serious damage to the local tourism industry and spurred growth in local support for independence from France. These tests, like earlier series, brought condemnation from the Pacific nations and countries on the Pacific Rim. This latest protest was more intense, however, because the tests came during a moratorium that had been honoured by all of the other nuclear powers except China. There was debate over whether these tests were a necessary preparation for a shift to computer simulation or the final, defiant gesture of French colonialism. There was also a sense of an opportunity lost in the subsequent dismantling of facilities that had served the nuclear testing and that might have been used to service a fishing fleet or the tourist industry or to assist the local economy in other ways.

France was the last of a series of nuclear powers that had conducted tests in the Pacific Islands. The United Kingdom had begun tests in Australia in 1956 before switching to Christmas Island, while a decade earlier the United States had begun testing in the Marshall Islands. The U.S. tests ultimately forced the relocation of the people of Bikini and Enewetak, while the residents of Rongelap and Utirik were seriously affected by the downwind drift of radioactive debris, especially from the Bravo test of 1954. In 1996 there remained a legacy of contaminated soils, uninhabitable environments, a high incidence of cancers and birth malformations, and a bitterness that neither time nor compensatory funds had removed. Yet the government of the Marshall Islands was considering a proposal to use one of its remote atolls as a waste dump for radioactive nuclear materials.

In international terms the Pacific Islands nations are small, remote, geographically fragmented, and poor in exploitable resources—factors that have encouraged their use for military purposes and restricted development options. Some industrial development has taken place by adding labour-intensive value to imported raw materials, but many countries do not have the option of developing manufacturing on a profitable scale. The processing of agricultural or marine commodities may founder on water shortages, lack of infrastructure, high transport costs, and a limited skills base. Despite many attempts, few nations have developed fishing or aquaculture industries for more than local supply. Rather, marine resources, especially tuna, are exploited by na-

tions from the Pacific Rim. The U.S. has a long-standing agreement that compensates island countries for the activities of its tuna-fishing industry, but surveillance and monitoring remain a problem unless support is provided by larger neighbours such as Australia and New Zealand. The filament-mesh "wall of death" nets that caused huge inroads into fish stocks in the 1980s were banned by international convention. The indications are that the fishing industry is now sustainable at present levels of activity and that, with improved monitoring and collective strength, revenues to island economies will increase.

The main focus of new resource developments is on mining and forestry, with both, except for modest and long-standing industries in Fiji, being focused on Papua New Guinea. Forestry is also of major importance in the neighbouring Solomon Islands and, to a lesser extent, Vanuatu. In many cases the weakness of governance, the narrow economic base, and political greed have destroyed major assets for political advantage and individual profit.

Although Papua New Guinea is rich in minerals, the development of these resources has been problematic. Bougainville is the site of the largest open-pit copper and gold mine in the world, but before its premature closing in 1989 at the hands of a secessionist guerrilla movement, it had a destructive effect on the local environment. Mining had not only polluted local land and waterways but also generated onshore overburden and tailings dumps of 3,300 ha (8,150 ac) and more than 900 ha (2,225 ac) of newly created delta on the adjacent coast. The exploitation of the resource, the dispossession of the landowners, and the distribution of profits between government and local landowners (the latter receiving less than 1%) provided the impetus for secessionism. Despite seven years of civil war, the Papua New Guinea government has remained unable to reestablish its control over its rebel province. The Ok Tedi and Porgera mines have provided a replacement national income for Bougainville (which used to contribute some 40% of export earnings and 20% of gross domestic product) but have generated their own environmental and political problems.

Forestry has proved an even more contentious issue in the Melanesian nations of the western Pacific. Through local business interests and Asian investors in particular, there has been a rapid development of the forestry industry concentrated heavily upon clear felling of tropical rain forests and the export of whole logs. With a growing level of government corruption, weak government controls, and a cultural climate that encourages and rewards entrepreneurial activity

Pacific Nuclear Testing

A mushroom cloud from a 1971 French nuclear bomb test rises over Mururoa atoll. In 1996 France announced that it would end its nuclear testing in the South Pacific.

Pacific Area Test Sites (Testing Party)	Nuclear Tests Conducted at Site
Bikini Atoll, Marshall Is. (U.S.)	23
Enewetak Atoll, Marshall Is. (U.S.)	43
Christmas Island, Kiribati (U.S. and U.K.)	30
Johnston Island (U.S.)	12
Amchitka Island, Alaska (U.S.)	3
Monte Bello Islands, Australia (U.K.)	3
Emu Field, Australia (U.K.)	2
Maralinga Test Range, Australia (U.K.)	7
Malden Island, Kiribati (U.K.)	3
Mururoa Atoll, French Polynesia (France)	114
Fangataufa Island, French Polynesia (France)	10
Other French Polynesia (France)	52
Other Pacific (U.S.)	4
TOTAL	306

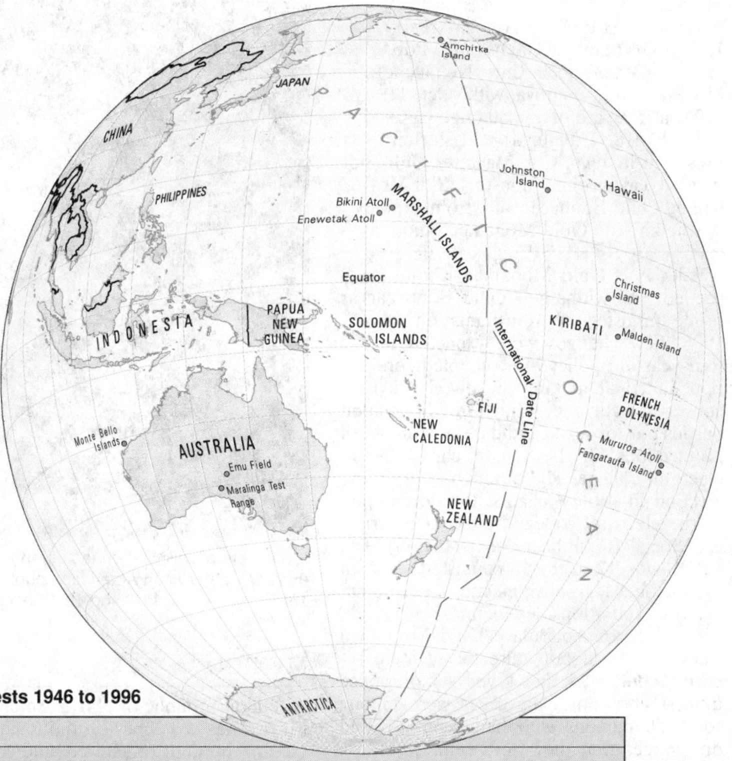

Pacific Nuclear Tests 1946 to 1996

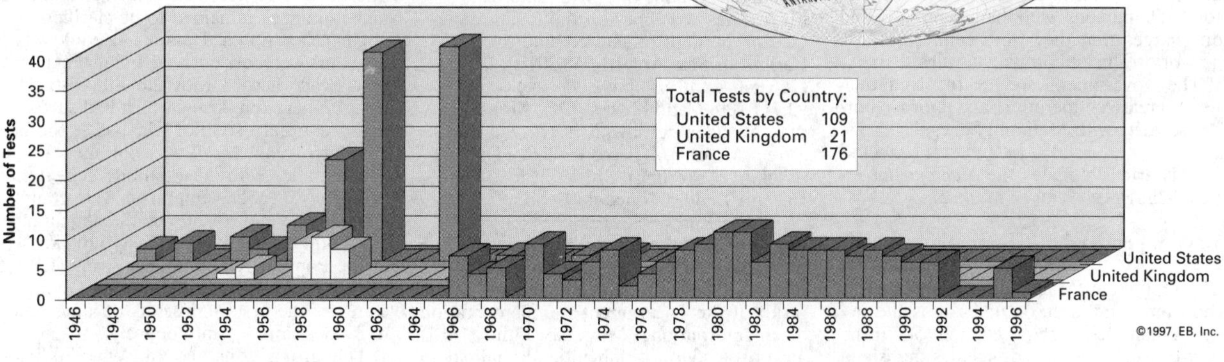

Total Tests by Country:
United States 109
United Kingdom 21
France 176

Number of Tests

United States
United Kingdom
France

© 1997, EB, Inc.

by politicians, forestry companies are operating the industry at unsustainable levels. In the Solomon Islands, for example, the current log yield of 850,000 cu m (1,112,000 cu yd) per annum is well ahead of the estimated sustainable annual yield of 280,000 metric tons, an estimate that is dropping steadily as high volumes of export continue. There, where the government has a stated intention of terminating all log exports by 1999, forestry exporters are encouraged to accelerate production. Moreover, the government has subverted its own taxation regime by discounting tax obligations for exporters; court actions are also pending on inducements paid by exporters to politicians and senior public servants. This level and nature of resource exploitation has generated concern among regional aid donors, who have tried to improve controls by linking the development policies of the islands to aid programs, but with little success. In January 1996 Australia refused to proceed with a forestry development aid program because of the Solomon Islands government's inability to develop a long-term policy for sustainable logging.

In the future the seafloor may prove to be a lucrative source of newly exploitable resources. Nodules of manganese and cobalt have been identified in a number of areas, most notably in the deep ocean between French Polynesia and the Cook Islands. These resources, however, will be difficult to exploit until new technology permits their recovery without serious damage to the environment.

While resource exploitation in Pacific Island nations is a matter of concern for regional organizations, island nations see few options at a time when aid funds are diminishing because of economic difficulties in the major donor nations of the Organisation for Economic Co-operation and Development and a post-Cold War redirection of funds away from the less-developed world and toward Eastern Europe. This has contributed to the largely unplanned and poorly monitored exploitation of commercial resources in the islands and has encouraged governments to seek quick-fix solutions through tax havens and doubtful investments.

Small Pacific island nations without large-scale commercial resources are dependent on overseas development assistance for providing basic services and meeting the social and economic aspirations of their people. At the same time, those with resources that currently offer a higher return have embarked on a development path that is unlikely to provide sustainable income and may well undermine the stability of governments and ensure low, short-term returns rather than long-term sustainable yields.

Barrie Macdonald is professor of history at Massey University, Palmerston, N.Z.

MAURITANIA

The republic of Mauritania is on the Atlantic coast of West Africa. Area: 1,030,700 sq km (398,000 sq mi). Pop. (1996 est.): 2,333,000. Cap.: Nouakchott. Monetary unit: ouguiya, with (Oct. 11, 1996) a free rate of 138.50 ouguiya to U.S. $1 (218.17 ouguiya = £1 sterling). President in 1996, Col. Maaouya Ould Sidi Ahmad Taya; prime ministers, Sidi Mohamed Ould Boubacar and, from January 2, Cheikh Afia Ould Mohamed Khouna.

Cheikh Afia Ould Mohamed Khouna succeeded Sidi Mohamed Ould Boubacar as prime minister of Mauritania on Jan. 2, 1996. Few changes were expected in the four-year-old policy of economic liberalization aimed at making the ouguiya a fully convertible currency. Only three opposition parties put forward candidates for the April 12 elections for the Senate, chosen by an electoral college. The others boycotted the election in protest against the domination of the electoral college by the Democratic and Social Republican Party (PRDS). The PRDS won 17 of the 18 contested seats. In the October legislative elections, the PRDS again scored a lopsided victory.

On July 16 Abdoulaye Ould Mohamed Mahoud, the deputy director of state security, confirmed that seven senior police officers and four magistrates were among some 50 persons who had been arrested on charges that they were connected to a network trafficking in illegal drugs.

The government sought to strengthen ties, increase cooperation, and improve border security with Mali and Senegal.

(NANCY ELLEN LAWLER)

This article updates the *Macropædia* article WESTERN AFRICA: *Mauritania*.

MAURITIUS

The republic of Mauritius, a member of the Commonwealth, occupies an island in the Indian Ocean about 800 km (500 mi) east of Madagascar and includes the island dependencies of Rodrigues, Agalega, and Cargados Carajos Shoals. Area: 2,040 sq km (788 sq mi). Pop. (1996 est.): 1,141,-000. Cap.: Port Louis. Monetary unit: Mauritian rupee, with (Oct. 11, 1996) a free rate of Mau Rs 20.65 to U.S. $1 (Mau Rs 32.53 = £1 sterling). President in 1996, Cassam Uteem; prime minister, Navin Ramgoolam.

A major electoral reversal occurred in December 1995 when the opposition alliance of the Mauritius Labour Party and the Mauritian Militant Movement ousted Sir Anerood Jugnauth's Mauritian Socialist Movement, which had led the nation since 1982, and won all 60 seats in the island's 20 constituencies. The Mauritius Labour Party leader, Navin Ramgoolam, became prime minister.

Social and economic conditions in Mauritius continued to improve. Life expectancy at birth was 70 years, the rate of adult literacy was 81.7%, and per capita gross national product was at $3,030; 100% of the population had access to health services, 99% to safe water, and 99% to sanitation.

(GUY ARNOLD)

This article updates the *Micropædia* article MAURITIUS.

Workers in a Volkswagen factory in Puebla state assemble vehicles for domestic sales and for export to other Latin American countries and to the U.S. Mexico began to show clear signs in 1996 of emerging from the 1995 recession.

MEXICO

A federal republic of North America, Mexico has coastlines on the Pacific Ocean, the Gulf of Mexico, and the Caribbean Sea. Area: 1,958,201 sq km (756,066 sq mi). Pop. (1996 est.): 92,711,000. Cap.: Mexico City. Monetary unit: Mexican peso, with (Oct. 11, 1996) a free rate of 7.62 pesos to U.S. $1 (12.01 pesos = £1 sterling). President in 1996, Ernesto Zedillo Ponce de León.

The year 1996 began in the shadow of the previous year's financial crisis. Although that crisis had been largely overcome as the result of the government's implementation of an International Monetary Fund (IMF) austerity program, difficulties remained to be tackled on both the political and economic fronts. At the end of December 1995, there had been a partial Cabinet reshuffle. Energy Minister Ignacio Pichardo Pagaza, a former head of the ruling Institutional Revolutionary Party (PRI) and widely viewed as belonging to the party's "old guard," was replaced by Jesús Reyes Heroles. Arsenio Farell Cubillas was appointed comptroller general in place of Norma Samaniengo, and Carlos Almeida López became head of the president's press office, a post formerly occupied by Carlos Salomon. These changes, though relatively minor, were seen as a prelude in the new year to further political reform, to which Pres. Ernesto Zedillo Ponce de León had pledged a firm commitment.

As the year began, Zedillo resumed this reform drive, seeking the cooperation of the two main opposition parties, the National Action Party (PAN) and the Party of the Democratic Revolution (PRD). Although both parties intermittently withdrew from the negotiations, Zedillo at the end of July managed to achieve an accord that, among other attributes, ended the ruling party's role at the head of the Federal Electoral Institute (IFE). Accordingly, Interior Minister Emilio Chuayffet resigned as president of the IFE in mid-October along with

other PRI members who had served on the board since it was established in 1990; the question of replacement and selection of new nominees remained to be clarified.

On other political matters Zedillo's endeavours were less positive. Finalizing terms of a peace accord with the Zapatista National Liberation Army, which had surfaced in the southern state of Chiapas at the beginning of January 1994, continued to be problematic, with negotiations repeatedly breaking down. Developments were complicated at the end of June by the appearance of another armed guerrilla group, known as the Popular Revolutionary Army (EPR), in the village of Aguas Blancas, Guerrero state, on the first anniversary of a massacre of 17 peasants by state police.

The group consisted of some 70 people, masked and carrying AK-47 and R-15 rifles. Their brief appearance at a commemoration for those killed the previous year, being held by members of the left-leaning PRD and peasant groups, was non-confrontational but called for the overthrow of the Zedillo government, which it alleged to be antidemocratic and illegitimate. The incident was initially played down by the authorities, but during the next few weeks and months, there were more incidents involving the EPR in a number of different states, which prompted a major counterinsurgency effort by the government.

The conflict appeared to simmer down to some degree when the EPR declared a cease-fire in the days preceding (and during) municipal and local legislative elections in the state of Guerrero on October 6. Just before the elections, tension was high as a result of some 15,000 government troops who had been posted to the state to flush out the EPR. On October 5 troops were ordered to temporarily suspend their counterinsurgency operations and remain confined to barracks until the elections had been held. This fostered an atmosphere of relative peace as the voting took place. There were, nevertheless, reports of irregularities perpetrated by the PRI in regard to voting lists, vote buying, and intimidation, compiled by the independent Civic Alliance (Alianza Cívica). Recriminations by the PRI and the PAN, however, were limited, given that both parties won significant numbers of seats. Also, in the weeks immediately after the elections, EPR hostilities did not resume.

At its convention in late September, the rank and file of the ruling PRI adopted a number of resolutions that unleashed additional controversy and threatened the prospects for internal party reform, which Zedillo was seeking. Two major resolutions were approved. One concerned rules covering the party's choice of presidential candidate in 2000, when Zedillo's term ended. Government technocrats with no experience of elected office (such as Zedillo) and fewer than 10 years of PRI membership would not be allowed to be candidates. A unanimous resolution of the party was to defend state ownership of the petrochemical industry (a part of the state oil concern, Pemex) and resist the privatization moves the government had been seeking to impose. This, in fact, led to the deferral in October of the planned government sell-off.

Throughout 1996 Zedillo continued to be dogged by the backlog of unfinished business from the administration of Pres. Carlos Salinas de Gortari. Not the least of these were the investigations into the murder of former PRI presidential candidate Luis Donaldo Colosio and the case against Salinas's brother, Raúl, concerning his alleged involvement in the assassination of the PRI secretary-general, José Francisco Ruiz Massieu, in September 1994. During October the discovery of a body believed to be that of a member of the legislature suspected in the Ruiz Massieu case, on the grounds of property owned by Raúl Salinas, appeared to provide more evidence of foul play.

In regard to the economy, the picture was significantly brighter than in 1995, as a modest recovery began after the almost 7% decline in gross domestic product (GDP) registered in 1995. Growth in the first quarter of 1996 was measured at 2.2%, and in the second quarter there was significant expansion year-on-year of 7.2%. By mid-1996 recovery was evident in both manufacturing and construction, which had declined sharply (by 6.4% and 22%, respectively) in 1995. Indeed, in June, when industrial output rose by 12% overall, manufacturing was up from the previous year by 12.6% and construction by 13.2%. The increases resulted largely from exports rather than domestic demand. Overall, GDP growth of about 3% in 1996 was officially expected.

Inflation, which surged to an annual rate of almost 52% in 1995 as a result of the devaluation of the peso and the impact of adjustment measures, was reduced significantly in 1996. The monthly consumer price index rose by 1.3–1.6% from June through September, compared with a 2.4% increase per month in the first half of the year.

Concerning the exchange rate, which had been altered to a floating regime in the wake of the 1995 financial crisis, the peso showed remarkable stability during the first nine months of 1996, tending to appreciate from its end-of-1995 level of about 7.7 to the U.S. dollar. Indeed, by the end of September, the rate—which then stood at

7.54 per $1—was comfortably within the target average of 7.7 envisioned for the year. During the second week of October, however, the rate declined to around 7.8 new pesos per $1, and the rate at the year's end was expected to be about 8 per $1.

The relative strength of the peso did not hamper the achievement of monthly trade surpluses during the first nine months of 1996. In fact, the accumulated surplus stood at approximately $5.5 billion by the end of September, and it appeared probable that the total at the end of the year would be at the upper end of the $6.5 billion to $7 billion range. The buoyant trade results led to further improvements in the current-account position.

(SUSAN M. CUNNINGHAM)

MICRONESIA, FEDERATED STATES OF

A republic in the western Pacific Ocean, the Federated States of Micronesia comprises more than 600 islands and islets in the Caroline Islands archipelago. Area: 701 sq km (271 sq mi). Pop. (1996 est.): 106,000. Cap.: Palikir, on Pohnpei. Monetary unit: U.S. dollar, with (Oct. 11, 1996) a free rate of U.S. $1.58 to £1 sterling. President in 1996, Bailey Olter.

At an economic summit attended by 500 delegates in December 1995, the Federated States of Micronesia started planning for the transition from its economic relationship with the United States. The summit proposed that the Federated States undertake fiscal reform and promote private-sector development. New expenditures were to be devoted to improved health and education services and to development initiatives that would be both environmentally sustainable and culturally sensitive. The nation was also seeking to diversify its sources of aid. To instill more fiscal discipline, the national government would commit funds to regional projects only on a dollar-for-dollar basis with state governments.

(BARRIE MACDONALD)

This article updates the *Macropædia* article PACIFIC ISLANDS: *Micronesia*.

MOLDOVA

A landlocked republic of the extreme northeastern Balkans, Moldova borders Ukraine on the north, northeast, and southeast and Romania on the west. Area: 33,700 sq km (13,000 sq mi). Pop. (1996 est.) 4,372,000. Cap.: Chisinau. Monetary unit: Moldovan leu, with (Oct. 11, 1996) a free rate of 4.61 lei = U.S. $1 (7.26 lei = £1 sterling). President in 1996, Mircea Snegur; prime minister, Andrei Sangheli.

With two rounds of presidential elections—on November 17 and December 1—Moldova experienced electoral fever through most of 1996. The campaigning began when in July 1995 Pres. Mircea Snegur quit the ruling Agrarian Democratic Party of Moldova (PDAM) to form the Party of Revival and Accord of Moldova. Subsequently, Snegur, Prime Minister Andrei Sangheli, and Parliament Chairman Petru Lucinschi engaged in a presidential race that became increasingly personal. Snegur repeatedly threatened to dismiss Sangheli's Cabinet for incompetence.

Snegur won the support of the right-wing parties, including the Christian Democratic Popular Front and the Moldovan Party of Democratic Forces, but this could not counterbalance the leftist coalition around Lucinschi, which included the PDAM, the socialists, and the communists. Lucinschi eventually won the election with 54% of the popular vote. His victory could bring a change in Moldova's policy of rapprochement with the West. Perceived as pro-Russian, Lucinschi was the ethnic Moldovan who had held the highest position in the hierarchy of the now defunct Communist Party of the Soviet Union; he was Central Committee secretary. (DAN IONESCU)

This article updates the *Macropædia* article BALKAN STATES: *Moldova*.

MONACO

A sovereign principality on the northern Mediterranean coast, Monaco is bounded on land by the French département of Alpes-Maritimes. Area: 1.95 sq km (0.75 sq mi). Pop. (1996 est.): 30,500. Monetary unit: French franc, with (Oct. 11, 1996) a free rate of F 5.18 to U.S. $1 (F 8.16 = £1 sterling). Chief of state, Prince Rainier III; minister of state in 1996, Paul Dijoud.

Monaco removed itself from the French telephone network early in 1996 and received its own country code—377. The Office Monegasque des Telephones, which was controlled by the royal family, joined with Global TeleSystems Group Inc. to create a joint venture, GTS Monaco Access SAM. The new company would offer international phone service to cellular phone companies and cable television companies at rates lower than those of established national phone companies, which had previously held protected monopolies for their international connections.

On October 4 Princess Stephanie was granted a divorce from Daniel Ducruet. The couple, the parents of two children, were married in July 1995. (ANNE ROBY)

This article updates the *Micropædia* article MONACO.

MONGOLIA

A landlocked republic between Russia and China in eastern Asia, Mongolia was formerly known as Outer Mongolia. Area: 1,566,500 sq km (604,800 sq mi). Pop. (1996 est.): 2,334,000. Cap.: Ulaanbaatar (Ulan Bator). Monetary unit: tugrik, with (Oct. 11, 1996) a free rate of Tug 466.67 to U.S. $1 (Tug 735.15 = £1 sterling). Presidents in 1996, Punsalmaagiyn Ochirbat; prime ministers, Puntsagiyn Jasray and, from July 19, Mendsaihan Enhsaihan.

The surprising victory of the Democratic Alliance over the ruling Mongolian People's Revolutionary Party (MPRP) in the June 1996 national election marked the end of 75 years of communist rule in Mongolia. The MPRP, brought to power by the Soviet-backed 1921 revolution, had managed to retain control of the country during the first democratic elections of 1990 and 1992.

For the 1996 election the system of representation was changed for the third time since 1990. The pact between the MPRP and the opposition National Democratic Party (NDP) and Social Democratic Party

A boy plays outside his home in a public-housing project in Ulaanbaatar, the capital of Mongolia. During 1996 the country continued to suffer a number of economic problems, including a budget crisis, a decline in revenue from copper exports, and price increases.

(SDP) on proportional representation was abandoned by the MPRP, which forced through the State Great Hural (national assembly) a bill changing the 26 multiseat constituencies of the 1992 election into 76 single-seat constituencies.

The Democratic Alliance, an electoral coalition formed in March 1996 by the NDP and the SDP, won 50 of the 76 seats in the Great Hural. The MPRP won 25, and one seat went to the United Heritage (conservative) Party, a small pro-MPRP party. Although more people voted for the MPRP than any other single party (41.9%), their number was smaller than the combined vote for the NDP (30.7%) and the SDP (13.6%).

On July 19 the Great Hural approved Pres. Punsalmaagiyn Ochirbat's nomination of Democratic Alliance leader Mendsaihan Enhsaihan for the post of prime minister. The MPRP minority then disrupted legislative proceedings for three days in an unsuccessful bid for some official posts, but the Democratic Alliance proceeded with the formation of its administration.

(ALAN J.K. SANDERS)

MOROCCO

A constitutional monarchy of North Africa, Morocco has coastlines on the Atlantic Ocean and the Mediterranean Sea. Area: 458,730 sq km (177,117 sq mi). Pop. (1996 est.): 26,736,000. (Area and population figures refer to Morocco as constituted prior to the purported division of Western Sahara between Morocco and Mauritania and the subsequent Moroccan occupation of the Mauritanian zone in 1979.) Cap.: Rabat. Monetary unit: dirham, with (Oct. 11, 1996) a free rate of 8.79 dirhams to U.S. $1 (13.84 dirhams = £1 sterling). King, Hassan II; prime minister in 1996, 'Abd al-Latif Filali.

On March 3, 1996, King Hassan announced that proposals for constitutional reforms would be presented later in the year. In essence the reforms, which had been fore- shadowed a year earlier, would provide for a bicameral legislature. Members of the lower house, the Majlis an-Nawwab, would be directly elected every five years and would enact the country's legislation. The upper chamber, the Majlis ash-Shura, would be a consultative body, with its members indirectly elected from the municipalities, the professional organizations, and the "salaried classes"; one-third of the members would be replaced every three years. The reforms were approved in a national referendum on September 13, and legislative elections were promised for April 1997, although they would probably be held later in the year.

In a further administrative move, this time in response to criticism from other countries, a major antidrug and antismuggling campaign was launched in January under the control of Interior Minister Driss Basri. The campaign led to the resignation of the minister for human rights, Muhammad Ziane, who had criticized the campaign as an "abuse of power." His responsibilities were assumed by the justice minister, Abderrahmane Amalou. The campaign also generated much complaint because of the delays it caused to importers and exporters alike, and there were accusations that it was really undertaken for the benefit of powerful figures. Nevertheless, the campaign muted French and Dutch criticisms of the $1.8 billion apparently earned from Moroccan drug sales in Europe.

Morocco's privatization program continued; 25% of the refining company Samir was sold in March, and the terms of the sale were eased in October so as to encourage foreign investors. Despite receiving $450 million of private foreign investment in 1995 and having the most highly deregulated financial sector in the Middle East and North Africa, Morocco continued to lag behind its target of gaining $1 billion in foreign investment annually. The South Korean company Daewoo, however, announced in September that it would invest $500 million over the next five years in tourism, telecommunications, and automobile manufacturing.   (GEORGE JOFFÉ)

This article updates the *Macropædia* article NORTH AFRICA: *Morocco*.

MOZAMBIQUE

A republic and member of the Commonwealth, Mozambique is located in eastern Africa, on the Indian Ocean. Area: 812,379 sq km (313,661 sq mi). Pop. (1996 est.): 17,878,000. Cap.: Maputo. Monetary unit: metical, with (Oct. 11, 1996) a free rate of 11,141 meticais to U.S. $1 (17,550 meticais = £1 sterling). President in 1996, Joaquim Chissano; prime minister, Pascoal Mocumbi.

The creation of a new and, it was hoped, mutually beneficial relationship with the postapartheid regime in South Africa was one of the important concerns of 1996 in Mozambique. On May 6 Pres. Joaquim Chissano chaired a meeting of investors aimed at obtaining funds to restore the flow of goods between Johannesburg and Maputo, which had declined from 40% of the region's exports to only 5% in the years since Mozambique became independent in 1975. Since Maputo was the nearest port to Johannesburg, it appeared to be a project that would benefit both countries. It would, however, involve much preparatory work, such as dredging the harbour at Maputo, rehabilitating the railway, and building a new toll road to shorten the journey between Maputo and Witbank, S.Af.

Also on May 6, Chissano and Pres. Nelson Mandela of South Africa signed an agreement that proved to be more controversial. The proposal was to lease 200,000 ha (494,000 ac) of land in northern Mozambique to white South African farmers. Members of the Mozambique National Resistance (Renamo) opposition party, as well as some of the residents in the area, did not agree that the payment of $800 million was adequate compensation for the loss of the land and were concerned that white South Africans might assume a prominent role in Mozambique. In an attempt to reassure critics, South African Gen. Constand Viljoen met the Renamo leader, Afonso Dhlakama, in July and stressed that there was no intention of creating South African colonies in Mozambique. What had been agreed upon, he said, formed part of the framework for the development of the whole southern African region, starting with the reorganization of agriculture.

South Africa had offered assistance in February to deal with a legacy of the recent civil war, the clearing of land mines. By the middle of the year, 11,000 of these explosive devices had been removed from three provinces, but an additional $460 million was needed to complete the work. (*See* MILITARY AFFAIRS: *Special Report.*)

Although the government was no longer engaged in armed conflict, it faced criticism from the Human Rights League, which urged Chissano to dismiss Interior Minister Manuel Antonio because, the league maintained, he had said that detainees who died in police cells had only themselves to blame. Again, in July, the league accused the police of torturing and killing civilians.

(KENNETH INGHAM)

This article updates the *Macropædia* article SOUTHERN AFRICA: *Mozambique*.

MYANMAR (BURMA)

Myanmar is a republic of Southeast Asia with coastlines on the Bay of Bengal and the Andaman Sea. Area: 676,577 sq km (261,228 sq mi). Pop. (1996 est.): 45,976,000. Cap.: Yangon (Rangoon). Monetary unit: kyat, with (Oct. 11, 1996) an official rate of K5.94 to U.S. $1 (K9.36 = £1 sterling) and (Jan. 1, 1996) unofficial free rate of K125 to U.S. $1 (K194 = £1 sterling). Chairman of the State Law and Order Restoration Council in 1996, Gen. Than Shwe.

In late May Myanmar's military junta, the State Law and Order Restoration Council (SLORC), arrested more than 250 members of the National League for Democracy (NLD). The NLD had planned to hold a three-day meeting on the anniversary of its 1990 landslide victory in the parliamentary elections, which the SLORC annulled. This was the most severe crackdown on the banned opposition since the release in 1995 of Daw Aung San Suu Kyi, the NLD leader who had been under house arrest for six years. The SLORC promulgated a new law banning rallies by the NLD and prohibiting it from drafting a new constitution.

Nevertheless, more than 10,000 supporters rallied at Suu Kyi's house, and the NLD held its meeting. It proceeded with the drafting of a new constitution that would deny the armed forces any role in a future civilian government. Suu Kyi's invitation to enter into a "constructive dialogue" with the government was rejected by the SLORC. Instead, the SLORC promised to present a new constitution in 1997 that would guarantee a role for the military in the country's political affairs.

In October in an attempt to prevent the NLD from holding a party congress, the SLORC arrested more than 500 NLD members and cut Suu Kyi's telephone and severely restricted outside access to her, particularly by diplomats. Hundreds of students demonstrated in the capital in December for the right to form a union and for the release of students held by the military authorities.   (CLAUDE RAKISITS)

This article updates the Macropædia article SOUTHEAST ASIA: Myanmar.

A youth works in an industrial shop in Yangon. Foreign investment in the booming Myanmar economy continued in 1996—attracted by plentiful natural resources, cheap labour, and governmental economic reforms—despite concerns about human rights abuses.

LE BACQUER—PRADO/GAMMA LIAISON

NAMIBIA

A republic and member of the Commonwealth, Namibia is situated in southern Africa, on the Atlantic Ocean. Area: 825,118 sq km (318,580 sq mi). Pop. (1996 est.): 1,709,000. Cap.: Windhoek. Monetary unit: Namibian dollar, at par with the South African rand (also legal currency), with (Oct. 11, 1996) a free rate of Nam$4.54 to U.S. $1 (Nam$7.16 = £1 sterling). President in 1996, Sam Nujoma; prime minister, Hage Geingob.

In March 1996 Pres. Sam Nujoma appeared on television to denounce a newly released book detailing the detention and torture of people by the South West Africa People's Organization during the 1980s as "false history" and to accuse those who were promoting it of threatening national reconciliation. He and the governing party were in turn accused of failing to face up to, and apologize for, what had happened. The government then published a listing of those who had died for liberation, including detainees.

In mid-1996 an agreement was finally reached with South Africa on how to cancel Namibia's preindependence debt. This followed President Nujoma's first state visit to South Africa, during which he pleaded for South African investment in his country.

The government was criticized for having agreed to large increases in pay for politicians and top civil servants, especially when a severe drought was showing no sign of ending. The country's terms of trade continued to deteriorate, and in order to diversify the economy and create jobs for the unemployed, the government pressed ahead with its Export Processing Zone strategy. Legislation was passed to provide that there could be no strikes at EPZ factories for five years.   (CHRISTOPHER SAUNDERS)

This article updates the Macropædia article SOUTHERN AFRICA: Namibia.

NAURU

An island republic within the Commonwealth, Nauru lies in the Pacific Ocean about 1,900 km (1,200 mi) east of New Guinea. Area: 21 sq km (8 sq mi). Pop.

(1996 est.): 10,600. Cap.: Government offices in Yaren district. Monetary unit: Australian dollar, with (Oct. 11, 1996) a free rate of $A 1.26 to U.S. $1 ($A 1.99 = £1 sterling). Presidents in 1996, Lagumot Harris, Bernard Dowiyogo from November 11, and, from November 26, Kennan Adeang.

In the face of economic downturn on Nauru, Lagumot Harris was elected on Nov. 22, 1995, to replace Bernard Dowiyogo as the nation's president. Accordingly, President Harris took strong measures in 1996 to redress deficiencies in the republic's economic condition, using the twin measures of reducing spending and increasing taxes. Wages of government workers were frozen for two years, some overseas consulates were closed, and some government departments were merged or privatized. To cut costs and improve revenue, a statutory authority was created to take control of the national airline.   (A.R.G. GRIFFITHS)

This article updates the Macropædia article PACIFIC ISLANDS: Nauru.

NEPAL

A constitutional monarchy, Nepal is a landlocked country in the Himalayas situated between India and the Tibetan Autonomous Region of China. Area: 147,181 sq km (56,827 sq mi). Pop. (1996 est.): 20,892,000. Cap.: Kathmandu. Monetary unit: Nepalese rupee, with (Oct. 11, 1996) a free rate of NRs 56.78 to U.S. $1 (NRs 89.44 = £1 sterling). King, Birendra Bir Bikram Shah Dev; prime minister in 1996, Sher Bahadur Deuba.

In February 1996 the police clashed with members of the Communist Party of Nepal-Maoist (CPN-Maoist) in western Nepal. Ten people were killed, and several were injured. According to the secretary-general of the CPN-Maoist, the party was seeking a revolutionary transformation of society.

Prime Minister Sher Bahadur Deuba in March successfully defeated a no-confidence motion against his six-month-old three-party coalition government in a special sitting of the national legislature. The United Communist Party of Nepal had accused the government of having made the country "directionless, motionless, and aimless" since the communists were voted out of office in September 1995.

In January India and Nepal signed the Makahali River Treaty, which allowed for the joint exploitation of that waterway. This was important for Nepal, as it opened the way for the development of the gigantic Pancheshwar hydroelectric project, the cost of which would be split equally between the two countries.   (CLAUDE RAKISITS)

NETHERLANDS, THE

A constitutional monarchy of northwestern Europe, The Netherlands, a Benelux country, is on the North Sea. Area: 41,526 sq km (16,033 sq mi). Pop. (1996 est.): 15,589,000. Cap., Amsterdam; seat of government, The Hague. Monetary unit: Netherlands guilder, with (Oct. 11, 1996) a free rate of 1.72 guilders to U.S. $1 (2.71 guilders = £1 sterling). Queen, Beatrix; prime minister in 1996, Wim Kok.

AD VAN DENDEREN

An illegal immigrant stands in a jail cell in The Netherlands, a country traditionally receptive to political refugees. The number of Europeans seeking asylum, which had risen dramatically in the early 1990s following the breakup of the Soviet bloc, generally continued to decline in 1996.

On Feb. 1, 1996, a parliamentary commission inquiring into the police methods against organized crime in The Netherlands presented its final report. The commission was established as a result of conflicts in the police force, which in 1994 caused the discharge of two government ministers. The main conclusions of the report were that the links between organized crime and the noncriminal were less extensive than was often suggested in the media and that the use of criminals to infiltrate operations involving large-scale drug trafficking did not prove effective and had dangerous side effects. The main recommendation was to create clear legal regulations for police inquiries.

On March 15 the Fokker aviation company was adjudged bankrupt after the Dutch government terminated further credit to it. During its lifetime of 77 years, Fokker aircraft were the pride of Dutch industry. Parts of the Fokker concern were transferred to a newly created holding company, wherein crucial activities could be continued. Despite this, more than 5,000 highly specialized employees lost their jobs.

The events leading to the bankruptcy began in December 1993 when Daimler-Benz AG of Germany became the controlling shareholder of Fokker, and the Dutch government withdrew from its financial responsibility for the firm. After severe financial losses on its investments in Fokker, Daimler-Benz eliminated its support. Rescue talks with Samsung of South Korea failed before the deadline from the government of March 15. In October talks were resumed between Samsung and the government, but delays on the Korean side caused Fokker to abandon hope in late November. The bankruptcy of Fokker resulted in part from the policy of the minister of economics, Hans Wijers, to strengthen the operation of the private market and to hold back public support for private companies as much as possible.

On June 28 Robin Linschoten was forced to resign as minister of state for social affairs and employment. His resignation was caused by a combination of two incidents. The first was the accusation that at the end of 1995 he deliberately held back information from Parliament concerning the possible consequences of the privatization of the national health regulations. The second and decisive factor was his failure to provide leadership to the supervising commission on institutions in order to implement regulations for social insurances. Although Linschoten was one of the leaders of the right-wing party of the governing coalition, his discharge did not affect the stability of the Cabinet under Prime Minister Wim Kok.

Queen Beatrix gave her traditional speech on September 15 to open the new parliamentary year. She noted that the growth rates of the nation's economy and of employment were higher than in the surrounding countries. The government deficit was reduced, and The Netherlands was expected to meet the criteria for accession to the European economic and monetary union in 1997.

A goal of the government for the future was to improve the transportation infrastructure of the very densely populated western part of The Netherlands. One of the issues to be decided was the route of the high-speed train from Paris to Amsterdam, which would have important environmental effects on the "green" areas between the cities of The Netherlands.

(KLAAS J. HOEKSEMA)

See also *Dependent States.*

NEW ZEALAND

New Zealand, a constitutional monarchy and member of the Commonwealth in the South Pacific Ocean, consists of North and South islands and Stewart, Chatham, and other minor islands. Area: 270,534 sq km (104,454 sq mi). Pop. (1996 est.): 3,619,000. Cap.: Wellington. Monetary unit: New Zealand dollar, with (Oct. 11, 1996) a free rate of $NZ 1.44 to U.S. $1 ($NZ 2.27 = £1 sterling). Queen, Elizabeth II; governors-general in 1996, Dame Catherine Tizard and, from March 21, Sir Michael Hardie Boys; prime minister, Jim Bolger.

At the end of two terms, the conservative National Party (NP) administration of Prime Minister Jim Bolger seemed about to reap the benefits of its own and the previous Labour Party (LP) government's privatizations of state services. The government had only to negotiate a referendum's requirement that it vary a two-party general election cycle by moving to mixed member proportional (MMP) voting, in which a party's representation in the legislature is proportional to the number of votes its candidates receive.

In the election, which was held on Oct. 12, 1996, the NP was ahead of the LP, its traditional opposition, 44 seats to 37, but secondary and minor parties held the balance for either major player to form a government in the enlarged 120-seat chamber. (For detailed election results, see *Political Parties,* above.) Other highlights of the first election under MMP were that Maori candidates changed their allegiance from the LP to the New Zealand First Party (NZFP) and doubled their participation to 14 seats, women MPs increased from 21 to 35, and 45 new MPs were elected.

LP leader Helen Clark looked for support to become the country's first woman prime minister, but the NZFP (17 seats) had not shown its hand, and the Alliance (13 seats) seemed full of rigid conditions for association with either main party. The NZFP was led by a charismatic part-Maori former NP Cabinet minister, Winston Peters. A defector from the LP, Jim Anderton, headed the Alliance—his own New Labour Party joined with a former social credit unit, green parties, the Liberal Party, and a tribal group. The question in the second week after the voting seemed to be whether Peters and his warriors would go with the NP, which already was linked to eight seats of two minor parties, or with the LP, and what price the NZFP would extract either way.

On December 10, more than eight weeks after election day, the NZFP completed talks with both the government and Labour to select a formal coalition partner. The NZFP decided to go with the NP. Bolger, in turn, said Peters would be deputy prime minister and have the new position of treasurer, which would be responsible for preparation of the annual budget and would be separate from the minister of finance. Bolger and Peters agreed on a Cabinet consisting of 15 members from the NP and 5 from the NZFP. Five NP ministers lost their Cabinet seats.

The first stage of government tax cuts combined with social help, provided for in the budget of May 23, took effect July 1; the package was worth $NZ 1,330,000,000 in 1996, with provision for increases to $NZ 2,930,000,000 by 1998–99. The government needed minor party help at that time in getting necessary law changes approved, but the LP and the Alliance opposed the measures.

In October a Maori tribal group, Ngai Tahu, won a $NZ 170 million award, to be assembled in land and other assets, in compensation for British Crown land dealings at the time of European settlement.

(JOHN A. KELLEHER)

See also *Dependent States.*

NICARAGUA

A republic of Central America, Nicaragua has coastlines on the Caribbean Sea and the Pacific Ocean. Area: 131,812 sq km (50,893 sq mi). Pop. (1996 est.): 4,272,000. Cap.: Managua. Monetary unit: córdoba oro, with (Oct. 11, 1996) a central bank rate of 8.68 córdobas oro to U.S. $1 (13.67 córdobas oro = £1 sterling). President in 1996, Violeta Barrios de Chamorro.

Presidential elections were held on Oct. 20, 1996, and were won by Arnoldo Alemán of the right-wing Liberal Alliance, a former mayor of Managua. With two-thirds of the votes counted, he had received 48% of the vote and thereby exceeded the 45% needed to avoid a second round. The results were disputed by his nearest rival, a former president, Daniel Ortega Saavedra of the Sandinista National Liberation Front, who won 39%. He alleged irregularities and refused to concede defeat, although international observers declared the elections free and fair.

Three candidates had previously been disqualified by the Supreme Electoral Council: Alvaro Robelo and Eden Pastora were barred because they had taken a foreign nationality, while Antonio Lacayo, the son-in-law of Pres. Violeta Chamorro, was ruled out because of an antinepotism clause in the constitution. Twenty candidates representing 30 political parties contested the presidency, although Alemán and Ortega were always in the lead. The Sandinistas attempted to present a moderate left-wing image. In September they changed their controversial anthem, which referred to

Arnoldo Alemán, elected president of Nicaragua in October, speaks to supporters. The head of the right-wing Liberal Alliance, he defeated former president Daniel Ortega.

"the Yankee as the enemy of humanity," and adopted Beethoven's "Ode to Joy" instead. After the election Alemán called on all parties to participate in a national government.

(SARAH CAMERON)

This article updates the *Macropædia* article CENTRAL AMERICA: *Nicaragua.*

NIGER

Niger is a landlocked republic of West Africa. Area: 1,267,000 sq km (489,000 sq mi). Pop. (1996 est.): 9,465,000. Cap.: Niamey. Monetary unit: CFA franc, with (Oct. 11, 1996) a par value of CFAF 100 to the French franc and a free rate of CFAF 518.24 to U.S. $1 (CFAF 816.38 = £1 sterling). President in 1996, Mahamane Ousmane until January 27; chairman of the National Salvation Council from January 27 and president from August 7, Col. (and later Gen.) Ibrahim Baré Maïnassara; prime ministers, Hama Amadou until January 27, Boukary Adji from January 30, and, from December 21, Amadou Boubacar Cissé.

Niger's six years of multiparty democracy ended abruptly on Jan. 27, 1996, when Col. Ibrahim Baré Maïnassara (*see* BIOGRAPHIES) overthrew the government of Pres. Mahamane Ousmane. Three days later Baré's new National Salvation Council (CSN) named economist Boukary Adji its new prime minister, along with an all-civilian Cabinet. On February 13 the ousted president, prime minister, and president of the National Assembly signed a joint declaration accepting the coup's legitimacy and agreeing to participate in a period of transition that would renew parliamentary democracy. The CSN suspended political parties and unions and dissolved the National Assembly, replacing it with a "Committee of Sages."

On April 1, 600 delegates attended a National Forum for Democratic Renewal. They adopted a new constitution that placed virtually all power in the hands of an elected president.

A national referendum on the new constitution passed overwhelmingly on May 12. The ban on political parties was lifted as the country prepared for presidential elections on July 7 and 8. In the election Baré won with 52.2% of the vote. Claiming massive vote fraud, opposition parties petitioned the Supreme Court to annul the results but were unsuccessful. After Baré suspended the Independent National Electoral Commission, opposition parties decided not to participate in the legislative elections on November 23.

At the end of August, a new independent electoral commission was appointed, political rallies were allowed, and access to the media was guaranteed to all candidates.

(NANCY ELLEN LAWLER)

This article updates the *Macropædia* article WESTERN AFRICA: *Niger.*

Desertification in Niger was one of several factors contributing to the country's economic woes and to the ever-present threat of famine. Early in the year a military coup against the elected government added to Niger's problems. It was widely condemned by both African and Western countries.

NIGERIA

A republic and suspended member of the Commonwealth, Nigeria is located in West Africa, on the Gulf of Guinea. Area: 923,768 sq km (356,669 sq mi). Pop. (1996 est.): 103,912,000. Cap.: Abuja. Monetary unit: naira, with (Oct. 11, 1996) an official par value of 22 naira to U.S. $1 (free rate of 34.66 naira = £1 sterling); a truer value of the naira was on the free market, where 79.70 naira = U.S. $1 (125.55 naira = £1 sterling). Chairman of the Provisional Ruling Council in 1996, Gen. Sani Abacha.

On Jan. 17, 1996, Ibrahim Abacha, the oldest son of the head of state, Gen. Sani Abacha, was killed in a plane crash; his death led to the postponement of the budget. He was close to his father and was regarded by some as a restraint upon him. The delayed budget was presented by General Abacha on February 15. He reported that there had been a 2.7% level of growth in 1995 and that the fiscal deficit of 81 billion naira in 1994 had been converted into a small surplus of 1 billion naira in 1995. The 1996 target was for a 4.94% level of growth. Of the total expected revenues of 340 billion naira, 214 billion would come from the sale of oil.

Political opposition to the military regime and moves toward a return to civilian politics became increasingly significant during 1996. The military accused foreign governments of supplying arms and financial assistance to its exiled opponents, and Wole Soyinka, the exiled winner of the 1986 Nobel Prize for Literature, was accused of involvement in bomb explosions in Kano and Kaduna during February because one of his books was found on the body of the Kaduna bomber (the only casualty). Following secret talks in Oslo and Johannesburg, S.Af., a new umbrella organization to oppose the regime was established on April 1; it was to be called the United Democratic Front of Nigeria, and its object was to work for the restoration of democracy and to enable opponents of the regime to speak with one voice.

Local government elections were held in mid-March, but only five days of campaigning were allowed, and voters had to line up behind their chosen candidates. This was not seen as a move toward democracy, although many candidates ran for election, either for personal advancement or in order to deprive the military of the right to impose candidates. At the end of March, General Abacha dismissed the army and air force commanders; no reason was given. Then in April dozens of military officers were reported to have been "retired," a move that was interpreted as a purge of those who opposed Abacha. A move by Chief Moshood ("MKO") Abiola's lawyers to facilitate his treason trial was not allowed by the Federal High Court. On June 4 Kudirat Abiola, Chief Abiola's senior wife, was murdered; the government offered a 1 million naira reward for the killer and was clearly fearful it might be accused of the murder. Abiola was not allowed to attend his wife's funeral. Bombs aimed at government officials in November further added to the turmoil.

On June 18 the National Electoral Commission of Nigeria (NECON) published rules to govern the registration of political parties, and organizations seeking recognition were given until June 26 to obtain registration forms that had to be submitted by July 26. Twenty-three organizations did so. Subsequently, NECON announced the registration of five political associations for the next republic. These were: the United Nigeria Congress Party, the Committee for National Consensus, the National Centre Party of Nigeria, the Democratic Party of Nigeria, and the Grassroots Democratic Movement. When General Abacha addressed the nation on October 1, he announced the creation of 6 new states to bring the total to 36 and appealed to the five newly recognized political parties to be disciplined and orderly; he again insisted that the program for a return to democracy was on track.

A UN fact-finding mission visited Nigeria at the end of March (at the request of the government) to evaluate progress toward democracy and to examine judicial procedures in the wake of the executions of nine members of the minority Ogoni ethnic group. A member of the mission was reported as saying that the "problems of human rights are terrible and the political problems are terrifying."   (GUY ARNOLD)

This article updates the *Macropædia* article WESTERN AFRICA: *Nigeria*.

NORWAY

A constitutional monarchy of northern Europe, Norway occupies the western part of the Scandinavian Peninsula, with coast-

A Nigerian steel mill opened in the 1970s with French, German, and Soviet help sits idle, a victim of the country's financial distress. Crime and corruption continued to poison Nigeria's economy, despite cleanup measures announced by the government.

lines on the Skagerrak, the North Sea, the Norwegian Sea, and the Arctic Ocean. Area: 323,878 sq km (125,050 sq mi), excluding the Svalbard Archipelago and Jan Mayen Island. Pop. (1996 est.): 4,382,000. Cap.: Oslo. Monetary unit: Norwegian krone, with (Oct. 11, 1996) a free rate of 6.51 kroner to U.S. $1 (10.25 kroner = £1 sterling). King, Harald V; prime ministers in 1996, Gro Harlem Brundtland and, from October 25, Thorbjørn Jagland.

Norway's oil-dependent economy continued to surge ahead in 1996, buoyed by an increase in petroleum output, higher oil prices, and a 2.6% strengthening of the dollar against the krone. The robust economy, however, prompted fears by the government of overheating, and fiscal tightening measures in the 1997 draft budget proposal were therefore introduced to combat this prospect.

Oil production from the Norwegian continental shelf was expected to rise by about 100,000 bbl a day in 1997 from the current 3.2 million bbl per day. Norway used just 150,000 bbl per day to meet domestic demand. The government forecast that annual sales of natural gas would expand to 41 billion cu m in 1997 from 35 billion cu m.

Because of the robust economy, there was no real challenger to the ruling Labour Party for the 1997 general election. Talks broke down between the Conservative Party and the right-wing Progress Party to form a coalition aimed to unseat Labour. Gro Harlem Brundtland, the dominant political figure in Norway since 1981, unexpectedly resigned as prime minister on October 23. She was succeeded by Thorbjørn Jagland, chairman of the Labour Party since 1992.

In foreign relations Norway continued its efforts to mediate between Israel and the Palestine National Authority in order to prevent the international peace agreement from derailing.

Norway mounted an aggressive campaign to import physicians and nurses from other Scandinavian countries to meet a massive domestic shortage. Paradoxically, the energy-rich country was also forced to import electricity from Denmark and Sweden, as unusually low rainfall left hydropower facilities with a deficit of water.

Europe remained a profitable market for Norwegian petroleum, pulp and paper, and fish. European Union members accounted for 80% of Norway's exports, which had risen 30% since 1991. The government forecast a balance of payments surplus of 48.3 billion kroner for 1996, an increase of about 4.1% over 1995.

The draft budget proposal for 1997 envisioned a 40.9 billion kroner surplus, or 5.1% of gross domestic product—including oil and gas—with the economy in a period of strong growth in terms of employment, production, and revenue. If projected petroleum revenues were excluded, however, the 1997 budget would have a deficit of 24.2 billion kroner. The government also upgraded its forecast 1996 budget surplus to 37.9 billion kroner. The budget surpluses were to be set aside in the Government Petroleum Fund for investment abroad in an effort to reduce Norway's dependence on oil and to provide a fund to meet the future social welfare obligations of an aging population.   (KAREN L. FOSSLI)

See also *Dependent States*.

SAEED KHAN—AFP

Imran Khan, a former cricket star who entered politics in 1996, waves to his supporters. In April Khan announced the formation of his own political party, Movement for Justice, and vowed to clean up the widespread corruption in Pakistan's government.

OMAN

The sultanate of Oman occupies the southeastern part of the Arabian Peninsula, facing the Persian Gulf, the Gulf of Oman, and the Arabian Sea. A small part of the country lies to the north and is separated from the rest of Oman by the United Arab Emirates. Area: 306,000 sq km (118,150 sq mi). Pop. (1996 est.): 2,251,000. Cap.: Muscat. Monetary unit: rial Omani, with (Oct. 11, 1996) a par value of 0.38 rial to U.S. $1 (free rate of 0.61 rial = £1 sterling). Sultan and prime minister in 1996, Qabus ibn Sa'id.

Oman's new minister of national economy, Ahmad Macki, announced in January 1996 a $26,200,000,000 five-year plan that would balance Oman's budget by the year 2000. The plan would shift the nation away from its dependence on oil, privatize the economy, and encourage foreign investment. Oil prices moved higher during the year, which allowed Oman to replenish its financial reserves. In October Oman shelved plans for a gas pipeline to India, but work continued on a major project to produce and ship 6.6 million tons of liquefied natural gas annually to Asian markets beginning in 2000.

In November Sultan Qabus ibn Sa'id promulgated a "basic law" that prohibited the use of public office for private purposes and established a procedure for succession; the royal family must agree on a successor within three days of a sultan's death or accept the (late) sultan's recommended candidate.   (DAVID J. DUNFORD)

This article updates the *Macropædia* article ARABIA: *Oman*.

PAKISTAN

A federal republic and member of the Commonwealth, Pakistan is situated in the northwestern part of the Indian subcontinent, on the Arabian Sea. Area: 796,095 sq km (307,374 sq mi), excluding

the 83,716-sq km Pakistani-administered section of Jammu and Kashmir. Pop. (1996 est., including 4.2 million residents of Pakistani-administered Jammu and Kashmir; excluding nearly one million Afghan refugees): 133.5 million. Cap.: Islamabad. Monetary unit: Pakistan rupee, with (Oct. 11, 1996) a free rate of PRs 36.93 to U.S. $1 (PRs 58.18 = £1 sterling). President in 1996, Farooq Ahmed Leghari; prime minister until November 4, Benazir Bhutto; acting prime minister from November 4, Meraj Khalid.

For Pakistan and for its prime minister, Benazir Bhutto, 1996 was another tumultuous year. After deftly weathering earlier political storms, Bhutto on November 5 was sacked by Pres. Farooq Leghari on charges of ineptitude, economic mismanagement, and corruption. Leghari appointed Meraj Khalid, a former speaker of the National Assembly, acting prime minister and promised elections within 90 days. He vowed to ban "corrupt" politicians from the polls.

Bhutto had put law and order on the top of her agenda for the year. Backed by her army generals, she began the year by cracking down on the Mohajir Qaumi Movement (MQM), the national organization for Muslim immigrants from India who fled to Pakistan after the 1947 partition. Clashes between the MQM and its rival faction, the moderate Haqiqi group; between police and the MQM; and between MQM and the native Sindhis in southern Sindh province continued unabated but with far fewer casualties than in 1995, when 2,500 people were killed in ethnic violence. The death toll in the first 10 months of 1996 was just under 800. Sectarian violence was also more subdued, though clashes between majority Sunnis and minority Shi'ite sects continued throughout the year.

But just as Bhutto was winning the war against violence, there was increasing pressure on her to step down as widespread corruption, rising unemployment, and economic mismanagement became rallying points for the opposition. In late April former cricket star Imran Khan formally announced that he was entering politics with his new political group, the Movement for Justice. A former prime minister, Nawaz Sharif, who headed a coalition of 15 opposition parties, also kept the pressure on Bhutto with his regular national rallies calling for her immediate dismissal.

Under Pakistan's constitution the only person who can dismiss an elected government is the president, who more often than not plays to the tune of military generals. For nearly three years President Leghari, a longtime ally of the Bhutto family, had turned a deaf ear to all the criticism. In late September, however, he surprised the nation when he filed a query in the nation's Supreme Court asking whether he was constitutionally bound by the prime minister's advice in appointing judges to the court. Bhutto had earlier refused to adhere to a ruling by the court, which had taken exception to the "political appointments" made by the Bhutto government. For her part, Bhutto said the judiciary was being used by "other forces" in a bid to destabilize her government.

For the first time since he became president, Leghari in September held discussions with opposition leaders. He appeared to be calling the shots when he met Bhutto in early October before her trip to the U.S., ostensibly to give her advice on talks with U.S. officials, her UN General Assembly speech, and her discussions with the International Monetary Fund on Pakistan's economic crisis. Ironically, Leghari in the past had advocated scrapping presidential powers, used several times by his predecessors, as an "inappropriate legacy" of former military ruler Gen. Zia ul-Haq.

Pakistan and India remained at odds over Kashmir, though for the first time in years there was a ray of hope that the two countries might start talking again on the issue. The U.S. was quietly pushing Pakistan to open direct talks with India on Kashmir. India privately agreed, so long as the talks were bilateral with no intermediaries.

In 1996 Pakistan received consignments of the long-delayed weapons and military spare parts released by the U.S. after the easing of an arms embargo. The equipment included parts that would help to keep Pakistan's existing fleet of F-16 aircraft operational but did not include any of the remaining 28 F-16s that Pakistan had paid for in 1988, before the U.S. halted military sales to Pakistan in 1990 because of its alleged program to develop nuclear weapons.

(ASSIF A. SHAMEEN)

PALAU

A republic in the Caroline Islands of the western Pacific Ocean, Palau comprises a 640-km (400-mi)-long chain of some 340 volcanic and coralline islands. The main islands of Babelthuap and Koror are situated about 900 km east of the Philippines. Area: 488 sq km (188 sq mi). Pop. (1996 est.): 17,000. Provisional cap.: Koror, on Koror; a site on Babelthuap was designated to be the eventual permanent capital. Monetary unit: U.S. dollar, with (Oct. 11, 1996) a free rate of $1.58 to £1 sterling. President in 1996, Kuniwo Nakamura.

Palau's first presidential election since independence took place in November 1996, with incumbent Kuniwo Nakamura easily winning, but only after his main rival, Johnson Toribiong, withdrew in the wake of a scandal over the collapse of the country's major transportation artery, the K-B bridge linking the capital and Babeldaob, the largest island in the chain.

Despite opposition from China, Palau informally allied itself with Taiwan by deciding to open a consulate in Taipei, the capital, which would issue tourist visas.

Palau, heavily dependent on tourism, also broadened its economic base. It entered into an agreement with JAL (Japan Airlines), which would assist Palau in establishing its own carrier in Micronesia. Palau hoped that when transportation links were firmly established in 1997, organically grown produce could be sent on returning flights to Japan. (A.R.G. GRIFFITHS)

This article updates the *Macropædia* article PACIFIC ISLANDS: *Palau.*

PANAMA

A republic of Central America, Panama lies between the Caribbean Sea and the Pacific Ocean on the Isthmus of Panama. Area: 75,517 sq km (29,157 sq mi). Pop. (1996 est.): 2,674,000. Cap.: Panama City. Monetary unit: balboa, at par with the U.S. dollar, with a free rate (Oct. 11, 1996) of 1.58 balboas to £1 sterling. President in 1996, Ernesto Pérez Balladares.

Although the 1977 Panama Canal Treaty calls for the handing over to Panama of all U.S.-held property in the Canal by the end of 1999, opinion polls in 1996 showed that the majority of Panamanians wanted some form of U.S. presence to remain. In July, Pres. Ernesto Pérez Balladares announced that the Howard Air Force Base would continue to be used by the U.S. to monitor the movements of drug traffickers. The statement was made after it was revealed that Pérez Balladares's 1994 election campaign had received $51,000 from a suspected money launderer associated with the Cali drug cartel. The president admitted that the money had been received but denied all personal knowledge of the contribution. He instigated a judicial review and the scrutiny of funding of all future election campaigns. The scandal came to light following the enforced closing in April of the Agro-Industrial and Commercial Bank of Panama (Banaico) because of its excessive debts and its involvement in the laundering of narcotics money. Fort Amador, at the Pacific end of the Canal, was handed over to Panama by the U.S. on October 1. Plans were drawn up for converting it into a cruise ship terminal. (BEN BOX)

This article updates the *Macropædia* article CENTRAL AMERICA: *Panama.*

PAPUA NEW GUINEA

A constitutional monarchy and Commonwealth member, Papua New Guinea is situated in the southwestern Pacific Ocean and comprises the eastern part of the island of New Guinea, the islands of the Bismarck, Kiriwina (Trobriand), Louisiade, and D'Entrecasteaux groups, Muyua (Woodlark) Island, and parts of the Solomon Islands group, including

Bougainville. Area: 462,840 sq km (178,-704 sq mi). Pop. (1996 est.): 4.4 million. Cap.: Port Moresby. Monetary unit: kina, with (Oct. 11, 1996) a free rate of 1.33 kinas to U.S. $1 (2.10 kinas = £1 sterling). Queen, Elizabeth II; governor-general in 1996, Wiwa Korowi; prime minister, Sir Julius Chan.

Prime Minister Sir Julius Chan worked in 1996 to cement links with Japan and China. He had a successful visit to Japan and in July welcomed Chinese Vice Premier and Foreign Minister Qian Qichen to Papua New Guinea. Relations with Australia, however, deteriorated when Australian Foreign Minister Alexander Downer threatened to review a $12 million defense cooperation project after Papua New Guinea government forces violated it by using Australian-supplied Iroquois helicopters against the secessionist Bougainville Revolutionary Army. The eight-year Bougainville conflict worsened, and in October Theodore Miriung, head of the government-backed Bougainville Transitional Government and a leading voice for peace, was assassinated.

(A.R.G. GRIFFITHS)

This article updates the *Macropædia* article PACIFIC ISLANDS: *Papua New Guinea.*

PARAGUAY

Paraguay is a landlocked republic of central South America. Area: 406,752 sq km (157,048 sq mi). Pop. (1996 est.): 4,964,000. Cap.: Asunción. Monetary unit: guaraní, with (Oct. 11, 1996) a free rate of 2,075 guaranies to U.S. $1 (3,269 guaranies = £1 sterling). President in 1996, Juan Carlos Wasmosy.

Democracy in Paraguay, established after the overthrow of Gen. Alfredo Stroessner in 1989, faced its biggest challenge when in April 1996 Pres. Juan Carlos Wasmosy dismissed the army commander, Gen. Lino César Oviedo, for breaking the constitutional ban on political activity by officers currently serving in the military. Oviedo, a candidate for presidential nomination by the ruling Colorado Party in 1998, had called for the postponement of internal party elections. With Oviedo refusing to accept dismissal and amid speculation of a coup, Wasmosy offered to appoint him minister of defense. Under pressure from demonstrators and the opposition majority in Congress, Wasmosy then changed his mind. In June Oviedo was arrested on charges of insurrection. In a newspaper interview from his cell, he claimed that Wasmosy's business interests were profiting from the award of public contracts and that the coup threat in April was an invention of the government.

Oviedo's defeat provided little relief for Wasmosy, as the Colorado Party winner was Luis María Argaña, a minister under Stroessner who favoured a return to the economic policies of the dictatorship. Argaña's victory forced Wasmosy to rely on him for support and put him in a strong position to win the 1998 nomination.

Earnings from cotton, Paraguay's most important agricultural export, were reduced by low prices and disease. Total exports were projected at $2.2 billion, compared with $2 billion in 1995, while imports were expected to rise from $3.3 billion to $3.6 billion. (CHARLIE NURSE)

PERU

The republic of Peru is located in western South America, on the Pacific Ocean. Area: 1,285,216 sq km (496,225 sq mi). Pop. (1996 est.): 23,947,000. Cap.: Lima. Monetary unit: nuevo sol, with (Oct. 6, 1995) a free rate of 2.25 nuevos soles to U.S. $1 (3.56 nuevos soles = £1 sterling). President in 1996, Alberto Fujimori; prime minister, Danté Cordova.

Peru suddenly became the focus of international attention on Dec. 17, 1996, when 20 or so heavily armed guerrillas invaded the Japanese embassy in Lima, the nation's capital. Hundreds of dignitaries who had been invited to celebrate the birthday of Japanese Emperor Akihito were taken hostage. The Marxist guerrillas, members of the Túpac Amaru Revolutionary Movement (MRTA), demanded, among other things, the release of hundreds of MRTA associates imprisoned in Peru and other countries. By the end of the year, all but about 80 of the hostages had been released, but there was no sign that the crisis would end soon.

Alberto Fujimori's decision to seek reelection in the year 2000, despite declining popularity, was welcomed by the business community because it believed he could introduce reforms while maintaining economic and political stability. Some Peruvians, however, were upset by Fujimori's decision to sell the nation's 29% interest in Telefonica de Peru, mainly because local investors were allowed only a limited interest in the enterprise.

Following the discovery of 100 kg (220 lb) of coca paste (which could be converted into cocaine) on board two navy ships in July, Fujimori suspended all commercial transportation by the army and navy as of August 1. A Mexican newspaper later charged that Fujimori's brother and his intelligence adviser, Vladimiro Montesinos, had ties to Mexican drug traffickers. Convicted drug baron Demetrio Chávez Peñaherrera alleged that he had paid Montesinos $50,000 a month during 1990–91. The police and intelligence services quickly denied the charge and Chávez recanted, but it did not restore confidence in Montesinos.

The Sendero Luminoso (Shining Path) guerrillas continued their terrorist activity with bombings in Lima and the occupation of a village in a coca-growing region in the upper Huallaga valley. In May Amnesty International published a report claiming that the government had imprisoned thousands of suspected terrorists unfairly.

Privatization measures continued amid growing protests, in particular against the selling of the government-owned Petroperu refinery. Spain's Repsol acquired control of the facility with a winning bid of $181 million. Yacimientos Petroleros Fiscales of Argentina and Mobil Corp. of the U.S. became minority partners in the consortium Refinadores de Peru.

Oil production during the first six months of 1996 declined 3.9% compared with the same period in 1995, although there was a slight increase over 1995 in July. Inflation rose in the first half of 1996 to 11.8% in July, compared with 10.2% in December 1995. This was due to high food prices, which reflected poor harvests.

(ALAN MURPHY)

PHILIPPINES

Situated in the western Pacific Ocean off the southeastern coast of Asia, the republic of the Philippines consists of an archipelago of about 7,100 islands. Area: 300,076 sq km (115,860 sq mi). Pop. (1996 est.): 71,750,000. Cap.: Manila (lower house of the legislature meets in Quezon City). Monetary unit: Philippine peso, with (Oct. 11, 1996) a free rate of 26.27 pesos to U.S. $1 (41.38 pesos = £1 sterling). President in 1996, Fidel V. Ramos.

Nur Misuari, the leader of a Muslim guerrilla group, signed a treaty with the government and on Sept. 30, 1996, became the governor of the Autonomous Region in Muslim Mindanao (ARMM). Misuari, head of the Moro National Liberation Front (MNLF), had begun a rebellion against the Philippine government in 1972.

The MNLF initially sought independence for areas of Mindanao island and other parts of the southern Philippines that were inhabited by Muslims, a minority in a predominately Roman Catholic nation. Fighting in those areas was estimated to have killed between 50,000 and 150,000 people. Despite aid from Muslim nations, MNLF

Women armed with guns supplied by the military guard a Peruvian village against attacks by Sendero Luminoso (Shining Path) guerrillas. Attention quickly switched to the Túpac Amaru guerrillas when they invaded the Japanese embassy on December 17 and seized hundreds of hostages.

WILLIAM ALBERT ALLARD—NATIONAL GEOGRAPHIC SOCIETY

A member of the Moro National Liberation Front passes a campaign poster for Nur Misuari, leader of the guerrilla group. After reaching an agreement with the Philippine government, in September Misuari was elected governor of the new Autonomous Region in Muslim Mindanao.

guerrillas failed to win control of a territory they could claim as a nation.

After years of sporadic negotiations, Misuari met in late August with Pres. Fidel Ramos to agree on a peace treaty that provided some autonomy and economic control for the ARMM. It was signed September 2. A week later Misuari was elected unopposed as governor of the ARMM, which comprised about a quarter of the Philippines' territory and was inhabited by some three million Muslims. In taking the oath as governor in Cotabato City, the ARMM headquarters, Misuari said that MNLF members would not give up their weapons. Some of the estimated 16,000 MNLF troops were to be integrated into the Philippine army and police.

The treaty was opposed by two groups. During the long civil war, Christians from other parts of the country moved into the south and had come to outnumber Muslims in many of the ARMM's 14 provinces. Some Christians planned to vote against an autonomous Muslim government in a referendum scheduled for 1998. Also, a hardline splinter group from the MNLF, the Moro Islamic Liberation Front, continued to fight for independence. Its forces, estimated at between 8,000 and 40,000, ambushed army troops and raided towns.

Another armed threat to Philippine stability that had arisen about the time of the Muslim rebellion also faded in 1996. It had come from the New People's Army (NPA), a communist insurgency that in the late 1970s and 1980s controlled large pockets of territory throughout the country. A combination of government military pressure, the worldwide decline of communism, and the aging of the NPA leadership eroded its strength. Some NPA guerrillas left rural bases to become urban terrorists. They claimed to protect workers from corrupt and abusive employers, but many regarded them as gangsters. Ramos announced on September 20 that formal peace talks were under way with the chairman of the Communist Party of the Philippines, José Maria Sison, who lived in exile in The Netherlands.

Although Ramos was not constitutionally eligible for another term and repeatedly said he did not want one, some lawyers and businessmen collected signatures for a referendum in 1997 to amend the constitution so as to abolish term limitations. Ramos was popular partly because of economic growth after years of stagnation. The International Monetary Fund said on September 10 that "the boom and bust cycles of the past have been broken and a solid foundation for sustained growth established." In 1996, for the third straight year, the government had a budget surplus.   (HENRY S. BRADSHER)

POLAND

A republic of eastern Europe, Poland is on the Baltic Sea. Area: 312,685 sq km (120,728 sq mi). Pop. (1996 est.): 38,731,000. Cap.: Warsaw. Monetary unit: zloty, with (Oct. 11, 1996) a free rate of 2.82 zlotys to U.S. $1 (4.43 zlotys = £1 sterling). President in 1996, Aleksander Kwasniewski; prime ministers, Jozef Oleksy to January 24 and, from February 7, Wlodzimierz Cimoszewicz.

The longevity of Poland's political divide between postcommunist and Solidarity forces was evident in 1996's biggest political scandal. Shortly before Lech Walesa left the presidency in late 1995, Internal Affairs Minister Andrzej Milczanowski (a presidential appointee and respected Solidarity activist) accused Prime Minister Jozef Oleksy, a former communist, of having served as an informant for the Soviet intelligence agency KGB and, later, for Russian intelligence. While hotly denying the charges, Oleksy conceded that Vladimir Alganov, the former first secretary of the Soviet embassy in Warsaw and, as it happened, an intelligence officer, had long been a close personal friend. The charges forced the prime minister to resign in late January, and he was replaced two weeks later by the less colourful but more credible Wlodzimierz Cimoszewicz. The Warsaw military prosecutor ultimately dropped all

charges against Oleksy but failed to dispel the widespread suspicion that the prime minister had been negligent in his contacts with Russian diplomats.

The postcommunist-dominated Sejm (parliament) launched an investigation to determine whether Poland's security forces had set out to frame Oleksy or even been duped by a Russian provocation. Eleven months later a special Sejm commission was still divided along partisan lines over its verdict; the postcommunist deputies wanted Milczanowski punished, whereas the opposition deputies saw no grounds.

Oleksy's resignation did not affect government policy (and the Social Democratic Party, in a gesture of defiance, promptly elected him its chairman). The postcommunist coalition that had taken over the reins of government after the 1993 elections continued to exercise power, although the two ruling parties—the Democratic Left Alliance and the Polish Peasant Party—were almost constantly at odds over privatization, fiscal policy, and, increasingly, the division of potentially lucrative government posts.

Poland's numerous right-wing parties managed to form a common political representation, Solidarity Electoral Action, led by Solidarity trade union chairman Marian Krzaklewski. Standing for a mix of anticommunism, conservative social policies, and populist economics, Poland's political right had previously engaged in incessant infighting, splintering a large potential electorate. The new organization, however, won immediate popularity; with more than 20% of voter support, at midyear Solidarity Electoral Action overtook the Democratic Left Alliance, which had topped all opinion polls since 1993. If Krzaklewski managed to hold his fractious coalition together, the 1997 elections could spell an end to the postcommunist domination of Polish politics.

In late November workers at the Gdansk shipyard went on strike and occupied local government offices in hopes of persuading the government to save their jobs by guaranteeing the future of the bankrupt shipyard. Another social problem focused on abortion. Fulfilling pledges made during the 1993 election campaign, the left in the Sejm succeeded in liberalizing the near-total ban on abortion adopted by the previous legislature. The new legislation would permit the termination of a pregnancy up to the 12th week if the woman faced difficult economic or personal circumstances. The hierarchy of the Roman Catholic Church argued that supporting abortion rights was grounds for excommunication. Opinion polls continued to suggest that a solid majority of Poles supported the more liberal provisions. The president signed the bill on November 20.

Poland recorded its fifth straight year of economic growth in 1996; gross domestic product rose by some 5%. Owing to recession in Germany, Poland's main trading partner, exports slowed, and the rate of growth was down from the 7% achieved in 1995. Imports and investments both reached record highs and, in a first for the countries of the former Soviet bloc, Poland surpassed the level of production achieved when the market transition began. The country also continued to gain international credibility: acceptance into the Organisation for Economic Co-operation and Development was an important milestone in 1996.

(LOUISA VINTON)

PORTUGAL

A republic of southwestern Europe, metropolitan Portugal is on the Atlantic coast of the Iberian Peninsula, which it shares with Spain. Area: 92,135 sq km (35,574 sq mi), including the Azores and Madeira Islands groups/archipelagoes in the Atlantic. Pop. (1996 est.): 9,927,000. Cap.: Lisbon. Monetary unit: Portuguese escudo, with (Oct. 11, 1996) a free rate of 154.90 escudos to U.S. $1 (244.01 escudos = £1 sterling). Presidents in 1996, Mário Soares and, from March 9, Jorge Sampaio; prime minister, António Guterres.

Portugal's Socialist government got off to a strong start in 1996, swiftly delivering a deficit-cutting budget that sought to meet Maastricht Treaty criteria for membership in the European economic and monetary union (EMU) but did not short-change social programs. Building on the solid economic foundation left by the Social Democratic Party (PSD), the government presented an ambitious privatization program and reinforced efforts to streamline the tax-collection process and crack down on tax evaders. In January former Lisbon mayor Jorge Sampaio gave the Socialists an extra stimulus by defeating former PSD prime minister Aníbal Cavaco Silva in the presidential elections. When Sampaio took office in early March, it was the first time in Portugal's postrevolutionary period that the president had been chosen from the same political party as the prime minister. Sampaio succeeded Mário Soares, a hero of the 1974 revolution, who closed out his two-term, 10-year presidency and started a foundation to promote democracy.

In October the government once again presented a deficit-cutting budget and declared that its primary goal was to join Europe's proposed single-currency bloc on time in 1999. Thought of as a dark horse in the race to meet the EMU criteria by the deadline, Portugal nevertheless boasted one of the most improved economies in Europe; inflation had fallen steadily, the deficit had been trimmed consistently, exchange rates had been mostly stable, and the ratio of public debt to gross domestic product had also followed a slow downward path in recent years.

While the Socialists shined, opposition parties across the political spectrum fell into disarray. The centre-right PSD elected university professor and political commentator Marcelo Rebelo de Sousa party leader and struggled to find a unified voice in the parliament. With many of their economic policies taken over by the Socialists, the PSD found it difficult to present a clear alternative program and capped the year by saying that in order to avoid political instability, they would not oppose the government's budget. The right-leaning Popular Party, meanwhile, suffered internal struggles for power, while the Portuguese Communist Party saw its electoral support remain stationary in opinion polls.

On the diplomatic front, Portugal achieved two major victories. In late October it triumphed over Australia in gaining a seat on the UN Security Council. Earlier in the month two activists fighting for peace and autonomy in the former Portuguese colony of East Timor—annexed by Indonesia in 1976 but not recognized by the UN—

had been awarded the 1996 Nobel Prize for Peace. Portuguese officials said both events reflected hard-won lobbying success and the growth of Portugal's influence.

In other developments work continued on the 1998 world exposition site in Lisbon, which would feature one of the world's largest aquariums. Construction started on a new automobile bridge across the Tagus River, linking the south bank to the exposition site, while the 25th of April Bridge farther west began renovation to add a rail link. Downtown Lisbon also embarked on an ambitious exposition-related facelift, which included the extension of the city's subway system and the renovation of a number of historic buildings.

(ERIK BURNS)

See also *Dependent States.*

QATAR

A monarchy (emirate) on the Arabian Peninsula, Qatar occupies a desert peninsula and the nearby small Hawar Islands (also claimed by Bahrain) on the west coast of the Persian Gulf. Area (including Hawar Islands): 11,427 sq km (4,412 sq mi). Pop. (1996 est.): 590,000. Cap.: Doha. Monetary unit: Qatar riyal, with (Oct. 11, 1996) an official rate of 3.64 riyals to U.S. $1 (5.73 riyals = £1 sterling). Emir and prime minister in 1996, Sheikh Hamad ibn Khalifah ath-Thani; prime minister from October 28, Sheikh Abdullah ibn Khalifa ath-Thani.

Although Qatar's emir, Sheikh Hamad ibn Khalifah ath-Thani, had deposed his father, Sheikh Khalifah ibn Hamad ath-Thani, in June 1995, the latter in 1996 continued to control much of Qatar's state reserves and to seek the aid of neighbouring countries to reinstate him as the country's ruler. On February 20 Qatari authorities announced they had foiled a coup attempt by "foreign-backed saboteurs" supporting Sheikh Khalifah. By the fall, however, father and son reportedly had reconciled, which allowed Sheikh Khalifah to return to Qatar but not as ruler.

While 1996 began with strained relations between Qatar and its neighbours, Qatar and Saudi Arabia agreed in April to demarcate their common border in accordance with an earlier agreement. A border dispute with Bahrain remained unresolved.

(DAVID J. DUNFORD)

This article updates the *Macropædia* article ARABIA: *Qatar.*

ROMANIA

A republic on the Balkan Peninsula in southeastern Europe, Romania has a coastline on the Black Sea. Area: 237,500 sq km (91,699 sq mi). Pop. (1996 est.): 22,670,000. Cap.: Bucharest. Monetary unit: leu, with (Oct. 11, 1996) a free rate of 3,285 lei to U.S. $1 (5,175 lei = £1 sterling). Presidents in 1996, Ion Iliescu and, from November 29, Emil Constantinescu; prime ministers, Nicolae Vacaroiu and, from December 12, Victor Ciorbea.

For Romania 1996 was a year of sweeping political changes that culminated in the victory of the democratic opposition in the November presidential and parliamentary elections. Those changes had been

heralded by the continuing disintegration of the ruling coalition, dominated by the left-wing Party of Social Democracy in Romania (PDSR). The alliance originally included the ultranationalist Romanian National Unity Party (PUNR) and Greater Romania Party (PRM), as well as the neo-communist Socialist Labour Party (PSM). The PDSR parted with the PRM and PSM in October 1995 and March 1996, respectively. In early September, after months of increasing friction, it broke with its last ally, the PUNR. Consequently, the PDSR, which did not have a parliamentary majority, found itself increasingly isolated politically. That the PDSR government, headed by Nicolae Vacaroiu, was able to survive for several more months was primarily due to its being tacitly tolerated by the democratic opposition.

The PDSR's efforts to rid itself of its former nationalist and far-left allies were clearly designed to improve the party's image both at home and abroad by stressing its commitment to balanced, centrist policies. Against the background of a protracted economic and social malaise, however, the party's popularity among Romanians continued to decline. The erosion was aggravated by massive price hikes for staples, energy, and fuel in June and July. The PDSR received an early warning signal in the June local elections, in which it lost in most big towns, including Bucharest. The Democratic Convention of Romania (CDR) won more county councillor posts than the PDSR, and almost as many mayoral offices. The CDR was an umbrella organization consisting of parties and associations of diverse political orientations.

PDSR leaders tried to explain the party's poor showing in the local elections as evidence of widespread frustration over the ongoing reforms. The opposition, in turn, spoke of the ruling party's innate inability to implement any serious reforms. It also accused the PDSR of condoning rampant corruption. In the parliamentary elections the CDR ranked first with 30% of the votes, followed by the PDSR (22%), the Social Democratic Union (USD, 13%), the Hungarian Democratic Union of Romania (UDMR, nearly 7%), and the PRM and PUNR, with more than 4% each. In the presidential election Ion Iliescu, Romania's acting president since May 1990, won the first round with over 32% but lost to his CDR rival, Emil Constantinescu, in a runoff on November 17. Thus, the CDR emerged victorious on all fronts. Its political offer in the form of a U.S.-style "contract with Romania" ultimately proved more attractive than that of the PDSR.

On September 16 Romania and Hungary signed a treaty that demarcated their common border and guaranteed the rights of ethnic minorities—a requirement for membership in the European Union and NATO.

Constantinescu was sworn in as Romania's president on November 29. He appointed Victor Ciorbea, the CDR mayor of Bucharest, prime minister and asked him to form a Cabinet based on a coalition consisting of the CDR, the USD, and the UDMR.

Romania was the last former communist country in Eastern Europe (with the exception of Yugoslavia) in which democrats could eventually replace a regime that had strong links with the communists. The changeover, which was met with sympathy

Youths hang out in a park in Bucharest. In Romania large numbers of children and young people lived on the streets. Most were outcasts from troubled families, and others came from orphanages and hospitals.

in the West, boosted Romania's chances to join the Euro-Atlantic structures, including NATO. (DAN IONESCU)

This article updates the *Macropædia* article BALKAN STATES: *Romania*.

RUSSIA

Russia is a federal republic occupying eastern and northeastern Europe and all of northern Asia. It is the world's largest country and covers more than 10% of the globe's total land mass. The name Russia is officially synonymous with the Russian Federation. Area: 17,075,400 sq km (6,592,800 sq mi). Pop. (1996 est.): 148,-070,000. Cap.: Moscow. Monetary unit: ruble, with (Oct. 11, 1996) a free rate of 5,437 rubles = U.S. $1 (8,564 rubles = £1 sterling). President in 1996, Boris Yeltsin; prime minister, Viktor Chernomyrdin.

Domestic Affairs. The first six months of 1996 in Russia were dominated by the presidential election campaign. There was alarm inside and outside Russia that incumbent Pres. Boris Yeltsin would be defeated by Communist challenger Gennady Zyuganov. (*See* BIOGRAPHIES.) Russia bucked the post-Soviet trend to elect reformed communists, however, and Yeltsin was reelected. (*See* SIDEBAR.) The election confirmed that Russia remained on track to implement a market economy and a democratic society. The effort of campaigning proved so strenuous, however, that in June, between the first and second rounds of the election, Yeltsin suffered a heart attack, his third in 15 months. He underwent heart bypass surgery in November; immediately before and after the operation, he was a virtual lame duck. Prime Minister Viktor Chernomyrdin was given state power while Yeltsin was incapacitated. As a result, the period until the summer was characterized by political uncertainty, which discouraged investment and held back economic growth, while the second half of the year was marked by a covert power struggle as Kremlin leaders maneuvered for position in the Yeltsin succession stakes.

On one level the struggle took the form of a clash of personalities. On a deeper level it was a power contest between Kremlin clans representing influential financial groups, oil and gas producers, heavy industry, and arms manufacturers. Losers in the struggle were Defense Minister Pavel Grachev and longtime Yeltsin confidant Aleksandr Korzhakov, who were ousted from power in June. A comeback was staged by Anatoly Chubais, who had been dismissed from the government in January and was appointed chief of the presidential staff in July. By year's end, with Yeltsin convalescing from his heart operation, Chubais, if not universally loved, was recognized as the driving force behind Kremlin policy.

The brightest meteor in the Kremlin firmament was the retired general Aleksandr Lebed (*see* BIOGRAPHIES), who captured the public imagination when he placed third in the presidential election in June. The ambitious Lebed was then co-opted by the Yeltsin campaign and appointed secretary of Russia's influential Security Council. Almost single-handedly, Lebed brought an end to Russia's war against the breakaway republic of Chechnya, where federal troops had been engaged in a bitter and bloody struggle since December 1994. Officials put the number of casualties at 30,000, Lebed at three times that figure.

In April separatist leader Dzhokhar Dudayev was killed (*see* OBITUARIES), probably by a Russian missile. Dudayev's departure from the scene, followed by Lebed's appointment to the Kremlin, facilitated a rapprochement between the warring sides. A cease-fire signed in August postponed a decision on Chechnya's status vis-à-vis the Russian Federation for five years and made it possible for federal troops to withdraw from Chechen territory and for elections to be planned. By the end of the year Chechnya was, in all but name, an independent state.

Lebed's abrasive personality won him powerful enemies, and in October Yeltsin sacked him. Lebed left with his popularity and the trust of the electorate intact, however, and his chances of replacing Yeltsin

as Russia's next president appeared strong.

The year was marked by little progress toward achieving a functioning multiparty system. Only the Communist Party of the Russian Federation, with half a million members, could boast a nationwide organization. Its support, at about one-third of the electorate, had remained more or less constant since 1991 but showed no sign of growing. Other parties were weak and confined to Moscow or St. Petersburg. The federal government was also weak, especially in comparison with the leaders of Russia's increasingly autonomous and differentiated regions. Fall elections gave many voters their first opportunity to elect local governors, who had until then been appointed by the president; this further enhanced the autonomy of regional leaders, some of whom ruled virtually private fiefdoms.

The Economy. Rumours of imminent economic crisis recurred throughout the year, and the long-awaited turnaround in the economy did not materialize. Gross domestic product (GDP) continued to decline, with output for the year as a whole 6% lower than in 1995. Although by year's end an increasing number of foreign investors seemed ready to commit funds to Russia, overall investment was too low to spark economic growth. The budget deficit remained a problem and threatened to be greater than planned. Nonetheless, Russia moved significantly closer to financial stabilization in 1996. Thanks to strict government austerity policies, the inflation rate fell steadily throughout the year and totaled 21.8% for the year as a whole.

The economic year began inauspiciously when, in January, President Yeltsin sacked Chubais, who had been the standard-bearer of market reform. Contrary to expectations, however, Chubais's ouster was not accompanied by a reversal of government economic policy, and, after Yeltsin's reelection in July, the balance tipped back to the reformers.

During the election campaign Yeltsin made lavish populist spending promises and tax concessions. These helped him win reelection but were almost all rescinded within a month of his inauguration. This did not make the government popular with the public. Austerity was offered as the reason for the late payment of wages and pensions and the axing of subsidies to industries, which in turn stoked unemployment. The most comprehensive figure for unemployment and underemployment (non-full-time workers and those on enforced leave) was 15% of the workforce by the summer of 1996. There were frequent strikes throughout the year.

Support for Russia from the West continued to flow as economic reforms were maintained. In February the government negotiated a three-year, $10.2 billion loan with the International Monetary Fund. The second largest loan in the IMF's history, this action signaled Western confidence in Russian economic reforms and support for Yeltsin's candidacy. Nonetheless, the IMF obligated Russia to meet a string of conditions concerning inflation levels, budget deficit, and removal of export tariffs. The loan was payable in monthly installments that could be withdrawn whenever (as happened in July and again in October and November) the IMF believed that Russia was not meeting its targets.

An envoy raises a white flag as he makes his way between Russian and Chechen troops in Grozny, scene of some of the fiercest fighting in the two-year-old war. In August the two sides negotiated a cease-fire that deferred for five years resolution of the question of Chechnya's status.

In April Russia made an important move toward entering international capital markets when it signed a rescheduling agreement on about $40 billion of its inherited (that is, ex-Soviet) debt to Western governments within the framework of the Paris Club of creditor governments. The hoped-for rescheduling of Russian debt to the London Club of Western creditor banks was not, however, finalized.

Considerable trade liberalization, including the abandonment of most direct administrative controls on exports and imports, took place during the year. The government announced its intention to make the ruble fully convertible for current-account transactions. The stronger ruble that resulted was one of the main planks of the government's stabilization program aimed at attracting investment. In the short term, however, the strength of the ruble was felt to work against domestic producers. One branch of industry that seemed unaffected was arms exports, which increased sharply.

The government successfully launched Russia's first Eurobond issue at the end of the year. As a precondition for the bond issue, U.S. and European agencies in October awarded Russia its first long-term credit rating since the 1917 revolution. Russia's higher-than-anticipated BB grading allowed the government to borrow at rates more favourable than the treasury bill market that had until then been Moscow's main source of financing.

Tax collection emerged as the government's main headache in the fall. Federal government tax receipts dropped in the first half of the year to half their 1995 levels. The decline in tax revenue relative to GDP was a long-term trend that partly reflected the disorganization and ineffectiveness of the government, and large firms with influential political patrons often got away without paying taxes.

President and the parliament waged an ongoing battle over private land ownership. The parliament introduced a land code explicitly designed to outlaw the free sale of arable land. This was vetoed by President Yeltsin, who signed a decree of his own giving farmers the right to freely sell and lease agricultural land. The presidential edict required supporting legislation that was not in the president's gift, however, and the impasse continued to impede agricultural reform.

Foreign Affairs. The year opened with the dismissal of Russia's long-serving foreign minister, Andrey Kozyrev, and his replacement by Yevgeny Primakov. Kozyrev was generally described as pro-Western, and the expectation was that Primakov, former director of Russia's foreign intelligence service (one of the KGB's successors), would adopt a more anti-Western policy. In fact, Primakov turned out to be a pragmatist with whom the West felt able to do business. This was partly because a hard-headed foreign policy consensus had emerged in Russia as early as 1992–93, and Kozyrev had already adapted to it. That consensus held that Russia could and should work in tandem with the West on a range of issues as long as its national interests were not challenged. In January, for example, Russia joined the Council of Europe (CE), but Russian politicians reacted angrily when the CE and the Organization for Security and Cooperation in Europe (OSCE) launched sustained criticism of human rights abuses in Chechnya—in particular, the unacceptably high rate of civilian casualties.

Throughout the year Russian leaders fulminated against the possibility of NATO expansion into Central and Eastern Europe. Russia continued to press for the OSCE—not NATO—to become the central pillar of a new European security architecture. By year's end, however, there were signs that Russian leaders were gradually and grudgingly moving toward acceptance of an enlarged NATO and that Russia itself might be preparing to cooperate more closely with the alliance.

Moscow continued to push for closer integration with the other members of the Commonwealth of Independent States. In April Russia signed an integration agreement with Belarus but steered clear of the full reunion of the two countries desired by Belarusian Pres. Alyaksandr Lukashenka, evidently fearing Belarus's economic problems would be a drain on Russia's budget.

The battle over NATO enlargement was paralleled inside Russia by a deepening conflict over Russia's armed forces. There was concern that drastic cuts in the defense budget were undermining military capability and destroying Russia's status as a great power. Military leaders charged that under-

Russia's Democratic Election

When campaigning opened at the beginning of 1996, Pres. Boris Yeltsin's popularity was close to zero. He himself did not at first want to run, since he had spent several months in 1995 convalescing after two heart attacks. Panic struck the Yeltsin team when opinion polls indicated that Yeltsin could not win; members of his staff urged him to find a pretext to cancel the election.

Instead, Yeltsin changed his team, assigning a key role to his daughter, Tatyana Dyachenko, and appointing

staunchly pro-capitalist Anatoly Chubais campaign manager. Chubais recruited a team of six leading Russian financiers and media moguls, who bankrolled the campaign to the tune of $3 million and guaranteed favourable coverage on television and in leading newspapers. In the outlying regions of the country, the Yeltsin campaign relied for support on local governors, most of whom had been appointed by the president.

The campaign of Gennady Zyuganov, the candidate of the Communist Party

of the Russian Federation, had a strong grass roots organization, particularly in rural areas and small towns, but it had nothing like the financial resources that the Yeltsin campaign could command.

Yeltsin threw himself into the campaign, stumping the country, dancing at rock concerts, exploiting all the advantages of the incumbent to maintain a high media profile. He vowed to abandon unpopular policies and increase welfare spending, end the war in Chechnya, pay wage and pension arrears, and abolish military conscription. His advertising campaign was fiercely anticommunist, playing up the threat of "civil war" and recalling the lean years following the 1917 revolution, with pictures of starving children and destroyed churches.

There were several attractive democratic candidates, notably the economist Grigory Yavlinsky. Seeing these candidates as a threat, the Yeltsin campaign worked to polarize the debate—to exclude the middle ground—and convince voters that only Yeltsin could defeat the Communist menace. The election soon became a two-horse race, but Zyuganov, who lacked Yeltsin's charisma and fought a lacklustre campaign, watched helplessly as his strong initial lead was whittled away.

Voter turnout in the first round on June 16 was 69.8%. Yeltsin won 35.3% of the vote; Zyuganov 32%; Aleksandr Lebed, the mercurial ex-general, an unexpectedly high 14.5%; Grigory Yavlinsky 7.3%; far-right Russian nationalist Vladimir Zhirinovsky 5.7%; and former Soviet president Mikhail Gorbachev 0.5%. With no candidate securing an absolute majority, Yeltsin and Zyuganov went into a second round of voting. In the meantime, Yeltsin cleverly annexed a large section of the voters by appointing Lebed to the posts of national security adviser and secretary of the Security Council.

His election tactics paid off. In the second round on July 3, with a turnout of 68.9%, Yeltsin won 53.8% of the vote and Zyuganov 40.3%, with 4.8% voting against both candidates. Moscow and St. Petersburg together provided over half of Yeltsin's support, but he also did well in large cities in the Urals and in the north and northeast. He lost in the traditional "red belt" in the south, but the Communists did not improve on the one-third of the national vote that they had commanded since 1991.

Many people sided with Yeltsin not because they liked his politics but because they liked the Communists even less and did not want to turn the clock back to the past. In addition, they voted for Yeltsin because he promised to abandon his government's unpopular austerity policies and increase public spending to help those suffering from the pain of economic reform. Within a month of the election, Yeltsin had issued a decree canceling almost all these promises.   (ELIZABETH TEAGUE)

At the May Day parade, a Russian citizen holds photographs of Lenin and of Communist Party candidate Gennady Zyuganov. Although Zyuganov denied Boris Yeltsin a victory in the first round of voting in June, the Russian president went on to win another term in the second round.

financing had humiliated the army to the point where armed mutiny was a real possibility. Military reform was hotly debated, the aim being a smaller army that would be cheaper to maintain. The transition to an all-volunteer force, which Yeltsin pledged during his campaign would be completed by the year 2000, was postponed until 2005. There was strong military opposition to the government's plans to reduce Russia's army from a nominal strength of 1.7 million soldiers in 1996 to 1.2 million by 1998.

In April Yeltsin visited Beijing. The warming of Sino-Russian relations was further accentuated after Yeltsin's heart surgery when Chinese Premier Li Peng in December became the first foreign leader to visit him.   (ELIZABETH TEAGUE)

RWANDA

The landlocked republic of Rwanda is situated in central Africa. Area: 26,338 sq km (10,169 sq mi). Pop. (1996 est.): 6.9 million, including 1,650,000 refugees, of whom 1.1 million are in Zaire and more than 500,000 are in Tanzania. Cap.: Kigali. Monetary unit: Rwanda franc, with (Oct. 11, 1996) a free rate of RF 327.21 to U.S. $1 (RF 515.45 = £1 sterling). President in 1996, Pasteur Bizimungu; prime minister, Pierre Celestin Rwigema.

Clashes between Rwanda's Tutsi-dominated army and the Burundian Hutu occurred in January 1996 and caused some 15,000 refugees to flee to Tanzania from camps in Burundi. In December 1995 Rwanda and Tanzania had agreed that 500,000 Rwandans would be repatriated from Tanzania and that refugees who obstructed this process were to be confined. In February Zaire announced plans to repatriate one million refugees; the Zaire government promised the UN High Commissioner for Refugees (UNHCR) that there would be no forced repatriation but deployed troops around the Kibumba camp of 200,000 to "encourage" the refugees to return. The UNHCR, which

faced dwindling funds and the reluctance of donors to provide more money, endorsed the Zaire action. In August the prime ministers of Zaire and Rwanda signed an agreement calling for the repatriation of a million refugees from over 30 camps in eastern Zaire. In mid-November hundreds of thousands of Rwandans began to leave Zaire voluntarily. The exodus surprised UN personnel who were organizing a humanitarian mission to avert starvation and death from deadly diseases. The whereabouts of hundreds of thousands of other refugees was unknown. Violence continued throughout the year, some carried out by government soldiers and some by Hutu extremists.

On June 1 a communiqué was issued by a new group, People Bearing Arms to Liberate Rwanda (PALIR), which claimed to have established a base in Cyangugu in southwestern Rwanda, near Zaire. It was thought to support rebel Hutu actions in the region; the government insisted it was no threat to security.   (GUY ARNOLD)

This article updates the *Macropædia* article CENTRAL AFRICA: *Rwanda.*

SAINT KITTS AND NEVIS

A constitutional monarchy and member of the Commonwealth, St. Kitts and Nevis comprises the islands of St. Kitts and Nevis in the eastern Caribbean Sea. Area: 269 sq km (104 sq mi). Pop. (1996 est.): 39,400. Cap.: Basseterre. Monetary unit: Eastern Caribbean dollar, with (Oct. 11, 1996) a par value of EC$2.70 to U.S. $1 (free rate of EC$4.25 = £1 sterling). Queen, Elizabeth II; governor-general in 1996, Cuthbert Sebastian; prime minister, Denzil Douglas.

In June 1996 St. Kitts-Nevis faced its most serious constitutional crisis since the secession of Anguilla 25 years earlier. Vance Amory, premier of Nevis, declared that he had instructed the territory's legal department to prepare a bill for secession from the twin-island federal state. His decision

appeared to have been influenced by the central government's insistence on asserting control over much of Nevis's affairs, including financial matters.

Prime Minister Denzil Douglas responded to Amory by warning of the risks of "fragmentation." Under the federal constitution a referendum in Nevis was required for secession to be legal.

(DAVID RENWICK)

This article updates the *Macropædia* article The WEST INDIES: *Saint Kitts and Nevis.*

SAINT LUCIA

A constitutional monarchy and member of the Commonwealth, St. Lucia is the second largest of the Windward Islands in the eastern Caribbean Sea. Area: 617 sq km (238 sq mi). Pop. (1996 est.): 144,000. Cap.: Castries. Monetary unit: Eastern Caribbean dollar, with (Oct. 11, 1996) a par value of EC$2.70 to U.S. $1 (free rate of EC$4.25 = £1 sterling). Queen, Elizabeth II; governors-general in 1996, Stanislaus A. James and, from June 1, George Mallet; prime ministers, John Compton and, from April 2, Vaughan Lewis.

Vaughan Lewis, a former director general of the Organization of Eastern Caribbean States, was endorsed as the new leader of the governing United Workers' Party (UWP) in January 1996 to replace John Compton, who retired from the party leadership after more than 30 years. Lewis later won a by-election made possible by the resignation from the parliament of the UWP's deputy leader, George Mallet, and was sworn in as prime minister on April 2.

In June Mallet was named governor-general of St. Lucia, an appointment strongly criticized by the opposition St. Lucia Labour Party (SLP) because of his former association with the UWP. The SLP threatened to boycott all events at which he served as host.   (DAVID RENWICK)

This article updates the *Macropædia* article The WEST INDIES: *Saint Lucia.*

SAINT VINCENT AND THE GRENADINES

A constitutional monarchy within the Commonwealth, St. Vincent and the Grenadines comprises the islands of St. Vincent and the northern Grenadines in the eastern Caribbean Sea. Area: 389 sq km (150 sq mi). Pop. (1996 est.): 113,000. Cap.: Kingstown. Monetary unit: Eastern Caribbean dollar, with (Oct. 11, 1996) a par value of EC$2.70 to U.S. $1 (free rate of EC$4.25 = £1 sterling). Queen, Elizabeth II; governor-general in 1996, Sir David Jack; prime minister, Sir James Fitz-Allen Mitchell.

In 1996 St. Vincent and the Grenadines was among those Caribbean countries that signed agreements with the U.S. that allowed U.S. Coast Guard personnel to pursue suspected drug smugglers into their territorial waters. This cooperation was further strengthened in August with an extradition treaty that provided for a rapid transfer of drug lords to U.S. jurisdiction.

(DAVID RENWICK)

This article updates the *Macropædia* article The WEST INDIES: *Saint Vincent and the Grenadines.*

A Rwandan boy is welcomed home. It was estimated that since 1994 at least 100,000 Rwandan children had been separated from their families, and only a few had been reunited.

ROCKY ROAD
TO CARIBBEAN UNITY

by David Renwick

illustration by Igor Kopelnitsky

The 14 member nations of the Caribbean Community and Common Market (Caricom) struggled in 1996 to advance their unification movement but with much less success than had been envisioned. Leaders in the Caribbean region generally agree that a single market and economy (SME) in Caricom is essential for the group's eventual integration into the huge Western Hemisphere trading bloc to be known as the Free Trade Area of the Americas (FTAA), which U.S. Pres. Bill Clinton proposed to the hemispheric summit conference in Miami, Fla., in December 1994.

Even an interim arrangement with the North American Free Trade Agreement (NAFTA), for which Caricom's leading members, Trinidad and Tobago and Jamaica, were pressing, would require a single or, at least, a coordinated Caricom voice. So would the group's ability to make the most of its membership in the 25-nation Association of Caribbean States, which linked Caricom with Central America, Mexico, Colombia, Venezuela, and the non-English-speaking Caribbean territories, including Cuba, in August 1995.

The FTAA, which would create the world's largest free-trade area, 750 million people, was scheduled to come into being by 2005. Unlike other similar trading agreements, it did not, at least as of 1996, include any preferential phasing-in period for the smaller economies of the hemisphere. As Luis Rodríguez, deputy permanent secretary of the Caracas, Venez.-based Latin American Economic System (SELA), to which some Caricom nations belong, pointed out, "Nothing so far in the set of principles enunciated by the ministers in the Americas suggests special or preferential treatment for the smaller and less developed countries of the hemisphere when FTAA is established."

Caricom, with 5.5 million people, is one of the hemisphere's smaller economies. The largest member is Jamaica, with 2.4 million people, and the smallest is Montserrat, with 10,000. Though small by world standards, Caricom is believed to have a good chance of competing with such powers as the U.S. and Brazil if it can function as an SME, along the lines of the European Union.

Caricom leaders have already decided that their countries should relate to the FTAA as a single bloc, but achieving this goal is difficult, as the lack of progress in 1996 demonstrated. While such leaders as Trinidad and Tobago's prime minister, Basdeo Panday, talk positively—"The SME will be an instrument for fostering economic development among Caricom states facing an increasingly open and competitive global environment"—actual achievements have been few. Such organizations as the UN Economic Commission for Latin America and the Caribbean, while conceding that the FTAA "holds the potential for increased economic growth, employment and social equity in Caricom," have reservations about the latter's ability to put its house in order first.

A few tentative steps were taken in 1996. The 14 Caricom countries (which include one non-English-speaking state, Suriname) managed to strip away tariffs among themselves, as well as quota restrictions on internal trade, and agreed on a uniform customs barrier to the outside world (a maximum of 20% on all nonagricultural goods, to be in place by 1998). Caricom also harmonized its incentives for industrial development throughout the region.

A much lengthier list, however, comprises what has not been done. The Caricom heads of government meeting in Barbados in July was marked more by wrangling over barriers to internal trade temporarily erected by one or two members than by the setting of a firm timetable for reaching milestones along the road to the SME. The basic elements on which agreement is required for the SME to begin to take shape include:

●Harmonization of macroeconomic policy, including monetary, exchange-rate, and interest-rate policy. The closest the countries have come to this is an agreement between some central banks to accept repatriated currency. Exchange-rate policy is complicated by the fact that the value of three Caricom currencies—the Trinidad and Tobago, Jamaica, and Guyana dollars—are market-determined, whereas the rest are set administratively. There are no fewer than eight different Caricom currencies. In any event, the basic criteria for monetary union—a stable exchange rate for a period of 36 months, a sustainable debt service ratio not exceeding 15%, and foreign exchange reserves equivalent to three months of imports maintained for at least 12 months—were in 1996 not met by most Caricom economies.

●Harmonization of fiscal policy, including broadly similar tax regimes and the avoidance of double taxation.

●Abandonment of nontariff barriers. Import licensing controlling the flow of some goods within Caricom still exists to a limited extent, as do regulations restricting the exchange of some agricultural products.

●Free movement of labour. This is traditionally one of the most difficult areas of agreement in single-market systems. Some Caricom nations removed barriers to the free movement of an elite group of professionals—physicians, dentists, lawyers, engineers, and accountants. Workers seeking better opportunities by relocating from one Caricom country to another have, however, not been granted free movement.

●Free movement of capital and the ability of investors from anywhere in Caricom to establish businesses on the same terms as local residents. Exchange control still exists in most Caricom countries, and investor rights are constrained by regulations that tend to favour nationals and by restrictions on foreign ownership of assets.

● Transferability of social benefits throughout the region. Only a handful of countries have passed legislation making provision for this.

● A regional transportation policy. This is regarded as critical to the SME's success but has been stymied by airline competition between Caricom nations and by the absence of reliable intraregional shipping services.

The challenges are therefore formidable, and few see them being overcome, even by 2005. As the UN Economic Commission pointed out, "The pace of convergence to a single Caricom market is such that it is unlikely to come into effect in time to allow for a smooth transition to the wider FTAA market."

David Renwick is a journalist in Trinidad and Tobago.

The Caribbean island of Nevis lies to the southeast of Saint Kitts (foreground). Saint Kitts and Nevis was one of the 14 members of Caricom that continued during 1996 to work toward agreements that would allow them to form a single market and economy.

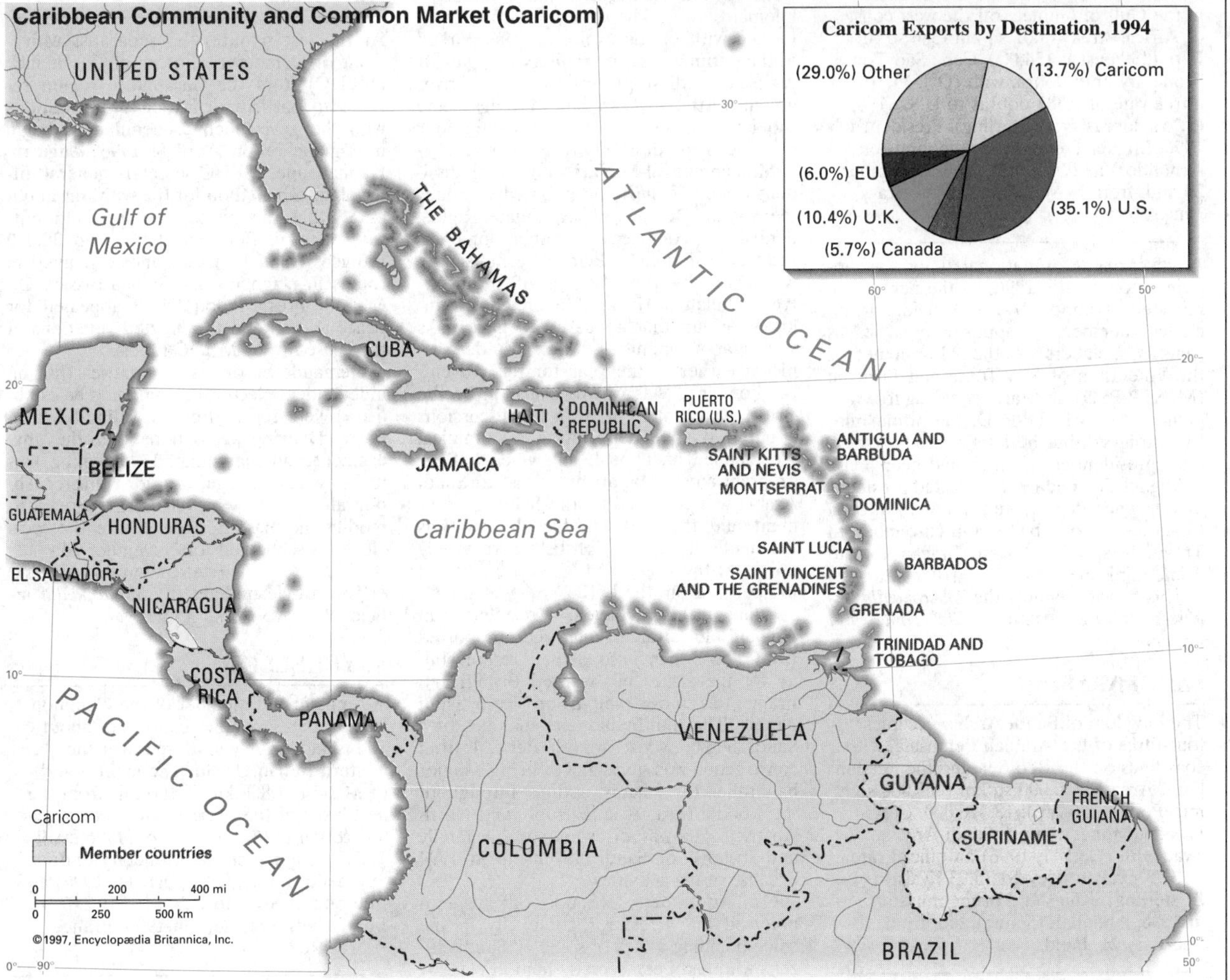

Caribbean Community and Common Market (Caricom)

UNITED STATES

Gulf of Mexico

THE BAHAMAS

ATLANTIC OCEAN

CUBA

MEXICO

HAITI   DOMINICAN REPUBLIC

PUERTO RICO (U.S.)

BELIZE

JAMAICA

GUATEMALA

HONDURAS

Caribbean Sea

SAINT KITTS AND NEVIS

ANTIGUA AND BARBUDA

MONTSERRAT

DOMINICA

EL SALVADOR

SAINT LUCIA

NICARAGUA

SAINT VINCENT AND THE GRENADINES

BARBADOS

GRENADA

COSTA RICA

PANAMA

TRINIDAD AND TOBAGO

PACIFIC OCEAN

VENEZUELA

GUYANA

FRENCH GUIANA

Caricom

☐ Member countries

COLOMBIA

SURINAME

0   200   400 mi
0   250   500 km

©1997, Encyclopædia Britannica, Inc.

BRAZIL

Caricom Exports by Destination, 1994

(29.0%) Other

(13.7%) Caricom

(6.0%) EU

(10.4%) U.K.

(5.7%) Canada

(35.1%) U.S.

SAN MARINO

The republic of San Marino is a landlocked enclave in northeastern Italy. Area: 61 sq km (24 sq mi). Pop. (1996 est.): 25,300. Cap.: San Marino. Monetary unit: Italian lira, with (Oct. 11, 1996) a free rate of 1,523 lire to U.S. $1 (2,399 lire = £1 sterling). The republic is governed by two *capitani reggenti*, or coregents, appointed every six months by a popularly elected Great and General Council. Executive power rests with the Congress of State, headed by the coregents and composed of three secretaries of state and seven ministers.

San Marino in 1996 engaged in diplomatic exchanges with a host of other countries, including Cuba, Germany, Finland, and—not least—one of Europe's other tiny sovereign states, Malta. Though small, San Marino made its presence felt, as witnessed by funds made available for the construction of a school and a clinic in Bosnia and Herzegovina and by its involvement in the International Labour Organization conference in Geneva.   (GREGORY O. SMITH)

This article updates the *Micropædia* article SAN MARINO.

SÃO TOMÉ AND PRÍNCIPE

The republic of São Tomé and Príncipe comprises two main islands and several smaller islets that straddle the Equator in the Gulf of Guinea, off the west coast of Africa. Area: 1,001 sq km (386 sq mi). Pop. (1996 est.): 134,000. Cap.: São Tomé. Monetary unit: dobra, with (Oct. 11, 1996) a free rate of 2,385 dobras to U.S. $1 (3,757 dobras = £1 sterling). President in 1996, Miguel Trovoada; prime ministers, Armindo Vaz d'Almeida until September 20 and, from November 13, Raul Bragança Neto.

A government of national unity was appointed on Jan. 5, 1996, by the new prime minister, Armindo Vaz d'Almeida; it included members of opposition parties as well as members of the Movement for the Liberation of São Tomé and Príncipe (MLSTP-PSD). In March, reacting to wrangling in the MLSTP-PSD, the prime minister resigned, but he later agreed to serve until presidential elections had been held.

Miguel Trovoada was reelected president in July when he defeated Manuel Pinto da Costa in a second ballot. On November 13 Trovoada appointed Raul Bragança Neto prime minister.   (GUY ARNOLD)

This article updates the *Macropædia* article CENTRAL AFRICA: *São Tomé and Príncipe.*

SAUDI ARABIA

The kingdom of Saudi Arabia occupies four-fifths of the Arabian Peninsula, with coastlines on the Red Sea and the Persian Gulf. Area: 2,240,000 sq km (865,000 sq mi). Pop. (1996 est.): 18,426,000. Cap.: Riyadh. Monetary unit: Saudi Arabian riyal, with (Oct. 11, 1996) an official rate of 3.75 riyals to U.S. $1 (5.93 riyals = £1 sterling). Kings and prime ministers in 1996, Abdullah (acting) and, from February 21, Fahd.

On Jan. 1, 1996, King Fahd handed over the reins of government to his half brother Crown Prince Abdullah, one of the 25 surviving sons of the dynasty's founder, 'Abd al-'Aziz (Ibn Sa'ud). Fahd, though in failing health, took power back on February 21, leaving Abdullah in charge of day-to-day affairs of government. Head of the 57,000 Saudi National Guard, Abdullah was not considered to be as pro-American as Fahd and would require the assent of his 24 half brothers to become king. At 72 years of age, Abdullah was considered by many to be too old for the job.

On April 22 the government announced the arrest of four Saudi men in connection with the bombing on Nov. 13, 1995, of the United States military training and communications facility in Riyadh in which 7 people, including 3 U.S. civilians and 2 soldiers, died and about 60 were injured. On May 31 the Saudi government announced that the men, 3 of whom were among the more than 20,000 Saudi veterans of the war in Afghanistan, had been beheaded. Before the execution the U.S. was warned that their deaths would provoke a violent anti-American response. When a truck bomb exploded on June 25 at a military compound near Az-Zahran housing U.S., British, and French military personnel, it was assumed to be a retaliatory measure. The blast caused the death of 19 U.S. servicemen and wounded almost 400 Saudis, Americans, and Bangladeshi. It left a crater 10.5 m (35 ft) deep and blew out windows almost a kilometre away. The large diesel fuel truck packed with plastic explosives was parked at the perimeter of the military complex. It aroused Saudi suspicions when the driver got into a nearby car, but warnings came too late; the bomb exploded within four minutes of the discovery of the truck.

Muhammad al-Mas'ari, the Saudi dissident leader of the London-based Committee for the Defence of Legitimate Rights, denied any complicity in either bomb attack, even though a claim of responsibility was made by the "Legion of the Martyr Abdullah al-Huzaifi," a previously unknown group that appeared to have links to Mas'ari's committee. Already under suspicion earlier in the year for the November bombing, Mas'ari was called in by the British government in April for discussions about his possible deportation to Dominica. He planned an appeal, and when a BBC program about Mas'ari broadcast to Saudi Arabia was censored by the Saudi government and the BBC Arabic channel was taken off the air, the British were visibly upset. At the year's end Mas'ari continued to operate from the U.K.

Osama bin Laden, resident in Afghanistan after having been deported from The Sudan, also denied responsibility for the attack but warned Britain and France to remove their troops from Saudi Arabia. The multimillionaire member of a Saudi family whose wealth derived from construction was suspected of being a major bankroller for Islamist groups throughout the Middle East, Asia, Europe, and North America. He was disowned by his family and stripped of Saudi citizenship in 1994 because of his activities.

On November 1 Saudi officials announced the arrest for complicity in the truck-bombing attack of some 40 Saudi citizens who had been secretly held in custody

for three months. This was in addition to the arrest of 80 to 100 members of the Saudi Hezbollah opposition party, which was reputed to be affiliated with the Iranian-backed Lebanese Hezbollah organization. The party, formed in 1993, had taken up Shi'ite grievances against the government.

Many of the dominant Sunni Saudis also objected to the government's policies. Though the official government-backed religious officials condemned the attack against the Americans, many religious groups opposed the U.S. military presence in Saudi Arabia, the U.S.'s pro-Israel policy, and the Saudi government for allowing foreign troops to be stationed on the soil of the sacred cities of Mecca and Medina. In December the Saudi government tightened security around U.S. military installations.

(REEVA S. SIMON)

This article updates the *Macropædia* article ARABIA: *Saudi Arabia.*

SENEGAL

The republic of Senegal is located in West Africa, on the Atlantic Ocean; it surrounds the country of The Gambia. Area: 196,712 sq km (75,951 sq mi). Pop. (1996 est.): 8,532,000. Cap.: Dakar. Monetary unit: CFA franc, with (Oct. 11, 1996) a par value of CFAF 100 to the French franc and a free rate of CFAF 518.24 to U.S. $1 (CFAF 816.38 = £1 sterling). President in 1996, Abdou Diouf; prime minister, Habib Thiam.

At the last minute, the separatist Movement of Democratic Forces of Casamance (MFDC) from the Casamance region refused to participate in peace negotiations with the government, scheduled to begin in Ziguinchor on April 8, 1996. Augustin Diamacoune, MFDC secretary-general, offered no explanation for the withdrawal but asked that the peace talks be held outside Senegal. Between 20,000 and 30,000 refugees from the Casamance remained in camps in neighbouring Guinea-Bissau. On May 17 Pres. Abdou Diouf appealed for peace and an end to reported violations of the cease-fire by MFDC rebels.

Demands by opposition parties that an independent electoral commission be established were rejected by the ruling Socialist Party. Denying accusations that the government had manipulated the voting lists to its own advantage, Interior Minister Abdourahmane Sow nevertheless agreed to modify the existing code before the local elections scheduled for November 24.

(NANCY ELLEN LAWLER)

This article updates the *Macropædia* article WESTERN AFRICA: *Senegal.*

SEYCHELLES

A republic and member of the Commonwealth, the Seychelles consists of about 100 islands widely scattered over the western Indian Ocean. The main island of Mahé is 1,800 km (1,100 mi) from the east coast of the African continent. Area: 455 sq km (176 sq mi). Pop. (1996 est.): 76,100. Cap.: Victoria. Monetary unit: Seychelles rupee, with (Oct. 11, 1996) a free rate of SR 5 to U.S. $1 (SR 7.87 = £1 sterling). President in 1996, France-Albert René.

The Seychelles enjoyed an uneventful year in 1996, with steady if moderate economic growth of about 3.9% over the previous year. International aid totaling $13 million a year helped the government finance a range of projects, including protection of the environment and the transport infrastructure and the rehabilitation of the Victoria Market.

The nation's steady progress in recent years was reflected in *Human Development Report 1996,* which ranked the Seychelles as 60th in world development terms. Some of the important human development statistics were as follows: life expectancy, 71 years; rate of adult literacy, 88%; and copies of daily newspapers per 100 people, 4. The government spent 12.9% of its total expenditure on education.   (GUY ARNOLD)

This article updates the *Micropædia* article SEYCHELLES.

SIERRA LEONE

A republic of West Africa and member of the Commonwealth, Sierra Leone lies on the Atlantic Ocean. Area: 71,740 sq km (27,699 sq mi). Pop. (1996 est.): 4,617,000.

Cap.: Freetown. Monetary unit: leone, with (Oct. 11, 1996) a free rate of 870 leones to U.S. $1 (1,371 leones = £1 sterling). Chairmen of the Supreme Council of State in 1996, Capt. Valentine E.M. Strasser and, from January 16 to March 29, Brig. Gen. Julius Maada Bio; president from March 29, Ahmad Tejan Kabbah.

On Jan. 16, 1996, a bloodless coup by army officers brought an end to Valentine Strasser's leadership; he was replaced by Brig. Gen. Julius Maada Bio, a former close associate of Strasser and vice-chairman of the Supreme Council of State. Strasser was allowed to leave the country for the U.K.

Despite the coup, elections for a return to civilian rule (which had been deferred from Dec. 5, 1995, to February 26–27) were held as planned. The Sierra Leone People's Party (SLPP) won 36% of the vote in a 60% turnout of voters. The leading presidential candidate was Ahmad Tejan Kabbah of the SLPP, although he obtained only 35.8% of the votes. Kabbah became president after a second round of voting, and on March 29 tens of thousands celebrated the return to civilian rule when Bio handed over power.

In the new National Assembly of 68 elected seats, the SLPP had 27. Six members of the armed forces attempted to mount a coup on September 8, but it was foiled. Some 20 military leaders, including Strasser and Bio, were retired by President Kabbah. Rebels in the Revolutionary United Front attacked several villages in October, killing at least 17 people. In November Kabbah signed a peace agreement with the RUF.

(GUY ARNOLD)

This article updates the *Macropædia* article WESTERN AFRICA: *Sierra Leone.*

SINGAPORE

Singapore, a republic of Southeast Asia and member of the Commonwealth, consists of the island of Singapore and 60 nearby islets, at the southern extremity of the Malay Peninsula. Area: 646 sq km (249 sq mi). Pop. (1996 est.): 3,045,000. Monetary unit: Singapore dollar, with (Oct. 11, 1996) a free rate of S$1.41 to U.S. $1 (S$2.22 = £1 sterling). President in 1996, Ong Teng Cheong; prime minister, Goh Chok Tong.

The year 1996 started on an upbeat note for Singapore. To the delight of policy makers, the Organisation for Economic Cooperation and Development in January reclassified the island republic as a "more advanced developing economy," a classification just below developed status. The island's economic indicators continued to be the envy of many industrialized countries. Overall economic growth was strong at about 8%, with unemployment averaging a low 2.7%. But the good news was tempered in the second half of the year as Singapore's disk drive and computer chip makers, hit by the slump in global electronics demand, reported declining profits.

Senior Minister Lee Kuan Yew raised speculation in June when he said he could foresee Singapore's eventual reunion with Malaysia, provided the latter adopted the meritocracy of Singapore. The island had left the Malaysian federation in 1965, and six years later Malaysia introduced its New Economic Policy, favouring indigenous Malays over other ethnic groups.

Rumours grew about the timing of national elections, due to take place by April 1997. Amid slowly eroding support for the ruling People's Action Party, Prime Minister Goh Chok Tong publicly asked voters to give his party at least 60% of the vote. The opposition was spread over eight separate parties, with the largest group, the Singapore Democratic Party, fractured by internal dissent.

On the international front, Singapore's ambition to achieve closer ties with Europe was realized with the first Asia-Europe Meeting, which took place in Bangkok in March. At the meeting the delegates decided, among other cooperative measures, to inaugurate an Asia-Europe Foundation, to be based in Singapore.

(MATTHEW FLETCHER)

This article updates the *Macropædia* article SOUTHEAST ASIA: *Singapore.*

SLOVAKIA

Slovakia is a landlocked state in central Europe. Area: 49,036 sq km (18,933 sq mi). Pop. (1996 est.): 5,372,000. Cap.:

After elections that took place in Sierra Leone in February and March, supporters of the United National People's Party, which was runner-up, celebrate the return to civilian rule. The elections were held despite the military government's attempts at intimidation.

Bratislava. Monetary unit: Slovak koruna, with (Oct. 11, 1996) a free rate of 31.19 koruny to U.S. $1 (49.13 koruny = £1 sterling). President in 1996, Michal Kovac; prime minister, Vladimir Meciar.

Politics in Slovakia in 1996 was played out against the backdrop of the continuing feud between Pres. Michal Kovac and Prime Minister Vladimir Meciar; the two men found themselves on opposing sides on practically every important issue. Kovac even initiated a slander suit against Meciar. Before a conference in August 1996, the two men had not met officially in 14 months.

The formal investigation of the kidnapping in August 1995 of Kovac's son, in which many believed Meciar's supporters had a role, slowly petered out during the year. Meciar had intimated that the abduction might have been a sham engineered by Kovac himself. A key witness, who might have implicated intelligence service chief Ivan Lexa in the kidnapping, died when his automobile was bombed on April 29. The police found no evidence to support allegations that Lexa and Interior Minister Ludovit Hudek had obstructed the investigation, and charges were dropped in July.

Eyebrows were raised in March when the National Council approved the Law on the Protection of the Republic, providing stiff penalties for the dissemination abroad of false information about the state and for the organizers of demonstrations harmful to the state. The law was vetoed by President Kovac in April, but the government was more successful in maintaining tight control over the media. In one visible case, Tatiana Repkova, editor and publisher of *Narodna obroda,* a newspaper that was uniquely independent of all political factions, was forced to quit in late November.

If Slovakia's political life was harsh, its economy was faring well. Western analysts expected a 6% growth rate in 1996, and the inflation rate was 5.2% in September. Unemployment was dropping. Still, the political jockeying between the two top Slovak leaders and the country's human rights record were poor recommendations abroad. Fears were expressed that Slovakia might be passed over in the expansion of the European Union and NATO. (EDITORS)

This article updates the *Macropædia* article CZECH AND SLOVAK REPUBLICS: *Slovakia.*

SLOVENIA

A republic at the northeastern head of the Adriatic Sea, Slovenia borders Austria to the north, Hungary to the east, Croatia to the southeast and south, the Adriatic to the southwest, and Italy to the west. Area: 20,255 sq km (7,820 sq mi). Pop. (1996 est.): 1,959,000. Cap.: Ljubljana. Monetary unit: tolar, with (Oct. 11, 1996) a free rate of 139.19 tolarji to U.S. $1 (219.26 tolarji = £1 sterling). President in 1996, Milan Kucan; prime minister, Janez Drnovsek.

On June 10, 1996, Slovenia signed an agreement of associate membership with the European Union (EU). The country's ultimate goal was full EU membership, with 2001 as the target date. Slovenia moved closer to membership when its legislature agreed to support changes in the nation's constitution to permit noncitizens to own property. This demand had been pressed strongly by Italy, which thereupon removed its veto against Slovenia. During the year Slovenia continued its efforts to be included in the first group of nations (Poland, Hungary, Czech Republic) to be invited to join in the expansion of NATO, winning important support for this in the U.S. Congress.

Pope John Paul II visited Slovenia May 17–19, the first pope ever to have visited the overwhelmingly Roman Catholic country. He was received enthusiastically despite major problems between the church and state authorities over the slow return of church properties seized during the communist regime. The Vatican, in late 1991, had been the first international entity to recognize the independence of Slovenia.

Quadrennial legislative elections held November 10 produced an even split between left-of-centre and right-of-centre parties. The centre-left Liberal Democracy of Slovenia won 25 of the 90 seats, followed by three more conservative parties: the Slovenian People's Party (19 seats), the Social Democratic Party (16), and the Slovenian Christian Democrats (10). In fifth place was the United List of Social Democrats, the reformed Communist Party. On December 8 a national referendum was held, with voters deciding whether to approve a change in the election law toward a majority system and away from proportional representation. In the referendum the voters rejected the proposed change.

Slovenia experienced a 3% increase in gross domestic product in 1996. The inflation rate was 10%. (RUDOLPH M. SUSEL)

This article updates the *Macropædia* article BALKAN STATES: *Slovenia.*

SOLOMON ISLANDS

A constitutional monarchy and member of the Commonwealth, the Solomon Islands comprises a 1,450-km (900-mi) chain of islands and atolls in the western Pacific Ocean. Area: 28,370 sq km (10,954 sq mi). Pop. (1996 est.): 396,000. Cap.: Honiara. Monetary unit: Solomon Islands dollar, with (Oct. 11, 1996) a free rate of SI$3.54 to U.S. $1 (SI$5.58 = £1 sterling). Queen, Elizabeth II; governor-general in 1996, Moses Pitakaka; prime minister, Solomon Mamaloni.

Despite serious economic problems, political controversy, and a Cabinet reshuffle, the government of Solomon Mamaloni remained in office in 1996. Forestry remained the mainstay of the economy (56% of export revenue). The government, however, planned to end log exports by 1999 in favour of processed products. This encouraged log exporters to accelerate their operations.

On the Papua New Guinea border, there was continued tension arising from the civil war on Bougainville, with allegations of border incursions. Measures taken to alleviate the tensions had little effect.

(BARRIE MACDONALD)

This article updates the *Macropædia* article PACIFIC ISLANDS: *Solomon Islands.*

SOMALIA

Situated in the Horn of northeastern Africa, Somalia lies on the Gulf of Aden and the Indian Ocean (the region on the Gulf of Aden [the self-declared Somaliland] claimed independence in 1991 but is not recognized internationally). Area: 637,000 sq km (246,000 sq mi). Pop. (1996 est.): 6,802,000 (excluding Somali refugees in neighbouring countries estimated to number about 500,000). Cap.: Mogadishu. Monetary unit: Somali shilling, with (Oct. 11, 1996) a free rate of 2,620 Somali shillings to U.S. $1 (4,128 Somali shillings = £1 sterling). Somalia had no functioning government in 1996.

In August 1996 Somalia lost the most commanding figure to emerge in that country since the government collapsed in 1991. Gen. Muhammad Farah Aydid (*see* OBITUARIES) died on August 1 after being mortally wounded in a battle near Mogadishu on July 24. A national hero to his followers and a dangerous megalomaniac to his opponents, he had differed from the other "warlords" by his determination to become the leader of a reunited Somalia. His death called into question the future of his Somali National Alliance (SNA), one of the two coalitions of clan-based groupings that divided Somalia, apart from the self-declared republic of Somaliland. The other coalition, the Somali Salvation Alliance, was headed by former businessman Ali Mahdi Muhammad. Both men were titled "president" and claimed to head governments. Mogadishu was divided between them.

The beginning of the year was marked by military successes for Aydid. He already held much of the southern Somali plain and its capital, Baydhabo, against the guerrilla attacks of the Rahanwayn Resistance Army (RRA). In January he captured the town of Xuddur, and in March he took Diinsoor and Doolow. The SNA was weakened, however, by the split with his fellow clansman and former right-hand man and financier, Osman Hassan Ali ("Ato"). Their conflict became violent in March, when their forces clashed near the port of Marka over control of the lucrative banana trade. In April the violence shifted to Mogadishu, where Ato occupied his own enclave. Intermittent fighting against an anti-Aydid coalition of Ato and Ali Mahdi continued there to the end of the year. In May the RRA recaptured Xuddur.

After Aydid's death, he was succeeded by his U.S.-educated son Hussein Aydid, who had served as interpreter to the U.S. command in Somalia in 1992–93 until his identity was discovered. Hopes of an early peace were dashed as fighting continued between Hussein's forces and the Ato-Ali Mahdi coalition. In December more than 100 were killed in street fighting between the rivals in Mogadishu.

In the north the self-declared independent Somaliland Republic of Pres. Muhammad Ibrahim Egal continued to establish itself in spite of failure to gain international recognition and continuing hostilities with those who favoured unity with the SNA. A constitution was under discussion, and there were plans for a general election. In November the mandate of President Egal's government reached its term, and a national conference was convened to appoint a new government.

(VIRGINIA R. LULING)

This article updates the *Macropædia* article EASTERN AFRICA: *Somalia.*

South African police and members of the Islamic group People Against Gangsterism and Drugs (Pagad) confront one another. Pagad was one of a number of vigilante groups that were being formed in South Africa in response to the country's rising rate of violent crime.

SOUTH AFRICA

South Africa, a member of the Commonwealth, occupies the southern tip of Africa, with the Atlantic Ocean to the west and the Indian Ocean to the east. Area: 1,219,090 sq km (470,693 sq mi). Pop. (1996 est.): 41,743,000. Executive cap., Pretoria; judicial cap., Bloemfontein; legislative cap., Cape Town. Monetary unit: South African rand, with (Oct. 11, 1996) a free rate of R 4.54 to U.S. $1 (R 7.16 = £1 sterling). President in 1996, Nelson Mandela.

Domestic Affairs. During 1996 the Constitutional Assembly drew up a new constitution for South Africa, replacing the interim constitution under which the country was functioning and consolidating the transition to democracy that took place in 1994. At the same time, the political honeymoon that the government of national unity (GNU), dominated by the African National Congress (ANC), had enjoyed since it was elected in 1994 came to a decisive end. The National Party (NP) left the GNU at the end of June—its first time out of government since 1948—and the regime came under criticism from a number of quarters. The rand began to fall in value in February and by the end of June had lost 20% of its value. An increase in crime, particularly violent crime, attracted attention throughout the year.

In January Pres. Nelson Mandela spelled out goals for the year, including the continuation of reconciliation, based on the ending of racial discrimination. He called for a "new patriotism" and a united crusade against crime and the "culture of rapacity." Criticizing a search for "short-lived quick solutions" and warning people not to expect entitlements from the state, he said that the government would have to improve on its delivery of services to the people. The Masekhane campaign, which aimed to end the widespread boycotting of rent and service payments, continued with varying

success through the year; in April 77% of the people in Soweto were reported as not paying for municipal services.

Among the accomplishments of the government was the enactment of a law permitting abortion on demand up to the 12th week of pregnancy; this was fiercely opposed by antiabortion groups and was due to be challenged in the Constitutional Court. Disadvantaged rural groups such as labour tenants had their legal right to own land acknowledged and promoted. A new health and safety act based on international standards and legislation promised to improve conditions in the mining industry. A national youth commission was established. With only approximately 4,000 houses a month under construction, there was a renewed emphasis on a state-private partnership in building rental housing stock for the poor. A new chief justice, Ismail Mahomed, the first black to occupy the post, was appointed.

Mandela said that the enactment of the new constitution "cleansed" the country "of a horrible past." The first draft of the constitution was passed in May. The Congress of South African Trade Unions (COSATU) called a general strike on April 30 to oppose the introduction in the constitution of a clause guaranteeing employers the right to lock out workers. The strike was supported by many workers in industrial areas and was accompanied by demonstrations of 300,000 people, and it succeeded in eliminating the clause. Among other changes from the interim constitution were a protection of property clause, which empowered the state to engage in land redistribution, and the replacement of the Senate by a National Council of Provinces. Compulsory power sharing among parties was abolished. Chief Mangosuthu Gatsha Buthelezi, home affairs minister and leader of the Inkatha Freedom Party (IFP), which had boycotted the Constitutional Assembly, labeled the draft constitution as that of a "totalitarian autocracy." KwaZulu/Natal enacted its own provincial constitution in March, with

9 of its 14 chapters frozen as "unresolved matters" in disputes between the IFP and the ANC.

The Constitutional Court considered the national and KwaZulu/Natal constitutions. It rejected the latter, regarding it as containing many provisions intended to usurp national power. It considered the former a "monumental achievement," taking issue with only nine of its provisions, including the fact that provincial powers were substantially less than those in the interim constitution. The Constitutional Assembly, again boycotted by the IFP, resubmitted a revised constitution to the court, which approved it in December. The IFP argued that the local government powers accorded to chiefs were insufficient.

While the levels of violence in Natal diminished in comparison with previous years, the situation there remained tense. Though booed by them, Mandela at a top-level meeting attended by King Goodwill Zwelithini and Buthelezi on March 15 chided chiefs in Natal for their support of violence. In April several of King Zwelithini's wives were assaulted and a relative was murdered, allegedly by supporters of the IFP, during an attack on one of the king's palaces. On May 4 police fought running gun battles in Durban with marchers of the pro-IFP National Hostels Residents Association.

Local elections were held in the Western Cape on May 29. The NP won 48.2% of the vote and thus consolidated at the local level the provincial victory it had won with 53.2% of the vote in the 1994 general election. Local elections took place in KwaZulu/Natal on June 26. The ANC won in Durban, Pietermaritzburg, and most other towns. The IFP, losing 6% support since the general election, still obtained a majority of votes in the province because of its strength in the rural areas.

In early February NP leader F.W. de Klerk complained of a breakdown of standards and of family life, of poor delivery of services, and of nonpayment of rent in the townships. He condemned the influence of radical trade unions and called for a new opposition alliance based on "Christian principles." When the NP departed from the government, it criticized the "pro-worker" labour relations clauses, the exclusion of the death penalty, and the abandonment of power sharing in the final constitution. The NP declared it would form a "dynamic but responsible" opposition.

Concern about crime was demonstrated by People Against Gangsterism and Drugs (Pagad), which burst onto the scene in the Western Cape in August when a mass demonstration that it organized resulted in the shooting and burning alive of a gangster leader outside his house. Pagad, which split into two factions, continued demonstrations at the houses of alleged gangsters. Gang leaders in the Western Cape claimed they were dissolving their gangs and working for peace.

A number of Cabinet changes took place during the year. In February the NP minister of welfare and population development, Abe Williams, resigned after allegations of corruption in his department. During the same month, the NP minister of constitutional development, Roelf Meyer, left the Cabinet to become secretary-general of the NP. Soon after presenting the budget in

March, the nonparty finance minister, Chris Liebenberg, resigned and was replaced by the ANC's Trevor Manuel. At the same time, the responsibility for overseeing the Reconstruction and Development Program was transferred from a minister without portfolio to the deputy president, Thabo Mbeki. Cyril Ramaphosa, the chairperson of the Constitutional Assembly and secretary-general of the ANC, resigned from both positions to become executive chairperson of the black-owned New Africa Investments. This company subsequently was involved in a takeover of the Anglo-American-owned Johnnic, which was seen as a step toward black economic empowerment. ANC legislators filled the Cabinet posts vacated by NP members in June, and Ben Magubane of the IFP left the Cabinet to enter the KwaZulu/Natal government.

After a 19-month trial, Col. Eugene de Kock, a former policeman in charge of "hit squads," was found guilty in August of 89 of the 121 charges against him, including 6 of murder and 2 of conspiracy to murder. In an effort to mitigate his sentence, he implicated many former senior officials of the regime in such "dirty tricks" as the planting of weapons caches, which was blamed on the ANC, and in hit squad activity, including operations previously alleged to have been committed by the liberation movements.

To the surprise of many, former defense minister Magnus Malan, Zakhele Khumalo, the deputy general secretary of the IFP, and 19 others were acquitted on charges stemming from the massacre of 13 United Democratic Front supporters at KwaMakhutha, Natal, in January 1987. The judge stated that the killings had been committed by (unknown) Inkatha members given military training by the former South African Defense Force.

During the year the Truth and Reconciliation Commission (TRC) began hearing evidence on human rights violations between 1960 and 1993; the TRC was chaired by Nobel Peace Prize winner Desmond Tutu, who retired as archbishop of Cape Town in June. Most of the testimony to the TRC was presented by victims of such violations, mainly at the hands of the state and its agents but also by liberation forces. Perpetrators of violations could apply for amnesty to the TRC provided they fully disclosed their responsibility for and role in such violations. By the year's end few perpetrators had testified. A former chief of police alleged that P.W. Botha while president of the country had in 1988 authorized the bombing by police of Khotso House, headquarters of the South African Council of Churches. Senior police officers also admitted their responsibility for the blowing up of the headquarters of COSATU as well as for the murders of activists in the 1980s. The TRC commissioners charged the police with having destroyed past files that provided evidence of violations. The TRC was scheduled to submit its final report by March 1998.

In May the former ruler of the Transkei, Gen. Bantu Holomisa, testified to the TRC and claimed that ANC Cabinet minister Stella Sigcau had received a R 50,000 bribe from millionaire hotel owner Sol Kerzner under the Transkei government of George Matanzima. Subsequently, Holomisa alleged that other ANC leaders had received favours from Kerzner and that the ANC had secretly received R 2 million for its 1994 election campaign from Kerzner (which was subsequently admitted by Nelson Mandela). This led to Holomisa's dismissal as deputy minister of environmental affairs and tourism in July and to his subsequent expulsion from the ANC. Many rank-and-file members of the ANC opposed these actions, and Holomisa announced that he would form a new political party.

There was conflict over economic policy between the ANC and its partners in the "triple alliance," COSATU and the South African Communist Party. In June the government announced a "macroeconomic strategy," targeting 6% growth and the creation of as many as 800,000 jobs by the year 2000 on the basis of attracting foreign investment. It aimed at budget deficit reduction, exchange control relaxation, wage and price "moderation," and labour market "flexibility." COSATU and the Communist Party described the strategy as "neoliberal" and opposed its calls for wage and fiscal restraint. Responding to the opposition of the unions in COSATU, Mandela declared in Germany in May that privatization was "the fundamental policy of the ANC." Several unions supported a one-day strike against privatization on July 2.

The Economy. The economic upswing that began in May 1993 continued into 1996, though there were signs of a slowdown. Gross domestic product (GDP) grew by 3.3% in 1995, the largest gain since 1988. Manufacturing grew 7.6%, while agriculture and mining declined. Anticipated GDP growth in 1996 was 3%. Gross domestic fixed investment rose 10.4% in 1995 and 6% in the first half of 1996. It was expected to increase by 4–7% in 1996 overall.

The economic upturn was, however, described as "jobless growth." Only 12,000 jobs had been created since May 1993, and since that time manufacturing, mining, and construction had lost 126,052 jobs. Employment in manufacturing had been stagnant since the mid-1980s. Unemployment in 1996 was estimated by the Central Statistical Services at 32.6%, and it was estimated that 280,000 were added to the unemployed in 1995–96.

In 1995 the rand depreciated only 2.66%, but during 1996 it lost some 20% of its value. Inflation reached a 24-year low of 5.5% in April, then rose to 7.5% by August, and was anticipated to be less than 8% for the year, compared with 8.7% in 1995.

The budget contained some tax relief for individuals and companies. There was a 10.4% increase in spending to R 173.7 billion, with interest repayments on debt accounting for 18.7%, education for 21.2%, health 9.9%, and welfare 9.6%.

Foreign Affairs. President Mandela was warmly greeted on his first official visit to the United Kingdom, and he shared a platform with French Pres. Jacques Chirac on Bastille Day (July 14) in Paris. Also, in July he met with Presidents Robert Mugabe of Zimbabwe, Sir Ketumile Masire of Botswana, and Joaquim Chissano of Mozambique to discuss the conflict over democratic reform in Swaziland. Mandela was elected chairperson of the Southern African Development Community in August. South Africa also became chair of the UN Conference on Trade and Development.

The second report of the Cameron Commission, appointed to investigate arms sales, recommended the disbandment of the Armscor board of directors and that Armscor no longer have the power to determine to whom arms were sold. To protests from the arms industry, the commission recommended that all future arms deals be authorized by Parliament and made public. The government accepted the recommendations. Despite evidence of illegal exports of arms to Rwanda and Burundi, the government, against the opposition of human rights groups, approved the sale of arms to the Rwandan government in October.

South Africa had been one of the few governments to maintain diplomatic relations with both Taiwan and China, but late in the year it severed ties with Taiwan. Its relations with the U.S. included a binational commission chaired by U.S. Vice Pres. Al Gore and Deputy President Mbeki. The South African government backed away from Mandela's call at the 1995 Commonwealth Conference for sanctions against Nigeria for human rights violations. Controversy arose over Mandela's meetings with Nation of Islam leader Louis Farrakhan and with a representative of the Palestine organization Hamas and over relations with Libya, Cuba, and Iran.

(MARTIN LEGASSICK)

This article updates the *Macropædia* article SOUTHERN AFRICA: *South Africa*.

SPAIN

A constitutional monarchy of southwestern Europe with coastlines on the Bay of Biscay, the Atlantic Ocean, and the Mediterranean Sea, Spain shares the Iberian Peninsula with Portugal; it includes the Balearic and Canary island groups, in the Mediterranean and the Atlantic, respectively, and enclaves in northern Morocco. Area: 505,990 sq km (195,364 sq mi). Pop. (1996 est.): 39,270,000. Cap.: Madrid. Monetary unit: Spanish peseta, with (Oct. 11, 1996) a free rate of 128.79 pesetas to U.S. $1 (202.88 pesetas = £1 sterling). King, Juan Carlos I; prime ministers in 1996, Felipe González Márquez, and from May 6, José María Aznar López.

The much-anticipated victory of the conservative Popular Party in the general elections on March 3 brought about a major shift in Spanish politics during 1996 after 13 years of Socialist rule. Prime Minister José María Aznar López (*see* BIOGRAPHIES) appointed a Cabinet, which took office in May. It reflected the range of his party's views—from Thatcherite free-marketers to more paternal, state interventionists in line with traditional Spanish conservatism.

Like his predecessor, Felipe González Márquez, Aznar was obliged to bargain with several regional parties in order to win a vote to install his minority government. Throughout the year backing for legislation came from the Basque Nationalist Party, the Canarian Coalition, and the Convergence and Union coalition from the northeastern Catalonia region. The kingmaker of Spanish politics became Jordi Pujol, the leader of the Catalan coalition and president of Catalonia, whose pro-business party won important concessions for greater autonomy for all Spanish regions.

CHRISTOPHER PILLITZ—STERN

Fishermen labour in rough seas off the coast of Galicia, in northwestern Spain. Although the coastal areas had been overfished and the European Union had imposed quotas, fishing remained one of the principal economic activities and mainstays of the region.

The Aznar government maintained the outgoing Socialists' commitment to joining the European Union's single currency and showed itself willing to take political risks in order to qualify for membership. In the summer it announced a decision to freeze the wages of civil servants in 1997 and stood by that decision throughout the fall, despite a series of union-led demonstrations that culminated in a march by tens of thousands of Spaniards throughout the nation on December 11.

The government, with the backing of regional parties, passed a strict 1997 budget on December 27, four days before time would have run out for a vote. The opposition Socialists and communist-led United Left coalition argued that the spending cuts and tax adjustments would hurt the disadvantaged and benefit the rich. The budget aimed to enable Spain to lower its deficit to within 3% of gross domestic product, a requirement for joining the EU's single currency.

The Basque separatist group Euskadi Ta Askatasuna (ETA) continued its battle for Basque independence and became a major problem for the new government. In January the ETA kidnapped José Antonio Ortega Lara, a prison employee from the northern city of Pamplona; at the year's end he had not been released. Ortega, the ETA's longest-held captive, became the focus of weekly demonstrations and candlelight vigils demanding his freedom.

The ETA said that it would not release Ortega until the government had moved some 450 ETA convicts to prisons in the Basque region. The convicts were spread throughout Spain to prevent them from working together. The government repeatedly refused the ETA's demand, which was also endorsed by a broad range of parties in the Basque region. In November the ETA also kidnapped Cosme Delclaux, heir of a prominent Basque business family, presumably to obtain the ETA's "revolutionary tax" ransom money, which would be used to finance the organization's campaign of terrorism.

In December the daily newspapers *El País* and *El Mundo* published what they claimed were excerpts of documents from the state intelligence agency, Cesid, concerning the government's secret war on Basque separatists in the 1980s. Defense Minister Eduardo Serra Rexach confirmed, then later denied, the authenticity of the reports.

In September a National Court judge began hearing evidence against dozens of Argentine officers accused of human rights violations during the 1976–83 military dictatorship in Argentina, including the torture and killing of Spaniards.

Spain marked the 60th anniversary of its civil war with the return in November of 370 members of the International Brigades, which fought for the Republic against Francisco Franco's Nationalists. The Cortes (parliament) voted to grant citizenship to any who requested it.

The government was forced to back down on a plan to reduce Spanish dependence on its own high-priced coal when hundreds of coal miners blocked highways and demonstrated in November. The miners persuaded the government to adjust a national elec-tricity plan that would have phased out the subsidy of Spanish coal, which made it more expensive than imports.

On December 3 a judge granted parole to Civil Guard Lieut. Col. Antonio Tejero Molina, who led a failed 1981 coup attempt in which the Cortes was stormed during the swearing-in ceremony of Prime Minister Leopoldo Calvo Sotelo. Tejero had served slightly more than half of his 30-year sentence.

Aznar's government distanced Spain from Fidel Castro's Cuba by trying to toughen the EU's policy toward the island. In November Cuba rejected Spain's proposed new ambassador after the Spaniard criticized Castro's human rights record. In late November Spain agreed to name a new ambassador.

As the year came to a close, the government announced the sale early in 1997 of the nation's remaining minority stake in the Telefónica telecommunications company and the petroleum group Repsol. The conservatives said all state enterprises were potentially for sale, markets permitting.

(GARY ABRAMSON)

SRI LANKA

A republic and member of the Commonwealth, Sri Lanka occupies an island in the Indian Ocean off the southeast coast of peninsular India. Area: 65,610 sq km (25,332 sq mi). Pop. (1996 est.): 18,318,-000. Legislative cap., Sri Jayawardenepura Kotte; administrative cap., Colombo. Monetary unit: Sri Lanka rupee, with (Oct. 11, 1996) a free rate of SL Rs 57.05 to U.S.

$1 (SL Rs 89.87 = £1 sterling). President in 1996, Chandrika Kumaratunga; prime minister, Sirimavo Bandaranaike.

Even though the Liberation Tigers of Tamil Eelam (LTTE), the guerrilla group that had been fighting the government since 1983 in its quest for an independent homeland for Sri Lanka's two million Tamils, suffered a severe military defeat with the loss of Jaffna Peninsula in December 1995, it still managed to inflict significant blows on government forces in 1996, as well as carry out terrorist acts against the Sinhalese civilian population. On January 31 the LTTE claimed responsibility for a massive bomb explosion in Colombo's financial district at the central bank building, where Sri Lanka's gold reserves are held. The explosion killed more than 200 people and wounded over 1,400 others. Similarly, in July two bombs ripped through separate cars of a commuter train, killing 64 people and wounding more than 450. Although the LTTE did not claim responsibility for the train explosions, the government accused it of the terrorist acts.

In July the LTTE conducted a weeklong operation against the military base of Mullaitivu, about 240 km (175 m), northeast of Colombo. An estimated 4,000 guerrillas attacked from the south and from the sea and eventually captured the fortified garrison, taking away large quantities of heavy weapons. Except for a handful of soldiers, all 1,200 military personnel in the base were killed. The LTTE lost about 200 fighters. This was the government's bloodiest and worst defeat in the civil war.

In late September government forces launched a major offensive against Kilinochchi, about 230 km (170 m) north of Colombo and the only major urban centre still under LTTE control. Approximately 15,000 army personnel, using conventional military tactics, attacked the LTTE's headquarters. The LTTE, unable to hold on to the town, was forced out into the jungle. The government lost about 250 men and the LTTE more than 1,000. This was a major military blow for the Tamil Tigers, because by losing their last urban centre, they were deprived of an important recruitment ground. Despite the LTTE's complete rejection of Pres. Chandrika Kumaratunga's 1995 peace plan, which would turn Sri Lanka into a loose federation of eight regions, Kumaratunga pledged to "restore complete peace" by the end of 1997.

(CLAUDE RAKISITS)

SUDAN, THE

A republic of North Africa, The Sudan has a coastline on the Red Sea. Area: 2,503,890 sq km (966,757 sq mi). Pop. (1996 est.): 31,065,000. Executive cap., Khartoum; legislative cap., Omdurman. Monetary unit: Sudanese dinar, with (Oct. 11, 1996) a free rate of Sd 146.50 to U.S. $1 (Sd 230.78 = £1 sterling). President of the Revolutionary Command Council for National Salvation, president, and prime minister in 1996, Lieut. Gen. Omar Hassan Ahmad al-Bashir.

The first presidential and legislative elections in The Sudan since the 1989 coup took place March 6–17, 1996. Opposition attempts to boycott the elections were ignored by the government, which main-

Herdsmen tend their cattle near Juba, the main town in the southern part of The Sudan. Civil war between the Christian black African south and the Arab Islamic-controlled government continued in 1996, and some Western nations accused The Sudan of supporting Islamic militants.

tained that 5.5 million votes had been cast, amounting to 70% of the electorate. Pres. Omar al-Bashir polled over four million votes, while his nearest opponent among some 40 candidates gained only 990,000. Hassan at-Turabi, leader of the National Islamic Front, was unanimously elected president of the 400-member National Assembly on April 1.

Although President Bashir was able to conclude an agreement in February securing the country's borders with Chad and the Central African Republic, fears that his government was supporting militant Islamic groups intent upon subverting the governments of other neighbouring countries aroused both anxiety and hostility. Egypt continued to demand the extradition of three Egyptian dissidents believed to have taken refuge in The Sudan after a failed assassination attempt against Pres. Hosni Mubarak in 1995. The Sudanese government denied that they were in the country.

Uganda during the year accused The Sudan of arming and training members of a Ugandan Christian fundamentalist group that had carried out damaging raids into northern Uganda. The Sudanese government responded by alleging that Uganda was assisting Sudanese rebels in the south of the country and that both Uganda and the rebels were armed and encouraged by Israel. On April 10 a peace treaty was signed with two of the rebel groups in the south, but John Garang's faction of the Sudan People's Liberation Army, the government's long-term opponent, remained determined to carry on the struggle.

The deterioration of the country's relations with the outside world was matched by the decline in the economy. The government itself admitted that the foreign debt stood at £12.4 billion, three times gross domestic product.   (KENNETH INGHAM)

SURINAME

The republic of Suriname is in northern South America, on the Atlantic Ocean.

Area: 163,820 sq km (63,251 sq mi), not including a 17,635-sq km area disputed with Guyana. Pop. (1996 est.): 436,000. Cap.: Paramaribo. Monetary unit: Suriname guilder, with (Oct. 11, 1996) a free rate of 410 guilders to U.S. $1 (645.87 guilders = £1 sterling). Presidents in 1996, Ronald Venetiaan until May 23 and, from September 5, Jules Wijdenbosch; chairman of the Council of Ministers from September 21, Pretaap Radhakishun.

General elections for the National Assembly were held on May 23, 1996. The main opposition party in the elections was the National Democratic Party (NDP), led by former military dictator Dési Bouterse. The outcome of the election was inconclusive. The New Front, a coalition of four parties that formed the government, won 45% of the vote and 24 seats in the Assembly, 6 fewer than in 1991 and 10 seats short of the two-thirds needed to appoint a president and to form a government. The NDP won 16 seats (a gain of 4 and 26% of the votes). Immediately after the election Pres. Ronald Venetiaan rejected an offer from Bouterse to form a coalition with the NDP, and he began coalition talks with some smaller parties.

On August 1 the buildings of the National Assembly and the Office of Foreign Affairs burned down. In this disaster almost all national political and historical archives were lost. This was the fifth destructive fire of an important government building since 1990.

On August 7 and 8 the new Assembly did not succeed in two elections to appoint a president. Venetiaan each time got only 23 of the 51 votes, and Jules Wijdenbosch, Bouterse's right-hand man, got 24. On September 5 Wijdenbosch was elected the new president of Suriname by a convention of representatives of all districts (such a convention becomes necessary when the Assembly, after two efforts, has not been able to elect a president).

(KLAAS J. HOEKSEMA)

SWAZILAND

Swaziland is a landlocked monarchy of southern Africa and a member of the Commonwealth. Area: 17,364 sq km (6,704 sq mi). Pop. (1996 est.): 934,000. Administrative and judicial caps., Mbabane; royal caps., Lozitha and Ludzidzini; legislative cap., Lobamba. Monetary unit: lilangeni (plural: emalangeni), at par with the South African rand, with (Oct. 11, 1996) a free rate of 4.54 emalangeni to U.S. $1 (7.16 emalangeni = £1 sterling). King, Mswati III; prime ministers in 1996, Prince Jameson Mbilini Dlamini until May 8 and, from July 26, Sibusiso Barnabas Dlamini.

The year 1996 proved one of mounting political tensions. The Swaziland Federation of Trade Unions called a week-long general strike on January 22 in support of 27 demands to end the absolute monarchy and establish multiparty politics. Violent clashes between the security forces and the protesters resulted in three deaths. On January 27 King Mswati III called for an end to the strike, and negotiations were promised.

At the opening of the parliament on February 16, the king said that a new constitution would be drafted over the next few months and that every citizen would be given an opportunity to contribute to the process. On February 27 the king said legislation banning political parties would be reconsidered. The king on May 8 dismissed Prime Minister Mbilini Dlamini, who had held the office since 1993; not until late July did he appoint a successor, Sibusiso Barnabas Dlamini. (GUY ARNOLD)

This article updates the *Macropædia* article SOUTHERN AFRICA: *Swaziland.*

SWEDEN

A constitutional monarchy of northern Europe, Sweden occupies the eastern side of the Scandinavian Peninsula, with coastlines on the North and Baltic seas and the Gulf of Bothnia. Area: 449,964 sq km (173,732 sq mi). Pop. (1996 est.): 8,858,000. Cap.: Stockholm. Monetary unit: Swedish krona, with (Oct. 11, 1996) a free rate of 6.60 kronor to U.S. $1 (10.39 kronor = £1 sterling). King, Carl XVI Gustaf; prime ministers in 1996, Ingvar Carlsson and, from March 21, Göran Persson.

An era in Swedish politics came to a close when Ingvar Carlsson, the Social Democratic prime minister, retired in March after a decade as party leader. Carlsson, who replaced the assassinated Olof Palme in 1986, handed the baton to Göran Persson, Sweden's finance minister. The appointment of Persson as only the fifth Social Democratic leader in 71 years was preceded by the fall from grace of Mona Sahlin, the youthful deputy prime minister. Widely expected to become the country's first female prime minister, she was forced to resign amid revelations that she used her government credit card for private purposes, although she was later cleared of any criminal offense.

Persson began where he left off as finance minister—by continuing to spearhead government efforts to alleviate Sweden's chronic budget deficit. When the Social Democrats came to power in 1994, the annual shortfall was about 13% of gross domestic product (GDP). But a prescription of welfare cuts and tax increases pruned it back to a projected 2.6% of GDP in 1997, which put Sweden in a position to qualify for the European economic and monetary union.

Completing the overhaul of the state's finances was a key achievement for the Social Democrats. But the cost was high; unemployment rose, hovering persistently around 13%—a distressing spectacle for many in a country weaned on a long tradition of near-full employment. Describing joblessness as its foremost challenge, the government pledged early in the year to reduce the "headline" rate (which excluded people employed on government-sponsored projects and training programs) from about 8% to 4% by the year 2000.

Measures to achieve this included the initiation in September of reforms to inject flexibility into Sweden's tightly regulated labour market. This, however, caused consternation in the country's most powerful trade union confederation, the Landsorganisation. The association, which had 2.2 million members and had been a close ally of the Social Democratic Labour Party for almost a century, condemned the proposals as an attack on worker security. It accused the government of lurching to the right and briefly threatened to withhold its 20 million kronor annual contribution to party funds.

The Social Democrats, heading a minority government, cemented an unofficial alliance with the agrarian-based Centre Party. Its leader, Olof Johansson, had been a prominent member of the previous rightwing coalition but declared his support for the Social Democrats in order, he said, for Sweden to have a stable parliamentary government.

Abroad the growing focus of Swedish foreign policy on the Baltic region continued in 1996. The government in May acted as host of the first international meeting of leaders of the nine countries that border the Baltic Sea. The event led to the creation of a Baltic council under Swedish stewardship, with a mandate to coordinate action against such problems as pollution and organized crime, as well as promoting cross-border business collaboration.

There was, however, embarrassment in Stockholm in September over the arrest and expulsion of two Swedes, including a high-ranking diplomat, from Russia in connection with alleged spying. Russian undercover agents caught on film one suspect, an employee of a Swedish defense company, receiving copies of secret documents from a contact in St. Petersburg.

In August Queen Silvia (*see* BIOGRAPHIES) welcomed delegates from more than 100 countries to Stockholm for the first World Congress Against Commercial Sexual Exploitation of Children.

(GREG MCIVOR)

SWITZERLAND

A landlocked federal state in west central Europe, Switzerland consists of a confederation of 26 cantons (6 of which are demicantons). Area: 41,285 sq km (15,940 sq mi). Pop. (1996 est.): 7,087,000. Administrative cap., Bern; judicial cap., Lausanne. Monetary unit: Swiss franc, with (Oct. 11, 1996) a free rate of Sw F 1.26 to U.S. $1 (Sw F 1.98 = £1 sterling). President in 1996, Jean-Pascal Delamuraz.

With apprehension regarding the economic outlook increasing throughout 1996, those Swiss still intent on upholding traditional neutrality by remaining outside the European Union (EU) were reminded that a country's affluence might not in itself protect it against the economic repercussions of developments elsewhere. Reports of financial scandals and a flood of allegations

A man throws additional footwear onto a pile of thousands of shoes and boots outside United Nations headquarters in Geneva in April as negotiators discussed further limits on the use of land mines. The pile symbolized the cost of land mines in human injuries and deaths.

that Swiss banks were still holding sizable deposits from Jews who later died in Nazi extermination camps added to the prevailing unease, as did mismanagement of the pension fund for the 120,000 federal government employees, previously regarded as a rock-solid financial bastion.

While many of those who had voted in a 1992 national referendum against the government's proposal to join the European Economic Area as a step toward EU membership were clearly having second thoughts, a further setback to the government's aspirations in that direction was the decisive rejection (67% against) of its new labour law in a December referendum. This legislation was intended to ensure increased "flexibility," whereby full equivalent time off for employees in compensation for working nights and Sundays (six a year) would no longer be mandatory; critics pointed out that the law did not necessarily apply to employers. Meanwhile, bilateral negotiations with the European Commission in Brussels inched toward a compromise on reciprocal employment opportunities for EU and Swiss nationals, Switzerland being given seven years in which to comply with the mandatory full freedom of movement. In autumn the government succeeded in edging away from neutral isolationism by securing parliamentary approval (98 votes to 16) for association with NATO's Partnership for Peace.

The year ended with the number of unemployed totaling 192,171 (a rate of 5.3%), with indications that the rise would continue through much of 1997. Thousands of foreign workers had gone back to their own countries. As was true everywhere in Western Europe, restructuring, computerization, and company mergers continued apace; news of layoffs seemed to come almost daily, and banks sometimes announced those and higher profits in practically the same breath.

As well as those of some private-sector companies, employees of Switzerland's federal, cantonal, and state enterprises, including the railways, were advised of wage reductions ranging up to 5%. The immediate reaction was large demonstrations coupled with strike threats. Air and ground personnel of Swissair, the national carrier, accepted both staff and salary reductions to bring the enterprise out of the red. Angry farmers protested outside the parliament building in Bern at what they considered inadequate government aid to offset the steep slump in beef prices after both Germany and Italy banned the importation of Swiss beef because of "mad cow" disease. Riot police used tear gas, rubber bullets, and a water cannon with a mixture of water and chemicals on the protesters, and several of them were hospitalized with severe second- and third-degree chemical burns. Eyebrows were raised at plans for an 800-strong military police volunteer battalion that could assist civil police in maintaining public order.   (ALAN MCGREGOR)

SYRIA

A republic of southwestern Asia, Syria is situated on the Mediterranean Sea. Area: 185,180 sq km (71,498 sq mi). Pop. (1996 est.): 14,798,000. Cap.: Damascus. Monetary unit: Syrian pound, with (Oct. 11, 1996) a par value (official rate) of LS

11.22 to U.S. $1 (LS 17.67 = £1 sterling) and a "primary trade" rate of LS 41.95 to U.S. $1 (LS 66.08 = £1 sterling). President in 1996, Gen. Hafez al-Assad; prime minister, Mahmoud Zuabi.

As 1996 began, Syria resumed peace talks with Israel. Two rounds of discussions between the Syrian and Israeli representatives took place in January, raising hopes that a breakthrough might be achieved on the issues of greatest concern to both sides: the final disposition of Syrian territory seized by Israel in June 1967 and the allocation of regional water resources. Syria hinted that the talks constituted a "golden chance" for peace but insisted that all land under Syrian control as of June 4, 1967, be returned before a peace agreement could be proposed. Israeli officials countered that several demilitarized zones along the shores of Lake Tiberias lay outside Syria's borders on that date, and the permanent status of those areas was open to negotiation. Talks collapsed when both parties refused to compromise.

Attacks on Israeli troops in southern Lebanon, followed by rocket strikes against the town of Qiryat Shemona within Israel, persuaded Israel to launch a large-scale military incursion into Lebanon in early April. As Israeli forces pounded Lebanese targets, Israel demanded that Syria publicly denounce terrorism as a means to pursue political objectives. The Syrian government refused to do so, and its uncompromising posture eventually persuaded France and the United States to give Syria a pivotal role in the international committee charged with monitoring the cease-fire that ended the fighting.

Buoyed by his success in handling the crisis, Pres. Hafez al-Assad traveled to Cairo to confer with his Egyptian counterpart. Assad told reporters there that Syria had "a feeling that things are not going ahead in a positive direction. That is why we need to remain vigilant so that we do not drop our guard and get taken for fools." To protect their forces from further Israeli offensives, Syrian commanders redeployed some 12,000 of their 35,000 troops in Lebanon to reinforced positions inside Syria. Even though the U.S. ambassador to Lebanon stated that the redeployment was "not alarming," the move prompted a barrage of Israeli warnings that it posed a threat to the Israeli-occupied Golan region.

Syria's relations with Turkey steadily deteriorated in 1996. Damascus announced in January that it would allow only 10% of the waters of the Orontes River to cross into the Turkish province of Hatay. Turkish authorities then announced that they would interrupt the flow of the Euphrates River so that repairs could be made to the Ataturk Dam. Syria and Iraq tried to work out a joint response to Turkey in regard to water issues, but the two nations could do little but submit their grievances to a summit of the Arab League. Syria also warned foreign engineering and construction companies that they faced lawsuits and boycotts if they continued to work on projects inside Turkey.

On a more positive note, Syria's economic prospects continued to improve. The nation began the year burdened by nonmilitary external debts totaling about $6 billion. The World Bank refused to consider requests

for loans until $400 million of outstanding interest had been repaid, and $240 million from the European Investment Bank remained frozen pending the settlement of arrears to European governments. In the spring, however, the European Union authorized the disbursement of $2.5 million to fund social programs, and the European Commission subsequently provided $22 million to upgrade municipal administration.

                    (FRED H. LAWSON)

TAIWAN

Taiwan, which consists of the island of Taiwan and surrounding islands off the coast of China, is the seat of the Republic of China (Nationalist China). Area: 36,179 sq km (13,969 sq mi), including the island of Taiwan and its 86 outlying islands, 22 in the Taiwan group and 64 in the Pescadores group. Pop. (1996 est.): 21,463,000. (Area and population figures include the Quemoy and Matsu groups, which are administered as an occupied part of Fujian [Fukien] province.) Cap.: Taipei. Monetary unit: New Taiwan dollar, with (Oct. 11, 1996) a free rate of NT$27.48 to U.S. $1 (NT$43.29 = £1 sterling). President in 1996, Lee Teng-hui; president of the Executive Yuan (premier), Lien Chan.

Taiwan completed its remarkable 10-year march toward democracy in 1996 with its first-ever direct presidential election. It was the first time in the history of China that ordinary citizens had had an opportunity to select their leader in a democratic election. Incumbent Pres. Lee Teng-hui, the Kuomintang (KMT, or Nationalist Party) candidate, easily won a second term in March by capturing 54% of the vote. He defeated Democratic Progressive Party (DPP) candidate Peng Ming-min, who garnered about 21% of the vote, and independent candidates Lin Yang-kang and Chen Li-an. An interview with President Lee is on pp. 7–9.

Lee's triumph was unwittingly aided by China's campaign of psychological warfare. Beijing threatened to use military force against Taiwan and test-fired live missiles into Taiwan's northern and southern coastal waters to drive home its point that under no circumstances would it allow the Republic of China on Taiwan, which it considered a renegade province, to declare formal independence. By standing firm against those threats, Lee enhanced his image. In the wake of its disappointing showing in the election, the DPP split apart as Peng Ming-min left the fold to establish a Taiwan Independence Party. After the election a public opinion poll showed that 40% of the respondents favoured independence for Taiwan, while 33% favoured eventual reunification with mainland China.

Following the election Lee announced that newly elected Vice Pres. Lien Chan would remain premier. John Chang became the new foreign minister and Wu Jing minister of education. Minister of Justice Ma Ying-jeou, whose anticorruption campaigns had embarrassed many KMT officials, was replaced. Lee still faced tough sledding in the Legislative Yuan, where the KMT retained a razor-thin majority. Both the DPP and the New Party vigorously criticized Lee and the KMT over domestic and foreign policy issues. The brutal murder of Liu

Protesters in Taipei demonstrate against Chinese war games in March that included the firing of live missiles into Taiwan's coastal waters. Shortly afterward, in Taiwan's first direct presidential election, incumbent Lee Teng-hui, who had stood firm against Chinese threats, won another term.

Pang-you, a provincial official, and seven others in November brought unwelcome attention on alleged ties between Taiwanese gangsters and President Lee's KMT.

Lee was moderately conciliatory toward China in his inauguration speech but reiterated his determination to expand Taiwan's international presence via vigorous diplomatic activity. Lien Chan traveled to the Dominican Republic as well as to Ukraine, where he met privately with Pres. Leonid Kuchma. For a fourth straight year, Beijing prevented the UN from considering Taiwan's application to rejoin the organization. Meanwhile, business executives in Taiwan, with investments in mainland China estimated at $25 billion, conducted a dialogue with Chinese leaders.

In August Lee called on Taiwan enterprises to limit their investments in the mainland to no more than 20–30% of their overall foreign investment and reserve 20% of such capital for Taiwan. In 1996 more than one-sixth of Taiwan's exports went to China, and more than 30,000 Taiwan companies invested there.

Taiwan's economy slumped in 1996 as exports of electronics flattened. A gross domestic product growth rate of below 6% was projected, and unemployment rose to a 10-year high of 3.2% in August. In an effort to stimulate the economy, Taiwan's central bank raised limits on foreign investment in companies listed on the Taipei stock market.

Taiwan tested an advanced air-to-air missile for its locally produced jet fighters and ordered $420 million worth of U.S. Stinger missiles, guided missile launchers, and military vehicles. (STEVEN I. LEVINE)

TAJIKISTAN

A landlocked republic of Central Asia, Tajikistan borders Kyrgyzstan on the north, Uzbekistan on the north and west, Afghanistan on the south, and China on the east. Area: 143,100 sq km (55,300 sq mi). Pop. (1996 est.): 5,945,000. Cap.: Dushanbe. Monetary unit: Tajik ruble, with (Oct. 11, 1996) a free rate of 298 Tajik rubles to U.S. $1 (469.44 Tajik

(continued on page 482)

Tajik soldiers load ammunition and weapons at a roadblock as they prepare to defend Dushanbe, the capital, against attacks by a rebel faction. In February Pres. Imomali Rakhmonov agreed to rebel demands that he dismiss three officials who had been accused of corruption.

CENTRAL ASIA'S NEXT "GREAT GAME"

by Bess Brown

illustration by Igor Kopelnitsky

The Central Asian republics gained their independence in the collapse of the U.S.S.R. at the end of 1991. There was considerable disquiet in Western foreign ministries at the time over the possibility that a power vacuum had been created and that these brand-new states would attract the political, cultural, economic, or religious ambitions of the key powers in the region: Iran, Turkey, Russia, and China. Of special concern were, on the one side, Iran, ruled by the ayatollahs, and, on the other, Kazakstan, which was being billed in the world press as the first nuclear-armed Muslim state.

Worries about Kazakstan may have been premature. In fact, Kazakstan had little or no control over the nuclear weapons left on its soil when the Soviet Union disintegrated; the warheads remained in the hands of Russian army units stationed in the newly independent state, and, while the Kazaks were traditionally Muslims, they made up less than half the country's population. Most of the remainder was Slavic. In the name of interethnic peace, Kazakstan had little choice but to follow the path it took, which was to become and to remain uncompromisingly secular while tilting politically toward Russia. Other states in the region found themselves in a different sort of cross fire.

Turkey. Even though the Central Asian leaders repeatedly said that secular Turkey was a more attractive development model for them than was Iran, during the first postindependence years Western officials still felt the need to urge the Central Asians to follow the Turkish model. Western journalists, who remembered the "Great Game" played in the Central Asian region between Russia and Great Britain in the 19th century, speculated on the outcome of a new Great Game between Iran and Turkey. The Turks themselves, delighted at the appearance in the international arena of five new Turkic-speaking countries (Kazakstan, Kyrgyzstan, Turkmenistan, and Uzbekistan in Central Asia, plus Azerbaijan in the Transcaucasus), set out to provide economic assistance and develop close cultural ties with their new brother countries. Even Tajikistan has been the recipient of Turkish support and encouragement, although it is not part of the Turkic family.

The Turks' initial excitement soon palled, however. Businessmen found that in most Central Asian states, ventures were complicated by attitudes deeply ingrained from the Soviet past. The Turkish aspiration to create a more or less unified Turkic cultural sphere was hailed as a desirable goal by most Central Asian intellectuals but was stymied by a rapidly developing sense of national identity in the new countries of Central Asia. Kazakstan's Pres. Nursultan Nazarbayev commented, for example, that the Central Asians did not propose to exchange one "big brother" (Russia) for another (Turkey). Turkish-led efforts to standardize the scripts used by all the Turkic states on the basis of Turkey's modified Latin alphabet were accepted by the Central Asian heads of state—but each then went ahead and introduced his own different Latin alphabet.

As the Central Asian states celebrated the fifth anniversary of their independence, their relationship with Turkey was still close, with Turkish businessmen and aid projects much in evidence and hundreds of Central Asian students studying in Turkey, but the post-Soviet euphoria had disappeared. Turkey and the four Turkic-speaking states of Central Asia recognized that they were part of a family, but it was increasingly a family of equals.

Early Western alarm about developments in Central Asia might have been greater had it been remembered that Turkmenistan, Uzbekistan, and Tajikistan had been part of the Persian cultural sphere for centuries. Even before the U.S.S.R. fell apart, Tajikistan, the one Central Asian republic that is Iranian-speaking, was developing close cultural ties with Iran and even described its own language as Farsi (Persian) rather than Tajik in official documents. These relationships did not extend to religious affairs, however. When the then leader of Tajikistan's official Muslim establishment was asked if he did not fear the spread of Iranian-style revolutionary Islamism in the republic, he replied that the Shi'ite fundamentalism of Iran had no attraction for the Sunni Muslims of Tajikistan. During Tajikistan's civil war, which started in mid-1992 and has continued sporadically since that time, Iran's cultural influence there declined, but during 1996 Iran began again to encourage the study of Farsi, for which it provided textbooks.

Iran. Iran had never disappeared from the scene in Turkic Central Asia either, though in the immediate postindependence years, it was a fairly minor player in the region. Iranian officials visited the Central Asian states, seeking to develop commercial ties, but they made no obvious effort to become involved in local politics or to encourage Islamic fundamentalism. The United States was concerned about Turkmenistan's close ties to Iran and pressured Kazakstan to give up plans for an oil pipeline through Iran to Persian Gulf ports, but most Central Asian countries sought to keep their relationship with Iran, if not particularly close, at least on a friendly footing. The exception was Uzbekistan, the only state in the region that supported the U.S. embargo against Iran.

Russia. By 1996 the most influential foreign power in the Central Asian region was, not surprisingly, Russia. In differing degrees, the Central Asian states looked to the

© 1997, Encyclopædia Britannica, Inc.

Russian Federation for trade, development funds, and help in setting up their own military forces. Socially and politically, several decades of Soviet assimilation policies are not easily undone, and Russian remains the language in which most Central Asians communicate with the outside world, though English is making inroads in the area. Moreover, Kazakstan and Kyrgyzstan joined a customs union with Russia and Belarus that caused disquiet in international lending organizations.

While the Central Asians recognized that geography and history dictated that they maintain close relations with the Russian Federation, the upsurge of Russian nationalist rhetoric, particularly during parliamentary and presidential election campaigns, alarmed Central Asians, and many of the region's leaders went on record as decisively rejecting a restoration of Russian dominance.

China. The other neighbouring nation that has been felt as a major presence in the Central Asian region is China. The Chinese leadership cannot have been happy about the independence of the Central Asian states, because of what it might suggest to the Turkic-speaking Uygur of Xinjiang, among whom a desire for independence had been stirring

even before the breakup of the U.S.S.R. China has been careful to cultivate good relations with the new states. The Central Asians have remained suspicious of Chinese intentions, though the flood of Chinese consumer goods into the new countries has been warmly welcomed. Kazakstan and Kyrgyzstan, in particular, feared that China might have designs on their territory, though both countries hailed the 1996 Shanghai treaty ratifying existing borders as having put their earlier fears to rest.

The first five years of independence were characterized by shifting outside influences in Central Asia. Given the continuing uncertainties in the former Soviet states of the region—especially Tajikistan—and the upheavals in Afghanistan, it may be expected that the next five will see a continuing interplay involving the same actors, with perhaps greater roles being played by countries such as Pakistan and India, both of which have been showing an increasing interest in their neighbours to the north.

Bess Brown is human dimensions specialist with the Organization for Security and Cooperation in Europe's Liaison Office for Central Asia.

(continued from page 479)
rubles = £1 sterling). President in 1996, Imomali Rakhmonov; prime ministers, Jamshed Karimov and, from February 8, Yahyo Azimov.

Fighting between the forces of Tajikistan's neocommunist government and armed Islamic opposition groups intensified in 1996. The opposition had had limited success in attacking government forces within Tajikistan and had concentrated on cross-border assaults from bases in northern Afghanistan.

Another round of UN-sponsored peace talks held in Ashgabat, the capital of Turkmenistan, between the government and the opposition ended inconclusively in February. Only after the talks were over did the opposition agree to an extension of a cease-fire that was having some effect on the border. It did not prevent the intensification of fighting in the important Tavildara region in the southern part of the country, however, and the opposition was able to capture the area in the summer. Talks were resumed in July and resulted in a new cease-fire agreement, which the two sides promptly accused each other of having violated. Although government forces claimed to have retaken Tavildara by late August, fighting continued into the autumn. Yet another cease-fire was signed in Moscow on December 23, with Russian Prime Minister Viktor Chernomyrdin looking on.

The government of Pres. Imomali Rakhmonov faced its first major internal challenge when two regional commanders mutinied in January. Both men, who were part of Rakhmonov's southern clique, demanded the resignation of the government and the removal from Tajikistan of Russian troops that had been a mainstay of Rakhmonov's regime in the fighting against the Islamic opposition and its Afghan allies. Rakhmonov compromised, dismissing several government officials and giving one of the rebellious commanders an important military post. The presidents of Russia and Turkey, both major aid donors, praised Rakhmonov's skill in ending the mutiny, but the Tajik president's position was visibly weakened. Later in the year he faced demands from the northern region of the country that the predominance of southerners in administrative posts be ended. In July three former prime ministers formed an opposition group calling for the creation of a government in which all parties and regions of the country would be represented.

In February Prime Minister Yahyo Azimov, appointed at the beginning of the month, declared that privatization was his first priority in trying to reverse the effects of four years of war on Tajikistan's economy.   (BESS BROWN)

This article updates the *Macropædia* article CENTRAL ASIA: *Tajikistan*.

TANZANIA

Tanzania, a member of the Commonwealth, consists of Tanganyika (mainland Tanzania), on the east coast of Africa, and Zanzibar and Pemba islands, just off the coast in the Indian Ocean. Area: 945,090 sq km (364,901 sq mi). Pop. (1996 est.): 29,058,000. Cap.: government in process of being transferred from Dar es Salaam; legislature meets in Dodoma, the new capital. Monetary unit: Tanzania shilling,

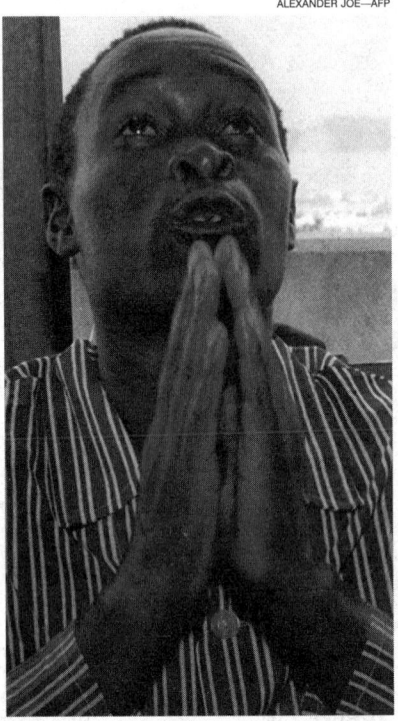

ALEXANDER JOE—AFP

A man gives thanks after having survived the capsizing of an overloaded ferry in Tanzania on May 21. The accident, which took place on Lake Victoria, killed 549 people.

with (Oct. 11, 1996) a free rate of 578 shillings to U.S. $1 (910.52 shillings = £1 sterling). President in 1996, Benjamin William Mkapa; prime minister, Frederick Tulway Sumaye.

Pres. Benjamin Mkapa began his term of office by appealing to opposition parties in 1996 not to oppose the government on every issue but to put the interests of their country before those of their party. He himself, he said, would deal fairly with members of all parties. His appeal fell on deaf ears in Zanzibar and Pemba. There the opposition persisted in boycotting the National Assembly, claiming that the government had come to power by employing fraudulent tactics in the recent elections.

In his attempts to introduce a free-market economy, Mkapa encountered the same problems that had plagued his predecessor. A preference for nationalization and state control of the economy died hard, not least among the bureaucrats who were staffing the government agencies. The delays caused by the slow working of the bureaucracy continued to encourage businessmen to resort to bribing officials in order to speed up their projects.

Mkapa himself, however, was held in high esteem by the International Monetary Fund (IMF) and private donors alike. Assistance, cut off in 1994, was resumed in November with a three-year IMF credit of $234 million. Remarkably, this went through despite the problems that began in September when a parliamentary select committee demanded that the finance minister, Simon Mbilinyi, be called to account for granting tax exemptions worth several billion shillings to four companies importing edible oil. At that moment Mbilinyi was engaged in negotiations with the IMF in New York; he resigned in November.

International interest in Tanzania had been demonstrated earlier in the year when the South African Iron and Steel Corp. signed an agreement with Pangea Goldfields of Canada to undertake jointly the exploration of three potential sources of gold. At the end of January, the Lake Victoria steamer passenger service between Tanzania and Kenya was reopened after 18 years. At a meeting in Kampala, Uganda, earlier in January, the presidents of Tanzania, Kenya, and Uganda agreed that every effort would be made to revive the economic links that had formerly existed between the three countries.

Some 550,000 Rwandan refugees who had crossed the border into northwestern Tanzania continued to receive help, but it became increasingly difficult to maintain adequate food supplies. In addition, about 100,000 refugees from Burundi were also in Tanzania. Although reluctant to add to the number of refugees already given sanctuary, President Mkapa pledged that his government would not forcibly repatriate those already in the country. In December, however, refugees were asked to return to their home countries.   (KENNETH INGHAM)

This article updates the *Macropædia* article EASTERN AFRICA: *Tanzania*.

THAILAND

Thailand is a constitutional monarchy in Southeast Asia, on the Andaman Sea and the Gulf of Thailand. Area: 513,115 sq km (198,115 sq mi). Pop. (1996 est.): 60,003,000. Cap.: Bangkok. Monetary unit: baht, with (Oct. 11, 1996) a free rate of 25.46 baht to U.S. $1 (40.10 baht = £1 sterling). King, Bhumibol Adulyadej; prime ministers in 1996, Banharn Silpa-archa and, from November 25, Chavalit Yongchaiyudh.

Allegations of corruption in the seven-party government of Prime Minister Banharn Silpa-archa paralyzed the legislative process in Thailand throughout 1996. Thai Nation (Chart Thai), the leading coalition party, was accused by the opposition in February of having solicited kickbacks from a Swedish manufacturer of submarines. The opposition also gathered evidence suggesting that prominent politicians had secured improper loans from a failed commercial bank that had been rescued by the government. The Cabinet survived a no-confidence vote on May 11 only after it used its majority to gag debate before opposition leader Chuan Leekpai could quiz Banharn about accusations of plagiarism in his academic attainments and alleged falsification of documents to conceal his father's Chinese nationality. Before a second no-confidence vote on September 21, the prime minister's daughter, herself a legislator, was accused by the legislature of having made huge profits in illegal land transactions with the Bank of Thailand. A week before the no-confidence motion was submitted, the Righteous Force Party quit the coalition, leaving Banharn with a slender majority. Then, citing alleged massive bribes in the awarding of new bank licenses, two more parties censured the prime minister. Chavalit Yongchaiyudh, defense minister and leader of the coalition's

New Aspiration Party, secured from Banharn a promise to resign in return for votes that would save the government. Chavalit and Amnuay Virawan, leader of the Nam Thai Party, jockeyed for support in order to succeed him. Instead, Banharn dissolved the National Assembly, dismissed Chavalit, and called elections for November 17.

Chavalit's New Aspiration Party secured moral support from the military, while Chuan's Democrat Party appealed to the business community and the urban middle classes. After a campaign marked by widespread charges of vote buying in rural areas, Chavalit emerged with 125 seats to Chuan's 123 in the 393-seat House of Representatives. Of Bangkok's 37 seats, 29 went to the Democrats. The Righteous Force Party gained only one seat nationwide. The morning after the elections, the stock market fell nearly 6%. In a week of intense jockeying, Chavalit created a comfortable majority by stitching together a coalition that excluded Banharn's Thai Nation (39 seats) but included Chart Pattana (52), led by former prime minister Chatichai Choonhavan, together with Social Action (20), Prachakorn Thai (18), plus two small parties. Chavalit was appointed prime minister on November 25, the day U.S. Pres. Bill Clinton arrived for a state visit after attending a regional summit in Manila that Banharn also had attended. Chavalit hoped to inspire confidence among businessmen by announcing that he was to retain the defense portfolio for himself, name Amnuay finance minister, and appoint able technocrats to key portfolios.

On June 2 Bangkok municipal elections for city governor resulted in a landslide win for Bhichit Rattakul, an independent candidate, and a humiliating defeat for former city governor Chamlong Srimuang. Bhichit promised to address the city's perennial woes of flooding and traffic congestion. In March the funeral of the revered mother of King Bhumibol Adulyadej provided Bangkok with some of the most spectacular pageantry in years. The state visit of Great Britain's Queen Elizabeth II and celebrations of the 50th anniversary of the king's accession to the throne added more royal splendour.

The economy seriously stumbled for the first time in a decade. Despite the confidence of the General Motors Corp., which in May announced an investment of $750 million in a Thai automobile assembly plant, followed by a $470 million commitment by Ford Motor Co., concern for the balance of payments steadily mounted as international institutional investors reassessed short-term deposits.   (ROBERT WOODROW)

This article updates the *Macropædia* article SOUTHEAST ASIA: *Thailand.*

TOGO

A republic of West Africa, Togo is situated on the Bight of Benin. Area: 56,785 sq km (21,925 sq mi). Pop. (1996 est.): 4,269,000. Cap.: Lomé. Monetary unit: CFA franc, with (Oct. 11, 1996) a par value of CFAF 100 to the French franc and a free rate of CFAF 518.24 to U.S. $1 (CFAF 816.38 = £1 sterling). President in 1996, Gen. Gnassingbé Eyadéma; prime ministers, Edem Kodjo and, from August 20, Klutse Kwassi.

Firefighters in Thailand control a bonfire of confiscated drugs that was set by officials on June 26 to mark the United Nations International Day Against Drug Abuse and Illicit Trafficking. Some 2,000 kg (4,400 lb) of drugs, including heroin, opium, morphine, and marijuana, were destroyed.

Prime Minister Edem Kodjo in 1996 continued his struggle to get legislation through the National Assembly. On January 3, 34 deputies from the opposition party, Action Committee for Renewal (CAR), joined 37 deputies from Pres. Gnassingbé Eyadéma's Rally of the Togolese People (RPT) in rejecting the 1996 budget for the second time in 15 days. Only the six members of Kodjo's Togolese Union for Democracy (UTD) voted for the measure. The CAR/RPT alliance proved temporary, for in late February 30 RPT deputies joined the 6 from UTD and passed the budget.

By July defections from CAR to the RPT had given the presidential party and its three allied independents a parliamentary majority in the 81-member Assembly, its first since the February 1994 legislative elections. In August CAR boycotted by-elections for three seats, the 1994 results of which had been annulled by the Supreme Court. All were won by the RPT. On August 19 Kodjo resigned. The next day Eyadéma named the minister of planning, Klutse Kwassi of the RPT, the new prime minister.   (NANCY ELLEN LAWLER)

This article updates the *Macropædia* article WESTERN AFRICA: *Togo.*

TONGA

A constitutional monarchy and member of the Commonwealth, Tonga comprises about 170 islands split into three main groups in the Pacific Ocean east of Fiji. Area: 750 sq km (290 sq mi). Pop. (1996 est.): 101,000. Cap.: Nuku'alofa. Monetary unit: pa'anga, with (Oct. 11, 1996) a free rate of 1.26 pa'anga (T$) to U.S. $1 (1.99 pa'anga = £1 sterling). King, Taufa'ahau Tupou IV; prime minister in 1996, Baron Vaea.

In January 1996 elections, the People's Party won six of the nine seats designated for commoners in the Legislative Assembly. In March two pro-democracy leaders were jailed for "threatening, abusive and insulting language" toward the minister of police. In July there were regional protests when a New Zealand journalist was denied entry to Tonga for a meeting of the Pacific Islands News Association. The Legislative Assembly in September imprisoned two journalists and an MP for contempt, but they were subsequently released by the chief justice.

The economy, and agriculture in particular, suffered through a drought that halved the production of squash, which usually accounted for 80% of official export earnings.   (BARRIE MACDONALD)

This article updates the *Macropædia* article PACIFIC ISLANDS: *Tonga.*

TRINIDAD AND TOBAGO

A republic and member of the Commonwealth, Trinidad and Tobago consists of two islands in the Caribbean Sea off the coast of Venezuela. Area: 5,128 sq km (1,980 sq mi). Pop. (1996 est.): 1,262,000. Cap.: Port of Spain. Monetary unit: Trinidad and Tobago dollar, with (Oct. 11, 1996) a free rate of TT$6.03 to U.S. $1 (TT$9.50 = £1 sterling). President in 1996, Noor Mohammed Hassanali; prime minister, Basdeo Panday.

The nation's new coalition government started 1996 briskly with its first budget in January, reducing the top rate of income tax from 38% to 35% and lowering the corporation tax by the same amount. Total expenditure was set at TT$9.6 billion for 1996.

Atlantic LNG, a consortium including Amoco and British Gas, was given permission in April to build a plant, at an estimated cost of about U.S.$1 billion, to supply liquefied natural gas (LNG) to the U.S. and Spain. When completed in mid-1999, it would be only the second LNG export plant in the Western Hemisphere.   (DAVID RENWICK)

This article updates the *Macropædia* article The WEST INDIES: *Trinidad and Tobago.*

TUNISIA

A republic of North Africa, Tunisia lies
on the Mediterranean Sea. Area: 164,150
sq km (63,378 sq mi). Pop. (1996 est.):
9,057,000. Cap.: Tunis. Monetary unit:
Tunisian dinar, with (Oct. 11, 1996) a free
rate of 0.98 dinar to U.S. $1 (1.54 dinars
= £1 sterling). President in 1996, Gen.
Zine al-Abidine Ben Ali; prime minister,
Hamed Karoui.

The regime of Pres. Zine al-Abidine Ben
Ali seemed to have succeeded in creating
a state of relative economic prosperity in
Tunisia and in April 1996 was reported to
be the leading nation in the Middle East
and North Africa in terms of social indicators. This success was not transferred to the
political scene, however. In February the
former leader of the Democratic Socialist
Movement (MDS), Mohamed Mouada, was
sentenced to 11 years in prison for maintaining secret contacts with a foreign power
(Libya). Earlier he had been sentenced to
a year in prison for currency offenses.

Mouada's trial was roundly condemned
by international observers, especially as
there had never been any secret about his
Libyan contacts. Informed opinion pointed
to an open letter he had written to President Ben Ali in October 1995, just before
his arrest. In the letter Mouada condemned
the political situation in Tunisia in terms
of both individual and political rights. The
Tunisian authorities were, however, not
bothered by criticism, either from Mouada
or from foreign observers, and in July condemned another MDS member and parliamentary deputy, Khemis Chamari, to five
years in prison for similar offenses.

During the year the Ben Ali regime
seemed to be losing its populist grasp of
the Tunisian scene and was coming to rely
increasingly on a group of advisers around
the president. In June, as part of a government reshuffle, the president appointed his
close colleague, Abdallah Kallel, defense
minister, and he also increasingly relied on
associates drawn from Tunisia's business
community and from the army. Ben Ali's
family also became involved in political life,
and in midyear his brother, Dourid, was
found dead in mysterious circumstances in
Tunis. He had previously been subject to
an international arrest warrant issued in
France for his alleged role in a drugs scandal in France in 1995.

In foreign affairs, in the wake of the election in Israel of the right-wing government
of Benjamin Netanyahu, Tunisia quietly
slowed down its normalization process with
Israel. Tunisia continued its rapprochement
with the Gulf States, which had become
tense after the Iraqi invasion of Kuwait,
and Kuwaiti investment in Tunisia was revived during 1996.   (GEORGE JOFFÉ)

This article updates the *Macropædia* article NORTH AFRICA: *Tunisia.*

TURKEY

A republic of Asia Minor and southeastern Europe, Turkey has coastlines on the
Aegean, Black, and Mediterranean seas.
Area: 779,452 sq km (300,948 sq mi),
including 23,764 sq km in Europe. Pop.
(1996 est.): 62,650,000. Cap.: Ankara.
Monetary unit: Turkish lira, with (Oct. 11,
1996) a free rate of 93,990 liras to U.S. $1

HURRIYET—EPA/AFP

Kurdish refugees leaving northern Iraq pass a Turkish border post. After fighting between rival
Kurdish factions escalated in September, Turkey assisted in the evacuation of U.S. government
personnel and of Kurds who had been associated with U.S. operations in Iraq.

(148,063 liras = £1 sterling). President in
1996, Suleyman Demirel; prime ministers,
Tansu Ciller until March 7, Mesut Yilmaz
until June 28, and, from June 28, Necmettin Erbakan.

The inconclusive results of elections for the
Turkish Grand National Assembly held on
Dec. 24, 1995, hindered the government's
effectiveness in 1996. The coalition between Prime Minister Tansu Ciller's centre-
right True Path Party (DYP) and Deniz
Baykal's centre-left Republican People's
Party (CHP) remained in power in a caretaker capacity until March 6, when Pres.
Suleyman Demirel approved a new coalition between the DYP and its centre-right
rival, Mesut Yilmaz's Motherland Party.
On March 11 the new government was
endorsed by 257 votes to 207 in the 550-
member parliament.

The coalition protocol provided for a
rotating premiership, filled first by Yilmaz
and then by Ciller after Jan. 1, 1997. But
the understanding broke down when Yilmaz failed to block a move by the Islamic
Welfare Party (RP) to set up a parliamentary inquiry into corruption charges against
Ciller. On June 5 the Constitutional Court
ruled that the parliamentary endorsement
of the new government by a simple majority
of members present had been invalid. Ciller
then instructed her party to vote against the
government in the vote of confidence that
it sought, and as a result, Yilmaz was forced
to resign. Alliances were then reversed.
Ciller agreed to become junior partner in
a coalition headed by Necmettin Erbakan
(*see* BIOGRAPHIES), leader of the Islamic
RP, against whom she had campaigned the
previous year. The RP-DYP coalition took
office on June 28 and was endorsed on
July 8 by 278 votes to 265. The accession
to power of an avowed Islamist as prime
minister was a milestone in the history of
Turkey's secular republic, although the sensitive portfolios of foreign affairs, defense,
and the interior were left in the hands of
the nominally secular DYP. That party's
Interior Minister Mehmet Agar was forced
to resign after a car accident in November
revealed suspicious ties between legislators,

top police officials, right-wing activists, and
gangsters and suggested longtime government support for death squads.

The troubled domestic scene was reflected in the conduct of foreign policy.
Ciller was caretaker prime minister at the
end of January when both Greece and
Turkey sent naval units to the eastern
Aegean in a dispute over the ownership of
uninhabited islets, known as Imia in Greek
and Kardak in Turkish. A clash was avoided
when both sides withdrew their forces in response to U.S. diplomacy. On March 24 Yilmaz, then prime minister, called on Greece
to agree to negotiations on all outstanding issues, which would include recourse to
third-party adjudication or arbitration. The
call was rejected by Greece.

Also during Yilmaz's premiership, Turkey
signed an agreement with Israel providing
for cooperation in the training of military
air crews and negotiated a wider defense
industry cooperation agreement.

Continuity in foreign policy was preserved
when Erbakan came to power; the permission given to the U.S., Great Britain, and
France to use bases in Turkey to fly over
northern Iraq was extended until the end
of the year, and the two agreements with
Israel were confirmed. Doubts were raised,
however, when Erbakan went to Iran and
on August 12 signed an agreement for the
purchase of Iranian natural gas and the
possible construction of a pipeline to carry
it. But by the end of the year, no move had
been made to implement this deal, which
was valued at $23 billion.

The cohesion of the coalition was then
strained when Erbakan decided to go to
Libya in October. The controversy increased when Libyan leader Muammar al-
Qaddafi told Erbakan that he favoured an
independent Kurdistan. Nevertheless, Ciller
instructed her party to vote for the government when the opposition sought to
censure Erbakan over the Libyan trip, and
the motion was rejected 275–265 on October 16.

Security operations against the armed
bands of the Kurdish Workers' Party continued. A suicide bomb attack and the
killing of 14 soldiers in an ambush on

Republic Day, October 29, showed that the problem was far from being solved. As the death toll in the 12-year-old insurgency rose above 20,000, allegations of violations of human rights in Turkey were cited by the European Parliament as one reason for suspending economic aid to Turkey. The parliament was also critical of Turkish policy in Cyprus. Both Erbakan and Ciller visited northern Cyprus to demonstrate their support for the Turkish Republic of Northern Cyprus, which Turkey was alone in recognizing.   (ANDREW MANGO)

TURKMENISTAN

A republic of Central Asia, Turkmenistan borders Uzbekistan on the northeast, Kazakstan on the northwest, the Caspian Sea on the west, Iran on the southwest, and Afghanistan on the southeast. Area: 488,100 sq km (188,500 sq mi). Pop. (1996 est.): 4,574,000. Cap.: Ashgabat. Monetary unit: manat, with (Oct. 11, 1996) an interbank rate (from February 1996) of 4,060 manat to U.S. $1 (6,396 manat = £1 sterling). President in 1996, Saparmurad Niyazov.

The opening in May 1996 of a rail line linking Tejen in southern Turkmenistan with Mashhad in northern Iran was hailed as a major step in providing access to ports on the Persian Gulf not only for Turkmenistan but for the Central Asian region as a whole.

Pres. Saparmurad Niyazov became the first Central Asian leader to take over the chairmanship of the Economic Cooperation Organization, a regional group set up in the 1960s by Pakistan, Iran, and Turkey and joined by the former Soviet Asian republics. Turkmenistan, however, rejected membership in the customs union set up by the Russian Federation, Belarus, and Kazakstan, on the grounds that it would be in conflict with Turkmenistan's "international legal status as a neutral state."

Economic reform was made a top priority, a reversal of Niyazov's postindependence policies that had put political stability above market reform. The president introduced fees for electric power and thereby ended one of his favourite policies for ensuring his own popularity.   (BESS BROWN)

This article updates the *Macropædia* article CENTRAL ASIA: *Turkmenistan*.

TUVALU

A constitutional monarchy within the Commonwealth, Tuvalu comprises five atolls and four coral islands in the western Pacific Ocean. Area: 24.4 sq km (9.4 sq mi). Pop. (1996 est.): 9,500. Cap.: Government offices in Vaiaku, on Fongafale islet, of Funafuti Atoll. Monetary unit: Australian dollar, with (Oct. 11, 1996) a free rate of $A 1.26 to U.S. $1 ($A 1.99 = £1 sterling). Queen, Elizabeth II; governor-general in 1996, Tulaga Manuella; prime minister, Kamuta Latasi.

In accordance with the recommendation of a widely representative convention in 1995, the government of Tuvalu devolved significant responsibility to island-based governing councils in 1996. The new councils (which would include traditional leaders, members of Parliament, and representatives of community organizations) would have respon-

A train on the so-called New Silk Road passes a camel on its way to the town of Sarakhs, Iran, located on the border with Turkmenistan. The rail line, which gave landlocked countries of Central Asia access to Iran and thus to the sea, was completed in 1996.

sibility for a centrally allocated budget, the appointment of local officials, and capital development programs. The whole scale of the economy remained modest, however, with a total government budget of $A 20 million, of which $A 12 million came from aid.   (BARRIE MACDONALD)

This article updates the *Macropædia* article PACIFIC ISLANDS: *Tuvalu*.

UGANDA

A landlocked republic and member of the Commonwealth, Uganda is located in eastern Africa. Area: 241,040 sq km (93,070 sq mi), including 44,000 sq km of inland water. Pop. (1996 est.): 20,158,000. Cap.: Kampala. Monetary unit: Uganda shilling, with (Oct. 11, 1996) an interbank rate of 1,080 shillings to U.S. $1 (1,701 shillings = £1 sterling). President in 1996, Yoweri Museveni; prime minister, Kintu Musoke.

The long-standing mutual mistrust between the governments of Uganda and Kenya, which had manifested itself as recently as late 1995, was set aside in January 1996 when the presidents of the two countries

A worker in Kampala, Uganda, checks bags of coffee beans before they are exported. The country, which had one of the lowest per capita incomes in the world, was seeking to expand its exports of coffee, cotton, and other products as a way of improving its economy.

met and agreed to work together to revive the East African economic community. Uganda badly needed a wider market for its produce. In spite of 10 years' rule by Pres. Yoweri Museveni and an average annual growth of 6% in gross domestic product over the last five years, the annual per capita income had reached only $200, one of the lowest in the world. The possibility of opening up a wider market for Uganda's coffee and cotton was announced by Museveni on his return from a visit to China in February. At the same time, he affirmed that the privatization of government-operated enterprises and the arrest of corrupt army officers had significantly reduced the incidence of corruption. In addition, an agreement with Iran paved the way for Iranian planes to land at the Entebbe airport.

Donor institutions, however, which poured in $800 million a year in aid, remained less than enthusiastic about the president's insistence upon maintaining restrictions on the activities of political parties. This was particularly significant because a presidential election was scheduled for May 9 and legislative elections in June.

Relations with The Sudan remained strained, a situation made worse by regular incursions into northern Uganda by members of the rebel Lord's Resistance Army. Based in The Sudan, these troops inflicted casualties among the Acholi villagers and made travel in the region hazardous. The villagers were critical of the government's failure to maintain law and order and of the absence of any of the benefits that Uganda had received from overseas aid.

Nevertheless, with strong support in the south and by reviving fears of a return to insecurity and economic decline, Museveni won a resounding electoral victory over his nearest rival, Paul K. Ssemogerere. In the parliamentary elections that followed, only about 20 known opposition candidates were among the 214 deputies elected as individuals. International observers determined that the elections were free and fair, and so in August the parliament was readmitted as a member of the Commonwealth club of parliaments. It had been excluded when Pres. Milton Obote's government was overthrown by the military in 1985.

Even before the legislative elections took place, the European Union granted Uganda $300 million under the terms of the Lome Convention, adding that the EU was satisfied with the country's commitment to respecting human rights and to the pursuit of democratic principles. Less than a month later, Amnesty International reported that despite human rights improvements, civilians continued to be tortured.

(KENNETH INGHAM)

This article updates the *Macropædia* article EASTERN AFRICA: *Uganda*.

UKRAINE

A republic in eastern Europe, Ukraine borders Russia to the north and east, the Black Sea to the south, Romania and Moldova to the southwest, and Hungary, Slovakia, and Poland to the west. Area: 603,700 sq km (233,100 sq mi). Pop. (1996 est.): 51,273,000. Cap.: Kiev. Monetary unit: hryvnia (a new currency introduced Sept. 2, 1996, to replace the karbovanets at a rate of 1 hryvnia = 100,000 karbovantsy; on September 16 the hryvnia

EPA/AFP

At a memorial service at Baby Yar, a large ravine in Kiev, Ukraine, a Jewish woman holds pictures of relatives who were among some 100,000 Jews massacred there by Nazi troops between 1941 and 1943. The site symbolizes the genocide of Jews during World War II.

became sole legal tender), with (Oct. 11, 1996) a free rate of 1.77 hryvny to U.S. $1 (2.78 hryvny = £1 sterling). President in 1996, Leonid Kuchma; prime ministers, Yevhen Marchuk and, from May 27, Pavlo Lazarenko.

In 1996 Ukraine marked its fifth year of independence as one of the most stable of the states created from the former Soviet Union. This was a country in which the lack of civil and ethnic strife seemed exceptionally notable against the background of turmoil in neighbouring states.

In June the Ukrainian parliament adopted a new constitution, despite sustained opposition from leftist deputies who had submitted an alternative draft on March 22 to restore a Soviet-style regime. The new constitution was accepted by 315 votes to 36 after an all-night sitting. It confirmed the authority of the president,

maintained a unicameral parliament, and affirmed Ukrainian as the state language while making allowances for the use of other languages (Russian and Crimean Tatar, for example) in areas where they were the primary languages spoken.

A new government was formed in September with a distinctly reformist hue. Earlier, on May 27, Prime Minister Yevhen Marchuk had been replaced with Pavlo Lazarenko, a close colleague of Pres. Leonid Kuchma's from the Dnipropetrovsk region, one of whose stated aims was to accelerate foreign investment in Ukraine.

Ukraine's economic performance was sluggish, with most revenue being used to pay off wage arrears amounting to $200 million in the state sector alone. The share of output from privatized firms was reportedly 48% by the middle of the year, however. With inflation under control, the government achieved a psychological breakthrough in September with the introduction of a new currency, the hryvnia. On March 25 the government raised the minimum wage by over 30% to $36 per month. Lazarenko's economic reforms suffered a setback in November, however, when the Supreme Council rejected his proposed budget.

The giant coal sector again endured a year of strikes and protests concomitantly with a very high accident rate. In March Marchuk announced that some 70 nonlucrative mines could be closed in the next few years. The next month, however, the World Bank stated that the optimal figure would be double this number and offered $300 million in credit for reforms in the Ukrainian coal industry, with a 17-year term of repayment. Although Ukraine was making significant progress toward democracy, its living standards remained low. The population showed a negative growth rate, and epidemics of hepatitis broke out in Donetsk and Sevastopol as a result of the pollution of the water supply by untreated industrial waste. Diphtheria was increasingly common.

The year marked the 10th anniversary of the accident at the Chernobyl nuclear power station. That event was marked by the G-7 summit meeting in Moscow on April 19–20, at which leaders of the Group of Seven leading industrial nations and Russia committed just over $3 billion worth of international assistance to Ukraine to close the station permanently by the year 2000 and to complete reactors under construction at the Khmelnytsky and South Ukraine stations.

The year was to have seen the signing of a Treaty of Friendship and Cooperation with Russia, scheduled for early April. That meeting was canceled by Russian Pres. Boris Yeltsin, then in the midst of his election campaign, on the grounds that the question of the Black Sea Fleet had yet to be resolved. Though Ukraine voluntarily gave up some 80% of the fleet to the Russian side, the two nations still differed over the status of the city of Sevastopol, the longtime base of the Black Sea Fleet. The question was exacerbated by a Russian Duma (parliament) declaration that Sevastopol was a Russian city, following a similar statement by Moscow's Mayor Yury Luzhkov on January 17.

While relations with Russia—particularly on energy issues and the use of the Druzhba oil pipeline link across Ukraine to the Czech Republic and Slovakia—were often difficult, relations with the U.S. and the European Union (EU) remained cordial. Ukraine kept its distance from the increased integration of the countries of the Commonwealth of Independent States, particularly the Russian-Belarusian "union" of April 2. In February Kuchma visited the U.S. and was offered more than $1 billion in financial assistance, which made Ukraine the third largest recipient of U.S. aid.

Ukraine moved cautiously on the question of the expansion of NATO. On July 7, at a meeting of Central and Eastern European leaders in Salzburg, Austria, Kuchma declared that Ukraine was seeking a "special partnership" with NATO and associate partnership with the Western European Union, the defense sector of the EU. By the middle of the year, the last of the 1,600 strategic warheads on Ukrainian territory had been moved to Russia.

Ukraine suffered a spate of terrorist attacks and individual assaults, including an attempt on July 16 to assassinate Lazarenko—while he was traveling to the airport on his way to Donetsk—and two bomb explosions in the centre of Sevastopol on September 18. The former governor of the Donetsk region, Volodymyr Shcherban, was dismissed after the attempt on Lazarenko and then was himself assassinated in early November. In September Kuchma announced the formation of an antiterrorist centre in a four-year program to combat crime.   (DAVID R. MARPLES)

UNITED ARAB EMIRATES

Consisting of Abu Dhabi, Ajman, Dubayy, al-Fujayrah, Ra's al-Khaymah, ash-Shariqah, and Umm al-Qaywayn, the United Arab Emirates is a federation of seven largely autonomous emirates located on the eastern Arabian Peninsula. Area: 83,600 sq km (32,280 sq mi). Pop. (1996 est.): 2,290,000. Cap.: Abu Dhabi. Monetary unit: United Arab Emirates dirham, with (Oct. 11, 1996) an official rate of 3.67 dirhams to U.S. $1 (5.78 dirhams = £1 sterling). President in 1996, Sheikh Zaid ibn Sultan an-Nahayan; prime minister, Sheikh Maktum ibn Rashid al-Maktum.

The United Arab Emirates (U.A.E.) economy continued to prosper in 1996, with gross domestic product growing about 6.5% to 155 billion dirhams by the year's end. Oil production rose to the OPEC quota ceiling of 2,161,000 bbl per day. The 1996 federal budget showed revenues of 4,730,000,000 dhirams and expenditures of 4,970,000,000.

The U.A.E. authorities sought to reduce the number of resident foreigners (highest ratio of any country—1.9 million, compared with 400,000 citizens). In the spring they announced that all immigrants illegally in the country would be punished, but they granted an amnesty for any who departed or obtained work and residence permits between July 1 and September 1 (later extended to October 31). By November nearly 170,000 had left the country and another 50,000 had found legitimate jobs.

(WILLIAM A. RUGH)
This article updates the Macropædia article ARABIA: United Arab Emirates.

UNITED KINGDOM

A constitutional monarchy in northwestern Europe and member of the Commonwealth, the United Kingdom comprises the island of Great Britain (England, Scotland, and Wales) and Northern Ireland, together with many small islands. Area: 244,110 sq km (94,251 sq mi), including 3,218 sq km of inland water but excluding the crown dependencies of the Channel Islands and Isle of Man. Pop. (1996 est.): 58,784,000. Cap.: London. Monetary unit: pound sterling, with (Oct. 11, 1996) a free rate of £0.63 to U.S. $1 (U.S. $1.58 = £1 sterling). Queen, Elizabeth II; prime minister in 1996, John Major.

Domestic Affairs. For the U.K.'s ruling Conservative Party, 1996 was a frustrating year. Despite low inflation, declining unemployment, rising house prices, and steady economic growth, the party remained unpopular with the voters. It also saw its majority in the House of Commons disappear. The general election in April 1992 had given the party a majority of 21 in the 651-seat Commons. Defections and by-election defeats, which had reduced the figure to five by the beginning of 1996, continued to take their toll. On February 23 it was cut to just two when one Tory MP, Peter Thurnham, resigned from the party and decided to sit as an independent; in October he joined the opposition Liberal Democrats. On April 11 the Conservative majority slipped to just one when the party lost the Midlands seat of Staffordshire South East to the Labour Party in a by-election. On December 13 the majority disappeared altogether following the death of Barry Porter, Conservative MP for Wirral South, and Labour's successful defense of a seat in a by-election in Barnsley.

The Conservatives found themselves consistently on the defensive throughout the year, facing charges of malpractice (or "sleaze") and incompetence. On February 15 Lord Justice Sir Richard Scott published his long-awaited report, which had been commissioned by the government, regarding the sale of British arms to Iraq in the 1980s. Although Scott acquitted government ministers of deliberately lying to Parliament, he did conclude that they had misled the MPs and the general public by concealing a change in policy; Britain had supplied some arms to Saddam Hussein's regime even though the declared policy of the British government at the time was to maintain a strict arms embargo. In a heated Commons debate on the Scott report on February 26, the government narrowly survived censure, winning by 320 votes to 319.

The government faced further embarrassment three weeks later, on March 20, when Stephen Dorrell, the health secretary, admitted that new scientific evidence established a "probable link" between bovine spongiform encephalopathy (BSE, or "mad cow" disease), which affected cattle, and Creutzfeldt-Jakob disease (CJD), which affected humans. This was the first official admission that BSE might have crossed the "species barrier." Sales of British beef plummeted as ministers faced accusations that they had done too little during the late 1980s and early 1990s to halt the spread of BSE in British herds. The government announced new measures to slaughter older cattle and to make sure that their flesh and carcasses would be incinerated and not allowed to enter the food chain. Consumer confidence in British beef remained low, and opinion polls showed that most voters distrusted government statements on the issue. Britain found itself in conflict with the rest of the European Union over an EU decision to ban the export of British beef. (See Foreign Affairs, below.)

In October the House of Commons voted to launch an inquiry into allegations against one current and one former government minister. These allegations arose from inquires by The Guardian, which had alleged that the former trade minister, Neil Hamilton, had violated the rules of Parliament by receiving cash and other benefits secretly from the owner of Harrods department store in London, Mohammed Al Fayed. Hamilton had launched a libel action against The Guardian's initial report two years earlier. On September 30 Hamilton dropped it, however. The Guardian's front-page headline the following day branded Hamilton a "a liar and a cheat." Six days later new evidence emerged of attempts by a current minister, David Willetts, to persuade the Conservative majority on the all-party House of Commons Committee on Standards and Privileges to block an inquiry into the original allegations. This revelation embarrassed the Conservative leadership and provoked the speaker of the House of Commons, Betty Boothroyd, to make an unusually forthright statement to the MPs on October 14, demanding a full and speedy inquiry into the full range of allegations prompted by the newspaper's reports. Following a short debate on October 16, the Commons agreed to her request. The inquiry reported on December 11. Its strongly worded criticisms of Willetts forced him to resign from the government.

Meanwhile, Labour continued to lead the Conservatives by more than 20 points in the opinion polls. In July, with the general election due by May 1997 at the latest, Labour leader Tony Blair launched a pre-election manifesto, "New Life for Britain." This shed the last remnants of Labour's historic devotion to public ownership and high government spending. It promised to keep inflation and interest rates down and to reduce government borrowing.

The Tories sought to counter Blair's popularity by launching an aggressive poster and newspaper advertising campaign in August, using the slogan "New Labour, New Danger." Labour complained that one of the advertisements, which portrayed Blair smiling but with his eyes coloured red and set behind a mask, was designed to make Labour's leader look like the devil. The Conservatives disputed this interpretation, but the Advertising Standards Association banned its future use. The Conservatives, however, repeated the "demon-eyes" motif in other advertisements, without associating them personally with Blair. Labour launched its own anti-Conservative advertisements, containing the slogan "Same Old Tories, Same Old Lies."

Although Labour remained well ahead of the Conservatives, the party encountered problems of its own. In January Harriet Harman, Labour's shadow cabinet health minister and one of Blair's closest senior allies, announced that she would send one of her sons to a selective grammar school, despite the fact that Labour's education policy was to oppose such schools. Blair backed Harman's right to make this decision, but it was criticized by many Labour MPs and seized on by the Conservatives as an example of Labour hypocrisy.

Labour also attracted fire from its opponents and some of its own MPs for changing its policy on Scottish devolution three times during the year. Labour had long advocated a new parliament for Scotland with wide legislative and limited tax-raising powers. Faced with Conservative charges that Labour was planning to impose an extra "tartan tax" on Scottish taxpayers, Blair and George Robertson, his shadow cabinet Scottish minister, promised a referendum on the party's plans for devolution should Labour win the next U.K.-wide general election. The details of their referendum strategy kept changing, however. Finally, on September 6, Labour announced that it would hold one referendum, in which Scottish voters would face two questions: Did

they want Scotland to have its own parliament, and should that parliament have the power to adjust tax rates relative to the standard national rates?

Outside politics, Scotland provided the year's grimmest headlines. On March 13 Thomas Hamilton, a former youth club worker, shot dead 16 young children, their teacher, and, finally, himself at the primary school in Dunblane, a small town 32 km (20 mi) north of Glasgow. The horrific attack prompted a debate about Britain's gun-licensing laws. Despite a well-documented history of mental instability, Hamilton had been able to obtain a license for the handgun he used in the shootings. The government established an inquiry into the country's gun laws. The inquiry, which reported on October 16, recommended the banning of the private ownership (outside strictly controlled gun clubs) of handguns over .22 calibre. The home secretary, Michael Howard, announced that the government would ban the private ownership of all such guns, including those held at gun clubs, and that privately owned single-shot .22-calibre guns and smaller pistols would have to be kept on gun club premises, not at home. These proposals, he said, would give the U.K. some of the tightest gun-control laws of any country in the world. Opposition MPs and some Conservatives urged the government to extend the total ban to .22-calibre guns.

The royal family continued to make news, to the despair of its supporters but to the delight of millions of tabloid newspaper readers. On April 17 Andrew, duke of York (the third of the queen's four children), obtained a divorce from Sarah, duchess of York, following widespread reports of her varied and exotic private life. The duchess, who lost the title "Her Royal Highness," continued to make news as former lovers found they could make money by giving their accounts of their affairs with her. On August 28 the divorce was also finalized between Charles and Diana, prince and princess of Wales. She, too, lost her right to be described as "Her Royal Highness." She was widely reported to have received £20 million as a divorce settlement. The divorce led to speculation that Charles might marry his mistress, Camilla Parker-Bowles (who had divorced her husband in 1995). While no formal announcements were made on the subject, Buckingham Palace officials advised the media that the prince would not marry again for the foreseeable future.

The Economy. For the fourth year in succession, the U.K. had the fastest economic growth of any major economy in Western Europe. The 2.5% growth rate was, however, less than the government had expected at the beginning of the year, although in November unemployment fell below two million for the first time since 1990.

For those at work the improvements in the economy were clear enough. Consumer price inflation remained subdued, fluctuating within the range of 2–3%. Interest rates fell to their lowest in 30 years; the Bank of England's base rate, which was 6.5% at the beginning of the year, was reduced in quarter-point stages to 5.75% by June. The last reduction was opposed by Eddie George, the governor of the Bank of England, but was insisted upon by Kenneth Clarke, the chancellor of the Exchequer, who wanted to prevent the economic

Diana, princess of Wales, leaves a meeting of a federation raising funds to combat leprosy, one of many charitable groups she supported. On August 28 her divorce from Prince Charles became final.

growth rate from slipping too far and also to maximize public support for the Conservative Party. In October, however, Clarke conceded a little ground to George and agreed to a slight increase; at the end of 1996, the base rate stood at 6%.

The combination of low inflation, falling interest rates, and declining unemployment had a marked effect on consumer confidence. Retail sales increased by more than 3% during the year, while house prices rose by 6–7%—the first significant increase since 1989. During the early 1990s up to two million homeowners had lived under the cloud of "negative equity"; that is, their mortgage debt exceeded the value of their home. In 1996 that cloud began to lift.

Foreign Affairs. On March 12 the government published a White Paper, *A Partnership of Nations,* setting out Britain's views on the future of the EU. The paper sought to satisfy both the pro- and anti-EU wings of the Conservative Party. It stated that Britain would "pursue our national interests, as our partners pursue theirs, yet with a strong sense of shared purpose and common enterprise." It argued that the call in the Treaty on European Union, agreed upon at Maastricht, Neth., in 1991, for "an ever closer union among the peoples of Europe" did not necessarily mean closer union between the nations of Europe. Specifically, the White Paper argued that Britain should retain its choice as to whether to join the EU's so-called Social Chapter, that there should be no extension to the powers of the European Parliament, and that Britain would resist any change in the decision-making rules that would limit further the power of the national veto and extend the range of decisions taken by majority voting.

The government's hopes of winning allies in the EU for its vision of Europe's future were dented by a dispute that erupted less than two weeks after the White Paper was published. On March 25 the European Commission imposed a worldwide ban on the export of all British beef products. On May 21, following a decision by the EU's standing veterinary committee to retain the ban in full, Prime Minister John Major announced that until that decision had been reversed, the U.K. would refuse to cooperate with the EU in any decision on any issue that required unanimity. One month later, on June 21, at the EU summit in Florence. Major agreed to end the non-cooperation policy in return for an agreement to lift the export ban in stages. Major failed, however, to secure a firm timetable for allowing British exports to resume. At year's end, the full ban was still in force, but the government had agreed to increase the cull by up to 100,000 cattle.

The last full year of British control of Hong Kong, prior to its reversion to Chinese rule in July 1997, was marked by attempts to repair relations between the U.K. and China. In January Malcolm Rifkind, the U.K.'s foreign secretary, visited China and promised that both the British and the Hong Kong governments would cooperate with China's Preparatory Committee and its chief executive designate. This had the effect of diminishing the significance of the Hong Kong Legislative Council (LegCo), which had been elected in 1995 but which China said it would dismantle after the end of British rule.

In September the tactics of Chris Patten, the governor of Hong Kong, were attacked by Sir Percy Craddock, a former British ambassador to China and one of Britain's key negotiators who produced the 1984 Sino-British agreement on the colony's future. In an article in Hong Kong's leading morning paper, the *South China Morning Post,* Craddock said that the 1984 agreement had said nothing about bringing democracy to Hong Kong while it remained under British rule. By championing democratic reform, Patten, he said, was "either deluding himself or wilfully misleading his followers." More lasting democratic institutions could have been created, Craddock argued, had Patten sought to negotiate more with China over the pace of reform rather than set up LegCo in the teeth of Chinese opposition.

Northern Ireland. The cease-fire that had come into force in September 1994 came to an abrupt end on February 9 when the Irish Republican Army (IRA) detonated a bomb at Canary Wharf, in London's Docklands area, which killed two people and injured another 100. A second bomb exploded 10 days later on a London bus, killing the IRA member who was carrying it. On June 15 a third bomb exploded at the Arndale shopping centre in Manchester. A telephone warning had allowed the centre to be evacuated. Nevertheless, 200 people were injured and the centre was destroyed.

The end of the cease-fire followed the publication of the Mitchell report on January 24. George Mitchell, a former U.S. senator, had been invited by the British and Irish governments in 1995 to lead an international group to propose how the arms used in the Northern Ireland conflict should be progressively decommissioned as part of the peace process. Mitchell's report sought to strike a compromise between the British government's insistence that the IRA give up its arms before peace negotiations took place and the IRA's insistence that negotiations come first.

Major's response was to accept the report in principle but not to hold peace talks until the election, in May, of a Northern Ireland peace forum. The unionist parties in Northern Ireland welcomed this idea, but it was opposed by the nationalist parties—the anti-IRA Social and Democratic Labour Party (SDLP) as well as the pro-IRA Sinn Fein—which condemned Major for delaying tactics. The Irish government also opposed Major's election plan; on February 7 it responded by proposing a peace conference of the kind that had been held in Dayton, Ohio, to end the war in Bosnia and Herzegovina. When Major rejected this plan, the IRA announced that it was ending its cease-fire. Within two hours the

Docklands bomb exploded. The breakdown in the cease-fire was not total. The IRA confined its bomb attacks initially to the British mainland and did not resume violence in Northern Ireland. The Protestant, "loyalist," paramilitary groups announced that they would maintain their cease-fire. For the time being, however, progress toward peace negotiations had been halted.

The election called by Major was held on May 30. Despite their opposition to it, Sinn Fein and the SDLP agreed to take part. The SDLP won 21% of the vote, while Sinn Fein won 15%. The two main unionist parties won 24% (Official Unionists) and 19% (Democratic Unionists). Sinn Fein, however, boycotted the peace forum following the election. This was largely symbolic, for the forum had no real powers. Meanwhile, multiparty peace talks chaired by Mitchell started on June 10; without a new IRA cease-fire, however, they had little chance of making progress. The British government consistently maintained that Sinn Fein could not take part in peace talks until the IRA had reinstated its cease-fire.

On October 7 the IRA resumed its bombing campaign inside Northern Ireland. Two bombs exploded at the British army's headquarters in Lisburn in County Antrim. Thirty-one people, including 24 soldiers and 2 children, were injured; four days later an injured soldier died from his wounds, the first British army death in Northern Ireland in more than two years. In the aftermath of the Lisburn bombing, John Burton, Ireland's prime minister, attacked the IRA as behaving like Germany's Nazis in the 1920s and '30s. Protestant loyalists ended their two-year cease-fire with a car bombing on December 22 in retaliation for an IRA attack in a children's hospital two days prior.

(PETER KELLNER)

See also *Commonwealth of Nations; Dependent States.*

A Protestant holding the Union Jack marches past vehicles set on fire by Roman Catholics in Northern Ireland to protest a police decision to allow the marchers, who were celebrating the victory of Protestant forces over Catholics in 1690, to pass through a Catholic area near Belfast in July.

UNITED STATES

The United States of America is a federal republic composed of 50 states. Area: 9,362,753 sq km (3,614,979 sq mi), including 203,679 sq km of inland water but excluding the 155,534 sq km of the Great Lakes that lie within U.S. boundaries. Pop. (1996 est.): 265,455,000. Cap.: Washington, D.C. Monetary unit: U.S. dollar, with (Oct. 11, 1996) a free rate of U.S. $1.58 to £1 sterling. President in 1996, Bill Clinton.

In 1996 Bill Clinton (*see* BIOGRAPHIES) showed that he was a master at gauging shifts in national mood, and indeed of helping to create them, as he maneuvered in Washington, D.C., and campaigned across the country to become the first two-term U.S. president from the Democratic Party since Franklin D. Roosevelt 60 years earlier. Clinton's victory over his Republican opponent, former senator Bob Dole (*see* BIOGRAPHIES), was all the more remarkable in that voters, in the lowest turnout since 1924, also returned a Republican-majority Congress for the first time since 1930. Never before had a Democrat won the nation's highest office with the Congress controlled by his opponents. Once again, however, the people had opted for the U.S. equivalent of minority government. (*See* Special Report.)

Nonetheless, Clinton could claim a clear victory. He won 49% of the popular vote, compared with 41% for his Republican rival; the remainder went to maverick populist Ross Perot, who ran as the Reform Party candidate. According to exit polls, Clinton

was particularly favoured by women, who endorsed him 54% to 38%; by African-Americans, who voted for him 83% to 12%; and by the elderly, who voted Democratic 50% to 43%. The Republican majority, by contrast, was shaved marginally in the House of Representatives and expanded slightly in the Senate. Nearly half of the Republican casualties came from among the more militant representatives who had first been elected in 1994.

Clinton won his victory by moving with agility to the right, a talent he had demonstrated throughout his national political career but never against such odds as those he faced in 1996. In the process he managed to emerge once again in the public eye as a moderate. To many he seemed more moderate than Dole and his fellow Republicans, especially the aggressive speaker of the House of Representatives, Newt Gingrich, whom Clinton brilliantly demonized in the presidential campaign as an avatar of mean-minded radical conservatism, threatening the poor, the elderly, and the middle class with cuts in federally mandated entitlements. The net result was that Clinton, who began the year almost passively, with the government paralyzed through a budget deadlock, emerged as a mediating chief executive who could urge his defeated adversaries to join him in seeking a "common ground" during his upcoming term.

Clinton, moreover, achieved this feat despite a continuing rain of scandals great and small upon his administration. They covered everything from the continuing investigation into the decade-old Whitewater

land deal to more sinister questions about the abuse of confidential FBI files on political opponents and the improper raising of campaign funds from non-U.S. sources. As the year closed, the U.S. Supreme Court was prepared to hear arguments on whether the president should be allowed, on account of his office, to postpone a civil suit leveled against him by Paula Corbin Jones, a former Arkansas state employee who alleged that Clinton had made sexual advances to her while he was governor. It was one sign of the administration's political skills that, although none of the scandals had gone away by the end of 1996 and some might return to hurt the president in his second term, none proved fatal to Clinton's reelection.

The Economy. The fact was that, however many questions were raised about the president's character or that of his administration, other, more fundamental factors weighed heavily in favour of his reelection. The nation was at peace, and, above all, it was prosperous. The monetary manipulations of the Federal Reserve System (Fed) chairman, Alan Greenspan, and his Open Market Committee ensured that economic growth continued. The Fed cut short-term rates just before the new year began, with the aim of keeping growth in the range of 2.5% for 1996. Any fears of flat growth or recession were thus dispelled, and the president signaled his approval for this course by renominating Greenspan, a Republican, for his third four-year term as Fed chairman and naming two other economic moderates to the seven-member board.

The steady growth put further downward pressure on the U.S. jobless rate, which was only 5.4% when the year began. By the time the year ended, it was 5.3%, not much changed but nonetheless at the lowest level since the 1970s. Inflation, too, was contained, staying at roughly 2.5%. Blue-collar workers registered a real, if marginal, rise in income, as wage increases averaged 2.8%, and white-collar workers saw a 3.1% increase in pay. Overall economic productivity rose at a 1.2% rate, while productivity in manufacturing rose 3.2%. Thus, the nation's economic progress was steady, if not muscular. One of the more negative signals, however, was the steady rise in personal bankruptcies, which reached more than one million during the year. There was also continued volatility in sectoral employment as large-scale corporate downsizing continued.

The most dynamic sector of the economy was the high-tech, particularly the computer-oriented, firms that continued to drive the stock market to new heights. In the first half of 1996, the sale of new public stock offerings continued to be one of the fastest avenues of growth for new companies, which went public at a rate of 70 or more per month. In the process many suddenly became worth 200 or 300 times their previous value, creating a steady procession of new millionaires. The same frothy optimism continued to affect more traditional stocks, as the Dow Jones industrial average continued its steady rise past 6,000. Among other things, the rise reflected a steady flow of money into equities from members of the baby-boomer generation, who were skeptical of the value of Social Security and were replacing it with contributions to such vehicles as 401(k) accounts. In midyear, however, there was a sudden correction in

Sitting on a Long Island beach, a woman mourns for victims of the crash of TWA Flight 800 on July 17. All 230 persons aboard the plane died when the aircraft exploded off Long Island, but at year's end investigators had not yet been able to determine the cause of the explosion.

CAROL GUZY—THE WASHINGTON POST

the upward rise of stocks, and the high-tech over-the-counter market, in particular, swooned. Nonetheless, by year's end the market had recovered, albeit selectively.

Developments in Government. If the November elections underlined anything, it was that the American people were eager to pull back from extremes that might erode their sense of stability, however transitory that might prove to be. The nation had been badly shocked in 1995 by signs that the social and political consensus was fraying in ways not seen since the Vietnam War. In Washington the tension was symbolized by the trench warfare between the White House and Congress over the 1996 budget, which had left the government essentially inoperative. Some 280,000 government workers were laid off, and another half million were working but not being paid. At issue were the differing ways in which the two sides proposed to close the budget deficit over seven years, chiefly in terms of taxes and in slowing the growth of such huge entitlement programs as Medicare and Medicaid. The Republicans wanted to cut $270 billion from Medicare growth, for example, while the president wanted to pare only $124 billion. Clinton had also rejected Republican efforts to give the military more than the $256 billion he had originally proposed.

The standoff, which had begun in mid-December 1995, continued for 18 days before the Republican wall began to crack. It was Clinton's soon-to-be presidential rival, Senator Dole, who first urged his party to begin providing funds on a continuing basis so that the government could get back to work. He was then joined by Speaker Gingrich, who broke with more radical members of his party to do so. Both men realized that the American people, while sympathetic to the goal of cutting the size and scope of the government, were profoundly uneasy at its paralysis. After 21 days the funding cutoff ended on January 6, with both sides submitting their proposals for seven-year reductions in spending. The squabbling over the actual 1996 budget continued until late April, however, with 13 separate temporary spending bills required for keeping the government functioning while the horse trading went on.

In general, the outcome of the exhausting battle confirmed the thinking that had propelled the congressional Republicans to power in 1994. In the final budget more than 200 federal programs were abolished, mostly in the Labor and the Health and Human Services departments. Funding for the Corporation for Public Broadcasting, a longtime target of conservative ire, was slashed, though the corporation survived. So did such Clinton programs as the subsidized national service for youth, funding to put 100,000 extra police on the streets, and extra money to improve the quality of education, viewed by conservatives as a federal prop to a pillar of the Democratic Party, the National Education Association.

The president was quick to turn the situation to political advantage and to articulate the theme that was to dominate the electoral politics of the year. "The era of big government is over," he told Congress and the nation in his annual state of the union address. He added, however, that "we cannot go back to the time when our citizens were left to fend for themselves." Clearly

RON HAVIV—SABA

Male and female recruits go through basic training together at the Aberdeen Proving Ground in Maryland. The Maryland base was only one of a number of U.S. military facilities where investigations of alleged sexual harassment were under way during 1996.

positioning himself as a moderate, he called for such achievements as bipartisan welfare reform, an increase in the minimum wage, and portability of health insurance so that workers would not lose coverage if they changed jobs. He also asked for a line-item veto of the kind already wielded by 43 of 50 state governors and endorsed by the Republican congressional majority.

The limited nature of Clinton's 1996 goals stood in sharp contrast to the grandiose first-term proposals he had outlined for health care reform, which died ignominiously in 1994. The fate of the new proposals was also different. In May Congress endorsed the first hike in the federally mandated minimum wage in five years, from $4.25 to $4.75 an hour, with another rise to $5.15 a year later. Some 3.6 million Americans were affected by the measure, most of them women. The change was fiercely opposed by small business lobbies, but in the end Republicans split over the issue.

At virtually the same time, Clinton won approval of the line-item veto, which allowed the president to strike a limited number of items from a budget bill rather than veto the entire document. The veto was highly limited, however. It applied only to items that affected no more than 100 taxpayers and specifically could not be used on entitlement programs like Medicare and Social Security. Nor could it be used to block major tax reductions, and it could be overturned by a two-thirds congressional majority. Nonetheless, the veto was decried by Sen. Mark Hatfield, chairman of the Senate Appropriations Committee and one of only three Senate Republicans to vote against it, as "the greatest effort to shift the balance of power to the White House since Franklin Roosevelt attempted to pack the Supreme Court." The veto was immediately promised a constitutional challenge.

If the president was able to win incremental victories that gave solace to the liberal constituencies within his party, he also made moves that set him apart from them. None was more symbolic, or fraught with more sweeping potential to affect American society, than his decision to sign the welfare

reform act passed by Congress, the first comprehensive overhaul of the system in 60 years. Momentum for some sort of change was clearly unstoppable. In polls the American people had frequently showed their unhappiness with welfare, particularly the $16 billion program known as Aid to Families with Dependent Children (AFDC). Clinton had already declared his willingness to accept a two-year limit on recipients in the program, but liberal members of his party had long argued that a welfare cutoff was meaningless, and perhaps dangerous, unless it was matched with expensive job-creation measures, probably in the public sector. The Republican Congress would have none of that. In the long wrangle over the bill, the White House was able to add a number of palliatives to the notion of a welfare cutoff: child nutrition programs, extra aid for recession-hit states, and money for child care and foster care. The overall direction of reform, however, was to take the federal government out of the social welfare business where possible and to hand its administration over to the states.

Under the provisions of the measure, states were to receive block grants for all welfare expenditures, set in relation to 1996 levels, with added money to take account of recessions or unusual population growth. The act abolished the AFDC program entirely and gave the states until July 1, 1997, to come up with plans that required welfare recipients to go to work within two years, while setting a total limit on welfare assistance of five years per family. After six years states that failed to put welfare families in work of some kind would lose their federal funds, although 20% of a state's caseload could be exempted. The law contained a number of clauses aimed at reinforcing the work ethic. Administrators could cut payments to teenage mothers who did not finish high school, for example, or who lived with an adult (a response to frequent criticisms that the AFDC program encouraged broken families and illegitimacy). State legislatures would need to provide a waiver to add payments for children born while their

(continued on page 495)

The U.S. Presidential Election

BY GEORGE RUSSELL

Election campaigns, like wars, are won through a combination of strategy, logistics, and the application of power. In 1996 Bill Clinton showed that while his style of governance may have been open to question, his political generalship was on a par with the military skills of the best. Through a brilliant bombardment with television imagery, and the most all-encompassing political poll-taking in U.S. history, the incumbent president smashed through the stratagems of his Republican opponent, Bob Dole, to win a victory that, for most of the year, was almost never in doubt. In the end, however, it was a resounding victory without coattails. Indeed, for much of the election year, the president campaigned without mentioning the name of the Democratic Party, while for their part the victorious Republicans who retained control of the House of Representatives and the Senate did so, at the end, with hardly an invocation of the beleaguered Dole. There was a reason for the symmetry of silences; both Clinton and the Republicans were campaigning more for rehabilitation in the eyes of the electorate than for a revolution of ideas or philosophies. In the end they proved to be running successfully against themselves, in two distinct branches of government.

This fact did not make the campaign cheap, however. Indeed, the elections of 1996 were the costliest in the history of the republic. By the end of the campaign, the Democrats were believed to have spent some $250 million and the Republicans $400 million—more than twice as much as in 1992. Immensely costly television campaigning and a saturation poll strategy caused the Democrats and the Clinton White House to construct a fund-raising machine of enormous ingenuity and rapacity—one whose dubious methods raised questions and investigations that would cast shadows

deep into the second Clinton administration. As the year came to a close, Attorney General Janet Reno rejected the notion of an investigation of the Democratic campaign-funding machine by an independent counsel, but congressional hearings were sure to keep the pot boiling.

A considerable amount of the Republican money, by contrast, had been spent in warring among themselves. One of the five major Republican primary candidates, the wealthy publisher Steve Forbes, alone spent an estimated $25 million, largely in "attack" television advertising against eventual standard-bearer Dole. Despite such intense opposition, Dole had virtually locked up his party's nomination by late March, long before the end of the exhausting string of Republican primaries ended in June. But Dole—73 years old in July, laconic, self-mocking, an inept orator more comfortable in Senate cloakrooms than on the hustings—proved unable to unite or inspire a party riven among conservative hard-liners and moderates, Christian fundamentalist activists and secular pragmatists, antiabortion campaigners and pro-choice supporters. His inability to inspire a coherent opposition drove away financial contributors and eventually revived the not-very-dormant presidential ambitions of the country's richest political maverick, billionaire populist Ross Perot, who had won almost 19% of the vote in 1992. Sensing Dole's weakness, Perot once again threw his hat into the ring as the Reform Party candidate, further dividing Dole's potential supporters.

President Clinton, by contrast, was an enthusiastic, flesh-pressing lover of crowds and personal contact who was by most accounts more in his element as a campaigner than as a chief executive, and his energy not so subtly conveyed the generational gap between himself and his main opponent. Dole's most eloquent appeal was at the Republican national convention in San Diego, Calif., when the wounded World War II veteran, whose right arm was permanently disabled, deliberately evoked the values of an earlier, simpler age by asking that voters consider him "a bridge to tranquillity." The ebullient Clinton, on the other hand, asked to be considered a "bridge to the 21st century."

The president's path to victory was a vindication of the strategy of "triangulation" propounded and, for much of the time, orchestrated by his chief political strategist, Dick Morris, who fell from influence in a sex scandal on the same day that Clinton delivered his acceptance speech at the Democratic national convention in Chicago. The strategy was based on the belief that after an erratic and disappointing first term, best symbolized by the failure of his ambitious and disastrous attempt to reform health care, Clinton had to present himself to American voters as standing both above and between the warring Democrats and Republicans.

The president made his first move in that direction in 1995 when, over the objections of many Democrats, he endorsed the notion of a balanced federal budget over seven years—a notion that had appeared in the successful 1994 Republican "Contract with America." Nearly a year and a half before election day, he followed that change with a series of television ads that took tough positions on anti-crime measures and penalties. Meanwhile, his pollsters took soundings across the country to discover the uncertainties that most concerned the American public—issues of crime, educational decline, environmental degradation, and medical care for the elderly, to name just a few. They also polled to discover, long in advance of the actual fact, that Americans would likely blame congressional Republicans, led by the controversial speaker of the House, Newt Gingrich, for any governmental paralysis that resulted from a budget deadlock in Washington, D.C. When the deadlock did occur, the Republicans, and Gingrich in particular, were marked as the proponents of radical risk and uncertainty. They were seen as making assaults on valued safety nets like Medicare that were considered vital entitlements by the middle-aged and elderly, despite the fact that the Republicans, as they frequently protested, were intent on merely slowing the rate of expansion of such programs, at least in the short term.

Under the circumstances the unfortunate strategy pursued by Dole during his primary campaign was tuned to buttress the Clinton plan. In the run-up to the early caucuses and primaries in Iowa and New Hampshire, Dole, a moderate deal maker by nature, abandoned his middle-of-the-road principles to fend off the challenge from a more conservative rival, Sen. Phil Gramm of Texas. Dole abandoned his longtime support for affirmative action, took tough stances on denying benefits to illegal immigrants, and backtracked in his support for one of Congress's rare restrictions on firearms, a selective ban on automatic weapons. Even as he did so, however, the consummate Washington insider was being outflanked on the economic right by dark horse Forbes and by another conservative populist, political commentator Patrick Buchanan.

Forbes harked back in policies and rhetoric to the supply-side economics of the Ronald Reagan administration. His salient campaign plank was a flat 17% income tax to replace the thicket of graduations and exemptions that had grown up since the last tax simplification, in 1986. An amateurish

but disciplined campaigner who could draw on his private wealth without the restrictions that governed donated funds, Forbes clearly struck a chord among Americans still resentful of the powers and prerogatives of Beltway Washington. He also had the support of such popular Reagan-era figures as Jack Kemp, who had been George Bush's secretary of housing and urban development. Buchanan represented another, more fundamentalist trend: the nativist, anticapitalist populism of the South and Midwest that had spawned radical movements in the 1930s. With Buchanan, a staunch Roman Catholic, this was allied with a hard-line antiabortion stance. Buchanan inveighed against immigration of all kinds, the loss of U.S. manufacturing jobs to Mexico and elsewhere, and the general climate of excessive social tolerance. A few of his economic themes were echoed, more pallidly, by another major primary candidate, Lamar Alexander, formerly the secretary of education in the Bush administration. All three candidates emphasized the fact to unhappy Republican voters that the party front-runner, still

(Opposite page) Bill Clinton waves to a crowd gathered in Little Rock, Ark., on November 5 to celebrate his reelection as president of the U.S. (Right) A delegate to the Democratic national convention, held in Chicago in August, sports a political pair of glasses.

(OPPOSITE PAGE) BOB STRONG—SIPA; (RIGHT) NAJLAH FEANNY—SABA

a sitting senator and the majority leader, was a "despised creature" of Washington.

Defeating his disparate rivals cost Dole time, energy, and, above all, money. By early March, when Dole had not yet managed to clinch the nomination, Perot had begun talking about entering the presidential race. Over the ensuing weeks, as he managed to tighten his grip on the nomination, Dole was still unable to articulate a campaign theme that went much beyond portraying Clinton as a classic "tax-and-spend" liberal—a position that Clinton had by this time long and fairly convincingly abandoned. At the same time, using the most powerful advantage of executive incumbency, the president had managed to push through such measures as a minimum-wage hike and portable health insurance that solidified his traditional blue-collar constituency, despite his generally conservative fiscal stance. Nor was Dole able to capitalize on the greatest uncertainty about Clinton: the continuing doubts about his character, as expressed in his evasive stance on avoiding the draft as a student, his elasticity on issues of principle, and the many questions that had arisen about the family's financial dealings during his gubernatorial tenure in Arkansas, collectively known as the Whitewater scandal.

As polls affirmed Dole's sorry electoral state (Clinton at times enjoyed leads of 20 percentage points), he took a dramatic step to change his image as a Washington insider. In mid-May Dole announced that he would resign his Senate seat and leadership role, and he shed his conservative suit-and-tie image for shirtsleeved campaigning. The positive effect was short-lived, however. Then, in a desperate bit of apostasy, Dole suddenly announced a complete reversal of course in his not-well-articulated economic policies. The apostle of fiscal moderation embraced a 15% tax cut, and just before the San Diego convention he announced that

Kemp, the party's most articulate and energetic supply-sider, was his choice for vice president. The energetic 61-year-old Kemp, a former professional football quarterback, was also chosen to help counter the active and youthful image projected by Clinton and his vice president, Al Gore. Both the ideological and the image-making changes failed to impress voters, however. Kemp was deemed unimpressive in his single televised debate with the vice president, while Dole was judged even worse in his two debates with Clinton.

The president's lead remained unassailable. In a final bid to rally an anti-Clinton majority, Dole appealed to independent Perot to withdraw from the race, but Perot called the plea "weird and inconsequential." In the final week of the campaign, the highly tuned Clinton machine sputtered only when revelations began to surface about the extent of the dubious fund-raising that had been undertaken, especially in Asian circles, to finance the juggernaut. Dole's standing began to rise—but too little, too late. In the end he lost by 8.4 percentage points—almost exactly the margin held by Perot.

The message of the campaign was exactly what Clinton and his inner circle of poll-taking political professionals had perceived. The American people were conservative in their fiscal attitudes, concerned with reinforcing their social values and institutions, and impatient with ideological intransigence. In an improving economy, however, their long-standing collective optimism also came to the fore. The largest American demographic group, the so-called baby boomers, ultimately chose one of their own to lead them forward, rather than turning back to the past.

George Russell, a senior editor at Time International, *is the author of* Eyewitness: A History of Photojournalism.

(continued from page 491)
mothers were on welfare. On the other side, the measure set aside $400 million in bonuses for states that reduced or contained rates of illegitimate birth, including $250 million for education in abstinence as a form of birth control. The bill also barred legal immigrants who had not applied for citizenship from receiving food stamps and other forms of assistance. The law recognized that many states had long been trying to find more workable formulas, and it gave 44 states a year to wind down various experiments already under way.

Some questioned whether this welfare reform was actually an answer to the problem or merely a means of shuffling the issue onto lower levels of government. Most experts agreed that without substantial levels of job training and placement, the two-year limit to federal funding might merely shift an immense burden onto state budgets. Many child-care advocates warned that the reforms would strike hardest at the children of those on welfare, perhaps adding millions to the rolls of a permanent underclass. Of course, the full impact of the welfare changes were not likely to be felt for several years, a point that was often made by its opponents, some of whom were closely aligned with the president's wife, Hillary Rodham Clinton. That, however, did not deter the president from signing the measure.

Clinton also took a variety of conservative postures on other social and so-called family-values issues, especially those related to crime and drugs. He appointed a four-star army general, Barry R. McCaffrey, previously commander of the Pentagon's Southern Command in Panama, as the nation's drug czar. He raised the possibility of a mandatory drug test for teenagers seeking to obtain a driver's license. The president caused a fierce storm of protest among homosexuals when he announced his support for legislation that would ban the provision of federal benefits to the partners in a same-sex marriage. When the Defense of Marriage Act passed, Clinton signed it.

The issue of same-sex partnerships proved a heated one across the country in an election year. The immediate reason for the furor was a series of court decisions in Hawaii, reaching to the state's Supreme Court, that ruled the prohibition of same-gender unions to be in violation of the state constitution's equal protection clause. The decisions led to conservative warnings that the ruling would usher in homosexual marriages across the nation as states were forced to recognize their legality under the "full faith and credit" provisions of the U.S. Constitution. In fact, the likelihood of such legitimacy was small, for 15 states had laws explicitly banning such marriages, and others were considering them.

Law Enforcement. While a looming election raised temperatures on some divisive social issues, the country clearly was in no mood to countenance a radicalism that threatened social war. The 1995 bombing of the Alfred P. Murrah Federal Building in Oklahoma City, Okla., which killed 169 people, had savagely underlined the horrors of extremism, and the nation clearly wanted no part of it. The two men charged with the crime, allegedly fringe members of a heavily armed antigovernment militia, awaited trial in 1996. There were no similar

bombings during the year, but in July the federal Bureau of Alcohol, Tobacco and Firearms arrested 10 men and 2 women—members of a little-known Phoenix, Ariz., splinter group called the Viper Militia—who seemingly had like plans. The authorities confiscated two machine guns, six rifles, hundreds of rounds of ammunition, and hundreds of kilograms of chemicals similar to those used in the Oklahoma City bombing. They also impounded videotape of sundry Vipers giving guided tours of nearby federal buildings, with detailed instructions on how to blow them up.

Federal authorities pulled off an even bigger coup when they staged a raid on a remote Montana mountain cabin and announced that they had arrested Theodore J. Kaczynski, thought to be the anonymous bomber who had eluded them for 18 years. Intermittently since 1978, the so-called Unabomber had mailed handmade explosive devices to a number of academics and business executives, killing 3 people and injuring 23. In the wake of the Oklahoma City bombing, he sent a bomb to the president of the California Forestry Association and threatened to blow up an aircraft leaving the Los Angeles airport unless the *New York Times* and *Washington Post* published his manifesto against industrialized society. The publication proved Kaczynski's undoing when his brother recognized the rhetoric and notified authorities. Kaczynski had no link to any organized causes.

The arrest won back some lustre for federal law-enforcement agencies, which had suffered a great loss of prestige as a result of their handling of the 1993 siege near

A young minimum wage earner bags groceries. The U.S. Congress voted to raise the minimum wage, unchanged since 1991, from $4.25 to $5.15 an hour in two stages.

JAMES LEYNSE—SABA

Waco, Texas, of the headquarters of the Branch Davidian sect, in which 82 members had died, and for the bungled 1992 arrest of a white separatist in Idaho, in which his wife and 14-year-old son had been killed. The FBI used different tactics in 1996 in outwaiting a group of self-described libertarian Freemen holed up on a ranch in Jordan, Mont. The Freemen were faced with federal charges of writing millions of dollars' worth of bad checks and money orders and of threatening to kidnap and kill a federal judge involved in foreclosure on the farm. Mindful of the innocent women and children in the beleaguered camp, the FBI simply outwaited the defenders until they surrendered.

The FBI's prestige was once again tarnished, however, this time in the midst of the year's most festive occasion, the Centennial Olympic Games in Atlanta, Ga. The Games had just finished their seventh day when, early in the morning, a homemade pipe bomb exploded in Centennial Olympic Park, killing one person and wounding 111. It was the first violence to occur at the Olympics since the massacre that had taken place in Munich, Ger., in 1972, and it happened despite unprecedented security. The bomb was contained in a knapsack left against a television broadcast tower in the park, a central meeting place. About 18 minutes before the explosion, an anonymous caller had phoned in a warning, and security personnel were trying to clear the area when the bomb went off. Official suspicion soon focused on Richard Jewell, an Olympics security guard, who was detained, interrogated, and investigated for months before being told that he was no longer a suspect. Jewell sued not only the authorities but also news media who publicized suspicions of his guilt. No other suspect was named in the bombing, despite a $500,000 FBI reward.

The Olympics bombing came on the heels of a much greater disaster. On July 17 a TWA flight from New York City to Paris suddenly exploded over the Atlantic Ocean near Long Island, with 230 passengers and crew aboard. All perished. A massive underwater search across 620 sq km (240 sq mi) of ocean eventually recovered most of the bodies and about 90% of the Boeing 747 aircraft. Authorities worked to determine whether a bomb or a mechanical problem had caused the calamity aboard Flight 800. By the end of the year, the investigation was far from over, but some authorities were venturing that the cause was a buildup of explosive vapour in a fuel tank.

Foreign Affairs. Terrorism, nonetheless, continued to strike a strong chord with Americans. A month before the TWA disaster, a small group of men wheeled a large tanker truck up against a link fence in front of an apartment building in Dhahran, Saudi Arabia, and then fled before an enormous explosion tore the face off the building. The edifice housed U.S. Air Force personnel involved in interdicting flights in southern Iraq in the wake of the 1990–91 Persian Gulf War. A total of 19 airmen were killed and 50 hospitalized by the blast. The explosion was believed to be the work of Saudi Islamic militants.

The Saudi attack was no doubt on President Clinton's mind two months later when he declared terrorism to be "the enemy of our generation" while signing a new law ordering sanctions against any nation investing in Iran and Libya, both considered terrorist states by the U.S. In fact, Clinton's action did nothing to lessen terrorist dangers, while it infuriated some of the closest U.S. allies. The law specifically penalized foreign firms that made investments in oil in the two countries, which were major petroleum suppliers to Europe. Clinton declared that the lesson for U.S. allies was "You cannot do business with countries that practice commerce with you by day while funding or protecting the terrorists who kill you and your innocent civilians by night." The allies said that this was posturing and an attempt to limit their sovereignty, and they filed a protest at The Hague.

In fact, when it came to actual outrages perpetrated by tyrants, the administration's policy seemed singularly feckless. In a test of U.S. will, Iraq's Saddam Hussein sent 50,-000 armoured troops north from Baghdad on an incursion into ethnic Kurdish territories specifically declared a "no-go" zone by the victors in the Gulf War. Hussein effectively installed a puppet regime beholden to himself, wiped out bases where the CIA had launched covert actions against his government, and then withdrew. In retaliation, Clinton ordered a strike of 44 cruise missiles against replaceable Iraqi air defenses far to the south and increased the no-go zone in the same region. The symbolic action did nothing to restore the status quo.

Clinton had irked allies earlier in the year with his posturing toward another old enemy, Fidel Castro. The U.S. was shocked when the Cuban dictator ordered the shooting down of two small, unarmed civilian planes that flew over Havana from airfields in Miami, Fla. The aircraft were flown by members of the so-called Brothers to the Rescue, who had earlier goaded Castro by dropping anticommunist leaflets on Havana. In the wake of the shootdown, Clinton threw his support behind the so-called Helms-Burton law, which allowed Cuban Americans whose businesses had been taken over during the 1959 revolution to file suit against foreign companies that bought or leased the assets from the Castro government. The law also mandated that the U.S. government deny a visa to any foreigner with a stake in such property. Clinton waived the more onerous sections of the law, but businesspeople from Canada and other countries were warned that they could face such sanctions. Their irate governments created countervailing sanctions in case the law was applied, and they filed suit against the U.S. before the World Trade Organization.

In a further bow to conservative sentiment that irked many U.S. allies, not to mention many in the Third World, the Clinton administration cast a veto against the reelection of UN Secretary-General Boutros Boutros-Ghali. The U.S. was vexed at his secretive style, slowness to implement financial reforms, and ill-advised efforts to make the UN into a peacemaker in areas such as Bosnia and Herzegovina where peace might not be had without force. Boutros-Ghali's successor, Kofi Annan of Ghana, was applauded in the U.S. as a more open and reform-minded choice, but the move was resented, particularly by France.

Such actions discomfited friends of the U.S., but in general the country's foreign policy during 1996 was aimed at avoiding

CHUCK KENNEDY—KRT

(From left) Palestinian Pres. Yasir Arafat, Israeli Prime Minister Benjamin Netanyahu, and Jordan's King Hussein listen as U.S. Pres. Bill Clinton discusses their October meeting in Washington, D.C. The U.S. sponsored the talks to try to salvage the Middle East peace agreements.

political harm. Clinton endured criticism for his administration's continued support for the government of Russian Pres. Boris Yeltsin, but it seemed justified after Yeltsin had won elections against the resurgent communist candidate, Gennady Zyuganov. (See BIOGRAPHIES.) Yeltsin's health, however, continued to make the Clinton policy an open issue after the Russian president later underwent quadruple bypass surgery. Clinton's 1995 gamble to send U.S. troops to Bosnia in the aftermath of the Dayton Accords that ended the slaughter in former Yugoslavia likewise paid off as peaceful elections were carried out. The results followed predictable ethnic lines, and virtually no action was taken before world courts against the authors of acknowledged genocide. Growing public protests against the Serbian dictator, Slobodan Milosevic, whose irredentist ambitions were a prime cause of the Bosnian catastrophe, further seemed to vindicate the Clinton approach. The major loss to the U.S. in the Balkans during the year was the death of Commerce Secretary Ron Brown (see OBITUARIES), who died in an air crash near Dubrovnik, Croatia, as he led a group of business executives exploring the possibilities of economic reconstruction in the shattered area.

The Middle East peace process, which Clinton had proudly midwifed, suffered a severe setback with the election in Israel of the conservative Likud government of Benjamin Netanyahu. The West Bank became embroiled in the worst Israeli-Palestinian violence in 30 years. Nonetheless, by the end of the year, an uneasy peace had returned, and it seemed that progress was being made. Late in the year, Clinton also shuffled his foreign policy team, among other changes replacing Warren Christopher with the first woman to serve as secretary of state, former UN ambassador Madeleine Albright, and naming Bill Richardson as chief delegate to the UN.

The area where U.S. foreign policy seemed to grow the most convoluted was in Asia, and once again election considerations lay at the bottom of it. The U.S.

launched no major initiatives across the Pacific, where Asia was the focus of an immense industrial boom. The administration, however, had not come to a clear view of how to deal with this rising economic power, much of it the result of investments by U.S. businesses, or with an increasingly assertive China. In 1996 China replaced Japan as the largest single source of the U.S. trade deficit, and the U.S. frequently locked horns with China over that country's alleged violation of copyright laws, software piracy, and other economic issues. Despite allegations that the Chinese had sold magnets to Pakistan that could be used in developing nuclear weapons and the charge that U.S. businesses lost $2 billion annually to factories that illicitly copied software, films, and other intellectual property, the administration backed the extension of most-favoured-nation trading status for China.

If Asian wealth was complicating foreign policy, it was also making a mockery of U.S. election law. As the election drew near, attention focused on the activities of John Huang, an Asian-American with connections to a wealthy Indonesian family that had business connections with China. Huang had raised more than $4 million for the Democratic Party during 1996. Possessed of a top security clearance, he had gathered in, among other things, an illegal $250,000 from a South Korean firm and $450,000 from an Indonesian couple. Another Asian-American fund-raiser and Clinton acquaintance, Taiwan-born Charles Yah Lin Trie, was revealed to have once taken a major Chinese arms dealer to the White House. Trie had also raised funds for the Clintons' steep legal bills in the Whitewater affair, some in the form of cash and checks in plain brown envelopes. Much of the money was returned, and there was no evidence of favours having been granted in return for the funds. Nonetheless, at year's end the Department of Justice had issued subpoenas to the White House for records on as many as 20 Democratic Party fundraisers.   (GEORGE RUSSELL)

See also *Dependent States.*

State and Local Affairs

States continued to be at the centre of national debates on public policy during 1996. The U.S. Congress, reacting in part to successful experimentation by a number of states, enacted a historic welfare-reform measure that relied on state and local oversight to reduce the dependency of recipients on government. The development was part of a continued trend toward increased state powers in a federalist system.

Continuing economic expansion allowed states to enact record tax reductions for the second consecutive year. Voters decided some 200 initiatives, referenda, and state bond issues in the November balloting, another national record. In the most highly publicized issue, California citizens ordered an end to government affirmative action programs, although enforcement of the measure was at least temporarily delayed by a federal judge.

Forty-nine states (all except Kentucky) held regular legislative sessions during the year, and 12 states held special sessions.

Party Strengths. Democrats made modest gains in the November state elections, winning a net increase of 70 seats among approximately 6,000 contested legislative races and holding even in governors' contests.

In 11 gubernatorial elections there were party changes in two; Republicans captured a Democratic-held office in West Virginia, and Democrats took the New Hampshire governorship from Republicans. The governors' lineup for 1997 thus remained at 32 Republicans, 17 Democrats, and 1 (Maine) independent.

Going into the 1996 elections, Republicans had two-party control of 18 state legislatures, Democrats dominated in 16 states, and 15 legislatures were split. Overall, Republicans controlled 50 of 99 legislative chambers. (Nebraska had a unicameral, nonpartisan legislature.) After November's legislative balloting in 45 states, Democrats controlled 50 of the 99 chambers and Republicans 46, with 2 tied. For 1997 Republicans maintained full control of 18 legislatures, Democrats held 20, and 11 state legislatures were split.

The election results confirmed a national trend toward divided government. For 1997 a record 31 states had at least one legislative chamber controlled by a party different from the governor's.

Government Structures and Powers. In the wake of a 1995 Supreme Court decision declaring federal term-limit measures by states to be unconstitutional, backers turned to other methods to generate turnover among elected officials. Voters in Alaska, Arkansas, Colorado, Idaho, Maine, Missouri, Nebraska, Nevada, South Dakota, and Wyoming required candidates to pledge their support for term limits or be identified on future ballots as having refused to do so. Similar initiatives were defeated in Montana, North Dakota, Oregon, and Washington.

States continued to experiment with ways of improving voter turnout. For the first time, presidential primary elections were held by mail in three states—Nevada, North Dakota, and Oregon. Although a federally mandated "motor-voter" law boosted registration by 11 million nationwide, the turnout in the November election was just above the historic low of 50%.

Fulfilling a 1994 campaign promise, the state treasurer of Texas pushed through the abolition of her agency during the year. Treasury operations were turned over to the state controller.

Finances. A strong national economy and a conservative political climate prompted states to reduce taxes in fiscal 1997 for the second consecutive year, this time by a net $4 billion, or 1.1% of the previous year's collections. With the $3.1 billion reduction in fiscal 1996, this action was the largest two-year state tax reduction in history and the first back-to-back drop in 17 years. Only two states, Missouri and Idaho, raised taxes overall, with both using gasoline levies to increase revenue.

Personal income taxes were again the primary focus of state tax-cutting efforts, with Connecticut, Delaware, New York, Ohio, and Utah cutting personal tax rates. Iowa, Kentucky, Massachusetts, New York, Ohio, and South Carolina increased the standard deduction or personal exemptions, which effectively reduced personal tax burdens.

Seventeen states modified business taxes during 1996, most by reducing corporate levies in an effort to retain or recruit jobs. For the second straight year, the most dramatic changes came in New York, which phased out its corporation income tax surcharge entirely. California, Connecticut, and North Carolina reduced corporate tax rates, Delaware and Rhode Island reduced bank tax rates, and Washington cut business taxes.

Georgia and North Carolina reduced sales taxes on the purchase of food for home consumption, but Louisiana and Vermont extended temporary sales tax increases. Connecticut, Illinois, and Kentucky reduced taxes on health care providers, while New York and Rhode Island extended similar taxes due to expire during the year.

Indiana halved its motor-vehicle excise tax, but motor-fuel taxes were increased in Connecticut, Idaho, Illinois, Missouri, and North Dakota. Massachusetts and Utah hiked tobacco taxes, while Delaware reduced levies on alcohol. Among miscella-neous tax actions, Arizona repealed its education property tax, New York ended the taxation of real-estate gains, and North Carolina phased out soft-drink levies. Florida reduced pari-mutuel gambling taxes, and North Carolina and Utah eased tax burdens on utilities and gas producers.

Voters in Florida, Nevada, and South Dakota approved measures requiring a two-thirds legislative or popular majority for enacting new taxes, bringing to 13 the number of states with so-called supermajority laws. Oregon voters went even farther, requiring that a majority of all registered voters approve any new state taxes or fees.

New Jersey staged a highly successful tax-amnesty program during the year, collecting $350 million in delinquent taxes. Michigan lawmakers enacted an experimental "renaissance zone" plan to eliminate both property and income taxes for businesses and residents of blighted areas.

Education. Colorado voters rejected a controversial initiative that sought to give parents "the natural, essential and inalienable right to direct and control the upbringing, education, values and discipline of their children."

In a case involving the Virginia Military Institute, the U.S. Supreme Court declared unconstitutional the "categorical exclusion" of one gender from any government-funded school or college.

Alabama approved a bill giving teachers who followed school-district guidelines immunity from lawsuits that arose from paddling students. Twenty-six states had laws prohibiting the use of corporal punishment on pupils.

Health and Welfare. Following years of experimentation by states, a historic federal welfare-reform act was signed into law by Pres. Bill Clinton in 1996. The legislation mandated work or job training, ordered a cutoff in benefits after two years for most recipients, and ended the financing of welfare for illegal aliens.

The new law was denounced by liberals as heartless and cheered by many Republican governors as overdue. Wisconsin Gov.

A heroin user shoots up. Longer sentences for drug use and for other crimes were a major factor in swelling the states' prison population in 1996 to a record 1.1 million and also in explaining why expenditures on corrections had become the fastest-growing item in state budgets.

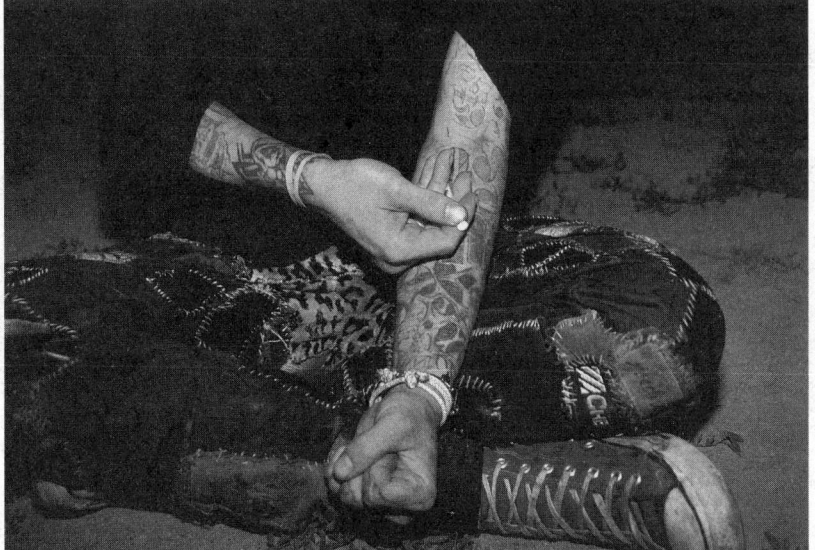

TODD YATES—BLACK STAR

CAROL GUZY—THE WASHINGTON POST

Children participate in a worship service at their church. A number of African-American churches in Southern states burned during the year in a continuing rash of fires, some of them arson, that prompted congressional hearings to determine if a civil rights conspiracy was behind the incidents.

Tommy Thompson announced in late 1996 that his state's welfare rolls had been cut in half during the previous four years after "Wisconsin Works," a state version of the federal law, was enacted.

In a controversial step designed to prevent the spread of AIDS, New York became the first state to require the mandatory testing of newborns for HIV. New York also joined Arizona, Nevada, Oregon, and Washington in requiring boxers to undergo HIV screening.

Reacting to advances in gene research, Illinois and New Jersey joined 13 other states in prohibiting health insurers and employers from discriminating on the basis of genetic findings.

The development of effective but expensive protease inhibitors threatened to exhaust state AIDS budgets during 1996. Federal rules required that all FDA-approved drugs be covered by Medicaid, with states picking up one-third of most program costs. States faced the funding shortage in a variety of ways, which included rationing and seeking additional legislative funding.

As a dozen states sued tobacco companies, seeking reimbursement for public health funds expended on tobacco-related illnesses, Massachusetts went farther; a new law there required the publication of the exact ingredients—from chocolate to ammonia—in each brand of cigarette, cigar, and chewing tobacco. In a corporate response that postponed enforcement, tobacco firms complained in a suit that the law would force them to reveal trade secrets.

Regulation of increasingly powerful health maintenance organizations (HMOs)

was argued in several states. Arizona and Wyoming became the first states to require the disclosure of HMO financial incentives with provider-doctors. Massachusetts enacted a law to prohibit HMOs from restricting communication between providers and patients. A number of states passed laws requiring insurance plans to cover a given minimum length of hospitalization for women giving birth. California voters, however, rejected two measures that would have imposed tough new HMO regulations.

Laws and Justice. States continued to wrestle with knotty end-of-life medical issues. Most states had enacted "advance-directive," or right-to-die, laws that allowed dying patients to order the withholding of heroic treatment. Iowa became the 34th state to explicitly prohibit suicide assistance by doctors. Two federal courts declared similar laws to be unconstitutional, and at the year's end the U.S. Supreme Court was preparing to address the issue.

Missouri adopted a new law that would keep repeat sexual offenders under lifetime parole by the corrections department. Voters in Arizona and California approved the medical use of marijuana, but the Clinton administration enjoined the measures as violating federal law.

A trend toward providing more rights for crime victims, including input into the sentencing of convicted criminals, continued during 1996. Voters in Connecticut, Indiana, Nevada, North Carolina, Oklahoma, Oregon, South Carolina, and Virginia approved new measures protecting crime victims.

Although courts continued to clear legal hurdles to capital punishment, only 45 con-

victs were executed by states during 1996, down from 56 the previous year. More than 200 persons were sentenced to death over the same period, and some 3,100 inmates were left on death row awaiting punishment at year-end.

Texas became the first state to employ neural network technology, which used electronic methods of recognizing suspicious patterns, to combat fraud in Medicaid claims. California voters rejected an initiative backed by trial lawyers that was designed to circumvent federal reforms in lawsuit abuse and to facilitate lawsuits for alleged securities fraud.

Ethics. Arkansas Gov. Jim Guy Tucker was convicted on two felony counts of conspiracy to defraud the Internal Revenue Service and other government agencies over cable television contracts. The charges had been brought by a federal independent counsel and grand jury investigating the Whitewater affair. Tucker, the 10th U.S. governor to be convicted of a crime in the 20th century, resigned his office.

The year produced few other major ethics scandals, although several legislatures grappled with a perception that special interests enjoyed inordinate influence over public processes. Continuing a trend, voters in California and Maine approved new limits on political campaign spending and contributions.

Prisons. States boosted corrections spending during 1996 by 6.8%, the fastest-growing category of state expenditures. The increase was made necessary by tougher anticrime laws, including "truth-in-sentencing" and "three-strikes" legislation.

Accelerated prison construction allowed the number of state prisoners to increase by 5.6% during the year, to a record 1.1 million.

The U.S. Supreme Court overturned an Arizona federal judge's ruling that would have required states to provide first-rate law libraries for inmates, including special help for illiterate and non-English-speaking prisoners.

Gambling. Michigan voters narrowly approved casino gambling for Detroit, but other pro-gambling ballot measures went down to defeat. Arkansas voters rejected a state lottery and casinos in Hot Springs; Nebraska voters said no to offtrack betting on horse races; Ohio turned down an initiative for riverboat casino gambling; and Washington voters defeated a proposal for electronic gambling on Indian lands.

In a victory for states rights, the U.S. Supreme Court effectively ruled that states did not have to negotiate with Indian tribes to establish casino gambling on reservations within their borders. In 1988 Congress had ordered states to allow reservation gaming where requested by Indian tribes, but in a case brought by Florida, the high court ruled that the 11th Amendment prohibited states from being sued to do so.

The Missouri Gaming Commission approved a novel plan aimed at protecting compulsive gamblers from themselves. After a gambler had registered as a "disassociated person," the gambler's photograph would be circulated to riverboat casinos. Casino employees were then required to escort the gambler off the premises immediately if he or she was recognized.

Environment. The Minnesota Senate approved a measure that would have established the nation's first constitutional right to hunt and fish, but the House failed to endorse it before adjourning. The proposed amendment was a response to antihunting and animal rights activists. After an animal-welfare group in New Jersey attempted to prosecute a man who had killed a rat in his garden, state legislators excluded rats and mice from protection under the state's animal cruelty laws.

Some 34 environmental initiatives and bond issues were decided by voters in 14 states in November. Voters in Florida rejected a "penny-a-pound" tax on sugarcane producers to combat water pollution in the Everglades. A billion-dollar environmental bond issue was approved in California, but an even larger bond issue for pollution cleanup was defeated in New York. Maine voters rejected a ban on timber clearcutting, but they voiced their approval of additional restrictions on logging operations.

Civil Rights. By a 54% to 46% margin, California voters approved a high-profile civil rights initiative that would eliminate state and local government affirmative action programs. Proposition 209 was stayed by a federal judge, however, following the November balloting. If enforced, the measure would end preferences based on race or sex in public hiring, the awarding of contracts, and college admissions.

A Hawaiian court ruled that the state had no legitimate interest in prohibiting same-sex marriages and set off a storm of controversy nationwide. States traditionally honoured other state determinations on such matters, but the U.S. Congress approved a "Defense of Marriage" measure, signed by the president, that allowed states to ignore same-sex marriages granted elsewhere.

A 1992 Colorado voter initiative prohibiting gays and lesbians from winning "any minority status, quota preferences, protected status or claim of discrimination" was struck down by the U.S. Supreme Court. The decision cast doubt on the legitimacy of numerous state laws that might discriminate on the basis of sexual orientation.

California approved a new law prohibiting gender-based differences in pricing for services such as haircuts and laundering. Citing a constitutional right to equality between the sexes, a Florida court struck down an 1895 law requiring a husband to pay for his wife's housing, food, clothing, and medical bills.

Consumer Protection. California moved to deregulate its electric utility industry, removing utilities' monopoly in power generation and allowing consumers eventually to choose their own power providers. The move was part of a nationwide trend, with, by year-end, some 47 states moving to reduce or eliminate such regulation.

Attempting to reduce expensive newspaper advertising, 20 states began listing the names of unclaimed-property owners on an Internet home page. Ohio became the 12th state to enact an agricultural disparagement, or "veggie-libel," law. The measure allowed farmers to sue critics who made false or degrading claims about their products.

Virginia approved a law preventing out-of-state telemarketers from pretending that they were locally based.

For the first time, the U.S. Supreme Court struck down the punitive damages verdict of a state court for being so "grossly excessive" as to violate the U.S. Constitution. The ruling overturned a $2 million award from an Alabama court to the buyer of a BMW who had not been notified that the paint on his supposedly new car had been touched up.   (DAVID C. BECKWITH)

Two women exchange marriage vows. A circuit court in Hawaii overturned that state's ban on same-sex marriages in December, but a number of other states had similar laws on their statute books, and still more states were considering such legislation.

CAROL GUZY—THE WASHINGTON POST

URUGUAY

A republic of eastern South America, Uruguay lies on the Atlantic Ocean. Area: 176,215 sq km (68,037 sq mi). Pop. (1996 est.): 3,140,000. Cap.: Montevideo. Monetary unit: peso uruguayo, with (Oct. 11, 1996) a free rate of 8.34 pesos uruguayos to U.S. $1 (13.13 pesos uruguayos = £1 sterling). President in 1996, Julio María Sanguinetti.

The Uruguayan legislature in October 1996 approved electoral reform abolishing the *ley de lemas,* which allowed political parties to combine the votes given to several candidates for the presidency and the legislature. Among new measures, each party had to select a single presidential candidate, and, if the winner did not gain a clear lead, there would have to be a runoff election. The National (Blanco) and Colorado parties supported the reform, but most of the Broad Front Party was opposed to a second election. Socialist, communist, and National Liberation Movement members of the Front maintained that as the third largest party, they could never field a candidate who could beat a Blanco/Colorado alignment in a runoff. The Front's leader, retired general Líber Seregni, had supported the full reform, however, and surprised his party by resigning over the issue at the party's 25th anniversary congress in February.

Admissions of human rights abuses during military rule in the 1970s revived demands for a full investigation. The armed forces responded in October by justifying its actions, refusing to admit guilt on the grounds that the matter had been closed by legislative amnesty and a referendum in the 1980s.   (BEN BOX)

UZBEKISTAN

A republic of Central Asia, Uzbekistan borders the Aral Sea to the north, Kazakstan to the north and west, Turkmenistan to the southwest, Afghanistan to the south, and Tajikistan and Kyrgyzstan to the east. Area: 447,400 sq km (172,700 sq mi). Pop. (1996 est.): 23,206,000. Cap.: Tashkent (Uzbek: Toshkent). Monetary unit: sum, with (Oct. 11, 1996) a free rate of 40.05 sumy to U.S. $1 (63.09 sumy = £1 sterling). President in 1996, Islam Karimov; prime minister, Otkir Sultonov.

Uzbekistan reaped the benefits in 1996 of policies that were far more responsive to Western concerns about human rights and the introduction of a market economy than had characterized the country in the first years of independence. In August Pres. Islam Karimov called on the parliament to adopt new legislation on human rights and admitted that human rights abuses had occurred in the past. The government's credibility was enhanced by the pardoning of a group of members of political opposition groups who had been sentenced to long prison terms and by the granting of permission for the Uzbek Human Rights Society to hold a conference in Tashkent in September. On his return to his homeland, the society's chairman, Abdumanob Pulatov, long an exile in the United States, spoke hopefully of the improved chances for the society to gain legal recognition.

Although Karimov said in January that he approved of the concept of a customs union of former Soviet states, he made it clear in April that Uzbekistan would not join the customs union of Kazakstan, Belarus, Kyrgyzstan, and the Russian Federation because it created a "bloc mentality" and limited the options of its members to look out for their national interests. Karimov was also critical of what he termed "the trend in the Commonwealth of Independent States" toward the creation of supranational bodies, such as the customs union, that he believed would undermine the independence of the CIS member states and cause Central Asia to revert to its old role in the U.S.S.R. as a supplier of raw materials to more developed areas.

Karimov underscored Uzbekistan's independent foreign policy with two major foreign visits in 1996. In April the president spent several days in France promoting trade and investment in Uzbekistan. Karimov's first official visit to the U.S. in late June was almost a triumphal progress, thanks in part to Uzbekistan's support of the U.S. embargo against Iran. Pres. Bill Clinton promised to help Uzbekistan establish strong ties with the West—Uzbekistan's top foreign policy priority—and achieve full integration in the world community. During the visit a number of oil and gas deals were signed with U.S. firms.   (BESS BROWN)

This article updates the *Macropædia* article CENTRAL ASIA: *Uzbekistan.*

VANUATU

The republic of Vanuatu, a member of the Commonwealth, comprises 12 main islands and some 60 smaller ones in the southwestern Pacific Ocean. Area: 12,190 sq km (4,707 sq mi). Pop. (1996 est.): 172,000. Cap.: Vila. Monetary unit: vatu, with (Oct. 11, 1996) a free rate of 111.01 vatu to U.S. $1 (174.87 vatu = £1 sterling). President in 1996, Jean-Marie Leye; prime ministers, Serge Vohor until February 8, Maxime Carlot Korman from February 23 to September 30, and, from September 30, Vohor.

Prime Minister Serge Vohor, who took power in December 1995, retained a majority for less than two months before resigning in February 1996 in anticipation of a vote of no confidence. Former prime minister Maxime Carlot Korman returned to office but was plagued by scandal. In July the ombudsman recommended a reprimand for Carlot. A further split within government ranks in September allowed Vohor to again become prime minister.

In August the Vanuatu Mobile Force (VMF), a paramilitary unit, went on strike over unpaid salary arrears totaling almost $1 million and in October briefly abducted Pres. Jean-Marie Leye before negotiating a settlement with the government. On November 12 the Vanuatu police arrested all VMF officers and did not release them until they had taken an oath of allegiance.
(BARRIE MACDONALD)

This article updates the *Macropædia* article PACIFIC ISLANDS: *Vanuatu.*

VATICAN CITY STATE

The independent sovereignty of Vatican City State is surrounded by but is not part of Rome. As a state with territorial limits, it is properly distinguished from the Holy See, which constitutes the worldwide administrative and legislative body for the Roman Catholic Church. Area: 44 ha (109 ac). Pop. (1996 est.): 850. As sovereign pontiff, John Paul II is the chief of state. Vatican City is administered by a pontifical commission of five cardinals headed by the secretary of state, in 1996 Angelo Cardinal Sodano.

News of the increasing numbers of Roman Catholic priests after more than 20 years of decline made 1996 a positive year for the Vatican City State. The finances of the Vatican also improved, which allowed Pope John Paul II a freer hand in conducting his worldwide apostolic mission.

The pope was active in pastoral visits to many parts of the world. In El Salvador he recalled the Vatican's role in helping to bring peace to that troubled country and stressed the Holy See's commitment to the socially disadvantaged.

(GREGORY O. SMITH)
See also RELIGION: *Roman Catholic Church.*

This article updates the *Micropædia* article VATICAN CITY.

VENEZUELA

A republic of northern South America, Venezuela lies on the Caribbean Sea. Area: 912,050 sq km (352,144 sq mi). Pop. (1996 est.): 22,311,000. Cap.: Caracas. Monetary unit: bolívar, with (Oct. 6, 1995) a free rate of 460 bolivares to U.S. $1 (268.75 bolivares = £1 sterling). President in 1996, Rafael Caldera.

In an address to the nation on April 15, 1996, Pres. Rafael Caldera announced a political U-turn for Venezuela, marking a decisive break with the interventionist policies he and his Cabinet had been following since he took office in January 1994. The initial phase of Venezuela's return to free-market policies was completed with a $1.4 billion standby loan from the International Monetary Fund (IMF), formally agreed to on July 12. An IMF team planned to visit the country every quarter to monitor progress. After their August visit they pledged to disburse the second part of the standby loan in October, which would amount to $225 million, the first installment of $500 million having been released in July.

Having implemented price and interest-rate controls and a fivefold increase in gasoline prices within one week (April 16–22), the government then faced more difficult challenges. The exchange rate set by the Brady Board Market rose to more than 500 bolivares to the dollar in the week before controls were lifted. As domestic interest rates increased following the removal of banking interest-rate limits, investors brought currency back into the country. This resulted in an appreciation of the exchange rate, which stabilized at 460–470 bolivares to the dollar. The exchange rate was allowed to float, with minimal official intervention.

The government was studying plans to increase transportation prices. It planned to maintain its subsidy to the poor and students for two years while the bus fleet was being converted to natural gas, a cheaper

A young man flees a burning barricade in Caracas, where students at the Central University of Venezuela held protests in June to demand that the government increase its funding for education. The demonstration ended in violence when police confronted the students.

fuel than gasoline. The new higher fares caused protests, which rekindled memories of the bloody riots of 1989 in response to increased fares. In early June six buses were firebombed in Caracas, and four people were killed. The government blamed subversive groups intent on destabilizing the country. A delay in wage bonuses promised in April and planned streamlining of the public-sector workforce resulted in a one-day strike on August 2. Unions threatened to strike unless the government addressed the 13,000 potential job losses after privatization of the aluminium, steel, and ferrosilicon industries.

Congress held extra sessions in late July to push through legislation before the August recess, approving the sale of 49% of the government's share in the national telecommunications utility. The legislature also passed two bills to stimulate Venezuelan capital markets. The first created an electronic settlement and clearance system to accelerate stock market transactions. The second strengthened the regulation of mutual and other investment funds, providing minimum capital requirement for investment funds (at least 20,000 tax units, or 54 million bolivares). The government hoped that these laws would also provide the framework for the introduction of private pension funds.

The oil sector was buoyant. In the first four months of 1996, production of crude oil, condensate, and liquid petroleum gas by the state oil company averaged 3,076,000 bbl per day, 7.1% higher than in 1995. With average prices for Venezuelan oil 12.9% above the 1995 levels, export earnings increased strongly.

Relations between Venezuela and Colombia continued to be tense following allegations by a Colombian National Security adviser that Venezuelan officials were trafficking arms to Colombian drug traders and guerrillas. A meeting between foreign ministers in August ended with a joint commitment to search for solutions to the problems of border security.

(ALAN MURPHY)

VIETNAM

The socialist republic of Vietnam occupies the eastern part of the Indochinese Peninsula in Southeast Asia and is bounded on the south and east by the South China Sea. Area: 331,041 sq km (127,816 sq mi). Pop. (1996 est.): 76,161,000. Cap.: Hanoi. Monetary unit: dong, with (Oct. 11, 1996) a free rate of 11,057 dong to U.S. $1 (17,418 dong = £1 sterling). President in 1996, Le Duc Anh; prime minister, Vo Van Kiet.

The political highlight of 1996 was the eighth National Congress of the Communist Party of Vietnam from June 28 to July 1. Held every five years, the party conference brought together top cadres and officials to consider policy and select leaders.

The 1996 gathering was preceded by intense speculation about the futures of the nation's top three leaders: Pres. Le Duc Anh, Communist Party General Secretary Do Muoi, and Prime Minister Vo Van Kiet. All in their 70s, the three were confirmed in their posts by the congress, despite talk that they would make way for younger figures. There were indications, however, that all three may step down before the next congress in 2001. In late November Anh was reported to be seriously ill.

The retention of the senior leadership eased investors' fears, which had been raised in April when the Communist Party's Central Committee released a report that called for an expanded government-operated sector of the economy that would generate 60% of gross domestic product by 2020. Already disillusioned by an overbearing bureaucracy that was slow to act, many investors were stung by the implications of the report, which left them wondering whether the reform movement was in jeopardy. At the party congress the final draft was watered down, and the 60% state-sector goal was dropped. The "state capitalist economy," which included joint ventures with foreign companies, was moved from fifth to third position on the list of priority sectors of the economy.

Perhaps the most welcome news to investors was that Kiet remained in power. The leading southerner in the top echelon of government, he was widely regarded as the prime mover of the economic reforms. Political jockeying among reformists and conservatives resulted in the dismissal of the army chief of staff, Gen. Dao Dinh Luyen, which was announced in January, and of Politburo member Nguyen Ha Phan, which was announced two months before the party congress. Infighting among the leadership took place amid a government campaign against "social evils" such as alcoholism, "cultural pollution," and even advertising.

The showdown at the congress resulted in a seemingly balanced 19-seat Politburo. The goal was clearly to bring in younger

A Vietnamese policeman questions one of a number of people surrendering videotapes containing pornographic or violent material. In February the government began a campaign against "social evils," including prostitution, drug use, gambling, and pornography.

people. Eight new members were included in the powerful policy-making body, and there were also a number of key promotions. Nong Duc Manh, the National Assembly chairman and a political moderate, rose from the 10th position in the government to the 4th, directly behind Kiet. Deputy Prime Minister Phan Van Khai, a Kiet protégé, rose to seventh.

The National Assembly passed amendments to the foreign investment law in an attempt to reverse the downturn in investor interest. The first half of 1996 saw a decline of about 20% in overseas investment from the same period a year earlier. Nonetheless, Vietnam's economy roared ahead, with growth of over 9%. Inflation moderated to just 3%.

In the international arena, the once-closed nation continued to expand its links with the outside world. In March Kiet visited Cambodia to cool a border dispute. Vietnam completed its first year as a member of the Association of Southeast Asian Nations, serving as host of ASEAN meetings and participating in the July ministerial conference and the November informal summit in Indonesia. U.S. Pres. Bill Clinton in May nominated Douglas Peterson, a former prisoner of war in Vietnam, to be the first U.S. ambassador to Hanoi since the North Vietnamese army took over the U.S. embassy in Saigon in 1975.

(ALEJANDRO REYES)

This article updates the *Macropædia* article SOUTHEAST ASIA: *Vietnam.*

WESTERN SAMOA

A constitutional monarchy and member of the Commonwealth, Western Samoa occupies an island group in the South Pacific Ocean. Area: 2,831 sq km (1,093 sq mi). Pop. (1996 est.): 167,000. Cap.: Apia. Monetary unit: Western Samoa tala, with (Oct. 11, 1996) a free rate of 2.44 tala to U.S. $1 (3.84 tala = £1 sterling). Head of state (*O le Ao o le Malo*) in 1996, Malietoa Tanumafili II; prime minister, Tofilau Eti Alesana.

In the April 1996 elections, there was a swing against the Human Rights Protection Party government of Prime Minister Tofilau Eti Alesana. The government survived, but three Cabinet ministers and the speaker lost their seats. (For detailed election results, see *Political Parties,* above.) With the support of independents, Alesana retained the prime ministership by 34 votes to 14. Issues that had told against the government included the introduction of a value-added goods and services tax and a 15% cut in public service expenditure to bail out the financially troubled and mismanaged Polynesian Airlines.   (BARRIE MACDONALD)

This article updates the *Macropædia* article PACIFIC ISLANDS: *Western Samoa.*

YEMEN

A republic of the southwestern Arabian Peninsula, Yemen has coastlines on the Red Sea, the Gulf of Aden, and the Arabian Sea. Area: 555,000 sq km (214,300 sq mi), including the undemarcated area bordered by Saudi Arabia and claimed by Yemen. Pop. (1996 est.): 16.6 million. Cap.: San'a'. Monetary unit: Yemen Rial, with (Oct. 11, 1996) a free rate of

YRls 100 to U.S. $1 (YRls 157.53 = £1 sterling). President in 1996, Maj. Gen. Ali Abdallah Salih; prime minister, 'Abd al-Aziz 'Abd al-Ghani.

Yemen and Saudi Arabia sought to improve their bilateral relations in 1996 with a series of high-level visits, but fundamental suspicions and border issues remained. Meanwhile, a confrontation with Eritrea broke out when Eritrean forces captured the Red Sea island of Greater Hanish in four days of fighting in mid-December 1995 that resulted in 16 casualties and some 160 captured Yemeni soldiers. Eritrea released the soldiers, but the sovereignty dispute continued, and Eritrea expelled the Yemeni ambassador in January. Egyptian Pres. Hosni Mubarak personally engaged in mediation of the dispute, and in March the two governments agreed to international mediation. By the year's end, however, the key issues had not been entirely resolved.

Sporadic tribal unrest continued. In January 1996 one tribe kidnapped 17 French tourists in retaliation for the arrest of one of their tribesmen for a 1995 abduction of an American.   (WILLIAM A. RUGH)

This article updates the *Macropædia* article ARABIA: *Yemen.*

YUGOSLAVIA

A federal republic comprising the republics of Serbia and Montenegro, Yugoslavia borders Hungary to the north, Romania to the northeast, Bulgaria to the southeast, Macedonia and Albania to the south, the Adriatic Sea to the southwest, and Croatia and Bosnia and Herzegovina to the west. Area: 102,173 sq km (39,449 sq mi). Pop. (1996 est.): 10,473,000. Cap.: Belgrade. Monetary unit: new dinar, with (Oct. 11, 1996) a free rate of 5.06 new dinars = U.S. $1 (7.97 new dinars = £1 sterling). President in 1996, Zoran Lilic; prime minister, Radoje Kontic.

The pivotal point in Yugoslav politics in 1996—and possibly for the career of Ser-

bian Pres. Slobodan Milosevic, came on November 17, when local elections were held. Surprisingly, in the elections Milosevic's ruling Socialists lost majorities to the centrist-right opposition alliance Zajedno ("Together") in at least 14 of the country's 18 largest cities, including the capital, Belgrade.

Devastated by international trade sanctions, years of mismanagement, failure to institute privatization, and halfhearted approaches to reform, the economy showed only slight signs of improvement during the year. Nearly one-third of the population was still unemployed, according to September 1996 figures, though the average annual wage reached $141, almost double the amount of a year earlier. Gross national product in 1996 was projected to be slightly higher than the 1995 total of $7.7 billion. Agriculture also continued to languish.

On May 8 an estimated 10,000 workers from the Nis Electronics Industry, one of the largest firms in Yugoslavia, went on strike, and in September–October the country's largest armaments and munitions manufacturer, in Kragujevac, was the scene of a strike involving 15,000 workers. With elections approaching, the opposition leaders backed the workers, and the government was obliged to meet most of their demands.

It was not at all certain, however, that the workers would support Zajedno at the polls. In fact, the opposition was given only the slimmest chance of winning. Early in the campaign Dragoslav Avramovic stepped down as Zajedno leader, and the alliance suffered from its inability to enunciate a clear political strategy and from a lack of access to the state-controlled mass media.

Nonetheless, by November 19 it was clear that the opposition had won in at least 32 municipalities and had swept a majority of the seats in the Belgrade city council. Jubilant demonstrations followed. The government, however, citing vague electoral "irregularities," announced that it would annul the election results and hold a third round.

Carrying a portrait of Vuk Draskovic, a leader of the opposition coalition Zajedno ("Together"), protesters march in Belgrade to denounce Serbian Pres. Slobodan Milosevic. When his opponents won a number of races in the November 17 elections, Milosevic annulled the results.

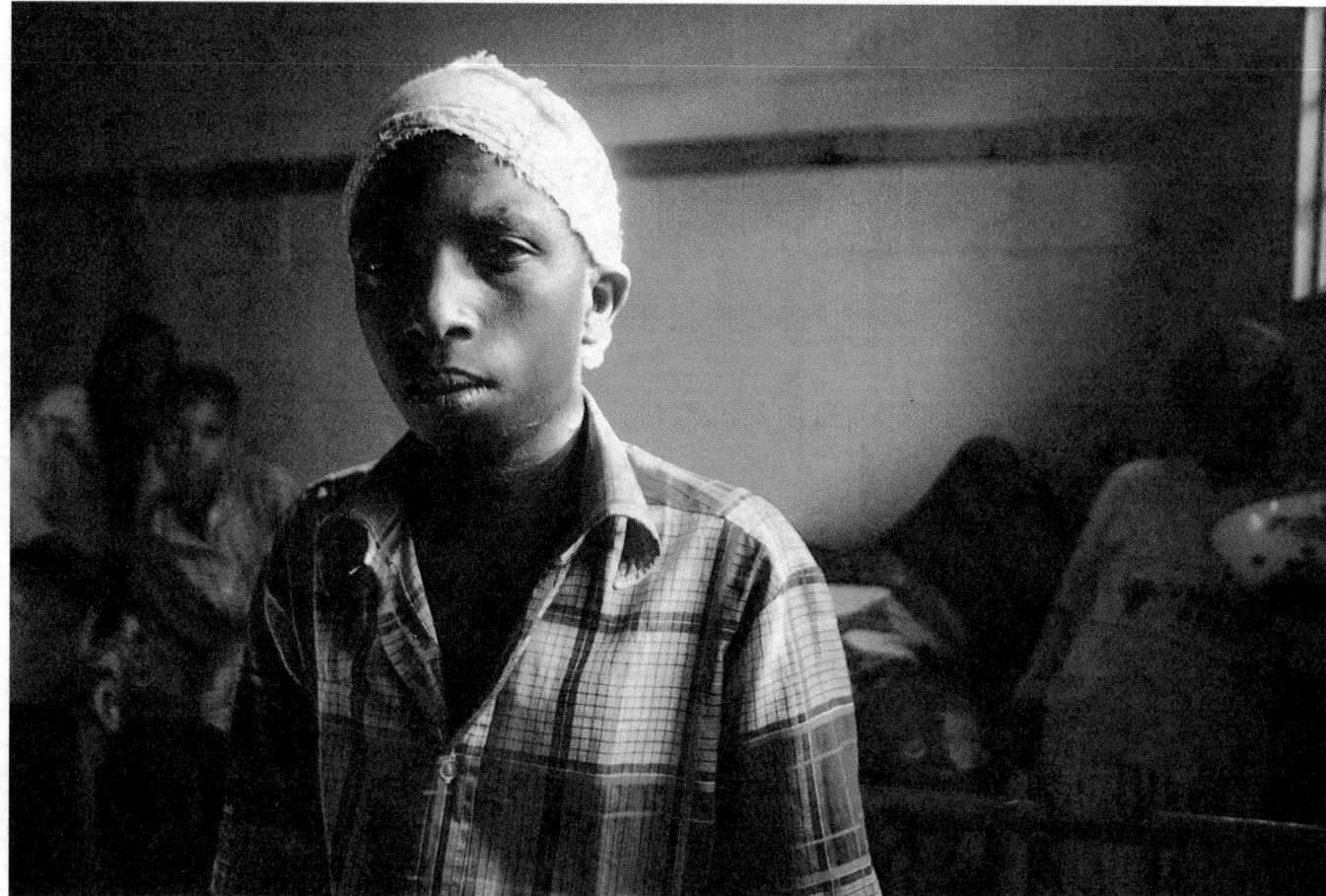

A Tutsi recovers from machete wounds received in a Hutu raid in eastern Zaire. Fighting between Hutu refugees from Rwanda and native Tutsi in Zaire's North Kivu province erupted into a civil war in which tens of thousands were killed and hundreds of thousands driven from their homes.

Protesting the government's action, the crowds began gathering daily, growing in size to as many as 200,000 by mid-December. Opposition deputies walked out of the federal parliament on December 10 and joined the demonstrators, and there were rumours that some military units were sympathetic to Zajedno as well.

Significantly, except in Nis, Serbia's second largest city, the demonstrators were not joined by the workers. Although riot police began to be sent in on December 24, at the same time that Milosevic supporters were bused into central Belgrade for a counterdemonstration, a violent government crackdown never materialized. The one notable episode of violence took place that same day; 58 people were injured, one later dying of gunshot wounds. Milosevic banned demonstrations from December 25 onward, but they were still occurring at the year's end.

On December 27 a mission from the Organization for Security and Cooperation in Europe led by former Spanish prime minister Felipe González Márquez publicly warned the Serbian strongman that he should accede to the election results. Milosevic's isolation at home and internationally deepened as Montenegro, the second constituent republic of Yugoslavia, too sought to distance itself from the events in Serbia.

Some small progress was made in resolving Serbia's differences with its predominantly ethnic Albanian province of Kosovo. Milosevic and Ibrahim Rugova, president

of the self-styled shadow government of the Republic of Kosovo, signed an agreement on September 1 calling for the reintegration of Kosovo schools and the return of some 300,000 Albanian children to classes. The agreement was hailed as the first major breakthrough in normalizing relations between Serbs and Albanians in the region.

Yugoslavia established full diplomatic relations with Macedonia in April, initiated bilateral ties with Croatia in August, and agreed with Bosnia and Herzegovina on inaugurating diplomatic relations in October.

(MILAN ANDREJEVICH)

This article updates the *Macropædia* article BALKAN STATES: *Yugoslavia.*

ZAIRE

The republic of Zaire is located in central Africa with a short coastline on the Atlantic Ocean. Area: 2,344,858 sq km (905,-354 sq mi). Pop. (1996 est.): 45,259,000 (excluding 500,000 Rwandan refugees). Cap.: Kinshasa. Monetary unit: new zaïre, with (Oct. 11, 1996) a free rate of 67,004 new zaïres to U.S. $1 (105,551 new zaïres = £1 sterling). President in 1996, Mobutu Sese Seko; first state commissioner (prime minister), Léon Kengo wa Dondo.

Government proposals for changes in the constitution, to be followed by presidential and legislative elections, met in 1996 with objections from part of the opposition coalition. The draft constitution, which provided

for a federal state with 26 instead of the original 11 provinces and a semipresidential parliamentary regime, was adopted by the Cabinet in May and by the High Council of the Republic-Transitional Parliament in October and was to be the subject of a referendum in December (later postponed until February 1997). Candidates for presidential and parliamentary office would then be registered, and elections would follow by July 1997. The leader of the opposition coalition, Étienne Tshisekedi, who regarded the existing government as unlawful, came into conflict with a section of his own supporters in May when he refused to agree to the proposed elections. His critics, who considered Tshisekedi's attitude unreasonable, appointed his deputy, Frédéric Kibassa-Maliba, in his place. Undaunted, Tshisekedi organized a protest calling for the resignation of the prime minister, Léon Kengo wa Dondo, in July and then rejected the new draft constitution in October.

With the opposition in some disarray, Pres. Mobutu Sese Seko's position should have been strengthened. An operation for prostate cancer, however, which took place in Switzerland in August, left the president's position in serious doubt. Yet even among those who longed for his overthrow, there was some anxiety lest there be no one else who could hold the country together.

The mineral-rich regions of Shaba (formerly Katanga) and Kasai, the source of Zaire's diamonds, were already exercising a measure of autonomy, but fears for the country's unity were more seriously roused by a rebellion in the eastern district of Kivu. Early in the year the government had made a weak attempt to encourage the Hutu refugees, more than a million in number, who had crossed the border from Rwanda into Kivu province in 1994, to return home. The effort came to nothing because the sympathies of the government lay with the Hutu, even though their presence was imposing an unbearable burden on the inhabitants and resources of the eastern region. In any event, the Hutu guerrilla leaders and their forces, who had been responsible for the massacre of hundreds of thousands of Tutsi in Rwanda, lived among the refugees and discouraged them from returning home.

At the same time, the refugees launched a campaign to drive some thousands of Tutsi, who had lived in Zaire for many years, over the border into Rwanda so that they themselves could settle permanently in the fertile Masisi region of northern Kivu. After some early success the Hutu turned their attention to southern Kivu, and the Banyamulenge, people of Tutsi descent who had inhabited the region for 200 years, began to arm in order to defend themselves. When in early October the deputy governor of southern Kivu told the Banyamulenge to leave or to be treated as rebels, the latter opened their campaign and quickly seized the town of Bukavu. Farther north other Tutsi turned on their attackers and captured the town of Goma.

Parliament responded by ordering that all ethnic Tutsi be expelled from the army, civil service, and state-owned companies, and a large mob attacked and looted Tutsi-owned property in Kinshasa. In Kivu the Hutu refugees and the Zairean army retired before the Tutsi advance, leaving the plight of the refugees more desperate than before the fighting began. Many began returning to Rwanda. (KENNETH INGHAM)

This article updates the *Macropædia* article CENTRAL AFRICA: *Zaire.*

ZAMBIA

A landlocked republic and member of the Commonwealth, Zambia is in eastern Africa. Area: 752,614 sq km (290,586 sq mi). Pop. (1996 est.): 9,715,000. Cap.: Lusaka. Monetary unit: kwacha, with (Oct. 11, 1996) a free rate of 1,265 kwacha to U.S. $1 (1,993 kwacha = £1 sterling). President in 1996, Frederick Chiluba.

Zambia began 1996 cheered by the December 1995 offer of substantial support from its external aid partners provided it maintained the momentum it had achieved in its management of the economy and its privatization program. In March the nation's Paris Club creditors took the further step of writing off 67% of the debt owed to them. Donor confidence was shaken in May, however, when the constitution was amended to prevent former president Kenneth Kaunda from running for reelection.

Creditors were also becoming concerned by evidence of increased corruption and by the delay in privatizing the copper-mining industry. In response to the latter charge, the privatization agency announced in August that Feb. 28, 1997, had been fixed as the date for receiving bids for the purchase of Zambia Consolidated Copper Mines.

Pres. Robert Mugabe addresses supporters at a rally in Zimbabwe's capital of Harare before the March election. His two opponents attempted to withdraw from the election, and fewer than one-third of those eligible voted, but Mugabe won another six-year term.

On the political front, Pres. Frederick Chiluba held meetings with opposition party leaders to try to deal with their criticisms of the forthcoming electoral system. Kaunda, the leader of the main opposition party, continued to threaten a boycott of the national elections if he was not allowed to be a candidate. In the parliamentary elections on November 18 President Chiluba's Movement for Multiparty Democracy won an overwhelming victory, gaining at least 127 of the 150 seats in the National Assembly.

In August eight members of Kaunda's party, including deputy party leader Inyambo Yeta, were put on trial on charges of treason. This did nothing to reduce the tension between political rivals, although two of the accused were soon conditionally released. Nor did the impending trial of two journalists, whose sentence of indefinite imprisonment by the speaker of the National Assembly had been overruled by the Supreme Court, enhance the government's reputation for upholding free speech.

(KENNETH INGHAM)

This article updates the *Macropædia* article SOUTHERN AFRICA: *Zambia.*

ZIMBABWE

A republic and member of the Commonwealth, Zimbabwe is a landlocked state in eastern Africa. Area: 390,757 sq km (150,872 sq mi). Pop. (1996 est.): 11,515,000. Cap.: Harare. Monetary unit: Zimbabwe dollar, with (Oct. 11, 1996) a free rate of Z$10.52 to U.S. $1 (Z$16.56 = £1 sterling). President in 1996, Robert Mugabe.

Robert Mugabe was reelected president of Zimbabwe for a six-year term in March 1996. His victory was marred by the fact that his two opponents attempted to withdraw from the contest only a few days before the election and because less than a third of the electorate took the trouble to vote. He nevertheless celebrated his success by promising to seize 23 white-owned farms for redistribution to blacks. He said

that unless Britain made money available to compensate the existing owners, his plan would go ahead without reimbursement because the government did not have the money with which to pay the farmers.

Herbert Murerwa, who became minister of finance in May, lacked the background in economics and business to arouse public confidence in his appointment, and government finance remained in a perilous condition in spite of a satisfactory rise in production in several important fields. Tobacco, the country's main foreign exchange earner, fetched prices nearly 40% higher than in 1995, while gold output in 1995 was the highest since 1916. Industrial share prices were up 80% in 1996. On the other hand, heavy losses were sustained in the state-owned enterprises, and inflation remained above 20%.

In August the civil service went on strike after being offered salary increases of only up to 9%, average real wages for civil servants having fallen 40% since 1990. The government, confident that an unemployment rate of 30% of the workforce would strengthen its negotiating position, served dismissal notices on 7,000 strikers but, faced with the threat of a general strike, backed down and offered an additional 20% increase. Nevertheless, the civil servants returned to work only when it had been agreed that those dismissed would be reinstated.

Trade relations with South Africa improved in August after many months during which Zimbabwe had argued that the tariffs its neighbour had imposed to avert the threat of competition from East Asia should be waived in its favour. The restrictions had weighed heavily upon Zimbabwe. Although final details were to be hammered out later, it was agreed in principle that South Africa would reduce its 90% tariff on Zimbabwean textiles to approximately 30%. A working group would also consider ways of reducing tariffs on other products.

(KENNETH INGHAM)

This article updates the *Macropædia* article SOUTHERN AFRICA: *Zimbabwe.*

Major New Revisions
from *Encyclopædia Britannica*

This section of the *Britannica Book of the Year* consists of articles or parts of articles that have recently been revised or rewritten for publication in the 1997 edition of *Encyclopædia Britannica* and have also been incorporated in *Britannica Online*™, an electronic version of the encyclopædia. The articles appearing here have been chosen by the yearbook editors for their general interest or their timeliness.

The selection from the article ENGLISH LITERATURE has been revised to include noteworthy new works of fiction, poetry, and drama. TELECOMMUNICATIONS SYSTEMS has been updated to describe recent devel-

opments in radiotelephones, videotelephones, modems, and facsimile transmission. The recent history of modern Turkey has been revised and selected from the article TURKEY AND ANCIENT ANATOLIA.

Subscribers desiring update sheets to put in their encyclopaedia to indicate that an article has been revised or added and owners of older sets wishing information about the exact articles being replaced by the reprints should address their requests to Britannica Home Library Service, Encyclopædia Britannica, Inc., 310 South Michigan Avenue, Chicago IL 60604. There is no charge for the article update sheets.

English Literature

LITERATURE AFTER 1945

Increased attachment to religion most immediately characterized literature after World War II. This was particularly perceptible in authors who had already established themselves before the war. W.H. Auden turned from Marxist politics to Christian commitment, expressed in poems that attractively combine classical form with vernacular relaxedness. Christian belief suffused the verse plays of T.S. Eliot and Christopher Fry. While Graham Greene continued the powerful merging of thriller plots with studies of moral and psychological ambiguity that he had developed through the 1930s, his Roman Catholicism loomed especially large in novels such as *The Heart of the Matter* (1948) and *The End of the Affair* (1951). Evelyn Waugh's *Brideshead Revisited* (1945) and his *Sword of Honour* trilogy (1965; published separately as *Men at Arms* [1952], *Officers and Gentlemen* [1955], and *Unconditional Surrender* [1961]) venerate Roman Catholicism as the repository of values seen as under threat from the advance of democracy. Less traditional spiritual solace was found in Eastern mysticism by Aldous Huxley and Christopher Isherwood.

Fiction. The two most innovatory novelists to begin their careers soon after World War II were also religious believers—William Golding and Muriel Spark. In novels of poetic compactness they frequently return to the notion of original sin—the idea that, in Golding's words, "man produces evil as a bee produces honey." Concentrating on small communities, Spark and Golding transfigure them into microcosms. Allegory and symbol set wide resonances quivering, so that short books make large statements. In Golding's first novel, *Lord of the Flies* (1954), schoolboys cast away on a Pacific island during a nuclear war reenact humanity's fall from grace as their relationships degenerate from innocent camaraderie to totalitarian butchery. In Spark's satiric comedy similar assumptions and techniques are discernible. Her best-known novel, *The Prime of Miss Jean Brodie* (1961), for example, makes events in a 1930s Edinburgh classroom replicate, in miniature, the rise of fascism in Europe.

In form and atmosphere *Lord of the Flies* has affinities with George Orwell's examinations of totalitarian nightmare, the fable *Animal Farm* (1945) and the novel

Golding
and Spark

Nineteen Eighty-four (1949). Spark's astringent portrayal of behaviour in confined little worlds is partly indebted to Dame Ivy Compton-Burnett, who, from the 1920s to the 1970s, produced a remarkable series of fierce but decorous novels, written almost entirely in mordantly witty dialogue, that dramatize tyranny and power struggles in secluded late Victorian households. The stylized novels of Henry Green, such as *Concluding* (1948) or *Nothing* (1950), also seem to be precursors of the terse, compressed fiction that Spark and Golding brought to such distinction. This kind of fiction, it was argued by Iris Murdoch, a philosopher as well as a novelist, ran antiliberal risks in its preference for allegory, pattern, and symbol over the social capaciousness and realistic rendition of character at which the great 19th-century novels excelled. Murdoch's own fiction, typically engaged with themes of goodness, authenticity, selfishness, and altruism, oscillates between these two modes of writing. *A Severed Head* (1961) is the most incisive and entertaining of her elaborately artificial works; *The Bell* (1958) best achieves the psychological and emotional complexity she finds so valuable in classic 19th-century fiction.

While restricting themselves to socially limited canvases, novelists such as Elizabeth Bowen, Elizabeth Taylor, and Barbara Pym continued the tradition of depicting emotional and psychological nuance. In contrast to their wry comedies of sense and sensibility, and to the packed parables of Golding and Spark, was yet another type of fiction, produced by a group of writers who became known as the Angry Young Men. From authors such as John Braine, John Wain, Alan Sillitoe, Stan Barstow, and David Storey (also a significant dramatist) came a spate of novels often ruggedly autobiographical in origin and near documentary in approach. The predominant subject of these books was social mobility, usually from the northern working class to the southern middle class. Social mobility was also inspected, from an upper-class vantage point, in Anthony Powell's 12-novel sequence *A Dance to the Music of Time* (1951–75), an attempt to apply the French novelist Marcel Proust's mix of irony, melancholy, meditativeness, and social detail to a chronicle of class and cultural shifts in England from World War I to the 1960s. Satiric watchfulness of social change was also the specialty

The Angry
Young
Men

of Kingsley Amis, whose deriding of the reactionary and pompous in his first novel, *Lucky Jim* (1954), led to his being labeled an Angry Young Man. As Amis grew older, though, his irascibility vehemently swiveled toward left-wing and progressive targets, and he established himself as a Tory satirist in the vein of Waugh or Powell. C.P. Snow's earnest 11-novel sequence, *Strangers and Brothers* (1940–70), about a man's journey from the provincial lower classes to London's "corridors of power," had its admirers. But the most inspired fictional cavalcade of social and cultural life in 20th-century Britain was Angus Wilson's *No Laughing Matter* (1967), a book that set a triumphant seal on his progress from a writer of acidic short stories to a major novelist whose work unites 19th-century breadth and gusto with 20th-century formal versatility and experiment.

The parody and pastiche that Wilson brilliantly deploys in *No Laughing Matter* and the book's fascination with the sources and resources of creativity constitute a rich, imaginative response to what had become a mood of growing self-consciousness in fiction. Thoughtfulness about the form of the novel and relationships between past and present fiction showed itself most stimulatingly in the works—generally campus novels—of the academically based novelists Malcolm Bradbury and David Lodge.

From the late 1960s onward the outstanding trend in fiction was enthrallment with empire. The first phase of this focused on imperial disillusion and dissolution. In his vast, detailed *Raj Quartet* (*The Jewel in the Crown* [1966], *The Day of the Scorpion* [1968], *The Towers of Silence* [1971], and *A Division of the Spoils* [1975]) Paul Scott charts the last years of the British in India; he followed it with *Staying On* (1977), a poignant comedy about those who remained after independence. Three half satiric, half elegiac novels by J.G. Farrell (*Troubles* [1970], *The Siege of Krishnapur* [1973], and *The Singapore Grip* [1978]) likewise spotlighted imperial discomfiture. Then, **Post-** in the 1980s, postcolonial voices made themselves audible. **colonial** Salman Rushdie's crowded comic saga about the gener- **voices** ation born as Indian independence dawned, *Midnight's Children* (1981), boisterously mingles material from Eastern fable, Hindu myth, Islāmic lore, Bombay cinema, cartoon strips, advertising billboards, and Latin American magic realism. For Rushdie, as *Shame* (1983) and *The Satanic Verses* (1988) further demonstrate, stylistic miscellaneousness—a way of writing that exhibits the vitalizing effects of cultural cross-fertilization—is especially suited to conveying postcolonial experience. (*The Satanic Verses* was understood differently in the Islāmic world, to the extent that the Iranian leader Ayatollah Ruhollah Khomeini pronounced a *fātwa*, in effect a death sentence, on Rushdie.) However, not all postcolonial authors followed his example. Vikram Seth's massive novel about India after independence, *A Suitable Boy* (1993), is a prodigious feat of realism, resembling 19th-century masterpieces in its combination of social breadth and emotional and psychological depth. Nor was India alone in inspiring vigorous postcolonial writing. Timothy Mo's novels report on colonial predicaments in East Asia with a political acumen reminiscent of Conrad. Particularly notable is *An Insular Possession* (1986), which vividly harks back to the founding of Hong Kong. Kazuo Ishiguro's spare, refined novel *An Artist of the Floating World* (1986) records how a painter's life and work became insidiously coarsened by the imperialistic ethos of 1930s Japan. Novelists such as Buchi Emecheta and Ben Okri wrote of postcolonial Africa, as did V.S. Naipaul in his most ambitious novel, *A Bend in the River* (1979). Nearer England, the strife in Northern Ireland provoked fictional response, among which the bleak, graceful novels and short stories of William Trevor and Bernard MacLaverty stand out.

Widening social divides in 1980s Britain were also registered in fiction, sometimes in works that purposefully imitate the Victorian "Condition of England" novel (the best is David Lodge's elegant, ironic *Nice Work* [1988]). The most thoroughgoing of such "Two Nations" panoramas of an England cleft by regional gulfs and gross inequities between rich and poor is Margaret Drabble's *The Radiant Way* (1987). With less documentary substantiality, Martin

Amis' novels, angled somewhere between scabrous relish and satiric disgust, offer prose that has the lurid energy of a strobe light playing over vistas of urban sleaze, greed, and debasement. *Money* (1984) is the most effectively focused of his books.

Just as some postcolonial novelists used myth, magic, and fable as a stylistic throwing-off of what they considered the alien supremacy of Anglo-Saxon realistic fiction, so numerous feminist novelists took to Gothic, fairy tale, **Feminist** and fantasy as countereffects to the "patriarchal discourse" **novelists** of rationality, logic, and linear narrative. The most gifted exponent of this kind of writing, which sought immediate access to the realm of the subconscious, was Angela Carter, whose exotic and erotic imagination unrolled most eerily and resplendently in her short-story collection *The Bloody Chamber and Other Stories* (1979). Jeanette Winterson also wrote in this vein. Having distinguished herself earlier in a realistic mode, as did authors such as Drabble and Pat Barker, Doris Lessing published a sequence of science fiction novels about issues of gender and colonialism, *Canopus in Argos—Archives* (1979–83).

Typically, though, fiction in the 1980s and '90s was not futuristic but retrospective. As the end of the century approached, an urge to look back—at starting points, previous eras, fictional prototypes—was widely evident. Many novels juxtaposed a present-day narrative with one set in the past. A.S. Byatt's *Possession* (1990) did so with particular intelligence. It also made extensive use of period pastiche, another enthusiasm of novelists toward the end of the 20th century. Adam Thorpe's striking first novel, *Ulverton* (1992), records the 300-year history of a fictional village in the styles of different epochs. William Golding's veteran fictional career came to a bravura conclusion with a trilogy whose story is told by an early 19th-century narrator (*To the Ends of the Earth* [1991]; published separately as *Rites of Passage* [1980], *Close Quarters* [1987], and *Fire Down Below* [1989]). In addition to the interest in remote and recent history, a concern with tracing aftereffects became dominatingly present in fiction. Most subtly and powerfully exhibiting this, Ian McEwan—who came to notice in the 1970s as an unnervingly emotionless observer of contemporary decadence—grew into imaginative maturity with novels largely set in Berlin in the 1950s (*The Innocent* [1990]) and in Europe in 1946 (*Black Dogs* [1992]). Their scenes of the 1990s were haunted by what were perceived as the continuing repercussions of World War II.

Poetry. The last flickerings of New Apocalypse poetry—the flamboyant, surreal, and rhetorical style favoured by Dylan Thomas, George Barker, David Gascoyne, and Vernon Watkins—died away soon after World War II. In its place emerged what came to be known with characteristic understatement as The Movement. Poets such as D.J. En- **The** right, Donald Davie, John Wain, Roy Fuller, Robert Con- **Movement** quest, and Elizabeth Jennings produced urbane, formally disciplined verse in an antiromantic vein characterized by irony, understatement, and a sardonic refusal to strike attitudes or make grand claims for the poet's role. The preeminent practitioner of this style was Philip Larkin. In Larkin's poetry (*The Less Deceived* [1955], *The Whitsun Weddings* [1964], *High Windows* [1974]) a melancholy sense of life's limitations throbs through lines of elegiac elegance. Suffused with acute awareness of mortality and transience, Larkin's poetry is also finely responsive to natural beauty, vistas of which open up even in poems darkened by fear of death or sombre preoccupation with human solitude. John Betjeman, poet laureate from 1972 to 1984, shared both Larkin's intense consciousness of mortality and his gracefully versified nostalgia for 19th- and early 20th-century life.

In contrast to the rueful traditionalism of their work is the poetry of Ted Hughes, who succeeded Betjeman as poet laureate in 1984. In extraordinarily vigorous verse, beginning with his first collection, *The Hawk in the Rain* (1957), Hughes captures the ferocity, vitality, and splendour of the natural world. In works such as *Crow* (1970) he adds a mythic dimension to his fascination with savagery (a fascination also apparent in the poetry Thom Gunn produced through the late 1950s and '60s). Much of Hughes's poetry is rooted in his experiences as a farmer in Yorkshire and Devon (as in his collection *Moortown* [1979]). It also shows a deep receptivity to the way the contemporary world is underlain by strata of history. This realization, along with strong regional roots, is something Hughes had in common with a number of poets writing in the second half of the 20th century. The work of Geoffrey Hill (especially *King Log* [1968], *Mercian Hymns* [1971], and *Tenebrae* [1978]) treats Britain as a palimpsest whose superimposed layers of history are uncovered in poems, which are sometimes written in prose. Basil Bunting's *Briggflatts* (1966) celebrates his native Northumbria. The dour poems of R.S. Thomas commemorate a harsh rural Wales of remote hill farms where gnarled, inbred celibates scratch a subsistence from the thin soil.

Britain's industrial regions received attention in poetry, too. In collections such as *Terry Street* (1969) Douglas Dunn wrote of working-class life in northeastern England. Tony Harrison, the most arresting English poet to find his voice in the later decades of the 20th century (*The Loiners* [1970], *From the School of Eloquence and Other Poems* [1978], *Continuous* [1981]), came, as he stresses, from a working-class community in industrial Yorkshire. Harrison's social and cultural journey away from that world by means of a grammar school education and a degree in classics provoked responses in him that his poetry conveys with imaginative vehemence and caustic wit: anger at the deprivations and humiliations endured by the working class; guilt over the way his talent had lifted him away from these. Trenchantly combining colloquial ruggedness with classic form, Harrison's poetry kept up a fiercely original and socially concerned commentary on such themes as inner-city dereliction (*V* [1985]) and the horrors of warfare (*The Gaze of the Gorgon* [1992]).

Also from Yorkshire was Blake Morrison, whose finest work, *The Ballad of the Yorkshire Ripper* (1987), was composed in taut, macabre stanzas thickened with dialect. Morrison's work also displayed a growing development in late 20th-century British poetry: the writing of narrative verse. Although there had been earlier instances of this verse after 1945 (John Betjeman's blank-verse autobiography *Summoned by Bells* [1960] proved the most popular), it was in the 1980s and '90s that the form was given renewed prominence by poets such as the Kipling-influenced James Fenton. An especially ambitious exercise in the narrative genre was Craig Raine's *History: The Home Movie* (1994), a huge semifictionalized saga, written in three-line stanzas, chronicling several generations of his own and his wife's families. Before this, three books of dazzling virtuosity (*The Onion, Memory* [1978], *A Martian Sends a Postcard Home* [1979], and *Rich* [1984]) established Raine as the founder, and most inventive exemplar, of what came to be called the Martian school of poetry. The defining characteristic of this school was a poetry rife with startling images, unexpected but audaciously apt similes, and rapid, imaginative tricks of transformation that set the reader looking at the world afresh.

From the late 1960s onward Northern Ireland, convulsed by sectarian violence, was particularly prolific in poetry. From a cluster of considerable talents—Michael Longley, Derek Mahon, Medbh McGuckian, Paul Muldoon—Seamus Heaney soon stood out. Born into a Roman Catholic farming family in County Derry, he began by publishing verse—in his collections *Death of a Naturalist* (1966) and *Door into the Dark* (1969)—that combines a tangible, tough, sensuous response to rural and agricultural life, reminiscent of that of Ted Hughes, with meditation about the relationship between the taciturn world of his parents and his own communicative calling as a poet. Since then, in increasingly magisterial books of poetry—*Wintering Out* (1972), *North* (1975), *Field Work* (1979), *Station Island* (1984), *The Haw Lantern* (1987), *Seeing Things* (1991)—Heaney became arguably the greatest poet Ireland has produced. Having spent his formative years amid the murderous divisiveness of Ulster, he wrote poetry particularly distinguished by its fruitful bringing together of opposites. Sturdy familiarity with country life goes along with delicate stylistic accomplishment and sophisticated literary allusiveness. Present and past coalesce in Heaney's

Tony Harrison

The Martian school of poetry

verses: Iron Age sacrificial victims exhumed from peat bogs resemble tarred-and-feathered victims of the atrocities in contemporary Belfast; elegies for friends and relatives slaughtered during the outrages of the 1970s and '80s are embedded in verses whose imagery and metrical forms derive from Dante. Surveying carnage, vengeance, bigotry, and gentler disjunctions such as that between the unschooled and the cultivated, Heaney made himself the master of a poetry of reconciliations.

Drama. Apart from the short-lived attempt by T.S. Eliot and Christopher Fry to bring about a renaissance of verse drama, theatre in the late 1940s and early 1950s was most notable for the continuing supremacy of the "well-made" play, which focused upon, and mainly attracted as its audience, the comfortable middle class. The most interesting playwright working within this mode was Terence Rattigan, whose carefully crafted, conventional-looking plays—in particular, *The Winslow Boy* (1946), *The Browning Version* (1948), *The Deep Blue Sea* (1952), and *Separate Tables* (1954)—affectingly disclose desperations, terrors, and emotional forlornness concealed behind reticence and gentility. In 1956 John Osborne's *Look Back in Anger* forcefully signaled the start of a very different dramatic tradition. Taking as its hero a furiously voluble working-class man and replacing staid mannerliness on stage with emotional rawness, sexual candour, and social rancour, *Look Back in Anger* initiated a move toward what critics called "kitchen-sink" drama. Shelagh Delaney (with her one influential play, *A Taste of Honey* [1958]) and Arnold Wesker (especially in his politically and socially engaged trilogy, *Chicken Soup with Barley* [1958], *Roots* [1959], and *I'm Talking About Jerusalem* [1960]) gave further impetus to this movement, as did Osborne in subsequent plays such as *The Entertainer* (1957), his attack on what he saw as the tawdriness of postwar Britain. Also working within this tradition was John Arden, whose dramas emulate some of Bertold Brecht's theatrical devices. Arden wrote historical plays (*Serjeant Musgrave's Dance* [1959], *Armstrong's Last Goodnight* [1964]) to advance radical social and political views and in doing so provided a model that several later left-wing dramatists followed.

An alternative reaction against drawing-room naturalism came from the Theatre of the Absurd. Through increasingly minimalist plays—from *Waiting for Godot* (1953) to such stark brevities as his 30-second-long drama, *Breath* (1969)—Samuel Beckett used character pared down to basic existential elements and symbol to reiterate his Stygian view of the human condition (something he also conveyed in similarly gaunt and allegorical novels such as *Molloy* [1951], *Malone Dies* [1958], and *The Unnamable* [1960], all originally written in French). Some of Beckett's themes and techniques are discernible in the drama of Harold Pinter. Characteristically concentrating on two or three people maneuvering for sexual or social superiority in a claustrophobic room, works such as *The Birthday Party* (1958), *The Caretaker* (1960), *The Homecoming* (1965), *No Man's Land* (1975), and *Moonlight* (1993) are potent dramas of menace in which a slightly surreal atmosphere contrasts with and undermines dialogue of tape-recorder authenticity. Joe Orton's anarchic black comedies—*Entertaining Mr. Sloane* (1964), *Loot* (1967), and *What the Butler Saw* (1969)—put theatrical procedures pioneered by Pinter at the service of outrageous sexual farce. Orton's taste for dialogue in the epigrammatic style of Oscar Wilde was shared by one of the wittiest dramatists to emerge in the 1960s, Tom Stoppard. In plays from *Rosencrantz and Guildenstern are dead* (1966) to later triumphs such as *Arcadia* (1993), Stoppard sets intellectually challenging concepts ricocheting in scenes glinting with the to-and-fro of polished repartee. The most prolific comic playwright from the 1960s onward was Alan Ayckbourn, whose often virtuoso feats of stagecraft and theatrical ingenuity made him one of Britain's most popular dramatists. Ayckbourn's plays showed an increasing tendency to broach darker themes and were especially scathing (for instance, in *A Small Family Business* [1987]) on the topics of the greed and selfishness that he considered to have been promoted by Thatcherism, the prevailing political philosophy in 1980s Britain.

"Kitchen-sink" drama

Plays for
television

Playwrights who had much in common with Arden's ideological beliefs and his admiration for Brechtian theatre—Edward Bond, Howard Barker, Howard Brenton—maintained a steady output of parable-like plays dramatizing radical left-wing doctrine. Their scenarios were remarkable for an uncompromising insistence on human cruelty and the oppressiveness and exploitativeness of capitalist class and social structures. In the 1980s agitprop theatre—antiestablishment, feminist, black, and gay—thrived. One of the more durable talents to emerge from it was Caryl Churchill, whose *Serious Money* (1987) savagely encapsulated the finance frenzy of the 1980s. David Edgar developed into a dramatist of impressive span and depth with plays such as *Destiny* (1976) and *Pentecost* (1994), his masterly response to the collapse of communism and rise of nationalism in eastern Europe. David Hare similarly widened his range with confident accomplishment; in the 1990s he completed a panoramic trilogy surveying the contemporary state of British institutions—the Anglican church (*Racing Demon* [1990]), the police and the judiciary (*Murmuring Judges* [1991]), and the Labour Party (*The Absence of War* [1993]).

Hare also wrote political plays for television, such as *Licking Hitler* (1978) and *Saigon: Year of the Cat* (1983).

Trevor Griffiths, author of dialectical stage plays clamorous with debate, put television drama to the same use (*Comedians* [1975] had particular impact). Dennis Potter deployed a wide battery of the medium's resources, including extravagant fantasy and sequences that sarcastically counterpoint popular music with scenes of brutality, class-based callousness, and sexual rapacity. Potter's works transmit his revulsion, semireligious in nature, at what he saw as widespread hypocrisy, sadism, and injustice in British society. One playwright, Alan Bennett, excelled in both stage and television drama. Bennett's masterpieces are dramatic monologues written for television—*A Woman of No Importance* (1982) and six works he called *Talking Heads* (1987). In these television plays Bennett's comic genius for capturing the rich waywardness of everyday speech combines with psychological acuteness, emotional delicacy, and a melancholy consciousness of life's transience. The result is a drama, simultaneously hilarious and sad, of exceptional distinction. Bennett's 1991 play, *The Madness of George III,* takes his fascination with England's past back to the 1780s and in doing so accords with the widespread mood of retrospection with which British literature approached the end of the 20th century.

(PETER KEMP)

Telecommunications Systems

In addition to the wireline telephones described above in *The telephone instrument,* there exist a number of wireless instruments that are connected to the public switched telephone network (PSTN). At the present time, these wireless telephones generally fall into one of three categories: cordless telephones, cellular radio systems, or personal communication systems. Eventually these systems will be expanded to include global satellite-based telephony.

Cordless telephones. Cordless telephones are devices that take the place of a telephone instrument within a home or office and permit very limited mobility (up to a hundred metres). Because they are plugged directly into an existing telephone jack, they essentially serve as a wireless extension to the existing home or office wiring. Cordless transceivers communicate with the plugged-in base unit over a pair of frequencies in the 46- and 48-megahertz bands or over a single frequency in the 902–928-megahertz band.

Cellular radio. Cellular telephones are transportable by vehicle or personally portable devices that may be used in motor vehicles or by pedestrians. Communicating by radiowave in the 800–900-megahertz band, they permit a significant degree of mobility within a defined serving region that may be hundreds of square kilometres in area. In this section, the concept of cellular radio and the development of cellular systems are discussed.

Cellular telecommunication. All cellular radio systems exhibit several fundamental characteristics, as summarized in the following:

1. As shown in Figure 8, the geographic area served by a cellular radio system is broken up into smaller geographic areas, or cells. Uniform hexagons most frequently are employed to represent these cells on maps and diagrams; in practice, though, radiowaves do not confine themselves to hexagonal areas, so that the actual cells have irregular shapes.

2. All communication with a mobile or portable instrument within a given cell is made to the base station that serves the cell.

3. Because of the low transmitting power of battery-operated portable instruments, specific sending and receiving frequencies assigned to a cell may be reused in other cells within the larger geographic area. Thus, the spectral efficiency of a cellular system (that is, the uses to which it can put its portion of the radio spectrum) is increased by a factor equal to the number of times a frequency may be reused within its service area.

4. As a mobile instrument proceeds from one cell to another during the course of a call, a central controller automatically reroutes the call from the old cell to the new cell without a noticeable interruption in the signal reception. This process is known as handoff. The central controller, or mobile telephone switching office (MTSO), thus acts as an intelligent central office switch that keeps track of the movement of the mobile subscriber.

5. As demand for the radio channels within a given cell increases beyond the capacity of that cell (as measured by the number of calls that may be supported simultaneously), the overloaded cell is "split" into smaller cells, each with its own base station and central controller. The radio-frequency allocations of the original cellular system are then rearranged to account for the greater number of smaller cells.

Cell
splitting

Frequency reuse between discontiguous cells and the splitting of cells as demand increases are the concepts that distinguish cellular systems from other radiotelephone systems. They allow cellular providers to serve large metropolitan areas that may contain hundreds of thousands of customers.

The first mobile and portable subscriber units for cellular systems were large and heavy. With significant advances in component technology, though, the weight and size of portable transceivers have been significantly reduced. For example, lightweight portables in 1990 may have weighed 310 grams (10 ounces); by 1994 they weighed as little as 120 grams.

Development of cellular systems. In the United States, interconnection of mobile radio transmitters and receivers (transceivers) with the PSTN began in 1946, with the introduction of mobile telephone service (MTS) by AT&T. The MTS system employed frequencies in either the 35-megahertz band or the 150-megahertz band. A mobile user who wished to place a call from a radiotelephone had to search manually for an unused channel before placing the call. The user then spoke with a mobile operator, who actually dialed the call over the PSTN. The radio connection was simplex—*i.e.,* only one party could speak at a time, the call direction being controlled by a push-to-talk switch in the mobile handset.

In 1964 AT&T introduced a second generation of mobile telephony, known as improved mobile telephone service (IMTS). This provided full-duplex operation, automatic dialing, and automatic channel searching. Initially 11 channels were provided in the 152–158-megahertz band, but in 1969 an additional 12 channels were added in the

454–459-megahertz band. Since only 11 (or 12) channels were available for all users of the system within a given geographic area (such as the metropolitan area around a large city) and since each frequency was used only once in that geographic area, the IMTS system faced a high demand for a very limited channel resource. For example, in New York City during 1976, the IMTS system served 545 customers with another 3,700 customers placed on a waiting list for service. Moreover, each base-station antenna was located on a tall structure and transmitted at high power in an attempt to provide coverage throughout the entire service area. Because of these high power requirements, all subscriber units in the IMTS system were mobile-based instruments that carried larger storage batteries.

During this time the American cellular radio system, known as the advanced mobile phone system, or AMPS, was developed primarily by AT&T and Motorola, Inc. AMPS was based on 666 paired voice channels, spaced every 30 kilohertz in the 800-megahertz region. The system employed an analog-modulation approach—frequency modulation, or FM—and was designed from the outset to support both mobile and portable subscriber units. It was publicly introduced in Chicago in 1983 and was a success from the beginning. At the end of the first year of service, there were a total of 200,000 AMPS subscribers throughout the United States; five years later there were more than 2,000,000. In response to this growth, an additional 166 voice channels were allocated to cellular carriers in each market. Still, the cellular system was expected to experience capacity shortages.

Although AMPS was the first cellular system to be developed, the first cellular system actually to be deployed was a Japanese system deployed in 1979. This was followed by the Nordic mobile telephone (NMT) system, deployed in 1981 in Denmark, Finland, Norway, and Sweden, and the total access communication system (TACS), deployed in the United Kingdom in 1983. A number of other cellular systems were developed and deployed in many more countries in the following years. All of them were incompatible with one another. In 1988 a group of government-owned public telephone bodies within the European Community announced the digital global system for mobile (GSM) communications, the first such system that would permit a cellular user in one European country to operate in another European country with the same equipment.

Airborne systems. In addition to the terrestrial cellular radiotelephone systems, there also exist several systems that permit the placement of telephone calls to the PSTN by passengers on commercial aircraft. These in-flight radiotelephones, known by the generic name aeronautical public correspondence (APC) systems, are of two types: terrestrial-based, in which telephone calls are placed directly from an aircraft to an en route ground station; and satellite-based, in which telephone calls are relayed via a geostationary satellite to a ground station. In the United States the North American terrestrial system (NATS) was introduced by GTE Corporation in 1984. Within a decade the system was installed in more than 1,700 aircraft, with ground stations in the United States providing coverage over most of the United States and southern Canada. A second-generation system, GTE GenStar, employs digital modulation. In Europe the European Telecommunications Standards Institute (ETSI) adopted a terrestrial APC system known as the terrestrial flight telephone system (TFTS) in 1992. This system employs digital modulation methods and operates in the 1,670–1,675 and 1,800–1,805-megahertz bands. In order to cover most of Europe, the ground stations must be spaced every 50 to 700 kilometres. The second type of APC system, based on satellite transmission, is available through the use of Inmarsat geostationary-orbit satellites. Because they do not depend on ground stations, satellite-based systems may be employed anywhere in the world.

Personal communication systems. Although cellular radio systems provide a high degree of mobility within a given service area, they do so at the expense of providing voice-only service usually at a significant monthly fee. In recognition of this shortcoming, in a number of countries throughout the world a new radiotelephone service has

been introduced that has been almost universally called the personal communication system (PCS). In the broadest sense, PCS includes all forms of radiotelephone communication that are interconnected to the PSTN, including cellular radio and aeronautical public correspondence, but the basic concept includes the following attributes: ubiquitous service to roving users, low subscriber terminal costs and service fees, and compact, lightweight, and unobtrusive personal portable units.

The first PCS to be implemented was the second-generation cordless telephony (CT-2) system, which entered service in the United Kingdom in 1991. The CT-2 system was designed at the outset to serve as a telepoint system. In telepoint systems, a user of a portable unit may originate telephone calls (but not receive them) by dialing a base station located within several hundred metres. The

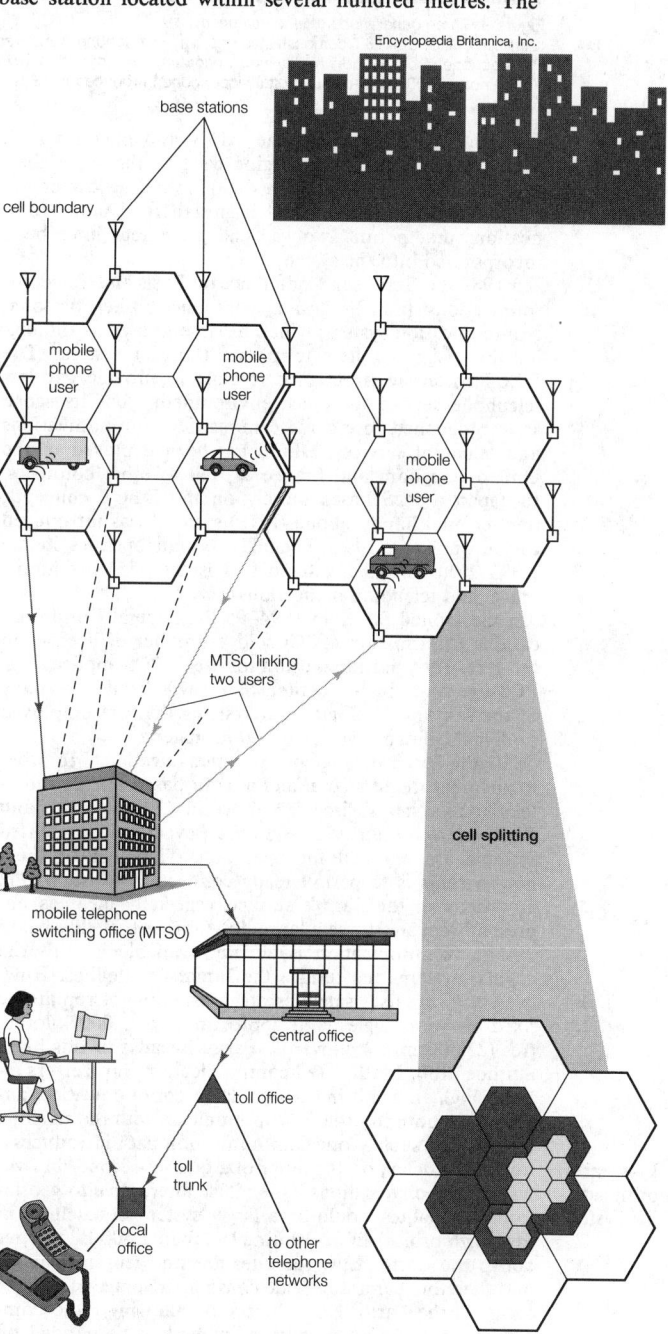

Encyclopædia Britannica, Inc.

Figure 8: *Operation of a cellular radiotelephone system.*
From a specific location within a geographic area, or cell, a subscriber places a call using a mobile radiotelephone. The call is relayed by the base station serving that cell to the mobile telephone switching office (MTSO). The MTSO in turn relays the call to another base station within the cellular system or to a central office in the public switched telephone system. When telephone traffic within a cell exceeds capacity, the cell is split into a number of smaller cells, each with its own base station.

Figure 9: *Three generations of videotelephony.*
(Left) An official of AT&T demonstrates one-way videophone transmission; (centre) the AT&T
Picturephone, a black-and-white analog videophone introduced in 1971; (right) the AT&T
VideoPhone 2500, a full-colour digital videophone introduced in 1992.
AT&T Archives

base unit is connected to the PSTN and operates as a public (pay) telephone, charging calls to the subscriber. The CT-2 system transmits a digital signal at low power (10 megawatts) in the 864–868-megahertz band. Modifications that permit two-way call placement have been incorporated into the system.

In 1988 the European Conference on Posts and Telecommunications (CEPT) began work on another personal communication system, which became known as the digital European cordless telephone (DECT) system. The DECT system was designed initially to provide cordless telephone service for office environments, but its scope soon broadened to include campuswide communications and telepoint services. DECT has been deployed in the United Kingdom and France as well as other countries. In Japan a PCS based loosely on the DECT concepts, the personal handy phone (PHP) system, was introduced to the public in 1994. The PHP system operates in the 1,895–1,907-megahertz band and is intended for home, office, and telepoint applications.

In the United States in 1994–95 the Federal Communications Commission (FCC) sold a number of licenses in the 1.85–1.99-gigahertz region for use in PCS applications. PCS operators in the United States will likely use many of the same technologies and systems that are employed in digital cellular systems at 800 megahertz.

Satellite-based radiotelephone communication. In order to augment the terrestrial and aircraft-based mobile radiotelephone systems discussed above in *Cellular radio* and *Personal communication systems,* several satellite-based systems are planned for operation. The goal of these new systems is to permit ready connection to the PSTN anywhere on the Earth's surface, especially in areas not presently covered by cellular radio. A form of satellite-based mobile communication is already available in airborne cellular systems that utilize the Inmarsat satellites. However, the Inmarsat satellites are geostationary, remaining fixed above a single point approximately 35,000 kilometres (22,000 miles) above the Earth. Because of this high-altitude orbit, Earth-based communication transceivers require high transmitting power, large communication antennas, or both in order to communicate with the satellite. In addition, such a long communication path introduces a noticeable delay, on the order of a quarter-second, in two-way voice conversations. One viable alternative to geostationary satellites would be a larger system of satellites in low earth orbit (LEO). Orbiting less than 1,600 kilometres above the Earth, LEO satellites are not geosynchronous and therefore cannot provide constant coverage of specific areas on the Earth. Nevertheless, by allowing radio communications with a mobile instrument to be handed off between satellites, an entire constellation of satellites can assure that no call will be dropped simply because a single satellite has moved out of range.

> Low earth orbit satellite systems

VIDEOTELEPHONE

In addition to the two-way speech transmission traditionally associated with the telephone, for many years there

has been an interest in transmitting two-way video signals over telephone circuits in order to facilitate communication between two parties. Two-way video communication systems employ a videotelephone, or videophone, at each end. The videophone incorporates a personal video camera and display, a microphone and speaker, and a data-conversion device. The data-conversion device permits transmission of video over telephone circuits through the use of two components: a compression/expansion circuit, which reduces the amount of information contained in the video signal, and a modem, which translates the digital video signal to the analog telephone line format.

Early videotelephones. The first public demonstration of a one-way videophone occurred on April 7, 1927, between Herbert Hoover (then secretary of commerce) in Washington, D.C., and officials of the American Telephone & Telegraph Company (AT&T) in New York City (see Figure 9). This was followed by the first public demonstration of a two-way videophone, on April 9, 1930, between Bell Laboratories and AT&T Headquarters, both in New York City. This two-way system employed early television equipment and a closed circuit; by 1956, Bell Laboratories had developed a videophone that could be employed over existing telephone circuits. Further studies led to the development of the first complete experimental videophone system, known as Picturephone, in 1963. By 1968, Bell engineers had developed a second-generation Picturephone, which was put into public service in 1971.

Analog videotelephone. The second-generation Picturephone was designed as a complete system. All aspects of the system—such as terminal equipment, local loop transmission, switching, long-distance transmission, and private branch exchange—were designed and developed to support two-way video communication over telephone circuits. Picturephone employed analog black-and-white video transmission similar to that used in television broadcasting. The crucial difference lay in the bandwidth of the video signals. Conventional television employs a 4.5-megahertz signal, which can transmit the information required to trace the standard American television picture of 525 lines per frame at a rate of 60 frames per second. In order to reduce the video signal to 1 megahertz—a bandwidth that could be supported by telephone lines— Picturephone employed a picture frame of approximately 250 lines. The screen was 14 by 12.5 centimetres (5 1/2 by 5 inches)—a screen size that was deemed to be appropriate for desktop use and was compatible with the resolution of the transmitted signal. The Picturephone terminal, shown in Figure 9, consisted of a free-standing microphone and a video display unit containing a speaker, an electron-tube camera, and a cathode-ray picture tube.

Despite the extensive development that went into the AT&T Picturephone system—more than 15 years of engineering effort and $500 million in development costs— market acceptance of Picturephone service was very poor. Ultimately AT&T concluded that the videotelephone was a "concept looking for a market," and service was discontinued in the late 1970s.

> Transmitting video signals over telephone lines

Digital videotelephone systems. In the late 1980s several companies began to develop and sell still-frame videophones that could operate directly over the PSTN. The still-frame videophone employs a video camera and a frame-capture system to capture a single video frame for transmission. Since still-frames exhibit no time dependency, they do not have to be transmitted in real time over the PSTN, permitting the use of standard, commercially available modems to transmit at 2.4 to 9.6 kilobits per second.

In 1992 AT&T introduced the VideoPhone 2500, the world's first colour videophone that could transmit over analog telephone lines (see Figure 9). Unlike the earlier Picturephones, the VideoPhone 2500 employs digital compression methods to enable a significant reduction of the bandwidth required for full-motion video transmission. A V.34 modem is employed to transmit the compressed video signal over an analog telephone line for access to the PSTN, where the signal may be readily circuited through central-office switches. Depending on the quality of the telephone line, the VideoPhone 2500 transmits at either 19.2 or 16.8 kilobits per second. The video compression algorithm employed in the VideoPhone 2500 is licensed to a number of Japanese manufacturers for employment in similar videophones. Other manufacturers in both the United States and Europe, including British Telecommunications and the Marconi Company, have developed similar videophone terminals for operation over the PSTN.

The videophones discussed above, being designed for transmission over standard telephone lines, operate at very low bit rates. In 1990 the International Telegraph and Telephone Consultative Committee (CCITT) adopted standards for "narrowband" videophone systems (operating in the range of 56 kilobits per second to 2 megabits per second) for transmission over multiple ISDN B channels. These systems would support full-motion colour video communications with a resolution of either 288 lines at 352 pixels per line (the common intermediate format, or CIF) or a resolution of 144 lines by 176 pixels per line.

MODEM

A voiceband modem is a device that is designed to transform digital electronic data from a source such as a personal computer, data terminal, or fax machine into a signaling format that is compatible with the telephone line.
Operating parameters. *Modulation/demodulation.* Modems are necessary for data communication over the public switched telephone network (PSTN) because ordinary analog telephone circuits are designed only to pass signals end-to-end that fall within the frequency range of voice communication—that is, 300 hertz to approximately 3,300 hertz, or 3.3 kilohertz. All other frequencies outside this limited bandwidth—especially the high frequencies associated with data transmission—are attenuated, or suffer a loss in amplitude and transmission speed. As a result, there occurs a phenomenon known as the "smearing" of signals over transmission time, and there is an overlapping of signals at the receiving end. In addition, telephone circuits are susceptible to other impairments that are unnoticeable or tolerable in voice communication but that would introduce an unacceptable number of errors into data communications. These impairments include signal "echoes," when voice paths are converted from two-wire to four-wire circuits, and various types of "noise," or interference, from other signals within the telephone system. All such impairments must be corrected by the modem.

One goal of a voiceband modem is to frequency-translate data signals in order to "fit" them within the nominal three-kilohertz bandwidth of the telephone circuit. It does this by a technique known as modulation. In modulation, the basic properties of an electromagnetic wave—for instance, its amplitude, frequency, or phase—are modified by another wave in such a manner that the original wave becomes a "carrier," bearing the recognizable imprint of the modifying wave. In the transmission of data signals over the PSTN, the carrier wave is the voiceband signal, and the modifying wave is the digital data signal. At the receiving end of the transmission path, a similar modem recognizes the modifications and separates the data signal

from the carrier signal. It is this dual function of modulation and demodulation that gives the modem its name.
One-way and two-way transmission. Voiceband modems may operate in a variety of transmission modes, including simplex, half-duplex, and full-duplex. Simplex transmission is one-way transmission between a transmitter and a corresponding receiver. In half-duplex transmission, two-way transmission is possible, but it cannot take place simultaneously; data must first be transmitted in one direction before transmission in the reverse direction is possible. Finally, full-duplex transmission is simultaneous transmission in both directions.

Depending on the nature of the data communications traffic, any one of these transmission modes may be required. In some instances, full-duplex transmission may be provided through two half-duplex modems operating over two independent telephone circuits. This arrangement is known as a four-wire circuit. In other cases, full-duplex capability over a single two-wire telephone circuit may be required, necessitating the use of a duplex arrangement within the modem to permit simultaneous transmission and reception.

Transmission rates. The information-carrying capacity of an analog voice signal is measured by its bandwidth, the range of frequencies that make up the signal. Data signals, on the other hand, are measured by the number of binary digits, or bits, required to encode the desired information. The rate of transmission in data communication is measured by the number of bits or kilobits (thousand bits) per second that can be passed through the system. During the course of their development, modems have risen in throughput from 300 bits per second to 28.8 kilobits per second and beyond.

Development of modems. *The first generation.* Although not strictly related to digital data communication, early work on telephotography machines by the Bell System during the 1930s did lead to methods for overcoming certain signal impairments inherent in telephone circuits. Among these developments were equalization methods for overcoming the smearing of fax signals as well as methods for translating fax signals to a 1,800-hertz carrier signal that could be transmitted over the telephone line.

The first development efforts on digital modems appear to have stemmed from the need to transmit data for North American air defense during the 1950s. By the end of that decade, data was being transmitted at 750 bits per second over conventional telephone circuits. The first modem to be made commercially available in the United States was the Bell 103 modem, introduced in 1962 by the American Telephone & Telegraph Company (AT&T). The Bell 103 permitted full-duplex data transmission over conventional telephone circuits at data rates up to 300 bits per second. In order to send and receive binary data over the telephone circuit, two pairs of frequencies (one pair for each direction) were employed. A binary "1" was signaled by a shift to one frequency of a pair, while a binary "0" was signaled by a shift to the other frequency of the pair. This type of digital modulation is known as frequency-shift keying, or FSK. Another modem, known as the Bell 212 modem, was introduced shortly after the Bell 103. Transmitting data at a rate of 1,200 bits, or 1.2 kilobits, per second over full-duplex telephone circuits, the Bell 212 made use of phase-shift keying, or PSK, to modulate a 1,800-hertz carrier signal. In PSK, data is represented as phase shifts of a single carrier signal. Thus, a binary "1" might be sent as a zero-degree phase shift, while a binary "0" might be sent as a 180-degree phase shift.

Between 1965 and 1980, significant efforts were put into developing modems capable of even higher transmission rates. These efforts focused on overcoming the various telephone line impairments that directly limited data transmission. In 1965 Robert Lucky at Bell Laboratories developed an automatic adaptive equalizer to compensate for the smearing of data symbols due to the mutual interference of signals being attenuated at various rates within the telephone system. Although the concept of equalization was well known and had been applied to telephone lines and cables for many years, older equalizers were fixed and often manually adjusted. The advent

The first digital modems

Carrier waves and modifying waves

of the automatic equalizer permitted the transmission of data at high rates over the PSTN without any human intervention. Moreover, while adaptive equalization methods compensated for imperfections within the nominal three-kilohertz bandwidth of the voice circuit, advanced modulation methods permitted transmission at still higher data rates over this bandwidth. One important modulation method was quadrature amplitude modulation, or QAM. In QAM, binary digits are conveyed as discrete amplitudes in two phases of the electromagnetic wave, each phase being shifted by 90 degrees with respect to the other. The frequency of the carrier signal was in the range of 1,800 to 2,400 hertz. QAM and adaptive equalization permitted data transmission of 9.6 kilobits per second over four-wire circuits. Further improvements in modem technology followed, so that by 1980 there existed commercially available first-generation modems that could transmit at 14.4 kilobits per second over four-wire leased lines.

The second generation. Beginning in 1980, a concerted effort was made by the International Telegraph and Telephone Consultative Committee (CCITT) to define a new standard for modems that would permit full-duplex data transmission at 9.6 kilobits per second over a single-pair circuit operating over the PSTN. Two breakthroughs were required in this effort. First, in order to fit high-speed full-duplex data transmission over a single telephone circuit, echo cancellation technology was required so that the sending modem's transmitted signal would not be picked up by its own receiver. Second, in order to permit operation of the new standard over unconditioned PSTN circuits, a new form of coded modulation was developed. In coded modulation, error-correcting codes form an integral part of the modulation process, making the signal less susceptible to noise. The first modem standard to incorporate both of these technology breakthroughs was the V.32 standard, issued in 1984. This standard employed a form of coded modulation known as trellis-coded modulation, or TCM. Seven years later, an upgraded V.32 standard was issued, permitting 14.4-kilobit-per-second full-duplex data transmission over a single PSTN circuit.

In mid-1990 the CCITT began to consider the possibility of full-duplex transmission over the PSTN at even higher rates than those allowed by the upgraded V.32 standard. This work resulted in the issuance in 1994 of the V.34 modem standard, allowing transmission at 28.8 kilobits per second.

Enhanced throughput. While modulation/demodulation technology was being standardized for the most recent modems, several other peripheral standards were also being developed. These peripheral standards fell into two categories: error control and compression. In 1988 the CCITT adopted a standard (V.42) that would permit errors in modem data to be flagged and retransmitted, thereby providing end-to-end error-free transmission. V.42 was a higher-level modem protocol; hence, it might be implemented in computer software without affecting the lower level modulator/demodulator functions. It was most often employed in file transfers between computers over telephone lines.

Beginning in 1990, the CCITT standard V.42*bis* incorporated the error-control mechanisms embedded in V.42 with a data-compression scheme that could provide a four-to-one reduction in the number of bits required to encode information. The throughput rate of a modem incorporating a data-compression scheme equals the data rate of the modem times the compression rate. Hence, a V.32*bis* modem, operating at 14.4 kilobits per second and also incorporating V.42*bis* data compression, could have an effective throughput rate of 57.6 kilobits per second.

FACSIMILE (FAX)

Facsimile, or fax, refers to the transmission of text or fixed images and drawings by wire or radio channels. Fax permits the transmission of a mix of documents—including handwriting, graphs, pictures, and maps—that often cannot be transmitted at all over other communications media. Although the concepts of fax were developed in the 19th century using contemporary telegraph technology, widespread employment of the method did not take place

until the 1980s, when inexpensive means of adapting digitized information to telephone circuits became common.

Early telegraph facsimile. Facsimile transmission over wires traces its origins to Alexander Bain, a Scottish mechanic. In 1843, less than seven years after the invention of the telegraph by Samuel F.B. Morse, Bain received a British patent for "improvements in producing and regulating electric currents and improvements in timepieces and in electric printing and signal telegraphs." Bain's fax transmitter was designed to scan a two-dimensional surface (Bain proposed metal type as the surface) by means of a stylus mounted on a pendulum. The invention was never demonstrated.

Frederick Blakewell, an English physicist, was the first actually to demonstrate facsimile transmission. The demonstration took place in 1851 at the World's Fair in London. Blakewell's system differed somewhat from Bain's in that images were transmitted and received on cylinders—a method that was widely practiced through the 1960s. At the transmitter, the image to be scanned was written with varnish or some other nonconducting material on tinfoil, wrapped around the transmitter cylinder, and then scanned by a conductive stylus that, like Bain's stylus, was mounted to a pendulum. The cylinder rotated at a uniform rate by means of a clock mechanism. At the receiver, a similar pendulum-driven stylus marked chemically treated paper with an electric current as the receiving cylinder rotated.

The first commercial facsimile system was introduced between Lyon and Paris, Fr., in 1863 by Giovanni Caselli, an Italian inventor. The first successful use of optical scanning and transmission of photographs was demonstrated by Arthur Korn of Germany in 1902. Korn's transmitter employed a selenium photocell to sense an image wrapped on a transparent glass cylinder; at the receiver the transmitted image was recorded on photographic film. By 1906

Marginal notes:
Development of the V.32 modem

The first facsimile transmission

(Top) AT&T Archives, (bottom) © Jon Feingersh/The Stock Market

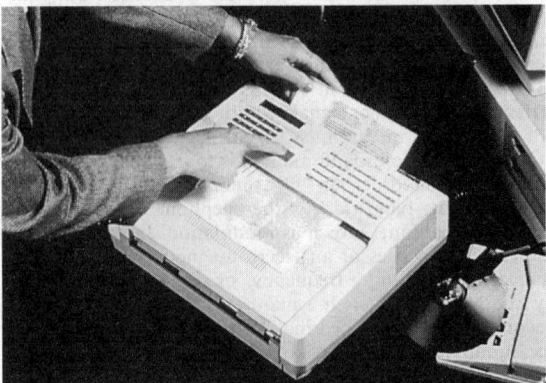

Figure 10: *Two generations of facsimile transmission.*
(Top) The analog telephotography machine, introduced in 1924; (bottom) the digital Group 3 fax machine, introduced in 1980.

Korn's equipment was put into regular service for transmission of newspaper photographs between Munich and Berlin via telegraph circuits.

Analog telephone facsimile. Further deployment of fax transmission had to await the development of improved long-distance telephone service. Between 1920 and 1923 the American Telephone & Telegraph Company (AT&T) worked on telephone facsimile technology, and in 1924 the telephotography machine was used to send pictures from political conventions in Cleveland, Ohio, and Chicago to New York City for publication in newspapers. The telephotography machine (shown in Figure 10) employed transparent cylindrical drums, which were driven by motors that were synchronized between transmitter and receiver. At the transmitter a positive transparent print was placed on the drum and was scanned by a vacuum-tube photoelectric cell. The output of the photocell modulated a 1,800-hertz carrier signal, which was subsequently sent over the telephone line. At the receiver an unexposed negative was progressively illuminated by a narrowly focused light beam, the intensity of which corresponded to the output of the photoelectric cell in the transmitter. The AT&T fax system was capable of transmitting a five-by-seven-inch photograph in seven minutes with a resolution of 100 lines per inch.

Further advancements in fax technology occurred during the 1930s and '40s. In 1948 Western Union introduced its desk-fax service, which was based on a small office machine. Some 50,000 desk-fax units were built until the service was discontinued in the 1960s.

Over the years, different manufacturers adopted operability standards that allowed their machines to communicate with one another, but there was no worldwide standard that enabled American machines, for example, to connect to European fax machines. In 1974 the International Telegraph and Telephone Consultative Committee (CCITT) issued its first worldwide fax standard, known as Group 1 fax. Group 1 fax machines were capable of transmitting a one-page document in about six minutes with a resolution of 100 lines per inch using an analog signal format. This standard was followed in 1976 by a CCITT Group 2 fax standard, which permitted transmission of a one-page document in about three minutes using an improved modulation scheme.

Digital facsimile. Although the Group 2 fax machines proved to be successful in business applications where electronic transmission of documents containing nontextual information such as drawings, diagrams, and signatures was required, the slow transmission rate and the cost of the terminals ultimately limited the growth of fax services. In response, the CCITT developed standards for a new class of fax machine, now known as Group 3, which would use digital transmission of images through modems. With the encoding of a scanned image into binary digits, or bits, various image compression methods (also known as source encoding or redundancy reduction) could be employed to reduce the number of bits required to represent the original image. By coupling a good source code with a high-speed modem, a Group 3 fax machine (see Figure 10) could reduce the time required to transmit a single page to less than one minute—a threefold improvement in transmission time over the older Group 2 fax machines.

The Group 3 standard was adopted by the CCITT in 1980. A schematic diagram of a modern Group 3 fax machine is shown in Figure 11. At the transmitter end the image of a page to be transmitted is focused on a charge-coupled device (CCD), a solid-state scanner that has 1,728 photosensors in a single row. The photosensors measure the brightness of spots, or pixels, in a line 0.01 inch high across the width of the page. After each line is scanned, the scanner is advanced by one line. The output of the scanner is supplied to an analog-to-digital converter where the spot intensity is converted to a single bit of information. Two lines are stored in a buffer memory, and a source compression algorithm then reduces the two lines of image information to a fraction of the original number of bits required to represent the image. The digital representation of the image is then transmitted over the public switched telephone network using a voiceband modem. At the

The Group 3 fax

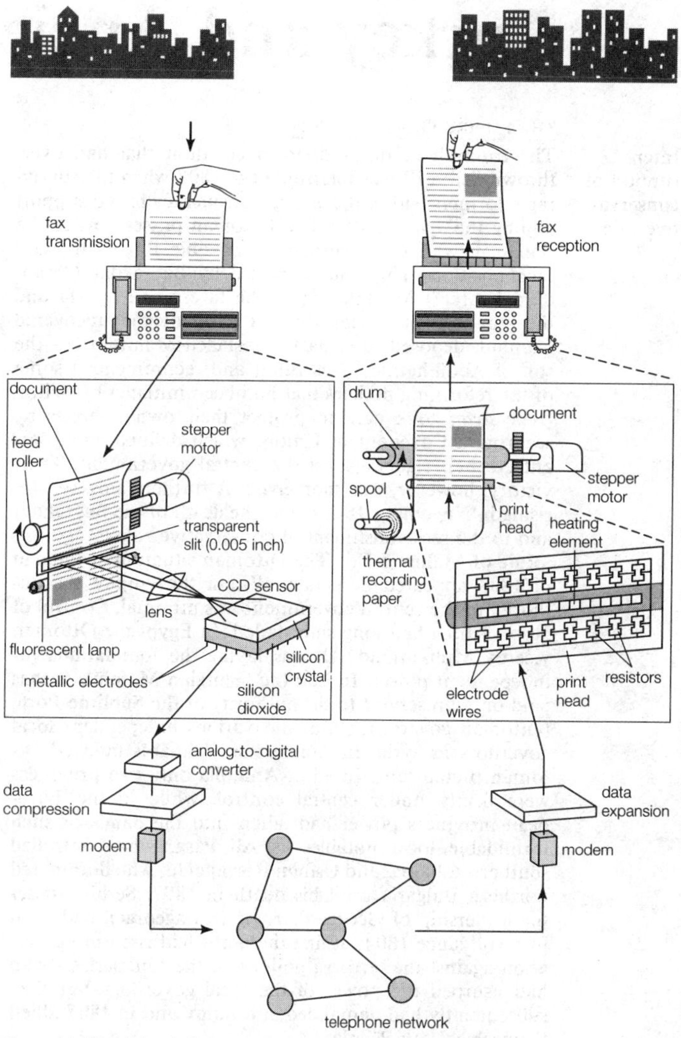

Figure 11: Digital facsimile transmission using Group 3 thermal fax machines.
Encyclopædia Britannica, Inc.

receiver another modem receives the signal, which then undergoes source decompression for reconstitution of the original image information. The received image may then be printed by a thermal printer on special temperature-sensitive recording paper, or it may be printed on plain paper via a xerographic process. Originally, Group 3 fax was intended for transmission at data rates between 2,400 and 9,600 bits per second. With more recent advances in voiceband modem technology, data transmission rates of 14,400 bits per second and above are common.

Since the Group 3 fax standard was adopted, the use of fax by large and small businesses and even in private homes has grown at a significant rate. There are now tens of millions of fax machines worldwide. This rapid growth has come about as the result of a decline in the price of fax machines and improvements in the quality and transmission speed of fax documents. Furthermore, inexpensive voiceband modems have become available that enable a personal computer to perform almost all the tasks of a fax machine.

Between 1981 and 1984 the CCITT sponsored the development of a high-speed fax service that was adopted as the Group 4 standard in 1984. Group 4 fax was intended to supplant Group 3 fax by permitting error-free transmission of documents over digital networks, such as the integrated services digital network (ISDN), at speeds up to 64,000 bits per second. At such rates, transmission time for a single page could be reduced to less than 10 seconds. At the present time, the limited availability of ISDN lines and the continued improvement in offered features and modem data rates for Group 3 fax have limited the deployment of Group 4 fax machines.　(DAVID E. BORTH)

The Group 4 fax

Turkey and Ancient Anatolia

THE EMPIRE FROM 1807 TO 1920

Inter-
ruption of
conserva-
tive rule

The triumph of the antireform coalition that had overthrown Selim III was interrupted in 1808 when the surviving reformers within the higher bureaucracy found support
among the *ayan* of Rumelia (Ottoman possessions in the
Balkans), who were worried by possible threats to their
own position. The *ayan* were led by Bayrakdar ("Standard Bearer") Mustafa Paşa. The forces of Mustafa and
the grand vizier Çelebi Mustafa Paşa together recovered
Istanbul, deposed Mustafa IV, installed Mahmud II—the
son of Abdülhamid I—as ruler, and recommenced some
of the reforming policies that had been initiated by Selim.

The *ayan* took care to protect their own interests by
securing a Covenant of Union, which defined and guaranteed their rights against the central government. Their
victory, however, was short-lived. A further Janissary uprising in November 1808 led to the death of the Bayrakdar
and to the reestablishment of conservative rule.

Rule of Mahmud II. The Ottoman situation at the end
of 1808 appeared desperate. Within the empire the authority of the central government was minimal. Control of
North Africa had long since faded. In Egypt the Ottoman
viceroy Muḥammad ʿAlī was laying the foundations for
independent power. In Iraq the Georgian Mamlūk pashas
paid only lip service to the authority of the Sublime Porte
(Ottoman government), as did various independent local
governors in Syria. In Arabia the Wahhābīs mocked Ottoman pretensions. In all of Anatolia only two provinces
were firmly under central control, while in the European provinces power had fallen into the hands of such
formidable local notables as Ali Paşa, who controlled
southern Albania, and Osman Pasvanoğlu, who dominated
northern Bulgaria until his death in 1807. Serbia, under
the leadership of George Petrović (Karageorge), had been
in revolt since 1804; at first the Serbs had risen in desper-
ation against the terrorist policies of the Janissaries—who
had usurped the power of the local governor—but they
subsequently had demanded autonomy and in 1807 allied
themselves with Russia.

The external threat to the empire was no less ominous.
Selim III had hoped to enlist French aid in order to recover
territory lost to Russia; as a result, the Ottomans found
themselves at war with both Russia, which invaded the
principalities (*i.e.,* Moldavia and Walachia; modern Romania) in November 1806, and Britain, which attempted
to seize the Dardanelles with a naval force (February 1807)
and invaded Egypt (March 1807). Meanwhile Napoleon,
through the agreements of Tilsit (July 7, 1807) and Erfurt
(Oct. 12, 1808), had abandoned active opposition to Russia and had accepted its occupation of the principalities.

The preoccupation of the European powers with other interests helped the Ottomans ameliorate their international
problems. Britain made peace on Jan. 5, 1809, in the
Treaty of Çanak. Through the Treaty of Bucharest (May
28, 1812) Russia returned the principalities to Ottoman
rule, although Russia retained most of Bessarabia.

Recon-
struction
of the
army

Internal reform. Mahmud II was then able to concentrate on internal reform. The basic element in Mahmud's
reforms was the reconstruction of the army to make it a
fit instrument for preserving the Ottoman Empire against
both the encroachments of European powers and the separatist ambitions of local potentates. This policy brought
him into conflict with the Janissaries. In 1826 Mahmud
set out his proposals for a new European-style army; on
June 15 the Istanbul Janissaries mutinied in protest and
were promptly and efficiently massacred by the sultan, an
episode known as "the Auspicious Incident."

As a tactician, Mahmud proved to be superior to Selim.
He had the support of most of the higher ulama. Whereas
in 1807 the Janissaries had enjoyed the approval of the
population of Istanbul, in 1826 only two guilds gave them
active help. Mahmud had built up a cooperative group
among the Janissary officers and had carefully arranged to
have loyal troops at hand. Perhaps most important of all,

Mahmud made sure his proposals were perceived not as
dangerous and infidel innovations but as a restoration of
the military system of the Ottoman golden age.

The destruction of the old army was completed in 1831
by the final abolition of the timar system. The remaining
timars were resumed by the government. Although the new
army was outfitted, equipped, and trained in the style of
European armies and helped by a succession of European
advisers (including the future chief of the German General
Staff, Helmuth von Moltke), it differed from the former
army in its greater loyalty to the sultan. It thus became an
instrument of political centralization, and it provided the
major motive for modernization. The continuing effort to
pay and equip the army and to train its officers and other
specialized personnel in a sustained, but ultimately vain,
attempt to keep pace with the European powers stimulated reform of the political and economic institutions of
the Ottoman Empire. For example, the modernization of
higher education began with the need to train officers,
army doctors, and veterinary surgeons; that of the taxation
system began with the need to pay the army; and that
of the administration, with the need to collect the taxes.
Ultimately the entire system of minimal government—by
which political, economic, and social decisions were left
to local organizations—was replaced by one in which the
state centralized decisions in its own hands.

Move toward centralization. Mahmud began by curbing
the power of rival claimants. He undermined the influence of the ulama and of popular religious organizations.
He created a new directorate of *evkâf* (charitable endow-
ments) in 1826, hoping to gain control of the hitherto
independent financial base of ulama power. To make his
power more effective, he built new roads and in 1834
inaugurated a postal service.

Adminis-
trative
reorgani-
zation

The central administration was reorganized. New European-style ministries were created to replace the ancient
bottleneck of power caused by the vesting of full administrative responsibility in the grand vizier. New councils
were established to assist in long-term planning; one, the
Supreme Council of Judicial Ordinances (1838), subsequently became the principal legislative body. Bureaucrats
were given greater security by the abolition of the practice
of confiscating their property at death, while the opening of a translation bureau (1833) and the reopening of
embassies abroad gave some the opportunity to learn European languages and encounter European ideas.

The reformed army and administration became the agents
by which the sultan extended his authority over the semi-
independent governors, local notables, valley lords, and
other groups that had wielded political power in various
parts of the empire. This process had begun immediately
after 1812. The Serbian revolt had been temporarily suppressed in 1813, although it broke out again in 1815.
Firm Ottoman governmental control was established over
Anatolia, Iraq, and much of Rumelia.

The only local ruler who succeeded in asserting his own
authority, unaided, against the Porte was Muḥammad ʿAlī
of Egypt, who was carrying through a still more radical program of modernization. In 1831 Egyptian forces
invaded Syria, routed the Ottomans at Konya (Dec. 27,
1832), and threatened Istanbul. Mahmud was forced to
seek Russian aid, and on July 8, 1833, he signed the Treaty
of Hünkâr İskelesi (Unkiar Skelessi); Muḥammad ʿAlī
was, for a time, left in possession of Syria, but Mahmud
had not abandoned his claims. In 1839 he attacked the
Egyptians; once more the Ottomans were defeated (June
24, 1839). With the help of the European powers (except
France) through the Treaty of London (July 15, 1840),
the Ottomans recovered Syria and eventually consolidated
their authority there; but Muḥammad ʿAlī obtained recognition as hereditary ruler of Egypt (1841).

Attempts to extend Ottoman control in the European
provinces, notably in Greece, Serbia, and the principalities, were frustrated. The Greek revolt was the product

of the economic prosperity of the Napoleonic Wars and exposure to western European ideas and was a reaction against Ottoman centralization. The revolt was the result of the opposition of peasants and bandits to Ottoman authority and was instigated by plots of certain intellectuals organized through the political society Philikí Etaireía and led by Alexander Ypsilantis, who invaded Moldavia in March 1821. Ypsilantis was defeated, but an uprising began in the Peloponnese. A stalemate developed, but the Ottomans were reinforced in 1825 by Egyptian troops and threatened to put down the revolt. The destruction of the combined Ottoman and Egyptian fleets by Russian, French, and British naval forces at Navarino in the southwestern Peloponnese (Oct. 20, 1827) prevented the Muslims from supplying their armies and made Greek independence inevitable. The Ottomans were forced to recognize Greek autonomy (1829) and independence (1832).

Similarly, Ottoman efforts to regain control of Serbia and the principalities were obstructed by Russian opposition, leading to the Russo-Turkish War (1828–29). By the Treaty of Edirne, on Sept. 14, 1829, the Ottomans ceded to Russia the mouth of the Danube and important territories in eastern Asia Minor and conceded new privileges to the principalities and Serbia. Serbian autonomy was recognized in 1830 and was extended over the full area of the state in 1833.

Changes in the empire

By the time of the death of Mahmud II in 1839, the Ottoman Empire was diminished in extent; it was more consolidated and powerful than it had been at its height but was increasingly subject to European pressures, with Russia supporting and Britain opposing separatist movements and the other powers oscillating between. The cure, however, had begun. Mahmud had established the respectability of change, and its symbol was the replacement of the turban with the fez (1828).

The Tanzimat reforms (1839–76). The Tanzimat is the name given to the series of Ottoman reforms promulgated during the reigns of Mahmud's sons Abdülmecid I (ruled 1839–61) and Abdülaziz (1861–76). The best-known of these reforms are the Hatt-ı Şerif of Gülhane ("Noble Edict of the Rose Chamber"; Nov. 3, 1839) and the Hatt-ı Hümayun ("Imperial Edict"; Feb. 18, 1856).

Purpose of the Tanzimat. The Tanzimat has been the subject of much controversy. Many Western writers have dismissed the promises of reform as merely an Ottoman desire to win European diplomatic support at critical moments, and some features of the Tanzimat appear to support such a view. The promises of equality for Christian subjects were not always implemented—for example, it was proposed in 1855 to end the poll tax paid by non-Muslims and to allow them to enter the army, but the old poll tax was merely replaced by a new exemption tax levied at a higher rate, and Christians were still excluded from the army. It is also true that the timing of reform announcements coincided with crises: the 1839 edict came when the Ottomans needed European help against Muḥammad ʿAlī, the 1856 edict when the Ottomans needed European acceptance in the wake of the Crimean War, and the 1876 constitution when European pressure for reforms was mounting.

This view of the Tanzimat is based, however, upon a misconception of its purpose. Europeans, who were principally concerned with improving conditions for Ottoman Christians, looked first at those elements of the Tanzimat that appeared to be directed toward this goal (*e.g.*, a proclamation in the 1839 edict of the principles of individual liberty, freedom from oppression, and equality before the law and a section of the 1856 edict that was concerned with the rights of Christians). To the Ottomans, however, the purpose of reform was to preserve the Ottoman state. Although the Ottomans found it necessary to make some concessions to European powers and to their own non-Muslim subjects and although some Tanzimat statesmen did consider equality to be an ultimate goal, it was the desire to preserve the state that brought about the mobilization of resources for modernization. The central reforms, therefore, were in the army, notably major reorganizations of 1842 and 1869 (the latter following the pattern of the successful Prussian conscript system); in the

administration, both at the centre and in the provinces; and in society, through changes in education and law.

Reform in education. Before the reforms, education in the Ottoman Empire had not been a state responsibility but had been provided by the various millets; education for Muslims was controlled by the ulama and was directed toward religion. The first inroads into the system had been made with the creation of naval engineering (1773), military engineering (1793), medical (1827), and military science (1834) colleges. In this way specialized Western-type training was grafted onto the traditional system to produce specialists for the army. Similar institutions for diplomats and administrators were founded, including the translation bureau (1833) and the civil service school (1859); the latter was reorganized in 1877 and eventually became the political science department of the University of Ankara and the major training centre for higher civil servants.

In 1846 the first comprehensive plan for state education was put forward. It provided for a complete system of primary and secondary schools leading to the university level, all under the Ministry of Education. A still more ambitious educational plan, inaugurated in 1869, provided for free and compulsory primary education. Both schemes progressed slowly because of a lack of money, but they provided a framework within which development toward a systematic, secular educational program could take place.

Comprehensive education plan

By 1914 there were more than 36,000 Ottoman schools, although the great majority were small, traditional primary schools. The development of the state system was aided by the example of progress among the non-Muslim millet schools, in which the education provided was more modern than in the Ottoman schools; by 1914 these included more than 1,800 Greek schools with about 185,000 pupils and some 800 Armenian schools with more than 81,000 pupils. Non-Muslims also used schools provided by foreign missionary groups in the empire; by 1914 there were 675 U.S., 500 French Catholic, and 178 British missionary schools, with more than 100,000 pupils among them. These foreign schools included such famous institutions as Robert College (founded 1863), the Syrian Protestant College (1866; later the American University of Beirut), and the Université Saint-Joseph (1874).

Reforms in law. Law, to a large extent, also had been the responsibility of the various millets. The Capitulations exempted foreigners and those Ottoman citizens on whom foreign consuls conferred protection from the application of criminal law. The Tanzimat reformers had two objects in the reform of law and legal procedure: to make Ottoman law acceptable to Europeans, so that the Capitulations could be abolished and sovereignty recovered, and to modernize the traditional Islāmic law. Their efforts resulted in the promulgation of a commercial code (1850), a commercial procedure code (1861), a maritime code (1863), and a penal code (1858). French influence predominated in these, as it did in the civil code of 1870–76. Increasingly, the laws were administered in new state courts, outside the control of the ulama. Although they failed to achieve the purposes intended, they provided the basis for future success.

Obstructions to reforms. The Tanzimat reforms moved steadily in the direction of modernization and centralization. The reformers were handicapped by a lack of money and skilled men, and they were opposed by traditionalists who argued that the reformers were destroying the empire's fundamental Islāmic character and who often halted the progress of reform. Centralization, meanwhile, was slowed by interference from the major European powers, who obstructed the Ottoman attempt to recover power in Bosnia and Montenegro in 1853, forced the granting of autonomy to Mount Lebanon in 1861, and considered, but eventually rejected, intervention to prevent the Ottomans from suppressing a Cretan revolt of 1868. Although Britain and France helped the Ottomans resist Russian pressure during the Crimean War (1853–56), the Ottomans derived no real benefits from the peace settlement; new arrangements helped to bring about the unification of the principalities (1859) and paved the way for the emergence of independent Romania.

European interference

The 1875–78 crisis. The success of the Tanzimat reformers, ironically, created a systemic weakness as centralization removed the checks on the power of the sultan. After the death of Ali Paşa, Abdülaziz so abused his unrestrained authority as to contribute to a major crisis in 1875–78.

Drought in 1873 and floods in 1874 had produced widespread discontent and even famine among the Ottoman peasantry, who already were disturbed by the increased burdens of a landholding system that had spread in the Balkans in the 19th century and by increased taxation and greater liability to conscription resulting from the 1869 military reorganization. The burden of taxation had been aggravated by the Ottoman debt burden. The first Ottoman foreign loan was in 1854; by 1875 the nominal public debt was £200,000,000, with annual interest and amortization payments of £12,000,000, more than half the national revenue. The Ottomans could meet only about half of their annual obligation, however, because a world financial crisis in 1873 had made new credit difficult to obtain.

Balkan discontent was fanned by nationalist agitation supported by Serbia and by émigré Slav organizations. It culminated in uprisings largely of Christian peasants against Muslim lords in Bosnia and Herzegovina (July 1875) and in Bulgaria (August 1876). Ottoman efforts to suppress the uprisings led to war with Serbia and Montenegro (July 1876) and to attempts by European powers to force Ottoman reforms.

Agreement among the European powers proved impossible, and, when the Ottomans rejected Russian demands, Russia decided to act alone and declared war (April 24, 1877). The war ended in defeat for the Ottomans, but their unexpected resistance at Plevna (modern Pleven, Bulg.; July–December 1877) allowed other European powers, led by Britain, to intervene. According to the Treaty of San Stefano (March 3, 1878), the Ottomans were to recognize the independence of Romania, Serbia, and Montenegro and cede territory to them, concede autonomy to an extensive new state of Bulgaria, cede territory to Russia in the Dobruja (west of the Black Sea) and eastern Asia Minor, introduce various administrative reforms, and pay an indemnity.

Russo-Turkish War, 1877–78

Diplomatic pressure from other European powers led to the modification of these terms at the Congress of Berlin (June–July 1878). The major changes concerned autonomous Bulgaria, which was substantially reduced in size and divided into two parts, the northern part to have political and the southern (eastern Rumelia) to have administrative autonomy. The independence of Serbia, Montenegro, and Romania was recognized, but their territorial gains were much reduced. Russia retained its acquisitions of Kars and Batum in Asia Minor. Austria-Hungary was given control of Bosnia and Herzegovina and the strategic district of Novi Pazar in Serbia. By a separate convention Cyprus was put under British rule.

The settlement was a major defeat for the Ottomans. Eastern Rumelia was soon lost when it united with Bulgaria in 1885. The Ottoman territories in Europe were reduced to Macedonia, Albania, and Thrace, and European influence had attained new dimensions. Britain now proposed to supervise governmental reforms in the Asian provinces, although this was skillfully frustrated by Abdülhamid II (ruled 1876–1909). In addition, the Ottomans were soon forced to accept new financial controls. By the Decree of Muharrem (December 1881) the Ottoman public debt was reduced from £191,000,000 to £106,000,000, certain revenues were assigned to debt service, and a European-controlled organization, the Ottoman Public Debt Administration (OPDA), was set up to collect the payments.

The OPDA subsequently played an important role in Ottoman affairs, acting as agent for the collection of other revenues and as an intermediary with European companies seeking investment opportunities. Its influence should not, however, be exaggerated. The OPDA remained under Ottoman political control, and its existence even enabled the Ottomans to add to the debt at the annual rate of £3,000,000 throughout the reign of Abdülhamid; nor was the burden of repayments a major drain on the country's resources. But taken in conjunction with the activities of European-controlled banks and with the tariff limitations imposed on the Ottomans by the Capitulations, the result was a distinct restriction on Ottoman ability to guide the allocation of resources.

The Ottoman constitution, 1876. Perhaps more significant than external changes were the internal political developments that brought about the first Ottoman constitution on Dec. 23, 1876. The Tanzimat had produced three types of criticism within the Muslim community. The first was a simple traditionalist opposition. The second was a more sophisticated critique elaborated by certain intellectuals, many of whom had bureaucratic training and some knowledge of Western ideas. The third expressed a determination to control, and if necessary to depose, the sultan.

The intellectuals were known as the Young Ottomans. Although some had taken part in a secret society (the "Patriotic Alliance") in 1865 and had some similarity of background, the Young Ottomans were not an organized political party; they are considered as a group largely through the accident of their assembly in Paris and London in 1867–71. Their political views ranged from secular, cosmopolitan revolutionism to profoundly Islāmic traditionalism. Because his views occupied a middle ground among these intellectuals and because of his lucidity of expression, Namık Kemal (1840–88) has often been regarded as the representative figure, although he is no more representative than the others. His views, however, had the greatest effect on later reformers.

The Young Ottomans

Kemal criticized the Tanzimat reformers for their indiscriminate adoption of Western innovations. While admiring much of Western civilization, he believed that the principles underlying its best institutions were to be found in Islām. In particular, he derived from early Islāmic precept and practice the idea of a representative assembly that could check the unbridled power of the sultan and his ministers. He helped to form and popularize the idea of a constitution and of loyalty to the Ottoman fatherland. Like others, he was assisted by the development of an Ottoman press, which had its origins in the 1830s but began to express opinions—occasionally critical of the government—in the 1860s. During this decade two influential newspapers were established, the *Tercüman-i Ahval* (1860) and the *Tasvir-i Efkâr* (1862); along with later newspapers, these became the vehicles for Young Ottoman ideas.

But it was the third line of criticism, that which sought to control the sultan, that was most important. Arising within the higher Ottoman bureaucracy itself, it was led by Midhat Paşa. Midhat and others became determined, because of their own exclusion from power and because of the disastrous results of Abdülaziz's policies, to impose some check on the sultan's power. The traditional check was deposition, and this was accomplished (May 30, 1876) following a riot by theological students and the removal of the hated grand vizier Mahmud Nedim Paşa. A new cabinet was formed, which included Midhat and other partisans of reform. A new sultan with a reputation for liberalism, Murad V (ruled 1876), was installed, but he quickly became insane and was deposed, replaced by Abdülhamid II. The experience convinced Midhat of the necessity of a permanent check upon the power of the sultan, such as could be provided by a representative assembly that would give ministers a basis of support independent of the sultan. Accordingly, Abdülhamid was persuaded to agree to a constitution.

Although earlier documents had had constitutional implications and although the development of councils—particularly provincial councils with their elected elements—had had parliamentary aspects, the December 23 document was the first comprehensive Ottoman constitution and (except for a Tunisian organic law of 1861) the first in any Islāmic country. The constitution was derived entirely from the will of the ruler, who retained full executive power and to whom ministers were individually responsible. In legislation the sultan was assisted by a two-chamber Parliament, the lower house indirectly elected and the upper house nominated by the ruler. Rights of ruler and ruled were set out, but the system it established might best

First Ottoman constitution

be described as attenuated autocracy. Midhat has been criticized for accepting certain amendments demanded by Abdülhamid, including the then-notorious article 113, which gave the sultan the right to deport persons harmful to the state; but it is clear that the majority of Midhat's colleagues were content with these amendments and that the amendments made little difference, so great were the sultan's powers within and outside the constitution. The Parliament summoned under the constitution in March 1877 was dissolved in less than a year and was not recalled until 1908. The liberals were exiled; some, including Midhat, were put to death.

Rule of Abdülhamid II. The reign of Abdülhamid II (1876–1909) is often regarded as having been a reaction against the Tanzimat, but, insofar as the essence of the Tanzimat reforms was centralization rather than liberalization, Abdülhamid may be seen as its fulfiller rather than its destroyer. The continued development of the army and administration, the formation of a gendarmerie, the growth of communications—especially the telegraph and railways—and the formation of an elaborate spy system enabled the sultan to monopolize power and crush opposition. His brutal repression of the Armenians in 1894–96 earned him the European title "red sultan." But Abdülhamid's reign also made positive advances in education (including the renovation of Istanbul University in 1900); legal reform, led by his grand vizier Mehmed Said Paşa; and economic development, through the construction of railways in Asia Minor and Syria with foreign capital and of the Hejaz Railway from Damascus to Medina with the help of subscriptions from Muslims in other countries.

Pan-Islāmism. The Hejaz Railway constituted one element in Abdülhamid's Pan-Islāmic policies. Political Pan-Islāmism had made its first appearance in Ottoman policy at the Treaty of Küçük Kaynarca (1774) with Russia, when the Ottoman sultan had made claims to religious jurisdiction over Muslims outside his territories, particularly those in the Crimea. Some years later the theory was elaborated by the addition of the baseless legend that in 1517 the 'Abbāsid Caliphate had been transferred to the Ottoman sultan. With the extinction of many independent Muslim states and their absorption into the empires of European powers, this myth of the Caliphate became

Power of the myth of the Caliphate

a useful weapon in the Ottoman diplomatic armoury and was exploited by Abdülhamid as a means of deterring European powers from pressing him too hard, lest he create dissension within their own territories. In addition, stress on popular Islām through the press and other publications and through the sultan's patronage of dervish orders served to rally Muslim opinion within the empire behind him.

Preservation of the empire. Abdülhamid had reasonable success in preserving the empire after 1878. Apart from eastern Rumelia, no further territories were lost until 1908 (Ottoman authority in Tunisia, occupied by France in 1881, and Egypt, occupied by Britain in 1882, was already insignificant). In Crete the Ottomans suppressed revolts and defeated Greece when it intervened in 1897 in support of the Cretans. The European powers, however, forced Abdülhamid to concede autonomy to Crete. He was more successful in obstructing European efforts to force the introduction of substantial reforms in Macedonia. In Arabia the Ottomans continued the expansion of their power that had begun in the early 1870s.

The Young Turk Revolution of 1908. Several conspiracies took place against Abdülhamid. In 1889 a conspiracy in the military medical college spread to other Istanbul colleges. These conspirators came to call themselves the Committee of Union and Progress (CUP; İttihad ve Terakki Cemiyeti) and were commonly known as the Young Turks. When the plot was discovered, some of its leaders went abroad to reinforce Ottoman exiles in Paris, Geneva, and Cairo, where they helped prepare the ground for revolution by developing a comprehensive critique of the Hamidian system. The most noteworthy among these were Murad Bey, Ahmed Rıza, and Prince Sabaheddin. As editor of *Mizan* ("Balance"), published first in Istanbul (1886) and later in Cairo and Geneva, Murad Bey preached liberal ideas combined with a strong Islāmic feeling; this may have contributed to his defection and

return to Istanbul in 1897. Ahmed Rıza in Paris edited *Meşveret* ("Consultation"), in which he set out ideas of reform, strongly flavoured by Auguste Comte's philosophy of positivism. His advocacy of a strong central government within the Ottoman Empire and the exclusion of foreign influence led to a major split within the Young Turk exiles at the 1902 Paris Congress; Ahmed Rıza clashed with Sabaheddin, who, with Armenian support, favoured administrative decentralization and European assistance to promote reform. Sabaheddin set up the League of Private Initiative and Decentralization.

The émigrés could supply literary sustenance to dissidents, but Abdülhamid could not be overthrown while the army remained loyal. The real origin of the Young Turk Revolution of 1908 lay in the discontent within the 3rd Army Corps in Macedonia, where officers acted independently of the CUP in Paris. It is still unclear if a coordinated conspiracy existed in Macedonia or if a number of separate centres of disaffection, linked haphazardly through individuals, dervish orders, Freemason lodges, and other means, coalesced in July 1908 under the banner of the CUP through the pressure of events. On July 3, 1908, Major Ahmed Niyazi, apparently fearing discovery by an investigatory committee, decamped from Resne with 200 followers, including civilians, leaving behind a demand for the restoration of the constitution. The sultan's attempt to suppress this uprising failed, and rebellion spread rapidly. Unable to rely on other troops, on July 24 Abdülhamid announced the restoration of the constitution.

The young officers who had instigated the revolution, like their civilian supporters, were primarily concerned with preserving the Ottoman Empire; they feared that Hamidian policies and European interventions were endangering its existence. Grievances concerning personal matters such as salary and rank, however, also may have played a part. Though some writers have argued that a new type of officer, of lower social origin than officers from earlier generations, influenced this discontent, there is little evidence to support such a theory. It is clear, however, that the officers had not thought much beyond their demand for the restoration of a constitution that had proved ineffectual in 1877–78. They had no program of action and were content to leave government to the established bureaucrats. Goals of rebel leaders

In April 1909, however, an army mutiny in Istanbul (known because of the Julian calendar as the "31st March Incident") exposed the weakness of the CUP and at the same time gave it a new opportunity. The mutiny resulted from the discontent of ordinary soldiers over their conditions and their neglect by college-trained and politically ambitious officers and from what they regarded as infidel innovations. They were encouraged by a religious organization known as the Mohammedan Union. The weakness of the government allowed the mutiny to spread, and, although order was eventually restored in Istanbul and more quickly elsewhere, a force from Macedonia (the Action Army), led by Mahmud Şevket Paşa, marched on Istanbul and occupied the city on April 24.

Dissolution of the empire. Abdülhamid was deposed and replaced by Sultan Mehmed V (ruled 1909–18), son of Abdülmecid. The constitution was amended to transfer real power to the Parliament. The army, and particularly Şevket Paşa, became the real arbiters of Ottoman politics.

Rise of the CUP. Although the removal of many of its political opponents had allowed the CUP to move into a more prominent position in government, it was still weak. It had a core of able, determined men but a much larger collection of individuals and factions whose Unionist affiliation was so weak that they easily merged into other parties. Although the CUP won an overwhelming majority in the election of April 1912, its support rapidly melted away following military losses to Italy. Evidence of army hostility finally forced the CUP out of office in July 1912, to be succeeded by a political coalition called the Liberal Union.

The Liberal Union, too, lost support following defeats in the Balkans. This provided the opportunity for a small group of CUP officers and soldiers to stage a coup (Jan. 23, 1913), known as the Sublime Porte Incident, to force

The
Sublime
Porte
Incident

the resignation of the grand vizier Mehmed Kâmil Paşa and establish a new cabinet under Şevket. Şevket, however, was not a Unionist, and it was only after his assassination (June 11, 1913) that the CUP at last succeeded in establishing a Unionist-dominated government under Said Halim Paşa.

Internal developments. The disastrous results of the Young Turks' external policies overshadowed the important internal developments of the years 1908–18. Further administrative reforms, particularly of provincial administration in 1913, led to more centralization, although by European standards the central Ottoman government remained relatively weak, particularly in the more distant provinces. The burden of taxation was well below that of European powers.

The Young Turks were the first Ottoman reformers to promote industrialization, with a Law for the Encouragement of Industry (1909, revised 1915). Although they had little success, they did build a framework for later state-directed economic planning. Considerable attention was given to education, especially to the neglected area of primary education. The process of secularization of the law was carried much further. A major development in national journalism took place, and the position of women improved. The whole period was one of intense social and political discussion and change.

Turkish nationalism. The basic ideologies of the state remained Ottomanism and Islām, but a new sense of Turkish identity began to develop. This new concept was fostered by educational work of the Turkish Society (formed 1908) and the Turkish Hearth (formed 1912). A political twist was given by the adherents of Pan-Turkism and Pan-Turanianism. Pan-Turkism, which aimed at the political union of all Turkish-speaking peoples, began among Turks in the Crimea and along the Volga River. Its leading exponent was İsmail Bey Gasprinski (Gaspirali), who attempted to create a common Turkish language. Many Pan-Turkists migrated to Ottoman lands, especially after 1905. One of them, Yusuf Akçuraoğlu, argued in *Üç tarz-ı siyaset* (1903; "Three Kinds of Policy") that Turkism provided a better basis for the Ottoman Empire than either Islām or Ottomanism. Pan-Turanianism developed from a much-disputed 19th-century theory of the common origin of Turkish, Mongol, Tungus, Finnish, Hungarian, and other languages; some of its advocates envisioned a great political federation of speakers of these languages, extending from Hungary eastward to the Pacific Ocean.

Pan-
Turkism
and Pan-
Turanian-
ism

These ideas, however, found little support within the Ottoman government. The accusation that the Young Turks pursued a deliberate policy of Turkification within the empire in order to alienate non-Turks and promote the rise of Arab and Albanian nationalism is an oversimplification. The extension of government activity inevitably brought with it the Turkish language, as it was the language of government. This produced some reaction from speakers of other languages, but the evidence suggests that it did not override basic feelings of Muslim solidarity, except among some small minorities. It was among the Christian groups that distinct separatist ideas were developed.

Foreign relations. The foreign relations of the Ottoman Empire under the Young Turks led to disaster. The 1908 revolution provided an opportunity for several powers to press their designs upon the empire. In October 1908 Austria-Hungary annexed Bosnia and Herzegovina, and Bulgaria proclaimed its independence. Italy seized Tripoli (Libya) and occupied the Dodecanese, a group of Aegean islands; by the Treaty of Lausanne (Oct. 18, 1912) Italy retained the former but agreed to evacuate the Dodecanese. In fact, however, it continued to occupy them.

The two Balkan Wars (1912–13) almost completed the destruction of the Ottoman Empire in Europe. In the first (October 1912–May 1913) the Ottomans lost almost all their European possessions, including Crete, to Bulgaria, Serbia, Greece, Montenegro, and the newly created state of Albania (Treaty of London, May 30, 1913). In the second (June–July 1913), fought between Bulgaria and the remaining Balkan states (including Romania) over the division of Macedonia, the Ottomans intervened against Bulgaria and recovered part of eastern Thrace, including

Edirne. The Ottomans had lost more than four-fifths of the territory and more than two-thirds of the population of their European provinces.

The people. In 1914 the total population of the Ottoman Empire was approximately 25 million, of which about 10 million were Turks, 6 million Arabs, 1.5 million Kurds, 1.5 million Greeks, and between 1.5 million and 2 million Armenians. The population of the empire (excluding such virtually independent areas as Egypt, Romania, and Serbia) in the period immediately prior to the losses of 1878 is estimated to have been about 26 million. Natural increases and Muslim immigration from Russia and the Balkans virtually made up the losses, and in 1914 the population was increasingly homogeneous in religion and language, though a variety of languages continued to be spoken.

Popula-
tion of the
empire

World War I, 1914–18. The Ottoman entry into World War I resulted from an overly hasty calculation of likely advantage. German influence was strong but not decisive; Germany's trade with the Ottomans still lagged behind that of Britain, France, and Austria, and its investments, which included the Baghdad railway, were smaller than those of France. A mission to Turkey led by the German military officer Otto Liman von Sanders in 1913 was only one of a series of German military missions, and Liman's authority to control the Ottoman army was much more limited than contemporaries supposed. Except for the interest of Russia in Istanbul and the Straits, no European power had genuinely vital interests in the Ottoman Empire. The Ottomans might have remained neutral, as a majority of the cabinet wished, at least until the situation became clearer. But the opportunism of the minister of war Enver Paşa, early German victories, friction with the Triple Entente (France, Russia, and Great Britain) arising out of the shelter given by the Ottomans to German warships, and long-standing hostility to Russia combined to produce an Ottoman bombardment of the Russian Black Sea ports (Oct. 29, 1914) and a declaration of war by the Entente against the Ottoman Empire.

The Ottomans made a substantial contribution to the Central Powers' war effort. Their forces fought in eastern Asia Minor, Azerbaijan, Mesopotamia, Syria and Palestine, and the Dardanelles, as well as on European fronts, and they held down large numbers of Entente troops. In September 1918 they dominated Transcaucasia. During the war the Young Turks also took the opportunity to attack certain internal problems—the Capitulations were abolished unilaterally (September 1914), the autonomous status of Lebanon was ended, a number of Arab nationalists were executed in Damascus (August 1915 and May 1916), and the Armenian community in eastern Asia Minor and Cilicia was massacred or deported to eliminate any domestic support for the pro-Christian tsarist enemy on the Eastern Front. Possibly 600,000 Armenians were killed, principally by Kurdish irregulars.

After 1916, army desertions took place on a massive scale, and economic pressures became acute. The surrender of Bulgaria (Sept. 28, 1918), which severed direct links with Germany, was the final blow. The CUP cabinet resigned on October 7, and a new government was formed under Ahmed Izzet Paşa on October 9. On October 30 the Ottomans signed the Armistice of Mudros.

Allied war aims and the proposed peace settlement. Entente proposals for the partition of Ottoman territories were formulated in a number of wartime agreements. By the Istanbul Agreements (March–April 1915) Russia was promised Istanbul and the Straits; France was to receive a sphere of influence in Syria and Cilicia. Britain had already annexed Cyprus and declared a protectorate over Egypt. By the Anglo-French Sykes-Picot Agreement (Jan. 3, 1916) the French sphere was confirmed and extended eastward to Mosul in Iraq. A British sphere of influence in Mesopotamia extended as far north as Baghdad, and Britain was given control of Haifa and 'Akko and of territory linking the Mesopotamian and Haifa-'Akko spheres. Palestine was to be placed under an international regime. In compensation, the Russian gains were extended (April–May 1916) to include the Ottoman provinces of Trabzon, Erzurum, Van, and Bitlis in eastern Asia Minor. By the

Partition of
Ottoman
territories

London Agreement (April 26, 1915) Italy was promised the Dodecanese and a possible share of Asia Minor. By the Agreement of St.-Jean-de-Maurienne (April 1917) Italy was promised a large area of southwestern Anatolia, including İzmir and an additional sphere to the north. Britain made various promises of independence to Arab leaders, notably in the Ḥusayn-MacMahon correspondence (1915–16), and in the Balfour Declaration (Nov. 2, 1917) promised to support the establishment of a national home for the Jewish people in Palestine.

The Russian withdrawal in 1917 and postwar bargaining led to some modifications of these agreements, and the Allied terms were not finally presented until 1920. By the Treaty of Sèvres (Aug. 10, 1920) the Ottomans retained Istanbul and part of Thrace but lost the Arab provinces, ceded a large area of Asia Minor to a newly created Armenian state with access to the sea, surrendered the islands of Gokçe and Bozca to Greece, and accepted arrangements that implied the eventual loss of İzmir to Greece. The Straits were internationalized, and strict European control of Ottoman finances was established. An accompanying tripartite agreement between Britain, France, and Italy defined extensive spheres of influence for the latter two powers. The treaty was ratified only by Greece and was abrogated by the Treaty of Lausanne (July 24, 1923) as the result of a determined struggle for independence waged under the leadership of the outstanding Ottoman wartime general Mustafa Kemal, later known as Atatürk.

The emergence of the modern Turkish state

KEMAL AND THE WAR OF INDEPENDENCE, 1919–23

Although the legal Ottoman government in Istanbul under the 36th and last Ottoman sultan Mehmed VI Vahideddin (ruled 1918–22) had decided that resistance to Allied demands was impossible, pockets of resistance remained in Asia Minor after the armistice. These included bands of irregulars and deserters, a number of intact Ottoman units, and various societies for the "defense of rights." Resistance was stimulated by the Greek occupation of İzmir (May 15, 1919). At this time Mustafa Kemal was sent on an official mission to eastern Asia Minor, landing at Samsun on May 19. He immediately began to organize resistance, despite official Ottoman opposition. Through the Association for the Defense of the Rights of Eastern Anatolia (founded March 3, 1919), he summoned a Congress at congress at Erzurum (July–August) followed by a second Erzurum congress at Sivas (September) with delegates representing the whole country. A new Association for the Defense of the Rights of Anatolia and Rumelia was established, and an executive committee with Mustafa Kemal as chairman was created to conduct resistance.

The official government yielded to Kemalist pressure. The unpopular grand vizier, Damad Ferid Paşa, resigned and was replaced by the more sympathetic Ali Riza Paşa. Negotiations with the Kemalists were followed by the election of a new parliament, which met in Istanbul in January 1920. A large majority in parliament was opposed to the official government policy and passed the National Pact, formulated at Erzurum and Sivas, which embodied the political aims of independence roughly within the October 1918 armistice lines. The Allies countered by extending the occupied area of Istanbul (March 16, 1920) and by arresting and deporting many deputies. Damad Ferid became grand vizier again on April 5 and, with religious support, set out to crush the Kemalists.

The Fundamental Law and abolition of the sultanate. The Kemalists were now faced with local uprisings, official Ottoman forces, and Greek hostility. The first necessity was to establish a legitimate basis of action. A parliament (the Grand National Assembly) met at Ankara on April 23 and asserted that the sultan's government was under infidel control and that it was the duty of Muslims to resist foreign encroachment. In the Fundamental Law of Jan. 20, 1921, the assembly declared that sovereignty belonged to the nation and that the assembly was the "true and only representative of the nation." The name of the state was declared to be Turkey (Türkiye), and executive power was entrusted to an executive council, headed by

Mustafa Kemal, who could now concentrate on the war.

The uprisings and the Ottoman forces were both defeated, principally by irregular forces, who at the end of 1920 were brought under Kemal's control. In 1920–21 the Greeks made major advances, almost to Ankara, but were defeated at the Battle of the Sakarya River (Aug. 24, 1921) and began a long retreat that ended in the Turkish occupation of İzmir (Sept. 9, 1922).

The Kemalists had already begun to gain European recognition. On March 16, 1921, the Soviet-Turkish Treaty gave Turkey a favourable settlement of its eastern frontier by restoring Kars and Ardahan. Domestic problems induced Italy to begin withdrawal from the territory it occupied; and, by the Treaty of Ankara (Franklin-Bouillon Agreement, Oct. 20, 1921), France agreed to evacuate Cilicia. Finally, by the Armistice of Mudanya, the Allies agreed to Turkish reoccupation of Istanbul and eastern Thrace.

A comprehensive settlement was eventually achieved at the Lausanne Conference (November 1922–July 1923). The Turkish frontier in Thrace was established on the New Maritsa River, and Greece returned the islands of Gokçe Turkish and Bozca. A compulsory exchange of populations was frontier arranged, as a result of which an estimated 1,300,000 Greeks left Turkey in return for 400,000 Turks. The question of Mosul was left to the League of Nations, which in 1925 recommended its retention by Iraq. The Lausanne Treaty also provided for the apportionment of the Ottoman public debt, for the gradual abolition of the Capitulations (Turkey regained tariff autonomy in 1929), and for an international regime for the Straits. Turkey did not recover complete control of the Straits until the 1936 Montreux Convention.

The result of the war and the peace settlement created a state in which the great majority spoke Turkish. Though there has been a tendency to see this as the almost inevitable consequence of the rise of Turkish and Arab nationalism, it seems in fact to have been the accident of war that broke off the Arab provinces. Whatever the views of Mustafa Kemal himself, it is clear that the majority of his followers thought of themselves primarily as Muslims; in the elaborate religious ceremony that preceded the opening of the Grand National Assembly, there was no mention of Turks or Turkey but only of the need to save "religion's last country." The creation of a sense of Turkish nationhood was the product of a long effort in which Mustafa Kemal played the dominant role.

Construction of a new political system began with the abolition of the sultanate and the declaration of a republic. Loyalty to the Ottoman dynasty was strong even among Kemalists; but Vahideddin's identification with the Allies weakened his support. An Allied invitation to the sultan to nominate representatives to Lausanne aided Kemal—a split Turkish delegation would be self-defeating. With a brilliant mixture of threats and persuasion, Kemal was able, therefore, to induce the assembly to abolish the sultanate (Nov. 1, 1922). Vahideddin left Turkey, and his cousin Abdülmecid was installed as the first and last Ottoman caliph who was not also sultan.

Declaration of the Turkish republic. On Oct. 29, 1923, the assembly declared Turkey to be a republic and elected Mustafa Kemal as first president. The caliphate was finally abolished on March 3, 1924, and all members of the Ottoman dynasty were expelled from Turkey. A full republican constitution was adopted on April 20, 1924; it retained Islām as the state religion, but in April 1928 this clause was removed and Turkey became a purely secular republic.

TURKEY UNDER KEMAL

Government. The assembly was the instrument of Kemal's will. The first assembly had contained large factions hostile to his policies, including religious conservatives, merchants, and former members of the CUP. In opposition to his 197 acknowledged supporters, who were known as the First Group, there were 118 opponents, members of the Second Group. The first assembly was dissolved on April 16, 1923, and Mustafa Kemal took care to keep his opponents out of the second assembly; only three of the Second Group were returned. Kemal's own party, which became the Republican People's Party (RPP), dominated all assemblies until 1950; this period saw a heavy preponderance in the assembly of urban professional men and of officials with a university education. With an outlook different from that of the illiterate Turkish peasants, they carried out a revolution from the top.

Opposition.   There was little opposition to Mustafa Kemal—the small Progressive Republican Party (November 1924–June 1925) had only 29 members and was suppressed because Kemal feared that its leading members, who included some of his most notable associates in the war of independence, might have too much influence in the army; the similarly short-lived Liberal Republican Party (August–December 1930) was an abortive attempt by Kemal to organize a moderate opposition to his own party. Otherwise, Kemal ruled quite autocratically. A plot against his life in 1926 gave him the chance to deal with his rivals, who were tried by a special court. Many of them were sentenced to death, imprisonment, or exile. Opposition outside the assembly, of which the most dangerous were the Kurdish revolts of 1925, 1930, and 1937, was suppressed vigorously.

Kemalist policies.   The bases of Mustafa Kemal's policies were enshrined in the RPP program of 1931, which was written into the Turkish constitution in 1937. Kemal's six fundamental principles were republicanism (the creation of the republic), nationalism, populism, statism, secularism, and revolution. Revolution was implicit in the radical reorganization of the political, social, and economic systems. Populism was the effort to mobilize popular support from the top through such characteristic devices as the People's Houses (1931–51), which spread the new concept of a national culture in provincial towns, and the village institutes, which performed the same educational and proselytizing role in the countryside. The creation of a sense of nationalism was encouraged by changes in school curricula, the rewriting of history to glorify the Turkish past, the "purification" of the language by a reduction of the number of words of foreign origin (sometime later, this effort appeared to be redundant in the light of a promulgation that all languages were descended from Turkish), and the renunciation of Pan-Islāmic, Pan-Turkish, and Pan-Ottoman goals in foreign policy.

Statism was the movement toward state-controlled economic development; the shortage of skilled labour and entrepreneurs (caused largely by the reduction of the Greek and Armenian communities, which in 1914 had controlled four-fifths of Ottoman finance, industry, and commerce), the lack of capital, and the intense nationalist desire for industrial self-sufficiency that would banish foreign influence all stimulated a movement in the 1930s toward state ownership or control. This was achieved through investment banks, monopolies, state industrial enterprises, and planning. A five-year plan was instituted in 1934. Although the immediate results were disappointing, the policy of state-inspired economic growth was important for future economic advance.

Secularism included the reform of law, involving the abolition of religious courts and schools (1924) and the adoption of a purely secular system of family law. The substitution of the Roman for the Arabic alphabet in writing Turkish was a significant step toward secularism and made learning easier; other measures included the adoption (1925) of the Gregorian calendar that had been jointly used with the Hijrī calendar since 1917, the replacement of Friday by Sunday as the weekly holiday (1935), the adoption of surnames (1934), and, most striking of all, the abolition of the fez (1925). The wearing of clerical garb outside places of worship was forbidden in 1934.

These changes, coupled with the abolition of the caliphate and the elimination of the dervish orders after a Kurdish revolt in 1925, dealt a tremendous blow to Islām's position in social life, completing the process begun in the Tanzimat. With secularism there came a steady improvement in the status of women, who were given the right to vote and to sit in parliament.

Vital as these changes were, in many cases they were primarily matters of appearance and style. Structural changes in society took longer. At the first census, in 1927, the

Mustafa Kemal's six principles (margin note)

population was put at 13.6 million, of which about one-fourth was urban. In 1940 the population was 17.8 million, but the urban proportion was almost unchanged. In 1938 the per capita income and literacy rate were both below comparable figures for developed countries.

Foreign policy was subordinated to internal change. The loss of Mosul was accepted (June 5, 1926). Hatay, however, was recovered. It was given internal autonomy by France in 1937, occupied by Turkish troops in 1938, and incorporated into Turkey in 1939. Turkey followed a neutralist policy, supported the League of Nations (which it joined in 1932), and sought alliances with other minor powers, leading to the Balkan Entente (1934) and the Sa'dābād Pact with Iran, Iraq, and Afghanistan (1937).

Neutralist policy (margin note)

TURKEY AFTER KEMAL

World War II and the postwar era, 1938–50.   Atatürk's autocratic, dominating, and inspiring personality had directed and shaped the Turkish republic. At his death in 1938 his closest associate, İsmet İnönü, was elected president. With the approach of war, foreign affairs assumed greater importance. An alliance with Britain and France (Oct. 19, 1939) was not implemented because of Germany's early victories. After Germany's invasion of Russia (June 1941), there was popular support for an alliance with Germany, which seemed to offer prospects of realizing old Pan-Turkish aims. Although a nonaggression pact was signed with Germany (June 18, 1941), Turkey clung to neutrality until an Axis defeat became inevitable; it entered the war on the Allied side on Feb. 23, 1945. The great expansion of Soviet power exposed Turkey in June 1945 to Soviet demands for control over the Straits and for the cession of territory in eastern Asia Minor. It was also suggested that a large area of northeastern Anatolia be ceded to Soviet Georgia. This caused Turkey to seek and receive U.S. assistance; U.S. military aid began in 1947 (providing the basis for a large and continuing flow of military aid), and economic assistance began in 1948.

The war also brought changes in domestic policy. The army had been kept small throughout the Atatürk period, and defense expenditure had been reduced to about one-fourth of the budget. The army was rapidly expanded in 1939, and defense expenditures rose to more than half the budget for the duration of the war. Substantial deficits were incurred, imposing a severe economic strain, which was aggravated by shortages of raw materials. By 1945 agricultural output had fallen to 70 percent of the 1939 figure, per capita income to 75 percent. Inflation was strong: official statistics show a rise of 354 percent between 1938 and 1945, but this figure probably understates the fall in the value of money, which in 1943 was less than one-fifth its 1938 purchasing power. One means chosen by the government to raise money was a capital levy, introduced in 1942, arranged to fall with punitive force upon the non-Muslim communities and upon the Dönmes (Jewish converts to Islām). The war did provide some stimulus to industry, however, and enabled Turkey to build up substantial foreign credits, which were used to finance postwar economic development.

The most notable change in the postwar years was the liberalization of political life. The investment in education was beginning to show some return, and the literacy rate had risen to nearly one-third of the adult population by 1945. A growing class of professional and commercial men demanded more freedom. The Allied victory had made democracy more fashionable; accordingly, the government made concessions allowing new political parties, universal suffrage, and direct election.

From a split within the RPP, the Democrat Party (DP) was founded in 1946 and immediately gathered support. Despite government interference, the DP won 61 seats in the 1946 general election. Some elements in the RPP, led by the prime minister Recep Peker (served 1946–47), wished to suppress the DP, but they were prevented by İnönü. In his declaration of July 12, 1947, İnönü stated that the logic of a multiparty system implied the possibility of a change of government. Prophetically, he renounced the title of "National Unchangeable Leader," which had been conferred upon him in 1938. Peker resigned and was

Political liberalization (margin note)

succeeded by more liberal prime ministers in Hasan Saka (1947–49) and Şemseddin Günaltay (1949–50).

Other restrictions on political freedom, including press censorship, were relaxed. The first mass-circulation, independent newspapers were established during the period. The formation of trade unions was permitted in 1947, although unions were not given the right to strike until 1963. A far-reaching land-redistribution measure was passed in 1945, although little was done to implement it before 1950. Other political parties were established, including the conservative National Party (1948); socialist and communist activities, however, were severely repressed.

In the more open atmosphere the DP was able to organize in the villages. The RPP, despite its local Village Institutes, had always been the government party and had had little real grass-roots organization. The Democrats were much more responsive to local interests. The DP won a massive victory in the 1950 elections, claiming 54 percent of the vote and 396 out of 487 seats. The RPP won 68 seats; the National Party, 1. The DP victory has been attributed variously to American influence, social change, a desire for economic liberalization, better organization, religious hostility to the RPP, and a bad harvest in 1949. Perhaps the ultimate reason, however, was simply that in 27 years the RPP had made too many enemies.

Turkey under the Democrats, 1950–60. In the DP government Celâl Bayar became president and Adnan Menderes prime minister, a post which for the first time came to surpass that of the president in importance.

The economy. The Democrats were committed to a program of economic growth, to be achieved through a reduction of state interference. At first they had much success. Good harvests in 1950 and 1953 and an economic boom caused by the Korean War assisted. But problems appeared after 1953. In 1954 another poor harvest obliged Turkey to import wheat again. A shortage of foreign exchange limited the purchase of essential materials and parts, which handicapped industry. After a sudden favourable surge in the early 1950s, the international balance of trade moved steadily against Turkey. Inflation, which averaged 15 percent or more annually, became a serious problem. The government attempted unsuccessfully to control prices through legislation, but its policies of continually rising public expenditure worsened inflation. Despite the problems, the DP achieved considerable success throughout the 1950s.

Political repressions. The political fortunes of the Democrat government closely reflected the economic changes. In the 1954 elections—the Democratic peak—the DP took a majority of the vote and most of the seats; the RPP took about one-third of the vote and many of the remaining seats. Subsequent economic difficulties led to mounting criticism within and outside the DP, to which the government responded with increasing repression. In 1953 much of the property of the RPP was confiscated, forcing the closure of the People's Houses. The RPP newspaper presses in Ankara were seized. In 1954 the National Party was dissolved because of its opposition to Kemalist principles, though it was immediately re-formed as the Republican Nation's Party and in 1958 united with the Peasants' Party to form the Republican Peasants' Nation Party. Laws passed in 1954 provided for heavy fines on journalists who were thought to have damaged the prestige of the state or the law; several prominent journalists were prosecuted under this law, which was made more severe in 1956, while other laws substantially abridged the independence of civil servants (including university teachers) and judges. In 1955 critics within the DP were expelled; these critics subsequently formed the Freedom Party, which in 1958 merged with the RPP. In 1956 limitations were placed upon public meetings.

The DP's declining popularity was reflected in the elections of October 1957. The three opposition parties attempted to form an electoral coalition, but a law passed that September had declared such coalitions illegal. The combined opposition vote was more than half the total, but the DP controlled a majority of the seats, and many believed that the law banning coalitions had deprived the

Seizure of RPP newspaper presses

opposition of victory. Opposition attacks upon the DP became stronger, and it was accused of unconstitutional action. At the same time the Democrats, fearing a revolution, redoubled control. In December 1959 an alleged plot (the so-called Nine Officers' Plot) was unearthed; some of the accused were so clearly innocent that punishment ultimately fell upon the accuser, but it appears that there indeed had been a conspiracy of some sort.

A charge on which the RPP laid great stress was that the DP was reversing the principles of secularism and was favouring conservative religious organizations. The DP had relaxed some of the secularist policies of pure Kemalism, following in the steps of the RPP in the years 1945–49. Religious instruction in schools had been extended and the organization of religious schools permitted. Arabic had been reinstated for the call to prayer, and radio readings of the Qur'ān had been allowed. These, however, were modest concessions in themselves, and the Democrats had clearly demonstrated their unwillingness to tolerate religious influence in politics by suppressing the activities of dervish orders in 1950–52.

The years 1958–60 saw a further worsening of the economy as the government reluctantly introduced restrictive measures. Returns on new investment fell and inflation continued. Serious problems of housing and unemployment were emerging in the large towns, whose population had been growing annually at the rate of about 10 percent, so that by 1960 the urban portion of the population had risen to nearly one-third. RPP attacks became more bitter, and the government's response stronger. In April 1960 the government ordered the army to prevent İnönü from campaigning in Kayseri and formed a committee to investigate the affairs of the RPP. It was widely believed that the government's next action would be to close the RPP. Student demonstrations followed, and martial law was declared on April 28. The army had been brought directly into the political arena.

Growth of economic problems

THE MILITARY COUP OF 1960

Relatively neglected from 1923 to 1939, the army had undergone a rapid expansion during World War II and, after the war, had been extensively modernized with the aid of U.S. advisers. Many officers feared that the DP threatened the principles of the secular, progressive Kemalist state. Some younger officers saw the army as the direct instrument of unity and reform. On May 3, 1960, the commander of the land forces, General Cemal Gürsel, demanded political reforms and resigned when his demands were refused. On May 27 the army acted; an almost bloodless coup was carried out by officers and cadets from the Istanbul and Ankara war colleges. The leaders established a 38-man National Unity Committee with Gürsel as chairman. The Democrat leaders were imprisoned.

The National Unity Committee. From the outset a clear division existed among the officers who had carried out the coup. One group, consisting predominantly of younger officers, believed that to restore national unity and carry out major social and economic reforms it would be necessary to retain power for an extended period; this group included both those who supported a nationalistic and Islāmist policy and those who favoured accelerated secularization. Another group, which included most of the senior officers, wanted to withdraw the army from politics as soon as possible. In November 1960 the dispute was decided in favour of the second group, and 14 members of the first group were expelled from the committee and sent into diplomatic exile.

The main work of the National Unity Committee was to destroy the DP and to prepare a new constitution. Substantial purges took place—5,000 officers, including 235 of the 260 generals, were dismissed or retired; 147 university teachers left their jobs; and 55 wealthy landowners were banished from eastern Anatolia, their lands confiscated. The DP was abolished (September 1960), and many Democrats were brought to trial at Yassi Ada on charges of corruption, unconstitutional rule, and high treason. Of 601 tried, 464 were found guilty. Three former ministers, including Menderes, were executed; 12 others, including Bayar, had their death sentences commuted.

Work of the National Unity Committee

Constitution of 1961. Work on the new constitution began immediately after the coup, when a committee of five law professors was appointed to prepare a draft. This document was submitted to the National Unity Committee on October 18. The Committee appointed a second committee to redraft the constitution; the new draft was presented to a Constituent Assembly, which met in January 1961. The constitution was completed in May and approved by 61 percent of the voters at a referendum in July.

The new constitution established a two-chamber parliament, consisting of a Senate and a National Assembly. A separate electoral law provided for proportional representation. The president was elected by the Senate and National Assembly together. The constitution also provided for a Constitutional Court and a State Planning Organization. The first elections were held in October 1961. The army then withdrew from direct political involvement, although the members of the National Unity Committee retained some influence as life members of the Senate.

THE ASCENDANCY OF THE RIGHT, 1961–71

No party won a majority in October 1961. The RPP won 38 percent of the votes and 173 of the 450 assembly seats. The newly formed Justice Party (JP), led by the retired general Ragıp Gümüşpala, received 35 percent and 158 seats. The remaining seats were divided between two smaller parties—the Republican Peasants' Nation Party, which took 54 seats, and the liberal New Turkey Party, which gained 65. The results demonstrated the enduring popularity of the old DP. Its votes had been divided among the three smaller parties, the majority going to the JP, which also emerged as the largest party in the Senate. The RPP had failed to hold all of its 1957 vote and had suffered by identification with the army coup.

The new Grand National Assembly elected General Gürsel as president. The RPP leader İnönü formed a coalition government with the JP, but the coalition survived only until June 1962, when it broke up over the question of an amnesty for the imprisoned Democrats. After some delay and splits within the parties, which led to the formation of the Nation Party by dissidents who withdrew from the Republican Peasants' Nation Party, the RPP formed a coalition with the two smaller parties. This accelerated the tendency for former Democrat voters to turn to the JP.

In the local elections of 1963 the JP made extensive gains at the expense of the two smaller parties. This led to the breakup of the coalition, and, because the JP was unable to form a government, İnönü formed a minority government from his own party alone, but with voting support from the New Turkey Party. The RPP government resigned after a defeat on the budget in February 1965 and was replaced by a coalition of all the other parties under the leadership of an independent, Suat Hayri Ürgüplü; this coalition acted as caretaker until the elections of Oct. 10, 1965.

In December 1964 a new electoral law introduced the principle of the "national remainder," by which a certain number of seats were distributed to parties according to their proportion of the vote. The law was intended to operate in favour of the smaller parties and against the JP, but in the election of 1965 the JP won a surprising majority with 53 percent of the votes and 240 seats. The RPP received 29 percent and 134 seats, the smaller parties 76 seats. The new JP leader, Süleyman Demirel, a former engineer, was able to form a government.

The "national remainder" principle

Political moderation had triumphed in the years 1961–65. The army had stood aloof while power came gradually to a party that drew its main support from the same groups and areas as the Democrats and that espoused a similar philosophy. Attempts to restore army rule had failed. Intervention proposed by senior officers in October 1961 had been rejected by others. Two projected coups had been foiled in February 1962 and May 1963. Members of a secret society within the army—the Young Kemalists—were arrested in April 1963. Criticism of the 1960 revolution was made illegal in 1962; army leaders contented themselves with occasional warnings against too rapid a rehabilitation of the Democrats. This peaceful political evolution can be ascribed partly to İnönü, who

used his personal influence and prestige to restrain the army even while power ebbed from his own party. The price was the postponement of several reforms. The only significant progressive initiative of the early 1960s was the labour law of 1963, which legalized strikes and promoted an expansion of trade unions; by the 1990s about half of Turkey's nonagricultural workers were members of a trade union.

The JP's program embraced political and economic liberalization. The DP prisoners had been released (1962–64), and their political rights were restored in 1969. The JP eschewed central economic planning and sought foreign investment in industry to provide growth. The policy had much success: Over the period 1963–77 the gross domestic product grew strongly, and industry replaced agriculture as the major contributor to national income. But the JP failed to address new political problems caused by the rise of extremist parties of the right and left and by political violence.

Industrial development, urbanization, and the growth of trade unions provided a base for the development of a radical left that included a new trade union federation, the Confederation of Reformist Workers' Unions (DISK; founded 1967); a revolutionary youth movement, Dev Genç (1969); a socialist political party, the Workers' Party of Turkey (WPT; 1961); and an armed guerrilla movement, the Turkish Peoples' Liberation Army (1970). These and similar groups espoused anticapitalist and anti-Western doctrines, and their followers, particularly in the universities, often supported them by violent action. The violence of the left was opposed by that of right-wing groups, of which the most prominent was the National Action Party (NAP), created in 1963 from the former Republican Peasants' Nation Party and led by an ex-officer, Alparslan Türkeş. The NAP's agenda combined Islām and Turkish nationalism and stressed education. As part of its organization, the NAP developed a paramilitary section, known as the Gray Wolves, that clashed with the leftists.

The JP's failure to deal with increasing violence during the late 1960s was caused in part by its own internal divisions. A coalition of diverse groups, including prosperous farmers from western Anatolia and big and small businessmen, the JP fell victim to personal rivalries. Its victory in the 1969 election, with slightly less than half the vote, was narrower than its 1965 victory; moreover, it lost votes not to the RPP—which was supported by only about one-fourth of the electorate—but to smaller parties. However, a change in the electoral system had made it more difficult for these smaller parties to win seats, and the JP thus increased its parliamentary representation. In the new parliament the right wing of the JP, led by Sadettin Bilgiç, disappointed at its exclusion from the government, defeated Demirel in February 1970; the Demirel government continued but was much weakened by these events.

POLITICAL DEVELOPMENTS SINCE 1971

Military intervention and coalition governments. Senior army officers, concerned by the uncontrolled spread of political violence and a revolt in Kurdistan and fearing that political divisions would spread to the army itself, delivered a warning to the government in March 1970 and a year later forced Demirel's resignation. During the next two years Turkey was ruled by supraparty coalitions of conservative politicians and technocrats who governed with the support of the army and were primarily concerned with restoring law and order. Martial law was established in several provinces and was not completely lifted until September 1973; there were armed clashes with guerrillas and many arrests and trials; extremist political parties, including the WPT and the Islāmic-based National Order Party (NOP), were shut down; and the constitution was amended to limit personal freedoms. Unlike in 1960–61, however, there was no sweeping political reorganization; the constitution, parliament, and the major political parties remained. In 1973 the army withdrew to barracks when its candidate for the presidency was defeated, leaving government once more to the politicians.

Martial law

From 1973 until 1980 the army and the politicians were faced with the consequences of their failure to address the political problems that had led to the 1971 military intervention. During these years Turkey was ruled mainly by weak coalition governments dependent on the support of minor parties, including the extremists; these extremists refused to agree to measures that would curb their own violence and introduced their supporters into state institutions. The annual death toll from political violence rose from 34 in 1975 to about 1,500 before the military intervention in September 1980.

In the 1973 election the RPP emerged as the strongest party with about one-third of the vote, narrowly defeating its principal rival, the JP. The RPP had changed its character since the early 1960s; its conservative wing, opposed to the leftist program adopted at the 1965 election, had departed. The party leader, İnönü, supported the radicals but in 1972 was discarded in favour of the radical leader, Bülent Ecevit. The RPP thus became a social democratic party, drawing its support primarily from workers and intellectuals in the major cities. The remainder of the vote was distributed among small parties, mainly of the right.

Lacking a majority, the RPP formed a coalition with the National Salvation Party (NSP), founded in 1972 as a successor to the banned NOP and led by Necmettin Erbakan. The electoral success of the NSP—which polled more than one-tenth of the vote—was striking. Although the constitution banned religious parties, the NSP was in all but name an Islāmic party; in 1980 it called for the restoration of Sharī'ah law. The coalition's principal domestic achievement was a land-reform measure that reduced ceilings on landholdings to about 250 acres (100 hectares) of irrigated and 500 acres of dry land. Implementation of the land reform was slow, however, and the law was eventually annulled by the constitutional court in 1977. In September 1974 Ecevit resigned, hoping to bring about an election in which he could profit from the popular Turkish invasion of Cyprus (see below *Foreign affairs since 1950*), but his gamble failed; nonpartisan and coalition governments of the right followed, and there was no election until 1977.

In the 1977 elections the RPP again emerged as the largest party, with about two-fifths of the vote, edging out the JP. The smaller parties, which had done so well in 1973, lost votes but still held the balance of power in the assembly. The NSP took about one-tenth of the vote and the NAP a smaller proportion. Demirel's ineffective coalition government continued and was succeeded in 1978 by an even more ineffective coalition under Ecevit. Inflation, unemployment, the trade deficit, and political violence all grew rapidly. The economy was seriously weakened by a rise in world oil prices and a fall in remittances from Turkish workers abroad. Ecevit resigned in 1979, and Demirel formed a minority JP government that announced a major new economic recovery program.

The 1980s. On Sept. 12, 1980, the senior command of the army, led by General Kenan Evren, carried out a bloodless coup. This coup, the third army intervention in 20 years, was generally supported by the public. The leading politicians were arrested, and parliament, political parties, and trade unions were dissolved. A five-member National Security Council took control, suspending the constitution and implementing a provisional constitution that gave almost unlimited power to military commanders. Martial law, which had been established in a number of provinces in 1979, was extended throughout Turkey, and a major security operation was launched to eradicate terrorism. There followed armed clashes, thousands of arrests, imprisonment, torture, and executions, but political violence by opponents of the government was greatly reduced.

As it had been in 1971, the army's intervention was prompted by disgust at the failure of the politicians to control violence, fear of the Islāmic upsurge (which drew strength from the Iranian revolution of 1979), concern at the spread of guerrilla warfare in Kurdistan, and renewed worries that the army might become infected by the politicization that had paralyzed the police force. In 1980, however, the army was determined not only to restore order but also to undertake a thorough reform of the political system.

The 1982 constitution. A new constitution, modeled on the French constitution of 1958, was approved by referendum in 1982. It provided for a strong president (elected for a seven-year term) who appointed the prime minister and senior judges and could dismiss parliament and declare a state of emergency. A unicameral parliament replaced the bicameral experiment of 1961, and—in an effort to reduce the influence of smaller parties—no party polling less than 10 percent of the votes cast was to receive seats in parliament. There were also close controls over political parties, the press, and trade unions.

The first elections under the new constitution were held in 1983 and were a disappointment to the army, which had intended that two parties—the centre-right National Democratic Party (NDP) and the centre-left Populist Party (PP)—should dominate the new parliament. Instead, a third party, the Motherland Party (MP), emerged as the clear winner, gaining more than half of the seats. The MP, a heterogeneous coalition of liberal, nationalist, social democratic, and Islāmic groups, owed its success to the unwillingness of Turks to accept the army's prescription for government and to the reputation of its leader, Turgut Özal. Özal was considered an authority on economic issues; he had been the author of the JP's economic reform package of 1980 and had been responsible for the successful stabilization program carried out after the army intervention. By the early 1980s, then, only the army upheld the principles of Atatürk.

The 1983 elections

Under Özal's leadership the MP ruled Turkey until 1991. From 1983 to 1987 its economic policies—based on removing state controls, encouraging foreign trade, and relying on free-market principles—had considerable success, helped by the fall in world oil prices and by opportunities created by the Iran-Iraq War. The inflation rate fell, and economic growth was strong. After 1987, however, the economic situation deteriorated as a result of the world recession of the late 1980s and early '90s and the government's failure to stem the rising budget deficit, largely the consequence of the continued burden of inefficient, heavily subsidized state industries. Inflation and unemployment rose, and a large foreign-trade deficit developed.

The Kurdish conflict. The public security situation also worsened, notably in the Kurdish provinces of the southeast. Following major social changes associated with the commercialization of agriculture since the 1950s, there had been outbreaks of violence in Kurdistan during the 1970s, generally linked with the activities of the revolutionary left. After 1980, however, the disturbances took on a specifically Kurdish character. Several groups emerged, espousing demands ranging from freedom of cultural expression to outright independence; some turned to violence to advance their cause. The most important of these groups was the Kurdish Workers' Party (Partiya Karkeran Kurdistan [PKK]) led by Abdullah Öcalan. The PKK, a leftist group founded in 1978 that in 1983 began a terrorist campaign from bases in Iraq, sought an independent Kurdish state, although it offered to accept full autonomy. The PKK, with between 5,000 and 10,000 armed fighters, directed attacks against government property, government officials, Turks living in the Kurdish regions, Kurds accused of collaborating with the government, foreigners, and Turkish diplomatic missions abroad. The PKK received support from Syria and from Kurds living abroad and also acquired money through criminal activities. From 1991 the existence of so-called safe havens in Iraqi Kurdistan—established following the Persian Gulf War and protected mainly by U.S. and British forces—provided new bases for PKK operations. Turkish governments sought to deal with the Kurdish problem by granting cultural concessions in 1991 and limited autonomy in 1993. Kurdish political parties, however, remained forbidden. The main government effort remained the military suppression of the uprising; martial law was imposed, and increasing numbers of troops and security forces were committed to the task. By 1993 the total number of security forces involved in the struggle in southeastern Turkey was about 200,000, and the conflict had become the largest civil war in the Middle East. It is estimated that between 1982 and 1995 some

15,000 people were killed, the great majority of whom were Kurdish civilians. Dozens of villages were destroyed and many of the inhabitants driven from their homes. Turkish forces also attacked PKK bases in Iraq, first from the air and then with ground forces; in an operation in late 1992 about 20,000 Turkish troops entered the safe havens, and in 1995 some 35,000 were employed in a similar campaign.

In the 1987 election the MP was returned to power. Its share of the vote fell to slightly more than one-third, but it expanded its representation in parliament. Prior to the election, the political rights of the old politicians had been restored, and they figured prominently in the campaign. Demirel reemerged as the leader of the True Path Party (TPP; founded 1983), which won about one-fifth of the vote. Erdal İnönü, the son of İsmet İnönü, led the Social Democratic and Populist Party (SDPP; founded 1985), which gained one-fourth of the vote. Necmettin Erbakan's new Welfare Party (WP), an Islāmic party, and Alparslan Türkeş's right-wing National Endeavour Party (NEP) also took part, although they failed to obtain 10 percent of the vote and thus were not represented in parliament.

After 1987 the popularity of the MP fell rapidly. Fractures developed—especially between liberals and Islāmists—and Özal was heavily criticized for nepotism and corruption. In October 1989 Özal was elected president, succeeding Evren, while within the MP the internal struggle continued and was eventually decided in favour of the liberals, whose young leader, Mesut Yılmaz, became prime minister.

The 1990s. The MP was defeated in the elections of 1991 but secured about one-fourth of the vote. The remainder of the centre-right vote went to the TPP, which emerged as the largest party in the new assembly. Mainly because of personality differences between Özal and Demirel, the obvious coalition government of the MP and TPP was not possible; instead, the TPP formed a coalition government with the third-largest party, the SDPP. The declining centre-left vote was divided between the SDPP and the Democratic Left Party (DLP) of Bülent Ecevit. The program of the new government, with Demirel as prime minister, represented a compromise between the economic liberalism of the TPP and the political liberalism of the SDPP, but the lack of fundamental agreement made it difficult to tackle the economic and political problems which troubled Turkey. In addition to the continuing Kurdish war there was a recrudescence of the political violence by the radical left and right. After Özal's death in 1993, Demirel was elected president. Tansu Çiller, a liberal economist, became Turkey's first woman prime minister. Çiller emphasized more rapid economic privatization and closer links with the European Union. The coalition government collapsed in September 1995 when the SDPP withdrew from the government after protracted internal divisions. Çiller failed to form a new coalition and called an election for December 1995.

The most striking feature of the 1995 election was the extent of support for the WP, which emerged as the largest single party with about one-fifth of the vote. The political success of the WP reflected the increasing role of Islām in Turkish life during the 1980s and '90s, as evidenced by changes in dress and appearance, segregation of the sexes, the growth of Islāmic schools and banks, and support for Şūfi orders. Support for the WP came not only from the smaller towns but also from major cities, where the WP drew support from the secular left parties. The WP stood for a greater role for Islām in public life, state-directed economic expansion, and a turning away from Europe and the West toward the Islāmic countries of the Middle East. Despite its electoral success, the WP was unable to find a coalition partner to form a government, and in March 1996 a coalition government of the MP and TPP was formed, although it was dependent on voting support from the centre left. Yılmaz and Çiller agreed to share the prime ministership, with Yılmaz taking first turn in 1996.

Despite considerable fluctuations from year to year, Turkey maintained the economic advance that had begun in 1950. Increasingly, Turkey was becoming an urbanized, industrialized country and a major exporter of manufactured goods, especially to Europe. The pace of economic change was an underlying cause of much of the social and political unrest in Turkey during the 1990s.

FOREIGN AFFAIRS SINCE 1950

Until the 1960s, Turkish foreign policy was wholly based on close relations with the West, particularly the friendship of the United States. Turkey sent troops to Korea and joined NATO (1952) and the Baghdad Pact (1955). This Western-oriented policy derived from fear of the Soviet Union, dependence on U.S. military and economic aid, and Turkey's desire to be accepted as a secular, democratic, Western state. After 1960, however, this policy came into question as a consequence of East-West détente, the rise of economic and political cooperation in western Europe, the growing economic importance of Middle Eastern countries, and doubts about the reliability of the United States as an ally, especially in consequence of events in Cyprus.

The independence of Cyprus was arranged through the Zürich and London agreements of 1959. Turkey sought to protect the interests of the Turkish community on Cyprus, and, when these were threatened by disputes between Turkish and Greek Cypriots in 1963 and again in 1967, Turkey contemplated intervention. In July 1974 the Greek government supported the leaders of a coup that overthrew the president, Makarios III, and proclaimed the union of Cyprus with Greece. Failing to persuade either Britain or the United States to take effective action, Turkey acted unilaterally and occupied the northern part of the island, refusing to withdraw until a new arrangement satisfactory to the Turkish Cypriots was agreed to and guaranteed. These events, which were followed by disputes over the extent of territorial waters, underwater resources in the Aegean Sea, sovereignty over uninhabited islands, and air space, led to bad relations with Greece and a cooling of relations with the United States, which Turks believed had favoured Greece. In 1987 and 1996 Turkey and Greece came to the brink of war over the Aegean.

Occupation of Cyprus

As a result, Turkey—while remaining faithful to the Western alliance—broadened its options. From 1964 it developed better relations with the Soviet Union, leading to a friendship agreement in 1978; following the disintegration of the Soviet Union in 1991, however, Turkey was quick to establish relations with the newly independent Transcaucasian and Central Asian states. Turkey recognized China in 1971, improved relations with the Balkan states (although relations with Bulgaria were disturbed by an exodus of 300,000 Turkish refugees from that country in 1989), and cultivated closer connections with the Arab and Islāmic worlds. In the former Yugoslavia, popular Turkish sympathy for the Bosnian Muslims led Turkey to advocate international action on their behalf, and Turkish forces took part in the UN and NATO operations there. Turkey cooperated with Iraq in suppressing Kurdish disorder, although it supported the UN against Iraq in the 1990–91 Persian Gulf War, allowing use of U.S. air bases in Turkey. In return, the United States extended the defense agreement that was due to expire in 1990 and increased military and economic aid. International sanctions against Iraq cost Turkey hundreds of millions of dollars a year in oil pipeline revenues. Turkey's relations with Syria were adversely affected by Syria's support for Kurdish rebels and by Syrian concern over the construction of the Atatürk Dam in southeastern Turkey, which threatened to divert the flow of the Euphrates River. Turkey applied to join the European Economic Community (EEC) in 1959, and an association agreement was signed in 1963. In 1987 Özal applied for full membership. The increasing economic links between Turkey and the European Union (EU)—more than half of Turkey's trade was with the EU in the 1990s—gave the application a stronger economic justification. However, doubts persisted in the EU, where Turkish policy on human rights and on Cyprus was criticized, and in Turkey, where the Islāmists opposed membership. Nevertheless, in 1996 a customs union between Turkey and the EU was inaugurated.

(MALCOLM EDWARD YAPP)

Bibliography: Recent Books

The following list encompasses more than 150 recent books in English that have been judged significant contributions to learning in their respective fields. Each citation includes a few lines of commentary to indicate the tenor of the work. The citations are organized by broad subject area, using the 10 parts of the *Propædia* as an outline.

Matter and Energy

David Arnett, *Supernovae and Nucleosynthesis: An Investigation of the History of Matter from the Big Bang to the Present* (1996), a description of the physics of galactic and stellar evolution from the origin of matter and the synthesis of helium and hydrogen to the creation of atomic nuclei.

Anatoly I. Burshtein, *Introduction to Thermodynamics and Kinetic Theory of Matter* (1996), a translation and update of a Russian text on molecular physics, describing the kinetic and equilibrium properties of gases, liquids, and solids.

Huw Price, *Time's Arrow and Archimedes' Point: New Directions for the Physics of Time* (1996), an application of the paradoxes of quantum theory to the symmetry of time and "backward causation," showing that the future influences the past.

Sidney Perkowitz, *Empire of Light: A History of Discovery in Science and Art* (1996), a history and appreciation of light from its oldest detectable manifestation (infrared cosmic background radiation) to its relation to the physiology of vision.

Giuseppe Bertin and C.C. Lin, *Spiral Structure in Galaxies: A Density Wave Theory* (1996), a theory that characterizes spiral galaxies as wave rather than material phenomena and takes note of similarities between these spirals and hurricanes.

The Earth

Jerry Dennis, *The Bird in the Waterfall: A Natural History of Oceans, Rivers, and Lakes* (1996), a medley of scientific observation, folklore, historical anecdote, and sailors' yarns about wave physics, the hydrosphere, and the phenomenon of biological adaptation as exemplified by the dipper, the bird in the waterfall.

Cindy Lee Van Dover, *The Octopus's Garden: Hydrothermal Vents and Other Mysteries of the Deep Sea* (1996), a firsthand account of Earth's last frontier, the unknown terrain 2,750–3,660 m (9,000–12,000 ft) below sea level, and its flora, fauna, and geologic profile, with a description of the rigours of deep-sea science.

Ralph Hardy, *Teach Yourself Weather* (1996), a summary of knowledge about weather and its relationship to Earth's motion, radiation balance, and distribution of water and the influence of this knowledge on ecology and on crop and weather forecasting.

David Laskin, *Braving the Elements: The Stormy History of American Weather* (1996), an account of efforts, from the rain dance to computer models, to influence or understand the U.S.'s turbulent weather, with a consideration of the effects of industrial pollution and other human interactions.

Eugen Seibold and Wolfgang H. Berger, *The Sea Floor: An Introduction to Marine Geology* (3rd ed., 1996; first published in 1993), a view of the evolution of Earth and its life, based on research in the fields of marine geophysics and stratigraphy.

Ian Thornton, *Krakatau: The Destruction and Reassembly of an Island Ecosystem* (1996), the description of a catastrophic volcanic eruption in 1883 and its aftermath as animal and plant species reestablished themselves.

J.D. MacDougall, *A Short History of Planet Earth: Mountains, Mammals, Fire, and Ice* (1996), an overview of the 4.5 billion-year life span of Earth's landmasses and seas, a history gleaned from rocks and fossils.

Norman MacLeod and Gerta Keller (eds.), *Cretaceous-Tertiary Mass Extinctions: Biotic and Environmental Changes* (1996), a group of essays by paleobiologists and paleontologists on the geochemical and other changes that may have foreshadowed the annihilation of dinosaurs some 65 million years ago.

Life on Earth

Steven J. Dick, *The Biological Universe: The Twentieth-Century Extraterrestrial Life Debate and the Limits of Science* (1996), a chronicle of the ongoing search for intelligent life elsewhere in the universe.

Susan Aldridge, *The Thread of Life: The Story of Genes and Genetic Engineering* (1996), a history and an explanation of biochemistry and molecular genetics, describing the "geography" of the genome, repository of an organism's DNA, and the fields of medical, agricultural, and environmental biotechnology.

Stephen L. Buchmann and Gary Paul Nabhan, *The Forgotten Pollinators* (1996), a description of the 100 million-year-old co-evolution of plants and insects that stresses the economic and ecological importance of insect pollinators and urges research leading to conservation.

David E. Fastovsky and David B. Weishampel, *The Evolution and Extinction of the Dinosaurs* (1996), current thinking on dinosaur origins, diversity, and extinction that calls into question traditional ideas.

David B. Weishampel and Luther Young, *Dinosaurs of the East Coast* (1996), a history of the 200-year search for dinosaur remains on the East Coast of the U.S., where footprints are plentiful but fossil remains are rare.

Alan Feduccia, *The Origin and Evolution of Birds* (1996), a detailed history and an analysis of avian evolution, presenting evidence for birds' relatively rapid development from tree-dwelling rather than ground-dwelling progenitors.

Alexander F. Skutch, *The Minds of Birds* (1996), a characterization of the mental and emotional lives of birds, based on 60 years of observation of 9,000 species, that, without anthropomorphizing, offers examples of a rich array of avian cognitive and emotional abilities, such as memory, counting, and a strong aesthetic sense.

Christopher Vaughan, *How Life Begins: The Science of Life in the Womb* (1996), a month-by-month narrative of fetal development, describing the fetus as a biochemical "stage manager" that signals its needs to the mother through the placenta and discussing brain development, genetics, and fetal sleep.

Frans de Waal, *Good Natured: The Origins of Right and Wrong in Humans and Other Animals* (1996), an argument that ethical and altruistic behaviours are neither exclusive to humans nor recent but rather are fundamental adaptive and decision-making characteristics essential to species survival.

David Quammen, *The Song of the Dodo: Island Biogeography in an Age of Extinctions* (1996), a description of islands as protectors of biodiversity and as laboratories for the study of species distribution that expresses concern over the escalating pace of species extinction and collapsing ecosystems.

John Leslie, *The End of the World: The Science and Ethics of Human Extinction* (1996), a philosopher-scientist's musings on the imminence of doomsday, both human-induced (pollution, nuclear war) and cosmic (asteroids).

Theo Colborn, *Our Stolen Future: Are We Threatening Our Fertility, Intelligence, and Survival?—A Scientific Detective Story* (1996), an account of the threat to plant and animal heredity caused by chemicals still in common use, warning of the dangers to the fetus from these endocrine-attacking substances.

Colin Tudge, *The Time Before History: 5 Million Years of Human Impact* (1996), a reflection on the symbiotic relationship between humans and ecological and planetary forces over time that comments on the effects of agriculture and "depletion hunting" (and, more recently, industrialization) on the Earth's deep planetary rhythms.

Tom Athanasiou, *Divided Planet: The Ecology of Rich and Poor* (1996), a skeptical view of the value of recycling and energy conservation as agents for halting environmental degradation without first controlling the growth of industrialized nations and mitigating the polarization of rich and poor.

William Cronon (ed.), *Uncommon Ground: Rethinking the Human Place in Nature* (1996; first published in 1995), a group of historians, scientists, and critics speak out in favour of preserving some authentic, untouched wilderness.

Human Life

Rick Potts, *Humanity's Descent: The Consequences of Ecological Instability* (1996), a dynamic view of human evolution, theorizing that the prehistoric climate was chaotic and unstable, rather than static, imposing on early humans the need to assume adaptive behaviours in order for the species to survive.

Alan Walker and Pat Shipman, *The Wisdom of the Bones: In Search of Human Origins* (1996), a story of the discovery and piecing together of a 1.5 million-year-old fossil skeleton, possibly the missing link, that folds into the narrative a concise history of paleoanthropology.

Paul Mellars, *The Neanderthal Legacy: An Archaeological Perspective from Western Europe* (1996), a reassessment of the genetic and other contributions made by the Neanderthals to the anatomically modern human populations that succeeded them.

Philip Kitcher, *The Lives to Come: The Genetic Revolution and Human Possibilities* (1996), an account of the revolution in genetics and its ethical implications, beginning with the identification of the role of DNA and culminating in the Human Genome Project.

Gina Maranto, *Quest for Perfection: The Drive to Breed Better Human Beings* (1996), a look at research by geneticists and reproductive endocrinologists whose discoveries have expedited assisted reproduction and also raised the spectre of genetic manipulation and the control of birth outcomes.

Gerald Weissmann, *Democracy and DNA: American Dreams and Medical Progress* (1996), a series of essays showing the parallels between 20th-century biomedical researchers who espouse meliorism and their 19th-century role models, for example, Oliver Wendell Holmes, Sr., and Margaret Fuller.

James Elkins, *The Object Stares Back: On the Nature of Seeing* (1996), a series of meditations and observations on sight and vision as a physiological, social, aesthetic, and emotional function that is subjective, ambiguous, incomplete, and uncontrollable.

Stanley Coren, *Sleep Thieves: An Eye-Opening Exploration into the Science and Mysteries of Sleep* (1996), a collection of facts, rumours, and folklore about sleep, with warnings on the economic and social costs of sleep deprivation and the threat to health and safety.

John J. Medina, *The Clock of Ages: Why We Age, How We Age: Winding Back the Clock* (1996), a molecular biologist's characterization of human aging that examines the ambiguity of death (Is "brain dead" dead?), the ethics of aging and death, and the way aging takes place in each human biological system.

Robert A. Weinberg, *Racing to the Beginning of the Road: The Search for the Origin of Cancer* (1996), the history of the search for answers to the basic questions What is cancer? How does it function? as prelude to the quest for a cure or cures.

Kevin Davies and Michael White, *Breakthrough: The Race to Find the Breast Cancer Gene* (1996), a history of the collaboration and competition that located the gene for breast cancer, a factor in a minority of cases of the disease.

Daniel C. Dennett, *Kinds of Minds: Toward an Understanding of Consciousness* (1996), a philosophical investigation of the properties and qualities of human and animal minds that speculates on the nature of consciousness and the place of language.

Daniel L. Schacter, *Searching for Memory: The Brain, the Mind, and the Past* (1996), an analysis of memory, what it is, how it works, and how factors such as aging or trauma affect it, with descriptions of varieties of memory and of the cognitive psychologists, clinicians, and neuroscientists who promote an understanding of its mechanics.

Mihaly Csikszentmihalyi, *Creativity: Flow and the Psychology of Discovery and Invention* (1996), a study of creativity based on the thoughts and philosophical observations of 90 contemporary scientists, writers, and actors.

Alan Soble, *Sexual Investigations* (1996), a study of human sexuality and love from a philosophical point of view, examining ethical and political issues related to sex and analyzing attitudes toward it.

Human Society

Heather Pringle, *In Search of Ancient North America: An Archaeological Journey to Forgotten Cultures* (1996), a visit to nine geographically and culturally diverse prehistoric sites in North America, where archaeologists have only recently begun to appreciate the social complexity of these early societies.

Charles Bergman, *Orion's Legacy: A Cultural History of Man as Hunter* (1996), a meditation on the "oldest male profession," hunting, with observations on its mythmakers, troubadours, and historians, describing its rituals throughout the ages and speculating that early hominids were probably scavengers before they became hunters.

Lawrence H. Keeley, *War Before Civilization: The Myth of the Peaceful Savage* (1996), an examination of prehistoric civilizations in light of the pervasiveness of war, characterizing "pacification of the past" as wishful thinking and enumerating the lessons that archaeology teaches about preventing war.

Martin Gardner, *The Universe in a Handkerchief: Lewis Carroll's Mathematical Recreations, Games, Puzzles, and Word Plays* (1996), a collection and description of the games, paradoxes, puns, riddles, and acrostics ubiquitous in Carroll's writings, especially *Through the Looking-Glass*.

Herbert Clark, *Using Language* (1996), a view of the phenomenon of language that describes its morphology and that sees it as a joint action between speaker and listener or text and reader requiring the communication of a particular kind of signal.

Alberto Manguel, *A History of Reading* (1996), a study of readers and what they read, from clay tablets to CD-ROMs, with an anecdotal but scholarly examination of 6,000 years of interaction between readers and written words.

Paul Chaat Smith and Robert Allen Warrior, *Like a Hurricane: The Indian Movement from Alcatraz to Wounded Knee* (1996), a chronicle of Native American activism in the late 1960s and early 1970s, including the storming of the Bureau of Indian Affairs building in Washington and the seizure of Alcatraz.

Donald R. Kinder and Lynn M. Sanders, *Divided by Color: Racial Politics and Democratic Ideals* (1996), an in-depth look at why white and black Americans believe what they do on the subject of race, examining how racial issues and attitudes affect politics and such social problems as welfare and school desegregation.

Gary Orfield, Susan F. Eaton, and the Harvard Project on School Desegregation, *Dismantling Desegregation: The Quiet Reversal of "Brown v Board of Education"* (1996), a history of school desegregation and the assumption of a policy-setting role by the courts, with an analysis of the resegregation that followed.

Charles M. Harr, *Suburbs Under Siege: Race, Space, and Audacious Judges* (1996), an assertion that lack of affordable housing in the suburbs is a national crisis and that judges should emulate the corrective action mandated by a court in New Jersey.

Kristin Luker, *Dubious Conceptions: The Politics of Teenage Pregnancy* (1996), a study that attempts to correct popular misconceptions about teenage parenthood by exploring teens' motivations and problems and arguing that teenage pregnancy is a symptom rather than a cause of poverty.

Unni Wikan, *Tomorrow, God Willing: Self-Made Destinies in Cairo* (1996), a portrait of a poor family in modern Cairo narrated by a member of the poorest class and told with dignity, humour, and a transcendent sorrow that inspires admiration and compassion.

Robert Heilbroner, *Teachings from the Worldly Philosophy* (1996), selected excerpts from representative economic texts illustrating the development of economic thought from the Bible to Joseph Schumpeter.

Guillermo Calvo, *Money, Exchange Rates, and Output* (1996), a collection of writings by a macroeconomist on theories of, for example, monetary policy, exchange rates, and public debt.

David Hackett Fischer, *The Great Wave: Price Revolutions and the Rhythm of History* (1996), an account of price fluctuations and patterns in Western history from the 11th century to the present.

Douglas Irwin, *Against the Tide: An Intellectual History of Free Trade* (1996), the evolution of ideas about free trade versus protectionism from Adam Smith to John Maynard Keynes, laying out the various arguments and relating economic analysis to doctrine.

William Julius Wilson, *When Work Disappears: The World of the New Urban Poor* (1996), an examination of the effects on the inner-city poor of vanishing low-skilled jobs, with proposals for both long- and short-term remedies.

Roger D. Masters, *Machiavelli, Leonardo, and the Science of Power* (1996), a reexamination and reevaluation of Machiavelli's thought, hypothesizing that, given evidence of Machiavelli's interest in science and Leonardo da Vinci's possible interest in politics, the two men might have been acquainted.

Eleanor Clift and Tom Brazaitis, *War Without Bloodshed: The Art of Politics* (1996), the dynamics of U.S. politics as personified by prominent individuals such as pollsters, lobbyists, a former senator's chief of staff, and members of both the House and Senate, with a description of the role of big money.

R.W. Johnson and Lawrence Schlemmer (eds.), *Launching Democracy in South Africa: The First Open Election, April 1994* (1996), an account of South Africa's first nonracial multiparty election, discussing the complexity of the election process and evaluating the chances of success for the new democratic government.

Richard A. Posner and Katharine B. Silbaugh, *A Guide to America's Sex Laws* (1996), the historical and constitutional background of federal and state laws governing sexual activity, revealing their anachronisms and inconsistencies.

Cass R. Sunstein, *Legal Reasoning and Political Conflict* (1996), an argument that most judges decide cases by employing a philosophy of legal pragmatism and attention to specifics rather than by engaging in sweeping theoretical generalities.

Ronald K.L. Collins and David M. Skover, *The Death of Discourse* (1996), an argument favouring a cultural approach to the First Amendment that would protect free speech but discourage amusement and commerce from undercutting traditional values of serious discourse and civic participation.

Donald Dworkin, *Freedom's Law: The Moral Reading of the American Constitution* (1996), essays on major constitutional issues of the past 20 years: abortion, affirmative action, race, homosexuality, and free speech, based on the principles enshrined in the Bill of Rights.

James Boyle, *Shamans, Software, and Spleens* (1996), an investigation of issues related to the ownership of information, discussing the pros and cons of treating information as a commodity but supporting restrictions on intellectual property rights.

Jerome Bruner, *The Culture of Education* (1996), essays that place education in a broad context of social and familial life, that urge understanding rather than performance as the foundation of a truly valuable and useful education, and that foresee a "cognitive revolution," with the teacher as enabler.

Irving B. Harris, *Children in Jeopardy: Can We Break the Cycle of Poverty?* (1996), an argument in favour of Head Start and other early-learning programs, showing that they are effective at combating inner-city problems.

Daniel McGroarty, *Break These Chains: The Battle for School Choice* (1996), an argument that education is a moral not a market issue, claiming that a voucher system for public education is, in fact, an extension of the civil rights movement because it makes the same rights (to a first-class education) available to the poor as to the rest of the population.

Art

Barbara Maria Stafford, *Good Looking: Essays on the Virtue of Images* (1996), studies of the relationship of art to the visualizing capabilities of computers, exploring the influence of science, philosophy, and ethics on what is viewed and how it is viewed.

David Denby, *Great Books: My Adventures with Homer, Rousseau, Woolf and Other Indestructible Writers of the Western World* (1996), a man's account of his return to the Western literary canon to find that its writings are as exciting as they were when he first encountered them 30 years ago.

Ian Watt, *Myths of Modern Individualism: Faust, Don Quixote, Don Juan, Robinson Crusoe* (1996), a literary analysis of four representative types of individualism and their influence on 20th-century morality and imagination.

Patrick Chabal with Moema Parente Augel, David Brookshaw, Ana Mafalda Leite, and Caroline Shaw, *The Postcolonial Literature of Lusophone Africa* (1996), a study of Creole and Portuguese literature in the modern Portuguese-speaking countries of Africa, with a substantial bibliography appended.

John Lahr, *Light Fantastic: Adventures in Theater* (1996), a collection of critical and historical essays on playwrights and productions, covering many of the distinguished personalities in the modern theatre and including memoirs, diary excerpts, and interviews.

Linda Hutcheon and Michael Hutcheon, *Opera: Desire, Disease, Death* (1996), an analysis of 19th-century society's changing attitudes toward disease and illness and how those changes were reflected in the way the invalid and the mortally ill were portrayed in grand opera over the course of the century.

Thierry Beauvert, *Opera Houses of the World* (1995), a lavishly illustrated history of opera houses and their performers and performances.

Robert Cantwell, *When We Were Good: The Folk Revival* (1996), a chronicle of the resurgence of folk music and its metamorphosis from the voice of the workingman and farmer to representative of the 1960s civil rights and peace movements.

Veit Erlmann, *Nightsong: Performance, Power, and Practice in South Africa* (1996), an ethnomusicologist's study of an a cappella song tradition that influenced American folk and pop music, in which black migrant workers perform and compete, with a videotape available of one of the all-night contests.

John Hix, *The Glasshouse* (1996), an account of the development of the glasshouse from its origins as a box for protecting a delicate plant to such virtuoso 19th-century structures as the Crystal Palace and large royal conservatories.

Christopher Reed (ed.), *Not at Home: The Suppression of Domesticity in Modern Art and Architecture* (1996), a series of essays criticizing the likes of Le Corbusier, Frank Lloyd Wright, and the Bloomsbury group for alienating modern art and architecture from the traditions of intimacy, security, and privacy that the home had stood for and anticipating a postmodern return to earlier values.

Richard T. LeGates and Frederic Stout (eds.), *The City Reader* (1996), an anthology of writings on urban studies and planning, from the evolution of cities since the Greek polis to the effect of computer-based technologies on urban politics and culture.

Victor Burgin, *Some Cities* (1996), an essay in words and photographs, part observation of the urban scene as an expression of human life and part personal history, describing the author's relationship with cities and their effect on him.

Jean Clottes and Jean Courtin (trans. Marilyn Garner), *The Cave Beneath the Sea: Paleolithic Images at Cosquer* (1996), an account, with photographs, of prehistoric paintings discovered in a cave near Marseille whose entrance has been submerged since sea levels rose at the end of the Ice Age.

Bernard Meehan, *The Book of Durrow* (1996), an iconographic and paleographic study of an early medieval Irish manuscript gospel book (possibly older than the Book of Kells), examining its decorations and calligraphy for evidence of provenance and date and place of creation.

Technology

Edward Tenner, *Why Things Bite Back: Technology and the Revenge of Unintended Consequences* (1996), an account of the unforeseen, often unfortunate, developments that stem from some of humankind's medical, chemical, biological, and mechanical achievements.

Stephen Fenichell, *Plastic: The Making of a Synthetic Century* (1996), a history of plastic, from its origins as Parkesine in England (1862), that describes present-day efforts to make it biodegradable and to reduce its toxicity.

Paul Higgins and Patrick Le Roy, *Manufacturing Planning and Control: Beyond MRP II* (1996), a description of the technology of manufacturing planning, pointing out the shortcomings of MRP (material requirements planning) and proposing a systems technology that emphasizes master planning so that business and manufacturing can keep their competitive edge.

Sophia Behling and Stefan Behling, *Sol Power: The Evolution of Solar Architecture* (1996), an argument in favour of emulating indigenous cultures by extracting maximum benefits from minimum resources and urging the use of solar auxiliaries to reduce depletion of the Earth's nonrenewable resources.

Richard Turton, *The Quantum Dot: A Journey into the Future of Microelectronics* (1996), a look into the past at the microchip, into the present at the quantum dot (a created crystal with the wavelike properties predicted by quantum physics), and into a future where "designer atoms" will have unimagined power and capabilities.

Gerhard Dohrn-van Rossum (trans. Thomas Dunlap), *History of the Hour: Clocks and Modern Temporal Orders* (1996), a study of "time consciousness," from antiquity, with the heavens as clock, to the invention of the mechanical clock and the varieties of time that developed as a consequence: working time, merchants' time, railroad time, and modern hour-zone time.

David Buisseret (ed.), *Rural Images: Estate Maps in the Old and New Worlds* (1996), an examination of privately commissioned maps, from 1570 to the 19th century, both as works of art and as historical records of prevailing social and economic systems.

Sophie D. Coe and Michael D. Coe, *The True History of Chocolate* (1996), an account of the 3,000-year history of chocolate, from its first cultivation in Central America to its vogue in 18th-century Great Britain, with descriptions of its religious, commercial, and medicinal applications.

Francisco Asensio Cerver, *New Bridges: Thematic Architecture* (1996), a collection of photographs and descriptions of 15 bridges built within the past decade, illustrating the harmony between architecture and engineering, aesthetics and pragmatism.

Robert Buderi, *The Invention That Changed the World: How a Small Group of Radar Pioneers Won the Second World War and Launched a Technological Revolution* (1996), an account of the combined research efforts of Great Britain and the U.S. that culminated in the development of radar.

Gregory J.E. Rawlins, *Moths to the Flame: The Seductions of Computer Technology* (1996), a discussion of computer technology and its long- and short-term effects on society and culture, speculating on the potential threat to privacy and ethics.

Michael Prestwich, *Armies and Warfare in the Middle Ages: The English Experience* (1996), a realist's view of medieval warfare, its challenging logistics, problems with public health, and conspicuous absence of pageantry, chivalry, or romance.

Leonard E. Phillips, *Parks: Design and Management* (1996), a detailed sourcebook about the design and management of parks, discussing such factors as low-maintenance vegetation and security and naming the principal features of successful parks.

Religion

Ninian Smart, *Dimensions of the Sacred: An Anatomy of the World's Beliefs* (1996), a cross-cultural analysis of world religions based on seven "dimensions," showing the applicability of these criteria to such secular belief systems as Marxism.

Denise Lardner Carmody and John Tully Carmody, *Mysticism: Holiness East and West* (1996), an examination of the lives and works of outstanding mystics of the Buddhist, Christian, Hindu, Jewish, and Muslim faiths and of the religious practices of Native Americans.

Tulku Thondup, *Masters of Meditation and Miracles: The Longchen Nyingthig Lineage of Tibetan Buddhism* (1996), biographical sketches of 35 teachers, with special emphasis on 16 little-known masters from a particular Tibetan Buddhist lineage who lived between the 9th and the 20th centuries, with a brief life of the Buddha.

Nelson Foster and Jack Shoemaker (eds.), *The Roaring Stream: A New Zen Reader* (1996), a compendium of writings by major poets, practitioners, and teachers of Zen Buddhism and its forerunner, Ch'an, from the 6th to the 19th century.

Karen Armstrong, *Jerusalem: One City, Three Faiths* (1996), an overview of Jerusalem's 3,000-year existence, describing the holy place from which Judaism, Christianity, and Islam each has departed or been expelled, only to return more bound to it than before.

José V. Malcioln, *The African Origins of Modern Judaism: From Hebrews to Jews* (1996), a claim that the Hebrews and monotheism originated in Africa, followed by a history of the Jews in Europe, the Americas, India, Africa, and China.

Scott L. Waugh and Peter D. Diehl (eds.), *Christendom and Its Discontents: Exclusion, Persecution, and Rebellion, 1000–1500* (1996), a collection of essays on the turbulence in the medieval church and its effects on secular life, including studies on the repression of heterodoxy, the fate of non-Christians in Europe, and the religious aspirations of women.

Francis Robinson (ed.), *The Cambridge Illustrated History of the Islamic World* (1996), a history of Islam from the birth of Muhammad to the present, with a description of the economy, politics, education, and the arts in Muslim countries.

The History of Mankind

Sandra Mackey, *The Iranians: Persia, Islam and the Soul of a Nation* (1996), an overview of 3,000 years of political, religious, and cultural history in a region whose strategic natural resources have returned it to a position of pivotal world significance.

Neal Ascherson, *Black Sea* (1995), a historical biography of the sea, describing how its unique oceanography has influenced and been affected by 3,000 years of warriors (male and female), emperors, and traders, from the Scythians to the Soviets.

Andrew Dalby, *Siren Feasts: A History of Food and Gastronomy in Greece* (1996), an account of what the ancient Greeks ate and how gastronomical writing developed among them.

Theodor Mommsen, *A History of Rome Under the Emperors, Based on the Lecture Notes of Sebastian and Paul Hensel, 1882–86* (1996; originally published in German, 1992), a transcription of the notes for a lecture on the period in Roman history following the fall of the Republic.

Kate Cooper, *The Virgin and the Bride: Idealized Womanhood in Late Antiquity* (1996), a study of Roman attitudes toward sexual morality and civic virtue, discussing the influence of the Christian ideal of virginity on Roman life and values.

E.A. Thompson, *The Huns* (1996; first published in 1948), a full reworking of *Attila the Hun* restating the author's assertion that the Hun empire existed before Attila and describing the Huns as little more than plunderers.

Johan Huizinga (trans. from the Dutch by Rodney J. Payton and Ulrich Mammitzsch), *The Autumn of the Middle Ages* (1996; first published in Dutch in 1919), a classic humanistic study of the waning of the Middle Ages, based on the accounts of historiographers, poets, theologians, and painters of the period.

Thomas Bartlett and Keith Jeffery (eds.), *A Military History of Ireland* (1996), chronologically arranged essays on 1,000 years of Irish military history demonstrating the central role of warfare in Irish life and culture from the Middle Ages to the 1990s.

Robert Ford Campany, *Strange Writing: Anomaly Accounts in Early Medieval China* (1996), a survey of ancient Chinese texts (206 BC–AD 618) dealing with the spirit world.

Frances Wood, *Did Marco Polo Go to China?* (1996; first published in Great Britain in 1995), a claim that Marco Polo never reached China, supported by internal evidence from his memoirs and considerable scholarly research.

Wheeler M. Thackston (ed. and trans.), *Baburnama: Memoirs of Babur, Prince and Emperor* (1996), an autobiography, the first in Islamic literature, by a 16th-century ruler of eastern Iran and Central Asia, now Uzbekistan and Tajikistan.

Henry Kamm, *Dragon Ascending: Vietnam and the Vietnamese* (1996), the 4,000-year history of the Vietnamese.

Frederick W. Lange (ed.), *Paths to Central American Prehistory* (1996), contributions by specialists in pre-Columbian art, history, and archaeology that attempt to fill in gaps in the history of Honduras, El Salvador, and Panama from the Paleo-Indian period to the Spanish invasion.

Nieves Mathews, *Francis Bacon: The History of a Character Assassination* (1996), a revisionist analysis of Bacon's exile from court and his resulting disgrace, suggesting that the charges of corruption against him were probably unfounded.

P.J. Marshall (ed.), *The Cambridge History of the British Empire* (1996), a concise political and cultural account of the empire, evaluating its influence on former colonies and the mother country and the effects of its dissolution on immigration and the economy.

William B. Taylor, *Magistrates of the Sacred: Priests and Parishioners in Eighteenth-Century Mexico* (1996), a study of the interaction between priests, their parishioners, and colonial government, including the role of priests as fighters for Mexican independence.

Jonathan D. Spence, *God's Chinese Son: The Taiping Heavenly Kingdom of Hong Xiuquan* (1996), a study of Hong, who claimed to be Jesus's younger brother, the mid-19th-century uprising he led, and the apocalyptic end of the Taiping movement.

Cary Nelson and Jefferson Hendricks (eds.), *Madrid 1937: Letters of the Abraham Lincoln Brigade from the Spanish "Civil War"* (1996), a personal perspective on the prologue to World War II, embodied in letters from some of the 2,800 American volunteers who saw the Spanish Civil War firsthand.

Jeff Chinn and Robert Kaiser, *Russians as the New Minority: Ethnicity and Nationalism in the Soviet Successor States* (1996), an analysis of the collapse of Russian hegemony that has turned former political kingpins into a minority that is ignored at best, exploring the likelihood of accommodation between current and former ruling elites.

James T. Patterson, *Grand Expectations: The United States, 1945–1974* (1996), a review of the personalities, events, trends, politics, and social philosophy in the United States from the end of World War II to the Watergate scandal.

Robert Kagan, *A Twilight Struggle: American Power and Nicaragua, 1977–1990* (1996), an exploration of U.S.-Nicaraguan relations during the Reagan administration, illustrating the complexity of political negotiations on the Cold War's last frontier.

Andres Oppenheimer, *Bordering on Chaos: Guerrillas, Stockbrokers, Politicians, and Mexico's Road to Prosperity* (1996), interviews with key individuals about Mexico's economic and political situation, which is complicated by corruption, violence, rebellion, trade issues, and relations with the United States.

Dali L. Yang, *Calamity and Reform in China: State, Rural Society, and Institutional Change Since the Great Leap Famine* (1996), an account of the 1958–61 famine, relating it to Mao Zedong's Great Leap Forward and the government's subsequent reversal of some of its rural policies.

Leslie Pincus, *Authenticating Culture in Imperial Japan: Kuki Shūzō and the Rise of National Aesthetics* (1996), a study of the historical and philosophical bases for the rejection of Western culture in favour of inward-turning thought.

Edward Alexander, *The Jewish Wars: Reflections by One of the Belligerents* (1996), a group of essays on the war of ideas against Zionism, relations between U.S. and Israeli Jews, strategies of discrimination against Israel, and other topics.

David McDowall, *A Modern History of the Kurds* (1996), a depiction of the 25 million Kurds, whose tribal traditions, lack of geographic, linguistic, or national commonality, and strategic importance have complicated their political situation.

Sam C. Nolutshungu, *Limits of Anarchy: Intervention and State Formation in Chad* (1996), a discussion of the dubious benefits of intervention in the creation of new nations such as Chad.

Charles Van Onselen, *The Seed Is Mine: The Life of Kas Maine, a South African Sharecropper, 1894–1985* (1996), an account of survival in apartheid South Africa by a representative of the humblest segment of the most oppressed class.

The Branches of Knowledge

Stefan Hildebrandt and Anthony Tromba, *The Parsimonious Universe: Shape and Form in the Natural World* (1996), a history of the mathematical and physical theories that illustrate the principle of economy of means.

Clifford Pickover (ed.), *Fractal Horizons: The Future Use of Fractals* (1996), essays on the variety of potential applications of fractals with examples of their contributions to fine art, music, medicine, and fashion.

Anthony Aveni, *Behind the Crystal Ball: Magic, Science, and the Occult from Antiquity Through the New Age* (1996), a survey of the occult, superstition, magic, and science from the era when they were part of the same discipline to modern times.

Martin Gardner, *The Night Is Large: Collected Essays, 1938–1995* (1996), a collection of 47 essays on such broad-ranging topics as pseudoscience, mathematics, the arts, philosophy, and religion.

John Horgan, *The End of Science: Facing the Limits of Knowledge in the Twilight of the Scientific Age* (1996), a hypothesis presented through interviews with distinguished scientists that there are no more unexplored scientific frontiers with the possible exception of the search for a Final Unifying Theory.

Nuccio Ordine (trans. Henryk Baranski with Arielle Saiber), *Giordano Bruno and the Philosophy of the Ass* (1996), an analytic history of the donkey as a symbol in science, epistemology, art, and philosophy as epitomized in the works of Renaissance philosopher Giordano Bruno.

Rocky (Edward W.) Kolb, *Blind Watchers of the Sky: The People and Ideas That Shaped Our View of the Universe* (1996), sketches of Western thinkers and observers whose hypotheses about the cosmos laid the foundations of modern astronomy.

David Lindley, *Where Does the Weirdness Go?: Why Quantum Mechanics Is Strange, but Not as Strange as You Think* (1996), an explanation of the operation of quantum systems, showing how traditional thinking about reality must be revised to affirm that "measuring" the smallest objects commits them irreversibly to a "size" they otherwise do not have.

David Oldroyd, *Thinking About the Earth: A History of Ideas in Geology* (1996), a synthesis of historical views of geology from the days of early maps to modern seismology and geochemistry.

Fritjof Capra, *The Web of Life: A New Scientific Understanding of Living Systems* (1996), a proposal for an interdisciplinary "systems" approach to new discoveries in the biological, physical, psychological, and social sciences that would integrate them into a single context more intelligible to the layperson.

David Philip Miller and Peter Hanns Reill (eds.), *Visions of Empire: Voyages, Botany, and Representations of Nature* (1996), a collection of essays on the sociology of scientific knowledge, describing the behaviour of 18th-century European scientists and explorers when they discovered the indigenous peoples and plants of the Pacific.

William Agosta, *Bombardier Beetles and Fever Trees: A Close-Up Look at Chemical Warfare and Signals in Animals and Plants* (1996), a study of chemical ecology and the uses of organic chemicals by plants and animals to poison, communicate, attract and repel, and camouflage, with suggestions that humans might substitute some of these natural chemicals for synthetics to reduce pollution.

Robert C. Solomon and Kathleen M. Higgins, *A Short History of Philosophy* (1996), a chronological survey of major Western and non-Western philosophies, pointing to their common underlying aim to organize knowledge and to discover the nature of being and of God's relation to humankind.

Thomas Molnar, *Return to Philosophy* (1996), a view of philosophy that would eliminate its arcane language and deconstructed thought and restore it to its role as investigator of the nature of knowledge and the world.

James Burke, *The Pinball Effect: How Renaissance Water Gardens Made the Carburetor Possible—and Other Journeys Through Knowledge* (1996), a view of life that makes survival a matter of knowing and participating in the interactive process that is called "the web of change."

Avishai Margalit, *The Decent Society* (1996), a description of the decent society as one in which honour rather than humiliation is the dynamic.

Joyce Coleman, *Public Reading and the Reading Public in Late Medieval England and France* (1996), a history of the spoken written word, contending that reading aloud, whether communal, devotional, or official, was emotionally engaging, not merely a compensation for illiteracy, and has a direct descendant in books on cassette.

(JEAN S. GOTTLIEB)

CONTRIBUTORS

Abramson, Gary. Reporter on Spain for *Business Week,* the *Chicago Tribune,* and the Associated Press. • WORLD AFFAIRS: *Spain*

Adams, Andy. Editor and Publisher, *Sumo World.* Author of *Sumo; Sumo World Record Book.* • SPORTS AND GAMES: *Judo; Wrestling:* Sumo

Alder, Phillip. Syndicated Bridge Columnist. Author of *Get Smarter at Bridge.* • SPORTS AND GAMES: *Contract Bridge*

Alexander, Steve. Freelance. • COMPUTERS AND INFORMATION SYSTEMS

Allaby, Michael. Writer and Lecturer. Author of *Basic Environmental Science; Facing the Future.* • THE ENVIRONMENT: *Environmental Issues; International Environmental Activities*

Allan, J.A. Professor of Geography, School of Oriental and African Studies, University of London. Author of *Water and Peace in the Middle East.* • WORLD AFFAIRS: *Libya*

Andrades, Jorge Adrián. • SPORTS AND GAMES: *Equestrian Sports:* Polo

Andrejevich, Milan. Writer and Journalist, Washington, D.C. • WORLD AFFAIRS: *Bosnia and Herzegovina; Yugoslavia*

Archibald, John J. Retired Feature Writer, *St. Louis* (Mo.) *Post-Dispatch;* Adjunct Professor, Washington University, St. Louis. Member of the American Bowling Congress Hall of Fame. • SPORTS AND GAMES: *Bowling:* U.S. Tenpins

Arnold, Guy. Freelance Writer. Author of *South Africa: Crossing the Rubicon; Modern Nigeria;* and others. • WORLD AFFAIRS: *Botswana; Burundi; Cape Verde; Chad; Comoros; Djibouti; Equatorial Guinea; Gambia, The; Ghana; Guinea-Bissau; Liberia; Madagascar; Maldives; Mauritius; Nigeria; Rwanda; São Tomé and Príncipe; Seychelles; Sierra Leone; Swaziland*

Arnold, Mavis. Freelance Journalist, Dublin. • WORLD AFFAIRS: *Ireland*

Arrington, Leonard J. Formerly Church Historian, Church of Jesus Christ of Latter-day Saints. Coauthor of *The Mormon Experience* and others. • RELIGION: *Church of Jesus Christ of Latter-day Saints*

Aurora, Vincent. Preceptor of French Literature, Columbia University, New York City. • LITERATURE: *French:* France

Baber, Bonnie. Senior Editor, *Footwear News* magazine. • BUSINESS AND INDUSTRY REVIEW: *Apparel:* Footwear

Backe, Everett E. Senior Scientist and Professor, Institute of Textile Technology. Author of *Cotton Ginners Handbook.* • BUSINESS AND INDUSTRY REVIEW: *Textiles:* Cotton; Wool

Bahry, Louay. Adjunct Professor of Political Science, Washington, D.C. Author of *The Baghdad Bahn.* • WORLD AFFAIRS: *Bahrain; Iraq*

Bailey, George. Author of *Galileo's Children; Germans.* • WORLD AFFAIRS: *Germany*

Bakker, Martinus A. Professor of Germanic Languages, Calvin College, Grand Rapids, Mich. Editor of *Studies in Netherlandic Culture and Literature.* • LITERATURE: *Netherlandic*

Balaban, Avraham. Professor of Modern Hebrew Literature, University of Florida. Author of *A Different Wave of Hebrew Fiction: Postmodernist Israel.* • LITERATURE: *Jewish:* Hebrew

Barford, Michael F. Editor and Director, *Tabacosmos.* • BUSINESS AND INDUSTRY REVIEW: *Tobacco*

Barrett, David B. Research Professor of Missiometrics, Regent University, Virginia Beach, Va. Author of *World Christian Encyclopedia; Schism and Renewal in Africa.* • RELIGION: *Tables* (in part)

Barrett, John C.A. Headmaster, the Leys School; Secretary, British Committee, World Methodist Council. Author of *Family Worship in Theory and Practice.* • RELIGION: *Methodist Churches*

Bass, Howard. Journalist and Author; formerly Editor, *Winter Sports;* Ice Hockey Correspondent, *Daily Telegraph;* Skiing and Skating Correspondent, *Daily Mail.* Author of 17 books on winter sports. • SPORTS AND GAMES: *Ice Hockey:* International; *Ice Skating; Skiing*

Bauer, Stephen. Professor of English Literature, Miami University, Oxford, Ohio. Author of *Daylight Savings,* winner of the Peregrine Smith Poetry Prize. • LITERATURE: *Introduction*

Beckwith, David C. Freelance Journalist, Washington, D.C. • WORLD AFFAIRS: *United States:* State and Local Affairs

Belaski, Ann M. Copy Editor, Encyclopædia Britannica. • BIOGRAPHIES *(in part)*

Berfield, Susan. Staff Writer, *Asiaweek* magazine. • WORLD AFFAIRS: *Indonesia*

Bickelhaupt, David L. Professor Emeritus, Fisher College of Business, Ohio State University. • BUSINESS AND INDUSTRY REVIEW: *Insurance*

Binczewski, George J. Principal Technical Adviser, S.C. Systems, Moraga, Calif. • BUSINESS AND INDUSTRY REVIEW: *Materials and Metals:* Light Metals

Bird, Thomas E. Co-director of the Jewish Studies Program and the Center for Jewish Studies, Queens College, City University of New York. • LITERATURE: *Jewish:* Yiddish

Bisman, Ronald W. North Island Editor, *New Zealand Harness Racing Weekly.* Author of *Cardigan Bay; Salute to Trotting.* • SPORTS AND GAMES: *Equestrian Sports:* Harness Racing

Bleibtreu, Hermann K. Professor of Anthropology, University of Arizona. • ANTHROPOLOGY AND ARCHAEOLOGY: *Anthropology:* Physical

Blum, Charlotte. Staff Writer, *Middle East Economic Digest,* London. • ARCHITECTURE AND CIVIL ENGINEERING: *Sidebar*

Boddy, William C. Founder and Editor, *Motor Sport,* London. Author of *Aero-Engined Racing Cars.* • SPORTS AND GAMES: *Automobile Racing:* Grand Prix Racing

Boden, Edward. Publications Adviser, British Veterinary Association. • HEALTH AND DISEASE: *Veterinary Medicine*

Boggan, Tim. Historian, U.S.A. Table Tennis Association (USATT). Author of *Winning Table Tennis.* • SPORTS AND GAMES: *Table Tennis*

Booth, John Nicholls. Lecturer and Writer. Author of *The Quest for Preaching Power; Psychic Paradoxes;* and others. • RELIGION: *Unitarian (Universalist) Churches*

Borth, David E. Manager, Communication Systems Research Laboratory, Corporate Research Laboratories, Motorola Inc. Coauthor of *Introduction to Spread Spectrum Communications.* • MACROPÆDIA: *Telecommunications Systems*

Boswall, Jeffery. Senior Lecturer in Biological Imaging, University of Derby, Eng. • LIFE SCIENCES: *Ornithology*

Box, Ben. Editor, Trade and Travel Handbooks. • WORLD AFFAIRS: *Costa Rica; Guatemala; Panama; Uruguay*

Boye, Roger. Formerly Coin Columnist, *Chicago Tribune.* • ART, ANTIQUES, AND COLLECTIONS: *Numismatics*

Boylan, Patrick J. Professor and Head, Department of Arts Policy and Management, City University, London. Author of *Museums 2000: Politics, People, Professionals and Profit* and others. • LIBRARIES AND MUSEUMS: *Museums* (international)

Bradsher, Henry S. Foreign Affairs Writer. • WORLD AFFAIRS: *Philippines*

Braidwood, Robert J. Professor Emeritus of Old World Prehistory, Oriental Institute and Department of Anthropology, University of Chicago. Author of *Prehistoric Men.* • ANTHROPOLOGY AND ARCHAEOLOGY: *Archaeology:* Eastern Hemisphere

Brant, Sara. Yearbooks Assistant, Encyclopædia Britannica. • BIOGRAPHIES *(in part)*

Brazee, Rutlage J. Geophysical Consultant. • EARTH SCIENCES: *Geophysics*

Brecher, Kenneth. Professor of Astronomy and Physics, Boston University. • MATHEMATICS AND PHYSICAL SCIENCES: *Astronomy*

Brokopp, John G. Specialist in publicity, public relations, and writing about equestrian racing. • SPORTS AND GAMES: *Equestrian Sports:* Thoroughbred Racing (U.S. and Canada)

Brown, Bess. Human Dimensions Specialist, Europe's Liaison Office for Central Asia. Author of *Authoritarianism in the New States of Central Asia.* • WORLD AFFAIRS: *Spotlight:* Central Asia's Next "Great Game"; *Kazakstan; Kyrgyzstan; Tajikistan; Turkmenistan; Uzbekistan*

Buchan, David. Correspondent, *Financial Times,* Paris. • WORLD AFFAIRS: *France*

Burks, Ardath W. Professor Emeritus of Asian Studies, Rutgers University, New Brunswick, N.J. Author of *Japan: A Postindustrial Power.* • WORLD AFFAIRS: *Japan*

Burns, Erik. Bureau Chief, AP–Dow Jones News Services, Lisbon. • WORLD AFFAIRS: *Portugal*

Butler, Frank. Formerly Sports Editor, *News of the World.* Author of *The Good, the Bad and the Ugly: A Story of Boxing.* • SPORTS AND GAMES: *Boxing*

Cafferty, Bernard. Associate Editor, *British Chess Magazine;* Chess Columnist, the *Sunday Times.* • SPORTS AND GAMES: *Chess*

Calvert, Michael T. Freelance Writer. • BIOGRAPHIES *(in part);* WORLD AFFAIRS: *Austria:* Sidebar

Cameron, Sarah. Freelance Writer and Editor, Trade and Travel Handbooks. • WORLD AFFAIRS: *Spotlight:* The Japanese in Latin America; *Cuba; Dominican Republic; El Salvador; Haiti; Honduras; Nicaragua*

Campbell, Robert. Architect and Architecture Critic. Author of *Cityscapes of Boston;* Coauthor of *American Architecture of the 1980s.* • ARCHITECTURE AND CIVIL ENGINEERING: *Architecture*

Carter, Robert W. Journalist, London. • SPORTS AND GAMES: *Equestrian Sports:* Show Jumping and Dressage; Steeplechasing; Thoroughbred Racing (Europe and Australia)

Chapman, Kenneth F. Formerly Editor, *Stamp Collecting* and *Philatelic Magazine.* • ART, ANTIQUES, AND COLLECTIONS: *Philately*

Chappell, Duncan. Deputy President, Federal Administrative Appeals Tribunal, Sydney, Australia. • LAW, CRIME, AND LAW ENFORCEMENT: *Crime; Law Enforcement*

Chapple, Abby. Writer and Consultant, Consumer Communications, Largent, W.Va. • BUSINESS AND INDUSTRY REVIEW: *Home Furnishings:* Furniture

Cheuse, Alan. Writing Faculty, English Department, George Mason University, Fairfax, Va.; Book Commentator, National Public Radio. Author of *The Light Possessed* and others. • LITERATURE: *English:* United States

Clapham, Christopher S. Professor of Politics and International Relations, University of Lancaster, Eng. Author of *Africa and the International System: The Politics of State Survival* and others. • WORLD AFFAIRS: *Eritrea; Ethiopia*

Clark, David D. Managing Editor, *World Literature Today.* • LITERATURE: *English:* Other Literature in English

Clarke, Douglas L. Captain, U.S. Navy (ret.); Military Analyst. Author of *The Missing Man: Politics and the MIA.* • MILITARY AFFAIRS; MILITARY AFFAIRS: *Special Report:* Combating the Land Mine Scourge

Clarke, R.O. Lecturer and Consultant on Industrial Relations, London. • ECONOMIC AFFAIRS: *Labour-Management Relations*

Cogle, T.C.J. Consultant, *Electrical Review.* • BUSINESS AND INDUSTRY REVIEW: *Electrical*

Corzine, Robert. Oil and Gas Correspondent, *Financial Times.* • BUSINESS AND INDUSTRY REVIEW: *Energy:* Alternative Energy; Natural Gas; Petroleum

Cosgrave, Bronwyn. Freelance Fashion Writer; Features Editor, *Zest* magazine. • BIOGRAPHIES *(in part);* FASHIONS

Coveney, Michael. Theatre Critic, *The Observer.* Author of *The World According to Mike Leigh* and others. • PERFORMING ARTS: *Theatre:* Great Britain and Ireland

Craine, Anthony G. Associate Editor, *Inside Sports* magazine. • BIOGRAPHIES *(in part)*

Crampton, Richard J. Fellow, St. Edmund Hall, Oxford. Author of *Eastern Europe in the Twentieth Century* and others. • WORLD AFFAIRS: *Bulgaria*

Crowell, George T. Senior Writer, *Asiaweek* magazine. • WORLD AFFAIRS: *Korea, Democratic People's Republic of; Korea, Republic of*

Crowley, Edward. Editor, Baltic Magazine Supplements; Director, Technical Writing Services. • BUSINESS AND INDUSTRY REVIEW: *Shipbuilding;* TRANSPORTATION: *Shipping and Ports*

Cunningham, Susan M. Economic and Political Analyst; Freelance Writer. Author of *Latin America Since 1945.* • WORLD AFFAIRS: *Argentina; Brazil; Mexico*

Curwen, Peter J. Professor of Business, Sheffield (Eng.) Business School. Author of *The U.K. Publishing Industry* and others. • MEDIA AND PUBLISHING: *Book Publishing* (international)

Deam, John B. Retired Technical Director, AMT—The Association for Manufacturing Technology, McLean, Va. • BUSINESS AND INDUSTRY REVIEW: *Machinery and Machine Tools*

Deanin, Rudolph D. Professor, Department of Plastics Engineering, University of Massachusetts at Lowell. Author of *Plastics Additives.* • BUSINESS AND INDUSTRY REVIEW: *Materials and Metals:* Plastics

de la Barre, Kenneth. Director, the Bridge Group. • WORLD AFFAIRS: *Arctic Regions*

Deeb, Marius K. Professor, George Washington University, Washington, D.C. Author of *Political Parties and Democracy in Egypt.* • WORLD AFFAIRS: *Egypt*

Denselow, Robin. Rock Music Critic, *The Guardian;* Current Affairs Reporter, BBC Television. Author of *When the Music's Over: The Politics of Pop.* • PERFORMING ARTS: *Music:* Popular (international)

de Puy, Norman R. Minister, American Baptist Churches; Editor and Publisher, *Cabbages and Kings* newsletter. • RELIGION: *Baptist Churches*

Dicks, Geoffrey R. U.K. Economist, NatWest Markets. Author of *Sources of World Financial and Banking Information.* • BUSINESS AND INDUSTRY REVIEW: *Introduction*

Dixon, Bernard. Science Writer; Consultant; Editor, *Medical Science Research.* Author of *Power Unseen: How Microbes Rule the World* and others. • HEALTH AND DISEASE: *Medicine* (international); *Mental Health*

Dooling, Dave. Consultant and Writer, D² Associates. • MATHEMATICS AND PHYSICAL SCIENCES: *Space Exploration*

Dowd, Siobhan. Director, PEN American Center Program; Columnist, *Literary Review* (London). Author of *This Prison Where I Live.* • LITERATURE: *English:* United Kingdom

Dunford, David J. Retired U.S. Ambassador; Adjunct Instructor, University of Arizona. • WORLD AFFAIRS: *Oman; Qatar*

Earp, John H. Director, Halcrow Fox and Associates. • TRANSPORTATION: *Introduction; Freight and Pipelines; Intercity Rail; Roads and Traffic; Urban Mass Transit*

Edmondson, Lesley. Freelance Writer. • BIOGRAPHIES *(in part)*

Ehringer, Gavin Forbes. Rodeo Columnist, *Western Horseman.* • SPORTS AND GAMES: *Rodeo*

Ellis, Roger. Editor, *Mining Journal,* London. • BUSINESS AND INDUSTRY REVIEW: *Mining*

Epstein, Thomas. Visiting Scholar, Brown University, Providence, R.I. Author of *Russian Postmodernism.* • LITERATURE: *Russian*

Fagan, Brian. Professor of Anthropology, University of California, Santa Barbara. Author of *Time Detectives.* • ANTHROPOLOGY AND ARCHAEOLOGY: *Archaeology:* Western Hemisphere

Farr, D.M.L. Professor Emeritus of History, Carleton University, Ottawa. • WORLD AFFAIRS: *Canada*

Fendell, Robert J. Columnist, *Sport Scene Florida.* Author of *Encyclopedia of Motor Racing Greats* and others. • SPORTS AND GAMES: *Automobile Racing:* U.S. Racing

Finch, Andrew. Assistant Director, Government and Public Affairs, American Association of Museums. • LIBRARIES AND MUSEUMS: *Museums* (U.S.)

Flagg, Gordon. Managing Editor, *American Libraries.* • LIBRARIES AND MUSEUMS: *Libraries* (U.S.)

Flanders, Douglas L. Development Officer, *The United Church Observer.* • RELIGION: *The United Church of Canada*

Fletcher, Charmaine. Media and Press Officer, the Salvation Army. • RELIGION: *Salvation Army*

Fletcher, Matthew. Staff Writer, *Asiaweek* magazine. • WORLD AFFAIRS: *Singapore*

Flink, Steve. Senior Correspondent, *Tennis Week* magazine; Formerly Editor, *World Tennis* magazine. • SPORTS AND GAMES: *Tennis*

Flores, Ramona Monette S. Professor, University of the Philippines; Editorial Consultant, *Masks and Voices;* Editor, *Pahinungód Newsletter.* • MEDIA AND PUBLISHING: *Radio* (international); *Television* (international)

Follett, Christopher. Denmark Correspondent, *The Times;* Danish Correspondent, Radio Sweden; Newscaster, Radio Denmark. Author of *Fodspor paa Cypern.* • WORLD AFFAIRS: *Denmark*

Fossli, Karen L. Oslo Correspondent, *Financial Times.* • WORLD AFFAIRS: *Norway*

Foster, David William. Regents' Professor of Spanish and Women's Studies, Arizona State University. Author of *Violence in Argentine Literature* and others. • LITERATURE: *Spanish:* Latin America

Frank, Stephen E. Staff Reporter, *The Wall Street Journal.* • ECONOMIC AFFAIRS: *Banking*

Frank, Steven. Senior Editor, *Asiaweek* magazine. • WORLD AFFAIRS: *Malaysia*

Freeman, Laurie. Freelance Writer and Editor. • BUSINESS AND INDUSTRY REVIEW: *Advertising*

Friday, Elbert W., Jr. Assistant Administrator for Weather Services, National Oceanic and Atmospheric Administration. • EARTH SCIENCES: *Meteorology and Climate*

Fridovich, Irwin. James B. Duke Professor of Biochemistry, Duke University Medical Center, Durham, N.C. • LIFE SCIENCES: *Molecular Biology (in part)*

Fridovich-Keil, Judith L. Assistant Professor, Department of Genetics and Molecular Medicine, Emory University School of Medicine, Atlanta, Ga. • LIFE SCIENCES: *Molecular Biology (in part)*

Friedrich, Mary Jane. Associate Editor, Encyclopædia Britannica. • BIOGRAPHIES *(in part);* THE ENVIRONMENT: *Zoos;* OBITUARIES *(in part)*

Friskin, Sydney E. Hockey Correspondent, *The Times.* • SPORTS AND GAMES: *Billiard Games:* Snooker; *Field Hockey*

Fuller, Amanda E. Assistant Editor, *The Great Ideas Today,* Encyclopædia Britannica. • BIOGRAPHIES *(in part);* MEDIA AND PUBLISHING: *Television and Radio:* Sidebar

Fuller, Elizabeth. Senior Research Analyst, Open Media Research Institute, Prague. • WORLD AFFAIRS: *Armenia; Azerbaijan; Georgia*

Gaddum, Anthony H. Chairman, H.T. Gaddum and Co.; Vice President, International Silk Association. • BUSINESS AND INDUSTRY REVIEW: *Textiles:* Silk

Ganado, Albert. Lawyer. Coauthor of *A Study in Depth of 143 Maps Representing the Great Siege of Malta of 1565* and others. • WORLD AFFAIRS: *Malta*

Garrod, Mark. Golf Correspondent, PA Sport, U.K. Contributor to *Golf World* and *Amateur Golf* magazines. • SPORTS AND GAMES: *Golf*

Gaughan, Thomas. Associate Director of Libraries, Illinois Institute of Technology, Chicago. • LIBRARIES AND MUSEUMS: *Libraries* (international)

Gibbons, Anne R. Freelance Writer. • LIFE SCIENCES: *Entomology*

Gibbons, J. Whitfield. Professor of Ecology, Savannah River Ecology Laboratory, University of Georgia. Author of *Keeping All the Pieces* and others. • LIFE SCIENCES: *Zoology*

Gibney, Frank B. President, Pacific Basin Institute, Santa Barbara, Calif.; Chairman, TBS Britannica Yearbook, Tokyo; Acting Chairman, Encyclopædia Britannica Board of Editors, Chicago. Author of *Senso: The Japanese Remember the Pacific War.* • Feature (interviewer): *A Conversation with Lee Teng-hui.*

Gill, Martin J. Editor, *World Fishing* magazine. • AGRICULTURE AND FOOD SUPPLIES: *Fisheries*

Girnius, Saulius A. Senior Research Analyst, Open Media Research Institute, Prague. • WORLD AFFAIRS: *Latvia; Lithuania*

Goldsmith, Arthur. Freelance Writer. Author of *The Camera and Its Images.* • ART, ANTIQUES, AND COLLECTIONS: *Photography;* BUSINESS AND INDUSTRY REVIEW: *Photography*

Gordon, Katherine I. Editorial Coordinator, Encyclopædia Britannica. • BIOGRAPHIES *(in part)*

Gottlieb, Jean S. Freelance Editor; Historian of Science. Author of *A Checklist of the Newberry Library's Printed Books in Science, Medicine, Technology, and the Pseudosciences, ca. 1460–1750.* • BIBLIOGRAPHY

Gould, Kira. Managing Editor, *Metropolis.* • BUSINESS AND INDUSTRY REVIEW: *Home Furnishings:* Housewares

Greeman, Adrian Lee. Editor, *Civil Engineer International.* • ARCHITECTURE AND CIVIL ENGINEERING: *Bridges*

Green, Anthony L. Copy Product Coordinator, Encyclopædia Britannica. • BIOGRAPHIES *(in part)*

Green, Theresa. Information Officer. • BUSINESS AND INDUSTRY REVIEW: *Materials and Metals:* Glass

Greskovic, Robert. Dance Reviewer, *Arts & Entertainment Monthly;* Freelance Writer. • PERFORMING ARTS: *Dance:* North America

Griffiths, A.R.G. Associate Professor in History, Flinders University of South Australia. Author of *Contemporary Australia; Beautiful Lies.* • BIOGRAPHIES *(in part);* WORLD AFFAIRS: *Australia; Nauru; Palau; Papua New Guinea*

Griggs, Richard A. Political Geographer, Department of Environmental and Geographical Science, University of Cape Town, S.Af. Author of *State Breakdown: The Role of Fourth World Nations.* • WORLD AFFAIRS: *Spotlight:* Fourth World Resurgence in Europe *(in part)*

Grumet, Robert S. Anthropologist, New Hope, Pa. • ANTHROPOLOGY AND ARCHAEOLOGY: *Anthropology:* Cultural

Gutek, Gerald Lee. Professor, Educational Leadership and Policy Studies, Loyola University, Chicago. Author of *A History of the Western Educational Experience* and others. • EDUCATION (U.S.)

Guthridge, Guy G. Manager, Polar Information Program, U.S. National Science Foundation. • WORLD AFFAIRS: *Antarctica*

Hafez, Sabry. Professor of Modern Arabic, School of Oriental and African Studies, University of London. Author of *The Genesis*

of Arabic Narrative Discourse; Arabic Cinema. • LITERATURE: *Arabic*

Halman, Talat S. Research Professor; Chairman, Department of Near Eastern Languages and Literatures, New York University. Author of *Poetry of Ancient Anatolia and Near East.* • LITERATURE: *Turkish*

Hannen, Mark. Competitions Officer, English Basket Ball Association. • SPORTS AND GAMES: *Basketball* (international)

Harakas, Stanley S. Emeritus Archbishop Iakovos Professor of Orthodox Theology, Holy Cross Greek Orthodox School of Theology. Author of *Health and Medicine in the Eastern Orthodox Tradition* and others. • RELIGION: *Oriental Orthodox Church; The Orthodox Church*

Haub, Carl V. Demographer, Population Reference Bureau. Author of *Population Change in the Former Soviet Union* and others. • POPULATION TRENDS: *Demography*

Hawkland, William D. Chancellor Emeritus of Law and Boyd Professor, Louisiana State University. • LAW, CRIME, AND LAW ENFORCEMENT: *Court Decisions*

Healy, Tim. Writer, *Asiaweek* magazine; *Seattle* (Wash.) *Times.* • WORLD AFFAIRS: *Brunei; Dependent States* (East Asia)

Heinzl, John. Business Reporter, *Toronto Globe and Mail.* • BUSINESS AND INDUSTRY REVIEW: *Retailing*

Hendershott, Myrl C. Professor of Oceanography, Scripps Institution of Oceanography, La Jolla, Calif. • EARTH SCIENCES: *Oceanography*

Hennelly, James. Assistant Editor, Encyclopædia Britannica. • BIOGRAPHIES *(in part)*

Henschel, Milton. President, Watchtower Bible and Tract Society. • RELIGION: *Jehovah's Witnesses*

Hering, Howard. Administrative Manager, Frederick Wildman and Sons. • BUSINESS AND INDUSTRY REVIEW: *Beverages:* Wine

Hobbs, Greg. Chief Writer, Australian Football League. Author of 12 books on Australian Football. • SPORTS AND GAMES: *Football:* Australian

Hocknell, Peter R. Research Officer, International Boundaries Research Unit, University of Durham, Eng. • WORLD AFFAIRS: *Spotlight:* Fourth World Resurgence in Europe *(in part)*

Hoeksema, Klaas J. Staff Member, Institute for Polytechnics, Amsterdam. • WORLD AFFAIRS: *Netherlands, The; Suriname*

Hoke, John. Publisher, *Amateur Wrestling News.* • SPORTS AND GAMES: *Wrestling*

Hollar, Sherman. Researcher, Encyclopædia Britannica. • BIOGRAPHIES *(in part)*; OBITUARIES *(in part)*

Homel, David. Author of *Rat Palms* and others. • LITERATURE: *French:* Canada

Hope, Thomas W. Chairman/CEO, Hope Reports, Inc. Author of *America's Top 100 Contract Producers.* • PERFORMING ARTS: *Motion Pictures:* Nontheatrical Films

Hoyt, Mike. Senior Editor, *Columbia Journalism Review.* • MEDIA AND PUBLISHING: *Newspapers* (U.S.)

Hunnings, Neville March. Editor, *Encyclopedia of European Union Laws—Constitutional Texts.* • LAW, CRIME, AND LAW ENFORCEMENT (international)

IEIS. International Economic Information Services. • ECONOMIC AFFAIRS: *World Economy; Stock Exchanges* (international)

Ingham, Kenneth. Emeritus Professor of History, University of Bristol, Eng. Author of *Politics in Modern Africa: The Uneven Tribal Dimension* and others. • WORLD AFFAIRS: *Spotlight:* Signs of Hope in Africa; *Angola; Kenya; Malawi; Mozambique; Sudan, The; Tanzania; Uganda; Zaire; Zambia; Zimbabwe*

Ingram, Derek. Consultant Editor, Gemini News Service. Author of *Commonwealth for a Colour-Blind World; The Imperfect Commonwealth.* • WORLD AFFAIRS: *Commonwealth of Nations*

Ionescu, Dan. Senior Research Analyst, Open Media Research Institute, Prague. • WORLD AFFAIRS: *Moldova; Romania*

Jackson, Peter S. Wyse. Secretary-General, Botanic Gardens Conservation International, U.K. • THE ENVIRONMENT: *Botanic Gardens*

Jamail, Milton. Lecturer, Department of Government, University of Texas at Austin. • SPORTS AND GAMES: *Baseball:* Latin America

Jardine, Adrian. Member, Guild of Yachting Writers. • SPORTS AND GAMES: *Sailing*

Jessell, Harry A. Executive Editor, *Broadcasting & Cable.* • MEDIA AND PUBLISHING: *Radio:* (U.S., *in part); Radio:* Amateur Radio *(in part); Television* (U.S., *in part)*

Joffé, George. Journalist and Writer on North African and Middle Eastern Affairs. • WORLD AFFAIRS: *Algeria; Morocco; Tunisia*

Johnson, Todd M. Senior Researcher, World Evangelization Research Center. Coauthor of *World Christian Encyclopedia.* • BIOGRAPHIES *(in part)*; RELIGION: Sidebar; Tables (in part)

Johnsson, William G. Editor, *Adventist Review.* Author of *Behold His Glory* and others. • RELIGION: *Seventh-day Adventist Church*

Jones, David G.C. Honorary Lecturer in Physics, University of Sussex, Brighton, Eng. Author of *Atomic Physics.* • MATHEMATICS AND PHYSICAL SCIENCES: *Physics;* Physics: Sidebar

Jones, W. Glyn. Professor Emeritus of Scandinavian Studies, University of East Anglia, Norwich, Eng. Author of *Colloquial Danish* and others. • LITERATURE: *Danish*

Jotischky, Helma. Head of Business Intelligence, Paint Research Association. Author of *The Americas* and others. • BUSINESS AND INDUSTRY REVIEW: *Paints and Varnishes*

Karimi-Hakkak, Ahmad. Associate Professor of Persian Languages and Literature, University of Washington. • LITERATURE: *Persian*

Katz, William A. Professor, School of Information Science and Policy, State University of New York at Albany. • MEDIA AND PUBLISHING: *Magazines* (U.S.)

Kelleher, John A. Journalist, New Zealand. Formerly Editor, the *Dominion* and *Dominion Sunday Times* (Wellington). • WORLD AFFAIRS: *New Zealand*

Kelling, George H. Historian and Media Relations Officer, Wilford Hall Air Force Medical Center. Author of *Countdown to Rebellion: British Policy in Cyprus 1939–1955.* • WORLD AFFAIRS: *Cyprus*

Kellner, Peter. Political Commentator, BBC Television; Columnist, *The Observer,* London. Author of *The Civil Servants: An Inquiry into Britain's Ruling Class* and others. • BIOGRAPHIES *(in part); WORLD AFFAIRS: United Kingdom*

Kemp, Peter. Fiction Editor, *Sunday Times,* London. Author of *H.G. Wells and the Culminating Ape* and others. • MACROPÆDIA: *English Literature*

Knapp, Rebecca. Managing Editor, *Art & Antiques.* • ART, ANTIQUES, AND COLLECTIONS: *Introduction*

Knox, Richard A. Editor, *Power Supply World.* • BUSINESS AND INDUSTRY REVIEW: *Energy:* Nuclear

Koberstein, Wayne. Editor, *Pharmaceutical Executive* magazine. • BUSINESS AND INDUSTRY REVIEW: *Pharmaceuticals*

Kolbe, Regina Galgano. Arts and Antiques Marketing Consultant, Regina Kolbe Promotions, New Orleans. • ART, ANTIQUES, AND COLLECTIONS: *Antiquarian Books; Art Auctions and Sales*

Kovel, Ralph and Terry. Authors; Publishers. Authors of *Kovels' Antiques & Collectibles Price List 1996.* • ART, ANTIQUES, AND COLLECTIONS: *Collectibles*

Kraar, Louis. Board of Editors, *Fortune* magazine. Coauthor of *Japanese Maverick.* • BIOGRAPHIES *(in part)*

Krause, Stefan. Assistant Research Analyst, Open Media Research Institute, Prague. • WORLD AFFAIRS: *Greece; Macedonia*

Kroll, Thomas E. Lecturer, Roosevelt University and Northwestern University, Chicago; President, Thomas Kroll Associates.

Author of *Introduction to Data Processing; C Language Programming.* • BUSINESS AND INDUSTRY REVIEW: *Microelectronics; Telecommunications*

Kuhn, Howard A. Vice President; Chief Technical Officer, Concurrent Technologies Corp. Author of *Powder Forging; Powder Processing.* • BUSINESS AND INDUSTRY REVIEW: *Materials and Metals:* Metalworking

Kuptsch, Christiane. Research Officer, ISSA. • SOCIAL PROTECTION (international)

Lamb, Kevin M. Special Projects Writer, Dayton (Ohio) *Daily News.* Author of *Quarterbacks, Nickelbacks & Other Loose Change.* • SPORTS AND GAMES: *Football:* Canadian, U.S.

Lambert, Philip. Associate Professor of Music, Baruch College, City University of New York. Author of *The Music of Charles Ives.* • PERFORMING ARTS: *Music:* Classical

Langeneckert, Sandra. Copy Editor, Encyclopædia Britannica. • BIOGRAPHIES *(in part)*

Laqueur, Walter. Chairman, International Research Council, Center for Strategic and International Studies, Washington, D.C. Author of *Europe in Our Time* and others. • WORLD AFFAIRS: *Introduction*

Latham, Arthur. Associate Editor, Encyclopædia Britannica. • CHRONOLOGY OF 1996

Lavallée, H.-Claude. Director, Pulp and Paper Research Centre, University of Quebec at Trois-Rivières. • BUSINESS AND INDUSTRY REVIEW: *Wood Products:* Paper and Pulp

Lawler, Nancy Ellen. Professor of Economics, Oakton Community College, Des Plaines, Ill. Author of *Soldiers of Misfortune* and others. • WORLD AFFAIRS: *Benin; Burkina Faso; Cameroon; Central African Republic; Congo; Côte d'Ivoire; Gabon; Guinea; Mali; Mauritania; Niger; Senegal; Togo*

Lawson, Fred H. James Irvine Professor of Government, Mills College, Oakland, Calif. • WORLD AFFAIRS: *Syria*

Lee Jai Seong. Research Fellow, Korea Institute for International Economic Policy (KIEP). • BIOGRAPHIES *(in part)*

Legassick, Martin. Professor, History Department, University of Western Cape, Bellville, S.Af. • WORLD AFFAIRS: *South Africa*

Lehman, Richard L. Professor, Rutgers University, New Brunswick, N.J. Author of *Handbook on Continuous Fiber Reinforced Ceramic Composites.* • BUSINESS AND INDUSTRY REVIEW: *Materials and Metals:* Ceramics

Levine, Beth. Freelance Writer. Author of *Divorce: Young People Caught in the Middle* and others. • MEDIA AND PUBLISHING: *Book Publishing* (U.S.)

Levine, Steven I. Senior Research Associate, Boulder Run Research. • WORLD AFFAIRS: *China; Taiwan*

Lindstrom, Sieg. Managing Editor, *Track & Field News.* • SPORTS AND GAMES: *Track and Field Sports*

Litsky, Frank. Sportswriter, *New York Times.* • SPORTS AND GAMES: *Ice Hockey:* North America

Litweiler, John. Jazz Critic; Contributor to *Down Beat, Chicago Tribune,* and others. Author of *Ornette Coleman: A Harmolodic Life.* • BIOGRAPHIES *(in part)*; OBITUARIES *(in part)*; PERFORMING ARTS: *Music:* Jazz

Logan, Robert G. Sportswriter, *Daily Herald* (Arlington Heights, Ill.). Author of *Cubs Win!* and others. • SPORTS AND GAMES: *Basketball* (U.S.)

Longmore, Andrew. Chief Sports Feature Writer, *The Times;* Formerly Assistant Editor, *The Cricketer.* • BIOGRAPHIES *(in part)*; SPORTS AND GAMES: *Cricket; Cricket:* Sidebar

Loy, Dennis. Senior Editor, *Textile Technology Digest.* • BUSINESS AND INDUSTRY REVIEW: *Textiles:* Introduction; Man-Made Fibres

Luling, Virginia R. Social Anthropologist. • WORLD AFFAIRS: *Somalia*

Macdonald, Barrie. Professor of History, Massey University, Palmerston, N.Z. • WORLD AFFAIRS: *Spotlight:* A Postnuclear Era in the Pacific; *Dependent States* (Pacific);

Fiji; Kiribati; Marshall Islands; Micronesia, Federated States of; Solomon Islands; Tonga; Tuvalu; Vanuatu; Western Samoa

McElroy, John. Editorial Director, *Automotive Industries.* • BUSINESS AND INDUSTRY REVIEW: *Automobiles*

McGregor, Alan. Freelance Contributor, *The Times; The Lancet;* Swiss Radio International; CBS Radio. • WORLD AFFAIRS: *Switzerland*

McIvor, Greg. Stockholm Correspondent, *Financial Times.* • WORLD AFFAIRS: *Sweden.*

McLachlan, Keith S. Professor, School of Oriental and African Studies, University of London. Author of *Boundaries of Modern Iran.* • WORLD AFFAIRS: *Iran*

Mango, Andrew. Foreign Affairs Analyst. Author of *Turkey: The Challenge of a New Role.* • WORLD AFFAIRS: *Turkey*

Marples, David R. Professor of History, University of Alberta. Author of *Belarus: From Soviet Rule to Nuclear Catastrophe* and others. • WORLD AFFAIRS: *Belarus; Ukraine*

Mathews, John H. Copy Editor, Encyclopædia Britannica. • BIOGRAPHIES *(in part);* ECONOMIC AFFAIRS: *Banking:* Sidebar

Matthíasson, Björn. Economist, Ministry of Finance, Iceland. • WORLD AFFAIRS: *Iceland*

Mazie, David M. Staff Writer, *Reader's Digest;* Freelance Writer. • SOCIAL PROTECTION (U.S.)

Mermel, T.W. Consulting Engineer; formerly Chairman, Committee on World Register of Dams, International Commission on Large Dams. • ARCHITECTURE AND CIVIL ENGINEERING: *Dams*

Michael, Tom. Assistant Editor, Encyclopædia Britannica. • BIOGRAPHIES *(in part);* NOBEL PRIZES *(in part);* OBITUARIES *(in part)*

Mihalisko, Kathleen. Government Marketing Analyst, Integrated Systems Group, Inc. • WORLD AFFAIRS: *Commonwealth of Independent States*

Millikin, Sandra. Freelance Art Historian. • ART, ANTIQUES, AND COLLECTIONS: *Special Report:* Blockbuster Art Exhibitions; *Art Exhibitions*

Monti, Steven. Senior Index Editor, Encyclopædia Britannica. • COMPUTERS AND INFORMATION SYSTEMS: Sidebar

Morgan, Paul. Writer, *Rugby World.* • SPORTS AND GAMES: *Football:* Rugby Football

Morris, Jacqui M. Editor, *Oryx.* • THE ENVIRONMENT: *Wildlife Conservation*

Morris, James. Calgary (Alta.) Staff Correspondent, *The Canadian Press.* • SPORTS AND GAMES: *Curling*

Morrison, Graham. Press Officer, British Fencing Federation; Correspondent, *Daily Telegraph; Country Life.* • SPORTS AND GAMES: *Fencing*

Mullen, Fiona. Deputy Editor, The Economist Intelligence Unit, London. • WORLD AFFAIRS: *Austria*

Munns, Thomas E. Senior Program Officer, National Materials Advisory Board, National Research Council. • BUSINESS AND INDUSTRY REVIEW: *Materials and Metals:* Advanced Composites *(in part)*

Murphy, Alan. Associate Editor, Trade and Travel Handbooks. • WORLD AFFAIRS: *Bolivia; Ecuador; Peru; Venezuela*

Naylor, Ernest. Lloyd Roberts Professor of Marine Zoology, University College of North Wales. • LIFE SCIENCES: *Marine Biology*

Neher, Stephen. Assistant Editor, Encyclopædia Britannica. • WORLD AFFAIRS: *Political Parties Table (in part)*

Newby, Donald J. Formerly Bowls Correspondent, *Daily Telegraph;* formerly Editor, *World Bowls.* Author of various bowls publications. • SPORTS AND GAMES: *Lawn Bowls*

Noble, Thomas F.X. Professor of History, University of Virginia. Author of *Soldiers of Christ: Saints and Saints' Lives.* • RELIGION: *Roman Catholic Church*

Nugent, Ann. Writer, Critic, and Editor, *Dance Theatre Journal.* Author of *Swan Lake: Stories of the Ballets.* • PERFORMING ARTS: *Dance:* Europe

Nurse, Charlie. Lecturer, Politics Department, Anglia Polytechnic University, England. • WORLD AFFAIRS: *Chile; Paraguay*

O'Donoghue, Michael. Lecturer in Gemology, London Guildhall University. • BUSINESS AND INDUSTRY REVIEW: *Gemstones*

Ogden, Shepherd. President, The Cook's Garden. Author of *Step by Step Organic Flower Gardening* and others. • THE ENVIRONMENT: *Gardening*

O'Quinn, Jim. Editor in Chief, *American Theatre* magazine. • PERFORMING ARTS: *Theatre:* U.S. and Canada

Orr, Jay. Music Writer, *Nashville* (Tenn.) *Banner.* • PERFORMING ARTS: *Music:* Popular (U.S.)

Osborne, K.L. Editor, *British Rowing Almanack.* Author of *Boat Racing in Britain, 1715–1975.* • SPORTS AND GAMES: *Rowing*

Palmer, John. European Editor, *The Guardian.* Author of *Europe Without America: The Crisis in Atlantic Relations.* • WORLD AFFAIRS: *European Union*

Park Chang Seok. Editor, Political-Economic Desk, *Korea Times.* Author of *A Ung San Report.* • BIOGRAPHIES *(in part)*

Parker, Ines. Freelance Writer. • WORLD AFFAIRS: *Belize*

Parker, Sandy. Publisher, newsletter on fur industry; Co-publisher, *Fur World.* • BUSINESS AND INDUSTRY REVIEW: *Apparel:* Furs

Parming, Tönu. President, Estonian Publishing Co. • WORLD AFFAIRS: *Estonia*

Paul, Charles Robert, Jr. Consultant, U.S. Olympic Committee. • SPORTS AND GAMES: *Gymnastics; Weight Lifting*

Pawlaczyk, Paul. Communications Director, United States Badminton Association. • SPORTS AND GAMES: *Badminton*

Pertile, Lino. Professor of Romance Languages and Literature, Harvard University. Author of *Cambridge History of Italian Literature.* • LITERATURE: *Italian*

Pfeffer, Irving. Attorney. Author of *The Financing of Small Business.* • ECONOMIC AFFAIRS: *Stock Exchanges* (North America)

Pinfold, Geoffrey M. Director, NCL Stewart Scott. Author of *Reinforced Concrete Chimneys and Towers.* • ARCHITECTURE AND CIVIL ENGINEERING: *Buildings*

Pojeta, John, Jr. Research Associate in Paleobiology, Smithsonian Institution, Washington, D.C. • LIFE SCIENCES: *Paleontology*

Pollard, Peter. Associate Editor, Trade and Travel Handbooks. • WORLD AFFAIRS: *Colombia*

Prasad, H.Y. Sharada. Formerly Information Adviser to the Prime Minister of India. • WORLD AFFAIRS: *India*

Primorac, Max. President, Center for Civil Society in Southeast Europe, Washington, D.C. • WORLD AFFAIRS: *Croatia*

Prince, Greg W. Executive Editor, *Beverage World.* • BUSINESS AND INDUSTRY REVIEW: *Beverages:* Beer; Soft Drinks; Spirits

Qian Zhongwen. Senior Research Fellow, Literature Institute, Chinese Academy of Social Sciences. • LITERATURE: *Chinese*

Rakisits, Claude. International Affairs Consultant. • WORLD AFFAIRS: *Bangladesh; Bhutan; Myanmar (Burma); Nepal; Sri Lanka*

Rauch, Robert. Freelance Editor and Writer. • BIOGRAPHIES *(in part);* MUSIC: *Classical:* Sidebar

Réamonn, Páraic. Communications Director, World Alliance of Reformed Churches. • RELIGION: *Reformed, Presbyterian, and Congregational Churches*

Rebelo, L.S. Reader Emeritus; Visiting Professor, Department of Portuguese Studies, King's College, University of London. • LITERATURE: *Portuguese:* Portugal

Reed, Arthur. Senior Editor, Europe, *Air Transport World.* Author of *Britain's Aircraft Industry;* coauthor of *RAE Farnborough.* • TRANSPORTATION: *Aviation*

Rengers, Maria Ottolino. Copy Editor, Encyclopædia Britannica. • BIOGRAPHIES *(in part)*

Renwick, David. Freelance Journalist. • WORLD AFFAIRS: *Spotlight:* Rocky Road

to Caribbean Unity; *Antigua and Barbuda; Bahamas, The; Barbados; Dependent States* (Caribbean and Bermuda); *Dominica; Grenada; Guyana; Jamaica; Saint Kitts and Nevis; Saint Lucia; Saint Vincent and the Grenadines; Trinidad and Tobago*

Reyes, Alejandro. Senior Correspondent, *Asiaweek* magazine. • WORLD AFFAIRS: *Vietnam*

Rhodes, Leara D. Assistant Professor, College of Journalism and Mass Communication, University of Georgia. • MEDIA AND PUBLISHING: *Magazines* (international); *Newspapers* (international)

Robinson, David. Film Critic and Historian. Author of *A History of World Cinema; Chaplin: His Life and Art.* • PERFORMING ARTS: *Motion Pictures*

Roby, Anne. Freelance Writer and Editor. • WORLD AFFAIRS: *Andorra; Liechtenstein; Luxembourg; Monaco*

Rollin, Jack. Association Football Columnist, *Sunday Telegraph.* Executive Editor, *Rothmans Football Yearbook.* Author of *World Cup 1930–1990* and others. • BIOGRAPHIES *(in part);* SPORTS AND GAMES: *Football:* Association (Soccer)

Romano, Frank J. Professor of Graphic Arts, School of Printing Management and Sciences, Rochester (N.Y.) Institute of Technology. • BUSINESS AND INDUSTRY REVIEW: *Printing*

Rugh, William A. President, AMIDEAST. • WORLD AFFAIRS: *United Arab Emirates; Yemen*

Rusch, William G. Director, Department for Ecumenical Affairs, ELCA. Author of *Reception: An Ecumenical Opportunity.* • RELIGION: *Lutheran Communion*

Russell, Cristine. Freelance Science Writer and Special Health Correspondent, *Washington Post.* • HEALTH AND DISEASE: *Medicine* (U.S.)

Russell, George. Senior Editor, *Time International.* Author of *Eyewitness: A History of Photojournalism.* • WORLD AFFAIRS: *Special Report:* The U.S. Presidential Election; *United States*

Rutherford, Andrew. Professor, University of Southampton, Eng. Author of *Transforming Criminal Policy* and others. • LAW, CRIME, AND LAW ENFORCEMENT: *Prisons and Penology*

Saeki, Shoichi. Professor Emeritus, Tokyo University. Author of *Japanese Autobiographies.* • LITERATURE: *Japanese*

Saludo, Ricardo L. Assistant Managing Editor, *Asiaweek* magazine. • WORLD AFFAIRS: *Spotlight:* Democracy and Development in Asia

Sanders, Alan J.K. Lecturer in Mongolian Studies, School of Oriental and African Studies, University of London. Author of *The Historical Dictionary of Mongolia* and others. • WORLD AFFAIRS: *Mongolia*

Sarahete, Yrjö. General Secretary, Fédération Internationale des Quilleurs. • SPORTS AND GAMES: *Bowling:* World Tenpins

Saunders, Christopher. Associate Professor, History Department, University of Cape Town, S.Af. Author of *The Making of the South African Past.* • WORLD AFFAIRS: *Namibia*

Schafrik, Robert E. Director, National Materials Advisory Board, National Research Council. • BUSINESS AND INDUSTRY REVIEW: *Materials and Metals:* Advanced Composites *(in part)*

Schoenfield, Albert. Formerly Member, U.S. Swimming Olympic International Committee. Formerly Publisher, *Swimming World.* Honouree, International Swimming Hall of Fame. Author of *The Saga of the Exterminators Squadron.* • SPORTS AND GAMES: *Swimming*

Sego, Stephen. Freelance Journalist; formerly Director, Radio Free Afghanistan. • WORLD AFFAIRS: *Afghanistan*

Shackleford, Peter. Chief of Environment, Planning, and Finance, World Tourism Organization. • BUSINESS AND INDUSTRY REVIEW: *Tourism*

Shallcross, Bożena. Assistant Professor, Indiana University, Bloomington. Author of *Homes of the Romantic Artists* and others. • LITERATURE: *Eastern European*

Shameen, Assif A. Correspondent for *Asiaweek* magazine. • WORLD AFFAIRS: *Pakistan*

Sharples, Jerry A. Private Consultant. Coauthor of *Imperfect Competition and Political Economy.* • AGRICULTURE AND FOOD SUPPLIES: *International Issues; Agricultural Commodities*

Shelley, Andrew. Chairman, JSM, London. • SPORTS AND GAMES: *Squash Rackets*

Shepherd, Melinda C. Associate Editor, Encyclopædia Britannica. • SPORTS AND GAMES: *Special Report:* The Centennial Olympic Games; *Introduction;* OBITUARIES *(in part);* WORLD AFFAIRS: *Dependent States* (Europe and the Atlantic); *Political Parties Table (in part)*

Sherry, Paul H. President, United Church of Christ. • RELIGION: *United Church of Christ*

Shimizu, Teiji. Freelance Reporter. • BIOGRAPHIES *(in part)*

Simon, Alissa. Associate Director for Programming, The Film Center, Chicago. • BIOGRAPHIES *(in part)*

Simon, Reeva S. Assistant Director, Middle East Institute, Columbia University, New York City. • WORLD AFFAIRS: *Lebanon; Saudi Arabia*

Simons, Paul. Writer; Television Producer. Author of *Weird Weather.* • LIFE SCIENCES: *Botany*

Simpson, Patricia A. Independent Scholar. • LITERATURE: *German*

Sklar, Morton. Director, World Organization Against Torture; Judge, Administrative Tribunal for OAS. Author of *Torture in the United States* and others. • SOCIAL PROTECTION: *Human Rights*

Smith, Donald. Editor, *Rubber World.* • BUSINESS AND INDUSTRY REVIEW: *Materials and Metals:* Rubber

Smith, Gregory O. Dean of Academic Affairs, American University of Rome. • WORLD AFFAIRS: *San Marino; Vatican City State*

Smith, Reuben W. Emeritus Professor of History, University of the Pacific, Stockton, Calif. • RELIGION: *Islam*

Solomon, Norman. Fellow, Oxford Centre for Hebrew and Jewish Studies. Author of *The Analytic Movement.* • RELIGION: *Judaism*

Sparks, Karen J. Managing Editor, Encyclopædia Britannica. • DISASTERS; OBITUARIES *(in part)*

Spencer, Peter L. Editor, *Consumers' Research.* • ECONOMIC AFFAIRS: *Consumer Affairs* (U.S.)

Steele, Bruce C. Executive Editor, *Out* magazine. • PERFORMING ARTS: *Special Report:* Computer Animation

Stern, Irwin. Senior Lecturer in Portuguese, Columbia University, New York City. • LITERATURE: *Portuguese:* Brazil

Stewart, Ian. Professor of Mathematics, University of Warwick, Coventry, Eng. • MATHEMATICS AND PHYSICAL SCIENCES: *Mathematics*

Stoffels, Robert E. Consultant. • BUSINESS AND INDUSTRY REVIEW: *Special Report:* Satellite TV

Støverud, Torbjørn. Honorary Research Fellow, University College, London. • LITERATURE: *Norwegian*

Styles, Margretta Madden. President, International Council of Nurses; President, American Nurses Credentialing Center. • HEALTH AND DISEASE: *Special Report:* For Nursing, New Responsibilities, New Respect

Sullivan, H. Patrick. Dean and Professor Emeritus of the College of Religion, Vassar College, Poughkeepsie, N.Y. • RELIGION: *Hinduism*

Summerhill, Edward M. Part-Time Staff Member, Reuters; Freelance Writer, Finnish News Agency. • WORLD AFFAIRS: *Finland*

Sumner, David E. Journalism Professor; Contributor to Episcopal Church periodicals. Author of *The Episcopal Church's History:*

1945–1985 and others. • RELIGION: *Anglican Communion*

Susel, Rudolph M. Editor, *American Home; Our Voice.* • WORLD AFFAIRS: *Slovenia*

Susser, Leslie D. Diplomatic Correspondent, *The Jerusalem Report.* Coauthor of *Shalom Friend: The Life and Legacy of Yitzhak Rabin.* • WORLD AFFAIRS: *Israel*

Suzuki, Toshihiko. Communication Officer, the Delegation of the European Commission, Japan. • SPORTS AND GAMES: *Baseball:* Japan.

Swan, Russ. Editor, *World Highways.* • ARCHITECTURE AND CIVIL ENGINEERING: *Roads*

Swift, Richard N. Professor Emeritus of Politics, New York University. • WORLD AFFAIRS: *Multinational and Regional Organizations; United Nations*

Synan, Vinson. Dean, School of Divinity, Regent University, Virginia Beach, Va. Author of *In the Latter Days; Pentecostal Churches.* • RELIGION: *Pentecostal Churches*

Taishoff, Lawrence B. Chairman Emeritus, *Broadcasting & Cable.* • MEDIA AND PUBLISHING: *Radio* (U.S., *in part); Radio:* Amateur Radio *(in part); Television* (U.S., *in part)*

Taylor, Thomas F. General Secretary, Friends World Committee for Consultation. Formerly Editor, *Friends World News.* • RELIGION: *Religious Society of Friends*

Teague, Elizabeth. Senior Analyst, Jamestown Foundation, The Netherlands. • WORLD AFFAIRS: *Russia; Russia:* Sidebar

Tesoro, José Manuel. Staff Writer, *Asiaweek* magazine. • WORLD AFFAIRS: *Cambodia*

Tétreault, Mary Ann. Professor of Political Science, Iowa State University. Author of *The Economics of the New World Order* and others. • WORLD AFFAIRS: *Kuwait*

Thomas, Robert Murray. Professor Emeritus of Education and Head, Program in International Education, University of California, Santa Barbara. • EDUCATION (international)

Tikkanen, Amy. Editorial Assistant, Encyclopædia Britannica. • BIOGRAPHIES *(in part);* OBITUARIES *(in part)*

Trickett, Anthony. General Manager, Economic Affairs, International Iron and Steel Institute. Author of *Indirect Trade in Steel.* • BUSINESS AND INDUSTRY REVIEW: *Materials and Metals:* Iron and Steel

Tugend, Alina. Press and Publications Officer, Consumers International. • ECONOMIC AFFAIRS: *Consumer Affairs* (international)

Turner, Darrell J. Religion Writer, *Journal Gazette,* (Fort Wayne, Ind.). • RELIGION: *Introduction*

Tutunji, Jenab. Assistant Professorial Lecturer, Political Science, George Washington University, Washington, D.C. • WORLD AFFAIRS: *Jordan*

UNHCR. The Office of the United Nations High Commissioner for Refugees. • POPULATION TRENDS: *Refugees and International Migration*

Utt, Roger L. Editor, *Puerta del Sol;* formerly Assistant Professor of Spanish, Department of Romance Languages and Literatures, University of Chicago. • LITERATURE: *Spanish:* Spain

Venzke, Bruce H. Associate Editor, *Pool & Billiard Magazine;* Past President, Billiard Congress of Wisconsin. • SPORTS AND GAMES: *Billiard Games:* Carom Billiards; Pocket Billiards

Verdi, Robert William. Sports Columnist, *Chicago Tribune.* Coauthor of *Once a Bum, Always a Dodger; Holy Cow!;* and others. • SPORTS AND GAMES: *Baseball:* U.S.

Vinton, Louisa. Specialist and Writer on Poland, Vienna. • WORLD AFFAIRS: *Poland*

Wallenfeldt, Jeff. Assistant Editor, Encyclopædia Britannica. • BIOGRAPHIES *(in part)*

Wallis, Shani. Independent Technical Journalist. • ARCHITECTURE AND CIVIL ENGINEERING: *Tunnels*

Walters, Jonathan S. Assistant Professor of Religion and Asian Studies, Whitman College, Walla Walla, Wash. Author of *History of Kelaniya.* • RELIGION: *Buddhism*

Wanninger, Richard S. • SPORTS AND GAMES: *Volleyball*

Warren, J. Robert. Editor, Asia-Pacific Report, *Chemical Market Reporter.* • BUSINESS AND INDUSTRY REVIEW: *Chemicals*

Watson, Rory. Deputy Editor, *European Voice.* Coauthor of *American Express Guide to Brussels.* • WORLD AFFAIRS: *Belgium*

Way, Diane Lois. Lawyer; Historical Researcher. • BIOGRAPHIES *(in part)*

Wechsler, Helen J. Program Manager, International Programs, American Association of Museums. • LIBRARIES AND MUSEUMS: *Museums* (international)

Weil, Eric. Sports Editor, *Buenos Aires Herald.* • SPORTS AND GAMES: *Football: Association (Soccer):* Latin America

Westberg, M. Victor. Manager of Committees on Publication, the First Church of Christ, Scientist, Boston. • RELIGION: *Church of Christ, Scientist*

Whitney, Barbara. Copy Supervisor, Encyclopædia Britannica. • BIOGRAPHIES *(in part);* BUSINESS AND INDUSTRY REVIEW: *Games and Toys;* OBITUARIES *(in part)*

Wiggins, Lee Anne. Copy Editor, Encyclopædia Britannica. • BIOGRAPHIES *(in part)*

Wilkinson, John R. Sportswriter, Coventry Newspapers. • SPORTS AND GAMES: *Cycling*

Willis, Clifford L. Director of News and Information, Office of Communication, Christian Church (Disciples of Christ). • RELIGION: *Christian Church (Disciples of Christ)*

Wilson, Derek. Correspondent, BBC, Rome. Author of *Rome, Umbria and Tuscany.* • WORLD AFFAIRS: *Italy*

Wilson, Michael. Freelance Aviation Writer and Consultant; Managing Editor, *Testimony.* • BUSINESS AND INDUSTRY REVIEW: *Aerospace*

Wise, Larry. Tournament Staff Director, Indian Industries. Author of *Tuning Your 3-D Bow* and others. • SPORTS AND GAMES: *Archery*

Wolf, Allison Wheeler. Director of Communications, American Apparel Manufacturers Association. • BUSINESS AND INDUSTRY REVIEW: *Apparel:* Clothing

Woodrow, Robert. Formerly Assistant Managing Editor, *Asiaweek* magazine. • WORLD AFFAIRS: *Laos; Thailand*

Woods, Elizabeth. Writer. Author of *If Only Things Were Different (I): A Model for a Sustainable Society; Bird Salad;* and others. • LITERATURE: *English:* Canada

Woods, Michael. Science Editor, Block News Alliance. Author of *Science on Ice: Research in Antarctica.* • MATHEMATICS AND PHYSICAL SCIENCES: *Chemistry;* NOBEL PRIZES *(in part)*

Woollen, Anthony. Former Editor, *Food Manufacture.* Former Editor, *Food Industries Manual.* • AGRICULTURE AND FOOD SUPPLIES: *Food Processing*

World Forest Institute. Information Specialists. • BUSINESS AND INDUSTRY REVIEW: *Wood Products:* Wood

Wright, Andrew G. Associate Editor, *Engineering News-Record.* • BUSINESS AND INDUSTRY REVIEW: *Building and Construction*

Wyllie, Peter John. Professor, Division of Geological and Planetary Sciences, California Institute of Technology. Author of *The Dynamic Earth; The Way the Earth Works.* • EARTH SCIENCES: *Geology and Geochemistry*

Wyllie, Robert J.M. Editor, *Engineering & Mining Journal.* • BUSINESS AND INDUSTRY REVIEW: *Energy:* Coal

Yapp, Malcolm Edward. Emeritus Professor of the Modern History of Western Asia, School of Oriental and African Studies, University of London. Author of *The Near East Since the First World War* and others. • MACROPÆDIA: *Turkey and Ancient Anatolia*

Young, M. Norvel. Chancellor Emeritus, Pepperdine University, Malibu, Calif. Author of *Preachers of Today.* • RELIGION: *Churches of Christ*

Zanga, Louis. Freelance Journalist. • WORLD AFFAIRS: *Albania*

1997
Britannica
World Data

Encyclopædia Britannica, Inc.

Chicago

Auckland/London/Madrid/Manila/Paris/Rome
Seoul/Sydney/Tokyo/Toronto

CONTENTS

538 Introduction

539 Glossary

544 The Nations of the World

544 Afghanistan	596 Dominican Republic	651 Liberia	702	St. Vincent and
545 Albania	597 Ecuador	652 Libya		the Grenadines
546 Algeria	598 Egypt	653 Liechtenstein	703	San Marino
547 Andorra	599 El Salvador	654 Lithuania	704	São Tomé and Príncipe
548 Angola	600 Equatorial Guinea	655 Luxembourg	705	Saudi Arabia
549 Antigua and Barbuda	601 Eritrea	656 Macedonia	706	Senegal
550 Argentina	602 Estonia	657 Madagascar	707	Seychelles
551 Armenia	603 Ethiopia	658 Malawi	708	Sierra Leone
552 Australia	604 Fiji	659 Malaysia	709	Singapore
554 Austria	605 Finland	660 Maldives	710	Slovakia
555 Azerbaijan	606 France	661 Mali	711	Slovenia
556 Bahamas, The	608 Gabon	662 Malta	712	Solomon Islands
557 Bahrain	609 Gambia, The	663 Marshall Islands	713	Somalia
558 Bangladesh	610 Georgia	664 Martinique	714	South Africa
559 Barbados	611 Germany	665 Mauritania	715	Spain
560 Belarus	613 Ghana	666 Mauritius	716	Sri Lanka
561 Belgium	614 Greece	667 Mexico	717	Sudan, The
562 Belize	615 Grenada	669 Micronesia	718	Suriname
563 Benin	616 Guadeloupe	670 Moldova	719	Swaziland
564 Bhutan	617 Guatemala	671 Mongolia	720	Sweden
565 Bolivia	618 Guinea	672 Morocco	721	Switzerland
566 Bosnia and Herzegovina	619 Guinea-Bissau	673 Mozambique	722	Syria
567 Botswana	620 Guyana	674 Myanmar (Burma)	723	Taiwan
568 Brazil	621 Haiti	675 Namibia	724	Tajikistan
570 Brunei	622 Honduras	676 Nepal	725	Tanzania
571 Bulgaria	623 Hong Kong	677 Netherlands, The	726	Thailand
572 Burkina Faso	624 Hungary	678 New Zealand	727	Togo
573 Burundi	625 Iceland	679 Nicaragua	728	Tonga
574 Cambodia	626 India	680 Niger	729	Trinidad and Tobago
575 Cameroon	628 Indonesia	681 Nigeria	730	Tunisia
576 Canada	629 Iran	682 Norway	731	Turkey
578 Cape Verde	630 Iraq	683 Oman	732	Turkmenistan
579 Central African	631 Ireland	684 Pakistan	733	Tuvalu
Republic	632 Israel	685 Palau	734	Uganda
580 Chad	633 Italy	686 Panama	735	Ukraine
581 Chile	635 Jamaica	687 Papua New Guinea	736	United Arab Emirates
582 China	636 Japan	688 Paraguay	737	United Kingdom
584 Colombia	639 Jordan	689 Peru	739	United States
585 Comoros	640 Kazakstan	690 Philippines	743	Uruguay
586 Congo	641 Kenya	691 Poland	744	Uzbekistan
587 Costa Rica	642 Kiribati	692 Portugal	745	Vanuatu
588 Côte d'Ivoire	643 Korea, North	693 Puerto Rico	746	Venezuela
589 Croatia	644 Korea, South	694 Qatar	747	Vietnam
590 Cuba	645 Kuwait	695 Réunion	748	Western Samoa
591 Cyprus	646 Kyrgyzstan	696 Romania	749	Yemen
592 Czech Republic	647 Laos	697 Russia	750	Yugoslavia
593 Denmark	648 Latvia	699 Rwanda	751	Zaire
594 Djibouti	649 Lebanon	700 St. Kitts and Nevis	752	Zambia
595 Dominica	650 Lesotho	701 St. Lucia	753	Zimbabwe

754 Comparative National Statistics

754 World and regional summaries	802 Agriculture and land use	856 Finance
756 Government and international organizations	808 Crops and livestock	862 Housing and construction
	814 Extractive industries	868 Household budgets and consumption
762 Area and population	820 Manufacturing industries	
768 Major cities and national capitals	826 Energy	874 Health services
776 Language	832 Transportation	880 Social protection and defense services (social security, crime, military)
781 Religion	838 Communications	
784 Vital statistics, marriage, family	844 Trade: external	
790 National product and accounts	850 Trade: domestic (wholesale and retail)	886 Education
796 Employment and labour		

892 Bibliography and sources

INTRODUCTION

Britannica World Data provides a statistical portrait of some 217 countries and dependencies of the world, at a level appropriate to the size and importance of each. It contains 194 country statements (the "Nations of the World" section), ranging in length from one to four pages, and permits, in the 24 major thematic tables (the "Comparative National Statistics" section), simultaneous comparisons among all of these larger countries and 23 additional smaller dependent states.

Updated annually, *Britannica World Data* can be consulted as a separate work of reference, but it is particularly intended as direct, structured support for many of Britannica's other reference works—encyclopaedias, yearbooks, atlases—at a level of detail that their editorial style or design do not permit.

Like the textual, graphic, or cartographic modes of expression of these other products, statistics possess their own inherent editorial virtues and weaknesses. Two principal goals in the creation of *Britannica World Data* were up-to-dateness and comparability, each possible to maximize separately, but not always possible to combine. If, for example, research on some subject is completed during a particular year (x), figures may be available for 100 countries for the preceding year ($x-1$), for 140 countries for the year before that ($x-2$), and for 180 countries for the year before that ($x-3$).

Which year should be the basis of a thematic compilation for 220 countries so as to give the best combination of up-to-dateness and comparability? And, should $x-1$ be adopted for the thematic table, ought up-to-dateness in the country table (for which year x is already available) be sacrificed for agreement with the thematic table? In general, the editors have opted for maximum up-to-dateness in the country statistical boxes and maximum comparability in the thematic tables, so as to take the best advantage of recent information.

Comparability, however, also resides in the meaning of the numbers compiled, which may differ greatly from country to country. The headnotes to the thematic tables explain many of these definitional problems; the Glossary serves the same purpose for the country statistical pages. Published data do not always provide the researcher or editor with a neat, unambiguous choice between a datum compiled on two different bases (say, railroad track length, or route length), one of which is wanted and the other not. More often a choice must be made among a variety of official, private, and external intergovernmental (UN, FAO, IMF) sources, each reporting its best data but each representing a set of problems: (1) of methodological variance from (or among) international conventions; (2) of analytical completeness (data for a single year may, successively, be projected [based on 10 months' data], preliminary [for 12 months], final, revised or adjusted, etc.); (3) of time frame, or accounting interval (data may represent a full Gregorian calendar year [preferred], a fiscal year, an Islamic or other national or religious year, a multiyear period or

average [when a one-year statement would contain unrepresentative results]); (4) of continuity with previous data; and the like. Finally, published data on a particular subject may be complete and final but impossible to summarize in a simple manner. The education system of a single country may include, for example, public and private sectors; local, state, or national systems; varying grades, tracks, or forms within a single system; or opportunities for double-counting or fractional counting of a student, teacher, or institution. When no recent official data exist, the tables may show unofficial estimates, a range (of published opinion), analogous data, or no data at all. For certain subjects, especially population, the editors have prepared their own estimates.

The published basis of the information compiled is the statistical collections of Encyclopædia Britannica, Inc., some of the principal elements of which are enumerated in the Bibliography. Usual holdings for a country with a well-developed statistical program may include any of the following kinds of documents: the national statistical abstract; the constitution; the most recent censuses of population; periodic or occasional reports on vital statistics, social indicators, agriculture, mining, labour, manufacturing, domestic and foreign trade, finance and banking, transportation, and communications. Those works are supplemented by data received in correspondence. Further information is received in a variety of formats—telephone communications, fax, microfilm and microfiche, and most recently, in electronic formats such as computer disks, CD-ROMs, and the on-line resources of the Internet. Though the primary sources remain print documents, the balance is changing rapidly and with it standards as to what constitutes the research process itself. Some two score national statistical offices were publishing on the Internet at this writing, but more will surely follow, as will other ministries and departments, intergovernmental and nongovernmental organizations, and institutional and commercial providers. The challenge of balancing the editorial goals and readers' expectations of the distinctly different print and on-line versions of *World Data, Book of the Year,* and the *Britannica* itself against the panoply of sources and media now available will provide a daunting editorial challenge for the coming years.

The great majority of the social, economic, and financial data contained in this work should not be interpreted in isolation. Interpretive text of long perspective, such as that of the *Encyclopædia Britannica* itself; political, geographic, and topical maps, such as those in the *Britannica Atlas;* and recent analysis of political events and economic trends, such as that contained in the articles of the *Book of the Year,* will all help to supply balance, physical framework, and analytic focus that numbers alone cannot provide. By the same token, study of those sources will be made more concrete by use of *Britannica World Data* to supply up-to-date geographic, demographic, and economic detail.

GLOSSARY

A number of terms that are used to classify and report data in the "Nations of the World" section require some explanation.

Those italicized terms that are used regularly in the country compilations to introduce specific categories of information (*e.g., birth rate, budget*) appear in this glossary in italic boldface type, followed by a description of the precise kind of information being offered and how it has been edited and presented.

All other terms are printed here in roman boldface type. Many terms have quite specific meanings in statistical reporting, and they are so defined here. Other terms have less specific application as they are used by different countries or organizations. Data in the country compilations based on definitions markedly different from those below will usually be footnoted.

Terms that appear in small capitals in certain definitions are themselves defined at their respective alphabetical locations.

Terms whose definitions are marked by an asterisk (*) refer to data supplied only in the larger two- to four-page country compilations.

access to services, a group of measures indicating a population's level of access to public services, including electrical power, treated public drinking water, sewage removal, and fire protection.*

activity rate, *see* participation/activity rates.

age breakdown, the distribution of a given population by age, usually reported here as percentages of total population in 15-year age brackets. When substantial numbers of persons do not know, or state, their exact age, distributions may not total 100.0%.

area, the total surface area of a country or its administrative subdivisions, including both land and inland (nontidal) water area. Land area is usually calculated from "mean low water" on a "plane table," or flat, basis.

area and population, a tabulation usually including the first-order administrative subdivisions of the country (such as the states of the United States), with capital (headquarters, or administrative seat), area, and population. When these subdivisions are especially numerous or, occasionally, nonexistent, a planning, electoral, census, or other nonadministrative scheme of regional subdivisions has been substituted.

associated state, *see* state.

atheist, in statements of religious affiliation, one who professes active opposition to religion; "nonreligious" refers to those professing only no religion, nonbelief, or doubt.

balance of payments, a financial statement for a country for a given period showing the balance among: (1) transactions in goods, services, and income between that country and the rest of the world, (2) changes in ownership or valuation of that country's monetary gold, SPECIAL DRAWING RIGHTS, and claims on and liabilities to the rest of the world, and (3) unrequited transfers and counterpart entries needed (in an accounting sense) to balance transactions and changes among any of the foregoing types of exchange that are not mutually offsetting. Detail of national law as to what constitutes a transaction, the basis of its valuation, and the size of a transaction visible to fiscal authorities

all result in differences in the meaning of a particular national statement.*

balance of trade, the net value of all international goods trade of a country, usually excluding reexports (goods received only for transshipment), and the percentage that this net represents of total trade.

Balance of trade refers only to the "visible" international trade of goods as recorded by customs authorities and is thus a segment of a country's BALANCE OF PAYMENTS, which takes all visible and invisible trade with other countries into account. (Invisible trade refers to imports and exports of money, financial instruments, and services such as transport, tourism, and insurance.) A country has a favourable, or positive (+), balance of trade when the value of exports exceeds that of imports and negative (−) when imports exceed exports.

barrel (bbl), a unit of liquid measure. The barrel conventionally used for reporting crude petroleum and petroleum products is equal to 42 U.S. gallons, or 159 litres. The number of barrels of crude petroleum per metric ton, ranging typically from 6.20 to 8.13, depends upon the specific gravity of the petroleum. The world average is roughly 7.33 barrels per ton.

birth rate, the number of live births annually per 1,000 of midyear population. Birth rates for individual countries may be compared with the estimated world annual average of 25.0 births per 1,000 population between 1990 and 1995.

budget, the annual receipts and expenditures—of a central government for its activities only; does not include state, provincial, or local governments or semipublic (parastatal, quasi-nongovernmental) corporations unless otherwise specified. Figures for budgets are limited

---

Abbreviations

Measurements

cu m	cubic metre(s)
kg	kilogram(s)
km	kilometre(s)
kW	kilowatt(s)
kW-hr	kilowatt-hour(s)
metric ton-km	metric ton-kilometre(s)
mi	mile(s)
passenger-km	passenger-kilometre(s)
passenger-mi	passenger-mile(s)
short ton-mi	short ton-mile(s)
sq km	square kilometre(s)
sq m	square metre(s)
sq mi	square mile(s)
troy oz	troy ounce(s)
yr	year(s)

Political Units and International Organizations

CACM	Central American Common Market
Caricom	Caribbean Community and Common Market
CFA	Communauté Financière Africaine
CFP	Comptoirs Françaises du Pacifique
CIS	Commonwealth of Independent States
CUSA	Customs Union of Southern Africa
E.Ger.	East Germany
EC	European Communities
EU	European Union
FAO	United Nations Food and Agriculture Organization
IMF	International Monetary Fund
OECS	Organization of Eastern Caribbean States
U.A.E.	United Arab Emirates
U.K.	United Kingdom
U.S.	United States
U.S.S.R.	Union of Soviet Socialist Republics
W.Ger.	West Germany

Months

Jan.	January	Oct.	October
Feb.	February	Nov.	November
Aug.	August	Dec.	December
Sept.	September		

Miscellaneous

AIDS	Acquired Immune Deficiency Syndrome
avg.	average
c.i.f.	cost, insurance, and freight
commun.	communications
CPI	consumer price index
est.	estimate(d)
excl.	excluding
f.o.b.	free on board
GDP	gross domestic product
GNP	gross national product
govt.	government
incl.	including
mo.	month(s)
n.a.	not available (in text)
n.e.s.	not elsewhere specified
NMP	net material product
no.	number
pl.	plural
pos.	position
pub. admin.	public administration
PVC	Polyvinyl Chloride
SDR	Special Drawing Right
SITC	Standard International Trade Classification
svcs.	services
teacher tr.	teacher training
transp.	transportation
voc.	vocational
$	dollar (of any currency area)
£	pound (of any currency area)
...	not available (in tables)
—	none, less than half the smallest unit shown, or not applicable (in tables)

to ordinary (recurrent) receipts and expenditures, wherever possible, and exclude capital expenditures—*i.e.,* funds for development and other special projects originating as foreign-aid grants or loans.

When both a recurrent and a capital budget exist for a single country, the former is the budget funded entirely from national resources (taxes, duties, excises, etc.) that would recur (be generated by economic activity) every year. It funds the most basic governmental services, those least able to suffer interruption. The capital budget is usually funded by external aid and may change its size considerably from year to year.

capital, usually, the actual seat of government and administration of a state. When more than one capital exists, each is identified by kind; when interim arrangements exist during the creation or movement of a national capital, the de facto situation is described.

Anomalous cases are annotated, such as those in which (1) the de jure designation under the country's laws differs from actual local practice (*e.g.,* Benin's designation of one capital in constitutional law, but another in actual practice), (2) international recognition does not validate a country's claim (as with the proclamation by Israel of a capital on territory not fully recognized as part of Israel), or (3) both a state and a capital have been proclaimed on territory recognized as part of another state (as with the Turkish Republic of Northern Cyprus).

capital budget, *see* budget.

causes of death, as defined by the World Health Organization, "the disease or injury which initiated the train of morbid events leading directly to death, or the circumstances of accident or violence which produced the fatal injury." This principle, the "underlying cause of death," is the basis of the medical judgment as to cause; the statistical classification system according to which these causes are grouped and named is the *International List of Causes of Death,* the latest revision of which is the Tenth. Reporting is usually in terms of events per 100,000 population. When data on actual causes of death are unavailable, information on morbidity, or illness rate, usually given as reported cases per 100,000 of infectious diseases (notifiable to WHO as a matter of international agreement), may be substituted.

chief of state/head of government, paramount national governmental officer(s) exercising the highest executive and/or ceremonial roles of a country's government. In general usage, the chief of state is the formal head of a national state. The primary responsibilities of the chief of state may range from the purely ceremonial—convening legislatures and greeting foreign officials—to the exercise of complete national executive authority. The head of government, when this function exists separately, is the officer nominally charged (by the constitution) with the majority of actual executive powers, though they may not in practice be exercised, especially in military or single-party regimes in which effective power may reside entirely outside the executive governmental machinery provided by the constitution. A prime minister, for example, usually the actual head of government, may in practice exercise only cabinet-level authority.

In communist countries an official identified as the chief of state may be the chairman of the policy-making organ, and the official given as the head of government the chairman of the nominal administrative/executive organ.

c.i.f. (trade valuation): *see* imports.

colony, an area annexed to, or controlled by, an independent state but not an integral part of it; a non-self-governing territory. A colony has a charter and may have a degree of self-government. A crown colony is a colony originally chartered by the British government.

commonwealth (U.K. and U.S.), a self-governing political entity that has regard to the common weal, or good; usually associated with the United Kingdom or United States. Examples include the Commonwealth of Nations (composed of independent states [from 1931 onward]), Puerto Rico since 1952, and the Northern Marianas since 1979.

communications, collectively, the means available for the public transmission of information within a country. Data are provided for daily newspapers, their number and total circulation, and the per capita rate of circulation implied by that total; for radio, television, and telephone receivers, total numbers and rates of availability are supplied. Telephone data refer to "main lines," or the number of subscriber lines (not the number of receivers) having access to the public switched network.

constant prices, an adjustment to the members of a financial time series to eliminate the effect of inflation year by year. It consists of referring all data in the series to a single year so that "real" change may be seen.

constitutional monarchy, *see* monarchy.

consumer price index (CPI), also known as the retail price index, or the cost-of-living index, a series of index numbers assigned to the price of a selected "basket," or assortment, of basic consumer goods and services in a country, region, city, or type of household in order to measure changes over time in prices paid by a typical household for those goods and services. Items included in the CPI are ordinarily determined by governmental surveys of typical household expenditures and are assigned weights relative to their proportion of those expenditures. Index values are period averages unless otherwise noted.

coprincipality, *see* monarchy.

current prices, the valuation of a financial aggregate as of the year reported.

daily per capita caloric intake (supply), the calories equivalent to the known average daily supply of foodstuffs for human consumption in a given country divided by the population of the country (and the proportion of that supply provided, respectively, by vegetable and animal sources). The daily per capita caloric intake of a country may be compared with the corresponding recommended minimum daily requirement. The latter is calculated by the Food and Agriculture Organization of the United Nations from the age and sex distributions, average body weights, and environmental temperatures in a given region to determine the calories needed to sustain a person there at normal levels of activity and health. The daily per capita caloric requirement ranges from 2,200 to 2,500.

de facto population, for a given area, the population composed of those actually present at a particular time, including temporary residents and visitors (such as immigrants not yet granted permanent status, "guest" or expatriate workers, refugees, or tourists), but excluding legal residents temporarily absent.

de jure population, for a given area, the population composed only of those legally resident at a particular time, excluding temporary residents and visitors (such as "guest" or expatriate workers, refugees, or tourists), but including legal residents temporarily absent.

deadweight tonnage, the maximum weight of cargo, fuel, fresh water, stores, and persons that may safely be carried by a ship. It is customarily measured in long tons of 2,240 pounds each, equivalent to 1.016 metric tons. Deadweight tonnage is the difference between the tonnage of a fully loaded ship and the fully unloaded tonnage of that ship.

See also gross ton.

death rate, the number of deaths annually per 1,000 of midyear population. Death rates for individual countries may be compared with the estimated world annual average of 9.3 deaths per 1,000 population between 1990 and 1995.

density (of population), usually, the DE FACTO POPULATION of a country divided by its total area. Special adjustment is made for large areas of inland water, desert, or other uninhabitable areas—*e.g.,* excluding the ice cap of Greenland.

department, a first-order civil administrative subdivision. The *overseas department* (France) is an overseas subdivision of the French Republic, almost equivalent to a department of metropolitan France, with elected representation in the French Parliament.

dependent state, constitutionally or statutorily organized political entity outside of and under

---

Dependent states[1]

Australia	**Portugal**
Christmas Island	Macau
Cocos (Keeling) Islands	**United Kingdom**
Norfolk Island	Anguilla
Denmark	Bermuda
Faroe Islands	British Virgin Islands
Greenland	Cayman Islands
France	Falkland Islands
French Guiana	Gibraltar
French Polynesia	Guernsey
Guadeloupe	Hong Kong
Martinique	Isle of Man
Mayotte	Jersey
New Caledonia	Montserrat
Réunion	Pitcairn Island
Saint Pierre and Miquelon	Saint Helena and Dependencies
Wallis and Futuna	Turks and Caicos Islands
Netherlands, The	**United States**
Aruba	American Samoa
Netherlands Antilles	Guam
New Zealand	Northern Mariana Islands
Cook Islands	Puerto Rico
Niue	Virgin Islands (of the U.S.)
Tokelau	
Norway	
Jan Mayen	
Svalbard	

[1]Excludes territories (1) to which Antarctic Treaty is applicable in whole or in part, (2) without permanent civilian population, (3) without internationally recognized civilian government (Western Sahara, Gaza Strip), or (4) representing unadjudicated unilateral or multilateral territorial claims.

the jurisdiction of an independent state (or a federal element of such a state) but not formally annexed to it (*see* Table).

direct taxes, taxes levied directly on firms and individuals, such as taxes on income, profits, and capital gains. The *immediate* incidence, or burden, of direct taxes is on the firms and individuals thus taxed; direct taxes on firms may, however, be passed on to consumers and other economic units in the form of higher prices for goods and services, blurring the distinction between direct and indirect taxation.

distribution of income/wealth, the portion of personal income or wealth accruing to households or individuals constituting each respective decile (tenth) or quintile (fifth) of a country's households or individuals.*

divorce rate, the number of legal, civilly recognized divorces annually per 1,000 population.

doubling time, the number of complete years required for a country to double its population at its current rate of natural increase.

earnings index, a series of index numbers comparing average wages in a collective industrial sample for a country or region with the same industries at a previous period to measure changes over time in those wages. It is most commonly reported for wages paid on a daily, weekly, or monthly basis; annual figures represent averages of these shorter periods. The scope of the earnings index varies from country to country; the index is often limited to earnings in manufacturing industries. The index for each country applies to all wage earners in a designated group and ordinarily takes into account basic wages (overtime is normally distinguished), bonuses, cost-of-living allowances, and contributions toward social security. Some countries include payments in kind. Contributions toward social security by employers are usually excluded, as are social security benefits received by wage earners.

economically active population, *see* population economically active.

education, tabulation of the principal elements of a country's educational establishment, classified as far as possible according to the country's own system of primary, secondary, and higher levels (the usual age limits for these levels being identified in parentheses), with total number of schools (physical facilities) and of teachers and students (whether full- or part-time). The student-teacher ratio is calculated whenever available data permit.

educational attainment, the distribution of the population age 25 and over with completed educations by the highest level of formal education attained or completed; it must sometimes be reported, however, for age groups still in school or for the economically active only.

emirate, empire, *see* monarchy.

enterprise, a legal entity formed to conduct a business, which it may do from more than one establishment (place of business or service point).

ethnic/linguistic composition, ethnic, racial, or linguistic composition of a national population, reported here according to the most reliable breakdown available, whether published in official sources (such as a census) or in external analysis (when the subject is not addressed in national sources).

exchange rate, the value of one currency compared with another, or with a standardized unit of account such as the SPECIAL DRAWING RIGHT, or as mandated by local statute when one currency is "tied" by a par value to another. Rates given usually refer to free market values when the currency has no, or very limited, restrictions on its convertibility into other currencies.

exports, material goods legally leaving a country (or customs area) and subject to customs regulations. The total value and distribution by percentage of the major items (in prefer-

ence to groups of goods) exported are given, together with the distribution of trade among major trading partners (usually single countries or trading blocs). Valuation of goods exported is free on board (f.o.b.) unless otherwise specified. The value of goods exported and imported f.o.b. is calculated from the cost of production and excludes the cost of transport.

external debt, public and publicly guaranteed debt with a maturity of more than one year owed to nonnationals of a country and repayable in foreign currency, goods, or services. The debt may be an obligation of a national or subnational governmental body (or an agency of either), of an autonomous public body, or of a private debtor that is guaranteed by a public entity. The debt is usually either outstanding (contracted) or disbursed (drawn).

external territory (Australia), *see* territory.

federal, consisting of first-order political subdivisions that are prior to and independent of the central government in certain functions.

federal republic, *see* republic.

federation, union of coequal, preexisting political entities that retain some degree of autonomy and (usually) right of secession within the union.

fertility rate, *see* total fertility rate.

financial aggregates, tabulation of seven-year time series, providing principal measures of the financial condition of a country, including: (1) the exchange rate of the national currency against the U.S. dollar, the pound sterling, and the International Monetary Fund's SPECIAL DRAWING RIGHT (SDR), (2) the amount and kind of international reserves (holdings of SDRs, gold, and foreign currencies) and reserve position of the country in the IMF, and (3) principal economic rates and prices (central bank discount rate, government bond yields, and industrial stock [share] prices). For BALANCE OF PAYMENTS, the origin in terms of component balance of trade items and balance of invisibles (net) is given.*

fish catch, the live-weight equivalent of the aquatic animals (including fish, crustaceans, mollusks, etc., but excluding whales, seals, and other aquatic mammals) caught in freshwater or marine areas by national fleets and landed in domestic or foreign harbours for commercial, industrial, or subsistence purposes.

f.o.b. (trade valuation): *see* exports.

food, see daily per capita caloric intake.

form of government/political status, the type of administration provided for by a country's constitution—whether or not suspended by extralegal military or civil action, although such de facto administrations are identified—together with the number of members (elected, appointed, and ex officio) for each legislative house, named according to its English rendering. Dependent states (*see* Table) are classified according to the status of their political association with the administering country.

gross domestic product (GDP), the total value of the final goods and services produced by residents and nonresidents within a given country during a given accounting period, usually a year. Unless otherwise noted, the value is given in current prices of the year indicated. The *System of National Accounts* (SNA), published under the joint auspices of the UN, IMF, OECD, EC, and World Bank) provides a framework for international comparability in classifying domestic accounting aggregates and international transactions comprising "net factor income from abroad," the measure that distinguishes GDP and GNP.

gross national product (GNP), the total value of final goods and services produced both from within a given country *and* from external (foreign) transactions in a given accounting period, usually a year. Unless otherwise noted, the value is given in current prices of the year indicated. GNP is equal to GROSS DOMESTIC

PRODUCT (*q.v.*) adjusted by net factor income from abroad, which is the income residents receive from abroad for factor services (labour, investment, and interest) less similar payments made to nonresidents who contribute to the domestic economy.

gross ton, volumetric unit of measure (equaling 100 cubic feet [2.83 cu m]) of the permanently enclosed volume of a ship, above and below decks available for cargo, stores, or passenger accommodation. Net, or register, tonnage exempts certain nonrevenue spaces—such as those devoted to machinery, bunkers, crew accommodations, and ballast—from the gross tonnage. *See also* deadweight tonnage.

head of government, see chief of state/head of government.

health, a group of measures including number of accredited physicians currently practicing or employed and their ratio to the total population; total hospital beds and their ratio; and INFANT MORTALITY RATE.

household, economically autonomous individual or group of individuals living in a single dwelling unit. A family household is one composed principally of individuals related by blood or marriage.

household income and expenditure, data for average size of a HOUSEHOLD (by number of individuals) and median household income. Sources of income and expenditures for major items of consumption are given as percentages.

In general, household income is the amount of funds, usually measured in monetary units, received by the members (generally those 14 years old and over) of a household in a given time period. The income can be derived from (1) wages or salaries, (2) nonfarm or farm SELF-EMPLOYMENT, (3) transfer payments, such as pensions, public assistance, unemployment benefits, etc., and (4) other income, including interest and dividends, rent, royalties, etc. The income of a household is expressed as a gross amount before deductions for taxes. Data on expenditure refer to consumption of personal or household goods and services; they normally exclude savings, taxes, and insurance; practice with regard to inclusion of credit purchases differs markedly.

immigration, usually, the number and origin of those immigrants admitted to a nation in a legal status that would eventually permit the granting of the right to settle permanently or to acquire citizenship.*

imports, material goods legally entering a country (or customs area) and subject to customs regulations; excludes financial movements. The total value and distribution by percentage of the major items (in preference to groups of goods) imported are given, together with the direction of trade among major trading partners (usually single countries), trading blocs (such as the European Union), or customs areas (such as Belgium-Luxembourg). The value of goods imported is given free on board (f.o.b.) unless otherwise specified; f.o.b. is defined above under EXPORTS.

The principal alternate basis for valuation of goods in international trade is that of cost, insurance, and freight (c.i.f.); its use is restricted to imports, as it comprises the principal charges needed to bring the goods to the customs house in the country of destination. Because it inflates the value of imports relative to exports, more countries have, latterly, been estimating imports on an f.o.b. basis as well.

incorporated territory (U.S.), *see* territory.

independent, of a state, autonomous and controlling both its internal and external affairs. Its date usually refers to the date from which the country was in effective control of these affairs within its present boundaries, rather than the date independence was proclaimed or the date recognized as a de jure act by the former administering power.

indirect taxes, taxes levied on sales or transfers of selected intermediate goods and services, including excises, value-added taxes, and tariffs, that are ordinarily passed on to the ultimate consumers of the goods and services. Figures given for individual countries are limited to indirect taxes levied by their respective central governments unless otherwise specified.

infant mortality rate, the number of children per 1,000 live births who die before their first birthday. Total infant mortality includes neonatal mortality, which is deaths of children within one month of birth.

invisibles (invisible trade), see balance of trade.

kingdom, see monarchy.

labour force, portion of the POPULATION ECONOMICALLY ACTIVE (PEA) comprising those most fully employed or attached to the labour market (the unemployed are considered to be "attached" in that they usually represent persons previously employed seeking to be reemployed), particularly as viewed from a short-term perspective. It normally includes those who are self-employed, employed by others (whether full-time, part-time, seasonally, or on some other less than full-time basis), and, as noted above, the unemployed (both those previously employed and those seeking work for the first time). In the "gross domestic product and labour force" table, the majority of the labour data provided refer to population economically active, since PEA represents the longer-term view of working population and, thus, subsumes more of the marginal workers who are often missed by shorter-term surveys.

land use, distribution by classes of vegetational cover or economic use of the land area only (excluding inland water, for example, but not marshland), reported as percentages. The principal categories utilized include: (1) forest, which includes natural and planted tracts, (2) meadows and pastures, which includes land in temporary or permanent use whose principal purpose is the growing of animal fodder, (3) agricultural and under permanent cultivation, which includes temporary and permanent cropland, as well as land left fallow less than five years, but capable of being returned to production without special preparation, and (4) other, which includes built-up, wasteland, watercourses, and the like.

leisure, the principal monetary expenditures, uses, or reported preferences in the use of the individual's free time for recreation, rest, or self-improvement.*

life expectancy, the number of years a person born within a particular population group (age cohort) would be expected to live, based on actuarial calculations.

literacy, the ability to read and write a language with some degree of competence; the precise degree constituting the basis of a particular national statement is usually defined by the national census and is often tested by the census enumerator. Elsewhere, particularly where much adult literacy may be the result of literacy campaigns rather than passage through a formal educational system, definition and testing of literacy may be better standardized.

major cities, usually the five largest cities proper whose population is at least one-tenth that of the primate (largest) city; fewer will be listed if the size disparity is very great or there are fewer urban localities in the country. For multipage tables, 10 or more will be listed without regard for the size of the primate city.* Populations for cities will usually refer to the city proper—*i.e.,* the legally bounded corporate entity, or the most compact, contiguous, demographically urban portion of the entity defined by the local authorities. Occasionally figures for METROPOLITAN AREAS are cited when the relevant civil entity at the core of a major agglomeration had an unrepresentatively small population.

manufacturing, mining, and construction enterprises/retail sales and service enterprises, a detailed tabulation of the principal industries in these sectors, showing for each industry the number of enterprises and employees, wages in that industry as a percentage of the general average wage, and the value of that industry's output in terms of value added or turnover.*

marriage rate, the number of legal, civilly recognized marriages annually per 1,000 population.

material well-being, a group of measures indicating the percentage of households or dwellings possessing certain goods or appliances, including automobiles, telephones, television receivers, refrigerators, air conditioners, and washing machines.*

merchant marine, the privately or publicly owned ships registered with the maritime authority of a nation (limited to those in Lloyd's of London statistical reporting of 100 or more GROSS TONS) that are employed in commerce, whether or not owned or operated by nationals of the country.

metropolitan area, a city and the region of dense, predominantly urban, settlement around the city; the population of the whole usually has strong economic and cultural affinities with the central city.

military expenditure, the apparent value of all identifiable military expenditure by the central government on hardware, personnel, pensions, research and development, etc., reported here both as a percentage of the GNP, with a comparison to the world average, and as a per capita value in U.S. dollars.

military personnel, see total active duty personnel.

mobility, the rate at which individuals or households change dwellings, usually measured between censuses and including international as well as domestic migration.*

monarchy, a government in which the CHIEF OF STATE holds office, usually hereditarily and for life, but sometimes electively for a term. The state may be a coprincipality, emirate, empire, kingdom, principality, sheikhdom, or sultanate. The powers of the monarch may range from absolute (*i.e.,* the monarch both reigns and rules) through various degrees of limitation of authority to nominal, as in a constitutional monarchy, in which the titular monarch reigns but others, as elected officials, effectively rule.

monetary unit, currency of issue, or that in official use in a given country; name, spelling, and abbreviation in English according to International Monetary Fund recommendations or local practice; name of the lesser, usually decimal, monetary unit constituting the main currency; and valuation in U.S. dollars and U.K. pounds sterling, usually according to free-market or commercial rates.
    See also exchange rate.

natural increase, also called natural growth, or the balance of births and deaths, the excess of births over deaths in a population; the rate of natural increase is the difference between the BIRTH RATE and the DEATH RATE of a given population. The estimated world average during 1990–95 was 15.7 per 1,000 population, or 1.57% annually. Natural increase is added to the balance of migration to calculate the total growth of that population.

net material product, see material product.

nonreligious, see atheist.

official language(s), that (or those) prescribed by the national constitution for day-to-day conduct and publication of a country's official business or, when no explicit constitutional provision exists, that of the constitution itself, the national gazette (record of legislative activity), or like official documents. Other languages may have local protection, may be permitted in parliamentary debate or legal action (such as a trial), or may be "national languages," for the protection of which special provisions have been made, but these are not deemed official. The United States, for example, does not yet formally identify English as "official," though it uses it for virtually all official purposes.

official name, the local official form(s), short or long, of a country's legal name(s) taken from the country's constitution or from other official documents. The English-language form is usually the protocol form in use by the country, the U.S. Department of State, and the United Nations.

official religion, generally, any religion prescribed or given special status or protection by the constitution or legal system of a country. Identification as such is not confined to constitutional documents utilizing the term explicitly.

organized territory (U.S.), see territory.

overseas department (France), see department.

overseas territory (France), see territory.

parliamentary state, see state.

part of a realm, a dependent Dutch political entity with some degree of self-government and having a special status above that of a colony (*e.g.,* the prerogative of rejecting for local application any law enacted by The Netherlands).

participation/activity rates, measures defining differential rates of economic activity within a population. Participation rate refers to the percentage of those employed or economically active who possess a particular characteristic (sex, age, etc.); activity rate refers to the fraction of the total population who *are* economically active.

passenger-miles, or **passenger-kilometres,** aggregate measure of passenger carriage by a specified means of transportation, equal to the number of passengers carried multiplied by the number of miles (or kilometres) each is transported. Figures given for countries are often calculated from ticket sales and ordinarily exclude passengers carried free of charge.

people's republic, see republic.

place of birth/national origin, if the former, numbers of native- and foreign-born population of a country by actual place of birth; if the latter, any of several classifications, including those based on origin of passport at original admission to country, on cultural heritage of family name, on self-designated (often multiple) origin of (some) ancestors, and on other systems for assigning national origin.*

political status, see form of government/political status.

population, the number of persons present within a country, city, or other civil entity at the date of a census of population, survey, cumulation of a civil register, or other enumeration. Unless otherwise specified, populations given are DE FACTO, referring to those actually present, rather than DE JURE, those legally resident but not necessarily present on the referent date. If a time series, noncensus year, or per capita ratio referring to a country's total population is cited, it will usually refer to midyear of the calendar year indicated.

population economically active, the total number of persons (above a set age for economic labour, usually 10–15 years) in all employment statuses—self-employed, wage- or salary-earning, part-time, seasonal, unemployed, etc. The International Labour Organisation defines the economically active as "all persons of either sex who furnish the supply of labour for the production of economic goods and services." National practices vary as regards the treatment of such groups as armed forces, inmates of institutions, persons seeking their first job, unpaid family workers, seasonal workers and persons engaged in part-time economic activities. In some countries, all or part of these groups may be included among the economically active, while in other countries the same groups may be treated as inactive. In general, however, the data on economically active population do not include students, persons occupied solely in family or household work, retired persons, persons living entirely on their own means, and persons wholly dependent upon others.

See also labour force.

population projection, the expected population in the years 2000 and 2010, embodying the country's own projections wherever possible. Estimates of the future size of a population are usually based on assumed levels of fertility, mortality, and migration. Projections in the tables, unless otherwise specified, are medium (*i.e.,* most likely) variants, whether based on external estimates by the United Nations, World Bank, or U.S. Department of Commerce or on those of the country itself.

price and earnings indexes, tabulation comparing the change in the CONSUMER PRICE INDEX over a period of seven years with the change in the general labour force's EARNINGS INDEX for the same period.

principality, *see* monarchy.

production, the physical quantity or monetary value of the output of an industry, usually tabulated here as the most important items or groups of items (depending on the available detail) of primary (extractive) and secondary (manufactured) production, including construction. When a single consistent measure of value, such as VALUE ADDED, can be obtained, this is given, ranked by value; otherwise, and more usually, quantity of production is given.

public debt, the current outstanding debt of all periods of maturity for which the central government and its organs are obligated. Publicly guaranteed private debt is excluded. For countries that report debt under the World Bank Debtor Reporting System (DRS), figures for outstanding, long-term EXTERNAL DEBT are given.

quality of working life, a group of measures including weekly hours of work (including overtime); rates per 100,000 for job-connected injury, illness, and mortality; coverage of labour force by insurance for injury, permanent disability, and death; workdays lost to labour strikes and stoppages; and commuting patterns (length of journey to work in minutes and usual method of transportation).*

railroads, mode of transportation by self-driven or locomotive-drawn cars over fixed rails. Length-of-track figures include all mainline and spurline running track but exclude switching sidings and yard track. Route length, when given, does not compound multiple running tracks laid on the same trackbed.

recurrent budget, *see* budget.

religious affiliation, distribution of nominal religionists, whether practicing or not, as a percentage of total population. This usually assigns to children the religion of their parents.

republic, a state with elected leaders and a centralized presidential form of government, local subdivisions being subordinate to the national government. A *federal republic* (as distinguished from a unitary republic) is a republic in which power is divided between the central government and the constituent subnational administrative divisions (*e.g.,* states, provinces, or cantons) in whom the central government itself is held to originate, the division of power being defined in a written constitution and jurisdictional disputes usually being settled in a court; sovereignty usually rests with the authority that has the power to amend the constitution. A *unitary republic* (as distinguished from a federal republic) is a republic in which power originates in a central authority and is not derived from constituent subdivisions. A *people's republic,* in the dialectics of Communism, is the

first stage of development toward a communist state, the second stage being a *socialist republic.* An *Islamic republic* is structured around social, ethical, legal, and religious precepts central to the Islamic faith.

retail price index, *see* consumer price index.

retail sales and service enterprises, *see* manufacturing, mining, and construction enterprises/retail sales and service enterprises.

roundwood, wood obtained from removals from forests, felled or harvested (with or without bark), in all forms.

rural, *see* urban-rural.

self-employment, work in which income derives from direct employment in one's own business, trade, or profession, as opposed to work in which salary or wages are earned from an employer.

self-governing, of a state, in control of its internal affairs in degrees ranging from control of most internal affairs (though perhaps not of public order or of internal security) to complete control of all internal affairs (*i.e.,* the state is autonomous) but having no control of external affairs or defense. In this work the term self-governing refers to the final stage in the successive stages of increasing self-government that generally precede independence.

service/trade enterprises, *see* manufacturing, mining, and construction enterprises/retail sales and service enterprises.

sex distribution, ratios, calculated as percentages, of male and female population to total population.

sheikhdom, *see* monarchy.

social deviance, a group of measures, usually reported as rates per 100,000, for principal categories of socially deviant behaviour, including specified crimes, alcoholism, drug abuse, and suicide.*

social participation, a group of measures indicative of the degree of social engagement displayed by a particular population, including rates of participation in such activities as elections, voluntary work or memberships, trade unions, and religion.*

social security, public programs designed to protect individuals and families from loss of income owing to unemployment, old age, sickness or disability, or death and to provide other services such as medical care, health and welfare programs, or income maintenance.

socialist republic, *see* republic.

sources of income, *see* household income and expenditure.

Special Drawing Right (SDR), a unit of account utilized by the International Monetary Fund (IMF) to denominate monetary reserves available under a quota system to IMF members to maintain the value of their national currency unit in international transactions.*

state, in international law, a political entity possessing the attributes of: territory, permanent civilian population, government, and the capacity to conduct relations with other states. Though the term is sometimes limited in meaning to fully independent and internationally recognized states, the more general sense of an entity possessing a *preponderance* of these characteristics is presumed here. It is, thus, also a first-order civil administrative subdivision, especially of a federated union. An *associated state* is an autonomous state in free association with another that conducts its external affairs and defense; the association may be terminated in full independence at the instance of the autonomous state in consultation with the administering power. A *parliamentary state* is an independent state of the Commonwealth that is governed by a parliament and that may recognize the British monarch as its titular head.

structure of gross domestic product and labour force, tabulation of the principal elements of the national economy, according to standard

industrial categories, together with the corresponding distribution of the labour force (when possible POPULATION ECONOMICALLY ACTIVE) that generates the GROSS DOMESTIC PRODUCT.

sultanate, *see* monarchy.

territory, a noncategorized political dependency; a first-order administrative subdivision; a dependent political entity with some degree of self-government, but with fewer rights and less autonomy than a colony because there is no charter. An *external territory* (Australia) is a territory situated outside the area of the country. An *organized territory* (U.S.) is a territory for which a system of laws and a settled government have been provided by an act of the United States Congress. An *overseas territory* (France) is an overseas subdivision of the French Republic with elected representation in the French Parliament, having individual statutes, laws, and internal organization adapted to local conditions.

ton-miles, or **ton-kilometres,** aggregate measure of freight hauled by a specified means of transportation, equal to tons of freight multiplied by the miles (or kilometres) each ton is transported. Figures are compiled from waybills (nationally) and ordinarily exclude mail, specie, passengers' baggage, the fuel and stores of the conveyance, and goods carried free.

total active duty personnel, full-time active duty military personnel (excluding militias and part-time, informal, or other paramilitary elements), with their distribution by percentages among the major services.

total fertility rate, the sum of the current age-specific birth rates for each of the child-bearing years (usually 15–49). It is the probable number of births, given present fertility data, that would occur during the lifetime of each woman should she live to the end of her child-bearing years.

tourism, service industry comprising activities connected with domestic and international travel for pleasure or recreation; confined here to international travel and reported as expenditures in U.S.$ by tourists of all nationalities visiting a particular country and, conversely, the estimated expenditures of that country's nationals in all countries of destination.

transfer payments, *see* household income and expenditure.

transport, all mechanical methods of moving persons or goods. Data reported for national establishments include: for railroads, length of track and volume of traffic for passengers and cargo (but excluding mail, etc.); for roads, length of network and numbers of passenger cars and of commercial vehicles (*i.e.,* trucks and buses); for merchant marine, the number of vessels of more than 100 gross tons and their total deadweight tonnage; for air transport, traffic data for passengers and cargo and the number of airports with scheduled flights.

unincorporated territory (U.S.), *see* territory.

unitary republic, *see* republic.

urban-rural, social characteristic of local or national populations, defined by predominant economic activities, "urban" referring to a group of largely nonagricultural pursuits, "rural" to agriculturally oriented employment patterns. The distinction is usually based on the country's own definition of urban, which may depend only upon the size (population) of a place or upon factors like employment, administrative status, density of housing, etc.

value added, also called value added by manufacture, the gross output value of a firm or industry minus the cost of inputs—raw materials, supplies, and payments to other firms—required to produce it. Value added is the portion of the sales value or gross output value that is actually created by the firm or industry. Value added generally includes labour costs, administrative costs, and operating profits.

The Nations of the World

Afghanistan

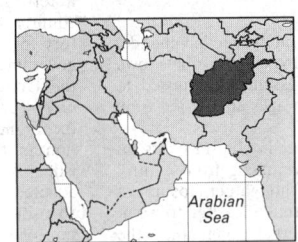

Official name: Islamic State of Afghanistan (Dowlat-e Eslāmī-ye Afghānestān [Persian]; Pashtu long-form name, n.a.).
Form of government[1]: Islamic state.
Chief of state: President.[2]
Head of government: Prime Minister[3].
Capital: Kabul.
Official languages: Pashto; Dari (Persian).
Official religion: Islam.
Monetary unit: 1 afghani (Af) = 100 puls (puli); valuation (Oct. 11, 1996) 1 U.S.$ = Af 4,750; 1 £ = Af 7,483.

Area and population[4]	area		population
	sq mi	sq km	1993 estimate
Regions			
Central	11,657	30,192	3,481,400
East	9,802	25,386	1,567,500
East-central	21,739	56,304	685,600
North	29,520	76,457	2,421,900
North-east	30,233	78,304	2,518,300
South	19,525	50,569	1,659,600
South-west	77,000	199,430	2,188,700
West	46,187	119,624	1,497,500
TOTAL	251,825[5]	652,225[5]	16,020,500

Demography

Population (1996): 22,664,000[6].
Density (1996): persons per sq mi 90.0, persons per sq km 34.7.
Urban-rural (1995): urban 20.0%; rural 80.0%.
Sex distribution (1995): male 51.30%; female 48.70%.
Age breakdown (1995): under 15, 40.7%; 15–29, 28.4%; 30–44, 16.1%; 45–59, 10.0%; 60–74, 4.1%; 75 and over, 0.6%.
Population projection: (2000) 26,668,000; (2010) 34,098,000.
Doubling time: 24 years.
Ethnic composition (early 1990[6]): Pashtun 38%; Tadzhik 25%; Ḥazāra 19%; Uzbek 6%; Chahar Aimak, Turkmen, Baluchi, and other 12%.
Religious affiliation (1990): Sunnī Muslim 84%; Shīʿī Muslim 15%; other 1%.
Major cities (1988): Kabul 700,000[7]; Kandahār (Qandahār) 225,500; Herāt 177,300; Mazār-e Sharīf 130,600.

Vital statistics

Birth rate per 1,000 population (1995): 42.7 (world avg. 25.0).
Death rate per 1,000 population (1995): 18.5 (world avg. 9.3).
Natural increase rate per 1,000 population (1995): 24.2 (world avg. 15.7).
Total fertility rate (avg. births per childbearing woman; 1995): 6.2.
Life expectancy at birth (1995): male 46.0 years; female 44.7 years.
Major causes of death per 100,000 population: n.a.; however, in the early 1990s, injuries and poisoning, infectious and parasitic diseases, and diseases of the respiratory system were the leading causes of death reported in hospitals.

National economy

Budget (1987–88). Revenue: Af 79,800,000,000 (1984–85; tax revenue 45.4%, nontax revenue 54.6%). Expenditures: Af 105,800,000,000 (1981–82; governmental ministries 50.0%, developmental budget 31.9%, debt service 13.9%).
Production (metric tons except as noted). Agriculture, forestry, fishing (1995): wheat 2,170,000, corn (maize) 530,000, grapes 330,000, rice 300,000, potatoes 280,000, barley 274,000, opium poppy 600–3,000; livestock (number of live animals) 18,000,000 sheep, 2,715,000 goats, 1,500,000 cattle, 300,000 horses, 265,000 camels, 9,000,000 chickens; roundwood (1994) 7,251,000 cu m; fish catch (1993) 1,200. Mining and quarrying (1994): salt 13,000; copper 5,000; gypsum 3,000; barite 2,000. Manufacturing (by production value in Af '000,000; 1988–89): food products 4,019; leather and fur products 2,678; textiles 1,760; printing and publishing 1,070; industrial chemicals (including fertilizers) 1,053; footwear 999. Construction (Af '000,000; 1985): 1,094. Energy production (consumption): electricity (kW-hr; 1992) 703,000,000 (834,000,000); coal (metric tons; 1992) 8,000 (8,000); petroleum products (metric tons; 1992) none (302,000); natural gas (cu m; 1992) 188,947,000 (188,947,000).
Population economically active (1994)[8]: total 5,557,000; activity rate of total population 29.4% (participation rates: female 9.0%; unemployed [1990] 3.4%).

Consumer price index (1990 = 100)							
	1988	1989	1990	1991	1992	1993	1994
Consumer price index	64.3	83.1	100.0	266.0	420.8	563.9	676.7

Public debt (external, outstanding; 1993): U.S.$5,381,000,000.
Tourism: receipts (1992) U.S.$1,000,000; expenditures (1987) U.S.$1,000,000.
Gross national product (1988): U.S.$3,100,000,000 (U.S.$220 per capita).

Structure of gross domestic product and labour force				
	1992–93			
	in value Af '000,000[9]	% of total value	labour force	% of labour force
Agriculture	61,400	48.5	4,276,100	67.2
Manufacturing	} 32,800	25.9	298,900	4.7
Mining and public utilities			81,400	1.3
Construction	12,400	9.8	81,400	1.3
Transp. and commun.	5,300	4.2	139,900	2.2
Trade	12,400	9.8	420,600	6.6
Pub. admin., services	} 2,400	1.9	929,300	14.6
Other			214,300	3.4
TOTAL	126,700	100.0[10]	6,360,500	100.0

Land use (1994): forested 2.9%; meadows and pastures 46.0%; agricultural and under permanent cultivation 12.4%; other 38.7%.

Foreign trade[11]

Balance of trade (current prices)						
	1989	1990	1991	1992	1993	1994
U.S.$'000,000	−249	−351	−265	−236	+234	−306
% of total	29.1%	38.7%	27.4%	24.7%	15.5%	34.1%

Imports (1994): U.S.$602,000,000 (1989–90; machinery 37.7%, basic manufactures 18.3%, minerals and fuels 10.9%). *Major import sources* (1994): Japan 14.4%; Singapore 7.1%; China 5.2%; India 5.0%; Pakistan 4.6%; Hong Kong 4.3%; Thailand 2.8%; France 2.7%; Germany 2.7%; United Kingdom 2.5%.
Exports (1994): U.S.$296,000,000 (1992; dried fruits and nuts 51.3%, carpets and rugs 13.1%, karakul wool and hides 4.9%, cotton 1.4%). *Major export destinations* (1994): Belgium-Luxembourg 3.8%; Pakistan 3.7%; Germany 3.6%; China 3.2%; United Kingdom 2.0%; Saudi Arabia 1.9%.

Transport and communications

Transport. Railroads (1995): length 25 km. Roads (1993): total length 17,579 km (paved 47%[12]). Vehicles (1994): passenger cars 31,000; trucks and buses 25,000. Merchant marine: none. Air transport (1992): passenger-km 265,000,000; metric ton-km cargo 11,000,000; airports (1995) 3.
Communications. Daily newspapers (1992): total number 16; total circulation 206,000; circulation per 1,000 population 12.8. Radio (1995): 1,670,000 receivers (1 per 13 persons). Television (1995): 100,000 receivers (1 per 215 persons). Telephones (main lines; 1993): 29,000 (1 per 769 persons).

Education and health

Education (1992–93)				
	schools	teachers	students	student/ teacher ratio
Primary	1,753	16,160	786,532	48.7
Secondary[12]	819	5,715	271,000	47.4
Voc., teacher tr.[12]	33	556	8,537	15.4
Higher[13]	5[12]	444[14]	9,367[14]	21.1

Educational attainment (1980). Percentage of population age 25 and over having: no formal schooling 88.5%; some primary education 6.8%; complete primary 0.3%; some secondary 1.2%; postsecondary 3.2%. *Literacy* (1995): percentage of total population age 15 and over literate 31.5%; males 47.2%; females 15.0%.
Health (1988–93): physicians 2,347 (1 per 6,690 persons); hospital beds 5,331 (1 per 2,945 persons); infant mortality rate (1995) 152.8.
Food (1992): daily per capita caloric intake 1,523 (vegetable products 89%, animal products 11%); 62% of FAO recommended minimum requirement.

Military

Total active duty personnel (1996): no identifiable military units appear to represent the central government. *Military expenditure as percentage of GNP* (1990): 15.0% (world 4.4%); per capita expenditure U.S.$29.

[1]In 1995 the central government in Kabul had united a number of Sunnī mujahideen guerrilla groups who, following traditional deliberative and legislative models, had established a state, a parliament, and a draft constitution. [2]The Taleban army, made up of former students, ousted the president, captured the capital city, Kabul, and gained a stronghold in the country on Sept. 27, 1996. In November 1996 other factional groups were negotiating a national coalition government. [3]Ousted by the Taleban army. [4]In 1993 an administrative reorganization created 32 provinces (*wilayah*), but detailed breakdown of area and population is unavailable. [5]Detailed breakdown does not account for 6,162 sq mi (15,960 sq km), which is included in the total. [6]Excluding. Afghan refugees estimated to number about 1.6 million in Pakistan and about 1.4 million in Iran. [7]1993 estimate. [8]Based on settled population only. [9]At prices of 1978–79. [10]Detail does not add to total given because of rounding. [11]Exports are f.o.b. and imports are c.i.f. [12]1988–89. [13]Includes universities only. [14]1989–90.

Albania

Official name: Republika e Shqipërisë (Republic of Albania).
Form of government: unitary multiparty republic with one legislative house (People's Assembly [140])[1].
Chief of state: President.
Head of government: Prime Minister.
Capital: Tiranë.
Official language: Albanian.
Official religion: none.
Monetary unit: 1 lek = 100 qindars; valuation (Oct. 11, 1996)
1 U.S.$ = 108.10 leks;
1 £ = 170.29 leks.

Area and population

Provinces	Capitals	area sq mi	area sq km	population 1990 estimate
Berat	Berat	396	1,027	180,489
Dibër	Peshkopi	605	1,568	153,775
Durrës	Durrës	327	848	251,029
Elbasan	Elbasan	572	1,481	248,676
Fier	Fier	454	1,175	251,115
Gjirokastër	Gjirokastër	439	1,137	67,392
Gramsh	Gramsh	268	695	44,791
Kolonjë	Ersekë	311	805	25,291
Korçë	Korçë	842	2,181	218,219
Krujë	Krujë	234	607	109,876
Kukës	Kukës	514	1,330	104,731
Lezhë	Lezhë	185	479	63,505
Librazhd	Librazhd	391	1,013	73,871
Lushnjë	Lushnjë	275	712	137,830
Mat	Burrel	397	1,028	78,754
Mirditë	Rrëshen	335	867	51,701
Përmet	Përmet	359	929	40,419
Pogradec	Pogradec	280	725	73,333
Pukë	Pukë	399	1,034	50,286
Sarandë	Sarandë	424	1,097	89,459
Shkodër	Shkodër	976	2,528	241,549
Skrapar	Çorovoda	299	775	47,605
Tepelenë	Tepelenë	315	817	51,022
Tiranë	Tiranë	478	1,238	374,483
Tropojë	Bajram	403	1,043	45,965
Vlorë	Vlorë	621	1,609	180,725
TOTAL		11,100[2]	28,748	3,255,891

Demography

Population (1996): 3,249,000[3].
Density (1996): persons per sq mi 292.7, persons per sq km 113.0.
Urban-rural (1995): urban 37.3%; rural 62.7%.
Sex distribution (1995): male 48.02%; female 51.98%.
Age breakdown (1995): under 15, 34.3%; 15–29, 24.0%; 30–44, 20.2%; 45–59, 12.7%; 60–74, 7.0%; 75 and over, 1.7%.
Population projection: (2000) 3,427,000; (2010) 3,860,000.
Doubling time: 47 years.
Ethnic composition (1989): Albanian 98.0%; Greek 1.8%; Macedonian 0.1%.
Religious affiliation (1992): a significant portion of the population are nonreligious; believers identify themselves as Muslim 65%, Orthodox 20%, Roman Catholic 13%, other 2%.
Major cities (1990): Tiranë 243,000; Durrës 85,400; Elbasan 83,300; Shkodër 81,800; Vlorë 73,800.

Vital statistics

Birth rate per 1,000 population (1995): 22.8 (world avg. 25.0).
Death rate per 1,000 population (1995): 7.7 (world avg. 9.3).
Natural increase rate per 1,000 population (1995): 15.1 (world avg. 15.7).
Total fertility rate (avg. births per childbearing woman; 1995): 2.7.
Marriage rate per 1,000 population (1990): 8.9.
Divorce rate per 1,000 population (1990): 0.8.
Life expectancy at birth (1995): male 64.6 years; female 70.8 years.
Major causes of death per 100,000 population: n.a.; however, principal health problems in the mid-1990s included malnutrition (especially of children), perinatal and child health care, and environmental pollution.

National economy

Budget (1994). Revenue: 46,049,000,000 leks (taxes 78.1%, of which excise taxes 20.6%, social security contributions 13.9%, import duties and export taxes 13.6%, income taxes 9.0%; nontax revenue 21.9%). Expenditures: 68,259,000,000 leks (current expenditure 76.4%, of which personnel costs 22.6%, social security 15.9%, government operations and maintenance 15.4%, service of public debt 6.5%; capital expenditure 17.2%).
Public debt (1994): U.S.$229,900,000.
Tourism (1994): receipts from visitors U.S.$5,000,000; expenditures by nationals abroad U.S.$4,000,000.
Production (metric tons except as noted). Agriculture, forestry, fishing (1995): cereals 662,900; vegetables and melons 469,500 (mainly beans, peas, onions, tomatoes, cabbage, eggplants, and carrots), potatoes 130,000, sugar beets 67,000, grapes 55,000, olives 39,000, apples 10,000, oranges 5,500; livestock (number of live animals) 2,480,000 sheep, 1,650,000 goats, 840,000 cattle, 138,000 mules and asses, 3,900,000 poultry; roundwood (1994) 409,000 cu m; fish catch (1993) 3,500. Mining and quarrying (value in '000,000 leks; 1994): chromium ore 2,547; copper ore 1,030. Manufacturing (value of production in '000 leks; 1993)[4]: food products 824,000; textiles 263,000; clothing 139,000; consumer products 93,000; tobacco 70,000; building materials 64,000; leather

63,000. Construction (1990): 12,428 units. Energy production (consumption): electricity (kW-hr; 1994) 3,903,000,000 (3,903,000,000); coal (metric tons; 1994) 179,000 (179,000); crude petroleum (barrels; 1994) 3,527,800 (2,703,-500); petroleum products (metric tons; 1994) 261,000 (261,000); natural gas (cu m; 1994) 77,000,000 (77,000,000).
Gross national product (1994): U.S.$1,229,000,000 (U.S.$360 per capita).

Structure of gross domestic product and labour force

	1994 value '000,000 leks	1994 % of total value	1991 labour force[3]	1991 % of labour force[3]
Agriculture	92,254	55.5	662,000	49.0
Manufacturing, mining, public utilities	20,966	12.6	300,000	22.2
Construction	15,732	9.5	99,000	7.3
Transp. and commun.	5,546	3.3	29,000	2.1
Trade			25,000	1.9
Pub. admin., defense	31,799	19.1	...	...
Services			236,000	17.5
Other			...	...
TOTAL	166,297	100.0	1,351,000	100.0

Population economically active (1993): total 1,540,000[3]; activity rate of total population 49.4% (participation rates: ages 15–64, 90.2%; female 49.0%; unemployed 17.5%).

Price and earnings indexes (December 1993 = 90.9)

	1992	1993	1994	1995
Consumer price index	49.1	90.9	114.4	120.0
Earnings index	...	...	...	...

Household income and expenditure. Average household size (1989) 4.7; annual income per rural household 80,835 leks (U.S.$ value, n.a.); sources of income: wages 53.0%, transfers from relatives abroad 21.5%, social insurance 11.4%; expenditure: n.a.
Land use (1994): forested 38.2%; meadows and pastures 15.5%; agricultural and under permanent cultivation 25.6%; other 20.7%.

Foreign trade

Balance of trade (current prices)

	1989	1990	1991	1992	1993	1994
'000,000 leks	−83	−150	−308	−454	−490	−460
% of total	12.1%	24.5%	60.3%	76.4%	68.6%	62.0%

Imports (1994): U.S.$601,000,000 (machinery and transport equipment 31.8%; food, beverages, live animals, and tobacco 25.5%; manufactured goods 18.9%; mineral fuels 10.9%, of which crude petroleum 8.2%; chemicals 6.5%). *Major import sources:* Italy 35.0%; Greece 24.0%; Bulgaria 8.2%; Germany 5.5%; Turkey 4.6%; states of the former Yugoslavia 4.5%.
Exports (1994): U.S.$141,300,000 (manufactured goods 45.3%; mineral fuels 26.7%; food, beverages, live animals, and tobacco 14.3%). *Major export destinations:* Italy 52.1%; United States 11.1%; Greece 10.4%; states of the former Yugoslavia 6.0%.

Transport and communications

Transport. Railroads: length (1992) 419 mi, 674 km; passenger-mi (1993) 139,000,000, passenger-km 223,000,000; short ton-mi cargo (1994) 342,000, metric ton-km cargo 500,000. Roads (1995): total length 15,500 km (paved 30%). Vehicles (1995): passenger cars 58,682; trucks and buses 34,441. Merchant marine (1992): vessels (100 gross tons and over) 24; total deadweight tonnage 80,954. Air transport: n.a.; airports (1996) with scheduled flights 1.
Communications. Daily newspapers (1992): total number 4; total circulation 165,000; circulation per 1,000 population 50. Radio (1995): 550,000 receivers (1 per 5.8 persons). Television (1995): 300,000[5] receivers (1 per 10.7 persons). Telephones (main lines; 1993): 49,000 (1 per 70 persons).

Education and health

Education (1993)

	schools	teachers	students	student/ teacher ratio
Primary (age 6–13)	1,777	32,098	535,713	16.7
Secondary (age 14–17)	476[6]	4,149	73,259	17.7
Voc., teacher tr.[6]	466	7,390	138,000	18.7
Higher	8[6]	1,774	30,185	17.0

Educational attainment (1989). Population age 10 and over having: primary education 65.3%; secondary 29.1%; higher 5.6%. *Literacy* (1989): total population age 10 and over literate 91.8%; males 95.5%; females 88.0%.
Health (1990): physicians 5,566[7] (1 per 585 persons); hospital beds 19,000 (1 per 172 persons); infant mortality rate per 1,000 live births (1995) 51.3.
Food (1992): daily per capita caloric intake 2,605 (vegetable products 83%, animal products 17%); 108% of FAO recommended minimum requirement.

Military

Total active duty personnel (1996): 54,000 (army 83.3%, navy 4.6%, air force 12.1%). *Military expenditure as percentage of GNP* (1993): 8.2% (world 3.2%); per capita expenditure U.S.$28.

---

[1]A transitional constitution was adopted on April 29, 1991. The proposed text of a permanent constitution was rejected in a referendum on Nov. 6, 1994. [2]Detail does not add to total given because of rounding. [3]At mid-year 1996, approximately 500,000 Albanians were believed to be working in neighbouring countries. [4]Value of production in constant prices of 1990. [5]Families that had a television receiver. [6]1990. [7]Includes dentists.

Algeria

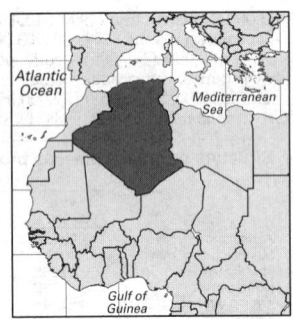

Official name: Al-Jumhūrīyah al-Jazā'irīyah ad-Dīmuqrāṭīyah ash-Sha'bīyah (Arabic) (Democratic and Popular Republic of Algeria).
Form of government: military-backed regime with one interim legislative body (National Transition Council [200])[1].
Chief of state: President.
Head of government: Prime Minister.
Capital: Algiers.
Official language: Arabic[1].
Official religion: Islam.
Monetary unit: 1 Algerian dinar (DA) = 100 centimes; valuation (Oct. 11, 1996) 1 U.S.$ = DA 55.83; 1 £ = DA 87.95.

Population (1987 census)

Wilāyat	population	Wilāyat	population
Adrar	217,678	Médéa	652,863
Aïn Defla	537,256	Mila	511,605
Aïn Temouchent	274,990	Mostaganem	505,932
Alger	1,690,191	M'Sila	604,693
Annaba	455,888	Naâma	113,700
Batna	752,617	Oran	932,473
El-Bayadh	153,254	Ouargla	284,454
Béchar	185,346	El-Oued	376,909
Bejaïa	700,952	Oum el-Bouaghi	403,936
Biskra	430,202	Relizane	544,877
Blida	702,188	Saïda	235,494
Bordj Bou Arreridj	424,828	Sétif	1,000,694
Bouira	526,900	Sidi bel-Abbès	446,277
Boumerdes	650,975	Skikda	622,510
Ech-Chleff	684,192	Souk Ahras	296,077
Constantine	664,303	Tamanrasset	95,822
Djelfa	494,494	Et-Tarf	275,315
Ghardaïa	216,140	Tébessa	410,233
Guelma	353,309	Tiaret	575,794
Illizi	18,930	Tindouf	16,428
Jijel	472,312	Tipaza	620,151
Khenchela	246,541	Tissemsilt	228,120
Laghouat	212,388	Tizi Ouzou	936,948
Mascara	566,901	Tlemcen	714,862
		TOTAL	23,038,942[2]

Demography

Area: 919,595 sq mi, 2,381,741 sq km.
Population (1996): 28,566,000[3].
Density (1996): persons per sq mi 31.1, persons per sq km 12.0.
Urban-rural (1995): urban 55.8%; rural 44.2%.
Sex distribution (1995): male 50.60%; female 49.40%.
Age breakdown (1995): under 15, 38.7%; 15–29, 29.7%; 30–44, 17.8%; 45–59, 8.1%; 60–74, 4.6%; 75 and over, 1.1%.
Population projection: (2000) 31,158,000; (2010) 37,489,000.
Doubling time: 30 years.
Ethnic composition (1992): Arab c. 80%; Berber c. 20%, of which Kabyle c. 13%, Shawia c. 6%.
Religious affiliation (1990): Muslim 99.9%, of which Sunnī 99.5%, Ibāḍīyah 0.4%; Roman Catholic 0.1%.
Major cities (1987): Algiers (1995) 2,168,000 (metro area; 3,702,000); Oran 609,823; Constantine 440,842; Annaba 222,518; Batna 181,601.

Vital statistics

Birth rate per 1,000 population (1995): 29.0 (world avg. 25.0).
Death rate per 1,000 population (1995): 6.1 (world avg. 9.3).
Natural increase rate per 1,000 population (1995): 22.9 (world avg. 15.7).
Total fertility rate (avg. births per childbearing woman; 1995): 3.7.
Marriage rate per 1,000 population (1993): 5.7.
Divorce rate per 1,000 population (1985): 2.1.
Life expectancy at birth (1995): male 66.9 years; female 69.1 years.
Notified cases of infectious diseases per 100,000 population (1990): hepatitis 15.1; typhoid fever 11.3; measles 7.2; cholera 5.2; tuberculosis 4.8.

National economy

Budget (1995). Revenue: DA 600,900,000,000 (export taxes on hydrocarbons 50.8%; value-added taxes 16.1%). Expenditures: DA 627,700,000,000 (current expenditure 70.8%; development expenditure 23.1%; other 6.1%).
Public debt (external, outstanding; 1994): U.S.$28,103,000,000.
Tourism: (1994) receipts from visitors U.S.$49,000,000; expenditures by nationals abroad U.S.$135,000,000.
Production (metric tons except as noted). Agriculture, forestry, fishing (1995): wheat 1,600,000, potatoes 720,000, tomatoes 700,000, barley 540,000, oranges 253,000, onions 248,000, dates 230,000, grapes 180,000, olives 172,500; livestock (number of live animals) 18,000,000 sheep, 1,300,000 cattle; roundwood (1994) 2,409,000 cu m; fish catch (1993) 90,460. Mining and quarrying (1994): iron ore (gross weight) 2,016,000; phosphate rock (gross weight) 738,000; mercury 475,000 kg. Manufacturing (1993): cement 6,940,000; flour and semolina 2,540,000[4]; bricks 1,676,000; crude steel 1,400,000; pig iron 1,300,000; phosphate fertilizer 204,000; refined sugar 201,000; methanol 90,000; beer 420,000 hectolitres. Construction: n.a. Energy production (consumption): electricity (kW-hr; 1994) 19,888,000,000 (18,764,000,000); coal (metric tons; 1994) 20,000 (1,280,000); crude petroleum (barrels; 1994) 280,-

379,000 (160,307,000); petroleum products (metric tons; 1994) 39,543,000 (10,862,000); natural gas (cu m; 1994) 50,452,000,000 (19,209,000,000).
Gross national product (1994): U.S.$46,115,000,000 (U.S.$1,690 per capita).

Structure of gross domestic product and labour force

	1994		1990	
	in value DA '000,000	% of total value	labour force	% of labour force
Agriculture	140,500	9.5	907,490	15.9
Petroleum and natural gas	334,200[5]	22.7[5]	55,000	1.0
Other mining	2,200	0.2	...	...
Manufacturing	137,000[5]	9.3[5]	646,390	11.3
Public utilities, construction	182,100	12.4	651,370	11.4
Pub. admin., defense	187,000	12.7	1,318,370	23.1
Transp. and commun.	}		252,230	4.4
Trade	488,400[6]	33.2[6]	444,970	7.8
Other	}		1,435,180[7]	25.1[7]
TOTAL	1,471,400	100.0	5,711,000	100.0

Population economically active (1990): total 5,711,000; activity rate of population 22.8% (participation rates [1987] ages 15–64, 44.3%; female 9.2%; unemployed [1994] 27.3%).

Price and earnings indexes (1990 = 100)

	1990	1991	1992	1993	1994	1995	1996
Consumer price index	100.0	125.9	165.8	199.8	257.8	334.6	374.8[8]
Earnings index[9]	100.0	131.1	170.2	199.1	203.8	224.2	246.6

Household income and expenditure. Average household size (1987) 6.9; income per household: n.a.; sources of income (1995): wages and salaries 43.1%, self-employment 38.3%, transfers 18.6%; expenditure (1988): food and beverages 52.3%, transportation and communications 12.0%, clothing and footwear 8.6%, housing and energy 6.7%, other 20.4%.
Land use (1994): forested 1.6%; meadows and pastures 13.3%; agricultural and under permanent cultivation 3.4%; other (mostly desert) 81.7%.

Foreign trade[10]

Balance of trade (current prices)

	1989	1990	1991	1992	1993	1994
U.S.$'000,000	+360	+3,215	+4,107	+2,489	+1,312	−1,005
% of total	1.9%	14.2%	21.1%	12.6%	7.0%	5.5%

Imports (1994): U.S.$9,599,000,000 (food 29.4%, of which cereals and preparations 13.8%; nonelectrical machinery 14.7%; iron and steel 9.5%). *Major import sources:* France 24.8%; U.S. 14.3%; Italy 9.7%; Spain 9.4%; Germany 5.4%.
Exports (1994): U.S.$8,594,000,000 (crude petroleum 45.7%, natural gas 31.2%, refined petroleum 18.8%). *Major export destinations:* Italy 17.9%; U.S. 16.5%; France 15.4%; The Netherlands 10.3%; Spain 7.6%.

Transport and communications

Transport. Railroads (1994): route length 2,965 mi, 4,772 km; passenger-km 2,524,000,000; metric ton-km cargo 2,400,000,000. Roads (1994): total length 99,974 km (paved 68.4%). Vehicles (1994): passenger cars 725,000; trucks and buses 480,000. Merchant marine (1992): vessels (100 gross tons and over) 149; total deadweight tonnage 1,093,363. Air transport (1995)[11]: passenger-km 3,070,000,000; metric ton-km cargo 20,346,000; airports (1996) 28.
Communications. Daily newspapers (1994): total number 8; total circulation 1,440,000; circulation per 1,000 population 53. Radio (1995): 3,500,000 receivers (1 per 8.0 persons). Television (1995): 2,000,000 receivers (1 per 14 persons). Telephones (main lines; 1993): 1,068,100 (1 per 25 persons).

Education and health

Education (1992–93)

	schools	teachers	students	student/ teacher ratio
Primary (age 6–11)	13,970	153,793	4,436,363	28.8
Secondary (age 12–17) }	3,402	130,413	2,255,276	17.3
Voc., teacher tr.		5,317	49,922	9.4
Higher	...	14,379	243,397	16.9

Educational attainment (1989). Percentage of economically active population age 16 and over having: no formal schooling 38.2%; Qur'ānic education 0.9%; primary 20.8%; secondary 11.1%; vocational 19.7%; higher 9.3%. *Literacy (1995):* total population age 15 and over literate 10,531,000 (61.6%); males literate 6,368,000 (73.9%); females literate 4,163,000 (49.0%).
Health (1992): physicians 25,304 (1 per 1,033 persons); hospital beds 57,879 (1 per 455 persons); infant mortality rate per 1,000 live births (1995) 50.3.
Food (1992): daily per capita caloric intake 2,897 (vegetable products 89%, animal products 11%); 121% of FAO recommended minimum requirement.

Military

Total active duty personnel (1996): 123,700 (army 86.5%, navy 5.4%, air force 8.1%). *Military expenditure as percentage of GNP (1994):* 3.3% (world 3.0%); per capita expenditure U.S.$49.

---

[1]Constitutional referendum was scheduled for late November 1996; Berber may become second official language. [2]De facto population. [3]Excludes about 1,200,000 Algerians abroad. [4]1992. [5]Petroleum and natural gas includes (and Manufacturing excludes) refined petroleum and manufacture of hydrocarbons. [6]Includes import duties of DA 119,100,000,000. [7]Includes 1,141,278 unemployed. [8]January. [9]Public workers only; all data based on January averages of gross income. [10]Imports c.i.f.; exports f.o.b. [11]Air Algérie.

Andorra

Official name: Principat d'Andorra;
(Principality of Andorra).
Form of government: parliamentary
coprincipality with one legislative
house (General Council [28]).
Chiefs of state: President of France;
Bishop of Urgell, Spain.
Head of government: Head of the
Government.
Capital: Andorra la Vella.
Official language: Catalan.
Official religion: none[1].
Monetary unit: There is no local
currency of issue; the French franc
and Spanish peseta are both in
circulation. 1 franc (F) = 100 centimes;
1 peseta (Pta) = 100 céntimos.
Valuation (Oct. 11, 1996)
1 U.S.$ = F 5.18, 1 £ = F 8.16;
1 U.S.$ = Ptas 128.79,
1 £ = Ptas 202.88.

Area and population

Parishes	Capitals	area sq mi	area sq km	population 1993[2] estimate
Andorra la Vella	Andorra la Vella	49[3]	127[3]	22,387
Canillo	Canillo	74	191	2,193
Encamp	Encamp			9,654
La Massana	La Massana	25	65	5,302
Les Escaldes–Engordany		—	3	13,177
Ordino	Ordino	33	85	1,652
Sant Julià de Lòria	Sant Julià de Lòria	3	3	7,234
TOTAL		181	468	61,599

Demography

Population (1996): 64,100.
Density (1996): persons per sq mi 354.1, persons per sq km 137.0.
Urban-rural (1995): urban 62.5%; rural 37.5%.
Sex distribution (1993): male 53.14%; female 46.86%.
Age breakdown (1993): under 15, 16.3%; 15–29, 27.7%; 30–44, 27.2%; 45–59,
15.1%; 60–74, 9.9%; 75 and over, 3.8%.
Population projection: (2000) 66,000; (2010) 71,000.
Doubling time: 92 years.
Ethnic composition (by nationality; 1995): Spanish 46.4%; Andorran 19.5%;
Portuguese 10.8%; French 6.7%; other nationality 5.3%; undeclared na-
tionality 11.3%.
Religious affiliation (1992): Roman Catholic 92.0%; Protestant 0.5%; Jewish
0.4%; other 7.1%.
Major cities (1993): Andorra la Vella 22,387; Les Escaldes 13,177; Encamp
9,654.

Vital statistics

Birth rate per 1,000 population (1995): 11.0[4] (world avg. 25.0).
Death rate per 1,000 population (1995): 3.4[4] (world avg. 9.3).
Natural increase rate per 1,000 population (1995): 7.6[4] (world avg. 15.7).
Total fertility rate (avg. births per childbearing woman; 1995): 1.7.
Marriage rate per 1,000 population (1994): 2.0.
Divorce rate per 1,000 population: n.a.
Life expectancy at birth (1995): male 75.6 years; female 81.7 years.
Major causes of death per 100,000 population: n.a.; however, health problems
are those of a developed country—cardiovascular disease, hypertension, ma-
lignant neoplasms (cancers).

National economy

Budget (1995). Revenue: Ptas 21,182,000,000 (excise taxes on goods [mostly
fuel] 51.8%; consumption taxes 31.0%; income from inheritance 11.5%).
Expenditures: Ptas 21,270,000,000 (current expenditure 58.6%; development
expenditure 41.4%).
Public debt (1994): about U.S.$125,000,000.
Production (value of recorded exported products in Ptas '000 except as noted).
Agriculture: traditional crops include tobacco, hay, potatoes, and grapes;
livestock (number of live animals; 1995) 6,541 cattle, 3,257 sheep[5], 899
horses. Quarrying (1992): marble 11,800. Manufacturing (1992): wearing apparel (primarily woolen goods and leather goods) 1,045,700; motor vehicles
and parts 816,100; mineral water 343,100; furniture 213,300; newspapers and
periodicals 204,700; electrical machinery and apparatus for industry 167,600;
other products include cigars and cigarettes and liqueurs. Construction
(approved new building construction; 1995): 159,800 sq m. Energy production (consumption): electricity (kW-hr; 1995) 89,000,000 (324,000,000[6]); coal,
none (n.a.); crude petroleum, none (n.a.); petroleum products, none (n.a.);
natural gas, none (n.a.).
Population economically active (1995): total 27,314; activity rate of total population 42.8% (participation rates: ages 15–64, 58.2%; female [1989] 45.6%;
unemployed, unofficially, none[7]).

Price and earnings indexes (1991 = 100)

	1990	1991	1992	1993	1994	1995	1996[8]
Consumer price index[9]	94.4	100.0	105.9	110.8	116.1	121.4	125.8
Annual earnings index[10]	...	100.0	107.6	114.4	117.1	121.2	...

Gross domestic product (at current market prices; 1995): U.S.$1,034,000,000
(U.S.$16,130 per capita)[11].

Structure of labour force

	1995 labour force	1995 % of labour force
Agriculture	174	0.6
Mining	...	...
Manufacturing	1,243	4.6
Construction	4,573	16.7
Public utilities	...	...
Transportation and communications	...	...
Trade	5,293	19.4
Restaurants, hotels	5,209	19.1
Finance, real estate, insurance	1,263	4.6
Pub. admin., defense	3,274	12.0
Services	4,738	17.3
Other	1,547	5.7
TOTAL	27,314	100.0

Land use (1993): forested 22.0%; meadows and pastures 56.0%; agricultural
and under permanent cultivation 2.0%; other 20.0%.
Household income and expenditure. Average household size: n.a.; income per
household: n.a.; sources of income: n.a.; expenditure: n.a.
Tourism (1993): more than 14,000,000 visitors; number of hotels and other
overnight residences (1995) 276.

Foreign trade

Balance of trade (current prices)

	1990	1991	1992	1993	1994	1995
Ptas '000,000	−117,280	...	−112,177	...	−117,846	−125,510
% of total	95.5%	...	93.0%	...	89.7%	91.1%

Imports (1995): Ptas 131,602,000,000 (food, beverages, and tobacco 29.6%;
machinery and apparatus 14.1%; chemicals and chemical products 8.9%;
transport equipment 7.9%; textiles and wearing apparel 7.5%; photographic
and optical goods and watches and clocks 4.4%). *Major import sources:* Spain
40.2%; France 31.1%; Germany 4.8%; United States 4.2%; Italy 3.6%.
Exports (1995): Ptas 6,095,000,000 (transport equipment 26.4%; textiles and
wearing apparel 21.5%; electrical machinery 8.7%; agricultural products
6.5%; chemicals and chemical products 6.2%). *Major export destinations:*
France 47.8%; Spain 47.0%; Germany 1.5%.

Transport and communications

Transport. Railroads: none; however, both French and Spanish railways stop
near the border. Roads (1993): total length 167 mi, 269 km (paved 74%).
Vehicles (1994): passenger cars 36,067; trucks and buses 4,208. Merchant
marine: vessels (100 gross tons and over) none. Airports (1996) with scheduled flights: none.
Communications. Daily newspapers (1993): total number 3; circulation 5,500;
circulation per 1,000 population 87. Radio (1995): total number of receivers
10,000 (1 per 6.8 persons). Television (1995): total number of receivers, n.a.
Telephones (main lines; 1993): 26,800 (1 per 2.3 persons).

Education and health

Education (1993–94)

	schools	teachers	students	student/ teacher ratio
Primary/Lower secondary (age 7–15)	12	...	5,405	...
Upper secondary	6	...	1,638	...
Higher	—	—	—	—

Educational attainment (mid-1980s). Percentage of population age 15 and
over having: no formal schooling 5.5%; primary education 47.3%; secondary
education 21.6%; postsecondary education 24.9%; unknown 0.7%. *Literacy:*
resident population is virtually 100% literate.
Health (1993): physicians 118 (1 per 538 persons); hospital beds 114 (1 per
556 persons); infant mortality rate per 1,000 live births (1995) 7.7.
Food (1992)[12]: daily per capita caloric intake 3,670 (vegetable products 64%,
animal products 36%); 147% of FAO recommended minimum requirement.

Military

Total active duty personnel (1995): none. France and Spain are responsible
for Andorra's external security; a 100-person police force maintains domestic security.

[1]Roman Catholicism enjoys special recognition in accordance with Andorran tradition.
[2]January 1. [3]Andorra la Vella includes Les Escaldes–Engordany and Sant Julià de
Lòria. [4]Official government figures. [5]Large herds of sheep and goats from Spain and
France feed in Andorra in the summer. [6]Estimated figure. [7]The restricted size of the
indigenous labour force necessitated high levels of immigration in the late 1980s and
early 1990s to serve the tourist trade; emigration exceeded immigration in 1994 and
1995 because of a labour force surplus. [8]June. [9]Consumer price index of Spain. [10]Per
Andorran Office of Social Security. [11]Tourism (including winter-season sports, fairs,
festivals, and income earned from low-duty imported manufactured items) and the
banking system (of some importance as a tax haven for foreign financial investment
and transactions) are the primary sources of GDP. [12]Composite values derived from
Spanish and French food data.

Angola

Official name: República de Angola (Republic of Angola).
Form of government: multiparty republic with one legislative house (National Assembly [220[1]]).
Head of state and government: President[2].
Capital: Luanda.
Official language: Portuguese.
Official religion: none.
Monetary unit: 1 readjusted Kwanza[3] = 100 lwei; valuation (Oct. 11, 1996) 1 U.S.$ = readjusted Kwanza 201,994; 1 £ = readjusted Kwanza 318,201.

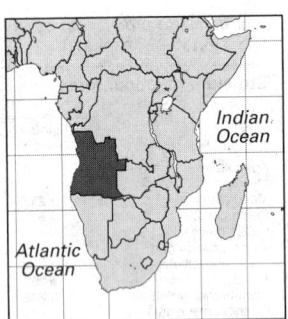

Area and population

Provinces	Capitals	area sq mi	area sq km	population 1996 estimate[4]
Bengo	Caxito	12,112	31,371	190,000
Benguela	Benguela	12,273	31,788	718,000
Bié	Kuito	27,148	70,314	1,280,000
Cabinda	Cabinda	2,807	7,270	199,000
Cunene	N'Giva	34,495	89,342	255,000
Huambo	Huambo	13,233	34,274	1,730,000
Huíla	Lubango	28,958	75,002	954,000
Kuando Kubango	Menongue	76,853	199,049	139,000
Kuanza Norte	N'Dalatando	9,340	24,190	440,000
Kuanza Sul	Sumbe	21,490	55,660	710,000
Luanda	Luanda	934	2,418	2,022,000
Lunda Norte	Lucapa	39,685	102,783	320,000
Lunda Sul	Saurimo	17,625	45,649	165,000
Malanje	Malanje	37,684	97,602	1,020,000
Moxico	Lwena	86,110	223,023	360,000
Namibe	Namibe	22,447	58,137	154,000
Uíge	Uíge	22,663	58,698	985,000
Zaire	M'Banza Kongo	15,494	40,130	262,000
TOTAL		481,354[5]	1,246,700	11,904,000[5]

Demography

Population (1996): 11,904,000.
Density (1996): persons per sq mi 24.7, persons per sq km 9.5.
Urban-rural (1992): urban 42.0%; rural 58.0%.
Sex distribution (1991): male 48.80%; female 51.20%.
Age breakdown (1996): under 15, 45.0%; 15–29, 25.5%; 30–44, 15.1%; 45–59, 8.9%; 60 and over, 5.5%.
Population projection: (2000) 13,400,000; (2010) 18,082,000.
Doubling time: 22 years.
Ethnic composition (1983): Ovimbundu 37.2%; Mbundu 21.6%; Kongo 13.2%; Luimbe-Nganguela 5.4%; Nyaneka-Humbe 5.4%; Chokwe 4.2%; Luvale (Luena) 3.4%; Luchazi 2.4%; Ambo (Ovambo) 2.4%; Lunda 1.2%; Mbunda 1.2%; Portuguese 0.5%; mestizo 0.5%; other 0.4%.
Religious affiliation (1980): Christian 90.0%, of which Roman Catholic 68.7%; Protestant 19.8%; traditional beliefs 9.5%; other 0.5%.
Major cities (1988): Luanda 1,134,000; Huambo 203,000[6]; Benguela 155,000[6]; Lobito 150,000[6]; Lubango 105,000[7].

Vital statistics

Birth rate per 1,000 population (1995): 45.1 (world avg. 25.0).
Death rate per 1,000 population (1995): 18.1 (world avg. 9.3).
Natural increase rate per 1,000 population (1995): 27.0 (world avg. 15.7).
Total fertility rate (avg. births per childbearing woman; 1995): 6.4.
Marriage rate per 1,000 population (1972): 4.5.
Divorce rate per 1,000 population: n.a.
Life expectancy at birth (1995): male 44.2 years; female 48.5 years.
Major causes of death (percentage of total deaths; 1990): diarrheal diseases 25.8%; malaria 19.4%; cholera 7.3%; acute respiratory infections 6.8%; measles 6.2%.

National economy

Budget (1994). Revenue: NKz 260,934,000,000[3] (tax revenue 98.4%, of which income taxes 71.8%, petroleum taxes 19.0%, import duties 4.3%; nontax revenue 1.6%). Expenditures: NKz 427,089,000,000[3] (defense and internal security 56.5%; administration 29.0%; health 3.4%; education 2.6%; other 8.5%).
Tourism: receipts from visitors (1994) U.S.$13,000,000; expenditures by nationals abroad (1993) U.S.$66,000,000.
Production (metric tons except as noted). Agriculture, forestry, fishing (1995): cassava 1,700,000, sugarcane 330,000, bananas 275,000, corn (maize) 211,000, sweet potatoes 200,000, millet 61,000, palm oil 52,000, dry beans 34,000, peanuts (groundnuts) 17,000, coffee 2,900; livestock (number of live animals) 3,280,000 cattle, 1,570,000 goats, 800,000 pigs, 255,000 sheep, 6,400,000 chickens; roundwood (1993) 6,583,000 cu m; fish catch (1993) 80,723. Mining and quarrying (1994): diamonds 1,350,000 carats. Manufacturing (1993): bread 15,452; sugar 3,190[8]; pasta 3,190[8]; wheat flour 2,452; laundry soap 1,542; corn flour 543; leather shoes 132,000 pairs[8]; beer 260,200 hectolitres; soft drinks 69,050 hectolitres[7]; fabric 3,038,000 sq m; matches 6,357,000 boxes[7]. Construction (value in NKz '000,000[3]; 1986): residential 608; nonresidential 1,977. Energy production (consumption): electricity (kW-hr; 1992) 1,855,-000,000 (1,855,000,000); coal, none (none); crude petroleum (barrels; 1992) 192,634,000 (10,373,000); petroleum products (metric tons; 1992) 1,317,000 (346,000); natural gas (cu m; 1992) 166,576,000 (166,576,000).
Gross national product (1989): U.S.$6,010,000,000 (U.S. $620 per capita).

Structure of gross domestic product and labour force

	1991 in value NKz '000,000,000[3]	1991 % of total value	labour force	% of labour force
Agriculture	85,567	11.9	2,892,000	69.4
Mining	367,436	51.1		
Manufacturing	24,448	3.4		
Construction	11,505	1.6		
Finance	3,595	0.5	438,000	10.5
Trade	72,624	10.1		
Public utilities	—	—		
Transportation and communications	15,100	2.1		
Pub. admin., defense	138,778	19.3	836,000	20.1
Services				
Other	...	...		
TOTAL	719,053	100.0	4,166,000	100.0

Public debt (external, outstanding; 1994): U.S.$8,450,000,000.
Population economically active (1991): total 4,166,000; activity rate of total population 40.3% (participation rates over age 10, 60.1%; female 38.4%; unemployed, n.a.).

Price and earnings indexes (1991 = 100)

	1991	1992	1993	1994
Consumer price index	100.0	595.0	11,534.0	123,639.0
Monthly earnings index	100.0	150.0	1,000.0	8,800.0

Household income and expenditure. Average household size (1980) 4.8; annual income per household: n.a.; sources of income: n.a.; expenditure: n.a.
Land use (1994): forested 18.4%; meadows and pastures 43.3%; agricultural and under permanent cultivation 2.8%; other 35.5%.

Foreign trade

Balance of trade (current prices)

	1989	1990	1991	1992	1993	1994
U.S.$'000,000	+1,191	+1,276	+2,080	+1,160	+1,551	+1,565
% of total	25.1%	25.1%	43.6%	19.0%	35.2%	37.6%

Imports (1994): U.S.$1,633,000,000 (1991; current consumption goods 50.2%, capital goods 20.2%, intermediate consumption goods 18.9%, transport equipment 6.8%). *Major import sources* (1991): Portugal 29.8%; United States 10.5%; France 9.7%; Japan 7.8%; Brazil 7.3%.
Exports (1994): U.S.$3,002,000,000 (mineral fuels 96.0%, diamonds 3.2%). *Major export destinations* (1991): United States 56.6%; Germany 5.6%; Brazil 4.9%; The Netherlands 4.2%; United Kingdom 3.4%; Belgium-Luxembourg 3.3%.

Transport and communications

Transport. Railroads (1988): route length 1,739 mi, 2,798 km; passenger-mi 203,000,000, passenger-km 326,000,000; short ton-mi cargo 1,178,000,000, metric ton-km cargo 1,720,000,000. Roads (1995): total length 45,128 mi, 72,626 km (paved 25%). Vehicles (1995): passenger cars 197,000; trucks and buses 26,000. Merchant marine (1992): vessels (100 gross tons and over) 113; total deadweight tonnage 123,479. Air transport (1991)[9]: passenger-mi 771,000,000, passenger-km 1,241,000,000; short ton-mi cargo 28,000,000, metric ton-km cargo 42,000,000; airports (1996) with scheduled flights 17.
Communications. Daily newspapers (1995): total number 5; total circulation 121,500[10]; circulation per 1,000 population 10[10]. Radio (1995): total number of receivers 450,000 (1 per 26 persons). Television (1995): total number of receivers 50,500 (1 per 229 persons). Telephones (main lines; 1993): 53,300 (1 per 204 persons).

Education and health

Education (1990–91)

	schools	teachers	students	student/ teacher ratio
Primary (age 7–10)	6,308[11]	31,062	990,155	31.9
Secondary (age 11–16)	5,276[11]	5,138[12]	166,812	...
Voc., teacher tr.	...	566[12]	19,687	...
Higher	1[11]	439	6,534	14.9

Educational attainment: n.a. *Literacy* (1990): percentage of population age 15 and over literate 41.7%; males literate 55.6%; females literate 28.5%.
Health (1990): physicians 662 (1 per 15,136 persons); hospital beds 11,857 (1 per 845 persons); infant mortality rate per 1,000 live births (1995) 142.1.
Food (1992): daily per capita caloric intake 1,839 (vegetable products 90%, animal products 10%); (1984) 84% of FAO recommended minimum requirement.

Military

Total active duty personnel (1996): 95,500 (army 92.8%, navy 1.5%, air force 5.7%). *Military expenditure as percentage of GNP* (1986): 23.9% (world 5.4%); per capita expenditure U.S.$173.

---

[1]Excludes 3 seats for Angolans abroad not filled at October 1992 elections. [2]President to be assisted by two vice presidents pending implementation of the November 1994 Lusaka Protocol, which had not taken place as of late 1996. [3]In July 1995 a readjusted Kwanza, equivalent to 1,000 New Kwanza (NKz) was introduced; previously in September 1990 the Kwanza (Kz) was replaced at par, by the New Kwanza (NKz). [4]Unified national estimates and projections based on sample surveys, partial censuses, and analysis of provincial vital statistics. [5]Detail does not add to total given because of rounding. [6]1983. [7]1984. [8]1989. [9]TAAG Airline only. [10]Circulation for four newspapers only. [11]1985–86. [12]1989–90.

Antigua and Barbuda

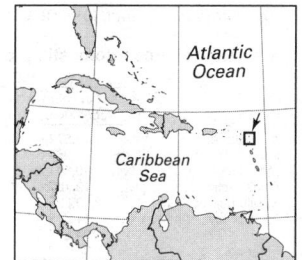

Official name: Antigua and Barbuda.
Form of government: constitutional monarchy with two legislative houses (Senate [17]; House of Representatives [17]).
Chief of state: British Monarch represented by Governor-General.
Head of government: Prime Minister.
Capital: Saint John's.
Official language: English.
Official religion: none.
Monetary unit: 1 Eastern Caribbean dollar (EC\$) = 100 cents; valuation (Oct. 11, 1996) 1 U.S.\$ = EC\$2.70; 1 £ = EC\$4.25.

Area and population	area		population
	sq mi	sq km	1991 census
Parishes[1]			
Saint George	9.3	24.1	4,473
Saint John's	28.5	73.8	35,635
Saint Mary	22.0	57.0	5,303
Saint Paul	18.5	47.9	6,117
Saint Peter	12.7	32.9	3,622
Saint Phillip	17.0	44.0	2,964
Islands[1]			
Barbuda	62.0	160.6	1,241
Redonda	0.5	1.3	2
TOTAL	170.5	441.6	59,355[3]

Demography

Population (1996): 64,400.
Density (1996): persons per sq mi 377.7, persons per sq km 145.8.
Urban-rural (1995): urban 36.5%; rural 63.5%.
Sex distribution (1991): male 48.20%; female 51.80%.
Age breakdown (1991): under 15, 30.4%; 15–29, 27.8%; 30–44, 20.5%; 45–59, 10.2%; 60–74, 7.7%; 75 and over, 3.4%.
Population projection: (2000) 65,000; (2010) 65,000.
Doubling time: 59 years.
Ethnic composition (1994): black 91.3%; mixed 3.7%; white 2.4%; Syrian/Lebanese 0.6%; Indo-Pakistani 0.4%; Amerindian 0.3%; other 1.3%.
Religious affiliation (1991): Protestant 73.7%, of which Anglican 32.1%, Moravian 12.0%, Methodist 9.1%, Seventh-day Adventist 8.8%; Roman Catholic 10.8%; Jehovah's Witness 1.2%; Rastafarian 0.8%; other religion/no religion/not stated 13.5%.
Major cities (1991)[4]: Saint John's 21,514.

Vital statistics

Birth rate per 1,000 population (1995): 17.1 (world avg. 25.0); (1988) legitimate 23.4%; illegitimate 76.6%.
Death rate per 1,000 population (1995): 5.4 (world avg. 9.3).
Natural increase rate per 1,000 population (1995): 11.7 (world avg. 15.7).
Total fertility rate (avg. births per childbearing woman; 1995): 1.7.
Marriage rate per 1,000 population (1988): 4.9.
Divorce rate per 1,000 population (1988): 0.2.
Life expectancy at birth (1995): male 71.3 years; female 75.6 years.
Major causes of death per 100,000 population (1988): diseases of the circulatory system 237.5; malignant neoplasms (cancers) 44.5; diseases of the respiratory system 44.5; endocrine and metabolic disorders 25.4; ill-defined conditions 68.6.

National economy

Budget (1994). Revenue: EC\$292,500,000 (current revenue 95.6%, of which consumption taxes 25.4%, taxes on goods and services 17.8%, import duties 16.1%, nontax revenue 14.9%; grants 3.4%; development revenue 1.0%). Expenditures: EC\$314,200,000 (current expenditures 87.0%; development expenditures 13.0%).
Public debt (external, outstanding; end of 1994): U.S.\$327,000,000.
Production (metric tons except as noted). Agriculture, forestry, fishing (1995): tropical fruit (including papayas, guavas, soursops, and oranges) 5,500, mangoes 1,300, eggplants 250, lemons and limes 220, carrots 210, "Antiguan Black" pineapples 150; livestock (number of live animals) 15,700 cattle, 12,-200 sheep; roundwood, n.a.; fish catch (1993) 2,400 (of which spiny lobster 300). Mining and quarrying: crushed stone for local use. Manufacturing (1994): beer and malt 166,000 cases; T-shirts 179,000 units; rum (1988) 4,000 hectolitres; other manufactures include cement, handicrafts, small appliances, and electronic components. Construction (1994): gross value of building applications EC\$209,300,000. Energy production (consumption): electricity (kW-hr; 1994) 117,500,000 (105,700,000); coal, none (none); crude petroleum, none (none); petroleum products (metric tons; 1993) negligible (99,000); natural gas, none (none).
Population economically active (1991): total 26,753; activity rate of total population 45.1% (participation rates: ages 15–64, 69.7%; female 45.6%; unemployed [1994] 6.7%).

Price and earnings indexes (1990 = 100)						
	1989	1990	1991	1992	1993	1994
Consumer price index	93.5	100.0	105.7	108.9	112.2	116.1
Earnings index	...	...	...	...	...	...

Household income and expenditure. Average household size (1991) 3.2; income per household: n.a.; sources of income: n.a.; expenditure (1974)[5]: food and nonalcoholic beverages 42.9%, housing 23.3%, transportation 10.0%, clothing and footwear 7.5%, energy 5.5%, alcoholic beverages and tobacco 3.6%, other 7.2%.
Gross national product (at current market prices; 1994): U.S.\$453,000,000 (U.S.\$6,970 per capita).

Structure of gross domestic product and labour force				
	1994		1991	
	in value EC\$'000,000	% of total value	labour force	% of labour force
Agriculture, fishing	42.6	3.7	1,040	3.9
Quarrying	17.0	1.5	64	0.2
Manufacturing	26.0	2.3	1,444	5.4
Construction	106.3	9.3	3,109	11.6
Public utilities	49.5	4.3	435	1.6
Transportation and communications	225.7	19.7	2,395	9.0
Trade, restaurants, and hotels	282.8	24.7	8,524	31.9
Finance, real estate	168.8	14.8	1,454	5.4
Pub. admin., defense	201.6	17.6	2,572	9.6
Services	80.9	7.1	5,207	19.5
Other	−57.7[6]	−5.0[6]	509	1.9
TOTAL	1,143.6[7]	100.0	26,753	100.0

Land use (1994): forested 11.0%; meadows and pastures 9.0%; agricultural and under permanent cultivation 18.0%; other 62.0%.
Tourism (1994): receipts from visitors U.S.\$293,000,000; expenditures by nationals abroad U.S.\$25,000,000.

Foreign trade[8]

Balance of trade (current prices)						
	1989	1990	1991	1992	1993	1994
U.S.\$'000,000	−316	−325	−326	−347	−375	−403
% of total	83.4%	83.0%	76.7%	71.4%	78.6%	83.1%

Imports (1992): U.S.\$417,000,000 ([9]agricultural products 9.0%, other [including petroleum products for reexport] 91.0%). *Major import sources* (1989)[9]: United States 27.0%; United Kingdom 16.0%; Canada 4.0%; OECS 3.0%; Italy 3.0%.
Exports (1992): U.S.\$70,000,000 ([9]reexports [significantly, petroleum products reexported to neighbouring islands] 78.0%, domestic exports 22.0%). *Major export destinations* (1989)[9]: United States 41.0%; United Kingdom 19.0%; Germany 19.0%.

Transport and communications

Transport. Railroads[10]. Roads (1993): total length 721 mi, 1,161 km (paved 33%). Vehicles (1994): passenger cars 14,800; trucks and buses 3,700. Merchant marine (1992): vessels (100 gross tons and over) 292; total deadweight tonnage 997,381. Air transport (1991): passenger-mi 121,000,000, passenger-km 195,000,000; short ton-mi cargo 137,000, metric ton-km cargo 200,000; airports (1996) with scheduled flights 2.
Communications. Daily newspapers (1994): 1; total circulation, n.a. Radio (1995): total number of receivers 40,000 (1 per 1.6 persons). Television (1995): total number of receivers 28,000 (1 per 2.3 persons). Telephones (main lines; 1993): 19,200 (1 per 3.3 persons).

Education and health

Education (1994–95)				
	schools	teachers	students	student/teacher ratio
Primary (age 5–10)	43[11]	439	11,506	26.2
Secondary (age 11–16)	12[11]	277	4,294	15.5
Higher	1	16	46	2.9

Educational attainment (1991). Percentage of population age 25 and over having: no formal schooling 1.1%; primary education 50.5%; secondary 33.4%; higher (not university) 5.4%; university 6.2%; other/unknown 3.4%.
Literacy (1990): total population age 15 and over literate 40,000 (90.0%).
Health (1992): physicians 59 (1 per 1,083 persons); hospital beds 369 (1 per 173 persons); infant mortality rate per 1,000 live births (1995) 17.8.
Food (1992): daily per capita caloric intake 2,458 (vegetable products 69%, animal products 31%); 105% of FAO recommended minimum requirement.

Military

Total active duty personnel (1994): a 90-member defense force is part of the Eastern Caribbean regional security system.

[1]Community councils on Antigua and the local government council on Barbuda are the organs of local government. [2]Uninhabited. [3]Unadjusted de jure population excluding institutionalized population; de jure population adjusted for undercount (including institutionalized population) is 63,896. [4]Large settlements include (1991): All Saints 2,230; Liberta 1,473; Codrington 814. [5]Weights of consumer price index components. [6]Less imputed bank service charges. [7]Detail does not add to total given because of rounding. [8]Exports f.o.b.; imports c.i.f. [9]Estimated percentages. [10]Privately owned tracks are mostly nonoperative. [11]1991–92.

Argentina

Official name: República Argentina
　(Argentine Republic).
Form of government: federal republic
　with two legislative houses (Senate
　[72]; Chamber of Deputies [257]).
Head of state and government:
　President[1].
Capital: Buenos Aires.
Official language: Spanish.
Official religion: Roman Catholicism.
Monetary unit: 1 peso (pl. pesos)[2]
　(Arg$) = 100 centavos; valuation
　(Oct. 11, 1996) 1 U.S.$ = Arg$1.00;
　1 £ = Arg$1.58.

Pacific Ocean

Atlantic Ocean

Area and population

Provinces	Capitals	area sq mi	area sq km	population 1995 estimate
Buenos Aires	La Plata	118,754	307,571	13,333,670
Catamarca	Catamarca	39,615	102,602	287,567
Chaco	Resistencia	38,469	99,633	890,548
Chubut	Rawson	86,752	224,686	396,800
Córdoba	Córdoba	63,831	165,321	2,914,972
Corrientes	Corrientes	34,054	88,199	852,685
Entre Ríos	Paraná	30,418	78,781	1,063,416
Formosa	Formosa	27,825	72,066	444,367
Jujuy	San Salvador de Jujuy	20,548	53,219	551,804
La Pampa	Santa Rosa	55,382	143,440	280,876
La Rioja	La Rioja	34,626	89,680	246,158
Mendoza	Mendoza	57,462	148,827	1,500,818
Misiones	Posadas	11,506	29,801	877,904
Neuquén	Neuquén	36,324	94,078	460,395
Río Negro	Viedma	78,384	203,013	556,674
Salta	Salta	60,034	155,488	952,174
San Juan	San Juan	34,614	89,651	550,641
San Luis	San Luis	29,633	76,748	320,109
Santa Cruz	Río Gallegos	94,187	243,943	180,115
Santa Fe	Santa Fe	51,354	133,007	2,934,220
Santiago del Estero	Santiago del Estero	52,645	136,351	696,092
Tierra del Fuego[3]	Ushuaia	8,329	21,571	96,917
Tucumán	San Miguel de Tucumán	8,697	22,524	1,209,716
Other federal entity				
Distrito Federal	Buenos Aires	77	200	2,988,006
TOTAL		1,073,518[4]	2,780,400	34,586,635[4]

Demography

Population (1996): 34,995,000.
Density (1996): persons per sq mi 32.6, persons per sq km 12.5.
Urban-rural (1991): urban 86.9%; rural 13.1%.
Sex distribution (1995): male 49.06%; female 50.94%.
Age breakdown (1995): under 15, 28.9%; 15–29, 24.8%; 30–44, 19.0%; 45–59, 14.1%; 60–74, 9.8%; 75 and over, 3.4%.
Population projection: (2000) 36,648,000; (2010) 40,755,000.
Doubling time: 63 years.
Ethnic composition (1986): European 85%; mestizo and Amerindian 15%.
Religious affiliation (1995): Roman Catholic 90.9%; other 9.1%.
Major cities (1991): Buenos Aires 2,960,976 (Greater Buenos Aires 12,582,-321); Córdoba 1,179,067; Rosario 1,078,374[5]; La Plata 542,567.

Vital statistics

Birth rate per 1,000 population (1995): 19.5 (world avg. 25.0); (1982) legitimate 67.5%; illegitimate 29.8%; unknown 2.7%.
Death rate per 1,000 population (1995): 8.6 (world avg. 9.3).
Natural increase rate per 1,000 population (1995): 8.6 (world avg. 15.7).
Total fertility rate (avg. births per childbearing woman; 1995): 2.7.
Marriage rate per 1,000 population (1990): 5.8.
Life expectancy at birth (1995): male 68.2 years; female 71.5 years.
Major causes of death per 100,000 population (1993): heart disease 247.1; neoplasms (cancers) 143.5; diseases of the brain 75.8; accidents 32.8.

National economy

Budget (1995). Revenue: U.S.$55,650,600,000 (current revenue 96.9%, of which tax revenue 90.0%, nontax revenue 6.5%, other 0.4%; capital revenue 3.1%). Expenditure: U.S.$55,560,600,000 (1989; social security 35.3%; economic services 16.0%; education 9.9%; defense 9.9%; transportation and communications 8.8%; debt service 7.4%).
Public debt (external, outstanding; 1994): U.S.$66,005,000,000.
Land use (1994): forested 18.6%; meadows and pastures 51.9%; agricultural and under permanent cultivation 9.9%; other 19.6%.
Production (metric tons except as noted). Agriculture, forestry, fishing (1995): sugarcane 16,500,000, soybeans 12,088,000, corn (maize) 11,395,000, wheat 8,656,000, sunflower seeds 5,520,000, grapes 1,930,000, potatoes 1,914,000, sorghum 1,623,000, tomatoes 920,000; livestock (number of live animals) 53,500,000 cattle, 21,780,000 sheep; roundwood (1994) 9,757,000 cu m; fish catch (1994) 938,602. Mining and quarrying (1994): silver 1,223,652 troy oz; gold 28,906 troy oz. Manufacturing (1994): cement 6,306,000; wheat flour 3,346,000; vegetable oil 3,027,000; sugar 1,110,000; paper 966,000; soda 22,-528,000 hectolitres; wine 14,179,000 hectolitres; beer 11,293,000 hectolitres. Construction (authorized; 1994): 15,081,456 sq m. Energy production (consumption): electricity (kW-hr; 1993) 63,038,000,000 (64,280,000,000); coal (metric tons; 1993) 167,000 (1,133,000); crude petroleum (barrels; 1993) 216,836,000 (186,053,000); petroleum products (metric tons; 1993) 22,134,000 (19,430,000); natural gas (cu m; 1993) 26,614,000,000 (28,602,000,000).

Gross national product (1994): U.S.$275,657,000,000 (U.S.$8,060 per capita).

Structure of gross domestic product and labour force

	1992 in value Arg$'000,000[2]	1992 % of total value	1980 labour force	1980 % of labour force
Agriculture	13,577.4	6.0	1,200,992	12.0
Mining	4,067.0	1.8	47,171	0.5
Manufacturing	49,541.1	21.9	1,985,995	19.9
Construction	12,107.4	5.3	1,003,175	10.1
Public utilities	3,825.8	1.7	103,256	1.0
Transp. and commun.	11,718.6	5.2	460,476	4.6
Trade	34,929.0	15.4	1,702,080	17.0
Finance	38,132.6	16.8	395,704	4.0
Pub. admin., defense }	59,021.5	26.0	2,399,039	24.0
Services }				
Other	−282.9[6]	−0.1[6]	691,302	6.9
TOTAL	226,637.6[4]	100.0	9,989,190	100.0

Population economically active (1995): total 14,345,171; activity rate of total population 41.5% (participation rates: ages 15–64, 64.5%; female 36.9%; unemployed [1996] 17.0%).

Price and earnings indexes (1990 = 100)[2]

	1990	1991	1992	1993	1994	1995
Consumer price index	100.0	272.0	339.0	375.0	391.0	404.0
Hourly earnings index	100.0	194.3	238.4	...	...	...

Household size and expenditure. Average household size (1991) 3.8; expenditure (1985–86): food 38.2%, transportation 11.6%, housing 9.3%, energy 9.0%, clothing and footwear 8.0%, health 7.9%, recreation and culture 7.5%, education 2.6%, other 5.9%.
Tourism: receipts (1994) U.S.$3,970,000,000; expenditures (1993) U.S.$2,445,-000,000.

Foreign trade[7]

Balance of trade (current prices)

	1990	1991	1992	1993	1994	1995
U.S.$'000,000	+ 8,627	+ 4,572	− 1,388	− 1,576	− 4,002	+ 2,985
% of total	53.7%	23.6%	5.4%	5.7%	11.3%	7.7%

Imports (1994): U.S.$21,590,000,000 (machinery and transport equipment 52.0%, chemical products 14.0%, manufactured products 12.9%, food products and live animals 4.6%, petroleum and petroleum products 2.9%). *Major import sources:* U.S. 22.8%; Brazil 19.9%; Italy 6.6%; Germany 6.4%; France 5.0%; Chile 3.9%; Uruguay 3.7%; Japan 2.9%.
Exports (1994): U.S.$15,839,000,000 (food products and live animals 35.2%, manufactured products 12.5%, machinery and transport equipment 11.2%, petroleum and petroleum products 10.4%, vegetable and animal oils 9.6%, chemical products 5.9%). *Major export destinations:* Brazil 23.1%; U.S. 11.0%; The Netherlands 7.5%; Chile 6.3%; Italy 4.1%; Uruguay 4.1%.

Transport and communications

Transport. Railroads (1994): route length (1995) 33,821 km; passenger-km 6,460,159,000; metric ton-km cargo 6,613,000,000. Roads (1992): total length 133,954 mi, 215,578 km (paved 29%). Vehicles (1994): passenger cars 4,426,-706; commercial vehicles and buses 1,239,625. Merchant marine (1992): vessels (100 gross tons and over) 423; total deadweight tonnage 1,173,105. Air transport (1994): passenger-km 11,438,000,000; metric ton-km cargo 1,285,000,000; airports (1996) with scheduled flights 43.
Communications. Daily newspapers (1992): total number 190; total circulation 4,780,000; circulation per 1,000 population 143. Radio (1995): 21,500,000 receivers (1 per 1.6 persons). Television (1995): 7,165,000 receivers (1 per 4.8 persons). Telephones (main lines; 1994): 4,834,073 (1 per 7.1 persons).

Education and health

Education (1994–95)

	schools	teachers	students	student/ teacher ratio
Primary (age 6–12)	24,511[8]	286,885	5,126,307	17.9
Secondary (age 13–17)[9]	7,224[10]	233,564	2,238,091	9.6
Higher	1,540[11]	118,695	926,793	7.8

Educational attainment (1991). Percentage of population age 25 and over having: no formal schooling 5.7%; less than primary education 22.3%; primary 34.6%; incomplete secondary 12.5%; complete secondary 12.8%; higher 12.0%. *Literacy* (1995): percentage of total population age 15 and over literate 96.2%; males literate 96.2%; females literate 96.2%.
Health (1992): physicians 88,800 (1 per 376 persons); hospital beds 147,000 (1 per 227 persons); infant mortality rate (1994) 20.3.
Food (1992): daily per capita caloric intake 2,880 (vegetable products 66%, animal products 34%); 109% of FAO recommended minimum requirement.

Military

Total active duty personnel (1995): 67,300 (army 60.0%, navy 26.8%, air force 13.2%). *Military expenditure as percentage of GNP* (1994): 1.7% (world 3.0%); per capita expenditure U.S.$139.

[1]Assisted by a ministerial coordinator who exercises general administration of the country. [2]On Jan. 1, 1992, the austral was replaced by the peso at a ratio of 10,000 to 1. [3]Area of Tierra del Fuego (province since 1991) excludes claims to British-held islands in the South Atlantic Ocean. [4]Detail does not add to total given because of rounding. [5]*Municipio.* [6]Import duties. [7]Import figures are f.o.b. in balance of trade and c.i.f. in commodities and trading partners. [8]1991–92. [9]Secondary includes vocational and teacher training. [10]1988–89. [11]1987.

Armenia

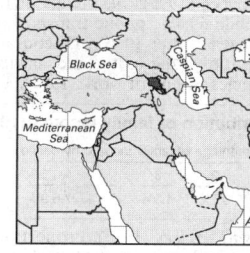

Official name: Hayastani Hanrape-tut'yun (Republic of Armenia).
Form of government: unitary multiparty republic with a single legislative body (National Assembly [190]).
Head of state: President.
Head of government: Prime Minister.
Capital: Yerevan.
Official language: Armenian.
Official religion: none[1].
Monetary unit[2]: 1 dram = 100 lumas; valuation (Oct. 11, 1996) official, 1 U.S.$ = 412.32 drams; 1 £ = 649.53 drams.

Area and population

Administrative sub-divisions (Capitals[3])	area	population		area	population
		1990			1990
	sq km[4]	estimate		sq km[4]	estimate
Cities[5]			**Rural districts**		
Gyumri	...	205,000	Hrazdan	923	121,000
Kirovakan	...	170,000	Ijevan	1,332	77,000
Yerevan	...	1,238,000	Kamo	636	62,000
			Kotayk	805	119,000
Rural districts			Krasnoselsk	697	18,000
Akhuryan	576	41,000	Martuni	1,185	77,000
Amasia	608	6,000	Masis	169	77,000
Anii (Maralik)	429	20,000	Meghri	664	15,000
Aparan	592	22,000	Nairii (Yeghvard)	344	55,000
Aragatsi (Tsaghkahovit)	382	14,000	Noyemberyan	538	34,000
Ararati (Vedi)	1,396	90,000	Sevan	387	45,000
Artashat	512	105,000	Sisian	1,719	31,000
Art'ik	478	50,000	Spitak	544	39,000
Ashotski (Ghukasyan)	457	11,000	Step'anavan	630	39,000
Ashtarak	679	64,000	T'alin	1,091	39,000
Baghramyan	453	20,000	Tashir	690	37,000
Ejmiatsin	359	134,000	Taushi (Berd)	824	35,000
Ghap'an	1,344	58,000	T'umanyani (Alaverdi)	1,109	59,000
Goris	747	42,000	Vardenis	1,151	39,000
Gugark'	771	24,000	Vayk	1,172	22,000
Hoktemberyan	421	124,000	Yeghegnadzor	1,134	37,000
			TOTAL	29,800[6]	3,515,000

Demography

Population (1996): 3,765,000.
Density (1996): persons per sq mi 327.2, persons per sq km 126.3.
Urban-rural (1995): urban 67.6%; rural 32.4%.
Sex distribution (1994): male 48.42%; female 51.58%.
Age breakdown (1993): under 15, 30.1%; 15–29, 24.4%; 30–44, 22.4%; 45–59, 12.3%; 60–74, 8.6%; 75 and over, 2.2%.
Population projection: (2000) 3,784,000; (2010) 3,888,000.
Doubling time: n.a.; doubling time exceeds 100 years.
Ethnic composition (1989): Armenian 93.3%; Azerbaijani 2.6%; other 4.1%.
Religious affiliation: believers are predominantly Armenian Apostolic.
Major cities (1991): Yerevan 1,283,000; Gyumri 163,000[7]; Kirovakan 76,000[7].

Vital statistics

Birth rate per 1,000 population (1995): 13.3 (world avg. 25.0); (1993) legitimate 86.0%; illegitimate 14.0%.
Death rate per 1,000 population (1995): 6.5 (world avg. 9.3).
Natural increase rate per 1,000 population (1995): 6.8 (world avg. 15.7).
Total fertility rate (avg. births per childbearing woman; 1993): 3.3.
Marriage rate per 1,000 population (1995): 4.2.
Divorce rate per 1,000 population (1995): 0.8.
Life expectancy at birth (1993): male 68.4 years; female 75.4 years.
Major causes of death per 100,000 population (1993): circulatory diseases 395.6; cancers 78.6; respiratory diseases 38.3; accidents and violence 24.2.

National economy

Budget (1994). Revenue: 51,756,000,000 drams (tax revenue 47.2%, of which enterprise profits tax 20.7%, value-added tax 9.8%, payroll tax 5.5%, income tax 4.4%, other taxes 6.8%; grants 42.8%; nontax 10.0%). Expenditures: 82,578,000,000 drams (current expenditures 77.7%, of which subsidies 29.1%, pensions and social welfare 6.8%, health and education 4.8%, interest 4.4%, wages 4.2%, other 28.4%; capital expenditure and net lending 22.3%).
Production (metric tons except as noted). Agriculture, forestry, fishing (1995): vegetables (except potatoes) 452,000, milk 427,000, potatoes 400,000, cereals 317,000, wheat 215,000, grapes 130,000; livestock (number of live animals) 636,000 sheep and goats, 503,000 cattle, 82,000 pigs, 3,000,000 poultry; roundwood 44,100 cu m; fish catch (1993) 4,300. Mining and quarrying (1994): copper 50,000; perlite 10,000; molybdenum 500. Manufacturing (value in '000,000 drams; 1994): machine-building and metalworking equipment 18,436; food products 13,842; chemicals and petrochemicals 5,330; ferrous and nonferrous metals 5,259; construction materials 3,154; textiles 2,500; leather products 2,335. Construction (1995): 284,000 sq m. Energy production (consumption): electricity (kW-hr; 1995) 5,560,000,000 (5,674,000,000); coal (metric tons; 1994) none (36,000); crude petroleum (barrels; 1994) none (1,195,000); petroleum products (metric tons; 1994) none (356,000); natural gas (cu m; 1994) none (883,773,000).
Land use (1994): forested 14.1%; pastures 23.1%; agricultural and under permanent cultivation 19.2%; other 43.6%.
Gross national product (at current market prices; 1994)[8]: U.S.$2,532,000,000 (U.S.$670 per capita).

Structure of net material product and labour force

	1994			
	in value '000,000 drams	% of total value	labour force	% of labour force
Agriculture	80,980	48.6	538,000	27.1
Manufacturing, mining }	60,618	36.4	323,000	16.3
Public utilities				
Construction	9,648	5.8	108,000	5.4
Transp. and commun.	1,595	1.0	28,000	1.4
Trade	3,644	2.2	65,000	3.3
Finance	—	—	...	...
Pub. admin., defense	—	—	30,000	1.5
Services	—	—	368,000	18.6
Other	10,208	6.1	523,000[9]	26.4[9]
TOTAL	166,693	100.0[10]	1,983,000	100.0

Population economically active (1994): total 1,983,000; activity rate of total population 52.8% (participation rates: ages 16–59 [male], 16–54 [female] 75.4%; female 45.0%; unemployed 4.0%).

Price and earnings indexes (1990 = 100)

	1989	1990	1991	1992	1993	1994	1995
Consumer price index	104.0	100.0	200.3	1,852	70,956	3,779,686	4,996,745
Monthly earnings index	91.2	100.0	142.8	581.4	4,615.7	...	...

Household income and expenditure. Average household size (1989) 4.7; income per household (1994) 47,352 drams (U.S.$153); sources of income (1994): salaries and wages 52.3%, agricultural income 7.7%, other 40.0%; expenditure (1994): goods and services 78.0%, taxes and payments to government 22.0%.

Foreign trade

Balance of trade (current prices)

	1990	1991	1992	1993
'000,000 drams	−869	−2,279	−5,499	−134,811
% of total	11.1%	18.8%	6.2%	30.2%

Imports (1994): U.S.$401,200,000 (food products 42.1%, mineral products 40.4%, jewelry 8.9%, machinery and equipment 2.9%). *Major import sources:* former Soviet Union (FSU) 54.7%, of which Russia 27.5%, Turkmenistan 17.3%, other FSU 9.9% non-FSU 45.3%, of which U.S. 24.0%, Iran 10.6%, France 2.7%, Germany 1.7%, other non-FSU 6.3%.
Exports (1994): U.S.$209,300,000 (jewelry 34.4%, machinery and equipment 16.8%, mineral products 8.3%, textiles and textile products 7.1%). *Major export destinations:* FSU 69.5%, of which Russia 44.3%, Turkmenistan 20.9%, other FSU 4.3%; non-FSU 30.6%, of which Belgium 9.9%, Iran 7.7%, Germany 3.4%.

Transport and communications

Transport. Railroads (1991): length 511 mi, 823 km; (1995) passenger-mi 196,000,000, passenger-km 316,000,000; short ton-mi cargo 3,345,000,000, metric ton-km cargo 4,884,000,000. Roads (1994): length 4,800 mi, 7,700 km (paved 97%). Vehicles (1991): passenger cars 2,782, trucks and buses 12,034. Air transport (1990): passenger-mi 3,453,000,000, passenger-km 5,556,900,000; short ton-mi cargo 34,000,000, metric ton-km cargo 49,000,000; airports (1996) 1.
Communications. Daily newspapers (1992): total number 7; total circulation 84,000; circulation per 1,000 population 23. Radio (1993): 642,000 receivers (1 per 5.6 persons). Television (1993): 722,000 receivers (1 per 5.0 persons). Telephones (main lines; 1993): 583,500 (1 per 6.4 persons).

Education and health

Education (1994–95)

	schools	teachers	students	student/teacher ratio
Primary (age 6–13) }	1,400	54,000[11]	574,500	11.0[11]
Secondary (age 14–17)				
Voc., teacher tr.	69[11]	...	25,200[11]	...
Higher	14	...	36,500	...

Educational attainment (1989). Percentage of population age 25 and over having: primary education or no formal schooling 7.4%; some secondary 18.6%; completed secondary and some postsecondary 57.7%; higher 13.8%.
Literacy (1989): total population age 15 and over literate 98.8%; males literate 99.4%; females literate 98.1%.
Health (1994): physicians 13,000 (1 per 288 persons); hospital beds 30,000 (1 per 125 persons); infant mortality rate 14.7.

Military

Total active duty personnel (1996): c. 57,400 (army 100%). *Military expenditure as percentage of GNP* (1994): 0.9% (world 3.0%); per capita expenditure (1994): U.S.$20.

[1]The constitution provides for the right to practice the religion of one's choice. In practice, the law imposes restrictions on religious freedom. The 1991 Law on Religious Organizations establishes the separation of church and state, but recognizes the Armenian Apostolic Church (the Armenian Orthodox Church) as having special status. The law requires all nonapostolic religious denominations to register with the Ministry of Justice and prohibits proselytizing. [2]The Armenian dram was introduced on Nov. 22, 1993, to replace the Russian ruble, at a rate of 200 Russian rubles to 1 dram. [3]If name of capital different from that of district. [4]One sq km = 0.386 sq mi. [5]18 additional cities of republic jurisdiction exist. [6]Totals include areas of Lake Sevan and cities. [7]1989; reduced in population by evacuation following Dec. 7, 1988, earthquake. [8]Ruble-area national accounts and GNP data are very speculative. [9]Includes 97,000 unemployed and 426,000 undistributed employed. [10]Detail does not add to total given because of rounding. [11]1993–94.

Australia

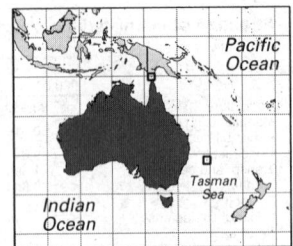

Official name: Commonwealth of Australia.
Form of government: federal parliamentary state (formally a constitutional monarchy) with two legislative houses (Senate [76]; House of Representatives [148]).
Chief of state: British Monarch represented by Governor-General.
Head of government: Prime Minister.
Capital: Canberra.
Official language: English.
Official religion: none.
Monetary unit: 1 Australian dollar ($A)=100 cents; valuation (Oct. 11, 1996) 1 U.S.$=$A 1.26; 1 £=$A 1.99.

Area and population		area		population
				1996[1]
States	**Capitals**	sq mi	sq km	estimate
New South Wales	Sydney	309,500	801,600	6,173,000
Queensland	Brisbane	666,900	1,727,200	3,339,000
South Australia	Adelaide	379,900	984,000	1,477,700
Tasmania	Hobart	26,200	67,800	473,200
Victoria	Melbourne	87,900	227,600	4,533,300
Western Australia	Perth	975,100	2,525,500	1,755,500
Territories				
Australian Capital Territory	Canberra	900	2,400	306,400
Northern Territory	Darwin	519,800	1,346,200	177,500
TOTAL		2,966,200	7,682,300	18,235,600

Demography

Population (1996): 18,287,000.
Density (1996): persons per sq mi 6.2, persons per sq km 2.4.
Urban-rural (1995): urban 85.0%; rural 15.0%.
Sex distribution (1996): male 49.78%; female 50.22%.
Age breakdown (1996): under 15, 21.3%; 15–29, 22.5%; 30–44, 23.1%; 45–59, 17.2%; 60–74, 10.9%; 75 and over, 5.0%.
Population projection: (2000) 19,201,000; (2010) 20,986,000.
Doubling time: 99 years.
Ethnic composition (1986): white 95.2%; aboriginal 1.5%; Asian 1.3%; other 2.0%.
Religious affiliation (1991): Christian 74.0%, of which Roman Catholic 27.3%, Anglican Church of Australia 23.8%, other Protestant 20.1% (Uniting Church and Methodist 8.2%, Presbyterian 4.3%), Orthodox 2.8%; Muslim 0.9%; Buddhist 0.8%; Jewish 0.4%; no religion 12.9%; other 11.0%.
Major cities (1995): Sydney 3,772,700; Melbourne 3,218,100; Brisbane 1,489,100; Perth 1,262,600; Adelaide 1,081,000; Newcastle 466,000; Canberra-Queanbeyan 331,800; Gold Coast–Tweed 326,900; Wollongong 253,600; Hobart 194,700.
Place of birth (1994): 77.2% native-born; 22.8% foreign-born, of which Europe 13.3% (United Kingdom 6.8%[2], Italy 1.5%, Yugoslavia 1.0%, Greece 0.8%, East and West Germany 0.7%, other Europe 2.5%), Asia and Middle East 4.5%, New Zealand 1.6%, Africa, the Americas, and other 3.4%.
Mobility (1995–96). Population age 15 and over living in the same residence as in 1994: 81.6%; different residence between states, regions, and neighbourhoods 18.4%.
Households (1993–94). Total number of households 6,616,800. Average household size 2.6; 1 person 21.8%, couples only 25.8%, couples with dependent children only 23.7%, nonfamily members 12.4%, single parent with children 6.6%, other 9.7%.
Immigration (1996): permanent immigrants admitted 96,970, from United Kingdom and Ireland 12.8%, New Zealand 11.8%, China 7.6%, Vietnam 4.8%, Hong Kong 4.6%, India 4.4%, Philippines 3.9%, South Africa 3.2%, Bosnia and Herzegovina 3.2%, Yugoslavia 3.1%, Sri Lanka 2.2%. Refugee arrivals (1994–95): 13,600.

Vital statistics

Birth rate per 1,000 population (1996): 14.1 (world avg. 25.0); (1993) legitimate 75.0%; illegitimate 25.0%.
Death rate per 1,000 population (1996): 6.9 (world avg. 9.3).
Natural increase rate per 1,000 population (1996): 7.2 (world avg. 15.7).
Total fertility rate (avg. births per childbearing woman; 1996): 1.82.
Marriage rate per 1,000 population (1996): 6.0.
Divorce rate per 1,000 population (1996): 2.7.
Life expectancy at birth (1996): male 75.4 years; female 81.1 years.
Major causes of death per 100,000 population (1994): diseases of the circulatory system 308.0; cancers 192.0; respiratory diseases 56.0; accidents, poisoning, and violence 40.0; endocrine, nutritional, and metabolic diseases 23.0; digestive system diseases 22.0; nervous system diseases 17.0.

Social indicators

Educational attainment (1995). Percentage of population age 15 to 69 having: no formal schooling 0.3%; incomplete secondary education 36.3%; completed secondary 17.8%[3,4]; postsecondary, technical, or other certificate/ diploma 33.7%; university 11.9%.
Quality of working life (1995). Average workweek: 40.9 hours (16.8%[4] overtime). Annual rate per 100,000 workers for: accidental injury and industrial disease, 3,200[5]; death, n.a. Proportion of employed persons insured for

damages or income loss resulting from: injury 100%[5]; permanent disability 100%[5]; death 100%[5]. Working days lost to industrial disputes per 1,000 employees (1995): 79. Means of transportation to work (1986): private automobile 69.4%; public transportation 10.1%; motorcycle and bicycle 3.2%; foot 6.6%; other 10.7%. Discouraged job seekers (considered by employers to be too young or too old, having language or training limitations, or no vacancies in line of work; 1995): 1.3% of labour force.

Distribution of family income (1990[6])									
percentage of family income by decile									
1	2	3	4	5	6	7	8	9	10 (highest)
1.4%	3.1%	4.2%	5.5%	6.9%	8.6%	10.6%	13.3%	17.2%	29.2%

Access to services (1976). Proportion of dwellings having access to: electricity 99.5%; bathroom 96.0%; flush toilet 92.2%; kitchen 97.9%; public sewer 73.4%.
Social participation. Eligible voters participating in last national election (1996): 95.8%; voting is compulsory. Population age 16 and over participating in voluntary work: n.a. Trade union membership in total workforce (1994): 35.0%.
Social deviance (1995). Offense rate per 100,000 population for: murder 1.8; sexual assault 71.0; assault 560.0; auto theft 703.0; burglary and housebreaking 2,132.0; armed robbery 37.0; fraud and forgery (1989) 760.4. Incidence per 100,000 in general population of: alcoholism, n.a.; prisoners with drug offenses (1993) 9.7; suicide (1994) 13.0.
Material well-being (1995). Households possessing: automobile 85%; telephone 95%; refrigerator 99.7%; air conditioner 32.3%[7]; personal computers 23.0%[4]; washing machine 90.0%; central heating 3.9%[7]; swimming pool 10.1%[7].

National economy

Gross national product (1994): U.S.$320,705,000,000 (U.S.$17,980 per capita).

Structure of gross domestic product and labour force				
	1994–95[8]		1995–96	
	in value $A '000,000	% of total value	labour force	% of labour force
Agriculture	13,592	3.3	421,900	4.7
Mining	17,983	4.4	85,300	0.9
Manufacturing	64,623	15.7	1,111,300	12.3
Construction	27,031	6.5	600,300	6.6
Public utilities	13,449	3.3	80,800	0.9
Transportation and communications	36,978	9.0	546,700	6.0
Trade[9]	78,442	19.0	2,106,500	23.2
Finance, real estate	91,176	22.1	1,111,400	12.3
Pub. admin., defense	15,226	3.7	378,700	4.2
Services	56,324	13.6	1,844,200	20.3
Other	−2,231[10]	−0.6[10]	779,200[11]	8.6[11]
TOTAL	412,593	100.0	9,066,300	100.0

Budget (1994–95). Revenue: $A 110,247,000,000 (income tax 68.6%, of which individual 54.5%, corporate 14.1%; excise duties and sales tax 21.4%). Expenditures: $A 121,877,000,000 (social security and welfare 35.5%; health 14.1%; economic and public services 13.3%; transfers to state governments 12.4%; interest on public debt 6.6%).
Public debt (1994–95): $A 99,962,000,000.
Tourism (1994): receipts from visitors U.S.$5,955,000,000; expenditures by nationals abroad U.S.$4,339,000,000.

Manufacturing, mining, and construction enterprises (1992–93)[12]				
	no. of establishments	no. of employees	Avg. annual wages[13] as a % of all wages	annual turnover ($A '000,000)
Manufacturing				
Food, beverages, and tobacco	3,327	159,282	91.7	36,999
Metal products	6,807	143,146	...	31,310
Machinery and equipment	7,483	188,379	99.3	30,781
Chemical, petroleum, and coal products	2,639	87,428	126.8	27,550
Printing and publishing	4,299	84,965	...	11,539
Miscellaneous manufacturing	5,149	47,910	...	4,800
Wood and paper products	3,372	57,772	...	9,909
Nonmetallic mineral products	1,586	38,394	107.6	8,362
Textile, clothing, footwear, and leather	3,623	75,223	...	8,849
Mining[14]				
Coal, oil, and gas	254	30,800	191.8[15]	17,655
Metallic minerals	261	25,640	163.9[15]	11,344
Nonmetallic minerals[15]	699	8,799	116.0	2,240
Construction[16]	98,100	518,200	...	34,407

Production (gross value in $A '000 except as noted). Agriculture, forestry, fishing (1994–95): livestock slaughtered 6,271,400 (cattle 3,960,000, poultry 927,200, sheep and lambs 738,400, pigs 609,200); wool 3,263,900, wheat 1,926,900, sugarcane 945,000[14], barley 845,000, cotton 652,000[14], grapes 570,200, potatoes 338,000, tomatoes 274,600[5], rice 262,000, apples 238,000, oranges 230,000, bananas 203,000, sorghum 173,000, oats 148,000, pears 108,000, carrots 65,700[5], onions 54,100[5], peaches 53,000, tobacco 51,000, pineapples 45,000, corn (maize) 41,000, cauliflower 33,700[5]; livestock (number of live animals; 1995) 120,651,000 sheep, 26,187,000 cattle, 2,640,000 pigs, 70,608,000[4] poultry; roundwood (1994) 21,362,000 cu m; fish catch (1993) 218,339 metric tons. Mining and quarrying (metric tons [tons of contained metal]; 1994–95): iron ore 136,991,000; bauxite 42,308,000; zinc 918,000; lead 463,000; copper 350,000; tin 7,300; gold 296,626 kg; diamonds 43,591,000 carats. Manufacturing (metric tons except as noted; 1995–96): pig iron 7,554,000; cement 6,397,000; beef and veal 1,706,400; lamb and mutton 555,300; pork 328,900;

woven cotton cloth 62,968,000 sq m; textile floor coverings 42,680,000 sq m; woven woolen cloth 8,624,000 sq m[17]; beer 17,410,000 hectolitres; electric motors 2,849,000 units; refrigerators 414,100 units; motor vehicles 302,500 units. Construction (buildings completed, by value in $A '000; 1995–96): new dwellings 12,105,700; alterations and additions to dwellings 2,283,500; nonresidential 10,728,400.

Retail and service enterprises (1991–92)

	no. of establishments	no. of employees	total wages and salaries ($A '000,000)	annual turnover ($A '000,000)
Retail				
Motor vehicle dealers, gasoline and tire dealers	37,305	220,661	2,572[18]	44,954
Food stores	53,166	406,299	2,461[18]	43,963[17]
Department and general stores	459	87,148	1,175[18]	11,209[17]
Clothing, fabrics, and furniture stores	21,688	91,138	965[18]	7,957[17]
Household appliances and hardware stores	14,268	75,355	629	12,588[17]
Recreational goods	...	...	...	6,299[17]
Services[5]				
Real estate agents	7,265	51,922	...	2,798.7
Architectural services	4,409	16,204	...	945.2
Surveying services	1,175	6,964	...	481.2
Consulting engineering services	5,454	28,208	...	2,325.2
Legal services	8,850	63,108	...	5,105.2
Accounting services	8,699	60,000	...	4,051.2
Computing services	4,894	30,062	...	3,928.8
Advertising services	858	9,083	...	842.1
Market research services	174	8,064	...	251.7
Business management services	686	4,933	...	506.6

Energy production (consumption): electricity (kW-hr; 1993) 155,300,000,000 (155,300,000,000); coal (metric tons; 1993) 183,230,000 (94,030,000); crude petroleum (barrels; 1993) 200,750,000 (2,774,000,000); petroleum products (metric tons; 1993) 32,318,000 (34,916,000); natural gas (cu m; 1993) 24,352,-000,000 (17,783,000,000).

Population economically active (1995–96): total 9,066,300; activity rate of total population 52.8% (participation rates: ages 15–64, 63.7%; female 53.8%; unemployed 8.5%).

Price and earnings indexes (1990 = 100)

	1990	1991	1992	1993	1994	1995	1996
Consumer price index	100.0	103.2	104.2	106.1	108.1	113.2	116.1[19]
Weekly earnings index	100.0	105.1	109.3	111.3	115.0	120.8	123.8[20]

Household income and expenditure (1993–94). Average household size 2.6; average annual income per household $A 37,700 (U.S.$27,585); sources of income: wages and salaries 72.7%, transfer payments 13.0%, self-employment 7.5%, other 6.8%; expenditure: food and beverages 18.7%, transportation and communications 15.3%, housing 13.9%, recreation 13.3%, household durable goods 6.6%, clothing and footwear 5.7%, health 4.6%, energy 2.8%, other 19.1%.

Financial aggregates

	1990	1991	1992	1993	1994	1995	1996[21]
Exchange rate, $A 1.00 per:							
U.S. dollar	0.78	0.78	0.74	0.68	0.73	0.74	0.79
£	0.44	0.44	0.42	0.45	0.48	0.47	0.51
SDR	0.54	0.53	0.50	0.49	0.53	0.50	0.53
International reserves (U.S.$)							
Total (excl. gold; '000,000)	16,265	16,535	11,208	11,102	11,285	11,896	16,024
SDRs ('000,000)	311	290	96	82	73	55	46
Reserve pos. in IMF ('000,000)	349	351	577	550	506	502	493
Foreign exchange ('000,000)	15,605	15,894	10,536	10,470	10,706	11,340	15,485
Gold ('000,000 fine troy oz)	7.93	7.93	7.93	7.90	7.90	7.9	7.9
% world reserves	0.8	0.8	0.8	0.9	0.9	0.9	0.9
Interest and prices							
Central bank discount (%)	15.24	10.99	6.96	5.83	5.75	5.75	5.75[22]
Govt. bond yield (short-term; %)	13.46	9.94	7.25	5.63	7.65	7.60[23]	...
Industrial share prices (1990 = 100)	100.0	96.4	100.3	104.7	112.9	114.2	117.8[20]
Balance of payments (U.S.$'000,000)							
Balance of visible trade	+358	+3,529	+1,640	−29	−3,280	−4,053	−146[20]
Imports, f.o.b.	39,284	38,833	41,173	42,666	50,611	57,149	14,254[20]
Exports, f.o.b.	39,642	42,362	42,813	42,637	47,331	53,096	14,108[20]
Balance of invisibles	−16,446	−14,949	−13,182	−10,481	−14,086	−15,138	−2,413[20]
Balance of payments, current account	−16,088	−11,420	−11,542	−10,510	−17,366	−19,191	−2,559[20]

Land use (1994): meadows and pastures 54.2%; agricultural and under permanent cultivation 6.2%; other 39.6%[24].

Foreign trade

Balance of trade (current prices)

	1991	1992	1993	1994	1995	1996[22]
$A '000,000	4,050	2,870	455	3,188	−5,849	466
% of total	3.9%	2.5%	0.4%	2.4%	3.9%	3.8%

Imports (1994–95): $A 72,882,000,000 (machinery 28.9%, of which office machines and automatic data-processing equipment 7.3%; basic manufactures 13.8%, of which textile yarn and fabrics 3.3%, paper and paper products 2.2%, nonferrous metals 1.6%; transport equipment 13.4%, of which road motor vehicles 11.2%; chemicals and related products 8.9%; mineral fuels and lubricants 4.5%; food and live animals 3.6%; crude materials [inedible] excluding fuels 2.3%; beverages and tobacco 0.7%). *Major import sources:* U.S. 23.3%; Japan 17.4%; U.K. 6.3%; Germany 5.9%; China 4.8%; New Zealand 4.6%; Singapore 3.0%; Italy 2.7%; South Korea 2.6%; France 2.4%.

Exports (1994–95): $A 64,899,000,000 (mineral fuels and lubricants 14.4%, of which coal, coke, and briquettes 10.1%; petroleum, petroleum products, and natural gas 4.2%; crude materials excluding fuels 13.7%, of which textile fibres and their waste 5.9%, metalliferous ores and metal scrap 5.8%; food and live animals 13.2%, of which meat and meat preparations 5.7%, dairy products 2.1%, fish and fish preparations 1.6%, vegetables and fruits 1.4%; basic manufactures 11.5%; machinery and transport equipment 11.1%; chemicals 3.3%). *Major export destinations:* Japan 23.5%; U.S. 8.1%; New Zealand 7.2%; South Korea 6.4%; Singapore 4.1%; U.K. 3.9%; China 4.5%; Indonesia 3.6%; Hong Kong 3.5%; Malaysia 2.7%; Germany 1.6%.

Trade by commodity group (1994–95)

SITC Group	imports U.S.$'000,000	imports %	exports U.S.$'000,000	exports %
00 Food and live animals	1,887	3.6	6,472	13.2
01 Beverages and tobacco	366	0.7	350	0.7
02 Crude materials, excluding fuels	1,207	2.3	6,707	13.7
03 Mineral fuels, lubricants, and related materials	2,339	4.5	7,091	14.4
04 Animal and vegetable oils, fat, and waxes	140	0.3	148	0.3
05 Chemicals and related products, n.e.s.	4,614	8.9	1,646	3.3
06 Basic manufactures	7,168	13.8	5,662	11.5
07 Machinery and transport equipment	22,594	43.4	5,464	11.1
08 Miscellaneous manufactured articles	7,428	14.3	1,653	3.4
09 Goods not classified by kind	4,338	8.3	13,905	28.3
TOTAL	52,082[25]	100.0[25]	49,097[25]	100.0[25]

Direction of trade (1994–95)

	imports U.S.$'000,000	imports %	exports U.S.$'000,000	exports %
Africa	272	0.5	693	1.5
Asia	19,392	37.6	26,051	57.1
Japan	8,950	17.4	10,735	23.5
South America	493	1.0	603	1.3
North and Central America	12,875	25.0	4,541	9.9
United States	12,011	23.3	3,688	8.1
Europe	13,263	25.7	5,870	12.9
EEC	12,321	23.9	5,436	11.9
Russia	16	0.03	202	0.4
Other Europe	926	1.8	232	0.5
Oceania	2,983	5.8	4,725	10.4
New Zealand	2,354	4.6	3,299	7.2
Other	2,237	4.3	3,136	6.9
TOTAL	51,515	100.0[25]	45,619	100.0

Transport and communications

Transport. Railroads[26]: route length (1994) 22,501 mi, 36,212 km; passenger journeys 407,170,000; short ton-mi cargo[17, 27] 67,333,000,000[17, 27], metric ton-km cargo 98,305,000,000[17, 27]. Roads (1993): total length 507,316 mi, 816,447 km (paved 36%). Vehicles (1995): passenger cars 8,391,500; trucks and buses 2,246,700. Merchant marine (1994): vessels (150 gross tons and over) 90; total deadweight tonnage 3,499,527. Air transport (1995[28]): passenger-mi 30,079,000,000, passenger-km 48,408,000,000; short ton-mi cargo 1,145,000,000, metric ton-km cargo 1,672,000,000; airports (1994) with scheduled flights 400.

Communications. Daily newspapers (1992): total number 69; total circulation 4,600,000; circulation per 1,000 population 261. Radio (1995): 21,000,000 receivers (1 per 0.9 persons). Television (1995): 8,000,000 receivers (1 per 2.3 persons). Telephones (main lines; 1993): 8,540,000 (1 per 2.1 persons).

Education and health

Education (1994)

	schools	teachers	students	student/ teacher ratio
Primary (age 6–12) } Secondary (age 13–17) }	9,679	200,074	3,099,380	15.5
Vocational[29]	234[30]	52,587[30]	985,942[31]	...
Higher	95[32]	25,916[32]	604,200	...

Literacy (1980): percentage of total population age 15 and over literate 99.5%.
Health: physicians (1991) 39,984 (1 per 434 persons); hospital beds (1994–95) 77,494 (1 per 226 persons); infant mortality rate (1996) 5.7.
Food (1992): daily per capita caloric intake 3,179 (vegetable products 62%, animal products 38%); 120% of FAO recommended minimum requirement.

Military

Total active duty personnel (1995): 56,100 (army 42.2%, navy 26.7%, air force 31.1%). *Military expenditure as percentage of GNP* (1994): 2.6% (world 3.0%); per capita expenditure U.S.$457.

[1]March 31. [2]Includes both Northern Ireland and Republic of Ireland. [3]Completed highest level of secondary school available. [4]1994. [5]1992–93. [6]December. [7]1983. [8]At 1989–90 prices. [9]Trade includes hotels and restaurants. [10]Less imputed bank service charges. [11]Mostly unemployed. [12]Excludes operations of single-establishment enterprises employing fewer than four persons. [13]Excludes the drawings of working proprietors; 1991–92. [14]1993–94. [15]1990–91. [16]1991–95. [18]1985–86. [19]Second quarter. [20]First quarter. [21]July. [22]June. [23]Fourth quarter. [24]Urban areas, state forests and mining leases, unoccupied land (mainly desert). [25]Detail does not add to total given because of rounding. [26]Government railways only. [27]Includes government and private freight. [28]June figure annualized. [29]Includes special education. [30]1986. [31]1992. [32]1989.

Austria

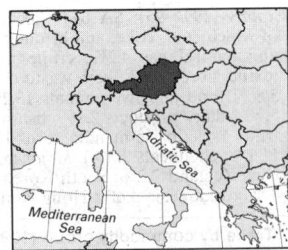

Official name: Republik Österreich (Republic of Austria).
Form of government: federal multiparty republic with two legislative houses (Federal Council [64]; National Council [183]).
Chief of state: President.
Head of government: Chancellor.
Capital: Vienna.
Official language: German.
Official religion: none.
Monetary unit: 1 Austrian Schilling (S) = 100 Groschen; valuation (Oct. 11, 1996) 1 U.S.$ = S 10.77; 1 £ = S 16.97.

Area and population		area		population
		sq mi	sq km	1994 estimate
States	**Capitals**			
Burgenland	Eisenstadt	1,531	3,965	273,613
Kärnten	Klagenfurt	3,681	9,533	559,696
Niederösterreich	Sankt Pölten	7,403	19,174	1,511,555
Oberösterreich	Linz	4,626	11,980	1,383,620
Salzburg	Salzburg	2,762	7,154	504,258
Steiermark	Graz	6,327	16,388	1,203,993
Tirol	Innsbruck	4,883	12,648	654,753
Vorarlberg	Bregenz	1,004	2,601	342,461
Wien (Vienna)	—	160	415	1,595,768
TOTAL		32,378[1]	83,858	8,029,717

Demography

Population (1996): 8,102,000.
Density (1996): persons per sq mi 250.2, persons per sq km 96.6.
Urban-rural (1991): urban 64.5%; rural 35.5%.
Sex distribution (1994): male 48.47%; female 51.53%.
Age breakdown (1994): under 15, 17.6%; 15–29, 22.0%; 30–44, 22.8%; 45–59, 17.8%; 60–74, 13.7%; 75 and over, 6.1%.
Population projection: (2000) 8,249,000; (2010) 8,357,000.
Doubling time: not applicable; population is stable.
Ethnic composition (national origin; 1991): Austrian 93.4%; citizens of former Yugoslavia 2.5%; Turkish 1.5%; German 0.7%; other 1.9%.
Religious affiliation (1991): Roman Catholic 78.0%; nonreligious and atheist 8.6%; Lutheran 4.8%; Muslim 2.0%; Jewish 0.2%; other (mostly Christian) 2.7%; unknown 3.7%.
Major cities (1991): Vienna 1,539,848; Graz 237,810; Linz 203,044; Salzburg 143,978; Innsbruck 118,112.

Vital statistics

Birth rate per 1,000 population (1995): 10.9 (world avg. 25.0); legitimate 73.2%; illegitimate 26.8%.
Death rate per 1,000 population (1995): 10.0 (world avg. 9.3).
Natural increase rate per 1,000 population (1995): 0.9 (world avg. 15.7).
Total fertility rate (avg. births per childbearing woman; 1994): 1.5.
Marriage rate per 1,000 population (1994): 5.4.
Divorce rate per 1,000 population (1994): 2.1.
Life expectancy at birth (1994): male 73.3 years; female 79.7 years.
Major causes of death per 100,000 population (1994): diseases of the circulatory system 531.2, of which ischemic heart diseases 206.0; malignant neoplasms (cancers) 242.9; diseases of the digestive system 49.5.

National economy

Budget (1993). Revenue: S 781,100,000,000 (tax revenue 91.1%, of which social-security contributions 37.4%, individual income taxes 16.3%, value-added taxes 15.7%; nontax revenue 8.2%). Expenditures: S 875,400,000,000 (social security and welfare 45.8%; health 13.2%; education 9.5%; general administration 5.3%; defense 2.2%).
National debt (end of year 1993): U.S.$91,610,000,000.
Production (metric tons except as noted). Agriculture, forestry, fishing (1994): sugar beets 2,800,000, corn (maize) 1,476,000, barley 1,368,000, wheat 1,265,000, potatoes 750,000, grapes 410,000, apples 334,000, rye 292,000, rapeseed 131,000, sunflower seed 95,000; livestock (number of live animals) 3,800,000 pigs, 2,430,000 cattle, 13,000,000 chickens; roundwood (1993) 12,857,000 cu m; fish catch (1993) 4,605. Mining and quarrying (1994): iron ore 1,644,000; magnesite 681,000; high-grade graphite 12,300. Manufacturing (value added in S '000,000,000; 1993): electrical machinery and apparatus 44.6; base metals and fabricated metals 42.3; nonelectrical machinery and apparatus 33.1; beverages and tobacco products 29.1; chemicals and chemical products 25.8; transport equipment 22.1. Construction (completed in S '000,000,000; 1993): residential 27.9; nonresidential 26.7. Energy production (consumption): electricity (kW-hr; 1994) 53,309,000,000 (52,485,000,000); coal (metric tons; 1994) 1,391,000 ([1993] 4,374,000); crude petroleum (barrels; 1994) 7,819,000 ([1993] 63,089,000); petroleum products (metric tons; 1993) 8,349,000 (10,475,000); natural gas (cu m; 1994) 1,343,000,000 ([1993] 6,836,000,000).
Land use (1993): forested 39.2%; meadows and pastures 23.6%; agricultural and under permanent cultivation 18.1%; other 19.1%.
Tourism (1994): receipts from visitors U.S.$13,160,000,000; expenditures by nationals abroad U.S.$9,330,000,000.
Population economically active (1993): total 3,734,200; activity rate of total population 46.7% (participation rates: ages 15–64, 69.3%; female 42.0%; unemployed [1995] 6.6%).

Price and earnings indexes (1990 = 100)						
	1989	1990	1991	1992	1993	1994	1995[2]
Consumer price index	96.8	100.0	103.3	107.5	111.4	114.7	118.2
Monthly earnings index	93.3	100.0	105.2	110.3	116.1	120.7	116.0

Gross national product (at current market prices; 1994): U.S.$197,475,000,000 (U.S.$24,950 per capita).

Structure of gross domestic product and labour force				
	1994		1993	
	in value S '000,000	% of total value	labour force	% of labour force
Agriculture	49,460	2.2	249,100	6.7
Mining	536,390 }	23.7	10,800	0.3
Manufacturing			952,700	25.5
Construction	178,850	7.9	325,800	8.7
Public utilities	62,070	2.7	36,400	1.0
Transportation and communications	143,910	6.4	237,400	6.4
Trade, restaurants	358,590	15.8	711,900	19.1
Finance, real estate	429,950	19.0	270,400	7.2
Pub. admin., defense	323,830	14.3 }	896,100	24.0
Services	102,640	4.5		
Other	77,230[3]	3.4[3]	43,900	1.2
TOTAL	2,262,920	100.0[1]	3,734,400[1]	100.0[1]

Household income and expenditure. Average household size (1993) 2.6; net median income per household (1993) S 291,930 (U.S.$25,110); sources of income (1992): wages and salaries 55.7%, transfer payments 24.4%, other 19.9%; expenditure (1992): food and beverages 18.8%, transportation 18.5%, housing 11.8%, cafe and hotel expenditures 9.7%, clothing and footwear 8.5%.

Foreign trade[4]

Balance of trade (current prices)						
	1989	1990	1991	1992	1993	1994
S '000,000	− 62,180	− 65,190	− 86,300	− 79,700	− 72,500	− 89,300
% of total	6.8%	6.5%	8.3%	7.6%	7.2%	8.0%

Imports (1994): S 628,900,000,000 (machinery and transport equipment 38.0%, of which road vehicles 11.4%, electrical machinery and apparatus 7.1%; chemicals and related products 10.4%; clothing 4.8%; food products 4.8%). *Major import sources:* Germany 40.0%; Italy 8.8%; France 4.7%; United States 4.4%; Japan 4.3%; Switzerland 4.1%.
Exports (1994): S 512,500,000,000 (machinery and transport equipment 39.0%, of which electrical machinery and apparatus 7.7%, road vehicles 7.0%; chemical products 9.2%; paper and paper products 5.8%; iron and steel 5.3%). *Major export destination:* Germany 38.1%; Italy 8.1%; Switzerland 6.4%; France 4.5%; Hungary 3.9%; United States 3.5%.

Transport and communications

Transport. Railroads (1994)[5]: length 3,502 mi, 5,636 km; passenger-mi 5,988,000,000, passenger-km 9,636,000,000; (1995) short ton-mi cargo 9,386,000,000, metric ton-km cargo 13,704,000,000. Roads (1994): total length 80,332 mi[6], 129,282 km[6] (paved 100%[7]). Vehicles (1994): passenger cars 3,479,595; trucks and buses 292,755. Merchant marine (1992): vessels (100 gross tons and over) 26; total deadweight tonnage 208,504. Air transport[8] (1995): passenger-mi 4,701,000,000, passenger-km 7,566,000,000; short ton-mi cargo 120,273,000, metric ton-km cargo 175,595,000; airports (1996) with scheduled flights 6.
Communications. Daily newspapers (1992): total number 27; total circulation 3,108,357; circulation per 1,000 population 394. Radio (1995): total receivers 4,710,000 (1 per 1.7 persons). Television (1995): total receivers 2,706,000 (1 per 3.0 persons). Telephones (main lines; 1994): 3,681,000 (1 per 2.2 persons).

Education and health

Education (1994–95)				
	schools	teachers	students	student/teacher ratio
Primary (age 6–10)	3,384	31,126	381,676	12.3
Secondary (age 11–18)	1,899	57,740	469,915	8.1
Voc., teacher tr.	1,028	24,956	308,091	12.3
Higher	44	14,322	228,147	15.9

Educational attainment (1993). Percentage of population age 25 and over having: lower-secondary education 37.5%; vocational education ending at secondary level 44.6%; completed upper secondary 6.1%; higher vocational 5.5%; higher 6.3%. *Literacy:* virtually 100%.
Health (1994): physicians 27,170 (1 per 296 persons); hospital beds 71,166 (1 per 113 persons); infant mortality rate per 1,000 live births (1995) 5.5.
Food (1992): daily per capita caloric intake 3,497 (vegetable products 64%, animal products 36%); 133% of FAO recommended minimum requirement.

Military

Total active duty personnel (1995): 55,750 (army 92.4%; navy, none; air force 7.6%). *Military expenditure as percentage of GNP* (1994): 1.0% (world 3.0%); per capita expenditure U.S.$232.

---

[1]Detail does not add to total given because of rounding. [2]July. [3]Value-added tax plus import duties (S 209,490,000,000) less imputed bank service charges (S 132,260,000,000). [4]Import figures are f.o.b. in balance of trade and c.i.f. in commodities and trading partners. [5]Federal railways only. [6]Includes some private roads. [7]Includes macadamized roads. [8]Austrian Airlines, Lauda Air, and Tyrolean Airways.

Azerbaijan

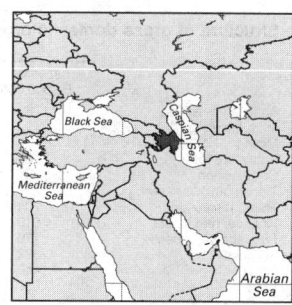

Official name: Azärbayjan Respublikasi (Azerbaijani Republic).
Form of government: federal multiparty republic with a single legislative body (National Assembly [125]).
Head of state: President.
Head of government: Prime Minister.
Capital: Baku (Azerbaijani: Bakı).
Official language: Azerbaijani.
Official religion: none.
Monetary unit: 1 manat (A.M.)[1] = 100 gopik; valuation (Oct. 11, 1996) free rate, 1 U.S.$ = A.M. 4,304; 1 £ = A.M. 6,780.

Area and population

Republics	Capitals	area sq mi	area sq km	population 1991 estimate
Naxçivan (Nakhichevan)	Naxçivan (Nakhichevan)	2,100	5,500	305,700
Qarabağ[2] (Nagorno Karabakh)	Xankändi (Stepanakert)	1,700	4,400	193,300
Regions under republican jurisdiction	—	29,600	76,700	4,924,300
Cities				
Baku (Bakı)	—	...	...	1,713,300
TOTAL		33,400	86,600	7,136,600

Demography

Population (1996): 7,570,200.
Density (1996): persons per sq mi 226.4, persons per sq km 87.4.
Urban-rural (1994): urban 53.0%; rural 47.0%.
Sex distribution (1992): male 49.31%; female 50.69%.
Age breakdown (1991): under 15, 33.2%; 15–29, 28.6%; 30–44, 18.8%; 45–59, 11.3%; 60–74, 5.1%; 75 and over, 3.0%.
Population projection: (2000) 7,796,614; (2010) 8,298,334.
Doubling time: 50 years.
Ethnic composition (1989): Azerbaijani 82.7%; Russian 5.7%; Armenian 5.6%; Lezgin 2.4%; Avar 0.6%; Ukrainian 0.5%; Tatar 0.4%; other 2.1%.
Religious affiliation (1993): Shīī Muslim 62.0%; Sunnī Muslim 26.0%; Russian and Armenian Orthodox 12.0%.
Major cities (1991): Baku 1,080,500; Gäncä (formerly Kirovabad) 282,200; Sumqayıt (Sumgait) 236,200; Mingacevir (Mingechaur) 90,900; Naxçıvan (Nakhichevan) 61,700.

Vital statistics

Birth rate per 1,000 population (1994): 21.4 (world avg. 25.0); legitimate 94.8%; illegitimate 5.2%.
Death rate per 1,000 population (1994): 7.4 (world avg. 9.3).
Natural increase rate per 1,000 population (1994): 14.0 (world avg. 15.7).
Total fertility rate (avg. births per childbearing woman; 1993): 2.8.
Marriage rate per 1,000 population (1994): 6.3.
Divorce rate per 1,000 population (1994): 0.8.
Life expectancy at birth (1993): male 66.7 years; female 74.6 years.
Major causes of death per 100,000 population (1993): diseases of the circulatory system 339.5; diseases of the respiratory system 98.1; accidents, poisoning, and violence 80.2; malignant neoplasms (cancers) 66.9; diseases of the digestive system 31.8; infectious and parasitic diseases 25.8; endocrine and metabolic disorders 12.2; diseases of the nervous system 11.8.

National economy

Budget (1994). Revenue: A.M. 552,500,000,000 (tax revenue 40.7%, of which enterprise profits tax 17.6%, value-added tax 11.3%, excise tax 6.7%, individual income tax 5.1%; nontax revenue 47.9%, of which foreign exchange revenue 45.6%, customs 2.3%; other 11.4%). Expenditures: A.M. 773,000,-000,000 (foreign currency outlays 32.5%; wages and salaries 11.1%; pensions 6.2%; subsidies 2.4%; capital expenditure 2.1%; other 45.7%).
Public debt (external, outstanding; 1994): U.S.$112,800,000.
Production (metric tons except as noted). Agriculture, forestry, fishing (1995): fruit 1,272,000, cereals 983,000, vegetables (except potatoes) 800,000, wheat 675,000, cotton 284,000, potatoes 200,000, tobacco 68,000, tea 4,000; livestock (number of live animals) 4,376,000 sheep and goats, 1,633,000 cattle, 33,000 pigs, 30,000 horses, 23,000,000 poultry; roundwood (1993) 17,000 cu m; fish catch (1993) 36,000. Mining and quarrying (1994): iron ore 100,000. Manufacturing (value of production in A.M. '000,000; 1994): textiles 110,265; processed foods 107,943; machine-building and metalworking equipment 82,939; chemical products 60,977; construction materials 34,164; ferrous and nonferrous metals 23,184; meat and dairy products 22,540; clothing 11,847. Construction (1991): 2,600,000 sq m. Energy production (consumption): electricity (kW-hr; 1994) 17,600,000,000 (17,800,000,000); coal (metric tons; 1994) none (8,000); crude petroleum (barrels; 1994) 70,393,000 (76,672,000); petroleum products (metric tons; 1994) 6,259,000 (6,208,000); natural gas (cu m; 1994) 5,549,000,000 (7,706,000,000).
Household income and expenditure. Average household size (1989) 4.8; income per household (1994): A.M. 71,443 (U.S.$, n.a.[3]); sources of income (1992): wages and salaries 70.2%, social benefits 19.0%, agricultural income 10.8%; expenditure: retail goods 85.8%, services 7.0%, taxes 3.9%, other 3.3%.

Gross national product (at current market prices; 1994): U.S.$3,730,000,000 (U.S.$500 per capita)[3].

Structure of gross domestic product and labour force

	1993 in value A.M. '000,000	1993 % of total value	1994 labour force	1994 % of labour force
Agriculture	42,562	26.5	1,011,000	37.8
Mining } Manufacturing }	39,127	24.4	350,000	13.1
Public utilities	6,307	3.9	...	...
Construction	11,759	7.3	202,000	7.6
Transportation and communications	12,542	7.8	167,000	6.2
Trade	8,451	5.3	160,000	6.0
Finance	13,486	8.4	91,000	3.4
Pub. admin., defense	9,415	5.9	52,000	1.9
Services	16,272	10.1	593,000	22.2
Other	633	0.4	48,000	1.8
TOTAL	160,554	100.0	2,674,000	100.0

Population economically active (1994): total 2,674,000; activity rate of total population 35.8% (participation rates: ages 16–59 [male], 16–54 [female] 71.5%; female 45.0%; unemployed [1995] 1.0%).

Price and earnings indexes (1990 = 100)

	1989	1990	1991	1992	1993	1994	1995
Consumer price index	...	100.0	205.6	2,082	25,602	451,722	...
Monthly earnings index	91.8	100.0	163.1	1,386	11,203	78,590	39,930

Tourism (1994): receipts from visitors U.S.$2,042,000; expenditures by nationals abroad, n.a.
Land use (1994): forest 11.0%; pasture 25.4%; agriculture 48.5%; other 15.1%.

Foreign trade

Balance of trade (current prices)

	1993	1994	1995
U.S.$'000,000	− 160	− 121	− 305
% of total	10.6%	4.0%	25.6%

Imports (1994): U.S.$778,000,000 (food products 26.3%, natural gas 24.8%, machinery and equipment 13.1%, metals 12.5%, chemical products 6.7%). *Major import sources:* Turkmenistan 25.2%; Russia 15.2%; Ukraine 11.1%; Turkey 9.8%; Iran 8.6%; Kazakstan 6.7%.
Exports (1994): U.S.$637,000,000 (petroleum products 32.5%, metals 16.5%, cotton 15.5%, machinery and equipment 14.2%, food products 10.0%, chemical products 5.2%). *Major export destinations:* Iran 38.0%; Russia 22.0%; United Kingdom 9.7%; Ukraine 9.1%; Turkey 2.5%.

Transport and communications

Transport. Railroads (1994): length 1,305 mi, 2,100 km; (1991) passenger-mi 3,025,400,000, passenger-km 4,868,900,000; short ton-mi cargo 20,877,000,-000, metric ton-km cargo 30,479,000,000. Roads (1995): total length 35,897 mi, 57,770 km (paved 93.8%). Vehicles (1995): passenger cars 289,000; trucks and buses 88,800. Merchant marine: vessels (100 gross tons and over) n.a.; total deadweight tonnage, n.a. Air transport (1991): passenger-mi 3,025,400,000, passenger-km 4,868,900,000; short ton-mi cargo 22,600,000, metric ton-km cargo 33,000,000; airports (1996) with scheduled flights 1.
Communications. Daily newspapers (1992): total number 6; total circulation 427,000; circulation per 1,000 population 58. Radio (1992): total number of receivers 1,174,000 (1 per 6.1 persons). Television (1992): total number of receivers 1,522,000 (1 per 4.8 persons). Telephones (main lines; 1993): 647,000 (1 per 11.0 persons).

Education and health

Education (1994–95)

	schools	teachers	students	student/ teacher ratio
Primary (age 6–13) } Secondary (age 14–17) }	4,500	139,000	1,462,000	9.9
Voc., teacher tr.	78	...	30,400	...
Higher	23	...	89,100	...

Educational attainment (1989). Percentage of population age 25 and over having: primary education or no formal schooling 12.2%; some secondary 19.2%; completed secondary and some postsecondary 58.1%; higher 10.5%.
Literacy (1989): percentage of total population 15 and over literate 97.3%; males literate 98.9%; females 95.9%.
Health (1994): physicians 29,000 (1 per 251 persons); hospital beds 79,000 (1 per 98 persons); infant mortality rate per 1,000 live births 25.2.

Military

Total active duty personnel (1996): 70,700 (army 81.0%, navy[4] 3.1%, air force 15.8%). *Military expenditure as percentage of GNP* (1994): c. 1.0% (world 3.0%); per capita expenditure (1994) U.S.$17.

---

[1]The manat was introduced on Aug. 15, 1992, at a 10-to-1 ratio with the Russian ruble and circulated parallel with it; on June 20, 1993, the manat became the sole legal tender. [2]In November 1991 the Azerbaijan Supreme Soviet abolished Nagorno Karabakh's autonomous status. [3]Ruble-area GNP and exchange-rate data are very speculative. [4]Azerbaijan shares a portion of the Caspian Flotilla.

Bahamas, The

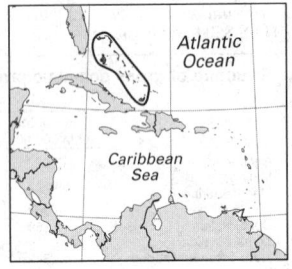

Official name: Commonwealth of The
  Bahamas.
Form of government: constitutional
  monarchy with two legislative
  houses (Senate [16]; House of
  Assembly [49]).
Chief of state: British Monarch
  represented by Governor-General.
Head of government: Prime Minister.
Capital: Nassau.
Official language: English.
Official religion: none.
Monetary unit: 1 Bahamian dollar
  (B$) = 100 cents; valuation
  (Oct. 11, 1996) 1 U.S.$ = B$1.00;
  1 £ = B$1.58.

Area and population

Islands and Island Groups[2]	area[1] sq mi	area[1] sq km	population 1990 census
Abaco, Great and Little	649	1,681	10,034
Acklins	192	497	405
Andros	2,300	5,957	8,187
Berry Islands	12	31	628
Bimini Islands	9	23	1,639
Cat Island	150	388	1,698
Crooked and Long Cay	93	241	412
Eleuthera	187	484	7,993
Exuma, Great and, and Exuma Cays	112	290	3,556
Grand Bahama	530	1,373	40,898
Harbour Island	3	8	1,219
Inagua, Great and Little	599	1,551	985
Long Island	230	596	2,954
Mayaguana	110	285	312
New Providence	80	207	172,196
Ragged Island	14	36	89
Rum Cay	30	78	53
San Salvador	63	163	465
Spanish Wells	10	26	1,372
Other uninhabited cays and rocks	9	23	—
TOTAL	5,382	13,939[3]	255,095

Demography

Population (1996): 280,000.
Density (1995)[4]: persons per sq mi 72.0, persons per sq km 27.8.
Urban-rural (1995): urban 86.0%; rural 14.0%.
Sex distribution (1995): male 48.91%; female 51.09%.
Age breakdown (1995): under 15, 29.3%; 15–29, 28.6%; 30–44, 23.2%; 45–59, 11.6%; 60–74, 5.1%; 75 and over, 2.2%.
Population projection: (2000) 295,000; (2010) 332,000.
Doubling time: 52 years.
Ethnic composition (1993): black 85.0%; white 12.0%; Asian or Hispanic 3.0%.
Religious affiliation (1980): non-Anglican Protestant 55.2%, of which Baptist 32.1%; Anglican 20.1%; Roman Catholic 18.8%; other 5.9%.
Major cities (1990): Nassau 172,196[5]; Freeport/Lucaya 26,574; Marsh Harbour 3,611; Bailey Town 1,490; Dunmore Town (Harbour Island) 1,219.

Vital statistics

Birth rate per 1,000 population (1995): 19.2 (world avg. 25.0); (1990) legitimate 42.8%; illegitimate 57.2%.
Death rate per 1,000 population (1995): 5.8 (world avg. 9.3).
Natural increase rate per 1,000 population (1995): 13.4 (world avg. 15.7).
Total fertility rate (avg. births per childbearing woman; 1995): 2.0.
Marriage rate per 1,000 population (1992): 9.1.
Divorce rate per 1,000 population (1992): 1.2.
Life expectancy at birth (1995): male 67.4 years; female 77.0 years.
Major causes of death per 100,000 population (1991): ischemic heart diseases 95.0; malignant neoplasms (cancers) 79.2; cerebrovascular disease 28.6; pneumonia 23.2.

National economy

Budget (1996–97). Revenue: B$714,900,000 (import taxes 47.2%, stamp taxes 17.8%, departure taxes 8.3%, fines and forfeits 6.3%, business and professional licenses 5.1%). Expenditures: B$765,800,000 (education 17.4%, health 13.8%, general administration 13.8%, public works and water supply 12.4%, interest on public debt 11.7%, public order 10.4%, defense 2.8%).
National debt (December 1995): U.S.$1,488,000,000.
Production (value of production in B$'000 except as noted). Agriculture, forestry, fishing (1994): crayfish 57,700, other marine products (mostly sponges, groupers, conchs) 4,800, poultry products (1993) 20,200, important agricultural products for export include (1995) grapefruits, cucumbers, and limes; roundwood 117,000 cu m. Mining and quarrying (value of export production; 1995): salt 13,400; aragonite 4,000. Manufacturing (value of export production; 1995): pharmaceuticals and other chemical products 74,200; rum 4,600. Construction (gross value of private buildings completed in B$'000,000; 1995–96)[6]: residential 85; nonresidential 34. Energy production (consumption): electricity (kW-hr; 1995) 1,254,000,000 ([1994] 1,053,000,-000); coal, none (none); crude petroleum, none (none); petroleum products (metric tons; 1993) negligible (562,000); natural gas, none (none).
Tourism (1995): receipts from visitors U.S.$1,344,000,000; expenditures by nationals abroad U.S.$213,000,000.
Gross national product (1994): U.S.$3,207,000,000 (U.S.$11,790 per capita).

Structure of gross domestic product and labour force

	1992 in value B$'000,000	1992 % of total value	1994 labour force[7]	1994 % of labour force
Agriculture, fishing	89	2.9	6,614	4.7
Manufacturing	105	3.4	5,060	3.6
Mining			2,010	1.4
Public utilities	88	2.9		
Construction	91	3.0	8,651	6.1
Transp. and commun.	227	7.4	10,821	7.7
Trade, restaurants	705	23.0	36,507	25.9
Finance, real estate	610	19.9	11,940	8.5
Pub. admin., defense	179	5.8	40,063	28.4
Services	523	17.1		
Other	443[8]	14.5[8]	19,348[9]	13.7[9]
TOTAL	3,059[3]	100.0[3]	141,014	100.0

Population economically active (1994)[10]: total 138,700; activity rate of total population 50.7% (participation rates: ages 15–64, 77.8%; female 46.8%; unemployed [1995] 10.7%).

Price and earnings indexes (1991 = 100)

	1989	1990	1991	1992	1993	1994	1995
Consumer price index	89.2	93.3	100.0	105.7	108.5	110.2	112.6[11]
Annual earnings index[12]	99.7	...	100.0	112.8	116.8[13]	...	...

Household income and expenditure. Average household size (1994) 3.9; income per household (1994) B$27,000 (U.S.$27,000); sources of income: n.a.; expenditure (1988)[14]: food and beverages 19.8%, housing 19.2%, transportation and communications 18.9%, household furnishings 10.2%.
Land use (1994): forested 32.4%; meadows and pastures 0.2%; agricultural and under permanent cultivation 1.0%; other 66.4%.

Foreign trade[15, 16]

Balance of trade (current prices)

	1990	1991	1992	1993	1994	1995
B$'000,000	−874	−866	−845	−792	−904	−1,067
% of total	64.7%	65.8%	68.7%	70.9%	73.0%	75.2%

Imports (1995): B$1,243,000,000 (machinery and transport equipment 24.8%; food products 16.8%; petroleum for domestic use 12.6%; chemicals and chemical products 8.1%). *Major import sources*[17]: U.S. 92.8%; EC 2.8%.
Exports (1995): B$176,000,000 (domestic exports 52.6%, of which crayfish 31.9%, salt 7.7%; reexports 47.4%, of which machinery and transport equipment 26.1%, chemical products 9.5%). *Major export destinations:* U.S. 81.1%; EC 9.2%; Canada 1.9%.

Transport and communications

Transport. Railroads: none. Roads (1993): total length 1,491 mi, 2,400 km (paved 56%). Vehicles (1994): passenger cars 46,089; trucks and buses 11,858. Merchant marine (1992): vessels (100 gross tons and over) 1,061; total deadweight tonnage 33,081,652. Air transport (1993): passenger-mi 119,000,000; passenger-km 191,000,000; short ton-mi cargo 274,000, metric ton-km cargo 400,000; airports (1996) with scheduled flights 23.
Communications. Daily newspapers (1992): total number 3; total circulation 35,000; circulation per 1,000 population 133. Radio (1995): total receivers 80,000 (1 per 3.5 persons). Television (1995): total receivers 50,000 (1 per 5.6 persons). Telephones (main lines; 1993): 79,500 (1 per 3.4 persons).

Education and health

Education (1993–94)

	schools	teachers	students	student/ teacher ratio
Primary (age 5–10)	115	1,581	33,343	21.1
Secondary (age 11–16)	...	1,775	28,363	16.0
Higher[18]	1	300	3,201	10.7

Educational attainment (1990). Percentage of population age 25 and over having: no formal schooling 3.5%; incomplete primary education 25.4%; complete primary/incomplete secondary 57.6%; complete secondary/higher 13.5%. *Literacy* (1995): total percentage age 15 and over literate 98.2%.
Health: physicians (1992) 373 (1 per 709 persons); hospital beds (1993) 1,081 (1 per 249 persons); infant mortality rate per 1,000 live births (1995) 24.3.
Food (1992): daily per capita caloric intake 2,624 (vegetable products 71%, animal products 29%); 108% of FAO recommended minimum requirement.

Military

Total active duty personnel (1995): 850 (coast guard 94.1%, other 5.9%).
Military expenditure as percentage of GNP (1993)[19]: 0.5% (world 3.2%); per capita expenditure U.S.$68.

---

[1]Includes areas of lakes and ponds, as well as lagoons and sounds almost entirely surrounded by land; area of land only is about 3,890 sq mi (10,070 sq km). [2]Family (Out) Islands (all islands other than New Providence) are administered by commissioners assigned by the central government. Extent of commissioner districts varies from part of an island to island groups. [3]Detail does not add to total given because of rounding. [4]Land area only. [5]Population cited is for New Providence Island. [6]New Providence and Grand Bahama islands only. [7]Survey date of official figures is unknown. [8]Includes net indirect taxes (B$430,000,000) and statistical discrepancy (B$13,000,000). [9]Includes 594 not adequately defined and 18,754 unemployed. [10]As of May 1. [11]Average of 2nd and 3rd quarters. [12]Annual mean household income. [13]May. [14]Domestic purchases by resident households only; data for expenditures in restaurants and hotels are not available. [15]Imports c.i.f.; exports f.o.b. [16]Official Bahamian statistics exclude trade data for crude petroleum imported for storage on behalf of foreign companies, hormones, and inorganic and organic chemicals. [17]Excludes all petroleum imports. [18]College of The Bahamas only. [19]Includes police.

Bahrain

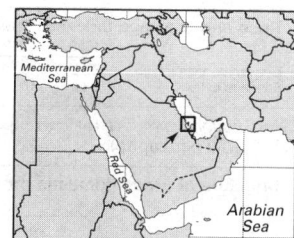

Official name: Dawlat al-Baḥrayn
(State of Bahrain).
Form of government: monarchy
(emirate)[1].
Chief of state: Emir.
Head of government: Prime Minister.
Capital: Manama.
Official language: Arabic.
Official religion: Islam.
Monetary unit: 1 Bahrain dinar
(BD) = 1,000 fils; valuation (Oct. 11,
1996) 1 BD = U.S.$2.65 = £1.68.

Area and population

Regions[2]	area sq mi	area sq km	population 1991 census
Al-Gharbīyah (Western)	60.3	156.1	22,034
Al-Hadd	2.3	6.0	8,610
Jidd (Judd) Ḥafṣ	8.3	21.6	44,769
Al-Manāmah (Manama)	10.0	25.8	136,999
Al-Muḥarraq	6.2	16.0	74,245
Ar-Rifāʿ	112.6	291.6	49,752
Ash-Shamālīyah (Northern)	14.2	36.8	33,763
Ash-Sharqīyah (Eastern)	...	...	3,242[3]
Sitrah	11.1	28.8	36,755
Al-Wusṭā (Central)	13.6	35.2	34,304
Towns with special status			
Ḥammād	5.1	13.1	29,055
Madīnat ʿĪsā	4.8	12.4	34,509
Islands			
Ḥawār[4] and other	19.5	50.6	2
TOTAL	268.0	694.2[5]	508,037

Demography

Population (1996): 598,000.
Density (1996): persons per sq mi 2,231.3, persons per sq km 861.4.
Urban-rural (1995): urban 90.3%; rural 9.7%.
Sex distribution (1994): male 57.78%; female 42.22%.
Age breakdown (1994): under 15, 31.5%; 15–29, 25.5%; 30–44, 30.8%; 45–59, 8.5%; 60–74, 3.0%; 75 and over, 0.6%.
Population projection: (2000) 690,334; (2010) 994,082.
Doubling time: 32 years.
Ethnic composition (1991): Bahraini Arab 63.6%; Persian, Indian, Pakistani, and other Asians 30.3%; other Arab 3.5%; European 1.2%; other 1.4%.
Religious affiliation (1995): Muslim 81.8%, of which Shīʿī 57.3%, Sunnī 24.5%; Christian 8.5%; other 9.7%.
Major cities (1991): Manama (1992) 140,401; Ar-Rifāʿ 45,956; Al-Muḥarraq 45,337; Madīnat ʿĪsā 34,509.

Vital statistics

Birth rate per 1,000 population (1994): 27.4 (world avg. 25.0); legitimate 100%.
Death rate per 1,000 population (1994): 5.4 (world avg. 9.3).
Natural increase rate per 1,000 population (1994): 22.0 (world avg. 15.7).
Total fertility rate (avg. births per childbearing woman; 1994): 3.6.
Marriage rate per 1,000 population (1993): 6.4.
Divorce rate per 1,000 population (1993): 1.3.
Life expectancy at birth (1994): male 69.0 years; female 72.4 years.
Major causes of death per 100,000 population (1991): diseases of the circulatory system 100.4; malignant neoplasms (cancers) 34.1; diseases of the respiratory system 29.7; accidents and violence 28.5; endocrine, nutritional, and metabolic diseases 17.4; congenital anomalies 13.8; diseases of the genitourinary system 13.4; diseases of the digestive system 10.7.

National economy

Budget (1994). Revenue: BD 513,900,000 (nontax revenue 62.6%, of which entrepreneurial and property income 56.9%; tax revenue 30.1%, of which import duties 9.9%, foreign grants 7.3%). Expenditures: BD 646,900,000 (general administration and public order 35.1%; defense 14.9%; education 12.0%; transportation and communications 9.7%; health 8.6%; fuel and energy 7.6%).
Public debt (external, outstanding; 1991): U.S.$1,810,000,000[6].
Population economically active (1991): total 226,448; activity rate of total population 44.6% (participation rates: ages 15–64, 66.1%; female 17.5%; unemployed 6.3%).

Price and earnings indexes (1990 = 100)

	1988	1989	1990	1991	1992	1993	1994
Consumer price index	97.6	99.1	100.0	100.8	100.6	103.1	104.0
Earnings index	...	...	...	...	...	...	...

Production (metric tons except as noted). Agriculture, forestry, roundwood, n.a.; fishing (1996): fruit (excluding melons) 25,095, cow's milk 20,000, dates 20,000, tomatoes 8,500, hen's eggs 3,500, onions 1,300, cucumbers and gherkins 500; livestock (number of live animals) 29,400 sheep, 18,000 goats, 16,500 cattle, 900 camels, 660,000 chickens; roundwood, n.a.; fish catch (1993) 8,958. Manufacturing (barrels; 1994): gas oil 28,900,000; fuel oil 20,900,000; kerosene 10,400,000; gasoline 7,700,000; jet fuel 7,100,000; naphtha 1,860,000; propane 1,500,000; butane 1,190,000; aluminum 447,514 metric tons; other manufactures include methanol, ammonia, plastics, and paper products. Construction (permits issued; 1991): residential 5,931; non-

residential 718. Energy production (consumption): electricity (kW-hr; 1994) 4,550,000,000 (4,550,000,000); coal, none (none); crude petroleum (barrels; 1994) 14,721,000 (89,516,000); petroleum products (metric tons; 1994) 10,651,000 (584,000); natural gas (cu m; 1994) 6,383,000,000 (6,383,000,000).
Gross national product (at current market prices; 1994): U.S.$4,114,000,000 (U.S.$7,500 per capita).

Structure of gross domestic product and labour force

	1994[7] value in BD '000,000[8]	1994[7] % of total value	1991 labour force	1991 % of labour force
Agriculture	20.5	1.1	5,108	2.3
Mining	269.3	15.1	3,638	1.6
Manufacturing	264.9	14.8	26,618	11.8
Construction	107.7	6.0	26,738	11.6
Public utilities	54.3	3.0	2,898	1.3
Transp. and commun.	200.1	11.2	13,789	6.1
Trade	151.2	8.5	29,961	13.2
Finance	397.5	22.3	17,256	7.6
Pub. admin., defense	355.4	19.9 }	83,944	37.1
Services	97.2	5.4 }		
Other	−131.9	−7.4	16,498	7.3
TOTAL	1,786.2	100.0[5]	226,448	100.0[5]

Household income and expenditure. Average household size (1991) 5.8; income per household: n.a.; sources of income: n.a.; expenditure (1984): food and tobacco 33.3%, housing 21.2%, household durable goods 9.8%, transportation and communications 8.5%, recreation 6.4%, clothing and footwear 5.9%, education 2.7%, health 2.3%, energy and water 2.2%.
Land use (1994): meadows and pastures 5.8%; agricultural and under permanent cultivation 2.9%; built-on and wasteland (mostly sand plains and salt marshes) 91.3%.
Tourism (1994): receipts from visitors U.S.$302,000,000; expenditures by nationals abroad U.S.$146,000,000.

Foreign trade[9]

Balance of trade (current prices)

	1990	1991	1992	1993	1994	1995
BD '000,000	+156.7	−73.1	−138.2	+88.2	+33.0	+157.1
% of total	5.9%	2.7%	5.1%	3.3%	1.3%	5.4%

Imports (1993): BD 1,450,600,000 (crude petroleum products 35.5%, transport equipment and machines 16.2%, chemicals 8.8%, food and live animals 7.8%). *Major import sources:* United States 14.1%; Japan 9.8%; Australia 9.7%; United Kingdom 9.4%; Germany 6.4%; Saudi Arabia 5.4%; not specified 15.0%.
Exports (1993): BD 1,394,900,000 (petroleum products 65.7%, basic manufactured goods 19.1%). *Major export destinations:* Saudi Arabia 15.8%; Japan 15.1%; South Korea 9.1%; United States 8.1%; not specified 5.5%.

Transport and communications

Transport. Railroads: none. Roads (1995): total length 1,762 mi, 2,835 km (paved 74.6%). Vehicles (1995): passenger cars 141,901; trucks and buses 29,584. Merchant marine (1992): vessels (100 gross tons and over) 87; total deadweight tonnage 192,487. Air transport (1995)[10]: passenger-mi 1,719,000,000, passenger-km 2,766,000,000; short ton-mi cargo 77,727,000, metric ton-km cargo 113,479,000; airports (1996) with scheduled flights 1.
Communications. Daily newspapers (1992): total number 3; total circulation 43,000; circulation per 1,000 population 60. Radio (1995): total number of receivers 320,000 (1 per 1.8 persons). Television (1995): total number of receivers 270,000 (1 per 2.1 persons). Telephones (main lines; 1993): 124,400 (1 per 4.4 persons).

Education and health

Education (1993–94)

	schools	teachers	students	student/ teacher ratio
Primary (age 6–11)	118	3,386	70,513	20.8
Secondary (age 12–17)	35[11]	2,343	47,417	20.2
Voc., teacher tr.	9[11]	823	6,776	8.2
Higher	4[11]	582[12]	7,763[12]	13.3[12]

Educational attainment (1991). Percentage of population age 25 and over having: no formal education 38.4%; primary education 26.2%; secondary 25.1%; higher 10.3%. *Literacy* (1991): percentage of population age 15 and over literate 69.7%; males literate 76.5%; females literate 58.6%.
Health (1993): physicians 482 (1 per 1,115 persons); hospital beds 1,529 (1 per 352 persons); infant mortality rate per 1,000 live births (1994) 23.8.
Food: n.a.

Military

Total active duty personnel (1996): 11,000 (army 77.3%, navy 9.1%, air force 13.6%). *Military expenditure as percentage of GNP* (1994): 6.4% (world 3.0%); per capita expenditure U.S.$456.

---

[1]Appointed 40-member Consultative Council is an advisory body only. [2]Regions have no administrative function; the six major cities of Bahrain are administered by a single municipal council. [3]Ash-Sharqīyah includes population of Ḥawār and other islands. [4]Also claimed by Qatar. [5]Detail does not add to total given because of rounding. [6]Includes long-term private debt not guaranteed by the government. [7]UN estimates. [8]In purchasers' value at current prices. [9]Import figures are f.o.b. in balance of trade and c.i.f. for commodities and trading partners. [10]One-fourth apportionment of international flights of Gulf Air (jointly administered by the governments of Bahrain, Oman, Qatar, and the United Arab Emirates). [11]1987–88. [12]1992–93.

Bangladesh

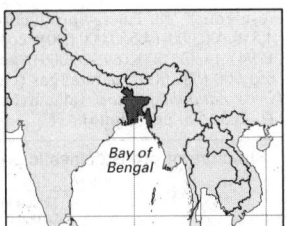

Official name: Gana Prajātantrī Bangladesh (People's Republic of Bangladesh).
Form of government: unitary multiparty republic with one legislative house (Parliament [330[1]]).
Chief of state: President.
Head of government: Prime Minister.
Capital: Dhākā.
Official language: Bengali.
Official religion: Islam.
Monetary unit: 1 Bangladesh taka (Tk) = 100 paisa; valuation (Oct. 11, 1996) 1 U.S.$ = Tk 42.10; 1 £ = Tk 66.32.

Area and population

Divisions[2]	Administrative centres	area		population 1991 census[3]
		sq mi	sq km	
Barisal	Barisal	5,134	13,297	7,757,334
Chittagong	Chittagong	17,902	46,367	29,015,222
Dhākā	Dhākā	12,015	31,119	33,939,848
Khulna	Khulna	8,600	22,274	13,243,054
Rājshāhi	Rājshāhi	13,326	34,513	27,499,727
TOTAL		56,977	147,570	111,455,185

Demography

Population (1996): 123,063,000.
Density (1996): persons per sq mi 2,159.9, persons per sq km 833.9.
Urban-rural (1995): urban 19.0%; rural 81.0%.
Sex distribution (1996): male 51.72%; female 48.28%.
Age breakdown (1996): under 15, 42.0%; 15–29, 26.4%; 30–44, 17.8%; 45–59, 8.9%; 60–74, 3.8%; 75 and over, 1.1%.
Population projection: (2000) 132,081,000; (2010) 153,195,000.
Doubling time: 30 years.
Ethnic composition (1991): Bengali 98.8%; tribal 1.1%, of which Chakmā 0.2%, Saontāl 0.2%, Marma 0.1%; other 0.1%.
Religious affiliation (1991): Muslim 88.3%; Hindu 10.5%; Buddhist 0.6%; Christian 0.3%; other 0.3%.
Major cities (1991)[4]: Dhākā 6,105,160; Chittagong 2,040,663; Khulna 877,388; Rājshāhi 517,136; Mymensingh 185,517[5].

Vital statistics

Birth rate per 1,000 population (1996): 33.7 (world avg. 25.0).
Death rate per 1,000 population (1996): 10.7 (world avg. 9.3).
Natural increase rate per 1,000 population (1996): 23.0 (world avg. 15.7).
Total fertility rate (avg. births per childbearing woman; 1996): 4.0.
Marriage rate per 1,000 population (1994): 10.7.
Divorce rate per 1,000 population (1981): 3.6.
Life expectancy at birth (1996): male 57.0 years; female 57.0 years.
Major causes of death (1990; percentage of recorded deaths): typhoid fever 19.8%; old age 14.8%; tetanus 10.1%; tuberculosis and other respiratory diseases 8.7%; diarrhea 6.4%; suicide, accidents, and poisoning 5.1%; high blood pressure and heart diseases 5.0%.

National economy

Budget (1993–94). Revenue: Tk 123,350,000,000 (sales tax 33.0%, customs duties 24.9%, business tax 11.5%, dividends and profits from public enterprises 9.2%, income taxes 3.9%, interest receipts 2.8%). Expenditures: Tk 93,620,000,000 (employee compensation 39.9%, transfer payments 31.4%, goods and services 24.4%, capital formation 4.2%).
Public debt (external, outstanding; 1994): U.S.$15,714,000,000.
Production (metric tons except as noted). Agriculture, forestry, fishing (1995): paddy rice 26,513,000, sugarcane 7,446,000, wheat 1,245,000, jute 770,000, bananas 630,000, pulses 545,000, oilseeds 462,000[6], mangoes 189,000, pineapples 150,000, tea 51,000; livestock (number of live animals) 30,330,000 goats, 24,340,000 cattle, 1,155,000 sheep, 882,000 buffalo, 123,000,000 chickens, 16,200,000 ducks; roundwood (1994) 31,346,000 cu m; fish catch (1993) 1,047,170. Mining and quarrying (1993): marine salt 340,000; industrial limestone 50,000. Manufacturing (1994–95): chemical fertilizers 2,142,301; jute manufactures 425,100; sugar 269,566; iron and steel 69,914; food products 69,480; newsprint 43,062; paper 39,733; glass sheet 808,000 sq m; cotton yarn 264,000 bales; matches 12,379,000 gross boxes. Construction: n.a. Energy production (consumption): electricity (kW-hr; 1994) 10,010,000,000 (10,010,-000,000); coal (metric tons; 1994) none (198,000); crude petroleum (barrels; 1994) 134,000 (8,966,000); petroleum products (metric tons; 1994) 1,104,000 (2,006,000); natural gas (cu m; 1994) 6,635,000,000 (6,635,000,000).
Household income. Average household size (1991) 5.5; average annual income per household (1991–92) Tk 40,092 (U.S.$1,061); sources of income (1988–89): self-employment 48.3%, wages and salaries 18.7%, transfer payments 7.5%, other 25.5%; expenditure (1991–92): food and drink 66.6%, housing and rent 10.4%, fuel and light 5.6%, clothing and footwear 4.7%, other 12.7%.
Land use (1994): forested 14.6%; meadows and pastures 4.6%; agricultural and under permanent cultivation 74.5%; other 6.3%.
Population economically active (1990): total 51,200,000; activity rate of total population 46.9% (participation rates: over age 10, 69.7%; female 39.3%; unemployed 1.0%[7]).

Price and earnings indexes (1990 = 100)

	1989	1990	1991	1992	1993	1994	1995
Consumer price index	92.5	100.0	107.2	111.8	111.8	115.8	122.5
Earnings index[8]	88.2	100.0	104.9	109.3	...	...	...

Gross national product (at current market prices; 1994): U.S.$26,636,000,000 (U.S.$230 per capita).

Structure of gross domestic product and labour force

	1993–94		1990	
	in value Tk '000,000	% of total value	labour force	% of labour force
Agriculture	314,945	30.4	33,303,000	65.0
Mining	} 103,012	} 9.9	15,000	—
Manufacturing			5,925,000	11.6
Construction	60,134	5.8	525,000	1.0
Public utilities	20,607	2.0	40,000	0.1
Transp. and commun.	129,221	12.5	1,611,000	3.1
Trade	82,213	7.9	4,285,000	8.4
Finance	21,395	2.1	296,000	0.6
Public admin., defense	55,148	5.3	} 5,200,000	} 10.2
Services and other	248,789	24.0		
TOTAL	1,035,464	100.0[9]	51,200,000	100.0

Tourism (1994): receipts from visitors U.S.$19,000,000; expenditures by nationals abroad U.S.$210,000,000.

Foreign trade

Balance of trade (current prices)

	1990	1991	1992	1993	1994	1995
Tk '000,000	−55,550	−48,564	−55,276	−52,113	−59,665	−107,719
% of total	32.4%	28.2%	25.3%	22.5%	21.9%	29.7%

Imports (1994–95): Tk 234,530,000,000 (textile yarn, fabrics, and made-up articles 22.6%; machinery and transport equipment 12.4%; petroleum and petroleum products 6.1%; chemicals 5.9%; cereals and cereal preparations 4.2%; iron and steel 3.5%). *Major import sources* (1993): Japan 12.5%; India 9.5%; Hong Kong 8.0%; South Korea 6.9%; China 5.1%; Singapore 4.6%; United States 4.3%.
Exports (1994–95): Tk 131,310,000,000 (ready-made garments 56.6%; jute manufactures 10.4%; fish and prawns 10.1%; hides, skins, and leather 6.7%; fertilizers 2.4%; raw jute 2.0%; tea 1.0%). *Major export destinations* (1993): Western Europe 40.2%; United States 33.6%; Association of Southeast Asian Nations (ASEAN) 4.0%; Hong Kong 2.7%; Japan 2.5%.

Transport and communications

Transport. Railroads (1992–93): route length 1,681 mi, 2,706 km; passenger-mi 3,176,000,000, passenger-km 5,112,000,000; short ton-mi cargo 439,000,000, metric ton-km cargo 641,000,000. Roads (1990): total length 120,100 mi, 193,283 km (paved 4%). Vehicles (1993): passenger cars 77,933; trucks and buses 101,349. Merchant marine (1992): vessels (100 gross tons and over) 301; total deadweight tonnage 566,775. Air transport (1993)[10]: passenger-mi 1,588,000,000, passenger-km 2,556,000,000; short ton-mi cargo 190,238,000, metric ton-km cargo 277,743,000; airports with scheduled flights (1996) 8.
Communications. Daily newspapers (1992): total number 51; total circulation 710,000; circulation per 1,000 population 6. Radio (1995): 8,000,000 receivers (1 per 15 persons). Television (1995): 600,000 receivers (1 per 200 persons). Telephones (main lines; 1993): 268,400 (1 per 435 persons).

Education and health

Education (1992–93)

	schools	teachers	students	student/ teacher ratio
Primary (age 6–10)	50,898	214,779	14,202,000	66.1
Secondary (age 11–17)	11,382	129,655	4,673,000	36.0
Voc., teacher tr.	153	1,856	30,275	16.3
Higher	1,031	26,263	912,985	34.8

Educational attainment (1991). Percentage of population age 25 and over having: no formal schooling 65.4%; primary education 17.1%; secondary 13.8%; postsecondary 3.7%. *Literacy* (1991): total population age 15 and over literate 34.8%; males literate 45.2%; females literate 23.7%.
Health (1993): physicians 22,400 (1 per 5,264 persons); hospital beds 35,280 (1 per 3,218 persons); infant mortality rate (1996) 100.0.
Food (1992): daily per capita caloric intake 2,019 (vegetable products 97%, animal products 3%); 87% of FAO recommended minimum requirement.

Military

Total active duty personnel (1996): 117,500 (army 86.0%, navy 8.5%, air force 5.5%). *Military expenditure as percentage of GNP* (1994): 1.7% (world 3.0%); per capita expenditure U.S.$4.

[1]Includes 30 seats reserved for women. [2]Geographic reorganization at the district level took place in 1993; each division is now divided into the following number of new districts: Barisal 6, Chittagong 15, Dhākā 17, Khulna 10, and Rājshāhi 16. [3]Adjusted for underenumeration. [4]Metropolitan population. [5]Municipal population. [6]1991–92. [7]Excluding underemployment. [8]Wage earnings in manufacturing. [9]Detail does not add to total given because of rounding. [10]Bangladesh Biman only.

Barbados

Official name: Barbados.
Form of government: constitutional monarchy with two legislative houses (Senate [21]; House of Assembly [28]).
Chief of state: British Monarch represented by Governor-General.
Head of government: Prime Minister.
Capital: Bridgetown.
Official language: English.
Official religion: none.
Monetary unit: 1 Barbados dollar (BDS$) = 100 cents; valuation (Oct. 11, 1996) 1 U.S.$ = BDS$2.01; 1 £ = BDS$3.17.

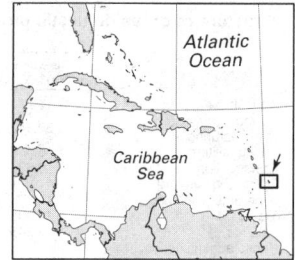

Area and population	area		population
			1990
Parishes[1]	sq mi	sq km	census
Christ Church	22	57	47,050
St. Andrew	14	36	6,346
St. George	17	44	17,905
St. James	12	31	21,001
St. John	13	34	10,206
St. Joseph	10	26	7,619
St. Lucy	14	36	9,455
St. Michael[2]	15	39	97,516
St. Peter	13	34	11,263
St. Philip	23	60	20,540
St. Thomas	13	34	11,590
TOTAL	166	430[3]	260,491

Demography

Population (1996): 265,000.
Density (1996): persons per sq mi 1,596, persons per sq km 616.
Urban-rural (1990): urban 37.9%; rural 62.1%.
Sex distribution (1995): male 47.88%; female 52.12%.
Age breakdown (1990): under 15, 24.1%; 15–29, 27.0%; 30–44, 22.1%; 45–59, 11.4%; 60 and over, 15.4%.
Population projection: (2000) 267,000; (2010) 271,000.
Doubling time: n.a.; doubling time exceeds 100 years.
Ethnic composition (1990): black 92.5%; white 3.2%; mixed 2.8%; other 1.5%.
Religious affiliation (1990): Anglican 33.0%; other Protestant 29.8%, of which Pentecostal 12.7%, Methodist 5.9%; nonreligious 20.2%; Roman Catholic 4.4%; not stated 2.7%; other 9.9%.
Major cities (1990): Bridgetown 6,070 (urban area 85,000); Speightstown, c. 3,500.

Vital statistics

Birth rate per 1,000 population (1995): 13.1 (world avg. 25.0); (1979) legitimate 26.9%; illegitimate 73.1%.
Death rate per 1,000 population (1995): 9.4 (world avg. 9.3).
Natural increase rate per 1,000 population (1995): 3.7 (world avg. 15.7).
Total fertility rate (avg. births per childbearing woman; 1992): 1.8.
Marriage rate per 1,000 population (1993): 8.5.
Divorce rate per 1,000 population (1993): 16.7.
Life expectancy at birth (1989–91): male 72.9 years; female 77.4 years.
Major causes of death per 100,000 population (1992): diseases of the circulatory system 366.8; malignant neoplasms (cancers) 178.5; endocrine and metabolic disorders 120.2; accidents, poisonings, and violence 40.3; diseases of the respiratory system 40.0; diseases of the digestive system 28.9; infectious and parasitic diseases 19.0; diseases of the nervous system 17.1.

National economy

Budget (1995–96). Revenue: BDS$1,148,900,000[4] (tax revenue 93.9%, of which goods and services taxes 38.5%, personal income and company taxes 31.7%, import duties 7.9%; nontax revenue 6.1%). Expenditures: BDS$1,-354,100,000 (current expenditure 91.0%, of which wages and salaries 33.3%, transfers 20.9%, public debt payments 13.9%; expenditure 9.0%).
Production (metric tons except as noted). Agriculture, forestry, fishing (1995): raw sugar 38,500, sweet potatoes 5,202, yams 2,570, lettuce 1,909, cabbage 1,823, onions 1,804, cucumbers 1,428, carrots 1,305, tomatoes 1,153, pumpkins 1,080, cassava 818; livestock (number of live animals; 1993) 66,000 sheep, 45,000 pigs, 38,000 goats, 33,000 cattle; roundwood, n.a.; fish catch 3,286. Manufacturing (value added in BDS$'000; 1995): food, beverages, and tobacco (mostly sugar, molasses, rum, beer, and cigarettes) 108,000; paper products, printing, and publishing 33,400; metal products and assembly-type goods (mostly electronic components) 28,000; textiles and wearing apparel 11,700. Construction (value added in BDS$; 1995): 150,500,000. Energy production (consumption): electricity (kW-hr; 1993) 511,900,000 (511,900,000); coal, none (none); crude petroleum (barrels; 1993) 462,450 (1,803,000); petroleum products (metric tons; 1996) 255,000 (314,000); natural gas (cu m; 1993) 28,000,000 (26,000,000).
Household income and expenditure. Average household size (1990) 3.5; income per household (1988) BDS$13,455 (U.S.$6,690); sources of income: n.a.; expenditure (1978–79): food 43.2%, housing 13.1%, household operations 9.6%, alcohol and tobacco 8.4%, fuel and light 6.2%, clothing and footwear 5.1%, transportation 4.6%, other 9.8%.
Population economically active (1995): total 136,800; activity rate of total population 51.7% (participation rates: ages 15 and over, 68.2%; female 62.7%; unemployed 19.7%).

Price and earnings indexes (1990 = 100)							
	1989	1990	1991	1992	1993	1994	1995
Consumer price index	97.0	100.0	106.3	112.7	114.0	114.1	116.2
Hourly earnings index	95.3	100.0	...	...	...	...	...

Gross national product (at current market prices; 1994): U.S.$1,704,000,000 (U.S.$6,260 per capita).

Structure of gross domestic product and labour force				
	1995			
	in value BDS$'000,000	% of total value	labour force	% of labour force
Agriculture, fishing	203.1	5.4	5,100	3.7
Mining	18.0[5]	0.5[5]	...	...
Manufacturing	216.5	5.8	11,700	8.6
Construction	150.5	4.0	8,800	6.4
Public utilities	108.6[5]	2.9[5]	1,000	0.7
Transportation and communications	291.4	7.7	5,100	3.7
Trade, restaurants	1,008.9	26.8	28,500	20.8
Finance, real estate	505.9	13.4	7,600	5.6
Pub. admin., defense	538.7	14.3	42,200	30.8
Services	131.8	3.5		
Other	591.8[6]	15.7[6]	26,900[7]	19.7[7]
TOTAL	3,765.2	100.0	136,900	100.0

Public debt (external, outstanding; 1994): U.S.$330,300,000.
Tourism: receipts from visitors (1994) U.S.$598,000,000; expenditures by nationals abroad (1993) U.S.$52,000,000.
Land use (1993): forested 11.6%; meadows and pastures 4.7%; agricultural and under permanent cultivation 37.2%; other 46.5%.

Foreign trade[8]

Balance of trade (current prices)						
	1990	1991	1992	1993	1994	1995
BDS$'000,000	−858.8	−984.6	−568.8	−689.3	−753.8	−917.0
% of total	50.5%	53.6%	42.6%	48.9%	50.9%	49.3%

Imports (1995): BDS$1,527,553,000 (retained imports 91.0%, of which food and beverages 16.3%, machinery 15.8%, construction materials 7.2%, chemicals 6.4%, fuels 2.9%; reexported imports 9.0%). *Major import sources* (1994): United States 33.5%; Trinidad and Tobago 16.4%; United Kingdom 9.8%; Canada 4.9%; Japan 4.7%; Venezuela 4.5%; Jamaica 3.2%; Germany 2.8%.
Exports (1995): BDS$463,900,000 (domestic exports 71.6%, of which chemicals 11.3%, sugar 11.0%, electrical components 10.7%, rum 4.1%, clothing 1.4%; reexports 28.4%). *Major export destinations* (1993): United States 20.6%; United Kingdom 14.2%; Trinidad and Tobago 12.2%; Jamaica 9.0%; Canada 7.1%; St. Lucia 6.5%; St. Vincent and the Grenadines 3.9%.

Transport and communications

Transport. Railroads: none. Roads (1989): total length 977 mi, 1,573 km (paved 95%). Vehicles (1994): passenger cars 40,120; trucks and buses 9,133[9]. Merchant marine (1992): vessels (100 gross tons and over) 37; total deadweight tonnage 84,000. Air transport (1994): passenger arrivals 649,-700, passenger departures 650,200; cargo unloaded 8,584 metric tons, cargo loaded 5,052 metric tons; airports (1996) with scheduled flights 1.
Communications. Daily newspapers (1994): total number 2; total circulation 41,405; circulation per 1,000 population 157. Radio (1995): total number of receivers 300,000 (1 per 1.2 persons). Television (1995): total number of receivers 65,000 (1 per 3.8 persons). Telephones (main lines; 1993): 82,500 (1 per 3.2 persons).

Education and health

Education (1989–90)				
	schools	teachers	students	student/ teacher ratio
Primary (age 3–11)[10]	106	1,553	26,662	17.2
Secondary (age 12–16)	33	1,406	21,259	15.1
Vocational[11]	8	79	996	12.6
Higher[12]	1	153	1,314	8.6

Educational attainment (1990). Percentage of population age 25 and over having: no formal schooling 0.4%; primary education 23.7%; secondary 60.3%[13]; higher 11.2%; other 4.4%. *Literacy* (1995): total population age 15 and over literate 97.4%; males literate 98.0%; females literate 96.8%.
Health (1992): physicians 312 (1 per 842 persons); hospital beds 1,966 (1 per 134 persons); infant mortality rate per 1,000 live births (1995) 13.2.
Food (1992): daily per capita caloric intake 3,207 (vegetable products 72%, animal products 28%); 133% of FAO recommended minimum requirement.

Military

Total active duty personnel (1995): 610 (army 82.0%, navy 18.0%). *Military expenditure as percentage of GNP* (1994): 0.8% (world 3.0%); per capita expenditure U.S.$51.

---

[1]Parishes and city of Bridgetown have no local administrative function. [2]Includes city of Bridgetown. [3]Detail does not add to total given because of rounding. [4]Current revenue only. [5]Mining excludes natural gas; Public utilities includes natural gas. [6]Net indirect taxes. [7]Unemployed. [8]Import figures are f.o.b. in balance of trade and c.i.f. in commodities and trading partners. [9]Includes taxis. [10]1991–92. [11]1987–88. [12]University of the West Indies, Cave Hill campus. [13]Includes composite senior.

Belarus

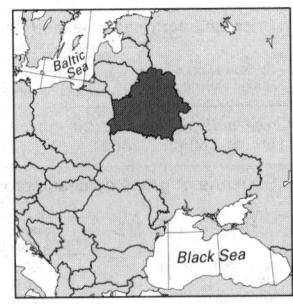

Official name: Respublika Belarus
(Republic of Belarus).
Form of government: unitary multiparty
republic with a single legislative body
(Supreme Soviet[1] [260]).
Head of state and government:
President.
Capital: Minsk.
Official languages: Belarusian; Russian.
Official religion: none.
Monetary unit[2]: rubel (Rbl; plural rubli)
valuation (Oct. 11, 1996) free rate,
1 U.S.\$ = Rbl 19,165; 1 £ = Rbl 30,191.

Area and population		area		population
				1992[3]
Provinces	Capitals	sq mi	sq km	estimate
Brest	Brest	12,500	32,300	1,494,000
Homel (Gomel)	Homel	15,600	40,400	1,611,000
Hrodno (Grodno)	Hrodno	9,700	25,000	1,199,000
Mahilyoŭ (Mogilyov)	Mahilyoŭ	11,200	29,000	1,267,000
Minsk (Mensk)	Minsk	15,700	40,800	3,272,000
Vitebsk	Vitebsk	15,500	40,100	1,438,000
TOTAL		80,200[4]	207,600[4]	10,281,000

Demography

Population (1996): 10,442,000.
Density (1996): persons per sq mi 130.3, persons per sq km 50.3.
Urban-rural (1995): urban 68.9%; rural 31.1%.
Sex distribution (1992): male 46.97%; female 53.02%.
Age breakdown (1991): under 15, 23.2%; 15–29, 21.5%; 30–44, 22.1%; 45–59, 16.5%; 60–69, 10.1%; 70 and over, 6.6%.
Population projection: (2000) 10,560,000; (2010) 10,939,000.
Doubling time: not applicable; population is declining.
Ethnic composition (1991): Belarusian 77.9%; Russian 13.5%; Ukrainian 3.0%; Jewish 0.7%; other 4.9%.
Religious affiliation: believers are predominantly Belarusian Orthodox; there is a Roman Catholic minority.
Major cities (1992): Minsk 1,671,000; Homel 517,000; Vitebsk 373,000; Mahilyoŭ 364,000; Hrodno 291,000.

Vital Statistics

Birth rate per 1,000 population (1994): 10.7 (world avg. 25.0); legitimate 87.9%; illegitimate 12.1%.
Death rate per 1,000 population (1994): 12.6 (world avg. 9.3).
Natural increase rate per 1,000 population (1994): −1.9 (world avg. 15.7).
Total fertility rate (avg. births per childbearing woman; 1993): 1.9.
Marriage rate per 1,000 population (1994): 7.3
Divorce rate per 1,000 population (1994): 4.3.
Life expectancy at birth (1994): male 64.0 years; female 74.0 years.
Major causes of death per 100,000 population (1993): diseases of the circulatory system 615.1; malignant neoplasms (cancers) 181.7; accidents and violence 130.6; diseases of the respiratory system 68.7; diseases of the digestive system 25.2.

National economy

Budget (1995). Revenue: Rbl 35,018,000,000,000[2] (value-added tax 28.4%, taxes on profits 23.8%, taxes on income 9.4%, excise taxes 8.0%, Chernobyl surcharges 7.9%, taxes on international trade 5.7%, other 16.8%). Expenditures: Rbl 37,888,000,000,000[2] (education 17.5%, health 15.2%, subsidies 10.8%, transfers 9.4%, Chernobyl expenditures 7.9%, lending minus repayments 5.1%, capital expenditure 4.1%, other 30.0%[5]).
Tourism: receipts from visitors, n.a.; expenditures by nationals abroad, n.a.
Land use (1994)[6]: forested 33.7%; meadows and pastures 14.1%; agricultural and under permanent cultivation 30.5%; other 21.7%.
Production (metric tons except as noted). Agriculture, forestry, fishing (1995): potatoes 8,570,000, grain 4,969,000, sugar beets 1,200,000, other vegetables 981,000, wheat 360,000, fruit 298,000; livestock (number of live animals) 5,403,000 cattle, 4,005,000 pigs, 284,000 sheep and goats, 215,000 horses, 45,000,000 poultry; roundwood 9,206,000 cu m; fish catch (1993) 14,000. Mining and quarrying (1995): potash 3,200,000; (1994) salt 300,000. Manufacturing (value of production in Rbl '000,000[2]; 1994): machine-building equipment 1,086,650; chemical products 659,438; food products 562,438; petroleum products 482,255; textiles 254,270; wood products 172,884; construction materials 142,555. Construction (1991): 5,395,000 sq m. Energy production (consumption): electricity (kW-hr; 1995) 24,918,000,000 (32,-113,000,000); coal (1994) none (1,199,000); crude petroleum (barrels; 1995) 14,162,000 (94,463,000); petroleum products (1994) 10,735,000 (10,002,000); natural gas (cu m; 1995) 266,000,000 (13,840,000,000).
Population economically active (1995): 4,636,000; activity rate of total population 45.2% (participation rate: ages 16–59 [male], 16–54 [female] 83.5%; female [1991] 53.3%; unemployed 2.4%).

Price and earnings indexes (1990 = 100)						
	1990	1991	1992	1993	1994	1995
Consumer price index	100.0	183.5	1,962	25,265	c. 586,000	c. 1,430,000
Monthly earnings index	100.0	300.0	3,150	40,950	c. 696,150	...

Gross national product (at current market prices; 1994)[7]: U.S.\$21,937,000,000 (U.S.\$2,160 per capita).

Structure of gross domestic product and labour force				
	1995			
	in value Rbl '000,000,000[2, 8]	% of total value	labour force	% of labour force
Agriculture	14,223	12.0	804,000	17.3
Mining } Manufacturing }	30,342	25.6	1,161,000	25.0
Public utilities	6,282	5.3	...	...
Construction	6,637	5.6	279,000	6.0
Transportation and communications	14,578	12.3	279,000	6.0
Trade	14,934	12.6	222,000	4.8
Finance	9,245	7.8	44,000	0.9
Public administration, defense	3,911	3.3	63,000	1.4
Services	11,141	9.4	827,000	17.8
Other	7,230[9]	6.1	957,000[10]	20.6
TOTAL	118,523	100.0	4,636,000	100.0[11]

Public debt (external, outstanding; 1994): U.S.\$1,272,000,000.
Household income and expenditure. Average household size (1989) 3.2; income per household (1995) Rbl 2,400,000[2]; sources of income (1994): wages and salaries 47.1%, transfers 45.6%, agricultural income 7.3%; expenditure (1994): retail goods 70.6%, taxes 4.6%, health services 3.8%, housing 1.3%, other 19.7%.

Foreign trade

Balance of trade (current prices)				
	1992	1993	1994	1995
U.S.\$'000,000	+377	−1,051	−710	−528
% of total	5.6%	15.7%	11.8%	5.4%

Imports (1995): Rbl 39,647,000,000,000[2] (Commonwealth of Independent States [CIS] 93.8%, mainly petroleum, natural gas, rolled metal, coal; non-CIS 6.2%, mainly intermediate inputs [rubber, paint, rolled metal] and consumer goods [cars, shoes, cotton textiles]). *Major import sources:* Russia and Ukraine constitute 91.5% of CIS-area trade; Europe, mainly Germany (30.6%), the majority of non-CIS imports.
Exports (1995): Rbl 33,664,000,000,000[2] (CIS 88.9%, mainly trucks, diesel fuel, synthetic fibres, refrigerators, tires, potassium fertilizer, milk and milk products, tractors; non-CIS commodities 11.1%, potassium and nitric fertilizers, trucks, refrigerators, tires, tractors, consumer durables). *Major export destinations:* Russia and Ukraine constitute 83.4% of CIS-area trade; Europe, mainly Germany and Poland, the majority of non-CIS exports.

Transport and communications

Transport. Railroads (1995): length 3,410 mi, 5,488 km; passenger-mi 9,900,-000,000, passenger-km 16,000,000,000; (1994) short ton-mi cargo 38,659,000,-000, metric ton-km cargo 56,441,000,000. Roads (1995): total length 32,030 mi, 51,547 km (paved 98.6%). Vehicles (1995): passenger cars 955,256; trucks and buses 9,289. Merchant marine (1992): vessels (100 gross tons and over) n.a.; total deadweight tonnage 18,373,000,000. Air transport (1992): passenger-mi 3,487,000,000, passenger-km 5,611,000,000; short ton-mi cargo 23,200,000, metric ton-km cargo 34,000,000; airports (1996) 2.
Communications. Daily newspapers (1992): total number 10; total circulation 1,899,000; circulation per 1,000 population 181. Radio (1993): 3,185,000 receivers (1 per 3.3 persons). Television (1993): 2,775,000 receivers (1 per 3.7 persons). Telephones (main lines; 1993): 1,814,400 (1 per 5.7 persons).

Education and health

Education (1994–95)				
	schools	teachers	students	student/ teacher ratio
Primary (age 6–13) } Secondary (age 14–17) }	5,000	122,700[12]	1,538,000	13.3[12]
Voc., teacher tr.	145	...	124,500	...
Higher	39	16,900[12]	173,800	10.5[12]

Educational attainment (1989). Percentage of population age 25 and over having: no formal schooling or primary education only 23.0%; some secondary 16.8%; completed secondary and some postsecondary 49.4%; higher 10.8%.
Literacy (1989): total population age 15 and over literate 7,690,000 (97.9%); males literate 3,661,000 (99.4%); females literate 4,029,000 (96.6%).
Health (1994): physicians 45,000 (1 per 230 persons); hospital beds 126,000 (1 per 82 persons); infant mortality rate per 1,000 live births 13.2.

Military

Total active duty personnel (1996): 85,500 (army 59.1%, air force and air defense 30.0%, CIS-controlled and other 10.9%). *Military expenditure as percentage of GNP* (1994): 0.3% (world 3.0%); per capita expenditure U.S.\$17.

[1]The Supreme Soviet represented the sole legal constitutional legislative body until Nov. 28, 1996; a disputed constitutional referendum on November 24 resulted in the abolition of the Supreme Soviet and the establishment of a second legislative house from Nov. 27, 1996. The dispute was to be decided by the Constitutional Court. [2]On Aug. 20, 1994, the rubel became the unit of account replacing the Belarusian ruble, which was formally recognized as the sole legal tender on May 18, 1994. The conversion took place at the rate of 10 Belarusian rubles per 1 rubel. [3]January. [4]Rounded area figures; exact area figures are 80,153 sq mi (207,595 sq km). [5]Includes expenditure arrears and statistical discrepancy. [6]25% of Belarusian territory severely affected by radioactive fallout from Chernobyl. [7]Ruble-area GNP and exchange rate data very speculative. [8]Provisional estimates. [9]Includes Rbl 1,256,000,000,000 and Rbl 5,884,000,000,000 of imputed payments to financial intermediaries. [10]Includes 131,000 unemployed and 692,000 undistributed employed. [11]Detail does not add to total given because of rounding. [12]1993–94.

Belgium

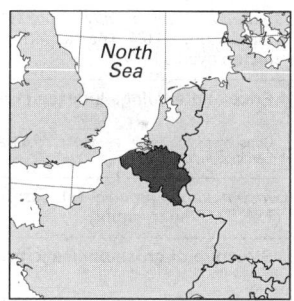

North Sea

Official name: Koninkrijk België (Dutch); Royaume de Belgique (French) (Kingdom of Belgium).
Form of government: federal constitutional monarchy with a Parliament composed of two legislative chambers (Senate [71[1]]; House of Representatives [150]).
Chief of state: Monarch.
Head of government: Prime Minister.
Capital: Brussels.
Official languages: Dutch; French; German.
Official religion: none.
Monetary unit: 1 Belgian franc (BF) = 100 centimes; valuation (Oct. 11, 1996) 1 U.S.$ = BF 31.55; 1 £ = BF 49.70.

Area and population

Regions[3] Provinces	Capitals	area sq mi	area sq km	population 1995[2] estimate
Brussels-Capital	—	62	161	951,580
Flanders	—	5,221[4]	13,522	5,866,106
Antwerp	Antwerp	1,107	2,867	1,628,710
East Flanders	Ghent	1,151	2,982	1,349,382
Flemish Brabant[5]	Leuven	813	2,106	995,266
Limburg	Hasselt	935	2,422	771,613
West Flanders	Brugge	1,214	3,145	1,121,135
Wallonia	—	6,504[4]	16,844	3,312,888
Hainaut	Mons	1,462	3,786	1,286,649
Liège	Liège	1,491	3,862	1,015,007
Luxembourg	Arlon	1,714	4,440	240,281
Namur	Namur	1,415	3,666	434,446
Walloon Brabant[5]	Wavre	421	1,091	336,505
TOTAL		11,787	30,528[4]	10,130,574

Demography

Population (1996): 10,185,000.
Density (1996): persons per sq mi 864.1, persons per sq km 333.6.
Urban-rural (1995): urban 96.7%; rural 3.3%.
Sex distribution (1995[2]): male 48.91%; female 51.09%.
Age breakdown (1994[2]): under 15, 18.1%; 15–29, 20.7%; 30–44, 22.7%; 45–59, 17.3%; 60–74, 15.1%; 75 and over, 6.1%.
Population projection: (2000) 10,331,000; (2010) 10,707,000.
Doubling time: not applicable; doubling time exceeds 100 years.
Nationality (1992): Belgian 91.0%; Italian 2.4%; Moroccan 1.4%; French 0.9%; Turkish 0.8%; Dutch 0.6%; other 2.9%.
Religious affiliation (1980): Roman Catholic 90.0%; Muslim 1.1%; Protestant 0.4%; nonreligious and atheist 7.5%; other 1.0%.
Major cities (1995[2]): Brussels 136,424[6] (951,580[7]); Antwerp 459,072; Ghent 227,072; Charleroi 206,491; Liège 192,393.

Vital statistics

Birth rate per 1,000 population (1994): 11.4 (world avg. 25.0); (1989) legitimate 88.7%; illegitimate 11.3%.
Death rate per 1,000 population (1994): 10.2 (world avg. 9.3).
Natural increase rate per 1,000 population (1994): 1.2 (world avg. 15.7).
Total fertility rate (avg. births per childbearing woman; 1990–95): 1.6.
Marriage rate per 1,000 population (1994): 5.1.
Divorce rate per 1,000 population (1994): 2.2.
Life expectancy at birth (1991–93): male 73.0 years; female 79.8 years.
Major causes of death per 100,000 population (1989): diseases of the circulatory system 412.8; malignant neoplasms (cancers) 274.6; accidents and violence 64.6%; diseases of the respiratory system 50.1.

National economy

Budget (1994). Revenue: BF 2,292,500,000,000 (direct taxes 52.3%, indirect taxes 40.8%). Expenditures: BF 2,668,700,000,000 (government departments 27.9%, debt service 27.7%, domestic transfers 16.3%).
Production (metric tons except as noted). Agriculture, forestry, fishing (1995[8]): sugar beets 5,729,000, potatoes 2,100,000, wheat 1,536,000, apples 454,930, barley 416,000, tomatoes 350,000; livestock (number of live animals) 7,060,-000 pigs, 3,365,000 cattle, 150,000 sheep, 23,000 horses; roundwood (1994) 4,340,000 cu m; fish catch (1993) 36,433. Mining and quarrying (1994): quartz 500,000; barite 30,000; granite (Belgium bluestone) 2,105,000 cu m; marble 330 cu m. Manufacturing (value added in BF '000,000; 1993): metal products and machinery 430,436; food, beverages, and tobacco 245,022; chemical and plastic products 195,571; textiles and wearing apparel 99,014; paper, printing, and publishing 92,275; pig iron, steel, and nonferrous metals 82,373; furniture and fixtures 54,198. Construction (1993): residential 33,063,000 cu m; nonresidential 42,864,000 cu m. Energy production (consumption): electricity (kW-hr; 1994) 72,236,000,000 (76,219,000,000); coal (metric tons; 1994) 753,000 (13,050,000); crude petroleum (barrels; 1994) none (206,706,000); petroleum products (metric tons; 1994) 25,373,000 (17,036,000); natural gas (cu m; 1994) 1,351,000 (11,531,000,000).
Household income and expenditure. Avg. household size (1991) 2.7; sources of income (1992): wages 49.6%, transfer payments 20.7%, property income 18.8%, self-employment 10.9%; expenditure (1992): food 18.0%, housing 17.0%, transp. 13.3%, health 11.8%, durable goods 10.7%, clothing 7.7%.
Gross national product (1994): U.S.$231,051,000,000 (U.S.$22,920 per capita).

Structure of gross domestic product and labour force

	1993 in value BF '000,000	1993 % of total value	1992 labour force	1992 % of labour force
Agriculture	120,000	1.8	109,200	2.7
Mining	15,500	0.2 }	872,800	21.4
Manufacturing	1,563,000	23.2 }		
Construction	362,800	5.4	246,600	6.0
Public utilities	179,800	2.7	44,300	1.1
Transp. and commun.	544,100	8.1	269,100	6.6
Trade	946,200	14.1	670,800	16.4
Finance	1,322,500	19.7	327,500	8.0
Pub. admin., defense	1,139,700	16.9 }	1,232,300	30.1
Services	681,200	10.1 }		
Other	−149,100[9]	−2.2[9]	316,000[10]	7.7[10]
TOTAL	6,725,700	100.0	4,088,600	100.0

Public debt (1996[2]): U.S.$314,300,000,000.
Population economically active (1992): total 4,088,600; activity rate of total population 40.6% (participation rates: ages 14–64, 61.1%; female 40.7%; unemployed 7.7%).

Price and earnings indexes (1990 = 100)

	1989	1990	1991	1992	1993	1994	1995
Consumer price index	96.7	100.0	103.2	105.7	108.6	111.2	112.8
Hourly earnings index	95.8	100.0	105.1	110.1	112.4	114.7	...

Land use (1994[8]): forest 21.3%; pasture 21.0%; agricultural 24.2%; other 33.5%.
Tourism (1994): receipts from visitors U.S.$5,182,000,000; expenditures by nationals abroad U.S.$7,782,000,000.

Foreign trade[8]

Balance of trade (current prices)

	1989	1990	1991	1992	1993	1994
BF '000,000	+176,000	+53,500	+30,900	+67,500	+370,500	+513,000
% of total	2.3%	0.7%	0.4%	0.9%	4.7%	5.9%

Imports (1994): BF 4,206,413,900,000 (machinery and transport equipment 25.6%; chemicals and chemical products 13.0%; food and live animals 8.9%; nonindustrial [gem] diamonds 7.2%; mineral fuels and lubricants 6.9%, of which petroleum and petroleum products 4.8%). *Major import sources:* Germany 20.2%; The Netherlands 17.7%; France 16.1%; U.K. 9.4%.
Exports (1994): BF 4,588,184,500,000 (machinery and transport equipment 28.1%; chemicals 16.7%, of which plastics 5.1%; food and live animals 9.1%; nonindustrial [gem] diamonds 6.8%; iron and steel 6.0%; textiles 5.0%; petroleum and petroleum products 2.8%). *Major export destinations:* Germany 21.0%; France 19.0%; The Netherlands 13.2%; U.K. 8.5%.

Transport and communications

Transport. Railroads (1994): route length 3,396 km; passenger-km 6,638,000,-000; metric ton-km cargo 8,084,000,000. Roads (1995): total length 142,555 km (paved 97%). Vehicles (1995): passenger cars 4,273,451; trucks and buses 417,056. Merchant marine (1992): vessels (100 gross tons and over) 232; total deadweight tonnage 218,506. Air transport (1994): passenger-km 7,496,412,000; metric ton-km cargo 422,249,000; airports (1996) with scheduled flights 2.
Communications. Daily newspapers (1995): total number 31; total circulation 3,089,200; circulation per 1,000 population 304. Radio (1994): 7,690,000 receivers (1 per 1.3 persons). Television (1994): 4,530,000 receivers (1 per 2.2 persons). Telephones (main lines; 1993): 4,395,700 (1 per 2.3 persons).

Education and health

Education (1993–94)

	schools	teachers	students	student/ teacher ratio
Primary (age 6–12)	4,453	72,589[11, 12]	731,527	...
Secondary (age 12–18)	1,950	110,599[13]	796,914	...
Voc., teacher tr.[12]	304	14,548[14]	155,192	...
Higher[12]	21	10,517[14]	123,320	...

Educational attainment (1981). Percentage of population age 15 and over having: less than secondary education 44.4%; lower secondary 26.5%; upper secondary 17.0%; vocational 2.9%; teacher's college 0.6%; university 3.5%.
Literacy (1995): virtually 99% literate.
Health: physicians (1995[2]) 37,792 (1 per 268 persons); hospital beds (1991) 80,549 (1 per 124 persons); infant mortality rate per 1,000 live births (1994) 7.6.
Food (1992): daily per capita caloric intake 3,681 (vegetable products 65%, animal products 35%); 139% of FAO recommended minimum requirement.

Military

Total active duty personnel (1996): 46,300 (army 65.0%, navy 5.7%, air force 26.6%, medical service 2.7%). Military expenditure as percentage of GNP (1994): 1.7% (world 3.0%); per capita expenditure U.S.$392.

---

[1]Excludes certain members of the royal family serving ex officio. [2]January 1. [3]Corresponding to three language-based federal community councils: Dutch (Flanders), French (Wallonia), and bilingual (Brussels-Capital) having authority in cultural affairs; a fourth (German) community council lacks expression as an administrative region. [4]Detail does not add to total given because of rounding. [5]Former Brabant province divided on Jan. 1, 1995. [6]1991. [7]Région Bruxelloise. [8]Includes Luxembourg. [9]Includes imputed bank service charges and statistical adjustments. [10]Unemployed. [11]Includes preschool teachers. [12]1992–93. [13]1991–92. [14]1987–88.

Belize

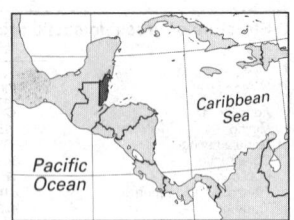

Official name: Belize.
Form of government: constitutional monarchy with two legislative houses (Senate [8[1]]; House of Representatives [29[2]]).
Chief of state: British Monarch represented by Governor-General.
Head of government: Prime Minister.
Capital: Belmopan.
Official language: English.
Official religion: none.
Monetary unit: 1 Belize dollar (BZ$) = 100 cents; valuation (Oct. 11, 1996) 1 U.S.$ = BZ$2.00[3]; 1 £ = BZ$3.15.

Area and population		area		population
		sq mi	sq km	1994 estimate
Districts	**Capitals**			
Belize	Belize City	1,663	4,307	62,939
Cayo	San Ignacio	2,006	5,196	41,594
Corozal	Corozal	718	1,860	31,412
Orange Walk	Orange Walk	1,790	4,636	33,855
Stann Creek	Dangriga	986	2,554	19,957
Toledo	Punta Gorda	1,704	4,413	19,243
TOTAL		8,867[4]	22,965[4, 5]	209,000

Demography

Population (1996): 219,000.
Density (1996): persons per sq mi 24.7, persons per sq km 9.5.
Urban-rural (1994): urban 47.5%; rural 52.5%.
Sex distribution (1994): male 50.72%; female 49.28%.
Age breakdown (1995): under 15, 42.5%; 15–29, 30.4%; 30–44, 14.9%; 45–59, 6.1%; 60–74, 4.2%; 75 and over, 1.9%.
Population projection: (2000) 242,000; (2010) 299,000.
Doubling time: 28 years.
Ethnic composition (1991): mestizo (Spanish-Indian) 43.6%; Creole (predominantly black) 29.8%; Mayan Indian 11.0%; Garifuna (black-Carib Indian) 6.7%; white 3.9%; East Indian 3.5%; other or not stated 1.5%.
Religious affiliation (1991): Roman Catholic 57.7%; Protestant 34.3%, of which Anglican 7.0%, Pentecostal 6.3%, Methodist 4.2%, Seventh-day Adventist 4.1%, Mennonite 4.0%; other Christian 1.7%; other 0.3%; none or not stated 6.0%.
Major cities (1994): Belize City 48,655; Orange Walk 12,155; San Ignacio/Santa Elena 9,891; Corozal 7,794; Belmopan 3,927.

Vital statistics

Birth rate per 1,000 population (1995): 33.7 (world avg. 25.0); (1992) legitimate 41.6%; illegitimate 58.4%.
Death rate per 1,000 population (1995): 5.9 (world avg. 9.3).
Natural increase rate per 1,000 population (1995): 27.8 (world avg. 15.7).
Total fertility rate (avg. births per childbearing woman; 1995): 4.2.
Marriage rate per 1,000 population (1993): 5.3.
Divorce rate per 1,000 population (1993): 0.6.
Life expectancy at birth (1995): male 66.4 years; female 70.4 years.
Major causes of death per 100,000 population (1990): accidents 92.6; heart diseases 84.7; diseases of the respiratory system 57.1; malignant neoplasms (cancers) 52.4; cerebrovascular disease 47.6; diabetes mellitus 37.0.

National economy

Budget (1996–97). Revenue: BZ$302,800,000 (current revenue 88.3%; development revenue 11.7%). Expenditures: BZ$375,000,000 (current expenditures 71.2%; development expenditures 28.8%, of which foreign grants and loans 27.0%).
Public debt (external, outstanding; 1994): U.S.$159,600,000.
Tourism (1994): receipts from visitors U.S.$71,400,000; expenditures by nationals abroad U.S.$18,600,000.
Production (metric tons except as noted). Agriculture, forestry, fishing (1994): sugarcane 1,210,000, oranges 82,500, grapefruits 30,200, corn (maize) 23,300, bananas 21,800, rice 6,500, red kidney beans 3,200, coconuts 3,000, cocoa (1993) 72, honey 72; livestock (number of live animals) 59,000 cattle, 26,000 pigs, 1,000,000 chickens; roundwood (1993) 188,000 cu m; fish catch (1993) 2,129, of which shrimp 1,060, lobsters 442, freshwater and marine fish 390, conchs 232. Mining and quarrying (1993): limestone 250,000; sand and gravel 200,000. Manufacturing (1994): sugar 107,000[6]; molasses 45,200[6]; fertilizer 24,900; flour 12,100; orange concentrate 59,300 hectolitres; beer 57,000 hectolitres[7]; grapefruit concentrate 25,900 hectolitres; cigarettes 105,000,000 units[7]; garments 4,276,000 units. Construction (publicly financed buildings under construction; 1991): residential 180 units; nonresidential, n.a. Energy production (consumption): electricity (kW-hr; 1993–94) 154,600,000 (138,-600,000); coal, none (none); crude petroleum, none (none); petroleum products (metric tons; 1993) none (86,000); natural gas, none (none).
Household income and expenditure. Average household size (1991) 4.9; average annual income of employed head of household (1993) BZ$6,450[8] (U.S.$3,225[8]); sources of income: n.a.; expenditure (1990): food, beverages, and tobacco 34.0%, transportation 13.7%, energy and water 9.1%, housing 9.0%, clothing and footwear 8.8%, household furnishings 8.0%, recreation 4.1%.

Population economically active (1994): total 69,670; activity rate of total population, 33.0% (participation rates: ages 15–64, 58.3%; female 32.1%; unemployed 11.6%).

Price and earnings indexes (1990 = 100)						
	1990	1991	1992	1993	1994	1995	1996
Consumer price index	100.0	102.3	104.7	106.2	109.0	112.1	115.2[9]
Earnings index	...	...	...	...	...	...	...

Gross national product (at current market prices; 1994): U.S.$535,000,000 (U.S.$2,550 per capita).

Structure of gross domestic product and labour force				
	1994			
	in value BZ$'000[10]	% of total value	labour force	% of labour force
Agriculture, fishing, forestry	181,513	19.3	13,857	19.9
Mining	4,565	0.5	369	0.5
Manufacturing	132,794	14.1	5,974	8.6
Construction	69,267	7.4	4,065	5.8
Public utilities	37,189	4.0	1,170	1.7
Transportation and communications	107,505	11.4	3,818	5.5
Trade, restaurants	161,565	17.2	12,625	18.1
Finance, real estate, insurance	104,976	11.2	2,094	3.0
Pub. admin., defense	123,689	13.2	} 15,950	22.9
Services	55,544	5.9		
Other	−38,375[11]	−4.1[11]	9,748[12]	14.0
TOTAL	940,232	100.0[4]	69,670	100.0

Land use (1993): forested 92.1%; meadows and pastures 2.1%; agricultural and under permanent cultivation 2.5%; other 3.3%.

Foreign trade[13]

Balance of trade (current prices)					
	1990	1991	1992	1993	1994	1995
BZ$'000,000	−118.2	−222.5	−217.2	−237.8	−170.6	−154.6
% of total	18.2%	31.4%	27.9%	30.3%	22.0%	19.7%

Imports (1994): BZ$519,900,000 (machinery and transport equipment 25.6%; food and beverages 17.7%; mineral fuels and lubricants 11.3%; chemicals and chemical products 10.7%). *Major import sources:* United States 53.1%; Mexico 9.6%; United Kingdom 7.3%; Netherlands Antilles 6.0%; Guatemala 3.0%.
Exports (1994): BZ$285,900,000 (domestic exports 83.5%, of which sugar 28.2%, garments 12.8%, orange and grapefruit concentrate 11.7%, bananas 10.4%, marine products 9.2%; reexports 16.5%). *Major export destinations:* United States 44.0%; United Kingdom 30.0%; Mexico 8.0%; Canada 7.0%.

Transport and communications

Transport. Railroads: none. Roads (1993): total length 1,684 mi, 2,710 km (paved 18%). Vehicles (1993): passenger cars 10,667; trucks and buses 6,108. Merchant marine (1992): vessels (100 gross tons and over) 32; total deadweight tonnage 45,706. Air transport (1994)[14]: passenger arrivals 158,778, passenger departures 163,478; cargo loaded 180 metric tons, cargo unloaded 943 metric tons. Airports (1996) with scheduled flights 11.
Communications. Daily newspapers: none[15]. Radio (1995): total number of receivers 29,620 (1 per 7.2 persons). Television (1995): total number of receivers 23,547 (1 per 9.1 persons). Telephones (main lines; 1993): 28,600 (1 per 7.2 persons).

Education and health

Education (1994–95)	schools	teachers	students	student/teacher ratio
Primary (age 5–12)	237	1,939	50,291	25.9
Secondary (age 13–16)	30	740	10,150	13.7
Higher	4[16]	...	1,216[17]	...

Educational attainment (1991). Percentage of population age 25 and over having: no formal schooling 13.0%; primary education 64.3%; secondary 14.9%; higher 6.6%; other 1.2%. *Literacy* (1991): total population age 15 and over literate 99,000 (93%).
Health (1993): physicians 120 (1 per 1,708 persons); hospital beds 585 (1 per 350 persons); infant mortality rate per 1,000 live births (1995) 34.7.
Food (1992): daily per capita caloric intake 2,662 (vegetable products 75%, animal products 25%); 118% of FAO recommended minimum requirement.

Military

Total active duty personnel (1995): 1,065 (army 93.9%, maritime wing 4.7%, air wing 1.4%); British troops 100. *Military expenditure as percentage of GNP* (1994): 1.7% (world 3.0%); per capita expenditure U.S.$43.

---

[1]Excludes president of the Senate, who may be elected by the Senate from outside its appointed membership. [2]Excludes speaker of the House of Representatives, who may be elected by the House from outside its elected membership. [3]The Belize dollar is officially pegged to the U.S. dollar. [4]Includes offshore cays totaling 266 sq mi (689 sq km). [5]Detail does not add to total given because of rounding. [6]1995. [7]1993. [8]Estimated figure for about 33,000 employed heads of household. [9]Average of 1st quarter. [10]At factor cost. [11]Less imputed bank service charges. [12]Includes 1,663 not adequately defined and 8,085 unemployed. [13]Import figures are f.o.b. in balance of trade and c.i.f. in commodities and trading partners. [14]Belize International Airport only. [15]Four weekly newspapers in 1994. [16]Colleges only. [17]Three colleges only.

Benin

Official name: République du Bénin (Republic of Benin).
Form of government: multiparty republic with one legislative house (National Assembly [82[1]]).
Head of state and government: President, assisted by Prime Minister.
Capital[2]: Porto-Novo.
Official language: French.
Official religion: none.
Monetary unit: 1 CFA franc (CFAF) = 100 centimes; valuation (Oct. 11, 1996) 1 U.S.$ = CFAF 518.24; 1 £ = CFAF 816.38.

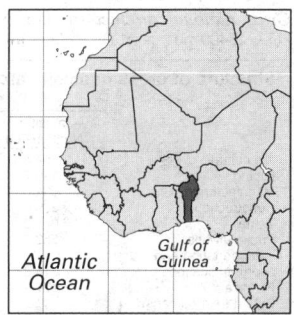

Atlantic Ocean   *Gulf of Guinea*

Area and population		area		population
		sq mi	sq km	1992 census
Provinces	Capitals			
Atacora	Natitingou	12,050	31,200	648,330
Atlantique	Cotonou	1,250	3,200	1,060,310
Borgou	Parakou	19,700	51,000	816,278
Mono	Lokossa	1,500	3,880	646,954
Ouémé	Porto-Novo	1,800	4,700	869,492
Zou	Abomey	7,200	18,700	813,985
TOTAL		43,500	112,680	4,855,349

Demography

Population (1996): 5,574,000.
Density (1996): persons per sq mi 128.1, persons per sq km 49.5.
Urban-rural (1994): urban 41.0%; rural 59.0%.
Sex distribution (1995): male 48.74%; female 51.26%.
Age breakdown (1995): under 15, 47.4%; 15–29, 25.5%; 30–44, 14.4%; 45–59, 8.1%; 60–74, 3.7%; 75 and over, 0.8%.
Population projection: (2000) 6,266,000; (2010) 8,300,000.
Doubling time: 21 years.
Ethnic composition (1992): Fon 39.7%; Yoruba (Nago) 12.1%; Adjara 11.1%; Bariba 8.6%; Aizo 8.6%; Somba (Otomary) 6.6%; Fulani 5.6%; other 7.7%.
Religious affiliation (1991): traditional beliefs 62.0%; Christian 23.3%, of which Roman Catholic 21.0%, Protestant 2.3%; Muslim 12.0%; other 2.7%.
Major cities (1992): Cotonou 533,212; Porto-Novo 177,660; Djougou 132,192; Abomey-Calavi 125,565; Parakou 106,708.

Vital statistics

Birth rate per 1,000 population (1995): 47.0 (world avg. 25.0).
Death rate per 1,000 population (1995): 14.0 (world avg. 9.3).
Natural increase rate per 1,000 population (1995): 33.0 (world avg. 15.7).
Total fertility rate (avg. births per childbearing woman; 1995): 6.7.
Marriage rate per 1,000 population (1980–85): 12.8.
Divorce rate per 1,000 population (1980–85): 0.8.
Life expectancy at birth (1995): male 50.3 years; female 54.2 years.
Major causes of death per 100,000 population (1994): n.a.; however, of the 8,165 reported cases of selected infectious diseases (notifiable to the World Health Organization), measles 73%, tuberculosis 26%, neonatal tetanus 0.9%, polio 0.1%.

National economy

Budget (1995). Revenue: CFAF 160,600,000,000 (current receipts 81.0%, of which nonpetroleum fiscal receipts and customs duties 67.4%, other current receipts 13.6%; foreign aid 19.0%). Expenditures: CFAF 208,100,000,000 (current expenditures 62.5%, of which debt service 13.8%; public-investment program 37.5%).
Production (metric tons except as noted). Agriculture, forestry, fishing (1996): cassava 1,342,600, yams 1,258,600, corn (maize) 470,000, seed cotton 368,600, sorghum 110,000, tomatoes 109,100, peanuts (groundnuts) 103,300, dry beans 63,300, sweet potatoes 61,300, millet 25,000, coconuts 20,000, sugarcane 16,-140, karité nuts (shea nuts) 15,500, paddy rice 15,000, palm kernels 13,300, bananas 13,000, mangoes 12,000, oranges 12,000, pineapples 3,000, tobacco 338; livestock (number of live animals; 1995) 1,223,000 cattle, 1,180,000 goats, 940,000 sheep, 555,000 pigs, 20,000,000 chickens; roundwood (1994) 5,444,-000 cu m; fish catch (1993) 40,983. Mining and quarrying (1993): limestone 500,000, marine salt 100. Manufacturing (1994): cement 380,000[3]; cotton fibre 103,000; meat 68,000; wheat flour 11,515; palm oil 9,432. Construction: n.a. Energy production (consumption): electricity (kW-hr; 1993) 5,000,000 (245,000,000); coal, none (none); crude petroleum (barrels; 1993) 2,214,000 (negligible); petroleum products (metric tons; 1993) none (136,000); natural gas, none (none).
Land use (1994): forested 30.7%; meadows and pastures 4.0%; agricultural and under cultivation 17.0%; other 48.3%.
Tourism (1994): receipts from visitors U.S.$55,000,000; expenditures by nationals abroad U.S.$19,000,000.
Population economically active (1992): total 2,085,400; activity rate of total population 43.0% (participation rates: ages 10–64, 67.7%; female 54.7%; unemployed, n.a.).

Price and earnings indexes (1991 = 100)						
	1990	1991	1992	1993	1994	1995	1996[4]
Consumer price index	...	100.0	104.0	104.5	144.7	165.7	168.9
Hourly earnings index[5]	100.0	100.0	100.0	100.0	144.1	...	...

Gross national product (at current market prices; 1994): U.S.$1,954,000,000 (U.S.$370 per capita).

Structure of gross domestic product and labour force				
	1994		1992	
	in value CFAF '000,000,000	% of total value	labour force	% of labour force[6]
Agriculture	281.8	33.4	1,147,746	55.0
Mining			661	0.0
Manufacturing }	71.4	8.4	160,406	7.7
Public utilities	6.2	0.7	1,176	0.1
Construction	37.6	4.5	51,655	2.5
Transportation and communications	70.3	8.3	52,837	2.5
Trade }	169.0	20.0	432,501	20.7
Finance			3,106	0.1
Pub. admin., defense	72.4	8.6 }	164,544	7.9
Services	93.6	11.1 }		
Other	42.3	5.0	70,814	3.4
TOTAL	844.5[7]	100.0	2,085,446	100.0[7]

Public debt (external, outstanding; 1994): U.S.$1,508,000,000.
Household income and expenditure. Average household size (1979) 5.4; income per household (1983) U.S.$240; sources of income: self-employment 73.7%, wages and salaries 26.3%; expenditure: n.a.

Foreign trade

Balance of trade (current prices)						
	1990	1991	1992	1993	1994	1995
CFAF '000,000,000	−38.3	−41.1	−50.1	−56.1	−36.1	−72.1
% of total	19.7%	17.8%	20.3%	22.5%	9.7%	15.4%

Imports (1995): CFAF 269,400,000,000 (1989; manufactured goods 30.7%, of which cotton yarn and fabric 16.9%; food products 19.4%, of which cereals 10.3%; machinery and transport equipment 14.5%, of which transport equipment 5.8%, nonelectrical equipment 5.3%, electrical equipment 3.4%; chemical products 7.1%; beverages and tobacco 7.1%). Major import sources (1994): France 24.3%; Thailand 11.9%; United Kingdom 9.8%; China 6.4%; Hong Kong 6.0%; United States 5.6%; The Netherlands 5.2%; Germany 5.2%; Japan 3.1%; Taiwan 2.3%.
Exports (1995): CFAF 197,300,000,000 (1993; reexports 67.2%; domestic exports 32.8%, of which cotton lint 21.6%, crude petroleum 4.7%, seed cotton 2.6%). Major export destinations (1994): Morocco 37.6%; Portugal 13.8%; Libya 7.9%; Italy 5.8%; United States 5.3%; India 3.7%.

Transport and communications

Transport. Railroads (1994): length 359 mi, 578 km; passenger-mi 66,500,000, passenger-km 107,000,000; short ton-mi cargo 172,000,000, metric ton-km cargo 253,000,000. Roads (1993): total length 3,770 mi, 6,070 km (paved 20.0%). Vehicles (1994): passenger cars 22,000; trucks and buses 12,300. Merchant marine (1992): vessels (100 gross tons and over) 12; total deadweight tonnage 210. Air transport (1995)[8]: passenger-mi 142,407,000, passenger-km 229,182,000; short ton-mi cargo 10,856,000, metric ton-km cargo 15,849,000; airports (1996) with scheduled flights 1.
Communications. Daily newspapers (1995): total number 2; total circulation 12,000[9]; circulation per 1,000 population 2.6[9]. Radio (1995): total number of receivers 400,000 (1 per 13 persons). Television (1995): total number of receivers 20,000 (1 per 270 persons). Telephones (main lines; 1993): 20,410 (1 per 260 persons).

Education and health

Education (1993–94)				
	schools	teachers	students	student/ teacher ratio
Primary	2,889	12,343	602,069	48.8
Secondary	145	2,384	97,480	40.9
Voc., teacher tr.	14	283	4,873	17.2
Higher	16	602	9,964	16.5

Educational attainment (1979). Percentage of population age 25 and over having: no formal schooling 89.2%; primary education 8.3%; some secondary 1.4%; secondary 0.8%; postsecondary 0.3%. Literacy (1995): total percentage of population age 15 and over literate 37.0%; males literate 48.7%; females literate 25.8%.
Health: physicians (1989) 323 (1 per 13,879 persons); hospital beds (1982) 4,902 (1 per 749 persons); infant mortality rate per 1,000 live births (1995) 108.0.
Food (1992): daily per capita caloric intake 2,532 (vegetable products 96%, animal products 4%); 110% of FAO recommended minimum requirement.

Military

Total active duty personnel (1996): 4,800 (army 93.8%, navy 3.1%, air force 3.1%). Military expenditure as percentage of GNP (1994): 2.3% (world 3.0%); per capita expenditure U.S.$6.

[1]83rd seat, provided for by the constitution, vacated by constitutional court. [2]Porto-Novo, the official capital established under the constitution, is the seat of the legislature, but the president and most government ministers reside in Cotonou. [3]1993. [4]March. [5]Minimum hourly industrial wage; January 1. [6]Age 10 years and over. [7]Detail does not add to total given because of rounding. [8]Represents ⅟₁₁ of the traffic of Air Afrique, which is operated by 11 West African states. [9]1992.

Bhutan

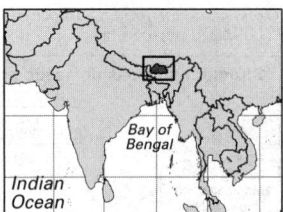

Official name: Druk-Yul (Kingdom of Bhutan).
Form of government: constitutional[1] monarchy with one legislative house (National Assembly [152[2]]).
Head of state and government: Monarch (*druk gyalpo*).
Capital: Thimphu.
Official language: Dzongkha (a Tibetan dialect).
Official religion: Mahāyāna Buddhism.
Monetary unit: 1 ngultrum[3] (Nu) = 100 chetrum; valuation (Oct. 11, 1996) 1 U.S.$ = Nu 35.65; 1 £ = Nu 56.16.

Area and population

Districts	Capitals	area sq mi	area sq km	population 1994 estimate
Bumthang	Jakar	1,150	2,990	...
Chhukha	Chhukha	...	...	...
Chirang	Damphu	310	800	...
Dagana	Dagana	540	1,400	...
Gaylegphug	Gaylegphug	1,020	2,640	...
Ha	Ha	830	2,140	...
Lhuntshi	Lhuntshi	1,120	2,910	...
Mongar	Mongar	710	1,830	...
Paro	Paro	580	1,500	...
Pema Gatsel	Pema Gatsel	150	380	...
Punakha	Punakha	2,330	6,040	...
Samchi	Samchi	830	2,140	...
Samdrup Jongkhar	Samdrup Jongkhar	900	2,340	...
Shemgang	Shemgang	980	2,540	...
Tashigang	Tashigang	1,640	4,260	...
Thimphu	Thimphu	630	1,620	...
Tongsa	Tongsa	570	1,470	...
Wangdi Phodrang	Wangdi Phodrang	1,160	3,000	...
TOTAL		18,150[4, 5]	47,000[4, 5]	800,000[6]

Demography

Population (1996): 842,000[6].
Density (1996): persons per sq mi 46.4, persons per sq km 17.9.
Urban-rural (1996): urban 7.0%; rural 93.0%.
Sex distribution (1988): male 50.97%; female 49.03%.
Age breakdown (1988): under 15, 40.3%; 15–29, 26.4%; 30–44, 16.5%; 45–59, 10.5%; 60–74, 5.2%; 75 and over, 1.1%.
Population projection: (2000) 916,000; (2010) 1,129,000.
Doubling time: 29 years.
Ethnic composition (1993): Bhutiā (Ngalops) 50.0%; Nepalese (Gurung) 35.0%; Sharchops 15.0%.
Religious affiliation (1980): Buddhist 69.6%; Hindu 24.6%; Muslim 5.0%; other 0.8%.
Major cities (1993): Thimphu 30,340; Phuntsholing 10,000[7].

Vital statistics

Birth rate per 1,000 population (1996): 37.8 (world avg. 25.0); legitimate, n.a.; illegitimate, n.a.
Death rate per 1,000 population (1996): 14.0 (world avg. 9.3).
Natural increase rate per 1,000 population (1996): 23.8 (world avg. 15.7).
Total fertility rate (avg. births per childbearing woman; 1996): 5.6.
Marital status of population 15 years and over (1985): married 71.2%; single 19.7%; widowed 7.5%; divorced 1.6%.
Divorce rate per 1,000 population: n.a.
Life expectancy at birth (1996): male 51.0 years; female 54.0 years.
Major causes of death (percentage distribution; 1989): respiratory tract infections 19.5%; diarrhea/dysentery 15.2%; skin infections 12.2%; parasitic worm infestations 10.0%; malaria 9.4%.

National economy

Budget (1995–96). Revenue: Nu 4,733,000,000 (internal revenue 40.1%, grants from government of India 30.5%, grants from UN and other international agencies 29.4%). Expenditures: Nu 4,935,000,000 (capital expenditures 62.1%, current expenditures 37.9%).
Public debt (external, outstanding; 1994): U.S.$86,700,000.
Production (metric tons except as noted). Agriculture, forestry, fishing (1995): oranges 58,000, rice 43,000, corn (maize) 40,000, potatoes 34,000, sugarcane 13,000, green peppers and chilies 9,000, millet 7,000, apples 6,000, wheat 6,000, barley 4,000, pulses 2,000; livestock (number of live animals) 435,000 cattle, 75,000 pigs, 59,000 sheep, 42,000 goats, 30,000 horses; roundwood (1994) 1,398,000 cu m; fish catch (1993) 350. Mining and quarrying (1993): limestone 198,000; dolomite 90,000; gypsum 20,000. Manufacturing (value in Nu '000,000; 1994): chemical products 419.0; cement 255.1; wood board products 230.6; distillery products 178.3; processed fruits 103.0. Construction (number of buildings completed; 1977–78): residential 10; nonresidential (guest house) 1. Energy production (consumption): electricity (kW-hr; 1993) 1,627,000,000 (185,000,000); coal (metric tons; 1993) 2,000 (19,000); crude petroleum, none (n.a.); petroleum products (metric tons; 1993) none (27,-000); natural gas, none (n.a.).
Household income and expenditure. Average household size (1980) 5.4[6]; income per household: n.a.; sources of income: n.a.; expenditure (1979): food 72.3%, clothing 21.2%, energy 3.7%, household durable goods 0.7%, personal effects and other 2.1%.

Gross national product (at current market prices; 1994): U.S.$272,000,000 (U.S.$400 per capita).

Structure of gross domestic product and labour force

	1994 in value Nu '000,000	1994 % of total value	1984 labour force	1984 % of labour force
Agriculture	3,154.4	37.9	303,000[8]	87.2
Mining	118.7	1.4		
Manufacturing	831.6	10.0		
Construction	989.0	11.9		
Trade	647.2	7.8	3,000[8]	0.9
Public utilities	553.5	6.7		
Transportation and communications	614.3	7.4		
Finance	477.4	5.7		
Pub. admin., defense	715.3	8.6	12,000[8]	3.4
Services			30,000[8]	8.5[9]
Other	216.0[10]	2.6[10]	...	...
TOTAL	8,317.4	100.0	348,000	100.0

Population economically active (1984)[6]: total 348,000; activity rate of total population 53.4% (participation rates: ages 15–64, 94.8%; female 55.0%; unemployed 6.5%).

Price and earnings indexes (1990 = 100)

	1988	1989	1990	1991	1992	1993	1994
Consumer price index	83.6	90.9	100.0	112.3	130.2	144.8	155.0
Earnings index	...	...	...	...	...	...	...

Land use (1994): forested 66.0%; meadows and pastures 5.8%; agricultural and under permanent cultivation 2.8%; other 25.4%.
Tourism (1994): receipts from visitors U.S.$4,000,000; expenditures by nationals abroad, n.a.

Foreign trade[11]

Balance of trade (current prices)

	1988–89	1989–90	1990–91	1991–92	1992–93	1993–94
Nu '000,000	−833.8	−481.6	−583.5	−687.9	−1,633.6	−966.2
% of total	28.6%	17.5%	18.3%	17.4%	30.8%	18.7%

Imports (1993–94): Nu 3,064,100,000 (1992–93[12]; petroleum products 5.9%, motor vehicles and parts 5.0%, rice 3.5%, iron and steel products 1.8%, fabrics 1.4%, machinery parts 0.5%). *Major import source:* India 60.1%.
Exports (1993–94): Nu 2,097,900,000 (1992–93[12]; electricity 29.4%, timber and wood manufactures 17.0%, fruit and vegetables 11.1%, cement 10.4%). *Major export destination:* India 87.0%.

Transport and communications

Transport. Railroads: none. Roads (1991): total length 1,502 mi, 2,418 km (paved 79%). Vehicles (1988): passenger cars 2,590; trucks and buses 1,367. Merchant marine: none. Air transport (1986): passenger-mi 2,722,-000, passenger-km 4,381,000; metric ton-km cargo, n.a.; airports (1996) with scheduled flights 1.
Communications. Daily newspapers: none[13]. Radio (1995): total number of receivers 23,000 (1 per 36 persons). Television (1985): total number of receivers 200 (1 per 3,325 persons). Telephones (main lines; 1993): 3,800 (1 per 400 persons).

Education and health

Education (1990)

	schools	teachers	students	student/ teacher ratio
Primary (age 7–11)[14]	235	1,859	56,773	30.5
Secondary (age 12–16)	31	662	15,984	24.1
Voc., teacher tr.	8	149	1,822	12.2
Higher	2	57	519	9.1

Educational attainment: n.a. *Literacy* (1977): total population age 15 and over literate 124,000 (18.0%); males literate 98,000 (31.0%); females literate 26,000 (9.0%).
Health: physicians (1991) 141 (1 per 5,335 persons); hospital beds (1993) 954 (1 per 822 persons); infant mortality rate per 1,000 live births (1996) 112.
Food (1975–77): daily per capita caloric intake 2,058 (vegetable products 98%, animal products 2%); 89% of FAO recommended minimum requirement.

Military

Total active duty personnel (1993): about 7,000 (army 100%).

---

[1]There is no formal constitution, but a form of constitutional monarchy is in place. [2]Includes 47 nonelective seats occupied by representatives of the King and religious groups. [3]Indian currency is also accepted legal tender; the ngultrum is at par with the Indian rupee. [4]2,700 sq mi (7,000 sq km) are not included in the district area totals. [5]Includes Chhukha area. [6]The figure stated is an estimate based on recent reported figures resulting from the repudiation of the 1980 census by the King and from the existence of a large number of Nepalese refugees; as such the actual population could range from 700,000 to 1,800,000. [7]1982. [8]Derived value. [9]Includes 6.5% with no occupation. [10]Less imputed bank service charges plus indirect tax. [11]Import figures are c.i.f. in balance of trade, commodities, and trading partners. [12]Trade data with India only. [13]A weekly newspaper is published from Thimphu in Dzongkha, Nepalese, and English, circulation (1995) 10,000. [14]1993.

Bolivia

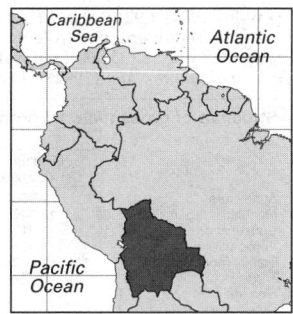

Official name: República de Bolivia (Republic of Bolivia).
Form of government: unitary multiparty republic with two legislative houses (Chamber of Senators [27]; Chamber of Deputies [130]).
Head of state and government: President.
Capitals: La Paz (administrative); Sucre (judicial).
Official languages: Spanish, Aymara, Quechua.
Official religion: Roman Catholicism.
Monetary unit: 1 boliviano (Bs) = 100 centavos; valuation (Oct. 11, 1996) 1 U.S.$ = Bs 5.17; 1 £ = Bs 8.14.

Area and population

Departments	Capitals	area sq mi	area sq km	population 1997 estimate[1]
Beni	Trinidad	82,458	213,564	322,656
Chuquisaca	Sucre	19,893	51,524	488,824
Cochabamba	Cochabamba	21,479	55,631	1,271,488
La Paz	La Paz	51,732	133,985	2,063,877
Oruro	Oruro	20,690	53,588	350,092
Pando	Cobija	24,644	63,827	39,286
Potosí	Potosí	45,644	118,218	642,023
Santa Cruz	Santa Cruz	143,098	370,621	1,672,796
Tarija	Tarija	14,526	37,623	334,879
TOTAL		424,164	1,098,581	7,185,921

Demography

Population (1996): 7,592,000.
Density (1996): persons per sq mi 17.9, persons per sq km 6.2.
Urban-rural (1992): urban 57.7%; rural 42.3%.
Sex distribution (1995): male 49.64%; female 50.36%.
Age breakdown (1995): under 15, 40.6%; 15–29, 27.5%; 30–44, 16.3%; 45–59, 9.6%; 60–74, 5.0%; 75 and over, 1.0%.
Population projection: (2000) 8,329,000; (2010) 10,229,000.
Doubling time: 29 years.
Ethnic composition (1982): mestizo 31.2%; Quechua 25.4%; Aymara 16.9%; white 14.5%; other 12.0%.
Religious affiliation (1992): Roman Catholic 85.0%; Protestant 11.0%; other 4.0%.
Major cities (1992): La Paz 711,036; Santa Cruz 694,616; El Alto 404,367; Cochabamba 404,102; Oruro 183,194; Sucre 130,952.

Vital statistics

Birth rate per 1,000 population (1994): 32.2 (world avg. 25.0).
Death rate per 1,000 population (1994): 8.4 (world avg. 9.3).
Natural increase rate per 1,000 population (1994): 23.8 (world avg. 15.7).
Total fertility rate (avg. births per childbearing woman; 1994): 4.2.
Marriage rate per 1,000 population (1980): 4.8.
Divorce rate per 1,000 population: n.a.
Life expectancy at birth (1994): male 60.9 years; female 65.9 years.
Major causes of death (percentage of total registered deaths; 1980–81): infectious and parasitic diseases 23.9%; diseases of the circulatory system 19.5%; diseases of the respiratory system 14.0%; accidents, homicides, and violence 9.8%; diseases of the digestive system 8.6%.

National economy

Budget (1994). Revenue: Bs 4,445,900,000 (taxes on goods and services 41.6%, income of government enterprises 23.7%, property taxes 8.4%, taxes on international trade 6.8%, social security contributions 6.3%, income taxes 3.1%). Expenditures: Bs 6,400,000,000 (education 18.5%, social security 14.6%, transportation and communications 13.4%, public services 12.6%, defense 8.2%, health 7.1%, public order and safety 6.1%).
Production (metric tons except as noted). Agriculture, forestry, fishing (1995): sugarcane 3,697,000, soybeans 887,000, potatoes 642,000, corn (maize) 521,000, bananas and plantains 423,000, cassava 299,000, rice 263,000, wheat 125,000, coffee 20,000; livestock (number of live animals) 7,784,000 sheep, 5,996,000 cattle, 2,405,000 pigs, 1,496,000 goats, 631,000 asses, 322,000 horses; roundwood (1994) 2,076,000 cu m; fish catch (1993) 6,167. Mining and quarrying (metric tons of pure metal; 1995): zinc 104,706; lead (1994) 19,678; tin 10,720; silver 316; gold 10.8. Manufacturing (value added in Bs '000; 1992): food products 1,459,318; petroleum products 856,675; wood products 517,201; textiles 299,955; beverages 288,796; nonferrous metals 210,903. Construction (1985)[2]: residential dwellings 226. Energy production (consumption): electricity (kW-hr; 1993) 2,445,000,000 (2,457,000,000); coal, none (none); crude petroleum (barrels; 1993) 7,637,000 (8,575,000); petroleum products (metric tons; 1993) 1,132,000 (1,253,000); natural gas (cu m; 1993) 2,872,000,000 (695,000,000).
Population economically active (1992): total 2,530,409; activity rate of total population 33.6% (participation rates: ages 15–64, 63.6%; female 39.0%; unemployed 2.5%).

Price and earnings indexes (1990 = 100)

	1989	1990	1991	1992	1993	1994	1995
Consumer price index	85.4	100.0	121.4	136.1	147.7	159.3	175.6
Monthly earnings index[3]	82.0	100.0	113.8	131.8	152.6	177.1	195.9

Public debt (external, outstanding; 1994): U.S.$4,113,000,000.
Gross national product (at current market prices; 1994): U.S.$5,601,000,000 (U.S.$770 per capita).

Structure of gross domestic product and labour force

	1995 in value Bs '000[4]	1995 % of total value	1992 labour force[5]	1992 % of labour force[5]
Agriculture	3,265,274	16.1	984,407	38.9
Mining	1,995,675	9.8	52,623	2.1
Manufacturing	2,826,679	13.9	222,485	8.8
Construction	798,387	3.9	129,409	5.1
Public utilities	385,600	1.9	6,086	0.2
Transportation and communications	2,262,358	11.1	116,800	4.6
Trade	2,167,907	10.7	232,429	9.2
Finance	2,192,922	10.8	54,711	2.2
Pub. admin., defense	1,756,278	8.7 }	406,928	16.1
Services	1,504,160	7.4 }		
Other	1,154,993[6]	5.7[6]	324,531	12.8
TOTAL	20,310,233	100.0	2,530,409	100.0

Household income and expenditure. Average household size (1992): 3.8; average annual income per household: n.a.; sources of income: n.a.; expenditure (1988): food 35.5%, transportation and communications 17.7%, housing 14.8%, household durable goods 7.3%, clothing and footwear 5.1%, beverages and tobacco 4.5%, recreation 2.7%, health 2.1%, education 0.3%.
Tourism (1994): receipts from visitors U.S.$135,000,000; expenditures by nationals abroad U.S.$140,000,000.
Land use (1994): forested 53.5%; meadows and pastures 24.4%; agricultural and under permanent cultivation 2.2%; other 19.9%.

Foreign trade[7]

Balance of trade (current prices)

	1990	1991	1992	1993	1994	1995
U.S.$'000,000	+326.6	+59.0	−294.4	−384.1	−89.3	−162.5
% of total	21.4%	3.6%	17.2%	20.9%	4.1%	6.9%

Imports (1995): U.S.$943,400,000 (capital goods 43.3%, of which capital goods for industry 21.8%, transport equipment 20.1%; raw materials 36.9%, of which raw materials for industry 27.4%; consumer goods 19.4%, of which durable consumer goods 10.3%, nondurable consumer goods 9.1%). *Major import sources:* United States 18.2%; Brazil 14.5%; Japan 13.8%; Argentina 10.4%; Chile 7.5%; Peru 5.0%; Germany 4.7%.
Exports (1995): U.S.$811,400,000 (zinc 13.8%; gold 12.1%; soybeans 10.9%; natural gas 8.6%; tin 7.9%; jewelry articles 6.9%; silver 6.6%; timber 5.8%; petroleum 4.8%; sugar 1.7%). *Major export destinations:* United States 23.3%; United Kingdom 15.1%; Peru 14.2%; Argentina 12.0%; Germany 5.4%; The Netherlands 4.3%; France 3.6%.

Transport and communications

Transport. Railroads (1993): route length 2,295 mi, 3,694 km; passenger-mi 216,800,000, passenger-km 348,900,000; short ton-mi cargo 521,900,000, metric ton-km cargo 761,900,000. Roads (1993): total length 26,370 mi, 42,438 km (paved 4%). Vehicles (1994): passenger cars 347,383; trucks and buses 189,846. Merchant marine (1992): vessels (100 gross tons and over) 1; total deadweight tonnage 15,765. Air transport (1994): passenger-mi 819,000,000, passenger-km 1,318,000,000; short ton-mi cargo 25,283,000, metric ton-km cargo 36,913,000; airports (1996) with scheduled flights 14.
Communications. Daily newspapers (1992): total number 16; total circulation 390,000; circulation per 1,000 population 52. Radio (1995): total number of receivers 4,250,000 (1 per 1.7 persons). Television (1992): total number of receivers 775,000 (1 per 8.9 persons). Telephones (main lines; 1993): 234,400 (1 per 33 persons).

Education and health

Education (1990–91)

	schools[8]	teachers	students	student/ teacher ratio
Primary (age 6–13)	9,758	51,763	1,278,775	24.7
Secondary (age 14–17)	724 }	12,434	219,232	17.6
Voc., teacher tr.	47 }			
Higher[9]	10	4,261	109,503	25.7

Educational attainment (1992). Percentage of population age 25 and over having: no formal schooling 23.3%; some primary 20.3%; primary education 21.7%; some secondary 9.0%; secondary 6.5%; some higher 5.0%; higher 4.8%; not specified 9.4%. *Literacy (1992):* total population age 15 and over literate 79.5%; males literate 87.7%; females literate 71.8%.
Health: physicians 1,976 (1 per 3,663 persons); hospital beds 7,203 (1 per 1,005 persons); infant mortality rate per 1,000 live births (1990–95) 75.1.
Food (1992): daily per capita caloric intake 2,094 (vegetable products 84%, animal products 16%); 88% of FAO recommended minimum requirement.

Military

Total active duty personnel (1996): 33,500 (army 74.6%, navy 13.4%, air force 12.0%). *Military expenditure as percentage of GNP (1994):* 2.4% (world 3.0%); per capita expenditure U.S.$18.

[1]Based on unadjusted 1992 census results. [2]National government sponsored only. [3]Private-sector earnings in La Paz. [4]In 1990 prices. [5]Population 7 years of age and over. [6]Net import duties. [7]Import figures are f.o.b. in balance of trade and c.i.f. for commodities and trading partners. [8]1986–87. [9]1991–92.

Bosnia and Herzegovina[1]

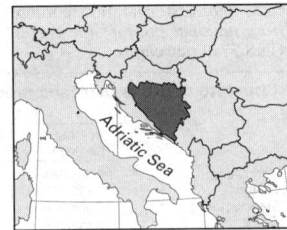

Official name: Republika Bosna i Hercegovina (Republic of Bosnia and Herzegovina).
Form of government: federal multiparty republic with bicameral legislature (Senate [15[2]]; House of Representatives [42]).
Heads of state and government: 2 cochairmen assisted by the Council of Ministers.
Capital: Sarajevo.
Official language: Serbo-Croatian.
Official religion: none.
Monetary unit: 1 Bosnian dinar (BD) = 100 para; valuation (Oct. 15, 1996) 1 U.S.$ = BD 153.78; 1 £ = BD 243.48.

Area and population (1991 census)[3]

Districts	population	Districts	population	Districts	population
Banja Luka	195,139	Grude	15,976	Pucarevo	30,624
Banovići	26,507	Han Pijesak	6,346	Rogatica	21,812
Bihać	70,896	Jablanica	12,664	Rudo	11,572
Bijeljina	96,796	Jajce	44,903	Sanski Most	60,119
Bileća	13,269	Kakanj	55,857	Šarajevo	525,980
Bosanska Dubica	31,577	Kalesija	41,795	Šekovići	9,639
Bosanska Gradiška	60,062	Kalinovik	4,657	Šipovo	15,553
Bosanska Krupa	58,212	Kiseljak	24,081	Skender Vakuf	19,416
Bosanski Brod	33,962	Kladanj	16,028	Sokolac	14,833
Bosanski Novi	41,541	Ključ	37,233	Srbac	21,660
Bosanski Petrovac	15,552	Konjic	43,636	Srebrenica	37,211
Bosanski Šamac	32,835	Kotor Varoš	36,670	Srebrenik	40,769
Bosansko Grahovo	8,303	Kreševo	6,699	Stolac	18,845
Bratunac	33,575	Kupres	10,728	Tešanj	48,390
Brčko	87,332	Laktaši	29,910	Teslić	59,632
Breza	17,266	Lištica	26,437	Titov Drvar	17,079
Bugojno	46,843	Livno	39,526	Tomislavgrad	29,261
Busovača	18,883	Ljubinje	4,162	Travnik	70,402
Čajniče	8,919	Ljubuški	27,182	Trebinje	30,879
Čapljina	27,852	Lopare	32,400	Tuzla	131,861
Cazin	63,406	Lukavac	56,830	Ugljevik	25,641
Čelinac	18,666	Maglaj	43,294	Vareš	22,114
Čitluk	14,709	Modriča	35,413	Velika Kladuša	52,921
Derventa	56,328	Mostar	126,067	Višegrad	21,202
Doboj	102,546	Mrkonjič Grad	27,379	Visoko	46,130
Donji Vakuf	24,232	Neum	4,268	Vitez	27,728
Foča	40,513	Nevesinje	14,421	Vlasenica	33,817
Fojnica	16,227	Odžak	30,651	Zavidovići	57,153
Gacko	10,844	Olovo	16,901	Zenica	145,577
Glamoč	12,421	Orašje	28,201	Žepče	22,840
Goražde	37,505	Posušje	16,659	Živinice	54,653
Gornji Vakuf	25,130	Prijedor	112,470	Zvornik	81,111
Gračanica	59,050	Prnjavor	46,894	TOTAL	4,365,639
Gradačac	56,378	Prozor	19,601		

Demography

Area: 19,741 sq mi, 51,129 sq km.
Population (1996)[4]: 3,200,000.
Density (1996)[4]: persons per sq mi 162.1, persons per sq km 62.6.
Urban-rural (1981): urban 36.2%; rural 63.8%.
Sex distribution (1991): male 49.79%; female 50.21%.
Age breakdown (1991): under 15, 23.4%; 15–29, 26.5%; 30–44, 22.8%; 45–64, 16.0%; 65 and over, 11.3%.
Population projection: (2000) 3,162,000; (2010) 3,436,000.
Doubling time: 99 years.
Ethnic composition (1991): Muslim 49.2%; Serb 31.3%; Croat 17.3%.
Religious affiliation (1992): Muslim 40%; Serbian Orthodox 31%; Roman Catholic 15%; Protestant 4%; other 10%.
Major cities (1991): Sarajevo 416,497; Banja Luka 143,079; Zenica 96,027; Tuzla 83,770; Mostar 75,865.

Vital statistics

Birth rate per 1,000 population (1995): 6.5 (world avg. 25.0); (1993) legitimate 92.6%; illegitimate 7.4%.
Death rate per 1,000 population (1995): 15.5 (world avg. 9.3).
Natural increase rate per 1,000 population (1995): −9.0 (world avg. 15.7).
Total fertility rate (avg. births per childbearing woman; 1995): 1.0.
Marriage rate per 1,000 population (1991): 6.0.
Divorce rate per 1,000 population (1991): 0.3.
Life expectancy at birth (1995): male 51.2 years; female 61.4 years.
Major causes of death per 100,000 population (1989): circulatory diseases 344.1; malignant neoplasms (cancers) 122.6; accidents, violence, and poisoning 47.1; digestive system diseases 29.2; respiratory diseases 29.0. During the early 1990s, violence and acts of war were principal causes of death.

National economy

Production (metric tons except as noted). Agriculture, forestry, fishing (1995): potatoes 377,000, corn (maize) 372,000, wheat 281,000, plums 35,000; livestock (head) 273,000 cattle, 260,000 sheep, 147,000 pigs; roundwood (1994) 1,538,000 cu m; fish catch (1993) 2,500. Mining (1994): iron ore 200,000; bauxite 75,000. Manufacturing (1994): cement 150,000; crude steel 100,000; pig iron 100,000; coke 100,000; alumina 50,000. Construction (residential units constructed; 1990): 26,568. Energy production (consumption): electricity

(kW-hr; 1994) 1,921,000,000 (2,081,000,000); coal (metric tons; 1994) 1,400,-000 (1,400,000); crude petroleum, none (none); petroleum products (metric tons; 1994) none (35,000); natural gas (cu m; 1994) none (378,000,000).
Gross national product (1992)[5]: U.S.$5,900,000,000 (U.S.$1,500 per capita).

Structure of gross material product and labour force

	1989		1990	
	in value Din '000,000[6]	% of total value	labour force[7]	% of labour force[7]
Agriculture	2,963	10.9	39,053	3.8
Manufacturing, mining	15,589	57.6	496,190	48.3
Construction	1,918	7.1	74,861	7.3
Public utilities	403	1.5	22,345	2.2
Transp. and commun.	1,600	5.9	68,798	6.7
Trade	3,777	13.9	130,914	12.8
Finance			38,686	3.8
Pub. admin., defense	834	3.1	155,411	15.1
Services				
Other				
TOTAL	27,084	100.0	1,026,258	100.0

Population economically active (1991): total 992,000; activity rate of total population 22.7% (participation rates: ages 15–64, 35.6%; female [1990] 37.7%; unemployed [1996] 75.0%).

Price and earnings indexes (1985 = 100)

	1984	1985	1986	1987	1988	1989	1990
Consumer price index	58	100	188	400	1,188	16,169	109,000
Monthly earnings index	...	...	...	...	...	...	...

Household income and expenditure. Average household size (1991) 3.4; income per household (1990) Din 72,850[6] (U.S.$6,437); sources of income (1990): wages 53.2%, transfers 18.2%, self-employment 12.0%, other 16.6%; expenditure (1988): food 41.3%, clothing 8.3%, fuel and lighting 7.8%, housing 7.8%, transportation 6.0%, beverages and tobacco 5.7%.
Land use (1994): forest 39.2%; pasture 23.5%; agricultural 15.7%.
Tourism: tourism has not been a significant element of the economy since 1991.

Foreign trade[5]

Balance of trade (current prices)

	1990	1991	1992	1993	1994	1995
U.S.$'000,000	...	...	...	−339	−608	−860
% of total	...	...	...	66.6%	89.4%	89.2%

Imports (1995)[5]: U.S.$912,000,000. Major import sources: Croatia 46%; Slovenia 14%; Russia 11%; Germany 9%; Italy 8%.
Exports (1995)[5]: U.S.$52,000,000. Major export destinations: Italy 29%; Germany 23%; Croatia 13%; Slovenia 13%.

Transport and communications

Transport. Railroads (1991): route length 634 mi, 1,021 km; passenger-mi 344,000,000, passenger-km 554,000,000; short ton-mi cargo 1,333,000,000, metric ton-km cargo 1,946,000,000. Roads (1991): total length 13,153 mi, 21,168 km (paved 54%). Vehicles (1990): passenger cars 438,080; trucks and buses 50,578. Airports (1996) with scheduled flights, n.a.[8]
Communications. Daily newspapers (1994): total number 4; circulation 160,-700; circulation per 1,000 population 46. Radio (1990): number of receivers 733,000 (1 per 5.9 persons). Television (1990): number of receivers 629,000 (1 per 6.8 persons). Telephones (main lines; 1993): 600,000 (1 per 6.2 persons).

Education and health

Education (1990–91)

	schools	teachers	students	student/ teacher ratio
Primary (age 7–14)	2,205	23,369	539,875	23.1
Secondary (age 15–18)	238	9,030	172,063	19.1
Higher	44	2,802	37,541	13.4

Educational attainment (1981). Percentage of population age 15 and over having: less than full primary education 49.5%; primary 24.2%; secondary 21.7%; postsecondary and higher 4.3%. *Literacy* (1981): total population age 10 and over literate 2,962,400 (85.5%); males 96.5%; females 76.6%.
Health: physicians (1996) 4,500[5] (1 per 711 persons); hospital beds (1990) 19,858 (1 per 217 persons); infant mortality rate per 1,000 live births (1995) 43.2.

Military

Total active duty personnel (1996): 92,000 (army 100%)[9].

---

[1]Government structure provided for by Dayton accords and constitutions of 1993 and 1994 is being implemented in stages since formal signing of peace accord on Dec. 14, 1995. [2]All seats are nonelective. [3]First-order subdivisions as of late 1996 comprised two autonomous regions: the c. 26,100 sq km Federation of Bosnia and Herzegovina (which is further divided into 10 cantons) and the c. 25,000 sq km Republika Srpska. [4]Excludes 1,300,000 refugees in adjacent countries and Western Europe. [5]Estimated figures. [6]Yugoslav new dinar (Din). [7]Excludes 28,000 workers in the private sector. [8]Sarajevo Airport reopened in August 1996. [9]Excludes 50,000 troops in the Croatian Defense Council, 85,000 troops in the Republika Srpska army, and 48,000 troops in the NATO peacekeeping forces.

Botswana

Official name: Republic of Botswana.
Form of government: multiparty
republic with one legislative body[1]
(National Assembly [46[2]]).
Head of state and government:
President.
Capital: Gaborone.
Official language: English[3].
Official religion: none.
Monetary unit: 1 pula (P) = 100 thebe;
valuation (Oct. 11, 1996)
1 U.S.$ = P 3.51; 1 £ = P 5.53.

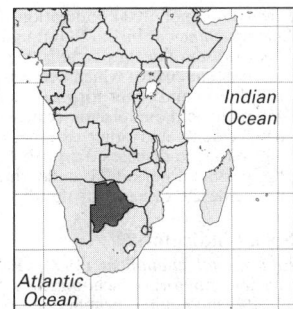

Area and population		area		population
				1991
Districts	Capitals	sq mi	sq km	census
Barolong	...	773	2,003	18,400
Central	Serowe	57,039	147,730	412,970
Ghanzi	Ghanzi	45,525	117,910	24,719
Kgalagadi	Tsabong	41,290	106,940	31,134
Kgatleng	Mochudi	3,073	7,960	57,770
Kweneng	Molepolole	13,857	35,890	170,437
Ngwaketse	Kanye	10,219	26,467	128,989
North East	Masunga	1,977	5,120	43,354
North West				
Chobe	Kasane	8,031	20,800	14,126
Ngamiland	Maun	33,359	86,400	57,811
Okavango	Orapa	8,776	22,730	36,723
South East	Ramotswa	687	1,780	43,584
Towns[4]				
Francistown	—	31	79	65,244
Gaborone	—	65	169	133,468
Jwaneng	—	39	100	11,188
Lobatse	—	16	42	26,052
Orapa	—	7	17	8,827
Selebi-Pikwe	—	19	50	39,772
Sowa	—	61	159	2,228
TOTAL		224,607[5]	581,730	1,326,796

Demography

Population (1996): 1,594,000.
Density (1996): persons per sq mi 7.1, persons per sq km 2.7.
Urban-rural (1991): urban 45.7%; rural 54.3%.
Sex distribution (1995): male 48.96%; female 51.04%.
Age breakdown (1995): under 15, 43.2%; 15–29, 28.5%; 30–44, 16.5%; 45–59, 7.9%; 60–74, 3.2%; 75 and over, 0.7%.
Population projection: (2000) 1,789,000; (2010) 2,318,000.
Doubling time: 23 years.
Ethnic composition (1983): Tswana 75.5%; Shona 12.4%; San (Bushman) 3.4%; Khoikhoin (Hottentot) 2.5%; Ndebele 1.3%; other 4.9%.
Religious affiliation (1980): traditional beliefs 49.2%; Protestant 29.0%; African Christian 11.8%; Roman Catholic 9.4%; other 0.6%.
Major cities (1993): Gaborone 156,803; Francistown 75,678; Selebi-Pikwe 42,-350; Molepolole 41,730; Kanye 34,233.

Vital statistics

Birth rate per 1,000 population (1991–95): 37.1 (world avg. 25.0); (1986) legitimate 28.8%[6]; illegitimate 71.2%[6].
Death rate per 1,000 population (1991–95): 6.6 (world avg. 9.3).
Natural increase rate per 1,000 population (1991–95): 30.5 (world avg. 15.7).
Total fertility rate (avg. births per childbearing woman; 1993): 4.8.
Marriage rate per 1,000 population (1987): 1.6.
Life expectancy at birth (1993): male 59.5 years; female 65.6 years.
Major causes of death (as percentage of total of inpatient deaths[7]; 1992): tuberculosis and other diseases of the respiratory system 14.3%; pneumonia 10.0%; diseases of the digestive system 8.9%; cerebrovascular disease 4.2%; AIDS 3.9%; kidney disease 3.0%.

National economy

Budget (1995–96). Revenue: P 5,039,700,000 (mineral royalties 48.7%, customs and excise taxes 19.9%, property income 19.6%, interest income 4.1%). Expenditures: P 5,458,900,000 (economic services 40.4%, education 20.8%, public order and safety 3.5%, social welfare 3.0%, health 2.5%).
Population economically active (1991): total 441,203; activity rate of total population 33.2% (participation rates: ages 15–64, 59.6%; female 38.4%; unemployed 13.9%).

Price and earnings indexes (1990 = 100)							
	1989	1990	1991	1992	1993	1994	1995
Consumer price index	89.8	100.0	111.8	129.8	148.4	164.1	181.3
Monthly earnings index	90.4	100.0	113.6	133.5	162.0	160.4[8]	...

Production (metric tons except as noted). Agriculture, forestry, fishing (1995): cereals 45,900 (of which sorghum 38,000, corn [maize] 5,000, millet 2,000), vegetables and melons 12,900, pulses 12,000, fruits 9,500, roots and tubers 9,000, seed cotton 3,000; livestock (number of live animals) 2,800,000 cattle, 1,900,000 goats, 250,000 sheep, 237,000 mules and asses, 31,500 horses; roundwood (1994) 1,447,000 cu m; fish catch (1993) 2,000. Mining and quarrying (1995): copper 19,140; nickel 15,294; cobalt 271; diamonds 16,802,438 carats. Manufacturing (value added in P '000,000; 1993): food products 222.3; paper and paper products 97.9; industrial chemicals 36.7; wood products

11.7. Construction (value added in P '000,000; 1994–95): 573,400. Energy production (consumption): electricity (kW-hr; 1991) 929,000,000 (929,000,-000); coal (metric tons; 1992) 901,452 (n.a.); crude petroleum, none (n.a.).
Public debt (external, outstanding; 1994): U.S.$680,800,000.
Tourism (1994): receipts U.S.$35,000,000; expenditures U.S.$52,000,000.
Gross national product (1994): U.S.$4,037,000,000 (U.S.$2,800 per capita).

Structure of gross domestic product and labour force				
	1994–95		1991	
	in value P '000,000	% of total value	labour force	% of labour force
Agriculture	572,400	4.9	97,626	22.1
Mining	4,098,300	35.5	13,264	3.0
Manufacturing	468,400	4.1	26,470	6.0
Construction	573,400	5.0	57,510	13.0
Public utilities	299,100	2.6	6,388	1.4
Transp. and commun.	355,300	3.1	11,398	2.6
Trade	1,817,200	15.7	35,194	8.0
Finance and business services	554,800	4.8	13,286	3.0
Pub. admin., defense	2,486,300	21.5	34,002	7.7
Services	322,400	2.8	72,064	16.3
Other	...	...	74,001[9]	16.8[9]
TOTAL	11,547,500[5]	100.0	441,203	100.0[5]

Household income and expenditure (1985–86). Average household size 5.0; average annual income per household P 3,910 (U.S.$2,080); sources of income (1987): wages and salaries 73.3%, self-employment 15.9%, transfers 10.8%; expenditure: food, beverages, and tobacco 39.4%, household durable goods 14.0%, rent and services 13.3%, transportation 13.1%, clothing 5.6%, health 2.3%.
Land use (1994): forested 46.8%; meadows and pastures 45.2%; agricultural and under permanent cultivation 0.7%; other 7.3%.

Foreign trade[10]

Balance of trade (current prices)						
	1989	1990	1991	1992	1993	1994
P '000,000	1,174.9	241.3	398.1	299.1	668.4	1,216.3
% of total	18.6%	3.8%	5.6%	4.2%	8.4%	14.0%

Imports (1994): P 4,394,593,000 (machinery and transport equipment 29.6%, of which transport equipment 12.0%; food, beverages, and tobacco 17.6%; chemical and rubber products 9.7%; metal and metal products 9.4%; textiles and footwear 8.9%; wood and paper 5.8%; mineral fuels 5.7%). *Major import sources* (1992): Customs Union of Southern Africa 85.0%; European countries 7.1%, of which U.K. 2.6%; U.S. 1.0%.
Exports (1994): P 4,653,833,000 (diamonds 79.9%; copper-nickel matte 5.6%; textiles 3.8%; meat products 3.7%). *Major export destinations* (1992): European countries 86.7%, of which U.K. 1.6%; Customs Union of Southern Africa 6.9%; U.S. 0.3%.

Transport and communications

Transport. Railroads (1994): length 603 mi, 971 km; passenger-km 257,000,-000[11]; metric ton-km cargo 1,710,000. Roads (1995): total length 11,388 mi, 18,327 km (paved 23%). Vehicles (1994): passenger cars 27,058; trucks and buses 42,696. Merchant marine: none. Air transport (1994)[12]: passenger-km 58,370,000; metric ton-km cargo 479,000; airports (1996) 4.
Communications. Daily newspapers (1993): total number 2; total circulation 49,700; circulation per 1,000 population 34.6. Radio (1994): total receivers 1,400,000 (1 per 1.1 persons). Television (1994): total receivers 13,800 (1 per 108 persons). Telephones (main lines; 1993): 43,500 (1 per 33 persons).

Education and health

Education (1994)				
	schools	teachers	students	student/teacher ratio
Primary (age 6–13)	781	9,552	301,370	31.6
Secondary (age 14–18)	199	5,192	99,560	19.2
Voc., teacher tr.	45	856	9,570	11.2
Higher	1	475	4,533	9.5

Educational attainment (1991). Percentage of population age 25 and over having: no formal schooling 42.9%; primary education 17.3%; some secondary 32.3%; complete secondary 3.9%; postsecondary 3.7%. *Literacy* (1990): total population over age 15 literate 486,500 (73.6%); males literate 253,300 (83.7%); females literate 233,200 (65.1%).
Health (1994): physicians 339 (1 per 4,395 persons); hospital beds (1993) 3,299 (1 per 434 persons); infant mortality rate 39.0.
Food (1992): daily per capita caloric intake 2,266 (vegetable products 79%, animal products 21%); 98% of FAO recommended minimum requirement.

Military

Total active duty personnel (1995): 7,500 (army 93.3%, navy, none [landlocked], air force 6.7%). *Military expenditure as percentage of GNP* (1994): 6.0% (world 3.0%); per capita expenditure U.S.$169.

[1]In addition, the House of Chiefs, a 15-member body consisting of chiefs, subchiefs, and associated members, serves in an advisory capacity to the government. [2]Including four specially elected members and two nonelective seats. [3]Tswana is the national language. [4]Areas are included with respective district totals; population figures are not included with district totals. [5]Detail does not add to total given because of rounding. [6]Registered births only. [7]Represents nearly 30% of all deaths. [8]March. [9]Includes 61,265 unemployed. [10]Import figures are f.o.b. in balance of trade and c.i.f. in commodities and trading partners. [11]1986–87. [12]Air Botswana only.

Brazil

Official name: República Federativa
do Brasil (Federative Republic
of Brazil).
Form of government: multiparty
federal republic with 2 legislative
houses (Senate [81]; Chamber of
Deputies [513]).
Chief of state and government:
President.
Capital: Brasília.
Official language: Portuguese.
Official religion: none.
Monetary unit: 1 real[1] = 100 centavos;
valuation (Oct. 11, 1996)
1 U.S.$ = 1.03 reais; 1 £ = 1.62 reais.

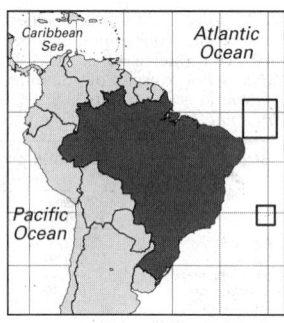

Area and population

States	Capitals	area sq mi	area sq km	population 1995 estimate[2]
Acre	Rio Branco	59,132	153,150	455,200
Alagoas	Maceió	10,785	27,933	2,685,400
Amapá	Macapá	55,388	143,454	326,200
Amazonas	Manaus	609,200	1,577,820	2,320,200
Bahia	Salvador	219,034	567,295	12,646,000
Ceará	Fortaleza	56,505	146,348	6,714,200
Espírito Santo	Vitória	17,836	46,194	2,786,700
Goiás	Goiânia	131,772	341,289	4,308,400
Maranhão	São Luís	128,713	333,366	5,231,300
Mato Grosso	Cuiabá	350,120	906,807	2,313,600
Mato Grosso do Sul	Campo Grande	138,286	358,159	1,912,800
Minas Gerais	Belo Horizonte	227,176	588,384	16,505,300
Pará	Belém	483,850	1,253,165	5,448,600
Paraíba	João Pessoa	21,848	56,585	3,340,000
Paraná	Curitiba	77,108	199,709	8,712,800
Pernambuco	Recife	38,200	98,938	7,445,200
Piauí	Teresina	97,444	252,379	2,725,000
Rio de Janeiro	Rio de Janeiro	16,954	43,910	13,296,400
Rio Grande do Norte	Natal	20,582	53,307	2,582,300
Rio Grande do Sul	Pôrto Alegre	108,905	282,062	9,578,600
Rondônia	Pôrto Velho	92,090	238,513	1,339,500
Roraima	Boa Vista	86,918	225,116	262,200
Santa Catarina	Florianópolis	36,851	95,443	4,836,600
São Paulo	São Paulo	96,066	248,809	33,699,600
Sergipe	Aracaju	8,514	22,050	1,605,300
Tocantins	Palmas	107,499	278,421	1,007,000
Federal District				
Distrito Federal	Brasília	2,248	5,822	1,737,800
Disputed areas[3]		1,149	2,977	—
TOTAL		3,300,171[4, 5]	8,547,404[4, 5]	155,822,400[4]

Demography

Population (1996): 157,872,000.
Density (1996): persons per sq mi 47.8, persons per sq km 18.5.
Urban-rural (1995): urban 78.2%; rural 21.8%.
Sex distribution (1995): male 49.38%; female 50.62%.
Age breakdown (1995): under 15, 31.8%; 15–29, 28.5%; 30–44, 21.2%; 45–59,
11.4%; 60–74, 5.7%; 75 and over, 1.4%.
Population projection: (2000) 165,715,000; (2010) 184,157,000.
Doubling time: 58 years.
Ethnic composition (1990): white 54.0%; mulatto and mestizo 39.0%; black
and black/Amerindian 5.9%; Asian 0.9%; Amerindian 0.2%.
Religious affiliation (1995): Roman Catholic *c.* 70%[6]; evangelical Protestant
c. 19%; other *c.* 11%.
Major cities (1991)[7] *and metropolitan areas/urban agglomerations* (1995): São
Paulo 9,393,753 (16,417,000[8]); Rio de Janeiro 5,473,909 (9,888,000[8]); Sal-
vador 2,070,296 (2,819,000[8]); Belo Horizonte 1,529,566 (3,899,000[8]); Brasília
1,492,542 (1,778,000[9]); Recife 1,296,995 (3,168,000[8]); Pôrto Alegre 1,237,223
(3,349,000[8]); Manaus 1,005,634 (1,189,000[9]); Goiânia 912,136 (1,033,000[9]);
Curitiba 841,882 (2,270,000[8]); Belém 765,476 (1,574,000[8]); Campinas 748,076
(1,607,000[9]); Fortaleza 743,335 (2,660,000[8]).

Other principal cities (1991)[7]

	population		population		population
Aracaju	401,676	Natal	459,827	São Bernardo	
Campo Grande	516,403	Niterói	400,586[10]	do Campo	550,030[11]
Guarulhos	544,698[11]	Nova Iguaçu	562,062[10]	São Jose dos	
João Pessoa	497,306	Osasco	566,949[11]	Campos	385,879
Juiz de Fora	377,538	Ribeirão Preto	416,186	Sorocaba	348,952
Londrina	355,062	Santo André	518,272[11]	Teresina	556,073
Maceió	554,727	Santos	415,554[12]	Uberlândia	354,710

Place of birth/national origin: n.a.
Mobility: n.a.
Families (1990)[13]. Average family size 3.9; 1–2 persons 26.2%, 3 persons
21.3%, 4 persons 21.5%, 5–6 persons 22.3%, 7 or more persons 8.7%.
Emigration: Emigration for economic opportunity accelerated in the 1980s.
By 1995 it was officially estimated that 1–2.5 million Brazilians lived outside
of Brazil. Emigrants' most popular destinations in order of preference are
the United States, Japan, and the United Kingdom.

Vital statistics

Birth rate per 1,000 population (1995): 21.2 (world avg. 25.0).
Death rate per 1,000 population (1995): 9.0 (world avg. 9.3).
Natural increase rate per 1,000 population (1995): 12.2 (world avg. 15.7).
Total fertility rate (avg. births per childbearing woman; 1995): 2.4.
Marriage rate per 1,000 population (1992): 5.0.

Divorce rate per 1,000 population (1992): 0.6.
Life expectancy at birth (1995): male 56.6 years; female 67.3 years.
Major causes of death per 100,000 population (1990)[14]: diseases of the circulatory system 206, of which cerebrovascular disease 70, diseases of pulmonary
circulation and other forms of heart disease 51, acute myocardial infarction
45; malignant neoplasms (cancers) 75; diseases of the respiratory system
64; accidents and other external causes (excluding homicide) 62; infectious
and parasitic diseases 37; birth trauma and other conditions originating in
the perinatal period 34; endocrine, metabolic, and nutritional disorders 31;
homicide 29; diseases of the digestive system 28; ill-defined conditions 133.

Social indicators

Educational attainment (1990). Percentage of population age 10 and over
having: no formal schooling or less than one year of primary education
18.1%; incomplete primary 56.8%; complete primary 6.9%; incomplete secondary 12.4%; complete secondary or higher 5.7%; unknown 0.1%.

Distribution of income (1988)[13, 15]

percentage of national income by decile

1	2	3	4	5	6	7	8	9	10 (highest)
0.7	1.7	2.2	3.4	3.9	5.0	6.8	9.9	15.9	50.5

Quality of working life. Annual estimated rate per 100,000 insured workers
(1990) for: on-the-job injury 2,032; industrial illness 17; death 4. Proportion
of labour force participating in national social insurance system (1990):
50.1%. Proportion of formally employed population receiving minimum
wage (1993): 25.0%.
Access to services. Proportion of households having access to: electricity (1990)
87.8%, of which urban households having access (1989) 97.2%, rural households having access (1989) 53.2%; safe public (piped) water supply (1992)
68.0%, of which urban households having access 89.6%, rural households
having access 33.5%; public refuse collection (1990) 64.5%; urban sewage
collection (1992) population connected to public system 40.2%, localized
disposal system 43.0%, other/unknown 16.8%.
Social participation. Voting is mandatory for national elections; in the October 1994 elections blank or otherwise invalid ballots accounted for as many
as 15% of all votes cast. Trade union membership in total workforce (1991):
16,748,155. Practicing Roman Catholic population in total affiliated Roman
Catholic population (1990): 25%.
Social deviance (1990). The incidence of crime is not accurately reported.
Crimes resulting in imprisonment: 159,071, of which murder 7.3%, assault
11.0%, theft, burglary, and housebreaking 26.6%, robbery and extortion
12.2%, narcotics trafficking 6.3%, narcotics usage 4.5%. Suicide: 5,142.
Leisure. Favourite leisure activities include: playing soccer, dancing, rehearsing all year in neighbourhood samba groups for celebrations of Carnival,
and competing in water sports, volleyball, and basketball.
Material well-being (1990)[13]. Households possessing: radio receiver 84.3%;
television receiver 73.7%; refrigerator 71.1%; stove 96.4%.

National economy

Gross national product (at current market prices; 1994): U.S.$536,309,000,000
(U.S.$3,370 per capita).

Structure of gross domestic product and labour force

	1994 in value R$'000,000,000[1, 16]	1994 % of total value	1990 labour force[13]	1990 % of labour force
Agriculture	43,436	14.3	14,180,519	22.0
Mining	3,588	1.2	860,453	1.3
Public utilities	16,744	5.5		
Manufacturing	69,578	22.9	9,410,712	14.6
Construction	23,496	7.7	3,823,154	5.9
Transportation and communications	17,369	5.7	2,439,920	3.8
Trade	21,470	7.0	7,975,670[17]	12.4[17]
Finance, real estate	27,617	9.1	1,715,598	2.7
Pub. admin., defense	31,684	10.4	3,117,005	4.8
Services	76,345	25.1	18,577,468[18]	28.8[18]
Other	−26,925[19]	−8.9[19]	2,367,482[20]	3.7[20]
TOTAL	304,402	100.0	64,467,981	100.0

Budget. Revenue (1993): CR$13,896,006,000,000[1] (development receipts
67.9%, of which credits 60.8%; current receipts 32.1%, of which social
contributions 13.4% [including social security 7.6%], taxes 12.1%). Expenditures (1994): R$214,827,000,000[1] (development expenditures 65.6%, of
which amortization of domestic debt 40.5%; current expenditures 33.9%;
contingency reserve 0.5%).
Public debt (external, outstanding; 1994): U.S.$94,512,000,000.
Production ('000 metric tons except as noted). Agriculture, forestry, fishing
(1995): sugarcane 301,585, corn (maize) 36,276, soybeans 25,581, cassava
25,538, oranges 19,639, rice 11,236, bananas 5,679, dry beans 2,913, tomatoes
2,734, potatoes 2,626, papayas 1,800, wheat 1,516, seed cotton 1,432, cashew
apples 1,250, coconuts 950, coffee 930, cottonseed 915, pineapples 913,
onions 907, grapes 829, apples 693, tangerines (1994) 670, sweet potatoes
630, cotton lint 515, lemons and limes 470, tobacco 453, mangoes 400, cacao
beans 319, peanuts (groundnuts) 168, cashews 164, maté 150, sisal 125,
natural rubber 30, brazil nuts 25; livestock (number of live animals; 1994)
151,600,000 cattle, 30,450,000 pigs, 20,500,000 sheep, 5,800,000 horses; roundwood (1994) 237,683,000 cu m, of which fuelwood 159,780,000 cu m, sawlogs
and veneer logs 41,171,000 cu m, pulpwood 30,701,000 cu m; fish catch
(1993) 780, of which freshwater fishes 208. Mining and quarrying (value of
export production in U.S.$'000; 1995): iron ore 2,519,000; semifinished cop-
per 230,392; bauxite 122,263; granite 80,000; semifinished tin 58,295; kaolin
(clay) 56,737; gemstones (1994) 27,000; magnesite 21,874; phosphate fertilizers 16,705; asbestos 14,780; manganese 14,493; gold production for both

domestic use and export 2,315,000 troy oz; Brazil is also a world-leading producer of high-quality grade quartz, columbium (niobium), and tantalum. Manufacturing (value added in CR$'000,000,000; 1993): industrial chemicals 1,050; food products 1,040; nonelectrical machinery 994; basic and fabricated metals 923; transport equipment 784; electrical machinery 591; textiles 379; nonmetallic mineral products 369; paper and paper products 296; clothing and footwear 272; printing and publishing 226. Construction (authorized[21]; 1987): residential 20,090,000 sq m; nonresidential 8,180,000 sq m.
Land use (1994): forested 57.7%; meadows and pastures 21.9%; agricultural and under permanent cultivation 6.0%; other 14.4%.

Manufacturing enterprises (1985)

	no. of enter- prises	number of labourers	wages of labourers as a % of avg. of all mfg. wages	value added in producer's prices (in CR$'000,000,000[1])[22]
Chemical products (excl. pharmaceuticals)	5,066	287,742	191.7	1,134
Food products	43,034	733,199	68.4	1,040
Nonelectrical machinery	11,088	552,163	146.5	994
Fabricated metals, iron and steel, and nonferrous metals	18,964	565,036	117.1	923
Transport equipment	4,184	341,621	154.8	784
Electrical machinery	4,573	315,767	138.5	591
Textiles	5,570	351,360	75.1	379
Nonmetallic mineral products	28,974	365,643	65.7	369
Paper and paper products	2,107	132,948	120.7	296
Clothing and footwear	23,200	655,234	49.6	272
Publishing and printing	9,053	164,523	100.1	226
Pharmaceuticals	930	49,048	173.7	217
Plastics	2,975	146,151	85.1	193
Beverages	2,798	77,167	...	178
Rubber products	1,421	71,656	136.3	91
Wood and wood products (excl. furniture)	17,129	218,059	48.4	91
Furniture	13,759	186,467	...	86

Population economically active (1990)[13]: total 64,467,981; activity rate of total population 43.8% (participation rates: ages 15–59, 68.5%; female 35.5%; unemployed [May 1996] 5.9%[23, 24]).

Price and earnings indexes (1990 = 100)

	1992	1993	1994	1995	1996[25]
Consumer price index	6,002	134,800	3,733,100	6,883,000	7,837,200
Monthly earnings index[26]	5,859	97,000	...	...	...

Tourism (1994): receipts U.S.$1,925,000,000; expenditures U.S.$2,931,000,000.

Retail trade enterprises (1990)

	no. of enterprises	total no. of employees	annual wage as a % of all trade wages	annual values of sales in Cr$'000,000
Vehicles, new and used; parts	45,385	406,568	152.1	1,685
General merchandise stores (including food products)	10,180	368,590	116.7	1,324
Clothing, footwear, and apparel	147,671	634,713	94.7	1,124
Gas stations	24,881	211,689	106.0	1,067
Food, beverages, and tobacco	228,922	606,341	53.1	1,059
Hardware, appliances, and construction materials	57,577	338,519	99.1	775
Domestic goods, equipment, kitchenware, and antiques	28,636	202,146	115.3	567
Pharmaceutical and cosmetic products	49,435	213,118	79.9	377
Agricultural and industrial equipment and machinery	9,897	90,900	154.1	289
Books, magazines, newspapers	14,383	69,771	81.8	116

Family income and expenditure (1987–88)[27]. Average family size 4.0; annual income per family Cz$450,000[1] (U.S.$1,074); sources of income: wages and salaries 62.4%, self-employed 14.7%, transfers 10.9%, other 12.0%; expenditure: food and beverages 25.3%, housing, energy, and household furnishings 21.3%, transportation and communications 15.0%, clothing and footwear 12.9%, health care 9.1%.

Financial aggregates[28]

	1991	1992	1993	1994	1995	1996[29]
Exchange rate, reais[1] per:						
U.S. dollar	—	.002	.049	.846	.973	.987
£	—	.003	.073	1.322	1.508	1.506
SDR	.001	.006	.163	1.235	1.446	1.443
International reserves (U.S.$)						
Total (excl. gold; '000,000)	8,033	22,521	30,604	37,070	49,708	53,606
SDRs ('000,000)	13	1	2	—	1	19
Reserve pos. in IMF ('000,000)						
Foreign exchange ('000,000)	8,020	22,520	30,602	37,069	49,707	53,587
Gold ('000,000 fine troy oz)	2.02	2.23	2.93	3.71	4.58	4.48
% world reserves	0.21	0.24	0.32	0.37	0.52[30]	...
Interest and prices						
Central bank discount (%)	2,494	1,489	5,757	56	39	30
Govt. bond yield (%)	...	...	...	...	...	...
Industrial share prices	...	...	...	...	...	...
Balance of payments (U.S.$'000,000)						
Balance of visible trade	+ 10,578	+ 15,239	+ 14,329	+ 10,861	– 3,157	...
Imports, f.o.b.	21,041	20,554	25,711	33,241	49,663	...
Exports, f.o.b.	31,619	35,793	39,630	44,102	46,506	...
Balance of invisibles	– 12,028	– 9,150	– 14,309	– 12,014	– 14,979	...
Balance of payments, current account	– 1,450	+ 6,089	+ 20	– 1,153	– 18,136	...

Energy production (consumption): electricity (kW-hr; 1994) 260,682,000,000 (292,339,000,000); coal (metric tons; 1994) 5,194,000 (16,434,000); crude petroleum (barrels; 1995) 251,008,000 ([1994] 469,227,000); petroleum prod-

ucts (metric tons; 1994) 55,111,000 (57,042,000); natural gas (cu m; 1994) 4,103,000,000 (4,103,000,000); carburant alcohol (cu m; 1992) 11,530,000 (8,052,000).

Foreign trade[31]

Balance of trade (current prices)

	1990	1991	1992	1993	1994	1995
U.S.$'000,000	+ 10,753	+ 10,578	+ 15,239	+ 13,117	+ 10,391	– 3,157
% of total	20.6%	20.1%	27.4%	20.5%	13.6%	3.3%

Imports (1994): U.S.$35,553,000,000 (nonelectrical machinery and apparatus 17.4%, electrical machinery and apparatus 10.8%, road vehicles 9.2%, food and live animals 9.0%, crude petroleum 7.2%). *Major import sources:* United States 23.1%; Argentina 10.7%; Germany 10.2%; Italy 5.8%; Japan 5.6%; Saudi Arabia 4.0%; France 2.6%; Canada 2.5%; United Kingdom 2.2%; Switzerland 2.0%.
Exports (1994): U.S.$43,558,000,000 (iron and steel fabricated products 9.5%, nonelectrical machinery and apparatus 9.1%, road vehicles 6.9%, coffee 5.9%, iron ore 5.3%, soy products 4.6%, leather footwear 3.4%, meat products 3.1%, soybeans 3.0%, aluminum 2.7%, textiles 2.3%). *Major export destinations:* United States 20.6%; Argentina 9.5%; The Netherlands 7.1%; Japan 6.0%; Germany 4.7%; Italy 3.8%; Belgium-Luxembourg 3.1%; United Kingdom 2.7%; Mexico 2.4%; Paraguay 2.4%.

Transport and communications

Transport. Railroads: route length (1994) 19,885 mi, 32,002 km; (1993) passenger-mi 8,723,000,000, passenger-km 14,038,000,000; (1993) short ton-mi cargo 85,439,000,000, metric ton-km cargo 124,738,000,000. Roads (1995): total length 1,205,000 mi, 1,939,000 km (paved 9%). Vehicles (1994): passenger cars 12,024,000; trucks and buses 3,316,000. Merchant marine (1992): vessels (100 gross tons and over) 635; total deadweight tonnage 9,348,339. Air transport (1995)[32]: passenger-mi 20,275,000,000, passenger-km 32,629,000,000; short ton-mi cargo 1,070,000,000, metric ton-km cargo 1,562,000,000; airports (1995) with scheduled flights 139.
Communications. Daily newspapers (1992): total number 373; total circulation 8,500,000; circulation per 1,000 population 55. Radio (1995): total number of receivers 55,000,000 (1 per 2.8 persons). Television (1995): total number of receivers 30,000,000 (1 per 5.2 persons). Telephones (main lines; 1993): 11,752,831 (1 per 13 persons).

Education and health

Education (1993)

	schools	teachers	students	student/ teacher ratio
Primary (age 7–14)	195,544	1,346,285	30,520,748	22.7
Secondary (age 15–18)	12,603	275,845	4,208,766	15.3
Higher	873	150,823	1,594,668	10.6

Literacy (1995)[33]: total population age 15 and over literate 91,100,000 (83.3%); males literate 45,200,000 (83.3%); females literate 45,900,000 (83.2%).
Health: physicians (1993) 222,658 (1 per 681 persons); hospital beds (1993) 509,270 (1 per 298 persons); infant mortality rate per 1,000 live births (1995) 57.2.
Food (1992): daily per capita caloric intake 2,824 (vegetable products 83%, animal products 17%); 118% of FAO recommended minimum requirement.

Military

Total active duty personnel (1996): 295,000 (army 66.0%, navy 17.0%, air force 17.0%). *Military expenditure as percentage of GNP* (1994): 1.1% (world 3.0%); per capita expenditure U.S.$42.

[1]The real (R$) replaced the cruzeiro real (CR$) on July 1, 1994, at a rate of 2,750 cruzeiros reais to 1 real (a rate par to the U.S.$ on that date). Previously, the cruzeiro real replaced the cruzeiro (Cr$) at a rate of 1,000 cruzeiros to 1 cruzeiro real on Aug. 2, 1993; the cruzeiro replaced the new cruzado (NCz$) at a rate of 1 to 1 on March 16, 1990, and the new cruzado replaced the (old) cruzado (Cz$) at a rate of 1,000 (old) to 1 new on Jan. 15, 1989. [2]Projection based on 1991 census. [3]Area in dispute between Ceará and Piauí. [4]Detail does not add to total given because of rounding. [5]Land area excluding inland water is 3,265,076 sq mi (8,456,508 sq km). [6]Includes syncretic Afro-Catholic cults having Spiritist beliefs and rituals. [7]Revised preliminary census. [8]Officially defined metropolitan area. [9]Officially defined urban agglomeration. [10]Within Rio de Janeiro metropolitan area. [11]Within São Paulo metropolitan area. [12]1995 population estimate of urban agglomeration is 1,173,000. [13]Excludes rural economically active population of Acre, Amapá, Amazonas, Pará, Rondônia, and Roraima states. [14]Projected rates based on about 75% of total deaths. [15]As of 1992, 33,000,000 Brazilians lived in extreme poverty (more than half of whom lived in the nine states of the northeast). [16]At factor cost. [17]Excludes restaurants and hotels. [18]Includes restaurants and hotels. [19]Less imputed bank service charges. [20]Unemployed. [21]Urban construction only for 74 cities. [22]1993. [23]Six largest metropolitan regions only. [24]Excludes workers in the extremely large informal sector. [25]February. [26]Minimum wages. [27]Based on 10,408,833 families in Brazil's nine largest metropolitan regions. [28]End-of-period figures. [29]March. [30]Third quarter of 1995. [31]Import figures are f.o.b. in balance of trade and c.i.f. for commodities and trading partners. [32]Transbrasil, VARIG, and VASP airlines only. [33]By official estimate; functional literacy, however, may be as low as 42% of total population over age 15.

Brunei

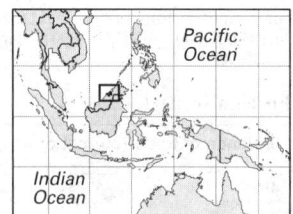

Official name: Negara Brunei
Darussalam (State of Brunei, Abode
of Peace).
Form of government: monarchy
(sultanate)[1].
Head of state and government: Sultan.
Capital: Bandar Seri Begawan.
Official language: Malay[2].
Official religion: Islam.
Monetary unit: 1 Brunei dollar
(B$) = 100 cents; valuation (Oct. 11,
1996) 1 U.S.$ = B$1.41;
1 £ = B$2.22.

Area and population

Districts	Capitals	area sq mi	area sq km	population 1994 estimate
Belait	Kuala Belait	1,052	2,724	57,800
Brunei and Muara	Bandar Seri Begawan	220	571	187,000
Temburong	Bangar	504	1,304	8,200
Tutong	Tutong	450	1,166	31,500
TOTAL		2,226	5,765	284,500

Demography

Population (1996): 300,000.
Density (1996): persons per sq mi 134.8, persons per sq km 52.0.
Urban-rural (1995): urban 58.0%; rural 42.0%.
Sex distribution (1994): male 52.72%; female 47.28%.
Age breakdown (1992): under 15, 34.5%; 15–29, 28.3%; 30–44, 24.7%; 45–59,
8.2%; 60–74, 3.2%; 75 and over, 1.1%.
Population projection: (2000) 331,000; (2010) 410,000.
Doubling time: 35 years.
Ethnic composition (1992): Malay 67.1%; Chinese 15.4%; other indigenous
6.0%; Indian and other 11.5%.
Religious affiliation (1991): Muslim 67.2%; Buddhist 12.8%; Christian 10.0%;
other religions and nonreligious 10.0%.
Major cities (1991): Bandar Seri Begawan 45,867[3]; Kuala Belait 21,163; Seria
21,082; Tutong 13,049.

Vital statistics

Birth rate per 1,000 population (1996): 23.2 (world avg. 25.0); (1982) legiti-
mate 99.6%; illegitimate 0.4%.
Death rate per 1,000 population (1996): 3.5 (world avg. 9.3).
Natural increase rate per 1,000 population (1996): 19.7 (world avg. 15.7).
Total fertility rate (avg. births per childbearing woman; 1996): 3.0.
Marriage rate per 1,000 population (1993): 6.8.
Divorce rate per 1,000 population (1989): 0.8.
Life expectancy at birth (1996): male 72.0 years; female 77.0 years.
Major causes of death per 100,000 population (1992): cardiovascular disease
55.3; malignant neoplasms (cancers) 37.3; accidents, poisoning, and violence
30.6; cerebrovascular diseases 19.0; pneumonia 12.3; hypertensive diseases
9.7; congenital anomalies 9.7.

National economy

Budget (1995). Revenue: B$3,538,000,000 (nontax revenue 68.4%, of which
property income 19.4%, commercial receipts 7.7%; tax revenue 31.6%, of
which corporate income tax 22.8%, import duty 2.8%). Expenditures: B$3,-
649,000,000 (current expenditure 62.1%; development expenditure 19.8%;
charged expenditure 12.6%).
Public debt (external, outstanding): none.
Tourism (1990): receipts from visitors U.S.$35,000,000; expenditures by na-
tionals abroad, n.a.
Production (metric tons except as noted). Agriculture, forestry, fishing (1995):
vegetables and melons 8,100, fruits (excluding melons) 5,000, eggs 3,300, cassava 1,000, rice 800, pineapples 680; livestock (number of live animals) 5,000
pigs, 5,000 buffalo, 5,000 goats, 1,500 cattle, 3,000,000 chickens; roundwood
295,000 cu m; fish catch (1993) 1,768. Mining and quarrying (1992): other
than petroleum and natural gas, none except sand and gravel for construction. Manufacturing (1993): gasoline 161,000; diesel oils 130,000; fuel oil
53,000; jet fuels 50,000; kerosene 3,000. Construction (value in B$'000,000;
1989): residential 26.2; nonresidential 5.1. Energy production (consumption):
electricity (kW-hr; 1993) 1,285,000,000 (1,285,000,000); coal, none (none);
crude petroleum (barrels; 1993) 57,758,000 (1,732,000); petroleum products
(metric tons; 1993) 836,000 (832,000); natural gas (cu m; 1993) 8,548,000,000
(1,867,000,000).
Population economically active (1991): total 111,955; activity rate of total
population 43.0% (participation rates: ages 15–64, 67.6%; female 32.9%;
unemployed 4.7%).

Price and earnings indexes (1990 = 100)

	1989	1990	1991	1992	1993	1994	1995
Consumer price index	98.0	100.0	101.6	102.9	107.3	109.9	116.5
Monthly earnings index[4]	...	...	76.9	87.5	...	...	...

Household income and expenditure. Average household size (1991) 5.8; income per household: n.a.; sources of income: n.a.; expenditure (1990): food
38.7%, transportation and communications 19.9%, housing 18.6%, clothing
6.4%, other 16.4%.

Gross national product (at current market prices; 1994): U.S.$3,975,000,000
(U.S.$14,240 per capita).

Structure of gross domestic product and labour force

	1995 in value B$'000,000	1995 % of total value	1991 labour force	1991 % of labour force
Agriculture	188	2.7	2,162	1.9
Mining Manufacturing }	2,756	39.0	9,397	8.4
Construction	405	5.7	14,145	12.6
Public utilities	74	1.1	2,223	2.0
Transportation and communications	299	4.2	5,392	4.8
Trade	596	8.4	15,404	13.8
Finance	549	7.8	5,807	5.2
Services	2,390	33.8	52,121	46.6
Other	–188	–2.7	5,304[5]	4.7[5]
TOTAL	7,069	100.0	111,955	100.0

Land use (1994): forested 85.4%; meadows and pastures 1.1%; agricultural
and under permanent cultivation 1.3%; other 12.2%.

Foreign trade

Balance of trade (current prices)

	1989	1990	1991	1992	1993	1994
B$'000,000	+1,998	+2,197	+2,417	+1,946	+1,672	+866
% of total	37.4%	37.7%	39.2%	33.7%	29.3%	14.7%

Imports (1994): B$2,517,000,000 (machinery and transport equipment 40.0%,
manufactured goods 21.5%, miscellaneous manufactured articles 17.2%,
food and live animals 11.2%, chemicals 4.9%, crude materials 2.3%, beverages and tobacco 2.1%). *Major import sources:* ASEAN 47.0%, of which
Singapore 28.9%, Malaysia 11.9%; EEC 17.3%; United States 11.3%; Japan
9.2%.
Exports (1994): B$3,383,200,000 (crude petroleum 45.8%, natural gas 41.8%,
petroleum products 3.1%). *Major export destinations:* Japan 54.6%; ASEAN
26.1%, of which Thailand 11.0%, Singapore 10.6%; South Korea 13.7%;
Taiwan 2.7%.

Transport and communications

Transport. Railroads (1993)[6]: length 12 mi, 19 km. Roads (1992): total length
1,502 mi, 2,417 km (paved 51%). Vehicles (1994): passenger cars 135,641;
trucks and buses 14,016. Merchant marine (1992): vessels (100 gross tons
and over) 51; total deadweight tonnage 349,718. Marine transport (1992):
cargo loaded 20,411,000 metric tons, cargo unloaded 1,377,000 metric tons.
Air transport (1995): passenger-mi 1,494,000,000, passenger-km 2,404,000,-
000; short ton-mi cargo 75,225,000, metric ton-km cargo 109,826,000; airports
(1996) with scheduled flights 1.
Communications. Daily newspapers (1993): total number 1; total circulation
30,000; circulation per 1,000 population 9.2. Radio (1995): total number of
receivers 120,000 (1 per 2.4 persons). Television (1995): total number of
receivers 90,000 (1 per 3.2 persons). Telephones (main lines; 1993): 55,200
(1 per 5.1 persons).

Education and health

Education (1993)

	schools	teachers	students	student/ teacher ratio
Primary (age 5–11)	158	2,646	41,134	15.5
Secondary (age 12–20)	237	1,948	26,199	13.4
Voc., teacher tr.	6[7]	389	2,011	5.2
Higher[7]	4	289	1,372	4.7

Educational attainment (1991). Percentage of population age 25 and over
having: no formal schooling 17.0%; primary education 43.3%; secondary
26.3%; postsecondary and higher 12.9%; not stated 0.5%. *Literacy* (1991):
total population age 15 and over literate 149,901 (87.8%); males literate
84,425 (92.5%); females literate 65,476 (82.5%).
Health (1993): physicians 197 (1 per 1,398 persons); hospital beds 967 (1 per
285 persons); infant mortality rate per 1,000 live births (1996) 8.0.
Food (1992): daily per capita caloric intake 2,745 (vegetable products 80%,
animal products 20%); 123% of FAO recommended minimum requirement.

Military

Total active duty personnel (1995): 4,900[8] (army 79.6%, navy 14.3%, air force
6.1%). *Military expenditure as percentage of GNP* (1994): 7.9% (world 3.0%);
per capita expenditure U.S.$1,086.

---

[1]A nonelective 21-member body advises the sultan on legislative matters. [2]All official
documents that must be published by law in Malay are, however, also required to
be issued in an official English version as well. [3]1988 metropolitan area population
estimate. [4]Nonagricultural sectors only; 1985 = 100. [5]Mostly unemployed. [6]Privately
owned. [7]1992. [8]All services form part of the army.

Bulgaria

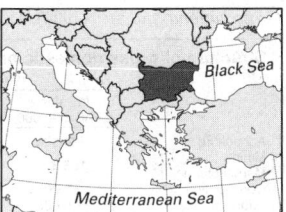
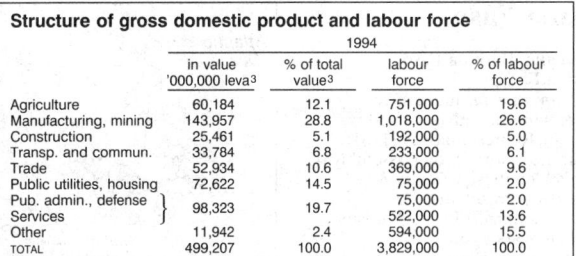

Official name: Republika Bŭlgaria
  (Republic of Bulgaria).
Form of government: unitary multiparty
  republic with one legislative body
  (Parliament [240]).
Chief of state: President.
Head of government: Prime Minister.
Capital: Sofia.
Official language: Bulgarian.
Official religion: none[1].
Monetary unit: 1 lev (leva) = 100 stotinki;
  valuation (Oct. 11, 1996)
  1 U.S.$ = 216.95 leva; 1 £ = 341.76 leva.

Area and population		area		population
				1995
Regions	Capitals	sq mi	sq km	estimate
Burgas	Burgas	5,659	14,657	849,046
Khaskovo	Khaskovo	5,364	13,892	901,572
Lovech	Lovech	5,849	15,150	999,051
Montana	Mikhaylovgrad	4,095	10,607	621,406
Plovdiv	Plovdiv	5,262	13,628	1,219,681
Ruse	Ruse	4,186	10,842	762,984
Sofiya	Sofia (Sofiya)	7,328	18,978	973,870
Varna	Varna	4,606	11,929	908,065
City Commune				
Sofiya	Sofia (Sofiya)	506	1,311	1,191,743
TOTAL		42,855	110,994	8,427,418

Demography

Population (1996): 8,366,000.
Density (1996): persons per sq mi 195.2, persons per sq km 75.4.
Urban-rural (1995): urban 67.8%; rural 32.2%.
Sex distribution (1995): male 49.00%; female 51.00%.
Age breakdown (1995): under 15, 18.1%; 15–29, 21.2%; 30–44, 20.7%; 45–59,
  18.9%; 60–74, 16.5%; 75 and over, 4.6%.
Population projection: (2000) 8,212,000; (2010) 7,892,000.
Doubling time: not applicable; population is declining.
Ethnic composition (1992): Bulgarian 85.7%; Turkish 9.4%; Gypsy 3.6%;
  other 1.3%.
Religious affiliation (1992)[2]: Bulgarian Orthodox 85.7%; Sunnī Muslim 12.1%;
  Shīʿī Muslim 1.0%; other 1.2%.
Major cities (1995): Sofia 1,116,454; Plovdiv 346,330; Varna 304,499; Burgas
  199,869; Ruse 168,609.

Vital statistics

Birth rate per 1,000 population (1995): 8.6 (world avg. 25.0); (1994) legitimate
  75.5%; illegitimate 24.5%.
Death rate per 1,000 population (1995): 13.6 (world avg. 9.3).
Natural increase rate per 1,000 population (1995): −5.0 (world avg. 15.7).
Total fertility rate (avg. births per childbearing woman; 1994): 1.5.
Marriage rate per 1,000 population (1994): 4.5.
Divorce rate per 1,000 population (1994): 0.9.
Life expectancy at birth (1995): male 68.9 years; female 75.3 years.
Major causes of death per 100,000 population (1994): diseases of the circula-
  tory system 824.4; malignant neoplasms (cancers) 192.8; accidents, poisoning,
  and violence 69.5; diseases of the respiratory system 64.4; diseases of the
  digestive system 42.0; endocrine and metabolic disorders 22.2.

National economy

Budget (1994). Revenue: 210,117,000,000 leva (tax 64.7%, social insurance
  23.7%, nontax revenue 11.6%). Expenditures: 244,312,100,000 leva (foreign
  debt service 29.9%, pensions and social insurance 27.7%, education 10.3%,
  health services 8.8%, economic development 6.6%, other 16.7%).
Public debt (external, outstanding; 1994): U.S.$9,014,000,000.
Tourism (1994): receipts from visitors U.S.$358,000,000; expenditures by na-
  tionals abroad U.S.$242,000,000.
Production (metric tons except as noted). Agriculture, forestry, fishing (1995):
  wheat 3,523,000, corn (maize) 1,200,000, barley 900,000, sunflower seeds
  650,000, potatoes 476,000, grapes 450,000, tomatoes 443,000; livestock (number of live animals) 3,117,000 sheep, 1,722,000 pigs, 745,000 goats, 673,000
  cattle, 338,000 beehives; roundwood 3,547,000 cu m; fish catch (1993) 21,-
  585. Mining and quarrying (1995): iron ore 285,000. Manufacturing (value
  of production in '000,000 leva; 1994): chemical and oil processing 109,592;
  food, beverages, and tobacco 105,208; metallurgy and ore mining 49,682;
  machine and metalworking 49,682; electronic and electrical equipment 23,-
  687; other goods 103,747. Construction (1994): residential 727,000 sq m.
  Energy production: electricity (kW-hr; 1994) 39,306,000,000; coal (metric
  tons; 1994) 30,833,000; crude petroleum (barrels; 1995) 343,100; petroleum
  products (metric tons; 1993) 4,010; natural gas (cu m; 1995) 60,094,000.
Household income and expenditure. Average household size (1992) 2.8; income
  per household (1994) 128,494 leva (U.S.$1,916); sources of income (1994):
  wages and salaries 34.7%, self-employment in agriculture 23.6%, transfer
  payments 14.8%; expenditure (1994): food 41.4%, housing and energy 7.8%,
  transportation 7.4%, clothing 6.8%, household durable goods 4.2%, health
  care 2.9%, education and culture 2.8%.
Gross national product (at current market prices; 1994): U.S.$10,255,000,000
  (U.S.$1,217 per capita).

Structure of gross domestic product and labour force				
	1994			
	in value '000,000 leva[3]	% of total value[3]	labour force	% of labour force
Agriculture	60,184	12.1	751,000	19.6
Manufacturing, mining	143,957	28.8	1,018,000	26.6
Construction	25,461	5.1	192,000	5.0
Transp. and commun.	33,784	6.8	233,000	6.1
Trade	52,934	10.6	369,000	9.6
Public utilities, housing	72,622	14.5	75,000	2.0
Pub. admin., defense }	98,323	19.7	75,000	2.0
Services			522,000	13.6
Other	11,942	2.4	594,000	15.5
TOTAL	499,207	100.0	3,829,000	100.0

Population economically active (1992): total 3,932,468; activity rate of total
  population 46.3% (participation rates: ages 16–59 [male], 16–54 [female]
  70.2%; female 48.4%; unemployed 16.4%).

Price and earnings indexes (1990 = 100)							
	1989	1990	1991	1992	1993	1994	1995
Consumer price index	80.8	100.0	438.5	786.6	1,228	2,296	3,722
Monthly earnings index	75.9	100.0	265.8	567.5	895.7	1,337	...

Land use (1994): forested 35.0%; meadows and pastures 18.7%; agricultural
  and under permanent cultivation 38.2%; other 8.1%.

Foreign trade

Balance of trade (current prices)						
	1990	1991	1992	1993	1994	1995
'000,000 leva	+ 244.6	+ 12,235.9	+ 1,049.1	− 20,245	− 8,652	− 3,935
% of total	1.2%	11.9%	0.6%	9.3%	1.8%	0.5%

Imports (1995): 339,402,300,000 leva (1994; fuels, mineral raw materials, and
  metals 36.8%; machinery and equipment 21.5%; chemical products and rubber 10.8%; food products 8.8%). *Major import sources* (1994): C.I.S. 33.1%;
  Germany 12.6%; Italy 5.8%; Greece 4.7%; Austria 2.8%.
Exports (1995): 343,337,700,000 leva (1994; fuels, minerals, and metals 30.4%;
  chemicals and rubber 16.6%; food and beverages 14.8%; machinery and
  equipment 12.2%). *Major export destinations* (1994): C.I.S. 17.0%; Germany
  8.4%; Italy 8.2%; Greece 6.9%.

Transport and communications

Transport. Railroads (1995): track length 4,044 mi, 6,508 km; passenger-mi
  2,916,000,000, passenger-km 4,693,000,000; short ton-mi cargo 5,887,000,000,
  metric ton-km cargo 8,595,000,000. Roads (1994): length 22,935 mi, 36,911
  km (paved 92%). Vehicles (1994): cars 1,587,873; trucks and buses 214,426.
  Merchant marine (1994): vessels (100 gross tons and over) 238; deadweight
  tonnage 2,604,000. Air transport (1994): passenger-mi 2,239,000,000, passenger-km 3,604,000,000; short ton-mi cargo 11,395,000, metric ton-km cargo
  16,637,000; airports (1996) with scheduled flights 3.
Communications. Daily newspapers (1992): total number 46; total circulation
  1,464,000; circulation per 1,000 population 174. Radio (1996): 3,920,000 receivers (1 per 2.1 persons). Television (1996): 3,127,000 receivers (1 per 2.7
  persons). Telephones (main lines; 1994): 2,087,000 (1 per 4.0 persons).

Education and health

Education (1994–95)				student/
	schools	teachers	students	teacher ratio
Primary (age 6–14) }	3,359	70,487	980,491	13.9
Secondary (age 15–17) }				
Voc., teacher tr.	522	19,019	216,595	11.3
Higher	88	24,274	221,207	9.1

Educational attainment (1992). Percentage of population age 7 and over having: no formal schooling 2.0%; incomplete primary education 6.8%; primary
  46.2%; secondary 33.6%; higher 11.4%. *Literacy* (1980): total population age
  15 and over literate 95.5%.
Health (1994): physicians 28,094 (1 per 300 persons); hospital beds 88,251 (1
  per 95 persons); infant mortality rate per 1,000 live births 14.8.
Food (1992): daily per capita caloric intake 2,831 (vegetable products 74%,
  animal products 26%); 113% of FAO recommended minimum requirement.

Military

Total active duty personnel (1995): 101,900 (army 75.9%, navy 2.9%, air force
  21.2%). *Military expenditure as percentage of GNP* (1994): 9.8% (world 3.0%);
  per capita expenditure U.S.$119.

---

[1]Bulgaria has no official religion; the 1991 constitution, however, refers to Eastern
Orthodoxy as the "traditional" religion. [2]Census data reflect the traditional religious
identity of Bulgaria but apparently disregard the nonreligious, who may exceed half
the adult population. [3]Data are based on estimates.

Burkina Faso

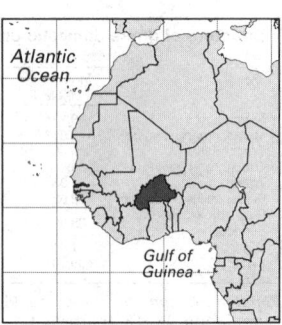

Official name: Burkina Faso (Burkina Faso).
Form of government: multiparty republic with one advisory body (House of Representatives [178[1]]) and one legislative body (Assembly of People's Deputies [107]).
Chief of state: President.
Head of government: Prime Minister.
Capital: Ouagadougou.
Official language: French.
Official religion: none.
Monetary unit: 1 CFA franc (CFAF) = 100 centimes; valuation (Oct. 11, 1996) 1 U.S.$ = CFAF 518.24; 1 £ = CFAF 816.38.

Area and population		area		population
				1991
Provinces	Capitals	sq mi	sq km	estimate
Bam	Kongoussi	1,551	4,017	173,516
Bazéga	Kombissiri	2,051	5,313	352,104
Bougouriba	Diébougou	2,736	7,087	242,986
Boulgou	Tenkodogo	3,488	9,033	465,845
Boulkiemde	Koudougou	1,598	4,138	393,900
Comoé	Banfora	7,102	18,393	296,083
Ganzourgou	Zorgho	1,578	4,087	223,555
Gnagna	Bogandé	3,320	8,600	272,203
Gourma	Fada N'Gourma	10,275	26,613	350,336
Houet	Bobo-Dioulasso	6,438	16,672	724,803
Kadiogo	Ouagadougou	451	1,169	652,377
Kénédougou	Orodara	3,207	8,307	162,010
Kossi	Nouna	5,088	13,177	389,360
Kouritenga	Koupéla	628	1,627	227,060
Mouhoun	Dédougou	4,032	10,442	329,115
Nahouri	Pô	1,484	3,843	119,144
Namentenga	Boulsa	2,994	7,755	214,564
Oubritenga	Ziniaré	1,812	4,693	328,682
Oudalan	Gorom Gorom	3,879	10,046	123,495
Passoré	Yako	1,575	4,078	232,278
Poni	Gaoua	4,000	10,361	258,647
Sanguie	Réo	1,994	5,165	234,079
Sanmatenga	Kaya	3,557	9,213	404,563
Sèno	Dori	5,202	13,473	269,892
Sissili	Léo	5,303	13,736	297,598
Soum	Djibo	5,154	13,350	217,972
Sourou	Tougan	3,663	9,487	313,355
Tapoa	Diapaga	5,707	14,780	187,785
Yatenga	Ouahigouya	4,746	12,292	558,318
Zoundwéogo	Manga	1,333	3,453	175,166
TOTAL		105,946	274,400	9,190,791

Demography

Population (1996): 10,615,000.
Density (1996): persons per sq mi 100.2, persons per sq km 38.7.
Urban-rural (1991): urban 14.0%; rural 86.0%.
Sex distribution (1995): male 49.54%; female 50.46%.
Age breakdown (1995): under 15, 44.9%; 15–29, 25.8%; 30–44, 15.2%; 45–59, 9.1%; 60–74, 4.2%; 75 and over, 0.8%.
Population projection: (2000) 11,884,000; (2010) 15,549,000.
Doubling time: 24 years.
Ethnic composition (1983): Mossi 47.9%; Mande 8.8%; Fulani 8.3%; Lobi 6.9%; Bobo 6.8%; Senufo 5.3%; Grosi 5.1%; Gurma 4.8%; Tuareg 3.3%.
Religious affiliation (1980): traditional beliefs 44.8%; Muslim 43.0%; Christian 12.2%, of which Roman Catholic 9.8%, Protestant 2.4%.
Major cities (1985): Ouagadougou 441,514; Bobo-Dioulasso 228,668; Koudougou 51,926; Ouahigouya 38,902; Banfora 35,319.

Vital statistics

Birth rate per 1,000 population (1995): 47.6 (world avg. 25.0).
Death rate per 1,000 population (1995): 19.7 (world avg. 9.3).
Natural increase rate per 1,000 population (1995): 27.9 (world avg. 15.7).
Total fertility rate (avg. births per childbearing woman; 1995): 6.9.
Life expectancy at birth (1995): male 44.5 years; female 43.8 years.
Major causes of death (ages 15 and under; 1991): malaria, respiratory diseases, intestinal infectious diseases, meningitis.

National economy

Budget (1994). Revenue: CFAF 199,797,000,000 (1993; import duties 23.4%, personal income taxes 18.8%, sales taxes 14.7%, export duties 11.6%). Expenditures: CFAF 234,866,000,000 (1993; wages and salaries 28.8%, goods and services 10.6%, debt service 6.8%).
Production (metric tons except as noted). Agriculture, forestry, fishing (1995): sorghum 1,232,000, millet 831,000, sugarcane 400,000, corn (maize) 350,000, peanuts (groundnuts) 203,000, seed cotton 177,000, pulses 62,000, rice 61,000, sweet potatoes 20,000, cassava 5,000, sesame 2,000; livestock (number of live animals) 7,242,000 goats, 5,800,000 sheep, 4,350,000 cattle, 19,300,000 chickens; roundwood (1994) 9,591,000 cu m; fish catch (1993) 7,000. Mining and quarrying (1994): gold 731 kg[2]; silver 100 kg[3]. Manufacturing (value added in CFAF '000,000; 1992): beer and soft drinks 6,405; cotton 5,382; sugar 5,172; cigarettes 2,095[4]; soap 1,843; textiles and clothing 1,294; flour 1,287; bicycles and mopeds 1,096; batteries 894. Construction (value added in CFAF; 1993): 42,400,000,000. Energy production (consumption): electricity (kW-hr; 1994) 216,000,000 (216,000,000); crude petroleum, none (n.a.); petroleum products (metric tons; 1994) none (309,000).

Gross national product (1994): U.S.$2,982,000,000 (U.S.$300 per capita).

Structure of gross domestic product and labour force				
	1994		1991	
	in value CFAF '000,000	% of total value	labour force	% of labour force
Agriculture	324,100	32.1	4,068,000	84.1
Mining	} 198,300	} 19.7		
Manufacturing			251,000	5.2
Construction	53,000	5.3		
Public utilities	9,000	0.9		
Transp. and commun.	38,000	3.8		
Trade	119,500	11.8		
Finance	...	...	517,000	10.7
Pub. admin., defense	} 218,600	} 21.7		
Services				
Other	47,900[5]	4.7[5]	...	...
TOTAL	1,008,400	100.0	4,836,000	100.0

Tourism: receipts (1994) U.S.$22,000,000; expenditures (1993) U.S.$35,000,000.
Public debt (external, outstanding; 1994): U.S.$1,037,000,000.
Population economically active (1991): total 4,836,000; activity rate 52.2% (participation rates [1985]: over age 15, 83.0%; female 49.1%; unemployed 0.9%).

Price and earnings indexes (1990 = 100)							
	1989	1990	1991	1992	1993	1994	1995
Consumer price index	100.8	100.0	102.5	100.5	101.1	126.5	135.8
Hourly earnings index[6]	100.0	100.0	100.0	100.0	...	...	...

Household income and expenditure. Average household size (1985) 6.2; average annual income per household CFAF 303,000 (U.S.$640); sources of income: n.a.; expenditure (1985)[7]: food 38.7%, transportation 18.6%, electricity and fuel 13.7%, beverages 9.0%, health 5.2%, housing 5.1%.
Land use (1994): forested 50.5%; meadows and pastures 21.9%; agricultural and under permanent cultivation 13.0%; other 14.6%.

Foreign trade

Balance of trade (current prices)						
	1990	1991	1992	1993	1994	1995
CFAF '000,000	−72.47	+137.03	+124.82	+103.79	+24.75	+53.72
% of total	46.7%	34.2%	35.7%	29.8%	6.8%	11.2%

Imports (1994): CFAF 202,700,000,000 (capital equipment 21.8%, food products 18.7%, raw materials 10.9%, petroleum products 9.6%). *Major import sources* (1991): France 24.4%; Côte d'Ivoire 19.4%; United States 4.9%; Japan 4.2%; The Netherlands 4.0%; Nigeria 2.8%.
Exports (1994): CFAF 125,200,000,000 (raw cotton 26.2%, live animals 17.8%, gold 7.7%, hides and skins 7.4%). *Major export destinations* (1991): Japan 20.3%; France 13.4%; Côte d'Ivoire 11.2%; Thailand 8.3%; Taiwan 6.2%; Togo 2.9%.

Transport and communications

Transport. Railroads (1984)[8]: route length[9] 386 mi, 622 km; passenger-km 679,790,000; metric ton-km cargo 469,675,000. Roads (1995): total length 7,771 mi, 12,506 km (paved 16%). Vehicles (1995): passenger cars 16,800; trucks and buses 17,222. Merchant marine: none. Air transport (1993): passenger-km 217,154,000; metric ton-km cargo 34,204,000; airports (1996) 2.
Communications. Daily newspapers (1995): total number 4; total circulation 17,000[10]; circulation per 1,000 population 1.7[10]. Radio (1995): 225,000 receivers (1 per 46 persons). Television (1995): 45,500 receivers (1 per 227 persons). Telephones (main lines; 1993): 21,900 (1 per 447 persons).

Education and health

Education (1992–93)				
	schools	teachers	students	student/ teacher ratio
Primary	2,741	9,412	562,644	59.7
Secondary	173[11]	2,419[11]	107,024	25.1[11]
Vocational	22[11]	493	8,329	16.9
Higher[11]	9	437	7,387	16.9

Educational attainment (1985). Percentage of population age 10 and over having: no formal schooling 86.1%; some primary 7.3%; general secondary 2.2%; specialized secondary and postsecondary 3.8%; other 0.6%. *Literacy* (1995): percentage of total population age 15 and over literate 18.2%; males literate 29.5%; females literate 9.2%.
Health (1991): physicians 341 (1 per 27,158 persons); hospital beds 5,041 (1 per 1,837 persons); infant mortality rate (1990–95) 130.0.
Food (1992): daily per capita caloric intake 2,387 (vegetable products 96%, animal products 4%); 101% of FAO recommended minimum requirement.

Military

Total active duty personnel (1996): 5,800 (army 96.6%, air force 3.4%). *Military expenditure as percentage of GNP* (1994): 2.4% (world 3.0%); per capita expenditure U.S.$4.

[1]Includes 114 elected seats chosen by traditional and religious authorities and 64 seats appointed by the government. [2]Officially marketed gold only; does not include substantial illegal production. [3]1992. [4]1990. [5]Includes indirect taxes less imputed bank service charges and subsidies. [6]January 1; index refers to the *S.M.I.G.* (*salaire minimum interprofessionnel garanti*), a form of minimum professional wage. [7]Weights of consumer price index components; Ouagadougou only. [8]Passenger-km and metric ton-km cargo figures are based on traffic between Abidjan, Côte d'Ivoire, and Ouagadougou. [9]1995. [10]Circulation for 3 newspapers only. [11]1991–92.

Burundi

Official name: Republika y'u Burundi
(Rundi); République du Burundi
(French) (Republic of Burundi).
Form of government: military regime
with one legislative house (National
Assembly [81])[1].
Head of state and government:
President, assisted by Prime Minister.
Capital: Bujumbura.
Official languages: Rundi; French.
Official religion: none.
Monetary unit: ,1 Burundi franc
(FBu) = 100 centimes; valuation (Oct.
11, 1996) 1 U.S.$ = FBu 220.46;
1 £ = FBu 347.29.

Area and population

Provinces	Capitals	area sq mi	area sq km	population 1990 census
Bubanza	Bubanza	420	1,089	222,953
Bujumbura	Bujumbura	509	1,319	608,931
Bururi	Bururi	952	2,465	385,490
Cankuzo	Cankuzo	759	1,965	142,707
Cibitoke	Cibitoke	631	1,636	279,843
Gitega	Gitega	764	1,979	565,174
Karuzi	Karuzi	563	1,457	287,905
Kayanza	Kayanza	476	1,233	443,116
Kirundo	Kirundo	658	1,703	401,103
Makamba	Makamba	757	1,960	223,799
Muramvya	Muramvya	593	1,535	441,653
Muyinga	Muyinga	709	1,836	373,382
Ngozi	Ngozi	569	1,474	482,246
Rutana	Rutana	756	1,959	195,834
Ruyigi	Ruyigi	903	2,339	238,567
TOTAL LAND AREA		10,019	25,949	
INLAND WATER		721	1,867	
TOTAL		10,740	27,816	5,292,793[2]

Demography

Population (1996): 5,943,000[3].
Density (1996)[4]: persons per sq mi 593.2, persons per sq km 229.0.
Urban-rural (1990): urban 6.3%; rural 93.7%.
Sex distribution (1990): male 48.63%; female 51.37%.
Age breakdown (1990): under 15, 46.4%; 15–29, 25.3%; 30–44, 15.4%; 45–59,
7.0%; 60–74, 4.0%; 75 and over, 1.7%; not determined 0.2%.
Population projection: (2000) 6,493,000; (2010) 8,229,000.
Doubling time: 25 years.
Ethnic composition (1983): Rundi 97.4%, of which Hutu 81.9%, Tutsi 13.5%;
Twa Pygmy 1.0%; other 1.6%.
Religious affiliation (1990): Roman Catholic 65.1%; Protestant 13.8%; Muslim
1.6%; nonreligious 18.6%; traditional beliefs 0.3%; other 0.6%.
Major cities (1990): Bujumbura 236,334; Gitega 20,708; Bururi 15,816; Ngozi
14,511; Cibitoke 8,280.

Vital statistics

Birth rate per 1,000 population (1995): 43.8 (world avg. 25.0).
Death rate per 1,000 population (1995): 15.2 (world avg. 9.3).
Natural increase rate per 1,000 population (1995): 28.6 (world avg. 15.7).
Total fertility rate (avg. births per childbearing woman; 1995): 6.6.
Marriage rate per 1,000 population: n.a.
Divorce rate per 1,000 population: n.a.
Life expectancy at birth (1995): male 48.7 years; female 50.7 years.
Major causes of death: n.a.; however, major health problems include malaria,
influenza, diarrheal diseases, measles, and AIDS.

National economy

Budget (1995). Revenue: FBu 59,600,000,000 (customs duties 37.1%, excise
duties 22.6%, income tax 19.2%, taxes on goods and services 14.6%, administrative receipts 2.4%). Expenditures: FBu 69,100,000,000 (wages and
salaries 27.5%, goods and services 18.4%, subsidies and transfers 9.8%,
public debt 6.3%).
Tourism (1994): receipts from visitors U.S.$3,000,000; expenditures by nation-
als abroad U.S.$4,000,000.
Production (metric tons except as noted). Agriculture, forestry, fishing (1995):
bananas 1,421,000, sweet potatoes 674,000, cassavas 501,000, dry beans
319,000, corn (maize) 153,000, sugarcane 138,000, yams and taros 110,000,
sorghum 66,000, potatoes 41,567, rice 27,000, coffee 26,000, millet 14,000,
peanuts (groundnuts) 13,000, wheat 9,000; livestock (number of live animals)
920,000 goats, 420,000 cattle, 350,000 sheep, 4,000,000 chickens; roundwood
(1994) 4,741,000 cu m; fish catch (1993) 24,100. Mining and quarrying (1991):
peat 10,026; kaolin clay 6,682; lime 86; gold 804 troy oz. Manufacturing
(1994): beer 1,382,670 hectolitres; carbonated beverages 201,400 hectolitres;
cigarettes 584,580,000 units; blankets 248,438 units; footwear 74,890 pairs.
Construction: n.a. Energy production (consumption): electricity (kW-hr;
1993) 117,000,000 (141,000,000); coal, none (n.a.); crude petroleum, none
(n.a.); petroleum products (metric tons; 1993) none (65,000); natural gas,
none (n.a.); peat (metric tons; 1993) 12,000 (12,000).
Land use (1994): forested 12.7%; meadows and pastures 38.6%; agricultural
and under permanent cultivation 45.9%; other 2.8%.
Gross national product (at current market prices; 1994): U.S.$904,000,000
(U.S.$150 per capita).

Structure of gross domestic product and labour force

	1995 in value FBu '000,000	1995 % of total value	1990 labour force	1990 % of labour force
Agriculture	126,664	47.8	2,574,443	93.1
Mining	} 1,296	0.5	1,419	—
Public utilities			1,672	0.1
Manufacturing	27,855	10.5	33,867	1.2
Construction	11,436	4.3	19,737	0.7
Transportation and communications	8,892	3.4	8,504	0.3
Trade	8,709	3.3	25,822	0.9
Finance	...	...	2,005	0.1
Pub. admin., defense	37,866	14.3 }	85,191	3.1
Services	4,648	1.7 }		
Other	37,623[5]	14.2[5]	13,270	0.5
TOTAL	264,990[2]	100.0	2,765,945[2]	100.0

Public debt (external, outstanding; 1994): U.S.$1,064,000,000.
Population economically active (1991): total 2,779,777; activity rate of total
population 52.9% (participation rates: ages 15–64, 91.4%; female 52.6%;
unemployed, n.a.).

Price and earnings indexes (1990 = 100)

	1989	1990	1991	1992	1993	1994	1995
Consumer price index	93.5	100.0	109.0	113.9	124.9	143.5	171.1
Earnings index	...	...	...	...	...	...	...

Household income and expenditure. Average household size (1990) 4.6; income per household: n.a.; sources of income: n.a.; expenditure[6]: food 59.6%,
clothing and footwear 11.1%, furniture and household goods 6.0%, energy
and water 5.8%, housing 4.4%, other 13.1%.

Foreign trade

Balance of trade (current prices)

	1990	1991	1992	1993	1994	1995
FBu '000,000	−26,583	−28,144	−30,751	−26,417	−22,603	−24,018
% of total	51.0%	45.8%	50.0%	44.0%	29.9%	31.1%

Imports (1995): FBu 52,082,000,000 (1994; machinery and transport equipment 21.3%, food and food products 17.9%, petroleum products 8.2%,
pharmaceutical products 6.4%). *Major import sources:* Belgium-Luxembourg
14.8%; France 9.2%; Germany 8.8%; Japan 6.1%; United States 5.7%; The
Netherlands 4.5%; Kenya 4.3%.
Exports (1995): FBu 28,872,000,000 (coffee 80.7%, tea 7.8%, cotton 1.6%,
animal hides and skins 1.2%). *Major export destinations:* Germany 21.6%;
Belgium-Luxembourg 17.6%; France 10.9%; United States 6.7%; Rwanda
3.6%; United Kingdom 3.6%; The Netherlands 2.3%; Zaire 1.6%.

Transport and communications

Transport. Railroads: none. Roads (1992): total length 8,993 mi, 14,473 km
(paved 7%). Vehicles (1992): passenger cars 14,483; trucks and other vehicles 14,914. Merchant marine (1979): vessels (100 gross tons and over)
1; total gross tonnage 385. Air transport (1994)[7]: passenger arrivals 28,-
762, departures 33,750; cargo loaded 1,760 short tons (1,597 metric tons),
unloaded 14,841 short tons (13,463 metric tons); airports (1996) with
scheduled flights 1.
Communications. Daily newspapers (1995): total number 1; total circulation
20,000; circulation per 1,000 population 3.4. Radio (1995): total number of
receivers 300,000 (1 per 20 persons). Television (1995): total number of
receivers 4,500 (1 per 1,316 persons). Telephones (main lines; 1993): 15,600
(1 per 363 persons).

Education and health

Education (1992–93)

	schools	teachers	students	student/ teacher ratio
Primary (age 6–11)	1,418	10,400	651,086	62.6
Secondary (age 12–18)	113[8]	2,562	55,713	21.7
Higher	8	556	4,256	7.6

Educational attainment: n.a. *Literacy* (1995): percentage of total population
age 15 and over literate 35.3%; males literate 49.7%; females literate 22.5%.
Health (1990): physicians 168 (1 per 31,777 persons); hospital beds 10,370 (1
per 515 persons); infant mortality rate per 1,000 live births (1995) 104.0.
Food (1992): daily per capita caloric intake 1,941 (vegetable products 97%,
animal products 3%); 83% of FAO recommended minimum requirement.

Military

Total active duty personnel (1995): 12,600 (army 99.2%, air force 0.8%). *Military expenditure as percentage of GNP* (1994): 3.7% (world 3.0%); per capita
expenditure U.S.$5.

[1]The new military government from July 1996 reinstated the National Assembly in
September 1996. [2]Detail does not add to total given because of rounding. [3]Population
is not adjusted for casualties or refugees of the recent civil war. [4]Based on land area.
[5]Indirect taxes less subsidies. [6]Weights of consumer price index components. [7]Figures
for Bujumbura airport only. [8]1990–91.

Cambodia

Official name: Preah Reach Ana
  Pak Kampuchea (Kingdom of
  Cambodia)[1].
Form of government: constitutional
  monarchy with one legislative house
  (National Assembly [120]).
Chief of state: King.
Heads of government: First Prime
  Minister assisted by Second Prime
  Minister.
Capital: Phnom Penh.
Official language: Khmer.
Official religion: Buddhism.
Monetary unit: 1 riel = 100 sen;
  valuation (Oct. 11, 1996)
  1 U.S.$ = 2,300 riels; 1 £ = 3,623 riels.

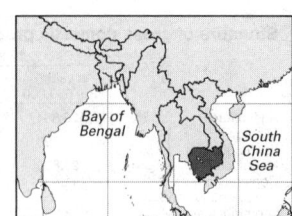

Area and population

Provinces	Capitals	area sq mi	area sq km	population 1987 estimate
Bântéay Méan Cheăy	...	2	2	2
Bătdâmbâng	Bătdâmbâng	7,353[2]	19,044[2]	837,000[2]
Kâmpóng Cham	Kâmpóng Cham	4,053	10,498	1,244,000
Kâmpóng Chhnăng	Kâmpóng Chhnăng	2,131	5,520	257,000
Kâmpóng Spœ	Kâmpóng Spœ	2,709	7,016	396,000
Kâmpóng Thum	Kâmpóng Thum	4,730	12,251	441,000
Kâmpôt	Kâmpôt	3,808	9,862	412,000
Kândal	...	1,472	3,813	838,000
Kaôh Kŏng	Krŏng Kaôh Kŏng	4,301	11,140	30,000
Krâchéh	Krâchéh	4,283	11,094	182,000
Môndôl Kiri	Senmonorom	5,517	14,288	18,000
Poŭthĭsăt	Poŭthĭsăt	4,900	12,692	204,000
Preăh Vihéar	Phnum Tbéng Meanchey	5,541	14,350	80,000
Prey Vêng	Prey Vêng	1,885	4,883	782,000
Rôtânăh Kiri	Lumphăt	4,163	10,782	52,000
Siĕmréab[3]	Siĕmréab	4,207	10,897	555,000
Stœng Trêng	Stœng Trêng	4,328	11,229	46,000
Svay Riĕng	Svay Riĕng	1,145	2,966	340,000
Takêv	Takêv	1,474	3,818	618,000
Municipalities				
TOTAL LAND AREA		68,045	176,238	
Phnom Penh		18	46	564,000
Preăh Seihânŭ		27	69	61,000
INLAND WATER		2,192	5,678	
TOTAL		70,238[4]	181,916	7,957,000

Demography

Population (1996): 10,081,000.
Density (1996)[5]: persons per sq mi 148.1, persons per sq km 57.2.
Urban-rural (1995): urban 21%; rural 79%.
Sex distribution (1995): male 48.17%; female 51.83%.
Age breakdown (1995): under 15, 44.9%; 15–29, 26.1%; 30–44, 16.6%; 45–59, 8.1%; 60–74, 3.5%; 75 and over, 0.7%.
Population projection: (2000) 11,158,000; (2010) 14,000,000.
Ethnic composition (1994): Khmer 88.6%; Vietnamese 5.5%; Chinese 3.1%; Cham 2.3%; other (Thai, Lao, and Kola) 0.5%.
Religious affiliation (1994): Buddhist 95%; Muslim 2%; other 3%.
Major cities (1987): Phnom Penh 920,000[6]; Bătdâmbâng 45,000; Kâmpóng Cham 33,000; Pursat 16,000; Kâmpóng Chhnăng 15,000.

Vital statistics

Birth rate per 1,000 population (1996): 39.2 (world avg. 25.0).
Death rate per 1,000 population (1996): 12.8 (world avg. 9.3).
Natural increase rate per 1,000 population (1996): 26.4 (world avg. 15.7).
Total fertility rate (avg. births per childbearing woman; 1996): 5.0.
Marriage rate per 1,000 population: n.a.
Divorce rate per 1,000 population: n.a.
Life expectancy at birth (1996): male 52 years; female 55 years.
Major causes of death per 100,000 population: n.a.; however, major health problems include tuberculosis, malaria, and pneumonia. Violence, acts of war, and military ordnance (especially unexploded mines) remain hazards.

National economy

Budget (1995). Revenue: 640,500,000,000 riels (1994; customs duties 47.6%; timber removal fees paid by state enterprises 17.1%; consumption taxes 7.9%). Expenditures: 1,149,000,000,000 riels (1994; current expenditure 67.1%, of which defense 34.1%, police 8.2%, education 5.9%, public health 2.9%; development expenditure 32.9%).
Public debt (external, outstanding; 1994): U.S.$1,774,000,000.
Tourism (1994): receipts U.S.$70,000,000; expenditures U.S.$7,000,000.
Production (metric tons except as noted). Agriculture, forestry, fishing (1996): rice 3,500,000, sugarcane 205,000, bananas 140,000, roots and tubers 138,000 (of which cassava 90,000, sweet potatoes 30,000), corn (maize) 60,000, oranges 60,000, rubber 40,000, mangoes 30,000, soybeans 18,000, tobacco leaves 10,000; livestock (number of live animals) 2,800,000 cattle, 2,050,000 pigs, 770,000 buffalo, 14,100,000 chickens and ducks; roundwood (1994) 7,149,000 cu m (the Khmer Rouge market additional quantities in Thailand); fish catch (1994) 103,200. Mining and quarrying (1994): legal mining is confined to fertilizers, salt, and construction materials; smuggling of gemstones from Khmer Rouge-controlled areas is believed to be extensive. Manufacturing (value of production in '000,000 riels; 1988): cigarettes 1,064.5; food 116.9; chemical products (including rubber) 83.5; light industries (including textiles) 63.2; mechanical equipment and parts 46.8; building materials 4.5.

Construction: n.a. Energy production (consumption): electricity (kW-hr; 1993) 180,000,000 (180,000,000); petroleum products (metric tons; 1993) none (155,000).
Household income and expenditure. Average household size (1980) 5.6.
Gross domestic product (1995): U.S.$2,758,000,000 (U.S.$287 per capita).

Structure of gross domestic product and labour force

	1994 in value '000,000,000 riels	1994 % of total value	1992 labour force	1992 % of labour force
Agriculture	3,140	51.2	2,495,000	69.4
Mining	18	0.3		
Manufacturing	325	5.3		
Construction	467	7.6		
Public utilities	43	0.7		
Transp. and commun.	195	3.2	} 1,100,000	30.6
Trade	909	14.8		
Public admin., defense	232	3.8		
Services }	802	13.1		
Other }				
TOTAL	6,131	100.0	3,595,000	100.0

Population economically active (1992): total 3,964,000; activity rate of total population 43.1% (participation rates: ages 16–60, 91.2%; female 55.7%).

Price and earnings indexes (1992 = 100)

	1990	1991	1992	1993	1994	1995	1996
Consumer price index	19.2	57.1	100.0	214.4	213.3	229.8	239.4[7]
Earnings index	...	...	...	...	...	...	...

Land use (1994): forested 69.1%; meadows and pastures 8.5%; agricultural and under permanent cultivation 21.7%; other 0.7%.

Foreign trade[8]

Balance of trade (current prices)

	1990	1991	1992	1993	1994	1995
U.S.$'000,000	−78.0	−33.0	−86.0	−203.0	−230.0	−332.6
% of total	31.2%	7.1%	14.0%	31.7%	18.7%	16.3%

Imports (1995): U.S.$1,188,000,000 (1994; cigarettes 14.4%; gold 11.7%; fabric 5.4%; diesel oil 4.5%; motorcycles 4.3%). *Major import sources* (1993)[9]: Singapore 24.3%; Vietnam 17.5%; Japan 8.2%; Australia 5.1%.
Exports (1995): U.S.$855,400,000 (1994; domestic exports 50.2%, of which logs 27.1%, sawn timber 15.9%, rubber 5.9%; reexports 49.8%). *Major export destinations* (1993)[10]: Singapore 65.8%; Japan 10.6%; Hong Kong 5.0%.

Transport and communications

Transport. Railroads (1995): length 380 mi, 612 km; passengers transported (1994) 500,000; cargo transported (1994) 100,000 metric tons. Roads (1995): total length 7,643 mi, 12,300 km (paved 34%). Vehicles (1995): passenger cars 36,924; trucks and buses 10,700. Merchant marine (100 gross tons and over) 3; total deadweight tonnage 3,839. Air transport (1977): passenger-mi 26,098,800, passenger-km 42,000,000; short ton-mi cargo 274,-000, metric ton-km cargo 400,000; airports (1996) with scheduled flights 7.
Communications. Daily newspapers (1996): total number 1. Radio (1995): 1,500,000 receivers (1 per 6 persons). Television (1995): 70,000 receivers (1 per 137 persons). Telephones (main lines; 1993): 5,900 (1 per 1,667 persons).

Education and health

Education (1994–95)

	schools	teachers	students	student/ teacher ratio
Primary (age 6–10)	4,539[11]	42,405[11]	1,640,000	...
Secondary (age 11–16)	440[11]	19,540[11]	266,000	...
Voc., teacher tr.	65[11]	2,618[11]	16,350	...
Higher[11]	9	268	22,182	82.8

Educational attainment: n.a. *Literacy* (1987): total population age 15 and over literate 3,778,042 (74.3%); males literate 2,001,084 (85.0%); females literate 1,776,958 (65.0%).
Health: physicians (1994) 1,200 (1 per 7,900 persons); hospital beds (1988) 12,953[12] (1 per 632[12] persons); infant mortality rate per 1,000 live births (1996) 106.
Food (1992): daily per capita caloric intake 2,021 (vegetable products 94%, animal products 6%); 91% of FAO recommended minimum requirement.

Military

Total active duty personnel (1996)[13]: 87,700 (army 41.0%, navy 1.4%, air force 0.6%, provincial 57.0%). *Military expenditure as percentage of GNP* (1994): 2.7% (world 3.0%); per capita expenditure U.S.$6.

---

[1]The United Nations Transitional Authority in Cambodia (UNTAC) assumed administrative responsibility for Cambodia in March 1992. Cambodian sovereignty, however, was retained by a Supreme National Council (SNC) until UN-supervised elections were held May 23–29, 1993. The Kingdom of Cambodia was proclaimed from Sept. 24, 1993. [2]Bântéay Méan Cheăy included in Bătdâmbâng. [3]The province of Ŏtdâr Méanchey has been combined with Siĕmréab, and area and population figures reflect the change. [4]Detail does not add to total given because of rounding. [5]Based on land area. [6]1994 estimate. [7]June. [8]Trade statistics do not indicate whether imports are c.i.f. or f.o.b.; illegal or undeclared trade is not accounted for in the foreign-trade figures shown here. [9]Estimated figures. [10]Domestic exports only (U.S.$37,700,000). [11]1992–93. [12]Public hospitals only. [13]Figures include provincial and exclude paramilitary forces.

Cameroon

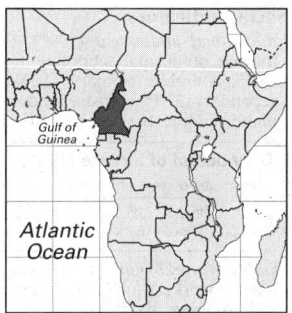

Official name: République du Cameroun (French); Republic of Cameroon (English).
Form of government: unitary multiparty republic with one legislative house (National Assembly [180]).
Chief of state: President.
Head of government: Prime Minister.
Capital: Yaoundé.
Official languages: French; English.
Official religion: none.
Monetary unit: 1 CFA franc (CFAF) = 100 centimes; valuation (Oct. 11, 1996) 1 U.S.$ = CFAF 518.24; 1 £ = CFAF 816.38.

Area and population		area		population
				1987
Provinces	Capitals	sq mi	sq km	census
Adamaoua	Ngaoundéré	24,591	63,691	495,200
Centre	Yaoundé	26,613	68,926	1,651,600
Est	Bertoua	42,089	109,011	517,200
Extrême-Nord	Maroua	13,223	34,246	1,855,700
Littoral	Douala	7,814	20,239	1,354,800
Nord	Garoua	25,319	65,576	832,200
Nord-Ouest	Bamenda	6,877	17,810	1,237,400
Ouest	Bafoussam	5,356	13,872	1,339,800
Sud	Ebolowa	18,189	47,110	373,800
Sud-Ouest	Buea	9,448	24,471	838,000
LAND AREA		179,519	464,952	
INLAND WATER		4,051	10,492	
TOTAL		183,569[1]	475,442[1]	10,495,700

Demography

Population (1996): 13,609,000.
Density (1996)[2]: persons per sq mi 74.1, persons per sq km 28.6.
Urban-rural (1991): urban 41.2%; rural 58.8%.
Sex distribution (1991): male 49.88%; female 50.12%.
Age breakdown (1991): under 15, 46.4%; 15–29, 24.4%; 30–44, 15.1%; 45–59, 8.6%; 60 and over, 5.5%.
Population projection: (2000) 15,245,000; (2010) 20,163,000.
Doubling time: 25 years.
Ethnic composition (1983): Fang 19.6%; Bamileke and Bamum 18.5%; Duala, Luanda, and Basa 14.7%; Fulani 9.6%; Tikar 7.4%; Mandara 5.7%; Maka 4.9%; Chamba 2.4%; Mbum 1.3%; Hausa 1.2%; French 0.2%; other 14.5%.
Religious affiliation (1990): Roman Catholic 34.7%; animist 26.0%; Muslim 21.8%; Protestant 17.5%.
Major cities (1987): Douala 810,000; Yaoundé 649,000; Garoua 142,000; Maroua 123,000; Bafoussam 113,000.

Vital statistics

Birth rate per 1,000 population (1995): 42.9 (world avg. 25.0).
Death rate per 1,000 population (1995): 13.5 (world avg. 9.3).
Natural increase rate per 1,000 population (1995): 29.4 (world avg. 15.7).
Total fertility rate (avg. births per childbearing woman; 1995): 6.1.
Life expectancy at birth (1996): male 51.9 years; female 54.0 years.
Major causes of death per 100,000 population: n.a.; however, major health problems include measles, malaria, tuberculosis of respiratory system, anemias, meningitis, and intestinal obstruction and hernia.

National economy

Budget (1995). Revenue: CFAF 533,600,000,000 (1992–93; sales tax 26.7%; petroleum royalties 25.9%; customs duties 19.1%). Expenditures: CFAF 737,100,000,000 (current expenditure 93.3%, of which debt services 45.2%, wages and salaries 26.3%, goods and services 14.1%).
Public debt (external, outstanding; 1994): U.S.$6,217,000,000.
Gross national product (at current market prices; 1994): U.S.$8,735,000,000 (U.S.$680 per capita).

Structure of gross domestic product and labour force				
	1991		1985	
	in value CFAF '000,000,000	% of total value	labour force	% of labour force
Agriculture	749	23.9	2,900,871	74.0
Mining	406	12.9	1,793	0.1
Manufacturing	424	13.5	174,498	4.5
Construction	165	5.3	66,684	1.7
Public utilities	38	1.2	3,522	0.1
Transp. and commun.	195	6.2	51,688	1.3
Trade	368	11.7	154,014	3.9
Finance	417	13.3	8,009	0.2
Public admin., defense	310	9.9 }	292,922	7.5
Services	66	2.1 }		
Other	...	...	263,634	6.7
TOTAL	3,138	100.0	3,917,635	100.0

Household income and expenditure. Average household size (1980) 5.2; average annual income per household (1983)[3] U.S.$420; sources of income: n.a.; expenditure (1993)[3]: food 49.1%, housing 18.0%, transportation and communications 13.0%, health 8.6%, clothing 7.6%, recreation 2.4%.
Tourism (1993): receipts from visitors U.S.$47,000,000; expenditures by nationals abroad U.S.$225,000,000.

Population economically active (1991): total 4,740,000; activity rate of total population 40.0% (participation rates [1985]: ages 15–69, 66.3%; female 38.5%; unemployed, n.a.).

Price and earnings indexes (1990 = 100)						
	1990	1991	1992	1993	1994	1995
Consumer price index	100.0	100.1	100.0	96.8	130.8	149.0
Earnings index	...	...	...	...	...	...

Production (metric tons except as noted). Agriculture, forestry, fishing (1996): sugarcane 1,350,000, cassava 1,300,000, bananas 980,000, plantains 970,000, corn (maize) 654,000, vegetables and melons 385,000, sweet potatoes 180,000, palm oil 110,000, cacao 120,000, yams 110,000, peanuts (groundnuts) 100,000, millet 100,000, rice 80,000, palm kernels 56,000; livestock (number of live animals) 4,900,000 cattle, 3,800,000 sheep, 3,800,000 goats, 1,410,000 pigs; roundwood (1994) 13,948,000 cu m; fish catch (1993) 80,000. Mining and quarrying (1994): marble 200,000; pozzolana 130,000; aluminum 85,000; limestone 57,000; tin ore and concentrate 4. Manufacturing (value added in CFAF '000,000; 1993): beverages and tobacco 24,615; petroleum and petroleum products 15,700; wood and wood products 14,026; rubber products 13,938; textiles 13,180; pottery, china, and earthenware 9,633; food products 8,615; iron and steel products 7,070. Construction (1983): residential 230,400 sq m; nonresidential 51,100 sq m. Energy production (consumption): electricity (kW-hr; 1994) 2,740,000,000 (2,740,000,000); coal (metric tons; 1994) 1,000 (1,000); crude petroleum (barrels; 1993) 39,462,000 (7,889,000); petroleum products (metric tons; 1994) 1,023,000 (1,014,000); natural gas, none (n.a.).
Land use (1994): forested 77.1%; meadows and pastures 4.3%; agricultural and under permanent cultivation 15.1%; other 3.5%.

Foreign trade[4]

Balance of trade (current prices)					
	1989	1990	1991	1992	1993	1994
CFAF '000,000,000	+40.3	+141.5	+198.6	+197.6	+249.7	+387.4
% of total	5.2%	14.8%	22.3%	25.9%	30.6%	34.5%

Imports (1991): CFAF 650,610,000,000 (machinery and transport equipment 27.2%, of which road vehicles 5.5%; chemical products 14.7%; food and live animals 13.6%; iron and steel 4.6%; paper and paper products 3.5%; textiles 3.5%; nonmetallic minerals 3.0%). *Major import sources* (1994): France 35.3%; Belgium-Luxembourg 6.6%; United States 6.1%; Germany 5.6%; Senegal 5.6%; Japan 4.0%; United Kingdom 4.0%; Italy 3.9%.
Exports (1994–95): CFAF 1,018,200,000,000 (crude petroleum 28.8%; lumber 15.1%; cocoa 6.0%; coffee 5.9%; cotton 3.7%). *Major export destinations* (1994): France 18.6%; Italy 13.9%; Spain 13.8%; Senegal 9.5%; The Netherlands 5.8%; Germany 5.1%; United Kingdom 3.7%; Nigeria 3.6%.

Transport and communications

Transport. Railroads (1992–93): route length 686 mi, 1,104 km; passenger-mi 247,000,000, passenger-km 398,000,000; short ton-mi cargo 405,000,000, metric ton-km cargo 592,000,000. Roads (1991): total length 30,074 mi, 48,400 km (paved 8%). Vehicles (1994): passenger cars 90,000; trucks and buses 79,000. Merchant marine (1992): vessels (100 gross tons and over) 47; total deadweight tonnage 39,797. Air transport (1992): passenger-mi 196,000,000, passenger-km 315,000,000; short ton-mi cargo 26,712,000, metric ton-km cargo 39,000,000; airports (1996) with scheduled flights 5.
Communications. Daily newspapers (1995): 1; total circulation 66,000; circulation per 1,000 population 5.0. Radio (1995): total number of receivers 1,500,000 (1 per 8.8 persons). Television (1995): total number of receivers 15,000 (1 per 907 persons). Telephones (main lines; 1993): 57,200 (1 per 219 persons).

Education and health

Education (1993–94)	schools	teachers	students	student/ teacher ratio
Primary (age 6–14)	6,763	34,146	1,823,556	53.4
Secondary (age 15–24)	388[5]	19,649	546,456	27.8
Voc., teacher tr.	220[5]	6,267[6]	90,543[7]	14.5[6]
Higher[7]	5[5]	1,086	33,177	30.5

Educational attainment (1976). Percentage of population age 15 and over having: no schooling 51.1%; primary education 41.7%; some postprimary 0.2%; secondary 5.7%; some postsecondary 0.3%; higher 0.2%; other 0.8%.
Literacy (1995): percentage of total population age 15 and over literate 63.4%; males literate 75.0%; females literate 52.1%.
Health: physicians (1989) 945 (1 per 11,848 persons); hospital beds (1988) 29,285 (1 per 371 persons); infant mortality rate (1990–95) 63.0.
Food (1992): daily per capita caloric intake 1,981 (vegetable products 93%, animal products 7%); 85% of FAO recommended minimum requirement.

Military

Total active duty personnel (1996): 13,100 (army 87.8%, navy 9.9%, air force 2.3%). *Military expenditure as percentage of GNP* (1994): 1.9% (world 3.0%); per capita expenditure U.S.$8.

---

[1]Detail does not add to total given because of rounding. [2]Based on land area. [3]Weights of consumer price index components. [4]Import figures are f.o.b. in balance of trade and c.i.f. for commodities and trading partners. [5]1986–87. [6]1989–90. [7]1990–91.

Canada

Official name: Canada.
Form of government: federal multiparty parliamentary state with two legislative houses (Senate [104]; House of Commons [295]).
Chief of state: Queen of Canada (British Monarch).
Representative of chief of state: Governor-General.
Head of government: Prime Minister.
Capital: Ottawa.
Official languages: English; French.
Official religion: none.
Monetary unit: 1 Canadian dollar (Can$) = 100 cents; valuation (Oct. 11, 1996) 1 U.S.$ = Can$1.35; 1 £ = Can$2.13.

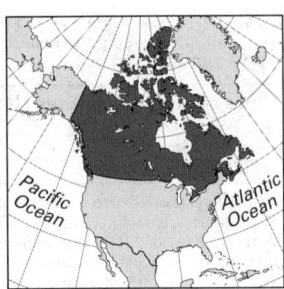

Area and population		area		population
		sq mi	sq km	1995 estimate
Provinces	**Capitals**			
Alberta	Edmonton	255,287	661,190	2,747,000
British Columbia	Victoria	365,948	947,800	3,766,000
Manitoba	Winnipeg	250,947	649,950	1,137,500
New Brunswick	Fredericton	28,355	73,440	760,100
Newfoundland	St. John's	156,649	405,720	575,400
Nova Scotia	Halifax	21,425	55,490	937,800
Ontario	Toronto	412,581	1,068,580	11,100,300
Prince Edward Island	Charlottetown	2,185	5,660	136,100
Quebec	Quebec	594,860	1,540,680	7,334,200
Saskatchewan	Regina	251,866	652,330	1,015,600
Territories				
Northwest Territories[1]	Yellowknife	1,322,910	3,426,320	65,800
Yukon Territory	Whitehorse	186,661	483,450	30,100
TOTAL		3,849,674	9,970,610	29,606,100[2]

Demography

Population (1996): 29,784,000.
Density (1996)[3]: persons per sq mi 8.4, persons per sq km 3.2.
Urban-rural (1995): urban 76.7%; rural 23.3%.
Sex distribution (1995): male 49.53%; female 50.47%.
Age breakdown (1995): under 15, 20.2%; 15–29, 21.1%; 30–44, 25.7%; 45–59, 16.8%; 60–74, 11.2%; 75 and over, 5.0%.
Population projection: (2000) 31,029,000; (2010) 33,946,000.
Doubling time: not applicable; doubling time exceeds 100 years.
Ethnic origin (1991): French 22.8%; British 20.8%; German 3.4%; Italian 2.8%; Chinese 2.2%; Amerindian and Inuktitut (Eskimo) 1.7%; Ukrainian 1.5%; Dutch 1.3%; multiple origin and other 43.5%[4].
Religious affiliation (1991): Roman Catholic 45.7%; Protestant 36.3%; Eastern Orthodox 1.5%; Jewish 1.2%; Muslim 1.0%; Buddhist 0.7%; Hindu 0.6%; nonreligious 12.4%; other 0.6%.
Major metropolitan areas (1995): Toronto 4,338,400; Montreal 3,328,300; Vancouver 1,826,800; Ottawa-Hull 1,026,900; Edmonton 882,900; Calgary 828,500; Quebec 695,200; Winnipeg 676,500; Hamilton 641,500; London 412,600.

Other metropolitan areas (1995)					
	population		population		population
Chicoutimi-Jonquière	167,200	Regina	198,700	Sherbrooke	148,000
Halifax	385,400	St. Catharines–Niagara	385,400	Sudbury	166,300
Kitchener	395,500	St. John's	177,300	Trois Rivières	143,000
Oshawa	276,200	Saskatoon	219,900	Victoria	311,200
				Windsor	286,200

Place of birth (1991): 84.6% native-born; 15.4% foreign-born, of which United Kingdom 2.6%, other European 5.9%, Asian countries 3.8%, United States 0.9%, other 2.2%.
Mobility (1991). Population living in the same residence as in 1986: 53.3%; different residence, same municipality 23.2%; same province, different municipality 15.9%; different province 3.9%; different country 3.7%.
Households (1991). Total number of households 10,018,267. Average household size 2.7; (1985) 1 person 22.9%, 2 persons 31.4%, 3 persons 17.4%, 4 persons 17.6%, 5 persons 7.3%, 6 or more persons 3.4%. Family households (1991): 7,356,168 (73.4%), nonfamily 2,662,099 (26.6%, of which 1 person 22.9%).
Immigration (1993): permanent immigrants admitted 255,819, from Hong Kong 14.3%, India 8.5%, Philippines 8.0%, China 7.7%, Sri Lanka 3.6%, Taiwan 3.6%, Vietnam 3.3%, Poland 2.7%, United States 2.5%; refugee arrivals 30,382.

Vital statistics

Birth rate per 1,000 population (1994–95): 12.9 (world avg. 25.0); (1985) legitimate 83.8%; illegitimate 16.2%.
Death rate per 1,000 population (1994–95): 6.8 (world avg. 9.3).
Natural increase rate per 1,000 population (1994–95): 6.1 (world avg. 15.7).
Total fertility rate (avg. births per childbearing woman; 1993): 1.9.
Marriage rate per 1,000 population (1995): 5.4.
Divorce rate per 1,000 population (1995): 2.7.
Life expectancy at birth (1994): male 74.7 years; female 81.7 years.
Major causes of death per 100,000 population (1994): diseases of the circulatory system 247.1; malignant neoplasms (cancers) 196.0; diseases of the respiratory system 55.4; accidents and violence 42.5 (including suicide 12.8).

Social indicators

Educational attainment (1991). Percentage of population age 25 and over having: no formal schooling 1.0%; less than complete primary education 4.0%; complete primary 11.7%; lower-level secondary 34.3%; upper-level secondary 27.7%; postsecondary 21.4%; graduates by level (1987): 4-year higher degree 101,960, master's 15,790, doctorate 2,385.

Distribution of income (1991)				
percentage of national income by quintile				
1	2	3	4	5 (highest)
5.3%	13.6%	19.7%	25.9%	35.5%

Quality of working life (1995). Average workweek: 38.4 hours. Annual rate per 100,000 workers for (1990): injury, accident, or industrial illness 3,320; death 5.1[5]. Average days lost to labour stoppages per 1,000 employee-workdays (1995): 0.5. Average duration of journey to work (1983): 23 minutes[6] (automobile 72.8%, public transportation 17.3%, other 9.9%). Rate per 1,000 workers of discouraged (unemployed no longer seeking work; 1983): 10.5.
Access to services (1990). Proportion of households having access to: electricity 100.0%; public water supply 99.8%; public sewage collection 99.3%.
Social participation. Eligible voters participating in last national election (October 1993): 69.7%. Population over 18 years of age participating in voluntary work (1987): 27.0%. Union membership in total workforce (1992): 29.7%. Practicing religious population in total affiliated population (1991): 87.6%.
Social deviance (1993). Offense rate per 100,000 population for: violent crime 1,079, of which assault 8.8[7], sexual assault 111.0[7], homicide 2.2; property crime 5,562, of which auto theft 510[7], burglary and housebreaking 1,589[7]. Incidence per 100,000 in general population of: alcoholism 2,285; drug abuse 258.
Leisure (1992). Favourite leisure activities (hours weekly): television 15.3; social time 12.7; reading 3.5; sports and entertainment 0.9.
Material well-being (1988). Households possessing: automobile 88.3%, of which two or more 25.1%; telephone 98.5%[8]; radio 99.1%[6]; television 99.0%[8]; refrigerator 99.6%; central air conditioner 24.6%[9]; cable television 69.0%; video recorder 58.8%[9]; microwave oven 63.4%[9].

National economy

Gross national product (1994): U.S.$569,949,000,000 (U.S.$19,570 per capita).

Structure of gross domestic product and labour force				
	1995			
	in value Can$'000,000[10]	% of total value	labour force	% of labour force
Agriculture	15,421	2.8	431,000	2.9
Mining	23,678	4.4	296,000	2.0
Manufacturing	102,384	18.9	2,061,000	13.8
Construction	27,221	5.0	724,000	4.9
Public utilities	17,632	3.2 }	1,033,000	6.9
Transp. and commun.	48,605	9.0 }		
Trade	65,494	12.1	2,307,000	15.5
Finance	86,772	16.0	809,000	5.4
Pub. admin., defense	32,690	6.0	810,000	5.4
Services	122,110	22.5	5,036,000	33.7
Other	—	—	1,422,000[11]	9.5[11]
TOTAL	542,007[12]	100.0[2]	14,928,000[2]	100.0

Budget (1994–95). Revenue: Can$146,566,000,000 (individual income taxes 58.6%, sales tax 20.6%, import duties 1.2%). Expenditures: Can$172,397,000,000 (1993–94; public debt interest 24.0%, defense 7.2%, health 4.6%, education 1.3%).
National debt (1994–95): Can$493,000,000,000.
Tourism (1994): receipts from visitors U.S.$6,309,000,000; expenditures by nationals abroad U.S.$11,676,000,000.

Manufacturing, mining, and construction enterprises (1993)				
	no. of estab-lishments	no. of employees	hourly wages as a % of avg. of all mfg. wages[8]	annual value added (Can$'000,000)
Manufacturing				
Food and beverages	3,202	216,000	91.3	20,110
Transport equipment	1,224	187,000	120.1	19,430
Chemicals and related products	1,396	97,000	115.0	12,860
Machinery	4,000	129,000	96.0	9,130
Electrical and electronic products	1,176	104,000	97.2	8,520
Printing, publishing, and related products	4,655	125,000	110.4	8,500
Paper and related products	651	101,000	133.0	7,890
Wood	2,201	100,000	100.9	7,880
Primary metals	417	85,000	150.8	7,790
Metal fabricating	3,287	106,000	94.1	6,290
Rubber and plastic	1,394	85,000	86.0	5,900
Textiles	1,057	60,000	76.2	3,600
Nonmetallic mineral products	1,519	44,000	103.3	3,440
Wearing apparel	1,923	85,000	59.2	3,220
Petroleum and coal products	170	16,000	150.2	2,560
Furniture and fixtures	1,965	50,000	73.1	2,310
Tobacco products industries	17	5,000	…	1,220
Mining[8]	1,232	113,000	149.3[13, 14]	29,650
Construction[15]	…	800,000	112.3[14]	28,182

Production (metric tons except as noted). Agriculture, forestry, fishing (1995): wheat 25,432,000, barley 13,035,000, corn (maize) 7,251,000, rapeseed 6,436,000, potatoes 3,774,300, oats 2,857,000, soybeans 2,280,000, vegetables 2,115,400 (of which tomatoes 605,000, carrots 315,000, onions 149,000, cabbage 143,000), dry peas 1,454,700, linseed 1,105,000, sugar beets 1,026,900, hops 490,000, apples 485,000, rye 300,000, pelts (1993) 1,811,263 units; livestock (number of live animals) 12,848,900 cattle, 11,673,000 pigs, 620,000 sheep, 350,000 horses; roundwood (1994) 187,951,000 cu m; fish catch (1993)

1,171,614. Mining and quarrying (1995): iron ore 37,130,000; zinc 1,093,541; copper 704,863; lead 203,050; nickel 166,842; uranium 10,094; molybdenum 8,482; silver 1,195; gold 4,791,200 troy oz; platinum group metals 485,800 troy oz. Manufacturing (value in Can$'000,000; 1993): transportation equipment 85,560; food 55,540; chemical products 29,070; paper products 22,080; metals 20,180; machinery 19,870; electrical products 19,120; wood products 18,990; petroleum and coal products 18,160; rubber and plastic products 14,600; metal products 14,330; printing and publishing 13,560; textiles 8,210; wearing apparel 6,990; furniture 4,570. Construction (value of building permits; 1995): residential Can$13,242,000,000; nonresidential Can$11,353,000,000.

Service enterprises (1988)

	no. of enterprises	no. of employees[16]	weekly wages as a % of all wages	annual sales (Can$'000,000)
Retail trade				
Motor vehicle dealers	...	79,800	...	35,917
Food stores	...	213,400	...	35,187
Service stations	...	63,700	...	14,612
Department stores	...	17	...	13,271
Clothing stores	...	50,200	...	7,486
Pharmacies	...	52,400	...	7,459
Furniture and appliance stores	...	62,100	...	4,447
Automotive stores	...	31,500	...	3,767
General merchandise	...	231,700[17]	...	3,109
Sporting goods	...	...	...	2,669
General stores	...	17	...	2,415
Hardware stores	...	17,300	...	1,824
Shoe stores	...	18,400	...	1,599
Jewelry stores	...	14,000	...	1,215
Variety stores	...	45,100	...	1,057

Energy production (consumption): electricity (kW-hr; 1994) 554,186,000,000 (510,272,000,000); coal (metric tons; 1994) 72,824,000 (52,229,000); crude petroleum (barrels; 1994) 638,633,000 (507,557,000); petroleum products (metric tons; 1994) 87,161,000 (77,264,000); natural gas (cu m; 1994) 148,-129,000,000 (78,223,000,000).

Population economically active (1995): total 14,928,000; activity rate of total population 50.4% (participation rates: ages 15–64, 64.8%; female 45.2%; unemployed 9.5%).

Price and earnings indexes (1990 = 100)

	1989	1990	1991	1992	1993	1994	1995
Consumer price index	95.5	100.0	105.6	107.2	109.2	109.4	129.6
Hourly earnings index[18]	94.6	100.0	105.5	108.2	110.5	111.5	113.1

Household income and expenditure (1995). Average household size 2.6; average annual income per family (1994) Can$54,153 (U.S.$39,655); sources of income (1995): wages and salaries 57.0%, transfer payments 20.7%, property and entrepreneurial income 13.7%, profits 8.6%; expenditure (1992): housing 24.7%[19], food 15.5%, transp. and commun. 15.3%, household durable goods 9.1%, recreation 8.4%, clothing 5.1%, health 4.3%, education 3.0%.

Financial aggregates

	1991	1992	1993	1994	1995	1996[20]
Exchange rate, Can$ per:						
U.S. dollar	1.14	1.21	1.29	1.36	1.37	1.37
£	2.03	2.14	1.94	2.09	2.17	2.14
SDR	1.65	1.75	1.82	2.05	2.03	1.96
International reserves (U.S.$)						
Total (excl. gold; '000,000)	16,252	11,431	12,481	12,286	15,049	19,337
SDRs ('000,000)	1,582	1,039	1,062	1,148	1,177	1,162
Reserve pos. in IMF ('000,000)	592	1,011	948	919	1,243	1,235
Foreign exchange ('000,000)	14,079	9,382	10,471	10,219	12,629	16,940
Gold ('000,000 fine troy oz)	12.96	9.94	6.05	3.89	3.41	3.10
% world reserves	1.38	1.07	0.65	0.43	0.38	0.34
Interest and prices						
Central bank discount (%)	7.67	7.36	4.11	7.00	5.79	4.25
Govt. bond yield (%)	9.76	8.77	7.85	8.63	8.28	7.48
Industrial share prices (1990 = 100)	101.4	99.5	114.1	125.2	129.6	154.7
Balance of payments (U.S.$'000,000)						
Balance of visible trade,	3,695	5,981	7,612	12,202	22,341	...
of which:						
Imports, f.o.b.	−122,308	−126,370	−136,418	−151,290	−167,513	...
Exports, f.o.b.	126,003	132,351	144,030	163,492	189,854	...
Balance of invisibles	−27,747	−27,951	−31,481	−29,590	−31,034	...
Balance of payments, current account	−24,052	−22,060	−23,869	−17,388	−8,693	...

Land use (1994): forested 53.6%; meadows and pastures 3.0%; agricultural and under permanent cultivation 4.9%; built-on, wasteland, and other 38.5%.

Foreign trade

Balance of trade (current prices)

	1990	1991	1992	1993	1994	1995
Can$'000,000,000	8.8	5.2	8.2	12.1	19.3	38.7
% of total	3.5%	2.1%	3.2%	3.4%	4.5%	7.9%

Imports (1995): Can$225,431,000,000 (machinery and transport equipment 55.6%, of which motor vehicles 22.2%; food, feed, beverages, and tobacco 5.9%; petroleum and energy products 3.2%; forestry products 0.9%). *Major import sources:* U.S. 66.7%; Japan 5.4%; Mexico 2.5%; U.K. 2.4%; Germany 2.1%; China 2.1%; South Korea 1.6%; Italy 1.5%.

Exports (1995): Can$253,821,000,000 (1993; machinery and transport equipment 39.4%, of which motor vehicles 26.2%; mineral fuels 10.5%, of which

crude petroleum 3.7%; food 6.4%, of which wheat 1.5%; lumber 5.0%; newsprint 3.2%; wood pulp 2.5%; office equipment 2.5%; aluminum 2.0%; refined petroleum products 1.4%). *Major export destinations:* U.S. 80.4%; Japan 4.5%; U.K. 1.4%; China 1.2%; Germany 1.2%; South Korea 1.0%; Belgium-Luxembourg 0.7%; France 0.7%; Italy 0.7%; The Netherlands 0.6%.

Trade by commodities (1994)

SITC Group	imports U.S.$'000,000	%	exports U.S.$'000,000	%
00 Food and live animals	7,888.0	5.3	10,148.5	6.1
01 Beverages and tobacco	685.0	0.5	894.1	0.5
02 Crude materials, excluding fuels	4,675.8	3.2	19,523.4	11.8
03 Mineral fuels, lubricants, and related materials	5,206.5	3.5	16,068.6	9.7
04 Animal and vegetable oils, fats, and waxes	...	...	...	...
05 Chemicals and related products, n.e.s.	11,290.0	7.6	8,779.2	5.3
06 Basic manufactures	19,252.2	13.0	25,421.4	15.4
07 Machinery and transport equipment	76,138.4	51.6	66,365.3	40.1
08 Miscellaneous manufactured articles	17,849.5	12.9	8,038.1	4.9
09 Goods not classified by kind	4,668.6	3.2	10,188.5	6.2
TOTAL	147,851.0[21]	100.0[21]	165,836.8[21]	100.0

Direction of trade (1995)

	imports U.S.$'000,000	%	exports U.S.$'000,000	%
Africa	1,302	0.8	1,094	0.6
Asia	23,029	14.1[2]	18,698	9.8
China	3,384	2.1	2,293	1.2
Japan	8,772	5.4	8,531	4.5
Taiwan	2,239	1.4	1,224	0.6
Other	8,634	5.3	6,650	3.5
Americas	116,434	71.3[2]	156,708	82.4
United States	108,988	66.7	152,896	80.4
Mexico	4,151	2.5	786	0.4
Other Americas	3,295	2.0	3,026	1.6
Europe	19,357	11.9[2]	12,680	6.7
EU	16,384	10.0	11,192	5.9
Other Europe	2,973	1.8	1,488	0.8
Oceania	1,176	0.7	910	0.5
TOTAL	163,295[21, 22]	100.0[21, 22]	190,187[21]	100.0

Transport and communications

Transport. Railroads (1994): length 39,174 mi, 63,045 km; passenger-mi 860,-600,000, passenger-km 1,385,000,000; short ton-mi cargo 191,145,000,000, metric ton-km cargo 279,510,000,000. Roads (1995): total length 634,400 mi, 1,021,000 km (paved 35%). Vehicles (1995): passenger cars 14,280,000; trucks and buses 3,895,600. Merchant marine (1993): vessels (100 gross tons and over) 1,049; total deadweight tonnage 1,910,000. Air transport (1995): passenger-mi 32,186,000,000, passenger-km 51,798,000,000; short ton-mi cargo 1,184,100,000, metric ton-km cargo 1,728,800,000; airports (1996) with scheduled flights 301.

Communications. Daily newspapers (1993): 108; total circulation 5,500,000; circulation per 1,000 population 195. Radio (1994): 26,878,000 receivers (1 per 1.1 persons). Television (1995): 19,400,000 receivers (1 per 1.5 persons). Telephones (main lines; 1993): 16,470,900 (1 per 1.7 persons).

Education and health

Education (1993–94)

	schools	teachers	students	student/ teacher ratio
Primary (age 6–14)[23]	16,231	300,797	5,360,900	17.8
Secondary (age 14–18)[23]	...	...	...	...
Postsecondary and higher	272	64,100	921,300	14.4

Literacy (1986): total population age 15 and over literate 18,745,000 (96.6%); males literate (1975) 8,003,000 (95.6%); females literate (1975) 8,182,000 (95.7%).

Health: physicians (1991) 60,559 (1 per 464 persons); hospital beds (1992) 165,907 (1 per 171 persons); infant mortality rate (1994) 6.2.

Food (1992): daily per capita caloric intake 3,094 (vegetable products 68%, animal products 32%); 116% of FAO recommended minimum requirement.

Military

Total active duty personnel (1996): 70,500 (army 30.5%, navy 13.5%, air force 23.3%, not identified by service 32.7%). *Military expenditure as percentage of GNP* (1994): 1.8% (world 3.0%); per capita expenditure U.S.$339.

[1]On May 25, 1993, the Prime Minister and Inuit representatives signed an agreement (following a number of territory-wide referendums), officially establishing Nunavut as a territory in 1999. It would comprise 2,201,400 sq km (844,960 sq mi) of the eastern part of Northwest Territories, with a population of 22,000 (17,500 Inuit). [2]Detail does not add to total given because of rounding. [3]Based on land area of 3,558,096 sq mi (9,215,430 sq km). [4]Includes 4.0% who are of both French and British origin. [5]1992. [6]Urban areas. [7]1991. [8]1990. [9]1989. [10]At prices of 1986. [11]Unemployed. [12]GDP at current values in 1993 is Can$776,299,000,000. [13]1986. [14]Percentage of all wages. [15]1988. [16]1984. [17]Department and General stores included with General merchandise. [18]Manufacturing only. [19]Includes energy and utilities. [20]September. [21]Detail does not add to total because of discrepancies in estimates. [22]Total for imports includes U.S.$3,-145,000,000 (1.9% of total imports; mostly special transactions) not distributable by region. [23]Primary includes Secondary.

Cape Verde

Official name: República de Cabo
Verde (Republic of Cape Verde).
Form of government: multiparty[1]
republic with one legislative house
(National People's Assembly [72]).
Chief of state: President.
Head of government: Prime Minister.
Capital: Praia.
Official language: Portuguese.
Official religion: none.
Monetary unit: 1 escudo (C.V.Esc.) =
100 centavos; valuation (Oct. 11, 1996)
1 U.S.$ = C.V.Esc. 82.97;
1 £ = C.V.Esc. 130.70.

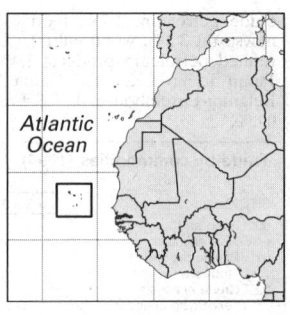

Area and population

Island Groups Islands/Counties[2] Counties	Capitals	area sq mi	area sq km	population 1990 census
Leeward Islands		696[3]	1,803	221,537
Brava	Nova Sintra	26	67	6,975
Fogo	São Filipe	184	476	33,902
Maio	Porto Inglês	104	269	4,969
Santiago		383	991	175,691
Praia	Praia	153	396	82,802
Santa Catarina	Assomada	94	243	41,584
Santa Cruz	Pedra Badejo	58	149	25,892
Tarrafal	Tarrafal	78	203	25,413
Windward Islands		861[3]	2,230	119,954
Boa Vista	Sal Rei	239	620	3,452
Sal	Santa Maria	83	216	7,715
Santo Antão		300	779	43,845
Paúl	Pombas	21	54	8,121
Porto Novo	Porto Novo	215	558	14,873
Ribeira Grande	Ponta do Sol	64	167	20,851
São Nicolau	Ribeira Brava	150	388	13,665
São Vicente[4]	Mindelo	88	227	51,277
TOTAL		1,557	4,033	341,491

Demography

Population (1996): 403,000.
Density (1996): persons per sq mi 258.8, persons per sq km 99.9.
Urban-rural (1990): urban 29.7%; rural 70.3%.
Sex distribution (1990): male 47.29%; female 52.71%.
Age breakdown (1990): under 15, 45.0%; 15–29, 27.3%; 30–44, 11.4%; 45–59,
7.9%; 60 and over, 8.4%.
Population projection: (2000) 448,000; (2010) 565,000.
Doubling time: 19 years.
Ethnic composition (1986): mixed 71.0%; black 28.0%; white 1.0%.
Religious affiliation (1991): Roman Catholic 93.2%; Protestant and other
6.8%.
Major cities (1990): Praia 61,644; Mindelo 47,109; São Filipe 5,616.

Vital statistics

Birth rate per 1,000 population (1995): 45.3 (world avg. 25.0); (1975) legiti-
mate 55.2%; illegitimate 44.8%.
Death rate per 1,000 population (1995): 8.6 (world avg. 9.3).
Natural increase rate per 1,000 population (1995): 36.7 (world avg. 15.7).
Total fertility rate (avg. births per childbearing woman; 1995): 6.2.
Marriage rate per 1,000 population (1990): 4.5.
Divorce rate per 1,000 population: n.a.
Life expectancy at birth (1995): male 61.1 years; female 65.0 years.
Major causes of death per 100,000 population (1987): enteritis and other
diarrheal diseases 97.4; heart disease 77.9; malignant neoplasms (cancers)
47.9; pneumonia 46.4; accidents, poisoning, and violence 44.0.

National economy

Budget (1994). Revenue: C.V.Esc. 6,929,000,000 (import duties 43.2%; income
taxes 19.6%; property income taxes 7.4%; transfers 7.1%; municipal taxes
1.8%). Expenditures: C.V.Esc. 19,037,000,000 (capital expenditure 63.5%;
current expenditure 36.5%, of which wages and salaries 19.5%, transfers
6.7%, goods and services 2.0%, public debt 1.7%).
Public debt (external, outstanding; 1994): U.S.$158,900,000.
Tourism (1994): receipts from visitors U.S.$10,000,000; expenditures by na-
tionals abroad U.S.$9,000,000.
Land use (1994): forested 0.2%; meadows and pastures 6.2%; agricultural
and under permanent cultivation 11.2%; other 82.4%.
Production (metric tons except as noted). Agriculture, forestry, fishing (1995):
sugarcane 18,000, fruits (except melons) 15,000, vegetables (including melons) 8,000, bananas 6,000, coconuts 5,000, cassava 3,000, potatoes 1,500,
sweet potatoes 200; livestock (number of live animals) 450,000 pigs, 130,000
goats, 19,000 cattle; roundwood, n.a.; fish catch (1993) 7,130. Mining and
quarrying (1992): salt 4,000. Manufacturing (1991): bread 3,926; canned
tuna 337; cigarettes 94; soft drinks 796,999 litres; rum 238,682 litres; other
items also manufactured are beer and flour. Construction (1982): residential
C.V.Esc. 365,800,000; nonresidential C.V.Esc. 1,700,000. Energy production
(consumption): electricity (kW-hr; 1994) 59,527,000 (46,570,000); coal, none
(none); crude petroleum, none (none); petroleum products (metric tons;
1993) none (65,383); natural gas, none (none).
Gross national product (at current market prices; 1994): U.S.$346,000,000
(U.S.$910 per capita).

Structure of gross domestic product and labour force

	1991 in value C.V.Esc. '000,000[5]	1991 % of total value	1990 labour force	1990 % of labour force
Agriculture	31	20.7	29,876	24.7
Manufacturing	9	6.0	5,520	4.6
Public utilities	4	2.7	883	0.7
Mining	...	...	410	0.3
Construction	30	20.0	22,722	18.9
Transportation and communications	18	12.0	6,138	5.1
Trade	42	28.0	12,747	10.6
Finance	6	6	821	0.7
Pub. admin., defense	13	8.7	17,358	14.4
Services	1[6]	0.7[6] }		
Other			24,090	20.0
TOTAL	150[3]	100.0[3]	120,565	100.0

Population economically active (1990): total 120,565; activity rate of total
population 35.3% (participation rates: ages 15–64, 64.3%; female 38.0%;
unemployed, 25.8%).

Price and earnings indexes (1990 = 100)

	1990	1991	1992	1993	1994	1995
Consumer price index	100.0	110.0	113.0	120.0	128.0	138.0
Earnings index	...	...	...	...	...	...

Household income and expenditure. Average household size (1990) 5.1; income
per household: n.a.; sources of income: n.a.; expenditure (1988): food 51.1%,
housing, fuel, and power 13.5%, beverages and tobacco 11.8%, transportation and communications 8.8%, household durable goods 6.9%, other 7.9%.

Foreign trade[7]

Balance of trade (current prices)

	1988	1989	1990	1991	1992	1993
C.V.Esc. '000,000	−7,416	−8,179	−9,097	−10,031	−11,907	−12,075
% of total	93.8%	88.6%	92.0%	92.0%	94.8%	95.1%

Imports (1993): C.V.Esc. 12,387,000,000 (foodstuffs and beverages 34.6%,
transport equipment 13.3%, machinery and apparatus 11.4%, nonmetallic
mineral products 10.3%, metal products 7.3%). *Major import sources:* Portugal 33.6%; The Netherlands 8.5%; Germany 4.9%; France 4.4%; United
States 3.5%.
Exports (1993): C.V.Esc. 312,200,000 (fish and fish preparations 62.6%, bananas 11.7%). *Major export destinations:* Portugal 48.8%; Angola 16.0%; The
Netherlands 3.4%.

Transport and communications

Transport. Railroads: none. Roads (1993): total length 680 mi, 1,095 km
(paved 78%). Vehicles (1993): passenger cars 6,479; trucks and buses 2,099.
Merchånt marine (1992): vessels (100 gross tons and over) 42; total deadweight tonnage 30,921. Air transport (1994)[8]: passenger-mi 106,000,000,
passenger-km 171,000,000; short ton-mi cargo 13,156,000, metric ton-km
cargo 19,207,000; airports (1996) with scheduled flights 9.
Communications. Daily newspapers: none. Radio (1995): total number of
receivers 57,000 (1 per 6.8 persons). Television (1992): total number of
receivers 1,000 (1 per 360 persons). Telephones (1994): 15,000 (1 per 25
persons).

Education and health

Education (1989–90)

	schools	teachers	students	student/ teacher ratio
Primary (age 7–12)	367	2,028	67,761	33.4
Secondary (age 13–17)	16[9]	238	7,114	29.9
Voc., teacher tr.	3[9]	56[10]	752	...
Higher	...	...	...	...

Educational attainment (1990). Percentage of population age 25 and over
having: no formal schooling 47.9%; primary 40.9%; incomplete secondary
3.9%; complete secondary 1.4%; higher 1.5%; unknown 4.4%. *Literacy*
(1990): total population age 15 and over literate 122,806 (65.3%); males
literate 64,698 (52.7%); females literate 58,108 (47.3%).
Health (1987): physicians 77 (1 per 4,208 persons); hospital beds 625 (1 per
550 persons); infant mortality rate per 1,000 live births (1995) 55.9.
Food (1992): daily per capita caloric intake 2,805 (vegetable products 88%,
animal products 12%); 119% of FAO recommended minimum requirement.

Military

Total active duty personnel (1996): 1,100 (army 90.9%, air force 9.1%). *Military
expenditure as percentage of GNP* (1994): 1.0% (world 3.0%); per capita
expenditure U.S.$8.

---

[1]Constitution revised Sept. 28, 1990, to adopt a multiparty system; first multiparty
elections took place on Jan. 13, 1991. [2]Island/county areas are coterminous except
Santiago and Santo Antão islands. [3]Detail does not add to total given because of
rounding. [4]Includes Santa Luzia Island, which is uninhabited. [5]At current factor
cost. [6]Finance included in Services. [7]Imports are c.i.f. [8]TACV airline only. [9]1986–87.
[10]Vocational teachers only.

Central African Republic

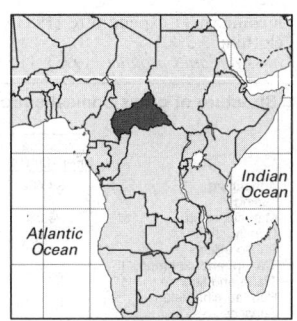

Official name: République Centrafricaine (Central African Republic).
Form of government: multiparty republic with one legislative body (National Assembly [85])[1].
Chief of state: President.
Head of government: Prime Minister.
Capital: Bangui.
Official languages: French; Sango.
Official religion: none.
Monetary unit: 1 CFA franc (CFAF) = 100 centimes; valuation (Oct. 11, 1996) 1 U.S.$ = CFAF 518.24; 1 £ = CFAF 816.38.

Area and population		area		population
		sq mi	sq km	1988 census
Prefectures	**Capitals**			
Bamingui-Bangoran	Ndélé	22,471	58,200	28,643
Basse-Kotto	Mobaye	6,797	17,604	194,750
Haut-Mbomou	Obo	21,440	55,530	27,113
Haute-Kotto	Bria	33,456	86,650	58,838
Kemo	Sibut	6,642	17,204	82,884
Lobaye	Mbaïki	7,427	19,235	169,554
Mambéré-Kadéï	Berbérati	11,661	30,203	230,364
Mbomou	Bangassou	23,610	61,150	119,252
Nana-Gribizi	Kaga-Bandoro	7,721	19,996	95,497
Nana-Mambéré	Bouar	10,270	26,600	191,970
Ombella-M'poko	Boali	12,292	31,835	180,857
Ouaka	Bambari	19,266	49,900	208,332
Ouham	Bossangoa	19,402	50,250	262,950
Ouham-Pendé	Bozoum	12,394	32,100	287,653
Sangha-Mbaéré	Nola	7,495	19,412	65,961
Vakaga	Birao	17,954	46,500	32,118
Autonomous commune				
Bangui	Bangui	26	67	451,690
TOTAL		240,324	622,436	2,688,426

Demography

Population (1996): 3,274,000.
Density (1996): persons per sq mi 13.6, persons per sq km 5.3.
Urban-rural (1996): urban 39.0%; rural 61.0%.
Sex distribution (1995): male 49.36%; female 50.64%.
Age breakdown (1995): under 15, 44.2%; 15–29, 26.6%; 30–44, 15.5%; 45–59, 8.4%; 60–74, 4.2%; 75 and over, 1.1%.
Population projection: (2000) 3,539,000; (2010) 4,177,000.
Doubling time: 30 years.
Ethnolinguistic composition (1988): Baya (Gbaya) 23.7%; Banda 23.4%; Mandjia 14.7%; Ngbaka 7.6%; Sara 6.5%; Mbum 6.3%; Kare 2.4%; French 0.1%; other 15.3%.
Religious affiliation (1995): Protestant 25.0%; Roman Catholic 25.0%; traditional 24.0%; Muslim 15.0%; other (Christian majority) 11.0%.
Major cities (1994): Bangui 524,000; Berbérati 47,000; Bouar 43,000; Bambari 41,000; Carnot 41,000; Bossangoa 33,000.

Vital statistics

Birth rate per 1,000 population (1995): 40.0 (world avg. 25.0); legitimate, n.a.; illegitimate, n.a.
Death rate per 1,000 population (1995): 17.0 (world avg. 9.3).
Natural increase rate per 1,000 population (1995): 23.0 (world avg. 15.7).
Total fertility rate (avg. births per childbearing woman; 1995): 5.5.
Marriage rate per 1,000 population: n.a.
Divorce rate per 1,000 population: n.a.
Life expectancy at birth (1996): male 47.0 years; female 52.0 years.
Mortality: n.a.; however, principal causes of death in the mid-1990s included respiratory infections (especially tuberculosis and pneumonia), diseases of the digestive system, meningitis, diarrheal diseases, malnutrition, cardiovascular diseases, malaria, viral hepatitis, and AIDS.

National economy

Budget (1995). Revenue: CFAF 52,120,000,000 (taxes 90.9%, nontax receipts 9.1%). Expenditures: CFAF 120,670,000,000 (capital expenditure 53.8%, current expenditure 46.2%).
Public debt (external, outstanding; 1994): U.S.$807,300,000.
Production (metric tons except as noted). Agriculture, forestry, fishing (1996): cassava 400,000, yams 250,000, bananas 100,000, peanuts (groundnuts) 85,000, plantains 78,000, corn (maize) 65,000, seed cotton 30,000, sesame seeds 29,000, pulses 26,000, sorghum 25,000, oranges 20,000, cottonseed 10,000[2], paddy rice 9,000, coffee 9,000, cotton lint 7,000[2]; livestock (number of live animals) 2,800,000 cattle, 1,350,000 goats, 550,000 pigs, 3,500,000 chickens; roundwood 3,762,000 cu m; fish catch (1993) 13,501. Mining and quarrying (1996): gold 138 kg[2], diamonds 560,000 carats[3]. Manufacturing (value added in CFAF '000,000; 1992): food, beverages, and tobacco 9,085; wood products 1,271; chemical products 964; textiles, wearing apparel, and leather products 344; metal products 321. Construction (1992)[4]: residential 10,052 sq m; nonresidential 82,411 sq m. Energy production (consumption): electricity (kW-hr; 1993) 97,000,000 (97,000,000); coal, none (none); crude petroleum, none (none); petroleum products (metric tons; 1993) none (73,000); natural gas, none (none).

Land use (1994): forested 75.0%; meadows and pastures 4.8%; agricultural and under permanent cultivation 3.2%; other 17.0%.
Gross national product (at current market prices; 1994): U.S.$1,191,000,000 (U.S.$370 per capita).

Structure of gross domestic product and labour force				
	1994		1988	
	in value[5] CFAF '000,000	% of total value	labour force	% of labour force
Agriculture	246,900	53.4	1,113,900	80.4
Mining	26,700	5.8	15,400	1.1
Manufacturing	32,200	7.0	22,400	1.6
Construction	18,800	4.1	7,000	0.5
Public utilities	1,900	0.4	1,500	0.1
Transp. and commun.	13,000	2.8	1,500	0.1
Trade	53,600	11.6	118,000	8.5
Other services	23,200	5.0	15,600	1.1
Pub. admin., defense	45,700	9.9	91,700	6.6
TOTAL	462,000	100.0	1,387,000	100.0

Tourism (1993): receipts U.S.$3,000,000; expenditures U.S.$55,000,000.
Population economically active (1988): total 1,186,972; activity rate of total population 48.2% (participation rates: ages 15–64, 78.3%; female 46.8%; unemployed 7.5%).

Price and earnings indexes (1990 = 100)							
	1989	1990	1991	1992	1993	1994	1995
Consumer price index	100.1	100.0	97.8	96.5	93.7	116.7	139.1
Earnings index	...	...	...	...	...	...	...

Household income and expenditure. Average household size (1988) 4.7; average annual income per household CFAF 91,985 (U.S.$435); sources of income: n.a.; expenditure (1991)[6]: food 70.5%, clothing 8.5%, other manufactured products 7.6%, energy 7.3%, services (including transportation and communications, recreation, and health) 6.1%.

Foreign trade

Balance of trade (current prices)						
	1990	1991	1992	1993	1994	1995
CFAF '000,000,000	−9.3	−13.0	−10.1	−4.5	+4.3	−0.7
% of total	12.4%	32.9%	15.2%	6.7%	2.7%	0.4%

Imports (1995): CFAF 94,203,000,000 (1992; food products 22.2%, transportation equipment 16.6%, chemical products 13.7%, energy products 11.0%).
Major import sources (1994): France 12.3%; Cameroon 4.4%; Namibia 2.1%; Japan 1.5%; Germany 1.1%; United States 1.1%; Belgium-Luxembourg 1.1%.
Exports (1995): CFAF 93,524,000,000 (diamonds 49.7%, coffee 15.7%, wood products 15.0%, cotton 12.1%). *Major export destinations* (1994): Belgium-Luxembourg 61.4%; Spain 8.6%; France 5.7%; Iran 5.7%; Italy 4.3%.

Transport and communications

Transport. Railroads: none. Roads (1996): total length 14,900 mi, 24,000 km (paved 2%). Vehicles (1994): passenger cars 14,000; trucks and buses 6,400. Merchant marine: vessels (100 gross tons and over) none. Air transport (1995)[7]: passenger-mi 138,400,000, passenger-km 222,800,000; short ton-mi cargo 10,461,000, metric ton-km cargo 15,273,000; airports[8] (1996) with scheduled flights 1.
Communications. Daily newspapers (1993): total number 1; total circulation 2,000[9]; circulation per 1,000 population 1.0[9]. Radio (1995): 180,000 receivers (1 per 17.4 persons). Television (1995): 7,500 receivers (1 per 419 persons). Telephones (main lines; 1993): 6,800 (1 per 431 persons).

Education and health

Education (1990–91)				
	schools	teachers	students	student/ teacher ratio
Primary (age 6–11)	930	4,004	308,409	77.0
Secondary (age 12–18) } Vocational	46	845	46,989	55.6
Higher[10]	1	139	3,783	27.2

Educational attainment (1988). Percentage of population age 10 and over having: no formal schooling 59.3%; primary education 29.6%; lower secondary 7.5%; upper secondary 2.3%; higher 1.3%. *Literacy* (1995): total population age 15 and over literate 60.0%; males literate 68.5%; females literate 52.4%.
Health (1991): physicians (1992) 157 (1 per 18,660 persons); hospital beds 4,258 (1 per 672 persons); infant mortality rate per 1,000 live births (1995) 113.0.
Food (1992): daily per capita caloric intake 1,690 (vegetable products 88%, animal products 12%); 75% of FAO recommended minimum requirement.

Military

Total active duty personnel (1996): 2,650[11] (army 94.3%; navy, none; air force 5.7%). *Military expenditure as percentage of GNP* (1994): 3.2% (world 3.0%); per capita expenditure U.S.$10.

---

[1]New constitution promulgated on Jan. 14, 1995. [2]1994. [3]An unknown but substantial amount is believed to be smuggled out of the country annually. [4]Bangui only. [5]At factor cost. [6]Weights of consumer price index components. [7]Represents ¹/₁₁ of the traffic of Air Afrique, which is operated by 11 West African states. [8]International air service only. [9]1992. [10]University of Bangui only. [11]Excludes 2,300 gendarmerie, who are part of the armed forces.

Chad

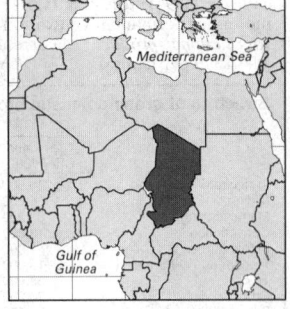

Official name: Jumhūrīyah Tshad (Arabic); République du Tchad (French) (Republic of Chad).
Form of government: unitary republic with one transitional legislative body (Higher Transitional Council [57])[1].
Chief of state: President.
Head of government: Prime Minister.
Capital: N'Djamena.
Official languages: Arabic; French.
Official religion: none.
Monetary unit: 1 CFA franc (CFAF) = 100 centimes; valuation (Oct. 11, 1996) 1 U.S.$ = CFAF 518.24; 1 £ = CFAF 816.38.

Area and population		area		population
Préfectures	Capitals	sq mi	sq km	1993 census
Batha	Ati	34,285	88,800	288,458
Biltine	Biltine	18,090	46,850	184,807
Borkou-Ennedi-Tibesti	Faya Largeau	231,795	600,350	73,185
Chari-Baguirmi	N'Djamena	32,010	82,910	1,251,906
Guéra	Mongo	22,760	58,950	306,253
Kanem	Mao	44,215	114,520	279,927
Lac	Bol	8,620	22,320	252,932
Logone Occidental	Moundou	3,357	8,695	455,489
Logone Oriental	Doba	10,825	28,035	441,064
Mayo-Kebbi	Bongor	11,625	30,105	825,158
Moyen-Chari	Sarh	17,445	45,180	738,595
Ouaddaï	Abéché	29,436	76,240	543,900
Salamat	Am Timan	24,325	63,000	184,403
Tandjilé	Laï	6,965	18,045	453,854
TOTAL		495,755[2]	1,284,000	6,279,931

Demography

Population (1996): 6,543,000.
Density (1996): persons per sq mi 13.2, persons per sq km 5.1.
Urban-rural (1995): urban 21.4%; rural 78.6%.
Sex distribution (1993): male 48.46%; female 51.54%.
Age breakdown (1993): under 15, 47.9%; 15–29, 24.5%; 30–44, 14.6%; 45–59, 7.1%; 60–74, 4.2%; 75 and over, 1.3%.
Population projection: (2000) 7,307,000; (2010) 9,319,000.
Doubling time: 27 years.
Ethnolinguistic composition (1993): Sara 27.7%; Sudanic Arab 12.3%; Mayo-Kebbi peoples 11.5%; Kanem-Bornu peoples 9.0%; Ouaddaï peoples 8.7%; Hadjeray (Hadjaraï) 6.7%; Tangale (Tandjilé) peoples 6.5%; Gorane peoples 6.3%; Fitri-Batha peoples 4.7%; Fulani (Peul) 2.4%; Bagirmi 1.5%; other 2.7%.
Religious affiliation (1993): Muslim 53.9%; Christian 34.7%, of which Roman Catholic 20.3%, Protestant 14.4%; traditional beliefs 7.4%; other 4.0%.
Major cities (1993): N'Djamena 530,965; Moundou 282,103; Bongor 196,713; Sarh 193,753; Abéché 187,936; Doba 185,461.

Vital statistics

Birth rate per 1,000 population (1995): 44.6 (world avg. 25.0); legitimate, n.a.; illegitimate, n.a.
Death rate per 1,000 population (1995): 17.7 (world avg. 9.3).
Natural increase rate per 1,000 population (1995): 26.9 (world avg. 15.7).
Total fertility rate (avg. births per childbearing woman; 1995): 5.9.
Marriage rate per 1,000 population: n.a.
Divorce rate per 1,000 population: n.a.
Life expectancy at birth (1995): male 44.9 years; female 49.6 years.
Major causes of death per 100,000 population: n.a.; however, major diseases include nutritional deficiencies, malaria, diseases of pregnancy and the neonatal period, sleeping sickness, leprosy, AIDS, venereal diseases, and respiratory diseases, especially tuberculosis.

National economy

Budget (1995). Revenue: CFAF 42,704,000,000 (taxes 43.6%, customs duties 22.3%, petroleum revenues 15.4%, other 18.7%). Expenditures: CFAF 61,652,000,000 (government salaries 39.3%, government operations 19.6%, debt service 11.9%, transfer payments 8.3%, other 20.9%).
Tourism: receipts from visitors (1994) U.S.$36,000,000; expenditures by nationals abroad (1993): U.S.$12,000,000.
Production (metric tons except as noted). Agriculture, forestry, fishing (1995): sorghum 437,448, sugarcane 308,000, yams 240,000, millet 227,735, cassava 195,000, seed cotton 170,000, rice 78,978, corn (maize) 62,501, peanuts (groundnuts) 54,700, sweet potatoes 47,000, pulses 34,000, mangoes 32,000, dates 18,000, onions 14,000, sesame seeds 13,088, potatoes 8,000; livestock (number of live animals) 4,539,000 cattle, 3,271,000 goats, 2,219,000 sheep, 600,000 camels, 4,400,000 chickens; roundwood (1994) 5,364,000 cu m; fish catch (1993) 80,000. Mining and quarrying: limited production of natron and salt. Manufacturing (1995): cotton fibre 52,100; refined sugar 25,900; salted, dried, or smoked fish 19,000[3]; soap 3,781; woven cotton fabrics 166,000 metres; beer 118,700 hectolitres; edible oil 73,028 hectolitres; cigarettes 22,944,000 packets; bicycles 1,481 units. Construction: n.a. Energy production (consumption): electricity (kW-hr; 1995) 89,128,000 (89,128,000); coal, none (n.a.); crude petroleum, none (n.a.); petroleum products (metric tons; 1994) none (31,000); natural gas, none (n.a.).
Household income and expenditure (1993). Average household size 5.0; average annual income per household CFAF 96,806 (U.S.$458); sources of

income: n.a.; expenditure (1983)[4]: food 45.3%, health 11.9%, energy 5.8%, clothing 3.3%.
Gross national product (1995): U.S.$1,153,000,000 (U.S.$190 per capita).

Structure of gross domestic product and labour force				
	1994		1993	
	in value CFAF '000,000	% of total value	labour force	% of labour force
Agriculture	94,482	21.1	1,903,492	83.0
Mining	5	5	756	—
Manufacturing	25,023	5.6	33,670	1.5
Construction	2,256	0.5	10,885	0.5
Public utilities	1,800[5]	0.4[5]	2,026	0.1
Transp. and commun. }	54,620	12.2	13,252	0.6
Trade and finance }			179,169	7.8
Pub. admin., defense }	21,249	4.8	61,875	2.7
Services }			79,167	3.4
Other	248,000[6]	55.4[6]	9,311	0.4
TOTAL	447,430	100.0	2,293,603	100.0

Public debt (external, outstanding; 1994): U.S.$743,600,000.
Population economically active (1993): total 2,719,497; activity rate of total population 43.9% (participation rates: over age 15, 72.0%; female 47.9%; unemployed 0.6%).

Price and earnings indexes (1990 = 100)							
	1989	1990	1991	1992	1993	1994	1995
Consumer price index	100.2	100.0	104.2	100.9	93.8	132.0	131.5
Earnings index	...	...	...	...	...	...	...

Land use (1994): forested 25.7%; meadows and pastures 35.7%; agricultural and under permanent cultivation 2.6%; other 36.0%.

Foreign trade

Balance of trade (current prices)						
	1989	1990	1991	1992	1993	1994
CFAF '000,000	−6,060	+364	−7,268	+606	−4,826	+10,707
% of total	5.8%	0.3%	6.2%	0.6%	6.1%	6.6%

Imports (1995): CFAF 111,200,000,000 (1983; petroleum products 16.8%; cereal products 16.8%; pharmaceutical products and chemicals 11.5%; machinery and transport equipment 8.5%, of which transport equipment 7.3%; electrical equipment 5.7%; textiles 2.9%; raw and refined sugar 2.3%). *Major import sources* (1989): France 36.2%; United States 20.4%; Cameroon 18.4%; Italy 5.6%; West Germany 3.7%.
Exports (1995): CFAF 115,000,000,000 (1994; raw cotton 33.2%; live cattle 17.8%; traditionally, other products have included frozen bovine meat and hides and skins). *Major export destinations* (1989): Portugal 21.0%; West Germany 16.9%; Japan 13.3%; France 9.9%; Spain 8.4%.

Transport and communications

Transport. Railroads: none. Roads (1995): total length 20,319 mi, 32,700 km (paved 1%). Vehicles (1995): passenger cars 9,630; trucks and buses 14,360. Merchant marine: vessels (100 gross tons and over) none. Air transport (1995)[7]: passenger-mi 138,455,000, passenger-km 222,822,000; short ton-mi cargo 10,461,000, metric ton-km cargo 15,273,000; airports (1996) with scheduled flights 4.
Communications. Daily newspapers (1992): total number 1; total circulation 2,000; circulation per 1,000 population 0.3. Radio (1995): total number of receivers 1,310,000 (1 per 4.9 persons). Television (1995): total number of receivers 50,000 (1 per 127.2 persons). Telephones (main lines; 1993): 4,600 (1 per 1,310 persons).

Education and health

Education (1991)	schools	teachers	students	student/ teacher ratio
Primary (age 6–12)	2,544	9,238	591,417	64.0
Secondary (age 13–19)	66[8]	2,062	72,641	35.2
Voc., teacher tr.	25[9]	285[8]	3,819[3]	15.1[8]
Higher[3]	4	59	2,969	50.3

Educational attainment (1993). Percentage of economically active population age 15 and over having: no formal schooling 81.1%; Qur'ānic education 4.2%; primary education 11.2%; secondary education 2.7%; higher education 0.3%; professional education 0.5%. *Literacy* (1993): percentage of total population age 15 and over literate 13.5%; males literate 23.0%; females literate 5.2%.
Health (1993): physicians 217 (1 per 27,765 persons); hospital beds 3,962 (1 per 1,521 persons); infant mortality rate per 1,000 live births (1995) 122.
Food (1992): daily per capita caloric intake 1,989 (vegetable products 93%, animal products 7%); 84% of FAO recommended minimum requirement.

Military

Total active duty personnel (1996): 30,350 (army 82.4%, navy, none, air force 1.2%, paramilitary 16.4%). *Military expenditure as percentage of GNP* (1994): 2.7% (world 3.0%); per capita expenditure U.S.$4.

[1]A 30-month national charter (transitional constitution) was adopted in February 1991. The transitional government ended in April 1996 with the adoption of a new constitution, but the transitional legislature (Higher Transitional Council) is to remain in office until the election of the permanent legislative body in January and February 1997. [2]Detail does not add to total given because of rounding. [3]1989. [4]Capital city only. [5]Mining included with public utilities. [6]Includes indirect taxes. [7]Chad's portion of total air transport of Air Afrique. [8]1988–89. [9]1987.

Chile

Official name: República de Chile
(Republic of Chile).
Form of government: multiparty
republic with two legislative
houses (Senate [47[1]]; Chamber of
Deputies [120]).
Head of state and government:
President.
Capital: Santiago[2].
Official language: Spanish.
Official religion: none.
Monetary unit: 1 peso (Ch$) = 100
centavos; valuation (Oct. 11, 1996)
1 U.S.$ = Ch$413.55;
1 £ = Ch$651.47.

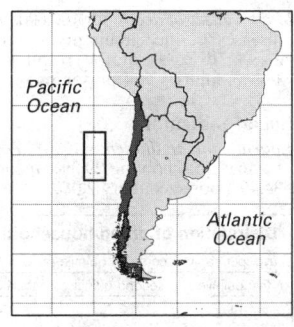

Area and population[3]

Regions	Capitals	area sq mi	area sq km	population 1995 estimate
Aisén del General Carlos				
Ibáñez del Campo	Coihaique	42,095	109,025	88,782
Antofagasta	Antofagasta	48,820	126,444	415,487
Araucanía	Temuco	12,300	31,858	853,187
Atacama	Copiapó	29,179	75,573	202,810
Bío-Bío	Concepción	14,258	36,929	1,753,662
Coquimbo	La Serena	15,697	40,656	525,432
Libertador General				
Bernardo O'Higgins	Rancagua	6,319	16,365	684,179
Los Lagos	Puerto Montt	25,868	66,997	957,212
Magallanes y la				
Antártica Chilena	Punta Arenas	50,979	132,034	181,551
Maule	Talca	11,700	30,302	902,646
Santiago,				
Región Metropolitana de	Santiago	5,926	15,349	5,783,703
Tarapacá	Iquique	22,663	58,698	410,343
Valparaíso	Valparaíso	6,331	16,396	1,478,281
TOTAL		292,135[4]	756,626[4]	14,237,275[5]

Demography

Population (1996): 14,376,000.
Density (1996): persons per sq mi 49.2, persons per sq km 18.9.
Urban-rural (1995): urban 85.8%; rural 14.2%.
Sex distribution (1995): male 49.40%; female 50.60%.
Age breakdown (1994): under 15, 30.5%; 15–29, 25.5%; 30–44, 22.1%; 45–59, 12.7%; 60–74, 6.9%; 75 and over, 2.3%.
Population projection: (2000) 15,057,000; (2010) 16,449,000.
Doubling time: 45 years.
Ethnic composition (1992): European and mestizo 89.7%; Araucanian (Mapuche) 9.6%; Aymara 0.5%; Rapa Nui Polynesian 0.2%.
Religious affiliation (1992): Roman Catholic 76.7%; Protestant 13.2%; atheist and nonreligious 5.8%; other 4.3%.
Major cities (1995): Greater Santiago 5,076,808; Concepción 350,268; Viña del Mar 322,220; Valparaíso 282,168; Talcahuano 260,915; Temuco 239,340.

Vital statistics

Birth rate per 1,000 population (1993): 21.0 (world avg. 25.0); (1990): legitimate 65.7%; illegitimate 34.3%.
Death rate per 1,000 population (1993): 5.3 (world avg. 9.3).
Natural increase rate per 1,000 population (1993): 15.7 (world avg. 15.7).
Total fertility rate (avg. births per childbearing woman; 1990): 2.6.
Marriage rate per 1,000 population (1993): 6.7.
Divorce rate per 1,000 population (1987): 0.4.
Life expectancy at birth (1990–95): male 71.5 years; female 77.4 years.
Major causes of death per 100,000 population (1993): diseases of the circulatory system 157.4; malignant neoplasms (cancers) 111.5; accidents and adverse effects 66.1; diseases of the respiratory system 64.9.

National economy

Budget (1993). Revenue: Ch$4,177,500,000,000 (income from taxes 84.4%, nontax revenue 15.6%). Expenditures: Ch$3,842,730,000,000 (social security and welfare 33.6%, economic affairs and services 14.6%, education 13.4%, health 11.5%, housing 5.6%).
Public debt (external, outstanding; 1994): U.S.$17,611,000.
Production (metric tons except as noted). Agriculture, forestry, fishing (1995): sugar beets 3,744,000, wheat 1,384,000, grapes 1,320,000, tomatoes 1,264,-000, corn (maize) 942,000, potatoes 870,000, apples 850,000, onions (dry) 350,000, oats 202,000, rice 146,000, barley 91,000; livestock (number of live animals) 4,625,000 sheep, 3,814,000 cattle, 1,490,000 pigs; roundwood (1994) 31,053,000 cu m; fish catch (1993) 6,190,600. Mining (1994): iron 8,644,000; copper 2,233,937; zinc 30,178; molybdenum 15,949; silver 964,075 kg; gold 37,774 kg. Manufacturing (1994): cement 2,617,880; cellulose 1,150,805; refined sugar 462,693; newsprint 183,115; noodles 55,200[6]; carbonated drinks 7,197,000 hectolitres[6]; tires 2,285,394 units; pressed-fibre panels 9,082,900 sq m[6]; flat glass 7,088,550 sq m. Construction (1994)[7]: residential 7,049,369 sq m; nonresidential 2,875,935 sq m. Energy production (consumption): electricity (kW-hr; 1993) 24,004,000,000 (24,004,000,000); coal (metric tons; 1993) 1,355,000 (2,667,000); crude petroleum (barrels; 1993) 4,383,000 (50,718,000); petroleum products (metric tons; 1993) 6,771,000 (7,477,000); natural gas (cu m; 1993) 1,802,000,000 (1,802,000,000).
Land use (1994): forested 22.0%; meadows and pastures 18.2%; agricultural and under permanent cultivation 5.7%; other 54.1%.
Gross national product (1994): U.S.$50,051,000,000 (U.S.$3,170 per capita).

Structure of gross domestic product and labour force

	1994 in value Ch$'000,000[8]	% of total value	labour force	% of labour force
Agriculture	486,595	8.3	834,190	15.0
Mining	470,974	8.0	91,110	1.6
Manufacturing	1,003,765	17.1	868,640	15.6
Construction	322,992	5.5	415,470	7.5
Public utilities	160,600	2.8	34,690	0.6
Transp. and commun.	454,329	7.8	388,190	7.0
Trade	993,408	17.0	993,360	17.8
Finance	972,559	16.6	313,890	5.6
Pub. admin., defense	159,952	2.7 }	1,315,860	23.6
Services	397,881	6.8 }		
Other	431,956[9]	7.4[9]	312,880[10]	5.6[10]
TOTAL	5,855,011	100.0	5,568,100[11]	100.0[11]

Population economically active (1994): total 5,568,100; activity rate of total population 38.6% (participation rates: ages 15–64, 59.8%; female 33.1%; unemployed 6.1%).

Price and earnings indexes (1990 = 100)

	1989	1990	1991	1992	1993	1994	1995
Consumer price index	79.0	100.0	122.0	141.0	158.0	177.0	191.0
Monthly earnings index	73.9	100.0	121.2	146.2	...	...	...

Household income and expenditure. Average household size (1992) 4.1; average annual income per family (household; 1985)[12] Ch$440,738 at June prices (U.S.$2,840); sources of income (1990): wages and salaries 75.1%, transfer payments 12.0%, other 12.9%; expenditure (1989): food 27.9%, clothing 22.5%, housing 15.2%, transportation 6.4%.
Tourism (1994): receipts U.S.$833,000,000; expenditures U.S.$639,000,000.

Foreign trade[13]

Balance of trade (current prices)

	1990	1991	1992	1993	1994	1995
U.S.$'000,000	+1,273	+1,575	+749	−979	+660	+1,384
% of total	8.3%	9.7%	3.9%	5.1%	2.9%	4.5%

Imports (1994): U.S.$11,359,400,000 (intermediate goods 51.8%; capital goods 28.7%; consumer goods 17.5%). *Major import sources:* U.S. 23.2%; Japan 8.9%; Brazil 8.8%; Argentina 8.4%; Germany 4.9%; France 3.2%.
Exports (1994): U.S.$11,645,100,000 (industrial products 44.9%, of which foodstuffs 18.6%, paper and paper products 7.9%, chemical and petroleum products 6.3%; mining 43.8%; fruits and vegetables 9.5%). *Major export destinations:* U.S. 17.3%; Japan 17.0%; Argentina 5.5%; Brazil 5.2%; Germany 5.0%; Taiwan 4.6%; U.K. 4.5%; France 3.5%.

Transport and communications

Transport. Railroads (1994): length 4,076 mi, 6,560 km; passenger-km 816,-240,000; metric ton-km cargo 2,329,246,000. Roads (1993): total length 49,270 mi, 79,293 km (paved 16%). Vehicles (1994): passenger cars 837,379; trucks and buses 497,855. Merchant marine (1992): vessels (100 gross tons and over) 392; total deadweight tonnage 854,850. Air transport (1994): passenger-km 5,634,152,000; metric ton-km cargo 1,429,903,000; airports (1996) with scheduled flights 18.
Communications. Daily newspapers (1994): total number 33; total circulation 887,200[14]; circulation per 1,000 population 63[14]. Radio (1995): 4,400,000 receivers (1 per 3.2 persons). Television (1995): 2,000,000 receivers (1 per 7.1 persons). Telephones (main lines; 1993): 1,520,300 (1 per 9.1 persons).

Education and health

Education (1993)

	schools	teachers	students	student/ teacher ratio
Primary (age 6–13)	8,338[15]	78,813	2,083,775	26.4
Secondary (age 14–17)	1,694[16]	...	391,457	...
Vocational	1,262[16]	...	261,358	...
Higher	201[16]	18,084[17]	315,653	...

Educational attainment (1992). Percentage of population age 25 and over having: no formal schooling 5.7%; primary education 44.2%; secondary 42.2%; higher 7.9%. *Literacy* (1992): total population age 15 and over literate 81.1%; males 81.3%; females 80.9%.
Health (1994): physicians 16,000 (1 per 875 persons); hospital beds 43,076 (1 per 326 persons); infant mortality rate per 1,000 live births (1993) 13.1.
Food (1992): daily per capita caloric intake 2,582 (vegetable products 81%, animal products 19%); 106% of FAO recommended minimum requirement.

Military

Total active duty personnel (1996): 89,700 (army 57.6%, navy 26.8%, air force 15.6%). *Military expenditure as percentage of GNP* (1994): 1.9% (world 3.0%); per capita expenditure U.S.$69.

---

[1]Includes 8 nonelective seats. [2]Legislative bodies meet in Valparaíso. [3]Excludes the 480,000-sq mi (1,250,000-sq km) section of Antarctica claimed by Chile (and administered as part of Magallanes y la Antártica Chilena region) and "inland" (actually tidal) water areas. The 1992 census population of Chilean-claimed Antarctica was 126. [4]Includes 205 sq mi (530 sq km) of waters, known as Laguna del Desierto, lost in a border dispute with Argentina, resolved on Oct. 21, 1994. [5]Population projection based on 1992 census. [6]1991. [7]Construction approved and already begun only. [8]In constant prices of 1986. [9]Less imputed bank service charges. [10]Includes 311,290 unemployed persons. [11]Detail does not add to total given because of rounding. [12]Greater Santiago area. [13]Import figures are f.o.b. in balance of trade and c.i.f. for commodities and trading partners. [14]Circulation for 31 newspapers only. [15]1992. [16]1988. [17]Universities only.

China

Official name: Chung-hua Jen-min Kung-ho-kuo (People's Republic of China).
Form of government: single-party people's republic with one legislative house (National People's Congress [2,978]).
Chief of state: President.
Head of government: Premier.
Capital: Peking (Beijing).
Official language: Mandarin Chinese.
Official religion: none.
Monetary unit: 1 Renminbi (yuan) (Y) = 10 jiao = 100 fen; valuation (Oct. 11, 1996) 1 U.S.$ = Y 8.30; 1 £ = Y 13.07.

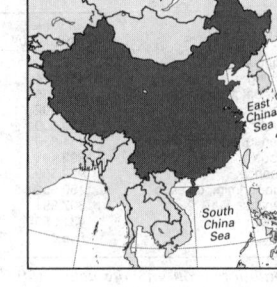

Major causes of death per 100,000 population (percentage distribution; 1994)[6]: diseases of the circulatory system 22.1%; malignant neoplasms (cancers) 21.8%; diseases of the respiratory system 16.1%; diseases of the heart 15.0%; injuries and poisoning 6.7%; digestive diseases 3.5%.

Social indicators

Educational attainment (1990). Percentage of population age 25 and over having: no schooling 29.3%; incomplete primary 34.3%; completed primary 34.4%; postsecondary 2.0%.

Distribution of urban household income (1994)

avg. per capita income by quintile (avg. Y 3,502)

first quintile	second quintile	third quintile	fourth quintile	fifth quintile
Y 1,986	Y 2,721	Y 3,304	Y 4,079	Y 5,923

Quality of working life (1991). Average workweek: 48 hours. Annual rate per 100,000 workers for: injury or accident, n.a.; industrial illness, n.a.; death, n.a. Funds for pensions and social welfare relief (1994): Y 121,890,000,000. Average days lost to labour stoppages per 1,000 workdays: n.a. Average duration of journey to work: n.a. Method of transport: n.a. Rate per 1,000 workers of discouraged (unemployed no longer seeking work): n.a.
Access to services. Proportion of communes having access to electricity (1979) 87.1%. Percentage of urban population with: safe public water supply (1994) 93.0%; public sewage collection, n.a.; public fire protection, n.a.
Social participation. Eligible voters participating in last national election: n.a. Population participating in voluntary work: n.a. Trade union membership in total labour force (1991): 17.9%. Practicing religious population in total affiliated population: n.a.
Social deviance. Annual reported arrest rate per 100,000 population (1986) for: property violation 20.7; infringing personal rights 7.2; disruption of social administration 3.3; endangering public security 1.0[7].
Leisure. Favourite leisure activities: n.a.
Material well-being (1994). Urban families possessing (number per family): bicycles 1.9; televisions 1.2; washing machines 0.9; sewing machines 0.6; cameras 0.3. Rural families possessing (number per family): bicycles 1.4; televisions 0.7.; sewing machines 0.6; washing machines 0.2; cameras 0.1.

National economy

Gross national product (at current market prices; 1994): U.S.$630,202,000,000 (U.S.$530 per capita).

Area and population[1, 2]

Provinces	Capitals	area sq mi	area sq km	population 1995[3] estimate
Anhwei (Anhui)	Ho-fei (Hefei)	54,000	139,900	59,550,000
Chekiang (Zhejiang)	Hang-chou (Hangzhou)	39,300	101,800	42,940,000
Fukien (Fujian)	Fu-chou (Fuzhou)	47,500	123,100	31,830,000
Hainan (Hainan)	Hai-k'ou (Haikou)	13,200	34,300	7,110,000
Heilungkiang (Heilongjiang)	Harbin	179,000	463,600	36,720,000
Honan (Henan)	Cheng-chou (Zhengzhou)	64,500	167,000	90,270,000
Hopeh (Hebei)	Shih-chia-chuang (Shijiazhuang)	78,200	202,700	63,880,000
Hunan (Hunan)	Ch'ang-sha (Changsha)	81,300	210,500	63,550,000
Hupeh (Hubei)	Wu-han (Wuhan)	72,400	187,500	57,190,000
Kansu (Gansu)	Lan-chou (Lanzhou)	141,500	366,500	23,780,000
Kiangsi (Jiangxi)	Nan-ch'ang (Nanchang)	63,600	164,800	40,150,000
Kiangsu (Jiangsu)	Nanking (Nanjing)	39,600	102,600	70,210,000
Kirin (Jilin)	Ch'ang-ch'un (Changchun)	72,200	187,000	25,740,000
Kwangtung (Guangdong)	Canton (Guangzhou)	76,100	197,100	66,890,000
Kweichow (Guizhou)	Kuei-yang (Guiyang)	67,200	174,000	34,580,000
Liaoning (Liaoning)	Shen-yang (Shenyang)	58,300	151,000	40,670,000
Shansi (Shanxi)	T'ai-yüan (Taiyuan)	60,700	157,100	30,450,000
Shantung (Shandong)	Chi-nan (Jinan)	59,200	153,300	86,710,000
Shensi (Shaanxi)	Sian (Xi'an)	75,600	195,800	34,810,000
Szechwan (Sichuan)	Ch'eng-tu (Chengdu)	219,700	569,000	112,140,000
Tsinghai (Qinghai)	Hsi-ning (Xining)	278,400	721,000	4,740,000
Yunnan (Yunnan)	K'un-ming (Kunming)	168,400	436,200	39,390,000
Autonomous regions				
Inner Mongolia (Nei Monggol)	Hu-ho-hao-t'e (Hohhot)	454,600	1,177,500	22,600,000
Kwangsi Chuang (Guangxi Zhuang)	Nan-ning (Nanning)	85,100	220,400	44,930,000
Ningsia Hui (Ningxia Hui)	Yin-ch'uan (Yinchuan)	25,600	66,400	5,040,000
Sinkiang Uighur (Xinjiang Uygur)	Wu-lu-mu-ch'i (Urumqi)	635,900	1,646,900	16,320,000
Tibet (Xizang)	Lhasa	471,700	1,221,600	2,360,000
Municipalities				
Peking (Beijing)	—	6,500	16,800	11,250,000
Shanghai (Shanghai)	—	2,400	6,200	13,560,000
Tientsin (Tianjin)	—	4,400	11,300	9,350,000
TOTAL		3,696,100[4]	9,572,900[4]	1,198,500,000[5]

Demography

Population (1996): 1,218,700,000.
Density (1996): persons per sq mi 329.7, persons per sq km 127.3.
Urban-rural (1994): urban 28.6%; rural 71.4%.
Sex distribution (1994): male 51.10%; female 48.90%.
Age breakdown (1990): under 15, 27.7%; 15–29, 31.0%; 30–44, 20.7%; 45–59, 12.0%; 60–74, 6.9%; 75 and over, 1.7%.
Population projection: (2000) 1,268,970,000; (2010) 1,371,580,000.
Doubling time: 67 years.
Ethnic composition (1990): Han (Chinese) 91.96%; Chuang 1.37%; Manchu 0.87%; Hui 0.76%; Miao 0.65%; Uighur 0.64%; Yi 0.58%; Tuchia 0.50%; Mongolian 0.42%; Tibetan 0.41%; Puyi 0.23%; Tung 0.22%; Yao 0.18%; Korean 0.17%; Pai 0.14%; Hani 0.11%; Kazak 0.10%; Tai 0.09%; Li 0.09%; other 0.51%.
Religious affiliation (1980): nonreligious 59.2%; Chinese folk-religionist 20.1%; atheist 12.0%; Buddhist 6.0%; Muslim 2.4%; Christian 0.2%; other 0.1%.
Major cities (1990): Shanghai 7,496,509; Peking 5,769,607; Tientsin 4,574,689; Shen-yang 3,603,712; Wu-han 3,284,229; Canton 2,914,281; Harbin 2,443,398; Chungking (Chongqing) 2,266,772; Nanking 2,090,204; Sian 1,959,044; Ta-lien (Dalian) 1,723,302; Ch'eng-tu 1,713,255; Ch'ang-ch'un 1,679,270; T'ai-yüan 1,533,884; Tsinan 1,480,915; Ch'ing-tao (Qingdao) 1,459,195; An-shan (Anshan) 1,203,986; Fu-shun 1,202,388; Lan-chou 1,194,640; Cheng-chou 1,159,679; Tzu-po (Zibo) 1,138,074; K'un-ming 1,127,411.
Households (1994). Average rural household size 4.5; urban household size 3.3. Family households (1990): 277,390,000 (99.4%); collective 1,671,000 (0.6%).

Vital statistics

Birth rate per 1,000 population (1995): 17.1 (world avg. 25.0).
Death rate per 1,000 population (1995): 6.6 (world avg. 9.3).
Natural increase rate per 1,000 population (1995): 10.5 (world avg. 15.7).
Total fertility rate (avg. births per childbearing woman; 1995): 2.0.
Marriage rate per 1,000 population (1994): 7.8.
Divorce rate per 1,000 population (1994): 0.8.
Life expectancy at birth (1992): male 69.1 years; female 72.4 years.

Structure of gross national product and labour force

	1994 in value Y '000,000,000	1994 % of total value	1994 labour force ('000)[8]	1994 % of labour force[8]
Agriculture	943.80	21.0	333,860	54.3
Mining	...	...	10,540	1.7
Manufacturing	1,835.86	40.9	96,130	15.6
Construction	290.04	6.4	31,880	5.2
Public utilities	...	...	2,460	0.4
Transp. and commun.	268.59	6.0	18,640	3.0
Trade	404.88	9.0	39,210	6.4
Finance	...	...	3,380	0.6
Pub. admin.	...	...	10,330	1.7
Services	757.41	16.9	26,720	4.3
Other	−8.78	−0.2	41,550	6.8
TOTAL	4,491.80	100.0	614,700	100.0

Budget (1995). Revenue: Y 652,300,000,000 (taxes 81.8%; funds collected for energy and transport projects 6.9%). Expenditures: Y 806,100,000,000 (culture, education, and public health 12.0%; debt service 10.8%; capital construction 9.2%; defense 7.8%; government administration 6.2%; enterprise development 5.8%).
Public debt (external, outstanding; 1994): U.S.$92,806,000,000.
Tourism: receipts from visitors (1995) U.S.$8,700,000,000; expenditures by nationals abroad (1992) U.S.$812,000,000.

Retail and service enterprises (1992)

	no. of enter-prises	no. of employees	annual wage as a % of all wages	annual gross output value (Y '000,000)
Retail trade	10,063,000	24,345,000	...	...
Grocery stores	171,000	1,213,000		
Department stores	174,000	2,120,000		
Other food shops	120,000	824,000		
Agricultural supplies stores	100,000	508,000		
Electrical appliances stores	96,000	930,000		
Household supplies stores	71,000	377,000		
Grain and oil shops	81,000	783,000		
Textile stores	40,000	288,000		
Drugstores	32,000	251,000		
Bookstores	28,000	151,000		
Coal stores	16,000	200,000		
Service trade	1,842,000	4,522,000		
Repair shops	742,000	1,110,000		
Barbershops	508,000	779,000		
Hotels	189,000	1,427,000		
Photo studios	98,000	225,000		

Production (metric tons except as noted). Agriculture, forestry, fishing (1994): grains—rice 178,251,000, corn (maize) 103,550,000, wheat 101,205,000, sorghum 4,915,000, barley 3,200,000, millet 3,001,000; oilseeds—soybeans 16,-329,000, peanuts (groundnuts) 9,718,000, rapeseed 7,460,000, sunflower seeds 1,350,000; fruits and nuts—apples 12,007,000, watermelons 6,760,000, oranges 6,175,000, pears 3,615,000, walnuts 200,000; other—sweet potatoes 105,180,-000, sugarcane 65,660,000, potatoes 40,039,000, seed cotton 12,750,000, sugar beets 12,530,000, cabbage 9,850,000, tomatoes 8,935,000, cucumbers 8,051,-

000, eggplants 5,421,000, garlic 4,986,000, onions 4,629,000, tobacco leaves 2,263,000, tea 600,000; livestock (number of live animals) 402,846,000 pigs, 111,649,000 sheep, 105,990,000 goats, 90,906,000 cattle, 22,416,000 water buffalo, 10,886,000 asses, 9,960,000 horses, 2,692,000,000 chickens, 443,000,000 ducks; roundwood (1993) 300,668,000 cu m; fish catch (1993) 17,567,907. Mining and quarrying (1994): metal concentrates—zinc 976,000, copper 684,000, lead 407,000, tin 54,000, tungsten 16,000; metal ores—iron ore 234,000,000, manganese ore 5,400,000, bauxite 3,700,000, silver 200, gold 160; nonmetals—salt 32,000,000, gypsum 11,000,000, phosphates 7,000,000, talc 2,700,000, fluorspar 2,400,000, barite 1,800,000, graphite 310,000, asbestos 240,000. Manufacturing (1995): cement 450,000,000; rolled steel 80,000,000; chemical fertilizer 24,500,000; paper and paperboard 24,000,000; sulfuric acid 17,410,000; sugar 5,656,000; cotton yarn 5,000,000; cotton fabrics 2,100,000,-000 m; cigarettes 34,910,000 cases; colour television sets 19,580,000 units; household washing machines 9,448,000 units; household refrigerators 9,296,-000 units; motor vehicles 1,503,000 units. Construction (1994): residential 957,660,000 sq m; nonresidential 484,590,000 sq m. Distribution of industrial production (percentage of total value of output by sector; 1978 [1994]): state-operated enterprises 80.6% (34.1%); collectives 19.2% (40.9%); privately operated enterprises 0.2% (25.0%). Retail sales (percentage of total sales by sector; 1978 [1994]): state-operated enterprises 90.5% (31.9%); collectives 7.4% (20.8%); privately operated enterprises 2.1% (47.3%).

Manufacturing and mining enterprises (1994)

	no. of enterprises	no. of employees[9]	annual wages as a % of avg. of all wages[10]	annual gross output value (Y '000,000)
Manufacturing				
Machinery, transport equipment, and metal manufactures,	120,707	17,630,000	96.7	1,382,879
of which,				
Metal products	29,311	...	...	170,799
Industrial equipment	26,360	4,420,000	...	239,175
Transport equipment	16,411	3,450,000	...	318,580
Electronic goods	6,877	1,630,000	...	199,986
Measuring equipment	5,165	900,000	...	42,445
Textiles	24,774	6,910,000	95.5	111,731
Garments	18,439	1,810,000	...	144,148
Foodstuffs,	56,673	4,690,000	87.5	531,400
of which,				
Food processing	27,819	1,920,000	...	250,901
Beverages	13,161	1,170,000	...	101,007
Tobacco manufactures	382	340,000	...	96,885
Chemicals,	51,541	7,250,000	92.1	615,391
of which,				
Pharmaceuticals	4,453	970,000	...	87,456
Plastics	16,826	1,010,000	...	92,664
Secondary forest products (including paper and stationery)	33,939	2,400,000	96.1	134,390
Primary forest products	1,103	1,120,000	114.3	16,750
Mining				
Nonferrous and ferrous metals	5,129	840,000	107.6	39,265
Crude petroleum	85	1,170,000	...	136,039
Coal	10,689	5,270,000	119.8	103,648

Energy production (consumption): electricity (kW-hr; 1993) 839,453,000,000 (844,653,000,000); coal (metric tons; 1993) 1,149,745,000 (1,129,095,000); crude petroleum (barrels; 1993) 1,063,135,000 (1,012,407,000); petroleum products (metric tons; 1993) 110,264,000 (113,379,000); natural gas (cu m; 1993) 16,932,000,000 (16,932,000,000).

Financial aggregates[11]

	1989	1990	1991	1992	1993	1994	1995
Exchange rate, Y per:							
U.S. dollar	4.72	5.22	5.43	5.75	5.80	8.45	8.32
£	7.58	10.06	10.16	8.70	8.59	13.18	12.90
SDR	6.21	7.43	7.77	7.91	7.97	12.33	12.36
International reserves (U.S.$)							
Total (excl. gold; '000,000)	17,960	29,586	43,674	20,620	22,387	52,914	75,377
SDRs ('000,000)	540	562	577	419	484	539	582
Reserve pos. in IMF ('000,000)	398	430	433	758	704	755	1,216
Foreign exchange	17,022	28,594	42,664	19,443	21,199	51,620	73,579
Gold ('000,000 fine troy oz)	12.7	12.7	12.7	12.7	12.7	12.7	12.7
% world reserves	1.4	1.4	1.4	1.4	1.4	1.4	1.4
Interest and prices							
Central bank discount (%)	...	...	...	...	...	...	...
Govt. bond yield (%)	...	...	...	...	...	...	...
Industrial share prices	...	...	...	...	...	...	...
Balance of payments (U.S.$'000,000)							
Balance of visible trade,	−5,620	+9,165	+8,743	+5,183	−10,654	+7,290	...
of which:							
Imports, f.o.b.	−48,840	−42,354	−50,176	−64,385	−86,313	−95,271	...
Exports, f.o.b.	43,220	51,519	58,919	69,568	75,659	102,561	...
Balance of invisibles	+1,303	+2,833	+5,022	+1,218	−955	−758	...
Balance of payments, current account	−4,317	+11,998	+13,765	+6,401	−11,609	+6,532	...

Household income and expenditure. Average household size (1994) 3.9; rural household 4.5, urban household 3.3. Average annual income per household Y 9,086; rural household Y 8,124, urban household Y 11,488. Sources of income: rural household (1994)—income from household businesses 72.2%, wages 21.6%, other 6.2%; urban household (1994)—wages 77.8%, business income 19.5%, other 2.7%. Expenditure (1994): rural household—food 58.9%, housing 14.0%, cultural activities 7.4%, clothing 6.9%, household materials 5.5%, health 3.2%, transportation 2.4%; urban household—food 50.0%, clothing 14.0%, cultural activities 8.8%, household materials 8.8%, transportation 4.7%, health 2.9%, utilities 2.3%.
Population economically active (1987): total 584,569,200; activity rate of total population 54.7% (participation rates: over age 15, 76.8%; female 49.7%; un-

employed 2.0%[12]). Urban workforce by sector of employment, 1978 (1994): state-run enterprises 74,500,000 (108,901,000); collectives 20,000,000 (32,113,-000); self-employment or privately run enterprises 150,000 (7,474,000).

Price and earnings indexes (1990 = 100)

	1989	1990	1991	1992	1993	1994	1995
Consumer price index	98.6	100.0	105.1	114.1	133.5	165.9	193.9
Annual earnings index[13]	90.4	100.0	109.3	126.7	157.5	212.1	...

Land use (1992): forested 14.0%; meadows and pastures 42.9%; agricultural and under permanent cultivation 10.3%; other 32.8%.

Foreign trade[14]

Balance of trade (current prices)

	1990	1991	1992	1993	1994	1995
Y '000,000	+62,570	+69,470	+57,730	−20,780	+126,800	+30,345
% of total	12.0%	10.2%	7.0%	1.9%	6.5%	11.4%

Imports (1994): U.S.$115,693,000,000 (machinery and transport equipment 44.6%; products of textile industries, rubber and metal products 24.3%; chemical and related products 10.5%; inedible raw materials 6.4%; mineral fuels and lubricants 3.5%; food and live animals 2.7%). *Major import sources:* Japan 22.8%; Taiwan 12.1%; United States 12.1%; Hong Kong 8.2%; South Korea 6.3%; Germany 6.2%; Russia 3.0%; Italy 2.7%; Singapore 2.1%; Australia 2.1%; United Kingdom 1.5%.
Exports (1994): U.S.$121,038,000,000 (products of textile industries, rubber and metal products 19.2%; machinery and transport equipment 18.1%; food and live animals 8.3%; chemicals and allied products 5.2%; mineral fuels and lubricants 3.4%; inedible raw materials 3.4%). *Major export destinations:* Hong Kong 26.7%; Japan 17.8%; United States 17.7%; Germany 3.9%; South Korea 3.6%; Singapore 2.1%; United Kingdom 2.0%; The Netherlands 1.9%; Taiwan 1.9%; Italy 1.3%; Russia 1.3%.

Transport and communications

Transport. Railroads (1994): length 44,040 mi, 70,876 km; (1995) passenger-mi 219,965,000,000, passenger-km 354,700,000,000; short ton-mi cargo 883,-576,000,000, metric ton-km cargo 1,290,000,000,000. Roads (1994): total length 694,580 mi, 1,117,821 km (paved 89%). Vehicles (1994): passenger cars 3,497,400; trucks and buses 5,603,300. Merchant marine (1992): vessels (100 gross tons and over) 2,390; total deadweight tonnage 20,657,996. Air transport (1995): passenger-mi 40,513,000,000, passenger-km 65,200,000,000; short ton-mi cargo 1,644,000,000, metric ton-km cargo 2,400,000,000; airports (1996) with scheduled flights 113.
Communications. Daily newspapers (1992): total number 74; total circulation 50,520,000; circulation per 1,000 population 43. Radio (1995): total number of receivers 215,950,000 (1 per 5.5 persons). Television (1995): total number of receivers 227,880,000 (1 per 5.3 persons). Telephones (1994): 28,874,424 (1 per 41 persons).

Education and health

Education (1994)

	schools	teachers	students	student/ teacher ratio
Primary (age 7–13)	857,245	6,473,000	154,529,000	23.9
Secondary (age 13–17)	82,358	3,234,000	49,817,000	15.4
Secondary specialized	14,204	524,000	7,254,000	13.8
Higher	1,080	396,000	2,799,000	7.1

Literacy (1990): total population age 15 and over literate 636,112,000 (77.7%); males literate 364,687,000 (87.0%); females literate 271,425,000 (68.0%).
Health (1994): physicians 1,882,000 (1 per 630 persons); hospital beds 3,134,-000 (1 per 378 persons); infant mortality rate per 1,000 live births (1993) 26.
Food (1992): daily per capita caloric intake 2,727 (vegetable products 87%, animal products 13%); 116% of FAO recommended minimum requirement.

Military

Total active duty personnel (1995): 2,930,000 (army 75.1%, navy 8.9%, air force 16.0%). *Military expenditure as percentage of GNP* (1994): 2.4% (world 3.0%); per capita expenditure U.S.$44.

[1]Names of the provinces, autonomous regions, and municipalities are stated in conventional form, followed by Pinyin transliteration; names of capitals are stated in conventional form or Wade-Giles transliteration, followed by Pinyin transliteration. [2]Data for Taiwan, Quemoy, and Matsu are excluded. [3]January 1. [4]Includes 4,600 sq mi (11,900 sq km) not shown separately. [5]Total includes servicemen not assigned to any political division. [6]Based on urban sample population. [7]Excludes arrests for anti-Communist activities. [8]Employed only. [9]In state-owned and collective-owned industries only. [10]1979. [11]Exchange rates and international reserves are end-of-year figures. [12]Rate of waiting for employment in cities and towns. [13]Average annual wage in industrial establishments in urban areas. [14]Imports and exports f.o.b.

Colombia

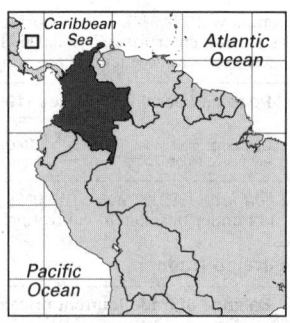

Official name: República de Colombia
  (Republic of Colombia).
Form of government: unitary,
  multiparty republic with two
  legislative houses (Senate [102];
  House of Representatives [163]).
Head of state and government:
  President.
Capital: Santafé de Bogotá, D.C.
Official language: Spanish.
Official religion: none.
Monetary unit: 1 peso (Col$) = 100
  centavos; valuation (Oct. 11, 1996)
  1 U.S.$ = Col$1,015; 1 £ = Col$1,599.

Area and population

Departments	Capitals	area sq mi	area sq km	population 1995 estimate
Amazonas	Leticia	42,342	109,665	59,378
Antioquia	Medellín	24,445	63,312	4,672,545
Arauca	Arauca	9,196	23,818	100,061
Atlántico	Barranquilla	1,308	3,388	1,818,367
Bolívar	Cartagena	10,030	25,978	1,534,820
Boyacá	Tunja	8,953	23,189	1,311,433
Caldas	Manizales	3,046	7,888	925,746
Caquetá	Florencia	34,349	88,965	332,948
Casanare	Yopal	17,236	44,640	191,502
Cauca	Popayán	11,316	29,308	972,846
Cesar	Valledupar	8,844	22,905	851,701
Chocó	Quibdó	17,965	46,530	370,140
Córdoba	Montería	9,660	25,020	1,167,353
Cundinamarca	Santafé de Bogotá, D.C.	8,735	22,623	1,756,135
Guainía	Puerto Inírida	27,891	72,238	13,389
Guaviare	Guaviare	16,342	42,327	72,592
Huila	Neiva	7,680	19,890	820,149
La Guajira	Riohacha	8,049	20,848	371,613
Magdalena	Santa Marta	8,953	23,188	1,025,536
Meta	Villavicencio	33,064	85,635	608,995
Nariño	Pasto	12,845	33,268	1,207,787
Norte de Santander	Cúcuta	8,362	21,658	1,057,482
Putumayo	Mocoa	9,608	24,885	245,564
Quindío	Armenia	712	1,845	425,799
Risaralda	Pereira	1,598	4,140	776,894
San Andrés y Providencia	San Andrés	17	44	44,088
Santander	Bucaramanga	11,790	30,537	1,715,423
Sucre	Sincelejo	4,215	10,917	637,369
Tolima	Ibagué	9,097	23,562	1,221,759
Valle	Cali	8,548	22,140	3,493,287
Vaupés	Mitú	25,200	65,268	38,760
Vichada	Puerto Carreño	38,703	100,242	19,673
Capital District				
Santafé de Bogotá, D.C.		613[1]	1,587[1]	5,237,635
TOTAL		440,762	1,141,568	35,098,736[1]

Demography

Population (1996): 35,652,000.
Density (1996): persons per sq mi 80.9, persons per sq km 31.2.
Urban-rural (1990): urban 70.3%; rural 29.7%.
Sex distribution (1993): male 49.59%; female 50.41%.
Age breakdown (1993): under 15, 33.9%; 15–29, 29.6%; 30–44, 20.4%; 45–59, 9.7%; 60–74, 4.9%; 75 and over, 1.5%.
Population projection: (2000) 37,822,000; (2010) 42,959,000.
Doubling time: 39 years.
Ethnic composition (1985): mestizo 58.0%; white 20.0%; mulatto 14.0%; black 4.0%; mixed black-Indian 3.0%; Amerindian 1.0%.
Religious affiliation (1993): Roman Catholic 93.1%; other 6.9%.
Major cities (1995): Santafé de Bogotá, D.C., 5,237,635; Cali 1,718,871; Medellín 1,621,356; Barranquilla 1,064,255; Cartagena 745,689.

Vital statistics

Birth rate per 1,000 population (1995): 21.9 (world avg. 25.0).
Death rate per 1,000 population (1995): 4.7 (world avg. 9.3).
Natural increase rate per 1,000 population (1995): 17.2 (world avg. 15.7).
Total fertility rate (avg. births per childbearing woman; 1995): 2.4.
Life expectancy at birth (1995): male 69.7 years; female 75.4 years.
Major causes of death per 100,000 population (1990)[2]: homicide with firearms 101.0; malignant neoplasms (cancers) 82.6; ischemic heart disease 70.4; accidents 49.0; infectious and parasitic diseases 25.5.

National economy

Budget (1994). Revenue: Col$12,487,873,000,000 (indirect taxes 35.4%, direct taxes 25.8%, credit resources 17.7%). Expenditures: Col$8,931,660,000,000 (finance and public credit 24.1%, education 18.3%, defense 11.0%, public works and transportation 8.6%, health 6.9%, police 6.0%).
Public debt (external, outstanding; 1994): U.S.$14,615,000,000.
Tourism (1994): receipts U.S.$794,000,000; expenditures U.S.$756,000,000.
Production (metric tons except as noted). Agriculture, forestry, fishing (1995): sugarcane 30,000,000, potatoes 3,200,000, plantains 2,890,000, bananas 2,500,000, rice 1,749,000, corn (maize) 1,084,000, coffee (green) 778,000, sorghum 560,000; livestock (number of live animals) 25,875,000 cattle, 3,708,000 vicuña[3], 2,635,000 pigs, 2,540,000 sheep; roundwood (1994) 17,833,000 cu m; fish catch (1993) 146,407. Mining and quarrying (1995): iron ore 609,615[4]; gold 710,013 troy oz; silver 169,252 troy oz; emeralds 6,305,903 carats. Manufacturing (value added in Col$'000,000; 1992): processed food 1,160,600; beverages 953,400; textiles and clothing 631,700; machinery and electrical

apparatus 351,200; paper and paper products 266,500; transport equipment 260,800; basic steel 203,900. Construction (1992)[5]: residential 9,436,277 sq m; nonresidential 2,180,763 sq m. Energy production (consumption): electricity (kW-hr; 1993) 40,298,000,000 (40,600,000,000); coal (metric tons; 1993) 21,713,000 (5,113,000); crude petroleum (barrels; 1993) 163,378,000 (92,056,000); petroleum products (metric tons; 1993) 13,852,000 (12,421,000); natural gas (cu m; 1993) 4,314,495,000 (4,314,495,000).
Gross national product (1994): U.S.$58,935,000,000 (U.S.$1,620 per capita).

Structure of gross domestic product and labour force

	1994 in value Col$'000,000	1994 % of total value	1980 labour force	1980 % of labour force
Agriculture	7,502,027	13.3	2,412,413	28.5
Mining	2,427,890	4.3	49,740	0.6
Manufacturing	10,616,579	18.9	1,136,735	13.4
Construction	3,560,161	6.3	242,191	2.9
Public utilities	1,815,596	3.2	44,233	0.5
Transp. and commun.	5,758,095	10.2	352,623	4.2
Trade	5,918,094	10.5	1,261,633	14.9
Finance			278,210	3.2
Pub. admin., defense	18,765,674	33.3	1,998,460	23.6
Services				
Other			690,762[6]	8.2[6]
TOTAL	56,364,116	100.0	8,467,000	100.0

Population economically active (1985): total 9,558,000; activity rate 34.3% (participation rates: over age 12, 49.4%; female 32.8%; unemployed 4.3%).

Price and earnings indexes (1990 = 100)

	1989	1990	1991	1992	1993	1994	1995
Consumer price index	77.4	100.0	130.4	165.6	203.1	251.5	304.2
Monthly earnings index[7]	79.4	100.0	126.1	158.9	198.7	...	...

Household income and expenditure. Average household size (1985) 4.7; sources of income (1992): wages 45.1%, self-employment 35.4%, transfer payments 14.2%; expenditure (1992): food 34.2%, transportation 18.5%, housing 7.8%, health care 6.4%, household durable goods 5.7%, clothing 4.5%.
Land use (1994): forest 22.0%; pasture 18.2%; agriculture 5.7%; other 54.1%.

Foreign trade[8]

Balance of trade (current prices)

	1990	1991	1992	1993	1994	1995
U.S.$'000,000	+1,621.0	+2,720.1	+920.1	−1,970.0	−2,640.7	−3,157.6
% of total	13.6%	23.2%	7.1%	12.2%	13.6%	13.9%

Imports (1994)[9]: U.S.$11,882,900,000 (machinery and transport equipment 46.7%, chemicals 19.1%, vegetable products 6.3%, metals 5.5%, petroleum 3.8%, food and tobacco 3.3%). *Major import sources:* U.S. 38.5%; Venezuela 9.6%; Japan 8.3%; Germany 5.7%; Brazil 2.8%; Mexico 2.5%.
Exports (1994)[9]: U.S.$8,401,100,000 (coffee 23.7%, forestry and fisheries 14.8%, petroleum products 14.7%, textiles and apparel 9.5%, coal 6.6%, chemicals 6.5%, food and tobacco 5.1%). *Major export destinations:* U.S. 36.5%; Germany 10.4%; Venezuela 6.3%; Japan 4.2%; The Netherlands 3.5%.

Transport and communications

Transport. Railroads (1992): route length (1994) 3,230 km; passenger-km 15,524,000; metric ton-km cargo 242,917,000. Roads (1992): total length 107,377 km (paved 12%). Vehicles (1992): cars 854,160; trucks and buses 430,611. Merchant marine (1992): vessels (100 gross tons and over) 101; deadweight tonnage 403,047. Air transport (1994): passenger-km 4,340,423,000; metric ton-km cargo 967,167,000; airports (1996) 63.
Communications. Daily newspapers (1994): 45; circulation 1,910,020[10]; circulation per 1,000 population 55[10]. Radio (1995): 5,400,000 receivers (1 per 6.5 persons). Television (1995): 5,500,000 receivers (1 per 6.4 persons). Telephones (main lines; 1993): 3,827,900 (1 per 8.9 persons).

Education and health

Education (1993)

	schools	teachers	students	student/ teacher ratio
Primary (6–10)	44,693	166,123	4,599,132	27.7
Secondary (11–16)[11]	6,134[12]	134,161	2,696,007	20.1
Higher[13]	235[14]	54,164	510,649	9.4

Educational attainment (1985). Percentage of population age 25 and over having: no schooling 15.3%; primary education 50.1%; secondary 25.4%; higher 6.8%; not stated 2.4%. *Literacy* (1990): population age 15 and over literate 86.7%; males literate 87.5%; females literate 85.9%.
Health: physicians (1992) 33,498 (1 per 1,078 persons); hospital beds (1989) 45,888 (1 per 693 persons); infant mortality rate (1995) 26.9.
Food (1992): daily per capita caloric intake 2,677 (vegetable products 84%, animal products 16%); 115% of FAO recommended minimum requirement.

Military

Total active duty personnel (1996): 146,300 (army 82.7%, navy 12.3%, air force 5.0%). *Military expenditure as percentage of GNP* (1994): 1.9% (world 3.0%); per capita expenditure U.S.$33.

---

[1]Detail does not add to total given because of rounding. [2]Estimates based on about 75% of total deaths. [3]1991. [4]1994. [5]Construction permits issued for 11 urban centres. [6]Includes unemployed. [7]Minimum legal wages revised annually January 2. [8]Import figures are f.o.b. in balance of trade and c.i.f. in commodities and trading partners. [9]Estimate. [10]Circulation for 26 newspapers only. [11]Secondary includes vocational and teacher training. [12]1988. [13]1992. [14]1987.

Comoros[1]

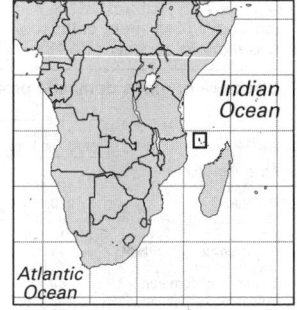

Official name: Jumhurīyat al-Qumur al-Ittihādīyah al-Islāmīyah (Arabic); République Fédérale Islamique des Comores (French) (Federal Islamic Republic of the Comoros).
Form of government[2]: federal Islamic republic with one legislative house (Federal Assembly [42]).
Chief of state: President.
Head of government: Prime Minister.
Capital: Moroni.
Official languages: Comorian; Arabic; French.
Official religion: Islam.
Monetary unit: 1 Comorian franc (CF) = 100 centimes; valuation (Oct. 11, 1996) 1 U.S.$ = CF 388.59; 1 £ = CF 612.15.

Area and population		area		population
				1994
Islands[3, 4]	Capitals	sq mi	sq km	estimate
Mwali (Mohéli)	Fomboni	112	290	28,200
Ndzuwani (Anjouan)	Mutsamudu	164	424	221,300
Ngazidja (Grande-Comore)	Moroni	443	1,148	286,100
TOTAL		719	1,862	535,600

Demography

Population (1996): 562,000.
Density (1996): persons per sq mi 781.6, persons per sq km 301.8.
Urban-rural (1995)[5]: urban 30.8%; rural 69.2%.
Sex distribution (1991): male 49.49%; female 50.51%.
Age breakdown (1995)[5]: under 15, 48.5%; 15–29, 26.4%; 30–44, 13.8%; 45–59, 7.3%; 60–74, 3.4%; 75 and over, 0.6%.
Population projection: (2000) 640,000; (2010) 883,000.
Doubling time: 20 years.
Ethnic composition (1995): nearly all Comorian (a mixture of Bantu, Arab, Malay, and Malagasy peoples).
Religious affiliation (1994): Sunnī Muslim 98.9%; Roman Catholic 1.1%.
Major cities (1991): Moroni 30,000; Mutsamudu 20,000; Domoni (1990) 8,000; Fomboni (1990) 5,600.

Vital statistics

Birth rate per 1,000 population (1995): 46.2 (world avg. 25.0).
Death rate per 1,000 population (1995): 10.6 (world avg. 9.3).
Natural increase rate per 1,000 population (1995): 35.6 (world avg. 15.7).
Total fertility rate (avg. births per childbearing woman; 1995): 6.8.
Marriage rate per 1,000 population: n.a.[6]
Divorce rate per 1,000 population: n.a.
Life expectancy at birth (1995): male 56.0 years; female 60.6 years.
Major causes of death per 100,000 population: n.a.; however, major diseases include malaria (afflicts 80–90% of the adult population), tuberculosis, leprosy, and kwashiorkor (a nutritional deficiency disease).

National economy

Budget (1995). Revenue: CF 25,583,000,000 (grants 39.2%, tax revenue 39.1%, loans 15.7%, nontax revenue 6.0%). Expenditures: CF 31,475,000,000 (current expenditures 70.6%, development expenditures 29.4%).
Production (metric tons except as noted). Agriculture, forestry, fishing (1995): bananas 56,000, coconuts 52,000[5], cassava 49,000, pulses 8,400, corn (maize) 3,700, rice 3,000, cloves 1,500, vanilla 150, ylang-ylang essence 50, other export crops grown in small quantities include coffee, cinnamon, and tuberoses; livestock (number of live animals[5]) 128,000 goats, 50,000 cattle, 14,500 sheep; roundwood, n.a.; fish catch 9,307, of which (1993) tuna c. 60%. Mining and quarrying (1994): sand, gravel, and crushed stone from coral mining for local construction. Manufacturing: products of small-scale industries include processed vanilla and ylang-ylang, cement, handicrafts, soaps, soft drinks, woodwork, and clothing. Construction: n.a. Energy production (consumption): electricity (kW-hr; 1995) 32,200,000 ([1994] 17,742,000); coal, none (none); crude petroleum, none (none); petroleum products (metric tons; 1993) none (21,000); natural gas, none (none).
Population economically active (1991): total 126,510; activity rate of total population 28.3% (participation rates: ages 15–64 [1985] 53.1%; female [1985] 26.2%; unemployed 20%).

Price and earnings indexes (1993 = 100)							
	1989	1990	1991	1992	1993	1994	1995
Consumer price index[7]	105.0	...	...	98.2	100.0	121.7	130.3
Monthly earnings index[8]	...	...	...	...	100.0	121.0	137.0

Tourism (1995): receipts from visitors U.S.$20,900,000; expenditures by nationals abroad U.S.$6,600,000.
Public debt (external, outstanding; 1994): U.S.$175,500,000.
Household income and expenditure. Average household size (1985) 5.6; income per household: n.a.; sources of income: n.a.; expenditure (1986)[9]: food and beverages 67.3%, clothing and footwear 11.6%, tobacco and cigarettes 4.1%, energy 3.8%, health care 3.2%, household furnishings 3.0%, other 7.0%.
Gross national product (at current market prices; 1994): U.S.$249,000,000 (U.S.$510 per capita).

Structure of gross domestic product and labour force				
	1995		1980	
	in value CF '000,000	% of total value	labour force[10]	% of labour force
Agriculture, fishing	32,883	39.1	53,063	53.3
Mining	...	...	62	0.1
Manufacturing	3,715	4.4	3,946	4.0
Construction	5,631	6.7	3,267	3.3
Public utilities	1,251	1.5	129	0.1
Transportation and communications	3,715	4.4	2,118	2.1
Trade, restaurants, hotels	22,686	27.0	1,873	1.9
Finance, insurance }	12,138	14.4	237	0.2
Public admin., defense }			2,435	2.5
Services	2,112	2.5	4,646	4.7
Other	—	—	27,687[11]	27.8[11]
TOTAL	84,131	100.0	99,463	100.0

Land use (1994)[5]: forested 17.9%; meadows and pastures 6.7%; agricultural and under permanent cultivation 44.9%; other 30.5%.

Foreign trade[12]

Balance of trade (current prices)						
	1990	1991	1992	1993	1994	1995
CF '000,000,000	−9.2	−9.4	−12.3	−10.6	−17.2	−19.2
% of total	48.4%	40.0%	50.4%	46.2%	64.8%	69.4%

Imports (1995): CF 23,400,000,000 (rice 22.4%, petroleum products 12.4%, cement 7.1%, meat and fish 7.1%, vehicles 7.0%, iron and steel 3.8%, other 30.2%). *Major import sources:* France 32.0%; India 17.3%; Saudi Arabia 9.4%; South Africa 6.7%.
Exports (1995): CF 4,200,000,000 (vanilla 54.8%, ylang-ylang 20.2%, cloves 3.2%, unspecified commodities 21.8%). *Major export destinations:* France 36.5%; United States 28.4%; Germany 8.0%.

Transport and communications

Transport. Railroads: none. Roads (1994): total length 529 mi, 851 km (paved 75%). Vehicles (1991)[5]: passenger cars 2,000; trucks and buses 5,000. Merchant marine (1992): vessels (100 gross tons and over) 6; total deadweight tonnage 3,579. Air transport (1993): passenger-mi 1,900,000, passenger-km 3,000,000; short ton-mi cargo, n.a., metric ton-mi cargo, n.a.; airports (1996) with scheduled flights 4.
Communications. Daily newspapers: none[13]. Radio (1995): total number of receivers 61,000 (1 per 8.9 persons). Television: no local television broadcasting in 1994. Telephones (main lines; 1995): 4,377 (1 per 124 persons).

Education and health

Education (1993–94)				
	schools	teachers	students	student/ teacher ratio
Primary (age 7–12)	275	1,737[14]	77,837	43.0[14]
Secondary (age 13–19)	...	613[15]	17,474	25.5[15]
Teacher training	...	...	163	...
Higher	...	...	400	...

Educational attainment (1980). Percentage of population age 25 and over having: no formal schooling 56.7%; Qur'anic school education 8.3%; primary 3.6%; secondary 2.0%; higher 0.2%; not specified 29.2%. *Literacy* (1995)[5]: total population age 15 and over literate 192,000 (57.0%); males literate 108,000 (64.0%); females literate 84,000 (50.0%).
Health: physicians (1993) 77[16] (1 per 6,600[16] persons); hospital beds (1990) 649 (1 per 715 persons); infant mortality rate per 1,000 live births (1995) 77.3.
Food (1992): daily per capita caloric intake 1,897 (vegetable products 95%, animal products 5%); 81% of FAO recommended minimum requirement.

Military

Total active duty personnel (1995): 800. *Military expenditure as percentage of GNP:* n.a.

[1]Excludes Mayotte, a *collectivité territoriale* ("territorial collectivity") of France, unless otherwise indicated. [2]A new constitution was approved by referendum on Oct. 20, 1996. Elections for new legislature to be held in November–December 1996. [3]Island names in Comorian (French), respectively. [4]Each island is administered locally by a governor and island council. [5]Includes Mayotte. [6]In the early 1990s, 20% of adult men had more than one wife. [7]Moroni only. [8]July average for government employees only. [9]Weights of consumer price index components for Moroni. [10]The wage labour force was very small in 1995; total of less than 7,000 including government employees, and less than 2,000 excluding them. [11]Not adequately defined. [12]Imports c.i.f.; exports f.o.b. [13]Weekly newspapers (1992): 2. [14]Public education only. [15]1991–92. [16]Estimated figure.

Congo

Official name: République du Congo
  (Republic of the Congo).
Form of government: multiparty
  republic with a Parliament consisting
  of two legislative chambers (Senate
  [60]; National Assembly [125]).
Chief of state: President.
Head of government: Prime Minister.
Capital: Brazzaville.
Official language: French[1].
Official religion: none.
Monetary unit: 1 CFA franc (CFAF) =
  100 centimes; valuation (Oct. 11,
  1996) 1 U.S.\$ = CFAF 518.24;
  1 £ = CFAF 816.38.

Area and population		area		population
		sq mi	sq km	1992 estimate
Regions	**Capitals**			
Bouenza	Madingou	4,733	12,258	177,357
Cuvette	Owando	28,900	74,850	151,839
Kouilou	Pointe-Noire	5,270	13,650	89,296
Lékoumou	Sibiti	8,089	20,950	74,420
Likouala	Impfondo	25,500	66,044	70,675
Niari	Loubomo	10,007	25,918	120,077
Plateaux	Djambala	14,826	38,400	119,722
Pool	Kinkala	13,110	33,955	182,671
Sangha	Ouesso	21,542	55,795	35,961
Communes				
Brazzaville	—	39	100	937,579
Loubomo	—	7	18	83,605
Mossendjo	—	2	5	16,405
Nkayi	—	3	8	42,465
Ouesso	—	2	5	16,171
Pointe-Noire	—	17	44	576,206
TOTAL		132,047	342,000	2,694,449

Demography

Population (1996): 2,665,000.
Density (1996): persons per sq mi 20.2, persons per sq km 7.8.
Urban-rural (1991): urban 41.1%; rural 58.9%.
Sex distribution (1995): male 48.92%; female 51.08%.
Age breakdown (1995): under 15, 45.6%; 15–29, 26.4%; 30–44, 14.6%; 45–59,
  8.1%; 60–74, 4.2%; 75 and over, 1.0%.
Population projection: (2000) 2,970,000; (2010) 3,853,000.
Doubling time: 23 years.
Ethnic composition (1983): Kongo 51.5%; Teke 17.3%; Mboshi 11.5%; Mbete
  4.8%; Punu 3.0%; Sango 2.7%; Maka 1.8%; Pygmy 1.5%; other 5.9%.
Religious affiliation (1980): Roman Catholic 53.9%; Protestant 24.9%; African
  Christian 14.2%; traditional beliefs 4.8%; other 2.2%.
Major cities (1992): Brazzaville 937,579; Pointe-Noire 576,206; Loubomo 83,-
  605; Nkayi 42,465; Mossendjo 16,405.

Vital statistics

Birth rate per 1,000 population (1990–95): 44.7 (world avg. 25.0); legitimate,
  n.a.; illegitimate, n.a.
Death rate per 1,000 population (1990–95): 14.9 (world avg. 9.3).
Natural increase rate per 1,000 population (1990–95): 29.8 (world avg. 15.7).
Total fertility rate (avg. births per childbearing woman; 1990–95): 6.3.
Marriage rate per 1,000 population: n.a.
Divorce rate per 1,000 population: n.a.
Life expectancy at birth (1990–95): male 48.9 years; female 53.8 years.
Major causes of morbidity and mortality in the early 1990s included malaria,
  acute respiratory infections, diarrhea, trauma, helminthiasis[2], and sexually
  transmitted diseases; major causes of death among adults included AIDS
  as well.

National economy

Budget (1995). Revenue: CFAF 249,300,000,000 (petroleum revenue 52.5%;
  nonpetroleum receipts 47.5%, of which customs duties 19.2%, income tax
  12.6%). Expenditures: CFAF 315,000,000,000 (debt service 47.3%; salaries
  35.3%; transfers, subsidies, goods, and services 8.9%).
Public debt (external, outstanding; 1994): U.S.\$4,667,000,000.
Tourism (1994): receipts from visitors U.S.\$3,000,000; expenditures by nation-
  als abroad U.S.\$36,000,000.
Production (metric tons except as noted). Agriculture, forestry, fishing (1995):
  cassava 630,000, sugarcane 440,000, plantains 95,000, bananas 44,000, corn
  (maize) 26,000, peanuts (groundnuts) 25,000, avocados 24,500, yams 16,000,
  palm oil 14,500, pineapples 12,200, cacao beans 1,500, coffee 1,400; livestock (number of live animals) 305,000 goats, 111,000 sheep, 68,000 cattle;
  roundwood (1994) 3,632,000 cu m; fish catch (1995) 35,024. Mining and
  quarrying (1993): gold 5 kg. Manufacturing (1993): residual fuel oil 268,000;
  cement 95,000; distillate fuel oils 92,000; aviation gas 58,000; gasoline 55,000;
  kerosene 50,000; wheat flour 15,131; dried, cured, or salted fish 4,000[3]; soap
  1,488; cigarettes 622,000,000 cartons; mechanical cultivators 294,404 units[3];
  beer 759,000 hectolitres; soft drinks 300,000 hectolitres; cotton textiles 1,800,-
  000 m; veneer sheets 35,000 cu m; footwear 300,000 pairs[4]. Construction:
  n.a. Energy production (consumption): electricity (kW-hr; 1994) 435,000,000
  (547,000,000); coal (metric tons; 1994) none (none); crude petroleum (barrels; 1994) 68,740,000 (8,040,000); petroleum products (metric tons; 1994)
  570,000 (540,000); natural gas (cu m; 1994) 5,125,000 (5,125,000).

Land use (1994): forested 58.3%; meadows and pastures 29.3%; agricultural
  and under permanent cultivation 0.5%; other 11.9%.
Gross national product (1994): U.S.\$1,607,000,000 (U.S.\$990 per capita).

Structure of gross domestic product and labour force				
	1995		1991	
	in value CFAF '000,000[5]	% of total value	labour force	% of labour force
Agriculture, forestry, fishing	107,800	10.7	471,000	59.1
Petroleum	329,400	32.8		
Manufacturing, mining	81,500	8.1	101,000	12.7
Construction	16,100	1.6		
Public utilities	14,800	1.5		
Trade	119,000	11.9		
Transp. and commun.	87,300	8.7	225,000	28.2
Pub. admin., defense	130,300	13.0		
Services	78,700	7.8		
Other	39,100	3.9	—	—
TOTAL	1,003,900[6]	100.0	797,000	100.0

Population economically active (1992): total 886,000; activity rate of total population 37.4% (participation rates [1984]: ages 15–64, 54.0%; female 45.6%;
  unemployed[7] 2.3%).

Price and earnings indexes (1990 = 100)						
	1990	1991	1992	1993	1994	1995
Consumer price index[8]	100.0	98.4	94.5	99.2	141.3	154.0
Earnings index	...	...	...	...	...	...

Household income and expenditure. Average household size (1984) 5.2; income per household: n.a.; sources of income: n.a.; expenditure (1977)[8, 9]:
  food, beverages, and tobacco 62.0%, housing 10.1%, transportation and
  recreation 8.6%, clothing and footwear 6.9%, fuel, energy, and water 5.7%,
  health and medical care 3.8%.

Foreign trade

Balance of trade (current prices)						
	1990	1991	1992	1993	1994	1995
CFAF '000,000,000	+238.4	+169.6	+195.9	+163.4	+192.1	+290.2
% of total	46.0%	37.2%	45.8%	34.8%	22.0%	30.3%

Imports (1995): CFAF 333,900,000,000 (1991[10]; machinery and transport
  equipment 38.0%, basic manufactures 27.4%, food and live animals 11.2%,
  chemicals and chemical products 8.4%, mineral fuels 3.2%, beverages and
  tobacco 2.3%). *Major import sources:* France 32.0%; U.S. 9.6%; The Netherlands 6.6%; Italy 4.4%; Belgium-Luxembourg 3.8%; Germany 3.3%.
Exports (1995): CFAF 624,100,000,000 (petroleum and petroleum products
  84.6%, wood and wood products 8.4%, other 7.0%). *Major export destinations:* U.S. 22.6%; Italy 15.4%; The Netherlands 12.5%; France 9.2%; Spain
  4.6%.

Transport and communications

Transport. Railroads: (1991) length 494 mi, 795 km; (1994) passenger-mi
  141,000,000, passenger-km 227,000,000; short ton-mi cargo 152,000,000, metric ton-km cargo 222,000,000. Roads (1993): total length 7,920 mi, 12,745
  km (paved 10%). Vehicles (1993): passenger cars 28,999; trucks and buses
  16,617. Merchant marine (1992): vessels (100 gross tons and over) 22; total
  deadweight tonnage 10,840. Air transport (1995)[11]: passenger-mi 138,460,-
  000, passenger-km 222,821,000; short ton-mi cargo 10,250,000, metric ton-
  km cargo 15,273,000; airports (1996) with scheduled flights 5.
Communications. Daily newspapers (1992): total number 6; total circulation
  19,000; circulation per 1,000 population 8.0. Radio (1995): 240,000 receivers
  (1 per 11 persons). Television (1995): 8,500 receivers (1 per 305 persons).
  Telephones (main lines; 1993): 19,200 (1 per 132 persons).

Education and health

Education (1993)				
	schools	teachers	students	student/ teacher ratio
Primary (age 6–13)	1,623	6,891	505,921	73.4
Secondary (age 14–18)	238[12]	6,048	192,229	31.8
Voc., teacher tr.	60[12]	1,813	20,621	11.4
Higher	12[12]	656[13]	13,806[13]	21.0

Educational attainment (1984). Percentage of population age 25 and over having: no formal schooling 58.7%; some primary education 21.4%; secondary
  education 16.9%; postsecondary 3.0%. *Literacy* (1995): total population age
  15 and over literate 74.9%; males literate 83.1%; females literate 67.2%.
Health (1989): physicians 567 (1 per 3,873 persons); hospital beds 4,817 (1
  per 456 persons); infant mortality rate per 1,000 live births (1990–95) 84.
Food (1992): daily per capita caloric intake 2,296 (vegetable products 92%,
  animal products 8%); 99% of FAO recommended minimum requirement.

Military

Total active duty personnel (1996): 10,000 (army 80.0%, navy 8.0%, air force
  12.0%). *Military expenditure as percentage of GNP* (1994): 2.4% (world 3.0%);
  per capita expenditure U.S.\$11.

---

[1]"Functional" national languages are Lingala and Monokotuba. [2]Parasitic infestation
by helminthic worms. [3]1992. [4]1990. [5]At current factor cost. [6]Detail does not add to
total given because of rounding. [7]Previously employed only. [8]African households only;
Brazzaville. [9]Cost-of-living components. [10]Based on c.i.f. valuation. [11]Represents 1/11
of the traffic of Air Afrique, which is operated by 11 African states. [12]1989. [13]1992.

Costa Rica

Official name: República de Costa Rica (Republic of Costa Rica).
Form of government: unitary multiparty republic with one legislative house (Legislative Assembly [57]).
Head of state and government: President.
Capital: San José.
Official language: Spanish.
Official religion: Roman Catholicism.
Monetary unit: 1 Costa Rican colón (₡) = 100 céntimos; valuation (Oct. 11, 1996) 1 U.S.$ = ₡214.48; 1 £ = ₡337.86.

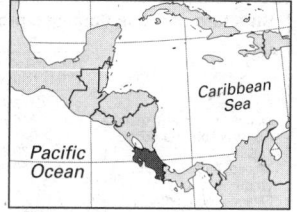

Area and population

Provinces	Capitals	area sq mi	area sq km	population 1995[1] estimate
Alajuela	Alajuela	3,766	9,753	595,174
Cartago	Cartago	1,207	3,125	374,651
Guanacaste	Liberia	3,915	10,141	263,845
Heredia	Heredia	1,026	2,657	267,369
Limón	Limón	3,548	9,188	251,482
Puntarenas	Puntarenas	4,354	11,277	371,657
San José	San José	1,915	4,959	1,209,045
TOTAL		19,730[2]	51,100	3,333,223

Demography

Population (1996): 3,400,000.
Density (1996): persons per sq mi 172.3, persons per sq km 66.5.
Urban-rural (1995): urban 44.0%; rural 56.0%.
Sex distribution (1995): male 50.55%; female 49.45%.
Age breakdown (1995): under 15, 34.9%; 15–29, 27.2%; 30–44, 20.9%; 45–59, 10.2%; 60–74, 5.3%; 75 and over, 1.5%.
Population projection: (2000) 3,680,000; (2010) 4,343,000.
Doubling time: 33 years.
Ethnic composition (1993): white 87.0%; mestizo 7.0%; black/mulatto 3.0%; East Asian (mostly Chinese) 2.0%; Amerindian 1.0%.
Religious affiliation (1992): Roman Catholic 80.0%; Evangelical Protestant 15.0%; other 5.0%.
Major cities (1995): San José 321,193[3] (metropolitan area 959,340); Limón 56,525; Alajuela 49,115; San Isidro 41,513; Desamparados 38,858[4].

Vital statistics

Birth rate per 1,000 population (1994): 25.4 (world avg. 25.0); (1992) legitimate 60.9%; illegitimate 39.1%.
Death rate per 1,000 population (1994): 4.2 (world avg. 9.3).
Natural increase rate per 1,000 population (1994): 21.2 (world avg. 15.7).
Total fertility rate (avg. births per childbearing woman; 1995): 3.0.
Marriage rate per 1,000 population (1994): 6.1.
Divorce rate per 1,000 population (1992): 1.1.
Life expectancy at birth (1990–95): male 71.9 years; female 77.5 years.
Major causes of death per 100,000 population (1992): diseases of the circulatory system 133.0, of which ischemic heart disease 87.6, cerebrovascular disease 30.2; malignant neoplasms (cancers) 80.5; diseases of the respiratory system 38.7; accidents 34.2; diseases of the digestive system 22.3.

National economy

Budget (1994). Revenue: ₡326,200,000,000 (tax revenue 88.2%, of which social security contributions 29.8%, sales tax 20.0%, import duties 12.0%; nontax revenue 11.6%). Expenditures: ₡399,670,000,000 (education 22.9%, health 20.5%, social security and welfare 17.7%, general public services 7.5%, public order 5.8%).
Public debt (external, outstanding; 1993): U.S.$3,139,000,000.
Gross national product (at current market prices; 1994): U.S.$7,856,000,000 (U.S.$2,380 per capita).

Structure of gross domestic product and labour force

	1994 in value ₡'000,000,000	1994 % of total value	1994 labour force	1994 % of labour force
Agriculture, forestry, fishing	212	16.2	252,232	21.3
Mining	247	18.9	2,160	0.2
Manufacturing			212,947	17.9
Construction	35	2.7	78,572	6.6
Public utilities	48	3.7	17,096	1.4
Transp. and commun.	71	5.4	60,190	5.1
Trade, restaurants	266	20.3	218,367	18.4
Finance, real estate	147	11.2	51,515	4.3
Public administration	187	14.3	276,626	23.3
Services	97	7.4		
Other	—	—	17,300	1.5
TOTAL	1,309[2]	100.0[2]	1,187,005	100.0

Production (metric tons except as noted). Agriculture, forestry, fishing (1994): sugarcane 2,950,000, bananas 1,932,000, pineapples 190,000, rice 180,000, oranges 169,000, coffee 138,000, plantains 104,000, palm oil 90,000, potatoes 56,000, corn (maize) 35,000, other products include other tropical fruits, cut flowers, and ornamental plants grown for export; livestock (number of live animals) 1,694,000 cattle, 252,000 pigs, 15,000,000 chickens; roundwood (1993) 4,315,000 cu m; fish catch (1992) 18,096, of which shrimp 3,994.

Mining and quarrying (1993): limestone 1,200,000; gold 19,300 troy oz.
Manufacturing (value added in ₡'000,000; 1992): food products 44,484, of which bakery products 10,348; malt liquors and malt 11,172; soft drinks and carbonated waters 8,978; paper and paper products 6,495; plastic products 5,835; fertilizers and pesticides 5,797. *Construction* (completed; 1994): 2,049,000 sq m. *Energy production* (consumption): electricity (kW-hr; 1994) 4,722,000,000 (4,209,000,000); coal, none (none); crude petroleum (barrels; 1993) none (3,878,000); petroleum products (metric tons; 1993) 503,000 (1,131,000); natural gas, none (none).
Population economically active (1994): total 1,187,005; activity rate of total population 38.7% (participation rates: ages 15–69, 59.7%; female 30.1%; unemployed [February 1995] 4.2%).

Price and earnings indexes (1990 = 100)

	1989	1990	1991	1992	1993	1994	1995
Consumer price index	84.0	100.0	128.7	156.8	172.1	195.4	240.7
Monthly earnings index[5]	84.9	100.0	122.6	150.7	183.5	...	...

Tourism (1994): receipts from visitors U.S.$626,000,000; expenditures by nationals abroad U.S.$300,000,000.
Household income and expenditure. Average household size (1994) 4.2; average annual household income (1994) ₡964,541 (U.S.$6,152)[6]; sources of income (1987–88): wages and salaries 61.0%, self-employment 22.6%, transfers 9.6%, other 6.8%; expenditure (1987–88): food and beverages 39.1%, housing and energy 12.1%, transportation 11.6%, household furnishings 10.9%, other 26.3%.
Land use (1993): forested 30.8%; meadows and pastures 45.8%; agricultural and under permanent cultivation 10.4%; other 13.0%.

Foreign trade[7]

Balance of trade (current prices)

	1990	1991	1992	1993	1994	1995
U.S.$'000,000	−349.2	−97.5	−375.2	−556.4	−517.4	−360.6
% of total	10.8%	3.0%	9.3%	12.0%	10.5%	6.5%

Imports (1993): U.S.$2,900,700,000 (raw materials for industry 31.1%; capital goods for industry 17.7%; nondurable consumer goods 17.0%; durable consumer goods 11.4%). *Major import sources:* United States 43.2%; Japan 7.6%; Venezuela 5.0%; Mexico 4.0%; Germany 3.6%.
Exports (1993): U.S.$1,944,600,000 (bananas 29.6%; coffee 10.4%; textiles, clothing, and footwear 5.7%; fish and shrimp 4.7%; ornamental plants, leaves, and flowers 4.6%). *Major export destinations:* United States 41.6%; Germany 8.9%; Italy 4.5%; Guatemala 4.5%; Nicaragua 3.9%.

Transport and communications

Transport. Railroads (1993): route length (1994) 590 mi, 950 km; passenger-mi 3,700,000, passenger-km 5,900,000; short ton-mi cargo 45,800,000, metric ton-km cargo 66,800,000[8]. Roads (1994): total length 22,110 mi, 35,583 km (paved 16%). Vehicles (1994): passenger cars 213,000; trucks and buses 127,000. Merchant marine (1992): vessels (100 gross tons and over) 24; total deadweight tonnage 8,368. Air transport (1994)[9]: passenger-mi 999,000,000, passenger-km 1,607,000,000; short-ton mi cargo 29,736,000, metric ton-km cargo 43,414,000; airports (1996) with scheduled flights 14.
Communications. Daily newspapers (1992): total number 4; total circulation 322,000; circulation per 1,000 population 103. Radio (1995): total number of receivers 760,000 (1 per 4.4 persons). Television (1995): total number of receivers 340,000 (1 per 9.8 persons). Telephones (main lines; 1993): 364,100 (1 per 8.8 persons).

Education and health

Education (1994)

	schools	teachers	students	student/teacher ratio
Primary (age 7–12)	3,472	...	497,845	...
Secondary (age 13–17)	257	...	196,553	...
Higher	25	...	76,964	...

Educational attainment (1994)[6]. Percentage of population age 5 and over having: no formal schooling 12.7%; incomplete primary education 29.5%; complete primary 25.1%; incomplete secondary 14.7%; complete secondary 8.7%; higher 7.8%; other/unknown 1.5%. *Literacy* (1995): total population age 15 and over literate 2,118,000 (94.8%); males literate 1,054,000 (94.7%); females literate 1,064,000 (95.0%).
Health (1995): physicians 3,799 (1 per 870 persons); hospital beds 5,860 (1 per 564 persons); infant mortality rate per 1,000 live births (1994) 13.0.
Food (1992): daily per capita caloric intake 2,883 (vegetable products 83%, animal products 17%); 129% of FAO recommended minimum requirement.

Military

Military expenditure as percentage of GNP (1991): 0.4% (world 4.1%); per capita expenditure U.S.$7. The army was officially abolished in 1948. Paramilitary and police forces had 7,500 members in 1995.

---

[1]July 1. [2]Detail does not add to total given because of rounding. [3]Population of San José canton. [4]Within San José metropolitan area. [5]Data for June average of each year. [6]Based on a July 1994 survey. [7]Import figures are f.o.b. in balance of trade and c.i.f. for commodities and trading partners. [8]Rail service suspended in June 1995 because of a lack of funds. [9]Lacsa (Costa Rican Airlines) only.

Côte d'Ivoire

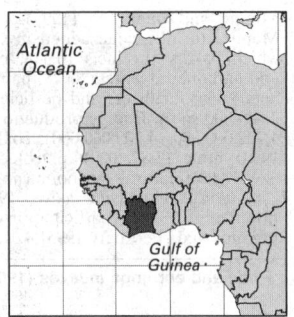

Official name: République de Côte
d'Ivoire (Republic of Côte d'Ivoire
[Ivory Coast][1]).
Form of government: multiparty
republic with one legislative house
(National Assembly [175]).
Chief of state: President.
Head of government: Prime Minister.
Capital: Abidjan (de facto; legislative).
　Capital designate: Yamoussoukro (de
jure; administrative).
Official language: French.
Official religion: none.
Monetary unit: 1 CFA franc
　(CFAF) = 100 centimes; valuation
　(Oct. 11, 1996) 1 U.S.$ = CFAF
　518.24; 1 £ = CFAF 816.38.

Area and population (1988 census)

Department	area sq km	population	Department	area sq km	population
Abengourou	5,200	216,058	Guiglo	11,220	170,321
Abidjan	8,550	2,485,847	Issia	3,590	195,663
Aboisso	6,250	225,895	Katiola	9,420	130,635
Adzopé	5,230	237,870	Korhogo	12,500	390,229
Agboville	3,850	203,493	Lakota	2,730	116,771
Agnibilékrou	1,700	84,349	Man	4,990	294,724
Bangolo	2,060	79,979	Mankono	10,660	123,362
Béoumi	2,820	90,327	M'bahiakro	5,460	102,531
Biankouma	4,950	98,236	Odiénné	20,600	169,764
Bondoukou	10,040	174,251	Oumé	2,400	141,268
Bongouanou	5,570	224,958	Sakassou	1,880	59,362
Bouaflé	3,980	165,822	San-Pédro	6,900	170,669
Bouaké	4,700	450,594	Sassandra	5,190	108,090
Bouna	21,470	135,813	Séguéla	11,240	121,235
Boundiali	7,895	127,847	Sinfra	1,690	121,903
Dabakala	9,670	81,820	Soubré	8,270	310,790
Daloa	5,450	359,753	Tabou	5,440	58,147
Danané	4,600	222,839	Tanda	6,490	204,070
Daoukro	3,610	86,494	Tengréla	2,200	54,847
Dimbokro	4,920	141,968	Tiassalé	3,370	133,708
Divo	7,920	387,106	Touba	8,720	107,886
Duékoué	2,930	102,168	Toumodi	2,780	80,802
Ferkessedougou	17,728	172,893	Vavoua	6,160	168,292
Gagnoa	4,500	276,217	Yamoussoukro	6,160	281,442
Grand-Lahou	2,280	52,559	Zuénoula	2,830	114,027
			TOTAL	320,763[2]	10,815,694

Demography

Population (1996): 14,733,000.
Density (1996): persons per sq mi 119.0, persons per sq km 45.9.
Urban-rural (1995): urban 43.6%; rural 56.4%.
Sex distribution (1993): male 50.77%; female 49.23%.
Age breakdown (1988): under 15, 48.8%; 15–29, 24.7%; 30–44, 14.1%; 45–59, 8.1%; 60–64, 1.7%; 65 and over, 2.6%.
Population projection: (2000) 16,761,000; (2010) 23,058,000.
Ethnolinguistic composition (1988)[3]: Akan 41.8%; Voltaic 16.3%; Malinke 15.9%; Kru 14.6%; Southern Mande 10.7%; other 0.7%.
Religious affiliation (1988): Muslim 38.7%; Catholic 20.8%; animist 17.0%; atheist 13.4%; Protestant 5.3%, excluding Harrism (1.4%); other 3.4%.
Major cities (1988): Abidjan (1990) 2,168,000; Bouaké 329,850; Daloa 121,842; Korhogo 109,445; Yamoussoukro 106,786.

Vital statistics

Birth rate per 1,000 population (1990–95): 49.9 (world avg. 25.0).
Death rate per 1,000 population (1990–95): 15.1 (world avg. 9.3).
Natural increase rate per 1,000 population (1990–95): 34.8 (world avg. 15.7).
Total fertility rate (avg. births per childbearing woman; 1990–95): 7.4.
Life expectancy at birth (1990–95): male 49.7 years; female 52.4 years.
Major causes of death per 100,000 population: n.a.; however, AIDS was a
　major cause of both morbidity and mortality among adults in the mid-1990s;
　other endemic diseases included yellow fever, trypanosomiasis, dracunculia-
　sis, childhood diseases, yaws, and tuberculosis.

National economy

Budget (1994). Revenue: CFAF 840,100,000,000 (current revenues 81.7%, of
　which duties 28.1%, taxes on income, goods, and services 16.8%). Expendi-
　tures: CFAF 789,800,000,000 (current expenses 79.1%; investments 20.9%).
Public debt (external, outstanding; 1994): U.S.$11,271,000,000.
Production (metric tons except as noted). Agriculture, forestry, fishing (1995):
　yams 2,823,650, cassava 1,564,080, plantains 1,300,000, sugarcane 1,171,288,
　paddy rice 1,045,452, cacao beans 860,000, corn (maize) 552,000, coconuts
　213,000, coffee 193,591; livestock (number of live animals) 1,282,000 sheep,
　1,258,000 cattle, 1,002,000 goats; roundwood (1994) 13,059,000 cu m; fish
　catch (1993) 70,174. Mining and quarrying (1994)[4]: gold 1,500 kg; diamonds
　15,000 carats. Manufacturing (value added in CFAF '000,000,000; 1993):
　food products 146, refined petroleum products 100, textiles 48, transport
　equipment 32, wood products 32, industrial chemicals 30, fabricated metal
　products 25. Construction (in CFAF; 1984): 62,000,000,000. Energy produc-
　tion (consumption): electricity (kW-hr; 1994) 1,917,000,000 (1,917,000,000);
　coal, none (n.a.); crude petroleum (barrels; 1994) 2,441,000 (24,623,000);
　petroleum products (metric tons; 1994) 2,320,000 (2,306,000).
Land use (1994): forest 34.3%; pasture 40.9%; agricultural 11.7%.
Gross national product (1994): U.S.$7,070,000,000 (U.S.$510 per capita).

Structure of gross domestic product and labour force

	1994			
	in value CFAF '000,000,000	% of total value	labour force	% of labour force
Agriculture	1,277.4	30.7	2,886,000	51.1
Manufacturing and mining	815.7	19.6	}	
Construction and public utilities	78.8	1.9	650,000	11.5
Transp. and commun.	260.6	6.3		
Trade	1,126.3	27.1	}	
Finance, pub. admin., defense, and services	413.6	9.9	2,112,000	37.4
Other (customs receipts)	185.3	4.5		
TOTAL	4,157.7	100.0	5,648,000	100.0

Population economically active (1994): total 5,648,000; activity rate of total
population 41.1% (participation rates: over age 10, 64.3%; female 33.8%;
unemployed, n.a.).

Price and earnings indexes (1990 = 100)

	1989	1990	1991	1992	1993	1994	1995
Consumer price index	100.8	100.0	101.7	106.0	108.3	136.5	156.0
Hourly earnings index[5]	100.0	100.0	100.0	100.0	...	...	...

Household income and expenditure. Average household size (1988) 5.4; average annual income per household (1980) CFAF 500,000; sources of income:
self-employment 49.9%, wages 44.9%, transfers and other resources 5.2%;
expenditure (1992)[6]: food 48.0%, clothing 10.1%, energy and water 8.5%,
housing 7.8%, transportation 6.8%.
Tourism (1994): receipts U.S.$43,000,000; expenditures U.S.$118,000,000.

Foreign trade

Balance of trade (current prices)

	1989	1990	1991	1992	1993	1994
U.S.$'000,000	+919.7	+1,093.8	+923.4	+994.7	+850.8	+1,308.5
% of total	20.6%	23.1%	20.6%	20.3%	19.1%	29.5%

Imports (1994): CFAF 868,200,000,000 (crude and refined petroleum 23.5%;
food and food products 18.8%; machinery and transport equipment 13.4%;
plastics 4.9%; pharmaceuticals 4.8%; paper and paper products 4.3%; iron
1.5%). *Major import sources:* France 28.2%; Nigeria 26.8%; U.S. 5.9%; Germany 3.3%; Italy 3.2%.
Exports (1994): CFAF 1,608,000,000,000 (food products 50.4%, of which cocoa
beans and products 32.3%, coffee and coffee products 7.5%, fish products
4.0%; wood and wood products 13.9%; petroleum products 9.6%; cotton
and cotton cloth 4.9%). *Major export destinations:* France 16.1%; Germany
9.8%; The Netherlands 8.9%; Italy 7.1%; Burkina Faso 6.0%; Mali 5.7%;
U.S. 5.1%; Belgium-Luxembourg 4.7%; U.K. 1.9%.

Transport and communications

Transport. Railroads (1992): route length 651 km; passenger-km 189,000,000;
metric ton-km cargo 266,000,000. Roads (1995): total length 31,168 mi, 50,-
160 km (paved 9.6%). Vehicles (1995): passenger cars 271,000; trucks and
buses 150,000. Merchant marine (1992): vessels (100 gross tons and over)
51; total deadweight tonnage 98,618. Air transport (1995)[7]: passenger-km
222,822,000; metric ton-km cargo 15,273,000; airports (1996) 11.
Communications. Daily newspapers (1992): total number 1; total circulation
90,000; circulation per 1,000 population 7. Radio (1995): 1,600,000 receivers
(1 per 8.9 persons). Television (1995): 810,000 receivers (1 per 17.6 persons).
Telephones (main lines; 1993): 93,880 (1 per 140 persons).

Education and health

Education (1993)

	schools	teachers	students	student/ teacher ratio
Primary (age 7–12)	7,249	39,691	1,553,540	39.1
Secondary (age 13–19)[8]	147	9,644	445,505	46.2
Voc., teacher tr.	15[9]	1,947[10]	3,094[9]	...
Higher	1	...	c. 40,000	...

Educational attainment (1988). Percentage of population age 6 and over
having: no formal schooling 60.0%; Koranic school 3.6%; primary education
24.8%; secondary 10.7%; higher 0.9%. *Literacy* (1995): percentage of population age 15 and over literate 40.1%; males 49.9%; females 30.0%.
Health: physicians (1990) 1,020 (1 per 11,745 persons); hospital beds (1993)
7,928 (1 per 1,698 persons); infant mortality rate (1990–95) 92.0.
Food (1992): daily per capita caloric intake 2,491 (vegetable products 96%,
animal products 4%); 107% of FAO recommended minimum requirement.

Military

Total active duty personnel (1996): 8,400[11] (army 81.0%, navy 10.7%, air force
8.3%). *Military expenditure as percentage of GNP* (1994): 1.1% (world avg.
3.0%); per capita expenditure U.S.$4.

---

[1]Since 1986, Côte d'Ivoire has requested that the French form of the country's
name be used as the official protocol version in all languages. [2]Total area per
more recent survey is 322,463 sq km; breakdown of that area by department is
not available. [3]"Ivoirian" nationals only, representing about 65% of the de facto
population. [4]Excludes production smuggled out of country. [5]January 1; index refers
to the S.M.I.G. (*salaire minimum interprofessionel garanti*), a form of minimum professional wage. [6]Weights of consumer price index components for a worker's family
living in the capital city. [7]Represents ¹⁄₁₁ share of traffic of Air Afrique, which is
operated by 11 West African states. [8]Data exclude 208 private schools, with (1992)
107,096 students. [9]1992. [10]1991. [11]Excluding about 700 French military personnel
stationed in Côte d'Ivoire.

Croatia

Official name: Republika Hrvatska
(Republic of Croatia).
Form of government: multiparty
republic with a two-chambered
legislature (House of Counties [68[1]];
House of Representatives [127[2]]).
Head of state: President.
Head of government: Prime Minister.
Capital: Zagreb.
Official language: Croatian.
Official religion: none.
Monetary unit: 1 kuna (plural kune)[3] =
100 lipa; valuation (Oct. 11, 1996)
1 U.S.$ = 5.45 kune; 1 £ = 8.56 kune.

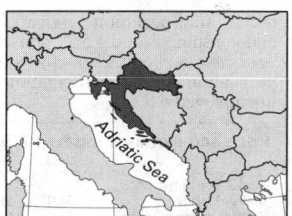

Price and earnings indexes (1990 = 100)

	1990	1991	1992	1993	1994	1995
Consumer price index	100	224	1,647	26,127	54,122	56,332
Annual earnings index[6]	100	168	697	11,187	26,089	38,008

Gross domestic product (1994): U.S.$11,855,800,000 (U.S.$2,482 per capita).

Structure of gross domestic product and labour force

	1994		1991	
	in value '000,000 kune[3]	% of total value	labour force	% of labour force
Agriculture	9,248.8	11.0	265,000	13.0
Mining } Manufacturing }	23,538.1	28.0	613,000	30.0
Construction	1,792.0	2.1	98,000	4.8
Public utilities	12,927.0	15.4	32,700	1.6
Transp. and commun.	3,750.9	4.5	120,000	5.9
Trade	10,057.3	12.0	163,000	8.0
Finance	6,741.0	8.0	60,400	3.0
Pub. admin., defense	12,541.6	15.0	315,000	15.4
Services } Other }	3,327.8	4.0	80,700 292,200[7]	4.0 14.3[7]
TOTAL	83,924.5	100.0	2,040,000	100.0

Area and population (1991 census)

City	Capitals	area sq mi	area sq km	population 1991 census
Zagreb	—	497	1,288	867,717
County				
Bjelovar-Bilogora	Bjelovar	1,019	2,640	144,042
Dubrovnik-Neretva	Dubrovnikvn	689	1,784	126,329
Istria	Pazin	1,087	2,815	204,346
Karlovac	Karlovac	1,278	3,311	174,105
Koprivnica-Križevci	Koprimica	688	1,783	129,907
Krapina-Zagorje	Krapina	477	1,235	149,534
Lika-Senj	Gospić	1,447	3,748	71,215
Medimurje	Čakovec	282	730	119,866
Osijek-Baranja	Osijek	1,397	3,619	331,979
Požega-Slavonija	Požega	917	2,374	134,548
Primorje-Gorski Kotar	Rijeka	1,381	3,578	323,130
Šibenik	Šibenik	722	1,871	109,171
Sisak-Moslavina	Sisak	1,976	5,117	287,002
Slavonski Brod-Posavina	Slavonski Brod	782	2,026	174,998
Split-Dalmatia	Split	1,745	4,520	474,019
Varaždin	Varaždin	478	1,238	187,343
Virovitica-Podravina	Virovitica	798	2,068	104,625
Vukovar-Srijem	Vukovar	943	2,442	231,241
Zadar-Knin	Zadar	2,453	6,352	272,003
Zagreb	Zagreb	800	2,071	167,145
TOTAL		21,359	55,322	4,784,265

Demography

Population (1996): 4,775,000.
Density (1996): persons per sq mi 218.1, persons per sq km 84.4.
Urban-rural (1991): urban 54.2%; rural 45.8%.
Sex distribution (1991): male 48.50%; female 51.50%.
Age breakdown (1991): under 15, 19.4%; 15–29, 20.7%; 30–44, 22.7%; 45–59, 18.3%; 60–74, 12.9%; 75 and over, 4.5%; not stated 1.5%.
Population projection: (2000) 4,771,000; (2010) 4,761,000.
Doubling time: not applicable; population is declining.
Ethnic composition (1991): Croat 78.1%; Serb 12.1%; Muslims 0.9%; Hungarians 0.5%; Slovene 0.5%; other 7.9%.
Religious affiliation (1991): Roman Catholic 76.5%; Eastern Orthodox 11.1%; Muslim 1.2%; other 11.2%[4].
Major cities (1991): Zagreb 867,717; Split 200,459; Rijeka 167,964; Osijek 129,792; Zadar 80,355.

Vital statistics

Birth rate per 1,000 population (1994): 10.2 (world avg. 25.0); legitimate 92.4%; illegitimate 7.6%.
Death rate per 1,000 population (1994): 10.4 (world avg. 9.3).
Natural increase rate per 1,000 population (1994): −0.2 (world avg. 15.7).
Total fertility rate (avg. births per childbearing woman; 1993): 1.5.
Marriage rate per 1,000 population (1994): 5.3.
Divorce rate per 1,000 population (1994): 1.0.
Life expectancy at birth (1991): male 68.6 years; female 76.0 years.
Major causes of death per 100,000 population (1993): diseases of the circulatory system 533.2; malignant neoplasms (cancers) 218.0; accidents, violence, and poisoning 95.0; diseases of the digestive system 49.7; diseases of the respiratory system 45.3.

National economy

Budget (1994). Revenue: 23,142,632,000 kune[3] (sales tax 56.8%, customs and import fees 15.1%, income tax 14.0%). Expenditures: 22,684,741 kune[3] (goods and services 41.7%, interest 27.8%, current transfers 12.4%).
Production (metric tons except as noted). Agriculture, forestry, fishing (1995): corn (maize) 1,600,000, wheat 1,007,500, sugar beets 580,000, potatoes 500,000, grapes 360,000, barley 109,000, plums 40,000; livestock (number of live animals) 1,347,000 pigs, 493,000 cattle, 453,000 sheep, 12,000,000 poultry; roundwood (1994) 3,303,000 cu m; fish catch (1993) 30,269, of which freshwater 4,446. Mining and quarrying (1994): lime 156,451[5]; bauxite 1,302. Manufacturing (1994): ammonia 350,184; crude steel 63,352; detergents 30,731; aluminum 25,993; cotton fibre 10,587. Construction (value in kune; 1994): residential 1,966,315; nonresidential 4,590,289. Energy production (consumption): electricity (kW-hr; 1993) 8,273,000,000 (9,939,000,000); coal (metric tons; 1994) 96,205 (793,000[5]); crude petroleum (barrels; 1994) 11,556,000 (36,474,000[5]); petroleum products (metric tons; 1994) 4,254,000 (3,084,000[5]); natural gas (cu m; 1994) 1,792,000,000 (2,373,000,000).
Land use (1994): forest 37.1%; pasture 19.3%; agricultural 21.6%; other 22.0%.
Population economically active (1991): total 2,040,000; activity rate 42.6% (participation rates: ages 15–64, 57.2%; female 42.8%; unemployed 11.2%).

Household income and expenditure. Average household size (1991) 3.1; income per household (1990) Din 165,813[3] (U.S.$14,650); sources (1990): self-employment 40.8%, wages 40.2%, transfers 12.1%, other 6.9%; expenditure (1988): food 34.2%, transportation 9.3%, clothing 8.6%, housing 8.3%, energy 7.6%, drink and tobacco 5.1%, durable goods 4.5%, health care 4.3%.

Foreign trade[8]

Balance of trade (current prices)[9]

	1990	1991	1992	1993	1994	1995
'000,000 kune[3]	−11,333	−7,160	−3,877	−1,636	−3,604	−5,962
% of total	13.7%	7.8%	2.2%	5.5%	10.0%	18.7%

Imports (1995): 30,399,052,000 kune[3] (1994; machinery and transport equipment 25.9%; products classified according to constituent material 15.2%; miscellaneous ready-made products 14.6%; mineral fuels, lubricants, and similar products 11.8%; chemical products 10.4%; food and live animals 9.5%; raw materials except fuel 2.9%; beverages and tobacco 1.2%). *Major import sources* (1994): Germany 20.2%; Italy 18.1%; Slovenia 9.9%; Austria 6.4%; Iran 5.5%.
Exports (1995): 49,739,202,000 kune[3] (1994; miscellaneous ready-made products 29.0%; machinery and transport equipment 17.5%; products classified according to constituent material 15.2%; chemical products 12.9%; mineral fuels, lubricants, and similar products 9.3%; food and live animals 9.3%; raw materials except fuel 5.0%; beverages and tobacco 1.6%). *Major export destinations* (1994): Germany 21.1%; Italy 20.3%; Slovenia 12.4%; former U.S.S.R. 3.9%; Sweden 3.8%.

Transport and communications

Transport. Railroads (1994): length 1,676 mi, 2,699 km; passenger-km 962,000,000; metric ton-km cargo 1,563,000,000. Roads (1994): total length 26,928 km (paved 81%). Vehicles (1994): passenger cars 698,391; trucks and buses 53,860. Merchant marine (1994): cargo ships 155. Air transport (1994): passenger-km 444,000,000; metric ton-km cargo 3,000,000; airports (1996) with scheduled flights 5.
Communications. Daily newspapers (1992): 9; total circulation 2,404,000; circulation per 1,000 population 503. Radio (1996): 1,100,000 receivers (1 per 4.3 persons). Television (1996): 750,000 receivers (1 per 6.4 persons). Telephones (main lines; 1993): 1,027,400 (1 per 4.7 persons).

Education and health

Education (1994–95)

	schools	teachers	students	student/ teacher ratio
Primary (age 7–14)	1,928	24,194	431,795	17.8
Secondary (age 15–18)	482	15,269	196,740	12.9
Voc., teacher tr.	3	79	2,660	33.7
Higher	61	5,814	77,525	13.3

Educational attainment (1991). Percentage of population age 15 and over having: no schooling or unknown 10.1%; less than full primary education 21.2%; primary 23.4%; secondary 36.0%; postsecondary and higher 9.3%.
Literacy (1991): total population age 10 and over literate 4,062,074 (97.0%); males 99.0%; females 95.8%.
Health (1994): physicians 9,138 (1 per 524 persons); hospital beds 28,230 (1 per 169 persons); infant mortality rate per 1,000 live births 10.2.

Military

Total active duty personnel (1995): 105,000 (army 97.9%, navy 1.1%, air force and air defense 1.0%). *Military expenditure as percentage of GNP* (1994): 9.0% (world 3.0%).

[1]Includes 5 nonelective seats. [2]Includes 12 seats reserved for Croatians abroad. [3]On Jan. 1, 1990, the Yugoslav new dinar (Din), equal to 10,000 Yugoslav old dinars (Din), was introduced. On Dec. 23, 1991, the Croatian dinar (HrD) was introduced at parity with the Yugoslav new dinar, which it replaced as Croatia's official currency. On May 30, 1994, the kuna, equal to 1,000 Croatian dinars, was introduced. [4]Includes a significant minority of adherents of the Croatian Old Catholic Church, as well as small communities of Protestant Christians and Jews. [5]1993. [6]Based on worker real net personal income. [7]Includes unemployed and private sector. [8]Import figures are f.o.b. in balance of trade and c.i.f. for commodities and trading partners. [9]Balance of trade recalculated to reflect currency changes.

Cuba

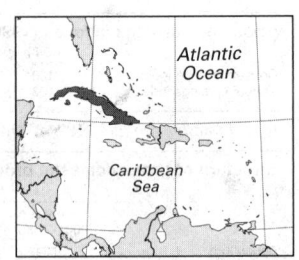

Official name: República de Cuba (Republic of Cuba).
Form of government: unitary socialist republic with one legislative house (National Assembly of the People's Power [589]).
Head of state and government: President.
Capital: Havana.
Official language: Spanish.
Official religion: none.
Monetary unit: 1 Cuban peso (CUP) = 100 centavos; valuation (Oct. 11, 1996) 1 U.S.$ = 1.00 CUP[1]; 1 £ = 1.58 CUP.

Area and population		area		population
				1990[2]
Provinces	Capitals	sq mi	sq km	estimate
Camagüey	Camagüey	6,174	15,990	744,744
Ciego de Avila	Ciego de Avila	2,668	6,910	367,489
Cienfuegos	Cienfuegos	1,613	4,178	366,531
Ciudad de la Habana[3]	—	281	727	2,107,557
Granma	Bayamo	3,232	8,372	793,868
Guantánamo	Guantánamo	2,388	6,186	499,182
Holguín	Holguín	3,591	9,301	997,735
La Habana[4]	Havana	2,213	5,731	647,280
Las Tunas	Las Tunas	2,544	6,589	495,133
Matanzas	Matanzas	4,625	11,978	612,268
Pinar del Río	Pinar del Río	4,218	10,925	694,306
Sancti Spíritus	Sancti Spíritus	2,604	6,744	430,662
Santiago de Cuba	Santiago de Cuba	2,382	6,170	995,370
Villa Clara	Santa Clara	3,345	8,662	810,249
Special municipality				
Isla de la Juventud	Nueva Gerona	926	2,398	73,319
TOTAL		42,804	110,861	10,635,693[5]

Demography

Population (1996): 11,117,000.
Density (1996): persons per sq mi 259.7, persons per sq km 100.3.
Urban-rural (1990): urban 72.8%; rural 27.2%.
Sex distribution (1994): male 50.20%; female 49.80%.
Age breakdown (1994): under 15, 22.8%; 15–29, 28.0%; 30–44, 21.8%; 45–59, 15.2%; 60–74, 8.4%; 75 and over, 3.8%.
Population projection: (2000) 11,385,000; (2010) 11,911,000.
Doubling time: over 100 years.
Ethnic composition (1994): mixed 51.0%; white 37.0%; black 11.0%; other 1.0%.
Religious affiliation (1980): nonreligious 48.7%; Roman Catholic 39.6%; atheist 6.4%; Protestant 3.3%; Afro-Cuban syncretist 1.6%; other 0.4%.
Major cities (1993): Havana 2,175,995; Santiago de Cuba 440,084; Camagüey 293,961; Holguín 242,085; Guantánamo 207,796.

Vital statistics

Birth rate per 1,000 population (1993): 14.0 (world avg. 25.0).
Death rate per 1,000 population (1993): 7.2 (world avg. 9.3).
Natural increase rate per 1,000 population (1993): 6.8 (world avg. 15.7).
Total fertility rate (avg. births per childbearing woman; 1990–95): 1.9.
Marriage rate per 1,000 population (1992): 17.7.
Divorce rate per 1,000 population (1993): 6.0.
Life expectancy at birth (1990–95): male 73.9 years; female 77.6 years.
Major causes of death per 100,000 population (1992): heart disease 173.4; malignant neoplasms (cancers) 115.5; cerebrovascular disease 60.9; accidents 45.8; diseases of the blood vessels 23.5; influenza and pneumonia 22.7.

National economy

Budget (1990). Revenue: CUP 12,463,200,000. Expenditures: CUP 14,448,400,-000 (capital investment 37.7%; education and public health 20.4%; social, cultural, and scientific activities 17.3%; defense, internal security 9.5%; housing, community services 6.0%).
Production (metric tons except as noted). Agriculture, forestry, fishing (1995): sugarcane 36,000,000, oranges and tangerines 423,000, grapefruit 280,000, bananas and plantains 260,000, cassava 250,000, potatoes 200,000, tomatoes 200,000, sweet potatoes 170,000, rice 95,000, tobacco leaves 42,000, coffee beans 18,000; livestock (number of live animals) 4,200,000 cattle, 1,550,000 pigs, 22,000,000 chickens; roundwood (1994) 2,756,000 cu m; fish catch (1993) 93,435. Mining and quarrying (1995): chromite (1993) 50,000; nickel (metal content of ores) 16,470[6]. Manufacturing (value added in U.S.$'000,-000; 1990): tobacco products 2,629; food products 1,033; beverages 358; chemical products 354; transport equipment 225; nonelectrical machinery 176; textiles (excluding ready-made clothing) 109; wearing apparel 88; rubber products 83. Construction (gross value of construction in CUP '000,000; 1989): residential 227; nonresidential 872. Energy production (consumption): electricity (kW-hr; 1994) 10,982,000,000 (10,982,000,000); coal (metric tons; 1994) none (153,000); crude petroleum (barrels; 1994) 6,552,000 (38,326,000); petroleum products (metric tons; 1994) 4,456,000 (7,905,000); natural gas (cu m; 1994) 39,004,000 (39,004,000).
Public debt (external, outstanding; 1993): U.S.$10,800,000,000.
Household income and expenditure. Average household size (1990) 3.7; average annual income per household (1982) CUP 3,680 (U.S.$4,330); sources of income (1982): wages and salaries 57.3%, bonuses and other payments 42.7%; personal consumption (1989): food 26.7%, other retail purchases

60.5%, transportation services 5.4%, energy 2.7%, value of self-produced and consumed food 1.5%, household repairs 1.3%, other 1.9%.
Population economically active (1988): total 4,570,236; activity rate of total population 43.7% (participation rates: over age 15, 56.9%; female 36.1%; unemployed 6.0%).

Price and earnings indexes (1985 = 100)							
	1983	1984	1985	1986	1987	1988	1989
Implicit consumer price deflator index	94.9	98.0	100.0	101.4	102.8	103.1	...
Monthly earnings index[7]	95.9	99.0	100.0	100.1	98.1	99.6	100.0

Tourism: receipts from visitors (1994) U.S.$850,000,000; expenditures by nationals abroad (1990) U.S.$48,000,000.
Gross national product (1991): U.S.$17,000,000,000 (U.S.$1,580 per capita).

Structure of global social product and labour force				
	1989			
	in value CUP '000,000	% of total value	labour force[7]	% of labour force
Agriculture	4,273	15.9	721,100	20.4
Mining[8]	1,039	3.9		
Manufacturing	10,617	39.4 }	767,500	21.8
Public utilities	733	2.7		
Construction	2,510	9.3	344,300	9.8
Transp. and commun.	2,151	8.0	235,900	6.7
Finance, insurance	—	—	21,700	0.6
Trade	5,401	20.1	395,300	11.2
Public administration	—	—	151,700	4.3
Services	—	—	835,700	23.7
Other	191	0.7	53,400	1.5
TOTAL	26,915	100.0	3,526,600	100.0

Land use (1994): forested 23.7%; meadows and pastures 27.0%; agricultural and under permanent cultivation 30.7%; other 18.6%.

Foreign trade[9]

Balance of trade (current prices)						
	1989	1990	1991	1992	1993	1994
U.S.$'000,000	−1,576	−1,599	−1,332	−412	−551	−797
% of total	32.1%	37.1%	38.4%	15.1%	19.2%	24.4%

Imports (1994): U.S.$2,032,000,000 (1992; mineral fuels and lubricants 39.4%, food and live animals 25.4%, machinery and transport equipment 15.8%, chemicals 6.9%, basic manufactures 6.6%, inedible crude materials 3.2%). *Major import sources:* Spain 15.7%; Russia 13.4%; China 8.0%; France 7.3%; Mexico 7.0%; Venezuela 6.7%; Netherlands Antilles 5.1%.
Exports (1994): U.S.$1,235,000,000 (1992; sugar 63.4%, minerals and concentrates 10.6%, fish products 5.9%, raw tobacco and tobacco products 4.6%, citrus and other agricultural products 3.4%). *Major export destinations:* Russia 22.1%; Canada 11.5%; China 8.9%; The Netherlands 7.1%; Spain 5.7%; Algeria 4.7%; Japan 4.6%.

Transport and communications

Transport. Railroads (1991): length 3,033 mi, 4,881 km; passenger-km 3,025,-000,000; metric ton-km cargo 1,368,000,000. Roads (1986): total length 28,928 mi, 46,555 km (paved 27%). Vehicles (1988): passenger cars 241,300; trucks and buses 208,400. Merchant marine (1992): vessels (100 gross tons and over) 393; total deadweight tonnage 924,591. Air transport (1994): passenger-km 2,153,000,000; metric ton-km cargo 237,998,000; airports with scheduled flights (1996) 14.
Communications. Daily newspapers (1992): total number 17; total circulation 1,315,000; circulation per 1,000 population 122. Radio (1995): 3,608,000 receivers (1 per 3.1 persons). Television (1995): 2,500,000 receivers (1 per 4.4 persons). Telephones (main lines; 1993): 344,200 (1 per 31 persons).

Education and health

Education (1993–94)				
	schools	teachers	students	student/ teacher ratio
Primary (age 6–11)	9,440	76,193	983,459	12.9
Secondary (age 12–17)	2,175[10]	53,423	459,140	8.6
Voc., teacher tr.	618[10]	31,671	266,660	8.4
Higher	35[10]	25,264[11]	198,474[11]	7.9[11]

Educational attainment (1981). Percentage of population age 25 and over having: no formal schooling or some primary education 39.6%; completed primary 26.6%; secondary 29.6%; higher 4.2%. *Literacy* (1995 est.): total population age 15 and over literate 95.7%; males literate 96.2%; females literate 95.3%.
Health (1992): physicians 46,860 (1 per 231 persons); hospital beds 80,684 (1 per 134 persons); infant mortality rate per 1,000 live births (1994) 9.4.
Food (1992): daily per capita caloric intake 2,833 (vegetable products 84%, animal products 16%); 123% of FAO recommended minimum requirement.

Military

Total active duty personnel (1996): 100,000 (army 85.0%, navy 5.0%, air force 10.0%). *Military expenditure as percentage of GDP* (1994): 1.6% (world 3.0%); per capita expenditure: U.S.$32.

[1]Official rate; the black-market rate is about 20–25 pesos (CUP) to 1 U.S.$. [2]January 1. [3]Province coextensive with the city of Havana. [4]Province bordering the city of Havana on the east, south, and west. [5]The 1993 census total was 10,900,000; detail, n.a. [6]Includes cobalt. [7]State sector only; excludes military and unemployed. [8]Mining includes metallurgy and refined petroleum products. [9]Imports c.i.f.; exports f.o.b. [10]1989–90. [11]1992–93.

Cyprus

Island of Cyprus

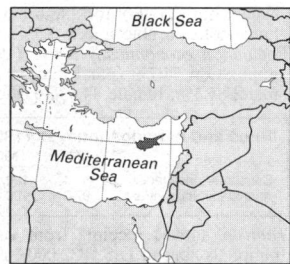

Area: 3,572 sq mi, 9,251 sq km.
Population (1996): 767,000[1].

Two de facto states currently exist on the island of Cyprus: the Republic of Cyprus (ROC), predominantly Greek in character, occupying the southern two-thirds of the island, which is the original and still the internationally recognized de jure government of the whole island; and the Turkish Republic of Northern Cyprus (TRNC), proclaimed unilaterally Nov. 15, 1983, on territory originally secured for the Turkish Cypriot population by the July 20, 1974, intervention of Turkey. Only Turkey recognizes the TRNC, and the two ethnic communities have failed to reestablish a single state. Provision of separate data below does not imply recognition of either state's claims but is necessitated by the continuing lack of unified data.

Republic of Cyprus

Official name: Kipriakí Dimokratía (Greek); Kıbrıs Cumhuriyeti (Turkish) (Republic of Cyprus).
Form of government: unitary multiparty republic with a unicameral legislature (House of Representatives [80[2]]).
Head of state and government: President.
Capital: Lefkosia (Nicosia).
Official languages: Greek; Turkish.
Monetary unit: 1 Cyprus pound (£C) = 100 cents; valuation (Oct. 11, 1996) 1 £C = U.S.$2.13 = £1.37.

Area and population

Census districts	Main towns	area sq mi	area sq km	population[3] 1994 estimate[4]
Ammochostos	Paralimni	...	...	32,000
Larnaca	Larnaca	433	1,121	105,200
Lefkosia	Lefkosia	...	...	255,700
Limassol	Limassol	538	1,393	182,000
Paphos	Paphos	539	1,396	54,900
TOTAL		2,276[5]	5,896[5]	629,800

Demography

Population (1996): 657,000[1].
Urban-rural (1994[4]): urban 68.0%; rural 32.0%.
Age breakdown (1994[4]): under 15, 25.3%; 15–29, 21.8%; 30–44, 22.4%; 45–59, 15.6%; 60–74, 10.2%; 75 and over, 4.7%.
Ethnic composition (1992): Greek Cypriot 95.1%; British 0.8%; other 4.1%.
Religious affiliation (1995): Cypriot Orthodox 92.0%; Maronite 1.3%; other 6.7%.
Urban areas (1994[4]): Lefkosia 186,400[6]; Limassol 143,400; Larnaca 64,000.

Vital statistics

Birth rate per 1,000 population (1994): 16.4 (world avg. 25.0).
Death rate per 1,000 population (1994): 7.8 (world avg. 9.3).
Natural increase rate per 1,000 population (1994): 8.6 (world avg. 15.7).
Life expectancy at birth (1992–93): male 74.6 years; female 79.1 years.

National economy

Budget (1994). Revenue: £C 1,144,300,000 (indirect taxes 39.3%, direct taxes 24.9%, social security contributions 20.4%). Expenditures: £C 1,196,100,000 (current expenditures 89.6%, development expenditures 10.4%).
Tourism (1994): receipts U.S.$1,653,000,000; expenditures U.S.$247,000,000.
Household expenditure (1992): food and beverages 22.7%, transportation and communications 15.6%, expenditures in cafes and hotels 13.6%.
Gross national product (1994): U.S.$7,254,000,000 (U.S.$11,440 per capita).

Structure of gross domestic product and labour force

	1995 in value £C '000,000	% of total value	labour force	% of labour force
Agriculture	204.0	5.3	34,000	11.4
Mining	10.7	0.3	800	0.3
Manufacturing	459.2	11.9	44,300	14.8
Construction	339.1	8.8	23,500	7.8
Public utilities	83.6	2.2	1,500	0.5
Transp. and commun.	299.7	7.7	17,500	5.8
Trade	751.0	19.4	72,000	24.0
Finance, insurance	628.8	16.3	21,500	7.2
Pub. admin., defense	502.7	13.0 }	62,900	21.0
Services	296.8	7.7 }		
Other	285.1	7.4	21,700[7]	7.2[7]
TOTAL	3,860.7	100.0	299,700	100.0

Production. Agriculture (value of production in £C '000,000; 1993): milk 27.9, potatoes 24.1, poultry 24.1, barley 21.8, grapes 15.6. Manufacturing (value added in £C '000,000; 1993): food 62.5; wearing apparel 46.9;

cement, bricks, and tiles 38.8; beverages 35.1; cigarettes and cigars 28.7. Energy production: electricity (kW-hr; 1994) 2,681,000,000.

Foreign trade[8]

Imports (1995): £C 1,670,400,000 (consumer goods 29.7%; transport equipment 11.9%; capital goods 10.7%; mineral fuels 7.7%). *Major import sources:* U.S. 13.0%; U.K. 11.8%; Italy 9.8%; Germany 8.2%; Greece 7.2%.
Exports (1995): £C 555,500,000 (reexports 50.0%[9]; domestic exports 41.8%, of which clothing 8.0%, potatoes 7.8%; ships' stores 8.2%). *Major export destinations:* Russia 13.7%; U.K. 13.3%; Bulgaria 9.1%; Greece 6.0%.

Transport and communications

Transport. Roads (1994): total length 10,117 km (paved 59%). Vehicles (1994): cars 210,365; trucks and buses 98,114. Merchant marine (1992): vessels 1,416; deadweight tonnage 36,198,083. Air transport (1995)[10]: passenger-km 2,667,000,000; metric ton-km cargo 36,187,000; airports (1996) 2.
Communications. Daily newspapers (1993): 9; total circulation 84,600; circulation per 1,000 population 135. Television (1995): 102,500 receivers (1 per 6.3 persons). Telephones (main lines; 1993): 311,000 (1 per 2.5 persons).

Education and health

Education (1994–95)

	schools	teachers	students	student/ teacher ratio
Primary (age 6–11)	383	3,498	64,884	18.5
Secondary (age 12–17)	107	3,832	53,738	14.0
Vocational	11	509	4,066	8.0
Higher	32	648	7,765	12.0

Educational attainment (1992). Percentage of population age 25 and over having: no formal schooling 5.1%; higher education 17.0%. *Literacy* (1992): population age 15 and over literate 95.2%; male 97.8%; female 92.8%.
Health (1993): physicians 1,455 (1 per 433 persons); hospital beds 3,297 (1 per 191 persons); infant mortality rate per 1,000 live births (1994) 9.0.

Turkish Republic of Northern Cyprus

Official name: Kuzey Kıbrıs Türk Cumhuriyeti (Turkish) (Turkish Republic of Northern Cyprus).
Capital: Lefkoşa (Nicosia).
Official language: Turkish.
Monetary unit: 1 Turkish lira (LT) = 100 kurush; valuation (Oct. 11, 1996) 1 U.S.$ = LT 93,990; 1 £ = LT 148,063.

Area and population

Districts	Administrative centres	area sq mi	area sq km	population[11] 1992 estimate
Lefkoşa	Lefkoşa	...	...	81,492
Gazimağusa (Famagusta)	Gazimağusa	...	...	66,408
Girne (Kyrenia)	Girne	247	640	27,218
TOTAL		1,295	3,355	175,118

Population (1996): 110,000[1] (Lefkoşa 41,815[11, 12]; Gazimağusa 21,722[11, 12]).
Ethnic composition (1985): Turkish 98.7%; other 1.3%.

Structure of gross domestic product and labour force

	1994 in value LT '000,000,000	% of total value	labour force	% of labour force
Agriculture and fishing	1,454	8.9	17,738	23.2
Mining and manufacturing	1,437	8.8	8,207	10.7
Construction	894	5.5 }	9,584	12.5
Public utilities	183	1.1 }		
Transp. and commun.	1,554	9.5	6,228	8.1
Trade, restaurants	3,612	22.2	8,004	10.5
Pub. admin.	3,578	22.0	16,589	21.7
Finance, real estate	2,367	14.5 }	9,460	12.4
Services	}			
Other	1,219[13]	7.5[13]	704[14]	0.9[14]
TOTAL	16,298	100.0	76,514	100.0

Budget (1994). Revenue: LT 4,641,000,000,000 (domestic sources 67.4%, loans 19.0%, aid from Turkey 13.4%). Expenditures: LT 6,261,000,000,000.
Imports (1994): U.S.$286,600,000 (machinery and transport equipment 22.1%, food 13.0%). *Major import sources:* Turkey 45.1%; U.K. 25.6%; other EC 10.8%.
Exports (1994): U.S.$53,400,000 (industrial products 51.3%, citrus fruits 30.0%). *Major export destinations:* U.K. 46.3%; Turkey 19.5%.

Education (1993–94)

	schools	teachers	students	student/ teacher ratio
Primary[15]	218	1,250	19,084	15.3
Secondary (age 15–17)	15	394	5,445	13.8
Vocational	12	341	2,498	7.3
Higher	7	...	5,710	...

Health (1993): physicians 252 (1 per 615 persons); hospital beds 1,047 (1 per 148 persons); infant mortality rate per 1,000 live births 4.3.

---

[1]Includes about 30,000 "settlers" from Turkey in the TRNC; excludes 35,000 Turkish military in the TRNC, 3,800 British military in the Sovereign Base Areas (SBA) in the ROC, and 1,200 UN peacekeeping forces. [2]Twenty-four seats reserved for Turkish Cypriots are not occupied. [3]Excludes British and UN military forces. [4]January 1. [5]Area includes 99 sq mi (256 sq km) of British military SBA and c. 107 sq mi (c. 278 sq km) of the UN Buffer Zone. [6]ROC only. [7]Includes 7,800 unemployed. [8]Imports c.i.f.; exports f.o.b. [9]Mainly cigarettes and consumer electronics. [10]Cyprus Airways. [11]Official TRNC figure(s). [12]1994. [13]Customs duties. [14]Unemployed. [15]Includes preprimary.

Czech Republic

Official name: Česká Republika.
Form of government: unitary multiparty republic with two legislative houses (Senate [81[1]]; Chamber of Deputies [200]).
Chief of state: President.
Head of government: Prime Minister.
Capital: Prague.
Official language: Czech.
Official religion: none.
Monetary unit[2]: 1 koruna (Kč) = 100 halura; valuation (Oct. 11, 1996) 1 U.S.$ = 27.18 Kč; 1 £ = 42.81 Kč.

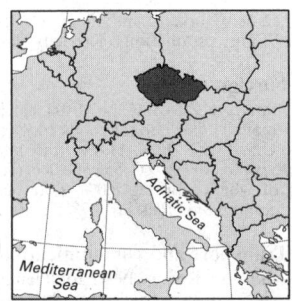

Area and population

		area		population
		sq mi	sq km	1993[3] estimate
Regions	**Capitals**			
Jižní Čechy	České Budějovice	4,380	11,345	699,329
Jižní Morava	Brno	5,802	15,027	2,055,674
Severní Čechy	Ústí nad Labem	3,003	7,777	1,176,707
Severní Morava	Ostrava	4,273	11,068	1,969,366
Střední Čechy	Prague	4,262	11,038	1,110,114
Východní Čechy	Hradec Králové	4,340	11,240	1,236,368
Západní Čechy	Plzeň	4,198	10,873	860,824
Capital city				
Prague	—	192	496	1,217,315
TOTAL		30,450	78,864	10,325,697

Demography

Population (1996): 10,315,842.
Density (1996): persons per sq mi 338.8, persons per sq km 130.8.
Urban-rural: n.a.
Sex distribution (1994): male 48.60%; female 51.40%.
Age breakdown (1994): under 15, 18.9%; 15–29, 23.1%; 30–44, 21.3%; 45–59, 18.7%; 60–74, 13.5%; 75 and over, 4.5%.
Population projection: (2000) 10,352,000; (2010) 10,439,451.
Doubling time: not applicable; population is declining.
Ethnic composition (1991): Czech 81.2%; Moravian 13.2%; Slovak 3.1%; Polish 0.6%; German 0.5%; Silesian 0.4%; Gypsy 0.3%; Hungarian 0.2%; Ukrainian 0.1%; other 0.4%.
Religious affiliation (1991): Roman Catholic 39.0%; Protestant 4.3%, of which Czechoslovak Brethren Reformed 2.0%, Czechoslovak Hussite 1.7%, Silesian Evangelical 0.3%; Eastern Orthodox 0.2%; Greek Catholic 0.1%; other Christian 0.3%; undenominational 39.9%; other 16.2%.
Major cities (1994): Prague 1,217,000; Brno 390,100; Ostrava 326,200; Plzeň 172,300; Olomouc 105,900.

Vital statistics

Birth rate per 1,000 population (1995): 9.3 (world avg. 25.0); (1992) legitimate 89.3%; illegitimate 10.7%.
Death rate per 1,000 population (1995): 11.4 (world avg. 9.3).
Natural increase rate per 1,000 population (1995): −2.1 (world avg. 15.7).
Total fertility rate (avg. births per childbearing woman; 1992): 1.7.
Marriage rate per 1,000 population (1995): 5.3.
Divorce rate per 1,000 population (1995): 3.0.
Life expectancy at birth (1993): male 68.9 years; female 76.6 years.
Major causes of death per 100,000 population (1992): diseases of the circulatory system 649.9; malignant neoplasms (cancers) 271.5; accidents, poisoning, and violence 84.2; diseases of the respiratory system 49.4; diseases of the digestive system 43.0; diseases of the genitourinary system 19.2; endocrine and metabolic disorders 16.0.

National economy

Budget (1995). Revenue: Kč 440,000,000,000[2] (taxes 58.0%, of which value-added tax 21.5%, income tax 16.5%, consumer tax 12.9%, external trade tax 4.0%, road tax 0.9%, property tax 0.7%, other taxes 1.5%; social security 35.1%; other revenue 15.1%). Expenditures: Kč 432,700,000,000[2] (current expenditures 84.9%, of which social security 34.0%, subsidies to organizations 20.2%, defense 9.5%, transfers to local budgets 7.7%, enterprise subsidies 6.4%, education 3.7%, health care 3.4%; capital expenditures 10.2%; other 4.9%).
Public debt (external, outstanding; 1994): U.S.$10,694,000,000.
Production (metric tons except as noted). Agriculture, forestry, fishing (1995): cereals 6,606,000 (of which wheat 3,823,000, barley 2,140,000, rye 262,000, corn [maize] 113,000); sugar beets 3,712,000, potatoes 1,330,119; livestock (number of live animals) 3,867,000 pigs, 2,030,000 cattle, 26,000,000 poultry; roundwood (1994) 11,404,000 cu m; fish catch (1993) 24,388. Mining and quarrying (1995): polymetallic ores 98,000; iron ores 36,000. Manufacturing (value of production in Kč '000,000[2]; 1993): machinery and transport equipment 60,766; metal products 48,151; textiles 19,330; chemical products 18,484; food products 16,638. Construction (value in Kč '000,000[2]; 1993): residential 19,496; nonresidential 236,611. Energy production (consumption): electricity (kW-hr; 1994) 58,705,000,000 (58,260,000,000); coal (metric tons; 1994) 10,886,000 (6,907,000); crude petroleum (barrels; 1994) 938,000 (48,312,000); petroleum products (metric tons; 1994) 4,384,000 (5,514,000); natural gas (cu m; 1994) 242,000,000 (7,339,000,000).
Household income and expenditure. Average household size (1996) 2.9; income per household (1996) Kč 243,043[2] (U.S.$8,942); sources of income (1996[3]): wages and salaries 66.7%, transfer payments 27.6%, other 5.7%;

expenditure (1996): food and beverages 25.6%, housing and utilities 11.3%, household durable goods 7.3%, clothing and footwear 7.2%, other 48.6%.
Population economically active (1996): total 5,642,700; activity rate of total population 54.7% (participation rates: [1992] ages 15–59 [male], 15–54 [female] 86.3%; female 44.4%; [1995] unemployed 3.3%).

Price and earnings indexes (1990 = 100)

	1989	1990	1991	1992	1993	1994	1995
Consumer price index	91.4	100.0	170.0	174.0	210.3	231.6	252.6
Annual earnings index	97.3	100.0	116.6	127.3	177.7	209.9	248.7

Tourism: (1994) receipts from visitors U.S.$1,966,000,000; expenditures by nationals abroad U.S.$832,000,000.
Gross national product (1994): U.S.$33,051,000,000 (U.S.$3,198 per capita).

Structure of net material product and labour force

	1993		1996	
	in value Kč '000,000[2]	% of total value	labour force	% of labour force
Agriculture	47,900	5.2	322,200	5.7
Mining and manufacturing	260,000	28.1	1,608,200	28.5
Construction	33,000	3.6	481,800	8.5
Public utilities	56,200	6.1	104,200	1.8
Transportation and communications	60,000	6.5	400,100	7.1
Trade	76,400	8.3	849,200	15.0
Finance			360,300	6.4
Pub. admin., defense }	265,100	28.7	277,100	4.9
Services			821,800	14.6
Other	124,500	13.5	417,800[4]	7.4
TOTAL	923,100	100.0	5,642,700	100.0[5]

Land use (1994): forested 33.3%; meadows and pastures 11.3%; agricultural and under permanent cultivation 43.0%; other 12.4%.

Foreign trade

Balance of trade (current prices)

	1990	1991	1992	1993	1994	1995
Kč '000,000[2]	−14,410	+41,680	−45,300	+10,100	−20,600	−93,892
% of total	2.8%	5.9%	8.4%	1.3%	2.4%	7.6%

Imports (1995): Kč 554,312,000,000[2] (machinery and transport equipment 35.6%, manufactured goods 17.9%, chemicals 13.2%, fuels and lubricants 9.4%). *Major import sources:* Germany 25.8%; Slovakia 13.1%; Russia 8.9%; Austria 6.9%; Italy 5.8%.
Exports (1995): Kč 453,450,000,000[2] (manufactured goods 32.4%, machinery and transport equipment 26.3%, miscellaneous manufactured articles 12.6%, inedible crude materials, except fuel 6.0%, food and live animals 5.8%). *Major export destinations:* Germany 31.8%; Slovakia 16.2%; Austria 6.5%; Italy 4.0%; Russia 3.5%.

Transport and communications

Transport. Railroads (1993): length 5,866 mi, 9,441 km; passenger-mi 5,311,000,000, passenger-km 8,548,000,000; short ton-mi cargo 17,520,000,000, metric ton-km cargo 25,579,000,000. Roads (1995): total length 77,528 mi, 124,770 km (paved 13%). Vehicles (1995): passenger cars 3,113,476; trucks and buses 204,238. Merchant marine (1993): vessels (oceangoing) 18; total deadweight tonnage 514,126. Air transport (1993): passenger-mi 1,588,000, passenger-km 2,555,062; short ton-mi 46,695,000, metric ton-km 68,174,000; airports (1996) with scheduled flights 2.
Communications. Daily newspapers (1992): total number 55; total circulation 6,000,000; circulation per 1,000 population 583. Radio (1996): total number of receivers 9,100,000 (1 per 1.1 persons). Television (1993): total number of receivers 4,905,000 (1 per 2.1 persons). Telephones (main lines; 1993): 1,961,100 (1 per 5.2 persons).

Education and health

Education (1993–94)

	schools	teachers	students	student/ teacher ratio
Primary (age 6–14)	4,199	63,767	1,061,396	16.6
Secondary (age 15–18)	324	8,456	122,171	14.4
Voc., teacher tr.	821	16,854	219,249	13.0
Higher	23	13,463	127,137	9.4

Educational attainment (1991). Percentage of adult population having: primary and incomplete secondary 33.1%; complete secondary 22.8%; higher 7.2%. *Literacy* (1990): total population age 15 and over literate 8,170,442 (100%); males literate 3,914,080 (100%); females literate 4,256,362 (100%).
Health (1993): physicians 37,068 (1 per 272 persons); hospital beds 103,556 (1 per 79 persons); (1995) infant mortality rate per 1,000 live births 7.4.
Food (1992): daily per capita caloric intake 3,303 (vegetable products 70%, animal products 30%); 128% of FAO recommended minimum requirement.

Military

Total active duty personnel (1996): 44,000 (army 63.6%, air force 36.4%). *Military expenditure as percentage of GNP* (1994): 2.7% (world 3.0%). Per capita expenditure (1994): U.S.$208.

---

[1]First Czech Senate elected November 1996. [2]The koruna (Kč) was introduced Feb. 8, 1993, at par with the former Czechoslovak koruna (Kčs), which it replaced. [3]January 1. [4]Includes 213,100 employed with second job, 188,300 people with disabilities, and 16,400 nondistributable. [5]Detail does not add to total given because of rounding.

Denmark

Official name: Kongeriget Danmark
 (Kingdom of Denmark).
Form of government: parliamentary
 state and constitutional monarchy
 with one legislative house (Folketing
 [179]).
Chief of state: Danish Monarch.
Head of government: Prime Minister.
Capital: Copenhagen.
Official language: Danish.
Official religion: Evangelical Lutheran.
Monetary unit: 1 Danish krone (Dkr;
 plural kroner) = 100 øre; valuation
 (Oct. 11, 1996) 1 U.S.$ = Dkr 5.87;
 1 £ = Dkr 9.25.

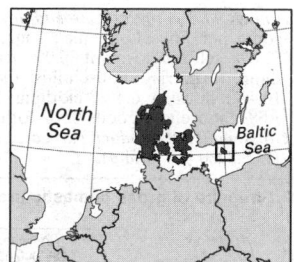

Area and population[1]

Counties	Capitals	area sq mi	area sq km	population 1995[2] estimate
Århus	Århus	1,761	4,561	619,232
Bornholm	Rønne	227	588	44,936
Frederiksborg	Hillerød	520	1,347	350,236
Fyn	Odense	1,346	3,486	467,695
København	—	203	526	605,868
Nordjylland	Ålborg	2,383	6,173	488,303
Ribe	Ribe	1,209	3,132	221,750
Ringkøbing	Ringkøbing	1,874	4,853	270,128
Roskilde	Roskilde	344	891	224,052
Sønderjylland	Åbenrå	1,520	3,938	251,992
Storstrøm	Nykøbing Falster	1,312	3,398	256,562
Vejle	Vejle	1,157	2,997	336,663
Vestsjælland	Sorø	1,152	2,984	288,221
Viborg	Viborg	1,592	4,122	230,778
Municipalities				
Copenhagen (København)	—	34	88	471,300
Frederiksberg	—	3	9	88,002
TOTAL		16,639[3]	43,094[3]	5,215,718

Demography

Population (1996): 5,244,000.
Density (1996): persons per sq mi 315.2, persons per sq km 121.7.
Urban-rural (1995): urban 85.2%; rural 14.8%.
Sex distribution (1995): male 49.34%; female 50.66%.
Age breakdown (1995): under 15, 17.3%; 15–29, 21.3%; 30–44, 21.9%; 45–59, 19.7%; 60–74, 12.9%; 75 and over, 6.9%.
Population projection: (2000) 5,318,000; (2010) 5,438,000.
Doubling time: not applicable; population is stable.
Ethnic composition (1994): Danish 96.4%; Asian 1.5%, of which Turkish 0.7%; other Scandinavian 0.5%; residents of former Yugoslavia 0.2%; British 0.2%; other 1.2%.
Religious affiliation (1994): Evangelical Lutheran 87.4%; other Christian 1.6%; Muslim 1.4%; other/nonreligious 9.6%.
Major cities (1992): Greater Copenhagen 1,342,679[4]; Århus 204,139; Odense 140,886; Ålborg 114,970; Frederiksberg 88,002[5, 6].

Vital statistics

Birth rate per 1,000 population (1995): 13.4 (world avg. 25.0); (1993) legitimate 53.2%; illegitimate 46.8%.
Death rate per 1,000 population (1995): 12.1 (world avg. 9.3).
Natural increase rate per 1,000 population (1995): 1.3 (world avg. 15.7).
Total fertility rate (avg. births per childbearing woman; 1993): 1.7.
Marriage rate per 1,000 population (1994): 6.8.
Divorce rate per 1,000 population (1994): 2.6.
Life expectancy at birth (1992–93): male 72.5 years; female 77.8 years.
Major causes of death per 100,000 population (1993): malignant neoplasms (cancers) 298.5; ischemic heart disease 277.3; cerebrovascular disease 114.1.

National economy

Budget (1994)[7]. Revenue: Dkr 559,073,000,000 (direct taxes 51.8%, indirect taxes 30.1%). Expenditures: Dkr 594,390,000,000 (social security assistance 32.4%, education 11.5%, welfare services 9.6%, health 8.5%, defense 2.9%).
National debt (end of year; 1993): Dkr 628,370,000,000.
Tourism (1994): receipts from visitors U.S.$3,174,000,000; expenditures by nationals abroad U.S.$3,583,000,000.
Population economically active (1994): total 2,908,303; activity rate of total population 56.0% (participation rates: ages 16–66, 79.6%; female 46.5%; unemployed [March 1995–February 1996] 9.8%).

Price and earnings indexes (1990 = 100)

	1990	1991	1992	1993	1994	1995	1996
Consumer price index	100.0	102.4	104.5	105.9	108.0	110.2	112.0[8]
Hourly earnings index	100.0	103.9	106.9	109.9	113.4	...	...

Household income and expenditure. Average household size (1995) 2.2; income per household (1988) Dkr 199,354 (U.S.$29,613); principal sources of income (1992): wages and salaries 63.3%, transfers 25.9%, self-employment 14.6%, other −3.8%; expenditure (1992): housing 22.7%, food and beverages 18.4%, transportation and communications 15.3%, recreation 8.0%, household furnishings 6.2%, cafe and hotel expenditures 6.1%.
Production (in Dkr ’000,000 except as noted). Agriculture, forestry, fishing (value added; 1994): pork 15,203, milk 11,525, beef 4,125, wheat 2,918, flowers and plants 2,599, barley 2,203, mink furs 1,259; roundwood (1993) 2,192,000

cu m; fish catch (1993) 1,534,058 metric tons. Mining and quarrying (1993): sand and gravel 25,000,000 cu m; chalk 400,000 metric tons. Manufacturing (value added; 1993): food products 29,445; nonelectrical machinery and apparatus 21,446; chemicals and chemical products 16,839; electrical machinery and apparatus 12,233; printing and publishing 9,546; fabricated metals 9,194; furniture 5,946. Construction (completed; 1994): residential 1,287,000 sq m; nonresidential 2,911,000 sq m. Energy production (consumption): electricity (kW-hr; 1994) 37,640,000,000 ([1993] 34,923,000,000); coal (metric tons; 1993) none (11,898,000); crude petroleum (barrels; 1994) 67,452,000 ([1993] 64,349,000); petroleum products (metric tons; 1993) 8,407,000 (8,121,000); natural gas (cu m; 1994) 4,565,000,000 ([1993] 2,659,000,000).
Gross national product (at current market prices; 1994): U.S.$145,384,000,000 (U.S.$28,110 per capita).

Structure of gross domestic product and labour force

	1994 in value Dkr '000,000[9]	1994 % of total value	1994 labour force[2]	1994 % of labour force[2]
Agriculture, fishing	28,981	3.6 }	132,885	4.6
Mining	7,334	0.9 }		
Manufacturing	155,259	19.4	462,993	15.9
Construction	43,703	5.5	139,660	4.8
Public utilities	15,331	1.9	17,829	0.6
Transp. and commun.	77,168	9.6	171,522	5.9
Trade, restaurants	110,900	13.9	439,807	15.1
Finance, real estate	155,066	19.4	278,090	9.6
Pub. admin., defense	176,052	22.0 }	920,824	31.7
Services	42,732	5.3 }		
Other	−12,585[10]	−1.6[10]	344,753[11]	11.9[11]
TOTAL	799,941	100.0[3]	2,908,303	100.0[3]

Land use (1993): forested 10.5%; meadows and pastures 4.6%; agricultural and under permanent cultivation 59.9%; other 25.0%.

Foreign trade[12]

Balance of trade (current prices)

	1990	1991	1992	1993	1994	1995
Dkr '000,000	+26,404	+32,060	+53,178	+51,783	+51,005	+43,171
% of total	6.5%	7.5%	12.0%	12.0%	10.8%	8.5%

Imports (1994): Dkr 215,009,000,000 (nonelectrical machinery and parts 12.3%, transport equipment and parts 11.7%, food products 11.1%). *Major import sources:* Germany 21.7%; Sweden 11.6%; The Netherlands 6.7%; United Kingdom 6.5%; France 5.4%; United States 5.2%.
Exports (1994): Dkr 252,287,000,000 (nonelectrical and electrical machinery 24.2%, fresh or frozen swine meat 6.4%, furniture 4.5%, textiles and clothing 4.3%, pharmaceuticals 4.3%). *Major export destinations:* Germany 22.4%; Sweden 10.4%; United Kingdom 8.2%; Norway 6.5%; France 5.5%; United States 5.5%.

Transport and communications

Transport. Railroads (1994): route length 1,763 mi, 2,838 km; passenger-mi 3,048,000,000, passenger-km 4,905,000,000; short ton-mi cargo 1,384,000,000, metric ton-km cargo 2,021,000,000. Roads (1994): total length 44,276 mi, 71,255 km (paved 100%). Vehicles (1994): passenger cars 1,668,278; trucks and buses 277,824. Merchant marine (1992): vessels (100 gross tons and over) 456; total deadweight tonnage 7,569,069. Air transport (1995)[13]: passenger-mi 3,214,000,000, passenger-km 5,172,000,000; short ton-mi cargo 91,376,000, metric ton-km cargo 133,407,000; airports (1996) with scheduled flights 13.
Communications. Daily newspapers (1994): total number 37; total circulation 1,616,000; circulation per 1,000 population 310. Radio (1995): 5,200,000 receivers (1 per 1.0 persons). Television (1995): 2,700,200 receivers (1 per 1.9 persons). Telephones (main lines; 1993): 3,059,800 (1 per 1.7 persons).

Education and health

Education (1993–94)

	schools	teachers	students	student/teacher ratio
Primary/lower secondary (age 7–15)	2,557	58,500	606,268	10.4
Upper secondary (age 16–18)	153	11,000	75,299	6.8
Vocational	242	12,000	162,637	13.6
Higher	158	8,000	156,264	19.5

Educational attainment (1994). Percentage of population age 25–69 having: completed lower secondary or not stated 41.9%; completed upper secondary or vocational 39.2%; advanced vocational 5.7%; undergraduate 8.5%; graduate 4.7%. *Literacy:* virtually 100%.
Health: physicians (1994) 14,497 (1 per 358 persons); hospital beds (1993) 26,463 (1 per 196 persons); infant mortality rate per 1,000 live births (1995) 5.3.
Food (1992): daily per capita caloric intake 3,664 (vegetable products 56%, animal products 44%); 136% of FAO recommended minimum requirement.

Military

Total active duty personnel (1995): 33,100 (army 57.7%, navy 18.1%, air force 24.2%). *Military expenditure as percentage of GNP* (1994): 1.9% (world 3.0%); per capita expenditure U.S.$522.

---

[1]Excludes the Faroe Islands and Greenland. [2]January 1. [3]Detail does not add to total given because of rounding. [4]1993. [5]Within Greater Copenhagen. [6]1995. [7]Includes both central and local governments. [8]March. [9]At factor cost. [10]Imputed bank service charges less other producers. [11]Includes 21,316 not adequately defined and 323,437 unemployed. [12]Import figures are f.o.b. in balance of trade and c.i.f. in commodities and trading partners. [13]Danish share of Scandinavian Airlines System (scheduled air service only) and Maersk Air.

Djibouti

Official name: Jumhūrīyah Jībūtī (Arabic); République de Djibouti (French) (Republic of Djibouti).
Form of government: multiparty republic with one legislative house (National Assembly [65]).
Head of state and government: President.
Capital: Djibouti.
Official languages: Arabic; French.
Official religion: none.
Monetary unit: 1 Djibouti franc (DF) = 100 centimes; valuation (Oct. 11, 1996) 1 U.S.$ = DF 177.72; 1 £ = DF 279.96.

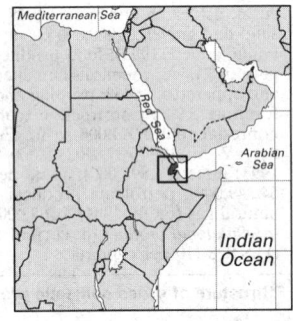

Area and population

Districts	Capitals	area[1] sq mi	sq km	population 1982 estimate
'Alī Sabīḥ (Ali-Sabieh)	'Alī Sabīḥ	925	2,400	15,000
Dikhil	Dikhil	2,775	7,200	30,000
Djibouti	Djibouti	225	600	200,000
Obock	Obock	2,200	5,700	15,000
Tadjoura (Tadjourah)	Tadjoura	2,825	7,300	30,000
TOTAL		8,950	23,200	335,000[2]

Demography

Population (1996): 603,600[3].
Density (1996): persons per sq mi 67.4, persons per sq km 26.0.
Urban-rural (1995): urban 82.8%; rural 17.2%.
Sex distribution (1995): male 49.39%; female 50.61%.
Age breakdown (1995): under 15, 41.8%; 15–29, 27.2%; 30–44, 15.9%; 45–59, 9.9%; 60–74, 4.3%; 75 and over, 0.7%.
Population projection: (2000) 679,969; (2010) 915,897.
Doubling time: 32 years.
Ethnic composition (1983): Somali 61.7%, of which Issa 33.4%, Gadaboursi 15.0%, Issaq 13.3%; Afar 20.0%; Arab (mostly Yemeni) 6.0%; European 4.0%; other (refugees) 8.3%.
Religious affiliation (1988): Sunnī Muslim 96%; Christian 4%, of which Roman Catholic 2%, Protestant 1%, Orthodox 1%.
Major city and towns (1989): Djibouti 450,000[4]; 'Alī Sabīḥ 4,000; Tadjoura 3,500; Dikhil 3,000.

Vital statistics

Birth rate per 1,000 population (1990–95): 38.1 (world avg. 25.0).
Death rate per 1,000 population (1990–95): 16.1 (world avg. 9.3).
Natural increase rate per 1,000 population (1990–95): 22.0 (world avg. 15.7).
Total fertility rate (avg. births per childbearing woman; 1990–95): 5.8.
Marriage rate per 1,000 population (1982): 6.7.
Divorce rate per 1,000 population (1982): 1.9.
Life expectancy at birth (1990–95): male 46.7 years; female 50.0 years.
Major causes of death (percentage of total deaths [infants and children to age 10, district of Djibouti only]; 1984): diarrhea and acute dehydration 16.0%; malnutrition 16.0%; poisoning 11.0%; tuberculosis 6.0%; acute respiratory disease 6.0%; malaria 6.0%; anemia 6.0%; heart disease 2.0%; kidney disease 1.0%; other ailments 19.0%; no diagnosis 11.0%.

National economy

Budget (1995)[5]. Revenue: DF 24,970,000,000 (tax revenue 94.3%, of which domestic taxes [construction, gambling, market fees, licenses] 31.5%, wages and salary tax 12.7%, surcharge on khat 9.4%, income and profit tax 6.8%; nontax revenue 5.7%). Expenditures: DF 35,293,000,000 ([1994] current expenditures 87.1%, of which defense and mobilization 28.9%, education 7.4%, health 5.4%; capital expenditures 12.8%).
Public debt (external, outstanding; 1994): U.S.$206,900,000.
Tourism: receipts from visitors (1993) U.S.$13,000,000; expenditures by nationals abroad U.S.$15,000,000.
Production (metric tons except as noted). Agriculture, forestry, fishing (1995): vegetables and melons 21,888, of which tomatoes 1,000, eggplant 45; livestock (number of live animals) 507,000 goats, 470,000 sheep, 190,000 cattle, 62,000 camels, 8,200 asses; roundwood, n.a.; fish catch (1993) 300. Mining and quarrying: mineral production limited to locally used construction materials and evaporated salt. Manufacturing (1991): structural detail, n.a.; main products include furniture, nonalcoholic beverages, meat and hides, light electromechanical goods, and mineral water. Construction (1989): 53,900 sq m. Energy production (consumption): electricity (kW-hr; 1994) 185,000,000 (185,000,000); firewood and charcoal, n.a. (n.a.)[6]; coal, none (n.a.); crude petroleum, none (n.a.); petroleum products (metric tons; 1994) none (127,000); natural gas, none (n.a.); geothermal, wind, and solar resources are substantial but largely undeveloped.
Population economically active (1991): total 282,000; activity rate of total population 54.2% (participation rates [1988]: over age 10, 67.0%; female 40.0%; unemployed [1987] c. 40–50%).

Price and earnings indexes (1990 = 100)

	1988	1989	1990	1991	1992	1993	1994
Consumer price index	90.1	92.8	100.0	106.8	112.1	118.6	120.7
Earnings index	...	...	...	...	...	...	...

Household income and expenditure. Average household size (1985)[7] 7.2; income per household: n.a.; sources of income (1976): wages and salaries 51.6%, self-employment 36.0%, transfer payments 10.5%, other 1.9%; expenditure (expatriate households; 1984): food 50.3%, energy 13.1%, recreation 10.4%, housing 6.4%, clothing 1.7%, personal effects 1.4%, health care 1.0%, household goods 0.3%, other 15.4%.
Gross national product (at current market prices; 1993): U.S.$448,000,000 (U.S.$780 per capita).

Structure of gross domestic product and labour force

	1995 in value DF '000,000	1995 % of total value	1991 labour force	1991 % of labour force
Agriculture	2,668	3.0	212,000	75.2
Mining	—	—		
Manufacturing	4,105	4.7	31,000	11.0
Construction	4,440	5.0		
Public utilities	6,967	7.9		
Transportation and communications	13,362	15.2		
Trade	13,637	15.5	39,000	13.8
Finance	8,197	9.3		
Pub. admin., defense	20,600	23.4		
Services	3,857	4.4		
Other	10,159	11.5	212,000	75.2
TOTAL	87,992	100.0[8]	282,000	100.0

Land use (1994): forested 0.9%; meadows and pastures 56.1%; agricultural and under permanent cultivation[9]; built-on, wasteland, and other 43.0%.

Foreign trade

Balance of trade (current prices)

	1991	1992	1993	1994	1995[5]
U.S.$'000,000	−186.6	−205.9	−183.9	−180.7	−171.5
% of total	56.5%	65.9%	56.4%	61.6%	71.9%

Imports (1994): U.S.$237,100,000 (food, beverages, and tobacco 29.4%; machinery and electric appliances 11.6%; clothing and footwear 9.7%; petroleum products 7.7%; transport equipment 7.1%; chemical products 6.8%; base metals and base metal products 4.6%). *Major import sources:* Thailand 13.8%; France 13.7%; Saudi Arabia 12.4%; Ethiopia 6.4%; Italy 5.9%; Japan 4.7%.
Exports (1994): U.S.$56,400,000 (1991: unspecified special transactions 71.7%; live animals [including camels] 15.5%; food and food products 12.8%). *Major export destinations:* Somalia 39.0%; Ethiopia 34.2%; Yemen 20.8%; Saudi Arabia 0.6%.

Transport and communications

Transport. Railroads (1995): length (1989) 66 mi, 106 km; passenger-mi 173,000,000, passenger-km 279,000,000; short ton-mile cargo 187,000,000[10], metric ton-km cargo 273,000,000[10]. Roads (1993): total length 1,805 mi, 2,905 km (paved 9.7%). Vehicles (1994): passenger cars 13,500; trucks and buses 3,000. Merchant marine (1992): vessels (100 gross tons and over) 10; total deadweight tonnage 4,090. Air transport (1995)[11]: passengers handled 120,141; metric tons of freight handled 11,953; airports (1996) with scheduled flights 1.
Communications. Weekly newspapers (1990): total number 1; total circulation 4,000; circulation per 1,000 population 7.6. Radio (1995): total number of receivers 35,000 (1 per 17 persons). Television (1995): total number of receivers 17,000 (1 per 35 persons). Telephones (main lines; 1994): 7,436 (1 per 77 persons).

Education and health

Education (1993)

	schools	teachers	students	student/ teacher ratio
Primary (age 6–11)	56	787	33,005	41.9
Secondary (age 12–18)[12]	26	362	9,363	28.6
Voc., teacher tr.	1	13	108	8.3
Higher[12]				

Educational attainment: n.a. *Literacy* (1995): percentage of population age 15 and over literate 46.2%; males literate 60.3%; females literate 32.7%.
Health (1989): physicians 97 (1 per 5,258 persons); hospital beds[13] 1,383 (1 per 369 persons); infant mortality rate per 1,000 live births (1990–95) 112.
Food (1992): daily per capita caloric intake 2,338 (vegetable products 89%, animal products 11%); 101% of FAO recommended minimum requirement.

Military

Total active duty personnel (1996): 9,600[14] (army 83.3%, navy 2.1%, air force 2.1%, paramilitary 12.5%). *Military expenditure as percentage of GNP* (1993): 6.0% (world 3.2%); per capita expenditure U.S.$69.

---

[1]Original figures are those given in sq km; sq mi equivalent is rounded to appropriate level of generality. [2]Includes 45,000 persons not distributed by district. [3]Excludes about 20,000 Somali and 5,000 Ethiopian refugees. [4]Excludes 20,000 transients. [5]Preliminary. [6]Represents about 15% of total energy consumption. [7]City of Djibouti only. [8]Detail does not add to total given because of rounding. [9]In 1988–89 only 1,005 acres (407 hectares) of land were cultivated. [10]Based on total weight of Ethiopian exports and imports transported to and from the port of Djibouti. [11]Djibouti International Airport only. [12]1991. [13]Public health facilities only. [14]Excludes 3,900 French troops.

Dominica

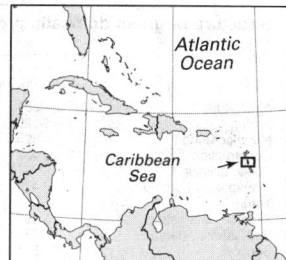

Atlantic Ocean

Caribbean Sea

Official name: Commonwealth of Dominica.
Form of government: multiparty republic with one legislative house (House of Assembly [32[1]]).
Chief of state: President.
Head of government: Prime Minister.
Capital: Roseau.
Official language: English.
Official religion: none.
Monetary unit: 1 East Caribbean dollar (EC$) = 100 cents; valuation (Oct. 11, 1996) 1 U.S.$ = EC$2.70; 1 £ = EC$4.25.

Area and population

Parishes	area sq mi	area sq km	population 1991 census
St. Andrew	69.3	179.6	11,106
St. David	49.0	126.8	6,977
St. George	20.7	53.5	20,365
St. John	22.5	58.5	4,990
St. Joseph	46.4	120.1	6,183
St. Luke	4.3	11.1	1,552
St. Mark	3.8	9.9	1,943
St. Patrick	32.6	84.4	8,929
St. Paul	26.0	67.4	7,495
St. Peter	10.7	27.7	1,643
TOTAL	285.3[2]	739.0[2]	71,183[3]

Demography

Population (1996): 73,800.
Density (1996): persons per sq mi 254.5, persons per sq km 98.4.
Urban-rural: n.a.
Sex distribution (1991): male 49.78%; female 50.22%.
Age breakdown (1991): under 15, 33.3%; 15–29, 28.3%; 30–44, 16.3%; 45–59, 9.7%; 60 and over, 11.8%; unknown, 0.6%.
Population projection: (2000) 74,000; (2010) 75,000.
Doubling time: 53 years.
Ethnic composition (1991): black 89.1%; mixed race 7.2%; Amerindian/Carib 2.4%; white 0.4%; other 0.7%; not stated 0.2%.
Religious affiliation (1991): Roman Catholic 70.1%; six largest Protestant groups 17.2%, of which Seventh-day Adventist 4.6%, Pentecostal 4.3%, Methodist 4.2%; other 8.9%; nonreligious 2.9%; unknown 0.9%.
Major towns (1991): Roseau 15,853; Portsmouth 3,621; Marigot 2,919; Atkinson 2,518; Mahaut 2,372.

Vital statistics

Birth rate per 1,000 population (1995): 18.6 (world avg. 25.0); (1991) legitimate 24.1%; illegitimate 75.9%.
Death rate per 1,000 population (1995): 5.3 (world avg. 9.3).
Natural increase rate per 1,000 population (1995): 13.3 (world avg. 15.7).
Total fertility rate (avg. births per childbearing woman; 1995): 1.9.
Marriage rate per 1,000 population (1990): 3.3.
Divorce rate per 1,000 population (1990): 0.4.
Life expectancy at birth (1995): male 74.4 years; female 80.2 years.
Major causes of death per 100,000 population (1990): diseases of the circulatory system 273.5, of which ischemic heart diseases 120.8, hypertensive disease 88.8; malignant neoplasms (cancers) 116.6; endocrine, metabolic, and nutritional disorders 51.4; diseases of the respiratory system 43.0; infectious and parasitic diseases 37.5.

National economy

Budget (1994–95). Revenue: EC$286,500,000 (current revenue 58.7%, external loans and sales of securities 22.9%, grants 15.1%, other 3.3%). Expenditures: EC$286,500,000 (current expenditures 54.7%, development expenditures 38.7%, debt repayment 3.5%, other 3.1%).
Public debt (external, outstanding; 1994): U.S.$86,500,000.
Tourism (1994): receipts from visitors U.S.$30,600,000; expenditures by nationals abroad U.S.$4,000,000.
Gross national product (at current market prices; 1994): U.S.$201,000,000 (U.S.$2,830 per capita).

Structure of gross domestic product and labour force

	1995 in value EC$'000,000	1995 % of total value	1991 labour force[4]	1991 % of labour force[4]
Agriculture	100.9	19.8	7,344	30.8
Mining	4.4	0.9	65	0.3
Manufacturing	35.8	7.0	1,947	8.2
Construction	44.4	8.7	2,819	11.8
Public utilities	21.0	4.1	304	1.3
Transportation and communications	88.4	17.3	1,202	5.0
Trade, hotels, restaurants	76.7	15.0	3,658	15.4
Finance, real estate }	82.7	16.2	810	3.4
Services }			3,446	14.5
Pub. admin., defense	92.9	18.2	1,520	6.4
Other	−36.8[5]	−7.2[5]	699	2.9
TOTAL	510.3[6]	100.0	23,814	100.0

Population economically active (1991): total 26,364; activity rate of total population 38.0% (participation rates: ages 15–64, 62.4%; female 34.5%; unemployed [1994] 23%).

Price and earnings indexes (1990 = 100)

	1989	1990	1991	1992	1993	1994	1995
Consumer price index	96.9	100.0	105.6	111.3	113.1	114.8	115.9
Earnings index	...	...	...	...	...	...	...

Household income and expenditure. Average household size (1991) 3.6; income per household: n.a.; sources of income: n.a.; expenditure (1984)[7]: food and nonalcoholic beverages 43.1%, housing and utilities 16.1%, transportation 11.6%, clothing and footwear 6.5%, household furnishings 6.0%.
Production (metric tons except as noted). Agriculture, forestry, fishing (1993): bananas 43,205[8], root crops 28,057 (of which dasheens 11,390, yams 7,985, tanias 6,176), coconuts 23,213, grapefruit 12,212, plantains 8,097, oranges 3,157, cacao 842, bay oil 46, cinnamon 39; livestock (number of live animals; 1994) 10,000 goats, 9,000 cattle, 8,000 sheep; roundwood, n.a.; fish catch 795 metric tons. Mining and quarrying: pumice, limestone, and sand and gravel are quarried primarily for local consumption. Manufacturing (value of production in EC$'000; 1994): laundry soap 15,661; toilet soap 13,382; crude coconut oil 3,281; copra 2,525; bottled spring water 323,000 cases[9]; other products include fruit juices, rum, garments, furniture, paint, and cardboard boxes. Construction (value of starts; 1993): U.S.$12,100,000. Energy production (consumption): electricity (kW-hr; 1994) 52,400,000 (43,500,000); coal, none (none); crude petroleum, none (none); petroleum products (metric tons; 1993) none (20,000); natural gas, none (none).
Land use (1993): forested 67.0%; meadows and pastures 3.0%; agricultural and under permanent cultivation 23.0%; other 7.0%.

Foreign trade[10]

Balance of trade (current prices)

	1990	1991	1992	1993	1994	1995
EC$'000,000	−129.3	−110.5	−140.3	−123.6	−137.3	−189.4
% of total	29.9%	26.9%	32.7%	32.3%	35.8%	44.0%

Imports (1992): EC$299,200,000 (machinery and transport equipment 28.5%; basic manufactures 25.1%; food 18.4%; chemicals and chemical products 12.8%). *Major import sources:* United States 27.0%; Caricom countries 24.2%; United Kingdom 15.3%; Japan 4.4%; Canada 3.8%.
Exports (1992)[11]: EC$151,400,000 (of which domestic exports 97.1%, of which bananas 55.7%, coconut-based laundry and toilet soaps 20.7%, fresh vegetables and roots and tubers 2.5%, plantains 2.1%, bay oil 1.5%; reexports 2.9%). *Major export destinations*[12]: United Kingdom 47.6%; Caricom countries 27.9%; Italy 9.3%.

Transport and communications

Transport. Railroads: none. Roads (1994): total length 466 mi, 750 km (paved 49%). Vehicles (1992): passenger cars 4,700; trucks and buses 5,500. Merchant marine (1992): vessels (100 gross tons and over) 7; total deadweight tonnage 3,153. Air transport (1991): passenger arrivals 43,312, passenger departures, n.a.; cargo unloaded 259 metric tons, cargo loaded 415 metric tons; airports (1996) with scheduled flights 2.
Communications. Daily newspapers: none[13]. Radio (1995): 65,000 receivers (1 per 1.1 persons). Television (1995): 5,200 receivers (1 per 14 persons). Telephones (main lines; 1994): 15,791 (1 per 4.6 persons).

Education and health

Education (1993–94)

	schools	teachers	students	student/ teacher ratio
Primary	64 }	674	12,822 }	28.6
Secondary	13[14] }		6,431 }	
Higher[14]	2	34	484	14.2

Educational attainment (1991). Percentage of population age 25 and over having: no formal schooling 4.2%; primary education 78.4%; secondary 11.0%; higher vocational 2.3%; university 2.8%; other/unknown 1.3%. *Literacy* (1990): total population age 15 and over literate, c. 42,000 (90.0%).
Health (1992): physicians 34 (1 per 2,112 persons); hospital beds 241 (1 per 298 persons); infant mortality rate per 1,000 live births (1995) 9.9.
Food (1992): daily per capita caloric intake 2,778 (vegetable products 83%, animal products 17%); 115% of FAO recommended minimum requirement.

Military

Total active duty personnel (1994): none[15].

---

[1]Includes 22 seats that are elective (including speaker if elected from outside of the House of Assembly) and 10 seats that are nonelective (including 9 appointees of the president and the attorney general serving ex officio). [2]Area breakdown by parish is based on 1961 census. Total area of Dominica per more recent survey is 290 sq mi (750 sq km). [3]Includes institutionalized population of 1,717. [4]Employed persons only. [5]Net of indirect taxes less imputed banking service charge. [6]Detail does not add to total given because of rounding. [7]Weights of consumer price index components. [8]1994. [9]1990. [10]Imports f.o.b. in balance of trade and c.i.f. in commodities and trading partners. [11]Exports (1994): EC$118,300,000 (domestic exports 98.1%, of which bananas 46.8%, coconut-based laundry and toilet soaps 30.4%; reexports 1.9%). [12]Excludes reexports. [13]Weekly newspapers (1992): total number 1; total circulation 5,000; circulation per 1,000 population 69. [14]1992–93. [15]300-member police force includes a coast guard unit.

Dominican Republic

Official name: República Dominicana (Dominican Republic).
Form of government: multiparty republic with two legislative houses (Senate [30]; Chamber of Deputies [120]).
Head of state and government: President.
Capital: Santo Domingo.
Official language: Spanish.
Official religion: none[1].
Monetary unit: 1 Dominican peso (RD$) = 100 centavos; valuation (Oct. 11, 1996) 1 U.S.$ = RD$13.78; 1 £ = RD$21.71.

Area and population

Provinces	Capitals	area sq mi	area sq km	population 1993 census[2]
Azua	Azua	978	2,532	193,966
Baoruco	Neiba	495	1,283	101,610
Barahona	Barahona	671	1,739	157,610
Dajabón	Dajabón	394	1,021	63,932
Duarte	San Francisco de Macorís	620	1,605	271,998
El Seíbo	El Seibo	690	1,786	94,159
Espaillat	Moca	323	838	198,406
Hato Mayor	Hato Mayor	513	1,329	76,670
Independencia	Jimaní	775	2,008	38,147
La Altagracia	Higüey	1,162	3,010	112,296
Elías Piña	Comendador	550	1,424	59,261
La Romana	La Romana	252	654	157,964
La Vega	La Vega	883	2,286	334,756
María Trinidad Sánchez	Nagua	491	1,271	122,069
Monseñor Nouel	Bonao	383	992	146,182
Monte Cristi	Monte Cristi	743	1,925	94,330
Monte Plata	Monte Plata	1,017	2,633	162,446
Pedernales	Pedernales	802	2,077	15,786
Peravia	Baní	636	1,648	199,449
Puerto Plata	Puerto Plata	717	1,857	254,795
Salcedo	Salcedo	170	440	99,854
Samaná	Samaná	330	854	73,026
San Cristóbal	San Cristóbal	488	1,265	408,918
San Juan	San Juan	1,379	3,571	246,758
San Pedro de Macorís	San Pedro de Macorís	485	1,255	212,654
Sánchez Ramírez	Cotuí	462	1,196	158,061
Santiago	Santiago	1,095	2,836	689,803
Santiago Rodríguez	Sabaneta	429	1,112	59,940
Santo Domingo[3]	—	541	1,401	2,138,262
Valverde	Mao	318	823	145,933
TOTAL		18,792	48,671	7,089,041

Demography

Population (1996): 7,502,000.
Density (1996): persons per sq mi 399.2, persons per sq km 154.1.
Urban-rural (1993): urban 55.5%; rural 44.5%.
Sex distribution (1993): male 49.90%; female 50.10%.
Age breakdown (1995): under 15, 35.1%; 15–29, 29.0%; 30–44, 19.8%; 45–59, 9.9%; 60–74, 4.9%; 75 and over, 1.3%.
Population projection: (2000) 8,021,000; (2010) 9,167,000.
Doubling time: 38 years.
Ethnic composition (1993): mixed 73%; white 16%; black 11%.
Religious affiliation (1994): Roman Catholic 91.3%; other 8.7%.
Major urban centres (1991): Santo Domingo 2,138,262[3, 4]; Santiago 375,000; La Vega 189,000; San Francisco de Macorís 162,000.

Vital statistics

Birth rate per 1,000 population (1995): 24.1 (world avg. 25.0).
Death rate per 1,000 population (1995): 5.7 (world avg. 9.3).
Natural increase rate per 1,000 population (1995): 18.4 (world avg. 15.7).
Total fertility rate (avg. births per childbearing woman; 1995): 2.7.
Marriage rate per 1,000 population (1992): 3.6.
Life expectancy at birth (1995): male 66.6 years; female 71.0 years.
Major causes of death per 100,000 population (1985)[5]: diseases of the circulatory system 165; infectious and parasitic diseases 85; malignant neoplasms (cancers) 45; diseases of the respiratory system 41.

National economy

Budget (1995). Revenue: RD$25,453,000,000 (tax revenue 87.9%, of which taxes on goods and services 45.0%, import duties 25.6%, income taxes 16.3%; nontax revenue 6.4%; grants and loans 5.7%). Expenditures: RD$24,107,-000,000 (development expenditure 53.6%; current expenditure 46.4%).
Public debt (external, outstanding; 1994): U.S.$3,681,000,000.
Production (metric tons except as noted). Agriculture, forestry, fishing (value of production in RD$'000,000; 1995): coffee 2,067, rice 1,781, chicken meat 1,692, sugarcane 1,586, milk 1,524, plantains 1,238, beef 1,077, beans 1,043, cacao beans 535, eggs 507, bananas 495, fish 110; roundwood (1994) 562,300 cu m. Mining (1995): nickel 30,890; gold 105,700 troy oz. Manufacturing (1995)[6]: cement 1,450,000; refined sugar 90,300; beer 2,082,000 hectolitres; rum 414,000 hectolitres; cigarettes 204,600,000 20-unit packs. Construction (value of authorized private construction in RD$'000,000; 1992): 2,519. Energy production (consumption): electricity (kW-hr; 1995) 5,534,000,000 (3,292,000,000); coal (metric tons; 1993) none (120,000); crude petroleum (barrels; 1993) none (14,286,000); petroleum products (metric tons; 1993) 1,907,000 (3,236,000); natural gas, none (none).
Gross national product (1994): U.S.$10,109,000,000 (U.S.$1,320 per capita).

Structure of gross domestic product and labour force

	1995[7] in value RD$'000,000	1995[7] % of total value	1981 labour force	1981 % of labour force
Agriculture	581	12.7	420,463	22.0
Mining	126	2.8	4,743	0.2
Manufacturing	805	17.5	224,437	11.7
Construction	437	9.5	80,850	4.3
Public utilities	87	1.9	13,891	0.7
Transp. and commun.	470	10.2	40,470	2.1
Trade	850	18.5	192,181	10.0
Finance, real estate	463	10.1	22,369	1.2
Pub. admin., defense	388	8.5 }	363,125	18.9
Services	381	8.3 }		
Other	—	—	552,859[8]	28.9[8]
TOTAL	4,588	100.0	1,915,388	100.0

Tourism (1994): receipts U.S.$1,148,000,000; expenditures U.S.$171,000,000.
Population economically active (1991)[9]: total 2,758,000; activity rate of total population 37.6% (participation rates: age 10 and over, 50.3%; female 29.0%; unemployed [1994] 28.0%).

Price and earnings indexes (1990 = 100)

	1990	1991	1992	1993	1994	1995	1996
Consumer price index	100.0	153.9	160.9	169.4	183.4	206.4	215.5[10]
Monthly earnings index	100.0	125.3	150.8	...	...	...	...

Household income and expenditure. Average household size (1981) 5.1; average income: n.a.; sources of income: n.a.; expenditure (1980–85): food and beverages 46.0%, housing 10.0%, household goods 8.0%.
Land use (1994): forested 12.4%; meadows and pastures 43.4%; agricultural and under permanent cultivation 30.6%; other 13.6%.

Foreign trade[11]

Balance of trade (current prices)

	1990	1991	1992	1993	1994	1995
U.S.$'000,000	−1,058	−1,071	−1,613	−1,607	−1,632	−2,058
% of total	41.9%	44.8%	58.9%	61.1%	55.9%	58.1%

Imports (1994): U.S.$2,276,000,000 (crude petroleum and petroleum products 22.9%; agricultural products 18.2%, of which cereals 5.8%; forest products 4.7%). *Major import sources*[9]: U.S. 41%; Venezuela 7%; Mexico 7%; Japan 6%; Netherlands Antilles 4%.
Exports (1995): U.S.$742,700,000[12] (ferronickel 30.1%; raw sugar 13.8%; raw coffee 10.9%; cacao 7.3%; gold 6.2%). *Major export destinations* (1994): U.S. 52.3%; The Netherlands 12.9%; Puerto Rico 6.3%; South Korea 5.8%; Belgium 5.1%.

Transport and communications

Transport. Railroads (1994)[13]: route length 1,083 mi, 1,743 km. Roads (1994): total length 7,450 mi, 12,000 km (paved 48%). Vehicles (1994): passenger cars 120,000; trucks and buses 80,000. Air transport (1994)[14]: passenger-mi 145,396,000, passenger-km 233,992,000; short ton-mi cargo 1,738,000, metric ton-km cargo 2,537,000; airports (1996) 4.
Communications. Daily newspapers (1992): total number 11; total circulation 265,000; circulation per 1,000 population 38. Radio (1995): 1,180,000 receivers (1 per 6.2 persons). Television (1995): 728,000 receivers (1 per 10 persons). Telephones (main lines; 1993): 552,400 (1 per 13 persons).

Education and health

Education (1993–94)

	schools	teachers	students	student/teacher ratio
Primary (age 7–14)	6,207	39,464	1,336,211	33.9
Secondary (age 15–18)	...	11,605	232,999	20.1
Higher[15, 16]	7	5,091[17]	73,461[17]	14.4[17]

Educational attainment (1981). Percentage of population age 25 and over having: no formal schooling 48.0%; incomplete primary education 31.7%; complete primary 4.0%; secondary 14.0%; higher 2.3%. *Literacy* (1995): total population age 15 and over literate, c. 4,164,000 (82.1%); males literate, c. 2,118,000 (82.0%); females literate, c. 2,046,000 (82.2%).
Health (1994): physicians[18] 6,869 (1 per 1,052 persons); hospital beds[18] 8,621 (1 per 838 persons); infant mortality rate per 1,000 live births (1995) 49.5.
Food (1992): daily per capita caloric intake 2,286 (vegetable products 86%, animal products 14%); 101% of FAO recommended minimum.

Military

Total active duty personnel (1995): 24,500 (army 61.2%, navy 16.3%, air force 22.5%). *Military expenditure as percentage of GNP* (1994): 1.1% (world 3.0%); per capita expenditure U.S.$16.

---

[1]Roman Catholicism is the state religion per concordat with Vatican City. [2]Preliminary figure. [3]National district. [4]1993. [5]Projected rates based on about 60% of total deaths. [6]Excludes free-zone sector for reexport (mostly ready-made garments) employing (1994) 164,000. [7]At prices of 1970. [8]Not adequately defined (421,628) and those seeking work for first time (131,231). [9]Estimated figures. [10]April. [11]Excludes free zones. [12]Excludes 1995 reexports of free zones equaling U.S.$1,904,000,000. [13]Most track is privately owned and serves the sugar industry only. [14]Dominicana and Dominair airlines. [15]1993–94. [16]Universities only. [17]Seven universities only. [18]Public sector only.

Ecuador

Official name: República del Ecuador (Republic of Ecuador).
Form of government: unitary multiparty republic with one legislative house (National Congress [82]).
Head of state and government: President.
Capital: Quito.
Official language: Spanish.
Official religion: none.
Monetary unit: 1 Sucre (S/.) = 100 centavos; valuation (Oct. 11, 1996) 1 U.S.$ = S/. 3,309; 1 £ = S/. 5,213.

Area and population

| | | area | | population |
| | | | | 1996 |
Regions Provinces	Capitals	sq mi	sq km	estimate
Amazonica				
Morona-Santiago	Macas	13,100	33,930	127,989
Napo	Tena	9,918	25,690	141,776
Pastaza	Puyo	11,496	29,774	55,739
Sucumbíos	Nueva Loja	7,076	18,327	123,070
Zamora-Chinchipe	Zamora	8,923	23,111	91,359
Costa				
El Oro	Machala	2,259	5,850	512,587
Esmeraldas	Esmeraldas	5,884	15,239	381,135
Guayas	Guayaquil	7,916	20,503	3,128,791
Los Ríos	Babahoyo	2,770	7,175	619,353
Manabí	Portoviejo	7,289	18,879	1,191,941
Insular				
Galápagos	Puerto Baquerizo Moreno	3,093	8,010	13,976
Sierra				
Azuay	Cuenca	3,137	8,125	588,014
Bolívar	Guaranda	1,521	3,940	177,025
Cañar	Azogues	1,205	3,122	208,079
Carchi	Tulcán	1,392	3,605	158,893
Chimborazo	Riobamba	2,536	6,569	407,876
Cotopaxi	Latacunga	2,344	6,072	298,046
Imbabura	Ibarra	1,760	4,559	312,420
Loja	Loja	4,257	11,026	414,652
Pichincha	Quito	4,987	12,915	2,238,527
Tungurahua	Ambato	1,288	3,335	421,746
TOTAL		105,037[1, 2]	272,045[2]	11,698,496[3]

Demography

Population (1996): 11,698,000.
Density (1996): persons per sq mi 111.4, persons per sq km 43.0.
Urban-rural (1995): urban 59.3%; rural 40.7%.
Sex distribution (1995): male 49.45%; female 50.55%.
Age breakdown (1995): under 15, 36.4%; 15–29, 29.0%; 30–44, 18.5%; 45–59, 9.6%; 60–74, 5.0%; 75 and over, 1.5%.
Population projection: (2000) 12,646,000; (2010) 14,899,000.
Doubling time: 34 years.
Ethnic composition (1989): Amerindian 40.0%; mestizo 40.0%; white 15.0%; black 5.0%.
Religious affiliation (1992): Roman Catholic 93.0%; other 7.0%.
Major cities (1995): Guayaquil 1,877,031; Quito 1,401,389; Cuenca 239,896; Machala 184,588; Santo Domingo 165,090.

Vital statistics

Birth rate per 1,000 population (1993): 26.5[4] (world avg. 25.0); (1982) legitimate 67.9%; illegitimate 32.1%.
Death rate per 1,000 population (1993): 5.8[4] (world avg. 9.3).
Natural increase rate per 1,000 population (1993): 20.7[4] (world avg. 15.7).
Total fertility rate (avg. births per childbearing woman; 1994): 3.1.
Marriage rate per 1,000 population (1992): 6.4[4, 5].
Divorce rate per 1,000 population (1992): 0.6[4, 5].
Life expectancy at birth (1994): male 67.5 years; female 72.6 years.
Major causes of death per 100,000 population (1992): circulatory diseases 93.1; accidents, poisoning, and violence 66.7; infectious and parasitic diseases 52.0; neoplasms (cancers) 50.0; respiratory diseases 40.6.

National economy

Budget (1994). Revenue: S/. 5,734,000,000,000 (income from petroleum 41.4%, production and sales tax 25.8%, import duties 10.4%, income taxes 7.0%). Expenditures: S/. 5,717,000,000,000 (general administration 46.8%, debt service 21.8%, subsidies 9.3%).
Production (metric tons except as noted). Agriculture, forestry, fishing (1995): sugarcane 6,750,000, bananas 5,403,000, rice 1,291,000, corn (maize) 688,000, plantains 680,000, potatoes 473,000, soybeans 91,000, cacao 86,000; livestock (number of live animals) 4,995,000 cattle, 2,618,000 pigs, 1,692,000 sheep, 61,512,000 chickens; roundwood (1994) 5,416,000 cu m; fish catch (1993) 330,720. Mining and quarrying (1992): limestone 3,078,000; gold 12,000 kg. Manufacturing (value added in S/. '000,000; 1990): food products 175,126, of which beverages (including liquors) 25,606; textiles 72,554; chemical products 71,241; metal products 33,686. Construction (in S/.; 1992)[6]: residential 93,166,704,000; nonresidential 58,102,274,000. Energy production (consumption): electricity (kW-hr; 1994) 8,163,000,000 (8,163,000,000); crude petroleum (barrels; 1994) 123,998,000 (35,436,000); petroleum products (metric tons; 1994) 6,499,000 (5,135,000); natural gas (cu m; 1994) 204,000,000 (204,000,000).
Tourism (1994): receipts U.S.$252,000,000; expenditures U.S.$203,000,000.
Public debt (external, outstanding; 1994): U.S.$10,384,000,000.

Gross national product (1994): U.S.$14,703,000,000 (U.S.$1,310 per capita).

Structure of gross domestic product and labour force

| | 1994 | | 1990 | |
	in value S/. '000,000[7]	% of total value	labour force	% of labour force
Agriculture	35,103	16.8	1,035,712	30.8
Mining	30,408	14.5	20,870	0.6
Manufacturing	32,163	15.3	370,338	11.0
Construction	5,299	2.5	196,716	5.9
Public utilities	3,072	1.5	12,660	0.4
Transp. and commun.	18,817	9.0	131,084	3.9
Trade	31,060	14.8	476,730	14.2
Finance	24,498	11.7	81,357	2.4
Pub. admin., defense	15,234	7.3 }	838,129	24.9
Services	12,446	5.9 }		
Other	1,405[8]	0.7[8]	196,171[9]	5.8[9]
TOTAL	209,505	100.0	3,359,767	100.0[1]

Population economically active (1990): total 3,359,767; activity rate of total population 34.8% (participation rates: ages 8 and over, 44.0%; female 26.4%; unemployed 1.3%).

Price and earnings indexes (1990 = 100)

	1989	1990	1991	1992	1993	1994	1995
Consumer price index	67.3	100.0	148.7	229.9	333.3	424.3	521.6
Hourly earnings index[10]	100.0	100.0	125.0	187.5	206.3	218.8	...

Household income and expenditure. Average household size (1990) 4.1; average annual income per household (1982) S/. 28,747 (U.S.$956); sources of income (1993): self-employment 76.9%, wages 17.4%, transfer payments 3.6%, other 2.1%; expenditure (1991): food and tobacco 38.2%, transportation and communications 12.4%, clothing 10.7%, household furnishings 7.7%, housing and utilities 5.3%, health care 4.1%.
Land use (1994): forested 56.3%; meadows and pastures 18.4%; agricultural and under permanent cultivation 11.0%; other 14.3%.

Foreign trade[11]

Balance of trade (current prices)

	1989	1990	1991	1992	1993	1994	1995
U.S.$'000,000	+719.7	+1,077.7	+736.0	+1,031.9	+680.7	+508.0	+532.4
% of total	18.0%	24.7%	14.1%	20.7%	13.3%	7.3%	6.6%

Imports (1994): U.S.$3,642,194,000 (industrial raw materials 33.4%, transport equipment 19.2%, industrial capital goods 17.9%, durable consumer goods 13.9%, nondurable consumer goods 9.7%). *Major import sources:* U.S. 25.2%; Japan 16.2%; Colombia 8.4%; Brazil 6.1%; Germany 5.8%; Venezuela 4.7%; Mexico 4.5%; Italy 3.3%.
Exports (1994): U.S.$3,717,240,000 (crude petroleum 31.9%, bananas and plantains 17.5%, shrimp 14.5%, coffee 10.7%, petroleum products 3.2%, cocoa 2.5%). *Major export destinations:* U.S. 42.4%; Colombia 5.9%; Germany 4.8%; Chile 4.4%; Peru 4.2%; Italy 3.8%; Spain 3.0%; Belgium 2.6%.

Transport and communications

Transport. Railroads (1993): route length 956 km; passenger-km 48,200,000; metric ton-km cargo 5,300,000. Roads (1993): total length 45,400 km (paved 14%). Vehicles (1994): passenger cars 195,000; trucks and buses 295,000. Merchant marine (1992): vessels (100 gross tons and over) 154; deadweight tonnage 504,127. Air transport (1993): passenger-km 1,255,000,000; metric ton-km cargo 64,200,000; airports (1996) 14.
Communications. Daily newspapers (1992): total number 36; total circulation 688,000; circulation per 1,000 population 62. Radio (1995): 3,240,000 receivers (1 per 3.5 persons). Television (1995): 900,000 receivers (1 per 13 persons). Telephones (main lines; 1993): 598,300 (1 per 19 persons).

Education and health

Education (1992–93)

	schools[12]	teachers	students	student/ teacher ratio
Primary (age 4–12)	16,146	63,347	1,986,753	31.4
Secondary (age 12–18) Vocational }	2,207	62,630	813,557	13.0
Higher	21	12,856[13]	206,541[13]	16.1[13]

Educational attainment (1990). Percentage of population age 25 and over having: no formal schooling 2.2%; incomplete primary 54.3%; primary 28.0%; postsecondary 15.5%. *Literacy* (1990): total population age 15 and over literate 5,217,543 (88.3%); males 2,616,192 (90.5%); females 2,601,351 (86.2%).
Health: physicians (1993) 12,149 (1 per 904 persons); hospital beds (1992) 17,253 (1 per 623 persons); infant mortality rate (1994) 39.3.
Food (1992): daily per capita caloric intake 2,583 (vegetable products 86%, animal products 14%); 113% of FAO minimum requirement.

Military

Total active duty personnel (1996): 57,100 (army 87.6%, navy 7.2%, air force 5.2%). *Military expenditure as percentage of GNP* (1994): 3.5% (world 3.0%); per capita expenditure U.S.$49.

[1]Detail does not add to total given because of rounding. [2]Includes 884 sq mi (2,289 sq km) in nondelimited areas. [3]Total includes 85,502 persons in nondelimited areas. [4]Excluding nomadic Indian tribes. [5]Based on incomplete registration. [6]Authorized construction in Cuenca, Guayaquil, and Quito only. [7]At constant 1975 prices. [8]Statistical discrepancy. [9]Includes unemployed persons not previously employed. [10]General minimum wage. [11]Import figures are f.o.b. in balance of trade and c.i.f. for commodities and trading partners. [12]1986–87. [13]1989–90.

Egypt

Official name: Jumhūrīyah Miṣr al-ʿArabīyah (Arab Republic of Egypt).
Form of government: republic with one legislative house (People's Assembly [454[1]]).
Chief of state: President.
Head of government: Prime Minister.
Capital: Cairo.
Official language: Arabic.
Official religion: Islam.
Monetary unit: 1 Egyptian pound (£E) = 100 piastres; valuation (Oct. 11, 1996) 1 U.S.$ = £E 3.40; 1 £ = £E 5.36.

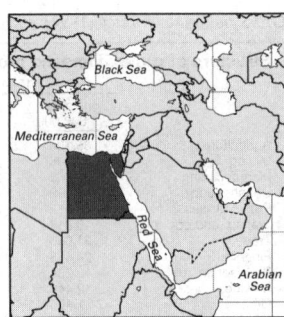

Area and population		area		population
Regions				1995
Governorates	**Capitals**	sq mi	sq km	estimate
Frontier				
Al-Baḥr al-Aḥmar	Al-Ghurdaqah	78,643	203,685	115,000
Janūb Sīnāʾ	Aṭ-Ṭūr	12,796	33,140	35,000
Maṭrūḥ	Marsā Maṭrūḥ	81,897	212,112	186,000
Shamāl Sīnāʾ	Al-ʿArīsh	10,646	27,574	219,000
Al-Wādī al-Jadīd	Al-Khārijah	145,369	376,505	136,000
Lower Egypt				
Al-Buḥayrah	Damanhūr	3,911	10,130	3,973,000
Ad-Daqahlīyah	Al-Manṣūrah	1,340	3,471	4,226,000
Dumyāṭ	Dumyāṭ	227	589	898,000
Al-Gharbīyah	Ṭanṭā	750	1,942	3,437,000
Al-Ismāʿīlīyah (Ismailia)	—	557	1,442	681,000
Kafr ash-Shaykh	Kafr ash-Shaykh	1,327	3,437	2,266,000
Al-Minūfīyah	Shibīn al-Kawm	592	1,532	2,672,000
Al-Qalyūbīyah	Banhā	387	1,001	3,045,000
Ash-Sharqīyah	Az-Zaqāzīq	1,614	4,180	4,220,000
Upper Egypt				
Aswān	Aswān	262	679	1,042,000
Asyūṭ	Asyūṭ	600	1,553	2,843,000
Banī Suwayf	Banī Suwayf	510	1,322	1,836,000
Al-Fayyūm	Al-Fayyūm	705	1,827	1,995,000
Al-Jīzah	Al-Jīzah	32,878	85,153	4,525,000
Al-Minyā	Al-Minyā	873	2,262	3,372,000
Qinā	Qinā	715[2]	1,851[2]	2,607,000
Sawhāj	Sawhāj	597	1,547	3,067,000
Urban				
Būr Saʿīd (Port Said)	—	28	72	467,000
Al-Iskandarīyah (Alexandria)	—	1,034	2,679	3,431,000
Al-Qāhirah (Cairo)	—	83	214	6,955,000
Al-Uqṣur (Luxor)	—	...[2]	...[2]	159,000
As-Suways (Suez)	—	6,888	17,840	411,000
TOTAL		385,229	997,739	58,819,000

Demography

Population (1996): 60,896,000.
Density (1996): persons per sq mi 158.1, persons per sq km 61.0.
Urban-rural (1995): urban 44.8%; rural 55.2%.
Sex distribution (1995): male 50.55%; female 49.45%.
Age breakdown (1995): under 15, 38.0%; 15–29, 26.4%; 30–44, 19.3%; 45–59, 9.8%; 60–74, 5.3%; 75 and over, 1.2%.
Population projection: (2000) 66,062,000; (2010) 75,717,000.
Doubling time: 29 years.
Ethnic composition (1986): Egyptian 99.9%; other 0.1%.
Religious affiliation (1990): Sunnī Muslim *c.* 90%; Christian *c.* 10%[3].
Major cities (1994): Cairo 6,849,000; Alexandria 3,382,000; Al-Jīzah 2,144,000[4].

Vital statistics

Birth rate per 1,000 population (1995): 29.0 (world avg. 25.0).
Death rate per 1,000 population (1995): 9.0 (world avg. 9.3).
Natural increase rate per 1,000 population (1995): 20.0 (world avg. 15.7).
Total fertility rate (avg. births per childbearing woman; 1995): 3.7.
Life expectancy at birth (1994): male 65.4 years; female 69.5 years.
Major causes of death per 100,000 population (1987): diseases of the circulatory system 314.4; diseases of the respiratory system 140.7; infectious and parasitic diseases 98.9; malignant neoplasms (cancers) 22.0.

National economy

Budget (1995–96). Revenue: £E 66,195,000,000 (1993–94; general taxes 60.3%, of which sales taxes 15.7%, customs duties 11.7%; oil revenue 8.9%; Suez Canal fees 5.0%). Expenditures: £E 71,492,000,000 (1993–94; debt servicing 29.7%; wages and salaries 19.9%; defense 10.6%; pensions 7.0%).
Public debt (external, outstanding; 1994): U.S.$30,538,000,000.
Production (metric tons except as noted). Agriculture, forestry, fishing (1995): sugarcane 13,827,000, wheat 5,722,400, corn (maize) 5,178,100, tomatoes 5,050,000, rice 4,789,100, oranges 1,550,000, cotton 828,000, sorghum 787,000; livestock (number of live animals) 3,382,000 sheep, 3,250,000 buffalo, 3,250,000 goats, 3,100,000 cattle, 39,000,000 chickens, 10,380,000 pigeons[5]; roundwood (1994) 2,643,000 cu m; fish catch (1993) 302,829. Mining and quarrying (1994): iron ore 2,100,000; salt 1,000,000; clay 590,000. Manufacturing (1994–95): cement 16,000,000; nitrate fertilizers 5,437,000[6]; reinforcing iron 1,681,000; sugar 1,311,000; phosphate fertilizers 900,000; cotton yarn 336,000[6]; refrigerators 373,000 units[6]; automobiles 6,800 units[6]. Construction (1992–93): urban residential units 123,098. Energy production (consumption): electricity (kW-hr; 1994) 47,920,000,000 (47,920,000,000); coal (metric tons; 1994) n.a. (1,852,000); crude petroleum (barrels; 1994) 323,676,000 (192,342,000); petroleum products (metric tons; 1994) 26,424,000 (16,630,000); natural gas (cu m; 1994) 10,544,000,000 (10,544,000,000).

Gross national product (1994): U.S.$40,950,000,000 (U.S.$710 per capita).

Structure of gross domestic product and labour force				
	1994–95[7]		1992	
	in value £E '000,000	% of total value	labour force	% of labour force
Agriculture	22,968	15.4	5,535,000	35.0
Mining (petroleum)			44,900	0.3
Manufacturing }	37,027	24.9	2,014,600	12.7
Construction	7,099	4.8	884,200	5.6
Public utilities	2,366	1.6	147,300	0.9
Transp. and commun.	15,451[8]	10.4[8]	777,700	4.9
Trade	25,334	17.0	1,332,100	8.4
Finance	8,074	5.4	237,100	1.5
Pub. admin., defense, services	10,579	7.1	3,420,200	21.6
Other	19,790	13.3	1,416,000[9]	8.9[9]
TOTAL	148,688	100.0[10]	15,814,800[11]	100.0[10, 11]

Population economically active (1993–94): total 16,013,000; activity rate 27.8% (participation rates: ages 15–64, 48.9%; unemployed 9.8%).

Price and earnings indexes (1990 = 100)							
	1989	1990	1991	1992	1993	1994	1995
Consumer price index	85.6	100.0	119.7	136.1	152.5	165.0	190.9
Annual earnings index[12]	95.3	100.0	119.9	133.9	155.4	...	...

Household income and expenditure. Average household size (1986) 4.9; expenditure (1986–87)[13]: food 55.7%, clothing 10.9%, housing 10.5%.
Tourism (1994): receipts U.S.$1,384,000,000; expenditures U.S.$1,067,000,000.
Land use (1994): agricultural 3.5%; other 96.5%.

Foreign trade[14]

Balance of trade (current prices)						
	1990	1991	1992	1993	1994	1995
U.S.$'000,000	–6,379	–5,667	–5,231	–6,378	–5,953	–7,597
% of total	44.8%	40.5%	41.6%	47.4%	42.4%	44.8%

Imports (1994–95): U.S.$12,267,000,000 (machinery and transport equipment 29.2%; foodstuffs 21.0%; chemical products 12.0%; iron and steel products 5.7%). *Major import sources:* U.S. 16.9%; Germany 9.5%; Italy 6.4%; France 6.2%; Australia 4.2%; Japan 4.2%; U.K. 3.6%.
Exports (1994–95): U.S.$4,670,000,000 (petroleum and petroleum products 38.0%; cotton yarn, textiles, and fabrics 14.4%; basic metals and manufactures 11.9%; clothing 6.6%). *Major export destinations:* Italy 12.3%; U.S. 10.5%; Germany 6.0%.

Transport and communications

Transport. Railroads (1993–94): length 7,726 km; passenger-km 47,992,000,000; metric ton-km cargo 2,336,000,000. Roads (1995): length 58,000 km (paved 78%). Vehicles (1995): passenger cars 1,280,000; trucks and buses 423,300. Merchant marine (1992): vessels (100 gross tons and over) 444; total deadweight tonnage 1,685,245. Inland water (1996): Suez Canal, number of transits 14,748; metric ton cargo 275,200,000. Air transport (1996)[15]: passenger-km 7,678,400,000; metric ton-km cargo 164,109,000; airports (1996) 14.
Communications. Daily newspapers (1992): total number 16; total circulation 2,426,000[16]; circulation per 1,000 population 44[16]. Radio (1995): 16,450,000 receivers (1 per 3.6 persons). Television (1995): 5,000,000 receivers (1 per 11.9 persons). Telephones (main lines; 1993): 2,374,800 (1 per 23.5 persons).

Education and health

Education (1993–94)				
	schools	teachers	students	student/ teacher ratio
Primary (age 6–11)[17]	17,799	288,939	7,732,308	26.8
Secondary (age 12–17)[17]	7,307	209,519	4,433,060	21.2
Vocational	1,351	91,647[6]	1,700,139[6]	18.5
Teacher training	56	650[6]	2,664[6]	4.1
Higher	12[18]	38,828[19]	620,145	16.0

Educational attainment (1986). Percentage of population age 25 and over having: no formal education 64.1%; some primary education 16.5%; primary and secondary 14.8%; higher 4.6%. *Literacy* (1995): total population age 15 and over literate 51.4%; males 63.6%; females 38.8%.
Health: physicians (1996) 129,000 (1 per 472 persons); hospital beds (1994) 113,020 (1 per 515 persons); infant mortality rate (1996) 73.0.
Food (1992): daily per capita caloric intake 3,335 (vegetable products 94%, animal products 6%); 125% of FAO recommended minimum requirement.

Military

Total active duty personnel (1996): 440,000 (army 70.4%, navy 4.5%, air force [including air defense] 25.1%). *Military expenditure as percentage of GNP* (1994): 4.1% (world 3.0%); per capita expenditure U.S.$29.

[1]Includes 10 nonelective seats. [2]The area of Al-Uqṣur (Luxor) is included with Qinā governorate. [3]According to the 1986 census, the Christian population of Egypt was 5.9% of the total; this figure is considered by some external authorities to understate the Christian population by as much as 60%. [4]1992. [5]1991. [6]1992–93. [7]At purchaser's value. [8]Transportation includes earnings from traffic on the Suez Canal. [9]Unemployed and those seeking work for the first time. [10]Detail does not add to total given because of rounding. [11]Total includes 5,700 persons not classifiable by sector. [12]Average nominal wages for each fiscal year (*e.g.,* 1990–91). [13]Weight of consumer price components; urban households only. [14]Import figures are f.o.b. except for commodities and trading partners. [15]Egypt Air only. [16]Partial circulation only. [17]Data exclude 1,770 primary and 1,449 secondary schools in the Al-Azhar education system. [18]Universities only. [19]Excludes Al-Azhar University.

El Salvador

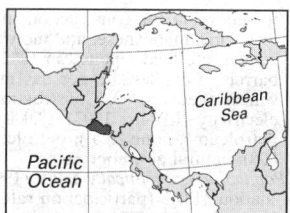

Official name: República de El
  Salvador (Republic of El Salvador).
Form of government: republic with
  one legislative house (Legislative
  Assembly [84]).
Chief of state and government:
  President.
Capital: San Salvador.
Official language: Spanish.
Official religion: none[1].
Monetary unit: 1 colón (₡) = 100
  centavos; valuation (Oct. 11, 1996)
  1 U.S.$ = ₡8.55; 1 £ = ₡13.48.

Area and population

Departments	Capitals	area sq mi	area sq km	population 1992 census
Ahuachapán	Ahuachapán	479	1,240	261,188
Cabañas	Sensuntepeque	426	1,104	138,426
Chalatenango	Chalatenango	779	2,017	177,320
Cuscatlán	Cojutepeque	292	756	178,502
La Libertad	Nueva San Salvador	638	1,653	513,866
La Paz	Zacatecoluca	473	1,224	245,915
La Unión	La Unión	801	2,074	255,565
Morazán	San Francisco	559	1,447	160,146
San Miguel	San Miguel	802	2,077	403,411
San Salvador	San Salvador	342	886	1,512,125
San Vicente	San Vicente	457	1,184	143,003
Santa Ana	Santa Ana	781	2,023	458,587
Sonsonate	Sonsonate	473	1,225	360,183
Usulután	Usulután	822	2,130	310,362
TOTAL		8,124	21,041[2]	5,118,599

Demography

Population (1996): 5,897,000.
Density (1996): persons per sq mi 725.9, persons per sq km 280.3.
Urban-rural (1992): urban 50.4%; rural 49.6%.
Sex distribution (1992): male 48.56%; female 51.44%.
Age breakdown (1992): under 15, 38.7%; 15–29, 28.7%; 30–44, 16.0%; 45–59, 9.2%; 60–74, 5.5%; 75 and over, 1.9%.
Population projection: (2000) 6,425,000; (2010) 7,772,000.
Doubling time: 31 years.
Ethnic composition (1993): mestizo (white and Indian) 89.0%; Amerindian 10.0%; white 1.0%.
Religious affiliation (1993): Roman Catholic 75.0%; other (mostly fundamentalist Protestant, Mormon, or Jehovah's Witness) 25.0%.
Major cities (1992)[3]: San Salvador 422,570 (metropolitan area 1,522,126); Soyapango 251,811[4]; Santa Ana 202,337; San Miguel 182,817; Mejicanos 145,000[4].

Vital statistics

Birth rate per 1,000 population (1995): 28.6 (world avg. 25.0); (1990) legitimate 30.6%; illegitimate 69.3%.
Death rate per 1,000 population (1995): 5.9 (world avg. 9.3).
Natural increase rate per 1,000 population (1995): 22.7 (world avg. 15.7).
Total fertility rate (avg. births per childbearing woman; 1995): 3.3.
Marriage rate per 1,000 population (1992): 4.3.
Divorce rate per 1,000 population (1992): 0.5.
Life expectancy at birth (1995): male 65.0 years; female 72.1 years.
Major causes of death per 100,000 population (1990)[5]: diseases of the circulatory system 120; violence 73; accidents 63; infectious and parasitic diseases 52; diseases of the respiratory system 49; ill-defined conditions 93.

National economy

Budget (1994). Revenue: ₡8,957,400,000 (sales taxes 38.7%, income taxes 20.4%, customs duties 14.2%, nontax revenue 10.6%). Expenditures: ₡10,264,300,000 (general public services 13.2%, education 13.2%, police 9.8%, fuel and energy 9.1%, health 8.3%, defense 8.1%).
Public debt (external, outstanding; 1994): U.S.$1,994,000,000.
Production (value added in ₡'000,000 except as noted). Agriculture, forestry, fishing (1993): coffee 1,492, corn (maize) 592, sugarcane 423, beans 418, aviculture 409, fish catch 261, *maicillo* (variety of millet) 202, forest products 96, rice 87, tobacco 61, oranges 126,000 metric tons[6], bananas 71,000 metric tons[6]; livestock (number of live animals; 1994) 1,256,000 cattle, 325,000 pigs. Mining and quarrying (1993): limestone 2,600,000 metric tons. Manufacturing (1993): food products 4,764; beverages 1,847; petroleum products 783; textiles 759; chemical products 691; nonmetallic mineral products 657; clothing and footwear 549; tobacco products 529. Construction (buildings completed; 1993): residential 650,000 sq m; nonresidential 296,000 sq m. Energy production (consumption): electricity (kW-hr; 1993) 2,718,000,000 (2,431,000,000); coal, none (none); crude petroleum (barrels; 1993) none (6,663,000); petroleum products (metric tons; 1993) 876,000 (1,195,000); natural gas, none (none).
Household income and expenditure. Average household size (1992): 4.7; average income per household (1990–91)[7]: ₡25,830 (U.S.$3,212); sources of income: n.a.; expenditure (1990–91)[7]: food and beverages 37.0%, housing 12.1%, transportation and communications 10.2%, clothing and footwear 6.7%, household furnishings 5.7%.
Population economically active (1992): total 1,762,002; activity rate of total population 34.4% (participation rates: ages 15–64, 55.4%; female 28.3%; urban unemployed [1993] 8.1%).

Price and earnings indexes (1990 = 100)

	1990	1991	1992	1993	1994	1995	1996[8]
Consumer price index	100.0	114.4	127.2	150.9	166.8	183.6	198.3
Annual earnings index[9]	100.0	111.9	128.6	...	...	...	...

Gross national product (at current market prices; 1994): U.S.$8,365,000,000 (U.S.$1,480 per capita).

Structure of gross domestic product and labour force

	1994 in value U.S.$'000,000[10]	1994 % of total value[10]	1992 labour force	1992 % of labour force
Agriculture	929	13.8	598,738	34.0
Mining	29	0.4	967	0.1
Manufacturing	1,424	21.2	245,800	13.9
Construction	247	3.7	82,664	4.7
Public utilities	38	0.6	9,984	0.6
Transportation and communications	514	7.6	62,209	3.5
Trade	1,112	16.5	275,518	15.6
Finance, real estate	804	12.0	51,544	2.9
Public admin., defense	391	5.8	100,800	5.7
Services	1,236	18.4	195,411	11.1
Other	—	—	138,367[11]	7.9[11]
TOTAL	6,724	100.0	1,762,002	100.0

Tourism (1994): receipts U.S.$86,000,000; expenditures U.S.$70,000,000.
Land use (1993): forested 5.0%; meadows and pastures 29.5%; agricultural and under permanent cultivation 35.2%; other 30.3%.

Foreign trade[12]

Balance of trade (current prices)

	1990	1991	1992	1993	1994	1995
U.S.$'000,000	−492.5	−518.2	−982.3	−1,141.9	−1,448.9	−1,855.3
% of total	37.6%	41.4%	46.9%	44.4%	47.1%	48.2%

Imports (1994): U.S.$2,261,600,000 (chemicals and chemical products 16.5%, transport equipment 12.4%, food and beverages 11.7%, nonelectrical machinery and equipment 11.6%). *Major import sources:* United States 41.5%; Guatemala 10.7%; Japan 6.3%; Venezuela 6.1%; Mexico 4.7%.
Exports U.S.$812,700,000 (coffee 32.5%, paper and paper products 7.0%, clothing 4.6%, pharmaceuticals 4.2%, raw sugar 4.2%). *Major export destinations:* United States 22.6%; Guatemala 21.9%; Germany 14.9%; Costa Rica 8.9%; Honduras 6.9%.

Transport and communications

Transport. Railroads (1994): route length 349 mi, 562 km; passenger-mi 3,442,000, passenger-km 5,540,000; short ton-mi cargo 20,302,000, metric ton-km cargo 29,640,000. Roads (1993): total length 9,670 mi, 15,562 km (paved 13%). Vehicles (1993): passenger cars 104,434; trucks and buses 152,778. Merchant marine (1993): vessels (100 gross tons and over) 15; total deadweight tonnage, n.a. Air transport (1993): passenger-mi 1,080,000,000, passenger-km 1,738,000,000; short ton-mi cargo 17,500,000, metric ton-km cargo 25,600,000; airports (1996) with scheduled flights 1.
Communications. Daily newspapers (1992): total number 8; total circulation 485,000; circulation per 1,000 population 90. Radio (1995): total number of receivers 2,080,000 (1 per 2.8 persons). Television (1995): total number of receivers 500,700 (1 per 12 persons). Telephones (main lines; 1993): 173,500 (1 per 32 persons).

Education and health

Education (1993)

	schools	teachers	students	student/ teacher ratio
Primary (age 7–15)	3,961	26,259[13]	1,042,256	39.7[13]
Secondary (age 16–18)	...	...	29,527	...
Voc. teacher tr.	...	...	88,588	...
Higher[14]	...	4,643	77,359	16.7

Educational attainment (1992): Percentage of population over age 25 having: no formal schooling 34.7%; incomplete primary education 37.6%; complete primary[15] 10.8%; secondary 9.4%; higher technical 2.4%; incomplete undergraduate 1.1%; complete undergraduate 2.9%; other/unknown 1.1%.
Literacy (1992): total population age 15 and over literate, 2,326,800 (74.1%); males literate, 1,141,007 (77.4%); females literate, 1,185,793 (71.3%).
Health (1993): physicians 4,525 (1 per 1,219 persons); hospital beds 9,379 (1 per 588 persons); infant mortality rate per 1,000 live births (1995) 33.0.
Food (1992): daily per capita caloric intake 2,663 (vegetable products 90%, animal products 10%); 116% of FAO recommended minimum requirement.

Military

Total active duty personnel (1995): 30,500 (army 91.8%, navy 1.6%, air force 6.6%). *Military expenditure as percentage of GNP* (1994): 1.2% (world 3.0%); per capita expenditure U.S.$19.

[1]Roman Catholicism, although not official, enjoys special recognition in the constitution. [2]Detail does not add to total given because of rounding. [3]Population of *municipios* (second-order administrative units). [4]Within San Salvador metropolitan area. [5]Projected rates based on about 75% of total deaths. [6]1994. [7]536,628 urban households only. [8]May. [9]Minimum wages in manufacturing and services in San Salvador metropolitan area. [10]At constant prices of 1990. [11]Includes 35,043 activities not defined and 103,324 unemployed. [12]Imports c.i.f., exports f.o.b. [13]Public schools only. [14]Universities and equivalent institutions only. [15]Education completed through ninth grade.

Equatorial Guinea

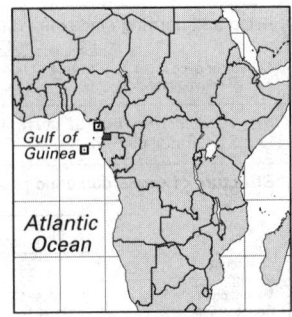

Official name: República de Guinea Ecuatorial (Republic of Equatorial Guinea).
Form of government: republic with one legislative house (Chamber of People's Representatives [80[1]]).
Chief of state: President.
Head of government: Prime Minister.
Capital: Malabo.
Official language: Spanish.
Official religion: none.
Monetary unit[2]: 1 CFA franc (CFAF) = 100 centimes; valuation (Oct. 11, 1996) 1 U.S.$ = CFAF 518.24; 1 £ = CFAF 816.38.

Area and population

Regions		area		population
		sq mi	sq km	1987 estimate
Provinces	Capitals			
Insular		785[3]	2,034	70,280
Annobón	Palé	7	17	2,360
Bioko Norte	Malabo	300	776	56,600
Bioko Sur	Luba	479	1,241	11,320
Continental		10,045[3]	26,017	259,950
Centro-Sur	Evinayong	3,834	9,931	55,970
Kie-Ntem	Ebebiyin	1,522	3,943	74,050
Litoral[4]	Bata	2,573	6,665	75,640
Wele-Nzas	Mongomo	2,115	5,478	54,290
TOTAL		10,831[3]	28,051	330,230

Demography

Population (1996): 406,000.
Density (1996): persons per sq mi 37.5, persons per sq km 14.5.
Urban-rural (1992): urban 29.4%; rural 70.6%.
Sex distribution (1995): male 49.25%; female 50.75%.
Age breakdown (1995): under 15, 43.2%; 15–29, 25.5%; 30–44, 15.6%; 45–59, 9.3%; 60–74, 5.3%; 75 and over, 1.1%.
Population projection: (2000) 448,000; (2010) 573,000.
Doubling time: 27 years.
Ethnic composition (1983): Fang 82.9%; Bubi 9.6%; Ndowe 3.8%; Annobonés 1.5%; Bujeba 1.4%; other 0.8%.
Religious affiliation (1980): Christian (mostly Roman Catholic) 88.8%; traditional beliefs 4.6%; atheist 1.4%; Muslim 0.5%; other 0.2%; none 4.5%.
Major cities (1983): Malabo 30,418; Bata 24,308; Ela-Nguema 6,179; Campo Yaunde 5,199; Los Angeles 4,079.

Vital statistics

Birth rate per 1,000 population (1994): 40.7 (world avg. 25.0); legitimate, n.a.; illegitimate, n.a.
Death rate per 1,000 population (1994): 14.7 (world avg. 9.3).
Natural increase rate per 1,000 population (1994): 26.0 (world avg. 15.7).
Total fertility rate (avg. births per childbearing woman; 1994): 5.3.
Marriage rate per 1,000 population: n.a.
Divorce rate per 1,000 population: n.a.
Life expectancy at birth (1994): male 50.0 years; female 54.3 years.
Major causes of death per 100,000 population: n.a.; however, major diseases include malaria (about 24% of total mortality), respiratory infections (12% of mortality), cholera, leprosy, trypanosomiasis (sleeping sickness), and waterborne (especially gastrointestinal) diseases.

National economy

Budget (1995). Revenue: CFAF 27,468,000,000 (domestic revenue 49.3%, of which tax revenue 32.1%, nontax revenue 9.9%, oil revenue 7.3%; foreign grants 50.7%). Expenditures: CFAF 29,452,000,000 (capital expenditure 64.2%; current expenditure 34.7%, of which interest 12.0%, salaries 9.0%).
Public debt (external, outstanding; 1994): U.S.$222,400,000.
Gross national product (at current market prices; 1994): U.S.$167,000,000 (U.S.$470 per capita).

Structure of gross domestic product and labour force

	1994		1983	
	in value CFAF '000,000	% of total value	labour force	% of labour force
Agriculture, forestry	33,893	47.4	59,390	57.9
Manufacturing, mining	15,280	21.4	1,616	1.6
Construction	3,391	4.7	1,929	1.9
Public utilities	2,452	3.4	224	0.2
Transportation and communications	1,452	2.0	1,752	1.7
Trade	6,567	9.2	3,059	3.0
Finance	1,497	2.1	409	0.4
Pub. admin., defense	3,472	4.9 }	8,377	8.2
Services	2,170	3.0 }		
Other	1,332	1.9	25,809	25.2
TOTAL	71,506	100.0	102,565	100.0[3]

Production (metric tons except as noted). Agriculture, forestry, fishing (1995): roots and tubers 82,000 (of which cassava 47,000, sweet potatoes 35,000), bananas 17,000, coconuts 8,000, coffee 7,000, palm oil 5,000, cacao beans 3,000, palm kernels 3,000; livestock (number of live animals) 36,000 sheep, 8,100 goats, 5,300 pigs, 4,800 cattle; roundwood (1994) 714,000 cu m; fish catch (1993) 3,800. Mining and quarrying: details, n.a.; however, in addition

to quarrying for construction materials, unexploited deposits of iron ore, lead, zinc, manganese, and molybdenum are present; the offshore Alba gas-condensate field, opened in 1992, achieved commercial production of 7,000 barrels of condensate per day in 1994 (11 months). Manufacturing (1993): veneer sheets 8,000. Construction: n.a. Energy production (consumption): electricity (kW-hr; 1993) 19,000,000 (19,000,000); coal, none (n.a.); crude petroleum[5], none (n.a.); petroleum products (metric tons; 1993) none (41,-000); natural gas, none (n.a.).
Population economically active (1991): total 148,000; activity rate of total population 41.0% (participation rates [1983]: ages 15–64, 66.7%; female 35.7%; unemployed 24.2%).

Price and earnings indexes (1990 = 100)

	1987	1988	1989	1990	1991	1992	1993
Consumer price index	92.3	93.4	98.9	100.0	96.8	89.9	93.5
Earnings index	...	...	...	...	...	...	...

Household income and expenditure. Average household size (1980) 4.5; income per household: n.a.; sources of income (1988): wages and salaries 57.0%, business income 42.0%, other 1.0%; expenditure (1988): food and beverages 62.0%, clothing and footwear 10.0%, medical care 6.0%.
Tourism: tourism is a government priority but remains undeveloped.
Land use (1994): forested 65.2%; meadows and pastures 3.7%; agricultural and under permanent cultivation 8.2%; built-on, wasteland, and other 22.9%.

Foreign trade

Balance of trade (current prices)

	1988	1989	1990	1991	1992	1993
CFAF '000,000	−2,949	−4,083	−8,522	−6,017	−10,932	+2,537
% of total	9.5%	12.1%	29.7%	11.4%	33.5%	7.7%

Imports (1994): CFAF 21,900,000,000 (capital equipment 21.0%; petroleum products 12.3%; other 66.7%). *Major import sources:* Cameroon 36.9%; Italy 16.7%; The Netherlands 14.3%; Spain 10.7%; France 8.3%; Belgium 4.8%; United States 2.4%.
Exports (1994): CFAF 32,900,000,000 (petroleum products 50.5%; wood 35.6%; food products 4.6%, of which cocoa 4.3%). *Major export destinations:* Japan 14.7%; Spain 11.8%; Côte d'Ivoire 10.7%; Nigeria 8.4%; Portugal 4.0%; France 3.9%; China 2.7%; Germany 2.3%.

Transport and communications

Transport. Railroads: none. Roads (1993): total length 1,667 mi, 2,682 km (paved 19%). Vehicles (1994): passenger cars 6,500; trucks and buses 4,000. Merchant marine (1992): vessels (100 gross tons and over) 3; total deadweight tonnage 6,699. Air transport (1990): passenger-mi 4,000,000, passenger-km 7,000,000; short ton-mi cargo (1985) 700,000, metric ton-km cargo (1985) 1,000,000; airports (1996) with scheduled flights 2.
Communications. Daily newspapers (1992): total number 1; total circulation 1,000; circulation per 1,000 population 3.0. Radio (1995): total number of receivers 200,000 (1 per 2.0 persons). Television (1995): total number of receivers 2,500 (1 per 158 persons). Telephones (main lines; 1993): 1,300 (1 per 333 persons).

Education and health

Education (1987–88)

	schools	teachers	students	student/ teacher ratio
Primary (age 6–11)	703	1,065	61,009	57.3
Secondary (age 12–17)	9	319	9,226	28.9
Voc., teacher tr.[6]	1	52	882	17.0
Higher	4	81	660	8.1

Educational attainment (1983). Percentage of population age 15 and over having: no schooling 35.4%; some primary education 46.6%; primary 13.0%; secondary 2.3%; postsecondary 1.1%; not specified 1.6%. *Literacy* (1983): percentage of total population age 15 and over literate 62.2%; males literate 77.8%; females literate 48.6%.
Health: physicians (1990) 99 (1 per 3,532 persons); hospital beds (1990) 992 (1 per 350 persons); infant mortality rate per 1,000 live births (1994) 102.6.
Food (latest): daily per capita caloric intake 2,230; 68% of FAO recommended minimum requirement.

Military

Total active duty personnel (1996): 1,320 (army 83.3%, navy 9.1%, air force 7.6%). *Military expenditure as percentage of GNP* (1994): 2.2% (world 3.0%); per capita expenditure U.S.$5.

---

[1]Conduct of November 1993 legislative elections was unacceptable to international observers. [2]As of Jan. 1, 1985, Equatorial Guinea became a member of the franc zone, substituting the CFA franc for the previous monetary unit, the ekwele; the CFA franc has a par value of 100 CFA francs to the French franc. [3]Detail does not add to total given because of rounding. [4]Includes three islets in Corisco Bay. [5]Equatorial Guinea announced an oil strike off Bioko in 1995 having an estimated production capacity of 10,000 barrels per day. [6]Efforts are being undertaken to provide the training necessary to qualify nondegree teachers for service. Also, teacher-training schools are to be expanded in order to increase the number of primary-school teachers.

Eritrea

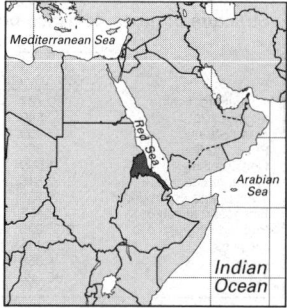

Official name: State of Eritrea.
Form of government: transitional regime[1] with one legislative house (National Assembly [150][2]).
Head of state and government: President.
Capital: Asmara.
Official language: none.
Official religion: none.
Monetary unit: Ethiopian birr (Br) = 100 cents; valuation (Oct. 11, 1996) 1 U.S.$ = Br 7.13; 1 £ = Br 10.88.

Area and population

Provinces[4]	Capitals	area[3] sq mi	area[3] sq km	population 1994 estimate[5]
Akele Guzai	Adi Qayeh	3,200	8,400	341,000
Asmara	Asmara (Asmera)	100	200	[6]
Barka	Agordat (Akordat)	10,700	27,800	232,000
Dankalia	Asseb (Aseb)	9,400	24,300	177,000
Gash and Setit	Barentu	7,200	18,600	304,000
Hamasien	...	1,000	2,700	731,000[6]
Sahel	Nakfa	6,300	16,400	224,000
Semhar	Massawa (Mitsiwa)	2,400	6,300	118,000
Senhit	Keren	2,300	5,900	254,000
Seraye	Mendefera	2,600	6,800	421,000
TOTAL		45,300[7]	117,400	2,802,000

Demography

Population (1996): 3,627,000.
Density (1996): persons per sq mi 77.6, persons per sq km 30.0.
Urban-rural (1992): urban 16.3%; rural 83.7%.
Sex distribution (1996): male 50.17%; female 49.83%.
Age breakdown (1996): under 15, 41.9%; 15–29, 29.6%; 30–44, 14.6%; 45–59, 9.1%; 60–74, 3.9%; 75 and over, 0.9%.
Population projection: (2000) 4,025,000; (2010) 5,153,000.
Doubling time: 25 years.
Linguistic composition (1976): Tigrinya 49.0%; Tigré 31.7%; Afar 4.3%; Hedareb 3.9%; Bilen 3.1%; Saho 3.0%; Kunama 2.7%; Nara 2.1%; Rashaida 0.3%.
Religious affiliation (1993): believers are *c.* 50% Christian and *c.* 50% Muslim; there are also a few animists.
Major cities (1992): Asmara 400,000; Asseb 50,000; Keren 40,000; Massawa 40,000; Mendefera 14,833[8].

Vital statistics

Birth rate per 1,000 population (1995): 44.3 (world avg. 25.0).
Death rate per 1,000 population (1995): 15.7 (world avg. 9.3).
Natural increase rate per 1,000 population (1995): 28.6 (world avg. 15.7).
Total fertility rate (avg. births per childbearing woman; 1995): 6.5.
Marriage rate per 1,000 population (1992): 6.8.
Divorce rate per 1,000 population: n.a.
Life expectancy at birth (1995): male 48.3 years; female 51.8 years.
Major causes of death per 100,000 population: n.a.; morbidity (principal causes of illness) arises mainly in malaria and other infectious diseases, parasitic infections, malnutrition, diarrheal diseases, and dysenteries.

National economy

Budget (1995). Revenue: Br 1,345,200,000 (taxes 53.2%, of which direct taxes 25.3%, import duties 16.7%, indirect taxes 11.2%; nontax revenue 46.8%). Expenditures: Br 2,657,100,000 (current expenditure 80.2%, of which materials 32.0%, wages and salaries 24.3%; capital 19.8%).
Public debt: n.a.
Tourism (1993): 12 major hotels.
Production (metric tons except as noted). Agriculture, forestry, fishing (1995): cereals 153,000, roots and tubers 109,000, sorghum 68,000, pulses 45,000, vegetables and melons 35,000, millet 30,000, barley 29,000, wheat 9,500, corn (maize) 7,800, sesame seeds 7,000, dry beans 4,000, chickpeas 4,000; livestock (number of live animals) 1,530,000 sheep, 1,400,000 goats, 1,315,000 cattle, 69,000 camels; fish catch (1995) 3,773, of which artisanal fisheries 746. Mining and quarrying (1995): salt 305,120; marble and granite are quarried, as are sand and aggregate (gravel) for construction; deposits of copper, zinc, mica, gold, iron, manganese, nickel, and lead exist but remain unexploited. Manufacturing (gross value in Br '000; 1995): beverages 163,400; food products 122,000; chemical products 101,900; leather products and shoes 57,900; textile products 54,300; metal products 47,000; nonmetallic products 31,300; paper and printing products 19,100; tobacco and matches 13,400. Construction: reconstruction, after some 30 years of civil war, is a principal concern of the government. Energy production: energy resources include hydroelectricity, fossil fuels, geothermal power, coal, biogas, solar power, and wind; commercial electricity production for 1986–87 was 148,664,000 kW-hr.
Persons economically active: n.a.

Price and earnings indexes (December 1992 = 100)

	1991	1992	1993	1994	1995
Consumer price index[9]	91.9	100.0	119.2	127.4	141.3
Earnings index	...	...	...	...	...

Gross national product (at current market prices; 1993): *c.* U.S.$393,415,000 (U.S.$115 per capita).

Structure of gross domestic product and labour force

	1995 in value Br '000,000	1995 % of total value	1992 labour force	1992 % of labour force
Agriculture	390.8	8.4	647	2.6
Manufacturing	571.3	12.2	11,894	48.3
Mining	2.1	0.1	292	1.2
Public utilities	59.8	1.3	2,284	9.3
Construction	235.6	5.0	298	1.2
Transp. and commun.	453.4	9.7	3,126	12.7
Trade	921.9	19.7	597	2.4
Finance	136.8	2.9	382	1.6
Public admin., defense	558.0	11.9	}	
Services	156.2	3.3	5,001	20.3
Other	1,195.7[10]	25.5[10]		
TOTAL	4,681.5[7]	100.0	24,621[7]	100.0[7]

Household income and expenditure. Average household size (1984) 4.5; average annual income per household: n.a.; sources of income: n.a.; expenditure: n.a.
Land use (1994): forested 7.3%; agricultural and under permanent cultivation 5.1%; meadows and pastures 69.0%; other (predominantly barren land) 18.6%.

Foreign trade

Balance of trade (current prices)

	1992	1993	1994	1995
U.S.$'000,000	−263.0	−239.0	−331.0	−323.0
% of total	89.8%	76.8%	71.9%	66.6%

Imports (1995): Br 2,608,500,000 (machinery and transport equipment 45.2%, manufactured goods 19.1%, food products 17.1%, chemical products 6.0%, raw materials 2.5%, petroleum and petroleum products 1.9%, animal and vegetable oils 1.2%). *Major import sources:* Saudi Arabia 19.6%[11]; Italy 17.5%; United Arab Emirates 9.2%; Germany 5.9%; United States 5.9%; Ethiopia 5.5%; United Kingdom 3.8%; The Sudan 3.0%.
Exports (1995): Br 529,500,000 (raw materials 29.8%, food products 26.2%, manufactured goods 19.3%, beverages and tobacco 3.8%, machinery and transport equipment 3.8%, chemical products 2.5%). *Major export destinations:* Ethiopia 63.3%; The Sudan 16.4%; Yemen 4.9%; Saudi Arabia 3.7%; Italy 2.2%; Germany 0.5%.

Transport and communications

Transport. Railroads (1996): none; a 217-mi (350-km) rail line that formerly connected Massawa and Agordat is under reconstruction. A rail line of 3 mi (5 km) inside Massawa was in service by late 1994. Roads (1995): total length 2,442 mi, 3,930 km (paved 21%). Vehicles (1995): automobiles 5,350, trucks and buses, n.a. Merchant marine: vessels (100 gross tons and over) n.a. Air transport (1993)[12]: passenger arrivals 47,645[13], passenger departures 42,548[13]; short ton cargo handled 25,907[14], metric ton cargo handled 28,557[14]; airports (1996) with scheduled flights 2.
Communications. Daily newspapers: none; (1994) 2 biweekly newspapers published; circulation *c.* 26,000[15]; circulation per 1,000 population 7.8[15]. Radio (1994): the government operates a station in Asmara. Television (1994): the government operates a station in Asmara. Telephones (main lines; 1993): 20,000 (1 per 167 persons).

Education and health

Education (1993–94)

	schools	teachers	students	student/ teacher ratio
Primary (age 7–12)	491	5,272	207,099	39.3
Secondary (age 13–18)	86[16]	1,993	65,537	32.9
Voc., teacher tr.	4[16]	102	987	9.7
Higher[17]	1	144	2,032	14.1

Literacy (1993): total population literate *c.* 20%.
Health (1993): physicians 69 (1 per 36,000 persons); hospital beds (1986–87): 2,449 (1 per 1,100 persons); infant mortality rate per 1,000 live births 135.
Food (1993): daily per capita caloric intake 1,750 (vegetable and animal products, n.a.); 93% of FAO recommended minimum requirement.

Military

Total active duty personnel (1996): estimated strength of Eritrean armed forces (predominantly former guerrillas) is some 55,000 to be reduced to 35,000.

[1]Transitional regime (independent May 24, 1993) to govern for up to four years pending the drafting of a constitution and holding of multiparty elections. [2]All seats appointive pending elections in 1997. [3]Approximate figures. The published total area is 46,774 sq mi (121,144 sq km); water area is 7,776 sq mi (20,140 sq km). [4]On May 20, 1995, a resolution was approved dividing the country into six administrative regions, which would then be divided into region, subregion, and village categories. [5]Agricultural population only. [6]Asmara population included in Hamasien. [7]Detail does not add to total given because of rounding. [8]1989. [9]Asmara only; year-end. [10]Including indirect taxes less subsidies. [11]Saudi Arabia is a transshipment point; not all goods included here are of Saudi Arabian origin. [12]Asmara airport only. [13]January to June only. [14]1987–88. [15]1992. [16]1992–93. [17]1993–94; full-time students only.

Estonia

Official name: Eesti Vabariik (Republic of Estonia).
Form of government: unitary multiparty republic with a single legislative body (Riigikogu[1] [101]).
Chief of state: President.
Head of government: Prime Minister.
Capital: Tallinn.
Official language: Estonian.
Official religion: none.
Monetary unit: 1 kroon (EEK) = 100 senti; valuation (Oct. 11, 1996)
1 U.S.$ = EEK 12.24;
1 £ = EEK 19.27.

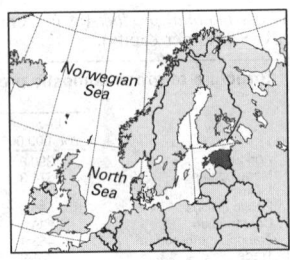

Area and population		area		population
				1995[2]
Counties	Capitals	sq mi	sq km	estimate
Harju	Tallinn	1,673	4,333	559,106
Hiiu	Kärdla	395	1,023	11,953
Ida-Viru	Jõhvi	1,299	3,364	206,418
Järva	Paide	1,013	2,623	43,639
Jõgeva	Jõgeva	1,005	2,604	42,146
Lääne	Haapsalu	920	2,383	32,586
Lääne-Viru	Rakvere	1,337	3,464	75,533
Pärnu	Pärnu	1,856	4,806	99,563
Põlva	Põlva	836	2,165	36,315
Rapla	Rapla	1,151	2,980	40,058
Saare	Kuressaare	1,128	2,922	40,759
Tartu	Tartu	1,193	3,090	154,483
Valga	Valga	790	2,047	40,014
Viljandi	Viljandi	1,386	3,589	64,377
Võru	Võru	890	2,305	44,633
TOTAL		17,462[3, 4]	45,227[3, 4]	1,491,583

Demography

Population (1996): 1,475,000.
Density (1996)[5]: persons per sq mi 84.5, persons per sq km 32.6.
Urban-rural (1995): urban 70.0%; rural 30.0%.
Sex distribution (1995): male 46.65%; female 53.35%.
Age breakdown (1995): under 15, 20.7%; 15–29, 21.0%; 30–44, 21.7%; 45–59, 18.1%; 60–74, 13.8%; 75 and over, 4.7%.
Population projection: (2000) 1,430,000; (2010) 1,401,000.
Ethnic composition (1994): Estonian 63.9%; Russian 29.0%; Ukrainian 2.7%; Belarusian 1.6%; Finnish 1.0%; other 1.8%.
Religious affiliation: believers are predominantly Evangelical Lutheran, with Orthodox and Baptist minorities.
Major cities (1995): Tallinn 434,763; Tartu 104,907; Narva 77,770; Kohtla-Järve 55,415; Pärnu 51,526.

Vital statistics

Birth rate per 1,000 population (1995): 9.1 (world avg. 25.0); (1994) legitimate 59.1%; illegitimate 40.9%.
Death rate per 1,000 population (1995): 14.2 (world avg. 9.3).
Natural increase rate per 1,000 population (1995): −5.1 (world avg. 15.7).
Total fertility rate (avg. births per childbearing woman; 1994): 1.3.
Marriage rate per 1,000 population (1994): 4.9.
Divorce rate per 1,000 population (1994): 3.7.
Life expectancy at birth (1993): male 62.4 years; female 73.8 years.
Major causes of death per 100,000 population (1993): diseases of the circulatory system 792.9, of which ischemic heart diseases 485.6, cerebrovascular disease 255.6; malignant neoplasms (cancers) 225.3; accidents 110.5; suicide 38.2.

National economy

Budget (1995). Revenue: EEK 15,952,000,000 (payments for social security and welfare 31.7%, value-added taxes 27.0%, personal income taxes 24.5%, corporate taxes 7.3%). Expenditures: EEK 15,498,000,000 (current expenditure 94.8%, capital expenditure 5.2%).
Public debt (external, outstanding; 1994): U.S.$108,600,000.
Production (metric tons except as noted). Agriculture, forestry, fishing (1994): hay 582,000, potatoes 563,000, barley 339,000, oats 58,000, wheat 57,000, rye 41,000, apples and pears 14,000; livestock (number of live animals) 460,000 pigs, 420,000 cattle; roundwood (1993) 1,073,000 cu m; fish catch 132,700. Mining and quarrying (value of production in EEK '000,000; 1994): oil shale 781; peat 121. Manufacturing (value of production in EEK '000,000; 1994): meat and meat products 1,502; chemicals and chemical products 1,502; dairy products 1,368; fish and fish products 1,156; beverages 1,091; cement, bricks, and tiles 923; wood and wood products (excluding furniture) 922; textiles 908. Construction (value of construction in EEK '000,000; 1994): residential 295; nonresidential 1,836. Energy production (consumption): electricity (kW-hr; 1994) 9,152,000,000 (5,288,000,000); oil shale (metric tons; 1994) 16,000,000[6] (16,299,000); coal and coke (metric tons; 1994) none (97,000); crude petroleum, none (n.a.); natural gas (cu m; 1994) none (645,000,000).
Household income and expenditure. Average household size (1994) 3.1[7]; average net income per household (1994) EEK 46,303 (U.S.$3,681)[7]; sources of income (1994)[8]: wages and salaries 53.0%, transfers 12.8%, self-employment 5.7%, other 28.5%; expenditure (1994)[8]: food and beverages 41.0%, housing 9.6%, transportation 9.2%, clothing and footwear 8.4%.
Gross national product (at current market prices; 1994): U.S.$4,351,000,000 (U.S.$2,820 per capita).

Structure of gross domestic product and labour force				
	1994		1993	
	in value EEK '000,000	% of total value	labour force	% of labour force
Agriculture, fishing	2,787	9.2	58,500[9]	7.8[9]
Mining	540	1.8	13,400	1.8
Manufacturing	5,059	16.7	127,300	17.0
Public utilities	883	2.9	11,700	1.6
Construction	1,666	5.5	33,200	4.4
Trade, restaurants	5,615	18.6	66,500	8.9
Transp. and commun.	2,734	9.1	47,400	6.4
Finance, real estate	2,452	8.1	29,100	3.9
Pub. admin., defense	1,216	4.0	27,800	3.7
Services	2,418	8.0	101,700	13.6
Other	4,858[10]	16.1	230,500[9]	30.9[9]
TOTAL	30,228	100.0	747,100	100.0

Population economically active (1989): total 856,000; activity rate of total population 54.7% (participation rates: ages 15–64, 79.7%; female 50.0%; unemployed [1994] 8.1%).

Price and earnings indexes (1992 = 100)						
	1990	1991	1992	1993	1994	1995	1996
Consumer price index	2.7	8.5	100.0	189.8	280.3	361.3	435.3[11]
Monthly earnings index	...	...	100.0	194.2	315.8	...	...

Tourism (1994): receipts from visitors U.S.$92,000,000; expenditures by nationals abroad U.S.$48,000,000.
Land use (1993): forested 47.8%; meadows and pastures 7.4%; agricultural and under permanent cultivation 27.1%; other 17.7%.

Foreign trade[12]

Balance of trade (current prices)					
	1991	1992	1993	1994	1995
EEK '000,000	+65	+79	−1,309	−4,594	−8,287
% of total	6.8%	0.8%	5.8%	12.0%	16.4%

Imports (1995): EEK 29,385,000,000 (nonelectrical and electrical machinery 21.4%, food products 14.1%, textiles and clothing 12.8%, chemicals and chemical products 12.4%, mineral fuels 11.4%). *Major import sources:* Finland 38.3%; Russia 15.4%; Sweden 9.0%; Germany 8.8%; The Netherlands 3.5%.
Exports (1995): EEK 21,098,000,000 (food products 16.4%, textiles and clothing 16.1%, wood, wood products, and paper products 13.4%, nonelectrical and electrical machinery 13.1%, chemicals and chemical products 10.2%). *Major export destinations:* Finland 21.3%; Russia 17.7%; Sweden 10.7%; Latvia 7.7%; Germany 7.2%; Lithuania 4.7%.

Transport and communications

Transport. Railroads (1994): route length 636 mi, 1,024 km; passenger-mi 334,000,000, passenger-km 537,000,000; short ton-mi cargo 2,474,000,000, metric ton-km cargo 3,612,000,000. Roads (1994): total length 9,168 mi, 14,755 km (paved 55%). Vehicles (1994): passenger cars 337,800; trucks and buses 60,300. Merchant marine (1992): vessels (100 gross tons and over) 234; total deadweight tonnage 680,367. Air transport (1995)[13]: passenger-mi 65,200,000, passenger-km 105,000,000; short ton-mi cargo 292,000, metric ton-km cargo 426,000; airports (1996) with scheduled flights 3.
Communications. Daily newspapers (1994): total number 6; total circulation 222,000; circulation per 1,000 population 148. Radio: n.a. Television (1995): total number of receivers 600,000 (1 per 2.5 persons). Telephones (main lines; 1993): 358,300 (1 per 4.2 persons).

Education and health

Education (1994–95)	schools	teachers	students	student/ teacher ratio
Primary } Secondary }	741	15,453	218,600	14.1
Vocational	84	1,585	27,806	17.5
Higher	22	...	23,169	...

Educational attainment (1989). Percentage of persons age 25 and over having: no formal schooling 2.2%; primary education 39.0%; secondary 45.1%; higher 13.7%. Literacy (1989): 99.7%.
Health (1994): physicians 4,680 (1 per 319 persons); hospital beds 12,521 (1 per 119 persons); infant mortality rate per 1,000 live births 14.5.
Food: daily per capita caloric intake, n.a.

Military

Total active duty personnel (1995): 3,450 (army 95.7%, navy 4.3%). *Military expenditure as a percentage of GNP* (1994): 0.9% (world 3.0%); per capita expenditure U.S.$64.

[1]Official legislation bans translation of parliament's name. [2]January 1. [3]Total includes 1,092 sq mi (2,827 sq km) of inland water, of which the Estonian portion of Lake Peipus (590 sq mi [1,529 sq km]) is not distributed by county. [4]Total includes 1,596 sq mi (4,133 sq km) of Baltic Sea islands. [5]Based on land area only. [6]Estimated figure. [7]Monthly average for December. [8]Annual average. [9]Agriculture, fishing excludes small farmers and Other includes 164,800 self-employed, small farmers, and others and 65,700 unemployed. [10]Includes taxes (EEK 4,076,000,000) less subsidies (EEK 675,000,000). [11]March. [12]Exports f.o.b.; imports c.i.f. [13]Estonian Air.

Ethiopia

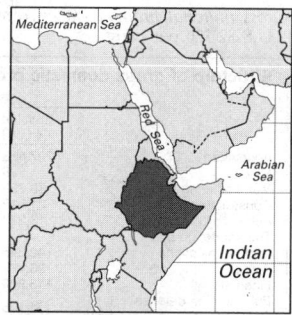

Official name: Federal Democratic
Republic of Ethiopia.
Form of government: federal republic[1]
with two legislative houses (Federal
Council [117]; Council of People's
Representatives [548]).
Chief of state: President.
Head of government: Prime Minister.
Capital: Addis Ababa.
Official language: none[2].
Official religion: none.
Monetary unit: 1 birr (Br) = 100 cents;
valuation (Oct. 11, 1996) 1 U.S.$ = Br
6.00; 1 £ = Br 9.45.

Area and population

Regions[3]	Capitals	area sq mi	area sq km	population 1993 estimate
Addis Ababa	...	2,003	5,188	2,657,559
Arsi	Asela	9,155	23,710	2,157,227
Asosa	...	8,906	23,067	570,910
Bale	Goba	25,996	67,330	1,063,382
Borena	...	36,301	94,018	723,746
Eastern Gojam	...	5,381	13,936	1,699,460
Eastern Harerge	...	34,981	90,600	2,774,346
Eastern Shewa	...	4,924	12,754	1,026,180
Gambela	...	10,064	26,065	195,023
Ilubabor	Mefa	12,905	35,059	3,117,220
Kefa	Jima	15,476	40,083	1,148,596
Metekel	...	11,768	30,481	416,380
Northern Gonder	...	23,946	62,020	2,038,164
Northern Omo	...	11,553	29,923	3,046,859
Northern Shewa	...	10,436	27,030	2,570,128
Northern Welo	...	11,906	30,835	1,621,520
Sidamo	Awasa	8,009	20,742	2,980,044
Southern Gonder	...	6,594	17,079	1,867,766
Southern Omo	...	8,494	22,000	269,197
Southern Shewa	...	6,486	16,799	3,235,768
Southern Welo	...	7,993	20,702	2,675,995
Welega	Nekemte	16,460	42,632	2,673,652
Western Gojam	...	6,675	17,289	2,210,466
Western Harerge	...	12,814	33,188	1,482,628
Western Shewa	...	8,964	23,218	2,934,434
Autonomous regions				
Aseb[4]	...	17,786	46,065	246,373
Dire Dawa	...	11,291	29,244	521,691
Ogaden	...	69,239	179,327	906,632
Tigray	Mekele	20,656	53,498	2,999,948
TOTAL		437,794[5]	1,133,882	51,831,290

Demography

Population (1996): 56,713,000.
Density (1996): persons per sq mi 129.5, persons per sq km 50.0.
Urban-rural (1995): urban 11.5%; rural 88.5%.
Sex distribution (1996): male 50.07%; female 49.93%.
Age breakdown (1995): under 15, 45.8%; 15–29, 26.2%; 30–44, 15.3%; 45–59, 8.3%; 60–74, 3.7%; 75 and over, 0.7%.
Population projection: (2000) 63,785,000; (2010) 85,078,000.
Ethnolinguistic composition (1983)[6]: Amhara 37.7%; Galla (Oromo) 35.3%; Tigrinya 8.6%; Gurage 3.3%; Ometo (Omotic) 2.7%; Sidamo 2.4%.
Religious affiliation (1980)[6]: Ethiopian Orthodox 52.5%; Muslim 31.4%; traditional beliefs 11.4%; other Christian 4.5%; other 0.2%.
Major cities (1993): Addis Ababa 2,200,186; Dire Dawa 173,588; Gonder 146,777; Nazret 131,585.

Vital statistics

Birth rate per 1,000 population (1995): 46.5 (world avg. 25.0).
Death rate per 1,000 population (1995): 17.5 (world avg. 9.3).
Natural increase rate per 1,000 population (1995): 29.0 (world avg. 15.7).
Total fertility rate (avg. births per childbearing woman; 1995): 7.1.
Life expectancy at birth (1995): male 45.9 years; female 48.2 years.
Major causes of death (1987–88)[6, 7]: infectious and parasitic diseases 33.1%; respiratory diseases 15.7%; digestive system diseases 10.7%.

National economy[6]

Budget (1994–95). Revenue: Br 6,817,700,000 (1993–94; taxes 79.1%, of which import duties 31.8%, income and profit tax 23.3%, sales tax 9.5%, export duties 1.3%; nontax revenue 20.9%). Expenditures: Br 8,136,900,000 (1993–94; general services 32.5%; social services 27.4%, of which education 16.6%; public health 6.2%; debt payment 21.3%).
Public debt (external, outstanding; 1994): U.S.$4,816,000,000.
Tourism: receipts (1994) U.S.$23,000,000; expenditures (1993) U.S.$11,000,000.
Production (metric tons except as noted). Agriculture, forestry, fishing (1995): corn (maize) 2,189,000, wheat 1,517,000, barley 1,417,000, sorghum 1,232,000, sugarcane 1,200,000, pulses 1,108,000, potatoes 350,000, yams 263,000, millet 248,000, coffee 228,000, seed cotton 45,500; livestock (number of live animals) 29,825,000 cattle, 21,700,000 sheep, 16,700,000 goats, 8,580,000 horses, mules, and asses, 1,000,000 camels; roundwood (1994) 45,378,000 cu m; fish catch (1993) 4,200. Mining and quarrying (1994): cement 400,000; limestone 200,000; salt 165,000; gold 128,603 troy oz; platinum 48 troy oz. Manufacturing (gross value in Br '000[8]; 1991–92): food and beverages 555,800; textiles 251,400; leather and shoes 162,300; cigarettes 106,000; chemicals 53,400. Construction (authorized; 1987–88)[9]: residential 260,251 sq m; nonresidential 63,346 sq m, of which commercial 16,994 sq m. Energy production (consumption): electricity (kW-hr; 1994) 1,284,000,000 (1,284,000,000); coal,

none (n.a.); crude petroleum (barrels; 1994) n.a. (5,637,000); petroleum products (metric tons; 1994) 746,000 (899,000); natural gas, n.a. (n.a.).
Land use (1994): forest 13.3%; pasture 20.0%; agriculture 11.0%; other 55.7%.
Gross national product (1994): U.S.$6,947,000,000 (U.S.$130 per capita).

Structure of gross domestic product and labour force

	1993–94 in value Br '000,000	1993–94 % of total value	1995[10] labour force	1995[10] % of labour force
Agriculture	13,754.1	54.4	21,605,317	88.6
Manufacturing, mining	1,932.3	7.6	401,535	1.6
Construction	736.0	2.9	61,232	0.3
Public utilities	254.8	1.0	17,066	0.1
Transp. and commun.	1,163.5	4.6	103,154	0.4
Trade	2,551.3	10.1	935,937	3.8
Finance	2,035.2	8.0	19,451	0.1
Pub. admin., defense	1,792.7	7.1	} 1,252,224	} 5.1
Services	1,008.2	4.0		
Other	66.6[11]	0.3[11]		
TOTAL	25,294.7	100.0	24,395,916	100.0

Population economically active (1995): total 24,606,100; activity rate of total population 43.4% (participation rates: ages 15–64, 72.2%; female 41.5%; unemployed [1993] 62.9%).

Price index (1990 = 100)

	1989	1990	1991	1992	1993	1994	1995
Consumer price index	95.1	100.0	135.7	150.0	155.3	167.1	183.9

Household income and expenditure. Average household size (1984) 4.5; income per household (1981–82) Br 1,728 (U.S.$835); sources of income (1981–82): self-employment 79.5%, wages and salaries 0.2%, other 20.3%; expenditure (1988): food 66.7%, fuel and power 15.9%, clothing and footwear 6.8%, health care 3.1%, education 2.5%, household goods 2.1%.

Foreign trade[6]

Balance of trade (current prices)

	1989	1990	1991	1992	1993	1994
Br '000,000	−747.6	−1,271.6	−433.1	−1,360.5	−2,325.1	−2,708.3
% of total	29.1%	50.8%	55.5%	60.3%	53.9%	39.6%

Imports (1992–93): Br 3,618,718,000 (1994; motor vehicles 17.8%, petroleum products 17.5%, food and live animals 10.9%, metal wares 7.3%, machinery [including aircraft] 6.8%, chemicals 5.3%, textiles 4.1%, pharmaceuticals 3.6%). *Major import sources* (1993): Saudi Arabia 18.8%; Germany 10.6%; Italy 10.3%; U.S. 9.5%; Djibouti 4.5%; U.K. 3.9%.
Exports (1992–93): Br 800,814,000 (coffee 67.1%, hides 16.8%, petroleum products 3.8%). *Major export destinations* (1993): Germany 19.7%; Japan 19.0%; Djibouti 12.1%; Saudi Arabia 9.9%; U.S. 9.1%; Italy 7.6%.

Transport and communications[6]

Transport. Railroads (1990–91)[12]: length 782 km; passenger-km 277,000,000; metric ton-km cargo 126,000,000. Roads (1995): total length 19,400 km (paved 15%). Vehicles (1995): passenger cars 45,559; trucks and buses 20,462. Merchant marine (1992): vessels (100 gross tons and over) 27; total deadweight tonnage 84,326. Air transport (1995)[13]: passenger-km 1,795,591,-000; metric ton-km cargo 173,079,000; airports (1996) 31.
Communications. Daily newspapers (1995): 3; circulation 77,000; circulation per 1,000 population 1.4. Radio (1995): 9,000,000 receivers (1 per 6.1 persons). Television (1995): 150,000 receivers (1 per 367 persons). Telephones (main lines; 1993): 132,500 (1 per 391 persons).

Education and health

Education (1992)

	schools	teachers	students	student/ teacher ratio
Primary (age 7–12)	8,120	69,743	1,855,894	26.6
Secondary (age 13–18)	1,209[14]	21,970	712,489	32.4
Voc., teacher tr.	...	602	8,290	13.8
Higher[15]	11[16]	1,697	26,218	15.4

Educational attainment: n.a. *Literacy* (1995): total population age 15 and over literate 35.5%; males 45.5%; females 25.3%.
Health: physicians (1988) 1,466 (1 per 30,195 persons); hospital beds (1986–87) 11,745 (1 per 3,873 persons); infant mortality rate (1995) 124.1.
Food (1992): daily per capita caloric intake 1,610 (vegetable products 93%, animal products 7%); 69% of FAO recommended minimum.

Military

Total active duty personnel (1996): the estimated strength of Ethiopian armed forces was some 120,000. *Military expenditure as percentage of GNP* (1994): 2.6% (world 3.0%); per capita expenditure U.S.$2.

---

[1]New republic formally established on Aug. 22, 1995. [2]Amharic is the "working" language of the Federal Democratic Republic of Ethiopia. [3]In December 1991 the Council of Representatives established a regional administrative system comprising 14 ethnically based "national local administrations" and a single region made up of the towns of Addis Ababa and Harare. [4]Estimates adjusted to exclude the Eritrean portion of Aseb area. [5]Detail does not add to total given because of rounding. [6]Includes Eritrea. [7]Percentage of illnesses in a sample population of hospital outpatients. [8]At constant prices of 1978–79. [9]Addis Ababa only. [10]For ages 10 and up. [11]Less imputed bank service charges. [12]Includes 62 mi (100 km) of the Chemin de Fer Djibouti-Ethiopiën (CDE) in Djibouti; excludes 190 mi (306 km) of Northern Ethiopia Railway, not in use since 1978. [13]Ethiopian Airlines only. [14]1985–86. [15]1991. [16]1983–84.

Fiji

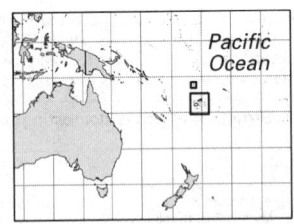

Pacific Ocean

Official name: Sovereign Democratic Republic of Fiji.
Form of government: republic with two legislative houses (Senate [34[1]]; House of Representatives [70]).
Chief of state: President.
Head of government: Prime Minister.
Capital: Suva.
Official language: English.
Official religion: none.
Monetary unit: 1 Fiji dollar (F$) = 100 cents; valuation (Oct. 11, 1996) 1 U.S.$ = F$1.40; 1 £ = F$2.20.

Area and population		area		population
Divisions Provinces	Capitals	sq mi	sq km	1986 census
Central	Suva			
Naitasiri	—	643	1,666	100,227
Namosi	—	220	570	4,836
Rewa	—	105	272	97,442
Serua	—	320	830	13,356
Tailevu	—	369	955	44,249
Eastern	Levuka			
Kadavu	—	185	478	9,805
Lau	—	188	487	14,203
Lomaiviti	—	159	411	16,066
Rotuma	—	18	46	2,688
Northern	Labasa			
Bua	—	532	1,379	13,986
Cakaudrove	—	1,087	2,816	40,433
Macuata	—	774	2,004	74,735
Western	Lautoka			
Ba	—	1,017	2,634	197,633
Nadroga-Navosa	—	921	2,385	54,431
Ra	—	518	1,341	31,285
TOTAL	—	7,055[2]	18,272[2]	715,375

Demography

Population (1996): 802,000.
Density (1996): persons per sq mi 113.7, persons per sq km 43.9.
Urban-rural (1987): urban 38.7%; rural 61.3%.
Sex distribution (1990): male 50.65%; female 49.35%.
Age breakdown (1990): under 15, 37.3%; 15–29, 28.5%; 30–44, 18.7%; 45–59, 10.0%; 60–74, 4.1%; 75 and over, 1.4%.
Population projection: (2000) 853,937; (2010) 998,000.
Doubling time: 38 years.
Ethnic composition (1996): Fijian 50.7%; Indian 43.5%[3]; other 5.8%.
Religious affiliation (1986): Christian 52.9%; Hindu 38.1%; Muslim 7.8%; Sikh 0.7%; other 0.5%.
Major cities (1986): Suva 69,665; Lautoka 28,728; Lami 8,601; Nadi 7,679; Ba 6,518.

Vital statistics

Birth rate per 1,000 population (1995): 24.6 (world avg. 25.0); (1978) legitimate 82.7%; illegitimate 17.3%.
Death rate per 1,000 population (1995): 6.2 (world avg. 9.3).
Natural increase rate per 1,000 population (1995): 18.4 (world avg. 15.7).
Total fertility rate (avg. births per childbearing woman; 1996): 2.8.
Marriage rate per 1,000 population (1988): 9.6.
Divorce rate per 1,000 population (1979): 0.7.
Life expectancy at birth (1996): male 70.0 years; female 75.0 years.
Major causes of death per 100,000 population (1987): diseases of the circulatory system 153.4; malignant neoplasms (cancers) 35.5; accidents, poisoning, and violence 32.2; diseases of the respiratory system 31.7; diabetes mellitus 27.3; infectious and parasitic diseases 18.2; birth trauma 16.5.

National economy

Budget (1995). Revenue: F$702,429,000 (income taxes, estate taxes, and gift duties 56.0%; customs duties and port dues 29.6%; fees, royalties, and sales 6.4%). Expenditures: F$681,048,000 (departmental expenditure 72.0%; public-debt charges 23.7%; pensions and gratuities 4.3%).
Public debt (external, outstanding; 1994): U.S.$282,800,000.
Production (metric tons except as noted). Agriculture, forestry, fishing (1995): sugarcane 4,110,000, paddy rice 18,496, copra 8,761, ginger 4,627; livestock (number of live animals) 354,000 cattle, 211,000 goats, 121,000 pigs; roundwood (1994) 528,339 cu m; fish catch (1993) 31,399. Mining and quarrying (1995): gold 3,477 kg; silver 1,572 kg. Manufacturing (1995): refined sugar 454,000; cement 91,000; flour 41,266; stock feed 28,120; soap 7,070; coconut oil 5,530; beer 150,000 hectolitres; paint 23,630 hectolitres. Construction (1995): residential 97,000 sq m; nonresidential 64,000 sq m. Energy production (consumption): electricity (kW-hr; 1993) 465,000,000 (465,000,000); coal (metric tons; 1993) none (20,000); crude petroleum, none (n.a.); petroleum products (metric tons; 1993) none (201,000); natural gas, none (n.a.).
Population economically active (1986): total 241,160; activity rate of total population 33.7% (participation rates: ages 15–64, 56.0%; female 21.2%; unemployed [1990] 6.4%).

Price and earnings indexes (1990 = 100)							
	1989	1990	1991	1992	1993	1994	1995
Consumer price index	92.4	100.0	106.5	111.7	117.5	118.2	120.8
Earnings index	...	...	...	...	...	...	...

Gross national product (at current market prices; 1994): U.S.$1,785,000,000 (U.S.$2,320 per capita).

Structure of gross domestic product and labour force				
	1994		1986	
	in value F$'000[4]	% of total value	labour force	% of labour force
Agriculture	207,468	22.0	106,305	44.1
Mining	1,528	0.2	1,345	0.5
Manufacturing	116,739	12.4	18,106	7.5
Construction	31,518	3.3	11,786	4.9
Public utilities	13,290	1.4	2,154	0.9
Transportation and communications	142,346	15.1	13,151	5.4
Trade	193,472	20.5	26,010	10.8
Finance	115,800	12.3	6,016	2.5
Pub. admin., defense	151,165	16.0	36,619	15.2
Services				
Other	−29,957[5]	−3.2[5]	19,668[6]	8.2[6]
TOTAL	943,369	100.0	241,160	100.0

Household income and expenditure. Average household size (1986) 5.7; income per household (1980) F$2,837 (U.S.$3,546); sources of income (1973): wages and salaries 81.5%, self-employment 9.1%, other 9.4%; expenditure (1991[7]): food, beverages, and tobacco 41.5%, housing and energy 21.4%, transportation and communications 12.9%, household durable goods 6.5%, clothing and footwear 5.4%.
Tourism (1994): receipts from visitors U.S.$298,000,000; expenditures by nationals abroad U.S.$55,000,000.
Land use (1993): forested 64.9%; agricultural and under permanent cultivation 14.2%; meadows and pastures 9.6%; other 11.3%.

Foreign trade

Balance of trade (current prices)						
	1990	1991	1992	1993	1994	1995
F$'000,000	−251.32	−279.57	−275.53	−521.42	−409.36	−454.45
% of total	14.1%	20.1%	20.9%	30.7%	20.4%	22.9%

Imports (1995): F$1,218,934,000 (durable manufactures 27.6%; machinery and transport equipment 22.8%; food, beverages, and tobacco 15.0%; mineral fuels 11.3%; miscellaneous manufactured consumer articles 9.8%; chemicals 7.6%). *Major import sources:* Australia 38.8%; New Zealand 16.9%; United States 15.9%; Japan 7.2%; Singapore 7.1%; Taiwan 3.1%; China 2.9%; Hong Kong 2.8%; United Kingdom 2.7%.
Exports (1995)[8]: F$764,481,000 (sugar 36.1%; clothing 24.2%; fish 8.3%; gold 7.8%; timber 6.9%; molasses 2.8%; coconut oil 0.5%). *Major export destinations*[9]: Australia 26.0%; United Kingdom 22.9%; United States 13.0%; Japan 6.6%; Malaysia 5.4%; New Zealand 5.3%; Canada 3.6%.

Transport and communications

Transport. Railroads (1995)[10]: length 370 mi, 595 km. Roads (1995): total length 3,200 mi, 5,100 km (paved 20%). Vehicles (1995): passenger cars 49,712; trucks and buses 33,928. Merchant marine (1992): vessels (100 gross tons and over) 64; total deadweight tonnage 60,444. Air transport (1994)[11]: passenger-mi 735,362,000, passenger-km 1,183,454,000; short ton-mi cargo 38,237,000[12], metric ton-km cargo 55,826,000[12]; airports (1996) with scheduled flights 13.
Communications. Daily newspapers (1995): total number 2; total circulation 54,000; circulation per 1,000 population 68. Radio (1995): total number of receivers 450,000 (1 per 1.7 persons). Television (1992): total number of receivers 12,000 (1 per 63 persons). Telephones (main lines; 1993): 53,997 (1 per 14.2 persons).

Education and health

Education (1992)	schools	teachers	students	student/teacher ratio
Primary (age 5–15)	693	4,644	145,630	31.4
Secondary (age 16–19)	142	3,045	60,237	19.8
Voc., teacher tr.	45	625	7,283	11.6
Higher[13]	5[14]	277	7,908	28.5

Educational attainment (1986). Percentage of population age 25 and over having: no formal schooling 28.3%; primary only 19.1%; some secondary 44.1%; secondary 4.1%; postsecondary 3.3%; other 1.1%. *Literacy* (1986): total population age 15 and over literate 87.0%; males literate 90.0%; females literate 84.0%.
Health (1993): physicians 354 (1 per 2,161 persons); hospital beds 1,747 (1 per 438 persons); infant mortality rate per 1,000 live births (1996) 21.0.
Food (1992): daily per capita caloric intake 3,089 (vegetable products 80%, animal products 20%); 116% of FAO recommended minimum requirement.

Military

Total active duty personnel (1995): 3,900 (army 92.3%, navy 7.7%, air force, none). *Military expenditure as percentage of GNP* (1994): 1.9% (world 3.0%); per capita expenditure U.S.$44.

[1]All seats are appointed. [2]Detail does not add to total given because of rounding. [3]The emigration of Indian population after the coup in 1987 has resulted in the reemergence of a Fijian majority. [4]Constant 1977 prices. [5]Less imputed bank service charges. [6]Not stated and unemployed. [7]Weights of consumer price index components based on 3,000 urban households. [8]Excludes reexports valued at F$105,460,000. [9]Based on exports of local products only. [10]Owned by the Fiji Sugar Corporation. [11]Air Pacific only. [12]1993. [13]1991. [14]1983.

Finland

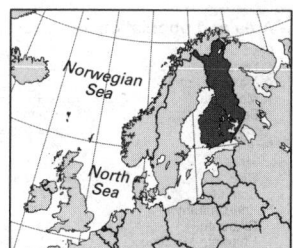

Official name: Suomen Tasavalta (Finnish); Republiken Finland (Swedish) (Republic of Finland).
Form of government: multiparty republic with one legislative house (Parliament [200]).
Chief of state: President.
Head of government: Prime Minister.
Capital: Helsinki.
Official languages: Finnish; Swedish.
Official religion: none[1].
Monetary unit: 1 markka (Fmk) = 100 penniä; valuation (Oct. 11, 1996) 1 U.S.$ = Fmk 4.58; 1 £ = Fmk 7.21.

Area and population		area		population
		sq mi	sq km	1995[2] estimate
Provinces	**Capitals**			
Häme	Hämeenlinna	8,590	22,248	727,418
Keski-Suomi	Jyväskylä	7,486	19,388	257,716
Kuopio	Kuopio	7,704	19,954	258,800
Kymi	Kouvola	4,951	12,824	333,411
Lappi	Rovaniemi	38,200	98,937	202,325
Mikkeli	Mikkeli	8,353	21,633	206,682
Oulu	Oulu	23,777	61,582	449,709
Pohjois-Karjala	Joensuu	8,334	21,585	177,917
Turku ja Pori	Turku	8,000	20,719	700,703
Uusimaa	Helsinki	4,017	10,404	1,309,549
Vaasa	Vaasa	10,548	27,319	449,366
Autonomous Province				
Åland (Ahvenanmaa)	Mariehamn (Maarianhamina)	599	1,552	25,158
TOTAL		130,559[3]	338,145[3]	5,098,754

Demography

Population (1996): 5,132,000.
Density (1996)[4]: persons per sq mi 43.6, persons per sq km 16.8.
Urban-rural (1995): urban 64.3%; rural 35.7%.
Sex distribution (1995): male 48.67%; female 51.33%.
Age breakdown (1995): under 15, 19.1%; 15–29, 19.4%; 30–44, 23.1%; 45–59, 19.5%; 60–74, 13.2%; 75 and over, 5.7%.
Population projection: (2000) 5,228,000; (2010) 5,289,000.
Doubling time: not applicable; population is stable.
Linguistic composition (1995): Finnish 93.0%; Swedish 5.8%; other 1.2%.
Religious affiliation (1995): Evangelical Lutheran 85.9%; Finnish (Greek) Orthodox 1.1%; nonreligious 12.0%; other 1.0%.
Major cities (1995[2]): Helsinki 515,765 (metro area 874,953); Espoo 186,507[5]; Tampere 179,251; Vantaa 164,376[5]; Turku 162,370.

Vital statistics

Birth rate per 1,000 population (1995): 12.4 (world avg. 25.0); (1994) legitimate 68.7%; illegitimate 31.3%.
Death rate per 1,000 population (1995): 9.7 (world avg. 9.3).
Natural increase rate per 1,000 population (1995): 2.7 (world avg. 15.7).
Total fertility rate (avg. births per childbearing woman; 1995): 1.8.
Marriage rate per 1,000 population (1994): 4.9.
Divorce rate per 1,000 population (1994): 2.7.
Life expectancy at birth (1993): male 72.1 years; female 79.5 years.
Major causes of death per 100,000 population (1993): ischemic heart diseases 280.4; malignant neoplasms (cancers) 198.4; cerebrovascular disease 124.4; diseases of the respiratory system 85.4; accidents 50.7.

National economy

Budget (1995). Revenue: Fmk 195,599,000,000 (tax revenue 53.6%, of which value-added taxes 19.3%, income and property taxes 17.0%, excise duties 11.8%; loans 31.5%). Expenditures: Fmk 195,596,000,000 (social security and health 24.9%; education 14.0%; state debt 12.5%; general administration 7.6%; agriculture 7.2%; defense 4.1%).
National debt (December 1995): U.S.$85,258,000,000.
Tourism (1994): receipts from visitors U.S.$1,436,000,000; expenditures by nationals abroad U.S.$1,727,000,000.
Production (metric tons except as noted). Agriculture, forestry, fishing (1994): silage 4,309,000, barley 1,858,000, oats 1,150,000, sugar beets 1,097,000, potatoes 726,000, turnips 108,000; livestock (number of live animals) 1,300,000 pigs, 1,230,000 cattle, 214,000 reindeer; roundwood 49,195,000 cu m; fish catch (1993) 152,491. Mining and quarrying (1994): chromite (gross weight) 573,000; nickel (concentrate) 107,000. Manufacturing (value added in Fmk '000,000; 1993): wood pulp, paper, and paperboard 16,473; electrical machinery 11,031; nonelectrical machinery 10,944; food products 9,955; chemicals and chemical products 7,159; printing and publishing 6,660; basic metal industries 6,555. Construction (completed; 1994): residential 10,380,000 cu m; nonresidential 15,660,000 cu m. Energy production (consumption): electricity (kW-hr; 1995) 60,574,000,000 ([1994] 65,420,000,000); coal (metric tons; 1993) none (6,002,000); crude petroleum (barrels; 1993) none (57,445,000); petroleum products (metric tons; 1993) 9,566,000 (8,472,000); natural gas (cu m; 1993) none (3,104,000,000).
Household income and expenditure (1993). Average household size 2.3; disposable income per household Fmk 129,400 (U.S.$22,653); sources of disposable income: wages and salaries 70.3%, transfer payments 9.7%, self-employment 7.4%, other 12.6%; expenditure (1994): housing and energy 25.0%, food, beverages, and tobacco 22.4%, transportation and communications 14.9%.

Gross national product (at current market prices; 1994): U.S.$95,817,000,000 (U.S.$18,850 per capita).

Structure of gross domestic product and labour force				
	1994			
	in value Fmk '000,000	% of total value	labour force	% of labour force
Agriculture, fishing	12,568	2.8 }	188,000	7.5
Forestry	11,439	2.6 }		
Mining	1,909	0.4	6,000	0.3
Manufacturing	111,855	25.2	466,000	18.6
Public utilities	12,076	2.7	25,000	1.0
Construction	23,558	5.3	179,000	7.2
Transp. and commun.	38,928	8.8	181,000	7.2
Trade, restaurants	50,012	11.3	354,000	14.2
Finance, real estate	85,546	19.3	198,000	7.9
Pub. admin., defense	86,825	19.5 }	809,000	32.3
Services	13,023	2.9 }		
Other	−3,728	−0.8	96,000[6]	3.8[6]
TOTAL	444,011	100.0	2,502,000	100.0

Population economically active (1994): total 2,502,000; activity rate of total population 49.2% (participation rates: ages 15–64, 73.1%; female 47.0%; unemployed [April 1995–March 1996] 17.0%).

Price and earnings indexes (1990 = 100)							
	1990	1991	1992	1993	1994	1995	1996
Consumer price index	100.0	104.1	106.8	109.1	110.3	111.3	112.0[7]
Annual earnings index	100.0	106.4	108.4	109.2	111.4	116.7	...

Land use (1993): forested 75.9%; meadows and pastures 0.3%; agricultural and under permanent cultivation 8.5%; other 15.3%.

Foreign trade[8]

Balance of trade (current prices)						
	1990	1991	1992	1993	1994	1995
Fmk '000,000	−1,700	+5,098	+12,516	+30,849	+33,659	+43,066
% of total	0.8%	2.8%	6.2%	13.0%	12.3%	14.2%

Imports (1995): Fmk 129,705,000,000 (raw materials 53.7%; consumer goods 18.9%; mineral fuels 7.0%). Major import sources: Germany 15.6%; Sweden 11.7%; United Kingdom 8.3%; Russia 7.1%; United States 7.1%; Japan 6.3%; Norway 4.1%.
Exports (1995): Fmk 172,771,000,000 (metal products and machinery 39.1%; paper, paper products, and publishing 27.4%; chemicals and chemical products 9.3%). Major export destinations: Germany 13.4%; United Kingdom 10.4%; Sweden 10.1%; United States 6.7%; Russia 4.8%; France 4.6%; The Netherlands 4.2%.

Transport and communications

Transport. Railroads: route length (1994) 3,641 mi, 5,859 km; (1995) passenger-mi 1,626,000,000, passenger-km 2,616,000,000; (1995) short ton-mi cargo 6,551,000,000, metric ton-km cargo 9,564,000,000. Roads (1995): total length[9] 48,246 mi, 77,644 km (paved 63%). Vehicles (1995): passenger cars 1,880,827; trucks and buses 254,578. Merchant marine (1992): vessels (100 gross tons and over) 263; total deadweight tonnage 989,270. Air transport (1994)[10]: passenger-mi 5,853,000,000, passenger-km 9,419,000,000; short ton-mi cargo 130,739,000, metric ton-km cargo 190,876,000; airports (1996) 24.
Communications. Daily newspapers (1994): total number 56; total circulation 2,400,000; circulation per 1,000 population 473. Radio (1995): 4,950,000 receivers (1 per 1.0 person). Television (1995): 1,900,000 receivers (1 per 2.7 persons). Telephones (main lines; 1993): 2,760,700 (1 per 1.8 persons).

Education and health

Education (1994–95)	schools	teachers	students	student/ teacher ratio
Primary (age 7–15)[11]	4,539	41,222[12]	587,523	14.2[12]
Secondary (age 16–18)[13]	456	6,322[12]	133,645	19.2[12]
Voc. (incl. higher)	495	21,245	202,859	9.5
Higher	21	7,790	127,846	16.4

Educational attainment (1994). Percentage of population age 25 and over having: incomplete upper-secondary education 46.1%; complete upper secondary or vocational 41.1%; higher 12.8%. Literacy: virtually 100%.
Health (1994): physicians 13,700[14] (1 per 371 persons); hospital beds (1993) 49,664[15] (1 per 102 persons); infant mortality rate per 1,000 live births 4.7.
Food (1992): daily per capita caloric intake 3,018 (vegetable products 60%, animal products 40%); 111% of FAO recommended minimum requirement.

Military

Total active duty personnel (1995): 31,100 (army 82.6%, navy 8.1%, air force 9.3%). Military expenditure as percentage of GNP (1994): 2.1% (world 3.0%); per capita expenditure U.S.$386.

---

[1]The Evangelical Lutheran and Finnish (Greek) Orthodox churches have special recognition. [2]January 1. [3]Total includes land area of 117,604 sq mi (304,593 sq km) and inland water area of 12,955 sq mi (33,552 sq km). [4]Based on land area only. [5]Within Helsinki urban area. [6]Includes 85,000 unemployed persons not previously employed and 11,000 not adequately defined. [7]April. [8]Imports c.i.f., exports f.o.b. [9]Excludes Åland Islands. [10]Traffic of Finnish airlines. [11]Includes lower secondary. [12]1992–93. [13]Excludes lower secondary. [14]Registered professionals of working age. [15]Excludes beds in hospitals operated by specialized institutions.

France

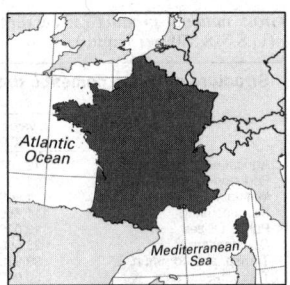

Official name: République Française (French Republic).
Form of government: republic with two legislative houses (Parliament; Senate [321], National Assembly [577]).
Chief of state: President.
Head of government: Prime Minister.
Capital: Paris.
Official language: French.
Official religion: none.
Monetary unit: 1 franc (F) = 100 centimes; valuation (Oct. 11, 1996) 1 U.S.$ = F 5.18; 1 £ = F 8.16.

Area and population

Regions Departments	Capitals	area sq mi	area sq km	population 1994[1] estimate
Alsace				
Bas-Rhin	Strasbourg	1,836	4,755	990,724
Haut-Rhin	Colmar	1,361	3,525	693,135
Aquitaine				
Dordogne	Périgueux	3,498	9,060	388,521
Gironde	Bordeaux	3,861	10,000	1,259,579
Landes	Mont-de-Marsan	3,569	9,243	317,828
Lot-et-Garonne	Agen	2,070	5,361	303,496
Pyrénées-Atlantiques	Pau	2,952	7,645	590,992
Auvergne				
Allier	Moulins	2,834	7,340	352,970
Cantal	Aurillac	2,211	5,726	155,587
Haute-Loire	Le Puy	1,922	4,977	206,578
Puy-de-Dôme	Clermont-Ferrand	3,077	7,970	600,725
Basse-Normandie				
Calvados	Caen	2,142	5,548	632,462
Manche	Saint-Lô	2,293	5,938	483,352
Orne	Alençon	2,356	6,103	294,596
Bourgogne				
Côte-d'Or	Dijon	3,383	8,763	505,896
Nièvre	Nevers	2,632	6,817	230,529
Saône-et-Loire	Mâcon	3,311	8,575	555,348
Yonne	Auxerre	2,868	7,427	330,794
Bretagne				
Côtes-d'Armor	Saint-Brieuc	2,656	6,878	536,320
Finistère	Quimper	2,600	6,733	840,103
Ille-et-Vilaine	Rennes	2,616	6,775	832,882
Morbihan	Vannes	2,634	6,823	631,290
Centre				
Cher	Bourges	2,793	7,235	321,337
Eure-et-Loir	Chartres	2,270	5,880	409,420
Indre	Châteauroux	2,622	6,791	234,531
Indre-et-Loire	Tours	2,366	6,127	543,973
Loir-et-Cher	Blois	2,449	6,343	311,779
Loiret	Orléans	2,616	6,775	606,652
Champagne-Ardenne				
Ardennes	Charleville-Mézières	2,019	5,229	292,642
Aube	Troyes	2,318	6,004	292,765
Haute-Marne	Chaumont	2,398	6,211	200,240
Marne	Châlons-sur-Marne	3,151	8,162	566,222
Corse[2]				
Corse-du-Sud	Ajaccio	1,550	4,014	123,869
Haute-Corse	Bastia	1,802	4,666	135,010
Franche-Comté				
Doubs	Besançon	2,021	5,234	493,133
Haute-Saône	Vesoul	2,070	5,360	229,448
Jura	Lons-le-Saunier	1,930	4,999	251,853
Territoire de Belfort	Belfort	235	609	136,795
Haute-Normandie				
Eure	Évreux	2,332	6,040	533,731
Seine-Maritime	Rouen	2,424	6,278	1,239,973
Île-de-France				
Essonne	Évry	696	1,804	1,141,679
Hauts-de-Seine	Nanterre	68	176	1,403,463
Paris	Paris	40	105	2,133,902
Seine-et-Marne	Melun	2,284	5,915	1,171,313
Seine-Saint-Denis	Bobigny	91	236	1,404,430
Val-de-Marne	Créteil	95	245	1,233,964
Val-d'Oise	Pontoise	481	1,246	1,102,804
Yvelines	Versailles	882	2,284	1,363,068
Languedoc-Roussillon				
Aude	Carcassonne	2,370	6,139	304,707
Gard	Nîmes	2,260	5,853	605,847
Hérault	Montpellier	2,356	6,101	853,594
Lozère	Mende	1,995	5,167	72,859
Pyrénées-Orientales	Perpignan	1,589	4,116	375,018
Limousin				
Corrèze	Tulle	2,261	5,857	236,353
Creuse	Guéret	2,149	5,565	127,470
Haute-Vienne	Limoges	2,131	5,520	355,524
Lorraine				
Meurthe-et-Moselle	Nancy	2,024	5,241	715,905
Meuse	Bar-le-Duc	2,400	6,216	194,384
Moselle	Metz	2,400	6,216	1,015,593
Vosges	Épinal	2,268	5,874	385,376
Midi-Pyrénées				
Ariège	Foix	1,888	4,890	136,667
Aveyron	Rodez	3,373	8,736	266,849
Gers	Auch	2,416	6,257	172,622
Haute-Garonne	Toulouse	2,436	6,309	985,030
Haute-Pyrénées	Tarbes	1,724	4,464	223,840
Lot	Cahors	2,014	5,217	156,881
Tarn	Albi	2,223	5,758	341,954
Tarn-et-Garonne	Montauban	1,435	3,718	204,732
Nord-Pas-de-Calais				
Nord	Lille	2,217	5,742	2,553,939
Pas-de-Calais	Arras	2,576	6,671	1,437,555

Area and population (continued)

Regions Departments	Capitals	area sq mi	area sq km	population 1994[1] estimate
Pays de la Loire				
Loire-Atlantique	Nantes	2,631	6,815	1,085,912
Maine-et-Loire	Angers	2,767	7,166	719,172
Mayenne	Laval	1,998	5,175	281,301
Sarthe	Le Mans	2,396	6,206	520,615
Vendée	La Roche-sur-Yon	2,595	6,720	524,069
Picardie				
Aisne	Laon	2,845	7,369	539,097
Oise	Beauvais	2,263	5,860	760,070
Somme	Amiens	2,382	6,170	552,398
Poitou-Charentes				
Charente	Angoulême	2,300	5,956	341,383
Charente-Maritime	La Rochelle	2,650	6,864	539,134
Deux-Sèvres	Niort	2,316	5,999	346,612
Vienne	Poitiers	2,699	6,990	388,701
Provence-Alpes-Côte d'Azur				
Alpes-de-Haute-Provence	Digne	2,674	6,925	137,903
Alpes-Maritimes	Nice	1,660	4,299	1,010,196
Bouches-du-Rhône	Marseille	1,964	5,087	1,793,876
Hautes-Alpes	Gap	2,142	5,549	118,220
Var	Toulon	2,306	5,973	866,747
Vaucluse	Avignon	1,377	3,567	487,338
Rhône-Alpes				
Ain	Bourg-en-Bresse	2,225	5,762	497,943
Ardèche	Privas	2,135	5,529	282,432
Drôme	Valence	2,521	6,530	425,476
Haute-Savoie	Annecy	1,694	4,388	613,176
Isère	Grenoble	2,869	7,431	1,060,252
Loire	Saint-Étienne	1,846	4,781	748,881
Rhône	Lyon	1,254	3,249	1,558,869
Savoie	Chambéry	2,327	6,028	365,392
TOTAL		210,026	543,965	57,899,566[3]

Demography

Population (1996): 58,392,000.
Density (1996): persons per sq mi 278.0, persons per sq km 107.3.
Urban-rural (1995): urban 72.8%; rural 27.2%.
Sex distribution (1995): male 48.76%; female 51.24%.
Age breakdown (1995): under 15, 19.7%; 15–29, 21.4%; 30–44, 22.2%; 45–59, 16.9%; 60–74, 13.6%; 75 and over, 6.2%.
Population projection: (2000) 59,455,000; (2010) 62,200,000.
Doubling time: not applicable; doubling time exceeds 100 years.
Ethnolinguistic composition (1990): French (mother tongue) 93.6%, of which fully or substantially bilingual in Occitan 2.7%, German (mostly Alsatian) 2.3%, Breton 1.0%, Catalan 0.4%; Arabic 2.5%; other 3.9%.
Religious affiliation (1980): Roman Catholic 76.4%; other Christian 3.7%; atheist 3.4%; Muslim 3.0%; other 13.5%.
Major cities (1990): Paris 2,152,423 (metropolitan area 9,060,257); Marseille 800,550 (1,231,082); Lyon 415,487 (1,262,223); Toulouse 358,688 (608,430); Nice 342,439 (475,507); Strasbourg 252,338 (338,483); Nantes 244,995 (492,-255); Bordeaux 210,336 (685,456); Montpellier 207,996 (236,788).
National origin (1990): French 93.6%, of which Martiniquais 0.2%, Guadeloupian 0.2%, Réunionese 0.2%; Portuguese 1.1%; Algerian 1.1%; Moroccan 1.0%; Italian 0.4%; Spanish 0.4%; Turkish 0.3%; other 2.1%.
Mobility (1990). Population living in same residence as in 1982: 51.4%; same region 89.0%; different region 8.8%; different country 2.2%.
Households (1993). Average household size 2.6; 1 person 27.7%, 2 persons 32.0%, 3 persons 17.4%, 4 persons 14.7%, 5 persons or more 8.2%. Family households (1990): 14,118,940 (72.1%); nonfamily 5,471,460 (27.9%, of which 1-person 24.6%).
Immigration (1993): permanent immigrants admitted 94,152 (Morocco 17.1%, Algeria 12.1%, Turkey 9.8%, Tunisia 4.1%, Sri Lanka 3.2%, Lebanon 1.7%, Vietnam 1.4%).

Vital statistics

Birth rate per 1,000 population (1995): 12.5 (world avg. 25.0); (1994) legitimate 63.8%; illegitimate 36.2%.
Death rate per 1,000 population (1995): 9.1 (world avg. 9.3).
Natural increase rate per 1,000 population (1995): 3.4 (world avg. 15.7).
Total fertility rate (avg. births per childbearing woman; 1995): 1.7.
Marriage rate per 1,000 population (1995): 4.4.
Divorce rate per 1,000 population (1993): 1.9.
Life expectancy at birth (1994): male 73.7 years; female 81.8 years.
Major causes of death per 100,000 population (1994): heart disease and other circulatory diseases 286.7; malignant neoplasms (cancers) 247.6; accidents and violence 76.9; respiratory diseases 63.7; digestive tract diseases 43.7.

Social indicators

Educational attainment (1990). Percentage of population age 25 and over having: primary 22.1%; lower secondary 7.8%; higher secondary and vocational 29.4%; postsecondary 11.6%; undeclared attainment 29.1%.

Distribution of income (1984)				
percentage of household income by quintile				
1	2	3	4	5 (highest)
7.1%	12.3%	17.1%	23.2%	40.3%

Quality of working life. Average workweek (1994): 38.9 hours. Annual rate per 100,000 workers (1992) for: injury or accident 3,386 (deaths 4.6); accidents in transit to work 847 (deaths 40.1); industrial illness 16.6[4]; death 4.8[4]. Proportion of labour force insured for damages or income loss resulting from: injury, permanent disability, or death, n.a. Average days lost to labour stoppages per 1,000 workers (1993): 23.0. Average length of journey to work (1990): 8.7 mi (14 km).
Access to services (1992). Proportion of dwellings having: central heating 86.0%; piped water 97.0%; indoor plumbing 95.8%.

Social deviance. Offense rate per 100,000 population (1993) for: murder 0.8; rape 9.7; other assault 254.4; theft (including burglary and housebreaking) 5,289.5. Incidence per 100,000 in general population of: alcoholism, n.a. (deaths related to alcoholism; 1991) 5.0; suicide (1993) 21.1.

Social participation. Eligible voters participating in last (May 1995) national election: 79.7%. Population over 15 years of age participating in voluntary associations: 28.0%.

Leisure (1987–88). Participation rate for favourite leisure activities: watching television 82%; reading magazines 79%; listening to radio 75%; entertaining relatives 64%; visiting relatives 61%; attending fairs/expositions 56%.

Material well-being (1994). Households possessing: automobile 79.5%; colour television receiver 92.4%; videocassette recorder 52.8%; refrigerator 99.0%; washing machine 89.4%.

National economy

Gross national product (1994): U.S.$1,317,950,000,000 (U.S.$22,760 per capita).

Structure of gross domestic product and labour force

	1995			
	in value F '000,000	% of total value	labour force	% of labour force
Agriculture	183,444	2.6	1,026,000	4.1
Mining	57,507	0.8	118,900	0.5
Manufacturing	1,542,442	21.8	3,992,700	15.8
Construction	342,836	4.8	1,466,600	5.8
Public utilities	178,069	2.5	162,900	0.6
Transp. and commun.	433,518	6.1	1,272,800	5.0
Trade[5]	1,012,441	14.3	3,482,000	13.8
Finance	320,501	4.5	601,900	2.4
Pub. admin., defense	1,323,570	18.7	6,248,100	24.7
Services	1,290,922	18.2	3,953,800	15.7
Other	403,238[6]	5.7[6]	2,934,600[7]	11.6[7]
TOTAL	7,088,488	100.0	25,260,300	100.0

Budget (1995). Revenue: F 1,448,500,000,000 (value-added taxes 46.5%; direct taxes 39.1%; customs taxes 11.0%). Expenditure: F 1,470,400,000,000 (current expenditures 88.0%, of which education 17.8%, defense 16.5%, health 4.2%; capital expenditure 12.0%).

Manufacturing enterprises (1995)

	no. of enter- prises[8]	no. of employees	annual salaries as a % of avg. of all salaries[8]	annual value added (F '000,000)
Food products	55,197	545,900	87	208,065
Transport equipment	4,293	508,700	108	167,357
Electrical machinery	15,620	433,600	118	156,221
Iron and steel	27,847	403,800	96	131,376
Mechanical equipment	32,134	390,300	104	127,637
Petroleum refineries	180	46,200	174	117,041
Printing, publishing	30,359	231,900	125	83,083
Textiles and wearing apparel	29,701	281,500	78	63,633
Rubber products	5,875	204,200	94	57,758
Chemical products	1,442	102,100	128	51,146
Paper and paper products	1,916	101,500	102	38,585
Metal products	442	43,700	103	28,115
Glass products	1,536	52,400	104	16,638
Footwear	4,236	55,400	75	12,970

Production (metric tons except as noted). Agriculture, forestry, fishing (1995): wheat 30,879,000, sugar beets 30,359,500, corn (maize) 12,784,000, barley 7,677,000, grapes 7,208,500, potatoes 5,753,800, rapeseed 2,782,000, dry peas 2,719,000, apples 2,488,000, sunflower seeds 1,993,000, tomatoes 803,000, carrots 641,000, oats 612,000, green peas 581,000, peaches 539,700, cauliflower 538,500, lettuce 515,500, pears 335,600, string beans 309,800, onions 287,900; livestock (number of live animals) 20,524,000 cattle, 14,593,000 pigs, 10,320,000 sheep, 1,069,000 goats; roundwood (1994) 42,850,000 cu m; fish catch (1993) 830,000. Mining and quarrying (1995): potash salts 900,000; iron ore 450,000[9]; uranium 875[9]; gold 144,693 troy oz[9]; silver 48,231 troy oz[9]. Manufacturing (1995): cement 19,896,000; crude steel 18,132,000; pig iron 12,876,000; paper products 8,700,000; aluminum 624,000[10]; rubber products 619,400, of which tires 59,268,000 units; automobiles 3,200,000 units. Construction (dwelling units completed; 1993) 299,000.

Retail trade enterprises (1992)

	no. of enter- prises	no. of employees	weekly wages as a % of all wages	annual turnover (F '000,000)
Large food stores	4,777	396,986	...	627,770
Clothing stores	73,840	233,602	...	139,596
Small food stores	80,404	210,235	...	132,028
butcher shops	38,411	110,658	...	65,447
Pharmacies	21,836	120,605	...	107,900
Department stores	1,419	63,776	...	71,858
Furniture stores	7,423	52,046	...	51,128
Electrical and electronics stores	9,673	53,174	...	48,295
Publishing and paper	20,010	54,899	...	30,729
Gas, coal, and other energy products	2,737	11,503	...	23,556

Energy production (consumption)[11]: electricity (kW-hr; 1994) 475,622,000,000 (412,454,000,000); coal (metric tons; 1994) 8,039,000 (21,809,000); crude petroleum (barrels; 1994) 20,297,000 (562,907,000); petroleum products (metric tons; 1994) 69,078,000 (66,994,000); natural gas (cu m; 1994) 2,517,200,000 (33,449,900,000).

Household income and expenditure. Average household size (1995) 2.6; average annual income per household (1995) F 302,560 (U.S.$60,610); sources of income (1992): wages and salaries 51.1%, social security 27.5%, self-employment 21.4%; expenditure (1994): housing 21.3%, food 18.3%, transportation 16.4%, health 10.2%, recreation 7.4%, clothing 5.7%.

Tourism (1994): receipts from visitors U.S.$25,629,000,000; expenditures by nationals abroad U.S.$13,875,000,000.

Population economically active (1995): total 25,260,300; activity rate of total population 43.4% (participation rates: ages 15–64, 67.6%[10]; female 45.0%; unemployed 11.7%).

Price and earnings indexes (1990=100)

	1989	1990	1991	1992	1993	1994	1995
Consumer price index	96.7	100.0	103.2	105.7	107.9	109.7	111.6
Earnings index	98.5	100.0	104.4	108.4	111.7	115.0	116.0

Public debt (1994): F 2,246,000,000,000 (U.S.$420,100,000,000).

Financial aggregates

	1991	1992	1993	1994	1995	1996[12]
Exchange rate, F per:						
U.S. dollar	5.18	5.51	5.90	5.35	4.90	5.17
£	9.67	9.37	8.73	8.35	7.60	8.08
SDR	7.41	7.57	8.10	7.80	7.28	7.44
International reserves (U.S.$)						
Total (excl. gold; '000,000)	31,284	27,028	22,649	26,257	26,853	26,843
SDRs ('000,000)	1,326	163	331	362	955	968
Reserve pos. in IMF ('000,000)	1,666	2,482	2,310	2,375	2,756	2,705
Foreign exchange	28,292	24,384	20,008	23,520	23,142	23,170
Gold ('000,000 fine troy oz)	81.85	81.85	81.85	81.85	81.85	81.85
% world reserves	8.7	8.7	8.7	8.7	9.1	9.0
Interest and prices						
Central bank discount (%)	9.50	9.50	9.50	9.50	...	...
Govt. bond yield (%)	9.05	8.60	6.91	8.52	7.59	6.29
Industrial share prices (1990=100)	96.7	102.3	112.6	112.5	102.5	117.4
Balance of payments (U.S.$'000,000)						
Balance of visible trade	−10,139	1,661	8,418	7,868	11,175	...
Imports, f.o.b.	217,233	223,561	187,873	215,593	259,225	...
Exports, f.o.b.	207,084	225,222	196,291	223,461	270,400	...
Balance of invisibles	3,991	1,819	3,503	263	5,268	...
Balance of payments, current account	−6,148	3,480	11,921	8,128	16,443	...

Land use (1994): forested 27.3%; meadows and pastures 19.3%; agricultural and under permanent cultivation 35.4%; other 18.0%.

Foreign trade

Balance of trade (current prices)

	1990	1991	1992	1993	1994	1995
F '000,000,000	−49.6	−29.6	+31.0	+101.7	+87.8	+107.0
% of total	3.1%	1.2%	1.3%	4.5%	3.5%	3.9%

Imports (1995): F 1,380,400,000 (machinery and transport equipment 38.5%, of which transport equipment 14.6%, electrical equipment 12.0%; agricultural products 11.9%; chemical products 8.4%; fuels 6.9%). *Major import sources:* Germany 18.3%; Italy 9.9%; U.K. 9.5%; Belgium-Luxembourg 8.8%; Spain 6.1%; U.S. 6.1%; The Netherlands 4.7%; Japan 2.1%.

Exports (1995): F 1,428,800,000 (machinery and transport equipment 42.6%, of which transport equipment 19.5%, electrical equipment 11.5%; agricultural products 15.1%; chemical products 8.4%; plastics 3.2%). *Major export destinations:* Germany 17.7%; Italy 9.5%; Belgium-Luxembourg 8.6%; U.K. 7.6%; U.S. 7.4%; Spain 6.2%; The Netherlands 5.0%.

Transport and communications

Transport. Railroads (1994): route length 34,074 km; passenger-km 58,930,000,000; metric ton-km cargo 49,740,000,000. Roads (1995): total length 812,700 km (paved [1985] 92%). Vehicles (1995): passenger cars 25,100,000; trucks and buses 5,005,000. Merchant marine (1992): vessels (100 gross tons and over) 729; total deadweight tonnage 4,981,027. Air transport (1993): passenger-km 59,200,000,000; metric ton-km cargo 3,700,000,000; airports (1996) with scheduled flights 61.

Communications. Daily newspapers (1993): number 116; circulation 10,096,000[13]; circulation per 1,000 population 175[13]. Radio (1995): 50,000,000 receivers (1 per 1.2 persons). Television (1993): 29,300,000 receivers (1 per 2.0 persons). Telephones (1994): 31,600,000 (1 per 1.8 persons).

Education and health

Education (1993–94)

	schools	teachers	students	student/ teacher ratio
Primary (age 6–10)	41,656	218,100[14]	4,060,607	...
Secondary (age 11–18)	11,325[15]	454,000	4,486,063	12.6
Voc., teacher tr.			1,251,295	
Higher	1,062[16]	57,429[17]	1,700,800[17]	29.6[17]

Literacy (1980): total population literate 41,112,000 (98.8%); males literate 19,933,000 (98.9%); females literate 21,179,000 (98.7%).

Health: physicians (1994) 160,235 (1 per 361 persons); hospital beds (1995) 679,731 (1 per 86 persons); infant mortality rate (1995) 4.9.

Food (1992): daily per capita caloric intake 3,633 (vegetable products 60%, animal products 40%); 144% of FAO recommended minimum requirement.

Military

Total active duty personnel (1996): 398,900 (army 59.3%, navy 15.9%, air force 22.2%, other 2.6%). *Military expenditure as percentage of GNP* (1994): 3.4% (world 3.0%); per capita expenditure U.S.$767.

---

[1]January 1. [2]In May 1992, Corse was granted local autonomy (with its own directly elected assembly), changing its regional status to "territorial collective." [3]Detail does not add to total given because of rounding. [4]1989. [5]Includes hotels. [6]Imputed rents and imputed bank service charges. [7]Unemployed. [8]1991. [9]Metal content of ores. [10]1993. [11]All energy statistics include Monaco. [12]September. [13]For 90 newspapers only. [14]Includes preprimary teachers. [15]1990–91. [16]1988–89. [17]1991–92.

Gabon

Official name: République Gabonaise (Gabonese Republic).
Form of government: unitary multiparty republic with one legislative house (National Assembly [120]).
Chief of state: President.
Head of government: Prime Minister.
Capital: Libreville.
Official language: French.
Official religion: none.
Monetary unit: 1 CFA franc (CFAF) = 100 centimes; valuation (Oct. 11, 1996) 1 U.S.$ = CFAF 518.24; 1 £ = CFAF 816.38.

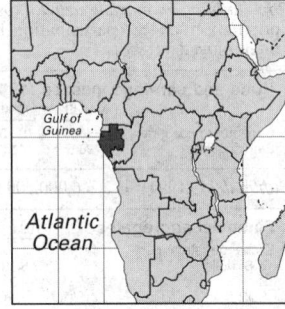

Area and population

Provinces	Capitals	area sq mi	area sq km	population 1993 census[1]
Estuaire	Libreville	8,008	20,740	463,187
Haut-Ogooué	Franceville	14,111	36,547	104,301
Moyen-Ogooué	Lambaréné	7,156	18,535	42,316
Ngounié	Mouila	14,575	37,750	77,781
Nyanga	Tchibanga	8,218	21,285	39,430
Ogooué-Ivindo	Makokou	17,790	46,075	48,862
Ogooué-Lolo	Koulamoutou	9,799	25,380	43,915
Ogooué-Maritime	Port-Gentil	8,838	22,890	97,913
Woleu-Ntem	Oyem	14,851	38,465	97,271
TOTAL		103,347[2]	267,667	1,014,976

Demography

Population (1996): 1,173,000.
Density (1996): persons per sq mi 11.4, persons per sq km 4.4.
Urban-rural (1993): urban 73.1%; rural 26.9%.
Sex distribution (1995): male 49.32%; female 50.68%.
Age breakdown (1995): under 15, 39.1%; 15–29, 22.3%; 30–44, 17.2%; 45–59, 12.4%; 60–74, 7.2%; 75 and over, 1.7%.
Population projection: (2000) 1,244,000; (2010) 1,445,000.
Doubling time: 32 years.
Ethnic composition (1983): Fang 35.5%; Mpongwe 15.1%; Mbete 14.2%; Punu 11.5%; other 23.7%.
Religious affiliation (1980): Christian 96.2%, of which Roman Catholic 65.3%, Protestant 18.8%, African indigenous 12.1%; traditional religion 2.9%; Muslim 0.8%; other 0.1%.
Major cities (1993): Libreville 362,386; Port-Gentil 80,841; Franceville 30,246; Oyem 22,669; Moanda 21,921.

Vital statistics

Birth rate per 1,000 population (1990–95): 37.2 (world avg. 25.0).
Death rate per 1,000 population (1990–95): 15.5 (world avg. 9.3).
Natural increase rate per 1,000 population (1990–95): 21.8 (world avg. 15.7).
Total fertility rate (avg. births per childbearing woman; 1990–95): 5.3.
Marriage rate per 1,000 population: n.a.
Divorce rate per 1,000 population: n.a.
Life expectancy at birth (1990–95): male 51.9 years; female 55.2 years.
Major causes of death per 100,000 population: n.a.; however, in the early 1990s major causes of morbidity and mortality included malaria, shigellosis (infection with dysentery), tetanus, cardiovascular diseases, trypanosomiasis, and tuberculosis.

National economy

Budget (1995). Revenue: CFAF 715,300,000,000 (oil revenues 60.1%; customs duties and other current revenues 39.9%). Expenditures: CFAF 653,800,000,000 (current expenditure 80.1%, of which service on public debt 31.8%, wages and salaries 27.2%; capital expenditure 19.9%).
Public debt (external, outstanding; 1994): U.S.$3,483,000,000.
Tourism (1994): receipts from visitors U.S.$5,000,000; expenditures by nationals abroad U.S.$143,000,000.
Production (metric tons except as noted). Agriculture, forestry, fishing (1995): roots and tubers 396,400 (of which cassava 210,000, yams 120,000, taro 64,000), plantains 250,000, sugarcane 220,000, corn (maize) 27,000, peanuts (groundnuts) 15,000, bananas 9,000, palm oil 2,800, cacao beans 1,200; livestock (number of live animals) 172,000 sheep, 165,000 pigs, 84,000 goats, 39,000 cattle, 2,600,000 chickens; roundwood (1994) 4,445,000 cu m; fish catch (1993) 28,289. Mining and quarrying (1995): manganese ore 1,950,000; uranium ore 640,000. Manufacturing (1992): cement 138,381; wheat flour 31,000; refined sugar 15,000; beer 785,000 hectolitres; soft drinks 410,000 hectolitres; cigarettes 399,000,000 units; textiles are also significant. Construction: n.a. Energy production (consumption): electricity (kW-hr; 1994) 933,000,000 (933,000,000); crude petroleum (barrels; 1994) 115,600,000 (11,600,000); petroleum products (metric tons; 1994) 776,000 (633,000); natural gas (cu m; 1994) 129,000,000 (129,000,000); fuelwood (cu m; 1994) 2,812,000 (2,812,000).
Population economically active (1993): total 376,000; activity rate of total population 37.0% (participation rates [1985]: ages 15–64, 68.2%; female 38.4%; unemployed [1996] 20%).
Household income and expenditure. Average household size (1993) 5.2; income per household: n.a.; sources of income (1983): private sector 73.4%, public sector 26.6%; expenditure (1969)[3]: food and tobacco 54.7%, clothing and footwear 17.5%, housing 13.0%, transportation and communications 6.3%.

Price and earnings indexes (1990 = 100)

	1989	1990	1991	1992	1993	1994	1995
Consumer price index	92.8	100.0	105.4	100.2	91.3	123.4	136.7
Earnings index	...	...	...	...	...	...	...

Land use (1994): forested 77.2%; meadows and pastures 18.2%; agricultural and under permanent cultivation 1.8%; other 2.8%.
Gross national product (at current market prices; 1994): U.S.$3,669,000,000 (U.S.$3,550 per capita).

Structure of gross domestic product and labour force

	1994 in value CFAF '000,000	1994 % of total value	1993 labour force	1993 % of labour force
Agriculture, forestry, fishing	195,100	9.3	156,000[4]	41.6
Mining	946,700	45.1		
Manufacturing	109,400	5.2	43,000[4]	11.5
Construction	82,700	3.9		
Public utilities	33,500	1.6		
Transportation and communications	110,900	5.3		
Trade	157,200	7.5	115,000[4]	30.7
Finance	13,100	0.6		
Services	210,200	10.0		
Pub. admin., defense	238,600	11.4	61,000[4]	16.2
TOTAL	2,097,300[2]	100.0[2]	376,000[2]	100.0

Foreign trade

Balance of trade (current prices)

	1990	1991	1992	1993	1994	1995
CFAF '000,000	+466,000	+397,000	+373,000	+411,200	+903,200	+903,700
% of total	52.6%	45.7%	44.3%	46.2%	51.8%	50.0%

Imports (1994): CFAF 267,600,000,000 (machinery and mechanical equipment 32.1%, food and agricultural products 17.5%, transport equipment 15.1%, construction materials 14.0%, chemical products 13.1%). *Major import sources* (1993): France 41.4%; Africa 25.3%; other EEC 15.0%; United States 5.0%; Japan 5.0%.
Exports (1994): CFAF 1,286,800,000,000 (crude petroleum and petroleum products 79.2%, wood 14.6%, manganese ore and concentrate 4.3%, uranium ore and concentrate 1.2%). *Major export destinations* (1993): United States 41.6%; France 18.2%; Japan 15.6%; other Americas 7.8%; Africa 4.1%.

Transport and communications

Transport. Railroads (1994): length 415 mi, 668 km; passengers carried 150,502; metric tons of cargo carried 2,427,026. Roads (1995): total length 4,850 mi, 7,800 km (paved 10%). Vehicles (1992): passenger cars 23,000; trucks and buses 17,000. Merchant marine (1992): vessels (100 gross tons and over) 29; total deadweight tonnage 30,186. Air transport (1993): passenger-mi 354,000,000, passenger-km 570,000,000; short ton-mi cargo 56,000,000, metric ton-km cargo 82,000,000; airports (1996) with scheduled flights 23.
Communications. Daily newspapers (1996): total number 1; total circulation 40,000; circulation per 1,000 population 23. Radio (1995): total number of receivers 200,000 (1 per 5.7 persons). Television (1995): total number of receivers 40,000 (1 per 29 persons). Telephones (main lines; 1993): 29,800 (1 per 41 persons).

Education and health

Education (1991)

	schools	teachers	students	student/teacher ratio
Primary	1,024	4,782	210,000	43.9
Secondary	51[5]	1,356[5]	42,871	...
Voc., teacher tr.	29[5]	476	8,477	11.8
Higher[6]	2	299	3,000	10.0

Educational attainment of economically active population (1993): none, or incomplete primary 37.7%; complete primary 32.1%; complete secondary 16.4%; postsecondary certificate or degree 13.8%. *Literacy* (1995): total population age 15 and over literate 63.2%; males literate 73.7%; females literate 53.3%.
Health: physicians (1989) 448 (1 per 2,337 persons); hospital beds (1984) 10,980 (1 per 103 persons); infant mortality rate per 1,000 live births (1990–95) 94.
Food (1992): daily per capita caloric intake 2,500 (vegetable products 88%, animal products 12%); 108% of FAO recommended minimum requirement.

Military

Total active duty personnel (1996): 4,700 (army 68.1%, navy 10.6%, air force 21.3%), excluding 600 French troops. *Military expenditure as percentage of GNP* (1994): 2.9% (world 3.0%); per capita expenditure U.S.$82.

[1]De jure; excludes nonnationals numbering 100,000 to 150,000 (mainly West African) prior to their large-scale expulsion in February 1995. [2]Detail does not add to total given because of rounding. [3]Libreville only. [4]Derived values. [5]1984–85. [6]Universities only.

Gambia, The

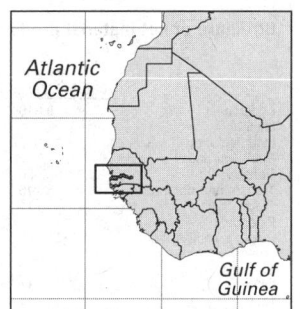

Atlantic Ocean

Gulf of Guinea

Official name: Republic of The Gambia.
Form of government: republic[1].
Head of state and government: President[1].
Capital: Banjul.
Official language: English.
Official religion: none.
Monetary unit: 1 dalasi (D) = 100 butut; valuation (Oct. 11, 1996)
1 U.S.$ = D 9.85; 1 £ = D 15.51.

Area and population

Divisions	Capitals	area sq mi	area sq km	population 1993 census[2]
Kombo St. Mary[3, 4]	Kanifing	29	76	228,214
Lower River	Mansakonko	625	1,618	65,146
MacCarthy Island	Kuntaur/Georgetown	1,117	2,894	156,021
North Bank	Kerewan	871	2,256	156,462
Upper River	Basse	799	2,069	155,059
Western	Brikama	681	1,764	234,917
City				
Banjul[4]	—	5	12	42,326
TOTAL		4,127[5]	10,689[5]	1,038,145

Demography

Population (1996): 1,148,000.
Density (1996)[6]: persons per sq mi 345.2, persons per sq km 133.3.
Urban-rural (1993): urban 36.7%; rural 63.3%.
Sex distribution (1993): male 50.08%; female 49.92%.
Age breakdown (1993): under 15, 43.8%; 15–29, 27.7%; 30–44, 15.1%; 45–59, 6.8%; 60–74, 3.5%; 75 and over, 1.4%; not stated 1.7%.
Population projection: (2000) 1,288,000; (2010) 1,607,000.
Doubling time: 29 years.
Ethnic composition (1993): Malinke 34.1%; Fulani 16.2%; Wolof 12.6%; Dyola 9.2%; Soninke 7.7%; other 20.2%.
Religious affiliation (1993): Muslim 95.0%; Christian 4.0%; traditional beliefs and other 1.0%.
Major cities/urban areas (1986): Serekunda 102,600[3]; Banjul 42,326 (Greater Banjul 270,540[4, 7]); Brikama 24,300; Bakau 23,600[3]; Farafenni 10,168[8].

Vital statistics

Birth rate per 1,000 population (1995): 43.0 (world avg. 25.0); legitimate, n.a.; illegitimate, n.a.
Death rate per 1,000 population (1995): 19.0 (world avg. 9.3).
Natural increase rate per 1,000 population (1995): 24.0 (world avg. 15.7).
Total fertility rate (avg. births per childbearing woman; 1995): 5.8.
Marriage rate per 1,000 population: n.a.
Divorce rate per 1,000 population: n.a.
Life expectancy at birth (1990–95): male 43.4 years; female 46.6 years.
Major causes of death per 100,000 population: n.a.; however, major infectious diseases include malaria, gastroenteritis and dysentery, pneumonia and bronchitis, measles, schistosomiasis, and whooping cough.

National economy

Budget (1994–95). Revenue: D 737,100,000 (tax revenue 81.4%, of which import duties and excises 34.8%, income taxes 18.4%, sales tax 6.6%; nontax revenue and grants 18.6%). Expenditures: D 887,500,000 (administrative expenses 23.2%; goods and services 16.1%; interest payments 14.5%; transportation and communications 9.0%; agriculture 8.2%; education and culture 8.0%; public services 2.9%).
Production (metric tons except as noted). Agriculture, forestry, fishing (1995): peanuts (groundnuts) 84,000, millet 53,000, corn (maize) 22,000, paddy rice 20,000, seed cotton 4,500, cassava 6,000, pulses (mostly beans) 4,000, palm oil 2,500, palm kernels 2,000; livestock (number of live animals) 400,000 cattle, 150,000 goats, 121,000 sheep; roundwood (1994) 812,700 cu m; fish catch (1993) 20,479, of which Atlantic Ocean 18,079, inland water 2,400. Mining and quarrying: sand and gravel are excavated for local use. Manufacturing (value of production in D '000; 1982): processed food, including peanut and palm-kernel oil 62,878; beverages 10,546; textiles 3,253; chemicals and related products 1,031; nonmetals 922; printing and publishing 358; leather 150. Construction: n.a. Energy production (consumption): electricity (kW-hr; 1993) 73,000,000 (73,000,000); coal, none (none); crude petroleum, none (none); petroleum products (metric tons; 1993) none (68,000); natural gas, none (none).
Public debt (external, outstanding; 1994): U.S.$364,300,000.
Population economically active (1992): total 412,000; activity rate of total population 47.2% (participation rates: [1983] ages 15–64, 78.2%; female 46.3%; unemployed, n.a.).

Price and earnings indexes (1990 = 100)

	1989	1990	1991	1992	1993	1994	1995
Consumer price index	89.1	100.0	108.6	118.9	126.6	128.7	137.7
Earnings index	...	...	...	...	...	...	...

Tourism (1994): receipts from visitors U.S.$27,000,000; expenditures by nationals abroad U.S.$14,000,000.

Household income and expenditure. Average household size (1983) 8.3; income per household: n.a.; sources of income: n.a.; expenditure (1986)[9]: food and beverages 58.0%, clothing and footwear 17.5%, energy and water 5.4%, housing 5.1%, education, health, transportation and communications, recreation, and other 14.0%.
Gross national product (at current market prices; 1994): U.S.$384,000,000 (U.S.$360 per capita).

Structure of gross domestic product and labour force

	1994–95 in value D'000,000[10]	1994–95 % of total value	1983 labour force	1983 % of labour force
Agriculture	117.8	20.9	239,940	73.7
Mining			66	0.0
Manufacturing	33.6	6.0	8,144	2.5
Construction	24.3	4.3	4,373	1.3
Public utilities	3.8	0.7	1,233	0.4
Transportation and communications	100.0	17.7	8,014	2.5
Trade	93.7	16.6	16,551	5.1
Finance	35.3	6.3	4,577	1.4
Public administration	59.6	10.6	8,295	2.5
Services	22.7	4.0	9,381	2.9
Other	72.6[11]	12.9[11]	25,049[12]	7.7[12]
TOTAL	563.4	100.0	325,623	100.0

Land use (1994): forested 10.0%; meadows and pastures 19.0%; agricultural and under permanent cultivation 17.2%; built-on area, wasteland, and other 53.8%.

Foreign trade[13]

Balance of trade (current prices)

	1989	1990	1991	1992	1993	1994
D '000,000	−1,023.0	−1,195.3	−1,561.4	−1,675.9	−1,428.1	−1,378.5
% of total	72.1%	61.2%	67.8%	59.7%	54.1%	67.1%

Imports (1993–94): D 1,999,414,000 (1992–93; food 29.1%; machinery and transport equipment 23.2%; basic manufactures 19.8%; mineral fuels and lubricants 5.9%; chemicals and related products 5.2%). *Major import sources* (1993): China 20.3%; Hong Kong 11.1%; United Kingdom 10.3%; France 7.9%; Belgium-Luxembourg 7.9%; Italy 3.2%.
Exports (1993–94): D 363,041,000 (1992–93; domestic exports 53.5%, of which fish and fish preparations 4.4%; reexports 46.5%[14]). *Major export destinations* (1993): Belgium-Luxembourg 50.9%; Japan 22.0%; Guinea 5.7%; United Kingdom 5.0%; Hong Kong 2.5%; Thailand 1.9%; Spain 1.3%.

Transport and communications

Transport. Railroads: none. Roads (1990): total length 1,483 mi, 2,386 km (paved 32%). Vehicles (1994): passenger cars 7,400; trucks and buses 3,100. Merchant marine (1992): vessels (100 gross tons and over) 11; total deadweight tonnage 2,029. Air transport (1991): passenger arrivals and departures 128,000; cargo 1,603 metric tons; airports (1996) with scheduled flights 1.
Communications. Daily newspapers (1992): total number 2; total circulation 2,000; circulation per 1,000 population 2.2. Radio (1995): total number of receivers 140,000 (1 per 8.0 persons). Television (1995): total number of receivers 6,000 (1 per 186 persons). Telephones (main lines; 1993): 16,300 (1 per 64 persons).

Education and health

Education (1992)

	schools	teachers	students	student/ teacher ratio
Primary (age 8–14)	245	3,193	97,262	30.5
Secondary (age 15–21)[15]	32	1,054	25,929	24.6
Postsecondary[16]	9	177	1,489	8.4

Educational attainment (1973). Percentage of population age 20 and over having: no formal schooling 90.8%; primary education 6.2%; secondary 2.6%; higher 0.4%. *Literacy* (1990): total population age 15 and over literate 27.2%; males literate 39.0%; females literate 16.0%.
Health (1990–91): physicians 61 (1 per 14,536 persons); hospital beds 601 (1 per 1,475 persons); infant mortality rate per 1,000 live births (1995) 123.
Food (1992): daily per capita caloric intake 2,360 (vegetable products 94%, animal products 6%); 103% of FAO recommended minimum requirement.

Military

Total active duty personnel (1996): 800. *Military expenditure as percentage of GNP* (1994): 3.7% (world 3.0%); per capita expenditure U.S.$14.

[1]New constitution approved by referendum on Aug. 7/8, 1996. Presidential elections of September 1996 did not meet international standards. [2]Preliminary. [3]Kombo St. Mary includes the urban areas of Serekunda and Bakau. [4]Kombo St. Mary and Banjul city make up Greater Banjul. [5]Includes inland water area of 2,077 sq km (802 sq mi). [6]Based on land area only. [7]1993. [8]1983. [9]Low-income population in Banjul and Kombo St. Mary only; weights of consumer price index components. [10]At constant prices of 1976–77. [11]Indirect taxes. [12]Not adequately defined. [13]Imports c.i.f.; exports f.o.b. [14]Mostly unofficial trade with Senegal. [15]Includes teacher training and vocational. [16]1984–85.

Georgia

Official name: Sakartvelos Respublika (Republic of Georgia).
Form of government: unitary multiparty republic with a single legislative body (Parliament [235]).
Head of state and government: President.
Capital: T'bilisi.
Official language: Georgian.
Official religion: none.
Monetary unit: lari[1] (decimal unit, 100 tetri); valuation (Oct. 14, 1996), 1 U.S.$ = 1.27 lari; 1 £ = 2.01 lari.

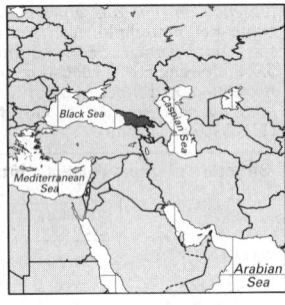

Area and population		area		population
		sq mi	sq km	1993[2] estimate
Autonomous republics	**Capitals**			
Abkhazia[3]	Sokhumi (Sukhumi)	3,343	8,660	516,600
Ajaria (Adzharia)	Bat'umi	1,120	2,900	386,700
Regions under republican jurisdiction				
Guria	...	785	2,033	160,800
Imereti	...	2,452	6,349	788,900
Kakheti	...	4,717	12,217	464,000
Kvemo Kartli	...	2,615	6,772	601,500
Racha-Lechkumi	...	1,245	3,224	45,400
Samegrelo	...	1,697	4,395	418,100
Samtskhe-Javakheti	...	2,017	5,224	198,800
Shida Kartli	...	3,043	7,882	485,900
Svaneti	...	1,694	4,389	23,200
Tianeti	...	1,569	4,063	43,800
Region under urban council jurisdiction				
T'bilisi		534	1,384	1,271,800
TOTAL		26,831	69,493[4]	5,405,400[4]

Demography

Population (1996): 5,360,625.
Density (1996): persons per sq mi 200.0, persons per sq km 77.1.
Urban-rural (1994): urban 55.7%; rural 44.3%.
Sex distribution (1994): male 47.60%; female 52.40%.
Age breakdown (1989): under 15, 24.8%; 15–29, 24.1%; 30–44, 19.2%; 45–59, 17.5%; 60–74, 10.8%; 75 and over, 3.6%.
Population projection: (2000) 5,238,000; (2010) 5,296,000.
Doubling time: 77 years.
Ethnic composition (1989): Georgian 70.1%; Armenian 8.1%; Russian 6.3%; Azerbaijani 5.7%; Ossetian 3.0%; Greek 1.9%; Abkhazian 1.8%; other 3.1%.
Religious affiliation: believers are predominantly Georgian Orthodox (65%); minorities include Sunnī and Shī'ī Muslim (11%), Russian Orthodox (10%), Armenian Apostolic (Orthodox) (8%), and smaller Jewish, Roman Catholic, Baptist, and Yazīdī communities.
Major cities (1994): T'bilisi 1,253,100; K'ut'aisi 240,600; Rust'avi 155,500; Bat'umi 137,100; Sokhumi (Sukhumi; 1993) 112,000.

Vital statistics

Birth rate per 1,000 population (1994): 10.7 (world avg. 25.0); (1989) legitimate 82.3%; illegitimate 17.7%.
Death rate per 1,000 population (1994): 8.6 (world avg. 9.3).
Natural increase rate per 1,000 population (1994): 2.1 (world avg. 15.7).
Total fertility rate (avg. births per childbearing woman; 1993): 2.5.
Marriage rate per 1,000 population (1994): 3.8.
Divorce rate per 1,000 population (1994): 0.5.
Life expectancy at birth (1994): male 69.0 years; female 76.0 years.
Major causes of death per 100,000 population (1992): diseases of the circulatory system 676.3; malignant neoplasms (cancers) 97.3; accidents, poisoning, and violence 63.5; diseases of the digestive system 34.7; diseases of the respiratory system 28.4; infectious and parasitic diseases 13.5.

National economy

Budget (1994). Revenue: 106,000,000,000,000 coupons[1] (grants 42.9%; tax revenue 41.1%, of which value-added tax 15.7%, company profit tax 10.9%, individual income tax 3.2%, customs duties 2.2%, other taxes 9.1%; nontax revenue 16.0%). Expenditures: 333,000,000,000,000 coupons[1] (current expenditure 88.9%, of which subsidies and transfers 57.1%, interest payments 10.2%, goods and services 7.5%, wages and salaries 3.3%, other 10.8%; capital expenditure 8.0%, of which local government 6.8%; net lending 3.1%).
Production (metric tons except as noted). Agriculture, forestry, fishing (1995): fruit (other than grapes) 1,265,000, vegetables (other than potatoes) 1,000,000, grapes 480,000, corn (maize) 450,000, potatoes 250,000, milk 121,000, wheat 50,000, barley 40,000, sugarbeets 12,000, sunflower seeds 10,000, soybeans 6,000; livestock (number of live animals) 944,000 cattle, 794,000 sheep and goats, 367,000 pigs, 17,000,000 poultry; roundwood, n.a.; fish catch (1993) 37,000. Mining and quarrying (1994): manganese ore 150,000. Manufacturing (value of production in '000,000 coupons; 1993): clothing 581; ferrous and nonferrous metals 498; food products 442; machinery 436; chemical products 222; textiles 142. Construction (1994): 12,100 sq m. Energy production (consumption): electricity (kW-hr; 1994) 6,803,000,000 (7,603,000,000); coal (metric tons; 1994) 34,000 (274,000); crude petroleum (barrels; 1994) 542,000 (2,008,000); petroleum products (metric tons; 1994) none (n.a.); natural gas (cu m; 1994) 8,969,000 (2,797,000,000).
Gross national product (1993): U.S.$3,055,000,000 (U.S.$560 per capita)[5].

Structure of net material product and labour force

	1993			
	in value '000,000,000 coupons[1]	% of total value	labour force	% of labour force
Agriculture	9,918	86.9	553,400	27.4
Mining	} 1,345	} 11.8		
Manufacturing			312,400	15.5
Public utilities				
Construction	80	0.7	125,300	6.2
Transp. and commun.	46	0.4	57,400	2.8
Trade	11	0.1	152,700	7.6
Finance	...	...	12,400	0.6
Public administration, defense	...	...	49,000	2.4
Services	...	...	485,200	24.0
Other	11	0.1	270,200	13.4
TOTAL	11,411	100.0	2,018,000	100.0[4]

Public debt (external; 1994): U.S.$1,227,000,000.
Population economically active (1993): total 2,018,000; activity rate of total population 37.4% (participation rates [1992]: ages 16–59 [male], 16–54 [female] 72.9%; female [1989] 45.9%; unemployed [1989] 3.5%).

Price and earnings indexes (1990 = 1)				
	1990	1991	1992	1993	1994
Consumer price index	1.0	1.8	15.0	478.0	28,319.0
Monthly earnings index	1.0	1.3	7.1	130.6	11,813.0

Household income and expenditure. Average household size (1989) 4.1; income per household: n.a.; sources of income (1993): wages and salaries 34.5%, benefits 21.9%, agricultural income 21.6%, other 22.0%; expenditure (1993): taxes 42.5%, retail goods 32.3%, savings 16.4%, transportation 4.2%, health care 3.9%, housing 0.7%.
Land use (1994): forest 33.3%; pasture 29.0%; agriculture 16.2%; other 21.5%.

Foreign trade

Balance of trade (current prices)					
	1988	1989	1990	1991	1992
'000,000 rubles	– 592	– 385	– 855	– 1,154	– 18,627
% of total	4.8%	3.1%	6.7%	8.6%	35.7%

Imports (1994): U.S.$324,554,000 (oil and gas 47.0%; textiles, clothing, shoes 28.5%; food products 16.1%; electricity 3.0%; petroleum products 2.9%). *Major import sources:* Turkmenistan 71.1%; Turkey 12.6%; Russia 4.2%; Azerbaijan 3.4%; Ukraine 1.2%.
Exports (1994): U.S.$147,837,000 (food products 30.0%; ferrous metals 29.7%; textiles 7.0%; chemicals 5.0%). *Major export destinations:* Russia 46.0%; Turkey 17.6%; Turkmenistan 8.8%; Kazakstan 6.5%; Azerbaijan 5.8%.

Transport and communications

Transport. Railroads (1996): length 983 mi, 1,583 km; (1989) passenger-mi 10,600,000, passenger-km 17,000,000; cargo traffic, n.a. Roads (1995): length 13,049 mi, 21,000 km (paved 93.5%). Vehicles (1995): passenger cars 441,828; trucks and buses 50,220. Merchant marine: vessels (1,000 gross tons and over) 54; total deadweight tonnage 1,108,068. Air transport (1989): passenger-mi 3,290,500,000, passenger-km 5,295,600,000; short ton-mi cargo, n.a., metric ton-km cargo, n.a.; airports (1996) with scheduled flights 2.
Communications. Daily newspapers (1989): total number 147; total circulation 3,677,000; circulation per 1,000 population 671. Radio and television (1990): total number of receivers 3,760,000 (1 per 1.5 persons). Telephones (main lines; 1993): 1,002,000 (1 per 5.5 persons).

Education and health

Education (1993–94)	schools	teachers	students	student/ teacher ratio
Primary (age 6–13)	} 3,788	...	815,000	...
Secondary (age 14–17)		...		...
Voc., teacher tr.	...	...	29,300	...
Higher	19	...	93,000	...

Educational attainment (1989). Percentage of population age 25 and over having: primary education or no formal schooling 12.3%; some secondary 15.2%; completed secondary and some postsecondary 57.4%; higher 15.1%.
Literacy (1989): percentage of total population age 15 and over literate 99.0%; males literate 99.5%; females literate 98.5%.
Health (1993): physicians 29,900 (1 per 182 persons); hospital beds 57,100 (1 per 95 persons); infant mortality rate per 1,000 live births (1994) 18.3.
Food: daily per capita caloric intake, n.a.

Military

Total active duty personnel (1996): 13,000 (army 76.9%, navy[6] 15.4%, air force 7.7%). About 8,500 Russian troops remained in Georgia in late 1996.
Military expenditure as percentage of GNP (1993): 3.1% (world 3.3%) per capita expenditure U.S.$17.

[1]The Georgian lari, introduced Sept. 25, 1995, replaced the Georgian coupon, at a rate of 1,000,000 coupons to 1 lari; on the same date, the Georgian lari became the sole legal tender, floating against all currencies. The Georgian coupon was introduced April 5, 1993, at par with the Russian ruble and circulated parallel with it; on Aug. 20, 1993, the coupon became the sole legal tender, floating against all currencies. [2]January 1. [3]Abkhazia adopted a constitution declaring it an independent state on Nov. 26, 1994; on Feb. 9, 1995, it was granted wider autonomy. [4]Detail does not add to total given because of rounding. [5]Ruble-area GNP and exchange-rate data are very speculative. [6]A portion of the former U.S.S.R. Black Sea Fleet has been allocated to Georgia.

Germany

Official name: Bundesrepublik
  Deutschland (Federal Republic of
  Germany).
Form of government: federal multiparty
  republic with two legislative houses
  (Federal Council [68]; Federal Diet
  [672]).
Chief of state: President.
Head of government: Chancellor.
Seat of government: Bonn (Berlin is
  capital designate).
Official language: German.
Official religion: none.
Monetary unit: 1 Deutsche Mark (DM)
  = 100 Pfennige; valuation (Oct. 11,
  1996) 1 U.S.$ = DM 1.53;
  1 £ = DM 2.41.

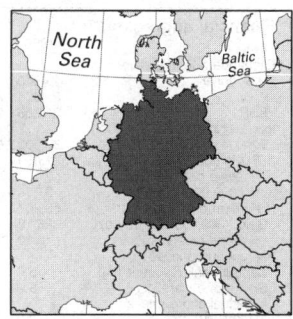

Area and population		area		population
				1995
States	**Capitals**	sq mi	sq km	estimate
Administrative districts				
Baden-Württemberg	Stuttgart	13,804[1]	35,752	10,272,100
Freiburg	Freiburg	3,613	9,357	2,071,100
Karlsruhe	Karlsruhe	2,671	6,919	2,645,100
Stuttgart	Stuttgart	4,076	10,558	3,841,600
Tübingen	Tübingen	3,443	8,918	1,714,300
Bayern	Munich	27,238[1]	70,546	11,921,900[1]
Mittelfranken	Ansbach	2,798	7,246	1,660,300
Niederbayern	Landshut	3,987	10,325	1,131,500
Oberbayern	Munich	6,768	17,529	3,959,400
Oberfranken	Bayreuth	2,792	7,231	1,104,500
Oberpfalz	Regensburg	3,741	9,690	1,047,300
Schwaben	Augsburg	3,859	9,994	1,710,800
Unterfranken	Würzburg	3,294	8,531	1,308,200
Berlin	—	343	889	3,472,000
Brandenburg	Potsdam	11,383	29,481	2,536,700
Bremen	Bremen	156	404	680,000
Hamburg	Hamburg	292	755	1,705,900
Hessen	Wiesbaden	8,152[1]	21,114	5,980,700
Darmstadt	Darmstadt	2,875	7,445	3,670,000
Giessen	Giessen	2,078	5,381	1,049,100
Kassel	Kassel	3,200	8,288	1,261,600
Mecklenburg-Vorpommern	Schwerin	8,946	23,170	1,832,300
Niedersachsen	Hannover	18,382	47,609	7,715,400[1]
Braunschweig	Braunschweig	3,126	8,097	1,678,700
Hannover	Hannover	3,492	9,045	2,130,500
Lüneburg	Lüneburg	5,987	15,505	1,581,100
Weser-Ems	Oldenburg	5,777	14,962	2,325,200
Nordrhein-Westfalen	Düsseldorf	13,156[1]	34,075[1]	17,816,100
Arnsberg	Arnsberg	3,089	8,000	3,817,300
Detmold	Detmold	2,517	6,518	1,991,100
Düsseldorf	Düsseldorf	2,042	5,289	5,287,400
Köln	Köln	2,844	7,365	4,162,000
Münster	Münster	2,666	6,904	2,558,300
Rheinland-Pfalz	Mainz	7,662[1]	19,846[1]	3,951,600
Koblenz	Koblenz	3,116	8,072	1,477,000
Rheinhessen-Pfalz	Mainz	2,646	6,852	1,972,100
Trier	Trier	1,901	4,923	502,500
Saarland	Saarbrücken	992	2,570	1,084,200
Sachsen	Dresden	7,109	18,412	4,584,300
Sachsen-Anhalt	Magdeburg	7,894[1]	20,446	2,759,200
Dessau	Dessau	1,652	4,280	577,300
Halle	Halle/Saale	1,633	4,228	917,200
Magdeburg	Magdeburg	4,532	11,738	1,264,700
Schleswig-Holstein	Kiel	6,077	15,739	2,708,400
Thüringen	Erfurt	6,244	16,171	2,517,800
TOTAL		137,830[1]	356,978[1]	81,538,600

Demography

Population (1996): 81,891,000.
Major cities (1994): Berlin 3,477,900; Hamburg 1,703,800; Munich 1,251,100;
  Cologne 963,300; Frankfurt am Main 656,200; Essen 619,600; Dortmund
  601,500; Stuttgart 592,000; Düsseldorf 573,100; Bremen 551,000; Duisburg
  536,300; Hannover 526,400; Nürnberg 498,200.

Other principal cities (1994)					
	population		population		population
Aachen	247,100	Heilbronn	122,600	Neuss	148,600
Augsburg	263,800	Herne	180,300	Oberhausen	225,800
Bergisch Gladbach	105,200	Hildesheim	106,200	Offenbach am Main	116,700
Bielefeld	324,200	Ingolstadt	110,600	Oldenburg	148,700
Bochum	401,600	Jena	100,200	Osnabrück	167,400
Bonn	295,300	Kaiserslautern	102,400	Paderborn	130,700
Bottrop	119,700	Karlsruhe	277,700	Pforzheim	117,600
Braunschweig	255,600	Kassel	201,900	Potsdam	139,200
Bremerhaven	131,200	Kiel	247,700	Recklinghausen	127,300
Chemnitz	278,700	Koblenz	109,600	Regensburg	125,400
Cottbus	127,200	Krefeld	249,700	Remscheid	123,400
Darmstadt	139,400	Leipzig	487,700	Reutlingen	107,400
Dresden	477,600	Leverkusen	161,800	Rostock	236,100
Erfurt	201,500	Lübeck	217,300	Saarbrücken	189,800
Erlangen	102,100	Ludwigshafen		Salzgitter	117,700
Freiburg		am Rhein	168,100	Schwerin	121,000
im Breisgau	197,800	Magdeburg	269,500	Siegen	111,900
Fürth	108,500	Mainz	185,300	Solingen	166,000
Gelsenkirchen	294,300	Mannheim	317,300	Ulm	115,200
Gera	125,600	Moers	106,900	Wiesbaden	266,600
Göttingen	127,900	Mönchenglad-		Witten	105,500
Hagen	214,200	bach	265,600	Wolfsburg	127,700
Halle an der Saale	294,000	Mülheim		Wuppertal	385,000
Hamm	184,600	an der Ruhr	177,000	Würzburg	128,400
Heidelberg	138,900	Münster	265,500	Zwickau	106,800

Density (1996): persons per sq mi 594.1, persons per sq km 229.4.
Urban-rural (1990): urban 85.3%; rural 14.7%.
Population projection: (2000) 82,840,000; (2010) 85,259,000.
Sex distribution (1995): male 48.62%; female 51.38%.
Age breakdown (1995): under 15, 16.3%; 15–29, 19.9%; 30–44, 23.4%; 45–59,
  19.7%; 60–74, 14.4%; 75 and over, 6.3%.
Doubling time: not applicable; doubling time exceeds 100 years.
Ethnic composition (by nationality; 1995): German 91.4%; Turkish 2.4%, of
  which (1990) Kurdish *c.* 0.5%; Yugoslav 1.0%; Italian 0.7%; Greek 0.4%;
  Polish 0.3%; Austrian 0.2%; Croatian 0.2%; Spanish 0.2%; other 3.2%.
Religious affiliation: (former West Germany; 1987) Roman Catholic 42.9%,
  Lutheran-Reformed and Lutheran traditions 41.6%, Muslim 2.7%, Reformed tradition 0.6%, Jewish 0.1%, other 12.1%; (former East Germany;
  1990) Protestant 47.0%, Roman Catholic 7.0%, unaffiliated and other 46.0%.
Households (1994). Number of households 36,695,000; average household size
  2.3; 1 person 34.7%, 2 persons 31.7%, 3 persons 16.1%, 4 persons 12.7%, 5
  or more persons 4.8%.

Vital statistics

Birth rate per 1,000 population (1995): 9.3 (world avg. 25.0); legitimate 87.6%;
  illegitimate 12.4%.
Death rate per 1,000 population (1995): 10.7 (world avg. 9.3).
Natural increase rate per 1,000 population (1995): −1.4 (world avg. 15.7).
Total fertility rate (avg. births per childbearing woman; 1994): 1.5.
Marriage rate per 1,000 population (1994): 3.4.
Divorce rate per 1,000 population (1994): 2.0.
Life expectancy at birth (1994): male 73.20 years; female 79.80 years.
Major causes of death per 100,000 population (1994): diseases of the circula-
  tory system 489.6; malignant neoplasms (cancers) 252.0, of which colon and
  rectum 56.1, bronchial, lung, and tracheal 42.3; diseases of the respiratory
  system 60.9, of which pneumonia 20.2, chronic bronchitis 13.1.

Social indicators

Educational attainment (1995). Percentage of population age 25 and over
  having: primary and lower secondary 57.1%; intermediate secondary 18.4%;
  vocational secondary 7.3%; post-secondary and higher (all levels) 17.2%.
Quality of working life. Average workweek (1995): 38.5 hours. Annual rate
  per 100,000 workers (1993) for: injuries or accidents at work 4,808; deaths,
  including commuting accidents, 6.7. Proportion of labour force insured for
  damages or income loss resulting from: injury, virtually 100%; permanent
  disability, virtually 100%; death, virtually 100%. Average days lost to labour
  stoppages per 1,000 workers (1993): 3.1.

Distribution of income (1984)[2]				
percentage of household income by quintile				
1	2	3	4	5 (highest)
6.8	12.7	17.8	24.0	38.7

Access to services. Proportion of dwellings (1994) having: electricity, virtually
  100%; piped water supply, virtually 100%; flush sewage disposal (1993)
  98.4%; public fire protection, virtually 100%.
Social participation. Eligible voters participating in last (October 1994) national election 79.1%. Trade union membership in total workforce (1994):
  c. 27%. Practicing religious population (1993): 7% of Protestants and 20%
  of Roman Catholics "regularly" attend religious services.
Social deviance (1994). Offense rate per 100,000 population for: murder and
  manslaughter 5; sexual abuse 56, of which child molestation 19, rape and
  forcible sexual assault 14; robbery 71; assault and battery 108; theft 4,749.
  Incidence per 100,000 in general population (late 1970s) of: alcoholism
  2,500–3,000; drug and substance abuse 650; suicide 16.5.
Material well-being (1995; median income)[2]. Households possessing: automobile 95.8%; telephone 99.3%; colour television receiver 96.3%; refrigerator 79.7%; washing machine 97.8%; home freezer 73.3%.

Recreational and leisure activities[2]		
(Monthly household expenditures, 1995; median income)		
Activity	DM	percentage
Vacations	215	27.2
Expenditures for motor vehicles	112	14.2
Sporting and camping equipment		
and sporting events	91	11.5
Televisions, radios, and their fees	84	10.6
Books, newspapers, and magazines	63	8.0
Gardening and pets	49	6.2
Games and toys	39	4.9
Visits to theatre and cinema	20	2.5
Photographic and moviemaking		
equipment and film	19	2.4
Tools	6	0.8
Other activities	93	11.5
TOTAL	791	100.0[1]

National economy

Budget (1995). Revenue: DM 1,745,750,000,000 (taxes 83.3%). Expenditures:
  DM 1,852,464,000,000 (pensions and other social security payments 33.8%,
  purchase of current goods and services 16.3%, personnel costs 14.9%).
Total national debt (1994)[3]: DM 1,003,480,000,000.
Production (value of production in DM except as noted; 1994–95). Agriculture, forestry, fishing: cereal grains 5,434,000,000, fruits 3,527,000,000,
  flowers and ornamental plants 2,595,000,000, potatoes 2,575,000,000, sugar
  beets 2,375,000,000, grapes for wine 2,226,000,000, vegetables 2,024,000,000,
  nurseries 1,610,000,000, oilseed crops 1,123,000,000; livestock (number of
  live animals) 24,515,900 pigs, 16,097,900 cattle, 109,878,000 poultry; roundwood (1993) 36,156,000 cu m; fish catch (metric tons; 1993) 316,373. Mining

and quarrying (metric tons; 1995): potash 35,200,000. Manufacturing (value added at factor cost in DM; 1994): capital equipment 295,000,000,000, of which electrical equipment 80,367,000,000, machinery 73,700,000,000, transport equipment 73,432,000,000; chemicals (including pharmaceuticals) 59,-144,000,000; food and beverages 40,665,000,000; calculators and computers 23,528,000,000; plastics and other synthetic products 20,837,000,000; furniture and other wood products 16,243,000,000; steel and light metal founding 15,113,000,000; printing and publishing 13,137,000,000; textiles 9,843,000,000; precision instruments 9,618,000,000; paper and cardboard products 8,889,-000,000; clothing 6,878,000,000; rubber products 6,830,000,000; office equipment 6,157,000,000[2]; glass products 5,190,000,000; musical instruments and toys 3,472,000,000; fine pottery and ceramic products 2,426,000,000. Construction (newly completed buildings, sq m; 1994): residential 66,588,000; nonresidential 42,394,000.

Service enterprises (1991)

	no. of enterprises	no. of employees	weekly wage as a % of all wages	annual turnover (DM '000,000)
Gas	151	37,000	...	42,228
Water	183	40,000	...	3,443
Electrical power	462	296,000	...	147,076
Transport				
air	133	57,390	...	20,270
buses	6,054	192,869	...	12,586
rail	1	416,199	...	14,697
shipping	1,449	9,076	...	
Communications				
press	2,452	240,075	...	31,096
film[4]	615	3,000	...	836
Postal services	17,616[5]	652,573	...	68,346
Hotels and restaurants	135,141	652,251	...	60,257
Wholesale trade	36,605[5]	1,214,000	...	1,015,984
Retail trade	152,629	2,241,000	...	605,755

Energy production (consumption): electricity (kW-hr; 1994) 528,221,000,-000 (530,558,000,000); hard coal (metric tons; 1994) 57,623,000 (66,255,-000); lignite (metric tons; 1994) 207,077,000 (209,308,000); crude petroleum (barrels; 1994) 21,535,000 (793,500,000); petroleum products (metric tons; 1994) 99,578,000 (113,839,000); natural gas (cu m; 1994) 20,904,000,000 (92,770,000,000).

Manufacturing, mining, and construction enterprises (1994)

	no. of enterprises	no. of employees	wages as a % of avg. of all wages[2]	annual gross production value (DM '000,000)
Manufacturing	42,111	6,857,000	100.0	1,960,573
of which				
Road motor vehicles	2,206	785,000	112.6	264,474
Machinery and appliances (electric)	3,471	997,000	106.9	237,185
Food and beverages	4,522	556,000	90.0	217,252
Chemical	1,395	575,000	102.7	211,519
Machinery (nonelectric)	5,931	962,000	99.6	204,112
Petroleum and natural gas	61	30,000	124.1	112,891
Calculators, computers	2,366	317,000	90.0	66,310
Plastics	2,446	277,000	89.4	64,819
Wood and wood products	3,442	274,000	83.8	60,278
Iron and steel	118	137,000	96.4	43,567
Textiles	1,183	167,000	81.8	34,019
Mining and quarrying	2,468	189,000	105.3	58,656
Construction	24,370	1,503,000	100.0	255,656

Gross national product (at current market prices; 1994): U.S.$2,075,452,000,-000 (U.S.$25,580 per capita).

Structure of gross domestic product and labour force

	1994			
	in value DM '000,000	% of total value	labour force	% of labour force
Agriculture	30,000	0.9	1,190,000	3.0
Public utilities, mining	74,050	2.2	602,000	1.5
Manufacturing	770,430	23.2	9,851,000	24.5
Construction	168,940	5.1	3,180,000	7.9
Transportation and communications	161,010	4.8	2,169,000	5.4
Trade	251,880	7.6	4,402,000	10.9
Finance, real estate	420,450	12.7	1,281,000	3.2
Services	614,680	18.5	9,033,000	22.5
Pub. admin., defense	302,160	9.1	3,493,000	8.7
Other (productive)	415,010	12.5	5,035,000	12.5
Other (accounting)	112,490	3.4	—	—
TOTAL	3,321,100	100.0	40,236,000	100.0[1]

Population economically active (1994): total 40,236,000; activity rate of total population 49.4% (participation rates: ages 15–64, 71.7%; female 42.7%; unemployed 10.3%).

Price and earnings indexes (1991 = 100)

	1991	1992	1993	1994	1995	1996[6]
Consumer price index	100.0	105.1	109.7	112.7	114.8	116.8
Hourly earnings index	100.0	107.1	113.5	115.3	87.6	...

Household income and expenditure. Average annual income per household (1994) DM 75,984 (U.S.$46,823); sources of take-home income (1995[2]): wages 81.4%, self-employment 11.6%, transfer payments 7.0%; expenditure (1995): rent 23.9%, food and beverages 21.1%, transportation 15.4%, entertainment, education, and leisure 11.3%, household operations, durables, and maintenance 6.7%, clothing and footwear 6.7%.
Tourism (1995): receipts U.S.$12,290,000,000; expenditures U.S.$48,101,000,-000.

Financial aggregates[7]

	1990	1991	1992	1993	1994	1995	1996 (Oct.)
Exchange rate, DM per:							
U.S. dollar	1.4940	1.5160	1.6140	1.7263	1.5488	1.4335	1.5126
£	2.8804	2.8360	2.4404	2.1988	2.4207	2.2219	2.4628
SDR	2.1255	2.1685	2.2193	2.3712	2.2610	2.1309	2.1876
International reserves (U.S.$)							
Total (excl. gold; '000,000)	67,902	63,001	90,967	77,640	77,363	85,005	85,846
SDRs ('000,000)	1,880	1,917	841	962	1,114	2,001	1,913
Reserve pos. in IMF ('000,000)	3,056	3,567	4,239	3,951	4,030	5,210	5,551
Foreign exchange	62,967	57,517	85,877	72,727	72,219	77,794	78,382
Gold ('000,000 fine troy oz)	95.18	95.18	95.18	95.18	95.18	95.18	95.18
% world reserves	10.12	10.13	10.24	10.43	10.46	10.48	10.52
Interest and prices							
Central bank discount (%)	6.0	8.0	8.3	4.8	4.5	3.0	2.5[8]
Govt. bond yield (%)	8.9	8.6	8.0	6.3	6.7	6.5	5.5[8]
Industrial share prices (1990 = 100)[9]	100.0	91.5	87.3	93.6	106.1	103.3	115.6[10]
Balance of payments (U.S.$'000,000,000)							
Balance of visible trade	69.04	19.92	28.72	41.75	51.68	66.12	15.68[11]
Imports, f.o.b.	341.88	383.48	401.51	340.73	378.59	457.10	125.00[11]
Exports, f.o.b.	410.92	403.37	430.23	382.49	430.27	523.22	109.32[11]
Balance of invisibles	−20.93	−37.80	−48.11	−55.15	−71.99	−87.10	−18.20[11]
Balance of payments, current account	48.11	−17.88	−19.39	−13.40	−20.31	−20.98	−2.52[11]

Land use (1994): forest 30.6%; pasture 15.1%; agriculture 19.9%; other 34.4%.

Foreign trade

Balance of trade (current prices)

	1991	1992	1993	1994	1995
DM '000,000,000	+ 37.03	+ 45.91	+ 75.81	+ 88.73	+ 103.40
% of total	2.9%	3.6%	6.4%	6.8%	7.4%

Imports (1995): DM 621,816,000,000 (machinery and transport equipment 34.4%, of which road transport equipment 9.9%, office equipment and computers 7.6%, electrical machinery other than office equipment 7.3%; chemicals and chemical products 9.4%, of which organic chemical products 2.2%, unfabricated plastics 1.9%; food and beverages 8.3%, of which fruits and vegetables 2.8%, meat and meat products 1.2%, coffee, tea, and cocoa 1.1%; mineral fuels 6.4%, of which crude petroleum and petroleum products 4.4%, natural gas 1.5%; clothing and wearing apparel 5.5%; iron and steel 3.4%; thread, yarn, and finished spinning goods 2.7%). *Major import sources:* France 10.7%; The Netherlands 8.4%; Italy 8.3%; U.S. 7.1%; Belgium-Luxembourg 6.5%; U.K. 6.4%; Japan 5.5%; Switzerland 4.4%; Austria 3.7%.
Exports (1995): DM 727,732,000,000 (machinery and transport equipment 49.6%, of which road transport equipment 16.2%, electrical machinery other than office equipment 7.1%, office equipment 2.4%; chemicals and chemical products 13.5%, of which organic chemical products 2.8%, unfabricated plastics 2.4%, medical and pharmaceutical products 2.0%). *Major export destinations:* France 11.6%; U.K. 8.0%; Italy 7.5%; U.S. 7.5%; The Netherlands 7.3%; Belgium-Luxembourg 6.5%; Switzerland 5.5%; Austria 5.4%; Japan 2.6%; Sweden 2.4%; Spain 2.2%.

Transport and communications

Transport. Railroads (1994): length (1993) 54,994 mi, 88,504 km; passengers carried 1,570,000,000; passenger-mi 38,502,000,000, passenger-km 61,962,-000,000; short ton-mi cargo 49,191,000,000, metric ton-km cargo 71,814,-000,000. Roads (1995): total length 404,337 mi, 650,700 km (paved 99%). Vehicles (1995): passenger cars 40,499,442; trucks and buses 2,336,760. Merchant marine (1995): vessels (100 gross tons and over) 1,476; total deadweight tonnage 5,721,000. Air transport (1994)[12]: passengers carried 85,000,000; passenger-mi 14,640,000,000, passenger-km 23,560,000,000; short ton-mi cargo 303,000,000, metric ton-km cargo 442,000,000; airports (1996) with scheduled flights 28.
Communications. Daily newspapers (1993): total number 386; total circulation 30,690,000; circulation per 1,000 population 376. Radio (1994): 36,186,000 receivers (1 per 2.3 persons). Television (1994): 32,314,000 receivers[13] (1 per 2.5 persons[13]). Telephones (main lines; 1994): 39,200,000 (1 per 2.1 persons).

Education and health

Education (1994–95)

	schools	teachers	students	student/ teacher ratio
Primary (age 6–10) } Secondary (age 10–19)	43,243	665,820	9,760,429	14.7
Voc., teacher tr.	9,178	106,820	2,427,751	22.7
Higher	332	227,124	1,858,428	8.2

Health (1995): physicians 273,880 (1 per 298 persons); dentists 60,616 (1 per 1,347 persons); hospital beds 628,658 (1 per 130 persons); infant mortality rate per 1,000 live births 5.6.
Food (1992): daily per capita caloric intake 3,344 (vegetable products 65%, animal products 35%); 126% of FAO recommended minimum requirement.

Military

Total active duty personnel (1996): 358,400 (army 70.5%, navy 8.0%, air force 21.5%). *Military expenditure as percentage of GNP* (1994): 1.8% (world 3.0%); per capita expenditure U.S.$448.

[1]Detail does not add to total given because of rounding. [2]Former West Germany only. [3]Provisional. [4]1984. [5]1990. [6]October. [7]End-of-period figures unless footnoted otherwise. [8]Through September. [9]Period averages. [10]Through 3rd quarter. [11]Through 1st quarter. [12]Domestic service only. [13]Data include officially registered sets only.

Ghana

Official name: Republic of Ghana.
Form of government: unitary multiparty republic with one legislative house (House of Parliament [200]).
Head of state and government: President.
Capital: Accra.
Official language: English.
Official religion: none.
Monetary unit: 1 cedi (₵) = 100 pesewas; valuation (Oct, 11, 1996) 1 U.S.$ = ₵1,703; 1 £ = ₵2,683.

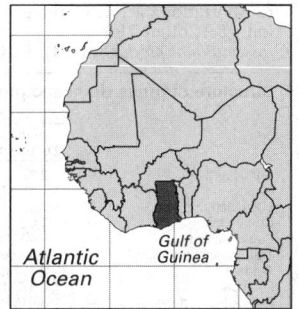

Atlantic Ocean
Gulf of Guinea

Area and population

Regions[2]	Capitals	area		population 1991[1] estimate
		sq mi	sq km	
Ashanti	Kumasi	9,417	24,389	2,485,766
Brong-Ahafo	Sunyani	15,273	39,557	1,432,971
Central	Cape Coast	3,794	9,826	1,359,861
Eastern	Koforidua	7,461	19,323	2,003,235
Greater Accra	Accra	1,253	3,245	1,696,170
Northern	Tamale	27,175	70,384	1,389,105
Upper East	Bolgatanga	3,414	8,842	921,196
Upper West	Wa	7,134	18,476	526,398
Volta	Ho	7,942	20,570	1,432,971
Western	Sekondi-Takoradi	9,236	23,921	1,374,483
TOTAL		92,098[3]	238,533	14,622,156

Demography

Population (1996): 16,904,000.
Density (1996): persons per sq mi 183.5, persons per sq km 70.8.
Urban-rural (1993): urban 35.4%; rural 64.6%.
Sex distribution (1995): male 49.67%; female 50.33%.
Age breakdown (1990): under 15, 46.8%; 15–29, 26.2%; 30–44, 14.4%; 45–59, 8.0%; 60–74, 3.8%; 75 and over, 0.8%.
Population projection: (2000) 18,407,000; (2010) 21,900,000.
Doubling time: 23 years.
Ethnolinguistic composition (1983): Akan 52.4%; Mossi 15.8%; Ewe 11.9%; Ga-Adangme 7.8%; Gurma 3.3%; Yoruba 1.3%; other 7.5%.
Religious affiliation (1980): Christian 62.6%, of which Protestant 27.9%, Roman Catholic 18.7%, African indigenous 16.0%; traditional beliefs 21.4%; Muslim 15.7%, of which Aḥmadīyah 7.9%; other 0.3%.
Major cities (1988[1]): Accra 949,100; Kumasi 385,200; Tamale 151,100; Tema 110,000; Sekondi-Takoradi 103,600.

Vital statistics

Birth rate per 1,000 population (1990–95): 41.7 (world avg. 25.0); legitimate, n.a.; illegitimate, n.a.
Death rate per 1,000 population (1990–95): 11.7 (world avg. 9.3).
Natural increase rate per 1,000 population (1990–95): 30.0 (world avg. 15.7).
Total fertility rate (avg. births per childbearing woman; 1993): 5.9.
Life expectancy at birth (1993): male 53.3 years; female 57.2 years.
Major causes of death per 100,000 population: n.a.; however, principal infectious diseases as a percentage of outpatients (1989): malaria 43.8%, respiratory infections (including tuberculosis) 8.0%, diarrheal diseases 6.7%, intestinal worms 3.1%.

National economy

Budget (1994). Revenue: ₵1,270,555,000,000 (import-export duties 28.5%, of which cocoa export duty 11.5%; excise and value-added taxes 24.3%, of which petroleum tax 15.9%; divestiture of government assets 20.6%; income taxes 13.4%). Expenditures: ₵896,851,000,000 (education 22.3%; debt service 20.1%; health 6.9%; transportation and communications 3.8%; social security and welfare 3.6%; defense 2.9%).
Public debt (external, outstanding; 1994): U.S.$4,075,000,000.
Production (metric tons except as noted). Agriculture, forestry, fishing (1995): roots and tubers 10,493,100 (of which cassava 6,899,100, yams 2,233,900, taro 1,360,100), cereals 1,834,600 (of which corn [maize] 1,041,600, sorghum 390,400, rice 201,700, millet 200,800), bananas and plantains 1,641,500, cacao 325,000, coconuts 263,800, green peppers 185,000[4], tomatoes 181,500, peanuts (groundnuts) 176,300, sugarcane 110,000, oranges 50,000, palm kernels 34,000, lemons and limes 30,000, pulses 20,000; livestock (number of live animals) 3,337,000 goats, 3,288,000 sheep, 1,680,000 cattle, 595,000 pigs, 11,500,000 chickens; roundwood (1994) 22,628,000 cu m; fish catch (1993) 371,227 (of which anchovies 81,350). Mining and quarrying (1995): bauxite 530,440; manganese ore 186,902; gold 53,881 kg; diamonds 293,880 carats. Manufacturing (value added in ₵; 1993): tobacco 71,474,700,000; footwear 60,350,600,000; chemical products 40,347,600,000; beverages 36,167,000,000; metal products 35,121,700,000; petroleum products 32,143,500,000; textiles 18,278,600,000; machinery and transport equipment 9,525,700,000. Construction (value added in ₵; 1994): 171,129,000,000. Energy production (consumption): electricity (kW-hr; 1993) 6,154,000,000 (5,870,000,000); coal (metric tons; 1993) none (3,000); crude petroleum (barrels; 1993) none (7,245,000); petroleum products (metric tons; 1993) 910,000 (1,082,000); natural gas, none (n.a.).
Household income and expenditure. Average household size (1984) 4.9; average annual income per household (1978) ₵9,600 (U.S.$[5]); sources of income: n.a.; expenditure (1978): food and beverages 57.4%, clothing and footwear 14.3%, housing and energy 11.5%, transportation and communications 3.3%, health care 1.3%.

Gross national product (1994): U.S.$7,311,000,000 (U.S.$430 per capita).

Structure of gross domestic product and labour force

	1994		1984	
	in value ₵'000,000	% of total value	labour force	% of labour force
Agriculture	2,452,851	47.3	3,310,967	59.4
Mining	103,715	2.0	26,828	0.5
Manufacturing	466,716	9.0	588,418	10.5
Construction	171,129	3.3	64,686	1.2
Public utilities	98,529	1.9	15,437	0.3
Transp. and commun.	228,172	4.4	122,806	2.2
Trade	995,660	19.2	792,147	14.2
Finance	197,058	3.8	27,475	0.5
Pub. admin., defense }	451,159	8.7	97,548	1.7
Services			376,168	6.7
Other	20,743[6]	0.4[6]	157,624[7]	2.8[7]
TOTAL	5,185,732	100.0	5,580,104	100.0

Tourism (1994): receipts from visitors U.S.$228,000,000; expenditures by nationals abroad U.S.$20,000,000.
Population economically active (1984): total 5,580,104; activity rate of total population 45.4% (participation rates: over age 15, 82.5%; female 51.2%; unemployed 2.8%).

Price and earnings indexes (1990 = 100)

	1989	1990	1991	1992	1993	1994	1995
Consumer price index	72.9	100.0	118.0	129.9	162.3	202.7	323.2
Monthly earnings index	80.7	100.0	117.2	...	...	...	...

Land use (1994): forested 42.2%; meadows and pastures 36.9%; agricultural and under permanent cultivation 19.0%; other 1.9%.

Foreign trade

Balance of trade (current prices)

	1989	1990	1991	1992	1993	1994
U.S.$'000,000	−197.8	−308.2	−320.7	−470.2	−664.3	−353.1
% of total	10.9%	14.7%	13.8%	19.2%	23.8%	12.6%

Imports (1994): U.S.$1,579,900,000 (1987; machinery and transport equipment 28.1%; mineral fuels and lubricants 14.0%; chemicals 12.0%; food and live animals 5.2%; beverages and tobacco 0.4%). *Major import sources:* Germany 13.7%; United Kingdom 12.1%; United States 11.7%; France 5.4%; Italy 4.8%.
Exports (1994): U.S.$1,226,800,000 (gold 44.7%; food and live animals 26.3%, of which cocoa 26.1%; logs and sawn timber 13.5%; electricity 4.6%; diamonds 1.7%). *Major export destinations:* United Kingdom 15.5%; Italy 7.9%; Japan 6.7%; United States 6.6%; Germany 5.5%; France 4.0%; The Netherlands 3.5%.

Transport and communications

Transport. Railroads (1993): route length 592 mi, 953 km; passenger-mi 731,400,000, passenger-km 1,177,000,000; short ton-mi cargo 93,906,000, metric ton-km cargo 137,100,000. Roads (1992): total length 22,800 mi, 36,700 km (paved 32%). Vehicles (1993): passenger cars 90,000; trucks and buses 44,200. Merchant marine (1992): vessels (100 gross tons and over) 155; total deadweight tonnage 130,977. Air transport (1993): passenger-mi 240,000,000, passenger-km 387,000,000; short ton-mi cargo 14,000,000, metric ton-km cargo 20,000,000; airports (1996) with scheduled flights 1.
Communications. Daily newspapers (1993): total number 4; total circulation 1,060,000; circulation per 1,000 population 68. Radio (1995): 4,300,000 receivers (1 per 3.8 persons). Television (1995): 250,000 receivers (1 per 66 persons). Telephones (main lines; 1993): 48,700 (1 per 321 persons).

Education and health

Education (1991–92)

	schools	teachers	students	student/ teacher ratio
Primary (6–12)	11,056	66,068	1,796,490	27.2
Secondary (13–20)	5,540	43,367	816,578	18.8
Voc., teacher tr.[8]	57	422	13,232	31.4
Higher[8]	16	700	9,274	13.2

Educational attainment (1984). Percentage of population age 25 and over having: no formal schooling 60.4%; primary education 7.1%; middle school 25.4%; secondary 3.5%; vocational and other postsecondary 2.9%; higher 0.6%. *Literacy* (1990): total population age 15 and over literate 4,960,000 (60.4%); males literate 2,835,000 (70.0%); females literate 2,125,000 (50.9%).
Health: physicians (1989) 628 (1 per 22,452 persons); hospital beds (1991) 18,477 (1 per 791 persons); infant mortality rate per 1,000 live births (1994) 83.
Food (1992): daily per capita caloric intake 2,199 (vegetable products 95%, animal products 5%); 96% of FAO minimum recommended requirement.

Military

Total active duty personnel (1995): 7,000 (army 71.4%, navy 14.3%, air force 14.3%). *Military expenditure as percentage of GNP* (1994): 0.7% (world 3.0%); per capita expenditure U.S.$2.

---

[1]January 1. [2]Government administration has been decentralized to the local level of 103 district assemblies, 4 municipal assemblies, and 3 metropolitan assemblies. [3]Detail does not add to total given because of rounding. [4]1994. [5]Unofficial 1978 exchange rate (7.5 to 9.9 times the official rate) does not permit meaningful conversion into other currencies. [6]Import duties and statistical adjustments less imputed bank service charges. [7]Unemployed only. [8]1989–90.

Greece

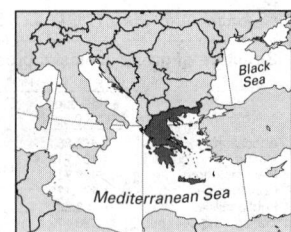

Official name: Ellinikí Dhimokratía (Hellenic Republic).
Form of government: unitary multiparty republic with one legislative house (Greek Chamber of Deputies [300]).
Chief of state: President.
Head of government: Prime Minister.
Capital: Athens.
Official language: Greek.
Official religion: Eastern Orthodox.
Monetary unit: 1 drachma (Dr) = 100 lepta; valuation (Oct. 11, 1996) 1 U.S.$ = Dr 239.98; 1 £ = Dr 378.04.

Area and population		area		population
		sq mi	sq km	1991 census
Regions				
Anatolikí Makedhonía kaí Thráki	(Eastern Macedonia and Thrace)	5,466	14,157	570,496
Attikí	(Attica)	1,470	3,808	3,523,407
Dhytikí Ellás	(Western Greece)	4,382	11,350	707,687
Dhytikí Makedhonía	(Western Macedonia)	3,649	9,451	293,015
Iónioi Nísoi	(Ionian Islands)	891	2,307	193,734
Ípiros	(Epirus)	3,553	9,203	339,728
Kedrikí Makedhonía[1]	(Central Macedonia)	7,393	19,147	1,710,513
Kríti	(Crete)	3,218	8,336	540,054
Nótion Aiyaíon	(Southern Aegean)	2,041	5,286	257,481
Pelopónnisos	(Peloponnesos)	5,981	15,490	607,428
Stereá Ellás	(Central Greece)	6,004	15,549	582,280
Thessalía	(Thessaly)	5,420	14,037	734,846
Vóreion Aiyaíon	(Northern Aegean)	1,481	3,836	199,231
TOTAL		50,949	131,957	10,259,900

Demography

Population (1996): 10,493,000.
Density (1996): persons per sq mi 206.0, persons per sq km 79.5.
Urban-rural (1995): urban 65.2%; rural 34.8%.
Sex distribution (1995): male 49.24%; female 50.76%.
Age breakdown (1994): under 15, 17.4%; 15–29, 22.6%; 30–44, 20.6%; 45–59, 18.1%; 60–74, 15.2%; 75 and over, 6.1%.
Population projection: (2000) 10,646,000; (2010) 11,037,000.
Doubling time: not applicable; doubling time exceeds 100 years.
Ethnic composition (1983): Greek 95.5%; Macedonian 1.5%; Turkish 0.9%; Albanian 0.6%; other 1.5%.
Religious affiliation (1980): Christian 98.1%, of which Eastern Orthodox 97.6%, Roman Catholic 0.4%, Protestant 0.1%; Muslim 1.5%; other 0.4%.
Major cities (1991): Athens 772,072; Thessaloníki 383,967; Piraeus (Piraiévs) 182,671; Pátrai 152,570; Peristérion 137,288.

Vital statistics

Birth rate per 1,000 population (1995): 9.8 (world avg. 25.0); (1994) legitimate 97.1%; illegitimate 2.9%.
Death rate per 1,000 population (1995): 9.4 (world avg. 9.3).
Natural increase rate per 1,000 population (1995): 0.4 (world avg. 15.7).
Total fertility rate (avg. births per childbearing woman; 1993): 1.4.
Marriage rate per 1,000 population (1994): 5.4.
Divorce rate per 1,000 population (1990): 0.6.
Life expectancy at birth (1990): male 74.6 years; female 79.8 years.
Major causes of death per 100,000 population (1994): malignant neoplasms (cancers) 206.9; diseases of pulmonary circulation and other forms of heart disease 185.2; cerebrovascular disease 178.5; ischemic heart disease 115.1.

National economy

Budget (1995). Revenue: Dr 12,792,300,000,000[2] (indirect and excise taxes 30.8%, direct taxes 17.4%, European Community 3.5%). Expenditures: Dr 12,801,276,000,000 (1993; health and social insurance 13.7%, defense 7.9%, education and culture 6.6%, police and other sectors 2.1%).
Public debt (1993): U.S.$16,193,000,000.
Tourism (1994): receipts from visitors U.S.$3,905,000,000; expenditures by nationals abroad U.S.$1,125,000,000.
Production (metric tons except as noted). Agriculture, forestry, fishing (1996): sugar beets 2,500,000, wheat 2,000,000, corn (maize) 2,000,000, tomatoes 1,920,000, olives 1,600,000, grapes 1,169,000, peaches and nectarines 1,040,000, potatoes 898,000, oranges 870,000, barley 440,000, apples 280,000, cabbages 180,000, rice 170,000, cucumbers 160,000; livestock (number of live animals) 9,559,000 sheep, 6,220,000 goats, 1,121,000 pigs, 600,000 cattle, 28,000,000 chickens; roundwood (1994) 2,779,000 cu m; fish catch (1993) 199,607. Mining and quarrying (1995): nickel ore 2,000,000; bauxite 1,916,000; zinc 25,000[3]; lead 20,000[3]; chromium ore 5,650[3, 4]. Manufacturing (value added in Dr; 1994): food, beverages, and tobacco 777,600,000,000; chemicals 353,000,000,000; textiles 254,600,000,000; transport equipment 193,919,000,000; paper and printing 181,709,000,000; clothing and footwear 144,300,000,000. Construction (value of completed buildings in Dr; 1992): residential 18,391,000,000; nonresidential 28,062,400,000. Energy production (consumption): electricity (kW-hr; 1994) 40,623,000,000 (41,005,000,000); coal (metric tons; 1994) 56,741,000 (59,569,000); crude petroleum (barrels; 1994) 3,589,000 (102,721,000); petroleum products (metric tons; 1994) 15,078,000 (14,311,000); natural gas (cu m; 1994) 55,047,000 (55,047,000).
Household income and expenditure. Average household size (1993–94) 2.9; income per household Dr 3,900,000 (U.S.$15,660); sources of income (1994): property and entrepreneurial income 54.5%, wages and salaries 27.9%, transfer payments 17.6%; expenditure: food, beverages, and tobacco 35.7%,

transportation 14.7%, clothing and footwear 13.0%, housing 8.6%, education 6.5%, other 21.5%.
Gross national product (1994): U.S.$80,194,000,000 (U.S.$7,710 per capita).

Structure of gross domestic product and labour force				
	1994			
	in value Dr '000,000	% of total value	labour force	% of labour force
Agriculture	2,387,103	14.9	789,700	18.8
Mining	186,238	1.2	15,600	0.4
Manufacturing	2,399,528	15.0	577,800	13.8
Construction	1,008,850	6.3	261,200	6.2
Public utilities	405,221	2.5	40,600	1.0
Transp. and commun.	1,142,953	7.2	252,300	6.0
Trade	2,162,625	13.5	814,200	19.4
Finance	477,150	3.0	231,000	5.5
Pub. admin., defense	3,015,986	18.9 }	807,300	19.2
Services	1,535,408	9.6 }		
Other	1,258,010[5]	7.9[5]	403,800[6]	9.6[6]
TOTAL	15,979,071[7]	100.0	4,193,400[7]	100.0[7]

Population economically active (1994): total 4,118,400; activity rate of total population 40.2% (participation rates: ages 15–64, 59.4%[8]; female 37.5%; unemployed 9.6%).

Price and earnings indexes (1990 = 100)							
	1989	1990	1991	1992	1993	1994	1995
Consumer price index	83.1	100.0	119.5	138.4	158.4	175.7	192.0
Hourly earnings index	83.8	100.0	116.7	132.8	146.7	165.9	187.9

Land use (1994): forested 20.3%; meadows and pastures 40.7%; agricultural and under permanent cultivation 27.2%; other 11.8%.

Foreign trade

Balance of trade (current prices)						
	1989	1990	1991	1992	1993	1994
Dr '000,000,000	−1,199.2	−1,613.3	−1,886.1	−2,113.5	−2,536.2	−2,331.9
% of total	30.8%	44.3%	37.3%	36.8%	39.6%	33.9%

Imports (1994): Dr 5,207,600,000,000 (machinery and transport equipment 31.9%, of which transport equipment 8.7%; food, beverages, and tobacco 14.7%, of which meat products 4.4%, dairy products 1.1%; chemical products 9.5%, of which plastic products 1.0%; crude petroleum 6.3%). *Major import sources:* Germany 18.3%; Italy 15.3%; U.S. 9.1%; France 8.2%; The Netherlands 7.3%; U.K. 6.6%; Belgium-Luxembourg 3.3%; Saudi Arabia 2.9%.
Exports (1994): Dr 2,276,600,000,000 (food, beverages, and tobacco 28.9%, of which olives and olive oil 3.7%, tobacco 2.3%; textiles 23.8%; petroleum products 11.6%; minerals and ores 4.5%; cotton 3.7%). *Major export destinations:* Germany 25.9%; U.S. 17.2%; Italy 11.3%; France 6.6%; U.K. 6.4%; The Netherlands 2.4%.

Transport and communications

Transport. Railroads (1993): route length 1,552 mi, 2,497 km; passenger-mi 1,072,000,000, passenger-km 1,726,000,000; short ton-mi cargo 358,000,000, metric ton-km cargo 523,000,000. Roads (1992): total length 72,170 mi, 116,150 km (paved 92%). Vehicles (1994): passenger cars 2,075,605; trucks and buses 873,647. Merchant marine (1994): vessels (100 gross tons and over) 2,149; total deadweight tonnage 30,536,000. Air transport (1994): passenger-mi 5,234,133,000, passenger-km 8,428,537,000; short ton-mi cargo 92,465,000, metric ton-km cargo 134,997,000; airports (1996) with scheduled flights 36.
Communications. Daily newspapers (1992): total number 145; total circulation 1,400,000; circulation per 1,000 population 136. Radio (1995): 4,200,000 receivers (1 per 2.5 persons). Television (1995): 2,300,000 receivers (1 per 4.5 persons). Telephones (1993): 5,571,293 (1 per 1.9 persons).

Education and health

Education (1992–93)	schools	teachers	students	student/ teacher ratio
Primary (age 6–12)	7,634	37,549	745,666	19.9
Secondary (age 12–18)	2,988	45,794	700,488	15.3
Voc., teacher tr.	695	14,319	190,443	13.3
Higher[9]	17	9,124	115,464	12.6

Educational attainment (1991). Percentage of population age 25 and over having: no formal schooling (illiterate) 6.8%; some primary education 10.6%; completed primary 39.7%; lower secondary 10.8%; higher secondary 20.6%; some postsecondary 4.9%; a degree from institution of higher education 6.6%. *Literacy* (1991): total population age 15 and over literate 7,870,000 (95.2%); males literate 3,900,000 (97.7%); females literate 3,970,000 (93.0%).
Health: physicians (1993) 40,116 (1 per 259 persons); hospital beds (1992) 51,422 (1 per 201 persons); infant mortality rate per 1,000 live births (1995) 7.9.
Food (1992): daily per capita caloric intake 3,815 (vegetable products 75%, animal products 25%); 153% of FAO recommended minimum requirement.

Military

Total active duty personnel (1996): 168,300 (army 72.5%, navy 11.6%, air force 15.9%). *Military expenditure as percentage of GNP* (1994): 5.6% (world 3.0%); per capita expenditure U.S.$411.

[1]Includes Mount Athos (Áyion Óros), an autonomous, self-governing monastic region; 1991 population 1,557. [2]Includes Dr 4,772,500,000,000 of domestic borrowing. [3]Metal content of ore. [4]1994. [5]Income from ownership of buildings. [6]Unemployed. [7]Detail does not add to total given because of rounding. [8]1993. [9]1991–92.

Grenada

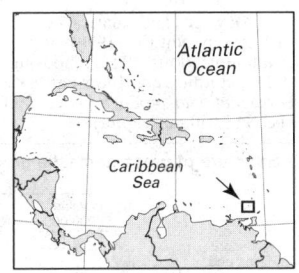

Official name: Grenada.
Form of government: constitutional monarchy with two legislative houses (Senate [13]; House of Representatives [15[1]]).
Chief of state: British Monarch represented by Governor-General.
Head of government: Prime Minister.
Capital: St. George's.
Official language: English.
Official religion: none.
Monetary unit: 1 East Caribbean dollar (EC$) = 100 cents; valuation (Oct. 11, 1996) 1 U.S.$ = EC$2.70; 1 £ = EC$4.25.

Area and population

Local Councils	Principal towns	area sq mi	area sq km	population 1991 census
Carriacou	Hillsborough	10	26	} 5,726
Petite Martinique	...	3	8	
St. Andrew	Grenville	38	99	24,135
St. David	...	17	44	11,011
St. George	...	25[2]	65[2]	27,373
St. John	Gouyave	14	35	8,752
St. Mark	Victoria	10	25	3,861
St. Patrick	Sauteurs	16	42	10,118
Town				
St. George's	—	2	2	4,621
TOTAL		133	344	95,597

Demography

Population (1996): 97,900.
Density (1996): persons per sq mi 736.1, persons per sq km 284.6.
Urban-rural (1991)[3]: urban 33.5%; rural 66.5%.
Sex distribution (1991): male 49.20%; female 50.80%.
Age breakdown (1991): under 15, 38.4%; 15–29, 25.8%; 30–44, 16.1%; 45–59, 8.9%; 60–74, 7.6%; 75 and over, 3.2%.
Population projection: (2000) 100,000; (2010) 104,000.
Doubling time: 29 years.
Ethnic composition (1991): black 84.9%; mixed 11.0%; Indo-Pakistani 3.0%; white 0.7%; other 0.4%.
Religious affiliation (1991): Roman Catholic 53.1%; Protestant 38.1%, of which Anglican 13.9%, Seventh-day Adventist 8.6%, Pentecostal 7.2%; other/not stated 7.4%; no religion 1.4%.
Major localities (1991): St. George's 4,621; Gouyave 3,000[4]; Grenville 2,000[4].

Vital statistics

Birth rate per 1,000 population (1995): 29.7 (world avg. 25.0); (1987) legitimate 18.1%; illegitimate 81.9%.
Death rate per 1,000 population (1995): 6.0 (world avg. 9.3).
Natural increase rate per 1,000 population (1995): 23.7 (world avg. 15.7).
Total fertility rate (avg. births per childbearing woman; 1995): 3.8.
Marriage rate per 1,000 population (1991): 4.3.
Divorce rate per 1,000 population (1991): 0.8.
Life expectancy at birth (1995): male 68.2 years; female 73.2 years.
Major causes of death per 100,000 population (1987): diseases of the circulatory system 264.3; malignant neoplasms (cancers) 82.8; endocrine and metabolic diseases 57.3; diseases of the respiratory system 45.6; diseases of the digestive system 38.2; ill-defined conditions 209.1.

National economy

Budget (1995). Revenue[5]: EC$179,300,000 (taxes on international trade 50.2%, personal income taxes 10.8%, corporate income taxes 8.4%). Expenditures[6]: EC$294,000,000 (public works 15.3%, education 12.9%, health 8.8%, agriculture and fisheries 7.1%).
Public debt (external, outstanding; 1994): U.S.$96,600,000.
Tourism (1994): receipts from visitors U.S.$72,400,000; expenditures by nationals abroad U.S.$4,000,000.
Gross national product (at current market prices; 1994): U.S.$241,000,000 (U.S.$2,620 per capita).

Structure of gross domestic product and labour force

	1995 in value EC$'000,000[7]	1995 % of total value	1991 labour force[8]	1991 % of labour force
Agriculture	61.7	11.9	4,223	17.1
Quarrying	2.6	0.5	126	0.5
Manufacturing	30.7	5.9	1,881	7.6
Construction	36.5	7.0	3,168	12.9
Public utilities	22.4	4.3	350	1.4
Transportation and communications	117.4	22.6	1,614	6.5
Trade, restaurants	109.5	21.1	5,149	20.9
Finance, real estate	67.6	13.0	866	3.5
Pub. admin., defense	89.1	17.1	1,738	7.1
Services	15.1	2.9	3,372	13.7
Other	−32.7[9]	−6.3[9]	2,163	8.8
TOTAL	519.9[10]	100.0	24,650	100.0

Production (metric tons except as noted). Agriculture, forestry, fishing (1995): coconuts 7,000, sugarcane 7,000, bananas 4,431, roots and tubers 4,000, nutmeg 2,140, mangoes 2,000, avocados 2,000, grapefruit 2,000, cacao 1,809, mace 95, other crops include cotton, limes, cinnamon, cloves, and pimiento; livestock (number of live animals) 12,000 sheep, 11,000 goats, 4,000 cattle; roundwood, n.a.; fish catch (1993) 2,093. Mining and quarrying: excavation of gravel for local use. Manufacturing (value of production in EC$'000; 1995): wheat flour 10,174; soft drinks 8,558; beer 7,172; animal feed 4,698; rum 4,520; other products include clothing, edible coconut oil, paints, pharmaceutical products, and cigarettes. Construction: n.a. Energy production (consumption): electricity (kW-hr; 1993) 65,000,000 (65,000,000); coal, none (none); crude petroleum, none (none); petroleum products (metric tons; 1993) none (43,000); natural gas, none (none).
Household income and expenditure. Average household size (1991) 3.7; income per household (1988) EC$7,097 (U.S.$2,629); sources of income: n.a.; expenditure (1987): food, beverages, and tobacco 40.7%, household furnishings and operations 13.7%, housing 11.9%, transportation 9.1%, personal effects and medical care 8.6%.
Population economically active (1988): total 38,920; activity rate of total population 39.9% (participation rates: ages 15–65, 72.7%; female 48.6%; unemployed [1994] 16.7%).

Price and earnings indexes (1990 = 100)

	1989	1990	1991	1992	1993	1994	1995
Consumer price index	97.3	100.0	102.7	106.5	109.5	112.4	114.9
Annual earnings index[11]	...	100.0	108.0	118.8	124.1	131.5	...

Land use (1993): forested 9.0%; meadows and pastures 3.0%; agricultural and under permanent cultivation 32.0%; other 56.0%.

Foreign trade[12]

Balance of trade (current prices)

	1990	1991	1992	1993	1994	1995
U.S.$'000,000	−82.6	−102.6	−94.5	−111.7	−123.1	−112.7
% of total	61.2%	67.3%	68.7%	72.2%	71.4%	72.3%

Imports (1995): U.S.$134,300,000 (food 23.8%; machinery and transport equipment 19.7%; basic manufactures 17.3%; chemicals and chemical products 7.9%). *Major import sources* (1994)[13]: Trinidad and Tobago 36%; United States 22%; United Kingdom 10%; Barbados 3%.
Exports (1995): U.S.$21,600,000 (domestic exports 89.4%, of which fish 15.7%, cocoa beans 15.3%, nutmeg 14.4%, bananas 8.8%, clothing 6.0%; reexports 10.6%). *Major export destinations* (1994)[13]: United States 28%; Venezuela 14%; United Kingdom 14%; St. Lucia 7%.

Transport and communications

Transport. Railroads: none. Roads (1993): total length 650 mi, 1,046 km (paved 66%). Vehicles (1991)[14]: passenger cars 4,739; trucks and buses 3,068. Merchant marine (1992): vessels (100 gross tons and over) 3; total deadweight tonnage 484. Air transport (1993)[15]: passenger arrivals and departures 277,000; cargo loaded and unloaded 2,300 metric tons; airports (1996) with scheduled flights 2.
Communications. Daily newspapers: none[16]. Radio (1995): total number of receivers 45,000 (1 per 2.2 persons). Television (1995): total number of receivers 15,000 (1 per 6.6 persons). Telephones (main lines; 1993): 20,100 (1 per 4.8 persons).

Education and health

Education (1993–94)

	schools	teachers	students	student/ teacher ratio
Primary (age 5–11)[17]	57	781	21,311	27.3
Secondary (age 12–16)	19	352	6,939	19.7
Vocational	...	...	...	...
Higher	1	66	651	9.9

Educational attainment (1991). Percentage of population age 25 and over having: no formal schooling 1.8%; primary education 74.9%; secondary 15.5%; higher 4.7%, of which university 2.8%; other/unknown 3.1%. *Literacy* (1992): total population age 15 and over literate 50,000 (85.0%).
Health: physicians (1991) 63 (1 per 1,517 persons); hospital beds (1992) 401 (1 per 240 persons); infant mortality rate per 1,000 live births (1995) 12.1.
Food (1992): daily per capita caloric intake 2,402 (vegetable products 79%, animal products 21%); 99% of FAO recommended minimum requirement.

Military

Total active duty personnel (1993): [18]. *Military expenditure as percentage of GNP:* n.a.; per capita expenditure, n.a.

[1]Excludes the speaker, who may be elected from outside its elected membership. [2]St. George local council includes St. George's town. [3]Urban defined as St. George's town and St. George local council. [4]1987. [5]Current revenue only. [6]Current and development expenditures. [7]At factor cost in 1990 prices. [8]Employed persons only. [9]Less imputed bank service charges. [10]Detail does not add to total given because of rounding. [11]Private sector only. [12]Imports c.i.f.; exports f.o.b. [13]Estimated figure(s). [14]Registered vehicles only. [15]Point Salines airport. [16]Weekly newspapers (1993): 5. [17]Excludes private schools. [18]The 750-member police force includes a paramilitary unit and a coast guard unit.

Guadeloupe

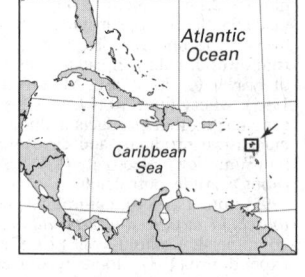

Atlantic Ocean

Caribbean Sea

Official name: Département de la Guadeloupe (Department of Guadeloupe).
Political status: overseas department (France[1]) with two legislative houses (General Council [43]; Regional Council [41]).
Chief of state: President of France.
Heads of government: Commissioner of the Republic (for France); President of the General Council (for Guadeloupe); President of the Regional Council (for Guadeloupe).
Capital: Basse-Terre.
Official language: French.
Official religion: none.
Monetary unit: 1 French franc (F)=100 centimes; valuation (Oct. 11, 1996) 1 U.S.$=F 5.18; 1 £=F 8.16.

Area and population

Arrondissements	Capitals	area sq mi	area sq km	population 1990 census
Basse-Terre[2]	Basse-Terre	332	861	151,979
Pointe-à-Pitre[3]	Pointe-à-Pitre	297	769	192,643
Saint-Martin–Saint-Barthélemy[4]	Marigot	29	75	33,556
TOTAL		687[5]	1,780[5]	378,178[6]

Demography

Population (1996): 427,000.
Density (1996): persons per sq mi 621.5, persons per sq km 239.9.
Urban-rural (1995)[7]: urban 99.4%; rural 0.6%.
Sex distribution (1995): male 48.83%; female 51.17%.
Age breakdown (1995): under 15, 26.1%; 15–29, 27.5%; 30–44, 22.3%; 45–59, 13.1%; 60–74, 7.7%; 75 and over, 3.3%.
Population projection: (2000) 454,000; (2010) 530,000.
Doubling time: 58 years.
Ethnic composition (1991): Creole (mulatto) 77.0%; black 10.0%; Guadeloupe mestizo (French–East Asian) 10.0%; white 2.0%; other 1.0%.
Religious affiliation (1994[8]): Roman Catholic 90.4%; other 9.6%.
Major communes (1990): Les Abymes 62,605; Saint-Martin 28,518; Pointe-à-Pitre 26,029 (141,000[9, 10]); Le Gosier 20,688; Basse-Terre 14,003 (53,000[9]).

Vital statistics

Birth rate per 1,000 population (1994): 17.4 (world avg. 25.0); legitimate 38.7%; illegitimate 61.3%.
Death rate per 1,000 population (1994): 5.6 (world avg. 9.3).
Natural increase rate per 1,000 population (1994): 11.8 (world avg. 15.7).
Total fertility rate (avg. births per childbearing woman; 1990–95): 2.2.
Marriage rate per 1,000 population (1994): 4.6.
Divorce rate per 1,000 population (1994): 1.3.
Life expectancy at birth (1990–95): male 71.1 years; female 78.0 years.
Major causes of death per 100,000 population (1991): diseases of the circulatory system 175.7; malignant neoplasms (cancers) 114.9; accidents, violence, and poisoning 70.1; diseases of the digestive system 29.4; diseases of the respiratory system 22.3.

National economy

Budget (1994). Revenue: F 2,971,000,000 (tax revenues 64.8%, of which direct taxes 33.7%; advances, loans, and transfers 29.8%; nontax revenues 4.6%). Expenditures: F 6,199,000,000 (current expenditures 65.6%; capital [development] expenditures 17.2%; advances and loans 17.1%).
Public debt (external, outstanding; 1990[11]): U.S.$58,000,000.
Tourism (1994): receipts from visitors U.S.$490,000,000; expenditures by nationals abroad, n.a.
Production (metric tons except as noted). Agriculture, forestry, fishing (1995): sugarcane 376,000, bananas 115,000, yams 7,000, plantains 6,000, sweet potatoes 5,000, pineapples 4,000, cucumbers 4,000, tomatoes 3,000, melons 3,000; livestock (number of live animals) 63,000 goats, 60,000 cattle, 14,000 pigs; roundwood (1994) 15,300 cu m; fish catch (1993) 7,990. Mining and quarrying (1993): pumice 210,000. Manufacturing (1994): cement 282,943; raw sugar 45,356; rum 49,224 hectolitres; other products include clothing, wooden furniture and posts, and metalware. Construction (buildings authorized; 1992): residential 358,474 sq m; nonresidential 160,084 sq m. Energy production (consumption): electricity (kW-hr; 1995) 1,053,500,000 (969,800,000); coal, none (none); crude petroleum, none (none); petroleum products (metric tons; 1994) none (446,000); natural gas, none (none).
Population economically active (1992): total 181,000; activity rate of total population 44.0% (participation rates [1990]: ages 15–64, 68.0%; female 45.5%; unemployed [1993] 26.1%).

Price and earnings indexes (1990 = 100)[12]

	1990	1991	1992	1993	1994	1995	1996[13]
Consumer price index	100.0	102.0	104.5	106.7	110.8	114.3	113.5
Monthly earnings index[14]	100.0	102.0	104.7	105.0	106.5	108.7[15]	109.6

Household income and expenditure. Average household size (1990) 3.4; income per household (1988) F 105,400 (U.S.$17,700); sources of income

(1988): wages and salaries 78.9%, self-employment 12.7%, transfer payments 8.4%; expenditure (1990): food and beverages 30.9%, transportation and communications 20.5%, housing and lighting 11.3%, household durables 9.3%, clothing and footwear 9.3%, energy and fuel 7.7%.
Gross national product (at current market prices; 1990): U.S.$1,160,000,000 (U.S.$2,970 per capita).

Structure of gross domestic product and labour force

	1989 in value F '000,000	1989 % of total value	1993 labour force	1993 % of labour force
Agriculture	1,177.4	9.2	9,079	5.2
Mining and manufacturing	758.4	5.9	10,376	5.9
Construction	949.3	7.4	15,564	8.9
Public utilities	38.7	0.3	...	...
Transportation and communications	773.3	6.1	54,474	31.0
Trade	2,499.6	19.6		
Finance, real estate	848.8	6.6		
Pub. admin., defense	4,242.4	33.2	40,207	22.9
Services	2,056.6	16.1		
Other	−563.3[16]	−4.4[16]	45,800[17]	26.1[17]
TOTAL	12,781.2	100.0	175,500	100.0

Land use (1994): forested 39.1%; meadows and pastures 14.2%; agricultural and under permanent cultivation 16.0%; other 30.7%.

Foreign trade

Balance of trade (current prices)

	1990	1991	1992	1993	1994	1995
F '000,000	−8,439	−8,209	−7,505	−7,309	−7,693	−8,655
% of total	86.3%	79.8%	83.8%	83.2%	82.0%	84.3%

Imports (1995): F 9,459,000,000 ([1994] consumer goods 27.8%, food and agriculture products 22.9%, machinery and equipment 17.8%, transport vehicles and parts 11.9%). *Major import sources* (1994): France 66.7%; other EEC 14.2%; United States 3.1%; Martinique 2.6%; Japan 2.4%.
Exports (1995): F 804,000,000 (bananas 25.4%, sugar 11.4%, rum 4.4%, melons 2.9%). *Major export destinations* (1994): France 75.5%; Martinique 13.4%; other EEC 4.4%; French Guiana 2.4%.

Transport and communications

Transport. Railroads: none. Roads (1996): total length 1,988 mi, 3,200 km (paved [1986] 80%). Vehicles (1992): passenger cars 94,700; trucks and buses 36,000. Merchant marine (1992): vessels (100 gross tons and over) 20; deadweight tonnage 4,430. Air transport (1995): passenger arrivals and departures 1,540,543; cargo loaded 9,140 metric tons, cargo unloaded 4,823 metric tons; airports (1996) with scheduled flights 7.
Communications. Daily newspapers (1995): total number 1; total circulation 20,000; circulation per 1,000 population 48. Radio (1995): total number of receivers 85,000 (1 per 5.1 persons). Television (1995): total number of receivers 150,000 (1 per 2.8 persons). Telephones (main lines; 1994): 152,435 (1 per 2.7 persons).

Education and health

Education (1992–93)

	schools	teachers	students	student/teacher ratio
Primary (age 6–10)	340	3,135	39,075	12.5
Secondary (age 11–17) Vocational	78	3,813	49,295	12.9
Higher[18]	1	310	4,296	13.9

Educational attainment (1990). Percentage of population age 25 and over having: incomplete primary, or no declaration 59.8%; primary education 14.5%; secondary 19.0%; higher 6.7%. *Literacy* (1982): total population age 15 and over literate 225,400 (90.1%); males literate 108,700 (89.7%); females literate 116,700 (90.5%).
Health: physicians 590 (1 per 680 persons); hospital beds 3,230 (1 per 122 persons); infant mortality rate per 1,000 live births (1994) 7.9.
Food (1992): daily per capita caloric intake 2,682 (vegetable products 77%, animal products 23%); 111% of FAO recommended minimum requirement.

Military

Total active duty personnel (1994): 535 French troops.

[1]Guadeloupe elects 4 deputies and 2 senators to French parliament. [2]Comprises Basse-Terre 327 sq mi (848 sq km), pop. 149,943, and Îles des Saintes 5 sq mi (13 sq km), pop. 2,036. [3]Comprises Grande-Terre 228 sq mi (590 sq km), pop. 177,570; Marie-Galante 61 sq mi (158 sq km), pop. 13,463; La Désirade 8 sq mi (20 sq km), pop. 1,610; and the uninhabited Îles de la Petite-Terre. [4]Comprises the French part of Saint-Martin 20 sq mi (52 sq km), pop. 28,518; Saint-Barthélemy 8 sq mi (21 sq km), pop. 5,038; and the small, uninhabited island of Tintamarre. [5]Total area includes 29 sq mi (75 sq km) not allocated by arrondissement. [6]Preliminary; final 1990 census total was 386,987. [7]Urban defined as locality with 2,000 or more inhabitants. [8]January 1. [9]Urban agglomeration. [10]Includes Les Abymes. [11]Includes external long-term private debt not guaranteed by the government. [12]Base and indexes are end of year unless footnoted. [13]March. [14]Based on minimum-level wage of public employees. [15]June. [16]Less imputed bank service charges. [17]Unemployed. [18]University of Antilles–French Guiana, Guadeloupe campus.

Guatemala

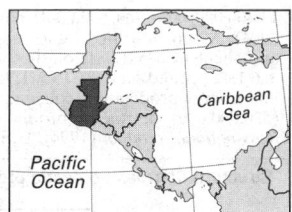

Official name: República de Guatemala (Republic of Guatemala).
Form of government: republic with one legislative house (Congress of the Republic [80]).
Head of state and government: President.
Capital: Guatemala City.
Official language: Spanish.
Official religion: none.
Monetary unit: 1 quetzal (Q) = 100 centavos; valuation (Oct. 11, 1996) 1 U.S.$ = Q 6.07; 1 £ = Q 9.56.

Area and population

Departments	Capitals	area sq mi	area sq km	population 1994 census[1]
Alta Verapaz	Cobán	3,354	8,686	543,777
Baja Verapaz	Salamá	1,206	3,124	155,480
Chimaltenango	Chimaltenango	764	1,979	314,813
Chiquimula	Chiquimula	917	2,376	230,767
El Progreso	Guastatoya (Progreso)	742	1,922	108,400
Escuintla	Escuintla	1,693	4,384	386,534
Guatemala	Guatemala City	821	2,126	1,813,825
Huehuetenango	Huehuetenango	2,857	7,400	634,374
Izabal	Puerto Barrios	3,490	9,038	253,153
Jalapa	Jalapa	797	2,063	196,940
Jutiapa	Jutiapa	1,243	3,219	307,491
Petén	Flores	13,843	35,854	224,884
Quetzaltenango	Quetzaltenango	753	1,951	503,857
Quiché	Santa Cruz del Quiché	3,235	8,378	437,669
Retalhuleu	Retalhuleu	717	1,856	188,764
Sacatepéquez	Antigua Guatemala	180	465	180,647
San Marcos	San Marcos	1,464	3,791	645,418
Santa Rosa	Cuilapa	1,141	2,955	246,698
Sololá	Sololá	410	1,061	222,094
Suchitepéquez	Mazatenango	969	2,510	307,187
Totonicapán	Totonicapán	410	1,061	272,094
Zacapa	Zacapa	1,039	2,690	157,008
TOTAL		42,042[2]	108,889	8,331,874

Demography

Population (1996): 10,928,000[3].
Density (1996): persons per sq mi 252.6, persons per sq km 97.5.
Urban-rural (1994): urban 35.0%; rural 65.0%.
Sex distribution (1994): male 49.25%; female 50.75%.
Age breakdown (1994): under 15, 44.0%; 15–29, 26.1%; 30–44, 15.8%; 45–59, 8.3%; 60 and over, 5.8%.
Population projection: (2000) 12,222,000; (2010) 15,827,000.
Doubling time: 24 years.
Ethnic composition (1994): Amerindian 42.8%; non-Amerindian 57.2%.
Religious affiliation (1986): Roman Catholic c. 75%, of which Catholic/traditional syncretist c. 25%; Protestant (mostly fundamentalist) c. 25%.
Major cities (1995): Guatemala City 1,167,495; Mixco 436,668; Villa Nueva 165,567; Chinautla 61,335; Amatitlán 40,229.

Vital statistics

Birth rate per 1,000 population (1994): 35.4 (world avg. 25.0).
Death rate per 1,000 population (1994): 7.5 (world avg. 9.3).
Natural increase rate per 1,000 population (1994): 27.9 (world avg. 15.7).
Total fertility rate (avg. births per childbearing woman; 1994): 4.8.
Marriage rate per 1,000 population (1991): 5.0.
Divorce rate per 1,000 population (1988): 0.2.
Life expectancy at birth (1994): male 61.9 years; female 67.1 years.
Major causes of death per 100,000 population (1988): infectious and parasitic diseases 121.6; diseases of the respiratory system 110.8; perinatal causes 58.7; malnutrition 50.2; dehydration 18.5.

National economy

Budget (1995). Revenue: Q 7,227,700,000 (tax revenue 91.0%, of which taxes on goods and services 46.5%, customs duties 23.1%, income taxes 19.1%; nontax revenue 8.6%). Expenditures: Q 6,648,200,000 (current expenditures 71.3%, of which disbursements for goods and services 47.2%, transfer payments 24.1%; capital expenditures 28.7%).
Public debt (external, outstanding; 1994): U.S.$2,368,000,000.
Tourism (1994): receipts from visitors U.S.$258,000,000; expenditures by nationals abroad U.S.$161,000,000.
Land use (1994): forested 53.6%; meadows and pastures 24.0%; agricultural and under permanent cultivation 17.6%; other 4.8%.
Production (metric tons except as noted). Agriculture, forestry, fishing (1995): sugarcane 12,499,000, corn (maize) 1,350,000, bananas 535,000, coffee 210,000, tomatoes 140,000, dry beans 109,000, sorghum 88,000, plantains 50,000, seed cotton 37,000; livestock (number of live animals) 1,700,000 cattle, 889,000 pigs, 440,000 sheep; roundwood (1994) 13,393,000 cu m; fish catch (1993) 8,147. Mining and quarrying (1994): gypsum (1993) 60,000; iron ore 3,498; antimony ore 494. Manufacturing (value added in Q '000,000; 1989[4]): food products 138.0; beverages 66.2; clothing and footwear 47.6; textiles 43.2; metal products 30.2. Construction (value of buildings authorized in Q '000,000; 1991)[5]: residential 170.2; nonresidential 127.5. Energy production (consumption): electricity (kW-hr; 1993) 3,084,000,000 (3,084,000,000); crude petroleum (barrels; 1993) 2,538,000 (5,472,000); petroleum products (metric tons; 1993) 690,000 (1,497,000).

Gross national product (1994): U.S.$12,237,000,000 (U.S.$1,190 per capita).

Structure of gross domestic product and labour force

	1995 in value Q '000[4]	% of total value	1995 labour force	% of labour force
Agriculture	1,003,621	24.0	1,798,227	58.1
Mining	15,500	0.4	3,095	0.1
Manufacturing	589,929	14.1	420,928	13.6
Construction	85,408	2.1	126,898	4.1
Public utilities	123,943	3.0	9,285	0.3
Transp. and commun.	360,440	8.6	77,377	2.5
Trade	1,037,052	24.8	225,940	7.3
Finance, real estate	395,671	9.5		
Pub. admin., defense	318,817	7.6	371,407	12.0
Services	244,044	5.9		
Other	—	—	61,901[6]	2.0[6]
TOTAL	4,174,425	100.0	3,095,058	100.0

Population economically active (1995): total 3,095,058; activity rate of total population 29.1% (participation rates [1994] ages 15–64, 51.0%; female 19.5%; unemployed 0.5%[7]).

Price and earnings indexes (1990 = 100)

	1989	1990	1991	1992	1993	1994	1995
Consumer price index	70.8	100.0	133.2	146.5	163.9	181.7	197.0
Annual earnings index[8]	86.9	100.0	126.6	162.3	203.8	232.7	291.1

Household income and expenditure. Average household size (1989) 5.4; income per household (1989) Q 4,306 (U.S.$1,529); sources of income: n.a.; expenditure (1981): food 64.4%, housing and energy 16.0%, transportation and communications 7.0%, household furnishings 5.0%, clothing 3.1%.

Foreign trade[9]

Balance of trade (current prices)

	1989	1990	1991	1992	1993	1994
U.S.$'000,000	−389.2	−207.4	−197.3	−1,190.8	−1,096.2	−755.3
% of total	14.9%	8.0%	7.5%	35.7%	29.0%	19.9%

Imports (1995): U.S.$3,292,460,900 (machinery 16.7%, transport equipment 14.8%, chemical products 14.0%, mineral products 13.0%, metal products 8.4%, plastic products 6.2%). *Major import sources:* United States 43.8%; Mexico 9.4%; El Salvador 4.9%; Venezuela 4.6%; Japan 3.8%; Germany 3.5%.
Exports (1995): U.S.$1,935,516,600 (coffee 27.9%, sugar 12.3%, bananas 7.2%, vegetable seeds 3.2%, legumes 3.0%). *Major export destinations:* United States 31.0%; El Salvador 13.9%; Honduras 6.4%; Germany 5.8%; Costa Rica 5.2%; Nicaragua 3.7%.

Transport and communications

Transport. Railroads (1993)[10]: route length 708 mi, 1,139 km; passenger-km (1990) 10,099,000; metric ton-km cargo 135,100,000. Roads (1993): total length 7,363 mi, 11,849 km (paved 26%). Vehicles (1994): passenger cars 102,000; trucks and buses 96,800. Merchant marine (1992): vessels (100 gross tons and over) 8; total deadweight tonnage 353. Air transport (1993)[11]: passenger-km 384,000,000; metric ton-km cargo 21,000,000; airports (1996) with scheduled flights 2.
Communications. Daily newspapers (1992): total number 5; total circulation 180,000; circulation per 1,000 population 18. Radio (1995): 570,000 receivers (1 per 19 persons). Television (1995): 475,000 receivers (1 per 22 persons). Telephones (main lines; 1993): 231,100 (1 per 43 persons).

Education and health

Education (1993)

	schools	teachers	students	student/ teacher ratio
Primary (age 7–12)	10,770	44,220	1,393,921	31.5
Secondary (age 13–18)	1,274[12]	20,942	334,883	16.0
Voc., teacher tr.	626[12]			
Higher[13]	5	4,346	69,532	16.0

Educational attainment (1994). Percentage of population age 25 and over having: no formal schooling 45.2%; incomplete primary education 20.8%; complete primary 18.0%; some secondary 4.8%; secondary 7.2%; higher 4.0%. *Literacy* (1994): total population age 15 and over literate 2,809,000 (64.2%); males literate 1,544,000 (71.7%); females literate 1,265,000 (57.3%).
Health (1987): physicians 3,579 (1 per 2,356 persons); hospital beds 13,667 (1 per 602 persons); infant mortality rate per 1,000 live births (1994) 53.9.
Food (1992): daily per capita caloric intake 2,255 (vegetable products 93%, animal products 7%); 103% of FAO recommended minimum requirement.

Military

Total active duty personnel (1996): 44,200 (army 95.0%, navy 3.4%, air force 1.6%). *Military expenditure as percentage of GNP* (1994): 1.4% (world 3.0%); per capita expenditure U.S.$17.

---

[1]Unadjusted for underenumeration. [2]Detail does not add to total given because of rounding. [3]Population of departments and cities taken from official projections based on 1973–81 intercensal growth rates and subsequent vital (birth and death) rates. [4]At prices of 1958. [5]Private construction in Guatemala City metropolitan area only. [6]Persons in activities not adequately defined. [7]Officially unemployed; majority of economically active population is estimated to be underemployed. [8]Based on employees entitled to social security. [9]Import figures are f.o.b. in balance of trade and c.i.f. for commodities and trading partners. [10]Guatemala Railways only. [11]Aviateca Airlines only. [12]1991. [13]1989.

Guinea

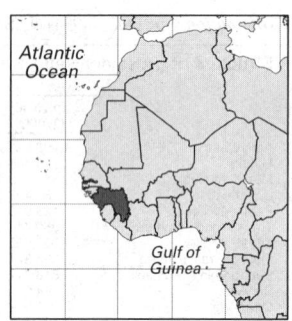

Official name: République de Guinée (Republic of Guinea).
Form of government: multiparty republic with one legislative house (National Assembly [114 seats][1]).
Head of state and government: President[2].
Capital: Conakry.
Official language: French.
Official religion: none.
Monetary unit: 1 Guinean franc (GF) = 100 cauris; valuation (Oct. 11, 1996) 1 U.S.$ = GF 997; 1 £ = GF 1,571.

Area and population

Regions	Capitals	area sq mi	area sq km	population 1983 census
Beyla	Beyla	6,738	17,452	161,347
Boffa	Boffa	1,932	5,003	141,719
Boké[3]	Boké	3,881	10,053	225,207
Conakry	Conakry	119	308	705,280
Coyah (Dubréka)	Coyah	2,153	5,576	134,190
Dabola	Dabola	2,317	6,000	97,986
Dalaba	Dalaba	1,313	3,400	132,802
Dinguiraye	Dinguiraye	4,247	11,000	133,502
Faranah[3]	Faranah	4,788	12,400	142,923
Forécariah	Forécariah	1,647	4,265	116,464
Fria	Fria	840	2,175	70,413
Gaoual	Gaoual	4,440	11,500	135,657
Guéckédou	Guéckédou	1,605	4,157	204,757
Kankan	Kankan	7,104	18,400	229,861
Kérouané	Kérouané	3,070	7,950	106,872
Kindia	Kindia	3,409	8,828	216,052
Kissidougou	Kissidougou	3,425	8,872	183,236
Koubia	Koubia	571	1,480	98,053
Koundara	Koundara	2,124	5,500	94,216
Kouroussa	Kouroussa	4,647	12,035	136,926
Labé	Labé	973	2,520	253,214
Lélouma	Lélouma	830	2,150	138,467
Lola	Lola	1,629	4,219	106,654
Macenta	Macenta	3,363	8,710	193,109
Mali	Mali	3,398	8,800	210,889
Mamou	Mamou	2,378	6,160	190,525
Mandiana	Mandiana	5,000	12,950	136,317
Nzérékoré	Nzérékoré	1,460	3,781	216,355
Pita	Pita	1,544	4,000	227,912
Siguiri	Siguiri	7,626	19,750	209,164
Télimélé	Télimélé	3,119	8,080	243,256
Tougué	Tougué	2,394	6,200	113,272
Yomou	Yomou	843	2,183	74,417
TOTAL		94,926[4]	245,857	5,781,014

Demography

Population (1996): 6,903,000.
Density (1996): persons per sq mi 72.7, persons per sq km 28.1.
Urban-rural (1990): urban 25.6%; rural 74.4%.
Sex distribution (1995): male 50.23%; female 49.77%.
Age breakdown (1995): under 15, 47.1%; 15–29, 25.9%; 30–44, 15.0%; 45–59, 7.8%; 60–74, 3.6%; 75 and over, 0.6%.
Population projection: (2000) 7,759,000; (2010) 10,301,000.
Doubling time: 27 years.
Ethnic composition (1990): Fulani 40.3%; Malinke 25.8%; Susu 11.0%; Kissi 6.5%; Kpelle 4.8%; other 11.6%.
Religious affiliation (1983): Muslim 86.9%; traditional beliefs 4.6%; Christian 4.3%; other 4.2%.
Major cities (1983): Conakry 650,000; Kankan 55,010; Nzérékoré 44,598; Kindia 39,121; Kissidougou 30,724.

Vital statistics

Birth rate per 1,000 population (1991): 47.0 (world avg. 25.0).
Death rate per 1,000 population (1991): 21.0 (world avg. 9.3).
Natural increase rate per 1,000 population (1991): 26.0 (world avg. 15.7).
Total fertility rate (avg. births per childbearing woman; 1990): 6.5.
Life expectancy at birth (1990–95): male 44.0 years; female 45.0 years.
Major causes of death per 100,000 population: n.a.; however, in the mid-1990s, the major causes of illness were (in order): malaria, acute respiratory infections, intestinal parasitic diseases, gastroenteritis, and malnutrition.

National economy

Budget (1995). Revenue: GF 564,900,000,000,000 (current revenues 74.0%, of which mining revenue 20.7%, other 53.3%; foreign aid 26.0%). Expenditures: GF 637,000,000,000,000 (current expenditure 50.8%, of which personnel 24.3%, other goods and services 11.4%; capital spending 49.2%).
Public debt (external, outstanding; 1994): U.S.$2,881,000,000.
Tourism (1993): receipts U.S.$6,000,000; expenditures U.S.$21,000,000.
Production (metric tons except as noted). Agriculture, forestry, fishing (1995): fruits 994,000 (of which plantains 429,000, bananas 151,000, pineapples 67,-000), roots and tubers 801,000 (of which cassava 512,000, sweet potatoes 143,000, yams 114,000), paddy rice 532,200, vegetables and melons 420,-000, sugarcane 220,000, peanuts (groundnuts) 170,000, corn (maize) 88,700, pulses 60,000, palm kernels 53,000, palm oil 50,000, coffee 30,000, eggs 14,490; livestock (number of live animals) 1,780,000 cattle, 580,000 goats, 475,000 sheep, 38,000 pigs, 13,500,000 chickens; roundwood (1994) 4,493,-000 cu m; fish catch (1993) 40,000. Mining and quarrying (1995): bauxite

14,400,000; alumina 642,000[5]; gold 500 kg[5]; diamond production ceased in 1994). Manufacturing (value of production in GF '000; 1985): corrugated and sheet iron 571,081; plastics 462,242; tobacco products 375,154; cement 326,138; printed matter 216,511; fruit juice 75,763; beer 69,934. Construction: n.a. Energy production (consumption): electricity (kW-hr; 1994) 530,000,000 (530,000,000); petroleum products (metric tons; 1994) none (355,000).
Gross national product (1994): U.S.$3,310,000,000 (U.S.$510 per capita).

Structure of gross domestic product and labour force

	1994 in value GF '000,000,000	1994 % of total value	1983 labour force	1983 % of labour force
Agriculture, forestry, fishing	415.7	24.1	1,423,615	78.2
Mining	328.6	19.1	12,241	0.7
Manufacturing	79.6	4.6	11,215	0.6
Construction	119.5	6.9	9,115	0.5
Public utilities	3.7	0.2	3,205	0.2
Transp. and commun.	88.4	5.1	29,496	1.6
Trade, finance	448.7	26.0	40,865	2.0
Pub. admin., defense	91.3	5.3 }	137,600	7.5
Services	102.6	6.0 }		
Other	45.7	2.7	155,679	8.5
TOTAL	1,723.6[4]	100.0	1,823,031	100.0

Population economically active (1992): total 2,590,000; activity rate of total population 42.3% (participation rates [1983]: ages 15–64, 63.5%; female 39.4%; unemployed, n.a.).

Price and earnings indexes (1990 = 100)

	1989	1990	1991	1992	1993	1994	1995[6]
Consumer price index	83.8	100.0	119.7	139.5	149.5	155.6	163.2
Annual salary index[7]	...	100.0	200.0	262.4	272.6	275.2	...

Household income and expenditure. Average household size (1983) 6.7; average annual income per capita (1984) GS 7,660 (U.S.$305); sources of income: n.a.; expenditure (1985): food 61.5%, health care 11.2%, clothing and footwear 7.9%, housing and energy 7.3%, transportation 5.1%.
Land use (1993): forest 27.3%; pasture 43.5%; agricultural 3.0%; other 26.2%.

Foreign trade[8]

Balance of trade (current prices)

	1990	1991	1992	1993	1994	1995
U.S.$'000,000	+85.5	−7.8	−91.2	−21.6	−169.7	−39.0
% of total	6.8%	0.6%	8.1%	1.9%	14.1%	3.2%

Imports (1994): U.S.$687,000,000 (goods for mining companies 22.2%; goods for public sector 20.1%; other private sector 57.7%). *Major import sources:* France 19.5%; Côte d'Ivoire 16.0%; U.S. 7.1%; Belgium-Luxembourg 6.9%; Hong Kong 6.3%; The Netherlands 3.8%; China 3.8%; Italy 3.3%.
Exports (1994): U.S.$625,900,000 (bauxite 43.4%; alumina 16.5%; gold 13.3%; coffee 9.1%; diamonds 6.4%; fish 3.1%). *Major export destinations:* Belgium-Luxembourg 26.7%; U.S. 15.1%; Ireland 10.0%; Spain 9.6%; France 4.6%.

Transport and communications

Transport. Railroads (1993): route length 411 mi, 662 km; (latest) passenger-mi 25,800,000, passenger-km 41,500,000; short ton-mi cargo 5,000,000, metric ton-km cargo 7,300,000. Roads (1992): total length 9,974 mi, 16,051 km (paved 9%). Vehicles (1995): passenger cars 23,155; trucks and buses 13,000. Merchant marine (1992): vessels (100 gross tons and over) 23; total deadweight tonnage 1,749. Air transport (1994): passenger-mi 20,408,000, passenger-km 32,842,000; short ton-mi cargo 850,000, metric ton-km cargo 1,241,000; airports (1996) with scheduled flights 2.
Communications. Daily newspapers (1988): 1; total circulation 13,000; circulation per 1,000 population 2.0. Radio (1995): 230,000 receivers (1 per 29 persons). Television (1995): 65,000 receivers (1 per 103 persons). Telephones (main lines; 1993): 11,580 (1 per 560 persons).

Education and health

Education (1993)

	schools	teachers	students	student/ teacher ratio
Primary (age 7–12)	2,849	9,718	471,792	48.5
Secondary (age 13–18)	225[9]	3,417	97,533	28.5
Voc., teacher tr.	35[9]	1,302	9,278	7.1
Higher	10[9]	805[10]	6,245[10]	7.8[10]

Educational attainment of those age six and over having attended school (1983): primary 55.2%; secondary 32.7%; vocational 3.4%; higher 8.7%. *Literacy* (1995): percentage of total population age 15 and over literate 35.9%; males 49.9%; females 21.9%.
Health: physicians (1990) 773 (1 per 7,445 persons); hospital beds (1988) 3,382 (1 per 1,934 persons); infant mortality rate (1990–95) 134.
Food (1992): daily per capita caloric intake 2,389 (vegetable products 96%, animal products 4%); 103% of FAO recommended minimum requirement.

Military

Total active duty personnel (1996): 9,700 (army 87.6%, navy 4.1%, air force 8.2%). *Military expenditure as percentage of GNP* (1994): 1.5% (world 3.0%); per capita expenditure U.S.$8.

---

[1]Met for first session Oct. 5, 1995. [2]President created office of Prime Minister July 1996. [3]The provinces of Boké and Faranah were reportedly abolished by presidential decree in January 1988. [4]Detail does not add to total given because of rounding. [5]1993. [6]Through third quarter. [7]Nonmilitary civil service employees. [8]Imports c.i.f.; exports f.o.b. in commodities and direction of trade. [9]1987–88. [10]Universities only.

Guinea-Bissau

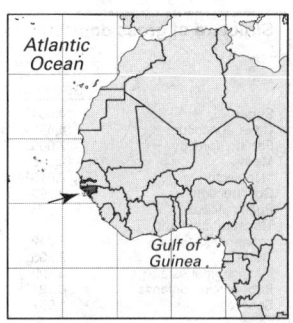

Official name: Républica da Guiné-Bissau (Republic of Guinea-Bissau).
Form of government: multiparty republic with one legislative house (National People's Assembly [100]).
Chief of state: President.
Head of government: Prime Minister.
Capital: Bissau.
Official language: Portuguese.
Official religion: none.
Monetary unit: 1 Guinea-Bissau peso (PG) = 100 centavos; valuation (Oct. 11, 1996) 1 U.S.$ = PG 18,036; 1 £ = PG 28,412.

Area and population		area		population
		sq mi	sq km	1991 census[1]
Regions	**Capitals**			
Bafatá	Bafatá	2,309	5,981	143,377
Biombo[2]	Bissau	324	840	60,420
Bolama	Bolama	1,013	2,624	26,691
Cacheu	Cacheu	1,998	5,175	146,980
Gabú	Gabú	3,533	9,150	134,971
Oio	Farim	2,086	5,403	156,084
Quinara	Fulacunda	1,212	3,138	44,793
Tombali	Catió	1,443	3,736	72,441
Autonomous Sector				
Bissau[2]	—	30	78	197,610
TOTAL		13,948[3]	36,125[3]	983,367

Demography

Population (1996): 1,096,000.
Density (1996)[4]: persons per sq mi 100.9, persons per sq km 39.0.
Urban-rural (1996): urban 22.0%; rural 78.0%.
Sex distribution (1995): male 49.21%; female 50.79%.
Age breakdown (1995): under 15, 41.7%; 15–29, 25.1%; 30–44, 16.2%; 45–59, 10.5%; 60–74, 5.4%; 75 and over, 1.1%.
Population projection: (2000) 1,192,000; (2010) 1,473,000.
Doubling time: 33 years.
Ethnic composition (1979): Balante 27.2%; Fulani 22.9%; Malinke 12.2%; Mandyako 10.6%; Pepel 10.0%; other 17.1%.
Religious affiliation (1992): traditional beliefs 54%; Muslim 38%; Christian 8%.
Major cities (1979): Bissau 197,610[5]; Bafatá 13,429; Gabú 7,803; Mansôa 5,390; Catió 5,179.

Vital statistics

Birth rate per 1,000 population (1990–95): 42.7 (world avg. 25.0); legitimate, n.a.; illegitimate, n.a.
Death rate per 1,000 population (1990–95): 21.3 (world avg. 9.3).
Natural increase rate per 1,000 population (1990–95): 21.4 (world avg. 15.7).
Total fertility rate (avg. births per childbearing woman; 1996): 5.8.
Marriage rate per 1,000 population (1981): 0.1.
Divorce rate per 1,000 population: n.a.
Life expectancy at birth (1990–95): male 41.9 years; female 45.1 years.
Major causes of death per 100,000 population: n.a.; however, major diseases include tuberculosis of the respiratory system, whooping cough, typhoid fever, cholera, bacillary dysentery and amebiasis, malaria, pneumonia, and meningococcal infections; malnutrition is widespread.

National economy

Budget (1992). Revenue: PG 168,490,000,000 (1989; grants from abroad 71.2%, nontax revenue 18.4%, tax revenue 10.4%). Expenditures: PG 555,900,000,-000 (1989; capital expenditures 58.0%, current expenditures 36.4%).
Public debt (external, outstanding; 1994): U.S.$735,600,000.
Tourism: n.a.
Production (metric tons except as noted). Agriculture, forestry, fishing (1996): rice 135,000, fruits 65,400, roots and tubers (sweet potatoes and cassava) 65,000, cashews 35,000, plantains 33,700, millet 30,000, coconuts 25,000, vegetables 20,000, peanuts (groundnuts) 18,000, sorghum 14,000, corn (maize) 13,000, palm kernels 8,000, sugarcane 5,500, bananas 5,000, palm oil 4,500, seed cotton 2,200; livestock (number of live animals) 475,000 cattle, 310,-000 pigs, 270,000 goats, 255,000 sheep, 850,000 chickens; roundwood (1994) 577,000 cu m; fish catch (1993) 5,350. Mining and quarrying: extraction of construction materials only. Manufacturing (1996): fresh pork 9,720; palm oil 5,000[6]; copra 5,000; fresh beef 3,850; animal hides 1,277[6], of which cattle 875[6], goat 194[6], sheep 158[6], sawlogs 40,000 cu m[6]; brewing of beer is also important. Construction: n.a. Energy production (consumption): electricity (kW-hr; 1993) 42,000,000 (42,000,000); coal, none (none); crude petroleum, none (none); petroleum products (metric tons; 1993) none (74,000); natural gas, none (none).
Population economically active (1992): total 471,000; activity rate of total population 46.9% (participation rates (1991): over age 10, 67.1%; female 40.5%; unemployed, n.a.).

Price and earnings indexes (1990 = 100)							
	1990	1991	1992	1993	1994	1995	1996[7]
Consumer price index	100.0	157.6	267.3	395.8	455.9	662.7	942.3
Earnings index	...	...	...	...	...	...	...

Gross national product (at current market prices; 1994): U.S.$253,000,000 (U.S.$240 per capita).

Structure of gross domestic product and labour force				
	1991		1994	
	in value PG '000,000	% of total value	labour force	% of labour force
Agriculture	382,400	44.7	365,000	77.2
Mining				
Manufacturing	72,556	8.5	21,000	4.5
Public utilities				
Construction	71,874	8.4		
Transportation and communications	33,364	3.9		
Trade	220,356	25.8	87,000	18.3
Finance, services	27,914	3.3		
Pub. admin., defense	46,522	5.4		
TOTAL	854.986	100.0	473,000	100.0

Land use (1994): forested 38.1%; meadows and pastures 38.4%; agricultural and under permanent cultivation 12.1%; other 11.4%.
Household income and expenditure. Average household size (1981) 4.1; income per household: n.a.; sources of income: n.a.; expenditure: n.a.

Foreign trade[8]

Balance of trade (current prices)						
	1990	1991	1992	1993	1994	1995
PG'000,000	−145,259	−202,920	−656,911	−459,028	−191,128	−845,647
% of total	63.3%	57.6%	92.9%	58.8%	29.8%	50.0%

Imports (1994): U.S.$152,000,000 (1991; foodstuffs 41.2%, transport equipment 25.9%, fuel and lubricants 11.4%, machinery 8.1%, building materials 5.5%). *Major import sources:* Thailand 30.3%; Portugal 21.7%; Hong Kong 5.9%; The Netherlands 5.9%; Côte d'Ivoire 5.3%; U.K. 4.6%; France 3.3%; Senegal 3.3%.
Exports (1994): U.S.$77,000,000 (1991; cashews 57.7%, frozen fish, including shrimp 10.8%, lumber 5.9%). *Major export destinations:* India 40.3%; Spain 37.7%; Portugal 5.2%; Italy 3.9%; Thailand 3.9%; Côte d'Ivoire 3.9%; Japan 2.6%.

Transport and communications

Transport. Railroads: none. Roads (1991): total length 2,579 mi, 4,150 km (paved 9%). Vehicles (1994): passenger cars 4,000; trucks and buses 2,800. Merchant marine (1992): vessels (100 gross tons and over) 19; total deadweight tonnage 1,846. Air transport (1993): passenger-mi 3,700,000, passenger-km 6,000,000; short ton-mi cargo 700,000, metric ton-km cargo 1,000,000; airports (1996) with scheduled flights 2.
Communications. Daily newspapers (1992): total number 1; total circulation 6,000; circulation per 1,000 population 6. Radio (1995): total number of receivers 40,000 (1 per 27 persons). Television: n.a. Telephones (main lines; 1993): 8,600 (1 per 122 persons).

Education and health

Education (1988)	schools	teachers	students	student/ teacher ratio
Primary (age 7–13)	632[9]	3,065[9]	79,035	24.6[9]
Secondary (age 13–18)	12[10]	824[10]	5,505	7.8[10]
Voc., teacher tr.	4[9]	107	825	7.7

Educational attainment (1979). Percentage of population age 7 and over having: no formal schooling or knowledge of reading and writing 90.4%; primary education 7.9%; secondary 1.0%; technical 0.5%; higher 0.2%. *Literacy* (1995): total population age 15 and over literate 54.9%; males literate 68.0%; females literate 42.5%.
Health: physicians (1986) 274 (1 per 3,245 persons); hospital beds (1993) 1,300 (1 per 797 persons); infant mortality rate per 1,000 live births (1990–95) 140.
Food (1992): daily per capita caloric intake 2,556 (vegetable products 93%, animal products 7%); 110% of FAO recommended minimum requirement.

Military

Total active duty personnel (1996): 7,250[11] (army 93.8%, navy 4.8%, air force 1.4%). *Military expenditure as percentage of GNP* (1994): 3.4% (world 3.0%); per capita expenditure U.S.$8.

[1]Preliminary. [2]Biombo region excludes Bissau city. [3]Includes water area of about 3,089 sq mi (8,000 sq km). [4]Based on land area of 10,859 sq mi (28,125 sq km). [5]1991. [6]1993. [7]June. [8]Import figures are c.i.f. in balance of trade and f.o.b. in commodities and trading partners. [9]1987. [10]1986. [11]Excludes 2,000 gendarmes, who are part of the armed forces.

Guyana

Official name: Co-operative Republic of Guyana.
Form of government: unitary multiparty republic with one legislative house (National Assembly [651]).
Head of state and government: President.
Capital: Georgetown.
Official language: English.
Official religion: none.
Monetary unit: 1 Guyana dollar (G$) = 100 cents; valuation (Oct. 11, 1996) 1 U.S.$ = G$138.90; 1 £ = G$218.81.

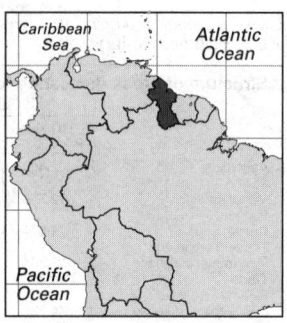

Structure of gross domestic product and labour force

	1995		1980	
	in value G$'000,000[7]	% of total value	labour force	% of labour force
Sugar	14,564[8]	19.8[8]		
Other agriculture	14,435[9]	19.7[9]	50,316	20.4
Fishing, forestry	7,009	9.6		
Mining	12,095	16.5	9,669	3.9
Manufacturing	2,846[10, 11]	3.9[10, 11]	28,980	11.8
Construction	3,098	4.2	7,024	2.8
Public utilities	[11]	[11]	2,850	1.2
Transportation and communications	3,742	5.1	9,412	3.8
Trade	3,205	4.4	15,231	6.2
Finance, real estate	5,122	7.0	2,944	1.2
Pub. admin., defense	6,187	8.4	29,948	12.1
Services	1,057	1.4	29,295	11.9
Other	—	—	61,002[12]	24.7[12]
TOTAL	73,360	100.0	246,671	100.0

Public debt (external, outstanding; 1994): U.S.$1,788,000,000.
Population economically active (1987): total 270,074; activity rate of total population 35.7% (participation rates: ages 15–64, 60.4%; female 29.9%; unemployed [1992] 12.9%).

Price and earnings indexes (1990 = 100)

	1989	1990	1991	1992	1993	1994	1995
Consumer price index[13]	96.4	100.0	183.1	208.4	224.4	260.5	281.5
Earnings index	...	...	...	...	...	...	...

Land use (1994): forested 83.8%; meadows and pastures 6.3%; agricultural and under permanent cultivation 2.5%; other 7.4%.

Foreign trade[14]

Balance of trade (current prices)

	1990	1991	1992	1993	1994	1995
U.S.$'000,000	−50.9	−40.7	−61.0	−68.3	−40.6	−40.8
% of total	8.9%	7.1%	7.4%	7.6%	4.2%	4.0%

Imports (1994): U.S.$504,000,000 (capital goods 24.7%; consumer goods 21.9%; fuels and lubricants 16.3%). *Major import sources*[15]: United States 29%; Trinidad and Tobago 17%; Netherlands Antilles 17%; United Kingdom 11%; Japan 4%.
Exports (1995): U.S.$495,700,000 (domestic exports 96.6%, of which sugar 25.3%, gold 19.1%, bauxite 16.7%, rice 15.4%, timber 1.7%; reexports 3.4%). *Major export destinations* (1994)[15]: Canada 33%; United States 24%; United Kingdom 22%; Germany 3%; The Netherlands 3%.

Transport and communications

Transport. Railroads: [16]. Roads (1993): total length 4,474 mi, 7,200 km (paved 10%). Vehicles (1994): passenger cars 24,000; trucks and buses 9,000. Merchant marine (1992): vessels (100 gross tons and over) 82; total deadweight tonnage 13,509. Air transport (1994): passenger-mi 200,000,000, passenger-km 322,000,000; short ton-mi cargo 2,100,000[17], metric ton-km cargo 3,000,-000[17]; airports (1996) with scheduled flights 1[18].
Communications. Daily newspapers (1995): total number 2; total circulation 44,500; circulation per 1,000 population 62. Radio (1995): total number of receivers 350,000 (1 per 2.1 persons). Television (1995): total number of receivers 15,000 (1 per 48 persons). Telephones (main lines; 1993): 41,000 (1 per 18 persons).

Education and health

Education (1994–95)

	schools	teachers	students	student/teacher ratio
Primary (age 6–11)	423[19]	3,453	100,806	29.2
Secondary (age 12–17)	93[19]	1,828	67,039	36.7
Voc., teacher tr. [19]	8	176	5,388	30.6
Higher[20]	1	204	3,357	16.5

Educational attainment (1980). Percentage of population age 25 and over having: no formal schooling 8.1%; primary education 72.8%; secondary 17.3%; higher 1.8%. *Literacy* (1995): total population age 15 and over literate, c. 511,000 (98.1%); males literate, c. 254,000 (98.6%); females literate, c. 257,000 (97.5%).
Health: physicians (1993) 244 (1 per 3,000 persons); hospital beds (1989) 2,488 (1 per 300 persons); infant mortality rate per 1,000 live births (1995) 51.4.
Food (1992): daily per capita caloric intake 2,384 (vegetable products 86%, animal products 14%); 105% of FAO recommended minimum requirement.

Military

Total active duty personnel (1995): 1,600 (army 86.6%, navy 7.2%, air force 6.2%). *Military expenditure as percentage of GNP* (1994): 1.5% (world 3.0%); per capita expenditure U.S.$9.

Area and population

		area		population
Administrative Regions	Capitals	sq mi	sq km	1986 estimate
Region 1 (Barima–Waini)	Mabaruma	7,853	20,339	18,516
Region 2 (Pomeroon–Supenaam)	Anna Regina	2,392	6,195	41,966
Region 3 (Essequibo Islands–West Demerara)	Vreed en Hoop	1,450	3,755	102,760
Region 4 (Demerara–Mahaica)	Paradise	862	2,233	310,758
Region 5 (Mahaica–Berbice)	Fort Wellington	1,610	4,170	55,556
Region 6 (East Berbice–Corentyne)	New Amsterdam	13,998	36,255	148,967
Region 7 (Cuyuni–Mazaruni)	Bartica	18,229	47,213	17,941
Region 8 (Potaro–Siparuni)	Mahdia	7,742	20,052	5,672
Region 9 (Upper Takutu–Upper Essequibo)	Lethem	22,313	57,790	15,338
Region 10 (Upper Demerara–Berbice)	Linden	6,595	17,081	38,598
TOTAL		83,044[2]	215,083[2]	756,072

Demography

Population (1996): 712,000.
Density (1996)[3]: persons per sq mi 9.4, persons per sq km 3.6.
Urban-rural (1995): urban 36.2%; rural 63.8%.
Sex distribution (1995): male 49.46%; female 50.54%.
Age breakdown (1995): under 15, 32.2%; 15–29, 30.1%; 30–44, 22.2%; 45–59, 9.5%; 60–74, 4.8%; 75 and over, 1.2%.
Population projection: (2000) 693,000; (2010) 695,000.
Doubling time: 54 years.
Ethnic composition (1992–93): East Indian 49.4%; black (African Negro and Bush Negro) 35.6%; mixed 7.1%; Amerindian 6.8%; Portuguese 0.7%; Chinese 0.4%.
Religious affiliation (1990): Christian 52.0%, of which Protestant 34.0% (including Anglican 17.0%), Roman Catholic 18.0%; Hindu 34.0%; Muslim 9.0%; other 5.0%.
Major cities (1992): Georgetown 248,500; Linden 27,200; New Amsterdam 17,700.

Vital statistics

Birth rate per 1,000 population (1995): 19.4 (world avg. 25.0).
Death rate per 1,000 population (1995): 9.1 (world avg. 9.3).
Natural increase rate per 1,000 population (1995): 10.3 (world avg. 15.7).
Total fertility rate (avg. births per childbearing woman; 1995): 2.2.
Marriage rate per 1,000 population: n.a.
Divorce rate per 1,000 population: n.a.
Life expectancy at birth (1995): male 58.2 years; female 63.9 years.
Major causes of death per 100,000 population (1990)[4]: diseases of the circulatory system 244.6, of which cerebrovascular disease 103.7, ischemic heart disease 56.8, diseases of pulmonary circulation and other forms of heart disease 49.3; diseases of the digestive system 39.0; endocrine and metabolic disorders 37.3; diseases of the respiratory system 37.3.

National economy

Budget (1995). Revenue: G$32,113,000,000 (current revenue 90.2%, of which consumption taxes 29.6%, income taxes on companies 19.1%, personal income taxes 13.2%, import duties 10.6%; development revenue 9.8%, of which external grants 5.4%). Expenditures: G$34,513,000,000 (current expenditure 65.0%, of which debt charges 26.5%, personal emoluments 17.0%; development expenditure 35.0%).
Production (metric tons except as noted). Agriculture, forestry, fishing (1995): rice 316,500, raw sugar 253,900, coconuts 63,600, roots and tubers 32,000, plantains 23,500, bananas 17,000, oranges 14,700, pineapples 6,600; livestock (number of live animals) 190,000 cattle, 130,000 sheep, 79,000 goats; roundwood 538,400 cu m; fish catch 38,200[5], of which shrimps and prawns 8,200[5]. Mining and quarrying (1995): bauxite 2,028,000; gold 289,514 troy oz[6]; diamonds 52,392 carats. Manufacturing (1995): flour 38,000; rum 179,000 hectolitres; beer and stout 84,700 hectolitres; cigarettes 317,000,000 units; soft drinks 3,032,000 cases; pharmaceuticals 16,100,000 tablets; other products include cotton cloth and dyed and printed fabrics. Construction: n.a. Energy production (consumption): electricity (kW-hr; 1995) 333,700,000 (217,200,000); coal, none (none); crude petroleum, none (none); petroleum products (metric tons; 1993) none (344,000); natural gas, none (none).
Tourism: receipts from visitors (1994) U.S.$24,000,000; expenditures by nationals abroad, n.a.
Household income and expenditure. Average household size (1980) 5.1; income per household, n.a.; sources of income, n.a.; expenditure, n.a.
Gross national product (at current market prices; 1994): U.S.$434,000,000 (U.S.$530 per capita).

---

[1]Includes 12 indirectly elected seats. [2]Includes inland water area equaling c. 7,000 sq mi (c. 18,000 sq km). [3]Based on land area only. [4]Based on incomplete data. [5]1994. [6]Including a declared production of 92,434 troy oz by individual prospectors. [7]At factor cost. [8]Includes sugar manufacturing. [9]Includes rice manufacturing. [10]Excludes sugar and rice manufacturing. [11]Manufacturing includes Public utilities. [12]Represents "not stated." [13]Weights of consumer price index components for Georgetown, Linden, and New Amsterdam only. [14]Imports c.i.f.; exports f.o.b. [15]Estimated figure. [16]No public railways. [17]1993. [18]International only; domestic air service is provided on a charter basis. [19]1989–90. [20]University of Guyana only.

Haiti

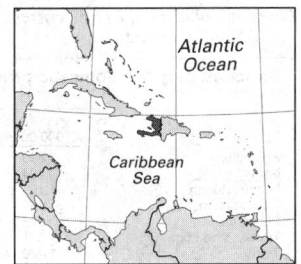

Official name: Repiblik Dayti (Haitian Creole); République d'Haïti (French) (Republic of Haiti).
Form of government: multiparty republic with two legislative houses (Senate [27]; Chamber of Deputies [83]).
Chief of state: President.
Head of government: Prime Minister.
Capital: Port-au-Prince.
Official languages: Haitian Creole; French.
Official religion: none[1].
Monetary unit: 1 gourde (G) = 100 centimes; valuation (Oct. 11, 1996) 1 U.S.$ = G 15.10; 1 £ = G 23.79.

Area and population

Departements	Capitals	area[2] sq mi	area[2] sq km	population 1995 estimate
Artibonite	Gonaïves	1,924	4,984	1,013,779
Centre	Hinche	1,419	3,675	490,790
Grand'Anse	Jérémie	1,278	3,310	641,399
Nord	Cap-Haïtien	813	2,106	759,318
Nord-Est	Fort-Liberté	697	1,805	248,764
Nord-Ouest	Port-de-Paix	840	2,176	420,971
Ouest	Port-au-Prince	1,864	4,827	2,494,862
Sud	Les Cayes	1,079	2,794	653,398
Sud-Est	Jacmel	781	2,023	457,013
TOTAL		10,695	27,700	7,180,294[3]

Demography

Population (1996): 6,732,000.
Density (1996): persons per sq mi 629.5, persons per sq km 243.0.
Urban-rural (1995): urban 32.6%; rural 67.4%.
Sex distribution (1995): male 49.09%; female 50.91%.
Age breakdown (1995): under 15, 40.2%; 15–29, 27.3%; 30–44, 17.0%; 45–59, 9.5%; 60–74, 4.8%; 75 and over, 1.2%.
Population projection: (2000) 7,223,000; (2010) 8,681,000.
Doubling time: 31 years.
Ethnic composition (1993): black 95.0%; mulatto/other 5.0%.
Religious affiliation (1982): Roman Catholic 80.3%[4]; Protestant 15.8%, of which Baptist 9.7%, Pentecostal 3.6%; nonreligious 1.2%; other 2.7%.
Major cities (1995): Port-au-Prince 846,247 (metropolitan area 1,425,594); Carrefour 277,662[5]; Delmas 232,142[5]; Cap-Haïtien 100,638; Pétionville 69,543[5].

Vital statistics

Birth rate per 1,000 population (1995): 39.0 (world avg. 25.0).
Death rate per 1,000 population (1995): 16.3 (world avg. 9.3).
Natural increase rate per 1,000 population (1995): 22.7 (world avg. 15.7).
Total fertility rate (avg. births per childbearing woman; 1995): 5.8.
Marriage rate per 1,000 population: n.a.
Divorce rate per 1,000 population: n.a.
Life expectancy at birth (1995): male 47.1 years; female 51.1 years.
Major causes of death per 100,000 population (1982)[6]: infectious and parasitic diseases 46.0; diseases of the circulatory system 11.9; diseases associated with malnutrition 8.5; diseases of the respiratory system 8.3; endocrine and metabolic disorders 8.0; ill-defined conditions 115.2.

National economy

Budget (1994–95). Revenue: G 3,342,300,000 (grants 25.9%, excise taxes 15.0%, turnover taxes 14.3%, customs duties 12.7%, income taxes 7.4%). Expenditures: G 4,106,500,000 (current expenditure 78.3%, development expenditure 8.6%, subsidies 7.1%, interest on public debt 6.0%).
Public debt (external, outstanding; 1994): U.S.$627,200,000.
Production (metric tons except as noted). Agriculture, forestry, fishing (1995): sugarcane 2,250,000, cassava (manioc) 350,000, plantains 270,000, mangoes 230,000, bananas 230,000, corn (maize) 213,000, sweet potatoes 185,000, rice 80,000, sorghum 80,000, dry beans 50,000, avocados 45,000, coffee 33,600, oranges 26,000, sisal 8,100, cacao 3,000; livestock (number of live animals) 1,200,000 cattle, 910,000 goats, 360,000 pigs; roundwood (1994) 5,687,000 cu m; fish catch (1993) 5,600. Mining and quarrying: insignificant amounts of limestone, calcareous clay, and marble. Manufacturing (1993–94): cement 84,000[7]; essential oils (mostly amyris, neroli, and vetiver) 227[7]; cigarettes 408,000,000 units; malt liquor 2,300,000 bottles; beer 1,000,000 bottles; articles assembled for reexport (export value in U.S.$'000,000) 105.7, of which garments 80.5, sports equipment and toys 9.2, electronic components 7.2, luggage and handbags 2.8. Construction: n.a. Energy production (consumption): electricity (kW-hr; 1992–93) 409,600,000 (230,000,000); coal (metric tons; 1993) none (10,000); crude petroleum, none (none); petroleum products (metric tons; 1993) none (185,000); natural gas, none (none).
Population economically active (1990): total 2,679,140; activity rate of total population 41.1% (participation rates: ages 15–64, 64.8%; female 40.0%; unemployed [1995] unofficially more than 50.0%).

Price and earnings indexes (1990 = 100)

	1990	1991	1992	1993	1994	1995	1996
Consumer price index	100.0	115.4	137.8	168.8	240.7	302.0	338.0[8]
Annual earnings index[9]	100.0	100.0	100.0	100.0	...	...	...

Household income and expenditure. Average household size (1982) 4.4; average annual income of wage earners (1984): urban (G 1,545 [U.S.$309]), rural (G 629 [U.S.$126]); expenditure (1986–87)[10]: food, beverages, and tobacco 51.1%, household furnishings 9.2%, clothing and footwear 8.7%, transportation and communications 7.6%.
Gross national product (1994): U.S.$1,542,000,000 (U.S.$220 per capita).

Structure of gross domestic product and labour force

	1993–94 in value G '000,000[11]	1993–94 % of total value	1990 labour force	1990 % of labour force
Agriculture	1,464	40.9	1,535,444	57.3
Mining	1	—	24,012	0.9
Manufacturing	392	10.9	151,387	5.6
Construction	70	1.9	28,001	1.0
Public utilities	18	0.5	2,577	0.1
Transp. and commun.	53	1.5	20,691	0.8
Trade, restaurants	390	10.9	352,970	13.2
Finance, real estate }	437	12.2 }	5,057	0.2
Services			155,347	5.8
Pub. admin., defense	719	20.1 }		
Other	38[12]	1.1[12]	403,654[13]	15.1[13]
TOTAL	3,582	100.0	2,679,140	100.0

Tourism (1993): receipts from visitors U.S.$46,000,000; expenditures by nationals abroad U.S.$25,000,000.
Land use (1994): forested 5.1%; meadows and pastures 18.0%; agricultural and under permanent cultivation 33.0%; other 43.9%.

Foreign trade[14, 15]

Balance of trade (current prices)

	1989–90	1990–91	1991–92	1992–93	1993–94	1994–95
U.S.$'000,000	−172.4	−156.1	−221.1	−233.5	−204.4	−378.7
% of total	33.8%	35.9%	43.9%	46.0%	55.8%	70.4%

Imports (1993–94): U.S.$285,300,000 (food and live animals 20.7%, mineral fuels 17.1%, basic manufactures 16.3%, chemicals and chemical products 12.9%). *Major import sources* (1994)[16]: United States 50%; Netherlands Antilles 17%; Malaysia 5%; France 3%; Germany 3%.
Exports (1993–94): U.S.$80,900,000 (local manufactures [mostly processed foods, electrical equipment, textiles, and clothing] 68.5%, coffee 9.0%, handicrafts [primarily wood carvings and masks and woven sisal products] 7.4%, essential oils 4.9%, sisal and twine 2.7%). *Major export destinations* (1994)[16]: United States 71%; France 7%; Germany 6%; Italy 5%.

Transport and communications

Transport. Railroad (1994): none. Roads (1994): total length 2,662 mi, 4,284 km (paved 14%). Vehicles (1993): passenger cars 32,000; trucks and buses 21,000. Merchant marine (1992): vessels (100 gross tons and over) 4; total deadweight tonnage 429. Air transport (1994)[17]: passenger arrivals 167,882, passenger departures 177,072; cargo unloaded 11,967 metric tons, cargo loaded 10,087 metric tons; airports (1996) with scheduled flights 2.
Communications. Daily newspapers (1994): total number 4; total circulation 44,000; circulation per 1,000 population 6.8. Radio (1995): total number of receivers 270,000 (1 per 24 persons). Television (1995): total number of receivers 25,000 (1 per 265 persons). Telephones (main lines; 1995): 55,302 (1 per 119 persons).

Education and health

Education (1992–93)

	schools	teachers	students	student/ teacher ratio
Primary (age 6–12)	6,111[18]	27,607	787,553	28.5
Secondary (age 13–18) }	630[18]	10,174	193,624	19.0
Voc., teacher tr.				
Higher[19, 20]	2	613	7,400	12.1

Educational attainment (1986–87). Percentage of population age 25 and over having: no formal schooling 59.5%; primary education 30.5%; secondary 8.6%; vocational and teacher training 0.7%; higher 0.7%. *Literacy* (1995): total population age 15 and over literate 1,930,000 (45.0%); males literate 992,000 (48.0%); females literate 938,000 (42.2%).
Health (1993–94): physicians 641[21] (1 per 10,041 persons); hospital beds 6,473 (1 per 994 persons); infant mortality rate per 1,000 live births (1995) 105.1.
Food (1992): daily per capita caloric intake 1,706 (vegetable products 95%, animal products 5%); 75% of FAO recommended minimum requirement.

Military

Total active duty personnel:[22].

[1]Roman Catholicism has special recognition. [2]Estimated. [3]Official population projection based on 1982 census. [4]About 80% of all Roman Catholics also practice voodoo. [5]Within Port-au-Prince metropolitan area. [6]Public health facilities only. [7]1992–93. [8]March. [9]Standard minimum wage. [10]Based on nationwide sample survey of 3,120 households. [11]At prices of 1975–76. [12]Import duties. [13]Includes 63,975 not adequately defined and 339,679 officially unemployed. [14]The import and export value of preassembled and assembled U.S.-made components is excluded. Virtually all components used in the export assembly plants are imported. [15]Import figures c.i.f., export figures f.o.b. for fiscal year ending March 31. [16]Estimated figures. [17]Port-au-Prince Airport only. [18]1991–92. [19]Port-au-Prince universities only. [20]1994–95. [21]Public health services only. [22]The Haitian army was disbanded in 1995. A 7,000-member UN force provided security between April 1995 and September 1996.

Honduras

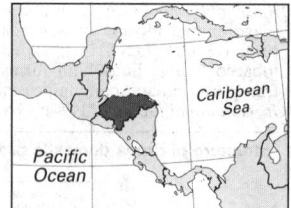

Official name: República de Honduras
 (Republic of Honduras).
Form of government: multiparty
 republic with one legislative house
 (Congress [128]).
Head of state and government:
 President.
Capital: Tegucigalpa[1].
Official language: Spanish.
Official religion: none.
Monetary unit: 1 Honduran lempira
 (L) = 100 centavos; valuation (Oct. 11,
 1996) 1 U.S.$ = L 12.07; 1 £ = L 19.01.

Area and population

Departments	Administrative centres	area sq mi	area sq km	population 1991 estimate
Atlántida	La Ceiba	1,641	4,251	255,000
Choluteca	Choluteca	1,626	4,211	309,000
Colón	Trujillo	3,427	8,875	164,000
Comayagua	Comayagua	2,006	5,196	257,000
Copán	Santa Rosa de Copán	1,237	3,203	226,000
Cortés	San Pedro Sula	1,527	3,954	706,000
El Paraíso	Yuscarán	2,787	7,218	277,000
Francisco Morazán	Tegucigalpa	3,068	7,946	878,000
Gracias a Dios	Puerto Lempira	6,421	16,630	37,000
Intibucá	La Esperanza	1,186	3,072	130,000
Islas de la Bahía	Roatán	100	261	24,000
La Paz	La Paz	900	2,331	112,000
Lempira	Gracias	1,656	4,290	180,000
Ocotepeque	Nueva Ocotepeque	649	1,680	77,000
Olancho	Juticalpa	9,402	24,351	309,000
Santa Bárbara	Santa Bárbara	1,975	5,115	291,000
Valle	Nacaome	604	1,565	121,000
Yoro	Yoro	3,065	7,939	355,000
TOTAL		43,277[2]	112,088[2]	4,708,000

Demography

Population (1996): 5,666,000.
Density (1996)[3]: persons per sq mi 130.5, persons per sq km 50.4.
Urban-rural (1994): urban 42.9%; rural 57.1%.
Sex distribution (1990): male 50.07%; female 49.93%.
Age breakdown (1990): under 15, 44.6%; 15–29, 28.3%; 30–44, 14.4%; 45–59, 7.8%; 60–74, 3.9%; 75 and over, 1.0%.
Population projection: (2000) 6,323,000; (2010) 7,998,000.
Doubling time: 24 years.
Ethnic composition (1987): mestizo 89.9%; Amerindian 6.7%; black (including Black Carib) 2.1%; white 1.3%.
Religious affiliation (1986): Roman Catholic 85.0%; Protestant (mostly fundamentalist, Moravian, and Methodist) 10.0%; other 5.0%.
Major cities (1994): Tegucigalpa 775,300[4]; San Pedro Sula 368,500; La Ceiba 86,000; El Progreso 81,200; Choluteca 72,800.

Vital statistics

Birth rate per 1,000 population (1993): 35.8 (world avg. 25.0); legitimate, n.a.; illegitimate, n.a.
Death rate per 1,000 population (1993): 6.4 (world avg. 9.3).
Natural increase rate per 1,000 population (1993): 29.4 (world avg. 15.7).
Total fertility rate (avg. births per childbearing woman; 1993): 4.9.
Marriage rate per 1,000 population (1983): 4.9.
Divorce rate per 1,000 population (1983): 0.4.
Life expectancy at birth (1993): male 64.8 years; female 69.2 years.
Major causes of death per 100,000 population (1983): diseases of the circulatory system 48.4; infectious and parasitic diseases 46.6; accidents and violence 42.2; diseases of the respiratory system 26.3.

National economy

Budget (1994). Revenue: L 7,972,900,000 (current revenue 57.9%, of which taxes on production and consumption 20.6%, import duties 14.9%, income taxes 13.3%; capital revenue 35.0%). Expenditures: L 9,289,600,000 (current expenditure 50.4%; public-debt service 15.7%; capital expenditure 15.3%).
Public debt (external, outstanding; 1994): U.S.$3,884,000,000.
Production (metric tons except as noted). Agriculture, forestry, fishing (1995): sugarcane 3,139,000, bananas 839,000, corn (maize) 672,000, plantains 189,-000, coffee 126,000, pineapples 96,000, palm oil 75,600, sorghum 63,000, dry beans 38,000, rice 35,000; livestock (number of live animals) 1,980,000 cattle, 600,000 pigs, 14,000,000 chickens; roundwood (1994) 6,312,000 cu m; fish catch (1993) 24,401. Mining and quarrying (1994): gypsum 25,500; salt 25,000; zinc 16,700; lead 2,810; copper 1,100. Manufacturing (1994): cement 999,600; raw sugar 347,400; wheat flour 227,700; beer 6,535,000 hectolitres; milk 614,530 hectolitres; cigarettes 2,406,220,000 units. Construction (value of private construction in L '000,000; 1994)[5]: residential 318.3; nonresidential 298.6. Energy production (consumption): electricity (kW-hr; 1994) 2,302,-000,000 (2,302,000,000); coal, none (none); crude petroleum (barrels; 1992) none (3,064,000); petroleum products (metric tons; 1993) 352,000 (812,000); natural gas, none (none).
Household income and expenditure. Average household size (1988) 5.4; income per household: n.a.; sources of income (1985): wages and salaries 58.8%, transfer payments 1.8%, other 39.4%; expenditure (1986): food 44.4%, utilities and housing 22.4%, clothing and footwear 9.0%, household furnishings 8.3%, health care 7.0%, transportation and communications 3.0%, other 5.9%.

Gross national product (at current market prices; 1994): U.S.$3,162,000,000 (U.S.$580 per capita).

Structure of gross domestic product and labour force

	1994 in value L '000,000[6]	1994 % of total value	1994 labour force	1994 % of labour force
Agriculture	5,593	23.9	749,700	43.5
Mining	464	2.0	4,200	0.2
Manufacturing	4,161	17.7	203,000	11.8
Construction	1,498	6.4	110,200	6.4
Public utilities	673	2.9	13,200	0.8
Transp. and commun.	1,271	5.4	48,200	2.8
Trade	2,420	10.3	183,900	10.7
Finance, real estate	3,410	14.5	34,300	2.0
Public admin., defense	1,565	6.7 }	376,000	21.8
Services	2,395	10.2 }		
TOTAL	23,450	100.0	1,722,700	100.0

Population economically active (1994): total 1,722,700; activity rate of total population 31.8% (participation rates: over age 15 [1992] 58.3%; female 31.7%; unemployed [1990] 40.0%).

Price and earnings indexes (1990 = 100)

	1989	1990	1991	1992	1993	1994	1995
Consumer price index	81.1	100.0	134.0	145.7	161.4	196.4	254.3
Weekly earnings index[7]	100.0	100.0	132.9	151.1	...	...	...

Land use (1994): forested 53.6%; meadows and pastures 13.8%; agricultural and under permanent cultivation 18.1%; other 14.5%.
Tourism (1994): receipts U.S.$33,000,000; expenditures U.S.$39,000,000.

Foreign trade[8]

Balance of trade (current prices)

	1990	1991	1992	1993	1994	1995
L '000,000	−29.8	+11.9	−129.3	−208.6	−113.1	−42.1
% of total	0.8%	0.7%	7.5%	11.4%	6.3%	1.9%

Imports (1994): U.S.$1,055,900,000 (machinery and electrical equipment 18.7%, mineral fuels 17.3%, industrial chemicals 15.5%, transport equipment 9.8%, metal products 7.2%, plastics and resins 6.9%). *Major import sources:* United States 42.5%; Guatemala 8.2%; Japan 4.7%; El Salvador 4.6%; Germany 3.5%; Mexico 3.0%; Costa Rica 2.3%.
Exports (1994): U.S.$834,300,000 (coffee 21.3%, bananas 18.6%, shrimp and lobsters 17.0%, frozen meats 4.6%, melons 2.9%, pineapples 2.4%). *Major export destinations:* United States 54.0%; Germany 7.2%; Belgium 5.0%; United Kingdom 4.6%; Japan 3.7%; Spain 2.8%; Italy 2.0%.

Transport and communications

Transport. Railroads (1989): length (1993) 614 mi, 988 km; passenger-km 7,700,000; metric ton-km cargo 30,200,000. Roads (1994): total length 8,825 mi, 14,203 km (paved 18%). Vehicles (1994): passenger cars 99,997; trucks and buses 128,575. Merchant marine (1992): vessels (100 gross tons and over) 966; total deadweight tonnage 1,437,321. Air transport (1993): passenger-mi 321,000,000, passenger-km 323,000,000; short ton-mi cargo 2,000,000, metric ton-km cargo 42,000,000; airports (1996) with scheduled flights 8.
Communications. Daily newspapers (1992): total number 4; total circulation 159,000; circulation per 1,000 population 29. Radio (1995): total number of receivers 1,910,000 (1 per 2.9 persons). Television (1995): total number of receivers 160,000 (1 per 34 persons). Telephones (main lines; 1993): 117,100 (1 per 48 persons).

Education and health

Education (1994)

	schools	teachers	students	student/ teacher ratio
Primary (age 7–13)	8,114	27,480	1,008,181	36.7
Secondary (age 14–19)	719	11,339	151,785	13.4
Voc., teacher tr.	5[9]	581[9]	58,154	13.7[9]
Higher	10	4,057	56,376	13.9

Educational attainment (1988). Percentage of population age 10 and over having: no formal schooling 33.4%; primary education 50.1%; secondary education 13.4%; higher 3.1%. *Literacy* (1990): total population age 15 and over literate 2,082,000 (73.1%); males literate 1,078,000 (75.5%); females literate 1,004,000 (70.6%).
Health: physicians (1990) 2,900 (1 per 1,586 persons); hospital beds (1994) 4,737 (1 per 1,126 persons); infant mortality rate per 1,000 live births (1993) 47.2.
Food (1992): daily per capita caloric intake 2,305 (vegetable products 88%, animal products 12%); 102% of FAO recommended minimum.

Military

Total active duty personnel (1995): 18,800 (army 85.1%, navy 5.3%, air force 9.6%). *Military expenditure as percentage of GNP* (1994): 1.6% (world 3.0%); per capita expenditure U.S.$8.

---

[1]Tegucigalpa and adjacent city of Comayagüela jointly form the capital according to the constitution. [2]The 1993 area is 43,433 sq mi (112,492 sq km); breakdown by department is not available. [3]Based on the revised area. [4]Population cited is for Central District (Tegucigalpa and Comayagüela). [5]Tegucigalpa, San Pedro Sula, and 10 other urban centres. [6]At factor cost. [7]Official minimum wages in all sectors. Minimum wages were fixed from June 1981 to Jan. 1, 1990, when new minimum wages were introduced. [8]Import figures are f.o.b. in balance of trade and c.i.f. for commodities and trading partners. [9]1989.

Hong Kong

Official name: Hsiang Kang (Chinese);
Hong Kong (English).
Political status: Crown Colony (United
Kingdom)[1] with one legislative house
(Legislative Council [60[2]]).
Chief of state: British Monarch.
Head of government: Governor.
Capital: none[3].
Official languages: Chinese; English.
Official religion: none.
Monetary unit: 1 Hong Kong dollar
(HK$) = 100 cents; valuation
(Oct. 11, 1996) 1 U.S.$ = HK$7.73;
1 £ = HK$12.18.

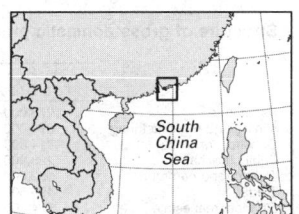

South
China
Sea

Area and population	area		population
			1994
Area	sq mi	sq km	estimate
Hong Kong Island	30.9	80.1	1,320,000
Kowloon and New Kowloon	18.0	46.5	1,990,000
New Territories	372.7	965.3	2,730,000
Marine	—	—	20,000
TOTAL	421.6	1,091.9	6,060,000

Demography

Population (1996): 6,304,000.
Density (1996): persons per sq mi 15,178.4, persons per sq km 5,860.0.
Urban-rural (1996): urban 100.0%.
Sex distribution (1995): male 50.84%; female 49.16%.
Age breakdown (1995)[4]: under 15, 18.9%; 15–29, 23.2%; 30–44, 29.9%; 45–59,
14.5%; 60–74, 10.1%; 75 and over, 3.4%.
Population projection: (2000) 6,780,000; (2010) 8,135,000.
Doubling time: not applicable; doubling time exceeds 100 years.
Linguistic composition (1991)[5]: Chinese 96.8%, of which Cantonese 88.7%;
English 2.2%; other 1.0%.
Religious affiliation (1995): predominantly Buddhist and Taoist; however,
there are about 260,000 Protestants, 254,100 Roman Catholics, 50,000 Mus-
lims, and 12,000 Hindus.
Major cities: no bounded localities exist within Hong Kong.

Vital statistics

Birth rate per 1,000 population (1995): 11.2 (world avg. 25.0); (1985) legiti-
mate 94.5%; illegitimate 5.5%.
Death rate per 1,000 population (1995): 5.1 (world avg. 9.3).
Natural increase rate per 1,000 population (1995): 6.1 (world avg. 15.7).
Total fertility rate (avg. births per childbearing woman; 1994): 1.2.
Marriage rate per 1,000 population (1995): 6.3.
Divorce rate per 1,000 population (1993): 1.3.
Life expectancy at birth (1995): male 75.7 years; female 81.3 years.
Major causes of death per 100,000 population (1995): malignant neoplasms
(cancers) 156.3; diseases of the circulatory system 142.8; diseases of the
respiratory system 87.5; accidents and poisoning 26.9; diseases of the di-
gestive system 22.1; infectious and parasitic diseases 19.5; diseases of the
genitourinary system 18.5.

National economy

Budget (1995–96). Revenue: HK$180,726,000,000 (earnings and profit taxes
43.2%; indirect taxes 22.9%, of which entertainment and stamp duties
12.6%, duties 4.4%; capital revenue 16.2%). Expenditures: HK$195,245,-
000,000 (education 17.3%; transportation and public works 13.8%; health
12.2%; housing 10.9%; law and order 8.8%; social welfare 7.5%; culture
and recreation 4.9%).
Public debt: n.a.
Gross domestic product (1994): U.S.$126,286,000,000 (U.S.$23,080 per capita).

Structure of gross domestic product and labour force				
	1994			
	in value HK$'000,000	% of total value	labour force	% of labour force
Agriculture	1,596	0.2	} 570,200	} 19.2
Mining	249	—		
Manufacturing	88,539	8.8		
Construction	49,863	4.9	225,600	7.6
Public utilities	22,168	2.2	[6]	[6]
Transp. and commun.	92,926	9.2	347,200	11.7
Trade	257,798	25.5	839,300	28.2
Finance, insurance, and real estate	248,750	24.7	331,100	11.1
Pub. admin., defense, and services	148,905	14.8	564,100	19.0
Other	98,327[7]	9.7[7]	95,000[6, 8]	3.2[6, 8]
TOTAL	1,009,121	100.0	2,972,500	100.0

Production (metric tons except as noted). Agriculture, forestry, fishing (1995):
vegetables 88,000, fruits and nuts 4,820, field crops 880, milk 407, eggs
30,800,000 units; livestock (number of live animals) 208,000 pigs[9], 190 cattle,
3,512,000 chickens; roundwood (1993) 193,000 cu m; fish catch 182,340.
Mining and quarrying: n.a.; clay, kaolin, and feldspar production ceased
after 1990. Manufacturing (value added in HK$; 1993): wearing apparel
16,011,000,000; textiles 13,180,000,000; electrical and electronic products
11,717,000,000; publishing and printed material 9,065,000,000; basic metals
and fabricated metal products 5,463,000,000; plastic products 3,804,000,000.

Construction (1995): residential 750,000 sq m; nonresidential 1,290,000 sq
m. Energy production (consumption): electricity (kW-hr; 1993) 36,394,000,-
000 (31,894,000,000); coal (metric tons; 1993) none (11,828,000); petroleum
products (metric tons; 1993) none (3,221,000); natural gas (cu m; 1990)
none (385,800,000).
Population economically active (1995): total 3,068,200; activity rate of total
population 49.6% (participation rates: over age 15, 62.8%; female 48.0%;
unemployed 3.2%).

Price and earnings indexes (1990 = 100)							
	1989	1990	1991	1992	1993	1994	1995
Consumer price index	91.2	100.0	111.6	122.0	132.5	143.2	155.7
Daily earnings index[10]	89.0	100.0	110.4	121.4	133.2	143.6	160.4

Household income and expenditure. Average household size (1994) 3.5;
monthly income per household (1991) HK$9,964 (U.S.$1,282); sources of
income: n.a.; expenditure (1989–90): food 34.2%, housing 25.6%, transportation and vehicles 7.6%, clothing and footwear 7.5%, durable goods 3.8%.
Tourism (1995): receipts from visitors U.S.$9,314,000,000; expenditures by
nationals abroad, n.a.
Land use (1995): forested 20.1%; agricultural and under permanent cultivation 5.8%; fishponds 1.5%; built-on, scrublands, and other 72.6%.

Foreign trade

Balance of trade (current prices)						
	1990	1991	1992	1993	1994	1995
HK$'000,000	−2,656	−13,096	−30,342	−26,347	−80,695	−146,994
% of total	0.2%	0.1%	1.6%	1.2%	3.3%	5.2%

Imports (1995): HK$1,491,121,000,000 (machinery and transport equipment
37.1%, of which electrical machinery 12.5%, telecommunications equipment
9.8%; textile yarn and fabrics 8.7%; chemicals and other related products
7.5%; apparel and accessories 6.6%; photographic apparatus, watches, and
clocks 4.2%; food and live animals 3.9%). *Major import sources:* China
36.2%; Japan 14.8%; Taiwan 8.7%; United States 7.7%; Singapore 5.2%;
South Korea 4.9%; Germany 2.1%; United Kingdom 2.0%.
Exports (1995): HK$231,657,000,000[11] (clothing accessories and apparel 31.9%;
electrical machinery 13.8%; office and automatic data-processing machines
7.7%; watches and clocks 7.4%; textile fabrics 6.1%; telecommunications
equipment 4.6%; articles of artificial resins and plastics 2.8%; metal products 2.7%; paper and paper products 1.3%). *Major export destinations:* China
33.3%; United States 21.7%; Japan 6.1%; Germany 4.3%; United Kingdom
3.2%; Taiwan 3.0%; Singapore 2.8%.

Transport and communications

Transport. Railroads (1994): route length 21 mi, 34 km; passenger-mi 2,119,-
000,000, passenger-km 3,411,000,000; short ton-mi cargo 68,000,000, metric
ton-km cargo 99,000,000. Roads (1995): total length 1,067 mi, 1,717 km
(paved 100%). Vehicles (1995): passenger cars 303,308; trucks and buses
130,916. Merchant marine (1992): vessels (100 gross tons and over) 387; total deadweight tonnage 11,688,605. Air transport (1995): passenger arrivals
10,630,704, passenger departures 10,739,254; airports (1996) with scheduled
flights 1.
Communications. Daily newspapers (1995): total number 59; total circulation 2,951,000[12]; circulation per 1,000 population 498[12]. Radio (1995): total
number of receivers 3,700,000 (1 per 1.7 persons). Television (1995): total
number of receivers 1,749,000 (1 per 3.5 persons). Telephones (main lines;
1995): 3,339,000 (1 per 1.9 persons).

Education and health

Education (1995–96)				
	schools	teachers	students	student/ teacher ratio
Primary (age 6–11)	860	19,493[13]	467,718	24.8[13]
Secondary (age 12–18)	507	22,257[13]	470,997	20.9[13]
Vocational	9	2,488[14]	48,421	18.5[14]
Higher	10	1,422[14]	76,357	32.4[14]

Educational attainment (1991). Percentage of population age 15 and over
having: no formal schooling 12.8%; primary education 25.2%; secondary
45.8%; matriculation 4.9%; nondegree higher 5.4%; higher degree 5.9%.
Literacy (1985): total population age 15 and over literate 3,668,000 (88.1%);
males literate 2,040,000 (94.7%); females literate 1,628,000 (80.9%).
Health (1995): physicians 8,122[15] (1 per 762 persons); hospital beds 29,342 (1
per 211 persons); infant mortality rate per 1,000 live births 4.7.
Food (1992): daily per capita caloric intake 3,129 (vegetable products 70%,
animal products 30%); 137% of FAO recommended minimum requirement.

Military

Total active duty personnel (1995): 880[16] (army 56.8%, navy 22.7%, air force
20.5%). *Military expenditure as percentage of GNP* (1984): 0.6% (world 5.9%);
per capita expenditure U.S.$39.

[1]On July 1, 1997, Hong Kong will revert to China as a Special Administrative Region
in which the existing socioeconomic system would remain unchanged for a period
of 50 years. [2]Includes 21 nonelective seats. [3]Victoria, for some time, had been
regarded as the capital because it is the seat of the British administration of the
Crown Colony. [4]Excludes transients and Vietnamese refugees. [5]Excludes about 59,900
Vietnamese refugees, about 1% of the population. [6]Other includes Public utilities.
[7]Indirect taxes less subsidies. [8]Includes 57,200 unemployed. [9]Excludes local pigs not
slaughtered in abattoirs. [10]September. [11]Excludes reexports valued at HK$1,112,470,-
000,000. [12]Thirty-two newspapers only. [13]1994–95. [14]1987–88. [15]Registered personnel;
all may not be present and working in the country. [16]British forces with a few locally
enlisted personnel.

Hungary

Official name: Magyar Köztársaság (Republic of Hungary).
Form of government: unitary multiparty republic with one legislative house (National Assembly [394[1]]).
Chief of state: President.
Head of government: Prime Minister.
Capital: Budapest.
Official language: Hungarian.
Official religion: none.
Monetary unit: 1 forint (Ft) = 100 filler; valuation (Oct. 11, 1996) 1 U.S.$ = Ft 155.50; 1 £ = Ft 244.95.

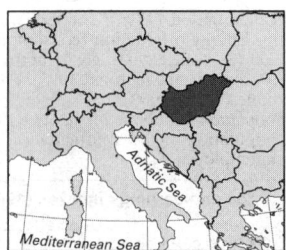

Area and population		area		population
				1996[2]
Counties	Capitals	sq mi	sq km	estimate
Bács-Kiskun	Kecskemét	3,229	8,362	540,000
Baranya	Pécs	1,732	4,487	411,000
Békés	Békéscsaba	2,175	5,632	402,000
Borsod-Abaúj-Zemplén	Miskolc	2,798	7,247	746,000
Csongrád	Szeged	1,646	4,263	427,000
Fejér	Székesfehérvár	1,688	4,373	426,000
Győr-Moson-Sopron	Győr	1,568	4,062	426,000
Hajdú-Bihar	Debrecen	2,398	6,211	550,000
Heves	Eger	1,404	3,637	328,000
Jász-Nagykun-Szolnok	Szolnok	2,165	5,607	420,000
Komárom-Esztergom	Tatabánya	869	2,251	312,000
Nógrád	Salgótarján	982	2,544	222,000
Pest	Budapest[3]	2,469	6,394	986,000
Somogy	Kaposvár	2,331	6,036	337,000
Szabolcs-Szatmár-Bereg	Nyíregyháza	2,292	5,937	572,000
Tolna	Szekszárd	1,430	3,704	249,000
Vas	Szombathely	1,288	3,336	272,000
Veszprém	Veszprém	1,791	4,639	378,000
Zala	Zalaegerszeg	1,461	3,784	301,000
Capital City				
Budapest[3]		203	525	1,909,000
TOTAL		35,919	93,030[4]	10,214,000

Demography

Population (1996): 10,201,000.
Density (1996): persons per sq mi 284.0, persons per sq km 109.7.
Urban-rural (1996): urban 62.6%; rural 37.4%.
Sex distribution (1996): male 47.82%; female 52.18%.
Age breakdown (1996): under 15, 18.0%; 15–29, 22.7%; 30–44, 21.1%; 45–59, 18.8%; 60–74, 14.4%; 75 and over, 5.0%.
Population projection: (2000) 10,086,000; (2010) 9,806,000. The population has declined at an average annual rate of 0.3% since 1980.
Ethnic composition (1993): Magyar 92%; Gypsy 3%; German 1%; Slovak 1%; Jewish 1%; Southern Slav 1%; other 1%.
Religious affiliation (1992): Christian 92.9%, of which Roman Catholic 67.8%, Protestant 25.1%; atheist and nonreligious 4.8%; other 2.3%.
Major cities (1996[2]): Budapest 1,909,000; Debrecen 211,000; Miskolc 180,000; Szeged 167,000; Pécs 163,000.

Vital statistics

Birth rate per 1,000 population (1995): 10.9 (world avg. 25.0); (1994) legitimate 80.6%; illegitimate 19.4%.
Death rate per 1,000 population (1995): 14.1 (world avg. 9.3).
Natural increase rate per 1,000 population (1995): −3.2 (world avg. 15.7).
Total fertility rate (avg. births per childbearing woman; 1995): 1.6.
Marriage rate per 1,000 population (1995): 5.3.
Divorce rate per 1,000 population (1995): 2.3.
Life expectancy at birth (1994): male 64.8 years; female 74.2 years.
Major causes of death per 100,000 population (1995): diseases of the circulatory system 676.4; malignant neoplasms (cancers) 317.2; accidents and self-inflicted injuries 110.3.

National economy

Budget (1996). Revenue: Ft 1,853,961,000,000 (value-added tax 27.7%, income tax 20.4%, payments by enterprises 17.8%, excise duties 12.9%). Expenditures: Ft 2,086,832,000,000 (debt service 26.2%, health 15.9%[5], education 15.7%[5], defense 11.3%[6], social security 9.6%).
Production (metric tons except as noted). Agriculture, forestry, fishing (1995): corn (maize) 4,680,000, wheat 4,614,000, sugar beets 4,198,700, barley 1,407,600, potatoes 1,099,200, sunflower seeds 789,000, grapes 544,200, apples 353,000, rye 171,300; livestock (number of live animals) 4,356,000 pigs, 947,000 sheep, 910,000 cattle; roundwood (1994) 4,527,000 cu m; fish catch (1993) 29,400. Mining and quarrying (1995): limestone 4,273,000[6]; bauxite 1,015,000; manganese ore 40,000[6]. Manufacturing (1995): cement 2,873,000; rolled steel 2,117,000; crude steel 1,865,000; pig iron 1,595,000[6]; fertilizers 265,000; aluminum 29,617[6]; cotton fabrics 65,000,000 sq m; ceramic tiles 5,170,000 sq m; leather footwear 11,300,000 pairs; televisions 274,000 units. Construction (in Ft '000,000; 1994): residential 20,807[7]; office buildings 22,494. Energy production (consumption): electricity (kW-hr; 1994) 33,486,000,000 (35,520,000,000); coal (metric tons; 1994) 14,111,000 (15,369,000); crude petroleum (barrels; 1994) 10,537,000 (47,138,000); petroleum products (metric tons; 1994) 6,356,000 (7,044,000); natural gas (cu m; 1994) 4,334,000,000 (9,350,000,000).
Tourism (1994): receipts U.S.$1,428,000,000; expenditures U.S.$925,000,000.
Public debt (external, outstanding; 1994): U.S.$22,090,000,000.
Gross national product (1994): U.S.$39,009,000,000 (U.S.$3,840 per capita).

Structure of gross domestic product and labour force

	1994		1995	
	in value Ft '000,000[8]	% of total value	labour force	% of labour force
Agriculture	276,000	6.3	348,200	7.6
Mining and manufacturing	870,000	20.0	923,700	20.2
Construction	214,600	4.9	190,500	4.2
Public utilities	128,900	3.0	105,700	2.3
Transp. and commun.	332,600	7.6	333,200	7.3
Trade	496,500	11.4	654,400	14.3
Finance, real estate	764,700	17.6	394,400	8.6
Services	834,900	19.2	1,095,100	24.0
Other	432,700[9]	9.9[9]	519,600[10]	11.4[10]
TOTAL	4,350,900	100.0[4]	4,564,800	100.0[4]

Population economically active (1996[11]): total 4,329,900; activity rate of total population 42.4% (participation rates: ages 15–74, 55.5%; female [1995] 47.8%; unemployed 9.8%).

Price and earnings indexes (1990 = 100)							
	1989	1990	1991	1992	1993	1994	1995
Consumer price index	77.6	100.0	135.0	166.1	203.4	241.6	309.7
Monthly earnings index	78.6	100.0	133.4	165.8	202.1	252.4	289.3

Household income and expenditure. Average household size (1991) 2.8; income per household (1990) Ft 376,195 (U.S.$5,900); sources of income (1994): wages 55.0%, social security benefits (cash) 19.2%, real estate 5.8%; expenditure (1994): food and beverages 40.2%, transportation, communications, and automobile maintenance 22.1%, housing 14.3%, household durable goods 8.0%, clothing 7.2%, culture and recreation 6.0%.
Land use (1994): forested 19.1%; meadows and pastures 12.4%; agricultural and under permanent cultivation 53.9%; other 14.6%.

Foreign trade[12]

Balance of trade (current prices)					
	1990	1991	1992	1993	1994	1995
Ft '000,000,000	+56.1	−76.2	−19.5	−317.7	−362.8	−284.8
% of total	4.9%	4.7%	1.1%	16.2%	13.8%	8.3%

Imports (1995): Ft 1,936,400,000,000 (intermediate industrial goods 42.2%, industrial consumer goods 20.9%, machinery and transport equipment 20.1%, fuels and electrical energy 10.8%, food and live animals 5.9%). *Major import sources:* Germany 23.4%; Russia 11.8%; Austria 10.7%; Italy 7.9%; France 3.9%; The Netherlands 3.1%; U.S. 3.1%.
Exports (1995): Ft 1,622,000,000,000 (intermediate industrial goods 39.4%, industrial consumer goods 24.9%, food and live animals 22.0%, machinery and transport equipment 11.3%, fuels and electrical energy 2.4%). *Major export destinations:* Germany 28.6%; Austria 10.1%; Italy 8.5%; Russia 6.4%; France 4.0%; U.S. 3.2%.

Transport and communications

Transport. Railroads (1994): length 8,190 mi, 13,180 km; (1995) passenger-mi 5,244,000,000, passenger-km 8,441,000,000; short ton-mi cargo 5,753,000,000, metric ton-km cargo 8,400,000,000. Roads (1995): total length 18,655 mi, 30,023 km (paved 99%). Vehicles (1995): passenger cars 2,245,395; trucks and buses 312,000. Merchant marine (1992): vessels (100 gross tons and over) 15; total deadweight tonnage 93,204. Air transport (1995)[13]: passenger-mi 1,489,000,000, passenger-km 2,396,000,000; short ton-mi cargo 20,261,000, metric ton-km cargo 29,581,000; airports (1996) with scheduled flights 1.
Communications. Daily newspapers (1993): total number 41; total circulation 2,215,000; circulation per 1,000 population 215. Radio (1993): 6,250,000 receivers (1 per 1.6 persons). Television (1993): 4,261,600 receivers (1 per 2.4 persons). Telephones (main lines; 1995): 1,711,500 (1 per 6.0 persons).

Education and health

Education (1995–96)				student/
	schools	teachers	students	teacher ratio
Primary (age 6–13)	3,809	86,891	974,800	11.2
Secondary (age 14–17)	936	28,684	349,300	12.2
Vocational	349	5,899	154,300	26.2
Higher	90	18,098	129,500	7.2

Educational attainment (1990). Population age 25 and over having: no formal schooling 1.3%; primary education 57.9%; secondary 30.7%; higher 10.1%.
Literacy (1984): population age 15 and over literate 8,269,850 (98.9%); males literate 3,934,250 (99.2%); females literate 4,335,600 (98.6%).
Health (1994): physicians 36,620 (1 per 280 persons); hospital beds 98,453 (1 per 104 persons); infant mortality rate per 1,000 live births (1995) 10.7.
Food (1992): daily per capita caloric intake 3,503 (vegetable products 64%, animal products 36%); 133% of FAO recommended minimum.

Military

Total active duty personnel (1996): 64,300 (army 74.6%, air force 25.4%).
Military expenditure as percentage of GNP (1994): 1.9% (world 3.0%); per capita expenditure U.S.$118.

---

[1]Includes 8 nonelective seats. [2]January 1. [3]Budapest has separate county status. The area and population of the city are excluded from the larger county (Pest), which it administers. [4]Detail does not add to total given because of rounding. [5]1993. [6]1994. [7]Includes hotel construction. [8]At purchaser's prices. [9]Taxes on products. [10]Unemployed. [11]First quarter. [12]Import figures are f.o.b. in balance of trade and c.i.f. for commodities and trading partners. [13]Malév airlines only.

Iceland

Official name: Lýdhveldidh Ísland (Republic of Iceland).
Form of government: unitary multiparty republic with one legislative house (Althing [63]).
Chief of state: President.
Head of government: Prime Minister.
Capital: Reykjavík.
Official language: Icelandic.
Official religion: Evangelical Lutheran.
Monetary unit: 1 króna (ISK) = 100 aurar; valuation (Oct. 11, 1996) 1 U.S.$ = ISK 67.12; 1 £ = ISK 105.73.

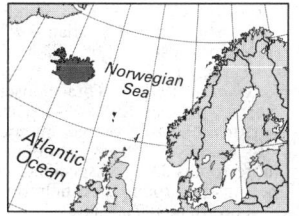

Area and population

Administrative units	Administrative centres	area sq mi	area sq km	population 1995[1] estimate
Austurland	Egilsstadhir	8,491	21,991	12,780
Nordhurland eystra	Akureyri	8,636	22,368	26,664
Nordhurland vestra	Saudhárkrókur	5,055	13,093	10,208
Reykjanes	...	765[2]	1,982[2]	69,955
Reykjavík	Reykjavík	[2]	[2]	104,276
Sudhurland	Selfoss	9,735	25,214	20,754
Vestfirdhir	Ísafjördhur	3,657	9,470	9,018
Vesturland	Borgarnes	3,360	8,701	14,154
TOTAL		39,699	102,819	267,809

Demography

Population (1996): 270,000.
Density (1996)[3]: persons per sq mi 29.4, persons per sq km 11.3.
Urban-rural (1995): urban 91.7%; rural 8.3%.
Sex distribution (1995): male 50.12%; female 49.88%.
Age breakdown (1995): under 15, 24.6%; 15–29, 23.4%; 30–44, 22.7%; 45–59, 14.3%; 60–74, 10.3%; 75 and over, 4.7%.
Population projection: (2000) 280,000; (2010) 306,000.
Doubling time: 68 years.
Ethnic composition (1994)[4]: Icelandic 96.0%; Danish 0.8%; Swedish 0.5%; persons born in the United States 0.4%; German 0.3%; other 2.0%.
Religious affiliation (1995): Protestant 95.8%, of which Evangelical Lutheran 91.5%, other Lutheran 3.3%; Roman Catholic 0.9%; nonreligious 1.5%; other 1.8%.
Major cities (1995): Reykjavík 104,276 (urban area [1994] 155,899); Kópavogur 17,660[5]; Hafnarfjördhur 17,538[5]; Akureyri 14,922; Sudhurnesjabær 10,223.

Vital statistics

Birth rate per 1,000 population (1994): 16.7 (world avg. 25.0); legitimate 40.4%; illegitimate 59.6%.
Death rate per 1,000 population (1994): 6.5 (world avg. 9.3).
Natural increase rate per 1,000 population (1994): 10.2 (world avg. 15.7).
Total fertility rate (avg. births per childbearing woman; 1994): 2.1.
Marriage rate per 1,000 population (1994): 4.9.
Divorce rate per 1,000 population (1994): 1.8.
Life expectancy at birth (1993–94): male 77.1 years; female 81.0 years.
Major causes of death per 100,000 population (1993): diseases of the circulatory system 294.6, of which ischemic heart diseases 177.7, cerebrovascular disease 67.0; malignant neoplasms (cancers) 171.0; diseases of the respiratory system 89.5.

National economy

Budget (1994). Revenue: ISK 109,602,000,000 (value-added tax 37.3%, income tax 20.7%, import duties 7.2%, taxes on alcohol and tobacco 6.0%). Expenditures: ISK 116,986,000,000 (health and welfare 47.6%, education 15.2%, general services 10.7%, communications 7.9%, agriculture 6.0%).
Production (metric tons except as noted). Agriculture, forestry, fishing (1995): potatoes 11,000, dried hay 1,676,000 cu m[6], silage 1,385,000 cu m[6]; livestock (number of live animals) 458,300 sheep, 78,200 horses, 73,200 cattle; fish catch (value in ISK '000,000; 1994) cod 12,350, redfish 7,603, shrimp 7,118, haddock 4,714, Greenland halibut 3,990. Mining and quarrying (1994): diatomite 25,200. Manufacturing (value added in ISK '000,000; 1992): preserved and processed fish 16,261; printing and publishing 5,337; fabricated metal products 4,118; wood furniture 2,810; meat 2,768. Construction (completed): residential (1994) 732,000 cu m; nonresidential (1993) 715,000 cu m. Energy production (consumption): electricity (kW-hr; 1994) 4,774,000,000 (4,774,000,000); coal (metric tons; 1993) none (53,000); crude petroleum, none (none); petroleum products (metric tons; 1993) none (636,000); natural gas, none (none).
Land use (1994): forested 1.2%; meadows and pastures 22.7%; agricultural and under permanent cultivation 0.1%; other 76.0%.
Population economically active (November 1995): total 149,600; activity rate of total population 55.9% (participation rates: ages 16–69, 85.9%; female 46.6%; unemployed [April 1995–March 1996] 4.7%).

Price and earnings indexes (1990 = 100)

	1990	1991	1992	1993	1994	1995	1996
Consumer price index	100.0	106.8	110.8	115.3	117.0	119.0	121.6[7]
Hourly wages index[8]	100.0	108.2	114.4	115.8	116.7	121.7	...

Tourism (1995): receipts from visitors U.S.$166,500,000; expenditures by nationals abroad U.S.$275,800,000.

Gross national product (at current market prices; 1995): U.S.$6,866,000,000 (U.S.$25,680 per capita).

Structure of gross domestic product and labour force

	1995 in value ISK '000,000[9]	1995 % of total value[9]	1995 labour force[10]	1995 % of labour force[10]
Agriculture	9,900	1.9	6,800	4.5
Fishing	38,600	7.4	6,800	4.5
Fish processing	22,400	4.3	9,000	6.0
Manufacturing	48,000	9.2	15,100	10.1
Construction	30,800	5.9	9,800	6.5
Public utilities	16,700	3.2	1,500	1.0
Transportation and communications	30,800	5.9	9,900	6.6
Trade, restaurants	54,300	10.4	24,400	16.3
Finance, real estate	77,800	14.9	13,700	9.2
Public administration	71,500	13.7	6,400	4.3
Health, education, other services	25,000	4.8	40,500	27.1
Other	96,000[11]	18.4[11]	5,800[12]	3.9[12]
TOTAL	521,800	100.0	149,600[13]	100.0

Public debt (external, outstanding; September 1995): U.S.$2,812,000,000.
Household income and expenditure. Average household size (1990)[14] 3.6; annual income per household (1990)[14] ISK 2,605,563 (U.S.$44,712); sources of income (1994): wages and salaries 73.1%, pension 10.2%, self-employment 2.7%, other 14.0%; expenditure (1992): food and beverages 24.2%, transportation and communications 15.3%, housing 13.4%, recreation 10.3%, household furnishings 8.2%, clothing and footwear 8.0%, expenditures in restaurants and hotels 7.3%.

Foreign trade

Balance of trade (current prices)

	1990	1991	1992	1993	1994	1995
ISK '000,000	+4,540	−3,253	−392	+12,188	+20,098	+13,068
% of total	2.5%	1.7%	0.2%	6.9%	9.7%	5.9%

Imports (1995): ISK 103,539,000,000 (nonelectrical machinery and apparatus 12.4%; electrical machinery and apparatus 10.0%; road vehicles 7.2%; crude petroleum and petroleum products 7.2%; plastics 4.2%). *Major import sources*[15]: Germany 11.4%; Norway 10.2%; United Kingdom 9.6%; Denmark 9.4%; United States 8.4%; Sweden 7.0%; The Netherlands 6.8%.
Exports (1995): ISK 116,607,000,000 (marine products 71.9%, of which frozen fish 30.9%, shrimp, lobster, and scallops 14.2%, salted fish 11.7%, fresh fish on ice 5.9%; aluminum 10.6%; ferrosilicon 2.8%). *Major export destinations:* United Kingdom 19.3%; Germany 13.7%; United States 12.3%; Japan 11.3%; Denmark 7.8%; France 6.8%.

Transport and communications

Transport. Railroads: none. Roads (1995): total length 7,668 mi, 12,340 km (paved 23%). Vehicles (1994): passenger cars 116,243; trucks and buses 15,597. Merchant marine (1992): vessels (100 gross tons and over) 394; total deadweight tonnage 114,851. Air transport (1995)[16]: passenger-mi 1,553,000,000, passenger-km 2,499,000,000; short ton-mi cargo 30,906,000, metric ton-km cargo 45,122,000; airports (1996) with scheduled flights 24.
Communications. Daily newspapers (1992): total number 5; total circulation 135,000; circulation per 1,000 population 517. Radio (1995): total number of receivers 197,000 (1 per 1.4 persons). Television (1995): total number of receivers 76,250 (1 per 3.5 persons). Telephones (main lines; 1994): 148,330 (1 per 1.8 persons).

Education and health

Education (1992–93)

	schools	teachers	students	student/teacher ratio
Primary/lower secondary (age 7–12)	...	...	25,234	...
Secondary (age 13–19)	...	...	24,368	...
Voc., teacher tr.	...	...	5,865	...
Higher	...	...	6,161[17]	...

Educational attainment: n.a. *Literacy:* virtually 100%.
Health: physicians (1992) 734 (1 per 357 persons); hospital beds (1993) 2,770[18] (1 per 95 persons); infant mortality rate per 1,000 live births (1994) 3.2.
Food (1992): daily per capita caloric intake 3,058 (vegetable products 60%, animal products 40%); 115% of FAO recommended minimum requirement.

Military

Total active duty personnel (1995): 130 coast guard personnel; NATO-sponsored U.S.-manned Iceland Defense Force (1995): 2,500 (navy 60.0%, air force 40.0%). *Military expenditure as percentage of GNP* (1994): none (world average 3.0%).

---

[1]December 1. [2]Reykjanes includes Reykjavík. [3]Population density calculated with reference to 9,191 sq mi (23,805 sq km) area free of glaciers, lava fields, and lakes. [4]By country of birth. [5]Within Reykjavík urban area. [6]1994. [7]July. [8]Based on weighted average of skilled and unskilled nonclerical workers. [9]Breakdown by sector is estimated. [10]November. [11]Indirect taxes, statistical discrepancy, and production of private nonprofit institution less imputed bank service charges and subsidies. [12]Unemployed. [13]Detail does not add to total given because of rounding. [14]Based on sample survey. [15]Import sources based on a c.i.f. total of ISK 113,616,000,000. [16]Icelandair only. [17]1991–92. [18]Excludes nursing wards in old-age homes.

India

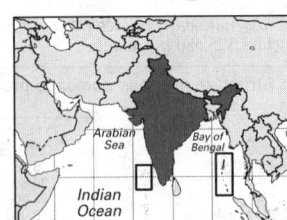

Official name: Bhārat (Hindī);
Republic of India (English).
Form of government: multiparty federal
republic with two legislative houses
(Council of States [245][1], House of
the People [545][2]).
Chief of state: President.
Head of government: Prime Minister.
Capital: New Delhi.
Official languages: Hindī; English.
Official religion: none.
Monetary unit: 1 Indian rupee
(Re, plural Rs) = 100 paise; valuation
(Oct. 11, 1996) 1 U.S.$ = Rs 35.65;
1 £ = Rs 56.16.

Religious affiliation (1991): Hindu 80.3%; Muslim 11.0%, of which Sunnī
8.2%, Shīʿī 2.8%; Christian 2.4%, of which Roman Catholic 1.4%, other
(mostly Protestant) 1.0%; Sikh 2.0%; Buddhist 0.7%; Jain 0.5%; Zoroastrian
0.01%; other 3.1%.
Households (1991)[15]. Total households 151,032,898. Average household size
5.6; 1–2 persons 12.1%, 3–5 persons 44.4%, 6–8 persons 30.5%, 9 or more
persons 13.0%. Average number of rooms per household 2.2; 1 room
40.5%, 2 rooms 30.6%, 3 rooms 13.8%, 4 rooms 7.1%, 5 rooms 3.2%, 6 or
more rooms 3.9%, unspecified number of rooms 0.9%. Average number of
persons per room 2.6. Shelterless (homeless) population estimated (1987)
at more than 100,000,000.
Emigration (1987 estimation): persons living abroad 12,697,000 (accepting
foreign citizenship 8,200,000), of which in Nepal (1980) 3,800,000 (2,388,-
000); Malaysia 1,170,000 (1,029,000); Middle Eastern countries 1,064,000
(102,000); Sri Lanka 1,028,000 (457,000); South Africa 850,000 (850,000);
United Kingdom 789,000 (395,000); Mauritius 701,000 (700,000); United
States 500,000 (287,000); Trinidad and Tobago 430,000 (430,000); Fiji 339,-
000 (339,000); Myanmar 330,000 (50,000); Canada 229,000 (129,000).

Vital statistics

Birth rate per 1,000 population (1995): 26.5 (world avg. 25.0).
Death rate per 1,000 population (1995): 9.8 (world avg. 9.3).
Natural increase rate per 1,000 population (1995): 16.7 (world avg. 15.7).
Total fertility rate (avg. births per childbearing woman; 1995): 3.3.
Marital status of male (female) population age 6 and over (1992–93): single
48.3% (37.1%); married 47.5% (55.2%); widowed 3.6% (7.2%); divorced or
separated 0.6% (0.5%).
Life expectancy at birth (1995): male 58.7 years; female 59.8 years.
Major causes of death per 100,000 population (1987)[16]: diseases of the circulatory system 227; infectious and parasitic diseases 215; diseases of the
respiratory system 108; certain conditions originating in the perinatal period
108; accidents, homicide, and other violence 102; diseases of the digestive
system 48; diseases of the nervous system 43; malignant neoplasms (cancers)
41; endocrine, metabolic, and nutritional disorders 30; diseases of the blood
and blood-forming organs 25; ill-defined conditions 129.

Social indicators

Educational attainment (1981)[17]. Percentage of population age 25 and over
having: no formal schooling (illiterate) 64.8%; no formal schooling (literate) 1.0%; some primary education 7.1%; completed primary 10.9%; some
secondary 6.2%; completed secondary 7.1%; higher vocational 0.4%; completed undergraduate degree 2.5%.

Distribution of expenditure (1989–90)

percentage of household expenditure by quintile

1	2	3	4	5 (highest)
8.8%	12.5%	16.2%	21.3%	41.2%

Quality of working life[18]. Average workweek (1989): 42 hours. Rate of fatal
(nonfatal) injuries per 100,000 workers: industrial workers (1989) 17 (3,625);
miners (1990) 32 (172); railway workers (1989) 15 (1,059). Employees covered under Employee's State Insurance Scheme (1991) 6,070,000; number
of beneficiaries 26,749,000.
Access to services (1991). Percentage of total (urban, rural) households having
access to: electricity for lighting purposes 42.4% (75.8%, 30.5%); attached
toilet or nearby latrine 23.7% (63.9%, 9.5%). Source of drinking water:
piped water 32.3%, well 32.2%, hand pump or tube well 30.0%, river or
canal 2.0%, public tank 1.3%, other 2.2%.
Social participation. Eligible voters participating in last (April/May 1996)
national election: 55%. Trade union membership (1989): 9,295,000.
Social deviance (1986)[19]. Offense rate per 100,000 population for: murder 3.5;
dacoity (gang robbery) 1.3; theft and housebreaking 57.9; riots 12.0. Rate of
suicide per 100,000 population (1991): 9.0.
Material well-being (1994). Households possessing: black and white television
receivers 18.8%, colour television receivers 6.3%, videocassette recorders
1.3%, refrigerators 6.9%, washing machines 2.3%.

National economy

Gross national product (1994): U.S.$278,739,000,000 (U.S.$310 per capita).

Area and population

States	Capitals	area sq mi	area sq km	population 1991 census
Andhra Pradesh	Hyderābād	106,204	275,068	66,508,008
Arunāchal Pradesh	Itānagar	32,333	83,743	864,558
Assam	Dispur	30,285	78,438	22,414,322
Bihār	Patna	67,134	173,877	86,374,465
Goa	Panaji	1,429	3,702	1,169,793
Gujarāt	Gāndhīnagar	75,685	196,024	41,309,582
Haryāna	Chandīgarh	17,070	44,212	16,463,648
Himāchal Pradesh	Shimla	21,495	55,673	5,170,877
Jammu and Kashmir	Srīnagar	38,830	100,569	7,718,700[3]
Karnātaka	Bangalore	74,051	191,791	44,977,201
Kerala	Trivandrum	15,005	38,863	29,098,518
Madhya Pradesh	Bhopāl	171,215	443,446	66,181,170
Mahārāshtra	Bombay (Mumbai)	118,800	307,690	78,937,187
Manipur	Imphāl	8,621	22,327	1,837,149
Meghālaya	Shillong	8,660	22,429	1,774,778
Mizoram	Āīzawl	8,140	21,081	689,756
Nāgāland	Kohīma	6,401	16,579	1,209,546
Orissa	Bhubaneshwar	60,119	155,707	31,659,736
Punjab	Chandīgarh	19,445	50,362	20,281,969
Rājasthān	Jaipur	132,140	342,239	44,005,990
Sikkim	Gangtok	2,740	7,096	406,457
Tamil Nādu	Madras	50,216	130,058	55,858,946
Tripura	Agartala	4,049	10,486	2,757,205
Uttar Pradesh[4]	Lucknow	113,673	294,411	139,112,287
West Bengal	Calcutta	34,267	88,752	68,077,965
Union Territories				
Andaman and Nicobar Islands	Port Blair	3,185	8,249	280,661
Chandīgarh	Chandīgarh	44	114	642,015
Dādra and Nagar Haveli	Silvassa	190	491	138,477
Damān and Diu	Damān	43	112	101,586
Lakshadweep	Kavaratti	12	32	51,707
Pondicherry	Pondicherry	190	492	807,785
National Capital Territory[5]				
Delhi	Delhi	572	1,483	9,420,644
TOTAL		1,222,243[6]	3,165,596[6]	846,302,688[7]

Demography

Population (1996): 952,969,000.
Density (1996)[6]: persons per sq mi 779.7, persons per sq km 301.0.
Urban-rural (1995): urban 26.8%; rural 73.2%.
Sex distribution (1995): male 51.64%; female 48.36%.
Age breakdown (1995): under 15, 35.2%; 15–29, 27.2%; 30–44, 19.1%; 45–59,
11.2%; 60–74, 5.9%; 75 and over, 1.4%.
Population projection: (2000) 1,022,021,000; (2010) 1,189,082,000.
Doubling time: 42 years.
Linguistic composition (1981)[8]: Hindī (including associated languages and
dialects) 38.77%; Telugu 7.96%; Bengalī 7.56%; Marāthī 7.28%; Tamil
6.56%; Urdū 5.18%; Gujarātī 4.87%; Kannada 3.95%; Malayālam 3.81%;
Oriya 3.36%; Punjābī 2.73%; Assamese 1.18%[9]; Bhīlī/Bhilodī 0.65%; San-
thālī 0.62%; Kashmirī 0.47%; Gondī 0.29%; Sindhī 0.29%; Konkanī 0.23%;
Dogrī 0.22%; Tulu 0.20%; Kurukh 0.19%; Nepālī 0.18%; Khandeshī 0.17%;
Manipurī 0.13%; other 3.15%. Hindī (45.00%) and English (2.50%) are also
spoken as lingua francas (second languages).
Major cities (1991): (urban agglomerations; 1995) Greater Bombay (Greater
Mumbai) 9,925,891 (15,093,000); Delhi 7,206,704 (9,882,000); Calcutta 4,399,-
819 (11,673,000); Madras 3,841,396 (5,906,000); Bangalore 3,302,296 (4,749,-
000); Hyderābād 3,145,939 (5,343,000); Ahmadābād 2,954,526 (3,688,000);
Kānpur 1,879,420 (2,356,000); Nāgpur 1,624,752 (1,847,000); Lucknow 1,619,-
115 (2,029,000); Pune 1,566,651 (2,940,000); New Delhi[10] 301,297.

Other principal cities (1991)

	population		population		population
Āgra	891,790	Indore	1,091,674	Rājkot	612,458
Allahābād	806,486	Jabalpur	764,586	Rānchi	599,306
Amritsar	708,835	Jaipur	1,458,183	Sholāpur	
Aurangābād	573,272	Jalandhar (Jullundur)	509,510	(Solāpur)	604,215
Bareilly	590,661	Jodhpur	666,279	Srīnagar	850,000[14]
Bhopāl	1,062,771	Kalyān[12]	1,014,557	Sūrat	1,505,872
Chandīgarh	510,565	Kota	537,371	Thāne (Thāna)[12]	803,389
Cochin (Kochi)	582,588	Ludhiāna	1,042,740	Trivandrum	699,872
Coimbatore	816,321	Madurai	940,989	Vadodara	
Farīdābād	617,717	Meerut	753,778	(Baroda)	1,061,598
Guwāhāti	584,342	Mysore	606,755	Vārānasi	
Gwalior	690,765	Nāshik (Nāsik)	656,925	(Benares)	932,399
Howrah (Hāora)[11]	950,435	Patna	917,243	Vijayawāda	701,827
Hubli-Dhārwād	648,298	Pimpri-Chinchwad[13]	517,083	Vishākhapatnam	752,037

Structure of gross domestic product and labour force

	1994–95 in value Rs '000,000,000[20]	1994–95 % of total value	1991 labour force[21]	1991 % of labour force[21]
Agriculture, forestry	2,659	31.1	191,340,829	60.9
Mining	189	2.2	1,751,275	0.6
Manufacturing	1,485	17.4	28,671,479	9.1
Construction	490	5.8	5,543,205	1.8
Public utilities	225	2.6	...	...
Transp. and commun.	655	7.7	8,017,746	2.5
Trade, restaurants	1,146	13.4	21,296,337	6.8
Finance, real estate	729	8.5	...	...
Pub. admin., defense	453	5.3 }	29,311,622	9.3
Services	510	6.0		
Other	—	—	28,198,877[22]	9.0[22]
TOTAL	8,541	100.0	314,131,370	100.0

Budget (1995–96). Revenue: Rs 1,605,900,000,000 (tax revenue 58.6%, of which
excise taxes 26.6%, customs duties 18.4%, corporation taxes 9.7%; nontax
revenue 41.4%, of which economic services 22.3%, interest receipts 11.5%).
Expenditures: Rs 1,961,300,000,000 (interest payments and debt servicing
26.5%; transportation 11.9%; grants to state governments 11.0%; defense
9.8%; communications 5.5%; agriculture 4.5%; industry and minerals 3.0%;
social services 3.0%).

Public debt (external, outstanding; 1994): U.S.$87,880,000,000.
Production (in '000 metric tons except as noted). Agriculture, forestry, fishing (1994–95): sugarcane 271,200, cereals 177,450 (of which rice 81,250, wheat 65,240, corn [maize] 9,300, sorghum 9,200, pearl millet 7,140, finger millet 2,680, barley 1,560), fruits 38,912[23] (of which mangoes 10,000[23], bananas 9,500[23], oranges 2,000[23], lemons and limes 1,700 [23], apples 1,200[23]), oilseeds 22,370 (of which peanuts [groundnuts] 8,560, rapeseed and mustard 6,290, soybeans 3,670, sunflower seeds 1,200, castor beans 860, sesame seeds 830, safflower seeds 420, linseed 320), pulses 14,460 (of which chickpeas 6,070, pigeon peas 2,340), coconuts 8,000, cotton lint 1,999, jute 1,489, tea 737, natural rubber 472, cashews 350, coffee 180, pepper 46; livestock (number of live animals; 1995) 194,655,000 cattle, 119,242,000 goats, 79,500,000 water buffalo, 45,000,000 sheep; roundwood (1994) 281,307,000 cu m; fish catch (metric tons; 1994) 4,789,000, of which freshwater fish 2,197,000. Mining and quarrying (1994–95): limestone 88,600; iron ore 60,700; bauxite 4,632; manganese 691[24]; chromium 292; zinc 152[24]; copper 57[24]; lead 36[24]; gold 76,400 troy oz; diamonds 23,800 carats. Manufacturing (in '000 metric tons except as noted; 1994–95): cement 62,400; finished steel 17,800; steel ingots 14,700; refined sugar 14,600; nitrogenous fertilizers 7,950; paper and paperboard 3,100; soda ash 1,450; jute textiles 1,364; aluminum 480; nylon and polyester yarns 357; bicycles 8,901,000 units; motorcycles and scooters 2,195,000 units; power-driven pumps 513,000 units; passenger cars and jeeps 310,500 units; passenger buses and trucks 195,000 units; cotton cloth 17,033,000,000 metres; other important manufactured products include drugs and pharmaceuticals, computer software, gold jewelry, and silk goods. Construction (value of new construction in Rs; 1989–90): 563,670,000,000.

Manufacturing enterprises (1990–91)[25, 26]

	no. of factories	no. of persons engaged	avg. wages as a % of avg. of all wages	annual value added (Rs '000,000)
Chemicals and chemical products,	6,914	552,500	150.5	60,870
of which drugs and medicine	1,794	134,500	157.1	13,226
basic industrial chemicals	1,377	92,900	143.1	12,576
fertilizers and pesticides	569	86,700	212.4	11,826
paints, soaps, and cosmetics	1,655	90,700	135.7	10,631
Textiles	12,837	1,403,000	89.7	57,129
Iron and steel	3,304	467,300	143.3	44,654
Transport equipment,	4,890	644,500	141.2	41,563
of which motor vehicles	2,832	299,500	156.5	24,005
Food products,	19,760	1,122,300	60.6	38,724
of which sugar	1,371	346,300	87.4	10,431
Nonelectrical machinery/apparatus	8,067	478,200	136.4	35,209
Electrical machinery/apparatus,	4,856	389,400	144.0	35,161
of which industrial machinery	1,706	154,900	172.2	16,875
Refined petroleum	79	22,200	242.5	18,768
Bricks, cement, plaster products	612	82,800	118.6	12,430
Nonferrous basic metals	2,710	161,700	108.7	11,442
Fabricated metal products	6,964	233,100	92.6	10,746
Paper and paper products	2,163	144,300	102.0	10,049
Rubber products	1,997	112,500	114.9	9,907
Tobacco products	7,878	434,300	28.9	8,566

Energy production (consumption): electricity (kW-hr; 1994–95) 351,000,000,-000 ([1994] 385,902,000,000); coal (metric tons; 1994) 273,859,000 (284,497,-000); crude petroleum (barrels; 1994–95) 244,743,000 ([1994] 434,149,000); petroleum products (metric tons; 1994) 43,575,000 (56,722,000); natural gas (cu m; 1994) 17,638,000,000 (17,638,000,000).

Financial aggregates[27]

	1990	1991	1992	1993	1994	1995	1996[28]
Exchange rate, Rs per:							
U.S. dollar	18.07	25.83	26.20	31.38	31.38	35.18	34.33
£	34.84	48.33	39.61	46.48	49.03	54.53	52.37
SDR	25.71	36.95	36.02	43.10	45.81	52.30	50.16
International reserves (U.S.$)							
Total (excl. gold; '000,000)	1,521	3,627	5,757	10,199	19,698	17,922	17,436
SDRs ('000,000)	316	46	4	100	2	139	82
Reserve pos. in IMF ('000,000)	—	—	292	292	310	316	311
Foreign exchange ('000,000)	1,205	3,580	5,461	9,807	19,386	17,467	17,044
Gold ('000,000 fine troy oz)	10.692	11.282	11.348	11.457	11.800	12.780	12.780
% world reserves	1.1	1.2	1.2	1.3	1.3	...	...
Interest and prices							
Central bank discount (%)	10.0	12.0	12.0	12.0	12.0	12.0	...
Advance (prime) rate (%)	16.5	17.9	18.9	16.3	...	...	...
Industrial share prices (1990 = 100)[29]	100.0	134.8	247.3	202.9	322.1	269.5	...
Balance of payments (U.S.$'000,000)							
Balance of visible trade	−5,151	−2,992	−2,130	...	...	...	...
Imports, f.o.b.	23,437	21,087	22,150	...	...	...	...
Exports, f.o.b.	18,286	18,095	20,019	...	...	...	...
Balance of invisibles	−1,785	−1,036	−1,977	...	...	...	...
Balance of payments, current account	−6,836	−4,028	−4,107	...	...	...	...

Land use (1994): forested 23.0%; meadows and pastures 3.8%; agricultural and under permanent cultivation 57.1%; other 16.1%.
Population economically active (1991): total 314,131,370; activity rate of total population 37.5% (participation rates: over age 15 [1981] 60.7%; female 28.6%; unemployed[30]).

Price and earnings indexes (1990 = 100)

	1989	1990	1991	1992	1993	1994	1995
Consumer price index	91.8	100.0	113.9	127.3	135.4	149.2	164.5
Earnings index	...	...	...	...	...	...	...

Household income and expenditure. Average household size (1991)[15] 5.6; income per household: n.a.; sources of income (1984–85): salaries and wages 42.2%, self-employed 39.7%, interest 8.6%, profits and dividends 6.0%, rent 3.5%; expenditure (1993–94): food and beverages 54.1%, transportation and communications 13.0%, housing and energy 9.9%, clothing and footwear 9.8%.
Service enterprises (net value added at factor cost in Rs '000,000; 1989–90): wholesale and retail trade 468,450; community, social, and personal services 226,320; construction 211,520; finance and insurance 172,770; transport and storage 169,630; real estate and business services 115,140; communication 30,780; electricity, gas, and water 29,050; restaurants and hotels 25,390.
Tourism: receipts from visitors (1994) U.S.$2,265,000,000; expenditures by nationals abroad (1990) U.S.$393,000,000.

Foreign trade[31, 32]

Balance of trade (current prices)

	1989–90	1990–91	1991–92	1992–93	1993–94	1994–95
Rs '000,000	−76,700	−106,450	−38,100	−96,870	−33,500	−72,970
% of total	12.2%	14.1%	4.1%	8.3%	2.3%	4.2%

Imports (1994–95): Rs 899,710,000,000 (mineral fuels and lubricants 20.7%; nonelectrical machinery 10.3%; industrial chemicals, soaps, and paints 8.2%; precious and semiprecious stones 5.7%; transport equipment 3.9%). *Major import sources:* U.S. 10.1%; Germany 7.6%; Japan 7.1%; Saudi Arabia 5.5%; U.K. 5.4%; Kuwait 5.2%; Belgium 4.2%; Australia 3.2%; France 2.1%; Iran 1.9%.
Exports (1994–95): Rs 826,740,000,000 (cut and polished diamonds and jewelry 17.1%; machinery, transport equipment, metal products, iron and steel, and electronic components 13.2%; ready-made garments 12.5%; chemicals and chemical products 9.2%; cotton yarn, fabrics, and thread 8.5%; leather and leather manufactures 6.1%; fish products 4.3%; oil cakes 2.2%). *Major export destinations:* U.S. 19.1%; Japan 7.7%; Germany 6.6%; U.K. 6.4%; Belgium 3.8%; Russia 3.1%; France 2.2%; The Netherlands 2.2%; Saudi Arabia 1.7%; Australia 1.3%.

Transport and communications

Transport. Railroads (1994–95): route length 38,935 mi, 62,660 km; passenger-mi 198,500,000,000, passenger-km 319,400,000,000; short ton-mi cargo 171,-213,000,000, metric ton-km cargo 249,966,000,000. Roads (1995): total length 1,248,700 mi, 2,009,600 km (paved 50%). Vehicles (1995): passenger cars 2,720,000; trucks and buses 2,207,000. Merchant marine (1992): vessels (100 gross tons and over) 888; total deadweight tonnage 10,365,939. Air transport (1994)[33]: passenger-mi 10,878,000,000, passenger-km 17,506,000,000; short ton-mi cargo 379,651,000, metric ton-km cargo 554,281,000; airports (1996) with scheduled flights 66.
Communications. Daily newspapers (1993): total number 3,805; total circulation 18,800,000; circulation per 1,000 population 21. Radio (1995): 65,000,000 receivers (1 per 14 persons). Television (1995): 20,000,000 receivers (1 per 47 persons). Telephones (main lines; 1995): 10,600,000 (1 per 89 persons).

Education and health

Education (1994–95)

	schools	teachers	students	student/teacher ratio
Primary (age 6–10)	581,305	1,714,395	109,043,663	63.6
Secondary (age 11–17)	231,670	2,008,218	56,614,505	28.2
Higher[34, 35]	7,958	215,234	4,804,773	22.3

Literacy (1995): total population age 15 and over literate 315,600,000 (52.0%); males literate 205,100,000 (65.5%); females literate 110,500,000 (37.7%).
Health (1992): physicians 410,875 (1 per 2,173 persons); hospital beds 642,103 (1 per 1,357 persons); infant mortality rate (1995) 73.0.
Food (1992): daily per capita caloric intake 2,395 (vegetable products 93%, animal products 7%); 108% of FAO recommended minimum requirement.

Military

Total active duty personnel (1996): 1,145,000 (army 85.6%, navy 4.8%, air force 9.6%); personnel in paramilitary forces for border security 282,000.
Military expenditure as percentage of GNP (1994): 2.9% (world 3.0%); per capita expenditure U.S.$9.

[1]Council of States can have a maximum of 250 members; a maximum of 12 of these members may be nominated by the president. [2]Includes 2 nonelective seats. [3]Census not conducted; population based on projection of 1989 official estimate. [4]Future creation of the new state of Uttarakhand from part of Uttar Pradesh was announced in August 1996. [5]Effective government of new national capital territory in place from December 1993. [6]Excludes 46,976 sq mi (121,667 sq km) of territory claimed by India as part of Jammu and Kashmir but occupied by Pakistan or China; inland water constitutes 9.0% of total area of India (including all of Indian-claimed Jammu and Kashmir). [7]Unadjusted for undercount; census total adjusted for undercount was officially estimated to be 858,997,000. [8]Mother tongue unless otherwise noted. [9]Estimated figure. [10]Within Delhi urban agglomeration. [11]Within Calcutta urban agglomeration. [12]Within Greater Bombay urban agglomeration. [13]Within Pune urban agglomeration. [14]1990 estimate. [15]Excludes Jammu and Kashmir. [16]Projected rates based on about 3.5% of total deaths (317,392 registered deaths out of an estimated total of nearly 9,000,000 deaths). [17]Excludes Assam. [18]Data apply to the workers employed in the "organized sector" only (28 million in 1994, of which 20 million are employed in the public sector and 8 million are employed in the private sector); few legal protections exist for the other 348 million workers in the "unorganized sector." [19]Crimes reported to National Crime Records Bureau by police authorities of state governments. [20]At factor cost. [21]All persons aged 5 years or older designated "workers" per 1991 census. [22]Not adequately defined. [23]1995. [24]Approximate metal content of ore. [25]Establishments with 10 or more workers using electrical power or 20 or more workers not using electrical power. [26]Excludes Arunāchal Pradesh, Mizoram, Sikkim, and Lakshadweep. [27]End-of-period unless otherwise noted. [28]March. [29]Annual average. [30]36,040,000 persons were registered at government unemployment offices in March 1994. [31]Imports c.i.f.; exports f.o.b. [32]Fiscal year beginning April 1. [33]Air-India, Indian Airlines, Jet Airways, and Modiluft only. [34]Excludes teacher training. [35]1993–94.

Indonesia

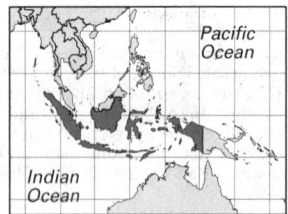

Official name: Republik Indonesia
(Republic of Indonesia).
Form of government: unitary multiparty
republic with two legislative houses
(House of People's Representatives
[500[1]]; People's Consultative
Assembly [1,000[2]]).
Head of state and government:
President.
Capital: Jakarta.
Official language: Bahasa Indonesia.
Official religion: monotheism.
Monetary unit: 1 Indonesian rupiah
(Rp) = 100 sen; valuation (Oct. 11,
1996) 1 U.S.$ = Rp 2,321;
1 £ = Rp 3,656.

Area and population		area		population
				1995
Metropolitan district	Capitals	sq mi	sq km	estimate
Jakarta Raya	Jakarta	228	590	9,160,500
Provinces				
Bali	Denpasar	2,147	5,561	2,902,200
Bengkulu	Bengkulu	8,173	21,168	1,415,000
Irian Jaya	Jayapura	162,928	421,981	1,956,300
Jambi	Jambi	17,297	44,800	2,383,400
Jawa Barat	Bandung	17,877	46,300	39,336,500
Jawa Tengah	Semarang	13,207	34,206	29,688,100
Jawa Timur	Surabaya	18,502	47,921	33,885,900
Kalimantan Barat	Pontianak	56,664	146,760	3,651,800
Kalimantan Selatan	Banjarmasin	14,541	37,660	2,900,400
Kalimantan Tengah	Palangkaraya	58,919	152,600	1,637,300
Kalimantan Timur	Samarinda	78,162	202,440	2,331,000
Lampung	Tanjung Karang	12,860	33,307	6,680,300
Maluku	Ambon	28,767	74,505	2,094,700
Nusa Tenggara Barat	Mataram	7,790	20,177	3,654,800
Nusa Tenggara Timur	Kupang	18,485	47,876	3,582,800
Riau	Pakanbaru	36,510	94,561	3,924,600
Sulawesi Selatan	Ujung Pandang	28,101	72,781	7,577,800
Sulawesi Tengah	Palu	26,921	69,726	1,947,500
Sulawesi Tenggara	Kendari	10,690	27,686	1,594,000
Sulawesi Utara	Menado	7,345	19,023	2,652,300
Sumatera Barat	Padang	19,219	49,778	4,328,200
Sumatera Selatan	Palembang	40,034	103,688	7,232,700
Sumatera Utara	Medan	27,331	70,787	11,145,300
Timor Timur[3]	Dili	5,743	14,874	843,100
Special autonomous districts				
Aceh	Banda Aceh	21,387	55,392	3,860,000
Yogyakarta	Yogyakarta	1,224	3,169	2,916,700
TOTAL		741,052	1,919,317	195,283,200

Demography

Population (1996): 198,189,000.
Density (1996): persons per sq mi 267.4, persons per sq km 103.3.
Urban-rural (1995): urban 35.0%; rural 65.0%.
Sex distribution (1990): male 49.88%; female 50.12%.
Age breakdown (1990): under 15, 36.5%; 15–29, 28.3%; 30–44, 18.1%; 45–59, 10.7%; 60–74, 5.3%; 75 and over, 1.1%.
Population projection: (2000) 210,249,000; (2010) 236,806,000.
Doubling time: 47 years.
Ethnolinguistic composition (1990): Javanese 39.4%; Sundanese 15.8%; Indonesian (Malay) 12.1%; Madurese 4.3%; Minang 2.4%; other 26.0%.
Religious affiliation (1990): Muslim 87.2%; Christian 9.6%, of which Roman Catholic 3.6%; Hindu 1.8%; Buddhist 1.0%; other 0.4%.
Major cities (1990): Jakarta 8,259,266; Surabaya 2,421,016; Bandung 2,026,893; Medan 1,685,972; Semarang 1,005,316.

Vital statistics

Birth rate per 1,000 population (1996): 22.9 (world avg. 25.0).
Death rate per 1,000 population (1996): 8.0 (world avg. 9.3).
Natural increase rate per 1,000 population (1996): 14.9 (world avg. 15.7).
Total fertility rate (avg. births per childbearing woman; 1996): 2.7.
Marriage rate per 1,000 population (1992–93): 7.6[4].
Divorce rate per 1,000 population (1992–93): 0.7[4].
Life expectancy at birth (1996): male 63.0 years; female 66.0 years.
Major causes of death (percent distribution, 1986): infectious and parasitic diseases 43.5%; diseases of the respiratory system 21.9%; cardiovascular diseases 9.7%; diseases of the nervous system 6.0%.

National economy

Budget (1994–95). Revenue: Rp 72,353,000,000,000 (income tax 25.4%, value-added tax 19.5%, oil and gas revenues 18.5%, development aid 15.2%, nontax revenue 8.3%). Expenditures: Rp 72,342,000,000,000 (general public services 37.1%, debt repayment 25.5%, development projects 18.7%).
Public debt (external, outstanding; 1994): U.S.$63,848,000,000.
Tourism (1994): receipts U.S.$4,785,000,000; expenditures U.S.$1,900,000,000.
Production (metric tons except as noted). Agriculture, forestry, fishing (1995): rice 49,860,000, sugarcane 30,272,000, cassava 15,438,000, maize 8,223,000, palm oil 4,300,000; livestock (number of live animals) 12,527,000 goats, 11,966,000 cattle, 6,507,000 sheep, 3,565,000 buffalo; roundwood (1994) 186,-274,000 cu m; fish catch (1993) 3,637,700. Mining and quarrying (1995): nickel ore 2,510,000; copper concentrate 1,510,257; bauxite 900,000. Manufacturing (value added in Rp '000,000; 1993)[5]: food products 13,035,392; machinery 8,891,670; textiles 8,450,944; chemicals products 7,127,707; wood products

4,904,761. Energy production (consumption): electricity (kW-hr; 1993) 58,-888,000,000 (58,888,000,000); coal (metric tons; 1993) 27,584,000 (9,003,000); crude petroleum (barrels; 1993) 557,561,000 (308,994,000); petroleum products (metric tons; 1993) 43,565,000 (34,785,000); natural gas (cu m; 1993) 52,841,000,000 (21,051,000,000).
Gross national product (1994): U.S.$167,632,000,000 (U.S.$880 per capita).

Structure of gross domestic product and labour force				
	1994			
	in value Rp '000,000,000	% of total value	labour force	% of labour force
Agriculture	65,821.2	17.5	37,857,499	46.2
Mining	31,381.0	8.3	741,283	0.9
Manufacturing	90,206.8	23.9	10,840,195	13.2
Construction	27,942.2	7.4	3,558,344	4.3
Public utilities	3,912.8	1.0	182,845	0.2
Transp. and commun.	26,962.0	7.1	3,376,711	4.1
Trade	62,561.5	16.6	13,967,234	17.0
Finance, real estate	28,110.2	7.5	623,899	0.8
Pub. admin., defense	17,140.2	4.5 }		
Services	23,351.4	6.2 }	10,755,020	13.1
Other	...	...	135,079	0.2
TOTAL	377,354.3	100.0	82,038,109	100.0

Population economically active: total (1994) 82,038,109; activity rate 42.7% (participation rates: over age 10, 58.0%; female [1990] 38.2%; unemployed 4.4%).

Price and earnings indexes (1990 = 100)							
	1989	1990	1991	1992	1993	1994	1995
Consumer price index	92.8	100.0	109.4	117.7	129.0	140.0	153.2
Earnings index[6]	92.5	100.0	109.6	...	...	...	...

Household income and expenditure. Average household size (1990) 4.5; income per household: n.a.; sources of income (1976): wages 42.1%, self-employment 41.5%, transfer payments 2.5%; expenditure (1993): food 49.8%, housing and utilities 21.3%, clothing 5.8%, durable goods 3.3%.
Land use (1994): forested 61.7%; meadows and pastures 6.5%; agricultural and under permanent cultivation 16.7%; other 15.1%.

Foreign trade

Balance of trade (current prices)						
	1990	1991	1992	1993	1994	1995
U.S.$'000,000	+6,240	+6,075	+4,937	+8,872	+11,496	+8,883
% of total	13.8%	11.6%	9.2%	13.4%	16.8%	10.8%

Imports (1995): U.S.$40,629,000,000 (machinery and transport equipment 40.1%, basic manufactures 16.4%, chemicals 15.4%, crude materials 9.0%, mineral fuels 7.4%). *Major import sources:* Japan 22.7%; U.S. 11.7%; Germany 6.9%; Singapore 5.8%.
Exports (1995): U.S.$45,418,000,000 (crude petroleum 11.3%, natural gas 8.9%, plywood 7.6%, garments 7.5%, preparation rubber 4.8%). *Major export destinations:* Japan 27.1%; U.S. 13.9%; Singapore 8.3%; Hong Kong 3.6%.

Transport and communications

Transport. Railroads (1994): route length 6,583 km; passenger-km (1993) 12,376,000,000; metric ton-km cargo 3,843,000,000. Roads (1992): length 319,758 km (paved 45%). Vehicles (1994): passenger cars 1,890,340; trucks and buses 1,903,594. Merchant marine (1992): vessels (100 gross tons and over) 2,014; deadweight tonnage 3,130,175. Air transport (1995): passenger-km 14,330,000,000; metric ton-km cargo 606,848,000; airports (1996) 81.
Communications. Daily newspapers (1992): total number 68; total circulation 4,591,000; circulation per 1,000 population 24. Radio (1995): 26,000,000 receivers (1 per 7.5 persons). Television (1995): 11,000,000 receivers (1 per 18 persons). Telephones (main lines; 1993): 1,713,000 (1 per 109 persons).

Education and health

Education (1992–93)				
	schools	teachers	students	student/ teacher ratio
Primary (age 7–12)	148,257	1,276,217	29,598,790	23.2
Secondary (age 13–18)	28,790	681,199	9,343,690	13.7
Voc., teacher tr.	3,557[7]	103,000[7]	1,429,657	13.1[7]
Higher	1,171	135,462	1,973,094	11.6

Educational attainment (1990). Percentage of population age 25 and over having: no schooling 34.6%; less than complete primary 28.2%; primary 23.3%; some secondary and secondary 12.5%; higher 1.4%. *Literacy* (1990): total population age 15 and over literate 59,134,871 (77.0%); males literate 31,716,520 (84.5%); females literate 27,418,351 (69.8%).
Health (1992): physicians 25,135 (1 per 7,402 persons); hospital beds 112,779 (1 per 1,650 persons); infant mortality rate (1996) 52.
Food (1992): daily per capita caloric intake 2,752 (vegetable products 96%, animal products 4%); 127% of FAO recommended minimum.

Military

Total active duty personnel (1995): 274,500 (army 78.0%, navy 14.7%, air force 7.3%). *Military expenditure as percentage of GNP* (1994): 1.4% (world 3.0%); per capita expenditure U.S.$12.

[1]Includes 100 nonelective seats reserved for the military. [2]Includes the 500 members of the House of People's Representatives plus 500 other delegates. [3]The legality of Indonesian administration of this province is disputed by the United Nations. [4]Muslim population only. [5]Medium and large manufacturing establishments only. [6]Based on daily wage rate of production workers in manufacturing. [7]1991.

Iran

Official name: Jomhūrī-ye Eslāmī-ye Īrān (Islamic Republic of Iran).
Form of government: unitary Islamic republic with one legislative house (Islamic Consultative Assembly [270]).
Supreme political/religious authority: Leader[1].
Head of state and government: President.
Capital: Tehrān.
Official language: Farsī (Persian).
Official religion: Islam.
Monetary unit: 1 rial (Rls); valuation (Oct. 11, 1996)
1 U.S.$ = Rls 3,000[2]; 1 £ = Rls 4,726[2].

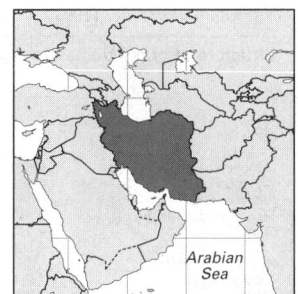

Area and population

Provinces	area sq km	population	Provinces	area sq km	population
Ardabīl	18,451	1,141,625	Kohkīlūyeh va		
Āzārbāyjān-e Gharbī	37,599	2,284,208	Būyer Aḥmadī	13,699	496,739
Āzārbāyjān-e Sharqī	44,767	3,278,718	Kordestān	27,858	1,233,480
Būshehr	25,360	694,252	Lorestān	28,560	1,501,778
Chahār Maḥāll va			Markazi[3]	29,530	1,182,611
Bakhtīārī	14,820	747,297	Māzandarān	46,645	3,793,149
Eşfahān	105,805	3,682,444	Semnān	91,544	458,125
Fārs	120,006	3,543,828	Sīstān va		
Gilan	14,820	2,204,047	Balūchestān	181,471	1,455,102
Hamadān	19,445	1,651,320	Tehrān	40,836	9,982,309
Hormozgān	65,379	924,433	Yazd	69,605	691,119
Ilām	19,086	440,693	Zanjān	23,767	1,776,133
Kermān	185,675	1,862,542	TOTAL LAND AREA	1,630,569	
Kermānshāhān	23,622	1,622,159	INLAND WATER	17,431[4]	
Khorāsān	315,687	6,013,200	TOTAL	1,648,000[4]	55,837,163
Khūzestān	66,532	3,175,852			

Demography

Population (1996): 62,231,000[5].
Density (1996): persons per sq mi 98.4, persons per sq km 38.0.
Urban-rural (1994–95): urban 58.6%; rural 41.4%.
Sex distribution (1991): male 51.52%; female 48.48%.
Age breakdown (1991): under 15, 44.3%; 15–29, 26.6%; 30–44, 15.1%; 45–59, 8.2%; 60–74, 4.8%; 75 and over 1.0%.
Population projection: (2000) 66,834,000; (2010) 79,887,000.
Doubling time: 25 years.
Ethnic composition (1983): Persian 45.6%; Azerbaijani 16.8%; Kurd 9.1%; Gilaki 5.3%; Lurī 4.3%; Māzandarānī 3.6%; Balochi 2.3%; Arab 2.2%; Bakhtyārī 1.7%; Turkmen 1.5%; Armenian 0.5%; other 7.1%.
Religious affiliation (1994): Muslim 99.1% (Shīʿī 93.4%, Sunnī 5.7%); Bahāʾī 0.6%; Christian 0.1%; Zoroastrian 0.1%; Jewish 0.1%.
Major cities (1991): Tehrān 6,475,527; Mashhad 1,759,155; Eşfahān 1,127,030; Tabriz 1,088,985; Shīrāz 965,117; Ahvāz 724,653; Qom 681,253.

Vital statistics

Birth rate per 1,000 population (1995): 34.9 (world avg. 25.0).
Death rate per 1,000 population (1995): 6.9 (world avg. 9.3).
Total fertility rate (avg. births per childbearing woman; 1995): 4.9.
Marriage rate per 1,000 population (1993): 7.9.
Divorce rate per 1,000 population (1993): 0.5.
Life expectancy at birth (1995): male 65.8 years; female 68.2 years.
Major causes of death per 100,000 population (1990)[6]: diseases of the circulatory system 304; accidents and violence 108; malignant neoplasms (cancers) 61; diseases of the respiratory system 48; infectious diseases 34.

National economy

Budget (1996–97). Revenue: Rls 54,369,000,000,000 (oil revenue 51.5%, taxes 19.6%, other 28.9%). Expenditures: Rls 54,619,000,000,000 (current expenditure 58.5%, development expenditure 41.5%).
Public debt (external, outstanding; 1994): U.S.$15,613,000,000.
Tourism (1993–94): receipts U.S.$71,000,000; expenditures U.S.$862,000,000.
Production (metric tons except as noted). Agriculture, forestry, fishing (1995): wheat 11,200,000, sugar beets 5,900,000, barley 3,100,000, rice 2,300,000, tomatoes 2,150,000, sugarcane 2,000,000, apples 2,000,000, grapes 1,900,000, oranges 1,600,000, cucumbers and gherkins 1,250,000, onions 1,150,000, dates 795,000, corn (maize) 700,000, lemons and limes 655,000, chickpeas 340,000, seed cotton 330,000, pistachios 220,000, pears 184,000; livestock (number of live animals) 50,000,000 sheep, 8,200,000 cattle; roundwood (1994) 6,939,000 cu m; fish catch (1993) 343,888, caviar (1992) 314. Mining and quarrying (1994): gypsum 8,430,000; iron ore (metal content) 4,300,000; copper ore (metal content) 130,000; zinc ore (metal content) 75,000; chromite (metal content) 64,000; lead ore (metal content) 30,000. Manufacturing (value added, in Rls '000,000; 1991–92): textiles (excluding wearing apparel) 653,400; transport equipment 587,400; food products 456,700; nonelectrical machinery 445,100; iron and steel 420,200; bricks, tiles, and cement 373,900. Energy production (consumption): electricity (kW-hr; 1994–95) 82,019,000,-000 (71,980,000,000[7]); coal (metric tons; 1993) 1,460,000 (7,567,000); crude petroleum (barrels; 1995–96) 1,318,000,000 (341,200,000[7]); petroleum products (metric tons; 1993) 45,012,000 (46,828,000); natural gas (cu m; 1994–95) 35,400,000,000 (35,300,000,000).
Gross national product (1994–95): U.S.$161,136,000,000 (U.S.$2,680 per capita).

Structure of gross domestic product and labour force

	1994–95		1991	
	in value Rls '000,000,000[8]	% of total value[8]	labour force	% of labour force
Agriculture	27,954	21.3	3,205,430	21.8
Petroleum, natural gas	24,433	18.7 }	100,545	0.7
Other mining	636	0.5 }		
Manufacturing	17,638	13.5	2,013,724	13.7
Construction	4,145	3.2	1,372,437	9.3
Public utilities	1,309	1.0	129,000	0.9
Transp. and commun.	8,199	6.3	762,178	5.2
Trade, restaurants	20,234	15.4	1,238,305	8.4
Finance, real estate	12,227	9.3	194,686	1.3
Pub. admin., defense	12,444	9.5 }	3,517,897	23.9
Services	2,798	2.1 }		
Other	−1,041[9]	−0.8[9]	2,202,502[10]	14.9[10]
TOTAL	130,976	100.0	14,736,704	100.0[4]

Population economically active (1991): total 14,736,704; activity rate 26.4% (participation rates: ages 15–64, 46.8%; female 11.1%; unemployed [1994] 30%).

Price and earnings indexes (1990–91 = 100)

	1990–91	1991–92	1992–93	1993–94	1994–95	1995–96
Consumer price index	100.0	120.7	150.2	184.5	249.3	372.5
Daily earnings index[11]	100.0	113.6	136.9	161.4	200.4	...

Household income and expenditure. Average household size (1991): 5.1; income per urban household (1988) Rls 1,339,970 (U.S.$19,536); sources of urban income (1988): wages 37.4%, self-employment 30.5%, other 32.1%; expenditure (1990–91)[12]: food and beverages 35.4%, housing 23.7%, clothing 11.2%, transportation and communications 7.9%, household furnishings 7.2%.
Land use (1994): forested 7.0%; meadows and pastures 26.9%; agricultural and under permanent cultivation 11.1%; other 55.0%.

Foreign trade

Balance of trade (current prices)

	1990–91	1991–92	1992–93	1993–94	1994–95	1995–96
U.S.$'000,000	+975	−6,529	−3,406	−1,207	+6,375	+5,557
% of total	2.6%	14.9%	7.9%	3.2%	20.1%	17.8%

Imports (1994–95): U.S.$12,683,000,000 ([13]nonelectrical machinery 28.9%, iron and steel 13.5%, transportation equipment 12.9%). *Major import sources* (1994)[14]: Germany 14.0%; U.A.E. 9.0%; Japan 8.0%; France 8.0%; Italy 7.0%.
Exports (1994–95): U.S.$19,058,000,000 (petroleum and natural gas 76.6%, carpets 8.8%, fresh and dried fruit 3.0%, iron and steel 1.5%, chemicals and chemical products 1.2%). *Major export destinations* (1994)[14]: Japan 13.0%; South Korea 6.0%; France 5.0%; Italy 5.0%; The Netherlands 5.0%; Greece 4.0%.

Transport and communications

Transport. Railroads (1994): route length 3,163 mi, 5,091 km; (1993) passenger-km 6,422,000,000; metric ton-km cargo 9,124,000,000. Roads (1991): length 94,130 mi, 151,488 km (paved [1989] 34%). Vehicles (1994): passenger cars 1,557,000; trucks and buses 588,900. Merchant marine (1992): vessels (100 gross tons and over) 403; total deadweight tonnage 8,345,269. Air transport (1995)[15]: passenger-km 5,400,000,000; metric ton-km cargo 107,900,000; airports (1996) with scheduled flights 19.
Communications. Daily newspapers (1992): 13; circulation 1,250,000; circulation per 1,000 population 22. Radio (1995): 13,000,000 receivers (1 per 4.7 persons). Television (1995): 7,000,000 receivers (1 per 8.8 persons). Telephones (main lines; 1993–94): 3,598,000 (1 per 16 persons).

Education and health

Education (1993–94)

	schools	teachers	students	student/teacher ratio
Primary (age 7–11)	61,683	311,531	9,862,817	31.7
Secondary (age 12–18) }	30,389	227,961	6,683,832	29.3
Voc., teacher tr. }		21,851	375,205	17.2
Higher }		32,934	436,564	13.3

Educational attainment (1986). Percentage of population age 25 and over having: no formal schooling 12.8%; secondary education 38.0%; higher 7.8%.
Literacy (1991): total population age 15 and over literate 20,275,521 (65.2%); males literate 11,891,113 (73.9%); females literate 8,384,408 (55.8%).
Health (1995): physicians (1994) 37,000 (1 per 1,600 persons); hospital beds 93,000 (1 per 650 persons); infant mortality rate 54.6.
Food (1992): daily per capita caloric intake 2,860 (vegetable products 91%, animal products 9%); 119% of FAO recommended minimum requirement.

Military

Total active duty personnel (1995): 513,000 (revolutionary guard corps 23.4%, army 67.3%, navy 3.5%, air force 5.8%). *Military expenditure as percentage of GNP* (1994): 2.4% (world 3.0%); per capita expenditure U.S.$51.

[1]Not required to be a supreme theological authority. [2]Fixed rate. [3]The Iranian parliament passed legislation in December 1995 making the religious city of Qom in Markazi a province. [4]Approximate figure. [5]De jure estimate excluding refugees. [6]Projected rates based on about 20% of total deaths. [7]1993. [8]At factor cost. [9]Less imputed bank service charge. [10]Includes 1,640,092 unemployed. [11]Construction sector only. [12]Relative weights of consumer price index for urban areas of Iran. [13]Based on 1991–92 imports equaling U.S.$29,677,000,000. [14]Estimated figures. [15]Iran Air.

Iraq

Official name: Al-Jumhūrīyah
al-'Irāqīyah (Republic of Iraq).
Form of government: unitary
multiparty[1] republic with one
legislative house (National Assembly
[220[2]]).
Head of state and government:
President.
Capital: Baghdad.
Official language: Arabic[3].
Official religion: Islam.
Monetary unit: 1 Iraqi dinar (ID) = 20
dirhams = 1,000 fils; valuation
(Oct. 11, 1996) 1 U.S.$ = 1,000 ID[4];
1 £ = 1,575 ID[4].

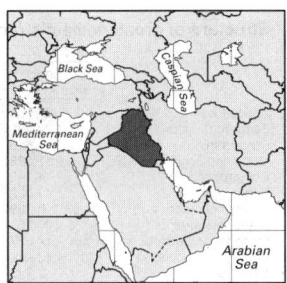

Area and population		area[5]		population
Governorates	**Capitals**	sq mi	sq km	1991 estimate
Al-Anbār	Ar-Ramādī	53,208	137,808	865,500
Bābil	Al-Ḥillah	2,163	5,603	1,221,100
Baghdād	Baghdad	1,572	4,071	3,910,900
Al-Baṣrah[5]	Basra	7,363	19,070	1,168,800
Dhī Qār	An-Nāṣirīyah	4,981	12,900	1,030,900
Diyālā	Ba'qūbah	6,828	17,685	1,037,600
Karbalā'	Karbalā'	1,944	5,034	567,600
Maysān	Al-'Amārah	6,205	16,072	524,200
Al-Muthannā	As-Samāwah	19,977	51,740	350,000
An-Najaf	An-Najaf	11,129	28,824	666,400
Nīnawā	Mosul	14,410	37,323	1,618,700
Al-Qādisīyah	Ad-Dīwānīyah	3,148	8,153	595,600
Ṣalāḥ ad-Dīn	Tikrīt	9,407	24,363	772,200
At-Ta'mīm	Karkūk (Kirkūk)	3,737	9,679	605,900
Wāsiṭ	Al-Kūt	6,623	17,153	605,700
Kurdish Autonomous Region[6]				
Dahūk	Dahūk	2,530	6,553	309,300
Irbīl	Irbīl	5,820	15,074	928,400
As-Sulaymānīyah	As-Sulaymānīyah	6,573	17,023	1,124,200
LAND AREA		167,618	434,128	
OTHER[7]		357	924	
TOTAL		167,975	435,052	17,903,000

Demography

Population (1996): 21,422,000.
Density (1996): persons per sq mi 127.5, persons per sq km 49.2.
Urban-rural (1995): urban 74.6%; rural 25.4%.
Sex distribution (1994): male 51.27%; female 48.73%.
Age breakdown (1994): under 15, 41.1%; 15–29, 30.5%; 30–44, 16.0%; 45–59, 7.6%; 60–74, 3.7%; 75 and over, 1.1%.
Population projection: (2000) 24,731,000; (2010) 34,545,000.
Doubling time: 29 years.
Ethnic composition (1983): Arab 77.1%; Kurd 19.0%; Azerbaijani 1.7%; Assyrian 0.8%; other 1.4%.
Religious affiliation (1994): Shī'ī Muslim 62.5%; Sunnī Muslim 34.5%; Christian (primarily Chaldean rite and Syrian rite Roman Catholic and Nestorian) 2.7%; other (primarily Yazīdī syncretist) 0.3%.
Major cities (1987): Baghdad (1995; urban agglomeration) 4,478,000; Mosul 664,221; Irbīl 485,968; Karkūk (Kirkūk) 418,624; Al-Baṣrah 406,296.

Vital statistics

Birth rate per 1,000 population (1994): 34.1 (world avg. 26.0).
Death rate per 1,000 population (1994): 9.8 (world avg. 9.2).
Natural increase rate per 1,000 population (1994): 24.3 (world avg. 16.8).
Total fertility rate (avg. births per childbearing woman; 1994): 4.9.
Marriage rate per 1,000 population (1992): 7.8.
Life expectancy at birth (1994): male 57.3 years; female 60.4 years.
Major causes of death (1995). Deprivation of medical care (because of acute medical supply shortages) and malnutrition.

National economy

Budget (1992). Revenue: ID 13,935,000,000. Expenditures: ID 13,935,000,000. Details of more recent budgets have not been released.
Tourism (1993): receipts U.S.$15,000,000; expenditures, n.a.
Public debt (external, outstanding; 1994): U.S.$20,000,000,000.
Production (metric tons except as noted). Agriculture, forestry, fishing (1995): wheat 1,320,000, barley 990,000, tomatoes 870,000, clover 840,000, dates 600,000, watermelons 470,000, potatoes 420,000, rice 403,000, grapes 350,000, oranges 318,000; livestock (number of live animals) 6,320,000 sheep, 1,250,000 cattle; roundwood (1994) 80,000 cu m; fish catch (1993) 23,500. Mining and quarrying (1994): phosphate rock 1,000,000; sulfur 800,000. Manufacturing (value added in ID '000,000; 1990): petroleum products and chemical products 668; nonmetal mineral products 152; food 114; textiles 91; paper products, printing, and publishing 78; beverages 56; footwear 56; electrical machinery 54; nonelectrical machinery 53; tobacco products 53. Construction (authorized; 1991): residential 4,558,000 sq m; nonresidential 410,000 sq m. Energy production (consumption): electricity (kW-hr; 1993) 26,300,000,000 (26,300,000,000); coal, none (none); crude petroleum (barrels; 1994) 212,800,000 ([1993] 186,000,000); petroleum products (metric tons; 1993) 22,056,000 (19,541,000); natural gas (cu m; 1994) 2,917,000,000 ([1993] 2,550,000,000).
Land use (1994): forested 0.4%; meadows and pastures 9.1%; agricultural and under permanent cultivation 13.1%; built-on, wasteland, and other 77.4%.

Gross national product (1993): U.S.$24,000,000,000 (U.S.$1,250 per capita).

Structure of gross domestic product and labour force				
	1992		**1988**	
	in value ID '000,000[8]	% of total value	labour force	% of labour force
Agriculture	20,844	35.1	477,264	11.6
Mining	230	0.4	60,701	1.5
Manufacturing	5,620	9.5	337,293	8.2
Construction	2,259	3.8	460,788	11.2
Public utilities	181	0.3	41,200	1.0
Transp. and commun.	5,947	10.0	266,233	6.4
Trade	15,190	25.6	281,877	6.8
Finance, real estate	4,692	7.9	41,532	1.0
Pub. admin., defense, and services	7,209	12.2	2,160,406	52.3
Other	−2,824	−4.8		
TOTAL	59,348[9]	100.0	4,127,294	100.0

Population economically active (1988): total 4,127,294; activity rate of total population 24.7% (participation rates: ages 15–64, 45.3%; female 12.0%).

Price and earnings indexes (1990 = 100)					
	1990	1991	1992	1993	1994
Consumer price index	100.0	287	860[10]	2,600[10]	10,000[10]
Earnings index	...	...	...	...	...

Household income and expenditure (1988). Average household size 8.9; sources of income: self-employment 33.9%, wages and salaries 23.9%, transfers 23.0%, rent 18.6%; expenditure: food and beverages 50.2%, housing and energy 19.9%, clothing and footwear 10.6%.

Foreign trade[11, 12]

Balance of trade (current prices)					
	1989[10]	1990[10]	1991[10]	1992[10]	1993[10]	1994[10]
U.S.$'000,000	+5,301	+5,587	−1,633	−2,199	−1,956	−1,450
% of total	27.6%	36.6%	66.3%	73.3%	68.8%	61.7%

Imports (1994): U.S.$1,900,000,000[10] (agricultural products 36.0%, of which cereals 10.5%; unspecified 64.0%). *Major import sources* (1993)[13]: Turkey 34.0%; Jordan 24.0%; Germany 9.0%; The Netherlands 4.0%; Switzerland 4.0%.
Exports (1994): U.S.$450,000,000[10] (mostly crude petroleum and petroleum products). *Major export destinations* (1993)[14]: Jordan 86.0%; Turkey 7.0%; Greece 5.0%.

Transport and communications

Transport. Railroads (1993): route length 1,263 mi, 2,032 km; passenger-mi 973,000,000, passenger-km 1,566,000,000; short ton-mi cargo 1,129,000,000, metric ton-km cargo 1,649,000,000. Roads (1989): total length 29,337 mi, 47,214 km (paved 77%). Vehicles (1994): passenger cars 672,000; trucks and buses 368,000. Merchant marine (1992): vessels (100 gross tons and over) 131; total deadweight tonnage 1,578,822. Air transport: 15.
Communications. Daily newspapers (1992): total number 6; total circulation 660,000; circulation per 1,000 population 35. Radio (1995): 3,700,000 receivers (1 per 5.6 persons). Television (1995): 1,000,000 receivers (1 per 21 persons). Telephones (main lines; 1993): 675,000 (1 per 29 persons).

Education and health

Education (1994–95)				
	schools	teachers	students	student/ teacher ratio
Primary (age 6–11)	8,035	132,030	2,977,800	22.6
Secondary (age 12–17)	2,635	48,961	1,062,204	21.7
Voc., teacher tr.	310	9,903	135,711	13.7
Higher	12	11,847	201,984	17.0

Educational attainment (1987). Percentage of population age 10 and over having: no formal schooling 52.8%; primary education 21.5%; secondary 11.6%; higher 4.1%; unknown 10.0%. *Literacy* (1995): total population age 15 and over literate 6,701,000 (58.0%); males literate 4,138,000 (70.7%); females literate 2,563,000 (45.0%).
Health (1993): physicians 8,787 (1 per 2,181 persons); hospital beds 27,202 (1 per 704 persons); infant mortality rate per 1,000 live births (1994) 91.9.
Food (1992): daily per capita caloric intake 2,121 (vegetable products 94%, animal products 6%); 88% of FAO recommended minimum requirement.

Military

Total active duty personnel (1996)[10]: 382,500 (army 91.5%, navy 0.7%, air force 7.8%). *Military expenditure as percentage of GDP* (1994): 18.0%[10] (world, n.a.); per capita expenditure U.S.$136.

[1]Multipartyism is officially authorized, but political power is in fact concentrated in a single-party apparatus. [2]Elective seats as of March 1996 elections; 30 additional seats allotted to the Kurdish Autonomous Region were filled by presidential appointment. [3]Kurdish is official in the Kurdish Autonomous Region only. [4]Exchange bureau rate. [5]Includes territory ceded to Kuwait as of Jan. 15, 1993. [6]De facto self-government from 1992 followed by Kurdish factional warfare in late 1996. [7]Territorial water at the mouth of the Shaṭṭ al-'Arab. [8]At factor cost. [9]Estimated gross domestic product (1994): U.S.$15,000,000,000. [10]Estimated figure(s). [11]Imports c.i.f.; exports f.o.b. [12]UN-imposed trade sanctions in place from August 1990 through October 1996. [13]Based on estimated imports equaling U.S.$520,000,000. [14]Based on estimated exports equaling U.S.$472,000,000. [15]No scheduled air service since June 1992.

Ireland

Official name: Éire (Irish); Ireland[1] (English).
Form of government: unitary multiparty republic with two legislative houses (Senate [60[2]]; House of Representatives [166]).
Chief of state: President.
Head of government: Prime Minister.
Capital: Dublin.
Official languages: Irish; English.
Official religion: none.
Monetary unit: 1 Irish pound (£Ir) = 100 new pence; valuation (Oct. 11, 1996) 1 £Ir = U.S.$1.61 = £1.02.

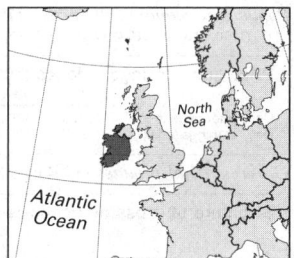

Area and population	area		population
Provinces Counties	sq mi	sq km	1991 census
Connacht	6,611	17,122	423,031
Galway[3]	2,293	5,940	180,364
Leitrim	581	1,525	25,301
Mayo	2,084	5,398	110,713
Roscommon	951	2,463	51,897
Sligo	693	1,796	54,756
Leinster	7,580	19,633	1,860,949
Carlow	346	896	40,942
Dublin[3]	356	922	1,025,304
Kildare	654	1,694	122,656
Kilkenny	796	2,062	73,635
Laoighis	664	1,719	52,314
Longford	403	1,044	30,296
Louth	318	823	90,724
Meath	902	2,336	105,370
Offaly	771	1,998	58,494
Westmeath	681	1,763	61,880
Wexford	908	2,351	102,069
Wicklow	782	2,025	97,265
Munster	9,315	24,127	1,009,533
Clare	1,231	3,188	90,918
Cork[3]	2,880	7,460	410,369
Kerry	1,815	4,701	121,894
Limerick[3]	1,037	2,686	161,956
Tipperary North Riding	771	1,996	57,854
Tipperary South Riding	872	2,258	74,918
Waterford[3]	710	1,838	91,624
Ulster (part of)	3,093	8,012	232,206
Cavan	730	1,891	52,796
Donegal	1,865	4,830	128,117
Monaghan	498	1,291	51,293
TOTAL LAND AREA	26,600	68,895[4]	
INLAND WATER	537	1,390	
TOTAL	27,137	70,285	3,525,719

Demography

Population (1996): 3,599,000.
Density (1996): persons per sq mi 132.6, persons per sq km 51.2.
Urban-rural (1991): urban 57.0%; rural 43.0%.
Sex distribution (1991): male 49.74%; female 50.26%.
Age breakdown (1991): under 15, 26.7%; 15–29, 24.1%; 30–44, 20.2%; 45–59, 13.8%; 60–74, 10.6%; 75 and over, 4.6%.
Population projection: (2000) 3,657,000; (2010) 3,805,000.
Place of birth (1991): native born 93.5%; Eng. and Wales 3.6%; N.Ire. 1.0%.
Religious affiliation (1991): Roman Catholic 91.6%; Church of Ireland (Anglican) 2.3%; Presbyterian 0.4%; other 5.7%.
Major cities (1991)[5]: Dublin 477,675; Cork 127,024; Limerick 52,040; Galway 50,842; Waterford 40,345.

Vital statistics

Birth rate per 1,000 population (1994): 13.4 (world avg. 26.0); legitimate 80.3%; illegitimate 19.7%.
Death rate per 1,000 population (1994): 8.6 (world avg. 9.2).
Natural increase rate per 1,000 population (1994): 4.8 (world avg. 16.8).
Total fertility rate (avg. births per childbearing woman; 1993): 1.9.
Life expectancy at birth (1990–92): male 72.3 years; female 77.9 years.
Major causes of death per 100,000 population (1994): heart and circulatory diseases 392.1, of which ischemic heart disease 218.2; malignant neoplasms (cancers) 205.6; respiratory disease 66.8, of which pneumonia 54.5.

National economy

Budget (1996). Revenue: £Ir 12,434,000,000 (income taxes 35.3%, value-added tax 25.1%, excise taxes 17.9%). Expenditures: £Ir 15,141,000,000 (social welfare 28.8%, debt service 15.3%, health 15.2%, education 13.9%).
Public debt (1994): U.S.$45,594,000,000.
Tourism (1994): receipts U.S.$1,765,000,000; expenditures U.S.$1,575,000,000.
Production (metric tons except as noted). Agriculture, forestry, fishing (1994): sugar beets 1,390,000, barley 910,000, potatoes 589,000, wheat 572,000, oats 128,000, milk 52,460,000 hectolitres; livestock (number of live animals) 8,433,000 sheep, 7,065,000 cattle, 1,530,000 pigs; roundwood 2,047,000 cu m; fish catch 291,215. Mining and quarrying (1994): gypsum 367,300; zinc ore 194,000[6]; lead ore 53,700[6]. Manufacturing (value added in £Ir; 1990): metals and engineering goods 3,237,500,000; food products 1,828,300,000; chemical products 1,492,600,000; paper, printing, and publishing 452,900,000; nonmetallic mineral products 441,400,000. Construction (1994): residential 2,969,000 sq m; nonresidential 2,673,000 sq m. Energy production (consumption): electricity (kW-hr; 1993) 16,416,000,000 (16,011,000,000); coal

(metric tons; 1993) 1,000 (2,888,000); crude petroleum (barrels; 1993) none (13,663,000); petroleum products (metric tons; 1993) 1,857,000 (4,347,000); natural gas (cu m; 1993) 2,521,000,000 (2,521,000,000).
Gross national product (1994): U.S.$48,275,000,000 (U.S.$13,630 per capita).

Structure of gross domestic product and labour force				
	1994		1995	
	in value £Ir '000,000[7]	% of total value	labour force	% of labour force
Agriculture	2,716	8.8	139,000	9.8
Mining			6,000	0.4
Manufacturing }	11,808	38.3	241,000	16.9
Construction			82,000	5.7
Public utilities			13,000	0.9
Transp. and commun. }	4,978	16.2	76,000	5.3
Trade			259,000[8]	18.2[8]
Pub. admin., defense	1,763	5.7	72,000	5.1
Services			345,000	24.2
Finance }	9,565	31.0	8	8
Other			192,000[9]	13.5[9]
TOTAL	30,830	100.0	1,425,000	100.0

Population economically active (1995): total 1,423,000; activity rate of total population 39.7% (participation rates: ages 15–64, 59.2%[10]; female 30.5%[10]; unemployed 13.5%).

Price and earnings indexes (1990 = 100)							
	1989	1990	1991	1992	1993	1994	1995
Consumer price index	96.8	100.0	103.2	106.4	107.9	110.4	113.2
Weekly earnings index	96.3	100.0	104.4	108.6	114.4	117.8	120.5

Household income and expenditure. Average household size (1991) 3.3; income per household: n.a.; sources of income (1987): wages and salaries 58.6%, self-employment 13.3%, interest and dividends 8.2%; expenditure (1994): food 26.6%, rent and household goods 11.5%, transportation 10.5%.
Land use (1993): forest 4.6%; pasture 68.1%; agricultural 13.4%; other 13.9%.

Foreign trade[11]

Balance of trade (current prices)						
	1990	1991	1992	1993	1994	1995
£Ir '000,000	2,458	2,784	4,062	5,563	6,291	8,103
% of total	9.4%	10.2%	13.9%	16.5%	16.0%	17.4%

Imports (1994): £Ir 17,191,100,000 (machinery and transport equipment 38.5%, chemicals 13.0%, manufactured goods 11.5%, food 8.1%, petroleum and petroleum products 3.8%, crude materials [inedible] 2.3%, beverages and tobacco 1.2%). *Major import sources:* U.K. 33.2%; U.S. 18.3%; Germany 7.1%; Japan 4.8%; France 3.8%; The Netherlands 2.8%.
Exports (1994): £Ir 22,789,600,000 (machinery and transport equipment 30.1%, chemical products 20.8%, food 18.6%, manufactured goods 5.5%). *Major export destinations:* U.K. 24.4%; Germany 14.1%; France 9.2%; U.S. 8.4%.

Transport and communications

Transport. Railroads (1995): route length 1,947 km; passenger-km 1,260,300,000; metric ton-km cargo 569,300,000. Roads (1993): length 92,345 km (paved 94%). Vehicles (1994): passenger cars 939,022; trucks and buses 147,719. Merchant marine (1992): vessels (100 gross tons and over) 189; total deadweight tonnage 208,573. Air transport (1995)[12]: passenger-km 4,660,790,000; metric ton-km cargo 106,999,000; airports (1996) 9.
Communications. Daily newspapers (1995): 6; total circulation 482,637; circulation per 1,000 population 135. Radio (1995): 2,150,000 receivers (1 per 1.7 persons). Television (1995): 1,000,000 receivers (1 per 3.6 persons). Telephones (main lines; 1995): 1,262,000 (1 per 2.8 persons).

Education and health

Education (1993–94)				
	schools	teachers	students	student/ teacher ratio
Primary (age 6–11)[13]	3,317	20,776	505,883	24.3
Secondary (age 12–18)	461	12,514	224,035	17.9
Voc., teacher tr.	325	7,854	143,889	18.3
Higher	29	4,700	86,973	18.5

Educational attainment (1991). Percentage of population age 15 and over having: primary education or no schooling 33.7%; secondary 42.7%; some postsecondary 12.6%; university or like institution 11.0%. *Literacy* (1987): virtually 100% literate.
Health: physicians (1984) 5,180 (1 per 681 persons); hospital beds (1993) 13,806[14] (1 per 255 persons); infant mortality rate (1994) 5.9.
Food (1988–90): daily per capita caloric intake 3,952 (vegetable products 62%, animal products 38%); 157% of FAO recommended minimum requirement.

Military

Total active duty personnel (1995): 12,900 (army 84.5%, navy 7.7%, air force 7.8%). *Military expenditure as percentage of GNP* (1994): 1.3% (world 3.0%); per capita expenditure U.S.$172.

[1]As provided by the constitution; the 1948 Republic of Ireland Act provides precedent for this longer formulation of the official name but, per official sources, "has not changed the usage *Ireland* as the name of the state in the English language." [2]Includes 11 nonelective seats. [3]Includes county borough(s). [4]Detail does not add to total given because of rounding. [5]County boroughs. [6]Metal content of ores. [7]At factor cost. [8]Trade includes Finance. [9]Unemployed. [10]1988. [11]Import figures are f.o.b. in balance of trade and c.i.f. for commodities and trading partners. [12]Aer Lingus only. [13]National schools only. [14]Acute-care public hospitals only.

Israel

Official name: Medinat Yisra'el (Hebrew); Isrā'īl (Arabic) (State of Israel).
Form of government: multiparty republic with one legislative house (Knesset [120]).
Chief of state: President.
Head of government: Prime Minister.
Capital: Jerusalem is the proclaimed capital of Israel (since Jan. 23, 1950) and the actual seat of government, but recognition of its status as capital by the international community has largely been withheld pending final settlement of territorial and other issues through peace talks between Israel and the Arab parties concerned.
Official languages: Hebrew; Arabic.
Official religion: none.
Monetary unit: 1 New (Israeli) sheqel (NIS) = 100 agorot; valuation (Oct. 11, 1996) 1 U.S.$ = NIS 3.19; 1 £ = NIS 5.03.

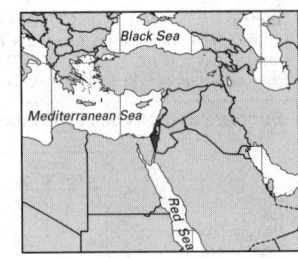

Area and population		area[1]		population
				1996[2]
Districts	Capitals	sq mi	sq km	estimate
Central (Ha Merkaz)	Ramla	479	1,242	1,213,200
Haifa (Hefa)	Haifa	330	854	740,300
Jerusalem (Yerushalayim)	Jerusalem	240	622	662,700
Northern (Ha Zafon)	Tiberias	1,284	3,325	952,100
Southern (Ha Darom)	Beersheba	5,447	14,107	770,200
Tel Aviv	Tel Aviv–Yafo	66	170	1,141,900
TOTAL		7,846	20,320	5,480,400[3, 4]

Demography

Population (1996): 5,481,000[3, 4].
Density (1996)[3, 4]: persons per sq mi 698.6, persons per sq km 269.7.
Urban-rural (1996)[2]: urban 91.0%; rural 9.0%.
Sex distribution (1995): male 49.5%; female 50.5%.
Age breakdown (1995): under 15, 29.6%; 15–29, 25.1%; 30–44, 19.8%; 45–54, 9.3%; 55–64, 6.8%; 65–74, 5.7%; 75 and over, 3.8%[5].
Population projection: (2000) 5,881,000; (2010) 6,713,000.
Ethnic composition (1996): Jewish 81.0%; Arab and other 19.0%.
Religious affiliation (1996): Jewish 81.0%; Muslim (mostly Sunnī) 14.5%; Christian 2.9%; Druze 1.7%[5].
Major cities (1996): Jerusalem 591,400; Tel Aviv–Yafo 355,900; Haifa 252,300; Rishon LeZiyyon 165,300; Holon 163,900; Petah Tiqwa 153,100.

Vital statistics

Birth rate per 1,000 population (1995): 21.1 (world avg. 25.0); (1994)[6] legitimate 98.2%; illegitimate 1.8%.
Death rate per 1,000 population (1995): 6.4 (world avg. 9.3).
Natural increase rate per 1,000 population (1995): 14.7 (world avg. 15.7).
Total fertility rate (avg. births per childbearing woman; 1995): 2.9.
Marriage rate per 1,000 population (1995): 6.5.
Divorce rate per 1,000 population (1995): 1.6.
Life expectancy at birth (1994): male 75.5 years; female 79.4 years.
Major causes of death per 100,000 population (1994): heart diseases 211.3; malignant neoplasms (cancers) 140.5; cerebrovascular diseases 59.5; accidents 25.5; diabetes mellitus 15.6.

National economy

Budget (1996). Revenue: NIS 123,543,000,000 (income tax, property tax, and land improvement tax 39.0%, value-added tax 28.0%, sales tax and fuel tax 9.5%, royalties and interest 2.7%). Expenditures: NIS 123,543,000,000 (defense 22.3%, labour and social welfare 16.8%, education and culture 16.2%, interest on loans 16.2%).
Public debt (1993): U.S.$64,112,000,000.
Production (metric tons except as noted). Agriculture, forestry, fishing (1995): tomatoes 503,700, grapefruit 404,400, potatoes 281,000, wheat 180,000, watermelons 125,000, seed cotton 113,200; livestock (number of live animals) 379,500 cattle, 351,700 sheep, 91,000 goats, 23,000,000 chickens; roundwood (1994) 113,000 cu m; fish catch (1993) 18,661. Mining and quarrying (1994): phosphate rock 2,642,000[7]; potash 1,300,000; lime 210,000; bromine 130,000; bromine compounds 121,000. Manufacturing (1995): cement 6,204,000; polyethylene 144,147[8]; sulfuric acid 130,000[8]; cardboard 119,740; paper 103,012; chlorine 37,760; ammonium sulfate 11,817[8]; wine 12,733,000 litres[8]. Construction (1995): residential 5,850,000 sq m; nonresidential 2,430,000 sq m. Energy production (consumption): electricity (kW-hr; 1994) 28,315,000 (27,985,000); coal (metric tons; 1994) none (6,026,000); crude petroleum (barrels; 1994) 29,000 (88,682,000); petroleum products (metric tons; 1994) 10,589,000 (8,122,000); natural gas (cu m; 1994) 22,025,000 (22,025,000).
Household income and expenditure (1995). Average household size 3.4; monthly income per household[9] NIS 6,125 (U.S.$2,034); sources of income (1993)[9]: salaries and wages 63.4%, allowances and assistance 18.9%, self-employment 14.6%, other 3.1%; expenditure (1995): food, beverages, and tobacco 22.9%, housing 22.3%, household durable goods 7.7%, clothing, footwear, and personal goods 6.5%, transportation 4.3%, energy 3.8%.

Population economically active (1995)[10]: total 2,110,000; activity rate 39.2% (participation rates: over age 15, 54.1%; female 43.2%; unemployed 6.9%).

Price and earnings indexes (1990 = 100)						
	1989	1990	1991	1992	1993	1994	1995
Consumer price index	85.3	100.0	119.0	133.2	147.8	166.0	182.7
Daily earnings index	85.2	100.0	112.8	125.9	140.6	155.6	178.5

Gross national product (1994): U.S.$78,113,000,000 (U.S.$14,410 per capita).

Structure of gross domestic product and labour force				
	1992		1995	
	in value NIS '000,000	% of total value	labour force	% of labour force
Agriculture	3,017	2.6	57,400	2.7
Manufacturing, mining	25,591	21.7	404,100	19.2
Construction	9,461	8.0	140,600	6.7
Public utilities	2,861	2.4	19,100	0.9
Transp. and commun.	9,573	8.1	114,900	5.4
Trade	12,230	10.4	329,600	15.6
Finance	29,365	24.9	244,000[11]	11.6[11]
Public and community services	5,083	4.3	607,900[12]	28.8[12]
Services	26,555	22.5	32,600[13]	1.5[13]
Other	−5,748[14]	−4.9[14]	159,800[15]	7.6[15]
TOTAL	117,988	100.0	2,110,000[10]	100.0[10]

Land use (1994): forest 6.1%; pastures 7.0%; agricultural 21.1%; other 65.8%.
Tourism (1994): receipts from visitors U.S.$2,266,000,000; expenditures by nationals abroad U.S.$2,896,000,000.

Foreign trade[16]

Balance of trade (current prices)						
	1990	1991	1992	1993	1994	1995
U.S.$'000,000	−3,245.7	−5,000.7	−5,654.8	−5,656.4	−6,695.4	−9,239.7
% of total	11.8%	17.4%	17.7%	16.0%	16.4%	19.5%

Imports (1995): U.S.$28,285,800,000 (investment goods 17.5%; diamonds 15.7%; consumer goods 12.9%; fuel and lubricants 7.1%). *Major import sources:* U.S. 18.6%; Belgium 12.2%; Germany 9.8%; U.K. 8.3%; Italy 7.8%; Switzerland 6.0%; France 4.1%; The Netherlands 3.4%.
Exports (1995): U.S.$19,046,100,000 (machinery and transport equipment 28.3%, of which electronic communications equipment 6.7%; diamonds 25.8%; chemicals 12.4%; textiles and leather apparel 5.4%; food, beverages, and tobacco 5.4%; rubber and plastic 3.9%). *Major export destinations:* U.S. 30.1%; Japan 6.9%; U.K. 6.1%; Germany 5.5%; Belgium 5.4%; Hong Kong 5.1%; The Netherlands 4.2%; France 3.7%; Italy 3.0%.

Transport and communications

Transport. Railroads (1995): route length 379 mi, 610 km; passenger-mi 166,000,000, passenger-km 267,000,000; short ton-mi cargo 805,000,000, metric ton-km cargo 1,176,000,000. Roads (1995): total length 9,134 mi, 14,700 km (paved 100%). Vehicles (1996): passenger cars 1,112,300; trucks and buses 246,700. Merchant marine (1992): vessels (100 gross tons and over) 58; total deadweight tonnage 723,418. Air transport (1995)[17]: passenger-mi 7,013,000,000, passenger-km 11,287,000,000; short ton-mi cargo 732,900,000; metric ton-km cargo 1,070,000,000; airports (1996) with scheduled flights 7.
Communications. Daily newspapers (1992): total number 31; total circulation 1,240,000; circulation per 1,000 population 242. Radio (1995): 2,250,000 receivers (1 per 2.4 persons). Television (1995): 1,500,000 receivers (1 per 3.6 persons). Telephones (main lines; 1993): 1,958,100 (1 per 2.7 persons).

Education and health

Education (1995–96)				
	schools	teachers	students	student/ teacher ratio
Primary (age 6–13)	1,937	57,618	693,365	12.0
Secondary (age 14–17)[18]	797	39,093[19]	357,653	...
Vocational, teacher tr.	435	17,141[19]	144,216	...
Higher	7	7,829[20]	101,700	...

Educational attainment (1991). Percentage of population age 25 and over having: no formal schooling 6.7%; primary 22.5%; secondary 39.6%; postsecondary, vocational, and higher 31.2%. *Literacy* (1992): total population age 15 and over literate 94.8%; males literate 97.1%; females literate 92.7%.
Health (1996): physicians (1993) 24,344 (1 per 212 persons); hospital beds 33,159 (1 per 165 persons); infant mortality rate per 1,000 live births (1995) 6.8.
Food (1992): daily per capita caloric intake 3,050 (vegetable products 80%, animal products 20%); 119% of FAO recommended minimum.

Military

Total active duty personnel (1996): 175,000 (army 76.6%, navy 5.1%, air force 18.3%). *Military expenditure as percentage of GNP* (1994): 8.6% (world 3.0%); per capita expenditure U.S.$1,304.

[1]Excluding West Bank (2,270 sq mi [5,879 sq km]), Gaza Strip (146 sq mi [378 sq km]), Golan Heights (454 sq mi [1,176 sq km]), and East Jerusalem (27 sq mi [70 sq km]). [2]January 1. [3]Includes population of Golan Heights (31,500) and East Jerusalem. [4]Excludes Israelis in Jewish localities (pop. 138,600) in the West Bank and Gaza Strip. [5]Percentages do not add to 100.0 because of rounding. [6]Jewish population only. [7]1995. [8]1993. [9]Urban population only. [10]Excludes armed forces; includes Israelis in occupied territories. [11]Finance includes other business activities. [12]Public and community services includes education, health, social, and personal services. [13]Services includes private households with domestic personnel. [14]Includes statistical discrepancies less imputed bank service charges. [15]Includes 145,000 unemployed. [16]Does not account for net imports and exports. [17]El Al only. [18]Includes intermediate schools. [19]1992–93. [20]1994–95.

Italy

Official name: Repubblica Italiana
 (Italian Republic).
Form of government: republic with
 two legislative houses (Senate [325[1]];
 Chamber of Deputies [630]).
Chief of state: President.
Head of government: Prime Minister.
Capital: Rome.
Official language: Italian.
Official religion: none.
Monetary unit: 1 lira (Lit, plural
 lire) = 100 centesimi; valuation (Oct.
 11, 1996) 1 U.S.$ = Lit 1,523;
 1 £ = Lit 2,399.

Area and population		area		population
Regions				1994[2]
Provinces[3]	**Capitals**	sq mi	sq km	estimate[4]
Abruzzi	L'Aquila	4,168	10,794	1,262,948
Chieti	Chieti	999	2,587	385,889
L'Aquila	L'Aquila	1,944	5,034	301,387
Pescara	Pescara	473	1,225	291,950
Teramo	Teramo	752	1,948	283,722
Basilicata	Potenza	3,858	9,992	611,155
Matera	Matera	1,331	3,447	209,057
Potenza	Potenza	2,527	6,545	402,098
Calabria	Catanzaro	5,823	15,080	2,079,588
Catanzaro	Catanzaro	924	2,392	744,135[5]
Cosenza	Cosenza	2,568	6,650	756,229
Crotone	Crotone	662	1,716	[5]
Reggio di Calabria	Reggio di Calabria	1,229	3,183	579,224
Vibo Valentia	Vibo Valentia	440	1,139	[5]
Campania	Naples	5,249	13,595	5,708,657
Avellino	Avellino	1,078	2,792	441,980
Benevento	Benevento	800	2,071	295,903
Caserta	Caserta	1,019	2,639	830,589
Napoli	Naples	452	1,171	3,061,423
Salerno	Salerno	1,900	4,922	1,078,762
Emilia-Romagna	Bologna	8,542	22,123	3,924,348
Bologna	Bologna	1,429	3,702	906,946
Ferrara	Ferrara	1,016	2,632	358,816
Forlì	Forlì	969	2,510	613,457[6]
Modena	Modena	1,039	2,690	608,911
Parma	Parma	1,332	3,449	391,909
Piacenza	Piacenza	1,000	2,589	268,338
Ravenna	Ravenna	718	1,859	350,527
Reggio nell'Emilia	Reggio nell'Emilia	885	2,292	425,444
Rimini	Rimini	154	400	[6]
Friuli-Venezia Giulia	Trieste	3,029	7,845	1,193,217
Gorizia	Gorizia	180	467	138,259
Pordenone	Pordenone	878	2,273	276,258
Trieste	Trieste	82	212	257,660
Udine	Udine	1,889	4,893	521,040
Lazio	Rome	6,642	17,203	5,185,316
Frosinone	Frosinone	1,251	3,239	486,328
Latina	Latina	869	2,251	489,656
Rieti	Rieti	1,061	2,749	148,919
Roma	Rome	2,066	5,352	3,774,746
Viterbo	Viterbo	1,395	3,612	285,667
Liguria	Genoa	2,092	5,418	1,662,658
Genova	Genoa	709	1,836	933,661
Imperia	Imperia	446	1,155	217,653
La Spezia	La Spezia	341	882	226,326
Savona	Savona	596	1,545	285,018
Lombardia	Milan	9,211	23,857	8,901,023
Bergamo	Bergamo	1,051	2,722	946,829[7]
Brescia	Brescia	1,846	4,782	1,055,881
Como	Como	497	1,288	805,424[7]
Cremona	Cremona	684	1,771	329,895
Lecco	Lecco	315	816	[7]
Lodi	Lodi	302	783	[8]
Mantova	Mantova	903	2,339	369,190
Milano	Milan	765	1,980	3,921,479[8]
Pavia	Pavia	1,145	2,965	491,988
Sondrio	Sondrio	1,240	3,212	176,371
Varese	Varese	463	1,199	803,966
Marche	Ancona	3,743	9,693	1,438,223
Ancona	Ancona	749	1,940	439,410
Ascoli Piceno	Ascoli Piceno	806	2,087	364,144
Macerata	Macerata	1,071	2,774	297,284
Pesaro e Urbino	Pesaro	1,117	2,892	337,385
Molise	Campobasso	1,713	4,438	331,990
Campobasso	Campobasso	1,123	2,909	239,694
Isernia	Isernia	590	1,529	92,296
Piemonte	Turin	9,807[9]	25,399	4,306,565
Alessandria	Alessandria	1,375	3,560	436,489
Asti	Asti	583	1,511	209,647
Biella	Biella	352	913	[10]
Cuneo	Cuneo	2,665	6,903	549,493
Novara	Novara	530	1,373	500,197[11]
Torino	Turin	2,637	6,830	2,236,325
Verbano-Cusio-Ossola	Verbania	858	2,221	[11]
Vercelli	Vercelli	806	2,088	374,414[10]
Puglia	Bari	7,470	19,348	4,065,603
Bari	Bari	1,980	5,129	1,547,227
Brindisi	Brindisi	710	1,838	413,579
Foggia	Foggia	2,774	7,185	698,776
Lecce	Lecce	1,065	2,759	814,346
Taranto	Taranto	941	2,437	591,675
Sardegna	Cagliari	9,301	24,090	1,657,375
Cagliari	Cagliari	2,662	6,895	767,617
Nuoro	Nuoro	2,720	7,044	273,768
Oristano	Oristano	1,016	2,631	157,693
Sassari	Sassari	2,903	7,520	458,297
Sicilia (Sicily)	Palermo	9,926	25,709	5,025,280
Agrigento	Agrigento	1,175	3,042	478,235
Caltanissetta	Caltanissetta	822	2,128	281,317

Area and population *(continued)*				
Catania	Catania	1,371	3,552	1,056,131
Enna	Enna	989	2,562	186,915
Messina	Messina	1,254	3,248	653,416
Palermo	Palermo	1,927	4,992	1,237,431
Ragusa	Ragusa	623	1,614	294,637
Siracusa	Siracusa	814	2,109	406,487
Trapani	Trapani	951	2,462	430,671
Toscana	Florence	8,877	22,992[9]	3,528,225
Arezzo	Arezzo	1,248	3,232	316,059
Firenze	Florence	1,365	3,536	1,178,731[12]
Grosseto	Grosseto	1,739	4,504	217,363
Livorno	Livorno	468	1,213	336,831
Lucca	Lucca	684	1,773	376,853
Massa-Carrara	Massa-Carrara	447	1,157	200,245
Pisa	Pisa	945	2,448	385,041
Pistoia	Pistoia	373	965	265,486
Prato	Prato	133	344	[12]
Siena	Siena	1,475	3,821	251,616
Trentino-Alto Adige	Bolzano	5,258	13,618	903,598
Bolzano-Bozen	Bolzano	2,857	7,400	446,621
Trento	Trento	2,401	6,218	456,977
Umbria	Perugia	3,265	8,456	819,172
Perugia	Perugia	2,446	6,334	595,695
Terni	Terni	819	2,122	223,477
Valle d'Aosta	Aosta	1,259	3,262	118,239
Veneto	Venice	7,090	18,364	4,415,309
Belluno	Belluno	1,420	3,678	212,229
Padova	Padova	827	2,142	827,631
Rovigo	Rovigo	691	1,789	246,799
Treviso	Treviso	956	2,477	751,101
Venezia	Venice	950	2,460	822,806
Verona	Verona	1,195	3,096	797,237
Vicenza	Vicenza	1,051	2,722	757,506
TOTAL		116,324[13]	301,277[13]	57,138,489

Demography

Population (1996): 57,500,000.
Density (1996): persons per sq mi 494.3, persons per sq km 190.8.
Urban-rural (1995[2]): urban 66.9%; rural 33.1%.
Sex distribution (1995): male 48.62%; female 51.38%.
Age breakdown (1991): under 15, 16.4%; 15–29, 23.9%; 30–44, 20.9%; 45–59, 18.2%; 60–74, 14.1%; 75 and over, 6.5%.
Population projection: (2000) 57,554,000; (2010) 56,278,000.
Doubling time: not applicable; population stable.
Ethnolinguistic composition (1983): Italian 94.1%; Sardinian 2.7%; Rhaetian 1.3%; other 1.9%.
Religious affiliation (1980): Roman Catholic 83.2%; nonreligious 13.6%; atheist 2.6%; other 0.6%.
Major cities (1994[2, 4]): Rome 2,687,881; Milan 1,334,171; Naples 1,061,583; Turin 945,551; Palermo 694,749; Genoa 659,754; Bologna 394,969; Florence 392,800; Bari 338,949; Catania 327,163; Venice 306,439.
National origin (1991): Italian 99.3%; foreign-born 0.7%, of which European 0.3%, African 0.2%, Asian 0.1%, other 0.1%.
Mobility (1991). Population living in the same commune as in 1986: 93.3%; another commune, same province 3.4%; different province 2.5%; abroad 0.8%.
Households. Average household size (1991) 2.7; composition of households: 1 person 19.5%, 2 persons 21.9%, 3 persons 25.2%, 4 persons 21.4%, 5 or more persons 12.0%. Family households (1991): 15,538,335 (73.8%); nonfamily 5,527,105 (26.2%), of which 1-person 19.5%.
Immigration (1992): immigrants admitted 113,916, from Europe 45.3%, of which EC countries 18.4%; Africa 19.8%; Western Hemisphere 18.1%; Asia 15.9%.

Vital statistics

Birth rate per 1,000 population (1994): 9.2 (world avg. 25.0); (1993) legitimate 92.7%; illegitimate 7.3%.
Death rate per 1,000 population (1994): 9.6 (world avg. 9.3).
Natural increase rate per 1,000 population (1994): −0.4 (world avg. 15.7).
Total fertility rate (avg. births per childbearing woman; 1992): 1.3.
Marriage rate per 1,000 population (1994): 5.0.
Divorce rate per 1,000 population (1994): 0.5.
Life expectancy at birth (1992): male 73.8 years; female 80.4 years.
Major causes of death per 100,000 population (1992): diseases of the circulatory system 415.6; malignant neoplasms (cancers) 265.9; diseases of the respiratory system 56.9; accidents and violence 50.4; diseases of the digestive system 48.0.

Social indicators

Educational attainment (1995). Percentage of labour force age 15 and over having: basic literacy or primary education 40.4%; secondary 30.5%; postsecondary technical training 5.1%; some college 19.2%; college degree 4.3%.
Quality of working life. Average workweek (1995): 37.0 hours. Annual rate per 100,000 workers (1988) for: injury or accident 3,697; industrial illness 405[14]; death 5.7. Percentage of labour force insured for damages or income loss (1992) resulting from: injury 100%; permanent disability 100%; death 100%. Number of working days lost to labour stoppages per 1,000 workers (1994): 383. Average duration of journey to work: n.a. Rate per 1,000 workers of discouraged (unemployed no longer seeking work; 1990): 1.1.
Material well-being. Rate per 1,000 of population possessing (1991): telephone 579; automobile 494; television 299 (colour 188[15]).
Social participation. Eligible voters participating in last national election (1994): 73.0%. Trade union membership in total workforce (1990): c. 28%.
Social deviance. Offense rate per 100,000 population for: murder 2.4; rape 3.0; assault 205.5; theft, including burglary and housebreaking 3,015.
Access to services (1981). Proportion of dwellings having access to: electricity 99.5%; safe water supply 98.7%; toilet facilities 98.5%; bath facilities 86.4%.

Leisure (1992). Favourite leisure activities (as percentage of household spending on culture): sporting events 17.8%; cinema 16.3%; theatre 14.0%.

National economy

Gross national product (1994): U.S.$1,101,258,000,000 (U.S.$19,270 per capita).

Structure of gross domestic product and labour force

	1994		1995	
	in value (Lit '000,000,000)	% of total value	labour force	% of labour force
Agriculture	47,319	2.9	1,490,000	6.6
Mining } Manufacturing }	339,244	20.7	4,622,000	20.3
Construction	83,806	5.1	1,615,000	7.1
Public utilities	96,005	5.8	257,000	1.1
Transp. and commun.	103,474	6.3	1,061,000	4.7
Trade	301,822	18.4	4,221,000	18.6
Finance	223,098	13.6	733,000	3.2
Pub. admin., defense	201,991	12.3	4,138,000	18.2
Services	224,307	13.7	1,873,000	8.2
Other	20,039[16]	1.2[16]	2,724,000[17]	12.0[17]
TOTAL	1,641,105	100.0	22,734,000	100.0

Budget (1994). Revenue: Lit 438,855,000,000,000 (income taxes 41.5%, of which individual 34.8%, corporate 6.7%; value-added and excise taxes 30.4%). Expenditures: Lit 642,286,000,000,000 (1992; social security and welfare 24.4%; debt service 23.7%; education and culture 9.9%; transportation 5.4%; defense 3.1%).
Public debt (1995): U.S.$1,314,200,000,000.
Tourism (1994): receipts U.S.$23,927,000,000; expenditures U.S.$12,181,000,000.

Manufacturing, mining, and construction enterprises (1992)

	no. of enterprises[18]	no. of employees[19]	hourly wages as a % of avg. of all wages	annual value added (Lit '000,000,000)
Manufacturing				
Electrical machinery	2,596	328,871	...	35,061
Machinery (nonelectrical)	4,391	348,354	...	24,781
Industrial chemicals	1,138	189,727	...	19,563
Transport equipment	1,095	305,462	...	16,217
Pottery, ceramics, and glass	2,264	162,696	...	13,107
Textiles	3,186	212,926	...	12,744
Printing, publishing[20]	1,907	147,609	...	12,704
Wearing apparel	5,556	266,835	...	11,684
Food products	1,547	126,321	...	10,044
Rubber and plastic products	1,974	138,764	...	9,933
Metal products	601	115,388	...	7,300
Paper and paper products[20]	...	...	...	...
Petroleum and gas	24	9,301	...	2,861
Mining and quarrying	...	14,263	...	1,041
Construction	...	1,688,400	...	87,635

Production (metric tons except as noted). Agriculture, forestry, fishing (1996): sugar beets 12,125,000; grapes 9,000,000; corn (maize) 8,712,000; wheat 8,191,000; tomatoes 4,786,500; olives 3,000,000; oranges 2,192,000; potatoes 2,120,000; apples 1,940,000; peaches and nectarines 1,688,000; rice 1,424,000; barley 1,405,000; pears 991,200; lettuce 930,600; livestock (number of live animals) 10,531,000 sheep, 7,984,000 pigs, 7,018,000 cattle, 130,000,000 chickens; roundwood (1994) 9,465,000 cu m; fish catch (1993) 552,024. Mining and quarrying (1994): rock salt 3,396,155; feldspar 1,806,935; potash 1,438,850[21]; barite 57,856; zinc 40,903; lead 20,455. Manufacturing (1994): cement 32,740,357; crude steel 26,072,585; pig iron 11,160,992; plastics 3,212,363[21]; sulfuric acid 1,975,482; caustic soda 958,898; textiles and yarns 454,685; wine 62,618,000 hectolitres[21]; beer 10,257,672 hectolitres; olive oil 6,290,000 hectolitres[21]; 6,251,283 washing machines; 5,033,314 refrigerators; 2,283,737 motorized road vehicles, of which 1,340,491 automobiles, 749,113 motorcycles, scooters, and mopeds, 194,133 trucks and buses; 2,780,353 colour televisions. Construction (1993): residential 77,470,366 cu m; commercial, industrial, and other 67,048,452 cu m.

Service enterprises (1994)

	no. of enterprises[18]	no. of employees[22]	hourly wage as a % of all wages	annual value added (Lit '000,000,000)
Public utilities	379	257,000	...	96,005
Transportation } Communications }	2,508	1,061,000	...	103,474
Finance	...	733,000	...	223,098
Wholesale and retail trade	9,173	4,221,000	...	301,822
Pub. admin., services	...	4,138,000	...	201,991

Energy production (consumption): electricity (kW-hr; 1994) 231,783,000,000 (269,382,000,000); coal (metric tons; 1994) 267,000 (16,672,000); crude petroleum (barrels; 1994) 33,422,000 (582,644,000); petroleum products (metric tons; 1994) 83,049,000 (89,500,000); natural gas (cu m; 1994) 20,209,000,000 (48,326,000,000).
Population economically active (1994): total 22,303,800; activity rate of total population 38.9% (participation rates: ages 15–64, 57.4%; female 36.9%; unemployed 11.3%).

Price and earnings indexes (1990=100)

	1989	1990	1991	1992	1993	1994	1995
Consumer price index	93.9	100.0	106.3	111.8	116.8	121.5	127.8
Earnings index	93.2	100.0	109.8	115.4	119.8	124.0	127.8

Household income and expenditure (1994). Average household size 2.6; average annual income per household (1984) Lit 19,692,000 (U.S.$11,208); sources of income (1991): salaries and wages 41.7%, property income and self-employ-

ment 38.0%, transfer payments 20.3%; expenditure: housing 21.9%, food and beverages 21.2%, transportation and communications 14.8%, recreation and education 9.1%.

Financial aggregates

	1991	1992	1993	1994	1995	1996[23]
Exchange rate, Lit per:						
U.S. dollar	1,240.6	1,232.4	1,573.7	1,612.4	1,628.9	1,516.6
£	2,195.1	2,175.8	2,363.7	2,469.6	2,571.2	2,350.3
SDR	1,646.5	2,022.4	2,340.5	2,379.2	2,355.7	2,206.8
International reserves (U.S.$)						
Total (excl. gold; '000,000)	48,679	27,643	27,545	32,265	34,905	47,526
SDRs ('000,000)	930	238	241	125	53[24]	80
Reserve pos. in IMF ('000,000)	2,255	2,439	2,164	2,033	1,963	1,909
Foreign exchange ('000,000)	45,495	24,966	25,140	30,107	32,942	45,537
Gold ('000,000 fine troy oz)	66.67	66.67	66.67	66.67	66.67	66.67
% world reserves	7.1	7.1	7.3	7.3	7.3	7.3
Interest and prices						
Central bank discount (%)	12.00	12.00	8.00	7.50	9.00	8.25[25]
Govt. bond yield (%)	11.37	13.67	11.21	10.57	11.98	8.92[25]
Industrial share prices (1990=100)	84.7	70.5	83.5	104.1	95.4	96.8[25]
Balance of payments (U.S.$'000,000)						
Balance of visible trade	−895	3,088	32,825	35,497	44,082	...
Imports, f.o.b.	−169,701	−175,067	−136,328	−154,308	−187,254	...
Exports, f.o.b.	168,806	178,155	169,153	189,805	231,336	...
Balance of invisibles	−20,556	−31,082	−21,763	−19,875	−18,378	...
Balance of payments, current account	−21,451	−27,994	11,062	15,622	25,704	...

Land use (1994): forested 23.0%; meadows and pastures 15.4%; agricultural and under permanent cultivation 37.9%; other 23.7%.

Foreign trade

Balance of trade (current prices)

	1990	1991	1992	1993	1994	1995
Lit '000,000,000	+724	−1,913	2,229	50,789	50,957	65,841
% of total	0.2%	0.4%	0.5%	10.6%	9.1%	9.6%

Imports (1994): Lit 270,063,385,000,000 (machinery and transport equipment 29.6%, of which transport equipment 11.2%, precision machinery 5.7%; chemicals 16.3%; metal and semiprocessed metal 7.8%; food and live animals 6.7%; crude petroleum 5.1%; textiles 4.3%). *Major import sources:* Germany 19.2%; France 13.0%; U.K. 6.3%; U.S. 4.6%; Spain 4.3%; Switzerland 3.9%.
Exports (1994): Lit 305,479,319,000,000 (machinery and transport equipment 41.1%, of which transport equipment 10.7%, electrical machinery 5.1%, precision machinery 3.8%; chemicals 10.1%; textiles 8.4%; wearing apparel 7.7%, of which shoes 2.8%; metal and processed metal 6.7%). *Major export destinations:* Germany 19.0%; France 13.1%; U.S. 7.8%; U.K. 6.5%.

Transport and communications

Transport. Railroads (1993): length 9,906 mi, 15,942 km; passenger-mi 29,270,000,000, passenger-km 47,100,000,000; short ton-mi cargo 14,120,000,000, metric ton-km cargo 20,620,000,000. Roads (1991): total length 188,597 mi, 303,518 km (paved 100%). Vehicles (1992): passenger cars 29,429,628; trucks and buses 2,684,127. Merchant marine (1993): vessels (100 gross tons and over) 1,591; total deadweight tonnage 7,529,052. Air transport (1993): passenger-mi 18,429,000,000, passenger-km 29,658,600,000; short ton-mi cargo 914,300,000, metric ton-km cargo 1,334,900,000; airports (1996) 31.
Communications. Daily newspapers (1995): total number 111; total circulation 7,236,800[26]; circulation per 1,000 population 126[26]. Radio (1994): 45,350,000 receivers (1 per 1.3 persons). Television (1994): 17,000,500 receivers (1 per 3.4 persons). Telephones (1992[2]): 32,945,122 (1 per 1.7 persons).

Education and health

Education (1994–95)

	schools	teachers	students	student/teacher ratio
Primary (age 6–10)	21,024	164,852	2,849,157	17.3
Secondary (age 11–18)	9,549	98,467	1,953,058	19.8
Voc., teacher tr.	7,886	128,032	2,736,445	21.4
Higher[27]	48	58,874	1,601,873	27.2

Literacy (1990): total population age 15 and over literate 47,507,000 (97.1%); males literate 22,832,000 (97.8%); females literate 24,675,000 (96.4%).
Health (1993): physicians 207,319 (1 per 193 persons); hospital beds 380,423 (1 per 147 persons); infant mortality rate per 1,000 live births (1994) 6.6.
Food (1992): daily per capita caloric intake 3,561 (vegetable products 75%; animal products 25%); 141% of FAO recommended minimum requirement.

Military

Total active duty personnel (1996): 325,150 (army 51.5%, navy 13.5%, air force 20.9%, central staff 14.1%). *Military expenditure as percentage of GNP* (1994): 2.0% (world 3.0%); per capita expenditure U.S.$350.

[1]Includes 10 nonelective seats. [2]January 1. [3]Six provinces were created in 1992. [4]Resident population only. [5]Catanzaro includes Crotone and Vibo Valentia. [6]Forlì includes Rimini. [7]Lecco is included partly in Bergamo and partly in Como. [8]Milano includes Lodi. [9]Detail does not add to total given because of rounding. [10]Vercelli includes Biella. [11]Novara includes Verbano-Cusio-Ossola. [12]Firenze includes Prato. [13]The total area for Italy, per the latest survey, is 301,323 sq km (116,341 sq mi). [14]1978. [15]1988. [16]Imputed bank charges less duties on imports. [17]Unemployed. [18]Enterprises with 20 or more persons engaged. [19]Total number of persons engaged. [20]Printing, publishing includes Paper and paper products. [21]1993. [22]1995. [23]August. [24]November. [25]July. [26]68 newspapers only. [27]Universities only.

Jamaica

Official name: Jamaica.
Form of government: constitutional
monarchy with two legislative
houses (Senate [21]; House of
Representatives [60]).
Chief of state: British Monarch
represented by Governor-General.
Head of government: Prime Minister.
Capital: Kingston.
Official language: English.
Official religion: none.
Monetary unit: 1 Jamaica dollar
(J$) = 100 cents; valuation (Oct. 11,
1996) 1 U.S.$ = J$34.00; 1 £ = J$53.56.

Area and population		area		population
		sq mi	sq km	1994[1] estimate
Parishes	Capitals			
Clarendon	May Pen	462	1,196	222,500
Hanover	Lucea	174	450	66,600
Kingston	[2]	8	22	[3]
Manchester	Mandeville	321	830	173,100
Portland	Port Antonio	314	814	78,500
Saint Andrew	[2]	166	431	697,000
Saint Ann	Saint Ann's Bay	468	1,213	154,500
Saint Catherine	Spanish Town	460	1,192	370,600
Saint Elizabeth	Black River	468	1,212	146,600
Saint James	Montego Bay	230	595	166,000
Saint Mary	Port Maria	236	611	113,700
Saint Thomas	Morant Bay	287	743	88,900
Trelawny	Falmouth	338	875	74,100
Westmoreland	Savanna-la-Mar	312	807	130,500
TOTAL		4,244	10,991	2,482,600

Demography

Population (1996): 2,505,000.
Density (1995): persons per sq mi 590.2, persons per sq km 227.9.
Urban-rural (1991): urban 50.2%; rural 49.8%.
Sex distribution (1995): male 49.74%; female 50.26%.
Age breakdown (1995): under 15, 32.3%; 15–29, 28.7%; 30–44, 19.7%; 45–59, 9.8%; 60 and over, 9.5%.
Population projection: (2000) 2,578,000; (2010) 2,802,000.
Doubling time: 39 years.
Ethnic composition (1982): black 74.7%; mixed black 12.8%; East Indian 1.3%; other 11.2%, of which not stated 9.5%.
Religious affiliation (1982): Protestant 55.9%, of which Church of God 18.4%, Baptist 10.0%, Anglican 7.1%, Seventh-day Adventist 6.9%, Pentecostal 5.2%; Roman Catholic 5.0%; nonreligious or atheist 17.7%; not stated 11.2%; other 10.2%, of which Rastafarian c. 5.0%.
Major cities (1991): Kingston 103,771[4] (metropolitan area 587,798); Spanish Town 92,383; Portmore 90,138; Montego Bay 83,446; May Pen 46,785.

Vital statistics

Birth rate per 1,000 population (1995): 23.2 (world avg. 25.0); (1987) legitimate 14.9%, illegitimate 85.1%.
Death rate per 1,000 population (1995): 5.0 (world avg. 9.3).
Natural increase rate per 1,000 population (1995): 18.2 (world avg. 15.7).
Total fertility rate (avg. births per childbearing woman; 1995): 3.0.
Marriage rate per 1,000 population (1993): 6.6.
Divorce rate per 1,000 population (1993): 0.6.
Life expectancy at birth (1990–95): male 71.4 years; female 75.8 years.
Major causes of death per 100,000 population (1991): diseases of the circulatory system 189.4; malignant neoplasms (cancers) 84.1; endocrine and metabolic disorders 51.3; diseases of the respiratory system 30.1.

National economy

Budget (1995–96). Revenue J$39,642,300,000 (tax revenue 85.6%, of which consumption taxes 32.3%, income taxes 30.6%, stamp duties 3.9%; nontax revenue 14.4%). Expenditures: J$48,334,200,000 (current expenditure 62.8%, of which debt interest 22.4%).
Production (metric tons except as noted). Agriculture, forestry, fishing (1995): sugarcane 2,295,000, yams 240,371, vegetables 183,873, bananas 85,223, citrus fruits 48,761, plantains 34,769, coffee 15,398, legumes 10,463, cacao beans 6,186; livestock (number of live animals) 440,000 goats, 440,000 cattle, 200,000 pigs; roundwood (1994) 464,900 cu m; fish catch (1995) 10,764. Mining and quarrying (1995): crude bauxite 3,532,800; alumina 3,030,200; gypsum 208,000. Manufacturing (value added in constant 1991–95 prices, J$'000,000; 1995): machinery and equipment 593.6; food processing 580.3; petroleum products 351.3; rubber and plastic products 324.1; textiles and clothing 257.0; tobacco and tobacco products 255.2; metal and nonmetallic products 223.6. Construction (1995): residential units completed 7,067[5]; factory space completed 6,989 sq m[6]. Energy production (consumption): electricity (kW-hr; 1993) 2,298,000,000 (2,298,000,000); coal, none (none); crude petroleum (barrels; 1993) none (5,373,000); petroleum products (metric tons; 1993) 733,000 (2,442,000); natural gas, none (none).
Household income and expenditure. Average household size (1991) 4.2; average annual income per household (1988) J$8,356 (U.S.$1,525); sources of income (1989): wages and salaries 66.1%, self-employment 19.3%, transfers 14.6%; expenditure (1988)[7]: food and beverages 55.6%, housing 7.9%, fuel and other household supplies 7.4%, health care 7.0%, transportation 6.4%, clothing and footwear 5.1%, household furnishings 2.8%, other 7.8%.

Gross national product (1994): U.S.$3,553,000,000 (U.S.$1,420 per capita).

Structure of gross domestic product and labour force				
	1995			
	in value J$'000,000	% of total value	labour force	% of labour force
Agriculture	15,323.1	9.4	223,200	19.4
Mining	11,711.7	7.2	7,000	0.6
Manufacturing	28,774.6	17.7	104,700	9.1
Construction	20,880.6	12.8	76,000	6.6
Public utilities	3,633.7	2.2	6,800	0.6
Transp. and commun.	13,918.9	8.6	44,500	3.9
Trade	38,505.0	23.7	201,400	17.5
Pub. admin., defense	13,960.2	8.6		
Finance, real estate	21,501.3	13.2	298,700	26.0
Services	6,454.5	4.0		
Other	−12,094.8[8]	−7.4[8]	187,800[9]	16.3[9]
TOTAL	162,568.8	100.0	1,150,000[10]	100.0

Population economically active (1995): total 1,150,000; activity rate of total population 46.0% (participation rates: ages 14 and over 58.7%; female 46.3%; unemployed 16.2%).

Price and earnings indexes (1990 = 100)							
	1989	1990	1991	1992	1993	1994	1995
Consumer price index	82.0	100.0	151.1	267.8	327.0	441.6	529.5
Earnings index	...	...	...	...	...	...	...

Public debt (external, outstanding; 1994): U.S.$3,518,000,000.
Tourism (1995): receipts U.S.$919,000,000; expenditures U.S.$81,000,000.
Land use (1993): forested 17.1%; meadows and pastures 23.7%; agricultural and under permanent cultivation 20.2%; other 39.0%.

Foreign trade[11]

Balance of trade (current prices)						
	1990	1991	1992	1993	1994	1995
U.S.$'000,000	−785	−654	−636	−1,121	−957.7	−1,342.6
% of total	25.3%	22.2%	23.2%	34.9%	28.7%	31.9%

Imports (1995): U.S.$2,772,900,000 (raw materials 55.8%, of which fuels 12.7%; consumer goods 24.7%, of which food 7.1%; capital goods 19.8%, of which machinery and apparatus 10.3%). *Major import sources* (1994): United States 52.3%; Mexico 6.2%; United Kingdom 4.2%; Trinidad and Tobago 4.2%; Japan 3.7%; Venezuela 3.7%; Netherlands Antilles 3.6%; Canada 2.8%.
Exports (1995): U.S.$1,430,300,000 (alumina 44.2%; raw sugar 6.7%; bauxite 5.0%; bananas 3.4%; coffee 2.0%; rum 1.6%). *Major export destinations* (1994): United States 43.9%; United Kingdom 11.4%; Canada 9.5%; Norway 5.9%; France 4.3%; Ghana 3.2%.

Transport and communications

Transport. Railroads (1991): route length 129 mi, 208 km; passenger-mi 12,127,000[6], passenger-km 19,516,000[6]; short ton-mi cargo 1,700,000, metric ton-km cargo 2,482,000. Roads (1991): total length 10,212 mi, 16,435 km (paved 29%). Vehicles (1994–95): passenger cars 86,791; trucks and buses 41,312. Merchant marine (1992): vessels (100 gross tons and over) 12; total deadweight tonnage 16,207. Air transport (1993)[12]: passenger-mi 450,996,000, passenger-km 725,809,000; short ton-mi cargo 51,844,000, metric ton-km cargo 75,691,000; airports (1996) with scheduled flights 5.
Communications. Daily newspapers (1993): total number 3; total circulation 130,400[13]; circulation per 1,000 population 53[13]. Radio (1995): 1,859,000 receivers (1 per 2.5 persons). Television (1995): 484,000 receivers (1 per 5.2 persons). Telephones (main lines; 1995): 286,555 (1 per 8.8 persons).

Education and health

Education (1994–95)				
	schools	teachers	students	student/ teacher ratio
Primary (age 6–11)[14]	788[15]	11,283	319,298	28.3
Secondary (age 12–16)	126	8,377	207,035	24.7
Voc., teacher tr.	18	950	15,898	16.7
Higher	15[16]	1,047[17]	24,200	17.9[17]

Educational attainment (1982). Percentage of population age 25 and over having: no formal schooling 3.2%; some primary education 79.8%; some secondary 15.0%; complete secondary and higher 2.0%. *Literacy* (1995): total population age 15 and over literate 85%; males literate 80.8%; females literate 89.1%.
Health (1995): physicians 417[18] (1 per 6,043 persons); hospital beds (1993) 5,023 (1 per 492 persons); infant mortality rate per 1,000 live births 28.6.
Food (1992): daily per capita caloric intake 2,240 (vegetable products 84%, animal products 16%); 116% of FAO recommended minimum requirement.

Military

Total active duty personnel (1995): 3,320 (army 90.4%; coast guard 4.5%; air force 5.1%). *Military expenditure as percentage of GNP* (1994): 0.7% (world 3.0%); per capita expenditure U.S.$11.

[1]January 1. [2]The parishes of Kingston and Saint Andrew are jointly administered from the Half Way Tree section of Saint Andrew. [3]Kingston included with Saint Andrew. [4]City of Kingston is coextensive with Kingston parish. [5]51% public sector. [6]1990. [7]Weights of consumer price index components. [8]Less imputed service charges. [9]Includes 186,700 unemployed. [10]Detail does not add to total given because of rounding. [11]Import figures are c.i.f. [12]Air Jamaica only. [13]Circulation for 2 newspapers only. [14]Includes lower-secondary students at all-age schools. [15]1991–92. [16]1988–89. [17]1987–88. [18]Public health only.

Japan

Official name: Nihon (Japan).
Form of government: constitutional monarchy with a National Diet consisting of two legislative houses (House of Councillors [252]; House of Representatives [500]).
Chief of state: Emperor.
Head of government: Prime Minister.
Capital: Tokyo.
Official language: Japanese.
Official religion: none.
Monetary unit: 1 yen (¥) = 100 sen; valuation (Oct. 11, 1996) 1 U.S.$ = ¥111.64; 1 £ = ¥175.86.

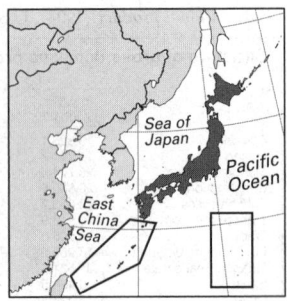

Area and population

Regions Prefectures	Capitals	area sq mi	area sq km	population 1995 census[1]
Chūbu				
Aichi	Nagoya	1,984	5,139	6,868,022
Fukui	Fukui	1,619	4,192	827,062
Gifu	Gifu	4,091	10,596	2,100,333
Ishikawa	Kanazawa	1,621	4,198	1,180,068
Nagano	Nagano	5,245	13,585	2,193,986
Niigata	Niigata	4,857	12,579	2,488,402
Shizuoka	Shizuoka	3,001	7,773	3,737,541
Toyama	Toyama	1,642	4,252	1,123,043
Yamanashi	Kōfu	1,723	4,463	882,005
Chūgoku				
Hiroshima	Hiroshima	3,269	8,467	2,881,707
Okayama	Okayama	2,738	7,092	1,951,159
Shimane	Matsue	2,559[2]	6,629[2]	771,483
Tottori	Tottori	1,349[2]	3,494[2]	614,954
Yamaguchi	Yamaguchi	2,358	6,107	1,555,538
Hokkaidō				
Hokkaidō (Territory)	Sapporo	32,247	83,520	5,692,217
Kantō				
Chiba	Chiba	1,989	5,151	5,797,787
Gumma	Maebashi	2,454	6,356	2,003,533
Ibaraki	Mito	2,353	6,094	2,955,512
Kanagawa	Yokohama	928	2,403	8,246,131
Saitama	Urawa	1,467	3,799	6,759,186
Tochigi	Utsunomiya	2,476	6,414	1,984,500
Kinki				
Hyōgo	Kōbe	3,236	8,381	5,401,899
Mie	Tsu	2,231	5,778	1,841,507
Nara	Nara	1,425	3,692	1,430,845
Shiga	Ōtsu	1,551	4,016	1,286,930
Wakayama	Wakayama	1,824	4,725	1,080,481
Kyūshū				
Fukuoka	Fukuoka	1,916	4,963	4,933,294
Kagoshima	Kagoshima	3,539	9,167	1,794,276
Kumamoto	Kumamoto	2,860	7,408	1,859,774
Miyazaki	Miyazaki	2,986	7,735	1,175,804
Nagasaki	Nagasaki	1,588	4,113	1,545,045
Ōita	Ōita	2,447	6,338	1,231,297
Saga	Saga	942	2,440	884,301
Ryukyu				
Okinawa	Naha	871	2,255	1,273,508
Shikoku				
Ehime	Matsuyama	2,190	5,672	1,506,598
Kagawa	Takamatsu	727	1,883	1,027,004
Kōchi	Kōchi	2,744	7,107	816,772
Tokushima	Tokushima	1,601	4,146	832,432
Tohoku				
Akita	Akita	4,484[3]	11,613[3]	1,213,772
Aomori	Aomori	3,714[3]	9,619[3]	1,481,602
Fukushima	Fukushima	5,322	13,784	2,133,491
Iwate	Morioka	5,898	15,277	1,419,510
Miyagi	Sendai	2,815	7,292	2,328,815
Yamagata	Yamagata	3,601	9,327	1,257,033
Metropolis				
Tōkyō[4]	Tokyo	836	2,166	11,771,819
Urban prefectures				
Kyōto[5]	Kyōto	1,781	4,613	2,629,379
Ōsaka[5]	Ōsaka	722	1,869	8,797,147
TOTAL		145,883[6,7]	377,835[6,7]	125,568,504

Demography

Population (1996): 125,612,000.
Density (1996): persons per sq mi 861.0, persons per sq km 332.4.
Urban-rural (1995): urban 77.6%; rural 22.4%.
Sex distribution (1996[8]): male 49.03%; female 50.97%.
Age breakdown (1996[8]): under 15, 15.8%; 15–29, 21.8%; 30–44, 19.6%; 45–59, 21.9%; 60–74, 15.0%; 75 and over, 5.9%.
Population projection: (2000) 127,287,000; (2010) 130,344,000.
Doubling time: not applicable; doubling time exceeds 100 years.
Composition by nationality (1995[9]): Japanese 98.9%; Korean 0.5%; Chinese 0.2%; Brazilian 0.1%; other 0.3%.
Place of birth (1995): 99.3% native-born; 0.7% foreign-born (mainly Korean).
Immigration (1995[9]): permanent immigrants/registered aliens admitted 1,354,011, from North and South Korea 50.0%, Taiwan, Hong Kong, and China 16.1%, Brazil 11.8%, Philippines 6.3%, United States 3.2%, Peru 2.6%, Thailand 1.0%, United Kingdom 0.9%, Vietnam 0.6%, Iran 0.6%, Canada 0.5%, Indonesia 0.5%, other 5.9%.
Major cities (1995): Tokyo 11,771,819; Yokohama 3,307,408; Ōsaka 2,602,352; Nagoya 2,152,258; Sapporo 1,756,968; Kyōto 1,463,601; Kōbe 1,423,830; Fukuoka 1,284,741; Kawasaki 1,202,811; Hiroshima 1,108,868; Kita-Kyūshū 1,019,522.

Other principal cities (1995)

	population		population		population
Akashi	287,613	Kakogawa	260,558	Okayama	616,056
Akita	312,035	Kanazawa	453,977	Okazaki	322,615
Amagasaki	488,574	Kashiwa	317,752	Ōmiya	433,768
Aomori	294,165	Kasugai	277,579	Ōtsu	276,331
Asahikawa	360,569	Kawagoe	323,345	Sagamihara	570,594
Chiba	856,882	Kawaguchi	448,801	Sakai	802,965
Fujisawa	368,636	Kōchi	322,077	Sendai	971,263
Fukui	255,601	Koriyama	324,831	Shimonoseki	259,791
Fukushima	285,745	Koshigaya	298,285	Shizuoka	474,089
Fukuyama	374,510	Kumamoto	650,322	Suita	342,794
Funabashi	540,814	Kurashiki	422,824	Takamatsu	330,997
Gifu	407,145	Machida	360,418	Takatsuki	362,259
Hachiōji	503,320	Maebashi	284,780	Tokorozawa	320,448
Hakodate	298,868	Matsudo	461,489	Tokushima	268,712
Hamamatsu	561,568	Matsuyama	460,870	Toyama	325,303
Higashi-Ōsaka	517,228	Miyazaki	300,054	Toyohashi	352,913
Himeji	470,986	Morioka	286,478	Toyonaka	398,912
Hirakata	400,130	Nagano	358,512	Toyota	341,038
Hiratsuka	253,818	Nagasaki	438,724	Urawa	453,300
Ibaraki	258,237	Naha	301,928	Utsunomiya	435,446
Ichihara	277,080	Nara	359,234	Wakayama	393,951
Ichikawa	440,527	Neyagawa	258,440	Yamagata	254,485
Ichinomiya	267,359	Niigata	494,785	Yao	276,658
Iwaki	360,497	Nishinomiya	390,388	Yokkaichi	285,777
Kagoshima	546,294	Ōita	426,981	Yokosuka	432,202

Religious affiliation (1992): Shintō and related religions 51.3%; Buddhism 38.3%; Christian 1.2%; other 9.2%.
Households (1995). Total households 43,447,100; average household size 2.9; composition of households 1 person 24.7%, 2 persons 23.1%, 3 persons 18.6%, 4 persons 19.0%, 5 persons 8.2%, 6 or more persons 6.4%. Family households 32,545,700 (74.9%); nonfamily 10,901,400 (25.1%), of which 1 person 10,768,000 (24.7%).

Type of household (1993)

Total number of occupied dwelling units: 40,835,000

	number of dwellings	percentage of total
by kind of dwelling		
exclusively for living	38,518,000	94.3
mixed use	169,000	0.4
combined with nondwelling	2,148,000	5.3
detached house	24,183,000	59.2
apartment building	14,253,000	34.9
tenement (substandard or overcrowded building)	2,205,000	5.4
other	194,000	0.5
by legal tenure of householder		
owned	24,410,000	59.8
rented	15,721,000	38.5
other	704,000	1.7
by kind of amenities		
flush toilet	30,524,000	74.7
bathroom	38,196,000	93.5
by year of construction		
prior to 1945	2,146,000	5.4
1945–70	9,700,000	24.3
1971–80	12,548,000	31.5
1981–87	9,258,000	23.2
1988–93	6,224,000	15.6

Mobility (October 1990). Population living in same residence as in October 1985, 74.7%; different residence, same town 9.5%; same prefecture 7.9%; different prefecture 7.6%; different country 0.3%.

Vital statistics

Birth rate per 1,000 population (1994): 10.0 (world avg. 25.0); (1985) legitimate 99.0%; illegitimate 1.0%.
Death rate per 1,000 population (1994): 7.1 (world avg. 9.3).
Natural increase rate per 1,000 population (1994): 2.9 (world avg. 15.7).
Total fertility rate (avg. births per childbearing woman; 1994): 1.5.
Marriage rate per 1,000 population (1994): 6.3; median age at first marriage men 28.5 years, women 26.2 years.
Divorce rate per 1,000 population (1994): 1.6.
Life expectancy at birth (1994): male 76.6 years; female 83.0 years.
Major causes of death per 100,000 population (1993): malignant neoplasms (cancers) 189.1; heart diseases 144.6; cerebrovascular diseases 95.3; pneumonia and bronchitis 70.1; accidents and adverse effects 27.8; senility without mention of psychosis 18.5; suicide 16.4; nephritis, nephrotic syndrome, and nephrosis 14.8; cirrhosis of the liver 13.6; diabetes mellitus 8.2.

Social indicators

Educational attainment (1990). Percentage of population age 25 years and over having: primary education 34.3%; secondary 44.5%; postsecondary 21.2%.

Distribution of income (1994)

percentage of average household income by quintile

1	2	3	4	5 (highest)
11.5	15.3	18.8	23.0	31.4

Quality of working life. Average workweek (1994): 38.1 hours. Annual rate of industrial deaths per 100,000 workers (1993): 2.6. Proportion of labour force insured for damages or income loss resulting from injury, permanent disability, and death (1991): 50.1%. Average man-days lost to labour stoppages per 1,000,000 workdays (1994): 1.8. Average duration of journey to work (1988)[10]: 26.8 minutes (1983; 26.7% private automobile, 67.4% public transportation, 5.5% taxi, 0.4% other). Rate per 1,000 workers of discouraged (unemployed no longer seeking work; 1993): 87.8.

Access to services (1989). Proportion of households having access to: gas supply 64.6%; safe public water supply 94.0%; public sewage collection 89.4%.

Social participation. Eligible voters participating in last national election (October 1996): 59.6%. Population 15 years and over participating in social-service activities on a voluntary basis (1987): 25.2%. Trade union membership in total workforce (1994): 19.1%.

Social deviance (1993). Offense rate per 100,000 population for: homicide 1.0; rape 1.3; robbery 2.0; larceny and theft 1,270.5. Incidence in general population of: alcoholism, n.a.; drug and substance abuse, n.a. Rate of suicide per 100,000 population: 16.2.

Leisure/use of personal time

Discretionary daily activities (1991)
(Population age 15 years and over)

	weekly average hrs./min.
Total discretionary daily time	5:56[7]
of which	
Hobbies and amusements	0:36
Sports	0:11
Learning (except schoolwork)	0:12
Social activities	0:05
Associations	0:29
Radio, television, newspapers, and magazines	2:23
Rest and relaxation	1:21
Other activities	0:21

Major leisure activities (1991)
(Population age 15 years and over)

	percentage of participation		
	male	female	total
Hobbies and amusements	93.0	90.8	91.9
Sports	84.2	72.1	78.0
Light exercises	30.8	34.1	32.0
Swimming	27.1	20.8	23.8
Bowling	33.0	23.1	27.9
Learning (except schoolwork)	36.3	37.0	36.7
Travel			
Domestic	72.7	68.3	70.4
Foreign	10.4	7.6	9.0

Material well-being (1994). Households possessing: automobile 79.7%; telephone, virtually 100%; colour television receiver 99.3%; refrigerator 98.9%; air conditioner 72.3%; washing machine 99.4%; vacuum cleaner 98.7%; videocassette recorder 82.8%; camera 86.8%; microwave oven 84.3%; compact disc player 53.8%.

National economy

Gross national product (at current market prices; 1995): U.S.$4,810,000,000,-000 (U.S.$38,420 per capita).

Structure of gross domestic product and labour force

	1993		1995	
	in value ¥'000,000,000	% of total value	labour force	% of labour force
Agriculture, fishing	9,977	2.1	3,670,000	5.5
Mining	1,235	0.3	60,000	0.1
Manufacturing	124,878	26.8	14,560,000	21.8
Construction	47,865	10.2	6,630,000	9.9
Public utilities	13,458	2.9	420,000	0.6
Transportation and communications	29,390	6.3	4,020,000	6.0
Trade	58,389	12.5	14,490,000	21.7
Finance	75,346	16.2	2,620,000	3.9
Pub. admin., defense	36,812	7.9	2,180,000	3.3
Services	85,856	18.4	15,660,000	23.5
Other	−17,233[11]	−3.7[11]	2,360,000[12]	3.5[12]
TOTAL	465,972[7]	100.0[7]	66,670,000	100.0[7]

Budget (1995). Revenue: ¥56,002,006,000,000 (income tax 34.9%; corporation tax 22.7%; value-added tax 10.3%; liquor and tobacco tax 5.7%; fuel taxes 4.4%; stamp duties 3.1%; customs duties 1.6%; carried-over surplus 1.1%). Expenditures: ¥78,034,006,000,000 (social security 18.6%; public works 18.2%; debt service 16.5%; culture, education, and science 8.7%; national defense 6.1%; pensions 2.2%).

Public debt (1995): U.S.$2,556,900,000,000.

Population economically active (1995): total 66,670,000; activity rate of total population 53.2% (participation rates: age 15 and over, 63.4%; female 40.5%; unemployed 3.2%).

Price and earnings indexes (1990 = 100)

	1990	1991	1992	1993	1994	1995	1996[13]
Consumer price index	100.0	103.3	105.1	106.4	107.1	107.0	107.3
Monthly earnings index	100.0	103.4	105.6	107.7	110.2	112.5	115.2

Household income and expenditure (1994). Average household size 3.0[14]; average annual income per household ¥6,849,600 (U.S.$61,597); sources of income (1992): wages and salaries 59.3%, transfer payments 19.5%, self-employment 10.1%, other 11.1%; expenditure: food 23.1%, transportation and communications 10.6%, recreation 9.8%, housing 6.3%, clothing and footwear 6.2%, fuel, light, and water charges 5.4%, education 5.4%, furniture and household utensils 3.7%, medical care 2.6%.

Tourism (1994): receipts from visitors U.S.$3,477,000,000; expenditures by nationals abroad U.S.$30,715,000,000.

Land use (1994): forested 66.4%; meadows and pastures 1.8%; agricultural and under permanent cultivation 11.7%; other 20.1%.

Manufacturing and mining enterprises (1993)

	no. of establishments	avg. no. of persons engaged	annual wages as a % of avg. of all mfg. wages	annual value added (¥'000,000,000)
Electrical machinery	33,937	1,845,000	99.5	18,008
Food, beverages, and tobacco	49,379	1,266,000	72.9	12,006
Transport equipment	15,287	957,000	124.4	12,003
Nonelectrical machinery	44,143	1,142,000	117.2	11,680
Chemical products	5,340	413,000	135.8	11,507
Fabricated metal products	50,281	854,000	102.2	8,296
Printing and publishing	28,623	561,000	121.5	6,587
Iron and steel	6,194	322,000	140.5	5,107
Ceramic, stone, and clay	20,165	445,000	99.9	4,959
Plastic products	19,865	445,000	91.9	4,137
Paper and paper products	11,064	281,000	101.4	3,115
Textiles	26,494	460,000	73.2	2,696
Apparel products	29,722	538,000	51.7	2,141
Nonferrous metal products	3,959	168,000	119.2	1,829
Precision instruments	6,488	217,000	100.1	1,775
Lumber and wood products	18,566	233,000	79.4	1,617
Furniture and fixtures	16,105	215,000	84.7	1,596
Rubber products	5,485	166,000	99.8	1,578
Petroleum and coal products	1,125	34,000	161.9	1,491
Leather products	5,379	72,000	69.8	429
Mining and quarrying	638	12,765	115.8	92

Energy production (consumption): electricity (kW-hr; 1993) 906,705,000,000 (906,705,000,000); coal (metric tons; 1993) 7,232,000 (118,900,000); crude petroleum (barrels; 1993) 4,152,000 (1,544,000,000); petroleum products (metric tons; 1993) 176,766,000, of which (by volume) diesel 32.9%, heavy fuel oil 29.6%, gasoline 19.9%, kerosene and jet fuel 15.3% (186,-458,000); natural gas (cu m; 1993) 2,202,600,000 (56,978,000,000). Composition of energy supply by source (1993): crude oil and petroleum products 57.0%, coal 16.7%, natural gas 11.0%, nuclear power 10.4%, hydroelectric power 3.9%, other 1.0%. Domestic energy demand by end use (1993): mining and manufacturing 42.3%, residential and commercial 25.9%, transportation 23.9%, other 7.9%.

Financial aggregates

	1990	1991	1992	1993	1994	1995	1996[15]
Exchange rate[16], ¥ per:							
U.S. dollar	134.40	125.20	124.75	111.85	99.74	102.30	108.44
£	258.41	234.21	188.62	172.27	157.59	158.56	168.86
SDR	191.21	179.09	171.53	153.63	145.61	152.86	158.07
International reserves (U.S.$)							
Total (excl. gold; '000,000)	78,501	72,059	71,623	98,524	125,860	183,250	212,792
SDRs ('000,000)	3,042	2,579	1,094	1,543	2,083	2,707	2,703
Reserve pos. in IMF ('000,000)	5,971	7,722	8,641	8,261	8,100	8,100	6,779
Foreign exchange ('000,000)	69,487	61,758	61,888	88,720	115,146	172,443	203,310
Gold ('000,000 fine troy oz)	24.23	24.23	24.23	24.23	24.23	24.23	24.23
% world reserves	2.6	2.6	2.6	2.6	2.6	2.7	2.7
Interest and prices							
Central bank discount (%)[16]	6.00	4.50	3.25	1.75	1.75	0.50	0.50[17]
Govt. bond yield (%)	7.36	6.53	4.94	3.69	3.71	2.27	2.40[13]
Industrial share prices (1990 = 100)	100.0	84.5	62.6	76.5	73.3	63.3	75.2[13]
Balance of payments (U.S.$'000,000,000)							
Balance of visible trade	63.6	103.1	132.4	141.6	145.9	132.1	...
Imports, f.o.b.	216.8	203.5	198.5	209.7	238.2	297.2	...
Exports, f.o.b.	280.4	306.6	330.9	351.3	384.2	429.3	...
Balance of invisibles	−22.2	−17.7	−14.8	−10.1	−16.7	−20.9	...
Balance of payments, current account	57.0	35.9	72.9	131.5	129.2	111.2	...

Retail and wholesale trade and services (1991)

	no. of establishments	avg. no. of employees	annual sales (¥'000,000,000)
Retail trade	1,519,186	6,936,000	140,634
Food and beverages	622,751	2,542,000	41,453
Grocery	68,913	643,000	16,404
Liquors	106,650	315,000	6,323
General merchandise	4,347	440,000	19,898
Department stores	2,004	427,000	19,574
Motor vehicles and bicycles	93,230	566,000	18,934
Apparel and accessories	240,989	809,000	14,844
Furniture and home furnishings	158,104	587,000	11,987
Gasoline service stations	72,807	385,000	11,234
Books and stationery	76,730	600,000	4,722
Wholesale trade	475,967	4,773,000	572,982
Machinery and equipment	111,046	1,286,000	130,512
General machinery except electrical	54,612	577,000	47,910
Motor vehicles and parts	17,318	222,000	32,019
General merchandise	705	51,000	98,548
Minerals and metals	22,657	264,000	61,300
Farm, livestock, and fishery products	43,331	416,000	60,273
Food and beverages	56,656	561,000	47,677
Textiles, apparel, and accessories	44,748	506,000	38,517
Building materials	63,885	444,000	35,698
Chemicals	18,140	179,000	24,457
Drugs and toilet goods	21,319	291,000	19,783
Medical services[18]	171,986	2,026,000	...
Educational services[18]	84,512	2,065,000	...

Production (metric tons except as noted). Agriculture, forestry, fishing (1996): rice 13,000,000, sugar beets 3,686,000, potatoes 3,400,000, cabbages 2,600,000, sugarcane 1,624,000, sweet potatoes 1,264,000, onions 1,200,-000, apples 900,000, cucumbers 865,500, tomatoes 760,000, carrots 680,000, watermelons 654,800, wheat 550,000, lettuce 540,000, eggplants 420,000, pears 395,000, cantaloupes 390,000, pumpkins 270,000, grapes 250,000, barley 220,000, strawberries 197,800, peaches 162,000, oranges 150,000, soybeans 99,000, tea 86,000, green beans 75,000, tobacco leaves 60,000, green peas 47,000; livestock (number of live animals) 10,200,000 pigs, 4,880,000 cattle, 31,000 goats, 28,000 horses, 25,000 sheep, 310,000,000 chickens; roundwood (1994) 18,887,000 cu m; fish catch (1993) 8,707,000, of which sardines 1,714,000, mackerel 665,000, Alaska pollack 382,000, squid 316,000, oysters 236,000, crabs 56,000, river eels 34,000, carp 13,000. Mining and quarrying (1995): limestone 201,089,000; silica stone 18,334,000; dolomite 3,773,000; silica sand 3,737,000; pyrophyllite 648,000; pyrophyllite clay 299,000; zinc 95,274; lead 9,659; copper 2,376; tungsten 578[19]; silver 100,080 kg; gold 9,190 kg. Manufacturing (1994): semifinished steel 102,727,-000[20]; crude steel 98,295,000; cement 91,624,000; hot-rolled steel products 87,982,000[20]; pig iron 73,776,000; sulfuric acid 6,594,000; fertilizers 6,047,000; plastic products 5,055,000; newsprint 2,971,800; spun yarn 656,000; synthetic fabrics 2,048,000,000 sq m; cotton fabrics 1,180,000,000 sq m; finished products (in number of units) 442,352,000 watches and clocks, 25,550,000 air conditioners, 20,171,000 electronic desk calculators, 19,202,000 videocassette recorders, 11,842,000 cameras, 9,445,000 colour television receivers, 7,997,-000 video cameras, 7,801,000 passenger cars, 6,702,000 bicycles, 5,288,000 facsimile machines, 5,042,000 automatic washing machines, 4,952,000 electric refrigerators, 3,960,000 computers, 3,167,000 microwave ovens, 2,725,000 motorcycles, 2,144,000 photocopy machines. Construction (value in ¥'000,-000; 1994): residential 26,870,000; nonresidential 54,559,000.

Foreign trade[21]

Balance of trade (current prices)

¥'000,000,000	1990	1991	1992	1993	1994	1995
	+10,398	+13,093	+15,922	+15,591	+14,736	+12,602
% of total	14.3%	18.3%	22.7%	24.1%	22.2%	17.9%

Imports (1995): ¥31,534,000,000,000 (machinery and transport equipment 25.3%, food products 15.2%, petroleum and petroleum products 8.9%, textiles 7.3%, chemicals and chemical products 7.3%). *Major import sources:* United States 22.4%; China 10.7%; South Korea 5.1%; Australia 4.3%; Taiwan 4.3%; Indonesia 4.2%; Germany 4.1%; Canada 3.2%; Malaysia 3.1%; Thailand 3.0%.
Exports (1995): ¥41,532,000,000,000 (electrical machinery 25.6%, motor vehicles 12.0%, chemicals 6.8%, scientific and optical equipment 4.7%, iron and steel products 4.0%, textiles and allied products 2.0%). *Major export destinations:* United States 27.3%; South Korea 7.1%; Taiwan 6.5%; Hong Kong 6.3%; Singapore 5.2%; China 5.0%; Germany 4.6%; Thailand 4.5%; Malaysia 3.8%; United Kingdom 3.2%.

Trade by commodity group (1994)

	imports		exports	
SITC group	U.S.$'000,000	%	U.S.$'000,000	%
00 Food and live animals	46,492	16.9	1,644	0.4
01 Beverages and tobacco				
02 Crude materials, excluding fuels	29,659[22]	10.8[22]	2,568[22]	0.6[22]
03 Mineral fuels, lubricants, and related materials	48,196	17.5	2,518	0.6
04 Animal and vegetable oils, fats, and waxes	22	22	22	22
05 Chemicals and related products, n.e.s.	19,606	7.1	22,863	5.8
06 Basic manufactures	31,294	11.4	42,851	10.8
07 Machinery and transport equipment	52,582	19.1	284,160	71.8
08 Miscellaneous manufactured articles	39,978	14.6	30,892	7.8
09 Goods not classified by kind	6,935	2.5	8,104	2.0
TOTAL	274,742	100.0[7]	395,600	100.0[7]

Direction of trade (1994)

	imports		exports	
	U.S.$'000,000	%	U.S.$'000,000	%
Africa	4,015	1.5	6,652	1.7
Asia	124,955	45.6	167,986	42.5
South America	7,055	2.6	5,598	1.4
North America and Central America	74,053	27.0	136,597	34.5
United States	63,067	23.0	118,693	30.0
other North and Central Am.	10,986	4.0	17,904	4.5
Europe	48,469	17.7	68,256	17.3
EU	36,168	13.2	60,056	15.2
Russia	3,481	1.3	1,167	0.3
other Europe	8,820	3.2	7,033	1.8
Oceania	16,771	6.1	10,676	2.7
TOTAL	274,123[7]	100.0[7]	395,201[7]	100.0[7]

Transport and communications

Transport. Railroads (1994): length 12,583 mi, 20,251 km; rolling stock—locomotives 5,879[14], passenger cars 43,753[14], freight cars 46,661[14]; passengers carried 22,598,000,000; passenger-mi 246,269,000,000, passenger-km 396,332,000,000; short ton-mi cargo 16,776,000,000, metric ton-km cargo 24,493,000,000. Roads (1994): total length 706,091 mi, 1,136,346 km (paved 73%). Vehicles (1994): passenger cars 42,956,000; trucks 20,472,000; buses 245,000. Merchant marine (1994): vessels (100 gross tons and over) 7,165; total deadweight tonnage 22,000,000. Air transport (1994): passengers carried 77,298,100,000; passenger-mi 71,227,000,000, passenger-km 114,602,900,000; short ton-mi cargo 4,101,400,000, metric ton-km cargo 5,987,900,000; airports (1996) with scheduled flights 73.

Distribution of traffic (1994)

	cargo carried ('000,000 tons)	% of national total	passengers carried ('000,000)	% of national total
Road	5,810.0	90.1	59,935.0	72.4
Rail (intercity)	79.0	1.2	22,598.0	27.3
Urban transport	—	—	17,445.0[19]	...
road	—	—	8,445.0[19]	...
rail	—	—	9,000.0[19]	...
Inland water	556.0	8.6	151.0	0.2
Air	0.9	0.0	74.0	0.1
TOTAL	6,445.9	100.0[7]	82,758.0[23]	100.0[23]

Communications. Daily newspapers (1995): total number 121; total circulation 72,518,000; circulation per 1,000 population 578. Radio (1994): 97,000,000 receivers (1 per 1.3 persons). Television (1994): 100,000,000 receivers (1 per 1.2 persons). Telephones (main lines; 1993): 58,459,000 (1 per 2.1 persons).

Other communications media (1994)

Print	titles		Electronic	traffic ('000)
Books (new)	53,890		Telegram	43,288
of which			Domestic	43,288
Social sciences	11,772		International	270
Fiction	10,490		Fax service	678[24]
Arts	6,705			
Natural sciences	4,194			
Engineering	4,363			
History	3,410		**Post**	
Philosophy	2,526		Mail	23,887,000
Magazines/journals[14]	3,895		Domestic	23,534,000
Weekly	107		International	353,000
Monthly	2,690		Parcels	384,000
			Domestic	378,000
Cinema[14]			International	6,000
Feature films	590			
Domestic	238			
Foreign	352			

Radio and television broadcasting (1993): total radio stations 1,324, of which commercial 464; total television stations 14,475, of which commercial 7,553. Commercial broadcasting hours (by percentage of programs; 1994): reports—radio 13.0%, television 21.0%; education—radio 3.4%, television 12.0%; culture—radio 14.9%, television 24.7%; entertainment—radio 67.6%, television 40.0%. Advertisements (daily average; 1993): radio 147, television 292.

Education and health

Education (1995)

	schools	teachers	students	student/ teacher ratio
Primary (age 6–11)	24,548	431,000	8,371,000	19.4
Secondary (age 12–17)	16,775	552,000	9,296,000	16.8
Higher	1,223	162,000	3,101,000	19.1

Literacy: total population age 15 and over literate, virtually 100%.
Health (1994): physicians 228,643 (1 per 546 persons); dentists 79,896 (1 per 1,564 persons); nurses 862,013 (1 per 145 persons); pharmacists 157,719 (1 per 792 persons); midwives 22,690[19] (1 per 5,476 persons); hospital beds (1992) 1,686,696 (1 per 74 persons), of which general 75.0%, mental 21.5%, tuberculosis 2.3%, other 1.2%; infant mortality rate per 1,000 live births 4.2.
Food (1992): daily per capita caloric intake 2,903 (vegetable products 78%, animal products 22%); 124% of FAO recommended minimum.

Military

Total active duty personnel (1996): 235,500 (army 62.9%, navy 18.2%, air force 18.9%). *Military expenditure as percentage of GNP* (1994): 1.0% (world 3.0%); per capita expenditure U.S.$366.

[1]Preliminary. [2]Excludes Lake Naka (38 sq mi [98 sq km]), which is part of both Shimane and Tottori prefectures. [3]Excludes Lake Towada (23 sq mi [60 sq km]), which is part of both Akita and Aomori prefectures. [4]Part of Kantō geographic region. [5]Part of Kinki geographic region. [6]1987 survey; includes Lake Naka and Lake Towada. [7]Detail does not add to total given because of rounding. [8]April 1. [9]January 1. [10]Applies to passengers carried within metropolitan areas only. [11]Import duties and statistical discrepancy less imputed bank service charge. [12]Includes 2,100,000 unemployed. [13]June. [14]1993. [15]August. [16]End of period. [17]July. [18]1985. [19]1992. [20]1991. [21]Import figures are f.o.b. in balance of trade and c.i.f. in commodities and trading partners. [22]Crude materials includes Animal and vegetable oils, fats, and waxes. [23]Totals do not include Urban transport. [24]Number of subscribers.

Jordan

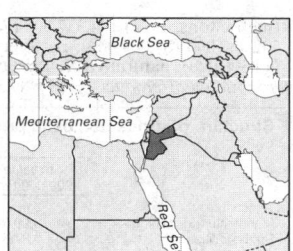

Official name: Al-Mamlakah al-Urdunnīyah al-Hāshimīyah (Al-Urdun) (Hashemite Kingdom of Jordan).
Form of government: constitutional monarchy[1] with a National Assembly comprising two legislative houses (Senate [40 appointed by king]; House of Deputies [80]).
Head of state and government: King assisted by Prime Minister.
Capital: Amman.
Official language: Arabic.
Official religion: Islam.
Monetary unit: 1 Jordan dinar (JD) = 1,000 fils; valuation (Oct. 11, 1996) JD 1.00 = U.S.$1.41 = £0.89.

Area and population

Governorates	Capitals	area sq mi	area sq km	population 1994 census[2]
'Ajlūn	'Ajlun	...[3]	...[3]	94,205
'Amman	Amman	4,097[4]	10,612[4]	1,567,908
Al-'Aqabah	Al-'Aqabah	...[5]	...[5]	79,745
Al-Balqā'	Aş-Şalt	425	1,100	273,489
Irbid	Irbid	985[3]	2,551[3]	745,774
Jarash	Jarash	...[3]	...[3]	123,195
Al-Karak	Al-Karak	1,548	4,010	169,552
Ma'ān	Ma'ān	13,954[5]	36,141[5]	79,401
Mādabā	Mādabā	...[4]	...[4]	106,308
Al-Mafraq	Al-Mafraq	10,475	27,129	170,903
Aţ-Ţafīlah	Aţ-Ţafīlah	850	2,202	61,156
Az-Zarqā'	Az-Zarqā'	2,008	5,201	623,943
TOTAL		34,342[6]	88,946[6]	4,095,579

Demography

Population (1996): 4,333,000.
Density (1996): persons per sq mi 126.2, persons per sq km 48.7.
Urban-rural (1994): urban 78.6%; rural 21.4%.
Sex distribution (1994): male 52.15%; female 47.85%.
Age breakdown (1994): under 15, 41.4%; 15–29, 31.6%; 30–44, 14.8%; 45–59, 8.0%; 60–74, 3.5%; 75 and over, 0.7%.
Population projection: (2000) 4,940,000; (2010) 6,601,000.
Doubling time: 23 years.
Ethnic composition (1995): Arab 98%, of which Palestinian c. 50%; Circassian 1%; Armenian 1%.
Religious affiliation (1995): Sunnī Muslim 92.0%; Christian 8.0%.
Major cities (1994): Amman 963,490; Az-Zarqā' 344,524; Irbid 208,201; Aş-Şalt 187,014; Ar-Ruşayfah 131,130; Al-Mafraq 109,841.

Vital statistics

Birth rate per 1,000 population (1994): 34.3 (world avg. 25.0).
Death rate per 1,000 population (1994): 3.0 (world avg. 9.3).
Natural increase rate per 1,000 population (1994): 31.3 (world avg. 15.7).
Total fertility rate (avg. births per childbearing woman; 1995): 5.9.
Marriage rate per 1,000 population (1994): 8.8.
Divorce rate per 1,000 population (1994): 1.5.
Life expectancy at birth (1995): male 64.4 years; female 69.9 years.
Major causes of death per 100,000 population: n.a.; however, major infectious diseases include mumps, chicken pox, hepatitis, rubella, scabies, and typhoid.

National economy

Budget (1995). Revenue: JD 1,672,700,000 (taxes 47.0%, of which sales tax 16.7%, custom duties 13.1%, income and profits taxes 9.3%; nontax 39.1%, of which licenses and fees 12.9%, postal, telegraph, and telephone 9.9%; external aid 10.4%). Expenditures: JD 1,758,800,000 (current 69.7%, of which general administration 26.9%, defense 22.8%; capital construction 30.3%).
Public debt (external, outstanding; 1994): U.S.$6,847,000,000.
Production (metric tons except as noted). Agriculture, forestry, fishing (1995): tomatoes 440,000, oranges and tangerines 114,500, wheat 75,000, lemons and limes 67,541, barley 50,000, eggplants 50,000, cauliflower and cabbage 45,860, olives 45,000, cucumbers 35,000, grapes 30,000, bananas 25,000; livestock (number of live animals) 2,100,000 sheep, 555,000 goats, 43,000 cattle, 18,000 camels, 78,000 chickens; roundwood (1994) 12,000 cu m; fish catch (1993) 62. Mining and quarrying (1995): phosphate ore 4,983,904; potash 1,780,004. Manufacturing (value added in JD '000; 1993): chemicals 148,100; nonmetallic mineral products, pottery, and china 111,454; food products 51,443, of which bakery products 17,030; beverages 34,454; refined petroleum 34,297; textiles 23,852; fabricated metal products, except machinery 23,645; furniture products 20,895; iron and steel 20,444; printing and publishing 20,309; plastic products 16,021; paper and paper products 14,392; clothing 10,484; nonelectrical machinery 8,567; electrical machinery 5,457. Construction (1995): 5,144,900 sq m. Energy production (consumption): electricity (kW-hr; 1993) 4,761,000,000 (4,761,000,000); crude petroleum (barrels; 1993) none (20,908,000); petroleum products (metric tons; 1993) 2,929,000 (3,455,000).
Land use (1994): forested 0.8%; meadows and pastures 8.9%; agricultural and under permanent cultivation 4.6%; other 85.7%.
Tourism (1994): receipts U.S.$582,000,000; expenditures U.S.$394,000,000.
Population economically active (1993): total 859,300; activity rate of total population 22.2% (participation rates: over age 15, 43.6%; female 14.0%; unemployed [1995] 7.9%).

Price and earnings indexes (1990 = 100)

	1989	1990	1991	1992	1993	1994	1995
Consumer price index	86.1	100.0	108.2	112.5	117.8	122.0	124.8
Daily earnings index	98.1	100.0	100.0	...	...	...	...

Gross national product (1994): U.S.$5,849,000,000 (U.S.$1,390 per capita).

Structure of gross domestic product and labour force

	1995 in value JD '000,000[7]	1995 % of total value	1993 labour force	1993 % of labour force
Agriculture	219.6	5.7	54,995	6.4
Mining	136.4	3.5 }	91,086	10.6
Manufacturing	522.7	13.6 }		
Construction	331.6	8.6	60,151	7.0
Public utilities	93.3	2.4	6,015	0.7
Transp. and commun.	603.0	15.7	57,573	6.7
Trade	402.4	10.5	129,754	15.1
Finance	710.4	18.5	24,920	2.9
Pub. admin., defense	730.0	19.0 }		
Services[8]	169.1	4.4 }	434,806	50.6
Other	−74.2[9]	−1.9[9]		
TOTAL	3,844.3	100.0	859,300	100.0

Household income and expenditure. Average household size (1995) 6.1; income per household (1995) JD 4,010 (U.S.$5,725); sources of income (1995): wages and salaries 51.4%, rent and property income 23.8%, transfer payments 13.7%, self-employment 11.1%; expenditure (1992): food and beverages 40.6%, housing and energy 26.9%, transportation 11.2%, clothing and footwear 8.2%, education 3.5%, health care 2.2%.

Foreign trade[10]

Balance of trade (current prices)

	1990	1991	1992	1993	1994	1995
JD '000,000	−829.3	−751.0	−1,140.5	−1,318.2	−1,106.8	−1,063.5
% of total	37.0%	32.8%	40.7%	43.3%	35.7%	23.7%

Imports (1995): JD 2,590,300,000 (machinery and transport equipment 24.5%; food and live animals 16.2%; mineral fuels 13.0%; chemicals and chemical products 12.3%; iron and steel 5.7%; miscellaneous manufactured articles 5.7%). *Major import sources:* Iraq 12.2%; United States 9.3%; Germany 8.4%; Italy 5.4%; United Kingdom 4.8%; France 4.6%; Japan 3.5%.
Exports (1995): JD 1,241,100,000 (domestic goods 80.9%, of which chemicals and chemical products 24.3%, potash 9.8%, phosphate fertilizers 8.5%, fruits, vegetables, and nuts 5.5%, machinery and transport equipment 3.7%; reexports 19.1%). *Major export destinations*[11]: Iraq 19.0%; India 11.4%; Saudi Arabia 7.0%; United Arab Emirates 4.3%; Syria 3.9%; Indonesia 2.7%; Lebanon 2.4%.

Transport and communications

Transport. Railroads (1994): route length 420 mi, 677 km; passenger traffic was negligible in 1993; short ton-mi cargo 463,000,000[12], metric ton-km cargo 676,000,000[12]. Roads (1994): total length 4,260 mi, 6,856 km (paved 100%). Vehicles (1994): passenger cars 167,828; trucks and buses 82,516. Merchant marine (1992): vessels (100 gross tons and over) 5; total deadweight tonnage 113,557. Air transport (1994)[13]: passenger-mi 2,731,000,000, passenger-km 4,395,000,000; short ton-mi cargo 182,000,000, metric ton-km cargo 265,226,000; airports (1996) with scheduled flights 2.
Communications. Daily newspapers (1992): total number 4; total circulation 250,000; circulation per 1,000 population 58. Radio (1996): 980,000 receivers (1 per 4.4 persons). Television (1996): 250,000 receivers (1 per 17.3 persons). Telephones (main lines; 1994): 317,330 (1 per 12.7 persons).

Education and health

Education (1993–94)

	schools	teachers	students	student/ teacher ratio
Primary (age 6–14)	2,482	48,158	1,036,079	21.5
Secondary (age 15–17)	741	7,150	93,773	13.1
Voc., teacher tr.	54	2,553	30,052	11.8
Higher	55[14]	4,280[15]	85,934[15]	20.1

Educational attainment (1995). Percentage of population age 25 and over having: no formal schooling 31.8%; primary education 34.5%; secondary 13.9%; postsecondary and vocational 8.4%; higher 11.4%. *Literacy* (1995): percentage of population age 15 and over literate 85.8%; males literate 91.4%; females literate 79.7%.
Health (1994): physicians 6,183 (1 per 893 persons); hospital beds 6,801 (1 per 651 persons); infant mortality rate per 1,000 live births 34.0.
Food (1994): daily per capita caloric intake 3,022 (vegetable products 88%, animal products 12%); 123% of FAO recommended minimum requirement.

Military

Total active duty personnel (1996): 98,650 (army 91.2%, navy 0.7%, air force 8.1%). *Military expenditure as percentage of GDP* (1994): 7.5% (world 3.0%); per capita expenditure U.S.$108.

[1]Political parties legalized July 1992; November 1993 legislative elections were multiparty. [2]Preliminary. [3]Irbid includes area of 'Ajlūn and Jarash governorates. [4]'Amman includes area of Mādabā governorate. [5]Ma'ān includes area of Al-'Aqabah governorate. [6]Excludes 116 sq mi (300 sq km) of territory per Israel-Jordan treaty of October 1994. [7]At factor cost. [8]Includes domestic help employed in households. [9]Less imputed bank service charges. [10]Imports f.o.b. in balance of trade and c.i.f. in commodities and trading partners. [11]Domestic exports only. [12]For Aqaba Railway Corporation only. [13]Royal Jordanian airlines only. [14]1988–89. [15]Includes community colleges.

Kazakstan

Official name: Qazaqstan Respublikasï
 (Republic of Kazakstan).
Form of government[1]: unitary republic
 with a Parliament consisting of
 two chambers (Senate [40[2]] and
 Assembly [67]).
Head of state and government[1]:
 President assisted by Prime Minister.
Capital: Almaty (formerly Alma-Ata);
 Aqmola (formerly Tselinograd) is the
 capital-designate[3].
Official language: Kazak.
Official religion: none.
Monetary unit[4]: 1 tenge (T) = 100 tiyn;
 valuation (Oct. 11, 1996) free rate,
 1 U.S.$ = 69.88 tenge; 1 £ = 110.07
 tenge.

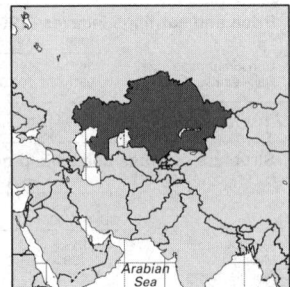

Area and population		area		population
				1995
Provinces	Capitals	sq mi	sq km	estimate
Almaty (Alma-Ata)	Almaty (Alma-Ata)	40,800[5]	105,700[5]	963,100
Aqmola	Aqmola	35,500	92,000	845,700
Aqtöbe	Aqtöbe	116,050	300,600	752,800
Atyraū	Atyraū	45,800	118,600	459,600
Batys Qazaqstan	Oral	58,400	151,300	669,800
Kökchetaū	Kökchetaū	30,200	78,200	657,000
Mangghystaū	Aqtaū	63,950	165,600	324,400
Ongtüstik Qazaqstan	Shymkent	45,300	117,300	1,987,800
Pavlodar	Pavlodar	48,200	124,800	943,600
Qaraghandy	Qaraghandy	44,550	115,400	1,270,100
Qostanay	Qostanay	44,000	113,900	1,055,300
Qyzylorda	Qyzylorda	87,250[6]	226,000[6]	606,100
Semey	Semey	71,750	185,800	811,000
Shyghys Qazaqstan	Shyghys Qazaqstan	37,650	97,500	939,500
Soltüstik Qazaqstan	Petropavl	17,400	45,000	600,900
Taldyqorghan	Taldyqorghan	45,750	118,500	721,500
Torghay	Arqalyq	43,150	111,800	305,900
Zhambyl	Zhambyl (Aullye-Ata)	55,700	144,300	1,039,600
Zhezkazghan	Zhezkazghan	120,700	312,600	484,400
Cities				
Almaty (Alma-Ata)	—	5	5	1,172,400
Leninsk	—	6	6	68,600
TOTAL		1,052,100	2,724,900	16,679,100

Demography

Population (1996): 16,677,000.
Density (1996): persons per sq mi 15.9, persons per sq km 6.1.
Urban-rural (1995): urban 56.0%; rural 44.0%.
Sex distribution (1994): male 49.00%; female 51.00%.
Age breakdown (1991): under 15, 31.4%; 15–29, 25.1%; 30–44, 21.3%; 45–59,
 12.2%; 60–69, 6.1%; 70 and over, 3.9%.
Population projection: (2000) 16,671,000; (2010) 17,283,000.
Doubling time: 77 years.
Ethnic composition (1995): Kazak 46.0%; Russian 34.8%; Ukrainian 4.9%;
 German 3.1%; Uzbek 2.3%; Tatar 1.9%; other 7.0%.
Religious affiliation: believers are predominantly Sunnī Muslims (Ḥanafīyah);
 there is a Christian minority (mainly Russian Orthodox and Baptist).
Major cities (1995): Almaty (Alma-Ata) 1,172,400; Qaraghandy (Karaganda)
 573,700; Shymkent (Chimkent) 397,600; Pavlodar 340,700.

Vital statistics

Birth rate per 1,000 population (1994): 18.2 (world avg. 25.0); (1994) legiti-
 mate 86.6%; illegitimate 13.4%.
Death rate per 1,000 population (1994): 9.6 (world avg. 9.2).
Natural increase rate per 1,000 population (1994): 8.6 (world avg. 15.7).
Total fertility rate (avg. births per childbearing woman; 1993): 2.5.
Marriage rate per 1,000 population (1994): 7.3.
Divorce rate per 1,000 population (1994): 2.5.
Life expectancy at birth (1994): male 64.0 years; female 73.0 years.
Major causes of death per 100,000 population (1994): diseases of the circula-
 tory system 459.0; malignant neoplasms (cancers) 134.3; accidents, poisoning,
 and violence 125.6; diseases of the respiratory system 87.9; infectious and
 parasitic diseases 30.5; diseases of the digestive system 30.4.

National economy

Budget (1994). Revenue: 104,103,000,000 tenge (profit tax 14.0%, value-added
 taxes 10.4%, taxes on international trade 8.2%, income tax 7.9%, nontax
 revenue 7.4%, economic development 6.6%, investment incentives 4.7%).
 Expenditures: 101,940,000,000 tenge (debt service 17.2%, national economy
 15.9%, education 14.1%, health 9.1%, social security 5.3%, defense 3.7%).
Public debt (external, outstanding; 1994): U.S.$2,704,000,000.
Production (metric tons except as noted). Agriculture, forestry, fishing (1995):
 wheat 6,490,000, grain 3,210,400, potatoes 1,720,000, fruit 427,000, sugar beets
 371,000, oats 315,400, seed cotton 180,250; livestock (number of live animals)
 25,132,000 sheep and goats, 8,073,000 cattle, 1,983,000 pigs, 1,800,000 horses;
 roundwood (1991) 1,974,000 cu m; fish catch (1993) 58,508. Mining and
 quarrying (1995): iron ore 23,000,000; chrome 2,900,000; manganese 280,-
 000; copper 260,000. Manufacturing (value of production in '000,000 tenge;
 1994): mineral products 139,105; metallurgy 81,585; food products 41,182;
 machinery 24,821; construction materials 13,995; chemical products 12,611.
 Construction (1994): residential 2,300,000 sq m. Energy production (consumption): electricity (kW-hr; 1994) 66,777,000,000 (78,277,000,000); coal

(metric tons; 1994) 104,357,000 (76,357,000); crude petroleum (barrels; 1994)
142,400,000 (87,004,000); petroleum products (metric tons; 1994) 13,372,000
(14,306,000); natural gas (cu m; 1994) 4,050,000,000 (9,588,000,000).
Gross national product (1994): U.S.$18,896,000,000 (U.S.$1,110 per capita)[7].

Structure of gross domestic product and labour force				
	1993			
	in value '000,000 tenge	% of total value	labour force	% of labour force
Agriculture	3,451	12.9	1,759,000	25.3
Manufacturing, mining	8,297	30.9 }	1,305,000	18.7
Public utilities	378	1.4 }		
Construction	2,484	9.3	620,000	8.9
Transp. and commun.	1,568	5.8	584,000	8.4
Trade	2,377	8.9	482,000	6.9
Finance	4,565	17.0	337,000	4.8
Pub. admin., defense	467	1.6	132,000	1.9
Services	1,384	5.2	1,356,000	19.5
Other	1,867	7.0	388,000	5.6
TOTAL	26,838	100.0	6,963,000	100.0

Population economically active (1995): total 6,448,000; activity rate of total
 population 38.4% (participation rates: ages 16–59 [male], 16–54 [female]
 80.1%; female [1994] 48.0%; unemployed 1.5%).

Price and earnings indexes (1990 = 100)					
	1988	1989	1990	1991	1992
Consumer price index	84.0	84.4	100.0	191.0	2,829
Monthly earnings index	80.8	88.1	100.0	166.0	1,743

Land use (1994): forested 3.5%; meadows and pastures 68.8%; agricultural
 and under permanent cultivation 12.9%; other 14.8%.
Household income and expenditure. Average household size (1989) 4.0; income per household (1991) 5,290 Russian rubles[4]: U.S.$ equivalent: n.a.[7];
 sources of income (1994): salaries and wages 67.7%, social benefits 16.9%,
 agricultural income 5.8%, other 9.6%; expenditure (1994): retail goods
 60.6%, taxes 16.8%, services 11.7%, other 10.9%.

Foreign trade

Balance of trade (current prices)				
	1992	1993	1994	1995[8]
U.S.$'000,000	−1,121	−414	−920	−193
% of total	13.6%	4.2%	12.3%	3.1%

Imports (1995)[9]: U.S.$4,513,000,000 (mainly electrical machinery and appli-
 ances, chemicals and pharmaceuticals, food products, and base metals).
Major import sources: Russia 64.7%; Germany 7.0%; Ukraine 5.3%; Kyrgyzstan 2.7%; Lithuania 2.1%; China 1.8%.
Exports (1995)[9]: U.S.$3,887,000,000 (mainly energy-related commodities [oil,
 coal, natural gas, and refined petroleum products]; base metals [copper,
 lead, zinc], ferrous metals, and chrome ores; chemical products [especially
 fertilizers]; and cotton textiles and clothing). *Major export destinations:* Russia 64.1%; China 7.4%; Ukraine 6.8%; Italy 3.1%; United States 2.8%.

Transport and communications

Transport. Railroads (1994): length 21,600 km; passenger-km 17,400,000,000;
 metric ton-km cargo 146,800,000,000. Roads (1995): total length 158,655 km
 (paved 68.4%). Vehicles (1995): passenger cars 1,030,000; trucks and buses
 516,000. Air transport (1994): passenger-km 4,600,000,000; metric ton-km
 cargo 100,000,000; airports (1996) with scheduled flights 12.
Communications. Newspapers (1989): total number 450; total circulation
 6,700,000; circulation per 1,000 population 405. Radio (1992): 4,188,000 receivers (1 per 4.1 persons). Television (1992): 4,795,000 receivers (1 per 3.6
 persons). Telephones (main lines; 1993): 1,559,300 (1 per 11.0 persons).

Education and health

Education (1994–95)				
	schools	teachers	students	student/ teacher ratio
Primary (age 7–13) }	8,710	270,300	2,758,700	10.1
Secondary (age 14–17) }				
Voc., teacher tr.	3,504	...	984,300	...
Higher	69	...	267,000	...

Educational attainment (1989). Population age 25 and over having: primary
 education or no formal schooling 16.2%; some secondary 19.8%; completed
 secondary and some postsecondary 54.1%; higher 9.9%. *Literacy* (1989):
 population age 15 and over literate 97.5%; males 99.1%; females 96.1%.
Health (1994): physicians 61,000 (1 per 276 persons); hospital beds 207,000 (1
 per 81 persons); infant mortality rate per 1,000 live births 27.4.

Military

Total active duty personnel (1996): about 40,000 (army 62.5%, air force 37.5%).
 Military expenditure as percentage of GNP (1994): 0.9% (world avg. 3.3%);
 per capita expenditure U.S.$26.

---

[1]According to a presidential edict of Oct. 16, 1995, implementing the new constitution
approved by referendum Aug. 30, 1995. [2]Elected seats only. [3]Government offices are
to be moved to Aqmola in 1997. [4]The Kazak tenge was introduced Nov. 18, 1993, to
replace the Russian ruble, at a rate of 500 Russian rubles to 1 tenge; on Nov. 25, 1993,
the Kazak tenge became the sole legal tender. [5]Area of Almaty city included with
Almaty province. [6]Area of Leninsk city included with Qyzylorda province. [7]Ruble-
area GNP and exchange-rate data for this period are very speculative. [8]Nine months.
[9]Total and source/destination data are IMF figures, compiled from sources in destination or source countries, rather than in the customs reports of the subject country.

Kenya

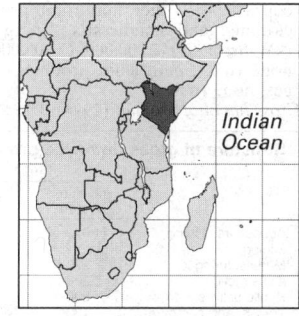

Indian Ocean

Official name: Jamhuri ya Kenya (Swahili); Republic of Kenya (English).
Form of government: unitary multiparty republic with one legislative house (National Assembly [202[1]]).
Head of state and government: President.
Capital: Nairobi.
Official languages: Swahili; English.
Official religion: none.
Monetary unit: 1 Kenya shilling[2] (K Sh) = 100 cents; valuation (Oct. 11, 1996) 1 U.S.$ = K Sh 55.99; 1 £ = K Sh 88.19.

Area and population

Provinces	Provincial headquarters	area sq mi	area sq km	population 1993 estimate
Central	Nyeri	5,087	13,176	3,626,000
Coast	Mombasa	32,279	83,603	2,155,000
Eastern	Embu	61,734	159,891	4,334,000
North Eastern	Garissa	48,997	126,902	408,000
Nyanza	Kisumu	6,240	16,162	4,041,000
Rift Valley	Nakuru	67,131	173,868	5,690,000
Western	Kakamega	3,228	8,360	3,035,000
Special area				
Nairobi	—	264	684	1,678,000
TOTAL		224,961[3]	582,646	24,967,000

Demography

Population (1996): 29,137,000.
Density (1996): persons per sq mi 129.5, persons per sq km 50.0.
Urban-rural (1995): urban 20.4%; rural 79.6%.
Sex distribution (1996): male 49.99%; female 50.01%.
Age breakdown (1996): under 15, 51.3%; 15–29, 26.5%; 30–44, 12.6%; 45–59, 6.4%; 60–74, 2.7%; 75 and over, 0.5%.
Population projection: (2000) 32,577,000; (2010) 43,552,000.
Doubling time: 28 years.
Ethnic composition (1989): Kikuyu 17.7%; Luhya 12.4%; Luo 10.6%; Kalenjin 9.8%; Kamba 9.8%; other 39.7%.
Religious affiliation (1987): Christian 73.0%, of which Roman Catholic 27.0%, Protestant 19.0%, other Christian (mostly African Indigenous, Anglican, and Eastern Orthodox) 27.0%; traditional beliefs 19.0%; Muslim 6.0%; other 2.0%.
Major cities (1989): Nairobi 1,504,900[4]; Mombasa 465,000; Kisumu 185,100; Nakuru 162,800; Machakos 92,300[5].

Vital statistics

Birth rate per 1,000 population (1995): 34.3 (world avg. 25.0).
Death rate per 1,000 population (1995): 9.8 (world avg. 9.3).
Natural increase rate per 1,000 population (1995): 25.3 (world avg. 15.7).
Total fertility rate (avg. births per childbearing woman; 1995): 4.6.
Life expectancy at birth (1995): male 56.9 years; female 56.8 years.
Major causes of death per 100,000 population: n.a.; however, major infectious diseases include AIDS, malaria, gastroenteritis, venereal diseases, diarrhea and dysentery, trachoma, amebiasis, and schistosomiasis.

National economy

Budget (1994–95). Revenue: K Sh 130,820,000,000 (goods and services 36.0%, income tax 34.5%, custom and excise duties 14.8%). Expenditures: K Sh 135,159,000,000 (recurrent expenditure 77.4%, development expenditure 22.6%).
Production (metric tons except as noted). Agriculture, forestry, fishing (1995): sugarcane 4,300,000, corn (maize) 2,750,000, cassava 840,000, sweet potatoes 630,000, plantains 370,000, wheat 330,000, pineapples 270,000, pulses 270,000, tea 245,000, bananas 220,000, potatoes 204,000, sorghum 130,000, coffee 93,000, millet 60,000, barley 60,000, coconuts 43,000, sisal 34,000, tomatoes 32,000, cashew nuts 15,000, sunflower seeds 15,000, seed cotton 12,000, cotton seeds 10,000, tobacco 10,000; livestock (number of live animals) 13,000,000 cattle, 7,400,000 goats, 5,600,000 sheep; roundwood (1994) 27,742,000 cu m; fish catch 241,064, of which freshwater fish 95.3%. Mining and quarrying (1994): soda ash 224,200; fluorite 89,155; salt 75,757. Manufacturing (value added in K£'000[2]; 1993): food products 456,000; beverages and tobacco 174,000; machinery and transport equipment 149,000; chemical products 141,000; metal products 94,000; paper and paper products 64,000; petroleum and petroleum products 62,000; clothing and footwear 44,000. Construction (1990): residential 411,000 sq m; nonresidential 182,000 sq m. Energy production (consumption): electricity (kW-hr; 1993) 3,396,000,000 (3,074,000,000); coal (metric tons; 1992) none (110,000); crude petroleum (barrels; 1993) none (16,668,000); petroleum products (metric tons; 1993) 1,975,000 (1,507,000).
Public debt (external, outstanding; 1994): U.S.$6,181,000,000.
Household income and expenditure. Average household size (1980) 6.2; average annual income per household: n.a.; sources of income: n.a.; expenditure (1980): food 46.5%, housing 10.0%, furniture and utensils 9.4%, transportation 8.4%, clothing and footwear 7.7%, energy 2.6%, health 2.2%, education 1.0%.

Population economically active (1992): total 10,633,000; activity rate of total population 41.1% (participation rates [1985]: ages 15–64, 76.2%; female 40.9%; unemployed, n.a.).

Price and earnings indexes (1990 = 100)

	1989	1990	1991	1992	1993	1994	1995
Consumer price index	86.5	100.0	119.8	155.2	226.3	292.0	294.3
Monthly earnings index	91.7	100.0	109.3	...	...	...	...

Gross national product (at current market prices; 1994): U.S.$6,643,000,000 (U.S.$260 per capita).

Structure of gross domestic product and labour force

	1994 in value K Sh '000,000	1994 % of total value	1993 labour force[6]	1993 % of labour force[6]
Agriculture	93,689	29.1	274,300	18.6
Mining	714	0.2	4,500	0.3
Manufacturing	33,930	10.5	193,600	13.1
Construction	16,954	5.3	72,600	4.9
Public utilities	4,481	1.4	22,100	1.5
Transp. and commun.	25,260	7.8	77,300	5.3
Trade	48,016	14.9	121,100	8.2
Finance	59,844	18.6	72,600	4.9
Pub. admin., defense } Services	39,354	12.2	636,800	43.2
Other	—	—	—	—
TOTAL	322,242	100.0	1,474,900	100.0

Tourism (1994): receipts from visitors U.S.$421,000,000; expenditures by nationals abroad U.S.$115,000,000.
Land use (1994): forested 29.5%; meadows and pastures 37.4%; agricultural and under permanent cultivation 8.0%; other 25.1%.

Foreign trade[7]

Balance of trade (current prices)

	1990	1991	1992	1993	1994	1995
K Sh '000,000	−18,164	−11,890	−5,923	−5,938	−16,738	−36,082
% of total	27.7%	16.4%	6.2%	3.7%	8.8%	15.6%

Imports (1994): K Sh 115,080,000,000 (machinery and transport equipment 27.7%, crude petroleum 16.4%, chemical products 15.6%, food and beverages 14.9%). *Major import sources:* United Kingdom 12.1%; United Arab Emirates 9.8%; South Africa 7.5%; Japan 7.3%; United States 6.8%; Germany 6.0%; Italy 3.5%; India 3.2%; Saudi Arabia 3.0%.
Exports (1994): K Sh 16,882,000,000 (tea 20.3%, coffee [not roasted] 15.7%, fruits and vegetables 8.6%, petroleum products 4.4%, cement 2.0%, hides and skins 2.0%, soda ash 1.1%). *Major export destinations:* Uganda 12.7%; United Kingdom 11.6%; Tanzania 10.6%; Germany 7.8%; The Netherlands 4.2%; United States 3.4%.

Transport and communications

Transport. Railroads (1993): route length 1,885 mi, 3,034 km; passenger-mi 288,000,000, passenger-km 464,000,000; short ton-mi cargo 898,600,000, metric ton-km cargo 1,312,000,000. Roads (1994): total length 39,400 mi, 63,400 km (paved 14%). Vehicles (1992): passenger cars 157,166; trucks and buses 133,968. Merchant marine (1992): vessels (100 gross tons and over) 29; total deadweight tonnage 11,649. Air transport (1995)[8]: passenger-mi 1,091,895,000, passenger-km 1,757,238,000; short ton-mi cargo 36,160,000, metric ton-km cargo 52,793,000; airports (1996) with scheduled flights 13.
Communications. Daily newspapers: total number (1995) 5; total circulation 402,000[9]; circulation per 1,000 population 28[9]. Radio (1995): 3,000,000 receivers (1 per 9.5 persons). Television (1995): 500,000 receivers (1 per 57 persons). Telephones (main lines; 1993): 214,800 (1 per 124 persons).

Education and health

Education (1993)

	schools	teachers	students	student/ teacher ratio
Primary (age 5–11)	15,804	173,002	5,428,600	31.4
Secondary (age 12–17)	2,639	31,657	517,577	16.3
Voc., teacher tr.	63	1,332[10]	29,593	13.4[10]
Higher	14	4,392[11]	88,180	8.1[11]

Educational attainment (1979). Percentage of population over age 25 having: no formal schooling 58.6%; primary education 32.2%; some secondary 7.9%; complete secondary and higher 1.3%. *Literacy* (1995): total population over age 15 literate 78.1%; males literate 86.3%; females literate 70.0%.
Health (1994): physicians 4,558 (1 per 5,999 persons); hospital beds 37,271 (1 per 734 persons); infant mortality rate per 1,000 live births (1995): 55.4.
Food (1992): daily per capita caloric intake 2,075 (vegetable products 88%, animal products 12%); 89% of FAO recommended minimum requirement.

Military

Total active duty personnel (1996): 24,200 (army 84.7%, navy 5.0%, air force 10.3%). *Military expenditure as percentage of GNP* (1994): 2.1% (world 3.0%); per capita expenditure U.S.$5.

---

[1]Includes 14 nonelective seats. [2]Kenya pound (K£) as a unit of account equals 20 K Sh. [3]Detail does not add to total given because of rounding. [4]1990. [5]1983. [6]Employed persons only. [7]Import figures are f.o.b. in balance of trade and c.i.f. in commodities and trading partners. [8]Kenya Airways only. [9]Circulation for four newspapers only. [10]1987–88; teacher training only. [11]1990–91; universities only.

Kiribati

Official name: Republic of Kiribati.
Form of government: unitary republic with a unicameral legislature (House of Assembly [41[1]]).
Head of state and government: President.
Capital: Bairiki, on Tarawa Atoll.
Official language: English.
Official religion: none.
Monetary unit: 1 Australian Dollar ($A) = 100 cents; valuation (Oct. 11, 1996) 1 U.S.$ = $A 1.26; 1 £ = $A 1.99.

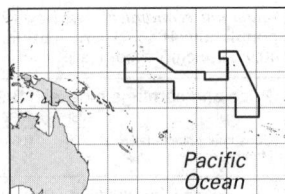

Pacific Ocean

Area and population		area[2]		population
Island Groups				1990
Islands	**Capitals**	sq mi	sq km	census
Gilberts Group	Bairiki Islet	110	286[3]	67,508
Abaiang	Tuarabu	7	18	5,233
Abemama	Kariatebike	11	27	3,218
Aranuka	Takaeang	5	12	1,002
Arorae	Roreti	3	9	1,440
Banaba	Anteeren	2	6	284
Beru	Taubukinberu	7	18	2,909
Butaritari	Butaritari	5	13	3,774
Kuria	Tabontebike	6	16	990
Maiana	Tebangetua	6	17	2,180
Makin	Makin	3	8	1,762
Marakei	Rawannawi	5	14	2,863
Nikunau	Rungata	7	19	1,994
Nonouti	Teuabu	8	20	2,814
Onotoa	Buariki	6	16	2,100
Tabiteuea North	Utiroa	10	26	3,201
Tabiteuea South	Buariki	5	12	1,331
Tamana	Bakaka	2	5	1,385
Tarawa North	Abaokoro	6	15	3,648
Tarawa South	Bairiki	6	16	25,380
Line Group	Kiritimati	192	496	4,782
Northern		167	432	
Kiritimati (Christmas)	London	150	388	2,537
Tabuaeran (Fanning)	Paelau	13	34	1,309
Teraina (Washington)	Washington	4	10	936
Southern		25	64	—
(Caroline, Flint, Malden, Starbuck, Vostok)				
Phoenix Group	Kanton	11	29	45
(Birnie, Enderbury, Kanton [Canton], McKean, Manra [Sydney], Nikumaroro [Gardner], Orona [Hull], Rawaki [Phoenix])				
TOTAL		313	811	72,335

Demography

Population (1996): 81,800.
Density (1996)[4]: persons per sq mi 292.1, persons per sq km 112.7.
Urban-rural (1995): urban 36.0%; rural 64.0%.
Sex distribution (1990): male 49.45%; female 50.55%.
Age breakdown (1990): under 15, 40.3%; 15–29, 27.5%; 30–44, 17.3%; 45–59, 9.2%; 60–74, 4.8%; 75 and over, 0.9%.
Population projection: (2000) 88,000; (2010) 106,000.
Doubling time: 36 years.
Ethnic composition (1990): I-Kiribati 97.4%; mixed (part I-Kiribati and other) 1.5%; Tuvaluan 0.5%; European 0.2%; other 0.4%.
Religious affiliation (1990): Roman Catholic 53.4%; Kiribati Protestant (Congregational) 39.2%; Baha'i 2.4%; Seventh-day Adventist 1.9%; Mormon 1.6%; other 1.5%.
Major cities (1990): urban Tarawa 25,154.

Vital statistics

Birth rate per 1,000 population (1994): 31.6 (world avg. 25.0); legitimate, n.a.; illegitimate, n.a.
Death rate per 1,000 population (1994): 12.3 (world avg. 9.3).
Natural increase rate per 1,000 population (1994): 19.3 (world avg. 15.7).
Total fertility rate (avg. births per childbearing woman; 1996): 3.3.
Marriage rate per 1,000 population (1988): 5.2.
Divorce rate per 1,000 population: n.a.
Life expectancy at birth (1996): male 62.0 years; female 67.0 years.
Major causes of death per 100,000 population (1993): senility without mention of psychosis 61.2; stroke 39.1; diarrhea 37.8; hepatitis 32.5; diabetes mellitus 28.6; malnutrition 23.4; meningitis 18.2.

National economy

Budget (1993). Revenue: $A 31,600,000 (1988; nontax revenue 46.0%, of which reserve fund drawdown 32.1%, fishing licenses 9.8%; tax revenue 28.4%, of which import duties 9.4%, income tax 4.9%; development revenue 25.6%). Expenditures: $A 61,000,000 (1988; education 16.1%; development 15.9%; health 13.0%; natural resources 7.3%; communications 7.0%; public works 6.6%).
Production (metric tons except as noted). Agriculture, forestry, fishing (1995): coconuts 65,000, copra (1994) 8,000, roots and tubers 7,700 (of which taro 1,500), vegetables and melons 4,900, bananas 4,300, seaweed (1994) 1,200; livestock (number of live animals) 9,000 pigs, 290,000 chickens; fish catch (1993) 29,295. Mining and quarrying: none. Manufacturing (1991): processed

copra 8,661; other important products are processed fish, baked goods, clothing, and handicrafts. Energy production (consumption): electricity (kW-hr; 1993) 7,000,000 (7,000,000); coal, none (n.a.); crude petroleum, none (n.a.); petroleum products (metric tons; 1993) none (7,000); natural gas, none (n.a.).
Gross national product (1994): U.S.$56,000,000 (U.S.$730 per capita).

Structure of gross domestic product and labour force				
	1992		1990	
	in value $A '000	% of total value	labour force	% of labour force
Agriculture, fishing	11,022	23.8	23,137[5]	71.0[5]
Mining	—	—	—	—
Manufacturing	920	2.0	622	1.9
Construction	2,300	5.0	339	1.0
Public utilities	800	1.7	301	0.9
Transp. and commun.	7,130	15.4	921	2.8
Trade	6,530	14.1	1,341	4.1
Finance	3,210	6.9	441	1.4
Pub. admin., defense }	11,935	25.8	2,123	6.5
Services			2,286	7.0
Other	2,413	5.2	1,099[6]	3.4[6]
TOTAL	46,260	100.0[3]	32,610	100.0

Public debt (external, outstanding; 1993): U.S.$18,000,000.
Population economically active (1990): total 32,610; activity rate of total population 45.1% (participation rates: over age 15, 75.6%; female 46.4%; unemployed 2.8%).

Price and earnings indexes (1985 = 100)							
	1988	1989	1990	1991	1992	1993	1994
Consumer price index	113.8	120.8	126.9	131.7	138.3	146.7	151.0
Earnings index	...	...	...	...	...	...	...

Household income and expenditure. Average household size (1990) 6.6; income per household: n.a.; sources of income (1978): wages 69.7%, self-employment 21.4%, transfer payments 6.0%, other 2.9%; expenditure (1982): food 50.0%, tobacco and alcohol 14.0%, clothing 8.0%, transportation 8.0%, housing, energy, and household operation 7.5%.
Tourism (1994): receipts from visitors U.S.$1,000,000; expenditures by nationals abroad, n.a.
Land use (1994): forested 2.7%; agricultural and under permanent cultivation 50.7%; other 46.6%.

Foreign trade

Balance of trade (current prices)						
	1988	1989	1990	1991	1992	1993
$A '000	−21,515	−22,161	−30,765	−29,529	−44,017	−29,478
% of total	61.7%	63.3%	80.7%	80.0%	77.2%	73.8%

Imports (1993): $A 133,953 (1992; machinery and transport equipment 47.3%; food 21.1%; manufactured goods 8.0%; mineral fuels 7.8%; beverages and tobacco 5.0%; chemicals 3.5%; crude materials 1.2%). *Major import sources:* United States 37.1%; Australia 13.2%; Japan 4.4%; New Zealand 2.5%; United Kingdom 0.7%.
Exports (1993): $A 8,675,000 (1992; domestic exports 86.7%, of which copra 66.8%, fish and fish preparations 11.3%; reexports 13.3%). *Major export destinations:* United States 28.8%; Germany 20.3%; Sweden 6.8%; Denmark 1.7%; Italy 1.7%; The Netherlands 1.7%.

Transport and communications

Transport. Roads (1991): total length 398 mi, 640 km (paved 5%). Vehicles (1982): passenger cars 307; trucks and buses 130. Merchant marine (1992): vessels (100 gross tons and over) 7; total deadweight tonnage 2,685. Air transport (1993): passenger-mi 6,000,000, passenger-km 10,000,000; short ton-mi cargo 514,000[7], metric ton-km cargo 750,000[7]; airports (1996) with scheduled flights 17.
Communications. Daily newspapers: none. Radio (1995): total number of receivers 6,050 (1 per 13 persons). Television (1995): total number of receivers 685 (1 per 117 persons). Telephones (main lines; 1993): 1,800 (1 per 43 persons).

Education and health

Education (1993)				
	schools	teachers	students	student/ teacher ratio
Primary (age 6–13)	92	537	16,316	30.4
Secondary (age 14–18)	9[7]	179	3,152	17.6
Voc., teacher tr.	6[7]	40	297	7.4
Higher[8]	—	—	—	—

Educational attainment (1990)[9]. Percentage of population age 15 and over having: no schooling 6.9%; primary 67.8%; secondary 24.5%; higher 0.6%; not stated 0.2%. *Literacy* (1985): total population age 15 and over literate 90%.
Health: physicians (1993) 10 (1 per 7,687 persons); hospital beds (1990) 283 (1 per 253 persons); infant mortality rate per 1,000 live births (1996) 54.
Food (1992): daily per capita caloric intake 2,651 (vegetable products 88%, animal products 12%); 116% of FAO recommended minimum requirement.

[1]Includes two nonelective members. [2]Includes uninhabited islands. [3]Detail does not add to total given because of rounding. [4]Based on inhabited island areas (280 sq mi, [726 sq km]) only. [5]Includes 20,568 persons engaged in "village work" (subsistence agriculture or fishing). [6]Includes 900 unemployed. [7]1990. [8]54 students overseas. [9]For indigenous population.

Korea, North

Official name: Chosŏn Minjujuŭi In'min Konghwaguk (Democratic People's Republic of Korea).
Form of government: unitary single-party republic with one legislative house (Supreme People's Assembly [687]).
Chief of state:[1].
Head of government: Premier.
Capital: P'yŏngyang.
Official language: Korean.
Official religion: none.
Monetary unit: 1 won = 100 chŏn; valuation (Oct. 11, 1996) 1 U.S.$ = 2.15 won[2]; 1 £ = 3.39 won.

Area and population

Provinces	Capitals	area sq mi	area sq km	population[3] 1987 estimate
Chagang-do	Kanggye	6,551	16,968	1,156,000
Hamgyŏng-namdo	Hamhŭng	7,324	18,970	2,547,000
Hamgyŏng-pukto	Ch'ŏngjin	6,784	17,570	2,003,000
Hwanghae-namdo	Haeju	3,090	8,002	1,914,000
Hwanghae-pukto	Sariwŏn	3,091	8,007	1,409,000
Kangwŏn-do	Wŏnsan	4,306	11,152	1,227,000
P'yŏngan-namdo	P'yŏngsan	4,470	11,577	2,653,000
P'yŏngan-pukto	Sinŭiju	4,707[4]	12,191[4]	2,380,000
Yanggang-do	Hyesan	5,528	14,317	628,000
Special cities				
Kaesŏng	—	485	1,255	331,000
Namp'o	—	291	753	715,000
P'yŏngyang	—	772	2,000	2,355,000
Special district				
Hyangsan-chigu	—	4	4	28,000
TOTAL		47,399	122,762	19,346,000

Demography

Population (1996): 23,904,000.
Density (1996): persons per sq mi 504.3, persons per sq km 194.7.
Urban-rural (1995): urban 61.3%; rural 38.7%.
Sex distribution (1995): male 49.28%; female 50.72%.
Age breakdown (1995): under 15, 29.1%; 15–29, 30.9%; 30–44, 21.9%; 45–59, 11.2%; 60–74, 5.5%; 75 and over, 1.5%.
Population projection: (2000) 25,491,000; (2010) 28,491,000.
Doubling time: 39 years.
Ethnic composition (1989): Korean 99.8%; Chinese 0.2%.
Religious affiliation (1980): atheist or nonreligious 67.9%; traditional beliefs 15.6%; Ch'ŏndogyo 13.9%; Buddhist 1.7%; Christian 0.9%.
Major cities (1987): P'yŏngyang 2,355,000; Hamhŭng 701,000; Ch'ŏngjin 520,-000; Namp'o 370,000; Sunch'ŏn 356,000.

Vital statistics

Birth rate per 1,000 population (1996): 22.5 (world avg. 25.0).
Death rate per 1,000 population (1996): 5.3 (world avg. 9.3).
Natural increase rate per 1,000 population (1996): 17.2 (world avg. 15.7).
Total fertility rate (avg. births per childbearing woman; 1996): 2.3.
Marriage rate per 1,000 population (1987): 9.3.
Divorce rate per 1,000 population (1987): 0.2.
Life expectancy at birth (1996): male 68.0 years; female 75.0 years.
Major causes of death per 100,000 population (1986): diseases of the circulatory system 224.9; malignant neoplasms (cancers) 69.0; diseases of the digestive system 51.6; diseases of the respiratory system 46.7; injuries and poisoning 38.2; infectious and parasitic diseases 19.4.

National economy

Budget (1994). Revenue: 41,525,200,000 won (1984; turnover tax 55.0%, payments by state enterprises 30.0%). Expenditures: 41,525,200,000 won (national economy 67.8%, social and cultural affairs 19.8%, defense 11.6%, administration 0.8%).
Public debt (external, outstanding; 1992): U.S.$8,000,000,000.
Tourism (1986): total number of tourist arrivals 85,000.
Population economically active (1994)[5]: total 12,486,000; activity rate of total population 53.2% (participation rates [1988–93]: ages 15–64, 49.5%; female 46.0%; unemployed, n.a.).
Price and earnings indexes: n.a.
Production (metric tons except as noted). Agriculture, forestry, fishing (1996): rice 2,800,000, corn (maize) 2,000,000, potatoes 1,600,000, cabbages 900,000, sweet potatoes 450,000, soybeans 400,000, pears 125,000, watermelons 110,-000, peaches and nectarines 110,000, wheat 100,000, cucumbers and gherkins 73,000, tomatoes 72,000, tobacco leaves 65,000, barley 55,000, millet 10,000, oats 10,000; livestock (number of live animals) 3,350,000 pigs, 1,350,000 cattle, 395,000 sheep, 305,000 goats, 22,500,000 chickens; roundwood 1994) 4,876,000 cu m; fish catch (1993) 1,780,000. Mining and quarrying (1994): iron ore 11,000,000; magnesite (metal content) 1,600,000; phosphate rock 510,000; sulfur 250,000; zinc 200,000; lead (metal content) 80,000; fluorspar 40,000; graphite 38,000; copper 16,000; gold 5,000 kg; silver 50 kg. Manufacturing (1994): cement 17,000,000; crude steel 8,100,000; pig iron 6,600,000; coke 3,000,000; steel semimanufactures 2,700,000; chemical fertilizers 2,500,-000; meat 259,200[6]; gasoline 8,600,000 barrels; textile fabrics 350,000,000 sq

m. Construction: n.a. Energy production (consumption): electricity (kW-hr; 1993) 38,000,000 (38,000,000); coal (metric tons; 1993) 72,000,000 (73,950,-000); crude petroleum (barrels; 1993) none (16,859,000); petroleum products (metric tons; 1993) 2,860,000 (4,390,000); natural gas, none (n.a.).
Household income and expenditure. Average household size (1987) 4.8; average annual income per household (1980) 3,677 won (U.S.$4,275); sources of income: n.a.; expenditure (1984)[7]: food 46.5%, clothing 29.9%, furniture 3.8%, energy 3.3%, housing 0.6%.
Gross national product (1994): U.S.$21,300,000,000 (U.S.$890 per capita).

Structure of gross domestic product and labour force

	1982 in value '000,000 won	1982 % of total value	1990–92 labour force	1990–92 % of labour force
Agriculture	...	...	4,987,000	43.0
Mining and manufacturing	...	...	} 3,479,000	30.0
Construction	...	...		
Public utilities	...	...		
Transportation and communications	...	...		
Trade	...	...		
Finance	...	...	} 3,131,000	27.0
Pub. admin., defense	...	...		
Services	...	...		
Other	...	...		
TOTAL	11,800	100.0	11,597,000	100.0

Land use (1994): forested 61.2%; meadows and pastures 0.4%; agricultural and under permanent cultivation 16.6%; other 21.8%.

Foreign trade[8]

Balance of trade (current prices)

	1990	1991	1992	1993	1994	1995
U.S.$'000,000	−420.5	−764.7	−600.0	−600.0	−429.5	−880.0
% of total	21.0%	35.6%	18.8%	22.7%	20.4%	42.7%

Imports (1995): U.S.$1,470,000,000 (crude petroleum, coal and coke, industrial machinery and transport equipment [including trucks], industrial chemicals, textile yarn and fabrics, and grain are among the major imports). *Major import sources* (1994): China 33.5%; Japan 13.5%; Italy 8.0%; Russia 7.9%; India 6.4%; Hong Kong 4.8%; Germany 4.6%.
Exports (1995): U.S.$590,000,000 (minerals [including lead, magnesite, zinc], metallurgical products [iron and steel, nonferrous metals], cement, agricultural products [including fish, grain, fruit and vegetables, tobacco], and manufactured goods [textile fabrics, clothing] are among the major exports). *Major export destinations* (1994): Japan 38.4%; China 23.7%; Germany 7.2%; Russia 4.8%; Hong Kong 3.9%; India 2.4%.

Transport and communications

Transport. Railroads (1990): length 5,302 mi, 8,533 km; (latest) passenger-mi 2,100,000,000, passenger-km 3,400,000,000; (latest) short ton-mi cargo 5,100,000,000, metric ton-km cargo 9,100,000,000. Roads (1992): total length 18,600 mi, 30,000 km (paved 6.2%). Vehicles (1990): passenger cars 248,-000. Merchant marine (1992): vessels (100 gross tons and over) 1; total deadweight tonnage 951,222. Air transport (1994): passenger-mi 52,200,000, passenger-km 84,000,000; short ton-mi cargo 1,370,000, metric ton-km cargo 2,000,000; airports (1996) with scheduled flights 1.
Communications. Daily newspapers (1992): total number 11; total circulation 5,000,000; circulation per 1,000 population 221. Radio (1995): total number of receivers 4,700,000 (1 per 5.0 persons). Television (1995): total number of receivers 2,000,000 (1 per 11.7 persons). Telephones (main lines; 1994): 1,089,300 (1 per 20.7 persons).

Education and health

Education (1987)

	schools	teachers	students	student/teacher ratio
Primary (age 6–9)	6,122	138,945	1,543,000	11.1
Secondary (age 10–15)	...	111,000	2,468,000	22.2
Voc., teacher tr.	473[9]	...	220,000	...
Higher	281	27,000	390,000	14.4

Educational attainment (1987–88). Percentage of population age 16 and over having attended or graduated from postsecondary-level school: 13.7%. *Literacy* (1992): 95%.
Health (1989): physicians 57,690 (1 per 370 persons); hospital beds 290,590 (1 per 74 persons); infant mortality rate per 1,000 live births (1996) 23.0.
Food (1992): daily per capita caloric intake 2,833 (vegetable products 93%, animal products 7%); 121% of FAO recommended minimum requirement.

Military

Total active duty personnel (1996): 1,054,000 (army 87.6%, navy 4.3%, air force 8.1%). *Military expenditure as percentage of GNP* (1994): 26.3% (world 3.0%); per capita expenditure U.S.$238.

---

[1]Kim Jong Il (son of the previous president Kim Il Sung, who died on July 8, 1994) had not assumed the title of president as of mid-October 1996. [2]Transfer rate; the black market rate (Jan. 1, 1996) was about 45 won to 1 U.S.$. [3]Civilian population only; UN cites a 1993 census total of 21,123,376, but details are not available. [4]P'yŏngan-pukto includes special district of Hyangsan-chigu. [5]The Democratic People's Republic of Korea categorizes economically active as including students in higher education, retirees, and heads of households, as well as those in the civilian labour force. [6]1996. [7]Workers and clerical workers only. [8]Imports are f.o.b. [9]1986.

Korea, South

Official name: Taehan Min'guk
(Republic of Korea).
Form of government: unitary multiparty
republic with one legislative house
(National Assembly [299]).
Head of state and government:
President, assisted by Prime Minister.
Capital: Seoul.
Official language: Korean.
Official religion: none.
Monetary unit: 1 won (W) = 100 chon;
valuation (Oct. 11, 1996)
1 U.S.$ = W 829; 1 £ = W 1,306.

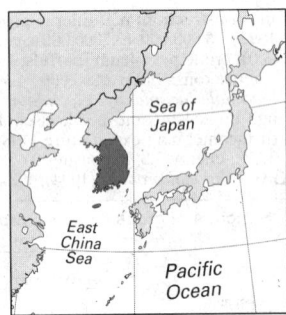

Area and population

Provinces	Capitals	area sq mi	area sq km	population 1995 census
Cheju-do	Cheju	705	1,827	505,442
Chŏlla-namdo	Kwangju	4,578	11,858	2,066,865
Chŏlla-pukto	Chŏnju	3,106	8,043	1,902,205
Ch'ungch'ŏng-namdo	Taejŏn	3,225	8,352	1,767,105
Ch'ungch'ŏng-pukto	Ch'ŏngju	2,871	7,436	1,396,481
Kangwŏn-do	Ch'unch'ŏn'	6,524	16,897	1,466,794
Kyŏnggi-do	Suwŏn	4,162	10,780	7,649,914
Kyŏngsang-namdo	Masan	4,548	11,779	3,845,569
Kyŏngsang-pukto	Taegu	7,510	19,451	2,676,344
Special cities				
Inch'ŏn-si	Inch'ŏn	131	339	2,307,618
Kwangju-si	Kwangju	193	501	1,257,504
Pusan-si	Pusan	205	531	3,813,814
Sŏul-t'ŭkpyŏlsi	Seoul	234	605	10,229,262
Taegu-si	Taegu	176	456	2,449,139
Taejŏn-si	Taejŏn	207	537	1,272,143
TOTAL		38,375	99,392	44,606,199

Demography

Population (1996): 45,232,000.
Density (1996): persons per sq mi 1,178.7, persons per sq km 455.1.
Urban-rural (1995): urban 81.0%; rural 19.0%.
Sex distribution (1995): male 50.21%; female 49.79%.
Age breakdown (1995): under 15, 23.2%; 15–29, 28.2%; 30–44, 25.1%; 45–59,
14.5%; 60–74, 7.3%; 75 and over, 1.7%.
Population projection: (2000) 46,789,000; (2010) 49,683,000.
Doubling time: 76 years.
Ethnic composition (1990): Korean 99.9%; other 0.1%.
Religious affiliation (1991): religious[1] 54.0%, of which Buddhist 27.6%, Protes-
tant 18.6%, Roman Catholic 5.7%, Confucian 1.0%, Wonbulgyo 0.3%,
Ch'ondogyo 0.2%, other 0.6%; nonreligious 46.0%.
Major cities (1995): Seoul 10,229,262; Pusan 3,813,814; Taegu 2,449,139;
Inch'ŏn 2,307,618; Taejon 1,272,143.

Vital statistics

Birth rate per 1,000 population (1996): 15.1 (world avg. 25.0).
Death rate per 1,000 population (1996): 5.9 (world avg. 9.3).
Natural increase rate per 1,000 population (1996): 9.2 (world avg. 15.7).
Total fertility rate (avg. births per childbearing woman; 1995): 1.8.
Marriage rate per 1,000 population (1994): 6.8.
Divorce rate per 1,000 population (1994): 1.1.
Life expectancy at birth (1995): male 68.0 years; female 76.0 years.
Major causes of death per 100,000 population (1994): diseases of the circula-
tory system 155.0; malignant neoplasms (cancers) 111.3; accidents, poison-
ing, and violence 72.0; diseases of the digestive system 39.6; diseases of the
respiratory system 25.2.

National economy

Budget (1995). Revenue: W 68,940,000,000,000 (taxes on goods and services
33.6%, income taxes 29.7%, nontax revenue 11.9%, social security contributions 7.2%, taxes on international trade 5.0%). Expenditures: W 62,-
030,000,000,000 (education 20.2%, defense 18.1%, general public services
10.5%, social security and welfare 10.2%, agriculture 8.9%, transportation
and communications 7.0%).
Public debt (external, outstanding; 1994): U.S.$27,103,000,000.
Production (metric tons except as noted). Agriculture, forestry, fishing (1995):
rice 6,519,000, cabbages 3,000,000, apples 650,000, tangerines 625,000, dry
onions 500,000, garlic 350,000, barley 300,000, soybeans 160,000; livestock
(number of live animals) 6,100,000 pigs, 3,075,000 cattle, 80,569,000 chickens;
roundwood (1993) 6,485,000 cu m; fish catch (1993) 2,648,977. Mining and
quarrying (1994): copper ore 224,000; iron ore 191,313; zinc concentrate
14,243; lead concentrate 4,345. Manufacturing (1994): cement 52,088,000;
pig iron 21,169,000; urea fertilizers 905,746; newsprint 867,171; polyvinyl
chloride resin 791,412; woolen fabrics 19,598,816 sq m; television receivers
16,999,000 units; passenger cars 1,755,000 units. Construction (1995): residential 62,614,000 sq m; nonresidential 54,713,000 sq m. Energy production
(consumption): electricity (kW-hr; 1995) 163,270,000,000 (163,270,000,000);
coal (metric tons; 1994) 7,438,000 (42,660,000); crude petroleum (barrels;
1994) none (544,639,000); petroleum products (metric tons; 1994) 103,580,-
000 (84,126,000); natural gas (cu m; 1994) none (3,864,000,000).
Household income and expenditure (1994)[2]. Average household size 3.8; income per household W 36,090,000 (U.S.$44,919); sources of income: wages
48.2%, other 51.8%; expenditure: food and beverages 29.7%, education and
recreation 14.2%, transportation and communications 11.3%, clothing and

footwear 7.7%, health care 5.0%, household durable goods 5.0%, housing
4.1%, energy 4.0%, other 20.0%.
Gross national product (1994): U.S.$366,484,000,000 (U.S.$8,220 per capita).

Structure of gross domestic product and labour force

	1994 in value W '000,000,000[3]	1994 % of total value	1994 labour force	1994 % of labour force
Agriculture	16,309.0	6.9	2,699,000	13.3
Mining	902.1	0.4	40,000	0.2
Manufacturing	69,536.4	29.5	4,695,000	23.1
Construction	26,806.0	11.4	1,777,000	8.7
Public utilities	5,660.9	2.4	71,000	0.3
Transp. and commun.	18,011.6	7.6	1,006,000	5.0
Trade	29,735.2	12.6	5,198,000	25.6
Finance	41,026.0	17.4	1,495,000	7.4
Pub. admin., defense	14,677.0	6.2	634,000	3.1
Services	13,709.7	5.8	2,222,000	10.9
Other	−442.9[4]	−0.2[4]	489,000[5]	2.4[5]
TOTAL	235,931.0	100.0	20,326,000	100.0

Population economically active (1994): total 20,326,000; activity rate 45.7%
(participation rates: ages 15 and over, 61.7%; female 40.1%; unemployed
2.4%).

Price and earnings indexes (1990 = 100)

	1989	1990	1991	1992	1993	1994	1995
Consumer price index	92.1	100.0	109.3	116.1	121.7	129.3	135.1
Monthly earnings index	83.2	100.0	116.9	135.2	149.9	173.1	190.2

Tourism (1994): receipts from visitors U.S.$3,806,000,000; expenditures by
nationals abroad U.S.$4,088,000,000.
Land use (1993): forested 65.4%; meadows and pastures 0.9%; agricultural
and under permanent cultivation 20.8%; other 12.9%.

Foreign trade

Balance of trade (current prices)

	1990	1991	1992	1993	1994	1995
U.S.$'000,000	−701	−3,968	−588	+2,880	−729	−2,896
% of total	0.8%	3.6%	0.4%	1.8%	0.5%	1.1%

Imports (1995): U.S.$135,118,900,000 (machinery and transport equipment
36.6%, manufactured goods 15.7%, mineral fuels and lubricants 14.1%,
chemicals 9.7%, inedible crude materials 8.7%). *Major import sources:* Japan
24.1%; United States 22.5%; Germany 4.9%; Saudi Arabia 4.0%; Australia
3.6%; Indonesia 2.5%; Canada 1.9%.
Exports (1995): U.S.$125,058,000,000 (machinery and transport equipment
52.5%, manufactured goods 22.0%, chemicals 7.2%, food and live animals
2.1%, mineral fuels 2.0%). *Major export destinations:* United States 19.3%;
Japan 13.6%; Hong Kong 8.5%; Singapore 5.3%; Germany 4.8%; Taiwan
3.1%; Indonesia 2.4%; Malaysia 2.4%.

Transport and communications

Transport. Railroads (1994): length 4,076 mi, 6,559 km; passenger-km 30,216,-
000,000; metric ton-km cargo 14,064,000,000. Roads (1994): total length 48,-
984 mi, 78,833 km (paved 78%). Vehicles (1994): passenger cars 5,148,713;
trucks and buses 2,255,634. Merchant marine (1992): vessels (100 gross tons
and over) 2,138; total deadweight tonnage 11,724,942. Air transport (1994):
passenger-km 39,260,000,000; metric ton-km cargo 4,825,626,000; airports
(1996) with scheduled flights 14.
Communications. Daily newspapers (1993): total number 63; total circulation
9,736,000[6]; circulation per 1,000 population 221[6]. Radio (1995): 42,000,000
receivers (1 per 1.1 persons). Television (1995): 10,430,000 receivers (1 per
4.3 persons). Telephones (main lines; 1993): 16,632,600 (1 per 2.6 persons).

Education and health

Education (1995)

	schools	teachers	students	student/ teacher ratio
Primary (age 6–13)	5,772	138,369	3,905,163	28.2
Secondary (age 14–19)	3,751	156,342	3,728,275	23.8
Vocational	789	43,045	923,942	21.5
Higher	708	56,237	1,889,933	33.6

Educational attainment (1990). Percentage of population age 25 and over
having: no formal schooling 11.0%; primary education or less 21.7%; some
secondary and secondary 53.9%; postsecondary 13.4%. *Literacy* (1990): total
population age 15 and over literate 96.3%; males literate 99.1%; females
literate 93.5%.
Health (1994): physicians 54,406 (1 per 817 persons); hospital beds 182,159 (1
per 244 persons); infant mortality rate per 1,000 live births (1996) 10.0.
Food (1992): daily per capita caloric intake 3,285 (vegetable products 86%,
animal products 14%); 140% of FAO recommended minimum requirement.

Military

Total active duty personnel (1995): 633,000 (army 82.1%, navy 9.5%, air force
8.4%). *Military expenditure as percentage of GNP* (1994): 3.7% (world 3.0%);
per capita expenditure U.S.$293.

---

[1]Refers to persons who have received commandments, accepted baptism, or entered
a faith and who participate in a religious function regularly or put the religious idea
into practice. [2]Excludes farm households. [3]At 1990 constant prices. [4]Import duties
less imputed bank service charges. [5]Unemployed. [6]Circulation for 20 newspapers only.

Kuwait

Official name: Dawlat al-Kuwayt (State of Kuwait).
Form of government: Constitutional monarchy with one legislative body (National Assembly [64[1]]).
Head of state and government: Emir[2].
Capital: Kuwait City.
Official language: Arabic.
Official religion: Islam.
Monetary unit: 1 Kuwaiti dinar (KD) = 1,000 fils; valuation (Oct. 11, 1996) 1 KD = U.S.$3.33 = £2.12.

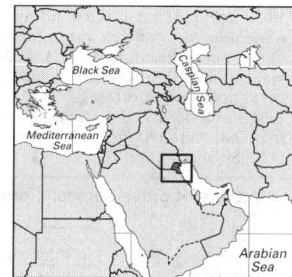

Area and population[3]

Governorates[5]	Capitals	area sq mi	area sq km	population[4] 1995 estimate
Al-Aḥmadī	Al-Aḥmadī	1,984	5,138	283,902
Al-Farwānīyah	Al-Farwānīyah	...	...	451,707
Al-Jahrā'	Al-Jahrā'	4,372	11,324	228,457
Capital	Kuwait City	38	98	276,915
Ḥawallī	Ḥawallī	138	358	449,554
Islands[6]	—	347	900	...
TOTAL		6,880[7]	17,818	1,690,535[4]

Demography

Population (1996): 2,070,000.
Density (1996): persons per sq mi 300.9, persons per sq km 116.2.
Urban-rural (1995): urban 97.0%; rural 3.0%.
Sex distribution (1994): male 61.36%; female 38.64%.
Age breakdown (1994): under 15, 29.4%; 15–29, 28.3%; 30–44, 30.5%; 45–59, 9.5%; 60–74, 2.0%; 75 and over, 0.3%.
Population projection: (2000) 2,458,041; (2010) 3,085,395.
Doubling time: 30 years.
Ethnic composition (by nationality; 1995): Kuwaiti 41.1%; non-Kuwaiti (including other Arab, South Asian, Palestinian, and Badoun [stateless immigrants]) 58.9%.
Religious affiliation (1995): Muslim 85%, of which Sunnī 45%, Shī'ah 30%; other Muslim 10%; other (mostly Christian and Hindu) 15.0%.
Major cities (1993): Al-Jahrā' 139,476; As-Sālimīyah 116,104; Ḥawallī 84,478; Al-Farwānīyah 47,106; Kuwait City 31,241.

Vital statistics

Birth rate per 1,000 population (1994): 26.9 (world avg. 25.0); legitimate, n.a.; illegitimate, n.a.
Death rate per 1,000 population (1994): 1.9 (world avg. 9.3).
Natural increase rate per 1,000 population (1994): 25.0 (world avg. 15.7).
Total fertility rate (avg. births per childbearing woman; 1994): 3.7.
Marriage rate per 1,000 population (1993): 8.0[8].
Divorce rate per 1,000 population (1993): 1.9[8].
Life expectancy at birth (1994): male 74.4 years; female 79.0 years.
Major causes of death per 100,000 population (1992): circulatory diseases 79.8; accidents, poisoning, and violence 40.3; malignant neoplasms (cancers) 22.6; respiratory diseases 17.1; congenital anomalies 9.2; endocrine, nutritional, and metabolic diseases 8.4; diseases of the nervous system 7.4; infectious and parasitic diseases 5.7; diseases of the digestive system 4.4.

National economy

Budget[9] (1995–96). Revenue: KD 2,910,000,000 (oil revenue 85.6%). Expenditures: KD 4,232,300,000 (current expenditures 71.0%, of which defense 19.5%, transfers 19.3%, education 7.0%, health 6.2%; development expenditure 9.7%).
Public debt (external, outstanding; 1991): U.S.$792,000,000[10].
Tourism (1994): receipts from visitors U.S.$101,000,000; expenditures by nationals abroad U.S.$2,146,000,000.
Gross national product (at current market prices; 1994): U.S.$31,433,000,000 (U.S.$19,040 per capita).

Structure of gross domestic product and labour force

	1995[8] in value KD '000,000[11]	1995[8] % of total value	1994 labour force[12]	1994 % of labour force[12]
Agriculture	34.1	0.4	15,985	1.6
Mining (oil sector)	3,137.5	39.5	7,071	0.7
Manufacturing	869.2	10.9	70,659	7.1
Construction	244.4	3.1	128,813	13.0
Public utilities	−9.9	−0.1	7,017	0.7
Transportation and communications	350.1	4.4	38,706	3.9
Trade[13]	607.6	7.6	184,284	18.6
Finance and business services	893.2	11.2	35,341	3.6
Pub. admin., defense	} 1,903.6	23.9	469,432	47.4
Services				
Other	−77.5[14]	−1.0[14]	33,210	3.4
TOTAL	7,952.3	100.0[7]	990,518	100.0

Production (metric tons except as noted). Agriculture, forestry, fishing (1996): cucumbers and gherkins 36,000, onions 16,000, tomatoes 12,000, eggplants 2,800, garlic 1,350; livestock (number of live animals) 308,010 sheep, 68,987 goats, 19,879 cattle, 8,000 camels, 20,480,000 chickens; fish catch (1993) 8,561. Mining and quarrying (1994): sulfur 175,000; lime 35,000. Manufacturing (value added in KD '000; 1992): refined petroleum products 307,047;

food products 33,629; clothing and apparel 30,015; fabricated metal products 28,925; cement, bricks, and tile 24,596; furniture and fixtures 13,627. Construction (floor area approved for construction; 1989): residential 2,563,000 sq m; nonresidential 416,000 sq m. Energy production (consumption): electricity (kW-hr; 1993) 18,200,000,000 (18,200,000,000); coal, none (none); crude petroleum (barrels; 1995) 657,000,000 ([1992] 117,400,000); petroleum products (metric tons; 1992) 16,059,000 (3,064,000); natural gas (cu m; 1994) 5,970,000,000 (5,970,000,000).
Population economically active (1995): total 746,408; activity rate of total population 47.4% (participation rates: ages 15–59, 70.7%; female [1988] 18.8%; unemployed 0.7%).

Price and earnings indexes (1990 = 100)

	1988	1989	1990	1991	1992	1993	1994
Consumer price index	94.8	98.1	100.0	116.9	116.9	108.9	111.6
Earnings index	...	...	...	...	...	...	...

Household income and expenditure. Average household size (1986) 7.4; annual income per household (1973)[15] KD 4,246 (U.S.$12,907); sources of income: wages and salaries 53.8%, self-employment 20.8%, other 25.4%; expenditure (1992): food, beverages, and tobacco 37.0%, housing and energy 18.7%, transportation 15.3%, household appliances and services 11.1%, clothing and footwear 10.0%, education and health 2.5%.
Land use (1994): forested 0.1%; meadows and pastures 7.7%; agricultural and under permanent cultivation 0.3%; other, built-up, and wasteland 91.9%.

Foreign trade[16]

Balance of trade (current prices)

	1990	1991	1992	1993	1994	1995
KD '000,000	+917	−1,135	−202	+969	+1,331	+1,731.8
% of total	29.4%	64.9%	5.0%	18.7%	25.2%	28.9%

Imports (1995): KD 2,323,100,000 (machinery and transport equipment 41.2%, manufactured goods 19.5%, miscellaneous manufactured articles 14.0%, food and live animals 13.7%, chemical products 7.3%, beverages and tobacco 1.2%). *Major import sources:* U.S. 16.1%; France 11.1%; Japan 9.4%; Germany 7.2%; Saudi Arabia 6.1%; U.K. 6.0%; Italy 5.9%; India 2.9%.
Exports (1995)[17]: KD 3,883,480,000 (crude petroleum and petroleum products 94.3%). *Major export destinations:* India 16.4%; Saudi Arabia 15.5%; China 11.9%; United Arab Emirates 10.4%; Philippines 3.6%; Egypt 2.7%; Pakistan 1.7%; Italy 1.0%.

Transport and communications

Transport. Railroads: none. Roads (1990): total length 2,655 mi, 4,273 km (paved 100%). Vehicles (1994): passenger cars 538,300; trucks and buses 154,900. Merchant marine (1992): vessels (100 gross tons and over) 209; total deadweight tonnage 3,188,526. Air transport (1995)[18]: passenger-mi 3,184,038,000, passenger-km 5,124,223,000; short ton-mi cargo 225,837,000, metric ton-km cargo 329,717,000; airports (1996) with scheduled flights 1.
Communications. Daily newspapers (1995): total number 9; total circulation 671,672; circulation per 1,000 population 672. Radio (1995): total number of receivers 1,000,000 (1 per 1.6 persons). Television (1996): total number of receivers 800,000 (1 per 2.0 persons). Telephones (main lines; 1993): 358,000 (1 per 4.1 persons).

Education and health

Education (1994–95)

	schools	teachers	students	student/ teacher ratio
Primary (age 6–9)	246	8,815	132,204	15.0
Secondary (age 10–17)	391	18,072	200,828	11.1
Voc., teacher tr.	34	683	2,936	4.3
Higher[19]	1	927[20]	11,284	...

Educational attainment (1988). Percentage of population age 25 and over having: no formal schooling 44.8%; primary education 8.6%; some secondary 15.1%; complete secondary 15.1%; higher 16.4%. *Literacy* (1988): total population age 15 and over literate 961,880 (79.7%); males literate 574,739 (83.3%); females literate 387,141 (74.9%).
Health: physicians 3,043 (1 per 533 persons); hospital beds 4,093[21] (1 per 357 persons); infant mortality rate per 1,000 live births 15.9.
Food (1993): daily per capita caloric intake 2,523 (vegetable products 79%, animal products 21%); 104% of FAO recommended minimum requirement.

Military

Total active duty personnel (1996): 15,300 (army [including central staff] 71.9%, navy 11.8%, air force 16.3%). *Military expenditure as percentage of GNP* (1994): 11.1% (world 2.6%); per capita expenditure U.S.$1,838.

[1]50 elected seats include 4 elected cabinet ministers; nonelected cabinet ministers serving ex officio occupy the other 14 seats. [2]Assisted by prime minister. [3]Area of governorates reflects situation prior to Amiri Decree No. 156 of 1988, which established Al-Farwānīyah governorate; but population estimate accounts for the reorganization. [4]Preliminary total of the census of April 23, 1995, was 1,575,983. [5]Governorates have no administrative function. [6]Bubian Island 333 sq mi (863 sq km) and Warba Island 14 sq mi (37 sq km). [7]Detail does not add to total given because of rounding. [8]Provisional. [9]Approved budget for 1995–96. [10]Includes external long-term debt not guaranteed by the government. [11]At purchaser's value. [12]Year-end estimates; April 1995 census indicated an economically active population of 746,408. [13]Trade includes restaurants and hotels. [14]Includes import duties of KD 86,500,000 and imputed bank service charges of KD −164,000,000. [15]Kuwaiti households only. [16]Imports are f.o.b. in balance of trade and c.i.f. in commodities and trading partners. [17]Total exports and reexports include oil and non-oil, but breakdown by destination is derived from non-oil exports. [18]Kuwait Airways only. [19]1992–93. [20]1989–90. [21]1993; public hospitals only.

Kyrgyzstan

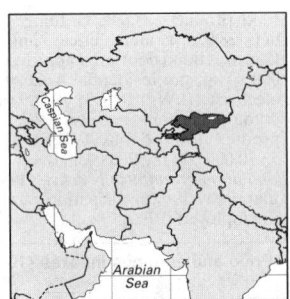

Official name: Kyrgyz Respublikasy (Kyrgyz Republic).
Form of government: unitary multiparty republic with two legislative houses (Assembly of People's Representatives [70]; Legislative Assembly [35]).
Head of state and government: President assisted by Prime Minister.
Capital: Bishkek (formerly Frunze).
Official languages: Kyrgyz; Russian.
Official religion: none.
Monetary unit: 1 som = 100 tiyiyn; valuation (Oct. 11, 1996) free rate, 1 U.S.$ = 13.40 som; 1 £ = 21.10 som.

Area and population

Provinces	Capitals	area sq mi	area sq km	population 1993[1] estimate
Chüy (Chu)	Kara-Balta	7,200	18,700	774,000
Jalal-Abad (Dzhalal-Abad)	Jalal-Abad (Dzhalal-Abad)	15,200	39,500	812,800
Naryn	Naryn	18,300	47,300	267,900
Osh	Osh	14,700	38,100	1,360,900
Talas	Talas	4,400	11,400	203,000
Ysyk-Köl (Issyk-Kul)	Ysyk-Köl (Issyk-Kul)	16,800	43,500	429,300
City of republic subordination				
Bishkek (Frunze)	—	...	...	634,100
TOTAL		76,600	198,500	4,482,000

Demography

Population (1996): 4,521,000.
Density (1996): persons per sq mi 59.0, persons per sq km 22.8.
Urban-rural (1995): urban 35.1%; rural 64.9%.
Sex distribution (1993): male 49.16%; female 50.84%.
Age breakdown (1989): under 15, 37.5%; 15–29, 27.0%; 30–44, 16.3%; 45–59, 10.9%; 60–74, 6.2%; 75 and over, 2.1%.
Population projection: (2000) 4,625,000; (2010) 5,358,000.
Doubling time: 44 years.
Ethnic composition (1989): Kyrgyz 52.4%; Russian 21.5%; Uzbek 12.9%; Ukrainian 2.5%; German 2.4%; Tatar 1.6%; other 6.7%.
Religious affiliation: believers are predominantly Sunnī Muslim (Ḥanafīyah).
Major cities (1991): Bishkek (Frunze) 631,300; Osh 218,700; Jalal-Abad 74,200; Tokmok 71,200; Kara-Köl 64,300.

Vital statistics

Birth rate per 1,000 population (1994): 24.6 (world avg. 25.0); legitimate 83.2%; illegitimate 16.8%.
Death rate per 1,000 population (1994): 8.3 (world avg. 9.3).
Natural increase rate per 1,000 population (1994): 16.3 (world avg. 15.7).
Total fertility rate (avg. births per childbearing woman; 1994): 3.1.
Marriage rate per 1,000 population (1994): 5.8.
Divorce rate per 1,000 population (1994): 1.2.
Life expectancy at birth (1994): male 64.0 years; female 72.0 years.
Major causes of death per 100,000 population (1993): diseases of the circulatory system 290.0; diseases of the respiratory system 125.0; accidents, poisoning, and violence 91.2; malignant neoplasms (cancers) 67.3; infectious and parasitic diseases 30.1; diseases of the digestive system 29.7.

National economy

Budget (1995). Revenue: 2,708,000,000 som (tax revenue 87.0%, of which value-added tax 26.0%, enterprise profits tax 15.3%, excise taxes 11.0%, personal income tax 10.5%, other 24.2%; nontax revenue 13.0%). Expenditures: 4,883,200,000 som (education 19.4%; social security 18.4%; health 10.9%; government services 7.4%; industrial expenditure 7.2%; public safety 6.8%; defense 4.9%).
Production (metric tons except as noted). Agriculture, forestry, fishing (1995): grain 979,334, potatoes 431,000, vegetables (other than potatoes) 344,000, fruit (other than grapes) 104,000, seed cotton 56,000, grapes 28,000; livestock (number of live animals) 5,076,000 sheep and goats, 920,000 cattle, 300,000 horses, 118,000 pigs; roundwood (1990) 6,000 cu m; fish catch (1993) 350. Mining and quarrying (1994): antimony 1,400; mercury 150; gold 2,000 kg. Manufacturing (value of production in '000,000 som; 1994): textiles 1,112; processed foods 729; ferrous and nonferrous metals 678; machinery and metalwork 650; construction materials 258; footwear and leather goods 89. Construction (1992): residential 1,232,000 sq m. Energy production (consumption): electricity (kW-hr; 1994) 12,932,000,000 (10,427,000,000); coal (metric tons; 1994) 298,000 (595,000); crude petroleum (barrels; 1994) 645,000 (154,000); petroleum products (metric tons; 1994) none (256,000); natural gas (cu m; 1994) 33,930,000 (1,008,000,000).
Population economically active (1995): total 1,641,000; activity rate of total population 36.7% (1993; participation rates: ages 16–59 [male], 16–54 [female] 81.1%; female 49.0%; unemployed 1.9%).

Price and earnings indexes (1990 = 100)

	1988	1989	1990	1991	1992	1993	1994
Consumer price index	95.2	97.1	100.0	185.0	1,766	23,122	89,534
Monthly earnings index	84.5	90.9	100.0	166.9	1,179	12,559	...

Public debt (external, outstanding; 1994): U.S.$441,300,000.
Household income and expenditure (1990). Average household size 4.7; income per household (1994) 4,359 som (U.S.$325.30); sources of income: wages and salaries 49.7%, pensions and stipends 11.1%, income from sale of agricultural products 3.5%, other 35.7%; expenditure: consumer goods 79.3%, services 11.7%, taxes 7.6%, other 1.4%.
Gross national product (at current market prices; 1994): U.S.$2,825,000,000 (U.S.$610 per capita)[2].

Structure of gross domestic product and labour force

	1994 in value '000,000 som	1994 % of total value	1995 labour force	1995 % of labour force
Agriculture	4,601	38.3	689,000	42.0
Mining	}			
Manufacturing	2,477	20.6	240,000	14.6
Public utilities	}			
Construction	409	3.4	77,000	4.7
Transportation and communications	494	4.1	86,000	5.2
Trade	1,209	10.1	112,000	6.8
Finance	602	5.0	8,000	0.5
Public administration, defense	...	...	58,000	3.5
Services	1,455	12.1	329,000	20.0
Other	773	6.4	42,000	2.6
TOTAL	12,020[3]	100.0	1,641,000	100.0[3]

Land use (1994): forested 3.5%; meadows and pastures 42.9%; agricultural and under permanent cultivation 7.2%; other 46.4%.
Tourism: receipts from visitors, n.a.; expenditures by nationals abroad, n.a.

Foreign trade

Balance of trade (current prices)

	1993	1994	1995
U.S.$'000,000	− 166.3	− 118.9	− 263.4
% of total	19.9%	14.9%	24.4%

Imports (1995): U.S.$672,400,000 (oil and gas 24.2%, machine-building equipment 15.4%, food products 14.4%, chemical products 4.5%, light industrial products 3.5%). *Major import sources:* Russian Federation 21.9%; Kazakstan 21.5%; Uzbekistan 17.0%; Turkey 7.3%; Cuba 4.3%.
Exports (1995): U.S.$409,000,000 (food products 20.2%, light industrial products 20.1%, metals 17.7%, machinery 10.8%, oil and gas 9.9%). *Major export destinations:* Russian Federation 25.6%; Uzbekistan 17.1%; China 16.8%; Kazakstan 16.3%; U.K. 6.7%.

Transport and communications

Transport. Railroads (1995): length 249 mi, 400 km; (1992) passenger-mi 81,500,000, passenger-km 131,200,000; short ton-mi cargo 987,000,000, metric ton-km cargo 1,588,900,000. Roads (1995): total length 11,533 mi, 18,560 km (paved 91%). Vehicles (1995): passenger cars 164,000; trucks and buses, n.a. Merchant marine: vessels (100 gross tons and over) none; landlocked state. Air transport (1992): passenger-mi 1,601,800,000, passenger-km 2,577,800,000; short ton-mi cargo 144,100,000, metric ton-km cargo 231,900,000; airports (1996) with scheduled flights 2.
Communications. Daily newspapers (1993): total number 128; total circulation 1,129,000; circulation per 1,000 population 250. Radio (1996): 825,000 receivers (1 per 5.5 persons). Television (1991): 875,000 receivers (1 per 19.6 persons). Telephones (main lines; 1993): 367,400 (1 per 12.3 persons).

Education and health

Education (1993–94)

	schools	teachers	students	student/ teacher ratio
Primary (age 6–13)	1,832 }	77,000	2,130,000	27.7
Secondary (age 14–17)	1,474 }		32,800	
Voc., teacher tr.	53	...	32,800	...
Higher	23	...	55,200	...

Educational attainment (1989). Percentage of population age 19 and over having: primary education 4.7%; some secondary 20.9%; completed secondary 44.4%; some postsecondary 19.3%; higher 10.7%. *Literacy* (1989): total population age 15 and over literate 4,130,562 (97.0%); males literate 2,048,536 (98.6%); females literate 2,082,026 (95.5%).
Health (1994): physicians 14,000 (1 per 319 persons); hospital beds 47,000 (1 per 95 persons); (1996) infant mortality rate per 1,000 live births 31.5.
Food: daily per capita caloric intake, n.a.

Military

Total active duty personnel (1996): 7,000 (army 100%). *Military expenditure as percentage of GNP* (1994): 0.7% (world 3.0%); per capita expenditure U.S.$12.

[1]January. [2]Ruble-area GNP and exchange-rate data are very speculative. [3]Detail does not add to total given because of rounding.

Laos

Official name: Sathalanalat Paxathipatai Paxaxôn Lao (Lao People's Democratic Republic).
Form of government: unitary single-party people's republic with one legislative house (National Assembly[1] [85]).
Chief of state: President.
Head of government: Prime Minister.
Capital: Vientiane (Viangchan).
Official language: Lao.
Official religion: none.
Monetary unit: 1 kip (KN) = 100 at; valuation (Oct. 11, 1996) 1 U.S.$ = KN 920; 1 £ = KN 1,449.

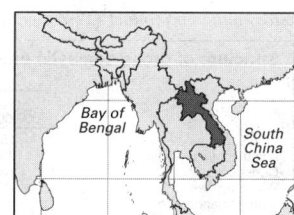

Area and population

Provinces	Capitals	area sq mi	area sq km	population 1990 estimate
Attapu	Attapu	3,985	10,320	80,000
Bokèo	Houayxay	1,919	4,970	64,000
Bolikhamxai	Pakxan	6,359	16,470	145,000
Champasak	Pakxé	5,952	15,415	469,000
Houaphan	Xam Nua	6,371	16,500	243,000
Khammouan	Thakhek	6,299	16,315	249,000
Louangnamtha	Louangnamtha	3,600	9,325	114,000
Louangphrabang	Louangphrabang	6,515	16,875	339,000
Oudomxay	Xay	8,182	21,190	291,000
Phôngsali	Phôngsali	6,282	16,270	142,000
Salavan	Salavan	4,010	10,385	211,000
Savannakhét	Savannakhét	8,525	22,080	640,000
Viangchan	Muang Phôn-Hông	7,718	19,990	312,000
Xaignabouli	Xaignabouli	4,554	11,795	182,000
Xékong	Thong	2,959	7,665	58,000
Xiangkhoang	Phônsavan	6,685	17,315	189,000
Municipalities				
Viangchan	Vientiane (Viangchan)	1,514	3,920	442,000
TOTAL		91,429	236,800	4,170,000

Demography

Population (1996): 5,023,000.
Density (1996): persons per sq mi 54.9, persons per sq km 21.2.
Urban-rural (1995): urban 22.0%; rural 78.0%.
Sex distribution (1995): male 49.46%; female 50.54%.
Age breakdown (1990): under 15, 43.7%; 15–29, 26.0%; 30–44, 16.2%; 45–59, 9.2%; 60–74, 4.2%; 75 and over, 0.7%.
Population projection: (2000) 5,602,000; (2010) 7,188,000.
Doubling time: 25 years.
Ethnic composition (1983): Lao-Lum (Lao) 67.0%; Lao-Theung (Mon-Khmer) 16.5%; Lao-Tai (Tai) 7.8%; Lao-Soung (Miao [Hmong] and Man [Yao]) 5.2%; other 3.5%.
Religious affiliation (1980): Buddhist 57.8%; tribal religionist 33.6%; Christian 1.8%, of which Roman Catholic 0.8%, Protestant 0.2%; Muslim 1.0%; atheist 1.0%; Chinese folk-religionist 0.9%; none 3.8%; other 0.1%.
Major cities (1985): Vientiane (Viangchan) 178,203; Savannakhét 96,652; Louangphrabang 68,399; Pakxé 47,323.

Vital statistics

Birth rate per 1,000 population (1996): 42.0 (world avg. 25.0).
Death rate per 1,000 population (1996): 13.8 (world avg. 9.3).
Natural increase rate per 1,000 population (1996): 28.2 (world avg. 15.7).
Total fertility rate (avg. births per childbearing woman; 1996): 6.2.
Marriage rate per 1,000 population: n.a.
Divorce rate per 1,000 population: n.a.
Life expectancy at birth (1996): male 51.0 years; female 54.0 years.
Major causes of death per 100,000 population (incomplete, 1990): malaria 7.6; pneumonia 3.0; meningitis 1.5; diarrhea 1.2; tuberculosis 0.8.

National economy

Budget (1995–96). Revenue: KN 295,510,000,000 (taxes 57.4%, foreign grants 30.5%, nontax revenue 12.1%). Expenditures: KN 355,973,000,000 (current expenditure 47.0%, capital expenditure 53.0%).
Public debt (external, outstanding; 1994): U.S.$2,022,000,000.
Tourism (1994): receipts from visitors U.S.$43,000,000; expenditures by nationals abroad U.S.$18,000,000.
Population economically active (1989): total 1,888,000; activity rate of total population 49.0% (participation rates [1985]: ages 15–64, 84.2%; female 45.3%; unemployed 3.0%).

Price and earnings indexes (1990 = 100)

	1989	1990	1991	1992	1993	1994	1995
Consumer price index	73.7	100.0	113.4	124.6	132.4	141.4	169.1
Earnings index	...	...	...	...	...	...	...

Production (metric tons except as noted). Agriculture, forestry, fishing (1995): rice 1,409,000, sugarcane 141,000, sweet potatoes 120,000, corn (maize) 82,000, cassava 69,000, pulses 43,000, potatoes 35,000, pineapples 35,000, melons 34,000, oranges 24,000, bananas 21,000, coffee 10,000; livestock (number of live animals) 1,653,000 pigs, 1,300,000 water buffalo, 1,190,000 cattle, 162,000 goats, 29,000 horses, 9,300,000 chickens; roundwood (1994) 4,296,000 cu m; fish catch (1993) 30,500. Mining and quarrying (1995): gypsum 110,000; rock

salt 12,000; tin (metal content) 687. Manufacturing (1992): detergent 769,000; soap 550,700; plastic products 147,200; nails 73,000; clothing 2,750,800 pieces; cigarettes 30,000,000 units; beer 95,900 hectolitres; soft drinks 63,700 hectolitres. Construction: n.a. Energy production (consumption): electricity (kW-hr; 1993) 900,000,000 (293,000,000); coal (metric tons; 1993) 1,000 (1,000); crude petroleum, n.a. (n.a.); petroleum products (metric tons; 1993) none (88,000); natural gas, n.a. (n.a.).
Gross national product (at current market prices; 1994): U.S.$1,496,000,000 (U.S.$320 per capita).

Structure of gross domestic product and labour force

	1995 in value KN '000,000[2]	1995 % of total value	1989 labour force	1989 % of labour force
Agriculture	461,600	55.2	1,359,000	72.0
Manufacturing	110,400	13.2		
Mining	1,600	0.2		
Construction	31,700	3.8		
Public utilities	10,800	1.3		
Transportation and communications	37,500	4.5	58,533	8.1
Trade	68,500	8.2		
Finance	39,700	4.7		
Pub. admin., defense Services	55,000	6.6		
Other	19,300	2.3		
TOTAL	836,400	100.0	1,888,000	100.0

Household income and expenditure. Average household size (1985) 6.0; average annual income per household KN 3,710 (U.S.$371); sources of income: n.a.; expenditure: n.a.
Land use (1994): forested 54.4%; meadows and pastures 3.5%; agricultural and under permanent cultivation 3.9%; other 38.2%.

Foreign trade[3]

Balance of trade (current prices)

	1990	1991	1992	1993	1994	1995
U.S.$'000,000	− 127.8	− 131.7	− 133.0	− 179.0	− 263.7	− 239.3
% of total	46.4%	45.8%	33.3%	27.8%	30.5%	25.6%

Imports (1995): U.S.$627,800,000 (consumption goods 45.2%; investment goods 30.1%, of which construction and electrical equipment 12.6%, machinery and equipment 7.0%, motor vehicles 5.7%; materials for garment assembly 10.6%). *Major import sources:* Thailand 45.2%; Japan 11.0%; Vietnam 3.9%; Singapore 3.8%; China 3.5%; France 1.3%.
Exports (1995): U.S.$348,200,000 (wood products 25.4%; garments 22.0%; electricity 6.9%; coffee 6.1%). *Major export destinations:* Thailand 40.9%; Vietnam 25.2%; France 6.8%; United States 3.2%; Russia 3.2%.

Transport and communications

Transport. Railroads: none. Roads (1992): total length 8,780 mi, 14,130 km (paved 16%). Vehicles (1994): passenger cars 10,000; trucks and buses 10,000. Merchant marine (1992): vessels (100 gross tons and over) 1; total deadweight tonnage 1,469. Air transport (1993): passenger-mi 29,000,000, passenger-km 46,000,000; short ton-mi cargo 3,000,000, metric ton-km cargo 4,000,000; airports (1996) with scheduled flights 11.
Communications. Daily newspapers (1992): total number 3; total circulation 14,000; circulation per 1,000 population 3.0. Radio (1995): total number of receivers 575,000 (1 per 8.5 persons). Television (1995): total number of receivers 80,000 (1 per 61 persons). Telephones (main lines; 1993): 8,600 (1 per 526 persons).

Education and health

Education (1993–94)

	schools	teachers	students	student/teacher ratio
Primary (age 6–10)	8,361	22,649	681,044	30.1
Secondary (age 11–16)	750[4]	11,066	143,673	13.0
Voc., teacher tr.	139[5]	1,647	11,693	7.1
Higher	9[4]	998	8,881	8.9

Educational attainment (1985). Percentage of population age 6 and over having: no schooling 49.3%; primary 41.2%; secondary 9.1%; higher 0.4%.
Literacy (1985): total population age 15 and over literate 83.9%; males literate 92.0%; females literate 75.8%.
Health (1990): physicians 1,173 (1 per 3,555 persons); hospital beds 10,364 (1 per 402 persons); infant mortality rate per 1,000 live births (1996) 89.0.
Food (1992): daily per capita caloric intake 2,259 (vegetable products 89%, animal products 11%); 102% of FAO recommended minimum requirement.

Military

Total active duty personnel (1996): 37,000 (army 89.2%, navy 1.4%, air force 9.4%). *Military expenditure as percent of GNP* (1994): 7.4% (world 3.0%); per capita expenditure U.S.$24.

[1]Formerly known as the Supreme People's Assembly. [2]At constant 1990 prices. [3]Import figures are c.i.f. in balance of trade and commodities. [4]1989–90. [5]1988–89.

Latvia

Official name: Latvijas Republika
  (Republic of Latvia).
Form of government: unitary multiparty
  republic with a single legislative body
  (Saeima, or Parliament [100]).
Chief of state: President.
Head of government: Prime Minister.
Capital: Rīga.
Official language: Latvian.
Official religion: none.
Monetary unit: 1 lats[1] (plural lati) =
  10 santimi; valuation (Oct. 11, 1996)
  1 U.S.$ = 0.55 lats; 1 £ = 0.87 lats.

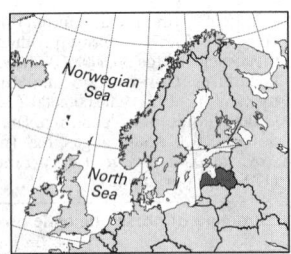

Area and population

Cities of republic jurisdiction	area sq km2	population 1995 estimate	Rural districts	area sq km2	population 1995 estimate
Daugavpils	72	120,152	Jelgava	1,613	37,473
Jelgava	60	71,129	Krāslava	2,288	39,438
Jūrmala	100	59,247	Kuldīga	2,503	41,047
Liepāja	60	100,271	Liepāja	3,589	51,677
Rēzekne	17	42,081	Limbaži	2,602	41,258
Rīga	295	839,670	Ludza	2,566	40,128
Ventspils	46	47,005	Madona	3,348	48,725
			Ogre	1,816	63,870
Rural districts			Preiļi	2,042	43,656
Aizkraukle	2,558	44,046	Rēzekne	2,654	42,485
Alūksne	2,246	27,670	Rīga	3,094	145,499
Balvi	2,384	32,715	Saldus	2,134	39,831
Bauska	1,884	53,890	Talsi	2,748	50,406
Cēsis	3,062	62,043	Tukums	2,457	56,748
Daugavpils	2,526	45,125	Valka	2,444	36,215
Dobele	1,680	41,513	Valmiera	2,377	61,901
Gulbene	1,876	29,797	Ventspils	2,471	14,363
Jēkabpils	2,998	58,469	TOTAL	64,610	2,529,543

Demography

Population (1996): 2,516,843.
Density (1996): persons per sq mi 100.9, persons per sq km 39.0.
Urban-rural (1995): urban 69.1%; rural 30.9%.
Sex distribution (1995): male 46.3%; female 53.7%.
Age breakdown (1995): under 15, 21.0%; 15–29, 20.3%; 30–44, 21.5%; 45–59, 18.5%; 60–74, 14.1%; 75 and over, 4.8%.
Population projection: (2000) 2,483,286; (2010) 2,401,339.
Ethnic composition (1995): Latvian 54.8%; Russian 32.8%; Belarusian 4.0%; Ukrainian 3.0%; Polish 2.2%; Lithuanian 1.3%.
Religious affiliation: believers are predominantly Evangelical Lutheran, Roman Catholic, or Russian Orthodox.
Major cities (1995): Rīga 839,670; Daugavpils 120,152; Liepāja 100,271; Jelgava 71,129; Jūrmala 59,247.

Vital statistics

Birth rate per 1,000 population (1994): 9.5 (world avg. 25.0); (1994) legitimate 73.6%; illegitimate 26.4%.
Death rate per 1,000 population (1994): 16.4 (world avg. 9.3).
Natural increase rate per 1,000 population (1994): −6.9 (world avg. 15.7).
Total fertility rate (avg. births per childbearing woman; 1994): 1.4.
Marriage rate per 1,000 population (1994): 4.5.
Divorce rate per 1,000 population (1994): 3.3.
Life expectancy at birth (1994): male 60.7 years; female 72.9 years.
Major causes of death per 100,000 population (1994): diseases of the circulatory system 917.0; accidents, poisoning, and violence 235.9; malignant neoplasms (cancers) 219.6; diseases of the respiratory system 52.8.

National economy

Budget (1994). Revenue: 561,272,000 lats (social security taxes 38.4%, value-added taxes 31.0%, profit tax 13.6%, income tax 5.3%[3], customs duties 5.2%). Expenditures: 599,202,000 lats (pensions 40.1%, education 13.7%, defense and law enforcement 10.4%, revenue from borrowing 6.2%, interest on foreign loans 1.5%).
Production (metric tons except as noted). Agriculture, forestry, fishing (1995): potatoes 927,000, barley 383,000, vegetables 232,000, sugar beets 222,000, wheat 160,000, fruits and berries 91,000; livestock (number of live animals) 551,000 cattle, 501,000 pigs, 86,000 sheep, 3,500,000 poultry; roundwood (1994) 4,590,000 cu m; fish catch (1994) 142,000. Mining and quarrying (1995): peat 421,000; gypsum 78,813. Manufacturing (1994): cement 244,000; steel 203,786[4]; processed meats 189,000; synthetic fibre 18,400; telephones 121,000 units; diesel engines 18,000 units; buses 4,800 units; rail passenger cars 118 units; beer 611,200 hectolitres; vodka 220,000 hectolitres[5]; textiles 14,000,000 sq m. Construction (1994): new residential 52,000,000 sq m. Energy production (consumption): electricity (kW-hr; 1994) 4,441,000,000 (4,975,000,000); coal (1993) none (599,000); crude petroleum, none (n.a.); petroleum products (1993) none (2,426,000); natural gas (1994) 995,000,000 ([1993] 1,219,000,000).
Household income and expenditure. Average household size (1989) 3.1; average annual income per household: n.a.; sources of income (1994): wages and salaries 67.0%, pensions and transfers 17.4%, self-employment 5.4%, other 10.2%; expenditure (1994): food, beverages, and tobacco 51.6%, housing and energy 13.9%, clothing and footwear 8.0%, transport and communications 7.4%, medical care and health services 3.2%, furniture, furnishings, and household equipment 2.8%, other goods and services 7.4%.

Gross national product (1994): U.S.$5,920,000,000 (U.S.$2,290 per capita).

Structure of gross domestic product and labour force

	1994 in value '000,000 lats[1]	1994 % of total value	1994 labour force	1994 % of labour force
Agriculture	150	6.2	232,000	19.3
Manufacturing and mining	358	14.9	235,000	19.5
Construction	109	4.5	62,000	5.1
Public utilities	77	3.2	18,000	1.5
Transportation and communications	371	15.4	106,000	8.8
Trade	168	7.0	162,000	13.4
Finance	128	5.3	73,000	6.1
Pub. admin., defense	245	10.2	142,000	11.8
Services	803	33.3	139,000	11.5
Other			36,000	3.0
TOTAL	2,409	100.0	1,205	100.0

Population economically active (1994): total 1,300,100; activity rate of total population 51.4% (participation rates: ages 16–59/55[6], 48.1%; female 51.9%; unemployed 6.5%).

Price and earnings indexes (1992 = 100)

	1991	1992	1993	1994	1995
Consumer price index	9.5	100.0	209.2	284.4	354.7
Monthly earnings index	14.0	100.0	223.3	355.7	420.3

Land use (1994): forested 44.4%; meadows and pastures 12.4%; agricultural and permanent cultivation 27.0%; other 16.2%.

Foreign trade

Balance of trade (current prices)

	1992	1993	1994
U.S.$'000,000	57	66	−257
% of total	2.8%	2.8%	11.3%

Imports (1994): U.S.$1,263,000,000 (mineral products 29.0%, machinery and equipment 10.1%, chemical products 8.2%, transport equipment 3.8%, food and agricultural products 3.3%). *Major import sources:* Russia 24.0%; Germany 13.5%; Finland 8.5%; Sweden 6.4%; Lithuania 5.9%.
Exports (1994): U.S.$1,006,000,000 (textiles 13.4%, food and agricultural products 10.3%, forestry products 9.5%, transport equipment 6.2%). *Major export destinations:* Russia 28.1%; Germany 10.5%; United Kingdom 9.7%; Sweden 6.9%; Ukraine 5.9%.

Transport and communications

Transport. Railroads (1994): length 2,413 km; passenger-km 1,794,000,000; metric-km cargo 9,520,000,000. Roads (1993): total length 64,693 km (paved 18.2%). Vehicles (1994): passenger cars 252,000; trucks and buses 73,600. Merchant marine (1992): cargo vessels 261; total deadweight tonnage 1,436,899. Air transport (1994): passenger-km 271,000,000; metric ton-km cargo 9,000,000; airports with scheduled flights (1996) 1.
Communications. Total newspapers (1992): total number 17; total circulation 258,000; circulation per 1,000 population 102. Radio (1996): 1,396,000 receivers (1 per 1.8 persons). Television (1996): 1,126,000 receivers (1 per 2.2 persons). Telephones (main lines; 1993): 694,300 (1 per 3.7 persons).

Education and health

Education (1994–1995)

	schools	teachers[7]	students	student/ teacher ratio
Primary	490	12,758	71,900	5.6
Secondary	381	18,344	240,700	13.2
Voc., teacher tr.	77	6,691	26,900	4.0
Higher	19	4,478	37,600	8.4

Educational attainment (1989). Percentage of persons age 25 and over having: primary or less 21.2%; complete secondary 46.3%; some higher 13.4%. *Literacy* (1989): percentage of total population age 15 and over literate 99.5%; males literate 99.8%; females literate 99.2%.
Health (1994): physicians 8,700 (1 per 291.4 persons); hospital beds 30,400 (1 per 83.2 persons); infant mortality rate per 1,000 live births (1994) 15.5.

Military

Total active duty personnel (1996): 6,950 (border guard 61.8%, army 21.6%, navy 14.4%, air force 2.2%). *Military expenditure as percentage of GNP* (1994): 1.2% (world 3.0%); per capita expenditure U.S.$33.

---

[1]The lats (pre-World War II Latvian currency), reintroduced in parallel with the Latvian ruble (LR; at 200 LR per lats) on March 5, 1993, became the sole official currency Oct. 18, 1993. From May 7, 1992, LR circulated in parallel at par with the Soviet ruble, serving temporarily as the sole legal tender until introduction of the lats on March 5, 1993. [2]One sq km is equal to approximately 0.3861 sq mi. [3]1993. [4]1995. [5]1991. [6]Males retire at age 59, females at 55. [7]1992–1996.

Lebanon

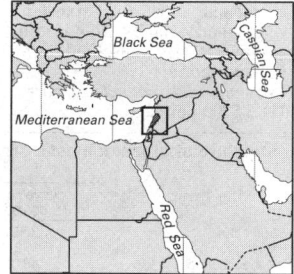

Official name: Al-Jumhūrīyah al-Lubnānīyah (Republic of Lebanon).
Form of government: unitary multiparty republic with one legislative house (National Assembly [128])[1].
Chief of state: President.
Head of government: Prime Minister.
Capital: Beirut.
Official language: Arabic.
Official religion: none.
Monetary unit: 1 Lebanese pound (£L) = 100 piastres; valuation (Oct. 11, 1996) 1 U.S.$ = £L 1,558; 1 £ = £L 2,454.

Area and population

Governorates	Capitals	area sq mi	area sq km	population 1970 estimate
Bayrūt	Beirut (Bayrūt)	7	18	474,870
Al-Biqā'	Zaḥlah	1,653	4,280	203,520
Jabal Lubnān	B'abdā	753	1,950	833,055
Al-Janūb	Sidon (Ṣaydā)	772	2,001	249,945
Ash-Shamāl	Tripoli (Ṭarābulus)	765	1,981	364,935
TOTAL		3,950	10,230	2,126,325

Demography

Population (1996): 3,800,000.
Density (1996): persons per sq mi 962.0, persons per sq km 371.5.
Urban-rural (1995): urban 87.2%; rural 12.8%.
Sex distribution (1994): male 50.32%; female 49.68%.
Age breakdown (1994): under 15, 33.2%; 15–29, 29.3%; 30–44, 18.6%; 45–59, 11.1%; 60–74, 6.3%; 75 and over, 1.5%.
Population projection: (2000) 4,115,000; (2010) 4,973,000.
Doubling time: during the 1970–75 prewar period the average growth rate was 2.6%; however, the dislocation of the population by the civil war between 1976 and 1991 rendered both the absolute size and principal components of population change (births, deaths, migration) highly problematic.
Ethnic composition (1993): Lebanese, *c.* 80%; Palestinian 12%; Armenian 5%; Syrian, Kurd, and other 3%.
Religious affiliation: no official data exist subsequent to the 1932 census, when Christians (predominantly Maronite Roman Catholic) were a slight majority; it is thought that Muslims today constitute the majority, but by what margin is highly uncertain. Unofficial and CIA estimates (1984/1986) indicated the main religious groups as follows: Shīʿī Muslim 32/41%; Maronite Christian 24.5/16%; Sunnī Muslim 21/27%; Druze 7/7%; Greek Orthodox 6.5/5%; Greek Catholic 4/3%; Armenian Christian 4%/n.a.; other 1/1%.
Major cities (1991): Beirut 1,100,000; Tripoli 240,000; Jūniyah 100,000; Zaḥlah 45,000[2]; Sidon (Ṣaydā) 38,000[2]; Tyre 14,000[2].

Vital statistics

Birth rate per 1,000 population (1994): 24.9 (world avg. 25.0).
Death rate per 1,000 population (1994): 4.4 (world avg. 9.3).
Natural increase rate per 1,000 population (1994): 20.5 (world avg. 15.7).
Total fertility rate (avg. births per childbearing woman; 1994): 2.9.
Life expectancy at birth (1994): male 72.5 years; female 77.9 years.
Major causes of death: normally, cardiovascular and gastrointestinal diseases, including typhoid fever and dysentery; but violence and acts of war were also among the principal causes of mortality between 1975 and 1991.

National economy

Budget (1994). Revenue: £L 2,195,795,000,000 (almost entirely taxation, direct and indirect). Expenditures: £L 4,206,705,000,000 (debt service 35%, government salaries 32%, defense 22%, education 10%).
Production (metric tons except as noted). Agriculture, forestry, fishing (1995): grapes 330,000, potatoes 325,000, tomatoes 236,000, oranges 180,000, cucumbers and gherkins 160,000, apples 135,000, lemons and limes 99,000, onions 71,000, olives 50,000; opium poppies and marijuana were important cash crops in the late 1980s and early '90s but were reportedly eradicated in 1993; livestock (number of live animals) 420,000 goats, 245,000 sheep, 79,000 cattle, 28,000,000 chickens; roundwood (1994) 393,150 cu m; fish catch (1993) 2,200. Mining and quarrying (1994): lime 15,000; salt 3,000; gypsum 2,000. Manufacturing (1993): cement 1,000,000; distillate fuel 85,000; gasoline 70,000; kerosene and jet fuel 5,000; dairying, curing of leather, meat cutting, and milling of flour are also significant. Construction (1996): 1,040,251 sq m[3]. Energy production (consumption): electricity (kW-hr; 1994) 5,150,000,000 (5,150,000,000); coal, n.a. (none); crude petroleum (barrels; 1993) none (2,602,000); petroleum products (metric tons; 1993) 323,000 ([1994] 3,493,000).
Public debt (external, outstanding; 1995): U.S.$3,200,000,000.
Household income and expenditure. Average household size (1987) 5.0; average annual income per household (1994) £L 2,400,000 (U.S.$1,430); sources of income (1974): wages 27.9%, transfers 3.0%, other 69.1%; expenditure (1966)[4]: food 42.8%, housing 16.8%, clothing 8.6%, health care 7.2%.
Land use (1994): forested 7.8%; meadows and pastures 1.0%; agricultural and under permanent cultivation 29.9%; wasteland and other areas 61.3%.
Population economically active (1994): total 938,000; activity rate of total population 32.2% (participation rates: over age 15 [1988] 44%; female [1993] 27.8%; unemployed [1993] reported by the national trade union at 35% but perhaps as low as 7–8% according to a 1987 study of 60,000 households).

Consumer price index (1990 = 100)

	1988	1989	1990	1991	1992	1993	1994
Consumer price index	22.7	57.9	100.0	151.5	333.3	430.3	475.6

Gross national product (1994): U.S.$15,800,000,000 (U.S.$4,360 per capita).

Structure of gross domestic product and labour force

	1994[5] in value[6] £L '000,000[7]	1994[5] % of total value	1986 labour force	1986 % of labour force
Agriculture	976,080	8.3	132,211	19.1
Mining	—	—	694	0.1
Manufacturing	1,461,600	12.4	123,647	17.8
Construction	613,200	5.2	43,357	6.2
Public utilities	640,080	5.4	6,668	1.0
Transp. and commun.	393,120	3.3	48,242	7.0
Trade	3,012,240	25.6	114,706	16.5
Finance	774,480	6.6	24,224	3.5
Real estate and business services	799,680	6.8	} 200,063	} 28.8
Services	907,200	7.7		
Pub. admin., defense	2,167,200	18.5		
TOTAL	11,744,880	100.0[8]	693,812	100.0

Tourism (1994): number of tourist arrivals 335,212.

Foreign trade[9]

Balance of trade (current prices)

	1990	1991	1992	1993	1994	1995
U.S.$'000,000	−2,073	−3,200	−3,633	−4,554	−5,364	−7,067
% of total	69.5%	74.5%	76.0%	77.0%	78.4%	76.1%

Imports (1995): U.S.$8,178,000,000 (1982; consumer goods 40.0%, machinery and transport equipment 35.0%, petroleum products 20.0%). *Major import sources:* Italy 12.0%; France 8.2%; U.S. 7.9%; Germany 6.9%.
Exports (1995): U.S.$1,111,000,000 (1993; food and beverages 21%, machinery and appliances 18%, textiles 17%, metal products 10%). *Major export destinations:* Saudi Arabia 7.7%; Switzerland 6.7%; U.A.E. 6.2%.

Transport and communications

Transport. Railroads (1995)[10]: length 222 km; passenger-km (1982) 8,570,000; metric ton-km cargo 42,010,000. Roads (1995): total length 6,359 km (paved 95%). Vehicles (1995): passenger cars 1,197,521; trucks and buses 84,736. Merchant marine (1992): vessels (100 gross tons and over) 163; total deadweight tonnage 438,165. Air transport (1995)[11]: passenger-km 1,720,063,000; metric ton-km cargo 43,009,000; airports (1996) with scheduled flights 1.
Communications. Daily newspapers (1992): total number 16; total circulation 500,000; circulation per 1,000 population 176. Radio (1995): 2,247,000 receivers (1 per 1.6 persons). Television (1995): 1,100,000 receivers (1 per 3.4 persons). Telephones (main lines; 1993): 350,000 (1 per 10.8 persons).

Education and health

Education (1993–94)

	schools	teachers	students	student/ teacher ratio
Primary (age 5–9)	2,100[12]	22,810[13]	360,858	...
Secondary (age 10–16)	1,405[13]	21,344[13]	234,341	...
Voc., teacher tr.	29	5,665	44,651	7.9
Higher	20	5,400[12]	74,810	...

Educational attainment (1970). Percentage of population age 25 and over having: no formal schooling 45.6%, of which, ability to read and write 35.6%; incomplete primary education 28.5%; complete primary 10.8%; incomplete secondary 7.1%; complete secondary 4.9%; higher 3.1%. *Literacy* (1995): total population age 15 and over literate 1,829,000 (92.4%); males literate 94.7%; females literate 90.3%.
Health (1994): physicians 5,300 (1 per 683 persons); hospital beds 11,000 (1 per 329 persons); infant mortality rate per 1,000 live births 28.0.
Food (1992): daily per capita caloric intake 3,317 (vegetable products 88%, animal products 12%); 134% of FAO recommended minimum requirement.

Military

Total active duty personnel (1996): Lebanese national armed forces 48,900 (army 97.1%, navy 1.2%, air force 1.7%). External regular military forces include: UN peacekeeping force in Lebanon 4,491; Syrian army 30,000. Most civilian militias were progressively disbanded after the civil war ended in 1991. However, only two factions were still active in 1996, though on a much-reduced scale[14]: Shīʿī Muslim (pro-Iran Hezbollah [Party of God]) 3,000; predominantly Maronite Christian and some Shīʿī and Druze (South Lebanese Army) 2,500. *Military expenditure as percentage of GDP* (1995): 3.2% (world 3.0%); per capita expenditure: U.S.$85.

[1]The current legislature was elected between August and October 1992; one-half of its membership is Christian and one-half Muslim/Druze. [2]1988 estimate. [3]Permits authorized in May 1996. [4]Weights based on consumer price index components. For capital city only. [5]UN estimates. [6]In purchasers' values at current prices. [7]Although the Lebanese pound continues to be the official currency, most financial transactions are done in U.S. dollars. Since the mid-1980s, foreign currency in circulation and foreign deposits in the domestic banking system were increasingly "dollarized." In the mid-1990s, about two-thirds of bank deposits in Lebanon were transacted in U.S. dollars. By 1993, however, the pound had once again stabilized against the dollar. [8]Detail does not add to total given because of rounding. [9]Imports are f.o.b. [10]Apart from a 14-mi (23-km) section delivering oil from the Zahrani refinery to a thermal power station serving Beirut, no passenger or general cargo track is currently in use. [11]MEA-Airliban international flights only. [12]1991–92. [13]1981–82. [14]Active personnel.

Lesotho

Official name: Lesotho (Sotho); Kingdom of Lesotho (English).
Form of government: multiparty republic[1] with 2 legislative houses (Senate [33[2]]; National Assembly [65]).
Chief of state: King.
Head of government: Prime Minister.
Capital: Maseru.
Official languages: Sotho; English.
Official religion: Christianity.
Monetary unit: 1 loti (plural maloti [M]) = 100 lisente; valuation (Oct. 11, 1996) 1 U.S.$ = M 4.54; 1 £ = M 7.16.

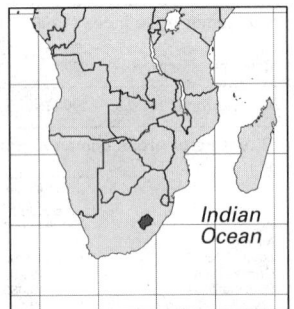

Area and population		area		population
		sq mi	sq km	1995 estimate[3]
Districts	Capitals			
Berea	Teyateyaneng	858	2,222	206,200
Butha-Buthe	Butha-Buthe	682	1,767	135,400
Leribe	Hlotse	1,092	2,828	349,500
Mafeteng	Mafeteng	818	2,119	259,000
Maseru	Maseru	1,652	4,279	400,200
Mohale's Hoek	Mohale's Hoek	1,363	3,530	231,300
Mokhotlong	Mokhotlong	1,573	4,075	100,300
Qacha's Nek	Qacha's Nek	907	2,349	86,800
Quthing	Quthing	1,126	2,916	151,900
Thaba-Tseka	Thaba-Tseka	1,649	4,270	136,200
TOTAL		11,720	30,355	2,056,800

Demography

Population (1996): 1,971,000[4].
Density (1996)[4]: persons per sq mi 168.2, persons per sq km 64.9.
Urban-rural (1992): urban 20.9%; rural 79.1%.
Sex distribution (1995): male 49.23%; female 50.77%.
Age breakdown (1995): under 15, 41.3%; 15–29, 27.0%; 30–44, 16.0%; 45–59, 9.1%; 60–74, 5.0%; 75 and over, 1.6%.
Population projection[4]: (2000) 2,114,000; (2010) 2,428,000.
Doubling time: 28 years.
Ethnic composition (1986): Sotho 85.0%; Zulu 15.0%.
Religious affiliation (1992): Christian 93.0%, of which Roman Catholic 42.8%, Protestant (mostly Lesotho Evangelical) 29.1%, other Christian 21.1%; other (mostly traditional beliefs) 7.0%.
Major urban centres (1986): Maseru 109,382; Maputsoe 20,000; Teyateyaneng 14,251; Mafeteng 12,667; Hlotse 9,595.

Vital statistics

Birth rate per 1,000 population (1990–95): 36.9 (world avg. 25.0); legitimate, n.a.; illegitimate, n.a.
Death rate per 1,000 population (1990–95): 10.0 (world avg. 9.3).
Natural increase rate per 1,000 population (1990–95): 26.9 (world avg. 15.7).
Total fertility rate (avg. births per childbearing woman; 1990–95): 5.2.
Marriage rate per 1,000 population: n.a.
Divorce rate per 1,000 population: n.a.
Life expectancy at birth (1990–95): male 58.0 years; female 63.0 years.
Major causes of death per 100,000 population: n.a.; however, major diseases include malaria, typhoid fever, and infectious and parasitic diseases.

National economy

Budget (1995–96). Revenue: M 1,790,300,000 (1993–94; tax revenue 78.8%, of which customs receipts 53.5%, sales tax 10.1%, income tax 7.3%, company tax 4.6%; grants and nontax revenue 21.2%). Expenditures: M 1,608,800,-000 (recurrent expenditure 67.5%, of which education 20.9%, public works [1994–95] 12.8%, health 6.7%, defense 6.4%; capital expenditure 32.5%).
Production (metric tons except as noted). Agriculture, forestry, fishing (1995): corn (maize) 63,445, roots and tubers 62,000, fruit 15,000, sorghum 6,458, pulses 5,575, beans 4,500, peas 1,075; livestock (number of live animals) 1,131,000 sheep, 749,000 goats, 580,000 cattle, 152,000 asses, 120,000 horses, 66,000 pigs, 1,500,000 chickens; roundwood (1994) 690,000 cu m; fish catch (1993) 35. Mining and quarrying (1988): sand and gravel 50,000 cu m. Manufacturing (total value added; 1992): M 246,200,000, of which textiles, apparel, and leather 49.9%, food and beverages 39.5%, nonmetal products 2.9%, chemical products 1.9%, printing and publishing 1.7%, furniture and fixtures 1.6%, iron and steel products 1.1%. Construction (permits issued in M '000,000; 1995): residential 13.23; nonresidential 265.61. Energy production (consumption): electricity (kW-hr; 1988) 1,000,000 (n.a.); coal, none (n.a.); petroleum, none (n.a.); natural gas, none (n.a.).
Public debt (external, outstanding; 1994): U.S.$516,000,000.
Tourism (1994): receipts from visitors U.S.$17,000,000; expenditures by nationals abroad U.S.$7,000,000.
Population economically active (1993): total 617,871; activity rate of total population 45.1% (participation rates: ages 15–64 [1986] 79.8%; female 23.7%; unemployed [1992] 35.0%).

Price and earnings indexes (1990 = 100)						
	1989	1990	1991	1992	1993	1994	1995
Consumer price index	89.6	100.0	117.7	137.9	156.0	168.9	184.5
Earnings index[5]	86.2	100.0	112.7	123.5	132.7	144.6	166.9

Household income and expenditure. Average household size (1986) 4.8; average annual income per household (1986–87) M 2,832 (U.S.$1,297); sources

of income (1986–87): transfer payments 44.7%, self-employment 27.8%, wages and salaries 22.4%, other 5.1%; expenditure (1989): food 48.0%, clothing 16.4%, household durable goods 11.9%, housing and energy 10.1%, transportation 4.7%.
Gross national product (at current market prices; 1994): U.S.$1,398,000,000 (U.S.$700 per capita).

Structure of gross domestic product and labour force				
	1994		1986	
	in value M '000,000	% of total value	labour force	% of labour force
Agriculture	335.1	11.3	474,171	66.2
Mining	2.7	0.1	6,446	0.9
Manufacturing	431.5	13.7	19,339	2.7
Construction	689.5	21.9	31,516	4.4
Public utilities	65.3	2.1	1,433	0.2
Transp. and commun.	88.5	2.8	5,014	0.7
Trade	269.9	8.6	22,204	3.1
Finance	361.9	11.5	3,581	0.5
Pub. admin., defense	359.5	11.4	17,907	2.5
Services	82.3	2.6	126,780	17.7
Other	439.2[6]	14.0[6]	7,879	1.1
TOTAL	3,145.4	100.0	716,270[7]	100.0[7]

Land use (1994): meadows and pastures 65.9%; agricultural and under permanent cultivation 10.5%; other 23.6%.

Foreign trade[8]

Balance of trade (current prices)						
	1990	1991	1992	1993	1994	1995
M '000,000	−1,523.0	−1,976.0	−2,374.7	−2,435.9	−2,384.0	−2,867.4
% of total	83.3%	84.2%	79.3%	73.8%	70.1%	71.2%

Imports (1995): M 2,880,930,000 (1990; manufactured goods [excluding chemicals, machinery, and transport equipment] 42.5%; food and live animals 19.1%; machinery and transport equipment 15.3%; petroleum products 8.6%). *Major import sources* (1994): Customs Union of Southern Africa 82.4%; Asia 12.6%; Europe 2.7%, of which European Economic Community 2.6%; the Americas 1.5%.
Exports (1995): M 395,110,000 (1994; manufactured goods 87.5%, of which clothing 54.8%, furniture 8.0%, footwear 6.9%, machinery and transport equipment 2.0%; crude materials 6.3%, of which wool 4.5%, mohair 1.7%; food and live animals 5.5%, of which cereals 1.5%, cattle 1.2%, vegetables 0.7%; chemicals 0.5%; diamonds 0.2%). *Major export destinations* (1994): Customs Union of Southern Africa 50.8%; the Americas 37.8%; Europe 10.5%, of which European Economic Community 10.1%; Asia 0.3%.

Transport and communications

Transport. Railroads (1996): length 1.6 mi, 2.6 km. Roads (1994): total length 3,308 mi, 5,324 km (paved 15%). Vehicles (1994): passenger cars 5,944; trucks and buses 17,785. Merchant marine: vessels (100 gross tons and over) none. Air transport (1995): passenger-mi 14,900,000, passenger-km 24,000,000; short ton-mi cargo 144,000, metric ton-km cargo 210,000; airports (1996) with scheduled flights 1.
Communications. Daily newspapers (1993): total number 6; total circulation 36,000; circulation per 1,000 population 19. Radio (1994): total number of receivers 118,000 (1 per 16.9 persons). Television (1994): total number of receivers 50,000 (1 per 40 persons). Telephones (main lines; 1993): 10,500 (1 per 190 persons).

Education and health

Education (1993–94)				
	schools	teachers	students	student/ teacher ratio
Primary (age 6–12)	1,209	7,292	354,275	48.6
Secondary (age 13–17)	187	2,526	55,312	21.9
Voc., teacher tr.	9	225	2,326	10.3
Higher	1	492	4,001	8.1

Educational attainment (1986–87). Percentage of population age 10 and over having: no formal education 22.9%; primary 52.8%; secondary 23.2%; higher 0.6%. *Literacy* (1995): total population age 15 and over literate 849,700 (71.3%); males literate 468,000 (81.1%); females literate 381,700 (62.3%).
Health (1993): physicians 136 (1 per 14,306 persons); hospital beds (1992) 2,400 (1 per 765 persons); infant mortality rate per 1,000 live births 71.5.
Food (1992): daily per capita caloric intake 2,201 (vegetable products 94%, animal products 6%); 97% of FAO recommended minimum requirement.

Military

Total active duty personnel (1996): 2,000[9]. *Military expenditure as percentage of GNP* (1994): 1.9% (world 3.0%); per capita expenditure U.S.$14.

[1]New constitution, effective April 1993, ended seven years of military rule. [2]Composed of 22 chiefs and 11 nominated members. [3]De jure population. [4]Excludes absentee miners working in South Africa. [5]Based on average annual wages, including overtime, of mine workers. [6]Indirect taxes less imputed bank service charges. [7]Approximately 117,600 persons (c. 40% of Lesotho's adult male labour force) were employed as mine workers in South Africa in 1993. [8]Import figures are f.o.b. in balance of trade and c.i.f. in commodities and trading partners. [9]Royal Lesotho Defence Force.

Liberia

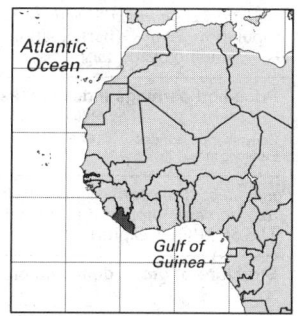

Official name: Republic of Liberia.
Form of government: transitional regime with one legislative body (Transitional Legislative Assembly [35][1]).
Head of state and government: President assisted by Council of State[1].
Capital: Monrovia.
Official language: English.
Official religion: none.
Monetary unit: 1 Liberian dollar (L$) = 100 cents; valuation (Oct. 11, 1996) 1 U.S.$ = L$1.00[2]; 1 £ = L$1.58.

Area and population		area		population
Counties	Capitals	sq mi	sq km	1986 estimate
Bomi	Tubmanburg	755	1,955	67,300
Bong	Gbarnga	3,127	8,099	268,100
Grand Bassa	Buchanan	3,382	8,759	166,900
Grand Cape Mount	Robertsport	2,250	5,827	83,900
Grand Gedeh	Zwedru	6,575	17,029	109,000
Grand Kru	Barclayville	3	3	3
Lofa	Voinjama	7,475	19,360	261,000
Margibi	Kakata	1,260	3,263	104,000
Maryland	Harper	2,066[3]	5,351[3]	137,700[3]
Montserrado	Bensonville	1,058	2,740	582,400
Nimba	Sanniquellie	4,650	12,043	325,700
Rivercess	Rivercess City	1,693	4,385	39,900
Sinoe	Greenville	3,959	10,254	65,400
TOTAL		38,250	99,067[4]	2,221,300[5]

Demography

Population (1996): 2,110,000[6].
Density (1995): persons per sq mi 55.2[6], persons per sq km 21.3[6].
Urban-rural (1995): urban 44.9%; rural 55.1%.
Sex distribution (1995): male 50.69%; female 49.31%.
Age breakdown (1995): under 15, 44.5%; 15–29, 25.6%; 30–44, 15.6%; 45–59, 9.0%; 60–74, 3.9%; 75 and over, 1.4%.
Population projection: (2000) 3,048,000; (2010) 4,540,000.
Doubling time: 23 years.
Ethnic composition (1984): Kpelle 19.4%; Bassa 13.8%; Grebo 9.0%; Gio 7.8%; Kru 7.3%; Mano 7.1%; other 35.6%.
Religious affiliation (1984): Christian 67.7%; Muslim 13.8%[7]; traditional beliefs and other 18.5%.
Major cities (1985): Monrovia 668,000[8]; Harbel 60,000; Gbarnga 30,000[9]; Buchanan 25,000; Yekepa 16,000.

Vital statistics

Birth rate per 1,000 population (1995): 43.0 (world avg. 25.0).
Death rate per 1,000 population (1995): 12.0 (world avg. 9.3).
Natural increase rate per 1,000 population (1994): 31.0 (world avg. 15.7).
Total fertility rate (avg. births per childbearing woman; 1995): 6.3.
Marriage rate per 1,000 population: n.a.
Divorce rate per 1,000 population: n.a.
Life expectancy at birth (1996): male 55.0 years; female 60.0 years.
Major causes of death per 100,000 population (1985)[10]: complications during pregnancy 632.6[11]; malaria 79.8; pneumonia 64.2; anemia 50.2; malnutrition 23.4; measles 12.7. Violence and acts of war were major causes of both morbidity and mortality from 1990 onward.

National economy

Budget (1993). Revenue: L$249,825,000 (1989; income and profits taxes 33.9%; import duties and consular fees 29.6%; excise tax 12.7%; property taxes 1.9%). Expenditures: L$273,930,000 (1988; current expenditure 91.1%, of which wages and salaries 34.1%, interest on public debt 13.1%, goods and services 7.8%, subsidies and grants 5.1%; development expenditure 8.9%).
Tourism: receipts from visitors (1986) U.S.$6,000,000; expenditures by nationals abroad, n.a.
Population economically active (1994): total 993,000; activity rate 43.5% (participation rates: ages 10–64, 64.0%; female 28.5%; unemployed 12.5%[11]).

Price and earnings indexes (1990 = 100)						
	1989	1990	1991	1992	1993	1994	1995
Consumer price index	79.8	100.0	110.0	121.0	133.1	146.4	161.0
Earnings index	...	...	...	...	...	...	...

Production (metric tons except as noted). Agriculture, forestry, fishing (1995): cassava 450,000, sugarcane 234,000, bananas 82,000, rice 56,000, plantains 45,000, natural rubber 31,000, yams 30,000, sweet potatoes 23,000, oranges 7,000, pineapples 7,000, peanuts (groundnuts) 3,800, pulses 3,000 (of which soybeans 2,000), cacao beans 365; livestock (number of live animals) 220,000 goats, 210,000 sheep, 120,000 pigs, 36,000 cattle, 3,500,000 chickens; roundwood (1994) 3,681,000 cu m; fish catch (1993) 7,782. Mining and quarrying (1993): iron ore[12]; diamonds 150,000 carats; gold 22,500 troy oz. Manufacturing (1992): palm oil 31,000; cement 8,300[13]; cigarettes 22,000,000 units; soft drinks 171,000 hectolitres[14]; beer 158,000 hectolitres[14]. Construction: n.a. Energy production (consumption): electricity (kW-hr; 1994) 485,000,000 (485,000,000); coal, none (n.a.); crude petroleum, none (n.a.); petroleum products (metric tons; 1994) none (101,000); natural gas, none (n.a.).

Public debt (external, outstanding; 1994): U.S.$1,137,000,000.
Household income and expenditure. Average household size (1983) 4.3; income per household: n.a.; sources of income: n.a.; expenditure: n.a.
Gross national product (1992): U.S.$973,000,000 (U.S.$354 per capita).

Structure of gross domestic product and labour force				
	1989		1994	
	in value L$'000,000	% of total value	labour force	% of labour force
Agriculture	410.7	34.4	676,000	68.1
Mining	122.3	10.2		
Manufacturing	81.6	6.8		
Construction	26.3	2.2		
Public utilities	19.0	1.6		
Transp. and commun.	79.1	6.6	77,000	7.7
Trade	63.3	5.3		
Finance	141.8	11.9		
Pub. admin., defense	139.4	11.7		
Services	35.5	3.0	240,000	24.2
Other	74.8[15]	6.3[15]		
TOTAL	1,193.6[4]	100.0	993,000	100.0

Land use (1993): forested 17.6%; meadows and pastures 58.9%; agricultural and under permanent cultivation 3.9%; other 19.6%.

Foreign trade

Balance of trade (current prices)						
	1990	1991	1992	1993	1994	1995
U.S.$'000,000	−2,316	−4,560	−4,985	−4,620	−5,471	−5,204
% of total	37.3%	82.5%	76.3%	79.8%	83.3%	79.6%

Imports (1995): U.S.$5,871,000,000 (1990; machinery and transport equipment 26.9%, petroleum and petroleum products 23.5%, food and live animals 21.1%, basic manufactures 13.9%, chemicals 5.8%). *Major import sources* (1995): Japan 32.7%; South Korea 20.4%; Italy 9.4%; Germany 8.3%; France 6.9%; Denmark 6.6%.
Exports (1995): U.S.$667,000,000 (1988; iron ore 55.1%, rubber 28.0%, logs and timber 8.4%, diamonds 2.1%, gold 1.8%, coffee 1.5%). *Major export destinations* (1995): Belgium-Luxembourg 55.6%; Ukraine 12.1%; Greece 6.4%; Singapore 5.7%; Denmark 4.5%; France 4.0%.

Transport and communications

Transport. Railroads (1993)[12, 16]: route length 306 mi, 493 km; short ton-mi cargo 137,000,000, metric ton-km cargo 200,000,000. Roads (1993): total length 2,703 mi, 4,350 km (paved 6.6%). Vehicles (1994): passenger cars 7,500; trucks and buses 3,000. Merchant marine (1992): vessels (100 gross tons and over) 1,672; total deadweight tonnage 97,373,965. Air transport (1992): passenger-mi 4,300,000, passenger-km 7,000,000; short ton-mi cargo 68,000, metric ton-km cargo 100,000; airports (1996) with scheduled flights 1.
Communications. Daily newspapers (1992): total number 8; total circulation 35,000; circulation per 1,000 population 14.8. Radio (1995): 600,000 receivers (1 per 3.6 persons). Television (1995): 45,000 receivers (1 per 48 persons). Telephones (main lines; 1993): 4,500 (1 per 528 persons).

Education and health

Education (1980)				
	schools	teachers	students	student/ teacher ratio
Primary (age 6–12)	1,651	9,099	167,000[13]	...
Secondary (age 13–18)	419	1,129	51,666	45.8
Voc., teacher tr.	6	63	2,322	36.9
Higher	3	472[17]	5,716[13]	...

Educational attainment (1974). Percentage of population age 25 and over having: no grade completed 87.1%; some primary education 4.8%; complete primary 1.5%; some secondary 5.1%; higher 1.5%. *Literacy* (1995): total population age 15 and over literate 705,000 (38.3%); males literate 523,000 (53.9%); females literate 182,000 (22.4%).
Health: physicians (1985) 227 (1 per 9,687 persons); hospital beds (1981) 3,000 (1 per 653 persons); infant mortality rate (1996) 113.0.
Food (1992): daily per capita caloric intake 1,640 (vegetable products 96%, animal products 4%); 71% of FAO recommended minimum requirement.

Military

Total active duty personnel (1996): The Armed Forces of Liberia (AFL), with a force of about 3,000, is confined to the capital city of Monrovia. A four-nation West African peacekeeping force of about 8,600 separates it and five guerrilla groups from each other. *Military expenditure as percentage of GNP* (1994): 2.0% (world 3.0%); per capita expenditure U.S.$10.

[1]Five years of multifactional warfare officially ended with the swearing in of the transitional government on Sept. 2, 1995. [2]Officially at par with the U.S.$; the unofficial parallel exchange rate (a truer value of the L$) was roughly L$59 = U.S.$1. [3]Figures for Grand Kru included in Maryland. [4]Detail does not add to total given because of rounding. [5]Includes 10,000 persons not allocated by county. [6]Excludes about 750,000 Liberian refugees in surrounding countries. [7]Some external sources estimate the Muslim population to exceed 30%. [8]1990 estimate; the 1996 population is estimated to be more than 1,000,000 (including many persons displaced because of war). [9]1986. [10]Hospital inpatient morbidity rates. [11]1984. [12]Mining ceased in late 1992. [13]1993. [14]1988. [15]Import duties less imputed bank service charges. [16]For iron-ore transport only. [17]1987.

Libya

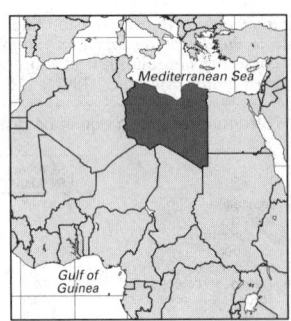

Official name: Al-Jamāhīrīyah al-'Arabīyah al-Lībīyah ash-Sha'bīyah al-Ishtirākīyah (Socialist People's Libyan Arab Jamahiriya).
Form of government: socialist state with one policy-making body (General People's Congress [750]).
Chief of state: Muammar al-Qaddafi (de facto)[1]; Secretary of General People's Congress (de jure).
Head of government: Secretary of the General People's Committee (prime minister).
Capital: Tripoli[2].
Official language: Arabic.
Official religion: Islam.
Monetary unit: 1 Libyan dinar (LD) = 1,000 dirhams; valuation[3] (Oct. 11, 1996) 1 Libyan dinar = U.S.$2.78 = £1.79.

Area and population

Baladīyāt	Capitals	area sq mi	area sq km	population 1988 estimate
Banghāzī	Banghāzī	5,800	15,000	512,200
Al-Jabal al-Akhḍar	Al-Bayḍā'	14,300	37,000	308,300
Al-Jabal al-Gharbī	Gharyān	33,600	87,000	204,300
Khalīj Surt	Surt	145,200	376,000	382,100
Al-Kufrah	Al-Kufrah	186,900	484,000	23,800
Margib	Al-Khums	11,200	29,000	408,900
Marzūq	Marzūq	135,100	350,000	45,200
Nikāt al-Khums	Zuwārah	39,000	101,000	196,000
Sabhā	Sabhā	31,700	82,000	121,700
Ṭarābulus	Tripoli (Ṭarābulus)	1,200	3,000	1,083,100
Ṭubruq	Ṭubruq	32,400	84,000	110,900
Wādī al-Ḥaiṭ	Awbārī	40,500	105,000	49,600
Az-Zāwiyah	Az-Zāwiyah	1,500	4,000	326,500
TOTAL		**678,400**	**1,757,000**	**3,772,600**

Demography

Population (1996): 5,445,000.
Density (1996): persons per sq mi 8.0, persons per sq km 3.1.
Urban-rural (1995): urban 86.0%; rural 14.0%.
Sex distribution (1995): male 52.10%; female 47.90%.
Age breakdown (1995): under 15, 45.4%; 15–29, 26.4%; 30–44, 14.7%; 45–59, 9.1%; 60–74, 3.7%; 75 and over, 0.6%.
Population projection: (2000) 6,293,749; (2010) 8,912,940.
Doubling time: 21 years.
Ethnic composition (1995): Libyan Arab and Berber 79%; other 21% (mostly Egyptians, Sudanese, and Chadians).
Religious affiliation (1992): Sunnī Muslim 97.0%; other 3.0%.
Major cities (1988): Tripoli 591,100; Banghāzī 446,250; Miṣrātah 121,700; Az-Zāwiyah 89,338.

Vital statistics

Birth rate per 1,000 population (1995): 44.9 (world avg. 25.0).
Death rate per 1,000 population (1995): 7.9 (world avg. 9.3).
Natural increase rate per 1,000 population (1995): 37.0 (world avg. 15.7).
Total fertility rate (avg. births per childbearing woman; 1995): 6.3.
Marriage rate per 1,000 population (1988): 4.5[4].
Divorce rate per 1,000 population (1988): 0.6[4].
Life expectancy at birth (1995): male 62.1 years; female 66.6 years.
Major causes of death per 100,000 population: n.a.; however, the major causes of death in the early 1990s were pneumonia, dysentery and diarrhea, cardiovascular disease, accidents, and malignant neoplasms (cancers).

National economy

Budget (1991–92). Revenue: LD 2,655,000,000 (1990–91; current revenue 55.7%, of which oil revenues 17.7%, income taxes 13.7%, customs duties 9.7%, stamp duties 2.4%; capital revenue 44.3%). Expenditures: LD 2,846,-000,000 (1990–91; current expenditures 55.7%, of which allocations to municipal people's committees 39.4%, education and scientific research 4.3%, health 2.7%; capital expenditures 44.3%, of which agriculture and land reclamation 13.6%, industry 5.3%).
Production (metric tons except as noted). Agriculture, forestry, fishing (1995): watermelons 180,000, wheat 167,000, barley 148,000, tomatoes 135,000, potatoes 127,000, oranges 80,000, onions 75,000, dates 68,000, olives 62,000, almonds 30,000, lemons and limes 3,000; livestock (number of live animals) 4,400,000 sheep, 800,000 goats, 130,000 camels, 100,000 cattle, 16,500,000 chickens; roundwood (1994) 650,000 cu m; fish catch (1993) 8,800. Mining and quarrying (1994): lime 260,000; gypsum 180,000; salt 12,000. Manufacturing (1993): distillate fuel 4,470,000; cement 2,300,000; gasoline 1,995,000; jet fuel 1,664,000; crude steel 920,000; meat 95,000. Construction (gross value in LD; 1982): residential 127,051,000; nonresidential 200,877,000. Energy production (consumption): electricity (kW-hr; 1994) 17,800,000,000 (17,800,-000,000); coal (metric tons; 1994) none (5,000); crude petroleum (barrels; 1994) 502,408,000 (112,725,000); petroleum products (metric tons; 1994) 13,-260,000 (7,480,000); natural gas (cu m; 1994) 6,390,000,000 (4,910,000,000).
Tourism: receipts from visitors (1994) U.S.$7,000,000; expenditures by nationals abroad (1993) U.S.$166,000,000.

Population economically active (1993): total 1,192,000; activity rate of total population 23.6% (participation rates: ages 10 and over, 35.2%; female 9.8%; unemployed, n.a.).

Price and earnings indexes (1990 = 100)

	1988	1989	1990	1991	1992	1993	1994
Consumer price index	67.5	88.5	100.0	111.7	128.5	154.1	200.4
Earnings index	...	...	...	...	...	...	...

Public debt (long-term debt; 1992): U.S.$2,592,000,000.
Gross domestic product (at current market prices; 1994): U.S.$32,900,000,000 (U.S.$6,510 per capita).

Structure of gross domestic product and labour force

	1992 in value[5] LD '000,000	1992 % of total value	1993 labour force	1993 % of labour force
Agriculture	638	7.5	119,000	10.0
Mining and quarrying	2,173	25.4		
Manufacturing	720	8.4	381,000	32.0
Construction	1,070	12.5		
Public utilities	193	2.3		
Transportation and communications	539	6.3		
Trade	770	9.0		
Finance, insurance	986	11.5	692,000	58.0
Pub. admin., defense	885	10.4		
Services	574	6.7		
TOTAL	**8,548**	**100.0**	**1,192,000**	**100.0**

Household income and expenditure. Average household size (1980) 5.1; income per household: n.a.; sources of income: n.a.; expenditure (1977): food 37.2%, housing and energy 32.2%, transportation 9.4%, education and recreation 8.5%, clothing 6.9%, health care 3.3%.
Land use (1994): forested 0.5%; meadows and pastures 7.6%; agricultural and under permanent cultivation 1.2%; desert and built-up areas 90.7%.

Foreign trade[6, 7]

Balance of trade (current prices)

	1990	1991	1992	1993	1994	1995
U.S.$'000,000	+8,215	+5,873	+4,768	+2,293	+3,440	+3,838
% of total	42.0%	35.5%	31.6%	17.5%	28.2%	28.3%

Imports (1995): U.S.$4,870,000,000 (1991; manufactured goods 78.3%, agricultural goods 20.3%). *Major import sources:* Italy 21.6%; Germany 13.7%; United Kingdom 8.1%; France 6.5%; Turkey 5.4%.
Exports (1995): U.S.$8,708,000,000 (1991; crude petroleum 99.8%). *Major export destinations:* Italy 39.0%; Germany 15.8%; Spain 12.4%; Turkey 3.7%; France 3.3%; Switzerland 3.1%; United Kingdom 2.2%.

Transport and communications

Transport. Railroads: none. Roads (1995): total length 50,704 mi, 81,600 km (paved 56%). Vehicles (1995): passenger cars 904,000; trucks and buses 322,000. Merchant marine (1992): vessels (100 gross tons and over) 150; total deadweight tonnage 1,223,589. Air transport (1995)[8]: passenger-mi 247,594,000, passenger-km 398,464,000; short ton-mi cargo 259,000, metric ton-km cargo 378,000; airports (1996) with scheduled flights 12.
Communications. Daily newspapers (1992): total number 4; circulation 71,-000; circulation per 1,000 population 14.6. Radio (1995): total number of receivers 1,000,000 (1 per 5.2 persons). Television (1995): total number of receivers 550,000 (1 per 9.5 persons). Telephones (main lines; 1993): 240,000 (1 per 21.0 persons).

Education and health

Education (1991–92)

	schools	teachers	students	student/ teacher ratio
Primary (age 6–12)	2,744[9]	99,623	1,238,986	12.4
Secondary (age 13–18)	1,555[9]	11,429	138,860	12.1
Voc., teacher tr.	195[9]	7,072	76,648	10.8
Higher	10[10]	...	72,899	...

Educational attainment (1984). Percentage of population age 25 and over having: no formal schooling (illiterate) 59.7%; incomplete primary education 15.4%; complete primary 8.5%; some secondary 5.2%; secondary 8.5%; higher 2.7%. *Literacy* (1995): percentage of total population age 15 and over literate 76.2%; males literate 87.9%; females literate 63.0%.
Health: physicians (1989–91) 4,749 (1 per 948 persons); hospital beds (1990) 18,503[11] (1 per 246 persons); infant mortality rate per 1,000 live births (1995) 61.4.
Food (1992): daily per capita caloric intake 3,308 (vegetable products 88%, animal products 12%); 140% of FAO recommended minimum requirement.

Military

Total active duty personnel (1996): 65,000 (army 53.9%, navy 12.3%, air force 33.8%). *Military expenditure as percentage of GNP* (1994): 4.3% (world 3.0%); per capita expenditure U.S.$277.

---

[1]No formal titled office exists. [2]Policy-making body (General People's Congress) meets in Surt. [3]Official exchange rate. [4]Registered events; incomplete to some degree. [5]At factor cost. [6]Dollar values based on IMF Direction of Trade Statistics (DOTS), which are compiled from available reports of trading partners (not the subject country's reports) and may, thus, be substantially incomplete. [7]Import figures are f.o.b. [8]Jamahiriya Libyan Arab Airlines. [9]1982–83. [10]1988–89. [11]Includes beds in clinics.

Liechtenstein

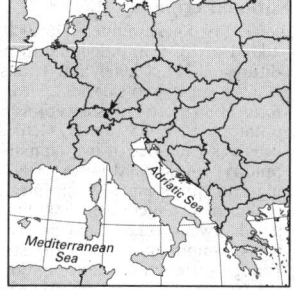

Official name: Fürstentum
Liechtenstein (Principality
of Liechtenstein).
Form of government: constitutional
monarchy with one legislative house
(Diet [25]).
Chief of state: Prince.
Head of government: Head of the
Government.
Capital: Vaduz.
Official language: German.
Official religion: none.
Monetary unit: 1 Swiss franc
(Sw F) = 100 centimes; valuation
(Oct. 11, 1996) 1 U.S.$ = Sw F 1.26;
1 £ = Sw F 1.98.

Area and population

Regions Communes	area		population 1996[1] estimate
	sq mi	sq km	
Oberland	48.3	125.2	20,817
Balzers	7.6	19.6	3,954
Planken	2.0	5.3	326
Schaan	10.3	26.8	5,106
Triesen	10.2	26.4	3,885
Triesenberg	11.5	29.8	2,461
Vaduz	6.7	17.3	5,085
Unterland	13.4[2]	34.8	10,106
Eschen	4.0	10.3	3,428
Gamprin	2.4	6.1	1,129
Mauren	2.9	7.5	3,049
Ruggell	2.9	7.4	1,621
Schellenberg	1.4	3.5	879
TOTAL	61.8[2]	160.0	30,923

Demography

Population (1996): 31,400.
Density (1996): persons per sq mi 506.5, persons per sq km 196.3.
Urban-rural: n.a.
Sex distribution (1996): male 48.83%; female 51.17%.
Age breakdown (1996): under 15, 19.0%; 15–29, 22.7%; 30–44, 25.5%; 45–59, 18.8%; 60–74, 9.7%; 75 and over, 4.2%.
Population projection: (2000) 33,300; (2010) 38,500.
Doubling time: n.a.; doubling time exceeds 100 years.
Linguistic composition (1990): German 90.0%; Italian 2.5%; other 7.5%.
Religious affiliation (1996): Roman Catholic 80.0%; Protestant 6.9%; other 5.6%; none, or not stated 7.5%.
Major cities (1996): Schaan 5,106; Vaduz 5,085.

Vital statistics

Birth rate per 1,000 population (1995): 13.9 (world avg. 25.0); legitimate 92.3%; illegitimate 7.7%.
Death rate per 1,000 population (1995): 7.3 (world avg. 9.3).
Natural increase rate per 1,000 population (1995): 6.6 (world avg. 15.7).
Total fertility rate (avg. births per childbearing woman; 1994): 1.5.
Marriage rate per 1,000 population (1995): 13.4.
Divorce rate per 1,000 population (1995): 1.7.
Life expectancy at birth (1995): male 66.5 years; female 77.5 years.
Major causes of death per 100,000 population (1995): diseases of the circulatory system 313.4; malignant neoplasms (cancers) 199.2; accidents, poisoning, and acts of violence 52.2; diseases of the respiratory system 39.2.

National economy

Budget (1994). Revenue: Sw F 546,100,000 (taxes and interest 66.5%, customs duties and repayments 20.4%, investment income 4.5%; other revenue sources include real estate capital-gains taxes and death and estate taxes). Expenditures: Sw F 516,900,000 (financial affairs 37.1%, education 15.3%, social affairs 14.5%, transportation 11.7%, general administration 8.1%).
Public debt: none.
Tourism (1995): 127,510 tourist overnight stays; receipts from visitors, n.a.; expenditures by nationals abroad, n.a.
Population economically active (1995[3]): total 15,431; activity rate of total population 49.9% (participation rates (1994): ages 15–64, 65.7%; female 38.1%; unemployed 2.3%).

Price and earnings indexes (1990 = 100)

	1989	1990	1991	1992	1993	1994	1995
Consumer price index[4]	94.9	100.0	105.8	110.2	113.7	114.7	117.0
Earnings index	...	...	...	...	...	...	...

Household income and expenditure. Average household size (1990) 2.7; income per household: n.a.; sources of earned income (1987): wages and salaries 92.9%, self-employment 7.1%; expenditure (1990)[5]: rent 20.9%, food 17.7%, transportation 11.0%, education and self-improvement 9.7%, clothing 7.0%, health 4.7%.
Production (metric tons except as noted). Agriculture, forestry, fishing (1995): silo corn (maize) 27,880[6], milk 12,590, potatoes 1,040[6], wheat 460[6], barley 416[6]; livestock (number of live animals) 5,862 cattle, 2,632 sheep, 2,429 pigs; commercial timber (1994) 26,315 cu m; fish catch, n.a. Mining and quarrying: n.a. Manufacturing (1994): processed milk 3,503; milk for whipped

cream 1,017; yogurt 60; cheese 1; wine (1993) 635.2 hectolitres; small-scale precision manufacturing includes optical lenses, electron microscopes, electronic equipment, and high-vacuum pumps; metal manufacturing, construction machinery, and ceramics are also important. Construction (1994): residential 276,336 cu m; nonresidential 341,087 cu m. Energy production (consumption): electricity (kW-hr; 1995) 81,077,000 (251,909,000); coal (metric tons; 1994) none (27); petroleum products (metric tons; 1994) none (53,019); natural gas (cu m; 1994) none (19,350,000).
Gross national product (at current market prices; 1991): c. U.S.$978,000,000 (U.S.$33,510 per capita).

Structure of gross domestic product and labour force

	1988		1995	
	in value Sw F '000	% of total value	labour force	% of labour force
Agriculture	...	...	326	2.1
Manufacturing	...	...	4,990	32.3
Construction	...	...	1,149	7.4
Public utilities	...	...	158	1.0
Transportation and communications	...	...	491	3.2
Trade, public accommodation	...	...	1,938	12.6
Finance, insurance, real estate	...	...	1,149	7.4
Pub. admin., defense	...	...	967	6.3
Services	...	...	4,263	27.6
TOTAL	1,700,000	100.0	15,431	100.0[2]

Land use (latest): forested 34.8%; meadows and pastures 15.7%; agricultural and under permanent cultivation 24.3%; other 25.2%.

Foreign trade

Balance of trade (current prices)

	1989	1990	1991	1992	1993	1994
Sw F '000,000	+742.8	+757.1	+822.8	+947.1	+1,024.2	+1,043.3
% of total	29.8%	27.8%	31.4%	30.6%	33.8%	33.1%

Imports (1994): Sw F 1,053,520 (machinery and transport equipment 31.0%; other finished goods 27.3%; limestone, cement, and other building materials 12.4%; metal products 11.9%; chemical products 6.0%; unrefined and semifabricated metal 5.9%). *Major import sources:* n.a.
Exports (1994): Sw F 2,096,807 (machinery and transport equipment 47.2%; metal products 16.3%; other finished goods 12.6%; chemical products 9.4%; limestone, cement, and other building materials 9.3%). *Major export destinations:* European Economic Community countries 39.6%; Switzerland 14.0%; other European Free Trade Association countries 6.0%; other 40.4%.

Transport and communications

Transport. Railroads (1993): length 11.5 mi, 18.5 km; passenger and cargo traffic, n.a. Roads (1995): total length 201 mi, 323 km. Vehicles (1995): passenger cars 18,820; trucks and buses 2,467. Merchant marine: none. Air transport: none.
Communications. Daily newspapers (1992): total number 2; total circulation 17,739; circulation per 1,000 population 611. Radio (1993): total number of receivers 20,000 (1 per 1.5 persons). Television (1994): total number of receivers 10,918 (1 per 2.8 persons). Telephones (main lines; 1994): 18,554 (1 per 1.7 persons).

Education and health

Education (1994–95)

	schools	teachers[7]	students	student/ teacher ratio
Primary (age 7–12)	14[8]	141	1,914	13.6
Secondary (age 13–19)	8[8]	159	1,858	11.7
Vocational	2	247	2,515	10.2

Educational attainment (1980). Percentage of population age 25 and over having: no formal schooling 0.2%; primary and lower secondary education 47.6%; higher secondary and vocational 41.0%; some postsecondary 6.6%; university 4.6%. *Literacy:* virtually 100%.
Health: physicians (1994) 32 (1 per 957 persons); hospital beds[9] (1985) 100 (1 per 269 persons); infant mortality rate per 1,000 live births (1995) nil (no deaths).
Food (1992)[10]: daily per capita caloric intake 3,440 (vegetable products 64%, animal products 36%); 129% of FAO recommended minimum requirement.

Military

Total active duty personnel: none. *Military expenditure as percentage of GNP:* none.

---

[1]January 1. [2]Detail does not add to total given because of rounding. [3]December 31. [4]The index is for Switzerland, which is united with Liechtenstein in a customs and monetary union. [5]Household expenditures are taken from a 1986 Swiss sample survey; a similarity of consumption patterns is assumed. [6]1987. [7]Full-time teachers only. [8]1993–94. [9]Liechtenstein has one hospital. Agreements with the Swiss cantons of St. Gallen and Graubünden and the Austrian Federal State of Vorarlberg allow use of certain hospitals. [10]Figures are derived from statistics for Switzerland and Austria.

Lithuania

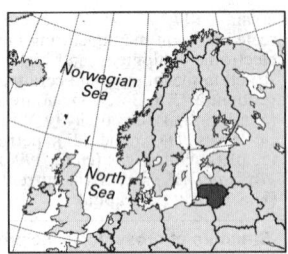

Official name: Lietuvos Respublika (Republic of Lithuania).
Form of government: unitary multiparty republic with a single legislative body, the Seimas (141).
Head of state: President.
Head of government: Prime Minister.
Capital: Vilnius.
Official language: Lithuanian.
Official religion: none.
Monetary unit: 1 litas (plural litai) = 100 centai; valuation (Oct. 11, 1996) 1 U.S.$ = 4.00 litai; 1 £ = 6.30 litai.

Area and population

Cities of republic jurisdiction	Capitals	area sq mi	area sq km	population 1989 estimate
Alytus	—	1	3	73,100
Birštonas	—	5	12	4,100
Druskininkai	—	8	22	22,500
Kaunas	—	46	120	422,600
Klaipėda	—	27	71	204,000
Marijampolė	—	8	20	50,500
Neringa	—	35	90	2,500
Palanga	—	27	69	19,400
Panevėžys	—	12	30	126,500
Šiauliai	—	27	69	145,000
Vilnius	—	110	286	582,400
Regions				
Akmenė	Naujoji Akmenė	407	1,055	37,800
Alytus	Alytus	545	1,411	32,700
Anykščiai	Anykščiai	681	1,765	38,300
Biržai	Biržai	570	1,476	38,600
Ignalina	Ignalina	581	1,505	59,000
Jonava	Jonava	364	944	54,000
Joniškis	Joniškis	445	1,152	32,900
Jurbarkas	Jurbarkas	582	1,507	40,200
Kaišiadorys	Kaišiadorys	451	1,169	40,200
Kaunas	Kaunas	588	1,522	85,500
Kėdainiai	Kėdainiai	647	1,677	69,400
Kelmė	Kelmė	660	1,710	42,900
Klaipėda	Gargždai	527	1,366	45,000
Kretinga	Kretinga	385	997	44,100
Kupiškis	Kupiškis	417	1,080	25,900
Lazdijai	Lazdijai	595	1,542	33,400
Marijampolė	Marijampolė	599	1,551	49,200
Mažeikiai	Mažeikiai	390	1,009	61,200
Molėtai	Molėtai	528	1,368	27,300
Pakruojis	Pakruojis	508	1,316	30,700
Panevėžys	Panevėžys	849	2,199	41,900
Pasvalys	Pasvalys	498	1,289	36,800
Plungė	Plungė	653	1,691	53,900
Prienai	Prienai	443	1,148	39,500
Radviliškis	Radviliškis	631	1,635	54,800
Raseiniai	Raseiniai	607	1,573	46,100
Rokiškis	Rokiškis	697	1,806	47,800
Šakiai	Šakiai	623	1,613	41,600
Šalčininkai	Šalčininkai	578	1,498	41,500
Šiauliai	Šiauliai	701	1,815	49,900
Šilalė	Šilalė	459	1,188	31,700
Šilutė	Šilutė	866	2,243	69,000
Širvintos	Širvintos	350	906	21,500
Škuodas	Škuodas	352	911	26,600
Švenčionys	Švenčionys	653	1,692	37,800
Tauragė	Tauragė	455	1,179	52,600
Telšiai	Telšiai	556	1,439	59,200
Trakai	Trakai	640	1,657	81,700
Ukmergė	Ukmergė	539	1,395	52,500
Utena	Utena	475	1,229	52,300
Varėna	Varėna	933	2,416	38,500
Vilkaviškis	Vilkaviškis	497	1,286	52,200
Vilnius	Vilnius	855	2,215	93,800
Zarasai	Zarasai	515	1,334	25,900
TOTAL		25,213[1]	65,301[1]	3,690,000

Demography

Population (1996): 3,707,000.
Density (1996): persons per sq mi 147.0, persons per sq km 56.8.
Urban-rural (1994): urban 68.3%; rural 31.7%.
Sex distribution (1994): male 47.29%; female 52.71%.
Age breakdown (1994): under 15, 22.2%; 15–29, 22.4%; 30–44, 21.7%; 45–59, 16.9%; 60–74, 12.3%; 75 and over, 4.5%.
Population projection: (2000) 3,681,000; (2010) 3,702,000.
Doubling time: not applicable.
Ethnic composition (1995): Lithuanian 81.3%; Russian 8.4%; Polish 7.0%; Belorussian 1.5%; Ukrainian 1.0%; other 0.8%.
Religious affiliation (1990): Roman Catholic, about 80%; Russian Orthodox, Old Believer, Evangelical Lutheran, and nonreligious minorities.
Major cities (1995): Vilnius 575,700; Kaunas 415,300; Klaipėda 202,800.

Vital statistics

Birth rate per 1,000 population (1995): 11.1 (world avg. 25.0).
Death rate per 1,000 population (1995): 12.2 (world avg. 9.3).
Natural increase rate per 1,000 population (1995): −1.1 (world avg. 15.7).
Total fertility rate (avg. births per childbearing woman; 1989): 2.0.
Marriage rate per 1,000 population (1994): 6.3.
Divorce rate per 1,000 population (1993): 3.7.
Life expectancy at birth (1993): male 63.3 years; female 75.0 years.
Major causes of death per 100,000 population (1993): circulatory diseases 674; malignant neoplasms (cancers) 201; accidents 168; respiratory diseases 48.

National economy

Budget (1995). Revenue: 7,760,000,000 litai (social security tax 26.2%, value-added tax 25.5%, individual income tax 21.8%, excise taxes 7.9%). Expenditures: 8,228,000,000 litai (transfer payments 29.1%, goods and services 27.6%, wages and salaries 27.6%, capital expenditures 11.2%).
Production (metric tons except as noted). Agriculture, forestry, fishing (1995): potatoes 1,594,000, barley 1,100,000, wheat 525,000, sugar beets 500,000; livestock (number of live animals) 1,260,000 pigs, 1,152,000 cattle, 8,849,000 poultry; roundwood (1994) 3,992,000 cu m; fish catch (1993) 119,852. Mining and quarrying (1994): limestone 830,000; peat 411,000. Manufacturing (value of production in '000 litai; 1993): processed foods 2,822,879; textile and knitwear 822,678; machinery 523,858; radio, television, and communications equipment 480,405. Construction (1993): residential 245,000,000 litai. Energy production (consumption): electricity (kW-hr; 1994) 10,055,000,000 (11,199,000,000); coal (metric tons; 1994) none (482,000); crude petroleum (barrels; 1994) 682,000 (27,000,000); petroleum products (metric tons; 1994) 3,819,000 (3,606,000); natural gas (cu m; 1994) none (1,871,000,000).
Gross national product (1994): U.S.$4,992,000,000 (U.S.$1,350 per capita).

Structure of gross national product and labour force

	1993 in value '000,000 litai	1993 % of total value	1994 labour force[2]	1994 % of labour force
Agriculture, forestry	1,219.3	14.6	391,500	23.4
Manufacturing, mining	2,188.9	26.2	339,800	20.2
Construction	560.5	6.7	110,900	6.6
Public utilities	410.3	4.9	37,700	2.3
Transp. and commun.	677.4	8.1	92,100	5.5
Trade	1,437.4	17.2	245,800	14.7
Finance	518.8	6.2	62,100	3.7
Pub admin., defense	559.5	6.7 }	395,000	23.6
Services	393.5	4.7 }		
Other	385.1	4.6	...	...
TOTAL	8,350.7	100.0[3]	1,675,000	100.0

Population economically active (1995): total 1,753,000; activity rate of total population 47.2% (participation rates: ages 16–60/55[4], 83.0%; female [1993] 48.5%; unemployed 6.2%).

Price and earnings indexes (1990 = 100)

	1989	1990	1991	1992	1993	1994	1995
Consumer price index	...	100.0	216.4	2,207	9,054	13,125	18,336
Monthly earnings index	86.1	100.0	259.9	2,008	2,226	3,798	5,283

Household income and expenditure (1993). Avg. household size (1989) 3.2; sources of income: wages 65.2%, pensions and grants 15.9%, self-employment in agriculture 10.4%, other 8.5%; expenditure: food 50.9%, nonfood goods 18.6%, services 11.3%, taxes 10.8%, agricultural expenses 5.1%.
Land use (1994): forest 30.9%; pasture 7.3%; agricultural 47.0%; other 14.8%.

Foreign trade

Imports (1995): U.S.$2,544,000,000 (petroleum and gas 26.6%, machinery 16.5%, textiles 9.3%, chemicals 8.9%, transport equipment 7.5%, base metals 6.6%, prepared foods 1.3%). Major import sources: Russia 31.1%; Belarus 3.6%; Latvia 3.5%; Ukraine 3.0%; Estonia 2.0%; Uzbekistan 0.7%.
Exports (1995): U.S.$2,210,000,000 (textiles 14.7%, chemicals 12.2%, mineral products 11.9%, machinery 10.8%, base metals 8.7%, live animals 8.4%, prepared foods 5.6%). Major export destinations: Russia 20.4%; Belarus 10.8%; Ukraine 7.5%; Latvia 7.1%; Estonia 2.2%; Kazakstan 1.0%.

Transport and communications

Transport. Railroads (1994): length 2,996 km; passenger-km 1,523,000,000; metric ton-km cargo 8,849,000,000. Roads (1995): total length 61,329 km (paved 74%). Vehicles (1994): passenger cars 652,810; trucks and buses 110,696. Merchant marine (1992): vessels (100 gross tons and over) 52; total deadweight tonnage 373,911. Air transport (1995): passenger-km 330,000,000; metric ton-km cargo 7,888,000; airports (1996) 3.
Communications. Daily newspapers (1992): 18; circulation 836,000; circulation per 1,000 population 223. Radio (1995): 1,420,000 receivers (1 per 2.6 persons). Television (1995): 1,570,000 receivers (1 per 2.4 persons). Telephones (main lines; 1993): 858,500 (1 per 4.4 persons).

Education and health

Education (1993–94)

	schools	teachers	students	student/ teacher ratio
Primary and secondary	2,317	41,052	511,000	12.4
Voc., teacher tr.	168	5,035	69,000	13.7
Higher	14	9,003[5]	53,000	7.3[5]

Educational attainment (1989). Percentage of population age 25 and over having: no schooling 9.1%; complete primary 21.3%; incomplete secondary 57.0%; postsecondary 12.6%. Literacy (1989): total population age 15 and over literate 98.4%; males literate 99.2%; females literate 97.8%.
Health (1993): physicians 16,622 (1 per 225 persons); hospital beds 43,600 (1 per 86 persons); infant mortality rate per 1,000 live births (1995) 12.5.

Military

Total active duty personnel (1996): 5,100 (army 82.3%, navy 6.9%, air force 10.8%). Military expenditure as percentage of GNP (1994): 0.6% (world 3.0%); per capita expenditure U.S.$19.

[1]Total includes 12 sq mi (30 sq km) not distributed by administrative subdivision. [2]Employed persons only. [3]Detail does not add to total given because of rounding. [4]Males retire at age 60, females at 55. [5]1987–88.

Luxembourg

Official name: Groussherzogtum Lëtzebuerg (Luxemburgian); Grand-Duché de Luxembourg (French); Grossherzogtum Luxemburg (German) (Grand Duchy of Luxembourg).
Form of government: constitutional monarchy with two legislative houses (Council of State [21][1]; Chamber of Deputies [60]).
Chief of state: Grand Duke.
Head of government: Prime Minister.
Capital: Luxembourg.
Official language: none: Luxemburgian (national); French (used for most official purposes); German (lingua franca).
Official religion: none.
Monetary unit: 1 Luxembourg franc (Lux F) = 100 centimes; valuation (Oct. 11, 1996) 1 U.S.$ = Lux F 31.55; 1 £ = Lux F 49.70.

Area and population	area		population
Districts Cantons	sq mi	sq km	1995[2] estimate
Diekirch	447	1,157	60,900
Clervaux	128	332	11,300
Diekirch	92	239	24,600
Redange	103	267	12,000
Vianden	21	54	2,900
Wiltz	102	265	10,100
Grevenmacher	203	525	46,700
Echternach	72	186	13,000
Grevenmacher	82	211	19,400
Remich	49	128	14,300
Luxembourg	349	904	298,000
Capellen	77	199	34,200
Esch	94	243	122,700
Luxembourg (Ville et Campagne)	92	238	120,500
Mersch	86	224	20,600
TOTAL	999	2,586	406,600[3]

Demography

Population (1996): 415,000.
Density (1996): persons per sq mi 415.4, persons per sq km 160.5.
Urban-rural (1993): urban 88.0%; rural 12.0%.
Sex distribution (1995[2]): male 49.09%; female 50.91%.
Age breakdown (1995): under 15, 18.3%; 15–29, 20.0%; 30–44, 24.6%; 45–59, 17.9%; 60–74, 13.6%; 75 and over, 5.6%.
Population projection: (2000) 433,000; (2010) 462,000.
Doubling time: not applicable; population stable.
Ethnic composition (nationality; 1995[2]): Luxemburger 67.4%; Portuguese 12.1%; Italian 4.8%; French 3.5%; Belgian 2.8%; German 2.3%; other 7.1%.
Religious affiliation (1990): Roman Catholic 94.9%; Protestant 1.1%; other 4.0%.
Major cities (1995[2]): Luxembourg 76,446; Esch-sur-Alzette 24,255; Differdange 16,196; Dudelange 15,833; Petange 13,066.

Vital statistics

Birth rate per 1,000 population (1994): 13.5 (world avg. 25.0); legitimate 87.3%; illegitimate 12.7%.
Death rate per 1,000 population (1994): 9.2 (world avg. 9.3).
Natural increase rate per 1,000 population (1994): 4.3 (world avg. 15.7).
Total fertility rate (avg. births per childbearing woman; 1994): 1.7.
Marriage rate per 1,000 population (1994): 5.8.
Divorce rate per 1,000 population (1994): 1.7.
Life expectancy at birth (1990–92): male 72.6 years; female 79.1 years.
Major causes of death per 100,000 population (1994): circulatory diseases 391.1, of which cerebrovascular disease 118.6, ischemic heart disease and myocardial infarction 128.3; malignant neoplasms (cancers) 234.6; accidents and suicide 62.7, of which suicide 18.3.

National economy

Budget (1995). Revenue: Lux F 145,150,800,000 (income and excise taxes 55.5%, customs taxes 16.8%). Expenditures: Lux F 146,433,000,000 (social security 20.9%, education 12.1%, transportation 9.2%, administration 7.4%, defense 2.6%, debt service 1.3%).
Public debt (1994): U.S.$334,810,000.
Production (metric tons except as noted). Agriculture, forestry, fishing (1994): barley 58,900, wheat 45,200, potatoes 23,000, rye 15,200, oats 12,400, sugar beets 11,600, apples 9,600; livestock (number of live animals; 1995) 213,887 cattle, 76,640 pigs; roundwood (1992) 372,000 cu m. Mining and quarrying (1987): metal ores, none; sand and gravel 956,810; gypsum 420,000; crushed stone 344,841. Manufacturing (1994): steel ingots and castings 3,073,268; pig iron 1,926,890; milk 261,600; beef and pork 23,120; wine 179,998 hectolitres. Construction (1993): residential and semiresidential 618,754 sq m; nonresidential 181,997 sq m. Energy production (consumption): electricity (kW-hr; 1993) 1,067,000,000 (5,118,000,000); coal (metric tons; 1993) none (277,000); crude petroleum, none (n.a.); petroleum products (metric tons; 1993) none (1,883,000); natural gas (cu m; 1993) none (576,000,000).

Gross national product (at current market prices; 1994): U.S.$15,973,000,000 (U.S.$39,850 per capita).

Structure of gross domestic product and labour force	1991		1995	
	in value Lux F '000,000	% of total value	labour force	% of labour force
Agriculture	4,477	1.4	1,378	0.7
Mining	997	0.3	...	...
Manufacturing	77,303	24.3	34,129	17.4
Construction	23,905	7.5	22,243	11.4
Public utilities	5,264	1.6	856	0.4
Transp. and commun.	22,139	6.9	14,060	7.2
Trade	52,285	16.4	37,104	19.0
Finance	44,236	13.9	34,751	17.8
Pub. admin., defense	46,800	14.7 }	51,079	26.1
Services	48,656	15.3 }		
Other	−7,258[4]	−2.3[4]	...	...
TOTAL	318,804	100.0	195,600	100.0

Population economically active (1991): total 164,713; activity rate of total population 42.8% (participation rates: ages 15–64, 61.6%; female 35.9%; unemployed 1.5%).

Price and earnings indexes (1990 = 100)	1990	1991	1992	1993	1994	1995
Consumer price index	100.0	103.1	106.4	110.2	112.6	114.8
Hourly earnings index	100.0	105.3	112.0	116.5	...	...

Household income and expenditure. Average household size (1991) 2.6; income per household (1992) Lux F 1,438,000 (U.S.$44,700); sources of income (1992): wages and salaries 67.1%, self-employment 4.8%, transfer payments 28.1%; expenditure (1991): transportation and communications 19.1%, housing 13.7%, food and beverages 12.9%, household goods and furniture 10.8%, health 7.3%, clothing and footwear 5.9%.
Tourism (1989): receipts from visitors U.S.$286,000,000.
Land use (1992): forested 34.2%; meadows and pastures 25.6%; agricultural and under permanent cultivation 23.2%; other 17.0%.

Foreign trade

Balance of trade (current prices)	1989	1990	1991	1992	1993	1994
Lux F '000,000	−31,900	−43,100	−60,500	−56,300	−55,400	−56,300
% of total	6.8%	9.3%	12.4%	11.9%	11.9%	11.6%

Imports (1994): Lux F 271,582,000,000 (metal products, machinery, and transport equipment 43.3%, of which transport equipment 9.5%; food, beverages, and tobacco 12.1%; mineral products 11.7%; chemical products 8.8%). *Major import sources:* Belgium 39.5%; Germany 28.7%; France 13.1%; The Netherlands 4.4%; Italy 2.3%; U.S. 2.2%.
Exports (1994): Lux F 215,275,000,000 (metal products, machinery, and transport equipment 55.0%, of which transport equipment 4.4%; plastic materials and rubber manufactures 13.7%; textile yarn, fabrics, and related products 7.4%; food, beverages, and tobacco 6.5%; chemical products 4.7%). *Major export destinations:* Germany 28.2%; France 18.9%; Belgium 13.8%; U.K. 6.1%; The Netherlands 5.4%; Italy 5.1%; U.S. 4.2%.

Transport and communications

Transport. Railroads (1993): route length 171 mi, 275 km; passenger-mi 176,000,000[5], passenger-km 284,000,000[5]; short ton-mi cargo 443,156,000, metric ton-km cargo 646,997,000. Roads (1995[2]): total length 3,190 mi, 5,134 km (paved 99%). Vehicles (1995[2]): passenger cars 229,037; trucks and buses 29,868. Merchant marine (1992): vessels (100 gross tons and over) 54; total deadweight tonnage 2,603,611. Air transport (1994): passenger arrivals 584,698, departures 590,928; short ton-mi cargo 606,902,000[6], metric ton-km cargo 886,062,000[6]; airports (1996) with scheduled flights 1.
Communications. Daily newspapers (1994): total number 5; total circulation 154,000; circulation per 1,000 population 381. Radio (1995): 240,000 receivers (1 per 1.7 persons). Television (1991): 134,845 receivers (1 per 2.9 persons). Telephones (main lines; 1994): 221,898 (1 per 1.8 persons).

Education and health

Education (1993–94)	schools	teachers	students	student/ teacher ratio
Primary (age 6–11)[7]	...	1,911	27,595	14.4
Secondary (age 12–18)	...	}	8,712[8]	...
Voc., teacher tr.	...	} 1,948	12,662	6.5
Higher	...		4,957[9]	...

Educational attainment: n.a. *Literacy* (1995): virtually 100% literate.
Health (1994[2]): physicians 848 (1 per 469 persons); hospital beds 4,560 (1 per 87 persons); infant mortality rate per 1,000 live births 5.3.
Food (1992): daily per capita caloric intake 3,681 (vegetable products 65%, animal products 35%); 139% of FAO recommended minimum.

Military

Total active duty personnel (1995): 800 (army 100.0%). *Military expenditure as percentage of GNP* (1994): 0.8% (world 3.0%); per capita expenditure U.S.$313.

[1]Has limited legislative authority. [2]January 1. [3]Detail does not add to total given because of rounding. [4]Imputed bank service charges. [5]1992. [6]1987. [7]Public schools only. [8]1992–93. [9]1990–91.

Macedonia

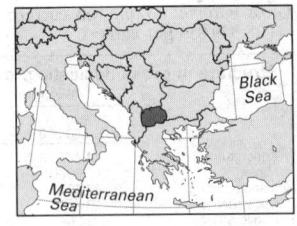

Official name[1]: Republika Makedonija (Republic of Macedonia).
Form of government: unitary multiparty republic with a unicameral legislature (Assembly [120]).
Head of state: President.
Head of government: Prime Minister.
Capital: Skopje.
Official language: Macedonian.
Official religion: none.
Monetary unit[2]: denar; valuation
(Oct. 11, 1996) 1 U.S.$ = 40.60 denar;
1 £ = 63.96 denar.

Area and population (1994 census)

Municipalities	area sq km[3]	population	Municipalities	area sq km[3]	population
Berovo	806	19,737	Negotino	734	23,094
Bitola	1,798	106,012	Ohrid	1,069	60,841
Brod	924	10,912	Prilep	1,675	93,248
Debar	274	26,449	Probištip	326	16,373
Delčevo	589	25,052	Radoviš	735	30,378
Demir Hisar	443	10,321	Resen	739	17,467
Gevgelija	757	34,767	Skopje[4]	1,818	541,280
Gostivar	1,341	108,189	Štip	815	50,531
Kavadarci	1,132	41,801	Struga	507	62,305
Kičevo	854	53,044	Strumica	952	89,759
Kočani	570	48,105	Sveti Nikole	649	21,391
Kratovo	376	10,855	Tetovo	1,080	174,748
Kriva Palanka	720	25,112	Titov Veles	1,536	65,523
Kruševo	239	11,981	Valandovo	331	12,049
Kumanovo	1,212	126,543	Vinica	432	19,010
			TOTAL	25,713[5]	1,936,877

Demography

Population (1996): 1,968,000.
Density (1996): persons per sq mi 198.2, persons per sq km 76.5.
Urban-rural (1994): urban 58.7%; rural 41.3%.
Sex distribution (1994): male 50.39%; female 49.61%.
Age breakdown (1994): under 15, 24.8%; 15–29, 24.1%; 30–44, 22.3%; 45–59, 15.8%; 60–74, 10.6%; 75 and over, 2.4%.
Population projection: (2000) 2,033,000; (2010) 2,206,000.
Doubling time: 75 years.
Ethnic composition (1994): Macedonian 66.4%; Albanian 23.1%; Turkish 3.9%; Gypsy 2.3%; Serb 1.9%; other 2.4%.
Religious affiliation (1991): most believers are Christians, predominantly of the Eastern Orthodox church; other Christians include members of the Macedonian Orthodox church and the Roman Catholic church; there are also a substantial Islamic community and a small Jewish community.
Major cities (1994): Skopje 440,577; Bitola 75,386; Prilep 67,371; Kumanovo 66,237; Tetovo 50,376.

Vital statistics

Birth rate per 1,000 population (1994): 17.3 (world avg. 25.0); legitimate 91.5%; illegitimate 8.5%.
Death rate per 1,000 population (1994): 8.1 (world avg. 9.3).
Natural increase rate per 1,000 population (1994): 9.2 (world avg. 15.7).
Total fertility rate (avg. births per childbearing woman; 1994): 2.2.
Marriage rate per 1,000 population (1994): 7.6.
Divorce rate per 1,000 population (1994): 0.3.
Life expectancy at birth (1993): male 70.1 years; female 74.4 years.
Major causes of death per 100,000 population (1993): diseases of the circulatory system 385.8; accidents, violence, and poisoning 35.3; diseases of the respiratory system 34.5; diseases of the digestive system 14.8; infectious and parasitic diseases 12.9%; malignant neoplasms (cancers) 6.2.

National economy

Budget (1994). Revenue: 63,157,000,000 denar[2] (excise tax 31.6%, income tax 25.8%, sales tax 19.6%, import duties 16.3%, enterprise profit tax 6.6%). Expenditure: 67,061,000,000 denar[2] (national economy 52.3%, transfers 23.8%, debt service 14.0%).
Tourism (1994): receipts from visitors U.S.$21,000,000; expenditures by nationals abroad U.S.$23,000,000.
External debt (1994): U.S.$924,000,000.
Production (metric tons except as noted). Agriculture, forestry, fishing (1995): wheat 381,000, grapes 191,000, corn (maize) 166,000, potatoes 154,000, plums 17,221; livestock (number of live animals) 2,044,000 sheep, 276,000 cattle, 195,000 pigs, 4,000,000 poultry; roundwood (1994) 166,000 cu m; fish catch (1994) 1,230 (all freshwater). Mining and quarrying (1994): copper ore 3,500,000; lead-zinc ore 955,000; gypsum 33,000; lime 14,100; iron ore 44,000; refined silver 13,000. Manufacturing (1994): cement 486,500; steel sheets 73,045; sulfuric acid 72,100; crude steel 25,000; cotton yarn 7,600; woolen yarn 4,856; cotton fabric 27,548,000 sq m; upper-shoe leather 1,307,000 sq m; distilled spirits 2,371,000 hectolitres; refrigerators 95,192 units. Construction (residential, 1994): 348,004 sq m. Energy production (consumption): electricity (kW-hr; 1994) 5,924,000,000 (5,359,000,000); coal (metric tons; 1994) 6,900,000 (6,959,000); crude petroleum (barrels; 1993) none (8,063,000); petroleum products (metric tons; 1992) 556,000 (823,000); natural gas (cu m; 1993) none (269,100,000).
Land use (1994): forested 38.9%; meadows and pastures 24.7%; agricultural and under permanent cultivation 25.7%; other 10.7%.
Gross national product (1994): U.S.$1,653,000,000 (U.S.$853 per capita).

Structure of gross domestic product and labour force

	1993		1994	
	in value '000,000 denar[2]	% of total value	labour force[6]	% of labour force
Agriculture	5,795	10.0	30,900	5.3
Mining and manufacturing	15,019	25.8	157,700	27.1
Construction	2,977	5.1	33,368	5.7
Public utilities	1,195	2.1	10,434	1.8
Transp. and commun.	3,433	5.9	21,000	3.6
Trade	3,959	6.8	29,900	5.1
Finance	3,201	5.5	11,400	2.0
Public admin., defense	11,330	19.5	84,717	14.1
Services	1,871	3.2	13,300	2.3
Other	9,363[7]	16.1[7]	189,281[8]	33.0
TOTAL	58,143	100.0	582,000	100.0

Population economically active (1994): total 582,000; activity rate 29.6% (participation rates: ages 15–64 [1991] 98.1%; female 25.5%; unemployed 32.0%).

Price and earnings indexes (1990 = 100)

	1990	1991	1992	1993	1994
Consumer price index	100.0	210.8	3,397	15,692	35,826
Earnings index[9]	100.0	184.4	1,984	11,819	24,231

Household income and expenditure (1994). Average household size 3.8; income per household Din 49,635[2] (U.S.$1,223); sources of income: wages and salaries 59.9%, transfer payments 17.0%, transfers from abroad 13.4%, other 9.7%; expenditure: food 42.2%, fuel and lighting 7.5%, clothing and footwear 7.4%, transportation and communications 7.2%, drink and tobacco 7.0%, health care 4.7%, education and entertainment 3.2%.

Foreign trade

Balance of trade (current prices)

	1990	1991	1992	1993	1994
U.S.$'000,000	−418	−225	−7	−172	−398
% of total	15.8%	8.9%	0.3%	7.5%	15.5%

Imports (1994): U.S.$1,484,000,000 (machinery and transport equipment 19.7%, food products 19.0%, manufactured products 13.7%, chemical products 13.3%, petroleum products 9.8%). *Major import sources:* Germany 17.1%; Bulgaria 16.3%; Slovenia 10.9%; Italy 7.4%; Austria 4.0%; former U.S.S.R. 3.1%.
Exports (1994): U.S.$1,086,000,000 (manufactured products 37.7%, machinery and transport equipment 12.3%, food products 10.1%, raw materials 7.1%, chemical products 4.4%). *Major export destinations:* Bulgaria 22.1%; Germany 13.4%; Italy 11.6%; former U.S.S.R. 7.0%; Slovenia 6.6%.

Transport and communications

Transport. Railroads (1994): length 573 mi, 922 km; passenger-mi 41,632,000, passenger-km 67,000,000; short ton-mi cargo 103,426,000, metric ton-km cargo 151,000,000. Roads (1994): length 5,233 mi, 8,422 km (paved 62%). Vehicles (1994): passenger cars 263,181; trucks and buses 22,825. Merchant marine: n.a. Air transport (1993)[10]: passenger-mi 181,671,190, passenger-km 292,372,000; metric tons cargo transported 625; airports (1996) with scheduled flights 1.
Communications. Daily newspapers (1994): total number 3; total circulation (1992) 55,000; circulation per 1,000 population 28. Radio (1992): 369,000 receivers (1 per 5.2 persons). Television (1992): 338,000 receivers (1 per 5.7 persons). Telephones (main lines; 1994): 331,874 (1 per 5.8 persons).

Education and health

Education (1994–95)

	schools	teachers	students	student/ teacher ratio
Primary (age 7–14)	1,050	13,102	258,955	19.9
Secondary (age 15–18)	95	4,520	77,754	16.5
Higher	27	1,122	26,959	24.0

Educational attainment (1981). Percentage of population age 15 and over having: less than full primary education 45.3%; primary 28.1%; secondary 21.2%; postsecondary and higher 5.1%; unknown 0.3%. *Literacy* (1981): total population age 10 and over literate 1,365,000 (89.1%); males literate 729,000 (94.2%); females literate 636,000 (83.8%).
Health (1994): physicians 4,505 (1 per 437 persons); hospital beds 10,664 (1 per 195 persons); infant mortality rate per 1,000 live births 22.4.

Military

Total active duty personnel (1996): 10,400 (army 100%). *Military expenditure as percentage of GNP* (1993): 1.8% (world 3.3%); per capita expenditure U.S.$14.

[1]Member of the United Nations under the name Former Yugoslav Republic of Macedonia. [2]Macedonia, as part of Yugoslavia, utilized the Yugoslav (old) dinar (Din) until Jan. 1, 1990, when it was replaced by the Yugoslav (new) dinar (Din) at a rate of 10,000 (old) for 1 new. Macedonia left the Yugoslav currency area in September 1991, utilizing a local coupon alone until May 1992, when a transitional local currency, the denar, was introduced. The denar (valued initially at denar 255 = 1 U.S.$) was established at par with the Yugoslav (new) dinar but circulated in parallel with the coupon until May 1993, when a differently defined denar was introduced, replacing both the transitional denar and the coupon. [3]One sq km is equal to approximately 0.3861 sq mi. [4]Skopje, a single administrative district, consists of 5 municipalities: Gazi Baba, Karpos, Kisela Voda, Centar, Cair. [5]Total includes 280 sq km of inland water not distributed by district. [6]Employed persons only. [7]Includes import duties, customs, imputed rents, and statistical discrepancy. [8]Persons actively seeking employment and the unemployed. [9]Based on nominal net wages per worker. [10]Palair Macedonian airline only.

Madagascar

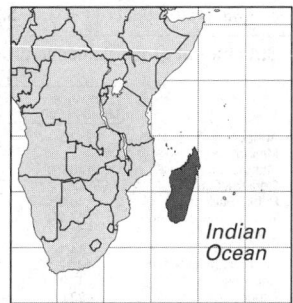

Official name: Repoblikan'i
  Madagasikara (Malagasy);
  République de Madagascar
  (French) (Republic of Madagascar).
Form of government: unitary
  multiparty republic with one
  legislative house (National Assembly
  [138]).
Chief of state: President.
Head of government: Prime Minister.
Capital: Antananarivo.
Official languages:[1].
Official religion: none.
Monetary unit: 1 Malagasy franc
  (FMG) = 100 centimes; valuation
  (Oct. 11, 1996) 1 U.S.$ = FMG 3,950;
  1 £ = FMG 6,222.

Area and population		area		population
		sq mi	sq km	1993 census[2]
Provinces	**Capitals**			
Antananarivo	Antananarivo	22,503	58,283	3,483,236
Antsirañana	Antsirañana	16,620	43,046	942,410
Fianarantsoa	Fianarantsoa	39,526	102,373	2,671,150
Mahajanga	Mahajanga	57,924	150,023	1,330,612
Toamasina	Toamasina	27,765	71,911	1,935,330
Toliary	Toliary	62,319	161,405	1,729,419
TOTAL		226,658	587,041	12,092,157

Demography

Population (1996): 13,671,000.
Density (1996): persons per sq mi 60.3, persons per sq km 23.3.
Urban-rural (1991): urban 24.4%; rural 75.6%.
Sex distribution (1993): male 49.55%; female 50.45%.
Age breakdown (1995): under 15, 46.1%; 15–29, 26.2%; 30–44, 15.2%; 45–59, 8.0%; 60–74, 3.8%; 75 and over, 0.7%.
Population projection: (2000) 17,529,000; (2010) 23,326,000.
Doubling time: 22 years.
Ethnic composition (1983): Malagasy 98.9%, of which Merina 26.6%, Betsimisaraka 14.9%, Betsileo 11.7%, Tsimihety 7.4%, Sakalava 6.4%, Antandroy 5.3%; Comorian 0.3%; Indian and Pakistani 0.2%; French 0.2%; Chinese 0.1%; other 0.3%.
Religious affiliation (1980): Christian 51.0%, of which Roman Catholic 26.0%, Protestant 22.8%; traditional beliefs 47.0%; Muslim 1.7%; other 0.3%.
Major cities (1993): Antananarivo 1,052,835; Toamasina 127,441; Antsirabe 120,239; Mahajanga 100,807; Fianarantsoa 99,005.

Vital statistics

Birth rate per 1,000 population (1990–95): 43.9 (world avg. 25.0); legitimate, n.a.; illegitimate, n.a.
Death rate per 1,000 population (1990–95): 11.8 (world avg. 9.3).
Natural increase rate per 1,000 population (1990–95): 32.1 (world avg. 15.7).
Total fertility rate (avg. births per childbearing woman; 1993): 6.1.
Marriage rate per 1,000 population: n.a.
Divorce rate per 1,000 population: n.a.
Life expectancy at birth (1990–95): male 55.0 years; female 58.0 years.
Major causes of death per 100,000 population: n.a.; however, major causes of death in the early 1990s included maternal and perinatal diseases, malaria, infectious and parasitic diseases, malnutrition, diarrhea, and respiratory diseases.

National economy

Budget (1995). Revenue: FMG 1,138,300,000,000 (taxes 97.6%, of which duties on trade 55.7%, value-added tax 20.4%, income tax 14.4%; nontax receipts 2.4%). Expenditures: FMG 1,888,700,000,000 (current expenditure 79.7%, of which debt service 31.6%, education 10.0%, general administration 7.7%, defense 6.1%, health 3.9%, agriculture 0.7%; capital expenditure 20.3%).
Tourism (1994): receipts from visitors U.S.$54,000,000; expenditures by nationals abroad U.S.$23,000,000.
Production (metric tons except as noted). Agriculture, forestry, fishing (1995): paddy rice 2,596,000, cassava 2,420,000, sugarcane 1,980,000, sweet potatoes 560,000, potatoes 270,000, bananas 225,000, mangoes 200,000, corn (maize) 168,600, taro 125,000, oranges 82,000, coconuts 80,000, coffee 78,510, dry beans 50,000, pineapples 50,000, seed cotton 33,300, peanuts (groundnuts) 28,000; livestock (number of live animals) 10,309,000 cattle, 1,592,000 pigs, 1,300,000 goats, 740,000 sheep, 23,000,000 chickens; roundwood (1994) 9,151,000 cu m; fish catch (1993) 115,029. Mining and quarrying (1995): salt 80,000; chromite ore 74,000; graphite 13,900; mica 387; gold 200 kg[3]; in addition, a wide variety of semiprecious stones and gemstones are produced. Manufacturing (1995): cotton cloth 25,000,000, refined sugar 89,474, cement 45,009, soap 15,000, tobacco products 1,936, beer 318,842 hectolitres, fuel oil 177,329 cu m, gas oil 129,227 cu m, kerosene 110,764 cu m, gasoline 87,905 cu m, shoes 972,000 pairs. Construction (1986)[4]: residential 19,700 sq m; nonresidential 5,700 sq m. Energy production (consumption): electricity (kW-hr; 1994) 605,000,000 (605,000,000); coal (metric tons; 1994) none (14,-000); crude petroleum (barrels; 1994) none (1,450,000); petroleum products (metric tons; 1994) 185,000 (348,000); natural gas, none (n.a.).
Household income and expenditure. Average household size (1993) 4.6[4]; average annual income per household: n.a.; sources of income (1975)[5]: wages and salaries 58.8%, self-employment 14.1%, other 27.1%; expenditure

(1983)[4, 6]: food 60.4%, fuel and light 9.1%, clothing and footwear 8.6%, household goods and utensils 2.4%.
Gross national product (1994): U.S.$3,058,000,000 (U.S.$230 per capita).

Structure of gross domestic product and labour force				
	1991		1993	
	in value FMG '000,000[7]	% of total value	labour force	% of labour force
Agriculture	1,488,350	32.6	5,100,000	86.2
Manufacturing	530,560	11.6	86,000	1.5
Mining	14,800	0.3 }		
Construction	52,600	1.2 }	46,000	0.8
Public utilities	86,950	1.9 }		
Transportation and communications	747,920	16.4	42,000	0.7
Trade	497,990	10.9 }	149,000	2.5
Finance	70,020	1.5 }		
Services[8]	791,890	17.4	243,000	4.1
Pub. admin., defense	284,430	6.2	208,000	3.5
Other	...	...	40,000	0.7
TOTAL	4,565,510	100.0	5,914,000	100.0

Population economically active (1993): total 5,914,000; activity rate of total population 48.9% (participation rates [1985]: ages 15–64, 74.9%; female 39.3%; unemployed [1982] 0.6%).

Price and earnings indexes (1990 = 100)							
	1989	1990	1991	1992	1993	1994	1995
Consumer price index	89.5	100.0	108.6	124.4	136.8	190.1	283.2
Annual earnings index[9]	91.7	100.0	127.1	134.5	146.1	189.0	264.6

Public debt (external, outstanding; 1994): U.S.$3,565,000,000.
Land use (1994): forested 39.9%; meadows and pastures 41.3%; agricultural and under permanent cultivation 5.3%; other 13.5%.

Foreign trade

Balance of trade					
	1990	1991	1992	1993	1994	1995
FMG '000,000,000	−327.9	−93.0	−175.1	−244.3	−77.7	−2,082.3
% of total	25.6%	7.7%	14.5%	19.6%	3.2%	37.7%

Imports (1994): FMG 1,150,780,000,000 (capital equipment 20.2%; food 16.8%, of which rice 6.9%; raw materials and spare parts 15.8%; nonfood consumer goods 15.3%; crude petroleum 11.4%). *Major import sources* (1992): France 30.3%; Germany 6.1%; U.S. 5.9%; Japan 5.8%; U.K. 5.0%; Italy 2.9%; The Netherlands 2.2%.
Exports (1994): FMG 849,960,000,000 (coffee 18.0%; vanilla 16.7%; shrimp 13.2%; cotton fabrics 2.9%; cloves and clove oil 2.6%; sugar 2.2%). *Major export destinations* (1992): France 26.6%; U.S. 15.5%; Germany 9.9%; Japan 8.6%; Belgium-Luxembourg 3.3%; Italy 3.1%; U.K. 2.6%; The Netherlands 2.2%.

Transport and communications

Transport. Railroads (1991): route length 640 mi, 1,030 km; passenger-mi 152,000,000, passenger-km 245,000,000; short ton-mi cargo 90,000,000, metric ton-km cargo 132,000,000. Roads (1992): total length 21,586 mi, 34,739 km (paved 15%). Vehicles (1992): passenger cars 47,711; trucks and buses 34,341. Merchant marine (1992): vessels (100 gross tons and over) 85; total deadweight tonnage 82,077. Air transport (1994): passenger-mi 390,208,000, passenger-km 627,962,000; short ton-mi cargo 12,120,000, metric ton-km cargo 17,700,000; airports (1996) with scheduled flights 19.
Communications. Daily newspapers (1992): total number 7; total circulation 48,000; circulation per 1,000 population 4. Radio (1995): total number of receivers 2,300,000 (1 per 5.8 persons). Television (1995): total number of receivers 130,000 (1 per 102 persons). Telephones (main lines; 1993): 34,810 (1 per 370 persons).

Education and health

Education (1993)	schools	teachers	students	student/teacher ratio
Primary (age 6–13)	13,624	37,676	1,504,668	39.9
Secondary (14–18)	1,142[10]	15,118	298,241	19.7
Voc., teacher tr.	61[11]	1,484[12]	17,419[12]	11.7[12]
Higher	5[10]	855[13]	42,681[13]	49.9[13]

Educational attainment: n.a. *Literacy* (1990): percentage of total population age 15 and over literate 80.2%; males literate 87.7%; females literate 72.9%.
Health: physicians (1990) 1,392 (1 per 8,628 persons); hospital beds (1989) 10,900 (1 per 1,067 persons); infant mortality rate per 1,000 live births (1990–95) 110.
Food (1992): daily per capita caloric intake 2,135 (vegetable products 89%, animal products 11%); 95% of FAO recommended minimum requirement.

Military

Total active duty personnel (1996): 21,000 (army 95.2%, navy 2.4%, air force 2.4%). *Military expenditure as percentage of GNP* (1994): 0.9% (world 3.0%); per capita expenditure U.S.$2.

---

[1]The 1992 constitution identifies Malagasy as the "national" language, although neither Malagasy nor French, the languages of the two official texts of the constitution, is itself "official." [2]Preliminary. [3]1994. [4]Antananarivo only. [5]Malagasy households only. [6]Weights of consumer price index components; excludes housing. [7]At factor cost. [8]Includes artisans and servants. [9]Average salary, all public employees, including military. [10]1988–89. [11]1987–88. [12]1990–91. [13]1992.

Malawi

Official name: Republic of Malawi.
Form of government: multiparty
republic with one legislative house
(National Assembly [177]).
Head of state and government:
President.
Capital:[1].
Official language: Chewa.
Official religion: none.
Monetary unit: 1 Malawi kwacha
(MK) = 100 tambala; valuation
(Oct. 11, 1996) 1 U.S.$ = MK 15.31;
1 £ = MK 24.11.

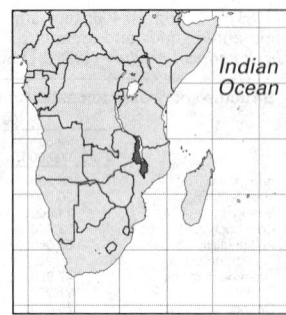

Area and population		area		population
Regions				1987
Districts	**Capitals**	sq mi	sq km	census
Central	Lilongwe	13,742	35,592	3,110,986
Dedza	Dedza	1,399	3,624	411,787
Dowa	Dowa	1,174	3,041	322,432
Kasungu	Kasungu	3,042	7,878	323,453
Lilongwe	Lilongwe	2,378	6,159	976,627
Mchinji	Mchinji	1,296	3,356	249,843
Nkhotakota	Nkhotakota	1,644	4,259	158,044
Ntcheu	Ntcheu	1,322	3,424	358,767
Ntchisi	Ntchisi	639	1,655	120,860
Salima	Salima	848	2,196	189,173
Northern	Mzuzu	10,398	26,931	911,787
Chitipa	Chitipa	1,353	3,504	96,794
Karonga	Karonga	1,141	2,955	148,014
Mzimba	Mzimba	4,027	10,430	433,696
Nkhata Bay	Nkhata Bay	1,579	4,090	138,381
Rumphi	Rumphi	2,298	5,952	94,902
Southern	Blantyre	12,260	31,753	3,965,734
Blantyre	Blantyre	777	2,012	589,525
Chikwawa	Chikwawa	1,836	4,755	316,733
Chiradzulu	Chiradzulu	296	767	210,912
Machinga	Machinga	2,303	5,964	515,265
Mangochi	Mangochi	2,422	6,272	496,578
Mulanje	Mulanje	1,332	3,450	638,062
Mwanza	Mwanza	886	2,295	121,513
Nsanje	Nsanje	750	1,942	204,374
Thyolo	Thyolo	662	1,715	431,157
Zomba	Zomba	996	2,580	441,615
TOTAL LAND AREA		36,400	94,276[2]	
INLAND WATER		9,347	24,208	
TOTAL		45,747	118,484	7,988,507

Demography

Population (1996): 9,453,000.
Density (1996)[3]: persons per sq mi 259.7, persons per sq km 100.3.
Urban-rural (1987): urban 10.7%; rural 89.3%.
Sex distribution (1987): male 48.40%; female 51.60%.
Age breakdown (1987): under 15, 46.0%; 15–29, 25.4%; 30–44, 14.5%; 45–59, 8.1%; 60 and over, 6.0%.
Population projection: (2000) 10,011,000; (2010) 10,662,000.
Doubling time: 23 years.
Ethnic composition (1983): Maravi (including Nyanja, Chewa, Tonga, and Tumbuka) 58.3%; Lomwe 18.4%; Yao 13.2%; Ngoni 6.7%; other 3.4%.
Religious affiliation (1980): Christian 64.5%, of which Protestant 33.7%, Roman Catholic 27.6%; traditional beliefs 19.0%; Muslim 16.2%; other 0.3%.
Major cities (1994): Blantyre 446,800[4]; Lilongwe 395,500; Mzuzu 62,700.

Vital statistics

Birth rate per 1,000 population (1995): 42.4 (world avg. 25.0).
Death rate per 1,000 population (1995): 23.9 (world avg. 9.3).
Natural increase rate per 1,000 population (1995): 18.5 (world avg. 15.7).
Total fertility rate (avg. births per childbearing woman; 1995): 6.1.
Marriage rate per 1,000 population (1987): 4.4.
Divorce rate per 1,000 population (1977): 1.4.
Life expectancy at birth (1995): male 37.0 years; female 37.3 years.
Major causes of death per 100,000 population (1986)[5]: infectious and parasitic diseases 711, of which malaria 270, diarrheal diseases 148, measles 128; malnutrition 267; diseases of the respiratory system 265.

National economy

Budget (1994–95). Revenue: MK 2,329,200,000 (tax revenue 84.2%, nontax revenue 8.2%, corn sales 7.6%). Expenditures: MK 5,940,700,000 (wages and salaries 17.2%, debt service 12.4%).
Public debt (external, outstanding; 1994): U.S.$1,889,000,000.
Production (metric tons except as noted). Agriculture (1995): sugarcane 2,200,000, corn (maize) 1,661,000, potatoes 376,000, cassava 200,000, plantains 200,000, tobacco 132,000, bananas 91,000, sorghum 45,000, tea 34,000, peanuts (groundnuts) 32,000; livestock (number of live animals) 980,000 cattle, 890,000 goats, 247,000 pigs, 196,000 sheep; roundwood (1994) 10,151,000 cu m; fish catch (1994) 65,000. Mining and quarrying (1994): limestone 173,000; rubies and sapphires 125 kg. Manufacturing (value added in MK '000; 1986): chemicals 30,805; textiles 19,630; food products 11,988; beverages 11,988; tobacco 9,480; printing and publishing 9,250. Construction (value in MK; 1994): 41,700,000[6]. Energy production (consumption): electricity (kW-hr; 1993) 795,000,000 (795,000,000); coal (metric tons; 1993) none (15,000); petroleum products (metric tons; 1993) none (189,000).
Land use (1994): forested 39.3%; meadows and pastures 19.6%; agricultural and under permanent cultivation 18.1%; other 23.0%.

Gross national product (1994): U.S.$1,560,000,000 (U.S.$140 per capita).

Structure of gross domestic product and labour force				
	1995		1987	
	in value MK '000,000[7]	% of total value	labour force	% of labour force
Agriculture	382.9	36.5	2,967,933	85.8
Mining	...	...	7,164	0.2
Manufacturing	140.0	13.3	97,776	2.8
Construction	42.2	4.0	46,875	1.4
Public utilities	30.3	2.9	8,833	0.2
Transp. and commun.	57.1	5.4	24,863	0.7
Trade	120.4	11.5	94,445	2.7
Finance	114.1	10.9	5,590	0.3
Public administration	137.7	13.1 }	147,039	4.3
Services	47.4	4.5 }		
Other	−22.0[8]	−2.1[8]	57,235	1.6
TOTAL	1,050.1	100.0	3,457,753	100.0

Population economically active (1987): total 3,457,753; activity rate 43.3% (participation rates: ages 15–64, 84.6%; female 51.5%; unemployed 5.4%).

Price and earnings indexes (1990 = 100)							
	1988	1989	1990	1991	1992	1993	1994
Consumer price index	79.5	89.4	100.0	112.6	138.2	163.7	222.6
Monthly earnings index	70.1	81.6	100.0	106.4	102.8	...	...

Household income and expenditure (1979–80). Average household size (1987) 4.3; income per household MK 1,934 (U.S.$2,419); sources of income: wages 83.3%, household enterprise 6.0%; expenditure (1990)[9]: food 55.5%, clothing and footwear 11.7%, housing 9.6%, household durable goods 8.4%, transportation 6.5%.
Tourism (1994): receipts U.S.$5,000,000; expenditures U.S.$15,000,000.

Foreign trade[10]

Balance of trade (current prices)						
	1989	1990	1991	1992	1993	1994
MK '000,000	−96.1	+180.1	+140.9	−103.4	−29.0	+247.3
% of total	6.1%	8.7%	5.6%	3.4%	1.0%	4.6%

Imports (1994): MK 3,295,700,000 (1990; transport equipment 9.2%, petroleum products 8.3%, clothing 3.8%, pharmaceutical products 2.2%). *Major import sources* (1990): South Africa 30.7%; U.K. 22.9%; Japan 7.5%; W.Ger. 6.0%.
Exports (1994): MK 3,098,460,000 (tobacco 70.5%, tea 7.5%, sugar 7.4%, cotton 0.5%). *Major export destinations* (1990): W.Ger. 16.2%; U.K. 15.6%; Japan 13.5%; U.S. 12.0%; South Africa 7.2%.

Transport and communications

Transport. Railroads (1994): route length 490 mi, 789 km; passenger-km 18,995,000; metric ton-km cargo 56,778,000. Roads (1990): total length 16,960 mi, 27,294 km (paved 22%[11]). Vehicles (1994): passenger cars 17,000; trucks and buses 12,000. Merchant marine (1991): vessels (100 gross tons and over) 1; total deadweight tonnage 300. Air transport (1993)[12]: passenger-km 265,913,000; metric ton-km cargo 14,768,000; airports (1996) 4.
Communications. Daily newspapers (1995): total number 7; total circulation 22,000[13]; circulation per 1,000 population 2.2[13]. Radio (1995): total number of receivers 1,060,000 (1 per 8.9 persons). Television (1995): total number of receivers, n.a. Telephones (main lines; 1993): 32,800 (1 per 326 persons).

Education and health

Education (1989–90)				student/
	schools	teachers	students	teacher ratio
Primary (age 6–13)[14]	3,118	26,333	1,795,451	68.2
Secondary (age 14–18)	94	1,096	29,326	26.8
Teacher tr., voc.	13	250	3,679	14.7
Higher	4	235	2,685	11.4

Educational attainment (1987). Percentage of population age 25 and over having: no formal education 55.0%; primary education 39.8%; secondary and higher 5.2%. *Literacy* (1995): total population age 15 and over literate 56.4%; males literate 71.9%; females literate 41.8%.
Health: physicians (1989) 186 (1 per 47,634 persons); hospital beds (1987) 12,617 (1 per 627 persons); infant mortality rate per 1,000 live births (1995) 140.9.
Food (1992): daily per capita caloric intake 1,825 (vegetable products 97%, animal products 3%); 79% of FAO recommended minimum requirement.

Military

Total active duty personnel (1996): 9,800 (army 100%, marines none, air force, none). *Military expenditure as percentage of GNP* (1994): 1.1% (world 3.0%); per capita expenditure U.S.$1.

---

[1]A capital is not designated in the 1994 constitution. Current government operations are divided among Lilongwe (ministerial and financial); Blantyre (executive and judicial); and Zomba (legislative). [2]Detail does not add to total given because of rounding. [3]Based on land area. [4]Includes Limbe. [5]Estimates based on reported inpatient deaths in hospitals, constituting an estimated 8% of total deaths. [6]Cities of Blantyre, Lilongwe, and Mzuzu only. [7]At constant prices of 1978. [8]Less imputed bank service charges. [9]Weights of consumer price index components, cities of Blantyre and Lilongwe only. [10]Import figures are f.o.b. in balance of trade and c.i.f. in commodities and trading partners. Reexports included in balance of trade, excluded from commodities and trading partners. [11]1989. [12]Air Malawi only. [13]Circulation for one newspaper only. [14]1992.

Malaysia

Official name: Malaysia.
Form of government: federal constitutional monarchy with two legislative houses (Senate [70[1]]; House of Representatives [192]).
Chief of state: Yang di-Pertuan Agong (Paramount Ruler).
Head of government: Prime Minister.
Capital: Kuala Lumpur.
Official language: Malay.
Official religion: Islam.
Monetary unit: 1 ringgit, or Malaysian dollar (RM) = 100 cents; valuation (Oct. 11, 1996) 1 U.S.$ = RM 2.51; 1 £ = RM 3.95.

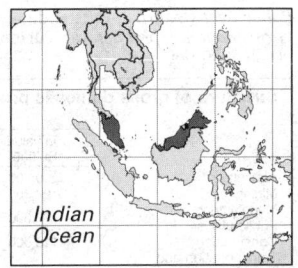

Area and population		area		population
Regions **States**	**Capitals**	sq mi	sq km	1991 census[2]
East Malaysia				
Sabah	Kota Kinabalu	28,425	73,620	1,736,902
Sarawak	Kuching	48,050	124,449	1,648,217
West Malaysia				
Johor	Johor Baharu	7,331	18,986	2,074,297
Kedah	Alor Setar	3,639	9,426	1,304,800
Kelantan	Kota Baharu	5,769	14,943	1,181,680
Melaka	Melaka	637	1,650	504,502
Negeri Sembilan	Seremban	2,565	6,643	691,150
Pahang	Kuantan	13,886	35,965	1,036,724
Perak	Ipoh	8,110	21,005	1,880,016
Perlis	Kangar	307	795	184,070
Pulau Pinang	George Town	398	1,031	1,065,075
Selangor	Shah Alam	3,072	7,956	2,289,236
Terengganu	Kuala Terengganu	5,002	12,955	770,931
Federal Territories				
Kuala Lumpur	—	94	243	1,145,075
Labuan	—	35	91	54,307
TOTAL LAND AREA		127,320	329,758	
INLAND WATER		264	684	
TOTAL		127,584	330,442	17,566,982

Demography

Population (1996): 20,359,000.
Density (1996): persons per sq mi 159.6, persons per sq km 61.6.
Urban-rural (1996): urban 54.0%; rural 46.0%.
Sex distribution (1995): male 50.36%; female 49.64%.
Age breakdown (1995): under 15, 35.8%; 15–29, 27.4%; 30–44, 19.9%; 45–59, 10.6%; 60–74, 5.1%; 75 and over, 1.2%.
Population projection: (2000) 22,087,000; (2010) 25,989,000.
Doubling time: 33 years.
Ethnic composition (1995): Malay and other indigenous (Orang Asli, or Bumiputera) 59.9%; Chinese 29.9%; Indian 9.5%; other nonindigenous 0.7%.
Religious affiliation (1980): Muslim 52.9%; Buddhist 17.3%; Chinese folk-religionist 11.6%; Hindu 7.0%; Christian 6.4%; other 4.8%.
Major cities (1991): Kuala Lumpur 1,145,075; Ipoh 382,633; Johor Baharu 328,646; Melaka 295,999; Petaling Jaya 254,849.

Vital statistics

Birth rate per 1,000 population (1996): 26.3 (world avg. 25.0).
Death rate per 1,000 population (1996): 4.9 (world avg. 9.3).
Natural increase rate per 1,000 population (1996): 21.4 (world avg. 15.7).
Total fertility rate (avg. births per childbearing woman; 1996): 3.4.
Marriage rate per 1,000 population: n.a.
Divorce rate per 1,000 population: n.a.
Life expectancy at birth (1996): male 70.0 years; female 74.0 years.
Major causes of death per 100,000 population (1993): diseases of the circulatory system 58.5; malignant neoplasms (cancers) 22.2; accidents, homicide, and other violence 17.4; birth injuries 11.6; infectious and parasitic diseases 8.6; congenital anomalies 5.4; pneumonia 5.4; vascular diseases 5.0.

National economy

Budget (1995). Revenue: RM 49,727,000,000 (income tax 34.1%, taxes on goods and services 23.7%, nontax revenue 22.0%, taxes on international trade 13.8%). Expenditures: RM 46,963,000,000 (education 21.8%, defense 12.7%, public services 10.0%, transportation and communications 8.5%, housing 6.1%, social security 5.7%).
Tourism (1994): receipts from visitors U.S.$3,189,000,000; expenditures by nationals abroad U.S.$1,737,000,000.
Production (metric tons except as noted). Agriculture, forestry, fishing (1995): palm oil 7,811,000, rice 2,126,000, sugarcane 1,601,000, rubber 1,089,000, bananas 530,000, pineapples 280,000, cacao beans 131,000; livestock (number of live animals) 3,282,000 pigs, 689,000 cattle, 312,000 goats, 100,000,000 chickens; roundwood (1994) 43,391,000 cu m; fish catch (1993) 680,000. Mining and quarrying (1995): kaolin 211,182; bauxite 184,433; iron ore 181,972; copper concentrates 87,728; tin concentrates 6,400. Manufacturing (1994): cement 9,928,000; refined sugar 1,002,000; wheat flour 673,000; fertilizer 292,000; plywood 2,958,000 cu m; radio receivers 36,310,000 units; automotive tires 10,156,000 units. Construction (completed; 1986)[3]: residential 8,809,100 sq m; nonresidential 959,900 sq m. Energy production (consumption): electricity (kW-hr; 1993) 35,579,000,000 (35,554,000,000); coal (metric tons; 1993) 260,000 (2,081,000); crude petroleum (barrels; 1993) 233,685,000 (82,477,000); petroleum products (metric tons; 1993) 11,089,000 (15,732,000); natural gas (cu m; 1993) 21,399,000,000 (6,150,000,000).

Gross national product (1994): U.S.$68,674,000,000 (U.S.$3,520 per capita).

Structure of gross domestic product and labour force				
	1995		1993	
	in value RM '000,000[4]	% of total value	labour force	% of labour force
Agriculture	16,721	13.9	1,580,000	20.7
Mining	8,851	7.3	35,000	0.4
Manufacturing	39,895	33.1	1,766,000	23.1
Construction	5,287	4.4	550,000	7.2
Public utilities	2,820	2.3	...	...
Transp. and commun.	8,787	7.3	342,000	4.5
Trade	14,635	12.2	...	...
Finance	12,884	10.7	315,000	4.1
Pub. admin., defense	11,463	9.5	862,000	11.3
Services	2,436	2.0	1,920,000[5]	25.1[5]
Other	−3,290[6]	−2.7[6]	276,000	3.6
TOTAL	120,489	100.0	7,646,000	100.0

Public debt (external, outstanding; 1994): U.S.$13,751,000,000.
Population economically active (1995): total 8,060,000; activity rate 40.1% (participation rates: ages 15–64 [1990] 66.5%; female [1990] 35.5%; unemployed 2.8%).

Price index (1990 = 100)							
	1989	1990	1991	1992	1993	1994	1995
Consumer price index	97.4	100.0	104.4	109.3	113.2	117.4	123.6

Household income and expenditure. Average household size (1991) 4.9; annual income per household (1987) RM 12,890 (U.S.$5,120); sources of income: n.a.; expenditure (1983): food 28.7%, transportation 20.9%, recreation and education 11.0%, housing 10.2%, household durable goods 7.7%, clothing and footwear 4.3%, health 2.5%.
Land use (1994): forested 67.9%; meadows and pastures 0.9%; agricultural and under permanent cultivation 23.1%; other 8.1%.

Foreign trade[7]

Balance of trade (current prices)						
	1990	1991	1992	1993	1994	1995
RM '000,000	+7,947	+3,165	+11,446	+15,095	+12,628	+8,794
% of total	5.3%	1.7%	5.9%	6.6%	4.3%	2.4%

Imports (1994): RM 155,919,400,000 (machinery and transport equipment 60.1%; basic manufactured goods 13.9%; chemicals 6.8%; food 4.3%; mineral fuels 2.6%; inedible crude materials 2.4%). *Major import sources:* Japan 26.7%; U.S. 16.7%; Singapore 14.1%; Taiwan 5.1%; Germany 4.2%; U.K. 3.2%; South Korea 3.2%; Australia 3.0%.
Exports (1994): RM 153,688,400,000 (machinery and transport equipment 53.5%; basic manufactures 9.1%; inedible crude materials 7.5%; mineral fuels 7.3%; animal and vegetable oils 6.8%; food, beverages, and tobacco 2.9%). *Major export destinations:* U.S. 21.2%; Singapore 20.7%; Japan 11.9%; Hong Kong 4.6%; U.K. 3.8%; Thailand 3.8%; Germany 3.3%.

Transport and communications

Transport. Railroads (1993): track length 2,222 km; passenger-km 1,848,000,-000[8]; metric ton-km cargo 1,380,000,000[8]. Roads (1994): total length 92,443 km (paved 75%). Vehicles (1994): passenger cars 2,291,199; trucks and buses 501,096. Merchant marine (1992): vessels (100 gross tons and over) 552; total deadweight tonnage 2,916,315. Air transport (1995): passenger-km 22,558,000,000; metric ton-km cargo 1,160,036,000; airports (1996) 36.
Communications. Daily newspapers (1992): total number 39; circulation 2,200,000; circulation per 1,000 population 117. Radio (1995): 7,460,000 receivers (1 per 2.7 persons). Television (1995): 9,400,000 receivers (1 per 2.1 persons). Telephones (main lines; 1993): 2,410,700 (1 per 7.9 persons).

Education and health

Education (1993)				
	schools	teachers	students	student/ teacher ratio
Primary (age 7–12)	6,968	134,579	2,718,906	20.2
Secondary (age 13–19)	1,336[9]	77,149[9]	1,531,893	18.1[9]
Voc., teacher tr.	75[9]	3,489[9]	40,944	9.5[9]
Higher	54[9]	11,471[10]	136,000[10]	11.9[10]

Educational attainment (1980). Percentage of population age 25 and over having: no formal schooling 36.6%; primary education 42.1%; secondary 19.4%; higher 1.9%. *Literacy* (1995): total population age 15 and over literate 83.5%; males literate 89.1%; females literate 78.1%.
Health (1994): physicians (1993) 8,279 (1 per 2,301 persons); hospital beds 33,-261 (1 per 586 persons); infant mortality rate per 1,000 live births (1996) 12.
Food (1992): daily per capita caloric intake 2,888 (vegetable products 84%, animal products 16%); 130% of FAO recommended minimum.

Military

Total active duty personnel (1996): 114,500 (army 78.6%, navy 10.5%, air force 10.9%). *Military expenditure as percentage of GDP* (1994): 3.2% (world 3.0%); per capita expenditure U.S.$109.

[1]Includes 40 appointees of the Paramount Ruler; the remaining 30 are indirectly elected at different times. [2]Preliminary results. [3]Results of the Central Bank Survey of four major towns: Kuala Lumpur, Shah Alam, Kelang, and Seberang Prai. [4]At constant prices of 1978. [5]Includes data for Public utilities and Trade. [6]Net bank service charges. [7]Import figures are f.o.b. in balance of trade. [8]Peninsular Malaysia and Singapore. [9]1992. [10]1991.

Maldives

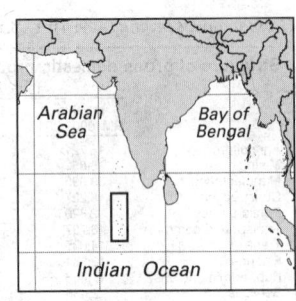

Official name: Divehi Jumhuriyya (Republic of Maldives).
Form of government: republic with one legislative house (Majlis[1] [48[2]]).
Head of state and government: President.
Capital: Male'.
Official language: Divehi.
Official religion: Islam.
Monetary unit: 1 Maldivian rufiyaa (Rf) = 100 laari; valuation (Oct. 11, 1996) 1 U.S.$ = Rf 11.77; 1 £ = Rf 18.54.

Area and population[3]

Administrative atolls	Capitals	area sq mi	area sq km	population 1990 census
North Thiladhunmathi (Haa-Alifu)	Dhidhdhoo	...	...	12,031
South Thiladhunmathi (Haa-Dhaalu)	Nolhivaranfaru	...	...	12,890
North Miladhunmadulu (Shaviyani)	Farukolhu-funadhoo	...	...	9,022
South Miladhunmadulu (Noonu)	Manadhoo	...	...	8,437
North Maalhosmadulu (Raa)	Ugoofaaru	...	...	11,303
South Maalhosmadulu (Baa)	Eydhafushi	...	...	7,716
Faadhippolhu (Lhaviyani)	Naifaru	...	...	7,224
Male' (Kaafu)	Thulusdhoo	...	...	6,726
Ari Atoll Uthuru Gofi (Alifu)	Rasdhoo	...	...	3,998
Ari Atoll Dhekunu Gofi (Alifu)	Mahibadhoo	...	...	5,029
Felidhu Atoll (Vaavu)	Felidhoo	...	...	1,579
Mulakatholhu (Meemu)	Muli	...	...	4,186
North Nilandhe Atoll (Faafu)	Magoodhoo	...	...	2,614
South Nilandhe Atoll (Dhaalu)	Kudahuvadhoo	...	...	4,199
Kolhumadulu (Thaa)	Veymandoo	...	...	8,189
Hadhdhunmathi (Laamu)	Hithadhoo	...	...	9,101
North Huvadhu Atoll (Gaafu-Alifu)	Viligili	...	...	7,295
South Huvadhu Atoll (Gaafu-Dhaalu)	Thinadhoo	...	...	10,417
Foammulah (Gnyaviyani)	Foahmulah	...	...	6,160
Addu Atoll (Seenu)	Hithadhoo	...	...	15,177
Male'		...	...	55,130
TOTAL		115	298	213,215[4]

Demography

Population (1996): 266,000.
Density (1996): persons per sq mi 2,313, persons per sq km 892.6.
Urban-rural (1996): urban 27.0%; rural 73.0%.
Sex distribution (1995): male 51.16%; female 48.84%.
Age breakdown (1995): under 15, 46.5%; 15–29, 26.8%; 30–44, 14.2%; 45–59, 7.6%; 60–74, 4.2%; 75 and over, 0.7%.
Population projection: (2000) 286,000; (2010) 345,000.
Doubling time: 22 years.
Ethnic composition: the majority is principally of Sinhalese and Dravidian extraction; Arab, African, and Negrito influences are also present.
Religious affiliation: virtually 100% Sunnī Muslim.
Major cities (1995): Male' 62,973.

Vital statistics

Birth rate per 1,000 population (1996): 39.4 (world avg. 25.0); legitimate, n.a.; illegitimate, n.a.
Death rate per 1,000 population (1996): 7.7 (world avg. 9.3).
Natural increase rate per 1,000 population (1996): 31.7 (world avg. 15.7).
Total fertility rate (avg. births per childbearing woman; 1996): 6.3.
Marriage rate per 1,000 population (1993): 11.7.
Divorce rate per 1,000 population (1993): 6.8.
Life expectancy at birth (1996): male 65.0 years; female 63.0 years.
Major causes of death per 100,000 population (1988): rheumatic fever 106.0; ischemic heart diseases 65.0; bronchitis, emphysema, and asthma 61.0; tetanus 23.5; tuberculosis 13.0; accidents and suicide 10.0.

National economy

Budget (1996). Revenue: Rf 1,968,900,000 (taxation 36.3%, nontax revenue 31.8%, loans for development 20.2%, foreign aid 11.1%). Expenditures: Rf 1,968,900,000 (social services 34.8%, social development 31.6%, economic development 23.9%).
Production (metric tons except as noted). Agriculture, forestry, fishing (1995): vegetables and melons 23,900, coconuts 13,000, fruits (excluding melons) 9,650, roots and tubers (including cassava, sweet potatoes, and yams) 7,760, copra (1994) 2,000; fish catch (1993) 89,938. Mining and quarrying: coral for construction materials. Manufacturing: details, n.a.; however, major industries include boat building and repairing, coir yarn and mat weaving, coconut and fish processing, lacquerwork, garment manufacturing, and handicrafts. Construction: n.a. Energy production (consumption): electricity (kW-hr; 1993) 40,000,000 (40,000,000); coal, none (n.a.); petroleum products (metric tons; 1993) none (35,000); natural gas, none (n.a.).
Tourism (1994): receipts from visitors U.S.$181,000,000; expenditures by nationals abroad U.S.$32,000,000.
Population economically active (1990): total 56,435; activity rate of total population 26.5% (participation rates: ages 15–64, 50.2%; female 19.9%; unemployed 0.9%).
Household income and expenditure (1990). Average household size 7.1; annual income per household Rf 2,616 (U.S.$274), sources of income: n.a.; expenditure (1981)[5]: food and beverages 61.8%, housing equipment 17.0%, clothing 8.0%, recreation and education 5.9%, transportation 2.6%, health 2.5%, rent 1.6%.

Public debt (external, outstanding; 1994): U.S.$125,800,000.
Gross national product (at current market prices; 1994): U.S.$221,000,000 (U.S.$900 per capita).

Structure of gross domestic product and labour force

	1994 in value Rf '000[6]	1994 % of total value	1990 labour force	1990 % of labour force
Agriculture[7]	250,700	19.8	14,117	25.0
Mining	22,300	1.8	496	0.9
Manufacturing	78,600	6.2	8,441	15.0
Public utilities			445	0.8
Construction	115,900	9.1	3,151	5.6
Transportation and communications	84,100	6.6	5,321	9.4
Trade	242,700	19.1	8,884	15.7
Finance	...	...	1,058	1.9
Public administration, defense	114,800	9.1	11,848	21.0
Services	359,500	28.3		
Other	...	...	2,674	4.7
TOTAL	1,268,600	100.0	56,435	100.0

Land use (1994): forested 3.3%; meadows and pastures 3.3%; agricultural and under permanent cultivation 10.0%; built-on, wasteland, and other 83.4%.

Foreign trade[8]

Balance of trade (current prices)

	1990	1991	1992	1993	1994	1995
U.S.$'000,000	−65.0	−83.3	−126.6	−133.7	−149.2	−186.1
% of total	38.4%	43.7%	61.3%	65.9%	61.9%	65.3%

Imports (1993): Rf 2,096,704,000 (consumer products 50.4%, intermediate and capital goods 36.8%, petroleum products 12.8%). *Major import sources:* Singapore 51.8%; India 8.6%; Sri Lanka 6.7%; United Arab Emirates 6.5%; Japan 3.9%; Thailand 3.3%.
Exports (1993): Rf 377,397,000 (canned tuna 26.9%, frozen skipjack tuna 21.4%, apparel and clothing 15.9%, fish meal 3.4%). *Major export destinations:* Sri Lanka 30.3%; United Kingdom 24.5%; Thailand 13.9%; United States 11.3%; Germany 5.9%; Japan 4.1%.

Transport and communications

Transport. Railroads: none. Roads: total length, n.a. Vehicles (1993): passenger cars 823; trucks and buses 869. Merchant marine (1992): vessels (100 gross tons and over) 44; total deadweight tonnage 78,994. Air transport (1993): passenger arrivals 348,853, passenger departures 344,061; cargo loaded 2,756 metric tons, cargo unloaded 7,216 metric tons; airports (1996) with scheduled flights 5.
Communications. Daily newspapers (1993): total number 2; total circulation 4,300; circulation per 1,000 population 18. Radio (1995): total number of receivers 25,000 (1 per 10 persons). Television (1995): total number of receivers 4,750 (1 per 53 persons). Telephones (1992): 8,523 (1 per 27 persons).

Education and health

Education (1986)

	schools	teachers	students	student/ teacher ratio
Primary (age 6–11)	243	1,138	41,812	36.7
Secondary (age 11–18)	9	291	3,581	12.3
Voc., teacher tr.	10	52	462	8.9
Higher	—	—	—	

Educational attainment (1990). Percentage of population age 15 and over having: no standard passed 25.6%; primary standard 37.2%; middle standard 25.9%; secondary standard 6.3%; preuniversity 3.4%; higher 0.4%; not stated 1.2%. *Literacy* (1985): total population age 15 and over literate 90,189 (90.4%); males literate 47,412 (90.6%); females literate 42,777 (90.1%).
Health (1993): physicians 45 (1 per 5,297 persons); hospital beds 200 (1 per 1,192 persons); infant mortality rate per 1,000 live births (1996) 52.
Food (1992): daily per capita caloric intake 2,580 (vegetable products 80%, animal products 20%); 117% of FAO recommended minimum requirement.

Military

Total active duty personnel: Maldives maintains a single security force numbering about 700–1,000; it performs both army and police functions.

[1]Also known or translated as Citizens' Majlis, Citizens' Council, or Citizens' Assembly. [2]Includes 8 nonelective seats. [3]Maldives is divided into 20 administrative districts corresponding to atoll groups; arrangement shown here is from north to south. Total area excludes 34,634 sq mi (89,702 sq km) of tidal waters. [4]Includes 4,792 people in resort and industrial islands. [5]Weights of consumer price index components. [6]At 1985 prices. [7]Primarily fishing. [8]Import figures are f.o.b. in balance of trade and c.i.f. for commodities and trading partners.

Mali

Official name: République du Mali (Republic of Mali).
Form of government: multiparty[1] republic with one legislative house (National Assembly [116]).
Chief of state: President.
Head of government: Prime Minister.
Capital: Bamako.
Official language: French.
Official religion: none.
Monetary unit: 1 CFA franc (CFAF) = 100 centimes; valuation (Oct. 11, 1996) 1 U.S.$ = CFAF 518.24; 1 £ = CFAF 816.38.

Area and population		area		population
				1995
Regions	Capitals	sq mi	sq km	estimate
Gao	Gao	65,858	170,572	408,000[2]
Kayes	Kayes	46,233	119,743	1,245,000
Kidal	Kidal	58,467	151,430	[2]
Koulikoro	Koulikoro	37,007	95,848	1,462,000
Mopti	Mopti	30,509	79,017	1,423,000
Ségou	Ségou	25,028	64,821	1,579,000
Sikasso	Sikasso	27,135	70,280	1,521,000
Tombouctou	Timbuktu (Tombouctou)	191,743	496,611	462,000
District				
Bamako	Bamako	97	252	913,000
TOTAL		482,077	1,248,574	9,013,000

Demography

Population (1996): 9,204,000.
Density (1996): persons per sq mi 19.1, persons per sq km 7.4.
Urban-rural (1995): urban 26.1%; rural 73.9%.
Sex distribution (1995): male 48.87%; female 51.13%.
Age breakdown (1991): under 15, 48.3%; 15–29, 22.5%; 30–44, 14.3%; 45–59, 8.8%; 60–74, 4.9%; 75 and over, 1.2%.
Population projection: (2000) 10,008,000; (2010) 12,338,000.
Doubling time: 22 years.
Linguistic composition (1987): Bambara-Malinké-Dyula (-Dioula) 50.3%; Fulani (Peulh-Foulfoulbe) 10.7%; Dogon-Kado 6.9%; Songhaï-Djerma 6.3%; Soninké-Marka 6.3%; Tamashek-Bella (Berber) 4.2%; Minianka 3.9%; Senufo 2.4%; Bwa- (Bobo-) Dafing 2.3%; Bozo-Somono 2.0%; other 4.7%.
Religious affiliation (1983): Muslim 90%; traditional beliefs 9%; Christian 1%.
Major cities (1987): Bamako 913,000[3]; Ségou 88,877; Mopti 73,979; Sikasso 73,050; Gao 54,874.

Vital statistics

Birth rate per 1,000 population (1995): 51.9 (world avg. 25.0); legitimate, n.a.; illegitimate, n.a.
Death rate per 1,000 population (1995): 19.9 (world avg. 9.3).
Natural increase rate per 1,000 population (1995): 32.0 (world avg. 15.7).
Total fertility rate (avg. births per childbearing woman; 1995): 7.3.
Marriage rate per 1,000 population: n.a.
Divorce rate per 1,000 population: n.a.
Life expectancy at birth (1995): male 44.7 years; female 48.1 years.
Major causes of death per 100,000 population: n.a.; morbidity ([notified cases of illness] by cause as a percentage of all reported infectious disease; 1985): malaria 62.1%; measles 10.3%; amebiasis 10.3%; syphilis and gonococcal infections 6.0%; influenza 4.9%; other principal causes in 1989 included polio and conditions originating in the perinatal period.

National economy

Budget (1996). Revenue: CFAF 250,500,000,000 (fiscal receipts 59.4%, nonfiscal receipts 8.0%). Expenditures: CFAF 319,900,000,000 (current expenditure 43.8%; capital expenditure 51.3%).
Public debt (external, outstanding; 1994): U.S.$2,623,000,000.
Tourism (1993): receipts from visitors U.S.$18,000,000; expenditures by nationals abroad U.S.$54,000,000.
Population economically active (1987): total 3,437,489; activity rate of total population 44.7% (participation rates: ages 15–64, 67.4%; female 37.4%; unemployed 0.8%).

Price and earnings indexes (1990 = 100)							
	1989	1990	1991	1992	1993	1994	1995[4]
Consumer price index	99.4	100.0	101.8	95.4	95.2	117.3	137.0
Hourly earnings index[5]	100.0	100.0	100.0	100.0	100.0	100.0	...

Production (metric tons except as noted). Agriculture, forestry, fishing (1995): millet 815,052, sorghum 807,314, rice 426,595, seed cotton 347,473, corn (maize) 286,076, peanuts (groundnuts) 144,305, sweet potatoes 10,000; livestock (number of live animals) 12,553,000 goats and sheep, 5,542,000 cattle, 611,000 asses, 260,000 camels, 101,000 horses, 63,000 pigs; roundwood (1994) 6,306,000 cu m; fish catch (1993) 64,354. Mining and quarrying (1994): limestone 10,000[6]; gypsum 700; gold 5,700 kg; silver 200 kg. Manufacturing (1995): sugar 34,213; cement 11,197; soap 10,097; soft drinks 68,609 hectolitres; beer 41,690 hectolitres; shoes 111,000 pairs; cigarettes 114,928 cartons. Construction: n.a. Energy production (consumption): electricity (kW-hr; 1993) 330,000,000 (330,000,000); coal, none (n.a.); crude petroleum,

none (n.a.); petroleum products (metric tons; 1993) none (146,000); natural gas, none (n.a.).
Gross national product (at current market prices; 1994): U.S.$2,421,000,000 (U.S.$250 per capita).

Structure of gross domestic product and labour force				
	1995		1987	
	in value CFAF '000,000	% of total value	labour force	% of labour force
Agriculture	440,950	40.5	2,802,722	82.2
Mining	34,143	3.1	1,524	—
Manufacturing	69,791	6.4	186,243	5.5
Construction	58,678	5.4	13,065	0.4
Public utilities	11,951	1.1	3,157	0.1
Transp. and commun.	45,742	4.2	6,174	0.2
Trade	209,765	19.3	158,892	4.7
Finance	9,222	0.9	320	—
Pub. admin., defense	62,515	5.8	158,704	4.6
Services	78,829	7.2	...	...
Other	66,378[7]	6.1[7]	78,470	2.3
TOTAL	1,087,964	100.0	3,409,271	100.0

Household income and expenditure. Average household size (1987) 5.6; average annual income per household: n.a.; sources of income: n.a.; expenditure (1986–87)[3, 8]: food 54.6%, clothing 14.2%, transportation and communications 11.9%, housing and energy 8.7%, household durable goods 4.2%.
Land use (1993): forested 5.7%; meadows and pastures 24.6%; agricultural and under permanent cultivation 2.0%; other 67.7%.

Foreign trade[9]

Balance of trade (current prices)					
	1989	1990	1991	1992	1993
CFAF '000,000,000	−24.9	−25.6	−26.1	−39.3	−32.1
% of total	12.6%	12.2%	11.5%	18.4%	14.3%

Imports (1994): CFAF 334,400,000,000 (machinery, appliances, and transport equipment 32.0%; food products 12.5%; chemicals 10.1%; construction products 10.1%; petroleum products 9.6%). *Major import sources:* Norway 28.1%; Côte d'Ivoire 18.3%; France 8.4%; Senegal 4.4%; Hong Kong 2.1%; Belgium-Luxembourg 2.1%; United States 1.7%; United Kingdom 1.4%; Germany 1.3%; Japan 1.2%; Italy 0.8%; The Netherlands 0.7%; Morocco 0.6%.
Exports (1994): CFAF 177,500,000,000 (raw cotton and cotton products 47.8%; live animals 29.2%; gold 15.7%). *Major export destinations:* Norway 28.8%; Thailand 18.3%; Brazil 13.7%; Ireland 9.6%; Belgium-Luxembourg 5.8%; China 2.2%; France 1.9%; Tunisia 1.4%; Côte d'Ivoire 1.1%; Spain 1.1%; Germany 1.1%; Japan 1.1%; United States 1.1%.

Transport and communications

Transport. Railroads (1994): route length 399 mi, 642 km; passenger-mi 304,155,000, passenger-km 489,491,000; short ton-mi cargo 187,176,000, metric ton-km cargo 273,273,000. Roads (1994): total length 9,321 mi, 15,000 km (paved 17%). Vehicles (1994): passenger cars 21,000; trucks and buses 8,600. Merchant marine: vessels (100 gross tons and over) none. Air transport (1993): passenger-mi 134,932,000, passenger-km 217,154,000; short ton-mi cargo 23,428,000, metric ton-km cargo 34,204,000; airports (1996) with scheduled flights 1.
Communications. Daily newspapers (1994): total number 1; total circulation 40,000; circulation per 1,000 population 4.5. Radio (1995): total number of receivers 1,600,000 (1 per 5.6 persons). Television (1995): total number of receivers 10,000 (1 per 901 persons). Telephones (main lines; 1993): 13,800 (1 per 639 persons).

Education and health

Education (1991–92)	schools	teachers	students	student/ teacher ratio
Primary (age 6–14)	1,514	7,963	375,131	47.1
Secondary (age 15–17)	307[11]	5,798	88,529	15.3
Higher	7[12]	701	6,703	9.6

Educational attainment (1987). Percentage of population age 6 and over having: no formal schooling 86.0%; primary education 12.5%; secondary 1.2%; postsecondary and higher 0.3%. *Literacy* (1987): percentage of total population age 6 and over literate 1,116,019 (18.8%); males literate 767,981 (26.7%); females literate 348,038 (11.4%).
Health: physicians (1988) 435 (1 per 18,046 persons); hospital beds (1987) 3,430 (1 per 2,253 persons); infant mortality rate per 1,000 live births (1995) 105.
Food (1992): daily per capita caloric intake 2,278 (vegetable products 91%, animal products 9%); 97% of FAO recommended minimum requirement.

Military

Total active duty personnel (1995): 7,350 (army 93.9%, navy 0.7%, air force 5.4%). *Military expenditure as percentage of GNP* (1994): 1.9% (world 3.0%); per capita expenditure U.S.$4.

---

[1]Multiparty legislative elections of February–March 1992 were boycotted by most opposition parties. [2]Population of Gao region includes Kidal region, established on May 15, 1991. Separate data not available. [3]1995 estimate. [4]Third quarter. [5]Minimum hourly wages of industrial workers. [6]1990. [7]Less imputed bank service charges. [8]Weights of consumer price index components. [9]Import figures are f.o.b. in balance of trade and c.i.f. in commodities and trading partners. [10]Air Afrique only. [11]Excludes vocational. [12]1990–91.

Malta

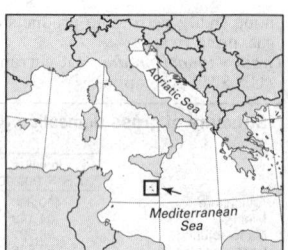

Official name: Malta (Maltese); Malta (English).
Form of government: unitary multiparty republic with one legislative house (House of Representatives [69[1]]).
Chief of state: President.
Head of government: Prime Minister.
Capital: Valletta.
Official languages: Maltese; English.
Official religion: Roman Catholicism.
Monetary unit: 1 Maltese lira (Lm) = 100 cents = 1,000 mils; valuation[2] (Oct. 11, 1996) 1 U.S.$ = Lm 0.36; 1 £ = Lm 0.57.

Area and population	area		population
			1995[4]
Census regions[3]	sq mi	sq km	estimate
Gozo and Comino	27	70	27,545
Inner Harbour	6	15	102,571
Northern	30	78	36,457
Outer Harbour	12	32	107,108
South Eastern	20	53	47,437
Western	27	69	48,333
TOTAL	122	316[5]	369,451

Demography

Population (1996): 372,000.
Density (1996): persons per sq mi 3,049, persons per sq km 1,177.
Urban-rural (1995): urban 89.3%; rural 10.7%.
Sex distribution (1995[4]): male 49.49%; female 50.51%.
Age breakdown (1995[4]): under 15, 22.0%; 15–29, 21.2%; 30–44, 23.1%; 45–59, 18.3%; 60–74, 11.5%; 75 and over, 3.9%.
Population projection: (2000) 380,000; (2010) 393,000.
Doubling time: 120 years.
Ethnic composition (by nationality; 1990): Maltese 95.7%; British 2.1%; other 2.2%.
Religious affiliation (1992): Roman Catholic 98.6%; other 1.4%.
Major cities (1995[4]): Birkirkara 21,903; Qormi 20,055; Hamrun 13,637; Sliema 13,505; Valletta 9,129.

Vital statistics

Birth rate per 1,000 population (1994): 13.1 (world avg. 25.0); legitimate 97.1%; illegitimate 2.9%.
Death rate per 1,000 population (1994): 7.3 (world avg. 9.3).
Natural increase rate per 1,000 population (1994): 5.8 (world avg. 15.7).
Total fertility rate (avg. births per childbearing woman; 1990–95): 2.1.
Marriage rate per 1,000 population (1994): 6.7.
Divorce rate per 1,000 population: n.a.
Life expectancy at birth (1994): male 74.9 years; female 79.1 years.
Major causes of death per 100,000 population (1994): diseases of the circulatory system 324.2; malignant neoplasms (cancers) 188.9; diseases of the respiratory system 63.6; diseases of the digestive system 32.6; accidents, poisoning, and violence 25.5; endocrine, nutritional, and metabolic diseases of the blood and blood-forming organs 25.5.

National economy

Budget (1996). Revenue: Lm 461,010,000 (indirect taxes 42.5%; direct taxes 35.6%; nontax revenue 18.7%; foreign grants 3.2%). Expenditures: Lm 515,025,000 (recurrent expenditures 84.3%, of which social security 23.9%, health 8.4%, education 6.0%, debt service 4.8%, defense 2.0%; capital expenditure 15.7%).
Public debt (1995): U.S.$1,163,100,000.
Production (wholesale value in Lm except where noted). Agriculture, forestry, fishing (1994): vegetables 5,768,176 (of which tomatoes 920,476, melons 804,672, lettuce 372,005, cauliflower 350,364, carrots 299,257, onions 263,247), fruits 765,537 (of which strawberries 239,994, grapes 113,448, peaches 104,108), potatoes 465,488; livestock (number of live animals; 1996) 103,000 pigs, 18,500 cattle, 17,600 sheep, 9,183 goats, 810,000 chickens; fish catch 1,089,188. Quarrying (1992): 4,344,000. Manufacturing (value of sales in Lm; 1994–95): machinery and transport equipment 402,993,000, of which transport equipment 3,171,000; food and beverages 103,733,000; textiles and wearing apparel 80,813,000; paper and printing 40,610,000; chemicals 35,151,000; metal manufacture 14,503,000. Construction (buildings completed; 1995): residential 3,168[6]; nonresidential 1,533. Energy production (consumption): electricity (kW-hr; 1994) 1,500,000,000 (1,500,000,000); coal (metric tons; 1994) none (300,000); crude petroleum, none (n.a.); petroleum products (metric tons; 1994) none (320,000); natural gas, none (n.a.).
Population economically active (1995): total 143,002; activity rate of total population 38.6% (participation rates: ages 15–64 [1985] 45.9%; female 27.4%; unemployed 3.5%).

Price and earnings indexes (1990 = 100)							
	1989	1990	1991	1992	1993	1994	1995
Consumer price index	97.1	100.0	102.5	104.2	108.5	113.0	117.5
Average weekly earnings	97.9	100.0	109.8	114.6	120.5	125.8	129.9

Household income and expenditure. Average household size (1985) 3.3; average annual income per household (1982) Lm 4,736 (U.S.$11,399); sources of income (1993): wages and salaries 63.8%, professional and unincorporated

enterprises 19.3%, rents, dividends, and interest 16.9%; expenditure (1993): food and beverages 27.9%, transportation and communications 15.7%, household furnishings and operations 9.5%, recreation, entertainment, and education 7.2%, clothing and footwear 6.9%, housing 5.5%, health 3.3%, tobacco 2.6%.
Tourism (1994): receipts from visitors U.S.$639,000,000; expenditures by nationals abroad U.S.$176,000,000.
Gross national product (1992): U.S.$2,606,000,000 (U.S.$7,210 per capita).

Structure of gross domestic product and labour force				
	1994		1995	
	in value Lm '000	% of total value	labour force	% of labour force
Agriculture	25,100	2.8	2,834	2.0
Manufacturing	215,100	24.0 }	35,063	24.5
Mining }	29,600	3.3 }	5,874	4.1
Construction }				
Public utilities	69,000	7.7	...	...
Transportation and communications	62,700	7.0	11,509	8.0
Trade	7	7	25,113[8]	17.6[8]
Finance	7	7	3,616	2.5
Pub. admin., defense	146,100	16.3	32,319	22.6
Services	348,700[7]	38.9[7]	17,291	12.1
Other	...	...	9,383[9]	6.6[9]
TOTAL	896,300	100.0	143,002	100.0

Land use (1993): agricultural and under permanent cultivation 40.6%; other (infertile clay soil with underlying limestone) 59.4%.

Foreign trade[10]

Balance of trade (current prices)						
	1989	1990	1991	1992	1993	1994
Lm '000,000	−169.0	−172.8	−214.5	−182.9	−229.5	−226.9
% of total	22.3%	18.3%	21.1%	15.7%	18.2%	16.2%

Imports (1995): Lm 1,042,516,000 (machinery and transport equipment 51.1%, manufactured and semimanufactured goods 24.5%, food and live animals 8.4%, chemicals and chemical products 6.8%, mineral fuels 4.3%, nonfuel materials 1.4%, beverages and tobacco 1.3%). *Major import sources* (1994): Italy 26.5%; Germany 17.6%; U.K. 15.3%; France 8.4%; U.S. 5.1%.
Exports (1995): Lm 672,325,000 (machinery and transport equipment 63.0%, manufactured and semimanufactured goods 26.7%, reexports 6.9%, chemicals 1.8%, food and live animals 1.2%, beverages and tobacco 0.2%). *Major export destinations* (1994): Italy 37.5%; Germany 14.2%; France 9.9%; U.S. 7.6%; U.K. 7.4%; Libya 3.6%.

Transport and communications

Transport. Railroads: none. Roads (1994): total length 997 mi, 1,604 km (paved 94%). Vehicles (1994): passenger cars 163,310; trucks and buses 27,978[11]. Merchant marine (1992): vessels (100 gross tons and over) 889; total deadweight tonnage 17,073,207. Air transport (1993): passenger-mi 776,940,000, passenger-km 1,250,370,000; short ton-mi cargo 5,006,000, metric ton-km cargo 7,308,000; airports (1996) with scheduled flights 1.
Communications. Daily newspapers (1993): total number 3; total circulation 68,000; circulation per 1,000 population 186. Radio (1995): 90,000 receivers (1 per 4.1 persons). Television (1995): 160,000 receivers (1 per 2.3 persons). Telephones (main lines; 1993): 157,500 (1 per 2.3 persons).

Education and health

Education (1995–96)				student/
	schools	teachers	students	teacher ratio
Primary (age 5–10)	111	1,990	35,479	17.8
Secondary (age 11–17)	59	2,679	29,907	20.9
Voc., teacher tr.	22	541	4,539	8.4
Higher[12]	1	284	3,679	13.0

Educational attainment (1967). Percentage of economically active population having: no formal schooling 10.8%; primary education 60.4%; lower secondary 3.4%; upper secondary 17.6%; technical secondary 3.9%; post-secondary and higher 3.9%. *Literacy* (1985): total population age 15 and over literate 250,419 (96.0%); males literate 121,899 (96.2%); females literate 128,520 (95.9%).
Health (1995): physicians 910 (1 per 407 persons); hospital beds 2,152 (1 per 172 persons); infant mortality rate per 1,000 live births (1994) 9.1.
Food (1992): daily per capita caloric intake 3,468 (vegetable products 75%, animal products 25%); 140% of FAO recommended minimum requirement.

Military

Total active duty personnel (1996): 1,950 (army 100%). *Military expenditure as percentage of GNP* (1993): 0.9% (world 3.2%); per capita expenditure U.S.$63.

---

[1]Normally a 65-member body; however, in the elections of Oct. 26, 1996, 4 additional seats were awarded to the minority party (by seats won), which had obtained a majority of the popular vote. [2]The Maltese lira is tied to the currencies of several principal trading partners. [3]Data are reported according to census regions as of January 1993; in late 1993 new administrative districts (Local Councils) were created. [4]January 1. [5]Detail does not add to total given because of rounding. [6]Dwellings completed. [7]Services includes Trade and Finance. [8]Includes hotels and catering. [9]Includes 4,956 unemployed. [10]Import figures are f.o.b. in balance of trade and c.i.f. for commodities and trading partners. [11]1992. [12]1992–93.

Marshall Islands

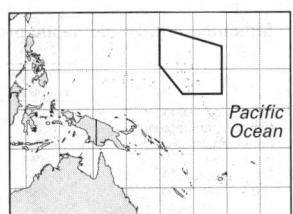

Official name: Majōl (Marshallese); Republic of the Marshall Islands (English).
Form of government: unitary republic with two legislative houses (Council of Iroij [12][1]; Nitijela [33]).
Head of state and government: President.
Capital: Majuro (Dalap-Uliga-Darrit).
Official languages: Marshallese (Kajin-Majōl); English.
Official religion: none.
Monetary unit: 1 U.S. dollar (U.S.$) = 100 cents; valuation (Oct. 11, 1996) 1 £ = U.S.$1.58.

Area and population

Election districts	area sq mi	area sq km	population 1988 census
Ailinglaplap	5.67	14.68	1,715
Ailuk	2.07	5.36	488
Arno	5.00	12.95	1,656
Aur	2.17	5.62	438
Bikini	2.32	6.01	10
Ebon	2.22	5.75	741
Enewetak	2.26	5.85	715
Jabat	0.22	0.57	112
Jaluit	4.38	11.34	1,709
Kili	0.36	0.93	602
Kwajalein	6.33	16.39	9,311
Lae	0.56	1.45	319
Lib	0.36	0.93	115
Likiep	3.96	10.26	482
Majuro	3.75	9.71	19,664
Maloelap	3.75	9.71	796
Mejit	0.72	1.86	445
Mili	6.15	15.93	854
Namorik	1.07	2.77	814
Namu	2.42	6.27	801
Rongelap	3.07	7.95	0
Ujae	0.72	1.86	448
Ujelang	0.67	1.74	0
Utrik	0.94	2.43	409
Wotho	1.67	4.32	90
Wotje	3.16	8.18	646
Other atolls	4.10	10.62	0
TOTAL	70.07	181.48[2]	43,380

Demography

Population (1996): 58,500.
Density (1996): persons per sq mi 834.8, persons per sq km 322.3.
Urban-rural (1988): urban 64.5%; rural 35.5%.
Sex distribution (1995): male 50.98%; female 49.02%.
Age breakdown (1995): under 15, 50.4%; 15–29, 25.6%; 30–44, 14.0%; 45–59, 6.3%; 60–74, 2.9%; 75 and over, 0.8%.
Population projection: (2000) 68,400; (2010) 100,000.
Doubling time: 18 years.
Ethnic composition (nationality; 1988): Marshallese 96.9%; other Pacific islanders 1.7%; Filipino 0.5%; all other 0.9%.
Religious affiliation (1973): Protestant 90.1%; Roman Catholic 8.5%; other 1.4%.
Major cities (1988): Majuro (Dalap-Uliga-Darrit) 14,649; Ebeye 8,324; no other urban localities.

Vital statistics

Birth rate per 1,000 population (1993): 46.6 (world avg. 25.0).
Death rate per 1,000 population (1993): 7.9 (world avg. 9.3).
Natural increase rate per 1,000 population (1993): 38.7 (world avg. 15.7).
Total fertility rate (avg. births per childbearing woman; 1993): 7.0.
Marriage rate per 1,000 population: n.a.
Divorce rate per 1,000 population: n.a.
Life expectancy at birth (1995): male 61.9 years; female 65.0 years.
Major causes of death per 100,000 population (1990–93)[3]: infectious and parasitic diseases 169.9; circulatory diseases 155.1; respiratory diseases 105.1; malignant neoplasms (cancers) 68.4; digestive diseases 63.3; accidents, injuries, and violence 36.7.

National economy

Budget (1995–96). Revenue: U.S.$80,100,000 (U.S. government grants 59.7%, income tax 9.4%, import tax 8.5%, value-added and excise taxes 6.1%, fishing rights 3.0%, interest income 2.7%). Expenditures: U.S.$77,400,000 (debt service 10.2%, education 9.9%, health services 8.8%, public works and social programs 4.9%, internal security 2.1%).
Production (metric tons except as noted). Agriculture, forestry, fishing (1991): copra 5,545, fruits 1,809 (of which pandanus 836, breadfruit 645, bananas 264, papaya 64), tubers 1,500 (of which taro 1,300, sweet potatoes 182), vegetables 136 (of which cabbage 36, pumpkins 36); livestock (number of live animals; 1994) 12,352 pigs, 59,086 chickens; roundwood, n.a.; fish catch (1993) 300. Mining and quarrying: high-grade phosphate mining on Ailinglaplap Atoll, quarrying of sand and aggregate for local construction only. Manufacturing (1994): copra 4,387; coconut oil and processed (chilled or frozen) fish are important products; the manufacture of handicrafts and personal items (clothing, mats, boats, etc.) by individuals is also significant. Construction (1994): value added U.S.$9,300,000. Energy production

(consumption): electricity (kW-hr; 1994) 57,891,000 (57,891,000); coal, none (n.a.); gasoline, oil, and lubricants (barrels; 1988)[4] n.a. (84,588).
Public debt (external, outstanding; 1994–95): U.S.$141,200,000.
Gross domestic product (1995): U.S.$105,300,000 (U.S.$1,870 per capita).

Structure of gross domestic product and labour force

	1995 in value U.S.$'000	1995 % of total value	1988 labour force	1988 % of labour force
Agriculture	15,700	14.9	2,150	18.7
Mining	300	0.3	2	—
Manufacturing	2,700	2.6	945	8.2
Public utilities	2,100	2.0	82	0.7
Construction	10,700	10.2	1,076	9.4
Transp. and commun.	6,500	6.2	537	4.7
Trade, restaurants, hotels	17,900	17.0	1,394	12.1
Finance, insurance, real estate	17,200	16.3	833	7.3
Public administration } Services	32,000	30.4	3,035	26.4
Other	200[5]	0.2[5]	1,434[6]	12.5[6]
TOTAL	105,300	100.0[2]	11,488	100.0

Land use (1989)[7]: forested 22.5%; meadows and pastures 13.5%; agricultural and under permanent cultivation 33.1%; other 30.9%.
Household income and expenditure. Average household size (1988) 8.7; income per household (1979) U.S.$3,366; sources of income: n.a.; expenditure (1982): food 57.7%, housing 15.6%, clothing 12.0%, personal effects and other 14.7%.
Population economically active (1988): total 11,488; activity rate of total population 26.5% (participation rates: over age 14, 54.1%; female 30.1%; unemployed 12.5%).

Price and earnings indexes (1990 = 100)

	1989	1990	1991	1992	1993	1994	1995
Consumer price index	99.4	100.0	103.4	116.8	119.5	125.6	134.4
Earnings index	...	...	...	...	...	...	...

Tourism (1994): receipts from visitors U.S.$2,000,000; expenditures by nationals abroad, n.a.

Foreign trade

Balance of trade (current prices)

	1990	1991	1992	1993	1994	1995
U.S.$'000,000	−53.9	−53.5	−52.6	−53.4	−49.3	−58.1
% of total	94.0%	90.3%	74.1%	77.7%	52.6%	27.2%

Imports (1995): U.S.$75,100,000 (food, beverages, and tobacco 28.2%, machinery and transport equipment 24.6%, mineral fuels and lubricants 24.0%, manufactured goods 8.9%, chemical products 2.5%). *Major import sources:* U.S. 51.0%; Guam 14.5%; Japan 7.5%; Australia 1.9%; Hong Kong 1.7%.
Exports (1995): U.S.$17,000,000 (chilled fish 38.8%, crude coconut oil 18.2%, pet fish 2.4%). *Major export destinations:* U.S. c. 80.0%; other c. 20.0%.

Transport and communications

Transport. Railroads: none. Roads: n.a. Vehicles (1994): passenger cars 1,418; trucks and buses 193. Merchant marine (1992): vessels (100 gross tons and over) 35; total deadweight tonnage 4,182,356. Air transport (1994): passenger-km 52,000,000[8]; metric ton-km cargo 30,433; airports (1996) with scheduled flights 23.
Communications. Daily newspapers (1993): there are no dailies, only weeklies, of which there are two with a total circulation of over 10,000. Radio (1995): receivers, n.a.; but there are two radio stations. Television (1995): n.a.; but there are two television stations. Telephones (main lines; 1993): 2,300 (1 per 23 persons).

Education and health

Education (1993–94)

	schools	teachers	students	student/ teacher ratio
Primary (age 6–14)	104	833	13,565	16.3
Secondary (age 15–18)	11	138	2,483	18.0
Voc., teacher tr.	...	...	...	...
Higher	...	...	...	...

Educational attainment (1988). Percentage of population age 25 and over having: no grade completed 5.1%; elementary education 43.2%; secondary 39.7%; higher 11.4%; not stated 0.6%. *Literacy* (latest): total population age 15 and over literate 19,377 (91.2%); males literate 9,993 (92.4%); females literate 9,384 (90.0%).
Health (1991): physicians 20 (1 per 2,309 persons); hospital beds (1985) 54 (1 per 698 persons); infant mortality rate per 1,000 live births (1994) 21.6.
Food: daily per capita caloric intake, n.a.

Military

Under the 1984 Compact of Free Association, the United States provides for the defense of the Republic of the Marshall Islands.

---

[1]Council of Iroij is an advisory body only. [2]Detail does not add to total given because of rounding. [3]Registered deaths only. [4]Imports only. [5]Import duties less imputed bank service charges. [6]Includes 1,432 unemployed. [7]Data are for the former Trust Territory of the Pacific Islands. [8]1990.

Martinique

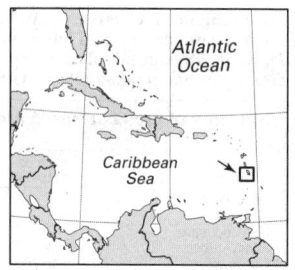

Official name: Département de la Martinique (Department of Martinique).
Political status: overseas department (France) with two legislative houses (General Council [45]; Regional Council [41]).
Chief of state: President of France.
Heads of government: Prefect (for France); President of the General Council (for Martinique); President of the Regional Council (for Martinique).
Capital: Fort-de-France.
Official language: French.
Official religion: none.
Monetary unit: 1 French franc (F) = 100 centimes; valuation (Oct. 11, 1996) 1 U.S.$ = F 5.18; 1 £ = F 8.16.

Area and population

Arrondissements	Capitals	area sq mi	area sq km	population 1990 census
Fort-de-France	Fort-de-France	147	381	187,275
Le Marin	Le Marin	158	409	93,411
La Trinité	La Trinité	131	338	78,893
TOTAL		436	1,128	359,579

Demography

Population (1996): 394,000.
Density (1996): persons per sq mi 903.7, persons per sq km 349.3.
Urban-rural (1995): urban 93.4%; rural 6.6%.
Sex distribution (1995): male 48.55%; female 51.45%.
Age breakdown (1995): under 15, 24.0%; 15–29, 25.8%; 30–44, 22.2%; 45–59, 14.0%; 60–74, 9.8%; 75 and over, 4.2%.
Population projection: (2000) 415,000; (2010) 458,000.
Doubling time: 77 years.
Ethnic composition (1983): mulatto 93.7%; French (metropolitan and Martinique white) 2.6%; East Indian 1.7%; other 2.0%.
Religious affiliation (1994): Roman Catholic 88.4%; other (mostly Seventh-day Adventist, Jehovah's Witness, Hindu, syncretist, and nonreligious) 11.6%.
Major urban areas (1990): Fort-de-France 100,080; Le Lamentin 30,028; Schoelcher 19,825; Sainte-Marie 19,682; Le Robert 17,713.

Vital statistics

Birth rate per 1,000 population (1994): 14.9 (world avg. 25.0); (1992) legitimate 34.1%; illegitimate 65.9%.
Death rate per 1,000 population (1994): 5.8 (world avg. 9.3).
Natural increase rate per 1,000 population (1994): 9.1 (world avg. 15.7).
Total fertility rate (avg. births per childbearing woman; 1993): 1.9.
Marriage rate per 1,000 population (1994): 3.9.
Divorce rate per 1,000 population (1993): 0.9.
Life expectancy at birth (1993): male 74.7 years; female 81.0 years.
Major causes of death per 100,000 population (1991): diseases of the circulatory system 205.5; malignant neoplasms (cancers) 129.0; accidents, poisoning, and violence 53.2; endocrine and metabolic disorders 30.7; diseases of the digestive system 27.1.

National economy

Budget (1994). Revenue: F 1,816,000,000 (general receipts from French central government and local administrative bodies 45.0%; tax receipts 34.0%, of which indirect taxes 19.5%, direct taxes 14.5%). Expenditures: F 1,816,-000,000 (health and social assistance 42.0%; wages and salaries 16.7%; other administrative services 7.2%; debt amortization 5.0%).
Public debt (1994): U.S.$186,700,000.
Production (metric tons except as noted). Agriculture, forestry, fishing (1995): sugarcane 209,365, bananas 172,953, pineapples 30,250, plantains 12,000, yams 6,000, cucumbers 3,000, tomatoes 2,740, melons 1,588[1], sweet potatoes 770, lemons and limes 365, avocados 342, pimientos 198[1], flowers and foliage 105[1]; livestock (number of live animals) 47,000 sheep, 34,000 pigs, 30,000 cattle; roundwood (1994) 12,000 cu m; fish catch (1993) 4,607. Mining and quarrying (1992): pumice 140,000; sand and gravel for local construction. Manufacturing (1995): cement 211,375; processed pineapples 17,489; sugar 8,041; rum 46,591 hectolitres; other products include clothing, fabricated metals, and yawls and sails. Construction (buildings authorized; 1994): residential permits 6,893; nonresidential 113,279 sq m. Energy production (consumption): electricity (kW-hr; 1995) 936,000,000 (843,000,000); coal, none (none); crude petroleum (barrels; 1994) none (5,805,000); petroleum products (metric tons; 1994) 718,000 (554,000); natural gas, none (none).
Household income and expenditure. Average household size (1990) 3.3; income per household (1989) F 147,150 (U.S.$24,525); sources of income (1989): wages and salaries 80%, other 20%; expenditure (1993): food and beverages 32.1%, transportation and communications 20.7%, housing and energy 10.6%, household durable goods 9.4%, clothing and footwear 8.0%, education and recreation 5.4%, health care 5.2%, other 8.6%.
Tourism (1994): receipts from visitors U.S.$379,000,000; expenditures by nationals abroad, n.a.
Gross domestic product (at current market prices; 1991): U.S.$3,375,000,000 (U.S.$9,210 per capita).

Structure of gross domestic product and labour force

	1991 in value F '000,000	1991 % of total value	1990 labour force	1990 % of labour force
Agriculture, fishing	1,152.2	5.5	8,445	5.2
Mining, manufacturing	1,592.0	7.7	9,706	6.0
Construction	1,078.6	5.2	} 9,298	5.7
Public utilities	493.7	2.4		
Transportation and communications	1,282.3	6.2	6,673	4.1
Trade, restaurants, hotels	4,556.1	21.9	13,965	8.6
Finance, real estate, insurance	1,017.6	4.9	26,489	16.2
Pub. admin. and defense	305.8	1.5	} 35,541	21.8
Services	3,424.5	16.4		
Other	5,883.2[2]	28.3[2]	52,900[3]	32.4[3]
TOTAL	20,786.0	100.0	163,017	100.0

Population economically active (1990): total 164,870[4]; activity rate of total population 45.9% (participation rates: ages 15–64, 68.1%; female 47.5%; unemployed [1994] 26.2%).

Price and earnings indexes (1990 = 100)

	1990	1991	1992	1993	1994	1995[5]	1996[5]
Consumer price index[6]	100.0	104.3	108.4	109.6	114.0	115.0	116.6
Monthly earnings index[7]	100.0	103.0	105.7	107.5	109.1	111.3	112.3

Land use (1994): forested 45.3%; meadows and pastures 13.2%; agricultural and under permanent cultivation 17.0%; other 24.5%.

Foreign trade[8]

Balance of trade (current prices)

	1990	1991	1992	1993	1994	1995
F '000,000	−7,970	−7,934	−7,982	−7,744	−7,877	−8,604
% of total	72.7%	78.4%	75.6%	78.0%	76.4%	78.2%

Imports (1995): F 9,805,500,000 (goods for intermediate consumption [inputs to the manufacturing process changed or destroyed in the final product] 24.0%, food products 19.7%, automobiles 14.1%, professional equipment 14.0%, energy products 7.2%). *Major import sources* (1994): France 61.6%; United States 2.7%; Guadeloupe 1.1%; Venezuela 0.7%; other Caribbean 1.9%.
Exports (1995): F 1,201,900,000 (bananas 40.4%, refined petroleum 17.8%, rum 9.8%, melons 1.7%). *Major export destinations* (1994): France 47.5%; Guadeloupe 37.4%; French Guiana 3.3%.

Transport and communications

Transport. Railroads: none. Roads (1994): total length 1,299 mi, 2,091 km (paved [1988] 75%). Vehicles (1985): passenger cars 135,269; trucks and buses 7,328. Merchant marine (1992): vessels (100 gross tons and over) 6; total deadweight tonnage 1,121. Air transport (1994): passenger arrivals and departures 1,566,253; cargo unloaded 8,272 metric tons, cargo loaded 5,572 metric tons; airports (1996) with scheduled flights 1.
Communications. Daily newspapers (1992): total number 1; total circulation 32,000; circulation per 1,000 population 86. Radio (1995): total number of receivers 71,000 (1 per 5.5 persons). Television (1995): total number of receivers 65,000 (1 per 6.0 persons). Telephones (main lines; 1993): 149,600 (1 per 2.5 persons).

Education and health

Education (1992–93)

	schools	teachers	students	student/ teacher ratio
Primary (age 6–11)	282	2,711	33,170	12.2
Secondary (age 12–18) } Vocational	79	3,830	47,295	12.3
Higher	1	71	3,670	51.7

Educational attainment (1990). Percentage of population age 25 and over having: incomplete primary, or no declaration 54.3%; primary education 18.0%; secondary 20.0%; higher 7.7%. *Literacy* (1982): total population age 15 and over literate 206,807 (92.5%); males literate 97,538 (91.8%); females literate 109,269 (93.2%).
Health (1991): physicians 625 (1 per 584 persons); hospital beds 3,747 (1 per 97 persons); infant mortality rate per 1,000 live births (1993) 4.0.
Food (1992): daily per capita caloric intake 2,829 (vegetable products 75%, animal products 25%); 117% of FAO recommended minimum requirement.

Military

Total active duty personnel (1994): 1,542 French troops.

---

[1]Production for export only. [2]Includes an estimated F 5,474,000,000 produced in the nonmoney economy. [3]Unemployed. [4]Includes military reserve personnel. [5]June. [6]Figures are end-of-year unless otherwise footnoted. [7]Based on minimum-level wage of public employees. [8]Imports c.i.f.; exports f.o.b.

Mauritania

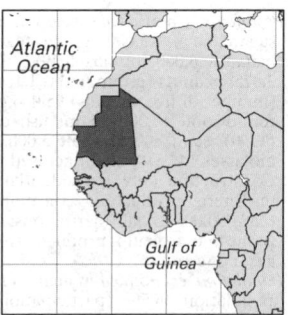

Official name: Al-Jumhūrīyah al-Islāmīyah al-Mūrītānīyah (Arabic) (Islamic Republic of Mauritania).
Form of government: unitary multiparty republic with two legislative houses (Senate [56]; National Assembly [79]).
Head of state and government: President.
Capital: Nouakchott.
Official languages: Arabic[1].
Official religion: Islam.
Monetary unit: 1 ouguiya (UM) = 5 khoums; valuation (Oct. 11, 1996) 1 U.S.\$ = UM 138.50; 1 £ = UM 218.17.

Area and population		area		population
				1992
Regions	Capitals	sq mi	sq km	estimate
El-'Açâba	Kiffa	13,900	36,000	185,574
Adrar	Atar	83,100	215,300	62,906
Brakna	Aleg	14,000	37,100	207,590
Dakhlet Nouadhibou	Nouadhibou	11,600	30,000	83,246
Gorgol	Kaédi	5,400	14,000	201,301
Guidimaka	Sélibaby	4,000	10,000	129,797
Hodh ech-Chargui	Néma	64,000	166,000	234,011
Hodh el-Gharbi	'Ayoûn el-'Atroûs	22,000	57,000	175,089
Inchiri	Akjoujt	19,000	49,000	13,630
Tagant	Tidjikdja	36,000	93,000	67,939
Tiris Zemmour	Zouérate	98,600	255,300	37,534
Trarza	Rosso	26,000	67,000	217,867
Capital District				
Nouakchott	Nouakchott	400	1,000	480,395
TOTAL		398,000	1,030,700	2,096,879[2]

Demography

Population (1996): 2,333,000.
Density (1996): persons per sq mi 5.9, persons per sq km 2.3.
Urban-rural (1995): urban 53.8%; rural 46.2%.
Sex distribution (1995): male 49.52%; female 50.48%.
Age breakdown (1995): under 15, 43.1%; 15–29, 27.3%; 30–44, 16.1%; 45–59, 8.3%; 60–74, 4.3%; 75 and over, 0.9%.
Population projection: (2000) 2,580,000; (2010) 3,283,000.
Doubling time: 22 years.
Ethnic composition (1993)[3]: Moor 70% (of which about 40% "black" Moor [Ḥarāṭīn, or African Sudanic] and about 30% "white" Moor [Bidan, or Arab-Berber]); other black African 30% (mostly Wolof, Tukulor, Soninke, and Fulani).
Religious affiliation (1994): Sunnī Muslim 99.5%; Roman Catholic 0.2%; other 0.3%.
Major cities (1992): Nouakchott 735,000[4]; Nouadhibou 72,305; Kaédi 35,241; Kiffa 29,292[5]; Rosso 27,783[5].

Vital statistics

Birth rate per 1,000 population (1995): 47.3 (world avg. 25.0); legitimate, n.a.; illegitimate, n.a.
Death rate per 1,000 population (1995): 15.7 (world avg. 9.3).
Natural increase rate per 1,000 population (1995): 31.6 (world avg. 15.7).
Total fertility rate (avg. births per childbearing woman; 1995): 6.9.
Marriage rate per 1,000 population: n.a.
Divorce rate per 1,000 population: n.a.
Life expectancy at birth (1995): male 45.7 years; female 51.5 years.
Major causes of death per 100,000 population: n.a.; however, mortality and morbidity arise mainly in diseases of the respiratory system, malaria, measles, and diarrhea.

National economy

Budget (1995). Revenue: UM 33,210,000,000 (tax revenue 71.0%, of which import taxes 14.2%, value-added taxes 13.6%, tax on wages 11.8%; nontax revenue 24.1%). Expenditures: UM 34,370,000,000 (current expenditures 71.6%, of which interest on public debt 13.0%, defense 10.6%; development expenditures 28.4%).
Tourism (1995): receipts from visitors U.S.\$2,700,000; expenditures by nationals abroad U.S.\$14,600,000.
Land use (1994): forested 4.3%; meadows and pastures 38.3%; agricultural and under permanent cultivation 0.2%; desert 57.2%.
Production (metric tons except as noted). Agriculture, forestry, fishing (1995): sorghum 156,500, rice 79,300, dates 25,000, pulses 17,000, millet 8,000; livestock (number of live animals) 5,288,000 sheep, 3,525,000 goats, 1,125,000 cattle, 1,087,000 camels; roundwood (1994) 13,000 cu m; fish catch (metric tons; 1994) 296,627. Mining and quarrying (gross weight; 1994): iron ore 10,439,000; gold 1,738 kg. Manufacturing (1994): cow's milk 91,000; goat's milk 77,000; meat 61,000, of which fresh beef and veal 18,000; hides and skins 4,318; cement, tiles, and bricks 5.9[6]; fabricated metal products 5.4[6]; paper and paper products 2.1[6]. Construction (1984): 42,478 sq m. Energy production (consumption): electricity (kW-hr; 1994) 148,000,000 (148,000,000); coal (metric tons; 1994) none (6,000); crude petroleum (barrels; 1994) none (6,905,000); petroleum products (metric tons; 1994) 835,000 (918,000); natural gas, none (none).
Household income and expenditure. Average household size (1980) 5.0; income per household: n.a.; sources of income: n.a.; expenditure (1990): food

and beverages 73.1%, clothing and footwear 8.1%, energy and water 7.7%, transportation and communications 2.0%.
Gross national product (at current market prices; 1994): U.S.\$1,063,000,000 (U.S.\$480 per capita).

Structure of gross domestic product and labour force				
	1994		1988	
	in value UM '000,000	% of total value	labour force	% of labour force
Agriculture	28,746	22.7	225,238	38.5
Mining	12,860	10.1	6,322	1.1
Manufacturing	12,311	9.7	5,630	1.0
Public utilities }	10,346	8.2	1,326	0.2
Construction			12,291	2.1
Transportation and communications	8,058	6.4	8,378	1.4
Trade and finance	18,045	14.2	73,451	12.5
Services	8,306	6.5 }	86,807	14.8
Pub. admin., defense	14,203	11.2 }		
Other	14,006[7]	11.0[7]	166,366[8]	28.4[8]
TOTAL	126,881	100.0	585,809	100.0

Population economically active (1992): total 654,000; activity rate of total population 30.5% (participation rates: over age 10 [1990] 49.7%; female 13.5%; unemployed 27%).

Price and earnings indexes (1990 = 100)						
	1989	1990	1991	1992	1993	1994	1995
Consumer price index[9]	93.8	100.0	105.6	116.3	127.1	132.3	140.9
Monthly earnings index[10]	100.0	100.0	100.0	114.6	129.2	129.2	...

Public debt (external, outstanding; 1994): U.S.\$2,081,000,000.

Foreign trade

Balance of trade (current prices)					
	1990	1991	1992	1993	1994
U.S.\$'000,000	+17.0	+53.2	-9.9	+25.0	+41.7
% of total	2.0%	6.5%	1.5%	3.2%	5.6%

Imports (1994): U.S.\$352,000,000 (goods to public mining/manufacturing sector 27.9%, food products 23.6%, petroleum products 9.0%). *Major import sources:* France 23.3%; United Kingdom 6.6%; Germany 6.1%; China 5.9%; Japan 5.6%; Spain 5.1%.
Exports (1994): U.S.\$393,700,000 (fish 52.6%, of which cephalopods 35.5%; iron ore 41.5%, gold 5.2%). *Major export destinations:* Japan 27.8%; Italy 14.9%; France 13.6%; Spain 11.4%; Côte d'Ivoire 6.3%.

Transport and communications

Transport. Railroads (1994): route length 437 mi, 704 km; passenger-mi, negligible; passenger-km, negligible; (1992) short ton-mi cargo 3,860,000,000, metric ton-km cargo 5,635,000,000. Roads (1995): total length 4,745 mi, 7,636 km (paved 23%). Vehicles (1994): passenger cars 8,000; trucks and buses 5,700. Merchant marine (1992): vessels (100 gross tons and over) 126; total deadweight tonnage 23,875. Air transport (1993)[11]: passenger-mi 128,560,000, passenger-km 206,898,000; short ton-mi cargo 9,738,000, metric ton-km cargo 14,218,000; airports (1996) with scheduled flights 10.
Communications. Daily newspapers (1992): total number 1[12]; total circulation 1,000; circulation per 1,000 population 0.5. Radio (1995): total number of receivers 1,000,000 (1 per 2.3 persons). Television (1995): total number of receivers 1,100 (1 per 2,067 persons). Telephones (main lines; 1993): 7,600 (1 per 286 persons).

Education and health

Education (1993–94)				student/
	schools	teachers	students	teacher ratio
Primary (age 6–11)	1,635	4,686	248,048	52.9
Secondary (age 12–17)	56[13]	1,776	43,861	24.7
Voc., teacher tr.	5[13]	162	1,949	12.0
Higher	4	72[14]	2,850[14]	39.6[14]

Educational attainment (1988). Percentage of population age 25 and over having: no formal schooling 60.8%; primary and incomplete secondary 34.1%; secondary 3.8%; higher 1.3%. *Literacy* (1995): percentage of total population age 15 and over literate 37.7%; males literate 49.6%; females literate 26.3%.
Health: physicians (1994) c. 200 (1 per 11,085 persons); hospital beds (1988) 1,556 (1 per 1,217 persons); infant mortality rate per 1,000 live births (1995) 83.5.
Food (1992): daily per capita caloric intake 2,685 (vegetable products 82%, animal products 18%); 116% of FAO recommended minimum requirement.

Military

Total active duty personnel (1996): 15,650 (army 95.8%, navy 3.2%, air force 1.0%). *Military expenditure as percentage of GNP* (1994): 3.8% (world 3.0%); per capita expenditure U.S.\$16.

---

[1]The 1991 constitution names Arabic as the official language and the following as national languages: Arabic, Fulani, Soninke, and Wolof. [2]Official population projection based on 1988 census. [3]Estimated figures; 1988 census data for ethnicity/race not released by the government. [4]1995. [5]1988. [6]1993 value added of production in U.S.\$'000,000. [7]Indirect taxes. [8]Statutory minimum wage rate of civil servants. [9]Nouakchott only. [10]Statutory minimum wage rate of civil servants. [11]Air Afrique scheduled traffic only. [12]A second daily newspaper began publishing in September 1995. [13]1991–92. [14]1994–95; University of Nouakchott only.

Mauritius

Official name: Republic of Mauritius.
Form of government: republic with
  one legislative house (National
  Assembly [66[1]]).
Chief of state: President.
Head of government: Prime Minister.
Capital: Port Louis.
Official language: English.
Official religion: none.
Monetary unit: 1 Mauritian rupee
  (Mau Re; plural Mau Rs) = 100 cents;
  valuation (Oct. 11, 1996) 1 U.S.$ =
  Mau Rs 20.65; 1 £ = Mau Rs 32.53.

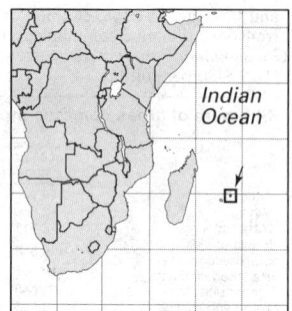

Indian
Ocean

Area and population

Islands Districts/Dependencies	area sq mi	area sq km	population 1995[2] estimate
Mauritius	720	1,865	1,082,972
Black River	100	259	48,790
Flacq	115	298	118,663
Grand Port	100	260	102,093
Moka	89	231	69,771
Pamplemousses	69	179	109,757
Plaines Wilhems	78	203	341,325
Port Louis	17	43	136,217
Rivière du Rempart	57	148	92,645
Savanne	95	245	63,711
Mauritian dependencies			
Agalega[3]			
Cargados Carajos Shoals (Saint Brandon)[3]	27	71	170
Rodrigues[4]	40	104	34,678
TOTAL	788[5]	2,040[5]	1,117,820

Demography

Population (1996): 1,141,000.
Density (1996): persons per sq mi 1,447.4, persons per sq km 559.1.
Urban-rural (1994): urban 43.6%; rural 56.4%.
Sex distribution (1994): male 50.06%; female 49.94%.
Age breakdown (1994)[6]: under 15, 28.0%; 15–29, 27.5%; 30–44, 24.4%; 45–59, 11.7%; 60–74, 6.6%; 75 and over, 1.8%.
Population projection: (2000) 1,199,000; (2010) 1,357,000.
Doubling time: 54 years.
Ethnic composition (1992): Indo-Pakistani 68.0%; Creole (mixed Caucasian, Indo-Pakistani, and African) 27.0%; Chinese 3.0%; white 2.0%.
Religious affiliation (1990): Hindu 50.6%; Roman Catholic 27.2%; Muslim 16.3%; Protestant 5.2%; Buddhist 0.3%; other 0.4%.
Major cities (1994): Port Louis 144,776; Beau Bassin–Rose Hill 96,621; Vacoas-Phoenix 94,042; Curepipe 76,610; Quatre Bornes 73,501.

Vital statistics

Birth rate per 1,000 population (1994): 19.6 (world avg. 25.0); (1985) legitimate 72.8%; illegitimate 27.2%.
Death rate per 1,000 population (1994): 6.7 (world avg. 9.3).
Natural increase rate per 1,000 population (1994): 12.9 (world avg. 15.7).
Total fertility rate (avg. births per childbearing woman; 1994): 2.3.
Marriage rate per 1,000 population (1994): 10.3.
Divorce rate per 1,000 population (1994): 0.9.
Life expectancy at birth (1991–93): male 66.4 years; female 73.9 years.
Major causes of death per 100,000 population (1994): diseases of the circulatory system 298.2; diseases of the respiratory system 68.8; malignant neoplasms (cancers) 67.1; homicide, suicide, and accidents 44.9.

National economy

Budget (1994–95). Revenue: Mau Rs 12,990,000,000 (tax revenue 92.0%, of which import and stamp duties 39.3%, income tax 13.8%, sales tax 10.1%, excise tax 8.5%). Expenditures: Mau Rs 14,672,000,000 (social services 35.0%, of which education, art, and culture 14.6%, social security 10.8%, health 8.1%; public-debt service 28.6%).
Tourism (1994): receipts from visitors U.S.$356,000,000; expenditures by nationals abroad U.S.$140,000,000.
Public debt (external, outstanding; 1994): U.S.$1,063,000,000.
Gross national product (at current market prices; 1994): U.S.$3,514,000,000 (U.S.$3,180 per capita).

Structure of gross domestic product and labour force

	1995 in value Mau Rs '000,000[7]	1995 % of total value	1994 labour force[8,9]	1994 % of labour force[8,9]
Agriculture	5,460	9.4	41,600	14.2
Mining	85	0.1	200	0.1
Manufacturing	12,830	22.1	104,700	35.8
Construction	4,315	7.4	13,400	4.6
Public utilities	1,375	2.4	3,500	1.2
Transportation and communications	7,000	12.1	14,200	4.9
Trade	10,365	17.9	23,300	8.0
Finance	6,810	11.7	...	...
Pub. admin., defense	6,470	11.2 }	76,800	26.3
Services	3,290	5.7 }		
Other	...	...	14,900	5.1
TOTAL	58,000	100.0	292,400	100.0[5]

Production (metric tons except as noted). Agriculture, forestry, fishing (1994): sugarcane 4,813,000, green tea 27,204, potatoes 16,850, tomatoes 9,000, bananas 6,000, onions 5,493, black tea 5,000, pineapples 4,050, cabbages 3,875, peanuts (groundnuts) 1,160, tobacco 1,025, corn (maize) 995; livestock (number of live animals) 95,000 goats, 34,000 cattle, 17,000 pigs, 7,000 sheep; roundwood 18,300 cu m; fish catch (1993) 20,102. Mining and quarrying (1990): sand 800,000; salt 3,000. Manufacturing (1994): raw sugar 500,209; molasses 144,510; manufactured tea 5,089; beer and stout 262,538 hectolitres. Construction (1994): residential 1,107,648 sq m; nonresidential 370,525 sq m. Energy production (consumption): electricity (kW-hr; 1993) 988,000,000 (988,000,000); coal (metric tons; 1993) none (58,000); crude petroleum, none (none); petroleum products (metric tons; 1993) none (440,000); natural gas, none (none).
Population economically active (1994)[10]: total 503,346; activity rate of total population 46.5% (participation rates: ages 15–64, 67.0%; female 34.5%; unemployed 7.1%).

Price and earnings indexes (1990 = 100)

	1989	1990	1991	1992	1993	1994	1995
Consumer price index	88.1	100.0	107.0	112.0	123.7	132.8	140.8
Monthly earnings index[9]	94.6	100.0	115.8	128.5	135.6	164.2	...

Household income and expenditure. Average household size (1990) 4.5[10]; income per household (1979) Mau Rs 15,540 (U.S.$2,430); sources of income (1990): salaries and wages 48.4%, entrepreneurial income 41.2%, transfer payments 10.4%; expenditure (1986–87)[11]: food, beverages, and tobacco 49.1%, housing 13.5%, transportation 9.3%, clothing and footwear 8.4%, recreation, entertainment, education, and cultural services 6.0%, energy 5.7%, health care 3.0%, other 5.0%.
Land use (1993): forested 21.7%; meadows and pastures 3.4%; agricultural and under permanent cultivation 52.2%; other 22.7%.

Foreign trade[12]

Balance of trade (current prices)

	1989	1990	1991	1992	1993	1994
U.S.$'000,000	−211.1	−280.0	−222.6	−170.8	−254.2	−392.8
% of total	9.6%	10.6%	8.4%	6.2%	8.9%	12.5%

Imports (1993): Mau Rs 34,473,000,000 (manufactured goods classified chiefly by material 36.4%, machinery and transport equipment 29.3%, food 14.0%, chemicals 8.1%, mineral fuels and lubricants 7.0%, inedible crude materials excluding fuels 3.3%, animal and vegetable oils and fats 1.4%). *Major import sources:* France 18.5%; South Africa 11.9%; United Kingdom 6.2%; Japan 5.1%; Hong Kong 5.1%; India 5.1%; Germany 4.2%; China 3.7%.
Exports (1994): Mau Rs 24,097,000,000 (clothing and textiles 53.4%, sugar 23.8%, yarn 2.9%, pearls and precious stones 1.9%). *Major export destinations:* United Kingdom 31.9%; France 20.1%; United States 18.1%; Germany 5.9%; Italy 4.2%.

Transport and communications

Transport. Railroads: none. Roads (1991): total length 1,138 mi, 1,831 km (paved 93%). Vehicles (1994): passenger cars 35,994; trucks and buses 10,286. Merchant marine (1992): vessels (100 gross tons and over) 35; total deadweight tonnage 152,197. Air transport (1995)[13]: passenger-mi 1,987,036,000, passenger-km 3,197,831,000; short ton-mi cargo 80,715,000, metric ton-km cargo 117,842,000; airports (1996) with scheduled flights 1.
Communications. Daily newspapers (1995): total number 7; total circulation 55,000[14]; circulation per 1,000 population 48[14]. Radio (1995): 150,000 receivers (1 per 7.5 persons). Television (1995) 156,850 receivers (1 per 7.2 persons). Telephones (main lines; 1994): 129,126 (1 per 8.6 persons).

Education and health

Education (1993)

	schools	teachers	students	student/ teacher ratio
Primary (age 5–12)	279	6,450	123,167	19.1
Secondary (age 12–20)	123	4,234	89,581	21.2
Voc., teacher tr.	19[15]	69[16]	2,052[17]	...
Higher	2	526[18]	2,556[17]	7.7[18]

Educational attainment (1990). Percentage of population age 25 and over having: no formal education 18.3%; incomplete primary 42.6%; primary 6.1%; incomplete secondary 18.0%; secondary 13.1%; higher 1.9%. *Literacy* (1990): percentage of total population age 15 and over literate 79.9%; males literate 85.2%; females literate 74.7%.
Health (1994): physicians 941 (1 per 1,182 persons); hospital beds (1993) 3,330 (1 per 351 persons); infant mortality rate per 1,000 live births 21.8.
Food (1988–90): daily per capita caloric intake 2,897 (vegetable products 87%, animal products 13%); 128% of FAO recommended minimum requirement.

Military

Total active duty personnel: none; however, a special 1,300-person paramilitary force ensures internal security. *Military expenditure as percentage of GNP* (1994): 0.3% (world 3.0%); per capita expenditure U.S.$10.

---

[1]Includes 4 nonelective seats. [2]January 1. [3]Administered directly from Port Louis. [4]Administered by resident commissioner assisted by local council. [5]Detail does not add to total given because of rounding. [6]Excludes Agalega and Cargados Carajos Shoals. [7]At factor cost. [8]Employed persons in establishments employing 10 or more persons. [9]March. [10]Island of Mauritius only. [11]Current weights of CPI components; Island of Mauritius only. [12]Import figures are f.o.b. in balance of trade and c.i.f. for commodities and trading partners. [13]Air Mauritius only. [14]Circulation for 5 newspapers only. [15]1992. [16]1982. [17]1993. [18]1991.

Mexico

Official name: Estados Unidos
  Mexicanos (United Mexican States).
Form of government: federal republic
  with two legislative houses (Senate
  [128]; Chamber of Deputies [500]).
Chief of state and head of government:
  President.
Capital: Mexico City.
Official language: Spanish.
Official religion: none.
Monetary unit: 1 Mexican
  peso[1] (Mex$) = 100 centavos;
  valuation (Oct. 11, 1996) 1
  U.S.$ = Mex$7.62;
  1 £ = Mex$12.01.

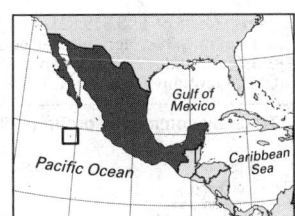

Social indicators

Access to services (1994). Proportion of dwellings having: electricity 91.1%;
  piped water supply 82.0%; drained sewage 67.7%.
Educational attainment (1992). Percentage of population age 15 and over
  having: no primary education 14.1%; some primary 22.3%; completed
  primary 20.7%; incomplete secondary 10.4%; complete secondary 24.2%;
  higher 8.3%.

Distribution of income (1994)
percentage of household income by quintile

1	2	3	4	5 (highest)
4.8	8.6	12.8	19.5	54.3

Quality of working life. Average workweek (1994) 44.8 hours[2]. Annual rate
  (1992) per 100,000 insured workers for: temporary disability 6,426; indemni-
  fication for permanent injury 239; death 18. Labour stoppages (1993): 155,
  involving 31,708 workers. Average duration of journey to work: n.a. Method
  of transport: n.a. Rate per 1,000 workers of discouraged (unemployed no
  longer seeking work): n.a.
Social participation. Eligible voters participating in last national election
  (1991): *c.* 60%. Population participating in voluntary work: n.a. Trade union
  membership in total workforce: n.a. Practicing religious population in total
  affiliated population: national average of weekly attendance (1993) 11%;
  (1970) weekly attendance 10% of urban dwellers, 25% of rural dwellers;
  yearly attendance 55% of urban dwellers, 73% of rural dwellers.
Social deviance (1991). Criminal cases tried by local authorities per 100,000
  population for: murder 60.3; rape 22.4; other assault 301.0; theft 703.8.
  Incidence per 100,000 in general population of: alcoholism, n.a.; drug and
  substance abuse, n.a.[3]; suicide (1994) 2.47.
Leisure (1985). Favourite leisure activities (average daily paid attendance):
  cinema 582,416; sporting events 31,518; live theatre 16,400; museums and
  archaeological sites 12,169; bullfights 3,049.
Material well-being (1985). Households possessing: radio 96%; television 73%;
  washing machine 33%; automobile 29%; telephone 27%; refrigerator 23%.

National economy

Gross national product (1994): U.S.$368,679,000,000 (U.S.$4,010 per capita).

Area and population

States	Capitals	area sq mi	area sq km	population 1995 estimate
Aguascalientes	Aguascalientes	2,112	5,471	862,335
Baja California Norte	Mexicali	26,997	69,921	2,108,118
Baja California Sur	La Paz	28,369	73,475	375,450
Campeche	Campeche	19,619	50,812	642,082
Chiapas	Tuxtla Gutiérrez	28,653	74,211	3,606,828
Chihuahua	Chihuahua	94,571	244,938	2,792,989
Coahuila	Saltillo	57,908	149,982	2,172,136
Colima	Colima	2,004	5,191	487,324
Durango	Durango	47,560	123,181	1,430,964
Guanajuato	Guanajuato	11,773	30,491	4,393,160
Guerrero	Chilpancingo	24,819	64,281	2,915,497
Hidalgo	Pachuca	8,036	20,813	2,111,782
Jalisco	Guadalajara	31,211	80,836	5,990,054
México	Toluca	8,245	21,355	11,704,934
Michoacán	Morelia	23,138	59,928	3,869,133
Morelos	Cuernavaca	1,911	4,950	1,442,587
Nayarit	Tepic	10,417	26,979	895,975
Nuevo León	Monterrey	25,067	64,924	3,549,273
Oaxaca	Oaxaca	36,275	93,952	3,224,270
Puebla	Puebla	13,090	33,902	4,624,239
Querétaro	Querétaro	4,420	11,449	1,248,844
Quintana Roo	Chetumal	19,387	50,212	703,442
San Luis Potosí	San Luis Potosí	24,351	63,068	2,191,712
Sinaloa	Culiacán	22,521	58,328	2,424,745
Sonora	Hermosillo	70,291	182,052	2,083,630
Tabasco	Villahermosa	9,756	25,267	1,748,664
Tamaulipas	Ciudad Victoria	30,650	79,384	2,526,387
Tlaxcala	Tlaxcala	1,551	4,016	883,630
Veracruz	Jalapa (Xalapa)	27,683	71,699	6,734,545
Yucatán	Mérida	14,827	38,402	1,555,733
Zacatecas	Zacatecas	28,283	73,252	1,336,348
Federal District				
Distrito Federal	—	571	1,479	8,483,623
TOTAL		756,066	1,958,201	91,120,433

Structure of gross domestic product and labour force

	1995 in value Mex$'000,000[1]	1995 % of total value	1993 labour force	1993 % of labour force
Agriculture	71,516.2	5.8	8,842,774	26.3
Mining	16,095.4	1.3	170,923	0.5
Manufacturing	216,438.4	17.6	5,077,678	15.1
Construction	46,056.7	3.8	1,879,231	5.6
Public utilities	19,605.5	1.6	99,123	0.3
Transportation and communications	111,539.7	9.1	1,362,350	4.0
Trade	230,694.2	18.7	6,892,693	20.5
Finance	192,383.9	15.6	1,080,051	3.2
Pub. admin., defense } Services	259,555.9	21.1	7,205,262	21.4
Other	64,897.5[4]	5.3[4]	1,041,727[5]	3.1[5]
TOTAL	1,230,784.0[6]	100.0[6]	33,651,812	100.0

Demography

Population (1996): 92,711,000.
Density (1996): persons per sq mi 122.6, persons per sq km 49.6.
Urban-rural (1990): urban 71.3%; rural 28.7%.
Sex distribution (1995): male 49.88%; female 50.12%.
Age breakdown (1995): under 15, 35.9%; 15–29, 30.1%; 30–44, 18.2%; 45–59,
  9.5%; 60–74, 4.8%; 75 and over, 1.5%.
Population projection: (2000) 98,881,000; (2010) 112,891,000.
Doubling time: 30 years.
Ethnic composition (1990): mestizo 60.0%; Amerindian 30.0%; Caucasian
  9.0%; other 1.0%.
Religious affiliation (1990): Roman Catholic 89.7%; Protestant (including
  Evangelical) 4.9%; Jewish 0.1%; other 2.1%; none 3.2%.
Major cities (1990): Mexico City 9,815,795; Guadalajara 1,650,042; Ciudad
  Netzahualcóyotl 1,255,456; Monterrey 1,068,996; Puebla 1,007,170; Juarez
  789,522; León 758,279; Tijuana 698,752; Mérida 523,422; Chihuahua 516,153.
Place of birth (1990): 93.1% native-born; 6.9% foreign-born and unknown.
Mobility (1990). Population 5 years and older living in the same state as in
  1985: 94.3%; different state 4.9%; unspecified 0.8%.
Households. Total households (1992) 17,152,000; distribution by size (1990):
  1 person 1.0%, 2 persons 4.3%, 3 persons 8.9%, 4 persons 14.9%, 5 persons
  17.4%, 6 persons 15.3%, 7 or more persons 38.2%. Family households (1990):
  17,064,507 (98.4%); nonfamily 1,039,738 (1.3%); unspecified 256,554 (0.3%).
Immigration (1987): permanent immigrants admitted 72,649.
Emigration (1994): legal immigrants into the United States 111,398.

Vital statistics

Birth rate per 1,000 population (1995): 27.6 (world avg. 25.0); (1983) legiti-
  mate 72.5%; illegitimate 27.5%.
Death rate per 1,000 population (1995): 4.7 (world avg. 9.3).
Natural increase rate per 1,000 population (1995): 22.9 (world avg. 15.7).
Total fertility rate (avg. births per childbearing woman; 1995): 3.1.
Marriage rate per 1,000 population (1994): 7.4.
Divorce rate per 1,000 population (1994): 0.4.
Life expectancy at birth (1994): male 69.0 years; female 75.0 years.
Major causes of death per 100,000 population (1994): heart diseases 67.8;
  malignant neoplasms (cancers) 51.8; accidents 41.6; diabetes mellitus 33.9;
  cerebrovascular diseases 25.3; cirrhosis of the liver 23.2; conditions originat-
  ing in the perinatal period 23.0; pneumonia and influenza 21.4; homicide
  17.7.

Budget (1994). Revenue: Mex$213,467,000,000[1] (petroleum revenues 24.8%).
  Expenditures: Mex$221,202,000,000[1] (transfers 53.7%, wages and salaries
  19.1%, interest on public debt 12.2%).
Public debt (external, outstanding; 1994): U.S.$92,843,000,000.
Tourism (1994): receipts from visitors U.S.$6,318,000,000; expenditures by
  nationals abroad U.S.$5,363,000,000.

Manufacturing, mining, and construction enterprises (1993)

	no. of enterprises	no. of employees ('000)	yearly wages as a % of avg. of all wages[7]	value added (Mex$'000,000[1,7])
Manufacturing	266,033	3,174.4	97.5	20,950,900
Metal products	46,667[8]	955.6[8]	114.2[8]	6,605,300[8]
Chemicals	7,321	371.2	152.3	4,228,000
Food, beverages, and tobacco	91,894	679.3	86.4	3,378,700
Textiles and apparel	44,071	530.6	80.0	2,414,800
Iron and steel	401	57.4	128.2	1,332,400
Nonmetallic mineral products	24,397	181.8	98.6	1,177,700
Paper and printing	15,022	193.2	100.0	1,127,900
Wood and wood products	31,549	162.6	62.8	497,000
Nonelectrical machinery and transport equipment	[8]	[8]	...[8]	[8]
Electrical machinery	[8]	[8]	...[8]	[8]
Other manufactures	4,711	42.7	...	189,200
Mining	2,845	95.6	161.0	1,643,800
Construction	5,308[7]	342.4[7]	62.1	1,414,800

Production (metric tons except as noted). Agriculture, forestry, fishing (1995):
  sugarcane 42,562,000, corn (maize) 16,187,000, sorghum 4,169,000, oranges
  3,572,000, wheat 3,468,000, bananas 2,033,000, tomatoes 1,935,000, mangoes
  1,342,000, dry beans 1,271,000, lemons and limes 984,000, grapes 476,000,
  soybeans 430,000, apples 413,223, rice 375,000, barley 325,000, pineapples
  280,000, cottonseed 190,000, strawberries 120,000, walnuts 18,000; livestock
  (number of live animals) 30,191,000 cattle, 18,000,000 pigs, 10,500,000
  goats, 6,200,000 horses, 6,000,000 turkeys, 5,987,000 sheep, 3,250,000 mules,
  3,230,000 asses, 330,000,000 chickens; roundwood (1994) 21,322,000 cu m;
  fish catch (1994) 1,260,019. Mining and quarrying (value of production
  [metal content] in Mex$'000; 1993): copper 2,236,437; silver 1,339,057; zinc
  1,321,759; gold 605,850; iron 530,658; lead 457,307; sulfur 219,833; gypsum
  160,139; dolomite 119,728; fluorite 110,838; molybdenum 88,043; manganese
  77,918; silica 68,956; bismuth 25,166; celestite 25,045. Manufacturing (gross
  value of production in Mex$'000[1]; 1994): machinery and equipment 82,169,-

495; food, beverages, and tobacco products 64,399,498; chemical products 50,455,651; metal products 25,363,292; mineral products 17,074,973; paper and paper products 9,209,617; textiles 8,555,146. Construction (gross value of new construction, in Mex$'000,000[1]; 1985): residential 154,835; nonresidential 168,096.

Trade and service enterprises (1993)

	no. of establishments	no. of employees	yearly wage as a % of avg. of all wages[9]	annual income (Mex$'000,000[1])
Trade	1,208,779	2,969,786	...	565,728,373
Wholesale	68,919	631,802	...	249,597,035
Retail	1,139,860	2,337,984	...	316,131,338
Boutiques (excluding food products)	422,299	922,890	...	108,507,889
Food and tobacco speciality stores	671,050	991,911	...	65,305,180
Automobile, tire, and auto parts dealers	32,138	152,821	...	47,888,576
Small supermarkets and grocery stores	8,719	168,752	...	48,769,283
Gasoline stations	3,042	35,340	...	32,517,091
Other	2,612	66,270	...	13,143,319
Services	711,843	2,766,750	85.2	200,001,682
Professional services	130,475	652,148	77.9	53,533,318
Food and beverage services	677	11,258	...	1,012,369
Transp. and travel agencies	9,967	62,767	133.4	11,858,406
Lodging	9,913	151,445	...	8,960,922
Automotive repair	112,293	252,950	...	7,263,560
Educational services (private)	20,622	247,086	134.3	10,815,238
Medical and social assistance	79,748	203,348	206.4	7,497,794
Amusement services (cinemas and theatres)	4,855	65,608	148.9	9,845,129
Recreation	20,973	65,936	...	3,065,672
Other repair	72,129	104,478	...	2,625,370
Commercial and professional organizations	1,946	11,946	77.9	264,770
Other	248,245	937,780	49.9	83,259,134

Energy production (consumption): electricity (kW-hr; 1994) 144,276,000,000 (143,447,000,000); coal (metric tons; 1994) 8,898,000 (9,188,000); crude petroleum (barrels; 1994) 972,000,000 (500,000,000); petroleum products (metric tons; 1994) 83,618,000 (89,164,000); natural gas (cu m; 1994) 26,378,000,000 (27,206,000,000).

Population economically active (1993): total 33,651,812; activity rate of total population 38.9% (participation rates: ages 15–64, 61.4%; female 31.6%; unemployed 2.4%).

Price and earnings indexes (1990 = 100)

	1989	1990	1991	1992	1993	1994	1995
Consumer price index	79.0	100.0	122.7	141.7	155.5	166.3	224.5
Monthly earnings index	76.6	100.0	129.1	292.9	164.7	174.6	192.1

Household income and expenditure. Average household size (1992) 4.8; income per household (1989) Mex$3,461[1] (U.S.$1,384); sources of income (1992): wages and salaries 61.5%, property and entrepreneurship 29.1%, transfer payments 7.8%, other 1.6%; expenditure (1992): food, beverages, and tobacco 36.9%, housing (includes household furnishings) 25.2%, transportation and communications 10.1%, clothing and footwear 8.5%, recreation and entertainment 5.5%, health and medical services 3.5%.

Financial aggregates[1, 10]

	1990	1991	1992	1993	1994	1995	1996 (7 mo.)
Exchange rate, Mex$ per:							
U.S. dollar	2.813	3.018	3.095	3.116	3.375	6.419	7.619
£	5.020	5.114	5.464	4.680	5.164	10.132	11.837
SDR	4.190	4.393	4.284	4.266	7.774	11.361	11.122
International reserves (U.S.$)							
Total (excl. gold; '000,000)	9,863	17,726	18,942	25,110	6,278	16,847	17,940
SDRs ('000,000)	417	586	548	223	177	1,597	723
Reserve pos. in IMF ('000,000)	—	—	—	—	—	—	—
Foreign exchange	9,446	17,140	18,394	24,886	6,101	15,250	17,217
Gold ('000,000 fine troy oz)	0.92	0.92	0.69	0.48	0.43	0.51	0.30
% world reserves	0.10	0.10	0.07	0.05	0.05	0.06	0.03
Interest and prices							
Treasury bill rate	34.76	19.28	15.62	15.03	14.10	48.44	24.25
Balance of payments (U.S.$'000,000)							
Balance of visible trade, of which:	−881	−7,279	−15,934	−13,481	−18,465	+7,089	...
Imports, f.o.b.	−41,592	−49,966	−62,130	−65,366	−79,347	−72,454	...
Exports, f.o.b.	40,711	42,687	46,196	51,885	60,882	79,543	...
Balance of invisibles	−6,570	−7,609	−8,508	−9,919	−10,953	+7,743	...
Balance of payments, current account	−7,451	−14,888	−24,442	−23,400	−29,418	−654	...

Land use (1994): forested 25.5%; meadows and pastures 39.0%; agricultural and under permanent cultivation 13.0%; other 22.5%.

Foreign trade

Balance of trade (current prices)

	1990	1991	1992	1993	1994	1995
Mex$'000,000,000	−7,494.0	−27,746	−57,138	−53,615	−80,166	+19,923
% of total		4.7%	14.4%	25.1%	22.2%	25.6%	3.4%

Imports (1995): U.S.$72,475,900,000 (intermediate goods 79.3%; capital goods 12.0%; consumer goods 7.4%). *Major import sources:* U.S. 74.5%; Japan 5.0%; Germany 3.7%; Canada 1.9%; France 1.4%; South Korea 1.3%; Italy 1.1%; Spain 1.0%.

Exports (1995): U.S.$79,823,300,000 (manufacturing goods 83.7%; crude petroleum 9.3%; agricultural goods 5.0%). *Major export destinations:* U.S. 83.6%; Canada 2.5%; Japan 1.2%; Spain 1.0%; Brazil 1.0%; Switzerland 0.8%; Germany 0.6%; U.K. 0.6%; Chile 0.6%; France 0.6%.

Trade by commodity group (1994)

SITC group	imports U.S.$'000,000	%	exports U.S.$'000,000	%
00 Food and live animals	4,888	6.1	3,756	6.1
01 Beverages and tobacco	343	0.4	484	0.8
02 Crude materials, excluding fuels	3,031	3.8	1,393	2.2
03 Mineral fuels, lubricants, and related materials	1,507	1.9	7,403	11.9
04 Animal and vegetable oils, fats, and waxes	496	0.6	—	—
05 Chemicals and related products, n.e.s.	6,765	8.4	2,725	4.4
06 Basic manufactures	12,978	16.2	6,032	9.7
07 Machinery and transport equipment	31,521	39.3	33,206	53.6
08 Miscellaneous manufactured articles	10,144	12.7	6,809	11.0
09 Goods not classified by kind	8,497	10.6	116	0.2
TOTAL[11]	80,170	100.0	61,964[6]	100.0[6]

Direction of trade (1995)

	imports U.S.$'000,000	%	exports U.S.$'000,000	%
Western Hemisphere	57,556	79.4	73,580	92.2
United States	54,017	74.5	66,757	83.6
Latin America and the Caribbean	2,165	3.0	4,844	6.1
Canada	1,374	1.9	1,979	2.5
Europe	7,318	10.1	4,042	5.1
EU	6,724	9.3	3,382	4.2
EFTA	414	0.6	624	0.8
Russia	—	—	—	—
Other Europe	180	0.2	36	0.1
Asia	7,296	10.1	1,896	2.4
Japan	3,608	5.0	928	1.2
Africa	120	0.2	33	—
Other	190	0.3	272	0.3
TOTAL	72,480	100.0[6]	79,823	100.0

Transport and communications

Transport. Railroads (1994): route length 16,432 mi, 26,445 km; passenger-mi 2,382,000,000, passenger-km 3,833,000,000; short ton-mi cargo 24,042,000,000, metric ton-km cargo 35,100,000,000. Roads (1995): total length 188,886 mi, 303,983 km (paved 36%[12]). Vehicles (1994): passenger cars 8,449,969; trucks and buses 3,950,456. Merchant marine (1992): vessels (100 gross tons and over) 635; total deadweight tonnage 1,495,311. Air transport (1994): passenger-mi 16,049,310,000, passenger-km 25,828,910,000; short ton-mi cargo 1,679,836,000, metric ton-km cargo 2,452,519,000; airports (1995) 83.
Communications. Daily newspapers (1992): total number 292; total circulation 11,256,000[13]; circulation per 1,000 population 142[13]. Radio (1995): 21,000,000 receivers (1 per 4.3 persons). Television (1992): 13,100,000 receivers (1 per 6.6 persons). Telephones (main lines; 1995): 8,736,000 (1 per 10 persons).

Education and health

Education (1994–95)

	schools	teachers	students	student/ teacher ratio
Primary (age 6–12)	91,857	507,669	14,572,202	28.7
Secondary (age 12–18)	22,255	256,831	4,493,173	17.5
Voc., teacher tr.[14]	6,571	77,347	1,076,700	13.9
Higher	10,341	319,551	3,763,938	11.8

Literacy (1992): total population age 15 and over literate 45,050,633 (85.9%); males literate 22,181,999 (88.7%); females literate 22,868,634 (83.5%).
Health (1994): physicians 146,021 (1 per 613 persons); hospital beds 74,891 (1 per 1,196 persons); infant mortality rate per 1,000 live births (1993) 17.5.
Food (1992): daily per capita caloric intake 3,146 (vegetable products 83%, animal products 17%); 135% of FAO recommended minimum requirement.

Military

Total active duty personnel (1996): 175,000 (army 74.3%, navy 21.1%, air force 4.6%). *Military expenditure as percentage of GNP* (1994): 0.6% (world 3.0%); per capita expenditure U.S.$24.

[1]The Mexican new peso, equivalent to 1,000 old Mexican pesos, was introduced on January 1, 1993. On January 1, 1996, the name of the currency was changed to Mexican peso. [2]Manufacturing only. [3]Through 1982, cannabis remained the most abused drug. [4]Imputed bank service charge. [5]Includes 819,132 unemployed persons. [6]Detail does not add to total given because of rounding. [7]1988. [8]Metal products includes Nonelectrical machinery and transport equipment and Electrical machinery. [9]1984. [10]Exchange rates and treasury bill rates are expressed in period averages; international reserves are expressed in end-of-period rates. [11]Totals include adjustments of unspecified nature. [12]1993. [13]1986. [14]1992–93.

Micronesia, Federated States of

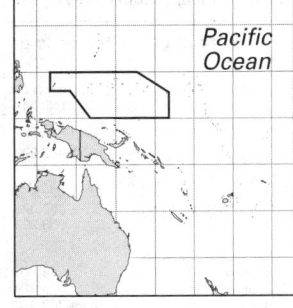

Pacific Ocean

Official name: Federated States of Micronesia.
Political status: federal republic in free association with the United States with one legislative house (Congress [14])[1].
Head of state and government: President.
Capital: Palikir, on Pohnpei.
Official language: none.
Official religion: none.
Monetary unit: 1 U.S. dollar (U.S.$) = 100 cents; valuation (Oct. 11, 1996) 1 £ = U.S.$1.58.

Area and population

States Major Islands	area sq mi	area sq km	population 1994 census
Chuuk (Truk)	49.1	127.2	52,870
Weno (Moen) Islands	7.0	18.1	15,253[2]
Kosrae	42.3	109.6	7,354
Kosrae Island	42.3	109.6	7,435[3]
Pohnpei	133.3	345.2	33,372
Pohnpei Island	129.0	334.1	33,372
Yap	45.9	118.9	11,128
Yap Island	38.7	100.2	6,650[4]
TOTAL	270.8[5]	701.4[5]	104,724

Demography

Population (1996): 106,000.
Density (1996): persons per sq mi 394.1, persons per sq km 151.7.
Urban-rural (1992): urban 26.0%; rural 74.0%.
Sex distribution (1994): male 51.09%; female 48.91%.
Age breakdown (1994): under 15, 42.7%; 15–29, 27.4%; 30–44, 17.1%; 45–59, 7.6%; 60 and over, 5.2%.
Population projection: (2000) 110,000; (2010) 120,000.
Doubling time: 24 years.
Ethnic composition (1980): Trukese 41.1%; Pohnpeian 25.9%; Mortlockese 8.3%; Kosraean 7.4%; Yapese 6.0%; Ulithian, or Woleaian, 4.0%; Pingelapese, or Mokilese, 1.2%; Western Trukese 1.0%; Palauan 0.4%; Filipino 0.2%; other 4.5%.
Religious affiliation: Christianity is the predominant religious tradition, with the Kosraeans, Pohnpeians, and Trukese being mostly Protestant and the Yapese mostly Roman Catholic.
Major cities (1989): Weno (Moen) 15,253; Tol 6,705[6]; Kolonia 6,169.

Vital statistics

Birth rate per 1,000 population (1992): 36.7 (world avg. 25.0); legitimate, n.a.; illegitimate, n.a.
Death rate per 1,000 population (1992): 7.8 (world avg. 9.3).
Natural increase rate per 1,000 population (1992): 28.9 (world avg. 15.7).
Total fertility rate (avg. births per childbearing woman; 1994): 5.1.
Marriage rate per 1,000 population: n.a.
Divorce rate per 1,000 population: n.a.
Life expectancy at birth (1991)[7]: male 70.6 years; female 77.3 years.
Major causes of death per 100,000 population (1991)[7]: diseases of the cerebrovascular system 89.6; diseases of the respiratory system 42.8, of which tuberculosis 8.9; malignant neoplasms (cancers) 38.8; homicide, suicide, and accidents 30.8; infectious and parasitic diseases 22.9 (with especially high morbidity rates for tuberculosis and leprosy).

National economy

Budget (1994–95). Revenue: U.S.$172,500,000 (external grants 65.1%; tax revenue 12.2%; fishing rights fees 12.1%). Expenditures: U.S.$169,100,000 (current expenditures 82.6%, of which government services 74.4%, transfer payments 7.0%, debt services 3.0%; capital expenditure 17.4%).
Public debt (external, outstanding; 1994–95): U.S.$119,500,000.
Production (metric tons except as noted). Agriculture, forestry, fishing: n.a.; however, Micronesia's major crops include coconuts (which provide annually more than 4,000 tons of copra), breadfruit, cassava, sweet potatoes, peppers, and a variety of tropical fruits (including bananas); livestock comprises mostly pigs and poultry; fish catch (1993) 1,555, of which skipjack tuna 450. Mining and quarrying: quarrying of sand and aggregate for local construction only. Manufacturing: n.a.; however, copra and coconut oil, traditionally important products, are being displaced by garment production; the manufacture of handicrafts and personal items (clothing, mats, boats, etc.) by individuals is also important. Construction: n.a. Energy production (consumption): electricity (kW-hr; 1990) 40,000,000 (40,000,000); coal, none (n.a.); crude petroleum, none (n.a.); petroleum products (metric tons; 1992) none (77,000); natural gas, none (n.a.).
Household income and expenditure. Average household size (1988–89) 8.5; annual income per household (1989) U.S.$3,435; sources of income (1994): wages and salaries 51.8%, operating surplus 23.0%, social security 2.1%; expenditure (1985): food and beverages 73.5%.
Land use (1984)[8]: forested 22.5%; meadows and pastures 13.5%; agricultural and under permanent cultivation 33.5%; other 30.5%.

Gross national product (at current market prices; 1994): U.S.$202,000,000 (U.S.$1,890 per capita).

Structure of gross domestic product and labour force

	1983 in value U.S.$'000,000	1983 % of total value	1990 labour force	1990 % of labour force
Agriculture and fishing	44.9	42.2	12,700	41.6
Trade	12.7	11.9	[9]	[9]
Public administration	31.5	29.6	6,300	20.7
Manufacturing			1,600	5.2
Construction			1,900	6.2
Transportation, communications, and public utilities	17.4	16.3	...	...
Finance			...	...
Services			3,700[9]	12.1[9]
Other			4,400[10]	14.4[10]
TOTAL	106.5	100.0	30,500[5]	100.0[5]

Population economically active (1990): total 30,500; activity rate of total population 60.6% (participation rates: ages 15–64, 60.6%; female 46.9%; unemployed 13.5%).

Price and earnings indexes (1992 = 100)

	1990	1991	1992	1993	1994	1995
Price index	91.6	95.2	100.0	106.0	110.2	114.6
Annual wage index[11]	...	...	100.0	109.4	110.3	115.8

Tourism (1990): number of visitors 23,171.

Foreign trade

Balance of trade (current prices)

	1989	1990	1991	1992	1993	1994
U.S.$'000,000	−55.4	−62.2	−59.9	−57.3	−80.3	−50.5
% of total	61.6%	58.9%	51.0%	40.8%	57.9%	24.3%

Imports (1994): U.S.$129,060,000 (manufactured goods 32.0%; food, beverages, and tobacco 24.3%; machinery and transport equipment 23.5%; mineral fuels 14.3%; chemicals 4.4%). *Major import sources:* United States (including Guam) 56.1%; Japan 32.0%; Australia 3.5%.
Exports (1994): U.S.$78,570,000 (marine products 94.3%; clothing and textiles 2.8%; agricultural products 2.1%, of which bananas 0.6%, copra 0.5%). *Major export destinations* (1992): Japan 80.0%; United States 9.3%; Guam 8.3%; South Pacific Region 2.4%.

Transport and communications

Transport. Railroads: none. Roads (1990): total length 140 mi, 226 km (paved 17%). Vehicles: passenger cars, trucks, and buses, n.a. Merchant marine (1992): vessels (100 gross tons and over) 17; deadweight tonnage 6,863. Air transport: n.a.; airports (1996) with scheduled flights 6.
Communications. Daily newspapers: there are no private daily newspapers. Radio (1995): total number of receivers 70,000 (1 per 1.5 persons). Television (1995): total number of receivers 7,000 (1 per 15 persons). Telephones (main lines; 1993): 6,015 (1 per 17 persons).

Education and health

Education (1987–88)

	schools	teachers	students	student/ teacher ratio
Elementary (age 6–12)	177	1,051[12]	25,139	22.2[12]
Secondary (age 13–18)	16	314[12]	5,385	13.2[12]
College	1	...	861[13]	...

Educational attainment (1980). Percentage of population age 25 and over having: no formal schooling 24.8%; some primary education 38.2%; primary 11.7%; some secondary 7.7%; secondary 9.6%; higher 8.0%. *Literacy* (1980): total population age 15 and over literate 30,074 (76.7%); males literate 13,710 (67.0%); females literate 16,364 (87.2%).
Health (1993): physicians 50 (1 per 2,069 persons); hospital beds 325 (1 per 318 persons); infant mortality rate per 1,000 live births (1994) 49.0.
Food: daily per capita caloric intake, n.a.

Military

External security is provided by the United States.

[1]On Nov. 3, 1986, the United States unilaterally terminated the UN trusteeship it held over the Federated States of Micronesia (FSM), thus formally initiating their free-association political status. On Dec. 22, 1990, the United Nations Security Council joined the Trusteeship Council, which had endorsed the termination of the trusteeship in May 1986. [2]1989. [3]1991. [4]1987. [5]Detail does not add to total given because of rounding. [6]1980. [7]Based on registered deaths only. [8]Includes all areas formerly constituting the U.S. Trust Territory of the Pacific Islands. [9]Services includes Trade. [10]Includes 4,100 unemployed. [11]Public sector only. [12]1983–84. [13]1986.

Moldova

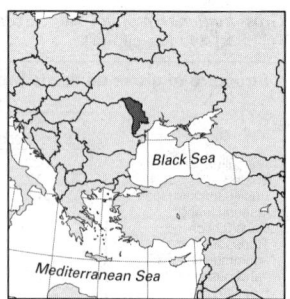

Official name: Republica Moldova
(Republic of Moldova).
Form of government: unitary multiparty
republic with a single legislative body
(Parliament [104]).
Head of state: President.
Head of government: Prime Minister.
Capital: Chişinău.
Official language: Romanian.
Official religion: none.
Monetary unit[1]: 1 Moldovan leu
(plural lei) = 100 bani; valuation (Oct.
11, 1996) free rate, 1 U.S.$ = 4.61
Moldovan lei; 1 £ = 7.26 Moldovan lei.

Area and population

Administrative subdivisions[2]

Cities	area sq km[3]	population 1991 est.	Rural districts	area sq km[3]	population 1991 est.
Bălţi	...	164,900	Drochia	780	80,200
Cahul	...	44,300	Dubăsari	670	47,300
Chişinău	160	753,500	Edineţ	860	90,800
Dubăsari	...	32,000	Făleşti	1,070	93,600
Orhei	...	39,100	Floreşti	830	77,200
Râbniţa	...	62,900	Glodeni	760	65,400
Soroca	...	42,700	Grigoriopol	820	52,700
Tighina (Bendery)	...	141,500	Hânceşti	1,350	115,700
Tiraspol	...	204,800	Ialoveni	930	85,800
Ungheni	...	39,400	Leova	720	50,900
			Nisporeni	760	79,800
Rural districts			Ocniţa	660	64,700
Anenil Noi	830	77,400	Orhei	1,100	95,500
Basarabeasca	660	43,800	Râbniţa	850	33,600
Brinceni	810	83,600	Rezina	670	55,000
Cahul	800	43,400	Rişcani	1,000	83,800
Cainari	...	41,900	Sângerei	1,020	90,500
Călăraş	760	84,500	Slobozia	960	115,700
Camenca	820	60,500	Şoldăneşti	560	46,500
Cantemir	860	59,700	Soroca	870	58,600
Căuşeni	1,120	73,500	Ştefan-Vodă	1,030	76,300
Ciadâr-Lunga	720	67,300	Străşeni	760	97,000
Cimişlia	1,170	60,400	Taraclia	620	44,800
Comrat	840	70,300	Teleneşti	860	74,700
Criuleni	850	91,100	Ungheni	1,070	78,500
Donduşeni	890	68,100	Vulcăneşti	930	61,100
			TOTAL	33,700[4]	4,366,300

Demography

Population (1996): 4,372,000.
Density (1996): persons per sq mi 208.8, persons per sq km 129.7.
Urban-rural (1995): urban 46.8%; rural 53.2%.
Sex distribution (1992): male 47.08%; female 52.92%.
Age breakdown (1989): under 15, 27.9%; 15–29, 22.9%; 30–44, 21.0%; 45–59, 15.6%; 60–74, 9.7%; 75 and over, 2.9%.
Population projection: (2000) 4,437,000; (2010) 4,706,000.
Doubling time: not applicable; doubling time exceeds 100 years.
Ethnic composition (1989): Moldovan 64.5%; Ukrainian 13.8%; Russian 13.0%; Gagauz 3.5%; Jewish 2.0%; Bulgarian 1.5%; other 1.7%.
Religious affiliation: believers are predominantly Eastern Orthodox.
Major cities (1991): Chişinău 753,500; Tiraspol 186,000; Bălţi 164,900; Tighina (Bendery) 141,500; Râbniţa 62,900.

Vital statistics

Birth rate per 1,000 population (1994): 14.3 (world avg. 25.0); legitimate 88.8%; illegitimate 11.2%.
Death rate per 1,000 population (1994): 11.8 (world avg. 9.3).
Natural increase rate per 1,000 population (1994): 2.5 (world avg. 15.7).
Total fertility rate (avg. births per childbearing woman; 1993): 2.5.
Marriage rate per 1,000 population (1994): 7.8.
Divorce rate per 1,000 population (1994): 3.2.
Life expectancy at birth (1994): male 64.0 years; female 71.0 years.
Major causes of death per 100,000 population (1993): diseases of the circulatory system 434.8; malignant neoplasms (cancers) 133.1; accidents and violence 105.8; diseases of the digestive system 91.6; diseases of the respiratory system 60.7; infectious and parasitic diseases 11.0.

National economy

Budget (1995). Revenue: 1,438,500,000,000 lei (enterprise profits tax 29.1%, value-added tax 16.1%, excise duties 10.5%, income tax 9.0%, property tax 1.5%). Expenditures: 1,718,800,000,000 lei (goods and services 41.4%, subsidies and transfers 10.7%, interest payments 5.7%).
Production (metric tons except as noted). Agriculture, forestry, fishing (1995): grain 2,026,000 (of which wheat 1,130,000), sugar beets 1,900,000, fruit (except grapes) 1,260,000, grapes 851,000, vegetables (except potatoes) 750,-000, potatoes 384,000; livestock (number of live animals) 1,425,000 sheep, 1,100,000 pigs, 832,000 cattle, 13,840,000 poultry; roundwood (1991) 125,000 cu m; fish catch (1993) 4,700. Mining and quarrying (1994): limestone 1,000,000; clay 250,000; gypsum 150,000. Manufacturing ('000,000 lei; 1994): food processing 1,339,373; machinery and metalworking 402,625; construction materials 168,585; textiles 111,459; clothing 55,368. Construction (1990): 490,900,000 lei. Energy production (consumption): electricity (kW-hr; 1994) 8,228,000,000 (8,579,000,000); coal (metric tons; 1994) none (2,141,000); crude petroleum (barrels; 1990) none (51,625,000); petroleum products (metric tons; 1994) none (1,085,000); natural gas (cu m; 1994) none (2,611,000,000).

Gross national product (1994): U.S.$3,853,000,000 (U.S.$870 per capita)[5].

Structure of gross domestic product and labour force

	1994			
	in value '000 lei	% of total value	labour force	% of labour force
Agriculture	1,877,607	43.3	767,000	45.1
Mining }			39,000	2.2
Manufacturing }	1,402,883	32.3	232,000	13.7
Public utilities	...	...	39,000	2.2
Construction	429,551	9.9	91,000	5.4
Transp. and commun.	350,028	8.1	73,000	4.3
Trade	253,969	5.8	107,000	6.3
Finance	...	...	20,000	1.2
Pub. admin., defense	...	...	32,000	1.9
Services	8,176	0.2	305,000	18.0
Other	15,879	0.4	33,000	1.9
TOTAL	4,339,079[6]	100.0	1,699,000	100.0

Population economically active (1994): total (1995) 1,693,000; activity rate of total population 44.8% (participation rates: ages 16–59 [male], 16–54 [female] 85.2%; female 53.0%; unemployed 1.4%).
Land use (1994): forest 12.5%; pasture 12.9%; agriculture 64.7%; other 9.9%.

Price and earnings indexes (1990 = 100)

	1990	1991	1992	1993	1994
Consumer price index	100.0	262.0	3,605	33,780	71,310
Earnings index	100.0	183.0	402.0	353.0	192.0

Household income and expenditure. Average household size (1989) 3.4; income per household (1990) 4,000 rubles[5]; sources of income (1994): wages and salaries 41.2%, social benefits 15.3%, agricultural income 10.4%, other 33.1%; expenditure (1994): consumer goods 69.3%, services 15.2%.

Foreign trade

Balance of trade (current prices)

	1993	1994
'000,000 lei	...	−352.0
% of total	...	9.5%

Imports (1994): 2,017,000,000 lei (1993; petroleum products 38.3%, food products 13.8%, machinery 8.4%, chemical products 7.8%, ferrous and nonferrous metals 4.3%, light industrial products 3.9%). *Major import sources* (1994): Russia 64.6%; Ukraine 25.1%; Belarus 4.1%; Azerbaijan 2.4%.
Exports (1994): 1,692,000,000 lei (1993; food 41.8%, machinery 19.6%, light industrial products 8.5%, metals 4.6%). *Major export destinations* (1994): Russia 69.9%; Ukraine 16.7%; Belarus 5.7%; Azerbaijan 3.1%.

Transport and communications

Transport. Railroads (1994): length 745 mi, 1,200 km; (1991) passenger-km 8,875,000,000; (1991) metric ton-km cargo 15,007,000,000. Roads (1995): total length 7,615 mi, 12,259 km (paved 87.2%). Vehicles (1994): passenger cars 169,387; trucks and buses 71,310. Air transport (1990): passenger-km 2,352,000,000; metric ton-km cargo 19,000,000; airports (1996) 1.
Communications. Daily newspapers (1992): total number 5; total circulation 205,000; circulation per 1,000 population 45. Radio (1996): 1,550,000 receivers (1 per 2.8 persons). Television (1991): 1,264,000 receivers (1 per 3.4 persons). Telephones (main lines; 1993): 523,900 (1 per 8.3 persons).

Education and health

Education (1994–95)

	schools	teachers	students	student/ teacher ratio
Primary (age 7–13) }	1,700	53,000[7]	731,000	13.7[7]
Secondary (age 14–17) }				
Voc., teacher tr.	64	...	41,800	...
Higher	18	...	49,400	...

Educational attainment (1989). Percentage of population age 15 and over having: no formal schooling or some primary education 24.5%; some secondary 20.4%; secondary or some postsecondary 46.4%; higher 8.7%. *Literacy* (1989): percentage of total population age 15 and over literate 96.4%; males literate 98.6%; females literate 94.4%.
Health (1994): physicians 17,400 (1 per 250 persons); hospital beds 53,070 (1 per 82 persons); infant mortality rate per 1,000 live births 22.6.

Military

Total active duty personnel (1996): 11,900 (army 89.1%, air force 10.9%). About 6,400 Russian troops remained in Moldova in late 1996. *Military expenditure as percentage of GNP* (1994): 0.8% (world 3.0%); per capita expenditure U.S.$21.

---

[1]The monetary unit of Moldova, at independence on Aug. 27, 1991, was the Russian ruble. On June 10, 1992, the national bank issued Moldovan ruble banknotes called coupons, valued at par with and circulated in parallel with Russian rubles. On Nov. 29, 1993, the Moldovan leu was introduced at a 1,000-to-1 ratio with the Moldovan coupon. On Nov. 29, 1994, the leu became the sole national currency. [2]Administrative subdivisions at independence in 1991. Area and population figures include the Gagauz autonomous region, recognized by the Moldovan government, and the separatist Transdniestrian republic, not recognized by the Moldovan government. Separate data for these regions is not available. [3]One sq km is equal to approximately 0.3861 sq mi. [4]Total includes approximately 320 sq km (125 sq mi) of area above the last total for the country published by Moldovan authorities. Source of discrepancy is unknown. [5]Ruble-area GNP and exchange-rate data are very speculative. [6]Detail does not add to total given because of rounding. [7]1991–92.

Mongolia

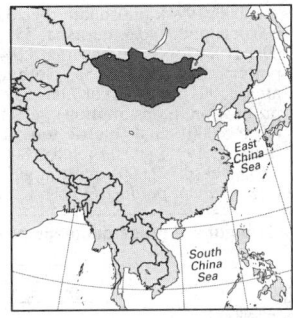

Official name: Mongol Uls
(Mongolia).
Form of government: unitary multiparty
republic with one legislative house
(State Great Hural [76]).
Chief of state: President.
Head of government: Prime Minister.
Capital: Ulaanbaatar (Ulan Bator).
Official language: Khalkha Mongolian.
Official religion: none.
Monetary unit: 1 tugrik (Tug) = 100
möngö; valuation (Oct. 11, 1996) 1
U.S.$ = Tug 466.67; 1 £ = Tug 735.15.

Area and population		area		population
				1991
Provinces	Capitals	sq mi	sq km	estimate
Arhangay	Tsetserleg	21,000	55,000	89,200
Bayan-Ölgiy	Ölgiy	18,000	46,000	99,300
Bayanhongor	Bayanhongor	45,000	116,000	78,700
Bulgan	Bulgan	19,000	49,000	56,700
Darhan-Uul	Darhan	100	200	88,600
Dornod	Choybalsan	47,700	123,500	82,600
Dornogovĭ	Saynshand	43,000	111,000	58,600
Dundgovĭ	Mandalgovi	30,000[1]	78,000[1]	51,900[1]
Dzavhan	Uliastay	32,000	82,000	93,600
Govĭ-Altay	Altay	55,000	142,000	65,100
Govĭ-Sümber	Choyr	[1]	[1]	[1]
Hentiy	Öndörhaan	32,000	82,000	76,700
Hovd	Hovd	29,000	76,000	81,100
Hövsgöl	Mörön	39,000	101,000	106,900
Ömnögovĭ	Dalandzadgad	64,000	165,000	43,500
Orhon	Erdenet	300	800	58,200
Övörhangay	Arvayheer	24,000	63,000	100,400
Selenge	Sühbaatar	16,000	42,000	92,000
Sühbaatar	Baruun-Urt	32,000	82,000	53,500
Töv	Dzüünmod	31,000	81,000	105,900
Uvs	Ulaangom	27,000	69,000	91,800
Autonomous municipality				
Ulaanbaatar	—	800	2,000	575,000
TOTAL		604,800[2]	1,566,500	2,149,300

Demography

Population (1996): 2,334,000.
Density (1996): persons per sq mi 3.9, persons per sq km 1.5.
Urban-rural (1995): urban 62.0%; rural 38.0%.
Sex distribution (1994): male 49.80%; female 50.20%.
Age breakdown (1995): under 15, 39.0%; 15–29, 29.5%; 30–44, 18.0%; 45–59, 7.8%; 60–69, 3.3%; 70 and over, 2.4%.
Population projection: (2000) 2,479,000; (2010) 2,879,000.
Doubling time: 47 years.
Ethnic composition (1989): Khalkha Mongol 78.8%; Kazak 5.9%; Dörbed Mongol 2.7%; Bayad 1.9%; Buryat Mongol 1.7%; Dariganga Mongol 1.4%; other 7.6%.
Religious affiliation: although formal freedom of worship exists, all traditional forms of religious practice (lamaistic Buddhism, shamanism, Islam, and others) have been greatly reduced during the 20th century; reliable data on the current situation do not exist.
Major cities (1994): Ulaanbaatar (Ulan Bator) 680,000; Darhan 85,800; Erdenet 63,000; Choybalsan 46,000; Ölgiy (1991) 29,400.

Vital statistics

Birth rate per 1,000 population (1996): 26.8 (world avg. 25.0).
Death rate per 1,000 population (1996): 6.9 (world avg. 9.3).
Natural increase rate per 1,000 population (1996): 19.9 (world avg. 15.7).
Total fertility rate (avg. births per childbearing woman; 1996): 3.4.
Marriage rate per 1,000 population (1989): 7.8.
Divorce rate per 1,000 population (1989): 0.5.
Life expectancy at birth (1996): male 64.0 years; female 67.0 years.
Major causes of death per 100,000 population: n.a.; however, in the early 1990s, major causes of mortality included diseases of the cardiovascular system, diseases of the respiratory system, diseases of the cerebrovascular system, malignant neoplasms (cancers), and injuries, accidents, and poisoning.

National economy

Budget (1996). Revenue: Tug 116,542,600,000 (taxes 75.4%, of which income tax 26.2%, social security contribution 16.9%, sales tax 11.9%, customs duties 9.6%; nontax revenue 24.6%). Expenditures: Tug 131,395,700,000 (social and cultural services 63.1%, of which social security 22.4%, education 20.8%, health 14.1%; capital investment 13.2%; salaries in state-run enterprises 9.5%; defense 8.9%).
Public debt (external; 1994): U.S.$382,400,000.
Tourism (1994): number of tourists 7,000.
Production (metric tons except as noted). Agriculture, forestry, fishing (1995): cereals 260,900 (of which wheat 256,700), potatoes 52,000, vegetables 10,-000; livestock (number of live animals) 13,718,600 sheep, 8,520,700 goats, 3,317,000 cattle, 2,150,000 horses, 390,000 camels, 23,500 pigs; roundwood (1994) 540,500 cu m; fish catch (1993) 130. Mining and quarrying (1995): fluorspar 526,900; copper 346,300; molybdenum 3,906; gold 4,504 kg. Manufacturing (value added by manufacturing in Tug '000,000; 1994): food products 30,802.7; textiles 14,333.7; chemicals 6,900.0; leather and footwear 5,880.0; construction materials 3,381.0; wood products 1,962.0; clothing and apparel 1,432.0; printing and publishing 450.2; glass and ceramics 53.8.

Construction (1994): residential 120,400 sq m; nonresidential, n.a. Energy production (consumption): electricity (kW-hr; 1994) 3,265,000,000 (3,472,-000,000); coal (metric tons; 1994) 635,000 (635,000); crude petroleum, none (n.a.); petroleum products (metric tons; 1994) none (595,000).
Gross national product (1994): U.S.$801,000,000 (U.S.$340 per capita).

Structure of gross domestic product and labour force				
	1995			
	in value Tug '000,000[3]	% of total value	labour force	% of labour force
Agriculture	1,430	16.1	345,300	39.8
Manufacturing and mining	2,404	27.0	101,300	11.7
Construction	208	2.3	27,700	3.2
Transp. and commun.	366	4.1	32,000	3.7
Trade	1,569	17.6	85,800	9.9
Services[4] }	2,931[5]	32.9[5]	110,800	12.8
Other }			165,300[6]	19.0[6]
TOTAL	8,908	100.0	868,200	100.0[2]

Population economically active (1995): total 868,200; activity rate of total population 37.7% (participation rates: ages 16–59 [1989] 77.9%; female [1992] 46.0%; unemployed 7.6%).

Price and earnings indexes (1990 = 100)							
	1989	1990	1991	1992	1993	1994	1995
Consumer price index	46.4	100.0	220.2	523.9	1,928.6	3,616.9	5,670.7
Monthly earnings index	96.7	100.0	184.0	260.1	991.4	2,071.8	2,781.3

Household income and expenditure. Average family size (1993) 4.4; income per household (1992)[7] Tug 5,500 (U.S.$140); sources of income (1993): wages and salaries 72.1%, transfer payments 9.7%, self-employment 9.5%[8], other 8.7%; expenditure (1991): food 48.6%, clothing 21.9%, housing 10.5%, transportation and communications 6.8%, household goods 4.1%, education and recreation 3.9%, healthcare 0.7%, other 3.5%.
Land use (1994): forested 8.8%; meadows and pastures 74.8%; agricultural and under permanent cultivation 0.8%; other 15.6%.

Foreign trade

Balance of trade (current prices)						
	1990	1991	1992	1993	1994	1995
U.S.$'000,000	−496	−101	−29	−21	+106	−22
% of total	35.8%	12.7%	3.9%	3.0%	19.5%	2.4%

Imports (1995): U.S.$473,000,000 (capital goods 31.5%, petroleum products 18.5%, consumer products 13.9%, raw materials 13.7%, food products 7.7%). *Major import sources:* Russia 52.0%; Japan 11.4%; China 10.1%; South Korea 5.2%; Germany 3.8%; U.S. 3.6%.
Exports (1995): U.S.$451,000,000 (copper concentrate 54.9%, cashmere products 8.7%, gold ore 5.6%, fluorite concentrate 3.4%, molybdenum concentrate and fluorite ore 2.3%). *Major export destinations:* Japan 18.7%; Kazakstan 15.2%; China 14.3%; Switzerland 13.2%; Russia 13.1%; U.S. 5.8%; U.K. 3.2%.

Transport and communications

Transport. Railroads (1994): length 1,294 mi, 2,083 km; passenger-km 789,-600,000; metric ton-km cargo 2,131,700. Roads (1996): total length 31,000 mi, 50,000 km (paved 3%). Vehicles (1996): passenger cars 28,000; trucks and buses 28,000. Merchant marine: vessels (100 gross tons and over) none. Air transport (1993): passenger-km 290,000,000; metric ton-km cargo 5,800,000; airports (1996) with scheduled flights 1.
Communications. Daily newspapers (1992): total number 3; total circulation 208,000; circulation per 1,000 population 90. Radio (1995): total number of receivers 280,000 (1 per 8 persons). Television (1995): total number of receivers 135,000 (1 per 17 persons). Telephones (main lines; 1995): 75,500 (1 per 30 persons).

Education and health

Education (1994–95)				
	schools	teachers	students	student/ teacher ratio
Primary and secondary (age 8–18)	659	19,097	381,204	20.0
Vocational	49	2,500[9]	29,900	19.0[9]
Higher	12	1,465[9]	13,800	9.4[9]

Educational attainment (1989). Percentage of population age 10 and over having: primary education 33.7%; some secondary 31.9%; complete secondary 16.9%; vocational secondary 9.4%; some higher and complete higher 8.1%.
Literacy (1988): percentage of total population age 15 and over literate 82.9%; males literate 88.6%; females literate 77.2%.
Health (1993): physicians 5,911 (1 per 401 persons); hospital beds 23,400 (1 per 101 persons); infant mortality rate per 1,000 live births (1996) 54.0.
Food (1992): daily per capita caloric intake 1,899 (vegetable products 56%, animal products 44%); 78% of FAO recommended minimum requirement.

Military

Total active duty personnel (1996): 21,100 (army 94.8%, air force 5.2%). *Military expenditure as percentage of GNP* (1994): 2.4% (world 3.0%); per capita expenditure (1994) U.S.$7.

[1]Dundgovĭ includes Govĭ-Sümber. [2]Detail does not add to total given because of rounding. [3]At constant prices of 1986. [4]Services includes finance, public administration, and defense. [5]Includes depreciation of fixed capital. [6]Includes 66,000 unemployed. [7]Urban households. [8]Includes income from agricultural cooperatives. [9]1990–91.

Morocco[1]

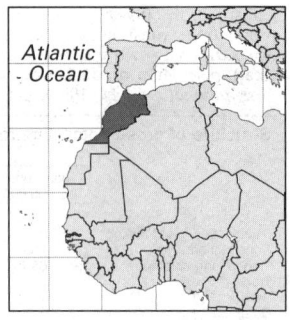

Atlantic Ocean

Official name: Al-Mamlakah al-Maghribīyah (Kingdom of Morocco).
Form of government: constitutional monarchy with one legislative house (House of Representatives [333]).
Chief of state: King.
Head of government: King assisted by Prime Minister.
Capital: Rabat.
Official language: Arabic.
Official religion: Islam.
Monetary unit: 1 Moroccan dirham (DH) = 100 Moroccan francs; valuation (Oct. 11, 1996) 1 U.S.$ = DH 8.79; 1 £ = DH 13.84.

Population (1994 census)

Region Province/Prefecture	Population	Region Province/Prefecture	Population
Centre		Larache	431,476
Azilal	454,914	Sidi Kacem	645,872
Ben Slimane	213,398	Tanger	627,963
Beni Mellal	869,748	Tétouan	537,290
El-Jadida	970,894	*Prefecture*	
Khouribga	480,839	Rabat	623,457
Settat	847,422	Salé	631,803
Prefecture		Skhirate-Témara	244,801
Aïn Chok–Hay Hassani	516,261	**Oriental**	
Aïn Sebaâ–Hay Mohemmedi	520,993	Berkane-Taourirt	399,017
Ben M'sik–Sidi Othmane	704,365	Figuig	117,011
Casablanca-Anfa	523,279	Jerada	149,686
Al Fida–Derb Sultan	386,700	Nador	683,914
Mechouar de Casablanca	3,956	*Prefecture*	
Mohammedia	170,063	Oujda-Angad	419,063
Sidi Bernoussi–Zenata	268,586	**Sud**	
Centre-Nord		Assa-Zag	21,848
Boulemane	161,622	Chtouka–Aït Baha	240,092
Al-Hoceïma	382,972	Guelmim	147,124
Sefrou	237,095	Laâyoune[1]	8,251
Taounate	628,840	Ouarzazate	694,884
Taza	708,025	Tan-Tan	58,079
Prefecture		Taroudannt	693,968
Fès El-Jadid–Dar Dbibagh	256,340	Tata	119,298
Fès-Médina	284,822	Tiznit	347,821
Zouagha–Moulay Yacoub	382,594	*Prefecture*	
Centre-Sud		Agadir–Ida-ou-Tanane	365,965
El-Hajeb	180,494	Inezgane–Aït Melloul	292,799
Ifrane	127,677	**Tensift**	
Khenifra	465,061	Chichaoua	311,800
Er-Rachidia	522,117	Essaouira	433,681
Prefecture		Al-Haouz	435,090
Al-Ismailia	314,916	El-Kelaâ des Sraghna	682,428
Meknès–El-Menzeh	293,525	Safi	822,564
Nord-Ouest		*Prefecture*	
Chefchaouen	439,303	Marrakech-Médina	189,367
Kenitra	979,210	Marrakech-Ménara	432,547
Khemisset	485,541	Sidi Youssef Ben Ali	239,291
		TOTAL	25,829,822

Demography

Area: 177,117 sq mi, 458,730 sq km.
Population (1996): 26,736,000.
Density (1996): persons per sq mi 151.0, persons per sq km 58.3.
Urban-rural (1994): urban 51.4%; rural 48.6%.
Sex distribution (1995): male 50.04%; female 49.96%.
Age breakdown (1995): under 15, 36.1%; 15–29, 29.8%; 30–44, 18.9%; 45–59, 9.0%; 60–74, 5.0%; 75 and over, 1.2%.
Population projection: (2000) 28,804,000; (2010) 33,908,000.
Ethnic composition (1986): Arab 70%; Berber 30%; other, less than 1%.
Religious affiliation (1993): Muslim (mostly Sunnī) 98.7%; Christian 1.1%.
Major urban areas (1994): Casablanca 2,941,000; Rabat-Salé 1,386,000; Fès 510,000.

Vital statistics

Birth rate per 1,000 population (1995): 27.9 (world avg. 25.0).
Death rate per 1,000 population (1995): 6.0 (world avg. 9.3).
Natural increase rate per 1,000 population (1995): 21.9 (world avg. 15.7).
Total fertility rate (avg. births per childbearing woman; 1995): 3.7.
Life expectancy at birth (1995): male 67.0 years; female 71.0 years.
Major causes of death (1989)[2]: childhood diseases 22.9%; circulatory diseases 15.4%; accidents 7.3%; infectious and parasitic diseases 6.3%; cancers 5.6%.

National economy

Budget. Revenue (1994): DH 89,790,000,000 (indirect taxes 26.4%, customs and stamp duties 18.0%). Expenditures (1994): DH 93,380,000,000 (current expenditure 50.4%, debt payments 29.1%, investment expenditure 20.4%).
Public debt (external, outstanding; 1993): U.S.$21,560,000,000.
Land use (1994): forest 20.1%; pasture 47.1%; agriculture 20.8%; other 12.0%.
Tourism (1994): receipts U.S.$1,265,000,000; expenditures U.S.$302,000,000.
Production (metric tons except as noted). Agriculture, forestry, fishing (1995): sugar beets 2,717,400, wheat 1,090,710, sugar cane 1,031,320, potatoes 774,400, oranges 672,000, tomatoes 623,580, barley 607,690, olives 436,360, dates 97,600; livestock (number of live animals) 16,586,200 sheep, 4,423,700 goats, 2,489,500 cattle, 85,000,000 chickens; roundwood (1994) 1,558,900 cu m; fish catch (1994) 608,939. Mining and quarrying (value of production in DH

'000,000; 1994): phosphate rock 3,600.0; zinc 276.9; lead 234.1; mineral water 200.0; copper 140.6; fluorspar 55.9. Manufacturing (value added in DH '000,000; 1993) food and beverages 9,435; chemical products 4,039; textiles 3,528; pottery and china 3,353; clothing 2,785. Construction (authorized, urban areas; 1994): residential 7,069,557 sq m, nonresidential 998,424 sq m. Energy production (consumption): electricity (kW-hr; 1994) 10,773,000,000 (11,693,000,000); coal (metric tons; 1994) 650,000 (2,200,000); crude petroleum (barrels; 1994) 60,800 (50,030,800); petroleum products (metric tons; 1994) 5,659,000 (6,792,000); natural gas (cu m; 1994) 25,100,000 (25,100,000).
Gross national product (1994): U.S.$30,330,000,000 (U.S.$1,150 per capita).

Structure of gross domestic product and labour force

	1994 in value DH '000,000	1994 % of total value	1993 labour force	1993 % of labour force
Agriculture	55,727	19.5	2,906,000	34.0
Mining	5,126	1.8		
Manufacturing	49,169	17.2	2,650,000	31.0
Construction	11,931	4.2		
Public utilities	21,737	7.6		
Transp. and commun.	17,221	6.0		
Trade	56,730	19.8		
Finance	...	...		
Pub. admin., defense	34,413	12.0	2,991,000	35.0
Services	33,976	11.9		
Other				
TOTAL	286,030	100.0	8,547,000	100.0

Population economically active (1994): total 8,694,000; activity rate 32.8% (participation rates [1993]: over age 15, 52.4%; female 21.4%; unemployed 16.0%).

Price index (1990 = 100)

	1990	1991	1992	1993	1994	1995	1996[3]
Consumer price index	100.0	108.0	114.2	120.1	126.3	134.0	138.2
Monthly earnings index[4]	100.0	110.0	130.0	130.0	140.0[5]	...	...

Household income and expenditure. Average household size (1994) 5.9; expenditure (1994)[6]: food 45.2%, housing 12.5%, transportation 7.6%.

Foreign trade[7]

Balance of trade (current prices)

	1990	1991	1992	1993	1994	1995
DH '000,000	−16,755	−13,576	−23,192	−28,740	−23,353	−26,519
% of total	19.3%	15.4%	25.5%	31.1%	24.1%	25.0%

Imports (1994): DH 65,963,000,000 (capital goods 25.7%; energy products and lubricants 15.5%, of which crude oil 10.5%; food, beverages, and tobacco 11.1%, of which wheat 2.3%; consumer goods 11.0%). *Major import sources:* France 22.6%; Spain 8.8%; U.S. 8.6%; Italy 7.0%; Germany 7.0%.
Exports (1994): DH 37,012,000,000 (food 28.0%; consumer goods 25.9%; minerals 11.0%). *Major export destinations:* France 31.7%; Spain 9.3%; Japan 6.6%; Italy 5.7%; Germany 4.3%; U.K. 3.9%; U.S. 3.5%.

Transport and communications

Transport. Railroads (1994): route length 1,768 km; passenger-km 1,884,000,000; metric ton-km cargo 4,740,000,000. Roads (1995): total length 60,513 km (paved 50%). Vehicles (1995): passenger cars 1,030,000; trucks and buses 273,100. Merchant marine (1992): vessels (100 gross tons and over) 492; total deadweight tonnage 586,221. Air transport (1995)[8]: passenger-km 4,602,444,000; metric ton-km cargo 57,705,000; airports (1996) 12.
Communications. Daily newspapers (1992): total number 14; total circulation 335,000; circulation per 1,000 population 13[9]. Radio (1995): 5,100,000 receivers (1 per 5.1 persons). Television (1995): 1,210,000 receivers (1 per 21.7 persons). Telephones (main lines; 1994): 993,000 (1 per 26.0 persons).

Education and health

Education (1994–95)

	schools	teachers	students	student/ teacher ratio
Primary (age 7–12)	6,205	154,650	3,914,282	25.3
Secondary (age 13–17)	451	29,364	391,639	13.3
Vocational[10]	562[11]	2,951	17,585	6.0
Higher	13[12]	9,038	266,032	29.4

Educational attainment (1982). Percentage of population age 25 and over having: no formal education 47.8%; some primary education 47.8%; some secondary 3.8%; higher 0.6%. *Literacy* (1995): total population over age 15 literate 43.7%; males literate 56.6%; females literate 31.0%.
Health (1994): physicians 8,838 (1 per 2,923 persons); hospital beds 26,407 (1 per 978 persons); infant mortality rate (1995) 45.8.
Food (1992): daily per capita caloric intake 2,984 (vegetable products 93%, animal products 7%); 123% of FAO recommended minimum requirement.

Military

Total active duty personnel (1996): 194,000 (army 90.2%, navy 3.1%, air force 6.7%). *Military expenditure as percentage of GDP* (1994): 4.1% (world 3.0%); per capita expenditure U.S.$43.

---

[1]Excludes area and population of Western Sahara except population of northern Laâyoune province. [2]Registered deaths of urban population only. [3]June. [4]Minimum wage. [5]July 1. [6]Weights of consumer price index components. [7]Import figures are f.o.b. in balance of trade and c.i.f. for commodities and trading partners. [8]Royal Air Maroc only. [9]Partial data. [10]Excludes teacher training. [11]1991–92. [12]Universities only.

Mozambique

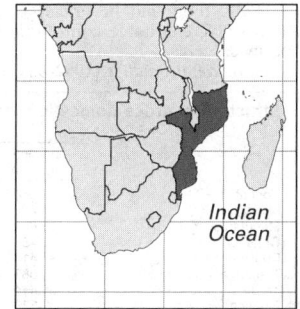

Indian Ocean

Official name: República de Moçambique (Republic of Mozambique).
Form of government: multiparty republic[1] with a single legislative house (Assembly of the Republic [250]).
Chief of state and head of government: President.
Capital: Maputo.
Official language: Portuguese.
Official religion: none.
Monetary unit: 1 metical (Mt; plural meticais) = 100 centavos; valuation (Oct. 11, 1996) 1 U.S.$ = Mt 11,141; 1 £ = Mt 17,550.

Area and population

Provinces	Capitals	area sq mi	area sq km	population 1991 estimate
Cabo Delgado	Pemba	31,902	82,625	1,202,221
Gaza	Xai-Xai	29,231	75,709	1,401,485
Inhambane	Inhambane	26,492	68,615	1,156,958
Manica	Chimoio	23,807	61,661	609,512
Maputo	Maputo	9,944	25,756	840,757
Nampula	Nampula	31,508	81,606	2,841,416
Niassa	Lichinga	49,828	129,055	686,650
Sofala	Beira	26,262	68,018	1,427,493
Tete	Tete	38,890	100,724	734,561
Zambézia	Quelimane	40,544	105,008	2,619,281
City				
Maputo	—	232	602	931,591
TOTAL LAND AREA		308,642[2]	799,379	
INLAND WATER		5,019	13,000	
TOTAL		313,661	812,379	14,451,925[3]

Demography

Population (1996): 17,878,000.
Density (1996)[4]: persons per sq mi 57.2, persons per sq km 22.1.
Urban-rural (1991): urban 28.1%; rural 71.9%.
Sex distribution (1995): male 48.53%; female 51.47%.
Age breakdown (1991): under 15, 46.0%; 15–29, 26.1%; 30–44, 15.3%; 45–59, 8.5%; 60–74, 3.5%; 75 and over, 0.6%.
Population projection: (2000) 19,829,000; (2010) 25,116,000.
Doubling time: 26 years.
Ethnolinguistic composition (1983): Makua 47.3%; Tsonga 23.3%; Malawi 12.0%; Shona 11.3%; Yao 3.8%; Swahili 0.8%; Makonde 0.6%; Portuguese 0.2%; other 0.7%.
Religious affiliation (1980): traditional beliefs 47.8%; Christian 38.9%, of which Roman Catholic 31.4%; Muslim 13.0%; other 0.3%.
Major cities (1991): Maputo 931,591; Beira 298,847; Nampula 250,473.

Vital statistics

Birth rate per 1,000 population (1995): 45.5 (world avg. 25.0).
Death rate per 1,000 population (1995): 18.3 (world avg. 9.3).
Natural increase rate per 1,000 population (1995): 27.2 (world avg. 15.7).
Total fertility rate (avg. births per childbearing woman; 1995): 6.4.
Marriage rate per 1,000 population (1974): 0.7.
Divorce rate per 1,000 population (1973): 0.01.
Life expectancy at birth (1995): male 46.8 years; female 49.5 years.
Major causes of death per 100,000 population: n.a.; however, major infectious diseases include cholera, malaria, diarrhea, acute respiratory infections, measles, tuberculosis, intestinal parasitoses and infestations, and AIDS.

National economy

Budget (1994). Revenue: Mt 1,525,700,000 (sales tax 48.4%, customs taxes 22.5%, individual income tax 17.9%). Expenditures: Mt 4,096,500,000 (defense and security 18.6%, goods and services 14.7%).
Production (metric tons except as noted). Agriculture, forestry, fishing (1995): cassava 4,178,000, corn (maize) 734,000, coconuts 438,000, sugarcane 300,000, sorghum 243,000, peanuts (groundnuts) 102,000, bananas 84,000; livestock (number of live animals) 1,280,000 cattle, 385,000 goats, 175,000 pigs, 121,000 sheep, 23,000,000 chickens; roundwood (1994) 15,441,000 cu m; fish catch (1994) 24,170. Mining and quarrying (1994): marine salt 40,000; bauxite 9,620; copper 135[5, 6]; garnet 3,000 kg; gemstones 6,865 carats. Manufacturing (value in Mt '000,000; 1994): food processing 263,761.9; beverages and tobacco 137,676.4; textiles 121,243.2; chemical products 92,014.9; nonmetallic mineral products 67,592.8; clothing 48,832.1; machinery and transport equipment 38,956.5; iron and steel products 36,223.3. Construction (value in Mt; 1994) 157,700,000. Energy production (consumption): electricity (kW-hr; 1994) 340,000,000 (728,000,000); coal (metric tons; 1994) 40,000 (60,000); crude petroleum (1993) none (none[7]); petroleum products (metric tons; 1994) none[7] (251,000); natural gas, none (none).
Population economically active (1980): total 5,671,290; activity rate 48.6% (participation rates: over age 15, 87.3%; female 52.4%; unemployed 1.7%).

Price and earnings indexes (1990 = 100)

	1989	1990	1991	1992	1993	1994	1995
Consumer price index	68.0	100.0	132.9	193.4	275.0	448.8	693.1
Monthly earnings index[8]	...	100.0	125.8	170.2	242.7	372.7	...

Public debt (external, outstanding; 1994): U.S.$5,047,000,000.
Household income and expenditure. Average family size (1992–93) 6.7[9]; income per household: n.a.; sources of income (1992–93)[9]: wages and salaries 51.6%, self-employment 12.5%, barter 11.5%, private farming 7.7%; expenditure (1992–93)[9]: food, beverages, and tobacco 74.6%, housing and energy 11.7%, transportation and communications 4.7%, clothing and footwear 3.7%, education and recreation 1.4%, health 0.8%.
Gross national product (at current market prices; 1994): U.S.$1,328,000,000 (U.S.$80 per capita).

Structure of gross domestic product and labour force

	1993 in value Mt '000,000	1993 % of total value	1980 labour force	1980 % of labour force
Agriculture	2,454,100	30.8	4,754,831	83.8
Mining	28,900	0.4	73,425	1.3
Manufacturing	642,900	8.1	273,369	4.8
Construction	848,600	10.6	42,121	0.7
Public utilities	162,900	2.0	10	10
Transportation and communications	1,157,200	14.5	77,025	1.4
Finance	...	...		
Trade	826,700	10.4	112,244	2.0
Pub. admin., defense	} 1,844,000	23.2	243,449[10]	4.3[10]
Services				
Other	...	...	94,826[11]	1.7[11]
TOTAL	7,965,300	100.0	5,671,290	100.0

Tourism: n.a.
Land use (1994): forested 22.1%; meadows and pastures 56.1%; agricultural and under permanent cultivation 4.0%; other 17.8%.

Foreign trade[12]

Balance of trade (current prices)

	1989	1990	1991	1992	1993	1994
U.S.$'000,000	−670	−648	−737	−716	−823	−868
% of total	76.1%	71.8%	69.5%	72.0%	75.7%	74.4%

Imports (1994): U.S.$1,018,000,000 (1990; foodstuffs 28.9%, capital equipment 22.9%, crude petroleum and derivatives 10.9%, machinery and spare parts 9.5%). *Major import sources* (1994): South Africa 35.4%; U.K. 8.4%; France 7.7%; Japan 6.7%; United States 6.4%; Portugal 5.0%; Italy 3.0%.
Exports (1994): U.S.$149,500,000 (shrimp 42.3%, cotton 12.6%, petroleum 9.2%, sugar 7.4%, cashew nuts 2.2%). *Major export destinations:* Spain 22.4%; South Africa 14.8%; Japan 13.1%; Portugal 9.9%; United States 9.5%.

Transport and communications

Transport. Railroads (1994): route length 1,946 mi, 3,131 km; passenger-mi 78,900,000, passenger-km 127,000,000; short ton-mi cargo 447,900,000, metric ton-km cargo 654,000,000. Roads (1994): total length 18,141 mi, 29,-195 km (paved 18.2%). Vehicles (1994): passenger cars 10,035; trucks and buses 29,500. Merchant marine (1992): vessels (100 gross tons and over) 107; total deadweight tonnage 31,645. Air transport (1994): passenger-mi 26,967,000, passenger-km 434,000,000; short ton-mi cargo 6,849,000, metric ton-km cargo 10,000,000; airports (1996) with scheduled flights 7.
Communications. Daily newspapers (1995): total number 3; total circulation 81,000[13]; circulation per 1,000 population 4.6[13]. Radio (1995): total number of receivers 620,000 (1 per 28 persons). Television (1995): total number of receivers 35,000 (1 per 499 persons). Telephones (main lines; 1993): 62,100 (1 per 263 persons).

Education and health

Education (1994)

	schools	teachers	students	student/teacher ratio
Primary (age 5–9)[14]	3,765	22,544	1,301,833	57.7
Secondary (age 10–16)[15]	239	3,889	150,683	38.7
Voc., teacher tr.	31	826	13,816	16.7
Higher	3	877[16]	5,250[16]	6.0[16]

Educational attainment (1980). Percentage of population age 25 and over having: no formal schooling 80.7%; primary education 18.2%; secondary 0.9%; higher 0.2%. *Literacy* (1995): percentage of total population age 15 and over literate 40.1%; males literate 57.7%; females literate 23.3%.
Health (1993): physicians 114 (1 per 143,351 persons); hospital beds 13,280 (1 per 1,231 persons); infant mortality rate per 1,000 live births (1995) 127.7.
Food (1992): daily per capita caloric intake 1,680 (vegetable products 97%, animal products 3%); 72% of FAO recommended minimum requirement.

Military

Total active duty personnel (1996): n.a.[17]. *Military expenditure as percentage of GNP* (1994): 8.7% (world 3.0%); per capita expenditure U.S.$6.

---

[1]Mozambique adopted a new multiparty constitution that became effective on Nov. 30, 1990; the first multiparty elections took place on Oct. 27–29, 1994. [2]Detail does not add to total given because of rounding. [3]Excludes refugees in neighbouring countries estimated at about 1,200,000 in 1991; most of these refugees were repatriated between June 1993 and the fall of 1994. [4]Based on land area. [5]1990. [6]Metal content only. [7]Internal disorder and a lack of foreign exchange have brought importation of crude petroleum and the production of refined petroleum products practically to a halt. [8]Agricultural workers only. [9]City of Maputo only. [10]Services includes Public utilities. [11]Unemployed. [12]Import figures are c.i.f. [13]Circulation for two newspapers only. [14]Includes initiation classes in which pupils learn Portuguese. [15]Includes the two stages of secondary education and the upper-level primary stage. [16]1993. [17]Under the terms of the 1992 peace agreement, government and Renamo forces are to merge, forming a new army some 30,000 strong.

Myanmar (Burma)

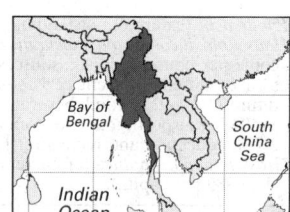

Official name: Pyidaungzu Myanma Naingngandaw (Union of Myanmar).
Form of government: military regime[1].
Head of state and government:
Chairman of the State Law and Order Restoration Council.
Capital: Yangôn (Rangoon).
Official language: Burmese.
Official religion: none.
Monetary unit: 1 Myanmar kyat (K) = 100 pyas; valuation (Oct. 11, 1996) 1 U.S.$ = K 5.94; 1 £ = K 9.36.

Area and population

Divisions	Capitals	area sq mi	area sq km	population 1994 estimate
Irrawaddy (Ayeyarwady)	Bassein (Pathein)	13,567	35,138	6,107,000
Magwe (Magway)	Magwe (Magway)	17,305	44,820	4,067,000
Mandalay	Mandalay	14,295	37,024	5,823,000
Pegu (Bago)	Pegu (Bago)	15,214	39,404	4,607,000
Sagaing	Sagaing	36,535	94,625	4,889,000
Tenasserim (Tanintharyi)	Tavoy (Dawei)	16,735	43,343	1,187,000
Yangôn	Yangôn (Rangoon)	3,927	10,171	5,037,000
States				
Chin	Hakha	13,907	36,019	438,000
Kachin	Myitkyinä	34,379	89,041	1,135,000
Karen	Pa-an (Hpa-an)	11,731	30,383	1,323,000
Kayah	Loi-kaw	4,530	11,733	228,000
Mon	Moulmein (Mawlamyine)	4,748	12,297	2,183,000
Rakhine (Arakan)	Sittwe (Akyab)	14,200	36,778	2,482,000
Shan	Taunggyi	60,155	155,801	4,416,000
TOTAL		261,228	676,577	43,922,000

Demography

Population (1996): 45,976,000.
Density (1996): persons per sq mi 176.0, persons per sq km 68.0.
Urban-rural (1996): urban 27.0%; rural 73.0%.
Sex distribution (1993): male 49.72%; female 50.28%.
Age breakdown (1990): under 15, 36.0%; 15–29, 29.7%; 30–44, 17.8%; 45–59, 10.1%; 60–74, 5.3%; 75 and over, 1.1%.
Population projection: (2000) 49,388,000; (2010) 58,236,000.
Doubling time: 33 years.
Ethnic composition (1983): Burman 69.0%; Shan 8.5%; Karen 6.2%; Rakhine 4.5%; Mon 2.4%; Chin 2.2%; Kachin 1.4%; other 5.8%.
Religious affiliation (1990): Buddhist 89.1%; Christian 4.9%; Muslim 3.8%; other 2.2%.
Major cities (1983): Yangôn (Rangoon) 2,513,023; Mandalay 532,949; Moulmein (Mawlamyine) 219,961; Pegu (Bago) 150,528; Bassein (Pathein) 144,096.

Vital statistics

Birth rate per 1,000 population (1996): 31.0 (world avg. 25.0).
Death rate per 1,000 population (1996): 10.2 (world avg. 9.3).
Natural increase rate per 1,000 population (1996): 20.8 (world avg. 15.7).
Total fertility rate (avg. births per childbearing woman; 1996): 3.9.
Marriage rate per 1,000 population: n.a.
Divorce rate per 1,000 population: n.a.
Life expectancy at birth (1996): male 58.0 years; female 61.0 years.
Major causes of death per 100,000 population (1987): infectious and parasitic diseases 29.5; respiratory diseases 14.8; circulatory diseases 10.0; malignant neoplasms (cancers) 7.9; malnutrition 2.2.

National economy

Budget (1992–93). Revenue: K 20,313,000,000 (revenue from taxes 61.8%, of which taxes on goods and services 31.8%, taxes on international trade 14.4%; nontax revenue 33.8%; capital revenue 4.4%). Expenditures: K 27,-931,000,000 (defense 32.7%; education 17.0%; general public service 12.2%; transportation 10.3%; health 7.4%; agriculture 7.1%).
Public debt (external, outstanding; 1994): U.S.$6,099,000,000.
Tourism: receipts from visitors (1994) U.S.$24,000,000; expenditures by nationals abroad (1991) U.S.$3,000,000.
Production (metric tons except as noted). Agriculture, forestry, fishing (1995): rice 20,109,000, sugarcane 2,167,000, pulses 1,228,000, peanuts (groundnuts) 501,000, sesame seeds 297,000, corn (maize) 272,000, plantains 260,000, onions 173,000, millet 150,000, potatoes 146,000, seed cotton 86,000, tobacco leaves 38,000, jute 35,000; livestock (number of live animals) 9,857,000 cattle, 4,200,000 ducks, 2,944,000 pigs, 2,203,000 buffalo, 1,492,000 sheep and goats, 27,981,000 chickens; roundwood (1994) 21,884,000 cu m; fish catch (1993) 836,878. Mining and quarrying (1994–95): gypsum 28,916; copper concentrates 24,036; refined lead 1,267; tin concentrates 530; jade 258; refined silver 97,350 troy oz. Manufacturing (1994): cement 469,582; urea 149,000; sugar 47,600; washing soap 36,431; noodles 25,065; stationery paper 14,315; cotton fabrics 10,804,000 metres; cigarettes 440,000,000 units; gunny-bags 26,769,-000 units; glass bottles 16,268,000 units. Construction (units; 1987–88)[2]: residential 1,193; nonresidential 1,483. Energy production (consumption): electricity (kW-hr; 1993) 3,030,000,000 (3,030,000,000); coal (metric tons; 1993) 71,000 (74,000); crude petroleum (barrels; 1993) 5,100,000 (5,285,000); petroleum products (metric tons; 1993) 618,000 (619,000); natural gas (cu m; 1993) 973,000,000 (973,000,000).
Household income and expenditure. Average household size (1994) 5.6; average annual income per household: n.a.; sources of income: n.a.; expenditure

---

(1994)[3]: food and beverages 67.1%, fuel and lighting 6.6%, transportation 4.0%, charitable contributions 3.1%, medical care 3.1%, clothing and footwear 2.8%.
Gross national product (1992–93): U.S.$30,707,000,000 (U.S.$700 per capita).

Structure of gross domestic product and labour force

	1993–94 in value K '000,000	1993–94 % of total value	1994–95 labour force[4]	1994–95 % of labour force[4]
Agriculture	150,068	60.5	11,551,000	68.7
Mining	1,462	0.6	87,000	0.5
Manufacturing	18,683	7.5	1,250,000	7.4
Construction	3,453	1.4	292,000	1.8
Public utilities	414	0.2	17,000	0.1
Transp. and commun.	5,080	2.1	420,000	2.5
Trade	55,414	22.3	1,450,000	8.6
Finance	375	0.2 }	1,264,000	7.5
Public admin., services	13,008	5.2 }		
Other	—	—	486,000	2.9
TOTAL	247,957	100.0	16,817,000	100.0

Population economically active (1990–91): total 15,737,000; activity rate of total population 37.2% (participation rates: ages 15–64 [1983] 64.2%; female [1987–88] 35.3%; unemployed [1987–88] 4.3%).

Price and earnings indexes (1990 = 100)

	1989	1990	1991	1992	1993	1994	1995
Consumer price index	85.0	100.0	132.3	161.3	212.6	263.8	330.3
Monthly earnings index[5]	107.2	100.0	92.8	129.4	144.8	...	...

Land use (1994): forested 49.3%; meadows and pastures 0.5%; agricultural and under permanent cultivation 15.3%; other 34.9%.

Foreign trade[6]

Balance of trade (current prices)

	1990	1991	1992	1993	1994	1995
K '000,000	+485.0	−1,055.4	−338.1	−948.4	−195.8	−2,050.7
% of total	13.5%	16.7%	4.9%	11.6%	2.1%	17.5%

Imports (1993–94): K 7,923,340,000 (machinery and transport equipment 31.4%; basic manufactures 17.1%; chemicals 13.3%; animal and vegetable oils 6.7%; mineral fuels and lubricants 4.1%). *Major import sources:* Japan 25.5%; China 15.9%; Thailand 10.9%; Singapore 10.4%; Malaysia 7.2%; Indonesia 4.1%; South Korea 3.7%.
Exports (1993–94): K 4,227,810,000 (inedible crude materials 36.8%; food, beverages, and tobacco 34.5%; basic manufactures 4.7%). *Major export destinations:* Singapore 19.4%; Thailand 17.4%; India 15.0%; Hong Kong 10.7%; China 5.5%; Japan 4.4%.

Transport and communications

Transport. Railroads (1992–93): track length (1994) 3,104 mi, 4,995 km; passenger-mi 2,908,000,000, passenger-km 4,680,000,000; short ton-mi cargo 403,000,000, metric ton-km cargo 648,000,000. Roads (1992–93): total length 15,118 mi, 24,330 km (paved 16%). Vehicles (1994): passenger cars 40,000; trucks and buses 40,000. Merchant marine (1992): vessels (100 gross tons and over) 144; total deadweight tonnage 1,354,005. Air transport: passenger-mi (1994–95) 252,000,000, passenger-km 406,000,000; short ton-mi cargo (1990–91) 5,649,000, metric ton-km cargo (1990–91) 8,248,000; airports (1996) with scheduled flights 19.
Communications. Daily newspapers (1993): total number 2; total circulation 414,000; circulation per 1,000 population 9. Radio (1995): total receivers 3,300,000 (1 per 14 persons). Television (1995): total receivers 1,000,000 (1 per 47 persons). Telephones (main lines; 1993): 80,000 (1 per 556 persons).

Education and health

Education (1993–94)

	schools	teachers	students	student/teacher ratio
Primary (age 5–9)	35,727	156,629	5,896,026	37.6
Secondary (age 10–15)	2,916	69,441	1,519,215	21.9
Voc., teacher tr.	111	2,473	26,789	10.8
Higher	40	5,970	235,184	39.4

Educational attainment (1983). Percentage of population age 25 and over having: no formal schooling 55.8%; primary education 39.4%; secondary 4.6%; religious 0.1%; postsecondary 0.1%. *Literacy* (1983): total population age 15 and over literate 16,472,494 (78.5%); males literate 8,816,031 (85.8%); females literate 7,656,463 (71.6%).
Health: physicians (1993–94) 12,245 (1 per 3,554 persons); hospital beds (1992–93) 27,830 (1 per 1,586 persons); infant mortality rate per 1,000 live births (1996) 76.
Food (1992): daily per capita caloric intake 2,598 (vegetable products 96%, animal products 4%); 120% of FAO recommended minimum requirement.

Military

Total active duty personnel (1995): 286,000 (army 92.7%, navy 4.2%, air force 3.1%). *Military expenditure as percentage of GNP* (1992): 4.0% (world 3.6%); per capita expenditure (1994) U.S.$57.

---

[1]The military government has refused to hand over power to the National League for Democracy, which won in the 1990 multiparty elections. [2]Construction Corporation activity only. [3]Yangôn only. [4]Employed only. [5]Wages in manufacturing. [6]Import figures are f.o.b. in balance of trade and c.i.f. in commodities and trading partners.

Namibia

Official name: Republic of Namibia.
Form of government: republic with two
legislative houses (National Assembly
[72[1]]; National Council[2] [26]).
Head of state and government:
President.
Capital: Windhoek.
Official language: English.
Official religion: none.
Monetary unit: 1 Namibian dollar
(N$) = 100 cents; valuation (Oct. 11,
1996) 1 U.S.$ = N$4.54;
1 £ = N$7.16.

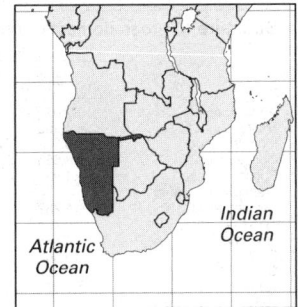

Area and population[3]

Regions	Chief towns	area sq mi	area sq km	population 1992 estimate
Erongo[3]	Omaruru	24,602	63,719	98,500
Hardap	Mariental	42,428	109,888	80,000
Karas	Keetmanshoop	62,288	161,324	73,000
Khomas	Windhoek	14,210	36,804	161,000
Kunene	Opuwo	55,697	144,254	58,500
Liambezi	Katima Mulilo	7,541	19,532	92,000
Ohangwena	Oshikango	4,086	10,582	178,000
Okavango	Rundu	16,763	43,417	136,000
Omaheke	Gobabis	32,715	84,731	55,600
Omusati	Ongandjera	5,265	13,637	158,000
Oshana	Oshakati	2,042	5,290	159,000
Oshikoto	Tsumeb	10,273	26,607	176,000
Otjozondjupa	Grootfontein	40,667	105,327	85,000
Other		2	6	1,000
TOTAL		318,580[4]	825,118	1,511,600

Demography

Population (1996): 1,709,000.
Density (1995): persons per sq mi 5.4, persons per sq km 2.1.
Urban-rural (1993): urban 35.2%; rural 64.8%.
Sex distribution (1995): male 49.74%; female 50.26%.
Age breakdown (1991): under 15, 41.7%; 15–29, 28.8%; 30–44, 14.7%; 45–59,
7.8%; 60–74, 5.3%; 75 and over, 1.7%.
Population projection: (2000) 1,957,000; (2010) 2,705,000.
Doubling time: 26 years.
Ethnic composition (1991): Ovambo 47.4%; Kavango 8.8%; Herero 7.1%;
Damara 7.1%; white 6.1%; Nama 4.6%; other 18.9%.
Religious affiliation (1981): Lutheran 51.2%; Roman Catholic 19.8%; Dutch
Reformed 6.1%; Anglican 5.0%; other 17.9%.
Major cities (1990): Windhoek 125,000; Swakopmund 15,500; Rundu 15,000;
Rehoboth 15,000; Keetmanshoop 14,000.

Vital statistics

Birth rate per 1,000 population (1990–95): 37.0 (world avg. 25.0).
Death rate per 1,000 population (1990–95): 10.5 (world avg. 9.3).
Natural increase rate per 1,000 population (1990–95): 26.5 (world avg. 15.7).
Total fertility rate (avg. births per childbearing woman; 1990–95): 5.7.
Life expectancy at birth (1990–95): male 57.5 years; female 60.0 years.
Major causes of death per 100,000 population: n.a.; however, in the early
1990s, tuberculosis had become a serious problem (especially in the south-
ern regions); AIDS cases, while few, were increasing exponentially.

National economy

Budget (1995–96). Revenue: N$3,521,700,000 (customs taxes 32.8%, individual
income taxes 18.7%, general sales tax 15.7%, nontax revenues 12.1%, mining
taxes 4.0%). Expenditures: N$4,339,900,000 (education 24.2%, health and
welfare 11.1%, transportation 6.2%, social security 5.7%, defense 5.3%).
Tourism (1994): receipts from visitors U.S.$184,000,000; expenditures by na-
tionals abroad U.S.$75,000,000.
Public debt (external, outstanding; 1993): U.S.$3,180,000.
Production (metric tons except as noted). Agriculture, forestry, fishing (1995):
roots and tubers 190,000, cereals 59,500 (of which millet 35,000, corn [maize]
15,300, sorghum 6,000), fruits 8,000, vegetables and melons 7,000, pulses
6,000, wool 3,026[5], karakul pelts 770,627 units[6]; livestock (number of live
animals) 2,620,000 sheep, 1,890,000 cattle, 1,640,000 goats; fish catch (1994)
329,990. Mining and quarrying (1995): diamonds 1,381,700 carats (mostly
gem quality); zinc 59,300; copper 29,800; lead 26,800; uranium 2,007; silver
2,218,600 troy oz; gold 67,459 troy oz. Manufacturing (1995): n.a.; products
include cut gems (primarily diamonds), fur products (karakul), processed
foods (fish, meats, and dairy products), textiles, carved wood products, refined metals (copper and lead). Construction (value of buildings completed
in N$'000,000; 1994): residential 347.7; nonresidential 160.4. Energy produc-
tion (consumption): electricity (kW-hr; 1992) 1,714,000,000 (1,714,000,000);
coal, none (n.a.); crude petroleum, none (n.a.).
Population economically active: total (1991) 493,580; activity rate of total
population, 34.9% (participation rates: ages 15–64, 61.3%; female 43.5%;
unemployed 20.1%).

Price and earnings indexes (1990 = 100)

	1989	1990	1991	1992	1993	1994	1995
Consumer price index	89.3	100.0	111.9	131.7	143.0	158.4	174.2
Earnings index	...	...	...	...	...	...	...

Household income and expenditure. Average household size (1991) 5.2; average annual income per household (1980) R 3,223 (U.S.$4,143); sources
of income (1992): wages and salaries 69.0%, income from property 25.6%,
transfer payments 5.4%; expenditure: n.a.
Gross national product (1994): U.S.$3,045,000,000 (U.S.$1,908 per capita).

Structure of gross domestic product and labour force

	1995 in value N$'000,000	1995 % of total value	1991 labour force[7]	1991 % of labour force
Agriculture	1,502	15.4	189,929	38.5
Mining	1,097	11.2	14,686	3.0
Manufacturing	872	8.9	22,884	4.6
Construction	347	3.6	18,638	3.8
Public utilities	187	1.9	2,974	0.6
Transportation and communications	566	5.8	9,322	1.9
Trade[8]	1,043	10.7	37,820	7.7
Finance	1,037	10.6	8,547	1.7
Services	135	1.4	} 89,541	18.1
Public administration and defense	2,697	27.7		
Other	267	2.7	99,239[9]	20.1[9]
TOTAL	9,750	100.0[4]	493,580	100.0

Land use (1994): forested 15.2%; meadows and pastures 46.2%; agricultural
and under permanent cultivation 0.8%; other 37.8%.

Foreign trade

Balance of trade (current prices)

	1990	1991	1992	1993	1994	1995
U.S.$'000,000	− 28	+ 102	+ 79	+ 122	+ 165	− 98
% of total	0.8%	4.3%	3.0%	5.0%	6.6%	3.5%

Imports (1994): N$4,467,700,000 (machinery and transport equipment 27.1%,
of which transport equipment 16.2%; food and live animals 22.3%; minerals
and fuels 11.4%; chemical products 8.1%). *Major import sources* (1993):
South Africa 87.0%[10]; Germany 3.0%; France 2.0%; Japan 2.0%.
Exports (1994): N$4,692,000,000 (minerals 50.1%, of which diamonds 31.4%;
food and live animals 47.0%, of which fish and fish products 28.6%, cattle
and meat products 12.6%; karakul pelts 0.2%). *Major export destinations*
(1993): United Kingdom 34.0%; South Africa 27.0%; Japan 10.0%; Spain
6.0%.

Transport and communications

Transport. Railroads: length (1995) 1,480 mi, 2,382 km; passenger-km 2,008,-
000,000[11]; metric ton-km 1,082,000. Roads (1995): total length 25,130 mi,
40,450 km (paved 12%). Vehicles (1995): passenger cars 62,500; trucks and
buses 66,500. Merchant marine (1992): vessels (100 gross tons and over)
30; total deadweight tonnage 5,874. Air transport (1995)[12]: passenger-km
844,116,000; metric ton-km cargo 75,970,000; airports (1996) with scheduled
flights 13.
Communications. Daily newspapers (1994): total number 6; total circulation
43,300; circulation per 1,000 population 54. Radio (1995): 240,000 receivers
(1 per 6.9 persons). Television (1995): 47,000 receivers (1 per 35 persons).
Telephones (main lines; 1996): 80,900 (1 per 21 persons).

Education and health

Education (1994)

	schools	teachers	students	student/ teacher ratio
Primary (age 6–12)	933	10,912[11]	366,666	32.0[11]
Secondary (age 13–19)	114	2,534[13]	101,838	29.3[13]
Voc., teacher tr.	17	140[14]	1,503	11.9[14]
Higher	7	213[15]	6,523	11.8[15]

Educational attainment (1991). Percentage of population age 25 and over
having: no formal schooling 35.1%; primary education 31.9%; secondary
28.5%; higher 4.5%. *Literacy* (1991): total population age 15 and over
literate 622,436 (75.8%); males literate 305,926 (77.7%); females literate
316,510 (73.9%).
Health: physicians (1992) 324 (1 per 4,594 persons); hospital beds (1989) 6,997
(1 per 216 persons); infant mortality rate per 1,000 live births (1993) 63.8.
Food (1992): daily per capita caloric intake 2,134 (vegetable products 87%,
animal products 13%); 94% of FAO recommended minimum requirement.

Military

Total active duty personnel (1996): 8,100 (army 98.8%, navy 1.2%). *Military
expenditure as percentage of GNP* (1994): 1.9% (world 3.0%); per capita
expenditure U.S.$35.

---

[1]72 elected and up to 6 appointed members. [2]Mostly an advisory body. [3]Includes the
434 sq mi (1,124 sq km) district of Walvis Bay (1992 population estimate, 23,000)
that was jointly administered with South Africa from November 1992 to March 1994.
[4]Detail does not add to total given because of rounding. [5]1994. [6]1987. [7]Includes more
than 140,000 nonwage (informal) workers. [8]Includes hotels. [9]Unemployed. [10]Includes
goods from other countries shipped via South Africa. [11]1992. [12]Namib Air only.
[13]1990. [14]1989. [15]1991.

Nepal

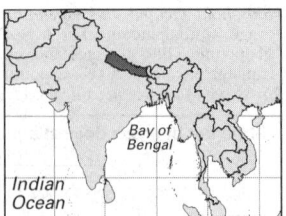

Official name: Nepāl Adhirājya
(Kingdom of Nepal).
Form of government: constitutional
monarchy with two legislative houses
(National Council [60[1]]; House of
Representatives [205]).
Chief of state: King.
Head of government: Prime Minister.
Capital: Kāthmāndu.
Official language: Nepālī.
Official religion: Hinduism.
Monetary unit: 1 Nepalese rupee
(NRs) = 100 paisa (pice); valuation
(Oct. 11, 1996) 1 U.S.$ = NRs 56.78;
1 £ = NRs 89.44.

Area and population		area		population
		sq mi	sq km	1991 census
Development regions Zones	Capitals			
Eastern	Dhankūtā	10,987	28,456	4,446,749
Koshī	Dharān	3,733	9,669	1,728,247
Mechī	Ilam	3,165	8,196	1,118,210
Sāgarmāthā	Rājbiraj	4,089	10,591	1,600,292
Central	Kāthmāndu	10,583	27,410	6,183,955
Bāgmatī	Bhaktapur	3,640	9,428	2,250,805
Janakpur	Sindhulimādī	3,733	9,669	2,061,816
Nārāyanī	Hetaudā	3,210	8,313	1,871,334
Western	Pokharā	11,351	29,398	3,770,678
Dhawalāgiri	Bagluri	3,146	8,148	490,877
Gandakī	Chāme	4,740	12,275	1,266,128
Lumbinī	Butawal	3,465	8,975	2,013,673
Mid-western	Surkhet	16,362	42,378	2,410,414
Bherī	Nepālganj	4,071	10,545	1,103,043
Karnālī	Mānma	8,244	21,351	260,529
Rāptī	Tulsipur	4,047	10,482	1,046,842
Far-western	Dipāyal	7,544	19,539	1,679,301
Mahākālī	Dadeldhurā	2,698	6,989	664,952
Setī	Silgadhī	4,846	12,550	1,014,349
TOTAL		56,827	147,181	18,491,097

Demography

Population (1996): 20,892,000.
Density (1996): persons per sq mi 367.6, persons per sq km 41.9.
Urban-rural (1995): urban 14.0%; rural 86.0%.
Sex distribution (1995–96): male 50.15%; female 49.85%.
Age breakdown (1991): under 15, 42.3%; 15–29, 25.7%; 30–44, 16.7%; 45–59, 9.7%; 60–74, 4.7%; 75 and over, 0.9%.
Population projection: (2000) 23,042,000; (2010) 28,698,000.
Doubling time: 25 years.
Ethnic composition (1991): Nepalese 53.2%; Bihārī (including Maithilī and Bhojpurī) 18.4%; Tharu 4.8%; Tamang 4.7%; Newār 3.4%; Magar 2.2%; Abadhi 1.7%; other 11.6%.
Religious affiliation (1991): Hindu 86.2%; Buddhist 7.8%; Muslim 3.8%; Christian 0.2%; Jain 0.1%; other 1.9%.
Major cities (1991): Kāthmāndu 419,073; Birātnagar 130,129; Lalitpur 117,203; Pokharā 95,311; Birganj 68,764.

Vital statistics

Birth rate per 1,000 population (1996): 37.2 (world avg. 25.0).
Death rate per 1,000 population (1996): 12.0 (world avg. 9.3).
Natural increase rate per 1,000 population (1996): 25.2 (world avg. 15.7).
Total fertility rate (avg. births per childbearing woman; 1996): 5.1.
Marriage rate per 1,000 population: n.a.
Divorce rate per 1,000 population: n.a.
Life expectancy at birth (1991): male 55.0 years; female 53.5 years.
Major causes of death per 100,000 population: n.a.; however, the leading causes of mortality are infectious and parasitic diseases, diseases of the respiratory system, diseases of the nervous system, diseases of the circulatory system, and injuries and poisoning.

National economy

Budget (1993–94). Revenue: NRs 22,412,900,000 (internal revenue 80.7%, of which tax on consumption 32.4%, customs 23.4%; foreign grants 19.3%). Expenditures: NRs 35,514,000,000 (development 63.7%, regular 36.3%).
Public debt (external, outstanding; 1994): U.S.$2,202,000,000.
Tourism (1994): receipts from visitors U.S.$172,000,000; expenditures by nationals abroad U.S.$112,000,000.
Production (metric tons except as noted). Agriculture, forestry, fishing (1995): rice 2,906,000, sugarcane 1,469,000, corn (maize) 1,302,000, wheat 942,000, potatoes 839,000, millet 253,000, pulses 188,000, barley 37,000, jute 12,000, tobacco 6,000; livestock (number of live animals) 6,838,000 cattle, 5,649,000 goats, 3,278,000 buffalo, 919,000 sheep, 636,000 pigs; roundwood (1994) 20,120,000 cu m; fish catch (1993) 16,582. Mining and quarrying (1993): limestone 350,000; magnesite 45,000; talc 7,000; garnet 25,000 kg. Manufacturing (1993–94): cement 102,595; sugar 58,249; jute goods 32,440; biscuits 7,030; cigarettes 9,042,000,000 units; processed leather 1,630,000 sq m; synthetic textiles 20,428,000 metres. Construction: n.a. Energy production (consumption): electricity (kW-hr; 1993) 936,000,000 (934,000,000); coal (metric tons; 1993) none (100,000); petroleum products (metric tons; 1993) none (310,-000); natural gas, none (none).
Gross national product (at current market prices; 1994): U.S.$4,174,000,000 (U.S.$200 per capita).

Structure of gross domestic product and labour force				
	1994–95		1991	
	in value NRs '000,000[2]	% of total value	labour force	% of labour force
Agriculture	87,072	41.9	5,961,788	81.2
Mining	1,268	0.6	2,367	—
Manufacturing	19,559	9.4	150,051	2.0
Construction	23,560	11.3	35,658	0.5
Public utilities	1,923	0.9	11,734	0.2
Transportation and communications	15,252	7.3	50,808	0.7
Trade	9,735	4.7	256,012	3.5
Finance	20,673	10.0	20,847	0.3
Services	19,563	9.4	752,019	10.3
Other	9,265[3]	4.5[3]	98,302	1.3
TOTAL	207,870	100.0	7,339,586	100.0

Land use (1994): forested 42.0%; meadows and pastures 14.6%; agricultural and under permanent cultivation 17.2%; other 26.2%.
Population economically active (1991): total 7,339,586; activity rate of total population 39.7% (participation rates: ages 10 years and over, 56.6%; female 40.4%; unemployed [1980] 5.5%).

Price and earnings indexes (1990 = 100)							
	1989	1990	1991	1992	1993	1994	1995
Consumer price index	92.4	100.0	115.6	135.4	145.5	157.7	169.7
Monthly earnings index[4]	115.7	100.0	136.7	113.2	123.3	...	...

Household income and expenditure (1984–85). Average household size (1991) 5.6; income per household NRs 14,796 (U.S.$853); sources of income: self-employment 63.4%, wages and salaries 25.1%, rent 7.5%, other 4.0%; expenditure: food and beverages 61.2%, housing 17.3%, clothing 11.7%, health care 3.7%, education and recreation 2.9%, transportation and communications 1.2%, other 2.0%.

Foreign trade[5]

Balance of trade (current prices)						
	1990	1991	1992	1993	1994	1995
NRs '000,000	– 13,037	– 17,059	– 16,255	– 21,781	– 37,402	– 49,843
% of total	51.4%	46.5%	33.7%	36.5%	51.0%	58.0%

Imports (1993–94): NRs 52,433,600,000 (basic manufactured goods 36.3%; machinery and transport equipment 19.3%; chemicals 10.8%; mineral fuels and lubricants 9.3%; food and live animals, chiefly for food 8.9%; crude materials except fuels 6.2%). *Major import sources:* other Asia 50.1%; India 34.1%; European Economic Community 4.8%; Oceania 4.2%.
Exports (1993–94): NRs 19,417,900,000 (basic manufactures 55.3%; miscellaneous manufactures 33.3%; food and live animals, chiefly for food 6.7%; crude materials except fuels 2.3%; chemicals and drugs 1.1%). *Major export destinations:* European Economic Community 47.7%; Americas 29.7%; India 13.3%; other European 5.3%.

Transport and communications

Transport. Railroads (1993–94): route length 33 mi, 53 km; passengers carried 653,000; freight handled 9,151 metric tons. Roads (1993): total length 5,924 mi, 9,534 km (paved 36%). Vehicles (1990–91): passenger cars 4,949; trucks and buses 3,363. Merchant marine: none. Air transport (1991): passenger-mi 439,000,000, passenger-km 706,000,000; short ton-mi cargo (1993–94) 63,786,000, metric ton-km cargo (1993–94) 93,126,000; airports (1996) with scheduled flights 24.
Communications. Daily newspapers (1992): total number 25; total circulation 140,000; circulation per 1,000 population 7.4. Radio (1995): 625,000 receivers (1 per 32 persons). Television (1995): 250,000 receivers (1 per 80 persons). Telephones (main lines; 1993): 72,000 (1 per 286 persons).

Education and health

Education (1993)	schools	teachers	students	student/ teacher ratio
Primary (age 6–10)	20,217	79,590	3,091,684	38.8
Secondary (age 11–15)	6,618	26,303	910,114	34.6
Vocational				
Higher	3	4,925[6]	102,018	22.4[6]

Educational attainment (1981). Percentage of population age 25 and over having: no formal schooling 41.2%; primary education 29.4%; secondary 22.7%; higher 6.8%. *Literacy* (1991): total population age 15 and over literate 4,255,000 (37.7%); males literate 2,975,000 (51.7%); females literate 1,280,000 (23.3%).
Health (1991–92): physicians 1,497 (1 per 12,623 persons); hospital beds 4,848 (1 per 3,898 persons); infant mortality rate per 1,000 live births (1996) 90.
Food (1992): daily per capita caloric intake 1,957 (vegetable products 93%, animal products 7%); 89% of FAO recommended minimum requirement.

Military

Total active duty personnel (1995): 35,000 (army 99.4%, air force 0.6%). *Military expenditure as percentage of GNP* (1994): 1.1% (world 3.0%); per capita expenditure U.S.$2.

---

[1]Includes 10 members nominated by the king. [2]Tentative estimate. [3]Includes indirect taxes. [4]Real wage rates for unskilled industrial workers in Kāthmāndu. [5]Import figures are f.o.b. in balance of trade and c.i.f. for commodities and trading partners. [6]1991.

Netherlands, The

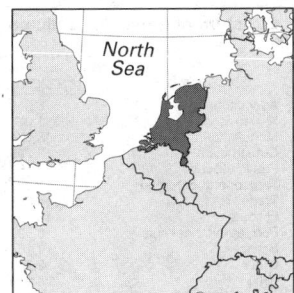

North Sea

Official name: Koninkrijk der Nederlanden (Kingdom of The Netherlands).
Form of government: constitutional monarchy with a parliament (States General) comprising two legislative houses (First Chamber [75]; Second Chamber [150]).
Chief of state: Monarch.
Head of government: Prime Minister.
Seat of government: The Hague.
Capital: Amsterdam.
Official language: Dutch.
Official religion: none.
Monetary unit: 1 Netherlands guilder (f.) = 100 cents; valuation (Oct. 11, 1996) 1 U.S.$ = f. 1.72; 1 £ = f. 2.71.

Area and population		area		population
				1995[1]
Provinces	Capitals	sq mi	sq km	estimate
Drenthe	Assen	1,024	2,652	454,864
Flevoland	Lelystad	551	1,426	262,325
Friesland	Leeuwarden	1,298	3,361	609,579
Gelderland	Arnhem	1,929	4,995	1,864,732
Groningen	Groningen	905	2,344	557,995
Limburg	Maastricht	837	2,167	1,130,050
Noord-Brabant	's-Hertogenbosch	1,907	4,938	2,276,207
Noord-Holland	Haarlem	1,027	2,660	2,463,611
Overijssel	Zwolle	1,288	3,337	1,050,389
Utrecht	Utrecht	524	1,356	1,063,460
Zeeland	Middelburg	692	1,792	365,846
Zuid-Holland	The Hague	1,104	2,860	3,325,064
TOTAL LAND AREA		13,085[2]	33,889[2]	
INLAND WATER		2,949	7,637	
TOTAL		16,033[2]	41,526[2]	15,424,122

Demography

Population (1996): 15,589,000.
Density (1996)[3]: persons per sq mi 1,189.6, persons per sq km 459.3.
Urban-rural (1994[1]): urban 90.4%; rural 9.6%.
Sex distribution (1995[1]): male 49.51%; female 50.49%.
Age breakdown (1994[1]): under 15, 18.4%; 15–29, 22.4%; 30–44, 23.8%; 45–59, 17.8%; 60–74, 12.1%; 75 and over, 5.5%.
Population projection: (2000) 16,023,000; (2010) 16,853,000.
Doubling time: not applicable; vital rates and net migration in near balance.
Ethnic composition (by nationality; 1994[1]): Netherlander 94.9%; Turkish 1.3%; Moroccan 1.1%; German 0.3%; other 2.4%.
Religious affiliation (1994): Roman Catholic 31.0%; Dutch Reformed Church 14.0%; Calvinist 8.0%; Muslim 3.9%; other 4.1%; no religion 39.0%.
Major cities (1995[1]): Amsterdam 722,245; Rotterdam 599,414; The Hague 442,105; Utrecht 235,357; Eindhoven 197,055.

Vital statistics

Birth rate per 1,000 population (1995): 12.3 (world avg. 25.0); (1994) legitimate 85.7%; illegitimate 14.3%.
Death rate per 1,000 population (1995): 8.8 (world avg. 9.3).
Natural increase rate per 1,000 population (1995): 3.5 (world avg. 15.7).
Total fertility rate (avg. births per childbearing woman; 1994): 1.6.
Marriage rate per 1,000 population (1994): 5.4.
Divorce rate per 1,000 population (1994): 2.4.
Life expectancy at birth (1994): male 74.6 years; female 80.3 years.
Major causes of death per 100,000 population (1994): malignant neoplasms (cancers) 241.0, of which lung cancer 55.4; ischemic heart diseases 132.2; cerebrovascular diseases 81.6; accidents, poisoning, and violence 33.1.

National economy

Budget (1994). Revenue: f. 170,927,000,000 (income and corporate taxes 43.7%; value-added and excise taxes 32.7%; property taxes 1.0%). Expenditures: f. 189,361,000,000 (social security and public health 21.5%; education, scientific research, and culture 18.6%; defense 7.6%; transportation 5.7%).
Public debt (1994): U.S.$215,924,000,000.
Tourism (1994): receipts from visitors U.S.$5,612,000,000; expenditures by nationals abroad U.S.$10,983,000,000.
Production (metric tons except as noted). Agriculture, forestry, fishing (1996): sugar beets 7,600,000, potatoes 7,363,000, wheat 1,213,000, apples 570,000, tomatoes 525,000, cucumbers 500,000, onions 453,000, barley 218,000; livestock (number of live animals; 1995) 14,100,000 pigs, 4,500,000 cattle, 2,000,-000 sheep; roundwood (1994) 1,072,000 cu m; fish catch (1993) 486,894. Manufacturing (value added in f. '000,000; 1993): foodstuffs 15,361; chemicals and chemical products 11,379; machinery and transport equipment 9,898; electrical machinery 9,226; publishing and printing 7,244. Construction (buildings completed by value in f. '000,000; 1994): residential 13,500; nonresidential 9,300. Energy production (consumption): electricity (kW-hr; 1993) 76,992,000,000 (87,295,000,000); coal (metric tons; 1993) none (13,124,-000); crude petroleum (barrels; 1993) 18,311,000 (384,663,000); petroleum products (metric tons; 1993) 60,656,000 (29,508,000); natural gas (cu m; 1993) 92,591,000,000 (50,190,000,000).
Household income and expenditure (1994). Average household size 2.4; income per household f. 59,739 (U.S.$32,824); sources of income: wages 81.6%, profits 12.8%, property income 5.6%; expenditure (1993): rent 25.4%, food,

beverages, and tobacco 18.3%, education and recreation 16.3%, transportation and communications 12.9%, clothing and footwear 7.0%, household furnishings and appliances 6.6%, health care 5.9%, other 7.6%.
Gross national product (at current market price; 1994): U.S.$338,144,000,000 (U.S.$21,970 per capita).

Structure of gross domestic product and labour force				
	1994			
	in value f. '000,000	% of total value	labour force	% of labour force
Agriculture	20,697	3.7	264,000	3.7
Mining	15,483	2.8	10,000	0.1
Manufacturing	106,525	19.2	1,075,000	15.0
Construction	31,824	5.7	393,000	5.5
Public utilities	9,996	1.8	47,000	0.6
Transp. and commun.	39,885	7.2	419,000	5.8
Trade	86,527	15.6	1,227,000	17.1
Finance	[4]	[4]	704,000	9.8
Pub. admin., defense	[4]	[4]	} 2,371,000	33.0
Services	266,122[4]	48.0[4]		
Other	−22,453[5]	−4.1[5]	675,000[6]	9.4[6]
TOTAL	554,610[2]	100.0[2]	7,184,000[2]	100.0

Population economically active (1994): total 7,184,000; activity rate of total population 46.7% (participation rates: ages 15–64, 68.6%; female 41.1%; unemployed 6.8%).

Price and earnings indexes (1990 = 100)						
	1989	1990	1991	1992	1993	1994	1995
Consumer price index	97.6	100.0	103.1	106.4	109.2	112.2	114.4
Hourly earnings index	97.2	100.0	103.7	108.2	111.7	113.8	115.0

Land use (1994): forested 10.3%; meadows and pastures 31.0%; agricultural and under permanent cultivation 28.0%; other 30.7%.

Foreign trade

Balance of trade (current prices)						
	1990	1991	1992	1993	1994	1995
f. '000,000	22,345	26,131	22,225	38,995	41,982	46,132
% of total	4.9%	5.6%	4.7%	8.2%	8.0%	7.9%

Imports (1994): f. 253,680,000,000 (machinery and transport equipment 29.4%, of which road vehicles 6.7%; foodstuffs, beverages, and tobacco 12.0%; chemicals and chemical products 11.8%; mineral fuels 7.7%, of which petroleum 4.6%; clothing 3.6%). *Major import sources:* Germany 23.5%; Belgium-Luxembourg 12.0%; U.K. 9.4%; U.S. 7.7%; France 7.6%.
Exports (1994): f. 282,207,000,000 (machinery and transport equipment 23.5%, of which road vehicles 3.2%; foodstuffs, beverages, and tobacco 18.8%; chemicals and chemical products 16.3%; mineral fuels 7.2%, of which petroleum products 4.7%; iron and steel 2.2%; clothing 1.7%). *Major export destinations:* Germany 28.9%; Belgium-Luxembourg 13.4%; France 10.8%; U.K. 9.7%; Italy 5.5%.

Transport and communications

Transport. Railroads (1994): length 2,757 km; passenger-km 14,439,000,000; metric ton-km cargo 2,830,000,000. Roads (1993): total length 118,943 km (paved 89%). Vehicles (1994): passenger cars 5,884,000; trucks and buses 662,000. Merchant marine (1993): vessels (100 gross tons and over) 399; total deadweight tonnage 2,874,000. Air transport (1994): passenger-km 41,767,000,000; metric ton-km cargo 3,273,400,000; airports (1996) 6.
Communications. Daily newspapers (1994): total number 64; total circulation 4,600,000; circulation per 1,000 population 296. Radio (1993): total number of receivers 13,400,000 (1 per 1.1 persons). Television (1994): total number of receivers 5,761,000 (1 per 2.7 persons). Telephones (main lines; 1993): 7,630,000 (1 per 1.9 persons).

Education and health

Education (1994–95)				
	schools	teachers[7]	students	student/ teacher ratio[7]
Primary (age 6–12)	8,854	99,031	1,450,400	15.7
Secondary (age 12–18)	1,332	89,370	852,600	7.7
Voc., teacher tr.	702	18,613	499,000	28.0
Higher	78	30,952[8]	419,200	10.2

Educational attainment (1994). Percentage of population ages 15–64 having: primary education 15.8%; secondary 65.9%; higher 18.3%. *Literacy* (1992): virtually 100% literate.
Health (1994): physicians (1993[1]) 39,069 (1 per 391 persons); hospital beds 86,573 (1 per 178 persons); infant mortality rate per 1,000 live births 5.9.
Food (1992): daily per capita caloric intake 3,222 (vegetable products 68%, animal products 32%); 120% of FAO recommended minimum requirement.

Military

Total active duty personnel (1995): 74,400 (army 58.1%, navy 19.2%, air force 16.8%, other[9] 5.9%). *Military expenditure as percentage of GNP* (1994): 2.2% (world 3.0%); per capita expenditure U.S.$464.

[1]January 1. [2]Detail does not add to total given because of rounding. [3]Based on land area only. [4]Services includes Finance and Pub. admin., defense. [5]Imputed bank service charge. [6]Includes 492,000 unemployed. [7]1990–91. [8]1985–86. [9]Includes 3,600 military police and 800 interservice personnel.

New Zealand

Official name: New Zealand (English); Aotearoa (Maori).
Form of government: constitutional monarchy with one legislative house (House of Representatives [120]).
Chief of state: British Monarch, represented by Governor-General.
Head of government: Prime Minister.
Capital: Wellington.
Official languages: English; Maori.
Official religion: none.
Monetary unit: 1 New Zealand dollar ($NZ) = 100 cents; valuation (Oct. 11, 1996) 1 U.S.$ = $NZ 1.44; 1 £ = $NZ 2.27.

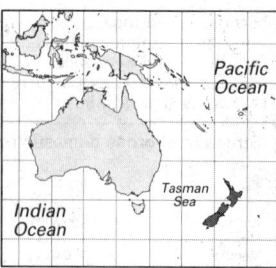

Area and population	area		population
Islands Regional Councils	sq mi	sq km	1996 census[1]
North Island	44,702	115,777	2,733,083
Auckland	...	...	1,073,220
Bay of Plenty	...	...	228,839
Gisborne[2]	...	...	45,811
Hawkes Bay	...	...	143,439
Manawatu-Wanganui	...	...	228,462
Northland	...	...	139,143
Taranaki	...	...	105,317
Waikato	...	...	356,267
Wellington	...	...	412,585
South Island	58,384	151,215	926,350
Canterbury	...	...	477,667
Marlborough	...	...	40,464
Nelson	...	...	40,941
Otago	...	...	191,684
Southland	...	...	100,342
Tasman	...	...	39,808
West Coast	...	...	35,444
Remainder[3, 4]			931
Offshore islands[5]	322	833	...
Stewart Island[6]	674	1,746	...
Chatham Islands[7]	372	963	...
TOTAL	104,454	270,534	3,660,364

Demography

Population (1996): 3,619,000.
Density (1996): persons per sq mi 34.6, persons per sq km 13.4.
Urban-rural (1995): urban 76.2%; rural 23.8%.
Sex distribution (1995): male 49.26%; female 50.74%.
Age breakdown (1995): under 15, 23.1%; 15–29, 23.2%; 30–44, 22.7%; 45–59, 15.6%; 60–74, 10.8%; 75 and over, 4.7%.
Population projection: (2000) 3,749,000; (2010) 4,025,000.
Doubling time: 81 years.
Ethnic composition (1991): New Zealand European 73.8%; New Zealand Maori 9.6%; Pacific Island Polynesian 3.6%; multiethnic 4.5%; other 8.5%.
Religious affiliation (1991): Anglican 21.4%; Presbyterian 16.0%; Roman Catholic 14.8%; Methodist 4.1%; nonreligious 19.7%; other 24.0%.
Major cities (1996): Auckland 353,670; Christchurch 313,969; Manukau 254,577; North Shore 170,913; Wellington 158,275.

Vital statistics

Birth rate per 1,000 population (1995): 16.1 (world avg. 25.0); legitimate 48.2%; illegitimate 51.8%.
Death rate per 1,000 population (1995): 7.8 (world avg. 9.3).
Natural increase rate per 1,000 population (1995): 8.3 (world avg. 15.7).
Total fertility rate (avg. births per childbearing woman; 1995): 2.0.
Marriage rate per 1,000 population (1995): 5.9.
Divorce rate per 1,000 population (1994): 2.6.
Life expectancy at birth (1996): male 74.0 years; female 80.0 years.
Major causes of death per 100,000 population (1993): diseases of the circulatory system 342.2, of which ischemic heart disease 199.4; malignant neoplasms (cancers) 205.1; diseases of the respiratory system 78.2.

National economy

Budget (1994–95): $NZ 33,990,000,000 (income taxes 56.9%, taxes on goods and services 27.6%, nontax revenue 11.3%). Expenditures: $NZ 31,428,000,000 (social services 36.9%, health 15.6%, education 15.2%).
Public debt (year ending June 30, 1995): $NZ 31,612,000,000.
Tourism (1994): receipts U.S.$1,357,000,000; expenditures U.S.$1,101,000,000.
Production (metric tons except as noted). Agriculture, forestry, fishing (1995): apples 475,000, barley 302,800, wheat 245,200, corn (maize) 160,800; livestock (number of live animals) 48,816,000 sheep, 9,273,000 cattle, 431,000 pigs, 337,000 goats; roundwood (1995) 16,495,000 cu m; fish catch (1995) 475,596. Mining and quarrying (1995): limestone 3,930,000; iron ore and sand concentrate 2,080,115; silver 27,589 kg; gold 10,118 kg. Manufacturing (1995–96): wood pulp 1,404,800; chemical fertilizers 1,266,000[8]; yarn 20,595[8]; beer 348,790,000 litres; carbonated soft drinks 245,393,000 litres; footwear 2,840,000 pairs[8]; carpets 9,884,000 sq m[8]. Construction ($NZ '000; 1995–96): residential 3,360,900; nonresidential 2,197,000. Energy production (consumption): electricity (kW-hr; 1994) 32,416,000,000 (32,416,000,000); coal (metric tons; 1994) 2,991,000 (2,191,000); crude petroleum (barrels; 1994) 14,401,000 (36,823,000); petroleum products (metric tons; 1994) 5,029,000 (4,504,000); natural gas (cu m; 1994) 4,442,300,000 (4,442,300,000).
Gross national product (1994): U.S.$46,578,000,000 (U.S.$13,190 per capita).

Structure of gross domestic product and labour force	1992–93		1996[9]	
	in value $NZ '000,000	% of total value	labour force	% of labour force
Agriculture	6,559	8.7	166,600	9.4
Mining	1,077	1.4	5,400	0.3
Manufacturing	13,674	18.2	296,100	16.6
Construction	2,299	3.1	111,400	6.3
Public utilities	2,153	2.9	14,100	0.8
Transp. and commun.	6,187	8.2	94,200	5.3
Trade	11,086	14.7	352,800	19.8
Finance	16,665	22.2	182,700	10.3
Pub. admin., defense	8,599	11.4	} 444,600	} 25.0
Services	4,154	5.5		
Other	2,767[10]	3.7[10]	112,600[11]	6.3[11]
TOTAL	75,220	100.0	1,780,500	100.0[12]

Population economically active (1996[9]): total 1,779,000; activity rate 49.5% (participation rates: over age 15, 65.5%; female 44.4%; unemployed 6.2%).

Price and earnings indexes (1990 = 100)							
	1989	1990	1991	1992	1993	1994	1995
Consumer price index	94.3	100.0	102.6	103.6	105.0	106.8	110.8
Weekly earnings index	95.8	100.0	103.0	104.8	105.5	108.5	111.8[13]

Household income and expenditure. Average household size (1996) 2.9; annual income per household (1995) $NZ 42,551 (U.S.$27,497); sources of income (1994–95): wages and salaries 65.8%, transfer payments 15.2%, self-employment 9.8%, other 9.1%; expenditure (1994–95): food 20.0%, housing 19.4%, transportation 17.1%, household durable goods 10.9%, clothing 4.4%.
Land use (1994): forested 27.9%; meadows and pastures 50.4%; agricultural and under permanent cultivation 14.2%; other 7.5%.

Foreign trade

Balance of trade (current prices)						
	1990	1991	1992	1993	1994	1995
$NZ '000,000	−607.0	+443.3	+2,356.9	+1,638.5	+1,358.2	−337.6
% of total	2.0%	1.4%	7.1%	4.5%	3.5%	0.8%

Imports (1995): $NZ 21,262,500,000 (machinery 24.5%; minerals, chemicals, and plastics 20.7%; transport equipment 17.2%; basic manufactures 7.3%; food, beverages, and tobacco 6.7%; metals and metal products 6.0%; textiles, clothing, and footwear 5.4%). *Major import sources:* Australia 19.5%; U.S. 18.9%; Japan 13.7%; U.K. 5.8%; Germany 4.3%.
Exports (1995): $NZ 20,924,900,000 (food and live animals 43.7%; basic manufactures 26.0%; minerals, chemicals, and plastics 11.1%; metals and metal products 7.1%). *Major export destinations:* Australia 20.8%; Japan 16.3%; U.S. 10.4%; U.K. 6.2%; South Korea 4.9%; Taiwan 3.0%; Hong Kong 2.8%.

Transport and communications

Transport. Railroads (1995): length 2,433 mi, 3,915 km; (1994) passenger journeys 10,300,000; short ton-mi cargo 1,918,000,000, metric ton-km cargo 2,800,000,000. Roads (1995): total length 57,089 mi, 91,876 km (paved 73%). Vehicles (1995): passenger cars 1,604,659; trucks and buses 347,883. Merchant marine (1992): vessels (100 gross tons and over) 139; total deadweight tonnage 279,805. Air transport[14] (1995): passenger-mi 11,012,000,000, passenger-km 17,723,000,000; short ton-mi cargo 395,000,000, metric ton-km cargo 577,000,000; airports (1996) 36.
Communications. Daily newspapers (1995): total number 28; total circulation 1,050,000[15]; circulation per 1,000 population 304[15]. Radio (1995): 3,100,000 receivers (1 per 1.2 persons). Television (1995): 1,100,000 receivers (1 per 3.2 persons). Telephones (main lines; 1994): 1,593,000 (1 per 2.2 persons).

Education and health

Education (1995)	schools	teachers	students	student/ teacher ratio
Primary (age 5–12)[16]	2,406	21,687	444,761	20.5
Secondary (age 13–17)	336	15,375	226,533	14.7
Voc., teacher tr.	30	5,337	107,034	20.1
Higher[17]	7	5,926	104,525	17.6

Educational attainment (1991). Percentage of population age 25 and over having: primary and some secondary education 54.9%; secondary 31.1%; higher 6.9%; not specified 6.1%[8]. *Literacy:* virtually 100.0%.
Health (1995): physicians 11,889 (1 per 301 persons); hospital beds (1994) 24,120 (1 per 146 persons); infant mortality rate per 1,000 live births (1995) 6.7.
Food (1992): daily per capita caloric intake 3,669 (vegetable products 61%, animal products 39%); 139% of FAO recommended minimum requirement.

Military

Total active duty personnel (1996): 9,870 (army 45.6%, air force 32.6%, navy 21.8%). *Military expenditure as percentage of GNP* (1994): 1.3% (world 3.0%); per capita expenditure U.S.$181.

[1]Preliminary. [2]Reorganized as a unitary authority that is administered by a district council with regional powers. [3]Includes the population of Kermadec Islands and persons on oil rigs. [4]Includes the population of Chatham Islands county and Campbell Island. [5]Excludes islands in Regional Councils. [6]Part of Southland Regional Council. [7]Chatham Islands county remains outside any Regional Council. [8]1994–95. [9]March. [10]Includes import duties less imputed bank service charges. [11]Includes 110,000 unemployed. [12]Detail does not add to total given because of rounding. [13]May. [14]Air New Zealand only. [15]1992. [16]Includes 94 composite schools that provide both primary and secondary education. [17]Universities only.

Nicaragua

Official name: República de Nicaragua
  (Republic of Nicaragua).
Form of government: unitary multiparty
  republic with one legislative house
  (National Assembly [93[1]]).
Head of state and government:
  President.
Capital: Managua.
Official language: Spanish.
Official religion: none.
Monetary unit: 1 córdoba oro
  (C$)[2] = 100 centavos;
  valuation (Oct. 11, 1996)
  1 U.S.$ = C$8.68; 1 £ = C$13.67.

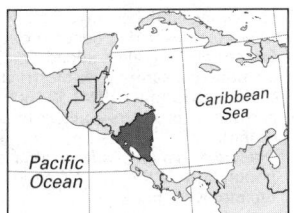

Area and population

Departments	Capitals	area[3] sq mi	sq km	population 1995 census[4]
Boaco	Boaco	1,639	4,244	124,513
Carazo	Jinotepe	405	1,050	141,831
Chinandega	Chinandega	1,902	4,926	348,971
Chontales	Juigalpa	2,463	6,378	137,477
Estelí	Estelí	902	2,335	168,936
Granada	Granada	359	929	153,183
Jinotega	Jinotega	3,766	9,755	214,070
León	León	1,972	5,107	330,168
Madriz	Somoto	619	1,602	99,842
Managua	Managua	1,418	3,672	1,056,702
Masaya	Masaya	228	590	236,107
Matagalpa	Matagalpa	3,291	8,523	364,790
Nueva Segovia	Ocotal	1,206	3,123	151,324
Río San Juan	San Carlos	2,885	7,473	70,875
Rivas	Rivas	832	2,155	141,792
Autonomous regions				
North Atlantic	...	12,417	32,159	175,405
South Atlantic	Bluefields	10,582	27,407	223,500
TOTAL LAND AREA		46,884[5]	121,428	
INLAND WATER		4,009	10,384	
TOTAL		50,893	131,812	4,139,486

Demography

Population (1996): 4,272,000.
Density (1996)[6]: persons per sq mi 91.1, persons per sq km 35.2.
Urban-rural (1995): urban 51.7%; rural 48.3%.
Sex distribution (1995): male 49.43%; female 50.57%.
Age breakdown (1994): under 15, 44.2%; 15–29, 28.7%; 30–44, 15.5%; 45–59, 7.2%; 60–74, 3.6%; 75 and over, 0.8%.
Population projection: (2000) 4,729,000; (2010) 5,863,000.
Doubling time: 25 years.
Ethnic composition (1991): mestizo (Spanish/Indian) 69.0%; white 17.0%; black 9.0%; Amerindian 5.0%.
Religious affiliation (1992): Roman Catholic 89.3%; other (mostly Baptist, Moravian, and Pentecostal) 10.7%.
Major cities (1995)[4]: Managua 819,731; León 124,117; Chinandega 84,281; Masaya 80,051; Granada 74,396; Estelí 65,036.

Vital statistics

Birth rate per 1,000 population (1995): 34.7 (world avg. 25.0).
Death rate per 1,000 population (1994): 6.2 (world avg. 9.3).
Natural increase rate per 1,000 population (1994): 28.5 (world avg. 15.7).
Total fertility rate (avg. births per childbearing woman; 1995): 4.2.
Marriage rate per 1,000 population (1991): 3.3.
Divorce rate per 1,000 population (1991): 0.4.
Life expectancy at birth (1995): male 63.0 years; female 67.7 years.
Major causes of death per 100,000 population (1991)[7]: diseases of the circulatory system 142.0; infectious and parasitic diseases 100.0; accidents and violence 93.0; diseases of the respiratory system 73.0; malignant neoplasms (cancers) 56.0.

National economy

Budget (1994–95). Revenue: C$5,541,000,000 (ordinary income [tax and non-tax revenue] 49.0%; loans 40.2%, of which external 22.2%; grants 10.8%). Expenditures: C$5,140,000,000 (current expenditure 53.0%, development expenditure 47.0%).
Public debt (external, outstanding; 1994): U.S.$9,006,000.
Production (value of production in C$'000,000[8] except as noted). Agriculture, forestry, fishing (1993): coffee 1,055; beef 1,044; poultry 626; corn (maize) 461; milk 437; rice 386; sugarcane 367; beans 317; pigs 136; sorghum 135; shrimp 123; lobster 80; sesame 73; tobacco 68; peanuts (groundnuts) 64; soybeans 54. Mining and quarrying (1993): gold 240. Manufacturing (1993): beef products 1,923; petroleum products 1,748; beverages 1,450; refined sugar and sugar products 528; cement, bricks, and tile 485; chemicals and chemical products 420; tobacco products 395; fish and crustacean products 294; sawlogs and wood products (excluding furniture) 170. Construction (completed; 1991): 569 cu m. Energy production (consumption): electricity (kW-hr; 1994) 1,643,000,000 (1,089,000,000); coal, none (none); crude petroleum (barrels; 1994) none (4,178,000); petroleum products (metric tons; 1994) 540,000 (582,000); natural gas, none (none).
Household income and expenditure. Average household size (1995) 5.7; income per household: n.a.; sources of income: n.a.; expenditure: n.a.
Tourism (1994): receipts from visitors U.S.$40,200,000; expenditures by nationals abroad U.S.$38,000,000.

Population economically active (1993): total 1,489,500; activity rate of total population 34.9% (participation rates: over age 15 [1991] 62.0%; female [1991] 33.2%; unemployed [1995] 18.0%).

Price and earnings indexes (1991 = 100)

	1991	1992	1993	1994	1995
Consumer price index	100.0	123.7	148.9	160.5	177.9
Annual earnings index[9]	100.0	150.5	172.5	...	...

Gross national product (at current market prices; 1994): U.S.$1,395,000,000 (U.S.$330 per capita).

Structure of gross domestic product and labour force

	1994 in value C$'000,000	% of total value	1991 labour force	% of labour force
Agriculture, forestry	4,088	32.8	415,400	30.0
Mining	81	0.6	9,000	0.6
Manufacturing	2,052	16.5	188,200	13.6
Construction	352	2.8	30,200	2.2
Public utilities	144	1.2	10,300	0.7
Transportation and communications	461	3.7	42,600	3.1
Trade	3,015	24.2	195,500	14.1
Finance, real estate	667	5.3	24,700	1.8
Pub. admin., defense	898	7.2	98,100	7.1
Services	707	5.7	183,900	13.3
Other			188,400[10]	13.6[10]
TOTAL	12,467[4]	100.0	1,386,300	100.0[4]

Land use (1994): forested 26.3%; meadows and pastures 45.3%; agricultural and under permanent cultivation 10.5%; other 17.9%.

Foreign trade[11]

Balance of trade (current prices)

	1990	1991	1992	1993	1994	1995
U.S.$'000,000	−236.8	−396.4	−547.8	−402.8	−433.5	−327.2
% of total	26.4%	42.1%	55.1%	43.0%	38.2%	23.8%

Imports (1994): U.S.$852,500,000 (food and live animals 14.4%, mineral fuels 12.8%, nonelectrical machinery 11.2%, electrical machinery 7.7%, road vehicles 6.4%). *Major import sources:* United States 25.2%; Venezuela 11.9%; Guatemala 8.1%; Costa Rica 8.0%; Japan 7.2%.
Exports (1994): U.S.$351,100,000 (coffee 21.0%, beef 18.0%, crustaceans 12.3%, oilseeds 5.0%, raw sugar 4.5%). *Major export destinations:* United States 42.9%; Germany 12.7%; El Salvador 10.7%; Costa Rica 7.3%; Honduras 3.6%.

Transport and communications

Transport. Railroads: [12]. Roads (1995): total length 10,654 mi, 17,146 km (paved 10%). Vehicles (1995): passenger cars 72,413; trucks and buses 68,090. Merchant marine (1992): vessels (100 gross tons and over) 25; total deadweight tonnage 1,295. Air transport (1994)[13]: passenger-mi 44,846,000, passenger-km 72,172,000; short ton-mi cargo 4,770,000, metric ton-km cargo 6,964,000; airports (1996) with scheduled flights 10.
Communications. Daily newspapers (1993): total number 3; total circulation 98,602; circulation per 1,000 population 25. Radio (1995): 925,000 receivers (1 per 4.4 persons). Television (1995): 210,000 receivers (1 per 20 persons). Telephones (main lines; 1994): 85,254 (1 per 47 persons).

Education and health

Education (1994)

	schools	teachers	students	student/teacher ratio
Primary (age 7–12)[14]	7,093	23,693	880,891	37.2
Secondary (age 13–18) } Voc., teacher tr.	451	5,356	211,606	39.5
Higher	10	2,005	22,120	11.0

Educational attainment: n.a. *Literacy* (1995): total population age 15 and over literate 1,574,000 (65.7%); males literate 727,000 (64.6%); females literate 847,000 (66.6%).
Health (1994): physicians 2,577 (1 per 1,566 persons); hospital beds 4,413 (1 per 914 persons); infant mortality rate per 1,000 live births (1995) 47.6.
Food (1992): daily per capita caloric intake 2,293 (vegetable products 90%, animal products 10%); 102% of FAO recommended minimum requirement.

Military

Total active duty personnel (1996): 17,000 (army 88.2%, navy 4.7%, air force 7.1%). *Military expenditure as percentage of GNP* (1994): 2.6% (world 3.0%); per capita expenditure U.S.$8.

---

[1]Includes three unsuccessful 1996 presidential candidates meeting special conditions. [2]The córdoba oro (gold cordoba), introduced in August 1990, circulated simultaneously with the new córdoba until April 30, 1991, when the new córdoba ceased to be legal tender; on April 30, 1 córdoba oro equaled 5,000,000 new córdobas. The new córdoba had been introduced in February 1988 at the rate of 1 new córdoba to 1,000 (old) córdobas. [3]Lakes and lagoons are excluded from the areas of departments and autonomous regions. [4]Preliminary figures. [5]Detail does not add to total given because of rounding. [6]Based on land area. [7]Projected rates based on about 45% of total deaths. [8]At prices of 1980. [9]Workers registered with the Nicaraguan Institute of Social Security and Welfare. [10]Unemployed persons previously employed. [11]Imports f.o.b. in balance of trade and c.i.f. in commodities and trading partners. [12]Railroad service ended in January 1994. [13]Nica only. [14]Includes preprimary.

Niger

Official name: République du Niger
  (Republic of Niger).
Form of government: republic[1, 2].
Head of state and government:
  President assisted by Prime Minister.
Capital: Niamey.
Official language: French.
Official religion: none.
Monetary unit: 1 CFA franc
  (CFAF) = 100 centimes;
  valuation (Oct. 11, 1996)
  1 U.S.$ = CFAF 518.24;
  1 £ = CFAF 816.38.

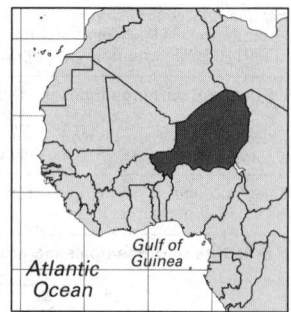

Area and population

Departments	Capitals	area[3] sq mi	sq km	population 1988 census
Agadez[4]	Agadez	244,869	634,209	208,828
Diffa	Diffa	54,138	140,216	189,091
Dosso	Dosso	11,970	31,002	1,018,895
Maradi	Maradi	14,896	38,581	1,389,433
Tahoua	Tahoua	41,188	106,677	1,308,598
Tillabéri	Tillabéri	34,863	90,293	1,725,720
Zinder	Zinder	56,151	145,430	1,411,061
TOTAL		458,075	1,186,408	7,251,626

Demography

Population (1996): 9,465,000.
Density (1996)[3]: persons per sq mi 19.4, persons per sq km 7.5.
Urban-rural (1995): urban 17.0%; rural 83.0%.
Sex distribution (1995): male 49.40%; female 50.60%.
Age breakdown (1995): under 15, 48.4%; 15–29, 25.7%; 30–44, 14.4%; 45–59, 7.5%; 60–74, 3.4%; 75 and over, 0.6%.
Population projection: (2000) 10,805,000; (2010) 14,751,000.
Doubling time: 23 years.
Ethnic composition (1988): Hausa 53.0%; Zerma- (Djerma-) Songhai 21.2%; Tuareg 10.4%; Fulani (Peul) 9.8%; Kanuri-Nanga 4.4%; Teda 0.4%; Arab 0.3%; Gurma 0.3%; other 0.2%.
Religious affiliation (1988): Muslim, primarily Sunnī, 98.7%; traditional beliefs 0.7%; Christian 0.4%; other 0.2%.
Major cities (1988): Niamey 391,876; Zinder 119,827; Maradi 110,005; Tahoua 49,948; Agadez 32,272.

Vital statistics

Birth rate per 1,000 population (1995): 55.2 (world avg. 25.0).
Death rate per 1,000 population (1995): 25.1 (world avg. 9.3).
Natural increase rate per 1,000 population (1995): 30.1 (world avg. 15.7).
Total fertility rate (avg. births per childbearing woman; 1995): 7.5.
Marriage rate per 1,000 population: n.a.
Divorce rate per 1,000 population: n.a.
Life expectancy at birth (1995): male 40.7 years; female 39.8 years.
Major causes of death: n.a.; however, among selected major causes of infectious disease registered at medical facilities were malaria, measles, diarrhea, meningitis, pneumonia, diphtheria, tetanus, viral hepatitis, and poliomyelitis; malnutrition and shortages of trained medical personnel are widespread.

National economy

Budget (1996). Revenue: CFAF 173,900,000,000 (current revenue 64.4%, of which taxes 47.0%; external aid and gifts 34.9%). Expenditures: CFAF 173,900,000,000 (current expenditures 54.1%; development expenditures 45.9%).
Public debt (external, outstanding; 1994): U.S.$1,311,000,000.
Tourism (1994): receipts from visitors U.S.$16,000,000; expenditures by nationals abroad U.S.$21,000,000.
Gross national product (at current market prices; 1994): U.S.$2,040,000,000 (U.S.$230 per capita).

Structure of gross domestic product and labour force

	1993 in value CFAF '000,000	1993 % of total value	1988 labour force	1988 % of labour force
Agriculture	233,300	37.1	1,764,049	76.2
Mining	35,100	5.6	5,295	0.2
Manufacturing	43,400	6.9	65,793	2.8
Construction	11,900	1.9	13,742	0.6
Public utilities	14,700	2.3	1,778	0.1
Transportation and communications	27,000	4.3	14,764	0.6
Trade and finance	116,100	18.5	210,354	9.1
Pub. admin., defense	69,300	11.0	59,271	2.6
Services	65,500	10.4	63,991	2.8
Other	12,400	2.0	116,657	5.0
TOTAL	628,700	100.0	2,315,694	100.0

Production (metric tons except as noted). Agriculture, forestry, fishing (1995): millet 1,725,000, beans and cowpeas 424,800[5], sorghum 420,000, cassava (manioc) 225,000, onions 178,000, sugarcane 142,000, rice 70,000, peanuts (groundnuts) 57,000, tomatoes 47,000, tobacco leaf 930; livestock (number of live animals) 5,716,000 goats, 3,789,000 sheep, 2,007,000 cattle, 450,000 asses, 380,000 camels, 82,000 horses; roundwood (1994) 5,671,000 cu m; fish catch (1993) 2,172. Mining and quarrying (1994): salt 3,000; uranium 2,183[6]. Manufacturing (percentage of total manufacturing value added; 1992): food

processing and beverages 44.1%; chemicals 31.9%; construction materials 8.9%; textiles 7.1%; paper products 6.3%; metal and wood products 1.1%. Construction (value added in CFAF; 1993): 11,900,000,000. Energy production (consumption): electricity (kW-hr; 1994) 178,000,000 (375,000,000); coal (metric tons; 1994) 133,500 (174,000); crude petroleum, none (none); petroleum products (metric tons; 1994) none (211,000); natural gas, none (none).
Population economically active (1988): total 2,315,694; activity rate of total population 31.9% (participation rates: ages 15–64, 55.2%; female 20.4%; unemployed, n.a.).

Price and earnings indexes (1985 = 100)

	1990	1991	1992	1993	1994	1995	1996[7]
Consumer price index	100.0	92.2	88.1	87.0	118.4	130.9	135.6
Hourly earnings index[8]	100.0	100.0	100.0	100.0	...	...	...

Household income and expenditure. Average household size (1988) 6.4; income per household: n.a.; sources of income (1977): self-employment 59.5%, family 30.1%, salary or wages 4.8%, employer 0.7%; expenditure (1987): food and beverages 43.1%, housing 22.8%, clothing 10.0%.
Land use (1994): forested 2.0%; meadows and pastures 8.2%; agricultural and under permanent cultivation 2.9%; other (largely desert) 86.9%.

Foreign trade

Balance of trade (current prices)

	1990	1991	1992	1993	1994	1995
CFAF '000,000,000	– 13,300	+ 1,000	– 13,100	– 3,600	– 12,300	– 7,200
% of total	8.0%	0.7%	6.9%	2.2%	4.8%	3.1%

Imports (1993): CFAF 67,500,000,000 (consumer goods 71.2%, of which grain 8.9%, petroleum products 8.3%; intermediate and capital goods 28.9%). *Major import sources:* France 21.8%; Côte d'Ivoire 8.7%; Germany 3.7%; Italy 2.6%; Japan 1.9%.
Exports (1994): CFAF 111,800,000,000 (uranium 70%; agricultural products 22%, of which live cattle 9%, live sheep and goats 5%). *Major export destinations* (1993): France 55.3%.

Transport and communications

Transport. Railroads: none[9]. Roads (1993): total length 8,580 mi, 13,808 km (paved [1990] 29%). Vehicles (1994): passenger cars 16,000; trucks and buses 18,000. Air transport (1995)[10]: passenger-mi 138,455,000, passenger-km 222,822,000; short ton-mi cargo 10,461,000, metric ton-km cargo 15,273,000; airports (1995) with scheduled flights 6.
Communications. Daily newspapers (1994): total number 3; total circulation 11,000; circulation per 1,000 population 1.2. Radio (1995): total number of receivers 440,000 (1 per 20 persons). Television (1995): total number of receivers 25,000 (1 per 366 persons). Telephones (main lines; 1993): 10,500 (1 per 830 persons).

Education and health

Education (1993–94)

	schools	teachers	students	student/ teacher ratio
Primary (age 7–12)	2,656	12,216	414,296	33.9
Secondary (age 13–19)	105[11]	2,219[12]	88,810	35.1[12]
Voc., teacher tr.	7[11]	175[12]	2,110	12.1[12]
Higher[13]	2	315	4,060	12.9

Educational attainment (1988). Percentage of population age 25 and over having: no formal schooling 85.0%; Koranic education 11.2%; primary education 2.5%; secondary 1.1%; higher 0.2%. *Literacy* (1995): percentage of total population age 15 and over literate 13.6%; males literate 20.9%; females literate 6.6%.
Health: physicians (1990) 142 (1 per 54,444 persons); hospital beds (1987) c. 3,500 (1 per 2,000 persons); infant mortality rate per 1,000 live births (1995) 119.2.
Food (1992): daily per capita caloric intake 2,257 (vegetable products 95%, animal products 5%); 95% of FAO recommended minimum requirement.

Military

Total active duty personnel (1996): 5,300 (army 98.1%, air force 1.9%). *Military expenditure as percentage of GNP* (1994): 0.9% (world 3.0%); per capita expenditure U.S.$2.

[1]Leader of military coup of January 1996 (now president) promulgated a new constitution on May 22, 1996; in July 1996 opposition parties were banned. [2]Appointed consultative body from February 1996 was to be replaced in November 1996 by an elected legislative body. [3]The departmental areas and total shown are obsolete. The total area, according to recent official estimates, is 489,000 sq mi (1,267,000 sq km); but subtotals distributing this total among the departments remain unpublished. [4]The peace accord signed in October 1994 provided for an eventual limited autonomy for the Tuaregs (a Berber-speaking people), who inhabit Agadez department. [5]1993–94. [6]1994–95. [7]April. [8]Guaranteed minimum wage for professionals. [9]Niger is a cofounder of the Common Benin-Niger Organization (OCBN) for Railroads and Transport, currently maintaining rail operations only in Benin but having the purpose of extending rail services from the sea at Cotonou, Benin, to Dosso and, ultimately, Niamey, Niger; in the interim, freight transported between the two countries is carried by truck. [10]Represents 1/11 of the traffic of Air Afrique, which is operated by 11 West African states. [11]1989–90. [12]1992–93. [13]Université de Niamey and École Nationale d'Administration du Niger only.

Nigeria

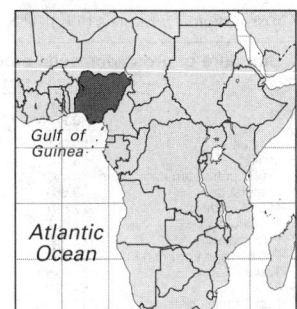

Official name: Federal Republic of Nigeria.
Form of government: military regime[1].
Head of state and government: President assisted by Provisional Council.
Capital: Abuja (Federal Capital Territory)[2].
Official language: English.
Official religion: none.
Monetary unit: 1 Nigerian naira (₦) = 100 kobo; valuation (Oct. 11, 1996) 1 U.S.$ = ₦22.00; 1 £ = ₦34.66.

Area and population		area		population
		sq mi	sq km	1992 estimate
States[3]	**Capitals**			
Abia	Umuahia	2,440	6,320	2,366,918
Adamawa	Yola	14,254	36,917	2,187,771
Akwa Ibom	Uyo	2,734	7,081	2,430,528
Anambra	Awka	1,870	4,844	2,850,940
Bauchi	Bauchi	24,944	64,605	4,423,246
Benue	Makurdi	13,150	34,059	2,863,810
Borno	Maiduguri	27,374	70,898	2,674,486
Cross River	Calabar	7,782	20,156	1,912,582
Delta	Asaba	6,833	17,698	2,647,286
Edo	Benin City	6,873	17,802	2,224,644
Enugu	Enugu	4,954	12,831	3,256,134
Imo	Owerri	2,135	5,530	2,560,064
Jigawa	Dutse	8,940	23,154	2,914,827
Kaduna	Kaduna	17,781	46,053	4,088,239
Kano	Kano	7,773	20,131	5,801,001
Katsina	Katsina	9,341	24,192	3,994,695
Kebbi	Birnin Kebbi	14,209	36,800	2,124,093
Kogi	Lokoja	11,519	29,833	2,162,017
Kwara	Ilorin	14,218	36,825	1,613,501
Lagos	Ikeja	1,292	3,345	5,847,355
Niger	Minna	29,484	76,363	2,556,838
Ogun	Abeokuta	6,472	16,762	2,408,727
Ondo	Akure	8,092	20,959	4,001,020
Osun	Oshogbo	3,572	9,251	2,269,101
Oyo	Ibadan	10,986	28,454	3,593,453
Plateau	Jos	22,406	58,030	3,382,215
Rivers	Port Harcourt	8,436	21,850	4,103,372
Sokoto	Sokoto	25,380	65,735	4,524,162
Taraba	Jalingo	21,032	54,473	1,525,008
Yobe	Damaturu	17,568	45,502	1,453,826
Federal Capital Territory				
Abuja	Abuja	2,824	7,315	390,031
TOTAL		356,669[4]	923,768	91,151,886[4]

Demography

Population (1996): 103,912,000.
Density (1996): persons per sq mi 291.3, persons per sq km 112.5.
Urban-rural (1995): urban 39.3%; rural 60.7%.
Sex distribution (1995): male 49.56%; female 50.44%.
Age breakdown (1995): under 15, 45.6%; 15–29, 25.7%; 30–44, 15.7%; 45–59, 8.5%; 60–74, 3.8%; 75 and over, 0.7%.
Population projection: (2000) 117,328,000; (2010) 157,375,000.
Doubling time: 23 years.
Ethnic composition (1983): Hausa 21.3%; Yoruba 21.3%; Igbo (Ibo) 18.0%; Fulani 11.2%; Ibibio 5.6%; Kanuri 4.2%; Edo 3.4%; Tiv 2.2%; Ijaw 1.8%; Bura 1.7%; Nupe 1.2%; other 8.1%.
Religious affiliation (1995): Muslim 50.0%; Christian 40.0%, of which Protestant 21.4%, Roman Catholic 9.9%, African indigenous 8.7%; other 10.0%.
Major cities (1992): Lagos 1,347,000; Ibadan 1,295,000; Kano 699,900; Ogbomosho 660,600; Oshogbo 441,600; Ilorin 430,600.

Vital statistics

Birth rate per 1,000 population (1990–95): 45.4 (world avg. 25.0).
Death rate per 1,000 population (1990–95): 15.4 (world avg. 9.3).
Natural increase rate per 1,000 population (1990–95): 30.0 (world avg. 15.7).
Total fertility rate (avg. births per childbearing woman; 1990–95): 6.4.
Life expectancy at birth (1993): male 53.5 years; female 55.9 years.

National economy

Budget (1995). Revenue: ₦350,660,000,000 (1992; petroleum royalties and rents 62.0%[5]; petroleum profit tax 12.8%; import duties 11.6%; company income tax 3.9%). Expenditures: ₦351,160,000,000 (1992; recurrent expenditure 64.3%, of which debt service 53.7%, defense 2.9%, education 2.8%, police 2.5%, health 1.4%; capital expenditure 35.7%).
Public debt (external, outstanding; 1994): U.S.$28,168,000,000.
Production (metric tons except as noted). Agriculture, forestry, fishing (1996): yams 23,640,000, cassava 21,000,000, corn (maize) 7,321,000, sorghum 6,800,-000, millet 5,159,000, rice 3,250,000, plantains and bananas 1,694,000, peanuts (groundnuts) 1,500,000, taro 1,204,000, green peppers 970,000, sugarcane 500,000; livestock (number of live animals) 24,500,000 goats, 17,790,000 cattle, 14,000,000 sheep; roundwood (1994) 99,083,000 cu m; fish catch (1993) 255,499. Mining and quarrying (1994): limestone 2,700,000; marble 30,661[6]; tin 300[7]. Manufacturing (value added in U.S.$'000,000; 1990): food and beverages 703; textiles 373; chemical products 165; metal products 160; machinery and transport equipment 159; paper products 62; rubber and plastic products 61. Construction (dwellings completed; 1982): 31,038. Energy production (consumption): electricity (kW-hr; 1994) 14,790,000,000 (14,790,-000,000); coal (metric tons; 1994) 50,000 (50,000); crude petroleum (bar-

rels; 1994) 665,994,000 (84,452,000); petroleum products (metric tons; 1994) 5,234,000 (5,974,000); natural gas (cu m; 1994) 9,798,000,000 (9,798,000,000).
Tourism (1994): receipts U.S.$34,000,000; expenditures U.S.$144,000,000.
Gross national product (1994): U.S.$29,995,000,000 (U.S.$280 per capita).

Structure of gross domestic product and labour force				
	1994		1986	
	in value ₦'000,000	% of total value	labour force	% of labour force
Agriculture	345,010	38.7	13,259,000	43.1
Mining[8]	240,480	27.0	6,800	0.1
Manufacturing	57,195	6.4	1,263,700	4.1
Construction	9,912	1.1	545,600	1.8
Public utilities	1,758	0.2	130,400	0.4
Transp. and commun.	28,379	3.2	1,111,900	3.6
Trade[9]	146,008	16.4	7,417,400	24.1
Finance	37,522	4.2	120,100	0.4
Pub. admin., defense	22,051	2.5 }	4,902,100	15.9
Services	3,477	0.4 }		
Other	...	...	2,008,500[10]	6.5[10]
TOTAL	891,790[4]	100.0[4]	30,765,500	100.0

Population economically active (1986): total 30,765,500; activity rate 31.1% (participation rates: ages 15–64, 58.8%; female 33.3%; unemployed [1992] 4.0%).

Price and earnings indexes (1990 = 100)							
	1989	1990	1991	1992	1993	1994	1995
Consumer price index	93.1	100.0	113.0	163.4	256.8	403.3	696.9
Earnings index	...	...	...	...	...	...	...

Household income and expenditure. Avg. household size (1983) 5.0; annual income per household (1981) ₦2,300 (U.S.$3,745)[11]; sources of income (1979): self-employment 49.4%, wages 36.2%, interest 5.4%, rent 4.7%, transfer payments 4.3%; expenditures (1979): food 53.0%, fuel and light 11.4%, clothing 6.0%, transportation 4.7%, household goods 3.8%, other 21.1%.
Land use (1994): forested 12.0%; pastures 43.9%; agricultural 35.9%; other 8.2%.

Foreign trade

Balance of trade (current prices)						
	1989	1990	1991	1992	1993	1994
₦'000,000	+29,730	+68,587	+40,696	+76,298	+69,145	+76,677
% of total	34.5%	45.4%	20.2%	22.8%	18.8%	22.8%

Imports (1994): ₦143,225,700,000 (machinery and transport equipment 31.2%; manufactured goods [mostly iron and steel products, textiles, and paper products] 26.8%; chemicals 25.2%; food 10.8%). *Major import sources* (1991): Germany 13.8%; U.K. 13.6%; U.S. 11.8%; France 8.9%.
Exports (1994): ₦206,285,100,000 (crude petroleum 97.4%; cocoa beans 0.9%; rubber 0.3%; other exports include cocoa products, textiles, and cashew nuts). *Major export destinations* (1991): U.S. 40.7%; Spain 12.6%; Germany 8.6%; The Netherlands 5.0%; France 5.0%; Italy 4.0%.

Transport and communications

Transport. Railroads (1993): length 3,557 km; passenger-km 555,000,000; metric ton-km cargo 161,000,000. Roads (1991): total length 112,140 km (paved 28%). Vehicles (1993): passenger cars 773,000; trucks and buses 606,000. Merchant marine (1992): vessels (100 gross tons and over) 271; total deadweight tonnage 733,329. Air transport (1993): passenger-km 913,000,000; metric ton-km cargo 11,484,000[6]; airports (1996) 12.
Communications. Daily newspapers (1994): total number 28; total circulation 1,533,000[12]; circulation per 1,000 population 16[12]. Radio (1995): 17,200,000 receivers (1 per 5.8 persons). Television (1995): 6,100,000 receivers (1 per 16 persons). Telephones (main lines; 1993): 342,300 (1 per 267 persons).

Education and health

Education (1993–94)				
	schools	teachers	students	student/ teacher ratio
Primary (age 6–12)	38,649	435,210	16,191,000	37.2
Secondary (age 12–17)	6,074	152,596	4,451,000	29.2
Voc., teacher tr.	376[13]	15,738[14]	391,583[14]	24.9[14]
Higher	31	12,103	228,000	18.8

Literacy (1995): total population age 15 and over literate 34,696,000 (57.1%); males literate 20,027,000 (67.3%); females literate 14,669,000 (47.3%).
Health (1994): physicians 21,739 (1 per 4,496 persons); hospital beds 91,346 (1 per 1,070 persons); infant mortality rate (1990–95) 84.2.
Food (1992): daily per capita caloric intake 2,124 (vegetable products 97%, animal products 3%); 90% of FAO recommended minimum requirement.

Military

Total active duty personnel (1996): 77,100 (army 80.4%, navy 7.3%, air force 12.3%). *Military expenditure as percentage of GNP* (1994): 0.8% (world 3.0%); per capita expenditure U.S.$3.

[1]Assumed control on Sept. 14, 1995. [2]Statutory transfer of capital from Lagos to Abuja took place in December 1991. [3]In October 1996 the creation of six new states was announced: Bayelsa, Ebonyi, Ekiti, Gombe, Nassarawa, and Zamfara. [4]Detail does not add to total given because of rounding. [5]Expected to be 57.2% in 1995. [6]1992. [7]Metal content. [8]Includes ₦238,987,000,000 from petroleum and natural gas. [9]Includes hotels. [10]Includes 1,263,000 unemployed. [11]Urban households only. [12]For 13 newspapers only. [13]1987–88. [14]1988–89.

Norway

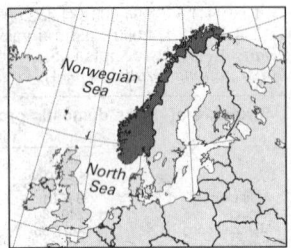

Official name: Kongeriket Norge (Kingdom of Norway).
Form of government: constitutional monarchy with one legislative house (Parliament [165]).
Chief of state: King.
Head of government: Prime Minister.
Capital: Oslo.
Official language: Norwegian.
Official religion: Evangelical Lutheran.
Monetary unit: 1 Norwegian krone (NKr) = 100 øre; valuation (Oct. 11, 1996) 1 U.S.$ = NKr 6.51; 1 £ = NKr 10.25.

Area and population

Counties	Capitals	area[1] sq mi	sq km	population 1996[2] estimate
Akershus	—	1,898	4,917	439,995
Aust-Agder	Arendal	3,557	9,212	100,219
Buskerud	Drammen	5,763	14,927	229,413
Finnmark	Vadsø	18,779	48,637	76,502
Hedmark	Hamar	10,575	27,388	186,337
Hordaland	Bergen	6,036	15,634	425,132
Møre og Romsdal	Molde	5,832	15,104	241,094
Nordland	Bodø	14,798	38,327	241,111
Nord-Trøndelag	Steinkjer	8,673	22,463	127,287
Oppland	Lillehammer	9,753	25,260	182,914
Oslo	Oslo	175	454	487,908
Østfold	Moss	1,615	4,183	240,213
Rogaland	Stavanger	3,529	9,141	356,968
Sogn og Fjordane	Leikanger	7,195	18,634	107,724
Sør-Trøndelag	Trondheim	7,271	18,831	257,079
Telemark	Skien	5,913	15,315	163,234
Troms	Tromsø	10,021	25,954	151,064
Vest-Agder	Kristiansand	2,811	7,281	150,443
Vestfold	Tønsberg	856	2,216	204,579
TOTAL		**125,050**	**323,878**	**4,369,216[3]**

Demography

Population (1996): 4,382,000.
Density (1996): persons per sq mi 35.0, persons per sq km 13.5.
Urban-rural (1990): urban 75.0%; rural 25.0%.
Sex distribution (1995): male 49.45%; female 50.55%.
Age breakdown (1994): under 15, 19.3%; 15–29, 22.0%; 30–44, 21.8%; 45–59, 16.6%; 60–74, 13.0%; 75 and over, 7.3%.
Population projection: (2000) 4,483,000; (2010) 4,681,000.
Doubling time: not applicable; doubling time exceeds 100 years.
Ethnic composition (by country of citizenship; 1994): Norway 96.3%; Denmark 0.4%; Sweden 0.3%; United Kingdom 0.3%; Pakistan 0.2%; United States 0.2%; Yugoslavia 0.2%; Iran 0.2%; other 1.9%.
Religious affiliation (1980): Lutheran 87.9%; nonreligious 3.2%; other 8.9%.
Major cities (1996)[4]: Oslo 487,908; Bergen 223,100; Trondheim 143,746; Stavanger 104,322; Baerum 97,019.

Vital statistics

Birth rate per 1,000 population (1995): 13.8 (world avg. 25.0); (1993) legitimate 55.6%; illegitimate 44.4%.
Death rate per 1,000 population (1995): 10.4 (world avg. 9.3).
Natural increase rate per 1,000 population (1995): 3.4 (world avg. 15.7).
Total fertility rate (avg. births per childbearing woman; 1994): 1.9.
Marriage rate per 1,000 population (1993): 4.5.
Divorce rate per 1,000 population (1993): 2.5.
Life expectancy at birth (1993): male 74.2 years; female 80.3 years.
Major causes of death per 100,000 population (1992): ischemic heart disease 242.6; malignant neoplasms (cancers) 224.5; cerebrovascular disease 126.1.

National economy

Budget (1995). Revenue: NKr 339,237,000,000 (social security taxes 24.6%, value-added taxes 24.2%, taxes on interest and dividends 9.2%, taxes on petroleum income and activity 3.1%, ordinary income tax 2.8%). Expenditures: NKr 339,144,000,000 (social security and welfare 25.2%, health 7.9%, debt service 6.0%).
Land use (1994): forested 27.2%; meadows and pastures 0.4%; agricultural and under permanent cultivation 2.9%; built-up and other 69.5%.
Tourism (1994): receipts from visitors U.S.$2,157,000,000; expenditures by nationals abroad U.S.$3,930,000,000.
Production (metric tons except as noted). Agriculture, forestry, fishing (1995): barley 576,000, potatoes 471,000, oats 352,000, wheat 326,000; livestock (number of live animals) 2,316,000 sheep, 1,003,100 cattle, 745,000 pigs; roundwood (1994) 8,744,000 cu m; fish catch (1995) 2,524,129, of which herring 687,185, cod 317,368, saithe 219,627, mackerel 202,107. Mining and quarrying (1995)[5]: iron ore 2,168,000, ilmenite-titanium 858,000, copper 29,000, zinc 22,000. Manufacturing (value added in NKr '000,000; 1994): machinery and equipment 27,803, of which transport equipment 12,495, electrical equipment 7,673; paper and paper products 15,851; food products 12,797; chemical products 8,850; wood and wood products 4,256. Construction (1995): residential 3,099,000 sq m; nonresidential 2,874,000 sq m. Energy production (consumption): electricity (kW-hr; 1993) 113,389,000,000 (113,256,000,000); coal (metric tons; 1994) 301,000 (914,000); crude petroleum (barrels; 1994) 977,367,000 (110,386,000); petroleum products (metric tons; 1994) 14,512,000 (7,703,000); natural gas (cu m; 1993) 31,347,000,000 (4,051,000,000).

Gross national product (1994): U.S.$114,328,000,000 (U.S.$26,480 per capita).

Structure of gross domestic product and labour force

	1991 in value NKr '000,000	1991 % of total value	1994 labour force	1994 % of labour force
Agriculture	20,052	2.9	106,000	4.8
Mining	3,908	0.6	23,000	1.1
Crude petroleum and natural gas	99,664	14.5	...	...
Manufacturing	92,591	13.5	308,000	14.1
Construction	24,705	3.6	126,000	5.8
Public utilities	26,386	3.8	22,000	1.0
Transp. and commun.	61,738	9.0	170,000	7.8
Trade	75,315[6]	11.0[6]	357,000	16.3
Finance	61,709	9.0	160,000	7.3
Pub. admin., defense	111,910	16.3 }	803,000	36.7
Services	67,231	9.8 }		
Other	41,479	6.0	107,000[7]	4.9[7]
TOTAL	**686,686[8]**	**100.0**	**2,186,000[8]**	**100.0[8]**

Public debt (1992): U.S.$29,233,000,000.
Population economically active (1995): total 2,186,000; activity rate of total population 50.0% (participation rates: ages 16–64 [1994] 79.6%; female 43.6%; unemployed 4.9%).

Price and earnings indexes (1990 = 100)

	1989	1990	1991	1992	1993	1994	1995
Consumer price index	96.0	100.0	103.4	105.8	108.2	109.8	112.5
Hourly earnings index	94.5	100.0	105.1	108.5	111.6	114.8	118.8

Household income and expenditure. Average household size (1993) 2.2; consumption expenditure per household (1992) NKr 206,908 (U.S.$33,294); sources of income (1991): wages and salaries 58.8%, social security 24.2%, self-employment and property income 16.9%; expenditure (1991): housing 19.4%, food 18.4%, transportation 12.4%, beverages and tobacco 7.0%, clothing and footwear 6.8%, household furniture and equipment 6.7%.

Foreign trade

Balance of trade (current prices)

	1990	1991	1992	1993	1994	1995
NKr '000,000	+48,231	+59,565	+61,730	+55,635	+51,512	+62,656
% of total	12.9%	15.9%	16.4%	14.0%	11.8%	11.9%

Imports (1995): NKr 208,626,000,000 (machinery and transport equipment 36.9%, of which road vehicles 7.7%, ships 2.9%; metals and metal products 10.6%, of which iron and steel 4.3%; food products 6.2%, of which fruits and vegetables 1.4%; petroleum products 3.1%). *Major import sources:* Sweden 15.5%; Germany 14.0%; U.K. 9.8%; Denmark 7.6%.
Exports (1995): NKr 265,883,000,000 (fuels and fuel products 51.0%; machinery and transport equipment 12.7%; metals and metal products 12.0%; food products 8.2%, of which fish 7.2%). *Major export destinations:* U.K. 20.3%; Germany 12.2%; Sweden 9.9%; The Netherlands 9.6%.

Transport and communications

Transport. Railroads (1994): route length 3,999 km; passenger-km 2,398,000,000; metric ton-km cargo 2,678,000,000. Roads (1995): total length 90,261 km (paved 74%). Vehicles (1995): passenger cars 1,684,664; trucks and buses 382,017. Merchant marine (1992): vessels (100 gross tons and over) 2,499; total deadweight tonnage 38,298,755. Air transport (1994): passenger-km 8,595,718,000; metric ton-km cargo 918,466,000; airports (1996) 50.
Communications. Daily newspapers (1994): total number 64; total circulation 2,858,935; circulation per 1,000 population 659. Radio (1995): 3,342,000 receivers (1 per 1.3 persons). Television (1995): 2,000,000 receivers (1 per 2.2 persons). Telephones (main lines; 1994): 2,392,042 (1 per 1.8 persons).

Education and health

Education (1993–94)

	schools	teachers	students	student/ teacher ratio
Primary (age 7–12)	3,325	36,196	466,991	12.9
Secondary (age 13–18) and vocational	771	21,780	240,506	11.0
Higher	195	10,213	172,574	16.9

Educational attainment (1993). Percentage of population age 16 and over having: lower secondary education 29.6%; higher secondary 51.6%; higher 18.8%. *Literacy* (1994): virtually 100% literate.
Health: physicians (1994) 14,497 (1 per 299 persons); hospital beds (1993) 22,961 (1 per 183 persons); infant mortality rate per 1,000 live births (1992) 5.9.
Food (1988–90): daily per capita caloric intake 3,221 (vegetable products 65%, animal products 35%); 120% of FAO recommended minimum requirement.

Military

Total active duty personnel (1995): 29,000 (army 50.7%, navy 22.1%, air force 27.2%). *Military expenditure as percentage of GNP* (1994): 3.1% (world avg. 3.0%); per capita expenditure U.S.$784.

[1]Excludes Svalbard and Jan Mayen (24,360 sq mi [63,080 sq km]). [2]January 1. [3]Includes the Norwegian population of Svalbard and Jan Mayen, registered as residents in municipalities on the mainland. [4]Population of municipalities. [5]Metal content of ore. [6]Includes hotels. [7]Unemployed. [8]Detail does not add to total given because of rounding.

Oman

Official name: Salṭanat 'Umān (Sultanate of Oman).
Form of government: monarchy[1].
Head of state and government: Sultan.
Capital: Muscat.
Official language: Arabic.
Official religion: Islam.
Monetary unit: 1 rial Omani (RO) = 1,000 baizas; valuation (Oct. 11, 1996) 1 RO = U.S.$2.63 = £1.64.

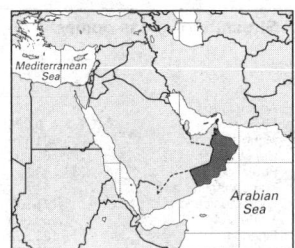

Area and population

Regions	Centres	area[2] sq mi	sq km	population 1993 census
Al-Bāṭinah	Ar-Rustāq; Ṣuḥār	5,100	13,200	538,763
Ad-Dākhilīyah	Nizwā; Samā'il	11,350	29,400	220,403
Masqaṭ	Muscat (Masqaṭ)	1,700	4,400	622,506
Ash-Sharqīyah	Ibrā; Sūr	13,850	35,800	247,551
Al-Wusṭa	Haymā'	30,650	79,400	16,101
Az-Ẓāhirah	Al-Buraymī; 'Ibri	15,900	41,200	169,710
Provinces				
Musandam	Khaṣab	800	2,000	27,669
Ẓufār (Dhofar)	Salālah	38,800	100,600	158,787
TOTAL		118,150	306,000	2,017,591

Demography

Population (1996): 2,251,000.
Density (1996): persons per sq mi 19.1, persons per sq km 7.4.
Urban-rural (1995): urban 13.2%; rural 86.8%.
Sex distribution (1993): male 51.00%; female 49.00%.
Age breakdown (1993): under 15, 41.0%; 15–29, 25.5%; 30–44, 22.0%; 45–59, 7.8%; 60–69, 2.1%; 70 and over, 1.6%.
Population projection: (2000) 2,626,000; (2010) 3,783,000.
Doubling time: 21 years.
Ethnic composition (1993): Omani Arab 73.5%; Pakistani (mostly Balochī) 18.7%; other 7.8%.
Religious affiliation (1994): Ibāḍiyah Muslim 75%; principal minorities are Sunnī Muslim and Shī'ī Muslim; smaller Hindu and Christian communities exist as well.
Major cities (1990): Muscat 51,969[3]; Nizwā 62,880; Samā'il 44,721; Salālah 10,000[4].

Vital statistics

Birth rate per 1,000 population (1990–95): 43.6 (world avg. 25.0).
Death rate per 1,000 population (1990–95): 4.8 (world avg. 9.3).
Natural increase rate per 1,000 population (1990–95): 38.8 (world avg. 15.7).
Total fertility rate (avg. births per childbearing woman; 1990–95): 7.2.
Marriage rate per 1,000 population: n.a.
Divorce rate per 1,000 population: n.a.
Life expectancy at birth (1990–95): male 67.7 years; female 71.8 years.
Major causes of death per 100,000 population: n.a.; however, major health concerns in the mid-1990s included malaria, tuberculosis, trachoma, dysentery, anemia, and diabetes.

National economy

Budget (1996). Revenue: RO 1,934,000,000 (oil revenue 76.2%; other 23.8%). Expenditures: RO 2,152,000,000 (current expenditure 82.2%, of which civil ministries 48.3%, defense 39.5%, interest paid on loans 6.8%; capital development projects and subsidies 17.1%).
Public debt (external, outstanding; 1994): U.S.$2,608,000,000.
Gross national product (at current market prices; 1994): U.S.$10,779,000,000 (U.S.$5,200 per capita).

Structure of gross domestic product and labour force

	1995 in value RO '000,000[5]	1995 % of total value	1990 labour force	1990 % of labour force
Agriculture[6]	152.0	2.9	146,400	27.7
Mining	2,038.2	38.5	2,800	0.5
Manufacturing	240.8	4.6	32,800	6.2
Construction	137.6	2.6	104,800	19.8
Public utilities	49.1	0.9	4,100	0.8
Transportation and communications	332.9	6.3	14,500	2.7
Trade	716.1[7]	13.5[7]	87,500	16.5
Finance	441.1[8]	8.3[8]	9,400	1.8
Pub. admin., defense	705.6	13.3	81,000	15.3
Services	429.6[9]	8.1[9]	45,800	8.7
Other	45.3[10]	0.9[10]	—	—
TOTAL	5,288.8	100.0	529,100	100.0[11]

Tourism (1994): receipts from visitors U.S.$88,000,000; expenditures by nationals abroad U.S.$47,000,000.
Household income and expenditure. Average household size (1993) 7.4; income per household: n.a.; sources of income: n.a.; expenditure (1990): housing and utilities 27.8%, food, beverages, and tobacco 26.4%, transportation 19.8%, clothing and shoes 7.8%, household goods and furniture 6.1%, education, health services, entertainment, and other 12.1%.
Production (metric tons except as noted). Agriculture, forestry, fishing (1995): vegetables and melons 166,800 (of which watermelons 30,000), dates 133,000, bananas 26,000, mangoes 10,500, onions 8,800, potatoes 5,500, papayas

2,650, tobacco leaf 2,300, wheat 1,300; livestock (number of live animals) 735,000 goats, 148,000 sheep, 142,000 cattle, 94,000 camels, 2,700,000 chickens; fish catch (1994) 118,571. Mining and quarrying (1994): copper 6,500; silver 3,300 kg; gold 75 kg. Manufacturing (value of production in RO '000; 1993): textiles and apparel 78,290; food products and beverages 72,930; chemical products 40,950; wood products 5,950; metal products 4,200; paper products 360; other major products include refined petroleum products. Construction (1989): number of residential permits 3,408; nonresidential permits 353. Energy production (consumption): electricity (kW-hr; 1994) 7,856,000,000 (7,856,000,000); coal, none (none); crude petroleum (barrels; 1994) 294,380,000 (26,615,000); petroleum products (metric tons; 1994) 3,884,000 (1,589,000); natural gas (cu m; 1994) 6,665,890,000 (6,665,890,000).
Population economically active (1993)[12]: total 704,030; activity rate of total population 34.9% (participation rates: over age 15, 59.2%; female 9.7%; unemployed, n.a.).

Price and earnings indexes (1990=100)

	1989	1990	1991	1992	1993	1994	1995
Consumer price index	99.4	100.0	104.6	105.6	106.9	106.1	104.7
Earnings index	...	...	...	...	...	...	...

Land use (1994): meadows and pastures 4.7%; agricultural and under permanent cultivation 0.3%; other (mostly desert and developed area) 95.0%.

Foreign trade[13]

Balance of trade (current prices)

	1990	1991	1992	1993	1994	1995
RO '000,000	+1,042	+594	+636	+411	+588	+648
% of total	32.6%	18.8%	17.5%	11.1%	16.0%	16.1%

Imports (1995): RO 1,633,200,000 (machinery and transport equipment 39.3%, basic manufactured goods 16.6%, food and live animals 13.6%, miscellaneous manufactured articles 9.7%, chemicals 6.2%, beverages and tobacco 5.4%). *Major import sources:* United Arab Emirates 23.8%; Japan 15.7%; United Kingdom 10.5%; United States 6.5%; Germany 5.1%; India 3.3%.
Exports (1995): RO 2,332,000,000 (petroleum 78.4%, metals and metal products 1.8%, live animals and products 1.5%, textiles 1.4%). *Major export destinations*[14]: United Arab Emirates 43.5%; Iran 9.5%; Hong Kong 9.2%; United States 5.8%; Tanzania 4.5%; Saudi Arabia 4.2%.

Transport and communications

Transport. Railroads: none. Roads (1994): total length 16,372 mi, 26,349 km (paved 20%). Vehicles: automobiles (1994) 201,200, trucks and buses (1993) 108,600. Merchant marine (1992): vessels (100 gross tons and over) 26; total deadweight tonnage 11,727. Air transport (1995)[15]: passenger-mi 1,718,585,000, passenger-km 2,765,800,000; short ton-mi cargo 77,726,700, metric ton-km cargo 113,479,000; airports (1996) with scheduled flights 6.
Communications. Daily newspapers (1992): total number 4; total circulation 79,000; circulation per 1,000 population 48. Radio (1995): total number of receivers 900,000 (1 per 2.4 persons). Television (1995): total number of receivers 1,500,000 (1 per 1.4 persons). Telephones (main lines; 1993): 147,800 (1 per 13.5 persons).

Education and health

Education (1993–94)

	schools	teachers	students	student/ teacher ratio
Primary (age 6–14)	415	11,158	297,209	26.6
Secondary (age 15–17)	128[16]	9,188	160,654	17.5
Voc., teacher tr.	25[16]	342	2,350	6.9
Higher	5[16]	732[17]	7,322[18]	...

Educational attainment: n.a. *Literacy* (1993): total population age 15 and over literate 59%; male and female literacy, n.a.; male literacy is approximately twice as high as female literacy.
Health (1993): physicians 2,381 (1 per 837 persons); hospital beds 3,625[19] (1 per 550 persons); infant mortality rate per 1,000 live births (1990–95) 30.0.
Food: daily per capita caloric intake, n.a.

Military

Total active duty personnel (1996): 43,500 (army 72.4%[20], navy 9.7%, air force 9.4%); foreign troops 3,700. *Military expenditure as percentage of GDP* (1994): 18.1% (world 3.0%); per capita expenditure U.S.$875.

---

[1]Appointed 80-member Consultative Council is an advisory body only. [2]Approximate; no comprehensive survey of surface area has ever been carried out in Oman. [3]1993 census. [4]1982. [5]In purchasers' values at current prices. [6]Agriculture includes fishing. [7]Trade includes restaurants and hotels. [8]Finance includes business services and real estate. [9]Services include education and health. [10]Other includes import taxes. [11]Detail does not add to total given because of rounding. [12]Non-Omani workers constitute 61.3% of the labour force. [13]Imports c.i.f.; exports f.o.b. [14]Non-oil exports only. [15]One-fourth apportionment of international flights of Gulf Air. [16]1989–90. [17]1990; universities and equivalent institutes. [18]1991–92. [19]Beds in hospitals, clinics, and dispensaries only. [20]Including personnel of Royal Household units not formally part of army table of organization.

Pakistan

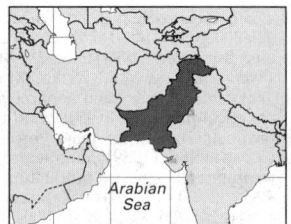

Official name: Islām-ī Jamhūrīya-e Pākistān (Islamic Republic of Pakistan).
Form of government: multiparty, federal Islamic republic with two legislative houses (Senate [87]; National Assembly [217]).
Chief of state: President.
Chief of government: Prime Minister.
Capital: Islāmābād.
Official language: Urdū.
Official religion: Islam.
Monetary unit: 1 Pakistan rupee (PRs) = 100 paisa; valuation (Oct. 11, 1996) 1 U.S.$ = PRs 36.93; 1 £ = PRs 58.18.

Area and population		area[1]		population
				1983
Provinces	Capitals	sq mi	sq km	estimate[2]
Balochistān	Quetta	134,051	347,190	4,611,000
North-West Frontier	Peshāwar	28,773	74,521	11,658,000
Punjab	Lahore	79,284	205,344	50,460,000
Sindh	Karāchi	54,407	140,914	20,312,000
Federally Administered				
Tribal Areas	...	10,509	27,220	2,329,000
Federal Capital Area				
Islāmābād	...	350	906	359,000
TOTAL		307,374	796,095	89,729,000

Demography

Population (1996)[3]: 133,500,000.
Density (1996)[4]: persons per sq mi 393.0, persons per sq km 151.7.
Urban-rural (1995): urban 31.5%; rural 68.5%.
Sex distribution (1995): male 52.50%; female 47.50%.
Age breakdown (1988): under 15, 46.3%; 15–29, 24.6%; 30–44, 14.0%; 45–59, 9.0%; 60–74, 4.8%; 75 and over, 1.3%.
Population projection: (2000) 144,560,000; (2010) 176,400,000.
Doubling time: 24 years.
Linguistic composition (1981): Punjābī 48.2%; Pashto 13.1%; Sindhī 11.8%; Saraiki 9.8%; Urdū 7.6%; other 9.5%.
Religious affiliation (1993): Muslim 95.0%[5]; Christian 2.0%; Hindu 1.8%; others (including Ahmadiyah) 1.2%.
Major cities (1981): Karāchi 5,208,132; Lahore 2,952,689; Faisalābād 1,104,209; Rāwalpindi 794,843; Islāmābād 204,364.

Vital statistics

Birth rate per 1,000 population (1996): 38.4 (world avg. 25.0).
Death rate per 1,000 population (1996): 8.3 (world avg. 9.3).
Natural increase rate per 1,000 population (1996): 30.1 (world avg. 15.7).
Total fertility rate (avg. births per childbearing woman; 1996): 5.8.
Marriage rate per 1,000 population (1975–80): 10.7.
Divorce rate per 1,000 population (1975–80): 0.3.
Life expectancy at birth (1996): male 62.0 years; female 64.0 years.
Major causes of death (percentage of total deaths; 1987): malaria 18.2%; childhood diseases 12.1%; diseases of digestive system 9.8%; diseases of respiratory system 9.2%; infection of intestinal tract 7.7%.

National economy

Budget (1994–95). Revenue: PRs 362,161,000,000 (customs duties 25.1%, nontax receipts 21.1%, income taxes 16.9%, sales tax 16.5%, excise taxes 13.2%). Expenditures: PRs 385,017,000,000 (public-debt service 35.3%, defense 26.5%, development 23.4%, general administration 4.0%, socioeconomic services 3.9%).
Public debt (external, outstanding; 1994): U.S.$22,993,000,000.
Production (metric tons except as noted). Agriculture, forestry, fishing (1994–95): sugarcane 45,659,000, wheat 16,699,000, rice 3,358,000, corn (maize) 1,318,000, gram 572,000, jowar 234,000, cotton 8,697,000 bales; livestock (number of live animals; 1995) 43,767,000 goats, 29,065,000 sheep, 20,000,000 buffalo, 19,000,000 cattle, 135,000,000 chickens; roundwood (1994) 28,635,000 cu m; fish catch (1993) 621,695. Mining and quarrying (1993–94): limestone 8,975,000; rock salt 895,000; gypsum 659,000; silica sand 177,000; chromite 10,630. Manufacturing (1993–94): cement 8,200,000; chemical fertilizers 3,875,000, of which urea 3,104,000; refined sugar 2,992,000; cotton yarn 1,288,000; vegetable products 700,000; chemicals 383,000; jute textiles 76,900; paper and paperboard 34,400; cotton textiles 307,000,000 sq m; cigarettes 37,500,000,000 units; motor-vehicle tires 1,594,000 units; bicycles 557,000 units. Construction (value in PRs; 1984): residential 8,490,000,000; nonresidential 14,579,000,000. Energy production (consumption): electricity (kW-hr; 1994) 57,147,000,000 (57,147,000,000); coal (metric tons; 1994) 3,534,000 (4,628,000); crude petroleum (barrels; 1994) 20,805,000 (50,063,000); petroleum products (metric tons; 1994) 5,778,000 (13,511,000); natural gas (cu m; 1994) 16,668,000,000 (16,668,000,000).
Household income and expenditure (1988). Average household size 6.3; income per household PRs 25,572 (U.S.$1,420); sources of income: self-employment 56.0%, wages and salaries 22.0%, other 22.0%; expenditure: food 47.0%, housing 12.0%, clothing and footwear 8.0%, other 33.0%.
Gross national product (at current market prices; 1994): U.S.$55,565,000,000 (U.S.$440 per capita).

Structure of gross domestic product and labour force				
	1994–95			
	in value PRs '000,000	% of total value	labour force	% of labour force
Agriculture	431,797	23.1	16,160,000	45.3
Mining	8,895	0.5	} 3,730,000	} 10.5
Manufacturing	301,176	16.1		
Construction	62,202	3.4	2,360,000	6.6
Public utilities	53,951	2.9	290,000	0.8
Transportation and communications	171,937	9.2	1,880,000	5.3
Trade	268,968	14.4	4,520,000	12.7
Finance	123,652	6.6	}	}
Pub. admin., defense	130,658	7.0	5,050,000	14.1
Services	131,761	7.1		
Other	181,523	9.7	1,690,000[6]	4.7[6]
TOTAL	1,866,520	100.0	35,680,000	100.0

Population economically active (1994–95): total 35,680,000; activity rate of total population 27.9% (participation rates: ages 15–64 [1992–93] 50.4%; female [1992–93] 14.2%; unemployed 4.7%).

Price index (1990 = 100)							
	1989	1990	1991	1992	1993	1994	1995
Consumer price index	91.7	100.0	111.8	122.4	134.6	151.3	170.0

Tourism (1994): receipts from visitors U.S.$117,000,000; expenditures by nationals abroad U.S.$398,000,000.
Land use (1994): forested 4.5%; meadows and pastures 6.5%; agricultural and under permanent cultivation 27.7%; built-on, wasteland, and other 61.3%.

Foreign trade[7]

Balance of trade (current prices)						
	1990	1991	1992	1993	1994	1995
PRs '000,000	−24,896	−28,537	−31,283	−54,352	−22,968	−78,506
% of total	9.3%	8.4%	7.9%	12.6%	4.9%	13.4%

Imports (1993–94): PRs 258,250,100,000 (petroleum products 16.3%, specialized machinery 9.1%, road vehicles 6.3%, vegetable oil and fats 5.7%, organic chemicals 4.1%, iron and steel manufactures 3.8%, electrical machinery 3.4%, general industrial machinery 3.2%). *Major import sources:* Japan 11.8%; U.S. 10.6%; Malaysia 5.5%; Saudi Arabia 5.4%; Kuwait 5.3%; China 5.1%; U.K. 4.9%; France 4.0%; Germany 3.9%.
Exports (1993–94): PRs 205,499,400,000 (textile fabrics 53.6%, ready-made garments 22.0%, rice 3.6%, leather and leather goods 3.5%, fresh fish 2.3%, cotton 2.1%, sugar and honey 1.8%). *Major export destinations:* U.S. 14.4%; Japan 8.0%; Germany 8.0%; U.K. 7.8%; Dubayy 6.3%; France 4.1%; Saudi Arabia 3.5%; The Netherlands 3.1%.

Transport and communications

Transport. Railroads (1993–94): route length 5,453 mi, 8,775 km; passenger-mi 10,208,000,000, passenger-km 16,428,000,000; short ton-mi cargo 4,011,000,000, metric ton-km cargo 5,856,000,000. Roads (1993–94): total length 122,875 mi, 197,749 km (paved 51%). Vehicles (1993): passenger cars 732,100; trucks and buses 252,023. Merchant marine (1992): vessels (100 gross tons and over) 73; total deadweight tonnage 513,823. Air transport (1995): passenger-km 10,573,000,000; metric ton-km cargo 445,046,000; airports (1996) with scheduled flights 34.
Communications. Daily newspapers (1992): total number 274; total circulation 809,000; circulation per 1,000 population 6. Radio (1995): total number of receivers 10,200,000 (1 per 14 persons). Television (1995): total number of receivers 2,080,000 (1 per 68 persons). Telephones (main lines; 1993): 1,604,800 (1 per 76 persons).

Education and health

Education (1994–95)	schools	teachers	students	student/ teacher ratio
Primary (age 5–9)	123,119	412,200	16,722,000	40.6
Secondary (age 10–14)	26,128	313,900	5,610,000	17.9
Voc., teacher tr.	724	6,924	93,000	13.4
Higher	826	30,162	794,000	26.3

Educational attainment (1981). Percentage of population age 25 and over having: no formal schooling 78.9%; some primary education 8.7%; some secondary 10.5%; postsecondary 1.9%. *Literacy* (1993): total population age 15 and over literate 35.0%; males literate 47.3%; females literate 22.3%.
Health (1994): physicians 66,199 (1 per 2,064 persons); hospital beds 80,908 (1 per 1,689 persons); infant mortality rate per 1,000 live births (1996) 79.
Food (1992): daily per capita caloric intake 2,315 (vegetable products 86%, animal products 14%); 100% of FAO recommended minimum requirement.

Military

Total active duty personnel (1996): 587,000 (army 88.6%, navy 3.7%, air force 7.7%). *Military expenditure as percentage of GNP* (1994): 6.0% (world 3.0%); per capita expenditure U.S.$24.

---

[1]Excludes 32,323 sq mi (83,716 sq km) area of Jammu and Kashmir (comprising both Azad Kashmir and the Northern Areas). [2]Excludes Afghan refugees and population of Jammu and Kashmir. [3]Excludes Afghan refugees; includes population (4,200,000) of Jammu and Kashmir. [4]Includes area and population of Jammu and Kashmir. [5]Mostly Sunnī, with Shīʿī comprising about 20% of total population. [6]Includes unemployed. [7]Import figures are f.o.b. in balance of trade and c.i.f. for commodities and trading partners.

Palau

Official name: Belu'u er a Belau
(Palauan); Republic of Palau
(English).
Form of government: unitary republic
with a national congress composed of
two legislative houses (Senate [14];
House of Delegates [16]).
Head of state and government:
President.
Capital: Koror.
Official languages[1]: Palauan; English.
Official religion: none.
Monetary unit: 1 U.S. dollar
(U.S.$) = 100 cents; valuation (Oct.
11, 1996) 1 £ = U.S.$1.58.

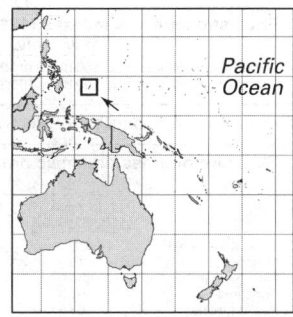

Pacific
Ocean

Area and population	area		population
			1990
States	sq mi	sq km	census
Aimeliik	20	52	439
Airai	17	44	1,234
Angaur	3	8	206
Hatohobei	1	3	22
Kayangel	1	3	137
Koror	7	18	10,501
Melekeok	11	28	244
Ngaraard	14	36	310
Ngarchelong	4	10	354
Ngardmau	18	47	149
Ngatpang	18	47	62
Ngchesar	16	41	287
Ngeremlengui	25	65	281
Ngiwal	10	26	234
Peleliu	5	13	601
Sonsorol	1	3	61
Other			
Rock Islands	18	47	—
TOTAL	188[2]	488	15,122

Demography

Population (1996): 17,000.
Density (1996): persons per sq mi 90.4, persons per sq km 34.8.
Urban-rural (1990): urban 59.6%; rural 40.4%.
Sex distribution (1990): male 53.82%; female 46.18%.
Age breakdown (1990): under 15, 30.3%; 15–29, 27.8%; 30–44, 22.8%; 45–59,
10.5%; 60–74, 6.4%; 75 and over, 2.2%.
Population projection: (2000) 18,100; (2010) 19,700.
Doubling time: 35 years.
Ethnic composition (1990): Palauan 83.2%; Filipino 9.8%; other Micronesian
2.0%; Chinese 1.2%; white 0.8%; other 3.0%.
Religious affiliation (1990): Roman Catholic 40.7%; Protestant 24.7% (includes
members of the Modekngei Church); traditional beliefs 27.1%; other 7.5%.
Major cities (1992): Koror 10,500.

Vital statistics

Birth rate per 1,000 population (1996): 22.0 (world avg. 25.0); legitimate, n.a.;
illegitimate, n.a.
Death rate per 1,000 population (1996): 8.0 (world avg. 9.3).
Natural increase rate per 1,000 population (1996): 14.0 (world avg. 15.7).
Total fertility rate (avg. births per childbearing woman; 1996): 3.1.
Marriage rate per 1,000 population: n.a.
Divorce rate per 1,000 population: n.a.
Life expectancy at birth (1995): male 69.1 years; female 73.0 years.
Major causes of death per 100,000 population (1993): diseases of the cir-
culatory system 192.9; malignant and benign neoplasms (cancers) 136.9;
accidents, poisoning, and violence 112.0; diseases of the respiratory system
43.6; infectious and parasitic diseases 43.6.

National economy

Budget (1993). Revenue: U.S.$48,157,000 (cash grants from the U.S. 36.9%,
tax revenue 35.4%). Expenditures: U.S.$37,503,000.
Tourism (1994): total number of visitors 44,073.
Gross national product (at current market prices; 1994)[3]: U.S.$81,800,000
(U.S.$5,000 per capita).

Structure of gross domestic product and labour force	1992		1990	
	in value U.S.$'000	% of total value	labour force	% of labour force
Agriculture, fisheries	25,800	28.8	445	7.3
Mining	11,930	13.3	14	0.2
Manufacturing			100	1.7
Public utilities	4,485	5.0	78	1.3
Construction	6,728	7.5	919	15.1
Transportation and communications			415	6.8
Trade			1,207	19.9
Finance	40,757	45.4	120	2.0
Public administration, defense			870	14.3
Services			1,672	27.6
Other			232	3.8
TOTAL	89,700	100.0	6,072	100.0

Production (metric tons except as noted). Agriculture, forestry, fishing: (value
of sales in U.S.$; 1993) eggs 262,701, fruit and vegetables 126,325, betel nuts
60,376, root crops (taro, cassava, sweet potatoes) 43,718; livestock (number
of live animals; 1984) pigs 1,343, cows 82, goats 52, poultry 9,500; roundwood,
n.a.; fish catch (1993) 1,490 (major species are parrot fish, snapper, unicorn
fish, and rabbitfish). Mining and quarrying: n.a. Manufacturing: includes
handicrafts and small items. Construction: Energy production (consumption): electricity (kW-hr; 1994) 203,000,000 (203,000,000); coal, none (n.a.);
crude petroleum, none (n.a.); petroleum products, none (75,000); natural
gas, none (n.a.).
Public debt (external, outstanding; 1993): U.S.$100,000,000.
Population economically active (1990): total 6,072; activity rate of total
population 40.2% (participation rates: ages 16–64, 64.1%; female 36.9%;
unemployed 7.8%).
Land use: n.a.
Household income and expenditure. Average household size (1990) 5.0; income per household (1989) U.S.$8,882; sources of income (1989): wages
63.7%, social security 12.0%, self-employment 7.4%, retirement 5.5%, interest, dividend, or net rental 4.3%, remittance 4.1%, public assistance 1.0%,
other 2.0%; expenditure: n.a.

Foreign trade

Imports (1993): U.S.$40,000,000 (1984; food and agricultural raw materials
28.9%, machinery and transport equipment 24.5%, chemicals and related
products 4.0%). *Major import sources* (1984): United States 41.8%; Japan
38.2%.
Exports (1989): U.S.$600,000 (1984; food and agricultural raw materials 69.1%,
manufactured goods 30.9%). *Major export destinations* (1984): Japan 58.8%;
United States 8.0%.

Transport and communications

Transport. Railroads: none. Roads (1993): total length 40 mi, 64 km (paved
59%). Vehicles (1994): passenger cars and trucks 4,271. Merchant marine
(1991): vessels (100 gross tons and over) 4; total deadweight tonnage, n.a.
Air transport (1993): passenger arrivals 50,366, passenger departures 49,376;
airports (1996) with scheduled flights 1.
Communications. Daily newspapers: none. Radio (1994): total number of
receivers 9,000 (1 per 1.8 persons). Television (1994): total number of receivers 1,600 (1 per 10.3 persons). Telephones (main lines; 1994): 2,615 (1
per 6.3 persons).

Education and health

Education (1993)	schools[4]	teachers[4]	students	student/ teacher ratio
Primary (age 6–13)	26	289	2,635	...
Secondary (age 14–18)	6	5	1,021	...
Higher[6]	1	...	509	...

Educational attainment (1990). Percentage of population age 25 and over having: no formal schooling 1.8%; some primary education 21.8%; completed
primary 5.5%; some secondary 13.3%; completed secondary 26.6%; some
postsecondary 11.1%; higher 19.9%. *Literacy* (1990): total population age
15 and over literate 10,288 (97.6%); males literate 5,677 (98.3%); females
literate 4,611 (96.6%).
Health (1990): physicians[7] 10 (1 per 1,518 persons); hospital beds 70 (1 per
200 persons); infant mortality rate per 1,000 live births (1996) 25.0.
Food: daily per capita caloric intake, n.a.

Military

The United States is responsible for the external security of Palau, as specified in the Compact of Free Association of Oct. 1, 1994.

[1]Sonsorolese-Tobian is also, according to official sources, considered an official language. [2]Detail does not add to total given because of rounding. [3]Gross national
product comprises U.S. government spending only. [4]1987. [5]Included with primary.
[6]Palau Community College. [7]Government-employed health personnel only.

Panama

Official name: República de Panamá (Republic of Panama).
Form of government: multiparty republic with one legislative house (Legislative Assembly [72]).
Head of state and government: President assisted by Vice Presidents.
Capital: Panama City.
Official language: Spanish.
Official religion: none.
Monetary unit: 1 balboa (B) = 100 cents; valuation (Oct. 11, 1996) 1 U.S.$ = B 1.00; 1 £ = B 1.58.

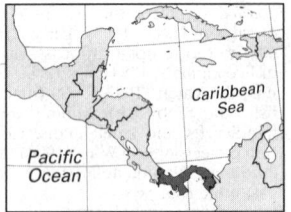

Area and population		area		population
				1994
Provinces	Capitals	sq mi	sq km	estimate
Bocas del Toro	Bocas del Toro	3,376	8,745	115,256
Chiriquí	David	3,341	8,653	402,441
Coclé	Penonomé	1,902	4,927	187,304
Colón	Colón	1,888	4,890	222,938[1]
Darién	La Palma	6,437	16,671	53,725
Herrera	Chitré	904	2,341	100,418
Los Santos	Las Tablas	1,470	3,806	79,805
Panamá	Panama City	4,590	11,887	1,203,124
Veraguas	Santiago	4,339	11,239	217,555
Special territory				
Comarca de San Blas	El Porvenir	910	2,357	[1]
TOTAL		29,157	75,517[2]	2,582,566

Demography

Population (1996): 2,674,000.
Density (1996): persons per sq mi 91.7, persons per sq km 35.4.
Urban-rural (1995): urban 53.3%; rural 46.7%.
Sex distribution (1994): male 50.58%; female 49.42%.
Age breakdown (1994): under 15, 33.8%; 15–29, 28.6%; 30–44, 19.3%; 45–59, 10.8%; 60–74, 5.6%; 75 and over, 1.9%.
Population projection: (2000) 2,856,000; (2010) 3,266,000.
Doubling time: 39 years.
Ethnic composition (1992): mestizo 64.0%; black and mulatto 14.0%; white 10.0%; Amerindian 8.0%; Asian (mostly Chinese) 4.0%.
Religious affiliation (1992): Roman Catholic 80.0%; Protestant (mostly evangelical) 10.0%; Muslim 5.0%; Bahā'ī 1.0%; Jewish 0.3%; other 3.7%.
Major cities (1990): Panama City 450,668[3]; San Miguelito 293,564[3, 4]; David 65,763[5]; Colón 54,654; Barú 46,093[5].

Vital statistics

Birth rate per 1,000 population (1995): 23.6 (world avg. 25.0); (1991) legitimate 25.5%; illegitimate 74.5%[6].
Death rate per 1,000 population (1995): 5.4 (world avg. 9.3).
Natural increase rate per 1,000 population (1995): 18.2 (world avg. 15.7).
Total fertility rate (avg. births per childbearing woman; 1995): 2.8.
Marriage rate per 1,000 population (1994): 4.8[7].
Divorce rate per 1,000 population (1994): 0.8[7].
Life expectancy at birth (1995): male 71.0 years; female 76.5 years.
Major causes of death per 100,000 population (1993): diseases of the circulatory system 113.9, of which ischemic heart diseases 47.8, cerebrovascular disease 41.3; malignant neoplasms (cancers) 60.4; accidents 32.9; diseases of the respiratory system 23.4; homicide, suicide, and violence 21.1.

National economy

Budget (1994). Revenue: B 1,928,600,000 (current revenue 73.4%, of which nontax revenue 25.0%; development revenue 26.6%, of which foreign loans 16.8%). Expenditures: B 1,928,600,000 (current expenditure 80.2%, of which public debt payments 25.6%, current transfers 14.0%, education 11.1%, administration 7.8%, health 7.2%; development expenditure 19.8%).
Public debt (external, outstanding; 1994): U.S.$3,923,000,000.
Production (metric tons except as noted). Agriculture, forestry, fishing (1995): sugarcane 1,720,000, bananas 910,000, rice 200,000, plantains 105,000, corn (maize) 120,000, oranges 26,900, pineapples 14,300, coffee 12,400, tobacco 2,100; livestock (number of live animals) 1,454,000 cattle, 257,000 pigs; roundwood (1994) 1,053,000 cu m; fish catch (value of production in B '000,000; 1994): shrimps 31, fish 20. Mining and quarrying (1993): limestone 725,000; gold 8,200 troy oz. Manufacturing (value of production in B '000,000; 1993): food products 890; refined petroleum 234; beverages 173; paints, soaps, and cosmetics 115; paper and paper products 102; plastic products 89. Construction (value of construction in B '000,000; 1994): residential 220; nonresidential 101. Energy production (consumption): electricity (kW-hr; 1994) 3,361,000,000 (2,674,000,000); coal (metric tons; 1993) none (58,000); crude petroleum (barrels; 1993) none (12,520,000); petroleum products (metric tons; 1993) 1,691,000 (1,136,000); natural gas (cu m; 1993) none (59,711,000).
Household income and expenditure. Average household size (1990) 4.4; average annual income per household (1990) B 5,450 (U.S.$5,450); sources of income (1983–84)[8]: wages and salaries 60.8%, transfer payments 13.2%, self-employment 12.8%, other 13.2%; expenditure (1983–84)[8]: food and beverages 34.9%, transportation and communications 15.1%, housing and energy 12.6%, education and recreation 11.7%.
Population economically active (1993)[7]: total 940,301; activity rate of total population 40.8%[9] (participation rates: ages 15–69, 62.8%[9]; female 34.0%[9]; unemployed [1994] 13.8%).

Price and earnings indexes (1990 = 100)

	1990	1991	1992	1993	1994	1995	1996
Consumer price index	100.0	101.3	103.1	103.6	104.9	105.9	106.8[10]
Monthly earnings index[11]	100.0	100.3	101.6	106.9	...	...	...

Gross national product (1994): U.S.$6,905,000,000 (U.S.$2,670 per capita).

Structure of gross domestic product and labour force

	1993		1994	
	in value B '000,000	% of total value	labour force[7]	% of labour force[7]
Agriculture, fishing	667.1	10.2	170,718	17.7
Mining	10.6	0.2	2,055	0.2
Manufacturing	534.6	8.1	102,545	10.6
Construction	401.3	6.1	62,282	6.4
Public utilities	253.6	3.9	10,860	1.1
Transp. and commun.	1,333.3[12]	20.3[12]	65,520	6.8
Trade, restaurants	830.8	12.7	199,267	20.6
Finance, real estate	1,269.5	19.3	49,945	5.2
Pub. admin.	876.7	13.3	68,663	7.1
Services	558.2	8.5	186,602	19.3
Other	−170.8[13]	−2.6[13]	48,169[14]	5.0[14]
TOTAL	6,564.9	100.0	966,616	100.0

Tourism (1994): receipts from visitors U.S.$243,000,000; expenditures by nationals abroad U.S.$131,000,000.
Land use (1994): forested 43.8%; meadows and pastures 19.8%; agricultural and under permanent cultivation 8.9%; other 27.5%.

Foreign trade[15, 16]

Balance of trade (current prices)

	1990	1991	1992	1993	1994	1995
B '000,000	−894	−1,071	−1,329	−1,426	−1,594	−1,655
% of total	50.1%	54.2%	57.0%	56.3%	57.7%	57.0%

Imports (1994): B 2,404,000,000 (machinery and apparatus 17.0%, mineral fuels 13.6%, transport equipment 13.0%, chemicals and chemical products 10.8%). *Major import sources:* U.S. 37.7%; Colón Free Zone 15.4%; Japan 7.2%; Ecuador 4.4%; Costa Rica 2.9%; South Korea 2.3%.
Exports (1994): B 533,000,000 (bananas 38.8%, shrimps 13.1%, clothing 3.9%, fish products 3.5%, raw sugar 3.2%). *Major export destinations:* U.S. 37.6%; Germany 12.2%; Sweden 9.1%; Costa Rica 7.1%; Belgium 6.9%.

Transport and communications

Transport. Railroads (1993): route length 220 mi, 354 km; passenger-km, n.a.; (1992)[17] metric ton-km cargo 673,000. Roads (1994): total length 6,402 mi, 10,303 km (paved 33%). Vehicles: passenger cars (1993) 161,500; trucks and buses 82,800. Merchant marine (1992): vessels (100 gross tons and over) 5,217; total deadweight tonnage 79,255,644. Panama Canal traffic (1994): oceangoing transits 12,478; cargo 170,836,000 metric tons. Air transport: passenger-km (1993) 380,000,000; metric ton-km cargo (1992) 5,268,000; airports (1996) with scheduled flights 10.
Communications. Daily newspapers (1992): total number 8; total circulation 223,000; circulation per 1,000 population 90. Radio (1995): 527,000 receivers (1 per 5.0 persons). Television (1995): 204,539 receivers (1 per 13 persons). Telephones (main lines; 1993): 261,500 (1 per 9.7 persons).

Education and health

Education (1994)

	schools	teachers	students	student/ teacher ratio
Primary (age 6–11)	2,765	14,512	358,410	24.7
Secondary (age 12–17) } Voc., teacher tr.	376	11,241	209,929	18.7
Higher	9	4,291	70,327	16.4

Educational attainment (1990). Percentage of population age 25 and over having: no formal schooling 11.6%; incomplete primary education 20.0%; complete primary 21.6%; secondary 28.7%; incomplete undergraduate 5.4%; complete undergraduate 7.0%; graduate 0.7%; other/unknown 5.0%. *Literacy* (1990): total population age 15 and over literate 1,385,000 (88.1%); males literate 705,000 (88.1%); females literate 680,000 (88.2%).
Health (1994): physicians 3,195 (1 per 808 persons); hospital beds 7,112 (1 per 363 persons); infant mortality rate per 1,000 live births (1995) 30.4.
Food (1992): daily per capita caloric intake 2,242 (vegetable products 80%, animal products 20%); 97% of FAO recommended minimum requirement.

Military

Total active duty personnel (1995): military abolished in 1991 was replaced by an 11,000-member national police force; U.S. forces in former Canal Zone number 9,100.

[1]Colón includes Comarca de San Blas. [2]Detail does not add to total given because of rounding. [3]1993. [4]Population of urban district. [5]Population of the *cabecera* (county seat) of the municipality. [6]Includes divorced and widowed mothers as well as mothers separated from the fathers. [7]Excludes indigenous population. [8]Panama City only. [9]Estimated figure. [10]May. [11]Public sector only. [12]Includes commission of Panama Canal. [13]Net of imputed bank service charges and import fees. [14]Includes 44,274 unemployed not previously employed. [15]Import figures are f.o.b. in balance of trade and c.i.f. in commodities and trading partners. [16]Excludes Colón Free Zone (1994 imports f.o.b. B 4,990,000,000; 1994 reexports f.o.b. B 5,735,000,000, of which textiles and clothing 25.8%, nonelectrical and electrical machinery and apparatus 22.3%). [17]Panama Railroad only.

Papua New Guinea

Official name: Independent State of
Papua New Guinea.
Form of government: constitutional
monarchy with one legislative house
(National Parliament [109]).
Chief of state: British Monarch
represented by Governor-General.
Head of government: Prime Minister.
Capital: Port Moresby.
Official language: English[1].
Official religion: none.
Monetary unit: 1 Papua New Guinea
kina (K) = 100 toea; valuation
(Oct. 11, 1996) 1 U.S.$ = K 1.33;
1 £ = K 2.10.

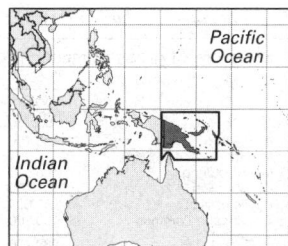

Area and population

Provinces	Administrative centres	area sq mi	area sq km	population 1990 census[2]
Central	Port Moresby (Central)	11,400	29,500	140,584
East New Britain	Rabaul	6,000	15,500	184,408
East Sepik	Wewak	16,550	42,800	248,308
Eastern Highlands	Goroka	4,300	11,200	299,619
Enga	Wabag	4,950	12,800	238,357
Gulf	Kerema	13,300	34,500	68,060
Madang	Madang	11,200	29,000	270,299
Manus	Lorengau	800	2,100	32,830
Milne Bay	Alotau (Samarai)	5,400	14,000	157,288
Morobe	Lae	13,300	34,500	363,535
National Capital District	Port Moresby	100	240	193,242
New Ireland	Kavieng	3,700	9,600	87,194
North Solomons (Bougainville)	Arawa (Buka)	3,600	9,300	3
Oro (Northern)	Popondetta	8,800	22,800	96,762
Sandaun (West Sepik)	Vanimo	14,000	36,300	135,185
Simbu (Chimbu)	Kundiawa	2,350	6,100	183,801
Southern Highlands	Mendi	9,200	23,800	302,724
West New Britain	Kimbe	8,100	21,000	127,547
Western	Daru	38,350	99,300	108,705
Western Highlands	Mount Hagen	3,300	8,500	291,090
TOTAL		178,704[4]	462,840	3,529,538[5]

Demography

Population (1996): 4,400,000.
Density (1996): persons per sq mi 24.6, persons per sq km 9.5.
Urban-rural (1995): urban 16.0%; rural 84.0%.
Sex distribution (1990)[2]: male 52.09%; female 47.91%.
Age breakdown (1990): under 15, 40.4%; 15–29, 28.8%; 30–44, 16.9%; 45–59,
9.3%; 60–74, 4.3%; 75 and over, 0.3%.
Population projection: (2000) 4,809,000; (2010) 5,918,000.
Doubling time: 31 years.
Ethnic composition (1983): New Guinea Papuan 84.0%; New Guinea Melane-
sian 15.0%; other 1.0%.
Religious affiliation (1980): Protestant 58.4%; Roman Catholic 32.8%; Angli-
can 5.4%; traditional beliefs 2.5%; Bahā'ī 0.6%; other 0.3%.
Major cities (1990)[2]: Port Moresby 193,242; Lae 80,655; Madang 27,057; We-
wak 23,224; Goroka 17,855.

Vital statistics

Birth rate per 1,000 population (1996): 32.6 (world avg. 25.0); legitimate, n.a.;
illegitimate, n.a.
Death rate per 1,000 population (1996): 10.1 (world avg. 9.3).
Natural increase rate per 1,000 population (1996): 22.5 (world avg. 15.7).
Total fertility rate (avg. births per childbearing woman; 1996): 4.8.
Marriage rate per 1,000 population: n.a.
Life expectancy at birth (1996): male 57.0 years; female 58.0 years.
Major causes of death per 100,000 population (1993): acute respiratory in-
fections 34.6; pneumonia 27.8; meningitis 7.6; conditions originating from
perinatal period 6.2; malaria 3.8.

National economy

Budget (1996). Revenue: K 1,661,200,000 (company tax 22.6%, import duties
18.7%, personal income tax 16.7%, nontax revenue 12.5%, foreign grants
10.0%, export tax 9.0%). Expenditures: K 1,728,600,000 (administrative
37.1%, interest payments 16.9%, transfers 16.4%, capital works 13.1%).
Public debt (external, outstanding; 1994): U.S.$1,622,000,000.
Production (metric tons except as noted). Agriculture, forestry, fishing (1995):
coconuts 700,000, bananas 650,000, sweet potatoes 450,000, sugarcane 300,-
000, palm oil 240,000, yams 222,000, taro 220,000, cassava 115,000, copra
(1994) 100,000, palm kernels 70,000, coffee 65,000, cacao 30,000, pineapples
14,000, tea 9,000; livestock (number of live animals) 1,030,000 pigs, 110,000
cattle, 3,250,000 chickens; roundwood (1994) 8,188,000 cu m; fish catch
(1993) 26,000. Mining and quarrying (1995): copper 212,737; silver 65,228 kg;
gold 51,721 kg. Manufacturing (value added, in K; 1985): food, beverages,
and tobacco 162,558,000; metals, metal products, machinery, and equipment
47,493,000; wood products 29,807,000. Construction (value in K; 1986)[6]:
residential K 19,369,000; nonresidential K 55,675,000. Energy production
(consumption): electricity (kW-hr; 1994) 1,790,000,000 (1,790,000,000); coal
(metric tons; 1994) none (1,000); crude petroleum (barrels) none (n.a.);
petroleum products (metric tons; 1994) none (720,000).
Tourism (1994): receipts from visitors U.S.$55,000,000; expenditures by na-
tionals abroad (1990) U.S.$70,000,000.
Gross national product (1994): U.S.$4,857,000,000 (U.S.$1,160 per capita).

Structure of gross domestic product and labour force

	1993 in value K '000,000	1993 % of total value	1980 labour force[7]	1980 % of labour force[7]
Agriculture	1,292.2	26.0	564,500	77.0
Mining	1,439.8	28.9	4,300	0.6
Manufacturing	437.9	8.8	14,000	1.9
Construction	181.7	3.6	21,600	2.9
Public utilities	69.8	1.4	2,800	0.4
Transp. and commun.	212.9	4.3	17,400	2.4
Trade	396.4	8.0	25,100	3.4
Finance	8	8	4,500	0.6
Pub. admin., defense	713.9	14.3	77,100	10.5
Services	233.9	4.7		
Other	—	—	1,500	0.2
TOTAL	4,978.5	100.0	732,800	100.0[4]

Land use (1994): forested 92.8%; agricultural and under permanent cultivation 0.9%; meadows and pastures 0.2%; other 6.1%.
Population economically active (1980)[7]: total 732,800; activity rate 24.6% (participation rates: over age 10, 35.2%; female 39.8%; unemployed 12.8%[9]).

Price and earnings indexes (1990 = 100)

	1989	1990	1991	1992	1993	1994	1995
Consumer price index	93.5	100.0	107.0	111.6	117.1	120.5	141.3
Weekly earnings index[10]	96.9	100.0	106.1	110.9	...	...	...

Household income and expenditure. Average household size (1980) 4.6; income per household (1975–76) K 2,771 (U.S.$3,483); sources of income
(1970): wages and salaries 57.3%, transfer payments 1.1%, self-employment
and other 41.6%; expenditure (1987)[11]: food and beverages 40.9%, transportation and communications 13.0%, housing 12.5%, clothing and footwear
6.2%, heating and lighting 4.9%, services and other 22.5%.

Foreign trade[12]

Balance of trade (current prices)

	1990	1991	1992	1993	1994	1995
K '000,000	+38.5	−52.7	+475.2	+1,318.9	+1,322.8	+1,769.9
% of total	1.8%	2.0%	15.7%	37.3%	33.1%	35.3%

Imports (1995): K 1,620,000,000 (1990; machinery and transport equipment
38.7%; basic manufactures 20.4%; food and live animals 17.9%; chemicals
7.5%; mineral fuels, lubricants, and related materials 2.7%). *Major import
sources* (1992): Australia 37.1%; Japan 15.0%; Singapore 14.4%; U.S. 6.4%;
New Zealand 4.5%; Hong Kong 3.0%; Malaysia 2.2%.
Exports (1995): K 3,399,800,000 (gold 24.7%; crude oil 24.3%; copper ore and
concentrates 22.2%; timber 12.8%; coffee 6.3%; palm oil and copra 5.9%;
cocoa beans 1.4%). *Major export destinations* (1993): Australia 35.8%; Japan
21.4%; South Korea 10.0%; China 6.6%; Germany 6.4%.

Transport and communications

Transport. Railroads: none. Roads (1986): total length 12,263 mi, 19,736
km (paved 6%). Vehicles (1994): passenger cars 13,000; trucks and buses
32,000. Merchant marine (1992): vessels (100 gross tons and over) 87; total
deadweight tonnage 40,855. Air transport (1993): passenger-mi 458,798,000,
passenger-km 738,366,000; short ton-mi cargo 56,418,000, metric ton-km
cargo 82,369,000; airports (1996) with scheduled flights 129.
Communications. Daily newspapers (1992): total number 2; total circulation
64,000; circulation per 1,000 population 16. Radio (1995): 300,000 receivers
(1 per 14 persons). Television (1995): 100,000 receivers (1 per 43 persons).
Telephones (main lines; 1993): 39,800 (1 per 104 persons).

Education and health

Education (1992)

	schools	teachers	students	student/ teacher ratio
Primary (age 7–12)	2,821	14,117	443,552	31.4
Secondary (age 13–16)	135[13]	2,415	58,226	24.1
Voc., teacher tr.	117[13]	878	11,370	12.9
Higher	2[13]	902[14]	5,007[13]	7.1[14]

Educational attainment (1990). Percentage of population age 25 and over having: no formal schooling 82.6%; some primary education 8.2%; completed
primary 5.0%; some secondary 4.2%. *Literacy* (1990): total population age
15 and over literate 52.0%; males literate 64.9%; females literate 37.8%.
Health: physicians (1993) 736 (1 per 5,584 persons); hospital beds (1989)
15,335 (1 per 234 persons); infant mortality rate (1996) 63.0.
Food (1992): daily per capita caloric intake 2,613 (vegetable products 91%,
animal products 9%); 115% of FAO minimum.

Military

Total active duty personnel (1996): 3,700 (army 86.5%, navy 10.8%, air force
2.7%). *Military expenditure as percentage of GNP* (1994): 1.1% (world 3.0%);
per capita expenditure U.S.$13.

---

[1]The national languages are English, Tok Pisin (English Creole), and Motu.
[2]Preliminary results. [3]Data unavailable because of civil insurrection. [4]Detail does not
add to total given because of rounding. [5]Excludes an estimated population of 160,000
in the North Solomons, 4,500 people in remote areas, and an estimated foreign
population of about 20,000–30,000. [6]Completed new buildings. [7]Citizens of Papua
New Guinea over age 10 involved in "money-raising activities" only. [8]Included with
Services. [9]1977; in six urban centres. [10]Minimum wage of urban labourers. [11]Weights
of retail price index components. [12]Import figures are f.o.b. in balance of trade and
c.i.f. for commodities and trading partners. [13]1990. [14]1986.

Paraguay

Official name: República del Paraguay (Spanish); Tetä Paraguáype (Guaraní) (Republic of Paraguay).
Form of government: multiparty republic with two legislative houses (Senate [45]; Chamber of Deputies [80]).
Head of state and government: President.
Capital: Asunción.
Official languages: Spanish; Guaraní.
Official religion: none[1].
Monetary unit: 1 Paraguayan Guaraní (G) = 100 céntimos; valuation (Oct. 11, 1996) 1 U.S.$ = G2,075; 1 £ = G3,269.

Area and population

Regions Departments	Capitals	area sq mi	area sq km	population 1992 census
Occidental		95,338	246,925	105,633
Alto Paraguay	Fuerte Olimpo	31,795	82,349	12,156
Boquerón	Filadelfia	35,393	91,669	29,060
Presidente Hayes	Pozo Colorado	28,150	72,907	64,417
Oriental		61,710	159,827	4,046,955
Alto Paraná	Ciudad del Este	5,751	14,895	406,584
Amambay	Pedro Juan Caballero	4,994	12,933	99,860
Asunción[2]	—	45	117	500,938
Caaguazú	Coronel Oviedo	4,430	11,474	386,412
Caazapá	Caazapá	3,666	9,496	129,352
Canindiyú	Salto del Guairá	5,663	14,667	103,785
Central	Asunción	952	2,465	866,856
Concepción	Concepción	6,970	18,051	167,289
Cordillera	Caacupé	1,910	4,948	198,701
Guairá	Villarrica	1,485	3,846	161,991
Itapúa	Encarnación	6,380	16,525	377,536
Misiones	San Juan Bautista	3,690	9,556	89,018
Ñeembucú	Pilar	4,690	12,147	69,770
Paraguarí	Paraguarí	3,361	8,705	208,527
San Pedro	San Pedro	7,723	20,002	280,336
TOTAL		157,048	406,752	4,152,588[3]

Demography

Population (1996): 4,964,000[3].
Density (1996): persons per sq mi 31.6, persons per sq km 12.2.
Urban-rural (1992): urban 50.5%; rural 49.5%.
Sex distribution (1992): male 50.19%; female 49.81%.
Age breakdown (1992): under 15, 40.1%; 15–29, 27.6%; 30–44, 18.7%; 45–59, 8.3%; 60–74, 4.2%; 75 and over, 1.1%.
Population projection: (2000) 5,480,000; (2010) 6,805,000.
Doubling time: 26 years.
Ethnic composition (1980): mestizo (Spanish-Guaraní) 90.8%; Amerindian 3.0%; German 1.7%; other 4.5%.
Religious affiliation (1995): Roman Catholic 92.9%; other 7.1%.
Major cities (1992): Asunción 502,426; Ciudad del Este 133,893; San Lorenzo 133,311; Lambaré 99,681; Fernando de la Mora 95,287.

Vital statistics

Birth rate per 1,000 population (1992): 35.5 (world avg. 25.0); (1985) legitimate 68.7%[4]; illegitimate 31.3%[4].
Death rate per 1,000 population (1992): 6.4 (world avg. 9.3).
Natural increase rate per 1,000 population (1992): 29.1 (world avg. 15.7).
Total fertility rate (avg. births per childbearing woman; 1992): 4.9.
Marriage rate per 1,000 population (1992): 3.9[4].
Life expectancy at birth (1993): male 64.8 years; female 69.1 years.
Major causes of death per 100,000 population (1993)[5]: diseases of the circulatory system 162.7; malignant neoplasms (cancers) 52.8; diseases of the respiratory system 38.1; infectious and parasitic diseases 32.7.

National economy

Budget (1995). Revenue: G2,713,119,000,000 (taxes on goods and services 35.9%, income on fixed assets 14.8%, customs duties 18.2%, royalty payments 12.7%, pension funds 6.3%, documentary tax 2.3%). Expenditures: G3,034,445,300,000 (education 19.1%, public works 14.7%, agriculture 9.3%, defense 8.8%, interior 6.9%, public health 6.3%, housing 5.2%).
Public debt (external, outstanding; 1994): U.S.$1,370,000,000.
Production (metric tons except as noted). Agriculture, forestry, fishing (1995): sugarcane 2,799,000, cassava 2,600,000, soybeans 2,300,000, corn (maize) 462,000, seed cotton 320,000, oranges 171,000, bananas 76,000, lint cotton 125,000, sweet potatoes 106,000; livestock (number of live animals) 8,100,000 cattle, 2,660,000 pigs, 13,253,000 chickens; roundwood (1994) 7,188,000 cu m; fish catch (1993) 16,000. Mining and quarrying (1993): limestone 600,000[6]; kaolin 74,000; gypsum 4,500. Manufacturing (value added in constant prices of 1982, G'000,000; 1995): food products 70,600; wood products and furniture 24,500; handicrafts 11,400; textiles 10,200; printing and publishing 7,800; nonmetal products 6,900; petroleum products 6,400; leather and hides 5,700. Construction (1985): residential 60,800 sq m; nonresidential 163,200 sq m. Energy production (consumption): electricity (kW-hr; 1993) 31,454,000,000 (3,334,000,000); coal, none (none); crude petroleum (barrels; 1993) none (1,840,000); petroleum products (metric tons; 1993) 284,000 (939,000); natural gas, none (none).
Tourism (1994): receipts from visitors U.S.$197,000,000; expenditures by nationals abroad U.S.$176,000,000.

Gross national product (1994): U.S.$7,606,000,000 (U.S.$1,570 per capita).

Structure of gross domestic product and labour force

	1995 in value G'000,000[7]	1995 % of total value	1982 labour force	1982 % of labour force
Agriculture	285,700	26.4	445,518	42.9
Mining	[8]	[8]	1,406	0.1
Manufacturing	160,500	14.8	124,658	12.0
Construction	58,000	5.4	69,900	6.7
Public utilities	57,000	5.3	2,605	0.3
Transp. and commun.	50,900	4.7	30,524	2.9
Trade }	282,400	26.1	85,961	8.3
Finance }			18,019	1.7
Pub. admin., defense	53,100	4.9	174,228	16.8
Services }	134,300[8]	12.4[8]	86,444	8.3
Other }				
TOTAL	1,081,900	100.0	1,039,258[9]	100.0

Population economically active (1992): total 1,390,580; activity rate 51.0% (participation rates; 1982: ages 15–64, 57.5%; female 19.7%; unemployed [1989] 9.2%).

Price and earnings indexes (1990 = 100)

	1989	1990	1991	1992	1993	1994	1995
Consumer price index	72.4	100.0	124.3	143.1	169.2	204.0	231.4
Earnings index	70.3	100.0	115.1	131.8	158.0	...	...

Household income and expenditure. Average household size (1992) 4.7; sources of income (1989): wages and salaries 33.9%, transfer payments 2.5%, other 63.6%; expenditure (1980): food 48.7%, housing 16.4%, clothing 9.7%, household durable goods 6.2%, transportation and communications 4.5%.
Land use (1994): forested 32.4%; meadows and pastures 54.6%; agricultural and under permanent cultivation 5.7%; other 7.3%.

Foreign trade

Balance of trade (current prices)

	1989	1990	1991	1992	1993	1994
U.S.$'000,000	+363.8	−234.7	−538.3	−580.6	−752.3	−1,323.6
% of total	21.8%	10.9%	26.7%	30.7%	34.2%	44.8%

Imports (1994): U.S.$2,140,400,000 (machinery and transport equipment 33.2%, of which transport equipment 12.9%; fuels and lubricants 7.4%; chemicals and pharmaceuticals 6.8%; iron products 5.5%). *Major import sources* (1995): Brazil 28.8%; U.S. 22.0%; Argentina 14.5%; Hong Kong 9.3%; Japan 4.6%; U.K. 2.5%; Germany 2.3%; Chile 1.7%; Italy 1.7%.
Exports (1995): U.S.$819,400,000 (cotton fibres 32.4%; soybean flour 24.1%; timber 7.5%; oilseed cakes 7.0%; vegetable oil 5.9%, of which soybean oil 5.7%; processed meats 5.0%; hides and skins 3.9%; perfume oils 0.8%; tobacco 0.7%). *Major export destinations* (1995): Brazil 45.8%; Germany 7.8%; Argentina 7.7%; U.S. 5.4%; Chile 5.2%; The Netherlands 3.9%; Italy 3.5%.

Transport and communications

Transport. Railroads (1994): route length 274 mi, 441 km; passenger-mi 2,900,000[10], passenger-km 4,600,000[10]; short ton-mi cargo 3,800,000, metric ton-km cargo 5,500,000. Roads (1995): total length 17,956 mi, 28,900 km (paved 9%). Vehicles (1993): passenger cars 174,212; trucks 76,565. Merchant marine (1992): vessels (100 gross tons and over) 38; total deadweight tonnage 38,513. Air transport (1993): passenger-mi 791,000,000, passenger-km 1,273,000,000; short ton-mi cargo 16,500,000, metric ton-km cargo 24,100,000; airports (1996) with scheduled flights 5.
Communications. Daily newspapers (1995): total number 5; total circulation 194,000; circulation per 1,000 population 40. Radio (1995): 700,000 receivers (1 per 6.9 persons). Television (1995): 350,000 receivers (1 per 14 persons). Telephones (main lines; 1993): 142,300 (1 per 33 persons).

Education and health

Education (1994–95)

	schools	teachers	students	student/ teacher ratio
Primary (age 7–12)	5,180	41,432[11]	827,857	19.1[11]
Secondary (age 13–18)[12]	1,102	20,793[11]	235,914	10.3[11]
Higher	2	742[11]	39,694	40.9[13]

Educational attainment (1982). Percentage of population age 25 and over having: no formal schooling 13.6%; primary education 64.7%; secondary 15.5%; higher 3.4%; not stated 2.8%. *Literacy* (1995): percentage of total population age 15 and over literate 92.1%; males literate 93%; females literate 90.6%.
Health (1993): physicians 3,341 (1 per 1,406 persons); hospital beds 5,435 (1 per 864 persons); infant mortality rate per 1,000 live births (1992) 47.1.
Food (1992): daily per capita caloric intake 2,670 (vegetable products 76%, animal products 24%); 116% of FAO recommended minimum requirement.

Military

Total active duty personnel (1996): 20,200 (army 73.8%, navy 17.8%, air force 8.4%). *Military expenditure as percentage of GNP* (1994): 1.2% (world 3.0%); per capita expenditure U.S.$18.

---

[1]Roman Catholicism, although not official, enjoys special recognition in the 1992 constitution. [2]Asunción is the capital city, not a department. [3]The 1992 census figure is not adjusted for undercount. The 1996 population figure is adjusted for estimated undercount. [4]Civil Registry records only. [5]Reporting areas only (constituting about 75 percent of the total population). [6]1992. [7]1982 prices. [8]Other includes mining. [9]Detail does not add to total given because of rounding. [10]1993. [11]1993–94. [12]Includes vocational education and teacher training. [13]1992–93.

Peru

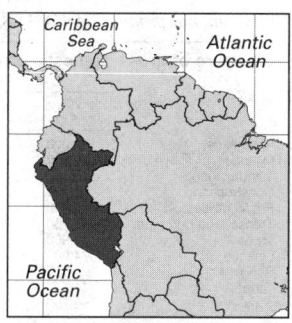

Official name: República del Perú (Spanish) (Republic of Peru).
Form of government[1]: unitary multiparty republic with one legislative house (Congress [120]).
Head of state and government: President.
Capital: Lima.
Official languages: Spanish; Quechua; Aymara.
Official religion: Roman Catholicism.
Monetary unit[2]: 1 nuevo sol (S/.) = 100 céntimos; valuation (Oct. 11, 1996) 1 U.S.$ = S/. 2.58; 1 £ = S/. 4.06.

Area and population		area		population
		sq mi	sq km	1995 estimate
Regions[3]	**Capitals**			
Andres Avelino Cáceres	...	40,707	105,430	2,169,086
Arequipa	...	24,458	63,345	981,272
Chavin	...	15,686	40,627	1,136,625
Grau	...	15,661	40,562	1,618,342
Inca	...	66,696	172,741	1,365,496
José Carlos Mariátegui	...	40,081	103,809	1,513,275
La Libertad	...	9,873	25,570	1,336,553
Loreto	...	142,414	368,852	777,388
Los Libertadores-Wari	...	34,340	88,939	1,515,099
Nor Oriental del Marañón	...	33,486	86,728	2,699,485
San Martín	...	19,789	51,253	624,525
Ucayali	...	39,541	102,411	367,844
Department				
Lima	...	13,437	34,802	6,742,576
Constitutional Province				
Callao	Callao	57	147	684,135
TOTAL		496,225[4]	1,285,216	23,531,701

Demography

Population (1996): 23,947,000.
Density (1996): persons per sq mi 48.3, persons per sq km 18.6.
Urban-rural (1995): urban 71.2%; rural 28.8%.
Sex distribution (1995): male 49.67%; female 50.33%.
Age breakdown (1993): under 15, 35.9%; 15–29, 29.0%; 30–44, 18.2%; 45–59, 10.2%; 60–74, 5.3%; 75 and over, 1.4%.
Population projection: (2000) 25,662,000; (2010) 30,506,000.
Doubling time: 34 years.
Ethnic composition (1981): Quechua 47.1%; mestizo 32.0%; white 12.0%; Aymara 5.4%; other Amerindian 1.7%; other 1.8%.
Religious affiliation (1989): Roman Catholic 92.5%; Protestant 5.5%.
Major cities (1995): metropolitan Lima 6,022,213; Arequipa 725,838; Callao 684,135; Chiclayo 668,066; Trujillo 627,553.

Vital statistics

Birth rate per 1,000 population (1990–95): 27.6 (world avg. 25.0); (1977) legitimate 57.8%; illegitimate 42.2%.
Death rate per 1,000 population (1990–95): 6.9 (world avg. 9.3).
Natural increase rate per 1,000 population (1990–95): 20.7 (world avg. 15.7).
Total fertility rate (avg. births per childbearing woman; 1993): 3.4.
Marriage rate per 1,000 population (1982): 6.0.
Life expectancy at birth (1990–95): male 64.4 years; female 69.2 years.
Major causes of death per 100,000 population (1989): diseases of the circulatory system 115.3; respiratory diseases 100.2; infectious diseases 84.5; malignant neoplasms 72.9; accidents, poisoning, and violence 53.6.

National economy

Budget (1994). Revenue: S/. 16,508,000,000 (taxes on goods and services 49.3%; income taxes 15.3%; import duties 9.8%; nontax revenue 8.7%). Expenditures: S/. 17,032,000,000 (current expenditure 81.5%, of which transfer payments 35.5%, wages and salaries 16.7%, interest payments 13.3%; capital expenditure 18.5%).
Tourism (1994): receipts U.S.$402,000,000; expenditures U.S.$323,000,000.
Production (metric tons except as noted). Agriculture, forestry, fishing (1995): sugarcane 6,500,000, potatoes 2,368,000, rice 1,142,000, plantains 1,066,000, corn (maize) 715,000, cassava 547,000, seed cotton 217,000, coffee 97,000; livestock (number of live animals) 12,570,000 sheep, 4,513,000 cattle, 2,401,000 pigs, 68,470,000 chickens; roundwood (1994) 12,496,000 cu m; fish catch (1993) 8,450,600. Mining and quarrying (1995): iron ore 3,835,000; zinc 689,000; copper 405,000; lead 233,000; silver 1,908. Manufacturing (value in S/. '000,000[6]; 1993): processed foods 180.5; base metal products 162.5; industrial chemicals 89.7; wood products 61.6; textiles 56.9; beverages and tobacco 53.4; apparel 36.6. Construction (value in S/. '000,000[6]; 1992): residential 22.4; nonresidential 14.6. Energy production (consumption): electricity (kW-hr; 1994) 15,163,000,000 (15,163,000,000); coal (metric tons; 1994) 109,000 (406,000); crude petroleum (barrels; 1994) 47,000,000 (54,000,000); petroleum products (metric tons; 1994) 7,227,000 (5,798,000); natural gas (cu m; 1994) 191,000,000 (191,000,000).
Household income and expenditure. Average household size (1993) 5.1; income per household (1988) I/. 1,086,620[2] (U.S.$2,173); sources of income (1988): business income 65.1%, wages 31.2%, transfers 3.7%; expenditure (1990): food 29.4%, recreation and education 13.2%, household durables 10.1%, clothing and footwear 8.5%, transportation 7.5%, health 7.0%, other 24.3%.
Gross national product (1994): U.S.$44,110,000,000 (U.S.$1,890 per capita).

Structure of gross domestic product and labour force				
	1993		1992	
	in value S/. '000,000[6]	% of total value	labour force	% of labour force
Agriculture	487.7	14.1	2,658,000	33.0
Mining	332.0	9.6	198,000	2.4
Manufacturing	782.3	22.6	840,000	10.4
Construction	233.4	6.7	300,000	3.7
Public utilities	54.9	1.6	25,000	0.3
Transp. and commun.	251.1	7.2	355,000	4.4
Trade	586.2	16.9	1,297,000	16.1
Finance	453.7	13.1	192,000	2.4
Services	283.4[7]	8.2[7]	2,199,000[7]	27.3[7]
TOTAL	3,464.7	100.0	8,064,000	100.0

Population economically active (1993): total 7,109,527; activity rate of total population 31.4% (participation rates: over age 15, 51.2%; female 50.9%; unemployed 7.1%).

Price and earnings indexes (1990 = 100)						
	1989	1990	1991	1992	1993	1994	1995
Consumer price index	...	100	510	884	1,314	1,626	1,806
Monthly earnings index[8]	...	100	706	1,163	2,059	...	...

Land use (1994): forest 66.3%; pasture 21.2%; agricultural 3.2%; other 9.3%.
Public debt (external, outstanding; 1994): U.S.$17,890,000,000.

Foreign trade

Balance of trade (current prices)						
	1990	1991	1992	1993	1994	1995
U.S.$'000,000	+585.3	−165.0	−566.7	−623.9	−1,095.2	−2,111.6
% of total	9.8%	2.4%	7.5%	8.2%	10.8%	15.9%

Imports (1994): U.S.$5,626,122,000 (raw and intermediate materials 30.2%, machinery 21.8%, transport equipment 15.6%, consumer goods 11.5%). *Major import sources:* U.S. 28.1%; Japan 8.7%; Brazil 6.6%; Argentina 5.3%; Germany 4.7%; Colombia 4.5%; Chile 3.8%.
Exports (1994): U.S.$4,048,390,000 (copper 19.1%, fish flour 18.4%, zinc 5.2%, clothing and accessories 4.7%, petroleum and derivatives 4.4%, textile yarn and fabric 3.7%, lead 3.5%). *Major export destinations:* U.S. 17.9%; Japan 9.5%; China 7.0%; Germany 6.6%; The Netherlands 5.7%; Italy 4.9%; Brazil 4.5%; U.K. 3.1%.

Transport and communications

Transport. Railroads (1993): route length 1,318 mi, 2,121 km; passenger-km 165,304,000; metric ton-km cargo 884,352,000. Roads (1995): total length 44,400 mi, 71,400 km (paved 11%). Vehicles (1994): passenger cars 470,000; trucks and buses 263,000. Merchant marine (1992): vessels (100 gross tons and over) 623; total deadweight tonnage 615,582. Air transport (1993): passenger-km 1,926,000,000; metric ton-km cargo 214,000,000; airports (1996) 27.
Communications. Daily newspapers (1992): total number 59; total circulation 1,590,000; circulation per 1,000 population 71. Radio (1995): 5,300,000 receivers (1 per 4.4 persons). Television (1995): 2,000,000 receivers (1 per 12 persons). Telephones (1992): 816,160 (1 per 28 persons).

Education and health

Education (1993)				
	schools[9]	teachers	students	student/ teacher ratio
Primary (age 6–11)	54,502	159,022	4,843,666	30.5
Secondary (age 12–16)	7,097	93,277	1,913,163	20.5
Voc., teacher tr.	1,952	11,919	270,668	22.7
Higher	655	46,983	730,987	15.6

Educational attainment (1993). Percentage of population age 15 and over having: no formal schooling 12.3%; less than primary education 0.3%; primary 31.5%; secondary 35.5%; higher 20.4%. *Literacy* (1993): total population age 15 and over literate 12,108,699 (87.2%); males 6,330,056 (92.9%); females 5,778,643 (81.7%).
Health (1992): physicians 20,124 (1 per 1,116 persons); hospital beds 44,100 (1 per 509 persons); infant mortality rate per 1,000 live births (1993) 58.3.
Food (1992): daily per capita caloric intake 1,882 (vegetable products 87%, animal products 13%); 80% of FAO recommended minimum requirement.

Military

Total active duty personnel (1996): 125,000 (army 68.0%, navy 20.0%, air force 12.0%). *Military expenditure as percentage of GNP* (1994): 1.6% (world 3.0%); per capita expenditure U.S.$35.

---

[1]A new constitution promulgated in December 1993 replaced the 1980 constitution, which was suspended in April 1992. [2]A new currency, the nuevo sol, was introduced in January 1991, replacing the inti (abbrev.: I/.) at the rate of one million intis for one nuevo sol. [3]The regional administrative structure established in 1987 has been made functional only very slowly because of financing problems. [4]Detail does not add to total given because of rounding. [5]Excludes Indian jungle population; based on incomplete information. [6]At 1979 prices. [7]Includes public administration and other. [8]Estimate for Lima metropolitan area only. [9]1992.

Philippines

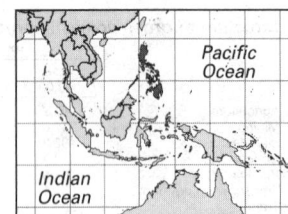

Official name: Republika ng Pilipinas (Pilipino); Republic of the Philippines (English).
Form of government: unitary republic with two legislative houses (Senate [24]; House of Representatives [204]).
Chief of state and head of government: President.
Capital: Manila.
Official languages: Pilipino; English.
Official religion: none.
Monetary unit: 1 Philippine peso (₱) = 100 centavos; valuation (Oct. 11, 1996) 1 U.S.$ = ₱ 26.27; 1 £ = ₱ 41.38.

Area and population

Regions	area sq mi	area sq km	population 1995 census
Bicol	6,808	17,633	4,325,307
Cagayan Valley	10,362	26,838	2,536,035
Caraga	7,277	18,847	1,942,687
Central Luzon	7,039	18,231	6,932,570
Central Mindanao	5,549	14,373	2,359,808
Central Visayas	5,773	14,951	5,014,588
Eastern Visayas	8,275	21,432	3,366,917
Ilocos	4,958	12,840	3,803,890
National Capital	246	636	9,454,040
Northern Mindanao	5,418	14,033	2,483,272
Southern Mindanao	10,479	27,141	4,604,158
Southern Tagalog	18,117	46,924	9,940,722
Western Mindanao	6,194	16,042	2,794,659
Western Visayas	7,808	20,223	5,776,938
Autonomous Regions			
Cordillera	7,063	18,294	1,254,838
Muslim Mindanao	4,493	11,638	2,020,903
TOTAL	115,860[1]	300,076	68,614,162[2]

Demography

Population (1996): 71,750,000.
Density (1996): persons per sq mi 619.3, persons per sq km 239.1.
Urban-rural (1995): urban 54.0%; rural 46.0%.
Sex distribution (1996): male 50.29%; female 49.71%.
Age breakdown (1996): under 15, 35.9%; 15–29, 28.8%; 30–44, 19.4%; 45–59, 10.2%; 60–74, 4.6%; 75 and over, 1.1%.
Population projection: (2000) 78,414,000; (2010) 94,503,000.
Doubling time: 30 years.
Ethnic composition (by mother tongue of households; 1990): Tagalog 27.9%; Cebuano 24.3%; Ilocano 9.8%; Hiligaynon Ilongo 9.3%; Bicol 5.8%; Waray 4.0%; Pampango 3.1%; Pangasinan 1.9%; other 13.9%.
Religious affiliation (1990): Roman Catholic 82.9%; Protestant 8.3%; Muslim 4.6%; Aglipayan (Philippine Independent Church) 2.6%; other 1.6%.
Major cities (1991): Manila 1,894,667; Quezon City 1,627,890; Davao 867,779; Cebu 641,042; Caloocan 629,473; Zamboanga 453,214.

Vital statistics

Birth rate per 1,000 population (1996): 28.7 (world avg. 25.0); (1982) legitimate 93.9%; illegitimate 6.1%.
Death rate per 1,000 population (1996): 5.9 (world avg. 9.3).
Natural increase rate per 1,000 population (1996): 22.8 (world avg. 15.7).
Total fertility rate (avg. births per childbearing woman; 1996): 3.7.
Marriage rate per 1,000 population (1991): 6.7.
Life expectancy at birth (1996): male 66.0 years; female 70.0 years.
Major causes of death per 100,000 population (1992): heart diseases 64.3; pneumonia 57.9; tuberculosis 25.0; accidents 19.6.

National economy

Budget (1995). Revenue: ₱ 350,200,000,000 (taxes on goods and services 31.0%, income taxes 29.5%, international duties 26.5%, nontax revenues 13.0%). Expenditures: ₱ 384,700,000,000 (debt service 28.4%, social services 27.8%, economic services 21.9%, general public administration 15.3%, defense 6.3%).
Public debt (external, outstanding; 1994): U.S.$29,577,000,000.
Production (metric tons except as noted). Agriculture, forestry, fishing (1995): sugarcane 25,700,000, rice 11,002,000, coconuts 10,300,000, corn (maize) 4,161,000, bananas 3,200,000, cassava 1,870,000, pineapples 1,360,000, mango 390,000, coffee 135,000, tobacco 64,000; livestock (number of live animals) 8,941,000 pigs, 2,825,000 goats, 2,508,000 buffalo, 2,021,000 cattle, 74,000,000 chickens; roundwood (1994) 38,630,000 cu m; fish catch (1993) 2,264,000. Mining and quarrying (1995): coal 1,293,369; nickel ore 647,267; copper concentrate 398,951; silver 28,480 kg; gold 12,393 kg. Manufacturing (gross value added in ₱ '000,000; 1994)[3]: food products 164,200; petroleum and coal products 34,500; chemicals 31,200; footwear and clothing 27,100; electrical machinery 22,700; beverages 17,200; nonmetallic mineral products 14,100; tobacco 10,100. Construction (authorized; 1992): residential 3,862,000 sq m; nonresidential 4,288,000 sq m. Energy production (consumption): electricity (kW-hr; 1994) 26,425,000,000 (26,425,000,000); coal (metric tons; 1994) 1,733,000 (2,503,000); crude petroleum (barrels; 1994) 2,186,000 (90,808,000); petroleum products (metric tons; 1994) 11,350,000 (12,559,000).
Tourism (1994): receipts U.S.$2,282,000,000; expenditures U.S.$196,000,000.
Land use (1994): forested 45.6%; meadows and pastures 4.3%; agricultural and under permanent cultivation 30.8%; other 19.3%.

Gross national product (1994): U.S.$63,311,000,000 (U.S.$960 per capita).

Structure of gross domestic product and labour force

	1994 in value ₱ '000,000[4]	% of total value	labour force	% of labour force
Agriculture	171,000	22.3	11,249,000	40.9
Mining	10,800	1.4	101,000	0.4
Manufacturing	190,500	24.9	2,582,000	9.4
Construction	42,500	5.5	1,187,000	4.3
Public utilities	23,000	3.0	100,000	0.4
Transp. and commun.	45,100	5.9	1,402,000	5.1
Trade	116,900	15.3	3,563,000	13.0
Finance	74,000	9.7	494,000	1.8
Services	91,900	12.0	4,480,000	16.3
Other			2,325,000[5]	8.4[5]
TOTAL	765,700	100.0	27,483,000	100.0

Population economically active (1994): total 27,483,000; activity rate 40.3% (participation rates: ages 15–64, 66.1%; female 36.9%; unemployed 8.4%).

Price and earnings indexes (1990 = 100)

	1989	1990	1991	1992	1993	1994	1995
Consumer price index	87.6	100.0	118.7	129.3	139.1	151.7	164.0
Daily earnings index[6]	...	100.0	128.5	128.5	128.5	145.7	...

Household income and expenditure (1992). Average household size (1995) 5.1; income per family (1994) ₱ 83,160 (U.S.$3,150); sources of income: wages 45.7%, business profits 42.5%, self-employment 8.4%, transfers 3.4%; expenditure: food, beverages, and tobacco 57.7%, household furnishings and operations 13.5%, transportation 5.0%, fuel and power 4.1%, clothing 3.7%.

Foreign trade[7]

Balance of trade (current prices)

	1990	1991	1992	1993	1994	1995
₱ '000,000	−86,604	−89,465	−121,250	−176,298	−212,086	−229,214
% of total	17.0%	15.6%	19.6%	22.5%	23.2%	20.3%

Imports (1995): U.S.$26,479,400,000 (machinery and transport equipment 26.3%, mineral fuels and lubricants 9.3%, chemicals 9.1%, textile yarns and fabrics 8.8%, base metals 6.2%, iron and steel 5.0%, food and live animals 2.0%). *Major import sources:* Japan 22.4%; United States 18.9%; Saudi Arabia 6.2%; Singapore 5.8%; Taiwan 5.4%; South Korea 5.1%; Hong Kong 4.8%; Germany 3.5%; United Kingdom 2.1%.
Exports (1995): U.S.$17,371,059,000 (electronics 36.2%, garments 14.8%, coconut oil 4.6%, ignition wiring sets 2.5%, woodcraft and furniture 2.3%, gold 1.5%). *Major export destinations:* United States 35.3%; Japan 15.7%; Singapore 5.7%; United Kingdom 5.3%; Hong Kong 4.7%; Thailand 4.6%; Germany 4.0%; Taiwan 3.3%; South Korea 2.5%.

Transport and communications

Transport. Railroads (1993): route length 658 mi, 1,059 km; passenger-mi 60,000,000, passenger-km 96,000,000; short ton-mi cargo 8,000,000, metric ton-km cargo 12,000,000. Roads (1993): total length 99,968 mi, 160,883 km (paved 16%). Vehicles (1993): passenger cars 1,078,895; trucks and buses 1,024,051. Merchant marine (1992): vessels (100 gross tons and over) 1,499; total deadweight tonnage 13,807,113. Air transport (1995)[8]: passenger-mi 8,948,000,000, passenger-km 14,401,000,000; short ton-mi cargo 255,902,000, metric ton-km cargo 373,611,000; airports (1996) with scheduled flights 21.
Communications. Daily newspapers (1992): total number 43; circulation 3,200,000; circulation per 1,000 population 49. Radio (1995): 8,300,000 receivers (1 per 8.4 persons). Television (1995): 7,000,000 receivers (1 per 10 persons). Telephones (main lines; 1993): 859,800 (1 per 76 persons).

Education and health

Education (1993–94)

	schools	teachers	students	student/teacher ratio
Primary (age 7–12)	35,087	320,634	10,731,453	33.5
Secondary (age 13–16)	5,880	134,898	4,590,037	34.0
Voc., teacher tr.	1,261[9]			
Higher	809[9]	56,880[10]	1,582,820	23.7[10]

Educational attainment (1990). Percentage of population age 25 and over having: no grade completed 6.7%; elementary education 46.9%; secondary 24.3%; postsecondary 11.0%; college 10.6%; not stated 0.5%. *Literacy* (1990): total population age 15 and over literate 34,215,672 (93.6%); males literate 17,080,157 (94.0%); females literate 17,135,515 (93.2%).
Health: physicians (1993) 78,445 (1 per 849 persons); hospital beds (1992) 83,-330 (1 per 780 persons); infant mortality rate per 1,000 live births (1996) 38.
Food (1992): daily per capita caloric intake 2,257 (vegetable products 88%, animal products 12%); 100% of FAO recommended minimum requirement.

Military

Total active duty personnel (1996): 107,500 (army 63.3%, navy 21.4%, air force 15.3%). *Military expenditure as percentage of GNP* (1994): 1.9% (world 3.0%); per capita expenditure U.S.$19.

---

[1]Detail does not add to total given because of rounding. [2]Includes 2,830 embassy employees abroad. [3]Manufacturing firms with 10 or more workers. [4]At 1985 prices. [5]Mostly unemployed. [6]Wages in nonagricultural activities. [7]Import figures are f.o.b. in balance of trade and c.i.f. for commodities and trading partners. [8]Philippines Airlines only. [9]1991–92. [10]1990–91.

Poland

Official name: Rzeczpospolita Polska (Republic of Poland).
Form of government: unitary multiparty republic with two legislative houses (Senate [100]; Diet [460]).
Chief of state: President.
Head of government: Prime Minister.
Capital: Warsaw.
Official language: Polish.
Official religion: none.
Monetary unit: 1 złoty (Zł)[1] = 100 groszy; valuation (Oct. 11, 1996) 1 U.S.$ = Zł 2.82; 1 £ = Zł 4.43.

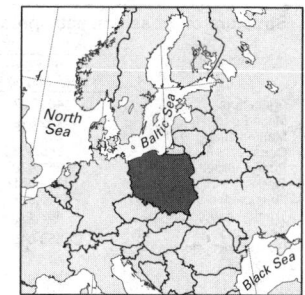

Area and population (1995[2] estimate)

Provinces	area sq km	population	Provinces	area sq km	population
Biała Podlaska	5,348	309,700	Opole	8,535	1,027,400
Białystok	10,055	700,100	Ostrołęka	6,498	407,500
Bielsko-Biała	3,704	915,100	Piła	8,205	492,100
Bydgoszcz	10,349	1,130,000	Piotrków	6,266	644,600
Chełm	3,866	250,100	Płock	5,117	521,900
Ciechanów	6,362	436,200	Poznań	8,151	1,351,000
Częstochowa	6,182	782,700	Przemyśl	4,437	414,100
Elbląg	6,103	490,400	Radom	7,294	763,000
Gdańsk	7,394	1,450,100	Rzeszów	4,397	743,900
Gorzów	8,484	509,500	Siedlce	8,499	661,500
Jelenia Góra	4,379	524,200	Sieradz	4,869	412,600
Kalisz	6,512	721,500	Skierniewice	3,960	423,800
Katowice	6,650	3,936,300	Słupsk	7,453	424,900
Kielce	9,211	1,137,200	Suwałki	10,490	484,700
Konin	5,139	478,800	Szczecin	9,982	989,200
Koszalin	8,470	520,100	Tarnobrzeg	6,283	609,200
Kraków	3,254	1,239,500	Tarnów	4,151	690,700
Krosno	5,702	505,300	Toruń	5,348	669,800
Legnica	4,037	522,600	Wałbrzych	4,168	741,200
Leszno	4,154	395,800	Warszawa	3,788	2,416,500
Łódź	1,523	1,121,200	Włocławek	4,402	435,000
Łomża	6,684	353,700	Wrocław	6,287	1,137,300
Lublin	6,792	1,025,100	Zamość	6,980	494,000
Nowy Sącz	5,576	728,100	Zielona Góra	8,868	672,200
Olsztyn	12,327	769,200	TOTAL	312,685	38,580,600

Demography

Population (1996): 38,731,000.
Density (1996): persons per sq mi 320.8, persons per sq km 123.9.
Urban-rural (1996): urban 61.8%; rural 38.2%.
Sex distribution (1996): male 48.66%; female 51.34%.
Age breakdown (1995): under 15, 22.8%; 15–29, 21.9%; 30–44, 23.6%; 45–59, 15.9%; 60–74, 12.1%; 75 and over, 3.7%.
Population projection: (2000) 39,134,000; (2010) 40,160,000.
Ethnic composition (1990): Polish 98.7%; Ukrainian 0.6%; other 0.7%.
Religious affiliation (1995): Roman Catholic 90.7%; Orthodox 1.4%; other 7.9%.
Major cities (1996[2]): Warsaw 1,638,300; Łódź 825,600; Kraków 745,400.

Vital statistics

Birth rate per 1,000 population (1995): 11.2 (world avg. 25.0); (1985) legitimate 95.0%; illegitimate 5.0%.
Death rate per 1,000 population (1995): 10.0 (world avg. 9.3).
Natural increase rate per 1,000 population (1995): 1.2 (world avg. 15.7).
Total fertility rate (avg. births per childbearing woman; 1996): 1.7.
Marriage rate per 1,000 population (1995): 5.4.
Divorce rate per 1,000 population (1995): 1.0.
Life expectancy at birth (1994): male 67.5 years; female 76.1 years.
Major causes of death per 100,000 population (1994): diseases of the circulatory system 512.7; malignant neoplasms (cancers) 201.0; accidents, poisoning, and violence 75.4; diabetes mellitus 14.2; infectious and parasitic diseases 6.8.

National economy

Budget (1995). Revenue: Zł 83,721,700,000 (income tax 38.6%, turnover tax 24.7%). Expenditures: Zł 91,163,000,000 (interest on debts 18.5%, social benefits 16.8%).
Public debt (external, outstanding; 1994): U.S.$39,110,000,000.
Gross national product (1994): U.S.$94,613,000,000 (U.S.$2,470 per capita).

Structure of gross domestic product and labour force

	1994 in value Zł '000,000[3]	1994 % of total value	1995 labour force	1995 % of labour force
Agriculture	13,228.2	6.3	4,045,900	23.8
Mining and manufacturing	60,070.6	28.5 }	3,728,800	21.9
Public utilities	7,635.5	3.6 }		
Construction	11,998.7	5.7	827,400	4.9
Transp. and commun.	12,531.0	6.0	838,100	4.9
Trade	29,740.2	14.1	2,089,000	12.3
Finance	14,717.5	7.0	268,200	1.6
Public administration	9,431.0	4.5	381,300	2.2
Services	27,558.3	13.1	2,234,900	13.1
Other	23,496.3[4]	11.2[4]	2,590,400[5]	15.2[5]
TOTAL	210,407.3	100.0	17,004,000	100.0[6]

Production (metric tons except as noted). Agriculture, forestry, fishing (1995): (value of production in Zł '000,000) potatoes 6,606, wheat 3,055, rye 1,421,

sugar beets 1,075; livestock (number of live animals) 20,418,000 pigs, 7,306,000 cattle; roundwood (1994) 18,388,000 cu m; fish catch 433,300. Mining and quarrying (1995): electrolytic copper 407,000; zinc 166,000; lead 66,400; aluminum 52,000. Manufacturing (value of production in Zł '000,000; 1995): food and beverages 52,558; machinery and transport equipment 33,372; chemicals 16,360. Construction (1995): 61,000 units, of which residential 31,100. Energy production (consumption): electricity ('000,000 kW-hr; 1994) 135,347 (132,668); coal ('000 metric tons; 1994) 200,700 (171,000); crude petroleum (barrels; 1994) 2,107,000 (99,757,000); petroleum products ('000 metric tons; 1994) 12,625 (13,807); natural gas ('000,000 cu m; 1994) 4,079 (10,908).
Population economically active (1995): total 17,004,000; activity rate of total population 44.0% (participation rates: over age 15, 58.4%; female 51.1%; unemployed 13.1%).

Price and earnings indexes (1990 = 100)

	1989	1990	1991	1992	1993	1994	1995
Consumer price index	15.3	100.0	176.7	256.8	351.5	468.4	593.9
Monthly earnings index	21.5	100.0	167.1	228.5	320.0	421.4	595.9

Household income and expenditure (1995). Average household size 3.1; average annual income Zł 8,431 (U.S.$2,990); sources of income: wages 55.7%, social security benefits 32.5% (of which pensions 26.6%), self-employment 6.9%, other 4.9%; expenditure: food 39.7%, housing 20.6%, clothing 7.0%.
Tourism (1994): receipts U.S.$6,150,000,000; expenditures U.S.$316,000,000.
Land use (1994): forest 28.8%; meadow 13.3%; agricultural and under permanent cultivation 47.0%; other 10.9%.

Foreign trade

Balance of trade (current prices)

	1990	1991	1992	1993	1994	1995
Zł '000,000	+4,554	−654	−4,026	−8,262	−9,826	−14,987
% of total	20.1%	2.0%	10.1%	13.8%	11.1%	11.9%

Imports (1995): Zł 70,502,000,000 (machinery and transport equipment 29.9%, manufactured goods 21.6%, chemicals 15.0%, miscellaneous manufactured articles 9.3%, mineral fuels and lubricants 9.1%, food 8.0%). *Major import sources:* Germany 26.6%; Italy 8.5%; Russia 6.7%; U.K. 5.2%; France 4.9%; The Netherlands 4.5%; U.S. 3.9%.
Exports (1995): Zł 55,515,000,000 (manufactured goods 27.6%, machinery and transport equipment 21.1%, miscellaneous manufactured articles 20.9%, food 9.2%, mineral fuels and lubricants 8.2%, chemicals 7.7%). *Major export destinations:* Germany 38.3%; The Netherlands 5.6%; Russia 5.6%; Italy 4.9%; U.K. 4.0%.

Transport and communications

Transport. Railroads (1996): length 23,986 km; passenger-km 26,635,000,000; metric ton-km cargo 69,116,000,000. Roads (1995): total length 372,479 km (paved 65%). Vehicles (1995): passenger cars 7,517,300; trucks and buses 1,472,300. Merchant marine (1992): vessels (100 gross tons and over) 644; total deadweight tonnage 4,314,308. Air transport (1996): passenger-km 4,633,000,000; metric ton-km cargo 74,000,000; airports (1996) 12.
Communications. Daily newspapers (1995): 66; circulation 5,404,000; circulation per 1,000 population 140. Radio (1995): total number of receivers 16,300,000 (1 per 2.4 persons). Television (1995): total number of receivers 10,000,000 (1 per 3.9 persons). Telephones (main lines; 1995): 5,006,000 (1 per 7.7 persons).

Education and health

Education (1995–96)

	schools	teachers	students	student/teacher ratio
Primary (age 7–14)	19,823	323,500	5,104,200	15.8
Secondary (age 15–18)	1,705	34,700	683,000	19.7
Voc., teacher tr.	8,887	88,700	1,729,300	19.5
Higher	179	71,300	794,600	11.1

Educational attainment (1988). Percentage of population age 15 and over having: no formal schooling or less than full primary education 6.4%; primary 38.8%; secondary 48.3%; higher 6.5%. *Literacy* (1988): 98.7%.
Health (1996): physicians 88,523 (1 per 436 persons); hospital beds 213,969 (1 per 180 persons); infant mortality rate per 1,000 live births 13.5.
Food (1992): daily per capita caloric intake 3,485 (vegetable products 63%, animal products 37%); 133% of FAO recommended minimum.

Military

Total active duty personnel (1996): 248,500 (army 71.9%, navy 7.2%, air force 20.9%). *Military expenditure as percentage of GNP* (1995): 2.5% (world 2.8%); per capita expenditure U.S.$66.

[1]On Jan. 1, 1995, the złoty was redenominated at a rate of 10,000 old złoty to 1 new złoty. [2]January 1. [3]In purchasers' values. [4]Includes import duties and value-added tax. [5]Includes 2,233,000 unemployed. [6]Detail does not add to total given because of rounding.

Portugal

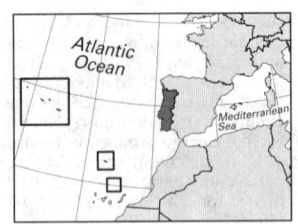

Official name: República Portuguesa (Portuguese Republic).
Form of government: parliamentary state with one legislative house (Assembly of the Republic [230]).
Chief of state: President.
Head of government: Prime Minister.
Capital: Lisbon.
Official language: Portuguese.
Official religion: none.
Monetary unit: 1 escudo (Esc) = 100 centavos; valuation (Oct. 11, 1996) 1 U.S.$ = Esc 154.90; 1 £ = Esc 244.01.

Area and population		area		population
				1993[1]
Continental Portugal Districts	Capitals	sq mi	sq km	estimate
Aveiro	Aveiro	1,081	2,800	658,400
Beja	Beja	3,947	10,223	166,500
Braga	Braga	1,041	2,695	754,700
Bragança	Bragança	2,547	6,597	154,700
Castelo Branco	Castelo Branco	2,555	6,616	211,800
Coimbra	Coimbra	1,533	3,971	425,400
Évora	Évora	2,856	7,396	172,400
Faro	Faro	1,925	4,986	342,000
Guarda	Guarda	2,139	5,540	185,400
Leiria	Leiria	1,354	3,508	426,200
Lisboa	Lisbon (Lisboa)	1,065	2,758	2,048,000
Portalegre	Portalegre	2,341	6,064	132,400
Porto	Porto	904	2,341	1,652,000
Santarém	Santarém	2,590	6,707	441,900
Setúbal	Setúbal	1,955	5,064	716,200
Viana do Castelo	Viana do Castelo	853	2,210	248,300
Vila Real	Vila Real	1,662	4,305	233,100
Viseu	Viseu	1,934	5,009	398,800
Azores (Açores) Autonomous Region	Ponta Delgada	868	2,247	237,800
Madeira Autonomous Region	Funchal	306	794	253,800
TOTAL		35,456[2]	91,831[2]	9,859,600[3]

Demography

Population (1996): 9,927,000.
Density (1996): persons per sq mi 280.0, persons per sq km 108.1.
Urban-rural (1995): urban 35.6%; rural 64.4%.
Sex distribution (1995[1]): male 48.29%; female 51.71%.
Age breakdown (1995): under 15, 18.9%; 15–29, 23.6%; 30–44, 21.6%; 45–59, 16.6%; 60–74, 13.9%; 75 and over, 5.4%.
Population projection: (2000) 9,967,000; (2010) 10,067,000.
Nationality (1990): Portuguese 99.5%; Cape Verdean 0.2%; Brazilian 0.1%; Spanish, British, and American 0.1%; other 0.1%.
Religious affiliation (1981): Christian 96.0%, of which Roman Catholic 94.5%, Protestant 0.6%, other Christian (mostly Apostolic Catholic and Jehovah's Witness) 0.9%; nonreligious 3.8%; Jewish 0.1%; Muslim 0.1%.
Major cities (1991): Lisbon 681,063; Porto 309,485; Vila Nova de Gaia 247,499; Amadora 176,137.

Vital statistics

Birth rate per 1,000 population (1995): 10.8 (world avg. 25.0); (1990) legitimate 85.5%; illegitimate 14.5%.
Death rate per 1,000 population (1995): 10.4 (world avg. 9.3).
Natural increase rate per 1,000 population (1994): 0.4 (world avg. 15.7).
Total fertility rate (avg. births per childbearing woman; 1995): 1.4.
Marriage rate per 1,000 population (1995): 6.6.
Divorce rate per 1,000 population (1995): 1.2.
Life expectancy at birth (1994–95): male 71.5 years; female 78.6 years.
Major causes of death per 100,000 population (1993): circulatory diseases 469.1, of which cerebrovascular diseases 250.6, ischemic heart disease 101.1; malignant neoplasms (cancers) 195.5; respiratory diseases 78.9.

National economy

Budget (1995). Revenue: Esc 6,110,600,000,000 (import duties and excise taxes 36.7%, social security taxes 29.0%, income and inheritance taxes 24.2%). Expenditures: Esc 6,332,900,000,000 (1988: education 12.4%, health 9.8%, defense 6.6%, administration 5.3%, public works 2.8%).
Public debt (1992): U.S.$39,922,000,000.
Production (metric tons except as noted). Agriculture, forestry, fishing (1996): potatoes 1,350,000, grapes 1,000,000, tomatoes 942,000, corn (maize) 750,000, wheat 372,000, olives 230,000, apples 213,000, oranges 160,000, cabbages 140,000, rice 120,000, cork 91,870[4], carrots 83,000; livestock (number of live animals) 6,200,000 sheep, 2,400,000 pigs, 1,316,000 cattle; roundwood (1994) 9,819,000 cu m; fish catch (1993) 274,174. Mining and quarrying (1995): salt 554,647; copper 134,180; kaolin 95,900[4]; tin 8,467; zinc 5,675[5]; tungsten 1,511. Manufacturing (value of production in Esc '000,000; 1991): textiles 227,941; wearing apparel 227,466; food products 188,619; fabricated metal products 147,049; electrical machinery 132,587; tobacco products 99,734; printing and publishing 88,594. Construction (1993): residential 4,793,000 sq m; nonresidential 2,045,167 sq m[6]. Energy production (consumption): electricity (kW-hr; 1994) 31,380,000,000 (32,268,000,000); coal (metric tons; 1994) 147,000 (5,225,000); crude petroleum (barrels; 1994) none (99,069,000); petroleum products (metric tons; 1994) 12,251,000 (10,159,000).
Gross national product (1994): U.S.$92,124,000,000 (U.S.$9,370 per capita).

Structure of gross domestic product and labour force				
	1990		1994	
	in value Esc '000,000	% of total value	labour force	% of labour force
Agriculture	490,787	10.8	490,200	10.8
Mining } Manufacturing	2,275,815	29.2	1,025,800	22.5
Construction	585,382	7.5	330,800	7.2
Public utilities	250,629	3.2	36,700	0.8
Trade	1,352,031	17.4		
Finance	720,037	9.2	1,442,300	31.6
Transp. and commun.	462,412	5.9		
Services } Pub. admin., defense	1,653,845	21.2	925,600	20.3
Other	...	...	310,000[7]	6.8[7]
TOTAL	7,790,937[3]	100.0[3]	4,561,400	100.0

Tourism (1994): receipts U.S.$4,087,000,000; expenditures U.S.$1,705,000,000.
Population economically active (1994): total 4,561,400; activity rate of total population 46.1% (participation rates: ages 15–64, 69.0%[5]; female 44.5%; unemployed 6.8%).

Price and earnings indexes (1990 = 100)							
	1989	1990	1991	1992	1993	1994	1995
Consumer price index	88.2	100.0	111.4	121.3	129.6	136.0	141.5
Annual earnings index[8]	85.0	100.0	114.2	129.8	140.1	146.7	...

Household income and expenditure. Average household size (1991) 3.1; income per household: n.a.; sources of income (1993): wages and salaries 46.4%, property and entrepreneurial income 31.8%, transfer payments 21.8%; expenditure (1986): food 34.7%, transportation and communications 15.4%, clothing and footwear 10.3%, cafes and hotels 9.7%, housing 5.0%, health 4.5%, recreation 4.3%, other 16.1%.
Land use (1994): forested 35.9%; meadows and pastures 10.9%; agricultural and under permanent cultivation 31.5%; other 21.7%.

Foreign trade

Balance of trade (current prices)						
	1990	1991	1992	1993	1994	1995
Esc '000,000	−918,600	−1,067,800	−1,144.6	−1,051.8	−1,099.9	−1,011.4
% of total	16.4%	18.5%	18.8%	17.5%	15.9%	14.7%

Imports (1994): Esc 4,595,200,000,000 (machinery and transport equipment 34.2%, of which road vehicles and parts 15.1%; food and live animals 11.6%; chemicals and chemical products 9.8%; mineral fuels 8.8%; textiles 6.1%; office machines 3.2%). *Major import sources:* Spain 19.8%; Germany 13.8%; France 12.8%; Italy 8.5%; United Kingdom 6.6%; The Netherlands 4.3%.
Exports (1994): Esc 3,057,600,000,000 (textiles and wearing apparel 25.9%; machinery and transport equipment 21.2%, of which transport equipment 6.0%; footwear 8.7%; cork and wood products 6.2%; chemicals and chemical products 4.7%). *Major export destinations:* Germany 18.7%; France 14.7%; Spain 14.4%; United Kingdom 11.7%; United States 5.2%.

Transport and communications

Transport. Railroads (1993): route length 1,906 mi, 3,068 km; passenger-km 4,471,000,000; metric ton-km cargo 1,539,000,000. Roads (1989): total length 43,605 mi, 70,176 km (paved 86%). Vehicles (1994[1]): passenger cars 4,360,447; trucks and buses 219,696. Merchant marine (1992): vessels (100 gross tons and over) 332; total deadweight tonnage 1,129,382. Air transport (1994): passenger-km 7,585,727,000; metric ton-km cargo 180,244,000; airports (1996) 14.
Communications. Daily newspapers (1995): total number 33; total circulation 465,000; circulation per 1,000 population 47. Radio (1993): 2,475,000 receivers (1 per 4.0 persons). Television (1994): 3,007,472 receivers (1 per 3.3 persons). Telephones (main lines; 1993): 3,260,300 (1 per 3.0 persons).

Education and health

Education (1993–94)				student/
	schools	teachers	students	teacher ratio
Primary (age 5–11)	13,263	71,467	929,471	13.0
Secondary (age 12–19)	663	64,479[9, 10]	839,144	14.0[9, 10]
Vocational	214	9	99,509	9
Higher[11]	273	30,998[10]	236,537	6.9[10]

Educational attainment (1981). Percentage of population age 25 and over having: no formal schooling 33.4%; some primary education 55.1%; some secondary 9.3%; postsecondary 2.2%. *Literacy* (1990): total population age 15 and over literate 6,769,270 (86.8%); males literate 3,208,634 (86.7%); females literate 3,560,636 (86.9%).
Health (1993): physicians 28,769 (1 per 343 persons); hospital beds 41,036 (1 per 241 persons); infant mortality rate per 1,000 live births (1995) 7.4.
Food (1992): daily per capita caloric intake 3,634 (vegetable products 74%, animal products 26%); 148% of FAO recommended minimum requirement.

Military

Total active duty personnel (1996): 54,200 (army 54.8%, navy 23.1%, air force 13.5%, paramilitary national guard 8.6%). *Military expenditure as percentage of GNP* (1994): 2.5% (world 3.0%); per capita expenditure U.S.$207.

[1]January 1. [2]Does not include 117 sq mi (304 sq km) of water areas comprising the Tagus and Sado estuaries and the Aveiro Lagoon. [3]Detail does not add to total given because of rounding. [4]1992. [5]1993. [6]1990. [7]Unemployed. [8]Based on average annual wage. [9]Secondary includes Vocational. [10]1992–93. [11]Includes teacher colleges.

Puerto Rico

Official name: Estado Libre Asociado de Puerto Rico; Commonwealth of Puerto Rico.
Political status: self-governing commonwealth in association with the United States, having two legislative houses (Senate [29[1]]; House of Representatives [53[1]]).
Chief of state: President of the United States.
Head of government: Governor.
Capital: San Juan.
Official languages: Spanish; English.
Official religion: none.
Monetary unit: 1 U.S. dollar (U.S.$) = 100 cents; valuation (Oct. 11, 1996) 1 £ = U.S.$1.58.

Population (1995 estimate)

Municipio	population	Municipio	population	Municipio	population
Adjuntas	19,974	Fajardo	37,820	Naguabo	23,894
Aguada	37,775	Florida	8,744	Naranjito	29,625
Aguadilla	66,189	Guánica	21,011	Orocovis	23,465
Agunas Buenas	29,754	Guayama	42,053	Patillas	20,967
Aibonito	26,065	Guayanilla	26,282	Peñuelas	25,716
Añasco	27,065	Guaynabo	103,866	Ponce	190,539
Arecibo	101,050	Gurabo	30,911	Quebradillas	24,490
Arroyo	19,409	Hatillo	38,122	Rincón	13,726
Barceloneta	25,270	Hormigueros	16,627	Río Grande	48,799
Barranquitas	27,945	Humacao	58,613	Sabana Grande	24,308
Bayamón	231,334	Isabela	40,709	Salinas	28,704
Cabo Rojo	45,597	Jayuya	16,612	San Germán	36,968
Caguas	139,778	Juana Díaz	47,475	San Juan	438,078
Camuy	32,181	Juncos	39,897	San Lorenzo	36,324
Canóvanas	49,205	Lajas	26,221	San Sebastián	42,148
Carolina	187,083	Lares	31,970	Santa Isabel	19,536
Cataño	32,663	Las Marías	9,636	Toa Alta	55,338
Cayey	50,414	Las Piedras	30,735	Toa Baja	91,144
Ceiba	18,278	Loíza	28,626	Trujillo Alto	72,320
Ciales	18,474	Luquillo	18,793	Utuado	35,229
Cidra	45,650	Manatí	39,770	Vega Alta	36,084
Coamo	35,326	Maricao	6,032	Vega Baja	60,320
Comerío	20,264	Maunabo	13,844	Vieques	8,975
Corozal	35,812	Mayagüez	101,684	Villalba	23,571
Culebra	1,598	Moca	36,014	Yabucoa	41,027
Dorado	32,121	Morovis	32,272	Yauco	43,219
				TOTAL	3,755,127

Demography

Area: 3,515 sq mi, 9,104 sq km.
Population (1996): 3,766,000.
Density (1996): persons per sq mi 1,071.4, persons per sq km 413.7.
Urban-rural (1990): urban 71.2%; rural 28.8%.
Sex distribution (1992): male 48.43%; female 51.57%.
Age breakdown (1992): under 15, 27.2%; 15–29, 25.1%; 30–44, 20.4%; 45–59, 14.1%; 60–74, 9.2%; 75 and over, 4.0%.
Population projection: (2000) 3,934,000; (2010) 4,386,000.
Doubling time: 69 years.
Ethnic composition (1980): white 80.0%; black 20.0%.
Religious affiliation (1984): Roman Catholic 85.3%; Protestant 4.7%; other 10.0%.
Major cities (1990): San Juan 426,832; Ponce 159,151; Caguas 92,429; Mayagüez 83,010; Arecibo 49,545.

Vital statistics

Birth rate per 1,000 population (1995): 17.4 (world avg. 25.0); (1993) legitimate 59.6%; illegitimate 40.4%.
Death rate per 1,000 population (1995): 7.6 (world avg. 9.3).
Natural increase rate per 1,000 population (1995): 9.8 (world avg. 15.7).
Total fertility rate (avg. births per childbearing woman; 1991): 2.2.
Marriage rate per 1,000 population (1992): 9.6.
Divorce rate per 1,000 population (1992): 4.0.
Life expectancy at birth (1991): male 69.6 years; female 78.5 years.
Major causes of death per 100,000 population (1993): heart disease 142.6; cancers 95.4; diabetes 55.1; cerebrovascular disease 38.0; pneumonia and influenza 29.2.

National economy

Budget. Revenue (1995): U.S.$7,437,900,000 (income taxes 43.6%, excise taxes 17.4%, nontax revenue 5.1%, property taxes 0.8%, other receipts 33.1%). Expenditures (1992): U.S.$5,607,000,000 (education 30.3%, public safety and protection 11.4%, welfare 10.8%, health 10.7%, debt service 6.2%).
Public debt (outstanding; 1995): U.S.$15,993,600,000.
Tourism: receipts from visitors (1995) U.S.$1,826,100,000; expenditures by nationals abroad (1994) U.S.$797,000,000.
Production (in U.S.$'000,000 except as noted). Agriculture, forestry, fishing (gross farm income; 1995): milk 194.9, poultry 94.5, vegetables 81.2, coffee 65.6, beef 37.1, pork 29.0, fruit 29.3, eggs 22.7, sugar 12.0; livestock (number of live animals; 1994) 429,000 cattle, 196,000 pigs; roundwood, n.a.; fish catch (1993) 1,946 metric tons. Mining (value of production in U.S.$'000; 1993): stone 50. Manufacturing (value added in U.S.$'000,000; 1995): chemicals, pharmaceuticals, and allied products 9,164; machinery and metal products 3,393; food products 2,269; clothing 510; printing and publishing 179; stone, clay, and glass products 171. Construction (authorized; 1985): residential 1,798,000 sq m; nonresidential 41,000 sq m. Energy production (consumption): electricity (kW-hr; 1993) 16,540,000,000 (16,540,000,000); coal (metric tons; 1993) none (160,000); crude petroleum (barrels; 1993) none (40,630,-000); petroleum products (metric tons; 1993) 4,977,000 (5,567,000); natural gas, none (none).
Gross national product (1993): U.S.$25,317,000,000 (U.S.$6,700 per capita).

Structure of gross domestic product and labour force

	1995			
	in value U.S.$'000,000	% of total value	labour force	% of labour force
Agriculture	365.6	0.9	34,000	2.8
Manufacturing	17,718.7	41.8	172,000	14.1
Mining } Construction	959.1	2.3	... 57,000	... 4.7
Public utilities } Transp. and commun. }	3,263.8	7.7	17,000 43,000	1.4 3.5
Trade	5,895.1	13.9	211,000	17.3
Finance, real estate	5,451.2	12.9	36,000	2.9
Pub. admin., defense	4,470.5	10.5	233,000	19.1
Services	4,545.5	10.7	249,000	20.4
Other	−305.8[2]	−0.7[2]	168,000[3]	13.8[3]
TOTAL	42,363.7	100.0	1,220,000	100.0

Population economically active (1995): total 1,220,000; activity rate 32.8% (participation rates: ages 16–64, 45.9%; female [1990] 37.1%; unemployed 13.8%).

Price and earnings indexes (1990 = 100)

	1989	1990	1991	1992	1993	1994	1995
Consumer price index	96.1	100.0	105.3	108.1	111.3	114.5	119.1
Hourly earnings index[4]	95.4	100.0	104.1	...	...	...	...

Household income and expenditure (1995). Average family size 3.6; income per family U.S.$27,017; sources of income: wages and salaries 56.3%, transfers 29.5%, self-employment 6.4%, rent 5.2%, other 2.6%; expenditure (1995): food and beverages 20.4%, transportation 13.6%, health care 13.4%, housing and energy 12.2%, household furnishings 12.0%, recreation 8.9%, clothing 7.7%, education 3.1%, other 8.7%.
Land use (1993): forested 16.5%; meadows and pastures 26.2%; agricultural and under permanent cultivation 8.9%; other 48.4%.

Foreign trade

Balance of trade (current prices)

	1990	1991	1992	1993	1994	1995
U.S.$'000,000	+3,584	+5,419	+5,857	+3,405	+5,098	+4,995
% of total	10.2%	14.6%	16.2%	9.4%	13.3%	11.7%

Imports (1995): U.S.$18,816,600,000 (chemicals [all forms] 19.3%, electrical machinery 16.7%, food 10.7%, transport equipment 9.7%, nonelectrical machinery 6.6%, petroleum and petroleum products 5.3%, clothing and textiles 4.2%, professional and scientific instruments 4.1%). *Major import sources* (1990): U.S. 68.7%; Venezuela 4.4%; Japan 3.2%; Dominican Republic 2.0%; The Bahamas 1.8%; U.K. 1.0%.
Exports (1995): U.S.$23,811,300,000 (chemicals and chemical products 46.9%, food 11.9%, electrical machinery 11.6%, nonelectrical machinery 9.6%, computers 8.5%). *Major export destinations* (1990): U.S. 86.9%; Dominican Republic 2.0%; U.S. Virgin Islands 1.4%; U.K. 0.8%; The Netherlands 0.7%.

Transport and communications

Transport. Railroads (1988)[5]: length 59 mi, 96 km. Roads (1994): total length 14,379 mi, 23,140 km (paved 87%). Vehicles (1994): passenger cars 1,432,000; trucks and buses 229,000. Merchant marine: n.a. Air transport (1990–91): passenger arrivals 4,245,137, passenger departures 4,262,164; cargo loaded and unloaded 222,172 metric tons[6]; airports (1996) with scheduled flights 7.
Communications. Daily newspapers (1994): total number 3; total circulation 506,930; circulation per 1,000 population 138. Radio (1995): 2,480,000 receivers (1 per 1.5 persons). Television (1995): 830,000 receivers (1 per 4.5 persons). Telephones (main lines, 1993): 1,207,200 (1 per 3.0 persons).

Education and health

Education (1985–86)

	schools	teachers	students	student/ teacher ratio
Primary (age 5–12)	1,542	18,359	427,582	23.3
Secondary (age 13–18)	395	13,612	334,661	24.6
Voc., teacher tr.	52	...	149,191	...
Higher	45	9,045	156,818	17.3

Educational attainment (1990). Percentage of population age 25 and over having: primary education 26.8%; some secondary 23.5%; complete secondary 21.0%; higher 28.7%. *Literacy* (1990): total population age 18 and over literate 2,122,860 (89.7%); males literate 1,001,878 (89.6%); females literate 1,120,982 (89.7%).
Health: physicians (1988) 9,422 (1 per 349 persons); hospital beds (1993–94) 9,598 (1 per 381 persons); infant mortality rate (1994) 11.5.

Military

Total active duty personnel (1992): 3,518 U.S. personnel.

---

[1]Includes (each house) 2 special at-large seats above usual legally mandated membership of body that were created under a constitutional provision to limit majority party's control of either house to two-thirds. [2]Statistical discrepancy. [3]Unemployed. [4]Manufacturing sector only. [5]Privately owned railway for sugarcane transport only. [6]Handled by the Luis Muñoz Marín International Airport only.

Qatar

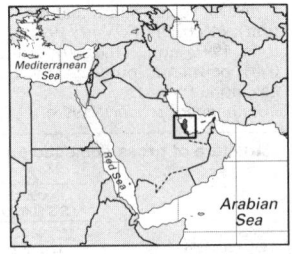

Official name: Dawlat Qaṭar (State of Qatar).
Form of government: monarchy (emirate)[1]; Islamic law is the basis of legislation in the state.
Head of state and government: Emir.
Capital: Doha.
Official language: Arabic.
Official religion: Islam.
Monetary unit: 1 riyal (QR) = 100 dirhams; valuation (Oct. 11, 1996) 1 U.S.$ = QR 3.64; 1 £ = QR 5.73.

Area and population		area		population
				1992
Municipalities	Capitals	sq mi	sq km	estimate
Ad-Dawḥah (Doha)	—	51	132	313,639
Al-Ghuwayrīyah	Al-Ghuwayrīyah	241	622	2,349
Jarayān al-Bāṭinah	Jarayān al-Bāṭinah	1,434	3,715	3,932
Al-Jumaylīyah	Al-Jumaylīyah	990[2]	2,565[2]	10,414
Al-Khawr	Al-Khawr	385	996	12,982
Ar-Rayyān	Ar-Rayyān	343	889	132,785
Ash-Shamāl	Madinat ash-Shamāl	348	901	6,323
Umm Ṣalāl	Umm Ṣalāl Muḥammad	190	493	16,110
Al-Wakrah	Al-Wakrah	430	1,114	34,185
TOTAL		4,416[3]	11,437[3]	532,719

Demography

Population (1996): 590,000.
Density (1996): persons per sq mi 133.6, persons per sq km 51.6.
Urban-rural (1995): urban 91.4%; rural 8.5%.
Sex distribution (1994): male 64.98%; female 35.02%.
Age breakdown (1994): under 15, 26.2%; 15–29, 21.5%; 30–44, 38.5%; 45–59, 11.7%; 60–74, 1.7%; 75 and over, 0.3%.
Population projection: (2000) 632,718; (2010) 754,805.
Doubling time: 44 years.
Ethnic composition (1995): Arab 40%; other (Pakistanis, Indians, and Iranians) 60%.
Religious affiliation (1995): Muslim (mostly Sunnī) 95%; other 5%.
Major cities (1987): Doha 236,131; Ar-Rayyān 99,939; Al-Wakrah 25,747; Umm Sa'īd 12,111.

Vital statistics

Birth rate per 1,000 population (1994): 17.8 (world avg. 25.0); legitimate, n.a.; illegitimate, n.a.
Death rate per 1,000 population (1994): 1.6 (world avg. 9.3).
Natural increase rate per 1,000 population (1994): 16.2 (world avg. 15.7).
Total fertility rate (avg. births per childbearing woman; 1994): 2.8.
Marriage rate per 1,000 population (1994): 2.8.
Divorce rate per 1,000 population (1994): 1.0.
Life expectancy at birth (1994): male 70.0 years; female 74.5 years.
Major causes of death per 100,000 population (1992): diseases of the circulatory system 56.9; injuries and poisoning 36.0; neoplasms (including benign neoplasms) 21.4; certain conditions originating in the perinatal period 11.1; diseases of the respiratory system 7.5; endocrine, metabolic, and nutritional diseases and immunity disorders 7.3; diseases of the digestive system 3.4; signs, symptoms, and ill-defined conditions 10.9.

National economy

Budget (1995–96)[4]. Revenue: QR 9,204,000,000 (crude oil about 75%). Expenditures: QR 12,731,000,000 (1994–95; wages and salaries 44.4%, state capital-development projects 41.7%, social and health services 8.1%, education 2.7%).
Public debt (external, outstanding; 1995): U.S.$3,900,000,000.
Production (metric tons except as noted). Agriculture, forestry, fishing (value of production in QR '000; 1994): milk and dairy products 142,898, forage 93,293, vegetables and other crops (except cereals) 73,172, beef 47,854, fruits and dates 29,413, poultry meat 28,036, eggs 12,345, cereals 1,748; livestock (number of live animals; 1995) 185,000 sheep, 160,000 goats, 46,500 camels, 13,000 cattle; roundwood, n.a.; fish catch (1993) 6,994. Mining and quarrying (1993): limestone 900,000; sulfur 60,000; gypsum, sand and gravel, and clay are also produced. Manufacturing (value added in QR; 1993): chemical products 2,698,700,000; metal products 799,700,000; nonmetallic mineral products 541,200,000; textiles and apparel 286,600,000; food, beverages, and tobacco 275,200,000; wood products and furniture 163,500,000; paper products 125,600,000. Construction (1992): residential 12,420 units; nonresidential 1,416 units. Energy production (consumption): electricity (kW-hr; 1994) 5,850,000,000 (5,850,000,000); coal, none (n.a.); crude petroleum (barrels; 1995) 159,870,000 (1994; 21,450,000); petroleum products (metric tons; 1994) 5,219,000 (701,000); natural gas (cu m; 1994) 13,500,000,000 (13,500,000,000).
Tourism (1993): receipts and expenditures, n.a.; total number of tourists staying in hotels 160,000.
Population economically active (1988): total 292,568; activity rate of total population 53.7% (participation rates: ages 15–64, 80.8%; female 11.2%; unemployed [1986] 0.5%).

Price and earnings indexes (1990 = 100)							
	1988	1989	1990	1991	1992	1993	1994
Consumer price index	94.0	97.1	100.0	104.4	107.5	110.9	114.2
Earnings index	...	...	...	...	...	...	...

Gross national product (at current market prices; 1994): U.S.$7,810,000,000 (U.S.$14,540 per capita).

Structure of gross domestic product and labour force				
	1994[4]		1988	
	in value QR '000,000	% of total value	labour force	% of labour force
Agriculture	290	1.1	4,544	1.6
Oil sector	8,100	31.0	7,657	2.6
Manufacturing	3,275	12.6	10,627	3.6
Construction	1,280	4.9	64,213	21.9
Public utilities	345	1.3	3,672	1.3
Transportation	965	3.7	11,877	4.1
Trade	1,830	7.0	34,246	11.7
Finance	3,065	11.8	6,172	2.1
Pub. admin., defense Services	} 6,950	26.6	149,560	51.1
Other				
TOTAL	26,100	100.0	292,568	100.0

Household income and expenditure. Average household size (1986) 6.4; income per household: n.a.; sources of income (1988): wages and salaries 80.8%, rents and royalties 10.6%, self-employment 5.6%, other 3.0%; expenditure (1993): food 28.7%, transportation 19.3%, housing 12.4%, clothing 10.6%, education 7.6%, health 1.2%.
Land use (1994): meadows and pastures 4.5%; agricultural and under permanent cultivation 0.7%; built-up, desert, and other 94.7%.

Foreign trade

Balance of trade (current prices)[5]					
	1989	1990	1991	1992	1993	1994
QR '000,000	+4,827	+7,992	+5,423	+6,644	+4,931	+5,451
% of total	33.9%	39.3%	30.2%	31.2%	26.4%	30.4%

Imports (1994): QR 7,016,000,000 (machinery and transport equipment 39.7%, manufactured goods 21.8%, food and live animals 13.2%, chemicals and chemical products 7.0%, raw materials 3.4%). *Major import sources:* Japan 13.4%; United States 10.6%; United Kingdom 10.3%; United Arab Emirates 6.9%; Germany 6.6%; Saudi Arabia 5.0%; Italy 4.3%; France 3.9%.
Exports (1994): QR 11,453,000,000 (mineral fuels and lubricants 81.2%, chemicals and chemical products 10.4%, manufactured goods 5.9%). *Major export destinations* (1989): Japan 54.4%; Thailand 5.0%; Singapore 4.0%; South Korea 3.6%; United Arab Emirates 3.4%; Italy 2.7%; India 2.7%; Saudi Arabia 2.5%.

Transport and communications

Transport. Railroads: none. Roads (1988): total length 671 mi, 1,080 km (paved 63%). Vehicles (1994): passenger cars 125,700; trucks and buses 63,800. Merchant marine (1992): vessels (100 gross tons and over) 65; total deadweight tonnage 635,580. Air transport (1995)[6]: passenger-mi 1,719,000,-000, passenger-km 2,766,000,000; short ton-mi cargo 77,400,000, metric ton-km cargo 113,000,000; airports (1996) with scheduled flights 1.
Communications. Daily newspapers (1992): total number 4; total circulation 70,000; circulation per 1,000 population 155. Radio (1995): total number of receivers 180,000 (1 per 3.2 persons). Television (1995): total number of receivers 250,500 (1 per 2.3 persons). Telephones (main lines; 1994): 130,000 (1 per 4.4 persons).

Education and health

Education (1993–94)[7]				student/
	schools	teachers	students	teacher ratio
Primary (age 6–11)	158	5,656	52,016	9.2
Secondary (age 12–17)	36[8]	3,695	35,518	9.6
Vocational	3[8]	128	774	6.0
Higher	1[8]	636	7,351	11.6

Educational attainment (1986). Percentage of population age 25 and over having: no formal education 53.3%, of which illiterate 24.3%; primary 9.8%; preparatory (lower secondary) 10.1%; secondary 13.3%; postsecondary 13.3%; other 0.2%. *Literacy* (1995): total population age 15 and over literate 460,000 (79.4%); males literate 298,000 (79.2%); females literate 122,000 (79.9%).
Health (1994): physicians 718 (1 per 793 persons); hospital beds 1,118 (1 per 509 persons); infant mortality rate per 1,000 live births 17.6.
Food: daily per capita caloric intake, n.a.

Military

Total active duty personnel (1996): 11,800 (army 72.0%, navy 15.3%, air force 12.7%). *Military expenditure as percentage of GNP* (1994): 3.9% (world 3.0%); per capita expenditure U.S.$582.

[1]Provisional constitution of 1970 provided limited constitutional forms but has not been fully implemented. [2]Includes area of unpopulated Hawar Islands (also claimed by Bahrain). [3]Includes approximately 4 sq mi (10 sq km) of area not distributed by municipalities. [4]Preliminary estimates. [5]After 1992, balance based on f.o.b. valuation of imports. [6]One-fourth apportionment of international flights of Gulf Air. [7]Public schools only; available detail for private schools (1991–92) included 17,728 primary students, 1,695 secondary students, and 1,465 teachers. [8]1992–93.

Réunion

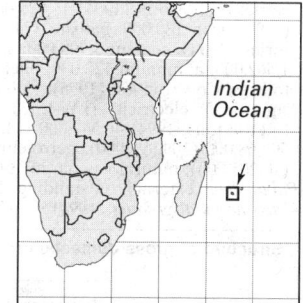

Indian Ocean

Official name: Département de la Réunion (Department of Réunion).
Political status: overseas department (France) with two legislative houses (General Council [47]; Regional Council [45]).
Chief of state: President of France.
Heads of government: Prefect (for France); President of General Council (for Réunion); President of Regional Council (for Réunion).
Capital: Saint-Denis.
Official language: French.
Official religion: none.
Monetary unit: 1 French franc (F) = 100 centimes; valuation (Oct. 11, 1996) 1 U.S.$ = F 5.18; 1 £ = F 8.16.

Area and population

Arrondissements	Capitals	area sq mi	area sq km	population 1990 census
Saint-Benoît	Saint-Benoît	284	736	85,132
Saint-Denis	Saint-Denis	164	423	207,158
Saint-Paul	Saint-Paul	180	467	113,071
Saint-Pierre	Saint-Pierre	339	878	192,462
TOTAL		970[1,2]	2,512[1,2]	597,823

Demography

Population (1996): 671,000.
Density (1996): persons per sq mi 691.8, persons per sq km 267.1.
Urban-rural (1995): urban 67.8%; rural 32.2%.
Sex distribution (1995): male 49.00%; female 51.00%.
Age breakdown (1995): under 15, 29.4%; 15–29, 27.7%; 30–44, 21.7%; 45–59, 12.2%; 60–74, 6.9%; 75 and over, 2.1%.
Population projection: (2000) 722,000; (2010) 866,000.
Doubling time: 46 years.
Ethnic composition (1983): mixed race 63.5%; East Indian 28.2%; Chinese 2.2%; white 1.9%; East African 1.1%; other 3.1%.
Religious affiliation (1993): Roman Catholic 88.3%; other (mostly Muslim) 11.7%.
Major cities (1990): Saint-Denis (1994) 104,454[3]; Le Port 29,190; Le Tampon 27,300; Saint-André 25,237; Saint-Pierre 23,899.

Vital statistics

Birth rate per 1,000 population (1994): 20.6 (world avg. 25.0); (1993) legitimate 46.0%; illegitimate 54.0%.
Death rate per 1,000 population (1994): 5.4 (world avg. 9.3).
Natural increase rate per 1,000 population (1994): 15.2 (world avg. 15.7).
Total fertility rate (avg. births per childbearing woman; 1994): 2.3.
Marriage rate per 1,000 population (1993): 5.5.
Divorce rate per 1,000 population (1993): 1.5.
Life expectancy at birth (1994): male 71.0 years; female 77.0 years.
Major causes of death per 100,000 population (1992): diseases of the circulatory system 173.0; malignant neoplasms (cancers) 87.2; diseases of the digestive system (including all deaths associated with alcoholism) 60.3; diseases of the respiratory system 43.1; homicide and violence 26.6.

National economy

Budget (1995). Revenue: F 4,067,000,000 (receipts from the French central government and local administrative bodies 49.8%, subsidies and related receipts 12.8%, new loans 8.6%). Expenditures: F 4,066,000,000 (current expenditures 69.0%, development expenditures 31.0%).
Public debt (external, outstanding; 1990)[4]: U.S.$61,000,000.
Tourism (1994): receipts U.S.$163,000,000; expenditures, n.a.
Gross national product (at current market prices; 1992): U.S.$5,500,000,000 (U.S.$8,800 per capita).

Structure of gross domestic product and labour force

	1992 in value F '000,000	1992 % of total value	1994 labour force	1994 % of labour force
Agriculture, fishing	1,200	3.6	12,015	5.0
Manufacturing	3,100	9.2	9,854	4.1
Construction	2,100	6.2	16,711	7.0
Public utilities	1,300	3.9	...	...
Transportation and communications	2,000[5]	6.0[5]	5,495	2.3
Trade, restaurants	6,000[5]	17.9[5]	22,587	9.4
Finance, real estate, business services	7,200	21.4	11,148	4.7
Pub. admin., defense	10,700	31.8	23,678	9.9
Services			50,986	21.3
Other	—	—	86,905[6]	36.3[6]
TOTAL	33,600	100.0	239,379	100.0

Production (metric tons except as noted). Agriculture, forestry, fishing (1995): sugarcane 1,817,000, corn (maize) 16,700, potatoes 15,000, pe-tsai (Chinese cabbage) and black nightshade 8,291[7], pineapples 6,300, green onions and shallots 5,800, bananas 4,000, tomatoes 4,000, eggplants 3,200, pimento 430, ginger 95, vanilla 33[8], tobacco 20, geranium essence 5.2; livestock (number of live animals) 83,000 pigs, 32,000 goats, 26,200 cattle; roundwood (1994) 36,000

cu m; fish (value of catch in F '000,000; 1994) lobster 40[9], other 44. Mining and quarrying: gravel and sand for local use. Manufacturing (value added in F '000,000; 1993): construction materials (mostly cement) 372; alcoholic and nonalcoholic beverages (excluding milk) 204; printing and publishing 192; fabricated metals 189; milk products 153. Construction (value of public construction; 1994): residential F 741,600,000; nonresidential, n.a. Energy production (consumption): electricity (kW-hr; 1995) 1,298,000,000 ([1994] 1,056,000,000); coal, none (none); crude petroleum, none (none); petroleum products (metric tons; 1995) none (507,000); natural gas, none (none).
Population economically active (1993): total 234,576; activity rate of total population 36.9% (participation rates: ages 15–64, 56.7%; female 41.7%; unemployed [January–March 1996] 38.5%).

Price and earnings indexes (December 1992 = 100)[10]

	1990	1991	1992	1993	1994	1995	1996[11]
Consumer price index	94.4	97.3	100.0	102.4	105.0	107.1	108.9
Monthly earnings index[12]	91.6	97.4	100.0	101.7	104.1	106.8	106.8

Household income and expenditure. Average household size (1994) 3.5; income per household (1994) F 114,900 (U.S.$20,695); sources of income (1994): wages and salaries and self-employment 68.9%, transfer payments 16.0%, interest, dividends, and self-employment 15.1%; expenditure (1986–87): transportation and communications 24.9%, food and beverages 22.4%, housing 11.8%, recreation and education 10.1%, clothing and footwear 7.9%, household furnishings 6.0%, other 16.9%.
Land use (1994): forested 35.2%; meadows and pastures 4.8%; agricultural and under permanent cultivation 19.6%; other 40.4%.

Foreign trade

Balance of trade (current prices)

	1990	1991	1992	1993	1994	1995
F '000,000	−10,747	−11,975	−11,542	−10,859	−12,109	−12,460
% of total	84.1%	87.6%	83.9%	84.5%	86.4%	85.8%

Imports (1995): F 13,495,000,000 (consumer goods 25.3%, food and agricultural products 20.1%, transport equipment 14.2%, fabricated metals 7.0%, mineral fuels 4.7%). *Major import sources* (1994): France 66.8%; other EC countries 12.3%; Bahrain 3.5%.
Exports (1995): F 1,035,000,000 (food products [mostly sugar; also includes lobster, rum, and geranium essence] 78.4%, machinery and apparatus 9.9%, transport equipment 4.5%). *Major export destinations* (1994): France 74.3%; other EC countries 6.0%.

Transport and communications

Transport. Railroads:[13]. Roads (1994): total length 1,711 mi, 2,754 km (paved [1991] 79%). Vehicles (1994): passenger cars 181,800; trucks and buses 61,700. Merchant marine (1992): vessels (100 gross tons and over) 7; total deadweight tonnage 33,476. Air transport (1995): passenger arrivals 566,668, passenger departures 562,605; cargo unloaded 13,526 metric tons, cargo loaded 4,605 metric tons; airports (1996) with scheduled flights 1.
Communications. Daily newspapers (1992): total number 3; total circulation 55,000; circulation per 1,000 population 88. Radio (1995): total number of receivers 170,000 (1 per 3.9 persons). Television (1995): total number of receivers 90,500 (1 per 7.3 persons). Telephones (main lines; 1993): 198,500 (1 per 3.2 persons).

Education and health

Education (1994–95)

	schools	teachers	students	student/teacher ratio
Primary (age 6–10)	343	...	73,220	...
Secondary (age 11–17)	102	4,591[14]	74,827[14]	16.3[14]
Voc., teacher tr.		1,108[14]	13,778[14]	12.4[14]
Higher[15]	1	242	8,058	33.3

Educational attainment (1986–87). Percentage of population age 25 and over having: no formal schooling 18.8%; primary education 44.3%; lower secondary 21.6%; upper secondary 11.0%; higher 4.3%. *Literacy* (1986–87): total population age 15 and over literate 298,965 (78.2%); males literate 141,006 (75.9%); females literate 157,959 (80.3%).
Health (1994): physicians 1,061 (1 per 605 persons); hospital beds 2,858 (1 per 225 persons); infant mortality rate per 1,000 live births 8.0.
Food (1992): daily per capita caloric intake 3,245 (vegetable products 77%, animal products 23%); 143% of FAO recommended minimum requirement.

Military

Total active duty personnel (1995): 4,000 French troops[16].

---

[1]Includes 3 sq mi (8 sq km) not distributed by arrondissement. [2]Indian Ocean islets administered by France from Réunion are excluded from total. Areas of these islets, which have no permanent population, are: Îles Glorieuses 1.7 sq mi (4.3 sq km), Île Juan de Nova 1.9 sq mi (4.8 sq km), Île Tromelin 0.3 sq mi (0.8 sq km), Bassas da India 0.1 sq mi (0.2 sq km), Île Europa 7.8 sq mi (20.2 sq km). [3]Urban population. [4]Includes long-term private debt not guaranteed by the government. [5]Transportation and communications includes hotels and restaurants. [6]Includes 2,621 not adequately defined and 84,284 unemployed. [7]1992. [8]1994. [9]Lobster are trapped around the islands of Saint-Paul and Nouvelle Amsterdam in the overseas territory of French Southern and Antarctic Lands. [10]Indexes refer to December. [11]March. [12]Minimum monthly wage in public administration. [13]No public railways; railways in use are for sugar industry. [14]1993–94. [15]University only. [16]Includes troops stationed on Mayotte.

Romania

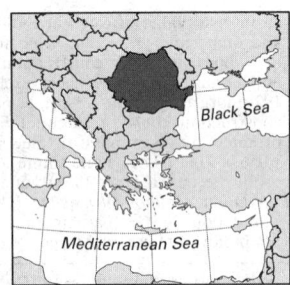

Official name: România (Romania).
Form of government: unitary republic
with two legislative houses (Senate
[143]; Assembly of Deputies [341[1]]).
Chief of state: President.
Head of government: Prime Minister.
Capital: Bucharest.
Official language: Romanian.
Official religion: none.
Monetary unit: 1 Romanian leu (plural
lei) = 100 bani; valuation (Oct. 11,
1996) 1 U.S.$ = 3,285 lei;
1 £ = 5,175 lei.

Area and population

Counties	Capitals	area sq mi	area sq km	population 1994 estimate
Alba	Alba Iulia	2,410	6,242	408,457
Arad	Arad	2,994	7,754	482,144
Argeş	Piteşti	2,636	6,826	679,868
Bacău	Bacău	2,556	6,621	742,901
Bihor	Oradea	2,913	7,544	633,629
Bistriţa-Năsăud	Bistriţa	2,068	5,355	328,786
Botoşani	Botoşani	1,925	4,986	462,370
Brăila	Brăila	1,840	4,766	391,923
Braşov	Braşov	2,071	5,363	642,764
Buzău	Buzău	2,356	6,103	515,202
Călăraşi	Călăraşi	1,964	5,088	336,657
Caraş-Severin	Reşiţa	3,290	8,520	370,058
Cluj	Cluj-Napoca	2,577	6,674	727,033
Constanţa	Constanţa	2,730	7,071	747,441
Covasna	Sfântu Gheorghe	1,432	3,710	232,951
Dâmboviţa	Târgovişte	1,565	4,054	558,518
Dolj	Craiova	2,863	7,414	758,895
Galaţi	Galaţi	1,724	4,466	642,983
Giurgiu	Giurgiu	1,361	3,526	305,661
Gorj	Târgu Jiu	2,163	5,602	397,927
Harghita	Miercurea-Ciuc	2,563	6,639	347,145
Hunedoara	Deva	2,727	7,063	547,180
Ialomiţa	Slobozia	1,719	4,453	305,454
Iaşi	Iaşi	2,114	5,476	815,368
Maramureş	Baia Mare	2,434	6,304	539,718
Mehedinţi	Drobeta-Turnu Severin	1,905	4,933	330,017
Mureş	Târgu Mureş	2,592	6,714	607,355
Neamţ	Piatra Neamţ	2,276	5,896	584,364
Olt	Slatina	2,123	5,498	520,871
Prahova	Ploieşti	1,821	4,716	874,219
Sălaj	Zalău	1,492	3,864	264,448
Satu Mare	Satu Mare	1,706	4,418	398,401
Sibiu	Sibiu	2,097	5,432	448,474
Suceava	Suceava	3,302	8,553	708,571
Teleorman	Alexandria	2,236	5,790	477,527
Timiş	Timişoara	3,358	8,697	691,797
Tulcea	Tulcea	3,281	8,499	269,311
Vâlcea	Râmnicu Vâlcea	2,226	5,765	436,989
Vaslui	Vaslui	2,053	5,318	463,832
Vrancea	Focşani	1,875	4,857	394,257
Muncipality				
Bucharest	Bucharest	703	1,821	2,339,156
TOTAL		92,043[2]	238,391	22,730,622

Demography

Population (1996): 22,670,000.
Density (1996): persons per sq mi 247.2, persons per sq km 95.4.
Urban-rural (1995): urban 55.4%; rural 44.6%.
Sex distribution (1995): male 49.27%; female 50.73%.
Age breakdown (1995): under 15, 20.4%; 15–29, 25.0%; 30–44, 20.5%; 45–59, 16.9%; 60–74, 13.6%; 75 and over, 3.6%.
Population projection: (2000) 22,615,000; (2010) 22,481,000.
Ethnic composition (1992): Romanian 89.4%; Hungarian 7.1%; Gypsy (Tigani) 1.8%; German 0.5%; Ukrainian 0.3%; other 0.9%.
Religious affiliation (1992): Romanian Orthodox 86.8%; Roman Catholic 5.0%; Greek Orthodox 3.5%; Pentecostal 1.0%; Muslim 0.2%; other 3.5%.
Major cities (1994): Bucharest 2,080,363; Constanţa 348,575; Iaşi 339,889; Timişoara 327,830; Galaţi 326,728; Cluj-Napoca 326,017; Braşov 324,210.

Vital statistics

Birth rate per 1,000 population (1995): 10.4 (world avg. 25.0).
Death rate per 1,000 population (1995): 12.0 (world avg. 9.3).
Natural increase rate per 1,000 population (1995): −1.6 (world avg. 15.7).
Total fertility rate (avg. births per childbearing woman; 1993): 1.5.
Marriage rate per 1,000 population (1994): 6.8.
Divorce rate per 1,000 population (1990): 1.4.
Life expectancy at birth (1995): male 69.3 years; female 75.4 years.
Major causes of death per 100,000 population (1992): circulatory disease 707.7; cancers 163.4; respiratory disease 94.0; diseases of the digestive system 57.9.

National economy

Budget (1994). Revenue: 8,318,838,000,000 lei (value-added tax 27.3%, corporate tax 22.9%, personal income tax 21.1%, customs 6.8%). Expenditures: 10,930,320,000,000 lei (culture 15.0%, defense 10.8%, health 9.1%, interest 5.8%).
Tourism (1994): receipts U.S.$414,000,000; expenditures U.S.$449,000,000.
Production (metric tons). Agriculture (1996): corn (maize) 10,000,000, potatoes 3,200,000, wheat 3,168,000, sugar beets 2,774,000, grapes 1,314,000, sunflower seeds 1,300,000, barley 1,140,000, cabbages 824,000, tomatoes 731,000; livestock (number of live animals) 10,381,000 sheep, 7,960,000 pigs, 3,496,000

cattle; roundwood (1994) 11,925,000 cu m; fish catch (1993) 34,919. Mining (1995): iron 180,000; bauxite 174,000; zinc 34,680; copper 24,000. Manufacturing (1994): cement 5,998,000; steel 5,800,000; pig iron 3,496,000; fertilizer 1,562,000; aluminum 122,000; beer 9,046,000 hectolitres; wine 8,425,000 hectolitres. Construction (1995): 9,300 dwelling units. Energy production (consumption): electricity (kW-hr; 1994) 55,136,000,000 (55,861,000,000); coal (metric tons; 1994) 40,547,000 (44,893,000); crude petroleum (barrels; 1994) 50,568,000 (109,995,000); petroleum products (metric tons; 1994) 13,066,000 (10,291,000); natural gas (cu m; 1994) 15,868,000,000 (20,214,000,000).
Public debt (external, outstanding; 1994): U.S.$2,942,000,000.
Gross national product (1994): U.S.$27,921,000,000 (U.S.$2,650 per capita).

Structure of gross domestic product and labour force

	1994 in value '000,000,000 lei	% of total value	labour force	% of labour force
Agriculture	10,001	20.1	3,653,000	32.5
Mining, manufacturing, and public utilities	16,091	32.3	2,881,700	25.6
Construction	3,010	6.0	562,700	5.0
Transp. and commun.	4,934	9.9	556,000	4.9
Trade	5,806	11.7	772,300	6.9
Finance	} 8,263	} 16.6	59,100	0.5
Pub. admin.			1,526,800	13.6
Services				
Other	1,690	3.4	1,237,400[3]	11.0[3]
TOTAL	49,795	100.0	11,249,000	100.0

Population economically active (1994): total 11,237,400; activity rate 49.4% (participation rates: ages 15–64, 67.2%[4]; female 44.2%[4]; unemployed 11.0%).

Price and earnings indexes (1990 = 100)

	1989	1990	1991	1992	1993	1994	1995
Consumer price index	96.0	100.0	274.4	854.0	3,033.1	7,181.2	9,496.6
Annual earnings index	90.5	100.0	221.3	597.4	1,804.8	4,142.0	...

Household income and expenditure. Average household size (1992) 3.1; income per household (1989) 73,500 lei (U.S.$4,940); sources of income (1982): wages 62.6%; expenditure (1989): food 51.1%, housing 16.4%, clothing 15.7%.
Land use (1994): forest 29.0%; pasture 21.2%; agricultural 43.1%; other 6.7%.

Foreign trade

Balance of trade (current prices)

	1990	1991	1992	1993	1994	1995
U.S.$'000,000	−3,244	−1,182	−1,420.5	−1,127.8	−411.1	−1,150.5
% of total	21.7%	12.5%	14.0%	10.3%	3.2%	7.1%

Imports (1994): 11,919,074,000,000 lei (machinery and transport equipment 47.2%, mineral fuels 23.7%, textiles 11.4%, chemicals 7.9%). *Major import sources:* Germany 18.0%; Russia 13.8%; Italy 11.8%; U.S. 6.5%; Iran 6.2%; France 5.1%.
Exports (1994): 10,272,827,000,000 lei (machinery 29.4%, textiles 18.8%, iron and steel 11.6%, mineral fuels 9.9%, chemicals 8.0%). *Major export destinations:* Germany 16.1%; Italy 12.9%; France 5.1%; China 4.5%; Turkey 4.1%.

Transport and communications

Transport. Railroads (1995): length 7,062 mi[5], 11,365 km[5]; passenger-km 18,880,000,000; metric ton-km cargo 27,180,000,000. Roads (1992): length 95,099 mi, 153,014 km (paved 51%). Vehicles (1994): cars 2,020,017; trucks and buses 370,239. Merchant marine (1992): vessels (100 gross tons and over) 439; total deadweight tonnage 4,845,539. Air transport (1994): passenger-km 2,580,000,000; metric ton-km cargo 19,404,000; airports (1996) 12.
Communications. Daily newspapers (1992): total number 76; total circulation 7,500,000; circulation per 1,000 population 324. Radios (1993): 4,640,000 (1 per 4.9 persons). Televisions (1993): 4,580,000 (1 per 5.0 persons). Telephones (main lines; 1993): 2,623,700 subscribers (1 per 8.7 persons).

Education and health

Education (1994–95)

	schools	teachers	students	student/ teacher ratio
Primary (age 6–9)[6]	13,963	168,702	2,532,169	15.0
Secondary (age 10–17)[7]	1,276	60,514	757,673	12.5
Voc., teacher tr.	1,530	9,360	345,394	36.9
Higher	63	20,452	255,162	12.5

Educational attainment (1992). Percentage of population age 25 and over having: no schooling 5.4%; some primary education 24.4%; some secondary 63.2%; postsecondary 6.9%. *Literacy* (1992): total population age 15 and over literate 16,920,000 (96.7%); males literate 8,280,000 (98.5%); females literate 8,640,000 (95.0%).
Health: physicians (1993) 40,265 (1 per 565 persons); hospital beds (1992) 215,629 (1 per 105 persons); infant mortality rate (1995) 21.2.
Food (1994): daily per capita caloric intake 2,953 (vegetable products 76%[4], animal products 24%[4]); 111% of FAO recommended minimum requirement.

Military

Total active duty personnel (1996): 228,400 (army 56.8%, navy 8.1%, air force 20.8%, other 14.3%). *Military expenditure as percentage of GNP* (1994): 2.6% (world 3.0%); per capita expenditure U.S.$75.

[1]Includes 13 nonelective seats. [2]Detail does not add to total given because of rounding. [3]Unemployed. [4]1992. [5]1994. [6]Includes lower secondary. [7]Upper secondary only.

Russia

Official name: Rossiyskaya Federatsiya (Russian Federation).
Form of government: federal multiparty republic with a bicameral legislative body (Federal Assembly comprising a Federation Council [178] and a State Duma [450]).
Head of state: President.
Head of government: Prime Minister.
Capital: Moscow.
Official language: Russian.
Official religion: none.
Monetary unit: 1 ruble (Rub) = 100 kopecks; valuation (Oct. 11, 1996) market rate, 1 U.S.$ = Rub 5,437; 1 £ = Rub 8,564.

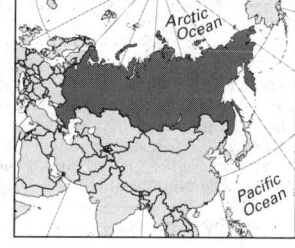

Area and population		area		population
				1995[1]
Federal Republics Other entities	Capitals	sq mi	sq km	estimate
Adygea	Maykop	2,900	7,600	450,000
Bashkortostan	Ufa	55,400	143,600	4,080,000
Buryatia	Ulan-Ude	135,600	351,300	1,053,000
Chechnia (Chechnya)[2, 3]	...	4	4	4
Chuvashia	Cheboksary	7,100	18,300	1,361,000
Dagestan	Makhachkala	19,400	50,300	2,067,000
Gorno-Altay	Gorno-Altaisk	35,700	92,600	200,000
Ingushetia[2]	Grozny	7,400[4]	19,300[4]	1,185,000[4]
Kabardino-Balkaria	Nalchik	4,800	12,500	790,000
Kalmykia (Khalmg Tangch)	Elista	29,400	76,100	320,000
Karachay-Cherkessia	Cherkessk	5,400	14,100	436,000
Karelia	Petrozavodsk	66,600	172,400	788,000
Khakassia	Abakan	23,900	61,900	585,000
Komi	Syktyvkar	160,600	415,900	1,202,000
Mari El	Yoshkar-Ola	9,000	23,200	766,000
Mordvinia	Saransk	10,100	26,200	960,000
North Ossetia	Vladikavkaz	3,100	8,000	658,000
Russia	Moscow	4,709,800[5]	12,198,300	124,527,000
Regions (Oblasts)				
Amur[6]	Blagoveshchensk	140,400	363,700	1,041,000
Arkhangelsk	Arkhangelsk	226,800	587,400	1,535,000
Astrakhan	Astrakhan	17,000	44,100	1,024,000
Belgorod	Belgorod	10,500	27,100	1,458,000
Bryansk	Bryansk	13,500	34,900	1,480,000
Chelyabinsk	Chelyabinsk	33,900	87,900	3,700,000
Chita	Chita	166,600	431,500	1,299,000
Irkutsk	Irkutsk	296,500	767,900	2,805,000
Ivanovo	Ivanovo	9,200	23,900	1,275,000
Kaliningrad[6]	Kaliningrad	5,800	15,100	926,400
Kaluga	Kaluga	11,500	29,900	1,095,000
Kamchatka	Petropavlovsk-Kamchatsky	182,400	472,300	424,000
Kemerovo	Kemerovo	36,900	95,500	3,078,000
Kirov	Kirov	46,600	120,800	1,645,000
Kostroma	Kostroma	23,200	60,100	809,000
Kurgan	Kurgan	27,400	71,000	1,117,000
Kursk	Kursk	11,500	29,800	1,349,000
Leningrad	St. Petersburg	33,200[7]	85,900[7]	1,674,000
Lipetsk	Lipetsk	9,300	24,100	1,250,000
Magadan	Magadan	178,100	461,400	279,000
Moskva (Moscow)	Moscow	18,100[8]	47,000[8]	6,626,000
Murmansk	Murmansk	55,900	144,900	1,067,000
Nizhny Novgorod	Nizhny Novgorod	28,900	74,800	3,741,000
Novgorod	Novgorod	21,400	55,300	746,000
Novosibirsk	Novosibirsk	68,800	178,200	2,749,000
Omsk	Omsk	53,900	139,700	2,180,000
Orenburg	Orenburg	47,900	124,000	2,223,000
Oryol (Orel)	Oryol	9,500	24,700	916,000
Penza	Penza	16,700	43,200	1,566,000
Perm	Perm	62,000	160,600	3,024,000
Pskov	Pskov	21,400	55,300	835,000
Rostov	Rostov-na-Donu	38,900	100,800	4,429,000
Ryazan	Ryazan	15,300	39,600	1,333,000
Sakhalin	Yuzhno-Sakhalinsk	33,600	87,100	673,000
Samara	Samara	20,700	53,600	3,305,000
Saratov	Saratov	38,700	100,200	2,739,000
Smolensk	Smolensk	19,200	49,800	1,173,000
Sverdlovsk[6]	Yekaterinburg	75,200	194,800	4,703,000
Tambov	Tambov	13,200	34,300	1,315,000
Tomsk	Tomsk	122,400	316,900	1,079,000
Tula	Tula	9,900	25,700	1,826,000
Tver	Tver	32,500	84,100	1,653,000
Tyumen	Tyumen	554,100	1,435,200	3,157,000
Ulyanovsk (Simbirsk)	Simbirsk	14,400	37,300	1,492,000
Vladimir	Vladimir	11,200	29,000	1,648,000
Volgograd	Volgograd	44,000	113,900	2,695,000
Vologda[6]	Vologda	56,300	145,700	1,355,000
Voronezh	Voronezh	20,200	52,400	2,507,000
Yaroslavl	Yaroslavl	14,100	36,400	1,456,000
Autonomous Region				
Yevreyskaya (Jewish)	Birobidzhan	13,900	36,000	216,000
Territories (Krays)				
Altay	Barnaul	65,300	169,100	2,697,000
Khabarovsk	Khabarovsk	304,500	788,600	1,588,000
Krasnodar	Krasnodar	29,300	76,000	5,004,000
Krasnoyarsk	Krasnoyarsk	903,400	2,339,700	3,117,000
Primorye (Maritime)[6]	Vladivostok	64,100	165,900	2,273,000
Stavropol	Stavropol	25,700	66,500	2,650,000
Autonomous cities				
Moscow	—	8	8	8,717,000
St. Petersburg[6]	—	7	7	4,837,000
Autonomous districts (Okrugs)[9]				
Aga-Buryat	Aginskoye	7,300	19,000	79,400
Chukchi (Chukotka)	Anadyr	284,800	737,700	99,700
Evenk	Tura	296,400	767,600	20,800
Khanty-Mansi	Khanty-Mansiysk	202,000	523,100	1,326,200
Komi-Permyak	Kudymkar	12,700	32,900	158,800

Area and population *(continued)*				
Koryak	Palana	116,400	301,500	33,800
Nenets	Naryan-Mar	68,100	176,400	49,300
Taymyr	Dudinka	332,900	862,100	47,300
Ust-Orda Buryat	Ust-Ordynsky	8,600	22,400	143,000
Yamalo-Nenets	Salekhard	289,700	750,300	479,700
Sakha (Yakutia)	Yakutsk	1,198,200	3,103,200	1,035,000
Tatarstan	Kazan	26,300	68,000	3,755,000
Tuva (Tyva)	Kyzyl-Orda	65,800	170,500	308,000
Udmurtia	Izhevsk	16,300	42,100	1,641,000
TOTAL		6,592,800	17,075,400	148,167,000

Demography

Population (1996): 148,070,000.
Density (1996): persons per sq mi 22.5, persons per sq km 8.7.
Urban-rural (1996): urban 73.0%; rural 27.0%.
Sex distribution (1994): male 46.96%; female 53.04%.
Age breakdown (1995): under 15, 21.5%; 15–29, 20.6%; 30–44, 24.6%; 45–59, 16.7%; 60–69, 9.9%; 70 and over, 6.7%.
Population projection: (2000) 147,829,000; (2010) 149,868,000.
Doubling time: not applicable; population is declining.
Ethnic composition (1996): Russian 81.5%; Tatar 3.8%; Ukrainian 3.0%; Chuvash 1.2%; Bashkir 1.0%; Belorussian 0.8%; Mordovian 0.7%; Chechen 0.6%; other 7.4%.
Religious affiliation: believers are predominantly Russian Orthodox; there are Catholic, Protestant, Muslim, Old Believer, and Jewish minorities.
Major cities (1996): Moscow 8,400,000; St. Petersburg 4,200,000; Nizhny Novgorod 1,400,000; Novosibirsk 1,400,000; Yekaterinburg 1,300,000; Samara 1,200,000; Omsk 1,200,000; Chelyabinsk 1,100,000; Kazan 1,100,000; Ufa 1,100,000; Perm 1,000,000; Rostov-na-Donu 1,000,000.

Other principal cities (1995)

	population		population		population
Astrakhan	486,000	Krasnoyarsk	868,800	Tolyatti	702,300
Barnaul	658,200	Naberezhnye Chelny	529,300	Tula	532,300
Irkutsk	585,000	Novokuznetsk	586,000	Ulyanovsk (Simbirsk)	699,300
Izhevsk	654,400	Orenburg	532,100	Vladivostok	631,800
Kemerovo	502,500	Penza	533,900	Volgograd	1,002,800
Khabarovsk	617,800	Ryazan	539,800	Voronezh	907,800
Krasnodar	645,700	Saratov	902,200	Yaroslavl	629,000

Mobility (1989). Population living in the same residence as in 1988: 78.8%; different residence, same oblast 11.5%; different republic 9.7%.
Emigration (1995): 339,591.
Households (1994). Total family households 52,930,000; average household size 2.8; 2 persons 26.2%; 3 persons 22.6%; 4 persons 20.5%; 5 persons or more 11.5%. Population in family households (1989): 128,787,000 (87.0%), nonfamily population 19,254,000 (13.0%).

Vital statistics

Birth rate per 1,000 population (1995): 9.3 (world avg. 25.0); (1992) legitimate 82.9%; illegitimate 17.1%.
Death rate per 1,000 population (1995): 15.0 (world avg. 9.3).
Natural increase rate per 1,000 population (1995): −5.7 (world avg. 15.7).
Total fertility rate (avg. births per childbearing woman; 1993): 1.8.
Marriage rate per 1,000 population (1995): 7.3.
Divorce rate per 1,000 population (1995): 4.5.
Life expectancy at birth (1995): male 58.0 years; female 72.0 years.
Major causes of death per 100,000 population (1995): circulatory diseases 784.0; accidents, poisoning, and violence 234.0, of which suicide 41.0, murder 31.0; malignant neoplasms (cancers) 203.0; respiratory diseases 75.0; digestive diseases 46.0; infectious and parasitic diseases 21.0.

Social indicators

Educational attainment (1995). Percentage of population age 15 and over having: primary or no formal education 10.0%; some secondary 20.2%; secondary and some postsecondary 77.8%; higher and postgraduate 15.1%.
Quality of working life (1990). Average workweek: 40 hours. Annual rate per 100,000 workers of: injury or accident 569; industrial illness 5.3; death 11.2. Proportion of labour force insured for damages or income loss resulting from: injury 100%; permanent disability 100%; death 100%. Average days lost to labour stoppages per 1,000 workdays (1992): 1.1.
Access to services (1990). Proportion of dwellings having access to: electricity, virtually 100%; safe public water supply 94%; public sewage collection 92%; central heating 92%; bathroom 87%; gas 72%; hot water 79%.
Social participation. Eligible voters participating in last national election (1993): 54.8%. Population participating in voluntary work: n.a. Trade union membership in total workforce (1989): 100%. Practicing religious population in total affiliated population (1991): 32%.
Social deviance. Offense rate per 100,000 population (1995) for: murder 21.4; rape 8.5; serious bodily injury 41.7; larceny-theft 1,020.0. Incidence per 100,000 in general population (1992) of: alcoholism 1,727.5; substance abuse 25.1; suicide 26.5.
Material well-being (1993). Goods possessed per 100 households: automobile 20; radio receiver 101; television receiver 112; refrigerator 95; camera 37; motorcycle 22; bicycle 54; tape recorder 59.

National economy

Budget (1996). Revenue: Rub 329,000,000,000,000 (1995; tax revenue 83.1%, of which profit tax 27.0%, value-added tax 22.0%, individual income tax 8.4%, excise tax 5.6%, other taxes 11.0%; nontax revenue 12.5%; transfers 4.4%). Expenditures: Rub 410,800,000,000,000 (current expenditure 74.3%, of which economy 23.3%, defense 20.9%, education 5.8%, health 3.0%, interest on foreign debt 2.4%; development expenditure 25.7%).

Gross national product (at current market prices; 1994): U.S.$392,496,000,000 (U.S.$2,650 per capita).

Structure of gross domestic product and labour force

	1994		1995	
	in value Rub '000,000	% of total value	labour force	% of labour force
Agriculture	41,022,100	6.5	10,500,000	14.4
Mining	}			
Manufacturing	181,000,000	28.7	17,200,000	23.5
Public utilities	}			
Construction	48,747,900	7.7	6,500,000	8.9
Transportation and communications	82,072,100	13.0	5,300,000	7.2
Trade	98,958,200	15.7	6,500,000	8.9
Finance	88,245,900	14.0	900,000	1.2
Services	60,505,200	9.6	17,100,000	23.4
Pub. admin., defense	29,486,300	4.7	1,700,000	2.3
Other	73,400	.01	7,440,000	10.2
TOTAL	630,111,100	100.05	73,140,000	100.0

Public debt (external, outstanding; 1995)[10]: U.S.$130,800,000,000.
Production (metric tons except as noted). Agriculture, forestry, fishing (1995): potatoes 39,900,000, wheat 30,100,000, sugar beets 19,100,000, barley 15,800,000, vegetables (other than potatoes) 11,675,000, oats 8,562,000, fodder crops 6,500,000, sunflower seeds 4,200,000, rye 4,100,000, corn (maize) 1,700,000, peas 1,212,000, buckwheat 597,000, millet 488,000, rice 462,000; livestock (number of live animals) 43,300,000 cattle, 31,818,000 sheep, 24,800,000 pigs, 2,400,000 horses; roundwood 115,000,000 cu m; fish catch 3,800,000. Mining and quarrying (1994): nickel 240,000,000; chrome ore 100,000,000; iron ore 73,300,000; tin 11,000,000; molybdenum 7,700,000; antimony 7,000,000; gold 4,713,000 troy oz. Manufacturing (1995): crude steel 51,600,000; pig iron 39,800,000; rolled steel 39,000,000; cement 36,400,000; mineral fertilizers 9,600,000; sulfuric acid 6,900,000; cellulose 4,193,000; synthetic resins and plastics 1,794,000; cardboard 1,298,000; caustic soda 1,156,000; detergents 296,000; synthetic fibres 216,000; cotton fabrics 1,235,000,000 sq m; silk fabrics 197,000,000 sq m; linen fabrics 131,000,000 sq m; wool fabrics 72,000,000 sq m; cigarettes 141,000,000,000 units; watches 29,800,000 units; paper 2,771,000 units; television receivers 1,888,000 units; refrigerators 1,766,000 units; washing machines 1,303,000 units; vacuum cleaners 911,000 units; passenger cars 835,000 units; bicycles 759,000 units; tape recorders 671,000 units; cameras 296,000 units; sewing machines 165,400 units; motorcycles 82,100 units; video recorders 20,900 units; forge press machines 2,100 units; leather footwear 67,300,000 pairs; beer 19,800,000 hectolitres; vodka and liquors 12,200,000 hectolitres; champagne 8,200,000 hectolitres; grape wine 1,460,000 hectolitres; brandy 171,400 hectolitres. Construction (1995): residential 14,600,000 sq m; nonresidential 26,400,000 sq m.

Manufacturing, mining, and construction enterprises (1995)

	no. of enter-prises	no. of employees	monthly wages as a % of avg. of all wages[11]	value added (Rub '000,000,000)
Manufacturing				
Machinery and metal products	48,905	4,842,000	98.2	27,234
Fuel and energy	1,758	1,554,000	133.3	44,211
Metallurgy	2,158	1,248,000	124.3	26,437
Chemicals, petrochemicals, pulp, and paper	23,027	2,432,000	94.1	17,934
Light industry	23,007	1,368,000	80.0	2,931
Food	14,713	1,514,000	100.1	12,886
Other industries	19,073	2,085,000	...	4,685
Building materials	8,359	994,000	108.2	3,761

Energy production (consumption): electricity (kW-hr; 1994) 875,914,000,000 (855,418,000,000); coal (metric tons; 1994) 176,754,000 (180,988,000); crude petroleum (barrels; 1994) 2,265,000,000 (1,375,000,000); petroleum products (metric tons; 1994) 162,085,000 (126,758,000); natural gas (cu m; 1994) 498,995,000,000 (327,275,000,000); peat (metric tons; 1994) 2,928,000 (4,007,000); oil shale (metric tons; 1994) 2,000,000 (1993; 3,300,000).
Energy production by source (1995): thermal 67.8%, hydroelectric 20.6%, nuclear and other 11.6%.
Population economically active (1995): total 73,140,000; activity rate of total population 49.5% (participation rates: ages 16–59 [male], 16–54 [female] 72.6%; female 46.7%; unemployed 8.3%).

Price and earnings indexes (1990 = 100)

	1991	1992	1993	1994	1995
Consumer price index	192.7	2,800	27,900	112,100	221,300
Monthly earnings index	180.9	1,978	19,361	71,494	101,700

Land use (1994): forested 44.9%; meadows and pastures 5.2%; agricultural and under permanent cultivation 7.7%; other 42.2%.
Household income and expenditure. Average household size (1995) 2.8; income per household: Rub 6,395,000 (U.S.$1,176); sources of income (1995): wages 77.8%, pensions and stipends 12.0%, other 10.2%; expenditure (1992): food 39.8%, clothing 19.4%, taxes and other financial payments 7.5%, furniture and household appliances 7.5%, culture 4.6%, alcoholic beverages 2.8%, housing 0.8%.

Foreign trade

Balance of trade (current prices; non-CIS)

	1991	1992	1993	1994	1995
U.S.$'000,000	+6,438	+4,986	+17,490	+21,800	+32,879
% of total	6.8%	6.7%	24.6%	27.9%	33.2%

Imports (1995): U.S.$33,138,000,000 (machinery and transport equipment 37.7%, food 28.9%, chemicals 11.2%, textiles 5.0%, ferrous and nonferrous metals 4.9%, fuels and lubricants 2.7%). *Major import sources:* Germany 19.7%; United States 8.0%; Finland 6.2%; Italy 5.6%; The Netherlands 5.0%; Poland 4.0%.
Exports (1995): U.S.$66,017,000,000 (fuels and lubricants 39.9%, ferrous and nonferrous metals 28.8%, chemicals 9.4%, machinery and transport equipment 7.8%, forestry products 5.8%, food 3.4%). *Major export destinations:* Germany 9.2%; United States 6.6%; Switzerland 5.4%; China 5.1%; Italy 5.0%; The Netherlands 4.8%.

Trade by commodity group (1995)

	imports		exports	
SITC group	U.S.$'000,000	%	U.S.$'000,000	%
00 Food and live animals	} 9,600	29.0	2,300	3.5
02 Raw materials, excl. fuels				
03 Mineral fuels, lubricants	900	2.7	26,400	40.0
05 Chemicals	3,700	11.2	6,200	9.4
65 Textile yarn, fabrics	1,600	4.8	800	1.2
07 Machinery and transport equip.	12,500	37.8	5,200	7.9
08 Misc. manufactured articles	4,800	14.5	25,117	38.0
09 Goods, n.e.s.	...	...	...	...
TOTAL	33,100	100.0	66,017	100.0

Direction of trade (1994)

	imports		exports	
	U.S.$'000,000	%	U.S.$'000,000	%
Africa	217	0.8	512	1.0
Asia	4,650	16.5	9,985	20.4
Japan	1,114	3.9	2,245	4.6
South America	791	2.8	1,021	2.1
North and Central America	2,263	8.0	3,619	7.4
United States	2,069	7.3	3,373	6.9
Europe	20,020	70.9	33,872	69.1
EU	15,278	54.1	22,211	45.3
EFTA	3,154	11.2	9,373	19.1
other Europe	1,588	5.6	2,288	4.7
Oceania	300	1.1	42	0.1
TOTAL	28,241	100.05	49,051	100.05

Transport and communications

Transport. Railroads (1995): length 151,000 km; passenger-km 192,200,000,000; metric ton-km cargo 1,213,000,000. Roads (1995): total length 949,000 km (paved 79%). Vehicles (1993): passenger cars 10,499,000; trucks and buses 407,000. Merchant marine (1993): vessels (100 gross tons and over) 24; total deadweight tonnage 91,000,000. Air transport (1995): passenger-km 71,700,000,000; metric ton-km cargo 1,800,000,000; airports (1996) 75.

Distribution of traffic (1995)

	cargo carried ('000,000 tons)	% of national total	passengers carried ('000,000)	% of national total
Intercity transport			26,549	56.2
Road	1,441	41.7	22,817	48.3
Rail	1,028	29.7	1,833	3.9
Sea and river	203	5.9	32	0.1
Air	1	...	34	0.1
Pipeline	783	22.7	—	—
Urban transport			20,684	43.8
Road	—	—	86	0.2
Rail	—	—	20,598	43.6
TOTAL	3,456	100.0	47,233	100.0

Communications. Daily newspapers (1992): total 339; total circulation 57,000,000; circulation per 1,000 population 386. Radio (1992): 48,800,000 receivers (1 per 3 persons). Television (1992): 54,200,000 receivers (1 per 2.7 persons). Telephones (main lines; 1993): 23,397,000 (1 per 6.3 persons).

Education and health

Education (1995–96)

	schools	teachers	students	student/ teacher ratio
Primary (age 6–13)	} 70,200	1,705,000	22,000,000	12.9
Secondary (age 14–17)				
Voc., teacher tr.	2,612	...	1,923,000	...
Higher	569	...	2,655,000	...

Health (1995): physicians 630,000 (1 per 235 persons); hospital beds 1,860,000 (1 per 80 persons); infant mortality rate per 1,000 live births (1995) 18.0.
Food (1992): daily per capita caloric intake 2,100 (vegetable products, n.a.; animal products, n.a.); 82% of FAO recommended minimum.

Military

Total active duty personnel (1996): 1,270,000 (army 73.6%, navy 15.0%, air force 11.4%). *Military expenditure as percentage of GNP* (1994): 12.4% (world 3.0%); per capita expenditure U.S.$647.

[1]January 1995. [2]The former Chechen-Ingush republic was split into two separate republics June 4, 1992; the final status of Chechnia was unresolved in December 1996. [3]Republic is not signatory to the March 31, 1992, treaty establishing the Russian Federation. [4]Ingushetia's area and population include Chechnia. [5]Detail does not add to total given because of rounding. [6]Entity has formally proclaimed itself a federal republic; final status remains undetermined. [7]Leningrad region includes area of autonomous city of St. Petersburg. [8]Moskva region includes area of autonomous city of Moscow. [9]With the exception of the Chukchi autonomous district (identified in Roman type), which has formally separated from Magadan region, all autonomous districts are administratively part of another national administrative subdivision, within which their area and population are included. [10]As of March 31, 1995; Russia has also assumed responsibility for the governmental and commercial debts of the former U.S.S.R., estimated to constitute a further U.S.$88,000,000,000. [11]1990.

Rwanda

Official name: Republika y'u Rwanda
(Rwanda); République Rwandaise
(French) (Republic of Rwanda).
Form of government: transitional
regime with one legislative body
(Transitional National Assembly[1]
[70]).
Head of state and government:
President assisted by Prime Minister
and Vice President (Minister of
Defense).
Capital: Kigali.
Official languages: Rwanda; French;
English.
Official religion: none.
Monetary unit: 1 Rwanda franc (RF);
valuation (Oct. 11, 1996)
1 U.S.$ = RF 327.21; 1 £ = RF 515.45.

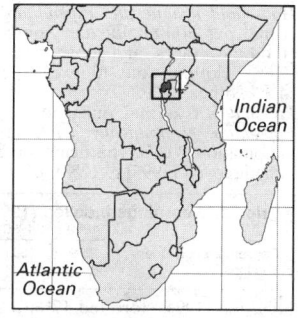

Indian
Ocean

Atlantic
Ocean

Area and population

Prefectures	Capitals	area sq mi	area sq km	population 1991 census
Butare	Butare	709	1,837	766,839
Byumba	Byumba	1,838	4,761	783,350
Cyangugu	Cyangugu	712	1,845	515,129
Gikongoro	Gikongoro	794	2,057	464,585
Gisenyi	Gisenyi	791	2,050	734,697
Gitarama	Gitarama	845	2,189	851,516
Kibungo	Kibungo	1,562	4,046	655,368
Kibuye	Kibuye	658	1,705	470,747
Kigali	Kigali (city)	1,159	3,002	918,869
Kigali (city)	—	45	116	237,782
Ruhengeri	Ruhengeri	642	1,663	766,112
TOTAL LAND AREA		9,757[2]	25,271	
TOTAL		10,169	26,338	7,164,994[3]

Demography

Population (1996): 6,853,000[4].
Density (1996): persons per sq mi 673.9, persons per sq km 260.2.
Urban-rural (1991): urban 5.4%; rural 94.6%.
Sex distribution (1996): male 49.56%; female 50.44%.
Age breakdown (1996): under 15, 46.1%; 15–29, 27.9%; 30–44, 15.1%; 45–59, 6.6%; 60–74, 3.5%; 75 and over, 0.8%.
Population projection: (2000) 8,900,000; (2010) 10,080,000.
Doubling time: 44 years.
Ethnic composition (1991)[4]: Hutu 85.0%; Tutsi 14.0%; Twa 1.0%.
Religious affiliation: In 1991 the largest organized religion was the Roman
Catholic church, representing approximately 44% of the population, fol-
lowed by Muslims at about 8–9%, with the remainder consisting of indige-
nous African Protestant churches or traditional animist believers.
Major cities (1991): Kigali 237,782[3]; Ruhengeri 29,578[5]; Butare 28,645[5];
Gisenyi 21,918[5].

Vital statistics

Birth rate per 1,000 population (1995): 39.2 (world avg. 25.0); (1978) legiti-
mate 94.9%; illegitimate 5.1%.
Death rate per 1,000 population (1995): 23.4 (world avg. 9.3).
Natural increase rate per 1,000 population (1995): 15.8 (world avg. 15.7).
Total fertility rate (avg. births per childbearing woman; 1995): 6.1.
Marriage rate per 1,000 population (1984)[6]: 2.5.
Divorce rate per 1,000 population: n.a.
Life expectancy at birth (1995): male 35.9 years; female 36.4 years.
Major causes of death per 100,000 population: n.a.; however, principal causes
in 1991 were malaria, bronchopneumonia, diarrhea, AIDS, pulmonary dis-
eases, cerebrospinal meningitis, kwashiorkor, road accidents, and cirrhosis
of the liver. Following the genocide of 1994 (equaling 3 years normal
mortality), malnutrition, cholera, and civil violence were also major causes.

National economy

Budget (1994). Revenue: RF 31,300,000,000 (grants 38.0%, import and export
duties 32.9%, taxes on goods and services 19.8%, income tax 5.7%). Expenditures: RF 39,800,000,000 (goods and services 38.7%, wages 32.7%, debt
payment 19.5%, transfer payments 9.1%).
Public debt (external, outstanding; 1994): U.S.$904,900,000.
Production (metric tons except as noted). Agriculture, forestry, fishing (1995):
plantains 2,600,000, roots and tubers 1,534,000 (of which sweet potatoes
1,100,000, cassava 250,000 potatoes 150,000), cereals 151,000 (of which
sorghum 72,000, corn [maize] 70,000), coffee 22,000, tea 6,000, tobacco 4,000;
livestock (number of live animals) 920,000 goats, 465,000 cattle, 250,000
sheep, 80,000 pigs; roundwood (1994) 5,660,000 cu m; fish catch (1993) 3,553.
Mining and quarrying (1990): cassiterite (tin ore) 730; wolframite (tungsten
ore) 175; gold (1992) 15,552 troy oz. Manufacturing (1994): cement 21,000;
lye soap 2,200; sugar 600; beer 45,800,000 bottles; nonalcoholic beverages
21,900,000 bottles; textiles 2,800,000 metres; corrugated iron sheets 2,200
sheets; blankets 406,876 units[7]; matches 70,942,000 boxes[7]. Construction
(1981): residential 59,600 sq m; nonresidential 34,400 sq m. Energy production (consumption): electricity (kW-hr; 1994) 166,000,000 (177,000,000);
coal, none (n.a.); petroleum products (metric tons; 1994) none (155,000);
natural gas (cu m; 1994) 179,389 (179,389).
Tourism: receipts from visitors (1993) U.S.$2,000,000; expenditures by nation-
als abroad (1992) U.S.$17,000,000.

Land use (1994): forested 10.1%; meadows and pastures 28.4%; agricultural
and under permanent cultivation 47.4%; other 14.1%.
Population economically active (1991): total 3,649,000; activity rate of total
population 50.2% (participation rates: ages 14–74 [1989] 46.3%; female
53.5%; unemployed, n.a.).

Price and earnings indexes (1990 = 100)

	1989	1990	1991	1992	1993	1994	1995
Consumer price index	96.0	100.0	119.6	131.1	147.3	...	293.0
Earnings index	...	...	...	...	...	...	...

Gross national product (1993): U.S.$1,499,000,000 (U.S.$200 per capita).

Structure of gross domestic product and labour force

	1994 in value RF '000,000	1994 % of total value	1989 labour force	1989 % of labour force
Agriculture	63,100	49.0	2,832,557	90.1
Mining	100	0.1	4,691	0.2
Manufacturing	6,600	5.1	45,089	1.4
Construction	3,600	2.8	38,237	1.2
Public utilities	300	0.2	2,562	0.1
Transp. and commun.	7,600	5.9	7,333	0.2
Trade	25,000	19.4	80,026	2.6
Finance			3,128	0.1
Pub. admin., defense Services	} 17,100	13.3	120,019	3.8
Other	5,400[8]	4.2[8]	9,414	0.3
TOTAL	128,800	100.0	3,143,056	100.0

Household income and expenditure. Average household size (1991) 4.7; average annual income per household (1983) RF 122,870 (U.S.$1,300); sources
of income (1977): self-employment 71.0%, salaries and wages 16.5%, transfers 9.5%; expenditure (1982)[9]: food 44.2%, housing 13.2%, clothing and
footwear 11.4%, transportation 10.3%, household equipment 8.4%.

Foreign trade[10]

Balance of trade (current prices)

	1989	1990	1991	1992	1993	1994
RF '000,000	−10,918	−6,834	−15,181	−17,729	−23,934	−3,068
% of total	41.7%	27.0%	39.6%	49.9%	55.9%	14.6%

Imports (1994): U.S.$458,900,000 (food 47.6%, capital goods 7.8%, energy
products 5.1%). *Major import sources* (1991): Belgium-Luxembourg 17.1%;
Kenya 13.4%; France 6.8%; Germany 6.0%; Italy 2.8%; The Netherlands
2.7%; U.K. 2.1%; U.S. 1.0%; Zaire 0.7%.
Exports (1994): U.S.$32,200,000 (coffee 54.0%, tea 18.0%, hides and skins
3.7%). *Major export destinations* (1991): Germany 21.3%; The Netherlands
18.8%; Belgium-Luxembourg 11.8%; U.K. 6.4%; U.S. 5.8%; Italy 1.7%.

Transport and communications

Transport. Railroads: none. Roads (1995): total length 9,050 mi, 14,565
km (paved 10%). Vehicles (1995): passenger cars 11,900; trucks 15,900.
Merchant marine: none. Air transport: (1993) passenger-mi 1,200,000, passenger-km 2,000,000; (1991) metric ton cargo loaded 2,674, metric ton cargo
unloaded 4,794; airports (1996) with scheduled flights 1.
Communications. Daily newspapers (1996): total number, none; total circulation per 1,000 population, n.a. Radio (1992): total number of receivers
650,000 (1 per 12 persons). Television: none. Telephones (main lines; 1993):
11,800 (1 per 634 persons).

Education and health

Education (1991–92)

	schools	teachers	students	student/ teacher ratio
Primary (age 7–15)	1,710	18,937	1,104,902	58.3
Secondary (age 16–19)[11]	...	3,413	94,586	27.7
Higher[12]	3[13]	646	3,389	5.2

Educational attainment (1978). Percentage of population age 25 and over having: no formal schooling 76.9%; some primary education 16.8%; complete
primary education 4.0%; some secondary and complete secondary education
2.0%; some postsecondary vocational and higher education 0.3%. *Literacy*
(1995): percentage of total population age 15 and over literate 60.5%; males
literate 69.8%; females literate 51.6%.
Health: physicians (1989) 272 (1 per 24,697 persons); hospital beds (1984)
9,046 (1 per 649 persons); infant mortality rate (1995) 119.7.
Food (1992): daily per capita caloric intake 1,821 (vegetable products 97%,
animal products 3%); 78% of FAO recommended minimum requirement.

Military

Total active duty personnel (1996): 33,000 (army 100%). *Military expenditure
as percentage of GNP* (1994): 7.6% (world 3.0%); per capita expenditure
U.S.$14.

[1]Transitional National Assembly was appointed on Nov. 25, 1994, for an interim
period of five years. [2]Detail does not add to total given because of rounding. [3]The
population of Kigali decreased to about 100,000–120,000 because of the 1994 civil
war. [4]Includes adjustments for (1) the loss of some 2,000,000 refugees to surrounding
countries, of whom the majority were Hutu; (2) the death of an estimated 500,000
Tutsi killed during the events of 1994; and (3) the return of 400,000–600,000 Tutsi
herdsmen from surrounding countries who had been in exile since 1959. [5]De jure
population only. [6]Excludes marriages not registered in court. [7]1990. [8]Indirect taxes
plus statistical adjustments. [9]Weights of consumer price index components. [10]Imports
f.o.b. in balance of trade and c.i.f. in commodities and trading partners. [11]Includes
vocational and teacher training. [12]1989–90. [13]1985.

Saint Kitts and Nevis

Official name: Federation of Saint Kitts and Nevis[1].
Form of government: constitutional monarchy with one legislative house (National Assembly [15[2]]).
Chief of state: British Monarch represented by Governor-General.
Head of government: Prime Minister.
Capital: Basseterre.
Official language: English.
Official religion: none.
Monetary unit: 1 Eastern Caribbean dollar (EC$) = 100 cents; valuation (Oct. 11, 1996) 1 U.S.$ = EC$2.70; 1 £ = EC$4.25.

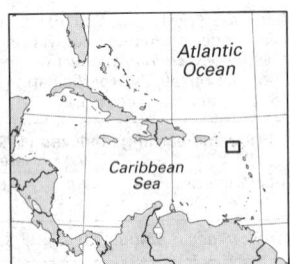

Area and population		area		population
		sq mi	sq km	1991 census[4]
Islands[3]	**Capitals**			
Nevis[5]	Charlestown	36.0	93.2	9,130
St. Kitts	Basseterre	68.0	176.2	32,696
TOTAL		104.0	269.4	41,826

Demography

Population (1996): 39,400.
Density (1996): persons per sq mi 378.8, persons per sq km 146.3.
Urban-rural (1995): urban 42.9%; rural 57.1%.
Sex distribution (1990): male 51.56%; female 48.44%.
Age breakdown (1990): under 15, 32.5%; 15–29, 25.6%; 30–44, 18.9%; 45–59, 10.1%; 60–74, 8.9%; 75 and over, 4.0%.
Population projection: (2000) 39,000; (2010) 39,000.
Doubling time: 50 years.
Ethnic composition (1991): black 94.9%; mixed/white/Indo-Pakistani 5.1%.
Religious affiliation (1985): Protestant 76.4%, of which Anglican 36.2%, Methodist 32.3%; Roman Catholic 10.7%; other 12.9%.
Major towns (1995): Basseterre 18,000; Charlestown 1,200[6].

Vital statistics

Birth rate per 1,000 population (1994): 24.0 (world avg. 25.0); (1983) legitimate 19.2%; illegitimate 80.8%.
Death rate per 1,000 population (1994): 10.0 (world avg. 9.3).
Natural increase rate per 1,000 population (1994): 14.0 (world avg. 15.7).
Total fertility rate (avg. births per childbearing woman; 1994): 2.6.
Marriage rate per 1,000 population: n.a.
Divorce rate per 1,000 population: n.a.
Life expectancy at birth (1994): male 63.0 years; female 69.0 years.
Major causes of death per 100,000 population (1985): diseases of the circulatory system 443.2, of which cerebrovascular disease 220.5, diseases of pulmonary circulation and other heart disease 122.7; malignant neoplasms (cancers) 95.5; diseases of the respiratory system 81.8; infectious and parasitic diseases 50.0; ill-defined conditions 102.3.

National economy

Budget (1995). Revenue: EC$141,100,000 (tax revenue 72.9%, of which taxes on international transactions 40.3%, income taxes 19.3%, consumption taxes 16.9%; nontax revenue 27.1%). Expenditures: EC$147,400,000 (wages and salaries 41.0%; goods and services 37.3%; debt service 12.5%; pensions 6.4%).
Production (metric tons except as noted). Agriculture, forestry, fishing (1994): sugarcane 180,285[7], coconuts 2,000, potatoes 240, cabbage 141, tomatoes 121, sweet potatoes 110; sea island cotton is grown on Nevis; livestock (number of live animals; 1995) 17,000 goats, 10,000 sheep, 1,800 cattle; roundwood, n.a.; fish catch (1993) 1,700. Mining and quarrying: excavation of sand for local use. Manufacturing (1994): raw sugar 19,961[7]; molasses 6,000; aerated beverages 47,000 hectolitres[8]; beer 17,200 hectolitres[8]; other manufactures include electronic components, garments, plastics, and ethanol. Construction (value added; 1994): EC$57,000,000. Energy production (consumption): electricity (kW-hr; 1994) 86,000,000 (86,000,000); coal, none (none); crude petroleum, none (none); petroleum products (metric tons; 1994) none (32,-000); natural gas, none (none).
Gross national product (1994): U.S.$195,000,000 (U.S.$4,760 per capita).

Structure of gross domestic product and labour force				
	1994		1984	
	in value EC$'000,000[9]	% of total value	labour force[10]	% of labour force[10]
Agriculture, fisheries	29.8	6.2	4,380	29.6
Mining	1.7	0.4	—	—
Manufacturing	51.0	10.7	2,170	14.7
Construction	57.0	11.9	400	2.7
Public utilities	8.5	1.8	1,030	7.0
Transportation and communications	71.9	15.0	450	3.0
Trade, restaurants	114.2	23.9	940	6.3
Finance, real estate	56.8	11.9	280	1.9
Pub. admin., defense	90.3	18.9 }	4,700	31.7
Services	20.8	4.3 }		
Other	−23.5[11]	−4.9[11]	460	3.1
TOTAL	478.4[12]	100.0[12]	14,810	100.0

Household income and expenditure. Average household size (1980) 3.7; income per household: n.a.; sources of income: n.a.; expenditure (1978)[13]: food, beverages, and tobacco 55.6%, household furnishings 9.4%, housing 7.6%, clothing and footwear 7.5%, fuel and light 6.6%, transportation 4.3%, other 9.0%.
Public debt (external, outstanding; 1994): U.S.$43,000,000.
Population economically active (1980): total 17,125; activity rate of total population 39.5% (participation rates: ages 15–64, 69.5%; female 41.0%; unemployed [1995] c. 12%[14]).

Price and earnings indexes (1990 = 100)							
	1989	1990	1991	1992	1993	1994	1995[15]
Consumer price index	95.9	100.0	104.2	107.2	109.1	112.0	115.4
Earnings index	...	...	...	...	...	...	...

Land use (1994): forested 17%; meadows and pastures 3%; agricultural and under permanent cultivation 39%; other 41%.
Tourism (1994): receipts from visitors U.S.$75,000,000; expenditures by nationals abroad U.S.$6,000,000.

Foreign trade[16]

Balance of trade (current prices)						
	1990	1991	1992	1993	1994	1995
U.S.$'000,000	−83.0	−79.1	−63.3	−72.2	−77.0	−81.9
% of total	60.0%	55.7%	49.5%	49.5%	52.1%	...

Imports (1994): U.S.$115,400,000 (basic and miscellaneous manufactures 36.6%, machinery 23.5%, food 17.3%, chemicals and chemical products 7.9%). *Major import sources:* United States 45.9%; Caricom countries 18.8%, of which Trinidad and Tobago 10.3%; United Kingdom 12.5%; Japan 4.2%; Canada 4.2%.
Exports (1994): U.S.$32,485,000 (electronic goods 38.0%, sugar [all forms] 33.2%, miscellaneous manufactures [mostly garments] 15.2%). *Major export destinations:* United States 46.6%; United Kingdom 26.4%; Caricom countries 9.3%, of which Antigua and Barbuda 2.6%.

Transport and communications

Transport. Railroads (1992)[17]: length 22 mi, 36 km. Roads (1995): total length 193 mi, 310 km (paved 43%). Vehicles (1990): passenger cars 4,000; trucks and buses, n.a. Merchant marine (1992): vessels (100 gross tons and over) 1; total deadweight tonnage 550. Cruise ship passenger overnights (1995) 88,827. Air transport: passenger arrivals (1992) 123,195[18]; passenger departures, n.a.; cargo handled, n.a.; airports (1996) with scheduled flights 2.
Communications (1992). Daily newspapers[19]: none. Radio (1995): total number of receivers 26,000 (1 per 1.5 persons). Television (1995): total number of receivers 9,500 (1 per 4.1 persons). Telephones (main lines; 1993): 12,200 (1 per 3.3 persons).

Education and health

Education (1991–92)	schools	teachers	students	student/ teacher ratio
Primary (age 5–12)	31	342	6,978	20.4
Secondary (age 13–17)	7	298	4,645	15.6
Voc., teacher tr.	2	35	189	5.4
Higher[20]	1	51	394	7.7

Educational attainment (1980). Percentage of population age 25 and over having: no formal schooling 1.1%; primary education 29.6%; secondary 67.2%; higher 2.1%. *Literacy* (1990): total population age 15 and over literate 25,500 (90.0%); males literate 13,100 (90.0%); females literate 12,400 (90.0%).
Health: physicians (1992) 39 (1 per 1,057 persons); hospital beds (1995) 276 (1 per 142 persons); infant mortality rate per 1,000 live births (1994) 20.0.
Food (1992): daily per capita caloric intake 2,419 (vegetable products 75%, animal products 25%); 101% of FAO recommended minimum requirement.

Military

Total active duty personnel (1994): the 340-member police force includes a 50-member paramilitary unit.

[1]Both Saint Christopher and Nevis and the Federation of Saint Christopher and Nevis are officially acceptable, variant, short- and long-form names of the country. [2]Includes 4 nonelective seats. [3]Parish subdivisions of both islands are for statistical purposes only. [4]Preliminary. [5]Nevis has full internal self-government. The Nevis legislature is subordinate to the National Assembly only with regard to external affairs and defense. [6]1990. [7]1995. [8]1991. [9]At factor cost. [10]Employed persons only. [11]Less imputed bank service charges. [12]Detail does not add to total given because of rounding. [13]Weights of consumer price index components. [14]IMF estimate. [15]Nine months. [16]Imports f.o.b. in balance of trade and c.i.f. in commodities and trading partners. [17]Light railway serving the sugar industry on Saint Kitts. [18]Saint Kitts airport only. [19]Total circulation of one weekly newspaper and one twice-weekly newspaper is 9,000. [20]1992–93.

Saint Lucia

Official name: Saint Lucia.
Form of government: constitutional monarchy with a Parliament consisting of two legislative chambers (Senate [11]; House of Assembly [18]).
Chief of state: British Monarch represented by Governor-General.
Head of government: Prime Minister.
Capital: Castries.
Official language: English.
Official religion: none.
Monetary unit: 1 Eastern Caribbean dollar (EC$) = 100 cents; valuation (Oct. 11, 1996) 1 U.S.$ = EC$2.70; 1 £ = EC$4.25.

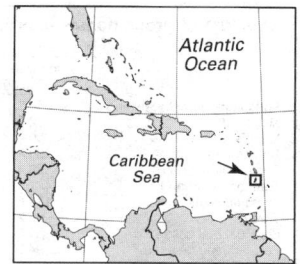

Area and population

Districts	Capitals	area sq mi	area sq km	population 1992 estimate
Anse-la-Raye	Anse-la-Raye	} 18	} 47	5,218
Canaries	Canaries			1,864
Castries	Castries	31	79	53,883
Choiseul	Choiseul	12	31	6,638
Dennery	Dennery	27	70	11,574
Gros Islet	Gros Islet	39	101	13,996
Laborie	Laborie	15	38	7,763
Micoud	Micoud	30	78	15,636
Soufrière	Soufrière	19	51	7,962
Vieux Fort	Vieux Fort	17	44	13,617
TOTAL		238[1]	617[1]	138,151

Demography

Population (1996): 144,000.
Density (1996): persons per sq mi 605.0, persons per sq km 233.4.
Urban-rural (1995): urban 48.1%; rural 51.9%.
Sex distribution (1992): male 48.49%; female 51.51%.
Age breakdown (1992): under 15, 36.7%; 15–29, 29.4%; 30–44, 16.3%; 45–59, 8.8%; 60–74, 6.3%; 75 and over, 2.5%.
Population projection: (2000) 151,000; (2010) 169,000.
Doubling time: 41 years.
Ethnic composition (1990): black 90.5%; mixed 5.5%; East Indian 3.2%; white 0.8%.
Religious affiliation (1991): Roman Catholic 79.0%; Protestant 15.5%, of which Seventh-day Adventist 6.5%, Pentecostal 3.0%; other 5.5%.
Major city (1992): Castries city proper 2,063 (urban area 13,615).

Vital statistics

Birth rate per 1,000 population (1995): 25.2 (world avg. 25.0); legitimate 14.2%; illegitimate 85.8%.
Death rate per 1,000 population (1995): 5.9 (world avg. 9.3).
Natural increase rate per 1,000 population (1995): 19.3 (world avg. 15.7).
Total fertility rate (avg. births per childbearing woman; 1994): 2.5.
Marriage rate per 1,000 population (1992): 3.2.
Divorce rate per 1,000 population (1992): 0.3.
Life expectancy at birth (1994): male 67.0 years; female 72.0 years.
Major causes of death per 100,000 population (1992): diseases of the circulatory system 205.6, of which ischemic heart diseases 133.2, cerebrovascular disease 34.7; malignant neoplasms (cancers) 64.4; diseases of the respiratory system 48.5; infectious and parasitic diseases 31.1; ill-defined conditions 130.3.

National economy

Budget (1995–96). Revenue: EC$361,500,000 (consumption duties on imported goods 26.2%; import duties 17.0%; taxes on domestic goods and services 12.1%; company taxes 11.9%). Expenditures: EC$399,300,000 (current expenditures 77.9%, of which wages and salaries 43.1%, goods and services 16.1%, pensions 3.8%, debt service 2.9%; development expenditures and net lending 22.1%).
Public debt (external, outstanding; 1994): U.S.$104,700,000.
Population economically active (1992): total 57,797; activity rate of total population 41.8% (participation rates: ages 15–64, 72.7%; female 46.5%; unemployed [1994] 19.2%).
Production. Agriculture, forestry, fishing (export value in EC$'000 except as noted; 1992): bananas 116,900[2], copra 2,603[3], breadfruit 713, mangoes 670, cacao beans 404[3], pepper 241, plantains 216, pineapple 189; livestock (number of live animals; 1995) 16,000 sheep, 12,800 pigs, 12,450 cattle, 12,400 goats; roundwood, n.a.; fish catch (1993) 1,114 metric tons. Mining and quarrying: excavation of sand for local construction and pumice. Manufacturing (value of production in EC$'000; 1992): food, beverages, and tobacco 72,379; paper products and cardboard boxes 41,029; garments 10,385; electrical and electronic components 9,501; refined coconut oil 6,981; textiles 4,359. Construction (buildings approved; 1992): residential 91,900 sq m; nonresidential 43,300 sq m. Energy production (consumption): electricity (kW-hr; 1994) 112,000,000 (112,000,000); coal, none (none); crude petroleum, none (none); petroleum products (metric tons; 1994) none (61,-000); natural gas, none (none).
Household income and expenditure. Average household size (1991) 4.0; income per household: n.a.; sources of income: n.a.; expenditure (1982)[4]: food 46.8%, housing 13.5%, clothing and footwear 6.5%, transportation and communications 6.3%, household furnishings 5.8%, fuel and light 4.5%, recreation and education 3.2%, beverages and tobacco 2.8%, health care 2.3%, other 8.3%.

Price and earnings indexes (1990 = 100)

	1989	1990	1991	1992	1993	1994	1995
Consumer price index	95.5	100.0	105.7	111.1	112.0	118.5	121.6
Earnings index[5]	97.1	100.0	103.0	...	...[6]	...	...

Tourism: receipts from visitors (1994) U.S.$224,000,000; expenditures by nationals abroad U.S.$24,000,000.
Gross national product (at current market prices; 1994): U.S.$501,000,000 (U.S.$3,450 per capita).

Structure of gross domestic product and labour force

	1993 in value EC$'000,000[7]	1993 % of total value[7]	1992 labour force[8]	1992 % of labour force[8]
Agriculture	126.0	12.3	2,824	8.9
Mining	6.9	0.7	...	...
Manufacturing	75.7	7.4	4,360	13.8
Construction	92.2	9.0	2,197	6.9
Public utilities	35.1	3.4	832	2.6
Transportation and communications	185.0	18.1	2,551	8.0
Trade, restaurants	251.3	24.6	8,714	27.5
Finance, real estate	143.1	14.0	3,488	11.0
Pub. admin., defense	134.6	13.2	6,758	21.3
Services	32.7	3.2	...	...
Other	−61.8[9]	−6.1[9]	...	...
TOTAL	1,020.7[10]	100.0[10]	31,724	100.0

Land use (1994): forested 13%; meadows and pastures 5%; agricultural and under permanent cultivation 30%; other 52%.

Foreign trade[11]

Balance of trade (current prices)

	1991	1992	1993	1994	1995
U.S.$'000,000	−151.1	−143.7	−140.5	−165.7	−154.7
% of total	...	...	...	...	...

Imports (1993): U.S.$300,300,000 (machinery and transportation equipment 22.8%; food and live animals 20.3%; basic manufactures 19.2%; chemicals and chemical products 9.1%; crude petroleum and petroleum products 7.6%). *Major import sources:* United States 37.3%; United Kingdom 12.5%; Trinidad and Tobago 10.1%; Japan 5.6%; Canada 3.4%.
Exports (1993): U.S.$119,700,000 (food and live animals 50.2%, of which bananas 47.7%; miscellaneous manufactures [primarily clothing] 24.8%; basic manufactures [primarily paper and paperboard] 9.0%). *Major export destinations:* United Kingdom 49.6%; United States 27.0%; Dominica 7.7%; Germany 2.4%; Barbados 1.9%.

Transport and communications

Transport. Railroads: none. Roads (1992): total length 500 mi, 805 km (paved 56%). Vehicles (1993): passenger cars 10,000; trucks and buses 9,200. Merchant marine (1992): vessels (100 gross tons and over) 7; total deadweight tonnage 2,070. Air transport (1994): passenger arrivals and departures 581,-539; cargo unloaded 2,002 metric tons, cargo loaded 3,918 metric tons; airports (1996) with scheduled flights 2.
Communications. Daily newspapers: none[12]. Radio (1995): total number of receivers 90,000 (1 per 1.6 persons). Television (1995): total number of receivers 25,000 (1 per 5.7 persons). Telephones (main lines, 1993): 24,200 (1 per 5.8 persons).

Education and health

Education (1992–93)

	schools	teachers	students	student/ teacher ratio
Primary (age 5–11)	88	1,204	32,545	27.0
Secondary (age 12–16)	14	524	9,550	18.2
Vocational	1	34	806	23.7
Higher	1	389	870	2.4

Educational attainment (1980). Percentage of population age 25 and over having: no formal schooling 17.5%; primary education 74.4%; secondary 6.8%; higher 1.3%. *Literacy* (1990): about 80%.
Health (1992): physicians 64 (1 per 2,235 persons); hospital beds 435 (1 per 318 persons); infant mortality rate per 1,000 live births (1995) 18.0.
Food (1992): daily per capita caloric intake 2,588 (vegetable products 73%, animal products 27%); 107% of FAO recommended minimum requirement.

Military

Total active duty personnel (1992): [13].

[1]Total includes the uninhabited 30 sq mi (78 sq km) Central Forest Reserve. [2]1994. [3]Value of production. [4]Castries administrative area only. [5]Public sector only. [6]No wage increases in public sector. [7]At constant prices of 1990. [8]Data exclude workers (all self-employed and many agricultural workers) not making contributions to the national insurance plan and all unemployed. [9]Less imputed bank service charges. [10]Detail does not add to total given because of rounding. [11]Imports c.i.f.; exports f.o.b. [12]In 1993 one newspaper was published twice a week and two others were published weekly. [13]The 497-member police force includes a specially trained paramilitary unit and a coast guard unit.

Saint Vincent and the Grenadines

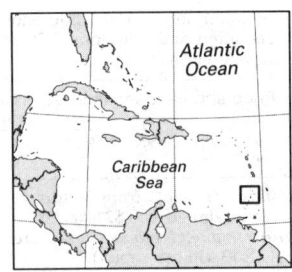

Official name: Saint Vincent and the Grenadines.
Form of government: constitutional monarchy with one legislative house (House of Assembly [21[1]]).
Chief of state: British Monarch represented by Governor-General.
Head of government: Prime Minister.
Capital: Kingstown.
Official language: English.
Official religion: none.
Monetary unit: 1 Eastern Caribbean dollar (EC$) = 100 cents; valuation (Oct. 11, 1996) 1 U.S.$ = EC$2.70; 1 £ = EC$4.25.

Area and population	area		population
			1994
Constituencies[2]	sq mi	sq km	estimate
Island of Saint Vincent			
Barrouallie	14.2	36.8	5,352
Bridgetown	7.2	18.6	7,755
Calliaqua	11.8	30.6	20,891
Chateaubelair	30.9	80.0	6,224
Colonarie	13.4	34.7	8,124
Georgetown	22.2	57.5	7,519
Kingstown (city)	1.9	4.9	15,924
Kingstown (suburbs)	6.4	16.6	11,075
Layou	11.1	28.7	6,171
Marriaqua	9.4	24.3	9,127
Sandy Bay	5.3	13.7	2,876
Saint Vincent Grenadines			
Northern Grenadines	9.0	23.3	5,678
Southern Grenadines	7.5	19.4	2,937
TOTAL	150.3	389.3[3]	109,653

Demography

Population (1996): 113,000.
Density (1996): persons per sq mi 753.3, persons per sq km 290.5.
Urban-rural (1994)[4]: urban 24.6%; rural 75.4%.
Sex distribution (1994): male 49.90%; female 50.10%.
Age breakdown (1991): under 15, 37.2%; 15–29, 29.5%; 30–44, 16.1%; 45–59, 8.3%; 60–74, 6.4%; 75 and over, 2.5%.
Population projection: (2000) 119,000; (2010) 133,000.
Doubling time: 39 years.
Ethnic composition (1986): black 65.5%; mulatto 19.0%; East Indian 5.5%; white (mostly Portuguese) 3.5%; Amerindian/black 2.0%; other 4.5%.
Religious affiliation (1985): Protestant 76.0%, of which Anglican 36.0%; Roman Catholic 10.0%; other/nonreligious 14.0%.
Major city (1994): Kingstown 15,924.

Vital statistics

Birth rate per 1,000 population (1995): 22.4 (world avg. 25.0); legitimate, n.a.; illegitimate, n.a.
Death rate per 1,000 population (1995): 6.6 (world avg. 9.3).
Natural increase rate per 1,000 population (1995): 15.9 (world avg. 15.7).
Total fertility rate (avg. births per childbearing woman; 1994): 2.1.
Marriage rate per 1,000 population (1994): 4.2.
Divorce rate per 1,000 population (1994): 0.8.
Life expectancy at birth (1994): male 71.0 years; female 74.0 years.
Major causes of death per 100,000 population (1994): diseases of the circulatory system 236.3, of which diseases of pulmonary circulation and other forms of heart disease 43.6, hypertensive disease 40.9; malignant neoplasms (cancers) 93.6; endocrine and metabolic disorders 68.2; accidents, homicide, suicide, and other violence 39.1.

National economy

Budget (1994). Revenue: EC$265,000,000 (current revenue 70.2%; development revenue 29.8%, of which domestic sources 15.8%, foreign loans and grants 14.0%). Expenditures: EC$263,600,000 (current expenditure 70.0%; development expenditure 30.0%).
Land use (1994): forested 36%; meadows and pastures 5%; agricultural and under permanent cultivation 28%; other 31%.
Tourism: receipts from visitors (1994) U.S.$51,000,000; expenditures by nationals abroad U.S.$3,000,000.
Production (metric tons except as noted). Agriculture, forestry, fishing (1995): bananas 55,000, coconuts 23,000, eddoes and dasheens[5] 6,252[6], sweet potatoes 3,950, plantains 1,500, mangoes 1,400, yams 1,100, oranges 960, lemons and limes 870, ginger 799[6], arrowroot starch 635[7], soursops, guavas, and papaws are other important fruits; livestock (number of live animals) 13,000 sheep, 9,400 pigs, 6,200 cattle; roundwood, n.a.; fish catch 770. Mining and quarrying: sand and gravel for local use. Manufacturing (value added in EC$'000; 1988): beverages and tobacco products 9,686; food products 9,499; textiles, clothing, and footwear 3,872; metal products and electrical machinery 2,510. Construction (gross floor area planned; 1993): 103,721 sq m. Energy production (consumption): electricity (kW-hr; 1994) 64,374,000 (64,374,000); coal, none (none); crude petroleum, none (none); petroleum products (metric tons; 1994) none (39,000); natural gas, none (none).
Gross national product (1994): U.S.$235,000,000 (U.S.$2,120 per capita).

Structure of gross domestic product and labour force

	1994		1991	
	in value EC$'000,000	% of total value	labour force	% of labour force
Agriculture, forestry, fishing	64.3	11.7	8,377	20.1
Mining	2.0	0.4	98	0.2
Manufacturing	50.9	9.2	2,822	6.8
Construction	68.3	12.4	3,535	8.5
Public utilities	26.4	4.8	586	1.4
Transportation and communications	114.6	20.8	2,279	5.5
Trade	96.2	17.5	6,544	15.7
Finance, real estate	54.8	9.9	1,418	3.4
Pub. admin., defense	94.2	17.1 }	7,696	18.5
Services	10.0	1.8 }		
Other	−30.5[8]	−5.5[8]	8,327[9]	20.0[9]
TOTAL	551.2	100.0[3]	41,682	100.0[3]

Public debt (external, outstanding; 1994): U.S.$64,100,000.
Population economically active (1991): total 41,682; activity rate of total population 39.1% (participation rates: ages 15–64, 67.5%; female 35.9%; unemployed [1995] c. 20%).

Price and earnings indexes (1990 = 100)						
	1989	1990	1991	1992	1993	1994	1995
Consumer price index	92.9	100.0	105.5	109.1	113.8	115.0	117.0
Daily earnings index[10]	100.0	100.0	100.0	100.0	100.0	100.0	...

Household income and expenditure. Average household size (1991) 3.9; income per household (1988) EC$4,579 (U.S.$1,696); sources of income: n.a.; expenditure (1975–76): food and beverages 59.8%, clothing 7.7%, household furnishings 6.6%, housing 6.3%, energy 6.2%, other 13.4%.

Foreign trade[11]

Balance of trade (current prices)						
	1989	1990	1991	1992	1993	1994
EC$'000,000	−111.5	−110.6	−161.2	−113.3	−173.6	−214.0
% of total	21.7%	19.8%	30.7%	21.4%	35.7%	47.9%

Imports (1993): EC$362,715,000 (basic manufactures 25.6%; food products 23.3%; machinery and transport equipment 18.1%; chemical products 11.9%). *Major import sources:* United States 36.1%; Trinidad and Tobago 15.4%; United Kingdom 11.7%; Barbados 3.9%; Canada 3.5%.
Exports (1993): EC$156,021,000 (domestic exports 93.8%, of which bananas 47.4%, flour 18.7%, varieties of taro roots 3.4%, sweet potatoes 2.2%; reexports 6.2%). *Major export destinations:* United Kingdom 40.7%; Saint Lucia 11.5%; Trinidad and Tobago 9.4%; United States 7.3%; Antigua and Barbuda 6.5%.

Transport and communications

Transport. Railroads: none. Roads (1995): total length 634 mi, 1,020 km (paved 31%). Vehicles (1993): passenger cars 5,473; trucks and buses 2,878. Merchant marine (1992): vessels (100 gross tons and over) 881; total deadweight tonnage 7,044,189. Air transport (1992): passenger arrivals 112,574, passenger departures 113,699; airports (1996) with scheduled flights 5.
Communications. Daily newspapers: none[12]. Radio (1995): total number of receivers 65,000 (1 per 1.7 persons). Television (1995): total number of receivers 17,700 (1 per 6.3 persons). Telephones (main lines; 1993): 16,500 (1 per 6.6 persons).

Education and health

Education (1993–94)	schools	teachers	students	student/ teacher ratio
Primary (age 5–11)	65	1,080	21,386	19.8
Secondary (age 12–18)	21[13]	395	9,870	25.0
Voc., teacher tr.	2[13]	49	414	8.4

Educational attainment (1980). Percentage of population age 25 and over having: no formal schooling 2.4%; primary education 88.0%; secondary 8.2%; higher 1.4%. *Literacy* (1991): total population age 15 and over literate 64,000 (96.0%).
Health (1992): physicians 40 (1 per 2,708 persons); hospital beds (1989) 500 (1 per 209 persons); infant mortality rate (1995) per 1,000 live births 19.0.
Food (1992): daily per capita caloric intake 2,347 (vegetable products 84%, animal products 16%); 97% of FAO recommended minimum requirement.

Military

Total active duty personnel (1992): 634-member police force includes a coast guard and paramilitary unit. *Military expenditure as percentage of central government expenditure* (1989–90): 5.6%[14].

[1]Includes 6 nonelective seats occupied by senators (rather than representatives); excludes speaker who may be elected from within or from outside of the House of Assembly membership. [2]For statistical purposes and the election of legislative representatives; St. Vincent and the Grenadines has no local administrative authority. [3]Detail does not add to total given because of rounding. [4]Urban defined as Kingstown and suburbs. [5]Varieties of taro roots. [6]1993. [7]1992–93. [8]Less imputed bank service charges. [9]Unemployed. [10]Agriculture and manufacturing sectors only. [11]Imports f.o.b. in balance of trade and c.i.f. in commodities and trading partners. [12]Weekly newspapers (1992): 2. [13]1991–92. [14]May not agree with military expenditure as percentage of GNP because of different bases used.

San Marino

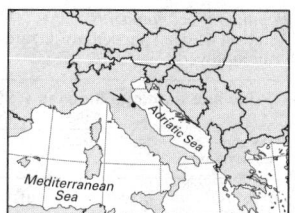

Official name: Serenissima Repubblica di San Marino (Most Serene Republic of San Marino).
Form of government: unitary multiparty republic with one legislative house (Great and General Council [60]).
Head of state and government: Captains-Regent (2).
Capital: San Marino.
Official language: Italian.
Official religion: none.
Monetary unit: 1 Italian lira (Lit; plural lire) = 100 centesimi; valuation (Oct. 11, 1996) 1 U.S.$ = Lit 1,523; 1 £ = Lit 2,399.

Area and population

Castles	Capitals	area sq mi	area sq km	population 1996[1] estimate
Acquaviva	Acquaviva	1.88	4.86	1,268
Borgo Maggiore	Borgo	3.48	9.01	5,238
Chiesanuova	Chiesanuova	2.11	5.46	863
Città	San Marino	2.74	7.09	4,357
Domagnano	Domagnano	2.56	6.62	2,171
Faetano	Faetano	2.99	7.75	829
Fiorentino	Fiorentino	2.53	6.56	1,763
Montegiardino	Montegiardino	1.28	3.31	684
Serravalle/Dogano	Serravalle	4.07	10.53	7,904
TOTAL		23.63[2]	61.19	25,077

Demography

Population (1996): 25,300.
Density (1996): persons per sq mi 1,070.7, persons per sq km 413.5.
Urban-rural (1996[1]): urban 89.4%; rural 10.6%.
Sex distribution (1996[1]): male 49.43%; female 50.57%.
Age breakdown (1996[1]): under 15, 14.6%; 15–29, 22.0%; 30–44, 24.8%; 45–59, 18.4%; 60–74, 14.1%; 75 and over, 6.1%.
Population projection: (2000) 26,900; (2010) 31,300.
Doubling time: not applicable; natural population growth is negligible.
Ethnic composition (1996[1]): Sammarinesi 75.4%; Italian 23.3%; other 1.3%.
Religious affiliation (1980): Roman Catholic 95.2%; no religion 3.0%; other 1.8%.
Major cities (1996[1]): Serravalle/Dogano 4,726; Borgo Maggiore 2,366; San Marino 2,316; Murata 1,540; Domagnano 1,036.

Vital statistics

Birth rate per 1,000 population (1991–95): 10.4 (world avg. 25.0); (1985) legitimate 95.2%; illegitimate 4.8%.
Death rate per 1,000 population (1991–95): 7.1 (world avg. 9.3).
Natural increase rate per 1,000 population (1991–95): 3.3 (world avg. 15.7).
Total fertility rate (avg. births per childbearing woman; 1995): 1.5.
Marriage rate per 1,000 population (1991–95): 8.1.
Divorce rate per 1,000 population (1991–95): 1.0.
Life expectancy at birth (1995): male 77.2 years; female 85.3 years.
Major causes of death per 100,000 population (1991–95): diseases of the circulatory system 324.8; malignant neoplasms (cancers) 229.4; accidents, violence, and suicide 45.2; diseases of the respiratory system 10.7.

National economy

Budget (1995). Revenue: Lit 521,000,000,000 (mainly receipts from postage stamp sales, tourism, and customs duties [collected by Italy and paid as a subsidy]). Expenditures: Lit 521,000,000,000 ([3]finance and economic planning 31.0%, internal affairs 11.3%, health and social security 9.0%, education and culture 7.1%, public works 6.3%).
Public debt: n.a.
Tourism: number of tourist arrivals (1995) 3,368,159; receipts from visitors (1983) U.S.$56,454,000; expenditures by nationals abroad, n.a.
Population economically active (1996[1]): total 16,073; activity rate of total population 63.5% (participation rates: ages 15–64, 88.4%; female 40.2%; unemployed 3.1%).

Price and earnings indexes (1990 = 100)

	1989	1990	1991	1992	1993	1994	1995
Consumer price index	94.0	100.0	108.0	115.7	121.9	128.0	134.3
Earnings index	...	...	...	...	...	...	...

Household income and expenditure. Total number of households (1996[1]) 9,494; average household size 2.6; income per household: n.a.; sources of income: n.a.; expenditure (1991)[4]: food, beverages, and tobacco 22.1%, housing, fuel, and electrical energy 20.9%, transportation and communications 17.6%, clothing and footwear 8.0%, furniture, appliances, and goods and services for the home 7.2%, education 7.1%, health and sanitary services 2.6%, other goods and services 14.5%.
Production (metric tons except as noted). Agriculture, forestry, fishing[3]: wheat *c.* 4,400, grapes *c.* 700, barley *c.* 500; livestock (number of live animals; 1995) 954 cattle, 694 pigs. Manufacturing (1995): processed meats 366,177 kg, of which beef 273,515 kg, pork 85,688 kg, veal 6,902 kg; cheese 78,803 kg; butter 13,739 kg; milk 1,097,890 litres; yogurt 5,722 litres; other major products include electrical appliances, musical instruments, printing

ink, paint, cosmetics, furniture, floor tiles, gold and silver jewelry, clothing, and postage stamps. Construction (new units completed; 1995): residential 145; nonresidential 123. Energy production (consumption): all electrical power is imported via electrical grid from Italy (consumption, n.a.); coal, none (n.a.); crude petroleum, none (n.a.); petroleum products, none (n.a.); natural gas, none (n.a.).
Gross national product (at current market prices; 1987): U.S.$188,000,000 (U.S.$8,590 per capita).

Structure of labour force (1996[1])

	labour force	% of labour force
Agriculture	249	1.6
Manufacturing	5,256	32.7
Construction and public utilities	1,440	9.0
Transportation and communications	311	1.9
Trade	2,641	16.4
Finance and insurance	417	2.6
Services	1,432	8.9
Public administration and defense	3,832	23.8
Other	495[5]	3.1[5]
TOTAL	16,073	100.0

Land use (1985): agricultural and under permanent cultivation 74%; meadows and pastures 22%; forested, built-on, wasteland, and other 4%.

Foreign trade

Balance of trade: n.a. San Marino and Italy form a single customs area; separate figures for San Marino are not available.
Imports (1995): manufactured goods of all kinds, oil, and gold. *Major import source:* Italy.
Exports (1995): wine, wheat, woolen goods, furniture, wood, ceramics, building stone, dairy products, meat, and postage stamps. *Major export destination:* Italy.

Transport and communications

Transport. Railroads: none (nearest rail terminal is at Rimini, Italy, 17 mi [27 km] northeast). Roads (1987): total length 147 mi, 237 km. Vehicles (1996[1]): passenger cars 23,561; trucks and buses 4,013. Merchant marine: vessels (100 gross tons and over) none. Air transport: airports with scheduled flights, none; there is, however, a heliport that provides passenger and cargo service between San Marino and Rimini, Italy, during the summer months.
Communications. Daily newspapers (1995): 5; circulation per 1,000 population, n.a. Radio (1994): total number of receivers 12,600 (1 per 1.9 persons). Television (1990): total number of receivers 8,000 (1 per 2.9 persons). Telephones (1992): 22,300 (1 per 1.1 persons).

Education and health

Education (1995–96)

	schools	teachers	students	student/teacher ratio
Primary (age 6–10)	14	217	1,134	5.2
Secondary (age 11–18)	3	134	771	5.8
Voc., teacher tr.	...	44[6]	428	6.2[6]
Higher	...	...	...	...

Educational attainment (1996[1]). Percentage of the adult labour force having: basic literacy or primary education 18.9%; secondary 40.3%; some postsecondary 34.1%; higher degree 6.7%. *Literacy* (1994): total population age 15 and over literate 20,913 (98.9%); males literate 10,154 (99.3%); females literate 10,759 (98.6%).
Health (1987): physicians 60 (1 per 375 persons); hospital beds 149 (1 per 151 persons); infant mortality rate per 1,000 live births (1990–94) 7.1.
Food (1992)[7]: daily per capita caloric intake 3,561 (vegetable products 75%, animal products 25%); 141% of FAO recommended minimum requirement.

Military

Total active duty personnel (1995): none[8]. *Military expenditure as percentage of national budget* (1987): 0.9% (world 5.4%); per capita expenditure (1987) U.S.$82.

---

[1]January 1. [2]Detail does not add to total given because of rounding. [3]Early 1980s. [4]Weighting coefficients for component expenditures are those of the 1991 official Italian consumer price index for the North-Central region of Italy. [5]Unemployed. [6]1993–94. [7]Figures are for Italy. [8]Defense is provided by a public security force of about 50; all fit males ages 16–55 constitute a militia.

São Tomé and Príncipe

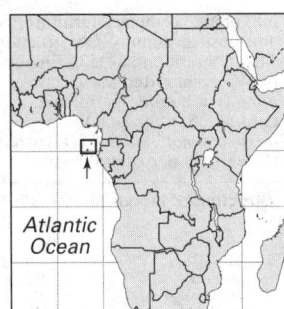

Atlantic Ocean

Official name: República democrática de São Tomé e Príncipe (Democratic Republic of São Tomé and Príncipe).
Form of government: Multiparty republic with one legislative house (National Assembly [55]).
Chief of state: President.
Head of government: Prime Minister.
Capital: São Tomé.
Official language: Portuguese.
Official religion: none.
Monetary unit: 1 dobra (Db) = 100 cêntimos; valuation (Oct. 11, 1996) 1 U.S.$ = Db 2,385; 1 £ = Db 3,757.

Area and population		area		population
		sq mi	sq km	1991 census[1]
Islands **Districts**	**Capitals**			
São Tomé		332	859	114,507
Aqua Grande	São Tomé	7	17	43,420
Cantagalo	Santana	46	119	11,421
Caué	São João Angolares	103	267	5,541
Lemba	Neves	88	229	9,448
Lobata	Guadalupe	41	105	13,101
Mé-Zóchi	Trindade	47	122	31,576
Autonomous Island		55	142	5,639
Príncipe	Santo António	55	142	5,639
TOTAL		386	1,001	120,146

Demography

Population (1996): 134,000.
Density (1996): persons per sq mi 346.5, persons per sq km 133.6.
Urban-rural (1994): urban 44.1%; rural 55.9%.
Sex distribution (1996): male 49.83%; female 50.17%.
Age breakdown (1996): under 15, 40.1%; 15–29, 29.8%; 30–44, 16.1%; 45–59, 7.2%; 60 and over, 5.4%; not stated, 1.4%.
Population projection: (2000) 146,000; (2010) 182,000.
Doubling time: 23 years.
Ethnolinguistic composition: mestiços, angolares (descendants of Angolan slaves), forros (descendants of freed slaves), serviçais (alien contract labourers), and tongas (children of serviçais) speak Portuguese; non-Portuguese-speaking Europeans speak French and Spanish.
Religious affiliation (1991): Roman Catholic, about 80.8%; remainder mostly Protestant, predominantly Seventh-day Adventist and an indigenous Evangelical Church.
Major cities (1991): São Tomé 43,420; Trindade 11,388[2]; Santana 6,190[2]; Neves 5,919[2]; Santo Amaro 5,878[2].

Vital statistics

Birth rate per 1,000 population (1995): 34.9 (world avg. 25.0); (1977) legitimate 9.8%; illegitimate 90.2%.
Death rate per 1,000 population (1995): 8.7 (world avg. 9.3).
Natural increase rate per 1,000 population (1995): 26.2 (world avg. 15.7).
Total fertility rate (avg. births per childbearing woman; 1995): 4.4.
Marriage rate per 1,000 population: n.a.
Divorce rate per 1,000 population: n.a.
Life expectancy at birth (1995): male 61.8 years; female 65.6 years.
Major causes of death per 100,000 population (1987): malaria 160.6; direct obstetric causes 76.7; pneumonia 74.0; influenza 61.5; anemias 47.3; hypertensive disease 32.1.

National economy

Budget (1994). Revenue: Db 12,329,000,000 (grants 60.9%; indirect taxes 25.2%, of which import taxes 10.3%, sales taxes 10.3%; nontax revenue 9.7%; direct taxes 4.2%). Expenditures: Db 26,421,000,000 (capital 57.3%; recurrent expenditure 42.7%, of which debt service 15.1%, personnel costs 7.1%, goods and services 5.0%).
Public debt (external, outstanding; 1994): U.S.$229,000,000.
Tourism (1990): receipts from visitors U.S.$2,000,000; expenditures by nationals abroad U.S.$2,000,000.
Production (metric tons except as noted). Agriculture, forestry, fishing (1996): coconuts 22,000, bananas 12,000, taro 6,000, cacao 3,000, cereals 3,000, palm kernels 3,000, vegetables and melons 3,000, corn (maize) 3,000, palmetto 3,000[3], cassava 2,500, fruits (other than melon) 1,700, copra 1,000[4]; livestock (number of live animals) 4,500 goats, 3,800 cattle, 2,200 sheep, 1,900 pigs; roundwood (1994) 9,000 cu m; fish catch (1993) 2,200, principally marine fish and shellfish. Mining and quarrying: some quarrying to support local construction industry. Manufacturing (value in Db; 1994): beer 628,000; clothing 604,000; lumber 328,000; bakery products 325,000; palm oil 182,000; soap 154,000; ceramics 77,000. Construction (1972): buildings authorized 44 (5,561 sq m, of which residential 3,698, mixed residential-commercial 1,361, commercial 502). Energy production (consumption): electricity (kW-hr; 1994) 16,000,000 (16,000,000); coal, none (n.a.); crude petroleum, none (n.a.); petroleum products (metric tons; 1993) none (25,000); natural gas, none (n.a.).
Household income and expenditure. Average household size (1981): 4.0; income per household: n.a.; sources of income: n.a.; expenditure (1990)[5]: food 65.7%, housing, transportation, and communications 14.6%, clothing and other items 11.4%, education and health 4.6%, housing and utilities 3.7%.

Population economically active (1991): total 49,216; activity rate of total population 41.0% (participation rates [1981]: ages 15–64, 61.1%; female 32.4%; unemployed [1994[6]] 22.0%).

Price and earnings indexes (1990 = 100)						
	1989	1990	1991	1992	1993	1994
Consumer price index	70.3	100.0	146.5	195.8	245.8	311.3
Earnings index	...	...	...	...	...	...

Gross national product (at current market prices; 1994): U.S.$31,000,000 (U.S.$250 per capita).

Structure of gross domestic product and labour force				
	1993		1991	
	in value Db '000,000	% of total value	labour force	% of labour force
Agriculture	4,663	27.7	13,592	27.6
Mining	...	...	...	...
Manufacturing }	1,326	7.9	1,510	3.1
Public utilities }			269	0.6
Construction	970	5.7	2,866	5.8
Transportation and communications }	4,642	27.6	2,186	4.4
Trade			4,451	9.0
Finance	...	...	176	0.4
Pub. admin., defense	3,870	23.0	5,592	11.4
Services	1,366	8.1	2,369	4.8
Other	...	...	16,205[7]	32.9[7]
TOTAL	16,837	100.0	49,216	100.0

Land use (1994): meadows and pastures 1.3%; agricultural and under permanent cultivation 54.0%; forest, built-on, wasteland, and other 44.7%.

Foreign trade[8]

Balance of trade (current prices)						
	1989	1990	1991	1992	1993	1994
U.S.$'000,000	−27.6	−22.2	−24.6	−22.7	−25.4	−23.9
% of total	70.1%	71.6%	67.2%	67.8%	65.8%	64.8%

Imports (1994): U.S.$30,400,000 (capital goods 40.2%, food and other agricultural products 21.5%, petroleum products 7.2%). *Major import sources* (1994): Portugal 28.3%; France 10.1%; Belgium 7.6%; Japan 5.5%; Angola 4.8%; Germany 2.6%; The Netherlands 2.4%; Gabon 1.8%; Italy 1.7%; United Kingdom 1.1%.
Exports (1994): U.S.$6,500,000 (cocoa 76.9%). *Major export destinations* (1994): The Netherlands 88.2%; Portugal 0.6%.

Transport and communications

Transport. Railroads: none. Roads (1991): total length 149 mi, 240 km (paved 41.7%). Vehicles (1987): passenger cars 2,600; trucks and buses 300. Merchant marine (1992): vessels (100 gross tons and over) 4; total deadweight tonnage 2,277. Air transport (1993): passenger-mi 5,000,000, passenger-km 8,000,000; short ton-mi cargo 700,000, short ton-km cargo 1,000,000; airports (1996) with scheduled flights 2.
Communications. Daily newspapers: none; 2 government weeklies (circulation, n.a.). Radio (1995): total number of receivers 31,000 (1 per 4.2 persons). Television (1995): total number of receivers 21,000 (1 per 6.2 persons). Telephones (main lines; 1993): 2,400 (1 per 52 persons).

Education and health

Education (1989)				
	schools	teachers	students	student/ teacher ratio
Primary (age 6–13)	64	559	19,822	35.5
Secondary (age 14–18)	11[9]	318	7,446	23.4
Voc., teacher tr.	2[9]	18[10]	289	...
Higher	...	...	700[11]	...

Educational attainment (1981). Percentage of population age 25 and over having: no formal schooling 56.6%; incomplete primary education 18.0%; primary 19.2%; incomplete secondary 4.6%; complete secondary 1.3%; post-secondary 0.3%. *Literacy* (1981): total population age 15 and over literate 28,114 (54.2%); males literate 17,689 (70.2%); females literate 10,425 (39.1%).
Health: physicians (1989) 61 (1 per 1,881 persons); hospital beds (1983) 640 (1 per 158 persons); infant mortality rate per 1,000 live births (1995) 62.1.
Food (1992): daily per capita caloric intake 2,129 (vegetable products 96%, animal products 4%); 91% of FAO recommended minimum requirement.

Military

Total active duty personnel: a gendarmerie of about 900 men was to be established in the early 1990s. *Military expenditure as percentage of GNP* (1980): 1.6% (world 5.4%); per capita expenditure U.S.$6.

[1]Preliminary. [2]1981. [3]1988. [4]1994. [5]Weights based on CPI components. [6]First 10 months. [7]Includes 15,148 unemployed. [8]Import figures are c.i.f. [9]1984–85. [10]Vocational teachers only. [11]Students abroad, 1982–83.

Saudi Arabia

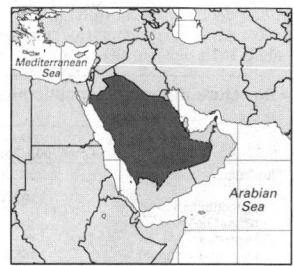

Official name: Al-Mamlakah
al-ʿArabīyah as-Saʿūdīyah (Kingdom
of Saudi Arabia).
Form of government: monarchy[1].
Head of state and government: King.
Capital: Riyadh.
Official language: Arabic.
Official religion: Islam.
Monetary unit: 1 Saudi riyal
(SRls) = 100 halalah; valuation (Oct.
11, 1996) 1 U.S.$ = SRls 3.75;
1 £ = SRls 5.93.

Area and population

Geographic Regions		area[2]		population
Administrative Regions[3]	Capitals	sq mi	sq km	1985 estimate
Al-Gharbīyah (Western)		—	—	3,043,189
Al-Bāḥah	Al-Bāḥah	6,000	15,000	...
Al-Madīnah al-Munawwarah	Medina (Al-Madīnah)	67,000	173,000	...
Makkah al-Mukarramah	Mecca (Makkah)	63,000	164,000	...
Al-Janūbīyah (Southern)		—	—	625,017
ʿAsīr	Abha	31,000	81,000	...
Jīzān	Jīzān	6,000	17,000	...
Najrān	Najrān	46,000	119,000	...
Ash-Shamālīyah (Northern)		—	—	679,476
Al-Ḥudūd ash-Shamālīyah (Northern Borders)	ʿArʿar	43,000	120,000	...
Al-Jawf	Sakākah	54,000	139,000	...
Tabūk	Tabūk	42,000	108,000	...
Ash-Sharqīyah (Eastern)		—	—	3,030,765
Ash-Sharqīyah (Eastern)	Ad-Dammām	274,000	710,000	...
Al-Wūsṭā (Central)		—	—	3,632,092
Ḥāʾil	Ḥāʾil	48,000	125,000	...
Al-Qaşīm	Buraydah	25,000	65,000	...
Ar-Riyāḍ	Riyadh (Ar-Riyāḍ)	159,000	412,000	...
TOTAL		864,000[4]	2,248,000[4]	11,010,539[5]

Demography

Population (1996): 18,426,000.
Density (1996): persons per sq mi 21.3, persons per sq km 8.2.
Urban-rural (1995): urban 80.2%; rural 19.8%.
Sex distribution (1995): male 55.72%; female 44.28%.
Age breakdown (1995): under 15, 41.9%; 15–29, 24.5%; 30–44, 19.7%; 45–59, 9.5%; 60–74, 3.6%; 75 and over, 0.8%.
Population projection: (2000) 21,257,000; (2010) 28,880,000.
Doubling time: 23 years.
Ethnic composition (1983): Saudi 82.0%; Yemeni 9.6%; other Arab 3.4%; other 5.0%.
Religious affiliation (1980): Sunnī Muslim 95.5%; Shīʿī Muslim 3.3%; Christian 0.8%; other 0.4%.
Major cities (1980): Riyadh (Ar-Riyāḍ) 1,800,000[6]; Jiddah 1,800,000[6]; Mecca (Makkah) 550,000; Aṭ-Ṭāʾif 300,000.

Vital statistics

Birth rate per 1,000 population (1990–95): 35.1 (world avg. 25.0).
Death rate per 1,000 population (1990–95): 4.7 (world avg. 9.3).
Natural increase rate per 1,000 population (1990–95): 30.4 (world avg. 15.7).
Total fertility rate (avg. births per childbearing woman; 1990–95): 6.4.
Life expectancy at birth (1990–95): male 68.4 years; female 71.4 years.
Major causes of death per 100,000 population: n.a.; however, principal infectious diseases include malaria, diarrheal diseases, cholera, trachoma, cerebrospinal meningitis, yellow fever, typhoid, tuberculosis, and lung infections. Parasitic infections, motor vehicle accidents, and metabolic disorders are also significant.

National economy

Budget (1996). Revenue: SRls 131,500,000,000 (oil revenues 81.2%). Expenditures: SRls 150,000,000,000 (defense and security [1995] 33.5%, education 18.4%, health and social development 8.9%, transportation and communications 4.1%, municipal services 3.6%).
Public debt (external, outstanding; 1991): U.S.$2,893,000,000.
Production (metric tons except as noted). Agriculture, forestry, fishing (1995): wheat 2,000,000, barley 1,200,000, dates 566,000, tomatoes 445,000, watermelons 400,000, potatoes 170,000, grapes 119,000, cucumbers and gherkins 115,000, eggplants 69,000, pumpkins, squash, and gourds 69,000, carrots 25,000, millet 12,000; livestock (number of live animals) 7,475,000 sheep, 4,200,000 goats, 418,000 camels, 204,000 cattle, 97,000 asses, 83,000,000 chickens; fish catch (1993) 49,920. Mining and quarrying (1995): gypsum (1994) 337,573; gold 8,080 kg. Manufacturing (1994): cement 17,012,815; steel 2,410,000; fuel oils 171,000,000 barrels; diesel oil 165,000,000 barrels; gasoline and naphtha 146,000,000 barrels; jet fuel 40,000,000 barrels; asphalt and related products 35,070,000 barrels[7]. Construction (1991): residential 16,077,677 sq m; nonresidential 2,204,894 sq m. Energy production (consumption): electricity (kW-hr; 1994) 66,760,000,000 (66,760,000,000); coal, n.a. (n.a.); crude petroleum (barrels; 1995) 2,871,000,000 (1994; 588,700,000); petroleum products (metric tons; 1994) 87,769,000 (34,482,000); natural gas (cu m; 1994) 37,701,000,000 (37,701,000,000).
Land use (1994): forested 0.8%; meadows and pastures 55.8%; agricultural and under permanent cultivation 1.8%; built-on, waste, and other 41.6%.
Population economically active (1994): total 5,614,000; activity rate of total population 32.2% (participation rates [1988] ages 15–64, 59.1%; female 3.5%).

Price and earnings indexes (1990 = 100)

	1989	1990	1991	1992	1993	1994	1995
Consumer price index	98.0	100.0	104.9	104.8	105.9	106.5	111.3
Earnings index	...	...	...	...	...	...	...

Gross national product (1994): U.S.$126,597,000,000 (U.S.$7,240 per capita).

Structure of gross domestic product and labour force

	1993		1990	
	in value[8] SRls '000,000	% of total value	labour force	% of labour force
Agriculture	28,300	6.1	569,200	9.9
Mining }			3,500	0.1
Oil sector }	157,900	34.6	46,800	0.8
Manufacturing	35,000	7.7	374,900	6.5
Construction	37,000	8.1	944,100	16.4
Public utilities	900	0.2	126,900	2.2
Transp. and commun.	30,000	6.6	262,300	4.5
Trade	31,800	7.0	898,300	15.6
Finance	28,800[9]	6.3[9]	99,000	1.7
Pub. admin., defense	90,000	19.7	624,800	10.8
Services	8,500	1.9 }	1,822,000	31.6
Other	7,800[10]	1.7[10] }		
TOTAL	456,000	100.0[4]	5,771,800	100.0[4]

Household income and expenditure. Average household size (1992) 6.1; income per household: n.a.; sources of income: n.a.; expenditure (1988)[11]: food 37%, housing 21%, transportation and communications 15%, clothing 8%, household furnishings 7%, education and entertainment 2%.
Tourism: receipts from visitors (1989) U.S.$2,050,000,000; expenditures by nationals abroad (1988) U.S.$2,000,000,000.
Pilgrims to Mecca from abroad (1996): more than 2,000,000.

Foreign trade[12]

Balance of trade (current prices)

	1989	1990	1991	1992	1993	1994
U.S.$'000,000	+7,228	+20,347	+18,718	+16,582	+14,198	+22,286
% of total	14.6%	29.7%	24.3%	19.7%	20.1%	32.3%

Imports (1994): SRls 87,422,000,000 (1993; machinery and appliances 21.3%, transport equipment 20.8%, metals and metal articles 10.1%, textiles and clothing 7.8%, chemicals 7.2%, vegetables 5.2%, live animals and products 3.5%). *Major import sources:* U.S. 21.3%; Japan 11.7%; U.K. 8.5%; Germany 8.3%; Italy 4.7%; France 4.3%; Switzerland 4.2%; S. Korea 2.8%.
Exports (1994): SRls 170,884,300,000 (1993; petroleum 97.0%, other 3.0%). *Major export destinations:* Japan 16.7%; U.S. 16.6%; S. Korea 7.9%; France 5.5%; The Netherlands 3.3%; Italy 2.9%; India 2.9%; U.K. 2.3%; Spain 2.2%.

Transport and communications

Transport. Railroads (1993): route length 864 mi, 1,390 km; (1992–93) passenger-mi 86,780,000, passenger-km 139,660,000; (1992–93) short ton-mi cargo 621,200,000, metric ton-km cargo 907,000,000. Roads (1995): total length 98,798 mi, 159,000 km (paved 42.7%). Vehicles (1995): passenger cars 1,710,000; trucks and buses 1,172,600. Merchant marine (1992): vessels (100 gross tons and over) 301; total deadweight tonnage 1,381,651. Air transport (1995)[13]: passenger-mi 11,500,000,000, passenger-km 18,501,400,000; short ton-mi cargo 613,000,000, metric ton-km cargo 894,900,000; airports (1996) with scheduled flights 25.
Communications. Daily newspapers (1992): total number 13; total circulation 729,000; circulation per 1,000 population 34. Radio (1995): 3,800,000 receivers (1 per 4.7 persons). Television (1995): 4,700,000 receivers (1 per 3.8 persons). Telephones (main lines; 1994): 1,530,000 (1 per 11.4 persons).

Education and health

Education (1994)

	schools	teachers	students	student/ teacher ratio
Primary (age 6–12)	10,699	142,760	2,114,736	14.8
Secondary (age 13–18)	6,346	84,512	1,156,590	13.7
Voc., teacher tr.[14]	293	7,359	84,611	11.5
Higher	77	10,280	155,390	15.1

Educational attainment (1986). Percentage of population age 25 and over having: no formal schooling 31.8%; primary, secondary, or higher education 68.2%. *Literacy* (1995): percentage of population age 15 and over literate 62.8%; males literate 71.5%; females literate 50.2%.
Health (1995): physicians 29,227 (1 per 612 persons); hospital beds 41,287 (1 per 433 persons); infant mortality rate per 1,000 live births (1990–95) 29.0.
Food (1994): daily per capita caloric intake 2,735 (vegetable products 82%, animal products 18%); 113% of FAO recommended minimum requirement.

Military

Total active duty personnel (1996): 105,500 (army 66.4%, navy 12.8%, air force 20.9%). *Military expenditure as percentage of GDP* (1994): 14.2% (world 3.0%); per capita expenditure U.S.$953.

[1]The Consultative Council, which consists of 60 appointed members and a speaker, acts as an advisory and reviewing body only. [2]Estimated. [3]13 administrative regions created September 1993. [4]Detail does not add to total given because of rounding. [5]Preliminary 1992 census total 16,929,294; detail, n.a. [6]1985 estimate. [7]1992. [8]In purchasers' value at current prices. [9]Finance includes real estate and business services. [10]Other equals import duties. [11]Urban middle-income households only. [12]Import figures are c.i.f. [13]Domestic and international operation of Saudi Arabian Airlines. [14]Includes intermediate colleges.

Senegal

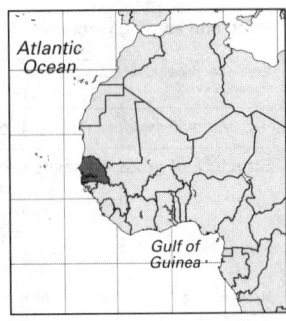

Official name: République du Sénégal (Republic of Senegal).
Form of government: multiparty republic with one legislative house (National Assembly [120]).
Chief of state: President.
Head of government: Prime Minister.
Capital: Dakar.
Official language: French.
Official religion: none.
Monetary unit: 1 CFA franc (CFAF) = 100 centimes; valuation (Oct. 11, 1996) 1 U.S.$ = CFAF 518.24; 1 £ = CFAF 816.38.

Area and population

Regions	Capitals	area sq mi	area sq km	population 1994 estimate
Dakar	Dakar	212	550	1,869,000
Diourbel	Diourbel	1,683	4,359	750,000
Fatick	Fatick	3,064	7,935	569,000
Kaolack	Kaolack	6,181	16,010	948,000
Kolda	Kolda	8,112	21,011	689,000
Louga	Louga	11,270	29,188	525,000
Saint-Louis	Saint-Louis	17,034	44,117	749,000
Tambacounda	Tambacounda	23,012	59,602	449,000
Thiès	Thiès	2,549	6,601	1,115,000
Ziguinchor	Ziguinchor	2,834	7,339	467,000
TOTAL		75,951	196,712	8,127,000[1]

Demography

Population (1996): 8,532,000.
Density (1996): persons per sq mi 112.3, persons per sq km 43.4.
Urban-rural (1995): urban 42.3%; rural 57.7%.
Sex distribution (1995): male 50.05%; female 49.95%.
Age breakdown (1995): under 15, 44.6%; 15–29, 26.9%; 30–44, 15.5%; 45–59, 8.3%; 60 to 74, 3.9%; 75 and over, 0.8%.
Population projection: (2000) 9,495,000; (2010) 12,241,000.
Doubling time: 23 years.
Ethnic composition (1988): Wolof 42.7%; Serer 14.9%; Peul (Fulani) 14.4%; Tukulor 9.3%; Diola 5.3%; Malinke (Mandingo) 3.6%; other 9.8%.
Religious affiliation (1988): Sunnī Muslim 94.0%; Christian, predominantly Roman Catholic, 4.9%; traditional beliefs and other 1.1%.
Major cities (1994): Dakar 785,071 (urban agglomeration 1,869,323[2]); Thiès 216,381; Kaolack 193,115; Ziguinchor 161,680; Rufisque 138,837[3]; Saint-Louis 132,444.

Vital statistics

Birth rate per 1,000 population (1995): 42.9 (world avg. 25.0).
Death rate per 1,000 population (1995): 11.6 (world avg. 9.3).
Natural increase rate per 1,000 population (1995): 31.3 (world avg. 15.7).
Total fertility rate (avg. births per childbearing woman; 1995): 6.0.
Marriage rate per 1,000 population: n.a.
Divorce rate per 1,000 population: n.a.
Life expectancy at birth (1995): male 55.6 years; female 58.7 years.
Major causes of death (percentage of officially confirmed deaths from infectious diseases only; 1988): malaria 44.8%; tetanus 17.8%; meningitis 15.3%; tuberculosis of respiratory system 10.4%.

National economy

Budget (1995). Revenue: CFAF 438,200,000,000 (tax revenue 75.4%, grants 16.8%, nontax revenue 7.8%). Expenditures: CFAF 453,900,000,000 (current expenditures 74.4%, development expenditure 25.6%).
Production (metric tons except as noted). Agriculture, forestry, fishing (1995): sugarcane 882,960, peanuts (groundnuts) 790,617, millet 666,805, paddy rice 155,152, sorghum 127,328, corn (maize) 106,509, cassava 55,515, seed cotton 37,000; livestock (number of live animals) 4,800,000 sheep, 3,250,000 goats, 2,850,000 cattle, 500,000 horses; roundwood (1994) 4,421,000 cu m; fish catch 314,800. Mining and quarrying (1994): calcium phosphate 1,587,000; salt 87,600; aluminum phosphate 19,200. Manufacturing (1993): cement 591,200; fertilizers 147,900; wheat flour 138,900; sugar 46,100; soap 35,700; canned fish 22,476; cigarettes (1992) 3,350,000,000 units; plastic footwear 507,500 pairs. Construction (authorized; 1993)[4]: residential 357,000 sq m; nonresidential 235,000 sq m. Energy production (consumption): electricity (kW-hr; 1994) 769,000,000 (408,000,000); coal, none (none); crude petroleum (barrels; 1994) none (6,392,000); petroleum products (metric tons; 1994) 856,000,000 (903,000,000); natural gas, none (none).
Population economically active (1988): total 2,347,556; activity rate of total population 34.0% (participation rates: ages 15–60, 53.1%; female 25.6%; unemployed [1992] 24.4%).

Price and earnings indexes (1990 = 100)

	1990	1991	1992	1993	1994	1995	1996
Consumer price index[4]	100.0	98.2	98.1	97.6	129.1	139.2	138.9[5]
Hourly earnings index[6]	100.0	100.0	100.0	100.0	...	...	...

Household income word expenditure. Average household size (1991) 8.7; average annual income per household: n.a.; sources of income: n.a.; expenditure (early 1980s): food 49%, clothing and footwear 11%, housing 7%, education 6%.

Public debt (external, outstanding; 1994): U.S.$3,070,000,000.
Gross national product (at current market prices; 1994): U.S.$4,952,000,000 (U.S.$610 per capita).

Structure of gross domestic product and labour force

	1994 in value CFAF '000,000,000[7]	1994 % of total value	1991 labour force	1991 % of labour force
Agriculture	332.6	21.8	1,789,467	65.3
Mining	} 199.0	13.0	1,998	0.1
Manufacturing			161,124	5.9
Public utilities	33.1	2.2	...	...
Construction	51.7	3.4	60,935	2.2
Transp. and commun.	145.7	9.5	58,081	2.1
Trade	} 321.5	21.1	378,241	13.8
Finance			4,623	0.2
Services	} 443.2	29.0	...	...
Pub. admin., defense			268,721	9.8
Other	—	—	16,286	0.6
TOTAL	1,526.6[1]	100.0	2,739,476	100.0

Tourism (1994): receipts from visitors U.S.$115,000,000; expenditures by nationals abroad U.S.$70,000,000.
Land use (1994): forested 39.5%; meadows and pastures 29.6%; agricultural and under permanent cultivation 12.2%; other 18.7%.

Foreign trade[8]

Balance of trade (current prices)

	1989	1990	1991	1992	1993	1994
U.S.$'000,000	−529	−553	−447	−489	−630	−522
% of total	27.6%	27.1%	25.5%	26.4%	35.5%	29.2%

Imports (1994): U.S.$1,154,000,000 (agricultural products 33.4%, of which rice 7.4%, fixed vegetable oils 5.1%; capital goods 13.0%[9]; refined petroleum 9.0%[9]. *Major import sources:* France 34.2%; Cameroon 7.9%; Nigeria 6.9%; Italy 5.4%; Thailand 4.6%.
Exports (1994): U.S.$632,000,000 (fish and crustaceans 23.3%; peanut [groundnut] oil 11.1%; phosphates 8.7%; manufactured phosphate derivatives 5.4%; cotton lint 3.7%). *Major export destinations:* France 26.0%; Italy 8.5%; Mali 7.9%; Cameroon 7.4%; Iran 3.6%; Spain 3.6%.

Transport and communications

Transport. Railroads: (1994) route length 562 mi, 904 km; (1991) passenger-mi 108,000,000, passenger-km 174,000,000; short ton-mi cargo 418,000,000, metric ton-km cargo 610,000,000. Roads (1994): total length 8,873 mi, 14,280 km (paved 28%). Vehicles (1993): passenger cars 102,000; trucks and buses 46,000. Merchant marine (1992): vessels (100 gross tons and over) 183; total deadweight tonnage 27,473. Air transport (1995)[10]: passenger-mi 138,455,000, passenger-km 222,822,000; short ton-mi cargo 10,461,000, metric ton-km cargo 15,273,000; airports (1996) with scheduled flights 7.
Communications. Daily newspapers (1992): total number 1; total circulation 50,000; circulation per 1,000 population 6.5. Radio (1995): total number of receivers 850,000 (1 per 9.8 persons). Television (1995): total number of receivers 61,000 (1 per 140 persons). Telephones (main lines; 1993): 64,100 (1 per 123 persons).

Education and health

Education (1992–93)

	schools	teachers	students	student/ teacher ratio
Primary (age 6–12)	2,454	12,711	738,550	58.1
Secondary (age 13–18)	359	5,509	182,140	33.1
Vocational	19	182	7,301	40.1
Higher[11]	2	784	16,733	21.3

Educational attainment (1988). Percentage of population age 6–34 having: no formal schooling 62.6%; primary education 25.7%; secondary 8.4%; higher 0.8%; other 2.5%. *Literacy* (1995): percentage of total population age 15 and over literate 1,523,000 (33.1%); males literate 985,000 (43.0%); females literate 538,000 (23.2%).
Health (1992): physicians 520 (1 per 14,825 persons); hospital beds 7,408 (1 per 1,041 persons); infant mortality rate per 1,000 live births (1995): 73.6.
Food (1992): daily per capita caloric intake 2,262 (vegetable products 91%, animal products 9%); 95% of FAO recommended minimum requirement.

Military

Total active duty personnel (1996): 13,400[12] (army 89.9%, navy 5.2%, air force 4.9%). *Military expenditure as percentage of GNP* (1994): 1.6% (world 3.0%); per capita expenditure U.S.$7.

[1]Detail does not add to total given because of rounding. [2]Urbanized area of Pikine (1994 population estimate 855,287) is within Dakar urban agglomeration. [3]Within Dakar urban agglomeration. [4]Capital region only. [5]March. [6]Index refers to the *S.M.I.G.* (*salaire minimum interprofessionnel garanti*), a form of minimum professional wage. [7]At constant 1987 prices. [8]Imports f.o.b.; exports c.i.f. [9]Estimated figure. [10]Represents ¹⁄₁₁ of total international scheduled traffic of Air Afrique (government-supported airline of 11 West African countries). [11]Universities only; 1994–95. [12]Excludes 1,500 French troops.

Seychelles

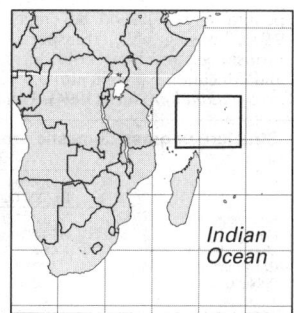

Official name: Repiblik Sesel (Creole);
  Republic of Seychelles (English);
  République des Seychelles (French).
Form of government: multiparty
  republic with one legislative house
  (National Assembly [33]).
Head of state and government:
  President.
Capital: Victoria.
Official languages: none[1].
Official religion: none.
Monetary unit: 1 Seychelles rupee
  (SR) = 100 cents; valuation (Oct. 11,
  1996) 1 U.S.$ = SR 5.00;
  1 £ = SR 7.87.

Indian Ocean

Area and population

Island Groups	Capital	area sq mi	area sq km	population 1987 census
Central (Granitic) group				
La Digue and satellites	—	6	15	1,926
Mahé and satellites	Victoria	61	158	61,183
Praslin and satellites	—	16	42	5,002
Silhouette	—	8	20	191
Other islands	—	2	4	0
Outer (Coralline) islands	—	83	214	296
TOTAL		176	455[2]	68,598

Demography

Population (1996): 76,100.
Density (1996): persons per sq mi 432.4, persons per sq km 167.3.
Urban-rural (1990): urban 59.3%; rural 40.7%.
Sex distribution (1995): male 48.61%; female 51.39%.
Age breakdown (1995): under 15, 31.2%; 15–29, 32.0%; 30–44, 20.1%; 45–59, 8.2%; 60–74, 6.0%; 75 and over, 2.5%.
Population projection: (2000) 80,900; (2010) 94,100.
Doubling time: 47 years.
Ethnic composition (1983): Seychellois Creole (mixture of Asian, African, and European) 89.1%; Indian 4.7%; Malagasy 3.1%; Chinese 1.6%; English 1.5%.
Religious affiliation (1996): Roman Catholic 88.6%; other Christian (mostly Anglican) 7.7%; Hindu 0.7%; other 3.0%.
Major city (1993): Victoria 25,000.

Vital statistics

Birth rate per 1,000 population (1995): 21.0 (world avg. 25.0); (1993) legitimate 21.6%; illegitimate 78.4%.
Death rate per 1,000 population (1995): 7.0 (world avg. 9.3).
Natural increase rate per 1,000 population (1995): 14.0 (world avg. 15.7).
Total fertility rate (avg. births per childbearing woman; 1995): 2.1.
Marriage rate per 1,000 population (1993): 11.3.
Divorce rate per 1,000 population (1993): 1.1.
Life expectancy at birth (1994): male 66.0 years; female 73.0 years.
Major causes of death per 100,000 population (1993): diseases of the circulatory system 239.4, of which cerebrovascular disease 72.0; malignant neoplasms (cancers) 141.2; diseases of the respiratory system 87.2, of which pneumonia 23.5; infectious and parasitic diseases 49.8; diseases of the digestive system 47.1; accidents and adverse effects 45.7.

National economy

Budget (1996). Revenue: SR 1,366,100,000 (customs taxes and duties 32.9%, transfers from Social Security Fund 11.0%, business taxes 9.6%, dividends and interest 6.5%, administrative fees 5.9%, fees and fines 4.5%, grants 1.1%). Expenditures: SR 1,330,400,000 (debt service 17.5%, capital projects 15.0%, education 10.3%, health 8.1%, tourism and transport 6.3%, social security 5.6%, defense 3.9%).
Tourism (1995): receipts from visitors SR 466,300,000; expenditures by nationals abroad U.S.$16,000,000[3].
Land use (1994): forested 11.1%; agricultural and under permanent cultivation 15.6%; built-on, wasteland, and other 73.3%.
Gross national product (at current market prices; 1994): U.S.$453,000,000 (U.S.$6,210 per capita).

Structure of gross domestic product and labour force

	1995 in value SR '000,000	1995 % of total value	labour force[4]	% of labour force
Agriculture	97.9	4.1	1,883	7.5
Mining, manufacturing, and construction	489.6	20.5	4,883	19.5
Tourism	293.8	12.3	4,662	18.6
Transportation and communications	623.3	26.1	3,626	14.5
Finance	303.3	12.7		
Public admin., defense	343.9	14.4	9,944	39.8
Other	236.4	9.9		
TOTAL	2,388.3[2]	100.0	24,998	100.0[2]

Production (metric tons except as noted). Agriculture, forestry, fishing (1995): coconuts 3,100, bananas 1,850, copra 1,000[5], cinnamon 470, tea 226; livestock (number of live animals) 18,200 pigs, 4,900 goats, 1,900 cattle, 600,000 chickens; fish catch (1995) 4,313, of which (1989) jack 36.9%, snapper 20.8%,

mackerel 6.7%, kawakawa 5.3%. Mining and quarrying (1994): guano 5,000. Manufacturing (1995): canned tuna 7,495; soft drinks 84,630 hectolitres; beer and stout 58,520 hectolitres; cigarettes 56,000,000 units. Energy production (consumption): electricity (kW-hr; 1994) 126,000,000 (126,000,000); coal, none (n.a.); crude petroleum, none (n.a.); petroleum products (metric tons; 1994) none (55,000); natural gas, none (n.a.).
Population economically active (1993): total 28,100; activity rate of total population 38.9% (participation rates: ages 15–64 [1989] 74.3%; female [1989] 42.5%; unemployed 11.5%).

Price and earnings indexes (1990 = 100)

	1989	1990	1991	1992	1993	1994	1995
Consumer price index	96.2	100.0	102.0	105.3	106.7	108.7	108.4
Monthly earnings index	...	100.0	100.6	117.3	115.0	115.4	...

Public debt (external, outstanding; 1994): U.S.$146,900,000.
Household income and expenditure. Average household size (1987) 4.5; average annual income per household (1978) SR 18,480 (U.S.$2,658); sources of income: wages and salaries 77.2%, self-employment 3.8%, transfer payments 3.2%; expenditure (1991–92): food and beverages 47.6%, housing 15.1%, clothing and footwear 8.6%, transportation 8.0%, energy and water 7.4%, recreation 6.7%, household and personal goods 6.6%.

Foreign trade

Balance of trade (current prices)

	1990	1991	1992	1993	1994	1995
SR '000,000	−692.3	−652.2	−735.2	−969.8	−786.7	−856.7
% of total	53.4%	55.8%	59.9%	64.7%	60.6%	62.9%

Imports (1995): SR 1,109,200,000 (machinery and transport equipment 29.5%, of which nuclear reactors, boilers, and other heavy machinery 11.0%, electrical machinery 9.4%; manufactured goods 25.0%, of which metal manufactures 6.2%, paper products 2.7%; food, beverages, and tobacco 22.0%; mineral fuels, lubricants, and related materials 14.0%, of which petroleum products 12.9%; chemicals 7.9%). *Major import sources* (1995): Singapore 15.1%; United Kingdom 14.7%; South Africa 12.9%; Yemen 11.9%; France 7.3%; Japan 5.8%; United States 3.9%; Italy 3.6%; The Netherlands 2.4%; Spain 2.2%; India 2.1%; Thailand 2.1%; Kenya 1.9%.
Exports (1995): SR 252,500,000[6] (petroleum products 47.2%[7]; canned tuna 34.8%; other fish 4.0%; frozen prawns 2.7%; cinnamon bark 1.4%; buttons 0.2%; copra 0.1%). *Major export destinations* (1995)[8]: China 15.0%; United Kingdom 12.4%; Thailand 11.5%; India 3.5%; Germany 2.6%; United States 1.8%; Japan 1.8%.

Transport and communications

Transport. Railroads: none. Roads (1995): total length 206 mi, 331 km (paved 76%). Vehicles (1994): passenger cars 5,000; trucks and buses 2,000. Merchant marine (1992): vessels (100 gross tons and over) 9; total deadweight tonnage 3,337. Air transport (1995): passenger arrivals 125,000, passenger departures 125,000; metric ton cargo unloaded 2,704, metric ton cargo loaded 782; airports (1996) with scheduled flights 2.
Communications. Daily newspapers (1992): total number 1; total circulation 3,000; circulation per 1,000 population 44. Radio (1995): total number of receivers 50,000 (1 per 1.5 persons). Television (1995): total number of receivers 13,000 (1 per 5.8 persons). Telephones (main lines; 1995): 13,100 (1 per 5.7 persons).

Education and health

Education (1996)

	schools[9]	teachers	students	student/ teacher ratio
Primary (age 6–15)	24	562	9,588	17.1
Secondary (age 16–18)	20	412	6,192	15.0
Voc., teacher tr.	1	145	1,437	9.9

Educational attainment (1987). Percentage of population age 12 and over having: no formal schooling 7.8%; primary education 51.5%; some secondary 12.2%; complete secondary 13.4%; vocational 9.9%; postsecondary 3.1%; unspecified 2.1%. *Literacy* (1987): total population age 15 and over literate 37,984 (84.2%); males literate 18,427 (82.9%); females literate 19,557 (85.7%).
Health[10] (1995): physicians 77 (1 per 974 persons); hospital beds 416 (1 per 180 persons); infant mortality rate per 1,000 live births 18.3.
Food (1992): daily per capita caloric intake 2,287 (vegetable products 85%, animal products 15%); 98% of FAO recommended minimum requirement.

Military

Total active duty personnel (1996): 300[11]. *Military expenditure as percentage of GNP* (1995): 3.9% (world 2.8%); per capita expenditure U.S.$192.

---

[1]Creole, English, and French are all national languages per 1993 constitution. [2]Detail does not add to total given because of rounding. [3]1992. [4]Excludes unemployed, self-employed, and domestic workers. [5]1993. [6]Includes SR 139,600,000 of reexports. [7]Items reexported. [8]Domestic export only. [9]1994. [10]Physicians and hospital beds in government hospitals only. [11]All services form part of the army.

Sierra Leone

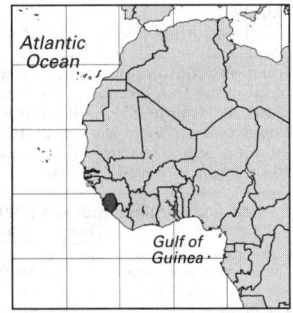

Official name: Republic of
Sierra Leone.
Form of government: multiparty
republic with one legislative house
(National Assembly [801]).
Head of state and government:
President.
Capital: Freetown.
Official language: English.
Official religion: none.
Monetary unit: 1 leone (Le) = 100
cents; valuation (Oct. 11, 1996)
1 U.S.$ = Le 870; 1 £ = Le 1,370.

Area and population		area		population
Provinces				1985
Districts	Capitals	sq mi	sq km	census[2]
Eastern Province	Kenema	6,005	15,553	960,551
Kailahun	Kailahun	1,490	3,859	233,839
Kenema	Kenema	2,337	6,053	337,055
Kono	Sefadu	2,178	5,641	389,657
Northern Province	Makeni	13,875	35,936	1,259,641
Bombali	Makeni	3,083	7,985	317,729
Kambia	Kambia	1,200	3,108	186,231
Koinaduga	Kabala	4,680	12,121	183,286
Port Loko	Port Loko	2,208	5,719	329,344
Tonkolili	Magburaka	2,704	7,003	243,051
Southern Province	Bo	7,604	19,694	741,377
Bo	Bo	2,015	5,219	268,671
Bonthe (incl. Sherbro)	Bonthe	1,339	3,468	105,007
Moyamba	Moyamba	2,665	6,902	250,514
Pujehun	Pujehun	1,585	4,105	117,185
Western Area[3]	Freetown	215	557	554,243
TOTAL		27,699	71,740	3,515,812

Demography

Population (1996): 4,617,000.
Density (1996): persons per sq mi 166.7, persons per sq km 64.4.
Urban-rural (1995): urban 36.2%; rural 63.8%.
Sex distribution (1995): male 49.10%; female 50.90%.
Age breakdown (1995): under 15, 44.2%; 15–29, 26.2%; 30–44, 15.7%; 45–59,
9.0%; 60–74, 4.2%; 75 and over, 0.7%.
Population projection: (2000) 5,069,000; (2010) 6,366,000.
Doubling time: 29 years.
Ethnic composition (1983): Mende 34.6%; Temne 31.7%; Limba 8.4%; Kono
5.2%; Bullom-Sherbro 3.7%; Fulani 3.7%; Kuranko 3.5%; Yalunka 3.5%;
Kissi 2.3%; other 3.4%.
Religious affiliation (1993): Sunnī Muslim 60.0%; traditional beliefs 30.0%;
Christian 10.0%[4].
Major cities (1985): Freetown 469,776; Koidu–New Sembehun 80,000; Bo
26,000; Kenema 13,000; Makeni 12,000.

Vital statistics

Birth rate per 1,000 population (1990–95): 49.1 (world avg. 25.0); legitimate,
n.a.; illegitimate, n.a.
Death rate per 1,000 population (1990–95): 25.1 (world avg. 9.3).
Natural increase rate per 1,000 population (1990–95): 24.0 (world avg. 15.7).
Total fertility rate (avg. births per childbearing woman; 1990–95): 6.5.
Marriage rate per 1,000 population: n.a.
Divorce rate per 1,000 population: n.a.
Life expectancy at birth (1990–95): male 41.4 years; female 44.6 years.
Major causes of death per 100,000 population: n.a.; however, the major dis-
eases are malaria, tuberculosis, leprosy, whooping cough, measles, tetanus,
and diarrhea.

National economy

Budget (1994–95). Revenue: Le 61,743,000,000 (customs duties 41.6%; excise
taxes 25.1%; company income tax 7.8%; personal income tax 7.7%). Expenditures: Le 102,279,000,000 (1993–94; recurrent expenditures 77.2%, of
which defense 20.0%, debt service 15.9%, education 11.3%, health 4.5%,
social security 1.2%; capital expenditures 22.8%).
Public debt (external, outstanding; 1994): U.S.$909,000,000.
Tourism (1994): receipts from visitors U.S.$10,000,000; expenditures by na-
tionals abroad U.S.$4,000,000.
Production (metric tons except as noted). Agriculture, forestry, fishing (1995):
rice 283,600, cassava 219,200, sweet potatoes 39,500, peanuts (groundnuts)
35,800, tomatoes 32,000, palm kernels 29,000, plantains 26,000, coffee 25,-
000, millet 23,800, sorghum 21,800, sugarcane 21,000, cacao beans 10,000;
livestock (number of live animals) 360,000 cattle, 301,900 sheep, 165,800
goats, 50,000 pigs, 6,000,000 chickens; roundwood (1994) 3,198,600 cu m;
fish catch 62,568. Mining and quarrying (1994–95): bauxite 728,000; rutile
and ilmenite (titanium ores) 203,000; diamonds 255,000 carats; gold 3,949
oz. Manufacturing (value added in Le '000,000; 1993): food, beverages, and
tobacco 36,117; industrial chemicals 10,560; earthenware 1,844; printing and
publishing 1,171; metal products 1,073; furniture 647; wearing apparel 502.
Construction (value added in Le; 1993–94): 15,788,200,000. Energy production (consumption): electricity (kW-hr; 1994) 237,000,000 (237,000,000); coal,
none (n.a.); crude petroleum (barrels; 1994) none (2,148,000); petroleum
products (metric tons; 1994) 168,000 (138,000); natural gas, none (n.a.).
Household income and expenditure. Average household size (1985) 6.6; average annual income per household (1984): U.S.$320; sources of income
(1984): self-employment 61.6%, wages and salaries 27.9%, other 10.5%; ex-

penditure (1989): food, beverages, and tobacco 66.2%, clothing and footwear
9.9%, housing 5.8%, transportation and communications 4.4%, furniture,
furnishings, and household durable goods 4.0%, recreation, entertainment,
and education 3.8%, health 3.5%.
Gross national product (1994): U.S.$698,000,000 (U.S.$150 per capita).

Structure of gross domestic product and labour force				
	1993–94		1991	
	in value Le '000,000	% of total value	labour force	% of labour force
Agriculture	275,327.5	38.8	945,000	61.7
Mining	119,229.2	16.8		
Manufacturing	61,475.3	8.6	275,000	18.0
Construction	15,788.2	2.2		
Public utilities	2,816.8	0.4		
Transportation and communications	61,267.5	8.6		
Trade[5]	98,270.1	13.8		
Finance	14,732.2	2.1	312,000	20.3
Pub. admin., defense	19,844.9	2.8		
Services	12,308.9	1.7		
Other	29,329.7[6]	4.2[6]		
TOTAL	710,389.3[7]	100.0	1,532,000	100.0

Population economically active (1991): total 1,532,000; activity rate of total
population 35.9% (participation rates: ages 10–64, 53.3%; female 32.4%;
unemployed [registered; 1992] 10.6%).

Price index (1990 = 100)							
	1989	1990	1991	1992	1993	1994	1995
Consumer price index	47.4	100.0	202.7	335.4	409.9	509.1	641.5

Land use (1994): forested 28.5%; meadows and pastures 30.7%; agricultural
and under permanent cultivation 7.5%; other 33.3%.

Foreign trade

Balance of trade (current prices)					
	1990	1991	1992	1993	1994	1995
Le '000,000	+1,475	+3,903	+14,449	−7,692	−9,511	−72,322
% of total	3.6%	4.6%	10.9%	5.4%	6.5%	67.1%

Imports (1994–95): Le 84,030,200,000 (food and live animals 34.8%; fuels
and lubricants 19.2%; machinery and transport equipment 18.0%; chemicals
7.4%; beverages and tobacco 2.5%; crude minerals 2.3%). *Major import
sources:* United States 42.7%; The Netherlands 14.2%; United Kingdom
5.7%; Indonesia 3.7%; Germany 3.0%.
Exports (1994–95): Le 45,216,100,000 (mineral exports 90.0%, of which rutile
and ilmenite [titanium ores] 46.8%, diamonds 25.6%, bauxite 13.9%; cocoa
2.5%, coffee 2.3%, reexports 0.8%). *Major export destinations:* United States
44.8%; United Kingdom 17.3%; Belgium 16.8%; The Netherlands 4.1%;
Germany 2.0%.

Transport and communications

Transport. Railroads (1990): length 52 mi, 84 km. Roads (1995): total length
7,254 mi, 11,674 km (paved 11%). Vehicles (1995): passenger cars 20,860;
trucks and buses 11,014. Merchant marine (1992): vessels (100 gross tons and
over) 62; total deadweight tonnage 18,384. Air transport (1985)[8]: passenger-
mi 68,290,000, passenger-km 109,903,000; short ton-mi cargo 1,400,000, metric ton-km cargo 2,044,000; airports (1996) with scheduled flights 1.
Communications. Daily newspapers (1993): total number 1; total circulation
10,000; circulation per 1,000 population 2.3. Radio (1995): 1,000,000 receivers (1 per 4.5 persons). Television (1995): 25,000 receivers (1 per 180
persons). Telephones (main lines; 1993): 14,500 (1 per 296 persons).

Education and health

Education (1992–93)				
	schools	teachers	students	student/ teacher ratio
Primary (age 5–11)	1,643	10,595	267,425	25.2
Secondary (age 12–18)	167	4,313	70,900	16.4
Voc., teacher tr.	44	709	7,756	10.9
Higher[9]	2	257	2,571	10.0

Educational attainment (1985). Percentage of population age 5 and over having: no formal schooling 64.1%; primary education 18.7%; secondary 9.7%;
higher 1.5%. *Literacy* (1995): total population age 15 and over literate 791,000
(31.4%); males literate 555,000 (45.4%); females literate 236,000 (18.2%).
Health: physicians (1992) 404 (1 per 10,832 persons); hospital beds (1988)
4,025 (1 per 980 persons); infant mortality rate per 1,000 live births (1990–
95) 166.
Food (1992): daily per capita caloric intake 1,694 (vegetable products 96%,
animal products 4%); 74% of FAO recommended minimum requirement.

Military

Total active duty personnel (1996): 14,200 (army 98.6%, navy 1.4%, air force,
none). *Military expenditure as percentage of GNP* (1994): 4.9% (world 3.0%);
per capita expenditure U.S.$8.

---

[1]Includes 12 paramount chiefs elected to represent each of the provincial districts.
[2]Preliminary figures exclude adjustment for underenumeration; adjusted total is
3,760,000. [3]Not officially a province; the administration of the Western Area is split
among Greater Freetown (the city and its suburbs) and other administrative bodies.
[4]Christian (1980) 9.1%, of which Protestant 4.7%, Roman Catholic 2.2%, Anglican
1.2%. [5]Includes hotels. [6]Import duties less imputed bank service charges. [7]Detail does
not add to total given because of rounding. [8]International flights only. [9]1990–91.

Singapore

Official name: Hsin-chia-p'o
  Kung-ho-kuo (Mandarin Chinese);
  Republik Singapura (Malay);
  Singapore Kudiyarasu (Tamil);
  Republic of Singapore (English).
Form of government: unitary multiparty
  republic with one legislative house
  (Parliament [87[1]]).
Chief of state: President.
Head of government: Prime Minister.
Capital: Singapore.
Official languages: Chinese; Malay;
  Tamil; English.
Official religion: none.
Monetary unit: 1 Singapore dollar
  (S$) = 100 cents; valuation (Oct. 11,
  1996) 1 U.S.$ = S$1.41; 1 £ = S$2.22.

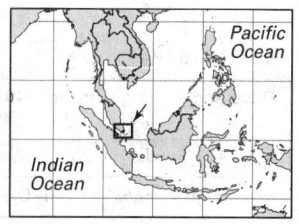

Population (1990 census)

Census division[2]	population	Census division[2]	population	Census division[2]	population
Alexandra	27,245	Henderson	18,445	Nee Soon East	58,651
Aljunied	51,669	Hong Kah Central	48,379	Nee Soon South	49,771
Ang Mo Kio	35,814	Hong Kah North	33,265	Pasir Panjang	35,824
Ayer Rajah	44,977	Hong Kah South	37,900	Paya Lebar	41,903
Bedok	22,032	Hougang	36,774	Potong Pasir	32,992
Boon Lay	39,249	Jalan Besar	28,298	Punggol	68,270
Boon Teck	22,652	Jalan Kayu	34,907	Queenstown	19,676
Braddell Heights	47,738	Joo Chiat	35,777	Radin Mas	35,730
Brickworks	10,593	Jurong	74,696	Sembawang	28,039
Bukit Batok	44,918	Kaki Bukit	32,782	Serangoon Gardens	44,702
Bukit Gombak	46,149	Kallang	34,178	Siglap	36,022
Bukit Merah	18,666	Kampong Chai Chee	33,928	Tampines East	41,474
Bukit Panjang	95,827	Kampong Glam	29,481	Tampines North	73,634
Bukit Timah	47,056	Kampong Kembangan	33,510	Tampines West	38,833
Buona Vista	23,873	Kampong Ubi	40,682	Tanah Merah	32,314
Cairnhill	48,445	Kebun Baru	36,878	Tanglin	43,544
Changi	50,003	Kim Keat	28,538	Tanjong Pagar	29,217
Changkat	41,995	Kim Seng	23,683	Teck Ghee	26,622
Cheng San	27,821	Kolam Ayer	22,420	Telok Blangah	29,157
Chong Boon	32,174	Kreta Ayer	29,631	Thomson	71,345
Chong Pang	38,613	Kuo Chuan	26,968	Tiong Bahru	27,468
Chua Chu Kang	43,465	Leng Kee	28,886	Toa Payoh	22,811
Clementi	37,635	Macpherson	23,764	Ulu Pandan	42,923
Eunos	52,976	Marine Parade	31,003	West Coast	46,052
Fengshan	27,285	Moulmein	33,872	Whampoa	18,285
Geylang Serai	36,800	Mountbatten	23,891	Yio Chu Kang	28,589
Geylang West	34,560	Nee Soon Central	47,032	Yuhua	32,733
				TOTAL	3,016,379

Demography

Area: 249.5 sq mi, 646.1 sq km.
Population (1996)[3]: 3,045,000.
Density (1996): persons per sq mi 12,204, persons per sq km 4,713.
Urban-rural: urban 100.0%.
Sex distribution (1995): male 50.32%; female 49.68%.
Age breakdown (1995): under 15, 23.0%; 15–29, 23.4%; 30–44, 28.8%; 45–59, 14.9%; 60–74, 7.4%; 75 and over, 2.5%.
Population projection: (2000) 3,292,000; (2010) 4,000,000.
Doubling time: 63 years.
Ethnic composition (1995): Chinese 77.4%; Malay 14.2%; Indian[4] 7.2%; other 1.2%.
Religious affiliation (1991): Buddhist, Taoist, and other traditional beliefs 53.9%; Muslim 15.4%; Christian 12.6%; Hindu 3.6%; nonreligious 14.5%.
Major cities: Singapore has no separately defined cities within its borders.

Vital statistics

Birth rate per 1,000 population (1995): 16.3 (world avg. 25.0).
Death rate per 1,000 population (1995): 5.2 (world avg. 9.3).
Natural increase rate per 1,000 population (1995): 11.1 (world avg. 15.7).
Total fertility rate (avg. births per childbearing woman; 1995): 1.7.
Marriage rate per 1,000 population (1995): 8.4.
Divorce rate per 1,000 population (1994): 1.3.
Life expectancy at birth (1995): male 74.2 years; female 78.7 years.
Major causes of death per 100,000 population (1994): diseases of the circulatory system 185.3; malignant neoplasms (cancers) 128.9; diseases of the respiratory system 87.0; accidents, poisoning, and violence 32.5; diseases of the genitourinary system 15.1.

National economy

Budget (1995). Revenue: S$24,782,200,000 (income tax 35.4%, nontax revenue 14.8%, assets taxes 7.4%, motor vehicle taxes 7.3%, goods and services tax 6.6%, customs and excise duties 6.4%). Expenditures: S$15,554,100,000 (security 36.2%, education 22.2%, general services 7.4%, health 6.5%, communications 5.6%, national development 4.7%).
Tourism (1994): receipts U.S.$7,067,000,000; expenditures U.S.$3,665,000,000.
Production (metric tons except as noted). Agriculture, forestry, fishing (1994): vegetables and fruits 5,000; livestock (number of live animals) 2,000,000 chickens; fish catch (1995) 9,941. Mining and quarrying (value of output in S$; 1994): granite 75,800,000. Manufacturing (value added in S$'000,000; 1994): machinery and appliances 16,383.1; chemical products 2,636.8; transport equipment 2,306.6; fabricated metal products 2,071.6; paper products 1,928.9; petroleum products 1,797.9; food, beverages, and tobacco 1,287.7. Construction (completed; 1994): residential 3,999,000 sq m; nonresidential

2,213,000 sq m. Energy production (consumption): electricity (kW-hr; 1993) 18,962,000,000 (18,910,000,000); crude petroleum (barrels; 1993) none (379,-855,000); petroleum products (metric tons; 1993) 44,620,000 (17,698,000).
Public debt (external, outstanding; 1994): U.S.$5,000,000.
Household income and expenditure. Average household size (1990) 4.2; income per household (1993) S$45,948 (U.S.$28,437); sources of income (1987–88): wages 81.2%, self-employment 16.8%, transfer payments and other 2.0%; expenditure (1991): food 18.7%, recreation and education 16.0%, transportation and communications 13.8%, rent and utilities 9.5%, furniture and household equipment 8.9%, clothing and footwear 7.3%, health 4.5%.
Gross national product (1994): U.S.$65,842,000,000 (U.S.$23,360 per capita).

Structure of gross domestic product and labour force

	1995 in value S$'000,000[5]	% of total value	labour force[6]	% of labour force[6]
Agriculture	179.7	0.2	4,600	0.3
Quarrying	48.6	...		
Manufacturing	28,601.6	28.0	408,000	24.0
Construction	7,575.6	7.4	112,700	6.6
Public utilities	1,741.0	1.7	5,800	0.4
Transp. and commun.	13,370.4	13.1	183,300	10.8
Trade	18,760.8	18.3	343,700	20.2
Finance	27,318.2	26.7	253,500	14.9
Services	10,537.9	10.3	378,400	22.2
Other	−5,834.7[7]	−5.7[7]	10,900[8]	0.6[8]
TOTAL	102,299.1	100.0	1,700,900	100.0

Population economically active (1994): total 1,693,100; activity rate of total population 57.8% (participation rates: ages 15 and over, 64.9%; female 40.2%; unemployed 2.6%).

Price and earnings indexes (1990 = 100)

	1989	1990	1991	1992	1993	1994	1995
Consumer price index	96.7	100.0	103.4	105.8	108.2	111.5	113.5
Monthly earnings index	91.5	100.0	109.2	118.1	125.5	136.5	144.8

Land use (1993): forested 4.5%; agricultural 1.1%; built-up 49.3%; other 45.1%.

Foreign trade[9]

Balance of trade (current prices)

	1990	1991	1992	1993	1994	1995
S$'000,000	−8,559	−5,770	−7,490	−10,338	−216	+1,178
% of total	4.3%	2.7%	3.5%	4.1%	0.1%	0.4%

Imports (1995): S$176,313,500,000 (office machines 10.6%, telecommunications apparatus 6.5%, crude petroleum 5.2%, electric power machinery 3.9%, scientific instruments 3.0%, petroleum products 2.8%, musical instruments 2.4%). *Major import sources:* Japan 21.1%; Malaysia 15.5%; U.S. 15.0%; Thailand 5.2%; Taiwan 4.1%; Germany 3.5%; Hong Kong 3.3%.
Exports (1995): S$167,514,700,000 (office machines 24.5%, telecommunications apparatus 9.1%, petroleum products 6.7%, optical instruments 2.2%, electrical circuit apparatus 2.1%, industrial machinery 1.6%, clothing 1.2%). *Major export destinations:* Malaysia 19.2%; U.S. 18.2%; Hong Kong 8.6%; Japan 7.8%; Thailand 5.8%; Taiwan 4.1%; Germany 3.4%; U.K. 2.6%.

Transport and communications

Transport. Railroads (1995): length 67 km. Roads (1994): total length 2,989 km (paved 97%). Vehicles (1995): passenger cars 363,906; trucks and buses 137,151. Merchant marine (1992): vessels (100 gross tons and over) 946; total deadweight tonnage 14,929,172. Air transport (1995): passenger-km 48,400,000,000; metric ton-km cargo 3,666,193,000; airports (1996) 1.
Communications. Daily newspapers (1994): total number 8; total circulation 1,008,100; circulation per 1,000 population 344. Radio (1995): 822,000 receivers (1 per 3.6 persons). Television (1995): 650,000 receivers (1 per 4.5 persons). Telephones (main lines; 1993): 1,245,000 (1 per 2.3 persons).

Education and health

Education (1994)

	schools	teachers	students	student/ teacher ratio
Primary (age 6–11)	194	10,553	251,097	23.8
Secondary (age 12–18)	173	9,675	197,981	20.5
Voc., teacher tr.	25	2,939	31,692	10.8
Higher	7	6,235	76,985	12.3

Educational attainment (1990). Percentage of population age 25 and over having: no schooling 64.0%; primary education 31.3%; postsecondary 4.7%.
Literacy (1990): total population age 10 and over literate 90.7%; males literate 95.7%; females literate 85.6%.
Health (1994): physicians 4,301 (1 per 681 persons); hospital beds 10,446 (1 per 281 persons); infant mortality rate per 1,000 live births (1995) 4.0.
Food (1988–90): daily per capita caloric intake 3,121 (vegetable products 76%, animal products 24%); 136% of FAO recommended minimum requirement.

Military

Total active duty personnel (1995): 53,900 (army 83.5%, navy 5.4%, air force 11.1%). Military expenditure as percentage of GNP (1994): 4.5% (world 3.0%); per capita expenditure U.S.$1,046.

[1]Includes 6 nonelected members. [2]The census divisions have no administrative function. [3]De jure population. [4]Includes Sri Lankan. [5]At prices of 1990. [6]Employed only. [7]Imputed bank service charges. [8]Includes agriculture, quarrying, public utilities, and activities not adequately defined. [9]Import figures are f.o.b. in balance of trade.

Slovakia

Official name: Slovenská Republika
  (Slovak Republic).
Form of government: unitary multiparty
  republic with one legislative house
  (National Council [150]).
Chief of state: President.
Head of government: Prime Minister.
Capital: Bratislava.
Official language: Slovak.
Official religion: none.
Monetary unit: 1 Slovak koruna
  (Sk) = 100 halura; valuation
  (Oct. 11, 1996) 1 U.S.$ = Sk 31.19;
  1 £ = Sk 49.13.

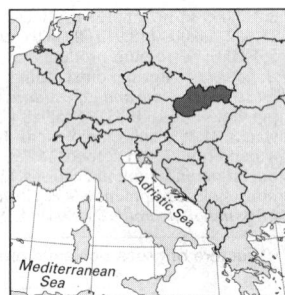

Area and population

Districts[1]	area sq km[2]	population 1995 estimate	Districts[1]	area sq km[2]	population 1995 estimate
Banská Bystrica	2,075	178,944	Prievidza	960	141,005
Bardejov	1,014	82,023	Považská Bystrica	1,196	173,183
Bratislava-vidiek	1,261	148,399	Rimavská Sobota	1,823	99,177
Čadca	934	124,588	Rožňava	1,621	87,574
Dolný Kubín	1,659	124,538	Senica	1,691	148,033
Dunajská Streda	1,075	110,887	Spišská Nová Ves	1,529	149,057
Galanta	965	143,869	Stará Ľubovňa	624	48,627
Humenné	1,909	114,361	Svidník	862	44,901
Komárno	1,100	109,329	Topoľčany	1,361	161,462
Košice	244	239,927	Trebišov	1,322	119,334
Košice-vidiek	1,533	101,315	Trenčín	1,310	180,992
Levice	1,551	121,113	Trnava	1,390	235,695
Liptovský Mikuláš	1,968	134,082	Veľký Krtíš	848	46,941
Lučenec	1,304	95,803	Vranov nad Topľou	847	76,091
Martin	1,128	114,551	Žiar nad Hronom	1,264	94,450
Michalovce	1,310	113,254	Žilina	1,097	185,124
Nitra	1,443	212,918	Zvolen	1,721	123,542
Nové Zámky	1,347	152,674			
Poprad	1,963	159,903	**Capital city**		
Prešov	1,418	207,675	Bratislava	368	450,776
			TOTAL	49,036[3]	5,356,107

Demography

Population (1996): 5,372,000.
Density (1996): persons per sq mi 283.7, persons per sq km 109.6.
Urban-rural (1991): urban 56.8%; rural 43.2%.
Sex distribution (1994): male 48.72%; female 51.28%.
Age breakdown (1995): under 15, 22.9%; 15–29, 23.6%; 30–44, 23.0%; 45–59, 15.4%; 60–74, 11.5%; 75 and over, 3.6%.
Population projection: (2000) 5,422,745; (2010) 5,550,664.
Doubling time: not applicable; population growth is negligible.
Ethnic composition (1994): Slovak 85.7%; Hungarian 10.6%; Gypsy 1.6%; Czech 1.1%; Ruthenian 0.3%; Ukrainian 0.3%; German 0.1%; other 0.3%.
Religious affiliation (1995): Roman Catholic 60.3%; nonreligious and atheist 9.7%; Protestant 7.9%, of which Slovak Evangelical 6.2%, Reformed Christian 1.6%; Greek Catholic 3.4%; Eastern Orthodox 0.7%; other 18.0%.
Major cities (1995): Bratislava 450,776; Košice 239,927; Prešov 92,013; Nitra 87,127; Žilina 86,373; Banská Bystrica 84,741.

Vital statistics

Birth rate per 1,000 population (1995): 11.5 (world avg. 25.0); legitimate 88.3%; illegitimate 11.7%.
Death rate per 1,000 population (1995): 9.8 (world avg. 9.3).
Natural increase rate per 1,000 population (1995): 1.7 (world avg. 15.7).
Total fertility rate (avg. births per childbearing woman; 1994): 0.8.
Marriage rate per 1,000 population (1994): 5.3.
Divorce rate per 1,000 population (1994): 1.6.
Life expectancy at birth (1992): male 66.6 years; female 75.4 years.
Major causes of death per 100,000 population (1994): diseases of the circulatory system 525.0; malignant neoplasms (cancers) 201.2; accidents, poisoning, and violence 65.5; diseases of the respiratory system 65.2; diseases of the digestive system 43.0; endocrine and metabolic disorders 13.0.

National economy

Budget (1994). Revenue: Sk 139,148,000,000 (tax revenue 66.8%; nontax revenue 15.5%; customs 3.1%; insurance 2.6%). Expenditures: Sk 162,002,-000,000 (education, health, and social welfare 39.0%; debt service 23.4%).
Public debt (external, outstanding; 1994): U.S.$4,172,000,000.
Tourism (1994): receipts U.S.$568,000,000; expenditures U.S.$284,000,000.
Production (metric tons except as noted). Agriculture, forestry, fishing (1995): cereals 3,528,000 (of which wheat 1,938,000, barley 794,000, corn [maize] 597,000, rye 89,300), sugar beets 1,176,000, potatoes 441,500; livestock (number of live animals) 2,037,000 pigs, 916,000 cattle, 428,-000 sheep, 7,300,000 poultry; roundwood (1994) 4,690,000 cu m; fish catch (1993) 2,773. Mining and quarrying (1995): iron ore 820,000; lead-zinc ore 300,000; copper ore 280,000. Manufacturing (1994): crude steel 3,921,000[4]; pig iron 3,207,000[4]; cement 2,879,000; plastic and resins 393,-800; flour 361,000; nitrogenous fertilizers 212,800; cotton yarn 13,736; beer 4,974,000 hectolitres; refrigerators and freezers 370,535 units. Construction (1991): residential 1,147,000 sq m. Energy production (consumption): electricity (kW-hr; 1994) 24,740,000,000 (25,898,000,000[5]); coal (metric tons; 1995) 3,725,000 (14,390,000[5]); crude petroleum (barrels; 1994) 492,850 (32,866,000); petroleum products (metric tons; 1993) 3,603,000 (2,323,000); natural gas (cu m; 1994) 288,000,000 (5,037,986,000[5]).

Population economically active (1994): total 2,510,600; activity rate of total population 46.9% (participation rates: ages 15–64, 70.8%; female 46.2%; unemployed [1995] 15.2%).

Price and earnings indexes (1990 = 100)

	1989	1990	1991	1992	1993	1994	1995
Consumer price index	90.5	100.0	156.1	171.7	218.5	247.7	272.3
Annual earnings index	95.8	100.0	115.0	136.5	161.1	190.8	228.3

Gross national product (1994): U.S.$11,914,000,000 (U.S.$2,200 per capita).

Structure of gross domestic product and labour force

	1994 in value Sk '000,000	1994 % of total value	1994 labour force[6]	1994 % of labour force
Agriculture	29,329	7.5	187,000	7.4
Mining and manufacturing	98,994	25.4	565,000	22.5
Construction	20,082	5.2	168,000	6.7
Public utilities	23,095	5.9	52,000	2.1
Transp. and commun.	38,233	9.8	173,000	6.9
Trade	63,105	16.2	300,000	11.9
Finance	35,196	9.0	28,000	1.2
Pub. admin., defense	41,463	10.6	380,000	15.1
Services	40,396	10.4	257,000	10.2
Other			400,600	16.0
TOTAL	389,893	100.0	2,510,600	100.0

Land use (1994): forested 40.6%; meadows and pastures 17.0%; agricultural and under permanent cultivation 32.9%; other 9.5%.
Household income and expenditure. Average household size (1994) 4.0; income per household (1994) Sk 48,190[7] (U.S.$1,545[7]); sources of income (1994): wages and salaries 76.7%, transfer payments 8.9%, other 14.4%; expenditure (1994): food and beverages 26.3%, taxes 18.4%, clothing and footwear 8.6%, housing 8.0%, household durable goods 3.1%, other 35.6%.

Foreign trade

Balance of trade (current prices)

	1993	1994	1995
Sk '000,000	−27,310	+2,858	+1,788
% of total	7.5%	1.0%	0.4%

Imports (1994): Sk 214,069,000 (machinery and transport equipment 27.6%; petroleum and petroleum products 19.3%; semimanufactured products 16.8%; chemical products 13.1%; manufactured products 9.1%). *Major import sources:* Czech Republic 29.7%; former U.S.S.R. 19.8%; Germany 13.4%; Austria 5.7%; Italy 4.4%; Poland 2.4%.
Exports (1994): Sk 214,375,000 (semimanufactured products 39.4%; machinery and transport equipment 19.0%; manufactured goods 13.4%; chemical products 12.9%; food, beverages, and tobacco 5.5%). *Major export destinations:* Czech Republic 37.4%; Germany 17.1%; former U.S.S.R. 6.1%; Hungary 5.5%; Austria 5.3%; Poland 2.8%.

Transport and communications

Transport. Railroads (1994): length 2,275 mi, 3,661 km; passenger-mi 2,826,-000,000, passenger-km 4,548,000,000; short ton-mi cargo 8,381,000,000, metric ton-km cargo 12,236,000,000. Roads (1994): total length 11,116 mi, 17,889 km (paved, n.a.). Vehicles (1994): passenger cars 994,046; trucks and buses 93,560. Merchant marine: n.a. Air transport (1994): passenger-mi 37,458,-000,000, passenger-km 60,283,000,000; short ton-mi cargo 3,806,000; metric ton-km cargo 5,557,000; airports (1996) with scheduled flights 2.
Communications. Daily newspapers (1992): total number 21; total circulation 1,680,000; circulation per 1,000 population 314. Radio (1996): 2,895,000 receivers (1 per 2.0 persons). Television (1996): 1,204,000 receivers (1 per 4.4 persons). Telephones (main lines; 1993): 892,800 (1 per 6.0 persons).

Education and health

Education (1994–1995)

	schools	teachers	students	student/ teacher ratio
Primary (age 6–14)	2,481	38,813	675,813	17.4
Secondary (age 15–18)	183	5,073	72,072	14.2
Voc., teacher tr.	722	17,654	234,284	13.3
Higher	14	7,781	66,900	8.6

Educational attainment (1991). Percentage of adult population having: incomplete primary education 0.5%; primary and incomplete secondary 30.6%; complete secondary 58.6%; higher 9.4%; unknown 0.9%. *Literacy* (1990): total population age 15 and over literate 3,980,202 (100%); males literate 1,916,410 (100%); females literate 2,063,792 (100%).
Health (1994): physicians 18,446 (1 per 290 persons); hospital beds 62,818 (1 per 85 persons); infant mortality rate per 1,000 live births (1995) 11.0.
Food (1990): daily per capita caloric intake 3,335 (vegetable products 63%, animal products 37%); 135% of FAO recommended minimum requirement.

Military

Total active duty personnel (1996): 47,000 (army 70.2%, air force 29.8%).
Military expenditure as percentage of GNP (1994): 2.4% (world 3.0%); per capita expenditure U.S.$160.

[1]Districts have the same names as district seats. [2]One sq km is equal to approximately 0.3861 sq mi. [3]Detail does not add to total given because of rounding. [4]1995. [5]1993. [6]Excluding women on regular and additional maternity leave and including employees with a second job. [7]Households of employees with two children and wife not economically active.

Slovenia

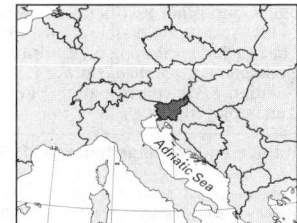

Official name: Republika Slovenija (Republic of Slovenia).
Form of government: multiparty republic with two legislative houses (State Council [40]; State Assembly [90]).
Head of state: President.
Head of government: Prime Minister.
Capital: Ljubljana.
Official language: Slovene.
Official religion: none.
Monetary unit: 1 Slovene tolar (SIT; plural tolarji) = 100 stotin; valuation (Oct. 11, 1996) 1 U.S.$ = 139.19 tolarji; 1 £ = 219.26 tolarji.

Area and population (1995 estimate)

Municipalities[1]	area sq km	population	Municipalities[1]	area sq km	population
Ajdovščina	352	22,736	Metlika	108	8,258
Brežice	268	24,530	Mozirje	507	16,745
Celje	230	64,360	Murska Sobota	692	63,340
Čerknica	482	15,434	Nova Gorica	605	59,292
Črnomelj	486	18,527	Novo Mesto	760	60,102
Domžale	240	46,676	Ormož	212	17,845
Dravograd	105	8,602	Pesnica	172	18,544
Gornja Radgona	210	21,614	Piran	45	17,463
Grosuplje	421	29,420	Postojna	492	19,498
Hrastnik	58	10,778	Ptuj	645	69,676
Idrija	425	17,157	Radlje ob Dravi	346	17,221
Ilirska Bistrica	480	14,518	Radovljica	641	34,777
Izola	28	14,340	Ravne na Koroškem	304	27,175
Jesenice	375	31,801	Ribnica	256	12,898
Kamnik	289	29,172	Ruše	209	15,506
Kočevje	766	18,852	Šentjur pri Celju	240	19,605
Koper	271	46,288	Sevnica	293	18,795
Kranj	453	73,766	Sežana	698	23,544
Krško	344	28,683	Škofja Loka	512	39,376
Lasko	250	19,130	Slovenj Gradec	286	21,359
Lenart	204	17,608	Slovenska Bistrica	369	33,631
Lendava	256	26,018	Slovenske Konjice	222	22,306
Litija	328	18,879	Šmarje pri Jelšah	400	32,429
Ljubljana-Bežigrad	46	58,257	Tolmin	940	20,643
Ljubljana-Center	5	27,670	Trbovlje	58	18,906
Ljubljana-Moste Polje	152	73,412	Trebnje	308	17,917
Ljubljana-Šiška	156	85,417	Tržič	155	15,087
Ljubljana-Vič Rudnik	544	82,840	Velenje	182	42,841
Ljutomer	179	18,895	Vrhnika	169	19,676
Logatec	173	10,131	Zagorje ob Savi	147	17,013
Maribor	357	152,326	Žalec	349	40,172
			TOTAL	20,256[2]	1,989,477

Demography

Population (1996): 1,958,746.
Density (1996): persons per sq mi 250.5, persons per sq km 96.7.
Urban-rural (1991): urban 50.5%; rural 49.5%.
Sex distribution (1994): male 48.50%; female 51.50%.
Age breakdown (1994): under 15, 17.5%; 15–29, 22.2%; 30–44, 23.8%; 45–59, 18.0%; 60–74, 13.4%; 75 and over, 4.1%.
Population projection: (2000) 1,963,000; (2010) 2,002,503.
Doubling time: not applicable; population is declining.
Ethnic composition (1991): Slovene 87.8%; Croat 2.8%; Serb 2.4%; Bosnian 1.4%; Magyar 0.4%; other 5.2%.
Religious affiliation (1991): Roman Catholic 83.6%; other (predominantly Christian adherents of the Slovene Old Catholic Church and the Eastern Orthodox Church) 16.4%.
Major cities (1995): Ljubljana 276,119; Maribor 134,979; Celje 50,155; Kranj 51,602; Velenje 33,436.

Vital statistics

Birth rate per 1,000 population (1995): 9.6 (world avg. 25.0); (1994) legitimate 71.2%; illegitimate 28.8%.
Death rate per 1,000 population (1995): 9.6 (world avg. 9.3).
Natural increase rate per 1,000 population (1995): 0.0 (world avg. 15.7).
Total fertility rate (avg. births per childbearing woman; 1994): 1.3.
Marriage rate per 1,000 population (1994): 4.2.
Divorce rate per 1,000 population (1994): 1.0.
Life expectancy at birth (1992–93): male 69.4 years; female 77.3 years.
Major causes of death per 100,000 population (1994): circulatory diseases 434.1; cancers 224.3; accidents 98.7; respiratory diseases 59.1; digestive diseases 58.4; endocrine and metabolic disorders 22.9.

National economy

Budget (1994). Revenue: SIT 424,654,000,000. Expenditures: SIT 416,818,000,000 (social activities 29.6%, work of provider organizations 27.4%, gross investments 25.3%, aid to communities 4.6%, financial obligations 2.2%).
Tourism (1994): receipts U.S.$932,000,000; expenditures U.S.$312,000,000.
Production (metric tons except as noted). Agriculture, forestry, fishing (1995): potatoes 430,000, corn (maize) 330,000, sugar beets 190,000, wheat 182,000, grapes 130,000; livestock (number of live animals) 592,000 pigs, 504,000 cattle, 9,900,000 poultry; roundwood (1994) 1,709,000 cu m; fish catch (1993) 2,969. Mining and quarrying (1994): lead-zinc ore 25,000; sea salt 11,230; alumina 3,000; mercury 6. Manufacturing (1994): cement 898,000; crude steel 424,000; aluminum ingots 84,809; soap and detergents 39,015; cotton yarn 15,394; leather footwear 8,913,000 pairs; refrigerators 797,000 units;

bicycles 182,000 units; telephones 316,000 units. Construction (in '000 sq m; 1993): residential 1,287; nonresidential 210. Energy production (consumption): electricity (kW-hr; 1994) 12,616,000,000 (9,376,000,000); coal (metric tons; 1994) 4,854,000 (4,915,000); crude petroleum (barrels; 1994) 12,578 (1993; 3,540,000); petroleum products (metric tons; 1993) 452,000 (1,966,000); natural gas (cu m; 1994) 12,595,000 (396,000,000).
Gross national product (1994): U.S.$14,246,000,000 (U.S.$7,161 per capita).

Structure of gross domestic product and labour force

	1992		1994	
	in value SIT '000,000	% of total value	labour force	% of labour force
Agriculture	49,631	4.9	12,690	1.4
Mining	17,156	1.7		
Manufacturing	298,095	29.7	244,883	26.2
Construction	38,621	3.8	34,427	3.7
Public utilities	24,362	2.4	8,415	1.0
Transp. and commun.	65,818	6.5	32,642	3.5
Trade	129,433	12.9	125,179	13.4
Finance	129,823	12.9	35,807	3.8
Pub. admin., defense	40,405	4.0	38,042	4.1
Services	139,875	13.9	115,251	12.3
Other	72,043[3]	7.3[3]	288,664[4]	30.6[4]
TOTAL	1,005,261[2]	100.0	936,000	100.0

Population economically active (1994): total 936,000; activity rate 47.0% (participation rates: ages 15–64, 66.3%; female 46.3%; unemployed 9.0%).

Price and earnings indexes (1990 = 100)

	1989	1990	1991	1992	1993	1994	1995
Consumer price index	15	100	215	659	867	1,040	1,172
Earnings index	21	100	165	546	826	1,059	1,256

Land use (1994): forest 54.0%; pasture 24.8%; agricultural 11.6%; other 9.6%.
Household income and expenditure. Average household size (1994) 3.1; income per household (1994) SIT 1,418,405 (U.S.$10,191); sources of income (1994): wages 52.4%, transfers 23.4%, self-employment 13.0%, other 11.2%; expenditure (1994): food 26.1%, housing 9.4%, transportation 13.3%, clothing 6.3%, health care 6.5%, education and entertainment 6.8%, energy 5.8%, household durable goods 4.2%.

Foreign trade

Balance of trade (current prices)

	1990	1991	1992	1993	1994	1995
U.S.$'000,000	−609	−257	+540	−410	−509	−1,166
% of total	6.9%	3.2%	4.2%	3.3%	3.6%	6.5%

Imports (1994): SIT 937,878,000,000 (machinery and transport equipment 31.8%, chemicals 12.2%, basic manufactures 10.9%, food 7.6%, mineral fuels 7.1%). *Major import sources:* Germany 23.7%; Italy 17.2%; Austria 10.3%; France 8.3%; Croatia 6.8%.
Exports (1994): SIT 876,800,000,000 (machinery and transport equipment 30.3%, basic manufactures 24.0%, chemicals 10.3%, food 4.0%, mineral fuels 1.1%). *Major export destinations:* Germany 30.3%; Italy 13.5%; Croatia 10.1%; France 8.6%; Austria 5.5%.

Transport and communications

Transport. Railroads (1994): length 746 mi, 1,201 km; passenger-km 590,000,000; metric ton-km cargo 2,448,000,000. Roads (1994): total length 9,158 mi, 14,739 km (paved 79%). Vehicles (1994): passenger cars 657,287; trucks and buses 36,607. Merchant marine (1993): vessels (100 gross tons and over) 13; total deadweight tonnage 586,680. Air transport (1993): passenger-mi 341,000,000, passenger-km 548,000,000; short ton-mi cargo 2,431,000, metric ton-km cargo 3,549,000; airports (1996) 1.
Communications. Daily newspapers (1992): total number 6; total circulation 308,000; circulation per 1,000 population 154. Radio (1992): 732,000 receivers (1 per 2.7 persons). Television (1992): 571,000 receivers (1 per 3.5 persons). Telephones (main lines; 1993): 516,300 (1 per 3.9 persons).

Education and health

Education (1993–94)

	schools	teachers	students	student/ teacher ratio
Primary (age 7–14)	846	15,341	214,832	14.0
Secondary (age 15–18)	221	9,579	110,426	11.5
Voc., teacher tr.	...	...	...	...
Higher	28	2,783	40,239	14.5

Educational attainment (1991). Percentage of population age 15 and over having: less than full primary education 17.1%; primary 29.9%; secondary 42.8%; postsecondary and higher 8.8%. *Literacy* (1991): virtually 100%.
Health (1994): physicians 2,110[5] (1 per 943 persons); hospital beds 11,496 (1 per 173 persons); infant mortality rate per 1,000 live births 5.5.

Military

Total active duty personnel (1996): 9,550 (army 100%). *Military expenditure as percentage of GNP:* 1.2% (world 3.3%); per capita expenditure (1994) U.S.$93.

[1]Table lists 62 municipalities in existence as of the end of 1994; 58 new first order administrative units were created at the beginning of 1995. [2]Detail does not add to total given because of rounding. [3]Includes imputed bank service charges, import duties, indirect taxes, and other adjustments. [4]Includes 85,000 unemployed and 203,664 nondistributable employed. [5]Physicians and dental physicians in hospitals only.

Solomon Islands

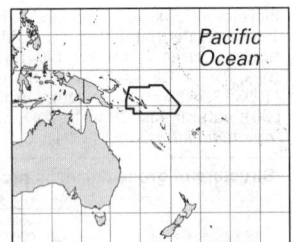

Pacific
Ocean

Official name: Solomon Islands.
Form of government: constitutional
monarchy with one legislative house
(National Parliament [47]).
Chief of state: British Monarch
represented by Governor-General.
Head of government: Prime Minister.
Capital: Honiara.
Official language: English.
Official religion: none.
Monetary unit: 1 Solomon Islands
dollar (SI$) = 100 cents; valuation
(Oct. 11, 1996) 1 U.S.$ = SI$3.54;
1 £ = SI$5.58.

Area and population		area		population
				1996
Provinces	**Capitals**	sq mi	sq km	estimate
Central Islands	Tulagi	237	615	28,968[1]
Choiseul	Taro	1,481	3,837	[2]
Guadalcanal	Honiara	2,060	5,336	59,064
Isabel	Buala	1,597	4,136	21,795
Makira	Kira Kira	1,231	3,188	28,064
Malaita	Auki	1,631	4,225	102,719
Rennell and Bellona	Tigoa	259	671	[1]
Temotu	Santa Cruz	334	865	20,472
Western	Gizo	2,114	5,475	91,321[2]
Capital Territory				
Honiara	—	8	22	43,643
TOTAL		10,954[3]	28,370	396,046

Demography

Population (1996): 396,000.
Density (1996): persons per sq mi 36.2, persons per sq km 14.0.
Urban-rural (1996): urban 23.3%; rural 76.7%.
Sex distribution (1996): male 51.65%; female 48.35%.
Age breakdown (1996): under 15, 43.7%; 15–29, 28.7%; 30–44, 15.2%; 45–59,
8.1%; 60–74, 3.6%; 75 and over, 0.7%.
Population projection: (2000) 459,000; (2010) 600,000.
Doubling time: 22 years.
Ethnic composition (1986): Melanesian 94.2%; Polynesian 3.7%; other Pacific
Islander 1.4%; European 0.4%; Asian 0.2%; other 0.1%.
Religious affiliation (1986): Christian 96.7%, of which Protestant 77.5%,
Roman Catholic 19.2%; Baha'i 0.4%; traditional beliefs 0.2%; other and
no religion 2.7%.
Major cities (1986)[4]: Honiara 43,643[5]; Gizo 3,727; Auki 3,262; Kira Kira
2,585; Buala 1,913.

Vital statistics

Birth rate per 1,000 population (1996): 36.5 (world avg. 25.0).
Death rate per 1,000 population (1996): 4.2 (world avg. 9.3).
Natural increase rate per 1,000 population (1996): 32.3 (world avg. 15.7).
Total fertility rate (avg. births per childbearing woman; 1996): 5.1.
Marriage rate per 1,000 population: n.a.
Divorce rate per 1,000 population: n.a.
Life expectancy at birth (1996): male 69.0 years; female 74.0 years.
Major causes of death per 100,000 population (1990): respiratory diseases
22.4; diarrheal diseases 13.6; malaria 10.0.

National economy

Budget (1994). Revenue: SI$274,400,000 (1991; taxes on foreign trade 46.8%,
income taxes 29.2%, nontax revenue 14.3%, foreign grants 9.7%). Expenditures: SI$338,900,000 (1991; administrative 33.2%, interest payments 12.6%,
capital expenditure 10.7%).
Tourism: receipts from visitors (1993) U.S.$6,000,000; expenditures by nation-
als abroad (1992) U.S.$11,000,000.
Land use (1994): forested 87.5%; meadows and pastures 1.4%; agricultural
and under permanent cultivation 2.0%; other 9.1%.
Gross national product (at current market prices; 1994): U.S.$291,000,000
(U.S.$800 per capita).

Structure of gross domestic product and labour force				
	1991		1993	
	in value SI$'000[6]	% of total value	labour force[7]	% of labour force
Agriculture	117,600	48.4	8,106	27.4
Mining	−700	−0.3	2,844	9.6
Manufacturing	9,000	3.7		
Construction	10,500	4.3	977	3.3
Public utilities	2,200	0.9	245	0.8
Transportation and communications	17,500	7.2	1,723	5.8
Trade	23,300	9.6	3,390	11.5
Finance	8,000	3.3	1,144	3.9
Pub. admin., defense	55,800	23.0	4,303	14.6
Services			6,845	23.1
Other	44,300	18.2	...	...
TOTAL	243,100[3]	100.0[3]	29,577	100.0

Household income and expenditure. Average household size (1996) 5.8; average annual income per household[8] (1983) SI$1,010 (U.S.$1,160); sources
of income (1983): wages and salaries 74.1%, self-employment, remittances,

gifts, and other assistance 25.9%; expenditure (1992)[9]: food 46.8%, housing
11.0%, household operations 10.9%, transportation 9.9%, recreation and
health 7.9%, clothing 5.7%, drinks and tobacco 5.0%.
Population economically active (1993): total 29,577[7]; activity rate of total population 8.3% (participation rates: ages 15–60 [1986] 98.6%; female 22.6%;
unemployed, n.a.).

Price and earnings indexes (1990 = 100)							
	1989	1990	1991	1992	1993	1994	1995
Consumer price index	92.0	100.0	115.1	118.3	138.7	157.6	172.7
Annual earnings index[7]	114.7	100.0	121.2	140.5	142.8	...	...

Production (metric tons except as noted). Agriculture, forestry, fishing (1995):
coconuts 225,000, sweet potatoes 63,000, palm oil and kernels 34,000, vegetables and melons 5,900; cacao beans 3,200; livestock (number of live animals)
55,000 pigs, 5,000 cattle; roundwood (1994) 468,000 cu m; fish catch (1994)
39,005. Mining and quarrying (1994): gold 997 troy oz. Manufacturing (1993):
processed fish 34,700; sawnwood 16,000 cu m; other major industries include
beer brewing, soap and tobacco manufacturing, garment manufacturing,
weaving, wood carving, fibreglass products, boatbuilding, and leatherwork-
ing. Construction (gross value in SI$ in Honiara; 1994): residential 9,508,-
000; nonresidential 11,151,000. Energy production (consumption): electricity
(kW-hr; 1993) 48,928,000 (43,473,000); coal, none (n.a.); petroleum products
(metric tons; 1993) none (51,000); natural gas, none (n.a.).
Public debt (external, outstanding; 1994): U.S.$99,600,000.

Foreign trade[10]

Balance of trade (current prices)							
	1988	1989	1990	1991	1992	1993	1994
SI$'000	+1,160	−47,300	−21,030	−23,770	+59,150	+33,520	−246
% of total	0.3%	12.1%	5.6%	11.0%	11.0%	5.6%	0.0%

Imports (1994): SI$468,121,000 (machinery and transport equipment 38.0%,
manufactured goods 19.9%, food 13.1%, mineral fuels and lubricants 8.2%).
Major import sources: Australia 37.2%; Japan 17.1%; New Zealand 9.6%;
Singapore 8.4%; United States 2.8%; Thailand 2.7%.
Exports (1994): SI$467,875,000 (timber products 59.2%, fish products 21.2%,
palm oil products 9.5%, copra 4.2%, cacao beans 2.7%). *Major export des-
tinations:* Japan 41.1%; South Korea 14.1%; United Kingdom 13.1%; The
Netherlands 8.5%; Thailand 4.5%; Singapore 3.4%; Australia 1.5%.

Transport and communications

Transport. Railroads: none. Roads (1993): total length 840 mi, 1,352 km
(paved 35%). Vehicles (1993): passenger cars 2,052; trucks and buses
2,574. Merchant marine (1992): vessels (100 gross tons and over) 33; total
deadweight tonnage 4,985. Air transport (1992): passenger-mi 117,100,000,
passenger-km 188,400,000; short ton-mi cargo 25,000[11], metric ton-km cargo
37,000[11]; airports (1996) with scheduled flights 30.
Communications. Daily newspapers[12]: none. Radio (1996): total number of
receivers 38,000 (1 per 10 persons). Television: none. Telephones (main
lines; 1993): 5,300 (1 per 65 persons).

Education and health

Education (1994)				
	schools	teachers	students	student/ teacher ratio
Primary (age 7–12)	520	2,510	73,120	29.1
Secondary (age 13–18)	23	364[13]	7,811	20.2[13]
Voc., teacher tr.[14]	1	...	...	...
Higher[14]	1	...	...	...

Educational attainment (1986)[15]. Percentage of population age 25 and over
having: no schooling 44.4%; primary education 46.2%; secondary 6.8%;
higher 2.6%. *Literacy* (1976): total population age 15 and over literate 55,500
(54.1%); males 33,600 (62.4%); females 21,900 (44.9%).
Health (1990): physicians 52 (1 per 6,154 persons); hospital beds 265 (1 per
1,208 persons); infant mortality rate per 1,000 live births (1996) 24.0.
Food (1992): daily per capita caloric intake 2,173 (vegetable products 89%,
animal products 11%); 95% of FAO recommended minimum requirement.

Military

Total active duty personnel: no military forces are maintained, but a police
force of 475 provides internal security.

---

[1]Central Islands includes Rennell and Bellona. [2]Western includes Choiseul. [3]Detail
does not add to total given because of rounding. [4]Ward populations. [5]1996. [6]At
1984 factor cost. [7]Persons employed in the monetary sector only. [8]Public-service
earnings. [9]Retail price index components. [10]Import figures are f.o.b. [11]1984. [12]In 1988
there were three weekly newspapers with a combined circulation of 10,000. [13]1993.
[14]Vocational and teacher training are carried out at the College of Higher Education.
[15]Indigenous population only.

Somalia[1]

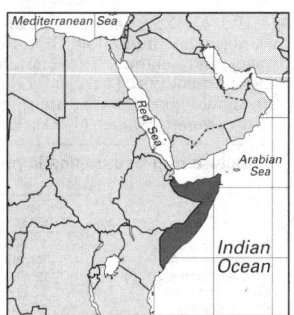

Official name: Soomaaliya
(Somali)(Somalia).
Form of government: republic[2, 3].
Head of state and government: [3].
Capital: Mogadishu.
Official languages: Somali; Arabic.
Official religion: Islam.
Monetary unit: 1 Somali shilling
(So.Sh.) = 100 cents; valuation (Oct.
11, 1996) 1 U.S.$ = So.Sh. 2,620;
1 £ = So.Sh. 4,128.

Price and earnings indexes (1985 = 100)

	1983	1984	1985	1986	1987	1988	1989[8]
Consumer price index	38.0	72.6	100.0	135.8	174.0	316.6	707.1
Earnings index	...	...	...	...	...	...	...

Gross national product (at current market prices; 1990): U.S.$946,000,000
(U.S.$150 per capita).

Structure of gross domestic product and labour force

	1991			
	in value So.Sh. '000,000	% of total value	labour force	% of labour force
Agriculture	867,500	64.5	2,275,000	70.8
Mining	2,700	0.2		
Manufacturing	59,200	4.4		
Construction	51,100	3.8	336,000	10.4
Public utilities	9,400	0.7		
Transportation and communications	80,700	6.0		
Trade	125,000	9.3		
Finance	45,700	3.4	604,000	18.8
Pub. admin., defense	80,700	6.0		
Services	30,900	2.3		
Other	−8,100	−0.6		
TOTAL	1,344,900[4]	100.0	3,215,000	100.0

Land use (1994): forested 25.5%; meadows and pastures 68.6%; agricultural
and under permanent cultivation 1.6%; other 4.3%.

Area and population

		area		population
Regions	Capitals	sq mi	sq km	1980 estimate
Bakool	Xuddur	10,000	27,000	148,700
Banaadir	Mogadishu (Muqdisho)	400	1,000	520,100
Bari	Boosaaso	27,000	70,000	222,300
Bay	Baydhabo	15,000	39,000	451,000
Galguduud	Dhuusamarreeb	17,000	43,000	255,900
Gedo	Garbahaarrey	12,000	32,000	235,000
Hiiraan	Beledweyne	13,000	34,000	219,300
Jubbada Dhexe	Bu'aale	9,000	23,000	147,800
Jubbada Hoose	Kismaayo	24,000	61,000	272,400
Mudug	Gaalkacyo	27,000	70,000	311,200
Nugaal	Garoowe	19,000	50,000	112,200
Sanaag	Ceerigaabo	21,000	54,000	216,500
Shabeellaha Dhexe	Jawhar	8,000	22,000	352,000
Shabeellaha Hoose	Marka	10,000	25,000	570,700
Togdheer	Burao	16,000	41,000	383,900
Woqooyi Galbeed	Hargeysa	17,000	45,000	655,000
TOTAL		246,000[4]	637,000	5,074,000

Demography

Population (1996): 6,802,000[5].
Density (1996): persons per sq mi 27.6, persons per sq km 10.7.
Urban-rural (1991): urban 37.2%; rural 62.8%.
Sex distribution (1996): male 51.21%; female 48.79%.
Age breakdown (1996): under 15, 44.4%; 15–29, 27.1%; 30–44, 16.1%; 45–59,
6.9%; 60–74, 4.0%; 75 and over, 1.5%.
Population projection: (2000) 7,079,000; (2010) 7,823,000.
Doubling time: 22 years.
Ethnic composition (1983): Somali 98.3%[6]; Arab 1.2%; Bantu 0.4%; other
0.1%.
Religious affiliation (1980): Sunnī Muslim 99.8%; Christian 0.1%; other 0.1%.
Major cities (1984): Mogadishu 570,000; Hargeysa 90,000; Kismaayo 86,000;
Berbera 83,000; Marka (1981) 60,000.

Vital statistics

Birth rate per 1,000 population (1995): 44.6 (world avg. 25.0); legitimate, n.a.;
illegitimate, n.a.
Death rate per 1,000 population (1995): 13.6 (world avg. 9.3).
Natural increase rate per 1,000 population (1995): 31.0 (world avg. 15.7).
Total fertility rate (avg. births per childbearing woman; 1995): 7.1.
Marriage rate per 1,000 population: n.a.
Divorce rate per 1,000 population: n.a.
Life expectancy at birth (1995): male 54.8 years; female 55.4 years.
Major causes of death per 100,000 population: n.a.; however, major diseases
include leprosy, malaria, tetanus, and tuberculosis; civil violence, malnutri-
tion, and poor health services remained epidemic in the mid-1990s.

National economy

Budget (1991). Revenue: So.Sh. 151,453,000,000 (domestic revenue sources,
principally indirect taxes and import duties 60.4%; external grants and transfers 39.6%). Expenditures: So.Sh. 141,141,000,000 (general services 46.9%;
economic and social services 31.2%; debt service 7.0%).
Public debt (external, outstanding; 1993): U.S.$1,897,000,000.
Production (metric tons except as noted). Agriculture, forestry, fishing (1995):
fruits (excluding melons) 210,000, sugarcane 200,000, corn (maize) 146,000,
sorghum 136,000, bananas 45,000, sesame seed 25,000, beans 13,000, dates
10,000, seed cotton 6,000, rice 2,000, other forest products include khat,
frankincense, and myrrh; livestock (number of live animals) 13,500,000
sheep, 12,500,000 goats, 6,200,000 camels, 5,200,000 cattle; roundwood (1994)
7,818,000 cu m; fish catch (1993) 14,850. Mining and quarrying (1992):
sepiolite 2,000 kilograms. Manufacturing (value added in So.Sh. '000,000;
1988): food 794; cigarettes and matches 562; hides and skins 420; paper and
printing 328; plastics 320; chemicals 202; beverages 144. Construction (value
added in So.Sh.; 1991): 51,100,000,000. Energy production (consumption):
electricity (kW-hr; 1994) 259,000,000 (259,000,000); coal, none (n.a.); crude
petroleum (barrels; 1991) n.a. (806,000); petroleum products (metric tons;
1991) none (59,000); natural gas, none (n.a.).
Household income and expenditure. Average household size (1980) 4.9; income
per household: n.a.; sources of income: n.a.; expenditure (1983)[7]: food and
tobacco 62.3%, housing 15.3%, clothing 5.6%, energy 4.3%, other 12.5%.
Tourism: receipts from visitors (1986) U.S.$8,000,000; expenditures by nation-
als abroad (1983) U.S.$13,000,000.
Population economically active (1991): total 3,215,000; activity rate of total
population 40.9% (participation rates [1987] over age 10, 63.1%; female
48.7%; unemployed, n.a.).

Foreign trade[9]

Balance of trade (current prices)

	1987	1988	1989	1990	1991	1992
U.S.$'000,000	−382	−373	−299	−274	−274	−305
% of total	64.3%	68.7%	62.4%	61.4%	61.4%	67.0%

Imports (1991): U.S.$360,000,000 (agricultural products 22.1%, of which rice
8.6%; unspecified 77.9%). *Major import sources* (1990): Italy 30.8%; The
Netherlands 8.8%; Bahrain 6.0%; United Kingdom 5.9%; Djibouti 5.9%;
China 4.9%; Germany 4.7%; Thailand 4.6%.
Exports (1991): U.S.$86,000,000 (agricultural products 46.1%, of which live
sheep and goats 23.3%, live camels 7.0%, live cattle 6.4%, bananas 5.8%;
fishery products 10.7%; other 43.2%). *Major export destinations* (1990): Italy
28.7%; Saudi Arabia 23.4%; Yemen 19.1%; United Arab Emirates 10.7%.

Transport and communications

Transport. Railroads: none. Roads (1992): total length 14,000 mi, 22,500
km (paved 25%). Vehicles (1994): passenger cars 11,800; trucks and buses
12,200. Merchant marine (1992): vessels (100 gross tons and over) 28; total
deadweight tonnage 18,496. Air transport (1991): passenger-mi 81,000,000,
passenger-km 131,000,000; short ton-mi cargo 3,000,000, metric ton-km
cargo 5,000,000; airports (1996) with scheduled flights 1.
Communications. Daily newspapers (1995): total number 1; total circulation,
n.a. Radio (1995): total number of receivers 300,000 (1 per 22 persons).
Television (1987): total number of receivers 3,000 (1 per 2,270 persons).
Telephones (main lines; 1993): 15,000 (1 per 434 persons).

Education and health

Education (1986–87)

	schools	teachers	students	student/teacher ratio
Primary (age 6–14)	1,125	8,208	171,830	20.9
Secondary (age 15–18)	82	2,109	42,764	20.3
Voc., teacher tr.	21	498	4,809	9.7
Higher	1	262[10]	1,692	...

Educational attainment: n.a. *Literacy* (1990): percentage of total population
age 15 and over literate 24.1%; males literate 42.7%; females literate 14.0%.
Health: physicians (1987) 323 (1 per 19,071 persons); hospital beds (1985)
5,536 (1 per 1,053 persons); infant mortality rate per 1,000 live births (1995)
123.
Food (1992): daily per capita caloric intake 1,499 (vegetable products 76%,
animal products 24%); 65% of FAO recommended minimum requirement.

Military

Total active duty personnel (1996): clan militias and armed gangs have fought
for control of the country since the 1991 revolution. *Military expenditure
as percentage of GNP* (1990): 0.9% (world 4.4%); per capita expenditure
U.S.$1.

---

[1]Proclamation of a "Republic of Somaliland" by the Somali National Movement in
May 1991 on territory corresponding to the former British Somaliland (which unified
with the former Italian Trust Territory of Somalia to form Somalia in 1960) has
received no international recognition. This entity would represent about a quarter of
Somalia's territory and a quarter to a third of its population; presidential elections
were scheduled for late 1996; a new currency, the Somaliland shilling, was introduced
in January 1995. [2]UN operation in Somalia (begun May 1992) ended March 1, 1995.
[3]No effective central government exists. [4]Detail does not add to total given because of
rounding. [5]Excluding Somali refugees in neighbouring countries, estimated to number
about 500,000 in early 1996. [6]The Somali are divided into six major clans, of which
four are predominantly pastoral (representing *c.* 70% of the population) and two are
predominantly agricultural (representing *c.* 20% of the population); the remainder
are urban dwellers with less clan identification. [7]Capital city only. [8]Third quarter.
[9]Imports are c.i.f. [10]1980–81.

South Africa

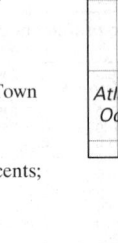

Official name: Republic of South
Africa (English).
Form of government: multiparty
republic with two legislative houses
(Senate [90]; National Assembly
[400])[1].
Head of state and government:
President[1].
Capitals: Pretoria (executive);
Bloemfontein (judicial); Cape Town
(legislative).
Official languages:[2].
Official religion: none.
Monetary unit: 1 rand (R) = 100 cents;
valuation (Oct. 11, 1996)
1 U.S.$ = R 4.54; 1 £ = R 7.16.

Area and population		area		population
		sq mi	sq km	1995 estimate
Provinces	**Capitals**			
Eastern	Bisho	65,475	169,580	6,481,000
Free State	Bloemfontein	49,993	129,480	2,782,000
Gauteng	Johannesburg	6,568	17,010	7,048,000
KwaZulu/Natal	Ulundi	35,560	92,100	8,713,000
Mpumalanga	Nelspruit	30,691	79,490	3,007,000
Northern	Pietersburg	47,842	123,910	5,397,000
Northern Cape	Kimberley	139,703	361,830	740,000
North-West	Mafikeng (Mmabatho)	44,911	116,320	3,352,000
Western Cape	Cape Town	49,950	129,370	3,721,000
TOTAL		470,693	1,219,090	41,241,000

Demography

Population (1996): 41,743,000.
Density (1996): persons per sq mi 88.7, persons per sq km 34.2.
Urban-rural (1995): urban 48.3%; rural 51.7%.
Sex distribution (1991): male 49.50%; female 50.50%.
Age breakdown (1995): under 15, 37.3%; 15–29, 27.1%; 30–44, 18.5%; 45–59, 10.4%; 60–74, 5.2%; 75 and over, 1.5%.
Population projection: (2000) 44,462,000; (2010) 49,200,000.
Doubling time: 38 years.
Ethnic composition (1995): black 76.3%, of which Zulu c. 22.0%, Xhosa c. 18.0%, Pedi c. 9.0%, Sotho c. 7.0%, Tswana c. 7.0%, Tsonga c. 3.5%, Swazi c. 3.0%, Ndebele c. 2.0%, Venda c. 2.0%; white 12.7%; Coloured 8.5%, of which Cape Malay 1.0%; Asian 2.5%.
Religious affiliation (1991)[3]: Christian 67.8%, of which black independent churches 22.2%, Afrikaans Reformed 11.8%, Roman Catholic 7.6%, Methodist 5.9%, Anglican 3.8%, Lutheran 2.5%; Hindu 1.3%; Muslim 1.1%; Jewish 0.4%; other/traditional beliefs 29.4%.
Major cities (1991)[4]: Cape Town 2,350,157; Johannesburg 1,916,063[5]; Durban 1,137,378; Pretoria 1,080,187; Port Elizabeth 853,204.

Vital statistics

Birth rate per 1,000 population (1995): 28.5 (world avg. 25.0).
Death rate per 1,000 population (1995): 10.0 (world avg. 9.3).
Natural increase rate per 1,000 population (1995): 18.5 (world avg. 15.7).
Marriage rate per 1,000 population (1994): 3.3.
Divorce rate per 1,000 population (1994): 0.7.
Total fertility rate (avg. births per childbearing woman; 1995): 3.5.
Life expectancy at birth (1995): male 62.7 years; female 68.2 years.
Major causes of death per 100,000 population (1993–94): accidents and violence 221.2; diseases of the circulatory system 102.0; infectious and parasitic diseases 51.7; ill-defined conditions 422.7.

National economy

Budget (1994–95). Revenue: R 113,550,000,000 (income taxes 51.3%, sales and value-added taxes 25.1%, nontax revenue 7.3%, excise duties 5.0%). Expenditures: R 152,195,000,000 (current expenditure 95.7%, development expenditure 4.3%).
Public debt (external, September 1995): U.S.$2,700,000,000.
Production (in R '000,000 except as noted). Agriculture, forestry, fishing (in value of production; 1994): corn (maize) 4,374, poultry 3,516, beef 3,180, temperate fruits 1,663, sugarcane 1,539, wheat 1,465, milk 1,369, sheep and goat meat 956, potatoes 842, grapes 780, citrus fruits 662, wool 489; roundwood (1994) 24,043,000 cu m; fish catch (1993) 563,228 metric tons. Mining and quarrying (in value of sales; 1994): gold 24,953; rough diamonds 15,495; coal 10,333; platinum-group metals 2,513[6]; iron ore 1,400; copper 1,255; manganese 645; lime and limestone 605; chrome 400. Manufacturing (in value added; 1992): food products 8,167; soaps, paints, pharmaceuticals, and refined petroleum 8,138; iron and steel 6,658; transport equipment 6,002; metal products 4,594; nonelectrical machinery 4,511; beverages 4,046; industrial chemicals 3,572. Construction (private buildings completed in value of construction; 1994): residential 5,172; nonresidential 2,266. Energy production (consumption): electricity (kW-hr; 1994) 182,448,000,000 (181,-290,000,000[7]); coal (metric tons; 1994) 182,496,000 (140,581,000[7]); crude petroleum (barrels; 1994) none (125,000,000[7]); petroleum products (metric tons; 1994) 16,425,000[7] (16,428,000[7]); natural gas (cu m; 1994): 1,896,000,-000[7] (1,896,000,000[7]).
Household income and expenditure. Average household size (1994) 4.6[3]; average annual income per household (1990–91) R 16,814 (U.S.$6,500), of which average black household R 9,348 (U.S.$3,614), average Coloured household

R 19,284 (U.S.$7,455), average Asian household R 29,712 (U.S.$11,487), average white household R 56,148 (U.S.$21,707); sources of income (1992)[3]: wages and salaries 73.6%, interest, dividends, rent, etc., 21.5%, transfers 4.9%; expenditure (1992)[3]: food and beverages 35.8%, transportation 14.7%, household goods 10.0%, housing and energy 9.6%.
Gross national product (1994): U.S.$118,961,000,000 (U.S.$2,930 per capita).

Structure of gross domestic product and labour force				
	1994			
	in value R '000,000[8]	% of total value	labour force	% of labour force
Agriculture	17,930	4.7	1,277,346	8.9
Mining	33,168	8.7	277,176	1.9
Manufacturing	89,766	23.4	1,614,596	11.3
Construction	12,265	3.2	437,167	3.1
Public utilities	15,751	4.1	95,046	0.7
Transp. and commun.	28,996	7.6	520,789	3.6
Trade	61,648	16.1	1,675,448	11.7
Finance, real estate	63,411	16.6	587,331	4.1
Pub. admin., defense	58,678	15.3 ⎫		
Services	7,573	2.0 ⎬	3,055,753	21.4
Other	−6,605	−1.7	4,756,396[9]	33.3[9]
TOTAL	382,561	100.0	14,297,048	100.0

Population economically active (1994): total 14,297,048; activity rate of total population 35.3% (participation rates: over age 15, 55.6%; female 44.2%; unemployed 32.6%).

Price and earnings indexes (1990 = 100)							
	1990	1991	1992	1993	1994	1995	1996[10]
Consumer price index	100.0	115.3	131.3	144.0	157.0	170.6	183.4
Monthly earnings index[11]	100.0	115.0	129.6	143.2	...	...	...

Tourism (1994): receipts U.S.$1,424,000,000; expenditures U.S.$1,678,000,000.
Land use (1994): forest 6.7%; pasture 66.7%; agriculture 10.8%; other 15.8%.

Foreign trade

Balance of trade (current prices)						
	1990	1991	1992	1993	1994	1995
R '000,000	+16,717	+16,146	+13,917	+20,500	+13,719	+3,013
% of total	15.9%	14.3%	11.6%	14.8%	8.3%	1.5%

Imports (1994): R 75,543,000,000 (machinery and apparatus 33.4%, motor vehicles 14.9%, chemicals and chemical products 11.0%). *Major import sources:* Germany 16.3%; U.S. 15.7%; U.K. 11.3%; Japan 9.9%.
Exports (1994): R 89,262,000,000 (gold 25.5%, base metals and metal products 12.3%, gem diamonds 11.0%, food 9.1%). *Major export destinations* (1994): Switzerland 6.7%; U.K. 6.6%; U.S. 4.9%; Japan 4.6%; Germany 4.1%.

Transport and communications

Transport. Railroads: route length (1994) 21,303 km; passenger-km (1992–93) 895,000,000[12]; metric ton-km cargo (1992–93) 91,402,000,000. Roads (1991): length 182,329 km (paved 30%). Vehicles (1994): passenger cars 3,814,904; trucks and buses 1,596,812. Merchant marine (1992): vessels 219; total deadweight tonnage 282,533. Air transport (1995)[13]: passenger-km 13,098,-000,000; metric ton-km cargo 254,880,000; airports (1996) 24.
Communications. Daily newspapers (1992): total number 20; total circulation 1,248,000; circulation per 1,000 population 32. Radio (1995): 11,200,000 receivers (1 per 3.7 persons). Television (1995): 3,485,000 receivers (1 per 12 persons). Telephones (main lines; 1993): 3,659,900 (1 per 11 persons).

Education and health

Education (1994)				
	schools	teachers	students	student/ teacher ratio
Primary/Secondary	22,260	349,436	11,782,324	35.7
Voc., teacher tr.	187	10,807	140,531	13.0
Tertiary vocational	15	7,341[6]	151,410	18.7[6]
University	21	32,047[6]	354,003	10.3[6]

Educational attainment (1994). Percentage of population age 25 and over having: no formal schooling 14.5%; primary education 19.6%; incomplete secondary 42.0%; complete secondary and incomplete higher 20.4%; complete higher 3.1%; other/unknown 0.4%. *Literacy:* total population age 15 and over literate (1991): 82.2%.
Health (1994): physicians 26,452 (1 per 1,523 persons); hospital beds 155,255 (1 per 260 persons); infant mortality rate (1995) 49.3.
Food (1992): daily per capita caloric intake 2,695 (vegetable products 86%, animal products 14%); 110% of FAO recommended minimum.

Military

Total active duty personnel (1996): 137,900 (army 85.6%, navy 4.0%, air force 6.1%, intraservice medical service 4.3%). *Military expenditure as percentage of GNP* (1994): 2.4% (world 3.0%); per capita expenditure U.S.$72.

---

[1]New constitution became effective with president's signature on Dec. 10, 1996. Complete implementation is expected by 1999. [2]Afrikaans; English; Ndebele; Pedi (North Sotho); Sotho (South Sotho); Swazi; Tsonga; Tswana (West Sotho); Venda; Xhosa; Zulu. [3]Excludes formerly nominally independent Transkei, Venda, Bophuthatswana, and Ciskei (TVBC). [4]Population of urban areas. [5]1991 population of the Witwatersrand (including East Rand [1,378,792] and West Rand [870,066] urban areas) is 4,164,921. [6]1993. [7]Includes Botswana, Lesotho, Namibia, and Swaziland. [8]At factor cost. [9]Includes 100,320 not adequately defined and 4,656,076 unemployed. [10]July. [11]Mining only. [12]Excludes suburban traffic. [13]SAA only.

Spain

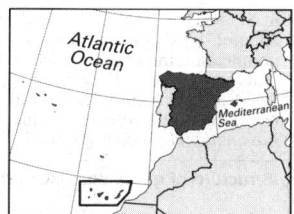

Official name: Reino de España (Kingdom of Spain).
Form of government: constitutional monarchy with two legislative houses (Senate [248[1]]; Congress of Deputies [350]).
Chief of state: King.
Head of government: Prime Minister.
Capital: Madrid.
Official language: Castilian Spanish[2].
Official religion: none.
Monetary unit: 1 peseta (Pta) = 100 céntimos; valuation (Oct. 11, 1996)
1 U.S.$ = Ptas 128.79;
1 £ = Ptas 202.88.

Area and population		area		population
				1994
Autonomous communities	Capitals	sq mi	sq km	estimate
Andalucía	Seville	33,822	87,599	7,053,043
Aragón	Zaragoza	18,425	47,720	1,183,576
Asturias	Oviedo	4,094	10,604	1,083,388
Baleares (Balearic Islands)	Palma de Mallorca	1,927	4,992	736,865
Canarias (Canary Islands)	Santa Cruz de Tenerife	2,875	7,447	1,534,897
Cantabria	Santander	2,054	5,321	526,090
Castilla–La Mancha	Toledo	30,680	79,461	1,656,179
Castilla y León	Valladolid	36,380	94,224	2,504,371
Cataluña	Barcelona	12,399	32,113	6,090,107
Ceuta	—	8	20	68,867
Extremadura	Mérida	16,075	41,634	1,050,590
Galicia	Santiago de Compostela	11,419	29,575	2,720,761
La Rioja	Logroño	1,948	5,045	263,437
Madrid	Madrid	3,100	8,028	5,034,548
Melilla	—	5	12	58,052
Murcia	Murcia	4,368	11,314	1,070,401
Navarra	Pamplona	4,012	10,391	523,614
País Vasco (Basque Country)	Vitoria (Gasteiz)	2,793	7,234	2,075,561
Valencia	Valencia	8,979	23,255	3,909,047
TOTAL		195,364[3, 4]	505,990[4]	39,143,394

Demography

Population (1996): 39,270,000[5].
Density (1996): persons per sq mi 201.0, persons per sq km 77.6.
Urban-rural (1990): urban 78.4%; rural 21.6%.
Sex distribution (1996): male 48.93%; female 51.07%.
Age breakdown (1996): under 15, 16.2%; 15–29, 24.4%; 30–44, 21.7%; 45–59, 16.6%; 60–69, 10.5%; 70 and over, 10.6%.
Population projection: (2000) 39,466,000; (2010) 39,917,000.
Doubling time: not applicable; doubling time exceeds 100 years.
Ethnolinguistic composition (1991): Spanish 74.4%; Catalan 16.9%; Galician 6.4%; Basque 1.6%; other 0.7%.
Religious affiliation (1993): Roman Catholic 94.9%; Muslim 1.2%; Protestant 0.5%; other 3.4%.
Major cities (1991): Madrid 3,010,492; Barcelona 1,641,656; Valencia 722,856; Seville 611,364; Zaragoza 570,541.

Vital statistics

Birth rate per 1,000 population (1994): 9.3 (world avg. 25.0); (1992) legitimate 89.5%; illegitimate 10.5%.
Death rate per 1,000 population (1994): 8.6 (world avg. 9.3).
Natural increase rate per 1,000 population (1994): 0.7 (world avg. 15.7).
Total fertility rate (avg. births per childbearing woman; 1995): 1.3.
Marriage rate per 1,000 population (1994): 5.0.
Divorce rate per 1,000 population (1990): 0.6.
Life expectancy at birth (1995): male 73.2 years; female 81.1 years.
Major causes of death per 100,000 population (1993): circulatory diseases 343.9; malignant neoplasms (cancers) 219.7; respiratory diseases 81.6.

National economy

Budget (1995)[6]. Revenue: Ptas 14,077,800,000,000 (direct taxes 46.1%; indirect taxes 38.9%, of which value-added tax on products 24.9%; other taxes on production 15.0%). Expenditures: Ptas 17,326,700,000,000 (public debt 16.9%; health 14.6%; labour and social security 8.8%; education 6.0%; defense 5.0%; pensions 4.9%; interior and justice 4.6%).
Tourism (1994): receipts U.S.$21,853,000,000; expenditures U.S.$4,188,000,000.
Production (metric tons except as noted). Agriculture, forestry, fishing (1995): sugar beets 7,629,000, barley 5,194,000, potatoes 4,195,000, grapes 3,085,000, wheat 2,958,000, tomatoes 2,706,000, corn (maize) 2,561,000, oranges 2,439,000, onions 1,032,000; livestock (number of live animals) 23,900,000 sheep, 18,332,000 pigs, 5,060,000 cattle, 2,678,000 goats; roundwood (1994) 13,815,000 cu m; fish catch (1993) 1,290,000. Mining and quarrying (metal content in metric tons; 1995): iron ore 1,982,000; zinc 172,000; lead 30,000. Manufacturing (value added in Ptas '000,000; 1992): machinery and transport equipment 2,515,900; food products 1,701,100; chemical products 981,500; paper products 734,600; wood and cork products 407,100; clothing and footwear 328,600; textiles 317,800. Construction (1995): dwellings 332,059. Energy production (consumption): electricity (kW-hr; 1994) 161,502,000,000 (163,377,000,000); coal (metric tons; 1994) 29,556,000 (42,808,000); crude petroleum (barrels; 1994) 6,057,000 (407,793,000); petroleum products (metric tons; 1994) 47,227,000 (40,591,000); natural gas (cu m; 1994) 206,650,000 (7,754,694,000).

Gross national product (1994): U.S.$525,334,000,000 (U.S.$13,280 per capita).

Structure of gross domestic product and labour force				
	1995			
	in value Ptas '000,000	% of total value	labour force	% of labour force
Agriculture	2,177,500	3.1	1,350,500	8.6
Mining	} 16,752,700	} 24.2	69,800	0.5
Manufacturing			2,693,000	17.2
Public utilities			101,300	0.6
Construction	5,734,500	8.2	1,474,100	9.4
Transp. and commun.	...	...	796,600	5.1
Trade			3,289,100	21.1
Finance	} 40,972,500	} 58.8	1,118,900	7.2
Services			3,217,800	20.6
Pub. admin., defense				
Other	3,921,000[7]	5.6[7]	1,513,900[8]	9.7[8]
TOTAL	69,722,000[3]	100.0[3]	15,625,400[3]	100.0

Public debt (1995)[9]: Ptas 38,697,700,000,000 (U.S.$312,000,000,000).
Population economically active (1995): total 15,625,400; activity rate of total population 39.9% (participation rates: ages [1993] 16–64, 60.3%; female 36.7%; unemployed 16.6%).

Price and earnings indexes (1990 = 100)							
	1989	1990	1991	1992	1993	1994	1995
Consumer price index	93.7	100.0	105.9	112.2	117.3	122.9	128.6
Monthly earnings index	92.0	100.0	108.2	116.5	124.4	124.4	136.2

Household income and expenditure. Average household size (1991) 3.4; income per household (1995) Ptas 2,925,116 (U.S.$23,637); sources of income (1991): wages and salaries 48.5%, profits and self-employment 27.5%, social security 19.5%; expenditure (1993): housing 25.5%, food 23.9%, transportation 13.3%, clothing and footwear 7.7%, household goods and services 6.0%.
Land use (1994): forested 32.3%; meadows and pastures 21.4%; agricultural and under permanent cultivation 40.3%; other 6.0%.

Foreign trade

Balance of trade (current prices)						
	1990	1991	1992	1993	1994	1995
Ptas '000,000	−2,765.4	−2,724.3	−3,022.5	−1,831.3	−1,853.9	−2,101.6
% of total	19.7%	19.6%	18.6%	10.2%	8.6%	8.4%

Imports (1995): Ptas 14,318,261,000,000 (machinery 11.6%; energy products 8.3%, of which crude petroleum 8.2%; agricultural products 7.9%; transportation equipment 7.3%). *Major import sources:* France 17.1%; Germany 15.3%; Italy 9.2%; U.K. 7.8%; Japan 3.3%.
Exports (1995): Ptas 11,423,085,000,000 (transport equipment 20.3%; agricultural products 12.7%; machinery 8.3%). *Major export destinations:* France 20.5%; Germany 15.4%; Italy 11.5%; U.K. 8.0%.

Transport and communications

Transport. Railroads (1994): route length 12,646 km; passenger-km 14,853,000,000; metric ton-km cargo 8,702,000,000. Roads (1994): length 341,230 km (paved 99%). Vehicles (1994): cars 13,733,794; trucks and buses 2,952,838. Merchant marine (1992): vessels 2,190; deadweight tonnage 5,077,275. Air transport (1994): passenger-km 39,750,579,000; metric ton-km cargo 4,153,315,000; airports (1996) with scheduled flights 25.
Communications. Daily newspapers (1994): total number 90; total circulation 4,000,000; circulation per 1,000 population 102. Radio (1995): 12,000,000 receivers (1 per 3.3 persons). Television (1995): 17,000,000 receivers (1 per 2.3 persons). Telephones (main lines; 1994): 14,080,000 (1 per 2.8 persons).

Education and health

Education (1993–94)				
	schools	teachers	students	student/ teacher ratio
Primary (age 6–11)	16,540	121,353	2,447,859	20.2
Secondary (age 12–18)[10]	25,775[11]	297,697	4,734,401	15.9
Higher[11]	1,415	73,412	1,370,689	18.7

Educational attainment (1986). Percentage of population age 25 and over having: no formal schooling 5.2%; less than primary education 40.3%; primary 29.9%; incomplete secondary 8.9%; completed secondary 8.7%; higher 7.0%.
Literacy (1991): total population age 10 and over literate 33,338,300 (85.4%); males literate 16,458,400 (85.1%); females literate 16,879,900 (84.3%).
Health (1994): physicians 159,291 (1 per 246 persons); hospital beds (1991) 168,514 (1 per 234 persons); infant mortality rate 6.0.
Food (1992): daily per capita caloric intake 3,708 (vegetable products 68%, animal products 32%); 151% of FAO recommended minimum requirement.

Military

Total active duty personnel (1996): 206,800 (army 68.8%, navy 17.4%, air force 13.8%). *Military expenditure as percentage of GNP* (1994): 1.6% (world 3.0%); per capita expenditure U.S.$189.

[1]At the June 1993 elections, 208 seats were directly elected and 47 indirectly elected by the parliaments of the autonomous communities. [2]The constitution states that "Castilian is the Spanish official language of the State," but that "all other Spanish languages will also be official in the corresponding Autonomous Communities." [3]Detail does not add to total given because of rounding. [4]Includes other enclaves (plazas de soberanía). [5]Estimate based on 1991 census. [6]Preliminary. [7]Import taxes and value-added tax on products. [8]Includes 813,600 unemployed persons not previously employed. [9]December. [10]Includes vocational. [11]1992–93.

Sri Lanka

Official name: Śrī Lankā Prajātāntrika
  Samājavādī Janarajaya (Sinhala);
  Ilangai Jananayaka Socialisa
  Kudiarasu (Tamil) (Democratic
  Socialist Republic of Sri Lanka).
Form of government: unitary multiparty
  republic with one legislative house
  (Parliament [225]).
Head of state and government:
  President.
Capitals: Colombo (administrative)
  and Sri Jayewardenepura Kotte
  (legislative).
Official languages: Sinhala; Tamil.
Official religion: none.
Monetary unit: 1 Sri Lanka rupee
  (SL Rs) = 100 cents; valuation
  (Oct. 11, 1996) 1 U.S.$ =
  SL Rs 57.05; 1 £ = SL Rs 89.87.

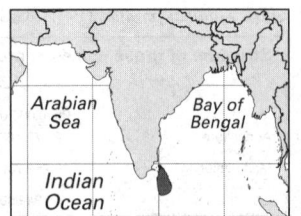

Area and population		area		population
Districts	**Capitals**	sq mi	sq km	1993 estimate
Amparai	Amparai	1,705	4,415	501,000
Anuradhapura	Anuradhapura	2,772	7,179	741,000
Badulla	Badulla	1,104	2,861	724,000
Batticaloa	Batticaloa	1,102	2,854	433,000
Colombo	Colombo	270	699	2,026,000
Galle	Galle	638	1,652	971,000
Gampaha	Gampaha	536	1,387	1,555,000
Hambantota	Hambantota	1,007	2,609	531,000
Jaffna	Jaffna	396	1,025	879,000
Kalutara	Kalutara	617	1,598	961,000
Kandy	Kandy	749	1,940	1,269,000
Kegalle	Kegalle	654	1,693	758,000
Kilinochchi	Kilinochchi	494	1,279	107,000
Kurunegala	Kurunegala	1,859	4,816	1,462,000
Mannar	Mannar	771	1,996	137,000
Matale	Matale	770	1,993	429,000
Matara	Matara	495	1,283	797,000
Monaragala	Monaragala	2,177	5,639	361,000
Mullaitivu	Mullaitivu	1,010	2,617	96,000
Nuwara Eliya	Nuwara Eliya	672	1,741	535,000
Polonnaruwa	Polonnaruwa	1,271	3,293	329,000
Puttalam	Puttalam	1,186	3,072	617,000
Ratnapura	Ratnapura	1,264	3,275	960,000
Trincomalee	Trincomalee	1,053	2,727	323,000
Vavuniya	Vavuniya	759	1,967	117,000
TOTAL		25,332	65,610	17,619,000

Demography

Population (1996): 18,318,000.
Density (1996): persons per sq mi 723.1, persons per sq km 279.2.
Urban-rural (1995): urban 22.0%; rural 78.0%.
Sex distribution (1993): male 50.97%; female 49.03%.
Age breakdown (1993): under 15, 35.2%; 15–29, 29.7%; 30–44, 17.9%; 45–59, 10.6%; 60–74, 5.2%; 75 and over, 1.4%.
Population projection: (2000) 19,258,000; (2010) 21,521,000.
Doubling time: 52 years.
Ethnic composition (1991)[1]: Sinhalese 82.7%; Tamil 8.9%; Sri Lankan Moor 7.7%; other 0.7%.
Religious affiliation (1981): Buddhist 69.3%; Hindu 15.5%; Muslim 7.6%; Christian 7.5%; other 0.1%.
Major cities (1990): Colombo 615,000; Dehiwala–Mount Lavinia 196,000; Moratuwa 170,000; Jaffna 129,000; Sri Jayewardenepura Kotte 109,000.

Vital statistics

Birth rate per 1,000 population (1996): 19.5 (world avg. 25.0); (1986) legitimate 96.3%; illegitimate 3.7%.
Death rate per 1,000 population (1996): 5.8 (world avg. 9.3).
Natural increase rate per 1,000 population (1996): 13.7 (world avg. 15.7).
Total fertility rate (avg. births per childbearing woman; 1996): 2.3.
Marriage rate per 1,000 population (1990): 8.9.
Divorce rate per 1,000 population (1988): 0.2.
Life expectancy at birth (1996): male 71.0 years; female 75.0 years.
Major causes of death per 100,000 population (1988): violence and poisoning 101.7; diseases of the circulatory system 98.7; diseases of the nervous system 37.0; respiratory diseases 32.1; infectious and parasitic diseases 29.6.

National economy

Budget (1994). Revenue: SL Rs 110,038,000,000 (sales and turnover tax 29.4%, import duties 20.5%, income taxes 13.9%, excise taxes 13.3%, nontax revenue 9.7%). Expenditures: SL Rs 157,475,000,000 (social security 16.7%, defense 12.3%, education 11.2%, transport 6.0%, health 5.8%, agriculture 5.2%, public order 4.5%, public services 4.1%).
Public debt (external, outstanding; 1994): U.S.$6,598,000,000.
Tourism (1994): receipts U.S.$224,000,000; expenditures U.S.$167,000,000.
Production (metric tons except as noted). Agriculture, forestry, fishing (1995): rice 2,684,000, coconuts 1,997,000, sugarcane 1,529,000, cassava 298,000, tea 242,000, rubber 105,000, potatoes 79,000, sweet potatoes 62,000; livestock (number of live animals) 1,703,000 cattle, 880,000 buffalo, 588,000 goats; roundwood (1994) 9,463,000 cu m; fish catch (1993) 220,900. Mining and quarrying (1993): quartz stone 1,133,000; limestone 650,000; titanium concentrate 79,600; gemstones U.S.$60,000,000. Manufacturing (value added,

in SL Rs '000,000; 1992): food, beverages, and tobacco 26,977; textiles and apparel 13,031; petrochemicals 7,205; paper and printed products 2,548; nonmetallic mineral products 1,888. Construction (1992): residential, 1,410 units completed. Energy production (consumption): electricity (kW-hr; 1993) 3,979,000,000 (3,979,000,000); crude petroleum (barrels; 1993) none (13,722,000); petroleum products (metric tons; 1993) 1,663,000 (1,507,000).
Gross national product (1994): U.S.$11,634,000,000 (U.S.$640 per capita).

Structure of gross domestic product and labour force				
	1993		1994	
	in value SL Rs '000,000	% of total value	labour force	% of labour force
Agriculture	103,440.5	20.7	2,132,489	34.7
Mining	5,432.8	1.1	31,990	0.5
Manufacturing	85,313.9	17.1	769,121	12.5
Construction	32,794.5	6.5	260,127	4.2
Public utilities	10,362.1	2.1	25,058	0.4
Transp. and commun.	47,339.0	9.5	295,519	4.8
Trade	107,154.5	21.4	643,072	10.5
Finance	32,453.8	6.5	61,210	1.0
Pub. admin., defense	37,429.4	7.5 }	1,080,485	17.6
Services	14,389.4	2.9 }		
Other	23,527.1	4.7	843,071[2]	13.8[2]
TOTAL	499,637.0	100.0	6,142,142	100.0

Population economically active: total (1994) 6,142,142; activity rate 41.0% (participation rates: ages 15 and over, 57.0%; female 33.9%; unemployed 13.7%).

Price and earnings indexes (1990 = 100)							
	1989	1990	1991	1992	1993	1994	1995
Consumer price index	82.3	100.0	112.2	125.0	139.6	151.4	163.1
Average wage index[3]	84.3	100.0	111.7	128.4	155.4	158.8	160.7

Household income and expenditure (1992). Average household size (1981) 5.2; income per household SL Rs 116,100 (U.S.$2,600); sources of income: wages 48.5%, property income and self-employment 41.8%, transfers 9.7%; expenditure: food and beverages 58.6%, transportation 16.0%, clothing 8.4%, housing and energy 4.6%, household furnishings 3.5%.
Land use (1994): forested 32.5%; meadows and pastures 6.8%; agricultural and under permanent cultivation 29.1%; other 31.6%.

Foreign trade

Balance of trade (current prices)						
	1990	1991	1992	1993	1994	1995
SL Rs '000,000	−17,485	−29,612	−27,128	−36,037	−53,894	−44,594
% of total	9.9%	14.9%	11.0%	11.5%	14.5%	10.3%

Imports (1994): SL Rs 221,525,900,000 (basic manufactures 37.3%, machinery and transport equipment 23.3%, food and live animals 14.0%, chemical products 8.5%, mineral fuels 6.2%). *Major import sources:* Japan 11.8%; India 9.1%; South Korea 7.3%; Hong Kong 7.1%; U.S. 6.4%; U.K. 5.3%.
Exports (1994): SL Rs 157,785,900,000 (clothing and accessories 46.2%, tea 13.0%, pearls 7.0%, fruits and vegetables 2.4%, natural rubber 2.3%, fish products 2.0%). *Major export destinations:* U.S. 34.7%; U.K. 8.9%; Germany 6.9%; Belgium 5.9%; Japan 5.1%; The Netherlands 3.5%; France 2.7%.

Transport and communications

Transport. Railroads (1994): route length 1,493 km; passenger-km 3,264,000,-000; metric ton-km cargo 144,000,000. Roads (1993): total length 26,004 km (paved 81%). Vehicles (1994): passenger cars 210,013; trucks and buses 231,713. Merchant marine (1992): vessels (100 gross tons and over) 66; total deadweight tonnage 472,625. Air transport (1995): passenger-km 4,035,000,-000; metric ton-km cargo 156,160,000; airports (1996) 1.
Communications. Daily newspapers (1992): total number 10; total circulation 480,000; circulation per 1,000 population 27. Radio (1995): 3,300,000 receivers (1 per 5.5 persons). Television (1995): 700,000 receivers (1 per 26 persons). Telephones (main lines; 1993): 157,800 (1 per 111 persons).

Education and health

Education (1993)	schools	teachers	students	student/ teacher ratio
Primary (age 5–10)	9,590[4]	70,008	2,012,702	28.7
Secondary (age 11–17)	9,041[4]	106,141	2,246,642	21.2
Voc., teacher tr.[4]	23	437	8,908	20.4
Higher[4]	8	1,937	31,447	16.2

Educational attainment (1981). Percentage of population age 25 and over having: no schooling 15.5%; less than complete primary education 12.1%; complete primary 52.3%; postprimary 14.7%; secondary 3.0%; higher 1.1%; unspecified 1.3%. Literacy (1991): percentage of population age 10 and over literate 86.9%; males literate 90.1%; females literate 83.8%.
Health (1992): physicians 3,345 (1 per 5,203 persons); hospital beds 48,061 (1 per 362 persons); infant mortality rate per 1,000 live births (1996) 16.
Food (1992): daily per capita caloric intake 2,273 (vegetable products 95%, animal products 5%); 102% of FAO recommended minimum.

Military

Total active duty personnel (1995): 125,300 (army 83.8%, navy 8.2%, air force 8.0%). *Military expenditure as percentage of GNP* (1994): 4.5% (world 3.0%); per capita expenditure U.S.$29.

[1]Excludes the Northern and Eastern provinces where Tamils are in the majority. [2]Mainly unemployed. [3]Agricultural minimum rates. [4]1991.

Sudan, The

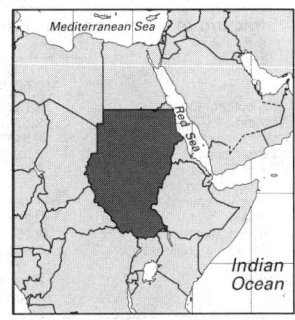

Official name: Jumhūrīyat as-Sūdān (Republic of the Sudan).
Form of government: Islamic military regime[1] with one legislative house (National Assembly [400][2]).
Head of state and government: President.
Capitals: Khartoum (executive); Omdurman (legislative).
Official language: Arabic.
Official religion: [3].
Monetary unit: 1 Sudanese dinar (Sd)[4]; valuation (Oct. 11, 1996) 1 U.S.$ = Sd 146.50; 1 £ = Sd 230.78.

Area and population

States[5]	Capitals	area sq mi	area sq km	population 1983 census
A'ālī an-Nīl (Upper Nile)	Malakāl	92,198	238,792	1,599,605
Baḥr al-Ghazāl (Bahr el-Ghazal)	Wāw	77,566	200,894	2,265,510
Dārfūr (Darfur)	al-Fāshir	196,404	508,684	3,093,699
al-Istiwā'īyah (Equatoria)	Juba	76,436	197,969	1,406,181
al-Kharṭūm (Khartoum)	Khartoum	10,874	28,165	1,802,299
Kurdufān (Kordofan)	al-Ubayyiḍ	146,817	380,255	3,093,294
ash-Shamālīyah (Northern)	ad-Dāmir	183,800	476,040	1,083,024
ash-Sharqīyah (Eastern)	Kassalā	128,987	334,074	2,208,209
al-Wusṭā (Central)	Wad Madanī	53,675	139,017	4,012,543
TOTAL		966,757[6, 7]	2,503,890[6, 7]	20,564,364[8]

Demography

Population (1996): 31,065,000.
Density (1996): persons per sq mi 32.1, persons per sq km 12.4.
Urban-rural (1995): urban 24.6%; rural 75.4%.
Sex distribution (1995): male 50.20%; female 49.80%.
Age breakdown (1995): under 15, 43.9%; 15–29, 27.0%; 30–44, 15.6%; 45–59, 8.8%; 60–74, 3.9%; 75 and over, 0.8%.
Population projection: (2000) 35,454,000; (2010) 46,512,000.
Doubling time: 23 years.
Ethnic composition (1983): Sudanese Arab 49.1%; Dinka 11.5%; Nuba 8.1%; Beja 6.4%; Nuer 4.9%; Azande 2.7%; Bari 2.5%; Fur 2.1%; Shilluk 1.7%; Lotuko 1.5%; other 9.5%.
Religious affiliation (1992): Sunnī Muslim 74.7%; traditional beliefs 17.1%; Christian 8.2%.
Major cities (1993): Omdurman 1,267,077; Khartoum 924,505; Khartoum North 879,105; Port Sudan 305,385; Kassalā 234,270.

Vital statistics

Birth rate per 1,000 population (1995): 41.3 (world avg. 25.0).
Death rate per 1,000 population (1995): 11.7 (world avg. 9.3).
Natural increase rate per 1,000 population (1995): 29.6 (world avg. 15.7).
Total fertility rate (avg. births per childbearing woman; 1995): 6.0.
Marriage rate per 1,000 population: n.a.
Divorce rate per 1,000 population: n.a
Life expectancy at birth (1995): male 53.8 years; female 55.6 years.
Major causes of death per 100,000 population: n.a.; however, principal causes of mortality and morbidity in the early 1990s included malaria, dysentery, tuberculosis, schistosomiasis, trypanosomiasis (sleeping sickness), violence, and AIDS; malnutrition was widespread and amounted, locally, to famine.

National economy

Budget (1994–95). Revenue: LSd 271,400,000,000[4] (nontax revenue 28.6%, taxes on business profits 21.4%, import duties 14.2%, defense taxes 8.5%). Expenditures: LSd 752,350,000,000[4] (interest on debt 48.5%, current expenditure 37.1%, development expenditure 14.4%).
Public debt (external, outstanding; 1994): U.S.$9,372,000,000.
Tourism (1993): receipts from visitors U.S.$3,000,000; expenditures by nationals abroad U.S.$33,000,000.
Population economically active (1992): total 8,559,000; activity rate of total population 32.0% (participation rates: ages 15–64 [1983] 57.4%; female 22.3%; unemployed [1993] c. 30.0%).

Price and earnings indexes (1990 = 100)

	1988	1989	1990	1991	1992	1993	1994
Consumer price index	36.3	60.5	100.0	223.6	486.6	979.9	2,057[9]
Monthly earnings index[10]	66.1	...	100.0	...	322.4	...	...

Production (metric tons except as noted). Agriculture, forestry, fishing (1995): sugarcane 4,800,000, sorghum 2,600,000, millet 650,000, peanuts (groundnuts) 630,000, wheat 520,000, seed cotton 400,000, cottonseed 260,000, sesame seeds 195,000, dates 140,000, cotton lint 131,000, gum arabic 40,000[11]; livestock (number of live animals) 23,000,000 sheep, 22,000,000 cattle, 16,500,000 goats, 2,903,000 camels; roundwood (1994) 9,148,000 cu m; fish catch (1993) 31,700. Mining and quarrying: salt (1994) 75,000; gold (1995) 119,000 troy oz. Manufacturing (1993–94): wheat flour 423,000; raw sugar 425,000; vegetable oils 90,000; cement 186,000; cattlehides and horsehides 38,000[12]; calfskins, goatskins, and sheepskins 18,000[12]; cigarettes 750,000,000 units[12]. Construction: n.a. Energy production (consumption): electricity (kW-hr; 1993) 1,328,000,000 (1,328,000,000); coal, none (none); crude petroleum (barrels; 1993) none (7,513,000); petroleum products (metric tons; 1993) 861,000 (1,041,000); natural gas, none (none).

Land use (1994): forested 18.1%; meadows and pastures 46.3%; agricultural and under permanent cultivation 5.5%; desert and other 30.1%.
Gross national product (1992): U.S.$8,176,000,000 (U.S.$300 per capita).

Structure of gross domestic product and labour force

	1993–94 in value LSd '000,000[13]	1993–94 % of total value	1983 labour force[14]	1983 % of labour force[14]
Agriculture	3,142	37.1	4,028,705	63.5
Mining	12	0.1	6,534	0.1
Manufacturing	794	9.4	266,693	4.2
Construction	465	5.5	139,282	2.2
Public utilities	209	2.5	43,728	0.7
Transportation and communications	3,135	37.1	215,474	3.4
Trade and finance			314,676	5.0
Services			550,409	8.7
Pub. admin., defense	704	8.3		
Other	...	...	777,480[15]	12.2[15]
TOTAL	8,461	100.0	6,342,981	100.0

Household income and expenditure. Average household size: n.a.; income per household: n.a.[16]; sources of income: n.a.; expenditure (1983): food and beverages 63.6%, housing 11.5%, household goods 5.5%, clothing and footwear 5.3%, health care 4.1%, energy 3.8%.

Foreign trade

Balance of trade (current prices)

	1989–90	1990–91	1991–92	1992–93	1993–94	1994–95
U.S.$'000,000	−592	−1,193	−941	−715	−463	−657
% of total	40.1%	63.6%	57.4%	50.3%	29.8%	42.5%

Imports (1994–95): U.S.$1,101,000,000 (petroleum products 17.2%; foodstuffs 17.0%, of which wheat flour 3.9%; electrical machinery 13.6%; chemicals and chemical products 10.0%; transport equipment 8.7%). *Major import sources:* Saudi Arabia 13.5%; U.K. 12.1%; Egypt 5.8%; Germany 4.4%; U.S. 3.6%.
Exports (1994–95): U.S.$444,000,000 (cotton 18.7%; sheep and lambs 14.0%; sesame seeds 12.8%; gum arabic 11.6%; gold 8.0%; peanuts [groundnuts] 5.1%). *Major export destinations:* Saudi Arabia 19.7%; U.K. 9.7%; Italy 9.0%; China 7.5%; Japan 5.3%; Switzerland 4.7%.

Transport and communications

Transport. Railroads (1993): route length (1992) 2,960 mi, 4,764 km; passenger-mi 735,000,000, passenger-km 1,183,000,000; short ton-mi cargo 1,534,000,000, metric ton-km cargo 2,240,000,000[17]. Roads (1993): total length 12,864 mi, 20,703 km (paved 10%). Vehicles (1992): passenger cars 116,000; trucks and buses 57,000. Merchant marine (1992): vessels (100 gross tons and over) 16; total deadweight tonnage 62,244. Air transport (1994)[18]: passenger-mi 382,136,000, passenger-km 614,990,000; short ton-mi cargo 26,785,000, metric ton-km cargo 39,105,000; airports (1996) with scheduled flights 10.
Communications. Daily newspapers (1992): total number 5; total circulation 620,000; circulation per 1,000 population 22. Radio (1995): 5,755,000 receivers (1 per 5.3 persons). Television (1995): 250,000 receivers (1 per 121 persons). Telephones (main lines; 1993): 64,000 (1 per 416 persons).

Education and health

Education (1991–92)

	schools	teachers	students	student/ teacher ratio
Primary (age 7–12)	8,016	64,227	2,168,180	33.8
Secondary (age 13–18)	2,578	29,208	683,982	23.4
Voc., teacher tr.	67	1,434	34,316	23.9
Higher	24	1,943	54,345	28.0

Educational attainment (1983). Percentage of population age 25 and over having: no formal schooling 76.7%; incomplete primary education 18.6%; incomplete secondary 1.9%; complete secondary 2.0%; higher 0.8%. *Literacy* (1995): total population age 15 and over literate 7,280,000 (46.1%); males 4,540,000 (57.7%); females 2,740,000 (34.6%).
Health: physicians (1990) 2,400 (1 per 10,000 persons); hospital beds (1986) 18,571 (1 per 1,222 persons); infant mortality rate (1995) 77.7.
Food (1992): daily per capita caloric intake 2,706 (vegetable products 89%, animal products 11%); 115% of FAO recommended minimum.

Military

Total active duty personnel (1995): 118,500 (army 97.1%, navy 0.4%, air force 2.5%). *Military expenditure as percentage of GNP* (1992): 17.1% (world 3.6%); per capita expenditure U.S.$83.

---

[1]Main opposition parties boycotted the March 1996 executive elections; the president (and military general) who was elected in March 1996 appointed himself president in 1989 after overthrowing a democratically elected government in a military coup. [2]Includes 10 nonelected seats filled by head of state for 10 local administrative units controlled by opposition forces in extreme southern Sudan. [3]Islam was being imposed in 1996. [4]A new currency, the Sudanese dinar (introduced May 1992 at a value equal to 10 Sudanese pounds [LSd]), is gradually replacing the Sudanese pound. [5]Local administrative reorganization into 26 new states was officially announced in February 1994; area and population breakdown was not available. [6]Total area per more recent survey is 967,499 sq mi (2,505,810 sq km). [7]Including c. 50,000 sq mi (130,000 sq km) of inland water area. [8]Preliminary unadjusted 1993 census figure was 24,940,683, including an estimated 3,850,000 in the southern Sudan. [9]June. [10]Manufacturing only. [11]1994–95. [12]1992. [13]In constant prices of 1981–82 at factor cost. [14]Excludes nomads, the homeless, and institutionalized persons. [15]Includes 592,759 unemployed not previously employed. [16]Average annual income of paid worker (1992) U.S.$216. [17]Sections of the Sudan Railways were closed in 1995 because of insufficient funds. [18]Sudan Airways only.

Suriname

Official name: Republiek Suriname
(Republic of Suriname).
Form of government: multiparty
republic with one legislative house
(National Assembly [51]).
Head of state and government:
President.
Capital: Paramaribo.
Official language: Dutch.
Official religion: none.
Monetary unit: 1 Suriname guilder
(Sf) = 100 cents; valuation (Oct.
11, 1996) 1 U.S.$ = Sf 410.00;
1 £ = Sf 645.87.

Area and population		area		population
				1980
Districts	Capitals	sq mi	sq km	census
Brokopondo	Brokopondo	2,843	7,364	6,621
Commewijne	Nieuw Amsterdam	908	2,353	20,063
Coronie	Totness	1,507	3,902	2,777
Marowijne	Albina	1,786	4,627	16,125
Nickerie	Nieuw Nickerie	2,067	5,353	32,690
Para	Onverwacht	2,082	5,393	12,827
Saramacca	Groningen	1,404	3,636	10,808
Sipaliwini	...	50,412	130,566	23,226
Wanica	Lelydorp	171	443	60,725
Town district				
Paramaribo	Paramaribo	71	183	167,798
TOTAL		63,251[1]	163,820[1]	355,240[2]

Demography

Population (1996): 436,000.
Density (1995): persons per sq mi 6.9, persons per sq km 2.7.
Urban-rural (1995): urban 49.6%; rural 50.4%.
Sex distribution (1995): male 49.64%; female 50.36%.
Age breakdown (1995): under 15, 35.2%; 15–29, 29.7%; 30–44, 19.0%; 45–59, 8.8%; 60–74, 5.9%; 75 and over, 1.4%.
Population projection: (2000) 465,000; (2010) 534,000.
Doubling time: 37 years.
Ethnic composition (1991): Suriname Creole 35.0%; Indo-Pakistani 33.0%; Javanese 16.0%; Bush Negro 10.0%; Amerindian 3.0%; other 3.0%.
Religious affiliation (1983): Hindu 26.0%; Roman Catholic 21.6%; Muslim 18.6%; Protestant (mostly Moravian) 18.0%; other 15.8%.
Major cities (1980): Paramaribo 200,970[3]; Nieuw Nickerie 6,078; Meerzorg 5,355; Marienburg 3,633.

Vital statistics

Birth rate per 1,000 population (1990–95): 24.5 (world avg. 25.0); legitimate, n.a.; illegitimate, n.a.
Death rate per 1,000 population (1990–95): 5.6 (world avg. 9.3).
Natural increase rate per 1,000 population (1990–95): 18.9 (world avg. 15.7).
Total fertility rate (avg. births per childbearing woman; 1993): 2.8.
Marriage rate per 1,000 population (1991): 4.9.
Divorce rate per 1,000 population (1991): 2.5.
Life expectancy at birth (1990–95): male 67.8 years; female 72.8 years.
Major causes of death per 100,000 population (1992): noncommunicable diseases 769.0; external and other causes 608.1; communicable and perinatal diseases 232.8; ill-defined diseases 279.0.

National economy

Budget (1994). Revenue: Sf 21,496,700,000 (grants 42.6%; corporate income taxes 20.1%; custom duties 14.1%; individual income taxes 6.0%, value-added taxes 2.7%). Expenditures: Sf 22,969,700,000 (current expenditures 90.6%, of which welfare and social services 6.7%; debt service 5.7%, defense 3.9%, health 1.2%, education 0.8%; capital expenditures 9.4%).
Public debt (external, outstanding; 1990): U.S.$138,000,000.
Production (metric tons except as noted). Agriculture, forestry, fishing (1995): rice 220,000, sugarcane 84,500, bananas 47,500, plantains 19,000, oranges 15,200, coconuts 11,000, watermelons 6,000, cassava 6,000, cucumbers 5,500, tomatoes 1,700, grapefruit 1,200, palm oil 1,000; livestock (number of live animals) 102,000 cattle, 20,000 pigs; roundwood (1994) 94,000 cu m; fish catch (1993) 9,503. Mining and quarrying (1994): bauxite 1,720,000; gold 9,645 troy oz[3]. Manufacturing (value of production at factor cost in Sf; 1993): food products 992,000,000; beverages 558,000,000; tobacco 369,000,000; chemical products 291,000,000; pottery and earthenware 258,000,000; wood products 180,000,000. Construction (value of buildings authorized; 1985): residential Sf 46,500,000; nonresidential Sf 8,100,000. Energy production (consumption): electricity (kW-hr; 1994) 1,683,000,000 (1,683,000,000); hard coal (metric tons) none (n.a.); crude petroleum (barrels; 1994) 1,686,000 (1,370,000); petroleum products (metric tons; 1992) none (461,000); natural gas, none (none).
Household income and expenditure. Average household size (1980) 3.9; income per household: n.a.; sources of income (1975): wages and salaries 74.6%, transfer payments 3.2%, other 22.2%; expenditure (1968–69): food and beverages 40.0%, household furnishings 12.3%, clothing and footwear 11.0%, transportation and communications 9.5%, recreation and education 8.4%, energy 6.9%, housing 4.4%, other 7.5%.
Gross national product (at current market prices; 1994): U.S.$364,000,000 (U.S.$870 per capita).

Structure of gross domestic product and labour force

	1994		1992	
	in value Sf '000,000	% of total value	labour force	% of labour force
Agriculture, forestry	8,738.5	13.7	29,000	21.0
Mining	8,574.6	13.4	2,210	1.6
Manufacturing	6,548.9	10.3	8,170	5.9
Construction	2,360.3	3.7	4,980	3.6
Public utilities	2,885.2	4.5	850	0.6
Transportation and communications	11,129.7	17.5	6,650	4.8
Trade[4]	12,877.3	20.2	13,570	9.8
Finance, real estate	13,257.3	20.8	3,180	2.3
Pub. admin., defense	3,441.7	5.4 }	41,350	30.0
Services	77.3	0.1 }		
Other	−6,181.8[5]	−9.7[5]	28,040[6]	20.3[6]
TOTAL	63,709.1[7]	100.0[7]	138,000	100.0[7]

Population economically active (1992): total 138,000; activity rate of total population 33.6% (participation rates[8]: ages 15–64, 56.0%; female 35.7%; unemployed 13.4%).

Price and earnings indexes (1990 = 100)							
	1989	1990	1991	1992	1993	1994	1995
Consumer price index	82.1	100.0	126.0	181.0	440.7	2,064.5	6,927.7
Earnings index	...	...	...	...	...	...	...

Tourism (1994): receipts from visitors U.S.$11,000,000; expenditures by nationals abroad U.S.$3,000,000.
Land use (1994): forested 96.2%; meadows and pastures 0.1%; agricultural and under permanent cultivation 0.4%; other 3.3%.

Foreign trade

Balance of trade (current prices)						
	1989	1990	1991	1992	1993	1994
U.S.$'000,000	+143.5	−7.7	−117.9	−110.8	−77.2	−99.3
% of total	13.1%	0.6%	11.3%	10.2%	8.0%	20.4%

Imports (1994): U.S.$350,200,000 (fuels and lubricants 18.2%; machinery and transport equipment 13.3%; food and live animals 7.3%, home appliances 4.2%). *Major import sources:* United States 39.8%; The Netherlands 24.1%; Trinidad and Tobago 11.2%; Japan 3.3%; Brazil 3.0%.
Exports (1994): U.S.$339,800,000 (alumina 63.6%, shrimp and fish 9.7%, rice 9.6%, aluminum 9.3%, petroleum 3.0%, bananas 2.9%). *Major export destinations:* Norway 32.6%; The Netherlands 26.9%; United States 13.1%; Japan 6.6%; Brazil 6.3%; France 2.9%.

Transport and communications

Transport. Railroads (1991): length 187 mi, 301 km; passengers, not applicable; cargo, n.a. Roads (1995): total length 2,778 mi, 4,470 km (paved 26%). Vehicles (1995): passenger cars 44,300; trucks and buses 17,050. Merchant marine (1992): vessels (100 gross tons and over) 24; total deadweight tonnage 15,721. Air transport (1995)[9]: passenger-mi 384,081,000, passenger-km 618,119,000; short ton-mi cargo 16,732,000, metric ton-km cargo 24,429,000; airports (1996) with scheduled flights 3.
Communications. Daily newspapers (1992): total number 3; total circulation 43,000; circulation per 1,000 population 103. Radio (1993): total number of receivers 290,256 (1 per 1.4 persons). Television (1993): total number of receivers 59,598 (1 per 7.0 persons). Telephones (main lines; 1994): 50,134 (1 per 8.3 persons).

Education and health

Education (1992–93)				
	schools	teachers	students	student/ teacher ratio
Primary (age 6–11)	223	3,695	79,162	21.4
Secondary (age 12–18)	86 }	2,487	17,709 }	12.6
Voc., teacher tr.	64[10]		12,307 }	
Higher[11]	1	155	1,478	9.5

Educational attainment: n.a. Literacy (1995): total population age 15 and over literate 271,000 (93.0%); males literate 137,000 (95.1%); females literate 134,000 (91.0%).
Health: physicians (1990) 299 (1 per 1,348 persons); hospital beds (1989) 1,901 (1 per 212 persons); infant mortality rate per 1,000 live births (1994) 27.9.
Food (1992): daily per capita caloric intake 2,547 (vegetable products 86%, animal products 14%); 113% of FAO recommended minimum requirement.

Military

Total active duty personnel (1996): 1,800[12] (army 77.8%, navy 13.3%, air force 8.9%). *Military expenditure as percentage of GNP* (1994): 3.9% (world 3.0%); per capita expenditure U.S.$112.

---

[1]Area excludes 6,809 sq mi (17,635 sq km) of territory disputed with Guyana. [2]Detail does not add to total given because of computational discrepancies. [3]1993. [4]Includes hotels. [5]Indirect taxes less subsidies and imputed bank service charges. [6]Includes 18,460 unemployed. [7]Detail does not add to total given because of rounding. [8]Districts of Wanica and Paramaribo only. [9]SLM (Suriname Airways) only. [10]1988–89. [11]1995–96. [12]All services are part of the army.

Swaziland

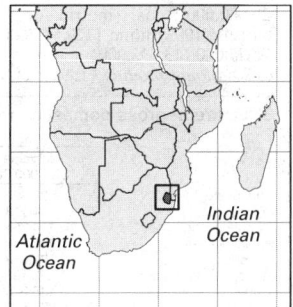

Official name: Umbuso weSwatini (Swazi); Kingdom of Swaziland (English).
Form of government[1]: monarchy with two legislative houses (Senate [30[2]]; House of Assembly [65[3]]).
Head of state and government: King, assisted by Prime Minister.
Capitals: Mbabane (administrative and judicial); Lozitha and Ludzidzini (royal); Lobamba (legislative).
Official languages: Swazi; English.
Official religion: none.
Monetary unit: 1 lilangeni[4] (plural emalangeni [E]) = 100 cents; valuation (Oct. 11, 1996) 1 U.S.$ = E 4.54; 1 £ = E 7.16.

Area and population		area		population
		sq mi	sq km	1986 census[5]
Districts	Capitals			
Hhohho	Mbabane	1,378	3,569	178,936
Lubombo	Siteki	2,296	5,947	153,958
Manzini	Manzini	1,571	4,068	192,596
Shiselweni	Nhlangano	1,459	3,780	155,569
TOTAL		6,704	17,364	681,059

Demography

Population (1996): 934,000.
Density (1996): persons per sq mi 139.3, persons per sq km 53.8.
Urban-rural (1991): urban 34.3%; rural 65.7%.
Sex distribution (1995): male 47.91%; female 52.09%.
Age breakdown (1995): under 15, 43.4%; 15–29, 29.7%; 30–44, 14.9%; 45–59, 7.9%; 60–74, 3.3%; 75 and over, 0.8%.
Population projection: (2000) 1,042,000; (2010) 1,332,000.
Doubling time: 22 years.
Ethnic composition (1983): Swazi 84.3%; Zulu 9.9%; Tsonga 2.5%; Indian 0.8%; Pakistani 0.8%; Portuguese 0.2%; other 1.5%.
Religious affiliation (1980): Christian 77.0%, of which Protestant 37.3%, African indigenous 28.9%, Roman Catholic 10.8%; traditional beliefs 20.9%; other 2.1%.
Major cities (1986): Manzini 52,000; Mbabane 38,290; Nhlangano 4,107; Piggs Peak 3,223; Siteki 2,271.

Vital statistics

Birth rate per 1,000 population (1995): 43.1 (world avg. 25.0); legitimate, n.a.; illegitimate, n.a.
Death rate per 1,000 population (1995): 10.8 (world avg. 9.3).
Natural increase rate per 1,000 population (1995): 32.3 (world avg. 15.7).
Total fertility rate (avg. births per childbearing woman; 1995): 6.1.
Marriage rate per 1,000 population (1989): 4.3.
Divorce rate per 1,000 population: n.a.
Life expectancy at birth (1995): male 52.8 years; female 61.0 years.
Major causes of death (1992)[6]: accidents and injuries 15.8%; infectious intestinal diseases 13.3%; tuberculosis 10.3%; malnutrition 6.2%; respiratory diseases 5.3%; circulatory diseases 5.0%; digestive diseases 4.6%.

National economy

Budget (1995–96). Revenue: E 1,422,000,000 (receipts from Customs Union of Southern Africa 52.3%; tax on income and profits 26.9%; sales tax 12.6%; foreign-aid grants 1.8%; property income 1.5%; fees, services, and fines 0.8%). Expenditures: E 1,506,000,000 (recurrent expenditure 75.1%, of which general administration 21.4%, education 18.0%, economic services 9.6%, justice and police 8.0%, defense 6.6%, health 6.5%, public-debt payments 2.1%).
Land use (1994): forested 7.0%; meadows and pastures 62.2%; agricultural and under permanent cultivation 11.1%; other 19.7%.
Tourism (1994): receipts from visitors U.S.$29,000,000; expenditures by nationals abroad U.S.$21,000,000.
Gross national product (at current market prices; 1994): U.S.$1,048,000,000 (U.S.$1,160 per capita).

Structure of gross domestic product and labour force					
	1994		1986		
	in value E '000	% of total value	labour force	% of labour force	
Agriculture	336,000	9.6	30,197	18.8	
Mining	53,000	1.5	5,245	3.3	
Manufacturing	1,027,000	29.3	14,742	9.2	
Construction	93,000	2.7	7,661	4.8	
Public utilities	41,000	1.2	1,315	0.8	
Transp. and commun.	170,000	4.8	7,526	4.7	
Trade	236,000	6.7	12,348	7.7	
Finance	187,000	5.3	1,931	1.2	
Pub. admin., defense	633,000	18.0 }	32,309	20.1	
Services	166,000	4.7 }			
Other	567,000[7]	16.2[7]	47,081[8]	29.4[8]	
TOTAL	3,509,000	100.0	160,355	100.0	

Population economically active (1986): total 160,355; activity rate of total population 23.5% (participation rates: ages 15 and over, 44.1%; female 34.2%; unemployed 27.0%).

Price and earnings indexes (1990 = 100)							
	1989	1990	1991	1992	1993	1994	1995
Consumer price index	90.1	100.0	110.8	119.9	140.3	160.4	184.0
Earnings index[9]	75.5	100.0	113.2	136.6	154.7	177.3	...

Public debt (external, outstanding; 1994): U.S.$227,500,000.
Production (metric tons except as noted). Agriculture, forestry, fishing (1995): sugarcane 3,798,000, corn (maize) 76,000, grapefruit and pomelo 45,000, lint cotton 16,000, roots and tubers 8,000 (of which potatoes 6,000, sweet potatoes 2,000), seed cotton 6,193, pulses 6,000; livestock (number of live animals) 597,000 cattle, 435,000 goats, 30,000 pigs, 24,000 sheep, 1,000,000 chickens; roundwood 2,279,000 cu m; fish catch (1993) 110. Mining and quarrying (1995): asbestos 28,570; diamonds 52,800 carats[10]. Manufacturing (value added in E; 1990): food and beverages 451,200,000, of which beverage processing 260,500,000; paper and paper products 103,500,000; textiles and garments 49,800,000; wood and wood products 15,700,000; machinery and equipment 12,700,000; nonmetallic mineral products 6,700,000. Construction (value in E; 1995)[11]: residential 43,900,000; nonresidential 17,900,000. Energy production (consumption): electricity (kW-hr; 1991) 387,000,000 (815,000,-000); coal (metric tons; 1992) 100,220 (1989; 28,454); crude petroleum, n.a. (n.a.); petroleum products, n.a. (n.a.); natural gas, n.a. (n.a.).
Household income and expenditure. Average household size (1986) 5.7; annual income per household (1985) E 332 (U.S.$151); sources of income (1985): wages and salaries 44.4%, self-employment 22.2%, transfers 12.2%, other 21.2%; expenditure (1985): food and beverages 33.5%, rent and fuel 13.4%, household durable goods 12.8%, transportation and communications 8.8%, clothing and footwear 6.0%, recreation 3.3%.

Foreign trade

Balance of trade (current prices)					
	1989	1990	1991	1992	1993	1994
E '000,000	−56.7	−77.5	−98.6	−362.7	−406.9	−943.4
% of total	2.1%	2.6%	2.9%	9.1%	8.7%	16.8%

Imports (1994): E 2,936,000,000 (machinery and transport equipment 26.1%; manufactured items 18.8%; foodstuffs 15.5%; chemicals 10.0%; minerals, fuels, and lubricants 9.7%). *Major import sources* (1993): South Africa 81.7%; United Kingdom 2.5%; The Netherlands 0.4%; Switzerland 0.3%; France 0.1%.
Exports (1994): E 2,832,000,000 (sugar 13.5%; wood and wood products 11.8%; cotton yarn 4.7%; asbestos 2.0%; citrus fruits 1.9%; canned fruits 1.7%). *Major export destinations* (1991): South Africa 47.0%; United States 3.3%; United Kingdom 3.3%; Mozambique 2.4%; South Korea 2.2%; Zimbabwe 2.2%.

Transport and communications

Transport. Railroads (1995): length 187 mi, 301 km; passenger-mi 752,000,-000[12], passenger-km 1,210,000,000[12]; short ton-mi cargo 1,993,000,000[13], metric ton-km cargo 2,910,000,000[13]. Roads (1995): total length 2,377 mi, 3,825 km (paved 28%). Vehicles (1995): passenger cars 27,300; trucks and buses 26,340. Merchant marine: none (landlocked state). Air transport (1995)[14]: passenger-mi 30,710,000, passenger-km 49,423,000; short ton-mi cargo 87,000, metric ton-km cargo 127,000; airports (1996) with scheduled flights 1.
Communications. Daily newspapers (1995): total number 2; total circulation 36,000; circulation per 1,000 population 41. Radio (1995): total number of receivers 117,000 (1 per 7.8 persons). Television (1995): total number of receivers 12,500 (1 per 73 persons). Telephones (main lines; 1993): 16,000 (1 per 53 persons).

Education and health

Education (1994)	schools	teachers	students	student/ teacher ratio
Primary (age 6–13)	535	5,887	192,599	32.7
Secondary (age 14–18)	165	2,872	52,571	18.3
Voc., teacher tr.[15]	5	228	2,958	13.0
Higher	1	190[15]	2,132	9.1[15]

Educational attainment (1986). Percentage of population age 25 and over having: no formal schooling 42.1%; some primary education 23.9%; complete primary 10.5%; some secondary 19.2%; complete secondary and higher 4.3%. *Literacy* (1995): total population age 15 and over literate 76.7%; males literate 78.0%; females literate 75.6%.
Health: physicians (1990) 83 (1 per 9,265 persons); hospital beds (1984) 1,608 (1 per 396 persons); infant mortality rate per 1,000 live births (1995) 90.7.
Food (1992): daily per capita caloric intake 2,706 (vegetable products 89%, animal products 11%); 117% of FAO recommended minimum requirement.

Military

Total active duty personnel (1983): 2,657. *Military expenditure as percentage of GNP* (1994): 1.7% (world 3.0%); per capita expenditure U.S.$17.

---

[1]In July 1996 the king announced that a 30-member Constitutional Review committee had been formed to prepare proposals for a new draft constitution. [2]Includes 20 nonelective seats. [3]Includes 10 nonelective seats. [4]The lilangeni is at par with the South African rand. [5]Preliminary. [6]Percentage of deaths of known cause at government, mission, and private hospitals. [7]Includes indirect taxes less imputed bank service charges and subsidies. [8]Includes 43,925 unemployed. [9]Manufacturing sector only. [10]1994. [11]Urban areas under the jurisdiction of the Manzini and Mbabane town councils only. [12]1988. [13]1991. [14]Royal Swazi National Airways only; international flights only. [15]1993–94.

Sweden

Official name: Konungariket Sverige (Kingdom of Sweden).
Form of government: constitutional monarchy and parliamentary state with one legislative house (Parliament [349]).
Chief of state: King.
Head of government: Prime Minister.
Capital: Stockholm.
Official language: Swedish.
Official religion: Church of Sweden (Lutheran).
Monetary unit: 1 Swedish krona (SKr) = 100 ore; valuation (Oct. 11, 1996 1 U.S.$ = SKr 6.60; 1 £ = SKr 10.39.

Area and population		area		population
		sq mi	sq km	1996[1] estimate
Counties	Capitals			
Älvsborg	Vänersborg	4,400	11,395	449,524
Blekinge	Karlskrona	1,136	2,941	152,737
Gävleborg	Gävle	7,024	18,191	288,509
Göteborg och Bohus	Göteborg	1,985	5,141	770,375
Gotland	Visby	1,212	3,140	58,120
Halland	Halmstad	2,106	5,454	269,338
Jämtland	Östersund	19,090	49,443	135,584
Jönköping	Jönköping	3,839	9,944	312,686
Kalmar	Kalmar	4,313	11,170	243,372
Kopparberg	Falun	10,886	28,194	289,956
Kristianstad	Kristianstad	2,350	6,087	294,709
Kronoberg	Växjö	3,266	8,458	180,377
Malmöhus	Malmö	1,907	4,938	817,022
Norrbotten	Luleå	38,191	98,913	266,011
Örebro	Örebro	3,289	8,519	276,417
Östergötland	Linköping	4,078	10,562	416,443
Skaraborg	Mariestad	3,065	7,937	279,511
Södermanland	Nyköping	2,340	6,060	258,700
Stockholm	Stockholm	2,505	6,488	1,725,756
Uppsala	Uppsala	2,698	6,989	288,475
Värmland	Karlstad	6,789	17,584	284,011
Västerbotten	Umeå	21,390	55,401	260,472
Västernorrland	Härnösand	8,370	21,678	258,290
Västmanland	Västerås	2,433	6,302	261,101
TOTAL LAND AREA		158,661[2]	410,929	
INLAND WATER		15,071	39,035	
TOTAL		173,732	449,964	8,837,496

Demography

Population (1996): 8,858,000.
Density (1996)[3]: persons per sq mi 55.8, persons per sq km 21.6.
Urban-rural (1995): urban 83.1%; rural 16.9%.
Sex distribution (1996[1]): male 49.40%; female 50.60%.
Age breakdown (1996[1]): under 15, 18.8%; 15–29, 19.3%; 30–44, 20.4%; 45–59, 19.4%; 60–74, 13.6%; 75 and over, 8.5%.
Population projection: (2000) 8,982,000; (2010) 9,199,000.
Ethnic composition (1996[1]): Swedish 89.4%; Finnish 2.3%; Iranian 0.5%; other 7.8%.
Religious affiliation (1994[1]): Church of Sweden 86.5% (nominally; about 30% nonpracticing); Roman Catholic 1.8%; Pentecostal 1.1%; other 10.6%.
Major cities (1996[1]): Stockholm 711,119; Göteborg 449,189; Malmö 245,699; Uppsala 183,472; Linköping 131,370.

Vital statistics

Birth rate per 1,000 population (1995): 11.7 (world avg. 25.0); (1994) legitimate 48.4%; illegitimate 51.6%.
Death rate per 1,000 population (1995): 10.6 (world avg. 9.3).
Natural increase rate per 1,000 population (1995): 1.1 (world avg. 15.7).
Total fertility rate (avg. births per childbearing woman; 1994): 1.9.
Marriage rate per 1,000 population (1995): 3.8.
Divorce rate per 1,000 population (1995): 2.6.
Life expectancy at birth (1990–94): male 75.3 years; female 80.8 years.
Major causes of death per 100,000 population (1993): heart disease 439.8; malignant neoplasms (cancers) 237.1; cerebrovascular disease 117.9.

National economy

Budget (1994–95). Revenue: SKr 423,183,000,000 (value-added and excise taxes 44.6%, income and capital gains taxes 21.5%, social security contributions 17.8%, nontax revenue 6.8%, property taxes 5.3%). Expenditures: SKr 579,421,000,000 (health and social affairs 23.0%, interest on national debt 21.3%, defense 6.7%, education and culture 5.1%).
Public debt (1995): U.S.$117,600,000,000.
Tourism (1994): receipts from visitors U.S.$2,826,000,000; expenditures by nationals abroad U.S.$4,878,000,000.
Production (metric tons except as noted). Agriculture, forestry, fishing (1995): sugar beets 2,507,800, barley 1,792,700, wheat 1,553,800, potatoes 1,073,800, oats 946,700; livestock (number of live animals) 2,313,137 pigs, 1,777,000 cattle, 461,000 sheep; roundwood 56,500,000 cu m; fish catch 347,741. Mining and quarrying (1995): iron ore 12,980,000[4]; copper 311,000; zinc 304,000; lead 137,000. Manufacturing (value added, in SKr '000,000; 1993): machinery and transport equipment 103,162; paper and paper products 35,528; food and beverages 23,783; wood and wood products 12,604; textiles and wearing apparel 3,603. Construction (dwellings completed; 1994): 21,630. Energy production (consumption): electricity (kW-hr; 1993) 144,311,000,000 (143,-

722,000,000); coal (metric tons; 1993) 4,000 (3,380,000); crude petroleum (barrels; 1993) none (129,547,000); petroleum products (metric tons; 1993) 17,577,000 (13,533,000); natural gas (cu m; 1993) none (835,950,000).
Gross national product (1994): U.S.$206,419,000,000 (U.S.$23,630 per capita).

Structure of gross domestic product and labour force				
	1994			
	in value SKr '000,000	% of total value	labour force	% of labour force
Agriculture	32,899	2.4	135,000	3.2
Mining	4,118	0.3	10,000	0.2
Manufacturing	294,755	22.0	720,000	16.9
Public utilities	45,250	3.4	32,000	0.7
Construction	77,058	5.8	219,000	5.1
Transp. and commun.	92,131	6.9	271,000	6.4
Trade	148,079	11.1	568,000	13.3
Finance	337,590	25.2	379,000	8.9
Pub. admin., defense } Services	379,129	28.3	1,593,000	37.5
Other	−71,715[5]	−5.4[5]	340,000[6]	8.0[6]
TOTAL	1,339,294	100.0	4,267,000	100.0[2]

Population economically active (1994): total 4,267,000; activity rate of total population 48.6% (participation rates: ages 16–64 77.6%; female 46.7%; unemployed 8.0%).

Price and earnings indexes (1990 = 100)							
	1989	1990	1991	1992	1993	1994	1995
Consumer price index	90.6	100.0	109.4	112.0	117.1	120.0	123.0
Hourly earnings index	91.0	100.0	105.0	110.0	113.0	118.0	123.0

Household income and expenditure. Average household size (1990) 2.1; median income per household SKr 119,000 (U.S.$18,400); sources of income (1992): wages and salaries 58.9%, transfer payments 25.8%, self-employment 15.3%; expenditure (1992): housing and energy 31.4%, food 19.8%, transportation 16.1%, education and recreation 9.8%.
Land use (1994): forested 68.0%; meadows and pastures 1.4%; agricultural and under permanent cultivation 6.8%; other 23.8%.

Foreign trade

Balance of trade (current prices)						
	1990	1991	1992	1993	1994	1995
SKr '000,000	26,863	38,343	42,062	63,285	82,735	82,735
% of total	4.1%	6.1%	6.9%	8.9%	9.6%	8.1%

Imports (1995): SKr 458,800,000,000 (machinery and transport equipment 40.7%, of which electrical machinery 12.7%, transport equipment 9.3%; chemicals 11.4%; food 6.4%; clothing 4.2%). *Major import sources:* Germany 16.0%; U.K. 8.3%; U.S. 7.4%; Denmark 5.9%; Finland 5.5%; Norway 5.3%.
Exports (1995): SKr 564,400,000,000 (machinery and transport equipment 45.6%, of which transport equipment 14.8%, electrical machinery 12.6%; paper products 9.6%; chemicals 9.0%; wood and wood pulp 6.2%; iron and steel products 6.0%). *Major export destinations:* Germany 11.1%; U.K. 8.5%; Norway 6.8%; U.S. 6.7%; Denmark 5.8%; Finland 4.0%.

Transport and communications

Transport. Railroads (1994): length 6,710 mi, 10,798 km; passenger-mi 3,759,-000,000, passenger-km 6,051,000,000; short ton-mi cargo 13,059,000,000, metric ton-km cargo 19,066,000,000. Roads (1992): total length 84,419 mi, 135,859 km (paved 72%). Vehicles (1995[1]): passenger cars 3,594,000; trucks and buses 318,000. Merchant marine (1993): vessels (100 gross tons and over) 417; total deadweight tonnage 2,339,474. Air transport (1994): passenger-mi 5,796,483,000, passenger-km 9,328,553,000; short ton-mi cargo 134,015,000, metric ton-km cargo 195,659,000; airports (1995) 48.
Communications. Daily newspapers (1995): total number 174; total circulation 4,544,000; circulation per 1,000 population 515. Radio (1994): 7,450,000 receivers (1 per 1.2 persons). Television (1994): 3,750,000 receivers (1 per 2.3 persons). Telephones (main lines; 1993): 5,907,000 (1 per 1.5 persons).

Education and health

Education (1993–94)				
	schools	teachers	students	student/ teacher ratio
Primary (age 7–12)	4,826	90,234	893,932	9.9
Secondary (age 13–18)	600	29,539	313,728	10.6
Higher[7]	...	27,523[8]	272,718	9.9

Educational attainment (1995). Percentage of population age 16–64 having: primary education 30.7%; lower secondary education 32.2%; higher secondary 14.3%; some postsecondary 22.8%. *Literacy* (1995): virtually 100%.
Health: physicians (1994) 22,400 (1 per 394 persons); hospital beds (1994) 52,-991 (1 per 166 persons); infant mortality rate per 1,000 live births (1995) 3.7.
Food (1992): daily per capita caloric intake 2,972 (vegetable products 62%, animal products 38%); 110% of FAO requirement.

Military

Total active duty personnel (1995): 64,000 (army 68.0%, navy 14.1%, air force 17.9%). *Military expenditure as percentage of GNP* (1994): 2.8% (world 3.0%); per capita expenditure U.S.$605.

[1]January 1. [2]Detail does not add to total given because of rounding. [3]Density based on land area only. [4]Metal content of ore. [5]Includes statistical discrepancies less imputed bank service charges. [6]Unemployed. [7]1989–90. [8]Includes graduate assistants.

Switzerland

Official name: Confédération
  Suisse (French); Schweizerische
  Eidgenossenschaft (German);
  Confederazione Svizzera (Italian)
  (Swiss Confederation).
Form of government: federal state with
  two legislative houses (Council of
  States [46]; National Council [200]).
Head of state and government:
  President.
Capitals: Bern (administrative);
  Lausanne (judicial).
Official languages: French; German;
  Italian.
Official religion: none.
Monetary unit: 1 Swiss Franc
  (Sw F) = 100 centimes; valuation (Oct.
  11, 1996) 1 U.S.$ = Sw F 1.26;
  1 £ = Sw F 1.98.

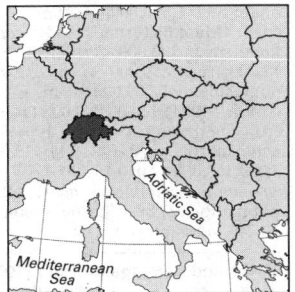

Area and population

Cantons	Capitals	area sq mi	area sq km	population 1995[1] estimate
Aargau	Aarau	542	1,404	523,114
Appenzell Ausser-Rhoden[2]	Herisau	94	243	54,227
Appenzell Inner-Rhoden[2]	Appenzell	67	173	14,742
Basel-Landschaft[2]	Liestal	200	517	251,259
Basel-Stadt[2]	Basel	14	37	197,054
Bern	Bern	2,302	5,961	941,747
Fribourg	Fribourg	645	1,671	222,227
Genève	Geneva	109	282	391,699
Glarus	Glarus	264	685	39,388
Graubünden	Chur	2,743	7,105	184,155
Jura	Delémont	323	836	68,979
Luzern	Luzern	576	1,493	337,941
Neuchâtel	Neuchâtel	310	803	164,176
Nidwalden[2]	Stans	107	276	35,983
Obwalden[2]	Sarnen	189	490	30,958
Sankt Gallen	Sankt Gallen	782	2,026	440,744
Schaffhausen	Schaffhausen	115	299	73,894
Schwyz	Schwyz	351	908	120,576
Solothurn	Solothurn	305	791	237,338
Thurgau	Frauenfeld	383	991	220,335
Ticino	Bellinzona	1,086	2,812	302,131
Uri	Altdorf	416	1,077	35,933
Valais	Sion	2,017	5,225	269,341
Vaud	Lausanne	1,240	3,212	602,099
Zug	Zug	92	239	90,412
Zürich	Zürich	668	1,729	1,168,567
TOTAL		15,940	41,285	7,019,019[3]

Demography

Population (1996): 7,087,000.
Density (1996): persons per sq mi 444.6, persons per sq km 171.7.
Urban-rural (1995): urban 67.8%; rural 32.2%.
Sex distribution (1995): male 48.84%; female 51.16%.
Age breakdown (1995): under 15, 17.6%; 15–29, 20.2%; 30–44, 23.7%; 45–59,
  18.9%; 60–74, 12.9%; 75 and over, 6.7%.
Population projection: (2000) 7,277,000; (2010) 7,539,000.
Linguistic composition (1990): German 63.6%; French 19.2%; Italian 7.6%;
  Spanish 1.7%; Portuguese 1.4%; Romansch 0.6%; other 5.9%.
Religious affiliation (1990): Roman Catholic 46.2%; Protestant 40.0%; Muslim
  2.2%; Orthodox Christian 1.0%; Jewish 0.3%; other 10.3%.
Major cities (1995[1]): Zürich 342,872 (940,180[4]); Basel 175,561 (406,391[4]);
  Geneva 172,737 (424,028[4]); Bern 128,422 (332,494[4]); Lausanne 116,795.

Vital statistics

Birth rate per 1,000 population (1995): 11.6 (world avg. 25.0); (1994) legiti-
  mate 93.6%; illegitimate 6.4%.
Death rate per 1,000 population (1995): 8.6 (world avg. 9.3).
Natural increase rate per 1,000 population (1995): 3.0 (world avg. 15.7).
Total fertility rate (avg. births per childbearing woman; 1994): 1.5.
Marriage rate per 1,000 population (1994): 6.1.
Life expectancy at birth (1993–94): male 75.1 years; female 81.6 years.
Major causes of death per 100,000 population (1993): heart disease 284.2, of
  which ischemic 149.7, other 134.5; malignant neoplasms (cancers) 242.2.

National economy

Budget (1996)[5]. Revenue: Sw F 39,864,000,000 (turnover taxes 29.4%, direct
  federal taxes 23.6%, motor fuel fees 11.5%). Expenditures: Sw F 44,154,-
  000,000 (social services 27.3%, transportation 14.0%, defense 12.9%).
National debt (end of year; 1995): Sw F 82,152,000,000.
Tourism (1994): receipts from visitors U.S.$7,570,000,000; expenditures by
  nationals abroad U.S.$6,325,000,000.
Production (metric tons except as noted). Agriculture, forestry, fishing (1994):
  milk 3,900,000, sugar beets 800,000, potatoes 800,000, wheat 550,000, barley
  370,000, apples 262,000, grapes 170,000; livestock (number of live animals)
  1,700,000 cattle, 1,680,000 pigs; roundwood (1993) 4,338,000 cu m; fish catch
  (1993) 3,157. Mining (1994): salt 300,000. Manufacturing (value added in
  Sw F '000,000; 1993): nonelectrical machinery and transport vehicles 12,670;
  chemical products 11,667; electrical goods, electronics, and optics 11,395;
  base metals and metal products 8,276. Construction (in Sw F '000,000; 1994):
  residential 20,576; nonresidential 28,325. Energy production (consumption):
  electricity (kW-hr; 1994) 62,390,000,000 ([1993] 53,871,000,000); coal (metric

tons; 1993) none (220,000); crude petroleum (barrels; 1993) none (33,161,-
000); petroleum products (metric tons; 1993) 4,620,000 (12,169,000); natural
gas (cu m; 1993) 2,400,000 (2,408,000,000).
Gross national product (1994): U.S.$264,974,000,000 (U.S.$37,180 per capita).

Structure of gross domestic product and labour force

	1992 in value Sw F '000,000	1992 % of total value	1995 labour force[6]	1995 % of labour force
Agriculture	9,845	2.9	154,000	3.9
Manufacturing	78,299	23.1	782,000	19.9
Mining			27,000	0.7
Public utilities	6,615	1.9		
Construction	25,079	7.4	286,000	7.3
Transp. and commun.	21,523	6.4	227,000	5.8
Trade	59,140	17.5	733,000	18.6
Finance, insurance[7]	83,144	24.5	485,000	12.3
Pub. admin., defense	70,346	20.8	160,000	4.0
Services			928,000	23.6
Other	−15,226[8]	−4.5[8]	154,000[9]	3.9[9]
TOTAL	338,765	100.0	3,936,000[10]	100.0

Population economically active (1994): total 3,943,000[6]; activity rate of total
  population 56.0% (participation rates: age 15 and over [1993] 60.8%; female
  40.5%; unemployed [March–May 1996] 4.5%).

Price and earnings indexes (1990 = 100)

	1990	1991	1992	1993	1994	1995	1996
Consumer price index	100.0	105.8	110.1	113.8	114.7	116.8	117.5[11]
Annual earnings index	100.0	106.9	111.9	114.8	116.6	117.6	...

Household income and expenditure. Average household size (1993) 2.2; average income per household (1993) Sw F 70,700 (U.S.$47,850); sources of
  income (1992): wages 63.6%, transfer payments 16.5%; expenditure (1992):
  food 19.2%, housing 15.8%, transportation 11.7%, health care 11.1%.
Land use (1993): forested 31.6%; meadows and pastures 28.2%; agricultural
  and under permanent cultivation 11.8%; other 28.4%.

Foreign trade[12]

Balance of trade (current prices)

	1990	1991	1992	1993	1994	1995
Sw F '000,000	−7,397	−6,144	+268	+3,721	+3,798	+1,679
% of total	4.0%	3.4%	0.2%	3.2%	2.2%	0.9%

Imports (1995): Sw F 90,775,000,000 (machinery and electronics 22.6%; chemical products 14.3%; vehicles 11.7%; food products 8.9%). *Major import
  sources:* Germany 34.8%; France 11.7%; Italy 10.5%; U.S. 5.8%; U.K. 4.4%.
Exports (1995): Sw F 92,012,000,000 (machinery and electronics 29.8%; chemical products 25.6%; precision instruments, watches, and jewelry 16.2%; base
  metals and finished products 9.1%). *Major export destinations:* Germany
  24.5%; France 9.7%; U.S. 8.4%; Italy 7.8%; U.K. 5.2%.

Transport and communications

Transport. Railroads: length (1993) 3,125 mi, 5,029 km; passenger-km (1994)
  12,300,000,000[13]; metric ton-km cargo (1994) 8,052,000,000[13]. Roads (1994):
  total length 44,334 mi, 71,348 km. Vehicles (1994): passenger cars 3,165,043;
  trucks and buses 270,915. Merchant marine (1992): vessels (100 gross tons
  and over) 24; total deadweight tonnage 602,084. Air transport (1995)[14]:
  passenger-km 19,725,000,000; metric ton-km cargo 1,508,000,000; airports
  (1996) with scheduled flights 5.
Communications. Daily newspapers (1994): total number 110; total circulation 3,427,801; circulation per 1,000 population 490. Radio (1995): 5,600,000
  receivers (1 per 1.3 persons). Television (1995): 2,602,000 receivers (1 per
  2.7 persons). Telephones (main lines; 1994): 4,258,000 (1 per 1.6 persons).

Education and health

Education (1994–95)

	schools	teachers	students	student/ teacher ratio
Primary (age 7–12)	...	...	437,444	...
Secondary (age 13–19)	...	...	373,986	...
Vocational	...	...	188,855	...
Higher	...	...	148,154	...

Educational attainment (1993). Percentage of resident Swiss and resident
  alien population age 25–64 having: lower secondary education or less 18%;
  vocational 50%; upper secondary 11%; higher technical 13%; university 8%.
Health: physicians (1992) c. 23,000 (1 per 299 persons); hospital beds (1993)
  51,685 (1 per 134 persons); infant mortality rate per 1,000 live births (1994)
  5.1.
Food (1992): daily per capita caloric intake 3,379 (vegetable products 62%,
  animal products 38%); 126% of FAO recommended minimum.

Military

Total active duty personnel (1995): 3,400[15]. *Military expenditure as percentage
  of GNP* (1994): 1.9% (world 3.0%); per capita expenditure U.S.$712.

---

[1]January 1. [2]Demicanton; functions as a full canton. [3]Includes 1,332,493 resident
aliens. [4]1990 population of urban agglomeration. [5]Confederation-level only. [6]Per revised official definition of June 1, 1995. [7]Includes consulting services. [8]Import duties
less imputed bank charges. [9]Unemployed. [10]Labour force includes 976,000 foreign
workers. [11]July. [12]Import figures are f.o.b. in balance of trade and c.i.f. in commodities and trading partners. [13]Swiss Federal Railways. [14]Swissair only. [15]Excludes
396,300 reservists.

Syria

Official name: Al-Jumhūrīyah al-'Arabīyah as-Sūrīyah (Syrian Arab Republic).
Form of government: unitary multiparty[1] republic with one legislative house (People's Council [250]).
Head of state and government: President.
Capital: Damascus.
Official language: Arabic.
Official religion: none[2].
Monetary unit: 1 Syrian pound (LS) = 100 piastres; valuation (official rate; Oct. 11, 1996) 1 U.S.$ = LS 11.22; 1 £ = LS 17.67[3].

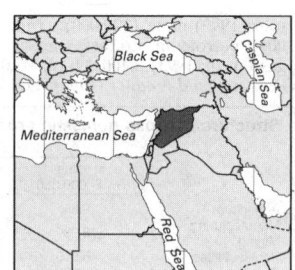

Area and population		area		population
				1995
Governorates	Capitals	sq mi	sq km	estimate
Darʿā	Darʿā	1,440	3,730	623,000
Dayr az-Zawr	Dayr az-Zawr	12,765	33,060	722,000
Dimashq	Damascus	6,962	18,032	1,730,000
Ḥalab	Aleppo	7,143	18,500	3,035,000
Ḥamāh	Ḥamāh	3,430	8,883	1,120,000
Al-Ḥasakah	Al-Ḥasakah	9,009	23,334	1,050,000
Ḥimṣ	Homs	16,302	42,223	1,247,000
Idlib	Idlib	2,354	6,097	922,000
Al-Lādhiqīyah	Latakia	887	2,297	766,000
Al-Qunayṭirah	Al-Qunayṭirah	719[4]	1,861[4]	50,000
Ar-Raqqah	Ar-Raqqah	7,574	19,616	566,000
As-Suwaydāʾ	As-Suwaydāʾ	2,143	5,550	270,000
Ṭarṭūs	Ṭarṭūs	730	1,892	596,000
Municipality				
Damascus	—	41	105	1,489,000
TOTAL		71,498[4]	185,180[4]	14,186,000

Demography

Population (1996): 14,798,000.
Density (1996): persons per sq mi 207.0, persons per sq km 79.9.
Urban-rural (1995): urban 52.4%; rural 47.6%.
Sex distribution (1995): male 50.71%; female 49.29%.
Age breakdown (1995): under 15, 44.7%; 15–29, 28.2%; 30–44, 14.8%; 45–59, 7.3%; 60 and over, 5.0%.
Population projection: (2000) 16,909,000; (2010) 23,019,000.
Doubling time: 21 years.
Ethnic composition (1981): Arab 88.8%; Kurdish 6.3%; other 4.9%.
Religious affiliation (1992): Muslim 86.0%, of which Sunnī 74.0%, 'Alawite (Shīʿī) 12.0%; Christian 8.9%; Druze 3.0%; other 2.1%.
Major cities (1994): Aleppo 1,591,400; Damascus 1,549,932; Homs 644,204; Latakia 306,535; Ḥamāh 229,000.

Vital statistics

Birth rate per 1,000 population (1995): 40.0 (world avg. 25.0).
Death rate per 1,000 population (1995): 6.0 (world avg. 9.3).
Natural increase rate per 1,000 population (1995): 34.0 (world avg. 15.7).
Total fertility rate (avg. births per childbearing woman; 1995): 6.1.
Marriage rate per 1,000 population (1994)[5]: 8.6.
Divorce rate per 1,000 population (1994)[5]: 0.7.
Life expectancy at birth (1994): male 68.4 years; female 71.3 years.
Major causes of death per 100,000 population (1981): diseases of the circulatory system 60.7; accidents 18.3; infectious diseases 15.1.

National economy

Budget (1995). Revenue: LS 125,718,000,000 (current revenues 81.3%, capital [development] revenues 18.7%). Expenditures: LS 162,040,000,000 (current expenditures 54.3%, capital [development] expenditures 45.7%).
Public debt (external, outstanding; 1994): U.S.$16,539,000,000.
Gross national product (1991): U.S.$16,204,000,000 (U.S.$1,170 per capita).

Structure of gross domestic product and labour force					
	1994[6]			1991	
	in value LS '000,000	% of total value		labour force	% of labour force
Agriculture	128,113	29.0		916,952	26.3
Mining	29,119	6.6		6,651	0.2
Manufacturing	22,319	5.0		456,162	13.1
Construction	18,128	4.1		340,779	9.8
Public utilities	2,500	0.6		8,422	0.2
Transportation and communications	42,014	9.5		166,965	4.8
Trade	127,017	28.7		378,250	10.9
Finance	16,099	3.6		24,651	0.7
Pub. admin.	42,031	9.5	}	951,104	27.3
Services	9,275	2.1	}		
Other	5,737	1.3		235,432[7]	6.8[7]
TOTAL	442,352	100.0		3,485,368	100.0[8]

Production (metric tons except as noted). Agriculture, forestry, fishing (1995): wheat 4,192,902, barley 1,722,201, seed cotton 600,100, tomatoes 430,000, grapes 380,000, apples 240,000, eggplants 155,000; livestock (number of live animals) 11,800,000 sheep, 1,200,000 goats, 750,000 cattle; roundwood (1994) 50,400 cu m; fish catch (1993) 7,500. Mining and quarrying (1994): phos-

phate rock 1,600,000; gypsum 235,000; salt 130,000; marble blocks 18,000,000 cu m. Manufacturing (1993): cement 3,667,000; wheat flour 1,218,000; refined sugar 183,000; fertilizers 89,639; olive oil 60,139; textiles 29,000; soap 17,000; rugs 656,000 sq m. Construction (1993): residential 628,000 sq m; nonresidential 209,000 sq m. Energy production (consumption): electricity (kW-hr; 1994) 14,800,000,000 (14,800,000,000); coal (metric tons) none (n.a.); crude petroleum (barrels; 1994) 198,244,000 (85,450,000); petroleum products (metric tons; 1994) 11,438,000 (10,044,000); natural gas (cu m; 1994) 2,050,160,000 (2,050,160,000).
Population economically active (1991): total 3,845,368; activity rate of total population 27.8% (participation rates: ages 15–64 [1986] 46.7%; female 10.2%; unemployed 6.1%).

Price and earnings indexes (1990 = 100)							
	1989	1990	1991	1992	1993	1994	1995[9]
Consumer price index	83.8	100.0	107.7	117.9	131.8	143.8	177.0
Earnings index	...	...	...	...	...	...	...

Average household size (1986): 5.7; income per household: n.a.; sources of income: n.a.; expenditure (1987)[10]: food 58.8%, rent, fuel, and light 16.0%, clothing 7.5%, household goods 5.8%, transportation 2.4%, education and recreation 2.1%.
Tourism (1994): receipts from visitors U.S.$800,000,000; expenditures by nationals abroad U.S.$400,000,000.
Land use (1994): steppe and pasture 45.2%; cultivable 30.1%; forested 2.6%; other 22.1%.

Foreign trade[11]

Balance of trade (current prices)						
	1990	1991	1992	1993	1994	1995
LS '000,000	+22,564	+9,995	−1,223	−7,312	−16,483	−2,981
% of total	31.3%	14.9%	1.7%	9.4%	17.1%	3.2%

Imports (1993): LS 46,468,900,000 (machinery and equipment 22.3%, food and beverages 15.4%, basic metals industries 13.4%, transportation equipment 11.8%, chemicals and chemical products 10.9%, textiles 8.3%). *Major import sources:* Germany 10.2%; Japan 8.2%; Italy 8.2%; France 7.1%; United States 6.4%; Turkey 5.4%; Romania 4.5%.
Exports (1993): LS 35,318,000,000 (crude petroleum and petroleum products 66.7%, fresh vegetables and fruits 9.3%, raw cotton 5.5%, live animals and meat 3.0%, textiles 2.9%). *Major export destinations:* Italy 30.8%; France 15.3%; Lebanon 10.5%; Spain 7.8%; Saudi Arabia 4.9%; United Kingdom 3.2%.

Transport and communications

Transport. Railroads (1995): route length 1,766 km; passenger-km 855,000,-000[12]; metric ton-km cargo 1,097,000,000[12]. Roads (1995): total length 39,243 km (paved 71%). Vehicles (1995): passenger cars 229,084; trucks and buses 218,900. Merchant marine (1992): vessels (100 gross tons and over) 94; total deadweight tonnage 210,369. Air transport (1995): passenger-km 948,490,000; metric ton-km cargo 15,965,000; airports (1996) with scheduled flights 5.
Communications. Daily newspapers (1992): total number 11; total circulation 290,000; circulation per 1,000 population 22.4. Radio (1995): 3,000,000 receivers (1 per 4.8 persons). Television (1995): 700,000 receivers (1 per 20.4 persons). Telephones (main lines; 1993): 550,312 (1 per 24.3 persons).

Education and health

Education (1993–94)				student/
	schools	teachers	students	teacher ratio
Primary (age 6–11)	10,219	110,580	2,624,594	23.7
Secondary (age 12–18)	2,354	49,951	846,550	16.9
Voc., teacher tr.	289	11,559	76,480	6.6
Higher[13]	47	3,723	173,486	46.6

Educational attainment (1984). Percentage of population age 10 and over having: no schooling 20.1%; knowledge of reading and writing 26.3%; primary education 29.3%; secondary 18.4%; certificate 3.3%; higher 2.7%.
Literacy (1995): percentage of population age 15 and over literate 70.8%; males literate 85.7%; females literate 55.8%.
Health (1993): physicians 13,863 (1 per 966 persons); hospital beds 14,698 (1 per 911 persons); infant mortality rate per 1,000 live births (1994) 29.6.
Food (1992): daily per capita caloric intake 3,175 (vegetable products 89%, animal products 11%); 128% of FAO recommended minimum requirement.

Military

Total active duty personnel (1996): 421,000 (army 74.8%, navy 1.4%, air force 23.8%). *Military expenditure as percentage of GNP* (1993): 8.3% (world 3.3%); per capita expenditure U.S.$178.

---

[1]Parties ideologically compatible with the Baʿth Party. [2]Islam is required to be the religion of the head of state and is the basis of the legal system. [3]The primary rate used in foreign exchange is 1 U.S.$ = LS 41.95; 1 £ = LS 66.08. [4]Includes territory in the Golan Heights recognized internationally as part of Syria (located between the 1949 Israel-Syria Armistice line [west] and the 1974 UN Disengagement of Forces zone [east]) that has been occupied by Israel since 1967. Israel's unilateral annexation of this territory in December 1981 has received no international recognition. [5]Syrian Arabs only. [6]UN estimates. [7]Unemployed. [8]Detail does not add to total given because of rounding. [9]November. [10]Weights of consumer price index components for Damascus only. [11]Import figures are f.o.b. in balance of trade and c.i.f. in commodities and trading partners. [12]1993. [13]University-level institutions only.

Taiwan

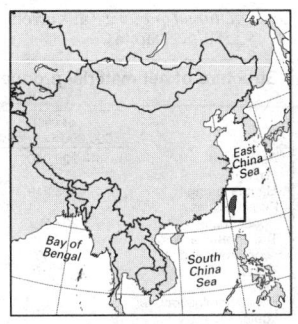

Official name: Chung-hua Min-kuo (Republic of China).
Form of government: multiparty republic with a National Assembly (334) and Legislative Yuan (164)[1].
Chief of state: President.
Head of government: Premier.
Capital: Taipei.
Official language: Mandarin Chinese.
Official religion: none.
Monetary unit: 1 New Taiwan dollar (NT$) = 100 cents; valuation (Oct. 11, 1996) 1 U.S.$ = NT$27.48; 1 £ = NT$43.29.

Area and population		area		population
Taiwan area Counties	Capitals	sq mi	sq km	1996[2] estimate
Chang-hua	Chang-hua	415	1,074	1,289,473
Chia-i	Chia-i	734	1,902	565,769
Hsin-chu	Hsin-chu	551	1,428	409,807
Hua-lien	Hua-lien	1,787	4,629	358,642
I-lan	I-lan	825	2,137	465,124
Kao-hsiung	Feng-shan	1,078	2,793	1,196,459
Miao-li	Miao-li	703	1,820	560,196
Nan-t'ou	Nan-t'ou	1,585	4,106	546,224
P'eng-hu	Ma-kung	49	127	90,470
P'ing-tung	P'ing-tung	1,072	2,776	912,103
T'ai-chung	Feng-yuan	792	2,051	1,409,560
T'ai-nan	Hsin-ying	778	2,016	1,083,805
T'ai-pei	Pan-ch'iao	792	2,052	3,314,855
T'ai-tung	T'ai-tung	1,357	3,515	254,248
T'ao-yüan	T'ao-yüan	471	1,221	1,532,431
Yün-lin	Tou-liu	498	1,291	753,254
Municipalities				
Chia-i	—	23	60	261,941
Chi-lung	—	51	133	370,049
Hsin-chu	—	40	104	341,128
Kao-hsiung	—	59	154	1,426,518
T'ai-chung	—	63	163	857,590
T'ai-nan	—	68	176	707,658
Taipei	—	105	272	2,626,138
non-Taiwan area Counties[3]				
Kinmen (Quemoy) }	—	69	179	53,237
Lienchiang (Matsu) }				
TOTAL		13,969[4]	36,179	21,386,679

Demography

Population (1996)[5]: 21,463,000.
Density (1996)[5]: persons per sq mi 1,536.5, persons per sq km 593.2.
Urban-rural (1991)[6]: urban 74.7%; rural 25.3%.
Sex distribution (1996)[6]: male 51.45%; female 48.55%.
Age breakdown (1996)[6]: under 15, 23.8%; 15–29, 26.5%; 30–44, 25.7%; 45–59, 13.0%; 60–69, 6.5%; 70 and over, 4.5%.
Population projection: (2000) 22,263,000; (2010) 24,395,000.
Doubling time: 79 years.
Ethnic composition (1986): Taiwanese 84.0%; mainland Chinese 14.0%; aborigine 2.0%.
Religious affiliation (1980): Chinese folk-religionist 48.5%; Buddhist 43.0%; Christian 7.4%; Muslim 0.5%; other 0.6%.
Major cities (1996)[6]: Taipei 2,626,138; Kao-hsiung 1,426,518; T'ai-chung 857,590; T'ai-nan 707,658; Chi-lung 370,049.

Vital statistics

Birth rate per 1,000 population (1996): 14.8 (world avg. 25.0); (1994)[6] legitimate 97.0%; illegitimate 3.0%.
Death rate per 1,000 population (1996): 6.0 (world avg. 9.3).
Natural increase rate per 1,000 population (1996): 8.8 (world avg. 15.7).
Total fertility rate (avg. births per childbearing woman; 1994)[6]: 1.8.
Life expectancy at birth (1994): male 71.8 years; female 77.7 years.
Major causes of death per 100,000 population (1994)[6]: malignant neoplasms 110.0; cerebrovascular diseases 64.5; accidents and suicide 62.5; heart disease 56.7; diabetes 28.8; liver diseases 19.7; kidney diseases 15.2; pneumonia 13.7.

National economy

Budget (1994)[7]. Revenue: NT$1,924,496,000,000 (income taxes 13.8%, land tax 10.7%, business tax 10.2%, surplus of public enterprises 10.1%, commodity tax 7.5%, customs duties 5.3%). Expenditures: NT$1,913,742,000,000 (administration and defense 28.1%, economic development 24.5%, education 20.0%).
Production (metric tons except as noted). Agriculture, forestry, fishing (1995): sugarcane 4,659,000, rice 1,687,000, citrus fruits 473,693, corn (maize) 321,322[8], pineapples 252,115, sweet potatoes 188,000, bananas 172,633; livestock (number of live animals) 10,508,502 pigs, 318,404 goats, 164,825 cattle; timber 35,603 cu m; fish catch 1,246,821. Mining and quarrying (1990): silver 3,926 kg. Manufacturing (1995): cement 22,478,018; steel ingots 12,320,863; paperboard 3,030,337; fertilizers 2,127,898; synthetic fibre 1,334,412; polyester filament 1,248,582; polyvinyl chloride plastics 975,927; electronic calculators 6,381,720 units; telephones 6,161,547 units. Construction (1995): total residential and nonresidential 46,221,000 sq m. Energy production (consumption): electricity (kW-hr; 1995) 138,647,000,000 (105,368,000,000); coal (metric tons; 1993) 328,000 ([1992] 16,500,000); crude petroleum (barrels; 1993) 400,000 ([1992] 215,400); natural gas (cu m; 1992) 767,000,000 (n.a.).

Gross national product (1995): U.S.$264,632,000,000 (U.S.$12,490 per capita).

Structure of gross domestic product and labour force[6]

	1995			
	in value NT$'000,000	% of total value	labour force[9]	% of labour force[9]
Agriculture	243,685	3.5	954,000	10.3
Mining	21,534	0.3	15,000	0.2
Manufacturing	1,948,519	28.2	2,449,000	26.6
Construction	361,574	5.2	1,003,000	10.9
Public utilities	175,954	2.6	36,000	0.4
Transp. and commun.	457,962	6.6	469,000	5.1
Trade	1,109,890	16.1	1,919,000	20.8
Finance	1,463,564	21.2	534,000	5.8
Pub. admin., defense	726,974	10.5 }	1,664,000	18.1
Services	533,348	7.7 }		
Other	−134,835[10]	−1.9[10]	165,000[11]	1.8[11]
TOTAL	6,907,676	100.0	9,210,000[4]	100.0

Public debt (1994): NT$638,575,000,000.
Tourism (1994): receipts from visitors U.S.$3,210,000,000.
Population economically active (1990): total 10,236,324; activity rate 50.5% (participation rates: ages 15–64, 72.5%; female 38.5%; unemployed [1995] 1.8%).

Price and earnings indexes (1990 = 100)[6]

	1989	1990	1991	1992	1993	1994	1995
Consumer price index	96.1	100.0	103.6	108.3	111.4	116.0	120.3
Monthly earnings index[12]	88.2	100.0	111.0	122.3	130.7	139.4	147.1

Household income and expenditure (1994). Average household size (1995) 3.7; income per household NT$906,890 (U.S.$34,280[13]); sources of income: wages 66.4%, self-employment and other 29.0%, transfer payments 4.6%; expenditure: food 27.1%, rent, fuel, and power 19.5%, education 17.0%, transportation 12.0%, health care 7.0%, furniture 4.9%, clothing 4.5%.
Land use (1980): forested 55.0%; agricultural 25.2%; other 19.8%.

Foreign trade

Balance of trade (current prices)

	1990	1991	1992	1993	1994	1995
NT$'000,000	330,980	350,013	231,668	199,604	194,360	206,730
% of total	10.1%	9.4%	6.0%	4.7%	4.1%	3.6%

Imports (1995): NT$2,742,850,000,000 (electronic machinery 21.6%, nonelectrical machinery 12.8%, chemicals 11.2%, iron and steel 7.0%, road motor vehicles 5.8%, crude petroleum 3.7%). *Major import sources:* Japan 28.2%; U.S. 20.9%; Germany 5.3%; Korea 4.1%; Malaysia 2.9%; Singapore 2.7%.
Exports (1995): NT$2,949,580,000,000 (nonelectrical machinery 21.7%, electrical machinery 21.5%, plastic articles 6.4%, synthetic fibres 5.6%, transportation equipment 4.8%). *Major export destinations:* U.S. 24.9%; Hong Kong 22.4%; Japan 11.0%; Singapore 3.7%; Germany 3.5%.

Transport and communications

Transport. Railroads (1995): track length 3,879 km; passenger-km 9,499,400,000; metric ton-km cargo 1,899,500,000. Roads (1994): total length 19,038 km (paved 89%). Vehicles (1995): passenger cars 3,874,200; trucks and buses 810,300. Merchant marine (1992): vessels (100 gross tons and over) 649; total deadweight tonnage 9,241,283. Air transport (1995): passenger-km 38,247,100,000; metric ton-km cargo 3,410,300,000; airports (1996) 13.
Communications. Daily newspapers (1988): total number 93; total circulation 4,000,000; circulation per 1,000 population 202. Radio (1995): 8,620,000 receivers (1 per 2.5 persons). Television (1995): 7,000,000 receivers (1 per 3.0 persons). Telephones (main lines; 1995): 9,174,800 (1 per 2.3 persons).

Education and health

Education (1994–95)

	schools	teachers	students	student/ teacher ratio
Primary (age 6–12)	2,528	84,150	2,032,361	24.2
Secondary (age 13–18)	920	74,465	1,423,040	19.1
Vocational	206	19,152	523,982	27.4
Higher	130	35,163	720,180	20.5

Educational attainment (1994). Percentage of population age 25 and over having: no formal schooling 9.6%; less than complete primary education 6.0%; primary 24.5%; incomplete secondary 26.1%; secondary 20.4%; some college 8.1%; higher 5.3%. *Literacy* (1994): population age 15 and over literate 15,006,668 (93.7%); males 8,011,056 (97.4%); females 6,995,612 (89.9%).
Health (1994): physicians 24,455 (1 per 864 persons); hospital beds 103,733 (1 per 204 persons); infant mortality rate per 1,000 live births 5.1.
Food: daily per capita caloric intake (1990) 3,020 (1988; vegetable products 77%, animal products 23%); 118% of FAO recommended minimum.

Military

Total active duty personnel (1995): 376,000 (army 63.8%, navy 18.1%, air force 18.1%). *Military expenditure as percentage of GNP* (1994): 4.8% (world 3.0%); per capita expenditure U.S.$542.

[1]National Assembly functions as an electoral college or constituent body; the legislative branch is the formal lawmaking body. [2]End of March. [3]The Nov. 7, 1992, constitutional reforms replaced the military administrations (established in 1949) on Quemoy and Matsu with civilian administrations. [4]Detail does not add to total given because of rounding. [5]Includes Quemoy and Matsu groups. [6]For Taiwan area only, excluding Quemoy and Matsu groups. [7]General government. [8]1991. [9]Civilian employed persons only. [10]Import duties less imputed bank service charge. [11]Unemployed. [12]In manufacturing. [13]Based on the average exchange rate.

Tajikistan

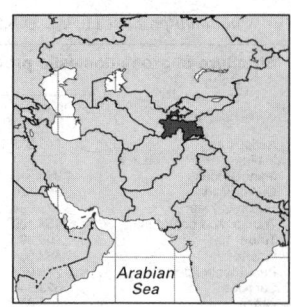

Official name: Jumhurii Tojikiston
(Republic of Tajikistan).
Form of government: parliamentary
republic with one legislative house
(Supreme Assembly [181]).
Chief of state: President.
Head of government: Prime Minister.
Capital: Dushanbe.
Official language: Tajik (Tojik).
Official religion: none.
Monetary unit: 1 Tajik ruble;
valuation (Oct. 11, 1996)
1 U.S.$ = 298.00 Tajik rubles;
1 £ = 469.44 Tajik rubles.

Area and population		area		population
		sq mi	sq km	1991 estimate
Autonomous republic	**Capitals**			
Badakhshoni Kuni (Gorno-Badakhshan)	Khorugh	24,600	63,700	167,100
Provinces				
Khujand	Khujand	10,100	26,100	1,635,900
Kŭlob	Kŭlob	4,600	12,000	668,100
Khatlon (Qŭrghonteppa)	Qŭrghonteppa	4,900	12,600	1,113,500
Regions under republican jurisdiction	—	11,000	28,400	1,181,800
City				
Dushanbe	—	100	300	591,900
TOTAL		55,300	143,100	5,358,300

Demography

Population (1996): 5,945,000.
Density (1996): persons per sq mi 107.5, persons per sq km 41.5.
Urban-rural (1995): urban 28.3%; rural 71.7%.
Sex distribution (1993): male 49.80%; female 50.20%.
Age breakdown (1989): under 15, 42.9%; 15–29, 28.1%; 30–44, 13.8%; 45–59, 9.0%; 60–74, 4.6%; 75 and over, 1.6%.
Population projection: (2000) 6,392,000; (2010) 8,029,000.
Doubling time: 33 years.
Ethnic composition (1991): Tajik 63.8%; Uzbek 24.0%; Russian 6.5%; Tatar 1.4%; Kyrgyz 1.3%; Ukrainian 0.7%; German 0.3%; other 2.0%.
Religious affiliation (1996): believers are predominantly Sunnī Muslim (Ḥanafīyah).
Major cities (1989): Dushanbe 582,400; Khujand (formerly Leninabad) 164,500; Kŭlob 79,300; Qŭrghonteppa 58,400; Urateppa 47,700.

Vital statistics

Birth rate per 1,000 population (1994): 28.2 (world avg. 25.0); (1994) legitimate 90.8%; illegitimate 9.2%.
Death rate per 1,000 population (1994): 7.0 (world avg. 9.3).
Natural increase rate per 1,000 population (1994): 21.2 (world avg. 15.7).
Total fertility rate (avg. births per childbearing woman; 1994): 5.0.
Marriage rate per 1,000 population (1994): 6.8.
Divorce rate per 1,000 population (1994): 0.8.
Life expectancy at birth (1993): male 65.7 years; female 71.5 years.
Major causes of death per 100,000 population (1993): diseases of the circulatory system 225.5; violence, poisoning, and accidents 184.0; diseases of the respiratory system 160.6; infectious and parasitic diseases 129.9; malignant neoplasms (cancers) 42.3; diseases of the digestive system 20.9.

National economy

Production (metric tons except as noted). Agriculture, forestry, fishing (1995): vegetables (except potatoes) 585,000, seed cotton 417,000, fruit (except grapes) 225,000, wheat 170,000, potatoes 110,000, grapes 85,000, barley 20,000, corn (maize) 20,000, rice 20,000; livestock (number of live animals) 2,700,000 sheep and goats, 1,199,000 cattle, 32,000 pigs, 4,500,000 poultry; roundwood, n.a.; fish catch (1993) 37,000. Mining and quarrying (1994): gypsum 300,000; aluminum (1995) 230,000; lead 1,200; antimony 1,000. Manufacturing (value of production in '000,000 Tajik rubles; 1994): ferrous and nonferrous metals 604,705; textiles 496,481; energy 330,078; food products 163,559; machinery 77,331; chemical products 68,892; construction materials 66,306. Energy production (consumption): electricity (kW-hr; 1994) 17,000,000,000 (1993; 17,000,000,000); coal (metric tons; 1994) 150,000 (1992; 136,000); crude petroleum (barrels; 1994) 219,900 (1992; 279,000); petroleum products, n.a. (n.a.); natural gas (cu m; 1994) 40,000,000 (1992; 1,771,000,000).
Public debt (external, outstanding; 1994): U.S.$594,400,000.
Tourism: receipts from visitors, n.a.; expenditures by nationals abroad, n.a.
Land use (1994): forest 3.8%; pasture 24.8%; agriculture 6.0%; other 65.4%.
Population economically active (1995): total 1,783,000; activity rate of total population 30.7% (participation rates: ages 16–59 [male], 16–54 [female] 67.8%; female [1994] 38.0%; unemployed [1995] 1.8%).

Price and earnings indexes (1990 = 100)							
	1988	1989	1990	1991	1992	1993	1994
Consumer price index	...	...	100.0	111.6	1,402	32,185	133,762
Monthly earnings index	85.6	90.9	100.0	164.2	922.7	...	...

Gross national product (at current market prices; 1994)[1]: U.S.$2,075,000,000 (U.S.$350 per capita).

Structure of net material product and labour force				
	1994		1993	
	in value '000,000 Tajik rubles	% of total value	labour force	% of labour force
Agriculture	326,040	25.4	949,000	51.2
Mining				
Manufacturing	595,219	46.4	219,000	11.8
Public utilities	...	...	25,000	1.3
Construction	206,527	16.1	116,000	6.3
Transportation and communications	58,393	4.5	72,000	3.9
Trade	51,979	4.0	87,000	4.7
Finance			18,000	1.0
Public administration, defense	...	...	21,000	1.1
Services			316,000	17.0
Other	46,834	3.6	31,016	1.7
TOTAL	1,284,992	100.0	1,854,016	100.0

Budget (1994). Revenue: 772,243,000,000 Tajik rubles (tax revenue 94.0%, of which domestic taxes 47.5%, income and profit taxes 35.8%, property taxes 8.7%, duties 7.5%; other 6.0%). Expenditures: 945,245,000,000 Tajik rubles (national economy 43.0%, social welfare and culture 30.0%, defense 4.0%).
Household income and expenditure. Average household size (1989) 6.1; income per household: n.a.; sources of income (1994): wages and salaries 64.3%, transfer payments 30.1%, self-employment (agriculture only) 5.6%; expenditure (1993): food and clothing 65.3%, services 9.3%, taxes and other payments 6.6%.

Foreign trade

Balance of trade (current prices)				
	1991	1992	1993	1994
U.S.$'000,000	– 200.0	...	– 100.0	– 400.0
% of total	25.0%	...	14.3%	33.0%

Imports (1994): 547,756,000,000 Tajik rubles (1993; minerals 40.3%, food products 39.0%, machinery 15.8%, chemical products 2.3%, textiles 0.9%). *Major import sources:* Uzbekistan 33.5%; Russia 24.4%; Turkmenistan 15.9%; Kazakstan 13.2%; Lithuania 5.5%; Ukraine 5.5%.
Exports (1994): 242,574,000,000 Tajik rubles (1993; base metals 85.0%, textiles 14.3%). *Major export destinations:* Russia 42.0%; Uzbekistan 20.6%; Lithuania 12.4%; Kazakstan 9.2%; Ukraine 4.6%; Latvia 3.1%.

Transport and communications

Transport. Railroads (1990): length 553.6 mi, 891.0 km; passenger-mi 6,094,400,000, passenger-km 9,808,000,000; short ton-mi cargo 7,617,000,000, metric ton-km cargo 11,121,000,000. Roads (1994): total length 8,078 mi, 13,000 km (1990; paved 93%). Vehicles (1994): passenger cars 184,900; trucks and buses, 3,600. Merchant marine: vessels (100 gross tons and over) n.a.; total deadweight tonnage, n.a. Air transport (1989): passenger-mi 3,214,600,000, passenger-km 5,173,400,000; short ton-mi cargo 22,124,000, metric ton-km cargo 32,300,000; airports (1996) with scheduled flights 1.
Communications. Daily newspapers (1992): total number 9; total circulation 361,370; circulation per 1,000 population 63.2. Radio (1992): total number of receivers 854,000 (1 per 6.7 persons). Television (1992): total number of receivers 860,000 (1 per 6.6 persons). Telephones (main lines; 1993): 259,600 (1 per 22 persons).

Education and health

Education (1993–94)	schools	teachers	students	student/ teacher ratio
Primary (age 6–13) } Secondary (age 14–17) }	3,300	97,000	1,227,000	12.6
Voc., teacher tr.	50	...	38,400	...
Higher	22	...	69,000	...

Educational attainment (1989). Percentage of population age 25 and over having: primary education or no formal schooling 16.3%; some secondary 21.1%; completed secondary and some postsecondary 55.1%; higher 7.5%.
Literacy (1989): percentage of total population age 15 and over literate 97.7%; males literate 98.8%; females literate 96.6%.
Health (1995): physicians 22,000 (1 per 265 persons); hospital beds 84,000 (1 per 70 persons); infant mortality rate per 1,000 live births (1994) 40.6.
Food: daily per capita caloric intake 2,760 (vegetable products 60%, animal products 40%); 113% of FAO recommended minimum requirement.

Military

Total active duty personnel (1996): 5,200 (army 100%); more than 12,000 Russian troops remained in Tajikistan in late 1996. *Military expenditure as percentage of GNP* (1994): 1.0% (world 3.0%); per capita expenditure U.S.$11.

[1]Preliminary estimates.

Tanzania

Official name: Jamhuri ya Muungano
wa Tanzania (Swahili); United
Republic of Tanzania (English).
Form of government: unitary multiparty
republic with one legislative house
(National Assembly [232[1]]).
Head of state and government:
President.
Seat of government: Dar es Salaam[2]
(Capital designate, Dodoma).
Official languages: Swahili; English.
Official religion: none.
Monetary unit: 1 Tanzania shilling
(T Sh) = 100 cents; valuation (Oct.
11, 1996) 1 U.S.$ = T Sh 578.00;
1 £ = T Sh 910.52.

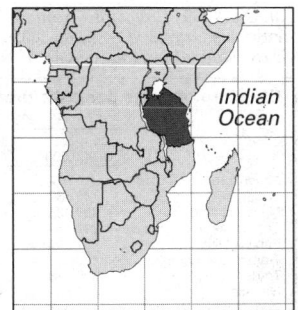

Indian
Ocean

Area and population		area		population
		sq mi	sq km	1994 estimate
Regions	**Capitals**			
Arusha	Arusha	31,778	82,306	1,596,000
Coast	Dar es Salaam	12,512	32,407	753,000
Dar es Salaam	—	538	1,393	1,606,000
Dodoma	Dodoma	15,950	41,311	1,461,000
Iringa	Iringa	21,955	56,864	1,427,000
Kagera	Bukoba	10,961	28,388	1,607,000
Kigoma	Kigoma	14,300	37,037	1,015,000
Kilimanjaro	Moshi	5,139	13,309	1,308,000
Lindi	Lindi	25,501	66,046	763,000
Mara	Musoma	7,555	19,566	1,146,000
Mbeya	Mbeya	23,301	60,350	1,742,000
Morogoro	Morogoro	27,336	70,799	1,483,000
Mtwara	Mtwara	6,451	16,707	1,050,000
Mwanza	Mwanza	7,564	19,592	2,217,000
Pemba North	Wete	222	574	163,000
Pemba South	Chake Chake	128	332	151,000
Rukwa	Sumbawanga	26,500	68,635	820,000
Ruvuma	Songea	24,517	63,498	924,000
Shinyanga	Shinyanga	19,607	50,781	2,092,000
Singida	Singida	19,051	49,341	934,000
Tabora	Tabora	29,402	76,151	1,223,000
Tanga	Tanga	10,351	26,808	1,546,000
Unguja (Zanzibar) North	Mkokotoni	182	470	115,000
Unguja (Zanzibar) South and Central	Koani	330	854	83,000
Unguja (Zanzibar) West	Zanzibar	89	230	246,000
TOTAL LAND AREA		341,217[3]	883,749	
INLAND WATER		22,800	59,050	
TOTAL		364,017[4]	942,799[4]	27,471,000

Demography

Population (1996): 29,058,000[5].
Density (1996)[6]: persons per sq mi 79.6, persons per sq km 30.7.
Urban-rural (1995): urban 24.4%; rural 75.6%.
Sex distribution (1995): male 49.18%; female 50.82%.
Age breakdown (1995): under 15, 45.3%; 15–29, 28.3%; 30–44, 14.0%; 45–59, 7.8%; 60–74, 3.7%; 75 and over, 0.9%.
Population projection: (2000) 31,045,000; (2010) 36,076,000.
Doubling time: 30 years.
Ethnolinguistic composition (1987): Nyamwezi and Sukuma 26.3%; Swahili 8.8%; Haya 5.3%; Hehet and Bena 5.0%; Chagga 4.4%; Gogo 4.4%; Makonde 3.7%; other 42.1%.
Religious affiliation (1984): Muslim 35%; animist 35%; Christian 30%.
Major cities (1988): Dar es Salaam 1,360,850; Mwanza 223,013; Dodoma 203,833; Tanga 187,155; Zanzibar 157,634.

Vital statistics

Birth rate per 1,000 population (1995): 42.0 (world avg. 25.0).
Death rate per 1,000 population (1995): 19.0 (world avg. 9.3).
Natural increase rate per 1,000 population (1995): 23.0 (world avg. 15.7).
Total fertility rate (avg. births per childbearing woman; 1995): 5.8.
Life expectancy at birth (1995): male 41.5 years; female 45.0 years.
Major causes of death per 100,000 population: n.a.; however, the major diseases include malaria, bilharziasis, tuberculosis, and sleeping sickness.

National economy

Budget (1995–96). Revenue: T Sh 627,000,000,000 (1994–95; import duties 30.4%, income tax 28.9%, sales and excise tax 24.2%). Expenditures: T Sh 627,688,000,000 (1994–95; interest payments on debt 30.8%, public administration 25.4%, other 43.8%).
Public debt (external, outstanding; 1994): U.S.$6,232,000,000.
Tourism (1994): receipts from visitors U.S.$192,000,000; expenditures by nationals abroad U.S.$102,000,000[7].
Production (metric tons except as noted). Agriculture (1995): cassava 5,968,-800, corn (maize) 2,566,600, sugarcane 1,410,000, sorghum 838,800, rice 722,700, bananas 651,000, plantains 651,000, sweet potatoes 450,700, millet 411,000, coconuts 365,000, potatoes 240,000; livestock (number of live animals) 13,376,000 cattle, 9,682,000 goats, 3,955,000 sheep, 335,000 pigs, 27,000,000 chickens; roundwood (1994) 35,140,000 cu m; fish catch (1993) 345,000. Mining and quarrying (1994): gemstones (including emeralds, sapphires, and rubies) 33,000 kg; gold 3,370 kg; diamonds 15,700 carats. Manufacturing (1994): cement 689,000; fresh meat and poultry 291,000[7]; sugar 121,000[7]; hides and skins 48,325[7]; soap 20,000[8]; wheat flour 3,000[9]; textiles 51,000,000 m. Construction: n.a. Energy production (consumption):

electricity (kW-hr; 1994) 912,000,000 (912,000,000); coal (metric tons; 1994) 4,000 (4,000); crude petroleum (barrels; 1994) none (4,288,000); petroleum products (metric tons; 1994) 579,000 (657,000).
Gross national product (1993)[10]: U.S.$2,521,000,000 (U.S.$100 per capita).

Structure of gross domestic product and labour force				
	1994		1991	
	in value T Sh '000,000	% of total value	labour force	% of labour force
Agriculture	947,980	52.0	10,540,000	80.3
Mining	26,842	1.5		
Manufacturing	126,397	6.9		
Construction	86,482	4.7	614,000	4.7
Public utilities	37,634	2.1		
Transp. and commun.	107,722	5.9		
Trade	254,458	14.0		
Finance	69,851	3.8	1,969,000	15.0
Pub. admin., defense	83,155	4.6		
Services				
Other	82,049	4.5	...	...
TOTAL	1,822,570	100.0	13,123,000	100.0

Population economically active (1994): total 13,852,000; activity rate 48.0% (participation rates [1991]: over age 10, 87.8%; female 40.0%).

Price index (1990 = 100)							
	1989	1990	1991	1992	1993	1994	1995
Consumer price index	73.6	100.0	128.7	156.8	196.4	263.4	335.7

Household income and expenditure. Average household size (1988) 5.2; income per household: n.a.; sources of income: n.a.; expenditure (1994): food 64.2%, clothing 9.9%, housing 8.3%, energy 7.6%, transportation 4.1%.
Land use (1994): forested 38.1%; meadows and pastures 39.6%; agricultural and under permanent cultivation 4.0%; other 18.3%.

Foreign trade[11]

Balance of trade (current prices)						
	1990	1991	1992	1993	1994	1995
T Sh '000,000	−161,606	−213,549	−258,245	−342,654	−385,977	−433,525
% of total	55.6%	58.8%	51.0%	48.6%	42.1%	35.7%

Imports (1994): T Sh 767,000,000,000 (1990; machinery and transport equipment 23.5%, basic manufactures 10.0%, chemicals 6.4%, food 1.4%). *Major import sources* (1995): U.K. 9.6%; Kenya 9.0%; Japan 7.2%; China 4.9%; India 4.7%; U.S. 4.4%; South Africa 4.2%; Belgium 3.8%.
Exports (1994): T Sh 265,000,000,000 (coffee 22.2%, cotton 20.2%, cashew nuts 9.8%, tea 7.6%). *Major export destinations* (1995): Germany 9.2%; Japan 8.2%; India 8.1%; Belgium 6.5%; U.K. 5.4%; Rwanda 5.0%; The Netherlands 5.0%.

Transport and communications

Transport. Railroads (1995): length 3,569 km; passenger-journeys 1,517,000[12]; metric ton-km cargo 1,160,000,000[12]. Roads (1995): length 88,100 km (paved 4.2%). Vehicles (1994): passenger cars 47,500; trucks and buses 38,000. Merchant marine (1992): vessels (100 gross tons and over) 43; deadweight tonnage 48,465. Air transport (1995)[13]: passenger-km 184,383,000; metric ton-km 2,904,000; airports (1996) with scheduled flights 11.
Communications. Daily newspapers: total number (1992) 3; total circulation 220,000; circulation per 1,000 population 8.6. Radio (1994): 565,000 receivers (1 per 48 persons). Television (1995): 80,000 receivers (1 per 357 persons). Telephones (main lines; 1994): 88,000 (1 per 314 persons).

Education and health

Education (1994)[14]				
	schools	teachers	students	student/ teacher ratio
Primary (age 7–13)	10,891	103,900	3,736,734[7]	...
Secondary (age 14–19)	491	10,612	180,899[7]	...
Teacher training	40	1,167[7]	15,824[7]	13.6
Higher	4[15]	1,206[15]	4,289	...

Educational attainment (1978). Percentage of population age 10 and over having: no schooling 48.6%; some primary education 40.7%; completed primary 8.7%; secondary and higher 1.9%. *Literacy* (1995): percentage of total population age 15 and over literate 67.8%; males literate 79.4%; females literate 56.8%.
Health (1991): physicians 1,112 (1 per 22,900 persons); hospital beds 25,470 (1 per 1,000 persons); infant mortality rate (1995) 107.
Food (1992): daily per capita caloric intake 2,018 (vegetable products 93%, animal products 7%); 87% of FAO recommended minimum requirement.

Military

Total active duty personnel (1996): 34,600 (army 86.7%, navy 2.9%, air force 10.4%). *Military expenditure as percentage of GNP* (1994): 3.3% (world 3.0%); per capita expenditure U.S.$3.

[1]Includes 43 nonelective seats. [2]Government in process of being transferred from Dar es Salaam to Dodoma; legislative branch meets in Dodoma. [3]Detail does not add to total given because of rounding. [4]A recent survey indicates a total area of 364,901 sq mi (945,090 sq km). [5]Data exclude about 650,000 refugees from Rwanda and Burundi. [6]Based on the total area of 364,901 sq mi. [7]1993. [8]1992. [9]1991. [10]Mainland Tanzania only. [11]Import figures are f.o.b. in balance of trade and c.i.f. in commodities and trading partners. [12]Tanzanian Railways only; 1994. [13]Air Tanzania only. [14]Excludes Zanzibar and Pemba. [15]1989.

Thailand

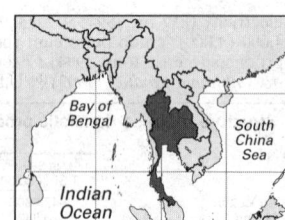

Official name: Muang Thai, or Prathet Thai (Kingdom of Thailand).
Form of government: constitutional monarchy with two legislative houses (Senate [260][1]; House of Representatives [391]).
Chief of state: King.
Head of government: Prime Minister[2].
Capital: Bangkok.
Official language: Thai.
Official religion: Buddhism.
Monetary unit: 1 Thai baht (B) = 100 stangs; valuation (Oct. 11, 1996) 1 U.S.$ = B 25.46; 1 £ = B 40.10.

Area and population	area		population
			1994
Regions[3]	sq mi	sq km	estimate[4]
Bangkok Metropolis	2,995	7,758	8,851,180
Central	6,407	16,594	2,857,293
Eastern	14,094	36,503	3,860,129
Northeastern	65,195	168,854	20,542,381
Northern	65,500	169,644	11,912,419
Southern	27,303	70,715	7,603,300
Western	16,621	43,047	3,468,717
TOTAL	198,115	513,115	59,095,419

Demography

Population (1996): 60,003,000[5].
Density (1996): persons per sq mi 302.9, persons per sq km 116.9.
Urban-rural (1994): urban 18.1%; rural 81.9%.
Sex distribution (1994): male 50.01%; female 49.99%.
Age breakdown (1995): under 15, 27.8%; 15–29, 28.6%; 30–44, 22.5%; 45–59, 13.0%; 60–74, 6.5%; 75 and over, 1.6%.
Population projection: (2000) 62,405,000; (2010) 67,754,000.
Doubling time: 63 years.
Ethnic composition (1983): Thai 79.5%, of which Siamese 52.6%, Lao 26.9%; Chinese 12.1%; Malay 3.7%; Khmer 2.7%; other 2.0%.
Religious affiliation (1992): Buddhist 94.8%; Muslim 4.0%; Christian 0.6%; other 0.6%.
Major cities (1991)[4]: Bangkok 5,620,591; Nonthaburi 264,201; Nakhon Ratchasima 202,503; Chiang Mai 161,541; Khon Kaen 131,478.

Vital statistics

Birth rate per 1,000 population (1996): 18.2 (world avg. 25.0).
Death rate per 1,000 population (1996): 7.3 (world avg. 9.3).
Natural increase rate per 1,000 population (1996): 10.9 (world avg. 15.7).
Total fertility rate (avg. births per childbearing woman; 1996): 2.0.
Marriage rate per 1,000 population (1994): 7.4.
Divorce rate per 1,000 population (1994): 0.8.
Life expectancy at birth (1996): male 67.0 years; female 72.0 years.
Major causes of death per 100,000 population (1993)[6]: accidents, homicide, and poisonings 13.7; diseases of the heart 10.7; malignant neoplasms (cancers) 9.1; hypertension and cerebrovascular disease 3.3; pneumonia and other lung diseases 2.8; diseases of the liver and the pancreas 2.6; nephritis and nephrosis 2.0.

National economy

Budget (1995). Revenue: B 760,755,000,000 (taxes 91.7%; state enterprises 4.9%; sale of property and services 1.0%). Expenditures: B 643,283,000,000 (current expenditure 67.7%, of which goods and services 58.1%, transfer payments 9.6%; capital expenditure 32.3%, of which government capital formation 29.8%, transfer payments 2.3%).
Production (metric tons except as noted). Agriculture, forestry, fishing (1995): sugarcane 54,616,000, rice 19,950,000, tapioca 17,340,000, corn (maize) 4,060,000, palm oil 2,140,000, rubber 1,810,000, soybean 451,000, coffee 82,000, kenaf 82,000, tobacco 49,600; livestock (number of live animals) 7,593,000 cattle, 4,507,000 pigs, 4,807,000 buffalo, 80,218,000 chickens; roundwood (1993) 38,039,000 cu m; fish catch (1993) 3,348,149. Mining and quarrying (1994): limestone 42,224,000; gypsum 8,140,000; kaolin clay 417,000; zinc ore 350,000; fluorite 23,705; lead ore 18,713; tin concentrates 3,926. Manufacturing (1993): cement 26,300,000; refined sugar 3,650,500; chemical fertilizer 458,103[7]; synthetic fibre 397,700; galvanized iron sheet 249,800; tin plate 222,400; jute products 118,900. Construction (1990): residential 16,343,000 sq m; nonresidential 13,449,000 sq m. Energy production (consumption): electricity (kW-hr; 1993) 66,305,000,000 (66,901,000,000); coal (metric tons; 1993) 15,546,000 (15,773,000); crude petroleum (barrels; 1993) 8,434,000 (117,941,000); petroleum products (metric tons; 1993) 18,291,000 (25,745,000); natural gas (cu m; 1993) 9,107,000,000 (9,107,000,000).
Land use (1993): forested 26.4%; meadows and pastures 1.6%; agricultural and under permanent cultivation 40.7%; other 31.3%.
Population economically active (1994): total 31,049,900; activity rate of total population 52.6% (participation rates: over age 13, 70.9%; female 44.5%; unemployed 2.1%).

Price and earnings indexes (1990 = 100)							
	1989	1990	1991	1992	1993	1994	1995
Consumer price index	94.4	100.0	105.7	110.1	113.7	119.5	126.4
Monthly earnings index	96.1	100.0	116.8	132.8	144.7	133.8	...

Tourism (1994): receipts from visitors U.S.$5,762,000,000; expenditures by nationals abroad U.S.$2,906,000,000.
Gross national product (1994): U.S.$129,864,000,000 (U.S.$2,210 per capita).

Structure of gross domestic product and labour force				
	1993		1994	
	in value B '000,000	% of total value	labour force[8]	% of labour force[8]
Agriculture	314,974	10.0	13,972,400	45.0
Mining	46,538	1.5	65,200	0.2
Manufacturing	899,435	28.4	4,530,600	14.6
Construction	217,159	6.9	2,295,400	7.4
Public utilities	77,294	2.4	182,900	0.6
Transp. and commun.	236,272	7.5	931,700	3.0
Trade	525,726	16.6	3,914,000	12.6
Finance	313,584	9.9		
Pub. admin., defense	120,402	3.8	3,904,100	12.6
Services	409,990	13.0		
Other	...	...	1,253,600[9]	4.0[9]
TOTAL	3,161,374	100.0	31,049,900	100.0

Public debt (external, outstanding; 1994): U.S.$16,672,000,000.
Household income and expenditure (1992). Average household size 3.9; average annual income per household B 84,744 (U.S.$3,336); sources of income: wages and salaries 70.1%, self-employment 22.6%, transfer payments 5.8%, other 1.5%; expenditure (1993): food, tobacco, and beverages 25.6%, housing 15.7%, transportation and communications 13.6%, education and recreation 12.2%, clothing 10.7%, medical and personal care 7.6%, other 14.6%.

Foreign trade[10]

Balance of trade (current prices)						
	1989	1990	1991	1992	1993	1994
B '000,000	−71,417	−172,323	−139,742	−107,887	−111,602	−231,424
% of total	6.5%	12.7%	8.8%	6.1%	5.6%	9.2%

Imports (1994): B 1,370,635,000,000 (electrical machinery 18.8%, nonelectrical machinery 18.6%, road vehicles 7.8%, iron and steel 6.8%, mineral fuels and lubricants 6.7%, plastics 3.7%, organic chemicals 3.3%). *Major import sources:* Japan 30.2%; U.S. 11.8%; Singapore 6.3%; Germany 5.8%; Taiwan 5.1%; Malaysia 4.9%; South Korea 3.6%; China 2.5%; U.K. 2.1%.
Exports (1994): B 1,152,011,000,000 (electrical machinery 17.3%, nonelectrical machinery 12.7%, garments 9.4%, fresh prawns 6.0%, rubber products 4.8%, precious jewelry 4.2%, rice 3.5%, canned seafoods 3.5%, footwear 3.5%). *Major export destinations:* U.S. 20.8%; Japan 16.9%; Singapore 13.5%; Hong Kong 5.2%; Germany 3.7%; U.K. 2.9%; The Netherlands 2.7%; Malaysia 2.4%; Taiwan 2.1%.

Transport and communications

Transport. Railroads (1994[11]): route length 2,405 mi, 3,870 km; passenger-mi 9,007,000,000, passenger-km 14,496,000,000; short ton-mi cargo (1993) 2,095,000,000, metric ton-km cargo (1993) 3,059,000,000. Roads (1994): total length 36,310 mi, 58,435 km (paved 79%). Vehicles (1994): passenger cars 1,325,477; trucks and buses 2,720,383. Merchant marine (1992): vessels (100 gross tons and over) 351; total deadweight tonnage 1,194,470. Air transport (1995): passenger-mi 16,859,000,000, passenger-km 27,132,000,000; short ton-mi cargo 896,674,000, metric ton-km cargo 1,309,122,000; airports (1996) with scheduled flights 25.
Communications. Daily newspapers (1992): total number 35; total circulation 4,150,000; circulation per 1,000 population 74. Radio (1995): 10,000,000 receivers (1 per 5.9 persons). Television (1995): 3,300,000 receivers (1 per 18 persons). Telephones (main lines; 1993): 2,184,900 receivers (1 per 27 persons).

Education and health

Education (1993)	schools	teachers	students	student/ teacher ratio
Primary (age 7–12)	34,412	445,542	8,583,525	19.3
Secondary (age 13–18)	2,318	107,025	2,118,767	19.8
Voc., teacher tr.	679	40,116	795,186	19.8
Higher	102	27,239	809,856	29.7

Educational attainment (1991). Percentage of population age 13 and over having: no formal schooling 7.4%; primary education 73.9%; secondary 10.4%; postsecondary 8.3%. *Literacy* (1985): total population age 15 and over literate 28,451,390 (88.8%); males literate 14,877,240 (93.2%); females literate 13,574,150 (84.5%).
Health: physicians (1993) 13,634 (1 per 4,245 persons); hospital beds (1991) 93,852 (1 per 599 persons); infant mortality rate per 1,000 live births (1996) 32.0.
Food (1992): daily per capita caloric intake 2,432 (vegetable products 90%, animal products 10%); 110% of FAO recommended minimum requirement.

Military

Total active duty personnel (1995): 259,000 (army 57.9%, navy 25.5%, air force 16.6%). *Military expenditure as percentage of GNP* (1994): 2.7% (world 3.0%); per capita expenditure U.S.$64.

---

[1]All members are appointed by the prime minister. [2]The new constitution requires that future prime ministers be elected members of Parliament. [3]Actual local administration is based on 76 provinces. [4]Based on registration records. [5]Based on 1990 census results, which are lower than the 1990 registration records estimate. [6]Percentage distribution. [7]1991. [8]February; economically active persons 13 years and over. [9]Mostly unemployed. [10]Import figures are f.o.b. in balance of trade and c.i.f. for commodities and trading partners. [11]Traffic data refer to fiscal year ending September 30.

Togo

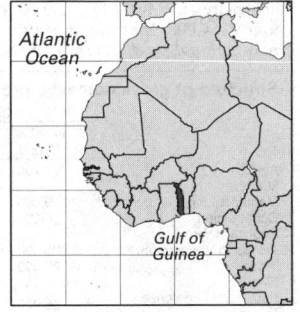

Official name: République Togolaise (Republic of Togo).
Form of government: multiparty republic[1] with one legislative body (National Assembly [81[2]]).
Chief of state: President[1].
Head of government: Prime Minister.
Capital: Lomé.
Official language: French.
Official religion: none.
Monetary unit: 1 CFA franc (CFAF) = 100 centimes; valuation (Oct. 11, 1996) 1 U.S.$ = CFAF 518.24; 1 £ = CFAF 816.38.

Area and population

Regions Prefectures	Capitals	area sq mi	area sq km	population 1989 estimate
Centrale	Sokodé			339,000
Sotouboua	Sotouboua	2,892	7,491	162,500
Tchamba	Tchamba	1,214	3,143	54,500
Tchaoudjo	Sokodé	984	2,549	122,000
De la Kara	Kara			531,500
Assoli	Bafilo	362	938	41,000
Bassar	Bassar	2,444	6,330	152,000
Binah	Pagouda	180	465	61,000
Doufelgou	Niamtougou	432	1,120	75,000
Kéran	Kandé	419	1,085	49,500
Kozah	Kara	653	1,692	153,000
Des Plateaux	Atakpamé			810,500
Amou	Amlamé	773	2,003	98,500
Haho	Notsé	1,406	3,641	139,000
Kloto	Kpalimé	1,072	2,777	233,500
Ogou	Atakpamé	2,349	6,083	204,000
Wawa	Badou	954	2,471	135,500
Des Savanes	Dapaong			410,500
Oti	Sansanné-Mango	1,453	3,762	98,500
Tône	Dapaong	1,869	4,840	312,000
Maritime	Lomé			1,300,000[3]
Golfe	Lomé	133	345	560,000
Lacs	Aného	275	713	172,500
Vo	Vogan	290	750	125,000
Yoto	Tabligbo	483	1,250	187,000
Zio	Tsévié	1,288	3,337	255,000
TOTAL		21,925	56,785	3,391,500

Demography

Population (1996): 4,269,000.
Density (1996): persons per sq mi 194.7, persons per sq km 75.2.
Urban-rural (1995): urban 30.8%; rural 69.2%.
Sex distribution (1995): male 49.54%; female 50.46%.
Age breakdown (1995): under 15, 45.7%; 15–29, 25.9%; 30–44, 14.9%; 45–59, 8.5%; 60–74, 4.1%; 75 and over, 0.9%.
Population projection: (2000) 4,818,000; (2010) 6,427,000.
Doubling time: 22 years.
Ethnic composition (1981): Ewe-Adja 43.1%; Tem-Kabre 26.7%; Gurma 16.1%; Kebu-Akposo 3.8%; Ana-Ife (Yoruba) 3.2%; non-African 0.3%; other 6.8%.
Religious affiliation (1981): traditional beliefs 58.9%; Roman Catholic 21.5%; Muslim 12.1%; Protestant 6.8%; other 0.7%.
Major cities (1983): Lomé 366,476; Sokodé 48,098[3]; Kpalimé 27,669[3].

Vital statistics

Birth rate per 1,000 population (1990–95): 44.5 (world avg. 25.0).
Death rate per 1,000 population (1990–95): 12.8 (world avg. 9.3).
Natural increase rate per 1,000 population (1990–95): 31.7 (world avg. 15.7).
Total fertility rate (avg. births per childbearing woman; 1990–95): 6.6.
Marriage rate per 1,000 population (1979): 2.3.
Life expectancy at birth (1990–95): male 53.2 years; female 56.8 years.
Morbidity (reported cases of illness; 1989): malaria 730,162; injury and trauma 218,949; diarrheal diseases 153,074; diseases of the respiratory system 90,061; intestinal parasites 52,064.

National economy

Budget (1994). Revenue: CFAF 66,600,000,000 (tax revenue 90.5%, of which taxes on international trade 40.8%, public enterprise taxes 19.4%; nontax revenue 9.5%). Expenditures: CFAF 137,000,000,000 (current expenditure 70.6%, of which 16.4%, defense 10.3%, health 4.2%; development/unclassified expenditures 29.4%, of which investment expenditures 9.1%).
Public debt (external, outstanding; 1994): U.S.$1,228,000,000.
Production (metric tons except as noted). Agriculture, forestry, fishing (1995): cassava 466,800, yams 411,242, corn (maize) 225,141, sorghum 191,100, cottonseed 140,000, millet 60,000, rice 39,718, pulses 33,204, peanuts (groundnuts) 27,200, kidney beans 22,476, bananas 16,100, coffee 16,000, coconuts 14,000, palm oil 14,000; livestock (number of live animals) 1,900,000 goats, 1,200,000 sheep, 850,000 pigs, 248,000 cattle, 5,685,000 chickens; roundwood (1994) 1,020,000 cu m; fish catch (1993) 17,114. Mining and quarrying (1995): phosphate rock 2,000,000; limestone is quarried for cement manufacture; marble production ceased in the early 1990s but resumed activity in 1995 at Gnaoulou and Pagola. Manufacturing (value added in CFAF '000,000; 1995): food products, beverages, and tobacco manufactures 36,393; nonmetallic manufactures 6,099; textiles, clothing, and leather 3,833; chemical products 3,625; paper, printing, and publishing 3,125; wood products 3,020; steel 330. Construction (value added in CFAF; 1995): 19,958,000,000. Energy

production (consumption): electricity (kW-hr; 1994) 93,000,000 (408,000,000); petroleum products (metric tons; 1994) none (184,000).
Gross national product (1994): U.S.$1,267,000,000 (U.S.$320 per capita).

Structure of gross domestic product and labour force

	1995 in value CFAF '000,000,000	1995 % of total value	1994 labour force	1994 % of labour force
Agriculture	210.5	33.9	1,041,000	67.7
Mining	36.6	5.9		
Manufacturing	62.6	10.1	177,000	11.5
Construction	20.0	3.2		
Public utilities	23.7	3.8		
Transp. and commun.	39.7	6.4		
Trade and finance	131.6	21.2		
Pub. admin., defense	49.4	7.9	318,000	20.7
Services	47.4	7.6		
TOTAL	630.3[4]	100.0	1,538,000[5]	100.0[5]

Population economically active (1994): total 1,538,000; activity rate of total population 33.8% (participation rates over age 10, 50.7%; female 35.6%; unemployed 16–18%).

Price and earnings indexes (1990 = 100)

	1989	1990	1991	1992	1993	1994	1995
Consumer price index	99.0	100.0	100.4	101.8	100.8	142.5	160.0
Hourly earnings index[6]	100.0	100.0	100.0	100.0	100.0	100.0	...

Household income and expenditure. Average household size (1980) 5.6; average annual income per household CFAF 102,000 (U.S.$452); sources of income: n.a.; expenditure (1970): food and beverages 60.9%, housing 9.9%, transportation 8.2%, clothing 7.7%, household durable goods 3.9%.
Tourism: receipts from visitors (1994) U.S.$7,000,000; expenditures by nationals abroad (1993) U.S.$30,000,000.
Land use (1994): forested 16.5%; meadows and pastures 3.7%; agricultural and under permanent cultivation 44.7%; other 35.1%.

Foreign trade[7]

Balance of trade (current prices)

	1990	1991	1992	1993	1994	1995
CFAF '000,000,000	−63.0	−36.1	−17.0	−5.1	−15.8	−60.6
% of total	30.2%	20.2%	10.4%	6.3%	8.1%	22.5%

Imports (1994): CFAF 134,500,000,000 (consumer goods 41.1%, capital equipment 27.8%, intermediate goods 16.8%, energy products 8.2%, other 6.1%).
Major import sources (1990): France 30.5%; W.Ger. 6.0%; U.S. 5.3%; Japan 4.3%; U.K. 3.8%; China 1.5%.
Exports (1994): CFAF 144,600,000,000 (raw materials 57.4%, of which phosphates 31.3%, cotton 19.3%, coffee 4.9%; reexports 27.7%; other 14.9%).
Major export destinations (1990): Africa 16.2%; France 9.8%; U.S.S.R. 4.7%; W.Ger. 3.7%; U.K. 1.5%; eastern Europe 1.2%.

Transport and communications

Transport. Railroads (1995): route length 395 km; (1994) passenger-km 14,000,000; metric ton-km cargo 5,600,000. Roads (1995): total length 12,040 km (paved 14%). Vehicles (1994): passenger cars 67,936; trucks and buses 31,986. Merchant marine (1992): vessels (100 gross tons and over) 8; total deadweight tonnage 20,633. Air transport (1995)[8]: passenger-km 222,822,000; metric ton-km cargo 15,273,000; airports (1996) 2.
Communications. Daily newspapers (1992): total number 2; total circulation 12,000; circulation per 1,000 population 3.0. Radio (1995): 720,000 receivers (1 per 5.7 persons). Television (1995): 150,000 receivers (1 per 27.6 persons). Telephones (main lines; 1993): 17,300 (1 per 233 persons).

Education and health

Education (1993)

	schools	teachers	students	student/ teacher ratio
Primary (age 6–11)	2,594	12,487	663,126	53.1
Secondary (age 12–18)	314[9]	2,918	126,335	43.3
Vocational	18[10]	261	8,392	32.2
Higher[11]	1[10]	276[12]	9,120[13]	26.6[12]

Educational attainment (1981). Percentage of population age 15 and over having: no formal schooling 76.5%; primary education 13.5%; secondary 8.7%; higher 1.3%. *Literacy* (1995): total population age 15 and over literate 51.7%; males 67.0%; females 37.0%.
Health: physicians (1988) 268 (1 per 12,299 persons); hospital beds (1990) 5,307 (1 per 640 persons); infant mortality rate (1990–95) 85.
Food (1992): daily per capita caloric intake 2,242 (vegetable products 95%, animal products 5%); 97% of FAO recommended minimum requirement.

Military

Total active duty personnel (1996): 6,950 (army 93.5%, navy 2.9%, air force 3.6%). *Military expenditure as percentage of GNP* (1994): 2.7% (world 3.0%); per capita expenditure U.S.$6.

[1]Personal military-supported rule from 1967 continues under constitution approved by referendum in September 1992. [2]A total of 34 opposition seats were not occupied for 18 months (February 1994–October 1995) because of a boycott. [3]1981. [4]Total includes statistical discrepancy of CFAF 8,800,000,000. [5]Detail does not add to total given because of rounding. [6]January 1. [7]Import figures are f.o.b. in total and balance of trade and c.i.f. for commodities and trading partners. [8]Represents ¹/₁₁ of the traffic of Air Afrique, which is operated by 11 West African states. [9]1990. [10]1987. [11]Universities only. [12]1988. [13]1989.

Tonga

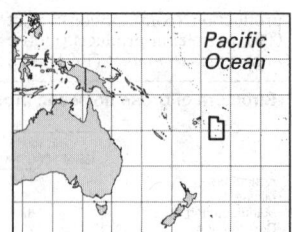

Pacific
Ocean

Official name: Pule'anga Fakatu'i 'o Tonga (Tongan); Kingdom of Tonga (English).
Form of government: constitutional monarchy with one legislative house (Legislative Assembly [30[1]]).
Head of state and government: King assisted by Privy Council.
Capital: Nuku'alofa.
Official languages: Tongan; English.
Official religion: none.
Monetary unit: 1 pa'anga[2] (T$) = 100 seniti; valuation (Oct. 11, 1996) 1 U.S.$ = T$1.26; 1 £ = T$1.99.

Area and population		area		population
Divisions				1986
Districts	**Capitals**	sq mi	sq km	census
'Eua	'Ohonua	33.7	87.4	4,393
'Eua Fo'ou		...	...	1,993
'Eua Motu'a		...	...	2,400
Ha'apai	Pangai	42.5	110.0	8,919
Foa		...	...	1,410
Ha'ano		...	...	891
Lulunga		...	...	1,584
Mu'omu'a		...	...	885
Pangai		...	...	2,850
'Uiha		...	...	1,299
Niuas	Hihifo	27.7	71.7	2,368
Niua Fo'ou		...	...	763
Niua Toputapu		...	...	1,605
Tongatapu	Nuku'alofa	100.6	260.5	63,794
Kolofo'ou		...	...	15,903
Kolomotu'a		...	...	13,115
Kolovai		...	...	4,031
Lapaha		...	...	7,005
Nukunuku		...	...	5,863
Tatakamotonga		...	...	6,773
Vaini		...	...	11,104
Vava'u	Neiafu	46.0	119.2	15,175
Hahake		...	...	2,299
Hihifo		...	...	2,093
Leimatu'a		...	...	2,884
Motu		...	...	1,384
Neiafu		...	...	5,268
Pangaimotu		...	...	1,247
TOTAL LAND AREA		278.1[3]	720.3[3]	
INLAND WATER		11.4	29.6	
TOTAL		289.5	749.9	94,649

Demography

Population (1996): 101,100.
Density (1996)[4]: persons per sq mi 363.5, persons per sq km 140.4.
Urban-rural (1995): urban 42.0%; rural 58.0%.
Sex distribution (1992): male 50.28%; female 49.72%.
Age breakdown (1986): under 15, 40.6%; 15–29, 29.0%; 30–44, 13.8%; 45–59, 10.2%; 60–74, 5.0%; 75 and over, 1.4%.
Population projection: (2000) 103,000; (2010) 105,000.
Doubling time: 32 years.
Ethnic composition (1986): Tongan 95.5%; part Tongan 2.8%; other 1.7%.
Religious affiliation (1986): Free Wesleyan 43.0%; Roman Catholic 16.0%; Mormon 12.1%; Free Church of Tonga 11.0%; Church of Tonga 7.3%; other 10.6%.
Major cities (1986): Nuku'alofa 21,383; Neiafu 3,879; Haveluloto 3,070; Vaini 2,697; Tofoa-Koloua 2,298.

Vital statistics

Birth rate per 1,000 population (1996): 27.8 (world avg. 25.0).
Death rate per 1,000 population (1996): 5.9 (world avg. 9.3).
Natural increase rate per 1,000 population (1996): 21.9 (world avg. 15.7).
Total fertility rate (avg. births per childbearing woman; 1996): 3.4.
Marriage rate per 1,000 population (1992): 8.2.
Divorce rate per 1,000 population (1992): 1.1.
Life expectancy at birth (1996): male 67.0 years; female 72.0 years.
Major causes of death per 100,000 population (1993)[5]: diseases of the circulatory system 58.1; diseases of the nervous system 51.0; senility 27.6; diabetes mellitus 17.3; renal failure 10.2.

National economy

Budget (1995–96). Revenue: T$58,210,000 (foreign-trade taxes 48.7%, government services revenue 19.6%, direct taxes 11.7%, indirect taxes 11.4%, interest and rent 7.3%). Expenditures: T$58,190,000 (general administration 20.3%, education 16.2%, law and order 12.0%, health 11.9%, public works and communications 9.7%, public debt 6.6%, agriculture 5.6%).
Tourism (1994): receipts U.S.$9,000,000; expenditures (1993) U.S.$3,000,000.
Production (metric tons except as noted). Agriculture, forestry, fishing (1995): yams 31,000, cassava 28,000, taro 27,200, coconuts 24,500, sweet potatoes 13,900, fruits 12,500, vegetables 7,600, copra (1994) 2,000; livestock (number of live animals) 93,500 pigs, 15,500 goats, 11,400 horses, 9,500 cattle; roundwood (1994) 4,600 cu m; fish catch (1993) 2,481. Mining and quarrying (1982): coral 150,000; sand 25,000. Manufacturing (output in T$; 1993): food products and beverages 7,673,000; chemical products 4,674,000; textile and wearing apparel 2,231,000; wood products 1,562,000; paper products 1,294,000; metal products 1,153,000. Construction (value in T$; 1984): residential 9,552,300; nonresidential 11,377,100. Energy production (consumption):

electricity (kW-hr; 1993) 27,000,000 (27,000,000); petroleum (barrels; 1989) none (154,000); petroleum products (metric tons; 1993) n.a. (30,000).
Gross national product (1994): U.S.$160,000,000 (U.S.$1,640 per capita).

Structure of gross domestic product and labour force				
	1993–94		1990	
	in value T$'000	% of total value	labour force	% of labour force
Agriculture	72,700	33.3	11,682	36.5
Mining	...	... }	4,665	14.6
Manufacturing	9,000	4.1 }		
Construction	8,000	3.7	1,257	3.9
Public utilities	...	...	408	1.3
Transp. and commun.	25,800	11.8	1,821	5.7
Trade	27,000	12.4	2,597	8.1
Finance	...	...	1,188	3.7
Pub. admin., defense }	26,900	12.3	7,052	22.0
Services				
Other	49,100	22.5	1,343	4.2
TOTAL	218,500	100.0[6]	32,013	100.0

Public debt (external, outstanding; 1994): U.S.$63,400,000.
Population economically active (1990): total 32,013; activity rate 33.6% (participation rates: ages 10 and over, 46.7%; female 33.0%; unemployed 4.2%).

Price and earnings indexes (1990 = 100)							
	1989	1990	1991	1992	1993	1994	1995
Consumer price index	91.1	100.0	110.6	119.4	120.5	121.8	123.5
Quarterly earnings index[7]	100.7	100.0	114.3	124.6	...	...	...

Household income and expenditure. Average household size (1986) 6.3; income per household: n.a.; sources of income: n.a.; expenditure (1984)[8]: food 49.3%, household operations 13.3%, housing 10.5%, tobacco and beverages 7.0%, transportation 5.8%, clothing and footwear 5.6%.
Land use (1994): forested 11.1%; meadows and pastures 5.6%; agricultural and under permanent cultivation 66.7%; other 16.6%.

Foreign trade[9]

Balance of trade (current prices)					
	1990	1991	1992	1993	1994	1995
T$'000,000	−64.5	−59.4	−67.7	−61.5	−72.8	−79.6
% of total	69.0%	63.0%	67.1%	56.8%	66.5%	68.3%

Imports (1995): T$98,050,000 (food and live animals 27.4%, machinery and transport equipment 21.0%, basic manufactures 19.5%, mineral fuels 12.7%, chemicals 7.0%). *Major import sources:* New Zealand 38.1%; Australia 27.8%; U.S. 10.5%; Fiji 7.6%; Japan 5.8%.
Exports (1995): T$18,020,000 (squash 46.7%, fish 24.1%, vanilla beans 15.6%, root crops 5.0%, coconut products 0.4%). *Major export destinations:* Japan 49.2%; U.S. 26.7%; New Zealand 8.4%; Australia 4.0%; Fiji 0.9%.

Transport and communications

Transport. Railroads: none. Roads (1993): total length 386 km (paved 76%). Vehicles (1993): passenger cars 3,400, commercial vehicles 3,900. Merchant marine (1992): vessels (100 gross tons and over) 15; total deadweight tonnage 13,740. Air transport (1994): passenger-km 9,397,000; metric ton-km cargo 16,000; airports (1996) with scheduled flights 6.
Communications. Daily newspapers (1992): 1; total circulation 7,000; circulation per 1,000 population 72. Radio (1995): 52,000 receivers (1 per 1.9 persons). Television (1995)[10]: 2,500 receivers (1 per 40 persons). Telephones (main lines; 1993): 5,900 (1 per 16 persons).

Education and health

Education (1993)				
	schools	teachers	students	student/ teacher ratio
Primary (age 6–11)	115	754	16,792	22.3
Secondary (age 12–18)	40[11]	847	15,573	18.4
Voc., teacher tr.	8[11]	65[12]	358	13.4[12]
Higher[11]	1	19	226	11.9

Educational attainment (1986). Percentage of population age 25 and over having: complete primary 38.3%; lower secondary 30.3%; secondary 23.4%; postsecondary 4.9%; higher 1.0%; not stated 2.1%. *Literacy* (1976): total population age 15 and over literate 46,456 (92.8%); males 23,372 (92.9%); females 23,084 (92.8%).
Health: physicians (1993) 45 (1 per 2,201 persons); hospital beds (1992) 307 (1 per 320 persons); infant mortality rate per 1,000 live births (1996) 16.
Food (1992): daily per capita caloric intake 2,946 (vegetable products 82%, animal products 18%); 129% of FAO recommended minimum requirement.

Military

Total active duty personnel (1991): Tonga has a national police (defense) force of about 300. *Military expenditure as percentage of GNP* (1989): 4.9% (world 4.9%); per capita expenditure U.S.$21.

---

[1]Includes 12 nonelective seats and 9 nobles elected by the 33 hereditary nobles of Tonga. [2]The pa'anga was pegged at par to the Australian dollar through Feb. 8, 1991, but beginning Feb. 11, 1991, it was linked to a weighted basket of foreign currencies. [3]Total includes 27.6 sq mi (71.5 sq km) of uninhabited islands. [4]Density is based on land area. [5]Reported inpatient deaths at all hospitals. [6]Detail does not add to total given because of rounding. [7]In manufacturing. [8]Current weight of consumer price index components. [9]Import data used in computing balance of trade is c.i.f. [10]Tonga has no authorized television service, but a "pirate" station began transmitting in mid-1984. [11]1992. [12]1990.

Trinidad and Tobago

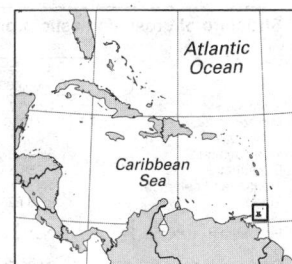

Official name: Republic of Trinidad and Tobago.
Form of government: multiparty republic with two legislative houses (Senate [31]; House of Representatives [36[1]]).
Chief of state: President.
Head of government: Prime Minister.
Capital: Port of Spain.
Official language: English.
Official religion: none.
Monetary unit: 1 Trinidad and Tobago dollar (TT$) = 100 cents; valuation (Oct. 11, 1996) 1 U.S.$ = TT$6.03; 1 £ = TT$9.50.

Area and population

| | | area | | population |
| | | | | 1990 |
Counties	Capitals	sq mi	sq km	census
Caroni	Chaguanas	191.0	494.7	120,508
Nariva/Mayaro	Rio Claro	349.0	903.9	36,781
St. Andrew/St. David	Sangre Grande	360.0	932.4	62,944
St. George	Tunapuna	354.0	916.9	445,620
St. Patrick	Siparia	252.0	652.7	120,129
Victoria	Princes Town	315.0	815.9	210,833
Unitary State				
Tobago	Scarborough	116.0	300.4	50,282
Cities				
Port of Spain	—	4.0	10.4	50,878
San Fernando	—	3.0	7.8	30,092
Boroughs				
Arima	—	4.0	10.4	29,695
Chaguanas	—	23.0	59.6	56,601
Point Fortin	—	9.0	23.3	20,025
TOTAL		1,980.1[2]	5,128.4	1,234,388

Demography

Population (1996): 1,262,000.
Density (1996): persons per sq mi 637.3, persons per sq km 246.1.
Urban-rural (1995): urban 71.8%; rural 28.2%.
Sex distribution (1995): male 49.46%; female 50.54%.
Age breakdown (1995): under 15, 31.7%; 15–29, 26.6%; 30–44, 22.1%; 45–59, 11.5%; 60–74, 6.0%; 75 and over, 2.1%.
Population projection: (2000) 1,264,000; (2010) 1,314,000.
Doubling time: 71 years.
Ethnic composition (1990): East Indian 40.3%; black 39.6%; mixed 18.4%; white 0.6%; Chinese 0.4%; other/not stated 0.7%.
Religious affiliation (1990): six largest Protestant bodies 29.7%, of which Anglican 10.9%, Pentecostal 7.5%; Roman Catholic 29.4%; Hindu 23.7%; Muslim 5.9%; other 11.3%.
Major cities (1990): Chaguanas 56,601; Port of Spain 52,451[3]; San Fernando 30,092; Arima 29,695; Point Fortin 20,025; Scarborough 4,000.

Vital statistics

Birth rate per 1,000 population (1995): 16.7 (world avg. 25.0).
Death rate per 1,000 population (1995): 6.9 (world avg. 9.3).
Natural increase rate per 1,000 population (1995): 9.8 (world avg. 15.7).
Total fertility rate (avg. births per childbearing woman; 1995): 2.0.
Marriage rate per 1,000 population (1993): 5.6.
Divorce rate per 1,000 population (1993): 0.9.
Life expectancy at birth (1995): male 67.8 years; female 72.6 years.
Major causes of death per 100,000 population (1992): diseases of the circulatory system 263.6, of which ischemic heart diseases 120.6, cerebrovascular disease 81.4; malignant neoplasms (cancers) 87.6; diabetes mellitus 84.6.

National economy

Budget (1995). Revenue: TT$8,409,000,000 (corporate taxes 26.4%, of which petroleum sector 17.5%; individual income taxes 17.8%; value-added taxes 14.8%; nontax revenues 9.0%; petroleum royalties 6.3%). Expenditures: TT$8,284,000,000 (current expenditures 92.1%; development expenditures 7.9%).
Tourism (1994): receipts from visitors U.S.$80,000,000; expenditures by nationals abroad U.S.$90,000,000.
Production (metric tons except as noted). Agriculture, forestry, fishing (1995): sugarcane 1,326,000, coconuts 20,000, oranges 14,906, rice 10,000, grapefruit and pomelo 7,297, bananas 6,000, corn (maize) 5,000, cucumbers 2,550, cocoa 1,865, coffee 831; livestock (number of live animals) 59,000 goats, 45,000 pigs, 9,500,000 chickens; roundwood (1994) 55,600 cu m; fish catch (1993) 10,565. Mining and quarrying (1994): natural asphalt 21,000. Manufacturing (1995): anhydrous ammonia and urea (nitrogenous fertilizers) 2,630,900; methanol 963,000; steel billets 676,100; cement 558,500; steel wire rods 594,400; raw sugar 117,200; beer and stout (1994) 481,600 hectolitres; rum 86,400 hectolitres. Construction (authorized; 1992): residential 253,600 sq m; nonresidential 50,700 sq m. Energy production (consumption): electricity (kW-hr; 1995) 4,229,000,000 (1993; 3,817,000,000); coal, none (none); crude petroleum (barrels; 1995) 47,817,000 (1993; 38,303,000); petroleum products (metric tons; 1993) 5,274,000 (1,523,000); natural gas (cu m; 1994) 5,214,000,000 (1993; 5,194,000,000).
Land use (1994): forested 45.8%; meadows and pastures 2.1%; agricultural and under permanent cultivation 23.8%; other 28.3%.

Public debt (external, outstanding; 1994): U.S.$1,682,000,000.
Gross national product (at current market prices; 1994): U.S.$4,838,000,000 (U.S.$3,740 per capita).

Structure of gross domestic product and labour force

| | 1995 | | 1993 | |
	in value TT$'000,000	% of total value	labour force	% of labour force
Agriculture	646	2.1	50,700	10.1
Petroleum[4], natural gas, quarrying	8,603	27.9	18,900	3.7
Manufacturing[5]	2,644	8.6	50,100	9.9
Construction	2,599	8.4	79,400	15.7
Public utilities	495	1.6	7,800	1.5
Transp. and commun.	2,641	8.6	33,800	6.7
Trade	4,446	14.4	87,000	17.3
Finance, real estate	3,594	11.7	32,200	6.4
Pub. admin., defense	2,994	9.7 }	143,900	28.5
Services	1,695	5.5 }		
Other	435[6]	1.4[6]	500	0.1
TOTAL	30,792	100.0[2]	504,500[2]	100.0[2]

Population economically active (1993): total 504,500; activity rate of total population 40.5% (participation rates: ages 15–64, 63.2%; female 37.0%; unemployed [1995] 17.2%).

Price and earnings indexes (1990 = 100)

	1989	1990	1991	1992	1993	1994	1995
Consumer price index	90.1	100.0	103.9	110.6	122.4	133.2	140.5[7]
Weekly earnings index[8]	94.5	100.0	100.1	103.0	104.6	100.9	...

Household income and expenditure. Average household size (1990) 4.1; income per household (1988) TT$17,083 (U.S.$4,444); sources of income: n.a.; expenditure (1993): food, beverages, and tobacco 25.5%, housing 21.6%, transportation 15.2%, household furnishings 14.3%, clothing and footwear 10.4%, other 13.0%.

Foreign trade[9]

Balance of trade (current prices)

	1990	1991	1992	1993	1994	1995
TT$'000,000	+4,089	+2,147	+4,720	+2,055	+5,426	+5,436
% of total	32.5%	16.6%	23.3%	13.2%	31.1%	22.9%

Imports (1994): TT$6,732,000,000 (nonelectrical machinery 17.7%, of which general industrial machinery 9.9%; food and live animals 15.0%; chemicals and chemical products 13.5%). *Major import sources:* United States 48.3%; United Kingdom 8.3%; Canada 5.7%; Brazil 5.3%; Japan 4.6%.
Exports (1994): TT$11,295,000,000 (refined petroleum 29.2%; crude petroleum 18.1%; urea 12.4%; anhydrous ammonia 11.8%; methanol 10.0%; iron and steel 8.3%). *Major export destinations:* United States 46.4%; Jamaica 6.1%; Canada 3.8%; Barbados 3.6%; French Guiana 3.1%.

Transport and communications

Transport. Railroads: none. Roads (1993): total length 4,970 mi, 8,000 km (paved 50%). Vehicles (1994): passenger cars 123,500; trucks and buses 24,500. Merchant marine (1992): vessels (100 gross tons and over) 53; total deadweight tonnage 17,533. Air transport (1993): passenger-mi 2,008,000,000, passenger-km 3,232,000,000; short ton-mi cargo 11,800,000, metric ton-km cargo 17,200,000; airports (1996) with scheduled flights 2.
Communications. Daily newspapers (1993): total number 3; total circulation 96,000; circulation per 1,000 population 76. Radio (1995): 550,000 receivers (1 per 2.3 persons). Television (1995): 250,000 receivers (1 per 5.1 persons). Telephones (main lines; 1993): 192,500 (1 per 6.5 persons).

Education and health

Education (1993–94)

	schools	teachers	students	student/ teacher ratio
Primary (age 5–11)	475	7,210	195,013	27.0
Secondary (age 12–16)	101[10]	4,882[11]	100,609[11]	20.6[11]
Higher[12]	1	438	5,191	11.9

Educational attainment (1990). Percentage of population age 25 and over having: no formal schooling 4.5%; primary education 56.4%; secondary 32.1%; higher 3.4%; other/not stated 3.6%. *Literacy* (1995): total population age 15 and over literate 886,000 (97.9%).
Health: physicians (1993) 1,051 (1 per 1,191 persons); hospital beds (1992) 3,653 (1 per 340 persons); infant mortality rate per 1,000 live births (1995) 18.5.
Food (1992): daily per capita caloric intake 2,585 (vegetable products 85%, animal products 15%); 107% of FAO recommended minimum requirement.

Military

Total active duty personnel (1996): 2,100 (army 66.7%, coast guard 33.3%).
Military expenditure as percentage of GNP (1994): 1.7% (world 3.0%); per capita expenditure U.S.$60.

---

[1]Excludes speaker, who may be elected from outside the House of Representatives. [2]Detail does not add to total given because of rounding. [3]1992. [4]Includes refined petroleum. [5]Excludes refined petroleum. [6]Net of value-added taxes less imputed bank service charges. [7]Average of 2nd and 3rd quarters. [8]Manufacturing sector only. [9]Imports f.o.b. in balance of trade and c.i.f. in commodities and trading partners. [10]1991–92. [11]Excludes vocational. [12]University of the West Indies, St. Augustine campus only.

Tunisia

Official name: Al-Jumhūrīyah
at-Tūnisīyah (Republic of Tunisia).
Form of government: multiparty
republic with one legislative house
(Chamber of Deputies [163]).
Chief of state: President.
Head of government: Prime Minister.
Capital: Tunis.
Official language: Arabic.
Official religion: Islam.
Monetary unit: 1 dinar (D) = 1,000
millimes; valuation (Oct. 11, 1996)
D 1.00 = U.S.$1.02 = £0.65.

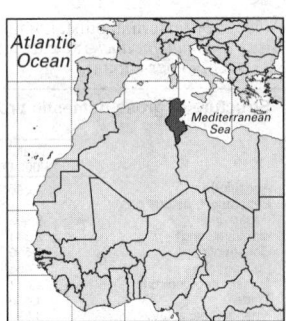

Area and population		area		population
		sq mi	sq km	1994 census
Governorates	**Capitals**			
Al-Ariānah	Al-Ariānah	602	1,558	570,700
Bājah	Bājah	1,374	3,558	306,500
Banzart	Bizerte (Banzart)	1,423	3,685	485,800
Bin 'Arūs	Bin 'Arūs	294	761	372,900
Jundūbah	Jundūbah	1,198	3,102	405,100
Al-Kāf	Al-Kāf	1,917	4,965	273,200
Madanīn	Madanīn	3,316	8,588	386,900
Al-Mahdīyah	Al-Mahdīyah	1,145	2,966	335,200
Al-Munastīr	Al-Munastīr	393	1,019	364,600
Nābul	Nābul	1,076	2,788	581,800
Qābis	Qābis	2,770	7,175	311,300
Qafşah	Qafşah	3,471	8,990	308,700
Al-Qaşrayn	Al-Qaşrayn	3,114	8,066	388,500
Al-Qayrawān	Al-Qayrawān	2,591	6,712	532,500
Qibilī	Qibilī	8,527	22,084	132,000
Şafāqis	Şafāqis	2,913	7,545	735,300
Sīdī Bū Zayd	Sīdī Bū Zayd	2,700	6,994	379,300
Siliānah	Siliānah	1,788	4,631	246,500
Sūsah	Sūsah	1,012	2,621	436,500
Tatāuīn	Tatāuīn	15,015	38,889	135,600
Tawzar	Tawzar	1,822	4,719	89,300
Tūnis	Tunis (Tūnis)	134	346	893,000
Zaghwān	Zaghwān	1,069	2,768	143,400
TOTAL		63,378[1]	164,150[1]	8,814,500[2]

Demography

Population (1996): 9,057,000.
Density (1996): persons per sq mi 142.9, persons per sq km 55.2.
Urban-rural (1985): urban 53.0%; rural 47.0%.
Sex distribution (1994): male 50.53%; female 49.47%.
Age breakdown (1994): under 15, 34.8%; 15–29, 28.5%; 30–44, 18.8%; 45–59, 9.6%; 60–74, 6.4%; 75 and over, 1.9%.
Population projection: (2000) 9,694,000; (2010) 11,209,000.
Doubling time: 44 years.
Ethnic composition (1983): Arab 98.2%; Berber 1.2%; French 0.2%; Italian 0.1%; other 0.3%.
Religious affiliation (1980): Sunnī Muslim 99.4%; Christian 0.3%; Jewish 0.1%; other 0.2%.
Major cities (commune; 1994): Tunis 674,100; Şafāqis 230,900; Aryānah 152,700; Ettadhamen 149,200; Sūsah 125,000.

Vital statistics

Birth rate per 1,000 population (1995): 20.9 (world avg. 25.0).
Death rate per 1,000 population (1995): 4.8 (world avg. 9.3).
Natural increase rate per 1,000 population (1995): 16.1 (world avg. 15.7).
Total fertility rate (avg. births per childbearing woman; 1990–95): 3.2.
Marriage rate per 1,000 population (1995): 6.0.
Divorce rate per 1,000 population (1993–94): 0.9.
Life expectancy at birth (1990–95): male 66.9 years; female 68.7 years.
Major causes of death per 100,000 population: n.a.; however, of approximately 12,000 deaths[3] for which a cause was reported in 1992, complications of pregnancy and childbirth represented 31.6%, circulatory diseases 22.4%, accidents and poisoning 14.9%, respiratory diseases 7.2%, endocrine and metabolic disorders 5.2%, infectious and parasitic diseases 4.8%.

National economy

Budget (1994). Revenue: D 6,275,800,000 (indirect taxes 37.7%, direct taxes 11.8%, investment 9.1%). Expenditures: D 5,987,000,000 (finance 20.4%, education 11.6%, interior affairs 6.5%, health 5.4%, national economy 4.3%).
Public debt (external, outstanding; 1994): U.S.$8,112,000,000.
Production (metric tons except as noted). Agriculture, forestry, fishing (1995): tomatoes 550,000, wheat 530,000, olives 475,000, watermelons 230,000, sugar beets 226,000, potatoes 205,000, grapes 112,000, oranges 101,000, dates 84,000; livestock (number of live animals) 7,600,000 sheep, 1,350,000 goats, 735,000 cattle; roundwood (1994) 2,634,000 cu m; fish catch (1994) 87,000. Mining and quarrying (1995): phosphate rock 6,301,598; iron ore 224,949; zinc 80,446. Manufacturing (1995): cement 3,033,200; phosphoric acid 1,365,200; flour 473,600; crude steel 192,000[4]. Construction (1982): residential building authorized 2,679,000 sq m. Energy production (consumption): electricity (kW-hr; 1994) 6,714,000 (5,701,000); coal (metric tons; 1993) none (14,000); crude petroleum (barrels; 1993) 35,754,000 (12,687,000); petroleum products (metric tons; 1994) 1,584,000 (3,884,000); natural gas (cu m; 1994) 354,000,000 (1993; 1,080,700,000).
Land use (1994): forested 4.3%; meadows and pastures 20.0%; agricultural and under permanent cultivation 31.9%; other 43.8%.
Gross national product (1994): U.S.$15,873,000,000 (U.S.$1,740 per capita).

Structure of gross domestic product and labour force

	1995		1994	
	in value D '000,000	% of total value	labour force	% of labour force
Agriculture	2,020.7	11.7	501,000	21.6
Mining	712.7	4.1 }	36,800	1.6
Public utilities	353.1	2.0 }		
Manufacturing	3,193.8	18.5	455,700	19.6
Construction	853.3	5.0	305,800	13.2
Transp. and commun.	1,437.1	8.3	[5]	[5]
Trade	4,159.2	24.1 }	315,600	13.6
Finance		}		
Pub. admin., defense	2,316.6	13.4 }	667,100[5]	28.7[5]
Services		}		
Other	2,226.5[6]	12.9[6]	38,600	1.7
TOTAL	17,256[3]	100.0	2,320,600	100.0

Population economically active (1989): total 2,360,000, activity rate of total population 28.8% (participation rates: ages 15–64, 42.2%; female 20.9%; unemployed 13.4%).

Price and earnings indexes (1990 = 100)						
	1989	1990	1991	1992	1993	1994	1995
Consumer price index	93.9	100.0	107.8	113.8	118.7	124.7	132.5
Hourly earnings index[7]	92.2	100.0	101.6	105.5	113.3	...	...

Household income and expenditure. Average household size (1994) 5.1; income per household: n.a.; sources of income: n.a.; expenditure (1985): food and beverages 39.0%, household durable goods 11.2%, housing 10.7%, transportation 9.0%, recreation 7.1%, clothing and footwear 6.0%, energy 5.1%, health care 3.0%, education 1.8%, other 7.1%.
Tourism (1994): receipts U.S.$1,302,000,000; expenditures U.S.$216,000,000.

Foreign trade

Balance of trade (current prices)						
	1990	1991	1992	1993	1994	1995
D '000,000	−1,439.7	−1,037.5	−1,726.1	−1,999.2	−1,504.2	−1,789.9
% of total	18.9%	13.1%	24.2%	20.7%	13.8%	14.7%

Imports (1994): D 6,647,300,000 (textiles 23.0%, machinery and electrical equipment 20.0%, petroleum and petroleum products 6.9%, transportation equipment 6.5%, iron and steel products 4.6%, plastics and plastic products 3.2%, pharmaceutical products 2.0%). *Major import sources:* France 27.4%; Italy 15.4%; Germany 12.2%; U.S. 6.6%; Belgium 4.3%; Spain 3.6%; United Kingdom 2.2%.
Exports (1994): D 4,696,600,000 (clothing and accessories 43.3%, petroleum and petroleum products 9.4%, olive oil 6.5%, machinery and electrical products 6.5%, chemical products 4.9%). *Major export destinations:* France 27.2%; Italy 19.6%; Germany 15.5%; Belgium 6.5%; Spain 4.7%.

Transport and communications

Transport. Railroads (1994): route length 1,337 mi, 2,152 km; passenger-mi 636,000,000, passenger-km 1,038,000,000; short ton-mi cargo 1,524,000,000, metric ton-km cargo 2,225,000,000. Roads (1989): total length 18,133 mi, 29,183 km (paved 60%). Vehicles (1994): passenger cars 183,700; trucks and buses 183,700. Merchant marine (1992): vessels (100 gross tons and over) 77; total deadweight tonnage 443,290. Air transport (1994)[8]: passenger-mi 1,338,165,000, passenger-km 2,153,573,000; short ton-mi cargo 139,456,000, metric ton-km cargo 203,602,000; airports (1996) 5.
Communications. Daily newspapers (1994): total number 7; total circulation 190,000[9]; circulation per 1,000 population 22[9]. Radio (1995): 1,700,000 receivers (1 per 5.2 persons). Television (1995): 650,000 receivers (1 per 14 persons). Telephones (main lines; 1993): 421,400 (1 per 20 persons).

Education and health

Education (1994–95)	schools	teachers	students	student/ teacher ratio
Primary (age 6–11)	4,286	58,279	1,472,844	25.3
Secondary (age 12–18)	712	27,785	662,222	23.8
Teacher tr.[10, 11]	...	237	3,839	16.2
Higher[12]	...	5,655	96,101	17.0

Educational attainment (1989). Percentage of population age 25 and over having: no formal schooling 54.9%; primary 26.9%; secondary 14.3%; higher 3.4%; unspecified 0.5%. *Literacy* (1995): total population age 15 and over literate 66.7%; males literate 78.6%; females literate 54.6%.
Health (1994): physicians 5,344 (1 per 1,640 persons); hospital beds 15,759 (1 per 556 persons); infant mortality rate (1990–95) 43.0.
Food (1992): daily per capita caloric intake 3,330 (vegetable products 92%, animal products 8%); 139% of FAO recommended minimum requirement.

Military

Total active duty personnel (1996): 35,000 (army 77.1%, navy 12.9%, air force 10.0%). *Military expenditure as percentage of GNP* (1994): 3.6% (world 3.0%); per capita expenditure U.S.$62.

---

[1]Total includes 3,714 sq mi (9,620 sq km) of territory in southwestern Tunisia that is not distributed by governorate. [2]Detail does not add to total given because of rounding. [3]Recorded deaths from urban areas only, including complete figures for Tunis. [4]1989. [5]Services includes transportation and communications. [6]Indirect taxes less subsidies. [7]Year-end; index refers to the *S.M.I.G.* (*salaire minimum interprofessionel garanti*), a form of minimum professional wage. [8]Tunis Air only. [9]Circulation for four dailies only. [10]1987–88. [11]Teacher training only. [12]1993–94.

Turkey

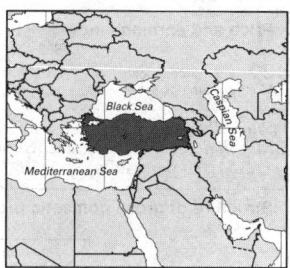

Official name: Türkiye Cumhuriyeti (Republic of Turkey).
Form of government: multiparty republic with one legislative house (Turkish Grand National Assembly [550]).
Chief of state: President.
Head of government: Prime Minister.
Capital: Ankara.
Official language: Turkish.
Official religion: none.
Monetary unit: 1 Turkish lira (LT) = 100 kurush; valuation (Oct. 11, 1996)
1 U.S.$ = LT 93,990;
1 £ = LT 148,062.

Area and population

Geographic regions[1]	area sq mi	area sq km	population 1990 census
Akdeniz kıyısı (Mediterranean Coast)	22,933	59,395	5,443,867
Batı Anadolu (West Anatolia)	29,742	77,031	3,864,661
Doğu Anadolu (East Anatolia)	68,074	180,180	6,867,415
Güneydoğu Anadolu (Southeast Anatolia)	15,347	35,880	2,699,776
İç Anadolu (Central Anatolia)	91,254	236,347	13,096,179
Karadeniz kıyısı (Black Sea Coast)	31,388	81,295	6,827,304
Marmara ve Ege kıyıları (Marmara and Aegean coasts)	33,035	85,560	11,698,384
Trakya (Thrace)	9,175	23,764	5,975,449
TOTAL	300,948	779,452	56,473,035

Demography

Population (1996): 62,650,000.
Density (1996): persons per sq mi 208.2, persons per sq km 80.4.
Urban-rural (1995): urban 68.8%; rural 31.2%.
Sex distribution (1995): male 50.63%; female 49.37%.
Age breakdown (1993): under 15, 32.9%; 15–29, 28.0%; 30–44, 18.2%; 45–59, 11.7%; 60–74, 7.5%; 75 and over, 1.7%.
Population projection: (2000) 66,842,000; (2010) 77,008,000.
Doubling time: 36 years.
Ethnolinguistic composition (1992)[2]: Turkish 92.0%; Kurdish 6.2%; Arabic 1.4%; other 0.4%.
Religious affiliation (1992): Sunnī Muslim c. 80.0%; Alevi (nonorthodox Shī'i sect) c. 19.8%; Christian c. 0.2%.
Major cities (1994): Istanbul 7,615,500; Ankara 2,782,200; İzmir 1,985,300; Adana 1,047,300; Bursa 996,600; Gaziantep 716,000; Konya 576,000.

Vital statistics

Birth rate per 1,000 population (1995): 25.3 (world avg. 25.0).
Death rate per 1,000 population (1995): 5.6 (world avg. 9.3).
Natural increase rate per 1,000 population (1995): 19.7 (world avg. 15.7).
Total fertility rate (avg. births per childbearing woman; 1995): 2.6.
Marriage rate per 1,000 population (1993): 7.7.
Divorce rate per 1,000 population (1993): 0.5.
Life expectancy at birth (1995): male 69.1 years; female 74.0 years.
Major causes of death per 100,000 population (1993)[3]: diseases of the circulatory system 369; malignant neoplasms (cancers) 80; accidents and violence 33; infectious and parasitic diseases 24; ill-defined conditions 60.

National economy

Budget (1995). Revenue: LT 1,404,071,000,000,000 (indirect taxes 45.8%, direct taxes 31.5%, nontax revenue 20.6%). Expenditures: LT 1,720,647,000,000,000 (interest payments 33.5%, personnel 29.2%, investments 5.9%).
Tourism (1995): receipts from visitors U.S.$4,957,000,000; expenditures by nationals abroad U.S.$911,000,000.
Production (in '000 metric tons except as noted). Agriculture, forestry, fishing (1995): wheat 18,015; sugar beets 11,680, barley 7,500, potatoes 4,750, grapes 3,550, apples 2,050, seed cotton 2,000, corn (maize) 1,900, cottonseed 1,180, oranges 900, sunflower seeds 900, cotton (lint) 755, olives 630, lentils 615, apricots 460, hazelnuts 450, pears 410, tobacco 210, sultana raisins 179, attar of roses 800 kg[4]; livestock (number of live animals) 35,646,000 sheep, 11,901,000 cattle; roundwood (1994) 16,845,000 cu m; fish catch (1993) 556,000. Mining (1994): boron (concentrate) 1,200; pumice 1,200; chromite 800; celestite (concentrate) 25. Manufacturing (1992)[5]: refined petroleum 35,038; textiles 27,199; food products 26,016; transport equipment 17,444; electrical machinery 13,690; iron and steel 12,789. Construction (completed; 1994): residential 45,714,000 sq m; nonresidential 11,610,000 sq m. Energy production (consumption): electricity (kW-hr; 1995) 86,341,000,000 (85,-552,000,000); coal (metric tons; 1995) 54,191,000 ([1993] 55,987,000); crude petroleum (barrels; 1995) 25,125,000 ([1993] 186,332,000); petroleum products (metric tons; 1993) 22,360,000 (23,379,000); natural gas (cu m; 1994) 199,500,000 ([1993] 4,771,000,000).
Land use (1994): forested 26.2%; meadows and pastures 16.1%; agricultural and under permanent cultivation 36.1%; other 21.6%.
Household income and expenditure. Average household size (1993) 4.5; income per household (1987) LT 3,680,500 (U.S.$4,294); sources of income (1987): self-employment 51.4%, wages and salaries 24.1%, rent and interest 13.7%, transfers 10.8%; expenditure (1994): food, tobacco, and cafe expenditures 38.5%, housing 22.8%, clothing 9.0%.
Gross national product (at current market prices; 1994): U.S.$149,002,000,000 (U.S.$2,450 per capita).

Structure of gross domestic product and labour force

	1995 in value LT '000,000'000[6]	1995 % of total value	1994 labour force[7]	1994 % of labour force[7]
Agriculture	1,078,720	15.9	9,023,000	40.8
Mining	86,297	1.3	159,000	0.7
Manufacturing	1,420,732	20.9	2,985,000	13.5
Construction	389,069	5.7	1,231,000	5.6
Public utilities	184,633	2.7	98,000	0.4
Transportation and communications	963,710	14.2	917,000	4.1
Trade	1,354,188	19.9	2,647,000	12.0
Finance, real estate	424,641	6.3	474,000	2.1
Pub. admin., defense	619,785	9.1 }	2,862,000	12.9
Services	272,102	4.0 }		
Other	—	—	1,740,000[8]	7.9[8]
TOTAL	6,793,877	100.0	22,136,000	100.0

Population economically active (1993)[7]: total 20,996,702; activity rate of total population 35.3% (participation rates: ages 15–64, 57.2%; female (1994) 28.9%; unemployed [1995] 7.2%).

Price and earnings indexes (1990 = 100)

	1990	1991	1992	1993	1994	1995	1996
Consumer price index	100.0	166.0	282.3	468.8	967.0	1,872.5	3,258.9[9]
Daily earnings index[10]	100.0	202.1	395.2	666.0	1,007	...	...

Public debt (external, outstanding; December 1994): U.S.$23,330,000,000.

Foreign trade[11]

Balance of trade (current prices)

	1990	1991	1992	1993	1994	1995
U.S.$'000,000	− 9,343	− 7,454	− 8,156	− 14,080	− 5,164	− 14,073
% of total	26.5%	21.5%	21.7%	31.4%	12.5%	24.5%

Imports (1995): U.S.$35,709,000,000 (nonelectrical machinery 16.1%; iron and steel 8.5%; crude petroleum 8.2%; electrical and electronic equipment 6.3%; organic chemicals 4.8%). *Major import sources:* Germany 15.5%; United States 10.4%; Italy 8.9%; Russia 5.8%; France 5.6%; United Kingdom 5.1%.
Exports (1995): U.S.$21,636,000,000 (textiles and clothing 26.1%; iron and steel 8.0%; edible fruits 5.7%; electrical and electronic machinery 4.6%). *Major export destinations:* Germany 23.3%; United States 7.0%; Italy 6.7%; Russia 5.7%; United Kingdom 5.3%; France 4.8%.

Transport and communications

Transport. Railroads (1994): length 5,252 mi, 8,452 km; passenger-mi 3,967,-000,000, passenger-km 6,385,000,000; short ton-mi cargo 5,654,000,000, metric ton-km cargo 8,254,000,000. Roads (1994): total length 236,759 mi, 381,028 km (paved [1992] 15%). Vehicles (1994): passenger cars 2,862,000; trucks and buses 942,000. Merchant marine (1992): vessels (100 gross tons and over) 880; total deadweight tonnage 7,114,289. Air transport (1995)[12]: passenger-mi 5,887,000,000, passenger-km 9,475,000,000; short ton-mi cargo 147,049,000, metric ton-km cargo 214,687,000; airports (1996) with scheduled flights 26.
Communications. Daily newspapers (1990): total number 399; total circulation 4,000,000; circulation per 1,000 population 71. Radio (1995): total number of receivers 8,800,000 (1 per 7.0 persons). Television (1995): total number of receivers 10,530,000 (1 per 5.9 persons). Telephones (main lines; 1994): 12,318,969 (1 per 4.9 persons).

Education and health

Education (1993–94)

	schools	teachers	students	student/ teacher ratio
Primary (age 6–10)	49,599	237,943	6,526,296	27.4
Secondary (age 11–16)	9,592	133,316	3,381,901	25.4
Voc., teacher tr.	3,239	66,199	1,142,191	17.3
Higher	625	42,475	1,083,063	25.5

Educational attainment (1993). Percentage of population age 25 and over having: no formal schooling 30.5%; incomplete primary education 6.6%; complete primary 40.4%; incomplete secondary 3.1%; complete secondary or higher 19.1%; unknown 0.3%. *Literacy* (1995): total population age 15 and over literate 33,605,000 (82.3%); males literate 19,191,000 (91.7%); females literate 14,414,000 (72.4%).
Health: physicians (1993) 61,050[13] (1 per 970 persons); hospital beds (1994) 134,665 (1 per 450 persons); infant mortality rate per 1,000 live births (1995) 45.6.
Food (1992): daily per capita caloric intake 3,429 (vegetable products 88%, animal products 12%); 136% of FAO recommended minimum requirement.

Military

Total active duty personnel (1996): 639,000 (army 82.2%, navy 8.0%, air force 9.8%). *Military expenditure as percentage of GNP* (1994): 4.1% (world 3.0%); per capita expenditure U.S.$87.

---

[1]Administratively divided into 76 provinces. [2]Official data based on mother tongue. Unofficially, Kurds as an ethnic group are estimated to constitute about 20% of the population. [3]Projected rates based on about 35% of total deaths. [4]1993. [5]Preliminary data; value added in LT '000,000,000. [6]At factor cost. [7]Civilian population only. [8]Unemployed. [9]June. [10]Based on June average. [11]Imports c.i.f.; exports f.o.b. [12]Turkish Airlines only. [13]Includes assistant physicians.

Turkmenistan

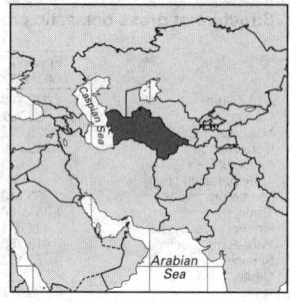

Official name: Türkmenistan Jumhuriyäti (Republic of Turkmenistan).
Form of government: unitary republic with one legislative body (Majlis [Parliament; 50]).
Head of state and government: President, assisted by a People's Council[1].
Capital: Ashgabat (formerly Ashkhabad).
Official language: Turkmen.
Official religion: none.
Monetary unit: manat; valuation (Oct. 11, 1996) 1 U.S.$ = 4,060 manat; 1 £ = 6,396 manat.

Area and population

		area		population
				1991
Provinces	**Capitals**	sq mi	sq km	estimate
Balkan	Nebitdag	90,300	233,900	925,500
Dashhovuse	Dashhovuse	28,400	73,600	738,000
Leban	Leban	36,200	93,800	774,700
Mary	Mary	33,500	86,800	859,500
City				
Ashgabat	—	...	...	416,400
TOTAL		188,500[2]	488,100	3,714,100

Demography

Population (1996): 4,574,000.
Density (1996): persons per sq mi 24.3, persons per sq km 9.4.
Urban-rural (1995): urban 45.1%; rural 54.9%.
Sex distribution (1992): male 49.32%; female 50.68%.
Age breakdown (1989): under 15, 40.5%; 15–29, 28.8%; 30–44, 15.5%; 45–59, 9.1%; 60–74, 4.7%; 75 and over, 1.4%.
Population projection: (2000) 4,922,000; (2010) 5,362,000.
Doubling time: 29 years.
Ethnic composition (1992): Turkmen 73.3%; Russian 9.8%; Uzbek 9.0%; Kazak 2.0%; Tatar 0.9%; other 5.0%.
Religious affiliation: believers are predominantly Sunnī Muslim (Şūfī).
Major cities (1991): Ashgabat 416,400; Chärjew 166,400; Dashhovuse 117,000; Mary 94,900; Nebitdag 89,100.

Vital statistics

Birth rate per 1,000 population (1994): 32.1 (world avg. 25.0); legitimate 96.2%; illegitimate 3.8%.
Death rate per 1,000 population (1994): 7.9 (world avg. 9.3).
Natural increase rate per 1,000 population (1994): 24.2 (world avg. 15.7).
Total fertility rate (avg. births per childbearing woman; 1993): 3.8.
Marriage rate per 1,000 population (1994): 8.7.
Divorce rate per 1,000 population (1994): 1.5.
Life expectancy at birth (1994): male 62.0 years; female 69.0 years.
Major causes of death per 100,000 population (1993): diseases of the circulatory system 309.7; diseases of the respiratory system 130.5; infectious and parasitic diseases 69.8; accidents, poisoning, and violence 58.2; malignant neoplasms (cancers) 57.9; diseases of the digestive system 26.2; endocrine and metabolic disorders 9.1; diseases of the nervous system 5.9.

National economy

Budget (1994). Revenue: 14,723,000,000 manat (tax revenue 76.6%, of which turnover tax 29.2%, company profit tax 19.7%, natural resource tax 7.5%, individual income tax 5.7%, excise tax 3.1%, other taxes 11.4%; nontax revenue 23.4%). Expenditures: 16,738,000,000 manat (national economy 40.5%, of which capital investment 9.5%, price subsidies 8.1%, operational costs 3.8%, other 19.1%; social and cultural affairs 39.1%, of which education 18.6%, health 9.3%, administration and defense 9.1%, social security 0.9%, other 1.2%; other expenditures 20.4%).
Production (metric tons except as noted). Agriculture, forestry, fishing (1995): seed cotton 1,293,000, vegetables 626,000, grain 269,000, fruit 249,000; livestock (number of live animals) 6,503,000 sheep and goats, 1,181,000 cattle, 128,000 pigs, 6,500,000 poultry; roundwood (1990) 4,000,000 cu m; fish catch (1993) 37,000. Mining and quarrying (1995): sulfur 200,000; sodium sulphate 200,000. Manufacturing (value of production in '000,000 manat; 1994): ferrous and nonferrous metals 278; machinery and metalworks 223; food products 129; chemical products 90; construction materials 52; wood products 31. Construction (1992): 20,754,000 sq m. Energy production (consumption): electricity (kW-hr; 1994) 10,496,000,000 (7,846,000,000); coal (metric tons; 1994) none (none); crude petroleum (barrels; 1994) 30,053,000 (30,053,000); petroleum products (metric tons; 1994) 2,765,000 (2,765,000); natural gas (cu m; 1994) 30,891,000,000 (8,332,000,000).
Household income and expenditure. Average household size (1989) 5.6; income per household: 3,853 manat (U.S.$ equivalent, n.a.[3]); sources of income (1993): wages and salaries 56.6%, self-employment 26.0%[4], pensions and grants 14.4%, nonwage income of workers 3.0%; expenditure (1993): goods 30.6%, taxes and other payments 5.4%, services 4.4%.
Population economically active (1995): total 1,680,000; activity rate of total population 37.4% (participation rates: ages 16–59 [male], 16–54 [female] 81.0%; female 41.0%; unemployed [1991] 20.0–25.0%).

Price and earnings indexes (1993 = 100)[5]

	1993	1994	1995
Consumer price index	100	4,607	46,634
Monthly earnings index	...	...	...

Public debt (external, outstanding; 1994): U.S.$418,100,000.
Gross national product (at current market prices; 1993): U.S.$4,898,390,000 (U.S.$1,270 per capita)[3].

Structure of gross domestic product and labour force

	1994		1992	
	in value '000,000 manat	% of total value	labour force	% of labour force
Agriculture	12,630	9.0	729,200	43.2
Mining	} 103,226	73.2	169,300	10.0
Manufacturing				
Public utilities	910	0.6	...	...
Construction	6,674	4.7	171,400	10.2
Transportation and communications	2,921	2.1	86,600	5.1
Trade	4,857	3.4	108,400	6.4
Finance	2,112	1.5	7,500	0.4
Public administration, defense	...	...	21,500	1.3
Services	2,906	2.1	348,300	20.7
Other	4,779	3.4	43,900	2.6
TOTAL	141,015	100.0	1,686,100	100.0[2]

Tourism: n.a.
Land use (1994): forested 8.2%; meadows and pastures 61.6%; agricultural and under permanent cultivation 3.0%; other 27.2%.

Foreign trade

Balance of trade (current prices)

	1993	1994	1995
U.S.$'000,000	+1,100	+485	+536
% of total	25.7%	12.5%	15.4%

Imports (1993): U.S.$1,593,000,000 (machinery and transport equipment 39.7%, chemicals 21.2%, food 20.2%, worked metal 14.4%). *Major import sources* (1995): Ukraine 21.2%; Georgia 11.3%; Turkey 10.5%; Armenia 6.2%; Iran 4.4%.
Exports (1994): U.S.$2,176,000 (natural gas and oil products 74.3%, cotton 16.7%). *Major export destinations* (1995): Ukraine 34.2%; Kazakstan 12.6%; Russia 8.0%; Turkey 7.2%; Armenia 6.5%.

Transport and communications

Transport. Railroads (1991): length (1996) 1,359 mi, 2,187 km; passengers transported 5,900,000; short ton-mi cargo 20,700,000, metric ton-km cargo 22,800,000. Roads (1995): total length 14,602 mi, 23,500 km (paved 81.2%). Vehicles (1988): passenger cars 170,600; trucks and buses, n.a. Merchant marine: vessels (100 gross tons and over) n.a.; total deadweight tonnage, n.a. Air transport (1989): passenger-mi 2,021,000,000, passenger-km 3,253,000,000; short ton-mi cargo 222,000,000, metric ton-km cargo 324,200,000; airports (1996) with scheduled flights 1.
Communications. Daily newspapers (1989): total number 66; total circulation 1,141,000; circulation per 1,000 population 319. Radio (1991): 823,000 receivers (1 per 5.2 persons). Televisions (1991): 705,000 receivers (1 per 6.1 persons). Telephones (main lines; 1993): 265,100 (1 per 14.9 persons).

Education and health

Education (1994–95)

	schools	teachers	students	student/ teacher ratio
Primary (age 6–13)	} 1,900	60,000[6]	902,500	14.0[6]
Secondary (age 14–17)				
Voc., teacher tr.	41	...	22,400	...
Higher	15	...	38,500	...

Educational attainment (1989). Percentage of population age 25 and over having: primary education or no formal schooling 13.6%; some secondary 21.3%; completed secondary and some postsecondary 56.8%; higher 8.3%.
Literacy (1989): total population age 15 and over literate 3,453,000 (97.7%); males literate 1,714,000 (98.8%); females literate 1,739,000 (96.6%).
Health (1994): physicians 14,000 (1 per 315 persons); hospital beds 47,000 (1 per 94 persons); infant mortality rate per 1,000 live births 46.4.

Military

Total active duty personnel (1996): 18,000 (100% army). *Military expenditure as percentage of GNP* (1994): 0.5% (world 3.0%); per capita expenditure U.S.$16.

---

[1]The People's Council is the ultimate representative organ of governmental supervision and is composed of the president, membership of the Majlis, elected members, and a variety of ex officio members of national, provincial, and local government; its purpose is to consider and render decisions about the constitution, national development, and national boundaries and treaties. [2]Detail does not add to total given because of rounding. [3]Ruble-area GNP and exchange-rate data for this period are very speculative. [4]Mainly agricultural income. [5]June. [6]1991–92.

Tuvalu

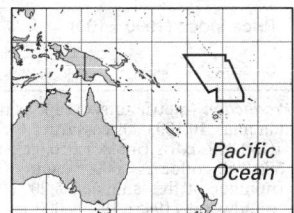

Official name: Tuvalu.
Form of government: constitutional monarchy with one legislative house (Parliament [12]).
Chief of state: British Monarch, represented by Governor-General.
Head of government: Prime Minister.
Capital: government offices are at Vaiaku, Fongafale islet, of Funafuti atoll.
Official language: none.
Official religion: none.
Monetary units[1]: 1 Tuvalu dollar = 1 Australian dollar ($T = $A) = 100 Tuvalu and Australian cents; valuation (Oct. 11, 1996) 1 U.S.$ = $A 1.26; 1 £ = $A 1.99.

Area and population

Islands[2]	area sq mi	area sq km	population 1987 estimate
Funafuti	0.91	2.36	2,718
Nanumaga	1.00	2.59	717
Nanumea	1.38	3.57	965
Niulakita	0.16	0.41	75
Niutao	0.82	2.12	867
Nui	1.27	3.29	622
Nukufetau	1.18	3.06	722
Nukulaelae	0.64	1.66	335
Vaitupu	1.89	4.90	1,437
TOTAL	9.25[3]	23.96[3]	8,458[4, 5]

Demography

Population (1996): 9,482.
Density (1996): persons per sq mi 1,025.1, persons per sq km 395.7.
Urban-rural (1995): urban 46.0%; rural 54.0%.
Sex distribution (1991): male 48.39%; female 51.61%.
Age breakdown (1991): under 15, 34.7%; 15–29, 24.1%; 30–44, 20.7%; 45–59, 11.4%; 60 and over, 9.2%.
Population projection: (2000) 9,856; (2010) 10,857.
Doubling time: 43 years.
Ethnic composition (1979): Tuvaluan (Polynesian) 91.2%; mixed (Polynesian/Micronesian/other) 7.2%; European 1.0%; other 0.6%.
Religious affiliation (1979): Church of Tuvalu (Congregational) 96.9%; Seventh-day Adventist 1.4%; Bahā'ī 1.0%; Roman Catholic 0.2%; other 0.5%.
Major locality (1990): Fongafale, on Funafuti atoll, 3,432.

Vital statistics

Birth rate per 1,000 population (1995): 24.9 (world avg. 25.0); (1989) legitimate 82.2%; illegitimate 17.8%.
Death rate per 1,000 population (1995): 9.0 (world avg. 9.3).
Natural increase rate per 1,000 population (1995): 15.9 (world avg. 15.7).
Total fertility rate (avg. births per childbearing woman; 1995): 3.1.
Marriage rate per 1,000 population: n.a.
Divorce rate per 1,000 population: n.a.
Life expectancy at birth (1995): male 61.9 years; female 64.3 years.
Major causes of death per 100,000 population (1985): diseases of the digestive system 170.0; diseases of the circulatory system 150.0; diseases of the respiratory system 120.0; diseases of the nervous system 120.0; malignant neoplasms (cancers) 70.0; infectious and parasitic diseases 40.0; endocrine and metabolic disorders 20.0; ill-defined conditions 430.0; in 1992 the leading causes of death included liver diseases, meningitis, tuberculosis, and still and perinatal deaths; other health problems included acute respiratory infections, diarrhea, filariasis, conjunctivitis, fish poisoning, diabetes, rheumatism, and hypertension.

National economy

Budget (1990). Recurrent revenue: $A 5,301,000 (local sources [including fisheries licenses, import duties, sales tax, and income and company taxes] 77.4%; Tuvalu Trust Fund[6] 22.6%). Expenditures: $A 10,826,000[7] (1987; capital [development] expenditures 68.9%, of which marine transport 20.7%, education 13.0%, fisheries 5.6%, health 3.1%; current expenditures 31.1%).
Gross national product (at current market prices; 1993): U.S.$7,400,000 (U.S.$800 per capita).

Structure of gross domestic product and labour force

	1994 in value[8] $A	1994 % of total value	1991 labour force	1991 % of labour force
Agriculture, fishing, forestry	2,974,000	22.2	4,020	68.0
Mining	299,000	2.2	—	—
Manufacturing[9]	427,000	3.2	60	1.0
Construction	1,852,000	13.9	240	4.0
Public utilities	320,000	2.4	—	—
Transportation and communications	549,000	4.1	60	1.0
Trade, hotels, and restaurants	1,892,000	14.2	240	4.0
Finance	1,323,000	9.9	—	—
Pub. admin., defense Services	3,735,000	27.9	1,290	22.0
TOTAL	13,371,000	100.0	5,910	100.0

Production (metric tons except as noted). Agriculture[10], forestry, fishing (1995): coconuts 1,800, fruits 1,040, hens' eggs 12, other agricultural products include breadfruit, pulaka (taro), bananas, pandanus fruit, sweet potatoes, and pawpaws; livestock (number of live animals) 12,600 pigs[11]; forestry, n.a.; fish catch (1993) 1,460, of which tuna 15.0%. Mining and quarrying: n.a.[12]. Manufacturing (1988): copra 90 metric tons; handicrafts and baked goods are also important. Construction: n.a.; however, the main areas of construction activity are roadworks, coastal protection, government facilities, and water-related infrastructure projects. Energy production (consumption): electricity (kW-hr; 1992) 1,300,000 (1,300,000); coal, none (none); crude petroleum, none (n.a.); petroleum products, none (n.a.); natural gas, none (none).
Public debt: n.a.
Tourism (1993): receipts from visitors U.S.$300,000; expenditures by nationals abroad, n.a.
Population economically active (1991): total 5,910; activity rate of total population 65.3% (participation rates: ages 15–64, 85.5%; female [1979] 51.3%; unemployed [1979] 4.0%).

Price and earnings indexes (1990 = 100)

	1987	1988	1989	1990	1991	1992	1993
Consumer price index	86.5	93.8	96.4	100.0	106.2	100.0	102.1
Earnings index[13]	91.1	93.3	97.8	100.0	...	...	...

Household income and expenditure. Average household size (1979) 6.4; average annual income per household $A 2,575 (U.S.$2,044); sources of income (1987): agriculture and other 45.0%, cash economy only 38.0%, overseas remittances 17.0%; expenditure (1992)[14]: food 45.5%, housing and household operations 11.5%, transportation 10.5%, alcohol and tobacco 10.5%, clothing 7.5%, other 14.5%.
Land use (1987): agricultural and under permanent cultivation 73.6%[15]; scrub 16.1%; other 10.3%.

Foreign trade

Balance of trade (current prices)

	1989	1990	1991	1992	1993	1994
$A '000	−5,894	−5,909	−6,200	−6,595	−9,129	−9,498
% of total	86.6%	90.2%	86.8%	91.7%	93.3%	93.4%

Imports (1994): U.S.$17,600,000 (1989; food 29.3%, manufactured goods 28.2%, petroleum and petroleum products 12.8%, machinery and transport equipment 12.2%, chemicals 7.1%, beverages and tobacco 3.9%). *Major import sources:* Australia 38.1%; New Zealand 4.0%; Japan 1.7%; United Kingdom 1.7%; United States 0.6%.
Exports (1994): U.S.$700,000 (1989; clothing and footwear 29.5%, copra 21.5%, fruits and vegetables 8.0%). *Major export destinations:* Germany 28.6%; France 14.3%.

Transport and communications

Transport. Railroads: none. Roads (1995): total length 5 mi, 8 km (paved, none). Vehicles[16]: passenger cars, n.a.; trucks and buses, n.a. Merchant marine (1992): vessels (100 gross tons and over) 6; total deadweight tonnage 16,005. Air transport (1977): passenger arrivals (Funafuti) 1,443; cargo, n.a.; airports (1996) with scheduled flights 1.
Communications. Daily newspapers (1995): none; 1 government newspaper published fortnightly; total circulation 260; circulation per 1,000 population 28. Radio (1995): total number of receivers 3,000 (1 per 3.1 persons). Television: none. Telephones (main lines; 1993): 120 (1 per 77 persons).

Education and health

Education (1990)

	schools	teachers	students	student/ teacher ratio
Primary (age 5–11)	9	72	1,485	20.6
Secondary (age 12–18)	1	21	314	15.0
Vocational	1	10	31	3.1
Higher	—	—	—	—

Educational attainment (1979). Percentage of population age 25 and over having: no formal schooling 0.4%; primary education 93.0%; secondary 6.1%; higher 0.5%. *Literacy* (1990): total population literate in Tuvaluan 8,593 (95.0%); literacy in English estimated at 45.0%.
Health (1993): physicians 8 (1 per 1,152 persons); hospital beds (1990) 30 (1 per 302 persons); infant mortality rate per 1,000 live births (1995): 27.9.
Food: daily per capita caloric intake, n.a.

Military

Total active duty personnel (1987): there is a police force numbering 32.

---

[1]The value of the Tuvalu dollar is pegged to the value of the Australian dollar, which is also legal currency in Tuvalu. [2]Local government councils have been established on all islands except Niulakita. [3]A recent survey puts the area at 9.4 sq mi (24.4 sq km). [4]De facto population. [5]1991 census total is 9,043. [6]The Tuvalu Trust Fund was capitalized in 1987 with $A 27,700,000 to replace recurrent grant aid from the United Kingdom; the fund was valued at $A 36,000,000 in late 1991. [7]Figure includes $A 5,200,000 of capital expenditures, paid for primarily by foreign-aid contributions that are not part of recurrent revenue. [8]At 1988 factor cost. [9]Including cottage industry. [10]Because of poor soil quality, only limited subsistence agriculture is possible on the islands. [11]Other livestock include goats. [12]Research into the mineral potential of Tuvalu's maritime exclusive economic zone (289,500 sq mi [750,000 sq km] of the Pacific Ocean) is currently being conducted by the South Pacific Geo-Science Commission. [13]Average minimum wage. [14]Weights of consumer price index components. [15]Capable of supporting coconut palms, pandanus, and breadfruit. [16]There are several cars, tractors, trailers, and light trucks on Funafuti; a few motorcycles are in use on most islands.

Uganda

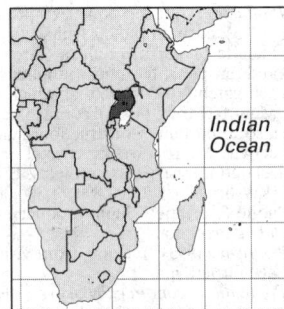

Official name: Republic of Uganda.
Form of government: republic with one
legislative house (National Assembly
[276[1]])[2].
Head of state and government:
President.
Capital: Kampala.
Official language: English.
Official religion: none.
Monetary unit: 1 Uganda
shilling (U Sh) = 100 cents;
valuation (Oct. 11, 1996)
1 U.S.$ = U Sh 1,080;
1 £ = U Sh 1,701.

Area and population

Regions Districts	Capitals	area sq mi	area sq km	population 1991 census[3]
Central				
Kalangala	...	...	...	16,400
Kampala	Kampala	70	180	773,500
Kiboga	...	...	...	140,800
Luwero	Luwero	3,550	9,200	449,200
Masaka	Kasawa Bukoto	6,310	16,330	831,300
Mpigi	Mpigi	2,400	6,220	915,400
Mubende	Bageza	3,980	10,310	497,500
Mukono	Kawuga Mukono	5,500	14,240	816,200
Rakai	Byakabanda	1,920	4,970	382,000
Eastern				
Iganga	Bulamogi	5,060	13,110	944,000
Jinja	Jinja	280	730	284,900
Kamuli	Namwendwa	1,680	4,350	480,700
Kapchorwa	Kaptanya	670	1,740	116,300
Kumi	Kumi	1,100	2,860	237,000
Mbale	Bunkoko	980	2,550	706,600
Pallisa	...	...	...	355,000
Soroti	Soroti	3,880	10,060	430,900
Tororo	Sukulu	1,780	4,550	554,000
Northern				
Apac	Apac	2,510	6,490	460,700
Arua	Olaki	3,020	7,830	624,600
Gulu	Bungatira	4,530	11,740	338,700
Kitgum	Labongo	8,230	16,140	350,300
Kotido	Kotido	5,100	13,210	190,700
Lira	Lira	2,800	7,250	498,300
Moroto	Katikekile	5,450	14,110	171,500
Moyo	Moyo	1,930	5,010	178,500
Nebbi	Nebbi	1,120	2,890	315,900
Western				
Bundibugyo	Busaru	900	2,340	116,000
Bushenyi	Bumbaire	2,080	5,400	734,800
Hoima	Hoima	3,820	9,900	197,800
Kabale	Rubale	960	2,490	412,800
Kabarole	Karambe	3,230	8,360	741,400
Kasese	Rukoki	1,240	3,200	343,000
Kibaale	...	...	...	219,300
Kisoro	...	...	...	184,900
Masindi	Nyangeya	3,720	9,640	253,500
Mbarara	Kakika	4,190	10,840	929,600
Rukungiri	Kagunga	1,060	2,750	388,000
TOTAL LAND AREA		76,080	197,040	
INLAND WATER[4]		16,990	44,000	
TOTAL		93,070[5]	241,040[5]	16,582,700[5]

Demography

Population (1996): 19,136,000.
Density (1996)[6]: persons per sq mi 251.5, persons per sq km 97.1.
Urban-rural (1995): urban 12.5%; rural 87.5%.
Sex distribution (1995): male 49.63%; female 50.37%.
Age breakdown (1995): under 15, 48.8%; 15–29, 26.5%; 30–44, 14.0%; 45–59,
6.9%; 60–74, 3.2%; 75 and over, 0.6%.
Population projection: (2000) 21,168,000; (2010) 27,244,000.
Doubling time: 18 years.
Ethnic composition (1983): Ganda 17.8%; Teso 8.9%; Nkole 8.2%; Soga
8.2%; Gisu 7.2%; Chiga 6.8%; Lango 6.0%; Rwanda 5.8%; other 31.1%.
Religious affiliation (1980): Roman Catholic 49.6%; Protestant 28.7%; Muslim
6.6%; other 15.1%.
Major cities (1991): Kampala 773,000; Jinja 61,000; Mbale 54,000.

Vital statistics

Birth rate per 1,000 population (1990–95): 51.8 (world avg. 25.0).
Death rate per 1,000 population (1990–95): 13.6 (world avg. 9.3).
Natural increase rate per 1,000 population (1990–95): 38.2 (world avg. 15.7).
Total fertility rate (avg. births per childbearing woman; 1993): 7.2.
Life expectancy at birth (1990–95): male 51.4 years; female 54.7 years.

National economy

Budget (1994–95). Revenue: U Sh 780,383,000,000 (taxes 62.3%, of which
customs duties 22.6%, sales taxes 16.5%, income taxes 9.9%; grants 32.5%).
Expenditures: U Sh 905,792,000,000 (current expenditures 54.4%, of which
security 13.9%, education 6.4%, health 2.4%; capital expenditures 44.3%).
Public debt (external, outstanding; 1994): U.S.$2,955,000,000.
Tourism (1994): receipts from visitors U.S.$61,000,000; expenditures by na-
tionals abroad U.S.$78,000,000.
Land use (1994): forest 31.5%; pasture 9.1%; agriculture 34.0%; other 25.4%.
Population economically active (1991): total 8,365,000; activity rate of total
population 49.6% (participation rates: ages 15–64, 78.9%[7]; female 35.2%).

Price index (1990 = 100)

	1989	1990	1991	1992	1993	1994	1995
Consumer price index	75.0	100.0	128.0	195.0	207.0	227.0	247.0

Production (metric tons except as noted). Agriculture, forestry, fishing (1995):
bananas 10,100,000, cassava 2,625,000, sweet potatoes 2,234,000, sugarcane
1,150,000, corn (maize) 950,000, millet 643,000, sorghum 398,000, potatoes
386,000, coffee 220,000, peanuts (groundnuts) 143,000, rice 80,000; livestock
(number of live animals) 5,200,000 cattle, 3,500,000 goats, 1,900,000 sheep;
roundwood (1995) 19,199,000 cu m; fish catch (1995) 217,300. Mining and
quarrying (1993): tungsten (wolfram) 60.0; tin ore 30.0; gold 57,900 troy
oz. Manufacturing (1993): cement 52,000; sugar 49,300; soap 47,600; metal
products 14,300; footwear 326,000 pairs; beer 239,000 hectolitres. Energy
production (consumption): electricity (kW-hr; 1994) 795,000,000 (681,000,-
000); petroleum products (metric tons; 1992) none (319,000).
Gross national product (1994): U.S.$3,718,000,000 (U.S.$200 per capita).

Structure of gross domestic product and labour force

	1994–95 in value U Sh '000,000	1994–95 % of total value	1991 labour force	1991 % of labour force
Agriculture	2,406,445	49.6	6,724,000	80.4
Mining	12,974	0.3	}	
Manufacturing	310,570	6.4	478,000	5.7
Construction	274,135	5.6	}	
Public utilities	60,672	1.2		
Transp. and commun.	187,463	3.9	}	
Trade[8]	610,697	12.6		
Finance	296,202	6.1	1,163,000	13.9
Pub. admin., defense	} 512,916	10.6		
Services				
Other	181,939	3.7	...	...
TOTAL	4,854,011[5]	100.0	8,365,000	100.0

Household size. Average household size (1983) 4.8; income per household:
n.a.; expenditure (1989–90)[9]: food 57.1%, rent, education, and health 15.7%,
fuel and lighting 7.3%, transportation 5.9%, clothing 5.5%.

Foreign trade

Balance of trade (current prices)

	1990	1991	1992	1993	1994	1995
U.S.$'000,000	−374.7	−369.6	−278.6	−416.1	−463.8	−504.1
% of total	47.2%	51.3%	44.7%	57.0%	47.7%	31.9%

Imports (1994–95): U.S.$1,041,000,000 (1993; machinery and transport equip-
ment 35.6%, basic manufactures 10.5%, food and live animals 7.6%, chemicals 5.7%). *Major import sources* (1992): Kenya 22.6%; U.K. 10.0%; Japan
9.8%; Germany 5.5%; U.S. 4.8%.
Exports (1994): U.S.$536,900,000 (unroasted coffee 76.0%, tea 1.7%, cotton
0.3%). *Major export destinations* (1992): U.K. 20.7%; Belgium-Luxembourg
12.3%; Spain 9.2%; U.S. 8.1%; France 6.4%; Germany 4.3%.

Transport and communications

Transport. Railroads (1993): route length 1,241 km; passenger-km 330,000,-
000[10]; metric ton-km cargo 135,000,000. Roads (1995): total length 26,800
km (paved 7.7%). Vehicles (1995): passenger cars 24,400; trucks and buses
25,246[11]. Merchant marine (1992): vessels (100 gross tons and over) 2; total
deadweight tonnage 8,600[12]. Air transport (1994)[13]: passenger-km 52,117,-
000; metric ton-km cargo 709,000; airports (1996) 1.
Communications. Daily newspapers (1993): total number 6; total circulation
80,000; circulation per 1,000 population 3.8. Radio (1993): 3,500,000 receivers (1 per 5.1 persons). Television (1995): 115,000 receivers (1 per 171
persons). Telephones (main lines; 1995): 43,039 (1 per 458 persons).

Education and health

Education (1994)

	schools	teachers	students	student/ teacher ratio
Primary (age 5–11)	8,431[11]	102,126	2,496,139	24.4
Secondary (age 12–15)	774[14]	16,245	244,248	15.0
Voc., teacher tr.	136[14]	2,766	46,238	16.7
Higher	9[14]	941	8,966	9.5

Educational attainment (1991). Percentage of population age 25 and over
having: no formal schooling or less than one full year 46.9%; primary
education 42.1%; secondary 10.5%; higher 0.5%. *Literacy* (1991): population
age 15 and over literate 4,927,000 (56.1%); males literate 2,892,000 (68.2%);
females literate 2,035,000 (40.3%).
Health (1989): physicians 774 (1 per 20,720 persons); hospital beds 20,136 (1
per 817 persons); infant mortality rate (1990–95) 115.4.
Food (1992): daily per capita caloric intake 2,159 (vegetable products 93%,
animal products 7%); 93% of FAO recommended minimum requirement.

Military

Total active duty personnel (1996): 50,000 (army 97.6%, navy 0.8%, air force
1.6%). *Military expenditure as percentage of GNP* (1994): 1.5% (world 3.0%);
per capita U.S.$3.

[1]62 of 276 elected seats are allocated to people with disabilities, women, workers, the
army, and the young. [2]New constitution promulgated on Oct. 8, 1995. [3]Preliminary.
[4]Includes swamps; excludes 11,950 sq mi (30,960 sq km) of Uganda's Lake Victoria
territorial waters. [5]Detail does not add to total given because of rounding. [6]Based
on land area. [7]1985. [8]Includes hotels. [9]Kampala and Entebbe only. [10]1991. [11]1993.
[12]1988. [13]Uganda Airlines only. [14]1989.

Ukraine

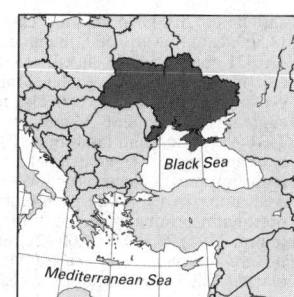

Official name: Ukrayina (Ukraine).
Form of government: unitary multiparty republic with a single legislative body (Supreme Council [450]).
Head of state: President.
Head of government: Prime Minister.
Capital: Kiev (Kyyiv).
Official language: Ukrainian.
Official religion: none.
Monetary unit: hryvnia (pl. hryvny)[1]; (no decimal unit); valuation (Oct. 11, 1996) free rate, 1 U.S.$ = 1.77 hryvny; 1 £ = 2.78 hryvny.

Area and population

Autonomous republic	Capitals	area sq mi	area sq km	population 1996[2] estimate
Crimea (Krym)	Simferopol	10,400[3]	27,000[3]	2,205,600
Cities				
Kiev	—	4	4	2,638,700
Sevastopol	—	3	3	406,900
Provinces				
Cherkasy	Cherkasy	8,100	20,900	1,504,600
Chernihiv	Chernihiv	12,300	31,900	1,349,500
Chernivtsi	Chernivtsi	3,100	8,100	943,600
Dnipropetrovsk	Dnipropetrovsk	12,300	31,900	3,852,000
Donetsk	Donetsk	10,200	26,500	5,198,500
Ivano-Frankivsk	Ivano-Frankivsk	5,400	13,900	1,467,100
Kharkiv	Kharkiv	12,100	31,400	3,088,400
Kherson	Kherson	11,000	28,500	1,265,700
Khmelnytsky	Khmelnytsky	8,000	20,600	1,508,800
Kirovohrad	Kirovohrad	9,500	24,600	1,224,800
Kyyiv (Kiev)	Kiev	11,200[4]	28,900[4]	1,895,800
Luhansk	Luhansk	10,300	26,700	2,788,500
Lviv	Lviv	8,400	21,800	2,761,500
Mykolayiv	Mykolayiv	9,500	24,600	1,343,300
Odessa	Odessa	12,900	33,300	2,586,500
Poltava	Poltava	11,100	28,800	1,739,100
Rivne	Rivne	7,800	20,100	1,194,200
Sumy	Sumy	9,200	23,800	1,397,900
Ternopil	Ternopil	5,300	13,800	1,175,400
Vinnytsya	Vinnytsya	10,200	26,500	1,876,000
Volyn	Volodymyr-Volynsky	7,800	20,200	1,075,200
Zakarpatska	Uzhhorod	4,900	12,800	1,288,100
Zaporizhzhya	Zaporizhzhya	10,500	27,200	2,077,800
Zhytomyr	Zhytomyr	11,600	29,900	1,480,600
TOTAL		233,100	603,700	51,334,100

Demography

Population (1996): 51,273,000.
Density (1996): persons per sq mi 221.8, persons per sq km 85.6.
Urban-rural (1996): urban 67.9%; rural 32.1%.
Sex distribution (1994): male 46.45%; female 53.55%.
Age breakdown (1995): under 15, 19.5%; 15–29, 20.6%; 30–44, 22.3%; 45–59, 18.2%; 60–69, 10.3%; 70 and over, 9.1%.
Population projection: (2000) 50,785,000; (2010) 50,320,000.
Ethnic composition (1991): Ukrainian 72.6%; Russian 22.2%; Belarusian 0.9%; Jewish 0.7%; Moldovan 0.6%; Tatar 0.4%; other 2.6%.
Religious affiliation: believers are predominantly Ukrainian Orthodox; there is a Ukrainian Catholic minority.
Major cities (1996): Kiev 2,630,200; Kharkiv 1,555,100; Dnipropetrovsk 1,147,200; Donetsk 1,088,200; Odessa 1,046,400.

Vital statistics

Birth rate per 1,000 population (1995): 9.6 (world avg. 25.0); (1993) legitimate 87.0%; illegitimate 13.0%.
Death rate per 1,000 population (1995): 15.4 (world avg. 9.3).
Natural increase rate per 1,000 population (1995): −5.8 (world avg. 15.7).
Total fertility rate (avg. births per childbearing woman; 1994): 1.5.
Marriage rate per 1,000 population (1995): 8.4.
Divorce rate per 1,000 population (1995): 3.8.
Life expectancy at birth (1994): male 62.0 years; female 73.0 years.
Major causes of death per 100,000 population (1993): circulatory diseases 783.0; neoplasms (cancers) 201.0; accidents 131.0; respiratory diseases 81.0; diseases of the digestive system (1992) 36.4; infectious diseases (1992) 13.1.

National economy

Budget (1995). Revenue: 20,922,000,000 hryvny (tax revenue 54.7%, of which corporate tax 23.1%, value-added tax 21.6%, income tax 7.7%, excise tax 1.9%, other 0.4%; nontax revenue 7.9%; unaccounted revenue 37.4%). Expenditures: 24,486,000,000 hryvny (social-cultural spending and education 39.7%; national economy 13.5%; defense 4.2%; expenditures relating to Chernobyl 3.9%; unaccounted expenditure 38.7%).
Public debt (external; 1994): U.S.$5,430,000,000.
Production (metric tons except as noted). Agriculture, forestry, fishing (1995): sugar beets 29,650,000, wheat 16,273,000, potatoes 14,279,000, barley 9,633,000, corn (maize) 3,392,000; livestock (number of live animals) 19,624,000 cattle, 13,946,000 pigs, 5,574,000 sheep and goats; roundwood (1993) 4,888,200 cu m; fish catch (1993) 371,343. Mining and quarrying (1994): iron ore 51,300,000; manganese 2,980,000. Manufacturing (value in '000 hryvny; 1994): metals 2,783,065; machinery 2,225,093; processed foods 1,285,328; chemicals 898,635. Construction (1995): residential 8,028,000 sq m. Energy production (consumption): electricity (kW-hr; 1994) 209,100,000,000 (208,100,000,000);

coal (metric tons; 1994) 91,800,000 (94,267,000); crude petroleum (barrels; 1994) 30,786,000 (137,900,000); petroleum products 10,678,000 (12,180,000); natural gas (cu m; 1994) 18,600,000,000 (18,800,000,000).
Gross national product (1994)[5]: U.S.$80,921,000,000 (U.S.$1,570 per capita).

Structure of gross domestic product and labour force

	1993 in value '000,000 hryvny	1993 % of total value	1995 labour force	1995 % of labour force
Agriculture	31,939	21.5	5,300,000	22.4
Mining	} 45,826	} 30.9	...	...
Manufacturing			} 5,800,000	} 24.5
Public utilities	1,303	0.9		
Construction	10,282	6.9	1,500,000	6.3
Transp. and commun.	17,425	11.8	1,400,000	5.9
Trade	16,482	11.1	1,600,000	6.8
Finance	17,784	12.0	200,000	0.8
Pub. admin., defense	5,304	3.6	700,000	3.0
Services	13,182	8.9	4,900,000	20.7
Other	−11,254[6]	−7.6[6]	2,427,000[7]	9.7[7]
TOTAL	148,273	100.0	23,627,000	100.0[8]

Population economically active (1995): total 23,627,000; activity rate of total population 46.0% (1993; participation rates: ages 16–59 [male], 16–54 [female] 82.4%; female [1994] 51.0%; unemployed 0.5%).

Price and earnings indexes (1992 = 100)

	1992	1993	1994	1995
Consumer price index	100.0	4,835	47,924	228,454
Monthly earnings index	100.0	2,432	21,561	115,180

Land use (1994): forest 17.1%; pasture 12.4%; agriculture 57.0%; other 13.5%.
Household income and expenditure (1992). Average household size 3.0; income per household 12,825 karbovantsy[1, 5]; sources of income (1995): wages and salaries 66.4%, sales of agricultural products 9.3%, subsidies 6.9%, pensions 6.5%, remuneration from abroad 5.3%, other 5.6%; expenditures (1995): food and nonalcoholic beverages 43.1%, consumer goods 27.5%, services 7.2%, housing 6.7%, taxes 6.2%, other 9.3%.

Foreign trade

Balance of trade (current prices)

	1992	1993	1994	1995
U.S.$'000,000	−622	−2,519	−2,360	−2,105
% of total	2.7%	9.0%	9.1%	7.9%

Imports (1995): U.S.$11,379,400,000 (mineral commodities 55.2%; machinery 14.8%; chemicals 5.4%; nonferrous metals 4.8%; plastics, rubber, and products 3.6%). *Major import sources:* Russia 51.2%; Turkmenistan 7.4%; Germany 5.3%; U.S. 2.8%.
Exports (1995): U.S.$11,566,700,000 (ferrous metals 36.2%; machinery 11.8%; mineral commodities 10.6%; chemicals 9.7%; food 8.5%). *Major export destinations:* Russia 43.5%; U.S. 4.8%; Germany 4.1%; Belarus 3.7%.

Transport and communications

Transport. Railroads (1994): length 22,700 km; passenger-km 70,900,000,000; metric ton-km cargo 200,400,000,000. Roads (1995): total length 172,257 km (paved 94.8%). Vehicles (1995): passenger cars 4,510,000. Air transport (1994): passenger-km 2,900,000,000; metric ton-km cargo 100,000,000; airports (1996) with scheduled flights 11.
Communications (1992). Daily newspapers: total number 90; total circulation 6,083,000; circulation per 1,000 population 52. Radio (1993): 41,700,000 receivers (1 per 1.3 persons). Television (1993): 17,500,000 receivers (1 per 3.0 persons). Telephones (main lines; 1993): 2,225,000 (1 per 6.7 persons).

Education and health

Education (1994–95)

	schools	teachers	students	student/teacher ratio
Primary (age 6–13)	} 22,300	576,000	7,125,000	12.4
Secondary (age 14–17)				
Voc., teacher tr.	778	...	618,000	...
Higher	232	...	888,500	...

Educational attainment (1989). Percentage of population age 15 and over having: some primary education 6.8%; completed primary 13.8%; some secondary 18.4%; completed secondary 31.1%; some postsecondary 19.5%; higher 10.4%. *Literacy* (1989): percentage of total population age 15 and over literate 98.4%; males literate 99.5%; females literate 97.4%.
Health (1995): physicians 230,000 (1 per 224 persons); hospital beds 639,000 (1 per 81 persons); infant mortality rate per 1,000 live births 14.4.

Military

Total active duty personnel (1996): 400,800[9] (army 46.9%, navy 4.0%, air force 30.9%, other 18.2%). *Military expenditure as percentage of GNP* (1994) 0.6% (world 3.0%); per capita expenditure U.S.$18. The Black Sea Fleet of the former U.S.S.R. remained to be divided among Russia, Ukraine, and Georgia at year-end 1996.

[1]On Sept. 2, 1996, the karbovanets, a transitional currency, was replaced by the hryvnia at a 100,000-to-1 ratio. Both currencies circulated in parallel until Sept. 16, 1996, when the hryvnia became the sole official currency. [2]January 1. [3]Crimea includes area of Sevastopol. [4]Kyyiv includes area of Kiev (city). [5]Ruble-area GNP and exchange-rate data are very speculative. [6]Less imputed bank service charges, net indirect taxes, and taxes on production. [7]Includes 126,900 unemployed. [8]Detail does not add to total given because of rounding. [9]Includes 73,000 in central staffs.

United Arab Emirates

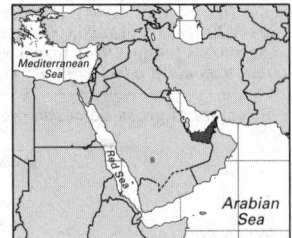

Official name: Al-Imārāt al-'Arabīyah al-Muttaḥidah (United Arab Emirates).
Form of government: federation of seven emirates with one appointive advisory body (Federal National Council [40[1]]).
Chief of state: President.
Head of government: Prime Minister.
Capital: Abu Dhabi.
Official language: Arabic.
Official religion: Islam.
Monetary unit: 1 U.A.E. dirham (Dh) = 100 fils; valuation (Oct. 11, 1996) 1 U.S.$ = Dh 3.67; 1 £ = Dh 5.78.

Area and population

Emirates	Capitals	area sq mi	area sq km	population 1993 census
Abu Dhabi (Abū Ẓaby)	Abu Dhabi	28,210[2]	73,060[2]	871,000
'Ajmān (Ajman)	'Ajmān	100	260	83,000
Dubayy (Dubai)	Dubayy	1,510	3,900	548,000
Al-Fujayrah (Fujairah)	Al-Fujayrah	500	1,300	68,000
Ra's al-Khaymah (Ras al-Khaimah)	Ra's al-Khaymah	660	1,700	148,000
Ash-Shāriqah (Sharjah)	Ash-Shāriqah	1,000	2,600	342,000
Umm al-Qaywayn (Umm al-Qaiwain)	Umm al-Qaywayn	300	780	23,000
TOTAL		32,280	83,600	2,083,000

Demography

Population (1996): 2,500,000.
Density (1996): persons per sq mi 77.4, persons per sq km 29.9.
Urban-rural (1995): urban 84.0%; rural 16.0%.
Sex distribution (1994): male 59.66%; female 40.34%.
Age breakdown (1994): under 15, 34.3%; 15–29, 25.3%; 30–44, 30.6%; 45–59, 7.8%; 60–74, 1.5%; 75 and over, 0.5%.
Population projection: (2000) 2,707,000; (2010) 3,212,000.
Doubling time: 32 years.
Ethnic composition (1993): expatriates of Bangladesh, India, Pakistan, and Sri Lanka 45.0%; Arabs 25.0%, of which non-UAE Arabs (primarily Egyptians) 13.0%, UAE Arabs 12.0%; Iranians 17.0%; other Asians and Africans 8.0%; Europeans and North Americans 5.0%.
Religious affiliation (1995): Muslim 96.0% (Sunnī 80.0%, Shī'ī 16.0%); other (mostly Christian and Hindu) 4.0%.
Major cities (1989): Dubayy 585,189; Abu Dhabi 363,432; Al-'Ayn 176,411; Ash-Shāriqah 125,000[3]; Ra's al-Khaymah 42,000[3].

Vital statistics

Birth rate per 1,000 population (1994): 25.0 (world avg. 25.0); legitimate, n.a.; illegitimate, n.a.
Death rate per 1,000 population (1994): 3.4 (world avg. 9.3).
Natural increase rate per 1,000 population (1994): 21.6 (world avg. 15.7).
Total fertility rate (avg. births per childbearing woman; 1994): 3.5.
Marriage rate per 1,000 population (1991): 2.7.
Divorce rate per 1,000 population (1991): 1.1.
Life expectancy at birth (1994): male 69.2 years; female 75.2 years.
Major causes of death per 100,000 population (1989)[4]: accidents and poisoning 43.7; diseases of the circulatory system 34.3; malignant neoplasms (cancers) 13.7; respiratory diseases 8.1.

National economy

Budget (1994). Revenue: Dh 16,200,000,000 (1993; current [domestic] grants 83.5%; other sources 16.5%, of which nontax revenue 12.5%, tax revenue 4.0%). Expenditures: Dh 17,600,000,000 (1993; current expenditures 96.2%, of which defense 37.8%, education 16.7%, public safety 13.1%, health 7.4%, economic services 4.5%; cultural and religious affairs 3.3%).
Gross national product (at current market prices; 1993): U.S.$38,720,000,000 (U.S.$22,470 per capita).

Structure of gross domestic product and labour force

	1994 in value[5] Dh '000,000	1994 % of total value	1990 labour force	1990 % of labour force
Agriculture	3,400	2.5	43,100	6.3
Petroleum	45,040	33.4	10,000	1.5
Manufacturing	11,160	8.3	63,400	9.2
Construction	13,210	9.8	119,200	17.3
Public utilities	3,100	2.3	20,600	3.0
Transportation and communications	8,530	6.3	71,700	10.4
Trade	14,870	11.0	101,400	14.7
Finance, real estate	16,830	12.5	18,800	2.7
Pub. admin., defense	16,280	12.1 }	241,300	35.0
Services	4,460[6]	3.36 }		
Other	−2,080[7]	−1.5[7]	—	—
TOTAL	134,800	100.0	689,500	100.0[8]

Public debt (external, outstanding; 1995): U.S.$3,900,000,000.
Tourism (1995): total number of tourist arrivals 2,200,000.
Production (metric tons except as noted). Agriculture, forestry, fishing (1995): tomatoes 442,826, dates 236,965, eggplants 69,000, cabbages 59,843, lemons

and limes 20,008, pumpkins and squash 16,900, cucumbers and gherkins 13,500, cauliflower 9,500, mangoes 8,820; livestock (number of live animals) 920,931 goats, 356,486 sheep, 155,000 camels, 69,183 cattle, 11,000,000 chickens; fish catch (1993) 92,500. Mining and quarrying (1994): sulfur 144,000; gypsum 100,000; lime 45,000; also marble, shale for ceramic applications, and aggregate for cement. Manufacturing (1994): cement 3,800,000; aluminum 247,000; mutton and lamb meat 24,000; goat's milk 19,000; cow's milk 6,000; beef and veal 6,000; goat meat 5,000. Construction: n.a. Energy production (consumption): electricity (kW-hr; 1994) 18,870,000,000 (18,870,000,000); coal, none (n.a.); crude petroleum (barrels; 1994) 778,300,000 (73,722,000); petroleum products (metric tons; 1994) 14,710,000 (7,625,000); natural gas (cu m; 1994) 25,409,000,000 (21,160,000,000).
Population economically active (1992): total 733,500; activity rate of total population 36.9% (participation rates [1986]: ages 15–64, 76.7%; female 6.6%; unemployed, n.a.).

Price and earnings indexes (1990 = 100)

	1988	1989	1990	1991	1992	1993	1994
Consumer price index	95.0	98.8	100.0	105.5	102.1	118.0	117.8
Earnings index	...	...	...	...	...	...	...

Household income and expenditure. Average household size (1986) 6.8; income per household: n.a.; sources of income: n.a.; expenditure (1991): rent, fuel, and light 23.9%, food 22.7%, transportation and communications 14.1%, durable household goods 11.6%, education, recreation, and entertainment 8.6%.
Land use (1994): forested, virtually none; meadows and pastures 2.4%; agricultural and under permanent cultivation 0.5%; built-on, wasteland, and other 97.1%.

Foreign trade

Balance of trade (current prices)

	1989	1990	1991	1992	1993	1994
U.S.$'000,000	+6,917	+10,200	+9,341	+4,460	+903	−2,977
% of total	26.6%	30.8%	25.3%	11.3%	2.3%	6.6%

Imports (1994): U.S.$23,883,000,000 (1993; machinery and transport equipment 38.4%, basic manufactures 24.8%, food and live animals 9.7%, chemicals 6.1%, crude minerals 1.6%, mineral fuels 1.4%). *Major import sources:* Japan 10.4%; United Kingdom 7.8%; Germany 7.5%; United States 7.3%; Italy 6.7%; South Korea 5.4%; India 4.9%; Hong Kong 4.5%; China 4.0%; France 3.9%; Singapore 3.7%; Taiwan 2.8%; Malaysia 2.3%; Saudi Arabia 2.0%; The Netherlands 1.8%.
Exports (1994): U.S.$20,906,000,000 (1991; crude petroleum and refined petroleum 80.7%, machinery and transport equipment 6.0%, food and live animals 2.4%). *Major export destinations:* Japan 39.7%; India 5.3%; Oman 4.9%; South Korea 4.7%; Iran 4.6%; Singapore 3.8%; Thailand 2.7%; Hong Kong 2.4%; United States 2.1%; United Kingdom 1.5%; Pakistan 1.3%; Kenya 1.2%; Taiwan 1.1%; Turkey 1.0%.

Transport and communications

Transport. Railroads: none. Roads (1995): total length 2,952 mi, 4,750 km (paved 100%). Vehicles (1995): passenger cars 197,000; trucks and buses 49,150. Merchant marine (1992): vessels (100 gross tons and over) 276; total deadweight tonnage 1,491,728. Air transport (1995)[9]: passenger-mi 1,719,-000,000, passenger-km 2,766,000,000; short ton-mi cargo 77,400,000, metric ton-km cargo 113,000,000; airports (1996) with scheduled flights 6.
Communications. Daily newspapers (1992): total number 11; total circulation 335,000[10]; circulation per 1,000 population 189[10]. Radio (1995): total number of receivers 490,000 (1 per 4.9 persons). Television (1995): total number of receivers 170,000 (1 per 14.0 persons). Telephones (main lines; 1993): 623,800 (1 per 2.8 persons).

Education and health

Education (1993–94)

	schools	teachers	students	student/ teacher ratio
Primary (age 6–11) }	354[11]	14,754	251,182	17.0
Secondary (age 12–18) }		11,637	145,143 }	12.6
Vocational	9[12] }		1,143 }	
Higher	1	510[13]	9,793[13]	19.2[13]

Educational attainment (1975). Percentage of population age 25 and over having: no formal schooling 72.2%; primary education 5.2%; secondary 16.6%; higher 6.0%. *Literacy* (1995): total population age 15 and over literate 79.2%; males literate 78.9%; females literate 79.8%.
Health (1993): physicians 2,523 (1 per 720 persons); hospital beds 6,118 (1 per 297 persons); infant mortality rate per 1,000 live births (1994) 18.2.
Food (1992): daily per capita caloric intake 3,384 (vegetable products 75%, animal products 25%); 140% of FAO recommended minimum requirement.

Military

Total active duty personnel (1996): 64,500 (army 91.5%, navy 2.3%, air force 6.2%). *Military expenditure as percentage of GDP* (1994): 5.7% (world 3.0%); per capita expenditure U.S.$1,149.

---

[1]All appointed seats. [2]Approximate, based on reported total and on reported partial areas for smaller emirates. [3]1980. [4]Registered; Abu Dhabi Emirate only. [5]At factor cost. [6]Services include domestic help. [7]Less imputed bank service charges. [8]Detail does not add to total given because of rounding. [9]One-fourth apportionment of international flights of Gulf Air. [10]Partial circulation only. [11]1987–88. [12]1985–86. [13]1992–93.

United Kingdom

Official name: United Kingdom of Great Britain and Northern Ireland.
Form of government: constitutional monarchy with two legislative houses (House of Lords [1,194]; House of Commons [651]).
Chief of state: Sovereign.
Head of government: Prime Minister.
Capital: London.
Official language: English.
Official religion: Churches of England and Scotland "established" (protected by the state, but not "official") in their respective countries; no established church in Northern Ireland or Wales.
Monetary unit: 1 pound sterling (£) = 100 new pence; valuation (Oct. 11, 1996) 1 £ = U.S.$1.58; 1 U.S.$ = £0.63.

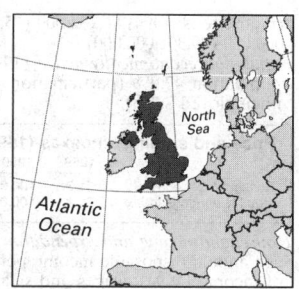

Area and population		area		population
		sq mi	sq km	1994 estimate
Countries	**Capitals**			
England	London	50,363	130,439	48,707,500[1]
Counties				
Avon	Bristol	520	1,346	978,700
Bedfordshire	Bedford	477	1,235	543,100
Berkshire	Reading	486	1,259	769,200
Buckinghamshire	Aylesbury	727	1,883	658,400
Cambridgeshire	Cambridge	1,316	3,409	686,900
Cheshire	Chester	899	2,329	975,600
Cleveland	Middlesbrough	225	583	560,100
Cornwall[2]	Truro	1,376	3,564	479,600
Cumbria	Carlisle	2,629	6,810	490,200
Derbyshire	Matlock	1,016	2,631	954,100
Devon	Exeter	2,591	6,711	1,053,400
Dorset	Dorchester	1,025	2,654	673,000
Durham	Durham	941	2,436	607,800
East Sussex	Lewes	693	1,795	726,500
Essex	Chelmsford	1,418	3,672	1,569,900
Gloucestershire	Gloucester	1,020	2,643	549,500
Greater London[3]	London	610	1,579	6,967,500
Greater Manchester[3]	Manchester	497	1,287	2,578,000
Hampshire	Winchester	1,458	3,777	1,605,700
Hereford & Worcester	Worcester	1,516	3,927	699,900
Hertfordshire	Hertford	631	1,634	1,005,400
Humberside	Hull	1,356	3,512	889,500
Isle of Wight	Newport	147	381	124,600
Kent	Maidstone	1,441	3,731	1,546,300
Lancashire	Preston	1,183	3,064	1,424,000
Leicestershire	Leicester	986	2,553	916,900
Lincolnshire	Lincoln	2,284	5,915	605,600
Merseyside[3]	Liverpool	252	652	1,434,400
Norfolk	Norwich	2,073	5,368	768,500
North Yorkshire	Northallerton	3,208	8,309	726,100
Northamptonshire	Northampton	914	2,367	594,800
Northumberland	Newcastle upon Tyne	1,943	5,032	307,700
Nottinghamshire	Nottingham	836	2,164	1,030,900
Oxfordshire	Oxford	1,007	2,608	590,200
Shropshire	Shrewsbury	1,347	3,490	416,500
Somerset	Taunton	1,332	3,451	477,900
South Yorkshire[3]	Barnsley	602	1,560	1,305,400
Staffordshire	Stafford	1,049	2,716	1,054,400
Suffolk	Ipswich	1,466	3,797	649,500
Surrey	Kingston upon Thames	648	1,679	1,041,200
Tyne and Wear[3]	Newcastle upon Tyne	208	540	1,134,000
Warwickshire	Warwick	765	1,981	496,300
West Midlands[3]	Birmingham	347	899	2,627,800
West Sussex	Chichester	768	1,989	722,100
West Yorkshire[3]	Wakefield	787	2,039	2,104,000
Wiltshire	Trowbridge	1,344	3,480	586,300
Northern Ireland[4]	Belfast	5,452	14,120	1,641,700
Scotland	Edinburgh	30,418	78,783	5,132,400
Regions				
Borders	Newton Saint Boswells	1,814	4,698	105,700
Central	Stirling	1,042	2,700	273,400
Dumfries and Galloway	Dumfries	2,481	6,425	147,800
Fife	Glenrothes	509	1,319	352,100
Grampian	Aberdeen	3,379	8,752	532,500
Highland	Inverness	10,092	26,137	207,500
Lothian	Edinburgh	683	1,770	758,600
Strathclyde	Glasgow	5,318	13,773	2,287,800
Tayside	Dundee	2,951	7,643	395,000
Island areas[5] (TOTAL)	—	2,149	5,566	72,000
Wales	Cardiff	8,019	20,768	2,913,000[1]
Counties				
Clwyd	Mold	937	2,427	417,400
Dyfed	Carmarthen	2,227	5,768	352,900
Gwent	Newport	531	1,376	452,200
Gwynedd	Caernarvon	1,494	3,869	240,300
Mid Glamorgan	Cardiff	393	1,018	544,500
Powys	Llandrindod Wells	1,960	5,077	120,200
South Glamorgan	Cardiff	161	416	414,600
West Glamorgan	Swansea	316	817	371,000
TOTAL		94,251	244,110	58,394,600

Demography

Population (1996): 58,784,000.
Density (1996): persons per sq mi 623.7, persons per sq km 240.8.
Urban-rural (1995): urban 89.5%; rural 10.5%.
Sex distribution (1996): male 49.09%; female 50.91%.
Age breakdown (1996): under 15, 19.5%; 15–29, 20.1%; 30–44, 21.9%; 45–59, 18.0%; 60–74, 13.3%; 75 and over, 7.2%.

Population projection: (2000) 59,595,000; (2010) 61,127,000.
Doubling time: not applicable; doubling time exceeds 100 years.
Ethnic composition (1991)[6]: white 94.5%; Asian Indian 1.5%; Pakistani 0.9%; West Indian 0.8%; African 0.3%; Chinese 0.3%; Bangladeshi 0.2%; Arab 0.1%; other and not stated 1.8%.
Religious affiliation (religious participation of about 8,400,000 active members only; 1990): Christian *c.* 80%, of which Roman Catholic *c.* 21%, Anglican *c.* 20%, Presbyterian *c.* 14%, Methodist *c.* 5%, Baptist *c.* 3%; Muslim *c.* 11%; Sikh *c.* 4%; Hindu *c.* 2%; Jewish *c.* 1%; other *c.* 2%.
Major cities (1994): Greater London 6,967,500; Birmingham 1,008,400; Leeds 724,400; Glasgow 680,000; Sheffield 530,100; Bradford 481,700; Liverpool 474,000; Edinburgh 443,600; Manchester 431,100; Bristol 399,200.
Place of birth (1991): U.K. 93.2% (52,721,000); foreign-born 6.8%, of which India 1.5%, Ireland 1.1%, Caribbean 0.9%, Pakistan 0.9%, other 2.2%.
Mobility (1991[6]): Population living in the same residence as 1990: 90.1%; different residence, same country (of Great Britain) 8.1%; different residence, different country of Great Britain 1.2%; from outside Great Britain 0.6%.
Households (1990–91)[6, 7]: Average household size 2.5 (3.1); 1 person 26% (20%), 2 persons 34% (26%), 3 persons 17% (16%), 4 persons 16% (17%), 5 persons 6% (10%), 6 or more persons 2% (11%). Family households (1987): 17,836,500 (77.4%), nonfamily 5,208,500 (22.6%, of which 1-person 9.9%).
Immigration (1994): permanent residents 253,000, from Australia 7.5%, United States 5.9%, Bangladesh, India, and Sri Lanka 4.0%, New Zealand 3.2%, South Africa 3.2%, Pakistan 2.4%.

Vital statistics

Birth rate per 1,000 population (1994): 12.9 (world avg. 25.0); legitimate 68.0%; illegitimate 32.0%.
Death rate per 1,000 population (1994): 10.7 (world avg. 9.3).
Natural increase rate per 1,000 population (1994): 2.2 (world avg. 15.7).
Total fertility rate (avg. births per childbearing woman; 1994): 1.7.
Marriage rate per 1,000 population (1993): 5.9.
Divorce rate per 1,000 population (1993[6]): 3.1.
Life expectancy at birth (1996): male 74.4 years; female 79.7 years.
Major causes of death per 100,000 population (1993): diseases of the circulatory system 507.3, of which ischemic heart disease 288.0, cerebrovascular disease 122.5; malignant neoplasms (cancers) 278.0; diseases of the respiratory system 175.3, of which pneumonia 104.7; diseases of the digestive system 36.1; diseases of the endocrine system 15.1, of which diabetes mellitus 11.7; diseases of the genitourinary system 13.5; suicide 7.4.

Social indicators

Educational attainment (1981). Percentage of population age 25 and over having: primary or secondary education only 89.7%; some postsecondary 4.8%; bachelor's or equivalent degree 4.9%; higher university degree 0.6%.

Distribution of disposable income (1994)				
percentage of household income by quintile				
1	2	3	4	5 (highest)
7.9	12.2	16.2	22.7	41.0

Quality of working life (1992). Average workweek (hours): male 43.3, female 30.2 (overtime [1986]: male 8.6%, female 2.1%). Annual rate per 1,000 workers for: injury or accident 752.6; industrial diseases 1.3[8, 9]; death 1.5. Proportion of labour force (employed persons) insured for damages or income loss resulting from: injury 100%; permanent disability 100%; death 100%. Average days lost to labour stoppages per 1,000 employee workdays 1993: 0.1. Principal means of transport to work (1991; London only): public transportation 81%, private automobile 15%, motor or pedal cycle 2%, other 2%.
Access to services (1991)[6]. Proportion of households having access to: bath or shower 98.7%; toilet 99.8%; central heating 81.1%.
Social participation. Eligible voters participating in last national election (April 1992): 76.9%. Population age 16 and over participating in voluntary work (1987)[6]: 22%. Trade union membership in total workforce (1992) 32.0%.
Social deviance (1994)[6]. Offense rate per 100,000 population for: theft and handling stolen goods 4,921.5; burglary 2,378.4; violence against the person 421.8; fraud and forgery 288.8; robbery 115.1; sexual offense 59.2. Incidence per 100,000 population of: registered drug addicts 36.5; suicide 7.9.
Leisure (1994). Favourite leisure activities (hours weekly): watching television 17.1; listening to radio 10.3; reading 8.8, of which books 3.8, newspapers 3.3; gardening 2.1.
Material well-being (1994). Households possessing: automobile 69.0%, telephone 91.1%, television receiver 98.3% (colour 95%), refrigerator 98.5%, central heating 84.3%, washing machine 89.0%, video recorder 76.4%.

National economy

Budget (1995–96). Revenue: £244,721,000,000 (income tax 37.4%, taxes on expenditures 17.6%, social security contributions 17.5%). Expenditures: £280,362,000,000 (social security benefits 26.3%, national health service 11.7%, defense 7.6%, debt interest 7.3%).
Production (metric tons except as noted). Agriculture, forestry, fishing (1995): wheat 14,400,000, sugar beets 8,125,000, barley 6,900,000, potatoes 6,445,000, rapeseed 1,330,000, cabbage 769,000, carrots 750,000, oats 600,000; livestock (number of live animals) 29,484,000 sheep, 11,868,000 cattle, 7,879,000 pigs; roundwood (1994) 8,155,000 cu m; fish catch (1993) 905,656. Mining and quarrying (1994): limestone 102,844,000; iron 2,000; tin 1,900; lead 1,800. Manufacturing (value added in £'000,000; 1995): food and beverages 17,364; paper, printing, and publishing 16,590; electrical and optical equipment 16,322; chemicals and chemical products 15,149; metals and metal products 14,218; transport equipment 12,321; machinery and equipment 11,015; textiles and leather products 7,097. Construction (value in £; 1994)[6]: res-

idential 7,417,000,000; nonresidential 12,521,000,000, of which commercial 5,648,000,000, industrial 2,489,000,000.
Gross national product (1994): U.S.$1,069,457,000,000 (U.S.$18,410 per capita).

Structure of gross domestic product and labour force

| | 1995 | | | |
	in value £'000,000	% of total value	labour force	% of labour force
Agriculture	11,896	2.0	313,000	1.1
Mining[10]	14,575	2.4	309,000	1.1
Manufacturing	131,658	21.8	3,942,000	14.1
Construction	31,815	5.3	838,000	3.0
Public utilities	15,787	2.6	171,000	0.6
Transp. and commun.	50,835	8.4	1,294,000	4.6
Trade	84,706	14.0	3,651,000	13.0
Finance	158,224	26.2	944,000	3.4
Pub. admin., defense	112,482	18.6	5,733,000	20.4
Services	23,255	3.8	4,958,000	17.7
Other	−30,974[11]	−5.1[11]	5,890,000[12]	21.0[12]
TOTAL	604,259	100.0	28,043,000	100.0

Total national debt (March 1994): £283,559,000,000.

Financial aggregates

	1990	1991	1992	1993	1994	1995	1996[13]
Exchange rate:							
U.S. dollar per £	1.78	1.77	1.76	1.50	1.53	1.58	1.54
SDRs per £	1.36	1.31	1.10	1.08	1.07	1.07	1.07
International reserves (U.S.$)							
Total (excl. gold; '000,000,000)	35.85	41.89	36.64	36.78	41.01	42.02	39.13[14]
SDRs ('000,000,000)	1.25	1.31	0.54	0.29	0.49	0.41	0.32
Reserve pos. in IMF ('000,000,000)	1.68	1.85	2.01	1.86	1.99	2.42	2.47
Foreign exchange ('000,000,000)	32.93	38.73	34.09	34.63	38.53	39.18	36.24[14]
Gold ('000,000 fine troy oz)	18.97	18.89	18.61	18.45	18.44	18.43	18.43[14]
% world reserves	2.0	2.0	2.0	2.0	2.0	2.0	2.0[14]
Interest and prices							
Central bank discount (%)	...	...	...	...	...	...	...
Govt. bond yield (%) long term	11.08	9.92	9.12	7.87	8.05	8.26	8.36
Industrial share prices (1990=100)	100.0	109.8	114.7	131.7	141.5	147.3	166.8
Balance of payments (U.S.$'000,000)							
Balance of visible trade,	−32,400	−17,990	−24,618	−20,570	−16,127	−18,266	...
Imports, f.o.b.	214,693	201,081	212,058	201,802	222,263	259,154	...
Exports, f.o.b.	182,293	183,091	187,440	181,232	206,136	240,888	...
Balance of invisibles	3,010	6,768	3,904	4,179	13,736	7,697	...
Balance of payments, current account	−29,390	−11,222	−20,714	−16,391	−2,391	−10,569	...

Manufacturing, mining, and construction enterprises (1992)

	no. of enter- prises[15]	no. of employees	annual wages as a % of avg. of all wages[16]	annual value added (£'000,000)
Manufacturing				
Food, beverages, and tobacco	8,916	564,000	103.0	15,616
Paper and paper products; printing and publishing	21,495	438,000	133.8	13,023
Mechanical engineering	23,322	521,000	108.4	12,491
Chemical engineering	3,137	278,000	118.1	11,894
Transport equipment	4,233	468,000	...	11,832
Electrical and data-processing equipment	9,644	504,000	96.8	11,389
Rubber and plastics	4,785	224,000	118.1	5,510
Clothing and footwear	11,207	258,000	85.6	3,405
Timber and wood products	13,794	186,000	98.1	3,137
Textiles	4,466	172,000	79.2	2,956
Metal manufacturing	1,188	112,000	102.8	2,943
Mineral-oil processing	123	13,000	118.1	1,434
Mining				
Extraction of coal, mineral oil, and natural gas	...	80,000	118.1	9,267
Extraction of minerals other than fuels	793	7,000	103.1	309
Construction	185,854	1,016,000	...	17,642

Land use (1994): forested 10.4%; meadows and pastures 45.9%; agricultural and under permanent cultivation 24.8%; other 18.9%.

Retail trade enterprises (1992)

	no. of enter- prises	no. of employees	weekly wage as a % of all wages	annual turnover (£'000,000)[17]
Food and grocery, of which	60,119	854,000	...	51,462
large grocery	71	579,000	...	40,837
other grocery	18,557	95,000	...	4,086
meats	12,149	58,000	...	2,523
Household goods, of which	45,532	299,000	...	20,881
electrical and musical goods	10,887	87,000	...	7,270
furniture	11,927	60,000	...	4,575
Drink, confectionery, and tobacco, of which	46,671	254,000	...	13,810
tobacco and confectionery	41,502	215,000	...	10,880
Clothing and footwear, of which	24,923	264,000	...	12,428
women's, girls', and infants' wear	13,624	102,000	...	4,771
footwear	3,098	67,000	...	2,589
men's and boys' wear	3,751	37,000	...	2,063
Pharmaceuticals	7,560	87,000	...	5,231
Mail order	129	33,000	...	4,076

Energy production (consumption): electricity (kW-hr; 1994) 325,383,000,000 (342,270,000,000); coal (metric tons; 1994) 47,717,000 (80,582,000); crude petroleum (barrels; 1994) 888,454,000 (629,354,000); petroleum products

(metric tons; 1994) 86,184,000 (75,021,000); natural gas (cu m; 1994) 76,680,-000,000 (79,391,000,000).
Population economically active (1995): total 28,043,000, activity rate of total population 47.9% (participation rates: ages 15–64, 76.2%[9]; female 45.9%; unemployed 8.2%).

Price and earnings indexes (1990 = 100)

	1989	1990	1991	1992	1993	1994	1995
Consumer price index	91.3	100.0	105.9	109.8	111.5	114.3	118.2
Monthly earnings index	91.1	100.0	108.0	114.6	118.5	123.3	...

Household income and expenditure (1993). Average household size 2.4; average annual disposable income per household £15,271 (U.S.$22,937); sources of income (1994): wages and salaries 64.4%, social security benefits 13.5%, dividends and interest 10.8%, income from self-employment 9.5%; expenditure (1994): food and beverages 22.1%, housing 16.4%, transport and vehicles 15.1%, household goods 8.0%, clothing 6.0%, energy 4.6%.
Tourism (1994): receipts from visitors U.S.$15,176,000,000; expenditures by nationals abroad U.S.$22,185,000,000.

Foreign trade

Balance of trade (current prices)

	1990	1991	1992	1993	1994	1995
£'000,000	−31,131	−17,990	−24,618	−20,570	−12,029	−10,621
% of total	7.8%	4.7%	6.2%	5.4%	4.3%	3.3%

Imports (1995): £168,335,000,000 (machinery and transport equipment 41.0%, of which electrical equipment 19.2%, road vehicles 10.8%; chemicals and chemical products 10.6%, of which plastics 2.8%, organic chemicals 2.8%; food and live animals 8.0%, of which vegetables and fruits 2.4%; meat and meat preparations 1.4%; paper and paperboard 3.1%; textile yarn and fabrics 2.9%; petroleum and petroleum products 2.8%; nonferrous metals 2.3%; iron and steel products 2.2%; beverages and tobacco 1.5%). *Major import sources:* Germany 15.5%; U.S. 12.0%; France 9.6%; The Netherlands 6.8%; Japan 5.7%; Italy 4.9%; Belgium-Luxembourg 4.7%; Ireland 4.2%; Switzerland 3.1%; Sweden 2.7%; Spain 1.5%.
Exports (1995): £153,761,000,000 (machinery and transport equipment 42.8%, of which electrical equipment 20.1%, road vehicles 7.7%; chemicals and chemical products 13.8%, of which organic chemicals 3.2%; petroleum and petroleum products 5.7%; food and live animals 4.6%; professional, scientific, and controlling instruments 3.9%; iron and steel products 2.8%). *Major export destinations:* Germany 13.1%; U.S. 11.7%; France 9.9%; The Netherlands 8.0%; Belgium-Luxembourg 5.4%; Italy 5.1%; Ireland 5.0%; Spain 3.9%; Sweden 2.7%; Japan 2.5%; Switzerland 1.8%.

Transport and communications

Transport. Railroads (1994–95)[18]: length 23,518 mi[19], 37,849 km[19]; passenger-mi 17,806,000,000, passenger-km 28,656,000,000; ton-mi cargo 8,073,000,000, metric ton-km cargo 13,764,000,000. Roads (1994): total length 241,804 mi, 389,147 km (paved 100%). Vehicles (1994)[6]: passenger cars 20,479,000; trucks and buses 2,753,000[9]. Merchant marine (1992): vessels (over 100 gross tons) 1,631; total deadweight tonnage 4,355,063. Air transport (1994): passenger-mi 60,582,000,000, passenger-km 97,498,000,000; short ton-mi cargo 2,017,152,000, metric ton-km cargo 2,944,992,000; airports (1996) 50.
Communications. Daily newspapers (1995): total number 104; total circulation 16,309,000; circulation per 1,000 population 278. Radio (1995): 70,000,000 receivers (1 per 0.8 person). Television (1994): 20,413,000 licenses (1 per 2.9 persons). Telephones (main lines; 1993): 28,680,900 receivers (1 per 2.0 persons).

Education and health

Education (1993–94)[20]

	schools	teachers	students	student/ teacher ratio
Primary (age 5–10)	23,673	225,500	4,997,700	22.2
Secondary (age 11–19)	4,496	228,400	3,587,500	15.7
Voc., teacher tr.	724[21]	93,000[22]	586,000[23]	...
Higher[24]	c. 90	34,497	470,565	13.6

Literacy (1990): total population literate, virtually 100%[25].
Health (1993)[6]: physicians 92,474 (1 per 629 persons); hospital beds 283,814 (1 per 205 persons); infant mortality rate (1994) 6.2.
Food (1992): daily per capita caloric intake 3,317 (vegetable products 68%, animal products 32%); 132% of FAO recommended minimum requirement.

Military

Total active duty personnel (1995): 236,900 (army 49.0%, navy 21.3%, air force 29.7%). *Military expenditure as percentage of GNP* (1994): 3.3% (world 3.0%); per capita expenditure U.S.$586.

[1]Detail does not add to total given because of rounding. [2]Includes separately administered Isles of Scilly (area 6 sq mi [16 sq km]; pop. 2,000). [3]Geographic entity only; since April 1, 1986, the administrative functions of the former metropolitan county councils have been dispersed among other local authorities. [4]Comprises 26 local government districts not shown separately. [5]Includes three separately administered island groups (Orkney 377 sq mi [976 sq km], pop. 19,810; Shetland 553 sq mi [1,432 sq km], pop. 22,880; Western Isles 1,119 sq mi [2,898 sq km], pop. 29,310). [6]Great Britain only. [7]Figures in parentheses are for Northern Ireland (1984). [8]Lung disease only. [9]1993. [10]Includes petroleum extraction. [11]Plus rent; less imputed bank service charges. [12]Includes 2,314,000 unemployed and 3,346,000 self-employed not distributed by sector and 230,000 military personnel. [13]June. [14]April. [15]1988. [16]1984. [17]Includes value-added taxes. [18]British Rail only. [19]1990. [20]Public sector only. [21]1987–88. [22]1984–85. [23]1992–93. [24]Universities only. [25]A survey in 1986–87, however, put the number of functional illiterates at 9–12% of the adult population.

United States

Official name: United States of America.
Form of government: federal republic with two legislative houses (Senate [100]; House of Representatives [435[1]]).
Head of state and government: President.
Capital: Washington, D.C.
Official language: none.
Official religion: none.
Monetary unit: 1 dollar (U.S.$) = 100 cents; valuation (Oct. 11, 1996) 1 U.S.$ = £0.63; 1 £ = U.S.$1.58.

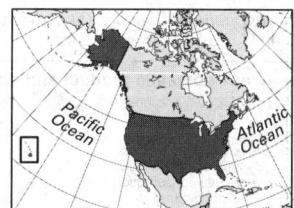

Area and population		area[2]		population
				1996
States	Capitals	sq mi	sq km	estimate
Alabama	Montgomery	51,718	133,950	4,273,084
Alaska	Juneau	587,875	1,522,595	607,007
Arizona	Phoenix	114,006	295,275	4,428,068
Arkansas	Little Rock	53,182	137,741	2,509,793
California	Sacramento	158,647	410,895	31,878,234
Colorado	Denver	104,100	269,619	3,822,676
Connecticut	Hartford	5,006	12,966	3,274,238
Delaware	Dover	2,026	5,247	724,842
Florida	Tallahassee	58,680	151,981	14,399,985
Georgia	Atlanta	58,930	152,629	7,353,225
Hawaii	Honolulu	6,459	16,729	1,183,723
Idaho	Boise	83,574	216,456	1,189,251
Illinois	Springfield	57,918	150,008	11,846,544
Indiana	Indianapolis	36,420	94,328	5,840,528
Iowa	Des Moines	56,276	145,755	2,851,792
Kansas	Topeka	82,282	213,110	2,572,150
Kentucky	Frankfort	40,411	104,664	3,883,723
Louisiana	Baton Rouge	47,719	123,592	4,350,579
Maine	Augusta	33,128	85,801	1,243,316
Maryland	Annapolis	10,455	27,078	5,071,604
Massachusetts	Boston	8,262	21,399	6,092,352
Michigan	Lansing	96,705	250,466	9,594,350
Minnesota	St. Paul	86,943	225,182	4,657,758
Mississippi	Jackson	47,695	123,530	2,716,115
Missouri	Jefferson City	69,709	180,546	5,358,692
Montana	Helena	147,046	380,849	879,372
Nebraska	Lincoln	77,359	200,360	1,652,093
Nevada	Carson City	110,567	286,368	1,603,163
New Hampshire	Concord	9,283	24,043	1,162,481
New Jersey	Trenton	7,790	20,176	7,987,933
New Mexico	Santa Fe	121,598	314,939	1,713,407
New York	Albany	53,013	137,304	18,184,774
North Carolina	Raleigh	52,672	136,420	7,322,870
North Dakota	Bismarck	70,704	183,123	643,539
Ohio	Columbus	44,828	116,104	11,172,782
Oklahoma	Oklahoma City	69,903	181,049	3,300,902
Oregon	Salem	97,052	251,364	3,203,735
Pennsylvania	Harrisburg	45,759	118,516	12,056,112
Rhode Island	Providence	1,213	3,142	990,225
South Carolina	Columbia	31,117	80,593	3,698,746
South Dakota	Pierre	77,121	199,743	732,405
Tennessee	Nashville	42,145	109,155	5,319,654
Texas	Austin	266,873	691,201	19,128,261
Utah	Salt Lake City	84,904	219,901	2,000,494
Vermont	Montpelier	9,615	24,903	588,654
Virginia	Richmond	40,598	105,149	6,675,451
Washington	Olympia	68,126	176,446	5,532,939
West Virginia	Charleston	24,232	62,761	1,825,754
Wisconsin	Madison	65,500	169,645	5,159,795
Wyoming	Cheyenne	97,819	253,351	481,400
District				
Dist. of Columbia	—	68	176	543,213
TOTAL		3,675,031	9,518,323	265,283,783[3]

Demography

Population (1996)[3]: 265,455,000.
Density (1996)[3]: persons per sq mi 72.2, persons per sq km 27.9.
Urban-rural (1995): urban 76.2%; rural 23.8%.
Sex distribution (1995): male 48.83%; female 51.17%.
Age breakdown (1995): under 15, 22.0%; 15–29, 20.9%; 30–44, 24.5%; 45–59, 16.0%; 60–74, 11.0%; 75 and over, 5.6%.
Population projection: (2000) 274,843,000; (2010) 297,943,000.
Doubling time: not applicable; doubling time exceeds 100 years.
Population by race and Hispanic[4] origin (1995): non-Hispanic white 73.7%; non-Hispanic black 12.0%; Hispanic 10.3%; Asian and Pacific Islander 3.3%; American Indian and Eskimo 0.7%.
Religious affiliation (1995): Christian 85.3%, of which Protestant 57.9%, Roman Catholic 21.0%, other Christian 6.4%; Jewish 2.1%; Muslim 1.9%; nonreligious 8.7%; other 2.0%.
Mobility (1994). Population living in the same residence as in 1993: 83.0%; different residence, same county 10.0%; different county, same state 3.0%; different state 3.0%; moved from abroad 1.0%.
Households (1995). Total households 98,990,000 (married-couple families 53,-858,000 [54.4%]). Average household size 2.6; 1 person 25.0%, 2 persons 32.1%, 3 persons 17.0%, 4 persons 15.5%, 5 or more persons 10.4%. Family households: 69,305,000 (70.0%); nonfamily 29,686,000 (30.0%), of which 1-person 83.3%.
Immigration (1994[5]): permanent immigrants admitted 804,416, from Mexico 13.8%, China 6.7%, Philippines 6.6%, Dominican Republic 6.4%, Vietnam 5.1%, India 4.3%, Poland 3.5%, Ukraine 2.6%, El Salvador 2.2%, Ireland 2.2%, United Kingdom 2.0%, Canada 2.0%, South Korea 2.0%, Russia 1.9%, Cuba 1.8%, Jamaica 1.8%, Haiti 1.6%, Iran 1.4%, Taiwan 1.2%. Refugee arrivals (1994[5]): 121,434.
Major cities (1994): New York 7,333,253; Los Angeles 3,448,613; Chicago 2,731,743; Houston 1,702,086; Philadelphia 1,524,249; San Diego 1,151,977; Phoenix 1,048,949; Dallas 1,022,830; San Antonio 998,905; Detroit 992,038.

Other principal cities (1994)					
	population		population		population
Akron	221,886	Fort Worth	451,814	Omaha	345,033
Albuquerque	411,994	Fresno	386,551	Pittsburgh	358,883
Anaheim	282,133	Honolulu	385,881	Portland (Ore.)	450,777
Anchorage	253,649	Indianapolis	752,279	Raleigh	236,707
Arlington (Tex.)	290,827	Jacksonville	665,070	Riverside	241,644
Atlanta	396,052	Kansas City (Mo.)	443,878	Rochester (N.Y.)	231,171
Aurora (Colo.)	250,717	Las Vegas	327,878	Sacramento	373,964
Austin	514,013	Lexington (Ky.)	237,612	St. Louis	368,215
Baltimore	702,979	Long Beach	433,852	St. Paul	262,071
Baton Rouge	227,022	Louisville	270,308	St. Petersburg	238,585
Birmingham	264,527	Memphis	614,289	San Francisco	734,676
Boston	547,725	Mesa	313,649	San Jose	816,884
Buffalo	312,965	Miami	373,024	Santa Ana	290,827
Charlotte	437,797	Milwaukee	617,044	Seattle	520,947
Cincinnati	358,170	Minneapolis	354,590	Tampa	285,523
Cleveland	492,901	Nashville	504,505	Toledo	322,550
Colorado Springs	316,480	New Orleans	484,149	Tucson	434,726
Columbus	635,913	Newark	258,751	Tulsa	374,851
Corpus Christi	275,419	Norfolk	241,426	Virginia Beach	430,295
Denver	492,901	Oakland	366,926	Washington, D.C.	567,094
El Paso	579,307	Oklahoma City	463,201	Wichita	310,236

Place of birth (1990): native-born 227,078,000 (91.3%); foreign-born 21,632,-000 (8.7%), of which Mexico 4,447,000, Germany (East and West) 1,163,000, Philippines 998,000, Canada 871,000, United Kingdom 765,000, Cuba 751,-000, South Korea 663,000, Italy 640,000, Vietnam 556,000, China 543,000, India 463,000, Japan 422,000, Poland 397,000, U.S.S.R. 337,000, Portugal 219,000, Greece 189,000, other 8,208,000.

Vital statistics

Birth rate per 1,000 population (1995): 14.8 (world avg. 25.0); (1993) legitimate 70.0%; illegitimate 30.0%.
Death rate per 1,000 population (1995): 8.8 (world avg. 9.3).
Natural increase rate per 1,000 population (1995): 6.0 (world avg. 15.7).
Total fertility rate (avg. births per childbearing woman; 1995): 2.1.
Marriage rate per 1,000 population (1995): 8.9; median age at first marriage (1991): men 26.3 years, women 24.1 years.
Divorce rate per 1,000 population (1995): 4.4.
Life expectancy at birth (1994): white male 73.2 years, black and other male 67.5 years; white female 79.6 years, black and other female 75.8 years.
Major causes of death per 100,000 population (1996[6]): cardiovascular diseases 355.5, of which ischemic heart disease 179.7, cerebrovascular diseases 59.1, atherosclerosis 9.8; malignant neoplasms (cancers) 203.8; diseases of the respiratory system 69.2, of which pneumonia 29.9; accidents and adverse effects 34.5, of which motor-vehicle accidents 16.8; diabetes mellitus 22.1; AIDS 15.5; suicide 11.3; chronic liver disease and cirrhosis 9.4.
Morbidity rates of infectious diseases per 100,000 population (1994): gonorrhea 160.3; chicken pox 58.0; syphilis 31.4; AIDS 30.0; salmonellosis 16.6; shigellosis 11.4; hepatitis A (infectious) 11.4; tuberculosis 9.4; lyme disease 5.0; hepatitis B (serum) 4.8; aseptic meningitis 3.4; pertussis 1.8.
Incidence of chronic health conditions per 1,000 population (1994): chronic sinusitis 133.9; arthritis 128.3; deformities or orthopedic impairments 119.2; hypertension 108.3; hay fever 100.3; hearing impairment 85.9; heart conditions 85.5; asthma 55.9; chronic bronchitis 53.8; migraine 43.2.

Social indicators

Educational attainment (1991). Percentage of population age 25 and over having: incomplete primary education 6.2%; primary 4.4%; incomplete secondary 11.0%; secondary 38.6%; some postsecondary 18.4%; 4-year higher degree or more 21.4%. Number of earned degrees (1995): bachelor's degree 1,192,000; master's degree 405,000; doctor's degree 43,000; first-professional degrees (in fields such as medicine, theology, and law) 77,000.

Distribution of income (1994)				
percentage of disposable household income by quintile				
1	2	3	4	5 (highest)
4.2	10.0	15.7	23.3	46.9

Quality of working life (1995). Average workweek: 39.2 hours. Annual rate per 100,000 workers for (1994): injury or accident 1,400; death 4.1. Proportion of labour force insured for damages or income loss resulting from: injury, permanent disability, and death (1988) 56.6%. Average days per 1,000 workdays lost to labour stoppages (1995): 1.9. Average duration of journey to work (1990): 22.4 minutes (private automobile 94.7%, of which drive alone 80.0%, carpool 14.7%; take public transportation 5.3%). Rate per 1,000 employed workers of discouraged workers (unemployed no longer seeking work; 1992): 6.9.
Access to services (1993). Proportion of occupied dwellings having access to: electricity, virtually 100.0%; safe public water supply 97.7% (13.0% from wells); public sewage collection 75.8%; septic tanks 23.6%.
Social participation. Eligible voters participating in last presidential election (1996): 49.0%. Population age 18 and over participating in voluntary work (1993): 47.7%. Trade-union membership in total workforce (1995): 14.9%. Practicing religious population in total affiliated population (church attendance; 1987): once a week 47%; once in six months 67%; once a year 74%.
Social deviance (1994). Offense rate per 100,000 population for: murder 8.9; rape 39.2; robbery 237.5; aggravated assault 429.7; motor-vehicle theft 590.4; burglary and housebreaking 1,040.4; larceny-theft 3,021.6; drug-abuse

violation 309.2[7]; drunkenness 260.1[7]. Drug and substance users (population age 26 and over; 1994): alcohol 41.2%; tobacco (cigarettes) 33.5%; marijuana 16.0%; cocaine 0.4%; analgesics 1.3%; tranquilizers 0.2%; stimulants 0.4%; hallucinogens 1.2%; heroin, n.a. Rate per 100,000 population of suicide (1996): 11.1.

Crime rates per 100,000 population in metropolitan areas[8] (1994)

		violent crime			
	total	murder	rape	robbery	assault
Atlanta	3,571	46.4	102.6	1,299	2,122
Baltimore	2,834	43.4	86.2	1,525	1,179
Boston	1,916	15.3	81.4	762	1,056
Chicago	...	33.1		1,210	1,440
Dallas	1,589	27.8	90.1	666	805
Detroit	2,687	52.9	109.2	1,249	1,276
Houston	1,308	21.3	53.0	568	666
Los Angeles	2,059	23.8	43.8	868	1,123
Miami	3,413	30.5	58.2	1,537	1,788
Minneapolis	1,908	18.7	155.9	929	806
New York	1,861	21.3	36.3	988	814
Philadelphia	1,322	25.9	46.2	814	436
Pittsburgh	1,113	17.4	70.8	670	356
St. Louis	3,751	63.5	77.9	1,543	2,066
San Francisco	1,461	12.3	39.4	893	516
Washington, D.C.	2,662	70.0	43.7	1,107	1,442

		property crime		
	total	burglary	larceny	auto theft
Atlanta	12,548	2,951	7,511	2,085
Baltimore	9,717	2,150	5,736	1,831
Boston	7,618	1,221	4,378	2,019
Chicago	7,315	1,564	4,323	1,428
Dallas	7,888	1,681	4,542	1,665
Detroit	9,230	2,167	4,170	2,892
Houston	5,978	1,452	3,239	1,287
Los Angeles	5,781	1,226	3,120	1,434
Miami	13,763	2,968	8,065	2,731
Minneapolis	9,259	2,388	5,738	1,134
New York	5,365	1,204	2,860	1,301
Philadelphia	5,112	904	2,588	1,620
Pittsburgh	6,035	1,178	3,410	1,449
St. Louis	12,600	3,207	7,106	2,287
San Francisco	6,880	1,086	4,547	1,247
Washington, D.C.	8,415	1,761	5,206	1,448

Leisure (1992). Favourite leisure activities (percentage of total population age 18 and over that undertook activity at least once in the previous year): movie 59.0%, amusement park 50.0%, sports event 37.0%, live theatre 31.0%, art museum 27.0%; exercising 60.0%, reading literature 54.0%, playing sports 39.0%.
Material well-being (1994). Occupied dwellings with householder possessing: automobile 84.9%[9]; telephone 93.9%; radio receiver 99.0%; television receiver 98.3%; air conditioner 68.4%[10]; washing machine 77.1%[10]; videocassette recorder 79.0%; cable television 62.4%.
Recreational expenditures (1994): U.S.$369,900,000,000 (television and radio receivers, computers, and video equipment 24.0%; nondurable toys and sports equipment 10.6%; sports supplies 10.3%; golfing, bowling, and other participatory activities 8.9%; magazines and newspapers 6.1%; books and maps 5.2%; spectator amusements 4.9%, of which theatre and opera 2.2%, spectator sports 1.3%; movies 1.3%; flowers, seeds, and potted plants 3.1%).

National economy
Budget (1996). Revenue: U.S.$1,453,400,000,000 (individual income tax 44.9%, social-insurance taxes and contributions 35.0%, corporation income tax 11.7%, other 8.4%). Expenditures: U.S.$1,570,100,000,000 (social security and medicare 33.6%, defense 16.9%, interest on debt 15.4%, income security 14.6%, health 7.6%, other 11.9%).
Total national debt (1995): U.S.$4,921,000,000,000.

Manufacturing, mining, and construction enterprises (1995)

	no. of enter-prises[11]	no. of employees	hourly wage as a % of all wages	value added (U.S.$'000,000)[12]
Manufacturing				
Chemical and related products	12,109	1,046,900	135.2	165,135
Transportation equipment	10,500	1,721,300	144.7	161,058
Food and related products	20,624	1,716,400	104.0	156,843
Machinery, except electrical	52,135	2,040,100	114.9	132,144
Electric and electronic machinery	15,962	1,615,900	101.1	121,950
Instruments and related products	10,326	843,800	111.2	89,806
Fabricated metal products	36,105	1,419,700	105.3	83,871
Paper and related products	6,342	691,200	125.5	59,923
Rubber and plastic products	14,515	958,300	95.8	58,477
Primary metals	6,771	706,700	127.8	51,816
Apparel and related products	22,872	892,500	66.3	36,357
Stone, clay, and glass products	16,166	549,400	108.4	34,558
Lumber and wood	33,982	762,200	88.9	33,352
Textile-mill products	6,412	646,400	81.8	29,862
Tobacco products	138	36,200	191.6	27,167
Petroleum and coal products	2,254	146,900	167.5	23,797
Furniture and fixtures	11,613	484,700	85.6	22,821
Leather and leather products	2,193	102,200	69.7	4,517
Miscellaneous manufacturing industries	16,544	385,700	87.2	19,999
Mining				
Oil and gas extraction	22,910	318,800	127.9	79,700
Coal mining	3,905	106,800	159.9	17,283
Nonmetallic, except fuels	5,775	108,900	117.3	9,619
Metal mining	1,027	52,800	145.5	7,180
Construction				
Special trade contractors	367,800[12]	3,453,000	134.6	122,422
Heavy construction contractors	37,300[12]	807,200	129.5	49,066
General contractors and operative builders	168,200[12]	1,295,600	123.4	63,743

Gross national product (at current market prices; 1995): U.S.$7,237,500,000,000 (U.S.$27,515 per capita).

Gross domestic product and national income
(in U.S.$'000,000,000)

	1991	1992	1993	1994	1995
Gross domestic product	5,677.5	6,038.6	6,377.9	6,738.4	7,245.8
By type of expenditure					
Personal consumption expenditures	3,887.7	4,139.9	4,391.8	4,628.4	4,924.3
Durable goods	446.1	497.3	537.9	591.5	606.4
Nondurable goods	1,251.5	1,300.9	1,350.0	1,394.3	1,486.1
Services	2,190.1	2,341.6	2,503.9	2,642.7	2,831.6
Gross private domestic investment	721.1	796.5	891.7	1,032.9	1,066.3
Fixed investment	731.3	789.1	876.1	980.7	1,028.2
Changes in business inventories	−10.2	7.3	15.6	52.2	33.7
Net exports of goods and services	−19.9	−30.3	−65.3	−98.2	−114.2
Exports	601.1	638.1	659.1	718.7	774.8
Imports	620.9	668.4	724.3	816.9	888.9
Government purchases of goods and services	1,090.5	1,131.8	1,158.1	1,175.3	1,260.7
Federal	447.3	448.8	443.4	437.3	472.7
State and local	643.2	313.8	714.6	738.0	788.8
By major type of product					
Goods output	2,182.5	2,312.8	2,421.9	2,584.7	2,697.4
Durable goods	888.4	977.9	1,047.9	1,153.6	1,179.8
Nondurable goods	1,294.1	1,334.9	1,374.0	1,431.1	1,517.6
Services	3,030.3	3,221.1	3,410.5	3,576.2	3,920.8
Structures	464.7	504.6	545.5	577.6	627.6
National income (incl. capital consumption adjustment)	4,544.2	4,836.6	5,140.3	5,458.4	5,799.2
By type of income					
Compensation of employees	3,390.8	3,582.0	3,772.2	4,004.6	4,209.1
Proprietors' income	368.0	414.3	321.0	473.7	478.3
Rental income of persons	−10.4	−8.9	12.6	27.7	122.2
Corporate profits	346.3	407.2	466.6	542.7	588.6
Net interest	449.5	442.0	445.6	409.7	401.0
By industry division (excl. capital consumption adjustment)					
Agriculture, forestry, fishing	90.9	100.9	105.3	101.9	94.0
Mining and construction	246.8	251.3	268.1	278.5	301.2
Manufacturing	841.0	895.3	929.0	979.7	1,026.3
Durable	464.2	501.7	523.0	562.4	597.1
Nondurable	376.8	393.6	406.1	417.3	429.3
Transportation	140.8	151.0	161.8	177.5	189.4
Communications	95.3	103.7	107.4	113.4	136.6
Public utilities	99.0	101.5	106.9	116.5	125.0
Wholesale and retail trade	669.3	700.3	742.8	785.8	805.6
Finance, insurance, real estate	685.0	748.9	815.6	894.2	991.9
Services	1,002.5	1,085.8	1,171.0	1,254.4	1,335.9
Government and government enterprise	699.5	734.5	765.3	793.4	820.3
Other	17.4	7.3	0.2	−11.4	−7.0

Structure of gross domestic product and labour force

	1993		1995	
	in value U.S.$'000,000,000	% of total value	labour force[13]	% of labour force[13]
Agriculture	107.3	1.7	3,440,000	2.6
Mining	89.4	1.4	627,000	0.5
Manufacturing	1,118.3	17.6	20,493,000	15.5
Construction	234.2	3.7	7,668,000	5.8
Public utilities	181.5	2.9 }	8,709,000	6.6
Transp. and commun.	377.7	6.0 }		
Trade	1,005.5	15.8	26,072,000	19.7
Finance	1,180.6	18.6	7,983,000	6.0
Public administration, defense	781.6	12.3 }	49,910,000	37.7
Services	1,264.8	19.9 }		
Other	2.5[14]	0.0	7,404,000[15]	5.6[15]
TOTAL	6,343.4	100.0[16]	132,304,000[16]	100.0

Business activity (1993): number of businesses 21,280,000 (sole proprietorships 74.5%, active corporations 18.6%, active partnerships 6.9%), of which services 9,131,000, wholesaling and retailing 4,090,000; business receipts $13,198,000,000,000 (active corporations 89.5%, sole proprietorships 5.7%, active partnerships 4.8%), of which wholesaling and retailing $3,979,000,000,000, services $1,337,000,000,000; net profit $721,000,000,000 (active corporations 69.1%, sole proprietorships 21.6%, partnerships 9.3%), of which services $151,000,000,000, wholesaling and retailing $68,000,000,000. New business concerns and business failures (1994): total number of new incorporations 705,537[10]; total failures 71,520, of which commercial service 20,595, retail trade 12,575; failure rate per 10,000 concerns 74.0; current liabilities of failed concerns $29,357,000,000; average liability $410,500. Business expenditures for new plant and equipment (1994): total $638,400,000,000, of which trade, services, and communications $336,900,000,000, manufacturing businesses $192,600,000,000 (nondurable goods 51.8%, durable goods 48.2%), public utilities $76,500,000,000, transportation $21,200,000,000, mining $11,200,000,000.
Production. Agriculture, forestry, fishing (value of production/catch in U.S.$'000,000 except as noted; 1995): corn (maize) 23,145, soybeans 14,564, hay 10,977, wheat 9,744, cotton lint 6,550, potatoes 2,799, tobacco 2,444, lettuce 1,913, grapes 1,812, apples 1,808, oranges 1,564, rice 1,514, sorghum 1,418, sugar beets 1,234[17], barley 1,027, peanuts (groundnuts) 1,018, sugarcane 901[17], almonds 888, tomatoes 852, strawberries 753, cottonseed 730, onions 634, dry beans 604, sunflower seeds 445, bell peppers 410, carrots 402, cantaloupes 383, broccoli 367, watermelon 358, grapefruit 301, cabbage 277, pears 270, celery 269, oats 265; livestock (number of live animals) 102,755,000 cattle, 59,992,000 pigs, 8,860,000 sheep, 6,000,000 horses, 1,808,000,000 chickens; roundwood (1994) 487,175,900 cu m; fish and shellfish catch (1993) 3,471, of which fish 1,884 (including salmon 423, Alaska pollack 358), shellfish

1,587 (including crabs 510, shrimp 413). Mining (metal content in metric tons except as noted; 1995): iron 39,342,000; copper 1,850,000; zinc 601,000; lead 384,000; molybdenum 47,000; vanadium 2,500; mercury 400; silver 1,500,000 kg; gold 320,000 kg; helium 102,000,000 cu m. Quarrying (metric tons; 1995): crushed stone 1,280,000,000; sand and gravel 907,000,000; cement 76,100,000; clay 46,600,000; phosphate rock 46,000,000; common salt 39,200,000; gypsum 17,200,000; lime 16,700,000. Manufacturing (metric tons except as noted; 1993): crude steel 87,343,000; paper and paperboard 76,688,000; wood pulp 57,189,000; pig iron 48,275,000; sulfuric acid 40,153,000; coke 21,237,000[11]; phosphoric acid 10,474,000; cheese 5,877,000; newsprint 5,833,000; aerospace vehicles (sales) U.S.$121,852,000,000[12]; machine tools (new orders for metal-cutting-type tools) U.S.$2,322,400,000; cotton fabric 4,402,000,000 sq m; carpets and rugs 1,134,300,000 sq m[12]; footwear 167,803,000 pairs[12]; motor-vehicle tires 237,448,000 units; major household appliances 51,277,000 units, of which 8,109,000 refrigerators, 7,703,000 microwave ovens, 6,793,000 washing machines, 5,074,000 clothes driers; television receivers 21,304,-000 units[12]; radio receivers 18,405,000 units; new passenger cars (factory sales) 5,955,000 units; new trucks and buses (factory sales) 4,786,000 units. Construction (completed; 1995): private U.S.$383,886,000,000, of which residential U.S.$236,111,000,000, nonresidential U.S.$109,721,000,000; public U.S.$129,180,000,000[17].

Retail and wholesale trade and services (1995)

	no. of establish-ments[12]	no. of employees	hourly wage as a % of all wages	annual sales or receipts (U.S.$'000,000)[17]
Retail trade	1,564,200	20,988,000	66.9	2,237,000
Automotive dealers	202,800	2,228,300	91.4	526,300
Food stores	190,300	3,376,600	70.5	397,800
General merchandise group stores	36,300	2,466,200	65.8	282,500
Eating and drinking places	430,100	7,432,500	46.6[18]	228,400
Gasoline service stations	100,100	647,100	60.5	142,200
Building materials, hardware, garden supply, and mobile home dealers	69,600	888,800	79.4	122,500
Furniture, home furnishings, equipment stores	113,100	937,900	88.4	119,600
Apparel and accessory stores	146,600	1,085,700	65.4	109,600
Drugstores and proprietary stores	48,700	607,800	77.5	81,500
Liquor stores	30,300	112,200	...	21,800
Wholesale trade	495,500	6,367,000	107.7	2,072,500
Durable goods	313,500	3,693,000	111.5	1,089,500
Machinery, equipment, and supplies	73,900	774,300	112.5	180,400
Motor vehicles, automotive equipment	47,300	498,000	98.1	201,200
Professional and commercial equipment	46,800	768,700	133.5	165,200
Electrical goods	39,300	477,400	116.2	147,400
Metals and minerals, except petroleum	11,200	140,300	110.5	95,500
Lumber and other construction materials	19,500	242,700	102.5	76,800
Hardware, plumbing, heating equipment and supplies	24,700	290,600	105.8	63,300
Furniture and home furnishings	16,500	149,600	97.7	36,000
Miscellaneous durable goods	34,300	327,200	88.5	150,400
Nondurable goods	182,000	2,674,000	102.3	983,000
Groceries and related products	42,900	890,700	105.4	286,500
Petroleum and petroleum products	16,100	166,400	96.6	138,300
Farm-products raw materials	11,600	109,000	78.1	95,800
Drugs, drug proprietaries, and druggists' sundries	6,100	197,100	128.2	78,400
Apparel and accessories	19,600	212,700	100.4	73,400
Paper and paper products	19,700	262,700	106.7	64,900
Beer, wine, and distilled alcoholic beverages	5,300	155,900	116.3	53,000
Chemicals and allied products	14,200	140,100	116.4	42,200
Miscellaneous nondurable goods	43,700	539,800	84.5	150,000
Services[19]	2,217,700	33,106,000	98.4	1,299,400
Health	464,900	9,280,900	108.0	285,000
Business, except computer services	306,500	6,628,100	92.9	201,900
Computer and data-processing services	54,700	1,043,300	154.0	100,700
Legal services	153,600	946,200	140.0	96,200
Automotive repair, services, garages	167,300	1,031,200	86.4	79,500
Management and public relations	49,500	813,200	125.5	70,000
Hotels and motels	42,700	1,724,400	68.1	62,100
Engineering services	39,200	579,000	154.7	61,500
Personal services	198,100	1,115,000	65.6	59,100
Amusement and recreation	84,300	1,720,600	73.2	51,100
Motion pictures	40,700	601,700	121.8	43,800

Energy production (consumption): electricity (kW-hr; 1994) 3,268,250,000,000 (3,312,888,000,000); coal (metric tons; 1994) 937,580,000 (843,873,000); crude petroleum (barrels; 1994) 2,464,000,000 (5,024,000,000); petroleum products (metric tons; 1994) 704,201,000 (737,681,000); natural gas (cu m; 1994) 530,014,000,000 (592,209,000,000). Domestic production of energy by source (1994): coal 31.2%, natural gas 27.6%, crude petroleum 19.9%, other[20] 21.3%.

Energy consumption by source (1994): petroleum and petroleum products 38.8%, natural gas 24.0%, coal 22.0%, other[20] 15.2%; by end use: industrial 38.0%, residential and commercial 35.0%, transportation 26.5%.

Household income and expenditure. Average household size (1993) 2.6; average (mean) annual income per household U.S.$41,428, of which average white household U.S.$43,285, average Hispanic[4] household U.S.$30,291, average black household U.S.$27,229; sources of income: wages and salaries 57.3%, transfer payments 17.0%, self-employment 7.4%, other 18.3%; expenditure:

transportation 17.8%, housing 17.6%, food 14.3%, fuel and utilities 6.9%, recreation 5.8%, health 5.8%, wearing apparel 5.5%, expenditures in restaurants and hotels 5.4%, household furnishings 4.0%, education 1.5%, other 15.4%.

Selected household characteristics (1994). Total number of households 97,-107,000, of which (by race) white 84.8%, black 11.6%, other 3.6%; in central cities 31.4%, in suburbs 46.3%, outside metropolitan areas 22.3%; (by tenure) owned 62,374,000 (64.2%), rented 34,732,000 (35.8%); family households 68,490,000, of which married couple 77.6%, female head with own children[21] under age 18, 11.2%, female head without own children[21] under 18, 6.9%; nonfamily households 28,617,000, of which female living alone 49.5%, male living alone 33.0%, other 17.5%.

Financial aggregates

	1990	1991	1992	1993	1994	1995	1996[22]
Exchange rate, U.S.$ per:							
£[23]	1.78	1.77	1.76	1.50	1.53	1.58	1.56
SDR[23]	1.36	1.37	1.41	1.40	1.43	1.52	1.45
International reserves (U.S.$)[24]							
Total (excl. gold; '000,000,000)	72.26	66.66	60.27	62.35	63.28	74.78	64.46
SDRs ('000,000,000)	10.99	11.24	8.50	9.02	10.04	11.04	10.18
Reserve pos. in IMF ('000,000,000)	9.08	9.49	11.76	11.80	12.03	14.65	15.42
Foreign exchange ('000,000,000)	52.19	45.93	40.01	41.53	41.22	49.10	38.86
Gold ('000,000 fine troy oz)	261.91	261.91	261.84	261.79	261.73	261.70	261.71
% world reserves	27.84	27.86	28.13	28.67	28.70	29.00	28.92
Interest and prices							
Central bank discount (%)[24]	6.50	3.50	3.00	3.00	4.75	5.25	5.00
Govt. bond yield (%)[23]	8.25	6.81	5.31	4.44	6.26	6.26	6.41
Industrial share prices[23] (1990 = 100)	100.0	114.1	125.5	132.3	138.0	164.1	204.3
Balance of payments (U.S.$'000,000,000)							
Balance of visible trade	-108.84	-73.44	-96.14	-112.74	-164.33	-158.78	...
Imports, f.o.b.	-497.55	-489.40	-536.28	-580.51	-668.87	-743.52	...
Exports, f.o.b.	388.71	415.96	440.14	467.77	504.54	584.71	...
Balance of invisibles	18.38	69.75	29.84	3.49	162.83	10.55	...
Balance of payments, current account	-90.46	-3.69	-66.30	-109.25	-1.50	-148.23	...

Population economically active (1995): total 132,304,000[13]; activity rate of total population 50.3% (participation rates: ages 15–64, 76.2%; female 47.8%; unemployed 5.6%).

Price and earnings indexes (1990 = 100)

	1990	1991	1992	1993	1994	1995	1996[22]
Consumer price index	100.0	104.2	107.4	110.6	113.4	116.6	120.8
Hourly earnings index[25]	100.0	103.3	105.8	108.5	111.4	114.2	119.1

Average employee earnings

	average hourly earnings in U.S.$		average weekly earnings in U.S.$	
	July 1994	July 1995	July 1994	July 1995
Manufacturing				
Durable goods	12.63	12.90	531.70	532.77
Lumber and wood products	9.87	10.22	404.67	407.78
Furniture and fixtures	9.57	9.83	383.76	380.42
Stone, clay, and glass products	12.16	12.46	533.82	538.27
Primary metal industries	14.39	14.68	637.48	628.30
Fabricated metal products	11.88	12.10	500.15	498.52
Machinery, except electrical	12.95	13.20	558.15	568.08
Electrical and electronic equipment	11.58	11.73	479.41	476.24
Transportation equipment	16.42	16.63	696.21	700.12
Instruments and related products	12.46	12.78	515.84	521.42
Miscellaneous manufacturing	9.58	10.02	378.41	388.78
Nondurable goods	11.29	11.67	460.63	467.97
Food and kindred products	10.70	10.93	445.12	450.32
Tobacco manufactures	20.38	22.02	772.40	865.39
Textile mill products	9.12	9.57	375.74	381.84
Apparel and other textile products	7.30	7.62	272.29	278.13
Paper and allied products	11.83	14.42	516.97	618.62
Printing and publishing	12.13	12.32	465.79	465.70
Chemicals and allied products	15.21	15.70	655.55	675.10
Petroleum and coal products	18.94	19.25	829.57	847.00
Rubber and miscellaneous plastics products	10.74	11.01	446.78	443.70
Leather and leather products	7.96	8.01	300.89	293.17
Nonmanufacturing				
Metal mining	16.03	15.33	708.53	682.19
Coal mining	17.54	18.37	747.20	771.54
Oil and gas extraction	13.92	14.70	623.62	649.74
Nonmetallic minerals, except fuels	13.14	13.48	632.03	648.39
Construction	14.72	15.10	585.86	604.00
Transportation and public utilities	13.82	14.23	556.95	570.62
Wholesale trade	11.99	12.42	460.42	476.93
Retail trade	7.44	7.66	220.97	227.50
Finance, insurance, and real estate	11.71	12.32	418.05	447.22
Hotels, motels, and tourist courts	7.58	7.72	239.53	248.58
Health services	12.12	12.41	398.75	409.53
Legal services	15.61	16.24	540.11	574.90
Miscellaneous services	14.55	15.90	568.91	567.63

Tourism (1995): receipts from visitors U.S.$76,485,000,000; expenditures by nationals abroad U.S.$57,900,000,000; number of foreign visitors 42,993,000 (13,668,000 from Canada, 9,610,000 from Mexico, 8,803,000 from Europe); number of nationals traveling abroad 47,419,000 (15,759,000 to Mexico, 12,-920,000 to Canada).

Land use (1994): forested 32.3%; meadows and pastures 26.1%; agricultural and under permanent cultivation 20.5%; other 21.0%.

Foreign trade

Balance of trade (current prices)

	1990	1991	1992	1993	1994	1995
U.S.$'000,000,000	−101.7	−99.2	−84.5	−115.7	−151.3	−158.8
% of total	11.4%	9.8%	8.6%	11.1%	12.9%	12.0%

Imports (1995): U.S.$743,505,000,000 (machinery and transport equipment 47.1%, of which motor vehicles and parts 14.6%; office and data-processing machines 8.5%; petroleum and petroleum products 7.1%; wearing apparel 6.9%; chemicals and related products 3.4%; food and live animals 3.4%). *Major import sources:* Canada 19.2%; Japan 16.5%; Mexico 8.1%; China 6.3%; Germany 4.9%; Taiwan 3.9%; United Kingdom 3.6%; South Korea 3.2%; Singapore 2.4%; France 2.3%; Malaysia 2.3%; Italy 2.2%; Thailand 1.5%; Hong Kong 1.4%; Brazil 1.2%.
Exports (1995): U.S.$583,031,000,000 (machinery and transport equipment 48.2%, of which motor vehicles and parts 13.2%; electrical machinery 11.2%; chemicals and related products 10.6%; food and live animals 6.7%; scientific and precision equipment 4.2%). *Major export destinations:* Canada 21.6%; Japan 11.0%; Mexico 7.8%; United Kingdom 4.9%; South Korea 4.4%; Germany 3.8%; Taiwan 3.4%; The Netherlands 2.8%; Singapore 2.6%; France 2.4%; Hong Kong 2.4%; Belgium 2.2%.

Trade by commodity group (1994)

	imports U.S.$'000,000	%	exports U.S.$'000,000	%
SITC Group				
00 Food and live animals	27,500[26]	4.0[26]	35,454[26]	6.9[26]
01 Beverages and tobacco	5,518	0.8	8,015	1.6
02 Crude materials, excluding fuels	19,141	2.8	27,257	5.3
03 Mineral fuels, lubricants, and related materials	60,151	8.7	9,211	1.8
04 Animal and vegetable oils, fat, and waxes	26	26	26	26
05 Chemicals and related products, n.e.s.	34,812	5.0	51,138	10.0
06 Basic manufactures	83,922	12.2	44,913	8.8
07 Machinery and transport equipment	314,381	45.6	252,062	49.2
08 Miscellaneous manufactured articles	118,657	17.2	56,497	11.0
09 Goods not classified by kind	24,948	3.6	27,790	5.4
TOTAL	689,030	100.0[16]	512,337	100.0

Direction of trade (1995)

	imports U.S.$'000,000	%	exports U.S.$'000,000	%
Africa	16,241	2.1	9,889	1.7
South Africa	2,311	0.3	2,751	0.5
Other Africa	13,930	1.8	7,138	1.2
Americas	256,359	33.2	221,455	38.0
Canada	148,304	19.2	126,024	21.6
Caribbean countries and Central America	15,552	2.0	17,364	3.0
Mexico	62,756	8.1	45,401	7.8
South America	29,747	3.9	32,666	5.6
Asia	337,246	43.7[16]	200,405	34.4[16]
China	48,521	6.3	11,749	2.0
Japan	127,195	16.5	64,298	11.0
Other Asia	161,530	21.0	124,358	21.3
Europe	161,796	21.0[16]	142,187	24.4
EU	136,872	17.8	123,615	21.2
Russia	4,270	0.6	2,826	0.5
Other Europe	20,654	2.7	15,746	2.7
Oceania	5,356	0.7	12,690	2.2[16]
Australia	3,546	0.5	10,788	1.8
Other Oceania	1,810	0.2	1,902	0.3
Other	−6,041	−0.8	−4,100	−0.7
TOTAL	770,947[16]	100.0[16]	582,526	100.0

Transport and communications

Transport. Railroads (1993): length 137,000 mi, 220,000 km; passenger-mi 13,138,000,000, passenger-km 21,144,000,000; short ton-mi cargo 1,183,000,000,000, metric ton-km cargo 1,727,000,000,000. Roads (1994): total length 3,906,544 mi, 6,286,985 km (paved 91.0%). Vehicles (1994): passenger cars 133,930,000; trucks and buses 75,783,000. Merchant marine (1995): vessels (1,000 gross tons and over) 543; total deadweight tonnage 11,945,000. Air transport (1994): passenger-mi 519,200,000,000, passenger-km 835,600,000,000; short ton-mi cargo 11,720,600,000, metric ton-km cargo 17,111,800,000; localities (1996) with scheduled flights 834[27]. Certified route passenger/cargo air carriers (1992) 77; operating revenue (U.S.$'000,000; 1991) 74,942, of which domestic 56,119, international 18,823; operating expenses 76,669, of which domestic 56,596, international 20,073.

Intercity passenger and freight traffic by mode of transportation (1993)

	cargo traffic ('000,000,000 ton-mi)	% of nat'l total	passenger traffic ('000,000,000 passenger-mi)	% of nat'l total
Rail	1,183	38.1	14	0.7
Road	871	28.0	1,718	81.7
Inland water	467	15.1	—	—
Air	12	0.4	370	17.6
Petroleum pipeline	572	18.4	—	—
TOTAL	3,105	100.0	2,102	100.0

Communications. Daily newspapers (1995): total number 1,710; total circulation 62,600,000; circulation per 1,000 population 238. Radio (1993): total number of receivers 538,000,000 (1 per 0.5 persons). Television (1994): total number of receivers 211,000,000 (1 per 1.2 persons). Telephones (access lines; 1993): 147,000,000 (1 per 1.8 persons).

Other communications media (1995)

Print	titles		titles
Books (new)	23,977	Home economics	90
of which		Industrial arts	106
Agriculture	288	Journalism and communications	90
Art	741	Labour and industrial	
Biography	1,285	relations	70
Business	825	Law	273
Education	484	Library and information	
Fiction	2,015	sciences	118
General works	868	Literature and language	158
History	1,285	Mathematics and science	238
Home economics	479	Medicine	182
Juvenile	3,009	Philosophy and religion	130
Language	250	Physical education and	
Law	481	recreation	151
Literature	1,058	Political science	136
Medicine	1,598	Psychology	138
Music	186	Sociology and anthropology	149
Philosophy, psychology	825	Zoology	94
Poetry, drama	420		
Religion	921	Cinema[17]	
Science	1,422	Feature films	462
Sociology, economics	3,053		
Sports, recreation	427		traffic
Technology	1,032	Cellular telephones	
Travel	125	Number of	
Periodicals[9]	3,731	subscribers	33,786,000
of which			
Agriculture	153		(pieces of mail)
Business and economics	262	Post	
Chemistry and physics	170	Mail	180,734,000,000
Children's periodicals	78	Domestic	179,933,000,000
Education	203	International	801,000,000
Engineering	265		
Fine and applied arts	145		
General interest	181		
History	151		

Education and health

Education (1995–96)

	schools	teachers	students	student/teacher ratio
Primary (age 5–13)[28]		1,784,000	33,410,000	18.7
Secondary and vocational (age 14–17)	85,393[29]	1,187,000	17,390,000	14.6
Higher, including teacher-training colleges	5,758[30]	833,000	14,210,000	17.1

Literacy: studies in the late 1980s indicated that adult "functional" literacy may not exceed 85%.
Health (1994): doctors of medicine 684,400[31] (1 per 381 persons), of which office-based practice 407,000 (including specialties in internal medicine 16.7%, general and family practice 14.3%, pediatrics 7.7%, obstetrics and gynecology 6.9%, general surgery 5.9%, psychiatry 5.6%, anesthesiology 5.4%, orthopedics 4.1%, ophthalmology 3.5%); doctors of osteopathy 35,000; nurses 2,044,000 (1 per 127 persons); dentists 157,000 (1 per 1,660 persons); hospital beds 1,128,000 (1 per 232 persons), of which nonfederal 92.6% (community hospitals 80.0%, psychiatric 10.7%, long-term general and special 1.7%), federal 7.4%; infant mortality rate per 1,000 live births (1995) 7.5.
Food (1992): daily per capita caloric intake 3,732 (vegetable products 67%, animal products 33%); 141% of FAO recommended minimum requirement. Per capita consumption of major food groups (pounds annually; 1994): milk 225.7; cereal products 198.7; sweeteners 147.6; potatoes 141.0; fresh fruits 126.7; red meat 114.8; fresh vegetables 113.9; fats and oils 66.9; poultry products 63.7; fish and shellfish 15.1.

Military

Total active duty personnel (1996): 1,483,800 (army 33.4%, navy 28.7%, air force 26.2%, marines 11.7%). *Military expenditure as percentage of GNP* (1994): 4.3% (world 3.0%); per capita expenditure U.S.$1,105. *Military aid* (1993): total $4,143,000,000 (Middle East 76.2%, of which Israel 43.4%, Egypt 31.4%; Europe 20.8%, of which Turkey 10.9%; Latin America 1.8%).

[1]Excludes 5 delegates having only committee voting privileges. [2]Total area excluding U.S. share of Great Lakes is 3,614,979 sq mi (9,362,788 sq km). [3]Includes military personnel residing overseas. [4]Persons of Hispanic origin may be of any race. [5]Fiscal year ending September 30. [6]Data for 12-month period ending March 31. [7]1991. [8]Estimated crime rates include unreported crimes. [9]1988. [10]1993. [11]1987. [12]1992. [13]Excludes military personnel overseas. [14]Statistical discrepancy. [15]Unemployed. [16]Detail does not add to total given because of rounding. [17]1994. [18]Excludes tips. [19]Annual receipts for 1992. [20]Includes hydroelectric, nuclear, and geothermal power. [21]"Own children" includes adopted children and stepchildren. [22]August. [23]Period average. [24]End-of-year. [25]Manufacturing sector only. [26]Animal and vegetable oils included in Food and live animals. [27]Includes 292 localities in Alaska. [28]Primary includes kindergarten. [29]1993–94. [30]1992–93. [31]619,800 professionally active.

Uruguay

Official name: República Oriental del Uruguay (Oriental Republic of Uruguay).
Form of government: republic with two legislative houses (Senate [31][1]; Chamber of Representatives [99]).
Head of state and government: President.
Capital: Montevideo.
Official language: Spanish.
Official religion: none.
Monetary unit: 1 peso uruguayo (Uruguayan peso)[2]; valuation (Oct. 11, 1996) 1 U.S.$ = Ur$8.34; 1 £ = Ur$13.13.

Area and population		area		population
		sq mi	sq km	1996 census
Departments	Capitals			
Artigas	Artigas	4,605	11,928	75,786
Canelones	Canelones	1,751	4,536	410,524
Cerro Largo	Melo	5,270	13,648	81,218
Colonia	Colonia del Sacramento	2,358	6,106	117,380
Durazno	Durazno	4,495	11,643	56,986
Flores	Trinidad	1,986	5,144	25,348
Florida	Florida	4,022	10,417	68,257
Lavalleja	Minas	3,867	10,016	60,618
Maldonado	Maldonado	1,851	4,793	113,884
Montevideo	Montevideo	205	530	1,378,705
Paysandú	Paysandú	5,375	13,922	107,706
Río Negro	Fray Bentos	3,584	9,282	48,730
Rivera	Rivera	3,618	9,370	97,959
Rocha	Rocha	4,074	10,551	71,492
Salto	Salto	5,468	14,163	115,244
San José	San José de Mayo	1,927	4,992	91,874
Soriano	Mercedes	3,478	9,008	83,741
Tacuarembó	Tacuarembó	5,961	15,438	84,078
Treinta y Tres	Treinta y Tres	3,679	9,529	49,846
TOTAL LAND AREA		67,574	175,016	
INLAND WATER		463	1,199	
TOTAL		68,037	176,215	3,139,376

Demography

Population (1996): 3,140,000.
Density (1996): persons per sq mi 46.2, persons per sq km 17.8.
Urban-rural (1996): urban 88.7%; rural 11.3%.
Sex distribution (1996): male 48.47%; female 51.53%.
Age breakdown (1990): under 15, 25.8%; 15–29, 23.0%; 30–44, 18.9%; 45–59, 15.8%; 60–74, 11.9%; 75 and over, 4.6%.
Population projection: (2000) 3,210,000; (2010) 3,389,000.
Doubling time: 90 years.
Ethnic composition (1990): white (mostly Spanish, Italian, or mixed Spanish-Italian) 86.0%; mestizo 8.0%; mulatto or black 6.0%.
Religious affiliation (1988): Roman Catholic 66.0%; Protestant 2.0%; Jewish 0.8%; nonreligious and atheist 31.2%.
Major cities (1985): Montevideo 1,311,976; Salto 80,823; Paysandú 76,191; Las Piedras 58,288; Rivera 57,316.

Vital statistics

Birth rate per 1,000 population (1994): 17.7 (world avg. 25.0); (1983) legitimate 73.8%; illegitimate 26.2%.
Death rate per 1,000 population (1994): 9.4 (world avg. 9.3).
Natural increase rate per 1,000 population (1994): 8.3 (world avg. 15.7).
Total fertility rate (avg. births per childbearing woman; 1994): 2.4.
Marriage rate per 1,000 population (1992): 6.2.
Divorce rate per 1,000 population (1992): 2.7.
Life expectancy at birth (1994): male 70.9 years; female 77.5 years.
Major causes of death per 100,000 population (1990): diseases of the circulatory system 378.4; malignant neoplasms (cancers) 222.8; respiratory diseases 76.3; accidents 47.0; diseases of the digestive system 39.1.

National economy

Budget (1995). Revenue: Ur$21,391,452,000 (direct taxes 78.7%, receipts from foreign trade 5.7%). Expenditures: Ur$23,868,032,000 (social security and welfare 60.8%, general public services 14.3%, capital investments 7.7%, interest on public debt 7.1%, subsidies 4.5%).
Public debt (external, outstanding; 1994): U.S.$3,774,000,000.
Tourism (1994): receipts U.S.$632,000,000; expenditures U.S.$190,000,000.
Production (metric tons except as noted). Agriculture, forestry, fishing (1995): rice 631,000, wheat 410,000, sugarcane 250,000, barley 200,000, potatoes 158,000, oranges 142,000, corn (maize) 109,000, sunflower seed 102,000; livestock (number of live animals) 22,685,000 sheep, 10,870,000 cattle, 480,000 horses; roundwood (1994) 3,517,000 cu m; fish catch 126,120. Mining and quarrying (1992): hydraulic cement 500,000; gypsum 145,000. Manufacturing (value added in NUr$'000,000[2]; 1993): food products (excluding beverages) 2,808,700; beverages 1,472,600; chemicals and chemical products 1,203,000; textiles 966,600; tobacco products 653,500; printing and publishing 578,600; wearing apparel, except footwear 437,400. Construction (approvals; 1994): residential 301,666 sq m; nonresidential 177,752 sq m. Energy production (consumption): electricity (kW-hr; 1994) 7,617,000,000 (5,957,000,000); coal, none (n.a.); crude petroleum, none (n.a.); petroleum products (metric tons; 1994) none (1,197,000); natural gas, none (n.a.).
Gross national product (1994): U.S.$14,725,000,000 (U.S.$4,650 per capita).

Structure of gross domestic product and labour force				
	1995		1993	
	in value Ur$'000[2]	% of total value	labour force	% of labour force
Agriculture	10,053,919	8.9	47,700	3.8
Mining	193,980	0.2	2,100	0.2
Manufacturing	19,953,405	17.6	254,300	20.2
Construction	5,393,547	4.8	86,400	6.9
Public utilities	4,082,148	3.6	16,900	1.3
Transp. and commun.	7,424,848	6.5	67,900	5.4
Trade	14,561,558	12.8	231,300	18.3
Finance	12,450,250	11.0	68,400	5.4
Pub. admin., defense	10,410,575	9.2 }	455,800	36.1
Services	13,256,882	11.7 }		
Other	15,528,500[3]	13.7[3]	30,200[4]	2.4[4]
TOTAL	113,309,612	100.0	1,261,000	100.0

Population economically active (1993): total 1,261,000; activity rate 44.7% (participation rates: ages 14 and over, 56.6%; female 42.4%; unemployed 2.4%).

Price and earnings indexes (1990=100)							
	1989	1990	1991	1992	1993	1994	1995
Consumer price index	47.1	100.0	202.0	340.2	524.3	758.9	1,079.5
Monthly earnings index[5]	51.3	100.0	212.0	363.7	588.1	858.3	1,185.5

Household income and expenditure. Avg. household size (1985) 3.3; avg. annual income per household (1985) NUr$266,261[2] (U.S.$2,625); sources of income[6]: wages 53.5%, self-employment 17.0%, transfer payments and other 29.5%; expenditure (1982–83)[7]: food 39.9%, housing 17.6%, transportation and communications 10.4%, health care 9.3%, clothing 7.0%, durable goods 6.3%, recreation 3.1%, education 1.3%, personal effects and other 5.1%.
Land use (1994): forested 5.3%; meadows and pastures 77.3%; agricultural and under permanent cultivation 7.5%; other 9.9%.

Foreign trade[8]

Balance of trade (current prices)						
	1990	1991	1992	1993	1994	1995
U.S.$'000,000	+435.4	+44.9	−248.9	−536.7	−732.2	−647.2
% of total	14.8%	1.4%	6.8%	14.0%	16.1%	13.4%

Imports (1995): U.S.$2,866,933,000 (machinery and appliances 20.9%; transport equipment 13.5%; chemical products 11.9%; mineral products 10.7%; synthetic plastics, resins, and rubber 7.0%; textile products 6.8%; processed foods 6.0%). *Major import sources* (1994): Brazil 25.6%; Argentina 23.5%; United States 9.4%; Italy 4.9%; Spain 4.4%; Germany 3.6%.
Exports (1995): U.S.$2,116,664,000 (live animals and live-animal products 26.6%; textiles and textile products 20.0%; vegetable products 14.6%; hides and skins 11.9%; synthetic plastics, resins, and rubber 3.6%; processed foods 3.5%). *Major export destinations* (1994): Brazil 25.7%; Argentina 20.0%; United States 6.8%; Germany 6.3%; United Kingdom 3.8%; Italy 3.2%.

Transport and communications

Transport. Railroads[9]: route length (1993) 3,004 km; passenger-km (1987) 140,600,000; metric ton-km cargo (1991) 203,200,000. Roads (1991): length 52,000 km (paved 23%). Vehicles (1993): passenger cars 310,833; trucks and buses 148,644. Merchant marine (1992): vessels (100 gross tons and over) 93; deadweight tonnage 172,520. Air transport (1993): passenger-km 490,000,000; metric ton-km cargo 46,000,000; airports (1996) 1.
Communications. Daily newspapers (1992): total number 32; total circulation 750,000; circulation per 1,000 population 240. Radio (1995): total receivers 1,850,000 (1 per 1.7 persons). Television (1995): total receivers 600,000 (1 per 5.3 persons). Telephones (main lines; 1993): 530,000 (1 per 5.9 persons).

Education and health

Education (1994)	schools	teachers	students	student/ teacher ratio
Primary (age 6–11)	2,423	16,821	337,889	20.1
Secondary (age 12–17)	348	20,061	184,083	9.2
Vocational	104	...	56,879	...
Higher	2	7,157	61,367	8.6

Educational attainment (1985). Percentage of population age 25 and over having: no formal schooling 7.5%; less than primary education 26.6%; primary 31.2%; secondary 19.9%; higher 14.8%. *Literacy* (1985): population age 15 and over literate 95.0%; males 975,200 (94.5%); females 1,074,300 (95.4%).
Health: physicians (1994) 11,241 (1 per 282 persons); hospital beds (1987) 14,133 (1 per 215 persons); infant mortality rate per 1,000 live births (1992) 18.7.
Food (1992): daily per capita caloric intake 2,750 (vegetable products 63%, animal products 37%); 103% of FAO recommended minimum requirement.

Military

Total active duty personnel (1996): 25,600 (army 68.8%, navy 19.5%, air force 11.7%). *Military expenditure as percentage of GNP* (1994): 2.6% (world 3.0%); per capita expenditure U.S.$130.

[1]Includes the vice president, who serves as ex officio presiding officer. [2]The peso uruguayo (Uruguayan peso [Ur$]) replaced the new Uruguayan peso (Nur$) on March 1, 1993, at the rate of 1 Uruguayan peso = 1,000 new Uruguayan pesos. [3]Includes indirect taxes less subsidies. [4]Includes unemployed not previously employed. [5]From urban areas only. [6]Salaried employees only. [7]Weights of consumer price index components in Montevideo. [8]Import figures are f.o.b. in balance of trade and c.i.f. for commodities and trading partners. [9]Passenger service ceased in 1988.

Uzbekistan

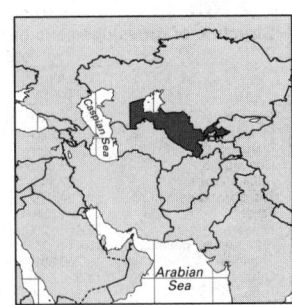

Official name: Ŭzbekiston Respublikasi
(Republic of Uzbekistan).
Form of government: multiparty
republic with a single legislative body
(Supreme Assembly [250]).
Head of state: President.
Head of government: Prime Minister.
Capital: Tashkent (Toshkent).
Official language: Uzbek.
Official religion: none.
Monetary unit: sum[1] (plural sumy);
valuation (Oct. 11, 1996) 1 U.S.$ =
40.05 sumy; 1 £ = 63.09 sumy.

Area and population

Autonomous Republic	Administrative centres	area sq mi	area sq km	population 1993 estimate
Qoraqalpoghiston	Nuqus	63,700	164,900	1,343,000
Provinces				
Andijon	Andijon	1,600	4,200	1,899,000
Bukhoro	Bukhara (Bukhoro)	15,200	39,400	1,262,000
Farghona	Fergana (Farghona)	2,700	7,100	2,338,000
Jizzakh	Jizzakh	7,900	20,500	831,000
Khorazm	Urganch	2,400	6,300	1,135,000
Namangan	Namangan	3,100	7,900	1,652,000
Nawoiy	Nawoiy	42,800	110,800	715,000
Qashqadaryo	Qarshi	11,000	28,400	1,812,000
Samarqand	Samarkand (Samarqand)	6,300	16,400	2,322,000
Sirdaryo	Guliston	2,000	5,100	600,000
Surkhondaryo	Termiz	8,000	20,800	1,437,000
Toshkent	Tashkent (Toshkent)	6,000	15,600	4,357,000
TOTAL		172,700	447,400	21,703,000

Demography

Population (1996): 23,206,000.
Density (1996): persons per sq mi 134.4, persons per sq km 51.9.
Urban-rural (1995): urban 38.70%; rural 61.30%.
Sex distribution (1995): male 49.50%; female 50.50%.
Age breakdown (1989): under 15, 40.8%; 15–29, 28.4%; 30–44, 15.0%; 45–59, 9.3%; 60–74, 4.7%; 75 and over, 1.8%.
Population projection: (2000) 25,015,000; (2010) 30,258,000.
Doubling time: 30 years.
Ethnic composition (1991): Uzbek 73.0%; Russian 7.7%; Tajik 4.8%; Tatar 2.3%; Kyrgyz 0.9%; Ukrainian 0.7%; Turkmen 0.6%; other 10.0%.
Religious affiliation (1996): believers are predominantly Sunnī Muslim (Ḥanafīyah) 88.0%; Russian Orthodox 9.0%; other 3.0%.
Major cities (1993): Tashkent 2,121,000; Samarkand 368,000; Namangan 341,000; Andijon 303,000; Bukhara 236,000.

Vital statistics

Birth rate per 1,000 population (1994): 29.4 (world avg. 25.0); (1994) legitimate 96.5%; illegitimate 3.5%.
Death rate per 1,000 population (1994): 6.6 (world avg. 9.3).
Natural increase rate per 1,000 population (1994): 22.8 (world avg. 15.7).
Total fertility rate (avg. births per childbearing woman; 1993): 3.8.
Marriage rate per 1,000 population (1994): 7.9.
Divorce rate per 1,000 population (1994): 1.1.
Life expectancy at birth (1994): male 66.0 years; female 72.0 years.
Major causes of death per 100,000 population (1993): diseases of the circulatory system 303.6; diseases of the respiratory system 115.0; accidents, poisoning, and violence 50.0; malignant neoplasms (cancers) 48.7; infectious and parasitic diseases 38.4; diseases of the digestive system 31.8; diseases of the nervous system 10.3; endocrine and metabolic disorders 10.3.

National economy

Budget (1995). Revenue: 89,914,000,000 sumy (taxes on income and profits 38.1%, excise taxes 27.6%, value-added tax 19.2%, property and land taxes 4.7%, other 10.4%). Expenditures: 100,262,000,000 sumy (social and cultural affairs 36.9%, investments 18.8%, national economy 13.3%, payments on interest 4.9%, administration 3.0%, other 23.1%).
Household income and expenditure (1995). Average household size (1989) 5.5; income per household 35,165 sumy (U.S.$1,040); sources of income: wages and salaries 63.0%, subsidies, grants, and nonwage income 34.9%, other 2.1%; expenditure: food and beverages 71%, clothing and footwear 14%, recreation 6%, household durables 4%, housing 3%.
Public debt (external, outstanding; 1994): U.S.$1,156,000,000.
Production (metric tons except as noted). Agriculture, forestry, fishing (1995): seed cotton 4,000,000, vegetables 3,089,000, fruit (except grapes) and berries 1,159,800, grapes 576,800, potatoes 440,300, rice 328,000, barley 250,000, corn (maize) 181,000, rye 10,000; livestock (number of live animals) 9,053,000 sheep, 5,500,000 cattle, 350,400 pigs, 30,000,000 chickens; roundwood (1990) 15,000 cu m; fish catch (1993) 23,401. Mining and quarrying (1995): copper 75,000; lead 10,000; gold 80. Manufacturing (value of production in '000,000 sumy; 1993): textiles 987; machine building and metalworking equipment 519; ferrous and nonferrous metals 484; processed foods 429; construction materials 294; chemical products 270; meat and dairy products 206; clothing 141. Construction (1992): residential 7,000,000,000 sq m. Energy production (consumption): electricity (kW-hr; 1994) 47,800,000,000 (47,400,000,000); coal (metric tons; 1995) 3,045,000 (1994; 4,200,000); crude

petroleum (barrels; 1994) 25,655,000 (43,980,000); petroleum products (metric tons; 1994) 7,880,000 (7,880,000); natural gas (cu m; 1995) 48,600,000,000 (1994; 38,564,000,000).
Gross national product (1994): U.S.$21,142,000,000 (U.S.$950 per capita).

Structure of gross domestic product and labour force

	1995 in value '000,000 sumy	% of total value	labour force	% of labour force
Agriculture	85,070	28.5	3,735,000	44.8
Manufacturing and mining	49,068	16.4	1,010,000	12.1
Construction	23,228	7.8	493,000	5.9
Transp. and commun.	25,119	8.4	218,000	2.6
Trade	16,821	5.6	566,000	6.8
Finance Pub. admin., defense Services	} 58,864	19.7	2,135,000	25.6
Other	40,360[2]	13.5	188,000[3]	2.2
TOTAL	298,530	100.0[4]	8,345,000	100.0

Population economically active (1995): total 8,345,000; activity rate of total population 36.8% (participation rates: ages 16–59 [male], 16–54 [female] 74.5%; female [1994] 43.0%; unemployed 2.2%).

Price and earnings indexes (1992 = 100)

	1991	1992	1993	1994	1995
Consumer price index	13.4	100.0	634.1	5,219	11,724
Monthly earnings index	11.8	100.0	1,196	10,791	41,952

Land use (1994): forested 2.9%; meadows and pastures 46.5%; agricultural and under permanent cultivation 10.1%; other 40.5%.

Foreign trade

Balance of trade (current prices)

	1992	1993	1994	1995
U.S.$'000,000	−39.1	+314.8	+26.1	−103.7
% of total	13.7%	11.5%	0.8%	3.1%

Imports (1995): 1,793,800,000 sumy (machinery and metalworking products 29.1%, chemical products 13.6%, ferrous and nonferrous metal products 12.4%, food products 5.5%, forestry and paper products 4.0%, light industrial products 2.9%). *Major import sources[5]:* Russia 58.9%; Kazakstan 16.9%; Ukraine 7.9%; Turkmenistan 5.1%; Tajikistan 4.0%.
Exports (1995): 1,690,100,000 sumy (light industrial products 34.7%, oil and gas 15.1%, machine-building equipment 5.9%, food products 5.8%, electricity 5.4%). *Major export destinations:* Russia 53.4%; Kazakstan 16.1%; Tajikistan 9.6%; Turkmenistan 9.0%; Kyrgyzstan 3.4%.

Transport and communications

Transport. Railroads (1996): length 2,100 mi, 3,380 km; (1991) passenger-mi 3,231,000,000, passenger-km 5,200,000,000; (1991) short ton-mi cargo 48,357,000,000, metric ton-km cargo 70,600,000,000. Roads (1995): total length 48,715 mi, 78,400 km (paved 86%). Vehicles (1994): passenger cars 865,300; buses 14,500. Merchant marine: vessels (100 gross tons and over) n.a.; total deadweight tonnage, n.a. Air transport (1991): passenger-mi 6,524,000,000, passenger-km 10,500,000,000; short ton-mi cargo 60,754,000,000; metric ton-km cargo 88,700,000,000; airports (1996) with scheduled flights 9.
Communications. Daily newspapers (1992): total number 12; total circulation 452,000; circulation per 1,000 population 21. Radio (1991): total number of receivers 3,677,000 (1 per 5.6 persons). Television (1991): total number of receivers 3,308,000 (1 per 6.3 persons). Telephones (main lines; 1993): 1,451,500 (1 per 15.1 persons).

Education and health

Education (1992–93)

	schools[5]	teachers	students	student/ teacher ratio
Primary (age 6–13) Secondary (age 14–17) }	9,100	91,500 300,800	1,852,841 2,893,058	20.3 9.6
Voc., teacher tr.	247	22,164	210,000[5]	11.0
Higher	55	...	230,100[5]	...

Educational attainment (1989). Percentage of population age 25 and over having: primary education or no formal schooling 13.3%; some secondary 19.8%; completed secondary and some postsecondary 57.7%; higher 9.2%.
Literacy (1989): percentage of total population age 15 and over literate 97.2%; males literate 98.5%; females literate 96.0%.
Health (1994): physicians 79,000 (1 per 284 persons); hospital beds 190,000 (1 per 118 persons); (1996) infant mortality rate per 1,000 live births 25.7.

Military

Total active duty personnel (1996): 29,000 (army 86.2%, air force 13.8%).
Military expenditure as percentage of GNP (1994): 0.7%; per capita expenditure U.S.$17.

---

[1]The sum was introduced on July 1, 1994, to replace the sum-coupon (an interim currency introduced in November 1993 to replace the Russian ruble) at a rate of 1 sum to 1,000 sum-coupons. The Russian ruble was banned from circulation in Uzbekistan from mid-April 1994. [2]Includes value-added taxes: excise taxes plus net import taxes minus subsidies. [3]Nondistributable unemployed. [4]Detail does not add to total given because of rounding. [5]1993–94.

Vanuatu

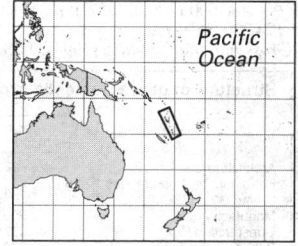

Pacific Ocean

Official name: Ripablik blong Vanuatu (Bislama); République de Vanuatu (French); Republic of Vanuatu (English).
Form of government: republic with a single legislative house (Parliament [50]).
Chief of state: President.
Head of government: Prime Minister.
Capital: Vila.
Official languages: Bislama; French; English.
Official religion: none.
Monetary unit: vatu (VT); valuation (Oct. 11, 1996) 1 U.S.$ = VT 111.01; 1 £ = VT 174.87.

Area and population

Local Government Regions	Capitals	area sq mi	area sq km	population 1989 census
Ambae/Maéwo	Longana	270	699	10,958
Ambrym	Eas	257	666	7,191
Banks/Torres	Sola	341	882	5,985
Éfaté	Vila	356	923	30,868
Épi	Ringdove	172	446	3,628
Malekula	Lakatoro	793	2,053	19,298
Paama	Liro	23	60	1,696
Pentecost	Loltong	193	499	11,341
Santo/Malo	Luganville	1,640	4,248	25,581
Shepherd	Morua	33	86	3,975
Taféa	Isangel	629	1,628	22,423
TOTAL		4,707	12,190	142,944

Demography

Population (1996): 172,000.
Density (1996): persons per sq mi 36.5, persons per sq km 14.1.
Urban-rural (1995): urban 20.0%; rural 80.0%.
Sex distribution (1989): male 51.60%; female 48.40%.
Age breakdown (1989)[1]: under 15, 45.5%; 15–29, 26.6%; 30–44, 15.2%; 45–59, 8.4%; 60–74, 3.7%; 75 and over, 0.6%.
Population projection: (2000) 189,000; (2010) 231,000.
Doubling time: 26 years.
Ethnic composition (1989): Ni-Vanuatu 97.9%; European 1.0%; other Pacific Islanders 0.4%; other 0.7%.
Religious affiliation (1989): Christian 77.2%, of which Presbyterian 35.8%, Roman Catholic 14.5%, Anglican 14.0%, Seventh-day Adventist 8.2%; Custom 4.6%; nonreligious 1.7%; unknown 4.0%; other 12.5%.
Major towns (1989): Vila (Port-Vila) 19,400; Luganville (Santo) 6,900; Port Olry 884[2]; Isangel 752[2].

Vital statistics

Birth rate per 1,000 population (1996): 33.5 (world avg. 25.0).
Death rate per 1,000 population (1996): 6.4 (world avg. 9.3).
Natural increase rate per 1,000 population (1996): 27.1 (world avg. 15.7).
Total fertility rate (avg. births per childbearing woman; 1996): 4.5.
Marriage rate per 1,000 population (1985): c. 7.4.
Divorce rate per 1,000 population (1985): less than 0.7.
Life expectancy at birth (1996): male 65.0 years; female 69.0 years.
Major causes of death per 100,000 population (1994)[3]: diseases of the circulatory system 39.0; diseases of the respiratory system 30.4; malignant neoplasms (cancers) 29.2; infectious and parasitic diseases 25.0; diseases of the digestive system 9.7.

National economy

Budget (1994). Revenue: VT 5,475,000,000 (taxes on international trade 53.8%, nontax revenue 20.7%, taxes on goods and services 18.2%). Expenditures: VT 8,554,000,000 (economic affairs and services 22.6%, general public services 20.4%, education 14.3%, health 7.2%, public order and safety 5.5%).
Public debt (external, outstanding; 1994): U.S.$41,500,000.
Tourism (1994): receipts from visitors U.S.$55,000,000; expenditures by nationals abroad U.S.$1,000,000.
Production (metric tons except as noted). Agriculture, forestry, fishing (1995): coconuts 280,000, roots and tubers 50,000, copra (1994) 30,000, bananas 12,500, vegetables and melons 8,200, cacao beans 1,783, peanuts (groundnuts) 1,750, corn (maize) 700; livestock (number of live animals) 151,000 cattle, 60,000 pigs, 12,000 goats; roundwood (1994) 63,200 cu m; fish catch (1993) 2,925. Mining and quarrying: small quantities of coral-reef limestone, crushed stone, sand, and gravel. Manufacturing (value added in VT '000,000; 1993): food, beverages, and tobacco 568; wood products 287; fabricated metal products 153; chemical, rubber, plastic, and nonmetallic products 118; paper products 68; textiles, clothing, and leather 48. Construction (approvals in Vila and Luganville; 1992): residential 20,386 sq m; nonresidential 19,876 sq m. Energy production (consumption): electricity (kW-hr; 1993) 29,000,000 (29,000,000); coal, none (none); crude petroleum, none (none); petroleum products (metric tons; 1993) none (20,000); natural gas, none (none).
Land use (1994): forested 75.0%; meadows and pastures 2.0%; agricultural 11.8%; other 11.2%.
Population economically active (1989): total 66,957; activity rate of total population 47.0% (participation rates: ages 15–64, 85.0%; female 46.3%; unemployed 0.5%).

Price and earnings indexes (1990 = 100)

	1989	1990	1991	1992	1993	1994	1995
Consumer price index	95.5	100.0	106.5	108.8	114.7	117.4	120.0
Earnings index	...	...	...	...	...	...	...

Gross national product (at current market prices; 1994): U.S.$189,000,000 (U.S.$1,150 per capita).

Structure of gross domestic product and labour force

	1993 in value VT '000,000[4]	1993 % of total value	1989 labour force	1989 % of labour force
Agriculture	2,783	20.8	49,811	74.4
Mining	...	...	1	
Manufacturing	863	6.5	891	1.3
Construction	697	5.2	1,302	1.9
Public utilities	326	2.4	109	0.2
Transportation and communications	939	7.0	1,031	1.5
Trade	4,128	30.9	2,713	4.1
Finance	1,465	11.0	646	1.0
Pub. admin., defense	1,597	11.9 }	7,892	11.8
Services	899	6.7 }		
Other	−331[5]	−2.5[5]	2,561	3.8
TOTAL	13,365[6]	100.0[6]	66,957	100.0

Household income and expenditure (1985)[7]. Average household size (1989) 5.1; income per household U.S.$11,299; sources of income: wages and salaries 59.0%, self-employment 33.7%; expenditure (1990)[7, 8]: food and nonalcoholic beverages 30.5%, housing 20.7%, transportation 13.2%, health and recreation 12.3%, tobacco and alcohol 10.4%.

Foreign trade[9]

Balance of trade (current prices)

	1990	1991	1992	1993	1994	1995
VT '000,000	−8,566	−7,364	−6,689	−6,409	−7,493	−7,486
% of total	66.0%	67.0%	56.8%	53.7%	56.3%	54.1%

Imports (1994): VT 10,043,000,000 (machinery and transport equipment 30.5%, basic manufactures 19.5%, food and live animals 15.6%, mineral fuels 6.7%, chemical products 6.7%, beverages and tobacco 4.7%). *Major import sources* (1993): Japan 35.4%; Australia 21.9%; Spain 13.0%; Italy 10.9%; New Zealand 4.2%; France 2.6%.
Exports (1994): VT 2,911,000,000 (copra 30.7%, beef and veal 15.5%, timber 10.6%, cacao beans and preparations 7.8%[10]). *Major export destinations* (1993)[11]: European Union 32.0%; Japan 29.0%; Australia 11.0%; New Caledonia 7.0%.

Transport and communications

Transport. Railroads: none. Roads (1993): total length 702 mi, 1,130 km (paved 21%). Vehicles (1994): passenger cars 4,000; trucks and buses 2,300. Merchant marine (1992): vessels (100 gross tons and over) 280; total deadweight tonnage 3,259,594. Air transport (1993): passenger-mi 88,000,000, passenger-km 142,000,000; short ton-mi cargo 9,600,000, metric ton-km 14,-000,000; airports (1996) with scheduled flights 29.
Communications. Daily newspapers: none. Radio (1995): total number of receivers 55,000 (1 per 3.1 persons). Television (1993): total number of receivers 2,000 (1 per 80 persons). Telephones (main lines; 1993): 4,100 (1 per 40 persons).

Education and health

Education (1992)

	schools	teachers	students	student/ teacher ratio
Primary (age 6–11)[12]	272	852	26,267	30.8
Secondary (age 11–18)	21[13]	220	4,269	19.4
Voc., teacher tr.	...	...	444	...
Higher	1	...	124[14]	...

Educational attainment (1989). Percentage of population age 6 and over having: no formal schooling or less than one year 22.3%; some primary education 52.6%; lower-level secondary 18.3%; upper-level secondary and higher 4.8%; not stated 2.0%. *Literacy* (1979): total population age 15 and over literate 32,120 (52.9%); males 18,550 (57.3%); females 13,570 (47.8%).
Health (1995): physicians 12 (1 per 14,025 persons); hospital beds 374 (1 per 450 persons); infant mortality rate per 1,000 live births (1996) 41.
Food (1992): daily per capita caloric intake 2,739 (vegetable products 85%, animal products 15%); 120% of FAO recommended minimum requirement.

Military

Total active duty personnel: Vanuatu has a paramilitary force of about 300.

---

[1]For indigenous population only. [2]1979. [3]Deaths reported to the Ministry of Health only. [4]At 1983 prices. [5]Imputed bank service charges. [6]Detail does not add to total given because of rounding. [7]Vila and Luganville only. [8]Weights of consumer price index components. [9]Imports c.i.f.; exports f.o.b. [10]1993. [11]Destination of domestic exports only. [12]Excludes independent private schools. [13]1986. [14]1991.

Venezuela

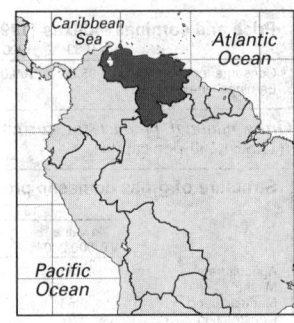

Official name: República de Venezuela (Republic of Venezuela).
Form of government: federal multiparty republic with two legislative houses (Senate [52[1]]; Chamber of Deputies [199]).
Head of state and government: President.
Capital: Caracas.
Official language: Spanish.
Official religion: none.
Monetary unit: 1 bolívar (B, plural Bs) = 100 céntimos; valuation[2] (Oct. 11, 1996) 1 U.S.$ = Bs 470.38; 1 £ = Bs 740.98.

Area and population

States	Capitals	area sq mi	area sq km	population 1995 estimate
Amazonas	Puerto Ayacucho	67,900	175,750	66,668
Anzoátegui	Barcelona	16,700	43,300	1,028,097
Apure	San Fernando de Apure	29,500	76,500	376,220
Aragua	Maracay	2,700	7,014	1,335,303
Barinas	Barinas	13,600	35,200	516,789
Bolívar	Ciudad Bolívar	91,900	238,000	1,122,975
Carabobo	Valencia	1,795	4,650	1,807,542
Cojedes	San Carlos	5,700	14,800	226,684
Delta Amacuro	Tucupita	15,500	40,200	110,838
Falcón	Coro	9,600	24,800	684,062
Guárico	San Juan de Los Morros	25,091	64,986	585,418
Lara	Barquisimeto	7,600	19,800	1,423,683
Mérida	Mérida	4,400	11,300	686,709
Miranda	Los Teques	3,070	7,950	2,326,143
Monagas	Maturín	11,200	28,900	551,015
Nueva Esparta	La Asunción	440	1,150	325,909
Portuguesa	Guanare	5,900	15,200	719,473
Sucre	Cumaná	4,600	11,800	771,580
Táchira	San Cristóbal	4,300	11,100	944,259
Trujillo	Trujillo	2,900	7,400	549,878
Yaracuy	San Felipe	2,700	7,100	463,911
Zulia	Maracaibo	24,400	63,100	2,752,431
Other federal entities				
Dependencias Federales	—	50	120	...
Distrito Federal	Caracas	745	1,930	2,268,534
TOTAL		352,144[3]	912,050	21,644,121

Demography

Population (1996): 22,311,000.
Density (1996): persons per sq mi 63.4, persons per sq km 24.5.
Urban-rural (1992): urban 84.6%; rural 15.4%.
Sex distribution (1994): male 50.40%; female 49.60%.
Age breakdown (1992): under 15, 37.4%; 15–29, 28.0%; 30–44, 19.0%; 45–59, 9.7%; 60 and over, 5.9%.
Population projection: (2000) 24,170,000; (2010) 28,716,000.
Doubling time: 33 years.
Ethnic composition (1993): mestizo 67%; white 21%; black 10%; Indian 2%.
Religious affiliation (1991): Roman Catholic 92.1%; other 7.1%.
Major cities (1990): Caracas 1,822,465; Maracaibo 1,249,670; Valencia 903,621; Barquisimeto 625,450; Ciudad Guayana 453,047.

Vital statistics

Birth rate per 1,000 population (1994): 25.7 (world avg. 25.0); (1974) legitimate 47.0%; illegitimate 53.0%.
Death rate per 1,000 population (1994): 4.6 (world avg. 9.3).
Natural increase rate per 1,000 population (1994): 21.1 (world avg. 15.7).
Total fertility rate (avg. births per childbearing woman; 1994): 3.1.
Marriage rate per 1,000 population (1992): 5.4.
Divorce rate per 1,000 population (1992): 0.9.
Life expectancy at birth (1994): male 70.1 years; female 76.0 years.
Major causes of death per 100,000 population (1992): heart diseases 79.9; malignant neoplasms (cancers) 53.7; accidents 43.6; perinatal problems 33.0; cerebrovascular diseases 29.7; pneumonia 17.3.

National economy

Budget (1994). Revenue: Bs 1,635,864,000,000 (tax revenues 78.3%, oil revenues 18.2%, nontax revenues 3.5%). Expenditures: Bs 1,627,732,000,000 (subsidies 32.0%, goods and services 29.9%, interest payments 20.7%, capital transfers 9.5%).
Public debt (external, outstanding; 1994): U.S.$28,039,000,000.
Tourism (1994): receipts U.S.$486,000,000; expenditures U.S.$1,429,000,000.
Production (metric tons except as noted). Agriculture, forestry, fishing (1995): sugarcane 6,607,000, bananas 1,210,000, corn (maize) 1,100,000, rice 643,000, plantains 535,000, oranges 454,000, sorghum 300,000, cassava 285,000; livestock (number of live animals) 14,231,000 cattle, 2,960,000 goats, 2,850,000 pigs, 95,000,000 chickens; roundwood (1994) 2,014,000 cu m; fish catch (1993) 390,333. Mining and quarrying (1995): iron ore 19,484,000; limestone 15,234,000; bauxite 5,183,000; gold 7,793 kg; diamonds 296,000 carats. Manufacturing (value added in Bs '000,000; 1993): food products 121,258; chemicals 112,822; base metals 84,289; beverages 73,095; transport equipment 65,635; nonmetallic mineral products 47,296; metal products 37,586; tobacco 34,872; paper and paper products 23,682. Construction (in Bs; 1992): residential 77,648,000,000; nonresidential 356,982,000,000. Energy production (consumption): electricity (kW-hr; 1994) 73,116,000,000 (72,796,000,000); coal (metric tons; 1994) 4,741,000 (354,000); crude petroleum (barrels; 1994)

986,468,000 (380,271,000); petroleum products (metric tons; 1994) 54,575,000 (24,229,000); natural gas (cu m; 1994) 24,675,000,000 (24,675,000,000).
Gross national product (1994): U.S.$59,025,000,000 (U.S.$2,760 per capita).

Structure of gross domestic product and labour force

	in value Bs '000,000[4] 1993	% of total value	labour force	% of labour force
Agriculture	25,738	4.6	749,700	9.9
Petroleum and natural gas } Mining	124,334	22.4	69,700	0.9
Manufacturing	90,655	16.3	1,080,700	14.3
Construction	40,037	7.2	653,800	8.7
Public utilities	9,329	1.7	52,100	0.7
Transp. and commun.	29,409	5.3	452,300	6.0
Trade	75,527	13.6	1,596,600	21.2
Finance	5	5	463,600	6.1
Pub. admin., defense	46,940	8.5 }	1,944,000	25.8
Services	103,705[5]	18.7[5]		
Other	9,569	1.7	483,700[6]	6.4[6]
TOTAL	555,243	100.0	7,546,200	100.0

Population economically active (1993): total 7,546,200; activity rate 36.3% (participation rates: over age 15, 57.9%; female 31.2%; unemployed 6.3%).

Price and earnings indexes (1990 = 100)

	1989	1990	1991	1992	1993	1994	1995
Consumer price index	71.1	100.0	134.2	176.4	243.6	391.8	626.5
Monthly earnings index[7]	67.1	100.0	...	...	...	...	...

Household income and expenditure. Average household size (1990) 5.1; average annual income per household (1981) Bs 42,492 (U.S.$9,899); sources of income: n.a.; expenditure (1990): food 37.1%, rent and utilities 9.4%, clothing 8.3%, transportation and communications 5.1%, education and recreation 4.9%, household furnishings and maintenance 2.8%.
Land use (1994): forested 34.0%; meadows and pastures 20.2%; agricultural and under permanent cultivation 4.4%; other 41.4%.

Foreign trade

Balance of trade (current prices)

	1990	1991	1992	1993	1994	1995
Bs '000,000	+529,115	+286,500	+154,700	+274,600	+1,159,400	+1,407.7
% of total	46.7%	20.1%	9.3%	12.1%	32.7%	27.2%

Imports (1994): Bs 1,192,700,000,000 (machinery 30.8%, transport equipment 13.8%, chemicals 13.5%, basic metal manufactures 7.9%, crude materials, excluding fuels 4.7%, cereals and preparations 4.4%, precision and photographic equipment 2.7%). *Major import sources:* U.S. 46.1%; Japan 5.6%; Germany 5.5%; Colombia 5.0%; Italy 3.7%; Canada 3.7%; Brazil 3.2%.
Exports (1994): Bs 2,349,499,000,000 (crude petroleum and petroleum products 75.2%, basic metal manufactures 9.0%). *Major export destinations:* U.S. 52.8%; Colombia 7.2%; Netherlands Antilles 6.4%; Suriname 5.4%; Brazil 3.5%; Germany 2.1%; Dominican Republic 1.9%; Japan 1.7%.

Transport and communications

Transport. Railroads (1993): route length 363 km; passenger-km 44,000,000; metric ton-km cargo 26,000,000. Roads (1993): total length 93,472 km (paved 32%). Vehicles (1993): passenger cars 1,507,309; trucks and buses 474,466. Merchant marine (1992): vessels (over 100 gross tons) 271; total deadweight tonnage 1,355,419. Air transport (1993): passenger-km 6,708,000,000; metric ton-km cargo 149,000,000; airports (1996) with scheduled flights 24.
Communications. Daily newspapers (1992): total number 82; total circulation 4,200,000; circulation per 1,000 population 208. Radio (1995): 8,300,000 receivers (1 per 2.6 persons). Television (1995): 3,700,000 receivers (1 per 5.9 persons). Telephones (main lines; 1993): 2,082,800 (1 per 10 persons).

Education and health

Education (1992–93)

	schools	teachers	students	student/ teacher ratio
Primary (age 7–12)	15,984	184,321	4,222,035	22.9
Secondary (age 13–17)[8]	1,621[9]	34,183	298,534	8.7
Higher	99[10]	43,833[9]	550,783[9]	12.6[9]

Educational attainment (1990). Percentage of population age 25 and over having: no formal schooling 23.5%; primary education or less 47.2%; some secondary and secondary 22.3%; postsecondary 7.0%. *Literacy* (1990): total population age 15 and over literate 13,371,743 (92.2%); males 6,742,992 (93.5%); females 6,628,751 (91.1%).
Health (1992): physicians (1989) 32,616 (1 per 576 persons); hospital beds 52,786 (1 per 382 persons); infant mortality rate (1994) 27.7.
Food (1992): daily per capita caloric intake 2,618 (vegetable products 85%, animal products 15%); 106% of FAO recommended minimum.

Military

Total active duty personnel (1996): 79,000 (army 72.1%, navy 19.0%, air force 8.9%). *Military expenditure as percentage of GNP* (1994): 1.3% (world 3.0%); per capita expenditure U.S.$35.

---

[1]Includes three former presidents holding lifetime membership; one former president was deprived of his seat because of a criminal conviction in mid-1996. [2]Free market rate; fixed exchange rate introduced in July 1994 was ended in December 1995. [3]Detail does not add to total given because of rounding. [4]At 1984 prices. [5]Services includes Finance. [6]Mostly unemployed. [7]Blue-collar workers. [8]Includes vocational and teacher training. [9]1991–92. [10]1990–91.

Vietnam

Official name: Cong Hoa Xa Hoi Chu Nghia Viet Nam (Socialist Republic of Vietnam).
Form of government: socialist republic with one legislative house (National Assembly [395]).
Chief of state: President.
Head of government: Prime Minister.
Capital: Hanoi.
Official language: Vietnamese.
Official religion: none.
Monetary unit: 1 dong (D) = 10 hao = 100 xu; valuation (Oct. 11, 1996) 1 U.S.$ = D 11,057; 1 £ = D 17,418.

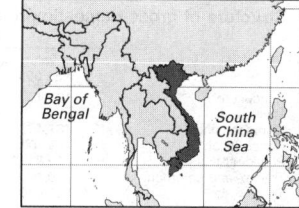

Area and population		area		population
Regions				1993
Provinces	Capitals	sq mi	sq km	estimate
Dong bang song Cuu Long		15,280	39,575[1]	15,531,600
An Giang	Long Xuyen	1,322	3,424	1,933,800
Ben Tre	Ben Tre	868	2,247	1,309,400
Can Tho	Can Tho	1,179	3,054	1,780,600
Dong Thap	Cao Lanh	1,265	3,276	1,462,900
Kien Giang	Rach Gia	2,410	6,243	1,326,600
Long An	Tan An	1,675	4,338	1,224,800
Minh Hai	Ca Mau	2,969	7,689	1,719,100
Soc Trang	Soc Trang	1,200	3,107	1,172,600
Tien Giang	My Tho	903	2,339	1,622,000
Tra Vinh	Tra Vinh	915	2,369	938,500
Vinh Long	Vinh Long	574	1,487	1,041,300
Dong bang song Hong		4,810[1]	12,457[1]	13,808,800
Ha Tay	Ha Dong	831	2,153	2,217,800
Hai Hung	Hai Duong	985	2,552	2,658,000
Haiphong (MUNICIPALITY)	—	580	1,503	1,583,900
Hanoi (CAPITAL)	—	355	920	2,154,900
Nam Ha	Nam Dinh	934	2,419	2,585,900
Ninh Binh	Ninh Binh	536	1,387	839,900
Thai Binh	Thai Binh	588	1,524	1,768,400
Dong Nam Bo		9,066[1]	23,481	8,692,900
Ba Ria–Vung Tau	Vung Tau	756	1,957	657,100
Dong Nai	Bien Hoa	2,264	5,864	1,762,900
Ho Chi Minh City (MUNICIPALITY)	—	807	2,090	4,322,300
Song Be	Thu Dau Mot	3,686	9,546	1,081,700
Tay Ninh	Tay Ninh	1,554	4,024	868,900
Duyen hai mien trung		17,692[1]	45,823	7,374,700
Binh Dinh	Quy Nhon	2,346	6,076	1,373,100
Binh Thuan	Phan Thiet	3,086	7,992	858,700
Khanh Hoa	Nha Trang	2,030	5,258	923,700
Ninh Thuan	Phan Rang Thap Cham	1,324	3,430	449,100
Phu Yen	Tuy Hoa	2,017	5,223	708,900
Quang Nam–Da Nang	Da Nang	4,629	11,988	1,911,700
Quang Ngai	Quang Ngai	2,261	5,856	1,149,500
Khu Bon cu		19,763	51,187	9,516,900
Ha Tinh	Ha Tinh	2,337	6,054	1,293,600
Nghe An	Vinh	6,325	16,381	2,680,600
Quang Binh	Dong Hoi	3,082	7,983	736,700
Quang Tri	Dong Ha	1,773	4,592	520,900
Thanh Hoa	Thanh Hoa	4,312	11,168	3,311,900
Thua Thien–Hue	Hue	1,934	5,009	973,200
Mien nui va trung du		39,749[1]	102,949	12,109,300
Bac Thai	Thai Nguyen	2,511	6,503	1,144,500
Cao Bang	Cao Bang	3,261	8,445	624,700
Ha Bac	Bac Giang	1,781	4,614	2,262,800
Ha Giang	Ha Giang	3,024	7,831	520,400
Hoa Binh	Hoa Binh	1,781	4,612	712,900
Lai Chau	Lai Chau	6,618	17,140	501,200
Lang Son	Lang Son	3,153	8,167	671,900
Lao Cai	Lao Cai	3,108	8,049	535,400
Quang Ninh	Hong Gai	2,293	5,939	889,600
Son La	Son La	5,487	14,210	776,000
Tuyen Quang	Tuyen Quang	2,240	5,801	628,500
Vinh Phu	Viet Tri	1,867	4,836	2,203,200
Yen Bai	Yen Bai	2,626	6,802	638,200
Tay Nguyen		21,455[1]	55,569	2,903,500
Dac Lac	Buon Ma Thuot	7,645	19,800	1,173,300
Gia Lai	Play Ku	6,047	15,662	737,700
Kon Tum	Kon Tum	3,835	9,934	249,600
Lam Dong	Da Lat	3,929	10,173	742,900
TOTAL		127,816[1]	331,041	70,982,500[2]

Demography

Population (1996): 76,151,000.
Density (1996): persons per sq mi 595.8, persons per sq km 230.0.
Urban-rural (1995): urban 20.8%; rural 79.2%.
Sex distribution (1995): male 49.24%; female 50.76%.
Age breakdown (1995): under 15, 37.5%; 15–29, 28.8%; 30–44, 18.5%; 45–59, 7.9%; 60–74, 5.8%; 75 and over, 1.5%.
Population projection: (2000) 82,648,000; (2010) 98,448,000.
Ethnic composition (1989): Vietnamese 87.1%; Tho (Tay) 1.8%; Chinese (Hoa) 1.5%; Tai 1.5%; Khmer 1.4%; Muong 1.4%; Nung 1.1%; other 4.2%.
Religious affiliation (1992): Buddhist c. 67.0%; Roman Catholic c. 8.0%.
Major cities (1993): Ho Chi Minh City 4,322,300; Hanoi 2,154,900.

Vital statistics

Birth rate per 1,000 population (1996): 26.1 (world avg. 25.0).
Death rate per 1,000 population (1996): 7.0 (world avg. 9.3).
Natural increase rate per 1,000 population (1996): 19.1 (world avg. 15.7).
Total fertility rate (avg. births per childbearing woman; 1996): 3.3.
Life expectancy at birth (1996): male 65.0 years; female 69.0 years.
Morbidity (cases of reportable infectious disease per 100,000 population; 1990): malaria 2,564; trachoma 241; diarrhea 183.

National economy

Budget (1995). Revenue: D 51,570,000,000 (transfers from state enterprises 39.1%; taxes 29.6%; nontax revenues 13.1%). Expenditures: D 55,970,000,000 (current expenditures 73.4%, of which social services 31.7%).
Public debt (external, outstanding; 1995): U.S.$26,800,000,000.
Gross national product (1994): U.S.$13,775,000,000[3] (U.S.$190 per capita[3]).

Structure of gross domestic product and labour force				
	1994			
	in value D '000,000,000	% of total value	labour force	% of labour force
Agriculture, forestry, fishing	48,865	28.7	24,587,000	73.0
Mining, manufacturing	} 50,481	29.6	3,595,000	10.7
Construction			875,000	2.6
Transp. and commun.	6,924	4.1	568,000	1.7
Trade and restaurants	23,072	13.6	1,825,000	5.4
Finance, insurance	3,450	2.0		
Pub. admin.	} 18,270	10.7	} 1,290,000	3.8
Services				
Other	19,196[1]	11.3[4]	929,000	2.8
TOTAL	170,258	100.0	33,669,000	100.0

Tourism (1993): receipts from visitors U.S.$85,000,000.
Production (metric tons except as noted). Agriculture, forestry, fishing (1995): rice 24,963,700, sugarcane 9,843,300, cassava 2,496,500, cashew nuts 100,000; livestock (number of live animals) 16,500,000 pigs, 3,604,200 cattle, 3,000,000 buffalo; roundwood (1994) 34,208,990 cu m; fish catch (1993) 1,100,000. Mining and quarrying (1994): phosphate rock 470,000; gold 10,000 kg. Manufacturing (1994): cement 5,161,000; fish sauce 131,700,000 litres[5]. Energy production (consumption): electricity (kW-hr; 1994) 12,020,000,000 (12,020,000,000); coal (metric tons; 1994) 5,600,000 (4,000,000); crude petroleum (barrels; 1994) 50,282,000 (283,300); petroleum products (metric tons; 1994) 38,000 (3,848,000).
Population economically active (1989): total 30,521,019; activity rate 47.4% (participation rates: ages 15–64, 79.9%; female 51.7%; unemployed 5.8%).
Household income and expenditure. Average household size (1989) 4.8; income per household (1990)[6] D 577,008 (U.S.$93); expenditure (1990): food 62.4%, clothing 5.0%, household goods 4.6%, education 2.9%, housing 2.5%.
Land use (1994): forest 29.6%; pasture 1.0%; agricultural 21.5%; other 47.9%.

Foreign trade

Balance of trade (current prices)						
	1990	1991	1992	1993	1994	1995
U.S.$'000,000	−317	−294	−109	−939	−1,772	−6,115
% of total	5.9%	6.3%	1.8%	13.6%	17.9%	35.9%

Imports (1995): U.S.$11,586,000,000 (1994; machinery and spare parts 18.2%, petroleum products 14.0%, fertilizers 5.0%, steel 3.0%). *Major import sources* (1995): Singapore 17.0%; North and South Korea 12.9%; Taiwan 9.6%.
Exports (1995): U.S.$5,471,000,000 (1994; crude petroleum 24.1%, fish and fish products 13.6%, agricultural and forestry products 13.3%, rice 11.9%). *Major export destinations* (1995): Japan 28.5%; Germany 9.4%; Singapore 7.5%.

Transport and communications

Transport. Railroads (1995): length 2,605 km; passenger-km 2,100,000,000[7]; metric ton-km cargo 1,062,000,000[7]. Roads (1995): total length 106,048 km (paved 26%). Vehicles (1994): passenger cars, trucks, and buses 200,000. Merchant marine (1992): vessels (100 gross tons and over) 230; total deadweight tonnage 872,752. Air transport (1993): passenger-km 209,000,000; metric ton-km cargo 19,000,000; airports (1996) with scheduled flights 12.
Communications. Daily newspapers (1994): 5. Radio (1995): 7,000,000 receivers. Television (1995): 2,500,000 receivers. Telephones (main lines; 1993): 260,000 (1 per 270 persons).

Education and health

Education (1993–94)				
	schools	teachers	students	student/ teacher ratio
Primary (age 7–12)	13,092[8]	275,640	9,725,095	35.3
Secondary (age 13–18)[9]	6,298	166,968	3,815,852	22.9
Vocational	451	12,197	137,405	11.3
Higher	104	20,648	118,589	5.7

Educational attainment (1989). Percentage of population 25 and over having: no formal education (illiterate) 16.6%; some primary 46.6%; complete primary 23.5%; secondary 6.5%; postsecondary and higher 6.8%. *Literacy* (1995): persons 15 and over literate 93.7%; males 96.5%; females 91.2%.
Health (1993): physicians 28,500 (1 per 2,502 persons); hospital beds 194,700 (1 per 366 persons); infant mortality rate (1996) 38.0.
Food (1992): daily per capita caloric intake 2,250; 104% of FAO recommended minimum requirement.

Military

Total active duty personnel (1996): 572,000 (army 87.4%, navy 7.3%, air force 5.3%). *Military expenditure as percentage of GNP* (1995): 4.3%.

[1]Detail does not add to total given because of rounding. [2]Total includes 1,044,800 persons in special enumeration groups not distributed in province and region estimates. [3]Figure indicates the World Bank's nominal assessment of the Vietnamese economy. [4]Includes housing and tourism. [5]1992. [6]Wage workers and government officials only. [7]1994. [8]Includes 2,955 institutions that provide primary and first cycle of secondary education. [9]Includes first and second cycles of secondary education.

Western Samoa

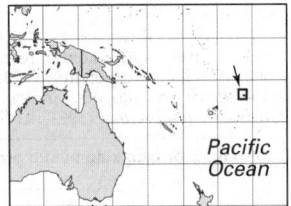

Official name: Malo Sa'oloto Tuto'atasi o Samoa i Sisifo (Samoan); Independent State of Western Samoa (English).
Form of government: constitutional monarchy[1] with one legislative house (Legislative Assembly [49]).
Chief of state: Head of State[2].
Head of government: Prime Minister.
Capital: Apia.
Official languages: Samoan; English.
Official religion: none.
Monetary unit: 1 tala (WS$, plural tala) = 100 sene; valuation (Oct. 11, 1996) 1 U.S.$ = WS$2.44; 1 £ = WS$3.84.

Area and population

Islands	area		population
Political Districts	sq mi	sq km	1986 census
Savaii	659	1,707	44,930
Fa'aseleleaga			...
Gaga'emauga			...
Gaga'ifomauga			...
Palauli			...
Satupa'itea			...
Vaisigano			...
Upolu	432	1,119	112,228
A'ana			...
Aiga-i-le-Tai			...
Atua			...
Tuamasaga			...
Vaa-o-Fonoti			...
TOTAL	1,093[3]	2,831[3]	157,158[4]

Demography

Population (1996): 167,400.
Density (1996): persons per sq mi 153.2, persons per sq km 59.1.
Urban-rural (1995): urban 21.0%; rural 79.0%.
Sex distribution (1991): male 52.45%; female 47.55%.
Age breakdown (1991): under 15, 40.6%; 15–29, 29.9%; 30–44, 14.6%; 45–59, 8.8%; 60–74, 5.0%; 75 and over, 1.1%.
Population projection: (2000) 174,200; (2010) 192,500.
Doubling time: 23 years.
Ethnic composition (1982): Samoan (Polynesian) c. 88%; Euronesian c. 10%; European c. 2%.
Religious affiliation (1991): Congregational 43.0%; Roman Catholic 21.0%; Methodist 17.0%; Mormon 10.0%; Seventh-day Adventist 3.0%; other 6.0%.
Major city (1991): Apia 34,126.

Vital statistics

Birth rate per 1,000 population (1996): 35.9 (world avg. 25.0); (1978) legitimate 43.5%; illegitimate 56.5%.
Death rate per 1,000 population (1996): 5.5 (world avg. 9.3).
Natural increase rate per 1,000 population (1996): 30.4 (world avg. 15.7).
Total fertility rate (avg. births per childbearing woman; 1996): 4.2.
Marriage rate per 1,000 population (1989)[5]: 5.3.
Divorce rate per 1,000 population (1989)[5]: 0.2.
Life expectancy at birth (1996): male 67.0 years; female 71.0 years.
Major causes of death per 100,000 population (1992)[5]: congestive heart failure 14.0%; malignant neoplasms (cancers) 11.0%; cerebrovascular diseases 8.0%; injury and poisoning 8.0%; pneumonia 6.0%; septicemia 6.0%; diabetes mellitus 4.0%; intestinal infectious diseases 2.0%.

National economy

Budget (1995–96). Revenue: WS$229,500,000 (tax revenue 46.4%; grants 38.6%; nontax revenue 15.0%). Expenditures: WS$244,500,000 (development expenditure 53.2%; current expenditure 46.8%, of which administration 19.3%, net lending 4.6%).
Production (metric tons except as noted). Agriculture, forestry, fishing (1995): coconuts 130,000, taro 36,900, copra (1994) 11,000, bananas 10,000, papayas 10,000, pineapples 5,700, mangoes 4,900, avocados 1,700, cow's milk 1,150; livestock (number of live animals) 178,800 pigs, 26,000 cattle; roundwood 131,000 cu m; fish catch (1993) 1,608. Mining and quarrying: n.a. Manufacturing (in WS$'000; 1990): beer 8,708; cigarettes 6,551; coconut cream 5,576; sawn wood 3,662; coconut oil 3,442; corned meat 2,905; soap 1,487; paints 1,457. Construction (permits issued in WS$; 1993): residential 12,-415,000; commercial, industrial, and other 19,346,000. Energy production (consumption; kW-hr; 1994) 64,000,000 (64,000,000); coal, none (n.a.); crude petroleum, none (n.a.); petroleum products (metric tons; 1994) none (40,000).
Household income and expenditure. Average household size (1981) 5.1; income per household (1972) WS$1,518 (U.S.$2,200); sources of income (1972): wages 49.4%, self-employment 22.8%, remittances, gifts, and other assistance 18.0%, land rent 8.7%, other 1.1%; expenditure (1987)[6]: food 58.8%, transportation 9.0%, housing and furnishings 5.1%, fuel and lighting 5.0%, clothing 4.2%, other goods and services 1.9%, other 16.0%.
Public debt (external, outstanding; 1994): U.S.$154,600,000.
Gross national product (at current market prices; 1994): U.S.$163,000,000 (U.S.$970 per capita).

Structure of gross domestic product and labour force

	1993		1986	
	in value WS$'000	% of total value	labour force	% of labour force
Agriculture	133,400	42.9	29,023	63.6
Mining	...	...	1,587	3.5
Manufacturing	37,400	12.0 }		
Construction	9,700	3.1	62	0.1
Public utilities	19,800	6.4	855	1.9
Transp. and commun.	9,100	2.9	1,491	3.3
Trade	25,800	8.3	1,710	3.7
Finance			842	1.8
Pub. admin., defense	44,800	14.4 }	9,436	20.7
Services	30,900	9.9 }		
Other	...	...	629	1.4
TOTAL	310,900	100.0[7]	45,635	100.0

Population economically active (1994): total 47,207; activity rate of total population 28.7% (participation rates: ages 15–64 [1981] 48.6%; female [1986] 18.8%).

Price and earnings indexes (1990 = 100)

	1989	1990	1991	1992	1993	1994	1995
Consumer price index	86.8	100.0	98.2	107.0	108.9	128.9	130.2
Earnings index	...	...	...	...	...	...	...

Tourism (1993): receipts from visitors U.S.$21,000,000; expenditures by nationals abroad U.S.$2,000,000.
Land use (1994): forested 47.3%; meadows and pastures 0.4%; agricultural and under permanent cultivation 43.1%; other 9.2%.

Foreign trade[8]

Balance of trade (current prices)

	1990	1991	1992	1993	1994	1995
WS$'000	−137,300	−196,994	−238,965	−228,318	−178,638	−192,293
% of total	77.0%	83.9%	89.3%	87.4%	90.7%	81.5%

Imports (1994): WS$206,347,000 (1993; industrial supplies 32.3%, food 23.4%, machinery 18.4%, petroleum products 10.8%, consumer goods 9.9%, transportation equipment 5.1%). *Major import sources* (1993): New Zealand 38.9%; Australia 16.4%; United States 11.5%; Japan 10.7%; Fiji 9.6%; Germany 2.0%; Singapore 1.3%.
Exports (1994): WS$9,122,000 (1993; taro 57.6%, coconut cream 21.0%, beer 7.9%, cigarettes 4.8%). *Major export destinations* (1993): New Zealand 51.6%; American Samoa 17.4%; United States 12.6%; Australia 12.1%.

Transport and communications

Transport. Railroads: none. Roads (1987): total length[9] 1,296 mi, 2,085 km (paved 19%). Vehicles (1994): passenger cars 1,000; trucks and buses 900. Merchant marine (1992): vessels (100 gross tons and over) 7; total deadweight tonnage 6,501. Air transport: passengers, n.a.; cargo, n.a.; airports (1996) with scheduled flights 2.
Communications. Daily newspapers: none. Radio (1995): 75,000 receivers (1 per 2.2 persons). Television (1995): 5,000 receivers (1 per 33 persons). Telephones (main lines; 1993): 6,500 (1 per 25 persons).

Education and health

Education (1986–87)

	schools	teachers	students	student/ teacher ratio
Primary (age 5–11)	164[10]	1,511[11]	40,755	27.0
Secondary (age 12–18)	38[12]	492	11,395	23.2
Voc., teacher tr.	4[10]	37	228	6.2
Higher[10]	6	25	271	10.8

Educational attainment (1981). Percentage of population age 25 and over having: some primary education 16.5%; complete primary 24.5%; some secondary 52.1%; complete secondary 3.1%; higher 2.0%; unknown 1.8%.
Literacy (1981): virtually 100%.
Health: physicians (1992) 60 (1 per 2,682 persons); hospital beds (1991) 863 (1 per 255 persons); infant mortality rate per 1,000 live births (1996) 60.0.
Food (1992): daily per capita caloric intake 2,828 (vegetable products 74%, animal products 26%); 124% of FAO recommended minimum requirement.

Military

No military forces are maintained; New Zealand is responsible for defense.

---

[1]According to the constitution, the current Head of State, paramount chief HH Malietoa Tanumafili II, will hold office for life. Upon his death, the monarchy will functionally cease, and future Heads of State will be elected by the Legislative Assembly. [2]Official title is O le Ao o le Malo. [3]Total includes 2 sq mi (5 sq km) of uninhabited islands. [4]The provisional total for the 1991 census is 159,862. [5]Registered only. [6]Consumer price index components. [7]Detail does not add to total given because of rounding. [8]Import figures are f.o.b. in balance of trade and c.i.f. in commodities and trading partners. [9]Total length includes 733 mi (1,180 km) of plantation roads. [10]1983. [11]Includes some secondary teachers. [12]1982.

Yemen

Official name: Al-Jumhūrīyah
al-Yamanīyah (Republic of Yemen).
Form of government: multiparty
republic with one legislative house
(Council of Representatives [301]).
Head of state: President[1].
Head of government: Prime Minister.
Capital: Ṣanʿāʾ.
Official language: Arabic.
Official religion: Islam.
Monetary unit: 1 Yemeni Rial
(YRls) = 100 fils; valuation (Oct. 11,
1996): 1 U.S.$ = YRls 100.00,
1 £ = YRls 157.53.

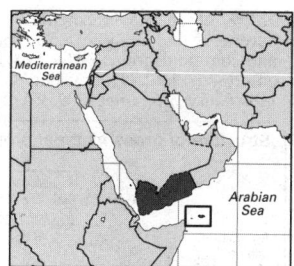

Area and population		area		population
				1994
Governorates	Capitals	sq mi	sq km	census
Northern Yemen				
Al-Baydạ̄'	Al-Baydạ̄'	4,310	11,170	509,265
Dhamār	Dhamār	3,430	8,870	1,050,346
Ḥajjah	Ḥajjah	3,700	9,590	1,262,590
Al-Ḥudaydah	Al-Ḥudaydah	5,240	13,580	1,749,944
Ibb	Ibb	2,480	6,430	1,959,313
Al-Jawf	Al-Jawf	...	...	157,096
Al-Maḥwīt	Al-Maḥwīt	830	2,160	403,465
Maʾrib	Maʾrib	15,400	39,890	167,388
Ṣaʿdah	Ṣaʿdah	4,950	12,810	486,059
Ṣanʿāʾ	Ṣanʿāʾ	7,840	20,310	1,910,286
Taʿizz	Taʿizz	4,020	10,420	2,205,947
Southern Yemen				
Abyān	Zinjibār	8,297	21,489	414,543
ʿAdan	Aden	2,695	6,980	562,162
Ḥaḍramawt	Al-Mukallā	59,991	155,376	870,025
Laḥij	Laḥij	4,928	12,766	634,652
Al-Mahrah	Al-Ghaydah	25,618	66,350	112,512
Shabwah	ʿAtāq	28,536	73,908	377,080
TOTAL		182,278[2, 3]	472,099[2]	14,832,673

Demography

Population (1996): 16,600,000.
Density (1996)[4]: persons per sq mi 77.5, persons per sq km 30.0.
Urban-rural (1994): urban 23.5%; rural 76.5%.
Sex distribution (1994): male 48.54%; female 51.46%.
Age breakdown (1994): under 15, 51.3%; 15–29, 22.9%; 30–44, 12.8%; 45–59, 7.7%; 60–74, 4.0%; 75 and over, 1.3%.
Population projection: (2000) 19,200,000; (2010) 25,800,000.
Doubling time: 21 years.
Ethnic composition (1986): predominantly Arab.
Religious affiliation (1980): Muslim 99.9%, of which Sunnī 53.0%, Shīʿī 46.9%; other 0.1%.
Major cities (1986): Ṣanʿāʾ 427,150; Aden 318,000[5]; Taʿizz 178,043; Al-Ḥudaydah 155,110; Al-Mukallā 59,100[5].

Vital statistics

Birth rate per 1,000 population (1994): 45.1 (world avg. 25.0).
Death rate per 1,000 population (1994): 11.8 (world avg. 9.3).
Natural increase rate per 1,000 population (1994): 33.3 (world avg. 15.7).
Total fertility rate (avg. births per childbearing woman; 1994): 7.4.
Marriage rate per 1,000 population: n.a.
Divorce rate per 1,000 population: n.a.
Life expectancy at birth (1994): male 55.9 years; female 59.1 years.
Major causes of death per 100,000 population: n.a.; however, major diseases include malaria, tuberculosis, leprosy, and intestinal infections.

National economy

Budget (1995). Revenue: YRls 87,951,000,000 (current revenue 75.7%, of which state property revenue 26.9%, international trade 18.4%, taxes on income and profits 15.6%; development revenue 19.7%; loans and grants 4.7%). Expenditures: YRls 124,140,409,000 (defense 25.2%; education 17.6%; public order and safety 8.1%; health 4.7%).
Production (metric tons except as noted). Agriculture, forestry, fishing (1995): sorghum 484,000, potatoes 200,000, tomatoes 192,000, wheat 170,000, grapes 147,000, watermelons 102,000, bananas 74,000, onions 56,500, papayas 55,000, millet 55,000; livestock (number of live animals) 3,715,000 sheep, 3,230,000 goats, 1,130,000 cattle, 500,000 asses, 172,900 camels, 21,500,000 chickens; roundwood (1994) 324,000 cu m; fish catch (1993) 86,811. Mining and quarrying (1994): salt 280,000; gypsum 80,000. Manufacturing (value-added YRls '000,000; 1994): food, beverages, and tobacco 27,226; chemicals and chemical products 5,619; nonmetallic mineral products 4,482; paper products 3,599; clothing and textiles 724; basic metal industries 632; wood products 242. Construction: n.a. Energy production (consumption): electricity (kW-hr; 1994) 1,958,000,000 (1,958,000,000); coal, none (n.a.); crude petroleum (barrels; 1994) 122,134,000 (25,945,000); petroleum products (metric tons; 1994) 3,330,000 (3,100,000).
Population economically active (1986): total 2,043,237; activity rate of total population 19.6% (participation rates: 15–64, 41.2%; female [1992] 14.0%; unemployed [1994] c. 50%).

Price index (1990 = 100)						
	1989	1990	1991	1992	1993	1994
Consumer price index	73.1	100.0	144.9	218.2	354.2	619.8

Gross national product (at current market prices; 1994): U.S.$3,884,000,000 (U.S.$280 per capita).

Structure of gross domestic product and labour force	1994		1986	
	in value YRls '000,000[6]	% of total value	labour force	% of labour force
Agriculture	39,718	18.2	1,151,348	56.3
Mining	21,476	9.8	11,771	0.6
Manufacturing	28,034	12.8	94,913	4.6
Public utilities	1,640	0.8	160,952	7.9
Construction	6,821	3.1	32,852	1.6
Transp. and commun.	23,797	10.9	107,611	5.3
Trade	31,289	14.3	248,979	12.2
Finance	13,578	6.2	8,757	0.4
Pub. admin., defense	44,593	20.4	226,054	11.1
Services	1,758	0.8	...	...
Other	5,572[7]	2.6[7]	...	...
TOTAL	218,276	100.0[3]	2,043,237	100.0

Household income and expenditure. Average household size (1994) 6.7; income per household: n.a.; sources of income: n.a.; expenditure: n.a.
Tourism: receipts from visitors (1994) U.S.$19,000,000; expenditures by nationals abroad U.S.$78,000,000.
Public debt (external, outstanding; 1994): U.S.$5,306,000.
Land use (1994): forested 3.8%; meadows and pastures 30.4%; agricultural and under permanent cultivation 2.9%; other 62.9%.

Foreign trade[8]

Balance of trade						
	1989	1990	1991	1992	1993	1994
YRls '000,000	−10,839	−13,797	−8,582	−18,238	−25,382	−29,389
% of total	44.5%	49.4%	37.7%	60.0%	69.0%	76.6%

Imports (1993): U.S.$2,821,200,000 (food and live animals 26.1%, basic manufactured goods 23.8%, machinery and transport equipment 22.6%, chemical products 7.5%, mineral fuels 6.7%, beverages and tobacco 1.8%). *Major import sources:* Europe 32.9%, of which EC 31.0%; Asia 27.5%, of which Japan 4.7%, India 1.7%; Arab countries 23.4%, of which Economic and Social Commission for Western Asia (ESCWA) countries 19.8%; the Americas 12.2%, of which U.S. 9.6%, Canada 0.1%; Oceania 1.8%; Africa 0.3%.
Exports (1993): U.S.$374,200,000 (mineral fuels 76.2%, food and live animals 12.6%, crude minerals 6.7%). *Major export destinations:* Asia 67.7%, of which Japan 26.2%, India 6.0%; Arab countries 17.3%, of which ESCWA countries 11.7%; Europe 12.3%, of which EC 6.9%; the Americas 1.0%, of which U.S. 0.9%; Africa 0.7%.

Transport and communications

Transport. Railroads: none. Roads (1995): total length 64,605 km (paved 7.9%). Vehicles (1995): passenger cars 229,084; trucks and buses 282,615. Merchant marine (1992): vessels (100 gross tons and over) 40; deadweight tonnage 13,653. Air transport (1992): passenger-km 1,124,000,000; metric ton-km cargo 114,000,000; airports (1996) with scheduled flights 11.
Communications. Daily newspapers (1992): total number 4; total circulation 236,000; circulation per 1,000 population 19. Radio (1995): 665,000 receivers (1 per 24.1 persons). Television (1995): 100,000 receivers (1 per 160.0 persons). Telephones (main lines; 1993): 162,100 (1 per 83.0 persons).

Education and health

Education (1993–94)[9]	schools	teachers	students	student/ teacher ratio
Primary (age 7–12)	8,045[10]	70,700	2,400,836	34.0
Secondary (age 13–18)	852[10]	8,617	194,663	22.6
Voc., teacher tr.	181[10]	875	48,415	55.3
Higher	2	2,185	80,026	36.6

Educational attainment (1986)[9]. Percentage of population age 10 and over having: no formal schooling 74.2%; reading and writing ability 19.8%; primary education 4.0%; secondary education 0.6%; higher 0.6%; not specified 0.8%. *Literacy* (1994): percentage of total population age 15 and over literate 43.2%; males literate 68.6%; females literate 23.1%.
Health (1994): physicians 2,785 (1 per 4,549 persons); hospital beds 9,169 (1 per 1,591 persons); infant mortality rate per 1,000 live births (1994) 80.9.
Food (1992): daily per capita caloric intake 2,203 (vegetable products 95%; animal products 5%); 91% of FAO recommended minimum requirement.

Military

Total active duty personnel (1996): 42,000 (army 88.1%, navy 3.6%, air force 8.3%). *Military expenditure as percentage of GNP* (1991): 15.7% (world 5.0%); per capita expenditure (1993) U.S.$25.

---

[1]Presidential Council assisting the President was abolished by a constitutional amendment of September 1994. [2]Yemeni territorial claims with regard to alignment of the long-undemarcated eastern boundary with Saudi Arabia (which increased Yemen's claimed total area to 214,300 sq mi [555,000 sq km]) were under negotiation with Saudi Arabia in 1996. [3]Detail does not add to total given because of rounding. [4]Based on the higher total area estimate of 214,300 sq mi (555,000 sq km). [5]1984. [6]In purchasers' value at current prices. [7]Includes import duties of 6.6 million Yemeni Rials less imputed bank service charges. [8]Imports are c.i.f. [9]Yemen Arab Republic only. [10]1992–93.

Yugoslavia

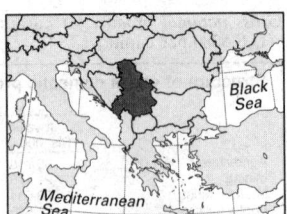

Official name: Savezna Republika Jugoslavija (Federal Republic of Yugoslavia).
Form of government: federal multiparty republic with two legislative houses (Chamber of Republics [40]; Chamber of Citizens [138]).
Chief of state: Federal President.
Head of government: Prime Minister.
Capital: Belgrade.
Official language: Serbo-Croatian.
Official religion: none.
Monetary unit[1]: 1 Yugoslav new dinar (second) = 100 paras; valuation (Oct. 11, 1996) 1 U.S.$ = 5.06 Yugoslav new dinars; 1 £ = 7.97 Yugoslav new dinars.

Area and population

Republics	Capitals	area		population 1995 estimate
		sq mi	sq km	
Montenegro	Podgorica	5,333	13,812	635,000
Serbia	Belgrade	21,609	55,968	5,806,000
Autonomous provinces[2]				
Kosovo and Metohia	Priština	4,203	10,887	1,989,000
Vojvodina	Novi Sad	8,304	21,506	2,114,000
TOTAL		39,449	102,173	10,544,000

Demography

Population (1996): 10,473,000.
Density (1996): persons per sq mi 265.5, persons per sq km 102.5.
Urban-rural (1991): urban 52.0%; rural 48.0%.
Sex distribution (1996): male 49.53%; female 50.47%.
Age breakdown (1991): under 15, 22.8%; 15–29, 21.6%; 30–44, 21.7%; 45–59, 17.1%; 60–74, 12.2%; 75 and over, 3.5%; unknown, 1.1%.
Population projection: (2000) 10,355,000; (2010) 10,731,000.
Doubling time: not applicable; doubling time exceeds 100 years.
Ethnic composition (1991): Serb 62.6%; Albanian 16.5%; Montenegrin 5.0%; Yugoslav 3.4%; Hungarian 3.3%; Muslim 3.2%; Romany (Gypsy) 1.4%; Croat 1.1%; other 3.5%.
Religious affiliation (1995): Serbian Orthodox 65.0%; Muslim 19.0%; Roman Catholic 4.0%; Protestant 1.0%; other, mostly nonreligious 11.0%.
Major cities (1991): Belgrade 1,168,454; Novi Sad 179,626; Niš 175,391; Kragujevac 147,305; Subotica 100,386.

Vital statistics

Birth rate per 1,000 population (1995): 13.2 (world avg. 25.0).
Death rate per 1,000 population (1995): 10.2 (world avg. 9.3).
Natural increase rate per 1,000 population (1995): 3.0 (world avg. 15.7).
Total fertility rate (avg. births per childbearing woman; 1994): 1.9.
Marriage rate per 1,000 population (1995): 5.7.
Divorce rate per 1,000 population (1995): 0.7.
Life expectancy at birth (1994): male 69.1 years; female 74.5 years.
Major causes of death per 100,000 population (1994): diseases of the circulatory system 565.4; malignant neoplasms (cancers) 161.4; accidents, violence, and poisoning 45.0; diseases of the respiratory system 38.7; diseases of the digestive system 28.4.

National economy

Budget (1996). Revenue: 32,098,000,000 Yugoslav new dinars (social security tax 42.9%, turnover tax 17.8%, income tax 14.3%). Expenditure[3]: 32,098,000,000 Yugoslav new dinars (social security 42.9%, current transfers and other 57.1%).
Production (metric tons except as noted). Agriculture, forestry, fishing (1995): corn (maize) 5,828,000, wheat 2,949,000, potatoes 986,000, grapes 433,000, plums 229,000; livestock (number of live animals; 1996) 4,446,000 pigs, 2,656,000 sheep, 1,926,000 cattle, 26,457,000 poultry; roundwood 3,501,000 cu m; fish catch (1994) 6,465. Mining and quarrying (1995): copper ore 20,206,000; lead ore 511,000; magnesite 75,000; aluminum and ingots 17,000; salt 13,500; asbestos ore 3,800; refined silver 31,054 kg. Manufacturing (1995): wheat flour 988,000; crude steel 180,000; nitric acid 148,800; sulfuric acid 87,100; electrolytic copper 78,400; canned fruit 63,200; welded pipes 15,000; rolled copper 13,700; medicines 13,300; rolled aluminum 12,800; canned meat 11,700; refined lead 11,500; cotton yarn 6,100; linoleum flooring 4,300; knitted clothing 2,900; woolen fabrics 13,391,000 sq m; liquor 26,031,000 hectolitres; hosiery 24,387,000 pairs; leather footwear 5,958,000 pairs; furniture 873,000 units; kitchen ranges 92,200 units; refrigerators 50,200 units; bicycles 42,600 units; washing machines and dryers 36,000 units; television receivers 30,600 units; gasoline engines 22,100 units; automobiles 8,400 units; telephones 3,000 units; tractors 1,800 units; trucks 693 units; radios 223 units; railway-goods cars 44 units. Construction (residential units constructed; 1994): 17,442. Energy production (consumption): electricity (kW-hr; 1994) 35,328,000,000 (35,328,000,000); coal (metric tons; 1994) 38,351,000 (38,401,000); crude petroleum (barrels; 1994) 7,997,000 (10,222,000); petroleum products (metric tons; 1994) 781,000 (881,000); natural gas (cu m; 1994) 787,222,000 (1,630,200,000).
Household income and expenditure. Average household size (1993) 3.9; income per household (1995) 11,042 Yugoslav new dinars (U.S.$7,780); sources of income (1995): wages and salaries 41.7%, self-employment 15.8%, pensions 12.7%, other 29.8%; expenditure (1995): food 47.7%, fuel and light 8.4%, beverages and tobacco 8.3%, clothing and footwear 7.4%, transportation and communications 5.7%, health care 5.2%; housing 2.8%, education and entertainment 2.4%, household durable goods 2.1%.
Gross national product (1995): U.S.$15,910,000,000 (U.S.$1,510 per capita).

Structure of gross material product and labour force

	1995			
	in value '000,000 Yugoslav new dinars	% of total value	labour force	% of labour force
Agriculture	8,859.3	22.9	111,000	3.5
Mining } Manufacturing }	16,001.5	41.3	870,000	27.6
Construction	2,561.6	6.6	137,000	4.3
Public utilities	91.6	0.2	53,000	1.7
Transp. and commun.	2,788.3	7.2	167,000	5.3
Trade	6,324.3	16.3	452,000	14.3
Finance	...	...	76,000	2.4
Pub. admin., defense } Services }	534.7	1.4	90,000 / 348,000	2.9 / 11.0
Other	1,602.6	4.1	850,000[4]	26.9[4]
TOTAL	38,764.5[5]	100.0	3,154,000	100.0[5]

Population economically active (1995): total 3,154,000; activity rate 30.0% (participation rates: over age 15, 59.0%; female 43.7%; unemployed 24.6%).

Price and earnings indexes (1992 = 100)

	1992	1993	1994	1995
Consumer price index	100.0	46.5	80.4	93.6
Annual earnings index	100.0	39.0	120.6	250.0

Tourism (1994): receipts from visitors U.S.$31,000,000; expenditures, n.a.
Land use (1994): forested 26.5%; meadows and pastures 20.8%; agricultural and under permanent cultivation 40.0%; other 12.7%.

Foreign trade

Balance of trade (current prices)

	1987	1988	1989	1990	1991	1992
Din '000,000[6]	−1,431	−1,027	−1,716	−2,647	−1,356	−2,105
% of total	8.9%	6.3%	9.3%	12.3%	8.0%	20.8%

Imports (1992): Din 6,119,000,000[6] (manufactured goods 23.4%, mineral fuels and lubricants 22.7%, machinery and transport equipment 18.7%, chemicals 16.4%, food and live animals 7.5%). *Major import sources:* Germany 15.1%; former U.S.S.R. 15.0%; Italy 9.6%; U.S. 3.7%.
Exports (1992): Din 4,014,000,000[6] (manufactured goods 47.2%, machinery and transport equipment 17.2%, food and live animals 17.0%, chemicals 7.0%). *Major export destinations:* former U.S.S.R. 21.1%; Germany 16.3%; Italy 12.0%; Greece 4.1%; U.S. 4.0%.

Transport and communications

Transport. Railroads (1995): length 2,505 mi, 4,031 km; passenger-mi 1,603,000,000, passenger-km 2,580,000,000; short ton-mi cargo 1,000,000,000, metric ton-km cargo 1,460,000,000. Roads (1995): total length 30,687 mi, 49,386 km (paved 58%). Vehicles (1994): passenger cars 1,400,000; trucks and buses 132,000. Merchant marine (1992): fishing vessels 12. Air transport (1995): passenger-mi 478,000,000, passenger-km 770,000,000; short ton-mi cargo 597,000,000, metric ton-km cargo 872,000,000; airports (1996) 5.
Communications. Daily newspapers (1995): total number 17; total circulation 2,294,650; circulation per 1,000 population 218. Radio (1995): 1,469,000 receivers (1 per 7.1 persons). Television (1995): 2,676,000 receivers (1 per 3.9 persons). Telephones (main lines; 1994): 2,315,000 (1 per 4.5 persons).

Education and health

Education (1994–95)

	schools	teachers	students	student/ teacher ratio
Primary (age 7–14)	4,439	51,685	903,088	17.5
Secondary (age 15–18)	557	26,513	338,721	12.8
Higher[7]	146	12,245	159,041	13.0

Educational attainment (1991). Percentage of population age 15 and over having: less than full primary education 33.5%; primary 25.0%; secondary 32.2%; postsecondary and higher 9.3%. *Literacy* (1991): total population age 10 and over literate 93.0%; males literate 97.2%; females literate 88.9%.
Health (1994): physicians 20,942 (1 per 502 persons); hospital beds 57,116 (1 per 184 persons); infant mortality rate per 1,000 live births (1995) 16.4.
Food (1990)[8]: daily per capita caloric intake 3,545 (1988–90; vegetable products 93%, animal products 7%); 140% of FAO recommended minimum.

Military

Total active duty personnel (1996): 113,900 (army 79.0%, air force 14.7%, navy 6.3%). *Military expenditure as percentage of government expenditure:* n.a.

[1]Yugoslavia experienced extreme hyperinflation between early 1993 and January 1994. The new dinar (second), or "super dinar," introduced on Jan. 24, 1994, was pegged to the Deutsche Mark at a rate of one-to-one and equaled 13,000,000,000,000,000,000,000 new dinars. The new dinar had been introduced Jan. 1, 1990, at the rate of 1 new dinar = 10,000 (old) dinars. Inflation was close to zero between January 1994 and September 1994. [2]The autonomous provinces are administratively part of the Republic of Serbia. [3]External analysts estimate defense expenditure at 76.7% of government expenditure. [4]Includes 73,000 workers in the private sector and 775,000 unemployed. [5]Detail does not add to total given because of rounding. [6]In new dinars before extreme hyperinflation. [7]1995–96. [8]Data refer to Yugoslavia as constituted prior to 1991.

Zaire

Official name: République du Zaïre (Republic of Zaire).
Form of government: Transitional regime with one legislative body (High Council of the Republic–Parliament of Transition [738])[1].
Chief of state: President[1].
Head of government: Prime Minister[1].
Capital: Kinshasa.
Official language: French.
Official religion: none.
Monetary unit: new zaïre (NZ)[2]; valuation (Oct. 11, 1996) 1 U.S.$ = NZ 67,004; 1 £ = NZ 105,551.

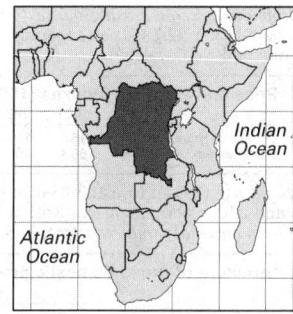

Area and population

Regions	Capitals	area sq mi	area sq km	population 1994 estimate
Bandundu	Bandundu	114,154	295,658	4,907,000
Bas-Zaïre	Matadi	20,819	53,920	2,578,000
Equateur	Mbandaka	155,712	403,292	4,789,000
Haute-Zaïre	Kisangani	194,302	503,239	5,432,000
Kasai-Occidental	Kananga	59,746	154,742	3,117,000
Kasai-Oriental	Mbuji-Mayi	65,754	170,302	3,778,000
Kinshasa	—	3,848	9,965	4,655,000
Maniema	Kindu	51,062	132,250	1,048,000[3]
Nord-Kivu	Goma	22,967	59,483	3,546,000[3]
Shaba	Lubumbashi	191,845	496,877	5,602,000
Sud-Kivu	Bukavu	25,147	65,130	3,093,000[3]
TOTAL		905,354[4]	2,344,858	42,545,000[3]

Demography

Population (1996): 45,259,000.
Density (1996): persons per sq mi 50.0, persons per sq km 19.3.
Urban-rural (1995): urban 29.1%; rural 70.9%.
Sex distribution (1995): male 49.41%; female 50.59%.
Age breakdown (1995): under 15, 47.3%; 15–29, 25.9%; 30–44, 14.1%; 45–59, 8.1%; 60–74, 3.8%; 75 and over, 0.8%.
Population projection: (2000) 51,136,000; (2010) 68,876,000.
Doubling time: 22 years.
Ethnic composition (1983): Luba 18.0%; Kongo 16.1%; Mongo 13.5%; Rwanda 10.3%; Azande 6.1%; Bangi and Ngale 5.8%; Rundi 3.8%; Teke 2.7%; Boa 2.3%; Chokwe 1.8%; Lugbara 1.6%; Banda 1.4%; other 16.6%.
Religious affiliation (1980): Roman Catholic 48.4%; Protestant 29.0%; indigenous Christian 17.1%; traditional beliefs 3.4%; Muslim 1.4%; other 0.7%.
Major cities (1994): Kinshasa 4,655,313; Lubumbashi 851,381; Mbuji-Mayi 806,475; Kisangani 417,517; Kananga 393,030.

Vital statistics

Birth rate per 1,000 population (1990–95): 47.5 (world avg. 25.0).
Death rate per 1,000 population (1990–95): 14.5 (world avg. 9.3).
Natural increase rate per 1,000 population (1990–95): 33.0 (world avg. 15.7).
Total fertility rate (avg. births per childbearing woman; 1990–95): 6.7.
Marriage rate per 1,000 population: n.a.
Divorce rate per 1,000 population: n.a.
Life expectancy at birth (1990–95): male 50.4 years; female 53.7 years.
Major causes of death per 100,000 population: n.a.; however, major causes in the early 1990s included malaria, measles, diarrhea, acute respiratory infections, and AIDS; malnutrition, parasitic diseases, and influenza were major causes of morbidity.

National economy

Budget (1994). Revenue: NZ 208,400,000,000[2] (tax revenue 88.4%, of which taxes on international trade 32.7%, taxes on goods and services 32.3%, taxes on income and profits 15.8%; nontax revenues 11.6%). Expenditures: NZ 529,400,000,000[2] (foreign-financed expenditure 32.0%; goods and services 28.3%, of which political institutions 16.2%, ministry of defense 2.0%; wages and salaries 16.9%).
Public debt (external, outstanding; 1994): U.S.$9,281,000,000.
Tourism (1993): receipts U.S.$6,000,000; expenditures U.S.$16,000,000.
Production (metric tons except as noted). Agriculture, forestry, fishing (1995): cassava 17,500,000, plantains 2,262,398, sugarcane 1,300,000, corn (maize) 1,170,027, peanuts (groundnuts) 581,144, rice 425,168, bananas 412,000, sweet potatoes 407,360, yams 315,000, mangoes 212,000, papayas 210,000, palm oil 181,000, oranges 156,000, pineapples 145,000, dry beans 125,000, seed cotton 77,000, coffee 76,200, palm kernels 72,000, natural rubber 11,000; livestock (number of live animals) 4,220,000 goats, 1,480,000 cattle, 1,200,000 pigs, 1,050,000 sheep, 35,500,000 chickens; roundwood (1994) 43,094,990 cu m; fish catch (1993) 147,250. Mining and quarrying (1995): copper (metal content) 34,000; cobalt (metal content) 4,100; zinc (metal content) 5,000; gold 763 kg; diamonds 17,300,000 carats. Manufacturing (1994): steel 861,000; cement 154,000; sugar 79,000; soap 37,400; tires 35,600; printed fabrics 25,900,000 sq m; cigarettes 2,535,000 cartons; shoes 1,061,000 pairs; beer 160,700 hectolitres. Construction (1985): residential 20,000 sq m; nonresidential 39,000 sq m. Energy production (consumption): electricity (kW-hr; 1994) 5,545,000,000 (4,523,000,000); coal (metric tons; 1994) 93,000 (136,000); crude petroleum (barrels; 1994) 9,845,000 (2,782,000); petroleum products (metric tons; 1994) 350,000 (1,024,000); natural gas, none (none).
Household income and expenditure. Average household size (1982) 6.0; average annual income per household Z 1,200[2] (U.S.$209); sources of income:

n.a.; expenditure (1985): food 61.7%, housing and energy 11.5%, clothing and footwear 9.7%, transportation 5.9%, furniture and utensils 4.9%.
Gross national product (1991): U.S.$8,123,000,000 (U.S.$220 per capita).

Structure of gross domestic product and labour force

	1995 in value Z '000,000[2]	1995 % of total value	1991 labour force	1991 % of labour force
Agriculture	21,248,000	58.0	9,021,000	65.1
Mining	1,591,000	4.3		
Manufacturing	2,365,000	6.5		
Construction	845,000	2.3	2,200,000	15.9
Public utilities	604,000	1.6		
Transp. and commun.	1,023,000	2.8		
Trade	6,114,000	16.7		
Finance	...	...		
Pub. admin., defense	483,000	1.3	2,627,000	19.0
Services	2,038,000	5.6		
Other	313,000	0.9		
TOTAL	36,622,000[4]	100.0	13,848,000	100.0

Population economically active (1991): total 13,848,000; activity rate 35.9% (participation rates [1987]: over age 10, 57.4%; female 40.8%; unemployed, n.a.).

Price and earnings indexes (1992 = 10)

	1992	1993	1994	1995
Consumer price index	10	199	47,501	304,915
Earnings index	...	...	...	...

Land use (1994): forested 76.7%; meadows and pastures 6.6%; agricultural and under permanent cultivation 3.5%; other 13.2%.

Foreign trade

Balance of trade (current prices)

	1990	1991	1992	1993	1994	1995
U.S.$'000,000	+234	+217	+64	+47	+90	+581
% of total	13.3%	15.0%	8.1%	6.0%	13.1%	25.0%

Imports (1995): U.S.$870,200,000 (non-oil 94.0%; oil 6.0%). *Major import sources*[5,6] (1995): Belgium-Luxembourg 15.0%; U.S. 6.7%; Germany 6.0%; France 4.2%; The Netherlands 4.0%; China 3.6%; Italy 3.3%.
Exports (1995): U.S.$1,451,500,000 (diamonds 17.2%, crude petroleum 11.4%, coffee 8.8%, copper 7.9%). *Major export destinations*[5] (1995): Belgium-Luxembourg 36.3%; U.S. 16.9%; Italy 9.7%; Japan 5.0%; Germany 4.0%; France 2.6%; Canada 2.2%.

Transport and communications

Transport. Railroads (1991)[7]: length 3,162 mi, 5,088 km; passenger-mi 360,000,000, passenger-km 580,000,000; short ton-mi cargo 1,258,000,000, metric ton-km cargo 1,836,000,000. Roads (1995): total length 95,708 mi, 154,027 km (paved 2%). Vehicles (1995): passenger cars 762,000; trucks and buses 550,000. Merchant marine (1992): vessels (100 gross tons and over) 27; total deadweight tonnage 30,692. Air transport (1991)[8]: passenger-mi 89,627,000, passenger-km 144,242,000; short ton-mi cargo 14,415,000, metric ton-km cargo 21,046,000; airports (1996) with scheduled flights 12.
Communications. Daily newspapers (1992): total number 9; total circulation 112,000; circulation per 1,000 population 2.7. Radio (1995): 3,480,000 receivers (1 per 13 persons). Television (1995): 22,000 receivers (1 per 1,994 persons). Telephones (main lines; 1993): 36,000 (1 per 1,140 persons).

Education and health

Education (1993)

	schools	teachers	students	student/ teacher ratio
Primary (age 6–11)	12,987	112,041	4,939,297	44.1
Secondary (age 12–17)	4,276[9]	59,325[9]	640,298	22.6[9]
Voc., teacher tr.	[9]	[9]	701,148	[9]
Higher[10]	...	3,873	61,422	15.9

Educational attainment: n.a. *Literacy* (1995): percentage of total population age 15 and over literate 77.3%; males literate 86.6%; females literate 67.7%.
Health: physicians (1990) 2,469 (1 per 15,584 persons); hospital beds (1986) 68,508 (1 per 487 persons); infant mortality rate per 1,000 live births (1990–95) 93.
Food (1992): daily per capita caloric intake 2,060 (vegetable products 97%, animal products 3%); 89% of FAO recommended minimum requirement.

Military

Total active duty personnel (1996): 49,100 (army 50.9%, navy 2.6%, air force 3.7%, paramilitary 42.8%). *Military expenditure as percentage of GNP* (1994): 2.1% (world 3.0%); per capita expenditure U.S.$3.

---

[1]The Transitional Constitutional Act promulgated in April 1994 allowed for a 15-month "transitional period to democracy" (later this transitional period was extended to 1997). [2]The new zaïre (NZ) replaced the (old) zaïre (Z) at a rate of 3,000,000 (old) zaïres to 1 NZ on Oct. 22, 1993. [3]Estimated to account for division of former Kivu province. [4]Detail does not add to total given because of rounding. [5]DOT (Direction of Trade) valuation; the valuation as the sum of all known trading partners, by external analysis, rather than as the reported sum of the country's own trade data (often withheld). [6]The DOT valuation is approximately 45% higher than values shown. [7]Traffic statistics are for services operated by the Zaire National Railways (SNCZ), which controls more than 90% of the country's total rail facility. [8]Air Zaire only; declared bankrupt 1995. [9]Secondary includes Voc., teacher tr. [10]1989.

Zambia

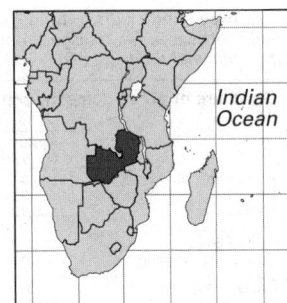

Official name: Republic of Zambia.
Form of government: multiparty republic with one legislative house (National Assembly [151[1]]).
Head of state and government: President.
Capital: Lusaka.
Official language: English.
Official religion: none.
Monetary unit: 1 Zambian kwacha (K) = 100 ngwee; valuation (Oct. 11, 1996) 1 U.S.$ = K 1,265; 1 £ = K 1,993.

Area and population		area		population
				1990
Provinces	Capitals	sq mi	sq km	census
Central	Kabwe	36,446	94,395	725,611
Copperbelt	Ndola	12,096	31,328	1,579,542
Eastern	Chipata	26,682	69,106	973,818
Luapula	Mansa	19,524	50,567	526,705
Lusaka	Lusaka	8,454	21,896	1,207,980
North-Western	Solwezi	48,582	125,827	383,146
Northern	Kasama	57,076	147,826	867,795
Southern	Livingstone	32,928	85,283	946,353
Western	Mongu	48,798	126,386	607,497
TOTAL		290,586	752,614	7,818,447

Demography

Population (1996): 9,715,000.
Density (1996): persons per sq mi 33.4, persons per sq km 12.9.
Urban-rural (1995): urban 43.1%; rural 56.9%.
Sex distribution (1995): male 49.45%; female 50.55%.
Age breakdown (1995): under 15, 47.4%; 15–29, 27.5%; 30–44, 14.3%; 45–59, 6.9%; 60–74, 3.2%; 75 and over, 0.7%.
Population projection: (2000) 10,754,000; (2010) 13,657,000.
Doubling time: 24 years.
Ethnolinguistic composition (1980): Bemba peoples 36.2%; Maravi (Nyanja) peoples 17.6%; Tonga peoples 15.1%; North-Western peoples 10.1%; Barotze peoples 8.2%; Mambwe peoples 4.6%; Tumbuka peoples 4.6%; other 3.6%.
Religious affiliation (1980): Christian 72.0%, of which Protestant 34.2%, Roman Catholic 26.2%, African Christian 8.3%; traditional beliefs 27.0%; Muslim 0.3%; other 0.7%.
Major cities (1990): Lusaka 982,362; Ndola 376,311; Kitwe 348,571; Mufulira 175,025.

Vital statistics

Birth rate per 1,000 population (1990–95): 44.6 (world avg. 25.0); legitimate, n.a.; however, marriage is both early and universal, suggesting that legitimate births are a relatively high proportion of all births.
Death rate per 1,000 population (1990–95): 15.1 (world avg. 9.3).
Natural increase rate per 1,000 population (1990–95): 29.5 (world avg. 15.7).
Total fertility rate (avg. births per childbearing woman; 1993): 5.9.
Marriage rate per 1,000 population: n.a.
Divorce rate per 1,000 population: n.a.
Life expectancy at birth (1993): male 45.0 years; female 46.2 years.
Major causes of death per 100,000 population: n.a.; however, the major causes of morbidity are respiratory infections, diarrheal diseases, malaria, malnutrition, measles, AIDS, and accidents.

National economy

Budget (1995). Revenue: K 739,091,000,000 (value-added and excise taxes 26.0%; customs duties 22.1%; grants 21.1%; personal income taxes 18.2%; company income taxes 5.2%). Expenditures: K 908,204,000,000 (current expenditures 86.2%, of which debt service 34.7%, health 9.5%, education 9.4%, defense 5.3%; capital expenditures 13.8%).
Public debt (external, outstanding; 1994): U.S.$4,858,000,000.
Production (metric tons except as noted). Agriculture, forestry, fishing (1995): sugarcane 1,310,000, corn (maize) 737,800, cassava 600,000, fruits and vegetables 334,800 (of which onions 20,000, tomatoes 20,000, oranges 3,500), sweet potatoes 57,000, millet 54,500, wheat 50,000, seed cotton 44,000, peanuts (groundnuts) 36,100, sorghum 26,500, soybeans 21,000, sunflower seeds 16,000, tobacco 7,000; livestock (number of live animals) 3,300,000 cattle, 620,000 goats, 295,000 pigs, 69,000 sheep, 22,000,000 chickens; roundwood (1994) 8,352,000 cu m; fish catch (1993) 65,307. Mining and quarrying (1995): copper 350,476; zinc 3,446[2]; cobalt 2,482; lead 2,002[2]; silver 10,007 kg; gold 3,987 troy oz. Manufacturing (1993): smelter copper 435,400; refined copper 424,800; cement 376,000[3]; raw sugar 147,000; wheat flour 50,400[4]; refined zinc 7,320; refined lead 2,400; cigarettes 1,500,000,000 units[3]. Construction (value added in K; 1995): 45,663,000,000. Energy production (consumption): electricity (kW-hr; 1994) 7,785,000,000 (6,305,000,000); coal (metric tons; 1994) 380,000 (375,000); crude petroleum (barrels; 1994) none (4,032,000); petroleum products (metric tons; 1994) 496,000 (435,000); natural gas, none (n.a.).
Household income and expenditure. Average household size (1981) 5.8; average annual income per household (1981) K 1,041 (U.S.$908); sources of income (1981): wages and salaries 94.0%, other 6.0%; expenditure (1977): food 37.7%, housing 11.0%, clothing 8.3%, transportation 4.3%, education 2.1%, health 1.0%.

Population economically active (1993): total 2,918,000; activity rate of total population 32.7% (participation rates: ages 15–64, 60.1%[5]; female 28.2%[5]; unemployed 17.4%[6]).

Price and earnings indexes (1990 = 100)							
	1989	1990	1991	1992	1993	1994	1995
Consumer price index	46.0	100.0	192.6	572.8	1,655.4	2,520.8	3,381.4
Earnings index	86.1	100.0	120.6	110.9	74.8	...	...

Land use (1994): forested 43.0%; meadows and pastures 40.4%; agricultural and under permanent cultivation 7.1%; other 9.5%.
Gross national product (1994): U.S.$3,206,000,000 (U.S.$350 per capita).

Structure of gross domestic product and labour force				
	1995		1990	
	in value K '000,000	% of total value	labour force	% of labour force
Agriculture	581,164	16.5	1,872,000	68.9
Mining	318,438	9.0	56,800	2.1
Manufacturing	1,286,745	36.5	50,900	1.9
Construction	65,335	1.9	29,100	1.1
Public utilities	45,663	1.3	8,900	0.3
Transportation and communications	172,969	4.9	25,600	0.9
Trade	338,513	9.6	30,700	1.1
Finance	251,767	7.1	24,200	0.9
Public admin., defense	371,801	10.6	111,600	4.1
Services }				
Other	89,328[7]	2.57	506,100	18.6
TOTAL	3,521,723	100.0[8]	2,716,000[8]	100.0[8]

Tourism (1994): receipts from visitors U.S.$43,000,000; expenditures by nationals abroad U.S.$56,000,000[9].

Foreign trade

Balance of trade (current prices)						
	1990	1991	1992	1993	1994	1995
U.S.$'000,000	−257	+420	−85	+202	+63	−88
% of total	9.3%	21.8%	5.3%	12.6%	3.0%	3.6%

Imports (1995): U.S.$1,278,000,000 (1988; machinery and transport equipment 38.3%; basic manufactures 19.8%; chemicals 16.9%; mineral fuels, lubricants, and electricity 12.3%; food 3.8%). *Major import sources:* South Africa 27.7%; United Kingdom 11.3%; Zimbabwe 9.2%; Japan 8.6%; United States 7.0%; India 4.9%; Germany 4.3%.
Exports (1995): U.S.$1,190,000,000 (copper 70.6%; cobalt 11.3%; zinc 0.8%[10]; lead 0.1%[10]). *Major export destinations:* Japan 17.9%; Saudi Arabia 12.9%; Thailand 12.8%; Taiwan 7.2%; India 5.3%; Belgium-Luxembourg 5.0%; France 4.5%.

Transport and communications

Transport. Railroads (1993): length 791 mi, 1,273 km; passenger-mi 166,690,000[4], passenger-km 268,262,000[4]; short ton-mi cargo 735,600,000, metric ton-km cargo 1,074,000,000. Roads (1995): total length 24,170 mi, 38,898 km (paved 18%). Vehicles (1995): passenger cars 142,000; trucks and buses 73,500. Merchant marine: vessels (100 gross tons and over) none. Air transport (1993): passenger-mi 191,595,000, passenger-km 308,343,000; short ton-mi cargo 6,771,000, metric ton-km cargo 9,886,000; airports (1996) with scheduled flights 4.
Communications. Daily newspapers (1992): total number 2; total circulation 70,000; circulation per 1,000 population 7.4. Radio (1994): total number of receivers 1,660,380 (1 per 5.5 persons). Television (1995): total number of receivers 200,000 (1 per 47 persons). Telephones (main lines; 1993): 78,000 (1 per 112 persons).

Education and health

Education (1989)	schools	teachers	students	student/ teacher ratio
Primary (age 7–13)	3,489	32,348[11]	1,446,847	44.1[11]
Secondary (age 14–18)	480	5,786[11]	161,349[9]	27.9[9]
Voc., teacher tr.	26	846	8,218	9.7
Higher	2	320	6,247	19.5

Educational attainment (1980). Percentage of population age 25 and over having: no formal schooling 54.7%; some primary education 34.4%; some secondary 10.5%; higher 0.4%. *Literacy* (1995): population age 15 and over literate 3,890,000 (77.8%); males literate 2,060,000 (85.6%); females literate 1,830,000 (71.3%).
Health: physicians (1985) 986 (1 per 6,959 persons); hospital beds (1989) 22,461 (1 per 349 persons); infant mortality rate per 1,000 live births (1990–95) 104.4.
Food (1992): daily per capita caloric intake 1,931 (vegetable products 95%, animal products 5%); 83% of FAO recommended minimum requirement.

Military

Total active duty personnel (1996): 21,600 (army 92.6%; navy, none; air force 7.4%). *Military expenditure as percentage of GNP* (1994): 1.2% (world 3.0%); per capita expenditure U.S.$4.

---

[1]President may appoint a maximum of 8 additional members. [2]1994. [3]1991. [4]1990. [5]1985. [6]1987. [7]Less imputed bank service charge. [8]Detail does not add to total given because of rounding. [9]1992. [10]1993. [11]1988.

Zimbabwe

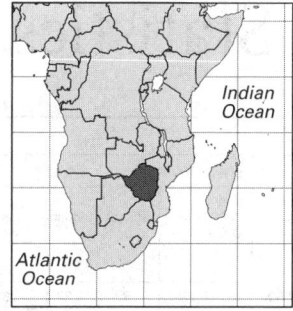

Official name: Republic of Zimbabwe.
Form of government: multiparty republic with one legislative house (House of Assembly [150[1]]).
Head of state and government: President.
Capital: Harare.
Official language: English.
Official religion: none.
Monetary unit: 1 Zimbabwe dollar (Z$) = 100 cents; valuation (Oct. 11, 1996) 1 U.S.$ = Z$10.52; 1 £ = Z$16.56.

Area and population

Provinces	Capitals	area sq mi	area sq km	population 1992 census[2]
Bulawayo	—	185	479	620,936
Harare	—	337	872	1,478,810
Manicaland	Mutare	14,077	36,459	1,537,676
Mashonaland Central	Bindura	10,945	28,347	857,318
Mashonaland East	Marondera	12,444	32,230	1,033,336
Mashonaland West	Chinhoyi	22,178	57,441	1,116,928
Masvingo	Masvingo	21,840	56,566	1,221,845
Matabeleland North	...	28,967	75,025	640,957
Matabeleland South	Gwanda	20,916	54,172	591,747
Midlands	Gweru	18,983	49,166	1,302,214
TOTAL		150,872	390,757	10,401,767

Demography

Population (1996): 11,515,000.
Density (1996): persons per sq mi 76.3, persons per sq km 29.5.
Urban-rural (1988): urban 26.4%; rural 73.6%.
Sex distribution (1992): male 48.80%; female 51.20%.
Age breakdown (1990): under 15, 45.5%; 15–29, 28.3%; 30–44, 15.1%; 45–59, 7.2%; 60–74, 3.1%; 75 and over, 0.8%.
Population projection: (2000) 12,514,000; (2010) 15,260,000.
Doubling time: 50 years.
Ethnolinguistic composition (1982): African 97.6%, of which Shona-speaking Bantu 70.8%, Ndebele-speaking Bantu 15.8%; European 2.0%; Asian 0.1%; other 0.3%.
Religious affiliation (1980): Christian 44.8%, of which Protestant (including Anglican) 17.5%, African indigenous 13.6%, Roman Catholic 11.7%; animist 40.4%; other 14.8%.
Major cities (1992): Harare 1,184,169; Bulawayo 620,936; Chitungwiza 274,035; Mutare 131,808; Gweru 124,735.

Vital statistics

Birth rate per 1,000 population (1996): 32.3 (world avg. 25.0).
Death rate per 1,000 population (1996): 18.2 (world avg. 9.3).
Natural increase rate per 1,000 population (1996): 14.1 (world avg. 15.7).
Total fertility rate (avg. births per childbearing woman; 1996): 4.1.
Marriage rate per 1,000 population: n.a.
Divorce rate per 1,000 population: n.a.
Life expectancy at birth (1992): male 58.0 years; female 62.0 years.
Major causes of death per 100,000 population (1990): infectious and parasitic diseases 64.7; accidents and poisoning 44.4; diseases of the circulatory system 40.9; diseases of the respiratory system 39.5; malignant neoplasms (cancers) 28.4; diseases of the digestive system 12.1; diseases of the nervous system 9.4; endocrine and metabolic disorders 4.9.

National economy

Budget (1996–97). Revenue: Z$23,350,355,000 (income tax 36.4%; sales tax 20.5%; customs duties 16.5%; excise tax 4.8%; revenue from investments and property 4.2%; stamp duties 1.0%). Expenditures: Z$30,173,080,000 (recurrent expenditures 85.8%, of which goods and services 46.4%, transfer payments 39.4%).
Population economically active (1992): total 3,600,000; activity rate of total population 34.6% (participation rates: over age 15, 63.4%; female 39.8%; unemployed 7.2%[3]).

Price and earnings indexes (1990 = 100)

	1989	1990	1991	1992	1993	1994	1995
Consumer price index	85.2	100.0	123.3	175.2	223.6	273.3	335.1
Earnings index	...	...	...	...	...	...	...

Production (metric tons except as noted). Agriculture, forestry, fishing (1995): sugarcane 3,943,000, corn (maize) 840,000, tobacco leaves 198,380, vegetables (including melons) 143,000, seed cotton 101,000, wheat 83,000, soybeans 77,000, peanuts (groundnuts) 52,000, sorghum 29,000; livestock (number of live animals) 4,500,000 cattle, 2,615,000 goats, 487,000 sheep, 277,000 pigs, 13,500,000 chickens; roundwood (1994) 8,067,000 cu m; fish catch (1993) 21,800 metric tons. Mining and quarrying (value of production in Z$; 1994): gold 2,039,300,000; nickel 631,600,000; asbestos 515,700,000; coal 453,100,000; copper 155,100,000; chrome 136,200,000. Manufacturing (value in Z$; 1993): foodstuffs 5,329,600,000; metals and metal products 4,107,100,000; chemicals and petroleum products 3,153,600,000; textiles 2,584,000,000; beverages and tobacco 2,523,400,000; clothing and footwear 1,394,600,000; transport equipment 1,387,500,000; paper, printing, and publishing 1,132,900,000; nonmetallic mineral products 740,200,000; wood and furniture 691,500,000; other manufactured goods 261,300,000. Construction (Z$; 1994): residential 635,-

657,000; commercial 155,129,000; industrial 190,172,000. Energy production (consumption): electricity (kW-hr; 1994) 7,334,000,000 (9,050,000,000); coal (metric tons; 1994) 5,469,000 (5,614,000); crude petroleum, none (none); petroleum products (metric tons; 1994) none (1,051,000); natural gas, none (none).
Public debt (external, outstanding; 1994): U.S.$3,496,000,000.
Household income and expenditure. Average household size (1992) 4.8; income per household Z$1,689 (U.S.$2,628); sources of income: n.a.; expenditure (1987): food, beverages, and tobacco 30.1%, household durable goods 11.1%, clothing, footwear, and textiles 10.3%, energy 7.3%, housing 6.5%, transportation 6.1%, education 6.0%, health service 3.8%, recreation 0.6%.
Gross national product (1994): U.S.$5,424,000,000 (U.S.$490 per capita).

Structure of gross domestic product and labour force

	1994 in value Z$'000,000	% of total value	labour force[4]	% of labour force[4]
Agriculture	4,004	10.1	328,700	25.7
Mining	2,739	6.9	50,500	3.9
Manufacturing	16,300	41.0	200,800	15.7
Construction	865	2.2	89,200	7.0
Public utilities	2,455	6.2	13,200	1.0
Transp. and commun.	2,125	5.3	51,800	4.1
Trade	4,357	10.9	104,300	8.2
Finance	1,973	5.0	22,400	1.8
Pub. admin., defense	902	2.3 }	416,700	32.6
Services	2,670	6.7 }		
Other	1,385[5]	3.4[5]	...	...
TOTAL	39,775	100.0	1,277,600	100.0

Land use (1994): forested 23.0%; meadows and pastures 44.3%; agricultural and under permanent cultivation 7.4%; other 25.3%.
Tourism (1993): receipts U.S.$138,000,000; expenditures U.S.$44,000,000.

Foreign trade

Balance of trade (current prices)

	1989	1990	1991	1992	1993	1994
Z$'000,000	277.6	−296.8	−1,867.4	−2,475.6	−95.3	−522.8
% of total	4.4%	3.4%	14.4%	14.4%	0.5%	1.7%

Imports (1994): Z$18,270,600,000 (machinery and transport equipment 41.4%, of which transport equipment 9.5%; manufactured goods 16.3%, of which textiles 2.5%, paper and paperboard 2.1%; fuels 9.9%, of which petroleum products 9.6%). *Major import sources:* South Africa 32.6%; United Kingdom 10.3%; Germany 5.9%; Japan 5.7%; United States 5.3%; Switzerland 2.9%; France 2.0%; Italy 1.9%; The Netherlands 1.9%.
Exports (1994): Z$15,365,200,000 (domestic exports 73.4%, of which tobacco 23.4%; gold sales 12.0%; ferroalloys 6.1%; nickel metal 4.3%; cotton 3.1%; corn [maize] 3.1%; asbestos 3.0%; cut flowers 1.0%). *Major export destinations*[6]: South Africa 11.6%; United Kingdom 11.6%; Germany 6.0%; United States 5.7%; Japan 5.1%; Botswana 5.0%; The Netherlands 4.0%; Zambia 3.3%; Italy 3.1%; Mozambique 2.9%; Malawi 2.4%; Belgium-Luxembourg 1.9%.

Transport and communications

Transport. Railroads (1991): route length 1,714 mi, 2,759 km; passenger-mi 355,057,000, passenger-km 571,410,000; short ton-mi cargo 3,695,000, metric ton-km cargo 5,394,000. Roads (1995): total length 57,048 mi, 91,810 km (paved 19%). Vehicles (1995): passenger cars 492,000; trucks and buses 108,000. Merchant marine: none. Air transport (1995)[7]: passenger-mi 521,-673,000, passenger-km 839,553,000; short ton-mi cargo 27,016,000, metric ton-km cargo 39,442,000; airports (1995) with scheduled flights 7.
Communications. Daily newspapers (1995): total number 2; total circulation 192,000; circulation per 1,000 population 17. Radio (1995): 801,000 receivers (1 per 14 persons). Television (1995): 137,090 receivers (1 per 82 persons). Telephones (main lines; 1993): 128,100 (1 per 84 persons).

Education and health

Education (1995)

	schools	teachers	students	student/ teacher ratio
Primary (age 7–13)	4,633	63,475	2,655,564	41.8
Secondary (age 14–19)	1,535	27,320	711,094	26.0
Voc., teacher tr.[8]	25	1,479	27,431	18.5
Higher[9]	28[8]	3,581	46,492	13.0

Educational attainment (1986–87). Percentage of employed population age 15 and over having: no formal schooling 24.5%; primary 42.9%; secondary and tertiary 31.7%. *Literacy* (1995): percentage of total population age 15 and over literate 85.1%; males literate 90.4%; females literate 79.9%.
Health: physicians (1993) 1,551 (1 per 6,909 persons); hospital beds (1995) 21,923 (1 per 514 persons); infant mortality rate (1996) 72.8.
Food (1992): daily per capita caloric intake 1,985 (vegetable products 92%, animal products 8%); 95% of FAO recommended minimum requirement.

Military

Total active duty personnel (1996): 43,000 (army 90.7%, air force 9.3%). *Military expenditure as percentage of GNP* (1994): 3.7% (world 3.0%); per capita expenditure U.S.$17.

---

[1]Includes 30 nonelective seats. [2]Preliminary results. [3]Does not take into consideration seasonal unemployment of communal workers; 1986–87. [4]Wage-earning workers only. [5]Less imputed bank service charges. [6]Excludes gold sales and reexports. [7]Air Zimbabwe only. [8]1992. [9]Includes postsecondary vocational and teacher training at the higher level.

Comparative National Statistics

World and regional summaries

region/bloc	area and population, 1996 — area square miles	area square kilometres	population total	per sq mi	per sq km	population projection, 2010	gross national product, 1994 — total ('000,000 U.S.$)	% agriculture	% industry	% services	growth rate, 1990–94	GNP per capita (U.S.$)	labour force, 1990 — total ('000)	% male	% female
World	52,512,080	136,005,610	5,752,539,000	109.5	42.3	6,917,773,000	26,099,730	5	33	62	1.6	4,670	2,353,806	63.8	36.2
Africa	11,717,230	30,347,400	720,363,000	61.5	23.7	1,009,616,000	468,800	20	30	50	0.6	670	242,784	65.6	34.4
Central Africa	2,552,970	6,612,160	84,967,000	33.3	12.9	126,670,000	26,550	30	31	39	−5.2	330	26,428	64.7	35.3
East Africa	2,473,640	6,406,670	223,700,000	90.4	34.9	311,503,000	49,210	35	22	43	1.5	230	85,082	58.8	41.2
North Africa	3,287,810	8,515,370	162,036,000	49.3	19.0	214,099,000	189,930	18	33	49	1.0	1,220	40,016	84.6	15.4
Southern Africa	1,032,300	2,673,660	47,835,000	46.3	17.9	57,263,000	134,770	5	31	64	0.2	2,840	14,532	64.3	35.7
West Africa	2,370,510	6,139,540	201,825,000	85.1	32.9	300,081,000	68,380	39	26	35	2.0	340	76,726	63.8	36.2
Americas	16,311,640	42,247,000	774,221,000	47.5	18.3	911,629,000	8,867,770	3	28	69	2.6	11,590	293,723	66.5	33.5
Anglo-America[3]	8,368,970	21,675,560	295,362,000	35.3	13.9	332,023,000	7,309,430	2	26	72	2.4	25,220	135,438	58.7	41.3
Canada	3,849,670	9,970,610	29,784,000	7.7	3.0	33,946,000	569,950	3	31	66	1.4	19,570	13,360	60.2	39.8
United States	3,679,190	9,529,060	265,455,000	72.2	27.9	297,943,000	6,737,370	2	26	72	2.5	25,860	122,005	58.6	41.4
Latin America	7,942,670	20,571,440	478,859,000	60.3	23.3	579,606,000	1,558,340	10	35	56	3.6	3,280	158,285	73.1	26.9
Caribbean	90,740	234,980	35,246,000	388.4	150.0	41,001,000	80,850	8	36	57	1.7	2,270	13,813	66.9	33.1
Central America	202,240	523,820	33,056,000	163.4	63.1	45,418,000	40,480	18	22	60	5.1	1,280	9,520	78.5	21.5
Mexico	756,070	1,958,200	92,711,000	122.6	47.3	112,891,000	368,680	7	33	60	2.5	4,010	30,487	72.9	27.1
South America	6,893,620	17,854,440	317,846,000	46.1	17.8	380,296,000	1,068,330	10	36	54	4.0	3,380	104,465	73.6	26.4
Andean Group	2,110,450	5,466,100	115,576,000	54.8	21.1	143,758,000	232,430	10	36	54	4.6	2,040	34,715	75.6	24.4
Brazil	3,300,170	8,547,400	157,872,000	47.8	18.5	184,157,000	536,310	13	39	49	2.2	3,370	55,026	72.6	27.4
Other South America	1,483,000	3,840,940	44,398,000	29.9	11.6	52,381,000	299,590	6	30	65	7.3	6,870	14,724	72.4	27.6
Asia	12,330,690	31,936,220	3,499,626,000	283.8	109.6	4,215,212,000	7,618,890	8	41	51	2.7	2,260	1,464,452	64.5	35.5
Eastern Asia	4,547,010	11,776,650	1,443,991,000	317.6	122.6	1,615,885,000	5,716,930	5	43	53	2.9	4,050	775,590	57.4	42.6
China	3,696,120	9,572,900	1,218,709,000	329.7	127.3	1,371,446,000	630,200	21	47	32	12.9	530	669,693	56.7	43.3
Japan	145,880	377,820	125,612,000	861.1	332.5	130,344,000	4,321,140	2	43	55	1.2	34,630	62,202	62.1	37.9
South Korea	38,380	99,390	45,232,000	1,178.5	455.1	49,683,000	366,480	8	43	49	6.6	8,220	18,664	66.2	33.8
Other Eastern Asia	666,630	1,726,540	54,438,000	81.7	31.5	64,412,000	399,110	4	31	65	6.0	7,560	25,031	58.8	41.2
South Asia	1,971,180	5,105,300	1,272,514,000	645.6	249.3	1,604,468,000	382,200	30	27	44	3.9	320	411,136	77.4	22.6
India	1,222,240	3,165,600	952,969,000	779.7	301.0	1,189,082,000	278,740	30	28	42	3.8	310	322,944	74.8	25.2
Pakistan	339,700	879,810	133,500,000	393.0	151.7	176,400,000	55,570	25	25	50	4.6	440	33,698	87.5	12.5
Other South Asia	409,240	1,059,890	186,045,000	454.6	175.5	238,986,000	47,890	32	22	46	3.9	280	54,494	86.2	13.8
Southeast Asia	1,735,800	4,495,720	490,877,000	282.8	109.2	607,334,000	561,450	18	37	46	6.9	1,190	189,297	63.0	37.0
ASEAN	1,312,900	3,400,420	429,797,000	327.4	126.4	527,910,000	513,070	13	39	47	7.0	1,250	164,976	63.2	36.8
Non-ASEAN	422,900	1,095,300	61,080,000	144.4	55.8	79,424,000	48,380	61	10	29	5.7	810	24,321	62.2	37.8
Southwest Asia	4,076,700	10,558,550	292,244,000	71.7	27.7	387,525,000	958,310	15	39	46	−0.5	3,370	88,429	69.4	30.6
Central Asia	1,545,180	4,002,000	54,923,000	35.5	13.7	66,290,000	46,830	36	36	27	−11.1	870	20,728	54.8	45.2
Gulf Cooperation Council	1,026,860	2,659,540	26,435,000	25.7	9.9	40,709,000	243,430	4	53	43	2.1	9,700	6,511	91.7	8.3
Iran	636,300	1,648,000	62,231,000	97.8	37.8	79,887,000	310,000	21	37	42	5.2	4,720	15,253	82.0	18.0
Other Southwest Asia	868,360	2,249,010	148,655,000	171.2	66.1	200,639,000	358,050	15	32	53	−4.2	2,560	45,936	68.7	31.3
Europe	8,868,710	22,969,920	729,370,000	82.2	31.8	746,952,000	8,760,800	3	31	65	−0.2	12,050	340,666	57.1	42.9
Eastern Europe	7,437,210	19,262,280	343,433,000	46.2	17.8	347,546,000	785,190	10	39	51	−9.1	2,280	171,080	50.6	49.4
Russia	6,592,850	17,075,400	148,070,000	22.5	8.7	149,868,000	392,500	7	38	55	−10.6	2,650	72,286	47.6	52.4
Ukraine	233,090	603,700	51,273,000	220.0	84.9	50,320,000	80,920	19	50	31	−14.4	1,570	25,401	48.0	52.0
Other Eastern Europe	611,270	1,583,180	144,090,000	235.7	91.0	147,358,000	311,770	11	38	51	−5.1	2,150	73,393	54.4	45.6
Western Europe	1,431,500	3,707,640	385,937,000	269.6	104.1	399,406,000	7,975,610	2	31	67	0.9	20,840	169,586	63.6	36.4
European Union (EU)	1,249,600	3,236,460	373,381,000	298.8	115.4	385,995,000	7,577,390	2	31	67	0.9	20,470	163,771	63.6	36.4
France	210,030	543,970	58,392,000	278.0	107.3	62,200,000	1,355,040	3	29	68	0.8	23,470	25,404	60.1	39.9
Germany	137,830	356,970	81,891,000	594.1	229.4	85,259,000	2,075,450	1	31	69	1.1	25,580	38,981	60.7	39.3
Italy	116,340	301,320	57,500,000	494.2	190.8	56,278,000	1,101,260	3	32	66	0.7	19,270	23,339	68.1	31.9
Spain	195,360	505,990	39,270,000	201.0	77.6	39,917,000	525,330	4	31	66	0.7	13,280	14,456	75.5	24.5
United Kingdom	94,250	244,110	58,784,000	623.7	240.8	61,127,000	1,069,460	2	31	67	0.8	18,410	27,766	61.4	38.6
Other EU	495,790	1,284,100	77,544,000	156.4	60.4	81,214,000	1,450,850	4	31	65	0.9	18,950	33,825	63.4	36.6
Non-EU	181,900	471,180	12,556,000	69.0	26.6	13,411,000	398,220	3	33	64	1.0	31,850	5,815	61.9	38.1
Oceania	3,283,800	8,505,070	28,956,000	8.8	3.4	34,364,000	383,470	4	27	68	3.4	13,360	12,181	63.0	37.0
Australia	2,966,150	7,682,300	18,287,000	6.2	2.4	20,986,000	320,710	3	28	69	3.4	17,980	7,963	61.9	38.1
Pacific Ocean Islands	317,650	822,770	10,669,000	33.6	13.0	13,378,000	62,760	9	26	65	3.6	6,130	4,218	65.0	35.0

[1]Refers only to the outstanding long-term external public and publicly guaranteed debt of the 136 countries that report under the World Bank's Debtor Reporting System (DRS). [2]World total contains

Africa

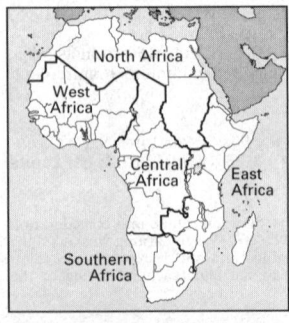

Americas

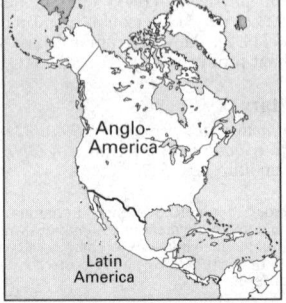

Asia

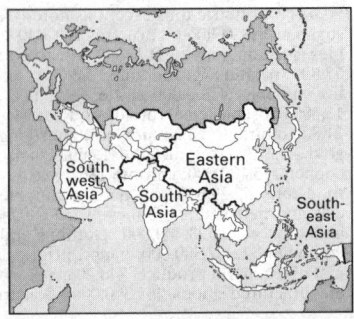

pop. per 1,000 ha of arable land, 1994	electricity consumption (kW-hr per capita), 1994	imports (c.i.f.)	exports² (f.o.b.)	balance²	total	% of GNP	male	female	pop. per doctor	infant mortality per 1,000 births	pop. having safe water (%)	food (% FAO recommended minimum), 1992	male	female	region/bloc
4,150	2,245	5,118,180	4,959,200²	−158,980²	1,281,688	25.1	64.1	68.3	720	57.6	77	115	83.7	71.1	World
4,100	494	129,720	116,610	−13,110	238,653	78.7	52.9	55.5	2,810	93.1	51	97	66.6	46.5	Africa
3,640	136	6,110	6,300	+190	33,853	127.6	46.1	49.5	12,820	110.8	32	89	77.5	56.2	Central Africa
5,150	126	19,310	16,970	−2,340	43,502	97.0	47.5	49.5	12,330	107.1	42	81	67.6	47.5	East Africa
4,200	663	50,180	46,530	−3,650	97,487	62.1	63.7	66.8	970	61.5	73	123	64.8	40.2	North Africa
3,300	3,913	28,690	24,410	−4,280	1,424	22.0	61.8	66.9	1,680	53.2	69	109	81.6	79.9	Southern Africa
3,610	129	25,440	22,400	−3,040	62,386	91.3	50.7	53.3	6,790	94.0	48	94	58.4	37.5	West Africa
2,120	5,993	1,197,670	1,169,870	−27,800	353,930	23.6	68.4	74.7	520	32.5	88	126	91.3	89.9	Americas
1,250	13,191	938,850	922,260	−16,590	—	—	72.4	79.2	390	7.8	100	139	95.8	95.4	Anglo-America³
640	17,510	167,380	167,010	−360	—	—	74.7	81.7	460	6.2	100	116	96.6	96.6	Canada
1,400	12,711	770,950	753,320	−17,630	—	—	72.1	78.9	390	8.0	100	141	95.7	95.3	United States
3,740	1,587	258,820	247,610	−11,210	353,930	23.6	66.0	71.9	650	41.7	80	116	88.0	85.8	Latin America
7,500	1,408	23,400	23,160	−230	10,155	43.9	66.6	70.9	490	52.6	74	106	83.7	82.6	Caribbean
5,670	608	24,990	29,690	+4,710	24,490	60.5	64.6	70.1	1,190	44.3	66	107	76.5	70.9	Central America
3,870	1,562	75,890	60,410	−15,480	79,097	21.5	66.5	73.1	580	27.1	83	135	91.8	87.4	Mexico
3,400	1,713	134,550	134,350	−200	240,188	22.5	66.0	71.8	670	46.0	81	113	88.5	87.0	South America
5,990	1,503	56,150	53,070	−3,080	82,977	35.7	68.2	73.7	870	37.6	78	103	92.6	88.7	Andean Group
3,560	1,837	49,500	48,100	−1,400	94,512	17.6	63.8	70.4	680	57.2	87	118	83.3	83.2	Brazil
1,490	1,804	28,910	33,180	+4,270	62,699	21.0	67.8	71.5	410	31.9	67	120	96.0	95.7	Other South America
7,130	1,035	1,508,050	1,406,570	−101,480	504,957	20.0	64.5	67.5	980	54.8	74	113	81.1	63.8	Asia
13,820	1,619	903,680	840,120	−63,560	112,039	11.2	69.7	73.6	620	24.0	71	117	91.4	77.0	Eastern Asia
12,880	780	132,010	147,040	+15,030	84,554	13.4	69.1	72.4	630	26.0	67	116	89.9	72.7	China
31,250	7,726	335,870	300,250	−35,620	—	—	76.6	83.0	550	4.2	100	124	100.0	100.0	Japan
23,680	4,174	135,150	119,020	−16,130	27,103	7.4	68.0	76.0	820	10.0	93	140	99.3	96.7	South Korea
13,560	3,867	300,650	273,810	−26,840	382	47.7	69.7	75.5	510	18.0	99	121	95.9	91.4	Other Eastern Asia
5,890	372	59,400	59,170	−230	135,600	35.9	58.7	59.8	2,360	78.8	80	104	62.4	35.5	South Asia
5,530	420	34,460	36,080	+1,620	87,880	31.5	58.7	59.8	2,170	73.0	81	108	65.5	37.7	India
6,070	418	11,460	10,930	−530	22,993	41.4	62.0	64.0	2,060	79.0	79	100	50.0	24.4	Pakistan
8,580	92	13,480	12,160	−1,320	24,727	57.6	56.5	56.7	5,620	102.1	76	86	53.1	30.3	Other South Asia
7,610	507	363,460	337,580	−25,880	155,969	29.8	63.5	67.1	2,600	49.0	62	116	91.9	83.6	Southeast Asia
8,650	571	358,960	333,490	−25,480	146,074	33.0	64.6	68.3	2,550	42.2	66	116	92.7	85.1	ASEAN
4,120	66	4,500	4,100	−400	9,895	12.3	56.3	59.2	2,990	83.2	38	114	86.7	73.1	Non-ASEAN
2,920	1,975	181,520	169,700	−11,820	101,349	16.3	66.1	70.5	590	46.3	84	120	85.7	72.3	Southwest Asia
1,260	2,965	8,330	8,560	+230	4,322	9.2	64.2	71.8	290	34.5	100	...	98.8	96.2	Central Asia
6,520	5,269	72,880	70,570	−2,310	2,608	24.2	68.1	71.3	640	26.5	93	115	72.8	53.2	Gulf Cooperation Council
3,620	1,203	12,310	11,150	−1,170	15,613	5.0	65.8	68.2	1,600	54.6	84	119	78.4	65.8	Iran
3,440	1,387	88,000	79,430	−8,570	78,807	31.1	66.5	70.9	680	50.4	76	122	86.2	68.3	Other Southwest Asia
2,440	5,517	2,202,340	2,139,800	−62,550	181,971	23.4	68.7	77.1	290	10.9	100	133	99.0	97.5	Europe
1,560	4,512	184,400	188,940	+4,540	181,814	23.5	63.3	73.9	280	16.4	100	123	99.3	96.7	Eastern Europe
1,140	5,805	46,360	48,800	+2,440	80,054	20.4	58.0	72.0	240	18.0	100	...	99.5	96.8	Russia
1,560	4,044	14,820	13,660	−1,160	4,603	5.7	65.3	74.7	230	14.0	100	...	99.5	97.4	Ukraine
2,530	3,361	123,220	126,480	+3,260	97,157	32.3	67.9	75.5	380	16.0	100	123	98.9	96.3	Other Eastern Europe
4,910	6,420	2,017,940	1,950,860	−67,080	158	4.0	73.4	80.0	300	6.1	100	135	98.9	98.2	Western Europe
4,830	6,163	1,901,450	1,827,900	−73,560	—	—	73.3	80.0	300	6.1	100	136	98.8	98.1	European Union (EU)
3,160	7,139	274,320	258,320	−16,000	—	—	72.9	81.1	360	6.1	100	144	98.9	98.7	France
6,900	6,528	443,780	421,430	−22,350	—	—	72.5	79.0	310	5.6	100	126	100.0	100.0	Germany
6,870	4,711	204,290	185,110	−19,180	—	—	73.8	80.4	190	6.6	100	141	97.8	96.4	Italy
2,510	4,129	114,830	106,660	−8,170	—	—	73.2	81.1	250	6.0	100	151	97.5	94.2	Spain
9,830	5,870	262,500	252,470	−10,030	—	—	74.4	79.7	450	6.2	100	132	100.0	100.0	United Kingdom
4,580	7,398	601,730	603,900	+2,180	—	—	73.3	79.5	340	6.3	100	133	98.1	97.4	Other EU
9,270	14,245	116,490	122,960	+6,480	158	4.0	74.8	81.0	310	5.2	100	124	99.9	99.9	Non-EU
560	7,278	80,400	71,470	−8,940	2,176	29.2	71.6	76.7	520	24.2	88	122	96.0	93.8	Oceania
380	9,363	61,350	54,670	−6,680	—	—	75.4	81.1	450	5.7	100	120	99.5	99.5	Australia
3,600	3,667	19,050	16,800	−2,250	2,176	29.2	65.2	69.1	710	41.4	65	126	89.1	82.0	Pacific Ocean Islands

U.S.$54,890,000,000 undistributable by continent or region.   ³Anglo-America includes Canada, the United States, Greenland, Bermuda, and St. Pierre and Miquelon.

Europe

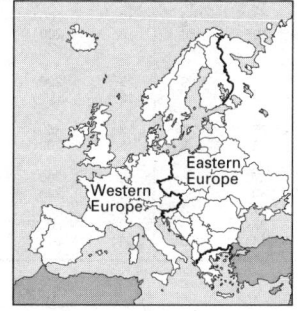

Eastern Europe

Oceania

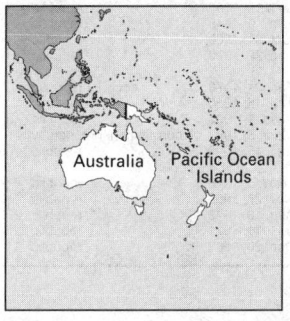

Government and international organizations

This table summarizes principal facts about the governments of the countries of the world, their branches and organs, the topmost layers of local government constituting each country's chief administrative subdivisions, and the participation of their central governments in the principal intergovernmental organizations of the world.

In this table "date of independence" may refer to a variety of circumstances. In the case of the newest countries, those that attained full independence after World War II, the date given is usually just what is implied by the heading—the date when the country, within its present borders, attained full sovereignty over both its internal and external affairs. In the case of longer established countries, the choice of a single date may be somewhat more complicated, and grounds for the use of several different dates often exist. The reader should refer to *Macropædia* and *Micropædia* articles on national histories and relevant historical acts. In cases of territorial annexation or dissolution, the date given here refers either to the final act of union of a state composed of smaller entities or to the final act of separation from a larger whole (*e.g.*, the separation of Bangladesh from Pakistan in 1971).

The date of the current, or last, constitution is in some ways a less complicated question, but governments sometimes do not, upon taking power, either adhere to existing constitutional forms or trouble to terminate the previous document and legitimize themselves by the installation of new constitutional forms. Often, however, the desire to legitimize extraconstitutional political activity by associating it with existing forms of long precedent leads to partial or incomplete modification, suspension, or abrogation of a constitution, so that the actual day-to-day conduct of government may be largely

unrelated to the provisions of a constitution still theoretically in force. When a date in this column is given in italics, it refers to a document that has been suspended, abolished by extraconstitutional action, or modified extensively.

The characterizations adopted under "type of government" represent a compromise between the forms provided for by the national constitution and the more pragmatic language that a political scientist might adopt to describe these same systems. For an explanation of the application of these terms in the Britannica World Data, *see* the Glossary at page 539.

The positions denoted by the terms "chief of state" and "head of government" are usually those identified with those functions by the constitution. The duties of the chief of state may range from largely ceremonial responsibilities, with little or no authority over the day-to-day conduct of government, to complete executive authority as the effective head of government. In certain countries, an official of a political party or a revolutionary figure outside the constitutional structure may exercise the powers of both positions.

Membership in the legislative house(s) of each country as given here includes all elected or appointed members, as well as ex officio members (those who by virtue of some other office or title are members of the body), whether voting or nonvoting. The legislature of a country with a unicameral system is shown as the upper house in this table.

The number of administrative subdivisions for each country is listed down to the second level. A single country may, depending on its size, complexity, and historical antecedents, have as many as five levels of administrative subordination or it may have none at all. Each level of subordination may have several kinds of subdivisions.

Government and international organizations

country	date of independence[a]	date of current or last constitution[b]	type of government	executive branch[c] chief of state	executive branch[c] head of government	legislative branch[d] upper house (members)	legislative branch[d] lower house (members)	admin. subdivisions first-order (number)	admin. subdivisions second-order (number)	seaward claims territorial (nautical miles)	seaward claims fishing/ economic (nautical miles)
Afghanistan	Aug. 19, 1919	—	Islamic state	—————————[1]		...	...	32	298	—	—
Albania	Nov. 28, 1912	April 29, 1991[2]	republic	president	prime minister	140	—	26	c. 200	12	3
Algeria	July 5, 1962	Nov. 28, 1996[5]	republic[6]	president	prime minister	200[7]	—	48	1,541	12	12
American Samoa	—	July 1, 1967	territory (U.S.)	U.S. president	governor	18	21	3	14	12	200
Andorra	Dec. 6, 1288	May 4, 1993	parl. coprincipality	[8]	head of the govt.	28	—	7	...	—	—
Angola	Nov. 11, 1975	Aug. 27, 1992	republic	———— president ————		220	—	18	163	20	200
Antigua and Barbuda	Nov. 1, 1981	Nov. 1, 1981	constitutional monarchy	British monarch	prime minister	17	17	30	—	12[9]	200[9]
Argentina	July 9, 1816	Aug. 24, 1994[10]	federal republic	———— president[11] ————		72	257	24	503	12	200
Armenia	Sept. 23, 1991	July 5, 1995[5]	republic	president	prime minister	190	—	10	...	...	...
Aruba	—	Jan. 1, 1986	overseas territory (Neth.)	Dutch monarch	[12]	21	—	...	...	12	200
Australia	Jan. 1, 1901	July 9, 1900	federal parl. state[14]	British monarch	prime minister	76	148	8	c. 900	12	200
Austria	Oct. 30, 1918	Oct. 1, 1920	federal republic	president	chancellor	64	183	9	99	—	—
Azerbaijan	Aug. 30, 1991	Nov. 12, 1995[5]	republic	———— president[15] ————		125	—	2	...	...	...
Bahamas, The	July 10, 1973	July 10, 1973	constitutional monarchy	British monarch	prime minister	16	49	—	21	3	200
Bahrain	Aug. 15, 1971	June 1973	monarchy (emirate)	emir	prime minister	40[7]	—	1	—	12	17
Bangladesh	March 26, 1971	Dec. 16, 1972	republic	president	prime minister	330	—	5	64	12	200
Barbados	Nov. 30, 1966	Nov. 30, 1966	constitutional monarchy	British monarch	prime minister	21	28	—	—	12	200
Belarus	Aug. 25, 1991	March 30, 1994[18]	republic	———— president ————		...	...	6	118	—	—
Belgium	Oct. 4, 1830	May 5, 1993	fed. const. monarchy	monarch	prime minister	71[19]	150	20	589	12	17
Belize	Sept. 21, 1981	Sept. 21, 1981	constitutional monarchy	British monarch	prime minister	8	29	6	...	12[21]	200
Benin	Aug. 1, 1960	Dec. 2, 1990	republic	———— president[15] ————		83	—	6	77	200	200
Bermuda	March 24, 1910	June 8, 1968	colony (U.K.)	British monarch	[22]	11	40	11	—	12	200
Bhutan		[23]		———— king ————		152	—	20	—	—	—
Bolivia	Aug. 6, 1825	Feb. 2, 1967	republic	———— president ————		27	130	9	112	—	—
Bosnia and Herzegovina	March 3, 1992	Dec. 4, 1995[24]	federal republic	——— cochairmen CM (2) ———		15	42	2	...	...	...
Botswana	Sept. 30, 1966	Sept. 30, 1966	republic	———— president ————		15[7]	46	19	—	—	—
Brazil	Sept. 7, 1822	Oct. 5, 1988	federal republic	———— president ————		81	513	27	4,491	12	200
Brunei	Jan. 1, 1984	Sept. 29, 1959	monarchy (sultanate)	———— sultan ————		21[7]	—	4	...	12	200
Bulgaria	Oct. 5, 1908	July 12, 1991	republic	president	prime minister	240	—	9	278	12	200
Burkina Faso	Aug. 5, 1960	June 11, 1991	republic	president	prime minister	178[7]	107	30	109	—	—
Burundi	July 1, 1962	March 13, 1992	republic[6]	———— president[15] ————		81	—	15	122	—	—
Cambodia	Nov. 9, 1953	Sept. 24, 1993	constitutional monarchy	king	[25]	120	—	21	...	12	200
Cameroon	Jan. 1, 1960	Dec. 23, 1995[26]	republic	president	prime minister	180	—	10	58	50	3
Canada	July 1, 1867	April 17, 1982	federal parl. state[14]	Canadian GG[27]	prime minister	104	295	12	...	12	200
Cape Verde	July 5, 1975	Sept. 25, 1992	republic	president	prime minister	72	—	14	31	12[9]	200[9]
Central African Republic	Aug. 13, 1960	Jan. 14, 1995	republic	president	prime minister	85	—	17	66	—	—
Chad	Aug. 11, 1960	April 1996	republic	president	prime minister	57	—	14	53	—	—
Chile	Sept. 18, 1810	March 11, 1981	republic	———— president ————		47	120	13	51	12	200
China	1523 BC	Dec. 4, 1982	people's republic	president	premier SC	2,978	—	30	335	12	3
Colombia	July 20, 1810	July 5, 1991	republic	———— president ————		102	163	33	1,011	12	200
Comoros	July 6, 1975	Oct. 20, 1996[5]	federal Islamic republic	president	prime minister	42	—	3	7	12[9]	200[9]
Congo	Aug. 15, 1960	March 15, 1992[5]	republic	president	prime minister	60	125	15	47	200	3
Costa Rica	Sept. 15, 1821	Nov. 9, 1949	republic	———— president ————		57	—	7	82	12	200
Côte d'Ivoire	Aug. 7, 1960	Oct. 31, 1960	republic	president	prime minister	175	—	10	50	12	200
Croatia	June 25, 1991	Dec. 22, 1990	republic	president	prime minister	68	127	21	489	...	...
Cuba	May 20, 1902	Feb. 24, 1976	socialist republic	———— president ————		589	—	15	169	12	200
Cyprus[29]	Aug. 16, 1960	Aug. 16, 1960	republic	———— president ————		80[30]	—	...	...	12	3
Czech Republic	Jan. 1, 1993	Jan. 1, 1993	republic	president	prime minister	81	200	75	...	—	—
Denmark	c. 800	June 5, 1953	constitutional monarchy	monarch	prime minister	179	—	16	275	3	200
Djibouti	June 27, 1977	Sept. 15, 1992	republic	———— president ————		65	—	5	9	12	200
Dominica	Nov. 3, 1978	Nov. 3, 1978	republic	president	prime minister	32	—	37	—	12	200
Dominican Republic	Feb. 27, 1844	Nov. 28, 1966	republic	———— president ————		30	120	30	154	6	200
Ecuador	May 24, 1822	Aug. 10, 1979	republic	———— president ————		82	—	21	193	200	200
Egypt	Feb. 28, 1922	Sept. 11, 1971	republic	president	prime minister	454	—	27	...	12[31]	200[31]
El Salvador	Jan. 30, 1841	Dec. 20, 1983	republic	———— president ————		84	—	14	262	200	200

Finally, in the second half of the table are listed the memberships each country maintains in the principal international intergovernmental organizations of the world. This part of the table may also be utilized to provide a complete membership list for each of these organizations as of Dec. 1, 1996.

Notes for the column headings

a. The date may also be either that of the organization of the present form of government or the inception of the present administrative structure (federation, confederation, union, etc.).
b. Constitutions whose dates are in italic type had been wholly or substantially suspended or abolished as of late 1996.
c. For abbreviations used in this column see the list on the facing page.
d. When a legislative body has been adjourned or otherwise suspended, figures in parentheses indicate the number of members in the legislative body as provided for in constitution or law.
e. Vatican City also a member.
f. States contributing funds to or receiving aid from UNICEF in 1996.
g. Palestine (Liberation Organization) also a member.

International organizations, conventions

ACP	African, Caribbean, and Pacific (Lomé IV) convention
ADB	Asian Development Bank
APEC	Asia-Pacific Economic Cooperation Council
CARICOM	Caribbean Community and Common Market
EU	The European Union
ECOWAS	Economic Community of West African States
EEC	European Economic Community
FAO	Food and Agriculture Org.
GCC	Gulf Cooperation Council
I-ADB	Inter-American Development Bank
IAEA	International Atomic Energy Agency
IBRD	International Bank for Reconstruction and Development
ICAO	International Civil Aviation Org.
ICJ	International Court of Justice
IDA	International Development Association
IDB	Islamic Development Bank
IFC	International Finance Corporation
ILO	International Labour Org.
IMF	International Monetary Fund
IMO	International Maritime Org.
ITU	International Telecommunication Union
LAS	League of Arab States
OAS	Organization of American States
OAU	Organization of African Unity
OPEC	Organization of Petroleum Exporting Countries
SPC	South Pacific Commission
UNCTAD	United Nations Conference on Trade and Development
UNESCO	United Nations Educational Scientific and Cultural Org.
UNICEF	United Nations Children's Fund
UNIDO	United Nations Industrial Development Org.
UPU	Universal Postal Union
WHO	World Health Org.
WIPO	World Intellectual Property Org.
WMO	World Meteorological Org.
WTO	World Trade Org.

Abbreviations used in the executive-branch column

CM	Council of Ministers
CS	Council of State
FC	Federal Council
GG	Governor-General
GPC	General People's Committee
PNA	Palestine National Authority
PRC	Provisional Ruling Council
SC	State Council
SLORC	State Law and Order Restoration Council

membership in international organizations

UN (date of admission)	UNCTAD	UNICEF	ICJ	FAO	IAEA	IBRD	ICAO	IDA	IFC	ILO	IMF	IMO	ITU	UNESCO	UNIDO	UPU	WHO	WIPO	WMO	WTO	Commonwealth of Nations	EU	GCC	LAS	OAS	OAU	SPC	ACP	ADB	APEC	CARICOM	ECOWAS	EEC	I-ADB	IDB	OPEC	country
1946	●	●	●	●	●	●	●	●	●	●	●	●	●	●	●	●	●	●	●										●						●		Afghanistan
1955	●	●	●	●	●	●	●	●	●	●	●	●	●	●	●	●	●	●	●	●[4]															●		Albania
1962	●	●	●	●	●	●	●	●	●	●	●	●	●	●	●	●	●	●	●					●		●									●	●	Algeria
—																●			●								●										American Samoa
1993	●											●	●	●		●	●																				Andorra
1976	●	●	●	●	●	●	●	●	●	●	●	●	●	●	●	●	●	●	●							●		●									Angola
1981	●	●	●	●		●	●	●	●	●	●	●	●	●	●	●	●	●	●		●				●			●			●			●			Antigua and Barbuda
1945	●	●	●	●	●	●	●	●	●	●	●	●	●	●	●	●	●	●	●						●				●					●			Argentina
1992	●	●	●	●	●	●	●	●	●	●	●	●	●	●	●	●	●	●	●	●[4]																	Armenia
—														●[13]																							Aruba
1945	●	●	●	●	●	●	●	●	●	●	●	●	●	●	●	●	●	●	●		●						●		●	●							Australia
1955	●	●	●	●	●	●	●	●	●	●	●	●	●	●	●	●	●	●	●			●											●	●			Austria
1992	●	●	●	●	●	●	●	●	●	●	●	●	●	●	●	●	●	●	●	●[4]															●		Azerbaijan
1973	●	●	●	●	●	●	●	●	●	●	●	●	●	●	●	●	●	●	●	●[16]	●				●						●			●			Bahamas, The
1971	●	●	●	●	●	●	●	●	●	●	●	●	●	●	●	●	●	●	●				●	●											●		Bahrain
1974	●	●	●	●	●	●	●	●	●	●	●	●	●	●	●	●	●	●	●		●								●						●		Bangladesh
1966	●	●	●	●		●	●	●	●	●	●	●	●	●	●	●	●	●	●		●				●			●			●			●			Barbados
1945	●	●	●	●	●	●	●	●	●	●	●	●	●	●	●	●	●	●	●	●[4]																	Belarus
1945	●	●	●	●	●	●	●	●	●	●	●	●	●	●	●	●	●	●	●			●											●	●			Belgium
1981	●	●	●	●		●	●	●	●	●	●	●	●	●	●	●	●	●	●		●				●			●			●			●			Belize
1960	●	●	●	●		●	●	●	●	●	●	●	●	●	●	●	●	●	●							●						●		●	●		Benin
—																																					Bermuda
1971	●	●	●	●		●	●	●	●		●		●	●	●	●	●	●	●										●								Bhutan
1945	●	●	●	●	●	●	●	●	●	●	●	●	●	●	●	●	●	●	●						●									●			Bolivia
1992	●	●	●	●	●[16]	●	●	●	●	●	●	●	●	●	●	●	●	●	●																		Bosnia and Herzegovina
1966	●	●	●	●		●	●	●	●	●	●	●	●	●	●	●	●	●	●	●	●					●		●						●			Botswana
1945	●	●	●	●	●	●	●	●	●	●	●	●	●	●	●	●	●	●	●						●					●				●			Brazil
1984	●	●	●	●		●	●	●	●	●	●	●	●	●		●	●	●	●		●								●	●					●		Brunei
1955	●	●	●	●	●	●	●	●	●	●	●	●	●	●	●	●	●	●	●	●[4]																	Bulgaria
1960	●	●	●	●		●	●	●	●	●	●	●	●	●	●	●	●	●	●							●		●				●		●	●		Burkina Faso
1962	●	●	●	●		●	●	●	●	●	●	●	●	●	●	●	●	●	●	●[16]						●		●						●			Burundi
1955	●	●	●	●	●	●	●	●	●	●	●	●	●	●	●	●	●	●	●	●[16]									●								Cambodia
1960	●	●	●	●	●	●	●	●	●	●	●	●	●	●	●	●	●	●	●							●		●						●	●		Cameroon
1945	●	●	●	●	●	●	●	●	●	●	●	●	●	●	●	●	●	●	●		●				●				●	●				●			Canada
1975	●	●	●	●		●	●	●	●	●	●	●	●	●	●	●	●	●	●	●[16]						●		●				●		●			Cape Verde
1960	●	●	●	●		●	●	●	●	●	●	●	●	●	●	●	●	●	●							●		●						●	●		Central African Republic
1960	●	●	●	●		●	●	●	●	●	●	●	●	●	●	●	●	●	●							●		●						●	●		Chad
1945	●	●	●	●	●	●	●	●	●	●	●	●	●	●	●	●	●	●	●						●					●				●			Chile
1945	●	●	●	●	●	●	●	●	●	●	●	●	●	●	●	●	●	●	●										●	●							China
1945	●	●	●	●	●	●	●	●	●	●	●	●	●	●	●	●	●	●	●						●									●			Colombia
1975	●	●	●	●		●	●	●	●	●	●	●	●	●	●	●	●	●	●	●[16]				●		●		●							●		Comoros
1960	●	●	●	●		●	●	●	●	●	●	●	●	●	●	●	●	●	●							●		●						●	●		Congo
1945	●	●	●	●		●	●	●	●	●	●	●	●	●	●	●	●	●	●						●									●			Costa Rica
1960	●	●	●	●		●	●	●	●	●	●	●	●	●	●	●	●	●	●							●		●				●		●	●		Côte d'Ivoire
1992	●	●	●	●	●	●	●	●	●	●	●	●	●	●	●	●	●	●	●	●[4]														●			Croatia
1945	●	●	●	●	●	●	●	●	●	●	●	●	●	●	●	●	●	●	●						●[28]												Cuba
1960	●	●	●	●	●	●	●	●	●	●	●	●	●	●	●	●	●	●	●		●												●[13]				Cyprus[29]
1993	●	●	●	●	●	●	●	●	●	●	●	●	●	●	●	●	●	●	●																		Czech Republic
1945	●	●	●	●	●	●	●	●	●	●	●	●	●	●	●	●	●	●	●			●											●				Denmark
1977	●	●	●	●		●	●	●	●	●	●	●	●	●	●	●	●	●	●	●[16]				●		●		●							●		Djibouti
1978	●	●	●	●		●	●	●	●	●	●	●	●	●	●	●	●	●	●		●				●			●			●[4]			●			Dominica
1945	●	●	●	●		●	●	●	●	●	●	●	●	●	●	●	●	●	●						●									●			Dominican Republic
1945	●	●	●	●	●	●	●	●	●	●	●	●	●	●	●	●	●	●	●						●									●			Ecuador
1945	●	●	●	●	●	●	●	●	●	●	●	●	●	●	●	●	●	●	●	●[4]				●		●									●		Egypt
1945	●	●	●	●	●	●	●	●	●	●	●	●	●	●	●	●	●	●	●						●									●			El Salvador

Government and international organizations (continued)

country	date of independence[a]	date of current or last constitution[b]	type of government	executive branch[c] chief of state	head of government	legislative branch[d] upper house (members)	lower house (members)	admin. subdivisions first-order (number)	second-order (number)	seaward claims territorial (nautical miles)	fishing/ economic (nautical miles)
Equatorial Guinea	Oct. 12, 1968	Nov. 16, 1991[5]	republic	president	prime minister	80	—	7	18	12	200
Eritrea	May 24, 1993	May 1993[32]	republic[6]	——— president ———		150[33]	—	33	...	...	...
Estonia	Aug. 20, 1991	July 3, 1992	republic	president	prime minister	101	—	15	198	12	...
Ethiopia	c. 1000 BC	Aug. 22, 1995[34]	republic	president	prime minister	117	548	10	...	—	—
Faroe Islands	—	April 1, 1948	part of Danish realm	Danish monarch	[35]	32	—	7	50	3	200
Fiji	Oct. 10, 1970	July 25, 1990	republic	president	prime minister	34	70	4	15	12[9]	200[9]
Finland	Dec. 6, 1917	July 17, 1919	republic	president	prime minister	200	—	12	455	4	12
France	August 843	Oct. 4, 1958	republic	president	prime minister	321	577	22	96	12	200
French Guiana	—	Feb. 28, 1983	overseas dept. (Fr.)	French president	[36]	19	31	2	21	12	200
French Polynesia	—	Sept. 6, 1984	overseas territory (Fr.)	French president	[37]	41	—	5	48	12	200
Gabon	Aug. 17, 1960	March 26, 1991	republic	president	prime minister	120	—	9	37	12	200
Gambia, The	Feb. 18, 1965	Aug. 8, 1996[5]	republic	——— president ———		45	—	7	35	12	200
Gaza Strip	—	May 4, 1994[38]	interim authority	——— chairman PNA ———		88	—	...	...	...	...
Georgia	April 9, 1991	Oct. 17, 1995	republic	——— president ———		235	—	13	67	...	...
Germany	May 5, 1955	May 23, 1949	federal republic	president	chancellor	68	672	16	29	12[31]	200
Ghana	March 6, 1957	Jan. 7, 1993	republic	——— president ———		200	—	110	...	12	200
Gibraltar	—	May 23, 1969	colony (U.K.)	British monarch	governor	18	—	—	—	3	3
Greece	Feb. 3, 1830	June 11, 1975	republic	president	prime minister	300	—	13	53	6/10	3
Greenland	—	May 1, 1979	part of Danish realm	Danish monarch	[35]	31	—	18	...	3	200
Grenada	Feb. 7, 1974	Feb. 7, 1974	constitutional monarchy	British monarch	prime minister	13	15	9	...	12	200
Guadeloupe	—	Feb. 28, 1983	overseas dept. (Fr.)	French president	[36]	43	41	3	34	12	200
Guam	—	Aug. 1, 1950	territory (U.S.)	U.S. president	governor	21	—	...	—	12	...
Guatemala	Sept. 15, 1821	Jan. 14, 1986	republic	——— president ———		80	—	22	330	12	200
Guernsey	—	Jan. 1, 1949[39]	crown dependency (U.K.)	British monarch[40]	bailiff	60	—	1	2	...	...
Guinea	Oct. 2, 1958	Dec. 23, 1990[2]	republic	——— president[41] ———		114	—	31	...	12	200
Guinea-Bissau	Sept. 10, 1974	May 11, 1991	republic	president	prime minister	100	—	9	37	12	200
Guyana	May 26, 1966	Oct. 6, 1980	cooperative republic	——— president ———		65	—	10	71	12	200
Haiti	Jan. 1, 1804	March 29, 1987	republic	president	prime minister	27	83	9	41	12	200
Honduras	Nov. 5, 1838	Jan. 20, 1982	republic	——— president ———		128	—	18	292	12	200
Hong Kong	—	[39]	crown colony (U.K.)	British monarch	governor	60	—	...	18	12	3
Hungary	Nov. 16, 1918	Oct. 18, 1989[2]	republic	president	prime minister	386	—	20	184	—	—
Iceland	June 17, 1944	June 17, 1944	republic	president	prime minister	63	—	8	171	12	200
India	Aug. 15, 1947	Jan. 26, 1950	federal republic	president	prime minister	245	545	32	506	12	200
Indonesia	Aug. 17, 1945	Aug. 17, 1945	republic	——— president ———		1,000	500	27	303	12[9]	200[9]
Iran	Oct. 7, 1906	Dec. 2–3, 1979	Islamic republic	——— president[42] ———		270	—	26	229	12	50[43]
Iraq	Oct. 3, 1932	Sept. 22, 1968[44]	republic	——— president ———		250	—	16[45]	96	12	3
Ireland	Dec. 6, 1921	Dec. 29, 1937	republic	president	prime minister	60	166	32	86	12	200
Isle of Man	—	1961[39]	crown dependency (U.K.)	British monarch[40]	chief minister	11	24	...	—	12[46]	3
Israel	May 14, 1948	June 1950[39]	republic	president	prime minister	120	—	6	15	12	3
Italy	March 17, 1861	Jan. 1, 1948	republic	president	prime minister	325	630	20	102	12	3
Jamaica	Aug. 6, 1962	Aug. 6, 1962	constitutional monarchy	British monarch	prime minister	21	60	13	—	12	200
Japan	c. 660 BC	May 3, 1947	constitutional monarchy	emperor	prime minister	252	500	47	3,233	12[47]	200
Jersey	—	Jan. 1, 1949[39]	crown dependency (U.K.)	British monarch[40]	bailiff	58	—	—	—	3	...
Jordan	May 25, 1946	Jan. 8, 1952	constitutional monarchy	——— king[15] ———		40	80	12	...	3	3
Kazakhstan	Dec. 16, 1991	Sept. 6, 1995	republic	——— president[15] ———		47	67	21	218	—	—
Kenya	Dec. 12, 1963	Dec. 12, 1963	republic	——— president ———		202	—	8	40	12	200
Kiribati	July 12, 1979	July 12, 1979	republic	——— president ———		41	—	21	—	12[9]	200[9]
Korea, North	Sept. 9, 1948	Dec. 27, 1972	socialist republic	supreme commander	premier	687	—	13	172	12	200
Korea, South	Aug. 15, 1948	Feb. 25, 1988	republic	——— president[15] ———		299	—	15	193	12[48]	12
Kuwait	June 19, 1961	Nov. 16, 1962	const. mon. (emirate)	——— emir[15] ———		64	—	—	—	12	3
Kyrgyzstan	Aug. 31, 1991	May 5, 1993	republic	——— president[15] ———		70	35	7	89	—	—
Laos	Oct. 23, 1953	Aug. 15, 1991	republic	president	prime minister	85	—	17	114	—	—
Latvia	Aug. 21, 1991	Nov. 7, 1922	republic	president	prime minister	100	—	33	...	12	...
Lebanon	Nov. 26, 1941	Sept. 21, 1990	republic	president	prime minister	128	—	6	26	12	3
Lesotho	Oct. 4, 1966	April 2, 1993	constitutional monarchy	king	prime minister	33[7]	65	10	...	—	—
Liberia	July 26, 1847	Aug. 20, 1995[49]	republic[6]	——— chairman CS ———		35	—	...	...	200	3
Libya	Dec. 24, 1951	March 2, 1977	socialist state[50]	rev. leader	sec. GPC	750	—	13	c. 1,500	12[51]	3
Liechtenstein	July 12, 1806	Oct. 5, 1921	constitutional monarchy	prince	head of govt.	25	—	11	—	—	—
Lithuania	Sept. 6, 1991	Nov. 6, 1992	republic	president	prime minister	141	—	10	56	12	...
Luxembourg	May 10, 1867	Oct. 17, 1868	constitutional monarchy	grand duke	prime minister	21[7]	60	3	12	—	—
Macau	—	May 10, 1990	special terr. (Port.)[52]	——— governor ———		23	—	...	...	6	12
Macedonia	Nov. 17, 1991	Nov. 17, 1991	republic	president	prime minister	120	—	30	...	—	—
Madagascar	June 26, 1960	Sept. 21, 1992	republic	president	prime minister	138	—	6	113	12	200
Malawi	July 6, 1964	May 18, 1994	republic	——— president ———		177	—	3	24	—	—
Malaysia	Aug. 31, 1957	Aug. 31, 1957	fed. const. monarchy	paramount ruler	prime minister	70	192	15	145	12	200
Maldives	July 26, 1965	Nov. 11, 1968	republic	——— president ———		48	—	21	201	12[9]	31
Mali	Sept. 22, 1960	Jan. 5, 1992	republic	president	prime minister	116	—	9	46	—	—
Malta	Sept. 21, 1964	Dec. 13, 1974	republic	president	prime minister	69	—	3	—	12	25
Marshall Islands	Dec. 22, 1990	May 1, 1979	republic	——— president ———		12[7]	33	24	—	12[9]	200
Martinique	—	Feb. 28, 1983	overseas dept. (Fr.)	French president	[36]	45	41	3	34	12	200
Mauritania	Nov. 28, 1960	July 21, 1991	republic	——— president ———		56	79	13	53	12	200
Mauritius	March 12, 1968	March 12, 1992	republic	president	prime minister	66	—	11	105	12	200
Mayotte	—	Dec. 24, 1976	terr. collectivity (Fr.)	French president	[53]	17	—	17	...	12	200
Mexico	Sept. 16, 1810	Feb. 5, 1917	federal republic	——— president ———		128	500	32	2,378	12	200
Micronesia	Dec. 22, 1990	Jan. 1, 1981	federal republic	——— president ———		14	—	4	...	12	200
Moldova	Aug. 27, 1991	Aug. 27, 1994	republic	president	prime minister	104	—	50	...	—	—
Monaco	Feb. 2, 1861	Dec. 17, 1962	constitutional monarchy	prince	min. of state	18	—	1	—	12	3
Mongolia	March 13, 1921	Feb. 12, 1992	republic	president	prime minister	76	—	21	299	—	—
Morocco	March 2, 1956	Oct. 9, 1992	constitutional monarchy	——— king[15] ———		333	—	61[54]	151[54]	12	200
Mozambique	June 25, 1975	Nov. 30, 1990	republic	president		250	—	11	112	12	200
Myanmar (Burma)	Jan. 4, 1948	Jan. 4, 1974	republic	——— chairman SLORC ———		(492)	—	14	58	12	200
Namibia	March 21, 1990	March 21, 1990	republic	——— president ———		26	78	13	—	12	200
Nauru	Jan. 31, 1968	Jan. 31, 1968	republic	——— president ———		18	—	1	—	12	200
Nepal	Nov. 13, 1769	Nov. 9, 1990	constitutional monarchy	king	prime minister	60	205	14	75	—	—
Netherlands, The	March 30, 1814	Feb. 17, 1983	constitutional monarchy	monarch	prime minister	75	150	12	633	12	200

membership in international organizations																																										country
United Nations (date of admission)	UN organs★ and affiliated intergovernmental organizations																				Commonwealth of Nations	regional multipurpose						economic										
	UNCTAD★[e]	UNICEF★[f]	ICJ★	FAO	IAEA[e]	IBRD	ICAO	IDA	IFC	ILO	IMF	IMO	ITU[e]	UNESCO	UNIDO	UPU[e]	WHO	WIPO[e]	WMO	WTO		EU	GCC	LAS[g]	OAS	OAU	SPC	ACP	ADB	APEC	CARICOM	ECOWAS	EEC	I-ADB	IDB[g]	OPEC	

UN date	Country
1968	Equatorial Guinea
1993	Eritrea
1991	Estonia
1945	Ethiopia
—	Faroe Islands
1970	Fiji
1955	Finland
1945	France
—	French Guiana
—	French Polynesia
1960	Gabon
1965	Gambia, The
—	Gaza Strip
1992	Georgia
1973	Germany
1957	Ghana
—	Gibraltar
1945	Greece
—	Greenland
1974	Grenada
—	Guadeloupe
—	Guam
1945	Guatemala
—	Guernsey
1958	Guinea
1974	Guinea-Bissau
1966	Guyana
1945	Haiti
1945	Honduras
—	Hong Kong
1955	Hungary
1946	Iceland
1945	India
1950	Indonesia
1945	Iran
1945	Iraq
1955	Ireland
—	Isle of Man
1949	Israel
1955	Italy
1962	Jamaica
1956	Japan
—	Jersey
1955	Jordan
1992	Kazakhstan
1963	Kenya
—	Kiribati
1991	Korea, North
1991	Korea, South
1963	Kuwait
1992	Kyrgyzstan
1955	Laos
1991	Latvia
1945	Lebanon
1966	Lesotho
1945	Liberia
1955	Libya
1990	Liechtenstein
1991	Lithuania
1945	Luxembourg
—	Macau
1993	Macedonia
1960	Madagascar
1964	Malawi
1957	Malaysia
1965	Maldives
1960	Mali
1964	Malta
1991	Marshall Islands
—	Martinique
1961	Mauritania
1968	Mauritius
—	Mayotte
1945	Mexico
1991	Micronesia
1992	Moldova
1993	Monaco
1961	Mongolia
1956	Morocco
1975	Mozambique
1948	Myanmar (Burma)
1990	Namibia
—	Nauru
1955	Nepal
1945	Netherlands, The

Government and international organizations (continued)

country	date of independence[a]	date of current or last constitution[b]	type of government	executive branch[c] chief of state	head of government	legislative branch[d] upper house (members)	lower house (members)	admin. subdivisions first-order (number)	second-order (number)	seaward claims territorial (nautical miles)	fishing/ economic (nautical miles)
Netherlands Antilles	—	Dec. 29, 1954	overseas territory (Neth.)	Dutch monarch [12]		22	—	5	—	12	200
New Caledonia	—	Nov. 9, 1988	overseas territory (Fr.)	French president [56]		54	—	3	33	12	200
New Zealand	Sept. 26, 1907	June 30, 1852[39]	constitutional monarchy	British monarch	prime minister	120	—	12	74	12	200
Nicaragua	April 30, 1838	Jan. 9, 1987	republic	president		93	—	17	143	200	200
Niger	Aug. 3, 1960	May 22, 1996	republic	president[15]		83	—	7	38	—	—
Nigeria	Oct. 1, 1960	*Oct. 1, 1979*	federal republic	chairman PRC		(91)	(593)	31	593	30	200
Northern Mariana Is.	—	Jan. 9, 1978	commonwealth (U.S.)	U.S. president	governor	9	18	4	—	12	200
Norway	June 7, 1905	May 17, 1814	constitutional monarchy	king	prime minister	165	—	19	435	4	200
Oman	Dec. 20, 1951	Nov. 1996[57]	monarchy (sultanate)	sultan		80[6]	—	8	59	12	200
Pakistan	Aug. 14, 1947	Aug. 14, 1973	federal Islamic republic	president	prime minister	87	217	16[58]	...	12	200
Palau	Oct. 1, 1994	Jan. 1, 1981	republic	president		14	16	16	...	...	...
Panama	Nov. 3, 1903	May 20, 1983[59]	republic	president[60]		72	—	10	67	200	3
Papua New Guinea	Sept. 16, 1975	Sept. 16, 1975	constitutional monarchy	British monarch	prime minister	109	—	20	267	12[9]	200[9]
Paraguay	May 14, 1811	June 22, 1992	republic	president		45	80	20	217	—	—
Peru	July 28, 1821	Dec. 29, 1993	republic	president		120	—	25	...	200	200
Philippines	July 4, 1946	Feb. 11, 1987	republic	president		24	204[61]	15	76	30	200[9]
Poland	Nov. 10, 1918	Dec. 8, 1992	republic	president	prime minister	100	460	49	2,483	12	62
Portugal	c. 1140	April 25, 1976	parliamentary state	president	prime minister	230	—	20	305	12	200
Puerto Rico	—	July 25, 1952	commonwealth (U.S.)	U.S. president	governor	27[63]	51[63]	78	...	12	200
Qatar	Sept. 3, 1971	July 1970[44]		emir		35[7]	—	9	—	12	64
Réunion	—	Feb. 28, 1983	overseas dept. (Fr.)	French president [36]		47	45	4	24	12	200
Romania	May 21, 1877	Dec. 13, 1991	republic	president	prime minister	143	343	41	...	12[31]	200[31]
Russia	Dec. 8, 1991	Dec. 24, 1993	federal republic	president	prime minister	178	450	89	1,863	12	...
Rwanda	July 1, 1962	May 5, 1995[65]	republic[6]	president[66]		70	—	11	...	—	—
St. Kitts and Nevis	Sept. 19, 1983	Sept. 19, 1983	constitutional monarchy	British monarch	prime minister	15	—	1	—	12	200
St. Lucia	Feb. 22, 1979	Feb. 22, 1979	constitutional monarchy	British monarch	prime minister	11	17	10	—	12	200
St. Vincent	Oct. 27, 1979	Oct. 27, 1979	constitutional monarchy	British monarch	prime minister	21	—	—	—	12	200
San Marino	855	Oct. 8, 1600	republic	captains-regent (2)		60	—	9	—	—	—
São Tomé and Príncipe	July 12, 1975	Sept. 10, 1990	republic	president	prime minister	55	—	1	6	12[9]	200[9]
Saudi Arabia	Sept. 23, 1932	[67]	monarchy	king		61[7]	—	13	103	12	3
Senegal	Aug. 20, 1960	March 7, 1963	republic	president	prime minister	120	—	10	48	12[31]	200[31]
Seychelles	June 29, 1976	June 18, 1993	republic	president		33	—	...	...	12	200
Sierra Leone	April 27, 1961	Oct. 1, 1991	republic	president		80	—	4	12	200	3
Singapore	Aug. 9, 1965	June 3, 1959[39]	republic	president	prime minister	83	—	—	—	3	12
Slovakia	Jan. 1, 1993	Jan. 1, 1993	republic	president	prime minister	150	—	38	...	—	—
Slovenia	June 25, 1991	Dec. 23, 1991	republic	president	prime minister	40	90	58	...	12[9]	200[9]
Solomon Islands	July 7, 1978	July 7, 1978	constitutional monarchy	British monarch	prime minister	47	—	10	...	200	200
Somalia	July 1, 1960	July 1, 1960	republic	[68]		...	...	...	...	200	200
South Africa	May 31, 1910	Dec. 10, 1996[69]	republic	president		90	400	9	360	12	200
Spain	1492	Dec. 29, 1978	constitutional monarchy	king	prime minister	248	350	19	50	12	200
Sri Lanka	Feb. 4, 1948	Sept. 7, 1978	republic	president		225	—	...	...	12	200
Sudan, The	Jan. 1, 1956	*Oct. 10, 1985*	Islamic military regime	president		400	—	26	275	12	3
Suriname	Nov. 25, 1975	Nov. 25, 1987	republic	president		51	—	10	...	12	200
Swaziland	Sept. 6, 1968	*Sept. 6, 1968*	monarchy	king[15]		30[7]	65[7]	4	55	—	—
Sweden	before 836	Jan. 1, 1975	constitutional monarchy	king	prime minister	349	—	24	288	12	17
Switzerland	Sept. 22, 1499	May 29, 1874	federal state	president FC		46	200	26	2,915	—	—
Syria	April 17, 1946	March 14, 1973	republic	president		250	—	14	47	35	3
Taiwan	Oct. 25, 1945	Dec. 25, 1947[39]	republic	president	premier	334	164	2	25	24	200
Tajikistan	Sept. 9, 1991	Nov. 6, 1994	republic	president	prime minister	181	—	5	...	—	—
Tanzania	Dec. 9, 1961	April 25, 1977	republic	president		275	—	25	99	12	200
Thailand	1350	Dec. 9, 1991	constitutional monarchy	king	prime minister	260	393	76	711	12	200
Togo	April 27, 1960	Sept. 27, 1992[5]	republic	president	prime minister	81	—	5	21	30	200
Tonga	June 4, 1970	Nov. 4, 1875	constitutional monarchy[70]	monarch[71]		30	—	2	23	12	200
Trinidad and Tobago	Aug. 31, 1962	July 27, 1976	republic	president	prime minister	31	36	12	124	12[9]	200[9]
Tunisia	March 20, 1956	June 1, 1959	republic	president	prime minister	163	—	23	254	12	3
Turkey	Oct. 29, 1923	Nov. 7, 1982	republic	president	prime minister	550	—	76	829	12[72]	17
Turkmenistan	Oct. 27, 1991	May 18, 1992	republic	president		73	50	5	...	—	—
Tuvalu	Oct. 1, 1978	Oct. 1, 1986	constitutional monarchy	British monarch	prime minister	12	—	8	—	12[9]	200[9]
Uganda	Oct. 9, 1962	Oct. 8, 1995	republic[6]	president[15]		276	—	39	...	—	—
Ukraine	Aug. 24, 1991	June 28, 1996	republic	president	prime minister	450	—	27	485	12	200
United Arab Emirates	Dec. 2, 1971	Dec. 2, 1971	federation of emirates	president	prime minister	40[7]	—	7	—	12	200
United Kingdom	Oct. 14, 1066	[74]	constitutional monarchy	monarch	prime minister	1,194	651	...	...	12[46]	200
United States	July 4, 1776	March 4, 1789	federal republic	president		100	435	51	3,043	12	200
Uruguay	Aug. 25, 1828	Feb. 15, 1967	republic	president		31	99	19	...	200	200
Uzbekistan	Aug. 31, 1991	Dec. 8, 1992	republic	president	prime minister	250	—	12	...	—	...
Vanuatu	July 30, 1980	July 30, 1980	republic	president	prime minister	50	—	11	...	12[9]	200[9]
Venezuela	July 5, 1811	Jan. 23, 1961	federal republic	president		52	199	24	202	12	200
Vietnam	Sept. 2, 1945	April 15, 1992	socialist republic	president	prime minister	395	—	53	479	12	200
Virgin Islands (U.S.)	—	July 22, 1954	territory (U.S.)	U.S. president	governor	15	—	1	—	12	200
West Bank	—	May 4, 1994[38]	interim authority[75]	chairman PNA		88	—	...	...	—	—
Western Sahara	—	—	annexure of Morocco	—	—	—	—	5	—	12	200
Western Samoa	Jan. 1, 1962	Oct. 28, 1960	[77]	head of state	prime minister	49	—	330[78]	—	12	200
Yemen	December 1918	Sept. 29, 1994[59]	republic	president	prime minister	301	—	18	...	12	200
Yugoslavia	Dec. 1, 1918	April 27, 1992	federal republic	federal president	prime minister	40	138	2	...	12	200
Zaire	June 30, 1960	April 9, 1994[80]	republic[6]	president	prime minister	738	—	11	...	12	200
Zambia	Oct. 24, 1964	May 28, 1996[81]	republic	president		150[61]	—	9	57	—	—
Zimbabwe	April 18, 1980	April 18, 1980	republic	president		150	—	10	80	—	—

[1]No effective central government because of warfare. [2]Transitional constitution. [3]Territorial sea claim assumed to claim fishing/economic rights within the same zone. [4]Observer status. [5]Date of referendum approving new constitution. [6]Transitional government. [7]Body with limited or no legislative authority. [8]President of France and Bishop of Urgell, Spain. [9]Measured from claimed archipelagic baselines. [10]Promulgation date of significant amendments to July 9, 1853, constitution. [11]Assisted by ministerial coordinator who exercises general administration of country. [12]Executive responsibilities divided between (for The Netherlands) the governor and (locally) the prime minister. [13]Associate member. [14]Formally a constitutional monarchy. [15]Assisted by the prime minister. [16]Full membership pending. [17]Defined by equidistant line. [18]Significant constitutional amendments of November 1996 did not meet international standards. [19]Excludes certain members of the royal family. [20]10 provincial councils; 5 region/community councils. [21]3 nautical miles from mouth of Sarstoon River (southern boundary with Guatemala) to Ranguana Caye. [22]Executive responsibilities divided between (for the U.K.) the governor and (locally) the premier of the cabinet. [23]Resembles a constitutional monarchy without a formal constitution. [24]Date of formal signing of peace accord. [25]First prime minister assisted by second prime minister. [26]Constitution adopted by national assembly. [27]Governor-general can exercise all the powers of the reigning monarch of the Commonwealth. [28]Suspended membership. [29]Republic of Cyprus only. [30]Includes unoccupied seats. [31]Zone defined by geographic coordinates. [32]Official proclamations organizing government. [33]Creation began in 1995. [34]Date new republic was formally established. [35]Executive responsibilities divided between (for Denmark) the high commissioner and (locally) the prime minister. [36]Executive responsibilities divided among (for France) the prefect and (locally) the president of the General Council and the president of the Regional Council. [37]Executive responsibilities divided between (for France) the high commissioner and (locally) the president of the territorial government. [38]Date of agreement providing for Palestinian self-rule. [39]Evolving body of constitutional law. [40]Represented by the lieutenant governor. [41]Assisted by extraconstitutional prime minister. [42]Shares coexecutive authority with spiritual leader. [43]Sea of Oman only; median line boundaries in Persian Gulf.

membership in international organizations

United Nations (date of admission)	UN organs★ and affiliated intergovernmental organizations																				Commonwealth of Nations	regional multipurpose						economic									country
	UNCTAD★[e]	UNICEF★[f]	ICJ★	FAO	IAEA[e]	IBRD	ICAO	IDA	IFC	ILO	IMF	IMO	ITU[e]	UNESCO	UNIDO	UPU[e]	WHO	WIPO[e]	WMO	WTO		EU	GCC	LAS[g]	OAS	OAU	SPC	ACP	ADB	APEC	CARICOM	ECOWAS	EEC	I-ADB	IDB[g]	OPEC	
—														•[13]		•			•												•[4]						Netherlands Antilles
—																•			•								•										New Caledonia
1945	•	•	•	•	•	•	•	•	•	•	•	•	•	•	•	•	•	•	•	•	•						•			•							New Zealand
1945	•	•	•	•	•	•	•	•	•	•	•	•	•	•	•	•	•	•	•	•					•									•			Nicaragua
1960	•	•	•	•	•	•	•	•	•	•	•	•	•	•	•	•	•	•	•	•						•		•				•			•		Niger
1960	•	•	•	•	•	•	•	•	•	•	•	•	•	•	•	•	•	•	•	•	•[28]					•		•				•				•	Nigeria
—																•											•										Northern Mariana Is.
1945	•	•	•	•	•	•	•	•	•	•	•	•	•	•	•	•	•	•	•	•									•					•			Norway
1971	•	•	•	•		•	•	•	•	•	•	•	•	•	•	•	•		•				•	•											•		Oman
1947	•	•	•	•	•	•	•	•	•	•	•	•	•	•	•	•	•	•	•	•	•								•						•		Pakistan
1994		•														•											•										Palau
1945	•	•	•	•	•	•	•	•	•	•	•	•	•	•	•	•	•	•	•	•[4]					•									•			Panama
1975	•	•	•	•		•	•	•	•	•	•	•	•	•	•	•	•		•	•[16]	•						•	•	•	•							Papua New Guinea
1945	•	•	•	•	•	•	•	•	•	•	•	•	•	•	•	•	•	•	•	•					•									•			Paraguay
1945	•	•	•	•	•	•	•	•	•	•	•	•	•	•	•	•	•	•	•	•					•									•			Peru
1945	•	•	•	•	•	•	•	•	•	•	•	•	•	•	•	•	•	•	•	•									•	•							Philippines
1945	•	•	•	•	•	•	•	•	•	•	•	•	•	•	•	•	•	•	•	•																	Poland
1955	•	•	•	•	•	•	•	•	•	•	•	•	•	•	•	•	•	•	•	•		•											•	•			Portugal
—				•[13]												•	•[13]														•[4]						Puerto Rico
1971	•	•	•	•	•	•	•			•	•	•	•	•	•	•	•	•	•	•			•	•											•	•	Qatar
—																•																					Réunion
1955	•	•	•	•	•	•	•	•	•	•	•	•	•	•	•	•	•	•	•	•																	Romania
1991	•	•			•	•	•	•	•	•	•	•	•	•	•	•	•	•	•	•[4]																	Russia
1962	•	•	•	•		•	•	•	•	•	•		•	•	•	•	•	•	•	•						•		•									Rwanda
1983	•	•	•	•		•		•			•			•	•	•	•			•	•				•			•			•						St. Kitts and Nevis
1979	•	•	•	•		•	•	•	•	•	•	•		•	•	•	•	•	•	•	•				•			•			•						St. Lucia
1980	•	•	•	•		•	•	•			•	•	•	•	•	•	•			•	•				•			•			•						St. Vincent
1992	•	•	•				•			•	•		•	•		•	•	•	•																		San Marino
1975	•	•	•	•		•	•	•		•	•	•	•	•	•	•	•		•	•[16]						•		•									São Tomé and Príncipe
1945	•	•	•	•	•	•	•	•	•	•	•	•	•	•	•	•	•	•	•	•[4]			•	•											•	•	Saudi Arabia
1960	•	•	•	•	•	•	•	•	•	•	•	•	•	•	•	•	•	•	•	•						•		•				•			•		Senegal
1976	•	•	•	•		•	•		•	•	•	•		•	•	•	•		•	•[16]	•					•		•									Seychelles
1961	•	•	•	•	•	•	•	•	•	•	•	•	•	•	•	•	•	•	•	•	•					•		•				•			•		Sierra Leone
1965	•	•	•		•	•	•		•	•	•	•	•			•	•	•	•	•	•								•	•							Singapore
1993	•	•		•	•	•	•	•	•	•	•	•	•	•	•	•	•	•	•	•																	Slovakia
1992	•	•		•	•	•	•	•	•	•	•	•	•	•	•	•	•	•	•	•														•			Slovenia
1978	•	•	•	•		•	•	•	•	•	•	•	•	•		•	•		•	•[16]	•						•	•	•								Solomon Islands
1960	•	•	•	•		•	•	•	•	•	•	•	•	•	•	•	•	•	•					•		•		•							•		Somalia
1945	•	•	•	•	•	•	•	•	•		•		•	•		•	•	•	•	•	•					•											South Africa
1955	•	•	•	•	•	•	•	•	•	•	•	•	•	•	•	•	•	•	•	•		•							•				•	•			Spain
1955	•	•	•	•	•	•	•	•	•	•	•	•	•	•	•	•	•	•	•	•	•								•								Sri Lanka
1956	•	•	•	•	•	•	•	•	•	•	•	•	•	•	•	•	•	•	•					•		•		•							•		Sudan, The
1975	•	•	•	•		•	•			•	•	•	•	•	•	•	•	•	•	•					•			•			•			•			Suriname
1968	•	•	•	•		•	•	•	•	•	•		•	•	•	•	•	•	•	•	•					•		•									Swaziland
1946	•	•	•	•	•	•	•	•	•	•	•	•	•	•	•	•	•	•	•	•		•							•				•	•			Sweden
—	•	•	•	•	•	•	•	•	•	•	•	•	•	•	•	•	•	•	•	•									•					•			Switzerland
1945	•	•	•	•	•	•	•	•	•	•	•	•	•	•	•	•	•		•					•											•		Syria
—																				•[4]									•	•							Taiwan
1992	•	•		•		•	•	•		•	•			•	•	•	•	•	•																		Tajikistan
1961	•	•	•	•	•	•	•	•	•	•	•	•	•	•	•	•	•	•	•	•	•					•		•									Tanzania
1946	•	•	•	•	•	•	•	•	•	•	•	•	•	•	•	•	•	•	•	•									•	•							Thailand
1960	•	•	•	•		•	•	•	•	•	•	•	•	•	•	•	•	•	•	•						•		•				•					Togo
—	•	•		•		•	•	•	•		•		•	•	•	•	•			•[16]	•						•	•	•								Tonga
1962	•	•	•	•		•	•	•	•	•	•	•	•	•	•	•	•	•	•	•	•				•			•			•			•			Trinidad and Tobago
1956	•	•	•	•	•	•	•	•	•	•	•	•	•	•	•	•	•	•	•	•				•		•									•		Tunisia
1945	•	•	•	•	•	•	•	•	•	•	•	•	•	•	•	•	•	•	•	•									•				•[13]		•		Turkey
1992	•	•		•		•	•	•[16]		•	•	•	•	•		•	•		•	•[4]															•		Turkmenistan
—		•												•		•	•			•[16]	•[55]						•	•	•								Tuvalu
1962	•	•	•	•	•	•	•	•	•	•	•		•	•	•	•	•	•	•	•	•					•		•							•		Uganda
1945	•	•			•	•	•	•[16]		•	•	•	•	•	•	•	•	•	•	•[4]																	Ukraine
1971	•	•	•	•	•	•	•	•	•	•	•	•	•	•	•	•	•	•	•	•			•	•											•	•	United Arab Emirates
1945	•	•	•	•	•	•	•	•	•	•	•	•	•	•[4]	•	•	•	•	•	•	•	•					•		•				•	•			United Kingdom
1945	•	•	•	•	•	•	•	•	•	•	•	•	•	•[4]	•	•	•	•	•	•					•		•		•	•				•			United States
1945	•	•	•	•	•	•	•		•	•	•	•	•	•	•	•	•	•	•	•					•									•			Uruguay
1992	•	•			•	•	•	•	•	•	•		•	•	•	•	•	•	•	•[4]																	Uzbekistan
1981	•	•	•	•		•	•	•	•		•	•	•	•	•	•	•		•		•						•	•	•								Vanuatu
1945	•	•	•	•	•	•	•		•	•	•	•	•	•	•	•	•	•	•	•					•						•[4]			•		•	Venezuela
1977	•	•	•	•	•	•	•	•	•	•	•	•	•	•	•	•	•	•	•	•[4]									•								Vietnam
—																•															•						Virgin Islands (U.S.)
—		•																																			West Bank
—																										•[76]											Western Sahara
1976	•	•	•	•		•		•	•		•		•	•		•	•				•						•	•	•								Western Samoa
1947	•	•	•	•		•	•	•	•	•	•	•	•	•	•	•	•	•	•	•[16]				•											•		Yemen
1945[79]	•	•	•	•	•	•[16]	•[16]	•[16]	•	•	•	•	•	•	•	•	•	•	•	•																	Yugoslavia
1960	•	•	•	•	•	•	•	•	•	•	28	•	•	•	•	•	•	•	•	•						•		•									Zaire
1964	•	•	•	•	•	•	•	•	•	•	•		•	•	•	•	•	•	•	•	•					•		•									Zambia
1980	•	•	•	•	•	•	•	•	•	•	•		•	•	•	•	•	•	•	•	•					•		•									Zimbabwe

[44]Provisional constitution. [45]De facto administration. [46]Median line between the Isle of Man and the United Kingdom. [47]3 nautical miles in 5 straits. [48]3 nautical miles in Korea Strait. [49]Date of peace accord. [50]Formally a *jamahiriya,* translated as "the masses of people." [51]Based on Gulf of Sidra closing line (32° 30′ N), in part. [52]Macau will revert to Chinese sovereignty on Dec. 20, 1999. [53]Executive responsibilities divided between (for France) the prefect and (locally) the president of the General Council. [54]Excludes claims in the Western Sahara. [55]Special member. [56]Executive responsibilities divided between (for France) the high commissioner and (locally) the president of the General Council. [57]Basic law promulgated by sultan. [58]Includes 11 federally administered tribal areas, excludes Jammu and Kashmir. [59]Effective date of significant amendments. [60]Assisted by vice presidents. [61]Elective seats only. [62]Defined by international treaties. [63]Excludes additional seats for both houses of the legislature to meet ⅓ total representation requirements for minority parties per constitution. [64]Limits of continental shelf or median line boundaries. [65]Date constitution adopted by transitional legislature. [66]Assisted by vice president (minister of defense) and prime minister. [67]Royal decrees since March 1, 1992, provide a formal description of the king's governance. [68]No effective central government. [69]Permanent constitution (announced May 8, 1996) became effective with president's signature on Dec. 10, 1996. [70]In practice resembles a system of monarchical absolutism. [71]Assisted by Privy Council. [72]Black Sea and Mediterranean Sea; 6 nautical miles in Aegean Sea. [73]Second representative body is a supervisory organ. [74]Based on evolving body of statutes and common law. [75]Urban areas only (excluding Hebron). [76]Membership held by Sahrawi Arab Democratic Republic. [77]Mixed political system approximating a constitutional monarchy. [78]Number of villages. [79]Suspended from participation in UN proceedings from September 1992; however, Yugoslavia is permitted to participate in the work of UN organs other than General Assembly bodies. [80]Date of Transitional Constitutional Act. [81]Date president signed new constitution.

Area and population

This table provides the area and population for each of the countries of the world and for all but the smallest political dependencies having a permanent civilian population. The data represent the latest published and unpublished data for both the surveyed area of the countries and their populations, the latter both as of a single year (1996) to provide the best comparability and as of the most recent census to provide the fullest comparison of certain demographic measures that are not always available between successive national censuses. The 1996 midyear estimates represent a combination of national, United Nations (UN) or other international organizations, and *Encyclopædia Britannica* estimates so as to give the best fit to available published series, to take account of unpublished information received in correspondence, and to incorporate the results of very recent censuses for which published analyses are not yet available.

One principal point to bear in mind when studying these statistics is that all of them, whatever degree of precision may be implied by the exactness of the numbers, are estimates—all of varying, and some of suspect, accuracy—even when they *contain* a very full enumeration. The United States—which has a long tradition both of census taking and of the use of the most sophisticated analytical tools in processing the data—is unable to determine within 2.1% (the estimated 1990 undercount) its total population nationally. And that is an *average* underenumeration. In states and larger cities, where enumeration of particular populations, both legal and illegal, is most difficult, the accuracy of the enumerated count may be off as much as 4% at a state level and as much as 10% for a single city. The high accuracy attained by census operations in China may approach 0.25% of rigorously maintained civil population registers. Other national census operations not so based, however, are inherently less accurate. For

example, Ethiopia's first-ever census in 1984 resulted in figures that were 30% or more above prevailing estimates; Nigeria's 1991 census corrected decades of miscounts and was well below prevailing estimates. An undercount of 2–8% is more typical, but even census operations offering results of 30% or more above or below prevailing estimates can still represent well-founded benchmarks from which future planning may proceed. The editors have tried to take account of the range of variation and accuracy in published data, but it is difficult to establish a value for many sources of inaccuracy unless some country or agency has made a conscientious effort to establish both the relative accuracy (precision) of its estimate and the absolute magnitude of the quantity it is trying to measure—for example, the number of people in Cambodia who died at the hands of the Khmer Rouge. If a figure of 2,000,000 is adopted, what is its accuracy: ± 1%, 10%, 50%? Are the original data documentary or evidentiary, complete or incomplete, analytically biased or unbiased, in good agreement with other published data?

Many similar problems exist and in endless variations: What is the extent of southern European immigration to western Europe in search of jobs? How many refugees from Afghanistan, Liberia, Rwanda, or Burundi are there in surrounding countries? How many undocumented aliens are there in the United States? How many Palestinians are there in the Middle East (they are politically inconvenient to enumerate everywhere)? How many Amerindians exist (remain, preserving their original language and a mode of life unassimilated by the larger national culture) in the countries of South America? How many people have died or emigrated as a result of the civil violence in Central America?

Still, much information is accurate, well founded, and updated regularly.

Area and population

country	area			population (latest estimate)				population (latest census)				
	square miles	square kilometres	rank	total midyear 1996	rank	density		% annual growth rate 1991–96	census year	total	male (%)	female (%)	urban (%)
						per sq mi	per sq km						
Afghanistan	251,825	652,225	41	22,264,000	42	90.0	34.7	8.7	1979	13,051,358[1]	51.4	48.6	15.1
Albania	11,100	28,748	142	3,249,000	128	292.7	113.0	−0.1	1989	3,182,417	51.5	48.5	35.7
Algeria	919,595	2,381,741	11	28,566,000	36	31.1	12.0	2.3	1987	23,038,942	49.9	50.1	49.7
American Samoa	77	199	205	58,800	206	763.6	295.5	3.7	1990	46,773	51.4	48.6	33.4
Andorra	181	468	193	64,100	203	354.1	137.0	2.5	1992[2]	61,599	53.1	46.9	62.5[3]
Angola	481,354	1,246,700	24	11,904,000	62	24.7	9.5	2.9	1970	5,673,046	52.1	47.9	14.2
Antigua and Barbuda	171	442	195	64,400	202	376.6	145.7	0.2	1991	63,896	48.2	51.8	36.2
Argentina	1,073,518	2,780,400	8	34,995,000	31	32.6	12.6	1.2	1991	32,615,528	48.9	51.1	88.4
Armenia	11,500	29,800	141	3,765,000	120	327.4	126.3	0.8	1989	3,287,677	49.3	50.7	67.8
Aruba	75	193	206	73,300	199	977.3	379.8	2.1	1991	66,687	49.2	50.8	...
Australia	2,966,200	7,682,300	6	18,287,000	51	6.2	2.4	1.1	1991	17,284,036	49.6	50.4	85.3
Austria	32,378	83,858	115	8,102,000	84	250.2	96.6	0.7	1991	7,795,786	48.2	51.8	64.5
Azerbaijan	33,400	86,600	113	7,570,000	86	226.6	87.4	0.9	1989	7,037,867	48.7	51.3	53.8
Bahamas, The	5,382	13,939	158	280,000	174	52.0	20.1	1.5	1990	255,095	49.0	51.0	64.3
Bahrain	268	694	186	598,000	161	2,231.3	861.7	3.3	1991	508,037	57.9	42.1	88.4
Bangladesh	56,977	147,570	93	123,063,000	9	2,159.5	833.9	1.9	1991	111,455,185	51.4	48.6	20.2
Barbados	166	430	196	265,000	178	1,596.4	616.3	0.2	1990[4]	257,083	47.7	52.3	37.9[5]
Belarus	80,153	207,595	85	10,442,000	70	130.3	50.3	0.3	1989	10,199,709	46.9	53.1	65.5
Belgium	11,787	30,528	139	10,185,000	73	864.1	333.6	0.4	1991	9,978,681	48.9	51.1	96.6[6]
Belize	8,867	22,965	150	219,000	180	24.7	9.5	2.5	1991	189,392	50.9	49.1	47.5
Benin	43,500	112,680	101	5,574,000	99	128.1	49.5	3.1	1992	4,855,349	48.7	51.3	39.6
Bermuda	21	54	212	61,400	204	2,923.8	1,137.0	0.6	1991[4]	58,460	48.5	51.5	100.0
Bhutan	18,150	47,000	131	842,000	154	46.4	17.9	2.3	...	...	50.6[5]	49.4[5]	5.3[5]
Bolivia	424,164	1,098,581	28	7,593,000	85	17.9	6.9	2.4	1992	6,420,792	49.4	50.6	57.5
Bosnia and Herzegovina	19,741	51,129	127	3,524,000	125	178.5	68.9	−3.3	1991	4,377,033	49.9	50.1	36.2[8]
Botswana	224,607	581,730	47	1,478,000	145	6.6	2.5	2.0	1991	1,326,796	47.8	52.2	23.9
Brazil	3,300,171	8,547,404	5	157,872,000	5	47.8	18.5	1.4	1991	146,825,475	49.4	50.6	75.6
Brunei	2,226	5,765	167	300,000	173	134.8	52.0	2.8	1991	260,482	52.8	47.2	90.0[9]
Bulgaria	42,855	110,994	103	8,366,000	83	195.2	75.4	−0.7	1992	8,487,317	49.1	50.9	67.2
Burkina Faso	105,946	274,400	73	10,615,000	67	100.2	38.7	2.8	1985[4]	7,964,705	48.1	51.9	11.7
Burundi	10,740	27,816	145	5,943,000	96	553.4	213.7	0.5	1990[4]	5,292,793	48.6	51.4	6.3
Cambodia	70,238	181,916	89	10,081,000	74	143.5	55.4	2.7	1993	9,307,597	48.3	51.7	21.0[10]
Cameroon	183,569	475,442	53	13,609,000	61	74.1	28.6	2.8	1987	10,516,232	49.0	51.0	38.3
Canada	3,849,674	9,970,610	2	29,784,000	33	7.7	3.0	1.2	1991	27,296,859	49.3	50.7	76.6
Cape Verde	1,557	4,033	169	403,000	169	258.8	99.9	2.9	1990	341,491	47.3	52.7	44.1
Central African Republic	240,324	622,436	43	3,274,000	127	13.6	5.3	2.6	1988	2,688,426	49.1	50.9	36.5
Chad	495,755	1,284,000	21	6,543,000	93	13.2	5.1	2.8	1993	6,279,931	47.9	52.1	21.4
Chile	292,135	756,626	38	14,375,000	59	49.2	19.0	1.5	1992	13,348,401	49.1	50.9	85.1[7]
China	3,696,100	9,572,900	3	1,218,709,000	1	329.7	127.3	1.2	1990	1,133,682,501	51.6	48.4	26.4
Colombia	440,762	1,141,568	26	35,652,000	30	80.9	31.2	1.7	1993	33,109,840	49.2	50.8	70.3[5]
Comoros	719	1,862	175	562,000	163	781.6	301.8	3.3	1991	446,817	49.5	50.5	27.8[5]
Congo	132,047	342,000	63	2,665,000	132	20.2	7.8	3.0	1984[4]	1,909,248	48.7	51.3	52.0
Costa Rica	19,730	51,100	128	3,400,000	126	172.3	66.5	2.1	1984	2,416,809	50.0	50.0	43.9
Côte d'Ivoire	124,504	322,463	68	14,733,000	58	118.3	45.7	3.5	1988	10,815,694	51.1	48.9	39.0
Croatia	21,857	56,610	126	4,775,000	108	218.5	84.3	0.0	1991	4,784,265	48.5	51.5	54.3
Cuba	42,804	110,861	104	11,117,000	65	259.7	100.3	0.8	1993	10,900,000	50.3	49.7	72.8[5]
Cyprus[11]	3,572	9,251	164	767,000	157	214.7	82.9	−0.2	1992[4, 12]	615,013	49.8	50.2	67.7
Czech Republic	30,450	78,864	117	10,316,000	71	338.8	130.8	0.0	1991	10,302,215	48.5	51.5	...
Denmark	16,639	43,094	133	5,244,000	104	315.2	121.7	0.3	1995[2]	5,215,718	49.3	50.7	84.9[7]
Djibouti	8,950	23,200	149	604,000	160	67.5	26.0	3.0	1960–61	81,200	51.6[10]	48.4[10]	82.8[10]
Dominica	290	750	183	73,800	198	254.5	98.4	0.6	1991	71,183	49.8	50.2	...
Dominican Republic	18,792	48,671	130	7,502,000	87	399.2	154.1	1.9	1993	7,089,041	50.1[8]	49.9[8]	52.0[8]
Ecuador	105,037	272,045	74	11,698,000	63	111.4	43.0	2.2	1990	9,648,189	49.7	50.3	55.4
Egypt	385,229	997,739	30	60,896,000	17	158.1	61.0	2.3	1986	48,205,049	51.1	48.9	43.9
El Salvador	8,124	21,041	151	5,897,000	97	725.9	280.3	2.2	1992	5,118,599	48.6	51.4	50.4

The sources of these data are censuses; national population registers (cumulated periodically); registration of migration, births, deaths, and so on; sample surveys to establish demographic conditions; and the like.

The statistics provided for area and population by country are ranked, and the population densities based on those values are also provided. The population densities, for purposes of comparison within this table, are calculated on the bases of the 1996 midyear population estimate as shown and of total area of the country. Elsewhere in individual country presentations the reader may find densities calculated on more specific population figures and more specialized area bases: land area for Finland (because of its many lakes) or ice-free area for Greenland (most of which is ice cap). The data in this section conclude with the estimated average annual growth rate for the country (including both natural growth and net migration) during the five-year period, 1991–96.

In the section containing census data, information supplied includes the census total (usually de facto, the population actually present, rather than de jure, the population legally resident, who might be anywhere); the male-female breakdown; the proportion that is urban (according to the country's own definition of the term "urban," which differs very much from country to country); and finally an analysis of the age structure of the population by 15-year age groups. This last analysis may be particularly useful in distinguishing the type of population being recorded—young, fast-growing nations show a high proportion of people under 30 (most countries in sub-Saharan Africa and the Middle East have nearly one-half of their population under 15 years), while other nations (for example Sweden, which suffered no age-group losses in World War II) exhibit quite uniform proportions.

Finally, a section is provided giving the population of each country at 10-year intervals from 1940 to 2010. The data for years past represent the best available analysis of the published data by the country itself, by the demographers of the United Nations, or by the editors of Britannica. The projections for 2000 and 2010 similarly represent the best fit of available data through the mid-1990s with projected population structure and growth rates during the next two decades. The evidence of the last 25 years with respect to similar estimates published about 1970, however, shows how cloudy is the glass through which these numbers are read. In 1970 no respectable Western analyst would have imagined proposing that mainland China could achieve the degree of birth control that it apparently has since then (as evidenced by the results of 1982 and 1990 censuses); on the other hand, even the Chinese admit that their methods have been somewhat Draconian and that they have already seen some backlash in terms of higher birth rates among those who have so far postponed larger families. How much is "some" by 2000? Compound that problem with all the social, economic, political, and biological factors that can affect 217 countries' populations, and the difficulty facing the prospective compiler of such projections may be appreciated.

Specific data about the vital rates affecting the data in this table may be found in great detail in both the country statistical boxes in "The Nations of the World" section and in the *Vital statistics, marriage, family* table, beginning at page 784.

Percentages in this table for male and female population will always total 100.0, but percentages by age group may not, for reasons such as nonresponse on census forms, "don't know" responses (which are common in countries with poor birth registration systems), and the like.

age distribution (%)						population (by decade, '000s)								country
0–14	15–29	30–44	45–59	60–74	75 and over	1940	1950	1960	1970	1980	1990	2000 projection	2010 projection	
44.5	26.9	15.8	8.6	3.6	0.6	...	8,150	9,829	12,431	14,985	14,767	26,668	34,098	Afghanistan
33.0	28.9	18.5	11.7	5.9	1.9	1,088	1,227	1,623	2,157	2,699	3,273	3,427	3,858	Albania
43.9	28.0	13.9	8.4	4.2	1.6	7,688	8,956	10,800	14,330	18,666	25,012	31,158	37,489	Algeria
38.1	29.0	18.1	9.4	4.3	1.1	13	19	20	27	33	47	67	86	American Samoa
16.3	27.7	27.2	15.1	9.9	3.8	5	6	8	19	33	53	66	71	Andorra
41.7	23.2	17.0	7.4	3.8	1.0	3,738	4,131	4,816	5,588	7,722	10,020	13,400	18,082	Angola
30.4	27.8	20.5	10.2	7.7	3.4	34	45	55	66	69	64	65	65	Antigua and Barbuda
30.6	23.3	19.3	13.9	9.6	3.3	14,169	17,150	20,616	23,962	28,114	32,547	36,648	40,755	Argentina
30.3	25.7	20.8	13.6	6.4	3.2	1,320	1,354	1,867	2,520	3,067	3,545	3,784	3,888	Armenia
24.4	22.0	27.0	16.1	7.2	3.0	31	51	57	61	60	63	76	83	Aruba
22.1	24.2	23.4	15.0	11.1	4.4	7,079	8,219	10,315	12,552	14,741	17,065	19,201	20,968	Australia
17.4	23.7	21.6	17.2	13.4	6.7	6,684	6,935	7,048	7,447	7,549	7,718	8,249	8,357	Austria
32.8	29.7	16.8	12.8	5.7	2.2	3,274	2,896	3,895	5,172	6,165	7,159	7,797	8,298	Azerbaijan
32.2	30.8	19.7	10.6	5.0	1.8	70	79	110	170	210	256	295	332	Bahamas, The
31.7	28.4	28.2	8.0	3.1	0.6	90	110	149	210	334	503	690	994	Bahrain
41.5	25.2	16.2	8.1	4.3	1.1	41,259	45,646	54,622	67,403	88,077	110,118	132,081	153,195	Bangladesh
24.1	27.1	22.1	11.4	9.9	5.4	179	209	232	235	249	261	267	271	Barbados
23.0	22.4	20.6	18.0	11.5	4.5	9,046	7,745	8,190	9,040	9,650	10,260	10,560	10,939	Belarus
18.2	21.8	22.5	16.9	14.1	6.6	8,301	8,639	9,153	9,690	9,859	9,967	10,331	10,707	Belgium
43.9	27.9	14.9	7.2	4.4	1.6	56	68	90	120	146	189	242	299	Belize
48.3[7]	26.9[7]	13.3[7]	7.4[7]	3.2[7]	0.8[7]	...	2,046	2,273	2,693	3,459	4,633	6,266	8,300	Benin
19.5	24.0	26.8	16.4	—13.3—		31	37	43	53	55	59	63	67	Bermuda
40.6[5]	26.5[5]	17.1[5]	10.4[5]	4.6[5]	0.8[5]	...	...	...	...	600	737	916	1,129	Bhutan
41.2	26.2	16.8	8.9	—6.5—		2,508	2,714	3,351	4,212	5,355	6,573	8,329	10,229	Bolivia
23.5[6]	26.3[6]	22.6[6]	16.2[6]	8.9[6]	2.7[6]	...	2,662	3,240	3,703	4,107	4,308	4,330	4,420	Bosnia and Herzegovina
42.8	27.3	14.3	7.3	4.1	2.2	278	430	497	584	903	1,304	1,557	1,598	Botswana
34.7	28.1	19.3	10.6	5.7	1.6	41,525	53,444	72,594	95,847	118,563	144,723	165,715	184,157	Brazil
34.5	29.3	24.2	7.9	—4.1—		36	45	83	128	185	254	331	410	Brunei
20.5	19.2	—39.8—		—20.5—		6,344	7,251	7,867	8,490	8,862	8,718	8,212	7,892	Bulgaria
48.3	23.4	13.4	8.7	4.7	1.4	3,036	3,584	4,350	5,412	6,599	9,012	11,884	15,549	Burkina Faso
46.4	25.3	15.4	7.0	4.0	1.7	1,887	2,363	2,812	3,513	4,138	5,633	6,493	8,229	Burundi
47.0	—53.0—					3,400	4,346	5,433	6,938	6,400	8,592	11,158	14,000	Cambodia
46.4	24.5	14.6	8.7	4.1	1.6	...	4,466	5,296	6,612	8,655	11,526	15,245	20,163	Cameroon
20.9	22.7	25.1	15.3	11.3	4.7	11,693	13,737	17,909	21,324	24,593	27,791	31,029	33,946	Canada
45.0	27.3	11.4	8.0	5.5	2.9	181	146	196	267	289	341	448	565	Cape Verde
43.2	27.5	15.0	9.2	4.1	0.8	991	1,260	1,467	1,827	2,244	2,806	3,539	4,177	Central African Republic
43.9[9]	26.0[9]	16.0[9]	9.3[9]	4.1[9]	0.7[9]	2,351	2,658	3,064	3,652	4,477	5,553	7,307	9,319	Chad
29.9[7]	26.1[7]	21.5[7]	13.1[7]	7.1[7]	2.2[7]	5,063	6,082	7,608	9,496	11,147	13,100	15,057	16,449	Chile
27.7	31.0	20.7	12.1	6.9	1.7	530,000	556,613	667,070	818,316	981,242	1,133,683	1,268,847	1,371,446	China
33.1[9]	30.0[9]	20.6[9]	9.9[9]	5.2[9]	1.3[9]	9,097	11,268	15,321	20,884	26,906	32,300	37,822	42,959	Colombia
47.6[6]	27.0[6]	13.1[6]	7.7[6]	3.5[6]	1.0[6]	119	148	177	245	333	464	640	883	Comoros
44.7	27.2	13.3	9.1	4.6	0.7	...	808	988	1,263	1,669	2,232	2,970	3,853	Congo
37.9	31.5	15.8	9.2	4.4	1.2	619	862	1,236	1,731	2,246	2,994	3,680	4,393	Costa Rica
46.8	27.3	15.0	7.5	2.8	0.6	2,350	2,776	3,799	5,515	8,194	11,974	16,761	23,058	Côte d'Ivoire
19.4	20.7	22.7	18.3	12.9	4.5	...	3,851	4,140	4,411	4,588	4,778	4,771	4,761	Croatia
22.2[9]	29.8[9]	21.1[9]	14.6[9]	8.4[9]	3.9[9]	4,566	5,850	6,985	8,520	9,710	10,598	11,385	11,911	Cuba
25.4	22.0	22.3	15.4	10.2	4.7	413	494	573	615	631	757	832	982	Cyprus[11]
21.0	21.8	22.6	16.8	12.7	5.1	...	8,925	9,539	9,830	10,292	10,298	10,352	10,439	Czech Republic
17.3	21.0	21.9	19.8	12.9	7.1	3,832	4,271	4,581	4,929	5,123	5,141	5,318	5,438	Denmark
42.9[10]	25.3[10]	15.8[10]	11.7[10]	3.8[10]	0.5[10]	44	60	78	158	355	505	680	916	Djibouti
33.3	28.3	16.3	9.7	—11.8—		45	51	60	70	75	72	74	75	Dominica
40.6[8]	30.1[8]	15.1[8]	8.7[8]	—5.5[8]—		1,759	2,353	3,231	4,423	5,697	6,698	8,021	9,167	Dominican Republic
38.8	28.5	17.3	9.0	4.7	1.7	2,546	3,307	4,421	5,958	8,123	10,264	12,646	14,899	Ecuador
39.5	26.4	16.9	10.6	5.2	1.0	16,942	20,461	26,085	33,329	40,546	53,051	66,062	75,717	Egypt
38.7	28.7	16.0	9.2	5.4	1.9	1,550	1,931	2,527	3,534	4,525	5,172	6,425	7,772	El Salvador

Area and population (continued)

country	area			population (latest estimate)					population (latest census)				
	square miles	square kilo-metres	rank	total midyear 1996	rank	density		% annual growth rate 1991–96	census year	total	male (%)	female (%)	urban (%)
						per sq mi	per sq km						
Equatorial Guinea	10,831	28,051	144	406,000	168	37.5	14.5	2.5	1983	300,000	48.3	51.7	28.2
Eritrea	46,774	121,144	99	3,627,000	122	77.5	29.9	2.7	1984	2,703,998	49.9	50.1	15.1
Estonia	17,462	45,227	132	1,475,000	146	84.5	32.6	–1.2	1989	1,572,916	46.9	53.1	71.6
Ethiopia	437,794	1,133,882	27	56,713,000	22	129.5	50.0	3.0	1984	39,480,954	50.0	50.0	9.9
Faroe Islands	540	1,399	177	43,500	209	80.6	31.1	–1.7	1996[2]	43,495	51.6	48.4	...
Fiji	7,055	18,272	155	802,000	156	113.7	43.9	1.6	1986	715,375	50.7	49.3	38.7
Finland	130,559	338,145	64	5,132,000	105	39.3	15.2	0.5	1990	4,998,478	48.5	51.5	79.7
France	210,026	543,965	48	58,392,000	20	278.0	107.3	0.5	1990	56,625,026	48.7	51.3	74.3[5]
French Guiana	33,399	86,504	114	149,000	186	4.5	1.7	3.2	1990	114,808	52.1	47.9	79.4
French Polynesia	1,544	4,000	170	223,000	179	144.4	55.8	2.0	1988	188,814	52.1	47.9	55.0
Gabon	103,347	267,667	76	1,173,000	149	11.4	4.4	1.5	1993	1,011,710	49.3	50.7	73.2
Gambia, The	4,127	10,689	162	1,148,000	150	278.2	107.4	3.8	1993	1,038,145	50.1	49.9	36.7
Gaza Strip	140	363	199	816,000	155	5,828.6	2,247.9	4.2	1993[2]	716,200	50.2	49.8	...
Georgia	26,831	69,492	121	5,361,000	103	199.8	77.1	–0.4	1989	5,443,359	47.2	52.8	55.7
Germany	137,828	356,974	62	81,891,000	12	594.2	229.4	0.5	1987[13]	61,077,042	48.0	52.0	85.3[5]
Ghana	92,098	238,533	81	16,904,000	53	183.5	70.9	2.6	1984	12,296,081	49.3	50.7	32.0
Gibraltar	2.2	5.8	216	27,100	213	12,318.2	4,672.4	–1.7	1991[14]	26,703	51.0	49.0	...
Greece	50,949	131,957	96	10,493,000	68	206.0	79.5	0.5	1991	10,264,156	49.3	50.7	58.9
Greenland	840,000	2,175,600	14	56,000	208	0.1	0.0	0.2	1996[2]	55,863	53.4	46.6	81.1
Grenada	133	344	201	97,900	193	736.1	284.6	0.5	1991	95,597	48.8	51.2	33.5
Guadeloupe	687	1,780	176	427,000	166	621.5	239.9	1.5	1990	387,034	48.9	51.1	48.4
Guam	209	541	190	153,000	185	732.1	282.8	2.3	1990	133,152	53.3	46.7	38.2
Guatemala	42,042	108,889	105	10,928,000	66	259.9	100.4	2.9	1994	8,331,874	49.3	50.7	35.0
Guernsey	30	78	210	65,800	201	2,193.3	843.6	1.2	1991[15]	58,867	48.1	51.9	...
Guinea	94,926	245,857	78	6,903,000	89	72.7	28.1	3.1	1983	5,781,014	48.6	51.4	26.0
Guinea-Bissau	13,948	36,125	137	1,096,000	152	78.6	30.3	2.2	1991	983,367	48.4	51.6	20.3[6]
Guyana	83,044	215,083	84	712,000	158	8.6	3.3	–0.8	1980	758,619	49.5	50.5	31.0[7]
Haiti	10,695	27,700	146	6,732,000	92	629.5	243.0	1.8	1982	5,053,792	48.5	51.5	20.6
Honduras	43,433	112,492	102	5,666,000	98	130.5	50.4	3.2	1988	4,376,839	49.6	50.4	43.7[5]
Hong Kong	415	1,076	179	6,304,000	94	15,191.3	5,858.7	1.8	1996[4]	6,218,000	50.0	50.0	100.0
Hungary	35,919	93,030	110	10,201,000	72	284.0	109.7	–0.3	1990	10,375,323	48.1	51.9	61.8
Iceland	39,699	102,819	106	270,000	176	6.8	2.6	0.9	1994[2]	266,978	50.2	49.8	91.4
India	1,222,243	3,165,596	7	952,969,000	2	779.7	301.0	1.9	1991	846,302,688	51.9	48.1	25.7
Indonesia	741,052	1,919,317	16	198,189,000	4	267.4	103.3	1.6	1990	179,378,946	49.9	50.1	30.9
Iran	636,296	1,648,000	18	62,231,000	16	97.8	37.8	2.4	1991[4]	55,473,189	51.5	48.5	57.3
Iraq	167,975	435,052	58	21,422,000	45	127.5	49.2	3.6	1987	16,335,199	51.4	48.6	70.2
Ireland	27,137	70,285	120	3,599,000	124	132.6	51.2	0.4	1996	3,621,035	49.7	50.3	57.0
Isle of Man	221	572	189	69,800	200	315.8	122.0	0.0	1991[4]	69,788	48.3	51.7	51.1
Israel[17, 18]	7,876	20,400	152	5,481,000	100	695.9	268.7	2.5	1995[4, 19]	5,643,500	49.8[20]	50.2[20]	86.9[20]
Italy	116,341	301,323	71	57,500,000	21	494.5	190.8	0.3	1991	57,103,833	48.6	51.4	67.1
Jamaica	4,244	10,991	161	2,505,000	133	590.2	227.9	1.0	1991	2,374,193	49.0	51.0	50.4
Japan	145,877	377,819	61	125,612,000	8	861.1	332.5	0.3	1995	125,570,000	49.0	51.0	77.4[21]
Jersey	45	116	209	88,400	195	1,964.4	762.2	1.0	1991	84,082	48.6	51.4	...
Jordan[22]	34,489	89,326	112	4,333,000	115	125.6	48.5	4.1	1994	4,095,579	52.2	47.8	78.6
Kazakstan	1,052,090	2,724,900	9	16,677,000	54	15.9	6.1	–0.2	1989	16,536,511	48.5	51.5	57.2
Kenya	224,961	582,646	46	29,137,000	34	129.5	50.0	3.5	1989	21,443,636	49.6	50.4	23.6[5]
Kiribati	313	811	181	81,800	196	261.3	100.9	2.2	1990	72,335	49.2	50.8	35.1
Korea, North	47,399	122,762	98	23,904,000	39	504.3	194.7	1.8	1993	21,213,378	48.7	51.3	61.3[10]
Korea, South	38,376	99,394	108	45,232,000	26	1,178.7	455.1	0.9	1995[4]	44,606,199	50.2	49.8	74.4[21]
Kuwait	6,880	17,818	156	2,070,000	140	300.9	116.2	28.0	1995	1,575,983	56.9[23]	43.1[23]	100.0[23]
Kyrgyzstan	76,600	198,500	86	4,512,000	111	59.0	22.8	0.3	1989	4,290,442	48.9	51.1	38.2
Laos	91,429	236,800	83	5,023,000	106	54.9	21.2	3.0	1995	4,581,258	49.5	50.5	22.0[10]
Latvia	24,946	64,610	124	2,490,000	135	99.8	38.5	–1.3	1989	2,680,029	46.6	53.4	71.1
Lebanon	3,950	10,230	163	3,776,000	118	955.9	369.1	1.9	1970	2,126,325	50.8	49.2	60.1
Lesotho	11,720	30,355	140	1,971,000	141	168.2	64.9	2.1	1986[4]	1,577,536	48.2	51.8	16.0
Liberia	38,250	99,067	109	2,110,000	139	55.2	21.3	1.0	1984	2,101,628	50.6	49.4	38.8
Libya	678,400	1,757,000	17	5,445,000	101	8.0	3.1	3.8	1984	3,637,488	53.6	46.4	64.5[16]
Liechtenstein	62	160	208	31,400	211	506.5	196.3	1.4	1980	25,215	49.6	50.4	...
Lithuania	25,213	65,301	123	3,707,000	121	147.0	56.8	–0.3	1989	3,689,779	47.4	52.6	68.0
Luxembourg	999	2,586	172	415,000	167	415.4	160.5	1.4	1991	384,634	49.0	51.0	85.9[6]
Macau	7.5	19.3	215	433,000	165	57,733.3	22,435.2	4.2	1991	339,464	48.5	51.5	97.0
Macedonia	9,928	25,713	148	1,968,000	142	198.2	76.5	–0.6	1994	1,936,877	50.4	49.6	58.7
Madagascar	226,658	587,041	45	13,671,000	60	60.3	23.3	2.9	1993[4]	12,092,157	49.5	50.5	21.9[5]
Malawi	45,747	118,484	100	9,453,000	78	206.0	79.8	0.0	1987	7,988,507	48.4	51.6	10.7
Malaysia	127,584	330,442	66	20,359,000	47	159.6	61.6	2.3	1991	17,566,982	50.4	49.6	50.6
Maldives	115	298	203	266,000	177	2,313.0	892.6	3.5	1995	244,644	51.1	48.9	25.9[21]
Mali	482,077	1,248,574	23	9,204,000	79	19.1	7.4	2.1	1987	7,696,348	48.9	51.1	22.0
Malta	122	316	202	373,000	172	3,057.4	1,180.4	0.8	1985	345,418	49.2	50.8	85.3
Marshall Islands	70	181	207	58,500	207	835.7	323.2	4.0	1988	43,380	51.1	48.9	64.5
Martinique	436	1,128	178	394,000	171	903.7	349.3	1.5	1990	359,579	48.4	51.6	80.5
Mauritania	398,000	1,030,700	29	2,333,000	137	5.9	2.3	2.6	1988	1,864,236	49.5	50.5	39.1
Mauritius	788	2,040	174	1,141,000	151	1,448.0	559.3	1.3	1990	1,056,827	49.9	50.1	39.3
Mayotte	144	373	198	123,000	189	854.2	329.8	5.6	1991	94,385	52.0	48.0	59.7[23]
Mexico	756,066	1,958,201	15	92,711,000	11	122.6	47.3	1.8	1990	81,249,645	49.1	50.9	71.3
Micronesia	271	701	185	106,000	191	391.1	151.2	0.9	1994	105,506	51.1	48.9	19.4[24]
Moldova	13,000	33,700	138	4,372,000	114	336.3	129.7	0.0	1989	4,337,592	47.5	52.5	46.9
Monaco	0.75	1.95	217	30,500	212	40,666.7	15,461.0	0.3	1990	29,972	47.5	52.5	100.0
Mongolia	604,800	1,566,500	19	2,334,000	136	3.9	1.5	1.5	1989	2,043,100	48.9	51.1	57.1
Morocco	177,117	458,730	55	26,736,000	37	151.0	58.3	1.9	1994	25,821,571	49.7	50.3	51.7
Mozambique	313,661	812,379	36	17,878,000	52	57.0	22.0	4.6	1980	11,673,725	48.6	51.4	13.2
Myanmar (Burma)	261,228	676,577	40	45,976,000	24	176.0	68.0	1.9	1983	35,307,913	49.6	50.4	24.0
Namibia	318,580	825,118	35	1,709,000	144	5.4	2.1	3.8	1991	1,401,711	48.6	51.4	32.8
Nauru	8.2	21.2	214	10,600	216	1,292.7	500.0	2.0	1992	9,919	51.2	48.8	100.0
Nepal	56,827	147,181	94	20,892,000	46	367.6	141.9	2.5	1991	18,491,097	49.9	50.1	9.6
Netherlands, The	16,033	41,526	134	15,589,000	56	972.3	375.4	0.7	1994[2]	15,341,553	49.4	50.6	90.4

0–14	15–29	30–44	45–59	60–74	75 and over	1940	1950	1960	1970	1980	1990	2000 projection	2010 projection	country
41.7	25.1	15.7	11.2	5.3	1.0	...	211	244	291	255	350	448	573	Equatorial Guinea
46.1	23.0	15.9	8.9	4.4	1.6	...	1,140	1,420	1,831	2,382	3,082	4,025	5,153	Eritrea
22.2	21.4	21.0	18.5	11.7	5.1	1,054	1,101	1,216	1,365	1,473	1,571	1,430	1,401	Estonia
46.6	22.7	15.6	8.9	4.5	1.7	...	18,434	22,771	28,791	36,368	47,423	63,785	85,078	Ethiopia
24.4	—57.9—			—17.8—		27	31	35	39	43	48	44	44	Faroe Islands
38.2	29.5	17.8	9.6	3.8	0.8	218	289	394	520	634	732	854	998	Fiji
19.3	20.5	24.6	17.1	12.9	5.7	3,698	4,009	4,430	4,606	4,800	4,986	5,228	5,289	Finland
19.1	22.6	22.8	15.6	12.8	7.1	41,300	41,736	45,684	50,770	53,880	56,735	59,455	62,200	France
33.4	27.3	23.2	10.2	4.4	1.5	30	27	33	49	68	117	163	201	French Guiana
36.0	29.7	18.9	10.4	4.1	0.9	50	62	84	109	151	197	238	274	French Polynesia
33.8[9]	23.7[9]	17.0[9]	17.4[9]	6.9[9]	1.2[9]	...	416	446	514	808	1,078	1,244	1,445	Gabon
43.8	27.7	15.1	6.8	3.5	1.4	193	232	357	458	632	917	1,288	1,607	Gambia, The
51.2	—38.7—			—10.1—		...	...	370	456	630	926	1,272		Gaza Strip
24.8	24.1	19.2	17.5	10.8	3.6	3,612	3,527	4,160	4,708	5,075	5,460	5,239	5,296	Georgia
14.6	24.0	20.1	20.6	13.6	7.2	57,400	68,373	72,673	77,772	78,289	79,433	82,840	85,259	Germany
45.0	26.4	14.6	8.1	4.1	1.8	3,636	5,297	6,958	8,789	11,222	14,470	18,407	21,900	Ghana
19.6	21.3	22.6	18.2	12.9	5.3	14	23	24	26	30	31	27	27	Gibraltar
19.3	22.2	20.3	18.3	14.1	5.9	7,319	7,566	8,327	8,793	9,643	10,161	10,646	11,037	Greece
27.7	22.3	27.7	15.0	—7.4—		19	23	33	41	50	56	57	60	Greenland
42.5[6]	30.4[6]	12.9[6]	6.6[6]	5.5[6]	2.1[6]	71	76	90	95	89	95	100	104	Grenada
24.9	29.5	21.4	12.5	8.3	3.4	180	206	265	320	327	390	454	530	Guadeloupe
30.0	30.0	22.6	10.8	5.5	1.1	22	59	67	85	107	133	167	198	Guam
44.0	26.1	15.8	8.3	—5.8—		2,201	2,969	3,964	5,246	6,917	9,197	12,222	15,827	Guatemala
17.0	23.3	22.2	16.8	13.5	7.2	44	44	45	51	55	61	69	78	Guernsey
46.3[16]	26.1[16]	14.9[16]	8.4[16]	3.7[16]	0.6[16]	...	2,550	3,136	3,900	4,461	5,755	7,759	10,301	Guinea
43.9[6]	26.5[6]	16.1[6]	8.8[6]	3.7[6]	1.0[6]	341	505	542	525	795	964	1,192	1,473	Guinea-Bissau
40.8	30.5	14.0	8.8	4.4	1.2	344	428	571	715	759	747	693	695	Guyana
39.2	26.9	15.6	10.0	5.4	2.9	2,827	3,097	3,723	4,605	5,068	6,060	7,223	8,681	Haiti
46.8	25.8	14.4	7.9	3.8	1.4	1,146	1,390	1,873	2,553	3,316	4,681	6,323	7,998	Honduras
19.4[10]	22.7[10]	28.2[10]	14.7[10]	10.9[10]	4.1[10]	1,786	1,974	3,074	3,942	5,063	5,705	6,780	8,135	Hong Kong
21.3	19.4	22.5	17.9	13.4	5.6	9,280	9,338	9,984	10,337	10,693	10,365	10,086	9,806	Hungary
24.8	23.7	22.7	13.9	10.2	4.7	121	143	176	204	228	255	280	306	Iceland
36.0[6]	28.7[6]	18.5[6]	10.8[6]	5.1[6]	1.0[6]	317,000	357,561	442,344	554,911	688,856	850,638	1,022,021	1,189,082	India
36.6	28.3	18.1	10.6	5.2	1.1	70,500	75,449	92,701	119,467	146,449	178,302	210,249	236,806	Indonesia
44.3	26.6	15.0	8.2	4.8	0.8	14,000	16,913	21,554	28,359	38,783	54,051	66,834	79,887	Iran
45.2	27.2	14.2	7.0	3.7	1.4	3,745	5,163	6,822	9,413	13,233	18,425	24,731	34,545	Iraq
26.7	24.1	20.2	13.8	10.6	4.6	2,958	2,969	2,834	2,954	3,421	3,526	3,657	3,805	Ireland
17.3	20.7	20.4	17.0	15.3	9.2	52	55	49	52	64	69	70	72	Isle of Man
32.6[20]	26.4[20]	18.0[20]	12.3[20]	9.4[20]	3.1[20]	...	...	2,114	2,958	3,862	4,613	5,881	6,713	Israel[17, 18]
15.7[7]	23.6[7]	21.1[7]	18.5[7]	14.7[7]	6.4[7]	43,840	47,104	50,200	53,822	56,434	56,749	57,554	56,278	Italy
34.4	30.6	16.6	9.0	—9.4—		1,212	1,403	1,629	1,891	2,133	2,369	2,578	2,802	Jamaica
18.2[21]	21.7[21]	22.2[21]	20.1[21]	12.6[21]	4.8[21]	73,075	83,200	93,419	103,720	116,807	123,478	127,287	130,344	Japan
15.5	24.9	23.9	17.0	11.9	6.8	51	57	63	71	76	84	92	101	Jersey
42.2	31.4	13.8	8.1	—4.5—		...	1,095	1,384	1,795	2,174	3,271	4,940	6,601	Jordan[22]
31.9	26.3	19.4	13.2	6.9	2.3	6,148	6,703	9,996	13,110	14,940	16,742	16,671	17,283	Kazakhstan
47.8	27.6	13.1	6.6	3.4	1.5	4,470	6,265	8,332	11,498	16,632	23,613	32,577	43,552	Kenya
40.3	27.5	17.3	9.2	4.8	0.9	29	33	41	49	57	72	88	106	Kiribati
29.5	31.9[9]	21.3[9]	11.0[9]	5.0[9]	1.2[9]	...	9,740	10,568	14,388	17,999	21,412	25,491	28,491	Korea, North
25.7[21]	30.4[21]	22.9[21]	13.4[21]	6.1[21]	1.5[21]	...	21,147	25,142	32,976	38,124	42,869	46,789	49,683	Korea, South
36.8[23]	28.3[23]	24.1[23]	8.6[23]	1.8[23]	0.4[23]	...	145	292	748	1,358	2,141	2,458	3,085	Kuwait
37.5	27.0	16.3	10.9	6.2	2.1	1,528	1,740	2,173	2,965	3,631	4,395	4,625	5,358	Kyrgyzstan
45.4[10]	26.5[10]	14.9[10]	8.1[10]	4.2[10]	1.0[10]	1,075	1,755	2,177	2,713	3,205	4,202	5,602	7,188	Laos
21.4	21.7	20.3	19.2	12.0	5.3	1,886	1,949	2,129	2,374	2,544	2,671	2,389	2,302	Latvia
42.6	23.8	16.7	9.1	—7.7—		965	1,364	1,786	2,383	3,137	3,367	4,115	4,973	Lebanon
40.7	25.1	16.6	10.7	5.6	1.3	566	726	859	1,067	1,346	1,735	2,114	2,428	Lesotho
43.2	28.2	14.7	7.7	4.4	1.8	...	824	1,055	1,397	1,900	2,265	3,048	4,540	Liberia
46.4[16]	25.0[16]	16.2[16]	8.6[16]	3.3[16]	0.6[16]	900	961	1,338	2,056	3,119	4,355	6,294	8,913	Libya
23.0	26.5	24.1	14.1	9.2	3.1	11	14	16	21	26	29	33	39	Liechtenstein
22.6	23.8	20.0	17.9	10.9	4.8	2,925	2,567	2,779	3,148	3,439	3,737	3,681	3,702	Lithuania
17.3	21.5	23.8	17.5	12.8	7.1	296	296	314	339	364	382	433	462	Luxembourg
24.1	27.2	29.4	9.6	7.3	2.3	375	188	169	221	243	332	473	512	Macau
24.8	24.1	22.3	15.8	10.6	2.4	...	1,229	1,392	1,629	1,900	2,024	2,033	2,206	Macedonia
45.1[9]	26.8[9]	15.1[9]	7.7[9]	4.3[9]	1.0[9]	4,034	4,620	5,482	6,766	8,678	11,525	15,295	20,096	Madagascar
46.1	25.4	14.5	8.0	—6.0—		1,696	2,817	3,450	4,489	6,129	9,136	10,011	10,662	Malawi
36.5[6]	28.4[6]	19.3[6]	10.0[6]	4.6[6]	1.2[6]	...	6,187	7,908	10,466	13,764	17,756	22,087	25,989	Malaysia
46.9[21]	26.7[21]	12.3[21]	9.0[21]	4.0[21]	0.8[21]	81	82	106	128	155	213	286	345	Maldives
46.1	23.9	15.0	8.9	4.9	1.2	3,388	3,426	4,224	5,690	6,816	8,130	10,008	12,338	Mali
24.1	23.2	23.0	15.4	10.5	3.8	270	308	329	326	324	354	380	393	Malta
51.0	24.5	14.6	5.5	3.6	0.8	...	11	15	22	32	46	68	100	Marshall Islands
23.1	28.9	20.5	13.5	9.7	4.3	200	222	252	287	326	361	415	458	Martinique
44.1	26.6	15.0	8.1	4.7	1.4	666	825	991	1,221	1,551	2,003	2,580	3,283	Mauritania
29.7	28.9	22.3	10.9	6.6	1.6	428	479	662	829	966	1,059	1,199	1,357	Mauritius
47.0	27.4	15.0	6.5	3.0	1.2	16	17	25	35	52	89	150	250	Mayotte
38.3	29.4	16.6	8.9	4.5	1.7	19,815	27,737	36,945	50,596	67,570	83,226	98,881	112,891	Mexico
46.4[24]	26.8[24]	12.6[24]	8.5[24]	4.5[24]	1.1[24]	...	30	40	57	73	101	110	120	Micronesia
27.9	22.9	21.0	15.6	9.7	2.9	2,468	2,341	3,004	3,595	4,002	4,364	4,437	4,706	Moldova
12.3	16.7	21.2	20.4	17.9	10.8	20	22	23	24	27	30	31	31	Monaco
41.9	29.2	14.6	8.5	—5.8—		750	747	931	1,248	1,663	2,122	2,479	2,879	Mongolia
37.0[3]	29.6[3]	17.3[3]	9.2[3]	5.4[3]	1.5[3]	7,750	8,953	11,640	15,126	19,177	23,837	28,804	33,909	Morocco
46.4	23.9	15.6	8.6	4.0	1.2	...	6,250	7,472	9,304	12,103	14,056	19,829	25,116	Mozambique
38.6	28.7	15.5	10.9	5.2	1.1	...	19,488	22,836	27,386	33,766	41,078	49,388	58,236	Myanmar (Burma)
41.7	28.8	14.7	7.8	—6.9—		336	405	522	761	1,002	1,387	1,957	2,705	Namibia
41.8	25.0	20.7	8.2	—2.8—		3	4	5	7	8	9	11	13	Nauru
42.3	25.7	16.7	9.7	4.7	0.9	7,000	8,000	9,180	11,232	14,634	18,111	23,042	28,698	Nepal
18.4	22.4	23.8	17.8	12.1	5.5	8,834	10,027	11,417	12,958	14,150	14,952	16,023	16,853	Netherlands, The

Area and population (continued)

country	area			population (latest estimate)					population (latest census)				
	square miles	square kilo-metres	rank	total midyear 1996	rank	density		% annual growth rate 1991–96	census year	total	male (%)	female (%)	urban (%)
						per sq mi	per sq km						
Netherlands Antilles	308	800	182	208,000	181	675.3	260.0	1.9	1992	189,474	47.9	52.1	...
New Caledonia	7,172	18,576	154	191,000	182	26.6	10.3	1.9	1989	164,173	51.1	48.9	59.4
New Zealand	104,454	270,534	75	3,619,000	123	34.6	13.4	1.2	1996	3,660,364	49.3[25]	50.7[25]	75.9[25]
Nicaragua	50,893	131,812	97	4,272,000	116	83.9	32.4	2.9	1971	1,877,952	48.3	51.7	48.0
Niger	489,000	1,267,000	22	9,465,000	77	19.4	7.5	3.4	1988[4]	7,228,552	49.5	50.5	15.3
Nigeria	356,669	923,768	32	103,912,000	10	291.3	112.5	3.1	1991	88,514,501	50.3	49.7	37.7[9]
Northern Mariana Islands	184	477	192	59,300	205	322.3	124.3	3.9	1990	43,345	52.6	47.4	28.0
Norway	125,050	323,878	67	4,382,000	113	35.0	13.5	0.6	1990	4,247,546	49.4	50.6	75.0[6]
Oman	118,150	306,000	70	2,251,000	138	19.1	7.4	4.2	1993	2,017,591	52.6[9]	47.4[9]	11.0[5]
Pakistan	339,697	879,811	34	133,500,000	7	393.0	151.7	2.8	1981[26]	84,253,644	52.5	47.5	28.3
Palau	188	488	191	17,000	215	90.4	34.8	2.0	1990	15,122	53.8	46.2	69.4
Panama	29,157	75,517	118	2,674,000	131	91.7	35.4	1.8	1990	2,329,329	50.6	49.4	53.7
Papua New Guinea	178,704	462,840	54	4,400,000	112	24.6	9.5	2.3	1990[27]	3,607,954	52.7	47.3	15.2
Paraguay	157,048	406,752	59	4,964,000	107	31.6	12.2	2.8	1992	4,123,550	50.2	49.8	50.5
Peru	496,225	1,285,216	20	23,947,000	38	48.3	18.6	2.0	1993	22,639,443	49.7	50.3	70.1
Philippines	115,860	300,076	72	71,750,000	14	619.3	239.1	2.5	1990	60,703,206	50.3	49.7	48.6
Poland	120,728	312,685	69	38,731,000	29	320.8	123.9	0.3	1988	37,878,641	48.7	51.3	61.2
Portugal	35,574	92,135	111	9,927,000	75	279.1	107.7	0.1	1991	9,862,540	48.2	51.8	29.7[7]
Puerto Rico	3,515	9,104	165	3,766,000	119	1,071.4	413.7	1.2	1990	3,522,037	48.4	51.6	71.2
Qatar	4,412	11,427	160	590,000	162	133.7	51.6	3.2	1986	369,079	67.2	32.8	88.0[16]
Réunion	970	2,512	173	671,000	159	691.8	267.1	1.8	1990	597,828	49.2	50.8	73.4
Romania	91,699	237,500	82	22,670,000	41	247.2	95.5	-0.3	1992	22,760,449	49.1	50.9	54.4
Russia	6,592,800	17,075,400	1	148,070,000	6	22.5	8.7	-0.1	1989	147,400,537	46.9	53.1	73.6
Rwanda	10,169	26,338	147	6,853,000	90	673.9	260.2	-1.4	1991	7,164,994	48.7	51.3	5.4
St. Kitts and Nevis	104	269	204	39,400	210	378.8	146.5	-1.2	1991	40,618	49.1	50.9	48.9[5]
St. Lucia	238	617	188	144,000	187	605.0	233.4	1.2	1991	133,308	48.5	51.5	44.1[5]
St. Vincent and the Grenadines	150	389	197	113,000	190	753.3	290.5	1.2	1991	106,499	49.9	50.1	24.6
San Marino	24	61	211	25,300	214	1,070.7	413.5	1.5	1976	19,149	50.4	49.6	90.1[6]
São Tomé and Príncipe	386	1,001	180	134,000	188	347.2	133.9	2.2	1991	117,504	49.4	50.6	44.1[7]
Saudi Arabia	865,000	2,240,000	13	18,426,000	49	21.3	8.2	2.4	1992	16,929,294	55.9	44.1	77.3[5]
Senegal	75,951	196,712	87	8,532,000	82	112.3	43.4	2.6	1988	6,928,405	48.7	51.3	38.6
Seychelles	176	455	194	76,100	197	432.4	167.3	1.6	1987	68,598	49.7	50.3	35.5
Sierra Leone	27,699	71,740	119	4,617,000	109	166.7	64.4	2.4	1985	3,517,530	49.6	50.4	31.8
Singapore	249	646	187	3,045,000	130	12,228.9	4,713.6	2.0	1990[4]	2,705,115	50.6	49.4	100.0
Slovakia	18,933	49,036	129	5,372,000	102	283.7	109.6	0.3	1991	5,268,935	48.9	51.1	56.8
Slovenia	7,820	20,255	153	1,959,000	143	250.5	96.7	-0.4	1991	1,974,839	48.5	51.5	48.9
Solomon Islands	10,954	28,370	143	396,000	170	36.2	14.0	3.7	1986	285,176	51.9	48.1	15.7
Somalia	246,000	637,000	42	6,802,000	91	27.7	10.7	0.4	1975	4,089,203	50.1	49.9	25.4
South Africa[28]	470,693	1,219,090	25	41,743,000	27	88.7	34.2	1.9	1991[29]	30,986,922	50.0	50.0	60.3
Spain	195,364	505,990	51	39,270,000	28	201.1	77.6	0.2	1991	38,999,181	49.1	50.9	75.3
Sri Lanka	25,332	65,610	122	18,318,000	50	723.1	279.2	1.2	1981	14,848,364	50.8	49.2	21.5
Sudan, The	966,757	2,503,890	10	31,065,000	32	32.1	12.4	2.5	1993	24,940,683	50.2	49.8	22.5[5]
Suriname	63,251	163,820	92	436,000	164	6.9	2.7	1.5	1980	354,860	49.5	50.5	49.0[9]
Swaziland	6,704	17,364	157	934,000	153	139.3	53.8	3.3	1986	681,059	47.2	52.8	22.8
Sweden	173,732	449,964	56	8,858,000	81	51.0	19.7	0.6	1994[2]	8,816,381	49.4	50.6	84.3[7]
Switzerland	15,940	41,285	135	7,087,000	88	444.6	171.7	0.8	1990[30]	6,873,687	49.3	50.7	59.7[6]
Syria	71,498	185,180	88	14,798,000	57	207.0	79.9	3.4	1994	13,800,000	51.1[8]	48.9[8]	47.1[8]
Taiwan	13,969	36,179	136	21,463,000	44	1,536.5	593.2	0.9	1990[4]	20,393,628	52.1	47.9	74.5
Tajikistan	55,300	143,100	95	5,945,000	95	107.5	41.5	1.7	1989	5,108,576	49.7	50.3	32.6
Tanzania	364,901	945,090	31	28,838,000	35	79.6	30.7	2.7	1988	23,174,336	48.9	51.1	32.8[5]
Thailand	198,115	513,115	50	60,003,000	18	302.9	116.9	1.2	1990	54,532,300	49.6	50.4	18.7
Togo	21,925	56,785	125	4,269,000	117	194.7	75.2	3.2	1981	2,719,567	48.7	51.3	15.2
Tonga	290	750	184	101,000	192	348.3	134.7	0.7	1986[4]	94,649	50.3	49.7	30.7
Trinidad and Tobago	1,980	5,128	168	1,262,000	148	637.4	246.1	0.4	1990	1,234,388	50.1	49.9	64.8
Tunisia	63,378	164,150	91	9,057,000	80	142.9	55.2	2.0	1994	8,785,364	50.6	49.4	61.0
Turkey	300,948	779,452	37	62,650,000	15	208.2	80.4	1.8	1990	56,473,035	50.7	49.3	59.0
Turkmenistan	188,500	488,100	52	4,574,000	110	24.3	9.4	4.0	1995	4,000,460	49.6	50.3	46.0
Tuvalu	9.4	24.4	213	9,500	217	1,010.6	389.3	1.0	1991	9,043	48.4	51.6	42.5
Uganda	93,070	241,040	80	20,158,000	48	216.6	83.6	2.8	1991	16,671,705	49.1	50.9	11.3
Ukraine	233,100	603,700	44	51,273,000	23	220.0	84.9	-0.3	1989	51,706,746	46.3	53.7	66.9
United Arab Emirates	32,280	83,600	116	2,500,000	134	77.4	29.9	5.5	1995	2,377,000	66.4	33.6	84.0[10]
United Kingdom	94,251	244,110	79	58,784,000	19	623.7	240.8	0.3	1991[2]	56,467,000	48.4	51.6	89.1[5]
United States	3,679,192	9,529,063	4	265,455,000	3	72.2	27.9	1.0	1990[32]	248,709,873	48.7	51.3	75.2
Uruguay	68,037	176,215	90	3,140,000	129	46.2	17.8	0.3	1996	3,139,376	48.5	51.5	88.7
Uzbekistan	172,700	447,400	57	23,206,000	40	134.4	51.9	2.1	1989	19,905,158	49.3	50.7	40.7
Vanuatu	4,707	12,190	159	172,000	183	36.5	14.1	2.6	1989	142,630	51.6	48.4	17.7
Venezuela	352,144	912,050	33	22,311,000	43	63.4	24.5	2.2	1990	19,405,429	49.7	50.3	84.0
Vietnam	127,816	331,041	65	76,151,000	13	595.8	230.0	2.2	1989	64,411,713	48.7	51.3	20.1
Virgin Islands (U.S.)	136	352	200	97,600	194	717.6	277.3	-0.7	1990	101,809	48.3	51.7	37.2
West Bank[33]	2,270	5,900	166	1,316,000	147	579.7	223.1	4.3	1993[2]	1,051,300	50.4	49.6	...
Western Sahara	97,344	252,120	77	271,000	175	2.8	1.1	4.0	1994	252,146	...	...	90.7
Western Samoa	1,093	2,831	171	167,000	184	152.8	59.0	1.0	1991	161,298	52.5	47.5	21.2
Yemen	203,850	527,970	49	16,600,000	55	81.4	31.4	7.4	1994	14,587,807	51.1	48.9	33.6[10]
Yugoslavia	39,449	102,173	107	10,473,000	69	265.5	102.5	0.1	1991	10,394,026	49.6	50.4	46.8[8]
Zaire	905,354	2,344,858	12	45,259,000	25	50.0	19.3	3.2	1984	29,671,407	49.2	50.8	36.6[16]
Zambia	290,586	752,614	39	9,715,000	76	33.4	12.9	2.9	1990	7,818,447	49.2	50.8	42.0
Zimbabwe	150,872	390,757	60	11,515,000	64	76.3	29.5	2.5	1992	10,401,767	48.8	51.2	28.5[5]

[1]Settled population only. [2]Civil register; not a census. [3]1994 estimate. [4]Data are for de jure population. [5]1990 estimate. [6]1991 estimate. [7]1992 estimate. [8]1981 census. [9]1993 estimate. [10]1995 estimate. [11]Except census, data are for the island of Cyprus. [12]Republic of Cyprus only. [13]Former West Germany only. [14]Excludes visitors, transients, and family members of British servicemen. [15]Data exclude Alderney (population 2,297) and Sark (population 604). [16]1985 estimate. [17]Area figures exclude the West Bank, East Jerusalem, Gaza Strip, and Golan Heights. [18]Population figures include the Golan Heights and East Jerusalem, and exclude Israelis in the West Bank and Gaza Strip. [19]Includes East Jerusalem and Israelis in the West Bank, Gaza Strip, and Golan Heights. [20]1983

age distribution (%)						population (by decade, '000s)								country
0–14	15–29	30–44	45–59	60–74	75 and over	1940	1950	1960	1970	1980	1990	2000 projection	2010 projection	
26.0	23.9	25.5	14.3	7.3	3.0	77	112	136	163	174	188	223	267	Netherlands Antilles
32.6	28.6	19.8	12.1	5.4	1.6	53	59	79	110	140	170	206	249	New Caledonia
23.2[25]	24.6[25]	22.4[25]	14.4[25]	10.9[25]	4.5[25]	1,637	1,909	2,377	2,820	3,144	3,363	3,749	4,025	New Zealand
48.1	25.6	14.1	7.4	3.8	1.1	825	1,098	1,493	2,053	2,776	3,591	4,729	5,863	Nicaragua
48.7	24.8	14.6	6.8	3.6	1.5	1,700	2,400	3,028	4,165	5,586	7,731	10,805	14,751	Niger
45.0[6]	25.5[6]	15.6[6]	9.3[6]	4.0[6]	0.7[6]	...	31,797	39,230	49,309	65,699	86,488	117,328	157,375	Nigeria
23.8	33.5	30.7	9.1	2.3	0.5	48	6	9	10	17	45	65	83	Northern Mariana Islands
18.8	22.9	22.1	15.1	13.9	7.2	2,973	3,265	3,581	3,877	4,086	4,241	4,483	4,681	Norway
46.7[9]	24.1[9]	16.5[9]	8.4[9]	3.5[9]	0.7[9]	...	456	558	723	1,101	1,751	2,626	3,783	Oman
44.5	23.9	15.4	9.3	5.3	1.6	28,300	39,513	49,955	65,706	85,299	112,857	144,560	176,400	Pakistan
30.3	27.8	22.8	10.5	6.4	2.2	25	7	9	12	13	15	18	20	Palau
34.8	29.2	18.2	10.2	5.5	2.0	620	893	1,148	1,531	1,950	2,398	2,856	3,266	Panama
41.9	28.5	16.6	8.7	—3.2—		1,308	1,613	1,920	2,422	3,086	3,839	4,809	5,918	Papua New Guinea
40.1	27.6	18.7	8.3	4.2	1.1	1,111	1,351	1,774	2,351	3,136	4,220	5,480	6,805	Paraguay
37.0	28.6	17.7	9.8	—7.0—		6,784	7,632	9,931	13,193	17,295	21,307	25,662	30,506	Peru
39.6	28.7	17.3	9.2	4.2	1.1	16,459	20,988	27,561	36,850	48,286	62,049	78,414	94,503	Philippines
25.4	21.2	23.3	15.5	10.4	4.2	31,500	24,824	29,561	32,526	35,578	38,111	39,134	40,160	Poland
19.9[6]	23.7[6]	20.3[6]	16.9[6]	13.7[6]	5.3[6]	7,696	8,405	8,826	9,040	9,766	9,896	9,967	10,067	Portugal
27.2	25.1	20.4	14.1	9.2	4.0	1,878	2,218	2,360	2,721	3,204	3,528	3,934	4,386	Puerto Rico
27.8	29.3	32.3	8.6	1.6	0.4	...	47	59	151	229	484	633	755	Qatar
29.5	29.8	20.3	11.7	6.5	2.1	221	244	338	447	507	602	722	866	Réunion
22.4	22.9	20.8	17.1	—16.8—		15,907	16,311	18,403	20,253	22,201	23,201	22,616	22,481	Romania
23.1	22.0	21.9	17.6	11.2	4.2	110,098	105,018	119,906	130,392	138,914	148,292	147,829	149,868	Russia
45.6	28.6	12.4	8.4	3.9	0.9	1,910	2,429	3,083	3,813	5,170	7,145	8,900	10,080	Rwanda
36.9[6]	31.8[6]	14.5[6]	6.0[6]	6.9[6]	3.8[6]	43	49	51	46	43	42	39	39	St. Kitts and Nevis
36.8	29.4	16.3	8.7	6.3	2.5	70	79	86	101	122	134	151	169	St. Lucia
37.2	29.5	16.1	8.3	6.4	2.5	61	67	80	86	99	105	119	133	St. Vincent and the Grenadines
24.4	23.0	19.9	17.4	11.4	3.9	10	13	15	19	21	23	27	31	San Marino
46.9	26.2	12.2	8.0	—6.7—		60	60	64	74	94	117	146	182	São Tomé and Príncipe
42.1[7]	22.8[7]	21.6[7]	9.9[7]	3.0[7]	0.6[7]	...	3,201	4,075	5,745	9,604	16,048	21,257	28,880	Saudi Arabia
47.5	26.1	13.6	7.8	—5.0—		1,857	2,500	3,187	4,158	5,538	7,327	9,495	12,241	Senegal
33.6	30.3	15.3	10.7	7.1	2.9	32	34	42	54	63	70	81	94	Seychelles
43.9[16]	25.6[16]	15.7[16]	9.6[16]	4.5[16]	0.7[16]	1,700	1,944	2,241	2,656	3,236	3,999	5,069	6,366	Sierra Leone
23.2	27.3	27.7	12.7	6.9	2.2	751	1,022	1,639	2,075	2,282	2,705	3,292	4,000	Singapore
25.0	22.7	22.8	14.6	10.7	4.2	3,553	3,463	3,994	4,528	4,984	5,298	5,423	5,551	Slovakia
20.0	22.4	23.7	17.4	11.9	4.6	1,450	1,467	1,580	1,727	1,901	1,998	1,963	2,003	Slovenia
47.3	25.7	13.9	8.1	—4.9—		94	104	125	163	230	319	459	600	Solomon Islands
45.6	24.9	15.5	7.4	—5.4—		...	2,438	2,956	3,667	5,799	6,753	7,079	7,823	Somalia
34.6	28.5	19.6	10.8	5.1	1.4	10,353	13,596	17,417	22,740	29,252	37,191	44,462	49,200	South Africa[28]
19.1[6]	24.9[6]	20.1[6]	16.5[6]	13.7[6]	5.7[6]	25,757	27,868	30,303	33,779	37,636	38,798	39,466	39,917	Spain
35.3	29.6	17.9	10.6	5.2	1.4	5,972	7,678	9,889	12,514	14,747	16,993	19,258	21,521	Sri Lanka
46.2[9]	27.3[9]	14.4[9]	8.5[9]	3.0[9]	0.7[9]	...	8,051	10,589	13,788	19,064	26,628	35,454	46,512	Sudan, The
39.3	29.5	13.8	10.0	4.5	2.8	193	215	247	292	355	403	465	534	Suriname
47.3	26.6	13.4	7.4	3.4	1.3	154	253	320	409	550	769	1,042	1,332	Swaziland
18.9	19.7	20.4	19.0	13.9	8.2	6,371	7,041	7,498	8,081	8,310	8,559	8,982	9,199	Sweden
16.8	22.8	23.2	18.0	12.5	6.7	4,234	4,715	5,429	6,270	6,362	6,712	7,277	7,539	Switzerland
48.5[8]	25.8[8]	12.5[8]	8.3[8]	3.7[8]	1.2[8]	2,597	3,495	4,561	6,305	8,704	12,116	16,909	23,019	Syria
27.1	27.8	23.1	12.3	7.9	1.8	5,987	7,619	10,668	14,583	17,705	20,279	22,263	24,395	Taiwan
42.9	28.1	13.8	9.0	4.6	1.6	1,525	1,532	2,083	2,942	3,968	5,303	6,392	8,029	Tajikistan
47.2[5]	26.7[5]	14.2[5]	7.8[5]	3.3[5]	0.7[5]	...	8,909	10,876	14,038	18,689	24,826	31,045	36,076	Tanzania
28.8	30.4	21.2	12.3	5.7	1.6	15,296	20,010	26,392	35,037	46,538	56,096	62,405	67,754	Thailand
49.8	24.8	13.1	6.8	3.3	2.0	834	1,329	1,514	2,020	2,615	3,531	4,818	6,427	Togo
40.6	29.0	13.8	10.1	5.0	1.4	37	50	65	80	92	97	103	105	Tonga
33.7[5]	27.9[5]	20.0[5]	10.5[5]	5.9[5]	2.0[5]	503	668	828	941	1,082	1,227	1,264	1,314	Trinidad and Tobago
35.2[3]	29.0[3]	18.1[3]	9.8[3]	6.3[3]	1.6[3]	2,887	3,530	4,221	5,137	6,392	8,074	9,694	11,209	Tunisia
35.0	28.6	18.4	10.9	5.6	1.6	17,723	20,809	27,509	35,321	44,438	56,098	66,842	77,008	Turkey
40.5[31]	28.8[31]	15.5[31]	9.1[31]	4.7[31]	1.4[31]	1,302	1,211	1,594	2,189	2,860	3,668	4,922	5,362	Turkmenistan
34.6	24.0	20.7	11.3	—9.2—		4	5	5	6	8	9	10	11	Tuvalu
47.3	27.7	13.1	6.9	3.7	1.3	4,233	5,522	7,262	9,724	12,252	17,040	21,891	26,355	Uganda
21.5	21.0	20.6	18.5	10.7	7.7	41,340	36,906	42,783	47,317	50,034	51,892	50,785	50,320	Ukraine
34.9[10]	18.7[10]	31.6[10]	12.7[10]	1.9[10]	0.2[10]	...	70	90	223	1,015	1,844	2,707	3,212	United Arab Emirates
19.1	21.9	21.2	16.7	14.1	7.0	48,226	50,290	52,372	55,632	56,330	57,561	59,595	61,127	United Kingdom
21.5	23.4	23.9	14.4	11.5	5.3	132,594	152,271	180,671	204,879	227,726	249,911	274,843	297,943	United States
26.6[23]	22.8[23]	18.3[23]	16.5[23]	11.4[23]	4.3[23]	1,974	2,194	2,531	2,824	2,914	3,079	3,210	3,389	Uruguay
40.8	28.4	15.0	9.3	4.7	1.8	6,551	6,314	8,559	11,973	15,977	20,515	25,015	30,258	Uzbekistan
45.5	26.6	15.2	8.4	3.7	0.6	43	52	65	86	115	148	189	231	Vanuatu
38.3	28.1	18.6	9.3	4.5	1.2	3,740	5,094	7,579	10,721	15,091	19,502	24,170	28,716	Venezuela
39.0	28.7	16.0	9.1	5.6	1.6	...	29,954	34,743	42,729	53,711	66,689	82,648	98,448	Vietnam
28.9	23.7	22.0	16.0	7.3	2.2	25	27	32	75	97	102	99	107	Virgin Islands (U.S.)
48.3	—40.4—		—11.3—			...	...	...	608	734	1,011	1,533	2,244	West Bank[33]
...	...	...	...	—6.0—		...	14	32	76	155	214	294	350	Western Sahara
40.5	30.0	14.6	8.7	—6.0—		61	82	111	143	155	159	174	192	Western Samoa
47.6[3]	28.7[3]	11.9[3]	7.4[3]	3.6[3]	0.7[3]	...	4,316	5,247	6,332	8,219	11,230	19,200	25,800	Yemen
22.8	21.6	21.7	17.1	12.2	3.5	...	7,131	8,050	8,910	9,842	10,529	10,355	10,731	Yugoslavia
45.2[16]	25.9[16]	15.5[16]	8.7[16]	3.9[16]	0.7[16]	10,370	13,055	16,151	21,368	27,009	37,460	51,136	68,876	Zaire
47.3	28.2	12.9	7.3	3.5	0.7	1,484	2,440	3,141	4,189	5,738	8,150	10,754	13,657	Zambia
46.6[7]	28.6[7]	13.5[7]	7.1[7]	3.3[7]	0.9[7]	1,940	2,730	3,812	5,260	7,126	9,903	12,514	15,260	Zimbabwe

census. [2]1990 census. [22]Excludes the West Bank. [23]1985 census. [24]1980 census. [25]1991 census. [26]Excludes Afghan refugees and residents of Pakistani-occupied Jammu and Kashmir. [27]Excludes an estimated 155,000 persons in North Solomons province and five remote census districts. [28]Includes the former black independent states of Bophuthatswana, Ciskei, Transkei, and Venda. [29]Excludes the former black independent states of Bophuthatswana, Ciskei, Transkei, and Venda. [30]Includes resident aliens; excludes seasonal workers. [31]1989 census. [32]Excludes 515,000 armed forces overseas. [33]Excludes East Jerusalem.

Major cities and national capitals

The following table lists the principal cities or municipalities (those exceeding 100,000 in population [75,000 for Anglo-America]) of the countries of the world, together with figures for each national capital (indicated by a ★), regardless of size.

Most of the populations given refer to a so-called city proper, that is, a legally defined, incorporated, or chartered area defined by administrative boundaries and by national or state law. Some data, however, refer to the municipality, or commune, similar to the medieval city-state in that the city is governed together with its immediately adjoining, economically dependent areas, whether urban or rural in nature. Some countries define no other demographic or legal entities within such communes or municipalities, but many identify a centre, seat, head (*cabecera*), or locality that corresponds to the most densely populated, compact, contiguous core of the municipality. Because the amount of work involved in carefully defining these "centres" may be considerable, the necessary resources usually exist only at the time of a national census (generally 5 or 10 years apart). Between censuses, therefore, it may be possible only to track the growth of the municipality as a whole. Thus, in order to provide the most up-to-date data for cities in this table, figures referring to municipalities or communes may be given (identified by the abbreviation "MU"), even though the country itself may define a smaller, more closely knit city proper. Specific identification of municipalities is provided in this table *only* when

the country also publishes data for a more narrowly defined city proper; it is *not* provided when the sole published figure is the municipality, whether or not this is the proper local administrative term for the entity.

Problems also exist in the identification of cities in terms of named legal entities. There is, for example, a single municipality (*commune*) named Brussel (Brussels) at the centre of the Brussels agglomeration in Belgium; the *commune* numbers only about 136,000 population, while the agglomeration, which is understood by most people to constitute the city, numbers nearly a million. Both are shown so as to apprise the reader of the existence of a problem.

For certain countries, more than one form of the name of the city is given, usually to permit recognition of recent place name changes or of *forms* of the place name likely to be encountered in press stories if the title of the city's entry in the *Encyclopædia Britannica* is spelled according to a different romanization or spelling policy. Chinese names, for example, are given first in their Wade-Giles spelling (the scholarly system used by Britannica) and then, parenthetically, in their Pinyin spelling, the official Chinese system now encountered in press reports, official documents, and maps.

Sources for this data were usually the national census and statistical abstracts of the countries concerned, supplemented by the Internet and correspondence with most national statistical offices to solicit unpublished data.

Major cities and national capitals

country city	population	country city	population	country city	population	country city	population	country city	population
Afghanistan (early 1990s est.)		San Nicolás		Naogaon	110,000	**Brazil** (1991)		Mossoró	117,020
Herāt	186,800	de los Arroyos	119,302	Nārāyanganj	296,000	Alvorada	132,582	Natal	459,827
★ Kābul	700,000[1]	San Salvador de		Narsinghdi	106,000	Americana	153,592	Nilópolis	104,671
Kandahār		Jujuy	180,102[4]	Nawābganj		Anápolis	222,400	Niterói	400,586
(Qandahār)	237,500	Santa Fe	406,388[4]	(Nowābgonj)	141,000	Aracaju	401,676	Nova Friburgo	111,020
Mazār-e Sharīf	127,800	Santiago del Estero		Pābna	112,000	Araçatuba	145,751	Nova Iguaçu	562,062
Albania (1991 est.)		La Banda	263,471	Rājshāhi	318,000	Arapiraca	124,790	Novo Hamburgo	199,479
★ Tiranë	300,000	Vicente López	289,142[4]	Rangpur	207,000	Araraquara	101,302	Olinda	341,059
Algeria (1987)		**Armenia** (1994 est.)		Saidpur	105,000	Barra Mansa	145,112	Osasco	566,949
★ Algiers	1,507,241	Gyumri (Kumayri;		Savar	115,000	Bauru	254,211	Parnaíba	105,131
Annaba	222,518	Leninakan)	120,000[6]	Sirājganj	108,000	Belém	765,476	Passo Fundo	135,158
Batna	181,601	★ Yerevan	1,226,000	Sylhet	109,000	Belo Horizonte	1,529,566	Pelotas	260,510
Béchar	107,311	**Aruba** (1991)		Tangail	114,000	Betim	152,846	Petrolina	123,857
Bejaïa	114,534	★ Oranjestad	20,046	Tongi	181,000	Blumenau	185,200	Petrópolis	164,849
Biskra	128,280	**Australia** (1995 est.)		**Barbados** (1990)		Boa Vista	118,928	Piracicaba	223,170
Blida (el-Boulaida)	127,284	Adelaide	1,081,000[7]	★ Bridgetown	6,070	★ Brasília	1,492,542	Poços de Caldas	104,800
Constantine		Bankstown	162,600[8]	**Belarus** (1996 est.)		Cachoeiro de		Ponta Grossa	219,648
(Qacentina)	440,842	Blacktown	228,400[8]	Baranovichi		Itapemirim	112,099	Porto Alegre	1,237,223
Mostaganem	114,037	Brisbane	1,489,100[7]	(Baranavichy)	172,000	Campina Grande	298,331	Porto Velho	226,198
Oran (Wahran)	609,823	Cairns	100,900	Bobruysk (Babrujsk)	227,100	Campinas	748,076	Presidente Prudente	157,618
Sétif	170,182	Campbelltown	149,100[8]	Borisov (Barysau)	153,000	Campo Grande	516,403	Recife	1,296,995
Sidi bel Abbès	152,778	★ Canberra	303,700[7]	Brest (Bierascie)	293,000	Campos	275,528	Ribeirão Prêto	416,186
Skikda	128,747	Canterbury	134,500[8]	Gomel (Homiel)	512,000	Canoas	269,234	Rio Branco	167,457
Tébessa	107,559	Fairfield	186,100[8]	Grodno (Horadnia)	301,000	Carapicuíba	207,264	Rio Claro	130,364
Tlemcen (Tilimsen)	107,632	Geelong	152,600[9]	Lida	101,000	Caruaru	180,654	Rio de Janeiro	5,473,909
American Samoa (1990)		Gold Coast-Tweed	326,900[9]	★ Minsk	1,700,000	Cascavel	175,294	Rio Grande	157,608
★ Fagatogo (legislative		Gosford	142,150[8]	Mogilyov (Mahilou)	367,000	Caxias do Sul	262,983	Salvador	2,070,296
and judicial)	2,323[2]	Hobart	194,700[7]	Mozyr (Mazyr)	108,000	Colombo	105,464	Santa Bárbara d'Oeste	140,208
★ Utulei (executive)	930[2]	Keilor	114,639[8]	Orsha (Vorsha)	134,000	Contagem	195,705	Santa Maria	193,294
Andorra (1994 est.)		Knox	132,686[8]	Pinsk	130,000	Cuiabá	252,784	Santarém	168,153
★ Andorra la Vella	22,821	Lake Macquarie	175,510[8]	Soligorsk	101,000	Curitiba	841,882	Santo André	518,272
Angola (1993 est.)		Liverpool	106,750[8]	Vitebsk (Viciebsk)	365,000	Diadema	305,068	Santos	415,554
Huambo	400,000	Melbourne	3,218,100[7]	**Belgium** (1995 est.)		Divinópolis	141,984	São Bernardo	
★ Luanda	2,000,000	Moorabbin	100,389[8]	Antwerp	459,072	Dourados	116,754	do Campo	550,030
Lubango	105,000[3]	Newcastle	466,000[9]	Brugge (Bruges)	116,273	Duque de Caxias	325,903	São Caetano do Sul	149,203
Antigua and Barbuda		Parramatta	137,450[8]	★ Brussels	136,424[11]	Embu	155,851	São Carlos	100,502
(1991)		Penrith	163,500[8]	Agglomeration	951,580	Feira de Santana	340,034	São Gonçalo	296,021
★ Saint John's	21,514	Perth	1,262,600[7]	Charleroi	206,491	Florianópolis	191,664	São João de Meriti	220,742
Argentina (1991)		Randwick	117,600[8]	Ghent	227,483	Fortaleza	743,335	São José	
Avellaneda	346,620[4]	Stirling	178,734[1]	Liège (Luik)	192,393	Foz do Iguaçu	186,362	do Rio Prêto	263,454
Bahía Blanca	260,096	Sydney	3,772,700[7]	Namur	105,014	Franca	227,613	São José dos	
★ Buenos Aires	2,988,006[4, 5]	Townsville	124,900[9]	**Belize** (1994 est.)		Goiânia	912,136	Campos	385,879
Catamarca	110,269	Wanneroo	190,965[1]	★ Belmopan	3,927	Governador Valadares	210,396	São Leopoldo	160,228
Comodoro		Wollongong	253,600[9]	**Benin** (1992)		Gravataí	166,954	São Luís	164,334
Rivadavia	124,104	**Austria** (1991)		Abomey-Calavi	125,565	Guarapuava	107,046	São Paulo	9,393,753
Concordia	116,485	Graz	237,810	★ Cotonou (official)	533,212	Guarulhos	544,698	São Vicente	268,467
Córdoba	1,208,713[4]	Innsbruck	118,112	Djougou	132,192	Ilhéus	135,117	Sapucaia do Sul	104,626
Corrientes	258,103	Linz	203,044	Parakou	106,708	Imperatriz	209,970	Sete Lagoas	137,537
Formosa	148,074	Salzburg	143,978	★ Porto-Novo		Ipatinga	120,025	Sorocaba	348,952
General San Martín	407,506[4]	★ Vienna	1,539,848	(de facto)	177,660	Itabuna	170,434	Susano (Suzano)	110,414
La Matanza	1,111,811	**Azerbaijan** (1991 est.)		**Bermuda** (1994 est.)		Itajaí	114,558	Taboão da Serra	159,894
La Plata	642,979[4]	★ Baku (Baky)	1,087,000[8]	★ Hamilton	1,100	Itapevi	107,983	Taubaté	185,790
La Rioja	103,727	Gäncä (Gyandzha)	282,200	**Bhutan** (1993 est.)		Itaquaquecetuba	164,665	Teresina	556,073
Lanús	466,755[4]	Sumqayit (Sumgait)	236,200	Paro	3,000[12]	Jaboatão	217,905	Uberaba	198,565
Lomas de Zamora	572,769[4]	**Bahamas, The** (1990)		★ Thimphu	30,340	Jacareí	143,468	Uberlândia	354,710
Mar del Plata	512,880	★ Nassau	172,196[10]	**Bolivia** (1993 est.)		Jequié	114,542	Uruguaiana	103,160
Mendoza	773,113[4]	**Bahrain** (1992 est.)		Cochabamba	448,756	João Pessoa	497,306	Vila Velha	263,897
Morón	641,541[4]	★ Al-Manāmah	140,401	El Alto	446,189	Joinville	326,208	Vitória	258,243
Neuquén	243,803[4]	**Bangladesh** (1991)		★ La Paz		Juàzeiro do Norte	163,527	Vitória da	
Paraná	211,936[4]	Barisāl	188,000	(administrative)	784,976	Juiz de Fora	377,538	Conquista	179,868
Posadas	210,755[4]	Bogra	130,000	Oruro	201,831	Jundiaí	253,177	Volta Redonda	219,988
Quilmes	509,445[4]	Brāhmanbāria	125,000	Potosí	123,327	Lages	137,169	**Brunei** (1991)	
Resistencia	292,350[4]	Chittagong	1,599,000	Santa Cruz	767,260	Limeira	177,016	★ Bandar Seri	
Río Cuarto	138,853[4]	Comilla	156,000	★ Sucre (judicial)	144,994	Londrina	355,062	Begawan	21,484
Rosario	1,118,984[4]	★ Dhākā (Dacca)	3,839,000	**Bosnia and Herzegovina**		Luziânia	194,128	**Bulgaria** (1996 est.)	
Salta	370,904[4]	Dinājpur	138,000	(1991)		Macapá	146,523	Burgas	199,470
San Fernando	132,626[4]	Gāzipur	104,000	Banja Luka	143,079	Maceió	554,727	Dobrich	103,532
San Isidro	299,022[4]	Jamālpur	111,000	★ Sarajevo	250,000[5]	Manaus	1,005,634	Pleven	125,029
San Juan	352,691[4]	Jessore	154,000	**Botswana** (1993 est.)		Marabá	102,364	Plovdiv	344,326
San Luis	110,136	Khulna	731,000	★ Gaborone	156,803	Maracanaú	133,206	Ruse	168,051
San Miguel de		Mymensingh	202,000			Marília	144,906	Sliven	107,011
Tucumán	622,324[4]					Maringá	225,516	★ Sofia	1,116,823
						Mauá	294,631	Stara Zagora	149,666
						Mogi das Cruzes	125,992	Varna	301,421
						Montes Claros	223,046		

country city	population
Burkina Faso (1993 est.)	
Bobo Dioulasso	300,000
Koudougou	105,000
★ Ouagadougou	690,000
Burundi (1994 est.)	
★ Bujumbura	300,000
Gitega	101,827[13]
Cambodia (1994 est.)	
★ Phnom Penh	920,000
Cameroon (1992 est.)	
Bafoussam	120,000
Bamenda	110,690[14]
Douala	1,200,000
Garoua	160,000
Maroua	140,000
★ Yaoundé	800,000
Canada (1991)	
Brampton	234,445
Brantford	81,997
Burlington	129,575
Burnaby	158,858
Calgary	710,677
Cambridge	92,772
Coquitlam	84,021
Delta	88,978
East York	102,696
Edmonton	616,741
Etobicoke	309,993
Gatineau	92,284
Gloucester	101,677
Guelph	87,976
Halifax	114,455
Hamilton	318,499
Kelowna	75,950
Kitchener	168,282
Laval	314,398
London	303,165
Longueuil	129,874
Markham	153,811
Mississauga	463,388
Montreal	1,017,666
Montreal-Nord	85,516
Nepean	107,627
Niagara Falls	75,399
North York	562,564
Oakville	114,670
Oshawa	129,344
★ Ottawa	313,987
Quebec	167,517
Regina	179,178
Richmond	126,624
Richmond Hill	80,142
Saanich	95,577
Saint Catharines	129,300
Saint John's	95,770
Saskatoon	186,058
Sault Sainte Marie	81,476
Scarborough	524,598
Sherbrooke	76,429
Sudbury	92,884
Surrey	245,173
Thunder Bay	113,746
Toronto	635,395
Vancouver	471,844
Vaughan	111,359
Windsor	191,435
Winnipeg	616,790
York	140,525
Cape Verde (1990)	
★ Praia	61,644
Central African Republic (1994 est.)	
★ Bangui	524,000
Chad (1993; MU)	
Abéché	187,936
Bongor	196,713
Doba	185,461
Moundou	282,103
★ N'Djamena	530,965
Sarh	193,753
Chile (1995 est.; MU)	
Antofagasta	236,730
Arica	173,336
Calama	120,602[1]
Chillán	157,083
Concepción	350,268
Copiapó	100,946[15]
Coquimbo	122,872[15]
Curicó	103,919[15]
Iquique	152,592
La Serena	117,983
Los Angeles	142,136[15]
Osorno	123,055
Puente Alto	318,898
Puerto Montt	122,399
Punta Arenas	117,206
Quilpué	110,340
Rancagua	193,755
San Bernardo	206,315
★ Santiago (administrative)	5,076,808
Talca	169,448
Talcahuano	260,915
Temuco	239,340
Valdivia	119,431
★ Valparaíso (legislative)	282,168
Viña del Mar	322,220
China (1990 est.)[16]	
A-ch'eng (Acheng)	197,595
A-k'o-su (Aksu)	164,092
An-ch'ing (Anqing)	250,718
An-k'ang (Ankang)	142,170
An-shan (Anshan)	1,390,000[17]
An-shun (Anshun)	174,142
An-ta (Anda)	136,446
An-yang (Anyang)	420,332
Canton (Guangzhou)	3,580,000[17]
Chan-chiang (Zhanjiang)	400,997
Ch'ang-chi (Changji)	132,260
Chang-chia-k'ou (Zhangjiakou)	529,136
Ch'ang-chih (Changzhi)	317,144
Ch'ang-chou (Changzhou)	531,470
Chang-chou (Zhangzhou)	181,424
Ch'ang-ch'un (Changchun)	2,110,000[17]
Ch'ang-sha (Changsha)	1,330,000[17]
Ch'ang-shu (Changshu)	181,805
Ch'ang-te (Changde)	301,276
Chao-ch'ing (Zhaoqing)	194,784
Ch'ao-chou (Chaozhou)	313,469
Ch'ao-hsien (Chaoxian)	123,676
Chao-tung (Zhaodong)	179,976
Ch'ao-yang (Chaoyang)	222,394
Chen-chiang (Zhenjiang)	368,316
Cheng-chou (Zhengzhou)	1,710,000[17]
Ch'eng-te (Chengde)	246,799
Ch'eng-tu (Chengdu)	2,810,000[17]
Chi-an (Ji'an)	148,583
Chi-hsi (Jixi)	683,885
Chi-lin (Jilin)	1,270,000[17]
Chi-nan (Jinan)	2,320,000[17]
Chi-ning (Jining) (*Inner Mongolia*)	163,552
Chi-ning (Jining) (*Shantung*)	265,248
Ch'i-t'ai-ho (Qitaihe)	214,957
Ch'i-tung (Qidong)	126,872
Chia-hsing (Jiaxing)	211,526
Chia-mu-ssu (Jiamusi)	493,409
Chiang-men (Jiangmen)	230,587
Chiang-yin (Jiangyin)	213,659
Chiang-yu (Jiangyou)	175,753
Chiao-hsien (Jiaoxian)	153,364
Chiao-nan (Jiaonan)	121,397
Chiao-tso (Jiaozuo)	409,100
Ch'ien-chiang (Qianjiang)	205,504
Ch'ih-feng (Chifeng)	350,077
Chin-ch'ang (Jinchang)	105,287
Chin-ch'eng (Jincheng)	136,396
Chin-chou (Jinzhou)	569,518
Ch'in-chou (Qinzhou)	114,586
Chin-hsi (Jinxi)	357,052
Chin-hua (Jinhua)	144,280
Ch'in-huang-tao (Qinhuangdao)	364,972
Ch'ing-chou (Qingzhou)	128,258
Ch'ing-tao (Qingdao)	2,060,000[17]
Ching-te-chen (Jingdezhen)	281,183
Ch'ing-yüan (Qingyuan)	164,641
Chiu-chiang (Jiujiang)	291,187
Chiu-t'ai (Jiutai)	180,130
Chou-k'ou (Zhoukou)	146,288
Chou-shan (Zhoushan)	156,317
Chu-ch'eng (Zhucheng)	102,134
Ch'ü-ching (Qujing)	178,669
Ch'u-chou (Quzhou)	112,373
Chu-chou (Zhuzhou)	409,924
Chu-hai (Zhuhai)	164,747
Ch'u-hsien (Chuxian)	125,341
Chu-ma-tien (Zhumadian)	123,232
Ch'üan-chou (Quanzhou)	185,154
Chung-shan (Zhongshan)	278,829
Chungking (Chongqing)	2,980,000[17]
Feng-ch'eng (Fengcheng)	193,784
Fo-shan (Foshan)	303,160
Fu-chin (Fujin)	103,104
Fu-chou (Fuzhou) (*Fukien*)	874,809
Fu-chou (Fuzhou) (*Kiangsi*)	1,290,000[17]
Fu-hsin (Fuxin)	635,473
Fu-ling (Fuling)	173,878
Fu-shun (Fushun)	1,350,000[17]
Fu-yang (Fuyang)	179,572
Fu-yü (Fuyu)	192,981
Ha-mi (Hami)	161,315
Hai-ch'eng (Haicheng)	205,560
Hai-k'ou (Haikou)	280,153
Hai-la-erh (Hailar)	180,650
Hai-lun (Kailun)	133,565
Hai-ning (Haining)	100,478
Han-chung (Hanzhong)	169,930
Han-tan (Handan)	1,110,000[17]
Hang-chou (Hangzhou)	1,340,000[17]
Harbin	2,830,000[17]
Heng-shui (Hengshui)	104,269
Heng-yang (Hengyang)	487,148
Ho-fei (Hefei)	1,000,000[17]
Ho-kang (Hegang)	522,747
Ho-pi (Hebi)	212,976
Ho-tse (Heze)	189,293
Ho-yuan (Heyuan)	120,101
Hsi-ch'ang (Xichang)	134,419
Hsi-ning (Xining)	551,776
Hsia-men (Xiamen)	368,786
Hsiang-fan (Xiangfan)	410,407
Hsiang-t'an (Xiangtan)	441,968
Hsiao-kan (Xiaogan)	166,280
Hsiao-shan (Xiaoshan)	162,930
Hsien-ning (Xianning)	136,811
Hsien-t'ao (Xiantao)	222,884
Hsien-yang (Xianyang)	352,125
Hsin-hsiang (Xinxiang)	473,762
Hsin-t'ai (Xintai)	281,248
Hsin-yang (Xinyang)	192,509
Hsin-yu (Xinyu)	173,524
Hsing-ch'eng (Xingcheng)	102,384
Hsing-hua (Xinghua)	161,910
Hsing-t'ai (Xingtai)	302,789
Hsü-ch'ang (Xuchang)	208,815
Hsü-chou (Xuzhou)	805,695
Hsuan-ch'eng (Xuancheng)	112,673
Hu-chou (Huzhou)	218,071
Hu-ho-hao-t'e (Hohhot)	652,534
Hua-tien (Huadian)	175,873
Huai-an (Huai'an)	131,149
Huai-hua (Huaihua)	126,785
Huai-nan (Huainan)	1,200,000[17]
Huai-pei (Huaibei)	366,549
Huai-yin (Huaiyin)	239,675
Huang-shan (Huangshan)	102,628
Huang-shih (Huangshi)	457,601
Hui-chou (Huizhou)	161,023
Hun-chiang (Hunjiang)	482,043
Hung-hu (Honghu)	190,772
I-ch'ang (Yichang)	371,601
I-cheng (Yizheng)	109,268
I-ch'un (Yichun)	795,789
I-ch'un (Yichun) (*Kiangsi*)	151,585
I-hsing (Yixing)	200,824
I-ning (Yining)	177,193
I-pin (Yibin)	241,019
I-yang (Yiyang)	185,818
Jen-ch'iu (Renqiu)	114,256
Jih-chao (Rizhao)	185,048
Jui-an (Rui'an)	156,468
K'ai-feng (Kaifeng)	507,763
K'ai-li (Kaili)	113,958
K'ai-yuan (Kaiyuan)	124,219
Kan-chou (Ganzhou)	220,129
Kashgar (Kashi)	174,570
Ko-chiu (Gejiu)	214,294
K'o-la-ma-i (Karamay)	197,602
K'u-erh-le (Korla)	159,344
Kuang-shui (Guangshui)	102,770
Kuang-yüan (Guangyuan)	182,241
Kuei-hsien (Guixian)	114,025
Kuei-lin (Guilin)	364,130
K'uei-t'un (Kuitun)	118,553
Kuei-yang (Guiyang)	1,530,000[17]
K'un-ming (Kunming)	1,520,000[17]
K'un-shan (Kunshan)	102,052
Kung-chu-ling (Gongzhuling)	226,569
Lai-chou (Laizhou)	198,664
Lai-wu (Laiwu)	246,833
Lai-yang (Laiyang)	137,080
Lan-chou (Lanzhou)	1,510,000[17]
Lang-fang (Langfang)	148,105
Lao-ho-k'ou (Laohekou)	123,366
Le-shan (Leshan)	341,128
Lei-yang (Leiyang)	130,115
Leng-shui-chiang (Lengshuijiang)	137,994
Lhasa	106,885
Li-ling (Liling)	108,504
Li-yang (Liyang)	109,520
Liang-ch'eng (Liangcheng)	156,307
Liao-ch'eng (Liaocheng)	207,844
Liao-yang (Liaoyang)	492,559
Liao-yüan (Liaoyuan)	354,141
Lien-yüan (Lianyuan)	118,858
Lien-yün-kang (Lianyungang)	354,139
Lin-ch'ing (Linqing)	123,958
Lin-fen (Linfen)	187,309
Lin-ho (Linhe)	133,183
Lin-i (Linyi)	324,720
Liu-chou (Liuzhou)	609,320
Liu-p'an-shui (Liupanshui)	363,954
Lo-ho (Luohe)	126,438
Lo-yang (Luoyang)	1,190,000[17]
Long-yen (Longyan)	134,481
Lou-ti (Loudi)	128,418
Lu-an (Lu'an)	144,248
Lu-chou (Luzhou)	262,892
Lung-ching (Longjing)	139,417
Lung-k'ou (Longkou)	148,362
Ma-an-shan (Ma'anshan)	305,421
Man-chou-li (Manzhouli)	120,023
Mao-ming (Maoming)	178,683
Mei-ho-k'ou (Meihekou)	209,038
Mei-hsien (Meixian)	132,156
Mi-shan (Mishan)	132,744
Mien-yang (Mianyang)	262,947
Mu-tan-chiang (Mudanjiang)	571,705
Nan-ch'ang (Nanchang)	1,350,000[17]
Nan-ch'ung (Nanchong)	180,273
Nan-ning (Nanning)	1,070,000[17]
Nan-p'ing (Nanping)	195,064
Nan-t'ung (Nantong)	343,341
Nan-yang (Nanyang)	243,303
Nanking (Nanjing)	2,500,000[17]
Nei-chiang (Neijiang)	256,012
Ning-po (Ningbo)	1,090,000[17]
O-ch'eng (Echeng)	190,123
Pai-ch'eng (Baicheng)	217,987
Pai-yin (Baiyin)	204,970
P'an-chih-hua (Panzhihua) (Tu-k'ou [Dukou])	415,466
P'an-shan (Panshan)	362,773
Pang-pu (Bengbu)	449,245
Pao-chi (Baoji)	337,765
Pao-ting (Baoding)	483,155
Pao-t'ou (Baotou)	1,200,000[17]
Pei-an (Bei'an)	204,899
Pei-hai (Beihai)	112,673
Pei-p'iao (Beipiao)	194,301
★ Peking (Beijing)	7,000,000[17]
Pen-hsi (Benxi)	768,778
Pin-chou (Binzhou)	133,555
P'ing-hsiang (Pingxiang)	425,579
P'ing-ting-shan (Pingdingshan)	410,775
P'ing-tu (Pingdu)	150,123
Po-chou (Bozhou)	106,346
P'u-ch'i (Puqi)	117,264
P'u-yang (Puyang)	175,988
San-men-hsia (Sanmenxia)	120,523
San-ming (Sanming)	160,691
San-ya (Sanya)	102,820
Sha-shih (Shashi)	281,352
Shan-t'ou (Shantou)	578,630
Shan-wei (Shanwei)	107,847
Shao-hsing (Shaoxing)	179,818
Shao-kuan (Shaoguan)	350,043
Shao-yang (Shaoyang)	247,227
Shang-chih (Shangzhi)	215,373
Shang-ch'iu (Shangqiu)	164,880
Shang-jao (Shangrao)	132,455
Shanghai	7,830,000[17]
Shen-chen (Shenzhen)	350,727
Shen-yang (Shenyang)	4,540,000[17]
Shih-chia-chuang (Shijiazhuang)	1,320,000[17]
Shih-ho-tzu (Shihezi)	299,676
Shih-shou (Shishou)	104,571
Shih-tsui-shan (Shizuishan)	257,862
Shih-yen (Shiyan)	273,786
Shuang-ch'eng (Shuangcheng)	142,659
Shuang-ya-shan (Shuangyashan)	386,081
Sian (Xi'an)	2,760,000[17]
Ssu-p'ing (Siping)	317,223
Su-ch'ien (Suqian)	105,021
Su-chou (Suzhou) (*Anhwei*)	151,862
Su-chou (Suzhou) (*Kiangsu*)	706,459
Sui-hua (Suihua)	227,881
Sui-ning (Suining)	146,086
Ta-an (Da'an)	138,963
Ta-ch'ing (Daqing)	657,297
Ta-hsien (Daxian)	188,101
Ta-li (Dali)	136,554
Ta-lien (Dalian)	2,400,000[17]
Ta-t'ung (Datong)	1,110,000[17]
T'ai-an (Tai'an)	350,696
T'ai-chou (Taizhou)	152,442
T'ai-yüan (Taiyuan)	1,960,000[17]
Tan-chiang (Danjiang)	103,211
Tan-tung (Dandong)	523,699
Tan-yang (Danyang)	169,603
T'ang-shan (Tangshan)	1,500,000[17]
T'ao-nan (Taonan)	150,168
Te-chou (Dezhou)	195,485
Te-yang (Deyang)	182,488
T'eng-hsien (Tengxian)	315,083
T'ieh-fa (Tiefa)	131,807
T'ieh-li (Tieli)	265,683
T'ieh-ling (Tieling)	254,842
T'ien-men (Tianmen)	186,332
T'ien-shui (Tianshui)	244,974
Tientsin (Tianjin)	5,770,000[17]
Tsa-lan-t'un (Zalantun)	130,031
Ts'ang-chou (Cangzhou)	242,708
Tsao-chuang (Zaozhuang)	380,846
Tsao-yang (Zaoyang)	162,198
Tsitsihar (Qiqihar)	1,380,000[17]
Tsun-i (Zunyi)	261,862
Tu-chiang-yen (Dujiangyan)	123,357
Tu-yun (Duyun)	132,971
Tun-hua (Dunhua)	235,100
T'ung-ch'uan (Tongchuan)	280,657
T'ung-hua (Tonghua)	324,600
Tung-kuan (Dongguan)	308,669
T'ung-liao (Tongliao)	255,129
T'ung-ling (Tongling)	228,017
Tung-t'ai (Dongtai)	192,247
Tung-ying (Dongying)	281,728
Tz'u-hsi (Cixi)	107,329
Tzu-hsing (Zixing)	110,048
Tzu-kung (Zigong)	393,184
Tzu-po (Zibo)	2,460,000[17]
Wa-fang-tien (Wafangdian)	251,733
Wan-hsien (Wanxian)	156,823
Wei-fang (Weifang)	428,522
Wei-hai (Weihai)	128,888
Wei-nan (Weinan)	140,169
Wen-chou (Wenzhou)	401,871
Wen-teng (Wendeng)	133,910
Wu-chou (Wuzhou)	210,452
Wu-hai (Wuhai)	264,081
Wu-han (Wuhan)	3,750,000[17]
Wu-hsi (Wuxi)	826,833
Wu-hu (Wuhu)	425,740
Wu-lan-hao-t'e (Ulanhot)	159,538
Wu-lu-mu-ch'i (Ürümqi)	1,160,000[17]
Wu-wei (Wuwei)	133,101
Ya-k'o-she (Yakeshi)	377,869
Yang-chiang (Yangjiang)	215,196
Yang-chou (Yangzhou)	312,892
Yang-ch'üan (Yangquan)	362,268
Yen-an (Yan'an)	113,277
Yen-ch'eng (Yancheng)	296,831
Yen-chi (Yanji)	230,892
Yen-t'ai (Yantai)	452,127
Yin-ch'uan (Yinchuan)	356,652
Ying-k'ou (Yingkou)	421,589
Yü-lin (Yulin)	144,467
Yü-men (Yumen)	109,234
Yü-shu (Yushu)	131,861
Yü-tz'u (Yuci)	191,356
Yu-yao (Yuyao)	114,065
Yüan-chiang (Yuanjiang)	107,004
Yüeh-yang (Yueyang)	302,800
Yun-ch'eng (Yuncheng)	108,359
Yung-an (Yong'an)	111,762
Colombia (1995 est.)	
Armenia	220,303
Barrancabermeja	180,653
Barranquilla	1,064,255
Bello	304,819
Bucaramanga	351,737

Major cities and national capitals (continued)

country city	population
Buenaventura	266,988
Cali	1,718,871
Cartagena	745,689
Cartago	117,166
Ciénaga	144,340
Cúcuta	479,309
Dosquebradas	163,599
Envigado	109,240
Florencia	118,027
Floridablanca	246,834
Ibagué	346,632
Itagüí	169,374
Magangué	104,496
Malambo	112,289
Manizales	335,125
Medellín	1,621,356
Montería	276,074
Neiva	248,178
Palmira	256,823
Pasto	325,540
Pereira	352,530
Popayán	223,128
Quibdó	130,921
Ríohacha	142,455
Santa Marta	309,372
★ Santafé de Bogotá, D.C.	5,237,635
Sincelejo	180,076
Soacha	266,817
Soledad	264,583
Tuluá	138,124
Tumaco	114,802
Tunja	120,210
Turbo	127,045
Valledupar	265,505
Villavicencio	252,711
Comoros (1991)	
★ Moroni	30,000
Congo (1992 est.)	
★ Brazzaville	937,579
Pointe-Noire	576,206
Costa Rica (1995 est.)	
★ San José	321,193[18]
Côte d'Ivoire (1988)	
★ Abidjan (de facto; legislative)	2,797,000[5]
Bouaké	329,850
Daloa	121,842
Korhogo	109,445
★ Yamoussoukro (de jure; administrative)	106,786
Croatia (1991)	
Osijek	129,792
Rijeka	167,964
Split	200,459
★ Zagreb	867,717
Cuba (1994 est.)	
Bayamo	137,663
Camagüey	293,961
Cienfuegos	132,038
Guantánamo	207,796
★ Havana	2,241,000[5]
Holguín	242,085
Las Tunas	126,930
Manzanillo	107,650[19]
Matanzas	123,843
Pinar del Río	128,570
Santa Clara	205,400
Santiago de Cuba	440,084
Cyprus (1994 est.)	
Limassol	143,400
★ Nicosia (Lefkosia)	186,400[20]
Czech Republic (1995 est.)	
Brno	389,576
Hradec Králové	100,671
Liberec	100,698
Olomouc	106,278
Ostrava	325,827
Plzen	171,908
★ Prague	1,213,299
Denmark (1995 est.; MU)	
Ålborg	159,056
Århus	277,477
★ Copenhagen	1,353,333[21]
Odense	182,617
Djibouti (1991 est.)	
★ Djibouti	317,000
Dominica (1991)	
★ Roseau	15,853
Dominican Republic (1993)	
La Romana	136,000[22]
La Vega	189,000[22]
San Francisco de Macorís	162,000[22]
San Pedro de Macorís	137,000[22]
Santiago	375,000[17]
★ Santo Domingo	2,138,262[23]
Ecuador (1996 est.)	
Ambato	155,690
Cuenca	247,421
Duran	127,832
Esmeraldas	115,017
Guayaquil	1,925,479
Ibarra	113,791
Loja	114,198
Machala	190,924
Manta	149,353
Milagro	114,229
Portoviejo	163,758
Quevedo	116,287
★ Quito	1,444,363
Riobamba	114,322
Santo Domingo	165,090
Egypt (1992 est.)	
Alexandria	3,382,000[8]
Aswān	220,000
Asyūṭ	321,000
Banhā	136,000
Banī Suwayf	179,000
Būr Saʿīd (Port Said)	460,000[8]
★ Cairo	6,849,000[8]
Damanhūr	222,000
al-Fayyūm	250,000
Hulwan (Helwan)	352,300[24]
Al-Ismāʿīlīyah	255,000
Al-Jīzah (Giza)	2,144,000
Kafr ad-Dawwar	226,000
Kafr ash-Shaykh	102,910[25]
Al-Maḥallah al-Kubrā	408,000
Al-Manṣūrah	371,000
Al-Minyā	208,000
Qinā	141,000
Sawhāj	156,000
Shibīn al-Kawm	158,000
Shubrā al-Khaymah	834,000
As-Suways (Suez)	388,000
Ṭanṭā	380,000
Al-Uqṣur (Luxor)	155,000[8]
Az-Zaqāzīq	287,000
El Salvador (1992; MU)	
Apopa	100,763
Delgado	104,790
Mejicanos	145,000[21]
Nueva San Salvador	116,575
San Miguel	182,817
★ San Salvador	422,570
Santa Ana	202,337
Soyapango	251,811[21]
Equatorial Guinea (1991 est.)	
★ Malabo	58,040
Eritrea (1991 est.)	
★ Asmara	367,300
Estonia (1995 est.)	
★ Tallinn	434,763
Tartu	104,907
Ethiopia (1994 est.)	
★ Addis Ababa	2,316,400
Bahir Dar	115,531
Debrezit	105,963
Dese	117,268
Dire Dawa	194,587
Gonder	166,593
Harer	122,932
Jima	119,717
Mekele	119,779
Nazret	147,088
Faroe Islands (1995 est.)	
★ Tórshavn	13,687
Fiji (1990 est.)	
★ Suva	200,000[21]
Finland (1996 est.; MU)	
Espoo	191,247
★ Helsinki	525,031
Oulu	109,094
Tampere	182,742
Turku	164,744
Vantaa	166,480
France (1990)	
Aix-en-Provence	126,854
Amiens	136,234
Angers	146,163
Besançon	119,194
Bordeaux	213,274
Boulogne-Billancourt	101,971
Brest	153,099
Caen	115,624
Clermont-Ferrand	140,167
Dijon	151,636
Grenoble	153,973
Le Havre	197,219
Le Mans	148,465
Lille	178,301
Limoges	136,407
Lyon	422,444
Marseille	807,726
Metz	123,920
Montpellier	210,866
Mulhouse	109,905
Nancy	102,410
Nantes	252,029
Nice	345,674
Nîmes	133,607
Orléans	107,965
★ Paris	2,175,200
Perpignan	108,049
Reims	185,164
Rennes	203,533
Rouen	105,470
Saint-Étienne	201,569
Strasbourg	255,937
Toulon	170,167
Toulouse	365,933
Tours	133,403
Villeurbanne	119,848
French Guiana (1990)	
★ Cayenne	41,659
French Polynesia (1988)	
★ Papeete	23,555
Gabon (1993)	
★ Libreville	362,386
Gambia, The (1993)	
★ Banjul	42,407
Serekunda	102,600[26]
Gaza Strip (early 1990s est.)	
Gaza (Ghazzah)	293,000
Khan Younis	160,463
Rafah	101,926
Georgia (1991 est.)	
Bat'umi (Batumi)	137,500
K'ut'aisi (Kutaisi)	238,200
Rust'avi (Rustavi)	161,900
Sukhumi	120,000
★ T'bilisi (Tbilisi)	1,279,000
Germany (1995 est.)	
Aachen	247,113
Augsburg	262,110
Bergisch Gladbach	105,122
Berlin	3,472,009
Bielefeld	324,067
Bochum	401,129
★ Bonn	293,072
Bottrop	119,669
Braunschweig	254,130
Bremen	549,182
Bremerhaven	130,847
Chemnitz	274,162
Cologne (Köln)	963,817
Cottbus	125,643
Darmstadt	139,063
Dortmund	600,918
Dresden	474,443
Duisburg	536,106
Düsseldorf	572,638
Erfurt	213,472
Erlangen	101,450
Essen	617,955
Frankfurt am Main	652,412
Freiburg im Breisgau	198,496
Fürth	107,799
Gelsenkirchen	293,542
Gera	126,035
Göttingen	127,519
Hagen	213,747
Halle	290,051
Hamburg	1,705,872
Hamm	184,020
Hannover	525,763
Heidelberg	138,964
Heilbronn	122,253
Herne	180,029
Hildesheim	106,095
Ingolstadt	110,910
Jena	102,204
Kaiserslautern	101,910
Karlsruhe	277,011
Kassel	201,789
Kiel	246,586
Koblenz	109,550
Krefeld	249,662
Leipzig	481,121
Leverkusen	161,832
Lübeck	216,854
Ludwigshafen	167,883
Magdeburg	265,379
Mainz	184,627
Mannheim	316,223
Moers	107,011
Mönchengladbach	266,073
Mülheim an der Ruhr	176,513
Munich (München)	1,244,676
Münster	264,887
Neuss	148,870
Nürnberg	495,845
Oberhausen	225,443
Offenbach am Main	116,482
Oldenburg	149,691
Osnabrück	168,050
Paderborn	131,513
Pforzheim	117,960
Potsdam	138,268
Recklinghausen	127,139
Regensburg	125,608
Remscheid	123,069
Reutlingen	107,782
Rostock	232,634
Saarbrücken	189,012
Salzgitter	117,842
Schwerin	118,291
Siegen	111,541
Solingen	165,973
Stuttgart	588,482
Ulm	115,123
Wiesbaden	266,081
Witten	105,423
Wolfsburg	126,965
Wuppertal	383,776
Würzburg	127,946
Zwickau	104,921
Ghana (1988 est.)	
★ Accra	1,781,100[19, 21]
Kumasi	385,192
Sekondi-Takoradi	103,653
Tamale	151,069
Tema	109,975
Gibraltar (1996 est.)	
★ Gibraltar	27,100[27]
Greece (1991)	
★ Athens	748,110
Iráklion	117,167
Kallithéa	110,738
Larissa	113,426
Pátrai (Patras)	155,180
Peristérion	145,854
Piraiévs (Piraeus)	169,622
Thessaloníki	377,951
Greenland (1996 est.)	
★ Nuuk (Godthåb)	12,882
Grenada (1991)	
★ Saint George's	4,621
Guadeloupe (1990)	
★ Basse-Terre	14,107
Guam (1990)	
★ Agana	1,139
Guatemala (1994; MU)	
★ Guatemala City	823,301
Mixco	209,791
Villa Nueva	101,295
Guernsey (1991)	
★ St. Peter Port	16,648
Guinea (1995 est.)	
★ Conakry	1,508,000
Guinea-Bissau (1991)	
★ Bissau	197,610
Guyana (1992 est.)	
★ Georgetown	248,500
Haiti (1995 est.)	
Cap-Haïtien	100,638
Carrefour	277,662
Delmas	232,142
★ Port-au-Prince	846,247
Honduras (1994 est.; MU)	
San Pedro Sula	368,500
★ Tegucigalpa	775,300[28]
Hong Kong (1996)	
Hong Kong	6,218,000[28]
Hungary (1996 est.)	
★ Budapest	1,909,000
Debrecen	211,000
Győr	127,000
Kecskemét	105,000
Miskolc	180,000
Nyíregyháza	113,000
Pécs	163,000
Szeged	167,000
Székesfehérvár	107,000
Iceland (1995 est.)	
★ Reykjavík	104,276
India (1991)	
Abohar	107,163
Ādoni	136,182
Agartala	157,358
Āgra	891,790
Ahmadābād	2,876,710
Ahmadnagar	181,339
Āizawl	155,240
Ajmer	402,700
Akola	328,034
Alandur	125,244
Alībāg	328,640
Alīgarh	480,520
Allahābād	792,858
Alleppey (Alappuzha)	174,666
Alwar	205,086
Ambāla	119,338
Ambattur	215,424
Amrāvati	421,576
Amritsar	708,835
Amroha	137,061
Anand	110,266
Anantapur	174,924
Āra (Arrah)	157,082
Āsansol	262,188
Aurangābād (Shambājinagar)	573,272
Āvadi	183,215
Baharampur	115,144
Bahraich	135,400
Bally	184,474
Bālurghāt	119,796
Bangalore	2,660,088
Bānkura	114,876
Barāhanagar	224,821
Bārāsat	102,660
Barddhamān (Burdwān)	245,079
Bareilly	587,211
Barrackpore	133,265
Basīrhāt	101,409
Bathinda (Bhatinda)	159,042
Beāwar	105,363
Belgaum	326,399
Bellary	245,391
Bhāgalpur	253,225
Bharatpur	148,519
Bharūch (Broach)	133,102
Bhātpāra	304,952
Bhāvnagar	402,338
Bhilainagar	395,360
Bhīlwāra	183,965
Bhīmavaram	121,314
Bhind	109,755
Bhiwandi	379,070
Bhiwāni	121,629
Bhopāl	1,062,771
Bhubaneshwar	411,542
Bhuj	102,176
Bhusāwal	145,143
Bīd (Bhīr)	112,434
Bīdar	108,016
Bidhān Nagar	100,048
Bihār Sharīf	201,323
Bijāpur	186,939
Bīkaner	416,289
Bilāspur	179,833
Bokāro	333,683
Brahmapur	210,418
Budaun	116,695
Bulandshahr	127,201
Burhānpur	172,710
Burnpur	174,933
Calcutta	4,399,819
Calicut (Kozhikode)	419,831
Chāmpdānī	101,067
Chandannagar	120,378
Chandīgarh	504,094
Chandrapur	226,105
Chennai (Madras)	3,841,396
Chhapra	136,877
Chittoor	133,462
Cochin (Kochi)	564,589
Coimbatore	816,321
Cuddalore	144,561
Cuddapah	121,463
Cuttack	403,418
Darbhanga	218,391
Dāvangere	266,082
Dehra Dūn	270,159
Delhi	7,206,704
Dewās	164,364
Dhānbād	151,789
Dhūle (Dhūlia)	278,317
Dibrugarh	120,127
Dindigul	182,447
Durg	150,645
Durgāpur	425,836
Elūru	212,866
Erode	159,232
Etāwah	124,072
Faizābād	124,437
Farīdābād	617,717
Farrukhābād-cum-Fatehgarh	194,567
Fatehpur	117,675
Fīrozābād	215,128
Gadag-Betigeri	134,051
Gāndhīdhām	104,585
Gāndhīnagar	123,359
Gangānagar	161,482
Gaya	291,675
Ghāziābād	454,156
Gondia	109,470
Gorakhpur	505,566
Gudivāda	101,656
Gulbarga	304,099
Guna	100,490
Guntakal	107,592
Guntūr	471,051
Gurgaon	121,486
Guwāhāti (Gauhāti)	584,342
Gwalior	690,765
Hābra	100,223
Haldia	100,347
Haldwāni-cum-Kāthgodam	104,195
Hālisahar	114,028
Hāpur	146,262
Haridwār (Hardwār)	147,305
Hāthras	113,285
Hindupur	104,651
Hisār (Hissār)	172,677
Hoshiārpur	122,705
Howrah (Hāora)	950,435
Hubli-Dhārwād	648,298

country city	population
Hugli-Chunchura	151,806
Hyderābād	3,145,939
Ichalkaranji	214,950
Imphāl	198,535
Indore	1,091,674
Ingrāj Bāzār	139,204
Jabalpur	741,927
Jaipur	1,458,183
Jalandhar (Jullundur)	509,510
Jalgaon	242,193
Jālna	174,985
Jammu	206,135[12]
Jāmnagar	341,637
Jamshedpur	478,950
Jaunpur	136,062
Jhānsi	300,850
Jodhpur	666,279
Jūnāgadh	130,484
Kākināda	279,980
Kalyān	1,014,557
Kāmārhāti	266,889
Kānchipuram	144,955
Kānchrāpāra	100,194
Kānpur	1,874,409
Karīmnagar	148,583
Karnāl	173,751
Katihār	135,436
Khammam	127,992
Khandwa	143,133
Kharagpur	177,989
Kolhāpur	406,370
Kota	537,371
Krishnanagar	121,110
Kukatpalle	186,963
Kulti-Barākar	108,518
Kumbakonam	139,483
Kurnool	236,800
Lālbāhādur Nagar	155,514
Lātūr	197,408
Lucknow	1,619,115
Ludhiāna	1,042,740
Machilīpatnam (Masulipatam)	159,110
Madurai	940,989
Mahbūbnagar	116,833
Mālegaon	342,595
Mālkājgiri	127,178
Mandya	120,265
Mangalore	273,304
Māngo	108,100
Mathura	226,691
Maunāth Bhanjan	136,697
Medinīpur (Midnāpore)	125,498
Meerut	753,778
Mira-Bhayandar	175,605
Miraj	121,593
Mirzāpur-cum-Vindhyāchal	169,336
Modinagar	101,660
Moga	108,304
Morādābād	429,214
Morena	147,124
Mumbāi (Bombay)	9,925,891[21]
Munger (Monghyr)	150,112
Murwāra (Katni)	163,431
Muzaffarnagar	240,609
Muzaffarpur	241,107
Mysore	480,692
Nadiād	167,051
Nāgercoil	190,084
Nāgpur	1,624,752
Naihāti	132,701
Nānded (Nānder)	275,083
Nandyāl	119,813
Nāshik (Nāsik)	656,925
Navadwīp	125,037
Navsāri	126,089
Nellore	316,606
New Bombay	307,724
★ New Delhi	301,297
Neyveli	118,080
Nizāmābād	241,034
Noida	146,514
North Barrackpore	100,606
North Dum Dum	149,965
Ongole	100,836
Pālghāt (Palakkad)	123,289
Pāli	136,842
Pallavaram	111,866
Pānihāti	275,990
Pānīpat	191,212
Parbhani	190,255
Pathānkot	123,930
Patiāla	238,368
Patna	917,243
Pīlībhīt	106,605
Pimpri-Chinchwad	517,083
Pondicherry	203,065
Porbandar	116,671
Proddatūr	133,914
Pune	1,566,651
Puri	125,199
Pūrnia (Pūrnea)	114,912
Quilon (Kollam)	139,852
Qutubullapur	106,591
Rāe Bareli	129,904
Rāichūr	157,551
Rāiganj	151,045
Raipur	438,639
Rāj Nāndgaon	125,371
Rājahmundry	324,851
Rājapālaiyam	114,202
Rājkot	559,407
Rāmagundam	214,384
Rāmpur	243,742
Rānchi	599,306
Ratlām	183,375
Raurkela Steel Township	215,509
Rewa	128,981
Rishra	102,815
Rohtak	216,096
Sāgar	195,346
Sahāranpur	374,945
Salem	366,712
Sambalpur	131,138
Sambhal	150,869
Sāngli	193,197
Satna	156,630
Shāhjahānpur	237,713
Shāntipur	109,956
Shiliguri (Silīguri)	216,950
Shillong	131,719
Shimoga	179,258
Shivpuri	108,277
Sholāpur (Solapur)	604,215
Shrīrāmpur	137,028
Sīkar	148,272
Silchar	115,483
Sirsa	112,841
Sitāpur	121,842
Sonīpat (Sonepat)	143,922
South Dum Dum	232,811
Srīnagar	586,038[12]
Sūrat	1,498,817
Surendranagar	106,110
Tāmbaram	107,187
Tellicherry (Thalassery)	103,579
Tenāli	143,726
Thāne (Thāna)	803,389
Thanjāvūr	202,013
Tiruchchirāppalli	387,223
Tirunelveli	135,825
Tirupati	174,369
Tirupper (Tiruppūr)	235,661
Tiruvannāmalai	109,196
Tiruvottiyūr	168,642
Titāgarh	114,085
Tonk	100,079
Trivandrum (Thiruvananthapuram)	524,006
Tumkūr	138,903
Tuticorin	199,854
Udaipur	308,571
Ujjain	362,266
Ulhāsnagar	369,077
Uluberia	155,172
Unnāo	107,425
Uttarpāra-Kotrung	101,268
Vadodara (Baroda)	1,031,346
Vārānasi (Benares)	929,270
Vellore	175,061
Vijayawāda	701,827
Vishākhapatnam	752,037
Vizianagaram	160,359
Warangal	447,657
Wardha	102,985
Yamunanagar	144,346
Yavatmāl (Yeotmāl)	108,578
Indonesia (1990)	
Ambon	206,260
Balikpapan	309,492
Banda Aceh	143,409
Bandar Lampung	458,215
Bandung	2,026,893
Banjarmasin	443,738
Bengkulu	146,439
Binjai	127,222
Blitar	113,064
Bogor	271,711
Cilacap	113,893[29]
Cimahi	105,940[29]
Cirebon	245,307
Denpasar	261,263[29]
★ Jakarta	8,259,266
Jambi	301,359
Jayapura	149,618[29]
Jember	140,105[29]
Kediri	235,602
Madiun	165,999
Magelang	123,213
Malang	650,295
Manado	275,374
Mataram	141,387[29]
Medan	1,685,972
Padang	477,344
Palembang	1,084,483
Pangkal Pinang	108,411
Pasuruan	134,019
Pekalongan	227,535
Pekanbaru	341,328
Pematangsiantar	203,834
Pontianak	387,112
Probolinggo	131,291
Purwokerto	105,395[29]
Samarinda	335,016
Semarang	1,005,316
Sukabumi	119,981
Sumba	355,073[29]
Surabaya	2,421,016
Surakarta	504,176
Tanjung Balai	102,095
Tanjung Karang-Telukbetung	284,275[29]
Tasikmalaya	165,297[29]
Tebing Tinggi	116,767
Tegal	225,770
Ujung Pandang	913,196
Yogyakarta	412,392
Iran (1991)	
Ahvāz	724,653
Āmol	139,923
Arāk	331,354
Ardabīl	311,022
Bābol	137,348
Bandar 'Abbās	249,504
Bandar-e Būshehr	132,824
Bīrjand	101,177
Bojnūrd	112,426
Borūjerd	201,016
Dezfūl	181,309
Eşfahān (Isfahan)	1,127,030
Gonbad-e Kavus	102,768
Gorgān	162,468
Hamadān	349,653
Īlām	116,428
Islāmshahr (Eslāmshahr)	230,183
Karaj	442,387
Kāshān	155,188
Kermān	311,643
Kermānshāh (Bākhtarān)	624,084
Khomeynīshahr	118,348
Khorramābād	249,258
Khorramshahr	197,241
Khvoy	137,885
Malāyer	130,458
Marāgheh	117,388
Mashhad (Meshed)	1,759,155
Masjed-e Soleymān	107,539
Najafābād	160,004
Neyshābūr	135,681
Orūmīyeh	357,399
Qā'emshahr	123,684
Qazvīn	278,826
Qom	681,253
Rājaishahr	160,362
Rasht	340,637
Sabzevār	148,065
Sanandaj	244,039
Sārī	167,602
Shīrāz	965,117
Sīrjān	107,887
Tabrīz	1,088,985
★ Tehrān	11,000,000[8]
Yazd	275,298
Zāhedān	361,623
Zanjān	254,100
Iraq (1987)	
Al-'Amārah	208,797
★ Baghdad	4,478,000[5, 21]
Ba'qūbah	114,516[30]
Al-Başrah	406,296
Al-Ḥillah	268,834
Dīwānīyah	196,519
Irbīl	485,968
Karbalā'	296,705
Karkūk	418,624
Al-Kūt	183,183
Mosul	664,221
An-Najaf	309,010
An-Nāşirīyah	265,937
Ar-Ramādī	192,556
As-Sulaymānīyah	364,096
Ireland (1991)	
Cork	127,253[31]
★ Dublin	478,389[31]
Isle of Man (1991)	
★ Douglas	22,214
Israel (1996 est.)	
Ashdod	128,400
Bat Yam	142,300
Beersheba (Be'er Sheva')	152,600
Bene Beraq	128,600
Haifa (Ḥefa)	252,300
Ḥolon	163,900
★ Jerusalem (Yerushalayim, Al-Quds)	591,400
Netanya	148,400
Petaḥ Tiqwa	153,100
Ramat Gan	121,700
Rishon LeZiyyon	165,300
Tel Aviv–Yafo	355,900
Italy (1994 est.; MU)	
Ancona	100,597
Bari	338,949
Bergamo	115,889
Bologna	394,969
Brescia	191,875
Cagliari	178,063
Catania	327,163
Ferrara	137,384
Florence (Firenze)	392,800
Foggia	155,892
Forlì	108,693
Genoa (Genova)	659,754
Latina	108,819
Lecce	100,474
Livorno	165,536
Messina	233,845
Milan (Milano)	1,334,171
Modena	176,588
Monza	120,882
Naples (Napoli)	1,061,583
Novara	102,768
Padua (Padova)	212,589
Palermo	694,749
Parma	169,299
Perugia	147,489
Pescara	120,613
Piacenza	101,692
Prato	166,305
Ravenna	133,604
Reggio di Calabria	178,736
Reggio nell'Emilia	134,169
Rimini	130,006
★ Rome (Roma)	2,687,881
Salerno	146,546
Sassari	122,010
Siracusa (Syracuse)	127,496
Taranto	213,933
Terni	108,294
Trento	103,063
Trieste	226,707
Turin (Torino)	945,551
Venice (Venezia)	306,439
Verona	256,756
Vicenza	108,013
Jamaica (1991)	
★ Kingston	103,771[32]
Japan (1995)	
Abiko	124,255
Ageo	206,099
Aizuwakamatsu	119,632
Akashi	287,613
Akishima	107,289
Akita	312,035
Amagasaki	488,574
Anjō	149,459
Aomori	294,165
Asahikawa	360,569
Asaka	110,793
Ashikaga	165,830
Atsugi	208,622
Beppu	128,251
Chiba	856,882
Chigasaki	212,944
Chōfu	198,524
Daitō	128,840
Ebetsu	115,491
Ebina	113,416
Fuchu	216,202
Fuji	229,189
Fujieda	124,822
Fujinomiya	119,536
Fujisawa	368,636
Fukaya	100,271
Fukui	255,601
Fukuoka	1,284,741
Fukushima	285,745
Fukuyama	374,510
Funabashi	540,814
Gifu	407,145
Habikino	117,728
Hachinohe	242,657
Hachiōji	503,320
Hadano	164,703
Hakodate	298,868
Hamamatsu	561,568
Handa	106,451
Higashi-Hiroshima	113,935
Higashi-Kurume	111,076
Higashi-Murayama	135,115
Higashi-Ōsaka	517,228
Hikone	103,508
Himeji	470,986
Hino	166,429
Hirakata	400,130
Hiratsuka	253,818
Hirosaki	177,971
Hiroshima	1,108,868
Hitachi	199,241
Hōfu	118,802
Hoya	100,259
Ibaraki	258,237
Ichihara	277,080
Ichikawa	440,527
Ichinomiya	267,359
Iida	106,774
Ikeda	104,292
Ikoma	106,727
Imabari	120,215
Iruma	144,401
Ise	102,631
Isesaki	120,235
Ishinomaki	121,209
Itami	188,436
Iwaki	360,497
Iwakuni	107,386
Iwatsuki	109,551
Izumi	157,301
Joetsu	132,202
Kadoma	140,507
Kagoshima	546,294
Kakamigahara	131,955
Kakogawa	260,558
Kamakura	170,319
Kanazawa	453,977
Kariya	125,307
Kashihara	121,987
Kashiwa	317,752
Kasugai	277,579
Kasukabe	200,130
Kawachi-Nagano	117,082
Kawagoe	323,345
Kawaguchi	448,801
Kawanishi	144,539
Kawasaki	1,202,811
Kiryū	120,375
Kisarazu	123,499
Kishiwada	194,820
Kita-Kyūshū	1,019,562
Kitami	110,449
Kobe	1,423,830
Kochi	322,077
Kodaira	173,032
Kofu	201,123
Koganei	109,275
Kokubunji	105,781
Komaki	137,163
Komatsu	107,964
Koriyama	326,831
Koshigaya	298,285
Kumagaya	156,395
Kumamoto	650,322
Kurashiki	422,824
Kure	209,477
Kurume	234,433
Kusatsu	101,827
Kushiro	199,325
Kuwana	103,049
Kyōto	1,463,601
Machida	360,418
Maebashi	284,780
Matsubara	134,457
Matsudo	461,489
Matsue	147,414
Matsumoto	205,532
Matsusaka	122,449
Matsuyama	460,870
Minō	127,540
Misato	133,601
Mishima	107,890
Mitaka	165,739
Mito	246,350
Miyakonojō	132,712
Miyazaki	300,054
Moriguchi	157,290
Morioka	286,478
Muroran	109,767
Musashino	135,026
Nagano	358,512
Nagaoka	190,470
Nagareyama	146,250
Nagasaki	438,724
Nagoya	2,152,258
Naha	301,928
Nara	359,234
Narashino	152,884
Neyagawa	258,440
Niigata	494,785
Niihama	127,916
Niiza	144,735
Nishinomiya	390,388
Nobeoka	126,628
Noda	119,791
Numazu	212,245
Obihiro	171,714
Odawara	200,092
Ōgaki	149,758
Ōita	426,981
Okayama	616,056
Okazaki	322,615
Okinawa	115,342
Ōme	137,208
Ōmiya	433,768
Ōmuta	145,085
Ōsaka	2,602,352
Ōta	143,067
Otaru	157,024
Ōtsu	276,331
Oyama	150,114
Saga	171,219
Sagamihara	570,594
Sakai	802,965
Sakata	101,224
Sakura	162,624
Sapporo	1,756,968
Sasebo	244,879
Sayama	162,232
Sendai	971,263
Seto	129,396
Shimizu	240,172
Shimonoseki	259,791
Shizuoka	474,089
Sōka	217,912

Major cities and national capitals (continued)

country city	population
Suita	342,794
Suzuka	179,795
Tachikawa	157,892
Tajimi	101,274
Takamatsu	330,997
Takaoka	173,612
Takarazuka	202,547
Takasaki	238,132
Takatsuki	362,259
Tama	148,127
Tokorozawa	320,448
Tokushima	268,712
Tokuyama	108,675
★ Tokyo	7,966,195
Tomakomai	169,324
Tondabayashi	121,690
Tottori	146,336
Toyama	325,303
Toyohashi	352,913
Toyokawa	114,379
Toyonaka	398,912
Toyota	341,038
Tsu	163,309
Tsuchiura	132,246
Tsukuba	156,009
Tsuruoka	100,538
Ube	175,113
Ueda	123,282
Uji	184,829
Urawa	453,300
Urayasu	123,660
Utsunomiya	435,446
Wakayama	393,951
Yachiyo	154,507
Yaizu	115,932
Yamagata	254,485
Yamaguchi	135,581
Yamato	203,920
Yao	276,658
Yatsushiro	107,708
Yokkaichi	285,777
Yokohama	3,307,408
Yokosuka	432,202
Yonago	134,769
Zama	118,146
Jersey (1991)	
★ St. Helier	28,123
Jordan (1994)	
★ Amman	963,490
Irbid	208,201
Al-Mafraq	109,841[21]
Ar-Ruṣayfah	131,130
As-Salṭ	187,014[21]
Az-Zarqāʾ	344,524
Kazakstan (1995 est.)	
Aktau (Aqtaū; (Shevchenko)	151,300
★ Almaty (Alma-Ata)	1,150,500
Aqmola (Akmola; Tselinograd)	280,200
Aqtöbe (Aktyubinsk)	258,900
Atyraū (Guryev)	146,900
Auliye-Ata (Dzhambul)	310,600
Ekibastuz	141,100
Kökshetaū (Kokchetav)	141,400
Oral (Uralsk)	219,100
Öskemen (Ust-Kamenogorsk)	326,300
Pavlodar	340,700
Petropavl (Petropavlovsk)	239,000
Qaraghandy (Karaganda)	573,700
Qostanay (Kustanay)	232,100
Qyzylord (Kzyl-Orda)	162,000
Rūdny	125,700
Semey (Semipalatinsk)	320,200
Shymkent (Shimkent; Chimkent)	397,600
Taldyqorghan (Taldy-Kurgan)	116,100
Temirtaū	206,100
Zhezqazghan (Zhezkazgan; Dzhezkazgan)	108,700
Kenya (1991 est.)	
Kisumu	201,100
Mombasa	600,000
★ Nairobi	2,000,000
Nakuru	124,200
Kiribati (1990)	
★ Bairiki	2,226
Korea, North (1987 est.)	
Anju	186,000
Ch'ŏngjin	520,000
Haeju	195,000
Hamhŭng-Hungnam	701,000
Hŭich'ŏn	163,000
Kaesŏng	120,000
Kanggye	211,000
Kimch'aek (Songjin)	179,000
Kusŏng	177,000
Namp'o	370,000
★ P'yŏngyang	2,355,000
Sinp'o	158,000
Sinŭiju	289,000
Sunch'ŏn	356,000
Tanch'ŏn	284,000
Tŏkch'ŏn	217,000
Wŏnsan	274,000
Korea, South (1995)	
Andong	188,452
Ansan	510,317
Anyang	590,996
Asan	154,635
Ch'angwŏn	481,678
Chech'ŏn	137,065
Cheju	258,509
Chinhae	125,997
Chinju	329,913
Ch'ŏnan	330,509
Ch'ŏngju	531,195
Chŏng-ŭp	139,084
Chŏnju	563,406
Ch'unch'ŏn	235,067
Ch'ungju	205,131
Hanam	115,805
Iksan	322,749
Inch'ŏn	2,307,618
Iri	203,382
Kangnŭng	220,430
Kimch'ŏn	146,996
Kimhae	256,270
Kimje	115,430
Kŏje	147,551
Kongju	131,220
Koyang	518,269
Kumi	311,488
Kunp'o	235,194
Kunsan	266,517
Kuri	142,299
Kwangju	1,257,504
Kwangmyŏng	350,902
Kwangyang	122,061
Kyŏngju	273,819
Kyŏngsan	173,762
Masan	441,358
Miryang	121,502
Mokp'o	247,524
Naju	107,831
Namwon	103,538
Namyangju	228,931
P'ohang	508,983
Poryŏng	122,631
Puch'ŏn	779,476
Pusan	3,813,814
P'yŏngt'aek	312,938
Sach'ŏn	113,492
Sangju	124,136
★ Seoul (Sŏul)	10,229,262
Shihŭng	133,411
Sŏngnam	869,243
Sŏsan	134,758
Sunch'ŏn	249,241
Suwŏn	755,502
Taegu	2,449,139
Taejŏn	1,272,143
Tongyŏng	131,716
Ŭijŏngbu	276,255
Ŭiwang	108,761
Ulsan	967,394
Wŏnju	237,423
Yŏngch'ŏn	113,510
Yŏngju	131,090
Yŏsu	183,557
Kuwait (1993 est.)	
Al-Jahra	139,476
★ Kuwait (Al-Kuwayt)	31,241
As-Sālimīyah	116,104
Kyrgyzstan (1994 est.)	
★ Bishkek (Frunze)	597,000
Osh	238,200[17]
Laos (1990 est.; MU)	
★ Vientiane (Viangchan)	442,000
Latvia (1995 est.)	
Daugavpils	120,152
Liepāja	100,271
★ Rīga	839,670
Lebanon (1991 est.)	
★ Beirut (Bayrūt)	1,100,000[21]
Jūniyah	100,000
an-Nabaṭīyah	100,000[30]
Sidon (Ṣaydā)	100,000[30]
Tripoli (Ṭarābulus)	240,000
Zaḥlah	200,000[30]
Lesotho (1990 est.)	
★ Maseru	170,000[21]
Liberia (1990 est.)	
★ Monrovia	668,000[21]
Libya (1988 est.)	
Banghāzī	446,250
Misrātah	121,669
★ Tripoli (Ṭarābulus)	591,062
Liechtenstein (1995 est.)	
★ Vaduz	5,067
Lithuania (1993 est.)	
Kaunas	429,000
Klaipėda	206,400
Panevėžys	132,000
Šiauliai	147,800
★ Vilnius	590,100
Luxembourg (1995 est.)	
★ Luxembourg	76,446
Macau (1991)	
★ Macau (Santo Nome de Deus)	326,460
Macedonia (1994; MU)	
Bitola	106,012
Giostivar	108,189
Kumanovo	126,543
★ Skopje (Skopije)	541,280
Tetovo	174,748
Madagascar (1993)	
★ Antananarivo	1,052,835
Antsirabe	120,239
Mahajanga	100,807
Toamasina	127,441
Malaŵi (1994 est.)	
★ Blantyre (executive; judicial)	446,800[33]
★ Lilongwe (ministerial; financial)	395,500
★ Zomba (legislative)	62,700
Malaysia (1991)	
Alor Setar	125,026
George Town (Pinang)	219,376
Ipoh	382,633
Johor Baharu	328,646
Kelang	243,698
Kota Baharu	219,713
Kota Kinabalu	208,484
★ Kuala Lumpur	1,145,075
Kuala Terengganu	228,659
Kuantan	198,356
Kuching	147,729
Melaka	295,999
Petaling Jaya	254,849
Port Kelang	192,080
Sandakan	223,432
Seloyang Baru	124,606
Seremban	182,584
Shah Alam	101,733
Sibu	126,384
Taiping	183,165
Tawai	244,765
Maldives (1995 est.)	
★ Male'	62,973
Mali (1995 est.)	
★ Bamako	800,000
Malta (1995 est.)	
★ Valletta	9,129
Marshall Is. (1990 est.)	
★ Majuro	20,000
Martinique (1990)	
★ Fort-de-France	101,540
Mauritania (1995 est.)	
★ Nouakchott	735,000
Mauritius (1994 est.)	
★ Port Louis	144,776
Mayotte (1991; MU)	
★ Mamoudzou	20,274
★ Dzaoudzi	8,268
Mexico (1990)	
Acapulco	515,374
Aguascalientes	440,425
Atizapán de Zaragoza (Ciudad López Mateos)	315,059
Campeche	150,518
Cancún	167,730
Celaya	214,856
Chihuahua	516,153
Ciudad Apodaca	103,364
Ciudad Madero	160,331
Ciudad Obregón	219,980
Ciudad Santa Catarina	162,707
Ciudad Victoria	194,996
Coatzacoalcos	198,817
Colima	106,967
Córdoba	130,695
Cuautla	110,242
Cuernavaca	279,187
Culiacán	415,046
Durango	348,036
Ensenada	169,426
Gómez Palacio	164,092
Guadalajara	1,650,042
Guadalupe	535,332
Hermosillo	406,417
Heroica Nogales	105,873
Irapuato	265,042
Juárez	789,522
La Paz	137,641
León	758,279
Los Mochis	162,659
Matamoros	266,055
Mazatlán	262,705
Mérida	523,422
Mexicali	438,377
★ Mexico City	9,815,795
Minatitlán	142,060
Monclova	177,792
Monterrey	1,068,996
Morelia	428,486
Nezahualcóyotl	1,255,456
Nuevo Laredo	218,413
Oaxaca	212,818
Orizaba	114,216
Pachuca	174,013
Poza Rica	151,739
Puebla	1,007,170
Querétaro	385,503
Reynosa	265,663
Salamanca	123,190
Saltillo	420,947
San Luis Potosí	488,238
San Nicolás de los Garza	436,603
San Pedro Garza García	113,017
Soledad de Graciano Sanchez	123,943
Tampico	272,690
Tapachula	138,858
Tehuacán	139,450
Tepic	206,967
Tijuana	698,752
Tlaquepaque	328,031
Toluca	327,865
Tonala	151,190
Torreón	439,436
Tuxtla	289,626
Uruapan	187,623
Veracruz	438,821
Villahermosa	261,231
Xalapa (Jalapa) Enríquez	279,451
Zacatecas	100,051
Zamora de Hidalgo	109,751
Zapopan	668,323
Micronesia	
★ Palikir	—
Moldova (1991 est.)	
Bălţi (Beltsy)	164,900
★ Chişinău (Kishinyov)	662,000[8]
Tighina (Bendery)	141,500
Tiraspol	186,000
Monaco (1996 est.)	
★ Monaco	30,500[27]
Mongolia (1993 est.)	
★ Ulaanbaatar (Ulan Bator)	619,000
Morocco (1993 est.)	
Agadir	137,000
Beni-Mellal	139,000
Casablanca (Dar el-Beida)	2,943,000
Fès (Fez)	564,000
el-Jadida (Mazagan)	125,000
Kenitra	234,000
Khouribga	190,000
Marrakech	602,000
Meknès	401,000
Mohammedia	156,000
Oujda	331,000
★ Rabat	1,220,000
Safi	278,000
Salé	521,000
Tanger	307,000
Tétouan	272,000
Mozambique (1991 est.)	
Beira	298,847
Chimoio	108,818
★ Maputo (Lourenço Marques)	931,591
Matala	337,239
Nacala	125,208
Nampula	250,473
Quelimane	146,206
Tete	112,221
Myanmar (Burma) (1983)	
Bassein (Pathein)	144,096
Mandalay	532,949
Monywa	106,843
Moulmein (Mawlamyine)	219,961
Pegu (Bago)	150,528
Sittwe (Akyab)	107,621
Taunggye	108,231
★ Yangon (Rangoon)	3,851,000[5]
Namibia (1992 est.)	
★ Windhoek	161,000
Nauru (1983)	
★ Yaren	559
Nepal (1993 est.; MU)	
Bhaktapur (Bhādgāon)	130,000
Birātnagar	132,000
★ Kāthmāndu	535,000
Lalitpur (Patan)	190,000
Netherlands, The (1995 est.)	
Almere	104,621
Amersfoort	112,288
★ Amsterdam (capital)	722,245
Apeldoorn	149,904
Arnhem	134,499
Breda	129,957
Dordrecht	114,152
Eindhoven	197,055
Enschede	147,924
Groningen	170,748
Haarlem	148,947
Haarlemmermeer	104,364
Leiden	115,473
Maastricht	118,341
Nijmegen	147,365
Rotterdam	599,414
★ The Hague (seat of government)	442,105
Tilburg	164,144
Utrecht	235,357
Zaanstad	133,536
Zoetermeer	105,126
Zwolle	100,196
Netherlands Antilles (1993 est.)	
★ Willemstad	197,019[21]
New Caledonia (1989)	
★ Nouméa	65,110
New Zealand (1996)	
Auckland	353,670
Christchurch	313,969
Dunedin	121,100[5]
Hamilton	106,700[5]
Manukau	254,577
North Shore	170,913
Waitakere	147,500[5]
★ Wellington	158,275
Nicaragua (1994 est.; MU)	
Chinandega	101,211
León	171,375
★ Managua	1,195,000[5]
Masaya	100,646
Niger (1988)	
Maradi	110,005
★ Niamey	391,876
Zinder	119,827
Nigeria (1995 est.)[34]	
Aba	291,600
Abeokuta	416,800
★ Abuja (capital designate)	339,100[35]
Ado-Ekiti	350,500
Agege	100,300
Akure	158,200
Awka	108,400
Benin City	223,900
Bida	122,500
Calabar	170,000
Deba Habe	135,400
Ede	299,500
Effon-Alaiye	149,300
Ejigbo	103,300
Enugu	308,200
Gombe	105,200
Gusau	154,000
Ibadan	1,365,000
Ife	289,500
Igboho	104,100
Ijebu-Ode	152,500
Ikare	137,300
Ikerre	238,500
Ikire	120,200
Ikirun	177,000
Ikorodu	180,300
Ila	257,400
Ilawe-Ekiti	179,900
Ilesha	369,000
Ilobu	194,400
Ilorin	464,000
Inisa	116,800
Ise-Ekiti	127,100
Iseyin	211,800
Iwo	353,000
Jos	201,200
Kaduna	333,600
Kano	657,300
Katsina	201,500
Kumo	144,400
Lafia	119,500
★ Lagos	1,484,000
Maiduguri	312,100
Makurdi	120,100
Minna	133,600
Mushin	324,900
Offa	192,300
Ogbomosho	711,900
Oka	139,600
Ondo	165,400
Onitsha	362,700
Oshogbo	465,000
Owo	178,900
Oyo	250,100
Port Harcourt	399,700
Sapele	135,800
Shagamu	114,300
Shaki	169,700
Shomolu	144,100
Sokoto	199,900
Ugep	100,000

country city	population
Warri	122,900
Zaria	369,800
Northern Mariana Is. (1990)	
★ Saipan	38,896
Norway (1996 est.; MU)	
Bergen	223,100
★ Oslo	487,908
Stavanger	104,322
Trondheim	143,746
Oman (1993)	
★ Muscat	51,969
Pakistan (1981)	
Bahāwalpur	180,263
Chiniot	105,559
Dera Ghāzi Khān	102,007
Faisalābād (Lyallpur)	1,875,000[5]
Gujrānwāla	1,663,000[5]
Gujrāt	155,058
Hyderābād	1,107,000[5]
★ Islamābād	204,364
Jhang	195,558
Jhelum	106,462
Karāchi	9,863,000[5]
Kasūr	155,523
Lahore	5,085,000[5]
Lahore Cantonment	237,000
Lārkāna	123,890
Mardān	147,977
Mīrpur Khās	124,371
Multān	1,257,000[5]
Nawābshāh	102,139
Okāra	153,483
Peshāwar	1,676,000[5]
Quetta	285,719
Rahīm Yār Khān	119,036
Rāwalpindi	1,290,000[5]
Sāhiwāl	150,954
Sargodha	291,362
Sheikhūpura	141,168
Siālkot	302,009
Sukkur	190,551
Wāh Cantonment	122,335
Palau (1992 est.)	
Koror	10,500
Panama (1994 est.)	
Colón	137,825[36]
★ Panama City	445,902
San Miguelito	282,428
Papua New Guinea (1990)	
★ Port Moresby (National Capital District)	193,242
Paraguay (1992)	
★ Asunción	502,426
Ciudad del Este	133,893
San Lorenzo	133,311
Peru (1993)	
Arequipa	619,156
Ayacucho	105,918
Callao	615,046
Chiclayo	411,536
Chimbote	268,979
Chincha Alta	110,016
Cuzco	255,568
Huancayo	258,209
Huánuco	118,814
Ica	161,406
Iquitos	274,759
Juliaca	142,576
★ Lima	421,570[19]
Metro Lima-Callao	5,706,127
Piura	277,964
Pucallpa	172,286
Sullana	147,361
Tacna	174,336
Trujillo	509,312
Philippines (1994 est.)	
Angeles	276,545
Bacolod	343,048
Bago	139,771
Baguio	169,565
Batangas	190,627
Butuan	244,900
Cabanatuan	185,728
Cadiz	143,299
Cagayan de Oro	413,689
Calbayog	130,321
Caloocan	642,670
Cavite	103,422
Cebu	688,196
Cotabato	112,934
Dagupan	116,936
Davao	960,910
General Santos	279,343
Gingoog	111,326
Iligan	209,639
Iloilo	302,200
Lapu-Lapu	141,009
Las Piñas	380,482
Legaspi	125,128
Lipa	159,769
Lucena	161,049
Makati	453,000[13]
Malabon	277,000[13]
Mandaluyong	247,000[13]
Mandaue	212,987
★ Manila	1,894,667[17]
Metro Manila	8,594,150
Marikina	308,000[13]
Muntilupa	275,056
Naga	102,545
Navotas	187,000[13]
Olongapo	208,633
Ormoc	142,092
Pagadian	113,905
Parañaque	308,000[13]
Pasay	388,129
Pasig	395,000[13]
Quezon City	1,676,644
Roxas	111,649
San Carlos (*Negros Occidental*)	106,000[13]
San Carlos (*Pangasinan*)	123,473
San Juan del Monte	127,000[13]
San Pablo	163,297
Silay	140,175
Tacloban	153,068
Tagig	267,000[13]
Toledo	125,978
Valenzuela	340,000[13]
Zamboanga	464,466
Poland (1995 est.)	
Białystok	277,100
Bielsko-Biała	180,300
Bydgoszcz	385,700
Bytom	228,200
Chorzów	126,500
Czestochowa	259,800
Dąbrowa Górnicza	131,000
Elbląg	128,500
Gdańsk	463,100
Gdynia	251,400
Gliwice	214,200
Gorzów Wielkopolski	124,800
Grudziadz	103,700
Jastrzębie-Zdrój	103,500
Kalisz	106,800
Katowice	355,100
Kielce	213,800
Koszalin	111,700
Kraków	746,000
Legnica	107,800
Łódź	828,500
Lublin	352,500
Olsztyn	167,000
Opole	130,600
Płock	126,500
Poznań	582,300
Radom	232,300
Ruda Śląska	166,600
Rybnik	144,000
Rzeszów	159,900
Słupsk	102,800
Sosnowiec	248,900
Szczecin	419,600
Tarnów	121,600
Toruń	203,800
Tychy	134,700
Wałbrzych	140,000
★ Warsaw (Warszawa)	1,640,700
Włocławek	123,100
Wrocław	642,900
Zabrze	201,800
Zielona Góra	115,800
Portugal (1991)	
★ Lisbon	677,790
Porto	310,600
Puerto Rico (1995 est.; MU)	
Arecibo	101,050
Bayamón	231,334
Caguas	139,778
Carolina	187,083
Guaynabo	103,866
Mayaguez	101,684
Ponce	190,539
★ San Juan	438,078
Qatar (1992 est.)	
★ Doha	313,639[13]
Réunion (1994 est.)	
★ Saint-Denis	104,454
Romania (1993 est.)	
Arad	188,609
Bacău	206,995
Baia Mare	150,018
Botoşani	127,337
Brăila	236,344
Braşov	324,104
★ Bucharest	2,343,824
Buzău	149,032
Cluj-Napoca	321,850
Constanţa	348,985
Craiova	303,033
Drobeta-Turnu Severin	118,086
Focşani	101,414
Galaţi	324,234
Iaşi	337,643
Oradea	221,559
Piatra Neamţ	125,157
Piteşti	182,931
Ploieşti	254,304
Râmnicu Vâlcea	114,165
Satu Mare	131,386
Sibiu	168,619
Suceava	116,232
Timişoara	325,359
Tirgu Mureş	165,502
Russia (1995 est.)	
Abakan	161,000
Achinsk	123,000
Almetyevsk	138,000
Angarsk	267,000
Anzhero-Sudzhensk	101,000
Arkhangelsk	374,000
Armavir	164,000
Arzamas	112,000
Astrakhan	486,000
Balakovo	206,000
Balashikha	136,000
Barnaul	596,000
Belgorod	322,000
Berezniki	184,000
Biysk	228,000
Blagoveshchensk	214,000
Bratsk	257,000
Bryansk	462,000
Cheboksary	450,000
Chelyabinsk	1,086,000
Cherepovets	320,000
Cherkessk	119,000
Chita	322,000
Dimitrovgrad	135,000
Dzerzhinsk	285,000
Elektrostal	150,000
Engels	186,000
Glazov	107,000
Grozny	364,000[1]
Irkutsk	585,000
Ivanovo	474,000
Izhevsk	654,000
Kaliningrad	419,000
Kaliningrad (*Moscow oblast*)	134,000
Kaluga	347,000
Kamensk-Uralsky	197,000
Kamyshin	128,000
Kansk	109,000
Kazan	1,085,000
Kemerovo	503,000
Khabarovsk	618,000
Khimki	134,000
Kineshma	103,000
Kirov	464,000
Kiselyovsk	116,000
Kislovodsk	120,000
Kolomna	154,000
Kolpino	143,000
Komsomolsk-na-Amure	309,000
Kostroma	285,000
Kovrov	162,000
Krasnodar	646,000
Krasnoyarsk	869,000
Kurgan	363,000
Kursk	442,000
Kuznetsk	100,000
Leninsk-Kuznetsky	121,000
Lipetsk	474,000
Lyubertsy	166,000
Magadan	128,000
Magnitogorsk	427,000
Makhachkala	339,000
Maykop	165,000
Mezhdurechensk	105,000
Miass	167,000
Michurinsk	108,000
★ Moscow	8,717,000
Murmansk	407,000
Murom	126,000
Mytishchi	152,000
Naberezhnye Chelny (Brezhnev)	526,000
Nakhodka	163,000
Nalchik	239,000
Neftekamsk	117,000
Nevinnomyssk	131,000
Nikolo-Beryozovka (Neftekamsk)	117,000
Nizhnekamsk	210,000
Nizhnevartovsk	238,000
Nizhny Novgorod (Gorky)	1,383,000
Nizhny Tagil	409,000
Noginsk	119,000
Norilsk	159,000
Novgorod	233,000
Novocheboksarsk	123,000
Novocherkassk	190,000
Novokuybyshevsk	115,000
Novokuznetsk	572,000
Novomoskovsk (*Tula oblast*)	144,000
Novorossiysk	202,000
Novoshakhtinsk	107,000
Novosibirsk	1,369,000
Novotroitsk	110,000
Obninsk	108,000
Odintsovo	129,000
Oktyabrsky	110,000
Omsk	1,163,000
Orekhovo-Zuyevo	126,000
Orenburg	532,000
Orsk	275,000
Oryol	348,000
Penza	534,000
Perm	1,032,000
Pervouralsk	137,000
Petropavlovsk-Kamchatsky	210,000
Petrozavodsk	280,000
Podolsk	202,000
Prokopyevsk	253,000
Pskov	207,000
Pyatigorsk	133,000
Rostov-na-Donu	1,026,000
Rubtsovsk	170,000
Ryazan	536,000
Rybinsk (Andropov)	248,000
Saint Petersburg (Leningrad)	4,838,000
Salavat	156,000
Samara (Kuybyshev)	1,184,000
Saransk	320,000
Sarapul	109,000
Saratov	895,000
Sergiev Posad (Zagorsk)	114,000
Serov	100,000
Serpukhov	139,000
Severodvinsk	241,000
Seversk	110,000
Shakhty	230,000
Shchyolkovo	108,000
Simbirsk (Ulyanovsk)	678,000
Smolensk	355,000
Sochi	355,000
Solikamsk	108,000
Stary Oskol	198,000
Stavropol	342,000
Sterlitamak	259,000
Surgut	263,000
Syktyvkar	229,000
Syzran	177,000
Taganrog	292,000
Tambov	316,000
Tolyatti	702,000
Tomsk	470,000
Tula	532,000
Tver (Kalinin)	455,000
Tyumen	494,000
Ufa	1,094,000
Ukhta	106,000
Ulan-Ude	366,000
Usolye-Sibirskoye	106,000
Ussuriysk	162,000
Ust-Ilimsk	110,000
Velikiye Luki	116,000
Vladikavkaz (Ordzhonikidze)	312,000
Vladimir	339,000
Vladivostok	632,000
Volgodonsk	183,000
Volgograd	1,003,000
Vologda	299,000
Volzhsky	288,000
Vorkuta	104,000
Voronezh	908,000
Votkinsk	104,000
Yakutsk	192,000
Yaroslavl	629,000
Yekaterinburg (Sverdlovsk)	1,280,000
Yelets	119,000
Yoshkar-Ola	251,000
Yuzhno-Sakhalinsk	160,000
Zelenodolysk	101,000
Zelenograd	191,000
Zlatoust	203,000
Rwanda (1991)	
★ Kigali	232,733
St. Kitts and Nevis (1990 est.)	
★ Basseterre	15,000
St. Lucia (1992 est.)	
★ Castries	13,615[37]
St. Vincent and The Grenadines (1991)	
★ Kingstown	15,466
San Marino (1996 est.)	
★ San Marino	2,316
São Tomé and Príncipe (1990 est.)	
★ São Tomé	43,420
Saudi Arabia (1980 est.)	
Ad-Dammām	200,000
Jiddah	1,800,000[30]
Mecca (Makkah)	550,000
Medina (Al-Madinah)	290,000
★ Riyadh (Ar-Riyad)	1,800,000[30]
Aṭ-Ṭā'if	300,000
Senegal (1994 est.)	
★ Dakar	785,071
Kaolack	193,115
Mboure	106,046
Rufisque	138,837
St.-Louis	132,444
Thiès	216,381
Ziguinchor	161,680
Seychelles (1993 est.)	
★ Victoria	25,000
Sierra Leone (1990 est.)	
★ Freetown	669,000[21]
Singapore (1996 est.)[27]	
★ Singapore	3,045,000
Slovakia (1995 est.)	
★ Bratislava	450,776
Košice	239,927
Slovenia (1995 est.)	
★ Ljubljana	276,119
Maribor	134,979
Solomon Islands (1996 est.)	
★ Honiara	43,643
Somalia (1990 est.)	
★ Mogadishu	900,000
South Africa (1991)	
Alexandra	124,586
Benoni	113,501
★ Bloemfontein (judicial)	126,867
Boksburg	119,890
Botshabelo	177,926
★ Cape Town (legislative)	854,616
Carletonville	118,699
Daveyton	151,659
Diepmeadow	241,099
Durban	715,669
East London	102,325
Evaton	201,026
Germiston	134,005
Ibhayi	257,054
Johannesburg	712,507
Kathlehong (Katlehong)	201,785
Kempton Park	106,606
Khayelitsa	189,586
Kwamashu (Kwa Mashu)	156,679
Lekoa	217,582
Mamelodi	154,845
Manguang (Mangaung)	125,545
Mdantsane	242,823
Ntuzuma	102,310
Pietermaritzburg	156,473
Port Elizabeth	303,353
★ Pretoria (executive)	525,583
Roodepoort	162,632
Sandton	101,197
Soshanguve	146,334
Soweto	596,632
Tembisa	209,238
Umlazi	299,275
Spain (1994 est.; MU)	
Albacete	141,179
Alcalá de Henares	166,250
Alcorcón	142,165
Algeciras	103,787
Alicante	274,964
Almería	167,361
Badajoz	130,153
Badalona	219,340
Barakaldo	103,594
Barcelona	1,630,867
Bilbao	371,787
Burgos	166,251
Cádiz	155,438
Cartagena	179,659
Castellón de la Plana	139,094
Córdoba	315,948
Coruña, La	255,087
Donostia (San Sebastián)	177,929
Elche (Elx)	191,305
Fuenlabrada	158,212
Getafe	144,368
Gijón	269,644
Granada	271,180
Hospitalet de Llobregat	266,242
Huelva	145,049
Jaén	112,772
Jerez de la Frontera	190,390
Leganés	178,162
León	147,311
Lleida (Lérida)	114,234
Logroño	124,823
★ Madrid	3,041,101
Málaga	531,443
Mataró	102,117
Móstoles	199,141
Murcia	341,531
Ourense (Orense)	108,547
Oviedo	201,712
Palma (de Mallorca)	322,008
Palmas de Gran Canaria, Las (Is. Canarias)	371,787

Major cities and national capitals (continued)

country / city	population
Pamplona	182,465
Sabadell	189,006
Salamanca	167,382
Santa Coloma de Gramanet	131,764
Santa Cruz de Tenerife	203,929
Santander	194,822
Sevilla (Seville)	714,148
Tarragona	114,630
Terrassa	161,428
Valencia	764,293
Valladolid	336,917
Vigo	288,573
Vitoria (Gasteiz)	214,148
Zaragoza (Saragossa)	606,620
Sri Lanka (1990 est.)	
★ Colombo (administrative)	615,000
Dehiwala-Mount Lavinia	196,000
Jaffna	129,000
Kandy	104,000
Moratuwa	170,000
★ Sri Jayawardenepura Kotte (legislative and judicial)	109,000[38]
Sudan, The (1993)	
Juba	114,980
Kassalā	234,270
★ Khartoum (executive)	924,505
Khartoum North	879,105
Nyala	228,778
★ Omdurman (legislative)	1,267,077
Port Sudan	305,385
al-Qaḍārif	189,384
al-Ubayyiḍ	228,096
Wad Madanī	218,714
Wāw	116,000[39]
Suriname (1993 est.)	
★ Paramaribo	200,970
Swaziland (1990 est.)	
★ Lobamba (legislative)	...
★ Lozitha (royal)	...
★ Ludzidzini (royal)	...
★ Mbabane (administrative)	47,000
Sweden (1996 est.; MU)	
Göteborg	449,189
Helsingborg	114,339
Jönköping	115,429
Linköping	131,370
Malmö	245,699
Norrköping	123,795
Örebro	119,635
★ Stockholm	711,119
Umeå	101,337
Uppsala	183,472
Västerås	123,728
Switzerland (1995 est.)	
Basel (Bâle)	175,561
★ Bern (Berne)	128,422
Geneva (Genève)	172,737
Lausanne	116,795
Zürich	342,872
Syria (1994 est.)	
Aleppo (Ḥalab)	1,591,400
★ Damascus (Dimashq)	1,549,932
Dar'ā	180,093
Dayr az-Zawr	174,085
Dūmā	131,158
Ḥamāh	229,000[36]
Al-Ḥasakah	106,000[36]
Homs (Ḥims)	644,204
Jaramānah	138,469
Latakia (al-Ladhiqiyah)	306,535
Al-Qāmishlī	151,000[36]
Ar-Raqqah	219,016
Ṭarṭūs	136,812
Taiwan (1996 est.)	
Chang-hua	221,090[8]
Chi-lung (Keelung)	370,049
Chia-i	261,941
Chung-ho	387,123[5]
Chung-li	295,825[5]
Feng-shan (Kao-hsiung-hsien)	301,374[5]
Fêng-yüan	157,548[5]
Hsin-chu	341,128
Hsin-chuang	328,758[5]
Hsin-tien	248,822[5]
Hua-lien	107,824[5]
Kao-hsiung	1,426,518
Pan-ch'iao (T'ai-pei-hsien)	539,115[5]
P'ing-tung	214,728[5]
San-chu'ung	382,880[5]
T'ai-chung	857,590
T'ai-nan	707,658
T'ai-tung	109,189[5]
★ Taipei (T'ai-pei)	2,626,138
T'ao-yuan	260,680[5]
Yung-ho	241,104[5]
Tajikistan (1994 est.)	
★ Dushanbe	524,000
Khujand (Khudzhand; Leninabad)	164,500[17]
Tanzania (1988)	
Arusha	134,708
★ Dar es Salaam	1,360,850
★ Dodoma (legislative)	203,833
Mbeya	152,844
Morogoro	117,760
Mwanza	223,013
Shinyanga	100,724
Tanga	187,155
Zanzibar	157,634
Thailand (1993 est.)	
★ Bangkok	5,584,228[8]
Chiang Mai	170,397
Hat Yai	148,632
Nakhon Ratchasima	188,171
Nonthaburi	261,335
Ubon Ratchathani	105,936
Togo (1990 est.)	
★ Lomé	513,000[21]
Tonga (1990 est.)	
★ Nuku'alofa	34,000
Trinidad and Tobago (1992 est.)	
★ Port-of-Spain	52,451
Tunisia (1994)	
Aryānah	152,700
Ettadhamen	149,200
Kairouan	102,600
Ṣafāqis (Sfax)	230,900
Sūsah	125,000
★ Tunis	674,100
Turkey (1994 est.)	
Adana	1,047,300
Adapazari	186,000
Adıyaman	128,000
★ Ankara	2,782,200
Antakya	137,200
Antalya	497,200
Aydın	121,200
Balıkesir	187,600
Batman	182,800
Bursa	996,600
Çorum	116,810[13]
Denizli	234,500
Diyarbakır	448,300
Edirne	115,500
Elaziğ	222,800
Erzurum	250,100
Eskişehir	451,000
Gaziantep	716,000
Gebze	237,300
Hatay	133,474[1]
İçel	422,357[13]
İskenderun	156,800
Isparta	120,900
İstanbul	7,615,500
İzmir	1,985,300
İzmit	275,800
Kahramanmaraş	242,200
Karabük	113,900
Kayseri	454,000
Kırıkkale	170,300
Kocaeli	256,882[13]
Konya	576,000
Kütahya	140,700
Malatya	319,700
Manisa	187,500
Mersin	523,000
Ordu	121,300
Osmaniye	138,000
Samsun	326,900
Sivas	240,100
Tarsus	225,000
Trabzon	145,400
Urfa (Şanlıurfa)	357,900
Uşak	119,900
Van	194,600
Zonguldak	115,900
Turkmenistan (1994 est.)	
★ Ashkhabad (Ashgabat)	518,000
Chärjew (Chardzhev; Chardzhou)	166,400[17]
Dashhowuz (Dashkhovuz; Tashauz)	117,000[17]
Tuvalu (1991)	
★ Funafuti	3,839
Uganda (1991)	
★ Kampala	773,463
Ukraine (1996 est.)	
Alchevsk	124,000
Berdyansk	135,000
Bila Tserkva (Belaya Tserkov)	216,000
Cherkasy (Cherkassy)	312,000
Chernihiv (Chernigov)	312,000
Chernivtsi (Chernovtsy)	261,000
Dniprodzerzhynsk (Dneprodzerzhinsk)	281,000
Dnipropetrovsk (Dnepropetrovsk)	1,147,000
Donetsk	1,088,000
Horlivka (Gorlovka)	322,000
Ivano-Frankivsk (Ivano-Frankovsk)	237,000
Kamyanets-Podilsky (Kamenets-Podolsky)	108,000
Kerch	175,000
Kharkiv (Kharkov)	1,555,000
Kherson	363,000
Khmelnytsky (Khmelnitsky)	259,000
★ Kiev (Kyyiv)	2,630,000
Kirovohrad	276,000
Kostyantynivka (Konstantinovka)	102,000
Kramatorsk	197,000
Krasny Luch	109,000
Kremenchuk (Kremenchug)	246,000
Kryvy Rih (Krivoy Rog)	720,000
Luhansk (Voroshilovgrad)	487,000
Lutsk	219,000
Lviv (Lvov)	802,000
Lysychansk (Lisichansk)	123,000
Makiyivka (Makeyevka)	409,000
Mariupol (Zhdanov)	510,000
Melitopol	174,000
Mykolayiv (Nikolayev)	508,000
Nikopol	157,000
Odesa (Odessa)	1,046,000
Oleksandriya (Aleksandriya)	103,000
Pavlohrad	134,000
Poltava	321,000
Rivne (Rovno)	246,000
Sevastopol	365,000
Severodonetsk	132,000
Simferopol	348,000
Slovyansk (Slavyansk)	133,000
Stakhanov	109,000
Sumy	304,000
Ternopil (Ternopol)	235,000
Uzhhorod	126,000
Vinnytsya (Vinnitsa)	388,000
Yenakiyeve (Yenakiyevo)	114,000
Yevpatoriya	115,000
Zaporizhzhya (Zaporozhye)	882,000
Zhytomyr (Zhitomir)	301,000
United Arab Emirates (1989 est.)	
★ Abu Dhabi (Abū Ẓaby)	363,432
Al-'Ayn	176,441
Dubai (Dubayy)	585,189
Sharjah (Ash-Shāriqah)	125,123[23]
United Kingdom (1994 est.)[40]	
Aberdeen	219,100[5]
Aylesbury	151,600[1]
Barnsley	226,500
Basildon	161,700[1]
Basingstoke/Deane	146,500[1]
Bedford	137,300[1]
Belfast	297,100
Beverley	115,800[1]
Birmingham	1,008,400
Blackburn	139,500[1]
Blackpool	153,600[1]
Bolton	265,200
Bournemouth	159,900[1]
Bracknell	101,900[1]
Bradford	481,700
Braintree	121,800[1]
Brighton	154,400[1]
Bristol	399,200
Bury	181,400[1]
Cambridge	113,800[1]
Canterbury	132,400[1]
Cardiff	300,000
Carlisle	102,900[1]
Chelmsford	155,700[1]
Cheltenham	106,700[1]
Chester	120,800[1]
Chesterfield	101,200[1]
Chichester	102,500[1]
Colchester	149,100[1]
Coventry	302,500
Crewe/Nantwich	109,500[1]
Darlington	100,200[1]
Derby	230,500
Doncaster	292,500
Dover	106,100[1]
Dudley	312,200
Dundee	167,600[5]
Eastleigh	109,600[1]
Edinburgh	447,600[5]
Elmbridge	117,300[1]
Epping Forest	118,200[1]
Exeter	105,100[1]
Fareham	101,000[1]
Gateshead	202,400
Glasgow	674,800[5]
Gloucester	104,800[1]
Guildford	126,200[1]
Harrogate	146,500[1]
Havant	117,500[1]
Horsham	112,300[1]
Huddersfield	148,544[1]
Huntingdon	148,800[1]
Ipswich	114,800[1]
King's Lynn/West Norfolk	131,600[1]
Kingston upon Hull	269,100
Kirklees	386,900
Knowsley	155,300[1]
Lancaster	133,600[1]
Leeds	724,400
Leicester	293,400
Liverpool	474,000
★ London	6,967,500
Luton	178,600[1]
Macclesfield	151,400[1]
Maidstone	138,500[1]
Manchester	431,100
Mansfield	102,100[1]
Middlesbrough	145,800[1]
Milton Keynes	184,400[1]
Newark-on-Trent	104,400[1]
Newbury	141,000[1]
Newcastle under Lyme	123,000[1]
Newcastle upon Tyne	283,600
Newport	137,000[1]
Northampton	187,200[1]
Norwich	128,100[1]
Nottingham	282,400
Nuneaton/Bedworth	118,500[1]
Oldham	220,400
Oxford	132,000[1]
Peterborough	156,400[1]
Plymouth	255,800
Poole	137,200[1]
Portsmouth	189,100[1]
Preston	132,200[1]
Reading	137,700[1]
Reigate/Banstead	118,800[1]
Renfrew	201,700
Rhymney Valley	104,300[1]
Rochdale	207,100
Rochester upon Medway	146,200
Rotherham	256,300
St. Albans	127,700[1]
St. Helens	180,200[1]
Salford	230,700
Salisbury	109,800[1]
Sandwell	293,700
Scarborough	108,700[1]
Sefton	292,400
Sevenoaks	109,400[1]
Sheffield	530,100
Slough	103,500[1]
Solihull	202,000
Southampton	211,700
Southend-on-Sea	167,500[1]
Stafford	121,500[1]
Stockport	291,400
Stockton-on-Tees	177,800[1]
Stoke-on-Trent	254,200
Stratford-on-Avon	108,600[1]
Stroud	105,400[1]
Sunderland	292,200
Sutton in Ashfield	109,800[1]
Swale	117,200[1]
Swansea	189,300[1]
Swindon	128,493[36]
Tameside	221,800
Tonbridge/Malling	102,100[1]
Trafford	218,100
Tunbridge Wells	101,800[1]
Wakefield	317,300
Walsall	263,900
Warrington	185,000[1]
Warwick	118,600[1]
West Bromwich	154,500[36]
Wigan	310,000
Winchester	100,500[1]
Windsor/Maidenhead	136,700[1]
Wirral	331,100
Wokingham	142,900[1]
Wolverhampton	245,100
Wrexham Maelor	117,100[1]
Wycombe	161,400[1]
York	104,000[1]
United States (1994 est.)	
Abilene (*Texas*)	110,034
Akron (*Ohio*)	221,886
Alameda (*Calif.*)	78,672
Albany (*Ga.*)	81,062
Albany (*N.Y.*)	104,828
Albuquerque (*N.M.*)	411,994
Alexandria (*Va.*)	112,879
Alhambra (*Calif.*)	84,411
Allentown (*Pa.*)	105,339
Amarillo (*Texas*)	165,036
Anaheim (*Calif.*)	282,133
Anchorage (*Alaska*)	253,649
Ann Arbor (*Mich.*)	108,817
Arlington (*Texas*)	286,922
Arlington (*Va.*)	174,603[41]
Arlington Heights (*Ill.*)	77,438
Arvada (*Colo.*)	95,446
Atlanta (*Ga.*)	396,052
Aurora (*Colo.*)	250,717
Aurora (*Ill.*)	112,313
Austin (*Texas*)	514,013
Bakersfield (*Calif.*)	191,060
Baltimore (*Md.*)	702,979
Baton Rouge (*La.*)	227,482
Beaumont (*Texas*)	115,022
Bellevue (*Wash.*)	84,239
Berkeley (*Calif.*)	99,830
Billings (*Mont.*)	86,578
Birmingham (*Ala.*)	264,527
Boise City (*Idaho*)	145,987
Boston (*Mass.*)	547,725
Boulder (*Colo.*)	85,613
Bridgeport (*Conn.*)	132,919
Brockton (*Mass.*)	87,411
Brownsville (*Texas*)	112,904
Buffalo (*N.Y.*)	312,965
Burbank (*Calif.*)	99,665
Cambridge (*Mass.*)	99,890
Camden (*N.J.*)	82,866
Canton (*Ohio*)	84,188
Cape Coral (*Fla.*)	84,968
Carrollton (*Texas*)	94,261
Carson (*Calif.*)	90,025
Cedar Rapids (*Iowa*)	113,438
Chandler (*Ariz.*)	119,227
Charleston (*S.C.*)	76,854
Charlotte (*N.C.*)	437,797
Chattanooga (*Tenn.*)	152,259
Chesapeake (*Va.*)	180,577
Chicago (*Ill.*)	2,731,743
Chula Vista (*Calif.*)	149,255
Cincinnati (*Ohio*)	358,170
Clarksville (*Tenn.*)	92,116
Clearwater (*Fla.*)	99,838
Cleveland (*Ohio*)	492,901
Colorado Springs (*Colo.*)	316,480
Columbia (*S.C.*)	104,101
Columbus (*Ga.*)	186,470
Columbus (*Ohio*)	635,913
Compton (*Calif.*)	96,477
Concord (*Calif.*)	111,889
Coral Springs (*Fla.*)	92,612
Corona (*Calif.*)	92,898
Corpus Christi (*Texas*)	275,419
Costa Mesa (*Calif.*)	98,427
Cranston (*R.I.*)	77,323
Dallas (*Texas*)	1,022,830
Daly City (*Calif.*)	94,036
Davenport (*Iowa*)	96,964
Dayton (*Ohio*)	178,540
Dearborn (*Mich.*)	86,187
Decatur (*Ill.*)	83,105
Denver (*Colo.*)	493,559
Des Moines (*Iowa*)	193,965
Detroit (*Mich.*)	992,038
Downey (*Calif.*)	99,889
Duluth (*Minn.*)	83,990
Durham (*N.C.*)	143,439
El Cajon (*Calif.*)	92,658
El Monte (*Calif.*)	104,661
El Paso (*Texas*)	579,307
Elgin (*Ill.*)	85,339
Elizabeth (*N.J.*)	106,298
Erie (*Pa.*)	108,398
Escondido (*Calif.*)	116,349
Eugene (*Ore.*)	118,122
Evansville (*Ind.*)	129,452
Everett (*Wash.*)	76,685
Fairfield (*Calif.*)	83,776
Fall River (*Mass.*)	89,425
Fargo (*N.D.*)	79,715
Farmington Hills (*Mich.*)	79,144
Fayetteville (*N.C.*)	83,999
Flint (*Mich.*)	138,164
Fontana (*Calif.*)	103,737
Fort Collins (*Colo.*)	98,954
Fort Lauderdale (*Fla.*)	162,842
Fort Wayne (*Ind.*)	183,359
Fort Worth (*Texas*)	451,814
Fremont (*Calif.*)	183,575
Fresno (*Calif.*)	386,551
Fullerton (*Calif.*)	116,863

[1]1993 estimate. [2]Eight villages, including Fagatogo, Utulei, and Pago Pago, are collectively known as Pago Pago (1990 census pop. 10,559). [3]1984 estimate. [4]Population of municipality. [5]1995 estimate. [6]1989 census. [7]Population of the statistical division containing the city. [8]1994 estimate. [9]Statistical district. [10]Population cited is for New Providence Island. [11]1991 census. [12]1982 estimate. [13]1990 census. [14]1987 census. [15]1992 census. [16]Excludes the agricultural population of the named civil division. [17]1991 estimate. [18]San José canton. [19]Mid-1990s estimate. [20]Excludes population of Lefkosia (Turkish-occupied Nicosia), estimated at 37,400 in 1985. [21]Population refers to widest officially defined agglomeration or metropolitan area. [22]1989 estimate.

country / city	population	country / city	population	country / city	population	country / city	population	country / city	population
Gainesville (Fla.)	87,806	Montgomery (Ala.)	195,471	San Bernardino		Winston-Salem (N.C.)	155,128	My Tho	108,404
Garden Grove (Calif.)	147,958	Moreno Valley (Calif.)	139,311	(Calif.)	181,718	Worcester (Mass.)	165,387	Nam Dinh	171,699
Garland (Texas)	194,218	Naperville (Ill.)	101,163	San Buenaventura		Yonkers (N.Y.)	183,490	Nha Trang	221,331
Gary (Ind.)	114,256	Nashua (N.H.)	79,631	(Ventura) (Calif.)	96,769	Youngstown (Ohio)	91,775	Phan Thiet	114,236[6]
Glendale (Ariz.)	168,439	Nashville-Davidson		San Diego (Calif.)	1,151,977			Qui Nhon	163,385
Glendale (Calif.)	178,481	(Tenn.)	504,505	San Francisco (Calif.)	734,676	Uruguay (1996)		Rach Gia	141,132
Grand Prairie (Texas)	108,908	New Bedford (Mass.)	94,623	San Jose (Calif.)	816,884	★ Montevideo	1,378,707	Thai Nguyen	127,643
Grand Rapids (Mich.)	190,395	New Haven (Conn.)	119,604	San Mateo (Calif.)	87,836			Vinh	112,455
Green Bay (Wis.)	102,708	New Orleans (La.)	484,149	Sandy (Utah)	85,406	Uzbekistan (1993 est.)		Vung Tau	145,145
Greensboro (N.C.)	196,167	New York City (N.Y.)	7,333,253	Santa Ana (Calif.)	290,827	Andijon (Andizhan)	303,000		
Gresham (Ore.)	78,594	Newark (N.J.)	258,751	Santa Barbara (Calif.)	85,626	Angren	132,000	Virgin Islands (U.S.)	
Hammond (Ind.)	82,837	Newport News (Va.)	179,127	Santa Clara (Calif.)	94,562	Bukhoro (Bukhara)	236,000	(1990)	
Hampton (Va.)	139,628	Newton (Mass.)	85,358	Santa Clarita (Calif.)	123,676	Chirchiq (Chirchik)	156,000	★ Charlotte Amalie	12,331
Hartford (Conn.)	124,196	Norfolk (Va.)	241,426	Santa Monica (Calif.)	87,047	Farghona (Fergana)	191,000		
Hawthorne (Calif.)	75,329	Norman (Okla.)	87,290	Santa Rosa (Calif.)	116,962	Jizzakh (Dzhizak)	116,000	West Bank (1987 est.)	
Hayward (Calif.)	115,590	Norwalk (Calif.)	100,744	Savannah (Ga.)	140,597	Marghilon (Margilan)	129,000	Nābulus	106,944
Henderson (Nev.)	101,997	Norwalk (Conn.)	78,710	Scottsdale (Ariz.)	152,439	Namangan	341,000	★ —	—
Hialeah (Fla.)	194,120	Oakland (Calif.)	366,926	Scranton (Pa.)	77,964	Nawoiy (Navoi)	115,000		
Hollywood (Fla.)	124,992	Oceanside (Calif.)	146,229	Seattle (Wash.)	520,947	Nukus	185,000	Western Sahara	
Honolulu (Ha.)	385,881	Odessa (Texas)	94,763	Shreveport (La.)	196,982	Olmaliq (Almalyk)	116,000	(1982)	
Houston (Texas)	1,702,086	Oklahoma City		Simi Valley (Calif.)	106,949	Qarshi (Karshi)	177,000	★ El Aaiún (Laayoune)	93,875
Huntington Beach		(Okla.)	463,201	Sioux City (Iowa)	82,735	Quqon (Kokand)	184,000		
(Calif.)	189,220	Omaha (Neb.)	345,033	Sioux Falls (S.D.)	109,174	Samarqand		Western Samoa (1991)	
Huntsville (Ala.)	160,325	Ontario (Calif.)	134,825	South Bend (Ind.)	105,092	(Samarkand)	368,000	★ Apia	32,859
Independence (Mo.)	111,669	Orange (Calif.)	116,785	South Gate (Calif.)	91,907	★ Tashkent			
Indianapolis (Ind.)	752,279	Orlando (Fla.)	176,948	Southfield (Mich.)	79,789	(Toshkent)	2,106,000[8]	Yemen (1986)	
Inglewood (Calif.)	110,085	Overland Park (Kan.)	125,225	Spokane (Wash.)	192,781	Urganch (Urgench)	135,000	Aden	294,430[42]
Irvine (Calif.)	125,624	Oxnard (Calif.)	145,863	Springfield (Ill.)	105,938			Al-Ḥudaydah	155,110
Irving (Texas)	164,917	Palm Bay (Fla.)	75,139	Springfield (Mass.)	149,164	Vanuatu (1993 est.)		★ Şan'ā'	503,600[19]
Jackson (Miss.)	193,097	Palmdale (Calif.)	103,423	Springfield (Mo.)	149,727	★ Vila	26,100	Ta'izz	178,430
Jacksonville (Fla.)	665,070	Parma (Ohio)	85,792	Stamford (Conn.)	107,199				
Jacksonville (N.C.)	79,494	Pasadena (Calif.)	134,170	Sterling Heights		Venezuela (1990)		Yugoslavia (1991)	
Jersey City (N.J.)	226,022	Pasadena (Texas)	129,292	(Mich.)	119,505	Acarigua	116,551	★ Belgrade (Beograd)	1,168,454
Joliet (Ill.)	79,492	Paterson (N.J.)	138,290	Stockton (Calif.)	222,633	Barcelona	221,792	Kragujevac	147,305
Kalamazoo (Mich.)	81,644	Pembroke Pines		Sunnyvale (Calif.)	119,584	Barinas	153,630	Niš	175,391
Kansas City (Kan.)	142,630	(Fla.)	81,498	Sunrise (Fla.)	75,038	Barquisimeto	625,450	Novi Sad	179,626
Kansas City (Mo.)	443,878	Peoria (Ill.)	112,878	Syracuse (N.Y.)	159,895	Baruta	182,941[21]	Podgorica	
Kenosha (Wis.)	85,122	Philadelphia (Pa.)	1,524,249	Tacoma (Wash.)	183,060	Cabimas	165,755[21]	(Titograd)	117,875
Killeen (Texas)	82,856	Phoenix (Ariz.)	1,048,949	Tallahassee (Fla.)	133,718	★ Caracas	1,822,465	Priština	155,499
Knoxville (Tenn.)	169,311	Pittsburgh (Pa.)	358,883	Tampa (Fla.)	285,523	Catia la Mar	100,104	Subotica	100,386
Lafayette (La.)	102,281	Plano (Texas)	157,394	Tempe (Ariz.)	144,289	Ciudad Bolívar	225,340		
Lakewood (Calif.)	79,416	Pomona (Calif.)	143,870	Thousand Oaks		Ciudad Guayana		Zaire (1994 est.)	
Lakewood (Colo.)	126,031	Pompano Beach (Fla.)	75,719	(Calif.)	110,981	(San Felix		Boma	135,284
Lancaster (Calif.)	119,186	Portland (Ore.)	450,777	Toledo (Ohio)	322,550	de Guayana)	453,047	Bukavu	201,569
Lansing (Mich.)	119,590	Portsmouth (Va.)	103,464	Topeka (Kan.)	120,646	Cumaná	212,432	Butembo	109,406
Laredo (Texas)	149,914	Providence (R.I.)	150,639	Torrance (Calif.)	138,219	Guacara	100,766	Goma	109,094
Las Vegas (Nev.)	327,878	Provo (Utah)	88,519	Trenton (N.J.)	84,441	Guarenas	134,158	Kalemi	101,309
Lawton (Okla.)	86,078	Pueblo (Colo.)	100,471	Troy (Mich.)	79,029	Los Teques	140,617	Kananga	393,030
Lexington-Fayette (Ky.)	237,612	Quincy (Mass.)	84,040	Tucson (Ariz.)	434,726	Maracaibo	1,249,670	Kikwit	182,142
Lincoln (Neb.)	203,076	Racine (Wis.)	86,014	Tulsa (Okla.)	374,851	Maracay	354,196	★ Kinshasa	4,655,313
Little Rock (Ark.)	178,136	Raleigh (N.C.)	236,707	Tuscaloosa (Ala.)	79,797	Maturín	206,654	Kisangani	417,517
Livonia (Mich.)	100,415	Rancho Cucamonga		Tyler (Texas)	80,194	Mérida	170,902	Kolwezi	417,810
Long Beach (Calif.)	433,852	(Calif.)	114,799	Vacaville (Calif.)	83,008	Petare	338,417	Likasi	299,118
Los Angeles (Calif.)	3,448,613	Reading (Pa.)	78,246	Vallejo (Calif.)	111,484	Puerto Cabello	128,825	Lubumbashi	851,381
Louisville (Ky.)	270,308	Reno (Nev.)	145,029	Virginia Beach (Va.)	430,295	Puerto La Cruz	155,731	Matadi	172,730
Lowell (Mass.)	96,054	Rialto (Calif.)	83,519	Visalia (Calif.)	85,073	San Cristóbal	220,675	Mbandaka	169,841
Lubbock (Texas)	194,467	Richardson (Texas)	78,989	Vista (Calif.)	79,816	Santa Ana de Coro	124,506	Mbuji-Mayi	806,475
Lynn (Mass.)	78,312	Richmond (Calif.)	87,944	Waco (Texas)	105,892	Turmero	174,280	Mwene-Ditu	137,459
McAllen (Texas)	95,299	Richmond (Va.)	201,108	Warren (Mich.)	142,625	Valencia	903,621	Tshikapa	180,860
Macon (Ga.)	109,191	Riverside (Calif.)	241,644	Warwick (R.I.)	86,006			Uvira	115,590
Madison (Wis.)	194,586	Roanoke (Va.)	96,643	★ Washington, D.C.	567,094	Vietnam (1992 est.)			
Manchester (N.H.)	96,640	Rochester (Minn.)	75,769	Waterbury (Conn.)	103,523	Bien Hoa	273,879[6]	Zambia (1990)	
Memphis (Tenn.)	614,289	Rochester (N.Y.)	231,170	West Covina (Calif.)	103,298	Buon Ma Thuot	282,095	Chingola	167,954
Mesa (Ariz.)	313,649	Rockford (Ill.)	143,263	West Palm Beach		Cam Pha	209,086	Kabwe	166,519
Mesquite (Texas)	113,631	Sacramento (Calif.)	373,964	(Fla.)	75,456	Cam Rahn	114,041[6]	Kitwe	338,207
Miami (Fla.)	373,024	St. Louis (Mo.)	368,215	West Valley City		Can Tho	215,587	Luanshya	146,275
Miami Beach (Fla.)	90,153	St. Paul (Minn.)	262,071	(Utah)	94,663	Da Lat	106,409	★ Lusaka	982,362
Midland (Texas)	96,163	St. Petersburg (Fla.)	238,585	Westland (Mich.)	85,221	Da Nang	382,674	Mufulira	152,944
Milwaukee (Wis.)	617,044	Salem (Ore.)	115,912	Westminster (Calif.)	79,751	Haiphong	783,133	Ndola	376,311
Minneapolis (Minn.)	354,590	Salinas (Calif.)	119,814	Westminster (Colo.)	87,045	★ Hanoi	2,154,900[1]		
Mission Viejo (Calif.)	83,813	Salt Lake City (Utah)	171,849	Whittier (Calif.)	79,813	Ho Chi Minh City		Zimbabwe (1992)	
Mobile (Ala.)	204,490	San Angelo (Texas)	88,726	Wichita (Kan.)	310,236	(Saigon)	4,322,300[1]	Bulawayo	620,936
Modesto (Calif.)	176,357	San Antonio (Texas)	998,905	Wichita Falls (Texas)	97,766	Hong Gai	127,484	Chitungwiza	274,035
						Hue	219,149	Gweru	124,735
						Long Xuyen	132,681	★ Harare	1,184,169
								Mount Darwin	164,362
								Mutare	131,808

Language

This table presents estimated data on the principal language communities of the countries of the world. The countries, and the principal languages (occasionally, language families) represented in each, are listed alphabetically. A bullet (●) indicates those languages that are official in each country. The sum of the estimates equals the 1996 population of the country given in the "Area and population" table.

The estimates represent, so far as national data collection systems permit, the distribution of mother tongues (a mother tongue being the language spoken first and, usually, most fluently by an individual). Many countries do not collect any official data whatever on language use, and published estimates not based on census or survey data usually span a substantial range of uncertainty. The editors have adopted the best-founded distribution in the published literature (indicating uncertainty by the degree of rounding shown) but have also adjusted or interpolated using data not part of the base estimate(s). Such adjustments have not been made to account for large-scale refugee movements, as these are of a temporary nature.

A variety of approaches have been used to approximate mother-tongue distribution when census data were unavailable. Some countries collect data on ethnic or "national" groups only; for such countries ethnic distribution often had to be assumed to conform roughly to the distribution of language communities. This approach, however, should be viewed with caution, because a minority population is not always free to educate its children in its own language and because better economic opportunities often draw minority group members into the majority-language community. For some countries, a given individual may be visible in national statistics only as a passport-holder of a foreign country, however long he may remain resident. Such persons, often guest workers, have sometimes had to be assumed to be speakers of the principal language of their home country. For other countries, the language mosaic may be so complex, the language communities so minute in size, scholarly study so inadequate, or

the census base so obsolete that it was possible only to assign percentages to entire groups, or families, of related languages, despite their mutual unintelligibility (Papuan and Melanesian languages in Papua New Guinea, for instance). For some countries in the Americas, so few speakers of any single indigenous language remain that it was necessary to combine these groups as *Amerindian* so as to give a fair impression of their aggregate size within their respective countries.

No systematic attempt has been made to account for populations that may legitimately be described as bilingual, unless the country itself collects data on that basis, as does Bolivia or the Comoros, for example. Where a nonindigenous official or excolonial language constitutes a lingua franca of the country, however, speakers of the language as a second tongue are shown in italics, even though very few may speak it as a mother tongue. No comprehensive effort has been made to distinguish between dialect communities *usually* classified as belonging to the same language, though such distinctions were possible for some countries—*e.g.*, between French and Occitan (the dialect of southern France) or among the various dialects of Chinese.

In giving the names of Bantu languages, grammatical particles specific to a language's autonym (name for itself) have been omitted (the form *Rwanda* is used here, for example, rather than *kinyaRwanda*, and *Tswana* instead of *seTswana*). Parenthetical alternatives are given for a number of languages that differ markedly from the name of the people speaking them (such as Kurukh, spoken by the Oraon tribes of India) or that may be combined with other groups sometimes distinguishable in national data but appearing here under the name of the largest member—*e.g.*, "Tamil (and other Indian languages)" combining data on South Asian Indian populations in Singapore. The term *creole* as used here refers to distinguishable dialectal communities related to a national, official, or former colonial language (such as the French creole that survives in Mauritius from the end of French rule in 1810).

Language

Major languages by country	Number of speakers	Major languages by country	Number of speakers	Major languages by country	Number of speakers	Major languages by country	Number of speakers	Major languages by country	Number of speakers
Afghanistan[1]		● Spanish	33,890,000	**Bahrain**[2]		● Dzongkha (Bhutiä)	420,000	Marka	180,000
Indo-Aryan languages		Other	390,000	● Arabic	430,000	Nepāli (Hindī)	290,000	Samo	250,000
Pashai	140,000	**Armenia**		English	420,000	**Bolivia**		Tamashek (Tuareg)	100,000
Iranian languages		● Armenian	3,360,000	Other	170,000	● Aymara	240,000	Voltaic (Gur) languages	
Balochi	210,000	Azeri (Azerbaijani)	90,000	**Bangladesh**[1]		Guaraní	10,000	Bobo group	
● Dari (Persian)	640,000	Other	150,000	● Bengali	120,270,000	● Quechua	620,000	Bobo	240,000
Chahar Aimak	640,000	**Aruba**		Chakmā	460,000	● Spanish	3,170,000	Bwamu	230,000
Hazāra	2,000,000	● Dutch	4,000	● English	3,200,000	Spanish-Amerindian		Dogon	40,000
Tajik	4,620,000	English	7,000	Gāro	110,000	(multilingual)	3,490,000	Gouin (Cerma)	60,000
Nūristāni group	170,000	Papiamento	56,000	Khāsī	100,000	Spanish-Aymara	1,500,000	Gurunsi (Grusi) group	
Pamir group	140,000	Spanish	5,000	Marma (Magh)	230,000	Spanish-Guaraní	30,000	Ko	20,000
● Pashto	11,870,000	Other	1,000	Mro	40,000	Spanish-Quechua	1,970,000	Lyele	260,000
Turkic languages		**Australia**		Santhālī	90,000	Other	60,000	Nuni	130,000
Turkmen	440,000	Aboriginal languages	51,000	Tripurī	90,000	**Bosnia and Herzegovina**		Sissala	10,000
Uzbek	2,000,000	Arabic	183,000	Other	1,690,000	● Serbo-Croatian	3,490,000	Lobi	200,000
Other	430,000	Cantonese	183,000	**Barbados**		Other	30,000	Mossi group	
Albania[1]		Dutch	53,000	Bajan (English		**Botswana**[1]		Dagara	330,000
● Albanian	3,183,000	● English	15,538,000	Creole)	238,000	● English (lingua franca)	590,000	Gurma	610,000
Greek	60,000	English (lingua		● English	27,000	Khoikhoin (Hottentot)	37,000	Kusaal	10,000
Macedonian	5,000	franca)	17,700,000	**Belarus**		Ndebele	19,000	Mossi	5,330,000
Other	1,000	French	51,000	● Belarusian	6,780,000	San (Bushman)	51,000	Senufo group	
Algeria		German	126,000	Polish	60,000	Shona	183,000	Minianka	—
● Arabic	23,710,000	Greek	320,000	● Russian	3,300,000	Tswana	1,115,000	Senufo	150,000
Berber	4,820,000	Hindī	26,000	Ukrainian	130,000	Tswana (lingua		Other	760,000
French	13,000,000	Hungarian	33,000	Other	60,000	franca)	1,180,000	**Burundi**[1]	
Other	40,000	Indonesian Malay	33,000	**Belgium**[2, 3]		Other	72,000	● French	550,000
American Samoa		Italian	468,000	Arabic	160,000	**Brazil**[1]		● Rundi	5,790,000
● English	2,000	Japanese	24,000	● Dutch (Flemish;		Amerindian		Hutu	4,870,000
English (lingua franca)	58,000	Korean	22,000	Netherlandic)	6,040,000	languages	270,000	Tutsi	800,000
● Samoan	53,000	Macedonian	71,000	● French (Walloon)	3,330,000	German	870,000	Twa	60,000
Tongan	2,000	Mandarin	60,000	● German	90,000	Italian	660,000	Other[5]	160,000
Other	2,000	Maltese	59,000	Italian	240,000	Japanese	600,000	**Cambodia**[1]	
Andorra[2]		Philippine languages	66,000	Spanish	50,000	● Portuguese	154,000,000	Cham	230,000
● Catalan (Andorran)	20,000	Polish	75,000	Turkish	90,000	Other	1,470,000	Chinese	310,000
English	1,000	Portuguese	29,000	Other	180,000	**Brunei**		● Khmer	8,930,000
French	5,000	Russian	27,000	**Belize**		Chinese	28,000	Vietnamese	550,000
Portuguese	8,000	Serbo-Croatian	99,000	● English	111,000	English	10,000	Other[6]	50,000
Spanish	33,000	Spanish	101,000	English Creole (lingua		● Malay	136,000	**Cameroon**[1]	
Other	3,000	Turkish	48,000	franca)	170,000	Malay-Chinese	2,000	Chadic languages	
Angola[1]		Vietnamese	123,000	Garifuna (Black Carib)	15,000	Malay-English	87,000	Buwal	270,000
Ambo (Ovambo)	290,000	Other	419,000	German	3,000	English-Chinese	7,000	Hausa	160,000
Chokwe	500,000	**Austria**		Mayan languages	21,000	Malay-Chinese-		Kotoko	150,000
Herero	90,000	Czech	19,000	Spanish	69,000	English	12,000	Mandara (Wandala)	770,000
Kongo	1,570,000	● German	7,454,000	Spanish (lingua franca)	120,000	Other	16,000	Masana (Masa)	530,000
Luchazi	290,000	Hungarian	34,000	**Benin**[1]		**Bulgaria**[1]		● English	2,720,000
Luimbe-Nganguela	640,000	Polish	19,000	Adja	610,000	● Bulgarian	6,960,000	● French	2,050,000
Lunda	140,000	Romanian	17,000	Aizo (Ouidah)	480,000	French	230,000	Niger-Congo	
Luvale (Luena)	430,000	Serbo-Croatian	176,000	Bariba	470,000	Macedonian	210,000	languages	
Mbunda	140,000	Slovene	30,000	Dendi	120,000	Romany	310,000	Adamawa-Eastern	
Mbundu	2,570,000	Turkish	123,000	Djougou	170,000	Turkish	790,000	languages	
Nyaneka-Nkhumbi	640,000	Other	230,000	Fon	2,180,000	Other	100,000	Baya (Gbaya)	160,000
Ovimbundu (Umbundu)	4,430,000	**Azerbaijan**		● French	860,000	**Burkina Faso**[4]		Chamba	330,000
● Portuguese	4,200,000	Armenian	360,000	Fulani (Peul)	310,000	● French	30,000	Mbum	180,000
Other	180,000	● Azeri (Azerbaijani)	6,260,000	Somba (Ditamari)	360,000	French (lingua		Benue-Congo	
Antigua and Barbuda		Lezgi (Lezgian)	170,000	Yoruba (Nago)	660,000	franca)	630,000	languages	
● English	61,000	Russian	570,000	Other	210,000	Fulani	1,030,000	Bamileke (Medumba)-	
English/English Creole	61,000	Other	250,000	**Bermuda**		Kru languages		Widikum (Mogha-	
Other	3,000	**Bahamas, The**		● English	61,000	Siamou (Seme)	20,000	mo)-Bamum	
Argentina		● English		**Bhutan**[1]		Mande languages		(Mum)	2,520,000
Amerindian languages	100,000	English/English Creole	230,000	Assamese	130,000	Busansi (Bisa)	380,000	Basa (Bassa)	150,000
Italian	610,000	French (Haitian)				Dyula	280,000	Duala	1,480,000
		Creole	50,000					Fang (Pangwe)-	
								Beti-Bulu	2,670,000

Major languages by country	Number of speakers
Ibibio (Efik)	20,000
Jukun	90,000
Lundu	370,000
Maka	670,000
Tikar	1,010,000
Tiv	360,000
Wute	40,000
Kwa languages	
Igbo	70,000
West Atlantic languages	
Fulani	1,310,000
Saharan languages	
Kanuri	40,000
Semitic languages	
Arabic	130,000
Other	100,000
Canada	
• English	18,112,000
• French	7,148,000
English-French	238,000
English-other	441,000
French-other	51,000
English-French-other	33,000
Aboriginal (Amerindian and Eskimo [Inuktitut]) languages	214,000
Arabic	48,000
Chinese	313,000
Czech	27,000
Danish	24,000
Dutch	146,000
Finnish	30,000
German	515,000
Greek	131,000
Hungarian	80,000
Italian	536,000
Pilipino (Filipino)	51,000
Polish	146,000
Portuguese	182,000
Punjābī	74,000
Russian	30,000
Serbo-Croatian	48,000
Spanish	98,000
Ukrainian	244,000
Vietnamese	48,000
Yiddish	27,000
Other	751,000
Cape Verde	
Crioulo (Portuguese Creole)	403,000
• Portuguese	...
Central African Republic	
Banda	770,000
Baya (Gbaya)	780,000
• French	*380,000*
Mandjia	480,000
Mbum	210,000
Ngbaka	250,000
Nzakara	50,000
• Sango (lingua franca)	*2,910,000*
Sara	210,000
Zande (Azande)	70,000
Other	460,000
Chad[1]	
• Arabic	1,710,000
Daju (Dagu)	150,000
• French	*850,000*
Hausa	150,000
Kanuri	150,000
Kotoko	140,000
Masa	150,000
Masalit, Maba, and Mimi	410,000
Mbum	420,000
Mubi	270,000
Sara, Bagirmi, and Kreish	1,990,000
Tama	410,000
Teda (Tubu)	480,000
Other	110,000
Chile[1]	
Araucanian (Mapuche)	1,390,000
Aymara	70,000
Rapa Nui	33,000
• Spanish	12,940,000
China[1]	
Achang	30,000
Bulang (Blang)	90,000
Ch'iang (Qiang)	210,000
Chinese (Han)	1,120,670,000
Cantonese (Yüeh [Yue])	*56,000,000*
Hakka	*41,000,000*
Hsiang (Xiang)	*54,000,000*
Kan (Gan)	*27,000,000*
• Mandarin	*801,000,000*
Min	*46,000,000*
Wu	*95,000,000*
Ching-p'o (Jingpo)	130,000
Chuang (Zhuang)	16,650,000
Daghur (Daur)	130,000
Evenk (Ewenki)	30,000
Gelo	470,000
Hani (Woni)	1,350,000
Hui	9,250,000
Kazak	1,200,000
Korean	2,060,000
Kyrgyz	150,000
Lahu	440,000
Li	1,190,000
Lisu	620,000
Manchu	10,560,000
Maonan	80,000
Miao	7,950,000
Mongol	5,170,000
Mulam	170,000
Na-hsi (Naxi)	300,000
Nu	30,000
Pai (Bai)	1,710,000
Pumi	30,000
Puyi (Chung-chia)	2,740,000
Salar	90,000
She	680,000
Shui	370,000
Sibo (Xibe)	190,000
Tai (Dai)	1,100,000
Tajik	40,000
Tibetan	4,940,000
Tu (Monguor)	210,000
T'u-chia (Tujia)	6,130,000
Tung (Dong)	2,700,000
Tung-hsiang (Dongxiang)	400,000
Uighur	7,760,000
Wa (Va)	380,000
Yao	2,290,000
Yi	7,060,000
Other	960,000
Colombia[1]	
Amerindian languages	300,000
Arawakan	40,000
Cariban	20,000
Chibchan	150,000
Other	100,000
English Creole	50,000
• Spanish	35,300,000
Comoros	
• Arabic	...
• Comorian	422,000
Comorian-French	73,000
Comorian-Malagasy	31,000
Comorian-Arabic	9,000
Comorian-Swahili	3,000
Comorian-French-other	22,000
• French	*30,000*
Other	3,000
Congo[1]	
Bobangi	30,000
• French	*780,000*
Kongo	1,370,000
Kota	20,000
Lingala (lingua franca)	...
Maka	50,000
Mbete	130,000
Mboshi	310,000
Monokutuba (lingua franca)	*1,600,000*
Punu	80,000
Sango	70,000
Teke	460,000
Other	140,000
Costa Rica	
Chibchan languages	10,000
Bribrí	6,000
Cabécar	4,000
Chinese	6,000
English Creole	68,000
• Spanish	3,315,000
Côte d'Ivoire[1]	
Akan (including Baule and Anyi)	4,430,000
• French	*5,200,000*
Kru (including Bete)	1,550,000
Malinke (including Dyula and Bambara)	1,680,000
Southern Mande (including Dan and Guro)	1,130,000
Voltaic ([Gur] including Senufo and Lobi)	1,730,000
Other (non-Ivoirian population)	4,210,000
Croatia	
• Serbo-Croatian	4,590,000
Other	190,000
Cuba	
• Spanish	11,117,000
Cyprus[1]	
• Greek	630,000
• Turkish	110,000
Other	30,000
Czech Republic[1]	
Bulgarian	3,000
• Czech	8,406,000
German	49,000
Greek	3,000
Hungarian	20,000
Moravian	1,333,000
Polish	60,000
Romanian	1,000
Romany	33,000
Russian	5,000
Ruthenian	2,000
Silesian	45,000
Slovak	317,000
Ukrainian	8,000
Other	70,000
Denmark[2]	
• Danish	5,053,000
English	19,000
German	10,000
Iranian languages	8,000
Norwegian	11,000
South Slavic languages	12,000
Swedish	9,000
Turkish	35,000
Other	88,000
Djibouti[1]	
Afar	120,000
• Arabic	40,000
• French	*50,000*
Somali	370,000
Gadaboursi	90,000
Issa	200,000
Issaq	80,000
Other	70,000
Dominica	
• English	...
English Creole	74,000
French Creole	*66,000*
Dominican Republic	
French (Haitian) Creole	150,000
• Spanish	7,350,000
Ecuador	
Quechuan (and other Amerindian languages)	820,000
• Spanish	10,880,000
Egypt[1]	
• Arabic	60,170,000
French	*270,000*
Other	730,000
El Salvador	
• Spanish	5,897,000
Equatorial Guinea[1]	
Bubi	40,000
Fang	340,000
French	...
Krio (English Creole)	...
• Spanish	...
Other	30,000
Eritrea	
Cushitic languages	
Afar	150,000
Bilin	110,000
Hadareb (Beja)	140,000
Saho	110,000
Nilotic languages	
Kunama	100,000
Nara	70,000
Semitic languages	
Arabic (Rashaida)	10,000
Tigré	1,150,000
Tigrinya	1,780,000
Estonia[1]	
Belarusian	20,000
• Estonian	940,000
Finnish	10,000
Russian	430,000
Ukrainian	40,000
Other	30,000
Ethiopia[1]	
• Amharic	17,040,000
Gurage	2,660,000
Oromo (Oromifa)	17,590,000
Sidamo	1,810,000
Somali	2,300,000
Tigrinya	4,080,000
Walaita	1,570,000
Other	9,670,000
Faroe Islands	
• Danish	...
• Faroese	44,000
Fiji[1]	
• English	*160,000*
Fijian	406,000
Hindī	349,000
Other	47,000
Finland	
Estonian	8,000
• Finnish	4,773,000
Russian	14,000
Sami (Lapp)	2,000
• Swedish	297,000
Other	38,000
France	
Arabic[7]	1,480,000
English[7]	80,000
• French[7, 8, 9]	54,680,000
Basque	*80,000*
Breton	*580,000*
Catalan (Rousillonais)	*210,000*
Corsican	*170,000*
Dutch (Flemish)	*110,000*
German (Alsatian)	*1,330,000*
Occitan	*1,580,000*
Italian[7]	260,000
Polish[7]	50,000
Portuguese[7]	670,000
Spanish[7]	220,000
Turkish[7]	200,000
Other[7]	740,000
French Guiana	
Amerindian languages	4,000
English Creole	2,000
• French	...
French Creoles	135,000
Other	7,000
French Polynesia[10]	
Chinese	12,000
• French	180,000
Polynesian languages	204,000
• Tahitian	...
Other	44,000
Gabon[1]	
Fang	420,000
• French	*390,000*
Kota	40,000
Mbete	170,000
Mpongwe (Myene)	180,000
Punu, Sira, Nzebi	200,000
Teke	20,000
Other	160,000
Gambia, The	
• English	...
Gambians	
Aku (Krio)	7,000
Mande languages	
Bambara	8,000
Malinke	391,000
Soninke	88,000
West Atlantic languages	
Dyola	105,000
Fulani	186,000
Manjak	18,000
Serer	27,000
Wolof	144,000
Other	14,000
non-Gambians	158,000
Gaza Strip	
Arabic	811,000
Hebrew	5,000
Georgia	
Abkhaz	90,000
Armenian	360,000
Azeri (Azerbaijani)	290,000
• Georgian	3,730,000
Ossetian	120,000
Russian	460,000
Other	160,000
Germany[2]	
• German	77,370,000
Greek	350,000
Italian	560,000
Polish	290,000
Portuguese	100,000
South Slavic languages	1,030,000
Spanish	140,000
Turkish	1,880,000
Kurdish	*400,000*
Other	180,000
Ghana[1]	
Akan	8,860,000
• English	...
Ewe	2,010,000
Ga-Adangme	1,310,000
Gurma	560,000
Hausa (lingua franca)	*10,100,000*
Mole-Dagbani (Mossi)	2,680,000
Yoruba	230,000
Other	1,250,000
Gibraltar[2]	
Arabic	2,000
• English	24,000
Spanish	...
Other	1,000
Greece[1]	
Albanian	60,000
• Greek	10,050,000
Macedonian	160,000
Turkish	100,000
Other	150,000
Greenland[2]	
• Danish	7,000
• Greenlandic	49,000
Grenada	
• English	...
English/English Creole	98,000
Guadeloupe	
French Creole/French	406,000
• French	...
Other	21,000
Guam	
• Chamorro	45,000
Chinese	2,000
Chuukese (Trukese)	2,000
• English	57,000
English (lingua franca)	*151,000*
Japanese	4,000
Korean	5,000
Palauan	2,000
Philippine languages	31,000
Other	6,000
Guatemala	
Garifuna (Black Carib)	30,000
Mayan languages	3,830,000
Cakchiquel	980,000
Kekchí	530,000
Mam	300,000
Quiché	1,110,000
• Spanish	7,070,000
Guernsey	
English	66,000
French	...
Guinea[1]	
• French	*580,000*
Mande languages	
Kpelle	320,000
Loma	160,000
Malinke	1,600,000
Susu	760,000
Yalunka	200,000
Other	480,000
West Atlantic languages	
Basari-Koniagi	80,000
Fulani (Peul)	2,670,000
Kissi	410,000
Other	210,000
Other	10,000
Guinea-Bissau	
Balante	159,000
Crioulo (Portuguese Creole)	47,000
Crioulo-Portuguese	24,000
Crioulo-other (except Portuguese)	327,000
Fulani	182,000
Malinke	76,000
Mandyako	54,000
Pepel	30,000
• Portuguese	—
Portuguese-other (except Crioulo)	88,000
Other	107,000
Guyana	
Amerindian languages	
Arawakan	10,000
Cariban	10,000
• English	...
English/English Creoles	692,000
Haiti	
• French	60,000
French-Haitian (French) Creole	810,000
• Haitian (French) Creole	5,860,000
Honduras	
English Creole	12,000
Garifuna (Black Carib)	77,000
Miskito	11,000
• Spanish	5,564,000
Other	2,000
Hong Kong	
Chinese	
• Cantonese	5,590,000
Cantonese (lingua franca)	*6,040,000*
Chiu Chau	88,000
Fukien (Min)	120,000
Hakka	101,000
Putonghua (Mandarin)	70,000
Putonghua (lingua franca)	*1,140,000*
Sze Yap	25,000
• English	139,000
English (lingua franca)	*1,990,000*
Japanese	13,000
Pilipino (Filipino)	6,000
Other	152,000
Hungary	
German	40,000
• Hungarian	10,050,000
Romanian	10,000
Romany	50,000
Serbo-Croatian	20,000
Slovak	10,000
Other	20,000

Language (continued)

Major languages by country	Number of speakers
Iceland[2]	
● Icelandic	259,000
Other	11,000
India	
Austroasiatic languages	
Ho	1,130,000
Khaṛiā	280,000
Khāsī	890,000
Korkū	510,000
Muṇḍā	490,000
Muṇḍārī	1,060,000
Santhālī	5,950,000
Savara (Sora)	330,000
Dravidian languages	
Goṇḍī	2,760,000
Kannaḍa	38,000,000
Khond	290,000
Koyā	340,000
Kui	720,000
Kurukh (Oraon)	1,790,000
Malayālam	36,680,000
Tamil	63,210,000
Telugu	76,630,000
Tuḷu	1,950,000
English	330,000
● English (lingua franca)	*31,000,000*
Indo-Iranian (Indo-Aryan) languages	
Assamese	15,760,000
Bengali	72,790,000
Bhīlī (Bhilodī)	6,290,000
Barel	*400,000*
Bhilalī	*400,000*
Dogrī	2,150,000
Gujarātī	46,900,000
Halabī	740,000
● Hindī	373,360,000
Aṅga (Aṅgikā)	*700,000*
Baghelkhaṇḍī	*400,000*
Bāgṛī	*1,900,000*
Banjārī	*800,000*
Bhojpurī	*25,200,000*
Bundelkhaṇḍī	*700,000*
Chhattīsgaṛhī	*11,800,000*
Gaṛhwālī	*2,200,000*
Gojrī	*600,000*
Hāṛautī	*600,000*
Khorthā (Khottā)	*900,000*
Kumaunī	*2,200,000*
Lamanī (Banjārī)	*2,100,000*
Magahī (Magadhī)	*11,700,000*
Maithilī	*10,800,000*
Mālvī	*1,100,000*
Maṇḍealī	*400,000*
Māṛwāṛī	*8,300,000*
Mewārī	*1,400,000*
Nagpurī	*600,000*
Nīmāḍī	*1,400,000*
Pahāṛī	*2,200,000*
Rājasthānī	*3,700,000*
Sadānī (Sadrī)	*1,400,000*
Surgujiā	*900,000*
Hindī (lingua franca)	*433,000,000*
Kashmirī	4,490,000
Khandeshī	1,680,000
Kiṣan	220,000
Koṅkanī	2,240,000
Marāṭhī	70,130,000
Nepālī (Gorkhalī)	1,770,000
Oṛiyā	32,340,000
Punjābī	26,270,000
Sindhī	2,750,000
Kachchhī	*800,000*
Urdū	49,920,000
Sino-Tibetan languages	
Ādi	170,000
Āo	150,000
Gāro	580,000
Meithei (Manipurī)	1,280,000
Mizo (Lushai)	540,000
Nissī	200,000
Tripurī	690,000
Other	16,220,000
Indonesia	
Balinese	3,290,000
Banjarese	3,470,000
Batak	4,400,000
Buginese	4,360,000
● Indonesian Malay	24,000,000
Javanese	78,150,000
Madurese	8,580,000
Minangkabau	4,680,000
Sundanese	31,250,000
Other	36,010,000
Iran[1]	
Armenian	300,000
Iranian languages	
Bakhtyārī (Lurī)	1,050,000
Balochi	1,420,000
● Farsī (Persian)	28,400,000
Farsī (lingua franca)	*51,500,000*
Gīlakī	3,290,000
Kurdish	5,680,000
Lurī	2,690,000
Māzandarānī	2,240,000
Other	1,350,000
Semitic languages	
Arabic	1,340,000
Other	150,000
Turkic languages	
Afshari	700,000
Azeri (Azerbaijani)	10,460,000
Qashqa'i	790,000
Shahsavani	370,000
Turkish (mostly Pishaghchi, Bayat, and Qajar)	450,000
Turkmen	970,000
Other	120,000
Other	460,000
Iraq[1]	
● Arabic	16,520,000
Assyrian	180,000
Azeri (Azerbaijani)	360,000
Kurdish	4,060,000
Persian	180,000
Other	120,000
Ireland	
● English	3,540,000
● Irish[11]	60,000
Irish	*1,170,000*
Isle of Man	
● English	70,000
Israel[12]	
● Arabic	1,010,000
English	70,000
French	40,000
German	40,000
● Hebrew	3,770,000
Hungarian	30,000
Romanian	90,000
Russian	90,000
Spanish	50,000
Yiddish	120,000
Other	180,000
Italy[1]	
Albanian	120,000
Catalan	30,000
French	300,000
German	300,000
Greek	40,000
● Italian	54,080,000
Rhaetian	740,000
Friulian	710,000
Ladin	30,000
Romany	110,000
Sardinian	1,520,000
Slovene	120,000
Other	130,000
Jamaica	
● English	...
English/English Creoles	2,390,000
Hindī and other Indian languages	50,000
Other	100,000
Japan[2]	
Ainu	25,000
Chinese	220,000
English	70,000
● Japanese	124,420,000
Korean	680,000
Philippine languages	90,000
Other	110,000
Jersey	
English	88,000
● French	...
Jersey Norman French	*6,000*
Jordan[1]	
● Arabic	4,300,000
Other	40,000
Kazakstan	
German	530,000
● Kazak	6,590,000
Russian	7,950,000
Tatar	230,000
Uighur	180,000
Ukrainian	330,000
Uzbek	320,000
Other	640,000
Kenya[1]	
Bantu languages	
Bajun (Rajun)	70,000
Basuba	110,000
Embu	340,000
Gusii (Kisii)	1,790,000
Kamba	3,280,000
Kikuyu	6,090,000
Kuria	170,000
Luhya	4,030,000
Mbere	120,000
Meru	1,600,000
Nyika (Mijikenda)	1,390,000
Pokomo	80,000
Swahili	10,000
● Swahili (lingua franca)	*19,000,000*
Taita	290,000
Cushitic languages	
Oromo languages	
Boran	130,000
Gabbra	60,000
Gurreh	160,000
Orma	60,000
Somali languages	
Degodia	180,000
Ogaden	50,000
Somali	300,000
English (lingua franca)	*2,200,000*
Nilotic languages	
Kalenjin	3,140,000
Luo	3,720,000
Masai	460,000
Sambur	140,000
Teso	250,000
Turkana	390,000
Semitic languages	
Arabic	80,000
Other	650,000
Kiribati[1]	
● English	...
Kiribati (Gilbertese)	80,900
Tuvaluan (Ellice)	400
Other	500
Korea, North[1]	
Chinese	40,000
● Korean	23,870,000
Korea, South[1]	
Chinese	50,000
● Korean	45,180,000
Kuwait	
● Arabic	1,610,000
Other	460,000
Kyrgyzstan	
● Kyrgyz	2,360,000
Russian	1,150,000
Uzbek	570,000
Other	410,000
Laos[1]	
● Lao-Lum (Lao)	3,370,000
Lao-Soung (Miao [Hmong] and Man [Yao])	260,000
Lao-Tai (Tai)	390,000
Lao-Theung (Mon-Khmer)	830,000
Other[13]	170,000
Latvia[1]	
Belarusian	100,000
● Latvian	1,380,000
Lithuanian	30,000
Polish	60,000
Russian	830,000
Ukrainian	70,000
Other	50,000
Lebanon[1]	
● Arabic	2,870,000
Armenian	190,000
French	*740,000*
Other	30,000
Lesotho[1]	
● English	...
● Sotho	1,800,000
Zulu	320,000
Liberia[1]	
● English	*570,000*
Krio (English Creole)	*2,600,000*
Kwa (Kru) languages	
Bassa	340,000
Belle (Belleh)	15,000
De (Dey)	10,000
Grebo	255,000
Krahn	108,000
Kru	209,000
Mande (Northern) languages	
Gbandi	80,000
Kpelle	553,000
Loma	161,000
Malinke (Mandingo)	145,000
Mende	22,000
Vai	102,000
Mande (Southern) languages	
Gio (Dan)	223,000
Mano	202,000
West Atlantic (Mel) languages	
Gola	113,000
Kissi	115,000
Other	141,000
Libya[1]	
● Arabic	5,230,000
Berber	160,000
Other[14]	50,000
Liechtenstein[2]	
● German	27,600
Italian	900
Turkish	800
Other	2,100
Lithuania	
● Lithuanian	2,960,000
Polish	220,000
Russian	430,000
Other	80,000
Luxembourg[2]	
Belgian	12,000
Danish	2,000
Dutch	4,000
English	5,000
French	15,000
German	10,000
Greek	1,000
Italian	20,000
Luxemburgian	280,000
Portuguese	50,000
Spanish	3,000
Other	14,000
Macau	
Chinese	
● Cantonese	370,000
Mandarin	5,000
Other Chinese languages	40,000
English	2,000
● Portuguese	10,000
Other	5,000
Macedonia[1]	
Albanian	450,000
● Macedonian	1,309,000
Romany	44,000
Serbo-Croatian	40,000
Turkish	79,000
Vlach	9,000
Other	37,000
Madagascar[1]	
● French	*1,400,000*
● Malagasy	13,530,000
Other	140,000
Malaŵi[1]	
Chewa (Maravi)	6,250,000
● English	*540,000*
Lomwe	1,970,000
Ngoni	720,000
Yao	1,420,000
Other	370,000
Malaysia	
Bajau	130,000
Chinese	1,180,000
Chinese-others	670,000
Dusun	210,000
English	100,000
English-others	230,000
English (lingua franca)	*6,200,000*
Iban	480,000
Iban-others	80,000
● Malay	8,780,000
Malay-others	3,120,000
Tamil	790,000
Tamil-others	10,000
Other	4,580,000
Maldives	
● Divehi (Maldivian)	266,000
Mali[1]	
Afro-Asiatic languages	
Berber languages	
Tamashek (Tuareg)	670,000
Semitic languages	
Arabic (Mauri)	150,000
● French	*730,000*
Niger-Congo languages	
Mande languages	
Bambara	2,930,000
Bambara (lingua franca)	*5,500,000*
Bobo Fing	10,000
Dyula	270,000
Malinke, Khasonke, and Wasulunka	610,000
Samo (Duun)	60,000
Soninke	810,000
Voltaic (Gur) languages	
Bwa (Bobo)	220,000
Dogon	370,000
Mossi	40,000
Senufo and Minianka	1,100,000
West Atlantic languages	
Fulani and Tukulor	1,280,000
Nilo-Saharan languages	
Songhai	660,000
Other	20,000
Malta[1]	
● English	8,000
● Maltese	357,000
Other	8,000
Marshall Islands[2]	
● English	...
● Marshallese	56,700
Other	1,800
Martinique	
French Creole/French	381,000
● French	...
Other	13,000
Mauritania[1]	
● Arabic	...
French	*130,000*
Fulani	30,000
Ḥassānīyah Arabic	1,900,000
Soninke	70,000
Tukulor	120,000
Wolof	160,000
Zenaga	30,000
Other	30,000
Mauritius	
Bhojpurī	218,000
Bhojpurī-other	24,000
Chinese	4,000
● English	2,000
French	39,000
French Creole	704,000
French Creole-other	101,000
Hindī	14,000
Marāṭhī	8,000
Tamil	9,000
Telugu	7,000
Urdū	7,000
Other	3,000
Mayotte[15]	
● Arabic	...
Mahorais (local dialect of Comorian Swahili)	108,000
Other Comorian Swahili dialects	47,000
Malagasy	42,000
● French	52,000
Other	8,000
Mexico	
Amerindian languages	7,310,000
Amuzgo	40,000
Aztec (Nahuatl)	1,660,000
Chatino	40,000
Chinantec	150,000
Chocho	20,000
Chol	180,000
Chontal	50,000
Cora	20,000
Cuicatec	20,000
Huastec	170,000
Huave	20,000
Huichol	30,000
Kanjobal	20,000
Mame	20,000
Mayo	50,000
Mazahua	190,000
Mazatec	230,000
Mixe	130,000
Mixtec	530,000
Otomí	400,000
Popoluca	40,000
Purepecha	130,000
Tarahumara	80,000
Tepehua	10,000
Tepehuan	30,000
Tlapanec	100,000
Tojolabal	50,000
Totonac	290,000
Trique	20,000
Tzeltal	370,000
Tzotzil	320,000
Yaqui	10,000
Yucatec (Mayan)	980,000
Zapotec	540,000
Zoque	60,000
Other	330,000
● Spanish	85,330,000
Spanish-Amerindian languages	*5,940,000*
Micronesia	
Chuukese (Trukese)	44,100
● English	500
Kosraean	7,700
Mortlockese	8,100
Palauan	400
Pohnpeian	25,200
Woleaian	3,900
Yapese	6,100
Other	10,000
Moldova	
Bulgarian	70,000
Gagauz	140,000
● Romanian (Moldovan)	2,690,000
Russian	1,010,000
Ukrainian	370,000
Other	60,000
Monaco[2]	
English	2,000
● French	12,000
Italian	5,000
Monegasque	5,000
Other	6,000
Mongolia[1]	
Bayad	45,000
Buryat	40,000
Darhat	16,000

Major languages by country	Number of speakers
Dariganga	33,000
Dörbed	63,000
Dzakhchin	26,000
Kazak	138,000
● Khalkha (Mongolian)	1,849,000
Ould	9,000
Torgut	12,000
Uryankhai (Tuvan)	23,000
Other	91,000
Morocco	
● Arabic	17,380,000
Berber	8,820,000
Other[16]	530,000
Mozambique	
Chopi	510,000
Chuabo	1,020,000
Koti	60,000
Kunda	10,000
Lomwe	1,400,000
Makonde	350,000
Makua	4,990,000
Marendje	620,000
Mwani	80,000
Ngulu	20,000
Nguni	
Swazi	20,000
Zulu	10,000
Nsenga	40,000
Nyanja	600,000
Nyungwe	410,000
Phimbi	20,000
● Portuguese	220,000
Ronga	650,000
Sena	1,680,000
Shona	1,170,000
Swahili	10,000
Tonga	350,000
Tsonga	2,230,000
Tswa	1,070,000
Yao	300,000
Other	120,000
Myanmar (Burma)[1]	
● Burmese	32,760,000
Burmese (lingua franca)	*38,000,000*
Chin	1,040,000
Kachin (Ching-p'o)	650,000
Karen	2,960,000
Kayah	190,000
Mon	1,150,000
Rakhine (Arakanese)	2,140,000
Shan	4,020,000
Other	2,600,000
Namibia	
Afrikaans	162,000
Caprivi	80,000
● English	13,000
English (lingua franca)	*142,000*
German	16,000
Herero	137,000
Kavango (Okavango)	166,000
Nama	213,000
Ovambo (Ambo [Kwanyama])	866,000
San (Bushman)	33,000
Tswana	7,000
Other	16,000
Nauru	
Chinese	900
English	800
English (lingua franca)	*10,500*
Kiribati (Gilbertese)	1,900
● Nauruan	6,100
Tuvaluan (Ellice)	900
Nepal	
Austroasiatic (Munda) languages	
Santhālī	40,000
Indo-Aryan languages	
Bengali	30,000
Bhojpurī	1,530,000
Dhanwar	30,000
Hindī	190,000
Hindī (Awadhī dialect)	420,000
Maithilī	2,430,000
● Nepālī (Eastern Pahāṛī)	10,320,000
Rājbanśī	90,000
Tharu	1,100,000
Urdū	220,000
Tibeto-Burman languages	
Bhutiā (Sherpa)	140,000
Chepang	30,000
Gurung	250,000
Limbū	280,000
Magar	480,000
Newārī	770,000
Rai and Kirāntī	490,000
Tamāng	1,000,000
Thakali	10,000
Thami	20,000
Other	660,000
Netherlands, The[2]	
Arabic	162,000
● Dutch	14,808,000
Dutch and Frisian	*590,000*
Turkish	186,000
Other	433,000
Netherlands Antilles	
● Dutch	...
English	17,000
Papiamento	179,000
Other	12,000
New Caledonia[1]	
● French	64,000
Melanesian languages	88,000
Polynesian languages (mostly Wallisian)	22,000
Other	17,000
New Zealand	
● English	3,290,000
English-Maori	154,000
● Maori	51,000
Other	123,000
Nicaragua	
English Creole	40,000
Misumalpan languages	
Miskito	170,000
Sumo	10,000
● Spanish	4,050,000
Niger[1]	
Berber languages	
Tamashek (Tuareg)	980,000
Chadic languages	
Hausa	5,010,000
Hausa (lingua franca)	*6,630,000*
● French	*1,420,000*
Saharan languages	
Kanuri	420,000
Teda (Tubu)	40,000
Semitic languages	
Arabic	30,000
Songhai and Zerma	2,010,000
Voltaic (Gur) languages	
Gurma	30,000
West Atlantic languages	
Fulani (Fulfulde)	920,000
Other	20,000
Nigeria[1]	
Arabic	300,000
Bura	1,600,000
Edo	3,500,000
● English (lingua franca)	*16,000,000*
English Creole (lingua franca)[17]	*36,000,000*
Fulani	11,700,000
Hausa	22,200,000
Hausa (lingua franca)	*52,000,000*
Ibibio	5,800,000
Igbo (Ibo)	18,700,000
Ijo (Ijaw)	1,900,000
Kanuri	4,300,000
Nupe	1,300,000
Tiv	2,300,000
Yoruba	22,200,000
Other	8,100,000
Northern Mariana Islands	
Carolinian	2,800
Chamorro	17,700
Chinese	4,200
Chuukese (Trukese)	1,400
● English	2,800
English (lingua franca)	*53,700*
Japanese	1,200
Korean	3,800
Palauan	2,000
Philippine languages	20,200
Other	3,000
Norway[2]	
Danish	18,000
English	24,000
● Norwegian	4,230,000
Swedish	12,000
Other	98,000
Oman	
● Arabic (Omani)	1,650,000
Balochī	420,000
Farsi (Persian)	60,000
Swahili	40,000
Urdū	50,000
Other	20,000
Pakistan	
Balochī	4,350,000
Brāhūī	1,730,000
English (lingua franca)	*16,000,000*
Pashto	18,990,000
Punjābī	
Punjābī	69,610,000
Hindko	3,510,000
Sindhī	
Sindhī	17,010,000
Siraikī	14,210,000
● Urdū	10,980,000
Other	4,120,000
Palau	
Chinese	300
● English	500
English (lingua franca)	*16,900*
● Palauan	14,000
Philippine languages	1,600
Other	600
Panama	
Amerindian languages	223,000
Bokotá	4,000
Chibchan	199,000
Cuna	54,000
Guaymí	142,000
Teribe	2,000
Chocó	20,000
Embera	17,000
Waunana	3,000
Chinese	8,000
English	...
English Creoles	374,000
● Spanish	2,069,000
Papua New Guinea[1]	
● English	*70,000*
Melanesian languages	880,000
Motu	*140,000*
Papuan languages	3,430,000
Tok Pisin (English Creole)	*2,920,000*
Other	90,000
Paraguay	
German	43,000
● Guaraní	1,992,000
Guaraní-Spanish	2,414,000
Portuguese	157,000
● Spanish	322,000
Other	36,000
Peru	
Amerindian languages	4,650,000
Aymara	550,000
● Quechua	3,940,000
Other	160,000
● Spanish	19,110,000
Other	190,000
Philippines	
Aklanon	470,000
Bicol	4,170,000
Bilaan	130,000
Binisaya	160,000
Cebuano	17,430,000
Chavacano	350,000
Cuyonon	150,000
Davaweno	170,000
● English (lingua franca)	*37,300,000*
Hiligaynon	6,700,000
Ibaloi (Nabaloi)	130,000
Ibanag	370,000
Ifugao	200,000
Ilocano	7,020,000
Itawit	140,000
Kalinga	110,000
Kankanai	260,000
Kinaray-a (Hamtikanon)	630,000
Maguindanao	910,000
Manobo	190,000
Maranao	920,000
Masbateño	410,000
Pampango	2,250,000
Pangasinan	1,380,000
● Pilipino (Filipino; Tagalog)	20,040,000
Romblon	150,000
Samal	300,000
Sambal	140,000
Subanon	170,000
Surigaonon	410,000
Tau Sug	770,000
Waray-Waray	2,890,000
Yakan	130,000
Other	2,120,000
Poland	
Belarusian	190,000
German	500,000
● Polish	37,800,000
Ukrainian	230,000
Portugal[2]	
● Portuguese	9,830,000
Other	100,000
Puerto Rico	
● English	19,000
● Spanish	1,933,000
Spanish-English	1,766,000
Other	48,000
Qatar[2]	
● Arabic	240,000
Other[18]	350,000
Réunion	
● French	*200,000*
French Creole	610,000
Other[19]	60,000
Romania	
Bulgarian	9,000
Czech	5,000
German	98,000
Hungarian	1,629,000
Polish	3,000
● Romanian	20,556,000
Romany (Tigani)	166,000
Russian	31,000
Serbo-Croatian	33,000
Slovak	18,000
Tatar	23,000
Turkish	27,000
Ukrainian	63,000
Other	8,000
Russia	
Adyghian	120,000
Armenian	360,000
Avar	530,000
Azeri (Azerbaijani)	280,000
Bashkir	980,000
Belarusian	440,000
Buryat	360,000
Chechen	880,000
Chuvash	1,370,000
Dargin	340,000
Georgian	90,000
German	350,000
Ingush	210,000
Kabardian	380,000
Kalmyk	150,000
Karachay	150,000
Kazak	560,000
Komi-Permyak	100,000
Komi-Zyryan	240,000
Kumyk	270,000
Lak	100,000
Lezgi (Lezgian)	240,000
Mari	520,000
Mordvin	740,000
Ossetian	370,000
Romanian	110,000
Romany	130,000
● Russian	126,790,000
Tabasaran	90,000
Tatar	4,700,000
Tuvan	200,000
Udmurt	500,000
Ukrainian	1,860,000
Uzbek	100,000
Yakut	360,000
Other	1,440,000
Rwanda	
● English	...
● French	*470,000*
● Rwanda	6,850,000
St. Kitts and Nevis	
● English	...
English/English Creole	39,000
St. Lucia	
● English	29,000
English/French Creole	115,000
St. Vincent and the Grenadines	
● English	...
English/English Creole	112,000
Other	1,000
San Marino[1]	
● Italian (Romagnolo)	25,000
São Tomé and Príncipe	
Crioulo (Portuguese Creole)	115,000
English	...
French	1,000
● Portuguese	...
Other	17,000
Saudi Arabia[1]	
● Arabic	17,500,000
Other	920,000
Senegal	
● French	*430,000*
Senegalese	
Diola (Dyola)	420,000
Fulani (Peul)-Tukulor	1,850,000
Malinke (Mandingo)	320,000
Serer	1,070,000
Soninke	110,000
Wolof	4,100,000
Wolof (lingua franca)	*6,800,000*
Other	460,000
non-Senegalese	190,000
Seychelles	
English	2,000
French	1,000
● Seselwa (French Creole)	70,000
Other	3,000
Sierra Leone[1]	
● English	*700,000*
Krio (English Creole [lingua franca])	*4,400,000*
Mande languages	
Kono-Vai	240,000
Kuranko	160,000
Mende	1,600,000
Susu	70,000
Yalunka	160,000
West Atlantic languages	
Bullom-Sherbro	170,000
Fulani	170,000
Kissi	110,000
Limba	390,000
Temne	1,460,000
Other	80,000
Singapore[1]	
Chinese	2,357,000
● English	*1,139,000*
● Malay	432,000
● Mandarin Chinese	...
● Tamil (and other Indian languages)	219,000
Other	38,000
Slovakia[1]	
Czech, Moravian, and Silesian	58,000
German	5,000
Hungarian	571,000
Polish	3,000
Romany	84,000
Russian	2,000
Ruthenian and Ukrainian	32,000
● Slovak	4,604,000
Other	13,000
Slovenia	
Hungarian	9,000
Serbo-Croatian	154,000
● Slovene	1,721,000
Other	74,000
Solomon Islands[1]	
● English	...
Melanesian languages	339,000
Papuan languages	34,000
Polynesian languages	15,000
Other[20]	8,000
Somalia[1]	
● Arabic	...
English	...
● Somali	6,690,000
Other	120,000
South Africa	
● Afrikaans	6,300,000
Afrikaans/English	80,000
● English	3,800,000
Nguni	
● Ndebele	630,000
● Swazi	1,090,000
● Xhosa	7,310,000
● Zulu	9,350,000
Sotho	
● North Sotho (Pedi)	4,090,000
● South Sotho	2,880,000
● Tswana (Western Sotho)	3,010,000
● Tsonga	1,750,000
● Venda	710,000
Other	750,000
Spain	
Basque (Euskera)	620,000
● Castilian Spanish	29,220,000
Catalan (Català)	6,630,000
Galician (Gallego)	2,510,000
Other	290,000
Sri Lanka	
English	10,000
English-Sinhala	1,010,000
English-Sinhala-Tamil	660,000
English-Tamil	210,000
● Sinhala	11,050,000
Sinhala-Tamil	1,710,000
● Tamil	3,600,000
Other	60,000
Sudan, The[1]	
● Arabic	15,330,000
Azande (Zande)	840,000
Bari	760,000
Beja	1,980,000
Dinka	3,580,000
Fur	640,000
Lotuko	460,000
Nubian languages	2,520,000
Nuer	1,530,000
Shilluk	530,000
Other	2,890,000
Suriname	
● Dutch	...
English	...
Sranantonga	170,000
Sranantonga-other	170,000
Other (mostly Hindī, Javanese, and Saramacca)	90,000

Language (continued)

Major languages by country	Number of speakers
Swaziland[1]	
● English	...
● Swazi	840,000
Zulu	20,000
Other	70,000
Sweden[2]	
Arabic	68,000
Danish	41,000
English	32,000
Finnish	209,000
German	45,000
Iranian languages	49,000
Norwegian	46,000
Polish	39,000
South Slavic languages	116,000
Spanish	55,000
● Swedish	7,932,000
Turkish	29,000
Other	197,000
Switzerland	
● French	1,360,000
● German	4,510,000
● Italian	540,000
Romansch	40,000
Other	630,000
Syria[1]	
● Arabic	13,320,000
Kurdish	1,330,000
Other	150,000
Taiwan	
Austronesian languages	
Ami	129,000
Atayal	82,000
Bunun	40,000
Paiwan	63,000
Puyuma	8,000
Rukai	8,000
Saisiyat	4,000
Tsou	6,000
Yami	4,000
Chinese languages	
Hakka	2,180,000
● Mandarin	2,830,000
Min (South Fuklen)	16,100,000
Other	20,000
Tajikistan	
Russian	580,000
● Tajik	3,690,000
Uzbek	1,370,000
Other	300,000
Tanzania[1]	
Chaga (Chagga), Pare	1,420,000
● English	900,000
Gogo	1,130,000
Ha	990,000
Haya	1,700,000
Hehet	1,980,000
Iramba	820,000
Luguru	1,420,000
Luo	240,000
Makonde	1,700,000
Masai	280,000
Ngoni	380,000
Nyakyusa	1,560,000
Nyamwezi (Sukuma)	6,080,000
Shambala	1,230,000
● Swahili	2,550,000
Swahili (lingua franca)	26,000,000
Tatoga	210,000
Yao	710,000
Other	4,440,000
Thailand[1]	
Chinese	7,280,000
Karen	220,000
Malay	2,180,000
Mon-Khmer languages	
Khmer	760,000
Kuy	640,000
Other	210,000
Thai languages	
Lao	16,130,000
● Thai (Siamese)	31,540,000

Major languages by country	Number of speakers
Other	410,000
Other	620,000
Togo[1]	
● French	730,000
Chadic languages	
Hausa	12,000
Kwa languages	
Adja-Ewe group	
Adja	133,000
Ane (Mina)	242,000
Anlo	3,000
Ewe	990,000
Fon	43,000
Hwe	5,000
Kpessi	4,000
Peda-Hula (Pla)	17,000
Watyi (Ouatchi)	440,000
Ana-Ife group	
Ahlo	8,000
Ana (Ana-Ife)	107,000
Anyana	9,000
Nago	11,000
Yoruba	8,000
Kebu-Akposo group	
Adele	9,000
Akposo	114,000
Kebu	49,000
Voltaic (Gur) languages	
Kabre-Tem group	
Kabre	589,000
Kotokoli (Tem)	246,000
Namba (Lamba)	130,000
Naudemba (Losso)	175,000
para-Gurma group	
Basari	75,000
Chekossi (Akan)	50,000
Chamba	41,000
Dye (Gangam)	40,000
Gurma	145,000
Konkomba	60,000
Moba	229,000
Mossi	11,000
Tamberma	24,000
Yanga	12,000
West Atlantic (Mel) languages	
Fulani (Peul)	58,000
Other	181,000
Tonga	
● English	...
● Tongan	99,000
Other	2,000
Trinidad and Tobago	
● English	...
English Creole[21]	36,000
Hindī	44,000
Trinidad English	1,189,000
Other	3,000
Tunisia	
● Arabic	6,330,000
Arabic-French	2,380,000
Arabic-French-English	290,000
Arabic-other	10,000
Other-no Arabic	30,000
Other	30,000
Turkey[1]	
Arabic	870,000
Kurdish[22]	6,770,000
● Turkish	55,960,000
Other	290,000
Turkmenistan	
Russian	500,000
● Turkmen	2,990,000
Uzbek	360,000
Other	310,000
Tuvalu	
● English	...
Kiribati (Gilbertese)	700
Tuvaluan (Ellice)	8,800
Uganda[1]	
Bantu languages	
Ganda (Luganda)	3,400,000

Major languages by country	Number of speakers
Gisu	1,370,000
Gwere	550,000
Kiga (Chiga)	1,310,000
Konjo	260,000
Nkole	1,570,000
Nyoro	630,000
Rundi	590,000
Rwanda	1,110,000
Soga	1,570,000
Swahili (lingua franca)	6,700,000
Toro	610,000
Central Sudanic languages	
Lugbara	730,000
Madi	260,000
English	190,000
Nilotic languages	
Acholi	890,000
Alur	330,000
Karamojong	390,000
Kumam	200,000
Lango	1,150,000
Padhola	310,000
Teso	1,700,000
Other	190,000
Ukraine	
Belarusian	160,000
Bulgarian	160,000
Hungarian	160,000
Polish	30,000
Romanian	340,000
Russian	17,030,000
● Ukrainian	33,530,000
Other	450,000
United Arab Emirates[2]	
● Arabic	1,050,000
Other[18]	1,450,000
United Kingdom	
● English	57,190,000
Scots-Gaelic	80,000
Welsh	560,000
Other	960,000
United States	
Amharic	40,000
Arabic	410,000
Armenian	170,000
Bengali	40,000
Cajun	40,000
Chinese (including Formosan)	1,490,000
Czech	110,000
Danish	40,000
Dutch	160,000
● English	228,770,000
English (lingua franca)	258,000,000
Finnish	60,000
French	1,960,000
French Creole (mostly Haitian)	220,000
German	1,780,000
Greek	450,000
Gujarātī	120,000
Hebrew	170,000
Hindī (including Urdū)	380,000
Hungarian	170,000
Ilocano	50,000
Italian	1,510,000
Japanese	490,000
Korean	720,000
Kru (Gullah)	80,000
Lithuanian	60,000
Malayālam	40,000
Miao (Hmong)	90,000
Mon-Khmer (mostly Cambodian)	150,000
Navajo	170,000
Norwegian	90,000
Pennsylvania Dutch	100,000
Persian	230,000
Polish	830,000
Portuguese	500,000
Punjābī	60,000
Romanian	80,000

Major languages by country	Number of speakers
Russian	280,000
Samoan	40,000
Serbo-Croatian	130,000
Slovak	90,000
Spanish	19,970,000
Swedish	90,000
Syriac	40,000
Tagalog	970,000
Thai (including Laotian)	240,000
Turkish	50,000
Ukrainian	110,000
Vietnamese	580,000
Yiddish	250,000
Other	780,000
Uruguay	
● Spanish	3,090,000
Other	110,000
Uzbekistan	
Crimean Tatar	210,000
Karakalpak	460,000
Kazak	890,000
Korean	120,000
Kyrgyz	170,000
Russian	2,540,000
Tajik	1,030,000
Tatar	430,000
Turkish	120,000
Turkmen	130,000
Ukrainian	90,000
● Uzbek	16,660,000
Other	520,000
Vanuatu[23]	
● Bislama (English Creole)	110,000
● English	60,000
● French	30,000
Other	2,000
Venezuela	
Amerindian languages	
Goajiro	80,000
Warrau (Warao)	30,000
Other	110,000
● Spanish	21,610,000
Other	480,000
Vietnam[1]	
Bahnar	160,000
Cham	110,000
Chinese (Hoa)	1,070,000
French	370,000
Hre	110,000
Jarai	290,000
Khmer	1,060,000
Koho	100,000
Man (Mien, or Yao)	560,000
Miao (Meo, or Hmong)	660,000
Mnong	80,000
Muong	1,080,000
Nung	840,000
Rade (Rhadé)	230,000
Roglai	80,000
San Chay (Cao Lan)	140,000
San Diu	110,000
Sedang	110,000
Stieng	60,000
Tai	1,230,000
Tho (Tay)	1,410,000
● Vietnamese	66,120,000
Other	520,000
Virgin Islands (U.S.)	
● English	79,000
French	3,000
Spanish	13,000
Other	3,000
West Bank[24]	
Arabic	1,200,000
Hebrew	120,000
Western Sahara	
Arabic	271,000
Western Samoa	
● English	1,000
● Samoan	79,000
Samoan-English	87,000

Major languages by country	Number of speakers
Yemen[1]	
● Arabic	16,300,000
Other	300,000
Yugoslavia[1]	
Albanian	1,730,000
Hungarian	350,000
Macedonian	50,000
Romanian	40,000
Romany	140,000
● Serbo-Croatian	7,880,000
Slovak	70,000
Vlach	20,000
Other	200,000
Zaire[1]	
Azande (Zande)	2,760,000
Boa	1,060,000
Chokwe	830,000
● French	3,500,000
Kongo	7,260,000
Kongo (lingua franca)	14,000,000
Lingala (lingua franca)	31,000,000
Luba	8,140,000
Lugbara	730,000
Mongo	6,100,000
Ngala and Bangi	2,620,000
Rundi	1,740,000
Rwanda	4,650,000
Swahili (lingua franca)	22,000,000
Teke	1,240,000
Other	8,140,000
Zambia[25]	
Bemba group	
Aushi (Ushi)	170,000
Bemba	2,430,000
Bisa	140,000
Lala	270,000
Lamba	230,000
Other	290,000
● English	800,000
Lozi (Barotse) group	
Lozi (Barotse)	580,000
Luyi (Luyana)	150,000
Nkoya	60,000
Other	10,000
Mambwe group	
Lungu	90,000
Mambwe	160,000
Mwanga (Winamwanga)	180,000
Other	20,000
North-Western group	
Chokwe	60,000
Kaonde	260,000
Luchazi	60,000
Lunda	250,000
Luvale (Luena)	200,000
Mbunda	140,000
Nyanja (Maravi) group	
Chewa	510,000
Ngoni	190,000
Nsenga	440,000
Nyanja (Maravi)	500,000
Other	60,000
Tonga (Ila-Tonga) group	
Ila	80,000
Lenje	170,000
Soli	70,000
Tonga	1,060,000
Other	80,000
Tumbuka group	
Senga	80,000
Tumbuka	360,000
Other	350,000
Zimbabwe	
● English	260,000
Ndebele (Nguni)	1,870,000
Nyanja	260,000
Shona	8,310,000
Other	820,000

[1]Figures given represent ethnolinguistic groups.　[2]Data refer to nationality (usually resident aliens holding foreign passports).　[3]Data are partly based on place of residence.　[4]Majority of population speak Moré (language of the Mossi); Dyula is language of commerce.　[5]Swahili also spoken.　[6]English and French also spoken.　[7]Based on "nationality" at 1982 census.　[8]Includes naturalized citizens.　[9]French is the universal language throughout France; traditional dialects and minority languages are retained regionally in the approximate numbers shown, however.　[10]Data reflect multilingualism; 1996 population estimate is 223,000.　[11]Refers to Irish speakers in Gaeltacht areas.　[12]Includes the population of the Golan Heights and East Jerusalem; excludes the Israeli population in the West Bank and Gaza Strip.　[13]English and French also spoken.　[14]English and Italian also spoken.　[15]Data reflect ability to speak the language, not mother tongue; 1996 population estimate is 123,000.　[16]French also spoken.　[17]Includes speakers of standard English.　[18]Mostly Pakistanis, Indians, and Iranians.　[19]Gujarātī and Chinese also spoken.　[20]Solomon Islands Pidgin (English) is the lingua franca.　[21]Spoken on Tobago only.　[22]Other estimates of the Kurdish population range from 6 percent to 20–25 percent.　[23]Data reflect multilingualism; 1996 population is 172,000.　[24]Excludes East Jerusalem.　[25]Groups are officially defined geographic divisions; elements comprising them are named by language.

Religion

The following table presents statistics on religious affiliation for each of the countries of the world. An assessment was made for each country of the available data on distribution of religious communities within the total population; the best available figures, whether originating as census data, membership figures of the churches concerned, or estimates by external analysts in the absence of reliable local data, were applied as percentages to the estimated 1996 midyear population of the country to obtain the data shown below.

Several concepts govern the nature of the available data, each useful separately but none the basis of any standard of international practice in the collection of such data. The word "affiliation" was used above to describe the nature of the relationship joining the religious bodies named and the populations shown. This term implies some sort of formal, usually documentary, connection between the religion and the individual (a baptismal certificate, a child being assigned the religion of its parents on a census form, maintenance of one's name on the tax rolls of a state religion, etc.) but says nothing about the nature of the individual's personal religious practice, in that the individual may have lapsed, never been confirmed as an adult, joined another religion, or may have joined an organization that is formally atheist.

The user of these statistics should be careful to note that not only does the nature of the affiliation (with an organized religion) differ greatly from country to country, but the social context of religious practice does also. A country in which a single religion has long been predominant will often show more than 90% of its population to be *affiliated,* while in actual fact, no more than 10% may actually *practice* that religion on a regular basis. Such a situation often leads to undercounting of minority religions (where someone [head of household, communicant, child] is counted at all), blurring of distinctions seen to be significant elsewhere (a Hindu country may not distinguish Protestant [or even Christian] denominations; a Christian country may not distinguish among its Muslim or Buddhist citizens), or double-counting in countries where an individual may conscientiously practice more than one "religion" at a time.

Until 1989 communist countries had for long consciously attempted to ignore, suppress, or render invisible religious practice within their borders. Countries with large numbers of adherents of traditional, often animist, religions and belief systems usually have little or no formal methodology for defining the nature of local religious practice. On the other hand, countries with strong missionary traditions, or good census organizations, or few religious sensitivities may have very good, detailed, and meaningful data.

The most comprehensive work available is DAVID B. BARRETT (ed.), *World Christian Encyclopedia* (1982); it examines both the theoretical and practical problems of collecting and analyzing religious statistics, assembles a mine of national detail, and establishes a basis for further study.

Religion

Religious affiliation	1996 population	Religious affiliation	1996 population	Religious affiliation	1996 population	Religious affiliation	1996 population	Religious affiliation	1996 population
Afghanistan		**Azerbaijan**		Serbian Orthodox	1,090,000	**Central African Republic**		**Cyprus**	
Sunnī Muslim	19,040,000	Muslim (mostly Shīʿī)	7,070,000	Roman Catholic	530,000	Protestant	820,000	Greek Orthodox	630,000
Shīʿī Muslim	3,400,000	Russian Orthodox	190,000	Protestant	140,000	Roman Catholic	820,000	Muslim (mostly Sunnī)	110,000
other	230,000	Armenian Apostolic		other	350,000	traditional beliefs	790,000	other (mostly Christian)	30,000
		(Orthodox)	170,000			Muslim	490,000		
Albania		other	130,000	**Botswana**		other	360,000	**Czech Republic**	
Muslim	2,270,000			traditional beliefs	730,000			Roman Catholic	4,030,000
Albanian Orthodox	650,000	**Bahamas, The**		Protestant	390,000	**Chad**		Evangelical Church of	
Roman Catholic	320,000	Protestant	155,000	African Christian	170,000	Muslim	3,520,000	Czech Brethren	200,000
		Anglican	56,000	Roman Catholic	140,000	Roman Catholic	1,330,000	Czechoslovak	
Algeria		Roman Catholic	53,000	other	50,000	Protestant	940,000	Hussite	180,000
Sunnī Muslim	28,430,000	other	16,000			traditional beliefs	480,000	Silesian Evangelical	30,000
Ibāḍīyah Muslim	110,000			**Brazil**		other	270,000	Eastern Orthodox	20,000
other	30,000	**Bahrain**		Roman Catholic				atheist and	
		Shīʿī Muslim	340,000	(including syncretic		**Chile**		nonreligious	4,120,000
American Samoa		Sunnī Muslim	150,000	Afro-Catholic cults		Roman Catholic	11,030,000	other	1,740,000
Congregational	33,000	other	110,000	having Spiritist		Evangelical			
Roman Catholic	12,000			beliefs and rituals)	111,000,000	Protestant	1,780,000	**Denmark**	
other	14,000	**Bangladesh**		Evangelical Protestant	30,000,000	other	1,570,000	Evangelical Lutheran	4,626,000
		Muslim	108,670,000	other	17,000,000			other	618,000
Andorra		Hindu	12,940,000			**China**			
Roman Catholic	64,000	other	1,450,000	**Brunei**		nonreligious	696,000,000	**Djibouti**	
other	6,000			Muslim	202,000	Chinese folk-		Sunnī Muslim	568,000
		Barbados		other	98,000	religionist	245,000,000	Christian[1]	36,000
Angola		Anglican	87,000			atheist	146,000,000		
Roman Catholic	8,180,000	Protestant	79,000	**Bulgaria**		Buddhist	103,000,000	**Dominica**	
Protestant	2,360,000	Roman Catholic	12,000	Christian (mostly		Muslim	18,000,000	Roman Catholic	52,000
traditional beliefs	1,130,000	other	87,000	Bulgarian Orthodox)	7,240,000	Christian	9,000,000	Protestant	12,000
other	230,000			Muslim (mostly		traditional beliefs	1,000,000	other	10,000
		Belarus		Sunnī)	1,090,000				
Antigua and Barbuda		Belarusian Orthodox	9,060,000	other	30,000	**Colombia**		**Dominican Republic**	
Protestant	27,000	Roman Catholic	1,330,000			Roman Catholic	33,200,000	Roman Catholic	6,850,000
Anglican	21,000	other	50,000	**Burkina Faso**		other	2,450,000	other	650,000
Roman Catholic	7,000			Muslim	5,310,000				
other	9,000	**Belgium**		traditional beliefs	4,250,000	**Comoros**		**Ecuador**	
		Roman Catholic	8,790,000	Christian	1,060,000	Sunnī Muslim	558,000	Roman Catholic	10,910,000
Argentina		other	1,400,000			Christian	4,000	other	790,000
Roman Catholic	31,820,000			**Burundi**					
other	3,180,000	**Belize**		Roman Catholic	3,870,000	**Congo**		**Egypt**	
		Roman Catholic	126,000	nonreligious	1,110,000	traditional beliefs	1,280,000	Sunnī Muslim	54,810,000
Armenia		Protestant	60,000	other (mostly Protestant)	960,000	Roman Catholic	1,110,000	Christian (mostly	
Armenian Apostolic		Anglican	15,000			Protestant	230,000	Coptic[2])	6,090,000
(Orthodox)	3,540,000	other	18,000	**Cambodia**		Muslim	50,000		
other (mostly Roman				Buddhist	9,580,000			**El Salvador**	
Catholic and Muslim)	230,000	**Benin**		Muslim	220,000	**Costa Rica**		Roman Catholic	4,420,000
		Voodoo		other	290,000	Roman Catholic	2,760,000	other (mostly	
Aruba		(traditional beliefs)	3,460,000			other	640,000	Protestant)	1,470,000
Roman Catholic	64,000	Roman Catholic	1,170,000	**Cameroon**					
other	9,000	Muslim	670,000	Roman Catholic	4,730,000	**Côte d'Ivoire**		**Equatorial Guinea**	
		other	270,000	traditional beliefs	3,540,000	Muslim	5,700,000	Roman Catholic	390,000
Australia				Muslim	2,970,000	Roman Catholic	3,060,000	other	10,000
Roman Catholic	5,000,000	**Bermuda**		Protestant	2,380,000	traditional beliefs	2,510,000		
Anglican	4,360,000	Anglican	23,000			nonreligious	1,980,000	**Eritrea**	
Uniting Church	1,510,000	Methodist	10,000	**Canada**		Protestant	780,000	Christian (mostly	
Presbyterian	790,000	Roman Catholic	9,000	Roman Catholic	13,460,000	other	710,000	Ethiopian Orthodox)	1,810,000
other Protestant	1,200,000	other	19,000	Protestant	8,460,000			Muslim	1,810,000
Orthodox	520,000			Anglican	2,390,000	**Croatia**			
nonreligious	2,360,000	**Bhutan**		Eastern Orthodox	420,000	Roman Catholic	3,650,000	**Estonia**	
other	2,550,000	Buddhist	630,000	Jewish	350,000	Serbian Orthodox	530,000	*Believers are predominantly*	
		Hindu	210,000	Muslim	280,000	Sunnī Muslim	60,000	*affiliated with the Evangeli-*	
Austria				Buddhist	180,000	Protestant	20,000	*cal Lutheran Church of*	
Roman Catholic	6,320,000	**Bolivia**		Hindu	170,000	other	520,000	*Estonia; Russian Orthodox*	
Evangelical		Roman Catholic	6,020,000	Sikh	160,000			*and Protestant minorities.*	
Lutheran	390,000	Evangelical Protestant	770,000	nonreligious	3,730,000	**Cuba**			
atheist and		other	800,000	other	180,000	Roman Catholic	4,400,000	**Ethiopia**	
nonreligious	700,000					nonreligious	5,410,000	Ethiopian Orthodox	29,880,000
other	690,000	**Bosnia and Herzegovina**		**Cape Verde**		atheist	710,000	Muslim (mostly	
		Sunnī Muslim	1,410,000	Roman Catholic	387,000	other	600,000	Sunnī)	17,060,000
				Protestant	16,000				

Religion   (continued)

Religious affiliation	1996 population
traditional beliefs	6,920,000
other	2,760,000
Faroe Islands	
Evangelical Lutheran	32,000
other	12,000
Fiji	
Christian (mostly Methodist and Roman Catholic)	424,000
Hindu	306,000
Muslim	63,000
other	9,000
Finland	
Evangelical Lutheran	4,410,000
other	722,000
France	
Roman Catholic	43,150,000
nonreligious	7,120,000
Muslim	3,210,000
atheist	1,990,000
Protestant	1,170,000
Jewish	640,000
other	1,750,000
French Guiana	
Roman Catholic	117,000
other	32,000
French Polynesia	
Protestant	104,000
Roman Catholic	88,000
other	31,000
Gabon	
Roman Catholic	750,000
traditional beliefs	270,000
African Christian	120,000
other	30,000
Gambia, The	
Muslim (mostly Sunnī)	1,090,000
other	50,000
Gaza Strip	
Muslim (mostly Sunnī)	805,000
other	11,000
Georgia	
Georgian Orthodox	3,480,000
Sunnī Muslim	590,000
Russian Orthodox	540,000
Armenian Apostolic (Orthodox)	430,000
other (mostly nonreligious)	320,000
Germany	
Protestant (mostly Evangelical Lutheran)	36,850,000
Roman Catholic	30,300,000
Muslim	1,740,000
other (mostly nonreligious or unaffiliated)	13,000,000
Ghana	
African Christian	4,960,000
Protestant	3,390,000
traditional beliefs	2,970,000
Roman Catholic	2,490,000
Muslim	2,430,000
other	660,000
Gibraltar	
Roman Catholic	21,000
other	6,000
Greece	
Greek Orthodox	10,280,000
Muslim	140,000
other	70,000
Greenland	
Evangelical Lutheran	55,000
other	1,000
Grenada	
Roman Catholic	52,000
Anglican	14,000
other	32,000
Guadeloupe	
Roman Catholic	390,000
other	40,000

Religious affiliation	1996 population
Guam	
Roman Catholic	122,000
Protestant	24,000
other	7,000
Guatemala	
Roman Catholic	8,200,000
Evangelical Protestant	2,730,000
Guernsey	
Anglican	43,000
other	23,000
Guinea	
Muslim	6,000,000
traditional beliefs	320,000
Christian	300,000
other	290,000
Guinea-Bissau	
traditional beliefs	710,000
Muslim	330,000
Christian	50,000
Guyana	
Hindu	242,000
Roman Catholic	130,000
Protestant	123,000
Anglican	118,000
Muslim	64,000
other	36,000
Haiti	
Roman Catholic	5,410,000
Baptist	650,000
Pentecostal	240,000
other	430,000
Honduras	
Roman Catholic	4,820,000
Evangelical Protestant	570,000
other	280,000
Hong Kong	
Buddhist and Taoist	4,650,000
Protestant	270,000
Roman Catholic	260,000
other	1,120,000
Hungary	
Roman Catholic	6,920,000
Protestant	2,560,000
nonreligious and atheist	490,000
other	230,000
Iceland	
Evangelical Lutheran	248,000
other	22,000
India	
Hindu	765,000,000
Sunnī Muslim	79,000,000
Shīʿī Muslim	26,000,000
Sikh	19,000,000
Roman Catholic	14,000,000
Protestant	9,000,000
Buddhist	7,000,000
Jain	5,000,000
Zoroastrian (Parsi)	130,000
other	29,000,000
Indonesia	
Muslim	172,840,000
Protestant	11,970,000
Roman Catholic	7,100,000
Hindu	3,630,000
Buddhist	2,040,000
other	610,000
Iran	
Shīʿī Muslim	58,220,000
Sunnī Muslim	3,520,000
other	490,000
Iraq	
Shīʿī Muslim	13,390,000
Sunnī Muslim	7,390,000
other (mostly Christian)	640,000
Ireland	
Roman Catholic	3,300,000
other	300,000
Isle of Man	
Anglican	43,000
other	27,000

Religious affiliation	1996 population
Israel	
Jewish[3]	4,470,000
Muslim (mostly Sunnī)	770,000
other	240,000
Italy	
Roman Catholic	47,780,000
Muslim	700,000
other (mostly nonreligious and atheist)	9,020,000
Jamaica	
Protestant	1,230,000
Anglican	180,000
Roman Catholic	120,000
other	980,000
Japan	
Shintoist[4]	117,670,000
Buddhist[4]	90,520,000
Christian	1,550,000
other	11,380,000
Jersey	
Anglican	54,000
Roman Catholic	20,000
other	14,000
Jordan	
Sunnī Muslim	3,990,000
Christian	350,000
Kazakstan	
Muslim (mostly Sunnī)	7,840,000
Russian Orthodox	7,340,000
Protestant	330,000
other (mostly nonreligious)	1,160,000
Kenya	
Roman Catholic	7,690,000
Protestant	5,620,000
traditional beliefs	5,510,000
African Christian	5,130,000
Anglican	2,100,000
Muslim	1,750,000
other	1,340,000
Kiribati	
Roman Catholic	44,000
Congregational	32,000
other	6,000
Korea, North	
atheist and nonreligious	16,230,000
traditional beliefs	3,730,000
Ch'ŏndogyo	3,320,000
other	630,000
Korea, South	
nonreligious	22,660,000
Buddhist	11,010,000
Protestant	8,210,000
Roman Catholic	2,660,000
Confucian	180,000
Wonbulgyo	140,000
Ch'ŏndogyo	50,000
other	310,000
Kuwait	
Sunnī Muslim	930,000
Shīʿī Muslim	620,000
other Muslim	210,000
other	310,000
Kyrgyzstan	
Muslim (mostly Sunnī)	3,160,000
other (mostly non-religious and Russian Orthodox)	1,350,000
Laos	
Buddhist	2,900,000
traditional beliefs	1,690,000
other	430,000
Latvia	
Believers are predominantly affiliated with the Latvian Evangelical Lutheran Church; Russian Orthodox, Roman Catholic, and Protestant minorities.	
Lebanon	
Shīʿī Muslim	1,370,000
Sunnī Muslim	890,000
Maronite Christian	760,000

Religious affiliation	1996 population
Druze	250,000
Greek Orthodox	210,000
Greek Catholic	130,000
Armenian Apostolic (Orthodox)	130,000
other	40,000
Lesotho	
Roman Catholic	860,000
Protestant	590,000
other	520,000
Liberia	
Christian	1,430,000
traditional beliefs	390,000
Muslim	290,000
Libya	
Sunnī Muslim	5,280,000
other	160,000
Liechtenstein	
Roman Catholic	25,000
other	6,000
Lithuania	
Roman Catholic	2,980,000
other (mostly Russian Orthodox, Old Believer, Evangelical Lutheran, and nonreligious)	730,000
Luxembourg	
Roman Catholic	395,000
other	20,000
Macau	
nonreligious	263,000
Buddhist	73,000
other	97,000
Macedonia	
Serbian (Macedonian) Orthodox	1,320,000
Sunnī Muslim	590,000
other	60,000
Madagascar	
traditional beliefs	7,520,000
Protestant	2,730,000
Roman Catholic	2,730,000
Muslim	680,000
Malaŵi	
Protestant (mostly Presbyterian)	4,730,000
Roman Catholic	1,890,000
Muslim	1,890,000
traditional beliefs	950,000
Malaysia	
Muslim	10,770,000
Buddhist	3,520,000
Chinese folk-religionist	2,360,000
Hindu	1,430,000
Christian	1,300,000
other	980,000
Maldives	
Sunnī Muslim	266,000
Mali	
Muslim	8,280,000
traditional beliefs	830,000
Christian	90,000
Malta	
Roman Catholic	364,000
other	9,000
Marshall Islands	
Protestant (mostly Congregational)	54,000
Roman Catholic	5,000
Martinique	
Roman Catholic	350,000
other	50,000
Mauritania	
Sunnī Muslim	2,320,000
other	10,000
Mauritius	
Hindu	580,000
Roman Catholic	310,000
Muslim	190,000
other	60,000

Religious affiliation	1996 population
Mayotte	
Sunnī Muslim	119,000
Christian	4,000
Mexico	
Roman Catholic	83,150,000
Protestant and Evangelical Catholic	4,530,000
nonreligious	3,000,000
other	2,020,000
Micronesia	
Roman Catholic	63,000
Protestant (mostly Congregational)	43,000
Moldova	
Russian (Moldovan) Orthodox	4,350,000
other	20,000
Monaco	
Roman Catholic	28,000
other	3,000
Mongolia	
Tantric Buddhist (Lamaist)	2,240,000
Muslim	90,000
Morocco	
Muslim (mostly Sunnī)	26,660,000
other	80,000
Mozambique	
traditional beliefs	8,550,000
Roman Catholic	5,610,000
Muslim	2,320,000
Protestant	1,340,000
other	60,000
Myanmar (Burma)	
Buddhist	40,960,000
Christian	2,250,000
Muslim	1,750,000
traditional beliefs	530,000
Hindu	230,000
other	70,000
Namibia	
Lutheran	875,000
Roman Catholic	338,000
Dutch Reformed	104,000
Anglican	85,000
other	306,000
Nauru	
Congregational	5,800
other	4,800
Nepal	
Hindu	18,070,000
Buddhist	1,630,000
Muslim	740,000
other	450,000
Netherlands, The	
Roman Catholic	4,830,000
Dutch Reformed Church (NHK)	2,180,000
Reformed Churches	1,250,000
Muslim	600,000
nonreligious	6,080,000
other	650,000
Netherlands Antilles	
Roman Catholic	154,000
other	54,000
New Caledonia	
Roman Catholic	106,000
other	85,000
New Zealand	
Anglican	790,000
Presbyterian	580,000
Roman Catholic	530,000
Methodist	150,000
Baptist	80,000
Ratana	50,000
Mormon	50,000
nonreligious	720,000
other	670,000
Nicaragua	
Roman Catholic	3,770,000
other (mostly Protestant)	500,000

Religious affiliation	1996 population

Niger
Sunnī Muslim — 9,340,000
other — 130,000

Nigeria
Muslim — 51,960,000
Protestant — 22,310,000
traditional
  beliefs — 10,390,000
Roman Catholic — 10,260,000
African Christian — 8,990,000

Northern Mariana Islands
Roman Catholic — 46,000
other — 13,000

Norway
Evangelical Lutheran
  (Church of Norway) — 3,850,000
other — 530,000

Oman
Believers are predominantly Ibāḍīyah or Sunnī Muslim; Hindu, Christian, and Shīʿī Muslim minorities.

Pakistan
Sunnī Muslim — 100,130,000
Shīʿī Muslim — 26,700,000
Christian — 2,670,000
Hindu — 2,400,000
other — 1,600,000

Palau
Roman Catholic — 7,000
traditional beliefs — 5,000
Protestant — 4,000
other — 1,000

Panama
Roman Catholic — 2,140,000
Protestant — 270,000
other — 260,000

Papua New Guinea
Protestant — 2,640,000
Roman Catholic — 1,250,000
Anglican — 170,000
other — 340,000

Paraguay
Roman Catholic — 4,610,000
other (mostly
  Protestant) — 350,000

Peru
Roman Catholic — 21,210,000
Evangelical
  Protestant — 1,720,000
nonreligious — 340,000
other — 680,000

Philippines
Roman Catholic — 59,500,000
Protestant — 3,900,000
Muslim — 3,280,000
Aglipayan — 1,890,000
Church of Christ
  (Iglesia ni Cristo) — 1,680,000
other — 1,500,000

Poland
Roman Catholic — 35,140,000
nonreligious — 2,650,000
Polish Orthodox — 550,000
other — 390,000

Portugal
Roman Catholic — 9,380,000
other — 550,000

Puerto Rico
Roman Catholic — 3,030,000
other — 730,000

Qatar
Muslim (mostly
  Sunnī) — 561,000
other — 30,000

Réunion
Roman Catholic — 590,000
other (mostly
  Muslim) — 80,000

Romania
Romanian Orthodox — 19,680,000
Roman Catholic — 1,140,000
other — 1,850,000

Russia
Believers are predominantly affiliated with the Russian Orthodox Church; Roman Catholic, Protestant, Muslim, Jewish, and Buddhist minorities.

Rwanda
Roman Catholic — 4,450,000
traditional beliefs — 1,710,000
Protestant — 620,000
Muslim — 70,000

St. Kitts and Nevis
Anglican — 13,000
Methodist — 11,000
other — 15,000

St. Lucia
Roman Catholic — 114,000
other — 30,000

St. Vincent and the Grenadines
Anglican — 47,000
Methodist — 24,000
Roman Catholic — 13,000
other — 29,000

San Marino
Roman Catholic — 24,000
other — 1,000

São Tomé and Príncipe
Roman Catholic — 110,000
Protestant — 30,000

Saudi Arabia
Sunnī Muslim — 17,590,000
Shīʿī Muslim — 620,000
other — 220,000

Senegal
Sunnī Muslim — 8,020,000
Christian — 420,000
other — 90,000

Seychelles
Roman Catholic — 67,000
other — 9,000

Sierra Leone
Sunnī Muslim — 2,770,000
traditional beliefs — 1,390,000
Christian — 460,000

Singapore
Buddhist and Taoist — 1,642,000
Muslim — 468,000
Protestant — 238,000
Roman Catholic — 147,000
Hindu — 108,000
nonreligious — 426,000
other — 16,000

Slovakia
Roman Catholic — 3,240,000
Slovak Evangelical — 330,000
atheist — 520,000
other — 1,280,000

Slovenia
Roman Catholic — 1,840,000
other — 120,000

Solomon Islands
Protestant — 165,000
Anglican — 134,000
Roman Catholic — 76,000
other — 21,000

Somalia
Sunnī Muslim — 6,790,000
other — 10,000

South Africa[5]
Christian — 22,490,000
Protestant — 11,080,000
  Dutch (Afrikaans)
  Reformed
  Churches — 3,980,000
  Nederduitse
  Gereformeerde — 3,510,000
  Gereformeerde — 180,000
  Nederduitsch
  Hervormde — 290,000
other Protestant — 7,110,000
Methodist — 1,980,000
Presbyterian — 440,000
United
  Congregational — 420,000
Lutheran — 850,000
Apostolic Faith
  Mission of South
  Africa — 440,000
New Apostolic
  Church — 160,000
other Apostolic — 460,000
Baptist — 270,000
Pentecostal
  Protestant — 80,000
African Protestant
  Church — 30,000
Full Gospel — 220,000
Pentecostal — 20,000
Salvation Army — 40,000
Seventh-day
  Adventist — 90,000
Swiss — 50,000
Assemblies of
  God — 170,000
other — 1,390,000
Roman Catholic — 2,560,000
Anglican — 1,280,000
Greek Orthodox — 30,000
black independent
  churches — 7,520,000
Zion Christian
  Church — 1,660,000
other — 5,860,000
Mormon — 10,000
Hindu — 430,000
Muslim — 370,000
Jewish — 70,000
other beliefs — 30,000
nonreligious — 410,000
not stated — 10,050,000

Spain
Roman Catholic — 37,520,000
Muslim — 450,000
other — 1,300,000

Sri Lanka
Buddhist — 12,690,000
Hindu — 2,840,000
Muslim — 1,380,000
Roman Catholic — 1,260,000
other — 150,000

Sudan, The
Sunnī Muslim — 22,680,000
traditional beliefs — 5,190,000
Christian[1] — 2,830,000
other — 370,000

Suriname
Hindu — 119,000
Roman Catholic — 99,000
Muslim — 86,000
Protestant — 82,000
other — 50,000

Swaziland
Christian[1] — 720,000
traditional beliefs — 200,000
other — 20,000

Sweden
Church of Sweden
  (Lutheran) — 7,660,000
other — 1,200,000

Switzerland
Roman Catholic — 3,270,000
Protestant — 2,830,000
other — 990,000

Syria
Sunnī Muslim — 10,950,000
Shīʿī Muslim — 1,780,000
Christian — 1,480,000
Druze — 440,000
other — 150,000

Taiwan
Chinese folk-
  religionist — 10,410,000
Buddhist — 9,230,000
Christian[1] — 1,590,000
other — 240,000

Tajikistan
Sunnī Muslim — 4,760,000
Shīʿī Muslim — 300,000
other (mostly
  nonreligious) — 890,000

Tanzania
Muslim — 10,090,000
traditional beliefs — 10,090,000
Christian — 8,650,000

Thailand
Buddhist — 56,880,000
Muslim — 2,420,000
Christian — 330,000
other — 370,000

Togo
traditional beliefs — 2,510,000
Roman Catholic — 920,000
Sunnī Muslim — 520,000
Protestant — 290,000
other — 30,000

Tonga
Free Wesleyan — 44,000
Roman Catholic — 16,000
other — 41,000

Trinidad and Tobago
Roman Catholic — 371,000
Hindu — 299,000
Protestant — 237,000
Anglican — 138,000
Muslim — 74,000
other — 143,000

Tunisia
Sunnī Muslim — 9,010,000
other — 50,000

Turkey
Muslim (mostly
  Sunnī) — 62,530,000
other — 120,000

Turkmenistan
Muslim (mostly
  Sunnī) — 3,980,000
Russian Orthodox — 500,000
other — 90,000

Tuvalu
Congregational — 9,200
other — 300

Uganda
Roman Catholic — 9,490,000
Anglican — 5,010,000
traditional beliefs — 2,410,000
Muslim (mostly
  Sunnī) — 1,260,000
other — 970,000

Ukraine
Believers are predominantly affiliated with the Ukrainian Orthodox Church; Ukrainian Autocephalous Orthodox and Ukrainian Catholic (Uniate) minorities.

United Arab Emirates
Sunnī Muslim — 2,000,000
Shīʿī Muslim — 400,000
other — 100,000

United Kingdom
Christian[1] — 51,230,000
Church of
  England — 33,540,000
Protestant — 8,820,000
Roman Catholic — 7,700,000
Eastern Orthodox — 350,000
other Christian — 820,000
Muslim — 820,000
Hindu — 410,000
Jewish — 320,000
Sikh — 240,000
nonreligious and
  atheist — 5,580,000
other — 180,000

United States
Christian (professing) — 227,020,000
Christian (affiliated) — 197,480,000
  Protestant — 121,310,000
  Roman Catholic — 59,950,000
  Eastern Orthodox — 5,680,000
  Anglican — 2,370,000
  other Christian — 10,510,000
  multiply affiliated
    Christians — -3,330,000
Christian
  (unaffiliated) — 29,540,000
nonreligious — 22,870,000
Jewish — 5,560,000
Muslim — 3,800,000
Buddhist — 1,880,000
atheist — 880,000
Hindu — 800,000
Baha'i — 690,000
New-Religionist — 610,000
Sikh — 190,000
other — 1,150,000

Uruguay
Roman Catholic — 2,110,000
other — 1,090,000

Uzbekistan
Muslim (mostly
  Sunnī) — 20,420,000
Russian Orthodox — 2,090,000
other (mostly
  nonreligious) — 700,000

Vanuatu
Presbyterian — 60,000
Roman Catholic — 24,000
Anglican — 24,000
other — 60,000

Venezuela
Roman Catholic — 20,680,000
other — 1,630,000

Vietnam
Buddhist — 50,760,000
Roman Catholic — 6,430,000
New-Religionist
  Cao Dai — 2,860,000
  Hoa Hao — 1,610,000
other — 14,490,000

Virgin Islands (U.S.)
Protestant — 45,000
Roman Catholic — 33,000
other — 20,000

West Bank
Muslim (mostly
  Sunnī) — 1,080,000
Jewish[6] — 130,000
Christian and other — 110,000

Western Sahara
Sunnī Muslim — 271,000

Western Samoa
Congregational — 79,000
Roman Catholic — 36,000
other — 52,000

Yemen
Muslim (mostly
  Sunnī) — 16,580,000
other — 20,000

Yugoslavia
Serbian Orthodox — 6,810,000
Sunnī Muslim — 1,990,000
Roman Catholic — 420,000
Protestant — 110,000
other — 1,150,000

Zaire
Roman Catholic — 21,910,000
Protestant — 13,130,000
African Christian — 7,740,000
traditional beliefs — 1,540,000
Muslim — 630,000
other — 320,000

Zambia
Christian[1] — 6,990,000
traditional beliefs — 2,620,000
other — 100,000

Zimbabwe
Christian[1] — 6,680,000
traditional beliefs — 4,660,000
other — 170,000

---

[1]Includes affiliated and nominal Christians. [2]Official 1986 census figure is 5.9 percent. [3]Includes the Golan Heights and East Jerusalem; excludes the West Bank and Gaza Strip. [4]Many Japanese practice both Shintoism and Buddhism. [5]Excludes the former black independent states of Bophuthatswana, Ciskei, Transkei, and Venda, in which there are about 5,810,000 Christians and 2,090,000 practicers of traditional beliefs. [6]Excludes East Jerusalem.

Vital statistics, marriage, family

This table provides some of the basic measures of the factors that influence the size, direction, and rates of population change within a country. The accuracy of these data depends on the effectiveness of each respective national system for registering vital and civil events (birth, death, marriage, etc.) and on the sophistication of the analysis that can be brought to bear upon the data so compiled.

Data on birth rates, for example, depend not only on the completeness of registration of births in a particular country but also on the conditions under which those data are collected: Do all births take place in a hospital? Are the births reported comparably in all parts of the country? Are the records of the births tabulated at a central location in a timely way with an effort to eliminate inconsistent reporting of birth events, perinatal mortality, etc.? Similar difficulties attach to death rates but with the added need to identify "cause of death." Even in a developed country such identifications are often left to nonmedical personnel, and in a developing country with, say, only one physician for every 10,000 population, there will be too few physicians to perform autopsies to assess accurately the cause of death after the fact and also too few to provide ongoing care at a level where records would permit inference about cause of death based on prior condition or diagnosis.

Calculating natural increase, which at its most basic is simply the difference between the birth and death rates, may be affected by the differing degrees of completeness of birth and death registration for a given country. The total fertility rate may be understood as the average number of children that would be borne per woman if all childbearing women lived to the end of their childbearing years and bore children at each age at the average rate for that age. Calculating a meaningful fertility rate requires analysis of changing age structure of the female population over time, changing mortality rates among mothers and their infants, and changing medical practice at births, each improvement of natural survivorship or medical support leading to greater numbers of live-born children and greater numbers of children who survive their first year (the basis for measurement of infant mortality, another basic indicator of demographic conditions and trends within a population).

As indicated above, data for causes of death are not only particularly difficult to obtain, since many countries are not well equipped to collect the data, but also difficult to assess, as their accuracy may be suspect and their meaning may be subject to varying interpretation. Take the case of a citizen of a less developed country who dies of what is clearly a lung infection: Was the death complicated by chronic malnutrition, itself complicated by a parasitic infestation, these last two together so weakening the subject that he died of an infection that he might have survived had his general health been better? Similarly, in a developed country: Someone may die from what is identified in an autopsy as a cerebrovascular accident, but if that accident occurred in a vascular system that was weakened by diabetes, what was the actual cause of death? Statistics on causes of death seek to identify the "underlying" cause (that which sets the final train of events leading to death in motion) but often must settle for the most proximate cause or symptom. Even this kind of analysis may be misleading for those charged with interpreting the data with a view to ordering health-care priorities for a particular country. The eight groups of causes of death utilized here include most, but not all, of the detailed

Vital statistics, marriage, family

country	vital rates						causes of death (rate per 100,000 population)								
	year	birth rate per 1,000 population	death rate per 1,000 population	infant mortality rate per 1,000 live births	rate of natural increase per 1,000 population	total fertility rate	year	infectious and parasitic diseases	malignant neoplasms (cancers)	endocrine and metabolic disorders	diseases of the nervous system	diseases of the circulatory system	diseases of the respiratory system	diseases of the digestive system	accidents, poisoning, and violence
Afghanistan	1995	42.7	18.5	152.8	24.2	6.2	...	...	...	...	...	...	...	...	...
Albania	1991	23.8	5.5	32.9	18.3	2.9[2]	1992	7.1	53.5	4.7	15.8	187.9	75.0	17.2	31.7
Algeria	1992	30.3	6.1	52.0[3]	24.2	3.8[3]	...	...	...	...	...	...	...	...	...
American Samoa	1991	35.7	4.3	11.0	31.4	5.4	1990	16.4[5]	46.8	16.4[6]	...	131.1[7]	65.6[8]	...	58.5
Andorra	1995	11.0	3.4	7.7	7.6	1.7	...	...	...	...	...	...	...	...	...
Angola	1995	45.1	18.1	142.1	27.0	6.4	...	...	...	...	...	...	...	...	...
Antigua and Barbuda	1995	17.1	5.4	17.8	11.7	1.7	1988	14.0	44.5	25.4	7.6	237.5	44.5	15.2	5.1
Argentina	1995	19.5	8.6	28.8	10.9	2.7	1991	27.3	143.0	26.3	13.7	337.3	49.0	33.5	51.6
Armenia	1994	13.5	6.5	17.1[11]	7.0	3.3[11]	1993	11.0	93.8	21.6[12]	4.9[12]	369.7	51.4	27.8	62.8
Aruba	1992	18.1	5.8	9.6[13]	12.3	1.8[14]	1991	9.8	124.9	47.7	4.2	189.5	30.9	23.9	11.2
Australia	1996	14.1	6.9	5.7	7.2	1.8	1994	5.7	192.0	23.0	17.0	308.0	56.0	22.0	40.0
Austria	1995	10.9	10.0	5.5	0.9	1.5[3]	1994	2.8	242.9	23.1	15.3	531.2	43.2	49.5	63.8
Azerbaijan	1995	21.0	6.0	27.0	15.0	2.4	1993	26.4	68.2	8.6[13]	9.7[13]	347.1	100.3	32.5	81.9
Bahamas, The	1995	19.2	5.8	24.3	13.4	2.0	1990	18.0	80.4	72.2	11.0	126.3	52.2	29.0	40.8
Bahrain	1994	27.4	5.4	23.8	22.0	3.6	1991	2.8	32.3	16.8	3.8	86.6	27.7	10.2	19.0
Bangladesh	1996	33.7	10.7	100.0	23.0	4.0	...	...	...	...	...	...	...	...	...
Barbados	1995	13.1	9.4	13.2	3.7	1.8[12]	1992	19.0	178.5	120.2	17.1	366.8	39.9	28.9	40.3
Belarus	1994	12.0	11.0	12.0	1.0	1.7	1993	8.0	184.5	9.0[15]	14.7	624.7	69.7	8.9	132.6
Belgium	1995	11.4	10.5	7.6	0.9	1.6[16]	1990	11.1	270.1	23.1	38.0	398.9	88.1	38.8	65.1
Belize	1995	33.7	5.9	34.7	27.8	4.2	1990	...	52.4	37.0[6]	...	164.0	57.1	32.8	92.6[17]
Benin	1995	47.0	14.0	108.0	33.0	6.7	...	...	...	...	...	...	...	...	...
Bermuda	1992	15.1	7.4	8.8	7.7	1.8[13]	1990	...	181.5	...	...	344.4	25.2	...	38.6
Bhutan	1996	37.8	14.0	112.0	23.8	5.6	...	...	...	...	...	...	...	...	...
Bolivia	1994	34.4	9.6	75.0	24.8	4.8	...	...	...	...	...	...	...	...	...
Bosnia and Herzegovina	1994	14.0	7.0	15.2	7.0	1.6	1989	9.9	122.6[19]	12.6	11.9	344.1	29.0	29.2	47.1
Botswana	1991–95	37.1	6.6	39.0[3]	30.5	4.8	...	...	...	...	...	...	...	...	...
Brazil	1995	21.2	9.0	57.2	12.2	2.4	1990[20]	37	75	31[15]	8	206	64	28	91
Brunei	1996	23.2	3.5	8.0	19.7	3.1	1986	5.3	27.0	...	...	80.0	23.4	...	39.8
Bulgaria	1995	8.6	13.6	14.8[3]	-5.0	1.6[3]	1994	9.0	192.8	22.2	7.3	824.4	64.4	42.0	69.5
Burkina Faso	1995	47.6	19.7	119	27.9	6.9	...	...	...	...	...	...	...	...	...
Burundi	1995	43.8	15.2	104.0	28.6	6.6	...	...	...	...	...	...	...	...	...
Cambodia	1996	39.2	12.8	106.0	26.4	5.0	...	...	...	...	...	...	...	...	...
Cameroon	1995	42.9	13.5	79.9	29.4	6.1	...	...	...	...	...	...	...	...	...
Canada	1994	13.2	7.2	6.2	6.0	1.7	1993	10.9	196.7	22.2	19.9	274.4	62.8	26.3	47.2
Cape Verde	1995	45.3	8.6	55.9	36.7	6.2	1980	153.7	43.8	20.6	16.5	135.8	72.3	27.7	30.1
Central African Republic	1995	40.0	17.0	113.0	23.0	5.5	...	...	...	...	...	...	...	...	...
Chad	1995	44.6	17.7	122.1	26.9	5.9	...	...	...	...	...	...	...	...	...
Chile	1993	21.0	5.3	13.1	15.7	2.6	1993	15.1	111.5	16.2	8.0	157.4	64.9	34.2	66.1
China	1995	17.1	6.6	26.0[11]	11.5	2.0	1992[21]	17.9	115.9	8.4[15]	3.9	199.4	131.9	26.9	55.6
Colombia	1995	21.9	4.7	26.9	17.2	2.4	1991	18.3	62.9	12.5	7.4	144.7	37.9	16.7	132.3
Comoros	1995	46.2	10.6	77.3	35.6	6.8	...	...	...	...	...	...	...	...	...
Congo	1995	39.6	17.4	110.1	22.2	5.2	...	...	...	...	...	...	...	...	...
Costa Rica	1994	25.4	4.2	13.0	21.2	3.0	1992	9.0	80.5	13.2	7.8	133.0	38.7	22.3	47.4
Côte d'Ivoire	1995	39.6	17.4	110.1	22.2	5.2	...	...	...	...	...	...	...	...	...
Croatia	1994	10.2	10.4	10.2	-2.0	1.5[11]	1993	3.2	218.0[19]	11.0[15]	3.1	533.2	49.7	49.7	95.0
Cuba	1993	14.0	7.2	9.4[3]	6.8	1.8[18]	1990	9.4	128.7	23.3	10.6	294.7	58.0	26.3	79.9
Cyprus	1994	16.4	7.8	9.0	8.6	2.2	...	...	...	...	...	...	...	...	...
Czech Republic	1993	11.7	11.5	8.5	0.2	1.9[18]	1993	3.0	270.5	15.4	9.1	638.9	46.6	40.2	82.3
Denmark	1995	13.4	12.1	5.3	1.3	1.7	1993	10.2	298.5	24.2	14.0	513.9	98.9	43.3	74.1
Djibouti	1995	42.8	15.5	108.8	27.0	6.1	...	...	...	...	...	...	...	...	...
Dominica	1995	18.6	5.3	9.9	13.3	1.9	1990	37.5	116.6	51.4	9.7	273.5	43.0	20.8	18.0
Dominican Republic	1995	24.1	5.7	49.5	18.4	2.7	1985	51.4	27.4	12.3	8.6	100.3	35.4	22.3	33.7
Ecuador	1995	28.3	6.2	49.7	22.1	3.2[11]	1992	52.0	50.0	11.8[6]	1.9[24]	93.1	40.6	13.2	66.7
Egypt	1994	26.0	6.2	58.2	19.8	3.7	1987	98.9	22.0	9.1	13.6	314.4	140.7	45.8	39.1
El Salvador	1995	28.6	5.9	33.0	22.7	3.3	1990[20]	52	43	17	12	120	49	38	137

causes classified by the World Health Organization and would not, thus, aggregate to the country's crude death rate for the same year. Among the lesser causes excluded by the present classification are: benign neoplasms; nutritional disorders; anemias; mental disorders; kidney and genitourinary diseases not classifiable under the main groups; maternal deaths (for which data *are* provided, however, in the "Health services" table); diseases of the skin and musculoskeletal systems; congenital and perinatal conditions; and general senility and other ill-defined (ill-diagnosed) conditions, a kind of "other" category.

Expectation of life is probably the most accurate single measure of the quality of life in a given society. It summarizes in a single number all of the natural and social stresses that operate upon individuals in that society. The number may range from as few as 40 years of life in the least developed countries to as much as 80 years for women in the most developed nations. The lost potential in the years separating those two numbers is prodigious, regardless of how the loss arises—wars and civil violence, poor public health services, or poor individual health practice in matters of nutrition, exercise, stress management, and so on.

Data on marriages and marriage rates probably are less meaningful in terms of international comparisons than some of the measures mentioned above because the number, timing, and kinds of social relationships that substitute for marriage depend on many kinds of social variables—income, degree of social control, heterogeneity of the society (race, class, language communities), or level of development of civil administration (if one must travel for a day or more to obtain a legal civil ceremony, one may forgo it). Nevertheless, the data for a single country say specific things about local practice in terms of the age at which a man or woman typically marries, and the overall rate will at least define the number of legal civil marriages, though it cannot say anything about other, less formal arrangements (here the figure for the legitimacy rate for children in the next section may identify some of the societies in which economics or social constraints may operate to limit the number of marriages that are actually confirmed on civil registers). The available data usually include both first marriages and remarriages after annulment, divorce, widowhood, or the like.

The data for families provide information about the average size of a family unit (individuals related by blood or civil register) and the average number of children under a specified age (set here at 15 to provide a consistent measure of social minority internationally, though legal minority depends on the laws of each country). When well-defined family data are not collected as part of a country's national census or vital statistics surveys, data for households are substituted on the assumption that most households worldwide represent families in some conventional sense. In the older countries of Europe and North America, increasing numbers of households are composed of unrelated individuals (unmarried heterosexual couples, aged [or younger] groups sharing limited [often fixed] incomes for reasons of economy, or homosexual couples); such arrangements are not yet so common in the rest of the world that they represent great numbers overall. Very few census programs, even in developed countries, make adequate provision for distinguishing these households.

expectation of life at birth (latest year)		nuptiality, family, and family planning														country
		marriages			age at marriage (latest)						families (F), households (H) (latest)					
					groom (percent)			bride (percent)			families (households)		children		induced abortions	
male	female	year	total number	rate per 1,000 population	19 and under	20–29	30 and over	19 and under	20–29	30 and over	total ('000)	size	number under age 15	percent legiti- mate	number	ratio per 100 live births	
44.0	43.0	1991	...	...	1.5	80.4	18.1	24.0	71.4	4.6	H 2,110	H 6.2	H 2.8[1]	...	...	...	Afghanistan
69.3	75.4	1991	24,853	7.6	0.7[4]	67.1[4]	32.2[4]	29.8[4]	61.4[4]	8.8[4]	F 675	F 4.7	F 1.6	...	...	...	Albania
67.0	69.0	1990	139,930	5.9	...	...	...	...	...	...	H 3,322	H 6.9	H 3.0	...	...	...	Algeria
69.0	74.0	1990	370	7.8	...	...	...	...	...	...	H 7	H 7.0	H 2.7	72.0	...	...	American Samoa
75.6	81.7	1994	132	2.0	...	...	...	...	...	...	...	...	...	...	...	...	Andorra
44.2	48.5	...	...	...	...	...	...	...	...	...	...	H 4.8	...	...	...	...	Angola
71.3	75.6	1988	382	4.9	1.0[9]	37.4[10]	61.6	3.7[9]	52.4[10]	43.9	H 20	H 3.5	H 1.2	23.4	...	...	Antigua and Barbuda
68.2	71.5	1983	177,010	6.0	5.6	71.5	22.9	26.0	58.6	15.4	H 10,097	H 3.2	H 1.0	67.5	...	...	Argentina
68.4	75.4	1994	17,300	4.6	3.7[2]	75.4[2]	20.9[2]	38.0[2]	50.6[2]	11.4[2]	H 559	H 4.7	H 1.8	87.7	27,958	39.6	Armenia
71.1	77.1	1992	566	7.9	...	...	...	...	...	...	H 19	H 3.6	...	63.2	...	...	Aruba
75.4	81.1	1993	113,255	6.6	0.8	55.6	43.6	4.1	64.2	31.7	H 6,636	H 2.7	H 0.6	75.0	...	...	Australia
73.3	79.7	1994	43,284	5.4	1.2	55.1	43.7	5.3	64.9	29.8	H 3,058	H 2.6	H 0.5	75.2	...	...	Austria
66.7	74.6	1993	60,028	8.3	1.2[13]	80.4[13]	18.4[13]	24.8[13]	63.9[13]	11.3[13]	H 1,381	H 4.8	H 1.7	97.5	42,134	23.2	Azerbaijan
67.7	75.5	1992	2,407	9.1	19.0	53.0	27.7	34.0	48.3	17.1	H 68	H 3.9	...	41.2	...	...	Bahamas, The
69.0	72.4	1992	3,048	5.9	2.2[2]	72.1[2]	24.6[2]	29.4[2]	58.6[2]	10.5[2]	H 67	H 6.5	H 2.2	...	...	...	Bahrain
57.0	57.0	1992	1,200,000	10.7	...	...	...	...	...	...	H 19,700	H 5.3	...	...	...	...	Bangladesh
72.9	77.4	1993	2,310	8.5	0.1	40.2	59.7	1.4	53.6	44.9	H 67	H 3.5	H 1.5	26.9	723	19.6	Barbados
66.0	75.7	1993	82,326	7.9	6.1[12]	71.6[12]	22.3[12]	31.1[12]	64.3[12]	18.6[12]	H 2,796	H 3.2	H 0.8	91.0	95,853	74.9	Belarus
73.0	79.8	1994	51,962	5.1	0.7[11]	64.9[11]	34.4[11]	4.9[11]	69.5[11]	25.6[11]	F 3,613	F 2.7	F 0.5	90.8	...	...	Belgium
66.0	70.0	1993	1,094	5.3	6.5	57.2	36.3	24.2	51.6	24.2	H 38	H 4.9	H 2.2	41.6	990	15.1	Belize
50.3	54.2	1980–85	...	12.8	...	...	...	...	...	...	...	H 5.4	...	...	...	...	Benin
73.0	79.0	1992	909	15.1	0.2[18]	37.4[18]	62.4[18]	1.5[18]	49.4[18]	49.1[18]	H 22	H 2.6	H 0.5	63.9	92	11.0	Bermuda
51.2	50.0	...	...	...	...	...	...	...	...	...	...	H 5.4	...	...	...	...	Bhutan
60.9	65.9	1980	26,990	4.8	8.3	75.1	16.6	26.1	55.4	18.5	H 1,655	H 3.8	H 1.6	80.9	...	...	Bolivia
72.1	77.7	1990	31,449	7.0	2.3[13]	76.0[13]	21.7[13]	28.5[13]	59.3[13]	12.2[13]	H 1,203	H 3.6	H 1.1	...	...	...	Bosnia and Herzegovina
59.5	65.6	1986	1,638	1.5	—	33.0	67.0	5.0	69.2	25.8	H 125	H 5.7	H 2.0	28.8	17	0.1	Botswana
56.6	67.3	1992	748,020	5.0	7.7[2]	71.7[2]	20.6[2]	34.3[2]	54.5[2]	12.1[2]	F 31,888	F 4.2	...	...	...	...	Brazil
72.0	77.0	1993	1,971	7.1	10.6[12]	50.1[12]	39.3[12]	11.4[12]	54.7[12]	33.9[12]	H 45	H 5.8	H 2.0	99.6	...	...	Brunei
68.9	75.3	1994	37,910	4.5	5.9[18]	76.6[18]	17.5[18]	38.0[18]	51.8[18]	10.2[18]	F 2,627	F 3.3	F 0.7	75.5	132,891	149.1	Bulgaria
44.5	43.8	...	...	...	...	...	...	...	...	...	...	H 6.2	...	...	...	...	Burkina Faso
48.7	50.7	...	...	...	...	...	...	...	...	...	...	H 4.6	...	...	...	...	Burundi
51.0	54.0	...	...	...	...	...	...	...	...	...	...	H 5.6	...	...	...	...	Cambodia
51.9	54.0	...	...	...	...	...	...	...	...	...	...	H 5.2	...	...	...	...	Cameroon
74.7	81.7	1993	159,316	5.5	0.9	52.1	47.0	3.9	60.2	35.9	H 10,018	H 2.7	H 0.6	83.8	99,971	25.7	Canada
60.7	64.6	1992	1,360	3.8	2.3[14]	62.4[14]	35.3[14]	17.0[14]	61.1[14]	21.9[14]	F 59	F 5.1	...	55.2	...	...	Cape Verde
47.0	52.0	...	...	...	...	...	...	...	...	...	...	H 4.7	...	...	...	...	Central African Republic
44.9	49.6	...	...	...	...	...	...	...	...	...	...	H 3.9	...	...	...	...	Chad
71.5	77.4	1993	92,821	6.7	5.5	70.2	24.3	20.1	63.4	16.5	H 3,261	H 4.1	H 1.2	65.7	67	—	Chile
69.1	72.4	1994	9,290,021	7.8	...	...	...	...	...	...	H 278.6[22]	H 4.1	H 1.1	...	10,500,000	47.7	China
69.7	75.4	1986	70,350	2.3	4.0	64.1	31.5	22.3	58.5	19.0	F 4,772	F 5.4	F 2.5	75.2	...	...	Colombia
56.0	60.6	...	...	...	...	...	...	...	...	...	...	H 5.6	...	...	...	...	Comoros
44.2	47.5	...	...	...	...	...	...	...	...	...	H 326	H 4.7	H 2.0	...	...	...	Congo
71.9	77.5	1994	20,073	6.1	7.5[18]	65.6[18]	26.9[18]	27.8[18]	54.6[18]	17.6[18]	H 786.6	H 4.2	H 4.2	60.9	...	...	Costa Rica
44.2	47.5	...	...	...	...	...	...	...	...	...	...	H 5.4	...	...	...	...	Côte d'Ivoire
68.6	76.0	1993	23,021	4.8	1.2[13]	72.4[13]	26.4[13]	19.5[13]	64.8[13]	15.7[13]	H 1,544	H 3.1	H 0.6	...	...	...	Croatia
73.9	77.6	1991	161,160	15	6.3	54.1	39.6	18.8	51.0	30.2	F 2,860	F 3.7	F 1.6	...	124,059	71.3	Cuba
74.6	79.1	1994	6,097	9.6	0.6	61.0	38.4	11.0	64.7	24.3	H 160	H 3.5	H 1.0	99.6	...	...	Cyprus
68.9	76.6	1993	66,033	6.4	12.0[12]	79.3[12]	8.7[12]	42.2[12]	54.4[12]	3.4[12]	H 3,984	H 2.7	H 0.5	90.3	70,634	58.4	Czech Republic
72.5	77.8	1994	35,362	6.8	0.4[11]	40.8[11]	58.8[11]	1.8[11]	52.7[11]	45.5[11]	H 2,358	H 2.2	...	53.2	18,833	27.8	Denmark
47.8	51.6	...	...	...	...	...	...	...	...	...	...	H 5.6	...	96.8	...	...	Djibouti
74.4	80.2	1990	228	3.3	—	41.2	58.8	3.1	58.3	38.6	H 19	H 3.6	H 2.2	...	...	...	Dominica
66.6	71.0	1992	25,351	3.6	8.0[23]	63.0[23]	29.0[23]	29.7[23]	51.0[23]	19.3[23]	H 753	H 2.5	H 2.5	32.8	562	0.5	Dominican Republic
67.3	72.5	1993	68,193	6.2	12.6	63.9	23.5	33.4	52.3	14.3	...	H 4.1	...	67.9	...	...	Ecuador
65.4	69.5	1993	479,000	8.3	4.8[13]	61.4[13]	33.8[13]	37.6[13]	50.6[13]	11.8[13]	H 9,733	H 4.9	H 2.1	100.0	...	...	Egypt
65.0	72.1	1992	23,084	4.2	6.6	54.8	38.6	21.5	51.4	27.1	H 1,101	H 4.7	...	30.6	...	...	El Salvador

Vital statistics, marriage, family (continued)

country	vital rates						causes of death (rate per 100,000 population)								
	year	birth rate per 1,000 population	death rate per 1,000 population	infant mortality rate per 1,000 live births	rate of natural increase per 1,000 population	total fertility rate	year	infectious and parasitic diseases	malig- nant neo- plasms (cancers)	endocrine and metabolic disorders	diseases of the nervous system	diseases of the circula- tory system	diseases of the respira- tory system	diseases of the digestive system	accidents, poisoning, and violence
Equatorial Guinea	1995	40.2	14.4	100.2	25.8	5.2	...	...	...	...	...	...	...	...	...
Eritrea	1995	44.3	15.7	120.6	28.6	6.5	...	...	...	...	...	...	...	...	...
Estonia	1995	9.1	14.2	14.5	−5.1	1.3	1994	11.4	218.1	10.1	13.6	816.0	44.3	34.5	233.2
Ethiopia	1995	46.5	17.5	124.1	29.0	7.1	...	...	...	...	...	...	...	...	...
Faroe Islands	1992	16.8	8.4	8.5[2]	8.4	2.7[18]	1992	4.3	191.3	14.9[6]	—	352.8	59.5	14.9	57.4
Fiji	1995	24.6	6.2	21.0	18.4	2.8	1987	18.2	35.5	27.3[6]	2.4[24]	153.4	31.7	15.5	32.2
Finland	1995	12.4	9.7	4.7	2.7	1.8	1993	6.7	198.9	13.4	20.6	485.2	85.6	37.5	85.2
France	1994	12.2	9.0	6.1	3.2	1.6	1992	12.2	245.7	26.0	19.6	298.2	65.8	45.5	81.1
French Guiana	1993	29.2	4.1	15.4	25.1	3.7[2]	1989	61.7	58.1	16.3	10.9	114.3	20.9	13.6	98.0
French Polynesia	1994	23.5	4.9	9.4	18.6	3.9[18]	1986–92	22.0	83.0	12.0	12.0	118.0	35.0	14.0	69.0
Gabon	1995	28.3	13.7	92.4	14.6	3.9	...	...	...	...	...	...	...	...	...
Gambia, The	1995	43.0	19.0	82.3	24.0	5.8	...	...	...	...	...	...	...	...	...
Gaza Strip	1994	56.0	6.0	43.0	50.0	7.7	...	...	...	...	...	...	...	...	...
Georgia	1994	17.0	9.0	16.0	8.0	2.2	1989	13.5	98.6	12.0	4.1	553.2	51.4	32.1	58.2
Germany	1995	9.3	10.7	5.6	−1.4	1.3[3]	1992	7.0	263.7	35.0	16.8	543.1	65.2	52.1	52.6
Ghana	1990–95	41.7	11.7	81.0	30.0	6.0	...	...	...	...	...	...	...	...	...
Gibraltar	1994	18.8	9.6	5.7[2]	9.2	2.8[2]	1987	17.0	203.9	—	—	601.4	34.0	23.8	3.4
Greece	1995	9.8	9.4	7.9	0.4	1.4[11]	1993	6.5	202.3	12.4	13.1	460.2	53.9	27.1	41.5
Greenland	1994	20.7	8.0	13.0	12.7	2.9[12]	1993	27.1	186.3	...	...	188.2	47.0	12.7	152.0
Grenada	1995	29.7	6.0	12.1	23.7	3.8	1987	9.6	82.8	57.3	7.4	264.3	45.6	38.2	...
Guadeloupe	1992	17.8	5.6	10.4	12.2	2.2[16]	1990	20.8[14]	121.2	23.0[14]	12.3[14]	186.8	30.5	29.7	72.9
Guam	1995	24.0	4.0	8.0	20.0	3.1	1992	4.9	65.2	29.5[6]	9.8	123.4	14.7[28]	11.2	68.7
Guatemala	1994	35.4	7.5	53.9	27.9	4.8	1984	211.5	29.8	29.6	9.0	57.2	145.7	21.7	52.0
Guernsey	1993	10.7	9.5	1.3[18]	1.2	1.6[13]	1990	8.4	314.3	11.8	15.1	430.3	112.6	30.3	20.2
Guinea	1995	43.3	19.2	136.6	24.1	5.8	...	...	...	...	...	...	...	...	...
Guinea-Bissau	1995	40.2	16.6	117.9	23.6	5.4	...	...	...	...	...	...	...	...	...
Guyana	1995	19.4	9.1	51.4	10.3	2.2	1984	19.3	37.1	33.3	11.6	202.5	39.8	74.0	56.5
Haiti	1995	39.0	16.3	105.1	22.7	5.8	...	...	...	...	...	...	...	...	...
Honduras	1993	35.8	6.4	47.2	29.4	4.9	1983	46.6	12.4	5.3	7.8	48.4	26.3	16.7	42.2
Hong Kong	1995	11.2	5.1	4.8	6.1	1.2[3]	1995	19.5	156.3	8.4	4.5	142.8	87.5	22.1	26.9
Hungary	1995	10.9	14.1	10.7	−3.2	1.6	1993	9.1	312.8	19.2	11.6	751.7	68.8	116.3	119.5
Iceland	1994	16.7	6.5	3.2	10.2	2.1	1993	4.1	171.0	12.1	13.6	294.6	89.5	14.0	38.3
India	1995	26.5	9.8	73.0	16.7	3.3	...	...	...	...	...	...	...	...	...
Indonesia	1996	22.9	8.0	52.0	14.9	2.7	...	...	...	...	...	...	...	...	...
Iran	1995	34.9	6.9	54.6	28.0	4.9	1990[30]	34	61	12[15]	26	304	48	24	108
Iraq	1994	44.0	7.0	67.0	37.0	6.7	...	...	...	...	...	...	...	...	...
Ireland	1994	13.4	8.6	5.9	4.8	1.9	1994	4.8	205.6	11.6	—	392.1	66.8	...	62.2
Isle of Man	1994	12.7	12.9	5.7	−0.2	1.8[13]	1994	107.9	217.4	8.6[6]	—	552.7	204.4	20.2	95.0
Israel	1995	21.2	6.4	7.8	14.8	2.9[18]	1992	14.6	130.5	23.2	9.7	268.4	44.1	18.6	38.4
Italy	1994	9.2	9.6	6.6	−0.4	7.4[11]	1992	3.4	265.9	34.2	18.2	415.6	56.9	48.0	50.4
Jamaica	1995	23.2	5.0	28.6	18.2	3.0	1991	8.1	84.1	51.3	7.5	189.5	30.2	14.1	8.4
Japan	1994	10.0	7.1	4.2	2.9	1.5	1993	11.2	189.1	10.3	5.8	253.4	93.6	32.0	47.3
Jersey	1991	12.5	9.9	6.0[13]	2.6	1.3[13]	...	...	...	...	...	...	...	...	...
Jordan	1994	34.3	3.0	34.0	31.3	5.9[31]	...	...	...	...	...	...	...	...	...
Kazakhstan	1994	20.0	8.0	27.0	12.0	2.5	1993	26.5	135.2	9.6	8.7	425.1	85.5	29.3	133.0
Kenya	1995	34.3	9.8	55.4	25.3	4.6	...	...	...	...	...	...	...	...	...
Kiribati	1994	31.6	12.3	98.4	19.3	3.8	...	...	...	...	...	...	...	...	...
Korea, North	1996	22.5	5.3	23.0	17.2	2.3	1986	19.4	69.0	3.0[15]	6.5	224.9	46.7	51.6	38.2
Korea, South	1996	15.1	5.9	10.0	9.2	1.8[31]	1994	12.8	111.3	17.9	5.3	155.0	25.2	39.6	72.0
Kuwait	1994	26.9	1.9	15.9	25.0	3.7	1993	9.6	27.4	6.6	5.7	82.1	13.7	4.3	41.3
Kyrgyzstan	1994	24.6	8.3	29.1	16.3	3.1	1994	32.7	67.9	8.0	8.9	330.8	131.5	34.3	95.7
Laos	1996	42.0	13.8	89.0	28.2	6.2	...	...	...	...	...	...	...	...	...
Latvia	1994	9.5	16.4	15.5	−6.9	1.4	1994	20.3	219.6	12.4	9.3	917.0	52.8	39.9	235.9
Lebanon	1994	24.9	4.3	28.0	20.6	2.9	...	...	...	...	...	...	...	...	...
Lesotho	1995	33.2	13.6	82.8	19.6	4.4	...	...	...	...	...	...	...	...	...
Liberia	1995	43.3	12.1	110.6	31.2	6.3	...	...	...	...	...	...	...	...	...
Libya	1995	44.9	7.9	61.4	37.0	6.3	...	...	...	...	...	...	...	...	...
Liechtenstein	1995	11.7	6.7	5.5	5.0	1.5	1994	23.0	134.6	...	6.6	328.2	36.1	26.3	36.1
Lithuania	1993	12.5	12.4	16.0	0.1	2.0[13]	1993	13.2	200.8	7.9	9.7	670.2	48.2	27.3	167.2
Luxembourg	1994	13.5	9.2	5.3	4.3	1.7	1994	8.9	234.5	18.8	13.6	391.1	68.4	44.8	62.7
Macau	1994	15.2	3.3	6.2	11.9	1.6[2]	1994	9.5	81.4	7.2	2.6	128.6	39.9	11.3	23.2
Macedonia	1994	17.3	8.1	22.4	9.2	2.2	1993	12.9	6.2	16.4	4.7	385.8	34.5	14.8	35.3
Madagascar	1995	43.0	14.6	95.0	23.9	6.0	...	...	...	...	...	...	...	...	...
Malaŵi	1995	42.4	23.9	140.9	18.5	6.1	1986[32]	711	27	25	60	50	265	34	78
Malaysia	1996	26.3	4.9	12.0	21.4	3.4	1992	13.2	21.0	4.4	6.4[15]	54.1	7.5	1.9	28.5
Maldives	1996	39.4	7.7	52.0	31.7	6.3	1988	31.3	—	—	—	170.1	66.2	—	9.9
Mali	1995	51.9	19.9	105.0	32.0	7.3	...	...	...	...	...	...	...	...	...
Malta	1994	13.1	7.3	9.1	5.8	2.1[12]	1994	4.3	188.9	25.5	9.0	324.2	63.6	32.6	25.5
Marshall Islands	1993	46.6	7.9	53.0	38.7	7.0	1993	169.9	68.4	...	—	155.1	105.1	63.3	36.7
Martinique	1993	15.8	6.0	6.2[12]	9.8	1.9	1990	22.0	135.5	30.7	10.7[25]	208.0	34.2	31.3	54.8
Mauritania	1995	47.3	15.7	83.5	31.6	6.9	...	...	...	...	...	...	...	...	...
Mauritius	1994	19.6	6.7	18.1	12.9	2.3	1994	13.7	64.0	23.3	3.8	297.1	68.6	32.1	44.7
Mayotte	1991	43.7	6.0	38.0	37.7	6.8[13]	...	...	...	...	...	...	...	...	...
Mexico	1993	31.5	4.7	27.1[12]	26.7	3.7[18]	1992	28.5	50.6	42.6	6.8	101.2	45.9	40.6	69.5
Micronesia	1996	36.7	7.8	22.0	28.9	4.2	1984	20.4	27.1	6.8	4.5	53.2	47.5	5.7	23.8
Moldova	1994	16.0	10.0	19.0	6.0	2.1	1993	11.0	133.1	8.3[13]	8.2[13]	434.5	60.7	91.6	105.7
Monaco	1988	22.9	18.5	9.0[13]	4.4	1.2[13]	...	...	...	...	...	...	...	...	...
Mongolia	1994	34.0	7.7	48	26.3	4.5	...	...	...	...	...	...	...	...	...
Morocco	1995	27.9	6.0	45.8	21.9	3.7	1992	10.2	14.0	12.2	4.9	35.5	9.5	7.9	19.2
Mozambique	1995	45.5	18.3	127.7	27.2	6.4	...	...	...	...	...	...	...	...	...
Myanmar (Burma)	1996	31.0	10.2	76.0	20.8	3.9	...	...	...	...	...	...	...	...	...
Namibia	1990–95	37.0	10.5	84.0	26.5	5.7	...	...	...	...	...	...	...	...	...
Nauru	1996	24.0	5.0	26.0	19.0	2.5[13]	1976–81[33]	33.0	38.0	24.0	13.0	89.0	16.0	53.0	116.0
Nepal	1996	37.2	12.0	90.0	25.2	5.1	...	...	...	...	...	...	...	...	...
Netherlands, The	1995	12.3	8.8	5.9[3]	3.5	1.6[3]	1994	6.7	241.0	29.4	14.5	334.1	73.4	32.5	33.1

expectation of life at birth (latest year)		nuptiality, family, and family planning															country
		marriages			age at marriage (latest)						families (F), households (H) (latest)						
		year	total number	rate per 1,000 population	groom (percent)			bride (percent)			families (households)		children		induced abortions		
male	female				19 and under	20–29	30 and over	19 and under	20–29	30 and over	total ('000)	size	number under age 15	percent legitimate	number	ratio per 100 live births	
50.4	54.8	...	...	...	...	...	...	...	...	...	...	H 4.5	...	...	...	...	Equatorial Guinea
48.3	51.8	...	...	...	...	...	...	...	...	...	...	[25]	...	...	...	...	Eritrea
65.0	75.0	1994	7,378	4.9	5.3	53.7	41.0	17.2	47.8	35.0	H 427	H 3.1	H 0.8	66.1	28,403	157.7	Estonia
45.9	48.2	...	...	...	...	...	...	...	...	...	...	H 4.5[25]	...	...	...	...	Ethiopia
72.8	79.6	1990	203	4.3	1.0[26]	68.8[26]	30.2[26]	8.8[26]	70.7[26]	20.5[26]	F 14	F 3.0	F 0.9	57.5	26	3.3	Faroe Islands
70.0	74.0	1988	6,892	9.6	6.6[26]	68.7[26]	24.7[26]	31.0[26]	55.8[26]	13.2[26]	F 97	F 6.0	F 2.5	82.7	...	...	Fiji
72.1	79.5	1994	24,898	4.9	1.2[18]	58.9[18]	39.9[18]	4.7[18]	66.7[18]	28.6[18]	H 2,218	H 2.3	H 0.4	71.1	12,232	18.7	Finland
72.9	81.1	1992	269,940	4.7	0.4[9]	61.7	37.9	3.3[9]	69.5	27.2	H 20,899	H 2.6	H 1.0	68.1	161,129	21.2	France
63.4	69.7	1992	716	5.3	...	...	...	...	...	...	H 33	H 3.4	H 1.2	20.3	388	16.8	French Guiana
68.4	72.8	1994	1,263	5.9	11.3[26, 27]	75.8[26, 27]	12.9[26, 27]	41.5[26, 27]	52.5[26, 27]	6.0[26, 27]	H 40	H 4.7	H 1.7	37.2	...	...	French Polynesia
52.3	58.0	...	...	...	...	...	...	...	...	...	H 136	H 4.0	...	...	...	...	Gabon
50.3	54.7	...	...	...	...	...	...	...	...	...	...	H 8.3	...	...	...	...	Gambia, The
66.5	69.2	...	...	...	...	...	...	...	...	...	...	...	...	...	...	...	Gaza Strip
68.9	76.5	1993	24,105	4.9	5.7[13]	66.2[13]	28.1[13]	27.8[13]	55.7[13]	16.5[13]	H 1,244	H 4.1	H 1.1	82.3	68,883	75.6	Georgia
72.5	79.0	1993	441,261	5.4	0.6	51.6	47.8	3.7	62.7	33.6	H 36,230	H 2.2	H 0.3	86.6	111,236	13.9	Germany
53.3	57.2	...	...	...	...	...	...	...	...	...	H 2,355	H 4.9	H 2.2	...	...	...	Ghana
73.4	80.4	1994	697	5.2	...	...	...	...	...	...	H 8	H 3.2	H 0.7	97.1	...	...	Gibraltar
74.6	79.8	1993	62,195	6.0	0.9	56.3	42.8	11.9	68.7	19.4	H 2,990	H 3.3	H 0.7	97.1	11,977	11.5	Greece
60.7	68.4	1991	451	8.1	1.1	44.6	54.3	2.7	59.6	37.7	F 31	F 1.8	F 0.5	28.0	962	80.7	Greenland
68.2	73.2	...	...	...	...	...	...	...	...	...	H 24	H 3.7	H 2.2	...	...	...	Grenada
70.0	77.0	1992	1,880	4.7	0.5[2]	51.4[2]	48.0[2]	7.2[2]	61.4[2]	31.4[2]	H 112	H 3.4	H 0.9	39.3	561	8.7	Guadeloupe
73.0	79.0	1992	1,477	10.6	3.0	55.5	41.5	9.2	59.3	31.5	H 31	H 4.0	H 1.3	67.8	...	...	Guam
61.9	67.1	1991	47,732	5.0	15.9[14]	55.7[14]	28.4[14]	41.5[14]	38.0[14]	20.5[14]	H 1,611	H 5.4	H 5.4	34.8	...	...	Guatemala
...	...	1990	403	6.8	...	...	...	...	...	...	H 21	H 2.6	H 0.5	80.2	...	...	Guernsey
42.3	46.9	...	...	...	...	...	...	...	...	...	H 1,064	H 4.7	...	...	...	...	Guinea
46.2	49.6	...	...	...	...	...	...	...	...	...	H 124	H 4.1	H 2.8	11.3	...	...	Guinea-Bissau
58.2	63.9	...	...	...	...	...	...	...	...	...	H 150	H 5.1	H 2.1	...	...	...	Guyana
47.1	51.1	...	...	...	...	...	...	...	...	...	H 1,147	H 4.4	H 1.8	...	...	...	Haiti
64.8	69.2	1983	19,875	4.9	7.7	65.1	27.2	27.9	58.5	13.6	H 463	H 5.7	H 2.8	...	...	...	Honduras
75.7	81.3	1993	41,681	7.0	0.9	46.2	52.9	3.6	67.3	29.1	H 1,582	H 3.4	H 0.7	94.5	17,600	25.2	Hong Kong
64.8	74.2	1995	54,000	5.3	4.2	65.2	24.6	19.6	64.3	16.1	F 3,058	F 2.9	F 0.8	81.5	77,000	64.9	Hungary
77.1	81.0	1994	1,310	4.9	0.2	43.4	56.4	1.7	56.0	42.3	H 85	H 2.9	H 1.3	40.4	743	16.1	Iceland
58.7	59.8	...	...	...	...	...	...	...	...	...	H 119,231	H 5.6	H 2.4	...	581,215	...	India
63.0	66.0	1992–93[29]	1,423,774	7.6	...	...	...	...	...	...	H 39,695	H 4.5	H 1.8	...	...	...	Indonesia
65.8	68.2	1993	460,888	7.9	...	...	...	...	...	...	H 9,759	H 5.1	H 2.2	...	...	...	Iran
57.3	60.4	1990	143,518	8.1	...	...	...	...	...	...	H 1,873	H 8.9	H 4.1	...	...	...	Iraq
72.3	77.9	1994	16,297	4.6	0.9[2]	69.4[2]	29.6[2]	3.2[2]	78.5[2]	18.1[2]	H 541	H 3.3	H 1.3	80.3	...	...	Ireland
...	...	1994	452	6.5	0.4	42.7	56.9	2.2	54.0	43.8	...	...	...	76.1	...	...	Isle of Man
75.1	78.5	1995	33,365	6.4	3.5[12]	73.5[12]	23.0[12]	22.1[12]	67.1[12]	10.8[12]	H 1,355	H 3.7	H 1.1	98.5	18,444	16.8	Israel
73.8	80.4	1994	286,512	5.0	0.8[18]	67.3[18]	31.9[18]	8.1[18]	75.9[18]	16.0[18]	F 19,766	F 2.6	F 0.5	92.7	146,639	26.1	Italy
74.4	75.8	1994	15,171	6.1	...	...	...	...	...	...	H 554	H 4.2	H 1.4	14.9	...	...	Jamaica
76.6	83.0	1994	782,735	6.3	1.3	61.7	37.0	3.1	78.6	18.3	H 40,670	H 3.0	...	99.0	386,807	32.6	Japan
...	...	...	...	...	...	...	...	...	...	...	H 29	H 2.6	H 0.4	88.1	313	29.2	Jersey
64.4	69.9	1992	37,216	8.0	5.2	72.4	22.4	39.2	54.3	6.5	H 11,891	H 6.1	H 3.4	...	...	...	Jordan
63.2	72.7	1993	146,161	8.6	6.0[12]	73.4[12]	20.6[12]	31.0[12]	53.6[12]	15.4[12]	H 3,824	H 4.0	H 1.4	87.6	296,586	87.6	Kazakstan
56.9	56.8	...	...	...	...	...	...	...	...	...	H 1,938	H 6.2	H 2.7	...	...	...	Kenya
62.0	67.0	1988	352	5.2	...	...	...	...	...	...	H 11	H 6.6	H 2.5	...	...	...	Kiribati
67.0	73.3	1987	188,007	9.3	...	...	...	...	...	...	H 4,054	H 4.8	H 1.7	...	...	...	Korea, North
68.0	76.0	1994	304,146	6.8	0.3[11]	70.2[11]	29.5[11]	2.3[11]	87.4[11]	10.3[11]	H 11,355	H 3.8	H 1.0	99.5	...	...	Korea, South
73.0	77.0	1993	11,418	7.8	6.1[12]	72.2[12]	21.7[12]	35.9[12]	53.3[12]	10.8[12]	H 246	H 7.4	H 1.6	100.0	...	...	Kuwait
63.9	72.6	1994	26,097	5.8	6.3	79.3	14.4	40.6	50.1	9.3	H 856	H 4.2	H 1.9	83.2	59,394	46.2	Kyrgyzstan
51.0	54.0	...	...	...	...	...	...	...	...	...	...	H 6.0	...	...	...	...	Laos
64.2	74.6	1994	11,572	4.5	6.5	64.9	28.8	19.8	56.1	24.1	H 732	H 3.1	H 0.8	73.6	31,348	117.1	Latvia
72.5	77.9	...	...	...	...	...	...	...	...	...	H 405	H 5.3	H 2.2	...	...	...	Lebanon
50.7	54.4	...	...	...	...	...	...	...	...	...	H 330	H 4.8	H 2.0	...	...	...	Lesotho
55.7	60.8	...	...	...	...	...	...	...	...	...	H 474	H 5.0	...	...	...	...	Liberia
62.1	66.6	...	...	...	...	...	...	...	...	...	F 383	F 5.4	F 2.9	...	...	...	Libya
66.5	79.5	1994	202	13.1	—	54.5	44.5	0.0	66.3	29.2	H 8	H 3.0	H 0.7	85.3	...	...	Liechtenstein
65.3	76.1	1993	23,709	6.4	8.4	70.7	20.9	27.9	55.0	17.1	H 1,000	H 3.2	H 0.8	93.3	42,023	89.9	Lithuania
72.6	79.1	1993	2,379	6.3	1.1	53.2	45.7	4.9	65.0	30.1	H 145	H 2.6	H 0.5	87.3	...	...	Luxembourg
68.1	71.8	1994	2,742	6.8	0.6	38.5	60.9	2.6	62.4	35.0	H 99	H 3.5	H 0.9	99.3	...	...	Macau
70.1	74.4	1994	15,736	7.6	5.1	75.4	19.5	27.7	62.5	9.8	H 468	H 3.8	H 1.3	91.5	18,754	57.9	Macedonia
50.8	52.9	...	...	...	...	...	...	...	...	...	H 1,709	H 4.7	H 2.0	...	...	...	Madagascar
37.0	37.0	...	...	...	...	...	...	...	...	...	...	H 4.3	...	...	...	...	Malaŵi
69.0	73.0	...	...	...	...	...	...	...	...	...	H 3,580	H 4.9	...	...	...	...	Malaysia
65.0	63.0	1993	2,778	11.7	13.7	58.2	29.1	...	...	...	...	H 7.1	...	...	...	...	Maldives
44.7	48.1	1987	33,646	4.4	...	...	...	...	...	...	H 1,364	H 5.6	...	...	...	...	Mali
74.9	79.1	1994	2,483	6.7	2.5[11]	73.1[11]	23.8[11]	9.9[11]	76.9[11]	13.2[11]	H 76	H 3.6	H 1.2	97.1	...	...	Malta
61.9	65.0	...	...	...	...	...	...	...	...	...	H 5	H 8.7	...	...	...	...	Marshall Islands
74.7	81.0	1993	1,555	4.2	0.1[14]	46.8[14]	53.1[14]	3.3[14]	61.5[14]	35.2[14]	H 107	H 3.3	H 0.8	34.1	1,753	30.6	Martinique
45.7	51.5	...	...	...	...	...	...	...	...	...	H 246	H 5.0	...	...	...	...	Mauritania
66.4	73.9	1994	11,414	10.3	1.9	59.9	38.2	25.5	55.9	18.6	F 155	F 5.3	F 2.0	72.8	...	...	Mauritius
54.0	58.0	...	...	...	...	...	...	...	...	...	H 19	H 4.9	H 2.3	89.2	...	...	Mayotte
66.5	73.1	1993	659,567	7.2	16.5	65.1	18.4	36.0	52.9	11.1	H 17,152	H 5.1	H 2.0	72.5	...	...	Mexico
72.0	72.0	...	...	...	...	...	...	...	...	...	H 11	H 7.0	...	...	...	...	Micronesia
67.9	71.5	1993	39,469	9.1	5.9[2]	74.6[2]	19.5[2]	37.6[2]	46.9[2]	15.5[2]	H 1,144	H 3.4	H 1.1	89.6	52,003	74.7	Moldova
72.0	80.0	1987	...	7.5	...	...	...	...	...	...	H 14	H 2.2	H 0.3	96.8	...	...	Monaco
60.0	63.5	1989	16,100	7.8	...	...	...	...	...	...	F 428	F 4.8	...	...	...	...	Mongolia
67.0	71.0	...	...	...	...	...	...	...	...	...	H 2,819	H 5.8	H 2.5	...	...	...	Morocco
46.8	49.5	...	...	...	...	...	...	...	...	...	F 1,860	F 4.4	F 2.0	73.1	...	...	Mozambique
58.0	61.0	...	...	...	...	...	...	...	...	...	...	H 5.6	...	...	...	...	Myanmar (Burma)
57.5	60.0	...	...	...	...	...	...	...	...	...	...	H 5.2	...	...	...	...	Namibia
64.0	69.0	1976	43	6.1	...	...	...	...	...	...	H 1	H 8.0	H 2.6	...	...	...	Nauru
55.0	53.5	...	...	...	...	...	...	...	...	...	H 3,345	H 5.5	H 2.3	...	...	...	Nepal
74.0	80.0	1993	88,273	5.8	0.3	54.0	45.7	2.1	65.8	32.1	H 6,185	H 2.4	H 0.4	85.7	19,804	10.1	Netherlands, The

Vital statistics, marriage, family (continued)

country	vital rates						causes of death (rate per 100,000 population)								
	year	birth rate per 1,000 population	death rate per 1,000 population	infant mortality rate per 1,000 live births	rate of natural increase per 1,000 population	total fertility rate	year	infectious and parasitic diseases	malignant neoplasms (cancers)	endocrine and metabolic disorders	diseases of the nervous system	diseases of the circulatory system	diseases of the respiratory system	diseases of the digestive system	accidents, poisoning, and violence
Netherlands Antilles	1991	18.3	5.8	6.3[13]	12.5	2.2[12]	1995[34]	16.7	149.0	61.7	9.9	71.6	40.8	21.4	47.6
New Caledonia	1995	22.7	5.5	7.8	17.2	2.9[3]	1992	19.3	129.0	10.8	9.1	115.3	45.4	15.3	80.7
New Zealand	1994	16.3	7.7	7.1	8.6	2.0	1992	5.9	199.9	17.8	12.7	351.1	81.7	23.2	52.6
Nicaragua	1994	35.0	7.0	53.0	28.0	4.3	1991[35]	100	56	18	13	142	73	34	93
Niger	1995	55.2	25.1	119.2	30.1	7.5	...	...	...	...	...	...	...	...	...
Nigeria	1990–95	45.4	15.4	84.2	30.0	6.4	...	...	...	...	...	...	...	...	...
Northern Mariana Islands	1992	29.0	3.0	9.0[2]	26.0	2.4[18]	1987	18.7	70.2[19]	23.4	14.0	135.7	70.2	9.4	145.1
Norway	1995	13.8	10.3	5.0[11]	3.5	1.9[11]	1992	6.6	228.4	16.8	18.4	482.9	106.7	28.3	57.0
Oman	1992	61.3	4.5	24.2	56.8	7.9	...	...	...	...	...	...	...	...	...
Pakistan	1996	38.4	8.3	79.0	30.1	5.8	...	...	...	...	...	...	...	...	...
Palau	1995	22.1	6.6	25.1	15.5	2.9	...	...	...	...	...	...	...	...	...
Panama	1995	23.6	5.4	30.4	18.2	2.8	1993	18.3	60.4	13.8[6]	2.1[24]	113.9	23.4	8.5	54.0
Papua New Guinea	1996	32.6	10.1	22.5	4.8	...	...	...	...	...	...	...	...	...	...
Paraguay	1992	35.5	6.4	47.1	29.1	4.9	1993[37]	33	53	22	8	162	38	17	45
Peru	1995	26.2	6.6	50.0	19.6	3.2	1989[35]	85	73	19	11	115	100	36	67
Philippines	1996	28.7	5.9	38.0	22.8	3.7	1991	65.9	35.2	17.9	124.9	82.2	20.5	20.5	71.8
Poland	1995	12.0	10.1	14.0	1.9	2.1[2]	1993	7.2	196.8	15.8	8.1	529.7	35.8	32.3	73.0
Portugal	1993	11.5	10.7	8.6	0.8	1.5	1993	10.4	195.5	37.3	9.8	469.1	78.9	50.4	61.2
Puerto Rico	1995	17.4	7.6	12.8	9.8	2.0	1993	59.4	122.2	66.7	19.2	242.3	80.5	43.9	34.1
Qatar	1994	16.7	3.7	17.6	13.0	2.8	1992	3.4	21.4[19]	7.3[18]	2.6	59.9	7.5	3.4	36.0
Réunion	1994	20.6	5.4	8.0	15.2	2.3	1992	14.7	87.2	21.8[2]	22.6	173.0	43.1	60.3[39]	58.0
Romania	1995	10.4	12.0	21.2	–1.6	2.2[13]	1992	12.4	163.4	11.7	8.2	707.7	94.0	57.9	74.3
Russia	1995	9.3	15.0	18.0	–5.7	37.6[3]	1995	21.0	203.0	11.0[3]	10.9[3]	784.0	75.0	46.0	234.0
Rwanda	1995	39.2	23.4	119.7	15.8	6.1	...	...	...	...	...	...	...	...	...
St. Kitts and Nevis	1994	24.0	10.0	20.0	14.0	2.6	1985	50.0	95.5	20.5[6]	11.4	443.2	81.8	25.0	29.5
St. Lucia	1994	23.0	6.0	19.0	17.0	2.5	1992	31.1	64.4	22.4	5.8	205.6	48.5	21.0	34.7
St. Vincent and the Grenadines	1993	24.5	6.2	14.5	10.0	2.1[12]	1992	17.5	99.7	55.4	13.9	222.5	33.2	25.9	62.8
San Marino	1991–95	10.4	7.1	7.1[40]	3.3	1.5[31]	1991–95	...	229.4	2.4[6]	...	324.8	10.7	...	45.2
São Tomé and Príncipe	1995	34.9	8.7	62.1	26.2	4.4	1987	240.7	19.6	5.3[6]	2.7[24]	143.5	86.5	15.2	14.3
Saudi Arabia	1994	37.8	4.4	28.0	33.4	2.9	...	...	...	...	...	...	...	...	...
Senegal	1995	42.9	11.6	68	31.3	6.0	...	...	...	...	...	...	...	...	...
Seychelles	1995	21.0	7.0	18.3	14.0	2.6[3]	1994	43.3	128.6	16.2	16.2	288.4	98.8	39.3	43.3
Sierra Leone	1995	47.6	18.7	138.8	28.9	6.4	...	...	...	...	...	...	...	...	...
Singapore	1995	16.3	5.2	4.0	11.1	1.7	1994	12.3	128.0	12.8	2.4	185.3	86.9	13.3	32.5
Slovakia	1995	11.5	9.8	11.0	1.7	0.8[3]	1994	4.1	201.1	13.0	6.0	525	65.2	43.0	68.5
Slovenia	1995	9.6	9.6	5.5[3]	0.0	1.3[3]	1994	3.1	224.3	22.9	10.4	434.1	59.1	58.4	98.7
Solomon Islands	1996	36.5	4.2	24.0	32.3	5.1	...	...	...	...	...	...	...	...	...
Somalia	1995	44.6	13.6	123.0	31.0	7.0	...	...	...	...	...	...	...	...	...
South Africa	1995	28.5	10.0	49.3	18.5	3.5	1993	42.4	48.0	19.1	7.7	91.2	38.2	12.4	99.3
Spain	1994	9.3	8.6	6.0	0.7	1.3	1993	10.9	219.7	36.9	13.7	343.9	81.6	47.0	42.0
Sri Lanka	1996	19.5	5.8	16.0	13.7	2.3	1989	26.0	26.7	8.4	36.9	101.4	31.1	17.4	135.7
Sudan, The	1995	41.3	11.7	83.0	29.6	6.0	...	...	...	...	...	...	...	...	...
Suriname	1995	24.7	5.9	30.2	18.8	2.7	1987[41]	35	57	42	10	179	34	25	69
Swaziland	1995	43.1	10.8	90.7	32.3	6.1	...	...	...	...	...	...	...	...	...
Sweden	1995	11.7	10.6	3.7	1.1	1.9	1993	8.8	235.8	24.4	14.7	554.7	94.9	34.0	21.1
Switzerland	1996	11.6	8.6	5.1[3]	3.0	1.5[3]	1993	16.0	236.1	24.1[15]	17.6	390.8	68.2	27.3	68.7
Syria	1995	40.0	6.0	29.6	34.0	6.1	1981[20]	22	12	7	13	86	19	8	27
Taiwan	1996	14.8	6.0	5.1[3]	8.8	1.8[3]	1992	...	101.5	23.7[6]	...	140.1[11]	24.3[41]	18.2[42]	63.7[42]
Tajikistan	1994	35.0	6.0	40.0	29.0	4.5	1993	128.3	40.7	8.8[2,15]	7.9[2]	222.8	158.7	20.7	181.3
Tanzania	1995	45.3	19.8	109.0	25.5	6.1	...	...	...	...	...	...	...	...	...
Thailand	1996	18.2	7.3	32.0	10.9	2.0	1991	...	162.0	...	...	250.0	55.0	73.0	104.0
Togo	1995	18.2	7.3	32.0	10.9	6.8	...	...	...	...	...	...	...	...	...
Tonga	1996	27.8	5.9	16.0	21.9	3.4	1992	16.3	54.9	15.2	6.1	158.5	31.5	18.3	4.1
Trinidad and Tobago	1995	16.7	6.9	18.5	9.8	2.0	1992	29.8	87.6	84.6[6]	2.4[24]	263.6	31.7	13.6	52.7
Tunisia	1995	20.9	4.8	43.0[16]	16.1	3.2[16]	...	...	...	...	...	...	...	...	...
Turkey	1995	25.3	5.6	45.6	19.7	2.6	1993[42]	24	80	9[6]	2[3]	369	19	10	33
Turkmenistan	1994	33.0	7.0	45.0	26.0	4.1	1993	75.3	62.3	8.0[13]	9.1[13]	333.8	140.7	28.2	62.7
Tuvalu	1993	25.5	9.1	73.6	16.4	3.0	1985	40.0	70.0	20.0	120.0	150.0	120.0	170.0	...
Uganda	1995	46.9	20.5	100.3	26.4	6.7	...	...	...	...	...	...	...	...	...
Ukraine	1994	12.0	13.0	14.0	–0.2	1.7	1993	14.5	198.9	8.2[12,15]	8.9[12]	782.6	81.3	38.3	131.2
United Arab Emirates	1994	25.0	3.4	18.2	21.6	2.7	...	...	...	...	...	...	...	...	...
United Kingdom	1994	12.9	10.7	6.2	2.2	1.7	1993	5.8	278.0	15.1	16.0	507.3	175.3	36.1	...
United States	1995	15.2	8.7	8.0	9.7	2.0[2]	1995	29.3[43]	204.1	22.2[6]	0.3[24]	358.7	70.1[28]	12.8	55.0
Uruguay	1994	17.7	9.4	18.7[44]	8.3	2.4	1990	16.0	222.8	25.5	16.2	378.4	76.3	39.1	61.7
Uzbekistan	1994	33.0	6.0	35.0	27.0	4.0	1993	38.0	48.2	9.4[12]	8.9[12]	300.3	113.8	31.4	49.5
Vanuatu	1996	33.5	6.4	41.0	27.1	4.5	1994[45]	25.0	29.2	9.1	5.5	39.0	30.4	9.7	9.1
Venezuela	1994	25.7	4.6	27.7	21.1	3.1	1989	30.0	51.1	18.6	7.4	115.0	29.0	18.8	61.4
Vietnam	1996	26.1	7.0	39.0	19.1	3.3	1979	48.0	54.0	...	...	123.8	...	...	...
Virgin Islands (U.S.)	1993	24.3	5.5	12.3	18.8	2.6[13]	1989	10.8	78.9	36.5[5]	—	232.7	14.8[28]	12.8	56.2
West Bank	1994	46.0	7.0	40.0	39.0	5.7	...	...	...	...	...	...	...	...	...
Western Sahara	1995	46.9	18.5	149.0	28.4	6.9	...	...	...	...	...	...	...	...	...
Western Samoa	1996	35.9	5.5	60.0	30.4	4.2	1992	3.1	11.2	9.9	3.1	24.2	9.9	6.8	2.5
Yemen	1994	45.0	11.8	82.5	33.2	7.4	...	...	...	...	...	...	...	...	...
Yugoslavia	1993	13.5	10.2	21.9	3.3	1.9	1993	9.9	160.1[19]	19.9	9.8	583.4	40.6	29.0	45.5
Zaire	1995	48.5	17.1	110.2	31.4	6.7	...	...	...	...	...	...	...	...	...
Zambia	1995	45.2	23.1	95.8	22.1	6.6	...	...	...	...	...	...	...	...	...
Zimbabwe	1996	32.3	18.2	72.8	14.1	4.1	1990	64.7	28.4	4.9	9.4	40.8	39.5	12.1	44.9

[1]Excludes nomadic tribes. [2]1991. [3]1994. [4]1986. [5]Septicemia only. [6]Diabetes mellitus only. [7]Cerebrovascular disease and heart disease only. [8]Chronic obstructive pulmonary diseases, pneumonia, and influenza only. [9]Under 21 years of age. [10]21–29 years of age. [11]1993. [12]1992. [13]1989. [14]1988. [15]Includes nutritional disorders. [16]1990–95. [17]Accidents only. [18]1990. [19]Includes benign neoplasms (cancers). [20]Projected rates based on about 75 percent of the total deaths. [21]Results based on a sample population of about 100,000. [22]Millions of households. [23]1985. [24]Meningitis only. [25]Ethiopia includes Eritrea. [26]1987. [27]First marriages only. [28]Bronchitis, pneumonia, and influenza only. [29]Muslims only. [30]Projected rates based on about 20 percent of the total deaths.

expectation of life at birth (latest year)		nuptiality, family, and family planning															country
		marriages			age at marriage (latest)						families (F), households (H) (latest)						
					groom (percent)			bride (percent)			families (households)		children		induced abortions		
male	female	year	total number	rate per 1,000 population	19 and under	20–29	30 and over	19 and under	20–29	30 and over	total ('000)	size	number under age 15	percent legitimate	number	ratio per 100 live births	
71.1	75.8	1993	1,223	6.3	...	...	...	...	...	...	H 41	H 3.7	H 2.1	51.6	...	...	Netherlands Antilles
69.0	76.0	1993	896	5.0	0.7[14]	54.3[14]	45.0[14]	8.8[14]	63.9[14]	27.3[14]	...	H 4.1	...	48.1	...	...	New Caledonia
73.4	79.1	1994	21,858	6.2	0.8	50.6	48.6	3.2	60.8	36.0	H 1,178	H 2.9	H 0.7	63.3	11,460	19.3	New Zealand
60.7	66.4	1991	13,122	3.3	18.1[9,23]	—81.9[23,36]—		48.2[9,23]	—51.8[23,36]—		...	H 6.9	...	...	...	...	Nicaragua
40.7	39.8	...	...	...	...	...	...	...	...	...	H 1,130	H 6.4	...	...	...	...	Niger
53.5	55.9	...									H 14,441	H 5.0	...	...	...	...	Nigeria
59.0	64.0	1987	685	31.2	2.5	50.2	47.3	5.7	70.4	23.9	H 7	H 4.6	H 1.5	53.9	...	...	Northern Mariana Islands
74.2	80.3	1994	20,000	4.6	0.6[12]	53.7[12]	45.7[12]	3.2[12]	67.6[12]	29.2[12]	F 1,983	F 2.2	F 0.4	55.6	14,909	25.0	Norway
68.3	72.3	...	...	...							H 350	H 3.7	...	...	...	...	Oman
62.0	64.0	...									...	H 6.3					Pakistan
69.1	73.0	...									...					...	Palau
71.0	76.5	1994	13,537	5.2	2.7[12]	52.4[12]	43.8[12]	12.3[12]	55.2[12]	31.1[12]	H 524	H 4.4	H 1.5	25.5	...	...	Panama
57.0	58.0	...									H 674	H 4.6				...	Papua New Guinea
64.8	69.1	1991	16,379	3.8	4.6	64.5	30.9	33.5	46.9	19.6	H 868	H 4.7	1.9	68.7	...	...	Paraguay
65.2	70.0	1993	90,000	4.1	5.5[38]	60.4[38]	34.1[38]	25.9[38]	51.4[38]	22.6[38]	H 3,099	H 5.1	...	57.8			Peru
66.0	70.0	1991	445,526	7.1	5.5	68.1	26.4	19.5	64.3	16.2	F 9,566	F 5.7	F 2.4	93.9	2,315	...	Philippines
67.5	76.1	1994	208,900	5.4	4.4[2]	76.6[2]	19.0[2]	21.8[2]	65.0[2]	13.2[2]	F 9,435	F 3.6	F 0.9	95.0	11,640	2.3	Poland
70.8	78.0	1993	68,176	6.9	4.0	79.0	17.0	18.0	71.0	11.0	H 2,954	H 3.8	H 0.8	85.5	...	...	Portugal
70.8	79.7	1993	33,262	12.6	10.1	54.7	35.2	21.1	50.1	28.8	H 1,005	H 3.6	H 1.0	59.6	...	...	Puerto Rico
70.0	74.5	1993	1,570	2.8	5.0	69.8	25.2	29.9	59.7	10.4	H 61	H 6.4	...	...	...	...	Qatar
71.0	77.0	1993	3,503	5.5	1.2[18]	65.2[18]	33.6[18]	12.5[18]	66.8[18]	20.7[18]	H 185	H 3.5	...	46.0	4,302	31.7	Réunion
69.3	75.4	1994	154,000	6.8	3.3[11]	77.3[11]	19.4[11]	31.0[11]	57.3[11]	11.7[11]	H 7,115	H 3.1	...	...	585,761	234.3	Romania
58.0	72.0	1995	1,074,900	7.3	9.7[3]	79.4[3]	10.9[3]	41.0[3]	51.6[3]	7.4[3]	H 40,426	H 3.2	H 0.8	85.4	3,243,957	235.2	Russia
35.9	36.4	1982	14,313	2.6	...	...	...	...	...	...	H 1,509	H 4.7	2.3	94.9	...	...	Rwanda
63.0	69.0	...									H 12	H 3.7	H 1.4	19.2	...	...	St. Kitts and Nevis
67.0	72.0	1992	436	3.2	0.8[13]	34.4[13]	64.8[13]	3.5[13]	45.1[13]	51.4[13]	H 33	H 4.0	H 2.0	14.2	...	...	St. Lucia
71.0	74.0	1993	417	3.8	1.0[12]	37.0[12]	62.0[12]	4.8[12]	46.3[12]	48.9[12]	H 27	H 3.9	H 2.0	...	...	...	St. Vincent and the Grenadines
77.2	85.3	1989	169	7.4	0.6	75.1	24.3	5.3	85.3	9.5	H 9	H 2.6	H 0.4	95.2	...	...	San Marino
61.8	65.6	...	...	...	...	...	...	...	...	...	...	H 4.0	...	9.8			São Tomé and Príncipe
67.0	70.1	...									H 1,513	H 6.6					Saudi Arabia
55.6	58.7	...									...	H 8.7					Senegal
66.0	73.0	1994	937	12.7	2.0	45.8	42.2	11.2	51.5	29.6	H 13	H 4.8	H 1.9	27.2	387	22.8	Seychelles
44.1	49.9	...									H 749	H 4.7					Sierra Leone
74.2	78.7	1995	24,965	8.4	0.6[3]	56.3[3]	43.1[3]	3.7[3]	74.9[3]	21.4[3]	H 662	H 4.2	H 1.3	...	16,476	32.8	Singapore
66.6	75.4	1994	28,155	5.3	8.3[2]	77.5[2]	14.2[2]	35.9[2]	55.0[2]	9.1[2]	H 1,778	H 3.0	H 0.7	88.3	45,919	61.5	Slovakia
69.4	77.3	1994	8,314	4.2	0.8	65.6	33.6	7.6	73.2	19.2	H 637	H 3.1	...	71.2	13,263	66.4	Slovenia
69.0	74.0	...									H	H 5.8					Solomon Islands
55.4	54.8	...										H 4.9					Somalia
62.7	68.0	1993	120,159	3.0	...	...	...	...	...	...	8,688	H 4.6	...	75.9	...	...	South Africa
73.2	81.1	1994	196,062	5.0	1.8[2]	71.5[2]	26.7[2]	8.2[2]	76.7[2]	15.1[2]	F 10,665	F 3.5	...	89.5	...	...	Spain
71.0	75.0	1992	152,154	8.7	0.6	67.0	32.4	15.7	70.9	13.4	H 2,721	H 5.2	H 1.9	96.3	...	...	Sri Lanka
53.8	55.6	...									H 3,471	H 5.3				...	Sudan, The
67.2	72.4	1991	1,974	4.6	...	...	...	...	...	...	...	H 3.9	...	...	...	...	Suriname
52.8	61.0	...									H 122	H 5.7	...	...	1,145	...	Swaziland
75.3	80.8	1993	34,005	3.9	0.4	39.4	60.2	2.2	52.0	45.8	H 3,670	H 2.2	H 0.5	48.4	34,169	28.9	Sweden
75.1	81.6	1994	42,411	6.1	0.3	47.3	52.4	2.2	62.5	35.3	H 3,250	H 2.2	0.4	93.6	...	...	Switzerland
68.4	71.3	1993	114,979	8.6	...	...	...	...	...	...	F 1,151	F 6.2	F 2.4	...			Syria
71.8	77.7	1994	170,580	8.1	1.5[18]	62.3[18]	36.2[18]	6.0[18]	77.7[18]	16.3[18]	H 5,636	H 3.8	H 1.0	97.0	...	...	Taiwan
65.7	71.5	1993	53,946	9.6	2.1	86.8	11.1	39.0	54.3	6.7	H 799	H 6.1	H 2.7	93.0	54,494	27.2	Tajikistan
41.5	45.0	...									H 3,435	H 5.1	H 2.3	...			Tanzania
67.0	72.0	1994	435,425	7.4	...	...	...	...	...	...	H 10,418	H 5.3	H 1.9	...	...	...	Thailand
55.3	59.6	...									H 479	H 5.6					Togo
67.0	72.0	1992	806	8.2	...	...	...	...	...	...	F 15	F 6.1	F 2.7	80.6			Tonga
67.8	72.6	1993	7,012	5.6	5.9[2]	61.0[2]	33.1[2]	25.5[2]	52.6[2]	21.9[2]	H 301	H 4.1	H 1.3	...	9	—	Trinidad and Tobago
66.9	68.7	1995	52,203	6.0	0.4[13]	63.6[13]	36.0[13]	21.5[13]	66.8[13]	11.7[13]	H 1,703	H 5.1	H 1.9	99.8	23,300	10.9	Tunisia
69.1	74.0	1993	460,002	7.7	7.4[12]	75.3[12]	17.3[12]	34.1[12]	57.7[12]	8.2[12]	...	H 4.5	...	...	...	...	Turkey
61.4	68.6	1993	42,106	10.7	3.0[13]	87.4[13]	9.6[13]	16.1[13]	77.1[13]	6.8[13]	H 598	H 5.6	H 2.4	96.5	39,068	31.3	Turkmenistan
67.2	64.0	...									H 1	H 6.4	H 2.2	82.2			Tuvalu
43.6	46.2	...									H 2,766	H 4.8					Uganda
65.3	74.7	1993	427,882	8.2	7.0[12]	70.5[12]	22.5[12]	37.3[12]	44.2[12]	18.5[12]	H 14,507	H 3.2	H 0.8	89.2	957,022	159.5	Ukraine
70.4	74.7	...									H 247	H 6.8					United Arab Emirates
74.4	79.7	1992	356,013	6.1	24.0	50.8	25.2	37.9	43.2	18.9	H 21,672	H 2.7	H 1.7	68.0	171,260	21.9	United Kingdom
72.0	78.9	1995	2,335,000	8.9	4.5[14]	54.1[14]	41.4[14]	11.8[14]	55.7[14]	32.5[14]	H 96,391	H 2.6	F 1.0	70.5	1,354,000	35.5	United States
70.9	77.5	1992	54,754	6.2	7.2[18]	59.8[18]	33.0[18]	23.6[18]	52.3[18]	24.1[18]	H 863	H 3.3	H 0.9	73.8	...	...	Uruguay
65.1	71.8	1993	225,451	10.3	2.3	87.4	10.3	37.9	55.2	6.9	H 3,415	H 5.5	H 2.4	95.8	226,276	33.8	Uzbekistan
65.0	69.0	1989	49,460	34.0	...	...	...	...	...	...	H 28	H 5.1	H 2.2	...	113	2.4	Vanuatu
70.1	76.0	1992	108,955	5.4	10.7[2]	61.3[2]	28.0[2]	30.4[2]	51.7[2]	17.9[2]	H 2,707	H 5.3	H 2.2	47.0	...	...	Venezuela
63.7	67.9	...									H 12,958[46]	H 4.8[46]	H 1.9[46]	...			Vietnam
66.7	70.7	1993	3,646	35.1	0.4	33.6	66.0	1.9	45.9	52.2	H 32	H 3.1	H 1.0	38.4	...	...	Virgin Islands (U.S.)
65.7	67.5	...									...						West Bank
45.3	47.6	...															Western Sahara
67.0	71.0	1993	759	4.7	0.5	51.0	48.5	8.0	65.0	27.0	F 20	F 7.8	F 3.8	43.5	...	...	Western Samoa
61.6	63.5	...									H 1,848	H 5.6					Yemen
69.1	74.3	1994	59,599	5.7	2.4[11]	66.8[11]	30.8[11]	21.0[11]	62.8[11]	16.2[11]	H 2,870	H 3.6	H 0.9	...	...	...	Yugoslavia
44.8	48.0	...									...	H 6.0				...	Zaire
45.0	46.2	...									H 1,370	H 4.4	H 2.1	...	...	...	Zambia
58.0	62.0	...									H 2,166	H 4.8	1.1	95.8			Zimbabwe

[31]1995. [32]Projected rates based on about 10 percent of total deaths. [33]Average annual rates for the period. [34]Includes Aruba. [35]Projected rates based on about 45 percent of total deaths. [36]Over 21 years of age. [37]Reporting areas only (constituting about 75 percent of the total population). [38]1982. [39]Includes all deaths associated with alcoholism. [40]1990–94. [41]Projected rates based on about 70 percent of total deaths. [42]Projected rates based on about 35 percent of total deaths. [43]Of which AIDS, 16.1. [44]1991–92 average. [45]Registered events only. [46]Private households only.

National product and accounts

This table furnishes, for most of the countries of the world, breakdowns of (1) gross national product (GNP)—its global and per capita values, purchasing power parity (PPP), and growth rates (1985–94), (2) principal industrial and accounting components of gross domestic product (GDP), and (3) principal elements of each country's balance of payments, including international goods trade, invisibles, and tourism payments.

Measures of national output. The two most commonly used measures of national output are GDP and GNP. Each of these measures represents an aggregate value of goods and services produced by a specific country. The GDP, the more basic of these, is a measure of the total value of goods and services produced entirely within a given country. The GNP, the more comprehensive value, is composed of both domestic production (GDP) and the net income from current (short-term) transactions with other countries. When the income received from other countries is greater than payments to them, a country's GNP is greater than its GDP. In theory, if all national accounts could be equilibrated, the global summation of GDP would equal GNP.

In the first section of the table, data are provided for the nominal and real GNP. ("Nominal" refers to value in current prices for the year indicated and is distinguished from a "real" valuation, which is one adjusted to eliminate the effect of recent inflation [most often] or, occasionally, of deflation between two given dates.) Both the total and per capita values of this product are denominated in U.S. dollars for ease of comparison, as is a new value for GNP per capita adjusted for purchasing power parity.

The latter is a concept that provides a better approximation of the ability of equivalent values of two (or more) national currencies to purchase comparable quantities of goods and services in their respective domestic markets and may differ substantially from two otherwise equal GNP per capita values based solely on currency exchange rates. Beside these are given figures for average annual growth of total and per capita real GNP. GNP per capita provides a rough measure of annual national income per person, but values should be compared cautiously, as they are subject to a number of distortions, notably of exchange rate, but also of purchasing power parity and in the existence of elements of national production that do not enter the monetary economy in such a way as to be visible to fiscal authorities (e.g., food, clothing, or housing produced and consumed within families or communal groups or services exchanged). For reasons of comparability, the majority of the data in this section are taken from the World Bank's *The World Bank Atlas* (annual).

The internal structure of the national product. GDP/GNP values allow comparison of the relative size of national economies, but further information is provided when these aggregates are analyzed according to their industrial sectors of origin, component kinds of expenditure, and cost components.

The distribution of GDP for ten industrial sectors, usually compiled from national sources, is aggregated into three major industrial groups:

1. The primary sector, composed of agriculture (including forestry and fishing) and mineral production (including fossil fuels).

National product and accounts

country	gross national product (GNP), 1994 nominal, ('000,000 U.S.$)	per capita nominal (U.S.$)	per capita purchasing power parity (PPP; U.S.$)	real GNP (%)	population (%)	real GNP per capita (%)	primary agriculture	primary mining	secondary manufacturing	secondary construction	secondary public utilities	tertiary transp., communications	tertiary trade	tertiary financial svcs.	tertiary other svcs.	tertiary government
Afghanistan	4,956[1]	280[1]	...	...	...	...	52[2]	3	26[2,3]	7[2]	3	4[2]	9[2]	— 2[2] —		
Albania	1,229	360	...	-4.4	1.6	-6.0	40	4	— 13[4] —			—	— 47 —			
Algeria	46,115	1,690	5,330	0.1	2.5	-2.4	11	4	33[4]	11	1	— 30 —				14
American Samoa	128[5,6]	2,600[5,6]	...	...	...	...	...	...	...	...	...	...	...	...	...	...
Andorra	760[5,6]	14,000[5,6]	...	...	...	...	...	...	...	...	...	...	...	...	...	...
Angola	4,706[6]	420[6]	...	...	...	...	20	35	5	2	—	3	14	— 19 —		
Antigua and Barbuda	453	6,970	...	3.2	0.5	2.7	3	1	2	8	4	17	20	13	6	14
Argentina	275,657	8,060	8,920	3.3	1.4	1.9	6[8]	2	22[8]	5[8]	2[8]	5[8]	15[8]	17[8]	— 26[8] —	
Armenia	2,532	670	2,170	-11.4	1.5	-12.9	49	3	22[3]	4	3	6	3	2	8	3
Aruba	1,256	15,890	...	7.3	1.1	6.2	...	...	...	...	...	...	...	...	...	...
Australia	320,705	17,980	19,000	2.7	1.5	1.2	3	4	15	7	3	7	17	24	17	4
Austria	197,475	24,950	20,230	2.8	0.5	2.3	2	4	24[4]	7	3	7	16	19	5	15
Azerbaijan	3,730	500	1,720	-10.9	1.3	-12.2	27	3	25[3]	7	3	8	5	9	14	6
Bahamas, The	3,207	11,790	15,250	1.0	1.7	-0.7	3[8]	4	3[4,8]	3[8]	3[8]	7[8]	23[8]	20[8]	17[8]	6[8]
Bahrain	4,114	7,500	12,070	2.2	3.1	-0.9	1	17	15	6	4	11	9	18	6	21
Bangladesh	26,636	230	1,350	4.1	2.0	2.1	30	4	10[4]	6	2	12	8	2	24	5
Barbados	1,704	6,530	10,760	0.2	0.3	-0.1	5	1	8	4	4	9	31	16	4	18
Belarus	21,937	2,160	5,010	-1.5	0.2	-1.7	18	3	32[3]	8	3	10	11	10	11	2
Belgium	231,051	22,920	20,450	2.5	0.2	2.3	2	—	23	5	3	8	14	20	10	17
Belize	535	2,550	5,600	7.9	2.6	5.3	19[10]	—	14[10]	7[10]	4[10]	11[10]	17[10]	11[10]	6[10]	13[10]
Benin	1,954	370	1,660	2.2	3.0	-0.8	33[10]	4	8[4,10]	4[10]	1[10]	8[10]	20[10]	— 11[10] —		9[10]
Bermuda	1,894	26,280	...	0.9	0.7	0.2	...	...	...	...	...	...	...	...	...	...
Bhutan	272	400	1,270	...	...	...	41	1	11	10	6	8	8	7	— 9 —	
Bolivia	5,601	770	2,520	4.1	2.2	1.9	17	8	16	5	1	11	10	9	— 16 —	
Bosnia and Herzegovina	10,667[2]	2,450[2]	...	...	...	...	...	...	...	...	...	...	...	...	...	...
Botswana	4,037	2,800	5,320	9.9	3.3	6.6	5	35	6	4	3	4	15	6	3	21
Brazil	536,309	3,370	5,630	1.4	1.8	-0.4	12	2	25	7	4	6	8[11]	17	18[11]	11
Brunei	3,975	14,240	...	0.8	2.3	-1.5	3	4	45[4]	5	1	4	8	7	— 30 —	
Bulgaria	10,255	1,160	4,230	-3.4	-0.2	-3.2	13	4	28[4]	5	12	7	11	— 33[12] —		
Burkina Faso	2,982	300	770	2.5	2.7	-0.2	34	4	15[4]	5	1	4	13	— 25 —		
Burundi	904	150	580	2.0	3.0	-1.0	49	1[13]	12	4	13	3	4	— 2 —		15
Cambodia	6,400[6]	630[6]	...	...	...	...	51[10]	— 10	5[10]	8[10]	1[10]	3[10]	15[10]	— 13[10] —		4[10]
Cameroon	8,735	680	1,970	-3.8	2.8	-6.6	24[5]	13[5]	14[5]	5[5]	1[5]	6[5]	12[5]	13[5]	2[5]	10[5]
Canada	569,949	19,570	21,320	1.7	1.3	0.4	3	4	18	5	3	9	12	17	22	7
Cape Verde	346	910	1,850	4.1	2.3	1.8	21[5]	—	6[5]	20[5]	3[5]	12[5]	28[5]	— 15 —		9[5]
Central African Republic	1,191	370	1,060	-0.4	2.4	-2.8	53[10]	6[10]	7[10]	4[10]	—	3[10]	12[10]	— 5[10] —		10[10]
Chad	1,153	190	740	3.2	2.3	0.9	44[5]	—	9[5]	2[5]	15	2[5]	31[5]	— 15 —		10[5]
Chile	50,051	3,560	9,060	7.9	1.7	6.2	8	8	17	6	3	7	17	17	— 10 —	
China	630,202	530	2,510	8.3	1.4	6.9	21	3	45[3]	7	3	6	6	— 15 —		
Colombia	58,935	1,620	5,970	4.1	2.2	1.9	14	6	19	6	3	11	16	12	— 14 —	
Comoros	249	510	1,130	1.4	2.7	-1.3	39	...	5	6	1	5	28	14	3	14[14]
Congo	1,607	640	2,000	0.3	3.0	-2.7	15[5]	21[5]	9[5]	1[5]	2[5]	11[5]	13[5]	1[5]	10[5]	17[5]
Costa Rica	7,856	2,380	5,760	5.3	2.5	2.8	16	4	20[4]	3	4	6	21	11	7	13
Côte d'Ivoire	7,070	510	1,340	-1.6	3.6	-5.2	34	4	6	2	6	8	7	— 9 —		13
Croatia	12,093	2,530	...	...	...	...	13	4	31[4]	3	3	9	2	12	21	5
Cuba	14,000[6]	1,260[6]	...	...	...	...	...	...	...	...	...	...	...	...	...	...
Cyprus[15]	7,240	11,350	...	6.7	2.1	4.6	5[10]	—	13[10]	9[10]	2[10]	8[10]	19[10]	16[10]	7[10]	13[10]
Czech Republic	33,051	3,210	7,910	-2.1	0.0	-2.1	6	3	34[3]	6	3	7	8	— 25 —		14
Denmark	145,384	28,110	20,800	1.4	0.1	1.3	4	1	19	5	2	9	14	19	5	27
Djibouti	500[6]	1,200[6]	...	...	...	...	3	...	5	5	8	16	15	16	4	24
Dominica	201	2,830	...	4.0	-0.2	4.2	18[10]	1[10]	6[10]	7[10]	4[10]	15[10]	12[10]	12[10]	1[10]	16[10]
Dominican Republic	10,109	1,320	3,790	4.2	2.1	2.1	13	1	19	9	2	10	17	11	9	9
Ecuador	14,703	1,310	4,380	3.3	2.3	1.0	17	18	11	2	1	9	15	17	14	8
Egypt	40,950	710	3,610	3.6	2.0	1.6	17	10	17	5	2	11	18	5	8	7
El Salvador	8,365	1,480	2.510	3.5	1.9	1.6	9	—	19	3	3	5	37	8	10	7

2. The secondary sector, composed of manufacturing, construction, and public utilities.
3. The tertiary sector, which includes transportation and communications, trade (wholesale and retail), restaurants and hotels, financial services (including banking, real estate, insurance, and business services), other services (community, social, and personal), and government services.

Percentages in this section of the table may not add to 100 because the value of each economic sector is calculated as a percentage of the total GDP, which may contain adjustments such as import duties and bank service charges that are not distributed by sector.

There are three major domestic components of GDP expenditure: private consumption (analyzed in greater detail in the "Household budgets and consumption" table), government spending, and gross domestic investment. The fourth, nondomestic, component of GDP expenditure is net foreign trade; values are given for both exports (a positive value) and imports (a negative value, representing obligations to other countries). The sum of these five percentages, excluding statistical discrepancies and rounding, should be 100% of the GDP.

The structure of GDP as accounted by cost components here comprises four general categories: indirect taxes (excise or value-added taxes), net of subsidies; consumption of fixed capital (depreciation); and two income categories: (a) compensation of employees (salaries, wages, etc.) and (b) net operating surplus ("profits," interests, rent, etc.).

Balance of payments (external account transactions). The external account records the sum (net) of all economic transactions of a current nature between one country and the rest of the world. The account shows a country's net of overseas receipts and obligations, including not only the trade of goods and merchandise but also such invisible items as services, interest and dividends, short- and long-term investments, tourism, transfers to or from overseas residents, etc. Each transaction gives rise either to a foreign claim for payment, recorded as a deficit (*e.g.,* from imports, capital outflows), or a foreign obligation to pay, recorded as a surplus (*e.g.,* from exports, capital inflows) or a domestic claim on another country. Any international transaction automatically creates a deficit in the balance of payments of one country and a surplus in that of another. Values are given in U.S. dollars for comparability.

Tourist trade. Net income or expenditure from tourism (in U.S. dollars for comparability) is often a significant element in a country's balance of payments. Receipts from foreign nationals reflect payments for goods and services from foreign currency resources by tourists in the given country. Expenditures by nationals abroad are also payments for goods and services, but in this case made by the residents of the given country as tourists abroad. The majority of the data in this section are compiled by the World Tourism Organization.

gross domestic product (GDP) by type of expenditure, 1993(%)					cost components of gross domestic product (GDP), 1993 (%)				balance of payments, 1994 (current external transactions; '000,000 U.S.$)			tourist trade, 1994 ('000,000 U.S.$)		country
consumption		gross domestic	foreign trade		indirect taxes	consump- tion of	compen- sation of	net operating	net transfers		current balance	receipts from	expendi- tures by	
private	govern- ment	invest- ment	exports	imports	net of subsides	fixed capital	employ- ees	surplus	goods, merchan- dise	invisibles	of payments	foreign nationals	nationals abroad	
...	...	...	...	...	...	...	...	...	...	...	...	1[2]	1[2]	Afghanistan
—170—		10	12	−92	...	13[2]	62[2]	25[2]	−460	448	−12	5	4	Albania
54	18	27	23	−23	...	...	...	...	5,468[5]	−3,101[5]	2,3671[5]	49	135	Algeria
...	...	...	...	...	...	...	...	...	...	...	...	10[5]	...	American Samoa
...	...	...	...	...	...	...	...	...	...	...	...	...	...	Andorra
54	33	15	45	−46	7[2]	[7]	39[2]	54[2, 7]	1,369	−2,241	−872	13	66[1]	Angola
56	19	24	112	−112	15[8]	—85[8]—			−254	236	−18	394	24	Antigua and Barbuda
—84—		18	6	−8	...	...	...	...	−2,428[1]	−5,024[1]	−7,452[1]	3,790	2,445[1]	Argentina
87	16	9	44	−57	...	...	...	...	−181[1]	114[1]	−67[1]	...	...	Armenia
58	17	23	42	−39	...	...	...	...	−311	392	81	451	65	Aruba
62	18	20	19	−19	12	15	49	24	−3,372	−14,109	−17,481	5,955	4,339	Australia
55	19	25	38	−37	13	13	53	21	−8,869	6,417	−2,452	13,160	9,330	Austria
87	11	18	40	−56	6	4	54	36	...	...	...	2,042	...	Azerbaijan
76	15	21	44	−56	14[8]	[7]	51[8]	36[7, 8]	−782	662	−119	1,333	192	Bahamas, The
32	25	20	115	−92	3	17	44	35	−282	193	−89	302	146	Bahrain
80	14	14	11	−18	7	7	—86—		−1,434	1,678	244	19	210	Bangladesh
62	22	13	48	−46	...	...	...	...	−330[1]	394[1]	64[1]	598	52[1]	Barbados
56	19	36	56	−66	9	20	49	22	−542	−3	−545	...	...	Belarus
63	15	18	69	−64	10	10	54	27	6,930[9]	6,091[9]	13,021[9]	5,182	7,782	Belgium
62	16	33	54	−65	15[8]	6[8]	—78[8]—		−119[1]	70[1]	−49[1]	74	21[1]	Belize
83	12	15	23	−33	...	...	...	...	−65	101	36	55	19	Benin
67	12	13	62	−53	...	...	...	...	−536	580	44	524	140[1]	Bermuda
72	19	28	35	−55	3	9	—88—		−12	−3	−15	3[1]	...	Bhutan
86	12	19	16	−33	...	...	...	...	−137	−82	−218	135	140	Bolivia
...	...	...	...	...	...	...	...	...	...	...	...	...	...	Bosnia and Herzegovina
44	31	27	48	−50	10	13	31	45	528	−280	249	35	52	Botswana
61	17	20	10	−8	12[2]	—88[2]—			10,861	−12,014	−1,153	1,925	2,931	Brazil
...	...	...	...	...	...	...	...	...	...	...	...	...	...	Brunei
66	17	20	50	−54	6	13	52	27	...	...	...	358	242	Bulgaria
81	16	23	12	−31	4[8]	[7]	27[8]	69[7, 8]	−139	148	9	22	35[1]	Burkina Faso
87	19	13	8	−28	11[2]	5[2]	22[2]	62[2]	−101	86	−14	3	4	Burundi
86	7	14	9	−16	...	...	...	...	−236	−4	−240	70	7	Cambodia
72	8	16	28	−23	...	...	...	...	502[1]	−1,068[1]	−565[1]	47[1]	225[1]	Cameroon
61	21	18	29	−30	13	12	56	18	12,202	−29,590	−17,388	6,309	11,676	Canada
85	13	43	11	−53	...	..	...	...	−148[1]	137[1]	−10[1]	10	9	Cape Verde
84	12	12	14	−23	...	...	...	...	15	−40	−25	9[2]	41[2]	Central African Republic
95	16	11	18	−40	...	...	...	...	−64[1]	−53[1]	−117[1]	36	12[1]	Chad
64	10	29	27	−29	...	...	...	...	659	−1,416	−757	833	639	Chile
51	9	41	24	−25	...	...	...	...	7,290	−758	6,532	7,323	3,036	China
70	12	20	17	−19	10[8]	[7]	39[8]	51[7, 8]	−2,284	−749	−3,033	794	756	Colombia
78	21	15	18	−33	...	...	...	...	−29	20	−9	8[8]	6[8]	Comoros
70	22	14	44	−51	...	...	...	...	393	−1,261	−868	3	36	Congo
61	17	30	39	−46	13	2	50	35	−686	223	−463	626	300	Costa Rica
62	14	5	40	−21	...	...	...	...	1,309	−1,295	13	43	118	Côte d'Ivoire
78	21	2	—1—		11[2]	13[2]	62[2]	14[2]	−446	547	101	1,427	552	Croatia
...	...	...	...	...	...	...	...	...	...	...	...	850	...	Cuba
59	17	24	48	−48	7	11	—83—		−1,736	1,779	44	1,700	176	Cyprus[15]
56	23	18	56	−55	...	...	...	...	−918	837	−81	1,966	832	Czech Republic
52	26	14	34	−27	14	10	54	23	7,739	−5,080	2,659	3,174	3,583	Denmark
76	38	13	71	−98	...	...	...	...	−191[1]	103[1]	−88[1]	13[1]	7[1]	Djibouti
66	24	24	48	−52	16[8]	—84[8]—			−52	16	−36	31	4	Dominica
76	6	23	23	−28	12	6	—82—		−1,632	1,473	−156	1,148	118[1]	Dominican Republic
71	8	21	26	−26	12	[7]	14	74[7]	435	−1,242	−807	252	203	Ecuador
73	10	20	28	−31	4	4	27	64	−5,953	5,984	31	1,384	1,067	Egypt
87	9	19	20	−34	6[8]	4[8]	—90[8]—		−1,115	1,137	−18	86	70	El Salvador

National product and accounts

country	gross national product (GNP), 1994 nominal, ('000,000 U.S.$)	per capita nominal (U.S.$)	per capita purchasing power parity (PPP; U.S.$)	real GNP (%)	population (%)	real GNP per capita (%)	agriculture	mining	manufacturing	construction	public utilities	transp., communications	trade	financial svcs.	other svcs.	government
Equatorial Guinea	167	430	...	4.1	2.5	1.6	45	14	2	5	4	2	11	2	4	7
Eritrea	1,800[6]	500[6]	...	...	...	...	18[10]	—	12[10]	4[10]	1[10]	13[10]	28[10]	4[10]	3[10]	10[10]
Estonia	4,351	2,820	...	-6.4	0.0	-6.4	11	2	24	6	4	14	16	11	6	2
Ethiopia	6,947	130	410	2.3	2.9	-0.6	54	4	8[4]	3	1	5	10	8	4	7
Faroe Islands	758[1,6]	16,450[1,6]	...	...	...	...	15	—	13	4	1	9	11	7	24	16
Fiji	1,785	2,320	5,590	3.4	1.4	2.0	21	—	12	5	1	15	20	13	—17—	
Finland	95,817	18,850	16,390	0.1	0.4	-0.3	5	—	24	5	5	9	11	20	3	20
France	1,355,039	23,470	19,820	2.2	0.5	1.7	3[10]	1[10]	20[10]	5[10]	3[10]	6[10]	14[10,16]	6[10]	18[10,16]	19[10]
French Guiana	800[1,6]	6,000[1,6]	...	...	...	...										
French Polynesia	1,500[1,6]	7,000[1,6]	...	...	...	...	5[2]	—	7[2]	6[2]	2[2]	17	23[2]	—29[2,17]—		29[2]
Gabon	3,669	3,550	...	-0.5	1.8	-2.3	9	30	22	5	2	7	9	1	13	14
Gambia, The	384	360	1,150	4.6	4.1	0.5	19	—	6	6	1	16	19	6	3	10
Gaza Strip	1,700[1,6]	2,400[1,6]	...	...	...	...	25	2	10[2]	21	2	—26—				18
Georgia	6,000[6]	1,060[6]	...	...	0.4	...	58	4	—22[4]—			—20—				
Germany	2,075,452	25,580	19,890	2.4	0.5	1.9	1[10]	2[10,13]	23[10]	5[10]	13	5[10]	8[10]	13[10]	19[10]	9[10]
Ghana	7,311	430	2,020	4.5	3.1	1.4	48	2	9	3	2	4	19	4	1	8
Gibraltar	205[1,6]	6,600[1,6]	...	...	...	...										
Greece	80,194	7,710	11,400	1.8	0.5	1.3	14	1	15	7	3	7	14	3	9	19
Greenland	920[1]	16,650[1]	...	...	...	...										
Grenada	241	2,620	...	4.1	0.2	3.9	12	—	7	7	4	22	20	13	3	19
Guadeloupe	3,800[1,6]	9,000[1,6]	...	...	...	...										
Guam	2,998	20,550	...	...	...	...										
Guatemala	12,237	1,190	3,490	3.8	2.9	0.9	24[10]	—	14[10]	2[10]	3[10]	9[10]	24[10]	9[10]	6[10]	8[10]
Guernsey[18]	1,531[8]	26,000[8]	...	...	...	...										
Guinea	3,310	510	...	4.1	2.9	1.2	24	19	5	7	—	5	—26—		6	6
Guinea-Bissau	253	240	900	4.0	2.1	1.9	45	4	—19[4]—			—36—				
Guyana	434	530	2,000	0.8	0.6	0.3	50[8]	12[8]	10[8,19]	3[8]	19	6[8]	5[8]	9[8]	28	9[8]
Haiti	1,542	220	930	-3.0	2.0	-5.0	39	—	13	3	1	2	10	—12—		17
Honduras	3,162	580	1,900	2.9	3.0	-0.1	20	2	18	7	4	6	11	15	11	7
Hong Kong	126,286	21,650	23,080	6.0	0.7	5.3	—	—	11	5	2	9	25	24	—14—	
Hungary	39,009	3,840	6,310	-1.3	-0.4	-0.9	7[8]	4	23[4,8]	5[8]	4[8]	7[8]	16[8]	9[8]	—15[8]—	
Iceland	6,545	24,590	18,900	1.4	1.1	0.3	13	—	17	8	4	7	12	19	6	18
India	278,739	310	1,290	4.9	2.0	2.9	30	2	17	6	3	8	13	8	6	6
Indonesia	167,632	880	3,690	7.6	1.6	6.0	18	10	22	6	1	7	16	8	4	7
Iran	310,000	4,720	4,650	2.3	3.3	-1.0	21	18	14	3	1	7	16	10	2	9
Iraq	12,640[5]	710[5]	...	...	...	...	28[5]	—	4[5]	3[5]	—	13[5]	20[5]	16[5]	—24[5]—	
Ireland	48,275	13,630	14,550	5.2	0.0	5.2	9	20	37[20]	20	20	—17—		—31—		6
Isle of Man	780[6]	10,800[6]	...	...	...	...	2[5]	—	12[5]	8[5]	3[5]	9[5]	21	27[5]	33[5,21]	6[5]
Israel	78,113	14,410	15,690	5.2	2.7	2.5	3[8]	4	22[4,8]	8[8]	2[8]	8[8]	10[8]	25[8]	4[8]	23[8]
Italy	1,101,258	19,270	18,610	1.9	0.1	1.8	3	4	20[4]	6	6	6	18	14	14	13
Jamaica	3,553	1,420	2,970	2.6	0.9	1.7	10[10]	8[10]	20[10]	13[10]	2[10]	9[10]	25[10]	14[10]	5[10]	4[10]
Japan	4,321,136	34,630	21,350	3.6	0.4	3.2	2	—	30	9	4	6	14[11]	16	19[11]	4
Jersey	2,884[5]	34,200[5]	...	...	...	...	5[2]	—	—22—			—93[2]—				
Jordan	5,849	1,390	4,290	-1.1	5.2	-6.3	8[10]	3[10]	14[10]	7[10]	2[10]	16[10]	10[10]	17[10]	4[10]	19[10]
Kazakstan	18,896	1,110	2,830	-5.7	0.8	-6.5	13	3	31[3]	9	2	6	9	17	10	2
Kenya	6,643	260	1,350	2.9	2.9	0.0	29	—	10	6	1	8	14	17	1	15
Kiribati	56	730	...	0.5	1.5	-1.0	24[8]	—	2[8]	5[8]	2[8]	15[8]	14[8]	7[8]	—26[8]—	
Korea, North	21,300[6]	920[6]	...	...	...	...										
Korea, South	366,484	8,220	10,540	8.8	1.0	7.8	7	—	29	11	2	7	13	17	6	7
Kuwait	31,433	19,040	24,500	-1.8	-0.5	-1.3	—	39[10]	11[10]	3[10]	—	4[10]	7[10]	12[10]	—25[10]—	
Kyrgyzstan	2,825	610	1,710	-3.7	1.7	-5.4	37	3	28[3]	6	3	4	7	12	—7—	
Laos	1,496	320	...	5.2	3.1	2.1	56	—	13	3	1	5	8	9	—4—	
Latvia	5,920	2,290	5,170	-6.3	-0.1	-6.2	15	4	22[4]	4	5	—54—				
Lebanon	8,400	2,880	...	...	...	...	9	—	13	3	5	4	30	17	8	10
Lesotho	1,398	700	1,720	3.2	2.7	0.5	11[10]	—	14[10]	22[10]	2[10]	3[10]	9[10]	12[10]	3[10]	11[10]
Liberia	2,300[6]	770[6]	...	...	...	...										
Libya	32,900[6]	6,510[6]	...	...	...	...	8[5]	26[5]	8[5]	12[5]	2[5]	6[5]	9[5]	11[5]	7[5]	11[5]
Liechtenstein	978[5]	33,510[5]	...	...	...	...										
Lithuania	4,492	1,350	3,240	-7.4	0.4	-7.8	15	4	26[4]	7	5	8	17	6	5	7
Luxembourg	15,973	39,850	31,090	2.3	1.0	1.3	1[5]	—	24[5]	7[5]	2[5]	7[5]	16[5]	14[5]	15[5]	15[5]
Macau	6,627	16,160	...	...	...	...										
Macedonia	1,653	790	...	...	...	...	19[10]	—	38[4,10]	6[10]	—	4[10]	25[10]	—7[10]—		
Madagascar	3,058	230	670	1.3	3.0	-1.7	34	4	—14[4]—			—52—				
Malawi	1,560	140	600	2.5	4.5	-2.0	31	...	14	4	3	5	12	11	5	16
Malaysia	68,674	3,520	8,610	8.2	2.5	5.7	16	8	30	4	2	7	12	11	2	10
Maldives	221	900	...	9.7	3.2	6.5	21	2	6[19]	9	19	7	19		28	9
Mali	2,421	250	520	3.7	2.8	0.9	44	2	9	5[22]	22	5	17	—7—		7
Malta	3,900[6]	10,760[6]	...	...	...	...	3[8]	23	25[8]	3[8,23]	24	7[8]	14[8]	15[8]	10[8]	23[8,24]
Marshall Islands	88	1,680	...	...	...	...										
Martinique	3,900[1,6]	10,000[1,6]	...	...	...	...										
Mauritania	1,063	480	1,570	2.7	2.5	0.2	24	9	11	—7—		6	14	—14—		12
Mauritius	3,514	3,180	13,130	6.5	0.9	5.6	10	—	23	8	3	12	17	12	6	10
Mayotte	54	600	...	...	...	...										
Mexico	368,679	4,010	7,050	2.8	2.2	0.6	7	3	22	5	2	7	26	11	—17—	
Micronesia	202	1,890	...	...	...	...										
Moldova	3,853	870	...	...	...	...	48[10]	3	25[3,10]	2[10]	3	1[10]	4[10]	—20[10]—		
Monaco	558[1,6]	18,000[1,6]	...	...	...	...										
Mongolia	801	340	2,020	-0.9	2.4	-3.3	21	4	—46[4]—			—33—				
Morocco	30,330	1,150	3,440	3.3	2.2	1.1	14	2	18	5	8	7	21	...	13	13
Mozambique	1,328	80	550	5.5	2.0	3.5	31	—	8	11	2	15	10	—23—		
Myanmar (Burma)	40,483[6]	900[6]	...	...	...	...	63	1	6	2	—	2	22	—4—		
Namibia	3,045	2,030	3,950	6.1	2.7	3.4	14[10]	16[10]	9[10]	3[10]	1[10]	5[10]	10[10]	12[10]	4[10]	26[10]
Nauru	100[1,6]	10,000[1,6]	...	...	...	...										
Nepal	4,174	200	1,080	4.8	2.6	2.2	49	1	9	10	1	6	11	9	—9—	
Netherlands, The	338,144	21,970	18,080	2.6	0.7	1.9	4	3	19	6	2	7	16	—48—		

private	government	gross domestic investment	exports	imports	indirect taxes net of subsides	consumption of fixed capital	compensation of employees	net operating surplus	goods, merchandise	invisibles	current balance of payments	receipts from foreign nationals	expenditures by nationals abroad	country
77	29	27	27	−60	...	...	...	...	31	−32	−2	...	...	Equatorial Guinea
...	...	...	...	...	...	...	...	...	−132	176	44	...	...	Eritrea
61	17	25	69	−72	12	12	50	25	−361	190	−171	92	48	Estonia
86	11	13	9	−18	...	...	...	...	−507[1]	456[1]	−52[1]	23	11[1]	Ethiopia
...	...	...	...	...	...	...	...	...	114[1]	−3[1]	111[1]	...	...	Faroe Islands
67	20	15	56	−59	13	7	34	46	−210	223	13	298	55	Fiji
57	24	14	33	−28	11	17	53	18	7,651	−6,583	1,068	1,436	1,727	Finland
61	20	17	22	−20	12	13	53	22	8,109	−21	8,088	25,629	13,875	France
...	...	...	...	...	8[8]	7	61[8]	31[7,8]	...	...	...	...	...	French Guiana
60[2]	40[2]	21[2]	9[2]	−31[2]	...	...	...	...	...	...	...	235	...	French Polynesia
48	16	22	47	−32	...	...	...	...	1,593	1,273	320	5	143	Gabon
74	18	20	53	−65	18[5]	10[5]	——— 72[5] ———		−57	65	8	27	14	Gambia, The
149[8]	16[8]	41[8]	19[8]	−84[8]	...	...	...	...	...	...	...	...	...	Gaza Strip
89	9	32	36	−66	...	...	...	...	−363	172	−191	...	...	Georgia
56	18	24	32	−29	12	13	54	21	48,320	−72,200	−23,880	11,091	43,398	Germany
80	14	22	20	−36	...	...	...	...	−353	89	−264	228	20	Ghana
...	...	...	...	...	...	...	...	...	...	...	...	90[1]	...	Gibraltar
73	19	19	22	−32	14	9	36	41	−11,273	11,127	−146	3,905	1,125	Greece
...	...	...	...	...	...	...	...	...	...	...	...	...	...	Greenland
66	20	35	39	−59	18[8]	——— 82[8] ———			−99	66	−33	55	4	Grenada
...	...	...	...	...	11[8]	7	78[8]	11[7,8]	...	...	...	490	...	Guadeloupe
...	...	...	...	...	...	...	...	...	...	...	...	950[1]	...	Guam
85	7	17	17	−26	6[2]	2[2]	——— 92[2] ———		−997	371	−625	258	161	Guatemala
...	...	...	...	...	...	...	...	...	...	...	...	146[1]	...	Guernsey[18]
84	7	16	21	−28	...	...	...	...	−170	−116	−286	6[1]	28[1]	Guinea
95	9	23	12	−39	...	...	83		−38	−28	−66	6[1]	...	Guinea-Bissau
51	13	52	91	−107	17	——— 83 ———			13	−54	−41	47	...	Guyana
104	7	4	7	−23	7	1	——— 92 ———		−84	88	4	46	15	Haiti
66	11	32	34	−42	14	6	48	32	−91	−218	−309	33	39	Honduras
67	8	29	207	−211	6	7	47	46[7]	...	...	...	8,317	...	Hong Kong
72	13	23	27	−35	13[5]	8[5]	59[5]	20[5]	−3,716	−338	−4,054	1,428	925	Hungary
61	21	16	33	−30	18[8]	13[8]	53[8]	16[8]	284	−160	125	137	249	Iceland
66	11	24	11	−12	10	10	——— 80 ———		−2,310[8]	−1,719[8]	−4,107[8]	2,265	393[2]	India
56	9	33	26	−24	7	5	——— 88 ———		7,901	−10,691	−2,790	4,785	1,900	Indonesia
55	15	29	24	−23	2[2]	15[2]	——— 83[2] ———		6,817	−2,040	−4,777	153	1,109[8]	Iran
48[5]	35[5]	19[5]	3[5]	−5[5]	−7[5]	10[5]	45[5]	52[5]	...	...	...	55[2]	...	Iraq
58	16	14	65	−53	10	9	50	31	9,561	−6,349	3,212	1,765	1,575	Ireland
...	...	...	...	...	...	...	...	...	...	...	...	...	...	Isle of Man
63	29	24	34	−50	17	14	49	20	−5,930	2,207	−3,723	2,266	2,896	Israel
62	18	17	21	−18	10	12	44	34	35,497	−20,904	14,593	23,927	12,181	Italy
61	13	35	60	−68	...	...	...	...	−644	693	48	919	81	Jamaica
58	10	30	9	−7	7	16	55	22	145,930	−16,690	129,240	3,477	30,715	Japan
...	...	...	...	...	...	...	...	...	...	...	...	526[2]	...	Jersey
71	23	37	51	−83	16	9	39	36	−1,579	1,181	−389	582	394	Jordan
43	14	49	33	−39	...	...	...	...	−414[1]	−241[1]	−438[1]	...	...	Kazakstan
62	15	18	42	−37	15	7	35	50[7]	−239[1]	364[1]	125[1]	421	115	Kenya
...	...	...	...	...	...	...	...	...	...	...	...	1	2[5]	Kiribati
...	...	...	...	...	...	...	...	...	...	...	...	...	...	Korea, North
54	11	36	30	−31	11	10	47	31	−3,146	−709	−3,855	3,806	4,088	Korea, South
45	36	14	50	−45	...	...	...	...	4,483	−1,458	3,025	101	2,146	Kuwait
66	11	30	31	−38	...	...	...	...	−96	−22	−118	...	...	Kyrgyzstan
90[5]	10[5]	13[5]	13[5]	−25[5]	...	...	...	...	−219	−4	−223	...	...	Laos
52	22	9	73	−57	11	10	47	32	−301	502	201	...	...	Latvia
110[2]	44[2]	10[2]	32[2]	−96[2]	...	...	...	...	...	...	...	...	...	Lebanon
105	17	76	19	−118	17	——— 83 ———			−667	775	108	17	7	Lesotho
58[2]	13[2]	10[2]	42[2]	−23[2]	...	...	...	...	...	...	...	...	...	Liberia
34[5]	27[5]	22[5]	46[5]	−28[5]	...	...	...	...	3,777[2]	−1,576[2]	2,201[2]	7	154[8]	Libya
...	...	...	...	...	...	...	...	...	...	...	...	...	...	Liechtenstein
76	13	18	71	−78	10[8]	2[8]	39[8]	50[8]	−205	111	−94	70	50	Lithuania
55	13	26	86	−80	16[8]	11[8]	66[8]	8[8]	9	9	9	290[2]	...	Luxembourg
30	8	31	74	−43	...	...	...	...	...	...	...	2,688	103	Macau
55	6	42	——— −3 ———		11	7	67	22[7]	−433	106	327	29	...	Macedonia
106	9	14	——— −2 ———		...	...	...	...	−98	−99	−197	54	37[8]	Madagascar
86	17	12	16	−32	8	——— 92 ———			−276	2	−274	5	15	Malawi
51	13	35	81	−81	14[8]	——— 86[8] ———			1,581	−5,728	−4,147	3,189	1,737	Malaysia
49[2]	22[2]	19[2]	62[2]	−53[2]	...	...	...	...	−139[1]	92[1]	−48[1]	181	32	Maldives
86	16	19	17	−38	...	...	...	...	−102	−63	−164	18	54	Mali
61	20	30	96	−106	11	6	46	38	−560	475	−86	639	176	Malta
...	...	...	...	...	4[5]	45	70[5]	22[5]	−51	55	4	2	...	Marshall Islands
...	...	...	...	...	10[8]	7	71[8]	19[7,8]	...	...	...	379	...	Martinique
79	11	23	46	−59	...	...	...	...	47	−117	−70	15[2]	31[2]	Mauritania
64	12	31	61	−67	15	7	41	44[7]	−393	163	−230	356	140	Mauritius
47[2]	92[2]	3[2]	——— −42[2] ———		...	...	...	...	...	...	...	...	...	Mayotte
71	11	22	12	−17	10	10	28	52	−18,465	−10,319	−28,784	6,318	5,363	Mexico
...	...	...	...	...	...	...	...	...	−112	110	−2	...	...	Micronesia
46	23	49	43	−61	...	...	...	...	−128	−55	−183	2	...	Moldova
...	...	...	...	...	...	...	...	...	...	...	...	...	...	Monaco
66	18	19	63	−66	25	22[2]	39[2]	40[2,25]	−8	40	32	...	...	Mongolia
65	18	23	23	−29	...	...	...	...	−2,107	1,387	−720	1,265	302	Morocco
68	16	67	21	−71	...	...	...	...	−869	564	−305	...	...	Mozambique
——— 89 ———		12	1	−2	3	3	45	48	−737	563	−174	24	1[5]	Myanmar (Burma)
57	35	14	58	−64	16	7	46	38[7]	165	25	190	184	75	Namibia
...	...	...	...	...	...	...	...	...	...	...	...	...	...	Nauru
80	9	21	18	−28	6	——— 94 ———			−790	438	−352	172	112	Nepal
61	15	19	51	−45	10	12	53	25	16,425	−3,052	13,373	5,612	10,983	Netherlands, The

National product and accounts

country	gross national product (GNP), 1994 nominal ('000,000 U.S.$)	per capita nominal (U.S.$)	per capita purchasing power parity (PPP; U.S.$)	real GNP (%)	population (%)	real GNP per capita (%)	agriculture	mining	manufacturing	construction	public utilities	transp., communications	trade	financial svcs.	other svcs.	government
Netherlands Antilles	1,850[1,6]	10,000[1,6]	...	...	...	...	...	...	...	...	...	...	...	...	...	...
New Caledonia	2,919[8]	15,900[8]	...	...	...	...	2[2]	4[2]	13[2]	6[2]	3[2]	6[2]	23[2]	—20[2]—	...	25[2]
New Zealand	46,578	13,190	16,780	1.4	0.9	0.5	7[5]	1[5]	17[5]	4[5]	3[5]	8[5]	16[5]	23[5]	3[5]	12[5]
Nicaragua	1,395	330	1,850	-3.3	3.1	-6.4	30	1	17	2	1	4	25	6	6	8
Niger	2,040	230	800	1.0	3.2	-2.2	37	6	7	2	2	4	—18—	...	10	11
Nigeria	29,995	280	1,430	4.1	2.9	1.2	34	36	6	1	—	2	15	4	—	3
Northern Mariana Is.	524[6]	10,500[6]	...	...	...	...	...	...	...	...	...	...	...	...	...	...
Norway	114,328	26,480	21,120	1.8	0.4	1.4	3[5]	15[5]	13[5]	4[5]	4[5]	9[5]	11[5]	9[5]	10[5]	16[5]
Oman	10,779	5,200	9,150	5.0	4.4	0.6	3[10]	38[10]	5[10]	4[10]	1[10]	5[10]	15[10]	4[10]	12[10]	18[10]
Pakistan	55,565	440	2,210	4.4	2.8	1.6	22	1	15	4	3	9	14	7	7	7
Palau	90[6,8]	5,640[6,8]	...	...	...	...	...	...	...	...	...	...	...	...	...	...
Panama	6,905	2,670	6,080	2.0	2.0	0.0	10	...	9	6	3	25	12	15	10	11
Papua New Guinea	4,857	1,160	2,430	4.3	2.2	2.1	26	29	9	4	1	4	8	—5—	...	14
Paraguay	7,606	1,570	3,540	4.0	3.0	1.0	25	—	17	6	3	4	30	2	—13—	...
Peru	44,110	1,890	3,690	-0.5	2.0	-2.5	14	10	23	7	2	7	17	13	—8—	...
Philippines	63,311	960	2,800	3.9	2.1	1.8	22	1	24	5	2	5	14	4	—22—	...
Poland	94,613	2,470	5,380	1.2	0.3	0.9	7	4	33	6	2	5	14	—31—	...	...
Portugal	92,124	9,370	12,400	3.9	-0.1	4.0	6[2]	4	29[2,4]	8[2]	3[2]	6[2]	17[2]	9[2]	8[2]	13[2]
Puerto Rico	26,647	7,230	...	2.6	0.9	1.7	1	23	39	2[23]	26	8[26]	15	13	11	11
Qatar	7,810	14,540	19,100	3.7	4.5	-0.8	1	32	11	5	1	3	7	12	—27—	...
Réunion	2,500[1,6]	3,900[1,6]	...	...	...	...	6[2]	...	12[2]	8[2]	7[2]	—67[2]—	...	...	...	...
Romania	27,921	1,230	2,920	-6.0	0.2	-6.2	19[8]	3	45[3,8]	4[8]	3	6[8]	13[8]	5[8]	4[8]	8[8]
Russia	392,496	2,650	5,260	-3.9	0.5	-4.4	10	3	49[3]	8	3	8	11	8	7	3
Rwanda	624	80	330	0.5	2.7	-2.2	41	4	—21[4]—	...	...	—38—	...	...	...	...
St. Kitts	195	4,760	9,330	4.2	-0.5	4.7	7	—	12	12	2	15	23	12	4	17
St. Lucia	501	3,450	...	5.7	1.7	4.0	12	1	7	9	3	18	25	14	3	13
St. Vincent	235	2,120	...	5.3	0.9	4.4	16	—	9	11	5	20	16	10	2	16
San Marino	380[1,6]	15,800[1,6]	...	...	...	...	...	...	...	...	...	...	...	...	...	...
São Tomé and Príncipe	31	250	...	-0.4	2.1	-2.5	28	...	8[19]	6	19	—28—	...	...	8	23
Saudi Arabia	126,597	7,240	9,480	2.4	3.6	-1.2	6	35	8	8	—	7	7	6	2	20
Senegal	4,952	610	1,660	2.2	2.7	-0.5	22[10]	4	13[4,10]	3[10]	2[10]	10[10]	—21[10]—	...	—29[10]—	...
Seychelles	453	6,210	...	5.8	1.3	4.5	4	4	11[4]	8	1	28	9	9	2	14
Sierra Leone	698	150	770	0.6	2.5	-1.9	41	7	11	2	—	8	17	4	2	4
Singapore	65,842	23,360	21,430	8.0	1.1	6.9	—	3	28	7	2	15	18	27	—10—	...
Slovakia	11,914	2,230	6,660	-2.9	0.4	-3.3	6[5]	3	53[3,5]	7[5]	3	8[5]	10[5]	2[5]	12[5]	3[5]
Slovenia	14,246	7,140	6,230	...	...	...	5[8]	2[8]	30[8]	4[8]	2[8]	7[8]	13[8]	14[8]	4[8]	13[8]
Solomon Islands	291	800	2,040	5.2	3.4	1.8	48[8]	—	4[8]	4[8]	1[8]	7[8]	10[8]	3[8]	—23[8]—	...
Somalia	3,300[6]	500[6]	...	...	1.6	...	65[5]	—	4[5]	4[5]	5	6[5]	9[5]	3[5]	2[5]	6[5]
South Africa	125,225	3,010	5,130	1.0	2.4	-1.4	5	9	23	3	4	8	16	13	2	15
Spain	525,334	13,280	14,040	3.0	0.3	2.7	3	3	23[3]	8	3	—60—	...	...	...	...
Sri Lanka	11,634	640	3,150	4.1	1.3	2.8	21	1	17	7	2	9	21	6	7	7
Sudan, The	23,700[6]	780[6]	...	...	...	...	36	—	11	5	2	—38—	...	...	...	8
Suriname	364	870	3,680	1.7	1.1	0.6	22	2	14	5	2	7	26	15	—	9
Swaziland	1,048	1,160	2,880	2.1	3.4	-1.3	10	2	29	3	1	5	7	6	5	19
Sweden	206,419	23,630	17,850	0.5	0.5	0.0	2	—	22	6	3	7	11	23	—29—	...
Switzerland	264,974	37,180	24,390	1.5	1.0	0.5	3[8]	4	23[4,8]	7[8]	2[8]	6[8]	17[8]	25[8]	—21[8]—	...
Syria	74,400[6]	5,000[6]	...	...	...	...	18	4	39[4]	4	—	11	13	3	2	10
Taiwan	244,090	11,600	...	8.0	1.0	7.0	3	1	32	6	3	6	16	20	7	11
Tajikistan	2,075	350	1,160	-8.8	2.9	-11.7	27[8]	3	36[3,8]	9[8]	3	5[8]	5[8]	5[8]	15[8]	3[8]
Tanzania	3,440	130	620	4.2	3.1	1.1	52	1	7	5	2	6	14	4	—4—	...
Thailand	129,864	2,210	6,870	9.8	1.6	8.2	12[8]	2[8]	28[8]	7[8]	2[8]	7[8]	17[8]	9[8]	13[8]	4[8]
Togo	1,267	320	1,060	0.4	3.1	-2.7	49	4	7	2	6	4	13	—7—	...	10
Tonga	160	1,640	3,740	0.9	0.8	0.1	33	4	4[4]	4	...	12	12	—12—	...	...
Trinidad and Tobago	4,838	3,740	8,440	-1.1	1.2	-2.3	2	23	9	8	2	13	16	9	7	11
Tunisia	15,873	1,800	4,960	4.1	2.3	1.8	13[10]	4[10]	18[10]	4[10]	2[10]	8[10]	27[10]	—14[10]—	...	...
Turkey	149,002	2,450	4,610	3.6	2.1	1.5	15	1	19	7	3	13	18	7	4	12
Turkmenistan	1,880[6]	470[6]	...	...	...	...	9[10]	66[10]	7[10]	5[10]	1[10]	2[10]	1[10]	—6[10]—	...	...
Tuvalu	9[1,6]	920[1,6]	...	...	...	...	22	2	3	14	2	4	14	10	—28—	...
Uganda	3,718	200	940	5.5	2.5	3.0	49	—	7	6	2	4	12	6	—11—	...
Ukraine	80,921	1,570	3,330	-5.0	0.1	-5.1	22[5]	4	43[4,5]	10[5]	2[5]	8[5]	7[5]	3[5]	14[5]	4[5]
United Arab Emirates	62,700[6]	22,480[6]	...	...	...	...	2	39	8	9	2	6	10	11	3	11
United Kingdom	1,069,457	18,410	18,170	1.7	0.3	1.4	2[10]	2[10]	21[10]	5[10]	3[10]	8[10]	14[10]	27[10]	4[10]	19[10]
United States	6,737,367	25,860	25,860	2.3	1.0	1.3	2[8]	1[8]	18[8]	4[8]	3[8]	6[8]	16[8]	18[8]	20[8]	13[8]
Uruguay	14,725	4,650	6,850	3.6	0.6	3.0	8[10]	—	17[10]	5[10]	3[10]	7[10]	14[10]	10[10]	12[10]	9[10]
Uzbekistan	21,142	950	2,390	-0.1	2.3	-2.4	26	3	30[3]	10	3	6	9	—19—	...	...
Vanuatu	189	1,150	2,640	1.6	2.5	-0.9	21	—	6	5	2	7	31	17	1	12
Venezuela	59,025	2,760	7,890	3.1	2.5	0.6	5	22	16	7	2	5	14	—19—	...	8
Vietnam	13,775	190	...	...	...	...	29[10]	4	—30[4,10]—	...	...	4[10]	14[10]	2[10]	—11[10]—	...
Virgin Islands (U.S.)	1,246[6,27]	11,740[6,27]	...	...	...	...	...	...	...	...	...	...	...	...	...	...
West Bank	4,000[6]	2,800[6]	...	...	...	...	...	...	...	...	...	...	...	...	...	...
Western Sahara	60[5,6]	300[5,6]	...	...	...	...	...	...	...	...	...	...	...	...	...	...
Western Samoa	163	970	2,060	...	...	...	43	...	12	3	6	3	8	—55—	10	14
Yemen	3,884	280	...	...	...	...	21	4	—24—	...	...	4[28]	19[28]	—14[28]—	...	...
Yugoslavia	14,570	1,390	...	...	...	...	26[28]	3	29[3,28]	7[28]	2	4[28]	19[28]	14[28]	...	...
Zaire	5,276[6]	120[6]	...	...	...	...	51	6	7	1	2	4	21	—3—	...	3
Zambia	3,206	350	1,000	2.0	3.3	-1.3	34	4	—36[4]—	...	...	—30—	...	...	...	...
Zimbabwe	5,424	490	2,040	2.4	3.0	-0.6	10[10]	7[10]	41[10]	2[10]	6[10]	5[10]	11[10]	5[10]	7[10]	2[10]

[1]1993. [2]1990. [3]Manufacturing includes mining and public utilities. [4]Manufacturing includes mining. [5]1991. [6]Gross domestic product (GDP). [7]Net operating surplus includes consumption of fixed capital. [8]1992. [9]Data refer to the Belgium-Luxembourg Economic Union (BLEU). [10]1994. [11]Services includes restaurants and hotels. [12]Services includes public utilities. [13]Mining includes public utilities. [14]Government includes finance, insurance. [15]Republic of Cyprus only. [16]Services includes hotels. [17]Services includes transportation, communications. [18]Excludes Alderney

gross domestic product (GDP) by type of expenditure, 1993 (%)					cost components of gross domestic product (GDP), 1993 (%)				balance of payments, 1994 (current external transactions; '000,000 U.S.$)			tourist trade, 1994 ('000,000 U.S.$)		country
consumption		gross domestic invest-ment	foreign trade		indirect taxes net of subsides	consump-tion of fixed capital	compen-sation of employ-ees	net operating surplus	net transfers		current balance of payments	receipts from foreign nationals	expendi-tures by nationals abroad	
private	govern-ment		exports	imports					goods, merchan-dise	invisibles				
...	...	...	...	...	8[8]	10[8]	51[8]	30[8]	−921	823	−98	721[1]	...	Netherlands Antilles
60	16	21	31	−28	14	10	43	33				102		New Caledonia
90	17	19	20	−46	...	...	...	...	1,336	−3,342	−2,006	1,357	1,101	New Zealand
82	17	6	13	−17	...	...	...	...	−434	−295	−729	40	38	Nicaragua
									−19	−59	−78	16	21	Niger
82	4	12	28	−25	1	2	11	86	2,948	−5,076	−2,128	34	144	Nigeria
...	...	...	...	...	...	...	...	...				584	...	Northern Mariana Is.
52	22	19	43	−36	11	15	51	23	8,321	−4,676	3,645	2,157	3,930	Norway
45	30	19	48	−43	25	7	33[8]	67[7,8,25]	1,336[1]	−2,405[1]	−1,069[1]	88	47	Oman
72	13	21	16	−22	10	6	——83——		−2,552[1]	−383[1]	−2,935[1]	117	398	Pakistan
...	...	...	...	...	...	...	...	...						Palau
60	15	28	100	−104	10	7	41	42	−444	−765	−1,209	244	131	Panama
52	21	19	49	−40	11[5]	12[5]	37[5]	40[5]	1,326	−757	569	55	70	Papua New Guinea
81	7	23	37	−48	7[8]	8[8]	30[8]	56[8]	−1,277	528	−749	197	176	Paraguay
78	7	19	11	−14	7[5]	4[5]	20[5]	69[5]	−1,108	−1,147	−2,255	402	323	Peru
74	10	24	31	−39	10	9	26	55	−7,850	5,010	−2,840	2,282	196	Philippines
65	22	16	19	−22	14	7	44	42[7]	−1,809	−736	−2,545	6,150	316	Poland
65	17	27	24	−33	12	4	48	36	−6,730	5,694	−1,036	4,087	1,705	Portugal
63[8]	14[8]	17[8]	69[8]	−63[8]	5	7	41	49	1,730[5]	−5,131[5]	−3,401[5]	1,737	797	Puerto Rico
32	34	19	46	−31	1	12	36	52	...	...	...	...	...	Qatar
79[8]	29[8]	27[8]	4[8]	−39[8]	9[8]	7	59[8]	31[7,8]				157[8]	...	Réunion
66	12	27	23	−28	5	7	36	59[7]	−411	−9	−420	414	449	Romania
44	17	31	39	−31	9	17	39	35	19,713	−8,344	11,369	...	...	Russia
87	22	15	7	−32	...	...	...	...	−172[8]	87[8]	−85[8]	2[1]	17[8]	Rwanda
49	25	39	——−13——		13[8]	——87[8]——			−69	43	−26	75	6	St. Kitts
69	15	25	66	−74	16[8]	——84[8]——			−166	101	−65	224	23	St. Lucia
68	18	35	44	−66	15[8]	——85[8]——			−74	12	−61	51	3	St. Vincent
...	...	...	...	...	...	...	...	...						San Marino
98	16	62	30	−107	...	...	...	...	−18	3	−15	1[2]	2[2]	São Tomé and Príncipe
44	29	24	40	−37	2	9	30	60	20,483	−29,549	−9,066	1,884[2]	...	Saudi Arabia
80	12	14	22	−29	...	...	...	...	−233	455	222	115	70	Senegal
53	30	29	54	−65	22[5]	11[5]	38[5]	29[5]	139	−167	−28	116[1]	16[8]	Seychelles
82	14	9	28	−33	8[2]	6[2]	14[2]	73[2]	−69[1]	−167	−58[1]	10	4	Sierra Leone
43	9	44	169	−165	...	...	...	...	2,106	9,844	11,950	7,067	3,665	Singapore
58	26	22	67	−73	13[5]	14[5]	48[5]	25[5]	109	610	719	568	284	Slovakia
55	22	19	61	−57	13	17	61	9	−180	637	457	932	312	Slovenia
...	...	...	...	...	...	...	...	...	14[8]	−16[8]	−2[8]	6[8]	11[5]	Solomon Islands
75[2]	9[2]	20[2]	1[2]	−5[2]	...	...	...	...						Somalia
60	20	16	24	−20	11[10]	14[10]	53[10]	22[10]	3,656	−4,229	−573	1,424	1,678	South Africa
63	18	20	19	−20	7	11	46	35	−14,581	8,154	−6,427	21,853	4,188	Spain
75	9	26	34	−43	14	5	44	37	−871	325	−546	224	167	Sri Lanka
71[5]	18[5]	17[5]	5[5]	−105	...	...	...	...	−522	−79	−601	3[1]	33[8]	Sudan, The
60	17	23	5	−6	7[8]	11[8]	45[8]	36[8]	99	−41	58	11	3	Suriname
75	23	18	70	−86	...	...	...	...	−30	54	−24	29	21	Swaziland
55	28	13	33	−29	10	14	59	16	9,561	−8,745	816	2,826	4,878	Sweden
59	14	21	37	−32	5	11	64	21	3,330	15,165	18,495	7,570	6,325	Switzerland
74	14	26	29	−43	−9	4	——105——		−1,015	378	−637	800	400	Syria
57	16	25	44	−42	11[8]	5[8]	58[8]	26[8]	11,984	−5,830	6,154	3,210	7,885	Taiwan
...	...	...	...	...	...	...	...	...	−208[1]	41	−204[1]	...	...	Tajikistan
82	9	51	31	−72	8	3	8	81	−838[1]	429[1]	−409[1]	192	102[1]	Tanzania
54	10	40	37	−41	12	11	26	51	−3,709	−4,710	−8,419	5,762	2,906	Thailand
86	17	6	23	−31	...	...	...	...	−50	−20	−69	7	30[1]	Togo
...	...	...	...	...	...	...	...	...	−41	35	−6	9	3[1]	Tonga
61	16	13	39	−30	10	11	50	29	741	−523	218	80	90	Trinidad and Tobago
62	16	29	41	−48	...	...	...	...	−1,574	1,270	−304	1,302	216	Tunisia
67	13	26	14	−20	10	6	49	35	−4,216	6,847	2,631	4,321	866	Turkey
44	23	46	——−13——		...	...	...	...	485	−401	84	...	...	Turkmenistan
...	...	...	...	...	...	...	...	...				0.3[1]	...	Tuvalu
87	12	14	5	−18	...	...	...	...	−259	172	−87	61	78	Uganda
80	13	8	17	−18	−5[5]	15[5]	77[5]	13[5]	−2,519[1]	1,670[1]	−849[1]	...	...	Ukraine
49	18	27	69	−64	−1	15	24	62	...	...	...	...	...	United Arab Emirates
64	22	15	26	−27	13	10	56	20	−16,127	13,736	−2,319	15,176	22,185	United Kingdom
69	16	17	10	−11	8	12	61	19	−164,320	13,390	−150,930	60,406	43,562	United States
73	13	14	21	−22	19[8]	7	44[8]	37[7,8]	−672	282	−390	632	190	Uruguay
58	25	15	——3——		−1[8]	3[8]	65[8]	33[8]	−378[1]	−511[1]	−429[1]	...	...	Uzbekistan
56	29	32	47	−64	...	...	...	...	−63	34	−28	55	1	Vanuatu
73	9	19	26	−27	4	8	34	54	7,691	−5,241	2,450	486	1,429	Venezuela
70	16	19	28	−33	...	...	...	...	−900	−66	−966	85[2]	...	Vietnam
...	...	...	...	...	...	...	...	...				919		Virgin Islands (U.S.)
...	...	...	...	...	...	...	...	...						West Bank
...	...	...	...	...	...	...	...	...						Western Sahara
...	...	...	...	...	...	...	...	...	−811[1]	42[1]	−39[1]	21[1]	2[1]	Western Samoa
68	29	20	15	−32	11	5	——84——		...	...	...	19	78	Yemen
...	...	...	...	...	...	...	...	...				31		Yugoslavia
75	11	15	35	−36	...	...	...	...	643	−1,058	−415	6[1]	16[1]	Zaire
81	9	11	40	−41	7[2]	9[2]	57[2]	26[2]	−11[1]	−86[1]	−87[1]	43	56[8]	Zambia
64	19	22	34	−40	10[5]	——90[5]——			226	−485	−259	138[1]	44[1]	Zimbabwe

and Sark.   [19]Manufacturing includes public utilities.   [20]Manufacturing includes mining, construction, and public utilities.   [21]Services includes trade.   [22]Construction includes public utilities.   [23]Construction includes mining.   [24]Government includes public utilities.   [25]Net operating surplus includes indirect taxes net of subsidies.   [26]Transportation includes public utilities.   [27]1987.   [28]1995.

Employment and labour

This table provides international comparisons of the world's national labour forces—giving their size; composition by demographic component and employment status; and structure by industry.

The table focuses on the concept of "economically active population," which the International Labour Organisation (ILO) defines as persons of all ages who are either employed or looking for work. In general, "economically active population" does not include students, persons occupied solely in domestic duties, retired persons, persons living entirely on their own means, and persons wholly dependent on others. Persons engaged in illegal economic activities—smugglers, prostitutes, drug dealers, bootleggers, black marketeers, and others—also fall outside the purview of the ILO definition. Countries differ markedly in their treatment, as part of the labour force, of such groups as members of the armed forces, inmates of institutions, the unemployed (both persons seeking their first job and those previously employed), seasonal and international migrant workers, and persons engaged in informal, subsistence, or part-time economic activities. Some countries include all or most of these groups among the economically active, while others may treat the same groups as inactive.

Three principal structural comparisons of the economically active total are given in the first part of the table: (1) participation rate, or the proportion of the economically active who possess some particular characteristic, is given for women and for those of working age (usually ages 15 to 64), (2) activity rate, the proportion of the total population who are economically active, is given for both sexes and as a total, and (3) employment status, usually (and here) grouped as employers, self-employed, employees, family workers (usually unpaid), and others.

Each of these measures indicates certain characteristics in a given national labour market; none should be interpreted in isolation, however, as the meaning of each is influenced by a variety of factors—demographic structure and change, social or religious customs, educational opportunity, sexual differentiation in employment patterns, degree of technological development, and the like. Participation and activity rates, for example, may be high in a particular country because it possesses an older population with few children, hence a higher proportion of working age, or because, despite a young population with many below working age, the economy attracts eligible immigrant workers, themselves almost exclusively of working age. At the same time, low activity and participation rates might be characteristic of a country having a young population with poor employment possibilities or of a country with a good job market distorted by the presence of large numbers of "guest" or contract workers who are not part of the domestic labour force. An illiterate woman in a strongly sex-differentiated labour force is likely to begin and end as a family or

Employment and labour

| country | year | economically active population | | | | | | | | | | distribution by economic sector | | | |
| | | total ('000) | participation rate (%) | | activity rate (%) | | | employment status (%) | | | | agriculture, forestry, fishing | | manufacturing; mining, quarrying; public utilities | |
			female	ages 15–64	total	male	female	employers, self-employed	employees	unpaid family workers	other	number ('000)	% of econ. active	number ('000)	% of econ. active
Afghanistan	1979	3,941	7.9	49.1	30.3	54.2	4.9	...	...	...	...	2,369	60.1	494	12.5
Albania	1994	1,340	47.0[3]	92.0[3,4]	57.4[3]	60.8[3]	54.0[3]	...	...	...	...	534	39.9	84[5]	6.3[5]
Algeria	1987	5,341	9.2	44.3	23.6	42.4	4.4	16.8	61.7	2.6	18.9	725	13.6	622	11.6
American Samoa	1990	14.2	41.1	52.6[8]	30.4	34.8	25.7	2.1	92.6	0.2	5.1	0.3	2.3	4.8	33.7
Andorra	1989	25	45.6	74.3	55.1	...	...	...	...	...	...	0.3	1.2	2.7	11.0
Angola	1991	4,166	38.4	60.1[10]	40.3	50.4	30.4	...	...	...	...	2,892	69.4	438[11]	10.5[11]
Antigua and Barbuda	1991	26.8	45.6	69.7	45.1	50.9	39.6	12.1	82.8	0.7	4.4	1.0	3.9	1.9	7.3
Argentina	1995	14,345	36.7	64.5	41.5	53.5	29.9	28.0[13]	60.4[13]	5.0[13]	6.6[13]	1,201[14]	12.0[14]	2,136[14]	21.3[14]
Armenia	1994	1,618	...	74.5[16]	43.1	...	...	...	...	...	...	538	33.3	323	20.0
Aruba	1991	31.1	42.5	67.1	46.7	54.5	39.0	7.0	86.4	0.4	6.3	0.2	0.5	2.3	7.3
Australia	1994[18]	8,684	42.3	73.3	48.5	56.1	41.0	14.0	75.8	0.9	9.2	423	4.9	1,385	16.0
Austria	1993[18]	3,734	42.0	69.3	46.7	56.3	37.8	9.7	87.4	3.0	—	249	6.7	1,000	26.8
Azerbaijan	1994	2,674	...	64.4[16,19]	36.5	...	...	...	...	...	...	1,011	37.8	350	13.1
Bahamas, The	1994	139	47.5	77.8	50.7	54.8	46.8	11.6[20]	85.1[20]	0.3[20]	3.0[20]	6.4[19]	4.7[19]	6.7[19]	4.9[19]
Bahrain	1991	226	17.5	66.8	44.6	63.5	18.5	5.1	88.5	0.1	6.3	5	2.3	33	14.6
Bangladesh	1990–91[18]	51,155	39.3	76.9	46.0	54.2	38.9	26.3	11.5	46.2	16.0	33,033	65.1	5,980	11.7
Barbados	1994[18]	129	48.7	79.3	50.8	53.6	48.1	8.8[22]	76.4[22]	0.2[23]	14.6[23]	5.3[19]	4.2[19]	11.3[19]	8.9[19]
Belarus	1994	4,798	...	77.7[16]	46.5	...	...	...	...	...	...	917	19.1	1,365	28.4
Belgium	1992	4,237	42.3	51.5[23]	42.2	49.8	34.9	12.7	72.4	3.4	11.5	95	2.2	788	18.6
Belize	1994	69.3	32.1	79.3	33.0	45.4	20.9	26.2[19]	59.2[19]	4.9[19]	9.8[19]	18.3[13]	31.4[13]	7.0[13]	12.0[13]
Benin	1992	2,085	42.6	73.4	43.0	50.6	35.7	58.4	5.3	30.5	5.8	1,148	55.0	162	7.8
Bermuda	1994	34.1	49.8	63.5[13]	60.2[13]	65.8[13]	55.0[13]	9.7[13]	84.0[13]	0.1[13]	6.2[13]	0.5	1.5	1.6	4.7
Bhutan	...	...	...	...	...	...	...	...	...	...	...	...	...	...	...
Bolivia	1992	2,530	38.2	64.0	39.4	48.7	30.4	41.2	31.5	7.1	20.2	984	38.9	281	11.1
Bosnia and Herzegovina	1990[5]	1,026	36.9	...	22.7	...	...	...	...	...	...	39	3.8	519	50.5
Botswana	1991[18]	441	38.5	59.4	33.3	42.8	24.5	6.5	62.5	17.1	13.9	98	22.1	47	10.7
Brazil	1990[18]	64,468	35.5	63.6[23]	43.8	57.5	30.5	26.3	62.3	7.7	3.7	14,181	22.0	10,217	15.9
Brunei	1991	112	32.9	67.6	43.0	54.6	30.0	3.5	91.4	0.4	4.7	2.2	1.9	11.6	10.4
Bulgaria	1994	3,799	48.4[24]	68.8[24]	46.3[24]	48.7[24]	44.1[24]	6.8	71.8	0.7	20.7	751	19.8	1,018	26.8
Burkina Faso	1991	4,679	48.7	78.1[10,25]	50.9	53.5	48.5	...	...	...	...	4,294	91.8	58	1.2
Burundi	1990	2,780	52.6	91.4	52.7	51.2	53.8	62.8	5.1	30.3	1.8	2,574	92.6	37	1.3
Cambodia	1993	4,010	55.8	86.2	43.1	39.5	46.4	...	...	...	...	2,454[14]	74.4[14]	220[11,14]	6.7[11,14]
Cameroon	1991	4,740	33.2	58.9[10]	40.0	53.9	26.3	60.2[22]	14.6[22]	18.0[22]	7.1[22]	2,856	60.3	628[11]	13.2[11]
Canada	1993[18]	13,946	45.2	74.9	51.7	57.2	46.3	9.6	89.0	0.5	0.9	481	3.4	2,343	16.8
Cape Verde	1990	121	37.1	64.3	35.3	46.9	24.9	24.7	53.7	2.0	19.6	29.9	24.8	6.8	5.7
Central African Republic	1988	1,187	46.8	78.3	48.2	52.2	44.3	75.3	8.0	8.1	8.6	881	74.2	31	2.6
Chad	1991	2,016	18.2	51.6[10]	35.3	56.5	14.7	...	...	...	...	1,489	73.9	149[11]	7.4[11]
Chile	1994[18]	5,300	32.7	59.8	38.6	53.1	24.7	26.4	64.6	3.2	5.8	809	15.3	939	17.7
China	1990	657,290	44.9	85.0	57.9	61.8	53.7	...	...	...	...	467,926	71.2	87,275	13.3
Colombia	1985	9,558	32.8	49.4[26]	34.3	46.6	22.2	...	...	...	...	2,412[14]	28.5[14]	1,231[14]	14.5[14]
Comoros	1991	215	40.0	57.8[10]	44.4	53.7	35.2	47.6[14]	25.6[14]	—26.8[14]—		171	79.4	14[11]	6.5[11]
Congo	1984	563	45.6	54.0	29.5	33.0	26.2	64.3	31.4	1.2	3.1	294	52.2	50	8.8
Costa Rica	1994	1,187	30.1	57.0[23]	38.7	53.9	23.3	24.0	72.2	3.3	0.6	252	21.2	232	19.6
Côte d'Ivoire	1988	4,263	32.3	66.6	39.4	52.2	26.0	...	...	...	...	2,628	61.6	100	2.3
Croatia	1991	2,040	42.9	65.2	45.3	53.9	37.4	12.7	73.7	2.0	11.6	341	16.7	571	28.0
Cuba	1988	4,570	36.1	56.9[23]	44.2	56.2	32.1	...	...	...	...	791[27]	22.3[27]	668[27]	18.9[27]
Cyprus[28,29]	1994	294	38.7[24]	70.5[24]	46.3[24]	57.0[24]	35.7[24]	18.7[24]	73.1[24]	6.1[24]	2.1[24]	34	11.5	48	16.2
Czech Republic	1991	5,421	47.6	77.9	52.6	56.8	48.7	2.2	88.7	7.6	1.5	628	11.6	2,021	37.3
Denmark	1993	2,893	46.7	81.4	55.8	60.4	51.4	8.3	89.7	1.6	0.3	144	5.0	603	20.9
Djibouti	1991	282	40.8	70.4[10]	61.5	74.1	50.3	...	...	...	...	212	75.2	31[11]	11.0[11]
Dominica	1991	26.4	34.5	62.4	38.0	50.0	26.1	29.2[31]	50.6[31]	1.9[31]	18.3[31]	7.3	27.9	2.3	8.8
Dominican Republic	1981	1,915	28.9	53.6	33.9	48.1	19.7	36.5	51.3	3.3	8.9	420	22.0	243	12.7
Ecuador	1990	3,360	26.4	55.7	34.8	51.5	18.3	45.7	42.5	4.4	7.4	1,036	30.8	404	12.0
Egypt	1992[18]	16,290	23.8	49.0	29.2	43.5	14.2	24.7	50.0	16.4	9.0	5,535	35.0	2,207	14.0
El Salvador	1992	1,762	28.3	55.4	34.4	50.8	19.0	27.8	52.3	5.1	14.7	599	34.0	257	14.6
Equatorial Guinea	1983	103	35.7	66.7	39.2	52.5	26.9	29.0	16.0	29.9	25.1	59.4	57.9	1.8	1.8
Eritrea	...	...	...	...	...	...	...	...	...	...	...	...	...	...	...
Estonia	1989	856	50.0	79.7	54.7	58.5	51.3	...	...	...	...	100	11.7	270	31.5
Ethiopia	1995	24,606	41.1	72.2	43.3	50.3	36.5	58.5[32]	6.5[32]	34.0[32]	1.0[32]	21,605	87.8	419	1.7
Faroe Islands	1977	17.6	27.2	64.0	41.9	58.2	23.9	11.9	86.1	...	2.0	3.3	18.8	3.9	21.9

traditional agricultural worker. Loss of working-age men to war, civil violence, or emigration for job opportunities may also affect the structure of a particular labour market.

The distribution of the economically active population by employment status reveals that a large percentage of economically active persons in some less developed countries falls under the heading "employers, self-employed." This occurs because the countries involved have poor, largely agrarian economies in which the average worker is a farmer who tills his own small plot of land. In countries with well-developed economies, "employees" will usually constitute the largest portion of the economically active.

Caution should be exercised when using the economically active data to make intercountry comparisons, as countries often differ in their choices of classification schemes, definitions, and coverage of groups and in their methods of collection and tabulation of data. The population base containing the economically active population, for example, may range, in developing countries, from age 9 or 10 with no upper limit to, in developed countries, age 18 or 19 upward to a usual retirement age of from 55 to 65, with sometimes a different range for each sex. Data on female labour-force participation, in particular, often lack comparability. In many less developed countries, particularly those dominated by the Islamic faith, a cultural bias favouring traditional roles for women results in the undercounting of economically active women. In other less developed countries, particularly those in which subsistence workers are deemed economically active, the role of women may be overstated.

The second major section of the table provides data on the distribution by economic (also conventionally called industrial) sector of the "economically active population." The data usually include such groups as unpaid family workers, members of the armed forces, and the unemployed, the last distributed by industry as far as possible.

The categorization of industrial sectors is based on the divisions listed in the *International Standard Industrial Classification of All Economic Activities*. The "other" category includes persons whose activities were not adequately defined and the unemployed who were not distributable by industrial sector.

A substantial part of the data presented in this table is summarized from various issues of the ILO's *Year Book of Labour Statistics,* which compiles its statistics both from official publications and from information submitted directly by national census and labour authorities. The editors have supplemented and updated ILO statistical data with information from Britannica's holdings of relevant official publications and from direct correspondence with national authorities.

construction		transportation, communications		trade, hotels, restaurants		finance, real estate		public administration, defense		services		other		country
number ('000)	% of econ. active	number ('000)	% of econ. active	number ('000)	% of econ. active	number ('000)	% of econ. active	number ('000)	% of econ. active	number ('000)	% of econ. active	number ('000)	% of econ. active	
51	1.3	66	1.6	138	3.5	1	1	1	1	749[1]	19.0[1]	78[2]	2.0[2]	Afghanistan
33[5]	2.5[5]	19[5]	1.4[5]	3[5]	0.2[5]	3[5]	0.2[5]	16[5]	1.2[5]	145[5]	10.8[5]	505[6]	37.7[6]	Albania
690	12.9	216	4.1	391	7.3	143	2.7	7	7	1,180[7]	22.1[7]	1,374	25.7	Algeria
1.2	8.3	0.8	5.5	1.8	13.0	0.3	2.1	1.4	10.0	2.8	19.8	0.7[9]	5.1[9]	American Samoa
2.9	11.8	...	...	6.0	24.2	1.3	5.4	2.6	10.3	4.1	16.7	0.1	0.5	Andorra
11	11	12	12	12	12	12	12	12	12	836[12]	20.1[12]	—	—	Angola
3.1	11.6	2.4	9.0	8.5	31.9	1.5	5.4	7	7	6.4[7]	23.9[7]	1.9	7.0	Antigua and Barbuda
1,003[14]	10.0[14]	460[14]	4.6[14]	1,702[14]	17.0[14]	396[14]	3.9[14]	7	7	2,399[7,14]	23.9[7,14]	736[14,15]	7.3[14,15]	Argentina
108	6.7	49	30.0	65	4.0	29	1.8	30	1.9	350	21.6	126[17]	7.8[17]	Armenia
3.2	10.4	2.3	7.5	11.0	35.4	2.4	7.8	7	7	8.6[7]	27.7[7]	1.1[17]	3.5[17]	Aruba
609	7.0	525	6.0	2,114	24.3	1,063	12.2	7	7	2,136[7]	24.6[7]	429[9]	4.9[9]	Australia
326	8.7	237	6.4	712	19.1	270	7.2	7	7	896[7]	24.0[7]	44	1.2	Austria
202	7.6	167	6.2	160	6.0	91	3.4	52	1.9	593	22.2	48	1.8	Azerbaijan
7.7[19]	5.6[19]	9.1[19]	6.6[19]	36.7[19]	26.8[19]	11.2[19]	8.2[19]	7	7	40.5[7,19]	29.6[7,19]	18.5[17,19]	13.5[17,19]	Bahamas, The
27	11.8	14	6.1	30	13.2	17	7.6	41	18.1	43	19.0	16[17]	7.3[17]	Bahrain
525	1.0	1,611	3.1	4,285	8.4	296	0.6	7	7	1,909[7]	3.7[7]	3,245[21]	6.3[21]	Bangladesh
6.9[19]	5.5[19]	4.5[19]	3.6[19]	14.5[19]	11.5[19]	5.5[19]	4.4[19]	7	7	38.1[7,19]	30.2[7,19]	40.2[17,19]	31.8[17,19]	Barbados
370	7.7	318	6.6	459	9.6	97	2.0	90	1.9	952	19.8	230[21]	4.8[21]	Belarus
245	5.8	257	6.1	634	15.0	342	8.1	7	7	1,393[7]	32.9[7]	484[17]	11.4[17]	Belgium
4.1[13]	7.0[13]	2.9[13]	5.0[13]	10.0[13]	17.2[13]	1.8[13]	3.1[13]	5.4[13]	9.2[13]	6.0[13]	10.3[13]	2.8[13]	4.8[13]	Belize
52	2.5	53	2.5	433	20.7	3	0.1	7	7	165[7]	7.9[7]	71[21]	3.4[21]	Benin
1.6	4.8	2.3	6.8	10.7	31.4	5.1	14.9	7	7	12.3[7]	35.9[7]	—	—	Bermuda
...	...	...	...	...	...	...	...	...	...	...	...	...	...	Bhutan
129	5.1	117	4.6	232	9.2	54	2.1	59	2.3	350	13.8	323[15]	12.7[15]	Bolivia
75	7.3	69	6.7	131	12.8	39	3.8	7	7	155[7]	15.1[7]	—	—	Bosnia and Herzegovina
58	13.2	11	2.6	35	8.0	13	3.0	7	7	107[7]	24.2[7]	72[17]	16.2[17]	Botswana
3,823	5.9	2,440	3.6	7,976	12.4	1,716	2.7	7	7	21,694[7]	33.7[7]	2,367[9]	3.7[9]	Brazil
14.1	12.6	5.4	4.8	15.4	13.8	5.8	5.2	7	7	52.1[7]	46.6[7]	5.3[17]	4.7[17]	Brunei
192	5.1	233	6.1	369	9.7	44	1.2	75	2.0	522	13.7	594[17]	15.6[17]	Bulgaria
11	0.2	1.5	0.3	120	2.6	2	—	7	7	112[7]	2.4[7]	67[17]	1.4[17]	Burkina Faso
20	0.7	9	0.3	26	0.9	2.0	0.1	7	7	85[7]	3.1[7]	27[17]	1.0[17]	Burundi
11	11	12	12	12	12	12	12	12	12	625[12,14]	18.9[12,14]	—	—	Cambodia
11	11	12	12	12	12	12	12	12	12	1,256[12]	26.5[12]	—	—	Cameroon
851	6.1	992	7.1	2,391	17.1	817	5.9	7	7	5,949[7]	42.7[7]	122[9]	0.9[9]	Canada
22.7	18.8	6.1	5.1	12.7	10.6	0.8	0.7	7	7	17.4[7]	14.4[7]	24.1	20.0	Cape Verde
6	0.5	7	0.6	92	7.8	0.7	0.1	7	7	70[7]	5.9[7]	100[17]	8.5[17]	Central African Republic
11	11	12	12	12	12	12	12	12	12	377[12]	18.7[12]	—	—	Chad
361	6.8	371	7.0	941	17.8	299	5.6	7	7	1,268[7]	23.9[7]	312[17]	5.9[17]	Chile
11,890	1.8	11,814	1.8	25,631	3.9	8,268	1.3	7	7	34,053[7]	5.2[7]	10,434	1.6	China
242[14]	2.9[14]	353[14]	4.2[14]	1,262[14]	14.9[14]	278[14]	3.3[14]	7	7	1,998[7,14]	23.6[7,14]	691[14,15]	8.2[14,15]	Colombia
11	11	12	12	12	12	12	12	12	12	30[12]	14.1[12]	—	—	Comoros
25	4.5	29	5.1	67	11.8	3	0.5	7	7	85[7]	15.1[7]	10	2.0	Congo
79	6.6	60	5.1	218	18.4	52	4.3	7	7	277[7]	23.3[7]	17[15]	1.5[15]	Costa Rica
85	2.0	118	2.8	530	12.4	1	1	1	1	591[1]	13.9[1]	210[2]	4.9[2]	Côte d'Ivoire
93	4.5	112	5.5	223	10.9	58	2.8	104	5.1	204	10.0	329[17]	16.1[17]	Croatia
313[27]	8.8[27]	249[27]	7.0[27]	306[27]	8.6[27]	1	1	1	1	1,086[1,27]	30.7[1,27]	128[27]	3.6[27]	Cuba
23	7.8	17	5.8	70	23.6	21	7.0	7	7	61[7]	20.6[7]	22[21]	7.5[21]	Cyprus[28,29]
412	7.6	366	6.8	544	10.0	86	1.6	238	4.4	957	17.7	169	3.1	Czech Republic
185	6.4	200	6.9	445	15.5	276	9.5	189	6.5	830	28.7	18[30]	0.6[30]	Denmark
11	11	12	12	12	12	12	12	12	12	39[12]	13.8[12]	—	—	Djibouti
2.8	10.7	1.2	4.6	3.7	13.9	0.8	3.1	1.5	5.8	3.4	13.1	3.2[17]	12.3[17]	Dominica
81	4.3	40	2.1	192	10.0	22	1.2	7	7	363[7]	18.9[7]	553[15]	28.9[15]	Dominican Republic
197	5.9	131	3.9	477	14.2	81	2.4	7	7	838[7]	24.9[7]	196[15]	5.8[15]	Ecuador
884	5.6	778	4.9	1,332	8.4	237	1.5	7	7	3,420[7]	21.6[7]	1,416[17]	9.0[17]	Egypt
83	4.7	62	3.5	276	15.6	52	2.9	101	5.7	195	11.1	137[17]	7.8[17]	El Salvador
1.9	1.9	1.8	1.7	3.1	3.0	0.4	0.4	7	7	8.4[7]	8.2[7]	25.8[17]	25.2[17]	Equatorial Guinea
...	...	...	...	...	...	...	...	...	...	...	...	...	...	Eritrea
73	8.5	73	8.5	75	8.8	4	0.5	19	2.2	182	21.3	60	7.0	Estonia
61	0.2	103	0.4	936	3.8	19	0.1	7	7	1,252[7]	5.1[7]	210[2]	0.9[2]	Ethiopia
2.0	11.1	1.9	11.1	2.1	11.9	0.3	1.9	7	7	3.5[7]	20.1[7]	0.6	3.2	Faroe Islands

Employment and labour (continued)

country	year	economically active population						employment status (%)				distribution by economic sector			
		total ('000)	participation rate (%)		activity rate (%)							agriculture, forestry, fishing		manufacturing; mining, quarrying; public utilities	
			female	ages 15-64	total	male	female	employers, self-employed	employees	unpaid family workers	other	number ('000)	% of econ. active	number ('000)	% of econ. active
Fiji	1986	241	21.2	56.0	33.7	52.4	14.5	33.6	42.2	16.3	7.9	106	44.1	22	9.0
Finland	1994	2,503	47.0	73.1	49.2	53.6	45.1	12.7	83.3	0.6	3.4	188	7.5	497	19.9
France	1994[18]	25,871	44.9	67.7	44.8	50.6	39.2	10.2	77.4	—	12.4	1,048	4.1	4,432	17.4
French Guiana	1990	48.8	38.2	67.3	42.5	50.5	33.9	10.6	62.7	2.5	24.2	4.2	8.6	3.1	6.4
French Polynesia	1988	75	37.1	64.8	39.9	48.2	30.9	13.0	55.0	4.0	28.0	7.6	10.0	5.4	7.2
Gabon	1991	504	36.9	56.0[10]	43.9	53.9	30.7	...	...	...	...	338	67.1	71[11]	14.1[11]
Gambia, The	1983	326	46.3	78.2	47.3	51.1	43.6	0.5	78.0	14.3	7.1	240	73.7	9	2.9
Gaza Strip	1993	120	2.7	34.2[23]	16.1	32.0	0.9	...	...	...	...	21.1	17.6	12.2[33]	10.1[33]
Georgia	1993	1,920	...	58.1[16,24]	35.7	...	...	...	...	...	...	562	29.3	303	15.8
Germany	1993	40,179	42.5	72.4[24]	49.5	58.6	41.0	7.8	91.0	1.2	—	1,128	2.9	10,183	26.1
Ghana	1984	5,580	51.2	82.5[23]	45.4	44.9	45.8	67.7	15.7	12.2	4.4	3,311	59.3	631	11.3
Gibraltar	1994	12.9	38.0	66.9[13,23]	47.5	58.7	36.2	6.6[27]	89.7[27]	...	3.6[27]	—	—	0.7	5.7
Greece	1992[18]	4,034	37.0	63.9	40.6	52.7	29.1	32.5	51.6	11.1	4.8	812	20.1	815	20.2
Greenland	1976	21.4	33.4	63.5[23]	43.1	53.0	31.4	12.6	82.5	0.4	4.5	3.2	15.1	3.3	15.3
Grenada	1988	38.9	48.6	72.7[34]	39.9	42.9	37.2	...	...	...	...	5.6	14.3	3.3	8.6
Guadeloupe	1990	172	45.5	66.4	44.5	49.6	39.7	13.2	53.7	2.0	31.1	8.4	4.9	9.6	5.6
Guam	1990	66.1	37.4	75.7[8]	49.7	58.4	39.7	2.4	94.4	0.1	3.1	0.5	0.8	3.5	5.3
Guatemala	1989[18]	2,898	25.5	59.1	33.5	50.8	16.7	32.7	47.6	16.2	3.5	1,416	48.9	405	14.0
Guernsey[35]	1991	30.2	43.2	74.2	51.2	60.6	42.6	13.7	86.3	...	...	2.4	7.9	2.4	7.9
Guinea	1983	1,823	39.4	63.5	39.1	48.7	30.1	36.2	15.6	37.6	10.6	1,424	78.1	27	1.5
Guinea-Bissau	1991	464	40.5	67.1[10]	45.9	56.2	36.1	...	...	...	...	362	78.0	21[11]	4.5[11]
Guyana	1987[36]	270	29.9	60.4	35.7	50.9	21.0	14.3[14]	63.8[14]	1.9[14]	20.0[14]	50[14]	20.4[14]	41[14]	16.8[14]
Haiti	1990	2,679	40.0	64.8	41.1	50.3	32.3	59.1	16.5	10.4	14.0	1,535	57.3	178	6.6
Honduras	1992[18]	1,729	31.2	58.3[23]	34.8	49.0	21.2	36.5	48.7	10.7	4.1	640	37.0	264	15.3
Hong Kong	1994[18]	2,973	36.9	69.6	50.3	62.0	38.1	9.9	87.4	0.7	1.9	18	0.6	590	19.8
Hungary	1993	5,015	48.5	82.8[16]	48.6	52.3	45.3	...	...	...	...	431	8.6	1,304	26.0
Iceland	1994	146	47.3	84.3[38]	54.6	57.3	51.8	...	...	...	...	12.2	8.4	25.8	17.7
India	1991	314,131	28.6	60.7[23,27]	37.5	51.6	22.3	8.8[27]	16.3[27]	3.6[27]	71.3[27]	191,341	60.9	30,423	9.7
Indonesia	1992	79,451	38.2	67.0	42.9	53.1	32.7	43.2	28.7	25.7	2.4	42,048	52.9	8,816	11.1
Iran	1991	14,737	11.1	46.8	26.4	45.6	6.0	39.7	45.4	2.3	12.6	3,205	21.8	2,243	15.2
Iraq	1988	4,127	12.0	45.3	24.7	42.3	6.1	25.4[39]	59.5[39]	11.4[39]	3.7[39]	477	11.6	439	10.6
Ireland	1991	1,334	32.2	59.7	37.8	51.4	24.3	18.2	77.8	1.4	2.6	155	11.6	246	18.4
Isle of Man	1991	33.2	42.3	73.2	47.6	56.9	38.9	15.8	80.1	—	4.1	1.2	3.7	3.9	11.6
Israel	1994[18]	2,030	42.8	60.3	39.1	45.1	33.3	14.6	76.8	0.8	7.8	65	3.2	434	21.4
Italy	1994[18]	22,680	36.9	57.4	40.1	52.1	28.8	21.4	62.8	4.0	11.8	1,573	6.9	4,837	21.3
Jamaica	1994	1,091	47.3	71.6[20,40]	43.7	46.1	41.3	32.7	49.5	2.0	15.8	218	20.0	107	9.8
Japan	1994	66,450	40.5	71.4	53.1	64.4	42.3	12.0	78.8	6.1	3.1	3,730	5.6	15,410	23.2
Jersey	1991	47.5	43.2	66.9[23]	56.5	66.1	47.5	12.6	84.0	...	3.4	2.2	4.7	3.8	8.0
Jordan	1993	859	11.4[25]	43.2[25]	22.2	...	...	22.8[41]	67.2[41]	0.8[41]	9.2[41]	55	6.4	97	11.3
Kazakstan	1993	6,963	...	71.8[16]	41.2	...	...	...	...	...	...	1,759	25.3	1,305	18.7
Kenya	1991	10,260	39.4	64.4[10]	39.0	47.4	30.7	...	...	...	...	7,857	76.6	816[11]	8.0[11]
Kiribati	1990	32.6	46.4	75.6[23]	45.1	48.9	41.4	71.9	25.3	...	2.8	23.1	71.0	0.9	2.8
Korea, North	1985	9,084	46.0	75.3	44.6	48.6	40.6	...	...	...	...	3,726[22]	44.1[22]	2,790[11,22]	33.0[11,22]
Korea, South	1993[18]	19,803	40.0	61.1[23]	44.9	53.6	36.2	27.4	59.3	10.5	2.8	2,828	14.3	4,769	24.1
Kuwait	1988	730	24.3	61.5	38.9	53.5	21.0	3.9	94.1	0.1	1.9	9	1.3	69	9.4
Kyrgyzstan	1994	1,592	...	...	35.9	...	...	...	...	...	...	702	44.1	254	16.0
Laos	1985	2,014	45.3	84.2	48.9	53.1	44.6	...	...	...	...	1,393[14]	75.7[14]	130[11,14]	7.1[11,14]
Latvia	1994	1,301	48.7	...	51.4	...	...	...	...	...	...	232	17.8	253	19.5
Lebanon	1988	904	16.6	44.0	26.5	43.9	8.9	...	...	...	...	132[42]	19.1[42]	131[42]	18.9[42]
Lesotho	1986	504	27.0	44.0	31.6	47.3	16.7	16.8	55.7	20.5	7.0	131	25.9	142	28.2
Liberia	1984	704	41.0	56.3	33.5	39.1	27.8	59.1	21.6	14.4	5.0	481	68.3	31	4.4
Libya	1991	1,169	9.3	37.1[10]	24.8	42.9	4.9	...	...	...	...	129	11.0	372[11]	31.8[11]
Liechtenstein	1994	15.1	38.1	70.0	49.3	62.8	36.5	6.2	91.3	0.1	2.4	0.3	2.2	4.8	32.1
Lithuania	1994	1,937	...	81.8[16,19]	52.1	...	...	...	...	...	...	390	20.1	378	19.5
Luxembourg	1991[43]	168	36.5	62.5	43.5	56.4	31.2	9.2	85.3	1.1	4.4	5	3.2	26	15.8
Macau	1993[18]	175	41.8	63.4	44.3	52.8	36.2	10.6	86.2	1.1	2.1	0.3	0.2	44	24.9
Macedonia	1993	937	...	...	45.2	...	...	...	...	...	...	215	22.9	168	17.9
Madagascar	1991	5,311	39.3	63.9[10]	42.8	52.4	33.0	...	...	...	...	4,043	76.1	632[11]	11.9[11]
Malawi	1987	3,458	51.0	89.4	43.3	43.9	42.8	4.9	16.2	77.6	1.3	2,968	85.8	114	3.3
Malaysia	1993[18]	7,383	34.3	57.3[13]	35.1[13]	47.3[13]	22.6[13]	21.1	71.4	7.5	—	1,559	21.1	1,825	24.7
Maldives	1990	56.4	19.9	50.2	26.5	41.3	10.8	39.7	49.3	4.5	6.5	14.1	25.0	9.4	16.6
Mali	1987	3,438	37.4	67.4	44.7	57.2	32.7	35.4	5.2	57.6	1.8	2,803	81.5	191	5.6
Malta	1990	132	25.4	47.4[13]	37.2	56.1	18.7	14.1[46]	77.4[46]	...	8.5[46]	3	2.5	38	28.8
Marshall Islands	1988	11.5	30.1	54.1[24]	26.5	37.7	14.8	21.6	58.9	7.1	12.5	2.2	18.7	1.0	9.0
Martinique	1990	165	47.5	68.1	45.9	49.8	42.2	9.5	56.9	1.5	32.1	8.4	5.1	9.7	5.9
Mauritania	1991	638	22.3	45.5[10]	30.8	48.1	13.8	...	...	...	...	410	64.3	70[11]	11.0[11]
Mauritius[47]	1991	463	35.2	68.0	44.5	57.9	31.2	12.2[20]	80.1[20]	1.9[20]	5.9[20]	81	17.5	146	31.5
Mayotte	1991	27.3	29.4	56.4	28.9	39.2	17.7	12.0	42.9	7.3	37.8	3.1	11.4	1.3	4.7
Mexico	1993	33,652	30.9	61.4	38.9	54.6	23.6	30.1	53.8	13.6	2.6	8,843	26.3	5,348	15.9
Micronesia	1990	30.5	29.8[14]	60.6	30.3	...	...	2.7[14]	74.4[14]	0.1[14]	22.7[14]	12.7	41.5	1.6	5.2
Moldova	1994	1,699	...	68.7[16]	39.1	...	...	...	...	...	...	767	45.1	232	13.7
Monaco	1990	12.6	39.7	...	42.0	53.2	31.8	17.4	75.1	0.3	7.2	—	0.3	2.7	21.8
Mongolia	1993	845	47.2[31]	77.9[31,49]	39.3[31]	41.6[31]	37.1[31]	...	...	...	...	300	35.5	124	14.7
Morocco	1982	5,999	19.7	48.9	29.3	47.1	11.6	27.1	40.5	17.6	14.8	2,352	39.2	1,016	16.9
Mozambique	1980	5,671	52.4	87.3[23]	48.6	47.6	49.5	...	...	...	...	4,755	83.8	347	6.1
Myanmar (Burma)	1991–92[18]	16,510	35.3[46]	64.2[46]	40.2[46]	52.4[46]	28.2[46]	41.4[46]	27.4[46]	30.2[46]	1.0[46]	11,076	67.1	1,220	7.4
Namibia	1991	494	43.6	61.3	35.2	39.9	30.5	17.8	49.1	17.9	15.2	190	38.5	41	8.2
Nauru	1977	2.2	...	...	30.5	...	...	...	...	...	...	...	...	...	...
Nepal	1991	7,340	40.4	57.0[10]	40.0	47.8	32.2	75.8	21.4	2.3	0.4	5,962	81.2	164	2.2
Netherlands, The	1994	7,184	41.1	68.6	46.7	55.6	38.0	10.1	81.8	1.2	6.8	264	3.7	1,132	15.8
Netherlands Antilles	1992	87.8	45.1	68.6	46.3	53.1	40.1	...	...	...	...	0.5	0.6	8.4	9.6
New Caledonia	1989	66	37.5	70.7[50]	40.2	49.1	30.8	16.3	64.3	1.6	17.8	7.8	11.8	6.2	9.3
New Zealand	1993[18]	1,653	43.6	73.0	48.7	55.7	41.9	18.2	71.3	1.0	9.5	158	9.5	270	16.3
Nicaragua	1993	1,490	33.2[13]	51.6[10]	34.7[13]	47.8[13]	22.3[13]	...	...	...	...	430	28.8	183	12.3
Niger	1988[51]	2,316	20.4	55.2	31.9	51.1	13.0	51.4	5.0	40.3	3.3	1,764	76.2	73	3.1

construction		transportation, communications		trade, hotels, restaurants		finance, real estate		public administration, defense		services		other		country
number ('000)	% of econ. active	number ('000)	% of econ. active	number ('000)	% of econ. active	number ('000)	% of econ. active	number ('000)	% of econ. active	number ('000)	% of econ. active	number ('000)	% of econ. active	
12	4.9	13	5.5	26	10.8	6	2.5	7	7	377	15.2[7]	20[17]	8.2[17]	Fiji
179	7.2	181	7.2	354	14.1	198	7.9	115	4.6	694	27.7	96[30]	3.8[30]	Finland
1,443	5.7	1,397	5.5	3,716	14.6	2,340	9.2	7	7	7,733[7]	30.3[7]	3,376[17]	13.2[17]	France
4.4	9.1	1.9	3.8	4.2	8.5	1.7	3.5	7	7	17.5[7]	35.9[7]	11.8[9]	24.2[9]	French Guiana
5.5	7.4	2.8	3.7	10.3	13.7	1.2	1.5	7	7	21.5[7]	28.6[7]	21.1[17]	28.0[17]	French Polynesia
11	11	12	12	12	12	12	12	12	12	95[12]	18.8[12]	—	—	Gabon
4	1.3	8	2.5	17	5.1	5	1.4	8	2.5	9	2.9	25	7.7	Gambia, The
36.4	30.3	7.1	5.9	18.4	15.3	33	33	7	7	14.0[7]	11.6[7]	11.1[21,33]	9.2[21,33]	Gaza Strip
125	6.5	107	5.6	117	6.1	20	1.0	49	2.6	479	24.9	158[17]	8.2[17]	Georgia
2,691	6.9	2,141	5.5	5,721	14.7	3,044	7.8	7	7	10,355[7]	26.5[7]	3,747[9]	9.6[9]	Germany
65	1.2	123	2.2	792	14.2	27	0.5	98	1.7	376	6.7	158[9]	2.8[9]	Ghana
1.2	9.6	0.9	7.4	3.2	24.7	1.6	12.4	1.9	14.8	3.3	25.5	—	—	Gibraltar
261	6.5	262	6.5	722	17.9	205	5.1	7	7	762[7]	18.9[7]	194[30]	4.8[30]	Greece
3.1	14.6	1.8	8.6	2.7	12.6	0.3	1.6	7	7	6.3[7]	29.5[7]	0.6	2.8	Greenland
3.5	9.1	1.7	4.4	5.4	13.9	0.8	2.0	7	7	5.9[7]	15.3[7]	12.7[17]	32.5[17]	Grenada
14.0	8.1	7.0	4.0	15.0	8.7	2.8	1.6	7	7	60.8[7]	35.2[7]	54.9[17]	31.8[17]	Guadeloupe
8.0	12.1	4.5	6.8	11.5	17.5	3.9	6.0	17.7	26.7	14.5	21.9	2.0[9]	3.1[9]	Guam
114	3.9	72	2.5	375	12.9	38	1.3	7	7	417[7]	14.4[7]	60[17]	2.1[17]	Guatemala
3.2	10.5	1.4	4.5	7.4	24.6	5.8	19.3	1.9	6.4	5.3	17.7	0.4	1.3	Guernsey[35]
9	0.5	29	1.6	37	2.0	4	0.2	7	7	138[7]	7.5[7]	156	8.5	Guinea
11	11	12	12	12	12	12	12	12	12	81[12]	17.5[12]	—	—	Guinea-Bissau
7[14]	2.8[14]	9[14]	3.8[14]	15[14]	6.2[14]	3[14]	1.2[14]	30[14]	12.1[14]	29[14]	11.9[14]	61[14,17]	24.7[14,17]	Guyana
28	1.0	21	0.8	353	13.2	5	0.2	7	7	155[7]	5.8[7]	404[17]	15.1[17]	Haiti
72	4.2	52	3.0	282	16.3	30	1.7	7	7	334[7]	19.3[7]	55[17]	3.2[17]	Honduras
226	7.6	347	11.7	839	28.2	331	11.1	7	7	564[7]	19.3[7]	57[17]	1.9[17]	Hong Kong
271	5.4	369	7.4	654	13.0	37	37	274	5.5	1,049[37]	20.9[37]	663[9]	13.2[9]	Hungary
11.1	7.6	8.6	5.9	22.8	15.7	12.4	8.5	6.0	4.1	39.8	27.3	6.9[9]	4.8[9]	Iceland
5,543	1.8	8,108	2.6	21,296	6.8	1	1	1	1	29,312[1]	9.3[1]	28,199	9.0	India
2,414	3.0	2,566	3.2	11,650	14.7	527	0.7	7	7	9,492[7]	11.9[7]	1,937[17]	2.4[17]	Indonesia
1,372	9.3	762	5.2	1,238	8.4	195	1.3	7	7	3,518[7]	23.9[7]	2,203[17]	14.9[17]	Iran
461	11.2	266	6.4	282	6.8	42	1.0	7	7	2,160[7]	52.3[7]	—	—	Iraq
80	6.0	65	4.9	201	15.0	95	7.1	7	7	286[7]	21.5[7]	209[30]	15.7[30]	Ireland
3.4	10.3	2.4	7.3	6.1	18.4	4.4	13.1	7	7	10.4[7]	31.4[7]	1.4[9]	4.1[9]	Isle of Man
127	6.2	112	5.5	296	14.6	213	10.5	7	7	685[7]	33.7[7]	97[30]	4.8[30]	Israel
1,641	7.2	1,080	4.8	4,221	18.6	1,514	6.7	7	7	5,134[7]	22.6[7]	2,676[9]	11.8[9]	Italy
66	6.1	40	3.7	196	17.9	47	4.3	7	7	237[7]	21.7[7]	180[17]	16.5[17]	Jamaica
6,550	9.9	3,920	5.9	14,430	21.7	2,620	3.9	7	7	17,570[7]	26.4[7]	2,220[17]	3.3[17]	Japan
4.4	9.3	2.4	5.0	6.8	14.4	7.4	15.6	3.1	6.5	15.7	33.1	1.6[17]	3.4[17]	Jersey
60	7.0	58	6.7	130	15.1	25	2.9	7	7	435[7]	50.6[7]	—	—	Jordan
620	8.9	584	8.4	482	6.9	337	4.8	132	1.9	1,356	19.5	388[21]	5.6[21]	Kazakstan
11	11	12	12	12	12	12	12	12	12	1,587[12]	15.5[12]	—	—	Kenya
0.3	1.0	0.9	2.8	1.3	4.1	0.4	1.4	2.1	6.5	2.3	7.0	1.1[17]	3.4[17]	Kiribati
11	11	12	12	12	12	12	12	12	12	1,939[12,22]	22.9[12,22]	—	—	Korea, North
1,685	8.5	1,005	5.1	4,837	24.4	1,360	6.9	7	7	2,769[7]	14.0[7]	550[9]	2.8[9]	Korea, South
115	15.7	38	5.2	83	11.4	22	3.0	7	7	384[7]	52.6[7]	11[2]	1.5[2]	Kuwait
88	5.5	89	5.2	70	4.4	30	1.9	50	3.1	277	17.4	39	2.4	Kyrgyzstan
11	11	12	12	12	12	12	12	12	12	316[12,14]	17.2[12,14]	—	—	Laos
62	4.8	106	8.2	198	15.2	73	5.6	50	3.8	231	17.8	96[9]	7.3[9]	Latvia
43[42]	6.2[42]	48[42]	7.0[42]	115[42]	16.5[42]	24[42]	3.5[42]	7	7	200[7,42]	28.8[7,42]	—	—	Lebanon
28	5.5	8	1.6	24	4.7	2	0.5	7	7	157[7]	31.1[7]	13	2.6	Lesotho
4	0.6	14	2.0	47	6.7	1	1	1	1	63[1]	9.0[1]	64[17]	9.1[17]	Liberia
11	11	12	12	12	12	12	12	12	12	668[12]	57.1[12]	—	—	Libya
1.2	7.7	0.5	3.2	2.1	13.8	1.1	7.4	0.9	6.0	3.7	24.2	0.5[17]	3.5[17]	Liechtenstein
111	5.7	92	4.7	246	12.7	63	3.3	60	3.1	335	17.3	262[9]	13.5[9]	Lithuania
14	8.4	11	6.3	29	17.5	15	9.2	21	12.8	31	18.7	14[21]	8.1[21]	Luxembourg
17	9.8	10	6.0	45	25.4	9	5.3	7	7	45[7]	26.0[7]	4[17]	2.5[17]	Macau
37	3.9	21	2.3	54	5.8	20	2.2	15	1.6	69	7.4	338[44]	36.1[44]	Macedonia
11	11	12	12	12	12	12	12	12	12	636[12]	12.0[12]	—	—	Madagascar
46	1.4	25	0.7	94	2.7	6	0.2	7	7	147[7]	4.3[7]	57	1.7	Malawi
539	7.3	344	4.7	1,266	17.1	330	4.5	7	7	1,521[7]	20.6[7]	—	—	Malaysia
3.2	5.6	5.3	9.4	8.9	15.7	1.1	1.9	7	7	11.8[7]	21.0[7]	2.7[45]	4.7[45]	Maldives
13	0.4	6	0.2	159	4.6	0.3	—	75	2.2	84	2.4	107	3.1	Mali
6	4.4	9	6.9	13	9.8	5	3.7	7	7	53[7]	40.0[7]	5[9]	3.8[9]	Malta
1.1	9.4	0.5	4.7	1.4	12.1	0.8	7.3	7	7	3.1[7]	26.4[7]	1.4[17]	12.5[17]	Marshall Islands
9.3	5.6	6.7	4.0	14.0	8.5	3.0	1.8	7	7	59.1[7]	35.8[7]	54.8[17]	33.2[17]	Martinique
11	11	12	12	12	12	12	12	12	12	158[12]	24.8[12]	—	—	Mauritania
24	5.2	32	6.9	61	13.2	11	2.4	7	7	94[7]	20.3[7]	14[17]	3.1[17]	Mauritius[47]
3.1	11.4	1.5	5.4	2.0	7.2	0.1	0.4	7	7	5.7[7]	21.0[7]	10.5[17]	38.4[17]	Mayotte
1,879	5.6	1,362	4.0	6,893	20.5	1,080	3.2	7	7	7,205[7]	21.4[7]	1,041[17]	3.1[17]	Mexico
1.8	6.1	48	48	48	48	48	48	6.3	20.8	3.7[48]	12.1[48]	4.1[9]	13.5[9]	Micronesia
91	5.4	73	4.3	107	6.3	20	1.2	32	1.9	344	20.2	33[17]	1.9[17]	Moldova
0.7	5.3	...	...	2.5	20.2	1.0	8.0	2.8	22.4	1.9	14.9	0.9[21]	7.1[21]	Monaco
33	3.9	38	4.4	62	7.3	1	1	1	1	123[1]	14.5[1]	166[21]	19.7[21]	Mongolia
437	7.3	141	2.3	498	8.3	37	37	533	8.9	474[37]	7.9[37]	548[2]	9.1[2]	Morocco
42	0.7	7.7	1.4	112	2.0	1	1	1	1	243[1]	4.3[1]	95[9]	1.7[9]	Mozambique
283	1.7	394	2.4	1,355	8.2	1,205	7.3	7	7	474[7]	2.9[7]	503[9]	3.0[9]	Myanmar (Burma)
19	3.8	9	1.9	38	7.7	9	1.7	7	7	6[7]	1.2[7]	183[17]	37.1[17]	Namibia
...	...	...	...	...	...	...	...	...	...	...	...	...	...	Nauru
36	0.5	51	0.7	256	3.5	20	0.3	7	7	752[7]	10.3[7]	98	1.3	Nepal
393	5.5	419	5.8	1,227	17.1	704	9.8	7	7	2,371[7]	33.0[7]	675[17]	9.4[17]	Netherlands, The
6.5	7.4	5.0	5.7	20.9	23.8	8.2	9.3	7	7	24.8[7]	28.2[7]	13.4[9]	15.3[9]	Netherlands Antilles
4.5	6.8	3.1	4.7	9.5	14.3	2.5	3.8	7	7	22.0[7]	33.4[7]	13.5[9]	16.0[9]	New Caledonia
81	4.9	91	5.5	316	19.1	149	9.0	7	7	429[7]	26.0[7]	160[17]	9.7[17]	New Zealand
30	2.0	33	2.2	195	13.1	19	1.3	86	5.7	190	12.7	325[9]	21.8[9]	Nicaragua
14	0.6	15	0.6	209	9.0	2	0.1	7	7	123[7]	5.3[7]	117[21]	5.0[21]	Niger

Employment and labour (continued)

country	year	economically active population total ('000)	participation rate (%) female	participation rate (%) ages 15–64	activity rate (%) total	activity rate (%) male	activity rate (%) female	employment status (%) employers, self-employed	employment status (%) employees	employment status (%) unpaid family workers	employment status (%) other	distribution by economic sector — agriculture, forestry, fishing number ('000)	agriculture, forestry, fishing % of econ. active	manufacturing; mining, quarrying; public utilities number ('000)	manufacturing; mining, quarrying; public utilities % of econ. active
Nigeria	1986[18]	30,766	33.3	58.8	31.1	41.1	20.9	64.6	18.8	10.7	5.9	13,259	43.1	1,401	4.6
Northern Mariana Islands	1990	26.6	43.2	83.6[8]	61.3	66.2	55.9	1.4	96.1	0.2	2.3	0.6	2.3	6.0	22.5
Norway	1994	2,151	45.5	76.5[8]	49.9	55.0	44.9	8.1	85.3	0.9	5.7	111	5.2	363	16.9
Oman	1988	644	6.3	57.2	38.2	60.7	5.9	...	...	...	...	399	62.0	33	5.1
Pakistan	1993–94[18]	34,748	14.9	50.4	27.9	45.9	8.6	41.2[52]	32.4[52]	20.2[52]	6.2[52]	15,770	45.4	3,960	11.4
Palau	1990	6.1	36.9	64.1[8]	40.2	47.1	32.1	2.5	89.5	0.2	7.8	0.4	7.1	0.2	3.0
Panama	1993	940	34.0	60.4[23]	37.3	48.5	25.7	26.2	65.9	3.6	4.4	193	20.5	105	11.2
Papua New Guinea	1980[53]	733	39.8	35.2[10]	24.6	28.3	20.5	72.7	26.4	—	0.9	564	77.0	21	2.9
Paraguay	1982	1,039	19.7	57.5	34.3	54.8	13.6	43.1	37.7	9.2	9.9	446	42.9	129	12.4
Peru	1993	8,293	38.3[54]	56.9[23]	36.2	...	...	39.8[27]	41.8[27]	8.4[27]	10.0[27]	2,693	32.5	1,091	13.2
Philippines	1994[18]	27,483	36.9	66.1	38.6	49.0	28.3	36.2	41.7	13.7	8.4	11,429	40.9	2,783	10.1
Poland	1994[18]	17,122	46.2	67.7	44.4	49.1	40.0	19.9	62.8	4.9	12.5	3,988[19]	23.0[19]	4,348[19]	25.0[19]
Portugal	1993[18]	4,715	44.7	67.5	47.9	55.2	41.2	23.1	74.2	1.8	0.9	528	11.2	1,173	24.9
Puerto Rico	1995[18]	1,128	39.4	52.9[8]	32.2	40.1	24.8	13.6	85.2	0.7	0.6	42	3.4	220	17.9
Qatar	1988	293	11.2	80.8	53.7	77.3	22.2	1.8[42]	97.7[42]	—	0.5[42]	4.5	1.6	22.0	7.5
Réunion	1990[18]	234	41.1	60.3	39.1	46.8	31.6	8.4	53.1	1.1	37.4	11	4.8	11	4.8
Romania	1992	10,465	44.7	68.3	45.9	51.6	40.4	13.9	79.7	2.0	4.4	2,417	23.1	4,016	38.4
Russia	1994	70,987	...	...	48.0	...	...	...	...	...	...	10,350	14.6	19,200	27.0
Rwanda	1991	3,649	47.5	79.1[10]	50.2	53.3	47.2	...	...	...	...	3,313	90.8	129[11]	3.5[11]
St. Kitts and Nevis	1980	17.1	41.0	69.5	39.5	48.4	31.2	9.7	78.5	0.4	11.4	4.5	26.1	3.8	22.3
St. Lucia	1991	53.1	40.3	67.6	39.9	49.1	31.2	21.0[14]	55.8[14]	1.6[14]	21.6[14]	11.6	21.8	7.5	14.0
St. Vincent	1991	41.7	35.9	67.5	39.1	50.3	28.0	18.2	59.6	2.1	20.1	8.4	20.1	3.5	8.4
San Marino	1993	14.9	40.8	74.8	55.4	63.5	46.8	22.2	77.3	0.5	—	0.3	2.0	4.7	31.9
São Tomé and Príncipe	1991	35	33.6	59.1	30.1	40.5	20.0	25.8	68.6	0.7	4.9	13.6	38.4	1.8	5.0
Saudi Arabia	1988	5,369	3.6	59.1	36.3	54.9	3.6	...	...	...	...	192	3.6	595	11.1
Senegal	1991	3,249	39.1	64.2[10]	42.6	52.6	32.9	...	...	...	...	2,543	78.3	228[11]	7.0[11]
Seychelles	1993[55]	28.1	...	...	38.9	...	...	...	...	...	...	2.2	7.7	4.6[11]	16.4[11]
Sierra Leone	1991	1,532	32.4	53.3[10]	35.9	49.4	22.8	...	...	...	...	945	61.7	275[11]	18.0[11]
Singapore	1993[18]	1,636	40.2	68.7	49.6	58.7	40.3	12.3	84.1	0.9	2.7	4	0.2	437	26.7
Slovakia	1993[18]	2,509	46.1	71.9	47.2	52.2	42.5	5.7	90.0	0.1	4.2	226	9.0	691	27.5
Slovenia	1991	946	46.7	66.7	48.1	52.9	43.6	2.2	88.8	1.9	7.1	121	12.8	335	35.4
Solomon Islands	1993[56]	29.6	25.6[42]	24.9[42,57]	13.7[42]	19.7[42]	7.3[42]	29.6[42]	68.6[42]	—	1.8[42]	8.1	27.4	3.1	10.4
Somalia	1991	3,215	40.5	64.3[10]	40.9	51.1	31.0	...	...	...	...	2,275	70.8	336[11]	10.5[11]
South Africa[58]	1991	11,624	39.4	69.3[50]	37.5	45.5	29.5	7.0	74.8	—	18.2	1,224	10.5	2,361	20.3
Spain	1993[18]	15,319	36.8	60.3[8]	39.4	51.1	28.3	17.1	71.0	3.6	8.3	1,410	9.2	3,060	20.0
Sri Lanka	1994	6,142	33.9	57.0[23]	41.0	53.7	28.0	24.3	54.9	7.1	13.7	1,833	29.8	826	13.5
Sudan, The	1983[51]	6,343	29.1	57.4	35.1	50.0	20.4	...	...	...	...	4,029	63.5	317	5.0
Suriname	1992[59]	107	37.8	56.0	48.2	61.4	35.7	...	...	...	...	3.8	3.5	11.2	10.5
Swaziland	1991	326	39.0	62.3[10]	39.8	49.5	30.3	...	...	...	...	215	66.0	39[11]	12.0[11]
Sweden	1994	4,267	48.0	77.6[8]	48.6	51.1	46.1	9.8	81.8	0.5	8.0	135	3.2	762	17.9
Switzerland	1994[18]	3,852	43.3	65.5[23]	54.1	62.1	46.7	12.8	84.3	2.9	—	153	4.0	740	19.2
Syria	1991[18]	3,485	18.0	46.7[42]	27.8	44.6	10.2	31.0	49.3	13.0	6.7	917	26.3	471	13.5
Taiwan	1995[18]	9,210	38.6	58.7[23]	43.2	51.6	34.3	21.9	68.0	8.3	1.8	954	10.4	2,500	27.1
Tajikistan	1994	1,984	...	63.5[16,19]	34.4	...	...	...	...	...	...	1,005	50.7	205	10.4
Tanzania	1991	13,123	40.0	87.8[10]	46.0	48.9	43.2	...	...	...	...	10,540	80.3	614[11]	4.7[11]
Thailand	1994[18,60]	31,050	44.5	74.4[23]	52.6	58.9	46.4	31.2	40.3	19.5	9.1	13,972[61]	45.0[61]	4,779	15.4
Togo	1991	1,432	36.2	58.8[10]	40.0	51.8	28.5	70.3[27]	10.4[27]	11.3[27]	8.0[27]	991	69.2	161[11]	11.2[11]
Tonga	1990	32.0	33.0	57.0	33.6	45.2	22.0	33.7	45.4	16.8	4.1	11.7	36.5	5.1	15.8
Trinidad and Tobago	1993	505	37.0	63.2	40.5	50.5	30.2	18.3	77.4	3.1	1.2	51	10.0	77	15.2
Tunisia	1989	2,361	20.9	52.8	29.8	46.5	12.7	20.9	54.9	7.4	16.8	510	21.6	418	17.7
Turkey	1993[18]	20,997	30.8	57.2	35.3	48.5	21.9	27.6	41.5	27.7	3.2	8,437	40.2	3,164	15.1
Turkmenistan	1992	1,582	...	78.3[16]	41.5	...	...	...	...	...	...	695	43.9	154	9.7
Tuvalu	1991	5.9	51.3[41]	85.5	65.3	...	...	0.3[41]	22.2[41]	—77.5[41]—		4.2	68.0	0.1	2.0
Uganda	1991	8,365	40.8	67.3[10]	43.6	52.2	35.2	...	...	...	...	6,724	80.4	478[11]	5.7[11]
Ukraine	1994	22,270	...	...	43.5	...	...	...	...	...	...	4,821	21.6	6,249	28.1
United Arab Emirates	1990	690	10.4[25]	69.0[25]	47.0[25]	67.6[25]	12.9[25]	6.8[14]	92.7[14]	0.1[14]	0.5[14]	43	6.3	94	13.6
United Kingdom	1993	28,271	43.8	76.2	49.4	56.8	42.3	11.2	76.7	0.5	11.6	522	1.8	5,775	20.4
United States	1994[18]	131,056	46.0	76.2	51.3	57.0	45.8	8.3	91.0	0.1	0.5	3,862	2.9	23,628	18.0
Uruguay	1992	1,259	42.4	68.3[40]	45.0	55.4	35.9	22.9	72.3	2.3	2.5	56	4.5	280	22.2
Uzbekistan	1994	8,235	...	...	37.3	...	...	...	...	...	...	3,754	45.6	1,225	14.9
Vanuatu	1989	67.0	46.3	85.0	47.0	49.0	44.9	...	...	...	...	49.8	74.4	1.0	1.5
Venezuela	1993[18]	7,546	31.2	60.0	36.3	49.5	22.8	30.2	61.8	1.7	6.3	750	9.9	1,203	15.9
Vietnam	1989	30,521	51.7	79.9	47.4	47.0	47.7	...	...	...	...	20,471	67.1	3,390	11.1
Virgin Islands (U.S.)	1990[18]	47.4	47.8	70.3	46.6	50.3	43.1	7.6	85.5	0.2	6.7	0.6	1.2	3.7	7.8
West Bank	1993	218	11.5	40.2[23]	20.1	35.4	4.7	...	...	...	...	41.0	18.8	28.1[33]	12.9[33]
Western Sahara	...	...	...	...	...	...	...	...	...	...	...	...	...	...	...
Western Samoa	1986	45.6	18.8	48.6[27]	29.0	44.5	11.6	21.1[27]	43.5[27]	35.0[27]	0.4[27]	29.0	63.6	2.4	5.4
Yemen	1988	3,029	31.6	52.6	26.4	36.8	16.4	...	...	...	...	2,152	71.1	129	4.3
Yugoslavia	1994	3,139	43.4	58.7[23,63]	29.9	...	...	...	...	...	...	116	3.7	947	30.2
Zaire	1991	13,848	35.2	64.2[10]	36.1	47.2	25.2	...	...	...	...	9,021	65.1	2,200[11]	15.9[11]
Zambia	1991	2,928	29.6	52.6[10]	33.4	47.4	19.6	22.9[14]	42.5[14]	3.6[14]	31.0[14]	2,010	68.6	333[11]	11.4[11]
Zimbabwe	1992	3,601	39.6	63.4	34.6	42.8	26.7	24.1	43.9	9.2	22.8	2,110[65]	64.7[65]	179[65]	5.5[65]

[1]Services includes finance, real estate and public administration, defense. [2]Unemployed, not previously employed only. [3]Includes emigrant workers (352,000). [4]Ages 15–59 (male) and 15–54 (female). [5]State sector only. [6]Includes nonagricultural private sector (241,000) and unemployed (261,000). [7]Services includes public administration, defense. [8]Ages 16–64. [9]Unemployed only. [10]Over age 10. [11]Manufacturing; mining, quarrying; public utilities includes construction. [12]Services includes transportation, communications; trade, hotels, restaurants; finance, real estate; and public administration, defense. [13]1991. [14]1980. [15]Includes unemployed, not previously employed. [16]Ages 16–59 (male) and 16–54 (female). [17]Mostly unemployed. [18]Excludes all or some classes or elements of the military. [19]1993. [20]1990. [21]Includes unemployed. [22]1982. [23]Over age 15. [24]1992. [25]1988. [26]Over age 12. [27]1981. [28]Republic of Cyprus only. [29]1993 population economically active for Turkish Republic of Northern Cyprus is 75,947. [30]Mostly unemployed, not previously employed. [31]1989. [32]1984. [33]Other includes public utilities and finance, real estate. [34]Ages 15–65. [35]Excludes

construction		transportation, communications		trade, hotels, restaurants		finance, real estate		public administration, defense		services		other		country
number ('000)	% of econ. active	number ('000)	% of econ. active	number ('000)	% of econ. active	number ('000)	% of econ. active	number ('000)	% of econ. active	number ('000)	% of econ. active	number ('000)	% of econ. active	
546	1.8	1,112	3.6	7,417	24.1	120	0.4	7	7	4,902[7]	15.9[7]	2,009[17]	6.5[17]	Nigeria
5.8	21.7	1.4	5.3	5.3	19.8	1.0	3.8	1.4	5.3	4.5	16.9	0.6[9]	2.3[9]	Northern Mariana Islands
126	5.9	168	7.8	360	16.7	163	7.6	150	7.0	650	30.2	573[30]	2.6[30]	Norway
52	8.0	26	4.0	23	3.6	1	0.2	7	7	110[7]	17.1[7]	—	—	Oman
2,314	6.7	1,843	5.3	4,423	12.7	273	0.8	7	7	4,631[7]	13.3[7]	1,534[30]	4.4[30]	Pakistan
0.9	14.2	0.4	6.6	1.1	18.7	0.2	2.9	0.8	13.7	1.6	26.1	0.5[9]	7.8[9]	Palau
58	6.2	63	6.8	187	19.9	47	5.0	7	7	246[7]	26.2[7]	41[30]	4.4[30]	Panama
22	2.9	1.7	2.4	25	3.4	4	0.6	7	7	77[7]	10.5[7]	2	0.2	Papua New Guinea
70	6.7	31	2.9	86	8.3	18	1.7	7	7	174[7]	16.8[7]	86[15]	8.3[15]	Paraguay
308	3.7	364	4.4	1,352	16.3	197	2.4	7	7	2,287[7]	27.6[7]	—	—	Peru
1,187	4.3	1,402	5.1	3,563	13.0	494	1.8	7	7	4,480[7]	16.3[7]	2,325[17]	8.5[17]	Philippines
1,160[19]	6.7[19]	921[19]	5.3[19]	2,028[19]	11.7[19]	248[19]	1.4[19]	331[19]	1.9[19]	3,756[19]	21.6[19]	586[19,30]	3.4[19,30]	Poland
384	8.2	216	4.6	923	19.6	312	6.6	7	7	1,137[7]	24.1[7]	42[2]	0.9[2]	Portugal
84	6.8	42	3.4	250	20.4	34	2.8	7	7	550[7]	44.8[7]	7	0.6	Puerto Rico
64.2	22.0	11.9	4.1	34.2	11.7	6.2	2.1	7	7	149.6[7]	51.1[7]	—	—	Qatar
17	7.1	7	3.1	18	7.7	3	1.3	7	7	79[7]	33.9[7]	87[17]	37.4[17]	Réunion
583	5.6	634	6.1	779	7.4	306	2.9	7	7	1,244[7]	11.9[7]	486[30]	4.6[30]	Romania
7,050	9.9	5,300	7.5	6,450	9.1	3,640	5.1	1,450	2.0	13,590	19.1	3,957[21]	5.6[21]	Russia
11	11	12	12	12	12	12	12	12	12	207[12]	5.7[12]	—	—	Rwanda
0.4	2.5	0.3	1.6	1.3	7.3	0.8	4.7	1.0	5.7	2.9	17.0	2.2[17]	12.8[17]	St. Kitts and Nevis
5.0	9.3	2.7	5.0	11.1	20.8	1.9	3.6	7	7	9.2[7]	17.2[7]	4.3	8.2	St. Lucia
3.5	8.5	2.3	5.5	6.5	15.7	1.4	3.4	7	7	7.7[7]	18.5[7]	8.3[9]	20.0[9]	St. Vincent
1.2	8.0	0.3	1.9	2.5	16.8	0.4	2.6	3.6	24.4	1.2	8.3	0.6[9]	4.1[9]	San Marino
2.9	8.1	2.2	6.2	4.5	12.6	0.2	0.5	7	7	8.0[7]	22.5[7]	2.4	6.7	São Tomé and Príncipe
1,181	22.0	321	6.0	964	18.0	151	2.8	7	7	1,965[7]	36.6[7]	—	—	Saudi Arabia
11	11	12	12	12	12	12	12	12	12	477[12]	14.7[12]			Senegal
11	11	3.4	12.2	5.2	18.6	1.0	3.4	2.6	9.1	5.6	20.0	3.6[17]	12.6[17]	Seychelles
11	11	12	12	12	12	12	12	12	12	312[12]	20.4[12]	—	—	Sierra Leone
102	6.2	167	10.2	364	22.2	173	10.6	7	7	344[7]	21.0[7]	45[17]	2.7[17]	Singapore
194	7.7	172	6.8	266	10.6	21	0.9	85	3.4	385	15.4	486[21]	18.7[21]	Slovakia
42	4.4	53	5.6	103	10.9	44	4.7	7	7	177[7]	18.7[7]	71[17]	7.5[17]	Slovenia
1.0	3.3	1.7	5.8	3.4	11.5	1.1	3.9	4.3	14.6	6.8	23.1	—	—	Solomon Islands
11	11	12	12	12	12	12	12	12	12	604[12]	18.8[12]	—	—	Somalia
526	4.5	497	4.3	1,358	11.7	504	4.3	7	7	2,641[7]	22.7[7]	2,513[17]	21.6[17]	South Africa[58]
1,530	10.0	787	5.1	3,185	20.8	1,081	7.1	7	7	3,066[7]	20.0[7]	1,200[30]	7.8[30]	Spain
260	4.2	296	4.8	643	10.5	61	1.0	7	7	1,080[7]	17.6[7]	1,142[17]	18.6[17]	Sri Lanka
139	2.2	215	3.4	294	4.6	21	0.3	7	7	550[7]	8.7[7]	777[30]	12.3[30]	Sudan, The
5.0	4.7	6.6	6.2	13.6	12.7	3.2	3.0	7	7	41.3[7]	38.6[7]	22.4[17]	20.9[17]	Suriname
11	11	12	12	12	12	12	12	12	12	72[12]	20.1[12]	—	—	Swaziland
219	5.1	271	6.4	568	13.3	379	8.9	198	4.6	1,391	32.6	344[17]	8.1[17]	Sweden
254	6.6	225	5.8	781	20.3	562	14.6	7	7	979	25.4	158[17]	4.1[17]	Switzerland
341	9.8	167	4.8	378	10.9	25	0.7	7	7	951[7]	27.3[7]	235[9]	6.8[9]	Syria
1,003	10.9	469	5.1	1,919	20.8	534	5.8	317	3.4	1,347	14.6	165[9]	1.8[9]	Taiwan
105	5.3	63	3.2	112	5.6	37	37	21	1.1	326[37]	16.5[37]	146[17]	7.4[17]	Tajikistan
11	11	12	12	12	12	12	12	12	12	1,969[12]	15.0[12]	—	—	Tanzania
2,295	7.4	932	3.0	3,914	12.6	1	1	1	1	3,904[1]	12.6[1]	1,253[17]	4.0[17]	Thailand
11	11	12	12	12	12	12	12	12	12	280[12]	19.6[12]	—	—	Togo
1.3	3.9	1.8	5.7	2.6	8.1	1.2	3.7	7	7	7.1[7]	22.0[7]	1.3[9]	4.2[9]	Tonga
79	15.7	34	6.7	87	17.2	32	6.4	7	7	144[7]	28.5[7]	1	0.1	Trinidad and Tobago
248	10.5	96	4.1	217	9.2	15	0.7	7	7	444[7]	18.8[7]	412[17]	17.5[17]	Tunisia
1,137	5.4	954	4.5	2,477	11.8	471	2.2	7	7	2,699[7]	12.9[7]	1,659[9]	7.9[9]	Turkey
164	10.4	56	3.5	89	5.6	38	2.4	74	4.7	275	17.4	36[21]	2.3[21]	Turkmenistan
0.2	4.0	0.1	1.0	0.2	4.0	—	—	7	7	1.3[7]	22.0[7]	—	—	Tuvalu
11	11	12	12	12	12	12	12	12	12	1,163[12]	13.9[12]	—	—	Uganda
1,640	7.4	1,491	6.7	1,629	7.3	176	0.8	681	3.1	5,023	22.6	560[21]	2.5[21]	Ukraine
119	17.3	72	10.4	101	14.7	19	2.7	7	7	241[7]	35.0[7]	—	—	United Arab Emirates
1,679	5.9	1,626	5.8	5,031	17.8	3,210	11.4	7	7	7,214[7]	25.5[7]	3,214[17]	11.4[17]	United Kingdom
8,297	6.3	7,498	5.7	27,658[62]	21.1[62]	14,377	11.0	7	7	45,048[7,62]	34.4[7,62]	652[30]	0.5[30]	United States
86	6.8	68	5.4	224	17.7	68	5.4	7	7	446[7]	35.4[7]	32[30]	2.5[30]	Uruguay
550	6.7	330	4.0	501	6.1	29	0.4	90	1.1	1,690	20.5	66	0.8	Uzbekistan
1.3	1.9	1.0	1.5	2.7	4.1	0.6	1.0	7	7	7.9[7]	11.8[7]	2.6	3.8	Vanuatu
654	8.7	452	6.0	1,597	21.2	464	6.1	7	7	1,944[7]	25.8[7]	484[17]	6.4[17]	Venezuela
581	1.9	576	1.9	1,880	6.2	90	0.3	305	10.0	1,374	4.5	1,854[17]	6.1[17]	Vietnam
5.7	12.0	3.7	7.8	10.3	21.8	3.6	7.7	5.1	10.8	7.8	16.4	6.9	14.6	Virgin Islands (U.S.)
58.9	27.0	11.1	5.1	27.7	12.7	33	33	7	7	23.9[7]	11.0[7]	27.5[17,33]	12.6[17,33]	West Bank
...	...	...	...	...	...	...	...	...	...	...	...	...	...	Western Sahara
0.1	0.1	1.5	3.3	1.7	3.7	0.8	1.8	7	7	9.4[7]	20.7[7]	0.6	1.4	Western Samoa
178	5.9	90	3.0	84	2.8	4	0.1	7	7	391[7]	12.9[7]	—	—	Yemen
147	4.7	170	5.4	454[64]	14.5[64]	83	2.6	90	2.9	342	10.9	790[17]	25.2[17]	Yugoslavia
11	11	12	12	12	12	12	12	12	12	2,627[12]	19.0[12]	—	—	Zaire
11	11	12	12	12	12	12	12	12	12	585[12]	20.0[12]	—	—	Zambia
51[65]	1.6[65]	76[65]	2.3[65]	128[65]	3.9[65]	24[65]	0.7[65]	7	7	397[7,65]	12.2[7,65]	277[17,65]	8.5[17,65]	Zimbabwe

Alderney and Sark. [36]Data are for the economically active population ages 15–64 only. [37]Services includes finance, real estate. [38]Ages 16–69. [39]1977. [40]Ages 14–64. [41]1979. [42]1986. [43]Excludes about 30,000 foreign border workers. [44]Includes unemployed, emigrant workers, and employees in private nonagricultural sector. [45]Includes unemployed, previously employed. [46]1983. [47]Island of Mauritius only. [48]Services includes transportation, communications; trade, hotels, restaurants; and finance, real estate. [49]Ages 16–59. [50]Ages 20–64. [51]Excludes nomadic population. [52]1992–93. [53]Citizens over age 10 involved in money-raising activities only. [54]1985–86. [55]Excludes domestic workers (private households), self-employed, and family workers. [56]Wage earners only. [57]Over age 14. [58]Excludes the former black independent states of Bophuthatswana, Ciskel, Transkel, and Venda. [59]Districts of Wanica and Paramaribo only. [60]February survey. [61]Includes seasonally inactive labour force (1,572,000). [62]Services includes hotels. [63]1995. [64]Includes arts and crafts. [65]1986–87.

Agriculture and land use

This table provides data on the structure of national agricultural sectors from the perspective of farms and farmland use. The data are taken mainly from national agricultural censuses and surveys, supplemented by reports of the United Nations Food and Agriculture Organization's (FAO's) *World Census of Agriculture.* Many of these national censuses, of course, are taken under guidelines established by the FAO for the *World Census of Agriculture* programs (the 1990 census is the fifth and will include national censuses taken during the decade 1986–95). It represents a cooperative effort by FAO member countries to collect agricultural data within a general framework that permits international harmonization of concepts and definitions; transfer of technical expertise; and increased effectiveness in the collection, analysis, publication, and policy-related use of such statistics. More than 100 countries participated in the 1990 census.

All agricultural statistics are subject to quality-control problems, including errors or biases arising from such factors as incomplete or inaccurate lists of holdings, ambiguous questions, respondents who inadvertently or willfully give inaccurate information, failure to record data for all parts of fragmented holdings, respondents' misunderstandings of the definitions of land use and cropping methods, or a failure to report livestock temporarily absent from the holding on public or common pasture land or in transit. Frequently, subjects studied, classificational schemes, and definitions vary from the FAO guidelines (economic planners need different information

about a commercial, high-technology, multicrop agricultural sector than they do for a family-subsistence, low-technology, one-crop sector). When a complete census of agriculture is impossible, a sample survey may be taken. This is a limited census of a predetermined number of carefully screened holdings. From these results, nationwide projections may be prepared.

With respect to the first section of the table, number and size of farms, many countries impose a minimum size limit for holdings that may be covered in their census reports, and this cutoff, if not sufficiently low, can result in a substantial undercount of smaller holdings; conversely Soviet-bloc nations formerly published statistics only on state collective or cooperative farms and excluded production from privately held plots of land, even though these often represented a significant fraction of agricultural output.

The land tenure statistics classify farms (a single parcel of land, or holding, or a group of holdings operated as a single farm) according to the rights under which the farmer holds the land or operates the enterprise represented by the farm. Owner-operated includes two types of ownership: outright ownership in which the holder has title and has the right to determine use and transfer of the land; and ownerlike possession in which the holder lacks the legal title but uses it under perpetual lease, hereditary tenure, or leases of 30 years or more with nominal, or no, rent. Farms classed as owner-operated are divided into individual and family, corporate or state, and socialized or collective proprietorships. Rented includes

Agriculture and land use

country	year	number of farms ('000)	average (ha)	under 1 ha	1–5 ha	5–10 ha	10–20 ha	20–50 ha	50–200 ha	over 200 ha	individual/ family	corporate/ state	socialized/ collective	rented (including share-croppers)	tribal/ communal	other[b]
Afghanistan	1994	126[1]	3.5[1]	44.8[1]	35.2[1]	20.0[1]					55.1[1]	—	—	25.1[1]	—	19.8[1]
Albania	1990	0.5[3]	1,182[2,3]								100.0[4]	—	—	—	...	...
Algeria	1987	899[6]	6.2[6]	1.1[6]	12.7[6]	15.8[6]	21.7[6]	25.6[6]	18.0[6]	5.1[6]	...	...	...	...	...	...
American Samoa	1990	1.1	2.9	44.7[8]	40.0[9]	13.8[10]		1.6[11]			93.9	...	—	2.2	—	3.9
Andorra	—	—	—													
Angola	1970–71	1,067	3.9	3.3	13.5	9.3	11.3	13.7	19.2	29.7	80.5	1.1	...	—	18.2	0.2
Antigua and Barbuda	1984	2.3	2.1	61.7	33.8	2.9	0.6	0.6	0.4	—	32.1[14]	22.9[14]		40.5[14]	—	4.5[14]
Argentina	1988	421	469	15.1		8.4	14.0[15]	12.0[16]	25.1	25.5	85.1[14]	—	...	8.3[14]	—	6.6[14]
Armenia	1993	243[18,19]	2[18]			...					...	...	...	...	...	...
Aruba	...	...	...								...	...	...	...	...	...
Australia	1994–95	150	3,710[7]	15.7					9.2[20]	75.1[21]	...	...	...	...	...	...
Austria	1993	267	26.4[26]	3.3[26]	32.2[26]	17.8[26]	20.0[26]	21.5[26]	4.6[26]	0.7[26]	38.9[26]	1.5[26]	...	59.5[26]	...	0.1[26]
Azerbaijan	1993	0.2[18,19]	39[18]								...	...	...	...	...	...
Bahamas, The	1994	1.8	8.5	43.6[27,28]	34.5[29]	9.7	6.2	2.3	3.7		25.7	...	—	20.1	39.7	14.5
Bahrain	1980	0.8	4.4	19.4	52.9	17.4	8.2	2.0	0.1		37.9	0.1	—	62.0	—	—
Bangladesh	1983–84	10,045	0.9	70.3	27.0[30]	2.5[31]	0.2[32]				62.8	...	...	1.4	...	35.8
Barbados	1989	17.2	95.8[35]	95.0[27]	3.9	0.3	0.2	0.1	0.3	0.2	76.2[14]	...	...	7.5[14]	16.3[14]	
Belarus	1994	7.7	18[18]								52.1	13.1	34.8	...	—	—
Belgium	1991	84	16.5	13.9	24.1	14.8	19.1	22.1	6.0		33.4[14]	...	...	65.7[14]	—	0.9[14]
Belize	1996	11.0[37]	26.7[17]	9.3[37]	15.2[37]	56.3[37]			19.1[37]		43.6[17]	56.4[17]	—	...	...	...
Benin	1992	408	...	...	...	...	...	...	...	...	...	...	...	...	...	...
Bermuda	1990	0.08[38]	3.1[38]	...	...	...	...	...	...	...	...	...	...	...	...	...
Bhutan	1984	160	0.8	51.3[38,39]	42.9[9,39]	5.8[39,40]					...	...	...	...	...	...
Bolivia	1996	519	72.1	27.1	41.1	11.8	6.6	6.0	4.8	2.7	78.0	...	...	2.0	4.1	15.9
Bosnia and Herzegovina[18]	1981	540	...	33.4	48.9	13.7	2.3	0.6			100.0	—	—	—	—	—
Botswana	1990	90.3[41]	5.0	9.1	56.1	26.9	7.9				—	0.4	—	—	99.6	—
Brazil	1985	5,835	64.5	11.1	28.6	13.2	14.0	15.6	12.4	4.9	63.2	—	...	17.9	—	18.4[43]
Brunei	1964	6.3	2.6	44.1[8]	40.4[9]	15.5[40]					52.3	1.0	—	22.0	—	24.7
Bulgaria	1991	2.2[45,46]	2,467[45,46]	...	...	...	...	...	...	...	19.0[47]	40.0[47]	41.0[47,48]	...	...	...
Burkina Faso	1984	1,860	4.8	...	...	...	...	...	...	...	...	...	...	...	...	...
Burundi	1983	...	...	...	...	...	...	...	...	...	...	...	...	...	...	...
Cambodia	1962[49]	840	3.6	30.7	54.9	10.4	3.4	0.6			...	...	...	...	...	...
Cameroon	1973	926	1.6	42.7	53.8	3.2	0.3	—			2.4	...	...	5.2	59.5	32.9
Canada	1996	280[50]	242[50]	1.4[8]	3.5[9]	24.2[51]		70.9[52]			...	63.5[14]		36.5[14]	...	...
Cape Verde	1988	32.2	...	...	...	...	...	...	...	...	...	...	...	...	...	...
Central African Republic	1980	283[17]	1.7[17]	32.2[17]	65.2[17]	2.5[17]	0.8		—	—	0.3[14]	...	...	0.1[14]	98.6[14]	1.2[14]
Chad	1973	366	2.6	19.7	69.5	10.0	0.8				...	...	...	...	...	...
Chile	1983–84	306[55]	94.1[55]	16.0[55]	32.5[55]	13.4[55]	12.3[55]	11.8[55]	9.2[55]	4.8[55]	84.0			7.2	8.8	
China	1987	1,650[56]	...	...	...	...	...	...	...	...	...	10.0[57]	90.0[57]	...	...	...
Colombia	1988	1,548	26.3[57]	19.2[27]	32.4	15.0	11.8	10.8	8.8	2.0	77.6	...	...	5.6	3.7	13.1
Comoros	1982	...	...	...	...	...	...	...	...	...	...	...	...	...	...	...
Congo	1986	143[6]	1.4[6]	37.3[6]	62.2[6]	0.5[6]					91.7[14]	8.3[14]	...	0.1	—	0.3
Costa Rica	1973	82	38.3	23.3	25.5	11.2	10.8	15.2	10.7	3.3	97.9	1.7	...	...	—	0.3
Côte d'Ivoire	1975	550	5.0	9.5	54.4	24.9	9.4	1.7	0.1	—	...	...	...	...	...	...
Croatia[58]	1981	569	...	30.7	51.1	14.7	2.3	0.3			100.0	—	—	—	—	—
Cuba	1988	1.8[46]	1,047[46]	...	...	...	...	...	...	...	...	...	...	...	...	...
Cyprus	1985	48.0	3.8	24.4	56.8	15.0	2.9	0.9			79.0			9.4	—	11.6[59]
Czech Republic[60]	1980	1,391	8.1	89.9[61]	9.9[62]			0.2[63]			49.0[64]	3.0[64]	48.0[48,64]	—	—	—
Denmark	1994[65]	69.3	35.9[50]	17.8		22.6	35.9	23.7			64.4[3]			35.6[3]		
Djibouti	1988–89	1.2	0.4	c. 100							...	...	...	...	...	...
Dominica	1986–88	1.9	...	89[66]		9[67]		2			33	...	...	15	...	52
Dominican Republic	1981	385	6.3	16.0	65.7	8.5	5.4	2.6	1.5	0.3	53.2	18.5	4.5	1.6	—	17.4
Ecuador[17]	1991	517	15.4	27.8	38.8	10.6	8.0	8.2	5.6	0.9	70.3	0.3	...	7.7	7.4	14.3
Egypt	1990	3,896	0.7[38]	95.8[68]	2.3[69]	1.9[70]					...	...	...	...	...	...
El Salvador	1970–71	271	5.4	48.9	37.9	5.8	3.4	2.6	1.2	0.2	41.5	...	...	28.2	6.3	24.1

sharecropping; communal/tribal includes types of customary or traditional arrangements in which title or goods do not change hands. "Other" usually includes farms operated on several parcels of land and held under multiple forms of tenure.

Statistics on types of farms by commodities produced refer to FAO categories. The terms "mainly crops" and "mainly livestock" indicate that more than half of the for-sale production was that indicated.

The section on technology provides some measures of the role modern technology plays in the farm activities of each country (although, of course, irrigation may employ technology developed in ancient times). Ratios referred to area mean area of "arable" (cultivated and cultivable) land, roughly "cropland," less area of permanent crops (see below).

The classification of farmland by economic use is also subject to differing treatment internationally. For purposes of this table, "cropland" comprises: (1) land under temporary crops (those requiring replanting after each harvest), (2) land under permanent crops (those *not* requiring replanting, including tree, bush and shrub, and vine crops), and (3) land temporarily (less than five years) fallow (unused, but capable of being returned to cultivation with no special preparation). "Meadows and pastures" includes land (both permanent and temporary use) whose principal purpose is the raising of animal fodder or forage. "Woodland and forest" includes both natural and planted tracts of timber (*e.g.*, plantings of Christmas trees),

whether harvested or not. "Other" comprises: (1) mixed and multiple use lands, (2) residue of farmland holdings not classifiable according to categories listed above (including areas of farm buildings, roads, ornamental gardens, watercourses and flooded land, wasteland, etc.), (3) land not classified by respondents in census, or (4) detail not distinguishable as one of the categories above by reason of its summarization in a published source. When "cropland" is indicated to compose 100 percent of farmland, it should usually be understood to mean only that woodland, pasture, etc., were not part of the published data, rather than that those classes of land use do not exist.

Measurements of area are given in hectares (ha; 1 hectare is equal to 2.471 acres). A kilogram (kg) is equal to 2.205 pounds (1 kg/ha = 0.89 lb/ac). The following notes further define the column headings:
a. All properties used wholly or partly for agricultural production. A property need not have agricultural land to be considered a farm; piggeries, hatcheries, and poultry batteries are farms because they engage in agricultural production, *i.e.*, raise livestock and produce livestock products.
b. All forms of tenure not included in the preceding categories. Includes land operated by schools, religious bodies, squatters, seasonally by nomads, and built-on, waste, and similar types of alienation.
... Not available, or no agricultural census or survey ever taken.
—None, less than half the smallest unit shown, or not applicable.

mainly crops	mainly live-stock	mixed/ other	tractors (per 1,000 ha)	electricity (% of farms having)	irrigation (% of land irrig.)	artificial fertilizer (kg/ha)	total ('000 ha)	% of total land area	permanent crops	temporary crops	fallow	total cropland	meadows and pastures	woodland and forest	other	country
...	51.1[5]	...	0.1	...	38	7	38,054[2]	58.4[2]	1.8	46.3	51.9	19.9	75.4	4.8	—	Afghanistan
48.9[5]	51.1[5]	—	15.7	...	59	158	1,126[2]	41.1[2]	17.8	—82.2—		24.0	15.0[4]	36.0[4]	25.0[4]	Albania
12.5	...	—	12.5	...	8	13	39,640	16.6	6.9[7]	55.2[7]	37.9[7]	20.4[7]	77.2[7]	...	2.4[7]	Algeria
55.7[5]	44.3[5]	—	15	38.5	...	...	3.2	16.4	—88.7—		11.3	71.4	5.3	...	23.3	American Samoa
...	...	...	...	...	...	...	...	2.0	...	...	...	2.2	55.6	22.2	20.0	Andorra
...	...	...	3.4	...	89[12]	7	3,500[13]	2.8[13]	36.8	63.2	—	1.7	82.0	...	16.2	Angola
32.9	44.1	23.0	30.0	...	...	...	2.5	9.0	26.0	57.1	16.9	62.6	36.0	—1.4—		Antigua and Barbuda
10.6[17]	78.9[17]	10.5[17]	11.2	...	7	4	177,437	64.8	4.8	71.5	23.7	15.4	56.4	21.3	6.9	Argentina
...	...	...	33.4	...	59	...	1,261[2]	44.7[2]	12.6	84.3	3.1	30.8	61.5	...	7.7	Armenia
...	...	...	...	...	...	...	...	...	...	...	...	...	...	...	...	Aruba
26.7[22]	58.9	14.4[23]	6.8	...	5	28	469,100[24]	61.1[24]	1.1	—98.9—		3.8	6.6	...	89.6[25]	Australia
59.8[26]	—	40.2[26]	242	...	0.3	201	7,530	91.0	5.3	93.5	1.2	20.0	26.0	43.0	11.0	Austria
...	...	...	20.6	...	62	...	4,200[2]	48.5[2]	28.9	63.9	7.2	37.2	53.5	...	9.3	Azerbaijan
...	...	...	9.2	...	10[12]	...	20.3	2.0	50.0	17.8	32.2	38.5	11.0	28.3	22.0	Bahamas, The
...	...	...	...	21.3	100	333	3.5	5.2	50.7	49.3	...	45.9	...	...	54.1	Bahrain
91.3[33]	8.7[33]	—	0.6	...	33	98	9,137[34]	70.2[34]	—88.2[34]—		11.8[34]	89.5[34]	—10.5[34]—			Bangladesh
...	...	...	38.0	...	...	91	21.6	50.2	3.0	82.9	14.1	78.7	8.9	...	11.8	Barbados
79.1	19.4	1.5	20.2	...	2	...	9,346	45.0	...	...	...	65.3	—34.7—			Belarus
...	2.5[36]	...	145.3	...	0.1	496	1,392	45.6	1.2	98.4	0.4	51.9	45.2	0.5	2.4	Belgium
...	...	...	25.6	...	4	88	233[17]	10.0[17]	13.1[17]	81.1[17]	5.8[17]	36.5[17]	15.9[17]	36.1[17]	11.6[17]	Belize
...	...	...	0.1	...	0.7	2	3,300	29.3	...	...	...	100.0	—	—	—	Benin
...	...	...	12.5	...	...	...	2.4	4.4	18.6	72.9	8.5	91.1	8.9	—	—	Bermuda
...	...	...	...	...	30	1	156	3.4	11.7	—88.3—		100.0	—	—	...	Bhutan
...	...	...	2.5	...	8	3	22,670	20.6	3.6	96.4	—	5.0	47.4	41.6	6.0	Bolivia
...	...	...	214	...	0.3	...	2,525[26]	49.4[26]	8.9[26]	70.9[26]	20.2[26]	44.2[26]	55.4[26]	...	0.4[26]	Bosnia and Herzegovina[18]
13.6[38]	27.9[38]	58.5[38]	14.3	...	0.5	1	343[42]	5.9[42]	—	100.0[42]	—	83.5[42]	—	—	—	Botswana
80.0[44]	16.2[44]	3.8[44]	17.5	4.1[44]	7	43	376,287	44.5	18.2[42]	66.9[42]	14.9[42]	15.8[42]	47.8[42]	24.2[42]	12.2[42]	Brazil
...	...	...	24.0	...	33	57	16.4	2.8	78.0	22.0	—	54.8	0.1	16.4	28.7	Brunei
46.8[47]	53.2[47]	—	11.7	...	30	195	6,018[2]	54.4[2]	6.3[47]	—93.7[47]—		75.4[47]	24.6[47]	—	—	Bulgaria
...	...	...	0.04	...	0.6	6	9,565[2]	35.0[2]	...	...	...	...	...	...	...	Burkina Faso
...	...	...	0.1	...	1.2	4	2,170[2]	84.5[2]	—73.8—		26.2	56.7	37.7	5.6	...	Burundi
...	...	...	0.6	...	4	1	2,984	16.5	94.9	3.5	1.6	96.1	—	3.9	...	Cambodia
...	...	...	0.1	...	0.3	6[3]	1,490	3.3	...	...	...	100.0	—	—	—	Cameroon
43.9	42.9	13.2	16.3	...	1.6	47	67,754	7.3	20.8[53]	—80.9—		19.1	61.1	6.1	—32.7—		Canada
...	...	...	0.4	...	7	—	41	10.2	20.8[53]	79.1[53]	...	100.0[53]	—	—	—	Cape Verde
...	...	...	0.1	...	...	2	491	0.8	11.8	88.2	—	100.0	—	—	—	Central African Republic
...	...	...	0.05	...	0.4	2	23,877[54]	45.8[54]	50.0[54]	—50.0[54]—		23.7[54]	76.3[54]	—	—	Chad
...	...	...	10.5	...	32	69	8,746[19]	11.7[19]	26.5[19]	59.5[19]	14.0[19]	15.3[19]	52.4[19]	...	32.3[19]	Chile
...	...	...	8.0	...	54	261	166,902	17.4	4.1	—95.9—		100.0	—	—	—	China
...	...	...	9.3	...	13	101	36,034	34.7	47.3	34.6	18.1	14.7	48.5	14.0	22.8	Colombia
...	...	...	...	...	...	...	100	44.8	56.4	—43.6—		100.0	—	—	—	Comoros
6.2[5]	93.8[5]	—	4.9	...	0.7	3	226	0.7	14.8	85.2	—	100.0	—	—	—	Congo
...	...	...	24.6	...	42	203	2,870	56.2	42.2	57.8	—	15.7	49.9	22.9	11.4	Costa Rica
...	...	...	1.5	...	3	11	2,753	8.6	65.9	34.1	—	100.0	—	—	—	Côte d'Ivoire
...	...	...	3.4	...	0.3	...	3,220	57.0	8.8	81.8	9.4	50.4	48.5	...	1.1	Croatia[58]
...	...	...	30.0	...	35	199	8,679	78.3	...	...	...	33.9	32.1	31.9	2.1	Cuba
51.5[5,47]	37.0[5,47]	11.5[5,47]	125	...	35	144	210	35.6	34.7	54.3	11.0	74.9	—	—25.1—		Cyprus
45.0[5,64]	55.0[5,64]	...	24.6[64]	100.0	0.8	314	4,282[64]	54.3[64]	2.9[64]	—97.1[64]—		74.7[64]	20.4[64]	—4.9[64]—		Czech Republic[60]
50.0	31.9	18.1	61.4	...	17	255	2,691	62.4	...	92.7	7.3	71.4	28.6	...	...	Denmark
...	...	...	...	...	...	...	1	0.5	...	6.8	...	100.0	—	—	—	Djibouti
...	...	...	12.9	...	...	259	19[2]	25.3[2]	...	...	...	...	...	...	...	Dominica
44.0	56.0	—	2.4	60.0	23	50	2,412	49.8	38.0	40.2	21.8	34.1	51.6	13.0	0.9	Dominican Republic
67.8	12.4	19.8	5.5	...	34	29	7,954[32]	30.5[32]	50.1[32]	20.7[32]	29.2[32]	34.7[32]	62.0[32]	—3.2[32]—		Ecuador[17]
...	...	...	24.9	...	132	384	5,216[2,4]	5.2[2,4]	7.3[4]	92.7[4]	...	100.0[4]	—	—	—	Egypt
95.3	4.7	—	6.1	...	21	106	1,340[2]	64.7[2]	25.1	58.6	16.4	44.9	38.2	11.6	5.3	El Salvador

Agriculture and land use (continued)

country	farms (latest census of agriculture)[a]															
	year	number of farms ('000)	size of holding								tenure (% of farms)					
			average (ha)	size class (%)							owner-operated			rented (including share-croppers)	tribal/ com-munal	other[b]
				under 1 ha	1–5 ha	5–10 ha	10–20 ha	20–50 ha	50–200 ha	over 200 ha	individual/ family	corporate/ state	socialized/ collective			
Equatorial Guinea	...	...	...	...	...	...	...	...	...	...	...	...	...	...	...	...
Eritrea[71]	—	—	...	...	...	...	...	...	...	...	...	...	...	...	...	...
Estonia[18]	1994	10.4	...	—8.0[4]—		12.8[4]	27.8[4]	42.2[4]	—9.2[4]—		93.5[4]	—6.5[4]—		...	...	...
Ethiopia[71]	1994–95[72]	6,092[72]	1.3[72]	49.9[33]	46.5[33]	3.4[33]	0.2[33]				98.4[33]	1.6[33]		...	...	...
Faroe Islands	...	...	...	...	...	...	...	...	...	...	...	...	...	...	...	...
Fiji	1991	95	4.2[73]	43.3	31.4	13.3	6.6	3.3	1.5[20]	0.6[21]	15.8	0.4	—	49.5	32.2	2.1
Finland	1994[75]	190	12.8[26]	—	34.2	20.8	22.7	19.2	—3.1—		—84.5—			15.5	—	—
France	1994	801[4]	26.6[42]	—37.3—			27.8[76]	10.7[77]	—24.1—		45.0[36]			55.0[36]	—	—
French Guiana	1989	4.5	4.6	16.5	73.6	6.0	1.5	—2.4—			17.0[2]			57.2[2]	—	25.8[2]
French Polynesia	1987	5.6	...	37.7			—62.3—				36.5			6.3	...	57.1
Gabon	1975	71	1.0	68.0	—32.0—		—	—	—	—	81.8			0.3	5.3	12.5
Gambia, The	1989–90	...	...	...	...	...	...	...	...	...	...	...	...	...	...	...
Gaza Strip	1968	...	...	...	...	...	...	...	...	...	...	...	...	...	...	...
Georgia	1990	17.0[18, 19]	...	...	...	...	...	...	...	...	...	...	...	...	...	...
Germany	1994[2, 75]	578	28.0[19]	12.6[66]	16.7[79]	16.2	18.5	24.0	—12.0—		89.1			10.9	...	...
Ghana	1970	805	3.2	36.6	48.7	9.0	3.9	1.8	—	—	...	...	...	...	...	...
Gibraltar	—	—	...	...	...	...	...	...	...	...	...	...	...	...	...	...
Greece	1991	862	0.8	25.7[80]	50.6	14.4	6.2	—2.0—			79.9			18.7	...	1.4
Greenland	—	...	...	...	...	...	...	...	...	...	...	...	...	...	...	...
Grenada	1995	8	1.7	88.3[66]	6.9[81]	3.3[82]	0.7	0.4[83]	—0.3[84]—		—73.2—			14.1	—	12.7
Guadeloupe	1988–89	17	2.8	32.1	58.3	7.0	1.6	—0.9—			57.7[2, 14]		—	18.8[2, 14]	—	23.5[2, 14]
Guam	1992	0.2	4.0	58.8[8]	17.69	—19.6[10]—		—4.0[11]—			53.8			30.1	—	16.1[85]
Guatemala	1979	600	6.8	39.7[86]	49.8[87]	—8.2[88]—			—2.2[89]—		—74.0[90]—			6.3[90]	5.8[90]	13.9[90]
Guernsey	1993	0.089	16.2[50]	6.7[17]	24.0[17]	23.1[17]	—46.1[17]—				32.4[3, 14]		—	67.6[3, 14]	—	—
Guinea	1989[2]	431	2.4[56]	...	...	...	...	...	...	...	...	...	...	...	...	...
Guinea-Bissau	1988	84	3.0[1]	13.4[1]	73.3[1]	10.0[1]	3.0[1]	0.3[1]	—	—	...	...	...	...	...	...
Guyana	1993	25[91]	...	—90.0—			—10.0—		—	—	...	90.0	...	...	...	10.9
Haiti	1987	667	1.4[57]	61.8	36.6	1.5	0.1	—	—	—	93.4			5.9	—	0.7
Honduras	1992–93	318	13.5	25.2	46.5	11.0	7.2	6.3	3.1	0.6	39.9	23.1	—	16.6	—	20.4
Hong Kong	1986	11	0.3	97.5	2.3	0.1	—0.1—				—9.0—			77.0	—	14.0
Hungary	1995	3.2[4, 48]	...	90[50]	—9.9[50]—				—0.1[50]—		38.0[47]	7.0[47]	55.0[48]	—	—	—
Iceland	1981	7.0	...	15.7	9.3	11.7	23.7	35.8	—3.7—		...	...	...	...	...	...
India	1990–91	105,300	1.6	59.0	32.2	7.2	—1.6—				94.1	—	—	0.5	—	5.4
Indonesia	1993	21,737	1.0	70.8	27.8	1.2	—0.2—				74.8[45]	—6	—6	3.2[6]	—6	22.1[6]
Iran	1988	3,326	...	26.8	39.3	17.1	10.9	4.8	1.0	0.1	...	...	...	...	...	...
Iraq	1979	470	13.3	25.9[93]	27.6[94]	23.2[95]	11.5[96]	9.4	1.9[97]	0.5[98]	52.5[12]	—	—	40.9[12]	—	6.6[12]
Ireland	1991	171	26.0	0.9	10.3	14.1	28.3	34.8	11.1	0.4	95.9	0.4	—	3.7	—	—
Isle of Man	1992	0.8	59.7	—26.7[99]—			16.2[100]	17.0[83]	12.4[101]	27.9[102]	72.4[45]			27.6[45]	—	—
Israel	1981	52	11.3	26.5	57.6	8.3	4.0	2.0	—1.8—		84.0		1.4	—	—	14.6
Italy	1990	2,941	7.5[34]	33.0[34]	43.0[34]	11.7[34]	6.7[34]	3.8[34]	—1.8[34]—		88.0			3.1	—	8.9
Jamaica	1978–79	184	2.9	32.5[103]	60.7[104]	4.8[82]	0.9	0.4[83]	0.3[101]	0.4[102]	99.5[35]	0.2[35]		—	—	0.3[35]
Japan	1994	2,787	1.5	57.4	40.7	—1.9—					99.7[26]	—0.2[26]—		—	—	0.1[26]
Jersey	1990	0.6	11.1	—45.0[105]—		16.4[106]	19.7[107]	—19.0[108]—			31.4[38]			68.6[38]	...	—
Jordan	1983	57	6.3	25.3	44.6	15.6	8.6	4.5	1.3	0.1	80.5	—	—	13.1	0.3	6.1
Kazakstan	1993	8.5[18, 19]	412[18, 19]	...	...	...	...	...	...	...	...	...	...	...	...	...
Kenya	1976–79[112]	2,750	2.5	65.5	27.3	2.7[113]	—4.4[114]—				...	...	...	...	...	...
Kiribati	...	...	...	...	...	...	...	...	...	...	...	...	...	...	...	...
Korea, North	...	...	...	...	...	...	...	...	...	...	...	...	...	...	...	...
Korea, South	1994[2]	1,558[91]	3.7[91]	59.4[27]	25.4[44]	—40.6—					82.5[26, 43]	—	—	17.4[26, 44]	—	0.1[26, 44]
Kuwait	1992–93	2.3[7]	2.4[115]	48.6[44]	25.4[44]	10.2[44]	8.7[44]	4.0[44]	3.1[44]	—	95.3[7]			—	—	4.7[7]
Kyrgyzstan	1993	8.6[18, 19]	44[18, 19]	...	...	...	...	...	...	...	...	...	...	...	...	...
Laos	1983	...	...	...	...	...	...	...	...	...	...	...	...	...	...	...
Latvia	1993	64.3[18, 47]	16.5[18, 19]	...	...	...	...	...	...	...	64.0[47]	2.0[47]	17.0[47, 48]	...	...	17.0[47]
Lebanon	1970	143	4.3	47.7	—44.5—		—6.5—		1.2	0.1	...	...	...	...	...	...
Lesotho	1989–90	229	1.5	46.8	49.6	—3.6—			—	—	87.0			10.0	...	3.0
Liberia	1971[117]	122	3.0	52.8	31.0	12.0	—3.7—		—0.5—		40.0[14]		—	—	43.3[14]	16.7[14]
Libya	1987	176	14.0	8.2	37.5	24.7	17.3	9.8	—2.5—		...	...	...	...	...	...
Liechtenstein	1990	0.42	8.7	33.8	25.7	10.3	10.8	18.7	—0.7—		31.7			24.5	—	43.8
Lithuania	1994	5.9[18, 19]	161[18, 19]	...	...	...	...	...	...	...	—57.2[4]—			—42.8[4]—		
Luxembourg	1995	3.2	40	14.1	10.9	8.9	8.0	20.8	—37.3—		50.1[26]			49.4[26]	...	0.5[26]
Macau	—	...	...	...	...	...	...	...	...	...	...	...	...	...	...	...
Macedonia[58]	1981	176	...	44.7	43.0	6.7	1.2	—0.2—			100.0	—	—	—	—	—
Madagascar	1984–85	1,453	1.3	54.8	44.2	1.0	0.2	0.1	—0.1—		—87.3[14]—			4.9[14]	—	7.4[14]
Malawi	1980–81[112]	1,136	1.2	54.9	40.1[120]	—5.0[121]—					...	...	...	...	...	...
Malaysia	1980[112, 122]	920	2.2	...	...	...	...	...	...	...	53.2[44]	18.2[44]		19.6[44]	—	9.0[44]
Maldives	1985	...	...	...	...	...	...	...	...	...	...	...	...	...	...	...
Mali	1982–83	562	4.0	20.1	54.1	17.4	—8.4—				96.8[124]	3.2	—	70.4	—	13.6[59]
Malta	1982–83	12	1.1	67.8	30.0	2.0	—0.2—				16.0	—	—	70.4	—	13.6[59]
Marshall Islands	...	...	...	...	...	...	...	...	...	...	...	...	...	...	...	...
Martinique[2]	1988–89	16.0	2.3	63.6	29.2	4.1	1.6	—1.5—			65.3[14]			22.5[14]	...	12.2[14]
Mauritania	1984–85	100	2.0	49.2	41.0[30]	7.0[82]	2.0	0.5[83]	—0.3[84]—		68.4			4.4	10.4	17.0
Mauritius	1980	32.5	1.1	61.3	36.2	1.9	0.3	0.2	—0.1—		95.8			4.2	—	—
Mayotte	1987	5.9[118]	1.7[109]	...	...	...	...	...	...	...	...	...	...	...	...	...
Mexico	1991	4,408[126]	50	23.5[44]	39.4[44]	21.1[44]	8.8[44]	2.7[44]	2.9[44]	1.5[44]	—95.8—			1.1	—	3.1
Micronesia	...	...	...	...	...	...	...	...	...	...	...	...	...	...	...	...
Moldova	1991	0.5[18, 19]	3[18, 19]	...	...	...	...	...	...	...	—	30.8	55.2	—	—	14.0
Monaco	...	...	...	...	...	...	...	...	...	...	...	...	...	...	...	...
Mongolia	1985	0.3	385,000	...	...	...	...	...	...	...	—	16.0	84.0	...	...	...
Morocco	1996	1,900[109]	3.9[109]	29.8[6]	44.0[6]	14.9[6]	7.7[6]	3.0[6]	—0.7[6]—		...	...	...	...	...	...
Mozambique	1973	1,605	3.1	...	...	...	...	...	...	...	0.2	0.1	—	—	99.7	—
Myanmar (Burma)	1992–93	2,925	2.3	53.6[66]	27.8[81]	15.2[128]	3.3[100]	—0.1[11]—			...	...	...	...	...	...
Namibia	1989	6.3[129]	...	...	...	...	...	...	...	...	45.0			55.0	—	—
Nauru	...	...	...	...	...	...	...	...	...	...	...	...	...	...	...	...
Nepal	1992	2,736	1.1[39]	69.8[27]	28.7	1.2	—0.3—				82.6			1.8	—	15.6
Netherlands, The	1995[65]	113[130]	15.5[36]	9.3	24.0	15.9	18.3	26.2	—6.3—		—31.5[14, 36]—			12.2[14, 36]	—	56.4[14, 36]

activity (% of farms)			technology (latest)				land in farms		land use (%) — cropland				meadows and pastures	woodland and forest	other	country
mainly crops	mainly live-stock	mixed/ other	tractors (per 1,000 ha)	electri-city (% of farms having)	irriga-tion (% of land irrig.)	artificial fertilizer (kg/ha)	total ('000 ha)	% of total land area	perma-nent crops	tempo-rary crops	fallow	total crop-land				
...	...	...	0.8	...	...	...	...	...	...	...	...	...	...	...	...	Equatorial Guinea
...	...	...	0.7	...	2	...	395	3.2	...	...	...	...	10.0	34.0	12.0	Eritrea[71]
...	...	...	13.3	...	...	...	252.3	22.7	...	...	...	44.0	...	...	...	Estonia[18]
16.5[72]	2.0[72]	81.5[72]	0.3	...	2	7	7,042[72]	6.4[72]	6.9[72]	82.0[72]	11.1[72]	87.0[72]	8.7[72]	0.8[72]	3.5[72]	Ethiopia[71]
...	...	...	...	...	...	...	...	...	...	...	...	...	...	...	...	Faroe Islands
26.5	29.3	44.2[74]	39.4[73]	...	1[73]	96[73]	260[13]	14.2[13]	...	...	...	37.8	34.0	19.1	9.1	Fiji
52.3	——47.6——		89.9	100.0	3	210	14,535	47.7	1.4	78.5	20.1	18.0	0.8	61.0	20.2	Finland
36.6[26,78]	38.0[26]	25.4[26]	80.0	...	8	319	30,052	54.5	7.2	81.8	11.0	55.1	35.6	——9.3——		France
...	...	...	32.5	...	20	64	22.0[2]	0.2[2]	22.8[2]	76.3[2]	0.9[2]	57.6[2]	42.4[2]	...	...	French Guiana
...	...	...	31.2	...	19.4	33	36.8	10.4	90.0	7.1	2.9	62.0	8.5	1.9	27.6	French Polynesia
...	...	...	5.1	...	1	3	73.0	0.3	...	...	...	...	...	...	...	Gabon
...	...	...	0.2	...	8	11	172[13]	17.2[13]	...	100.0	...	100.0	...	...	—	Gambia, The
...	...	...	83.3	...	133	...	16.5[19]	50.0[19]	68.8[19]	31.2[19]	...	100.0	...	...	—	Gaza Strip
...	...	...	28.6	...	57	...	3,200	45.7	24.6	——75.4——		32.6	62.5	—	4.9	Georgia
...	...	...	111.3	...	4	384	19,011[4]	54.4[4]	1.7[4]	——98.3[4]——		61.2[4]	27.1[4]	7.7[4]	4.0[4]	Germany
...	...	...	1.5	...	0.2	3	2,574	10.8	61.4	38.6	—	100.0	—	—	—	Ghana
...	...	...	...	...	...	4	...	...	...	...	...	...	...	...	...	Gibraltar
69.2	1.1	29.7	89.3	...	54	175	3,351	26.0	32.5	63.5	4.0	90.1	9.9	...	...	Greece
...	c. 100	...	...	...	...	...	...	...	...	...	...	...	...	...	...	Greenland
...	...	...	6.0	...	...	...	12.5	36.8	...	...	...	...	...	...	...	Grenada
...	...	...	34.8	...	13	307	51.0[2]	30.2[2]	14.5[19]	39.1[19]	46.5[19]	56.7[19]	43.3[19]	...	...	Guadeloupe
38.2	29.6	32.2	181.5	...	20.7	...	0.8	1.4	——51.0——		49.0	71.6	9.5	6.5	12.4	Guam
...	...	...	3.2	...	9	66	4,510[2]	41.6[2]	27.6	——72.4——		42.0	27.3	27.2	3.4	Guatemala
...	71.9	...	...	...	...	...	2	27.6	—	100.0	—	12.3	87.7	...	...	Guernsey
...	...	...	0.5	...	15	1	727	3.0	...	...	...	...	...	...	...	Guinea
...	...	...	0.1	...	6	3	96[2]	3.4[2]	...	...	...	...	...	...	...	Guinea-Bissau
...	...	...	7.6	...	27	33	10,652	26.2	...	...	...	8.4	91.6	...	...	Guyana
...	...	...	0.4	...	13	4	1,405[2]	51.0[2]	...	...	...	33.5	18.0	1.5	47.0	Haiti
...	...	...	2.9	...	4	18	3,337	29.8	23.9	33.7	42.5	41.7	45.9	10.9	1.5	Honduras
56.3	37.3	6.4	0.7	...	33	100.0[38]	8.0[2]	8.1[2]	7.4	37.0	55.6	100.0	—	—	—	Hong Kong
43.4[5,19]	44.3[5,19]	12.3[5,19]	8.2	...	4	231	8,010	86.1	4.1	95.9	—	58.9[47]	14.3[47]	22.0[47]	4.8[47]	Hungary
...	...	...	1,809	87.0[53]	...	2,529	...	...	...	...	...	...	...	...	...	Iceland
...	...	...	7.2	...	29	75	165,600	55.7	——84.4[92]——		15.6[92]	97.9[92]	——2.1[92]——			India
86.8[6]	—[6]	13.2[6]	1.9	...	24	110	48,583[45]	25.3[45]	27.0[45]	45.2[45]	27.8[45]	60.7[45]	5.1[45]	18.9[45]	15.3[45]	Indonesia
...	...	...	7.1	...	56	80	104,900[39]	63.8[39]	6.4	62.4	31.2	10.2	89.8	...	...	Iran
87.9	11.2	0.8	6.1	...	49	39	5,750[13]	13.1	3.0	62.4	34.6	87.2	0.7	0.2	11.9	Iraq
2.9	93.2	3.9	182	...	...	741	5,692	82.6	65.1	—	34.9	13.5	54.8	——31.7——		Ireland
...	...	...	...	...	...	...	47	81.4	3.4	——96.6——		11.3	88.7	...	...	Isle of Man
...	...	...	72.6	...	51	252	435[13]	21.1[13]	25.0[19]	——75.0[19]——		81.5[19]	...	——18.5[19]——		Israel
81.2	13.2	5.6	158	...	30	151	22,702	75.3	25.5	——74.5——		48.1	18.2	24.7	9.0	Italy
...	...	...	19.9	...	23	116	476[2]	44.0[2]	22.2[35]	72.2[35]	5.6[35]	41.3[35]	21.6[35]	13.5[35]	23.6[35]	Jamaica
80.8[42]	——19.2[42]——		507	...	69	414	5,083	13.4	10.3	——89.7——		87.7	——12.3——			Japan
85.1[109]	14.9[109]	—	...	...	...	...	6.5	56.2	——98.9——		1.1	63.4	——36.6——			Jersey
58.2[110,111]	14.9[110,111]	26.9[110,111]	18.4	1.5	20	63	405	4.5	13.3	63.0	23.7	87.7	1.0	0.3	11.0	Jordan
...	...	...	5.2	...	6	...	181,300	66.7	1.5	86.4	12.1	19.1	80.6	—	0.3	Kazakhstan
...	...	...	3.5	...	2	48	6,922	11.9	11.5	——88.5——		71.0	23.8	1.9	3.3	Kenya
...	...	...	...	...	...	...	...	...	...	...	...	...	...	...	...	Kiribati
...	...	...	44.2	...	86	407	...	...	...	...	...	...	...	...	...	Korea, North
77.6[5]	22.4[5]	—	40.9	...	71	454	2,145[2]	21.7[2]	6.7	——93.3——		100.0	—	...	...	Korea, South
38.9[7]	61.1[7]	—	20.0	100.0	40	167	7.9	0.4	20.6[7]	79.4[7]		70.0[7]	——30.0[7]——			Kuwait
...	...	...	16.4	...	64	...	10,100	50.9	6.1	90.9	3.0	13.9	86.1	...	...	Kyrgyzstan
...	...	...	1.1	...	16	2	1,700[2]	7.4[2]	2.3	——97.7——		52.4	47.6	...	...	Laos
...	...	...	31.0	...	...	...	2,540	39.3	...	...	...	68.5[116]	——31.5[116]——			Latvia
77.0[110]	8.1[110]	14.9[110]	13.9	...	40	79	316[2]	30.9[2]	36.7[42]	39.7[42]	23.6[42]	100.0[42]	—	—	—	Lebanon
56.0[5]	3.0[5]	41.0[5]	5.8	...	0.9	14	320[13]	10.5[13]	...	...	...	76.4	...	...	23.6	Lesotho
...	...	...	2.6	...	2	7	375	3.9	66.2[118]	33.8[118]	—	98.3[118]	...	1.7[118]	...	Liberia
...	...	...	19.0	...	26	39	15,470[2]	8.8[2]	——28.7——		71.3	49.5	11.7	—	38.8	Libya
23.9[38]	61.6[38]	14.5[38]	112	...	...	...	4.0[13]	25.0[13]	1.1	——98.9——		39.9	57.5	1.1	1.5	Liechtenstein
...	...	...	20.0	...	...	...	3,519	53.9	38.3	60.9	0.8	76.2	13.5	——10.3——		Lithuania
25.0[119]	57.7	17.3	143	...	...	...	137	53.3	——96.9——		3.1	42.4	49.4	6.3	1.9	Luxembourg
...	...	...	...	...	...	...	...	...	...	...	...	...	...	...	...	Macau
...	...	...	83.8	...	14	...	1,320	51.3	9.3	65.4	25.3	46.4	53.4	—	1.2	Macedonia[58]
...	...	...	1.1	...	42	2	3,105[13]	5.3[13]	15.4	84.6	—	100.0	—	...	—	Madagascar
22.1	...	77.9	0.8	...	2	23	1,700[13]	18.1[13]	0.2	99.8	—	94.8	—	5.2	—	Malawi
...	...	...	12.0[123]	...	33[123]	170[123]	7,604[13]	23.1[13]	84.8[38]	15.2[38]	—	100.0[38]	...	...	...	Malaysia
...	...	...	...	...	...	...	19	63.5	...	...	...	...	...	...	...	Maldives
...	...	...	0.3	...	3	9	2,503[13]	2.0[13]	—	100.0	—	100.0	—	—	—	Mali
...	...	...	37.5	...	8	39	13.0	40.6	5.0	——95.0——		87.5	——12.5——			Malta
...	...	...	...	...	...	...	...	...	...	...	...	...	...	...	...	Marshall Islands
...	...	...	115	...	50	945	37.2[19]	35.1[19]	46.6[19]	50.7[19]	2.7[19]	52.1[19]	47.9[19]	...	—	Martinique[2]
...	...	...	1.6	...	24	12	208[2]	0.2[2]	—	56.2	43.8	100.0	—	—	—	Mauritania
...	...	...	3.7	...	17	304	106[2]	52.2[2]	4.2[125]	95.8[125]	—	90.0[125]	——10.0[125]——			Mauritius
...	...	...	...	...	...	...	14.6	39.0	33.3	66.7	—	...	...	...	...	Mayotte
83.9	12.9	3.2	7.4	...	26	70	99,229[2]	52.0[2]	6.3	58.1	35.6	16.5	53.3	14.2	16.0	Mexico
61.4[5]	15.7[5]	22.9[5]	7.4	45	0	...	5.8	12.2	——9.3——		90.7	32.9	30.2	——36.9——		Micronesia
67.4[5,47]	32.6[5,47]	—	31.0	...	18	...	2,614[2]	79.3[2]	26.5[19]	——73.5[19]——		68.0[19]	12.0[19]	—	20.0[19]	Moldova
...	...	...	...	...	...	...	...	...	...	...	...	...	...	...	...	Monaco
13.6[5,47]	86.4[5,47]	—	8.4	...	6	12	118,470[2]	75.6[2]	—	66.8	33.2	100.0	99.1	...	...	Mongolia
...	...	...	4.5	...	14	36	9,256[66,127]	20.7[66,127]	7.2[66,127]	63.8[66,127]	29.0[66,127]	100.0[66,127]	...	...	...	Morocco
...	...	...	1.9	...	4	1	13,626	17.8	——44.9——		55.1	55.0	45.0	...	...	Mozambique
93.3	6.7	—	1.1	...	11	8	6,887	10.5	3.3	93.3	3.4	99.7	...	...	0.3	Myanmar (Burma)
1.3[5]	94.4[5]	4.3[5]	4.8	...	0.9	...	662[13]	0.8[13]	0.3	——99.7——		100.0	...	...	...	Namibia
...	...	...	...	...	...	...	...	...	...	...	...	...	...	...	...	Nauru
...	...	...	2.0	...	37	25	2,599	19.0	1.7	97.1	1.2	90.6	1.4	4.2	3.8	Nepal
32.1	57.4	10.5	201	...	62	628	1,965	58.0	——99.4——		0.6	47.3	52.7	—	—	Netherlands, The

Agriculture and land use (continued)

country	year	number of farms ('000)	average (ha)	under 1 ha	1–5 ha	5–10 ha	10–20 ha	20–50 ha	50–200 ha	over 200 ha	individual/family	corporate/state	socialized/collective	rented (including share-croppers)	tribal/communal	other[b]
Netherlands Antilles		...	...	...	...	...	...	...	...	...	...	...	...	...	...	...
New Caledonia	1991	10.3	23[131]	71.2[66,131]	13.8[79,131]	3.7[131]	2.3[131]	2.5[131]	3.8[131]	2.8[131]	...	...	...	...	84.5	15.5
New Zealand	1995	69.5	217[50]	—13.3—		11.6	9.9	—44.7—		20.5	85.7[38]	10.9[38]	—	—	—	3.4[38]
Nicaragua	1991	...	...	—26.2[56]—			—30.6[56]—			43.3[56]	64.4[14,39]	—35.6[14,39]—		...	...	...
Niger	1980[2]	699	4.9	3.8	54.1	37.8	—4.3—									
Nigeria	1971	...	...	92.0	7.8	0.2	—	—								
Northern Mariana Is.	1990	0.1	49.1	26.1[134]	35.3[135]	—24.4[10]—		—14.3—			56.3	...	...	23.5	...	20.2
Norway	1994[65]	85.7[136]	10.2[3]	—29.6—		24.7	28.9	15.3	—1.5—		—65.4[3]—			34.6[3]	...	
Oman	1992–93	95	1.6	71.0	24.3	3.8	0.5	0.3	0.1	—	99.3	—	—	0.4	—	0.3
Pakistan	1990	5,071	...	27.0	54.0	12.2	4.7	—2.1—			68.8	—	—	18.8	—12.4[137]—	
Palau[138]	1989	0.3	...	79.1[14]	—	—								12.7[14]	8.2[14]	—
Panama	1991	214	13.8	46.7	24.8	7.6	7.1	7.7	5.3	0.8	28.6	—	—	1.4	—	70.0[43]
Papua New Guinea	1985[139]	0.8	483	—26.8[65]—					28.3[88]	44.9[88]	26.9[14,88]	71.0[14,88]	—	2.1[14,88]	—	—
Paraguay	1991	307	88[118]	7.3	31.0	22.3	22.1	10.5	4.0	2.8	52.4	—	—	7.4	—	40.2[43]
Peru	1984	1,574	9.5	24.1	47.7	13.2	6.7	5.5	—2.8—		75.5	—	—	0.8	6.8	16.9
Philippines	1991	4,610	2.2	22.7	63.3	10.5	—3.5—				58.3	—	—	27.4	—	14.3
Poland[18]	1994	2,030	7.6	21.7[66]	32.8[79]	26.7	11.0[140]	—7.8[141]—			78.3[4,14]	13.9[4,14]	3.3[4,14]	—	—	4.5[4,14]
Portugal[4]	1995	489	10.5	24.9	53.2	—17.0—		3.0	—1.9—		92.0	—	—	—8.0—		
Puerto Rico	1992	22	14.5	—5.1[142]—		7.5[143]	14.3[144]	14.2[145]	—58.9[84]—		—79.5—			10.6	—	9.9
Qatar	1990	0.8	7.0	20.5	41.8	18.0	12.6	5.8	—1.4—		...	...	...	...	...	...
Réunion[2]	1989	15	4.1	35.6	47.9	12.5	2.7	—1.3—			46.1[6]	—	—	22.5[6]	—	31.4[6]
Romania	1996	3.6[46]	3,900[46]	...	...	...	...	...	...		51.0[14]	14.0	35.0[48]	...		—
Russia	1996	280[18]	43[18]	...	...	...	...	...	...		45.0[116]	55.0[116]	—	...		—
Rwanda	1984	1,112	1.2	56.8	26.8[146]	—16.4[147]—					50.9	—	—	1.4	—	47.7[59]
St. Kitts and Nevis	1987	3.4	...	90.1[28]	8.7[29]	0.5[31]	—0.7—				82.0[14]	—	—	7.7[14]	—	10.3[43]
St. Lucia	1986	12	2.0	75.9[66]	10.3[81]	4.9[82]	0.9	0.3[83]	0.2[101]	0.4[102]	72.0	—	—	15.5	—	12.5
St. Vincent	1988	9	1.8[148]	78.4[27]	18.6[30]	2.0[82]	0.4[149]	—0.6—			53.8	—	—	12.3	—	33.9[43]
San Marino	1975	0.7	7.0	21.3	47.8	—24.7—		5.1	—1.1—		39.9[14]	15.5[14]	—	29.9[14]	—	14.7[14]
São Tomé and Príncipe	1989	13.8	8.7[150]	88.5[150]	9.8[150]	0.7[150]	0.2[150]	0.2[150]	0.2[150]	0.4[150]	77.2[150]	—	—	20.5[150]	—	2.3[150]
Saudi Arabia	1982–83	212	10.1	36.6	35.8	11.3	8.2	5.0	2.6	0.5	85.9	—	—	2.6	—	11.5
Senegal	1976	362	7.0	—99.4—					—0.6—		...	...	0.6	...	...	99.4
Seychelles	1993	0.9[151]	...	...							98.9	—1.1—		...	...	
Sierra Leone	1971	286	1.8	38.8	55.0	—6.1—			—0.1—		93.6	—	—	6.4	—	—
Singapore	1973	16	0.8	77.4	22.2	0.3	—0.1—				7.4	—	—	88.8	—	3.8
Slovakia	1991	...	...	...							13.0[14,47]	6.0[14,47]	63.0[14,47]	—		8.0[14,47]
Slovenia[58]	1991	157	...	28.4	36.0	18.0	—17.6—				93.0[14,47]	7.0[14,47]	—	...		—
Solomon Islands	1975[112]	92	1.0	...	...	...	...				—	—	100.0	—		
Somalia	1984	198	3.6	...	...	...	...				99.9	0.1	—	...	...	
South Africa[154]	1996	62[155]	1,319	—0.8[105]—		1.5	1.9	6.4	13.7	75.7	89.6[85]	...	...	...	...	10.4
Spain	1989	2,285	19.0	27.7	36.6	13.2	9.5	6.8	3.9	2.3	72.5	...	—	19.8	—7.7—	
Sri Lanka	1982	1,817	1.1	77.5[8]	—22.2[157]—		0.1[158]	0.1[83]	—0.1[84]—		59.0[159]	27.2[159]	—	8.2[159]	—	5.6[159]
Sudan, The	1982	...	...	...	...	...					22.3	2.2	—	28.0	42.0	5.5
Suriname	1981	22	7.5	21.9[35]	61.2[35]	11.1[35]	3.6[35]	1.6[35]	0.3[35]	0.3[35]	20.2[35]	0.9[35]	—	49.5[35]	—	29.4[35]
Swaziland[160]	1992–93	0.4	51	41.2	29.5	10.3	6.1	—12.9—			84.4[34]	—	—	—15.6[34]—		
Sweden	1995	87	29.5[26]	...	14.7	19.1	21.1	26.9	—18.2—		46.4	—	—	14.5	—	39.1[59]
Switzerland	1990	108	9.9	21.7	19.0	17.4	29.1	12.3	0.6	—	59.1[14,162]	—	—	39.9[14,162]	—	1.0[14,162]
Syria	1994	444	8.9	16.7	36.8[30]	22.8[82]	13.1	8.5	2.0[163]	0.2[164]	65.8[14,124]	1.8[14]	32.5[14]	3.8	—	12.7
Taiwan	1994	808[91]	1.1[91]	72.6[3]	27.4[3]						83.5	—	—	3.8	—	12.7
Tajikistan	1993	...	...													
Tanzania	1993–94	5,440	0.5	70.1	28.8	1.0	—0.1—				49.0[165]	—	—	3.0	38.2	9.8
Thailand	1993	5,647	3.7	14.3	72.0[166]	—13.1[167]—		—0.5[168]—			86.7	—	—	7.4	—	5.9
Togo	1982–83	263	1.5	48.8	38.6[120]	—12.7[121]—					70.7[14]	—	—	21.1[14]	8.2[14]	—
Tonga	1985	10.1	3.3	18.9	67.9	12.7	—	0.5	—		—97.2—			—		2.8
Trinidad and Tobago	1987	30.6	4.3	35.1	50.7	9.6	4.1	—	0.4	0.1	52.1	—	—	36.5	—	11.4
Tunisia	1988	376	13.6	—45.7—		20.6	17.9	11.4	—4.4—							
Turkey	1991	4,068	...	16.0[170]	51.1	18.0	9.7	4.4	—0.8—		95.9	—	—	1.1	—	3.0
Turkmenistan	1993	0.1[18,19]	10[18,19]	...	...	...	...									
Tuvalu	1976	1.5	1.7	...	...	...					99.9	—	—	0.1	—	
Uganda	1991	1,704	3.9	49.2	41.5	5.7	—3.6—				13.2[14]	—	—	...	17.3[14]	69.5[14,43]
Ukraine	1993	14.4[18,19]	20[18,19]	...												
United Arab Emirates	1986–87	17.9	2.3	45.4	38.8[171]	—15.9[172]—										
United Kingdom	1993	242[19]	107.3[19,173]	5.6[19,66]	8.4[19,67]	11.9[19]	15.2[19]	24.7[19]	28.0[19]	6.2[19]	—74.3[174]—		—	25.7[174]	—	—
United States	1992	2,073[175]	190[175]	—8.6[104]—		—20.1[10]—		30.3[176]	22.2[177]	18.7[178]	57.7	—	—	11.3	—	31.0[85]
Uruguay	1990	55	280.5[125]	...	8.2	12.1	13.2	16.5	23.3	26.7	—59.1[42]—		...	17.3[42]	—	23.6[42]
Uzbekistan[18]	1993	17.7[116]	14.5[116]	...							9.0	55.0	35.0	—1.0—		
Vanuatu[179]	1993	22	6.9[131]	...							65.3[42]	34.7[42]	—	...		—
Venezuela	1984–85	381	82.0	8.3	36.3	15.7	13.0	10.4	9.3	7.1	61.5[57]	—	—	6.1[57]	—	31.3[19,57]
Vietnam	1991	31[45]	28.0[2]	...							—100—		—	—		—
Virgin Islands (U.S.)	1992	0.3[45]	27.0[45]	30.0[45,180]	30.3[45,181]	12.0[45]	13.9[45]	6.0[45]	3.7[45,182]	4.1[45,183]	75.3[45]	...	—	8.6[45]	—	16.1[45]
West Bank	1965	55	3.4	49.8	34.4	10.6	4.0	1.0	0.2	0.0	7.16	—	—	6.4	—	22.0
Western Sahara	1983	...														
Western Samoa	1989	11	6.1	...	...	...	...				0.1	—	—	2.6[14]	94.2[14]	3.1[14]
Yemen[184]	1977–83	591	2.3	57.5	30.9	7.4	3.3	0.8	0.1	—	90.3[14]	—	—	9.4[14]	—	0.3[14]
Yugoslavia	1991	1,176	...	•24.7	48.8	19.9	4.4	—0.7—			83.0	—17.0—		—	—	—
Zaire	1990	4,480	2.3	86.7	—13.3—						19.7	—	—	2.7	69.5	8.1
Zambia	1990	520	3.1[57]	—92.2—		7.4	—0.4—				99.9	0.1	—	...	...	
Zimbabwe[187]	1996	1,000[116]	38.7[17]	—16.7[17,99]—		—82.6[17,188]—		—0.7[17,21]—			—2.0[17]—		—	—	98.0[17]	—

[1]1967. [2]Cultivated area only. [3]1989. [4]1993. [5]Based on value of output by sector. [6]1973. [7]1991–92. [8]Less than 1.6 ha. [9]1.6 to 4.0 ha. [10]4.0 to 20 ha. [11]20 ha or more. [12]Percentage of farms having irrigation. [13]Arable and permanent crops only. [14]Based on area, not number, of holdings. [15]10 to 25 ha. [16]25 to 50 ha. [17]1974. [18]Private farms only. [19]1992. [20]50 to 100 ha. [21]100 ha or more. [22]Includes fruits and vegetables. [23]Includes houseplants and cut flowers. [24]1993–94. [25]Includes fallow and grazing lands. [26]1990. [27]Includes holdings without land. [28]Less than 1.2 ha. [29]1.2 to 4.0 ha. [30]1.0 to 4.0 ha. [31]0.1 to 10.1 ha. [32]10.1 ha or more. [33]1977. [34]1990–91. [35]1969. [36]1988. [37]1984–85. [38]1985. [39]1982. [40]4.0 ha or more. [41]Includes about 21,000 farms without land; distribution by size refers to traditional farms with land only. [42]1980. [43]More than one-half squatters. [44]1970. [45]1987. [46]State farms and cooperatives only. [47]1994. [48]Agricultural cooperatives only. [49]Precollectivization. [50]1981. [51]4.0 to 52.2 ha. [52]52.2 ha and over. [53]Irrigated land only. [54]1968. [55]1975–76. [56]1984. [57]1971. [58]Holdings and tenure refer to private plots only; size and tenure 1990. [59]Owned and rented holdings. [60]Data for Czech Republic include Slovakia unless otherwise noted. [61]Less than 0.5 ha. [62]0.5 to 50 ha. [63]350 to 1,000 ha. [64]Excludes Slovakia; 1994. [65]Arable area only. [66]Less than 2.0 ha. [67]2.0 to 20 ha. [68]2.1 ha or less. [69]2.1 to 4.2 ha. [70]4.2 ha or more. [71]Data for Ethiopia include Eritrea, unless otherwise stated. [72]Excludes Eritrea. [73]1978–79. [74]Includes 28 percent under forests. [75]Excludes holdings of less than 1.0 ha. [76]10 to 35 ha. [77]35 to 50 ha. [78]Includes fruit-growing and viticulture. [79]2.0 to 5.0 ha. [80]Excludes 1.1 percent of holdings with no agricultural land. [81]2.0 to 4.0 ha. [82]4.0 to 10 ha. [83]20 to 40 ha. [84]40 ha or more. [85]Includes part-owners. [86]Less than 0.7 ha. [87]0.7 to 7.1 ha. [88]7.1 to 45 ha. [89]45 ha or more. [90]Excludes holdings of 0.04 ha (500 sq m) or less. [91]Farm households only. [92]1986–87. [93]Less than 2.5 ha. [94]2.5 to 7.5 ha. [95]7.5 to 12.5 ha. [96]12.5 to 20 ha. [97]20 to 250 ha. [98]250 ha or more. [99]Less than 8.0 ha. [100]8.0 to 20 ha. [101]40 to 61 ha. [102]61 ha or more. [103]Less than 0.4 ha. [104]0.4 to 4.0 ha. [105]Less than 4.5 ha. [106]4.5 to 9.0 ha.

activity (% of farms)			technology (latest)				farmland use: land in farms		farmland use: land use (%)							country
									cropland							
mainly crops	mainly live-stock	mixed/ other	tractors (per 1,000 ha)	electri-city (% of farms having)	irriga-tion (% of land irrig.)	artificial fertilizer (kg/ha)	total ('000 ha)	% of total land area	perma-nent crops	tempo-rary crops	fallow	total crop-land	mead-ows and pastures	wood-land and forest	other	
...	...	...	2.5	...	...	...	...	...	...	...	...	...	...	...	...	Netherlands Antilles
...	...	...	200	...	...	60	314	17.2	39.9	—60.1—		4.8	68.2	10.6	16.4	New Caledonia
15.4[22]	63.7	20.9	197	...	74	741	16,607	62.0	—80.1[47]—		19.9[47]	1.9[47]	80.1[47]	9.0[47, 132]	9.0[47, 133]	New Zealand
52.7[5, 47]	38.0[5, 47]	9.3[5, 47]	2.4	...	8	28	5,651	47.7	...	...	...	...	...	...	...	Nicaragua
...	...	...	0.05	...	2	1	3,605[13]	2.8[13]	...	...	...	...	...	...	...	Niger
...	...	...	0.4	...	3	12	32,700[13]	35.9[13]	—20.0—		80.0	31.4	27.5	41.1	...	Nigeria
64.3[5]	35.7[5]	—	22	45	...	...	5.8	12.2	...	...	...	32.9	30.2	—36.9—		Northern Mariana Is.
24.3[5]	70.6[5]	3.9[5]	175	...	11	242	1,030[2]	3.4[2]	—95.7—		4.3	42.7	—57.3—			Norway
28.0	34.0	38.0	9.4	...	92	83	106	0.4	68.5	31.5	—	59.1	—40.9—			Oman
...	...	...	13.6	...	82	91	22,440	28.2	—76.9—		23.1	95.4	—4.6—			Pakistan
...	...	...	2.2	...	...	...	...	...	—78.5—		21.5	43.3	—56.7—			Palau[138]
88.1	11.9	—	10.1	0.5[57]	6	58	2,942	39.5	23.7	41.3	35.0	22.2	50.0	24.1	3.6	Panama
...	...	...	28.5	...	...	40	415[13]	0.9[13]	100.0	—	—	33.7	26.4	...	39.9	Papua New Guinea
33.0[118]	—67.0[118]—		7.5	...	3	9	23,818	59.9	1.9	85.5	12.6	19.1	43.1	32.8	5.0	Paraguay
4.9	93.0	2.1	4.9	6.5	38	41	14,893	11.6	24.1	75.9	—	27.1	47.5	19.8	5.6	Peru
98.2	1.5	0.3	2.1	...	29	67	9,190[13]	30.8[13]	57.5	42.5	—	86.3	6.8	—6.9—		Philippines
53.8[5]	46.2[5]	—	80.8	...	0.7	219	18,648	59.6	1.9	—98.1—		78.3	21.7	...	...	Poland[18]
66.7	19.4	13.9	55.5	...	27	73	4,822	52.4	28.0	50.1	21.9	56.0	18.9	18.3	6.8	Portugal[4]
61.0[5]	33.4[5]	5.6[5]	61.5	...	60	...	325	36.7	—78.9—		21.1	33.3	50.1	9.4	7.2	Puerto Rico
50.4[5]	49.6[5]	—	9.9	...	114	200	8.0[13]	0.7[13]	25.2	74.8	—	100.0	—	—	—	Qatar
...	...	...	37.2	...	14	282	61[2]	24.4[2]	7.8[4]	88.7[4]	3.5[4]	79.4[4]	20.6[4]	...	...	Réunion[3]
...	...	...	15.7	...	33	133	14,797[2]	64.2[2]	6.0	94.0	—	67.2	32.8	—	—	Romania
52.1	47.9	—	9.3	...	3	17	209,600	12.4	—86.4[116]—		13.6[116]	60.9[116]	37.5[116]	—	1.6[116]	Russia
...	...	...	0.1	...	0.5	1	1,170[13]	47.4[13]	—85.6—		14.4	63.7	10.6	5.2	20.5	Rwanda
...	...	...	27.0	...	...	...	8.9	24.7	17.3	70.7	12.0	65.5	18.3	10.9	5.3	St. Kitts and Nevis
25.0[17]	—75.0[17]—		17.4	...	20	...	21	34.4	68.5[17]	—31.5[17]—		57.9[17]	10.2[17]	26.4[17]	5.5[17]	St. Lucia
...	...	...	20.0	...	25	...	12	30.8	64.3	16.1	19.6	84.2	...	12.3	3.5	St. Vincent
...	...	...	...	...	...	...	4.7	76.5	60.9	6.5	32.6	69.2	6	8.2	16.4	San Marino
...	...	...	62.5	...	...	...	76	79.2	94.9	—5.1—		54.3	—45.7—			São Tomé and Príncipe
...	...	...	0.6	...	27	398	2,135	1.0	4.1	18.7	77.2	88.5	—11.5—			Saudi Arabia
...	...	...	0.2	...	8	2	8,050	41.8	0.1	—99.9—		22.4	77.6	...	...	Senegal
1.8[152]	32.4	65.8[153]	40.0	...	...	...	7.0[2]	15.6[2]	89.6	—10.4—		100.0	—	—	—	Seychelles
50.3	—49.7—		1.1	...	6	1	2,740[2]	38.3[2]	20.7	—79.3—		19.3	80.7	...	...	Sierra Leone
12.5	6.2	81.3	65.0	...	100	5,600	5.6[56]	9.0[56]	75.0	25.0	—	66.7	...	33.3	...	Singapore
...	...	...	13.6[47]	...	5.4	44[47]	2,446	49.9	3.2	92.1	4.7	60.6[47]	34.1[47]	—5.3[47]—		Slovakia
50.7	11.9	37.4	204	...	0.8	...	862	42.6	12.1[47]	—87.9[47]—		28.5[47]	17.5[47]	54.0[47]	—	Slovenia[58]
43.4	—56.6—		...	...	...	...	96[2]	3.4[2]	40.0	45.2	14.8	100.0	—	—	—	Solomon Islands
20.0	60.0	20.0	2.1	...	18	3	...	...	...	...	...	...	...	...	...	Somalia
26.2	52.5	21.3[156]	9.8	...	10	59	94,557[2]	77.4[2]	...	...	...	12.5[36]	83.7[36]	2.1[36]	1.7[36]	South Africa[154]
...	...	...	51.7	...	23	101	30,816[2]	61.7[2]	—79.4—		20.6	48.9	34.3	16.8	—	Spain
...	...	...	35.5	...	59	111	2,323[2]	35.9[2]	56.4	43.6	—	86.0	1.0	2.7	8.8	Sri Lanka
...	...	...	0.8	...	15	4	31,500	13.3	0.8	88.7	10.5	23.8	76.2	...	...	Sudan, The
33.0[35]	12.5[35]	54.5[35]	23.3	...	105	26	165	1.0	15.0	53.0	32.0	40.4	23.1	19.1	17.4	Suriname
45.8[131]	25.3[131]	28.9[131, 132]	24.1	...	36	46	527	30.6	6.3	70.8	22.9	10.2	57.2	17.9	14.7	Swaziland[160]
14.6	41.7	43.7[161]	59.3	...	4	127	7,800	19.0	—98.1—		1.9	35.5	5.4	49.3	9.8	Sweden
58.0	—42.0—		288	...	6	430	1,071	27.1	6.2	93.8	—	31.2	68.1	—	0.7	Switzerland
...	...	...	13.9	...	18	46	5,527[13]	30.1[13]	—83.2[4]—		16.8[4]	32.1[4]	44.4[4]	3.2[4]	20.3[4]	Syria
41.9[3]	30.3[3]	27.8[3]	...	...	38	400[109]	2,827	78.5	27.5[3]	72.5[3]	—	31.7[3]	...	65.7[3]	2.4[3]	Taiwan
66.3[47]	33.7[47]	—	37.0	...	79	...	4,300	30.1	43.1	56.6	0.3	20.9	76.7	—	2.4	Tajikistan
65.0	0.4	35.0	2.2	...	5	9	7,545[148]	8.5[148]	19.1[148]	72.5[148]	8.4[148]	49.8[148]	10.2[148]	24.7[148]	15.3[148]	Tanzania
...	...	...	9.6	...	26	36	17,464	34.2	15.3	—84.7—		93.3	1.1	1.6	4.0	Thailand
...	...	...	0.2	...	0.3	8	406	7.1	17.3[33]	—82.7[33]—		71.0[33]	29.0[33]	...	...	Togo
...	...	...	6.8	...	...	2	48[13]	66.7[13]	—62.7—		37.3	81.2	6.7	10.1	1.9	Tonga
63.7[169]	—36.3[169]—		35.3	40.7	29	57	133[2]	25.9[2]	55.9	—44.1—		62.3	4.4	6.1	27.2	Trinidad and Tobago
...	...	...	9.2	...	13	20	10,040[19]	64.6[19]	—87.1[19]—		12.9[19]	74.5[19]	25.5[19]	...	...	Tunisia
—	3.6[26]	96.4[26]	30.5	...	15	64	23,896	31.0	11.1[47]	69.9[47]	19.0[47]	91.5	3.9	0.8	3.8	Turkey
...	...	...	37.4	...	93	...	32,300	66.2	48.3	—51.7—		4.3	95.4	—	0.3	Turkmenistan
...	...	...	...	...	...	...	...	...	...	...	...	...	...	...	...	Tuvalu
...	...	...	0.9	...	0.2	...	3,683	15.3	29.8[150]	70.2[150]	—	100.0[150]	—	—	—	Uganda
47.9[5, 47]	52.1[5, 47]	—	12.8	...	8	...	40,400	69.7	7.7	88.2	4.1	80.9	16.3	—	2.8	Ukraine
...	...	...	6.4	...	17	120	39.0[13]	0.5[13]	64.8[109]	18.2[109]	17.1[109]	97.6[109]	...	1.3[109]	1.1[109]	United Arab Emirates
...	...	...	82.2	...	2	376	18,482	76.7	0.8[47]	98.5[47]	0.7[47]	32.3[47]	60.0[47]	—7.7[47]—		United Kingdom
44.8	55.2	—	25.9	68.8	11	99	393,471[175]	41.1[175]	—88.5—		11.5	46.0	43.5	7.8	2.7	United States
37.1[42]	58.7[42]	4.2[42]	26.2	...	11	54	15,682	88.4	6.6	—93.4—		4.3	—95.7—			Uruguay
...	...	...	41.5	...	98	...	25,500	57.0	43.9	55.6	0.5	16.1	82.0	—	1.9	Uzbekistan[18]
92.2[131]	7.2[131]	0.6[131]	3.8	...	...	...	183	15.0	62.5[131]	3.0[131]	34.5[131]	84.9[131]	15.1[131]	...	...	Vanuatu[179]
27.6	9.0	63.4	15.2	...	6	138	31,278	34.3	19.0[57]	59.0[57]	22.0[57]	13.2[57]	57.0[57]	22.8[57]	7.0[57]	Venezuela
74.5[5]	25.5[5]	—	6.7	...	34	82	9,060	27.4	7.4	—92.6—		100.0				Vietnam
48.3[45]	40.8[45]	10.9[45]	15.6	15.6	...	...	7.2	20.9	18.3[45]	13.7[45]	68.0[45]	10.7[45]	75.3[45]	10.3[45]	3.7[45]	Virgin Islands (U.S.)
61.9[5, 47]	38.1[5, 47]	—	14.1[39]	...	5	...	185[42]	31.4[42]	62.2[42]	37.8[42]	—	100.0[42]	—	—	—	West Bank
...	...	...	...	...	...	...	5,002[2]	18.8[2]	—	—	—	—	100.0	...	...	Western Sahara
...	...	...	1.4	...	...	...	67	23.7	71.2[111]	28.8[111]	—	93.8[111]	6.2[111]	...	...	Western Samoa
35.5[14, 185]	56.9[14, 185]	7.6[14, 185]	4.0	...	26	12	1,545[13]	2.9[13]	6.7	69.7	23.6	98.8	...	...	1.2	Yemen[184]
12.7[35, 186]	—87.3[35, 186]—		108	...	2	221	6,243	61.2	8.6[47]	88.8[47]	2.6[47]	65.4[47]	33.9[47]	—	0.7[47]	Yugoslavia
92.3	—9.7—		0.3	...	0.1	1	7,900[13]	3.5[13]	7.7	—92.3—		70.6	20.1	2.0	7.3	Zaire
15.8[57]	9.7[57]	74.5[57]	1.1	...	0.9	15	938	1.3	4.5[57]	—95.5—		14.2[57]	38.1[57]	...	47.7[57]	Zambia
74.2[5, 116]	25.8[5, 116]	—	5.9	...	7	53	32,800	84.8	2.5[17]	—97.5—		34.5[17]	65.7[17]	...	...	Zimbabwe[187]

[107]9.0 to 18 ha. [108]18 ha or more. [109]1978. [110]Commercial farms only. [111]1975. [112]Excludes large commercial farms. [113]5.0 to 8.0 ha. [114]8.0 ha or more. [115]1985–86. [116]1995. [117]Excludes temporary rangeland available for agricultural use to subsistence farms. [118]1981. [119]Two-fifths under horticulture and viticulture. [120]1.0 to 3.0 ha. [121]3.0 ha or more. [122]West Malaysia except as noted. [123]Malaysia. [124]Includes some rented farms. [125]1986. [126]Farms in rural areas only. [127]1992–93. [128]4.0 to 8.0 ha. [129]Commercial farms owned mostly by whites. [130]Includes agricultural and horticultural farms. [131]1983–84. [132]Includes timber plantations. [133]Includes conservation planting and plantations of native trees. [134]Less than 0.8 ha. [135]0.8 to 4.0 ha. [136]Excludes holdings of less than 0.5 ha. [137]Excludes 149 government holdings. [138]Partial data. [139]Large holdings only. [140]10 to 15 ha. [141]15 ha or more. [142]1.0 to 3.9 ha. [143]3.9 to 7.5 ha. [144]7.5 to 19.3 ha. [145]19.3 to 39 ha. [146]1.0 to 2.0 ha. [147]2.0 ha or more. [148]1972. [149]10.0 to 20.1 ha. [150]1964. [151]Includes 700 part-time farmers. [152]Includes root crops. [153]Includes fruits, vegetables, coconuts, and cinnamon. [154]Data excludes Transkei, Bophuthatswana, Venda, and Ciskei states. [155]Total indicates white commercial farmers, of which 60 percent have viable farming units. [156]Includes horticulture. [157]1.2 to 12 ha. [158]12 to 20 ha. [159]1988–89. [160]Includes individual-tenured farms and large estates. [161]Includes 36 percent of small farms not identified by activity. [162]Data excludes tenure of communal grazing lands. [163]50 to 300 ha. [164]300 ha or more. [165]Includes 5 percent multiple tenure. [166]1.0 to 6.4 ha. [167]6.4 to 22.4 ha. [168]22.4 ha or more. [169]1963. [170]Excludes approximately 102,000 holdings without land. [171]1.0 to 7.5 ha. [172]7.5 ha or more. [173]Full-time operations only. [174]Excludes Northern Ireland. [175]July 1995. [176]20 to 72 ha. [177]72 to 202 ha. [178]202 ha or more. [179]Tanna Island only. [180]Less than 3.0 ha. [181]3.0 to 10 ha. [182]100 to 260 ha. [183]260 ha or more. [184]Former Yemen Arab Republic only. [185]1976. [186]Data refer to Yugoslavia as constituted prior to 1991. [187]Total number of farms includes resettlement schemes and commercial land holdings. [188]8.0 to 100 ha.

Crops and livestock

This table provides comparative data for selected categories of agricultural production for the countries of the world. The data are taken mainly from the United Nations Food and Agriculture Organization's (FAO) annual *Production Yearbook.*

The FAO depends largely on questionnaires supplied to each country for its statistics, but, where no official or semiofficial responses are returned, the FAO makes estimates, using incomplete, unofficial, or other similarly limited data. And, although the FAO provides standardized guidelines upon which many nations have organized their data collection systems and methods, persistent, often traditional, variations in standards of coverage, methodology, and reporting periods reduce the comparability of statistics that *can* be supplied on such forms. FAO data are based on calendar-year periods; that is, data for any particular crop refer to the calendar year in which the harvest (or the bulk of the harvest) occurred.

In spite of the often tragic food shortages in a number of countries in recent years, worldwide agricultural production is probably more often underreported than overreported. Many countries do not report complete domestic production. Some countries, for example, report only crops that are sold commercially and ignore subsistence crops produced for family or communal consumption, or barter; others may limit reporting to production for export only, to holdings above a certain size, or represent a sampling only.

Methodological problems attach to much smaller elements of the agricultural whole, however. The FAO's cereals statistics relate, ideally, to weight or volume of crops harvested for dry grain (excluding cereal crops used for grazing, harvested for hay, or harvested green for food, feed, or silage). Some countries, however, collect the basic data they report to the FAO on sown or cultivated areas instead and calculate production statistics from estimates of yield. Millet and sorghum, which in many European and North American countries are used primarily as livestock or poultry feed, may be reportable by such countries as animal fodder only, while elsewhere many nations use the same grains for human consumption and report them as cereals. Statistics for tropical fruits are frequently not compiled by producing countries, and coverage is not uniform, with some countries reporting only commercial fruits and others including those consumed for subsistence as well. Figures on wild fruits and berries are seldom included

Crops and livestock

country	grains production ('000 metric tons) 1979–81 avg	1995	grains yield (kg/hectare) 1979–81 avg	1995	roots and tubers[a] production ('000 metric tons) 1979–81 avg	1995	roots yield (kg/hectare) 1979–81 avg	1995	pulses[b] production ('000 metric tons) 1979–81 avg	1995	pulses yield (kg/hectare) 1979–81 avg	1995	fruits[c] production ('000 metric tons) 1979–81 avg	1995	vegetables[d] production ('000 metric tons) 1979–81 avg	1995
Afghanistan	4,060	3,307	1,337	1,377	265	280	14,879	16,667	41	44	989	967	807	615	516	587
Albania	916	657	2,499	2,546	112	70	6,957	5,512	23	27	456	808	154	97	333	460
Algeria	1,958	2,194	660	877	540	720	6,861	9,474	52	39	430	349	1,197	1,157	824	2,205
American Samoa	...	...	...	...	3	2	4,130	3,361	...	...	...	...	2	1	...	...
Andorra	...	—	...	—	...	—	...	—	...	—	...	—	...	—	...	—
Angola	379	321	533	286	1,354	1,943	3,725	4,396	42	34	385	252	430	417	231	249
Antigua and Barbuda	—	—	1,848	1,607	...	...	4,724	4,811	...	...	...	...	9	7	1	2
Argentina	24,457	23,456	2,204	2,878	2,328	2,410	14,063	19,195	239	307	920	1,108	6,186	5,759	2,280	3,138
Armenia	270	259	1,783	1,519	240	400	12,213	13,333	...	4	...	2,097	407	275	468	452
Aruba	...	...	...	...	...	...	...	...	...	...	...	...	...	...	...	...
Australia	21,150	26,560	1,323	1,770	843	1,152	23,418	26,784	192	2,381	923	1,164	2,125	2,560	1,044	1,668
Austria	4,388	4,477	4,131	5,542	1,356	724	25,381	26,795	23	77	2,879	2,970	950	789	666	437
Azerbaijan	1,105	939	2,253	1,550	142	200	7,359	10,000	2,167	...	...	9	1,647	972	852	800
Bahamas, The	1	—	1,142	1,793	1	1	8,081	5,435	1	—	1,238	720	12	10	28	22
Bahrain	...	...	...	...	...	...	19,000	12,222	—	...	929	1,091	35	25	15	16
Bangladesh	20,983	25,931	1,939	2,424	1,705	1,864	10,062	10,591	637	545	647	750	1,303	1,381	1,066	1,461
Barbados	2	2	2,537	2,500	11	3	11,411	8,827	1	1	1,209	1,254	3	3	10	7
Belarus	4,108	5,927	1,438	2,304	12,672	8,570	16,085	11,427	101	173	496	1,362	510	298	799	981
Belgium[1]	2,069	2,311	4,857	6,654	1,468	2,100	39,163	40,385	7	24	3,107	3,927	386	665	912	1,635
Belize	27	38	1,934	1,824	3	4	20,000	21,765	1	3	531	811	72	220	3	5
Benin	366	648	697	956	1,363	2,447	7,452	9,211	34	71	446	634	142	161	121	253
Bermuda	...	...	...	...	1	1	8,982	23,941	...	...	...	...	1	—	2	3
Bhutan	159	106	1,439	1,088	40	56	6,767	10,750	2	2	592	800	29	64	11	10
Bolivia	663	1,110	1,186	1,583	1,063	1,044	5,187	5,580	18	33	1,016	1,004	547	785	317	434
Bosnia and Herzegovina	...	717	...	2,841	...	377	...	7,500	...	17	...	1,221	...	89	...	605
Botswana	35	46	228	372	7	9	5,513	6,000	19	12	622	462	9	10	16	13
Brazil	30,805	49,653	1,495	2,504	27,265	29,009	11,571	12,963	2,206	2,941	462	581	18,607	32,301	4,089	6,246
Brunei	3	1	1,659	2,133	1	1	1,499	3,563	...	...	...	...	5	5	8	8
Bulgaria	8,129	5,739	3,852	3,053	376	476	10,212	10,068	69	52	990	976	1,975	810	2,022	1,307
Burkina Faso	1,166	2,492	576	795	126	75	8,918	5,012	46	62	1,004	861	56	73	155	254
Burundi	219	269	1,081	1,287	1,036	1,326	6,778	6,395	317	358	957	1,021	1,243	1,506	151	220
Cambodia	1,334	1,867	1,074	1,374	178	60	6,693	7,059	14	15	512	625	125	277	368	488
Cameroon	866	1,260	848	1,346	1,663	2,080	3,866	5,794	105	78	542	566	1,715	2,142	370	467
Canada	42,727	49,693	2,184	2,705	2,626	3,774	23,829	26,273	199	2,090	1,550	1,674	697	747	1,751	2,115
Cape Verde	6	10	473	302	11	5	4,096	9,592	4	...	345	200	12	15	1	8
Central African Republic	103	112	530	777	1,106	718	3,268	3,023	7	26	556	963	165	222	44	66
Chad	508	963	560	650	424	528	4,509	4,448	47	34	412	576	94	100	59	74
Chile	1,742	2,804	2,125	4,533	901	907	10,289	15,603	171	92	842	1,178	1,657	3,152	1,760	2,828
China	286,457	416,797	3,027	4,664	144,354	152,813	13,579	15,342	6,648	5,511	1,223	1,211	8,662	39,538	83,172	128,588
Colombia	3,339	3,509	2,453	2,560	4,144	5,164	11,041	12,926	128	217	604	836	3,905	6,478	1,362	1,264
Comoros	18	21	1,058	1,323	48	66	5,556	5,946	5	8	1,239	833	36	61	3	5
Congo	15	27	789	937	679	710	6,683	6,651	5	9	572	789	126	198	33	44
Costa Rica	337	160	2,471	2,424	45	181	5,742	24,805	12	45	497	692	1,362	2,585	58	168
Côte d'Ivoire	866	1,685	858	1,104	3,414	4,761	5,071	5,792	8	8	667	667	1,549	1,773	317	532
Croatia	...	2,764	...	4,223	...	500	...	7,519	...	23	...	1,031	...	493	...	261
Cuba	551	181	2,458	1,392	997	652	6,080	4,559	12	22	307	306	810	1,210	466	474
Cyprus	87	144	1,795	2,267	182	223	23,104	25,883	6	2	1,043	1,447	358	330	102	125
Czech Republic	...	6,598	...	4,185	...	1,330	...	17,082	...	137	...	2,293	...	443	...	550
Denmark	7,346	8,968	4,041	6,126	913	1,480	26,964	37,000	14	403	3,397	3,336	124	112	263	311
Djibouti	—	—	2,500	1,625	...	...	...	...	...	...	...	...	...	...	13	22
Dominica	—	—	1,427	1,308	26	23	10,243	9,272	...	...	467	476	46	73	7	6
Dominican Republic	447	589	3,003	4,109	214	256	5,804	6,318	73	79	951	953	1,333	1,499	209	234
Ecuador	686	2,032	1,639	2,009	552	562	9,640	6,326	39	49	548	524	3,769	6,751	243	315
Egypt	8,134	17,182	4,052	6,048	1,330	1,734	18,338	21,603	283	362	2,001	2,275	2,310	5,245	7,345	10,191
El Salvador	719	893	1,702	2,026	27	107	12,347	18,388	41	51	840	841	257	319	96	129
Equatorial Guinea	...	...	...	...	53	82	2,926	2,645	...	...	...	...	11	17	...	...
Eritrea	...	153	...	517	...	109	...	2,804	...	45	...	604	...	5	...	35
Estonia	796	740	1,862	2,114	1,031	700	14,257	14,286	1	—	1,333	1,375	46	53	117	83
Ethiopia	...	8,245	...	1,505	...	2,018	...	3,679	...	1,108	...	892	...	227	...	565
Faroe Islands	...	...	...	...	1	2	13,684	13,636	...	...	...	...	...	...	...	...

in national reports at all. FAO vegetable statistics include vegetables and melons grown for human consumption only. Some countries do not make this distinction in their reports, and some exclude the production of kitchen gardens and small family plots, although in certain countries, such small-scale production may account for 20 to 40 percent of total output.

Livestock statistics may be distorted by the timing of country reports. Ireland, for example, takes a livestock enumeration in December that is reported the following year and that appears low against data for otherwise comparable countries because of the slaughter and export of animals at the close of the grazing season. It balances this, however, with a June enumeration, when numbers tend to be high. Milk production as defined by the FAO includes whole fresh milk, excluding milk sucked by young animals but including amounts fed by farmers or ranchers to livestock, but national practices vary. Certain countries do not distinguish between milk cows and other cattle, so that yield per dairy cow must be estimated. Some countries do not report egg production statistics (here given in metric tons), and external estimates must be based on the numbers of chickens and reported or assumed egg-laying rates. Other countries report egg pro-

duction by number, and this must be converted to weight, using conversion factors specific to the makeup by species of national poultry flocks.

Metric system units used in the table may be converted to English system units as follows:

metric tons × 1.1023 = short tons
kilograms × 2.2046 = pounds
kilograms per hectare × 0.8922 = pounds per acre.

The notes that follow, keyed by references in the table headings, provide further definitional information.

a. Includes such crops as potatoes and cassava.
b. Includes beans and peas harvested for dry grain only. Does not include green beans and green peas.
c. Excludes melons.
d. Includes melons, green beans, and green peas.
e. From milk cows only.
f. From chickens only.

cattle stock ('000 head) 1979–81 average	1995	sheep stock ('000 head) 1979–81 average	1995	hogs stock ('000 head) 1979–81 average	1995	chickens stock ('000 head) 1979–81 average	1995	milk[e] production ('000 metric tons) 1979–81 average	1995	milk[e] yield (kg/animal) 1979–81 average	1995	eggs[f] production (metric tons) 1979–81 average	1995	country
3,723	1,500	18,667	18,000	...	...	6,467	9,000	552	300	491	395	14,000	18,120	Afghanistan
606	670	1,232	2,500	174	90	3,464	3,100	296	814	1,326	1,600	8,403	16,560	Albania
1,356	1,300	13,111	18,000	4	6	24,237	80,000	514	530	975	952	24,550	150,000	Algeria
—	—	...	...	10	11	25	37	—	—	800	800	34	30	American Samoa
...	...	...	...	...	...	...	...	...	...	...	...	...	...	Andorra
3,083	3,280	225	255	600	800	5,400	6,400	153	160	497	488	3,650	3,900	Angola
14	16	12	12	2	2	66	80	6	6	959	969	138	160	Antigua and Barbuda
55,620	53,500	31,473	21,780	3,751	3,100	38,167	69,000	5,311	7,400	1,746	2,622	253,731	270,000	Argentina
766	503	2,242	623	231	82	9,000	3,000	501	420	1,677	741	25,367	10,600	Armenia
...	...	...	...	...	...	...	...	...	...	...	...	...	...	Aruba
26,161	26,187	134,871	120,651	2,416	2,640	45,508	67,000	5,598	8,556	2,994	4,725	197,870	155,000	Australia
2,553	2,430	193	325	3,906	3,800	14,531	12,543	3,434	3,200	3,509	3,902	96,804	95,000	Austria
1,765	1,633	5,128	4,376	179	33	17,000	23,000	800	826	1,208	929	40,200	28,000	Azerbaijan
4	2	35	37	14	13	1,250	1,600	1	1	1,000	1,000	347	430	Bahamas, The
6	17	7	29	...	...	343	660	6	20	2,703	2,600	3,238	3,500	Bahrain
25,053	24,340	750	1,155	...	...	59,158	123,000	833	782	221	206	39,745	82,000	Bangladesh
18	28	50	41	44	30	1,717	3,200	7	7	1,495	1,783	1,489	1,300	Barbados
6,760	5,403	525	258	4,520	4,005	35,000	45,000	6,082	5,300	2,215	2,356	166,267	185,000	Belarus
3,104	3,369	110	150	5,083	7,053	28,530	35,000	4,042	3,500	3,876	4,667	200,655	220,000	Belgium[1]
50	60	3	3	16	22	387	1,300	4	7	1,021	1,015	1,034	1,225	Belize
810	1,223	972	940	400	555	10,952	20,000	12	16	120	130	7,860	18,720	Benin
1	1	...	...	2	1	47	50	2	1	2,836	2,400	435	350	Bermuda
299	435	10	59	55	75	149	310	26	29	257	257	159	350	Bhutan
4,570	5,985	8,967	7,884	1,553	2,405	17,465	55,676	71	140	1,396	1,401	22,500	60,900	Bolivia
...	273	...	260	...	147	...	3,000	...	239	...	1,453	...	6,900	Bosnia and Herzegovina
2,906	2,800	147	250	5	16	873	2,100	90	117	350	350	786	1,890	Botswana
116,645	156,500	18,414	21,000	34,102	35,350	426,342	700,000	11,378	17,400	712	789	765,117	1,400,000	Brazil
3	2	...	...	12	5	1,106	3,000	...	...	...	...	1,787	3,300	Brunei
1,782	600	10,358	3,117	3,803	1,722	39,124	15,416	1,843	1,000	2,638	2,714	131,679	75,600	Bulgaria
2,760	4,350	3,200	5,800	198	560	11,042	19,300	81	121	175	175	7,448	16,500	Burkina Faso
614	420	301	350	44	80	3,100	3,800	42	32	350	350	2,356	2,888	Burundi
809	2,589	...	...	162	2,154	2,975	10,500	14	19	170	170	5,400	10,400	Cambodia
3,521	4,900	2,167	3,800	1,139	1,410	8,264	20,000	88	125	500	500	8,400	13,000	Cameroon
12,096	12,849	480	620	9,548	11,881	96,011	132,000	7,354	7,770	4,137	6,077	330,863	328,580	Canada
12	19	1	4	40	450	250	600	1	2	500	524	200	550	Cape Verde
1,662	2,797	84	172	243	547	1,534	3,422	23	50	200	222	966	1,377	Central African Republic
4,360	4,539	2,620	2,219	9	18	3,167	4,400	118	123	270	270	2,850	3,960	Chad
3,650	3,814	6,059	4,625	1,068	1,490	25,667	62,000	1,111	1,873	1,561	1,922	66,046	95,000	Chile
52,567	100,849	101,864	117,446	313,660	424,681	906,231	2,797,827	1,143	5,838	1,802	1,545	2,325,749	12,340,040	China
24,110	26,018	2,399	2,540	2,013	2,635	30,029	80,000	2,187	4,690	965	998	176,972	315,000	Colombia
70	50	8	15	...	...	280	430	3	4	500	500	564	680	Comoros
64	68	69	111	28	56	1,100	1,800	1	1	500	500	825	1,230	Congo
2,183	1,860	2	3	223	350	5,100	15,000	318	506	1,067	1,488	16,760	23,500	Costa Rica
664	1,258	1,020	1,282	315	414	17,333	26,670	12	22	110	94	10,253	16,068	Côte d'Ivoire
...	493	...	453	...	1,347	...	12,000	...	600	...	1,818	...	46,000	Croatia
5,166	4,200	356	310	1,443	1,550	23,714	22,000	1,045	850	1,579	1,458	98,936	70,000	Cuba
22	64	290	255	162	356	2,133	3,300	33	135	4,305	4,874	5,309	8,000	Cyprus
...	2,030	...	165	...	3,867	...	25,522	...	3,134	...	4,087	...	152,353	Czech Republic
2,970	2,060	55	82	9,699	11,190	10,118	18,954	5,126	4,640	4,920	6,195	77,130	91,000	Denmark
47	190	417	470	...	...	...	...	2	7	350	350	...	...	Djibouti
7	12	6	8	8	5	109	190	3	5	1,000	1,000	177	225	Dominica
1,918	2,302	65	135	298	950	19,467	33,500	427	429	1,742	1,704	19,267	45,178	Dominican Republic
2,987	4,995	1,148	1,692	3,417	2,618	32,588	61,512	924	1,870	1,446	2,207	43,056	55,000	Ecuador
1,906	3,100	1,791	3,382	21	27	27,597	39,000	648	1,000	674	675	78,100	158,000	Egypt
1,234	1,262	4	5	455	372	5,037	5,400	268	280	958	903	36,822	52,500	El Salvador
4	5	33	36	4	5	137	245	...	...	...	...	116	190	Equatorial Guinea
...	1,312	...	1,530	...	...	...	4,300	...	31	...	194	...	5,934	Eritrea
821	435	164	62	1,038	460	6,000	3,055	1,149	812	3,633	3,587	29,267	25,000	Estonia
...	29,825	...	21,700	...	20	...	54,200	...	738	...	209	...	73,370	Ethiopia
2	2	67	68	...	...	...	...	...	...	...	...	...	...	Faroe Islands

Crops and livestock (continued)

country	grains production ('000 metric tons) 1979–81 average	grains production ('000 metric tons) 1995	grains yield (kg/hectare) 1979–81 average	grains yield (kg/hectare) 1995	roots and tubers[a] production ('000 metric tons) 1979–81 average	roots and tubers[a] production ('000 metric tons) 1995	roots and tubers[a] yield (kg/hectare) 1979–81 average	roots and tubers[a] yield (kg/hectare) 1995	pulses[b] production ('000 metric tons) 1979–81 average	pulses[b] production ('000 metric tons) 1995	pulses[b] yield (kg/hectare) 1979–81 average	pulses[b] yield (kg/hectare) 1995	fruits[c] production ('000 metric tons) 1979–81 average	fruits[c] production ('000 metric tons) 1995	vegetables[d] production ('000 metric tons) 1979–81 average	vegetables[d] production ('000 metric tons) 1995
Fiji	19	18	2,002	2,388	22	37	11,787	3,529	—	1	519	1,111	11	12	4	19
Finland	2,993	3,333	2,514	3,408	629	798	15,669	22,105	13	11	2,149	948	107	89	130	232
France	46,078	53,606	4,700	6,457	6,735	5,754	28,250	33,717	340	2,792	3,319	4,709	14,120	11,019	6,774	7,554
French Guiana	1	26	1,317	3,317	13	28	10,827	11,440	...	...	...	...	2	11	3	8
French Polynesia	...	...	...	...	17	13	13,873	12,547	...	...	...	...	4	7	6	6
Gabon	11	28	1,714	1,805	372	396	5,209	5,408	—	—	528	667	181	270	22	33
Gambia, The	78	108	1,196	1,207	6	6	3,000	3,000	4	4	267	267	4	4	7	8
Gaza Strip	5	1	2,811	529	5	35	18,039	21,875	—	—	2,321	...	200	137	61	158
Georgia	573	554	1,942	1,530	412	250	12,400	12,500	10	—	711	...	1,678	1,265	960	1,250
Germany	32,044	39,870	4,166	6,051	19,465	10,382	23,625	30,010	116	205	1,904	2,859	4,448	3,289	3,206	2,009
Ghana	726	1,835	805	1,354	3,183	10,493	6,714	11,339	14	20	101	100	966	1,789	299	531
Gibraltar	...	...	...	...	...	...	...	...	...	...	...	...	...	...	...	...
Greece	4,951	4,690	3,093	3,694	1,041	900	16,378	22,005	94	41	1,254	1,605	3,437	3,790	3,636	3,936
Greenland	...	...	...	...	...	...	...	...	...	...	...	...	...	...	...	...
Grenada	—	—	943	1,000	3	4	4,578	5,227	1	1	1,546	1,139	29	22	2	2
Guadeloupe	...	...	...	...	22	16	8,472	7,568	—	—	514	756	115	130	17	25
Guam	...	...	3,000	2,000	2	2	13,753	14,904	...	...	...	...	2	2	2	5
Guatemala	1,122	1,516	1,567	1,614	52	79	3,552	5,613	77	122	843	801	734	852	277	332
Guernsey	...	...	...	...	...	...	...	...	...	...	...	...	...	...	...	...
Guinea	678	773	957	1,071	644	801	7,116	7,402	42	60	646	857	664	994	410	420
Guinea-Bissau	102	201	718	1,408	47	65	5,957	7,303	2	3	970	650	45	65	21	20
Guyana	267	493	2,906	3,724	16	32	6,629	7,273	1	1	491	591	41	67	9	12
Haiti	419	373	1,007	871	689	772	3,778	3,831	90	88	471	680	1,007	882	281	219
Honduras	492	771	1,169	1,543	18	30	5,576	8,386	38	38	518	560	1,647	1,291	95	311
Hong Kong	—	—	1,681	—	—	—	25,362	42,667	...	...	...	...	3	3	189	88
Hungary	13,001	11,042	4,517	4,054	1,507	1,151	15,792	16,262	127	130	1,516	2,369	2,389	1,557	1,841	1,443
Iceland	...	...	...	...	11	11	12,138	13,750	...	...	...	...	...	...	1	3
India	138,182	214,893	1,324	2,134	16,777	26,300	12,925	16,386	10,509	14,820	461	595	20,409	38,912	43,866	64,613
Indonesia	33,605	58,083	2,842	3,840	16,153	18,603	9,053	11,790	352	310	876	892	4,941	7,295	2,434	5,469
Iran	8,855	17,312	1,098	1,767	1,284	3,200	14,445	20,644	247	650	789	674	3,234	9,775	4,966	9,850
Iraq	1,803	2,845	835	908	96	420	18,148	16,471	36	39	796	1,160	1,161	1,605	1,992	3,072
Ireland	2,009	1,811	4,731	6,657	822	620	20,872	27,434	—	19	3,478	4,524	22	20	283	245
Isle of Man	...	...	...	...	...	...	...	...	...	...	...	...	...	...	...	...
Israel	239	253	1,856	2,204	201	288	36,582	37,392	8	7	935	1,129	1,913	1,525	762	1,438
Italy	18,025	19,713	3,547	4,666	2,962	2,076	18,260	23,281	321	174	1,335	1,614	20,661	17,150	13,401	13,147
Jamaica	7	4	1,659	1,362	230	337	11,667	15,228	8	9	882	1,077	332	372	104	194
Japan	14,318	13,437	5,256	5,737	5,342	5,157	22,839	26,651	108	103	1,264	1,376	6,330	3,867	15,230	13,540
Jersey	...	...	...	...	...	...	...	...	...	...	...	...	...	...	...	...
Jordan	88	127	556	774	9	90	16,902	27,273	8	5	547	773	90	292	436	787
Kazakhstan	26,790	10,583	1,063	564	1,918	1,950	10,220	9,142	...	55	...	654	379	177	1,185	1,065
Kenya	2,281	3,394	1,348	1,884	1,257	1,685	7,978	8,101	185	270	430	386	650	984	490	655
Kiribati	...	...	...	...	9	8	8,012	7,857	...	...	...	...	5	5	4	5
Korea, North	5,536	5,241	3,406	3,386	1,909	2,050	12,479	12,059	280	300	848	882	851	1,385	2,630	3,988
Korea, South	8,452	6,923	5,004	5,864	1,653	848	17,790	22,316	56	26	940	1,002	994	2,232	9,070	10,313
Kuwait	—	2	3,109	4,841	—	1	16,978	18,571	...	...	...	...	1	2	36	93
Kyrgyzstan	1,413	782	2,452	1,432	272	431	12,348	17,240	2	—	1,000	...	247	132	396	344
Laos	1,056	1,491	1,405	2,664	184	223	10,115	8,669	17	43	1,729	1,890	89	161	26	154
Latvia	859	701	1,278	1,835	1,371	927	12,979	15,214	7	6	1,167	1,735	106	88	229	232
Lebanon	41	77	1,204	1,933	130	222	16,805	21,982	10	39	940	1,903	704	1,383	354	943
Lesotho	198	41	975	666	17	62	15,000	14,762	10	4	739	318	16	15	21	20
Liberia	254	50	1,252	1,111	346	523	6,894	7,356	3	3	500	500	121	144	64	76
Libya	225	318	419	689	97	127	6,671	7,257	9	12	1,079	1,111	203	250	527	624
Liechtenstein	...	...	...	...	...	...	...	...	...	...	...	...	...	...	...	...
Lithuania	1,742	2,500	1,642	2,192	1,832	1,594	13,022	13,279	110	35	...	1,416	202	136	333	280
Luxembourg[1]	...	...	...	...	...	...	...	...	...	...	...	...	...	...	...	...
Macau	...	...	...	...	4	8	11,154	13,879	—	1	...	...	...	...	2	1
Macedonia	...	726	...	3,002	...	154	...	10,897	...	26	...	1,736	...	312	...	464
Madagascar	2,178	2,780	1,663	1,984	2,267	3,375	5,703	6,874	53	60	853	832	719	760	283	333
Malawi	1,341	1,778	1,161	1,293	562	576	6,389	4,593	204	273	609	588	376	509	212	252
Malaysia	2,061	2,169	2,828	3,077	468	530	8,950	9,701	...	...	...	...	931	1,233	314	494
Maldives	—	—	783	1,000	7	8	5,227	5,123	—	—	600	641	8	10	15	24
Mali	1,064	2,433	790	812	123	29	8,348	4,954	47	67	338	214	13	16	173	267
Malta	8	9	3,257	3,431	21	27	9,058	22,333	1	1	2,315	2,295	11	12	47	60
Marshall Islands	...	...	...	...	...	...	...	...	...	...	...	...	...	...	...	...
Martinique	...	...	...	...	22	21	10,446	10,472	...	...	...	...	178	217	27	23
Mauritania	48	246	384	838	7	5	2,898	2,000	29	17	407	321	15	27	7	9
Mauritius	1	2	2,543	4,339	12	20	17,632	17,845	1	2	491	714	6	11	26	57
Mayotte	...	...	...	...	...	...	...	...	...	...	...	...	...	...	...	...
Mexico	20,692	25,344	2,167	2,463	1,120	1,252	12,859	18,312	1,265	1,428	710	664	7,316	11,638	3,947	6,210
Micronesia	...	...	...	...	...	...	...	...	...	...	...	...	...	...	...	...
Moldova	2,565	1,698	3,221	3,185	324	400	7,969	9,877	53	65	1,463	1,042	1,994	1,282	1,609	1,590
Monaco	...	...	...	...	...	...	...	...	...	...	...	...	...	...	...	...
Mongolia	320	261	572	677	50	52	7,768	8,387	—	1	258	667	3	...	26	10
Morocco	3,583	1,823	812	453	504	783	14,232	14,476	229	118	591	373	1,623	1,979	1,320	2,878
Mozambique	649	1,127	603	653	3,679	4,310	4,157	4,304	59	134	373	367	327	312	186	126
Myanmar (Burma)	12,984	20,690	2,530	2,962	167	244	8,209	8,626	365	1,228	582	659	838	1,015	1,872	2,235
Namibia	73	60	626	601	180	190	8,167	7,917	6	6	944	1,000	8	8	6	7
Nauru	...	...	...	...	...	...	...	...	...	...	...	...	...	...	...	...
Nepal	3,640	5,440	1,617	1,795	349	984	5,454	7,709	140	188	536	609	135	565	517	1,250
Netherlands, The	1,280	1,590	5,686	8,112	6,329	7,363	37,733	41,002	24	30	3,144	4,041	535	770	2,527	3,397
Netherlands Antilles	...	...	...	...	...	...	...	...	...	...	...	...	...	...	...	...
New Caledonia	3	1	2,122	2,744	21	23	5,692	6,209	—	—	792	567	9	4	3	3
New Zealand	789	855	4,076	5,740	220	282	26,292	26,111	63	78	2,863	2,600	342	648	381	668
Nicaragua	392	592	1,473	1,871	28	81	9,083	11,571	39	80	592	666	313	248	47	59
Niger	1,702	2,221	440	307	212	260	7,227	7,429	292	433	265	170	37	47	142	264

livestock														country
cattle		sheep		hogs		chickens		milk[e]				eggs[f]		
stock ('000 head)		stock ('000 head)		stock ('000 head)		stock ('000 head)		production ('000 metric tons)		yield (kg/animal)		production (metric tons)		
1979–81 average	1995	1979–81 average	1995	1979–81 average	1995	1979–81 average	1995	1979–81 average	1995	1979–81 average	1995	1979–81 average	1995	
212	354	—	7	64	121	1,210	3,400	54	65	1,701	1,703	1,976	2,900	Fiji
1,747	1,185	107	80	1,430	1,394	8,803	5,561	3,236	2,491	4,572	6,087	77,967	66,000	Finland
23,825	20,524	12,133	10,320	11,472	14,593	177,148	217,990	27,084	25,800	3,707	5,314	849,667	1,026,000	France
6	9	3	3	6	9	123	150	—	—	2,080	2,545	292	500	French Guiana
8	7	2	—	24	42	490	270	2	2	2,771	2,135	923	1,250	French Polynesia
5	39	105	172	126	165	1,587	2,600	—	1	250	250	1,050	1,500	Gabon
293	400	136	121	10	11	273	550	5	7	175	175	402	894	Gambia, The
5	3	15	24	...	...	990	3,600	11	8	4,185	4,100	2,265	7,500	Gaza Strip
1,552	800	1,961	720	926	270	17,000	17,000	643	350	1,055	753	35,900	14,700	Georgia
20,672	15,962	3,148	2,340	34,768	24,698	136,705	101,139	31,725	28,000	4,178	5,320	1,123,574	843,000	Germany
804	1,680	1,942	3,288	379	595	11,461	11,500	16	23	130	130	12,203	14,310	Ghana
...	...	...	...	...	...	...	...	...	...	...	...	...	...	Gibraltar
929	600	8,040	9,604	944	1,121	29,554	28,000	666	690	1,867	3,644	122,540	126,500	Greece
...	...	20	22	...	...	...	...	...	...	...	...	...	...	Greenland
7	4	14	12	2	3	268	280	1	1	769	887	948	920	Grenada
91	60	3	3	44	14	147	280	1	—	507	500	778	1,656	Guadeloupe
1	—	...	...	13	4	185	200	...	...	...	...	1,071	700	Guam
1,886	1,700	615	440	640	889	14,012	19,000	263	260	749	77	40,590	69,740	Guatemala
...	...	...	...	...	...	...	...	9	—	4,202	...	...	...	Guernsey
1,500	1,780	436	475	39	38	7,083	13,500	41	46	185	185	7,420	14,490	Guinea
290	475	177	255	256	310	417	850	9	12	170	170	300	612	Guinea-Bissau
193	190	115	130	90	50	10,833	11,300	13	9	832	933	8,033	8,300	Guyana
1,000	1,200	88	85	1,533	360	5,067	5,600	20	36	229	252	2,943	3,750	Haiti
1,980	1,980	5	13	418	600	4,718	14,000	224	444	538	967	19,093	32,300	Honduras
7	2	—	—	520	107	6,309	3,512	4	—	3,022	2,405	2,737	1,030	Hong Kong
1,936	910	2,960	947	8,232	4,356	61,824	33,665	2,559	1,915	3,727	4,537	250,000	180,000	Hungary
60	71	838	470	11	21	358	165	121	105	3,635	3,483	3,000	2,300	Iceland
186,500	194,655	44,987	45,000	9,433	11,900	160,000	610,000	13,420	32,000	530	984	568,333	1,540,000	India
6,502	11,966	4,124	6,507	3,234	9,069	168,423	650,000	79	449	762	1,184	177,767	452,636	Indonesia
5,411	8,200	34,740	50,000	17	—	91,667	186,000	1,580	3,170	700	760	172,000	525,000	Iran
1,690	1,250	10,842	6,320	...	...	26,333	45,000	290	245	750	702	48,362	45,000	Iraq
6,043	6,410	2,374	5,772	1,122	1,498	8,389	11,906	4,729	5,689	3,178	3,741	35,000	31,700	Ireland
...	...	...	...	...	...	...	...	...	...	...	...	...	...	Isle of Man
299	379	243	352	120	109	25,016	23,000	702	1,136	6,817	9,389	91,675	117,450	Israel
8,697	7,164	9,120	10,682	8,885	8,023	138,333	129,000	10,546	10,674	3,478	3,887	659,163	631,000	Italy
279	440	4	2	208	200	5,100	7,400	48	53	1,000	1,000	15,500	28,000	Jamaica
4,261	4,916	13	25	9,851	10,250	284,477	315,000	6,526	8,500	4,526	6,044	1,998,041	2,571,000	Japan
...	...	...	...	...	...	...	...	...	...	...	...	...	...	Jersey
29	43	950	2,100	...	...	28,000	78,000	18	90	1,000	3,000	19,000	54,250	Jordan
8,349	9,347	34,162	33,524	3,017	2,445	44,000	50,000	4,490	5,300	1,546	1,683	187,867	185,000	Kazakstan
10,418	13,000	5,100	5,600	75	104	16,803	25,000	958	2,170	460	493	19,896	42,000	Kenya
...	...	...	...	10	...	167	290	...	...	...	...	105	135	Kiribati
945	1,350	292	395	2,100	3,350	17,950	22,500	55	90	2,244	2,310	103,833	150,000	Korea, North
1,634	3,070	6	2	2,153	6,100	41,417	80,569	449	1,986	4,864	6,829	255,786	442,000	Korea, South
17	20	250	250	...	...	9,343	25,000	24	30	2,653	3,550	8,573	7,500	Kuwait
968	1,061	9,853	7,077	320	165	9,000	12,000	676	864	1,803	1,705	23,283	8,300	Kyrgyzstan
437	1,190	...	...	1,117	1,653	4,890	9,300	6	11	200	200	22,167	37,000	Laos
1,413	551	207	86	1,623	501	10,000	3,500	1,668	937	2,898	1,767	40,467	22,891	Latvia
56	79	152	400	18	41	18,748	18,000	85	135	2,290	2,770	41,275	65,000	Lebanon
581	640	1,062	1,300	75	45	790	1,000	20	26	290	290	789	826	Lesotho
39	36	200	210	103	120	2,433	3,500	1	1	130	130	2,336	3,600	Liberia
156	100	5,046	4,400	...	...	6,366	16,500	63	85	1,499	1,375	16,233	33,000	Libya
6	6	2	3	3	3	...	...	9	12	3,310	4,444	...	...	Liechtenstein
2,195	1,152	61	40	2,568	1,260	13,600	8,530	2,565	2,400	2,955	3,265	54,000	55,000	Lithuania
...	...	...	...	...	...	...	...	...	...	...	...	...	...	Luxembourg[1]
...	...	...	...	...	...	450	430	...	...	...	...	575	635	Macau
...	276	...	2,044	...	195	...	4,000	...	265	...	1,345	...	25,500	Macedonia
10,147	10,309	695	740	1,175	1,592	17,804	23,000	440	483	255	275	13,483	18,200	Madagascar
817	980	84	196	192	247	8,050	8,750	35	42	458	460	10,503	11,500	Malawi
539	689	65	269	1,869	3,282	50,667	100,000	25	32	549	559	131,100	354,869	Malaysia
...	...	...	...	...	...	...	...	...	...	...	...	...	...	Maldives
5,670	5,542	6,247	5,173	48	63	12,433	23,250	139	136	245	245	6,720	11,880	Mali
13	19	5	17	12	104	1,284	810	29	40	4,111	3,810	6,256	7,100	Malta
...	...	...	...	...	...	...	...	...	...	...	...	...	...	Marshall Islands
57	30	55	47	37	34	487	330	5	2	754	613	1,500	1,510	Martinique
1,262	1,125	5,166	5,288	...	...	3,090	3,900	85	106	350	350	2,720	4,590	Mauritania
27	34	10	7	7	17	1,500	2,800	25	25	2,500	2,500	2,800	4,500	Mauritius
...	...	...	...	...	...	...	...	...	...	...	...	...	...	Mayotte
27,706	30,162	6,484	5,987	16,895	18,000	176,935	288,224	6,949	7,820	1,284	1,165	636,256	1,208,080	Mexico
...	...	...	...	...	...	...	...	...	...	...	...	...	...	Micronesia
1,138	832	1,208	1,432	2,020	1,061	16,000	13,840	1,189	759	2,780	2,061	48,633	45,000	Moldova
...	...	...	...	...	...	...	...	...	...	...	...	...	...	Monaco
2,452	3,317	14,261	13,719	32	24	267	160	210	281	355	316	983	180	Mongolia
3,362	2,490	15,228	16,586	7	10	24,333	156,522	753	830	640	571	72,900	190,000	Morocco
1,400	1,280	106	121	120	175	16,833	23,000	64	59	170	170	8,733	12,000	Mozambique
8,565	9,857	235	328	2,263	2,944	23,279	27,981	283	448	245	368	31,435	46,082	Myanmar (Burma)
2,318	1,890	4,084	2,620	15	18	1,200	2,000	68	70	412	410	900	1,500	Namibia
...	...	...	...	2	3	3	5	...	...	...	...	8	16	Nauru
6,893	6,838	730	919	375	636	5,700	9,500	190	288	325	376	14,300	18,500	Nepal
5,071	4,500	856	2,000	10,058	14,100	81,425	91,905	11,832	10,900	5,025	6,289	540,409	597,000	Netherlands, The
2	1	8	7	7	2	120	135	1	—	1,262	1,250	517	510	Netherlands Antilles
113	113	4	4	16	39	217	650	3	3	600	600	887	1,400	New Caledonia
8,063	8,729	67,393	47,144	433	425	6,691	12,700	6,586	9,684	3,016	2,940	56,855	50,000	New Zealand
2,373	1,750	3	4	625	400	4,500	7,300	234	187	814	688	28,833	27,500	Nicaragua
3,343	2,008	3,007	3,789	31	39	10,100	20,000	97	164	200	400	6,800	9,180	Niger

Crops and livestock (continued)

country	grains production ('000 metric tons) 1979–81 average	1995	grains yield (kg/hectare) 1979–81 average	1995	roots and tubers[a] production ('000 metric tons) 1979–81 average	1995	roots and tubers[a] yield (kg/hectare) 1979–81 average	1995	pulses[b] production ('000 metric tons) 1979–81 average	1995	pulses[b] yield (kg/hectare) 1979–81 average	1995	fruits[c] production ('000 metric tons) 1979–81 average	1995	vegetables[d] production ('000 metric tons) 1979–81 average	1995
Nigeria	7,480	20,943	1,229	1,124	18,789	56,006	8,795	10,613	647	1,850	442	833	5,238	7,094	3,355	5,830
Northern Mariana Islands	...	...	...	...	...	...	...	...	...	...	...	...	...	...	...	...
Norway	1,129	1,435	3,633	3,952	524	471	25,898	25,480	—	—	...	...	117	112	186	166
Oman	2	5	962	2,180	1	6	13,659	22,917	...	...	...	...	111	202	105	167
Pakistan	17,200	24,586	1,609	2,017	537	1,497	11,127	14,471	595	781	396	513	2,552	4,501	1,857	3,971
Palau	...	...	...	...	...	...	...	...	...	...	...	...	...	...	...	...
Panama	253	333	1,523	1,800	76	66	7,767	5,726	5	12	434	502	1,192	1,088	44	92
Papua New Guinea	4	3	2,048	1,698	1,125	1,267	7,087	7,073	2	2	500	522	875	1,154	286	381
Paraguay	459	1,133	1,511	2,164	2,080	2,708	12,906	14,442	69	56	795	722	623	514	225	265
Peru	1,429	2,142	1,951	2,633	2,477	3,369	7,574	9,292	111	126	857	946	1,501	2,512	720	1,215
Philippines	10,942	15,163	1,611	2,214	3,100	2,820	6,636	6,784	37	37	652	786	6,816	6,970	3,470	4,451
Poland	18,466	25,106	2,345	2,940	39,508	24,891	16,831	16,351	216	250	1,227	1,487	1,584	2,001	4,573	5,853
Portugal	1,210	1,306	1,102	1,862	1,141	1,477	8,962	14,937	76	44	229	228	2,055	1,622	1,524	1,999
Puerto Rico	6	1	8,915	8,046	39	10	6,438	6,443	6	1	827	527	296	194	28	33
Qatar	1	6	2,635	2,979	—	—	13,367	10,833	...	...	...	...	6	12	18	41
Réunion	12	17	5,071	6,124	11	17	13,288	12,058	1	1	2,617	737	23	35	15	58
Romania	18,109	19,885	2,856	3,210	4,317	3,020	14,737	12,080	115	96	255	1,545	2,952	2,977	4,202	3,637
Russia	82,466	61,796	1,147	1,165	37,632	37,300	9,962	10,941	2,659	1,435	815	831	3,075	2,416	12,696	9,957
Rwanda	271	151	1,132	1,632	1,743	1,534	8,772	6,864	221	130	727	634	2,162	2,655	169	120
St. Kitts and Nevis	...	...	...	...	2	1	3,690	3,659	—	—	1,000	1,000	1	2	—	1
St. Lucia	—	—	703	714	10	12	4,249	4,109	—	—	2,187	2,000	90	164	1	1
St. Vincent and the Grenadines	1	1	3,292	3,910	24	18	8,039	4,656	—	—	913	1,000	35	98	2	4
San Marino	...	...	...	...	...	...	...	...	...	...	...	...	...	...	...	...
São Tomé and Príncipe	—	4	1,505	2,105	14	11	8,928	6,848	...	...	...	...	4	14	3	3
Saudi Arabia	303	3,420	781	4,196	4	170	9,525	17,989	6	7	1,814	1,850	499	926	682	2,171
Senegal	850	1,059	699	874	43	68	4,345	3,661	21	42	401	430	74	122	82	134
Seychelles	...	...	...	...	...	...	5,000	5,000	...	...	...	...	2	2	1	2
Sierra Leone	542	338	1,247	1,145	124	262	3,305	4,942	31	41	579	672	128	156	153	192
Singapore	...	...	...	...	2	—	11,338	10,000	...	...	...	...	9	...	39	5
Slovakia	...	3,528	...	4,109	...	442	...	11,065	...	147	...	2,356	...	150	...	476
Slovenia	...	570	...	5,029	...	430	...	17,200	...	6	...	1,050	...	229	...	89
Solomon Islands	13	—	3,520	—	87	112	15,040	17,077	2	2	840	1,000	11	15	5	6
Somalia	305	285	477	378	39	44	10,858	10,000	10	13	493	236	182	210	27	73
South Africa	14,036	7,440	2,112	1,244	793	1,524	12,015	21,925	110	72	1,048	719	3,140	3,932	1,662	2,076
Spain	14,709	11,487	1,990	1,730	5,670	4,219	15,987	19,834	365	155	710	476	12,603	10,796	8,506	10,143
Sri Lanka	2,130	2,722	2,464	2,903	717	440	9,683	8,852	47	41	858	781	1,717	738	379	587
Sudan, The	2,962	3,821	672	473	296	156	3,328	2,833	99	107	1,259	1,004	754	805	789	943
Suriname	258	220	3,971	3,661	3	7	4,821	11,853	—	—	869	727	52	86	6	32
Swaziland	92	79	1,317	1,271	13	8	1,995	1,930	3	6	575	729	121	98	12	12
Sweden	5,407	4,819	3,593	4,450	1,191	1,074	28,931	30,679	32	78	2,258	2,378	207	102	228	238
Switzerland	843	1,281	4,884	5,971	924	680	37,844	39,535	1	10	3,378	4,000	724	549	306	287
Syria	3,069	6,136	1,162	1,665	279	553	15,133	22,120	180	259	819	1,009	733	1,596	2,973	1,948
Taiwan	...	...	...	...	...	...	...	...	...	...	...	...	...	...	...	...
Tajikistan	285	251	1,295	930	152	140	16,926	10,769	6	6	792	600	431	225	495	595
Tanzania	3,010	4,617	1,062	1,419	6,158	6,670	9,460	7,448	315	378	454	532	1,953	1,861	973	1,001
Thailand	20,316	25,358	1,912	2,385	15,512	18,382	14,268	13,955	342	365	684	811	6,453	6,851	2,711	2,686
Togo	301	466	723	691	922	865	8,717	5,857	23	33	238	321	41	48	65	159
Tonga	...	...	...	...	91	101	5,970	6,549	...	...	...	...	14	13	7	8
Trinidad and Tobago	13	15	3,204	3,659	20	12	12,206	10,222	4	2	1,638	1,662	57	75	30	18
Tunisia	1,146	637	810	627	127	205	12,795	13,141	89	79	559	768	518	725	1,044	1,554
Turkey	25,232	28,163	1,869	1,977	2,958	4,750	16,656	24,356	817	1,824	1,140	967	7,682	9,767	13,041	21,319
Turkmenistan	281	1,249	2,142	2,210	16	11	7,833	3,667	...	...	...	...	90	249	279	496
Tuvalu	...	...	...	...	...	—	...	...	...	...	...	...	—	1	...	...
Uganda	1,171	2,080	1,557	1,551	3,548	5,246	5,842	5,861	236	510	643	675	6,300	10,147	290	424
Ukraine	33,181	32,429	2,208	2,522	18,429	14,729	11,017	9,621	1,551	1,518	1,238	1,412	3,973	2,277	7,773	6,377
United Arab Emirates	3	7	6,053	7,396	2	4	14,595	20,000	...	...	...	...	62	297	130	581
United Kingdom	18,840	21,987	4,794	6,978	6,601	6,445	32,908	39,405	240	721	3,170	3,162	524	480	3,762	3,742
United States	301,405	276,999	4,150	4,647	15,487	20,764	28,812	35,131	1,466	1,724	1,613	1,915	26,527	29,695	25,476	33,596
Uruguay	1,012	1,492	1,644	2,643	197	208	5,508	9,469	5	6	910	981	275	439	153	137
Uzbekistan	2,597	2,803	2,208	1,691	264	500	10,409	9,634	7	—	952	...	1,284	899	2,718	4,137
Vanuatu	1	1	514	538	32	50	19,592	10,000	...	...	...	...	11	19	6	8
Venezuela	1,550	2,043	1,905	2,577	599	655	8,043	8,802	37	50	508	653	2,029	2,768	402	721
Vietnam	12,222	25,206	2,049	3,523	6,355	5,077	6,709	7,351	117	216	549	671	2,584	4,332	2,504	4,163
Virgin Islands (U.S.)	...	...	...	...	...	...	...	...	...	...	...	...	...	...	...	...
West Bank	53	45	1,293	...	8	17	25,594	...	...	2	731	...	181	153	164	228
Western Sahara	2	2	682	774	...	...	...	...	...	...	...	...	...	...	...	...
Western Samoa	...	...	...	...	39	41	6,927	6,164	...	...	...	...	53	43	...	1
Yemen	897	825	1,037	1,091	134	200	12,099	13,327	80	70	1,072	1,330	173	365	335	472
Yugoslavia	...	8,388	...	3,581	...	931	...	8,096	...	113	...	1,537	...	1,381	...	1,125
Zaire	900	1,697	807	799	13,595	18,358	6,899	8,101	155	200	604	626	2,624	3,529	479	575
Zambia	990	881	1,665	1,330	333	668	5,457	5,562	7	24	346	573	76	93	209	242
Zimbabwe	2,273	980	1,392	532	76	162	3,824	4,539	23	43	566	603	109	182	136	143

livestock								milk[e]				eggs[f]		country
cattle		sheep		hogs		chickens								
stock ('000 head)		stock ('000 head)		stock ('000 head)		stock ('000 head)		production ('000 metric tons)		yield (kg/animal)		production (metric tons)		
1979–81 average	1995	1979–81 average	1995	1979–81 average	1995	1979–81 average	1995	1979–81 average	1995	1979–81 average	1995	1979–81 average	1995	
12,066	17,791	8,022	14,000	1,000	6,926	79,823	124,000	289	380	239	233	198,333	320,000	Nigeria
...	...	...	...	...	...	...	...	...	...	...	...	...	...	Northern Mariana Islands
989	1,003	2,033	2,316	675	745	3,738	3,729	1,926	1,863	5,125	5,533	44,665	50,779	Norway
141	142	114	148	...	...	471	2,700	18	19	420	420	710	6,160	Oman
15,268	19,000	22,580	29,065	...	...	43,733	135,000	2,189	4,223	864	891	96,367	290,000	Pakistan
...	...	...	...	...	...	...	...	...	...	...	...	...	...	Palau
1,425	1,454	...	...	205	257	5,242	10,543	94	155	988	1,265	11,142	14,435	Panama
130	110	2	4	870	1,030	1,700	3,250	—	—	228	96	1,810	3,600	Papua New Guinea
5,966	8,100	387	386	1,090	2,660	11,862	13,253	163	291	1,903	1,894	26,025	46,792	Paraguay
4,276	4,513	13,767	12,570	2,116	2,401	40,174	68,470	796	857	1,298	1,496	59,700	144,200	Peru
1,885	2,021	30	30	7,712	8,941	53,268	74,000	14	18	994	1,037	201,285	305,000	Philippines
12,494	7,306	4,105	713	20,343	20,418	76,956	46,395	16,250	11,705	2,778	3,161	488,642	301,408	Poland
1,332	1,288	4,440	6,200	3,367	2,416	18,333	26,000	750	1,500	2,123	1,177	62,008	101,000	Portugal
497	429	6	8	225	196	6,973	14,000	420	373	2,324	4,088	21,902	18,000	Puerto Rico
9	12	48	175	...	...	515	3,400	4	4	1,561	1,510	281	3,400	Qatar
20	26	2	2	61	83	3,405	7,700	5	5	526	520	3,040	5,000	Réunion
6,351	3,481	15,766	10,857	10,926	7,758	91,847	70,157	3,987	3,900	1,914	2,000	323,833	270,000	Romania
58,414	39,696	63,566	23,345	36,218	22,631	507,000	482,500	46,953	39,098	2,113	2,200	2,193,000	1,869,000	Russia
625	465	303	250	124	80	1,064	1,400	61	80	510	607	860	2,000	Rwanda
5	4	14	14	2	2	78	60	...	...	...	...	297	350	St. Kitts and Nevis
10	12	13	16	10	13	187	250	1	1	1,390	1,527	497	540	St. Lucia
8	6	13	13	6	9	153	255	1	1	1,362	1,340	530	640	St. Vincent and the Grenadines
...	...	...	...	...	...	...	...	...	...	...	...	...	...	San Marino
3	4	2	2	2	2	90	250	—	—	170	170	130	262	São Tomé and Príncipe
374	204	4,040	7,475	...	...	19,333	83,000	64	350	443	6,832	40,791	132,000	Saudi Arabia
2,424	2,850	1,966	4,800	180	320	8,378	40,000	87	103	357	360	6,353	31,500	Senegal
3	- 2	...	...	10	19	178	500	1	—	519	529	811	2,400	Seychelles
349	360	268	302	36	50	4,060	6,000	18	17	250	250	4,669	6,900	Sierra Leone
1	—	...	...	1,017	190	14,162	2,000	...	...	...	...	26,870	18,260	Singapore
...	916	...	428	...	2,037	...	7,300	...	1,186	...	3,122	...	89,400	Slovakia
...	504	...	20	...	592	...	9,900	...	570	...	1,652	...	22,000	Slovenia
23	5	...	...	45	55	142	145	1	2	600	860	284	292	Solomon Islands
4,437	5,200	10,467	13,500	9	9	2,900	3,000	477	560	414	407	2,320	2,400	Somalia
13,647	13,015	31,625	28,784	1,339	1,628	30,000	52,000	2,553	2,495	2,809	2,554	159,952	237,000	South Africa
4,608	5,060	14,721	23,900	10,392	18,322	80,333	83,000	5,984	6,000	3,255	4,295	665,560	694,000	Spain
1,662	1,703	27	20	71	94	6,173	10,000	182	212	448	353	28,857	48,950	Sri Lanka
18,376	22,000	17,628	23,000	...	...	27,000	36,500	1,352	2,592	500	480	31,745	38,000	Sudan, The
46	102	3	7	19	20	4,533	3,400	7	18	1,209	1,753	2,638	4,000	Suriname
658	597	32	24	17	30	626	1,000	36	42	252	273	272	335	Swaziland
1,928	1,777	392	461	2,711	2,313	12,830	12,564	3,452	3,304	5,257	6,590	113,633	103,112	Sweden
2,008	1,762	350	437	2,113	1,611	6,146	6,000	3,653	3,900	4,194	5,000	43,186	33,300	Switzerland
778	750	9,311	11,800	—	1	14,637	18,500	504	775	1,353	2,344	68,759	105,000	Syria
135	165	...	...	5,021	10,509	41,411	101,838	47	318	4,127	4,802	...	...	Taiwan
1,177	1,250	2,377	2,000	130	40	6,000	4,500	452	450	1,025	968	19,000	16,000	Tajikistan
12,616	13,376	3,754	3,955	160	335	17,633	27,000	374	590	160	160	35,302	54,080	Tanzania
4,228	7,593	25	130	3,344	4,507	59,949	80,218	19	265	1,950	2,144	145,500	538,063	Thailand
229	248	592	1,200	231	850	2,018	5,685	7	10	225	225	1,677	6,325	Togo
10	10	...	...	105	94	166	215	—	—	2,106	1,500	229	260	Tonga
77	36	10	12	59	45	7,367	9,500	6	9	1,169	1,618	7,433	9,500	Trinidad and Tobago
583	735	4,651	7,600	4	6	24,167	45,000	216	565	878	1,698	36,383	62,500	Tunisia
15,467	11,901	46,199	35,646	13	8	54,805	183,684	7,737	9,133	1,300	1,459	217,164	493,600	Turkey
606	1,104	4,277	6,000	159	159	5,000	6,500	311	666	1,372	816	13,550	14,000	Turkmenistan
...	...	...	...	6	13	14	27	...	...	...	...	11	12	Tuvalu
4,919	5,200	1,319	1,900	187	920	13,233	22,500	344	455	350	350	10,587	18,000	Uganda
25,433	19,624	8,912	4,792	20,197	13,946	209,000	136,000	21,044	17,060	2,272	2,241	850,167	532,971	Ukraine
26	65	132	350	...	...	1,792	11,000	4	7	446	201	2,533	11,955	United Arab Emirates
13,321	11,868	21,643	29,484	7,856	7,879	115,967	125,718	15,917	14,668	4,755	5,506	834,000	618,000	United Kingdom
112,152	102,755	12,670	8,860	64,045	59,992	1,063,667	1,808,000	58,139	70,598	5,377	7,277	4,116,200	4,398,500	United States
10,965	10,870	19,219	22,685	308	300	5,892	9,800	811	1,328	1,442	1,759	16,903	22,500	Uruguay
3,391	5,291	7,949	8,600	441	391	22,000	30,000	2,123	3,686	1,627	1,529	81,567	88,000	Uzbekistan
94	151	...	...	68	60	270	320	2	3	201	261	237	280	Vanuatu
10,527	14,231	333	1,160	2,241	2,850	41,984	95,000	1,356	1,611	1,163	1,268	128,745	140,000	Venezuela
1,694	3,604	...	...	9,778	16,500	55,327	95,000	26	43	800	800	55,317	136,000	Vietnam
8	8	4	3	5	3	63	35	3	2	3,477	2,738	196	160	Virgin Islands (U.S.)
15	12	232	352	...	...	...	...	...	27	...	...	2,550	14,300	West Bank
...	...	18	29	...	...	...	...	...	...	...	...	...	...	Western Sahara
26	26	...	...	71	179	450	350	1	1	1,000	1,000	152	200	Western Samoa
973	1,130	3,002	3,715	...	...	4,517	21,500	70	155	361	600	7,083	18,300	Yemen
...	1,950	...	2,671	...	4,192	...	23,491	...	1,900	...	1,500	...	82,500	Yugoslavia
1,159	1,480	726	1,050	685	1,200	13,500	35,500	6	8	827	849	7,247	9,000	Zaire
2,238	3,300	29	69	217	295	18,338	22,000	60	89	300	300	27,880	35,200	Zambia
5,378	4,500	481	487	155	277	8,300	13,500	455	420	431	450	10,400	17,400	Zimbabwe

[f]Belgium includes Luxembourg.

Extractive industries

Extractive industries are generally defined as those exploiting in situ natural resources and include such activities as mining, forestry, fisheries, and agriculture; the definition is often confined, however, to nonrenewable resources only. For the purposes of this table, agriculture is excluded; it is covered in the two tables immediately preceding.

Extractive industries are divided here into three parts: mining, forestry, and fisheries. These major headings are each divided into two main subheadings, one that treats production and one that treats foreign trade. The production sections are presented in terms of volume except for mining, and the trade sections are presented in terms of U.S. dollars. Volume of production data usually imply output of primary (unprocessed) raw materials only, but, because of the way national statistical information is reported, the data may occasionally include some processed and manufactured materials as well, since these are often indistinguishably associated with the extractive process (sulfur from petroleum extraction, cured or treated lumber, or "processed" fish). This is also the case in the trade sections, where individual national trade nomenclatures may not distinguish some processed and manufactured goods from unprocessed raw materials.

Mining. In the absence of a single international source publication or standard of practice for reporting volume or value of mineral production, single-country sources predominantly have been used to compile mining production figures, supplemented by U.S. Bureau of Mines data, by the United Nations' *National Accounts Statistics* (annual; 2 parts), and by industry sources, especially *Mining Journal*'s *Mining Annual Review*. Each

country has its own methods of classifying mining data, which do not always accord with the principal mineral production categories adopted in this table—namely, "metals," "nonmetals," and "energy." The available data have therefore been adjusted to accord better with the definition of each group. Included in the "metal" category are all ferrous and nonferrous metallic ores, concentrates, and scrap; the "nonmetal" group includes all nonmetallic minerals (stone, clay, precious gems, etc.) except the mineral fuels; the last group, "energy," is composed predominantly of the natural hydrocarbon fuels, though it may also include manufactured gas.

The contribution (value) of each national mineral sector to its country's gross domestic product is given, as is the distribution by group of that contribution (to gross domestic product and to foreign trade), although statistics regarding the value of mineral production are less readily available in country sources than those regarding trade or volume of minerals produced. Figures for value added by mineral output, though not always available, were sought first, as they provide the most consistent standard to compare the importance of minerals both within a particular national economy and among national mineral sectors worldwide. Where value added to the gross domestic product was not available, gross value of production or sales was substituted and the exception footnoted. Figures for value of production are reported here in millions of U.S. dollars to permit comparisons to be made from country to country. Comparisons can also be made as to the relative importance of each mineral group within a given country.

Extractive industries

country	mining % of GDP, 1994	mineral production (value added)					trade (value)								
		year	total ('000,000 U.S.$)	by kind (%) metals[a]	non-metals[b]	energy[c]	year	exports total ('000,000 U.S.$)	by kind (%) metals[a]	non-metals[b]	energy[c]	imports total ('000,000 U.S.$)	by kind (%) metals[a]	non-metals[b]	energy[c]
Afghanistan	...	1988[1]	16.2	—	17.7	82.3	1992	5.4	72.6	27.4	—	0.1	—	100.0	—
Albania	...	1994[1]	81.4	46.1	0.8	53.1	1993	18.1	55.2	3.5	41.3	—	—	—	—
Algeria	23.4	1994	9,880.5	—0.6—		99.4	1994	6,617.6	—	0.2	99.8	57.9	17.2	43.0	39.9
American Samoa	...	1994	...	—	100.0	—	1989	0.1	100.0	—	—	0.1	—	—	100.0
Andorra	...	...	...	...	...	...	1992	0.3	—	100.0	—	7.8	—	100.0	—
Angola	52.1	1994	2,610.9	—	2.0	98.0	1992	3,801.2	—	9.9	90.1	—	—	—	—
Antigua and Barbuda	1.5	1994	6.3	—	100.0	—	1994	1,197.7	—	—	100.0	460.2	42.1	9.7	48.1
Argentina	1.8[2]	1992	4,108.1	2.7[3]	3.9[3]	93.4[3]	1993	5.4	—	100.0	—				
Armenia	...	...	...	...	...	...									
Aruba	...	1994	...	—	100.0	—	1991	0.1	100.0	—	—	0.5	...	97.9	2.1
Australia	4.4	1994–95	14,150.8	37.5[4]	7.1[4]	55.4[4]	1994	9,039.8	30.4	3.8	65.8	1,910.4	6.2	11.7	82.1
Austria	0.2[2]	1992	385.0	5.3[3]	30.8[3]	63.9[3]	1994	321.6	39.8	59.6	0.6	2,316.4	18.7	11.1	70.2
Azerbaijan	...	...	...	...	...	...	1994	1.2	100.0	—	—				
Bahamas, The	...	1994	...	—	100.0	—	1991	25.0	—	100.0	—	8.4	—	—	100.0
Bahrain	15.1	1992[1]	1,974.5	—	3.9	96.1	1993	2,439.6	0.4	1.8	97.8	1,432.6	1.9	2.4	95.7
Bangladesh	...	1994	...	—	—100.0[5]—		1993	...	—	—	—	382.3	0.1	32.0	67.9
Barbados	...	1994	...	—	—100.0[6]—		1993	...	—	—	—	5.2	—	18.4	81.6
Belarus	0.1[2]	1992	2.0	—	—100.0—		1994	10.5	65.5	1.5	33.0				
Belgium	0.2[7]	1993	433.6	—	—100.0—		1994[8]	10,682.6	5.2	92.9	2.0	17,144.8	13.2	57.6	29.2
Belize	0.5	1994	2.3	—	100.0	—	1994	—	—	—	—	3.1	—	32.9	67.1
Benin	0.8	1994	12.2[9]	—	—100.0[9]—		1990	22.5	—	—	100.0	—	—	—	—
Bermuda	...	...	...	...	...	...	1993	72.2	—	100.0	—	31.4	—	1.3	98.7[10, 11]
Bhutan	1.4	1994	3.8	—	100.0	—	1987	1.5	13.8	85.9	0.3[10, 11]	0.9	—	9.7	90.3[10, 11]
Bolivia	9.8	1994	629.0	—58.1[7]—		41.9[7]	1994	283.3	63.8	1.5	34.7	24.2	78.1	21.9	—
Bosnia and Herzegovina	...	...	...	...	...	...	...	...	...	...	...				
Botswana	35.5	1994[1]	1,452.9	11.4	88.0	0.7	[12]	...	...	...	...	...	...	...	...
Brazil	1.2	1994	6,321.4	...	...	...	1994	2,776.9	91.6	8.4	—	6,094.4	8.1	2.7	89.2
Brunei	57.9	1994	1,437.7	—3.0—		97.0	1994	1,898.3	—	—	100.0	5.3	—	100.0	—
Bulgaria	...	1991[1]	582.1	24.6	28.2	47.2	1993	77.5	73.1	26.9	—	1,498.0	4.8	1.7	93.5
Burkina Faso	0.9[7]	1992	28.4	—100.0—		—	1990	—	—	—	—	3.2	—	100.0	—
Burundi	0.6	1994	5.4	...	...	...	1993	...	—	—	—	1.2	—	100.0	—
Cambodia	0.3	1994	7.1	—	100.0	—						...	...	...	...
Cameroon	12.9[13]	1991	1,439.2	—	100.0	—	1991	1,371.9	—	—	100.0	143.0	90.7	9.3	—
Canada	4.2[7]	1990	25,411.4	24.6	6.4	69.0	1994	16,588.8	16.0	4.8	79.2	6,426.9	30.2	8.4	61.4
Cape Verde	0.3[13]	1991	0.8	—	100.0	—	1990	—	—	—	—	1.3	—	—	100.0
Central African Republic	5.8	1994	48.1[14]	—100.0[14]—		—	1989	60.7	—	100.0	—	1.0	—	100.0	—
Chad	0.5[13]	1991	5.0	—	100.0	—									
Chile	8.0	1994	2,440.0	...	...	...	1994	1,518.6	95.8	4.2	—	985.7	6.0	3.1	90.9
China	2.7[13]	1991	9,885.2	10.7	11.8	77.5	1994	3,972.4	3.0	27.2	69.8	4,402.2	48.9	7.9	43.2
Colombia	4.3	1994	2,873.8	...	...	...	1994	1,913.8	0.2	22.3	77.5	87.4	33.0	67.0	—
Comoros	—	1994	...	—	100.0	—						...	...	...	...
Congo	33.4	1994	580.7[9]	...	...	...	1994	827.3	—	28.4	71.6	...	...	...	...
Costa Rica	...	1990	3.8	12.8	87.2	—	1992	—	—	—	—	89.1	—	10.4	89.6
Côte d'Ivoire	2.5[13]	1991	248.1[9]	...	...	...	1990–91[16]	149.0	—	100.0	—	...	...	...	...
Croatia	...	1991	119.7	1.3	71.3	27.4	1993	50.1	19.3	24.8	55.9	499.0	6.2	9.1	84.7
Cuba	...	...	...	...	...	...	1989	485.3	99.3	0.7	—	1,799.4	—	2.1	97.9
Cyprus	0.3[17]	1994[17]	22.6	—	100.0	—	1994[17]	11.2	69.8	30.2	—	127.2	—	18.9	81.1
Czech Republic	...	1991[1]	2,225.4	—8.4—		91.6	1994	673.5	27.0	10.9	62.1	1,425.9	14.5	5.5	80.0
Denmark	0.9	1995	1,289.7	—	14.5[2]	85.5[2]	1994	593.9	26.7	14.9	58.4	792.7	6.3	14.8	78.9
Djibouti	—	1994	...	—	100.0	—	1989	...	—	—	—	14.6[11]	0.2	9.7	90.1[11]
Dominica	0.7	1994	1.4	—	100.0	—	1991	0.2	—	100.0	—	1.6	—	21.1	78.9
Dominican Republic	2.4	1995	126.0	...	...	...	1991	261.6	99.6	0.4	—	...	...	...	...
Ecuador	14.5	1993	1,217.0	—6.8—		93.2	1993	1,159.3	0.1	0.1	99.8	26.8	—	25.0	75.0
Egypt	9.8	1988	1,960.0	0.4	6.7	92.9	1994	813.2	—	1.8	98.2	241.7	41.6	14.3	44.1
El Salvador	0.4	1994	29.0	100.0	—	—	1994	—	—	—	—	133.0	—	5.5	94.5

Since the data for value of mineral production are obtained mostly from country sources, there is some variation (from a standard calendar year) in the time periods to which the data refer. In addition, the time period for which production data are available does not always correspond with the year for which mineral trade data are available.

The Standard International Trade Classification (SITC), Revision 3, was used to determine the commodity groupings for foreign trade statistics. The actual trade data for these groups is taken largely from the United Nations' *International Trade Statistics Yearbook* (2 vol.) and national sources.

Forestry. Data for the production and trade sections of forestry are based on the Food and Agriculture Organization (FAO) of the United Nations' *Yearbook of Forest Products.* Production of roundwood (all wood obtained in removals from forests) is the principal indicator of the volume of each country's forestry sector; this total is broken down further (as percentages of the roundwood total) into its principal components: fuelwood and charcoal, and industrial roundwood. The latter group was further divided to show its principal component, sawlogs and veneer; lesser categories of industrial roundwood could not be shown for reasons of space. These included pitprops (used in mining, a principal consumer of wood) and pulpwood (used in papermaking and plastics). Value of trade in forest products is given for both imports and exports, although exports alone tend to be the significant indicator for producing countries, while imports of wood are rarely a significant fraction of the trade of most importing countries.

Fisheries. Data for nominal (live weight) catches of fish, crustaceans, mollusks, etc., in all fishing areas (marine areas and inland waters) are taken from the FAO *Yearbook of Fishery Statistics (Catches and Landings).* Total catch figures are given in metric tons; the catches in inland waters and marine areas are given as percentages of the total catch, as are the main kinds of catch—fish, crustaceans, and mollusks. The total catch figures exclude marine mammals, such as whales and seals; and such aquatic animal products as corals, sponges, and pearls; but include frogs, turtles, and jellyfish. The subtotals by kind of catch, however, exclude the last group, which do not belong taxonomically to the fish, crustaceans, or mollusks.

Figures for trade in fishery products (including processed products and preparations like oils, meals, and animal feeding stuffs) are taken from the FAO's *Yearbook of Fishery Statistics (Fishery Commodities).* Value figures for trade in fish products are given for both imports and exports.

The following notes further define the column headings:
a. Includes ferrous and nonferrous metallic ores, concentrates, and scraps, such as iron ore, bauxite and alumina, copper, zinc, gold (except unwrought or semimanufactured), lead, or uranium.
b. Includes natural fertilizers; stone, sand, and aggregate; and pearls, precious and semiprecious stones, worked and unworked.
c. Includes hydrocarbon solids, liquids, and gases.

1 cubic metre = 35.3147 cubic feet
1 metric ton = 1.1023 short tons

forestry, 1994						fisheries, 1993								country
production of roundwood				trade (value, '000 U.S.$)		catch (nominal)						trade (value, '000 U.S.$)		
total ('000 cubic metres)	fuelwood, charcoal (%)	industrial roundwood (%)		exports	imports	total ('000 metric tons)	by source (%)		by kind of catch (%)			exports	imports	
		total	sawlogs, veneer				marine	inland	fish	crustaceans	mollusks			
7,251	77.5	22.5	11.8	119	1,149	1.2	—	100.0	100.0	—	—	...	...	Afghanistan
409	84.5	15.5	15.5	6,169	6,848	3.5	59.7	40.3	87.9	0.5	11.6	2,590	420	Albania
2,409	86.4	13.6	2.7	369	168,693	90.5	99.5	0.5	96.7	2.4	0.9	2,320	1,210	Algeria
...	...	...	...	...	416	0.1	100.0	—	100.0	—	—	...	...	American Samoa
...	...	...	...	122	6,413	—	—	100.0	100.0	—	—	...	...	Andorra
5,720	83.1	16.9	1.2	877	5,282	80.7	91.3	8.7	97.8	1.9	0.3	15,120	13,400	Angola
...	...	...	...	246	4,607	2.4	100.0	—	87.5	12.5	—	420	1,840	Antigua and Barbuda
9,757	39.9	60.1	24.5	113,600	430,163	930.6	98.6	1.4	77.0	2.0	21.0	709,292	44,763	Argentina
...	...	...	...	...	46	4.3	—	100.0	100.0	—	—	...	...	Armenia
...	...	...	...	6	7,206	0.3	100.0	—	100.0	—	—	190	5,450	Aruba
21,362	12.6	87.4	45.8	632,702	1,559,954	218.3	97.8	2.2	65.2	20.2	19.2	670,432	360,421	Australia
14,960	21.8	78.2	57.1	3,231,033	1,693,809	4.6	—	100.0	99.9	0.1	—	4,451	157,688	Austria
...	...	...	...	1,496	141	36.0	—	100.0	100.0	—	—	...	...	Azerbaijan
117	—	100.0	14.5	463	22,235	10.1	100.0	—	16.3	78.5	5.2	47,124	7,000	Bahamas, The
—	—	—	—	49	22,602	9.0	100.0	—	64.7	33.8	1.5	3,769	5,506	Bahrain
31,346	97.7	2.3	1.0	282	46,820	1,047.2	29.9	70.1	89.7	10.2	—	168,290	160	Bangladesh
5	—	100.0	100.0	546	21,191	2.9	100.0	—	100.0	—	—	253	6,466	Barbados
10,015	8.1	91.9	39.1	46,918	3,296	14.0	—	100.0	100.0	—	—	5,885	3,670	Belarus
4,340[8]	12.7[8]	83.7[8]	62.7[8]	2,229,922[8]	3,313,830[8]	36.4	97.7	2.3	93.4	4.6	2.0	228,837[8]	730,459[8]	Belgium
188	67.2	32.8	32.8	6,398	3,065	2.1	99.9	0.1	18.3	70.8	10.9	12,452	780	Belize
5,444	94.3	5.7	0.9	791	1,115	39.0	23.1	76.9	81.5	18.5	—	165	8,110	Benin
...	...	...	...	832	8,997	0.4	100.0	—	97.4	2.6	—	—	8,600	Bermuda
1,398	95.5	4.5	1.8	38	497	0.4	—	100.0	100.0	—	—	...	...	Bhutan
2,076	59.3	40.7	21.3	85,619	23,812	6.2	—	100.0	100.0	—	—	341	1,481	Bolivia
5,379[3]	...	...	...	357	327	2.5	—	100.0	100.0	—	—	...	4,630	Bosnia and Herzegovina
1,538	93.8	6.2	—	...	...	2.0	—	100.0	100.0	—	0.8	31	5,599	Botswana
237,683	67.2	32.8	17.3	2,574,281	414,831	780.0	72.4	27.6	89.1	10.1	0.8	191,633	200,567	Brazil
295	26.8	73.2	69.8	280	7,959	1.8	96.4	3.6	78.3	19.7	2.0	510	6,380	Brunei
3,547	48.2	51.8	22.6	38,295	43,090	21.6	55.7	44.3	95.1	—	4.9	8,009	5,333	Bulgaria
9,591	95.4	4.6	—	126	2,027	7.0	—	100.0	100.0	—	—	...	4,292	Burkina Faso
4,741	97.7	2.3	1.0	8	2,015	22.0	—	100.0	100.0	—	—	243	726	Burundi
7,149	90.7	9.3	0.5	81,877	846	108.9	30.4	69.6	92.4	6.3	1.3	...	...	Cambodia
13,948	78.6	21.4	15.1	473,894	15,923	80.0	75.0	25.0	81.2	18.8	—	1,430	20,100	Cameroon
187,951	3.7	96.3	75.6	21,916,210	2,186,790	1,171.6	96.9	3.1	75.4	12.3	12.2	2,055,438	821,404	Canada
...	...	...	...	80	1,107	7.1	100.0	—	98.8	1.1	—	2,715	180	Cape Verde
3,762	86.4	13.6	6.1	16,506	271	13.5	—	100.0	100.0	—	—	—	870	Central African Republic
1,634	61.3	38.7	0.9	573	570	80.0	—	100.0	100.0	—	—	...	...	Chad
31,053	31.1	68.9	32.2	1,351,706	136,138	6,038.0	99.7	0.3	97.1	0.5	1.8	1,124,679	18,505	Chile
303,381[15]	67.2[15]	32.8[15]	17.3[15]	1,262,413[15]	5,466,960[15]	17,567.9	57.3	42.7	73.7	8.9	16.6	1,542,426	575,930	China
17,833	79.3	20.7	15.1	25,381	223,950	146.4	67.8	32.2	92.3	7.3	0.4	161,209	71,925	Colombia
...	...	...	...	426	2,035	7.0	100.0	—	99.4	0.6	—	...	1,160	Comoros
3,632	62.8	37.2	17.5	119,371	701	41.5	53.5	46.5	99.0	1.0	—	6,200	32,120	Congo
4,279	74.1	25.9	20.3	5,489	119,692	17.7	87.2	12.8	70.5	29.2	0.3	63,730	13,175	Costa Rica
13,059	74.8	25.2	18.5	319,658	27,040	70.2	78.9	21.1	98.3	1.7	—	116,944	110,420	Côte d'Ivoire
2,958	39.0	61.0	42.6	248,262	136,770	30.3	85.3	14.7	91.8	2.2	6.0	49,357	23,422	Croatia
2,756	77.8	22.2	7.0	352	9,672	93.4	81.3	18.7	78.4	16.7	4.5	73,332	18,921	Cuba
47	23.9	76.1	54.8	257	96,061	2.9	96.9	3.1	84.2	0.1	15.7	3,474	28,283	Cyprus
12,304	7.3	92.7	44.6	631,512	309,116	24.4	—	100.0	100.0	—	—	22,132	52,498	Czech Republic
2,282	21.3	78.7	38.3	506,998	1,771,366	1,534.1	97.7	2.3	97.4	0.7	1.9	2,150,665	1,094,253	Denmark
—	—	—	—	314	1,603	0.3	100.0	—	100.0	—	—	80	1,150	Djibouti
...	...	...	...	9	3,511	0.8	99.9	0.1	99.9	0.1	—	—	1,420	Dominica
562	98.9	1.1	0.6	248	124,717	14.1	77.5	22.5	70.0	11.2	18.8	940	34,990	Dominican Republic
5,416	71.1	28.9	16.3	31,497	131,514	330.7	98.4	1.6	68.3	30.9	0.8	573,775	3,723	Ecuador
2,643	95.3	4.7	—	5,078	666,359	302.8	31.5	68.5	97.0	2.6	0.4	5,277	50,158	Egypt
6,504	97.8	2.2	1.4	104	58,902	13.0	64.7	35.3	57.3	36.3	6.4	21,699	4,615	El Salvador

Extractive industries (continued)

country	% of GDP, 1994	mineral production (value added)				trade (value)								
		year	total ('000,000 U.S.$)	metals[a]	non-metals[b]	energy[c]	year	exports total ('000,000 U.S.$)	exports metals[a]	exports non-metals[b]	exports energy[c]	imports total ('000,000 U.S.$)	imports metals[a]	imports non-metals[b]	imports energy[c]
Equatorial Guinea	20.2	1994	26.0	—	—	100.0	1990	...	...	...	...	2.1	—	100.0	—
Eritrea	—	1994	0.2	...	...	...						...	...	...	...
Estonia	1.8	1994	41.6	—	100.0	—	1994	80.0	71.1		28.9	...	...	...	...
Ethiopia	0.3[2]	1992	11.1	— 100.0 —			1993	...	...	...	...	72.3	—	1.3	98.7
Faroe Islands	...	...	...	...	...	...	1994	...	—	—	—	1.5	—	100.0	—
Fiji	0.2	1994	1.7	...	...	...	1994	0.8	100.0	—	—	2.4	—	100.0	—
Finland	0.4	1994	365.5	21.2[2]	78.8[2]	—	1994	153.6	32.2	60.7	7.1	2,732.0	21.0	10.1	68.9
France	0.8	1994	9,184.4	3.0[2]	21.2[2]	75.8[2]	1994	2,196.2	52.9	33.9	13.2	15,476.9	10.0	6.9	83.1
French Guiana		1994	...	— 100.0 —			1990	—	—	—	—	2.0	—	—	100.0
French Polynesia	...	...	...	...	...	...	1994	111.2	—	100.0	—	...	...	...	...
Gabon	43.6	1994	1,705.2	4.5	—	95.5	1994	2,255.4	9.1	—	90.9	...	...	...	...
Gambia, The	—	1994	...	—	100.0	—	1986	3.3	—	100.0	—	...	...	...	...
Gaza Strip	...	...	...	...	...	...						...	...	...	...
Georgia	...	...	...	...	...	...	1993	0.2	—	—	100.0	29.5	—	100.0	—
Germany	...	1989[18]	11,803.2	0.6	20.0	79.4	1994	3,910.4	49.6	31.5	18.9	25,105.8	16.5	7.2	76.3
Ghana	2.0	1994	107.8	— 100.0 —			1994	394.8	9.9	90.1	—	...	...	...	...
Gibraltar	...	...	...	...	...	...	1986	1.0	—	100.0	—	0.3	—	100.0	—
Greece	1.2	1990	666.2	13.6	34.6	51.8	1994	242.6	42.9	42.9	14.2	1,587.7	3.1	3.6	93.3
Greenland	—	1994	—	—	—	—	1993	...	...	...	...	1.1	—	100.0	—
Grenada	0.5	1994	0.9	—	100.0	—	1991	—	—	—	—	1.6	—	11.2	88.8
Guadeloupe	...	1994	...	—	100.0	—	1992	0.7	100.0	—	—	3.5	—	—	100.0
Guam	...	1987[1]	2.3	—	100.0	—						...	...	...	...
Guatemala	0.3	...	...	...	...	...	1994	22.2	—	—	100.0	136.1	—	—	100.0
Guernsey	...	...	...	...	...	...						...	...	...	...
Guinea	19.1	1994	336.5[20]	— 100.0[20] —			1994	387.2	79.2	20.8	...	...	...	...	...
Guinea-Bissau	—	1994	...	—	100.0	—	1986	1.0	—	100.0	—	...	...	...	...
Guyana	21.7	1994	98.1	— 100.0 —			1994	85.1	100.0	—	—	...	...	...	...
Haiti	—	1994	0.2	—	100.0	—	1994	...	...	...	...	...	...	...	...
Honduras	2.0	1994	49.4	— 100.0 —			1994	6.4	100.0	—	—	15.7	—	13.3	86.7
Hong Kong	—	1994	32.2	—	100.0	—	1994	1,818.8	18.7	80.4	0.9	4,089.3	5.9	85.9	8.2
Hungary	...	1989	939.5	4.8	4.3	90.9	1994	158.4	87.8	3.5	8.7	198.0	32.1	27.6	40.3
Iceland	...	1994	...	—	100.0	—	1994	15.2	—	100.0	—	49.1	66.0	22.7	11.3
India	2.2[21]	1991–92	4,827.9	9.6	11.2	79.2	1994	4,956.5	11.4	87.0	1.6	6,805.9	11.0	29.9	59.1
Indonesia	8.3	1994	14,522.9[6]	...	...	...	1994	10,857.0	10.6	1.2	88.2	1,660.1	20.8	14.6	64.6
Iran	19.2[21]	1994–95	14,341.5	— 2.5 —		97.5	1994	12,226.1	0.7	0.2	99.1	89.2	58.8	14.1	27.1
Iraq	0.4[2]	1992	739.9	...	...	...	1994	356.3	—	—	100.0	—	—	—	—
Ireland	...	1989	512.1[22]	30.3	68.7	1.0[22]	1994	464.7	72.3	18.9	8.8	1,151.4	10.0	8.9	81.1
Isle of Man	...	1994	...	—	100.0	—						...	...	...	...
Israel	...	1990	352.6	...	...	...	1994	5,179.8	0.5	97.9	1.6	5,476.4	—	77.3	22.7
Italy	...	1989	2,554.5	3.4	25.2	71.4	1994	656.6	25.6	63.6	10.8	13,396.4	17.9	9.3	72.8
Jamaica	7.7	1994	285.3	99.2[13]	0.8[13]	—	1994	671.2	100.0	—	—	138.0[13]	0.1[13]	—	99.9[13]
Japan	0.3[7]	1993	11,106.1	...	...	...	1994	769.1	42.5	56.7	0.8	54,750.5	13.7	8.9	77.4
Jersey	...	...	...	...	...	...						...	...	...	...
Jordan	3.1	1995	194.7	—	100.0	—	1994	288.1	3.7	96.3	—	371.3	0.5	7.4	92.1
Kazakstan	...	...	...	...	...	...	1993	55.3	64.5	3.5	32.0	0.4	100.0	—	—
Kenya	0.2	1994	12.7	— 100.0 —			1993	4.4	—	100.0	—	332.6	0.2	—	99.8
Kiribati	—	1994	...	...	...	...	1991	0.3	100.0	—	—	...	...	...	...
Korea, North	...	...	...	...	...	...	1994	89.7	59.1	21.5	19.4	...	...	...	...
Korea, South	0.4	1994	1,274.6	3.9[3]	41.3[3]	54.8[3]	1994	157.4	4.0	83.7	12.3	15,395.8	16.8	3.8	79.4
Kuwait	39.2	1994	9,509.5	—	—	100.0	1992	5,202.6	0.4	—	99.6	2.9	—	100.0	—
Kyrgyzstan	...	...	...	...	...	...						...	...	...	...
Laos	0.2	1995	2.3	— 100.0 —								...	...	...	...
Latvia	0.2	1991	30.9	—	100.0	—	1994	9.7	28.0	—	72.0	100.7	—	4.0	96.0
Lebanon	...	...	...	...	...	...	1986	45.8	28.3	71.7	—	28.9	2.2	78.3	19.5
Lesotho	0.2[13]	1991	1.1	—	100.0	—	12								
Liberia	3.0[3]	1989	122.3[23]	— 100.0[23] —			1990–91[16]	80.8	72.7	13.0	14.3	...	...	...	...
Libya	26.3[13]	1991	9,988.9[6]		— 100.0[6] —		1994	9,453.6	—	—	100.0	67.4	89.6	10.4	...
Liechtenstein	...	...	...	...	...	...						...	...	...	...
Lithuania	...	...	...	...	...	...	1994	75.5	39.0	6.2	54.8	203.7	—	12.8	87.2
Luxembourg	0.3[13]	1991	29.2	—	100.0	—	8								
Macau	...	1991	1.8	—	100.0	—	1994	—	—	—	—	28.3	—	62.7	37.3
Macedonia	...	...	...	...	...	...						...	...	...	...
Madagascar	0.3[13]	1991	8.1	— 100.0 —			1994	14.9	25.7	74.3	—	...	...	...	...
Malawi	...	1986	0.1	—	100.0	—	1991	—	—	—	—	6.6	—	100.0	—
Malaysia	7.4	1990	5,542.9	2.1	2.4	95.5	1994	3,839.3	3.5	3.1	93.4	1,081.9	37.7	30.7	31.6
Maldives	1.8	1994	2.0	—	100.0	—	1991	—	—	—	—	4.9	—	100.0	—
Mali	2.3	1995	68.4	— 100.0 —			1992	35.0	—	100.0	—	0.3	—	100.0	—
Malta	...	1992	6.7	—	100.0	—	1993	3.3	100.0	—	—	18.0	—	51.1	48.9
Marshall Islands	0.2	1994	0.2	—	100.0	—	1994	—	—	—	—	...	...	...	...
Martinique	...	1994	...	—	100.0	—	1994	3.2	—	39.9	60.1	103.8	—	—	100.0
Mauritania	10.1	1994	104.1	— 100.0 —			1994	216.2	100.0	—	—	...	...	...	...
Mauritius	0.1	1995	4.9	—	100.0	—	1994	25.5	—	100.0	—	38.3	—	71.8	28.2
Mayotte	...	...	...	...	...	...						...	...	...	...
Mexico	3.4	1991	5,946.9[11]	18.9	27.9	53.2[11]	1994	7,494.1	4.8	3.2	92.0	738.9	32.1	31.2	36.7
Micronesia	—	—	—	—	—	—						...	...	...	...
Moldova	...	1994	...	—	100.0	—	1994	5.9	99.8	—	0.2	230.4	—	—	100.0
Monaco	...	...	...	...	...	...						...	...	...	...
Mongolia	...	...	...	...	...	...						...	...	...	...
Morocco	1.8	1994	557.0	...	...	...	1994	447.9	28.1	71.9	—	1,061.8	—	13.5	86.5
Mozambique	0.4[25]	1994[1]	7.2	...	...	...	1993	1.1	—	—	100.0	...	...	...	...
Myanmar (Burma)	0.6[26]	1993–94	269.2[6]	...	...	...	1991	39.2	17.7	82.3	—	...	...	...	...
Namibia	15.9	1995	302.4	— 100.0 —			12								
Nauru	...	1994	...	—	100.0	—	1994	32.0	—	100.0	—	...	...	...	...
Nepal	0.6[21]	1994–95	25.4	— 100.0 —			1993	...	...	...	...	21.8	74.3	—	25.7
Netherlands, The	2.8	1994	8,507.1	—	5.5[2]	94.5[2]	1994	5,259.6	21.3	8.6	70.1	9,778.0	12.6	7.5	79.9

forestry, 1994 — production of roundwood — total ('000 cubic metres)	fuelwood, charcoal (%)	industrial roundwood (%) total	industrial roundwood (%) sawlogs, veneer	trade exports	trade imports	fisheries, 1993 — catch total ('000 metric tons)	by source (%) marine	inland	by kind of catch (%) fish	crusta-ceans	mollusks	trade exports	imports	country
714	62.6	37.4	37.4	24,041	72	3.8	89.5	10.5	83.7	11.3	3.7	—	1,850	Equatorial Guinea
...	...	...	...	...	...	2.5	80.0	20.0	100.0	—	...	...	...	Eritrea
2,439	43.0	57.0	23.0	119,283	28,872	146.9	98.2	1.8	99.1	—	0.9	49,778	2,609	Estonia
45,378	96.2	3.8	0.1	544	6,854	4.2	—	100.0	100.0	—	—	—	140	Ethiopia
				221	4,345	261.6	100.0	—	94.9	3.8	1.3	312,338	10,845	Faroe Islands
282	13.1	86.9	86.6	27,155	17,293	31.4	90.2	9.8	83.5	1.8	13.7	28,143	37,080	Fiji
47,928	8.6	91.4	46.9	9,302,073	655,647	152.5	63.8	36.2	99.8	0.2	—	13,364	102,624	Finland
42,850	22.9	77.1	50.9	4,289,536	5,931,484	830.0	93.2	6.8	64.8	2.7	32.5	857,752	2,556,151	France
120	49.8	50.2	42.6	1,636	3,415	7.0	98.9	1.1	47.4	52.6	—	30,504	3,898	French Guiana
...	...	...	...	37	18,745	8.1	99.9	0.1	99.1	0.9	—	748	8,243	French Polynesia
4,445	63.3	36.7	36.7	363,249	3,714	28.3	91.2	8.8	96.2	3.6	0.2	6,360	13,280	Gabon
813	86.1	13.9	13.0	39	715	20.5	88.3	11.7	96.9	3.1	—	2,538	470	Gambia, The
...	...	...	...	...	...	...	...	...	...	...	...	...	...	Gaza Strip
...	...	...	...	97	225	37.0	92.2	7.8	99.9	—	0.1	...	...	Georgia
37,012	10.3	89.7	56.9	6,822,310	10,870,300	316.4	84.4	15.6	87.5	4.3	8.2	654,212	1,883,684	Germany
22,628	91.4	8.6	8.0	229,208	13,062	371.2	86.0	14.0	99.0	0.5	0.5	20,164	16,403	Ghana
...	...	...	...	267	827	—	100.0	—	100.0	—	—	...	...	Gibraltar
2,779	54.7	45.3	23.4	45,085	483,770	199.6	93.4	6.6	80.7	2.9	16.4	132,065	162,957	Greece
—	...	...	...	141	7,251	113.6	100.0	—	30.6	68.0	1.4	290,037	4,270	Greenland
...	...	...	...	—	3,160	2.1	100.0	—	97.7	1.2	0.5	130	2,250	Grenada
15	98.0	2.0	2.0	160	37,391	8.0	99.5	0.5	90.2	3.5	6.0	268	21,199	Guadeloupe
...	...	...	...	14	2,563	0.6	70.2	29.8	96.9	3.1	—	...	...	Guam
13,393	94.5	5.5	5.2	23,539	83,937	8.1	41.2	58.8	67.3	32.5	0.2	23,940	4,010	Guatemala
...	...	...	...	...	...	[19]	[19]	[19]	[19]	[19]	[19]	...	...	Guernsey
4,493	86.8	13.2	3.1	6,279	3,155	40.0	90.0	10.0	96.2	1.3	2.5	4,390	5,070	Guinea
577	73.1	26.9	6.9	675	209	5.4	95.3	4.7	79.6	20.2	0.2	960	430	Guinea-Bissau
176	5.7	94.3	85.8	21,646	1,371	40.0	98.0	2.0	91.5	8.5	—	17,222	—	Guyana
5,678	95.9	4.1	3.9	18	5,509	5.6	89.3	10.7	75.9	17.0	7.1	1,920	3,960	Haiti
6,312	90.3	9.7	9.4	24,337	51,766	24.4	98.8	1.2	24.2	52.6	23.2	76,129	6,407	Honduras
19	100.0	—	—	784,330	2,804,335	226.8	97.5	2.5	87.9	4.4	7.7	561,573	1,376,856	Hong Kong
4,527	45.6	54.4	26.8	120,869	308,566	23.4	—	100.0	100.0	—	—	4,745	31,372	Hungary
...	...	...	...	1,648	56,090	1,718.5	99.9	0.1	95.9	3.4	0.7	1,137,638	23,374	Iceland
281,307	91.2	8.8	6.5	35,376	279,889	4,324.2	57.5	42.5	91.2	7.4	1.4	810,645	4,497	India
186,274	79.5	20.5	18.8	4,730,688	689,256	3,637.7	75.1	24.9	87.1	10.5	2.0	1,419,492	99,820	Indonesia
6,939	28.8	71.2	5.9	502	104,066	343.9	71.8	28.2	97.3	2.0	0.7	23,190	33,700	Iran
65	23.1	76.9	30.8	159	414	23.5	19.1	80.9	100.0	—	—	...	...	Iraq
2,008	3.0	97.0	66.6	157,157	533,663	305.0	99.7	0.3	88.4	3.4	8.2	271,885	75,609	Ireland
...	...	...	...	...	...	4.6	100.0	—	22.1	3.7	74.2	...	...	Isle of Man
113	11.5	88.5	31.9	21,715	449,864	18.7	17.7	82.3	98.9	0.8	0.3	7,180	101,790	Israel
9,465	57.9	42.1	23.0	2,172.818	6,419,655	552.0	90.0	10.0	56.4	4.5	39.0	261,607	2,131,181	Italy
465	86.0	14.0	13.7	354	90,824	11.0	68.2	31.8	98.2	1.6	0.2	8,250	25,490	Jamaica
25,834	0.5	99.5	68.5	1,491,974	16,980,960	8,128.1	97.8	2.2	78.1	1.9	18.7	766,952	14,187,149	Japan
...	...	...	...	...	...	2.9[19]	100.0[19]	—[19]	19.2[19]	77.7[19]	3.1[19]	...	...	Jersey
12	66.7	33.3	—	7,141	113,938	0.1	3.2	96.8	100.0	—	—	845	19,690	Jordan
...	...	...	...	437	3,353	75.0	—	100.0	100.0	—	—	3,911	...	Kazakhstan
27,742	93.2	6.8	1.7	1,368	18,770	185.4	2.6	97.4	99.7	0.2	0.1	38,440	905	Kenya
...	...	...	...	...	769	29.3	100.0	—	85.3	0.7	14.0	550	280	Kiribati
4,876	87.7	12.3	12.3	7,245	38,717	1,780.0	93.7	6.3	96.2	0.7	3.1	65,815	1,700	Korea, North
6,383	68.8	31.2	16.7	1,002,764	3,631,409	2,649.0	98.9	1.1	59.0	4.6	35.3	1,335,419	545,518	Korea, South
...	...	...	...	27	101,007	8.6	100.0	—	66.1	33.9	—	7,259	15,538	Kuwait
...	...	...	...	24	66	1.1	—	100.0	100.0	—	—	410	...	Kyrgyzstan
4,296	83.4	16.6	13.8	56,979	730	30.5	—	100.0	100.0	—	—	...	210	Laos
6,190	25.8	74.2	38.8	202,436	38,692	142.2	99.4	0.6	96.7	0.1	3.2	30,686	3,232	Latvia
372	98.1	1.9	1.9	815	113,335	2.2	90.9	9.1	97.8	1.1	1.1	...	...	Lebanon
690	100.0	—	—	...	...	—	—	100.0	100.0	—	—	12	12	Lesotho
3,681	73.3	26.7	21.7	68,080	325	7.8	48.6	51.4	96.7	3.0	0.2	1,440	2,030	Liberia
650	82.5	17.5	9.7	26	25,944	8.8	99.1	0.9	99.5	0.5	—	21,900	19,520	Libya
...	...	...	...	...	...	—	—	100.0	100.0	—	—	24	24	Liechtenstein
3,992	43.5	56.5	31.9	67,544	10,527	119.9	98.6	1.4	87.3	—	12.7	8,651	6,292	Lithuania
8[8]	8[8]	8[8]	8[8]	8[8]	8[8]	8[8]	—	100.0	100.0	—	—	8[8]	8[8]	Luxembourg
...	...	...	...	4,038	20,481	1.9	100.0	—	63.2	35.7	1.1	5,963	15,091	Macau
166	...	100.0	92.8	26,765	31,317	1.4	—	100.0	100.0	—	—	398	6,696	Macedonia
9,151	94.9	5.1	1.4	2,545	7,617	115.0	73.9	26.1	89.4	9.7	0.5	50,388	300	Madagascar
10,151	94.8	5.2	1.3	77	3,128	65.0	—	100.0	100.0	—	—	360	800	Malawi
43,391	16.0	84.0	80.4	4,280,304	698,068	680.0	97.1	2.9	72.0	12.1	14.6	306,845	265,032	Malaysia
...	...	...	...	74	8,175	90.0	100.0	—	99.9	—	—	28,685	—	Maldives
6,307	93.6	6.4	0.2	114	2,289	64.4	—	100.0	100.0	—	—	514	3,700	Mali
...	...	...	...	40	58,182	5.6	100.0	—	99.8	0.1	0.1	2,290	17,870	Malta
...	...	...	...	...	1,923	0.3	100.0	—	100.0	—	—	625	230	Marshall Islands
12	83.3	16.7	8.3	51	30,527	4.6	97.7	2.3	96.1	3.5	—	261	31,406	Martinique
13	61.5	38.5	7.7	100	1,201	92.8	94.6	5.4	48.0	0.3	51.7	121,859	1,000	Mauritania
18	41.0	59.0	37.7	309	49,986	21.1	99.7	0.3	97.5	0.4	2.1	23,108	19,698	Mauritius
...	...	...	...	...	...	0.4	100.0	—	100.0	—	—	2	...	Mayotte
21,322	71.6	28.4	23.0	258,004	1,386,490	1,200.7	86.3	13.7	86.0	8.1	5.8	430,774	128,026	Mexico
...	...	...	...	...	2,110	1.6	99.7	0.3	98.1	1.0	0.6	430	1,140	Micronesia
...	...	...	...	1,796	22,223	4.7	—	100.0	100.0	—	—	...	...	Moldova
...	...	...	...	...	...	—	100.0	—	100.0	—	—	...	...	Monaco
541	69.6	30.4	30.4	6,526	825	0.1	—	100.0	100.0	—	—	...	1,820	Mongolia
1,473	62.3	37.7	5.4	78,985	310,793	622.4	99.7	0.3	84.1	1.1	14.8	538,688	7,775	Morocco
15,441	93.4	6.6	0.4	4,172	4,033	30.2	84.5	15.5	59.0	40.2	0.8	70,887	11,280	Mozambique
21,884	88.8	11.2	4.9	182,202	4,988	836.9	74.7	25.3	99.1	0.9	—	46,362	—	Myanmar (Burma)
27[27]	27[27]	27[27]	27[27]	27[27]	27[27]	329.8	99.7	0.3	99.9	—	—	12	12	Namibia
...	...	...	...	50	212	0.5	100.0	—	100.0	—	—	...	...	Nauru
20,120	96.9	3.1	3.1	140	616	16.9	—	100.0	100.0	—	—	...	...	Nepal
1,072	19.0	81.0	42.6	2,093,640	3,997,901	486.9	99.7	0.3	83.8	2.0	14.2	1,289,136	802,444	Netherlands, The

Extractive industries (continued)

country	mining % of GDP, 1994	mineral production (value added) year	total ('000,000 U.S.$)	metals[a]	non-metals[b]	energy[c]	trade (value) year	exports total ('000,000 U.S.$)	metals[a]	non-metals[b]	energy[c]	imports total ('000,000 U.S.$)	metals[a]	non-metals[b]	energy[c]
Netherlands Antilles	...	1988	7.4	—	100.0	—	1992	112.2	—	9.0	91.0	986.4	—	—	100.0
New Caledonia	10.4[3]	1990	262.4	100.0	—	—	1995	490.3[28]	100.0[28]	—	—	7.7[2]	—	—	100.0[2]
New Zealand	1.4[29]	1992–93	608.5	—17.3[30]—		82.7[30]	1994	254.2	14.6	6.5	78.9	721.5	19.6	14.9	65.5
Nicaragua	0.7[7]	1993	12.6	82.2[13]	17.8[13]	—	1994	2.4	100.0	—	—	85.4	—	—	100.0
Niger	5.6[7]	1993	124.0	—100.0—		—	1994	85.7[31]	100.0[31]	—	—	...			
Nigeria	37.6[13]	1991	12,196.0	—	0.6	99.4	1994	10,897.0	—	—	100.0	10.7	—	100.0	—
Northern Mariana Islands	—	—	—	...	...	...	...	...	...	...	...	...	...	...	...
Norway	15.1[13]	1991	13,949.0	0.4	1.2	98.4	1994	16,105.3	1.0	1.5	97.5	1,620.1	72.0	11.3	16.7
Oman	38.4	1993	4,382.1	—	0.7	99.3	1994	4,118.4	0.3	—	99.7	62.7	82.2	17.8	—
Pakistan	0.5[21]	1994–95	286.9	...	...	...	1994	42.9	—	14.9	85.1	823.4	13.4	3.4	83.2
Palau	...	...	...	...	...	...	...	...	...	...	...	...	...	...	...
Panama	0.2[7]	1993	5.0	—100.0—		—	1994	1.6	100.0	—	—	147.3	2.5	—	97.5
Papua New Guinea	28.9[7]	1993	1,471.6	100.0	—	—	1994	525.6	100.0	—	—	...			
Paraguay	0.4[7]	1993	25.3	—	100.0	—	1994	—	—	—	—	66.7	2.8	15.5	81.7
Peru	9.6[7]	1991	1,098.1	—52.9[33]—		47.1	1994	667.3	99.8	0.2	—	158.6	3.5	—	96.5
Philippines	1.4	1994	580.4	67.3[2]	29.1[2]	3.6[2]	1994	349.3	64.9	2.5	32.6	1,987.3	16.0	5.1	78.9
Poland	...	1990	1,903.5	17.9	17.6	64.5	1994	1,305.9	6.9	12.1	81.0	2,219.1	12.5	6.6	80.9
Portugal	...	1986	129.2	14.4	77.7	7.9	1994	395.4	66.4	33.6	—	2,067.7	0.4	7.9	91.7
Puerto Rico	0.1[29]	1992–93	31.0	—	100.0	—	...	...							
Qatar	31.0	1994	2,225.3[6]	...	...	...	1993	2,432.3	—	0.1	99.9	32.2	34.5	65.5	—
Réunion	...	1994	—	—	100.0	—	1994	0.3	100.0	—	—	11.8	—	—	100.0
Romania	...	1991	1,315.6	1.7	7.8	90.5	1994	44.0	64.9	35.1	—	1,723.1	9.7	3.7	86.6
Russia	...	1989[1,35]	90,630.0	21.6	12.4	65.8	1994	17,269.4	7.4	6.2	86.4	211.0	90.5	9.5	—
Rwanda	0.2[13]	1991	2.2	...	...	...	1990	5.1	100.0	—	—	5.7	—	100.0	—
St. Kitts and Nevis	0.4[2]	1992	0.5	—	100.0	—	1988	...				0.6	—	—	100.0
St. Lucia	0.7[7]	1993	2.6	—	100.0	—	1991	—	—	—	—	5.0	—	61.5	38.5
St. Vincent	0.3[7]	1993	0.7	—	100.0	—	1990	—	—	—	—	1.4	—	—	100.0
San Marino				...	...	...	...	...							
São Tomé and Príncipe	0.1[13]	1994	—	—	100.0	—	...	...							
Saudi Arabia	34.6[7]	1993	42,162.9	—1.4[3]—		98.6[3]	1992	41,824.4	0.1	0.2	99.7	182.9	76.7	23.3	...
Senegal	0.7[2]	1992	42.3	—	100.0	—	1991	57.7	3.1	96.9	—	95.3	—	4.0	96.0
Seychelles	...	1994	—	—	100.0	—	1993	—	—	—	—	34.4[11]	—	—	100.0[11]
Sierra Leone	7.1[26]	1993–94	59.4	—100.0—		—	1993	99.0	27.1	72.9	—	3.3	—	100.0	—
Singapore	—	1994	26.8	—	100.0	—	1994	515.7	38.8	34.6	26.6	6,404.7	1.6	7.0	91.4
Slovakia	...	...	...	...	...	...	...	...	...	...	...	...	...	...	...
Slovenia	1.7[2]	1991	207.7	0.7	15.2	84.1	1994	10.1	—	—	100.0	296.0	34.1	16.9	49.0
Solomon Islands	-0.3[13]	1991	-0.5	—100.0—		—	1988	0.7[37]	100.0[37]	—	—	0.7	—	51.1	48.9
Somalia	0.2[13]	1991	1.0	—	100.0	—	1990–91[16]	0.5	100.0	—	—	...			
South Africa	8.7	1994	9,345.7	...	...	...	1994[12]	4,815.5[22]	13.6	59.6	26.8[22]	642.2[22]	13.2	82.3	4.5[22]
Spain	...	1990	3,786.9	8.6	32.3	59.1	1994	525.1	38.5	56.0	5.5	9,385.3	18.2	4.3	77.5
Sri Lanka	1.1[7]	1993	112.4[38]	—100.0[38]—		—	1994	245.2	5.3	94.7	—	360.2	—	41.2	58.8
Sudan, The	0.1	1994	13.5	—100.0—		—	1992	1.3	100.0	—	—	...			
Suriname	2.3[7]	1993	85.0[39]	...	...	...	1994	225.3	100.0	—	—	...			
Swaziland	1.5	1994	14.9	...	...	...	[12]	...				...			
Sweden	0.3	1994	533.7	55.2[2]	44.8[2]	—	1994	859.2	81.7	13.5	4.8	3,117.2	15.2	8.1	76.7
Switzerland	...	1994	—	—	100.0	—	1994	2,660.1	7.0	92.7	0.3	3,800.8	2.3	72.7	25.0
Syria	6.6	1994	2,594.1[9]	—100.0[9]—		—	1992	1,895.5	—	2.4	97.6	54.5	23.2	15.3	61.5
Taiwan	0.3	1994	794.5	—	80.1	19.9	1995	843.7	...	...	...	8,035.8	—35.8—		64.2
Tajikistan	...	...	...	...	...	...	...	...	...	...	...	...	...	...	...
Tanzania	1.1[13]	1991	22.0	...	...	...	1988	8.4	—	100.0	—	113.5	—	24.1	75.9
Thailand	1.5[7]	1993	1,838.1	1.3[7]	36.2[7]	62.5[7]	1994	1,336.8	1.5	88.9	9.6	3,551.5	8.7	29.5	61.8
Togo	5.4	1994	52.1	—	100.0	—	1991	124.7	—	100.0	—	3.1	—	100.0	—
Tonga	0.3	1993–94	0.4	—	100.0	—	1992	—	—	—	—	0.8	—	44.9	55.1
Trinidad and Tobago	26.6	1994	1,273.9	...	...	...	1994	388.2	—	—	100.0	63.5	89.1	10.9	—
Tunisia	4.4	1994	690.3	...	...	...	1994	394.2	0.1	10.5	89.4	336.8	0.7	34.9	64.4
Turkey	1.3	1995	1,882.4	10.6[3]	19.9[3]	69.5[3]	1994	315.8	29.3	68.1	2.6	4,427.7	20.5	1.8	77.7
Turkmenistan	...	...	...	...	...	...	...	...	...	...	...	...	...	...	...
Tuvalu	...	1994	...	...	...	...	1986	—	—	—	—	...	—	—	100.0
Uganda	0.3	1993–94	11.8	—100.0—		—	1992	—	—	—	—	8.0	—	100.0	—
Ukraine	...	...	...	...	...	...	1993	317.2	30.1	1.2	68.7	...			
United Arab Emirates	33.4	1994	12,269.1	—	0.5[7]	99.5[7]	1992	13,142.4	0.3	—	99.7	95.4	92.9	7.1	—
United Kingdom	2.2	1995	23,006.6	—	31.6	62.0	1994	15,555.0	6.4	31.6	62.0	12,218.4	14.4	37.2	48.4
United States	1.4[7]	1993	89,400.0	6.2[13]	7.7[13]	86.1[13]	1994	10,923.4	34.5	34.3	31.2	58,293.7	6.0	13.3	80.7
Uruguay	0.2	1995	30.8	—	100.0	—	1994	3.1	—	100.0	—	26.2	0.8	41.0	58.2
Uzbekistan	...	...	...	...	...	...	...	...	...	...	...	...	...	...	...
Vanuatu	...	1994	—	—	100.0	—	1986	—	—	—	—	0.5	—	38.0	62.0
Venezuela	15.3[7]	1993	9,156.9	3.0[2]	1.5[2]	95.5[2]	1994	8,372.4	2.7	0.3	97.0	94.0	40.4	59.4	0.2
Vietnam	...	1989	1,062.9	...	...	...	1993	896.6	1.0	1.0	98.0	90.1	0.1	9.5	90.4
Virgin Islands (U.S.)	...	1987[1]	2.7	—	100.0	—	...	...							
West Bank	...	...	...	...	...	...	...	...	...	...	...	...	...	...	...
Western Sahara	...	...	...	...	...	...	...	...	...	...	...	...	...	...	...
Western Samoa	—	1993	—	...	...	...	...	...							
Yemen	5.5[2]	1992	551.5	—100.0—		—	1992	8.8	84.3	15.7	—	76.2	—	19.3	80.7
Yugoslavia	9.5	1990	981.7	12.0	3.1	84.9	1990[40]	369.7	90.5	6.5	3.0	3,313.8	8.7	5.3	86.0
Zaire	24.2[13]	1991	708.0	...	...	...	1994	197.7	—	85.9	14.1	...			
Zambia	15.3[13]	1991	546.8	...	...	—	1994	17.9	—	100.0	—	...			
Zimbabwe	6.9	1994	336.1	...	...	...	1993	97.4	16.8	82.5	0.7	45.1	72.8	27.2	—

[1]Gross value of production (output). [2]1992. [3]1990. [4]1988–89. [5]Mostly natural gas. [6]Mostly crude petroleum and natural gas. [7]1993. [8]Belgium includes Luxembourg. [9]Mostly crude petroleum. [10]Includes coke and briquettes. [11]Includes petroleum products. [12]South Africa includes Botswana, Lesotho, Namibia, and Swaziland. [13]1991. [14]Mostly diamonds, some gold. [15]China includes Taiwan. [16]Average for the two-year period. [17]Republic of Cyprus only. [18]Data refer to former West Germany only. [19]Jersey includes Guernsey. [20]Mostly bauxite and diamonds. [21]1994–95.

forestry, 1994						fisheries, 1993								country
production of roundwood				trade (value, '000 U.S.$)		catch (nominal)						trade (value, '000 U.S.$)		
total ('000 cubic metres)	fuelwood, charcoal (%)	industrial roundwood (%)		exports	imports	total ('000 metric tons)	by source (%)		by kind of catch (%)			exports	imports	
		total	sawlogs, veneer				marine	inland	fish	crusta-ceans	mollusks			
5	...	100.0	58.3	733	20,802	1.2	100.0	—	100.0	—	—	260	8,250	Netherlands Antilles
...	...	...	...	11	8,181	3.5	100.0	—	55.7	19.2	2.8	7,121	5,497	New Caledonia
16,833	0.3	99.7	68.2	1,445,325	229,571	470.4	99.7	0.3	82.2	0.9	16.7	648,254	36,107	New Zealand
3,716	95.0	5.0	3.6	5,139	11,540	8.8	93.7	6.3	41.7	57.4	0.9	28,545	1,460	Nicaragua
5,671	93.8	6.2	—	116	1,042	2.2	—	100.0	—	—	—	340	1,130	Niger
99,083	91.7	8.3	6.0	24,201	82,744	255.5	56.2	43.8	93.1	6.9	—	31,690	154,240	Nigeria
...	...	...	...	...	51	0.1	100.0	—	99.2	0.8	—	30	...	Northern Mariana Islands
8,744	5.4	94.6	49.1	1,397,744	833,052	2,561.8	100.0	—	97.6	2.0	0.4	2,302,346	310,352	Norway
...	...	...	...	750	34,779	116.5	100.0	—	97.4	0.9	1.7	51,462	3,563	Oman
28,635	93.2	6.8	5.2	882	182,453	621.7	80.3	19.7	93.2	5.8	1.0	184,591	185	Pakistan
...	...	...	...	990	1,143	1.5	100.0	—	99.0	0.9	—	...	190	Palau
1,053	88.8	11.2	5.5	3,498	101,378	158.2	99.7	0.3	90.9	7.9	1.2	93,220[32]	11,951[32]	Panama
8,188	67.6	32.4	30.3	644,075	6,382	26.0	48.1	51.9	90.5	6.0	—	13,880	47,800	Papua New Guinea
7,188	56.8	43.2	37.5	39,291	27,491	16.0	—	100.0	100.0	—	—	24	1,605	Paraguay
12,496	84.8	15.2	15.1	23,542	103,458	8,450.6	99.5	0.5	98.4	0.1	1.5	685,004	818	Peru
38,630	91.7	8.3	1.1	90,116	354,415	2,263.8	74.6	25.4	80.9	7.9	11.1	478,086	94,601	Philippines
18,388	9.6	90.4	50.9	492,125	417,255	423.0	88.2	11.8	93.8	3.8	2.4	70,312	128,633	Poland
9,819	5.1	94.9	42.9	1,245,630	808,257	274.2	99.5	0.5	90.5	0.9	8.6	210,426	627,713	Portugal
...	...	...	...	...	...	1.9	79.8	20.2	74.4	18.8	6.8	[34]	[34]	Puerto Rico
...	...	...	...	28	11,296	7.0	100.0	—	98.1	1.2	0.7	50	2,620	Qatar
36	85.9	14.1	11.6	237	60,609	2.7	99.9	0.1	84.6	15.0	—	7,995	34,922	Réunion
11,925	19.2	80.8	36.1	220,821	83,893	34.9	15.1	84.9	99.9	—	0.1	653	14,813	Romania
120,000	21.1	78.9	48.8	3,021,671	93,904	4,461.4	93.1	6.9	96.3	1.4	2.2	1,471,446	19,074	Russia
5,660	95.3	4.7	1.1	242	316	3.6	—	100.0	100.0	—	—	...	355	Rwanda
...	...	...	...	33	1,797	1.7	100.0	—	88.2	11.8	—	180[36]	1,200[36]	St. Kitts and Nevis
...	...	...	...	—	11,706	1.1	100.0	—	98.7	1.3	—	8	3,290	St. Lucia
...	...	...	...	14	4,476	1.8	100.0	—	93.8	—	6.2	1,494	900	St. Vincent
...	...	...	...	...	...	...	—	100.0	100.0	—	—	...	...	San Marino
9	—	100.0	100.0	15	103	2.2	100.0	—	99.2	0.1	0.7	...	390	São Tomé and Príncipe
...	...	...	...	1,633	543,725	49.4	95.6	4.4	95.6	4.3	0.1	4,520	77,060	Saudi Arabia
4,421	84.1	15.9	0.9	103	30,487	377.7	92.7	7.3	94.7	1.0	4.3	147,680	24,918	Senegal
...	...	...	...	99	1,415	7.0	100.0	—	99.0	0.3	0.6	14,323	6,987	Seychelles
3,199	96.1	3.9	0.1	162	1,267	62.0	77.4	22.6	97.9	0.5	1.6	16,750	1,800	Sierra Leone
120	100.0	—	—	701,231	1,135,073	11.7	99.8	0.2	70.4	13.6	16.0	482,312	566,502	Singapore
5,318	11.8	88.2	40.0	108,154	32,229	2.8	—	100.0	100.0	—	—	...	...	Slovakia
1,944	12.1	87.9	53.8	422,480	302,593	3.0	69.1	30.9	100.0	—	—	5,914	19,653	Slovenia
468	29.5	70.5	70.5	113,699	757	45.4	100.0	—	98.7	—	0.2	33,760	185	Solomon Islands
7,818	98.7	1.3	0.4	30	186	14.9	98.3	1.7	95.9	2.4	1.7	7,170	270	Somalia
24,008[27]	29.2[27]	70.8[27]	17.8[27]	502,008[27]	391,077[27]	563.2	99.6	0.4	97.8	0.5	1.7	199,030[12]	90,038[12]	South Africa
13,815	16.9	83.1	43.3	1,179,844	2,664,032	1,290.0	97.6	2.4	81.4	2.5	16.1	813,750	2,629,799	Spain
9,463	92.8	7.2	0.4	5,955	100,459	220.9	91.9	8.1	96.5	3.4	0.1	31,378	34,463	Sri Lanka
9,148	75.0	25.0	0.1	425	13,046	31.7	4.7	95.3	100.0	—	—	172	2,500	Sudan, The
94	1.1	98.9	94.7	2,083	1,127	9.5	98.0	2.0	99.3	0.7	—	3,440	520	Suriname
2,297	24.4	75.6	13.9	59,665	—	0.1	—	100.0	100.0	—	—	[12]	[12]	Swaziland
56,500	6.7	93.3	51.2	8,995,668	1,172,013	347.8	98.5	1.5	98.9	0.9	0.2	122,586	371,756	Sweden
4,974	23.2	76.8	65.0	1,427,266	2,242,033	3.2	—	100.0	100.0	—	—	5,426[24]	353,668[24]	Switzerland
50	31.5	68.5	31.7	278	96,441	5.6	28.6	71.4	98.6	1.4	—	60	1,560	Syria
44	7.5	92.5	—	...	...	1,415.8	87.5	12.5	...	...	...	...	...	Taiwan
...	...	...	...	24	100	3.7	—	100.0	100.0	—	—	...	...	Tajikistan
35,140	94.0	6.0	0.9	6,391	5,777	345.0	13.0	87.0	99.1	0.5	0.1	6,435	226	Tanzania
35,044	92.1	7.9	0.2	319,255	1,630,235	3,348.1	91.5	8.5	77.1	11.9	18.1	3,404,268	830,480	Thailand
1,020	80.0	20.0	0.7	434	1,281	17.0	96.9	3.1	99.8	—	0.2	2,700	12,833	Togo
5	—	100.0	100.0	—	2,529	2.5	100.0	—	96.8	3.2	—	1,630	350	Tonga
56	18.0	82.0	77.3	1,440	57,250	10.6	100.0	—	87.7	12.3	—	6,128	4,219	Trinidad and Tobago
2,634	92.1	7.9	0.8	16,665	213,346	83.8	100.0	—	83.3	2.9	13.8	85,857	2,238	Tunisia
16,845	45.3	54.7	27.8	106,307	512,233	550.6	90.9	9.1	90.6	0.9	8.2	29,067	18,490	Turkey
...	...	...	...	92	780	37.0	—	100.0	100.0	—	—	2,118	...	Turkmenistan
...	...	...	...	—	325	1.5	100.0	—	100.0	—	—	...	...	Tuvalu
15,698	85.9	14.1	1.0	11	2,035	219.8	—	100.0	100.0	—	—	15,794	...	Uganda
...	...	...	...	14,075	11,498	371.3	78.7	21.3	95.5	1.6	2.9	11,387	46,812	Ukraine
...	...	...	...	16,126	277,101	92.5	100.0	—	99.9	0.1	—	19,450	23,700	United Arab Emirates
8,155	2.8	97.2	48.0	1,612,605	8,802,504	898.1	98.3	1.7	89.1	4.5	6.4	1,036,916	1,628,852	United Kingdom
487,176	18.0	82.0	47.9	13,965,250	18,262,930	5,939.3	94.2	5.8	77.2	8.2	14.0	3,179,474[34]	6,290,233[34]	United States
3,517	70.3	29.7	22.3	26,652	57,120	118.8	99.5	0.5	96.4	0.2	3.4	74,476	6,028	Uruguay
...	...	...	...	108	6,706	23.4	—	100.0	100.0	—	—	...	...	Uzbekistan
63	38.0	62.0	62.0	1,785	412	2.9	100.0	—	63.8	13.5	21.3	55	1,140	Vanuatu
2,014	40.9	59.1	57.7	32,445	190,060	390.3	93.7	6.3	86.2	5.0	8.8	89,150	16,768	Venezuela
34,209	87.1	12.9	7.1	34,950	49,159	1,100.0	75.0	25.0	66.8	27.8	5.4	368,435	—	Vietnam
...	...	...	...	...	...	0.9	100.0	—	87.4	8.4	4.2	...	...	Virgin Islands (U.S.)
...	...	...	...	...	...	...	...	...	...	...	...	...	...	West Bank
...	...	...	...	...	...	—	100.0	—	...	...	...	...	...	Western Sahara
131	53.4	46.6	44.3	60	1,783	1.6	100.0	—	98.1	0.4	1.5	25	3,960	Western Samoa
324	100.0	—	—	11	22,723	86.8	99.0	1.0	95.3	2.1	2.5	10,600	3,600	Yemen
3,110	...	...	...	22,507	25,978	6.5	4.4	95.6	99.4	0.2	0.4	2,600	24,141	Yugoslavia
43,095	92.3	7.7	0.9	52,580	9,500	147.3	1.5	98.5	100.0	—	—	...	28,850	Zaire
8,352	86.4	13.6	7.3	1,321	2,551	65.3	—	100.0	100.0	—	—	250	2,080	Zambia
8,067	77.6	22.4	6.5	12,270	9,806	21.8	—	100.0	100.0	—	—	250	2,900	Zimbabwe

[22]Excludes crude petroleum and natural gas. [23]Mostly iron ore. [24]Switzerland includes Liechtenstein. [25]1995. [26]1993–94. [27]South Africa includes Namibia. [28]Mostly nickel. [29]1992–93. [30]1990–91. [31]Radioactive materials only. [32]Excludes the Free Zone of Colón and the Canal Zone. [33]Includes coal mining. [34]United States includes Puerto Rico. [35]Data refer to the former U.S.S.R. [36]Includes Anguilla. [37]Gold only. [38]Mostly precious and semiprecious stones. [39]Mostly bauxite. [40]Data refer to former Socialist Federal Republic of Yugoslavia only.

Manufacturing industries

This table provides a summary of manufacturing activity by industrial sector for the countries of the world, providing figures for total manufacturing value added, as well as the percentage contribution of 29 major branches of manufacturing activity to the gross domestic product. U.S. dollar figures for total value added by manufacturing are given but should be used with caution because of uncertainties with respect to national accounting methods, purchasing power parities, price structures and preferments, exchange rates, and so on, especially for countries having nonconvertible currencies.

Manufacturing activity is classified here according to a modification of the International Standard Industrial Classification (ISIC), revision 2, published by the United Nations. A summary of the 2-, 3-, and 4-digit ISIC codes (groups) defining these 29 sectors follows, providing definitional detail beyond that possible in the column headings.

The collection and publication of national manufacturing data is usually carried out by one of three methods: a full census of manufacturing (usually done every 5 to 10 years for a given country), a periodic survey of manufacturing (usually taken at annual or other regular intervals between censuses), and the onetime sample survey (often limited in geographic, sectoral, or size of enterprise coverage). The full census is, naturally, the

most complete, but, since up to 10 years may elapse between such censuses, it is sometimes necessary to substitute a survey of more recent date but less complete coverage. In other instances, data published by the United Nations Industrial Development Organization (UNIDO), especially its *International Yearbook of Industrial Statistics;* occasional publications of the International Monetary Fund (IMF); and other sources have been used.

ISIC code(s)	Products manufactured
31	Food, beverages, and tobacco
311 + 312	food including prepared animal feeds
313	alcoholic and nonalcoholic beverages
314	tobacco manufactures
32	Textiles, wearing apparel, and leather goods
321	spinning of textile fibres, weaving and finishing of textiles, knitted articles, carpets, rope, etc.
322	wearing apparel (including leather clothing; excluding knitted articles and footwear)
323 + 324	leather products (including footwear; excluding wearing apparel), leather substitutes, and fur products

Manufacturing industries

country	year	total manufacturing value added ('000,000 U.S.$)	(31) food (311+312)	(31) beverages (313)	(31) tobacco manufactures (314)	(32) textiles (exc. wearing apparel) (321)	(32) wearing apparel (322)	(32) leather and fur products (323+324)	(33) wood products (exc. furniture) (331)	(33) wood furniture (332)	(34) paper, paper products (341)	(34) printing and publishing (342)	(35) industrial chemicals (351)	(35) paints, soaps, etc. (352 exc. 3522)	(35) drugs and medicines (3522)
Afghanistan	1988–89[1]	435	18.3	1.9	—	8.0	0.4	16.7	—0.5—		0.9	4.9	4.8	0.2	2.7
Albania	1993[2]	224	42.5	0.9	3.7	4.6	2.0	2.3	2.1	1.3	0.2	1.3	1.7	0.9	...
Algeria	1990	5,739	14.2	3.0	3.8	7.3	6.4	3.5	3.3	1.6	3.9	0.4	0.4	—3.0—	
American Samoa	1993[3,4]	326	99.5[5]	...	...	...	...	...	...	...	...	...	...	...	...
Andorra	1992[6]	38	2.3	9.0	0.1	0.3	30.2	0.9	—0.6—		2.6	5.9	1.0	1.8	0.1
Angola	1989	319	20.0	—12.2—		—11.6—			—3.7—		—0.3—		9.1[7]	[7]	[7]
Antigua and Barbuda	1994	27	...	...	...	...	...	...	...	...	...	...	...	...	...
Argentina	1990	31,156	15.1	3.0	1.5	7.1	1.6	1.7	0.8	0.8	2.8	2.2	5.9	—5.7—	
Armenia	1994[2,3]	300	17.7	...	...	3.2	2.1	3.0	—0.8[9]—		—9—		6.8[7]	[7]	[7]
Aruba	...	...	...	...	...	...	...	...	...	...	...	...	...	...	...
Australia	1992–93	47,563	15.7	3.8	0.7	2.9	2.2	0.7	3.1	1.9	2.8	9.7	3.4	2.8	2.1
Austria	1993[10]	30,935	8.6	3.5	4.7	4.1	1.4	0.9	2.4	4.2	3.6	3.8	3.5	1.9	2.2
Azerbaijan	1994[2,3,11]	947	19.9	...	...	11.6	1.3	0.9	—0.5[9]—		—9—		6.4[7]	[7]	[7]
Bahamas, The	1991[3,12]	96	8.0	49.3	—	0.6	2.6	—	...	3.1	—8.7—		—13.3—		
Bahrain	1992[2]	1,730	6.8	1.2	...	—	4.8	0.2	0.1	5.0	0.5	3.0	4.4	0.2	0.1
Bangladesh	1989–90[12,13]	1,819	15.0	0.2	8.7	24.9	9.0	3.6	0.8	0.3	3.0	1.3	7.6	3.4	6.0
Barbados	1993[10]	82[14]	28.1[14]	—15.8—		0.8[15]	2.9	[15]	—0.3—		—8.1—		16.7[16]	—3.5—	
Belarus	1994[2,3,11]	3,006	16.2	...	...	7.0	2.1	2.6	—5.4[9]—		—9—		16.3[7]	[7]	[7]
Belgium	1994[3]	45,230	—16.1—		2.9	4.5	2.4	0.1	0.6	3.9	2.1	4.3	14.6[7]	[7]	[7]
Belize	1992[10]	59	45.9	7.5	3.9	—3.8—			5.5	2.7	1.1	1.5	—14.1—		
Benin	1990	59	20.6	13.1	...	3.2	5.5	6.9	3.6	5.2	—	2.5	—	—9.5—	
Bermuda	1990	173	...	...	...	...	...	...	...	...	...	...	...	...	...
Bhutan	1989[10]	21	6.0	10.1	...	—5.6—			18.1	2.7	0.4	1.0	21.5	—1.7—	
Bolivia	1992[10,19]	754	18.9	12.0	0.8	2.9	0.5	1.5	1.5	0.2	0.5	2.2	0.3	1.0	1.3
Bosnia and Herzegovina	1989	4.252	8.3	9.9	1.1	3.5	10.5	6.5	—12.0—		3.3	1.0	7.3[20]	[20]	[20]
Botswana	1990	132	39.6	15.5	...	8.9	2.0	1.0	1.1	0.6	2.0	0.8	2.2	—0.8—	
Brazil	1993[3,12]	94,932[21]	12.4	2.1	1.3	4.5	—3.8—		1.1	1.0	3.5	2.7	12.5	1.0	2.6
Brunei	1990	582	...	...	...	...	...	...	...	...	...	...	...	...	...
Bulgaria	1992[2]	8,082	16.6	3.8	5.7	4.9	1.9	1.7	1.4	1.1	1.5	0.5	5.9	—4.5—	
Burkina Faso	1990	257	50.9	14.9	1.2	14.9	1.7	2.7	0.2	1.5	0.1	1.0	0.5	—0.1—	
Burundi	1990	104	47.2	23.2	13.0	1.0	1.4	0.5	0.1	0.1	—	1.4	3.8	—1.1—	
Cambodia	1994	128	...	...	...	...	...	...	...	...	...	...	...	...	...
Cameroon	1992–93[10]	469	6.7	13.7	5.5	10.2	1.2	0.5	—10.9—		2.9	1.6	—7.9—		
Canada	1993[10]	103,690	11.9	3.2	0.9	2.7	2.1	0.4	5.9	1.7	5.9	6.4	3.7	3.4	2.5
Cape Verde	1990	14	33.1	0.6	26.8	...	8.0	2.0	...	...	...	9.2	...	...	...
Central African Republic	1990	27	29.8	13.9	25.4	—25.0	—3.7	—0.5	25.6	1.9	—	5.9	4.1	—8.9—	
Chad	1992[3]	95	...	...	...	29.0[24]	—	—	...	...	—	...	...	...	...
Chile	1992[10,25]	10,847	19.0	5.7	3.4	3.6	2.1	1.8	2.8	0.8	6.6	3.0	3.4	4.8	2.6
China	1994	141,789	6.8	2.7	4.5	9.1	2.9	1.6	0.8	0.5	1.6	1.7	—7.9—		2.1
Colombia	1992[10,13]	9,370	16.3	13.4	1.5	8.9	3.1	2.2	0.7	0.6	3.7	4.5	5.2	—9.4—	
Comoros	1993	11	...	...	...	...	...	...	...	...	...	...	...	...	...
Congo	1990	104	22.3	23.3	8.7	1.9	1.0	1.9	6.8	3.9	1.0	1.0	7.8	—3.9—	
Costa Rica	1993[10]	1,218	30.0	13.8	2.0	2.6	4.0	1.3	1.9	1.4	3.8	4.1	3.0	4.1	3.3
Côte d'Ivoire	1993[10]	1,646	31.3[26]	4.1	[26]	—10.3—		0.8	—6.9—		...	...	6.4[20]	[20]	[20]
Croatia	1992	5,066	16.8	3.5	3.3	5.2	5.0	2.2	3.5	2.6	2.2	3.2	3.5	—7.4—	
Cuba	1990	5,990[21]	17.2	6.0	43.9	1.8	1.5	1.2	0.9	0.7	0.2	1.4	1.1	—4.8—	
Cyprus[27]	1993	840	15.0	8.4	6.9	4.0	11.2	3.9	5.4	4.5	2.0	4.9	0.4	3.6	1.2
Czech Republic	1993[2,3]	22,520	—26.7—			—6.3—		2.1	—1.7—		—3.6—		—5.8—		
Denmark	1993[12,29]	23,984	18.8	3.7	1.1	2.0	1.3	0.4	2.2	3.9	2.5	6.2	2.7	—8.3—	
Djibouti	1991	11	...	...	—	...	...	—	...	...	...	...	...	...	...
Dominica	1993	13	...	...	...	...	...	...	...	...	...	...	...	...	...
Dominican Republic	1990	1,298	31.9	13.8	5.2	3.5	1.2	3.0	0.2	1.5	2.9	1.7	1.6	—3.4—	
Ecuador	1993[10,13]	1,937	17.0	7.3	0.4	4.9	0.7	0.6	1.1	0.4	3.5	2.1	1.8	4.1	1.8
Egypt	1989–90[12,30]	7,012	13.6	1.4	2.6	21.4	0.5	0.7	0.2	0.2	1.4	1.6	4.1	2.6	2.2
El Salvador	1993[3]	1,438	37.7	14.6	4.2	6.0	—5.9—		1.4	2.2[31]	1.5	1.5	—5.5—		
Equatorial Guinea	1990[2]	1.9	27.6	4.1	...	...	2.6	...	...	49.3	...	1.2	—13.8—		
Eritrea	1983–84	151	17.1	19.4	2.0	7.6	0.3	2.2	...	0.1	0.6	1.3	0.1	3.1	...
Estonia	1994[2,3]	1,254	35.0[26]	6.7	[26]	5.6	3.9	1.7	5.7	5.4	0.8	3.0	9.2[32]	[32]	[32]
Ethiopia[33]	1991–92[2]	507	23.2	17.7	7.2	14.5	2.5	13.5	—1.0—		—6.8—		—	2.0	...
Faroe Islands	1990[3,12]	120	69.3[34]	...	...	...	...	...	...	...	...	...	...	...	...

ISIC code(s)	Products manufactured
33	Wood and wood products
331	sawlogs, wood products (excluding furniture), cane products, and cork products
332	wood furniture
34	Paper and paper products, printing and publishing
341	wood pulp, paper, and paper products
342	printing, publishing, and bookbinding
35	Chemicals and chemical, petroleum, coal, rubber, and plastic products
351	basic industrial chemicals (including fertilizers, pesticides, and synthetic fibres)
352 minus 3522	chemical products not elsewhere specified (including paints, varnishes, and soaps and other toiletries)
3522	drugs and medicines
353 + 354	refined petroleum and derivatives of petroleum and coal
355	rubber products
356	plastic products (excluding synthetic fibres)
36	Glass, ceramic, and nonmetallic mineral products
361 + 362	pottery, china, glass, and glass products
369	bricks, tiles, cement, cement products, plaster products, etc.

ISIC code(s)	Products manufactured
37	Basic metals
371	iron and steel
372	nonferrous basic metals and processed nickel and cobalt
38	Fabricated metal products, machinery and equipment
381	fabricated metal products (including cutlery, hand tools, fixtures, and structural metal products)
382 minus 3825	nonelectrical machinery and apparatus not elsewhere specified
3825	office, computing, and accounting machinery
383 minus 3832	electrical machinery and apparatus not elsewhere specified
3832	radio, television, and communications equipment (including electronic parts)
384 minus 3843	transport equipment not elsewhere specified
3843	motor vehicles (excluding motorcycles)
385	professional and scientific equipment; photographic and optical goods; watches and clocks
39	Other manufactured goods
390	jewelry, musical instruments, sporting goods, artists' equipment, toys, etc.

refined petroleum and products (353+354)	rubber products (355)	plastic products (356)	pottery, china, and glass (361+362)	bricks, tiles, cement, etc. (369)	iron and steel (371)	nonferrous metals (372)	fabricated metal products (381)	nonelectrical machinery (382 exc. 3825)	office equip., computers (3825)	electrical equip. (383 exc. 3832)	radio, television (3832)	transport equip. exc. motor vehicles (384 exc. 3843)	motor vehicles (3843)	professional equip. (385)	jewelry, musical instruments (390)	country
—	—	2.1	—1.1—		0.4	—							0.1		37.1	Afghanistan
21.6	—	1.2	0.1	7.9	2.5	—	1.2	0.7	—	0.5	0.7	—	0.1		—	Albania
2.9	0.4	1.0	1.2	8.9	10.0	0.6	10.0	—1.6—		—4.6—		—5.5—		1.2	1.3	Algeria
																American Samoa
...	0.3	0.4	0.6	0.3	1.7	0.2	0.5	—3.8—		—4.3—		—	21.1	9.1	2.9	Andorra
20.0	[7]	[7]	—11.3—		—1.9—			—5.0—			—4.7—			[8]	0.3[8]	Angola
																Antigua and Barbuda
19.9	1.2	1.4	1.3	3.0	5.3	1.0	5.2	—2.7—		—3.3—		—6.9—		0.4	0.3	Argentina
...	[7]	[7]	—4.0—		—6.7—			—23.6—							...	Armenia
																Aruba
2.5	0.9	3.5	2.0	3.3	4.4	4.2	7.8	4.1	0.6	3.8	1.9	2.5	4.8	1.1	0.8	Australia
1.6	1.0	2.3	2.2	4.9	4.5	1.1	8.2	—9.1—		10.8	2.5	1.1	4.3	0.8	0.8	Austria
40.2	[7]	[7]	—3.6—		—2.4—			—8.8—							...	Azerbaijan
			—6.8—		2.3	—									...	Bahamas, The
11.2	—	1.1	—	5.7	2.4	36.0	2.4	—	—	6.0	—	3.6	—	0.1	5.2	Bahrain
0.6	0.3	0.8	1.0	1.8	2.4	—	1.3	0.4	—	2.2	1.3	1.0	2.1	—	1.0	Bangladesh
[16]	[16]	[16]	—2.7—		—		9.8	—9.6—			—1.5—			0.2	Barbados
7.6	[7]	[7]	—5.5—		—3.0—			—26.8—							...	Belarus
1.0	[7]	[7]	—4.6—		4.5	1.7		—30.6—							...	Belgium
—	—0.3[17]—		[17]	6.2	—	—	2.0			—0.1—		—4.2—		—	1.1	Belize
			0.5	24.6	—	—	4.8								—	Benin
																Bermuda
...	0.7	2.2	—29.0—		...	...	...			—1.0[18]—					[18]	Bhutan
44.2	—	1.2	0.5	4.0	0.4	2.0	0.9	—0.2—		0.3	0.1		0.2	0.1	2.3	Bolivia
-0.7	0.2	[20]	—2.4—		5.8	7.0	11.6	—5.8—		—6.3—		—7.1—		...	0.3	Bosnia and Herzegovina
	0.3	0.2	—	—	—11.0[22]—		6.9	—0.9—		—0.7—		—0.8—		—	15.7	Botswana
	1.1	2.3	—4.4—		[22]		—11.8—		—7.0—		—9.3—			...	Brazil
																Brunei
9.6	1.4	1.5	1.4	2.5	4.6	2.8	4.3	—6.3[23]—		—6.0—		—4.1—		[23]	5.9	Bulgaria
	1.5	0.8	0.1	0.1	0.8	0.3	0.3	—0.2—		—0.4—		—1.0—			4.8	Burkina Faso
—	—	0.5	—	1.0	—	—	5.6	—	—	0.1	—				—	Burundi
																Cambodia
12.2	—10.8—		—7.5—		—5.5—		...	—0.6—		—0.4—		—0.1—			1.9	Cameroon
1.9	1.6	2.8	0.6	2.0	3.2	2.6	4.7	5.8	1.0	2.5	3.9	3.7	10.8	0.8	1.4	Canada
...	...	...	...	...	...	...	...	...	...	...	...	—20.1—			0.2	Cape Verde
—	—	—	—	—	—	—	0.9	—	—	0.2	—	—4.8—		—	7.7	Central African Republic
																Chad
6.3	0.8	2.0	0.8	3.5	2.3	15.2	3.8	1.9	—	1.2	0.1	1.0	1.2	0.1	0.2	Chile
3.5	1.1	1.8	—7.7—		10.6	2.1	3.6	—9.6—		4.8	4.0	—6.2—		1.1	1.7	China
2.9	1.4	3.4	2.2	4.0	2.9	0.5	2.8	—1.9—		—3.1—		—3.7—		0.9	0.9	Colombia
															—	Comoros
1.9	1.0	1.0	1.0	—	—	—	4.9	—1.9—		—1.9—		—2.9—		—	0.3	Congo
3.0	1.3	3.9	1.2	3.4	...	0.1	2.4	—1.8—		1.3	4.3	0.9	0.7	...	0.3	Costa Rica
21.5	1.3	[20]	—1.9—		—0.2—		—5.4—			—6.0—		—6.9—		...	3.0	Côte d'Ivoire
4.9	0.4	1.6	1.5	3.7	2.6	1.0	4.6	—5.7—		—6.8—		—8.1—		0.4	0.3	Croatia
	1.4	1.2	0.4	1.9	0.6	1.1	1.3	—2.9—		—0.9—		—3.8—		0.2	3.6	Cuba
1.2	0.4	3.4	0.5	9.3	—	—	6.6	3.0	—	1.4	—	0.3	0.6	—	1.9	Cyprus[27]
5.7	—2.1—		—4.5—		—16.8[22]—		[22]	—8.6—		—4.3[28]—		—8.5—		...	...	Czech Republic
0.8	—4.4—		—4.7—		—2.3—		6.0	—14.0—		—8.0—		—4.4—		...	2.3	Denmark
		...		...											...	Djibouti
																Dominica
16.2	0.8	1.6	0.7	3.5	1.8	0.2	3.7	—0.5—		—0.8—		—0.1—		0.2	0.2	Dominican Republic
33.4	1.3	2.7	0.9	4.1	0.9	0.6	4.5	0.2	—	2.3	0.2	—	2.9	0.1	0.2	Ecuador
18.2	0.4	1.0	1.5	5.0	5.3	3.0	4.1	2.7	—	2.5	0.2	1.3	1.8	0.3	0.1	Egypt
6.2	0.5		—5.2—		—2.6—		0.9	—0.7—		—1.7—		—0.3—		...	...	El Salvador
	...	...	...	0.8	...		0.6		...						...	Equatorial Guinea
38.4		3.0	1.0	1.6	0.8		1.2		0.1						...	Eritrea
[32]	—1.3—		—5.7—		...		3.8	—3.1—		2.2	0.3	—5.0—		0.9	0.3	Estonia
—	1.7	1.5	0.2	5.2	...	...	3.1	...	...	...	...	...	...	...	—	Ethiopia[33]
...	...	...	...	...	...	...	...	...	...	...	...	...	...	...	...	Faroe Islands

Manufacturing industries (continued)

country	year	total manufacturing value added ('000,000 U.S.$)	(31) food (311+312)	beverages (313)	tobacco manufactures (314)	(32) textiles (exc. wearing apparel) (321)	wearing apparel (322)	leather and fur products (323+324)	(33) wood products (exc. furniture) (331)	wood furniture (332)	(34) paper, paper products (341)	printing and publishing (342)	(35) industrial chemicals (351)	paints, soaps, etc. (352 exc. 3522)	drugs and medicines (3522)
Fiji	1991[10]	150	37.3	—9.5—		—12.0—		2.8	8.1	2.6	2.9	4.3		—6.6—	
Finland	1993[10,36]	17,308	10.7	2.5	0.5	1.4	1.0	0.5	5.4	1.2	16.7	6.4	5.3	1.8	1.1
France	1993[10]	247,350	11.6	2.6	1.0	2.5	2.2	0.9	1.6	1.8	2.2	6.3	3.0	—6.1—	
French Guiana	1991[13]	45	...	...	...	—37—			—38.2[37]—		...	...	...	...	...
French Polynesia	1993[3]	214	—27.2—			...	...	...	...	...	...	...	...	...	...
Gabon	1990	268	9.7	7.5	6.3	1.1	1.9	0.7	19.8	2.6	0.7	1.5	2.6	—1.1—	
Gambia, The	1990	22	58.1	5.3	—	4.1	—	0.1	—	6.3	—	3.8	—	—2.0—	
Gaza Strip	1994	50	...												
Georgia	1992	150	...												
Germany[39]	1993[10,29]	538,381	6.4	2.5	2.4	2.0	1.0	0.4	1.4	1.8	2.6	2.1	5.4	3.8	2.3
Ghana	1993[10,29]	610	8.4	9.1	18.1	4.6	—0.5—		15.2	0.8	1.8	1.3	0.9	—8.9—	
Gibraltar		...													
Greece	1992[12,13]	10,660	17.0	5.9	3.6	10.2	5.3	1.7	1.8	1.0	3.0	3.2	2.2	4.9	2.4
Greenland	1991	27	...												
Grenada	1993[2,41]	17	30.4	51.6	3.7	—	—	—	...	...	5.6	—	—	8.7	...
Guadeloupe	1991[13]	95	...	...	...	—37—			—25.8[37]—		...	...	...	...	...
Guam	1986	9.1	...												
Guatemala	1988[10,36]	842	24.1	5.3	2.5	6.5	3.2	2.7	1.2	0.6	1.4	4.8	4.9	9.1	6.8
Guernsey	1993[4]	61	—5.1—			—1.5—		—	...	...		17.6	—	—	7.8
Guinea	1993	123	...												
Guinea-Bissau	1991[12]	13	...												
Guyana	1995[43]	20	...												
Haiti	1993[3,44]	152	...	...	...	1.6	70.9	5.0	—1.2—		...	...	...	...	...
Honduras	1992[10,36]	533	27.1	16.6	6.3	2.9	10.1	1.0	5.0	1.3	2.4	2.7	0.4	3.0	1.0
Hong Kong	1992	12,570	3.9	1.4	1.9	15.2	20.1	0.5	0.3	0.4	2.6	8.0	—2.0—		
Hungary	1993	6,563	16.4	3.8	0.6	3.1	3.5	1.6	1.6	1.6	1.7	4.5	3.1	—7.1—	
Iceland	1992[10]	940	48.0	2.4	...	2.1	1.5	0.9	0.2	5.2	1.0	9.9	1.8	2.2	—
India	1991–92[12,45]	19,237	9.5	1.2	2.3	11.3	1.8	1.0	0.4	—	2.2	1.7	6.6	4.5	3.9
Indonesia	1992[12,29]	20,406[21]	14.0	1.0	10.2	9.9	3.7	3.0	9.3	1.1	3.5	1.3	6.3	1.7	1.2
Iran	1991–92[12,13]	3,098[46]	10.4	1.5	1.8	14.8	0.6	1.4	1.0	0.4	1.8	1.2	2.6	—3.8—	
Iraq	1992[12,47]	11,258[48]	7.1	3.3	0.1	2.2	0.7	0.5	—0.1—		2.0	0.8	21.4	—0.7—	
Ireland	1990[49]	14,780	20.5	5.4	1.1	2.3	1.4	0.3	1.2	0.6	1.3	3.8	2.8	1.4	12.6
Isle of Man	1990–91[3,12]	98	—15.7—			...	...	...	...	...	...	...	...	...	...
Israel	1992[10,36]	10,685	10.7	—1.4—		3.8	4.3	0.8	1.2	1.3	2.1	4.7	5.2	—5.7 —	
Italy	1991[29]	146,179	7.4	1.3	0.4	7.2	3.8	2.5	1.1	2.1	2.7	4.4	3.6	2.8	...
Jamaica	1990	734	16.6	12.3	11.5	0.7	3.8	2.3	0.6	1.9	1.4	3.6	7.6	—1.4—	
Japan	1993[50]	1,140,051	8.7	1.2	0.3	2.8	1.3	0.3	1.6	0.9	2.6	5.7	4.3	2.7	3.1
Jersey	1991	45	...												
Jordan	1993[10]	802	9.3	6.2	12.5	2.1	1.9	1.3	0.7	3.8	2.6	3.6	3.1	3.6	6.7
Kazakstan	1994[2,3,11]	6,867	14.9	...	...	3.1	1.0	0.6	—1.3[9]—		—9—		4.6[7]	7	7
Kenya	1993[12]	521	30.2	10.1	1.4	5.5	1.6	1.8	1.7	1.2[31]	4.2	2.8	1.8	—7.5—	
Kiribati	1992	0.68	...												
Korea, North															
Korea, South	1993[10,36]	135,089	6.5	1.6	2.0	7.1	3.5	2.2	1.0	1.2	2.3	2.8	3.8	2.7	2.0
Kuwait	1992[10]	1,871	6.1	1.6	—	1.3	5.5	0.2	0.8	2.5	0.9	2.0	1.5	0.9	...
Kyrgyzstan	1994[2,3,11]	444	20.4	...	...	23.1	2.2	1.8	—0.7[9]—		—9—		0.3[7]	7	7
Laos	1990[2]	66	4.5	7.4	16.3	—	5.1	0.3	40.1	5.0	—	1.2	—4.0—		
Latvia	1994[2,3]	1,536	—38.9—		0.8	6.2	1.9	2.0	7.8	3.8	0.5	2.4	—7.3—		
Lebanon	1992	481	...												
Lesotho	1993[3]	93	—50.9—			—34.8—			—2.4—		...	2.4	...	—2.4—	
Liberia	1985[2,10,29]	64	10.8	42.7		—	—	0.3	—	4.5	0.6	1.3	0.4	—7.2—	
Libya	1990	1,211	5.5	2.8	10.8	2.7	0.7	7.1	0.9	0.7	0.4	0.3	7.2	—5.8—	
Liechtenstein		...													
Lithuania	1993[2]	1,782	31.1	5.3	0.6	10.6	1.9	2.7	1.6	2.8	1.1	0.6	4.1	0.5	0.5
Luxembourg	1993	1,932	5.1	—6.9—		—6.8—			—0.8—		—5.4—		—7.5—		
Macau	1993[10]	444	1.7	0.6	0.3	19.5	54.2	1.8	0.1	0.9	0.5	3.3	—	0.6	0.4
Macedonia	1993	867	14.8	2.9	11.9	9.6	8.4	5.0	0.5	2.6	1.0	2.4	0.4	—3.4—	
Madagascar	1990	125	14.5	17.5	1.2	33.5	2.2	3.6	0.2	0.2	4.0	1.0	0.3	—7.6—	
Malawi	1990	133	14.6	7.2	5.4	13.9	0.9	3.3	1.5	0.6	0.4	6.5	4.8	—23.5—	
Malaysia	1992[12]	13,778	8.5	1.1	1.1	3.1	2.7	0.2	5.5	1.0	1.7	2.9	8.5	2.3	0.3
Maldives	1993	10[52]	...												
Mali	1990	96	18.4	1.2	13.1	36.5	10.3	0.1	0.1	...	0.4	0.8	0.8	—0.7—	
Malta	1992	568	10.8	8.1	1.5	2.7	13.3	3.0	0.4	5.2	1.6	9.8	0.5	—3.6[53]—	
Marshall Islands	1994	1.1	...												
Martinique	1991[13]	191	...	...	...	—37—			—16.8[37]—		...	...	...	...	...
Mauritania	1993	35	—42.9—		—	—	—	—	—	—	6.0	—	—18.8—		
Mauritius	1992[10,13]	680	17.3	10.0	5.0	2.9	40.9	1.6	0.5	1.4	1.0	2.4	2.1	1.9	0.1
Mayotte	1992	...													
Mexico	1993	59,513	—25.3—			—8.3—			—1.9—		—5.5—		—23.1—		
Micronesia	1992	2.2[4]	55	...	...	...	91.0			...	...	...	...	1.6[55]	
Moldova	1994[2,3,56]	759	56.2	...	...	3.6	1.8	2.1	—5.3[9]—		—9—		0.8[7]	7	7
Monaco															
Mongolia	1994[2,3]	564	—24.6—			7.7	0.9	4.6	—1.5—		...	0.3	5.8[7]	7	...
Morocco	1993[3,13]	3,953	6.8	—19.6—		9.9	7.8	1.5	—2.0—		—3.5—		—11.3—		
Mozambique	1994[2]	152	29.1	17.0	1.5	8.1	1.0	0.4	0.6	0.8	2.1	3.4	2.2	8.9	—
Myanmar (Burma)	1993–94	3,080	...												
Namibia	1994[3]	234	63.6[58]	...											
Nauru	1989														
Nepal	1991–92[10,13]	341	14.3	6.1	10.2	29.9	8.4	1.3	2.0	1.4	0.7	0.7	—2.8—		0.8
Netherlands, The	1993[10,29]	43,948	15.0	3.8	4.7	2.1	0.5	0.3	1.1	0.9	3.5	8.3	7.8	3.3	2.3
Netherlands Antilles	1992	132	...												
New Caledonia	1993[3]	371	...												
New Zealand	1990–91	7,352	22.8	—9.2—		3.2	—4.1—		—6.1—		7.5	7.3	3.4	—2.9—	
Nicaragua	1993[23]	406	37.2	25.1	9.3	3.4	0.2	1.3	2.2	0.6	0.5	1.9	—2.8—		
Niger	1990	33	5.2	24.7	...	21.5	3.2	...	—	...	0.3	4.3	...	—27.3—	

refined petroleum and products	rubber products	plastic products	(36) pottery, china, and glass	bricks, tiles, cement, etc.	(37) iron and steel	non-ferrous metals	(38) fabricated metal products	nonelectrical machinery	office equip., computers	electrical equip.	radio, television	transport equip. exc. motor vehicles	motor vehicles	professional equip.	(39) jewelry, musical instruments	country
(353+354)	(355)	(356)	(361+362)	(369)	(371)	(372)	(381)	(382 exc. 3825)	(3825)	(383 exc. 3832)	(3832)	(384 exc. 3843)	(3843)	(385)	(390)	
—	0.5	2.4	—	4.3[35]	35		3.9	— 1.1 —				0.7	0.2	—	0.8	Fiji
2.3	0.6	1.4	1.0	2.0	5.0	1.3	5.6	9.1	1.2	4.2	4.2	4.3	1.0	1.5	0.8	Finland
6.9	1.4	2.7	1.1	2.8	2.2	1.7	7.4	— 7.9 —		— 10.4 —		— 10.4 —		1.5	1.8	France
...	...	...	— 61.8[38] —		— 38 —		— 38 —			— 35.4 —					...	French Guiana
																French Polynesia
11.6	—	—	1.1	6.3	1.5	1.5	7.5	— 1.1 —		— 4.5 —		— 6.3 —		0.4	2.6	Gabon
—	1.3	—	—	0.9	—	—	3.5								14.6	Gambia, The
																Gaza Strip
...	...	...	...	...	...	...	...	...	...	...	...	...	...	...	...	Georgia
4.6	1.1	3.5	1.2	2.8	2.5	1.2	7.6	12.2	1.6	6.5	7.2	1.6	10.3	1.5	0.5	Germany[39]
8.1	0.6	2.6	— 4.4 —		0.7	8.2	3.4	— 0.3 —		— 1.5 —		— 0.6[40] —		—	40	Ghana
																Gibraltar
5.5	0.7	3.1	1.0	6.0	1.9	2.7	4.7	1.6	—	3.4	1.6	3.8	1.2	0.2	0.5	Greece
...	...	...	...	...	...	...	—	—	—	—	—	—	—	—	...	Greenland
...	...	...	...	...	...	...	...	...	...	...	...	...	...	...	...	Grenada
—	...	...	— 42 —		— 42 —		64.1[42]	— 10.0 —							...	Guadeloupe
																Guam
1.1	2.3	3.6	3.4	5.9	3.1	0.1	2.8	0.7	0.1	2.4	0.4	0.1	0.2	0.2	0.5	Guatemala
—	—	10.9	—	1.9	—	—	—	— 7.4 —		—	40.3	3.0	—	—	4.6	Guernsey
...	...	...	...	...	...	...	...	...	...	...	...	...	...	...	...	Guinea
...	...	...	...	...	...	...	...	...	...	...	...	...	...	...	...	Guinea-Bissau
...	...	...	...	...	...	...	...	...	...	...	...	...	...	...	...	Guyana
—	— 1.1 —		—	—	—	—	—	—	—	— 5.6 —		—	...	1.6	9.2	Haiti
4.6	1.1	2.7	0.1	4.7	0.6	0.2	3.1	0.7	—	0.8	0.1	0.1	0.2	0.1	1.1	Honduras
0.1	0.1	4.9	— 0.9 —		— 0.7 —		6.3	6.9	4.6	1.3	6.9	— 3.5 —		4.1	3.4	Hong Kong
15.2	0.5	2.5	1.8	2.6	2.1	1.1	4.0	— 7.3 —		— 6.3 —		— 5.2 —		2.2	0.6	Hungary
0.1	—	3.2	0.5	4.2	0.7	2.6	7.6	—	—	—	—	2.7	—	—	3.2	Iceland
3.7	2.0	1.3	0.9	6.1	5.3	3.3	2.8	7.9	1.0	5.9	2.8	3.7	5.5	0.8	0.6	India
...	3.0	2.2	1.4	2.4	4.6	1.6	3.6	1.3	—	2.1	2.6	5.3	2.6	0.1	1.0	Indonesia
0.6	1.4	1.7	2.0	8.5	9.5	3.8	4.2	— 10.1 —		— 2.6 —		— 13.4 —		0.4	0.5	Iran
24.0	0.4	0.8	0.5	22.5	— 4.3 —		2.6	— 1.4 —		— 4.1 —		— 0.3 —		—	—	Iraq
0.2	0.8	2.2	1.2	3.8	0.6	0.1	3.2	2.6	11.2	2.9	9.5	1.5	0.6	4.1	0.9	Ireland
																Isle of Man
—	0.7	5.3	0.7	3.8	1.4	0.7	11.3	— 2.7 —		— 22.7 —		— 7.1 —		0.6	1.8	Israel
1.8	1.6	3.4	3.1	3.1	4.9	1.2	5.9	13.0	1.0	7.5	2.9	3.1	6.1	1.2	1.0	Italy
11.0	2.1	3.3	1.6	3.7	1.2	—	2.6	— 1.8 —		— 1.9 —		— 6.0 —		—	1.1	Jamaica
1.4	1.3	3.7	1.2	3.1	4.7	1.2	7.5	9.5	3.0	6.5	7.8	1.6	9.1	1.3	1.6	Japan
																Jersey
6.2	0.1	2.9	— 20.1 —		3.7	1.5	4.2	1.5	—	1.0	—	—	1.2	0.2	—	Jordan
27.0	7	7	— 5.1 —		— 29.5 —		— 9.0 —								...	Kazakstan
0.8	3.3	3.2	0.5	4.3	...	...	6.2	— 0.5 —		— 5.4 —		— 4.0 —		8	2.0[8]	Kenya
																Kiribati
...	...	...					...								...	Korea, North
3.3	1.1	4.2	1.2	4.1	5.8	1.1	5.2	7.4	0.9	3.4	11.0	3.0	7.6	0.7	1.3	Korea, South
56.1	—	1.6	0.6	4.5	0.9	—	5.3	2.4	—	1.4	—	2.5	0.3	—	1.0	Kuwait
4.5	7	7	— 5.4 —		— 14.1 —		— 13.5 —								...	Kyrgyzstan
—	— 0.5 —		0.1	3.8	—	—	10.8	— 0.5 —		— 0.2 —					0.1	Laos
...	— 0.7 —		— 3.1 —		— 4.4 —		1.4	— 4.7 —		2.6	2.1	4.8	3.0	0.3	...	Latvia
...	...	...	...	...	...	...	...	...	...	...	...	...	...	...	...	Lebanon
...	...	...	— 3.8 —		1.4	...	...	...	...	...	...	...	...	...	...	Lesotho
...	...	0.6	0.2	20.7	—	—	9.5	— 0.3 —		— 0.7 —		—	—	—	—	Liberia
30.9	0.1	0.8	0.1	18.3	—	—	1.7	—	—	—	—	—	—	—	3.2	Libya
																Liechtenstein
5.8	—	0.3	0.6	4.8	0.5	...	1.1	2.1	0.2	5.6	6.2	1.4	0.5	1.2	6.3	Lithuania
...	— 13.4 —		— 10.9 —		20.5	3.3	6.4	8.0	—	— 4.2[51] —		— 0.6 —		51	0.2	Luxembourg
—	—	1.5	0.2	1.7	—	—	1.8	0.3	—	1.3	—	0.8	—	0.4	8.0	Macau
5.5	—	1.0	1.4	0.7	6.3	1.1	4.7	— 2.6 —		— 6.8 —		— 5.5 —		0.2	1.2	Macedonia
4.1	0.4	1.0	0.3	1.8	—	—	3.2	—	—	— 1.9 —		— 1.2 —		—	0.2	Madagascar
—	0.3	4.2	—	6.7	—	—	3.1	— 1.8 —		— 0.4 —		— 0.7 —		—	—	Malawi
1.7	4.9	3.3	1.0	4.6	2.8	0.8	4.3	3.8	0.7	3.8	22.3	1.6	2.9	1.2	1.4	Malaysia
—	—	—	—	—	—	—	—	—	—	—	—	—	—	—	—	Maldives
0.7	0.3	0.4	—	1.3	—	—	6.2	— 0.5 —		— 1.7 —		— 6.5 —		—	...	Mali
53	3.7	2.4	0.5	3.9	—	54	4.6[54]	— 2.1 —		4.8	6.9	2.4	0.2	4.1	3.9	Malta
52.2	...	...	— 42 —		— 42 —		28.8[42]	— 2.2 —							...	Martinique
																Mauritania
—	0.3	1.2	—	16.8	—	—	15.5	—	—	—	—	—	—	—	—	Mauritius
			0.1	3.5	0.8	—	1.7	—	—	0.7	0.3	0.5	0.2	1.2	2.3	Mayotte
—	—	—	— 6.5 —		— 3.3 —		— 25.3 —								0.8	Mexico
...	...	...	...	...	...	...	...	...	...	...	...	...	...	...	7.4	Micronesia
...	7	7	— 5.5 —		...	...	— 13.1 —								...	Moldova
...	...	...	...	...	...	...	...	...	...	...	...	...	...	...	...	Monaco
...	7	7	—	3.6	...	38.4[57]	1.3	...	...	...	...	...	...	...	0.1	Mongolia
...	— 2.8 —		— 9.4 —		...	...	5.2	— 1.6 —		— 2.9 —		— 3.9 —		0.2	0.1	Morocco
0.4	1.7	0.9	2.1	9.4	2.9	1.1	2.8	0.4	—	1.5	—	— 1.7 —		—	0.1	Mozambique
...	...	...	...	...	...	...	...	...	...	...	...	...	...	...	...	Myanmar (Burma)
...	...	...	...	...	...	...	...	...	...	...	...	...	...	...	...	Namibia
...	...	...	...	...	...	...	...	...	...	...	...	...	...	...	...	Nauru
—	0.9	1.6	—	11.9	2.7	—	2.3	—	—	1.1	0.3	—	—	—	0.4	Nepal
2.3	0.6	3.1	1.6	2.4	— 3.9 —		6.7	— 8.3 —		— 11.4 —		— 4.8 —		0.9	0.4	Netherlands, The
...	...	...	...	...	...	80.8	...	— 7.1 —							...	Netherlands Antilles
																New Caledonia
2.0	0.8	3.1	— 3.6 —		— 3.4 —		6.5	— 4.6 —		— 3.5 —		— 4.4 —		0.3	1.2	New Zealand
5.4	0.1	...	— 6.3 —		—	—	1.1	— 0.3 —		— 0.2 —		— 0.2 —		—	...	Nicaragua
...	...	...	...	4.9	...	...	8.6	...	...	...	...	...	...	...	...	Niger

Manufacturing industries (continued)

country	year	total manufacturing value added ('000,000 U.S.$)	(31) food (311+312)	beverages (313)	tobacco manufactures (314)	(32) textiles (exc. wearing apparel) (321)	wearing apparel (322)	leather and fur products (323+324)	(33) wood products (exc. furniture) (331)	wood furniture (332)	(34) paper, paper products (341)	printing and publishing (342)	(35) industrial chemicals (351)	paints, soaps, etc. (352 exc. 3522)	drugs and medicines (3522)
Nigeria	1990	3,606	14.0	12.0	2.0	12.4	0.1	3.0	0.7	0.9	3.2	3.0	0.5	—12.8—	
Northern Mariana Islands	1987[1,3]	58	—3.3—			26.0	—62.7[59]—		...	1.3	...	1.3	...	...	...
Norway	1993[13]	12,531	13.0	—9.5—		1.4	0.5	0.2	3.3	1.9	4.4	10.0	5.4	1.4	2.0
Oman	1993[2]	689	—27.5—			—29.6—			—2.2—		—0.1—		—15.5—		
Pakistan	1990–91	4,987	14.2	1.4	6.4	26.7	1.4	1.6	0.3	0.2	1.6	2.3	7.9	2.6	4.7
Palau	1983	0.13													
Panama	1992[36]	717	35.0	11.5	4.3	0.6	5.1	1.3	0.8	0.9	5.0	3.9	1.1	4.2	1.3
Papua New Guinea	1989	451	48.4	13.1	4.9	—	0.4	—	11.6	2.0	1.1	2.4	1.1	—1.1—	
Paraguay	1990	633	35.4	8.7	1.4	6.5	0.5	5.1	14.5	1.4	0.2	5.1	0.3	—0.9—	
Peru	1994	3,586	24.9	—7.1—		7.8	5.2	0.9	—7.1—		0.5	3.8	—6.9—		1.2
Philippines	1992	12,076	40.7	4.8	2.7	2.9	—6.8—		1.8	1.5	0.9	1.3	8.3[20]	20	20
Poland	1994	22,523	—20.6—		3.8	3.7	4.6	1.7	3.6	3.7	1.6	3.6			—18.1—
Portugal	1991[10]	13,933	9.4	2.7	5.0	11.3	8.0	4.2	4.4	2.3	3.7	4.4	2.1	2.6	1.9
Puerto Rico	1992[3]	22,737	4.6	11.6	...	0.5	4.0	1.0	...	0.5	0.8	1.4	2.7	1.9	43.9
Qatar	1993[10]	790	2.1	0.6	...	0.2	—5.1—		0.5	2.4	...	2.6	24.1	—0.4—	
Réunion	1993	352	33.4	10.3		—0.6—			—4.7—		4.3[60]	9.6		—3.4—	
Romania	1992[61]	5,911	15.7	5.2	1.1	6.2	3.7	2.8	3.6	2.6	1.4	0.7	3.0	—5.4—	
Russia	1993	35,400[62]	17.3	1.6	0.6	5.0	2.4	1.9	2.3	1.6	1.5	0.7	8.1	1.5	0.6
Rwanda	1990	178	29.1	18.1	11.2	...	...	...	4.4	0.9	1.0	1.3	9.0	—	—
St. Kitts and Nevis	1993[3,12]	19	19.6[65]	...	...	...	...	...	...	...	...	...	...	...	...
St. Lucia	1991[2,41]	42	—44.7—			3.4	11.6	...	...	...	30.2	...	0.5	...	...
St. Vincent	1988[3,12]	14	24.9	—25.4—			—10.1—		—1.9—		—5.3—		...	...	...
San Marino	...	...	...	...	...	...	...	...	...	...	...	...	...	...	...
São Tomé and Príncipe	1993[2]	4.6	26.3	20.7	—	—	26.3	—	—15.1—		...	1.2	...	6.6	...
Saudi Arabia	1990	5,387	5.9	0.8	0.6	0.4	0.1	0.1	0.2	0.7	2.0	1.1	35.4	—3.1—	
Senegal	1993	340[67]	48.9[67]	4.9	4.4	0.9	1.4	—	0.2	0.1	1.6	2.5	8.0	—5.5—	
Seychelles	1989	26	—79.6—				—0.6—		—2.1—		—6.0—				—4.1—
Sierra Leone	1993[10]	92	37.0	21.6	10.5	—	1.0	0.1	0.3	1.2	0.2	2.2			—20.2—
Singapore	1993[12,13]	17,507	2.5	1.0	0.6	0.4	1.5	0.2	0.3	0.7	1.4	4.8	3.1	1.3	4.3
Slovakia	1993[2]	8,572	14.7	2.6	...	3.6	1.9	2.1	1.9	1.9	3.8	1.7	6.2	1.4	1.8
Slovenia	1993[10]	3,218	11.9	3.1	3.2	8.4	—10.1—		—3.4—		3.0	5.6	5.3	—5.4—	
Solomon Islands	1991	7.1	...	...	...	...	...	...	...	...	...	...	...	...	...
Somalia	1990	36	21.6	6.3	37.5	10.5	0.8	2.0	—	7.3	−0.6	0.3	0.4	—5.1—	
South Africa	1992[12,68]	25,871	11.1	5.5	0.5	3.3	3.0	1.3	1.4	1.1	4.7	3.4	4.8	—11.0[53]—	
Spain	1992[12,36]	94,549	13.2	4.4	1.2	3.3	2.7	1.3	2.3	1.9	2.3	5.3	3.3	3.4	3.4
Sri Lanka	1992[10,36]	1,280	18.5	8.2	21.3	8.1	14.1	1.0	0.7	—	1.4	3.2	0.6	7.4	0.3
Sudan, The	1990	1,179	40.0	3.0	16.7	11.9	0.4	5.4	0.2	0.2	2.1	6.4	0.7	—2.2—	
Suriname	1992[2,12,41]	700	33.4	22.3	12.3	...	1.5	1.6	8.7	1.4	0.7	1.6	...	—8.3—	
Swaziland	1990[12]	252	29.3	40.0	—		—7.7—		—2.4—		—15.9—				—0.8—
Sweden	1993[12,13]	29,964	8.5	1.1	0.6	1.1	0.3	0.1	4.5	1.0	8.8	6.2	3.9	1.8	5.3
Switzerland	1990	58,051	10.3	1.7	0.5	3.0	2.0	0.8	3.9	2.5	2.4	7.3	7.2	—7.8—	
Syria	1992[12,30,48]	2,308	—25.4—				—30.6—		—7.3—		—1.0—				—10.3—
Taiwan	1994	69,895	—7.5—		1.6	6.3	2.4	0.9	0.7	1.0	2.2	1.3	6.7	—2.5—	
Tajikistan	1994[2,3,11]	802	9.3	...	...	28.1	1.4	0.3	—0.4[9]—		—9—		3.9[7]	7	7
Tanzania	1990	106	21.4	8.0	6.3	14.6	1.1	3.9	1.3	0.6	3.1	4.7	3.7	—2.7—	
Thailand	1991[10,13]	65,413	4.1	2.3	2.9	3.1	5.0	1.4	0.6	0.4	0.2	33.9	1.5	0.7	0.6
Togo	1993[3]	87	—62.3—				—10.9—		—6.9—		—3.2—				—4.9—
Tonga	1992[2,10]	16	—39.0—			2.3	8.7	3.8	1.4	69	69	4.5		—22.2—	
Trinidad and Tobago	1992	717	20.3	8.7	6.3	0.7	1.2	0.4	—1.6—		2.3	3.7	17.2	3.0	0.1
Tunisia	1992[10]	3,136	10.2	3.0	5.9	6.6	12.1	3.2	—4.8—		—2.2—		2.3	2.4	0.4
Turkey	1991[10,72]	31,369	10.5	3.6	4.8	10.8	3.3	0.5	0.6	0.3	1.8	1.4	4.2	2.3	2.9
Turkmenistan	1992[2,3,11]	801	13.3	...	...	18.9	1.2	0.4	—0.3[9]—		—9—		3.2[7]	7	7
Tuvalu	1993[12]	0.5	...	...	...	...	...	...	...	...	...	...	...	...	...
Uganda	1989	155	42.8	11.9	8.9	8.0	1.3	1.5	0.1	4.0	0.9	1.4	0.3	0.7	5.1
Ukraine	1994[2,3,11]	17,982	21.1	...	...	2.5	1.0	1.4	—2.7[9]—		—9—		7.7[7]	7	7
United Arab Emirates	1993[2]	6,621	—8.7—			—4.7—			—2.8—		—2.8—				—53.8—
United Kingdom	1992[12]	192,962	10.3	2.8	1.2	2.7	2.4	0.6	1.2	1.7	3.3	8.6	5.1	2.2	4.0
United States	1993[12]	1,481,700	9.6	1.7	1.4	2.8	1.9	0.3	1.9	1.3	3.8	7.9	4.9	3.4	3.4
Uruguay	1993[10,36]	2,962	24.0	12.6	5.6	8.3	3.7	2.6	0.6	0.6	2.1	4.9	1.9	—8.4—	
Uzbekistan	1992[2,3,11]	2,147	12.6	...	...	21.4	3.1	1.9	—1.3[9]—		...	...	5.4[7]	7	7
Vanuatu	1993[3]	10	—44.5—				—3.8—		—22.5—		5.3	...			—9.2[73]—
Venezuela	1993[3,36]	11,292	11.8	7.1	3.4	1.7	−1.3	2.1	0.3	0.8	2.3	2.8	5.1	3.6	2.4
Vietnam	1992[2,3]	3,706	—36.5—			8.4	1.5	0.5	3.4	...	2.0	0.7	8.1[74]	74	74
Virgin Islands (U.S.)	...[76]		...	...	...	...	...	...	...	...	...	...	...	...	...
West Bank	1994	132	...	...	...	...	...	...	...	...	...	...	...	...	...
Western Sahara	...	...	...	...	...	...	...	...	...	...	...	...	...	...	...
Western Samoa	1990	15	36.0	25.5	19.2	...	...	...	10.7	...	...	...	...	8.6	...
Yemen	1994[2,48]	3,541	—64.0—				—1.7—		—0.6—		—8.5—				—13.2—
Yugoslavia	1994[3]	4,506	19.5	5.7	4.7	3.1	5.3	2.9	1.0	3.2	2.0	2.0	3.6	—9.2—	
Zaire	1990	808	86.7	5.4	1.9	0.6	0.2	0.6	0.1	0.2	—	0.1	0.9	—0.1—	
Zambia	1990	1,103	8.7	19.1	10.3	6.2	4.2	3.2	2.7	2.2	1.2	2.3	3.9	—7.8—	
Zimbabwe	1992–93[12]	1,921	18.0	10.7	4.7	7.8	2.9	2.6	1.9	1.0	2.6	2.7	4.5[77]	1.4	2.8

[1]Gross output in value of sales. [2]Gross output of production. [3]Complete ISIC detail is not available. [4]Value of manufactured exports. [5]Canned tuna and salmon. [6]Value of manufactured exports (excluding duty-free reexports). [7]351 includes 352, 355, and 356. [8]390 includes 385. [9]33 includes 34. [10]In producer's prices. [11]Includes extraction of petroleum, natural gas, metals, and nonmetals. [12]In factor values. [13]Establishments employing 10 or more persons. [14]Excludes sugar refining. [15]321 includes 323 + 324. [16]351 includes 353 + 354, 355, and 356. [17]355 and 356 include 361 + 362. [18]38 includes 39. [19]Establishments employing 15 or more persons. [20]351 includes 352 and 356. [21]Excludes petroleum refining. [22]37 includes 381. [23]382 includes 385. [24]Cotton fibre only. [25]Establishments employing 50 or more persons. [26]311 + 312 includes 314. [27]Republic of Cyprus only. [28]Includes optical goods. [29]Establishments employing 20 or more persons. [30]Private establishments employing 10 or more persons, and all public establishments. [31]Includes metal furniture. [32]351 includes 352, 353, and 354. [33]Ethiopia includes Eritrea. [34]Processed fish only. [35]369 includes 371. [36]Establishments employing five or more persons. [37]33 includes 32. [38]36 includes 37 and 38. [39]Former West Germany only. [40]384 includes 390. [41]Selected industries only. [42]381 includes 36 and 37. [43]Excludes sugar and rice manufacturing; includes public utilities. [44]Value of manufactured goods exported to the U.S. [45]Establishments

refined petroleum and products	rubber products	plastic products	(36) pottery, china, and glass	(36) bricks, tiles, cement, etc.	(37) iron and steel	(37) non-ferrous metals	(38) fabricated metal products	(38) nonelectrical machinery	(38) office equip., computers	(38) electrical equip.	(38) radio, television	(38) transport equip. exc. motor vehicles	(38) motor vehicles	(38) professional equip.	(39) jewelry, musical instruments	country
(353+354)	(355)	(356)	(361+362)	(369)	(371)	(372)	(381)	(382 exc. 3825)	(3825)	(383 exc. 3832)	(3832)	(384 exc. 3843)	(3843)	(385)	(390)	
1.2	1.8	3.0	0.5	6.3	0.7	2.0	5.6	1.2		2.2		10.7			0.3	Nigeria
...	[59]	[59]	4.9		...	...	...								...	Northern Mariana Islands
2.0	0.2	1.7	0.8	2.3	2.0	4.7	4.4	6.7	0.3	3.7	1.7	13.0	1.1	1.6	0.9	Norway
...	...	...	9.1		1.6			11.4							2.9	Oman
3.0	1.0	0.5	7.7		5.6	—	0.9	2.5		4.1		2.6		0.2	0.6	Pakistan
...	...	...	...		...	...	...								...	Palau
4.7	0.2	4.5	1.5	5.7	1.4	0.3	2.5	0.2		0.2	0.1	1.7	0.4	0.2	1.3	Panama
—	—	0.4	0.7	1.6	...	...	6.7	1.3		0.7		2.4			...	Papua New Guinea
9.8	—	1.9	0.3	4.1	...	...	1.9	0.2		0.9					0.5	Paraguay
1.0	2.3		6.2		2.1	15.7	1.9	0.7		1.2		1.4		[8]	2.1[8]	Peru
10.8	1.3	[20]	3.1		2.5		2.4	1.1		4.0		1.2		[8]	1.8[8]	Philippines
...	...	...	5.3		5.0		5.1	7.3	0.2	2.7	1.5	6.3		1.2	0.3	Poland
...	0.4	1.8	3.6	6.0	1.6	0.6	7.3	4.5	0.1	3.4	3.2	1.9	2.1	0.5	1.1	Portugal
0.5	0.1	1.0	0.3	1.1	...	...	1.4	1.1	2.1	3.2	4.3	—	0.4	5.7	0.9	Puerto Rico
37.1	...		6.9		15.5		1.4								0.1	Qatar
...	...	[60]	...	18.7	—		9.5			5.5					—	Réunion
4.8	1.7	1.9	7.2	0.3	5.7	0.4	4.7	10.9[23]		4.1		6.2		[23]	0.7	Romania
6.7	1.2	0.4	0.9	7.2	11.2	5.8	1.6	2.0	0.2	3.3[63]		1.5[64]	8.2	2.1	2.6	Russia
—	—	—	—	11.7	...	...	10.3	0.9		0.8		1.4			...	Rwanda
...	...	...	...		...	...	...								...	St. Kitts and Nevis
...	...	2.1	...		...	...	...			7.5					...	St. Lucia
...	...	0.4	...		...	...	6.6[66]		[66]		[66]				...	St. Vincent
...	...	...	...		...	...	...								...	San Marino
...	...	—	3.8		...	...	...								...	São Tomé and Príncipe
17.1	0.1	2.7	0.9	12.6	6.4	0.3	5.0	1.1		2.0		0.6		0.1	0.7	Saudi Arabia
3.9	—	2.2	...	8.7	—	—	3.4	0.4		0.7		2.3			—	Senegal
...	...	...	5.2		...	...	2.4								—	Seychelles
...	...	...	3.5		...	...	2.1								0.1	Sierra Leone
6.9	0.3	2.8	0.4	1.6	0.6	0.3	6.5	5.4	20.5	4.0	18.4	7.4	0.2	2.0	0.6	Singapore
9.3	2.2	1.7	1.5	3.5	13.7	2.6	2.9	6.6	0.1	4.3	1.6	2.2	2.5	1.3	0.4	Slovakia
0.4	2.5	2.0	4.7		1.4	1.4	6.2	8.2		4.8		6.2		2.0	0.8	Slovenia
...	...	...	...		...	...	...								...	Solomon Islands
1.6	—	0.5	—	3.0	—	—	1.1	—		—		0.9		—	1.7	Somalia
[53]	1.4	2.5	1.5	3.5	9.0	3.3	6.2	6.1		4.6		8.1		1.0	1.7	South Africa
2.8	1.8	3.0	1.7	5.0	3.3	1.2	6.3	5.9	0.3	4.1	1.8	2.9	10.5	0.5	1.0	Spain
0.1	3.6	0.8	1.8	3.4	0.7	0.2	0.4	—		0.5	0.1	0.7	0.4	—	2.5	Sri Lanka
1.3	0.8	1.2	0.1	0.5	0.1	0.7	2.6	0.1		1.2		2.1		—	0.1	Sudan, The
...	0.7	0.6	5.3		...	...	2.0			0.9		0.9		0.2	0.5	Suriname
...	...	...	1.0		...	...	2.0	0.9							—	Swaziland
1.6	0.3	1.5	0.7	1.8	4.0	1.3	7.1	12.4	1.7	3.7	5.0	3.2	9.4	2.7	0.4	Sweden
2.9	1.2	3.2	1.1	1.6	2.0	1.7	6.7	13.2		10.0		1.8		4.8	0.2	Switzerland
...	...	...	8.1		2.0			14.9							0.4	Syria
7.6	1.2	5.8	5.0		7.2		7.0	5.1		17.0		7.8		1.0	2.2	Taiwan
0.7	[7]	[7]	3.8		34.2		4.4								...	Tajikistan
2.2	4.9	0.4	—	1.2	3.3	1.7	4.8	1.3		2.8		8.7			0.4	Tanzania
7.9	1.6	0.3	0.9	3.5	1.7	0.5	1.7	10.3	0.1	1.5	5.6	0.2	5.8	0.2	1.5	Thailand
...	...	...	6.9		...	...	3.6	...							...	Togo
—	—	—	2.2		...	...	5.6	0.3				2.2			7.8[69]	Tonga
12.7	0.8	0.5	1.5	3.9	5.4	—	2.0	—		1.6	0.5	—	2.0		3.6	Trinidad and Tobago
24.2	0.8	1.2[70]	2.8	6.6	1.7	3.2[71]	[71]	0.3		2.7	0.7	0.1	1.7		0.9	Tunisia
15.7	1.6	1.2	2.9	4.1	5.7	1.3	3.1	4.4	—	2.6	3.2	0.9	5.8	0.3	0.2	Turkey
55.7	[7]	[7]	4.0		0.1		0.8								...	Turkmenistan
—	...	...	—		—		...								...	Tuvalu
—	0.2	—	...	2.5	3.0	...	4.7	0.7		1.3	0.5	—	0.1		...	Uganda
12.6	[7]	[7]	4.5		24.0		19.2								...	Ukraine
...	...	...	8.3		8.2		9.2								1.4	United Arab Emirates
1.3	1.3	3.8	1.6	2.3	1.9	0.8	5.2	11.4	1.6	3.9	4.9	5.4	5.4	1.7	1.3	United Kingdom
1.6	1.1	3.3	0.9	1.6	2.2	1.2	5.2	8.4	2.0	3.3	5.8	5.0	6.8	5.8	1.5	United States
3.0	1.2	2.9	1.6	2.3	0.9	0.4	3.6	1.2		2.8		3.5		0.7	0.6	Uruguay
12.4	[7]	[7]	5.4		12.2		13.2								...	Uzbekistan
...	...	...	[73]		12.0[22]		[22]								...	Vanuatu
26.3	1.6	1.9	1.8	3.2	4.3	3.9	3.7	1.8	0.1	1.8	0.3	0.1	6.3	0.4	0.4	Venezuela
17.7[75]	[74]	...	1.2	7.9	2.5		1.9	3.8		1.9					...	Vietnam
...	...	...	...		...	...	...								...	Virgin Islands (U.S.)
...	...	...	...		...	...	...								...	West Bank
...	...	...	...		...	...	...								...	Western Sahara
...	...	...	...		...	...	...								...	Western Samoa
...	...	...	10.5		1.5		...								1.4	Yemen
...	2.8	...	5.1		2.0	2.7	8.6	3.9		6.3		5.7		—	—	Yugoslavia
0.1	—	0.2	...		...	...	0.4	0.3		0.2		0.5			1.5	Zaire
0.9	2.4	1.2	0.5	5.5	0.8	0.1	8.9	1.8		1.9		4.1		—	0.1	Zambia
[77]	1.9	1.4	0.5	3.1	15.6	0.8	5.3	1.1		2.7	0.3	0.8	2.4	0.1	0.4	Zimbabwe

with electric power and 10 or more employees, or without electric power and with 20 or more employees. [46]Conversion to U.S.$ based on floating exchange rate. [47]Establishments employing 30 or more persons. [48]Conversion to U.S.$ based on official exchange rate. [49]Establishments employing three or more persons. [50]Establishments employing four or more persons. [51]3825 and 383 include 385. [52]Includes public utilities. [53]352 includes 353 + 354. [54]381 includes 372. [55]Coconut soap includes coconut oil. [56]Excludes Transdniester area and city of Tighina (Bendery). [57]Includes ore extraction. [58]Fish and meat processing. [59]322 and 323 + 324 includes 355 + 356. [60]341 includes 356. [61]State enterprises only; state enterprises account for about 80% of all industrial output. [62]Sum of available data. [63]Excludes radio, television, and communications equipment; data suppressed for reasons of confidentiality. [64]Excludes shipbuilding and aircraft; data suppressed for reasons of confidentiality. [65]Refined sugar only. [66]381 includes 383. [67]Excludes fish processing. [68]Excludes formerly nominally independent republics of Bophuthatswana, Ciskei, Venda, and Transkei. [69]39 includes 332 and 341. [70]Includes synthetic fibres. [71]372 includes 381. [72]Private establishments employing 25 or more persons, and all public establishments. [73]35 includes 36. [74]351 includes 352 and 355. [75]Includes crude petroleum production. [76]Data withheld for reasons of confidentiality. [77]351 includes 353 + 354.

Energy

This table provides data about the commercial energy supplies (reserves, production, consumption, and trade) of the various countries of the world, together with data about oil pipeline networks and traffic. Many of the data and concepts used in this table are adapted from the United Nations' *Energy Statistics Yearbook*.

Electricity. Total installed electrical power capacity comprises the sum of the rated power capacities of all main and auxiliary generators in a country. "Total installed capacity" (kW) is multiplied by 8,760 hours per year to yield "Total production capacity" (kW-hr).

Production of electricity comprises the total gross production of electricity by publicly or privately owned enterprises and also that generated by industrial establishments for their own use, but usually excludes consumption by the utility itself. Measured in millions of kilowatt-hours (kW-hr), annual production of electricity ranges generally between 50% and 60% of total production capacity. The data are further analyzed by type of generation: fossil fuels, hydroelectric power, and nuclear fuel.

The great majority of the world's electrical and other energy needs are met by the burning of fossil hydrocarbon solids, liquids, and gases, either for thermal generation of electricity or in internal combustion engines. Many renewable and nontraditional sources of energy are being developed worldwide (wood, biogenic gases and liquids, tidal, wave, and wind power, geothermal and photothermal [solar] energy, and so on), but collectively these sources are still negligible in the world's total energy consumption. For this reason only hydroelectric and nuclear generation are considered here separately with fossil fuels.

Trade in electrical energy refers to the transfer of generated electrical output via an international grid. Total electricity consumption (residential and nonresidential) is equal to total electricity requirements less transformation and distribution losses.

Coal. The term coal, as used in the table, comprises all grades of anthracite, bituminous, subbituminous, and lignite that have acquired or may in the future, by reason of new technology or changed market prices, acquire an economic value. These types of coal may be differentiated according to heat content (density) and content of impurities. Most coal reserve data are based on proven recoverable reserves only, of all grades of coal. Exceptions are footnoted, with proven in-place reserves reported only when recoverable reserves are unknown. Production figures include deposits removed from both surface and underground workings as well as quantities used by the producers themselves or issued to the miners. Wastes recovered from mines or nearby preparation plants are excluded from production figures.

Natural gas. This term refers to any combustible gas (usually chiefly methane) of natural origin from underground sources. The data for production cover, to the extent possible, gas obtained from gas fields, petroleum fields, or coal mines that is actually collected and marketed.

Energy

country	electricity												coal		
	installed capacity, 1994 ('000 kW)	production, 1994		power source, 1994			trade, 1994		consumption				reserves, latest ('000,000 metric tons)	production, 1994 ('000 metric tons)	consumption, 1994 ('000 metric tons)
		capacity ('000,000 kW-hr)	amount ('000,000 kW-hr)	fossil fuel (%)	hydro power (%)	nuclear fuel (%)	exports ('000,000 kW-hr)	imports ('000,000 kW-hr)	amount, 1994 ('000,000 kW-hr)	per capita, 1994 (kW-hr)	residential, 1990 (%)	non-residential, 1990 (%)			
Afghanistan	494	4,327	687	31.3	68.7	—	—	128	815	43	...	...	66	6	6
Albania	1,892	16,574	3,903	3.4	96.6	—	—	—	3,903	1,143	...	...	15[1]	179	179
Algeria	6,007	52,621	19,888	99.1	0.9	—	1,191	67	18,764	687	...	...	43	20	1,280
American Samoa	33	289	110	100.0	—	—	—	—	110	2,075	27.5[3]	72.5[3]	—	—	—
Andorra	...	...	...	...	...	...	...	...	...	...	...	...	—	—	...
Angola	617	5,405	1,865	26.0	74.0	—	—	—	1,865	175	27.5[2]	72.5[2]	...	...	—
Antigua and Barbuda	26	228	97	100.0	—	—	—	—	97	1,492	42.4[4]	57.6[4]	...	...	...
Argentina	19,610	171,784	66,196	46.0	41.4	12.6	11	977	67,162	1,965	45.9	54.1	130	348	1,596
Armenia	2,768	24,248	5,658	37.9	62.1	—	...	16	5,674	1,599	...	...	...	...	36
Aruba	90	788	355	100.0	—	—	—	—	355	5,145	...	...	...	...	...
Australia	38,829	340,142	167,151	89.9	10.1	—	—	—	167,151	9,363	30.1[2]	69.9[2]	90,940	226,058	102,658
Austria	17,426	152,652	53,359	30.9	69.1	—	9,042	8,219	52,536	6,635	23.1[2]	83.4[2]	59	1,391	4,397
Azerbaijan	5,239	45,894	17,600	89.8	10.2	—	300	500	17,800	2,382	...	...	...	...	8
Bahamas, The	401	3,513	985	100.0	—	—	—	—	985	3,621	33.6[4]	66.4[4]	...	...	...
Bahrain	1,050	9,198	4,550	100.0	—	—	—	—	4,550	8,288	...	...	...	...	...
Bangladesh	2,970	26,017	10,010	94.0	6.0	—	—	—	10,010	85	43.8	56.2	1,054[1]	—	198
Barbados	140	1,226	571	100.0	—	—	—	—	571	2,188	33.7	66.3	...	...	—
Belarus	7,205	63,116	31,397	99.9	0.1	—	3,944	7,764	35,217	3,465	...	...	...	...	1,199
Belgium	14,899	130,515	72,236	42.1	1.7	56.2	5,070	9,053	76,219	7,561	26.9[8]	73.1[8]	410	753	13,050
Belize	23	201	110	100.0	—	—	—	—	110	524	...	...	...	...	...
Benin	15	131	6	100.0	—	—	—	242	248	47	...	...	...	...	...
Bermuda	140	1,226	520	100.0	—	—	—	—	520	8,254	39.6	60.4	...	...	...
Bhutan	361	3,162	1,682	0.4	99.6	—	1,455	3	230	143	19.2[3]	69.8[3]	...	2	20
Bolivia	786	6,885	2,876	51.6	48.4	—	3	19	2,892	400	76.1	23.9	...	...	...
Bosnia and Herzegovina	2,327	20,385	1,921	34.9	65.1	—	412	572	2,081	590	21.8	78.2	...	1,400[6]	1,400[6]
Botswana	10	10	522[10, 11]	10	10	10	10	82[10, 11]	10	10	...	...	3,500	10	10
Brazil	57,640	504,926	260,682	6.8	93.2	0.0	—	31,657	292,339	1,837	46.2	53.8	2,845	5,194	16,434
Brunei	492	4,310	1,315	100.0	—	—	—	—	1,315	4,696	55.3[4]	44.7[4]	—	—	—
Bulgaria	12,087	105,882	38,133	55.9	3.9	40.2	1,245	1,173	38,061	4,316	41.2[3]	58.8[3]	3,730	28,757	32,540
Burkina Faso	78	683	216	66.2	33.8	—	—	—	216	22	...	...	...	...	...
Burundi	43	377	149	1.4	98.6	—	—	43	192	31	...	...	...	...	...
Cambodia	35	307	187	61.5	38.5	—	—	—	187	19	...	...	...	...	...
Cameroon	627	5,493	2,740	3.0	97.0	—	—	—	2,740	213	...	...	...	1	1
Canada	113,828	997,133	554,186	21.3	59.2	19.5	50,919	7,005	510,272	17,510	28.8[4]	71.2[4]	8,623	72,824	52,229
Cape Verde	7	61	39	100.0	—	—	—	—	39	102	...	...	...	...	...
Central African Republic	43	377	101	20.8	79.2	—	—	—	101	31	...	...	4	...	...
Chad	29	254	85	100.0	—	—	—	—	85	14	...	...	...	...	...
Chile	5,504	48,215	25,250	32.9	67.1	—	—	—	25,250	1,798	32.7	67.3	1,181	1,222	3,185
China	190,100	1,665,276	928,083	80.4	18.1	1.5	3,893	1,847	926,037	780	7.7	92.3	114,500	1,239,902	1,231,928
Colombia	10,781	94,442	43,474	25.7	74.3	—	—	143	43,617	1,263	69.8	30.2	4,539	22,527	6,476
Comoros	5	44	17	88.2	11.8	—	—	—	17	27	...	...	...	...	...
Congo	118	1,034	435	0.7	99.3	—	—	112	547	217	...	...	...	...	...
Costa Rica	1,094	9,583	4,772	25.2	74.8	—	6	...	4,766	1,424	72.1	27.9	...	...	...
Côte d'Ivoire	1,173	10,275	1,917	42.5	57.5	—	—	—	1,917	139	29.6	70.4	...	...	...
Croatia	3,593	31,475	8,275	40.4	59.6	—	982	4,547	11,840	2,629	50.6	49.4	...	103	640
Cuba	3,988	34,935	10,982	99.0	1.0	—	—	—	10,982	1,002	56.0	44.0	...	—	153
Cyprus	666	5,834	2,681	100.0	—	—	—	—	2,681	3,653	77.3	22.7	...	—	27
Czech Republic	13,852	121,344	58,705	74.9	3.0	22.1	5,860	5,415	58,260	5,659	23.6[3, 13]	76.4[3, 13]	5,370[13]	76,944	67,244
Denmark	10,212	89,457	41,096	97.1	0.1	2.8[14]	6,623	1,779	36,252	7,008	32.5[8]	67.5[8]	63[5]	—	13,087
Djibouti	85	745	185	100.0	—	—	—	—	185	327	...	...	...	...	...
Dominica	8	70	34	50.0	50.0	—	—	—	34	479	53.5[4]	46.5[4]	...	...	...
Dominican Republic	1,447	12,676	6,182	69.7	30.3	—	—	—	6,182	805	...	...	...	...	104
Ecuador	2,278	19,955	8,163	21.9	78.1	—	—	—	8,163	728	68.2	31.8	24	...	...
Egypt	13,040	114,230	47,920	82.2	17.8	—	—	—	47,920	777	29.6	70.4	53	—	1,852
El Salvador	751	6,579	3,324	22.8	62.2	15.0[14]	14	105	3,415	605	68.8	31.2	...	...	...

(Much natural gas in Middle Eastern and North African oil fields is flared [burned] because it is often not economical to capture and market it.) Manufactured gas is generally a by-product of industrial operations such as gasworks, coke ovens, and blast furnaces. It is usually burned at the point of production and rarely enters the marketplace. Production of manufactured gas is, therefore, only reported as a percentage of domestic gas consumption.

Crude petroleum. Crude petroleum is the liquid product obtained from oil wells; the term also includes shale oil, tar sand extract, and field or lease condensate. Production and consumption data in the table refer, so far as possible, to the same year so that the relationship between national production and consumption patterns can be clearly seen; both are given in barrels.

Proven reserves are that oil remaining underground in known fields whose existence has been "proved" by the evaluation of nearby producing wells or by seismic tests in sedimentary strata known to contain crude petroleum, and that is judged recoverable within the limits of present technology and economic conditions (prices). The published proven reserve figures do not necessarily reflect the true reserves of a country, because government authorities or corporations often have political or economic motives for withholding or altering such data.

The estimated exhaustion rate of petroleum reserves is an extrapolated ratio of published proven reserves to the current rate of withdrawal/production. Present world published proven reserves will last about 40 to 45 years at the present rate of withdrawal, but there are large country-to-country variations above or below the average.

Data on petroleum and refined product pipelines are provided because of the great importance to both domestic and international energy markets of this means of bringing these energy sources from their production or transportation points to refineries, intermediate consumption and distribution points, and final consumers. Their traffic may represent a very significant fraction of the total movement of goods within a country. Available data for petroleum pipelines are often incomplete and their basis varies internationally, some countries reporting only international shipments, others reporting domestic shipments of 50 kilometres or more, and so on.

For data in the hydrocarbons portions of the table (coal, natural gas, and petroleum), extensive use has been made of a variety of international sources, such as those of the United Nations, the International Energy Agency (of the Organization for Economic Cooperation and Development), the World Energy Council (in its *World Energy Resources* [triennial]); the U.S. Department of Energy (especially its *International Energy Annual*); and of various industry surveys, such as those published by the *International Petroleum Encyclopedia,* the *Oil and Gas Journal,* and *World Oil.*

natural gas						crude petroleum							country
published proven reserves, 1996 ('000,000,-000 cu m)	production		consumption			reserves, 1996		produc-tion, 1995 ('000,000 barrels)	consump-tion, 1994 ('000,000 barrels)	refining capacity, 1996 ('000 barrels per day)	pipelines (latest)		
	natural gas, 1995 ('000,000 cu m)	manufac-tured gas, 1994 (% of total gas con-sumption)	amount, 1994 ('000,000 cu m)	resi-dential, 1990 (%)	non-resi-dential, 1990 (%)	published proven ('000,000 barrels)	years to exhaust proven reserves				length (km)	traffic ('000,000 metric ton-km)	
99	294	...	175	...	...	...	...	—	4	3	...	...	Afghanistan
2	136	...	77	...	...	165	41	4	3	40	200	...	Albania
3,625	51,817	27.6	19,208	26.8[2]	73.2[2]	9,200	33	277	160	465	6,910	...	Algeria
...	...	...	...	...	...	...	...	—	—	—	—	—	American Samoa
...	...	...	...	...	...	...	...	—	—	—	—	—	Andorra
51	561	10.9	167	...	...	5,412	24	223	12	32	179	...	Angola
...	...	...	...	...	...	...	...	—	—	—	—	—	Antigua and Barbuda
526	17,336	9.9	31,293	49.2	50.8	2,226	8	263	174	661	6,990	...	Argentina
...	170[5]	...	884	...	...	...	...	—	1	—	...	...	Armenia
...	...	...	...	...	...	...	...	—	2	...	...	—	Aruba
569	29,554	30.3	17,438	...	...	1,560	8	185	202	733	3,000	...	Australia
22	1,475	13.3	7,459	25.7[2]	74.3[2]	101	14	7	63	210	725	6,701	Austria
100	3,896	0.9	7,706	...	...	3,300[6]	38[6]	67	77	442	1,760	1,705	Azerbaijan
...	...	—	...	...	...	...	...	—	—	—	—	—	Bahamas, The
150	5,250	4.9	6,383	...	...	210	14	15	90	250	72	...	Bahrain
286	7,365	0.2	6,635	34.2	65.8	5,439	13,598	0.4	9	31	—	—	Bangladesh
0.1	17	6.9	22	62.6	37.4	3	6	0.5	2	4	—	—	Barbados
...	262[7]	1.5	13,061	...	...	...	...	14	94	725	2,570	...	Belarus
...	1.4[7]	20.4	14,141	43.4[8]	56.6[8]	...	...	—	207[9]	610	1,328	1,168	Belgium
...	...	...	...	...	...	...	...	—	—	—	—	—	Belize
1.2	...	...	...	...	...	29	32	0.9	0.04	—	—	—	Benin
...	...	...	...	...	...	...	...	—	—	—	—	—	Bermuda
...	...	...	...	...	...	...	...	—	—	—	—	—	Bhutan
126	3,279	18.7	1,159	—	100.0	139	14	10	9	45	2,380	...	Bolivia
...	—	7.4[6]	378	...	...	...	...	—	15[6]	...	174	—	Bosnia and Herzegovina
...	...	10	...	...	...	—	...	—	10	—	—	—	Botswana
146	2,880	62.5	4,103	—	100.0	4,200	17	253	467	1,256	5,804	...	Brazil
396	9,922	0.9	1,938	...	...	1,350	21	64	2	9	553	...	Brunei
7	11	16.2	4,554	...	...	15	50	0.3	51	300	718	259	Bulgaria
...	...	...	...	...	...	...	...	—	—	—	—	—	Burkina Faso
...	...	...	...	...	...	...	...	—	—	—	—	—	Burundi
...	...	...	...	...	...	...	...	—	—	—	—	—	Cambodia
110	—	100.0	...	...	...	400	11	37	8	42	—	—	Cameroon
1,898	175,897	22.8	78,223	20.6[2]	79.4[2]	4,898	9	565	508	1,848	23,564	99,908	Canada
...	...	...	...	...	...	...	...	—	—	—	—	—	Cape Verde
...	...	...	...	...	...	...	...	—	—	—	—	—	Central African Republic
...	...	...	...	...	...	...	...	—	—	—	—	—	Chad
110	1,164	34.1	1,865	23.4	76.6	300	75	4	54	178	1,540	...	Chile
1,671	17,300	51.0	17,540	12.2	87.8	24,000	22	1,090	1,024	2,867	16,800	61,200	China
283	4,437	25.0	5,111	12.8	87.2	3,500	16	213	94	249	4,935	...	Colombia
...	...	...	...	...	...	...	...	—	—	—	—	—	Comoros
122	2[12]	47.6	5	...	...	1,506	22	69	8	21	25	—	Congo
...	—	6.3	—	...	...	...	...	—	5	15	176	—	Costa Rica
23	—	56.7	—	—	—	100	25	4	25	64	...	—	Côte d'Ivoire
35	1,869	44.5	938	...	...	150	11	14	37	294	690	89	Croatia
3	31[5]	85.2	39	3.4	96.6	100	9	11	38	301	—	—	Cuba
—	—	74.8	—	...	...	...	...	—	6	22	—	—	Cyprus
4	290	25.4	7,339	...	...	6	5	1.1	45	187	...	...	Czech Republic
114	4,936	15.5	2,992	...	...	1,032	15	68	66	189	688	2,212	Denmark
...	...	...	...	...	...	...	...	—	—	—	—	—	Djibouti
...	...	...	...	...	...	—	...	—	—	—	—	—	Dominica
...	...	11.6	...	...	...	—	...	—	15	50	104	—	Dominican Republic
108	102	43.8	204	...	...	2,115	15	141	35	148	2,158	...	Ecuador
626	12,233	12.1	10,544	5.3	94.7	3,879	12	332	192	532	1,767	...	Egypt
—	—	49.4	—	—	—	...	...	—	7	19	—	—	El Salvador

Energy (continued)

country	electricity installed capacity, 1994 ('000 kW)	production, 1994 capacity ('000,000 kW-hr)	production, 1994 amount ('000,000 kW-hr)	power source, 1994 fossil fuel (%)	power source, 1994 hydro-power (%)	power source, 1994 nuclear fuel (%)	trade, 1994 exports ('000,000 kW-hr)	trade, 1994 imports ('000,000 kW-hr)	consumption amount, 1994 ('000,000 kW-hr)	consumption per capita, 1994 (kW-hr)	consumption residential, 1990 (%)	consumption non-residential, 1990 (%)	coal reserves, latest ('000,000 metric tons)	coal production, 1994 ('000 metric tons)	coal consumption, 1994 ('000 metric tons)
Equatorial Guinea	5	44	20	90.0	10.0	—	—	—	20	51	...	...	...	...	...
Eritrea	...														
Estonia	3,287	28,794	9,151	99.9	0.1	—	2,146	3,874	10,879	7,060	...	...	...	14,530	16,395
Ethiopia	464	4,065	1,284	6.3	88.4	5.3[14]	—	—	1,284	24	...	...	11	—	—
Faroe Islands	91	797	199	57.8	42.2	—	—	—	199	4,234	...	...	...	...	...
Fiji	200	1,752	520	21.2	78.8	—	—	—	520	674	10.5	89.5	...	—	20
Finland	14,143	123,893	65,546	52.4	18.0	29.6	630	7,171	72,087	14,182	18.6[2]	81.3[2]	...	—	7,501
France	107,229[16]	939,326[16]	475,622[16]	7.3[16]	17.0[16]	75.7[16]	66,886[16]	3,718[16]	412,454[16]	7,139[16]	30.3[8]	69.7[8]	139	9,039[16]	21,809[16]
French Guiana	165	1,445	446	100.0	—	—	—	—	446	3,163	...	58.7[2,17]	...	...	...
French Polynesia	79	692	335	71.0	29.0	—	—	—	335	1,558	...	...	...	...	...
Gabon	310	2,716	933	23.0	77.0	—	—	—	933	727	55.1	44.9	...	...	...
Gambia, The	29	254	75	100.0	—	—	—	—	75	69	...	...	...	...	...
Gaza Strip	...	...	...	...	...	...			...	...					
Georgia	4,558	39,928	6,803	30.7	69.3	...	200	1,000	7,603	1,395	...	...	...	34	274
Germany	114,355	1,001,750	528,221	66.9	4.3	28.8	33,571	35,908	530,558	6,528	26.3[8,18]	73.7[8,18]	67,300	264,700	275,563
Ghana	1,187	10,398	6,167	0.7	99.3	—	310	...	5,857	346	...	...	...	...	3
Gibraltar	30	263	88	100.0	—	—	—	—	88	3,143	...	...	...	...	...
Greece	8,921	78,148	40,623	92.9	7.0	0.1	434	816	41,005	3,937	30.6[8]	69.4[8]	3,000	56,741	59,569
Greenland	106	929	255	100.0	—	—	—	—	255	4,397	35.3[19]	64.7[19]	183	...	...
Grenada	9	79	70	100.0	—	—	—	—	70	761	46.8[4]	53.2[4]	...	...	...
Guadeloupe	388	3,399	1,005	100.0	—	—	—	—	1,005	2,387	...	32.9[17,19]	...	...	...
Guam	302	2,646	800	100.0	—	—	—	—	800	5,442	39.7	60.3	...	...	...
Guatemala	766	6,710	3,161	35.4	64.6	—	—	—	3,161	306	27.0[2]	73.0[2]	...	...	...
Guernsey	...	...	227[6]	100.0[6]	...	...	...	...	227[6]	4,997[6]	...	...	...	...	...
Guinea	176	1,542	530	66.0	34.0	—	—	—	530	82	...	...	...	...	...
Guinea-Bissau	11	96	45	100.0	—	—	—	—	45	43	...	...	...	...	...
Guyana	114	999	242	97.9	2.1	—	—	12	254	308	...	...	...	...	...
Haiti	153	1,340	362	54.4	45.6	—	—	—	362	51	...	...	13[1]	...	...
Honduras	305	2,672	2,655	7.8	92.2	—	—	17	2,672	486	51.7	48.3	21[1]	...	...
Hong Kong	10,323	90,429	26,741	100.0	—	—	1,758	8,253	33,236	5,490	70.8	29.2	...	—	8,450
Hungary	6,979	61,136	33,486	57.6	0.4	42.0	921	2,955	35,520	3,496	30.7[3]	69.3[3]	4,461	14,111	15,369
Iceland	1,083	9,487	4,780	0.1	94.5	5.4[14]	—	—	4,780	17,970	20.9[2]	79.1[2]	...	—	71
India	91,555	802,022	384,422	80.0	18.5	1.5	120	1,600	385,902	420	45.8	54.2	69,947	273,859	284,497
Indonesia	16,265	142,481	61,370	78.2	20.0	1.8[14]	—	—	61,370	315	55.0	45.0	32,063	28,549	3,461
Iran	25,117	220,025	79,128	90.6	9.4	—	—	—	79,128	1,122	21.1[11]	78.9[11]	193	980	1,280
Iraq	7,260	63,598	27,060	97.9	2.1	—	—	—	27,060	1,358	...	...	...	—	—
Ireland	3,910	34,252	17,105	92.9	7.0	0.1[14]	—	—	17,105	4,833	41.4[8]	58.6[8]	14	1	2,738
Isle of Man	...	...	188[4]	100.0	—	—	—	—	172[3]	2,530[3]	48.1[8]	51.9[8]	...	—	...
Israel	4,280	37,493	28,315	99.9	0.1	—	330	—	27,985	5,127	68.4	31.6	...	—	6,026
Italy	64,067[20]	561,227[20]	231,783[20]	77.9[20]	20.6[20]	1.5[4,20]	1,096[20]	38,695[20]	269,382[20]	4,711[20]	25.0[8]	75.0[8]	34	267[20]	16,672[20]
Jamaica	1,182	10,354	3,927	98.0	2.0	—	—	—	3,927	1,617	25.6	74.4	...	—	64
Japan	220,743	1,933,709	964,328	64.0	7.8	28.2	—	—	964,328	7,281	20.8[2]	79.2[2]	821	6,933	123,099
Jersey	...	...	440[6]	...	...	...	—	—	440[6]	6,579[6]	...	...	...	...	...
Jordan	1,066	9,338	5,075	99.7	0.3	—	—	...	5,075	976	60.0	40.0	...	...	...
Kazakstan	18,900	165,564	66,777	85.7	13.7	0.6	54,000	65,500	78,277	4,597	...	...	25,000	109,257	81,257
Kenya	808	7,078	3,538	5.9	86.7	7.4[14]	—	264	3,802	139	35.1	64.9	...	—	109
Kiribati	2	18	7	100.0	—	—	—	—	7	91	...	...	...	...	...
Korea, North	9,500	83,220	37,000	36.5	63.5	—	—	—	37,000	1,576	...	...	600	98,000	99,925
Korea, South	31,665	277,385	185,993	66.3	2.2	31.5	—	—	185,993	4,174	34.0	66.0	183	7,438	43,892
Kuwait	6,988	61,215	23,152	100.0	—	—	—	—	23,152	14,178	92.1	7.9	...	...	...
Kyrgyzstan	3,632	31,816	12,932	9.4	90.6	—	8,227	5,722	10,427	2,234	...	...	...	848	1,145
Laos	256	2,243	905	4.8	95.2	—	637	26	294	62	...	...	...	1	1
Latvia	2,035	17,827	4,440	25.6	74.4	—	830	2,648	6,258	2,423	...	...	...	—	425
Lebanon	1,220	10,687	5,150	81.4	18.6	—	—	—	5,150	1,767	...	...	...	—	112
Lesotho	10	10	10	10	10	10	10	10	10	10	...	...	...	10	10
Liberia	332	2,908	485	63.3	36.7	—	—	—	485	165	...	...	...	...	...
Libya	4,600	40,296	17,800	100.0	—	—	—	—	17,800	3,407	...	...	...	...	5
Liechtenstein	22	22	22	22	22	22	22	22	22	22	...	...	—	—	22
Lithuania	5,463	47,856	10,055	16.2	7.2	76.6	6,015	7,159	11,199	3,022	...	...	...	—	482
Luxembourg	1,238	10,845	1,190	42.2	57.8	—	564	5,019	5,645	14,077	15.3[8]	84.7[8]	...	—	323
Macau	260	2,278	1,277	100.0	—	—	—	140	1,417	3,560	75.0[4]	25.0[4]	...	...	—
Macedonia	1,366	11,966	5,511	87.4	12.6	—	54	221	5,678	2,651	27.4	72.6	...	6,860	7,235
Madagascar	220	1,927	605	42.3	57.7	—	—	—	605	42	...	...	1,075[1]	—	14
Malawi	185	1,621	802	2.0	98.0	—	—	—	802	74	52.8	47.2	12	—	15
Malaysia	7,830	68,591	39,975	86.2	13.8	—	50	102	40,027	2,032	51.6	48.4	4	174	1,876
Maldives	14	123	46	100.0	—	—	—	—	46	187	50.9[3]	49.1[3]	...	...	...
Mali	87	762	289	22.5	77.5	—	—	—	289	28	...	...	...	...	...
Malta	250	2,190	1,500	100.0	—	—	—	—	1,500	4,121	25.1[11]	74.9[11]	...	...	300
Marshall Islands	99[8]	867[8]	...	...	...	...	...	...	...	...	...	...	...	...	...
Martinique	115	1,007	903	100.0	—	—	—	—	903	2,408	...	40.9[17,19]	...	...	...
Mauritania	105	920	148	82.4	17.6	—	—	—	148	67	...	...	...	...	6
Mauritius	361	3,162	1,000	89.4	10.6	—	—	—	1,000	906	...	...	...	...	65
Mayotte	11	96	27	100.0	—	—	—	—	27	241	...	...	...	...	...
Mexico	35,466	310,682	144,276	74.5	18.4	7.1[14]	1,845	1,016	143,447	1,562	17.4[11]	82.6[11]	1,211	8,898	9,188
Micronesia	...														
Moldova	2,635	23,083	8,228	96.6	3.4	—	5,003	5,354	8,579	1,941	...	...	...	—	2,141
Monaco	16	16	16	16	16	16	16	16	16	16	...	...	...	16	16
Mongolia	901	7,893	3,265	100.0	—	—	—	207	3,472	1,469	29.8[3]	70.2[3]	24,000[1]	7,585	7,075
Morocco	3,788	33,183	10,773	92.2	7.8	—	—	920	11,693	441	66.6	33.4	45	650	2,200
Mozambique	2,358	20,656	490	89.8	10.2	—	—	325	815	52	...	...	240	40	60
Myanmar (Burma)	1,212	10,617	3,500	54.8	45.2	—	—	—	3,500	77	...	59.1[2,17]	3	76	78
Namibia	10	10	10	10	10	10	10	10	10	10	...	...	...	10	10
Nauru	10	88	30	100.0	—	—	—	—	30	2,727	...	...	...	...	...
Nepal	292	2,558	908	3.6	96.4	—	63	95	940	44	67.3	32.7	...	...	115
Netherlands, The	18,348	160,728	79,677	94.6	0.1	5.3	288	10,850	90,239	5,861	25.0[4]	75.0[4]	497	—	14,240

natural gas						crude petroleum							country
published proven reserves, 1996 ('000,000,000 cu m)	production natural gas, 1995 ('000,000 cu m)	production manufactured gas, 1994 (% of total gas consumption)	consumption amount, 1994 ('000,000 cu m)	consumption residential, 1990 (%)	consumption non-residential, 1990 (%)	reserves, 1996 published proven ('000,000 barrels)	reserves, 1996 years to exhaust proven reserves	production, 1995 ('000,000 barrels)	consumption, 1994 ('000,000 barrels)	refining capacity, 1996 ('000 barrels per day)	pipelines (latest) length (km)	pipelines (latest) traffic ('000,000 metric ton-km)	
37	...	...	...	...	...	12	2	7	...	—	—	—	Equatorial Guinea
...	...	...	...	...	...	...	...	...	...	18	...	...	Eritrea
...	...	4.1[15]	548	...	...	...	...	...	...	...	...	...	Estonia
25	—	100.0	—	...	...	0.4	...	—	6	—	—	—	Ethiopia
...	...	...	...	...	...	—	—	—	—	—	—	—	Faroe Islands
...	...	...	—	...	...	...	...	...	...	...	...	—	Fiji
—	—	30.6	3,433	0.6[8]	99.4[8]	...	...	—	67	200	—	—	Finland
30	3,395	20.6[16]	33,450[16]	32.4[8]	67.6[8]	138	7	21	563[16]	1,782	7,546	22,501	France
...	...	...	...	...	...	...	...	...	...	...	...	...	French Guiana
...	...	...	...	...	...	...	...	...	...	...	...	...	French Polynesia
14	102	9.7	88	19.7	80.3	1,340	10	133	12	17	284	...	Gabon
...	...	...	...	...	...	...	...	—	—	—	—	—	Gambia, The
...	...	...	...	...	...	...	...	...	...	...	...	...	Gaza Strip
...	45[12]	...	2,797	...	...	...	...	1.5	2	106	670	...	Georgia
320	18,998	18.3	92,770	36.6[8,18]	63.4[8,18]	339	16	21	784	2,126	7,590	13,872	Germany
23	—	94.8	—	...	...	16	8	2	7	25	—	...	Ghana
...	...	...	...	...	...	...	...	—	—	—	—	—	Gibraltar
8	119	106.6	55	...	...	14	5	3	101	401	573	...	Greece
...	...	...	...	...	...	...	...	—	—	—	—	—	Greenland
...	...	...	...	...	...	...	...	—	—	—	—	—	Grenada
...	...	...	—	...	...	...	...	—	—	—	—	—	Guadeloupe
...	...	100.0[5]	—	...	...	...	...	—	—	—	...	...	Guam
0.3	8	9.0	9	...	...	488	122	4	7	20	275	...	Guatemala
...	...	...	...	...	...	...	...	—	—	—	—	—	Guernsey
24[6]	...	...	...	...	...	...	...	—	—	—	—	—	Guinea
...	...	...	...	...	...	...	...	—	—	—	—	—	Guinea-Bissau
...	...	...	...	...	...	...	...	—	—	—	—	—	Guyana
...	...	...	...	...	...	...	...	—	—	—	—	—	Haiti
—	—	30.7[6]	—	—	—	...	...	—	3[6]	14	—	—	Honduras
...	...	81.5	...	...	...	...	...	—	—	—	—	—	Hong Kong
95	5,479	8.4	9,530	14.0[8]	86.0[8]	129	5	26	47	232	1,204	2,607	Hungary
...	...	...	...	...	...	...	...	—	—	—	—	—	Iceland
707	19,595	15.3	17,638	53.7	46.3	5,814	23	251	441	1,086	5,200	...	India
1,951	61,864	39.0	23,191	—	100.0	5,167	9	547	309	805	2,961	...	Indonesia
21,000	31,857	9.9	40,056	—	100.0[4]	88,200	65	1,353	343	1,168	9,800	...	Iran
3,101	3,426	29.4	3,170	...	...	100,000	391	256	207	348	5,075	...	Iraq
12	2,500	3.0	2,566	13.9[8]	86.1[8]	...	...	—	17	55	—	—	Ireland
...	...	—	...	...	...	...	...	—	...	—	—	—	Isle of Man
0.4	23	108.1	22	—	100.0	4	40	0.1	89	220	998	...	Israel
374	20,499	14.7[20]	49,513[20]	45.6[8]	54.4[8]	621	17	36	545[20]	2,284	3,851	11,348	Italy
—	—	36.5	—	...	...	...	...	—	6	36	10	...	Jamaica
27	2,192	40.8	58,029	61.3[8]	38.7[8]	49	8	6	1,637	4,867	406	...	Japan
...	...	...	—	—	...	...	...	—	—	—	—	—	Jersey
6	294	75.4	—	—	—	0.3	3	0.1	22	100	209	...	Jordan
1,800	5,500	...	9,588	...	...	...	...	151	87	394	4,350	22,300	Kazakhstan
—	—	103.4	—	—	—	...	...	—	16	90	483	...	Kenya
...	...	...	...	...	...	...	...	—	—	—	—	—	Kiribati
...	...	...	...	...	...	...	...	—	16	71	37	...	Korea, North
...	...	31.2	8,013	...	...	...	...	—	562	1,244	455	...	Korea, South
1,498	5,975	59.1	5,970	25.0	75.0	96,500	129	748	44	801	917	...	Kuwait
...	34[7]	...	1,008	...	...	...	...	0.7	0.2	...	...	...	Kyrgyzstan
...	...	...	...	...	...	...	...	—	—	...	136	...	Laos
...	...	...	886	...	...	...	...	—	—	...	1,530	...	Latvia
—	—	2.7[15]	...	...	...	...	...	—	3[15]	38	72	...	Lebanon
...	...	10	...	...	...	...	...	—	10	—	—	...	Lesotho
—	—	50.5[21]	—	...	...	...	...	—	—	15	—	—	Liberia
1,297	6,298	13.1	4,910	...	...	29,500	57	515	113	348	4,826	...	Libya
—	—	22	22	...	...	...	...	—	22	—	—	...	Liechtenstein
...	...	9.0	1,871	...	...	...	...	0.8	27	263	105	...	Lithuania
...	...	33.1	570	48.0[8]	52.0[8]	...	...	—	10	—	48	...	Luxembourg
...	...	...	...	...	...	...	...	—	1	51	—	—	Macau
...	—	13.3	269[15]	...	...	...	...	—	1	51	—	—	Macedonia
2	—	33.6	—	...	...	...	...	—	1.5	15	—	—	Madagascar
...	...	...	...	...	...	...	...	—	—	—	—	...	Malawi
1,926	26,193	7.4	13,166	6.6	93.4	4,300	17	258	100	321	1,307	...	Malaysia
...	...	...	...	...	...	...	...	—	—	—	—	...	Maldives
...	...	...	...	...	...	...	...	—	—	—	—	—	Mali
—	...	...	...	...	...	...	...	—	—	—	—	—	Malta
...	...	...	...	...	...	...	...	—	—	...	—	...	Marshall Islands
—	...	153.9	...	...	...	...	...	—	6	16	—	—	Martinique
...	...	88.4	...	...	...	...	...	—	7	—	—	—	Mauritania
...	...	...	...	...	...	...	...	—	—	—	—	—	Mauritius
...	...	...	...	...	...	...	...	—	—	—	—	—	Mayotte
1,937	38,454	26.6	27,206	3.9[11]	96.1[11]	49,775	50	994	500	1,520	38,350	...	Mexico
...	...	...	...	...	...	...	...	—	—	...	...	...	Micronesia
...	—	...	2,612	...	...	...	...	—	52[5]	...	...	...	Moldova
...	...	16	16	...	...	...	...	—	16	—	—	—	Monaco
...	...	...	...	...	...	...	...	—	—	—	—	—	Mongolia
1.1	17	28.5	25	—	100.0	1.2	12	0.1	50	155	362	...	Morocco
49	—	—	—	...	...	...	...	—	...	...	595	...	Mozambique
283	1,430	0.9	1,359	—	100.0[4]	50	8	6	7	32	1,343	...	Myanmar (Burma)
57	...	10	...	...	...	...	...	—	10	—	—	...	Namibia
...	...	...	...	...	...	...	...	—	—	—	—	—	Nauru
...	...	...	...	...	...	...	...	—	—	—	—	...	Nepal
1,845	78,778	18.5	48,841	46.8[4]	53.4[4]	107	4	27	377	1,187	1,383	5,503	Netherlands, The

Energy (continued)

country	electricity												coal		
	installed capacity, 1994 ('000 kW)	production, 1994		power source, 1994			trade, 1994		consumption				reserves, latest ('000,000 metric tons)	production, 1994 ('000 metric tons)	consumption, 1994 ('000 metric tons)
		capacity ('000,000 kW-hr)	amount ('000,000 kW-hr)	fossil fuel (%)	hydro-power (%)	nuclear fuel (%)	exports ('000,000 kW-hr)	imports ('000,000 kW-hr)	amount, 1994 ('000,000 kW-hr)	per capita, 1994 (kW-hr)	resi-dential, 1990 (%)	non-resi-dential, 1990 (%)			
Netherlands Antilles	200	1,752	883	100.0	—	—	—	—	883	4,482	...	...	...	...	165
New Caledonia	253	2,216	1,170	70.5	29.5	—	—	—	1,170	6,573	...	...	2	...	...
New Zealand	7,520	65,875	32,416	24.7	71.8	3.5[14]	—	—	32,416	9,180	37.5[4]	62.5[4]	117	3,241	2,441
Nicaragua	457	4,003	1,740	51.4	18.7	29.9[14]	13	—	1,727	404	67.1	32.9	...	...	...
Niger	63	552	178	100.0	—	—	—	197	375	42	50.0	50.0	70	174	174
Nigeria	5,881	51,518	14,790	59.4	40.6	—	...	—	14,790	136	80.4	19.6	190	50	50
Northern Mariana Islands	114[6]	999[6]	...	...	...	...	...	...	...	...	...	...	...	...	...
Norway	27,498	240,882	113,389	0.5	99.5	—	4,968	4,835	113,256	26,205	27.0[2]	73.0[2]	13	301	914
Oman	1,744	15,277	7,856	100.0	—	—	—	—	7,856	3,782	...	...	...	...	...
Pakistan	13,169	115,360	57,147	65.1	34.0	0.9	—	—	57,147	418	64.5	35.5	524	3,534	4,628
Palau	62	543	203	85.2	14.8	—	—	—	203	857	...	...	—	—	—
Panama	957	8,383	3,500	31.7	68.3	—	—	33	3,533	1,367	26.8[11]	73.2[11]	...	—	52
Papua New Guinea	490	4,292	1,790	74.3	25.7	—	—	—	1,790	426	27.5	72.5	...	...	1
Paraguay	6,533	57,229	35,862	0.1	99.9	—	32,773	1	3,090	640	...	...	—	—	—
Peru	4,187	36,678	15,163	23.2	76.8	—	—	—	15,163	650	35.8	64.2	1,060	109	406
Philippines	7,640	66,926	26,425	53.9	24.1	22.0[14]	—	—	26,425	399	53.0	47.0	262	1,733	2,503
Poland	29,636	259,611	135,347	97.2	2.8	—	7,242	4,563	132,668	3,460	33.5[3]	66.5[3]	42,100	200,703	170,961
Portugal	8,831	77,360	31,380	65.7	34.1	0.2	1,369	2,257	32,268	3,283	36.3[2]	63.6[2]	36	147	5,225
Puerto Rico	4,465	39,113	17,880	98.2	1.8	—	—	—	17,880	4,904	31.0[11]	69.0[11]	...	—	172
Qatar	1,303	11,414	5,850	100.0	—	—	—	—	5,850	10,833	83.0	17.0	...	...	...
Réunion	299	2,619	1,137	55.9	44.1	—	—	—	1,137	1,766	...	...	—	—	—
Romania	22,060	193,246	55,136	76.3	23.7	—	1,065	1,790	55,861	2,437	23.6[3]	76.4[3]	3,118	40,547	44,893
Russia	214,687	1,880,658	875,914	68.6	20.2	11.2	44,147	23,651	855,418	5,805	21.6[3, 23]	78.4[3, 23]	241,000[23]	275,346	279,057
Rwanda	34	298	166	2.4	97.6	—	3	14	177	23	...	...	...	...	...
St. Kitts and Nevis	16	140	86	100.0	—	—	—	—	86	2,098	...	...	...	...	...
St. Lucia	22	193	112	100.0	—	—	—	—	112	794	26.6[3]	73.4[3]	...	...	...
St. Vincent and the Grenadines	14	123	64	67.2	32.8	—	—	—	64	577	45.3[4]	54.7[4]	...	...	...
San Marino	20	20	20	20	20	20	20	20	20	20	...	...	...	20	20
São Tomé and Príncipe	6	53	16	50.0	50.0	—	—	—	16	123	...	...	...	...	...
Saudi Arabia	20,900	183,084	66,760	100.0	—	—	—	—	66,760	3,826	69.3[19]	30.7[19]	...	...	...
Senegal	231	2,024	769	100.0	—	—	—	—	769	95	...	...	...	...	...
Seychelles	28	245	126	100.0	—	—	—	—	126	1,726	...	...	...	...	...
Sierra Leone	126	1,104	237	100.0	—	—	—	—	237	54	...	...	...	...	...
Singapore	4,513	39,534	20,676	100.0	—	—	91	—	20,585	7,297	48.0	52.0	...	—	1
Slovakia	7,115	62,327	24,740	32.3	18.6	49.1	2,099	1,260	23,901	4,482	...	...	...	2,363	11,161
Slovenia	2,524	22,110	12,630	36.6	26.9	36.5	2,382	448	10,696	5,508	18.0	82.0	...	4,854	5,018
Solomon Islands	12	105	30	100.0	—	—	—	—	30	82	69.4	30.6	...	...	...
Somalia	70	613	259	100.0	—	—	—	—	259	29	...	...	...	...	...
South Africa	26,739[10]	234,234[10]	183,790[10]	94.3[10]	0.5[10]	5.2[10]	2,600[10]	100	181,290[10]	3,913[10]	...	...	55,333	183,581[10]	140,581[10]
Spain	44,444	389,329	161,502	47.7	18.1	34.2	3,251	5,106	163,357	4,129	16.7[2]	83.2[2]	1,450	29,556	42,808
Sri Lanka	1,557	13,639	4,386	6.8	93.2	—	—	—	4,386	242	65.1	34.9	...	—	1[6]
Sudan, The	500	4,380	1,333	29.4	70.6	—	—	—	1,333	49	...	...	...	—	—
Suriname	425	3,723	1,683	15.8	84.2	—	—	—	1,683	4,026	...	...	...	—	—
Swaziland	10	10	10	10	10	10	10	10	10	10	...	...	999	10	10
Sweden	35,889	314,388	142,889	7.2	41.5	51.3	6,419	6,680	143,150	16,382	26.4[2]	73.6[2]	1	...	3,305
Switzerland	16,405[22]	143,708[22]	65,636[22]	2.0[22]	60.9[22]	37.1[22]	28,093[22]	16,250[22]	53,793[22]	7,512[22]	26.6[8]	73.4[8]	...	—	229[22]
Syria	4,157	36,415	14,800	54.0	46.0	—	—	—	14,800	923	21.2[8]	78.8[8]	...	—	—
Taiwan	20,983	183,811	110,276	61.6	8.0	30.4	—	—	98,561	4,665	31.9	68.1	99	285	...
Tajikistan	4,443	38,921	17,000	3.5	96.5	...	5,800	4,900	16,100	2,714	...	...	...	140	140
Tanzania	439	3,846	912	31.1	68.9	—	—	—	912	32	...	...	200	4	4
Thailand	15,838	138,741	74,452	93.9	6.1	—	58	884	75,278	1,294	51.0	49.0	999	17,095	17,198
Togo	34	298	93	94.6	5.4	—	—	315	408	102	...	...	...	—	—
Tonga	7	61	29	100.0	—	—	—	—	29	296	...	...	...	...	...
Trinidad and Tobago	1,150	10,074	3,978	100.0	—	—	—	—	3,978	3,079	41.0	59.0	—	—	—
Tunisia	1,414	12,387	6,473	99.0	1.0	—	122	135	6,486	743	42.8	57.2	—	9	31
Turkey	20,858	182,716	78,322	60.8	39.1	0.1[14]	570	31	77,783	1,280	14.2[11]	85.8[11]	7,148	54,342	60,359
Turkmenistan	3,950	34,602	10,496	100.0	0.0	—	3,690	1,040	7,846	1,957	...	...	...	...	...
Tuvalu	...	...	...	...	...	...	...	...	...	...	...	...	...	...	...
Uganda	162	1,419	795	0.9	99.1	—	114	—	681	33	...	...	...	...	...
Ukraine	54,243	475,169	209,100	61.2	0.0	38.8	13,400	12,400	208,100	4,044	...	...	...	94,400	96,867
United Arab Emirates	5,290	46,340	18,870	100.0	—	—	—	—	18,870	10,140	...	...	...	—	—
United Kingdom	68,937	603,888	325,383	70.8	2.0	27.2	—	16,887	342,270	5,870	35.4[8]	64.6[8]	2,500	47,717	80,582
United States	769,989	6,745,104	3,268,250	71.1	8.6	20.3	7,592	52,230	3,312,888	12,711	34.9[8]	65.1[8]	240,558	937,580	843,873
Uruguay	2,055	18,002	7,617	2.0	98.0	—	1,675	15	5,957	1,881	60.6	39.4	...	—	—
Uzbekistan	11,422	100,057	47,800	85.0	15.0	...	15,200	14,800	47,400	2,121	...	...	...	3,800	4,200
Vanuatu	11	96	29	100.0	—	—	—	—	29	176	...	...	...	...	...
Venezuela	18,975	166,221	73,116	29.7	70.3	—	320	—	72,796	3,405	42.0	58.0	417	4,741	354
Vietnam	5,320	46,603	12,200	15.8	79.0	5.2[14]	—	—	12,200	165	36.4[3]	63.6[3]	150	5,600	4,000
Virgin Islands (U.S.)	316	2,768	1,057	100.0	—	—	—	—	1,057	10,163	40.2[4]	59.8[4]	...	—	245
West Bank	...	...	...	...	...	...	...	...	...	...	...	...	...	...	...
Western Sahara	56	491	87	100.0	—	—	—	—	87	320	...	...	...	...	...
Western Samoa	19	166	64	60.9	39.1	—	—	—	64	379	...	...	...	...	...
Yemen	810	7,096	1,958	100.0	—	—	—	—	1,958	141	...	...	1[5]	...	...
Yugoslavia	11,779	103,184	35,328	68.5	31.5	—	—	—	35,328	3,282	26.0	74.0	16,570[24]	38,351	38,401
Zaire	2,831	24,800	5,545	0.4	99.6	—	1,077	55	4,523	106	...	89.1[2, 17]	600	93	136
Zambia	2,436	21,339	7,785	0.5	99.5	—	1,500	20	6,305	686	31.8	68.2	55	380	375
Zimbabwe	2,148	18,816	7,334	67.7	32.3	—	...	1,716	9,050	823	44.2	55.8	734	5,469	5,614

natural gas — published proven reserves, 1996 ('000,000,000 cu m)	production natural gas, 1995 ('000,000 cu m)	production manufactured gas, 1994 (% of total gas consumption)	consumption amount, 1994 ('000,000 cu m)	consumption residential, 1990 (%)	consumption non-residential, 1990 (%)	crude petroleum reserves, 1996 published proven ('000,000 barrels)	years to exhaust proven reserves	production, 1995 ('000,000 barrels)	consumption, 1994 ('000,000 barrels)	refining capacity, 1996 ('000 barrels per day)	pipelines length (km)	pipelines traffic ('000,000 metric ton-km)	country
—	—	119.6	...	...	...	...	...	—	100	490	—	—	Netherlands Antilles
...	...					...	...	—					New Caledonia
80	4,763	9.0	4,442	4.8[4]	95.2[4]	104	9	11	37	91	310	...	New Zealand
—	—	83.9	...	...	...	...	...	—	4	17	56	...	Nicaragua
...	...	...	...	...	...	...	...	—	...	...	—	...	Niger
3,107	4,131	0.7	9,798	—	100.0	20,828	29	711	84	433	5,042	...	Nigeria
													Northern Mariana Islands
1,345	27,663	36.3	4,051	...	...	8,422	9	988	110	307	53	11,019	Norway
714	4,361	1.0	6,666	...	...	5,138	16	314	27	85	1,300	...	Oman
765	17,840	0.6	16,668	41.5	58.5	203	10	21	50	137	1,135	...	Pakistan
—	—	—	...	...	...	—	—	—	9	60	—	—	Palau
		25.6	60	—	—				9	60	130	...	Panama
85	99	...	79	—	—	400	11	37	—	—	—	—	Papua New Guinea
—		6.1							2	8			Paraguay
200	1,303	45.5	191	61.4	38.6	808	17	47	54	182	800	...	Peru
110	—	54.3	—			216	196	1.1	91	323	357	...	Philippines
151	4,593	31.3	10,908	...	...	31	10	3	100	352	2,346	11,932	Poland
—	—	61.5	...	...	...	...	...	—	99	304	80	...	Portugal
—	—	166.7	...	...	...	...	...	—	44	127	—	—	Puerto Rico
7,079	13,499	10.0	13,500	—	100.0	3,700	22	170	21	58	235	...	Qatar
													Réunion
368	21,300	10.4	19,792	...	...	1,606	32	50	113	655	4,229	2,558	Romania
48,224	582,988	4.7	327,275	...	...	158,000	70	2,254	1,375	6,721	210,000	1,899,000	Russia
57	0.2[8]	—	0.2	...	...	...	...	—	—	—	—	—	Rwanda
...	...	...	...										St. Kitts and Nevis
													St. Lucia
...													St. Vincent and the Grenadines
...	...	...	...						20		—	—	San Marino
...		20	20								—	—	São Tomé and Príncipe
5,264	37,718	47.0	37,700	9.8[8]	90.2[8]	261,203	88	2,976	589	1,656	6,550	...	Saudi Arabia
—	—	14.3	...	...	...	...	...	—	6	17	—	—	Senegal
													Seychelles
—								—	2	10	—	—	Sierra Leone
—	...	353.1	...					—	410	1,170	—	—	Singapore
25	241[7]	15.3	5,101	...	...	9	18	0.5	33	115	...	...	Slovakia
4	11[7]	...	644	...	...	7	700	0.01	3	12	290	128	Slovenia
—	—	—						—			—	—	Solomon Islands
6	—	...	...					—	...	10	15	...	Somalia
27	...	67.0[10]	1,896	...	...	27	7	4	125[10]	401	2,679	...	South Africa
17	178	35.0	7,755	...	...	20	4	5	408	1,327	2,059	5,266	Spain
—	—	54.0	—					—	15	48	62	...	Sri Lanka
85	—	54.5	—	...	...	300	429	0.7	8	22	815	...	Sudan, The
—	...	...	...			74	25	3	1.4	—	—	—	Suriname
...	...	10	...					...	10	—	—	—	Swaziland
—	—	38.8	763	...	...	...	...	—	127	437	—	—	Sweden
—	—	15.4[22]	2,432[22]	38.3[8]	61.7[8]	...	...	...	35[22]	132	314	1,265	Switzerland
198	4,412	11.7	2,050	...	...	2,500	11	224	85	242	1,819	...	Syria
68	841	...	...	...	...	4	10	0.4	...	543	615	...	Taiwan
...	347[7]	...	1,212	...	...	...	...	0.8	1	...	...	...	Tajikistan
57	—	100.0	...					—	4	16	982	...	Tanzania
167	10,477	13.7	9,513	—	100.0	231	12	20	138	426	67	...	Thailand
—						...	...				—	—	Togo
													Tonga
299	6,071	3.5	5,962	1.8	98.2	490	10	48	36	245	1,051	...	Trinidad and Tobago
74	337	12.7	786	9.1	90.9	416	13	33	13	34	883	...	Tunisia
11	201	30.7	5,046	...	...	488	20	25	176	713	4,059	2,994	Turkey
2,900	30,100	...	8,332	...	...	740[6]	17	29	30	237	250	...	Turkmenistan
													Tuvalu
...	...	...	...			...	...	29	138	1,262			Uganda
1,100	16,900	0.6	75,467	...	...	...	...	29	138	1,262	3,930	38,402	Ukraine
5,794	25,429	22.3	21,017	52.7[8]	47.3[8]	98,100	122	804	74	213	830	...	United Arab Emirates
660	71,144	13.0	79,391	...	...	4,293	4	977	629	1,888	3,926	10,388	United Kingdom
4,639	559,261	16.9	591,754	33.4[11]	66.6[11]	22,457	9	2,505	5,024	15,354	276,000	843,586	United States
—	—	11.7	—					...	3[15]	37	—	—	Uruguay
1,900	45,300	...	38,564	...	...	...	...	59	44	175	290	200	Uzbekistan
													Vanuatu
3,962	25,406	18.6	24,675	9.1	90.9	64,477	71	913	380	1,177	6,850	...	Venezuela
113	697	...	3	...	...	500	9	55	0.3	—	150	...	Vietnam
—	—	104.2	...					...	117	545	—	—	Virgin Islands (U.S.)
...						...	...	...					West Bank
											—	—	Western Sahara
...	...					...	...				—	—	Western Samoa
425	...	100.0	...	...	...	4,000	33	123	26	120	676	—	Yemen
45	765	0.9	1,630	...	...	78	10	8	10	168	545	...	Yugoslavia
1.4	—	7.8				187	19	10	3	17	390	...	Zaire
—	—	100.0	—	—	—	...	...	...	4	25	1,724	...	Zambia
...	—	88.7	—	—	—	...	...	...	...	—	212	...	Zimbabwe

[1]Estimated reserves in place. [2]1981. [3]1985. [4]1984. [5]1990. [6]1992. [7]1994. [8]1983. [9]Belgium includes Luxembourg. [10]South Africa includes Botswana, Lesotho, Namibia, and Swaziland. [11]1982. [12]1991. [13]Data refer to former Czechoslovakia. [14]Geothermally generated electricity. [15]1993. [16]France includes Monaco. [17]Transportation and industry only; excludes agricultural, commercial, and public-service sectors. [18]Data refer to former West Germany only. [19]1988. [20]Italy includes San Marino. [21]1989. [22]Switzerland includes Liechtenstein. [23]Data refer to former U.S.S.R. [24]Data refer to Yugoslavia as constituted prior to 1991.

Transportation

This table presents data on the transportation infrastructure of the various countries and dependencies of the world and on their commercial passenger and cargo traffic. Most states have roads and airports, with services corresponding to the prevailing level of economic development. A number of states, however, lack railroads or inland waterways because of either geographic constraints or lack of development capital and technical expertise. Pipelines, one of the oldest means of bulk transport if aqueducts are considered, are today among the most narrowly developed transportation modes worldwide for shipment of bulk materials. Because the principal contemporary application of pipeline technology is to facilitate the shipment of hydrocarbon liquids and gases, coverage of pipelines will be found in the "Energy" table. It is, however, also true that pipelines now find increasing application for slurries of coal or other raw materials.

While the United Nations' *Statistical Yearbook* and *Monthly Bulletin of Statistics* provide much data on infrastructure and traffic and have established basic definitions and classifications for transportation statistics, the number of countries covered is limited. Several commercial publications maintain substantial databases and publishing programs for their particular areas of interest: highway and vehicle statistics are provided by the International Road Federation's annual *World Road Statistics;* the International Union of Railways' *International Railway Statistics* and Jane's *World Railways* provide similar data for railways; Lloyd's *Register of Shipping Statistical Tables* summarizes the world's merchant marine; the *Official Airline Guide,* the International Civil Aviation Organization's *Digest of Statistics: Commercial Air Carriers,* and the International Air Transport Association's *World Air Transport Statistics* have also been used to supplement and update data collected by the UN. Because several of these agencies are commercially or insurance-oriented, their data tend to be more complete, accurate, and timely than those of intergovernmental organizations, which depend on periodic responses to questionnaires or publication of results in official sources. All of these international sources have been extensively supplemented by national statistical sources to provide additional data. Such diversity of sources, however, imposes limitations on the comparability of the statistics from country to country because the basis and completeness of data collection and the frequency and timeliness of analysis and publication may vary greatly. Data shown in italic are from 1991 or earlier.

The categories adopted in the table also have special problems of comparability. Total road length is subject to wide international variation of interpretation, as "roads" can mean anything from mere tracks to highly developed highways. Each country also has individual classifications that differ according to climate, availability of road-building materials, traffic patterns, administrative responsibility, and so on. "Paved roads," by contrast, is a much more tightly definable category, but the proportion of paved to total roads may be distorted by the less comparable total road statistics. Automobile and truck and bus fleet statistics, which are usually

Transportation

country	roads and motor vehicles (latest)								railroads (latest)					
	roads			motor vehicles			cargo		track length		traffic			
	length		paved (per-cent)	auto-mobiles	trucks and buses	persons per vehicle	short ton-mi ('000,000)	metric ton-km ('000,000)	mi	km	passengers		cargo	
	mi	km									passen-ger-mi ('000,000)	passen-ger-km ('000,000)	short ton-mi ('000,000)	metric ton-km ('000,000)
Afghanistan	10,923	17,579	47	31,000	25,000	364	1,993	2,910	16	25	...	...	...	...
Albania	9,631	15,500	30	58,682	34,441	34	55	80	447	720	484.2	779.2	400	584
Algeria	62,121	99,974	68	725,000	480,000	23	9,589	14,000	2,965[2]	4,772[2]	1,568	2,524	1,644	2,400
American Samoa	217	350	43	4,628	489	11	...	...	—	—	—	—	—	—
Andorra	167	269	74	36,067	4,208	1.6	...	...	—	—	—	—	—	—
Angola	45,128	72,626	25	197,000	26,000	52	...	...	1,739[2]	2,798[2]	203	326	1,178	1,720
Antigua and Barbuda	721	1,161	33	14,800	3,700	3.5	...	...	—	—	—	—	—	—
Argentina	133,954	215,578	29	4,426,706	1,239,625	6.0	...	...	21,015[2]	33,821[2]	4,014	6,460	4,530	6,613
Armenia	4,800	7,700	97	2,782	12,034	244	53	78	511	823	196	316	3,345	4,884
Aruba	236	380	100	32,060	814	2.1	...	...	—	—	—	—	—	—
Australia	507,316	816,447	36	8,391,500	2,246,700	1.7	60,416	88,206	22,501[2,7]	36,212[2,7]	7,152	11,510	67,333	98,305
Austria	80,332	129,282	100	3,479,595	292,755	2.1	7,362	10,749	3,502	5,636	5,988[7]	9,636[7]	9,386[7]	13,704[7]
Azerbaijan	35,897	57,770	94	289,000	88,800	20	1,190	1,740	1,305	2,100	3,025	4,869	20.9	30.5
Bahamas, The	1,491	2,400	56	46,089	11,858	4.7	...	...	—	—	—	—	—	—
Bahrain	1,751	2,818	75	133,071	28,847	3.4	...	...	—	—	—	—	—	—
Bangladesh	120,100	193,283	4	77,933	101,349	649	...	...	1,681[2]	2,706[2]	3,176	5,112	439	641
Barbados	977	1,573	95	40,120	9,133	5.4	...	...	—	—	—	—	—	—
Belarus	31,390	50,518	98	842,500	9,800	12	6,534	9,539	3,480	5,600	11,195	18,017	38,659	56,441
Belgium	88,579	142,555	97	4,273,451	417,056	2.2	18,800	27,500	2,110[2]	3,396[2]	4,125	6,638	5,537	8,084
Belize	1,684	2,710	18	10,667	6,108	12	...	...	—	—	—	—	—	—
Benin	3,770	6,070	20	22,000	12,300	153	...	...	359	578	66	107	173	253
Bermuda	140	225	100	20,148	3,300	2.6	...	...	—	—	—	—	—	—
Bhutan	1,502	2,418	79	2,590	1,367	348	...	...	—	—	—	—	—	—
Bolivia	26,370	42,438	4	347,383	189,846	13	1,133	1,654	2,295[2]	3,694[2]	216.8	348.9	521.9	761.9
Bosnia and Herzegovina	13,153	21,168	54	438,080	50,578	8.9	2,708	3,954	646	1,039	883	1,421	3,205	4,679
Botswana	11,388	18,327	23	27,058	42,696	20	...	...	603	971	160	257	1,171	1,710
Brazil	1,133,605	1,824,364	12	12,024,000	3,316,000	10	178,359	260,400	19,885[2]	32,002[2]	8,723	14,038	85,439	124,738
Brunei	1,502	2,417	51	135,641	14,016	1.9	...	...	12[13]	19[13]	—	—	—	—
Bulgaria	22,935	36,911	92	1,587,873	214,426	4.7	6,510	9,510	4,044	6,508	2,916	4,693	5,887	8,595
Burkina Faso	8,151	13,117	12	11,000	13,700	407	...	...	386[2]	622[2]	422	680	322	470
Burundi	8,993	14,473	7	14,483	14,914	188	...	...	—	—	—	—	—	—
Cambodia	7,643	12,300	34	36,924	10,700	206	1,360	1,990	380	612	33.6	54.0	6.9	10.0
Cameroon	30,074	48,400	8	90,000	79,000	76	175	255	686[2]	1,104[2]	247	398	405	592
Canada	634,400	1,021,000	35	14,280,000	3,895,600	1.6	29,033	42,388	44,182	71,104	861	1,385	191,448	279,510
Cape Verde	680	1,095	78	6,479	2,099	43	...	...	—	—	—	—	—	—
Central African Republic	14,900	24,000	2	14,000	6,400	158	62	90	—	—	—	—	—	—
Chad	20,319	32,700	1	9,630	14,360	265	580	850	—	—	—	—	—	—
Chile	49,270	79,293	16	837,379	497,855	11	...	...	4,076[2]	6,560[2]	507	816	1,595	2,329
China	694,580	1,117,821	89	3,497,400	5,603,300	131	335,000	489,000	44,040	70,876	219,965	354,700	883,576	1,290,000
Colombia	66,721	107,377	12	854,160	430,611	26	4,265	6,227	2,007[2]	3,230[2]	9.6	15.5	166.4	242.9
Comoros	529	851	75	2,000	5,000	68	...	...	—	—	—	—	—	—
Congo	7,919	12,745	10	28,999	16,617	54	46	67	494	795	141	227	152	222
Costa Rica	22,110	35,583	16	213,000	127,000	9.6	2,000	2,900	590[2]	950[2]	3.7	5.9	45.8	66.8
Côte d'Ivoire	31,168	50,160	10	271,000	150,000	34	...	...	405[2]	651[2]	117[15]	189[15]	182[15]	266[15]
Croatia	16,732	26,928	81	698,391	53,860	6.4	394	575	1,676	2,699	598	962	1,071	1,563
Cuba	28,928	46,555	27	241,300	208,400	23	2,482	3,623	3,033	4,881	1,880	3,025	937	1,368
Cyprus	6,286	10,117	59	210,365	98,114	2.5	...	...	—	—	—	—	—	—
Czech Republic	34,748	55,922	...	2,967,053	238,554	3.2	14,167	20,684	5,866	9,441	5,311	8,548	17,520	25,579
Denmark	44,276	71,255	100	1,668,278	277,824	2.7	7,300	10,600	1,763	2,838	3,048	4,905	1,384	2,021
Djibouti	1,805	2,905	10	13,500	3,000	34	...	...	66	106	173	279	187	273
Dominica	466	750	49	4,700	5,500	7.0	...	...	—	—	—	—	—	—
Dominican Republic	7,456	12,000	48	120,000	80,000	36	...	...	1,083[2]	1,743[2]	—	—	—	—
Ecuador	28,200	45,400	14	195,000	295,000	23	2,315	3,380	594[2]	956[2]	29.9	48.2	3.6	5.3
Egypt	29,445[19]	47,387[19]	73[19]	1,168,000	380,000	38	21,500	31,400	5,274	8,487	29,821	47,992	1,597	2,332
El Salvador	9,670	15,562	13	104,434	152,778	21	...	...	349[2]	562[2]	3.4	5.5	20.3	29.6

based upon registration, are relatively accurate, though some countries round off figures, and unregistered vehicles may cause substantial undercount. There is also inconsistent classification of vehicle types; in some countries a vehicle may serve variously as an automobile, a truck, or a bus, or even as all three on certain occasions. Relatively few countries collect and maintain commercial road traffic statistics.

Data on national railway systems are generally given for railway track length rather than the length of routes, which may be multitracked. Siding tracks usually are not included, but some countries fail to distinguish them. The United States data include only class 1 railways, which account for about 94 percent of total track length. Passenger traffic is usually calculated from tickets sold to fare-paying passengers. Such statistics are subject to distortion if there are large numbers of nonpaying passengers, such as military personnel, or if season tickets are sold and not all the allowed journeys are utilized. Railway cargo traffic is calculated by weight hauled multiplied by the length of the journey. Changes in freight load during the journey should be accounted for but sometimes are not, leading to discrepancies.

Merchant fleet and tonnage statistics collected by Lloyd's registry service for vessels over 100 gross tons are quite accurate. Cargo statistics, however, reflect the port and customs requirements of each country and the reporting rules of each country's merchant marine authority (although these, increasingly, reflect the recommendations of the International Mar-

itime Organization); often, however, they are only estimates based on customs declarations and the count of vessels entered and cleared. Even when these elements are reported consistently, further uncertainties may be introduced because of ballast, bunkers, ships' stores, or transshipped goods included in the data.

Airport data are based on scheduled flights reported in the commercial *Official Airline Guide* and are both reliable and current. The comparability of civil air traffic statistics suffers from differing characteristics of the air transportation systems of different countries; data for an entire country may be two to three years behind those for a single airport.

Outside of Europe, where standardization of data on inland waterways is necessitated by the volume of international traffic, comparability of national data declines markedly. Calculations as to both the length of a country's waterway system (or route length of river, lake, and coastal traffic) and the makeup of its stock of commercially significant vessels (those for which data will be collected) are largely determined by the nature and use of the country's hydrographic net—its seasonality, relief profile, depth, access to potential markets—and inevitably differ widely from country to country. Data for coastal or island states may refer to scheduled coastwise or interisland traffic.

merchant marine				air						canals and inland waterways (latest)				country
fleet, 1992 (vessels over 100 gross tons)	total dead-weight tonnage 1992 ('000)	international cargo (latest)		airports with sched-uled flights, 1996	traffic (latest)					length		cargo		
		loaded metric tons ('000)	off-loaded metric tons ('000)		passengers		cargo			mi	km	short ton-mi ('000,000)	metric ton-km ('000,000)	
					passenger-mi ('000,000)	passenger-km ('000,000)	short ton-mi ('000,000)	metric ton-km ('000,000)						
—	—	—	—	3	165[1]	265[1]	7.5[1]	11[1]		750	1,200	...	...	Afghanistan
24	81.0	1,065	664	1	...	...	...	...		27	43	24	35	Albania
149	1,093.4	57,607	14,284	28	1,908[3]	3,070[3]	13.9[3]	20.3[3]		...	...	...	...	Algeria
3	0.1	380	733	3	...	...	...	...		...	...	...	...	American Samoa
—	—	—	—	—	...	...	...	...		—	—	—	—	Andorra
113	123.5	23,288	1,261	17	1,803[4]	2,901[4]	203[4]	296[4]		805	1,295	...	...	Angola
292	997.4	28	113	2	140	225	14	20		...	...	...	...	Antigua and Barbuda
423	1,173.1	36,792	6,864	43	7,107[5]	11,438[5]	880[5]	1,285[5]		6,800	11,000	19,326	28,215	Argentina
...	...	...	...	1	3,453	5,557	34	49		...	...	...	...	Armenia
6	6	...	...	1	...	...	...	...		...	...	...	...	Aruba
695	3,857.3	332,124	40,284	400	30,079	48,408	1,145	1,672		5,200	8,368	66,439	97,000	Australia
26	208.5	1,068	4,901	6	4,701	7,566	120.3	175.6		277	446	1,247	1,820	Austria
...	...	...	...	1	1,299	2,091	133	194		...	...	3,600	5,300	Azerbaijan
1,061	33,081.7	5,920	5,705	23	119	191	0.3	0.4		...	...	...	...	Bahamas, The
87	192.5	13,285	3,512	1	1,719[8]	2,766[8]	77.7[8]	113.5[8]		...	...	...	...	Bahrain
301	566.8	1,728	9,456	8	1,588	2,556	190	278		5,000	8,046	...	...	Bangladesh
37	84.0	206	538	1	93[9]	149[9]	0.8[10]	1.1[10]		...	...	...	...	Barbados
...	18,373.0	...	...	2	3,487	5,611	23	34		...	...	91	133	Belarus
232	218.5	57,168	88,908	2	4,658	7,496	289.2	422.2		1,269	2,043	14,600	21,300	Belgium
32	45.7	178	241	11	...	...	...	...		513	825	...	...	Belize
12	0.2	246	1,489	1	142.4[11]	229.2[11]	10.8[11]	15.8[11]		...	...	...	...	Benin
94	5,206.5	130	470	1	...	...	...	...		...	...	...	...	Bermuda
—	—	—	—	1	2.7	4.4	...	...		—	—	—	—	Bhutan
1	15.8	—	—	14	819	1,318	25.3	36.9		6,214	10,000	90	132	Bolivia
...	...	...	...	1	...	...	...	...		...	...	...	...	Bosnia and Herzegovina
—	—	—	—	4	47[12]	76[12]	5[12]	8[12]		...	...	...	...	Botswana
635	9,348.3	168,026	52,570	139	20,275	32,629	1,070	1,562		31,069	50,000	56,030	81,803	Brazil
51	349.7	13,554	1,325	1	1,494	2,404	75.2	109.8		130	209	...	...	Brunei
222	1,938.2	5,290	20,080	3	2,239	3,604	11.4	16.6		292	470	247	360	Bulgaria
—	—	—	—	2	134.9	217.2	23.4	34.2		...	...	...	...	Burkina Faso
1	0.4	35	188	1	1.2	2.0	...	...		...	...	...	...	Burundi
3	3.8	11	95	7	...	...	...	...		2,300	3,700	51	75	Cambodia
47	39.8	1,260	2,328	5	196	315	27	39		1,299	2,090	...	...	Cameroon
1,185	2,896.8	169,879	77,191	301	28,942	46,577	3,986	5,819		1,860	3,000	...	...	Canada
42	30.9	87	580	9	106	171	13.2	19.2		...	...	...	...	Cape Verde
—	—	53	126	1	138.8[11]	222.8[11]	10.5[11]	15.3[11]		500	800	161	235	Central African Republic
—	—	—	—	4	138	223	10.5	15.3		1,240	2,000	...	...	Chad
392	854.9	21,768	13,464	18	3,501	5,634	979	1,430		450	725	5,629	8,218	Chile
2,390	20,658.0	105,852	101,688	113	40,513	65,200	1,644	2,400		86,100	138,600	1,164,000	1,700,000	China
101	403.0	26,280	13,812	63	2,697	4,340	662	967		8,900	14,300	7,038	10,276	Colombia
6	3.6	12	107	4	1.9	3.0	...	...		...	...	...	...	Comoros
22	10.8	8,987	736	5	139[11]	223[11]	10.5	15.3		696	1,120	...	...	Congo
24	8.4	1,605	1,892	14	999[14]	1,607[14]	29.7[14]	43.4[14]		454	730	...	...	Costa Rica
51	98.6	3,702	6,184	11	139[16]	223[16]	10.5[16]	15.3[16]		609	980	...	...	Côte d'Ivoire
203	140.9	3,948	7,776	5	276	444	2.1	3.0		488	785	160	230	Croatia
393	924.6	8,092	15,440	14	1,338	2,153	163	238		149	240	2,085	3,044	Cuba
1,416	36,198.1	2,232	5,028	2	1,657	2,667	24.8	36.2		...	...	...	...	Cyprus
22[17]	446.2[17]	...	...	2	1,588	2,555	46.7	68.2		295	475	221	322	Czech Republic
456	7,569.1	20,722	35,934	13	3,214[18]	5,172[18]	91.4[18]	133.4[18]		259	417	1,100	1,600	Denmark
10	4.1	414	958	1	42	67	4	6		...	...	...	...	Djibouti
7	3.2	103	181	2	...	...	...	...		...	...	...	...	Dominica
28	10.4	2,550	4,182	4	145	234	1.7	2.5		...	...	...	...	Dominican Republic
154	504.1	11,783	1,958	14	780	1,255	44.0	64.2		932	1,500	...	...	Ecuador
444	1,685.2	14,808	22,860	14	4,449	7,160	541	790		2,175	3,500	580	850	Egypt
15	...	221	1,023	1	1,080	1,738	17.5	25.6		...	...	...	...	El Salvador

Transportation (continued)

country	roads length mi	roads length km	paved (percent)	automobiles	trucks and buses	persons per vehicle	cargo short ton-mi ('000,000)	cargo metric ton-km ('000,000)	track mi	track km	passenger-mi ('000,000)	passenger-km ('000,000)	cargo short ton-mi ('000,000)	cargo metric ton-km ('000,000)
Equatorial Guinea	1,667	2,682	19	6,500	4,000	37	...	...	—	—	—	—	—	—
Eritrea	2,442	3,930	21	5,350	...	...	...	...	—	—	...	...	...	...
Estonia	9,168	14,755	55	337,800	60,300	3.8	1,061	1,549	636	1,024	334	537	2,474	3,612
Ethiopia	17,381	27,972	15	42,085	29,619	745	...	...	486[20]	782[20]	172	277	86	126
Faroe Islands	285	458	...	11,339	2,701	3.2	...	...	—	—	—	—	—	—
Fiji	3,200	5,100	20	49,712	33,928	9.4	...	...	370[13]	595[13]	...	...	—	—
Finland	48,246	77,644	63	1,880,827	254,578	2.4	15,900	23,200	3,641[2]	5,859[2]	1,626	2,616	6,551	9,564
France	504,987	812,700	92	25,100,000	5,005,000	1.9	104,500	152,500	21,173[2]	34,074[2]	36,276	58,380	31,414	45,864
French Guiana	706	1,137	40	25,000	9,000	3.4	...	...	—	—	—	—	—	—
French Polynesia	584	940	42	38,900	16,500	3.9	...	...	—	—	—	—	—	—
Gabon	4,850	7,800	10	24,000	17,500	27	...	...	415	668	21	34	126	184
Gambia, The	1,483	2,386	32	7,400	3,100	102	...	...	—	—	—	—	—	—
Gaza Strip	...	...	...	21,206	4,639	29	...	...	—	—	—	—	—	—
Georgia	13,000	21,000	94	441,828	50,220	11	67	98	976	1,570	1,552	2,497	8,462	12,355
Germany	404,325	650,700	99	40,499,442	2,336,760	1.9	138,975	202,900	54,994	88,504	36,041	58,003	45,649	66,646
Ghana	22,800	36,700	32	90,000	44,200	117	873	1,275	592[2]	953[2]	73.1	117.7	93.9	137.1
Gibraltar	27	43	100	18,404	1,064	1.4	...	...	—	—	—	—	—	—
Greece	72,170	116,150	92	2,075,605	873,647	3.5	11,400	16,700	1,552[2]	2,497[2]	1,072	1,726	358	523
Greenland	50	80	...	1,944	1,039	19	...	...	—	—	—	—	—	—
Grenada	650	1,046	66	4,739	3,068	12	...	...	—	—	—	—	—	—
Guadeloupe	2,000	3,200	80	86,000	34,000	3.2	...	...	—	—	—	—	—	—
Guam	419	674	100	74,728	30,739	1.4	...	...	—	—	—	—	—	—
Guatemala	7,363	11,849	26	102,000	96,800	52	...	...	708[2]	1,139[2]	6.3	10.1	92.5	135.1
Guernsey	...	...	...	33,037	7,522	1.6	...	...	—	—	—	—	—	—
Guinea	9,974	16,051	9	23,155	13,000	169	...	...	411[2]	662[2]	25.8	41.5	5.0	7.3
Guinea-Bissau	2,579	4,150	9	4,000	2,800	154	...	...	—	—	—	—	—	—
Guyana	4,474	7,200	10	24,000	9,000	22	...	...	116[13]	187[13]	...	...	...	...
Haiti	2,662	4,284	14	32,000	21,000	120	...	...	—	—	—	—	—	—
Honduras	8,825	14,203	18	99,997	128,575	23	...	...	614	988	4.8	7.7	20.7	30.2
Hong Kong	1,067	1,717	100	303,308	130,913	14	...	...	21	34	2,119	3,411	68	99
Hungary	18,655	30,023	99	2,245,395	312,000	4.0	495	723	8,190	13,180	5,244	8,441	5,753	8,400
Iceland	7,668	12,340	23	116,243	15,597	2.0	318	464	—	—	—	—	—	—
India	1,195,049	1,923,248	48	3,446,000	2,181,000	163	144,000	210,000	38,935[2]	62,660[2]	198,500	319,400	171,213	249,966
Indonesia	198,688	319,758	45	1,890,340	1,903,594	51	17,000	25,000	4,090	6,583	7,690	12,376	2,632	3,843
Iran	94,130	151,488	34	1,557,000	588,900	28	46,750	68,250	3,163[2]	5,091[2]	3,990	6,422	6,249	9,124
Iraq	29,337	47,214	77	672,000	368,000	19	...	...	1,263[2]	2,032[2]	973	1,566	1,129	1,649
Ireland	57,380	92,345	94	939,022	147,719	3.3	3,519	5,138	1,210[2]	1,947[2]	783	1,260	389.9	569.3
Isle of Man	357	574	58	38,917	4,925	1.6	...	...	37[2]	59[2]	...	...	...	...
Israel	9,134	14,700	100	1,112,300	246,700	3.9	...	...	379[2]	610[2]	166	267	805	1,176
Italy	188,597	303,518	100	29,429,628	2,684,127	1.8	138,000	202,000	9,906	15,942	29,270	47,100	14,120	20,620
Jamaica	10,212	16,435	29	86,791	41,312	19	...	...	129[2]	208[2]	12.1	19.5	1.7	2.5
Japan	706,091	1,136,346	73	42,956,000	20,472,000	2.0	188,000	274,000	12,583	20,251	246,269	396,332	16,776	24,493
Jersey	...	...	...	58,491	9,922	1.3	...	...	—	—	—	—	—	—
Jordan	4,260	6,856	100	167,828	82,516	16	19,133	27,934	420[2]	677[2]	3.7	6.0	463	676
Kazakhstan	98,537	158,581	78	940,656	541,960	11	9	13	13,422	21,600	10,812	17,400	100,550	146,800
Kenya	39,400	63,400	14	157,166	133,968	88	134	196	1,885[2]	3,034[2]	288	464	899	1,312
Kiribati	398	640	5	307	130	147	...	...	—	—	—	—	—	—
Korea, North	18,600	30,000	6	248,000	...	...	...	...	5,302	8,533	2,100	3,400	6,200	9,100
Korea, South	48,984	78,833	78	5,148,713	2,255,634	6.0	36,100	52,700	4,076	6,559	18,775	30,216	9,633	14,064
Kuwait	2,655	4,273	100	538,300	154,900	2.3	...	...	—	—	—	—	—	—
Kyrgyzstan	17,650	28,400	79	164,000	...	...	555	811	230	370	81.5	131.2	1,088	1,589
Laos	8,780	14,130	16	10,000	10,000	237	16	23	—	—	—	—	—	—
Latvia	40,198	64,693	18	252,000	73,600	7.8	1,200	1,700	1,499	2,413	1,115	1,794	6,521	9,520
Lebanon	4,579	7,370	85	1,035,085	80,833	3.2	...	...	138	222	5.3	8.6	29	42
Lesotho	3,308	5,324	15	5,944	17,785	82	...	...	1.6	2.6	...	...	...	...
Liberia	2,703	4,350	58	7,500	3,000	217	...	...	306[2]	493[2]	...	...	137[13]	200[13]
Libya	50,704	81,600	56	904,000	322,000	4.3	...	...	—	—	—	—	—	—
Liechtenstein	201	323	...	17,767	1,817	1.5	...	...	12	19	...	...	...	...
Lithuania	34,550	61,329	74	652,810	110,696	4.9	3,534	5,160	1,862	2,996	547	1,523	7,555	8,849
Luxembourg	3,190	5,134	99	229,037	29,868	1.6	164	239	171[2]	275[2]	176	284	443	647
Macau	60	97	100	32,580	5,824	10	...	...	—	—	—	—	—	—
Macedonia	5,233	8,422	62	263,181	22,825	6.8	807	1,178	573	922	41.6	67.0	103.4	151.0
Madagascar	21,586	34,739	15	47,711	34,341	149	220	321	640[2]	1,030[2]	152	245	90	132
Malawi	16,960	27,294	22	17,000	12,000	330	—	—	490[2]	789[2]	11.8	19.0	38.9	56.8
Malaysia	57,441	92,443	75	2,291,199	501,096	7.0	...	...	1,381	2,222	1,148[29]	1,848[29]	945[29]	1,380[29]
Maldives	...	...	...	823	869	141	...	...	—	—	—	—	—	—
Mali	9,321	15,000	17	21,000	8,600	298	...	...	399[2]	642[2]	304.2	489.5	187.2	273.3
Malta	997	1,604	94	163,310	27,978	1.9	...	...	—	—	—	—	—	—
Marshall Islands	...	...	...	1,418	193	34	...	...	—	—	—	—	—	—
Martinique	1,286	2,069	75	135,269	7,328	2.3	...	...	—	—	—	—	—	—
Mauritania	4,745	7,636	23	8,000	5,700	162	...	...	437[2]	704[2]	...	...	3,860	5,635
Mauritius	1,138	1,831	93	35,994	10,286	24	...	...	—	—	—	—	—	—
Mayotte	143	230	49	1,528		40	...	...	—	—	—	—	—	—
Mexico	188,886	303,983	36	8,449,969	3,950,456	7.2	107,000	156,000	16,432[2]	26,445[2]	2,382	3,833	24,042	35,100
Micronesia	146	235	18	...	...	...	...	...	—	—	—	—	—	—
Moldova	7,617	12,259	87	169,387	71,310	18	768	1,121	746	1,200	5,515	8,875	10,279	15,007
Monaco	27	43	100	20,715	2,702	1.3	...	...	1	2	...	...	...	...
Mongolia	31,000	50,000	3	28,000	28,000	42	183.8	268.4	1,294	2,083	490.6	789.6	1.4	2.1
Morocco	37,152	59,790	50	956,652	321,381	20	1,288	1,880	1,099[2]	1,768[2]	1,171	1,884	3,247	4,740
Mozambique	18,141	29,195	18	10,035	29,500	405	...	...	1,946	3,131	78.9	127.0	447.9	654.0
Myanmar (Burma)	15,118	24,330	16	40,000	40,000	554	71	103.7	3,104	4,995	2,908	4,680	444	648
Namibia	26,467	42,594	12	61,269	60,041	13	...	...	1,480	2,382	1,248	2,008	741	1,082
Nauru	17	28	79	1,448		6.3	...	...	3[13]	5[13]	...	...	4.7	6.8
Nepal	5,924	9,534	36	4,949	3,363	2,259	984	1,437	33[2]	53[2]	...	...	...	...
Netherlands, The	73,908	118,943	89	5,884,000	662,000	2.3	16,000	24,000	1,713	2,757	8,972	14,439	1,938	2,830

merchant marine				air					canals and inland waterways (latest)				country
fleet, 1992 (vessels over 100 gross tons)	total dead-weight tonnage, 1992 ('000)	international cargo (latest) loaded metric tons ('000)	off-loaded metric tons ('000)	airports with scheduled flights, 1996	traffic (latest) passengers passenger-mi ('000,000)	passenger-km ('000,000)	cargo short ton-mi ('000,000)	metric ton-km ('000,000)	length mi	km	cargo short ton-mi ('000,000)	metric ton-km ('000,000)	
3	6.7	100	60	2	4	7	0.7	1.0	...	...	...	...	Equatorial Guinea
...	...	...	...	2	...	...	...	...	...	...	...	...	Eritrea
234	680.4	10,968	3,420	3	65.2	105.0	0.3	0.4	311	500	0.7	1	Estonia
27	84.3	592	3,120	31	1,116	1,796	118	173	...	...	...	...	Ethiopia
191	59.8	190	350	1	...	...	...	...	...	...	...	...	Faroe Islands
64	60.4	568	625	13	735	1,183	38.2	55.8	126	203	...	...	Fiji
263	989.3	34,104	37,020	24	5,853	9,419	130.7	190.9	4,148	6,675	2,500	3,600	Finland
729	4,981.0	82,835	200,082	66	36,944[21]	59,455[21]	6,680[21]	9,753[21]	9,278	14,932	3,800	5,600	France
7	0.7	73	638	8	...	...	...	...	286	460	...	...	French Guiana
41	16.5	15	666	36	...	...	...	...	...	...	...	...	French Polynesia
29	30.2	12,828	212	23	354	570	56	82	994	1,600	...	...	Gabon
11	2.0	169	212	1	31	50	3	5	250	400	...	...	Gambia, The
—	—	...	...	—	...	...	...	...	...	...	...	...	Gaza Strip
...	...	...	...	1	3,291	5,296	...	...	...	...	17,561	25,638	Georgia
1,375	6,832.3	67,488	127,380	40	67,002	107,829	10,909	15,927	4,686	7,541	39,425	57,559	Germany
155	131.0	1,810	2,842	1	240	387	14	20	803	1,293	75	110	Ghana
49	1,136.1	5	400	1	...	...	...	...	—	—	...	...	Gibraltar
1,872	45,276.6	20,400	37,788	36	5,234	8,429	92	135	50	80	585	854	Greece
82	17.2	298	288	5	16.3	26.3	0.23	0.34	...	...	...	...	Greenland
3	0.5	25	190	2	...	...	...	...	...	...	...	...	Grenada
20	4.4	423	2,178	6	...	...	...	...	...	...	...	...	Guadeloupe
5	0.1	195	1,524	1	...	...	...	...	...	...	...	...	Guam
8	0.4	2,096	3,822	2	239	384	14	21	162	260	...	...	Guatemala
—	—	...	...	1	...	...	...	...	...	...	...	...	Guernsey
23	1.7	12,210	712	2	20.4	32.8	0.9	1.2	805	1,295	...	...	Guinea
19	1.8	40	315	2	3.7	6.0	0.7	1.0	...	...	...	...	Guinea-Bissau
82	13.5	1,730	673	1	200	322	2.1	3.0	3,700	6,000	...	...	Guyana
4	0.4	170	704	2	...	...	...	...	60	100	...	...	Haiti
966	1,437.3	1,316	1,002	8	201[22]	323[22]	29[22]	42[22]	289	465	...	...	Honduras
387	11,688.6	34,272[23]	76,668[23]	1	...	...	...	...	...	...	...	...	Hong Kong
15	134.5	...	...	1	1,489	2,396	20.3	29.6	1,008	1,622	14	20	Hungary
394	114.9	927	1,633	24	1,553	2,499	30.9	45.1	...	...	58	84	Iceland
888	10,365.9	53,220	75,000	66	10,878	17,506	379.7	554.3	10,054	16,180	202,000	295,000	India
2,014	3,130.2	247,908	56,316	81	8,904	14,330	415.6	606.8	13,409	21,579	17,000	25,000	Indonesia
403	8,345.3	113,207	16,719	19	3,355	5,400	73.9	107.9	562	904	...	...	Iran
131	1,578.8	97,830	8,638	...	976	1,570	37.4	54.6	631	1,015	...	...	Iraq
189	208.6	6,367	17,637	9	2,896	4,661	73	107	...	...	...	...	Ireland
101	2,836.5	6	203	1	115.5	185.9	0.2	0.3	...	...	...	...	Isle of Man
58	723.4	8,448	20,964	7	7,013[24]	11,287[24]	732.9[24]	1,070[24]	...	...	...	...	Israel
1,636	10,940.1	51,420	222,060	31	18,429[25]	29,659[25]	914.3[25]	1,335[25]	1,500	2,400	59	86	Italy
12	16.2	8,802	5,285	5	451[26]	726[26]	52[26]	76[26]	...	...	...	...	Jamaica
10,091	37,815.8	111,180	751,404	73	71,227	114,603	4,101	5,988	1,100	1,770	155,000	227,000	Japan
—	—	...	...	1	...	...	...	...	...	...	...	...	Jersey
5	113.6	8,868	6,168	2	2,731	4,395	181.6	265.2	...	...	19,202	28,035	Jordan
...	...	...	...	6	2,858	4,600	68	100	...	...	123	180	Kazakstan
29	11.6	1,596	3,228	13	1,092[27]	1,757[27]	36.2[27]	52.8[27]	...	...	...	...	Kenya
7	2.7	15	26	17	6	10	0.5	0.8	3	5	...	...	Kiribati
100	951.2	635	5,520	1	52.2	84.0	1.4	2.0	1,400	2,253	...	...	Korea, North
2,138	11,724.9	74,736	273,672	14	24,395	39,260	3,306	4,826	1,000	1,609	48,600	70,900	Korea, South
209	3,188.5	51,400	4,522	1	3,184	5,124	225.8	329.7	...	...	...	...	Kuwait
...	...	...	...	2	1,602	2,578	158.8	231.9	...	...	6	9	Kyrgyzstan
1	1.5	...	...	11	29	46	3.0	5.0	2,850	4,587	53	77	Laos
261	1,436.9	36,012	2,448	1	168	271	6	9	186	300	311	454	Latvia
163	438.2	152	1,150	1	1,069	1,720	29	43	...	...	...	...	Lebanon
—	—	—	—	1	14.9	24.0	0.1	0.2	—	—	—	—	Lesotho
1,672	97,374.0	14,900	1,520	1	4.3	7.0	0.7	1.0	...	...	...	...	Liberia
150	1,223.6	62,491	7,808	12	247.6[28]	398.5[28]	0.3[28]	0.4[28]	—	—	...	...	Libya
—	—	—	—	—	...	...	...	...	—	—	...	...	Liechtenstein
52	373.9	10,092	2,628	3	205	330	5.4	7.9	373	600	12	18	Lithuania
54	2,603.6	—	—	1	79.5	232	606.9	886.1	23	37	232	338	Luxembourg
6	0.1	755	3,935	—	...	...	...	...	...	...	...	...	Macau
...	...	...	...	1	181.7	292.4	...	...	...	...	...	...	Macedonia
85	82.1	540	984	19	390.2	627.9	12.1	17.7	...	...	...	...	Madagascar
1	0.3	...	...	4	165.2	265.9	10.1	14.8	891	1,434	6.7	9.8	Malawi
552	2,916.3	23,472	44,184	36	14,017	22,558	795	1,160	4,534	7,296	...	...	Malaysia
44	79.0	27	78	5	1.9	3.0	...	...	...	...	...	...	Maldives
—	—	—	—	1	134.9	217.2	23.4	34.2	1,128	1,815	18	27	Mali
889	17,073.2	90	2,458	1	777	1,250	5.0	7.3	...	...	...	...	Malta
35	4,182.4	29	123	23	30	49	7	10	...	...	...	...	Marshall Islands
6	1.1	564	1,620	2	...	...	...	...	...	...	...	...	Martinique
126	23.9	10,037	674	10	128.6	206.9	9.7	14.2	...	...	...	...	Mauritania
35	152.2	834	2,419	1	1,987	3,198	80.7	117.8	...	...	...	...	Mauritius
1	1.1	...	...	1	...	...	...	...	...	...	...	...	Mayotte
635	1,495.3	129,804	53,220	83	16,049[30]	25,829[30]	1,679[30]	2,453[30]	1,800	2,900	...	...	Mexico
17	6.9	...	...	4	...	...	...	...	...	...	...	...	Micronesia
...	...	...	...	1	1,461	2,352	13.0	19.0	...	...	172	251	Moldova
1	...	...	...	1	...	...	...	...	...	...	...	...	Monaco
—	—	—	—	1	180	290	4.0	5.8	247	397	613	895	Mongolia
492	586.2	19,476	21,120	12	2,860	4,602	39.5	57.7	...	...	...	...	Morocco
107	31.6	2,800	3,400	7	270	434	6.8	10.0	2,330	3,750	...	...	Mozambique
144	1,354.0	1,344	1,284	19	252	406	5.6	8.2	7,954	12,800	242	354	Myanmar (Burma)
30	5.9	483	260	13	524	844	52	76	...	...	...	...	Namibia
2	5.8	1,650	59	1	128[31]	206[31]	14[31]	20[31]	...	...	...	...	Nauru
—	—	—	—	24	478	769	63.8	93.1	...	...	...	...	Nepal
1,076	4,191.0	88,116	286,992	6	25,953	41,767	2,242	3,273	3,939	6,340	5,100	7,500	Netherlands, The

Transportation (continued)

country	roads length mi	km	paved (percent)	motor vehicles automobiles	trucks and buses	persons per vehicle	cargo short ton-mi ('000,000)	metric ton-km ('000,000)	track length mi	km	passengers passenger-mi ('000,000)	passenger-km ('000,000)	cargo short ton-mi ('000,000)	metric ton-km ('000,000)
Netherlands Antilles	368	592	51	69,321	21,194	2.2	...	...	—	—	—	—	—	—
New Caledonia	3,580	5,762	22	58,500	22,600	2.3	...	...	—	—	—	—	—	—
New Zealand	57,089	91,876	73	1,604,659	347,883	1.8	...	...	2,433	3,915	285	458	1,918	2,800
Nicaragua	9,498	15,286	11	72,046	74,527	28	...	...	—	—	—	—	—	—
Niger	8,580	13,808	29	16,000	18,000	260	1,044	1,524	—	—	—	—	—	—
Nigeria	69,680	112,140	28	773,000	606,000	66	...	...	2,210	3,557	345	555	110	161
Northern Mariana Islands	307	494	27	12,113	6,479	3.0	...	...	—	—	—	—	—	—
Norway	56,085	90,261	74	1,684,664	382,017	2.1	6,575	9,600	2,485[2]	3,999[2]	1,642	2,398	1,575	2,678
Oman	16,372	26,349	20	201,200	108,600	6.7	...	...	—	—	—	—	—	—
Pakistan	122,875	197,749	51	732,100	252,023	135	2,723	3,976	5,453[2]	8,775[2]	10,208	16,428	4,011	5,856
Palau	40	64	59	——2,945——		5.4	...	...	—	—	...	...	—	—
Panama	6,402	10,303	33	161,500	82,800	10	...	...	220[2]	354[2]	...	...	0.5	0.7
Papua New Guinea	12,263	19,736	6	13,000	32,000	93	...	...	—	—	—	—	—	—
Paraguay	18,217	29,317	10	174,212	76,565	18	...	...	274[2]	441[2]	2.9	4.6	4.3	6.3
Peru	44,400	71,400	11	470,000	263,000	31	...	...	1,318[2]	2,121[2]	102.7	165.3	605.8	884.4
Philippines	99,968	160,883	16	1,078,895	1,024,051	32	...	...	658	1,059	60	96	8	12
Poland	231,447	372,479	65	7,517,266	1,472,278	4.3	49,042	71,600	15,488	24,926	17,156	27,610	45,061	65,788
Portugal	43,605	70,176	86	4,360,447	219,696	2.2	7,665	11,190	1,906[2]	3,068[2]	2,778	4,471	1,054	1,539
Puerto Rico	14,379	23,140	87	1,432,000	229,000	2.2	...	...	—	—	—	—	—	—
Qatar	671	1,080	63	125,700	63,800	3.0	...	...	—	—	—	—	—	—
Réunion	1,711	2,754	79	181,800	61,700	2.7	...	...	—	—	—	—	—	—
Romania	95,099	153,014	51	2,020,017	370,239	9.5	13,526	19,748	7,062	11,365	11,731	18,880	18,617	27,180
Russia	590,000	949,000	79	10,499,000	407,000	14	987	1,441	94,400	152,000	119,200	191,900	830,900	1,213,100
Rwanda	9,050	14,565	10	11,900	15,900	216	140	200	—	—	—	—	—	—
St. Kitts and Nevis	193	310	43	4,000	700	10	...	...	—	—	—	—	—	—
St. Lucia	500	805	56	10,500	9,500	7.1	...	...	—	—	—	—	—	—
St. Vincent and the Grenadines	634	1,020	31	4,600	2,900	15	...	...	—	—	—	—	—	—
San Marino	147	237	...	23,561	4,013	0.9	...	...	—	—	—	—	—	—
São Tomé and Príncipe	149	240	42	2,600	300	39	...	...	—	—	—	—	—	—
Saudi Arabia	96,986	156,084	40	1,671,200	1,146,600	6.2	57,859	84,473	864[2]	1,390[2]	87	140	621	907
Senegal	8,873	14,280	28	102,000	46,000	53	375	547	562	904	108	174	418	610
Seychelles	206	331	76	5,000	2,000	11	...	...	—	—	—	—	—	—
Sierra Leone	7,254	11,674	11	20,860	11,014	141	36	53	52	84	...	...	...	...
Singapore	1,857	2,989	97	363,906	137,151	6.0	...	...	42	67	29	29	29	29
Slovakia	11,116	17,889	...	994,046	93,560	4.9	3,533	5,158	2,275	3,661	2,826	4,548	8,381	12,236
Slovenia	9,158	14,739	79	657,287	36,607	2.9	1,190	1,740	746	1,201	376	590	1,677	2,448
Solomon Islands	840	1,352	35	2,052	2,574	75	...	...	—	—	—	—	—	—
Somalia	14,000	22,500	25	11,800	12,200	278	...	...	—	—	—	—	—	—
South Africa	113,294	182,329	30	3,814,904	1,596,812	7.4	1,053	1,538	13,237[2]	21,303[2]	556	895	62,605	91,402
Spain	212,030	341,230	99	13,733,794	2,952,838	2.3	53,914	78,713	7,858[2]	12,646[2]	9,229	14,853	5,960	8,702
Sri Lanka	16,158	26,004	81	210,013	231,713	40	2,617	3,821	928[2]	1,493[2]	2,028	3,264	99	144
Sudan, The	12,864	20,703	10	116,000	57,000	143	...	...	2,960[2]	4,764[2]	735	1,183	1,534	2,240
Suriname	2,778	4,470	26	44,300	17,050	7.0	...	...	187	301	...	...	...	...
Swaziland	1,793	2,885	28	27,135	8,162	25	...	...	187	301	752	1,210	1,993	2,910
Sweden	84,419	135,859	72	3,594,000	318,000	2.3	20,800	30,400	6,710	10,798	3,759	6,051	13,059	19,066
Switzerland	44,334	71,348	96	3,165,043	270,915	2.0	7,108	10,378	3,125	5,029	7,643	12,300	5,515	8,052
Syria	22,528	36,255	77	119,400	160,500	49	1,075	1,570	1,097[2]	1,766[2]	531	855	751	1,097
Taiwan	11,830	19,038	89	3,874,200	810,300	4.5	9,326	13,616	2,410	3,879	5,902	9,499	1,300	1,900
Tajikistan	8,000	13,000	93	184,900	3,600	30	3,518	5,136	300	500	6,094	9,808	7,617	11,121
Tanzania	54,743	88,100	4	47,500	38,000	323	...	...	2,218	3,569	2,324	3,740	1,021	1,490
Thailand	36,310	58,435	79	1,325,477	2,720,383	15	...	...	2,405[2]	3,870[2]	9,007	14,496	2,095	3,059
Togo	4,672	7,519	32	67,936	31,986	41	...	...	326	525	82	132	12	17
Tonga	240	386	76	3,400	3,900	14	...	...	—	—	—	—	—	—
Trinidad and Tobago	4,970	8,000	50	123,500	24,500	8.5	...	...	—	—	—	—	—	—
Tunisia	18,133	29,183	60	320,000	183,700	17	678	990	1,337[2]	2,152[2]	636	1,038	1,524	2,225
Turkey	236,759	381,028	15	2,862,000	942,000	16	67,017	97,843	5,252	8,452	3,967	6,385	5,654	8,254
Turkmenistan	14,600	23,500	81	170,600	...	...	3,283	4,793	1,317	2,120	...	...	—	—
Tuvalu	5	8	—	...	...	...	...	...	—	—	—	—	—	—
Uganda	16,653	26,800	8	24,400	25,246	397	...	...	770[2]	1,240[2]	205	330	60	87
Ukraine	107,035	172,257	95	4,510,000	...	...	15,800	23,100	14,509	23,350	47,200	75,900	232,000	338,000
United Arab Emirates	2,830	4,555	100	300,000	75,000	5.9	...	...	—	—	—	—	—	—
United Kingdom	241,804	389,147	100	20,479,000	2,753,000	2.5	105,000	153,000	23,518[43]	37,849[43]	17,806	28,656	8,073	11,786
United States	3,906,544	6,286,985	91	133,930,000	75,783,000	1.2	1,096,000	1,600,000	137,000	220,000	13,138	21,144	1,183,000	1,727,000
Uruguay	32,311	52,000	23	310,833	148,644	6.8	500	730	1,867[2]	3,004[2]	87.4	140.6	139.2	203.2
Uzbekistan	26,843	43,200	83	865,300	14,500	25	15,037	21,954	2,200	3,500	3,300	5,200	48,400	70,600
Vanuatu	702	1,130	21	4,000	2,300	26	...	...	—	—	—	—	—	—
Venezuela	58,081	93,472	32	1,507,309	474,466	11	...	...	226[2]	363[2]	27	44	18	26
Vietnam	65,895	106,048	26	...	...	...	1,462	2,134	1,619	2,605	1,140	1,834	661	965
Virgin Islands (U.S.)	532	856	100	47,255	14,868	1.6	...	...	—	—	—	—	—	—
West Bank	...	...	...	69,200	20,723	13	...	...	...	...	...	...	—	—
Western Sahara	3,900	6,200	23	6,284	424	20	...	...	—	—	—	—	—	—
Western Samoa	1,296	2,085	19	1,000	900	86	...	...	—	—	—	—	—	—
Yemen	40,144	64,605	8	229,084	282,615	31	...	...	—	—	—	—	—	—
Yugoslavia	29,771	47,912	59	1,406,000	132,100	6.8	14,929[46]	21,796[46]	2,461	3,960	1,569	2,525	950	1,387
Zaire	95,708	154,027	...	94,000	86,000	236	...	...	3,162	5,088	360[47]	580[47]	1,258[47]	1,836[47]
Zambia	24,170	38,898	18	142,000	73,500	44	...	...	791	1,273	166.7	268.3	735.6	1,074
Zimbabwe	56,606	91,099	17	310,412	30,182	30	...	...	1,714[2]	2,759[2]	355.1	571.4	3.7	5.4

[1]Ariana Afghan Airlines only. [2]Route length. [3]Air Algérie international flights only. [4]TAAG airline only. [5]Aerolineas Argentinas only. [6]Included in Netherlands Antilles. [7]Government railways only. [8]Including Gulf Air international traffic. [9]Caribbean Airways only. [10]Caribbean Air Cargo only. [11]Air Afrique only. [12]Air Botswana only. [13]For industrial purposes only. [14]LASCA only. [15]Traffic between Ouagadougou, Burkina Faso, and Abidjan, Côte d'Ivoire. [16]Air Ivoire only. [17]Data refer to former Czechoslovakia. [18]Including SAS international and domestic traffic. [19]National roads only. [20]Includes 62 mi (100 km) of the Chemin de Fer Djibouti-Éthiopien (CDE) in Djibouti. [21]Air France and UTA only. [22]TAN and SAHSA airlines only. [23]Includes transshipments. [24]El Al only.

merchant marine				air					canals and inland waterways (latest)				country
fleet, 1992 (vessels over 100 gross tons)	total dead-weight tonnage, 1992 ('000)	international cargo (latest) loaded metric tons ('000)	off-loaded metric tons ('000)	airports with scheduled flights, 1996	traffic (latest) passengers passenger-mi ('000,000)	passenger-km ('000,000)	cargo short ton-mi ('000,000)	metric ton-km ('000,000)	length mi	km	cargo short ton-mi ('000,000)	metric ton-km ('000,000)	
154[32]	1,053.6[32]	18,560	18,715	5	234[33]	377[33]	1.2[33]	1.8[33]	...	...	...	...	Netherlands Antilles
17	18.1	1,040	930	10	145[34]	233[34]	3.4[34]	4.9[34]	...	...	...	...	New Caledonia
139	279.8	18,408	11,088	36	11,012	17,723	395	577	1,000	1,609	1,503	2,195	New Zealand
25	1.3	320	1,629	10	44.8	72.2	4.8	7.0	1,379	2,220	...	...	Nicaragua
—	—	—	—	6	138.5	222.8	10.5	15.3	186	300	13	19	Niger
271	733.3	80,607	10,812	12	567	913	66	96	5,328	8,575	...	...	Nigeria
2	0.9	...	...	3	...	...	...	...	...	...	...	...	Northern Mariana Islands
1,630	2,143.3	135,432	23,760	50	5,341[18]	8,596[18]	629[18]	918[18]	980	1,577	5,920	8,650	Norway
26	11.7	33,843	2,492	6	1,719[8]	2,766[8]	77.7[8]	113.5[8]	...	...	...	...	Oman
73	513.8	5,976	24,684	34	6,570	10,573	305	445	...	...	...	...	Pakistan
4	...	...	...	1	...	...	...	...	...	...	...	...	Palau
5,217	79,255.6	126,564	70,656	10	236	380	3.6	5.3	497	800	...	...	Panama
87	40.9	2,463	1,784	129	458.8	738.4	56.4	82.4	6,798	10,940	...	...	Papua New Guinea
38	38.5	...	...	5	791	1,273	16.5	24.1	1,900	3,100	...	...	Paraguay
623	615.6	10,197	5,077	27	1,197	1,926	147	214	5,300	8,600	...	...	Peru
1,499	13,807.1	12,864	34,128	21	8,948[35]	14,401[35]	255.9[35]	373.6[35]	2,000	3,219	...	...	Philippines
644	4,314.3	28,704	14,832	12	2,489	4,005	42	62	2,484	3,997	600	876	Poland
326	1,129.3	4,068	16,044	14	4,714	7,586	123	180	510	820	...	...	Portugal
13	...	...	...	7	...	...	...	...	...	...	...	...	Puerto Rico
65	635.6	18,145	2,588	1	1,719[8]	2,766[8]	77.4[8]	113.0[8]	...	...	...	...	Qatar
7	33.5	399	1,975	1	...	...	...	...	...	...	...	...	Réunion
439	4,845.5	14,676	21,684	12	1,603	2,580	13.3	19.4	1,071	1,724	2,128	3,107	Romania
4,543	16,592.3	22,488	1,632	58	47,649	76,683	5,360	7,825	63,380	100,000	96	140	Russia
—	—	—	—	3	1.2	2.0	...	...	...	...	...	...	Rwanda
1	0.6	24	36	2	...	...	...	...	...	...	...	...	St. Kitts and Nevis
7	2.1	150	234	2	...	...	...	...	...	...	...	...	St. Lucia
881	7,044.2	80	140	4	...	...	...	...	...	...	...	...	St. Vincent and the Grenadines
—	—	—	—	—	...	...	...	...	—	—	—	—	San Marino
4	2.3	16	45	2	5	8	0.7	1.0	...	...	...	...	São Tomé and Príncipe
301	1,381.7	214,070	46,437	25	11,500	18,501	556	895	...	...	...	...	Saudi Arabia
183	27.5	2,591	2,477	7	138.5[28]	222.8[28]	10.5[28]	15.3[28]	557	897	...	...	Senegal
9	3.3	11	348	2	389	626	48	70	...	...	...	...	Seychelles
62	18.4	1,802	533	1	34[36]	55[36]	3[36]	5[36]	500	800	447	652	Sierra Leone
946	14,929.2	129,996	174,996	1	30,074	48,400	2,511	3,666	...	...	...	...	Singapore
...	...	...	...	2	37.5	60.3	3.8	5.6	...	...	1,005	1,468	Slovakia
22	596.9	...	...	1	341	548	2,431	3,549	...	...	12,175	17,775	Slovenia
33	5.0	278	349	30	117.1[37]	188.4[37]	...	...	...	...	...	...	Solomon Islands
28	18.5	324	1,007	1	81	131	3.0	5.0	...	...	...	...	Somalia
219	282.5	104,889	16,449	24	8,139[38]	13,098[38]	174.6[38]	254.9[38]	...	...	...	...	South Africa
2,190	5,077.3	48,288	134,304	25	24,700	39,751	2,845	4,153	649	1,045	21,836[39]	31,880[39]	Spain
66	472.6	5,892	9,588	1	2,507	4,035	107	156	267	430	...	...	Sri Lanka
16	62.2	1,543	4,300	10	360[40]	580[40]	62[40]	91[40]	3,300	5,310	...	...	Sudan, The
24	15.7	5,776	1,286	2	375[41]	604[41]	48[41]	70[41]	746	1,200	...	...	Suriname
—	—	—	—	1	30.7	49.4	3	4	—	—	...	...	Swaziland
664	3,327.7	53,088	64,152	48	5,796[18]	9,329[18]	134[18]	196[18]	1,275	2,052	5,600	8,200	Sweden
24	602.8	...	...	5	12,257	19,725	1,033	1,508	40	65	127	186	Switzerland
94	210.4	17,868	5,676	5	589	948	11	16	541	870	...	...	Syria
649	9,241.3	148,371	254,248	13	23,766	38,247	2,336	3,410	...	...	234	341	Taiwan
...	...	...	...	1	1,386	2,231	140	205	...	...	...	...	Tajikistan
43	48.5	1,249	2,721	11	114	184	2.0	2.9	...	...	...	...	Tanzania
351	1,194.5	21,192	40,152	25	16,859	27,132	897	1,309	2,300	3,701	...	...	Thailand
8	20.6	148	709	1	134	215	10	14	31	50	...	...	Togo
15	13.7	15	104	6	5.8	9.4	0.01	0.01	...	...	...	...	Tonga
53	17.5	9,622	10,961	2	2,008	3,232	11.8	17.2	...	...	...	...	Trinidad and Tobago
77	443.3	7,500	11,880	5	1,338	2,154	139.5	203.6	...	...	...	...	Tunisia
880	7,114.3	21,089	46,374	26	5,887[42]	9,475[42]	147.0[42]	214.7[42]	750	1,200	209	305	Turkey
...	...	...	...	1	971	1,562	98	143	...	...	...	...	Turkmenistan
6	16.0	...	...	1	...	...	...	...	...	...	...	...	Tuvalu
2	...	...	...	1	32.4	52.1	0.5	0.7	...	...	...	...	Uganda
...	...	34,200	...	20	1,988	3,200	68	100	1,039	1,672	2,658	3,880	Ukraine
276	1,491.7	88,153	9,595	6	1,719[8]	2,766[8]	77.4[8]	113.0[8]	...	...	...	...	United Arab Emirates
1,631	4,687.3	177,408	178,944	50	60,582	97,498	2,017	2,945	1,424	2,291	34,400	50,200	United Kingdom
5,710	25,646.4	406,248[44]	582,024[44]	834	519,200	835,600	11,721	17,112	25,482	41,009	557,000	813,000	United States
93	172.5	710[45]	1,450[45]	1	304	490	32	46	1,000	1,600	...	...	Uruguay
...	...	...	...	9	3,017	4,855	306	447	...	...	...	...	Uzbekistan
280	3,259.6	80	55	29	88	142	9.6	14.0	...	...	...	...	Vanuatu
271	1,355.4	101,435	17,932	24	4,168	6,708	102	149	4,400	7,100	...	...	Venezuela
230	872.8	303	1,510	12	130	209	13	19	11,000	17,702	1,339	1,955	Vietnam
1	...	105.5	648.3	4	...	...	...	...	...	...	...	...	Virgin Islands (U.S.)
—	—												West Bank
—	—	40	15	1	...	...	...	...	...	...	...	...	Western Sahara
7	6.5	12	192	2	...	...	...	...	...	...	...	...	Western Samoa
40	13.7	1,936	7,829	11	756	1,217	85	124	...	...	...	...	Yemen
462[46]	5,173.1[46]	8	1	5	93	150	92	134	1,616[46]	2,600[46]	3,430[46]	5,007[46]	Yugoslavia
27	30.7	2,395	1,453	12	135[48]	218[48]	29[48]	42[48]	9,300	15,000	678	990	Zaire
—	—	—	—	4	192	308	6.8	9.9	1,398	2,250	...	...	Zambia
—	—	—	—	7	522	840	27	39	...	...	...	...	Zimbabwe

[25]Alitalia only. [26]Air Jamaica only. [27]Kenya Airways only. [28]International traffic only. [29]Peninsular Malaysia and Singapore. [30]Aeronaves de Mexico and Mexicana only. [31]Air Nauru only. [32]Includes Aruba. [33]Antillean Airlines only. [34]Air Caledonie only. [35]Philippines Air Lines only. [36]Sierra Leone Airlines international traffic only. [37]Solair only. [38]SAA only. [39]Coastal shipping only. [40]Sudan Airways only. [41]Suriname Airways only. [42]Turkish Airlines only. [43]British Railways only; excludes Northern Ireland. [44]Includes Puerto Rico. [45]Port of Montevideo only. [46]Data refer to Yugoslavia as constituted prior to 1991. [47]Zaire National Railways only. [48]Air Zaire only.

Communications

Virtually all the states of the world have a variety of communications media and services available to their citizens: book publishing and newspapers (although only daily papers are included in this table); postal services; radio and television broadcast systems; telephones; and cinema. Unfortunately, the availability of information about the structure and volume of these national services and sectors often runs behind the capabilities of the services themselves. Certain countries publish no official information; others publish data analyzed according to a variety of fiscal, calendar, religious, or other years; still others, while they possess such data almost simultaneously with the end of the business year, may not see them published except in company or parastatal reports of limited distribution. Even when such data are published in national statistical summaries, it may be only after a delay of up to several years. Figures in italics are from 1989 or earlier.

The data also differ in their completeness and reliability. Figures for book production, for example, generally include all works published in separate bindings except advertising works, timetables, telephone directories, price lists, catalogs of businesses or exhibitions, musical scores, maps, atlases, and the like. The figures include government publications, school texts,

theses, offprints, series works, and illustrated works, even those consisting principally of illustrations. Figures refer to works actually published during the year of survey, usually by a registered publisher, and deposited for copyright. A book is defined as a work of 49 or more pages, a pamphlet as a work of from 5 to 48 pages. A work published simultaneously in more than one country is counted as having been published in each. Newspaper statistics are especially difficult to collect and compare. Newspapers continually are founded, cease publication, merge, or change frequency of publication. Data on circulation, sales, and readership are often incomplete, slow to be aggregated at the national level, or regarded as proprietary. In some countries circulation data are virtually nonexistent. In others no daily newspaper exists.

Post office statistics are compiled mainly from the Universal Postal Union's annual summary *Statistique des services postaux*. Postal services, unlike the other media discussed earlier, tend most often to be operated by a single national service, to cover a country completely, and to record traffic data according to broadly similar schemes (although the details of *classes* of mail handled may differ). Some countries do not enumerate

Communications

country	publishing (latest)							daily newspapers (latest)		
	number of titles				number of copies ('000)					
	books		periodicals	pamphlets	books		periodicals	pamphlets	number	total circulation ('000)	circulation per 1,000 population
	total	school textbooks			total	school textbooks					
Afghanistan	1,776	150	*105*	1,019	...	...	...	...	16	206	12
Albania	363	190	*143*	18	3,498	3,110	*3,477*	270	4	165	49
Algeria	454	15	48	52	...	...	803	...	5	1,000	38
American Samoa	...	...	...	...	...	...	...	...	—	—	—
Andorra	56	5	...	...	...	...	...	...	3	4	67
Angola	...	...	...	...	...	...	...	...	4	116	12
Antigua and Barbuda	...	...	...	...	...	...	...	...	—	—	—
Argentina	5,628	736	...	...	49,293	4,720	...	...	190	4,780	143
Armenia	817[3]	...	40	3	10,100[3]	...	5,064	3	7	84	24
Aruba	...	...	...	...	...	...	...	...	5	...	...
Australia	*6,800*	*487*	...	3,923	...	...	...	...	69	4,600	265
Austria	3,786	...	2,481	...	...	...	...	...	27	3,108	398
Azerbaijan	530	29	49	69	7,961	2,276	801	993	6	427	59
Bahamas, The	15	...	...	...	16	...	...	...	3	35	133
Bahrain	...	...	26	...	...	...	73	...	3	43	83
Bangladesh	*1,209*	...	...	60	...	...	...	...	51	710	6
Barbados	17	...	52	60	...	...	...	...	2	41	160
Belarus	2,033	132	155	893	81,716	11,112	3,765	16,635	10	1,899	186
Belgium	13,913	...	13,706	...	...	...	...	...	33	3,100	310
Belize	43	—	...	91	43	—	...	76	—	—	—
Benin	647	6	...	...	874	9	...	...	1	12	2
Bermuda	...	...	...	...	...	...	...	...	1	16	258
Bhutan	...	...	...	...	...	...	...	...	—	—	—
Bolivia	*365*	...	...	82	*365*	...	...	46	16	390	57
Bosnia and Herzegovina	966	...	92	...	7,540	...	1,887	...	2	518	131
Botswana	97	4	14	61	...	...	177	...	1	40	29
Brazil	27,557	2,754	...	...	189,933	73,857	...	...	373	8,500	55
Brunei	45	...	15	...	...	...	132	...	1	20	74
Bulgaria	4,797	1,022	745	974	47,378	13,175	3,097	7,978	46	1,464	164
Burkina Faso	...	...	37	...	...	...	24	...	1	3	0.3
Burundi	...	...	...	...	...	...	...	...	1	20	3
Cambodia	...	...	...	...	...	...	...	...	1	20	3
Cameroon	...	...	58	...	...	...	127	...	1	50	4
Canada	22,208	1,240	1,400	...	...	...	37,108	...	106	5,800	204
Cape Verde	9	—	...	1	9	—	...	1	—	—	—
Central African Republic	...	...	...	...	...	...	...	...	1	2	1
Chad	...	...	*10*	...	...	...	...	...	1	2	0.4
Chile	1,493	148	417	327	...	...	3,450	...	45	2,000	147
China	92,972	11,107	6,486	...	5,855,140	2,657,140	205,060	...	74	50,520	43
Colombia	1,481	44	...	...	11,314	700	...	...	46	2,100	63
Comoros	...	...	...	...	...	...	...	...	—	—	—
Congo	...	...	3	...	...	...	34	...	6	19	8
Costa Rica	230	1	...	14	...	...	...	...	4	322	101
Côte d'Ivoire	...	...	...	...	...	...	...	...	1	90	7
Croatia	1,721	149	352	373	...	...	6,357	951	9	2,404	532
Cuba	273	100	160	295	1,150	538	2,797	937	17	1,315	122
Cyprus	499	48	37	443	575	256	167	779	9	77	107
Czech Republic	6,824	319	1,168	1,379	...	...	...	...	55	6,000	583
Denmark	7,791	789	205	3,701	...	...	7,838	...	42	1,710	332
Djibouti	...	...	7	...	...	...	6	...	—	—	—
Dominica	...	...	...	...	...	...	...	...	—	—	—
Dominican Republic	...	...	...	...	...	...	...	...	11	265	36
Ecuador	717	...	199	...	...	...	...	...	36	688	64
Egypt	2,327	646	266	272	108,772	50,283	1,815	19,028	16	2,426	41
El Salvador	*15*	6	...	...	*63*	21	...	...	8	485	90
Equatorial Guinea	...	*17*	...	...	...	*17*	...	...	1	1	3
Eritrea	83	64	...	23	360	323	...	60	—	—	—
Estonia	1,340	112	312	625	9,624	1,385	...	2,689	7	239	155
Ethiopia	147	23	*3*	93	426	69	*14*	248	4	70	1
Faroe Islands	*148*	...	...	...	...	...	...	...	—	—	—

domestic traffic or may record only international traffic requiring handling charges.

Data for some kinds of communications apparatus and traffic are relatively easy to collect; telephones, for example, must be installed, and service recorded so that it may be charged. But in most countries radios may be purchased by anyone and turned on whenever desired; car radios are seldom enumerated or licensed separately. As a result, data on distribution and use of radio and television apparatus may be collected in a variety of ways—on the basis of numbers of subscribers, licenses issued, periodic sample surveys, census or housing surveys, or private consumer surveys. Statistics on commercial cinema attendance (usually those of the United Nations Educational, Scientific and Cultural Organization [Unesco] or national data) may refer to a variety of screening facilities, including fixed, mobile, or drive-in facilities.

The *Statistical Yearbook* of Unesco contains extensive data on book publishing, newspapers, radio and television, and cinema that have been collected from standardized questionnaires. The quality and recency of its data, however, depend on the completion and timely return of each questionnaire by national authorities, and response rates depend on a variety of factors. In general, however, response rates for inquiries by international organizations in communications are better than in other fields because these organizations and the responsible authorities in each country must conduct day-to-day business and, hence, have a better ongoing relationship. The commercially published annual *World Radio TV Handbook* (Andrew G. Sennitt, editor) is a valuable source of information on broadcast media and has complete and timely coverage. It depends on data received from broadcasters, but, because some do not respond, local correspondents and monitors are used in many countries, and some unconfirmed or unofficial data are included as estimates. The statistics on telephones are derived mainly from the UN-affiliated International Telecommunication Union's *World Telecommunication Indicators* (annual) and refer to "main lines," or telephone lines that connect the subscriber's apparatus to the public, switched net.

... Not available.

—None, nil, or not applicable.

post offices, 1994				radio, 1995		television, 1995		telephones, 1993		cinema (latest)		country
number	persons per office	pieces of mail handled ('000)	pieces of mail handled per capita	receivers (all types; '000)	persons per receiver	receivers (all types; '000)	persons per receiver	main lines		annual attendance		
								receivers ('000)	persons per receiver	number ('000,000)	per 1,000 population	
...	...	...	...	1,670	11	100	181	29	770	...	...	Afghanistan
886	3,850	2,732	0.8	550	6.2	300[1]	111[1]	49	70	6.9	2,160	Albania
3,087	8,850	442,455	16	3,500	8.0	2,000	14	1,068	25	21.0	880	Algeria
...	...	...	...	20	2.9	8.0	7.1	6.0	6.5	...	...	American Samoa
...	...	...	...	10	6.3	22[1]	2.8[1]	29	2.4	...	...	Andorra
62	172,000	2,423	0.2	450	26	51	220	53	190	3.2	370	Angola
...	...	...	...	40	1.6	28	2.3	19	3.5	...	...	Antigua and Barbuda
5,187	6,590	352,261[2]	10[2]	21,500	1.6	7,165	4.8	4,115	8.1	18.0	550	Argentina
898[1,4]	3,840[1,4]	49,000[1,5]	14[1,5]	642[6]	5.6[6]	722[6]	4.7[6]	584	6.4	13.4	4,020	Armenia
...	...	...	...	40	1.8	19	3.8	20	3.3	...	...	Aruba
3,992	4,470	4,325,000	240	21,000	0.9	8,000	2.3	8,540	2.1	58.2	3,300	Australia
2,643	3,040	3,721,983	460	4,710	1.7	2,706	3.0	3,579	2.2	12.0	1,500	Austria
1,863	4,010	8,797	1.2	3,682[7]	1.9[7]	1,522[6]	4.7[6]	647	11	1.9	260	Azerbaijan
136	2,000	60,511	223	80	3.5	50	5.5	80	3.3	...	...	Bahamas, The
13	42,200	51,944[8]	95[8]	320	1.8	270	2.1	124	4.3	0.6	1,230	Bahrain
7,985[9]	13,100[9]	197,363[6]	1.8[6]	8,000	15	600	200	268	440	302.3	3,000	Bangladesh
17	15,400	1,052	4.0	300	0.9	65	4.1	83	3.2	...	...	Barbados
3,894	2,660	869,840[2,8]	84[2,8]	3,185[1]	3.3[1]	2,775[1]	3.7[1]	1,814	5.7	29.5	2,850	Belarus
1,639	6,150	3,533,196	351	5,000	2.0	4,200	2.4	4,396	2.3	18.6	1,840	Belgium
...	...	...	...	30	7.2	23	9.4	29	7.1	...	...	Belize
172	31,000	6,519	1.2	400	14	20	270	20	260	0.7	140	Benin
14[1]	4,290[1]	22,666[1]	378[1]	80	0.8	30	2.0	42	1.5	0.2	3,630	Bermuda
100[1]	16,000[1]	1,754[1]	1.1[1]	23	35	...	...	3.8	400	...	...	Bhutan
146	49,600	33,893	4.7	4,250	1.7	800[1]	8.8[1]	234	33	2.2	310	Bolivia
656[6]	6,630[6]	128,886[6]	30[6]	840	4.1	1,012	3.4	600[10]	7.3[10]	4.3	1,000	Bosnia and Herzegovina
173	8,340	36,358	25	300	5.2	14	111	44	32	...	...	Botswana
11,017	14,000	4,155,645[11]	27[11]	55,000	2.8	30,000	5.2	11,744	13	91.3	680	Brazil
6	46,700	15,653[8]	56[8]	120	2.4	90	3.2	55	5.1	2.3	11,900	Brunei
3,104	2,720	102,330[2,8]	12[2,8]	3,920	2.1	3,127	2.7	2,300	3.8	11.1	1,310	Bulgaria
66[12]	142,900[12]	13,689[12]	1.5[12]	225	46	46	244	22	460	6.0	720	Burkina Faso
27	227,000	7,602	1.2	300	20	4.5	1,320	16	390	0.1	24	Burundi
29	330,000	878	0.1	1,500	6.4	70	137	5.9	1,670	...	...	Cambodia
261	49,300	22,590[8,12]	1.8[8,12]	1,500	8.8	15	882	57	220	...	...	Cameroon
18,607	1,570	10,714,615[1,2]	370[1,2]	22,600	1.3	19,400	1.5	16,471	1.7	79.0	2,840	Canada
59	6,440	1,997[1]	5.4[1]	57	6.9	1.0[1]	371[1]	15	26	...	...	Cape Verde
33	98,200	...	...	180	17	7.5	419	6.7	480	...	...	Central African Republic
34	183,000	7,887	1.3	1,310	4.9	50	127	4.6	1,430	...	...	Chad
591	23,700	286,201[2]	20[2]	4,400	3.2	2,000	7.1	1,520	9.1	8.0	560	Chile
64,482	18,700	7,650,303[11]	6.3[11]	215,950	5.6	227,880	5.3	17,332	68	14,428.4	12,550	China
1,625	21,200	111,561	3.2	5,400	6.5	5,500	6.4	3,828	8.9	41.0	1,290	Colombia
36[1]	16,900[1]	901[1]	1.5[1]	61	8.9	0.2[1]	2,550[1]	4.0	130	...	...	Comoros
114	22,000	1,826	0.7	240	11	8.5	305	19	130	...	...	Congo
503	6,100	28,213[11]	9.2[11]	760	4.4	340	9.8	364	11	0.2	76	Costa Rica
287	47,700	26,980	2.0	1,600	8.9	810	18	94	140	7.3	550	Côte d'Ivoire
1,169	3,860	243,001	54	1,100	4.1	750	6.0	1,027	4.5	3.7	820	Croatia
1,545[1]	7,060[1]	27,868[1]	2.6[1]	3,608	3.1	2,500	4.4	344	31	23.8	2,180	Cuba
712	1,030	56,521	77	184	4.4	103	6.3	311	2.0	...	...	Cyprus
3,502	2,950	836,780	81	9,100	1.1	4,905[1]	2.1[1]	1,961	5.3	21.9	2,120	Czech Republic
1,291	4,030	1,848,124	355	5,200	1.0	2,700	10.2	3,060	1.7	10.2	1,970	Denmark
9[1]	62,200[1]	14,598[1]	26[1]	35	17	17	34	7.3	78	...	...	Djibouti
64	1,090	2,912	42	65	1.1	5.2	14	14	5.3	...	...	Dominica
206[1]	37,000[1]	9,800[1,8]	1.3[1,8]	1,180	6.6	728	11	552	13	...	...	Dominican Republic
374	30,000	18,820	1.7	3,240	3.5	900	13	598	19	6.8	650	Ecuador
7,162	8,140	242,132	4.2	16,450	3.6	5,000	12	2,375	24	16.5	300	Egypt
288	19,600	16,078	2.9	2,080	2.8	501	12	174	26	...	...	El Salvador
...	...	...	...	200	2.0	2.5	158	1.3[12]	290[12]	...	...	Equatorial Guinea
35	98,200	918	0.3	...	...	...	...	20	170	...	...	Eritrea
590	2,530	43,637[8]	29[8]	926[9]	1.7[9]	600	2.5	358	4.3	3.4	2,200	Estonia
481	114,000	28,905	0.5	9,000	6.1	150	367	133	400	...	...	Ethiopia
43	1,160	9,489	190	21	2.1	14	3.1	23	2.0	...	500	Faroe Islands

Communications (continued)

country	publishing (latest)								daily newspapers (latest)		
	number of titles				number of copies ('000)				number	total circulation ('000)	circulation per 1,000 population
	books		periodicals	pamphlets	books		periodicals	pamphlets			
	total	school textbooks			total	school textbooks					
Fiji	...	...	...	...	...	...	...	...	1	27	36
Finland	8,720	365	5,711	3,065	...	...	...	...	58	2,578	512
France	41,234	1,041	2,672	...	...	...	120,018	...	77	11,695	205
French Guiana	...	...	...	...	...	...	...	...	1	2	13
French Polynesia	...	...	...	...	...	...	...	...	4	24	117
Gabon	...	...	...	...	...	...	...	...	1	20	16
Gambia, The	15	...	10	6	6	...	885	1	2	2	2
Gaza Strip	...	...	...	...	...	...	...	...			
Georgia	1,659[3]	...	75	3	20,100[3]	...	29,700	3	147	3,677	671
Germany	67,206	3,311	9,010	...	...	...	395,036	...	357	25,952	323
Ghana	13	...	121	15	...	...	774	...	4	280	18
Gibraltar	...	...	...	...	...	...	...	...	2	4	150
Greece	4,066	...	309	...	...	...	...	...	145	1,400	135
Greenland	...	...	...	...	...	...	...	...	—	—	—
Grenada	...	...	...	...	...	...	...	...			
Guadeloupe	...	...	...	...	...	...	...	...	1	35	86
Guam	...	...	...	...	...	...	...	...	1	25	178
Guatemala	...	...	...	...	...	...	...	...	5	180	18
Guernsey	...	...	...	...	...	...	...	...	1	16	277
Guinea	...	...	3	...	...	...	5	...	1	13	2
Guinea-Bissau	...	...	...	...	...	...	...	...	1	6	6
Guyana	9	—	...	37	...	—	...	...	2	80	99
Haiti	188	17	...	83	...	...	...	...	4	45	7
Honduras	22	...	...	...	80	...	...	...	4	159	31
Hong Kong	...	...	598	...	...	...	...	...	49	4,750	822
Hungary	8,458	1,302	1,203	712	72,076	17,966	14,927	5,081	28	2,896	282
Iceland	943	133	629	384	...	...	...	...	5	135	519
India	11,658	311	...	1,110	...	...	...	...	2,300	27,500	31
Indonesia	6,128	715	117	175	...	...	3,985	...	68	4,591	24
Iran	6,822	...	318	...	26,275	...	6,166	...	13	1,250	20
Iraq	...	...	...	...	...	...	...	...	6	660	35
Ireland	...	...	...	...	...	...	...	...	8	652	186
Isle of Man	...	...	...	...	...	...	...	...	—	—	—
Israel	...	...	...	...	...	...	...	...	31	1,240	246
Italy	27,356	1,963	10,064	6,983	231,701	45,000	85,071	19,365	78	6,068	106
Jamaica	...	...	...	...	...	...	...	...	3	160	67
Japan	35,496	2,512	2,926	...	316,725	12,190	...	...	121	71,690	577
Jersey	...	...	...	...	...	...	...	...	1	24	300
Jordan	500	...	31	...	...	...	43	...	4	250	53
Kazakstan	1,226	...	88	...	30,512	...	33,300	...	450	6,700	405
Kenya	239	...	...	...	452	...	...	...	5	354	14
Kiribati	...	...	...	...	...	...	...	...	—	—	—
Korea, North	...	...	...	...	...	...	...	...	11	5,000	221
Korea, South	28,449	3,139	...	2,412	134,635	74,141	...	16,709	63	18,000	412
Kuwait	187	...	...	9	...	...	...	...	9	480	248
Kyrgyzstan	936[3]	...	50	3	9,700[3]	...	34,400	3	128	1,129	250
Laos	64	25	...	...	136	50	...	...	3	14	3
Latvia	1,298	112	170	316	12,148	1,346	1,912	2,262	17	258	98
Lebanon	...	...	...	...	...	...	...	...	16	500	185
Lesotho	...	...	...	...	...	...	...	...	2	14	7
Liberia	...	...	...	...	...	...	...	...	8	35	13
Libya	121	20	...	...	553	180	...	...	4	71	15
Liechtenstein	...	...	...	...	...	...	...	...	2	20	653
Lithuania	1,675	152	237	549	15,939	3,285	2,602	3,303	18	836	225
Luxembourg	417	...	508	...	...	...	...	...	5	145	372
Macau	...	...	16	...	...	...	...	...	9	250	510
Macedonia	492	178	74	67	1,537	810	347	146	2	56	27
Madagascar	86	31	63	57	178	62	191	359	7	48	4
Malawi	122	10	...	84	...	...	...	...	1	25	2
Malaysia	3,682	772	25	66	13,449	6,029	996	171	39	2,200	117
Maldives	...	...	...	...	...	...	...	...	2	3	13
Mali	...	...	...	...	...	...	...	...	2	41	4
Malta	320	14	359	97	...	...	...	...	3	54	150
Marshall Islands	...	...	...	...	...	...	...	...	—	—	—
Martinique	...	...	...	...	...	...	...	...	1	32	86
Mauritania	...	...	...	...	...	...	...	...	1	1	0.5
Mauritius	75	38	62	21	106	54	...	29	6	80	74
Mayotte	...	...	...	...	...	...	...	...	1	12	160
Mexico	2,587	101	182	21	...	...	28,016	...	292	10,231	116
Micronesia	...	...	...	...	...	...	...	...	—	—	—
Moldova	351	17	68	3	5,574	1,004	351	45	5	205	47
Monaco	41	...	3	...	722	...	38	...	1	8	258
Mongolia	121	37	45	164	438	370	6,361	521	3	208	92
Morocco	...	...	...	...	...	...	...	...	14	335	13
Mozambique	...	...	5	...	...	...	2,263	...	2	81	5
Myanmar (Burma)	673	...	...	...	...	...	...	...	2	324	7
Namibia	131	41	...	62	...	...	...	...	6	43	54
Nauru	...	...	...	...	...	...	...	...	—	—	—
Nepal	...	122	...	...	...	7,243	...	...	25	140	7
Netherlands, The	11,844	2,196	367	...	...	...	19,283	...	44	4,600	303
Netherlands Antilles	...	...	...	...	...	...	...	...	6	53	275
New Caledonia	11	...	...	3	...	...	...	...	3	23	133
New Zealand	...	...	...	...	...	...	...	...	31	1,050	305
Nicaragua	27	—	...	14	271	...	...	192	3	90	23
Niger	5	...	...	—	11	—	...	—	1	5	1

post offices, 1994				radio, 1995		television, 1995		telephones, 1993		cinema (latest)		country
number	persons per office	pieces of mail handled ('000)	pieces of mail handled per capita	receivers (all types; '000)	persons per receiver	receivers (all types; '000)	persons per receiver	main lines		annual attendance		
								receivers ('000)	persons per receiver	number ('000,000)	per 1,000 population	
261	2,950	28,757[8]	37[8]	450	1.8	13[1]	59[1]	54	11	...	...	Fiji
1,879	2,710	1,110,450[2]	218[2]	4,950	1.0	1,900	2.7	2,761	1.8	5.8	1,140	Finland
16,919	3,410	24,628,044	426	57,500	1.0	29,300	2.0	30,900	1.9	132.7	2,300	France
...	...	...	...	71	2.0	6.5	22	39	3.4	...	...	French Guiana
95	2,260	20,869	97	105	2.1	27	8.2	45	4.7	0.4	2,190	French Polynesia
59	21,700	5,071	4.0	155	7.5	40	29	30	41	2.0	1,810	Gabon
...	...	...	...	140	8.0	6.0	186	16	63	...	...	Gambia, The
...	...	...	...	...	...	...	...	...	...	...	...	Gaza Strip
...	...	1,026,922	188	...	...	...	...	571	9.6	30.4	5,530	Georgia
19,479	4,180	19,313,296	237	150,000	0.5	30,500	2.7	36,900	2.2	130.5	1,610	Germany
952	17,800	145,600	8.6	1,300	13	250	66	49	330	3.9	340	Ghana
3	10,000	10,368	346	17.2	1.6	7.5	3.7	14	2.1	0.17	5,830	Gibraltar
1,256	8,300	468,082	45	4,200	2.5	2,300	4.6	4,744	2.2	...	...	Greece
75	800	7,007	117	22	2.5	21	2.7	18	3.2	...	...	Greenland
58	1,590	...	...	45	2.0	15	6.1	20	4.5	...	...	Grenada
...	...	...	...	85	5.1	150	2.9	149	2.7	...	...	Guadeloupe
...	...	...	...	274	0.5	75	2.0	66	2.2	...	...	Guam
540	19,100	79,125	7.7	570	19	475	22	231	43	7.7	910	Guatemala
15	4,000	15,208[11]	253[11]	...	...	...	...	38	1.6	...	...	Guernsey
83	78,300	9,343	1.4	230	29	65	103	12	560	3.9	660	Guinea
24[12]	42,100[12]	410[12, 13]	0.4[2, 13]	40	27	...	...	8.6	120	...	...	Guinea-Bissau
85[1]	9,650[1]	4,582[1, 13]	5.6[1, 13]	350	2.2	15	51	41	20	13.0	17,200	Guyana
121	58,200	339,042	48	270	24	25	264	41	150	2.1	380	Haiti
64	90,200	13,810	2.4	1,910	2.9	160	34	117	48	...	...	Honduras
121	50,100	1,130,541	187	3,700	1.7	1,749	3.5	2,992	2.0	58.5	10,290	Hong Kong
3,223	3,180	1,296,344	126	6,250	1.6	4,262	2.4	1,498	6.9	14.8	1,440	Hungary
119	2,270	61,737	229	197	1.4	76	3.5	144	1.8	1.2	4,550	Iceland
152,786	6,010	13,215,938	14	65,000	14	20,000	47	8,037	110	4,300	4,960	India
13,629	14,100	774,520	4.0	26,000	7.5	11,000	18	1,713	110	133.2	770	Indonesia
6,721	8,890	264,200	4.4	13,000	4.7	7,000	8.8	3,598	17	29.0	500	Iran
343[12]	56,200[12]	48,807[12]	2.5[12]	3,700	5.5	1,000	20	675	29	...	...	Iraq
1,949	1,830	608,500	170	2,150	1.7	1,000	3.6	1,170	3.1	11.6	3,290	Ireland
32	2,190	20,411[8, 11]	292[8, 11]	...	...	...	...	...	...	...	...	Isle of Man
651	8,260	507,600	94	2,250	2.4	1,500	3.6	1,958	2.7	10.0	1,900	Israel
14,377[1]	3,970[1]	6,929,647[1]	120[1]	45,350	1.3	17,000	3.4	24,176	2.4	92.2	1,620	Italy
728[1]	3,310[1]	81,086[1]	34[1]	1,859	1.4	484	5.2	255	9.5	...	...	Jamaica
20,817	6,000	24,277,505	194	97,000	1.3	100,000	1.3	58,459	2.1	130.7	1,050	Japan
23[1]	3,650[1]	49,900[1]	594[1]	...	...	...	...	56	1.5	...	...	Jersey
946	5,490	124,681	24	980	4.3	250	17	288	14	0.2	52	Jordan
4,562	3,730	...	...	4,188[6]	4.0[6]	4,795[6]	3.5[6]	1,559	11	39.3	2,310	Kazakstan
1,072	27,300	385,798	13	3,000	9.5	500	57	215	120	5.8	220	Kenya
24[12]	3,130[12]	353[12]	4.7[12]	6.05	13	0.7	115	1.8	43	...	...	Kiribati
...	...	...	...	4,700	5.0	2,000	12	1,089	21	187.4	9,560	Korea, North
3,390	13,100	3,162,673	71	42,000	1.1	10,430	4.3	16,633	2.7	55.3	1,300	Korea, South
56	28,900	98,887[1]	68[1]	1,000	1.7	800	2.1	358	4.1	0.3	140	Kuwait
918	5,010	71,312	16	825	5.4	875[6]	5.1[6]	367	12	32.0	7,190	Kyrgyzstan
132	35,900	1,399	0.3	575	8.5	80	61	8.6	530	1.0	230	Laos
1,040	2,450	25,847	10	1,396	1.8	1,126	2.2	694	3.7	1.8	700	Latvia
...	...	...	...	2,247	1.3	1,100	2.7	350	11	99.3	35,200	Lebanon
140	14,200	87,448	44	1,100	1.9	250	8.2	10.5	179	...	...	Lesotho
...	...	...	...	600	4.0	45	53	3.8	590	...	...	Liberia
383	12,800	28,421[8]	5.8[8]	1,000	5.4	550	9.8	240	21	...	...	Libya
12	2,500	17,192[11, 12]	573[11, 12]	20[1]	1.5[1]	10[1]	3.0[1]	19	1.6	...	...	Liechtenstein
1,029[1]	3,620[1]	11,902	3.2	1,420	2.6	1,570	2.4	858	4.4	2.3	610	Lithuania
106	3,770	153,000	383	240	1.7	101	4.1	215	1.9	0.7	1,760	Luxembourg
14	28,400	14,006	35	115[14]	3.5[14]	70	6.1	135	2.9	2.7	6,400	Macau
266	8,050	26,514	12	382[1]	5.4[1]	350[1]	5.9[1]	324	6.8	0.3	150	Macedonia
921[1]	15,000[1]	29,048[1]	2.1[1]	2,300	6.4	130	114	35	370	0.4	31	Madagascar
305	35,600	102,723	9.5	1,060	9.4	...	...	33	290	...	...	Malawi
1,933	10,100	1,021,572	52	7,460	2.7	2,915[1]	6.5[1]	2,411	7.9	39.4	2,070	Malaysia
217	1,150	2,256	9.0	25	10	4.8	53	10	24	...	...	Maldives
122	85,800	2,040[1, 8]	0.2[1, 8]	1,600	5.6	10	901	14	670	...	...	Mali
50	7,280	135,754	373	90	4.1	145	2.6	158	2.3	0.3	830	Malta
...	...	...	...	...	...	...	...	2.3	23	...	...	Marshall Islands
...	...	...	...	71	5.5	65	6.0	150	2.5	1.1	3,150	Martinique
60	36,800	166	0.1	1,000	2.3	1.1	2,070	7.6	290	...	...	Mauritania
103	10,700	43,002	39	150	7.5	157	7.2	107	10	0.7	630	Mauritius
...	...	...	...	50	2.3	3.5	33	4.0	25	...	...	Mayotte
7,296	12,700	980,332	11	21,000	4.3	13,500[1]	6.5[1]	7,621	11	246.0	3,010	Mexico
...	...	...	...	70	1.5	7.0	15	6.1	18	...	...	Micronesia
1,309	3,320	96,241[11]	22[11]	1,421[6]	3.1[6]	1,264[6]	3.5[6]	524	8.3	4.7	1,090	Moldova
...	...	...	...	30	1.0	20	1.5	14	2.1	0.1	3,340	Monaco
358	6,600	3,181	1.3	280	8.2	135	17	66	36	20.1	9,720	Mongolia
1,378	19,300	227,746	8.6	5,100	5.3	1,210	22	281	32	20.4	790	Morocco
435	38,200	11,546	0.7	620	29	35	511	62	270	4.1	300	Mozambique
1,185	38,400	88,986	2.0	3,300	14	1,000	47	77[12]	560[12]	...	...	Myanmar (Burma)
90	16,700	89,743[12]	63[12]	230	7.2	39	42	70	22	...	...	Namibia
3	3,330	...	...	6.0	1.7	...	...	1.5[12]	6.7[12]	...	...	Nauru
2,461[1]	8,460[1]	327,602[1]	16[1]	625	32	250	80	72	290	...	...	Nepal
2,200	6,990	...	...	12,000	1.3	6,500	2.4	7,630	2.0	14.7	980	Netherlands, The
...	...	...	...	206	1.0	35	5.7	50[12]	3.8[12]	...	...	Netherlands Antilles
57	3,160	23,150	129	92	2.0	36	5.2	39	4.6	0.2	1,260	New Caledonia
...	...	...	...	3,100	1.2	1,100	3.2	1,593	2.2	...	...	New Zealand
202	21,800	11,411[13]	2.6[13]	925	4.7	210	21	67	60	5.0	1,750	Nicaragua
64	138,000	4,647[1]	0.5[1]	440	21	25	366	11	830	...	...	Niger

Communications (continued)

country	publishing (latest)								daily newspapers (latest)		
	number of titles				number of copies ('000)				number	total circulation ('000)	circulation per 1,000 population
	books total	books school textbooks	periodicals	pamphlets	books total	books school textbooks	periodicals	pamphlets			
Nigeria	1,022	340	92	540	...	...	495	...	26	1,850	18
Northern Mariana Islands	...	...	...	...			...	...	—	—	—
Norway	4,362	...	7,010	581	...	...	...	...	82	2,600	607
Oman	24	...	15	...	25	...	...	...	4	79	41
Pakistan	299	...	282	7	...	...	7,674	...	274	809	6
Palau	...	...	...	...	...	...	...	...	—	—	—
Panama	...	...	8	...	...	...	...	...	2	64	16
Papua New Guinea	58	3	...	64	...	...	...	...	5	168	37
Paraguay	129	25	...	23	...	...	...	...	59	1,590	71
Peru	1,371	14	45	735	...	...	90	...	8	223	90
Philippines	981	203	1,570	35	...	...	9,468	...	43	3,200	50
Poland	8,498	424	2,997	1,290	92,796	26,180	57,605	9,737	72	6,085	159
Portugal	6,089	1,391	866	...	21,234	10,602	7,050	...	25	465	47
Puerto Rico	...	...	...	...	...	...	...	...	3	507	141
Qatar	368	184	190	...	...	...	120	...	4	70	135
Réunion	50	1	...	19	...	...	...	...	3	55	88
Romania	3,662	...	1,379	...	66,598	...	...	...	76	7,500	324
Russia	22,088	807	2,592	6,929	851,638	143,377	918,218	98,223	339	57,367	387
Rwanda	131	42	15	76	746	552	101	2,109	1	0.5	0.1
St. Kitts and Nevis	—	—	10	3	—	—	44	3	—	—	—
St. Lucia	...	...	...	...	...	...	...	...	—	—	—
St. Vincent	...	...	...	...	...	...	...	...	—	—	—
San Marino	...	...	18	...	...	...	10	...	5	...	...
São Tomé and Príncipe	...	...	...	...	...	...	...	...			
Saudi Arabia	...	...	...	...	...	...	...	...	13	729	43
Senegal	...	...	123	...	...	...	381	...	1	50	6
Seychelles	...	...	...	...	...	...	...	...	1	3	45
Sierra Leone	...	...	...	...	...	...	...	...	1	10	2
Singapore	...	...	...	...	...	...	...	...	10	930	336
Slovakia	3,060	807	424	225	7,949	2,664	8,725	406	21	1,680	317
Slovenia	1,728	410	482	408	6,267	...	...	...	6	308	160
Solomon Islands	...	...	...	...	...	...	...	...	1	9	1
Somalia	...	...	...	...	...	...	...	...			
South Africa	3,002	254	11	1,749	28,359	13,234	2,149	8,454	20	1,248	32
Spain	36,236	2,282	...	4,522	165,339	24,787	...	17,890	148	4,100	104
Sri Lanka	1,515	93	...	1,689	11,888	8,502	...	5,043	10	480	27
Sudan, The	...	...	10	...	...	...	136	...	5	620	24
Suriname	...	...	...	...	...	...	...	...	3	43	105
Swaziland	...	...	...	...	...	...	...	...	3	12	15
Sweden	10,017	466	46	2,878	...	...	4,947	...	104	4,419	511
Switzerland	14,870	247	3,079	...	...	...	...	...	83	2,635	377
Syria	598	...	...	...	...	...	...	...	11	290	22
Taiwan	16,156	...	4,134	...	...	...	...	...	93	4,000	202
Tajikistan	787[3]	...	26	3	12,000[3]	...	481	3	9	116	21
Tanzania	127	23	...	45	275	46	...	89	3	220	8
Thailand	7,565	640	1,522	61	...	...	...	...	41	4,820	85
Togo	...	...	...	...	...	...	...	...	2	12	3
Tonga	...	...	...	...	...	...	...	...	1	7	72
Trinidad and Tobago	...	...	...	...	...	...	...	...	4	175	138
Tunisia	539	61	...	...	...	...	...	—	9	410	49
Turkey	5,568	603	1,325	410	...	...	1,325	...	399	4,000	71
Turkmenistan	386	27	33	179	4,435	1,678	12,800	2,169	66	1,141	319
Tuvalu	...	...	...	...	...	...	...	...	—	—	—
Uganda	162	—	26	...	...	—	158	...	6	80	4
Ukraine	4,145	156	321	857	74,151	17,667	3,491	13,416	90	6,083	118
United Arab Emirates	293	293	80	...	5,117	5,117	922	...	11	335	189
United Kingdom	88,032	2,157	...	6,983	...	...	...	...	101	22,100	383
United States	49,276	...	11,593	...	...	...	...	...	1,570	60,164	236
Uruguay	790	48	...	353	1,391	110	...	579	32	750	240
Uzbekistan	1,340	194	61	...	44,033	20,069	1,598	...	12	452	21
Vanuatu	...	...	...	...	...	...	...	...	—	—	—
Venezuela	3,934	...	...	...	...	...	...	...	82	4,200	205
Vietnam	...	...	...	...	...	...	...	...	4	570	8
Virgin Islands (U.S)	...	...	...	...	...	...	...	...	2	22	206
West Bank	...	...	...	...	...	...	...	...	—	—	—
Western Sahara	...	...	...	...	...	...	...	...	—	—	—
Western Samoa	...	...	...	...	...	...	...	...	4	236	19
Yemen	...	...	...	...	...	...	...	...	10	544	52
Yugoslavia	2,365	334	397	253	10,750	6,274	747	601	...	...	...
Zaire	64	14	...	...	535	112	...	...	9	112	3
Zambia	...	...	...	...	...	...	...	...	2	70	8
Zimbabwe	151	6	28	81	...	...	680	...	2	195	19

| post offices, 1994 | | | | radio, 1995 | | television, 1995 | | telephones, 1993 | | cinema (latest) | | country |
number	persons per office	pieces of mail handled ('000)	pieces of mail handled per capita	receivers (all types; '000)	persons per receiver	receivers (all types; '000)	persons per receiver	main lines receivers ('000)	persons per receiver	annual attendance number ('000,000)	per 1,000 population	
3,623	29,900	748,875	6.9	17,200	5.5	6,100	16	342	300	4.6	51	Nigeria
...	...	...	...	10.5	5.5	4.1	14	14	3.3	...	...	Northern Mariana Islands
2,414	1,790	2,107,318	488	3,342	1.3	2,000	2.2	2,335	1.8	10.9	2,530	Norway
76[6]	24,100[6]	61,321	30	900	2.4	1,500	1.4	148	8.6	...	...	Oman
13,285	9,530	411,443[11]	3.2[11]	10,200	14	2,080	68	1,605	76	25.3	230	Pakistan
...	...	...	...	9.0	1.9	1.6	11	...	...	...	...	Palau
205	12,500	17,434	6.8	527	5.0	205	13	262	9.8	...	...	Panama
108[6]	34,900[6]	38,686[6,13]	10[6,13]	300	14	100	43	40	100	...	...	Papua New Guinea
321	14,600	5,634	1.2	700	6.9	350	14	142	33	...	...	Paraguay
836	27,600	41,981[1]	1.9[1]	5,300	4.4	2,000	12	670	34	33.0	1,910	Peru
3,023	22,200	1,107,891	17	8,300	8.4	7,000	10	860	76	...	...	Philippines
7,468	5,160	1,315,218	34	16,300	2.4	10,000	3.9	4,419	8.7	14.9	390	Poland
7,053	1,390	994,007	101	2,495	4.0	1,771	5.6	3,260	3.2	7.8	790	Portugal
...	...	...	...	2,480	1.5	830	4.5	1,207	3.0	...	...	Puerto Rico
30	18,000	19,867[13]	37[13]	180	3.2	250	2.3	111	4.7	0.3	660	Qatar
...	...	...	...	170	3.9	91	7.2	199	3.1	...	...	Réunion
5,237	4,340	248,989	11	4,500	5.0	4,000	5.7	2,624	8.7	33.7	1,480	Romania
46,523	3,180	8,815,300[2]	60[2]	90,000[14]	1.6[14]	55,000[1]	2.7[1]	23,397	6.3	380.7	2,570	Russia
1	7,750,000	9,972[6]	1.4[6]	650[14]	12[14]	...	...	12	630	0.3	56	Rwanda
7	5,710	2,764	69	4.5	8.8	9.5	4.2	12	3.4	...	...	St. Kitts and Nevis
62[1]	2,260[1]	6,361[12]	45[12]	90	1.6	25	5.7	24	6.5	...	...	St. Lucia
103	1,080	526[6,13]	4.8[6,13]	65	1.7	18	6.2	17	6.7	...	...	St. Vincent
10	2,000	...	...	12.6	2.0	8[1]	3.0[1]	14	1.6	0.04	1,660	San Marino
10	12,000	246	2.0	31	4.2	21	6.2	2.4	52	...	...	São Tomé and Príncipe
1,266	13,800	636,134	36	3,800	4.7	4,700	3.8	1,575	11	...	...	Saudi Arabia
128	63,300	11,467	1.4	850	9.8	61	136	64	130	...	...	Senegal
5	14,000	4,507	64	50	1.5	13	5.8	11	6.2	...	...	Seychelles
71	62,000	1,645	0.4	1,000	4.5	25	180	15	310	...	...	Sierra Leone
1,110	2,640	613,177	209	822	3.6	650	4.6	1,246	2.3	30.7	20,600	Singapore
1,735	3,080	469,602	88	2,895	1.8	1,279[14]	4.2[14]	893	6.0	8.9	1,670	Slovakia
506	3,840	268,451	138	730[1]	2.7[1]	575[1]	3.5[1]	516	3.9	2.3	1,160	Slovenia
117[6]	2,820[6]	4,289[1]	12[1]	38	10	...	...	5.3	65	...	...	Solomon Islands
...	...	...	...	300	22	118[1]	55[1]	15	560	...	...	Somalia
2,198	18,400	2,465,620	61	11,200	3.3	3,485	12	3,660	11	26.0	680	South Africa
4,845	8,090	4,372,044	112	12,600	3.1	17,240	2.3	14,254	2.7	87.7	2,240	Spain
4,105	4,350	460,840	26	3,300	5.5	700	26	158	111	27.2	1,540	Sri Lanka
589	49,100	9,523[8]	0.3[8]	5,755	4.9	250	112	64	440	13.0	600	Sudan, The
...	...	...	...	262	1.6	43	10	47	8.6	...	...	Suriname
66	13,300	25,277	29	117	7.8	12.5	73	16	56	...	...	Swaziland
1,786	4,920	4,328,815	492	7,450	1.2	3,750	2.4	5,903	1.5	15.7	1,800	Sweden
3,642	1,920	4,229,598[12]	615[12]	5,600	1.3	2,602	2.7	4,266	1.6	15.9	2,290	Switzerland
637	21,800	17,392	1.3	3,000	4.8	700	20	550	24	4.0	300	Syria
14,079	1,500	2,032,127	96	8,620	2.5	7,000	3.0	7,951	2.6	64.2	3,200	Taiwan
738	7,790	...	...	854[12]	6.5[12]	860[12]	6.3[12]	260	22	12.7	2,250	Tajikistan
885[1]	31,700[1]	82,171[1]	2.9[1]	3,500	8.0	80	351	85	313	1.9	80	Tanzania
4,264	13,900	1,138,852	19	10,000	5.9	3,300	18	2,185	27	...	...	Thailand
51	77,100	3,511[1]	0.9[1]	720	5.7	150	28	17	230	...	...	Togo
108[12]	930[12]	4,014[12]	40[12]	52	1.9	2.5	40	5.9	16	...	...	Tonga
242	5,210	27,887	22	550	2.3	250	5.1	193	6.7	...	...	Trinidad and Tobago
947	9,230	144,522[12]	17[12]	1,700	5.2	650	14	421	20	...	...	Tunisia
34,692	1,760	1,428,990	23	8,800	7.1	10,530	5.9	10,936	5.4	16.5	290	Turkey
580[4,6]	6,490[4,6]	244,027[6]	65[6]	823[6]	4.6[6]	705[6]	5.3[6]	265	15	46.0	12,200	Turkmenistan
...	...	...	...	3.0	3.1	...	...	0.12	77	...	...	Tuvalu
319[12]	60,400[12]	17,239[1]	0.9[1]	1,800	10	115	162	21	830	...	...	Uganda
16,247	3,200	1,506,073[1]	29[1]	41,700[1]	1.2[1]	17,500[1]	3.0[1]	2,225	6.7	126.7	2,430	Ukraine
161	11,600	145,878	78	490	4.5	170	13	624	2.6	...	...	United Arab Emirates
19,603	2,980	17,468,000[11]	299[11]	65,400	0.9	20,000	2.9	28,681	2.0	113.4	1,950	United Kingdom
50,087	5,200	175,484,968	673	520,000	0.5	215,000	1.2	148,084	1.7	981.9	3,890	United States
168	18,900	18,210	5.7	1,850	5.7	600	5.3	530	5.9	6.2	2,110	Uruguay
3,800[4,6]	5,520[4,6]	1,537,874[6]	73[6]	3,677[6]	5.7[6]	3,308[6]	6.3[6]	1,452	15	29.0	1,320	Uzbekistan
...	...	...	...	55	3.1	2.0[1]	80[1]	4.1	39	...	...	Vanuatu
465	45,500	89,758	4.2	8,300	2.6	3,701	5.9	2,083	10	19.0	910	Venezuela
...	...	...	...	7,000	11	2,500	30	260	270	239.9	3,680	Vietnam
...	...	...	...	100	1.0	32	3.1	59	1.7	...	...	Virgin Islands (U.S.)
...	...	...	...	...	...	...	...	...	...	...	...	West Bank
...	...	...	...	...	...	...	...	...	...	...	...	Western Sahara
38	4,740	1,078	6.0	75	2.2	5.0	33	6.5	25	...	...	Western Samoa
269	47,100	5,320	0.4	665	20	100	131	162	83	...	...	Yemen
1,569[12]	6,650[12]	...	...	2,692	3.9	1,643	6.4	1,923	5.6	2.9	280	Yugoslavia
304	140,000	...	...	3,480	13	22	2,000	37	1,110	...	...	Zaire
421[1]	21,200[1]	25,131	2.7	603	16	200	47	78	110	...	...	Zambia
280	39,800	348,806	31	801	14	137	82	128	84	1.8	180	Zimbabwe

[1]1993. [2]Domestic only. [3]Books includes pamphlets. [4]Includes telephone and telegraph offices. [5]Letters dispatched only. [6]1991. [7]1988. [8]Letters only. [9]1989. [10]1990. [11]Domestic and foreign-dispatched only. [12]1992. [13]Foreign-dispatched and foreign-received only. [14]1994.

Trade: external

The following table presents comparative data on the international, or foreign, trade of the countries of the world. The table analyzes data for both imports and exports in two ways: (1) into several major commodity groups defined in accordance with the United Nations system called the Standard International Trade Classification (SITC) and (2) by direction of trade for each country with major world trading blocs and partners. These commodity groupings are defined by the SITC code numbers beneath the column headings. The single-digit numbers represent broad SITC categories (in the SITC, called "sections"); the double-digit numbers represent subcategories ("divisions") of the single-digit categories (27 is a subcategory of 2); the three-digit number is a subcategory ("group") of the double-digit (667 is a subcategory of 66). Where a plus or minus sign is used before one of these SITC numbers, the SITC category or subcategory is being added to or subtracted from the aggregate implied by the total of the preceding sections. The SITC commodity aggregations used here are listed in the table at the end of this headnote. The full SITC commodity breakdown—some 3,118 basic headings—is presented in the 1986 United Nations publication *Standard International Trade Classification, Revision 3*.

The SITC was developed by the United Nations through its Statistical Commission as an outgrowth of the need for a standard system of aggregating commodities of external trade to provide international comparability

of foreign trade statistics. The United Nations Statistical Commission has defined external merchandise trade as "all goods whose movement into or out of the customs area of a country compiling the statistics adds to or subtracts from the material resources of the country." Goods passing through a country for transport only are excluded, but goods entering for reexport, or deposited (as in a bonded warehouse, or free trade area) for reimport, are included. Statistics in this table refer only to goods and exclude purely financial transactions that are covered in the "Finance" and "National product and accounts" tables. Gold for fabrication (*e.g.*, as jewelry) is included; monetary and reserve gold are excluded.

For purposes of comparability of data, total value of imports and exports is given in this table in U.S. dollars. Conversions from currencies other than U.S. dollars are determined according to the average market rates for the year for which data are supplied; these are mainly as calculated by the International Monetary Fund (IMF) or other official sources. The commodity categories are given in terms of percentages of the total value of the country's import or export trade (with the exclusions noted above). Value is based on transaction value: for imports, the value at which the goods were purchased by the importer plus the cost of transportation and insurance to the frontier of the importing country (c.i.f. [cost, insurance, and freight] valuation); for exports, the value at which the goods were sold

Trade: external

country	year	imports total value ('000,000 U.S.$)	food and agricultural raw materials (0+1+2 −27−28 +4)	mineral ores and concentrates (27+28 +667)	fuels and other energy (3)	manufactured goods total[a] (5+6 −667 +7+8 +9)	of which chemicals and related products (5)	of which machinery and transport equipment (7)	of which other[a] (6−667 +8+9)	from European Union (EU)[b]	from United States	from Eastern Europe[c]	from Japan	from all other[d]
Afghanistan	1991[1]	936.4	15.0	—[2]	0.4	84.6[3]	2.1	48.2	34.3[3]	4.8[4]	0.2[4]	59.9[4,5]	7.9[4]	27.2[4]
Albania	1994	601.0	25.7[6]	—24.5[6]—		49.8[6]	9.3[6]	31.0[6]	9.5[6]	67.9[7]	0.2	9.9	—	22.0
Algeria	1994	9,598.7	36.4	0.4	0.6	62.7	11.0	27.0	24.7	59.7	14.3	1.7	2.6	21.7
American Samoa	1991	371.9	—6.3[2]—		15.9	77.8[3]	1.2	3.4	73.3[3,8]	—	28.7	—	3.8	67.5
Andorra	1995	1,055.5	30.6	3.0	3.5	62.9	10.1	21.9	30.8	85.7	4.2	0.1	3.4	6.6
Angola	1993	2,041.9	—32.4[2,6]—		0.7[6]	66.9[3,6]	10.6[6]	25.0[6]	31.3[3,6]	79.7[4]	7.2	0.9[4]	2.2	10.0[4]
Antigua and Barbuda	1991	245.9	—17.8[2]—		9.9	72.3[3]	6.2	26.8	39.3[3]	41.3[9]	29.5[9]	—[9]	—[9]	29.2[9]
Argentina	1994	21,581.1	6.8	1.1	2.9	89.2	14.0	52.0	23.1	30.0	22.8	0.7	2.9	43.6
Armenia	1994	393.8	—40.9[2]—		41.9	17.3[3]	2.0	3.3	11.9[3]	9.4	24.1	29.6	2.3	34.6
Aruba	1991	486.9	23.3	0.1	0.4	76.2	8.7	27.6	39.9	16.7	57.3	—	3.4	22.6
Australia	1995	61,286.0	—7.0[2]—		5.0	87.9[3]	11.1	47.0	29.9[3]	25.1	21.6	0.2	15.5	37.6
Austria	1994	55,058.5	8.4	1.2	4.4	85.9	10.4	38.0	37.5	68.4	4.4	7.5	4.3	15.5
Azerbaijan	1994	777.9	—29.3[2]—		32.0	38.6[3]	6.6	15.6	16.5[3]	9.0	1.3	29.9	—	59.8
Bahamas, The	1990	2,919.9	8.6	—	65.2	26.2	5.3	8.3	12.7	5.9	36.2	0.2[5]	0.5	57.3
Bahrain	1994	3,736.7	—11.8[2]—		33.4	54.8[3]	8.6	21.6	24.6[3]	18.5	10.9	—	5.6	65.0
Bangladesh	1993[10]	2,708.8	40.6	4.6	9.6	45.3	9.2	13.6	22.5	11.1	5.2	1.3	6.7	75.8
Barbados	1993	574.0	22.4	0.2	9.7	67.7	12.7	22.9	32.1	17.0	38.2	0.1	5.4	39.3
Belarus	1994	3,066.0	—37.3[2,11]—		11.1[11]	51.6[3,11]	10.0[11]	31.7[11]	10.0[3,11]	16.7	1.7	71.8	0.3	9.5
Belgium[12]	1994	125,762.3	13.3	9.6	6.8	70.2	13.2	25.5	31.5	75.0	5.3	2.3	2.7	14.7
Belize	1994	259.9	18.8	0.4	11.3	69.5	10.7	25.6	33.2	17.3	53.3	—	1.2	28.2
Benin	1991	408.0	—32.9[2]—		11.6	55.5[3]	7.5	13.7	34.4[3]	30.6	4.5	0.7	2.4	61.8
Bermuda	1993	588.9	20.5	0.1[2]	5.8	73.6[3]	13.9	23.3	36.3[3]	10.1[7]	70.2	—	5.4	14.3
Bhutan	1990	78.1	24.0	0.5	13.1	62.4	5.5	26.0	30.9	4.2	1.3	—	5.4	89.1[15]
Bolivia	1994	1,196.3	11.5	2.0	5.0	81.5	13.1	43.2	25.2	14.5	19.6	0.4	15.2	50.3
Bosnia and Herzegovina	1995	912.0[4]	...	...	31.6[6]	...	...	...	...	24.1[4]	3.4[4]	11.4[4]	—[4]	61.1[4]
Botswana	1994	1,636.6	21.1	2.7	5.7	70.5	7.7	29.6	33.2	7.5	1.9	0.1	2.1	88.5[18]
Brazil	1994	35,552.7	14.1	1.9	14.8	69.2	16.5	38.2	14.4	27.4	23.1	1.2	5.6	42.6
Brunei	1991	1,111.2	16.1	0.7	0.6	82.6	6.3	38.3	38.0	23.9	13.7	—	15.8	46.7
Bulgaria	1993	4,962.3	10.8	1.9[2]	35.1	52.2[3]	9.2	18.8	24.2[3]	29.8	3.6	37.4	1.3	27.9
Burkina Faso	1991	536.0	—25.6[2]—		11.6	62.8[3]	18.5	20.8	23.5[3]	40.4	4.9	0.3	4.2	50.1
Burundi	1993	204.5	13.0	0.6	12.4	74.0	14.1	21.3	38.6	45.4	1.8	0.4	9.2	43.3
Cambodia	1993	403.9	17.2[20]		11.7	...	6.5[20]	17.0[20]		9.2[4]	4.5[4]	2.5[4]	12.2[4]	71.6[4]
Cameroon	1991	2,306.2	16.8	6.2	3.4	73.6	14.7	27.1	31.7	64.6	6.6	0.4[5]	2.9	25.4
Canada	1995	164,333.6	7.4	1.9	3.6	87.1	8.1	51.5	27.5	10.0	66.8	0.4	5.4	17.4
Cape Verde	1990	136.3	30.7	—	7.5	61.8	6.1	30.7	24.9	68.7	2.4	3.0[5]	3.8	22.1
Central African Republic	1989	159.1	20.1	0.7	6.7	72.6	14.0	33.2	25.3	56.7	1.3	0.3	7.6	34.2
Chad	1992	243.0	25.1[24]	1.4[13,24]	1.6[24]	71.8[14,24]	15.1[24]	20.7[24]	36.0[14,24]	46.5[4]	2.5[4]	0.4[4]	1.6[4]	49.0[4]
Chile	1995	14,903.1	8.4	1.3	9.0	81.3	12.2	42.3	26.8	15.9	25.5	0.2	6.8	51.6
China	1995	132,083.5	12.2	2.6	3.9	81.3	12.9	39.9	28.6	16.1	12.2	3.7	22.0	46.1
Colombia	1994	11,889.5	11.1	0.7	2.7	85.5	16.3	41.0	28.2	20.4	32.0	1.1	9.5	37.0
Comoros	1993	67.8	25.9[20]	...	10.7	63.5	2.0[20]	9.0[20]		66.0[4]	—[4]	1.0[4]	2.0[4]	31.0[4]
Congo	1992	754.0[4]	18.9[25]	0.7[25]	1.7[25]	78.7[25]	9.1[25]	35.3[25]	34.3[25]	63.7[4]	8.8[4]	0.1[4]	2.9[4]	24.5[4]
Costa Rica	1992	2,789.1	8.9	0.3	8.7	82.0	16.3	25.5	40.3	11.0	49.7	0.3[5]	6.1	33.0
Côte d'Ivoire	1992	2,447.0[4]	—23.7[26]—		21.3[26]	55.0[26]	14.8[26]	16.4[26]	23.8[26]	56.0[4]	3.9[4]	0.1[4]	3.8[4]	36.2[4]
Croatia	1993	4,666.4	11.0	1.6	9.9	77.5	12.4	24.2	41.0	56.4	2.7	10.6	0.9	29.5
Cuba	1992	2,185.0	14.9[26]	0.5[2,26]	32.4[26]	52.2[3,26]	6.2[26]	27.5[26]	18.5[3,26]	30.0[4]	—[4]	9.0[4]	1.0[4]	60.0[4]
Cyprus	1995	3,712.3	21.7	0.4	7.7	70.1	8.8	27.6	33.7	51.6	13.0	6.4	6.7	22.3
Czech Republic	1994	14,787.5	11.6	1.9	10.1	76.3	13.1	34.9	28.3	55.6	3.4	27.8	2.0	11.2
Denmark	1995	41,626.4	15.6	0.5	3.4	80.4	11.6	33.2	35.7	68.7	4.7	3.7	2.7	20.3
Djibouti	1991	214.4	38.3	0.2	9.1	52.3	6.0	15.5	30.8	46.6	3.7	0.7[5]	7.2	41.8
Dominica	1991	109.6	27.6	0.3	7.9	64.2	12.0	21.6	30.5	21.2	31.4	0.3	5.6	41.5
Dominican Republic	1992	2,501.0	13.7[27]	0.3[27]	35.2[27]	50.7[27]	11.7[27]	23.2[27]	15.9[27]	15.8[4]	45.9[4]	0.1[4]	9.5[4]	28.7[4]
Ecuador	1993	2,552.7	7.4	0.3	1.7	90.6	15.5	49.1	26.1	24.3	31.7	1.2	13.5	29.2
Egypt	1994	9,592.1	33.2	1.4	1.4	63.9	12.2	29.1	22.6	40.0	16.9	6.3	4.2	32.7
El Salvador	1994	2,261.8	17.8	0.7	9.5	72.1	16.9	30.8	24.4	10.6	41.5	0.5	6.3	41.1

by the exporter, including the cost of transportation and insurance to bring the goods onto the transporting vehicle at the frontier of the exporting country (f.o.b. [free-on-board] valuation).

The largest part of the information presented here comes from the United Nations' *Commodity Trade Statistics* (including microfiche format) and *International Trade Statistics Yearbook*. These publications, however, cannot always provide the most recent data for all countries listed in this table and must be supplemented by national and regional sources. In some cases where the original data were only available for an alternative trade classification, an approximation has been made of the SITC commodity groupings.

The notes that follow further define the column headings.
a. Also includes any unallocated commodities.
b. EU of 15 countries (Austria, Belgium, Denmark, Finland, France, Germany, Greece, Ireland, Italy, Luxembourg, The Netherlands, Portugal, Spain, Sweden, and the United Kingdom).
c. Includes Albania, Bulgaria, Czech Republic, Hungary, Poland, Romania, Slovakia, and European republics of the former U.S.S.R. (Belarus, Estonia, Latvia, Lithuania, Moldova, Russia, and Ukraine).
d. May include value of trade shown as not available (...) in any of the four preceding columns. May include any unspecified areas or countries.

... Not available.
— None, less than 0.05%, or not applicable.
Detail may not add to 100.0 or indicated subtotals because of rounding.

SITC category codes

0	food and live animals
1	beverages and tobacco
2	crude materials, inedible, except fuels
27	crude fertilizers and crude minerals (excluding coal, petroleum, and precious stones)
28	metalliferous ores and metal scrap
3	mineral fuels, lubricants, and related materials (including coal, petroleum, natural gas, and electric current)
4	animal and vegetable oils, fats, and waxes
5	chemicals and related products not elsewhere specified
6	manufactured goods classified chiefly by material
667	pearls, precious and semiprecious stones, unworked or worked
7	machinery and transport equipment
8	miscellaneous manufactured articles
9	commodities and transactions not classified elsewhere

exports								direction of trade (%)					country
total value ('000,000 U.S.$)	Standard International Trade Classification (SITC) categories (%)												
	food and agricultural raw materials $(0+1+2 -27-28 +4)$	mineral ores and concentrates $(27+28 +667)$	fuels and other energy (3)	manufactured goods				to European Union (EU)[b]	to United States	to Eastern Europe[c]	to Japan	to all other[d]	
				total[a] $(5+6 -667 +7+8 +9)$	of which chemicals and related products (5)	of which machinery and transport equipment (7)	of which other[a] $(6-667 +8+9)$						
235.1	—— 63.0[2] ——		...	37.0[3]	...	...	...	7.3[4]	0.5[4]	70.2[4, 5]	0.3[4]	21.8[4]	Afghanistan
141.3	37.9[6]	—— 46.8[6] ——		15.3[6]	1.5[6]	0.8[6]	13.0[6]	76.2[7]	11.1	1.3	1.4	10.0	Albania
8,593.8	0.4	0.2	97.1	2.3	1.1	0.2	1.0	70.9	16.5	1.2	0.9	10.5	Algeria
326.9	65.9	—	—	34.1[8]	—	—	34.1[8]	—	100.0	—	—	—	American Samoa
48.9	8.6	2.7	0.2	88.6	5.9	40.2	42.5	99.6	—	0.1	—	0.3	Andorra
3,178.9	0.1	1.1	98.6	0.2[4]	—	—	0.2[4]	25.3[4]	64.4	0.5[4]	1.3	8.5[4]	Angola
39.8	—— 4.4[2] ——		25.0	70.6[3]	7.1	30.2	33.3[3]	15.0[9]	15.4[9]	—[9]	—[9]	69.5[9]	Antigua and Barbuda
15,838.7	55.2	0.2	10.4	34.2	5.9	11.2	17.1	24.8	11.0	0.5	2.8	60.9	Argentina
215.5	—— 6.0[2] ——		...	94.0[3]	6.0	20.0	67.9[3]	17.2	0.2	40.4	—	42.2	Armenia
37.5	12.6	1.0	3.1	83.3	3.8	11.9	67.5	6.7	9.7	—	—	83.6	Aruba
53,084.8	—— 39.8[2] ——		16.7	43.4[3]	4.0	12.8	26.6[3]	11.2	6.5	0.5	23.1	58.7	Australia
44,870.9	7.2	0.8	1.3	90.7	9.1	39.0	42.5	64.8	3.4	10.9	1.6	19.4	Austria
636.8	—— 11.0[2] ——		33.9	55.1[3]	6.0	15.5	33.6[3]	13.0	—	34.9	—	52.1	Azerbaijan
2,592.6	—— 4.9 ——		73.5	21.5	19.9	0.6	1.0	2.6	93.8	—	0.6	3.0	Bahamas, The
3,454.3	—— 2.5[2] ——		64.4	33.1[3]	2.2	1.6	29.2[3]	3.6[4]	4.3[4]	—	9.4[4]	82.7[4]	Bahrain
2,137.6	16.0	0.1	0.9	83.1	2.4	0.1	80.6	37.4	35.0	1.6	2.6	23.4	Bangladesh
181.0	29.2	0.4	16.1	54.3	14.4	18.0	21.8	18.1	18.6	—	0.6	62.6	Barbados
2,510.0	—— 14.1[2, 11] ——		2.1[11]	83.7[3, 11]	19.0[11]	45.9[11]	18.8[3, 11]	12.5	2.2	67.1	0.2	18.0	Belarus
137,393.5	11.9	7.6	3.0	77.4	17.0	28.1	32.3	75.3	5.0	2.0	1.3	16.4	Belgium[12]
142.9	73.3	0.1	2.4	24.1	1.4	5.8	16.9	35.4	44.3	—	0.1	20.2	Belize
43.0	—— 65.5[2] ——		29.0	7.5[3]	1.0	2.8	3.8[3]	18.6	18.7	—	0.4	62.3	Benin
35.3	5.6[11]	3.1[11, 13]	45.6[11]	45.8[11, 14]	9.5[11]	18.5[11]	17.8[11, 14]	27.0[11]	62.3[11]	—[11]	—[11]	10.6[11]	Bermuda
68.1	35.0	3.9	32.6[16]	28.4	16.6	0.1	11.8	0.2	—	—	—	99.8[17]	Bhutan
1,124.2	29.2	16.5	9.5	44.8	0.6	2.6	41.7	25.9	32.1	—	0.2	41.8	Bolivia
52.0[4]	...	...	...	...	9.4[6]	20.8[6]	...	61.5[4]	5.8[4]	...	—[4]	32.7[4]	Bosnia and Herzegovina
1,848.8	7.1	75.8	—	17.1	1.0	7.4	8.7	28.8	0.7	—	—	70.5[19]	Botswana
43,558.0	32.3	6.4	1.8	59.5	5.9	20.6	33.0	28.0	20.6	1.3	5.9	44.2	Brazil
2,466.5	0.5	—	96.7	2.7	0.1	1.3	1.3	0.5	1.1	—	62.6	35.8	Brunei
3,500.4	22.4	2.2[2]	8.7	66.7[3]	14.6	17.2	34.9[3]	28.2	3.4	22.4	0.4	45.6	Bulgaria
105.4	83.5	0.5	—	16.0	0.1	1.0	14.9	36.2	0.3	—	1.8	61.6	Burkina Faso
68.7	85.1	—	—	14.9	1.4	—	13.4	63.8[4]	2.0[4]	—[4]	0.7[4]	33.6[4]	Burundi
219.1[21]	88.9[22]	...	...	...	...	...	...	15.5[4]	0.5[4]	0.5[4]	37.6[4]	45.9[4]	Cambodia
2,892.5	35.3	...	47.5	17.2	0.7	7.5	9.0	61.3	0.4	0.3[5]	0.3	37.6	Cameroon
192,132.1	16.7	2.4	9.0	72.0	5.8	39.1	27.1	6.3	79.5	0.2	4.5	9.4	Canada
28.6	—— 18.4 ——		65.1	16.5	0.9	11.1	4.5	11.4	—	—	—	88.5[23]	Cape Verde
140.3	54.3	43.2	—	2.5	0.2	0.2	2.0	89.9	0.6	—	—	9.5	Central African Republic
261.0	88.2	—	—	11.9	6.5	3.1	2.3	42.9	0.8	0.8	7.3	48.2	Chad
15,901.1	37.2	16.1	0.2	46.4	3.5	1.8	41.1	22.0	13.4	0.5	17.9	46.3	Chile
148,779.6	10.1	1.1	3.6	85.2	6.1	21.1	58.0	12.9	16.6	2.0	19.1	49.4	China
8,916.8	41.5	5.1	20.1	33.4	5.9	5.8	21.7	30.7	35.8	0.4	4.0	29.1	Colombia
25.1	81.8	—	—	18.2	13.3	—	—	50.1	46.1	—	—	3.8	Comoros
910.0	18.1	2.1[2, 13]	66.0	13.7[3, 14]	—	0.2	13.5[3, 14]	51.5	36.5	0.25	—	11.8	Congo
1,833.7	65.3	0.1	0.5	34.0	5.6	3.3	25.1	24.8	48.4	0.2	0.7	25.9	Costa Rica
3,105.0	68.2	0.3[2, 13]	15.4	16.1[3, 14]	3.3	2.0	10.9[3, 14]	56.6	5.7	8.0	1.1	28.6	Côte d'Ivoire
3,903.8	17.7	0.6	9.7	72.1	14.5	14.2	43.5	57.5	2.1	7.7	—	32.6	Croatia
3,860.0	82.2	8.4[2, 13]	4.8	4.6[3, 14]	2.7	0.6	1.3[3, 14]	11.0[4]	—	76.2[5]	2.7	10.1	Cuba
1,237.4	51.0	1.2	3.7	44.1	6.4	12.2	25.6	34.7	1.2	29.4	0.2	34.5	Cyprus
14,318.5	11.9	2.0	5.7	80.4	9.9	26.1	44.5	54.4	2.1	29.0	0.6	13.8	Czech Republic
47,221.8	27.8	0.7	2.7	68.9	10.0	26.0	32.9	59.9	3.7	4.3	3.5	28.6	Denmark
17.3	32.5	—	—	67.5	0.4	8.3	58.7	62.6	0.8	—	0.9	35.7	Djibouti
54.2	67.2	0.4	—	32.4	23.7	4.2	4.4	61.2	5.2	—	—	33.6	Dominica
562.4	41.1	36.5[28]	—	22.4	1.2	2.9	18.3	21.4	53.9	0.1	3.0	21.6	Dominican Republic
3,020.0	49.3	0.1	41.4	9.3	1.1	2.3	5.9	16.3	46.3	1.8	1.7	33.9	Ecuador
3,474.5	16.3	0.5	39.2	44.1	4.6	0.5	38.9	44.0	10.5	3.3	1.4	40.8	Egypt
812.7	52.2	0.1	0.5	47.1	12.3	3.0	31.8	25.0	22.6	—	0.8	51.6	El Salvador

Trade: external (continued)

country	year	imports total value ('000,000 U.S.$)	food and agricultural raw materials (0+1+2-27-28+4)	mineral ores and concentrates (27+28+667)	fuels and other energy (3)	manufactured goods total[a] (5+6-667+7+8+9)	of which chemicals and related products (5)	of which machinery and transport equipment (7)	of which other[a] (6-667+8+9)	from European Union (EU)[b]	from United States	from Eastern Europe[c]	from Japan	from all other[d]
Equatorial Guinea	1990	61.6	13.5	3.4	7.7	75.4	3.9	58.2	13.3	31.5	39.9	—	0.3[4]	28.3
Eritrea	1993	204.6	—23.8—			76.2	5.5	37.3	33.3	32.6[7]	...	...	...	67.4
Estonia	1995	2,538.3	21.4	0.8	11.0	66.9	11.5	29.5	25.9	66.0	2.4	23.4	1.9	6.3
Ethiopia	1993	771.6	17.4	0.1	21.6	60.9	13.8	26.8	20.3	39.3	9.5	—	4.1	47.2
Faroe Islands	1994	238.2	30.7	0.6	11.8	56.8	8.5	19.8	28.5	67.5	1.4	3.6	2.0	25.5
Fiji	1994	830.5	15.9	0.3	11.2	72.5	7.3	30.9	34.3	3.9	14.8	0.1	8.0	73.3
Finland	1995	28,930.3	9.5	3.5	8.6	78.4	12.3	38.8	27.3	59.9	7.1	10.7	6.3	16.1
France[31]	1995	273,387.4	13.3	1.1	6.8	78.8	12.5	35.4	30.8	63.9	7.8	2.4	3.5	22.4
French Guiana	1995	783.3	18.8	0.1	5.3	75.8	8.0	42.2	25.6	76.9	3.3	0.5	1.4	17.9
French Polynesia	1988	808.3	20.4	0.2	5.4	74.1	6.4	35.9	31.8	65.5	11.3	0.1	4.4	18.6
Gabon	1992	1,072.0[4]	—12.1[2,6]—		1.9[6]	86.0[3,6]	8.3[6]	42.0[6]	35.7[3,6]	85.4[4]	5.6[4]	0.6[4]	5.4[4]	3.0[4]
Gambia, The	1992	234.2	—39.6[2]—		8.0	52.4[3]	5.8	19.9	26.7[4]	41.3[4]	2.9[4]	2.6[4,5]	2.9[4]	50.4[4]
Gaza Strip	1994	339.3	...	...	...	...	...	...	...	...	...	...	...	100.0[32]
Georgia	1992	216.0[4]	—21.4[2]—		61.2	17.4[3]	2.1	4.2	11.1[3]	5.1[4]	7.4[4]	34.7[4]	2.3[4]	50.5[4]
Germany	1994	377,992.3	12.5	1.6	7.0	79.0	8.8	33.7	36.5	55.5	7.3	7.2	5.6	24.5
Ghana	1992	2,174.7	—15.6[2]—		17.4	66.9[3]	11.1	33.6	22.2[3]	43.6	10.2	1.4	6.6	38.2
Gibraltar	1994	485.6[35]	—24.4[2,36]—		20.7[36]	54.9[3,36]	4.3[36]	21.4[36]	29.2[3,36]	74.9	...	...	3.4	21.7
Greece	1994	20,840.6	18.3	0.5	9.8	71.4	12.7	28.5	30.2	67.9	3.2	6.3	3.8	18.8
Greenland	1995	421.1	15.4	0.3	5.8	78.5	4.3	24.6	49.7	83.2	2.4	0.2	3.3	10.9
Grenada	1991	117.2	28.4	0.2	7.4	64.1	8.5	24.2	31.3	19.8	32.2	0.1	7.1	40.8
Guadeloupe	1995	1,901.3	22.6	0.3	5.8	71.3	9.5	32.0	29.8	77.8	3.3	0.3	2.2	16.5
Guam	1983	610.7	16.9	0.1	46.9	36.2	2.3	19.1	14.8	...	23.4	...	19.9	56.6
Guatemala	1994	2,647.2	14.5	0.2	11.5	73.8	17.6	31.3	24.8	11.8	44.2	1.3	3.8	38.9
Guernsey[38]	...	...	...	...	...	...	...	...	...	...	...	...	...	...
Guinea	1992	739.9	—12.8[2,36]—		13.7[36]	73.5[3,36]	...	17.0[36]	56.5[3,36]	53.1[4]	8.6	0.4[4]	3.3	34.6[4]
Guinea-Bissau	1990	85.7	20.1[24]	2.2[24]	6.2[24]	71.5[24]	5.6[24]	36.4[24]	29.5[24]	57.8[4]	1.0[4]	3.1[4]	10.6[4]	27.5[4]
Guyana	1991	306.6	—4.2—		21.9	73.9	1.1	48.1	24.7	25.1[4]	30.7[4]	0.7[4]	5.5[4]	38.0[4]
Haiti	1993[39]	226.0	—46.6[2]—		28.4	25.1[3]	6.9	5.4	12.8	18.1[4]	57.9[4]	...	4.8[4]	19.3[4]
Honduras	1994	1,334.6	15.5	0.2	13.0	71.3	17.2	29.0	25.2	11.7	47.5	0.6	4.2	36.1
Hong Kong	1995	196,071.8	7.0	2.3	1.9	88.8	7.4	36.5	44.9	10.7	7.9	0.3	14.6	66.5
Hungary	1994	14,553.7	9.5	0.8[2]	11.8	77.9[3]	12.7	34.1	31.2[3]	61.1	3.1	21.8	2.7	11.3
Iceland	1995	1,751.4	13.3	3.7	7.2	75.7	9.3	32.4	34.0	59.8	8.4	4.8	4.4	22.6
India	1995[1]	28,654.8	10.3	9.7	23.8	56.2	14.7	19.0	22.5	26.2	10.1	3.2	7.1	53.5
Indonesia	1994	31,983.5	13.4	1.8	7.6	77.2	15.2	42.1	20.0	20.7	11.2	1.1[5]	24.2	42.8
Iran	1992	30,712.1	—11.4[2]—		1.3	87.4[3]	9.8	50.3	27.3[3]	49.8	2.7	3.0	12.0	32.5
Iraq	1990	4,833.9	—31.5[2]—		0.4	68.1[3]	8.8	30.3	28.9	45.7[4]	10.8[4]	3.0[4]	4.6[4]	35.9[4]
Ireland	1995	32,323.1	9.7	0.7	3.3	86.3	12.8	42.3	31.3	56.1	17.7	0.6	5.3	20.3
Isle of Man[38]	...	...	...	...	...	...	...	...	...	...	...	...	...	...
Israel	1995	29,579.0	8.2	17.1	5.9	68.8	9.4	34.0	25.5	52.3	18.6	1.9	3.3	23.9
Italy[40]	1994	167,979.4	18.0	2.2	8.1	71.7	12.8	28.2	30.7	60.4	4.6	5.8	2.4	26.8
Jamaica	1992	1,692.8	16.7	0.1	17.4	65.8	12.7	21.7	31.4	10.0	52.3	0.2	5.0	32.5
Japan	1995	336,094.2	21.7	4.3	15.9	58.2	7.3	23.2	27.6	14.5	22.4	1.6	—	61.4
Jersey	1980	537.1	23.9	0.4	9.3	66.5	6.5	24.8	35.2	84.9[41]	...	...	...	15.1
Jordan	1994	3,382.3	23.6	0.9	12.6	63.0	12.0	25.4	25.6	35.5	9.8	5.6	4.0	45.1
Kazakhstan	1995	3,742.1	—19.2[2,6]—		9.9[6]	71.0[3,6]	9.7[6]	30.9[6]	30.4[3,6]	15.2[4]	1.6[4]	73.8[4]	0.4[4]	9.0[4]
Kenya	1992	1,793.0	18.8	0.9	25.2	55.1	15.4	23.9	15.8	33.2	8.2	0.5	7.1	51.1
Kiribati	1994	26.4	42.4	0.3	9.3	47.9	6.4	17.4	24.1	0.8	9.6	—	6.7	82.9
Korea, North	1995	1,785.0[1]	...	...	...	...	...	...	...	20.6[4]	0.3[4]	11.4[4]	15.8[4]	51.9[4]
Korea, South	1995	135,112.9	10.9	2.9	14.1	72.1	9.7	36.6	25.8	13.5	22.5	1.8	24.1	38.1
Kuwait	1994	6,680.4	18.0	0.5	0.7	80.9	7.6	38.1	35.2	36.3	14.5	0.9	11.7	36.6
Kyrgyzstan	1994	317.0	—20.5[2,11]—		26.5[11]	53.0[3,11]	11.9[11]	21.7[11]	19.4[3,11]	5.3	11.0	29.1	0.9	53.8
Laos	1993	431.9	—35.0[4]—		10.0[4]	55.0[4]	...	25.0[4]	30.0[4]	6.0[4]	1.4[4]	6.0[4]	11.6[4]	80.5[4]
Latvia	1995	1,817.5	12.2	0.4	21.2	66.2	12.7	25.4	28.2	49.9	1.9	41.9	0.6	5.8
Lebanon	1994	5,990.0	21.7	—13.3—		65.0	10.2	27.0	27.8	49.1[4]	9.3	4.6[4]	4.2	32.8[4]
Lesotho	1992	977.0	23.2[25]	0.4[25]	8.7[25]	67.8[25]	7.4[25]	16.7[25]	43.7[25]	4.8	...	—[4]	—[4]	95.2[43]
Liberia	1992	5,760.0[4]	—19.8[2,36]—		20.3[36]	59.9[3,36]	5.6[36]	30.2[36]	24.1[3,36]	22.6[4]	0.6[4]	0.8[4]	28.3[4]	47.7[4]
Libya	1991	5,357.5	25.7	0.3	0.4	73.7	7.6	33.8	32.2	62.6	1.3	0.9[5]	3.3	31.9
Liechtenstein	1994	770.3	4.0	0.4[2]	1.0	94.6[3]	6.0	31.0	57.5[3]	...	...	...	...	...
Lithuania	1994	2,589.0	12.4	1.0	31.6	55.1	10.5	21.9	22.7	32.3	2.0	58.5	0.2	7.0
Luxembourg	1994	8,117.6	13.3	—12.1—		74.6	14.3	26.2	34.1	92.9	2.2	...	1.0	3.9
Macau	1995	2,018.6	16.7	0.2	5.1	78.0	4.5	18.9	54.6	14.7	7.4	0.3	10.5	67.1
Macedonia	1994	1,484.1	24.4	1.5[2]	10.8	63.3[3]	13.3	19.7	30.4[3]	38.2	3.3	24.6	0.9	33.1
Madagascar	1994	709.0	16.6	0.1	14.8	68.5	13.8	30.1	24.6	46.8	4.5	1.4	9.9	37.4
Malawi	1991	647.4	8.6	1.0	10.9	79.5	20.0	33.1	26.3	35.6	3.3	0.1	7.4	53.7
Malaysia	1994	59,594.6	6.4	1.2	2.6	89.8	6.8	60.1	22.9	14.8	16.7	0.4	26.7	41.4
Maldives	1993	191.4	31.5	2.8	12.8	52.9	7.5	22.2	23.2	7.9	1.0	0.4	3.9	86.9
Mali	1990	601.8	26.2	0.9	19.5	53.5	10.7	22.2	20.6	46.8	4.8	1.3[5]	4.3	42.9
Malta	1993	2,173.4	10.8	0.4	4.7	84.1	6.8	50.1	27.2	72.5	8.7	1.3	2.7	14.8
Marshall Islands	1991	56.4	39.9	1.0[4]	11.1	48.0	2.7	16.3	29.0	—	83.7	—	9.6	6.6
Martinique	1995	1,969.8	20.4	0.2	7.5	71.9	10.3	32.4	29.2	76.8	2.9	0.2	2.2	17.9
Mauritania	1992	599.0	30.6[36]	...	7.0[36]	62.4[36]	...	51.0[36]	11.4[36]	58.4[4]	11.2[4]	1.8[4]	3.8[4]	24.7[4]
Mauritius	1994	1,894.9	16.8	1.6	6.2	75.3	7.1	25.7	42.5	36.9	2.2	0.2	5.1	55.6
Mayotte	1994	97.2	—25.2—		5.2	69.6	11.1	33.7	24.8	74.0[11,44]	...	...	3.3[11]	22.7[11]
Mexico	1994	80,170.3	10.4	0.6	1.8	87.2	9.0	39.4	38.9	11.2	69.2	0.4	6.0	13.2
Micronesia	1993	109.5	—34.9[2]—		10.2	54.9[3]	3.9	20.2	30.8[3]	...	65.3[45]	...	18.0	16.7
Moldova	1994	669.0	8.8	0.4	55.8	35.1	6.6	12.6	15.8	10.1	2.9	79.9	—	7.1
Monaco[31]	...	...	...	...	...	...	...	...	...	...	...	...	...	...
Mongolia	1995	388.7	8.8[6]	—27.2[6,13]—		64.0[6,14]	5.3[6]	31.1[6]	27.6[6,14]	8.7[7]	3.6	54.6[7]	11.4	21.6
Morocco	1995	8,551.5	25.9	2.6	13.7	58.3	11.9	23.3	22.6	56.6	6.5	7.8	1.5	28.1
Mozambique	1991	899.0	—37.3[2,36]—		8.5[36]	54.2[3,36]	6.5[36]	33.4[36]	14.3[3,36]	34.5[4]	12.3[4]	...	4.8[4]	48.4[4]
Myanmar (Burma)	1994[1]	1,290.4	—9.5[2]—		4.1	86.3[3]	13.3	31.4	41.6[3]	9.6[4]	1.0[4]	1.9[4]	8.8[4]	78.7[4]
Namibia	1994	1,374.3	23.8	1.1[2]	4.2	70.9[3]	7.1	31.4	32.5[3]	4.5	0.9	—	1.3	93.3[46]
Nauru	1991[48]	17.8	—24.2[2]—		4.8	70.9[3]	2.1	23.4[20]	45.4[3]	...	...	...	...	...
Nepal	1993[10]	696.0	17.9	2.4	11.8	67.8	12.0	16.6	39.3	7.3	0.7	3.0	8.0	80.9
Netherlands, The	1995	157,703.3	16.3	1.6	7.7	74.4	13.1	32.9	28.4	61.5	8.4	2.7	3.6	23.9

total value ('000,000 U.S.$)	Standard International Trade Classification (SITC) categories (%)							direction of trade (%)					country
	food and agricultural raw materials (0+1+2 -27-28 +4)	mineral ores and concentrates (27+28 +667)	fuels and other energy (3)	manufactured goods				to European Union (EU)[b]	to United States	to Eastern Europe[c]	to Japan	to all other[d]	
				total[a] (5+6 -667 +7+8 +9)	of which chemicals and related products (5)	of which machinery and transport equipment (7)	of which other[a] (6-667 +8+9)						
61.7	48.6	—	—	51.4	0.1	39.8[29]	11.5	47.2	—	—	—	52.8	Equatorial Guinea
41.8	——54.1——			46.0	3.0	1.7	41.3	4.0[7]	...	...	...	96.0[30]	Eritrea
1,835.2	22.8	1.3	7.1	68.8	9.7	20.0	39.1	54.0	2.4	37.9	0.5	5.2	Estonia
201.7	95.3	—	4.0	0.7	0.1	—	0.6	41.6	9.2	0.3	19.0	29.9	Ethiopia
321.3	96.8	—	—	3.2	0.1	2.5	0.6	88.0	2.9	0.1	2.7	6.3	Faroe Islands
544.5	49.3	0.1	7.4	43.2	1.0	8.0	34.3	20.3	17.9	—	6.8	55.0	Fiji
39,998.2	10.7	0.6	1.9	86.8	6.0	35.1	45.6	57.5	6.7	10.8	2.6	22.4	Finland
284,045.7	15.6	0.8	2.3	81.3	12.8	39.7	28.8	63.5	5.9	2.2	2.0	26.5	France[31]
158.2	33.6	0.1	0.2	66.1	1.4	33.0	31.7	77.6	1.0	—	—	21.3	French Guiana
74.7	5.9	31.3		62.8	1.6	38.6	22.6	40.0	18.9	—	22.5	18.6	French Polynesia
2,474.0	12.6	10.0[2,13]	74.1	3.3[3,14]	1.6	0.2	1.6[3,14]	48.7	31.8	3.2[5]	4.6	11.7	Gabon
63.7	63.8	—	—	36.2	—	—	36.2	56.5	1.4	2.9	27.5	11.7	Gambia, The
49.4	...	...	...	...	...	...	...	...	...	...	...	100.0[33]	Gaza Strip
121.0[4]	——16.3[2]——		1.2	82.6[3]	2.4	11.9	68.3[3]	28.1[4]	6.6[4]	47.1[4]	0.8[4]	17.4[4]	Georgia
423,994.8	6.4	0.8	1.1	91.8	13.4	49.1	29.3	57.7	7.9	6.8	2.6	24.9	Germany
1,252.0	——43.9[2]——		5.4	50.7[3]	0.2	1.2	49.3[3]	30.3	2.6	1.1	1.8	64.2[34]	Ghana
128.7[35]	——8.2[2,36]——		51.5[36]	40.3[3,36]	2.3	18.1[36]	19.4[3,36]	22.2[7,36]	...	...	...	77.8[37]	Gibraltar
9,118.7	33.4	2.3	10.3	54.0	4.3	6.2	43.6	57.0	4.8	12.9	1.0	24.3	Greece
363.6	95.7	—	0.8	3.5	—	0.3	3.2	93.3	0.6	—	4.6	1.4	Greenland
20.1	77.0	—	—	23.0	4.5	2.1	16.4	44.1	14.2	—	2.6	39.2	Grenada
162.0	52.3	0.6	—	47.0	1.1	36.5	9.4	77.0	3.4	—	—	19.6	Guadeloupe
39.2	23.5	2.7	3.5	70.3	5.6	11.5	53.2	...	24.9	...	4.8	70.4	Guam
1,502.4	66.4	0.4	1.8	31.4	11.9	1.8	17.7	12.1	32.2	0.3	2.6	52.8	Guatemala
...	...	...	...	...	...	...	...	...	...	...	...	...	Guernsey[38]
621.3	7.2	83.2	—	9.6	—	—	9.6	60.3[4]	19.3	0.2[4]	0.2[4]	20.0[4]	Guinea
19.3	87.1[24]	0.3[24]	—[24]	12.6[24]	0.3[24]	—[24]	12.3[24]	27.9[4]	0.4[4]	—[4]	0.6[4]	71.1[4]	Guinea-Bissau
265.9	40.9	28.6[2,13]	—	30.4[3,14]	3.6	7.2	19.6[3,14]	47.0[4]	34.2[4]	1.9[4]	6.4[4]	10.5[4]	Guyana
74.3	14.1	—	—	86.0	1.7	14.0	70.3	12.4[4]	78.8[4]	—[4]	0.8[4]	8.0[4]	Haiti
614.0	84.4	1.0	0.1	14.5	2.2	0.5	11.7	27.8	53.9	—	4.1	14.2	Honduras
173,870.8	4.3	1.3	1.0	93.5	6.2	32.4	54.9	15.0	21.8	0.5	6.1	56.6	Hong Kong
10,700.8	23.3	1.4[2]	4.0	71.4[3]	11.2	25.6	34.6[3]	63.7	4.0	18.3	0.9	13.2	Hungary
1,802.5	76.1	1.5	—	22.4	0.7	5.1	16.6	62.7	12.4	0.9	11.3	12.7	Iceland
26,330.0	16.7	18.5	1.9	62.8	8.2	7.2	47.5	27.9	19.1	3.9	7.7	41.5	India
40,053.4	17.6	3.2	26.3	52.9	2.5	7.6	42.8	14.9	14.6	0.7[5]	27.3	42.6	Indonesia
19,868.0	7.8	1.9[2,13]	80.9	9.3[3,14]	0.2	0.5	8.6[3,14]	39.8	0.8	10.4	13.5	35.5	Iran
6,659.0	0.8	0.3[13]	96.8	2.1[14]	1.2	0.2	0.7[14]	26.6[4]	33.6[4]	6.8[4,5]	9.5[4]	23.5[4]	Iraq
43,778.5	20.5	1.0	0.4	78.0	18.4	34.5	25.0	72.2	8.3	1.7	3.0	14.7	Ireland
...	...	...	...	...	...	...	...	...	...	...	...	...	Isle of Man[38]
19,046.0	7.3	31.0	0.5	61.2	14.6	28.4	18.2	32.2	30.1	3.3	6.9	27.4	Israel
190,008.1	7.4	0.3	1.6	90.7	7.6	36.8	46.4	57.2	7.8	4.3	2.1	28.6	Italy[40]
1,052.8	23.8	53.3	1.0	22.0	2.5	1.9	17.6	26.1	36.5	0.4	1.4	35.5	Jamaica
442,937.4	1.1	0.2	0.6	98.2	6.8	70.0	21.4	15.9	27.3	0.4	—	56.4	Japan
209.2	27.6	4.3[42]	—	68.0	1.2	31.1	35.7	67.3[41]	...	...	...	32.7	Jersey
1,424.3	18.4	20.2	0.1	61.2	27.8	15.8	17.6	8.7	3.3	1.2	1.3	85.5	Jordan
4,974.4	——27.8[2,6]——		14.3[6]	58.0[3,6]	11.6[6]	8.4[6]	38.0[3,6]	10.9[4]	2.8[4]	73.6[4]	1.0[4]	11.8[4]	Kazakhstan
1,361.7	48.4	2.3	11.2	38.1	3.3	1.5	33.3	33.4	2.9	—	1.1	62.6	Kenya
5.2	91.8	—	—	8.2	—	—	8.2	4.4	12.1	—	0.1	83.4	Kiribati
973.0[4]	...	...	...	...	...	...	...	26.3[4]	—[4]	3.1[4]	31.4[4]	39.2[4]	Korea, North
125,056.5	3.6	0.1	2.0	94.3	7.2	52.5	34.7	13.0	19.5	2.1	13.6	51.8	Korea, South
11,614.0	0.3	0.4	93.7	5.7	1.3	3.0	1.4	15.3[4]	15.6[4]	—[4]	20.3[4]	48.8[4]	Kuwait
340.1	——9.1[2,11]——		6.7[11]	84.2[3,11]	2.1[11]	35.4[11]	46.7[3,11]	12.3	0.2	22.5	—	65.0	Kyrgyzstan
241.0	——14.3[20]——		8.4[20]	77.3	...	21.0[20]	56.2	24.6[4]	3.9[4]	3.4[4]	5.4[4]	62.6[4]	Laos
1,303.8	37.4	0.7	1.7	60.1	6.9	16.3	36.9	44.0	1.3	47.7	0.3	6.6	Latvia
572.7	19.6	——10.5——		69.9	9.1	11.5	49.3	17.0[4]	3.7	4.9[4]	0.7	73.7[4]	Lebanon
109.1	14.8	1.3	—	83.9	0.5	10.2	73.2	22.7	23.0[4]	—	—	54.3[4]	Lesotho
389.0	32.4	33.7[2,13]	2.6	31.3[3,14]	—	26.0	5.3[3,14]	66.8	11.4[4]	1.5	—	20.3[4]	Liberia
11,211.7	0.7	—	95.4	3.9	3.4	—	0.5	86.2	—	1.6	—	12.2	Libya
1,533.1	3.7	—[2]	0.1	96.2[3]	9.4	47.2	39.5[3]	39.6[7]	...	...	...	60.4	Liechtenstein
2,028.8	27.4	1.7	15.9	55.0	12.7	15.6	26.7	30.1	0.6	59.1	0.1	10.0	Lithuania
6,434.6	7.0	——1.7——		91.3	18.5	19.4	53.4	84.7	4.2	...	0.9	10.2	Luxembourg
2,017.3	4.0	—	—	95.9	1.1	4.4	90.5	31.4	41.2	—	1.3	26.1	Macau
1,086.3	21.1	1.9[2]	0.1	76.8[3]	4.4	12.3	60.2[3]	33.6	3.6	35.0	0.1	27.7	Macedonia
545.1	82.0	4.6	0.6	12.8	1.3	0.3	11.2	64.8	8.0	1.7	8.1	17.5	Madagascar
472.4	96.4	—	—	3.6	0.3	0.2	3.1	47.3	15.0	—	12.0	25.7	Malawi
58,843.5	17.0	0.5	7.4	75.1	2.7	53.4	19.1	14.3	21.1	0.3	12.1	52.3	Malaysia
34.4	83.7	0.2	—	16.1	0.1	—	16.0	31.3	11.3	—	4.1	53.3	Maldives
330.3	98.4	—	—	1.6	—	0.9	0.8	26.0	0.6[4]	—	0.9[4]	72.5	Mali
1,355.4	3.3	0.2	2.2	94.2	2.5	57.1	34.5	72.0	7.5	1.8	0.6	18.1	Malta
2.9	99.9	—	—	0.1	—	—	0.1	—	100.0	—	—	—	Marshall Islands
241.9	62.3	1.0	17.8	18.9	2.1	13.0	3.8	78.0	2.6	—	—	19.3	Martinique
471.0	48.2	48.6[2,13]	1.9	1.3[3,14]	—	—	1.3[3,14]	58.2	4.5	10.8[5]	20.4	6.1	Mauritania
1,324.9	29.5	2.1	—	68.4	0.8	2.2	65.4	69.6	18.1	0.1	0.4	11.8	Mauritius
3.9	23.5[22]	—[22]	—[22]	76.5[22]	76.4[22]	—[22]	0.1[22]	70.0[11,44]	...	...	...	30.0[11]	Mayotte
61,964.3	8.2	1.0	11.9	78.9	4.5	53.6	20.8	4.3	85.2	—	1.6	8.9	Mexico
29.2	92.3	—	—	7.7	...	...	...	...	9.3[11]	...	80.0[11]	10.7[11]	Micronesia
566.0	68.3	1.1	2.5	28.1	2.1	11.5	14.5	6.9	0.3	86.7	—	6.1	Moldova
...	...	...	...	...	...	...	...	...	...	...	...	...	Monaco[31]
511.6	27.3[6]	——48.1[6,13]——		24.6[6,14]	...	...	...	8.6[7]	5.8	13.2[7]	18.7	53.7	Mongolia
4,728.1	34.8	10.0	2.2	53.0	20.8	3.2	28.9	62.1	3.4	1.5	7.7	25.4	Morocco
162.0	65.5	13.0[2,13]	1.2	20.4[3,14]	—	2.5	17.9[3,14]	50.0[4]	13.6[4]	2.5[4]	12.3[4]	21.6[4]	Mozambique
688.6	——71.3[2]——		0.2	28.5[3]	—	0.5	28.0[3]	7.1[4]	5.2[4]	0.1[4]	7.3[4]	80.4[4]	Myanmar (Burma)
1,321.4	47.0	50.1	—	2.8	...	...	...	...	3.0[4,47]	...	—[4,47]	97.0[4,47]	Namibia
28.9	—	99.4	—	0.6	...	...	0.6	...	...	...	...	...	Nauru
354.6	12.2	0.1	—	87.6	0.6	—	87.0	54.9	21.4	0.1	0.5	23.2	Nepal
177,351.0	23.8	1.1	7.1	68.1	16.4	26.6	25.1	71.4	3.2	2.7	1.0	21.7	Netherlands, The

Trade: external (continued)

country	year	imports total value ('000,000 U.S.$)	food and agricultural raw materials (0+1+2 −27−28 +4)	mineral ores and concentrates (27+28 +667)	fuels and other energy (3)	manufactured goods total[a] (5+6−667 +7+8 +9)	of which chemicals and related products (5)	of which machinery and transport equipment (7)	of which other[a] (6−667 +8+9)	from European Union (EU)[b]	from United States	from Eastern Europe[c]	from Japan	from all other[d]
Netherlands Antilles	1992	1,868.3	9.1	0.1	58.8	32.0	3.7	13.7	14.7	11.7	17.0	0.1	2.2	69.0
New Caledonia	1993	855.3	—19.7[2]—		9.8	70.5[3]	7.4	35.0	28.1[3]	59.2	5.4	0.3	5.3	29.8
New Zealand	1995	13,957.7	8.6	1.9	5.3	84.1	13.1	42.2	28.9	21.6	18.7	0.1	13.9	45.7
Nicaragua	1995	1,009.2	18.8	0.3	17.9	63.0	17.5	23.1	22.4	10.1	30.2	1.0	5.0	53.8
Niger	1991	355.3	—34.0[2]—		9.9	56.2[3]	11.3	21.5	23.4[3]	47.3[4]	3.1[4]	0.5[4]	3.8[4]	45.3[4]
Nigeria	1991	9,031.0	—10.6[2]—		0.7	88.7[3]	18.0	43.0	27.7[3]	56.0	10.4	1.3[5]	7.4	24.9
Northern Mariana Islands	1991	392.2	19.3	—	20.9	59.8	2.3	22.2	35.3	...	18.2	...	16.6	65.2
Norway	1995	32,705.9	9.5	4.7	2.9	83.0	9.6	37.7	35.7	71.4	6.7	3.4	3.8	14.6
Oman	1994	3,915.0	20.9	1.6	1.0	76.5	6.1	42.7	27.7	23.9	6.7	0.4	19.9	49.0
Pakistan	1995	11,703.6	23.0	1.2	16.1	59.7	17.0	28.9	13.8	23.5	9.3	2.5	10.7	53.9
Palau	1984	25.1[50]	28.9	0.1[2]	0.9[50]	70.0[3]	4.0	24.5	41.5[3]	—	41.8		38.2	20.0
Panama	1994	2,404.1	11.2	0.5	13.0	75.3	12.9	30.8	31.7	8.5	39.2	0.8	7.2	44.4
Papua New Guinea	1993	1,298.6	18.8[6]	0.3[6]	6.8[6]	74.1[6]	7.0[6]	38.3[6]	28.8[6]	4.0	3.9	0.9	14.5	76.7
Paraguay	1994	2,424.6	14.7	0.5	8.2	76.6	11.4	41.3	23.9	11.4	11.7	1.2[5]	9.3	66.3
Peru	1995	9,224.0	15.4	0.4	8.8	75.4	13.2	39.2	23.1	17.9	25.2	0.7	7.0	49.3
Philippines	1994	22,738.0	10.3	1.8	9.5	78.4	9.6	33.4	35.4	11.0	18.4	1.5	24.5	44.6
Poland	1994	21,433.5	13.5	2.0	10.5	74.0	14.8	29.0	30.2	64.0	3.5	13.0	1.6	18.0
Portugal	1995	32,636.3	17.1	0.6	8.4	73.9	10.4	33.7	29.8	74.0	3.3	1.3	2.3	19.1
Puerto Rico	1992[10]	15,387.3	17.3	0.3	10.6	71.8	25.4	21.8	24.7	4.8	68.1	0.1	3.7	23.2
Qatar	1993	1,890.7	15.5	1.7	0.6	82.2	7.8	42.4	32.0	32.3	11.6	0.9	16.4	38.7
Réunion	1995	2,711.1	21.5	0.2	4.7	73.6	10.7	29.8	33.1	80.1	0.6	0.1	2.1	17.2
Romania	1994	7,109.0	11.3	3.2	23.6	61.9	9.1	25.3	27.5	47.7	6.5	22.3	0.8	22.8
Russia	1994	38,649.6	27.9	—6.7—		65.3	9.9	31.2	24.2	39.1	5.4	27.0	2.9	25.7
Rwanda	1990	291.1	18.2	1.9	15.3	64.6	10.2	16.1	38.3	44.6	1.2	1.4[5]	7.7	45.1
St. Kitts and Nevis	1990	110.7	21.2	0.1	5.0	73.7	7.3	29.4	37.0	18.0	43.6	—	3.7	34.7
St. Lucia	1993	300.3	—26.8[2]—		7.6	65.6[3]	9.1	22.8	33.6[3]	19.1	37.3	—	5.6	38.0
St. Vincent and the Grenadines	1993	134.3	28.3	0.2[2]	5.8	65.6[3]	11.9	18.1	35.7[3]	24.0	36.1	0.2	2.6	37.1
San Marino[40]	...	...	...	...	...	...	...	...	...	...	...	...	...	...
São Tomé and Príncipe	1994	30.4	21.5[20]	...	7.2	71.3	...	40.2	31.1	53.8[7]	25.0[4]	...	5.5	15.7[4]
Saudi Arabia	1994	23,343.5	14.0	0.9	0.2	84.8	8.7	40.1	36.1	34.7	21.3	0.6	11.7	31.6
Senegal	1993	967.0	31.7[47]	0.3[47]	11.0[47]	57.0[47]	14.1[47]	22.7[47]	20.2[47]	58.7	5.4	1.7	3.7	30.5
Seychelles	1993	241.6	21.3	0.1	14.2	64.4	6.6	25.1	32.8	30.5	7.7	—	5.8	56.0
Sierra Leone	1994	149.9	—41.7[2]—		18.5	39.8[3]	7.3	18.0	14.5[3]	47.0[4]	10.0[4]	2.2[4]	5.6[4]	35.2[4]
Singapore	1995	124,503.5	5.5	0.6	8.1	85.9	6.5	57.9	21.5	13.3	15.1	0.6	21.1	49.9
Slovakia	1993	6,655.0	—14.2[2]—		21.1	64.7[3]	11.3	29.2	24.1[3]	27.9	1.8	62.1[5]	1.1	7.1
Slovenia	1994	7,303.9	13.1	2.1	7.1	77.7	12.2	31.8	33.7	69.2	2.7	9.0	1.7	17.4
Solomon Islands	1994	170.6	—16.2[2]—		8.2	75.6[3]	5.2	38.0	32.5[3]	2.8	2.8	—	17.1	77.4
Somalia	1992	228.0[4]	30.3[25]	0.2[25]	4.6[25]	64.9[25]	5.1[25]	37.1[25]	22.7[25]	27.2[4]	10.1[4]	—[4]	0.7[4]	62.0[4]
South Africa[53]	1995	27,737.0	8.7	2.2	10.2	79.0	12.1	43.9	23.0	44.5	11.8	0.5	9.9	33.4
Spain	1995	113,398.6	16.6	2.2	8.3	72.9	12.1	35.6	25.2	65.2	6.6	2.5	3.3	22.3
Sri Lanka	1994	4,483.6	17.7	3.4	6.2	72.7	8.7	23.4	40.6	17.9	6.3	0.7	11.7	63.2
Sudan, The	1992	820.9	15.2	0.7	28.0	56.2	6.6	30.6	19.1	23.8	7.9	2.6	3.5	62.3
Suriname	1992	639.8	8.5	1.0	13.5	76.9	12.8	38.7	25.4	22.5	39.7	—	15.6	22.2
Swaziland	1994	962.6	21.8[1]	0.4[1]	10.3[1]	67.4[1]	10.2[1]	26.7[1]	30.6[1]	7.6[1]	0.6[1]	—[1]	0.9[1]	90.9[1,55]
Sweden	1994	51,778.3	9.9	1.4	7.6	81.1	14.3	37.8	31.9	62.5	8.6	3.9	4.7	20.2
Switzerland[56]	1995	79,365.3	8.4	2.8	2.9	85.8	14.6	33.4	37.8	79.6	6.4	1.5	3.2	9.4
Syria	1994	5,467.6	19.8	0.4[2]	1.6	78.2[3]	8.5	37.2	32.5[3]	35.3	5.8	10.6	10.1	38.2
Taiwan	1995	103,698.0	10.0	2.7	6.9	80.4	13.9	40.3	26.2	14.4	20.1	2.1	29.2	34.2
Tajikistan	1994	531.0	—58.0[2,11,13]—		15.1[11]	26.9[3,11,14]	11.3[11]	7.0[11]	8.6[3,11,14]	24.5	6.0	16.6	—	52.9
Tanzania	1990	1,021.5	5.4	1.5	10.3	82.8	9.8	45.6	27.4	58.2	1.6	0.8[5]	7.7	31.8
Thailand	1994	54,340.0	8.5	2.5	6.8	82.2	10.5	46.9	24.9	15.0	11.8	2.4	30.2	40.5
Togo	1994	222.0	24.4[47]	0.7[47]	9.8[47]	65.1[47]	11.9[47]	28.3[47]	25.0[47]	53.1	5.5	0.6	3.5	37.3
Tonga	1992	62.6	29.9	0.5	12.8	56.8	6.2	19.3	31.4	2.6	8.3	—	12.5	76.6
Trinidad and Tobago	1994	1,136.2	20.5	5.6	0.6	73.2	13.7	29.8	29.7	16.2	48.3	0.3	4.6	30.6
Tunisia	1995	7,903.0	16.7	1.9	7.2	74.1	9.1	25.9	39.1	71.4	5.1	4.5	1.8	17.3
Turkey	1995	35,707.5	12.6	3.8	12.9	70.7	15.0	32.2	23.6	47.2	10.4	11.4	3.9	27.0
Turkmenistan	1992	1,009.0	—41.8[2]—		8.2	50.0[3]	10.2	22.3	17.4[3]	4.8[4,47]	0.5[4,47]	56.4[4,47]	0.5[4,47]	37.8[4,47]
Tuvalu	1992	6.7	36.1[47]	0.1[2,47]	14.6[47]	49.2[3,47]	6.8[47]	13.9[47]	28.5[3,47]	4.5[41]	35.8	...	11.9	47.8
Uganda	1992	524.4	13.0	1.5[2]	13.4	72.0[3]	8.3	32.2	31.5[3]	29.7	4.8	—	9.9	55.6
Ukraine	1994	9,989.2	4.6	—55.1—		40.3	9.4	18.3	12.6	12.3	2.3	68.2	0.3	16.8
United Arab Emirates	1992	17,410.0	11.6	0.7	1.7	86.1	5.5	35.1	45.4	33.5	8.9	0.5	16.6	40.5
United Kingdom[38]	1995	265,275.0	12.5	2.8	3.5	81.2	10.6	40.9	29.6	55.4	12.1	1.9	5.7	25.0
United States[57]	1995	770,944.2	6.9	1.6	8.2	83.3	5.5	46.4	31.4	17.7	—	0.9	16.5	64.8
Uruguay	1995	2,865.7	14.4	0.3	10.1	75.2	15.3	34.5	25.4	20.9	9.9	0.5	2.6	66.2
Uzbekistan	1994	2,475.0	—37.6[2]—		20.8	41.6[3]	7.9	17.6	16.0[3]	13.3	3.8	38.1	1.0	43.8
Vanuatu	1992	81.1	—22.8[2]—		9.0	68.2[3]	6.6	27.5	34.0[3]	40.0[4]	2.0[4]	—	15.0[4]	43.0[4]
Venezuela	1994	8,036.7	16.4	1.2	1.5	80.9	13.8	44.8	22.4	21.1	46.1	0.1	5.6	27.1
Vietnam	1993	3,924.0	—9.4[2,47]—		22.9[47]	67.8[3,47]	16.3[47]	26.1[47]	25.4[3,47]	10.4	0.1	4.8	11.5	73.2
Virgin Islands (U.S.)	1992	3,550.8	...	...	71.4	...	...	...	...	...	49.8	...	...	...
West Bank	1994	102.5[59]												
Western Sahara	...	...	...	...	...	...	...	...	...	...	...	...	...	...
Western Samoa	1990	81.7	29.0	0.5	11.4	59.0	4.7	28.9	25.4	5.9	8.9	—	11.2	74.0
Yemen	1992	2,589.6	35.2	0.6[2]	6.1	58.2[3]	6.6	21.8	29.7[3]	28.8	9.2	1.9[5]	7.0	53.1
Yugoslavia	1991	5,548.6	12.4	1.3	19.0	67.4	13.7	22.7	31.0	46.5[4]	4.2	24.5[5]	2.3	22.6
Zaire	1992	420.0	—20.0[9]—		13.8[9]	66.2[9]	4.4[9]	45.5[9]	16.3[9]	57.9[4]	4.9[4]	0.8[4]	2.7[4]	33.7[4]
Zambia	1990	1,237.7	3.7	1.1[2]	15.2	79.9[3]	12.6	47.0	20.3[3]	38.7	10.1	0.1	6.7	44.4
Zimbabwe	1993	1,817.8	13.3	2.5	14.7	69.6	15.3	35.0	20.8	28.6	8.9	1.7[4]	6.5	54.2[4]

[1]Year ending March. [2]Excluding precious stones, etc. (667). [3]Including precious stones, etc. (667). [4]Estimate. [5]Including also Asian republics of the former U.S.S.R. [6]1990. [7]Main countries only. [8]Includes special transactions: imports 51.0%, exports 34.1%. [9]1987. [10]Year ending June 30. [11]1992. [12]Figures for Belgium-Luxembourg Economic Union (Luxembourg is also shown separately). [13]Including metals. [14]Excluding metals. [15]Includes 83.6% from India. [16]Mainly electricity. [17]Includes 84.8% to India. [18]Includes 77.7% from South Africa. [19]Includes 48.7% to Switzerland. [20]Main items only. [21]Includes 82.8% for reexports. [22]Domestic exports only. [23]Includes ships' bunkers and stores. [24]1980. [25]1986. [26]1989. [27]1985. [28]Includes 31.9% for ferronickel. [29]Includes 38.7% for ships and boats. [30]Includes 68.7% for Ethiopia. [31]Figures for France include Monaco. [32]Includes 82.4% from Israel. [33]Includes 69.2% to Israel and 25.1% to Jordan. [34]Includes 41.5% to Switzerland. [35]Excluding petroleum products. [36]1988. [37]Includes 51.5% for ships' bunkers. [38]Figures for United Kingdom include Guernsey, Isle of Man, and Jersey (data for Jersey is also shown

exports total value ('000,000 U.S.$)	food and agricultural raw materials (0+1+2-27-28+4)	mineral ores and concentrates (27+28+667)	fuels and other energy (3)	manufactured goods total a (5+6-667+7+8+9)	of which chemicals and related products (5)	of which machinery and transport equipment (7)	of which other a (6-667+8+9)	to European Union (EU) b	to United States	to Eastern Europe c	to Japan	to all other d	country
1,558.9	3.0	0.8	91.2	5.0	0.9	3.0	1.0	8.1	25.0	—	3.1	63.8	Netherlands Antilles
376.7	—	32.6	—	67.4	—	—	67.4[49]	46.9[4]	7.6	0.3[4]	26.9	18.3[4]	New Caledonia
13,745.4	60.4	0.5	1.6	37.5	7.6	8.6	21.3	16.0	10.0	0.9	16.2	56.9	New Zealand
509.2	76.5	0.8	0.6	22.2	1.2	6.1	14.9	31.8	42.1	0.1	1.4	24.7	Nicaragua
311.9	—90.9[2]—		0.5	8.7[3]	0.2	1.5	7.0[3]	64.4[4]	1.6[4]	0.5[4]	—4	33.5[4]	Niger
12,265.0	—3.4[2]—		94.4	2.2[3]	0.4	0.1	1.7	39.5	45.3	0.1[5]	—	15.0	Nigeria
263.0	—	—	—	100.0	—	—	100.0	—	100.0	—	—	—	Northern Mariana Islands
41,740.3	9.9	0.9	47.3	41.9	3.1	13.3	25.5	77.2	6.2	1.9	1.8	12.9	Norway
5,418.3	4.9	0.3	76.5	18.3	0.4	12.8	5.1	0.9	1.0	—	34.8	63.2	Oman
8,157.9	15.6	0.2	1.0	83.2	0.7	0.5	82.0	30.5	15.1	0.6	6.8	47.1	Pakistan
0.5	69.1	—	—	30.9	—	—	30.9		8.0	—	58.8	33.2	Palau
524.3	78.3	0.3	2.5	18.9	5.3	—	13.6	33.4	40.1	0.5	0.4	25.6	Panama
2,624.6	26.8	19.5	30.6	23.1	—	2.5	20.6[51]	12.1	4.0	—	21.4	62.5	Papua New Guinea
816.8	78.2	0.2	0.3	21.3	2.5	0.9	17.9	27.8	7.0	0.1[5]	0.1	65.0	Paraguay
5,575.1	31.3	16.2	4.9	47.6	2.2	0.6	44.8	30.5	17.2	0.6	8.4	43.2	Peru
13,482.9	15.1	1.8	1.6	81.5	2.3	21.6	57.6	17.5	38.5	0.2	15.1	28.7	Philippines
17,194.4	14.8	1.5	9.1	74.6	6.7	19.8	48.1	68.4	3.4	13.2	0.2	14.9	Poland
22,786.9	11.8	2.0	3.3	83.0	4.9	26.9	51.1	80.3	4.6	0.8	0.8	13.5	Portugal
21,051.2	15.8	0.1	2.6	81.5	43.7	21.7	16.2	5.1	87.5	—	0.2	7.2	Puerto Rico
3,245.4	0.4	0.1	81.4	18.1	8.8	1.3	8.0	1.8[4]	2.0[4]	0.2[4]	59.4[4]	36.6[4]	Qatar
208.7	78.6	0.5	0.2	20.7	1.7	12.7	6.2	79.9	0.6	—	6.1	13.4	Réunion
6,151.2	10.0	0.8	10.0	79.2	9.6	14.3	55.3	48.2	3.2	11.8	0.9	36.0	Romania
63,243.0	4.9	—54.3—		40.8	8.7	8.5	23.6	34.7	5.3	27.5	3.5	28.9	Russia
131.9	72.8	3.9	—	23.3[52]	—	—	23.3[52]	64.1[4]	6.1[4]	—4	1.9[4]	27.9[4]	Rwanda
27.7	32.8	—	—	67.2	0.3	46.2	20.7	21.4	50.9	—	—	27.7	St. Kitts and Nevis
119.7	56.4	—	—	43.6	1.3	8.6	33.8	53.2	27.0	—	0.1	19.7	St. Lucia
57.8	84.4	—		15.6	0.6	5.0	10.0	44.4	7.3	—	—	48.2	St. Vincent and the Grenadines
...													San Marino [40]
6.5	76.9[20]	...	....	...	...	...	...	88.8[7]	1.9[4]	...	0.5[4]	8.8[4]	São Tomé and Príncipe
42,584.0	1.0[47]	0.2[47]	91.4[47]	7.4[47]	5.0[47]	0.9[47]	1.5[47]	22.6	18.5	—	16.0	42.9	Saudi Arabia
521.5	43.4	3.2	16.8	36.6	19.7	6.7	10.2	41.2	2.3	—	1.3	55.2	Senegal
51.6	30.4	—	55.1	14.5	0.3	7.8	6.4	28.7	7.0	—	—	64.3	Seychelles
115.8	4.8	84.2	...	11.0	—	—	11.0	51.0[4]	28.0[4]	1.1[4]	1.7[4]	18.2[4]	Sierra Leone
118,263.2	5.0	0.4	6.8	87.7	6.0	65.6	16.1	13.4	18.3	1.0	7.8	59.6	Singapore
5,450.9	—11.4[2]—		4.9	83.7[3]	12.0	19.4	52.3[3]	29.5	1.1	58.9[5]	0.1	10.3	Slovakia
6,827.8	6.5	0.2	1.1	92.1	10.3	30.3	51.5	65.6	3.7	9.5	0.3	20.9	Slovenia
142.2	—98.8[2]—		—	1.2[3]	—	—	1.2[3]	24.4	0.1	—	41.1	34.4	Solomon Islands
44.0	95.4	2.3	—	2.3	—	2.3	—	52.3	—	—	—	47.7	Somalia
27,339.9	12.3	14.3	8.1	65.4	7.7	8.8	48.9	28.3	6.6	0.7	5.8	58.6[54]	South Africa [53]
89,426.4	17.1	0.7	1.7	80.5	8.5	42.4	29.6	72.3	4.2	1.7	1.4	20.4	Spain
3,210.1	24.8	7.6	0.7	66.9	0.9	2.6	63.4	31.9	34.7	1.8	5.1	26.5	Sri Lanka
319.3	87.4	5.3	—	7.2	—	—	7.2	29.1	1.2	—	5.0	64.6	Sudan, The
357.1	18.1	67.6	1.3	13.0	—	0.1	12.9	47.5	10.7	—	5.3	36.5	Suriname
751.8	69.1[22]	3.3[22]	0.9[22]	26.7[22]	1.4[22]	8.3[22]	17.1[22]	19.8[22]	3.1[22]	—22	0.7[22]	76.4[22]	Swaziland
61,359.6	8.8	1.3	2.5	87.4	9.5	45.0	32.6	59.1	8.0	3.4	2.7	26.8	Sweden
80,454.9	3.7	2.8	0.1	93.3	25.7	31.6	36.1	60.6	8.5	2.4	3.9	24.6	Switzerland [56]
3,547.3	23.2	0.7[2]	56.2	19.9[3]	0.4	0.6	18.8[3]	55.8	1.2	8.8	0.3	33.9	Syria
111,585.0	11.8	0.3	0.7	87.3	9.3	48.6	29.4	13.9	23.7	0.5	11.8	50.1	Taiwan
485.0	—67.4[2,11,13]—		1.3[11]	31.3[3,11,14]	2.5[11]	14.6[11]	14.2[3,11,14]	53.0	5.6	15.1	2.3	24.1	Tajikistan
416.1	82.0	1.0	2.0	15.1	1.0	2.2	11.8	40.5	6.8	0.7[5]	3.9	48.2	Tanzania
45,167.3	25.6	2.7	0.8	70.9	2.8	33.3	34.8	15.6	21.0	1.8	17.1	44.4	Thailand
162.2	42.0[47]	49.2[47]	2.3[47]	6.5[47]	1.1[47]	1.0[47]	4.4[47]	19.6	0.1	2.5	—	77.7	Togo
12.8	83.4	—	—	16.6	—	4.0	12.7	0.7[4]	17.7	—	51.2	30.5	Tonga
1,960.4	8.2	0.1	49.2	42.6	26.7	1.7	14.2	7.7	46.4	—	0.2	45.7	Trinidad and Tobago
5,474.6	10.4	1.6	8.5	79.5	11.9	9.4	58.2	79.0	1.3	0.5	0.3	18.9	Tunisia
21,598.7	21.0	2.1	1.3	75.6	4.1	11.1	60.4	51.3	7.0	11.8	0.8	29.1	Turkey
2,149.0	—19.9[2]—		77.9	2.3[3]	1.1	0.2	1.0[3]	3.3[4,47]	0.1[4,47]	57.3[4,47]	0.3[4,47]	39.0[4,47]	Turkmenistan
5.2	92.2[26]	—26	—26	7.8[26]	—26	—26	7.8[26]	3.8[7]	55.8	...	...	40.4	Tuvalu
171.4	95.2	—	3.0	1.8	—	0.9	0.9	63.8	8.1	—	0.6	27.5	Uganda
9,708.2	11.5	—10.5—		78.0	13.7	21.4	42.9	11.6	4.0	48.9	0.3	35.2	Ukraine
24,756.0	0.3	0.1	96.6	3.0	0.2	0.2	2.6	7.0[4]	3.2[4]	0.1[4]	35.7[4]	53.9[4]	United Arab Emirates
242,067.1	8.4	2.7	6.0	82.8	13.7	42.8	26.3	57.9	11.7	2.2	2.5	25.8	United Kingdom [38]
583,030.5	13.8	1.7	1.8	82.8	10.6	48.3	23.9	21.2	—	0.9	11.0	66.9	United States [57]
2,116.5	59.3	0.3	0	39.4	5.6	5.9	27.9	21.0	5.9	0.3	0.9	72.0	Uruguay
3,084.0	—7.9[2]—		25.0	67.2[3]	2.7	5.4	59.0[3]	14.3	0.7	38.2	0.2	46.7	Uzbekistan
22.4	—78.5—		3.1	18.4	—	0.9	17.5	37.1	—	—	14.7	48.2	Vanuatu
16,649.7	3.0	1.5	75.9	19.5	3.0	3.1	13.4	9.0	51.9	0.1	1.7	37.3	Venezuela
2,985.2	—48.9[2,47]—		35.6[47]	15.5[3,47]	0.7[47]	0.1[47]	14.7[3,47]	7.2	...	5.4	31.4	56.0	Vietnam
2,303.5	...	...	84.2[58]	...	...	...	...	...	94.1	...	...	...	Virgin Islands (U.S.)
22.6[60]													West Bank
													Western Sahara
8.0	96.4	—	—	3.6	—	0.4	3.2	20.0	5.5	—	0.2	74.3	Western Samoa
474.4	20.5[22]	2.7[22]	74.4[22]	2.4[22]	1.5[22]	0.1[22]	0.8[22]	23.0[22]	35.3[22]	—22	16.9[22]	24.7[22]	Yemen
4,704.1	15.9	0.6	4.4	79.1	9.1	19.6	50.3	54.6[4]	4.5	29.1[5]	0.2	11.6	Yugoslavia
506.0	13.1	58.5[2,13]	11.1	17.3[3,14]	0.2	1.2	15.9[3,14]	58.7	15.7[4]	4.5	6.5	14.6[4]	Zaire
1,049.2	3.4	89.0[2,13]	—	7.5[3,14]	—	0.2	7.3[3,14]	30.6	1.6	—	31.0	36.8	Zambia
1,322.6	48.5	7.3	0.6	43.6	2.9	3.0	37.7	33.3	7.2	1.5[4]	7.3	50.7[4]	Zimbabwe

separately).   [39]Year ending September 30.   [40]Figures for Italy include San Marino.   [41]United Kingdom only.   [42]Including coins.   [43]Includes 83.8% from rest of Customs Union of Southern Africa.   [44]France only.   [45]Including Guam.   [46]Includes 85.0% from South Africa.   [47]1991.   [48]Based on trade with Australia and New Zealand only.   [49]Includes 56.4% for ferroalloys.   [50]Excluding bulk imports of fuels.   [51]Includes 19.7% for nonmonetary gold.   [52]Includes 19.8% for nonmonetary gold.   [53]Figures for South Africa refer to the Customs Union of Southern Africa (includes South Africa, Botswana, Lesotho, Namibia, and Swaziland, also shown separately).   [54]Including unspecified destinations of 21.2%.   [55]Includes 87.7% from South Africa; these imports may have had their origin from other countries.   [56]Figures for Switzerland include Liechtenstein also shown separately.   [57]Figures for United States include American Samoa, Guam, Puerto Rico, and Virgin Islands (U.S.), also shown separately.   [58]Exports of refined petroleum to United States only.   [59]Excluding imports from Israel ($580.7 million in 1987).   [60]Excluding exports to Israel ($160.5 million in 1987).

Trade: domestic

The following table presents data relating to domestic wholesale and retail trade for the countries of the world. The section on wholesale trade is based for the most part on establishments (service points from which a business enterprise operates [see note a]) engaged primarily in selling goods to retailers and distributors for resale or to purchasers who buy for business and farm uses. The retail trade section is based on businesses engaged in selling merchandise for personal or household consumption; restaurants are, when possible, included, hotels excluded.

The data presented here are based on information from a variety of country and international sources. The country sources include statistical abstracts, correspondence, annual reports, and censuses of business and trade.

Because there is no single published source or common international methodology for the compilation of data on wholesale and retail trade, nor a single current year on which, by common agreement, the various national reports would be based, allowance must be made for variations in the meaning and recency of the information provided for any single country and for its comparability internationally. Variations occur in part because of the ways in which countries define wholesale and retail trade; the conventional free-enterprise distinction between wholesale and retail activity (of a single enterprise or an entire national trade sector) may not exist in the business practice of some countries. Variations also exist in the kind and level of detail reported. For example, countries may design surveys differently according to the size (number of employees, sales, surface area) of establishments surveyed, their profitability, or other less direct criteria,

such as ownership or location. The depth of analysis to which the data are subjected may also vary. The structure of a national trade sector is also affected by the degree of government involvement, which may range from total control of wholesale distribution in some socialist countries to partial involvement in some strategic sectors, or to relative noninvolvement in fully private trade sectors of capitalist countries. In some smaller countries data may refer to a single trading enterprise.

At the table's extreme left, preceding the year to which the trade data refer, the combined value of the country's wholesale and retail trade as a percentage of gross domestic product or net material product is given. Unless otherwise noted, GDP data include restaurants and exclude hotels.

Both the wholesale and retail sections of the table provide similar detail: establishments or outlets, employees, sales, and certain derived values for relationships among these measures; the retail section provides an additional breakdown of sales by an end-use classification of retail sales outlets.

Although all sales figures are given in U.S. dollars, the comparability of these dollar figures may differ considerably; for instance, the purchasing power of various national currencies in domestic transactions may bear only a distant relationship to the exchange rate of the same currency in international transactions, especially for countries having nonconvertible currencies. The price of goods may also vary, depending on the degree to which they are subject to direct subsidies and artificial cost controls such as tax, investment, or free-trade preferences by a central government seeking to influence social or economic conditions.

Trade: domestic

country	domestic trade as percentage of GDP, 1993	year	wholesale trade					retail trade		
			establish-ments[a]	employees[b]	sales[c] (U.S.$'000,000)	employees per establishment	sales per establishment (U.S.$'000)	outlets[a]	employees[b]	sales[c] (U.S.$'000,000)
Afghanistan	10.5[1,2]	1981–82	...	3	...	...	...	...	126,100[3]	...
Albania	4.6[4]	1990						11,741[5]	62,000[3]	1,570[5]
Algeria	17.8[6]	1986	...	3				3,600[7,8]	390,990[1,3,9]	16,200
American Samoa	...	1990	177	255		1.4		583	1,495	
Andorra	24.2[6]	1988						592[10]	7,227	...
Angola	6.1[11]	1973	3					29,138[3]		
Antigua and Barbuda	22.8[1,12]	1980	25	350		14.0		199	1,000	23[13]
Argentina	15.4[12]	1985	54,452	351,087[14]	1,113	6.4[14]	20,435	500,342	1,055,071[14]	1,003
Armenia	2.3	1990	...	3					88,100[3]	
Aruba	37.2[1,15]	1990		723					5,700	
Australia	17.4[16]	1991–92	15,514	153,092	44,553	9.9	2,872	209,909	1,290,173	107,230
Austria	16.2[1]	1993	17,149[6]	188,000	75,378	10.2[6]	3,526[6]	33,601[6]	250,000	40,432
Azerbaijan	2.2		...							
Bahamas, The[17]	23.0[12]	1980	23	1,066	143	46.3	6,235	132	4,059	460[18]
Bahrain	10.6[1,12]	1983	3	3		3		255[3]	12,551[3]	1,601
Bangladesh	7.9[1,19]	1985	...	3	...			271,000	3,610,000[3]	5,500[18]
Barbados	26.6[1,20]	1990	...	3				1,911[21]	20,800[3]	264[13]
Belarus	7.7[20]	1991	3	3	3			22,300[3]	299,900[3]	19,900[3]
Belgium	14.1	1984	60,589	160,600	65,110	2.6	1,075	135,534	193,500	20,957
Belize	17.2[1]	1983	...	3					4,558[3]	33[19]
Benin	20.0[20,22]	1979						170[7]	1,910[14,18]	150[13]
Bermuda	32.8[23]	1985	60[23]	820				310[7,23]	4,342[14]	116[24,25]
Bhutan	7.8[1]	1982	...	3					9,000[3,5,14]	
Bolivia	10.1	1992	4,820	21,814	...	4.5		64,136	122,892	1,570[18]
Bosnia and Herzegovina	13.9[6]	1990	...	3	18,469[6]				130,914[3]	18,065[6]
Botswana	15.1[16]	1983–84	205	3,500	494[13]			1,660	10,700	165[13]
Brazil	7.5[22]	1990	45,278	652,054	22,706	14.1	501	680,634	4,102,638	39,312
Brunei	12.3[1,12]	1986	3	3		3		833[3,26]	4,261[3,26]	
Bulgaria	11.2[1]	1987	...	7,700[27]				41,339[24]	79,820[24]	34,700[24]
Burkina Faso	12.9	1975		3					19,354[3,14]	
Burundi	9.1[11]	1986	...	...	...	...	...	...	...	210
Cambodia	14.8[20]									
Cameroon	11.7[11]	1980	...	...				1,312[7]	13,776[14,18]	1,430[18]
Canada	12.1	1993	...	3	232,900[6]				2,428,000[3,4]	150,200
Cape Verde	28.0[11]	1980		3					3,930[3]	
Central African Republic	11.6[20]	1989	113	302		2.7		14,543	23,078	230
Chad	29.5[6]	1983	...	3	3				1,661[3,7,28]	497[3]
Chile	17.0	1983	561[7]	15,300[7]	2,312[7]	27.2[7]	4,121[7]	1,125[18,24]	21,700[18,24]	1,403[18,24]
China	5.7	1994	1,427,753	10,761,093[14]	196,241	7.5[14]	157	14,483,822[14]	33,871,181	188,710
Colombia	16.0	1985	...	...				1,110[30]	49,000[30]	8,600[18]
Comoros	28.0[1]	1980		3					1,873[3,7]	
Congo	12.3[11]	1984		3					13,240[3]	
Costa Rica	20.7	1975	332[31]	4,073[31]	35[31]	12.3[31]	104[31]	9,713	26,486	475[32]
Côte d'Ivoire	20.3[11]	1981	...					2,023[7]	16,720[7]	1,800[18]
Croatia	2.3	1994[33]	1,155	6,461	4,015	5.5	3,476	16,959	48,615	3,734
Cuba	20.1[6,34]	1989	...	...	15,174			56,916[27]	230,000[9,14]	8,124
Cyprus	19.4[1,20]	1993	1,559[25]	14,137	443	5.3[25]	720[25]	8,474[25]	39,676	1,102
Czech Republic[35]	8.3	1990	63,110[27]	251,000[27]	40,083[27]	4.0[27]	635[27]	62,667[6]	258,127	21,235
Denmark	14.5	1992	32,432	176,205	73,937	5.4	2,280	40,733	210,015	32,145
Djibouti	16.3[11]	1985	28	371[15]				431	1,877[15]	...
Dominica	12.1[1,20]	1989		3					3,700[3]	790[18]
Dominican Republic	17.5[20]	1983	670	...	3,136	...	4,681	11,220[15]		1,259[15]
Ecuador	14.9	1990	426	18,014	139	42.3	326	554	20,168	102
Egypt	18.2[19]	1983–84	2,552	45,500[14]	4,492	18.0[14]	1,760	2,545	55,800[14]	29,700[18]
El Salvador	36.6	1983	396	6,400	1,038	16.2	2,621	1,416	10,700	485

The data on distribution of retail sales by kind of consumer goods may have their origin in several different types of data or analysis. One country may aggregate sales data by kind of establishment only (this may be perfectly satisfactory in a country of small, independent outlets); another may aggregate data directly by kind of goods (most easily done in a country with well-developed statistical, tax-reporting, and commercial systems). Other countries may find it impolitic to publish data that reflect the poverty of their distribution network or their supply of consumer goods and may aggregate or publish data for only a few sectors: food or nonfood goods, for example. For countries with only a few trading enterprises in a particular sector, detail must often be withheld to preserve the confidentiality of individual businesses.

The notes that follow further define the column headings.
a. The number of establishments or outlets refers to economic units that operate at a single physical location in one principal kind of activity, whether singly owned or part of a multiunit firm. Such units are not necessarily identical with a company or enterprise.
b. Number of employees refers to full-time and part-time paid workers, including salaried managers and officers; it usually excludes owner-operators, partners, vendors, and unpaid relatives.
c. Total sales (also called turnover) includes the value of merchandise sold for cash or credit; amounts received from customers for layaway purchases; receipts from rental or leasing of vehicles, equipment, tools, instruments, etc.; receipts for delivery, installation, maintenance, repair, alteration, storage, and other services.

d. Outlets engaged primarily in the sale of food and nonalcoholic beverages, such as grocery stores, meat and fish markets, and bakeries.
e. Outlets engaged primarily in the sale of clothing and shoes; also includes outlets that sell accessory items, such as millinery, furs, and leather goods.
f. Outlets engaged primarily in the sale of home furnishings, including furniture, draperies, floor coverings, household appliances, and home entertainment equipment.
g. Outlets that primarily serve food and drink, including restaurants, lunchrooms, cafeterias, social caterers, refreshment places, contract feeders, ice cream parlors, and bars and taverns.
h. Outlets engaged primarily in the sale of pharmaceuticals, cosmetics, and perfumes.
i. Outlets engaged primarily in the sale of building materials, hardware, garden supplies, paint, electrical supplies, and farm equipment.
j. Outlets engaged primarily in the sale of motor vehicles, motorcycles, bicycles, and tires, batteries, and other automotive supplies and parts; includes service stations.
k. Outlets engaged in the sale of multiple lines of merchandise, such as department stores, variety stores, and rural general stores.
l. Miscellaneous specialized outlets such as those engaged primarily in the sale of liquors, sporting goods, books, jewelry, photographic and optical goods, gifts, flowers, tobacco products, home fuels, and newspapers.

food[d]	clothing, shoes[e]	home furnishings[f]	eating, drinking[g]	drugs, pharma-ceuticals[h]	building materials[i]	automobile parts[j]	general merchandise[k]	other[l]	employees per outlet	sales per outlet (U.S.$'000)	population per outlet	country
...	...	...	...	...	...	...	...	...	...	...	...	Afghanistan
62.4				37.6					...	134[5]	277[5]	Albania
...	...	...	...	...	...	...	...	...	5.0[7,8]	...	5,146[7,8]	Algeria
...	...	...	...	...	...	...	...	...	...	...	81	American Samoa
...	...	...	...	...	...	...	...	...	3.8[10]	...	39[10]	Andorra
...	...	...	...	...	...	...	...	...	...	...	...	Angola
...	...	...	...	...	...	...	...	...	5.0	100	378	Antigua and Barbuda
15.5	13.3	7.1	5.4	4.3	7.8	13.7	10.1	22.8	2.1[14]	2,004	61	Argentina
...	...	...	...	...	...	...	...	...	...	...	...	Armenia
...	...	...	...	...	...	...	...	...	...	...	...	Aruba
28.9	3.6	8.9	3.7	2.9	2.4	31.9	7.9	10.7	6.1	511	82.8	Australia
31.0	12.2	6.9	...	6.7	1.9	17.3	4.3	19.7	7.1[6]	857[6]	227[6]	Austria
...	...	...	...	...	...	...	...	...	...	...	...	Azerbaijan
24.4[15]	7.7[15]	7.1[15]	—	3.7[15]	8.4[15]	30.1[15]	7.6[15]	11.0[15]	30.8	1,881	1,026	Bahamas, The[17]
...	...	...	...	...	...	...	...	...	49.2[3]	...	1,507[3]	Bahrain
...	...	...	...	...	...	...	...	...	...	...	...	Bangladesh
...	...	...	...	...	...	...	...	...	...	...	130[21]	Barbados
...	...	...	...	...	...	...	...	...	13.4[3]	892[3]	460[3]	Belarus
35.1				64.9					1.4	155	73	Belgium
...	...	...	...	...	...	...	...	...	...	...	...	Belize
...	...	...	...	...	...	...	...	...	11.3[14,18]	...	19,871[18]	Benin
...	...	...	...	...	...	...	...	...	11.0[13,24]	...	178[7,23]	Bermuda
...	...	...	...	...	...	...	...	...	...	...	...	Bhutan
...	...	...	...	...	...	...	...	...	1.9	...	107	Bolivia
...	...	...	...	...	...	...	...	...	...	...	...	Bosnia and Herzegovina
...	...	...	...	...	...	...	...	...	6.4	99	604	Botswana
11.1	12.1	...	...	4.2	8.4	31.4	15.4	17.4	6.0	55	213	Brazil
...	...	...	...	...	...	...	...	...	5.1[3,26]	...	279[3,26]	Brunei
50.9	10.9	3.4	—	5.9	...	...	0.2	28.7	1.9[24]	839[24]	217[24]	Bulgaria
...	...	...	...	...	...	...	...	...	...	...	...	Burkina Faso
...	...	...	...	...	...	...	...	...	...	...	...	Burundi
...	...	...	...	...	...	...	...	...	...	...	...	Cambodia
...	...	...	...	...	...	...	...	...	10.5[7,14]	...	6,481[7]	Cameroon
26.1	5.8	5.5	...	6.1	...	34.3	10.8	11.4	...	...	...	Canada
...	...	...	...	...	...	...	...	...	...	...	...	Cape Verde
...	...	...	...	...	...	...	...	...	1.6	16	187	Central African Republic
...	...	...	...	...	...	...	...	...	...	...	...	Chad
28.3[15]	29	5.0[15]	1.6[15]	5.4[15]	4.7[15]	18.0[15]	17.1[15,29]	19.9[15]	19.3[18,24]	1,247[18,24]	10,210[18,24]	Chile
57.3	16.0			26.7					2.3[14]	13	82	China
...	...	...	...	...	...	...	...	...	44.1[30]	1,522[30]	...	Colombia
...	...	...	...	...	...	...	...	...	...	...	...	Comoros
...	...	...	...	...	...	...	...	...	...	...	...	Congo
37.7	13.5	6.9	...	8.2	7.0	15.1	5.9	5.7	2.7	59	202	Costa Rica
...	...	...	...	...	...	...	...	...	8.3[7]	...	4,257[7]	Côte d'Ivoire
25.2	5.5	1.6	...	—	3.2	19.1	28.5	16.9	2.9	220	282	Croatia
35.8	17.2	9.9	...	5.3	0.8	5.1	...	25.9	4.0[9,14]	184[27]	177[27]	Cuba
10.2	8.2	...	43.7	2.4	3.1	14.9	...	17.5	1.0[25]	124[25]	77[25]	Cyprus
42.9	15.1	12.8	...	3.6	2.9	10.0	...	12.7	4.2[6]	362[6]	249[6]	Czech Republic[35]
47.1	5.6	3.4	...	3.2	3.1	17.7	1.4	18.5	5.2	789	127	Denmark
...	...	...	...	...	...	...	...	...	...	...	998	Djibouti
...	...	...	...	...	...	...	...	...	...	...	...	Dominica
...	...	...	...	...	...	...	...	...	...	112[15]	519[15]	Dominican Republic
26.3	2.0	11.5	3.9	1.6	7.2	38.2	6.2	3.1	36.4	184	18,520	Ecuador
...	...	...	...	...	...	...	...	...	21.9[14]	1,278	17,756	Egypt
11.9[8,36]	7.6[8,36]	16.2[8,36]	...	7.9[8,36]	6.3[8,36]	12.4[8,36]	28.2[8,36]	9.5[8,36]	7.6	342	3,336	El Salvador

Trade: domestic (continued)

country	domestic trade as percentage of GDP, 1993	year	wholesale trade					retail trade		
			establishments[a]	employees[b]	sales[c] (U.S.$'000,000)	employees per establishment	sales per establishment (U.S.$'000)	outlets[a]	employees[b]	sales[c] (U.S.$'000,000)
Equatorial Guinea	7.1[11]	1983	...	36	...	...	...	...	2,701	...
Eritrea	c28.3[20]	[37]	...	...	...	...	...	...	...	...
Estonia	15.7	1994	17,629	...	1,357	...	77	821	70,000[4]	807
Ethiopia	10.1[1,19]	1984[37]	375[7,40]	3,200[7,40]	...	8.5[7,40]	...	7,416[7,40]	17,100[7,40]	273
Faroe Islands	13.1[12]	1987	78	3	19	...	241	430	1,484[1,3,32]	38
Fiji	20.5[1]	1991	342	3,245	388	9.5	1,134	1,188	8,158	556
Finland	11.4	1994	9,367[41]	80,394[41]	40,338	8.6[41]	4,946[41]	37,303[12]	137,609[12]	25,475
France	14.3[1,19]	1992	88,371	912,131	399,844	10.3	4,525	363,701	1,615,700	320,274
French Guiana	12.2[6]	1991	175	905	1,798	5.2	10,274	820	2,522	1,984
French Polynesia	17.7	1986	3	3	...	...	...	947[3]	5,038[3]	...
Gabon	9.6[11]	1982	...	3	...	...	...	...	12,683[3,14,23]	...
Gambia, The	19.5[16]	1983	...	3	...	...	...	...	16,551[3]	...
Gaza Strip	...	1986	...	3	...	...	...	...	13,400[3]	...
Georgia	2.7[12]	1988	...	3	...	...	...	...	172,400[3]	...
Germany	7.6[20]	1992	205,060	1,592,511	714,634	7.8	3,485	494,869	2,335,800	440,354
Ghana	19.0	1983	460[42]	1,100[42]	115[42]	2.4[42]	250[42]	1,500	16,000	252[18]
Gibraltar		1991	...	737	...	...	...	...	1,835	...
Greece	13.7[1]	1988	31,032	115,979	...	3.7	...	184,821	388,132	12,263[43]
Greenland	8.0[21]	1992	...	3	139	...	...	...	2,214[3,9]	211
Grenada	20.6[1,12]	1988	...	3	3	...	...	...	5,421[3]	6[3,13]
Guadeloupe	19.6[1,6]	1991	736	4,053	1,066	5.5	145	4,005	11,754	1,306
Guam	51.5[15]	1992	169	2,045	3	12.1	3	768	12,060	1,400[3]
Guatemala	24.3[20]	1989	...	3	...	...	...	88,200[15]	374,690[3]	1,200[18]
Guernsey	...	1991	...	642	...	...	...	...	2,573	...
Guinea	25.6[22]	1979	...	3	...	...	...	...	12,808[3,42]	...
Guinea-Bissau	25.8[1,11]	1979	3	3	...	...	...	685[3,42]	5,085[3]	44[3,26]
Guyana	4.4[20]	1980	...	3	...	...	...	147[7]	14,690[3]	93[13]
Haiti	10.4[16]	1983	...	3	...	...	...	653[7,44]	303,353[3]	500[18]
Honduras	11.2	1991	...	3	...	...	...	...	156,500[3]	401[13]
Hong Kong	24.9	1993	23,302	67,539	21,999	2.9	944	57,521	151,891	30,656
Hungary	15.9[12]	1994	206[15]	122,600[15]	13,121[23]	595[23]	...	217,861	467,400	19,470
Iceland	12.2	1992	1,509[13,45]	5,132[23]	598[32,45]	...	...	1,680	7,774[46]	825
India	13.0[19]	1980	3	3	...	...	...	3,132,000[3,24]	3,615,000[3,24]	108,300[13]
Indonesia	16.5	1980	3	3	3	3	3	54,632[3]	85,400[3]	3,451[3]
Iran	15.5[19]	1986–87	118,698	3	2,429[48]	...	133[48]	634,084	521,708[3,49]	37,350
Iraq	20.3[1]	1987–88[26]	1,942	3,902	130	2.0	67	108,460	165,594	7,077
Ireland	17.1[1]	1988	3,972	39,101	11,420	9.8	2,875	31,699	89,680	10,952
Isle of Man	10.5[2]	1991	...	851	...	...	...	...	2,993	...
Israel	9.4[11]	1988	17,967	67,300	16,875	3.8	939	43,844	103,100	10,763
Italy	18.2[1]	1983	...	3	...	...	...	1,033,725	1,369,200[3]	122,978
Jamaica	24.6[1,20]	1991	...	3	...	...	...	10,150[32]	173,500[3]	1,457[13]
Japan	14.1	1994	429,302	4,581,372	5,272,000	10.7	12,280	1,499,948[24]	7,384,177[24]	1,321,000[24]
Jersey	...	1986	...	855	...	...	...	...	7,046	...
Jordan	9.7[20]	1991	488	2,862	147	5.9	301	34,086	69,393	1,002
Kazakstan	5.0	1991	...	...	...	...	...	42,168	484,800	...
Kenya	14.1	1990	2,097	21,266	...	10.1	...	4,316	36,300	...
Kiribati	14.1[12]	1987	...	3	...	...	...	30	1,127[3,27]	3.8
Korea, North			...	...	...	...	...	...	...	...
Korea, South	12.7	1994	118,471	603,093	91,480	5.1	772	758,953	1,548,297	79,850
Kuwait	6.6[1,20]	1989	2,982	25,897	65	8.7	22	14,521	54,588	145
Kyrgyzstan	4.3[11]	1992	...	3	...	...	...	...	92,900[3,44]	138
Laos	8.1	1990	...	...	...	...	...	15,000	...	576
Latvia	13.6[4]	1994	...	...	...	...	...	7,214[11]	95,300[11]	986
Lebanon	28.4[11]	1986	...	3	...	...	...	...	114,706[3]	1,662[14]
Lesotho	8.6[20]	...	...	...	...	...	...	...	...	...
Liberia	5.3[6]	1984	...	3	...	3.7[14]	...	...	46,850[3]	115[18]
Libya	8.8[11]	1973	1,126	4,148[14]	...	3.7[14]	...	26,825	44,605[14]	9,205[13]
Liechtenstein	...	1975	67	216	...	3.2	...	228	740	...
Lithuania	17.2	1992	...	3	...	...	...	6,425	127,400[3]	236
Luxembourg	16.4[11]	1993	1,926	10,723	6,910	5.6	3,588	3,406	17,107	4,407
Macau	...	1991	...	3	...	...	...	...	47,706[3]	...
Macedonia	24.7[20]	1990	...	3	9,522[6]	...	...	...	65,593[3,6]	9,238[6]
Madagascar	10.9[11]	1976	1,104	...	...	...	...	1,570	...	696[23]
Malawi	11.5[20]	1984	439	23,000	522	52	1,189	500	8,600	127
Malaysia	12.4[20]	1980	19,663	116,200	15,461	5.9	786	95,993	73,000	8,200[18]
Maldives	19.0[1]	1990	...	3	...	...	...	...	8,844[3]	5[18]
Mali	17.5[1]	1979	...	3	...	...	...	...	5,200[3]	...
Malta	14.3[1,11]	1983	3	3	1.0	...	333	4[21]	11,936[3,7]	2.3
Marshall Islands	19.2[1,20]	1988	...	3	...	...	...	...	1,394[3]	...
Martinique	21.9[1,11]	1991	740	3	...	...	...	5,489	12,399[3,18]	234[13]
Mauritania	13.9[22]	1971[7]	23	100	102	4.3	4,445	59	700	103
Mauritius	17.8[1,20]	1986	3	3	...	3	...	207[1,3,7]	10,107[1,3,7]	164[1,3,7]
Mayotte		1983	3	3	...	...	3	41[3]	597[3,9]	27[3]
Mexico	25.5[20]	1988	36,512	3	23,506	...	644	713,315	3,875,100[3,4]	39,810
Micronesia	12.7	1980	...	348[14]	...	...	...	...	489[1,14]	...
Moldova	3.6[20]	1990	...	3	...	...	...	...	148,000[3]	...
Monaco	...	1975	...	273	...	...	...	...	1,439	...
Mongolia	18.5	1983[3,52]	...	...	...	...	...	4,828	21,100	1,235[27]
Morocco	20.9	1972	...	3	...	...	...	4,000[7]	20,000[7]	5,750[18]
Mozambique	10.4	1980	...	3	...	...	...	...	63,058[3]	...
Myanmar (Burma)	22.3[19]	1983	...	3	...	...	...	...	1,405,000[3,53]	2,116
Namibia	10.1[1,20]	1977	222	5,035	377	22.7	1,698	1,248	7,569	254
Nauru			...	...	...	...	...	...	...	...
Nepal	9.2[1,19]	1983	...	3	...	...	...	...	119,000[3,14,23]	736
Netherlands, The	16.0	1993	49,400	344,000[12]	176,870	6.8[12]	3,580	70,900	482,500[12]	58,482

retail trade (continued)

percentage breakdown of sales

food[d]	clothing, shoes[e]	home furnishings[f]	eating, drinking[g]	drugs, pharma-ceuticals[h]	building materials[i]	automobile parts[j]	general merchandise[k]	other[l]	employees per outlet	sales per outlet (U.S.$'000)	population per outlet	country
...	...	...	...	...	...	...	...	...	...	...	...	Equatorial Guinea
												Eritrea
46.0	10.1	6.8[38]	...	[39]	[38]	13.1	18.2	5.8[39]	...	984	1,826	Estonia
15.9	45.2	...	...	...	7.9	9.8	10.5	10.7	2.3[7,40]	277[7,40]	55,200[7,40]	Ethiopia
									...	89	109	Faroe Islands
11.9	10.2	7.6	8.5	2.6	12.3	9.6	36.1	1.2	6.9	468	625	Fiji
27.6	6.0	1.9	...	4.6	9.2	26.2	12.2	12.3	3.7[12]	940[12]	135[12]	Finland
38.2	15.7	17.6	...	6.4	...	6.1	6.3	9.7	4.4	881	158	France
									3.1	2,419	155	French Guiana
									5.3[3]	...	188[3]	French Polynesia
50.5	9.6	...	...	...	33.8	6.1			...	...	...	Gabon
...	...	...									...	Gambia, The
...	...	...									...	Gaza Strip
...	...	...						...		...	...	Georgia
26.9	12.4	7.5	...	7.1	...	19.1	16.0	11.0	4.7	890	163	Germany
...	...	...	...	...	...	...	...	...	1.1	108[42]	7,993	Ghana
										...		Gibraltar
60.0[43]	18.1[43]	9.5[43]	...	...	...	...	...	12.4[43]	2.1	...	54	Greece
...	...	...								...	...	Greenland
...	...	...								...	...	Grenada
44.8	13.4	19.6	...	7.1	...	...	...	15.1	2.9	326	91	Guadeloupe
11.6[9]	10.9[9]	4.9[9]	8.0[9]	0.3[9]	5.2[9]	26.9[9]	3.3[9]	28.9[9]	15.7	1,494[3]	181	Guam
											83[15]	Guatemala
...	...	...	...	...	...	...	...	...				Guernsey
												Guinea
									0.8[3,42]	...	1,080[3,42]	Guinea-Bissau
9.7	18.9	13.8	4.5	2.8	17.7	18.6		14.0	...	743	5,884	Guyana
...	...	...								...	7,034[7,44]	Haiti
...	...	...									...	Honduras
18.8	13.6	...	...	...	...	11.5	...	56.1	2.6	532	103	Hong Kong
11.4	5.2	7.6	6.8	2.1	13.6	19.1	23.4	10.8	2.1	89	47	Hungary
62.6[47]	8.8	...	...	...	...	...	[47]	28.6	4.6[46]	825	155	Iceland
...	...	...							1.2[3,24]	...	219[3,24]	India
...	...	...							1.6[3]	63[3]	2,681[3]	Indonesia
...	...	...							...	59	78	Iran
									1.5	20	158	Iraq
40.6	9.1	1.4	10.4	2.9	5.1	21.6	2.8	6.1	2.8	345	112	Ireland
...	...	...									...	Isle of Man
35.4	12.2	20.0	...	...	...	...	6.2	26.2	2.4	245	103	Israel
50.8	15.1	...	...	3.4	...	...	...	30.7	...	119	55	Italy
											214[32]	Jamaica
30.5	10.0	4.8	—	[50]	[50]	11.4	15.0	28.3[50]	4.9[24]	880[24]	83[24]	Japan
...	...	...										Jersey
28.9	12.1	6.6	...	1.6	7.4	22.6	9.5	11.3	2.0	29	108	Jordan
...	...	...							11.5	...	400	Kazakstan
									8.4	...	6,003	Kenya
									...	127	2,226	Kiribati
												Korea, North
29.7	17.8	13.7	—	4.5	2.9	...	12.0	19.4	2.0	105	58	Korea, South
18.4[47]	14.5	17.3	...	2.6	6.5	16.4	[47]	24.3	3.8	10	138	Kuwait
...	...	...							...	38	278	Kyrgyzstan
												Laos
53.9	9.1	2.1	8.1	...	1.2		...	25.6	13.2[11]	2,831[11]	373[11]	Latvia
...	...	...							...	...	...	Lebanon
...	...	...										Lesotho
												Liberia
...	...	...							1.7[14]	...	84	Libya
									3.2	...	105	Liechtenstein
59.2	10.9	3.7	...	...	1.3	0.8	...	24.1	19.8[3]	38	584	Lithuania
27.3	1.4	9.7	...	2.9	8.1	40.9	...	9.7	5.0	1,294	117	Luxembourg
...	...	...							...	...	...	Macau
...	...	...										Macedonia
											4,977	Madagascar
...	...	...							17.2	254	14,196	Malawi
32.9[51]	7.3[51]	10.8[51]	...	2.5[51]	1.1[51]	33.3[51]	4.4[51]	7.7[51]	0.8	64	143	Malaysia
												Maldives
												Mali
...	...	...							...	578[7]	83,378[7]	Malta
												Marshall Islands
											68	Martinique
									11.9	1,742	20,300	Mauritania
...	...	...							48.8[1,3,7]	792[1,3,7]	4,976[1,3,7]	Mauritius
										652[3]	1,477[3]	Mayotte
33.8	...	...	...	...	37.0	23.7	...	5.8	...	59	113	Mexico
												Micronesia
...	...	...							...	...	...	Moldova
...	...	...										Monaco
...	...	...							4.3	225	372	Mongolia
...	...	...							5.0[7]	...	c. 4,000[7]	Morocco
												Mozambique
												Myanmar (Burma)
31.4	11.9	5.3	...	2.8	1.7	...	41.9	5.0	5.9	196	713	Namibia
...	...	...									...	Nauru
										...	...	Nepal
41.6	12.7	6.9	...	38.8					5.9[12]	825	216	Netherlands, The

Trade: domestic (continued)

country	domestic trade as percentage of GDP, 1993	year	wholesale trade establishments[a]	employees[b]	sales[c] (U.S.$'000,000)	employees per establishment	sales per establishment (U.S.$'000)	retail trade outlets[a]	employees[b]	sales[c] (U.S.$'000,000)
Netherlands Antilles	21.8[4]	1988	...	3	...	...	...	...	15,890[3]	149[14]
New Caledonia	31.0[4]	1991	...	3	...	...	...	1,023	4,995[3]	...
New Zealand	16.4[1,54]	1994	8,263[54]	76,664[54]	16,295[54]	9.3[54]	1,972[54]	29,961[24,54]	116,301[24,54]	17,055
Nicaragua	24.5	1987	...	3	...	...	...	20,610[15]	94,600[3]	790[18]
Niger	18.5[1,22]	...	...							
Nigeria	14.8	1983[7]	154	16,000	2,220	104	14,415	421	20,000	2,202
Northern Mariana Islands	...	1987	28	187	49	6.7	1,777	383	2,304	155
Norway	11.0[1,11]	1992	18,390	101,385[46]	56,056	5.5[46]	3,048	40,154	121,677[46]	31,264
Oman	15.4[1,20]	1990	3	3	...	...	...	25,840[1,3,6]	87,500[3]	2,449[13]
Pakistan	14.3[1,19]	1983	...	...	...	...	...	276,701[44]	501,773[14,44]	12,848
Palau	20.0[27]	1984	...	124	...	...	...	...	133	...
Panama	11.8	1982[56]	560	13,115	1,491	23.4	2,662	7,561	15,765[7]	1,334
Papua New Guinea	8.0	1985	...	3	...	...	...	...	25,100[3,32]	669[1]
Paraguay	30.4[1]	1982	...	3	...	...	...	...	85,961[3]	2,645[18]
Peru	16.9	1973	4,210	34,100	2,163	8.1	514	103,010	72,200	8,500[18]
Philippines	14.1	1981	20,642	122,717	4,538	5.9	220	279,968	241,872	4,836
Poland	14.1	1994	...	15,945[57]	...	...	...	785,000	984,883	57,467
Portugal	17.4[4]	1983	4,522	135,400[14]	9,260	29.9[14]	2,048	4,889	74,400[14]	3,057
Puerto Rico	14.5[20]	1991	1,876	34,571	7,365[27]	18.4	3,165[27]	9,164	106,239	7,206[27]
Qatar	6.8	1990	134	3,801	85	28.4	636	4,956	18,238	1,048[41]
Réunion	19.2[4,24]	1992	1,313	6,732	2,664	5.1	203	3,506	12,927	2,114
Romania	13.2[1,12]	1989	...	...	...	...	...	82,035	465,200	19,926
Russia	10.7	1992	...	...	...	...	...	319,500	3,135,000	18,771
Rwanda	17.1[1,11]	1978	...	3	...	...	...	...	8,014[1,3]	350[18]
St. Kitts and Nevis	23.5[1]	1984	...	3	...	...	...	...	940[3]	...
St. Lucia	24.6	1980	...	3	...	...	...	...	4,770[1,3,14]	...
St. Vincent	16.1[1]	...								
San Marino	...	1994	209	3	...	...	...	1,126	2,531[3]	...
São Tomé and Príncipe	10.0[6]	1981	...	3	...	...	...	...	1,994[3]	...
Saudi Arabia	6.9[12]	1991[24]	4,460	31,481[14]	1,354	7.1[14]	304	80,266	174,187[14]	2,292
Senegal	27.4[12]	1987	977[7]	1,843[7]	...	19[7]	...	289[7]	4,964[7]	664[13]
Seychelles	11.3[4]	1989	3	3	...	3	...	243[3]	1,301[3]	...
Sierra Leone	15.9[19]	1983–84	...	3	...	...	...	...	7,211[3]	177[13]
Singapore	17.6[1,20]	1992	24,820	158,993	132,480	6.4	5,338	17,798[24]	78,152[24]	12,058[24]
Slovakia	8.9[11,34]	1992	...	...	...	...	...	5,590	24,638	1,313
Slovenia	14.1[11]	1994	849	5,150	665	6.1	665	6,021	29,768	4,060
Solomon Islands	9.6[11]	1991	...	3	...	...	...	405[18]	2,849[3]	139[18]
Somalia	9.3[11]	...								
South Africa	16.0	1991	...	...	46,541	...	...	58,100[32]	373,200[32]	35,592
Spain	20.5[1,27]	1984	40,000[21]	...	...	...	...	710,865[21]	1,400,000[21]	54,777
Sri Lanka	21.4[1]	1983[7]	190	15,000	3	78.9	...	1,348	44,300	1,116[3,25]
Sudan, The	12.8[6]	1981	...	...	...	...	...	...	...	3,278
Suriname	26.1	1985	...	3	...	...	...	13,000[58]	12,840[3]	110[18]
Swaziland	6.8[1]	1984	67	1,000	...	14.9	...	656	3,700	23[21]
Sweden	10.9	1993	31,960[25]	167,800[25]	37,518[25]	5.2[25]	1,174[25]	58,497	248,208[12]	30,159
Switzerland	17.5[12]	1991	22,094	176,857	...	8.0	...	55,080	245,443	23,620[25]
Syria	13.1	1983	2,827[44]	...	...	...	...	75,865[44]	110,000[14,44]	7,330[18]
Taiwan	15.3[1,20]	1987	55,654[13]	169,100	7,572[27]	2.9[13]	101[13]	355,760[13]	181,200	14,291[27]
Tajikistan	6.6	...	...	3	...	...	...	...	145,400[3]	...
Tanzania	14.6[1,11]	1983	...	...	...	...	...	1,620[7]	16,524[7]	3,975[18]
Thailand	16.6[12]	1988	16,740	139,252	14,535	8.3	868	260,030	280,886	13,683
Togo	12.8[22]	1980	...	...	...	...	...	181[7]	1,815[7]	112
Tonga	12.4[19]	1976	...	14[14]	...	...	...	...	654[14]	...
Trinidad and Tobago	14.3[1,20]	1977	124	6,786	509	54.7	4,102	370	15,986	1,670[18]
Tunisia	27.3[1,20]	1984	...	3	...	...	...	...	153,860[3,27]	2,814
Turkey	18.5[20]	1991	53,122	250,671	72,071	4.7	1,357	444,803	586,416	63,621
Turkmenistan	...	1990	...	3	...	...	...	...	90,000[3]	4,150
Tuvalu	14.1[1]	1979	...	3	...	...	...	...	113[3,14]	...
Uganda	12.1[19]	1977	226	4,100	...	18.1	...	251	3,200	5,285[24]
Ukraine	6.6[11]	1991	...	3	...	...	...	...	1,753,000[3,4]	70,800
United Arab Emirates	6.3[20]	1983	3	3	...	3	...	13,906[1,3,42]	121,278[3,42]	5,910[18]
United Kingdom	14.4[19]	1993[60]	114,738	850,000	401,941	7.4	3,503	305,827	2,337,000	213,114
United States	15.8[12]	1994	478,000[11]	6,113,000[57]	2,072,500	12.7[11]	3,686[11]	1,547,000[11]	19,743,000[57]	2,237,000
Uruguay	14.5[20]	1988	...	3	...	...	...	52,954[1,3]	161,285[1,3]	5,397[24,25]
Uzbekistan	6.7	1991	...	3	...	...	...	...	462,000[3]	...
Vanuatu	30.9	1983[49]	18	187[14]	...	10.4[14]	...	256	1,439[14]	...
Venezuela	13.6	1979	...	...	...	...	...	...	161,596	12,345[18]
Vietnam	13.6[20]	1990	...	...	...	...	...	25,723	419,400	4,414
Virgin Islands (U.S.)	...	1987	84	1,322	211	15.7	2,509	1,311	8,529	703
West Bank	...	1986	...	3	...	...	...	...	23,000[3]	...
Western Sahara	...	...								
Western Samoa	8.3	1986	...	3	...	...	...	...	842[3]	...
Yemen[61]	13.0[11]	1986	...	3	...	...	...	...	201,606[3]	...
Yugoslavia	22.5[12,34]	1992	5,723	17,693	8,671	3.1	1,515	51,159	125,348	8,958
Zaire	17.5[11]	1981	...	...	...	...	...	3,036[7]	33,398[7]	3,300[13]
Zambia	11.0[11]	1974	494[7]	15,500[7]	977[7]	31.4[7]	1,978[7]	1,636[7]	13,700[7]	768[13]
Zimbabwe	10.9[20]	1990	...	...	...	...	...	...	95,400[3]	693[27]

[1]Includes hotels. [2]1990–91. [3]Retail-trade data include wholesale trade. [4]1990. [5]Excludes retail-trade network of the agricultural cooperatives. [6]1989. [7]Data refer to larger establishments only. [8]1971. [9]1987. [10]1972. [11]1991. [12]1992. [13]1983. [14]All persons engaged, including proprietors. [15]1982. [16]1992–93. [17]Data refer to New Providence Island only. [18]1986. [19]1993–94. [20]1994. [21]1979. [22]Includes finance. [23]1981. [24]Excludes restaurants (eating and drinking establishments). [25]1984. [26]Privately owned establishments only. [27]1985. [28]1976. [29]General merchandise includes clothing and shoes. [30]For major cities only. [31]Wholesale selling directly to the public only. [32]1980. [33]Data exclude pharmacies. [34]Percentage of net material product. [35]Data refer to former Czechoslovakia. [36]Selected outlets in urban areas only. [37]Ethiopia includes Eritrea. [38]Home furnishings includes building materials. [39]Other includes drugs, pharmaceuticals.

retail trade   (continued)

food[d]	clothing, shoes[e]	home furnishings[f]	eating, drinking[g]	drugs, pharmaceuticals[h]	building materials[i]	automobile parts[j]	general merchandise[k]	other[l]	employees per outlet	sales per outlet (U.S.$'000)	population per outlet	country
…	…	…	…	…	…	…	…	…	…	…	…	Netherlands Antilles
…	…	…	…	…	…	…	…	…	…	…	169	New Caledonia
22.1	5.4	7.4	14.4	3.2	2.4	32.1	4.6	8.4	3.9[24,54]	346[24,54]	106[24,54]	New Zealand
…	…	…	…	…	…	…	…	…	…	…	143[15]	Nicaragua
…	…	…	…	…	…	…	…	…	…	…	…	Niger
27.0	[55]	2.3	8.8	…	7.2	[55]	4.7	50.0[55]	47.5	5,230	226,615	Nigeria
…	…	…	…	…	…	…	…	…	6.0	406	56	Northern Mariana Islands
34.9	9.9	7.3	…	…	4.8	27.0	4.0	12.1	3.0[46]	779	107	Norway
…	…	…	…	…	…	…	…	…	…	…	56[1,3,6]	Oman
64.0	12.0	4.0	…	…	…	…	…	20.0	1.8[14,44]	…	273[44]	Pakistan
…	…	…	…	…	…	…	…	…	…	…	…	Palau
…	…	…	…	…	…	…	…	…	13.9[7]	176	270	Panama
…	…	…	7.1	…	…	26.0	…	66.9	…	…	…	Papua New Guinea
…	…	…	…	…	…	…	…	…	…	…	…	Paraguay
…	…	…	…	…	…	…	…	…	0.7	20	145	Peru
25.4	12.3	6.7	…	…	11.3	29.5	…	14.8	0.9	17	177	Philippines
37.4	6.1	2.8	…	…	…	27.8	…	25.9	1.3	73	49	Poland
21.5[43]	14.1[43]	11.2[43]	…	3.3[43]	5.6[43]	35.2[43]	9.1[43]		15.3[14]	625	2,047	Portugal
30.5[15]	9.9[15]	4.5[15]	7.5[15]	4.3[15]	5.9[15]	23.2[15]	8.9[15]	5.3[15]	11.6	201[27]	387	Puerto Rico
9.0[41]	9.6[41]	13.2[41]	…	2.7[41]	7.2[41]	29.7[41]	9.1[41]	19.5[41]	3.7	177[10]	98	Qatar
54.4	11.5	17.8	…	6.9	…	…	…	9.4	3.7	603	178	Réunion
30.0[32]	10.0[32]	5.9[32]	25.0[32]	1.6[32]	0.8[32]	…	…	26.7[32]	5.7	243	282	Romania
…	…	…	…	…	…	…	…	…	9.8	59	563	Russia
…	…	…	…	…	…	…	…	…	…	…	…	Rwanda
…	…	…	…	…	…	…	…	…	…	…	…	St. Kitts and Nevis
…	…	…	…	…	…	…	…	…	…	…	…	St. Lucia
…	…	…	…	…	…	…	…	…	…	…	…	St. Vincent
…	…	…	…	…	…	…	…	…	2.2[3]	…	21.8[3]	San Marino
…	…	…	…	…	…	…	…	…	…	…	…	São Tomé and Príncipe
…	…	…	…	…	…	…	…	…	2.2[14]	29	201	Saudi Arabia
…	…	…	…	…	…	…	…	…	17.2[7]	…	23,430[7]	Senegal
…	…	…	…	…	…	…	…	…	54[3]	…	285[3]	Seychelles
…	…	…	…	…	…	…	…	…	…	…	…	Sierra Leone
17.7[47]	20.4	11.6	…	…	…	24.2	[47]	26.1	4.4	677	158	Singapore
42.1	7.7	9.3	…	1.9	0.8	3.7	1.7	32.8	1.4	235	948	Slovakia
15.2[3]	5.2[3]	1.0[3]	…	4.6[3]	8.1[3]	25.0[3]	35.1[3]	5.8[3]	4.9	674	329	Slovenia
…	…	…	…	…	…	…	…	…	…	…	…	Solomon Islands
…	…	…	…	…	…	…	…	…	…	…	…	Somalia
35.0	13.9	8.1	…	3.3	…	18.7	4.5	16.5	6.4[32]	383[32]	c. 540[32]	South Africa
39.2	10.5	16.7	…	…	…	4.2	…	29.4	2.0[21]	119[21]	52[21]	Spain
…	…	…	…	…	…	…	…	…	32.9	…	11,436	Sri Lanka
…	…	…	…	…	…	…	…	…	…	…	…	Sudan, The
…	…	…	…	…	…	…	…	…	…	…	…	Suriname
52.5[21]	25.1[18]	22.4[18]	…	…	…	…	…	…	5.6	…	969	Swaziland
35.5[12]	9.3[12]		…	…	…	…	…	55.2[12]	3.5[12]	515	149	Sweden
46.4[25]	13.5[25]	…	…	4.0[25]	…	…	…	36.1[25]	4.5	…	123	Switzerland
16.0	2.5	…	…	3.5	12.3	39.5[59]	3.5	22.7	1.4[14,44]	…	97[44]	Syria
21.5[23]	3.2[23]	8.8[23]	…	4.1[23]	3.1[23]	8.7[23]	3.1[23]	47.5[23]	0.3[13]	33[13]	52[13]	Taiwan
…	…	…	…	…	…	…	…	…	…	…	…	Tajikistan
…	…	…	…	…	…	…	…	…	10.0[7]	…	12,600[7]	Tanzania
10.5	3.4	4.6	…	1.0	7.2	43.2	12.4	17.7	1.1	53	209	Thailand
…	…	…	…	…	…	…	…	…	10.0[7]	…	15,600[7]	Togo
18.6	…	8.5	2.7	…	10.7	28.2	15.3	15.9	43.2	1,467	2,798	Trinidad and Tobago
…	…	…	…	…	…	…	…	…	…	…	…	Tunisia
15.0[4]	10.6[4]	15.5[4]	3.8[4]	2.8[4]	2.9[4]	27.3[4]	10.6[4]	11.5[4]	1.3	143	129	Turkey
…	…	…	…	…	…	…	…	…	…	…	…	Turkmenistan
…	…	…	…	…	…	…	…	…	…	…	…	Tuvalu
…	…	…	…	…	…	…	…	…	12.7	…	47,200	Uganda
…	…	…	…	…	…	…	…	…	…	…	…	Ukraine
…	…	…	…	…	…	…	…	…	…	…	49[1,3,42]	United Arab Emirates
44.1	14.4	8.0	…	3.9	3.7	…	6.8	19.1	7.6	697	190	United Kingdom
17.8	4.9	5.3	10.2	3.6	5.5	29.9	12.6	10.2	12.5[11]	1,177[11]	163[11]	United States
…	…	…	…	…	…	…	…	…	3.0[1,3]	…	…	Uruguay
…	…	…	…	…	…	…	…	…	…	…	…	Uzbekistan
…	…	…	…	…	…	…	…	…	5.6[14]	…	484	Vanuatu
50.2	10.1	7.6	…	…	…	5.0	…	27.1	…	…	…	Venezuela
…	…	…	…	…	…	…	…	…	16.6	171	2,575	Vietnam
17.6	7.9	6.4	12.0	2.3	4.8	11.4	1.9	35.7	6.5	536	81	Virgin Islands (U.S.)
…	…	…	…	…	…	…	…	…	…	…	…	West Bank
…	…	…	…	…	…	…	…	…	…	…	…	Western Sahara
…	…	…	…	…	…	…	…	…	…	…	…	Western Samoa
…	…	…	…	…	…	…	…	…	…	…	…	Yemen[61]
…	…	…	…	…	…	…	…	…	2.5	175	205	Yugoslavia
…	…	…	…	…	…	…	…	…	11.0[7]	…	9,676[7]	Zaire
…	…	…	…	…	…	…	…	…	8.4[7]	359[7]	2,873[7]	Zambia
…	…	…	…	…	…	…	…	…	…	…	…	Zimbabwe

[40]Excludes Addis Ababa and Asmera. [41]1988. [42]1977. [43]1978. [44]1975. [45]Excludes fuels, automobiles, alcohol and tobacco, and building materials. [46]Full-time equivalents. [47]Food includes general merchandise. [48]1972–73. [49]Urban establishments only. [50]Other includes drugs, pharmaceuticals, and building materials. [51]Peninsular Malaysia only. [52]State- and cooperative-owned establishments, including public catering. [53]1989–90. [54]1982–83. [55]Other includes clothing, shoes, and automobile parts. [56]Excludes Colón Free Zone. [57]1993. [58]1973. [59]Other includes machinery, transport equipment, and petroleum products. [60]Great Britain only. [61]Data refer to former Yemen Arab Republic only.

Finance

This table presents major statistical aggregates comprising national financial structure or constituting a basis for certain international financial comparisons. It includes such data as international reserves, money supply, central banking activity and discount rates, commercial (or "deposit money") banking activity, and external indebtedness of the central government. The country models are broadly similar and permit comparison of internal structure and external position at a high level of generalization.

One of the principal financial criteria of the relative economic position of a country is the size of its international reserves. International reserves as represented in this table comprise the sum of a country's (1) reserve position in the International Monetary Fund (IMF), a quota subscribed in the country's own currency, constituting a level up to which transactions may be effected within the IMF system, (2) holdings of foreign exchange, (3) holdings of gold, and (4) holdings of Special Drawing Rights (SDRs; an unconditional credit allocation, within a quota system set by the IMF, of currency needed by a country to maintain stability of foreign exchange transactions or markets). At appropriate accounting intervals these four elements are valued in a single unit of account (the SDR) and summed. The portion of this reserve total comprised by foreign exchange is very significant as an indication of the country's international liquidity (ability to pay its debts immediately in hard, or convertible, currencies). The ratio of external debt to total reserves, however, is less susceptible of interpretation in isolation: a low ratio, for example, may characterize the

situation of a country with little need to borrow or of one with substantial debt but also the means to repay it. Much higher ratios, on the other hand, may be manageable, despite small reserves, if a country's export earnings are also high.

The section on money supply for the country, both as a total and as a per capita amount, refers to one particular measure of money in circulation: M1, the sum of money in private sector demand deposit accounts and outside banks in circulation; it is distinguished from a broader measure of supply, M2, which is roughly M1 plus "quasi-money" (the time, savings, and foreign-currency deposits of residents).

The section of the table outlining banking activity and the principal monetary aggregates encompasses both central bank authorities and commercial (deposit) banks. For both, the principal component aggregates are grouped under assets and liabilities. For certain countries, the four principal aggregates under assets and liabilities do not comprise the entire total, and the percentages shown, therefore, may add to less than 100% (occasionally more, when the net of other liabilities [capital, reserves, undistributed profits, checks, and other transit items] is negative, reducing the total against which these percentages are calculated). The items excluded by the choice of categories are the least significant worldwide but may be important locally; they include such items as quasi-money, money seasonally adjusted, unused bank overdrafts, and so on. In the case of the central bank authority, data are also provided for the central bank discount

Finance

country	international reserves, 1996[a]			money supply, 1995[b]		central bank authority, 1995[b]									
						assets (%)				liabilities (%)				central bank discount rate, 1996[a]
	total ('000,000 SDRs)	% foreign exchange	ratio of external debt to total reserves, 1994[b]	stock ('000,000,000 national currency)	M1 per capita	claims on government	claims on private sector	claims on banks	claims on foreign assets	reserve money	government deposits	foreign liabilities	capital accounts	
Afghanistan	...	...	...	...	...	...	...	...	...	...	...	...	...	...
Albania	...	...	...	...	...	...	...	...	...	...	...	...	...	...
Algeria	1,924	89.7	9.5	520.3	18,400	59.9[1]	—	11.8[1]	28.2[1]	55.6[1]	2.2[1]	16.3[1]	—	...
American Samoa	...	...	...	...	...	...	...	...	...	...	...	...	...	...
Andorra	...	...	...	...	...	...	...	...	...	...	...	...	...	...
Angola	...	...	...	...	...	...	...	...	...	...	...	...	...	152.0[3]
Antigua and Barbuda	42	100.0	...	0.180	2,790	16.1	—	0.6	83.3	100.0	—	...	—	7.0[5]
Argentina	9,869	95.3	3.8	15.119[4]	440[4]	23.1[4]	—	45.6[4]	31.3[4]	30.3[4]	2.7[4]	7.4[4]	14.6[4]	7.0[3,7]
Armenia	...	...	...	...	...	...	...	...	...	...	...	...	...	...
Aruba	158	97.5	...	0.444	6,080	—	—	—	100.0	64.0	16.6	...	14.2	9.5
Australia	8,038	92.0	...	83.847	4,610	46.9	—	—	53.1	66.1	8.3	0.2	—	5.75
Austria	15,779	93.0	...	368.9	45,600	3.3	—	16.2	80.6	72.1	0.1	—	33.5	2.50
Azerbaijan	...	...	...	...	...	...	...	...	...	...	...	...	...	...
Bahamas, The	161	95.7	...	0.440	1,580	46.0	—	1.1	52.9	71.6	3.5	—	27.8	6.50
Bahrain	859	92.9	...	0.283	480	—	—	—	100.0	33.9	37.5	2.1	49.4	6.0[7]
Bangladesh	1,341	91.0	5.0	135.342	1,110	14.4[2]	—	25.1	60.5	65.5	2.5	20.5	4.1	6.50
Barbados	200	100.0	1.7	0.492	1,620	18.5	—	2.5	78.9	57.9	31.1	20.5	5.7	12.50
Belarus	...	...	...	...	...	...	...	...	...	...	...	...	...	...
Belgium	12,466	87.1	...	...	...	...	...	...	...	...	...	...	...	2.50
Belize	29	89.7	4.6	0.155	710	52.1	—	—	47.9	74.0	12.4	6.8	11.8	12.00
Benin	134[3]	97.8[3]	5.8	161.7	29,500	30.2	—	—	69.8	57.9	10.9	31.8	—	7.50
Bermuda	...	...	...	...	...	...	...	...	...	...	...	...	...	...
Bhutan	73[3]	98.6[3]	0.8	1.322	3,240	1.1	—	0.2	98.7	48.9	0.7	3.7	—	8.0[8]
Bolivia	600	88.8	8.3	3.916	520	36.6[2]	—	26.1	37.3	27.1	29.3	15.8	20.7	19.9[8]
Bosnia and Herzegovina	...	...	...	...	...	...	...	...	...	...	...	...	...	...
Botswana	3,328	95.6	0.2	0.830	530	—	—	—	100.0	15.4	53.7	—	24.3	13.00
Brazil	37,852	99.6	2.5	...	...	25.5[2]	—	28.7	45.8	33.6	18.5	4.6	1.2	27.0
Brunei	...	...	...	...	...	...	...	...	...	...	...	...	...	...
Bulgaria	...	...	...	...	...	...	...	...	...	...	...	...	...	...
Burkina Faso	234[3]	94.4[3]	4.4	214.1	20,400	24.3	—	1.2	74.4	65.4	16.2	17.0	—	7.50
Burundi	126	94.4	5.2	...	...	13.7[2]	1.9	4.6	79.8	28.7	14.0	11.5	20.7	...
Cambodia	...	...	...	279.139	28,000	28.7	—	4.7	66.6	47.5	8.6	24.9	20.2	...
Cameroon	3	33.3	1,363.1	319.2	23,800	92.1	—	5.8	2.1	40.2	15.4	96.2	0.7	8.60
Canada	12,836	85.6	...	134.6	4,540	32.4	—	—	67.6	95.7	—	—	—	5.00
Cape Verde	...	...	...	13.381	33,700	45.4[2]	9.2	5.1	40.3	95.2	—	0.4	21.5	5.00[8]
Central African Republic	158	99.4	3.8	111.2	34,300	23.8	—	1.0	75.1	65.1	1.0	11.1	0.5	8.60
Chad	130	100.0	9.8	87.9	13,600	39.4	—	0.8	59.8	59.2	8.5	19.2	1.3	8.60
Chile	9,338	94.5	0.7	2,312.9	161,000	29.5[2]	1.6	19.0	49.9	65.6	13.6	5.0	3.0	19.28[8]
China	58,154	97.0	1.6	2,557.8	2,110	7.7	3.3	56.7	32.3	100.7	4.7	—	1.9	9.18[8]
Colombia	5,270	94.7	1.8	8,057.0	228,000	8.2[2]	—	6.2	85.5	62.7	1.3	4.6	31.0	40.6
Comoros	...	...	...	...	...	...	...	...	...	...	...	...	...	...
Congo	42	97.6	91.3	134.9	51,300	69.5	—	3.7	26.8	80.1	13.7	8.8	1.2	8.60
Costa Rica	742	98.8	3.5	151.9	45,100	34.2[2]	—	11.4	54.4	86.7	7.9	66.9	8.0	37.00
Côte d'Ivoire	358[3]	99.2[3]	54.8	944.5	65,200	48.1	—	19.3	32.6	64.9	5.4	26.9	—	7.50
Croatia	...	...	...	8.270	1,730	3.6	—	2.1	94.3	55.5	3.7	11.0	18.9	8.50
Cuba	...	...	...	...	...	...	...	...	...	...	...	...	...	...
Cyprus[10]	767[3]	94.7[3]	...	0.613	930	52.9	—	2.0	45.1	72.7	19.8	3.6	...	6.00
Czech Republic	8,726	99.2	1.2	431.803	41,600	2.7[2]	—	14.7	82.6	87.5	8.5	9.9	5.2	9.50
Denmark	10,593	94.5	...	292.0	55,800	9.8	1.1	43.2	45.9	47.4	23.5	1.5	—	3.25
Djibouti	59	100.0	2.8	36.998	63,200	—	—	0.3	99.7	80.6	5.9	—	12.2	...
Dominica	15	100.0	5.4	0.092	1,240	24.9	—	—	75.1	93.3	0.9	5.8	—	6.4[5]
Dominican Republic	257	99.2	14.6	13.742[1]	1,880[1]	22.4[2]	—	19.2	58.4	173.1	—	148.6	-15.0	...
Ecuador	1,120	96.9	5.6	4,041.5[1]	356,000[1]	66.5[1,2]	0.4[1]	0.3[1]	32.9[1]	20.5[1]	13.5[1]	70.4[1]	5.7[1]	58.47
Egypt	11,374	98.1	2.2	41.540	690	40.5[2]	—	11.6	47.9	40.5	22.9	35.1	—	13.50
El Salvador	511	92.0	3.0	8.422	1,440	35.7[2]	—	17.1	47.2	69.5	10.2	8.8	11.4	14.39[8]

rate, generally the controlling interest rate for banking and commercial activity in the country.

The largest share of assets in the case of both central and commercial banks is usually either claims on government and government agencies or foreign assets and holdings, though some of the latter, such as the large outstanding loans to socialist and less developed countries, have become the chief liabilities. The chief liability of a central bank is usually reserve money (the currency and notes issued by the bank). When government deposits represent a substantial share, budgetary surpluses have usually been deposited by the central government. Large foreign liabilities imply extensive foreign investment. Among the deposit money banks, loans to the private sector normally represent the largest share of assets and savings deposits the largest share of liabilities.

Because the majority of the world's countries are in the less developed bloc, and because their principal financial concern is often external debt and its service, data are given for outstanding external public and publicly guaranteed long-term debt rather than for total public debt, which is the major concern in the developed countries. For comparability, the data are given in U.S. dollars. The volume of debt by itself does not create external payment problems. If the country's external debt service (interest payments plus principal repayment) needs can be met by a strong, dependable export market, by export of services, or, occasionally, by direct remittances from abroad (by residents working abroad and sending wages home in foreign currencies, for example), no debt problem need exist. Countries whose debt service ratio (total debt service as a percent of exports of goods and services) is relatively high, however, must often base their external borrowing policy on maintenance of domestic conditions of strict efficiency and, sometimes, austerity. The failure to adhere to such policies may lead to eventual crises of financial liquidity, deflation, and slower growth.

Ideally, the data presented here should be obtained by utilizing a single international methodology to provide a universally comparable set of international statistics. No international agency, however, can collect such data for all countries because of differences, both overall and in detail, in national definitions of financial aggregates, in accounting methodology, and in the completeness with which it is possible to survey a country's financial activity. The greater part of the data presented in the table comes from the IMF's *International Financial Statistics* and the World Bank's *World Debt Tables*. These sources are supplemented by other recent data from national, regional, or other international sources. In a few cases the desired data are negligible or unavailable, as noted.

Detailed percentages may not add to 100.0 because of rounding, statistical discrepancy, or nonaccounting of negligible quantities.
—None, less than half the last significant figure, or not applicable.
... Not available.
a. Latest month.
b. Year-end.

deposit money banks, 1995[b] assets (%) loans to government	loans to private sector	reserves	foreign assets	liabilities deposits ('000,000,000 national currency)	composition (%) demand depos.	savings depos.	govt. depos.	foreign liabilities	external public debt outstanding (long-term, disbursed only), 1994 total ('000,000 U.S.$)	creditors (%) official	private	debt service total ('000,000 U.S.$)	repayment (%) principal	interest	debt service ratio (%)	country
...	...	...	...	...	...	...	...	...	...	...	...	...	...	...	...	Afghanistan
...	...	...	...	...	...	...	...	...	229.9	68.0	32.0	11.1	73.9	26.1	2.1	Albania
80.2[2]	14.4	0.8	4.6	717.6	29.4	38.8	8.1	20.0	28,103	38.6	61.4	5,105	66.1	33.9	52.6	Algeria
...	...	...	...	...	...	...	...	...	...	...	...	...	...	...	...	American Samoa
...	...	...	...	...	...	...	...	...	...	...	...	...	...	...	...	Andorra
...	...	...	...	...	...	...	...	...	8,450	27.4	72.6	19	73.7	26.3	2.7[4]	Angola
15.1[2]	58.6	9.4	16.9	1.238	16.4	62.5[6]	5.3	10.2	...	...	...	...	...	...	...	Antigua and Barbuda
14.9[1,2]	70.2[1]	7.2[1]	7.7[1]	72.6[1]	8.6[1]	48.8[1,6]	4.6[1]	15.1[1]	55,785	33.6	66.4	4,522	37.1	62.9	21.5	Argentina
2.3	63.3	11.3	23.2	1.609	21.4	49.4	1.4	17.9	188.6	100.0	—	4.4	—	100.0	1.7	Armenia
...	...	...	...	...	...	...	...	...	...	...	...	...	...	...	...	Aruba
7.6[2]	85.5	1.4	5.4	415.513	15.6	52.1	0.8	16.0	...	...	...	...	...	...	...	Australia
30.7[1,2]	44.8[1]	2.1[1]	22.3[1]	3,826.7[1]	5.3[1]	45.0[1]	1.9[1]	24.2[1]	...	...	...	...	...	...	...	Austria
...	...	...	...	...	...	...	...	...	103.2	100.0	—	—	—	—	—	Azerbaijan
18.6[2]	87.8	6.3	-12.6	2.046	17.0	71.5[6]	2.1	...	...	...	...	...	...	...	...	Bahamas, The
5.0	34.4	5.3	55.3	2.346	7.7	47.5	19.7	22.3	...	...	...	...	...	...	...	Bahrain
22.0[2]	60.6	10.6	6.8	435.976	16.2	70.1	9.4	3.0	15,714	98.4	1.6	582	64.4	35.6	13.5	Bangladesh
25.7	54.4	5.2	14.7	2.776	7.5	61.3	7.8	19.8	330.3	55.1	44.9	79.7	65.9	34.1	11.4[4]	Barbados
...	...	...	...	...	...	...	...	...	1,100	65.3	34.7	109	79.8	20.2	3.9	Belarus
...	...	...	...	...	...	...	...	...	...	...	...	...	...	...	...	Belgium
10.9[2]	71.6	8.8	8.6	0.609	15.3	63.8[6]	3.9	13.0	159.6	85.5	14.5	25.9	73.7	26.3	5.7[4]	Belize
14.9	30.0	11.9	43.2	271.7	39.7	31.6	12.5	9.0	1,508	99.7	0.3	39	51.3	48.7	9.6	Benin
...	...	...	...	8.832[1]	...	...	...	...	...	...	...	...	...	...	...	Bermuda
13.7[2]	19.1	60.7	6.4	3.922	22.7	49.1[6]	8.8	—	86.7	89.6	10.4	6.8	75.0	25.0	6.9[9]	Bhutan
—	88.5	8.5	3.0	17.106	13.0	51.9[6]	—	15.7	4,113	98.0	2.0	285	53.7	46.3	23.8	Bolivia
...	...	...	...	...	...	...	...	...	...	...	...	...	...	...	...	Bosnia and Herzegovina
3.2[2]	56.5	33.7	6.6	2.974	20.4	60.8	—	3.3	680.8	92.7	7.3	92.0	65.1	34.9	3.9	Botswana
20.1[2,4]	63.4[4]	6.6[4]	9.8[4]	18.398[4]	2.7[4]	54.2[4]	7.7[4]	20.0[4]	94,512	31.3	68.7	8,792	55.7	44.3	17.4	Brazil
...	...	...	...	...	...	...	...	...	...	...	...	...	...	...	...	Brunei
...	...	...	...	...	...	...	...	...	9,014	31.7	68.3	634	77.9	22.1	11.5	Bulgaria
11.0	31.8	7.1	50.1	248.2	32.9	28.6	24.7	11.6	1,037	99.6	0.4	42	65.5	34.5	7.1[4]	Burkina Faso
18.6[2]	67.5	3.0	10.9	43.617	42.9	24.5	0.4	7.0	1,064	99.8	0.2	34	64.7	35.3	20.9	Burundi
0.6[2]	37.2	11.2	51.0	789.875	3.5	47.2[6]	0.1	21.5	1,774	100.0	—	—	—	—	—	Cambodia
32.3[2]	53.4	5.3	9.0	711.9	30.1	46.3	13.2	5.6	5,970	89.1	10.9	287	52.1	47.9	12.7	Cameroon
14.8[2]	71.9	0.7	12.6	660.2	16.6	51.9[6]	0.9	14.8	...	...	...	...	...	...	...	Canada
33.2[2]	38.4	25.0	3.4	23.929	36.5	52.5[6]	5.8	1.4	158.9	98.6	1.4	6.1	68.9	31.1	5.3[4]	Cape Verde
29.7[2]	57.4	5.1	7.8	40.4	30.4	22.2	17.9	9.6	807.3	95.7	4.3	15.8	49.1	50.9	8.5	Central African Republic
29.6[2]	45.8	16.6	8.0	60.7	38.2	13.0	17.9	14.0	743.6	99.0	1.0	11.9	36.1	63.9	6.6	Chad
1.6[1,2]	90.4[1]	6.2[1]	1.9[1]	11,572.5[1]	3.9[1]	57.4[1,6]	4.2[1]	14.9[1]	8,947	56.9	43.1	1,250	54.4	45.6	8.3	Chile
1.1	77.6	15.3	6.0	6,560.7	23.1	53.6	—	6.4	84,554	34.3	65.7	10,161	62.4	37.6	8.1	China
9.4[2]	75.3	13.0	2.1	20,421.5	20.8	35.6[6]	6.1	10.3	13,604	53.4	46.6	3,231	70.2	29.8	26.1	Colombia
...	...	...	...	...	...	...	...	...	175.5	100.0	—	2.7	74.1	25.9	4.6	Comoros
27.9[2]	56.6	4.8	10.6	152.9	32.2	15.9	7.2	9.3	4,667	78.8	21.2	532	59.5	40.5	49.4	Congo
5.5[2]	39.7	47.8	7.1	562.0	11.9	69.3[6]	2.7	5.8	3,155	80.3	19.7	380	56.4	43.6	11.2	Costa Rica
23.2	62.4	3.6	10.8	1,600.8	30.7	30.3	11.4	12.3	11,271	76.0	24.0	657	49.8	50.2	20.7	Côte d'Ivoire
29.2[2]	49.5	4.1	17.2	64.921	7.5	27.8[6]	1.4	23.6	902	86.8	13.2	164	55.8	44.2	2.3	Croatia
...	...	...	...	...	...	...	...	...	...	...	...	...	...	...	...	Cuba
8.2	56.9	9.9	25.0	5.629	6.3	55.6	—	30.3	...	...	...	...	...	...	...	Cyprus[10]
28.7[2]	53.7	10.8	6.7	1,492.093	20.8	40.3[6]	6.2	11.5	7,422	18.0	82.0	1,125	72.8	27.2	5.7	Czech Republic
11.2	49.2	4.4	35.2	891.0	29.2	31.7	—	20.7	...	...	...	...	...	...	...	Denmark
0.6[2]	49.3	1.4	48.7	76.626	27.6	35.0	0.9	21.1	206.9	99.9	0.1	5.9	77.1	22.9	1.5	Djibouti
18.7[2]	60.1	8.0	13.2	0.574	10.8	55.6[6]	9.8	16.2	86.5	100.0	—	6.3	67.5	32.5	5.4[4]	Dominica
6.0[1,2]	68.5[1]	20.1[1]	5.4[1]	33.549[1]	17.9[1]	59.5[1]	5.2[1]	7.6[1]	3,681	77.5	22.5	454	58.4	41.6	17.7	Dominican Republic
1.0[1]	83.4[1]	8.8[1]	6.8[1]	10,179.8[1]	21.8[1]	58.0[1]	—	12.8[1]	10,384	45.9	54.1	856	53.6	46.4	18.9	Ecuador
35.9[2]	32.7	13.4	17.9	209.091	8.3	58.0[6]	5.3	2.4	30,538	93.1	6.9	1,857	39.0	61.0	11.9	Egypt
3.9	70.3	24.1	1.7	35.084	11.2	63.2[6]	4.1	8.7	1,994	93.7	6.3	329	72.3	27.7	14.0	El Salvador

Finance (continued)

country	international reserves, 1996[a]			money supply, 1995[b]		central bank authority, 1995[b]									
	total ('000,000 SDRs)	% foreign exchange	ratio of external debt to total reserves, 1994[b]	stock ('000,000,000 national currency)	M1 per capita	assets (%)				liabilities (%)				central bank discount rate, 1996[a]
						claims on government	claims on private sector	claims on banks	claims on foreign assets	reserve money	government deposits	foreign liabilities	capital accounts	
Equatorial Guinea	1	100.0	...	4.7	11,700	99.9	—	—	0.1	22.5	0.4	104.1	1.7	8.60
Eritrea	...	...	...	...	...	...	...	...	...	...	...	...	...	...
Estonia	420	99.8	0.2	8.237	5,560	0.1[2]	0.2	2.9	96.8	76.0	—	16.9	28.2	4.1[11]
Ethiopia	571	98.1	8.8	9.280	170	60.0	—	3.4	36.5	58.9	13.4	9.7	6.5	12.00
Faroe Islands	...	...	...	...	...	...	...	...	...	...	...	...	...	...
Fiji	244	92.6	0.7	0.386	490	—	—	—	100.0	48.8	1.4	—	9.9	6.00
Finland	4,625	88.0	...	175.921	34,400	3.0	5.3	13.5	78.2	93.4	0.1	1.9	10.7	4.50
France	21,754	75.1	...	1,824.0	31,300	10.6	1.1	26.3	62.0	55.4	10.4	10.2	31.7	3.70[11]
French Guiana	...	...	...	5.407	36,700	...	...	...	...	...	...	...	...	...
French Polynesia	...	...	...	57.086	259,000	...	...	...	...	...	...	...	...	...
Gabon	79	98.7	19.9	217.2	187,000	56.4	—	2.1	41.5	70.0	6.9	26.4	0.7	8.60
Gambia, The	78	97.4	3.7	0.471	420	19.9[2]	—	—	80.1	30.2	43.9	21.6	6.6	14.00
Gaza Strip	...	...	...	...	...	...	...	...	...	...	...	...	...	...
Georgia	...	...	...	...	...	...	...	...	...	...	...	...	...	...
Germany	61,815	86.3	...	783.7	9,580	6.4	—	59.5	34.2	80.8	—	4.2	—	2.5
Ghana	479[3]	93.9[3]	6.8	925.3	55,500	58.1[2]	—	1.7	40.2	23.2	4.0	44.2	—	45.00
Gibraltar	...	...	...	...	...	...	...	...	...	...	...	...	...	...
Greece	8,399	97.2	...	3,385.8[1]	324,000[1]	48.4	—	5.0	46.6	39.0	6.4	31.7	...	17.5
Greenland	...	...	...	...	...	...	...	...	...	...	...	...	...	...
Grenada	23	100.0	3.2	0.146	1,490	18.4	—	0.1	81.5	98.6	1.4	—	—	6.5[5]
Guadeloupe	...	...	...	7.260	17,100	...	...	...	...	...	...	...	...	...
Guam	...	...	...	...	...	...	...	...	...	...	...	...	...	...
Guatemala	485	96.3	2.7	7.074[1]	680[1]	23.6[1,2]	—	16.0[1]	60.4[1]	353.1[1]	100.6[1]	24.1[1]	8.7[1]	...
Guernsey	...	...	...	...	...	...	...	...	...	...	...	...	...	...
Guinea	...	...	...	274.125	40,300	62.0[2]	—	1.7	36.3	36.5	46.0	18.2	10.2	18.0
Guinea-Bissau	16[3]	100.0[3]	38.8	469.2	433,000	25.7[2]	3.1	27.4	43.8	44.3	26.5	92.3	9.3	39.0
Guyana	182	99.5	7.2	15.310	21,400	76.7	—	—	23.3	11.9	12.9	76.3	2.0	14.5
Haiti	...	...	...	6.009	900	69.4[2]	—	0.9	29.7	78.3	17.3	6.9	10.8	...
Honduras	158	99.4	22.5	4.678	840	23.9[2]	—	21.3	54.8	60.4	28.0	120.2	31.9	17.0[8]
Hong Kong	...	...	...	189.641	30,400	...	...	...	...	...	...	...	...	6.00[11]
Hungary	7,447	99.2	3.2	895.6[1]	87,400[1]	48.4	0.2	17.5	33.9	50.8	6.3	104.4	1.4	27.0
Iceland	285	95.8	...	38.917	145,000	40.8	0.8	10.0	48.5	28.8	14.8	36.2	—	5.7
India	12,525	94.7	4.3	1,883.2	1,990	54.7	—	9.0	36.3	84.3	—	5.0	7.7	12.00
Indonesia	10,420	96.2	5.2	25,923.0[1]	428,000[1]	74.3[1,2]	—	4.3[1]	21.3[1]	48.9[1]	14.9[1]	6.4[1]	2.0[1]	...
Iran	...	...	...	...	...	...	...	...	...	...	...	...	...	...
Iraq	...	...	...	...	...	...	...	...	...	...	...	...	...	...
Ireland	5,591	93.9	...	5.361	1,490	3.2	—	—	96.8	58.0	19.1	—	22.4	6.25
Isle of Man	...	...	...	...	...	...	...	...	...	...	...	...	...	...
Israel	6,417	100.0	...	16.716	3,070	26.5	—	11.0	62.5	47.7	47.3	1.8	—	14.2
Italy	33,976	89.2	...	605,120.0	10,540,000	67.8[4]	—	0.8[4]	31.4[4]	72.9[4]	—	0.4[4]	—	9.00
Jamaica	489	99.6	4.7	29.320	11,600	36.7	—	—	63.3	75.7	67.7	18.9	5.6	43.65[5]
Japan	144,488	95.0	...	171,540.0	1,368,000	59.1	—	27.4	13.5	125.6	13.8	—	—	0.50
Jersey	...	...	...	...	...	...	...	...	...	...	...	...	...	...
Jordan	1,199	97.3	4.0	1.745	410	28.4	—	—	71.6	81.9	5.4	—	—	8.50
Kazakstan	...	...	...	...	...	...	...	...	...	...	...	...	...	...
Kenya	413	96.1	10.1	69.337	2,380	79.3	—	—	20.7	61.7	44.5	16.9	0.9	28.50
Kiribati	...	...	...	...	...	...	...	...	...	...	...	...	...	...
Korea, North	...	...	...	...	...	...	...	...	...	...	...	...	...	...
Korea, South	25,115	97.8	1.1	38,873.0	863,000	4.4[2]	—	50.3	45.3	52.5	12.4	0.1	—	5.0
Kuwait	2,781	89.5	...	1.168	680	0.4	—	—	99.6	41.7	14.5	—	17.2	7.3
Kyrgyzstan	...	...	...	...	...	...	...	...	...	...	...	...	...	...
Laos	...	...	...	67.177	13,600	7.3[2]	6.8	30.4	55.5	54.9	4.9	38.3	17.2	35.00
Latvia	...	...	...	0.345	140	10.5	—	5.9	83.6	73.0	0.5	23.1	2.9	19.00
Lebanon	3,646	90.3	0.1	1,560.6	512,000	0.4	0.8	2.2	96.6	34.6	18.2	0.9	1.0	18.81
Lesotho	317	98.7	1.4	0.521	250	8.0	—	—	91.9	17.0	72.1	7.9	3.8	15.50
Liberia	...	...	...	0.457[1]	190[1]	94.7[1,2]	1.1[1]	3.8[1]	0.4[1]	39.0[1]	5.4[1]	45.7[1]	4.3[1]	6.57[3,8]
Libya	...	...	...	...	...	...	...	...	...	...	...	...	...	...
Liechtenstein	...	...	...	...	...	...	...	...	...	...	...	...	...	...
Lithuania	...	...	...	3.505	950	0.6	—	4.8	94.6	71.5	3.2	30.3	—	25.0[11]
Luxembourg	...	...	...	...	...	36.6	—	1.5	61.9	36.6	25.4	6.7	31.3	3.50[8]
Macau	...	...	...	18.810[1]	45,600[1]	...	...	...	...	...	...	...	...	...
Macedonia	...	...	...	...	...	...	...	...	...	...	...	...	...	...
Madagascar	89	100.0	49.8	1,848.0	137,000	71.7[2]	—	9.0	19.3	59.8	16.4	29.1	3.1	...
Malawi	69	92.8	43.1	2.211	210	45.5[2]	—	—	54.5	77.1	19.3	25.6	—	50.00
Malaysia	16,785	96.1	0.5	63.594	3,160	2.9	0.8	9.2	87.1	65.5	11.4	—	—	7.00
Maldives	48	97.9	3.9	0.899	3,460	64.9[2]	—	0.3	34.7	61.4	10.8	11.4	3.8	...
Mali	218[3]	95.4[3]	11.8	200.2	32,300	29.2	—	—	70.8	58.1	11.3	32.7	—	7.50
Malta	1,116	93.8	0.1	0.499	1,340	10.2	—	—	89.8	77.6	6.4	—	—	5.5
Marshall Islands	...	...	...	...	...	...	...	...	...	...	...	...	...	...
Martinique	...	...	...	6.937	17,700	...	...	...	...	...	...	...	...	...
Mauritania	64	98.4	50.9	18.202	7,900	66.8[1,2]	2.2[1]	9.7[1]	21.3[1]	81.5[1]	29.8[1]	105.5[1]	18.1[1]	...
Mauritius	615	94.8	1.1	9.573	8,420	3.9	—	4.0	92.0	60.8	2.7	0.1	2.7	11.4
Mayotte	...	...	...	1.105	10,400	...	...	...	...	...	...	...	...	...
Mexico	11,709	94.6	12.6	150.572	1,640	-8.5	—	29.6	79.0	53.4	—	79.9	2.2	28.94[7]
Micronesia	...	...	...	...	...	...	...	...	...	...	...	...	...	...
Moldova	161	95.7	1.8	0.855	200	51.9	—	11.5	36.6	24.5	38.4	32.5	2.5	...
Monaco	...	...	...	...	...	...	...	...	...	...	...	...	...	...
Mongolia	66	95.5	4.6	54.576	23,500	7.5	—	10.2	82.3	49.5	12.5	48.2	11.0	108.0
Morocco	2,509	97.5	4.9	136.108	5,140	30.4	15.1	0.8	53.7	88.2	1.1	1.3	—	8.50[7]
Mozambique	...	...	...	...	...	...	...	...	...	...	...	...	...	...
Myanmar (Burma)	366	97.8	14.0	...	...	...	...	...	...	...	...	...	...	10.00[3,8]
Namibia	...	...	...	1.822	1,080	48.4	—	—	51.6	25.7	17.4	48.8	—	17.50
Nauru	...	...	...	...	...	...	...	...	...	...	...	...	...	...
Nepal	428	97.4	3.1	30.524[1]	1,530[1]	34.7[1]	0.9[1]	0.9[1]	63.5[1]	51.3[1]	13.9[1]	8.2[1]	21.5[1]	11.00[3]
Netherlands, The	22,565	86.6	...	172.9	11,100	5.0	—	11.9	83.1	62.4	17.7	—	—	2.00[11]

loans to govern-ment	loans to private sector	re-serves	foreign assets	deposits ('000,000,000 national currency)	demand depos.	savings depos.	govt. depos.	foreign liabilities	total ('000,000 U.S.$)	offi-cial	private	total ('000,000 U.S.$)	princi-pal	inter-est	debt service ratio (%)	country
11.0[2]	38.6	22.1	28.3	8.8	31.0	23.3	10.0	19.8	222.4	92.9	7.1	0.9	11.1	88.9	1.4	Equatorial Guinea
...	...	...	...	...	...	...	...	...	...	...	...	...	...	...	...	Eritrea
12.8[2]	47.8	10.2	29.2	12.645	34.8	17.7[6]	18.7	12.8	108.6	84.7	15.3	19.2	66.4	33.6	1.2[4]	Estonia
20.6	41.7	16.3	21.3	13.451	26.5	39.6	6.0	10.1	4,816	91.0	9.0	88	56.8	43.2	11.2	Ethiopia
...	...	...	...	...	...	...	...	...	...	...	...	...	...	...	...	Faroe Islands
12.6[2]	68.8	14.2	4.4	1.617	16.6	67.4	2.5	6.5	195.3	99.3	0.7	54.1	74.7	25.3	4.7	Fiji
6.9	65.0	8.5	19.6	538.445	30.3	26.5	3.5	23.7	...	...	...	...	...	...	...	Finland
10.3	58.4	0.4	30.9	11,256.0	13.9	29.9	—	28.8	...	...	...	...	...	...	...	France
...	...	...	...	...	...	...	...	...	...	...	...	...	...	...	...	French Guiana
...	...	...	...	...	...	...	...	...	...	...	...	...	...	...	...	French Polynesia
38.6[2]	46.9	6.1	8.4	442.0	26.7	31.6	3.5	8.9	3,483	92.0	8.0	182	47.3	52.7	7.5	Gabon
30.7[2]	46.1	15.9	7.3	0.743	30.1	59.7	—	3.3	364.3	99.9	0.1	26.0	77.3	22.7	15.9	Gambia, The
...	...	...	...	...	...	...	...	...	...	...	...	...	...	...	...	Gaza Strip
...	...	...	...	...	...	...	...	...	683	86.2	13.8	6.0	16.7	83.3	...	Georgia
19.6[2]	63.5	1.6	15.2	5,436.0	10.0	26.0	4.5	12.7	...	...	...	...	...	...	...	Germany
2.8[2]	24.8	42.3	30.0	1,584.0	23.4	27.4	4.8	24.3	4,075	91.4	8.6	217	64.3	35.7	15.6	Ghana
...	...	...	...	...	...	...	...	...	...	...	...	...	...	...	...	Gibraltar
39.7[1,2]	32.2[1]	18.0[1]	10.1[1]	14,334.2[1]	9.4[1]	53.8[1]	—	35.1[1]	...	...	...	...	...	...	...	Greece
...	...	...	...	...	...	...	...	...	...	...	...	...	...	...	...	Greenland
7.4[2]	62.2	8.0	22.4	0.712	12.8	63.9[6]	4.3	14.8	96.6	90.0	10.0	6.9	76.8	23.2	6.3[4]	Grenada
...	...	...	...	...	...	...	...	...	...	...	...	...	...	...	...	Guadeloupe
...	...	...	...	...	...	...	...	...	...	...	...	...	...	...	...	Guam
20.1[1]	64.0[1]	15.2[1]	0.7[1]	14.302[1]	23.3[1]	52.1[1]	0.5[1]	14.7[1]	2,368	82.7	17.3	232	62.1	37.9	9.0	Guatemala
...	...	...	...	...	...	...	...	...	...	...	...	...	...	...	...	Guernsey
9.1[2]	54.9	8.6	27.4	330.610	31.5	19.6[6]	5.0	24.1	2,881	96.6	3.4	88	54.5	45.5	12.8	Guinea
3.8[2]	31.1	22.7	42.4	964.320	19.4	29.6[6]	0.1	15.8	735.6	95.6	4.4	6.1	56.6	43.4	11.0	Guinea-Bissau
30.2[2]	41.9	20.4	7.5	50.597	12.5	72.5	4.1	5.7	1,788	96.0	4.0	71	54.9	45.1	20.5[4]	Guyana
0.1	49.0	34.9	16.0	10.222	23.4	78.3	0.4	0.8	627.2	92.7	7.3	—	—	—	...	Haiti
10.7[2]	68.3	9.8	11.2	11.376	20.8	49.3[6]	2.5	9.4	3,884	91.5	8.5	380	57.4	42.6	30.6	Honduras
...	...	...	...	7,837.9	...	...	...	...	...	...	...	...	...	...	...	Hong Kong
26.2[1,2]	42.0[1]	27.6[1]	4.2[1]	242.068[1]	17.3[1]	40.3[1,6]	1.1[1]	9.7[1]	22,090	19.4	80.6	4,638	68.8	31.2	42.5	Hungary
10.5	83.1	4.2	2.2	242.068	14.0	55.9	—	11.3	...	...	...	...	...	...	...	Iceland
27.8	58.3	13.9	—	4,651.9	14.8	50.9	—	—	87,880	71.2	28.8	8,132	53.8	46.2	20.3	India
...	...	...	...	...	...	...	...	...	63,848	77.9	22.1	9,319	63.5	36.5	18.9	Indonesia
2.5[1]	56.5[1]	29.1[1]	11.8[1]	48,712.0[1]	37.2[1]	60.3[1]	—	19.9[1]	15,613	3.8	96.2	3,682	90.0	10.0	18.6	Iran
...	...	...	...	...	...	...	...	...	...	...	...	...	...	...	...	Iraq
10.5	61.5	3.2	24.9	25.667	11.3	58.5	0.6	20.3	...	...	...	...	...	...	...	Ireland
...	...	...	...	...	...	...	...	...	...	...	...	...	...	...	...	Isle of Man
22.9	60.6	4.1	12.4	305.303	3.2	56.2	8.7	14.9	...	...	...	...	...	...	...	Israel
...	...	...	...	...	...	...	...	...	...	...	...	...	...	...	...	Italy
14.9[2]	42.7	24.2	18.3	106.004	18.7	53.8	6.6	12.6	3,440	89.9	10.1	469	61.4	38.6	17.5	Jamaica
9.2[2]	75.3	0.9	14.5	756,150.0	16.6	49.9	—	10.0	...	...	...	...	...	...	...	Japan
...	...	...	...	...	...	...	...	...	...	...	...	...	...	...	...	Jersey
3.4	44.9	25.3	26.5	7.115	9.3	42.7	7.7	29.2	6,837	55.9	44.1	463	57.2	42.8	11.2	Jordan
...	...	...	...	...	...	...	...	...	2,201	82.7	17.3	46	27.2	72.8	1.5	Kazakstan
14.4[2]	58.4	16.0	11.2	220.316	17.7	54.4[6]	2.5	8.8	5,651	86.8	13.2	709	65.3	34.7	26.6	Kenya
...	...	...	...	...	...	...	...	...	...	...	...	...	...	...	...	Kiribati
...	...	...	...	...	...	...	...	...	...	...	...	...	...	...	...	Korea, North
2.1	78.3	11.4	8.2	261,343.0	9.1	44.0[6]	5.5	9.3	27,103	34.7	65.3	4,462	63.2	36.8	3.8	Korea, South
46.4	26.0	1.6	26.1	6.867	12.2	76.5	2.0	9.2	...	...	...	...	...	...	...	Kuwait
...	...	...	...	...	...	...	...	...	350.8	100.0	—	13.1	—	100.0	3.9	Kyrgyzstan
13.6[2]	40.3	15.0	31.0	293.886	8.6	42.9[6]	5.2	13.5	2,022	99.8	0.2	20	75.0	25.0	7.7	Laos
21.6[2]	25.3	8.8	44.3	0.728	19.8	26.8[6]	10.5	33.4	197.6	88.2	11.8	19.9	53.8	46.2	1.6	Latvia
28.2	36.7	12.6	22.5	28,147.7	1.8	75.7[6]	0.9	11.7	621	53.6	46.4	122	78.3	21.7	8.0	Lebanon
12.7[2]	60.3	13.5	13.5	1.226	36.4	49.0	3.1	3.6	516.0	96.4	3.6	26.0	61.5	38.5	58.6	Lesotho
13.3[1,2]	43.2[1]	41.7[1]	1.8[1]	0.516[1]	29.9[1]	62.9[1]	6.8[1]	9.0[1]	1,137	81.7	18.3	14	100.0	—	...	Liberia
...	...	...	...	...	...	...	...	...	...	...	...	...	...	...	...	Libya
...	...	...	...	...	...	...	...	...	...	...	...	...	...	...	...	Liechtenstein
13.4[2]	68.3	9.5	8.8	5.585	28.5	38.9[6]	20.9	7.0	212.7	94.4	5.6	51.6	58.1	41.9	2.4	Lithuania
...	...	...	...	...	...	...	...	...	...	...	...	...	...	...	...	Luxembourg
...	...	...	...	101.277[1]	...	...	...	...	...	...	...	...	...	...	...	Macau
...	...	...	...	...	...	...	...	...	529	62.5	37.5	137	75.9	24.1	11.2	Macedonia
6.4	56.8	14.7	22.1	2,729.0	39.9	28.2	4.6	4.2	3,565	97.5	2.5	45	61.1	38.9	5.7	Madagascar
25.8[2]	31.0	32.2	11.0	4.076	29.9	47.5	—	3.7	1,889	98.5	1.5	60	60.8	39.2	15.7	Malawi
4.2	83.3	8.3	4.2	245.062	14.8	54.9	1.7	6.5	13,751	37.5	62.5	4,015	80.3	19.7	6.1	Malaysia
9.8[2]	40.1	37.5	12.6	1.635	24.1	34.9	3.6	16.2	125.8	94.1	5.9	9.4	68.1	31.9	3.4	Maldives
7.8	52.7	6.9	32.5	247.0	36.6	22.8	20.6	20.3	2,623	99.9	0.1	119	68.1	31.9	24.9	Mali
7.5	47.9	5.1	39.5	1.985	4.1	63.1	—	28.0	157.6	100.0	—	17.2	70.9	29.1	0.6	Malta
...	...	...	...	...	...	...	...	...	...	...	...	...	...	...	...	Marshall Islands
...	...	...	...	...	...	...	...	...	...	...	...	...	...	...	...	Martinique
1.5[1,2]	71.1[1]	21.4[1]	6.0[1]	59.752[1]	18.7[1]	12.7[1]	4.6[1]	22.7[1]	2,081	99.6	0.4	95	60.0	40.0	21.1	Mauritania
25.5	57.3	9.1	8.1	57.402	8.2	77.7	—	2.1	817	78.5	21.5	104	63.5	36.5	5.0	Mauritius
...	...	...	...	...	...	...	...	...	...	...	...	...	...	...	...	Mayotte
3.6[2]	75.3	14.9	6.2	768.312	11.2	53.6[6]	0.7	20.0	79,079	34.7	65.3	11,711	55.7	44.3	20.8	Mexico
...	...	...	...	...	...	...	...	...	...	...	...	...	...	...	...	Micronesia
66.7[2]	21.9	2.8	8.7	1.976	10.9	20.2	32.8	0.7	318.8	100.0	—	8.6	58.1	41.9	1.4	Moldova
...	...	...	...	...	...	...	...	...	...	...	...	...	...	...	...	Monaco
11.4[2]	51.2	12.4	25.1	101.307	16.8	58.6[6]	16.4	6.6	382.4	76.9	23.1	37.9	79.0	21.0	9.0	Mongolia
33.6	56.5	6.1	3.7	147.598	57.3	34.2	—	2.5	21,560	77.2	22.8	2,736	60.2	39.8	30.1	Morocco
...	...	...	...	...	...	...	...	...	5,033	98.5	1.5	75	34.0	66.0	19.0	Mozambique
...	...	...	...	...	...	...	...	...	6,099	94.7	5.3	172	30.2	69.8	15.3	Myanmar (Burma)
4.8	89.2	3.3	2.6	5.315	29.8	55.0[6]	1.4	9.4	...	...	...	...	...	...	...	Namibia
...	...	...	...	...	...	...	...	...	...	...	...	...	...	...	...	Nauru
16.7[1,2]	58.6[1]	11.8[1]	12.9[1]	62.269[1]	13.5[1]	67.7[1]	—	5.3[1]	2,202	97.2	2.8	74	59.5	40.5	11.5[9]	Nepal
11.7[2]	55.0	0.3	33.0	1,139.2	11.8	31.9[6]	—	31.1	...	...	...	...	...	...	...	Netherlands, The

Finance (continued)

country	international reserves, 1996[a]			money supply, 1995[b]		central bank authority, 1995[b]								central bank discount rate, 1996[a]
	total ('000,000 SDRs)	% foreign exchange	ratio of external debt to total reserves, 1994[b]	stock ('000,000,000 national currency)	M1 per capita	assets (%)				liabilities (%)				
						claims on government	claims on private sector	claims on banks	claims on foreign assets	reserve money	government deposits	foreign liabilities	capital accounts	
Netherlands Antilles	158	88.0	...	0.936	4,540	8.8	—	—	91.2	61.1	4.6	—	26.9	6.00
New Caledonia	...	...	...	62.453	331,000	...	...	...	...	...	...	...	...	...
New Zealand	3,510	96.6	...	33.354	9,270	29.4	...	4.6	66.1	19.4	59.3	2.6	...	10.75
Nicaragua	...	...	...	1.330	320	87.8[2]	2.8	4.4	4.9	7.6	0.8	90.8	0.9	10.2
Niger	64[3]	85.9[3]	11.8	100.6	10,800	50.6	—	4.7	44.7	65.9	8.0	25.3	—	7.50
Nigeria	1,595	98.5	19.8	...	...	...	...	...	...	...	...	...	...	13.50
Northern Mariana Islands	...	...	...	...	...	...	...	...	...	...	...	...	...	...
Norway	17,166	94.5	...	358.7	82,100	10.6	—	5.9	83.5	27.1	57.6	—	...	6.50
Oman	791	93.3	2.6	0.471	210	11.3	—	—	88.7	38.7	5.2	0.1	31.8	6.20[8]
Pakistan	1,140	92.9	7.6	490.961	3,450	57.9	—	22.4	19.7	75.9	7.8	12.3	—	12.72[7]
Palau	...	...	...	...	...	...	...	...	...	...	...	...	...	...
Panama	666	96.8	5.6	0.815	310	46.2[2]	15.6	—	38.2	12.2	90.8	22.2	14.6	7.25[3, 8]
Papua New Guinea	138	99.3	16.3	0.614[1]	150[1]	87.3[1]	—	—	12.7[1]	24.9[1]	74.6[1]	4.6[1]	15.8[1]	19.83[3, 5]
Paraguay	671	86.9	1.3	1,756.6	359,000	28.8[2]	0.2	18.2	52.9	48.6	12.9	5.1	8.5	18.00
Peru	5,904	99.3	2.5	7.549	320	3.1[2]	—	-0.6	97.5	49.3	27.4	19.2	2.3	15.8
Philippines	5,348	95.6	4.8	194.6	2,750	51.7[2]	—	2.4	45.9	50.6	22.3	27.6	6.7	11.81
Poland	11,468	99.2	6.7	37.439	970	20.1[2]	—	14.4	65.5	49.6	6.0	1.6	0.7	23.0
Portugal	11,328	91.8	...	4,351.6	439,000	6.6[2]	—	16.0	77.4	30.0	17.1	0.2	7.5	7.50
Puerto Rico	...	...	...	...	...	...	...	...	...	...	...	...	...	...
Qatar	488[3]	84.0[3]	...	3.720	6,360	12.5	—	5.9	81.7	60.9	10.9	—	33.6	...
Réunion	...	...	...	10.815	16,300	...	...	...	...	...	...	...	...	...
Romania	1,133	91.3	1.3	6,771.4	299,000	31.7	...	42.1	26.2	53.0	23.7	31.2	...	35.0[11]
Russia	10,185	95.2	18.2	151,267.0	1,030,000	53.9[2]	0.1	7.1	38.9	50.3	9.7	17.9	12.9	35.6[11]
Rwanda	...	...	...	25.041	3,250[4]	69.8[2, 4]	0.3[4]	2.3[4]	27.6[4]	33.8[4]	18.0[4]	14.4[4]	20.7[4]	16.00
St. Kitts and Nevis	23	100.0	1.3	0.083	2,110	4.7	—	—	95.3	97.9	2.1	—	—	6.5[5]
St. Lucia	40	95.0	1.8	0.264	1,840	7.0	—	—	92.9	97.4	2.6	—	—	7.0[5]
St. Vincent and the Grenadines	19	100.0	2.1	0.108	960	9.9	—	—	90.1	99.1	0.9	—	—	6.5[5]
San Marino	...	...	...	...	...	...	...	...	...	...	...	...	...	...
São Tomé and Príncipe	...	...	...	...	...	...	...	...	...	...	...	...	...	...
Saudi Arabia	7,804	84.7	...	124.5	6,860	...	...	...	...	...	...	...	...	...
Senegal	184[3]	100.0[3]	17.0	316.3	37,600	67.0	—	0.2	32.9	48.4	4.9	56.8	—	7.50
Seychelles	15	93.3	4.8	0.335	4,430	83.8	—	0.2	16.0	86.5	2.7	—	1.8	12.34[5]
Sierra Leone	17	82.4	14.8	49.902	10,900	16.7	—	—	83.3	60.1	18.7	596.4	—	35.94[5]
Singapore	48,095	99.5	...	25.350	8,410	—	—	—	100.0	17.5	45.7	—	—	2.31[7]
Slovakia	2,357	98.0	1.5	149.657	27,900	15.3[2]	—	21.5	63.2	45.2	9.5	32.9	4.9	8.80
Slovenia	...	...	...	176.9	90,000	4.9	—	13.9	81.1	32.6	15.4	0.2	10.4	10.00
Solomon Islands	18	94.4	5.7	0.171	440	59.7[2]	—	—	40.3	55.0	3.1	0.9	43.2	12.75[3, 5]
Somalia	...	...	...	...	...	...	...	...	...	...	...	...	...	...
South Africa	770	78.7	...	111.844	2,670	30.6	—	19.4	50.0	74.7	32.6	12.4	—	16.00
Spain	33,930	94.2	...	19,179.0	489,000	21.5	—	46.5	32.0	62.6	12.2	—	8.9	7.75
Sri Lanka	...	...	...	75.218	4,130	29.2	—	1.8	69.0	51.3	2.0	32.5	16.4	17.00
Sudan, The	64[3]	100.0[3]	118.9	242.8[1]	8,750[1]	86.5[1, 2]	—	1.4[1]	12.1[1]	78.6[1]	—	521.4[1]	0.9[1]	...
Suriname	82	86.6	...	57.724	133,000	7.0	—	—	93.0	79.3	14.0	3.1	6.6	...
Swaziland	189	95.2	0.8	0.363	390	1.9	—	2.8	95.3	28.7	51.7	7.2	3.9	15.00
Sweden	14,128	93.8	...	...	...	28.9	—	1.1	70.0	69.5	—	1.4	—	5.50
Switzerland	25,779	84.1	...	100.7	14,300	8.2	—	3.0	88.9	60.6	1.8	—	—	1.50
Syria	...	...	...	207.891[3]	15,270[3]	...	...	...	...	...	...	...	...	5.00[3]
Taiwan	61,809	99.2	...	3,173.3	149,000	0.1	—	13.7	86.2	50.5	5.1	—	—	5.00
Tajikistan	...	...	...	...	...	...	...	...	...	...	...	...	...	...
Tanzania	156	93.6	18.8	327.9[1]	11,800[1]	67.6	—	1.1	31.2	65.3	8.2	103.4	—	15.00
Thailand	26,441	98.3	0.6	388.3	6,570	4.2	—	5.4	90.4	39.3	32.0	—	31.0	10.50
Togo	88[3]	98.9[3]	12.9	131.6	31,300	51.8	—	1.7	46.6	59.0	5.9	37.8	—	7.50
Tonga	19	89.5	1.8	0.025	240	14.0	—	—	86.0	45.0	4.6	—	7.7	5.58[8]
Trinidad and Tobago	243	98.8	4.7	3.923	3,090	17.9	—	6.7	75.5	53.5	9.6	8.3	43.7	13.00
Tunisia	940	97.6	5.4	3.637	410	3.5	—	33.7	62.9	67.7	5.6	12.8	5.2	8.88
Turkey	10,813	98.4	6.6	384,391.0	6,080,000	48.9[1]	—	2.7[1]	48.5[1]	36.8[1]	2.9[1]	51.8[1]	1.8[1]	83.26[7]
Turkmenistan	...	...	...	...	...	...	...	...	...	...	...	...	...	60.0[3, 5]
Tuvalu	...	...	...	...	...	...	...	...	...	...	...	...	...	...
Uganda	306	100.0	9.2	419.151	22,200	71.5[2]	—	0.1	28.4	18.1	75.8	25.7	3.4	14.00
Ukraine	464	81.0	...	466,523.0	9,000,000	62.0[2]	—	9.4	28.6	50.2	1.4	39.6	5.3	63.00
United Arab Emirates	5,584	94.9	...	20.824	8,540	—	—	0.2	99.8	65.6	26.0	0.6	6.0	...
United Kingdom	27,470	90.5	...	...	...	43.4	—	—	56.6	50.0	—	54.6	—	6.13[7]
United States	59,375	53.9	...	1,221.1	4,620	82.3	—	—	17.7	93.8	7.8	0.1	—	5.00
Uruguay	867	91.1	3.6	7.589	2,380	45.8[2]	0.5	16.4	37.3	44.8	32.0	21.6	—	176.3
Uzbekistan	...	...	...	...	...	...	...	...	...	...	...	...	...	...
Vanuatu	30[3]	93.3[3]	0.9	6.306	37,000	11.8	1.5	—	86.7	57.7	31.0	0.1	10.1	...
Venezuela	5,034	82.6	3.2	1,449.8	65,700	20.2[2]	—	26.3	53.5	19.7	3.7	22.2	6.2	85.00
Vietnam	...	...	...	...	...	...	...	...	...	...	...	...	...	...
Virgin Islands (U.S.)	...	...	...	...	...	...	...	...	...	...	...	...	...	...
West Bank	...	...	...	...	...	...	...	...	...	...	...	...	...	...
Western Sahara	...	...	...	...	...	...	...	...	...	...	...	...	...	...
Western Samoa	35	94.3	3.0	0.061	370	0.1	—	0.1	99.9	52.6	40.5	—	—	5.58[8]
Yemen	367[3]	92.9[3]	20.7	139.590[1]	10,900[1]	97.5[1, 2]	—	—	2.5[1]	79.7[1]	9.9[1]	1.1[1]	0.6[1]	...
Yugoslavia	...	...	...	...	...	...	...	...	...	...	...	...	...	...
Zaire	97[3]	99.0[3]	75.7	373.0[1]	8,630[1]	24.0[1, 2]	0.4[1]	2.4[1]	73.2[1]	33.4[1]	4.3[1]	350.3[1]	58.5[1]	217.0
Zambia	...	...	...	227.9	23,800	...	...	...	...	...	...	...	...	37.40[3]
Zimbabwe	496	94.2	7.6	11.270	990	67.3[2]	—	—	32.7	18.2	72.0	22.6	—	29.50

deposit money banks, 1995[b]									external public debt outstanding (long-term, disbursed only), 1994							country
assets (%)				liabilities					total ('000,000 U.S.$)	creditors (%)		debt service				
loans to government	loans to private sector	reserves	foreign assets	deposits ('000,000,000 national currency)	composition (%)					official	private	total ('000,000 U.S.$)	repayment (%)		debt service ratio (%)	
					demand depos.	savings depos.	govt. depos.	foreign liabilities					principal	interest		
3.4[2]	65.4	6.5	24.7	3.203	19.2	52.9[6]	1.3	21.8	...	...	...	...	...	...	...	Netherlands Antilles
...	...	...	...	...	...	...	...	...	...	...	...	...	...	...	...	New Caledonia
5.8	89.2	3.4	1.7	90.742	35.1	39.8[6]	...	24.5	...	...	...	...	...	...	...	New Zealand
0.9[1,2]	77.2[1]	14.7[1]	7.2[1]	5.277[1]	7.7[1]	47.4[1,6]	10.2[1]	4.3[1]	9,006	79.0	21.0	172	36.3	63.7	35.8	Nicaragua
15.0	50.5	10.0	24.5	83.1	46.3	40.5	23.2	26.5	1,311	100.0	—	24	58.3	41.7	9.4	Niger
...	...	...	...	...	...	...	...	...	28,168	70.3	29.7	1,854	40.3	59.7	18.9	Nigeria
																Northern Mariana Islands
12.7[2]	79.9	0.7	6.7	703.0	45.0	23.4[6]	4.8	8.6	...	...	...	...	...	...	...	Norway
5.0	71.3	3.6	20.2	1.905	12.4	54.6	7.4	8.9	2,608	23.0	77.0	525	71.6	28.4	10.0[4]	Oman
29.5	52.1	12.3	6.2	892.573	28.4	36.1	5.3	12.9	22,993	95.0	5.0	2,804	71.7	28.3	28.5	Pakistan
																Palau
0.6	26.8	...	72.6	21.579	3.4	19.5	—	64.6	3,923	32.0	68.0	303	54.0	46.0	4.5	Panama
22.7[1]	64.7[1]	2.1[1]	10.5[1]	1.967[1]	22.0[1]	53.4[1]	3.7[1]	7.2[1]	1,622	84.3	15.7	303	75.2	24.8	10.1	Papua New Guinea
0.7[2]	64.9	20.4	14.0	5,890.3	11.0	50.8	11.7	13.0	1,352	91.2	8.8	229	67.7	32.3	8.6	Paraguay
3.6[2]	62.4	22.1	11.9	31.0	14.2	55.6[6]	5.2	11.8	17,890	77.6	22.4	855	56.2	43.8	16.3	Peru
16.0	60.3	10.1	13.6	1,231.0	5.9	62.2	3.2	13.7	29,577	76.3	23.7	3,519	57.5	42.5	14.4	Philippines
45.6[2]	28.0	12.9	13.5	130.917	13.6	51.1[6]	4.2	3.9	39,110	79.7	20.3	2,473	57.0	43.0	12.6	Poland
21.3[2]	46.0	9.2	23.5	22,789.4	15.4	35.9	3.0	33.0	...	...	...	...	...	...	...	Portugal
																Puerto Rico
31.9[2]	31.4	2.3	34.5	32.679	7.1	45.6	8.2	19.7	...	...	...	...	...	...	...	Qatar
																Réunion
71.9[2]	—	13.2	14.9	24,953.8	13.5	45.4[6]	7.3	8.5	2,942	66.0	34.0	330	49.7	50.3	4.4	Romania
35.5[2]	38.2	12.6	13.6	351,898.0	19.7	33.8	2.8	8.5	80,054	45.3	54.7	3,486	65.3	34.7	5.9	Russia
15.5[2,4]	53.4[4]	17.3[4]	13.9[4]	33.464[4]	38.5[4]	39.9[4]	8.5[4]	2.7[4]	904.9	99.8	0.2	5.4	69.4	30.6	10.6	Rwanda
20.1[2]	49.4	7.3	23.2	0.893	5.9	43.7[6]	18.9	23.4	43.0	99.5	0.5	4.4	65.9	34.1	3.3[4]	St. Kitts and Nevis
9.4[2]	76.3	7.8	6.5	1.251	15.0	53.8[6]	15.6	12.2	104.7	100.0	—	10.3	55.8	44.2	10.9[4]	St. Lucia
15.5[2]	56.2	8.6	19.7	0.629	12.7	48.3[6]	19.8	13.5	64.1	100.0	—	5.1	63.7	36.3	4.3[4]	St. Vincent and the Grenadines
...	...	...	...	...	...	...	...	...	...	...	...	...	...	...	...	San Marino
...	...	...	...	...	...	...	...	...	229.0	99.5	0.5	2.3	50.0	50.0	18.5	São Tomé and Príncipe
25.0[2]	39.5	3.6	31.9	307.0	26.5	37.6[6]	—	12.9	...	...	...	...	...	...	...	Saudi Arabia
11.7	67.5	5.9	14.9	526.7	30.4	35.0	25.9	12.3	3,070	96.5	3.5	143	62.6	37.4	10.6	Senegal
65.0[2]	14.7	32.1	2.9	1.670	11.2	52.4	6.8	3.0	146.9	85.2	14.8	17.5	69.1	30.9	6.0	Seychelles
22.8[2]	30.9	8.4	37.9	55.993	34.8	29.4	—	5.2	737	96.9	3.1	23	47.8	52.2	15.8	Sierra Leone
8.4	58.4	3.8	29.4	188.112	8.2	40.7	4.0	35.2	...	...	...	...	...	...	...	Singapore
36.4[2]	41.1	7.9	14.6	369.448	30.6	55.0[6]	5.2	7.8	2,659	27.7	72.3	677	66.9	33.1	7.4	Slovakia
21.5[2]	44.9	11.5	22.1	1,363.9	8.5	46.1[6]	6.7	13.7	1,358	54.9	45.1	207	70.5	29.5	2.4	Slovenia
51.9[2]	39.5	7.1	1.5	0.309	37.6	55.2	3.0	2.1	99.6	94.0	6.0	9.4	77.7	22.3	4.9[9]	Solomon Islands
...	...	...	...	...	...	...	...	...	1,935	98.1	1.9	...	...	...	...	Somalia
6.9	89.5	2.9	0.8	362.193	26.8	44.8	4.9	9.2	...	...	...	...	...	...	...	South Africa
23.6[2]	53.7	3.9	18.8	94,528.0	12.3	39.5	1.7	14.0	...	...	...	...	...	...	...	Spain
12.2[2]	64.7	13.0	10.1	271.846	12.1	56.4	3.5	16.4	6,598	93.1	6.9	372	64.2	35.8	9.1	Sri Lanka
0.8[1]	34.7[1]	21.9[1]	42.5[1]	254.1[1]	37.3[1]	53.8[1]	0.9[1]	6.0[1]	9,372	82.6	17.4	—	—	—	...	Sudan, The
0.7	25.9	37.4	36.0	77.780	39.7	27.4	1.6	23.9	...	...	...	...	...	...	...	Suriname
3.6	66.8	17.0	12.6	1.371	20.6	59.2	8.4	4.7	227.5	99.8	0.2	24.3	72.8	27.2	2.4	Swaziland
10.1	60.6	0.7	28.7	1,425.5	—46.0[6]—			0.1	39.9	...	...	...	...	...	...	Sweden
																Switzerland
3.9	68.0	0.9	27.2	899.3	5.8	39.8	—	23.7	...	...	...	...	...	...	...	
53.3[1,2]	19.7[1]	12.0[1]	12.9[1]	261.839[1]	27.6[1]	28.3[1]	2.6[1]	1.5[1]	16,539	92.9	7.1	229	56.3	43.7	3.3	Syria
12.8[2]	75.4	8.0	3.8	13,589.9	19.5	63.7	5.0	4.1	...	...	...	...	...	...	...	Taiwan
...	...	...	...	...	...	...	...	...	570.4	100.0	—	0.4	—	100.0	...	Tajikistan
24.9[1,2]	36.9[1]	8.9[1]	29.3[1]	572.890[1]	26.4[1]	27.5[1]	3.8[1]	2.0[1]	6,232	93.7	6.3	153	59.2	40.8	17.9	Tanzania
2.8[2]	89.7	2.5	5.0	4,789.9	2.0	61.0	2.8	24.3	16,672	63.9	36.1	2,650	71.1	28.9	4.5	Thailand
5.8	62.2	6.0	26.0	209.6	26.9	32.8	17.8	17.8	1,228	95.8	4.2	14	57.1	42.9	4.5	Togo
8.6[2]	56.1	35.3	—	0.106	16.3	43.9	12.8	—	63.4	84.1	15.9	2.7	77.8	22.2	3.2[4]	Tonga
17.1[2]	59.0	15.2	8.8	14.815	19.7	60.5	1.8	4.0	1,682	54.4	45.6	538	55.4	44.6	27.1	Trinidad and Tobago
3.3	89.9	2.7	4.2	10.319	20.3	40.4	—	16.0	7,914	86.0	14.0	1,314	65.7	34.3	17.0	Tunisia
21.3[1,2]	41.3[1]	13.1[1]	24.3[1]	1,379,826.0[1]	9.1[1]	31.5[1]	7.6[1]	9.1[1]	48,351	36.8	63.2	7,609	62.1	37.9	23.3	Turkey
...	...	...	...	30.241[1]	...	...	...	...	333.4	57.3	42.7	99.4	73.7	26.3	4.1	Turkmenistan
																Tuvalu
19.8[2]	39.6	15.1	25.4	526.103	38.8	28.2	7.4	23.5	2,955	96.7	3.3	123	72.4	27.6	35.8	Uganda
51.5[2]	10.8	12.8	24.9	751,233.0	27.2	29.7[6]	6.8	7.2	4,603	82.1	17.9	220	70.0	30.0	1.5	Ukraine
11.2[2]	44.0	7.3	37.8	168.964	8.5	35.8	9.0	16.6	...	...	...	...	...	...	...	United Arab Emirates
1.6[2]	48.5	0.4	49.4	1,708.8	—41.5[6]—			—	50.7	...	...	...	...	...	...	United Kingdom
11.0[2]	86.0	2.0	1.0	5,556.6	15.1	54.3	0.3	5.5	...	...	...	...	...	...	...	United States
8.1[1,2]	38.1[1]	14.7[1]	38.2[1]	53.612[1]	4.4[1]	45.8[1,6]	2.9[1]	34.8[1]	3,774	40.9	59.1	420	44.8	55.2	12.2	Uruguay
...	...	...	...	...	...	...	...	...	866	93.5	6.5	106	80.2	19.8	3.0	Uzbekistan
3.4[2]	27.4	6.1	63.1	33.176	14.1	66.1[6]	0.5	11.0	41.5	98.6	1.4	1.6	59.4	40.6	1.4[4]	Vanuatu
32.6[2]	38.1	23.4	6.0	3,145.1	28.7	66.1[6]	1.8	1.7	28,039	16.2	83.8	2,125	22.9	77.1	11.5	Venezuela
...	...	...	...	...	...	...	...	...	22,226	95.7	4.3	262	69.8	30.2	5.3	Vietnam
																Virgin Islands (U.S.)
																West Bank
																Western Sahara
3.2[2]	62.7	26.5	7.6	0.155	25.3	69.1	2.2	2.7	156.4	100.0	—	5.1	72.5	27.5	10.5	Western Samoa
6.6[1,2]	25.0[1]	58.2[1]	10.1[1]	56.490[1]	44.9[1]	34.3[1,6]	3.3[1]	11.7[1]	5,306	67.6	32.4	120	74.2	25.8	3.9	Yemen
...	...	...	...	...	...	...	...	...	8,963	53.9	46.1	...	...	...	...	Yugoslavia
6.7[1,2]	18.1[1]	6.7[1]	68.4[1]	368.000[1]	23.8[1]	36.5[1,6]	...	26.4[1]	9,281	90.7	9.3	—	—	—	...	Zaire
22.6[1]	36.3[1]	25.7[1]	15.3[1]	374.2[1]	22.0[1]	43.0[1]	3.3[1]	2.8[1]	4,858	96.0	4.0	305	62.0	38.0	25.8	Zambia
25.6[2]	55.3	9.3	9.8	26.038	35.9	20.1	2.7	26.6	3,253	80.0	20.0	442	64.4	35.6	19.5	Zimbabwe

[1]1994. [2]Includes claims on nonfinancial government (public) enterprises and/or local governments. [3]1995. [4]1993. [5]Treasury bill rate. [6]Includes foreign currency deposits. [7]Money market rate. [8]Short-term deposit rate. [9]1992. [10]Republic of Cyprus only. [11]Interbank rate.

Housing and construction

The present table summarizes data about the housing stock and the construction industries of the countries of the world. The principal focus is on the elements that are most comparable internationally: the age of the housing (by decade, so far as possible), the legal tenure of the householder, construction of exterior walls, principal physical amenities, sanitary arrangements, and the amount of space both absolutely (total area of the average dwelling in square metres [1 square metre equals 1.20 square yards, or 10.76 square feet]) and relatively (persons per room). The data on construction characterize the industry in terms of: (1) the portion of national gross domestic product (GDP) represented by each country's construction industry, (2) the number of new dwelling units constructed annually, their area, and the rate (in years) required to replace the total national stock of dwellings shown on the extreme left of the table, and (3) for nonresidential construction, the number of buildings or portions of buildings built for nonresidential purposes and their area in square metres.

Because housing patterns differ greatly from country to country, the portion of each country's housing stock for which data are compared was defined as specifically as possible. In general, the numbers refer to

permanent, private dwelling units that are usually occupied year-round, whether or not actually occupied on the date of the housing census or survey. That definition implies the exclusion of certain housing that is often part of national housing censuses: vacation homes, second homes occupied less than half the year, collective or communal dwellings, and so on. The housing unit to which the data on tenure refer may be either the individual dwelling or the household, according to the reporting practice of the country concerned.

The data are collected mostly from national housing censuses and surveys. The majority of countries combine the housing census with the population census at five- to ten-year intervals. Some countries, however, can conduct a meaningful housing census only in the capital city or in the few largest cities; others may be able to collect and process data for only a few of the most important housing characteristics even when national coverage is complete. These choices may be dictated by the lack of funding to collect data for the entire country or by the perception, particularly in a tropical, rural country where adequate dwellings can be built by hand, that no urgent housing problem exists. These choices may be complex, however, as

Housing and construction

country	year	dwelling units[a]	median age[b] (years)	1949 or earlier	1950–59	1960–69	1970–79	1980 or later	owned	rented	collective, vacant, other	traditional materials	sawn/framed wood	masonry or cement	other
Afghanistan	1979	3,940,000[1]	...	14.0[5]	20.3[6]	19.0[7]	24.3[8]	22.4[9]	55.2	23.5	21.3	...	...	...	...
Albania	1989	385,769[4]	22.6	...	...	...	...	...	91.2	8.8	...	...	...	...	...
Algeria	1987	3,050,812	...	—51.4[12]—		6.4[13]	18.6	23.6	63.0[14]	24.6[14]	12.4[14]	...	...	...	...
American Samoa	1990	6,959	13.9	4.4	7.5	21.9	22.7	43.5	78.1	21.9	...	4.1[16]	56.3[16]	34.9[16]	4.7[16]
Andorra	1990	...	18.1	18.0	5.7	20.8	—55.5—		...	...	...	...	...	...	...
Angola															
Antigua and Barbuda	1991	18,476	18.1	—39.6—		11.3	16.3	32.8	64.6	29.3	6.1	...	49.6	49.2	1.2
Argentina	1991	8,515,441[22]	21.6[16]	24.0[16]	17.3[16]	22.0[16]	18.3[16]	18.4[16]	78.0	16.0	6.0	6.1[16]	6.7[16]	84.2[16]	3.0[16]
Armenia	1989	559,000[25]	...												
Aruba	1991	19,224	27.7	17.0[27]	25.8[28]	12.1	16.8	28.3	70.6	26.7	2.7	—	7.7	90.6	1.7
Australia	1994	6,677,900	26.1[29]	37.9[29]	10.4[29]	18.6[29]	—33.1[29]—		70.1	27.6	2.3	...	...	...	...
Austria	1991	3,393,271	33.8	33.0[5]	14.7[6]	18.1[7]	18.5[8]	15.7[9]	50.0	38.7	11.3	...	5.1[4]	81.9[4]	13.0[4]
Azerbaijan	1989	1,381,000[25]	...												
Bahamas, The	1980	54,308	30.7	—54.7—		25.6	—19.7—		51.4	37.4	11.2	4.0[35]	32.3	54.7	9.0
Bahrain	1991	83,470	15.2[29]	58.3[29]	14.5[29]	—27.2[29]—			48.2[29]	33.6[29]	18.2[29]	...	...	93.6[29]	6.4[29]
Bangladesh	1991	19,020,489	...	...					86.3	6.5	7.2	78.9	2.4	8.0	10.7
Barbados	1990	75,211	19.1	—48.6—			22.9	28.5	76.1	20.4	3.5	0.2	61.2[38]	35.4	3.2
Belarus	1989	2,796,000[25]	...												
Belgium	1991	3,748,165	...	37.0[5]	21.5[39]	13.1[40]	18.5[8]	9.9[9]	64.5	34.2	1.3	...	...	...	...
Belize	1991	37,658	...	—26.3—			17.8	55.9	65.9	22.8	11.3	5.1	65.6	24.8	4.5
Benin	1979	612,041	...						76.8	10.1	13.1				
Bermuda	1991	22,061	...	—56.0—		15.8	12.0	16.2	43.4	52.4	4.2	—	1.7[16,38]	95.1[16]	3.2[16]
Bhutan	...	...	...												
Bolivia	1992	1,444,817	...						65.5	19.8	14.7	72.3[43]	2.3[43]	21.1[43]	4.2[43]
Bosnia and Herzegovina	1989														
Botswana	1991	276,209	...						59.2	22.9	17.9	48.7	—	49.3	2.0
Brazil	1990	35,578,857	...						67.0	17.7	15.3	...	...	...	...
Brunei	1991	40,351	...						83.8[29]	11.8[29]	4.4[29]	0.2[29]	54.8[29]	36.5[29]	8.5[29]
Bulgaria	1975	3,396,000[21]	17.9	—81.9—		11.1	—7.0—		77.3	22.7	—	...	...	...	...
Burkina Faso	1985	1,274,546[24]	...												
Burundi	1979	938,000[46]	...						98.7	1.1	0.2	...	...	...	...
Cambodia	...	...	...												
Cameroon	1987	1,787,835[25]	...						83.4[30]	11.2[30]	5.4[30]	66.0	13.0	17.0	4.0
Canada	1991	10,032,545	10.5	20.3[5]	20.0[6]	19.4[7]	—40.3[48]—		62.6	37.1	0.3	...	...	...	...
Cape Verde	1990	67,619	...	—73.6—				26.4	...	15.4[16]		36.1	—	60.1	3.8
Central African Republic	1975	519,314[43]	...						...	...	...	82.2	7.1	2.5	8.2
Chad	...	...	...												
Chile	1992	3,369,849	20.4[47]	—46.2[47]—		21.1[47]	—32.7[47]—		68.3	24.6	7.1	14.0	53.1	31.9	1.0
China	1990	276,947,962	20.6[50]	...					18.5[2,47]	81.5[2,47]	...	...	...	...	...
Colombia	1985	5,824,857	20.6[50]	54.6[50]	26.2[50]	19.2[50]	—		67.6	23.6	8.8	16.7	7.0	75.6	0.7
Comoros	1980	81,791	...	5.3	7.7	21.3	—63.7—		87.4	3.1	9.5	73.5	1.8	16.9	7.8
Congo	1984	363,140[25]	...						61.4	24.1	14.5	10.5	15.9	54.9	18.7
Costa Rica	1984	500,788	...						65.8	20.7	13.5	1.1	60.1	35.6	3.2
Côte d'Ivoire	1985	1,146,370[51]	...												
Croatia	1991	1,575,644	...						64.0	35.4	0.6	...	...	...	...
Cuba	1981	2,363,364	24.6	23.2[53]	21.3[54]	21.6	—25.6—		...	...	...	3.8	33.2	61.5	1.4
Cyprus	1982	168,588	22.8	—39.9—		15.4	—44.7—		60.0	16.5	23.5	11.9	—	87.6	0.5
Czech Republic	1991	3,705,691	42.4	41.7[5]	10.2[6]	14.5[7]	19.6[8]	14.0[9]	44.7[16]	41.7[16]	13.6[16]	...	32.0[55]	67.1	0.9
Denmark	1994[56]	2,412,671	36.6[11]	44.3[11]	10.0[11]	16.4[11]	18.1[11]	11.2[11]	52.4	45.8	1.8	...	...	...	...
Djibouti	1982	25,000[49]	27.6						...	...	...	...	73.0[57]	22.5	4.5
Dominica	1991	19,374[25]	18.6	—36.2—		11.6	12.8	31.8	71.9	19.7	8.4	—	50.5	48.4	1.1
Dominican Republic	1981	1,125,785[22]	...						72.0	17.0	11.0	31.1	31.3	31.4	6.2
Ecuador	1990	2,111,121	...						68.1	22.6	9.3	32.2	9.3	57.7	0.8
Egypt	1986	9,732,728	...	—37.1[2]—			—62.9[2]—		64.0	27.2	8.8	...	...	...	...
El Salvador	1992	1,236,866	...						69.6	17.9	12.5	39.8	2.9	52.6	4.7
Equatorial Guinea	...	...	...												
Eritrea	...	...	...												
Estonia	1995[56]	618,300	24.5	15.0[5]	12.8[6]	22.9[7]	25.5[8]	23.8[9]	18.3[24]	81.5[24]	0.2[24]	...	18.2[24]	77.4[24]	4.4[24]
Ethiopia	1984	9,300,000	...						48.8[2]	47.2[2]	4.0[2]	89.5	...	5.9	4.6
Faroe Islands	1977	11,172[14]	32.5	—60.1—		21.8	—15.0—		84.5	9.9	5.6	...	43.9	53.5	2.6
Fiji	1986	124,098	...						75.5	11.1	13.4	9.0	26.4	29.8	34.8
Finland	1994[56]	2,331,406	17.1	—25.5—		14.6	23.3	36.6	73.7	24.7	1.6	14.0[4,14]	81.8[4,14]	—4.2[4,14]—	
France	1990	21,535,677	19.1[20]	—43.5[20,61]—		11.6[20,62]	27.3[20,63]	17.7[20,64]	54.4	39.6	6.0	...	...	...	...
French Guiana	1990	38,324	...	—38.7[65]—			21.5[66]	39.8[67]	41.3	—58.7—		29.4	...	—70.6—	
French Polynesia	1988	39,513	10.8	—11.3—		16.0	27.6	45.1	68.5	21.2	10.3	36.9	15.8	45.2	2.2

planners are always aware that much housing is physically inadequate to protect dwellers from the elements, is disadvantageously placed in relation to tainted or disease-infested water supply or to the outfall of unprocessed sewage, or is built of materials (mud, skins, thatch, etc.) that may harbour pests or disease. In the developed countries, median age and the distribution of physical amenities provide strong indicators of the quality and availability of housing.

The data for the construction industry refer to the most recent year in which a broad range of countries could be surveyed.

The broadest indication of total activity in a national construction industry is its contribution to the national gross domestic product, since that figure, in addition to construction of buildings, also includes civil engineering projects, such as dams, roads and other transportation infrastructure, recreational facilities, irrigation and land reclamation works, and the like. The scope of the data relating to construction of buildings may be limited in several respects. It may be confined to activity capable of being surveyed in the modern or urban sectors only, may be limited to private new construction only or to government and government-financed

activity only, or may refer to construction mortgaged or financed through certain organizations only. Depending on national data-collection systems, it usually excludes remodeling of old premises but may include extensions or enlargements of existing buildings. The data for new construction are usually of two principal types: authorized new construction or certification after construction that newly built structures meet building and fire codes and the like. Data for construction completed are naturally more meaningful but are not available for every country, necessitating the substitution of authorized construction data, which are usually available only for areas regulated by certain types of governmental authorities.

The following notes further define the column headings:
a. Data refer to permanent, private dwelling units that are usually occupied year-round, whether or not occupied on the census date.
b. Data are estimates unless specifically provided by a country source.
c. Data may be either for dwellings or for households, depending on country reporting practice.
d. Data may be either for construction completed or for construction authorized, depending on country reporting practice.

physical amenities (percent)			sewage disposal (percent)			space[b]			construction industry (1993)							country
									percent of GDP	new residential[d]			new nonresidential[d]			
piped water	electricity	inside toilet or WC	closed public sewer or septic tank	open public sewer	other	average area (sq m)	rooms per dwelling unit	persons per room		total no. of dwellings	floor area ('000 sq m)	years to replace nat'l stock	number of units	floor area ('000 sq m)		
25.3[2]	66.5[2]	5.5[2]	5.5	77.9	16.6	...	5.5	2.1	4.1[3]	...	...	37.4[11]	...	...		Afghanistan
33.0	...	21.3	...	...	...	35.7	1.8	2.6	9.5[10]	12,428[11]	...	...	...	...		Albania
87.4	72.7	68.9	52.4	19.1	28.5	...	2.9	2.6	11.5	71,433[15]	...	42.6[15]	...	...		Algeria
96.2	94.4	93.4	68.5	—31.5—		...	4.5	1.6		218[17]	...	21.5[17]	...	...		American Samoa
—	...	—	...	...	...	...	...	...	19.9[18]	90[4, 19, 20]	84[19, 20]	...	19, 20	19, 20		Andorra
									1.9[11]	...	585[16]	...	210[16]	164.5[16]		Angola
91.5	...	...	53.0	—47.0—		...	3.6	0.9	10.5[21]	764[17]	...	20.2[17]	...	...		Antigua and Barbuda
77.4	93.5	95.1[16]	77.1[16]	—22.9[16]—		...	3.9[16]	1.3[16]	5.3[21]	67,528[23]	1,968[19]	105.2[24]	...	19		Argentina
									4.5	...	1,910[11, 26]	...	...	...		Armenia
97.9	98.7[29]	89.2[29]	...	...	...	...	5.2	0.7	8.2[21]	126	...	94.5[11]	50	...		Aruba
97.1[30]	98.4[31]	92.2[29]	99.0[29]	—1.0[29]—		...	5.1[29]	0.6[29]	6.9[32]	167,953[33]	11,170[3]	39.8[33]	23,340[14]	13,727[3]		Australia
95.0[29]	...	88.7	94.3[29]		5.7[29]	85.0	4.3[17]	0.6[17]	7.5	48,851[10]	4,616[10]	92.8[18]	500[14]	100[14]		Austria
									13.7[34]	...	2,600[19]	...	...	19		Azerbaijan
83.0[36]	77.9	...	63.2	2.2	34.6	...	4.0	1.2	3.0[21]	733[4, 10]	...	52.9[15]	19	...		Bahamas, The
92.8	97.1	78.2	99.8	...	0.2	...	4.2	1.4	5.6[21]	1,919[17]	...	27.5[17]	1,444[17]	...		Bahrain
56.8[29]	14.3	12.5	1.5[29]	—98.5[29]—		...	2.0[29]	2.9[29]	5.8[37]	300,900[23]	...	49.1	...	...		Bangladesh
94.0	92.6	66.2	66.8	0.4	32.8	...	4.3	0.8	3.8[10]	2,116[18]	...	...	...	...		Barbados
									8.7[10]	...	5,395[11, 19]	...	...	19		Belarus
99.6	100.0	91.9	62.5[41]	—37.5[41]—		86.3	4.3	0.6	5.4	29,136	27,096	129.0[11]	8,612	35,592		Belgium
54.9	67.2	34.7	34.7	—65.3—		...	...	...	7.4[10]	...	6,185[20]	...	...	...		Belize
									4.5[10]	...	...	...	...	...		Benin
97.4[16]	...	96.7[16]	96.7[16]	—3.3[16]—		...	3.2[16]	0.7[16]	4.9[42]	556[24]	268	36.6[24]	...	...		Bermuda
									10.1	...	...	...	...	...		Bhutan
57.5	55.5	42.8	22.5[43]	—77.5[43]—		...	...	...	5.1	24,980[24]	...	52.8[24]	...	...		Bolivia
66.2	94.2	53.2	...	...	...	56.0	...	...	7.1[24, 34]	26,568[11]	...	...	...	...		Bosnia and Herzegovina
77.0	5.4[29]	25.4[29]	8.6[29]	20.4[29]	71.0[29]	...	2.5	1.9	4.2[32]	...	96[15]	...	472[14]	132[15]		Botswana
73.4	87.8	...	60.1[17]	—39.9[17]—		...	5.1[16]	0.9[16]	7.4	...	20,090[2, 16]	...	5,017[14]	8,180[2, 15]		Brazil
90.3[29]	64.2[29]	94.2[29]	57.4[29]	—42.6[29]—		...	4.2[29]	1.6[29]	4.9[21]	195[4, 30]	...	147.0	5[20]	...		Brunei
74.6	99.8	33.2	33.2	—66.8—		45.3[44]	2.5[45]	1.1[45]	5.1	11,021	850	188.7[21]	...	...		Bulgaria
									5.3	...	...	...	...	...		Burkina Faso
11.0	0.6	...	1.6	—98.4—		37.2[47]	2.4[47]	0.6[47]	4.1[11]	...	...	...	...	...		Burundi
11.0	...	7.0	...	...	...	...	...	1.2	7.6[10]	...	...	...	...	...		Cambodia
32.0	22.0	7.0	2.2	70.4	27.6	...	4.1	1.2	5.3[11]	...	230[3]	...	53[1]	51.1[1]		Cameroon
99.9	100.0	99.5	98.9[29]	—1.1[17]—		...	5.7[17]	0.5[17]	5.3	160,020[11]	...	44.0[24]	14,846[14]	...		Canada
16.2	24.9	25.1	—3.4[16]—		96.6[16]	...	1.8[16]	2.8[16]	20.0[11]	...	31[47]	...	3[47]	0.5[47]		Cape Verde
...	...	...	...	...	...	...	...	...	4.1[10]	...	10[49]	...	11[18, 49]	82[49]		Central African Republic
									0.5[10]	...	...	...	...	...		Chad
88.2	90.2	...	70.3	—29.7—		59.9[43, 44]	4.4	1.0	5.6	117,384	7,056	32.1[24]	...	2,916		Chile
89.4[2, 15]	...	25.2[2, 15]	47.0[2, 15]	—53.0[2, 15]—		37.0[15]	2.2[15]	1.8[15]	6.7	...	850,170[21]	...	...	297,830[21]		China
70.5	78.5	77.9	69.6	—30.4—		...	3.3	1.6	6.0	11,052	9,436	70.2[15]	...	2,181		Colombia
12.9	5.7	...	2.1	—97.9—		33.7	2.5	2.1	5.6	...	...	...	...	...		Comoros
30.5	8.8	16.6	—86.2[2]—		13.8[2]	...	3.7[2]	1.7[2]	1.4[11]	...	...	...	...	...		Congo
86.9	97.3	...	66.5	—33.5—		...	4.0	1.4	2.8	...	1,914[24]	...	2,868[14]	178[14]		Costa Rica
23.0	39.6	23.9	—68.5—		31.5	...	...	...	4.7[11, 52]	...	...	...	...	...		Côte d'Ivoire
86.2	98.6	80.3	80.8	—19.2—		70.4	2.8	1.1	3.4	9,710[10]	820[10]	...	895	...		Croatia
74.1	82.9	45.2	60.9	9.3	30.1	71.0[44]	4.1	1.0	9.3[24, 34]	25,344[43]	1,800[43]	93.2[43]	469[14]	1,803[14]		Cuba
100.0	98.1	74.5	95.6	—4.4—		...	4.6	0.8	9.1[10]	6,639[15]	4,728	25.4[15]	1,103[14]	1,572		Cyprus
96.9	100.0	88.5	98.1	—1.9—		70.5	2.7	1.0	3.6[34]	69,300[11]	2,212	53.4[11]	...	...		Czech Republic
100.0	100.0	99.2[24]	98.6[29]	—1.4[29]—		107.8[11]	3.7	0.6	5.2	12,673[10]	...	190.4[10]	3,312	2,911[10]		Denmark
45.0	58.0	82.0	26.0	23.0	51.0	...	1.9	6.9	4.8[11]	...	54[24]	...	26[15]	13.7[15]		Djibouti
87.4	...	36.8	36.8	—63.2—		...	3.3	1.1	6.7[10]	...	...	...	...	...		Dominica
64.4	36.7[41]	44.6	52.1[41]	22.6[41]	25.3[41]	...	2.8[41]	1.5[41]	9.5[10]	...	648[15]	...	856[15]	508[15]		Dominican Republic
62.7	77.7	49.6	39.5	25.1	35.4	...	2.8	1.7	2.5	...	3,825[14]	...	596[14]	412.7[14]		Ecuador
73.1	87.0	...	...	...	...	...	3.3	1.5	5.1[37]	160,613[3]	...	53.0[3]	...	...		Egypt
46.4	69.3	39.7	39.7	—60.3—		...	1.5[58]	3.3[58]	3.1	694	341[14]	...	271	0.7[14]		El Salvador
									2.8[11]	...	...	...	...	...		Equatorial Guinea
									4.3[10]	...	...	...	...	...		Eritrea
93.8	99.9	89.6	...	...	...	34.5[24]	2.5[24]	0.9[24]	5.8	1,953[10]	159.2[10]	316.6[10]	...	...		Estonia
67.9[2]	...	55.2[2]	...	...	...	...	1.9	2.4	2.9[37]	...	260[59]	...	92[1]	63.3[59]		Ethiopia
99.7	99.5	95.0	89.7	8.1	2.2	...	5.5	1.1	10.6[21]	223[21]	...	37.5[15]	...	...		Faroe Islands
73.7	48.5	56.0	35.4[60]	—64.6[60]—		...	3.3	1.8	3.3[10]	1,344	64	72	105[15]	48		Fiji
94.0	95.9[4, 14]	96.3	97.3	—2.7—		75.1	3.6	0.6	4.7	30,412	2,443	41.6[18]	...	18,250[26]		Finland
99.7[43]	...	93.5	73.8[51]	—26.2[51]—		75.8[36]	3.8[21]	0.8[21]	4.9[10]	299,000	...	83.2[11]	...	31,156		France
77.0	86.7	62.0	34.3[47]	—65.7[47]—		...	2.8	1.2	9.3[24]	1,209	195	35.7[18]	...	28.5[14]		French Guiana
92.5	91.0	78.9	2.0[1]	67.0[1]	31.0[1]	...	3.8	1.3	6.1[18]	834[10]	85[17, 19]	59.3[15]	1,329[10]	19		French Polynesia

Housing and construction (continued)

country	housing stock			decade built (percent)					tenure[c] (percent)			construction of exterior walls (percent)			
	year	dwelling units[a]	median age[b] (years)	1949 or earlier	1950–59	1960–69	1970–79	1980 or later	owned	rented	collective, vacant, other	traditional materials	sawn/framed wood	masonry or cement	other
Gabon	1967	15,886[49]	...	...	...	...	...	...	——87.0——		13.0	...	...	...	...
Gambia, The	1983	202,199	...	...	...	...	...	...	63.9	21.9	14.2	82.9	—	12.9	4.2
Gaza Strip	1992	66,819[68]	23.0	4.7	31.2	14.3	25.8	23.9	89.1[14, 69]	7.6[14, 69]	3.3[14, 69]	—	—	96.0	4.0
Georgia	1989	1,244,000[25]	...	...	...	...	...	...	...	...	...	...	...	...	...
Germany	1993	34,988,753	39.4	——32.9[61]——		62.4[70]	——4.7[71]——		38.8	61.2	—	...	...	...	...
Ghana	1992	3,320,000[25]	...	...	...	...	...	...	37.0	19.6	43.4	62.6	1.3	33.6	2.5
Gibraltar	1991	7,604[22]	25.0	37.3[72]	16.7[73]	15.6[74]	23.0[75]	7.4[76]	15.2	84.8	—	...	...	...	...
Greece	1991	4,657,572	29.2[29]	30.2[5, 29]	27.4[6, 29]	20.7[7, 29]	——21.5[29]——		73.1[77]	26.9[77]	—	...	...	...	...
Greenland	1989	18,401	10.2	11.9[30]	18.8[30]	46.5[30]	——22.8[30]——		39.3[14]	——60.7[14]——		...	...	...	...
Grenada	1991	21,974	18.3[41]	48.0[41]	29.0[41]	22.2[41]	——0.8[41]——		78.7	13.8	7.5	—	68.5	30.2	1.3
Guadeloupe	1990	112,478	...	...	...	8.1[77]			62.6	——37.4——		29.5	——70.5——		
Guam	1990	35,223	15.8	2.3	7.1	19.2	41.5	29.9	45.6	54.4	—	0.0	5.1	85.8	9.1
Guatemala	1981	1,259,598	12.5	——62.0——		10.0	——28.0——		64.7	11.3	24.0	55.6	21.1	19.3	4.0
Guernsey	1991	21,215[22]	...	...	...	...	...	...	68.4	31.6	—	...	...	...	...
Guinea	1983	716,378	...	...	...	...	...	...	81.3	10.6	8.1	26.2	—	12.7	61.1
Guinea-Bissau	1979	123,936	...	...	...	...	...	...	...	...	...	95.7	0.1	2.3	1.9
Guyana	1980	149,734[25]	17.6	——43.5——		19.4	——37.1——		57.2	27.3	15.5	1.8	85.6	6.6	6.0
Haiti	1987	1,164,136	...	——75.9——			——24.1——		73.2	4.5	22.3	37.0	57.4	5.4	0.2
Honduras	1988	809,263	12.1[77]	——38.9[77]——		37.8[77, 78]	——23.3[77]——		71.8[77]	16.5[77]	12.7[77]	61.0[77]	26.4[77]	11.7[77]	0.9[77]
Hong Kong	1994	1,735,500	...	——48.1[29]——		13.6[29]	——38.3[29]——		45.1	50.1	4.8	...	...	...	...
Hungary	1995	3,971,000	16.4	32.9[5, 18]	11.8[18, 54]	14.9[18]	23.2[18]	17.2[18]	75.9	23.7	0.4	21.8	14.6	63.6	—
Iceland	1984	70,777	25.6	——46.0——			——54.1——		70.3[80]	——29.7[80]——		...	...	71.9[80]	...
India	1991	195,024,357	...	...	...	...	...	...	86.3	11.8	1.9	87.7	1.5	2.0	8.7
Indonesia	1993	42,016,761[24]	...	...	...	...	...	...	87.0[79]	5.0[79]	8.0[79]	...	...	...	...
Iran	1986	8,211,375	...	——82.5[30]——			——17.5[30]——		77.0	12.2	9.8	28.8	0.7	69.2	1.3
Iraq	1956	741,000	...	...	...	...	...	...	83.0	12.8	4.2	...	...	...	...
Ireland	1981	1,038,000[11]	47.2	——60.0——		12.8	——26.2——		67.9	20.9	11.2	...	...	...	...
Isle of Man	1991	27,316	...	...	...	...	...	...	66.5	32.5	1.0	...	...	...	...
Israel	1983	1,104,270	...	9.5[81]	——90.5[82]——				74.3	23.1	2.6	...	...	...	...
Italy	1991	19,509,362[24]	32.2	30.8[5]	19.7[39]	27.5[83]	——22.0[48]——		58.9[29]	35.5[29]	5.6[29]	...	...	...	...
Jamaica	1982	517,297[25]	17.0	——33.6——		28.8	——39.6——		46.7	32.6	20.7	7.1	28.4	54.4	10.1
Japan	1993	40,835,000	16.5	5.4[85]	10.9[86]	13.4[7]	31.5[8]	38.8[9]	59.8	38.5	1.7	—	68.1	——31.9——	
Jersey	1991	32,463	...	...	...	...	...	...	49.6	48.0	2.4	...	...	...	...
Jordan	1994	683,000	...	...	...	...	...	...	59.7	38.8	1.5	...	...	...	...
Kazakstan	1989	3,824,000[25]	...	...	...	...	...	...	...	...	...	...	...	...	...
Kenya	1989	4,352,751[25]	...	...	...	...	...	...	...	...	...	...	...	...	...
Kiribati	1990	11,301[25]	...	...	...	...	...	...	68.2[58]	17.9[58]	13.9[58]	64.4[58]	——35.6[58]——		
Korea, North	1987	4,054,027[25]	...	...	...	...	...	...	...	...	...	...	...	...	...
Korea, South	1990	7,160,386	13.1	13.2	6.6	12.7	23.7	43.8	79.0	17.7	3.3	7.8	18.9	73.0	0.3
Kuwait	1985	228,781	14.5[16]	——12.2[16]——		38.8[16]	——34.5[16]——		38.2	53.6	8.2	46.5[4]	—	36.5[4]	17.0[4]
Kyrgyzstan	1989	856,000[25]	...	...	...	...	...	...	...	...	...	...	...	...	...
Laos			...	...	...	...	...	...	...	...	...	...	...	...	...
Latvia	1991	1,024,188	...	...	...	...	...	...	...	...	...	...	...	...	...
Lebanon	1970	483,908[22]	...	30.1[87]	40.2[88]	——29.4——			...	...	...	...	...	...	...
Lesotho	1986	317,161[22]	...	...	...	...	...	...	...	...	...	...	...	...	...
Liberia	1974[49]	263,333	...	...	...	...	...	...	...	...	...	...	...	...	...
Libya	1984	569,679	...	...	...	...	...	...	62.5[50]	28.0[50]	9.5[50]	...	...	...	...
Liechtenstein	1990	10,386[18, 22]	29.4	27.1[87]	15.0[88]	27.1	——30.8——		53.6	41.7	4.7	...	...	...	...
Lithuania	1993	1,203,800	...	...	...	...	...	...	83.5	——16.5——		...	...	...	...
Luxembourg	1991	144,683	33.1	34.5[5]	17.6[6]	12.5[7]	17.8[8]	17.6[9]	66.1	28.3	5.6	...	...	...	...
Macau	1991	89,193	...	...	...	...	...	...	65.9	32.0	2.1	—	0.5[41]	99.3[41]	0.2[41]
Macedonia	1989	...	...	...	...	...	...	...	...	...	...	...	...	...	...
Madagascar	1993	2,688,951[25]	...	...	...	...	...	...	...	...	...	...	...	...	...
Malawi	1987	1,859,572	...	...	...	...	...	...	39.6	——60.4——		51.6	3.1	44.4	0.9
Malaysia	1991	3,447,597	...	...	...	...	...	...	63.4[16]	25.0[16]	11.6[16]	...	...	...	...
Maldives	1990	37,114	11.6	15.1	7.9	13.7	21.7	41.6	96.4	3.6	—	53.8	2.7	41.1	2.4
Mali	1987	1,364,079	...	——81.8[90]——			——18.2[91]——		84.2	8.5	7.3	75.9	8.5	10.3	5.3
Malta	1985	101,509	...	——81.8[90]——			——18.2[91]——		53.9	43.0	3.1	93.0[68]	...	92.9[68]	0.21[68]
Marshall Islands	1980[10]	4,923[43]	...	6.4	13.3	24.7	——55.5——		60.0	33.0	7.0	10.7	63.5	15.9	9.9
Martinique	1990	123,317	19.0	——54.5[65]——		17.9[64]	——27.6[76]——		60.9	32.5	6.6	20.4[47]	——79.6[47]——		
Mauritania	1977	246,462[25]	...	...	...	...	...	...	...	...	...	...	...	...	...
Mauritius	1990	236,885	...	——19.7[1]——		24.3[1, 93]	——56.0[1, 94]——		75.9	15.2	8.9	—	4.2[1]	66.8[1]	28.9[1]
Mayotte	1991	19,227	...	...	...	...	...	...	77.8	14.8	7.3	50.4	——48.2——		1.4
Mexico	1990	16,197,802	...	——51.4[16]——		15.4[16]	——33.2[16]——		77.9	14.6	7.5	19.0	8.1	69.5	3.4
Micronesia	1980	11,562	...	3.8	5.2	21.3	——69.7——		51.8	39.2	9.0	6.0	41.8	14.6	37.6
Moldova	1989	1,144,000[25]	...	...	...	...	...	...	...	...	...	...	...	...	...
Monaco	1990	16,122	30.0	——39.5[61]——		13.0[62]	19.7[63]	27.8[66]	23.3	60.5	16.2	...	...	...	...
Mongolia	1969	242,000	...	...	...	...	...	...	100.0	—	—	...	...	...	...
Morocco	1994	4,444,271[25]	...	...	...	...	...	...	69.3[14]	22.1[14]	8.6[14]	24.5[47]	—	73.5[47]	1.8[47]
Mozambique	1980	2,712,439[25]	...	...	...	...	...	...	...	...	...	86.5	2.3	8.3	2.9
Myanmar (Burma)	1983	6,750,884	...	...	...	...	...	...	...	...	...	80.3	14.8	3.2	1.7
Namibia	1991	254,389	...	...	...	...	...	...	69.2	16.9	13.9	52.0	...	36.2	11.8
Nauru	1977	508[95]	...	——88.6[95]——			——11.4[95]——		11.0[96]	80.6[96]	8.4[96]	...	...	...	...
Nepal	1981	2,585,154[25]	...	...	...	...	...	...	75.3[96]	10.7[96]	14.0[96]	...	...	...	...
Netherlands, The	1995[56]	6,195,100	27.5	25.7	11.0	16.8	20.4	26.1	47.6[10, 56]	52.4[10, 56]	—	...	...	...	...
Netherlands Antilles	1992	57,608	14.0	——28.4——		13.6	21.3	36.7	64.8[29]	35.2[29]	—	...	18.3[29]	78.8[29]	2.9[29]
New Caledonia	1989	44,047	...	——19.3——			——80.7——		56.4	29.7	13.9	6.4	11.7	61.7	20.2
New Zealand	1991	1,185,396	...	——64.1[29]——		19.2[29]	——16.2[29]——		72.4	22.7	4.9	...	...	...	...
Nicaragua	1971	330,422	...	...	...	...	...	...	64.4	20.3	15.3	30.8	45.6	21.8	1.8
Niger	1988	1,163,424[25]	...	...	...	...	...	...	...	...	...	66.5			
Nigeria	1982[97]	...	...	...	...	...	...	...	37.0	46.0	17.0	29.0	—	71.0	—
Northern Mariana Islands	1990	8,210	...	1.0	2.5	6.4	13.3	76.8	39.5	56.6	3.9	0.0	13.5	66.5	20.0
Norway	1990	1,769,000	25.3	44.1[5]	20.6[6]	17.8[7]	20.7[8]	16.0[9]	80.3	——19.7——		...	...	...	...
Oman	1989	2,469[47]	...	...	...	...	...	...	70.2	19.8	20.8	...	...	...	...
Pakistan[98]	1980	12,597,000	17.2	17.1[87]	36.7[99]	24.9[100]	——21.3[101]——		78.4	7.7	13.9	49.2	2.4	41.4	7.1

physical amenities (percent)			sewage disposal (percent)			space[b]			construction industry (1993) percent of GDP	new residential[d]			new nonresidential[d]		country
piped water	electricity	inside toilet or WC	closed public sewer or septic tank	open public sewer	other	average area (sq m)	rooms per dwelling unit	persons per room	percent of GDP	total no. of dwellings	floor area ('000 sq m)	years to replace nat'l stock	number of units	floor area ('000 sq m)	country
...	50.5	...	...	...	...	...	3.0	1.3	9.3[11]	...	216[51]	...	75[51]	119.4[51]	Gabon
21.9	...	...	...	...	...	...	2.0	2.0	6.0[32]	...	...	...	14[51]	...	Gambia, The
97.2[14]	97.6	98.4	...	...	...	144.3[44]	2.6[14]	2.5[14]	18.2[11]	1,247[15]	180[15]	53.6[15]	...	31.1[15]	Gaza Strip
...	...	...	...	...	...	...	...	...	6.2[21]	...	1,005[16]	...	...	...	Georgia
100.0	99.7	98.3	97.1[16]	—2.9[16]—		82.3	4.3	0.5	5.1[10]	404,413	36,148	86.5	38,025	36,368	Germany
36.0	28.5	7.0	...	...	...	23.7	1.9[24]	2.4	3.2	...	...	...	...	...	Ghana
96.7[29]	100.0[29]	99.2	100.0[29]	—	—	...	3.3	1.1	...	...	...	...	...	...	Gibraltar
81.3[31]	89.0[31]	93.0[31]	...	...	...	138.4[17]	2.6	0.8	6.6	100,332[11]	46,434[18,26]	46.4[11]	11,471[30]	12,536[18,26]	Greece
62.7[30]	84.2[30]	39.1[30]	39.1[30]	—60.9[30]—		72.0[44]	2.8	1.1	8.5[21]	325[11]	26[11]	71.1[24]	...	387	Greenland
88.1	...	36.1	36.1	—63.9—		...	2.9[29]	1.6[29]	6.7	...	...	...	...	...	Grenada
83.2	89.4	78.2	24.6[47]	—75.4[47]—		...	3.3	1.0	7.4[24]	676[24]	358	126.7[24]	...	160	Guadeloupe
99.2	98.4	97.0	97.0	—3.0—		...	5.0	0.8	7.9[47]	417[15]	...	67.4[15]	500[15]	...	Guam
52.0	37.0	14.3	20.1	3.4	76.5	...	2.4	2.2	2.1[10]	...	495[19,24]	...	...	19	Guatemala
96.5[30]	...	98.8	65.9	—34.1—		...	5.8[17]	0.5[17]	...	148	...	128.6[24]	...	...	Guernsey
11.9	12.5	...	...	...	...	...	...	...	6.9	...	...	...	...	...	Guinea
3.7	3.9	...	4.2	—95.8—		...	1.4	4.5	8.4[11]	...	...	...	...	...	Guinea-Bissau
38.1	69.0	29.0	10.4	—89.6—		...	2.9	1.8	3.6[10]	...	...	...	56[23]	...	Guyana
5.8	21.9	45.8	2.0[47]	—98.0[47]—		...	2.3	2.1	3.4[32]	...	...	...	...	...	Haiti
55.0[16]	25.0[16]	13.0[16]	14.4[16]	—85.6[16]—		...	2.4[16]	2.3[16]	6.8	1,442[20]	214[17]	...	148[17]	98[17]	Honduras
85.7[29]	...	69.2[50]	65.4[50]	—34.6[50]—		53.2[79]	3.1[50]	2.8[50]	4.7	56,042	1,428	30.9	303[15]	1,656	Hong Kong
84.1	98.8[31]	75.1	84.6	—15.4—		52.3	2.6	1.0	5.3[21]	20,947[10]	4,353[24]	78.3[43]	3,433[14]	21,886[14,26]	Hungary
99.1[31]	94.6[31]	93.6[31]	86.5[31]	—13.5[31]—		...	4.8[80]	0.9[80]	7.5	1,594[11]	568[26]	...	552[11]	729[11,26]	Iceland
32.3	42.4	23.7	...	...	...	...	2.2	2.7	5.6[37]	...	...	...	13,908[20]	...	India
14.7	55.2	51.5	24.7	—75.3—		59.0	3.3	1.7[79]	6.0[21]	406,987	15,818[3]	103.2	5,235[14]	853[38]	Indonesia
74.6	84.1	43.6	...	...	...	60.0[30]	2.8	1.8	3.3[37]	124,891[14]	...	65.0[14]	...	...	Iran
20.8	17.1	...	...	...	...	...	2.4	...	2.8[11]	...	4,558[11]	...	11,799[14]	410[11]	Iraq
94.8	94.7[79]	93.0	72.3[79]	—27.7[79]—		...	3.7[14]	1.0[14]	5.0[15]	21,396	2,246	44.0	...	2,067	Ireland
...	...	99.5	...	...	...	...	...	0.4[29]	9.8[15]	168[15]	...	161.0[15]	...	...	Isle of Man
96.5[79]	96.5[79]	98.8	99.0[77]	—1.0[77]—		149.8[44]	3.0	1.2	7.6[11]	42,336	5,340	25.9[11]	...	1,884	Israel
98.7[29]	99.0[29]	94.0[29]	95.7[30]	—4.3[30]—		85.3[29]	4.0[14]	0.8[29]	5.6	197,978[11]	93,214[26]	98.5[11]	29,235[24]	103,628[26]	Italy
76.9	48.6	35.2	61.2[1]	—38.8[1]—		...	2.4[41]	4.3	12.6[10]	5,286	...	136.4[11]	...	6,989[84]	Jamaica
94.0[1]	...	74.7	61.2[1]	—38.8[1]—		89.2[43]	4.9[43]	0.7[43]	8.8	1,485,684	131,683	27.5	...	230,654	Japan
94.0[31]	...	93.0[30]	96.0[31]	...	...	...	5.0	0.5	...	...	354[15]	82.5[15]	...	...	Jersey
95.8	93.9	55.4[31]	54.5	—84.3—		...	3.2	...	7.4[10]	4,200	4,206[19]	60.2[19]	820[17]	19	Jordan
50.0	...	...	...	—41.0—		...	...	...	12.4	...	6,125[11]	...	...	...	Kazakstan
...	...	...	...	...	...	...	...	...	5.6	...	828[11,19]	...	85[17]	19	Kenya
...	...	...	...	...	...	...	...	...	5.0[21]	...	...	...	...	...	Kiribati
33.1	23.7[58]	53.3	...	...	...	...	...	...	...	...	...	...	...	...	Korea, North
82.1[10]	49.9[31]	51.3	35.9[16]	—64.1[16]—		80.6	2.3	1.5	11.5	622,854[10]	69,300	9.5[18]	36,801[15]	48,487	Korea, South
53.9[16]	99.5[16]	...	...	...	...	...	4.0[16]	1.8[16]	3.4[10]	9,735[17,46]	4,716	23.5[17,46]	370[17]	408	Kuwait
...	...	...	...	...	...	...	...	...	3.2[21]	...	1,232	...	...	...	Kyrgyzstan
...	...	...	...	...	...	...	...	...	3.1	...	...	...	...	...	Laos
100.0	100.0	97.2	...	...	...	...	...	...	4.4	6,946[11]	819[11]	...	...	...	Latvia
...	93.4	82.9	...	...	...	...	...	...	3.3[21]	...	4,938[15,19]	...	...	19	Lebanon
...	...	...	...	...	...	...	...	...	21.9[10]	...	...	...	52[17]	...	Lesotho
...	...	...	...	...	...	...	2.3[14]	1.7	2.2[24]	...	...	...	...	...	Liberia
70.1[50]	72.1[50]	40.6[50]	40.6[50]	—59.4[50]—		...	3.3[50]	1.8[50]	11.8[11]	...	...	...	...	...	Libya
96.5	96.6	86.7	90.2	—9.8—		102.0	4.5[18]	0.6[18]	...	6,858[18]	299[26]	...	...	193[26]	Liechtenstein
95.7	...	...	...	...	...	58.5	...	...	6.7	8,200	610	147	...	...	Lithuania
99.4	...	99.4	90.4[41]	—7.0[41]—		114.2	5.4[16]	0.5[16]	7.5[11]	2,744[10]	1,931[10,26]	53.6[11]	282[10]	1,964[10,26]	Luxembourg
98.0	99.8	97.9	...	...	...	...	3.1	1.3	6.4[10]	9,553[10]	1,141[10,19]	20.2[11]	327[10]	19	Macau
72.0	96.4	56.3	...	...	...	68.6	...	...	...	6,583	...	...	953	...	Macedonia
...	...	...	...	...	...	...	...	...	1.2[11]	...	24[15,49]	...	...	8.9[15,49]	Madagascar
23.6	22.8[16]	33.4[16]	33.0[68]	—67.0[68]—		...	1.9	1.7	4.2[10]	...	8,809[17]	...	...	960[17]	Malawi
65.0[16]	64.4[16]	...	56.4[16]	4.4[16]	39.2[16]	...	2.3[41,89]	2.6[41,89]	4.1[10]	...	...	...	...	...	Malaysia
...	53.4[14]	...	43.2	—56.8—		...	4.4	1.5	9.3	680[15]	...	54.6[15]	...	...	Maldives
3.8	3.6	1.3	...	...	...	...	2.6	2.2	4.3[52]	10,025[23]	...	...	...	...	Mali
98.0	98.0	98.8	98.0	15.4[68]	6.1[68]	...	3.2[68]	1.3[68]	3.3[21,92]	4,605	...	22.5	2,024	...	Malta
49.8[43]	56.0[43]	43.7[43]	28.6	—71.4—		...	...	...	10.4[10]	...	...	...	...	...	Marshall Islands
94.1	90.2	89.0	41.8[47]	—58.2[47]—		...	3.2	0.9	5.2[21]	1,528[11]	...	55.8[11]	...	56.2[29]	Martinique
...	...	...	...	...	...	...	...	...	6.7[52]	...	42[19,20]	...	...	19	Mauritania
94.7	96.2	63.3	63.3	—36.7—		...	3.6[1]	1.4[1]	7.6[10]	4,592[23]	921[11]	48.7	552[15]	297[11]	Mauritius
42.5	32.2	6.7	54.4	—45.6—		...	2.2	2.2	...	616[17]	...	21.3[17]	...	...	Mayotte
79.4	87.5	45.0[16]	60.9	2.7	36.4	...	3.4	1.5	5.5[10]	...	...	...	61,386[27]	...	Mexico
40.0	28.3	...	8.0	—92.0—		...	...	...	...	...	...	...	...	...	Micronesia
...	...	...	...	...	...	...	...	...	2.2[10,34]	...	1,594[11]	...	...	...	Moldova
100.0	100.0	96.2	98.4[51]	—1.6[51]—		...	2.8	0.8	...	...	...	...	...	...	Monaco
0.3	47.5	...	...	...	...	...	...	...	2.1	...	112[11]	...	...	176[17]	Mongolia
32.1[14]	37.8[14]	52.5[14]	...	...	...	...	2.7[47]	2.2[47]	4.7	51,911[17]	2,156[14]	65.9[17]	1,014[14]	457[15]	Morocco
12.7	4.2	...	...	...	...	...	...	...	10.6	...	247[77]	...	...	121[77]	Mozambique
...	...	...	...	...	...	...	...	...	1.4[37]	1,193[59]	...	...	1,483[59]	...	Myanmar (Burma)
49.8	24.2	30.9	...	...	...	...	3.6	1.5	2.7[10]	...	...	...	...	...	Namibia
...	49.2	...	...	...	...	...	3.6[96]	1.6[96]	...	...	...	...	...	...	Nauru
47.7	30.2	6.1	...	...	...	...	3.7	2.0	10.4[37]	...	...	...	...	...	Nepal
100.0	100.0	100.0	90.0[15]	—10.0[15]—		...	4.1[14]	0.7[14]	5.7	87,369[10]	...	70.0[18]	15,091[24]	49,968[24,25]	Netherlands, The
79.6[29]	96.9[29]	82.0[29]	...	...	...	...	4.2[29]	1.0[29]	9.5[43]	547[11]	...	150.2[11]	361	...	Netherlands Antilles
90.1	85.3	70.9	76.7	—23.3—		...	3.3	1.2	4.9[43]	772	46[17]	57.1	1[20]	...	New Caledonia
92.7[79]	...	97.1[79]	19.2	—80.0—		126.3[15,44]	5.6	0.5	4.2[3]	12,937[37]	1,396[37]	61.2[24]	...	2,568[37]	New Zealand
27.9	40.9	19.3	19.2	—80.8—		...	2.2	2.1	2.4	...	569[11,19]	...	...	19	Nicaragua
...	...	...	...	...	...	...	...	...	1.9	...	...	...	...	...	Niger
...	81.3	7.0	...	...	...	...	1.4	3.0	1.2	31,038[47]	...	...	1,592[16]	...	Nigeria
91.0	94.1[16]	79.5	81.7	—18.3—		...	3.6	1.1	...	...	...	...	...	...	Northern Mariana Islands
97.5[41]	...	94.6	86.8[41]	—13.2[16]—		103.5	4.1	0.6	3.6[11]	17,748[14]	2,388	82.2[12]	4,954[14]	2,272	Norway
...	...	...	...	...	...	...	...	...	3.9[10]	1,043[17]	...	...	266[17]	...	Oman
20.3	30.6	25.1	...	...	...	...	1.9	3.3	3.5[37]	...	...	...	...	...	Pakistan[98]

Housing and construction (continued)

country	housing stock			decade built (percent)					tenure[c] (percent)			construction of exterior walls (percent)			
	year	dwelling units[a]	median age[b] (years)	1949 or earlier	1950– 59	1960– 69	1970– 79	1980 or later	owned	rented	collective, vacant, other	traditional materials	sawn/ framed wood	masonry or cement	other
Palau	1990	3,312	12.8	2.1	6.0	16.8	30.6	44.5	76.4	23.6	—	0.0	27.9	26.5	45.6
Panama	1990[102]	524,284[22]	18.0[16]	47.4[16]	12.8[16]	18.1[16]	—21.7[16]—		75.5	15.7	8.8	16.9	—	81.2	1.9
Papua New Guinea	1980	556,519[25]	...						40.0[51]	—60.0[51]—		...	...	...	...
Paraguay	1982	868,284[21]	21.1	—56.0—		17.0	—27.0—		80.4	10.5	9.1	21.5	29.7	47.6	1.2
Peru	1993	4,427,517	...	—30.9[29]—			69.1[29]—		82.0	11.0	7.0	55.7	7.0	35.7	1.6
Philippines	1990	11,380,000[25]	...	—78.5[41]—			21.5[41]—		83.0	8.0	9.0	35.3	27.3	33.5	3.9
Poland	1988	11,967,021	...	35.0[85]	—33.7[104]—		31.3[48]—		35.2	64.3	0.9	—14.1[58]—		—85.9[58]—	
Portugal	1981	4,188,655[11]	33.7	—53.3—		17.5	—29.2—		56.7	38.8	4.6	—	0.7	61.0	38.3
Puerto Rico	1990	1,188,985	18.0	9.0	12.8	22.9	29.5	25.8	72.1	27.9	—	...	15.1	83.6	1.3
Qatar	1986	64,543	...	...	...	...	...	...	21.9	72.0	6.1	...	...	...	...
Réunion	1990	157,853	14.3	—47.6[65]—		19.9[64]	—32.5[76]—		56.3	35.7	8.0	40.0	—	41.0	19.0
Romania	1992	7,632,000	...	...	...	...	...	...	78.6	20.8	0.6	...	...	...	...
Russia	1995	41,000,000	...	...	...	...	...	...	...	...	...	...	...	...	...
Rwanda	1978	1,055,950[25]	...	...	...	...	...	...	95.3	1.7	3.0	88.6	7.9	1.3	2.2
St. Kitts and Nevis	1980	11,615[25]	24.2	—63.5—		17.9	—14.7—		54.7	29.5	15.8	—	76.2	21.3	2.5
St. Lucia	1991	33,079	13.5	—17.0—		12.4	26.0	44.6	72.4	26.8	0.8	—	53.4	46.1	0.5
St. Vincent and the Grenadines	1980	27,110	...	...	...	...	...	...	72.1	16.0	11.9	—	53.8	42.9	3.3
San Marino	1991	8,518	...	...	...	...	...	...	73.5[106]	21.9[106]	4.6[106]	...	...	...	...
São Tomé and Príncipe	1981	30,056	...	...	...	...	...	...	...	...	...	2.2	29.8	67.2	0.8
Saudi Arabia	...	...	...	...	...	...	...	...	...	...	...	...	...	...	...
Senegal	1955[49, 108]	13,000	...	...	...	...	...	...	—84.6—		15.4	...	...	...	...
Seychelles	1987	15,050	...	...	...	...	...	...	63.7	25.1	11.2	1.0	40.0	52.0	7.0
Sierra Leone	1985	486,550	...	—63.2[16]—			—36.8[16]—		75.2	20.7	4.1	64.6	—	26.2	9.2
Singapore	1990	744,203	...	...	...	...	...	...	87.5	—12.5—		4.7[16]	—	95.3[16]	—
Slovakia	1991	1,617,829	26.9	17.1[5]	17.3[6]	20.3[7]	25.4[8]	19.9[9]	...	...	...	—	38.0[55]	61.4	0.6
Slovenia	1992	664,505	...	...	...	...	...	...	...	...	...	...	...	...	...
Solomon Islands	1986	43,842[25]	...	...	...	...	...	...	27.4[30]	43.0[30]	29.6[30]	...	...	...	...
Somalia	...	...	...	...	...	...	...	...	...	...	...	...	...	...	...
South Africa	1991	3,599,518[109]	18.6[41]	40.6[41]	24.2[41]	35.2[41]	—	—	54.5	34.0	11.5	...	...	...	...
Spain	1991	11,824,851[22]	39.4[16]	39.2[16 ,110]	23.4[16 ,111]	18.5[16, 112]	—18.9[16, 48]—		67.5	14.9	17.6	...	...	...	...
Sri Lanka	1981	2,811,406	...	...	...	...	...	...	69.4	10.1	20.5	...	...	...	...
Sudan, The	1983	...	...	...	...	...	...	...	86.2	8.1	5.7	76.5	4.4	16.7	2.4
Suriname	1980	77,744	...	—52.4—			—47.6—		...	...	...	38.9[113]	—61.1[113]—		
Swaziland	1986	122,369	...	...	...	...	...	...	...	...	...	65.9	—34.1—		
Sweden	1990	3,830,037	20.0	33.2	14.2	22.4	22.2	10.6	55.9	40.0	4.1	...	...	...	...
Switzerland	1990	2,800,953	28.5	33.2[87]	15.9[88]	19.4[7]	17.2[8]	14.3[9]	31.3	66.5	2.2	...	...	...	...
Syria	1987	1,836,195	...	—91.3[41]—			—8.7[41]—		81.6[41]	15.5[41]	2.8[41]	...	...	...	...
Taiwan	1990	4,237,174[22]	17.2	6.1[5]	6.7[6]	15.8[7]	42.6[8]	28.8[9]	78.5	12.8	8.7	...	...	...	...
Tajikistan	1989	799,000[25]	...	...	...	...	...	...	...	...	...	...	...	...	...
Tanzania	1978	3,554,793	...	—17.0—			—83.0—		75.4	19.4	5.2	83.0	—	16.3	0.7
Thailand	1990	12,305,197[25]	...	22.0[41]	25.0[41]	53.0[41]	...	...	86.0	11.2	2.8	8.4	68.2	22.3	1.1
Togo	1981	462,694	...	...	...	...	...	...	...	...	...	...	...	...	...
Tonga	1986	15,091	22.5	—59.4[114]—		20.3[115]	—20.3[116]—		82.0	3.5	14.5	35.1[30]	45.4[30]	15.3[30]	4.2[30]
Trinidad and Tobago	1990	271,871	15.3	—41.6—			17.9	40.5	64.6[16]	34.0[16]	1.4[16]	1.0	28.1	70.0[38]	0.9
Tunisia	1984	1,703,279[10]	...	...	...	...	...	...	78.9	12.6	8.5	...	...	...	...
Turkey	1986	10,855,495	8.4	16.2[114]	6.2[117]	19.6[100]	—58.0[102]—		77.2	12.0	10.8	—28.8—		—71.2—	
Turkmenistan	1989	598,000[25]	...	...	...	...	...	...	...	...	...	...	...	...	...
Tuvalu	1979	1,079	...	...	...	...	...	...	81.6	12.1	6.6	64.9	4.2	31.0	—
Uganda	...	...	...	...	...	...	...	...	...	...	...	...	...	...	...
Ukraine	1989	14,057,000[25]	...	...	...	...	...	...	...	...	...	...	...	...	...
United Arab Emirates	1980	153,009	15.0	0.8	1.3	11.4	—86.5—		36.2	45.2	18.6	2.9	7.3	87.3	2.5
United Kingdom[119]	1991	21,897,322	32.6[29]	54.0[29]	13.0[29]	16.6[29]	—16.4[29]—		66.4	33.6	—	...	...	...	...
United States	1990	102,263,678	25.0	32.9[14]	14.0[14]	16.6[14]	—36.5[14]—		64.2	35.8	—	...	...	...	...
Uruguay	1985	852,400	...	...	...	...	...	...	57.6	23.2	19.2	...	...	...	...
Uzbekistan	1989	3,415,000[25]	...	...	...	...	...	...	...	...	...	...	...	...	...
Vanuatu	1979	28,252[24, 25]	...	...	...	...	...	...	40.9[49]	25.7[49]	33.4[49]	61.4	7.7	13.6	17.2
Venezuela	1990	3,534,507	...	...	...	...	...	...	75.8	13.9	10.3	14.6	0.5	84.9	—
Vietnam	1989	12,958,041[25]	...	...	...	...	...	...	...	...	...	...	...	...	...
Virgin Islands (U.S.)	1990	39,290	14.7	10.0[16]	8.9[16]	42.7[16]	—38.4[16]—		44.6	55.4	—	...	...	...	...
West Bank	1992	119,165[68]	12.2	8.0	12.7	24.6	26.2	28.6	86.2[69]	11.5[69]	2.3[69]	23.0	—	75.3	1.7
Western Sahara	1982	19,559	...	...	...	...	...	...	32.2[53]	62.3[53]	5.5[53]	...	...	...	...
Western Samoa	1981	33,402	...	...	...	...	...	...	80.1	2.0	17.9	62.3	24.4	8.6	4.7
Yemen[120]	1988[121]	1,701,203	...	...	...	...	...	...	83.9	5.2	10.9	...	...	...	...
Yugoslavia	1993	3,039,000	...	...	...	...	...	...	...	...	...	...	...	...	...
Zaire	1984	5,669,600[25]	...	...	...	...	...	...	47.4[49, 68]	38.3[49, 68]	14.3[49, 68]	52.4[49]	—45.5[49]—		2.1[49]
Zambia	1980	1,128,356	...	...	...	...	...	...	78.8[122]	21.1[122]	...	...	...	...	...
Zimbabwe	1992	2,165,744[25]	...	...	...	...	...	...	65.1[109, 122]	32.6[109, 122]	2.3[109, 122]	55.9[122, 123]	—44.1[122, 123]—		

[1]1983. [2]Urban only. [3]1990–91. [4]Data refer to buildings. [5]1945 or earlier. [6]1946–60. [7]1961–70. [8]1971–80. [9]1981 or later. [10]1994. [11]1991. [12]1962 or earlier. [13]1963–69. [14]1985. [15]1987. [16]1980. [17]1986. [18]1990. [19]Residential includes nonresidential. [20]1984. [21]1992. [22]Occupied dwellings only. [23]Average annual gain in housing stock during intercensal interval. [24]1989. [25]Data refer to households. [26]Volume in cubic metres. [27]1939 or earlier. [28]1940–59. [29]1976. [30]1976. [31]Minimum. [32]1992–93. [33]1994–95. [34]Percentage of net material product. [35]Stucco. [36]1993. [37]1993–94. [38]Includes wood and brick, and wood and concrete. [39]1946–61. [40]1962–70. [41]1970. [42]1983–85 average. [43]1988. [44]Average size of dwelling unit in year to which new dwellings and floor area data refer. [45]1986–87. [46]Data refer to compound dwellings. [47]1982. [48]1971 or later. [49]Capital city only. [50]1973. [51]1975. [52]Includes Public utilities. [53]1934–45. [54]1946–59. [55]Includes prefabricated units. [56]January 1. [57]Includes corrugated steel. [58]1978. [59]1987–88. [60]1977. [61]1948 or earlier. [62]1949–61. [63]1962–74. [64]1975–81. [65]1974 or earlier. [66]1975–82. [67]1983 or later. [68]1967. [69]Excludes refugee camps. [70]1949–87.

| physical amenities (percent) | | | sewage disposal (percent) | | | space[b] | | | construction industry (1993) | | | | | | country |
piped water	electricity	inside toilet or WC	closed public sewer or septic tank	open public sewer	other	average area (sq m)	rooms per dwelling unit	persons per room	percent of GDP	new residential[d] total no. of dwellings	floor area ('000 sq m)	years to replace nat'l stock	new nonresidential[d] number of units	floor area ('000 sq m)	
87.9	75.7[16]	75.2	44.3	—55.7—		...	2.6	1.8	12.0[14]	...	...	...	...	...	Palau
80.7	65.7[16]	74.3[16]	44.2	—55.8—		...	2.8	1.6	6.4	2,496[21]	492[21]	34.6[15]	90[14]	276[21]	Panama
50.0	56.0	40.0	...	...	...	...	...	...	3.6	587[17]	...	...	...	...	Papua New Guinea
...	...	26.4	...	...	...	...	2.2[103]	2.4[103]	5.9	...	61[14]	...	2,715[15]	365[15]	Paraguay
46.7	54.9	35.7	40.0	22.2	37.8	42.4[29]	2.6[29]	2.0[29]	6.7	...	952[17]	...	...	...	Peru
38.8	55.1	35.0[16]	67.6	14.4	18.0	...	2.4	2.3[103]	5.5	129,492[11]	13,856[17]	56.9[24]	2,807[14]	4,288	Philippines
84.3	96.2[58]	68.9	67.0[58]	—33.0[58]—		55.6[20]	3.2	1.0	6.3	63,199	6,156[21]	62.5[11]	38,600[21]	...	Poland
99.1[11]	99.4[11]	78.1[11]	75.5	—24.5—		75.4[24,44]	5.0[38]	0.8	7.5[18]	...	1,872[21]	82.8[15]	4,292	1,772[21]	Portugal
95.6	97.4[37]	94.7	95.7	—4.3—		...	4.8[16]	0.8[16]	2.2[10,92]	10,212[21]	391[17]	58.9[17]	900[14]	41.0[14]	Puerto Rico
...	93.2	...	...	—50.5—	49.5	...	4.9	1.3	4.9	12,240	...	...	1,416	168[17]	Qatar
81.0	95.0	70.0	52.4[47]	—47.6[47]—		...	3.9	1.0	6.2[18]	7,272	...	17.6[18]	...	...	Réunion
...	48.6[105]	...	12.2[105]	—87.8[105]—		89.6[44]	2.6	1.4	4.4[21]	60,400[24]	5,409[24]	98.6[24]	...	...	Romania
...	...	...	...	...	...	...	...	...	7.7	...	31,500	...	...	...	Russia
...	...	...	...	...	...	...	...	...	7.1[11]	435[20]	60[29]	...	63[20]	34[29]	Rwanda
46.3	57.5	33.5	31.8[26]	—68.2[26]—		...	3.0	1.1	12.0	171[23]	...	68.0[23]	...	...	St. Kitts and Nevis
64.7	72.9	35.7	35.7	—64.3—		...	3.4	1.2	9.0	471[4,15]	92	57.2[24,15]	121[17]	43	St. Lucia
95.0[1]	...	...	22.0[1]	—78.0[1]—		...	2.8	1.8	9.8	465[15,19]	81[19]	...	19	19	St. Vincent and the Grenadines
100.0	100.0	100.0	98.3[106]	—1.7[106]—		...	3.8	0.7	...	145[107]	...	64.0[18]	123[107]	...	San Marino
...	22.0	9.2	9.8	...	...	...	...	...	5.7	...	...	...	...	...	São Tomé and Príncipe
...	...	...	...	...	...	...	...	...	8.6[21]	...	16,078[11]	...	2,205[11]	...	Saudi Arabia
87.7	95.9	...	33.1[60]	—66.9[60]—		...	2.3	1.5	3.4[10]	...	257[15]	...	34[15]	33[15]	Senegal
77.0	75.8	95.0	13.1	66.2	20.7	...	4.1	1.1	4.2[18]	4,802[19,60]	...	...	46[17]	19	Seychelles
15.9	8.3	7.3	...	...	...	...	...	...	1.9[37]	...	...	...	...	...	Sierra Leone
90.6[41]	98.3[16]	63.6[41]	63.6[41]	—36.4[41]—		...	1.8[41]	2.5[41]	7.1[10]	18,948	4,303	36.2[18]	1,991[11]	2,730	Singapore
91.8	...	80.1	87.6	—12.4—		71.7	2.9	1.1	7.7[11,18]	...	1,147[11]	...	...	...	Slovakia
97.4	99.5	86.8	...	...	...	69.0	3.0	1.0	4.6[10,18]	7,925	809	102[21]	280	200	Slovenia
92.7[30]	79.6[30]	89.2	89.2[30]	—10.8[30]—		10.8[30]	2.3[30]	2.0[30]	4.3[11]	...	...	...	...	...	Solomon Islands
...	...	...	...	...	...	...	...	...	3.8[11]	...	...	...	...	...	Somalia
66.4	55.9	54.9	...	...	...	117.5[44]	3.4[41]	...	3.2	39,266[24]	4,619[24]	34.5[24]	...	1,316[24]	South Africa
98.7	99.2	97.1	87.9[16]	—12.1[16]—		86.6	4.4[41]	...	8.0[10]	237,637	...	43.9[11]	...	...	Spain
18.2	14.9	4.7	4.7	—95.3—		18.6[41]	2.5	2.1	6.5	59,637[17]	...	47.2[17]	...	...	Sri Lanka
29.4	9.9	70.2[2,105]	2.6[2,105]	—97.4[2,105]—		...	2.2[105]	2.5[105]	5.1[32]	...	...	...	...	...	Sudan, The
62.9	82.0	40.4	19.6[113]	—80.4[113]—		...	2.1	1.9	5.3	...	355[14,26]	...	161[14]	...	Suriname
42.5	11.6	21.4	...	...	...	...	...	...	2.7	...	...	...	28[20]	...	Swaziland
99.0[14]	96.2[16]	98.0	96.3[16]	—3.7[16]—		...	3.4	0.6	6.4	21,630[10]	...	57.3[11]	...	3,818[20]	Sweden
100.0[16]	...	93.3[16]	92.2[17]	—	7.8[16]	93.0	3.7	0.6	7.4[21]	46,326[10]	...	84.6[11]	8,109[17]	...	Switzerland
40.2[1]	41.7[1]	...	36.0[1]	—64.0[1]—		93.0	3.0	2.0	4.4	24,297[21]	2,977[21]	33.0[15]	...	1,147[21]	Syria
79.4[16]	99.7[16]	94.2[16]	69.3[16]	...	...	30.5	4.1	1.2	5.3[10]	...	47,533[19,36]	...	...	19	Taiwan
...	...	...	...	...	...	...	...	...	16.4[34]	...	400	...	...	...	Tajikistan
37.2	6.3	...	...	...	...	...	2.5	1.9	3.0[11]	...	...	...	...	...	Tanzania
29.7	89.7	40.9[31]	40.9[30]	9.8[30]	49.3[30]	...	1.6	2.7	6.6[21]	...	16,343[11]	...	...	13,499[11]	Thailand
4.1[80]	10.3[80]	...	—	—100.0[80]—		...	1.8	3.4	1.6	...	...	...	...	...	Togo
61.3[30]	20.9[30]	42.3[30]	11.2[30]	—88.8[30]—		...	...	...	3.7[37]	...	...	...	...	...	Tonga
64.3[16]	83.3[16]	41.1[16]	41.0[16]	—59.0[16]—		...	3.3[16]	1.4[16]	7.5[10]	1,622[21]	298[21]	94.9[18]	57[21]	50.1[21]	Trinidad and Tobago
26.4	63.4	43.3	69.2[24]	—30.8[24]—		...	1.9	2.4	4.1[10]	34,566[15]	...	43.8[15]	...	...	Tunisia
68.0	56.8	70.6	42.0	52.0	6.0	110.5[44]	2.4[14]	2.2[41]	6.8[10]	245,449[10]	19,693[10]	43.3[23]	4,533[10]	17,336[10]	Turkey
...	...	...	...	...	...	...	...	...	11.0[34]	...	20,754[19,21]	...	...	19	Turkmenistan
65.4	7.4	37.3	...	...	...	...	...	...	13.7	...	...	...	...	...	Tuvalu
...	...	...	...	...	...	...	...	...	5.7[37]	...	...	...	65[103]	26.8[103]	Uganda
...	...	...	...	...	...	...	...	...	10.0[11]	...	14,454[11]	...	...	...	Ukraine
30.9[118]	24.2[118]	84.5	...	...	...	...	2.8	1.8	9.8[10]	...	...	...	133[20]	...	United Arab Emirates
...	...	99.8	...	...	...	...	5.0	0.5	5.4[10]	172,908	...	122.2[11]	...	...	United Kingdom[119]
98.5	96.9	98.9	99.2	—0.8—		147.1	5.2	0.5	3.7[21]	1,284,000	214,900[17]	78.2[11]	...	140,100[17]	United States
89.3	84.7	73.3	...	92.0	...	...	3.4	1.7	5.3[10]	...	160[14]	...	105[14]	21.4[14]	Uruguay
...	...	...	...	...	...	...	...	...	10.4	...	7,000	...	...	...	Uzbekistan
39.2[24]	14.2	27.5[24]	...	...	...	...	...	...	5.2	...	5.7[17]	...	...	15.3[17]	Vanuatu
86.2	89.8	84.4[29]	80.2	—19.8—		53.5[44]	4.2	1.3	7.2	91,666[17]	4,904[17]	29.5[17]	678[17]	1,067[17]	Venezuela
...	...	...	...	...	...	...	...	...	6.8	...	...	...	53[20]	59.3[20]	Vietnam
96.3[16]	98.1[16]	86.0[16]	93.6[16]	—6.4[16]—		...	4.3	0.6	...	...	...	...	262[16]	...	Virgin Islands (U.S.)
75.2[14]	75.3	98.4	...	...	...	127.2[44]	2.4[14]	2.7[14]	14.1[15]	5,740[11]	730[11]	20.8[11]	...	175.8[11]	West Bank
...	...	...	...	...	...	...	...	...	...	...	...	...	...	...	Western Sahara
78.5	95.3	...	...	...	...	...	4.5	1.2	4.4[24]	...	...	...	118[14]	...	Western Samoa
80.7	37.7	71.0	16.6	—83.4—		...	3.9[30,108]	1.5[30,108]	3.1	132[14]	...	...	...	...	Yemen[120]
5.7[51]	4.6[51]	...	...	...	...	...	2.0[51]	2.8[51]	5.0[21]	...	1,988[14]	...	73[14]	39[14]	Yugoslavia
79.1	98.0	67.8	...	...	...	67.4	2.8	1.3	7.1[21]	19,405	...	156.6	2,805[12]	2,073[25]	Zaire
...	...	...	...	...	...	...	...	...	5.5[11]	...	...	...	...	...	
12.4[122]	27.5[80]	15.1[122]	...	...	82.3[122]	...	1.9[122]	2.6[122]	5.0[11]	...	...	...	...	...	Zambia
9.3[122,123]	...	...	...	...	...	...	2.8[122]	1.9[123]	2.2[10]	...	...	...	...	...	Zimbabwe

[71]1988 or later.   [72]1952 or earlier.   [73]1953–62.   [74]1963–72.   [75]1973–81.   [76]1982 or later.   [77]1974.   [78]1969–78.   [79]1971.   [80]1960.   [81]1947 or earlier.   [82]1948–83.   [83]1961–71.   [84]Factory space only.   [85]1944 or earlier.   [86]1945–60.   [87]1946 or earlier.   [88]1947–60.   [89]Peninsular Malaysia only.   [90]1957 or earlier.   [91]1958–67.   [92]Includes Mining.   [93]1960–68.   [94]1969 or later.   [95]Dwellings of indigenous population only.   [96]1961.   [97]Lagos only.   [98]Excludes Islāmābād, North-West Frontier, and federally administered tribal lands.   [99]1947–65.   [100]1966–75.   [101]1976 or later.   [102]Excludes areas under U.S. military control in the provinces of Panama and Colón.   [103]1972.   [104]1945–70.   [105]1966.   [106]1979.   [107]1995.   [108]European-style dwellings only.   [109]White, Coloured, and Asian dwellings only; excludes Bantu.   [110]1940 or earlier.   [111]1941–60.   [112]1988–89.   [113]1964.   [114]1955 or earlier.   [115]1956–66.   [116]1967 or later.   [117]1956–65.   [118]1968.   [119]Excludes Northern Ireland.   [120]Former Yemen Arab Republic only.   [121]Combined from 1986 and 1988 census data.   [122]1969.   [123]Bantu dwellings only.

Household budgets and consumption

This table provides international data on household income, on the consumption expenditure of households for goods and services, and on the principal object of such expenditure (in most countries), food consumption (by kind). For purposes of this compilation, income comprises pretax monetary payments and payment in kind. The first part of the table provides data on distribution of income by households and by sources of income; the second part analyzes the largest portion of income use—consumption expenditure. Such expenditure is defined as the purchase of goods and services to satisfy current wants and needs. This definition excludes income expended on taxes, debts, savings and investments, and insurance policies. The third and last part of the table focuses on food, which usually, and often by a wide margin, represents the largest share of consumer spending worldwide. The data provided include daily available calories per capita and consumption of major food groups.

For both sources of income and consumption expenditure, the primary basis of analysis for most countries is the household, an economic unit that can be as small as a single person or as large as an extended family. For some of the countries that do not compile information by household, the table provides data on personal income and personal expenditure—i.e., the income and expenditure of all the individuals constituting a society's households. When no expenditure data at all is available, the table reports the weights of each major class of goods and services making up a given country's consumer (or retail) price index (CPI). The weighting of the components of the CPI usually reflects household spending patterns within the country or its principal urban or rural areas.

The data on distribution of income show, collectively for an entire country, the proportion of total income earned (occasionally, expended) by households constituting the lowest quintile and highest decile (poorest 20% and wealthiest 10%) within the country. These figures show the degree to which either group represents a disproportionate share of poverty or wealth.

The data on sources of income illuminate patterns of economic structure in the gaining of an income. They indicate, for example, that in poor, agrarian countries income often derives largely from self-employment (usually farming) or that in industrial countries, with well-developed systems of salaried employment and social welfare, income derives mainly from wages and salaries and secondarily from transfer payments (see note a). Because household sizes and numbers of income earners vary so greatly internationally, and because the frequency and methodology of household and CPI surveys do not permit single-year comparisons for more than a few countries at once, no summary of total *household* income or expenditure was possible. Instead, U.S. dollar figures are supplied for *per capita* private final consumption expenditure (for a single, recent year) that are more comparable internationally and refer to the same date. The figures on distribution of consumption expenditure by end use reveal patterns of personal and family use of disposable income and indicate, inter alia, that in developing countries food may absorb 50% or more of disposable income, while in the larger household budgets of the developed countries, by contrast, food purchases may account for only 20–30% of spending. Each category of expenditure betrays similar complexities of local habit, necessity, and aspiration.

The reader should exercise caution when using these data to make inter-country comparisons. Most of the information comes from single-country surveys, which often differ markedly in their coverage of economically or demographically stratified groups, in sample design, or in the methods

Household budgets and consumption

country	income (latest)						consumption expenditure						
	percent received by		by source (percent)				per capita private final, U.S.$ 1994	by kind or end use (percent of household or personal budget; latest)					
	lowest 20% of households	highest 10% of households	wages, salaries	self-employment	transfer payments[a]	other[b]		food[c]	housing[d]	clothing[e]	health care	energy, water	education
Afghanistan	...	...	20.7	28.0	8.2	43.1	...	33.9	3.0	...	1.1	0.7	...
Albania	...	...	53.0	4.0	11.5	31.5	570	...	...	...	...	...	...
Algeria	6.9[1]	31.5[1]	43.1	38.3	18.6	1.8	620	52.3	6.7[2]	8.6	2.8	2	3
American Samoa	...	...	...	...	...	...	1,880[4]	32.9	20.4[5]	5.2	...	...	...
Andorra	...	...	...	...	...	...	...	...	...	...	...	...	...
Angola	...	...	...	...	...	...	420[6]	74.1[7]	10.2[2,7]	5.5[7]	1.8[7]	2.7[7]	2.7[7]
Antigua and Barbuda	...	...	...	...	...	...	2,170[8]	42.9	23.3	7.5	...	5.5	...
Argentina	4.4	35.2	53.9	31.5	1.5	12.7	6,800	40.1	9.3	8.0	7.9	9.0	2.6
Armenia	...	...	24.5	13.6[9]	5.5	56.4	700	47.3	...	17.4	...	...	...
Aruba	...	...	...	...	...	...	...	26.9	9.9	8.4	2.9	8.5	1.9
Australia	3.8	28.0	72.7	7.5	13.0	6.8	11,280	18.7	18.5	5.6	7.1	2.2	1.6
Austria	4.0	28.7	55.7	[10]	24.4	19.9[10]	13,600	18.8	11.8	8.5	4.5	5.1	0.3
Azerbaijan	...	...	70.2	10.8[9]	19.0	...	460	42.2	—	13.6	4.8	—	...
Bahamas, The	3.6	32.1	...	...	...	—	3,950[6]	19.8	19.2	7.2	3.4	4.3	7.8
Bahrain	...	...	...	...	...	...	2,550	32.4	21.2	5.9	2.3	2.2	2.3
Bangladesh	9.4[1]	23.7[1]	18.7	48.3	7.5	25.5	170[11]	63.3	8.8	5.9	1.1	8.4	1.2
Barbados	7.0	44.0[12]	...	...	...	...	4,170	45.8	16.8	5.1	3.8	5.2	3
Belarus	11.1[13]	19.4[13]	47.1	7.3[9]	45.6	...	1,290	29.0	2.7	...	...	...	...
Belgium	7.9[14]	21.5[14]	49.6	10.9	20.7	18.8	14,620	18.3	11.4	7.0	10.5	6.2	3
Belize	...	...	84.1	——15.9——			1,690	34.0	9.0	8.8	1.6	9.1	2.3
Benin	8.0	39.0	26.3	——73.7——			200	37.0	10.0	14.0	5.0	2.0	4.0
Bermuda	7.2	24.7	65.3	9.0	3.3	22.4	12,690[15]	14.6	27.7	4.9	7.6	3.3	3.8
Bhutan	...	...	...	...	...	...	190[17]	72.3	...	21.2	...	3.7	...
Bolivia	5.6[13]	31.7[13]	...	...	...	...	650	46.6	7.8	5.1	2.1	4.7	0.3
Bosnia and Herzegovina	...	...	53.2	12.0	18.2	16.6	1,890[19]	44.7	1.6	8.3	3.4	7.8	3
Botswana	3.7	42.9	73.3	15.4	10.8	0.4	1,180	39.5[20]	11.8	5.6	2.3	2.5	4.9
Brazil	2.1[13]	51.3[13]	62.4	14.7	10.9	12.0	2,270	25.3	21.3[2]	12.9	9.1	2	...
Brunei	...	...	...	...	...	...	...	45.1	2.6	6.1	...	2.4	3
Bulgaria	8.3[13]	24.7[13]	34.7	23.6[9]	14.8	—	770	47.0	4.1	7.4	3.2	4.3	3
Burkina Faso	...	...	...	...	...	...	140	38.7[7]	5.1[7]	4.4[7]	5.2[7]	13.7[7]	3
Burundi	...	...	...	...	...	...	150	59.6[7]	4.4[7]	11.1[7]	...	5.8[7]	...
Cambodia	...	...	...	...	...	...	...	...	...	...	...	...	...
Cameroon	...	...	41.4	52.6	3.0	3.0	420	49.1	18.0[2]	7.6	8.6	2	...
Canada	5.7	24.1	57.0	13.7	20.7	8.6	11,370	13.4	24.5[2]	5.3	4.7	2	3.1
Cape Verde	...	...	...	...	...	...	880[19]	60.0	8.5	2.5	0.5	4.9	22
Central African Republic	...	...	...	...	...	...	220	70.5[7]	0.6[7]	9.5[7]	1.0[7]	6.5[7]	...
Chad	8.0	30.0	...	...	...	...	140	45.3[7]	...	3.5[7]	11.9[7]	5.8[7]	...
Chile	3.5[13]	46.1[13]	——75.1——		12.0	12.9	2,320	27.9	15.2	22.5	...	...	...
China	6.2[13]	26.8[13]	21.6	72.2	——6.2——		190	49.9[20,23]	6.8[23]	13.7[23]	2.9[23]	...	2.3[23]
Colombia	3.6[13]	39.5[13]	45.1	35.4	14.2	5.3	1,350	45.0	7.8	4.5	6.4	2.2	1.7
Comoros	...	...	25.6	64.5	8.7	1.2	430[19]	67.3	2.3	11.6	3.2	3.8	3
Congo	7.0	43.5	...	...	...	...	340	37.0	6.0	6.0	6.0	3.0	8.0
Costa Rica	4.0[13]	34.1[13]	61.0	22.6	9.6	6.8	1,520	39.1	12.1[2]	9.4	3.7	2	3
Côte d'Ivoire	7.3[1]	26.9[1]	44.9	49.9	——5.2——		290	48.0	7.8	10.0	0.7	8.5	...
Croatia	...	...	40.2	40.8	12.1	6.9	1,760[1]	37.8	2.9	8.6	4.3	7.6	3
Cuba	...	...	57.3	——42.7——			1,510[6]	26.7	...	...	...	2.5	...
Cyprus	7.9[23]	...	76.3	5.9	14.4	3.4	6,850	22.7	5.5	10.0	3.1	1.3	1.4
Czech Republic	10.5[13,24]	23.5[13,24]	——66.7——		27.6	5.7	2,010	26.1	5.5[2]	7.3	25	2	...
Denmark	3.5	25.6	63.3	14.6	25.9	-3.8	15,030	18.4	22.7	5.3	2.3	5.5	2.2
Djibouti	...	...	51.6	36.0	10.5	1.9	1,030[19]	50.3	6.4	1.7	2.4	13.1	...
Dominica	...	...	...	...	...	...	1,800[6]	43.1	16.1	6.5	...	5.4	...
Dominican Republic	4.2[13]	39.6[13]	41.7	31.8	1.5	25.0	1,080	46.0	10.0	3.0	8.0	5.0	3.0
Ecuador	5.4[1]	37.6[1]	17.4	76.9	3.6	2.1	1,020	36.1	9.0	10.1	4.2	3.3	22
Egypt	8.7[1]	26.7[1]	...	...	...	...	660	50.2	10.5[2]	10.9	2.7	2	3
El Salvador	5.5[14]	29.5[14]	...	...	...	...	1,250	37.0[23]	12.1[23]	6.7[23]	4.2[23]	3.6[23]	3.7[23]

employed for collection, classification, and tabulation of data. Further, the reference period of the data varies greatly; while a significant portion of the data is from 1980 or later, information for some countries dates from the 1970s. This older information is typeset in italic. Finally, intercountry comparisons of annual personal consumption expenditure may be misleading because of the distortions of price and purchasing power present when converting a national currency unit into U.S. dollars.

The table's food consumption data include total daily available calories per capita (food supply), which amounts to domestic production and imports minus exports, animal feed, and nonfood uses, and a percentage breakdown of the major food groups that make up food supply.

The data for daily available calories per capita provide a measure of the nutritional adequacy of each nation's food supply. The following list, based on estimates from the United Nations Food and Agriculture Organization (FAO), indicates the regional variation in recommended daily minimum nutritional requirements, which are defined by factors such as climatic ambience, physical activity, and average body weight: Africa (2,320 calories), formerly Centrally Planned Asia (2,300 calories), Far East (2,240 calories), Latin America (2,360 calories), Near East (2,440 calories).

The breakdown of diet by food groups describes the character of a nation's food supply. A typical breakdown for a low-income country might show a diet with heavy intake of vegetable foods, such as cereals, potatoes, or cassava. In the high-income countries, a relatively larger portion of total calories derives from animal products (meat, eggs, and milk). The reader should note that these data refer to total national *supply* and often do not reflect the differences that may exist within a single country.

In compiling this table, Britannica editors rely on both numerous national reports and principal secondary sources such as the World Bank's *World Development Report* (annual), the International Labour Organisation's *Sources and Methods: Labour Statistics vol. 1 Consumer Price Indices* (3rd ed.), the UN's *Yearbook of National Accounts Statistics* (annual) and *National Accounts Statistics: Compendium of Income Distribution Statistics,* and the FAO's *Food Balance Sheets 1988–90* and *Compendium of Food Consumption Statistics from Household Surveys in Developing Countries* (2 vol.).

The following terms further define the column headings:

a. Includes pensions, family allowances, unemployment payments, remittances from abroad, and social security and related benefits.

b. Includes interest and dividends, rents and royalties, and all other income not reported under the three preceding categories.

c. Includes alcoholic and nonalcoholic beverages and meals away from home when identifiable. Excludes tobacco except as noted.

d. Rent, maintenance of dwellings, and taxes only; excludes energy and water (heat, light, power, and water) and household durables (furniture, appliances, utensils, and household operations), shown separately.

e. Includes footwear.

f. Furniture, appliances, and utensils; usually includes expenditure on household operation.

g. Includes expenditure on cultural activities other than education.

h. May include data not shown separately in preceding categories, including meals away from home (*see* note c).

i. Represents pure fats and oils only.

j. Consists mainly of peas, beans, and lentils; spices; stimulants; alcoholic beverages (when combined with "other"); sugars and honey; and nuts and oilseeds.

transportation, communications	household durable goods[f]	recreation[g]	personal effects, other[h]	daily available calories per capita (1992)	cereals	potatoes, cassava	meat, poultry	fish	eggs, milk	fruits, vegetables	fats, oils[i]	other[j]	country
...	...	...	61.3	1,523	75.5	1.2	4.8	—	3.3	2.8	7.9	4.5	Afghanistan
...	...	...	...	2,605	63.4	1.6	5.3	0.2	7.4	3.5	7.7	10.9	Albania
12.0	4.5	4.6[3]	8.5	2,897	55.0	2.5	1.7	0.4	6.5	4.3	14.7	14.9	Algeria
17.8	5	1.1	22.6	...	...	...	...	...	...	...	...	...	American Samoa
...	...	...	...	*3,670*	*23.8*	*5.5*	*18.0*	*1.5*	*9.4*	*6.7*	*15.9*	*19.1*	Andorra
3.9[7]	...	...	1.8[7]	1,839	32.5	32.4	4.4	3.0	2.8	3.6	9.9	11.2	Angola
10.0	...	...	10.8	2,458	26.9	1.0	16.7	3.0	11.0	7.2	13.0	21.2	Antigua and Barbuda
11.6	...	7.5	5.9	2,880	30.9	5.5	18.1	0.3	9.0	4.1	12.8	19.4	Argentina
...	6.6	...	28.7	...	...	...	...	...	...	...	...	...	Armenia
15.5	9.1	3.1	11.9	...	...	...	...	...	...	...	...	...	Aruba
15.1	7.0	7.5	16.7	3,179	24.3	3.0	19.9	0.8	11.1	4.9	13.6	22.4	Australia
18.5	8.0	7.2	17.3	3,497	19.8	3.3	13.7	0.6	10.5	6.6	22.2	23.2	Austria
5.1	6.5	0.7	27.1	...	...	...	...	...	...	...	...	...	Azerbaijan
18.9	10.2	5.3	3.9	2,624	25.2	1.9	17.4	1.3	7.6	9.6	9.3	27.6	Bahamas, The
8.5	9.8	6.4	9.0	...	...	...	...	...	...	...	...	...	Bahrain
0.9	...	...	10.4	2,019	82.9	1.3	0.5	0.6	1.2	1.1	5.4	6.9	Bangladesh
10.5	8.1	4.8[3]	—	3,207	28.1	3.9	13.7	2.5	7.4	3.3	13.4	27.7	Barbados
...	...	...	68.3	...	...	...	...	...	...	...	...	...	Belarus
13.4	10.6	6.8[3]	15.8	3,681	19.0	4.7	18.6	1.0	9.1	5.6	21.3	20.7	Belgium
13.7	8.0	...	9.4	2,662	32.9	1.9	8.7	0.4	10.9	6.2	11.7	27.3	Belize
14.0	5.0	...	9.0	2,532	35.0	39.0	2.3	0.8	0.9	2.9	7.8	11.3	Benin
7.3	16.6	10.8	3.4	2,960[16]	20.5	2.3	19.7	2.7	8.9	9.5	13.4	23.0	Bermuda
...	0.7	...	2.1	2,058[18]	85.2	2.4	0.4	0.1	0.6	1.4	5.3	4.6	Bhutan
17.7	9.7	2.7	3.3	2,094	41.2	11.2	9.7	0.1	2.5	8.4	9.2	17.6	Bolivia
6.0	4.1	3.5[3]	2.3	...	...	...	...	...	...	...	...	...	Bosnia and Herzegovina
13.1	13.8	3.1	3.4	2,266	62.7	0.8	4.0	0.3	7.1	1.4	5.5	18.2	Botswana
15.0	...	...	16.4	2,824	34.4	6.4	6.8	0.4	6.4	5.0	15.0	25.5	Brazil
17.2	8.3	8.9[3]	9.4	2,745	47.6	1.0	11.9	1.6	5.7	4.0	7.0	21.1	Brunei
8.0	1.5	3.0[3]	21.5[16]	2,831	39.6	1.5	10.3	0.4	8.8	5.1	15.2	19.2	Bulgaria
18.6[7]	3.0[7]	2.3[3,7]	9.0[7]	2,387	71.8	1.4	2.3	0.2	1.4	0.8	4.1	17.6	Burkina Faso
...	6.0[7]	...	13.1[7,21]	1,941	21.1	29.0	1.0	0.2	0.8	9.6	2.6	35.8	Burundi
...	...	...	...	2,021	83.4	3.1	3.2	0.8	0.4	3.2	1.2	4.8	Cambodia
13.0	...	2.4	1.3	1,981	38.9	15.9	3.5	1.1	1.6	11.8	8.6	18.6	Cameroon
14.3	8.8	8.0	17.9	3,094	22.6	3.4	15.1	1.4	9.9	6.4	18.5	22.7	Canada
8.8	6.9	22	7.9[22]	2,805	51.5	5.0	3.7	0.9	3.0	2.4	13.9	19.6	Cape Verde
4.1[7]	0.8[7]	1.3[7]	5.7[7]	1,690	25.6	33.4	7.3	0.5	1.2	5.7	7.3	19.2	Central African Republic
...	...	...	33.5[7]	1,989	50.2	16.3	3.5	1.8	2.8	2.8	5.0	17.3	Chad
6.4	...	...	28.0	2,582	45.7	4.3	8.3	1.4	6.5	5.5	8.6	19.7	Chile
4.7[23]	5.3[23]	2.4[23]	12.0[23]	2,727	69.7	5.8	8.0	0.6	1.4	2.6	4.7	7.1	China
18.5	5.7	...	8.2	2,677	31.4	8.1	7.4	0.2	6.6	9.1	9.9	27.2	Colombia
2.2	3.0	2.5[3]	4.1	1,897	44.9	17.8	1.7	1.5	1.6	8.9	7.3	16.3	Comoros
15.0	4.0	...	15.0	2,296	18.6	43.9	2.7	3.2	1.0	7.4	11.6	11.6	Congo
11.6	10.9	4.4[3]	8.8	2,883	35.7	0.8	5.1	0.3	8.8	4.9	13.0	31.3	Costa Rica
12.2	3.4	...	9.4	2,491	36.7	27.2	2.5	1.2	1.4	9.4	9.9	11.6	Côte d'Ivoire
9.3	4.5	4.1[3]	1.5	...	...	...	...	...	...	...	...	...	Croatia
5.4	...	...	65.4	2,833	32.9	4.8	6.5	1.1	7.9	3.8	14.1	29.0	Cuba
15.6	10.5	6.3	23.6	...	40.0	2.5	13.7	0.4	7.9	7.0	10.1	18.4	Cyprus
3.1	4.5	0.8[25]	52.7	3,303	29.9[26]	4.2[26]	13.0[26]	0.5[26]	9.5[26]	4.2[26]	17.5[26]	21.2[26]	Czech Republic
15.3	6.2	8.0	14.1	3,664	20.4	3.6	23.7	2.0	8.7	3.9	17.7	20.1	Denmark
...	1.5	...	24.6	2,338	53.5	0.6	4.1	0.3	6.0	2.8	11.9	20.9	Djibouti
11.6	6.0	...	11.3	2,778	27.9	8.5	8.9	1.0	9.2	9.6	9.3	25.6	Dominica
4.0	8.0	...	13.0	2,286	32.7	3.5	5.2	0.3	5.2	15.2	14.1	23.7	Dominican Republic
12.8	5.5	22	19.0[22]	2,583	33.4	3.2	4.8	1.0	6.9	11.1	20.7	19.0	Ecuador
4.7	5.0	3.3[3]	12.7	3,335	63.2	1.8	2.8	0.4	1.8	6.3	11.1	12.6	Egypt
10.2[23]	5.7[23]	4.3[23]	12.5[23]	2,663	53.8	0.8	2.3	0.1	6.2	4.5	8.3	24.0	El Salvador

Household budgets and consumption (continued)

country	income (latest) percent received by		by source (percent)				consumption expenditure per capita private final, U.S.$ 1994	by kind or end use (percent of household or personal budget; latest)					
	lowest 20% of households	highest 10% of households	wages, salaries	self-employment	transfer payments[a]	other[b]		food[c]	housing[d]	clothing[e]	health care	energy, water	education
Equatorial Guinea	...	...	57.0[7]	42.0[7]	—	1.0[7]	350[27]	62.0[7]	...	10.0[7]	6.0[7]	...	...
Eritrea[29]	...	...	...	...	...	...	...	...	...	...	...	...	...
Estonia	6.6[13]	31.3[13]	53.0	5.7	12.8	28.5	910	41.0	9.6	8.4	25	6.5	3.1
Ethiopia[29]	8.6[1]	27.5[1]	0.2	79.5	—	20.3	85	49.0	7.0	6.0	3.0	7.0	4.0
Faroe Islands	...	...	88.3	11.7	—	—	...	40.9	11.0	8.0	...	18.9	...
Fiji	3.7	37.8	81.5	9.1	...	9.4	1,430[11]	34.7	15.6[2]	9.3	2.4	[2]	[3]
Finland	3.7	26.9	70.3	7.4	9.7	12.6	10,700	22.5	16.9	5.0	4.8	4.6	[3]
France	5.6	26.1	51.1	14.1	27.5	7.3	13,820	17.4	16.2	6.1	9.8	3.8	0.7
French Guiana	...	...	74.6	...	25.4		...	30.0[20]	16.1[2]	6.7	4.4	[2]	[3]
French Polynesia	...	...	61.9	18.5	16.6	3.0	4,310[30]	39.6	9.7	6.3	1.0	8.1	1.0
Gabon	3.3	54.4	...	...	...	...	1,390	54.7[7,20,31]	13.0[7,31]	17.5[7,31]	1.9[7,31]	...	...
Gambia, The	...	...	...	...	...	...	260	58.0[32]	5.1[32]	17.5[32]	...	5.4[32]	...
Gaza Strip	...	...	...	...	...	...	910[8]	...	...	...	...	...	...
Georgia	...	...	34.5	21.6[9]	21.7	22.0	530[11]	38.3	...	14.8	...	0.3	...
Germany	7.0[33]	24.4[33]	57.9	10	21.3	20.8[10]	14,400	19.0	16.9	7.9	3.5	4.1	[3]
Ghana	7.9[1]	27.3[1]	41.6[34]	47.1[34]	—	11.3[34]	310[11]	57.4	11.5[2]	14.3	1.3	[2]	[3]
Gibraltar	...	...	...	...	...	...	...	39.1[20]	12.6	11.0	...	...	...
Greece	...	...	34.0	22.8	17.0	26.2	7,030	29.9	14.1	6.5	3.1	3.3	0.5
Greenland	...	...	...	...	...	...	11,110	30.1	10.0	7.7	0.3	5.4	...
Grenada	...	...	...	...	...	...	1,340	40.7[20]	11.9	5.2	35	3.9	[3]
Guadeloupe	...	...	78.9	13.7	7.4	—	4,080[8]	31.6[20]	11.3[2]	9.3	4.6	[2]	[3]
Guam	...	...	...	...	...	...	...	24.1	28.6	10.6	4.8	...	...
Guatemala	2.1[13]	46.6[13]	...	...	...	...	1,080	64.4	16.0[2]	3.1	0.6	[2]	0.3
Guernsey	...	...	...	...	...	...	...	23.7	12.1	7.5	...	8.2	...
Guinea	3.0[1]	31.7[1]	...	...	...	...	430	61.5	7.3[2]	7.9	11.1	[2]	...
Guinea-Bissau	2.1[1]	42.4[1]	...	...	...	...	210	...	...	...	...	...	...
Guyana	4.0	40.0[12]	73.0	...	6.3	20.7	350	42.5[20]	21.4	8.6	...	5.2	[3]
Haiti	...	...	...	...	...	...	250	51.1[20]	4.3	8.7	2.2	...	[3]
Honduras	3.8[13]	41.9[13]	58.3	10	1.8	39.9[10]	360	44.4	22.4[2]	9.1	7.0	[2]	[3]
Hong Kong	5.4[24]	31.3[24]	...	...	...	...	12,840	15.1	15.7[2]	21.3	5.0	[2]	0.5
Hungary	9.5[1]	22.6[1]	55.0		19.2	5.8	2,920	38.1	5.7	7.4	1.5	6.1	0.7
Iceland	4.7	27.3	73.1	2.7	10.2	14.0	13,840	23.7	14.3	7.2	1.5	3.0	0.8
India	8.5[1]	28.4[1]	42.2	39.7	18.1		200	52.2	6.1[36]	10.0	2.4	4.7[36]	1.8
Indonesia	8.7[1]	25.6[1]	42.1	41.5	2.5	13.9	530	47.5[23]	20.1[2,23]	5.5[23]	...	[2]	...
Iran	3.8	41.7	37.4[23]	30.5[23]	32.1[23]		690	42.6[20]	24.9[2]	11.8	3.9	[2]	[3]
Iraq	2.1	...	23.9	33.9	23.0	18.6	1,710[14]	50.2	19.9[2]	10.6	1.6	[2]	[3]
Ireland	4.6	26.5	58.6	13.3	19.9	8.2	8,730	30.5	7.1	7.4	3.2	6.1	2.4
Isle of Man	6.4	26.6	64.1	6.6	16.9	12.4	...	31.0	7.9	7.0	...	11.0	...
Israel	8.4	23.1	63.4[23,31]	14.6[23,31]	18.9[23,31]	3.1[23,31]	8,950	23.8	19.8	5.3	6.2	2.4	2.9
Italy	6.8	25.3	41.7	25.9	20.3	12.1	11,170	19.5	10.0	9.8	6.7	3.8	0.7
Jamaica	5.8[1]	31.9[1]	86.3	13.9	14.0	8.5	1,100	35.7	5.7	4.6	2.8	4.9	0.2
Japan	10.9	31.6[12]	59.3	11.1	19.5	10.1	21,740	23.9	5.3	6.8	2.7	5.4	4.5
Jersey	...	...	...	...	...	...	...	28.3	14.9	8.3	...	6.5	...
Jordan	5.9[1]	34.7[1]	51.4	11.1	13.7	23.8	970	40.6	15.8	6.7	2.2	5.0	3.5
Kazakstan	...	...	67.7	5.8[9]	16.9	9.6	650	29.6	2.6	...	...	...	...
Kenya	3.4	47.9	...	...	...	...	160	46.5	10.0	7.7	2.2	2.6	1.0
Kiribati	...	...	69.7	21.4	6.0	2.9	370[4]	50.0[20]	7.5[2,5]	8.0	...	[2]	...
Korea, North	...	...	...	...	...	...	...	46.5[38]	0.6[38]	29.9[38]	...	3.3[38]	...
Korea, South	7.4	27.6	53.8	25.1	13.1	8.0	4,600	29.7	4.1	7.7	5.0	4.0	14.2
Kuwait	...	...	53.8	20.8	25.4		4,140	28.1[20]	15.5	8.1	0.7	9.6	[3]
Kyrgyzstan	3.0	57.0[12]	67.3		32.7		440	33.5	2.2	...	...	...	...
Laos	...	...	...	...	...	...	140[6]	...	...	...	...	...	...
Latvia	9.6[13]	22.1[13]	67.0	5.4[9]	17.4	10.2	1,210	51.6	...	...	...	...	...
Lebanon	5.0	45.0	27.9	...	3.0	69.1	780[4]	42.8[7]	16.8[7]	8.6[7]	7.2[7]	4.5[7]	3.9[7]
Lesotho	2.9[1]	43.6[1]	22.4	27.8	44.7	5.1	370	48.0[20]	10.1	16.4	...	...	...
Liberia	5.0	73.0[12]	...	...	...	...	330[6]	34.4[7]	14.9[7]	13.8[7]	...	5.0[7]	...
Libya	10.1	...	...	...	...	...	2,330[6]	37.2[20]	32.2[2]	6.9	3.3	[2]	[3]
Liechtenstein	...	...	92.9[39]	7.1[39]	...	...	...	21.3[20]	18.0	6.6	7.7	4.4	[3]
Lithuania	8.1[13]	21.0[13]	66.4	9.7	18.7	5.2	1,070	50.3	...	...	...	...	...
Luxembourg	10.0	34.0[12]	67.1	4.8	28.1	—	15,140[17]	12.8	13.7	5.9	7.3	6.1	[3]
Macau	...	...	65.0	18.1	7.0	9.9	4,160[27]	39.2[14]	17.5	6.8	4.0	5.2	[3]
Macedonia	...	...	57.7	17.2	16.2	9.0	1,800[1]	40.6	1.9	7.8	3.0	7.8	[3]
Madagascar	5.8[1]	34.9[1]	58.8[7,40]	14.1[7,40]	...	27.1[7,40]	210	59.0	6.0	6.0	2.0	6.0	4.0
Malawi	10.4	40.1	83.3	6.0	—	11.7	92	30.0	4.0	9.0	4.0	5.0	10.0
Malaysia	4.6[13]	37.9[13]	...	...	...	...	1,820	28.7	10.2[2]	4.3	2.5	[2]	0.6
Maldives	...	...	...	...	...	...	270[6]	57.4	1.6	8.0	2.5	...	[3]
Mali	...	...	...	...	...	...	170	57.0	2.0	6.0	2.0	6.0	4.0
Malta	...	...	63.8	19.3	—	16.9	4,080	31.2	3.5	7.6	3.5	2.0	0.4
Marshall Islands	...	...	...	...	...	...	...	57.7	15.6[2,5]	12.0	...	[2]	...
Martinique	...	...	80.0	...	...	20.0	4,840[7]	32.1[20]	10.6[2]	8.0	5.2	[2]	[3]
Mauritania	3.5[1]	30.2[1]	...	...	...	...	370	73.1	2.5	8.1	0.9	7.7	0.4
Mauritius	4.0	46.7	51.7	29.0	11.2	8.1	2,020	41.9	8.8	8.4	3.0	6.4	2.9
Mayotte	...	...	...	...	...	...	...	42.2	31.5	...	...	6.8	...
Mexico	4.3	39.1	61.5	29.1	7.8	1.6	2,950	36.6[20]	13.3[2]	8.4	3.4	[2]	[3]
Micronesia	...	...	51.8	23.0	2.1	23.1	...	73.5	...	...	...	...	...
Moldova	6.9[13]	25.8[13]	41.2	10.4	15.3	33.1	670	...	...	...	...	...	...
Monaco	...	...	...	...	...	...	...	...	...	...	...	...	...
Mongolia	...	...	72.1	9.5[9]	9.7	8.7	230	39.1	5.9[2]	23.4	0.5	[2]	2.9
Morocco	6.6[1]	30.5[1]	...	...	...	...	850	38.0	7.0	11.0	5.0	2.0	8.0
Mozambique	...	...	51.6		48.4		59	74.6	11.7	3.7	0.8	...	[3]
Myanmar (Burma)	8.0	40.0[12]	...	...	...	...	750[17]	49.1[7]	10.4[7]	15.3[7]	2.4[7]	4.0[7]	5.9[7]
Namibia	...	...	67.1	27.5	5.4	...	900	...	...	...	...	...	...
Nauru	...	...	...	...	...	...	...	...	...	...	...	...	...
Nepal	9.1[1]	25.0[1]	25.1	63.4	11.5		160	61.2	17.3	11.7	3.7	...	[3]
Netherlands, The	8.2	21.9	48.2	10.7	29.1	12.0	13,150	13.6	14.9	7.1	12.9	3.1	0.7

transportation, communications	household durable goods[f]	recreation[g]	personal effects, other[h]	daily available calories per capita (1992)	cereals	potatoes, cassava	meat, poultry	fish	eggs, milk	fruits, vegetables	fats, oils[i]	other[j]	country
...	...	...	22.0[7]	2,230[28]	...	...	...	...	...	...	...	...	Equatorial Guinea
...	...	...	...	1,750[11]	...	...	...	...	...	...	...	...	Eritrea[29]
9.2	2.3	5.0[25]	15.0	...	...	...	...	...	...	...	...	...	Estonia
8.0	2.0	...	14.0	1,610	71.5	4.1	3.1	—	2.4	-0.8	3.6	14.5	Ethiopia[29]
...	6.6	...	14.6	...	*29.3*	*5.5*	*15.8*	*3.9*	*7.0*	*3.3*	*18.0*	*17.2*	Faroe Islands
13.8	9.3	4.3[3]	10.6	3,089	38.7	6.1	3.9	3.1	4.6	1.5	14.1	27.9	Fiji
14.8	6.3	9.5[3]	15.6	3,018	23.4	4.9	16.7	1.9	15.4	4.9	12.8	20.0	Finland
16.1	7.7	6.9	15.3	3,633	23.9	3.7	16.0	1.2	12.5	4.9	18.9	18.9	France
17.5	7.9	6.2[3]	11.2	2,900	29.1	4.3	17.0	3.0	7.7	8.7	8.0	22.1	French Guiana
16.4	4.4	4.0	9.5	2,834	36.5	5.2	12.4	2.4	5.1	4.3	11.5	22.7	French Polynesia
6.3[7,31]	...	...	6.6[7,31]	2,500	24.4	25.5	6.3	2.1	1.4	14.7	7.9	17.7	Gabon
...	...	...	14.0[32]	2,360	67.2	1.0	2.4	1.3	1.7	1.1	9.7	15.5	Gambia, The
				...	*50.4*	*1.6*	*4.2*	*0.2*	*4.9*	*9.0*	*13.8*	*15.9*	Gaza Strip
...	5.9	...	40.7	...	...	...	...	...	...	...	...	...	Georgia
17.8	9.4	10.6[3]	10.8	3,344	22.3	4.8	13.9	0.8	10.1	6.0	18.8	23.3	Germany
3.3	3.8	3.9[3]	4.5	2,199	29.0	39.3	1.9	2.5	0.3	8.5	8.6	9.9	Ghana
13.3	10.0	...	14.0	...	...	...	...	...	...	...	...	...	Gibraltar
17.5	6.9	5.2	13.0	3,815	27.7	3.9	12.2	0.8	10.1	9.5	18.4	17.3	Greece
8.0	9.2	15.5	13.8	...	...	...	...	...	...	...	...	...	Greenland
9.1	13.7	4.6[3]	10.9[35]	2,402	26.5	2.4	7.6	2.4	12.3	8.3	10.0	30.6	Grenada
20.5	9.3	4.7[3]	8.7	2,777	34.4	3.3	11.2	3.2	7.5	8.0	11.2	21.3	Guadeloupe
18.0	...	5.1	8.8	...	...	...	...	...	...	...	...	...	Guam
7.0	5.0	0.9	2.7	2,255	60.5	0.4	1.4	—	2.9	2.1	7.2	25.4	Guatemala
15.7	8.3	...	24.7	...	...	...	...	...	...	...	...	...	Guernsey
5.1	*2.9*	*4.1*	*0.1*	2,389	48.2	13.2	1.5	0.7	1.2	14.4	12.0	8.7	Guinea
...	...	...	...	2,556	63.6	6.1	4.6	0.3	1.5	4.2	13,0	6.7	Guinea-Bissau
4.8	*2.9*	*6.4[3]*	*8.2*	2,384	48.4	2.1	4.5	3.0	5.6	5.0	6.9	24.6	Guyana
7.6	9.2	5.3[3]	11.6	1,706	37.4	12.4	3.5	0.3	1.7	9.8	6.1	28.7	Haiti
3.0	8.3	2.4[3]	3.1	2,305	50.9	0.5	2.3	0.3	5.1	6.8	13.3	20.9	Honduras
8.4	17.5	8.1	8.4	3,129	35.4	1.0	16.2	3.0	4.8	4.5	16.2	18.8	Hong Kong
15.2	8.8	5.9	10.6	3,503	29.1	2.8	12.6	0.3	8.8	4.5	20.8	21.1	Hungary
17.6	9.3	10.4	12.2	3,058	27.5	2.7	12.5	5.0	15.8	3.3	10.3	22.9	Iceland
10.6	3.1	1.8	5.7	2,395	63.1	1.8	0.7	0.3	4.8	3.2	7.2	18.9	India
...	2.9[23]	...	24.0	2,752	66.5	6.2	1.3	1.2	0.6	2.3	7.7	14.3	Indonesia
5.0	6.4	1.7[3]	3.7	2,860	62.8	2.1	3.3	0.3	3.2	7.1	10.8	10.3	Iran
6.5	6.7	0.8[3]	3.7	2,121	61.5	0.5	3.5	0.1	3.0	6.4	12.7	12.4	Iraq
14.0	7.2	8.9	13.1	3,952[16]	24.3	6.0	14.8	0.8	14.5	3.6	17.4	18.7	Ireland
14.9	5.7	...	22.5	...	...	...	...	...	...	...	...	...	Isle of Man
12.9	10.8	4.3	11.6	3,050	31.3	1.9	8.1	1.1	9.6	9.0	19.1	19.9	Israel
13.2	9.5	8.4	18.4	3,561	32.1	2.1	11.0	1.1	8.6	7.4	21.7	15.9	Italy
12.4	5.5	2.1	26.1	2,240	32.6	7.3	6.5	1.4	6.1	7.0	11.5	27.7	Jamaica
9.0	1.4	9.5	31.5	2,903	39.7	2.6	5.6	6.9	6.2	4.4	11.2	23.3	Japan
13.9	*7.1*	...	*21.0*	...	...	...	...	...	...	...	...	...	Jersey
11.2	6.1	4.0	4.9	3,022[37]	51.8	1.0	6.2	0.2	4.6	4.6	11.0	20.9	Jordan
...	...	...	67.8	...	...	...	...	...	...	...	...	...	Kazakstan
8.4	9.4	3.1	9.1	2,075	52.0	7.4	4.1	0.5	8.4	3.2	6.4	17.9	Kenya
8.0	5	...	26.5	2,651	39.0	10.9	3.7	5.7	1.2	5.8	8.2	25.5	Kiribati
...	3.8[38]	...	15.9	2,833	62.1	5.7	3.4	2.6	1.1	5.8	3.3	16.0	Korea, North
11.3	5.0	——19.0——		3,285	52.5	0.7	5.2	3.5	2.2	6.9	9.1	19.8	Korea, South
13.7	11.2	5.2[3]	7.9	2,523	36.0	1.2	10.7	0.7	9.5	8.1	15.8	17.9	Kuwait
...	...	...	64.3	...	...	...	...	...	...	...	...	...	Kyrgyzstan
...	...	...	...	2,259	74.7	4.6	7.0	0.4	1.7	2.5	1.9	7.2	Laos
...	...	...	54.8	2,490[16]	...	...	...	...	...	...	...	...	Latvia
5.4[7]	2.6[7]	1.9[7]	6.3[7]	3,317	37.6	3.1	6.0	—	5.9	11.4	15.7	20.3	Lebanon
4.7	11.9	...	8.8	2,201	75.3	0.6	4.2	0.2	1.5	1.7	3.9	12.5	Lesotho
...	6.1[7]	...	25.8[7]	1,640	46.7	22.6	2.0	1.1	0.5	4.9	14.4	7.7	Liberia
9.4	4.6	8.5[3]	2.5	3,308	45.4	1.7	5.6	0.2	6.7	7.5	16.5	16.3	Libya
13.3	5.8	16.3[3]	6.6	...	...	...	...	...	...	...	...	...	Liechtenstein
...	...	...	49.7	2,110[16]	...	...	...	...	...	...	...	...	Lithuania
19.1	10.8	4.2[3]	20.1	3,681	19.0	4.7	18.6	1.0	9.1	5.6	21.3	20.7	Luxembourg
8.2	3.0	8.8[3]	7.3	2,278	42.7	2.0	16.0	1.4	4.6	5.3	12.8	15.3	Macau
6.5	4.2	3.3[3]	1.8	...	...	...	...	...	...	...	...	...	Macedonia
4.0	1.0	...	12.0	2,135	55.8	19.2	6.2	0.7	3.3	4.2	3.5	7.1	Madagascar
10.0	3.0	...	25.0	1,825	68.8	4.0	1.5	0.9	0.7	4.6	1.7	17.9	Malaŵi
20.9	7.7	11.0	14.1	2,888	40.3	3.4	7.3	1.7	4.9	3.4	19.2	19.7	Malaysia
2.6	17.0	5.9[3]	5.0	2,580	52.6	3.9	0.6	12.6	—	4.2	4.8	21.4	Maldives
10.0	1.0	...	12.0	2,278	72.7	1.9	3.3	0.6	4.2	0.8	7.8	8.6	Mali
16.4	9.9	7.1	18.4	3,468	30.1	1.5	10.7	1.0	11.3	6.6	15.9	22.9	Malta
...	5	...	14.7	...	...	...	...	...	...	...	...	...	Marshall Islands
20.7	9.4	5.4[3]	8.6	2,829	31.2	3.7	11.3	2.7	7.7	10.9	11.2	21.2	Martinique
2.0	1.2	4.0	0.1	2,685	54.8	0.4	4.0	0.6	12.5	1.6	8.3	17.9	Mauritania
10.0	6.4	—	12.2	2,690	50.0	1.2	3.7	1.4	6.4	1.5	12.2	23.5	Mauritius
5.1	8.8	...	5.6	...	...	...	...	...	...	...	...	...	Mayotte
10.0	11.8	5.5[3]	11.0	3,146	46.7	0.7	8.5	0.6	5.8	3.3	12.5	21.8	Mexico
...	...	...	26.5	...	...	...	...	...	...	...	...	...	Micronesia
...	...	...	...	...	...	...	...	...	...	...	...	...	Moldova
...	...	...	...	3,593[16]	23.9	3.7	16.0	1.2	12.5	4.9	18.9	18.9	Monaco
3.5	8.0	0.4	16.2	1,899	46.5	2.0	24.1	0.1	6.4	0.8	6.2	13.8	Mongolia
8.0	5.0	...	16.0	2,984	54.5	1.7	2.1	0.6	1.8	4.4	10.9	24.0	Morocco
...	...	1.4[3]	7.9	1,680	32.0	43.3	1.5	0.3	0.7	1.8	12.7	7.7	Mozambique
3.8[7]	*0.5[7]*	*1.1[7]*	*7.5[7]*	2,598	79.5	0.4	1.8	1.0	1.0	2.5	6.3	7.5	Myanmar (Burma)
...	...	...	...	2,134	55.0	15.5	8.1	0.7	3.0	1.7	7.1	8.9	Namibia
...	...	...	...	...	...	...	...	...	...	...	...	...	Nauru
1.2	...	2.9[3]	2.0	1,957	80.9	3.0	1.2	—	4.1	0.9	4.4	5.4	Nepal
13.3	7.1	9.7	17.6	3,222	17.8	5.3	12.2	0.6	13.1	6.1	20.2	24.6	Netherlands, The

Household budgets and consumption (continued)

country	income (latest)						consumption expenditure						
	percent received by		by source (percent)				per capita private final, U.S.$ 1994	by kind or end use (percent of household or personal budget; latest)					
	lowest 20% of households	highest 10% of households	wages, salaries	self-employment	transfer payments[a]	other[b]		food[c]	housing[d]	clothing[e]	health care	energy, water	education
Netherlands Antilles	...	...	...	...	...	...	6,350[11]	24.4[41]	10.4[41]	8.7[41]	2.2[41]	8.3[41]	1.2[41]
New Caledonia	...	...	68.2	18.1	13.7	...	5,410[42]	25.9	23.3[2,5]	3.5	3.2	[2]	...
New Zealand	5.1[24]	28.7[24]	65.8	9.8	15.2	9.1	8,960	20.0	19.4	4.4	2.9	3.2	1.5
Nicaragua	4.2[1,43]	39.8[1,12]	...	...	...	...	400	...	...	...	...	...	...
Niger	7.5[1]	29.3[1]	...	...	...	...	220[11]	50.5	19.1[5]	7.3	...	...	...
Nigeria	4.0[1]	31.3[1,12]	30.2[23]	46.3[23]	0.9[23]	22.6[23]	350	48.0	3.0	5.0	3.0	1.0	4.0
Northern Mariana Islands	...	...	...	...	...	...	...	49.2[20]	19.5[2,5]	9.1	[25]	[2]	...
Norway	2.6	26.6	58.8	9.9	24.2	7.1	14,210	23.5	13.7	7.0	5.4	6.2	0.6
Oman	...	...	...	...	...	...	2,280	40.6	24.6	5.1	2.4	3.2	[3]
Pakistan	8.4[1]	25.2[1]	22.0	56.0	——22.0——		290	37.0	11.0	6.0	1.0	5.0	1.0
Palau	...	...	63.7	7.4	18.5	10.4	...	...	...	...	...	...	...
Panama	2.0[13]	42.1[13]	60.8[7]	12.8[7]	13.2[7]	13.2[7]	1,740	34.9	12.6[2]	5.1	3.5	[2]	[3]
Papua New Guinea	...	...	57.3	[10]	1.1	41.6[10]	700	40.9	12.5[5]	6.2	...	4.9	...
Paraguay	6.0	46.0[10]	33.9	[10]	2.5	63.6[10]	1,470	48.7	16.4	9.7	3.4	—	1.5
Peru	4.9[1]	34.3[1]	31.2	65.1	3.7	...	1,600	44.1[20]	6.8[2]	10.1	2.7	[2]	[3]
Philippines	6.5[1]	32.1[1]	45.7	42.5	3.4	8.4	700	56.8	4.1[2]	3.9	...	[2]	...
Poland	9.3[1]	22.1[1]	34.0	4.3	20.7	41.0	1,550	41.2	2.8	10.9	8.1	1.0	[3]
Portugal	5.2	33.4	46.4	[10]	21.8	31.8[10]	5,660	34.8	2.0	10.3	4.5	3.0	1.4
Puerto Rico	3.2	34.7	56.3	6.4	29.5	7.8	5,640[11]	20.6	11.8[2]	7.4	11.6	[2]	3.1
Qatar	...	...	80.8	5.6	...	13.6	3,600[4]	24.5	35.1[5]	9.1	1.0	1.9	4.3
Réunion	3.1[24]	51.4[24]	68.9	[10]	16.0	15.1[10]	4,820[42]	22.4	11.8	7.9	2.2	2.2	[3]
Romania	9.2[13]	20.2[13]	62.6		——37.4——		810	51.1	16.4[2,5]	15.7	1.2	[2]	[3]
Russia	5.5	46.9[10]	68.5	6.4	15.7	12.1	880	34.8	2.7	22.3	...	1.2[43]	...
Rwanda	9.7[1]	24.2[1]	10.4[43]	47.7[43]	13.9[43]	28.0[43]	120	32.1[43]	13.1[43]	9.4[43]	1.3[43]	1.2[43]	2,[43]
St. Kitts and Nevis	...	...	...	...	...	...	2,370[17]	55.6[13]	7.6	7.5	...	6.6	...
St. Lucia	...	...	...	...	...	...	...	49.6[20]	13.5	6.5	2.3	4.5	[3]
St. Vincent and the Grenadines	...	...	...	...	...	...	1,360[17]	59.8	6.3	7.7	...	6.2	...
San Marino	...	...	...	...	...	...	...	22.1[14]	20.9[2]	8.0	2.6	[2]	[3]
São Tomé and Príncipe	...	...	...	...	...	...	400[19]	...	...	...	...	...	...
Saudi Arabia	...	...	...	...	...	...	2,980	52.2[23,45]	17.2[23,45]	6.6[23,45]	2.1[23,45]	1.8[23,45]	1.1[23,45]
Senegal	3.5[1]	42.8[1]	51.6[7]		——48.4[7]——		380	49.0	7.0	11.0	2.0	4.0	6.0
Seychelles	4.1	35.6	77.2	3.8	3.2	15.8	3,410	53.9	13.6	4.2	0.4	9.1	...
Sierra Leone	5.6	37.8	27.9	61.6	——10.5——		150	63.8	5.8[2]	7.3	4.5	[2]	[3]
Singapore	5.1	33.5	76.7	16.8	——2.0——		10,340	18.7	10.2[2]	7.1	4.6	[2]	1.4
Slovakia	11.9[13]	18.2[12,13]	76.7	[8]	8.7	14.4[8]	1,300	26.8	7.6[2]	8.9	...	[2]	...
Slovenia	9.5[13]	23.8[13]	52.4	13.0	23.4	11.2	3,790	30.8	18.3	8.5	5.0	7.3	[3]
Solomon Islands	...	...	74.1		——25.9——		820[4]	46.8	21.9[2,5]	5.7	[25]	...	...
Somalia	...	...	...	...	...	...	17[1]	62.3[7,14]	15.3[7]	5.6[7]	...	4.3[7]	...
South Africa	3.3[1]	47.3[1,12]	73.6	[10]	4.9	21.5[10]	1,820	29.3	12.6[2]	7.5	4.5	[2]	1.4
Spain	8.3[14]	21.8[14]	48.5	27.5	19.5	4.5	7,750	21.6[20]	12.6[2]	8.6	4.7	[2]	[3]
Sri Lanka	8.9[1]	25.2[1]	48.5	[10]	9.7	41.8[10]	490	48.0	1.9	10.1	1.8	3.3	0.8
Sudan, The	4.0	34.6	...	...	...	...	1,050[27]	63.6	11.5	5.3	4.1	3.8	[3]
Suriname	9.3	...	74.6	[10]	3.2	22.2	5,880[11]	39.9[7]	4.4[7]	11.0[7]	3.6[7]	6.9[7]	2.6[7]
Swaziland	2.8	54.5	44.4	22.2	12.2	21.2	720	33.5[20]	13.4[2]	6.0	1.8	[2]	[3]
Sweden	5.3	18.6	58.9	9.7	25.8	5.6	12,220	21.3	19.9	8.6	3.2	4.9	0.1
Switzerland	6.0[46]	27.0[46]	63.6	[10]	16.5	19.9[10]	21,640	27.0[20]	13.1	4.4	9.9	7.7	[3]
Syria	6.0	...	40.7	...	25.1	34.2	2,230	58.8[20]	16.0[2]	7.5	...	[2]	[3]
Taiwan	7.1	25.5	64.5	19.7	4.5	11.3	6,770	26.8	22.5	5.6	7.8	3.0	5.6
Tajikistan	...	...	64.3	5.6[9]	30.1	—	440[17]	65.3	...	...	...	...	...
Tanzania	6.9[1]	30.2[1]	28.1	34.2	3.5	34.2	120	66.7	8.3	9.9	1.3	7.6	...
Thailand	5.6[1]	37.1[1]	36.4	45.0	0.9	17.7	1,340	29.0	6.3	11.6	8.0	1.7	0.5
Togo	8.0	30.5	...	...	...	...	190	42.5[7]	13.4[2,7]	11.5[7]	5.0[7]	2,7	3,7
Tonga	...	...	...	...	...	...	...	49.3	10.5	5.6	0.3	2.7	...
Trinidad and Tobago	2.6	33.6	...	...	...	...	2,180	25.5[20]	21.6	10.4	[22]	...	1.5
Tunisia	5.9[1]	30.7[1]	...	...	...	...	1,110	39.0	10.7	6.0	3.0	5.1	1.8
Turkey	3.5[14]	41.5[14]	24.1	51.4	10.8	13.7	1,430	38.5	22.8[2]	9.0	2.6	[2]	1.4
Turkmenistan	6.7[13]	26.9[13]	56.6	26.0[9]	14.4	3.0	570[11]	...	...	...	...	...	...
Tuvalu	...	...	17.9	76.1	...	6.0	...	45.5	11.5[5]	7.5	...	...	...
Uganda	6.8[1]	33.4[1]	...	...	...	...	230	57.1[7,20]	...	5.5[7]	...	7.3[7]	...
Ukraine	...	...	66.4	9.3	13.4	10.9	1,680[11]	41.3	1.7	...	...	...	[3]
United Arab Emirates	...	...	...	...	...	...	8,710	24.1	23.7	9.1	1.1	1.2	3.9
United Kingdom	4.6[14]	27.8[14]	66.2	9.8	13.9	11.0	11,210	17.1	21.7	6.0	...	4.6	[3]
United States	4.2	46.9[12]	64.4	9.0	19.3	7.3	18,030	15.4	14.9	6.9	17.0	3.5	2.2
Uruguay	6.0[14,21]	29.3[14,21]	53.5	17.0	——29.5——		3,820	39.9	17.6[2]	7.0	9.3	[2]	1.3
Uzbekistan	...	...	59.8	18.5	21.7	...	490	...	...	...	...	...	...
Vanuatu	...	...	59.0	33.7	——7.3——		600[11]	30.5[20]	29.0[2,5]	4.7	[25]	[2]	...
Venezuela	3.6[13]	42.7[13]	...	...	...	...	1,950	30.4	11.5	10.6	2.9	3.0	0.8
Vietnam	7.8[1]	29.0[1,12]	17.2	64.6	17.6	0.5	160	62.4	2.5	5.0	...	...	2.9
Virgin Islands (U.S.)	...	...	65.7	2.6	13.0	12.7	...	25.3[47]	24.9[47]	5.4[47]	...	6.5[47]	...
West Bank	...	...	...	...	...	...	1,380[8]	...	...	...	...	...	...
Western Sahara	...	...	...	...	...	...	...	...	...	...	...	...	...
Western Samoa	...	...	49.4	22.8	...	27.8	710[1]	58.8	5.1[5]	4.2	...	5.0	...
Yemen	...	...	...	...	...	...	630	61.0[48]	13.2[48]	...	1.1[48]	6.1[48]	...
Yugoslavia	5.3[13,49]	27.4[13,49]	41.7	15.8	12.7	29.8	2,480[27]	51.6	1.4	7.4	5.2	8.4	[3]
Zaire	...	...	...	...	...	...	190	61.7	11.5[2]	9.7	2.6	[2]	[3]
Zambia	3.9[1]	31.3[1]	79.9	17.8	1.3	1.0	330	36.0	7.0	10.0	8.0	4.0	14.0
Zimbabwe	4.0[1]	46.9[1]	92.0	1.0	...	7.0	320	30.1[14]	6.5	10.3	7.1	8.9	6.0

[1]Data refer to expenditure shares by fractiles of persons. [2]Housing includes energy, water. [3]Recreation includes education. [4]1988. [5]Housing includes household durable goods. [6]1989. [7]Capital city only. [8]1986. [9]Agricultural self-employment only. [10]Other includes self-employment. [11]1993. [12]Highest 20%. [13]Data refer to income shares by fractiles of persons. [14]Based on posttax income. [15]1985. [16]1988–90. [17]1992. [18]1977–78. [19]1990. [20]Includes tobacco. [21]Includes wage taxes. [22]Personal effects, other includes education and recreation. [23]Urban areas only. [24]Based on posttax per capita income. [25]Recreation includes health care. [26]Data refer to former Czechoslovakia. [27]1991. [28]Latest. [29]Ethiopia includes Eritrea. [30]1984. [31]Wage-earners only.

transpor-tation, com-munications	household durable goods[f]	recrea-tion[g]	personal effects, other[h]	daily available calories per capita (1992)	cereals	potatoes, cassava	meat, poultry	fish	eggs, milk	fruits, vegeta-bles	fats, oils[i]	other[j]	country
19.5[41]	10.0[41]	4.2[41]	10.1[41]	2,587	33.5	3.3	16.0	1.9	9.3	6.6	11.4	18.1	Netherlands Antilles
16.1	5	6.7	21.3	2,829	40.2	6.4	10.0	1.2	5.7	4.5	13.1	18.9	New Caledonia
17.1	10.9	—20.6—		3,669	22.3	2.8	16.8	1.6	10.8	6.3	16.4	23.0	New Zealand
...	...	...	...	2,293	51.1	1.6	2.1	—	4.7	2.9	8.3	29.3	Nicaragua
...	5	...	23.1	2,257	73.9	3.6	2.1	...	2.1	1.1	3.0	14.2	Niger
3.0	6.0	...	27.0	2,124	36.8	34.2	1.3	0.4	0.5	3.3	11.8	11.6	Nigeria
8.3	5	13.9[25]	—	3,200[11]	...	...	...	...	...	...	...	...	Northern Mariana Islands
12.8	6.9	8.8	15.1	3,244	27.0	5.3	10.6	4.2	13.2	4.9	16.9	18.0	Norway
8.9	7.1	4.1[3]	4.0	...	...	...	...	...	...	...	...	...	Oman
13.0	5.0	...	21.0	2,315	58.9	0.4	2.2	0.1	7.3	2.6	13.8	14.6	Pakistan
													Palau
15.1	8.4	11.7[3]	8.7	2,242	37.7	3.1	7.5	1.3	7.0	6.6	13.8	23.0	Panama
13.0	5	...	22.5	2,613	23.0	26.5	5.9	1.9	0.8	24.8	4.8	12.1	Papua New Guinea
4.5	6.2	2.3	7.3	2,670	29.2	17.0	11.7	0.2	4.2	8.0	10.7	19.0	Paraguay
7.3	7.5	7.6[3]	13.9	1,882	42.9	9.3	5.2	1.7	5.2	4.9	7.2	23.7	Peru
5.0	12.8	...	17.3	2,257	56.3	4.5	5.3	3.2	1.9	7.3	5.8	15.7	Philippines
8.9	8.3	15.0[3]	3.8	3,301	33.3	5.8	12.1	0.9	10.8	3.3	15.4	18.4	Poland
15.4	8.6	4.4	15.6	3,634	30.8	5.5	11.9	2.6	6.6	5.8	17.1	19.6	Portugal
11.8	11.2	7.9	14.7	...	...	...	...	...	...	...	...	...	Puerto Rico
13.0	5	—11.1—		...	...	...	...	...	...	...	...	...	Qatar
24.9	6.0	10.1[3]	12.5	3,245	47.8	2.3	10.5	1.5	5.3	5.1	10.3	17.2	Réunion
6.6	5	4.5[3]	4.5	2,953[37]	44.1	4.0	8.3	0.7	7.9	5.3	13.6	16.0	Romania
...	9.4	...	30.8	3,380[44]	36.8[44]	5.3[44]	10.6[44]	2.1[44]	8.8[44]	3.4[44]	13.2[44]	19.8[44]	Russia
1.7[43]	5.3[43]	0.4[43]	35.5[43]	1,821	18.0	31.0	1.0	—	1.4	16.0	2.5	30.1	Rwanda
4.3	9.4	...	9.0	2,419	18.7	3.8	11.3	3.4	7.9	4.2	18.6	32.1	St. Kitts and Nevis
6.3	5.8	3.2[3]	8.3	2,588	26.7	5.7	14.0	1.3	7.7	9.8	11.0	23.8	St. Lucia
3.7	6.6	...	9.7	2,347	34.6	10.6	8.8	0.4	5.2	4.1	7.4	28.9	St. Vincent and the Grenadines
17.6	7.2	7.1[3]	14.5	3,561	32.1	2.1	11.0	1.1	8.6	7.4	21.7	15.9	San Marino
...	...	...	...	2,129	31.3	13.9	1.3	2.5	1.2	2.9	16.4	30.5	São Tomé and Príncipe
4.5[23, 45]	5.9[23, 45]	...	8.6[23, 45]	2,735	49.5	0.8	6.9	0.5	6.7	10.5	11.4	13.6	Saudi Arabia
5.0	2.0	...	12.0	2,262	63.3	1.3	3.7	1.9	2.6	1.2	12.4	13.6	Senegal
6.4	6.6	1.4	4.4	2,287	48.9	1.1	5.3	2.4	5.9	3.5	11.6	21.3	Seychelles
4.4	3.9	3.8[3]	4.8	1,694	52.7	5.8	1.1	1.4	0.8	3.6	21.7	13.0	Sierra Leone
13.8	8.9	13.1	23.3	3,121	41.4	2.3	15.0	1.8	4.8	7.2	5.7	21.9	Singapore
...	3.9	...	26.2	3,335	...	...	...	...	...	...	...	...	Slovakia
12.7	3.3	6.1[3]	8.0	...	...	...	...	...	...	...	...	...	Slovenia
9.9	5	...[25]	15.7	2,173	25.3	36.6	3.6	5.4	0.7	2.9	8.7	16.8	Solomon Islands
...	...	...	12.1[7]	1,499	52.8	0.9	6.6	0.3	21.2	2.2	8.6	7.4	Somalia
16.7	10.0	6.3	11.7	2,695	53.9	1.7	7.6	0.7	4.0	2.4	9.5	20.3	South Africa
15.3	7.1	7.0[3]	23.1	3,708	21.3	5.2	20.0	1.6	8.6	7.3	17.5	18.5	Spain
17.0	3.9	2.4	10.8	2,273	57.5	3.1	0.4	1.4	2.8	4.7	3.8	26.1	Sri Lanka
1.5	5.5	0.7[3]	4.0	2,706	56.0	0.8	4.2	0.1	11.3	3.0	10.6	14.0	Sudan, The
9.5[7]	12.3[7]	5.8[7]	4.0[7]	2,547	52.1	2.0	6.5	0.5	6.2	4.1	9.9	18.8	Suriname
8.8	12.8	3.3[3]	20.4	2,706	53.9	1.1	4.7	—	3.7	3.6	7.5	25.5	Swaziland
15.7	6.6	10.9	8.8	2,972	21.1	4.4	10.1	2.3	15.3	5.5	20.1	21.3	Sweden
12.9	5.1	9.8[3]	10.1	3,379	20.3	2.4	17.6	0.7	12.9	5.8	18.3	22.0	Switzerland
2.4	5.8	2.1[3]	7.4	3,175	53.1	1.4	3.0	—	6.3	7.2	13.1	15.8	Syria
10.7	2.2	1.1[3]	4.7	3,020	36.8	2.5	14.3	1.9	3.1	8.3	14.4	18.7	Taiwan
...	...	...	34.7	2,760	...	...	...	...	...	...	...	...	Tajikistan
4.1	1.4	0.7	—	2,018	48.5	22.6	2.3	1.2	1.7	6.0	5.0	12.6	Tanzania
12.9	10.9	4.2	14.9	2,432	58.7	1.1	5.0	1.6	1.4	5.6	5.3	21.4	Thailand
9.5[7]	4.4[7]	5.1[3,7]	8.6[7]	2,242	47.7	29.0	2.3	1.2	0.6	1.8	9.3	8.0	Togo
5.8	10.6	0.5	14.7	2,946	15.7	35.1	12.2	2.0	2.1	4.5	8.0	20.5	Tonga
15.2	14.3	22	6.2[22]	2,585	42.1	2.5	5.0	0.5	6.5	3.4	13.1	26.9	Trinidad and Tobago
9.0	11.2	7.1	7.1	3,330	53.0	1.3	2.7	0.6	4.7	5.5	17.6	14.5	Tunisia
8.8	9.0	5.6	2.3	3,429	48.4	3.7	2.5	0.4	2.9	8.5	15.8	18.0	Turkey
...	...	...	...	...	...	...	...	...	...	...	...	...	Turkmenistan
10.5	5	...	25.0	...	...	...	...	...	...	...	...	...	Tuvalu
5.9[7]	...	...	24.2[7]	2,159	23.5	30.8	2.4	1.1	1.7	17.3	1.8	21.3	Uganda
...	6.8	6.3[3]	43.9	...	...	...	...	...	...	...	...	...	Ukraine
14.1	11.6	4.7	6.5	3,384	34.6	1.3	11.5	1.4	9.3	14.6	10.8	16.4	United Arab Emirates
15.1	8.0	15.9	11.6	3,317	22.1	6.1	14.7	0.9	11.8	4.5	17.8	22.1	United Kingdom
13.9	1.5	5.8	18.9	3,732	21.7	2.7	14.7	0.8	11.4	5.6	18.1	25.0	United States
10.4	6.3	3.1	5.1	2,750	36.8	3.9	18.3	0.2	13.0	3.7	9.6	14.4	Uruguay
...	...	...	...	...	...	...	...	...	...	...	...	...	Uzbekistan
13.2	5	12.3[25]	10.3	2,739	21.7	24.5	12.2	2.2	1.8	3.3	10.4	23.9	Vanuatu
7.1	4.5	2.7	26.4	2,618	36.4	2.0	5.9	1.2	7.4	7.3	16.1	23.6	Venezuela
...	4.6	...	22.6	2,250	72.7	7.5	6.0	0.9	0.5	4.3	1.8	6.2	Vietnam
11.7[47]	4.3[47]	...	21.9[47]	...	...	...	...	...	...	...	...	...	Virgin Islands (U.S.)
...	...	...	...	...	44.4	1.9	6.1	0.1	6.2	11.0	12.5	17.8	West Bank
													Western Sahara
9.0	5	...	17.9	2,828	20.1	19.1	12.0	3.6	1.2	13.2	8.4	22.4	Western Samoa
1.9[48]	3.0[48]	...	13.7[48]	2,203	66.9	1.0	3.5	0.4	3.7	3.5	6.5	14.4	Yemen
5.7	1.6	2.4[3]	16.3	3,545[49]	43.2[49]	2.3[49]	8.2[49]	0.2[49]	7.9[49]	3.7[49]	16.9[49]	17.7[49]	Yugoslavia
5.9	4.8	3.8[3]	—	2,060	16.4	55.8	1.8	0.7	0.1	7.7	7.0	10.4	Zaire
5.0	1.0	...	15.0	1,931	75.0	4.8	2.4	0.7	1.3	1.6	3.2	11.0	Zambia
1.1	12.9	0.6	16.5	1,985	59.4	1.4	2.5	0.2	1.5	1.1	9.6	24.3	Zimbabwe

[32]Low-income population in Banjul and Kombo St. Mary only. [33]Former West Germany only. [34]Urban areas of Eastern Region only. [35]Personal effects, other includes health care. [36]Housing includes water. [37]1994. [38]Workers and clerical workers only. [39]Earned income only. [40]Malagasy households only. [41]Curaçao only. [42]1987. [43]Rural areas only. [44]Data refer to former U.S.S.R. [45]Middle-income population only. [46]Excludes transfer payments and property income. [47]St. Thomas only. [48]Data refer to former Yemen Arab Republic. [49]Data refer to former Socialist Federal Republic of Yugoslavia.

Health services

The provision of health services in most countries is both a principal determinant of the quality of life and a large and growing sector of the national economy. This table summarizes the basic indicators of health personnel; hospitals, by kind and utilization; mortality rates that are most indicative of general health services; external controls on health (adequacy of food supply and availability of safe drinking water); and sources and amounts of expenditure on health care. Each datum refers more or less directly to the availability or use of a particular health service in a country, and, while each may be an accurate measure at a national level, each may also conceal considerable differences in availability of the particular service to different segments of a population or regions of a country. In the United States, for example, the availability of physicians ranges from about one per 769 persons in the least well-served states to one per 299 in the best-served, with a rate of one per 150 in the national capital. Such disparities are even more pronounced in most other countries, unless the government has made some special effort to achieve a more uniform distribution of personnel and facilities. In addition, even when trained personnel exist and facilities have been created, the country may lose health professionals via the "brain drain" to foreign countries; or low levels of financial support at the national level may leave facilities underserved; or lack of good transportation may prevent those most in need from reaching a clinic or hospital that could help them.

Definitions and limits of data have been made as specific as possible in the compilation of this table. For example, despite wide variation worldwide in the nature of the qualifying or certifying process that permits an individual to represent himself as a physician, organizations such as the World Health Organization (WHO) try to maintain more consistent international standards for training and qualification. International statistics presented here for "physicians" refer to persons qualified according to WHO standards and exclude traditional health practitioners, whatever the local custom with regard to the designation "doctor." Statistics for health personnel in this table uniformly include all those actually working in the health service field, whether in the actual provision of services or in teaching, administration, research, or other tasks. One group of practitioners for whom this type of guideline works less well is that of midwives, whose training and qualifications vary enormously from country to country but who must be included, as they represent, after nurses, perhaps the largest and most important category of health auxiliary worldwide. The statistics here refer to those midwives working in some kind of institutional setting (a hospital, clinic, community health-care centre, or the like) and exclude rural noninstitutional midwives and traditional birth attendants.

Hospitals also differ considerably worldwide in terms of staffing and services. In this tabulation, the term hospital refers generally to a permanent facility offering inpatient services and/or nursing care and staffed by at least one physician. Establishments offering only outpatient or custodial care are excluded. These statistics are broken down into data for general hospitals (those providing care in more than one specialty), specialized facilities (with care in only one specialty), local medical centres, and rural health-care centres; the last two generally refer to institutions that provide a more limited range of medical or nursing care, often less than full-time. Hospital data are further analyzed into three categories of administrative classification: public, private nonprofit, and private for profit. Statistics on number of beds refer to beds that are maintained and staffed on a full-time basis for a succession of inpatients to whom care is provided.

Data on hospital utilization refer to institutions defined as above. Admission and discharge, the two principal points at which statistics are normally

Health services

country	| health personnel							| hospitals									
	year	physicians	dentists	nurses	pharmacists	midwives	population per physician	year	number	kinds (%) general	specialized	medical centres	rural	ownership (%) government	private nonprofit	private for profit	hospital beds per 10,000 pop.
Afghanistan	1991	2,233	267	1,451	510	338	6,701	1988–93	...								3
Albania	1990	4,467	1,099	...	772[1]	9,936[1]	729	1989	895	—17.9—		—82.1—		100.0	...	—	57
Algeria	1992	25,304	7,563[2]	...	2,575[2]	...	1,033	1990[3]	181								12
American Samoa	1991	26	7[4]	140[4]	2[4]	1[4]	1,885	1990	1	100.0	—	—	—	100.0	—	—	27
Andorra	1993	118	...	...	...	...	538	1992	1	100.0	—	—	—	100.0	—	—	18[5]
Angola	1990	662	10	9,334	...	...	15,136	1990	58								12
Antigua and Barbuda	1992	59	13	179	13	...	1,083	1991	2	50.0	50.0	—	—	100.0	—	—	58[7]
Argentina	1992	88,800	21,900[2]	18,000[4]	...	...	376	1992	...								44
Armenia	1994	13,800[10]	10	34,900[11]	...	11	271[10]	1994	183					100.0	—	—	82
Aruba	1992	74	19	515[2]	13	3	936	1992	2	50.0	—	50.0	—	100.0	—	—	44
Australia	1991	38,800	4,720	139,375	10,880	...	445	1990	1,071[6]					65.5[6]	—34.5[6]—		93[7,12]
Austria	1994	27,170	3,607	38,455	2,064[13]	991	296	1994	325	38.8	61.9	—	—	...	...	...	96
Azerbaijan	1994	28,800[10]	10	70,100[11]	...	11	255[10]	1994	787					100.0	—	—	96
Bahamas, The	1992	373	58	1,067	52[14]	...	709	1995	5	60.0	20.0	20.0	—	60.0	—40.0—		40
Bahrain	1993	482	40	1,608	101	...	1,115	1991	12	58.3	42.7	—	—	75.0	16.7	8.3	28[5]
Bangladesh	1993	22,400	732	9,455	7,485[14]	10,104	5,196	1993	903	...	...	...	...	67.7	—32.3—		3
Barbados	1992	312	38	889	138	377	842	1992	10	70.0	30.0	—	—	80.0	—	20.0	75
Belarus	1995	45,000[10]	10	117,000[11]	...	11	222[10]	1995	880					100.0	—	—	122
Belgium	1994	37,792	7,070	...	13,657	...	267	1993	363	80.4	19.6	—	—	38.6	61.4	—	76
Belize	1993	120	12	300	17	233	1,708	1993	7					100.0	—	—	29
Benin	1989	323	16	1,384	86	453	13,879	...	...								
Bermuda	1994	106	23	560	31	...	572	1994	2	50.0	50.0	—	—	...	...	...	38
Bhutan	1990	141	9	233	5	70	5,418	1993	27					...	...	...	12
Bolivia	1993	3,392	1,643[7]	1,869	...	...	2,083	1995	336	10.7	8.9	23.5	56.8				10[5]
Bosnia and Herzegovina	1989	6,929	1,368	...	781	...	624	1989	...								46
Botswana	1994	339	...	3,329	...	...	4,395	1994	30	53.3	3.3	43.3	—				23
Brazil	1993	222,658	160,000	...	57,047[7]	...	681	1993	6,372	—100.0—							34
Brunei	1994	197	27	1,228	10	254	1,444	1994	10	90.0	—	—	10.0	90.0	—10.0—		34
Bulgaria	1994	28,094	5,540	50,773	2,075	6,720	300	1994	284	—79.2—	20.8	—	—	...	...	...	105
Burkina Faso	1991[16]	341	19	2,627	113	339	27,158	1993	78	—14.1—	85.9	—	—	100.0	—	—	5[2]
Burundi	1990	317	9	670[16]	55	97[16]	16,657	1990	...					100.0	—	—	19
Cambodia	1993	5,642	367[7]	9,950	262[7]	3,235	1,650	1988[3]	188	...	...	...	...	100.0	—	—	16
Cameroon	1989	945	55	6,053	206	...	11,848	1988	629	—27.0—		—73.0—		72.3	—27.7—		27
Canada	1994	64,110[12]	14,621[2]	262,288[2]	22,121[2]	...	455[12]	1989	1,079	81.8	16.6	1.6	—	95.8	—	4.2	50[5]
Cape Verde	1988	112	...	205	9	...	2,931	1987	75	6.7	—	93.3	—	100.0	—	—	15
Central African Republic	1992	157	8[14]	1,353[14]	22[14]	166[14]	18,660	1988	133	—21.1—		—78.9—		79.7	—20.3—		15
Chad	1993	217	5[4]	878	10	130	27,765	1993	...					...	...	...	7
Chile	1994	16,000	5,200[5]	5,653[5]	230[5,16]	1,924[5,16]	875	1994	198					89.4	—10.6—		31
China	1994	1,882,000[10,17]	10	1,094,000	417,000	51,000	630[17]	1994	67,857	15.6	6.2	—78.2—		100.0	—	—	26
Colombia	1992	36,551	13,815	46,376	...	...	914	1989	947					...	...	...	14
Comoros	1993	77	6[14]	155[14]	6[14]	86[14]	6,600	1989	...								25
Congo	1990	613	35	1,624	175	498	4,028	1990	...								33
Costa Rica	1995	3,799	1,255	7,021[5]	1,222	...	870	1995	33					87.9	—	12.1	18
Côte d'Ivoire	1990	2,020	219	3,691	135	1,533	5,931	1989	...					...	...	...	8
Croatia	1994	9,138	1,798	...	1,598	...	524	1994	84	38.1	61.9	—	—	...	...	...	59
Cuba	1992	46,860	8,057	73,943	...	...	231	1993	244					100.0	—	—	65[7]
Cyprus[18]	1993	1,455	498	2,536	423	120	433	1993[19]	110	39.1	58.2	—	2.7	10.0	0.9	89.1	52
Czech Republic	1993	31,897	6,015	...	...	...	324	1993	287	65.9	34.1	—	—	88.9	—11.1—		98
Denmark	1994	14,497	5,088	63,841	...	1,031[5]	358	1992	163	42.9	57.1	—	—	42.9	57.1	—	35
Djibouti	1989	97	10	...	14	...	5,258	1993	8	—25.0—		—75.0—		100.0	—	—	27[4]

collected, are the basis for the data on the amount and distribution of care by kind of facility. The data on numbers of patients exclude babies born during a maternal confinement but include persons who die before being discharged. The bed-occupancy and average length-of-stay statistics depend on the concept of a "patient-day," which is the annual total of daily censuses of inpatients. The bed-occupancy rate is the ratio of total patient-days to potential days based on the number of beds; the average length-of-stay rate is the ratio of total patient-days to total admissions. Bed-occupancy rates may exceed 100% because stays of partial days are counted as full days.

Two measures that give health planners and policy makers an excellent indication of the level of ordinary health care are those for mortality of children under age five and for maternal mortality. The former reflects the probability of a newborn infant dying before age five. The latter refers to deaths attributable to delivery or complications of pregnancy, childbirth, the puerperium (the period immediately following birth), or abortion.

Levels of nutrition and access to safe drinking water are two of the most basic limitations imposed by the physical environment in which health-care activities take place. The nutritional data are based on recommendations of the United Nations' Food and Agriculture Organization for the necessary daily intake (in calories) for a moderately active person of average size in a climate of a particular kind (fewer calories are needed in a hot climate) to remain in average *good* health. Excess intake in the many developed countries ranges to more than 40% above the minimum required to maintain health (the excess usually being construed to diminish, rather than raise, health). The range of deficiency is less dramatic numerically but far more critical to the countries in which deficiencies are chronic, because the deficiencies lead to overall poor health (raising health service

needs and costs), to decreased productivity in nearly every area of national economic life, and to the loss of social and economic potential through early mortality. By "safe" water is meant only water that has no substantial quantities of chemical or biological pollutants—*i.e.,* quantities sufficient to cause "immediate" health problems.

The data on health care expenditure represent a joint effort by the WHO and the World Bank to create better analytical tools by which the interrelations among health policy, health care delivery systems, and human health might be examined against the more general frameworks of government operations, resource allocation, and development process. First published in the World Bank's *World Development Report 1993: Investing in Health* and, the following year, in the World Health Organization's *Global Comparative Assessments in the Health Sector* (edited by C.J.L. Murray and A.D. Lopez), the database and underlying methodology are expected to provide a continuing basis for international comparisons and policy analysis.

Expenditures were tabulated for direct preventative and curative activities and for public health and public education programs having direct impact on health status—family planning, nutrition, and health education—but not more indirect programs like environmental, waste removal, or relief activities. Public, parastatal (semipublic, *e.g.,* social security institutions), international aid, and household expenditure reports and surveys were utilized to build up a comprehensive picture of national, regional, and world patterns of health care expenditures and investment that could not have been assembled from any single type of source. For reasons of space, public and parastatal are combined as the former.

admissions or discharges					mortality				popu-lation with access to safe water 1990–95 (%)	food supply (% of FAO require-ment) 1992	total health expenditures, 1990					country
rate per 10,000 pop.	by kinds of hospital (%)				bed occu-pancy rate (%)	aver-age length of stay (days)	under age 5 per 1,000 live newborn 1995	maternal mortality per 100,000 live births 1993			as percent of GDP	per capita (U.S.$)	by source (percent)			
	general	special-ized	medical centres	rural									public	private	inter-national aid	
...	...	...	...	...	...	...	251	1,700	12	62	4.00	...	84.0	16.0	...	Afghanistan
400	...	...	...	...	49.3	5	39	65	100	108	4.00	26	84.0	16.0	...	Albania
400	...	...	...	...	49.3	5	56	160	79	121	6.95	149	76.9	23.0	0.1	Algeria
965	100.0	—	—	—	38.4	4	...	...	...	...	...	...	...	...	...	American Samoa
...	...	...	...	...	...	...	...	...	...	...	...	...	...	...	...	Andorra
238	...	...	...	...	44.5[6]	16[6]	184	1,500	32	78	...	...	...	...	...	Angola
63[6]	...	...	...	...	49.9[6]	7[6]	23[8]	...	95[9]	105	4.55	241	59.1	37.3	3.6	Antigua and Barbuda
520[3]	...	...	...	...	51.9[3]	8[3]	26	100	71	123	4.21	137	60.1	39.7	0.2	Argentina
...	...	...	...	...	...	...	23	50	...	...	4.17	152	59.8	40.2	—	Armenia
...	...	...	...	...	92.2	...	...	...	...	...	...	...	...	...	...	Aruba
...	...	...	...	...	...	11[2,12]	8	9	100	120	7.67	1,294	69.6	30.4	—	Australia
2,649	...	...	...	...	77.6	10	8	10	100	132	8.38	1,711	66.4	33.6	—	Austria
...	...	...	...	...	...	...	38	22	...	...	4.27	99	61.2	38.8	—	Azerbaijan
822[2,3]	...	...	...	...	83.7[2,3]	8[2,3]	24	100	100	108	...	...	...	...	...	Bahamas, The
...	...	...	...	...	...	...	25	60	100	...	4.62	324	63.0	36.9	0.1	Bahrain
853[1]	...	...	...	...	...	...	148	850	97	87	3.19	6	24.8	56.7	18.5	Bangladesh
810	93.5	6.5	—	—	88.3	32	15	43	100	133	5.04	323	64.3	33.8	1.9	Barbados
...	...	...	...	...	...	...	19	37	...	...	3.19	157	68.7	31.3	—	Belarus
1,963	96.0	4.0	—	—	84.4	12	7	10	100	139	7.50	1,449	82.5	17.5	—	Belgium
...	...	...	...	...	...	...	38	...	82[9]	118	5.88	23	48.4	41.0	10.7	Belize
...	...	...	...	...	...	...	161	990	50	110	4.32	19	26.3	36.4	37.3	Benin
1,280	97.4	2.6	—	—	76.4	9	...	...	...	106	...	...	...	...	...	Bermuda
...	...	...	...	...	...	...	149	1,600	21[9]	...	5.05	10	41.1	30.4	28.5	Bhutan
252[2]	...	...	...	...	45.9[2]	5[2]	91	650	55	88	4.01	25	39.9	39.6	20.5	Bolivia
529[6]	...	...	...	...	82.4[6]	11[6]	20	...	...	...	...	...	...	...	...	Bosnia and Herzegovina
...	...	...	...	...	93.1[4]	...	60	250	93[15]	98	6.19	139	61.8	21.6	16.5	Botswana
970	...	...	...	...	...	7[4]	70	220	87	118	4.20	146	65.7	33.9	0.4	Brazil
...	...	...	...	...	...	...	14	60	100	123	...	...	...	...	...	Brunei
...	...	...	...	...	...	...	17	27	100	113	5.36	121	81.4	18.6	—	Bulgaria
...	...	...	...	...	...	...	189	930	78	101	8.46	7	9.8	17.9	72.3	Burkina Faso
...	...	...	...	...	...	...	146	1,300	70[15]	83	3.28	30	42.4	48.3	9.3	Burundi
...	...	...	...	...	...	...	142	900	36	91	...	...	...	...	...	Cambodia
...	...	...	...	...	...	...	113	550	50	85	2.62	27	26.4	61.7	11.9	Cameroon
...	...	...	...	14	...	...	8	6	100	116	9.05	1,945	74.1	25.9	—	Canada
...	...	...	...	...	...	...	62	...	71[15]	119	6.32	64	20.7	25.5	53.7	Cape Verde
...	...	...	...	...	...	...	152	700	18	75	4.19	18	26.5	37.5	36.0	Central African Republic
...	...	...	...	...	...	...	175	1,500	24	84	6.22	12	27.6	24.7	47.7	Chad
749[3]	—61.0—		—39.0—		69.9[3]	7[3]	17	65	85	106	4.73	100	70.1	29.1	0.7	Chile
419	...	...	...	...	69.0	15	44	95	67	116	3.51	11	58.5	40.9	0.6	China
614	41.4	16.7	—41.9—		57.2	6	41	100	87	115	3.98	51	44.0	54.4	1.6	Colombia
...	...	...	...	...	...	...	114	950	63[15]	81	5.40	28	46.3	29.2	24.5	Comoros
...	...	...	...	...	...	...	134	890	38[15]	103	3.99	50	47.1	40.7	12.1	Congo
958[2]	...	...	...	...	78.2[2]	6[2]	15	60	92	129	6.51	132	73.6	25.2	1.2	Costa Rica
...	...	...	...	...	...	...	138	810	72	108	3.35	28	48.7	47.9	3.4	Côte d'Ivoire
1,278	81.9	18.1	—	—	81.6	14	17	...	...	...	...	...	...	...	...	Croatia
1,376[2]	...	...	...	...	...	...	13	95	93	123	...	...	...	...	...	Cuba
747[3]	...	...	...	...	75.7[3]	7[3]	9	5	100	152	3.96	64	62.9	26.8	10.3	Cyprus[18]
1,938	96.6	3.4	—	—	73.8	14	9	15	100	...	5.94[20]	169[20]	84.9[20]	15.1[20]	—	Czech Republic
1,253	92.9	7.1	—	—	80.4	8	9	8	100	136	6.30	1,588	84.2	15.8	—	Denmark
...	...	...	...	...	...	...	166	570	45[15]	101	...	...	...	...	...	Djibouti

Health services (continued)

country	health personnel							hospitals									
	year	physicians	dentists	nurses	pharma-cists	midwives	popu-lation per physi-cian	year	number	kinds (%)				ownership (%)			hos-pital beds per 10,000 pop.
										gen-eral	spe-cial-ized	medical centres	rural	govern-ment	private non-profit	private for profit	
Dominica	1992	34	6	233	21	...	2,112	1994	53	1.9	—	—	98.1	100.0	—	—	25
Dominican Republic	1992	11,130	1,898	6,035	115[8]	...	671	1992[3]	723	—7.9—		—92.1—		...	...	...	12[8]
Ecuador	1993	12,149	1,524	4,215[7]	906	667[7]	836	1992	429	16.1	6.1	—77.8—		...	...	...	16
Egypt	1992	101,500	15,150	...	34,700	...	552	1991	6,418	5.1	—94.9—			...	...	...	19[8]
El Salvador	1993	4,525	1,182	5,094	...	1,940[2]	1,219	1993	78	...	...	...	...	61.5	1.3	37.2	17
Equatorial Guinea	1990	99	...	154	...	55	3,532	1988	...	...	...	...	...	...	...	...	29
Eritrea	1993	68	...	488	...	33	49,200	1993	10	...	...	...	...	...	...	...	9
Estonia	1994	4,680	820	7,302	930[2]	710	319	1994	107	...	...	...	...	96.3	—3.7—		84
Ethiopia	1988	1,466	...	3,496	364	...	30,195	1986–87	86	...	...	...	...	...	...	...	3
Faroe Islands	1993	82	39	301[7]	10[2]	17	574	1992	3	33.3	—	—	66.7	100.0	—	—	57
Fiji	1994	426	40	1,631	...	...	1,829	1994	25	...	...	...	...	...	...	...	22
Finland	1994	13,700	4,664	124,732	581[13]	3,928	371	1993	369	89.2	10.8	—	—	...	...	...	98
France	1993	158,968	38,868	320,505	52,673	11,479	362	1993	3,810	—91.7—			8.3	27.7	—72.3—		118
French Guiana	1992	200	32	489	33	31	644	1991	...	...	...	...	...	...	...	...	66
French Polynesia	1993	353	81	586	47	54	595	1993	34[2]	...	...	...	...	...	...	...	48
Gabon	1989	448	32	759	71	240	2,504	1988	27	...	...	...	...	...	...	...	51
Gambia, The	1991	61	...	430[4]	...	...	14,536	1994	13	15.4	—	—84.6—		83.3	—16.7—		7[3]
Gaza Strip	1993[21]	...	...	...	...	...	...	1993	6	...	...	...	...	...	...	...	13
Georgia	1994	29,900[10]	10	64,100[11, 14]	...	11	182[10]	1994	422[14]	...	...	...	...	100.0[14]	...	...	105
Germany	1994	267,186	59,211	708,000[7, 11]	43,822	11	305	1993	2,354	...	...	...	...	49.2	36.0	14.8	77
Ghana	1989[16]	628	39	11,808	67	1,736	22,452	1991	121	90.9	9.1	—	—	60.3	—39.7—		13
Gibraltar	1994	29	...	302[2]	...	...	951	1994	2	50.0	50.0	—	—	100.0	—	—	88
Greece	1993	40,116	10,731	34,314[22]	7,948[13]	1,916[22]	259	1992	372	46.5	53.5	—	—	...	...	...	50
Greenland	1993	78	30	356[2]	10[2]	17[2]	709	1990	16	6.3	—	—	93.7	100.0	—	—	75
Grenada	1995	64	8	365	28[14]	36[14]	1,523	1991[6]	3	100.0	—	—	—	100.0	—	—	38
Guadeloupe	1991	590	119	1,476	192	107	680	1991	30[4]	...	...	...	...	56.7[4]	—43.3[4]—		80
Guam	1986	147	...	594[11]	...	11	823	1985	...	...	...	...	...	...	...	...	...
Guatemala	1992	7,601	1,085[1]	14,401	...	...	1,282	1985	...	...	...	...	...	...	...	...	16[4]
Guernsey	1993	79	...	...	...	...	804	1993	1	100.0	—	—	—	100.0	—	—	...
Guinea	1991	920	...	...	197	371	6,448	1988	38	—100.0—			—	100.0	—	—	6
Guinea-Bissau	1986	274	13	...	12	...	3,245	1993	16	...	...	...	...	62.5	—37.5—		13
Guyana	1993	244	34	681	22	172[4]	3,000	1994	30	...	...	...	...	83.3	—16.7—		33[4]
Haiti	1994	641	95	2,725	...	...	10,041	1994	50	...	...	...	...	...	...	...	10
Honduras	1993	3,803	622	6,288	975	...	1,358	1994	61	...	...	...	...	47.5	—52.5—		9
Hong Kong	1995[23]	8,122	1,634	33,666	995	22	762	1994	87	...	...	...	...	77.0	—23.0—		45
Hungary	1994	36,620	4,942	56,012	4,806[7]	2,795	280	1994	148	74.1[24]	17.4[24]	—8.5[24]—		...	...	...	96
Iceland	1992	734	241	1,816	139	197	357	1992	26	88.5	11.5	—	—	...	...	...	105
India	1993[23]	410,875[7]	19,523	449,351	...	...	2,173[7]	1991	15,067	...	...	...	...	55.0	—45.0—		7[7]
Indonesia	1992	25,135	...	118,555[11]	3,520[13]	11	7,402	1992	971	...	...	...	...	70.9	—29.1—		6
Iran	1994	37,000	4,770[7]	48,639[2, 11]	3,223[7, 13]	11	1,600	1992	653	...	...	...	...	70.9	—29.1—		15[25]
Iraq	1993	8,787	1,656	13,206[2]	1,561	...	2,181	1993	185	...	...	...	...	...	...	...	14
Ireland	1994	7,146[12]	...	...	...	...	500[12]	1993[3, 6]	63	100.0	—	—	—	100.0	—	—	33
Isle of Man	1988	86	...	...	...	...	745	1986	3	33.3	33.3	—	33.3	100.0	—	—	...
Israel	1993	24,344	6,956	...	4,127	...	214	1994	244	19.7	80.3	—	—	12.7	50.0	37.3	63
Italy	1992	296,385	10,814[4]	170,409[4]	53,948[4]	...	193	1993	1,912	87.8	12.2	—	—	58.5	—41.5—		67
Jamaica	1995	1,589[7]	270[7]	1,836[16]	37[16]	250[16]	1,541[7]	1992	30	80.0	20.0	—	—	80.0	—20.0—		22[3]
Japan	1994	228,643	79,896	862,013	157,719	22,690[7]	547	1993	9,844	88.9	11.1	—	—	73.4	—26.6—		135
Jersey	1992	88	...	...	...	...	967	1990	6	16.7	83.3	—	—	100.0	—	—	88
Jordan	1994	6,183	2,718	6,466[2]	2,220[2]	538[16]	651	1994	63	...	...	...	...	42.9	—57.1—		17
Kazakstan	1993	67,103	7,075[7]	213,320[7]	8,722[7]	16,280[7]	253	1994	1,805[2]	...	...	...	...	100.0[2]	...	...	134
Kenya	1994	4,558	630	27,143[5]	605[5]	...	6,000	1993	877	—35.1—		—64.9—		...	...	...	14
Kiribati	1993	10	...	147	...	...	7,687	1990	1	...	...	...	...	...	...	...	40
Korea, North	1993	61,200	...	...	...	...	370	1989	...	...	...	...	...	...	...	...	135
Korea, South	1994	54,406	12,939	114,320	42,037	8,262	817	1994[22]	...	64.5[24]	35.5[24]	—	—	...	...	...	32
Kuwait	1994[16]	2,717	399	7,406	903	...	596	1994	22	63.6	36.4	—	—	63.6	—	36.4	26[3]
Kyrgyzstan	1994	14,674	226	41,939	1,122	3,414	305	1994	396	89.1	—	10.9	—	100.0	—	—	99
Laos	1990	1,173	...	5,593[11]	...	11	3,555	1990	1,074	0.7	—99.3—		—	100.0	—	—	25
Latvia	1994	7,714	968	12,559	292	981	330	1994	170	51.2	4.1	28.8	15.9	97.6	2.4	—	121
Lebanon	1989–91	6,638	1,015	1,248	1,390	153	407	1993	24	...	...	...	...	100.0	—	—	50
Lesotho	1993	136	...	874[14]	60[14]	...	14,306	1987	22	90.9	9.1	—	—	54.5	45.5	—	15
Liberia	1985	89	5	908	...	443	24,600	1988	92	—37.0—		—63.0—		...	...	...	...
Libya	1989–91	4,749	686	13,849	...	...	690	1990	...	...	...	...	...	...	...	...	41
Liechtenstein	1994	32	11	...	2	...	952	1989	1	...	...	...	...	...	...	...	35
Lithuania	1993	16,622	1,952	29,179	...	1,830	225	1993	198	...	...	...	...	100.0	—	—	117
Luxembourg	1994	870	203[5]	...	336[5]	143[5]	464	1994	34	50.0	50.0	—	—	...	...	...	110
Macau	1994	387	19	799	46	...	1,041	1994	30	6.7	—	93.3	—	46.7	—53.3—		22
Macedonia	1994	4,505	1,087	5,638[5]	357	1,436[5]	430	1994	62	27.4	24.2	—48.4—		100.0	—	—	56
Madagascar	1990	1,392	89	3,124	19	1,703	8,628	1990	...	...	...	...	...	...	...	...	9
Malawi	1989	186	...	284	5	...	49,118	1987	395	12.2	0.8	—87.0—		59.2	—40.8—		16
Malaysia	1993	8,279	1,562[7]	35,267	...	...	2,301	1992	306	...	...	...	...	...	...	...	18
Maldives	1993	45	1[14]	153	...	...	5,297	1993	5	20.0	—	80.0	—	100.0	—	—	8
Mali	1988	435	13	1,509	57	321	18,046	1987	...	...	...	...	...	...	...	...	4
Malta	1995	900	115	4,100	600	290	409	1995	7	...	...	...	...	...	...	...	58
Marshall Islands	1991	20	...	130	...	4	2,402	1985	2	100.0	—	—	—	100.0	—	—	14
Martinique	1992	625	121	1,567	199	130	590	1991	...	...	...	...	...	...	...	...	103
Mauritania	1991	135	20	819	6	141	14,259	1990	16	...	...	...	...	100.0	—	—	7
Mauritius	1994	941	148	2,575[11, 16]	206	11	1,182	1994	23	73.9	17.4	8.7	—	60.9	4.3	34.8	28[3]
Mayotte	1985	9	1	51	1	2	7,427	1991	2	100.0	—	—	—	100.0	—	—	11
Mexico	1992	149,432	4,730[16]	141,404[2, 16]	...	...	578	1993	1,539	...	...	...	...	53.9	—46.1—		10
Micronesia	1993	50	7	230	7	...	2,069	1993	4	100.0	—	—	—	100.0	—	—	31
Moldova	1994	17,400[10]	10	48,400[11]	...	11	251[10]	1994	339	...	...	...	...	100.0	—	...	125
Monaco	1994	124	31[4]	293[4]	64[4]	8[4]	244	1992	1	100.0	—	—	—	100.0	—	—	168
Mongolia	1993	5,911	299	9,183	1,113	...	376	1993	475	...	...	...	...	...	...	...	105
Morocco	1994	8,738	1,132[5]	13,358[5]	2,446	87[14]	2,945	1993[27]	201	48.8	—	51.2	—	100.0	—	—	10
Mozambique	1989	388	17	2,847	...	1,089	36,428	1990	238	4.2	0.8	—95.0—		100.0	—	—	8[5]

rate per 10,000 pop.	by kinds of hospital (%) general	special-ized	medical centres	rural	bed occu-pancy rate (%)	aver-age length of stay (days)	under age 5 per 1,000 live newborn 1995	maternal mortality per 100,000 live births 1993	popu-lation with access to safe water 1990–95 (%)	food supply (% of FAO require-ment) 1992	as percent of GDP	per capita (U.S.$)	public	private	inter-national aid	country
1,026	...	...	...	...	94.6	8	21[8]	...	77[15]	115	8.06	192	65.1	20.4	14.5	Dominica
470	...	...	...	...	...	...	48	110	76	101	3.72	38	52.7	43.3	4.0	Dominican Republic
518	...	...	...	...	57.5	7	58	150	71	113	4.14	44	55.9	37.3	6.8	Ecuador
...	...	...	...	...	...	...	73	170	80	133	2.61	28	30.3	62.0	7.7	Egypt
...	...	...	...	...	54.9[3,7]	63[3,7]	65	300	55	116	5.86	58	29.7	55.6	14.7	El Salvador
...	...	...	...	...	...	...	171	820	...	...	7.60	28	36.6	20.7	42.7	Equatorial Guinea
...	...	...	...	...	...	...	150	...	...	...	...	...	...	...	...	Eritrea
1,773	76.7	21.5	—	1.8	83.7	14	19	41	...	...	3.62	228	53.0	47.0	—	Estonia
...	...	...	...	...	...	...	174	1,400	25	69	3.80	4	41.3	39.9	18.8	Ethiopia
...	...	...	...	...	61.7	...	...	...	...	...	...	...	...	...	...	Faroe Islands
...	...	...	...	...	...	...	24	90	77[9]	135	3.76	70	54.9	38.3	6.9	Fiji
2,288	96.8	3.2	—	—	71.8	11	6	11	100	111	7.82	2,046	83.3	16.7	—	Finland
2,318[14]	...	...	...	...	...	...	9	15	100	144	9.40	1,869	74.2	25.8	—	France
1,903	...	...	...	...	75.1	10	...	...	...	128	...	...	...	...	...	French Guiana
...	...	...	...	...	...	...	...	...	...	124	...	...	...	...	...	French Polynesia
...	...	...	...	...	...	...	132	500	68[15]	107	4.10	164	52.7	40.9	6.4	Gabon
...	...	...	...	...	...	...	193	1,100	48	99	7.53	22	28.3	20.7	51.0	Gambia, The
1,375	...	...	...	...	97.9	3	...	...	...	...	...	...	...	...	...	Gaza Strip
...	...	...	...	...	...	...	21	33	...	...	4.45	152	62.5	37.5	—	Georgia
1,812	...	...	...	...	82.8	13	7	22	100	126	8.73	1,511	72.7	27.3	—	Germany
...	...	...	...	...	...	...	113	740	53	96	3.50	15	35.0	51.8	13.2	Ghana
1,730	...	...	...	...	40.6	8	...	...	...	...	...	...	...	...	...	Gibraltar
1,367	78.7	21.3	—	—	69.8	9	10	10	100	143	5.39	359	76.0	24.0	—	Greece
2,450	29.2	—	—	70.8	69.4	8	...	...	...	...	...	...	...	...	...	Greenland
774	100.0	—	—	—	59.1	7	34[8]	...	85[15]	99	5.96	133	68.8	27.8	3.5	Grenada
2,136	...	...	...	...	82.3	11	...	...	...	111	...	...	...	...	...	Guadeloupe
...	...	...	...	...	...	...	...	...	...	...	...	...	...	...	...	Guam
284	...	...	...	...	57.7	9	69	200	62	103	3.70	27	44.2	43.2	12.6	Guatemala
1,100	100.0	—	—	—	...	...	...	...	...	...	...	...	...	...	...	Guernsey
...	...	...	...	...	...	...	200	1,600	55	103	3.90	17	39.7	40.3	20.0	Guinea
...	...	...	...	...	...	...	207	910	53	111	8.15	16	31.3	18.9	49.8	Guinea-Bissau
...	...	...	...	...	...	...	63	...	65[9]	105	10.37	42	40.7	15.1	44.2	Guyana
...	...	...	...	...	...	...	107	1,000	28	75	6.99	27	26.3	54.8	19.0	Haiti
459[5]	...	...	...	...	...	...	52	220	65	102	4.54	52	56.7	35.7	7.7	Honduras
1,675	...	...	...	...	...	...	7	7	100	137	5.69	687	19.5	80.5	0.0	Hong Kong
2,241	...	...	...	...	74.2	11	17	30	100	133	5.95	185	84.4	15.6	—	Hungary
2,828	94.0	6.0	—	—	86.5	12	5	0	100	115	8.34	1,884	87.5	12.5	—	Iceland
...	...	...	...	...	...	...	102	570	81	108	6.00	21	20.0	78.4	1.6	India
...	...	...	...	...	...	...	65	650	62	127	2.01	12	25.6	66.7	7.7	Indonesia
...	...	...	...	...	...	...	62	120	84	119	2.54	244	56.9	43.1	0.0	Iran
645[14]	...	...	...	...	42.4[14]	4[14]	62	310	44	88	...	...	...	...	...	Iraq
1,464	100.0	—	...	...	81.1	7	7	10	100	153	7.22	876	81.1	18.9	—	Ireland
...	...	...	...	...	...	...	4[9]	...	...	...	...	...	...	...	...	Isle of Man
1,935	...	...	...	...	91.2	11	10	7	100	119	4.20	480	49.3	50.6	0.1	Israel
1,590	93.1	6.9	—	—	72.5	11	9	12	100	141	7.54	1,449	77.7	22.3	—	Italy
550[3]	81.7[3]	18.3[3]	—	—	63.8[3,6]	63[3,6]	21	120	86	116	5.04	83	57.4	33.2	9.5	Jamaica
...	...	...	...	...	...	...	6	18	100	124	6.45	1,538	74.5	25.5	—	Japan
1,718	84.0	16.0	—	...	...	...	...	...	...	...	...	...	...	...	...	Jersey
478[3]	...	...	...	...	68.1[3]	4[3]	41	150	89	123	3.77	55	36.9	52.3	10.8	Jordan
...	...	...	...	...	...	...	31	80	...	...	4.44	154	62.3	37.7	...	Kazakhstan
...	...	...	...	...	...	...	107	650	53	89	4.33	16	40.0	37.9	22.1	Kenya
...	...	...	...	...	...	...	78[8]	...	99[9]	116	...	...	...	...	...	Kiribati
...	...	...	...	...	...	...	27	70	100	121	...	...	...	...	...	Korea, North
657	97.4	2.6	—	—	73.7	13	13	130	93	140	6.61	365	40.9	58.9	0.2	Korea, South
950[3]	72.2[3]	27.8[3]	—	—	64.9[3]	7[3]	14	29	100	104	4.86	541	64.2	35.6	0.1	Kuwait
1,775	95.5	—	4.5	—	75.6	15	40	44.5	...	...	4.97	118	66.7	33.3	—	Kyrgyzstan
...	...	...	...	...	...	...	148	650	45	102	2.53	5	17.4	60.7	21.9	Laos
2,106	78.4	4.6	13.8	3.2	78.7	16	19	40	...	...	3.87	220	56.1	43.9	—	Latvia
...	...	...	...	...	...	...	37	300	94	134	...	...	...	...	...	Lebanon
221[6]	...	...	...	...	...	...	84	610	52	97	8.32	26	38.3	26.5	35.2	Lesotho
...	...	...	...	...	...	...	155	560	46	71	8.24	4	19.9	11.8	68.3	Liberia
...	...	...	...	...	...	...	84	220	97[15]	140	...	...	...	...	...	Libya
...	...	...	...	...	...	...	...	...	...	...	...	...	...	...	...	Liechtenstein
1,966	...	...	...	...	...	...	17	36	...	...	3.58	159	72.0	28.0	—	Lithuania
1,936	94.6	5.4	—	—	75.0	16	8	0	100	139	6.56	1,662	91.4	8.6	—	Luxembourg
329	...	...	...	...	64.4	16	...	...	...	99	...	...	...	...	...	Macau
995	67.2	6.1	—26.7—		68.5	14	37	...	...	...	...	...	...	...	...	Macedonia
...	...	...	...	...	...	...	125	490	29	94	2.56	7	29.0	49.6	21.4	Madagascar
...	...	...	...	...	...	...	215	560	54[15]	79	4.98	11	35.0	41.7	23.3	Malawi
717[3,4]	...	...	...	...	...	...	23	80	78	130	2.96	71	44.0	55.8	0.2	Malaysia
256[26]	...	...	...	...	71.4[26]	4[26]	71	...	88[15]	117	...	...	...	...	...	Maldives
...	...	...	...	...	...	...	188	1,200	37	97	5.19	15	24.9	46.7	28.4	Mali
...	...	...	...	...	...	...	11	0	100	141	5.38	349	68.3	31.7	0.0	Malta
...	...	...	...	...	...	...	92[8]	...	...	...	...	...	...	...	...	Marshall Islands
2,139	...	...	...	...	61.0	11	...	...	...	117	...	...	...	...	...	Martinique
...	...	...	...	...	...	...	145	930	66[15]	116	3.80	18	28.5	41.5	30.0	Mauritania
1,440[3]	...	...	...	...	74.6[3]	5[3]	18	120	99	119	4.40	100	47.8	39.0	13.3	Mauritius
...	...	...	...	...	...	...	...	...	...	...	...	...	...	...	...	Mayotte
403[2,3]	...	...	...	...	64.7[2,3]	5[2,3]	41	110	83	135	3.17	89	49.3	49.8	0.9	Mexico
...	...	...	...	...	...	...	29[8]	...	...	...	...	...	...	...	...	Micronesia
...	...	...	...	...	...	...	28	60	...	...	3.91	143	74.4	25.6	—	Moldova
...	...	...	...	...	...	...	...	...	...	...	...	...	...	...	...	Monaco
...	...	...	...	...	...	...	69	65	80	78	6.63	58	83.0	15.1	1.9	Mongolia
255	...	...	...	...	63.8	8	80	610	55	123	2.55	26	33.6	63.3	3.1	Morocco
...	...	...	...	...	...	...	179	1,500	33	72	5.86	5	21.0	25.7	53.3	Mozambique

Health services (continued)

country	health personnel							hospitals									hospital beds per 10,000 pop.
	year	physicians	dentists	nurses	pharmacists	midwives	population per physician	year	number	kinds (%) general	specialized	medical centres	rural	ownership (%) government	private non-profit	private for profit	
Myanmar (Burma)	1994	12,245	1,062	9,064	...	8,615	3,554	1994	717	...	...	...	...	...	...	...	6
Namibia	1992	324	51	4,471	91[2]	...	4,594	1992	47	...	...	...	...	91.5	—8.5—		45[2]
Nauru	...	...	...	...	...	...	...	...	...	...	...	...	...	...	...	...	...
Nepal	1992	1,497	...	2,781[11]	...	11	12,623	1992	114	...	...	...	...	...	...	...	3
Netherlands, The	1993	39,069	7,900[2]	121,000[4]	2,464	1,234[8]	391	1994	240	63.3	36.7	—	—	...	...	...	56
Netherlands Antilles	1994	291	63	1,225	31	11	677	1994	11	36.4	36.4	27.2	—	...	...	...	73
New Caledonia	1993	370	98	...	58	63	485	1990	8	12.5	12.5	75.0	—	62.5	—37.5—		62
New Zealand	1995	11,889	1,959	45,107[11]	3,532	11	301	1994	330	...	...	...	—	38.2	—61.8—		68
Nicaragua	1994	2,577	321	2,144	...	...	1,566	1994	56	46.4	7.1	46.4	—	...	...	...	11
Niger	1990	142	5	2,036	29	457	54,472	1987	...	...	...	...	...	...	...	...	5
Nigeria	1989	17,954	1,088	64,503	5,318	52,378	4,692	1985	11,588	6.6	0.5	—92.9—		81.4	—18.6—		12[1]
Northern Mariana Islands	1986	23	4	103	2	2	1,324	1988	1	100.0	—	—	—	100.0	—	...	19
Norway	1994	14,497	5,088	61,367	...	...	298	1993	350	19.1	80.9	—	—	...	...	...	53
Oman	1993[16]	2,381	152	4,728	388	...	837	1993[3]	46	...	...	...	...	100.0	—	...	18
Pakistan	1994	66,199	2,590	21,419	3,952[2]	18,641[5]	2,064	1992	10,905	—7.1—		—92.9—		...	...	...	6
Palau	1990	10	...	84	...	...	1,518	1986	1	...	...	...	...	...	...	...	50
Panama	1994	3,195	606	2,811	115[4]	...	808	1994	61	...	...	...	...	86.8[24]	—13.2[24]		28
Papua New Guinea	1990	301	...	2,447	...	...	12,874	1989	...	...	...	...	...	...	...	...	40
Paraguay	1993	3,341	1,160[7]	4,558[7]	...	...	1,406	1993	...	...	...	...	...	...	...	...	12
Peru	1992	23,771	7,945	15,026	5,940[2]	3,520[2]	944	1992	427	...	...	...	...	56.7	—43.3—		17
Philippines	1993	78,445	1,614[16]	14,853[16]	...	12,339[16]	849	1992	1,723	96.5	3.1	0.5	—	36.4	—63.6—		11
Poland	1994	87,712	17,490	208,571	18,716	24,287	439	1994	752	93.6	6.4	—	—	...	...	...	63
Portugal	1993	24,499	1,509	30,975	5,950	...	403	1993	335	43.0	18.8	38.2	—	74.3	14.7	11.0	42
Puerto Rico	1989	6,269	902	19,666	2,111	120	558	1994	72	83.3	8.3	8.3	—	36.1	30.6	33.3	26
Qatar	1993	693	107	1,718	160	...	807	1993	3	33.3	66.7	—	—	100.0	—	...	20
Réunion	1994	1,061	308	2,520	248[13]	166	605	1993	...	...	...	...	...	70.4[24]	—29.6[24]		44
Romania	1993[16]	40,265	6,326	...	6,432[4]	...	565	1992	...	...	...	...	...	...	...	...	95
Russia	1994	612,400	47,100	1,008,800	7,300	117,200	241	1994	12,265	37.4	17.2	—	45.4	99.8	—0.2—		119
Rwanda	1989	272	7	835	25	...	24,697	1985[3]	220	—13.6—		—86.4—		100.0	—	...	9[4]
St. Kitts and Nevis	1992	39	8	260	14	...	1,057	1992	4	50.0	—50.0—			...	...	...	67
St. Lucia	1992	64	6	256	...	...	2,235	1992	4	25.0	25.0	—	50.0	...	...	...	37
St. Vincent	1992	40	6	224	27[2]	...	2,708	1992	9	...	...	...	...	77.8	—22.2—		44
San Marino	1987	60	...	...	...	...	375	1987	...	...	...	...	...	...	...	...	66
São Tomé and Príncipe	1989	61	5	223	1	54	1,881	...	...	...	...	...	...	...	...	...	...
Saudi Arabia	1991	25,543	1,967	48,066	1,811	...	523	1995	279	...	...	...	...	74.2	—25.8—		23
Senegal	1992	520	...	...	...	...	14,825	1992	17	...	...	...	...	...	...	...	10
Seychelles	1994	72	11	344	5	...	1,026	1994	7	14.3	14.3	71.4	—	100.0	—	...	56
Sierra Leone	1992	404	...	...	...	...	10,832	1988	219	—25.6—		—74.4—		...	...	...	10
Singapore	1994	4,301	767	11,688	773	506	681	1994	22	...	...	...	...	50.0	9.1	40.9	36
Slovakia	1994	15,673	2,236	...	322[13]	...	341	1991	111	72.1	27.9	—	—	100.0	—	...	96[8]
Slovenia	1990	4,086	1,155[8]	...	1,019	...	489	1994	24	54.2	45.8	—	—	...	...	...	58
Solomon Islands	1990	52	...	447	...	...	6,154	1986	8	100.0	—	—	—	75.0	25.0	—	53
Somalia	1986	450	2	1,834	180	556	13,315	1988	...	...	...	...	...	...	...	...	7
South Africa	1994	26,452	4,029	158,538	9,622	...	1,523	1995	834	...	...	...	...	...	...	...	37
Spain	1993	159,291	12,247	167,894	39,608	6,210	246	1991	813	...	...	...	...	42.4	—57.6—		42
Sri Lanka	1993[16]	3,713	333[4]	11,818	520[4]	5,030[4]	4,745	1993[3]	426	...	...	...	...	100.0	—	...	28
Sudan, The	1990[16]	2,400	...	...	...	...	10,000	1986	...	...	...	...	...	...	...	...	8
Suriname	1994	251	...	995[7]	...	...	1,685	1989	...	...	...	...	...	...	...	...	33[8]
Swaziland	1990	83	7	1,264	13	...	9,265	1986	24	—41.7—		—58.3—		...	...	...	...
Sweden	1994	22,400	4,800	93,100[11]	5,786	11	394	1993	...	...	...	...	...	...	...	...	60
Switzerland	1993	21,500[12]	4,400[7]	...	1,543[13]	...	310[12]	1993	...	...	...	...	...	...	...	...	75
Syria	1993	13,863	6,238	18,396	4,775	4,551	966	1993	264	...	...	...	...	20.5	—79.5—		11
Taiwan	1995	27,495	7,131	56,743	19,224	842	774	1994	828	...	...	...	...	11.8	—88.2—		49
Tajikistan	1994	13,084	926	38,852	709	1,027	439	1994	449	...	...	...	...	98.2	—1.8—		88
Tanzania	1991	1,112[10]	10	...	...	...	22,568[10]	1991	173	...	...	...	...	...	...	...	10
Thailand	1993	13,634	2,786	87,026	4,721	10,525	4,259	1992	1,097	92.9	7.1	—	—	73.7	—26.3—		17
Togo	1991	319	22	1,187	65	222	11,270	1990	...	...	...	...	...	...	...	...	16
Tonga	1993	45	117	324[11]	2[4]	11	2,139	1992	4	...	...	...	...	...	...	...	31
Trinidad and Tobago	1993	1,051	136	2,260[11]	529	11	1,191	1992	...	...	...	...	...	...	...	...	29
Tunisia	1994	5,344	1,004	12,195	1,685	...	1,640	1994[3]	163	—13.5—		—86.5—		100.0	—	...	18
Turkey	1993	61,050	11,069	54,268	17,696	36,263	970	1994	982	75.3	8.8	—15.9—		84.3	—15.7—		22
Turkmenistan	1994	14,100[10]	10	43,000[11]	...	11	284[10]	1994	398	...	...	...	...	100.0	—	...	115
Tuvalu	1993	8	2[1]	39	...	...	1,152	1985	8	11.1	—	—	88.9	100.0	—	...	36
Uganda	1989	774	...	2,332	...	...	20,720	1989	81	...	...	...	...	...	...	...	12
Ukraine	1995	230,000[10]	10	598,000[11]	...	11	227[10]	1995	3,900	...	...	...	...	100.0	—	...	130
United Arab Emirates	1993	3,000	400	8,782[2]	686[2]	...	694	1993	35	...	...	...	...	82.9	—17.1—		21
United Kingdom	1993	87,300[12]	...	284,578[4]	37,832[14]	24,801[4]	667[12]	1993	...	...	...	...	...	...	...	...	51[12]
United States	1993	670,300	187,000	1,956,000	182,000	3,000	385	1993	6,580	82.1	17.9	—	—	31.1	51.2	17.7	46
Uruguay	1993	11,201	3,712	2,047	948	581	286	1993	112	...	...	...	...	61.6	—38.4—		45
Uzbekistan	1994	75,800	4,300	240,400	1,700	20,100	295	1994	1,355	...	...	...	...	100.0	—	...	97
Vanuatu	1995	12	3	259	6	33	14,025	1995	90	5.6	—	21.1	73.3	100.0	—	...	22
Venezuela	1992	32,616	7,945	52,260	5,615	...	626	1992	610	...	...	...	...	37.0	—63.0—		26
Vietnam	1993	28,500	...	53,700	6,500	12,000	2,490	1993	12,500	...	...	...	...	...	...	...	27
Virgin Islands (U.S.)	1985	167	...	...	...	...	622	1985	...	...	...	...	...	...	...	...	49
West Bank	1993[21]	1,344	445	2,279	149	56	1,536	1993	17	...	...	...	...	52.9	—47.1—		12
Western Sahara	1994	100	...	...	24	...	2,504	...	...	...	...	...	...	...	...	...	...
Western Samoa	1992	60	7	298	6	...	2,682	1992	36	2.8	—	—	97.2	100.0	—	—	34
Yemen	1994	2,785	167	5,772	295	385	4,549	1994	81	...	...	...	...	...	...	...	7
Yugoslavia	1994	20,942	4,278[5]	...	2,209[5]	...	514	1994	...	...	...	...	...	...	...	...	55
Zaire	1990	2,469	41	27,601	59	...	15,584	1986	400	...	...	...	...	52.5	—47.5—		21
Zambia	1990	713	26	1,503	24	311	11,414	1987	965	8.2	0.3	19.0	72.5	80.9	19.1	—	29[5]
Zimbabwe	1993	1,551	194	22,590	411	2,894	6,909	1993[3]	1,378	0.9	2.6	83.7	12.7	100.0	—	—	19[25]

[1]1987. [2]1991. [3]Government hospitals only. [4]1989. [5]1993. [6]General hospitals only. [7]1992. [8]1994. [9]1994–95. [10]Physicians includes dentists. [11]Nurses includes midwives. [12]OECD estimate. [13]Number of pharmacies. [14]1990. [15]Data refer to a year or period other than 1990–95, differ from the standard definition, or refer to only part of the country. [16]Government-employed health personnel only. [17]Includes doctors of traditional Chinese medicine (361,000 in 1994). [18]Republic of Cyprus only. [19]Excludes psychiatric hospitals. [20]Data refer to former Czechoslovakia. [21]West Bank includes Gaza Strip. [22]General

rate per 10,000 pop.	general	specialized	medical centres	rural	bed occupancy rate (%)	average length of stay (days)	under age 5 per 1,000 live newborn 1995	maternal mortality per 100,000 live births 1993	population with access to safe water 1990–95 (%)	food supply (% of FAO requirement) 1992	as percent of GDP	per capita (U.S.$)	public	private	international aid	country
...	...	...	...	...	...	...	99	580	38	120	...	...	...	...	...	Myanmar (Burma)
...	...	...	...	...	...	...	94	370	57	94	3.92	45	47.8	41.3	10.9	Namibia
...	...	...	...	...	...	...	...	...	...	...	...	...	...	...	...	Nauru
...	...	...	...	...	...	...	126	1,500	46	89	4.54	7	23.0	51.7	25.4	Nepal
1,070	97.4	2.6	—	—	78.0	15	8	12	100	120	8.03	1,501	72.6	27.4	—	Netherlands, The
...	...	...	...	...	...	...	...	...	...	107	...	...	...	...	...	Netherlands Antilles
1,165[6]	...	...	...	...	84.8[6]	8[6]	...	...	...	124	...	...	...	...	...	New Caledonia
1,379[3]	...	...	...	...	60.7[3]	8[3]	10	25	100	139	7.37	925	81.7	18.3	—	New Zealand
769	—76.2—		23.8		...	...	69	160	58	102	8.61	34	56.9	22.5	20.6	Nicaragua
...	...	...	...	...	...	...	186	1,200	54	96	4.98	16	24.5	31.3	34.1	Niger
...	...	...	...	...	...	...	149	1,000	40	90	2.72	10	36.5	57.4	6.1	Nigeria
1,550	100.0	—	—	—	54.7	4	...	...	...	...	...	...	...	...	...	Northern Mariana Islands
1,569	90.7	9.3	—	—	83.1	10	9	6	100	121	7.35	1,835	95.7	4.3	—	Norway
...	...	...	...	...	...	...	34	190	63	...	4.22	209	59.5	40.1	0.5	Oman
...	...	...	...	...	...	...	107	340	79	100	3.48	12	47.4	47.1	5.5	Pakistan
...	...	...	...	...	...	...	35[8]	...	...	...	...	...	...	...	...	Palau
913	...	...	...	...	59.8	7	29	55	83	97	7.13	142	72.6	23.1	4.3	Panama
...	...	...	...	...	...	...	84	930	28	115	4.44	37	59.1	36.1	4.8	Papua New Guinea
...	...	...	...	...	...	...	47	160	35	116	2.97	35	35.1	58.2	6.7	Paraguay
...	...	...	...	...	...	...	73	280	71	80	3.21	61	56.1	41.7	2.2	Peru
538	...	...	...	...	62.1	5	48	280	85	100	2.15	16	46.7	46.4	6.9	Philippines
1,288[7]	96.0[7]	4.0[7]	...	...	72.5[7]	14[7]	18	19	100	126	5.07	84	80.3	19.7	—	Poland
1,146	86.3	10.5	3.2	—	74.5	10	11	15	100	148	6.99	383	61.7	38.3	—	Portugal
1,101	94.0	4.3	1.7	—	63.1	5	...	...	...	...	...	...	...	...	...	Puerto Rico
...	...	...	...	...	71.7[7,28]	7[7,28]	24	...	100	...	4.73	630	63.0	36.9	0.0	Qatar
2,160	...	...	...	...	82.7	6	...	...	...	143	...	...	...	...	...	Réunion
...	...	...	...	...	...	...	29	130	100	115	3.87	58	61.4	38.6	—	Romania
2,150	...	...	...	...	83.2	17	26	75	...	...	3.02	159	66.8	33.2	—	Russia
85[22]	...	...	...	...	42.8[22]	7[22]	162	1,300	66	78	3.44	10	15.0	45.2	39.8	Rwanda
1,068[6]	...	...	...	...	49.3[6]	9[6]	41[8]	...	100	100	5.99	212	58.1	27.8	14.1	St. Kitts and Nevis
890[22]	...	...	...	...	...	...	22[8]	...	67[15]	107	7.18	169	75.6	23.0	1.4	St. Lucia
776[6]	...	...	...	...	67.9[6]	6[6]	23[8]	...	75[15]	97	5.69	102	68.5	28.8	2.7	St. Vincent
...	...	...	...	...	...	...	...	...	...	...	...	...	...	...	...	San Marino
...	...	...	...	...	...	...	82[8]	...	52[15]	91	9.22	38	28.8	17.0	54.2	São Tomé and Príncipe
...	...	...	...	...	...	...	31	130	95[15]	113	4.76	260	64.3	35.7	0.0	Saudi Arabia
...	...	...	...	...	...	...	160	1,200	52	95	3.66	29	45.1	38.0	16.9	Senegal
1,605[29]	...	...	...	...	75.2[29]	6[29]	20[8]	...	100	98	6.03	289	50.2	28.0	21.9	Seychelles
...	...	...	...	...	...	...	246	1,800	34	74	2.43	4	19.6	30.9	49.5	Sierra Leone
1,174	85.8	14.2	—	—	73.1	8	10	10	100	...	1.87	215	58.3	41.6	0.1	Singapore
1,679	94.9	5.1	—	—	73.2	14	14	...	100	...	...	...	...	...	...	Slovakia
1,585	...	...	...	...	80.7	11	12	...	...	...	...	...	...	...	...	Slovenia
...	...	...	...	...	...	...	30	...	82[15]	95	2.18	117	43.2	50.5	6.3	Solomon Islands
...	...	...	...	...	...	...	180	1,600	37[15]	65	1.51	8	7.3	41.1	51.6	Somalia
...	...	...	...	...	...	...	76	230	70	110	5.56	77	57.5	42.5	0.0	South Africa
997	...	...	...	...	76.7	12	8	7	100	151	6.59	831	78.4	21.6	—	Spain
1,464[14]	...	...	...	...	...	...	20	140	53	102	3.74	18	40.4	51.1	8.6	Sri Lanka
...	...	...	...	...	...	...	115	660	60	94	3.33	34	11.0	84.5	4.5	Sudan, The
766[30]	...	...	...	...	68.8[30]	10[30]	27	...	68[15]	113	2.88	93	37.9	58.0	4.1	Suriname
...	...	...	...	...	...	...	103	560	30[15]	117	7.22	64	43.6	22.2	34.2	Swaziland
1,954	...	...	...	...	83.0	9	6	7	100	110	8.79	2,343	89.3	10.7	—	Sweden
...	...	...	...	...	...	...	8	6	100	126	7.52	2,520	68.5	31.5	—	Switzerland
352[3]	...	...	...	...	75.5[3]	3[3]	44	180	85	128	2.07	41	16.6	79.4	4.0	Syria
...	...	...	...	...	...	...	8	8	...	...	4.30	323	53.0	47.0	0.0	Taiwan
1,492	...	...	...	...	70.2	15	57	74.0	...	...	5.98	100	72.6	27.4	—	Tajikistan
...	...	...	...	...	...	...	128	770	50	87	4.73	4	14.4	31.6	54.0	Tanzania
...	...	...	...	...	...	...	43	200	86[15]	110	4.98	72	20.4	78.7	0.9	Thailand
...	...	...	...	...	...	...	121	640	63	...	4.10	18	40.4	38.5	21.2	Togo
622	...	...	...	...	56.2	10	248[8]	...	100[15]	129	6.46	63	60.3	25.0	14.8	Tonga
1,114[3,6]	...	...	...	...	70.7[3,6]	6[3,6]	17	90	97	107	4.54	180	62.4	36.9	0.6	Trinidad and Tobago
...	...	...	...	...	...	...	51	170	99	139	4.91	76	63.8	33.3	3.0	Tunisia
568[14]	...	...	...	...	...	...	68	180	80	136	3.94	76	36.2	63.3	0.5	Turkey
...	...	...	...	...	...	...	68	55	...	...	4.99	125	66.4	33.2	0.4	Turkmenistan
1,368	40.9	—	—	59.1	51.5[6]	12.2[6]	56[8]	...	100[15]	...	...	...	...	...	...	Tuvalu
...	...	...	...	...	...	...	174	1,200	34	93	3.40	8	13.3	53.0	33.7	Uganda
...	...	...	...	...	...	...	20	50	...	...	3.30	131	69.7	30.3	—	Ukraine
...	...	...	...	...	...	...	20	26	95	140	2.66	472	34.0	66.0	0.1	United Arab Emirates
...	...	...	...	...	...	...	8	9	100	132	6.11	1,039	84.9	15.1	—	United Kingdom
1,191[31]	...	...	...	...	64.6[31]	7[31]	10	12	100	141	12.71	2,765	44.1	55.9	—	United States
401[3]	...	...	...	...	69.1[3]	15[3]	21	85	75[15]	103	4.62	123	53.8	44.8	1.4	Uruguay
...	...	...	...	...	...	...	48	55	...	...	5.90	116	72.1	27.9	—	Uzbekistan
567	...	...	...	...	41.9	6	51	280	100	120	5.68	67	51.5	25.7	22.8	Vanuatu
601[3]	...	...	...	...	69.7[3]	6[3]	25	120	79	106	3.60	88	54.2	45.6	0.1	Venezuela
...	...	...	...	...	...	...	59	160	36	104	2.11	3	39.3	47.4	13.3	Vietnam
...	...	...	...	...	...	...	...	...	...	...	...	...	...	...	...	Virgin Islands (U.S.)
809	...	...	...	...	81.0	4	...	...	...	...	...	...	...	...	...	West Bank
...	...	...	...	...	...	...	...	...	...	...	...	...	...	...	...	Western Sahara
894	70.8	—	—	29.2	32.9	5	74	...	83[15]	124	2.94	20	6.1	54.2	39.7	Western Samoa
...	...	...	...	...	...	...	159	1,400	55	91	3.19	20	34.7	54.1	11.3	Yemen
1,058	...	...	...	...	71.6	13	...	...	...	...	5.11[32]	264[32]	80.4[32]	19.6[32]	—	Yugoslavia
...	...	...	...	...	...	...	133	870	27	93	2.38	5	8.5	64.8	26.7	Zaire
1,249	—75.7—		—24.3—		68.5	7	141	940	50	84	3.16	17	65.4	30.6	4.1	Zambia
546	...	...	...	...	69.8	7	104	570	77	83	6.23	39	40.3	48.7	11.0	Zimbabwe

and specialized hospitals only. [23]Registered personnel; all may not be present and working in the country. [24]Based on bed ownership. [25]1995. [26]Central Hospital only. [27]Public sector only. [28]Hamad General Hospital only. [29]Victoria Hospital only. [30]Paramaribo hospitals (1,213 beds) only. [31]5,261 community hospitals only. [32]Data refer to the former Socialist Federal Republic of Yugoslavia.

Social protection

This table summarizes three principal areas of social protective activity for the countries of the world: social security, crime and law enforcement, and military affairs. Because the administrative structure, financing, manning, and scope of institutions and programmed tasks in these fields vary so greatly from country to country, no well-accepted or well-documented body of statistical comparisons exists in international convention to permit objective assessment of any of these subjects, either from the perspective of a single country or internationally. The data provided within any single subject area do, however, represent the most consistent approach to problems of international comparison found in the published literature for that field.

The provision of social security programs to answer specific social needs, for example, is summarized simply in terms of the existence or nonexistence of a specific type of benefit program because of the great complexity of national programs in terms of eligibility, coverage, term, age limits, financing, payments, and so on. Activities connected with a particular type of benefit often take place at more than one governmental level, through more than one agency at the same level, or through a mixture of public and private institutions. The data shown here are summarized from the U.S. Social Security Administration's *Social Security Programs Throughout the World* (biennial). A bullet symbol (●) indicates that a country has at least one program within the defined area; in some cases it may have several. A blank space indicates that no program existed providing the benefit shown; ellipses [...] indicate that no information was available as to whether a program existed.

Data given for social security expenditure as a percentage of total central governmental expenditure are taken from the International Monetary Fund's *Government Finance Statistics Yearbook,* which provides the most comparable analytic series on the consolidated accounts of central governments, governmentally administered social security funds, and independent national agencies, all usually separate accounting entities, through which these services may be provided in a given country.

Data on the finances of social security programs are taken in large part from the International Labour Office's *The Cost of Social Security* (triennial), supplemented by national data sources.

Figures for criminal offenses known to police, usually excluding civil offenses and minor traffic violations, are taken in part from Interpol's *International Crime Statistics* (biennial) and a variety of national sources. Statistics are usually based on the number of offenses reported to police, not the number of offenders apprehended or tried in courts. Attempted offenses are counted as the offense that was attempted. A person identified as having committed multiple offenses is counted only under the most serious offense. Murder refers to all acts involving the voluntary taking of life, including infanticide, but excluding abortion, or involuntary acts such as those normally classified as manslaughter. Assault includes "serious," or aggravated, assault—that involving injury, endangering life, or perpetrated with the use of a dangerous instrument. Burglary involves theft from the premises of another; although Interpol statistics are reported as "breaking and entering," national data may not always distinguish cases of forcible

Social protection

country	social security																
	programs available, 1995					expenditures, 1993 (% of total central govt.)	finances										
	old-age, invalidity, death[a]	sickness and maternity[b]	work injury[c]	unemployment[d]	family allowances[e]		year	receipts						expenditures			
								total ('000,000 natl. cur.)	insured persons (%)	employers (%)	government (%)	other (%)		total ('000,000 natl. cur.)	benefits (%)	administration (%)	other (%)
Afghanistan	●	●	●		●	...		...	...	...	...	...		...	...	...	...
Albania	●	●	●	●	●	...	1990	967.0	—	—	88.8	11.2		1,440.0	99.5	—0.5——	
Algeria	●	●	●		●	...	1990	27,700.0	...	...	...	...		28,748.0	61.8	30.6	7.6
American Samoa	●	...	...	...	...	...	1990	...	...	...	...	...		13.0	100.0	—	—
Andorra	...	...	...	...	...	...	1993	11,832.2	...	...	...	...		7,937.2	90.2	4.6	5.2
Angola	●	●				...	1983	13.0	29.2	48.7	—	22.1		4.2	66.1	33.9	—
Antigua and Barbuda	●	●				...											
Argentina	●	●	●	●	●	44.4[3]	1989	1,015,837.0	28.8	45.0	16.6	9.6		989,009.0	95.0	5.0	—
Armenia	●	●	●	●	●	...		...	...	...	...	...		...	...	...	...
Aruba	●	●	●			10	1992	66.3	...	...	...	...		60.4	...	...	...
Australia	●	●	●	●	●	29.7	1989	28,525.6	1.9	7.8	88.4	1.9		28,880.4	98.7	1.0	0.3
Austria	●	●	●	●	●	45.8[11]	1989	425,417.0	30.1	45.9	21.1	2.9		412,134.0	96.5	2.3	1.2
Azerbaijan	●	●	●	●	●	...		...	...	...	...	...		...	...	...	...
Bahamas, The	●	●	●		●	4.1[11]	1989	95.9	22.9	38.5	2.1	36.5		43.5	71.1	27.2	1.7
Bahrain	●		●			4.5[11]	1989	39.6	12.3	40.2	—	47.5		9.7	69.8	20.9	9.3
Bangladesh		●	●	●		9.8[11,14]	1989	73.6	12.4	37.5	2.4	47.7		34.1	94.0	6.0	—
Barbados	●	●	●	●		19.8[5]	1989	191.7	38.0	40.8	1.5	19.7		149.1	93.5	5.8	0.7
Belarus	●	●		●	●	11.0[13]	1986	3,199.0	—	—	93.2	6.8		3,199.0	100.0	—	—
Belgium	●	●	●	●	●	41.3[5]	1986	1,347,070.0	24.4	39.7	31.6	4.3		1,322,636.0	94.5	4.3	1.2
Belize	●	●	●			3.4	1989	15.3	8.9	53.2	—	38.0		3.9	56.7	43.3	—
Benin	●	●			●	8.7[11,15]	1989	3,551.9	16.8	81.4	—	1.8		4,500.9	69.3	28.1	2.6
Bermuda	●					...											
Bhutan	...	...	...	...	...	0.5[13]	1990	...	...	...	...	...		26.0[11]	...	...	...
Bolivia	●	●	●		●	11.6	1989	346.6	29.3	47.7	11.2	11.8		340.2	84.9	14.3	0.8
Bosnia and Herzegovina	●	●	●	●	●	...		...	...	...	...	...		...	...	...	...
Botswana			●			2.6[11,13]	1992	—						84.8[11]	...	...	...
Brazil	●	●	●	●	●	27.7[13]	1989	71,847.0	24.4	51.0	20.0	4.6		68,957.0	61.9	18.6	19.5
Brunei	●	...				...	1984	...	...	...	...	...		39.5	...	...	...
Bulgaria	●	●	●	●	●	32.3	1989	6,016.8	—	71.4	28.1	0.5		6,000.1	96.6	3.3	0.1
Burkina Faso	●	●	●		●	0.1[11,16]	1989	8,816.5	15.6	62.9	—	21.5		4,975.3	69.5	30.4	0.1
Burundi	●		●		●	0.7[17]	1989	1,991.5	31.6	47.6	—	20.8		1,563.9	74.8	16.8	8.4
Cambodia	...	...	...	...	...	...		...	...	...	...	...		...	...	...	...
Cameroon	●		●		●	5.5	1989	41,331.8	13.1	64.8	—	22.1		41,332.0	70.6	28.8	0.6
Canada	●	●	●	●	●	32.8[13]	1989	130,306.6	9.9	15.6	64.4	10.1		115,764.2	96.9	2.5	0.6
Cape Verde	●	●	●		●	...	1989	697.7	26.5	58.5	—	15.0		316.7	82.4	16.1	1.5
Central African Republic	●		●		●	6.2[4,11]	1989	3,604.0	8.4	76.0	—	15.6		3,247.0	64.6	32.9	2.5
Chad	●		●		●	1.9[18]	1989	1,172.8	12.6	77.6	—	9.8		634.5	43.0	51.4	5.6
Chile	●	●	●	●	●	31.1	1989	1,186,056.0	32.8	2.7	37.9	26.6		798,770.0	83.9	14.7	1.4
China	●	●	●	●		...	1989	57,446.2	—	99.4	—	0.6		54,654	98.4	0.6	1.0
Colombia	●	●	●		●	7.4	1989	294,438.0	24.8	56.0	0.2	19.0		257,455.0	85.5	11.5	3.0
Comoros	...	...	●	...	...	...	1983	40.7	100.0	—	—	—		54.3	17.4	62.3	20.3
Congo	●		●		●	0.4[21]	1983	15,272.8	12.1	80.2	—	7.7		7,256.7	66.6	21.3	12.1
Costa Rica	●	●	●		●	10.5[11]	1989	36,407.3	33.2	44.4	1.2	21.2		31,049.8	89.0	4.1	6.9
Côte d'Ivoire	●		●		●	3.6[4]	1989	27,288.4	19.3	75.4	—	5.3		20,593.5	100.0	—	—
Croatia	●	●	●	●	●	25.9		...	...	...	...	...		...	...	...	...
Cuba	●	●	●		●	...	1989	2,284.8	—	37.4	62.6	—		2,284.8	96.7	—	3.3
Cyprus[22]	●	●	●	●	●	19.8	1989	217.5	24.7	40.3	17.3	17.7		117.7	98.4	1.6	—
Czech Republic[23]	●	●	●	●	●	25.6	1989	132,748.0	—	3.9	96.1	—		132,748.0	99.7	0.3	—
Denmark	●	●	●	●	●	38.7[13]	1989	225,965.6	4.3	5.0	88.2	2.5		218,258.2	97.0	3.0	—
Djibouti	●	...	●		●	6.2[11,24]	1979	1,352.2	...	...	...	...		1,115.7	...	...	...
Dominica	●	●	●			1.4[15]	1986	12.3	22.6	50.9	—	26.5		4.4	68.0	32.0	—
Dominican Republic	●	●	●			4.2[11]	1986	77.9	20.1	72.9	—	6.8		74.3	75.9	24.1	—
Ecuador	●	●	●		●	1.9[3]	1988	71,286.0	37.0	50.0	—	13.0		52,032.4	86.0	14.0	—
Egypt	●	●	●	●		10.9	1989	2,443.5	22.8	41.0	2.0	34.2		1,685.6	93.4	6.6	—
El Salvador	●	●	●			3.1	1989	465.3	27.1	51.7	—	21.2		368.3	78.1	21.9	—

entry. Automobile theft excludes brief use of a car without the owner's permission, "joyriding," and implies intent to deprive the owner of the vehicle permanently. Criminal offense data for certain countries refer to cases disposed of in court, rather than to complaints. Police manpower figures refer, for the most part, to full-time, paid professional staff, excluding clerical support and volunteer staff. Personnel in military service who perform police functions are presumed to be employed in their principal activity, military service.

The figures for military manpower refer to full-time, active-duty military service and exclude reserve, militia, paramilitary, and similar organizations. Because of the difficulties attached to the analysis of data on military manpower and budgets (including problems such as data withheld on national security grounds, or the publication of budgetary data specifically intended to hide actual expenditure, or the complexity of long-term financing of purchases of military matériel [how much was actually spent as opposed to what was committed, offset by nonmilitary transfers, etc.]), extensive use is made of the principal international analytic tools: publications such as those of the International Institute for Strategic Studies (*The Military Balance* and *Strategic Survey*) and the U.S. Arms Control and Disarmament Agency (*World Military Expenditures and Arms Transfers*), both annuals.

The data on military expenditures are from the sources identified above, as well as from the IMF's *Government Finance Statistics Yearbook* and country statistical publications.

The following notes further define the column headings:

a. Programs providing cash payments for *each* of the three types of long-term benefit indicated to persons (1) exceeding a specified working age (usually 50–65, often 5 years earlier for women) who are qualified by a term of covered employment, (2) partially or fully incapacitated for their usual employment by injury or illness, and (3) qualified by their status as spouse, cohabitant, or dependent minor of a qualified person who dies.

b. Programs providing cash payments (jointly, or alternatively, medical services as well) to occupationally qualified persons for *both* of the short-term benefits indicated: (1) illness and (2) maternity.

c. Programs providing cash or medical services to employment-qualified persons who become temporarily or permanently incapacitated (fully or partially) by work-related injury or illness.

d. Programs providing term-limited cash compensation (usually 40–75% of average earnings) to persons qualified by previous employment (of six months minimum, typically) for periods of involuntary unemployment.

e. Programs providing cash payments to families or mothers to mitigate the cost of raising children and to encourage the formation of larger families.

f. A police officer is a full-time, paid professional, performing domestic security functions. Data include administrative staff but exclude clerical employees, volunteers, and members of paramilitary groups.

g. Includes all active-duty personnel, regular and conscript, performing national security functions. Excludes reserves, paramilitary forces, border patrols, and gendarmeries.

crime and law enforcement (latest)					military protection									country
offenses reported to the police per 100,000 population					population per police officer[f]	manpower, 1996[g]		expenditure, 1994				arms trade, 1994 ('000,000 U.S.$)		
total	personal		property			total ('000)	per 1,000 population	total '000,000	per capita	% of central government expenditure	% of GDP or GNP	imports	exports	
	murder	assault	burglary	automobile theft										
...	...	...	...	...	540[1]	[2]	[2]	408[3]	24[4]	64.4[4]	9.1[4]	20	20	Afghanistan
...	...	...	...	...	550	54.0	16.6	157[5]	56[5]	11.3[5]	4.1[5]	0	0	Albania
584	1.0	19.7	39.7	8.5	840	123.7	4.3	1,335	48	7.9	3.3	140	0	Algeria
3,448	11.8	579.6	1,060.9	21.6	460	—	[6]	—	—	—	—	...	...	American Samoa
7,000	2.0	46.0	1,204.0	150.0	220	—	—	...	...	...	...	...	...	Andorra
250	7.7	1.8	...	...	14[7]	97.0	8.1	1,127[8]	161[8]	28.8[9]	23.9[8]	600	0	Angola
4,977	4.7	475.0	1,984.4	35.9	120	0.2	2.3	...	...	...	...	...	...	Antigua and Barbuda
84	0.1	0.3	—	9.8	1,270	72.5	2.1	4,716	139	27.0	1.7	10	0	Argentina
437	9.7	6.0	11.6	14.7	...	57.4	15.3	71	20	...	0.9	10	0	Armenia
6,268	38.5	453.8	1,363.1	101.5	...	—	[6]	—	—	—	—	...	...	Aruba
5,319	7.1	369.6	1,962.8	1,005.5	450	57.8	3.2	8,270	457	9.4	2.6	430	20	Australia
6,421	2.6	2.5	1,307.3	42.4	470	55.8	6.9	1,863	234	2.3[12]	1.0	10	50	Austria
305	9.6	10.9	8.7	8.7	...	70.7	9.3	132	17	3.8[13]	1.0	60	0	Azerbaijan
6,752	17.6	115.7	1,336.5	...	125	0.9	3.1	9[4]	40[4]	2.5[4]	0.5[4]	...	...	Bahamas, The
3,457	0.8	...	...	...	180	11.0	18.4	245	430	15.3[13]	6.1	80	0	Bahrain
64	2.2	3.7	4.9	0.4	2,560	117.5	0.9	355	3	8.4[13]	1.5	10	0	Bangladesh
4,958	7.4	159.1	388.7	43.6	280	0.6	2.3	8[13]	34[13]	1.7[13]	0.6[13]	0	0	Barbados
650	2.9	7.0	...	...	...	85.5	8.2	...	...	...	...	0	0	Belarus
3,591	2.7	117.9	752.1	312.5	640	46.3	4.5	3,944	392	3.5[12]	1.7	40	30	Belgium
2,781	34.6	629.8	819.5	...	290	1.1	4.8	9	44	4.4	1.7	0	0	Belize
125	0.9	37.9	3.4	1.3	3,250	4.8	0.9	34	6	8.6[12]	2.3	0	0	Benin
8,871	5.1	221.7	1,949.2	...	370	—	[6]	—	—	—	—	...	...	Bermuda
...	...	...	...	...	...	4.0[14]	3.1[14]	...	...	...	...	0	0	Bhutan
...	...	...	...	...	...	33.5	4.4	130	17	9.6	2.4	0	0	Bolivia
558	...	...	...	...	...	92.0	26.1	...	...	...	...	100	0	Bosnia and Herzegovina
8,758	29.2	519.2	2.1	...	750	7.5	5.1	229	169	14.1	6.0	20	0	Botswana
116	...	...	...	...	...	295.0	1.9	6,427	40	3.5[13]	1.1	90	80	Brazil
520	0.1	85.0	96.2	28.5	100	5.0	16.7	309	1,087	20.1[3]	7.9	0	0	Brunei
2,255	9.5	8.4	1,202.5	136.7	...	103.5	12.4	1,001	114	6.1	2.7	0	50	Bulgaria
41	0.2	4.1	—	—	...	10.0	0.9	43	4	12.0[12]	2.3	5	0	Burkina Faso
87	3.3	7.4	...	...	...	18.5	3.1	32	5	19.2	3.7	5	0	Burundi
...	...	...	...	...	1,980	87.7	8.7	61	6	16.7	2.7	10	0	Cambodia
108	0.7	0.2	4.8	1.3	1,170	13.1	1.0	102	8	10.2[12]	1.9	5	0	Cameroon
13,296.6	2.7	159.7	1,674	556.7	8,640	70.5	2.4	9,525	339	7.9	1.8	170	230	Canada
...	...	...	...	...	110	1.1	2.7	3	8	2.8[16]	1.0	0	0	Cape Verde
135	1.6	22.8	2.7	...	2,740[1]	5.0	1.6	30	10	6.6[5]	3.2	0	0	Central African Republic
...	...	...	...	...	990	25.4	3.9	24	4	9.7[13]	2.7	40	0	Chad
1,125	5.0	93.3	...	15.2	470	89.7	6.2	966	69	9.1	1.9	90	0	Chile
201	1.9	4.1	17.5	...	1,360[19]	2,935.0	2.4	52,840	44	18.0	2.4	130	800	China
641	81.9	110.5	...	32.4	420	146.4	4.1	1,190	33	15.8[12]	1.9	30	0	Colombia
...	...	...	...	...	960	—	[20]	...	...	...	...	...	...	Comoros
32	1.5	4.7	0.2	0.2	870	10.0	3.7	28	11	11.1[3]	2.4	20	0	Congo
868	5.3	11.1	232.4	23.1	480	3.0	0.9	28	9	1.4[12]	0.4[12]	0	0	Costa Rica
67	2.5	73.1	19.5	11.9	4,640	8.4	0.6	61	4	...	1.1	0	0	Côte d'Ivoire
1,087	...	...	...	...	...	64.7	13.5	...	...	...	...	30	0	Croatia
...	...	...	...	...	650	100.0	9.0	350	32	...	1.6	0	0	Cuba
667	1.4	9.9	195.6	3.9	180	10.0	15.2	338	463	10.9[12]	3.6[12]	60	0	Cyprus[22]
1,911	2.0	89.4	621.5	95.7	640	70.0	6.8	2,165	208	7.4	2.7	90	300	Czech Republic[23]
10,399	4.6	169.2	2,381.0	619.7	600	32.9	6.3	2,719	524	4.2	1.9	40	10	Denmark
402	4.4	12.4	40.0	16.0	...	9.6	15.9	25	71[12]	13.9[12]	6.0[12]	0	0	Djibouti
1,956	4.2	25.2	1,078.1	33.6	300	[25]	[25]	...	...	...	...	...	...	Dominica
946	11.9	30.8	154.0	24.8	580	24.5	3.3	115	15	6.8	1.1	30	0	Dominican Republic
278	6.2	7.9	17.6	7.3	260	57.1	4.9	550	52	21.8	3.5	30	0	Ecuador
3,693	1.6	0.7	...	3.1	580	440.0	7.2	1,742	28	8.9	4.1	1,500	10	Egypt
...	...	...	...	...	1,000	28.4	4.8	106	18	9.1	1.2	30	0	El Salvador

Social protection (continued)

country	old-age, invalidity, death[a]	sickness and maternity[b]	work injury[c]	unemploy-ment[d]	family allow-ances[e]	expenditures, 1993 (% of total central govt.)	year	total receipts ('000,000 natl. cur.)	insured persons (%)	employers (%)	government (%)	other (%)	total expenditures ('000,000 natl. cur.)	benefits (%)	administration (%)	other (%)
Equatorial Guinea	•	•	•	...	•	...	1989	141.0	7.1	92.9	—	—	134.0	49.3	50.7	—
Eritrea[27]																
Estonia	•	•	•	•	•	34.0[11]	...	90.1	...	...	...	...	...	...	...	...
Ethiopia[27]	•	•	•	...	...	4.0[16]	1989	190.9	32.8	65.3	—	1.9	153.7	98.3	1.7	—
Faroe Islands	...	•	...	•	•											
Fiji	•	...	•	...	...	3.6	1989	153.5	20.9	33.8	0.8	44.5	75.47	95.3	4.7	—
Finland	•	•	•	•	•	45.6[11]	1989	118,589.0	7.7	41.1	44.0	7.2	106,235	96.3	3.7	—
France	•	•	•	•	•	43.9[13]	1989	1,700,202.0	77.7	—	20.4	1.9	1,669,096.0	95.5	3.7	0.8
French Guiana	•	•	•	•	•		1991	1,071.5	...	...	...	...	997.1	...	...	...
French Polynesia	•	•	•	...	•		1990	19,268.0	...	...	...	...	17,832.0	...	...	...
Gabon	•	•	•	...	•	...	1989	3,415.0	...	44.3	29.3	26.4	2,737.0	55.2	44.8	—
Gambia, The	•	...	•	...	...	2.9[3]	1982	—	...	...	...	...	5.6	...	...	...
Gaza Strip	...	...	•	...	...	—										
Georgia	•	•	•	•	•	...	...									
Germany	•	•	•	•	•	45.3[16]	1989[30]	522,172.0	36.9	34.3	26.1	2.7	507,604.0	97.1	2.8	0.1
Ghana	•	...	•	...	...	6.4	1989	17,920.8	21.1	52.9	—	26.0	4,147.7	13.3	64.0	22.7
Gibraltar	•	•	•	•	•											
Greece	•	•	•	•	•	12.2	1989	1,314,421.0	24.9	38.4	30.8	5.9	1,349,693.0	92.5	7.5	—
Greenland																
Grenada	•	...	•	...	...	5.0[11,17]	1989	24.1	20.1	60.3	3.2	16.3	13.5	93.1	6.9	—
Guadeloupe	•	...	...	...	•	...	1991	2,733.1	...	...	...	...	4,719.6	...	...	...
Guam							1989						7.3	...	...	...
Guatemala	•	•	•	...	...	5.2[5,11]	1989	348.5	29.1	54.8	—	16.1	279.7	82.7	14.6	2.7
Guernsey	...	•	...	•	•	...	1993	66,369	44.3		45.5	10.2	62,458	94.2	5.8	...
Guinea	•	•	•	...	•	...	1989	3,387.0	0.4	90.3	—	9.3	1,108.1	54.9	45.1	...
Guinea-Bissau	...	•	•	...	...	8.8[11]	1986	138.0	22.8	63.4	10.3	3.8	61.9	59.6	40.4	—
Guyana	•	...	•	...	...	3.7[9]	1989	294.7	17.1	22.6	0.5	59.7	137.3	67.2	32.1	0.7
Haiti	•	•	•	...	...	5.1[4]	1977	60.5	26.6		69.9	3.5	52.4	92.7	7.3	—
Honduras	•	•	•	...	...	4.5[15]	1986	166.2	23.9	40.8	3.3	32.0	76.8	84.6	15.4	—
Hong Kong	•	...	•	...	•	...	1993–94	...	...	...	...	...	8,780.7	74.7	25.3	—
Hungary	•	•	•	•	•	27.7[3]	1986	149,400.0	21.1	78.9	—	—	142,939.0	99.3	0.7	—
Iceland	•	•	•	•	•[32]	20.7	1993	10,188.0	—	—	—	—	77,817.0	97.8	2.2	—
India	•	•	•	•	...	...	1989	43,913.8	23.8	27.7	5.3	43.2	13,775.8	90.0	8.2	1.8
Indonesia	•	...	•	...	...	—	1989	239,477.0	50.7	49.3	—	—	181,499.0	12.3	15.8	71.9
Iran	•	•	•	•	•	12.9[12]	1986	346,460.0	83.2	0.1	8.2	8.5	167,879.0	43.4	6.3	50.0
Iraq	•	•	•	•	...	...	1977	107.8	9.9	55.6	21.9	12.6	71.0	94.0	2.4	3.6
Ireland	•	•	•	•	•	26.9	1989	4,627.5	16.3	24.8	57.7	1.2	4,612.9	95.2	4.7	0.1
Isle of Man	•	•	•	•	•	37.0[34]	1985	...	...	...	...	...	14.4	...	...	...
Israel	•	•	•	•	•	21.8	1989	13,851.1	31.1	27.7	35.0	6.2	13,593.3	81.7	15.4	2.9
Italy	•	•	•	•	•	28.5[35]	1989	278,383.0	16.5	51.4	30.0	2.1	100,251.0	89.3	2.0	8.7
Jamaica	•	...	•	...	...	3.2[17]	1989	374.3	11.5	13.6	43.8	31.1	273.6	92.6	7.4	—
Japan	•	•	•	•	•	32.7	1989	59,571,299.0	27.4	31.6	24.4	16.6	46,684,159.0	94.3	1.7	4.0
Jersey	•	•	•	•	•	9.5	1991	60.9	63.8		23.4	12.8	52.8	...	...	...
Jordan	•	...	•	...	...	9.8	1986	53.6	28.7	55.3	—	16.0	9.5	77.4	14.0	8.6
Kazakstan	•	•	•	•	•	...	...									
Kenya	•	...	•	...	...	0.1	1989	4,262.0	18.2	13.7	10.0	58.1	1,857.8	53.8	46.1	0.1
Kiribati	•	...	...	...	...											
Korea, North	...	...	•	...	...											
Korea, South	•	•	•	...	...	7.9	1994	4,570,500.0	—	34.8	—	—	6,287,600.0	...	...	...
Kuwait	•	...	...	...	...	9.7	1989	445.8	7.1	13.2	54.3	25.4	206.5	97.0	3.0	—
Kyrgyzstan	•	•	•	•	•	...	...									
Laos						...	...									
Latvia	•	•	•	•	•	34.8[38]	...									
Lebanon	•	•	•	...	•	...										
Lesotho	...	...	•	...	...	1.5[11,16]	1991	—	...	...	...	...	15.0[11]	...	...	...
Liberia	•	•	•	...	...	1.0[35]	1983	2.9	—	69.0	13.8	17.2	2.6	54.4	45.6	—
Libya	•	•	•	•	•	...	1989	314.3	21.6	25.4	50.2	2.8	260.0	77.5	19.5	3.0
Liechtenstein	•	•	•	•	•	...										
Lithuania	•	•	•	•	•	35.6	...						24,981.7	...	...	...
Luxembourg	•	•	•	•	•	48.5	1989	72,471.8	24.2	34.6	34.4	6.8	65,214.4	97.2	2.4	0.4
Macau	•	...	...	...	•	...	1994	145.7	...	...	...	...	128.0	...	...	...
Macedonia						...	1994						178.4			
Madagascar	•	...	•	...	•	1.5[11,16]	1989	15,229.0	22.2	77.8	—	—	14,542.0	81.2	18.8	—
Malawi	•	...	•	...	...	0.1[11,35]	1986	...	...	...	...	...	5.4	...	...	...
Malaysia	•	...	•	...	...	5.8[11]	1989	7,958.7	20.7	40.2	—	39.1	2,826.5	97.0	3.0	—
Maldives	...	...	•	...	...	1.0[16]	1990	—	...	...	...	...	7.1	...	...	...
Mali	•	•	•	...	•	3.0[35]	1986	8,128.8	16.6	74.3	—	9.1	7,924.6	63.7	34.7	1.6
Malta	•	•	•	•	•	33.2	1989	82.2	26.1	31.6	42.3	—	110.7	92.5	7.5	—
Marshall Islands	•	...	...	...	...											
Martinique	•	...	...	...	•	...	1991	2,958.8	...	...	...	...	4,873.3	...	...	...
Mauritania	•	...	•	...	•	3.7[15]	1989	808.4	1.5	90.4	—	8.1	735.2	63.5	31.2	5.3
Mauritius	•	...	•	•	•	16.2[11]	1989	1,733.5	2.9	47.9	31.7	17.5	1,072.7	95.2	3.0	1.8
Mayotte	...	...	...	...	...											
Mexico	•	•	•	...	•	12.3[3]	1989	16,011,795.0	20.9	54.8	12.9	11.4	14,562,293.0	79.9	15.5	4.6
Micronesia	•	...	...	...	...											
Moldova	•	•	•	•	•	...	...									
Monaco	•	•	•	•	•	...	...									
Mongolia	•	•	•	...	•	17.7	1989	2,431.6	—	—	20.8	79.2	2,304.6	100.0	—	—
Morocco	•	•	•	...	•	5.9[11,13]	1989	4,660.5	20.6	47.5	12.9	19.0	3,040.7	94.8	5.0	0.2
Mozambique	•	...	•	...	...	...	1986	228.2	—	86.2	13.7	0.1	145.0	100.0	—	—
Myanmar (Burma)	•	•	•	...	...	0.3	1986	44.3	19.9	59.6	18.5	2.0	35.9	51.5	15.6	32.9
Namibia	•	...	...	...	•	6.8[16]										
Nauru						...										
Nepal	•	...	...	...	...	0.7[14]	1985	—	...	...	...	...	59.3	...	...	...
Netherlands, The	•	•	•	•	•	34.6	1989	154,427.0	37.3	30.3	19.0	13.4	135,609.0	96.9	3.1	—

Table headers:
- **crime and law enforcement (latest)** — *offenses reported to the police per 100,000 population*: total; personal (murder, assault); property (burglary, automobile theft). **population per police officer[f]**
- **military protection** — *manpower, 1996[g]*: total ('000), per 1,000 population. *expenditure, 1994*: total '000,000, per capita, % of central government expenditure, % of GDP or GNP. *arms trade, 1994 ('000,000 U.S.$)*: imports, exports
- **country**

total	murder	assault	burglary	automobile theft	pop. per police officer[f]	manpower total ('000)	manpower per 1,000 pop.	exp. total '000,000	exp. per capita	% of central govt. expenditure	% of GDP or GNP	imports	exports	country
...	...	...	...	...	190	1.3	3.3	2	6	21.0[26]	2.2	0	0	Equatorial Guinea
						...[28]	...[28]					20	0	Eritrea[27]
2,750.3	15.9	25.1	399.7	116.3	...	3.5	2.3	96	60	2.9	0.9	30	5	Estonia
94	6.7	24.8	1.9	...	1,100	...[29]	...[29]	128	2	9.1	2.6	0	0	Ethiopia[27]
—	...	...	...	...	...	—	[6]							Faroe Islands
2,559	4.5	57.9	401.7	52.5	407	3.6	4.5	34	44	5.5	1.9	0	0	Fiji
8,388	0.6	38.8	1,921.9	79.6	640	32.5	6.3	1,966	388	4.2[12]	2.1	60	10	Finland
6,660	4.7	96.7	804.0	648.5	630	398.9	6.8	44,390	767	7.2	3.4	170	800	France
8,936	27.2	178.7	1,367.3	150.6	...	—	[6]	—				...	...	French Guiana
1,799	0.9	98.9	232.7	...	...	—	[6]							French Polynesia
114	1.4	17.9	2.3	7.5	1,290	4.7	4.0	93	82	9.6[12]	2.9	10	0	Gabon
...	...	...	...	...	3,310	0.8	0.7	14	14	17.4[12]	3.7	0	0	Gambia, The
4,355	...	...	...	...		—	—	—						Gaza Strip
...												0	0	Georgia
7,838	4.1	104.8	2,039.4	215.6	...	358.4	4.4	36,310	448	4.7	1.8	240	700	Germany
864	2.0	95.9	4.7	...	620	7.0	0.4	41	2	4.8[12]	0.8	0	0	Ghana
14,970	—	2,202	...	...	170	—	[6]					...	...	Gibraltar
3,699	2.5	66.4	301.9	83.2	380	168.3	16.0	4,339	411	11.5	5.6	270	5	Greece
9,360	18.1	845.0	1,883.5	...	340	—	[6]							Greenland
2,679	10.0	880.0	153.0	...	230	[25]	[25]	...						Grenada
4,533	10.2	154.8	554.5	146.9	...	—	[6]	—				...	...	Guadeloupe
10,080	7.9	169.3	634.2	333.6	...	—	[6]	—				...	...	Guam
510	27.4	77.1	27.9	58.1	670	44.2	4.3	175	16	15.2	1.4	0	0	Guatemala
...							[6]					0	0	Guernsey
18.4	0.5	0.7	0.7	0.1	1,140	9.7	1.4	50	8	7.0[13]	1.5	0	0	Guinea
129	0.5	8.7	4.0	0.2	...	9.3	8.4	8	7	7.6[12]	3.4	0	0	Guinea-Bissau
1,980	15.6	28.1	434.7	...	190	1.6	2.2	7	9	3.1	1.5	0	0	Guyana
701	...	...	...	...	400	[31]	[31]	30	5	24.8	1.9	50	0	Haiti
...	9.4	7.7	...	3.3	1,040	18.8	3.4	45	9	8.3	1.6	10	0	Honduras
1,482	1.2	102.0	212.3	70.7	221	—	[6]	—						Hong Kong
4,326	4.1	77.7	889.6	62.3	710	64.3	6.3	1,220	118	5.3	1.9	10	10	Hungary
1,550	0.9	64.3	704.8	112.8	940	—	—	—	—	—	—	0	0	Iceland
594	4.6	...	15.6	...	820	1,145.0	1.2	8,233	9	14.5	2.9	140	10	India
113	0.8	5.0	1.8	7.4	1,340	235.2	1.2	2,318	12	7.1	1.4	40	10	Indonesia
76.6	0.5	47.7	...	...	...	513.0	8.2	3,042	48	7.4	2.4	390	90	Iran
197	7.1	34.7	...	...	140	382.0	17.8	9,007[16]	528[16]	50.8[33]	74.9[16]	0	0	Iraq
2,710	0.7	18.0	913.3	67.3	310	12.7	3.5	608	172	3.4	1.3	60	0	Ireland
3,488	...	...	892.4	...	...	—	[6]					...	...	Isle of Man
5,982	1.8	229.4	1,008.1	410.5	210	175.0	31.9	6,588	1,304	19.2	8.6	1,000	470	Israel
4,165	5.8	36.2	...	566.6	680	325.2	5.7	20,360	350	3.9	2.0	110	90	Italy
2,006	25.6	18.2	252.2	13.9	430	3.3	1.3	27	11	3.4[16]	0.7	5	0	Jamaica
1,466	1.0	15.2	187.8	27.9	480	235.5	1.9	45,820	366	4.2[12]	1.0	650	10	Japan
...	...	...	...	...	...	—	[6]					...	...	Jersey
751	2.0	19.1	43.4	28.5	630	98.7	22.8	434	108	21.9	7.5	40	30	Jordan
815	...	...	...	...	...	[36]	[36]	450	26	...	0.9	0	0	Kazakstan
484	6.4	54.1	76.9	9.7	1,500	24.2	0.8	138	5	6.7	2.1	10	0	Kenya
285	12.4	5.5	73.3	...	330									Kiribati
...	...	...	...	...	460	1,054.0	44.1	5,500	238	40.7[35]	26.3	50	30	Korea, North
414	1.4	43.2	11.5	83.5	420	660.0	14.6	13,030	289	17.4	3.7	1,000	40	Korea, South
709	10.2[37]	92.2	66.8	17.1	80	15.3	7.4	3,086	1,838	22.2	11.1	250	40	Kuwait
987	10.4[37]	12.6	482.4	...	...	7.0	1.5	57	12	1.1[13]	0.7	0	0	Kyrgyzstan
...	...	...	...	...	280	37.0	7.4	114	24	21.3[4]	7.4	90	0	Laos
1,606	14.7	28.0	245.3	...	...	8.0	3.2	180	65	4.3	1.3	0	0	Latvia
366	13.2	14.7	65.7	67.3	530	48.9	15.9	310	85	9.7	3.2	40	0	Lebanon
1,885	33.9	170.6	221.5	...	1,130	2.0	0.9	26	13	6.5	1.9	0	0	Lesotho
...	...	...	...	...	1,570	[39]	[39]	30	235	13.3[5]	4.8[5]	0	0	Liberia
907	3.0	4.9	...	...	660	65.0	11.9	1,399	277	28.0[5]	4.3	0	0	Libya
...	...	114.3	614.3	153.6	...	—	[40]					...	...	Liechtenstein
1,199	6.9	9.1	325.2	28.1	660	5.1	1.4	71	18	3.1	0.6	0	0	Lithuania
7,044	1.3	131.1	731.5	275.5	730	0.8	1.9	126	313	3.1	0.8	0	0	Luxembourg
4,432	1.8	76.2	74.8	215.3	...	—	[6]					...	...	Macau
686	...	...	...	...	...	10.4	5.3	...	...	...	...	10	0	Macedonia
231	1.3	23.2	1.9	0.7	2,900	21.0	1.5	24	2	5.2	0.9	0	0	Madagascar
1,094	2.6	100.9	16.7	...	1,670	9.8	0.9	13	1	3.9[13]	1.1	0	0	Malawi
447	2.4	14.9	107.8	14.3	760	114.5	5.6	2,121	110	12.0	4.2	330	50	Malaysia
2,353	1.9	3.3	36.1	...	35,710	—	—	...	...	...	...	...	...	Maldives
33	—	1.1	3.9	—	160	7.4	0.8	34	4	9.4[13]	1.9	0	0	Mali
2,697	14.4	64.7	1,668.7	385.5	230	2.0	5.2	30	82	2.0	0.9[12]	0	0	Malta
2,273	...	...	...	...	400	—	[41]							Marshall Islands
3,924	7.9	156.4	689.0	102.6	...	—	[6]							Martinique
225	1.8	38	2.5	9.1	710	15.7	6.7	36	17	15.9[5]	3.8	0	0	Mauritania
3,219	3.3	13.6	66.0	...	240			11	10	1.4	0.3	0	0	Mauritius
...							[6]							Mayotte
108	7.3	30.2	...	...	...	175.0	1.9	2,246	24	3.4	0.6	80	20	Mexico
...							[41]							Micronesia
						11.9	2.7	92	21	...	0.8	0	80	Moldova
4,277	...	63.4	407.1	126.8		—						...	...	Monaco
453	0.7	41.9	17.0	...	120	21.1	9.0	17	7	9.8	2.4	0	0	Mongolia
366	1.4	6.7	...	...	840	194.0	7.3	1,228	43	13.8	4.1	130	0	Morocco
166	4.2	9.2	45.9	...	...	[42]	[42]	104	6	16.6[13]	8.7	0	0	Mozambique
309	4.1	31.2	0.1	0.1	650	321.0	6.6	2,618	59	32.9[13]	4.0[13]	90	0	Myanmar (Burma)
...	...	...	...	...	...	8.1	4.7	...	...	...	...	10	0	Namibia
...	25.0	400.0	100.0	...	110	—								Nauru
13	2.6	1.5	0.2	...	1,000	43.0	2.1	43	2	5.0	1.1	10	0	Nepal
10,181	24.9	191.8	3,803.0	316.8	510	63.1	4.0	7,137	464	4.4	2.2	220	110	Netherlands, The

Social protection (continued)

country	social security — programs available, 1995 old-age, invalidity, death[a]	sickness and maternity[b]	work injury[c]	unemployment[d]	family allowances[e]	expenditures, 1993 (% of total central govt.)	finances year	receipts total ('000,000 natl. cur.)	insured persons (%)	employers (%)	government (%)	other (%)	expenditures total ('000,000 natl. cur.)	benefits (%)	administration (%)	other (%)
Netherlands Antilles	●	...	●	●	...	31.9[10]	1994	182.2	100.0	—	—	—	174.6	...	...	...
New Caledonia	...	...	...	...	●		1987	15,834.0	...	...	...	...	14,598.0	...	...	...
New Zealand	●	●	...	●	●	37.3	1989	14,266.0	1.0	4.7	92.5	1.8	14,372.3	95.6	2.8	1.6
Nicaragua	●	●	●	...	●	10.3	1989	647,454.8	13.5	49.1	7.6	29.8	452,038.6	82.4	17.6	—
Niger	●	...	●	...	●	1.7[11,26]	1989	5,634.9	9.4	90.6	—	—	3,804.2	62.5	—	37.5
Nigeria	●	...	●			2.5[45]	1989	54.0	50.0	50.0	—	—	22.6	42.5	57.5	—
Northern Mariana Islands	●	...	...													
Norway	●	●	●	●	●	36.7[13]	1989	158,105.0	18.3	31.4	46.6	3.7	131,578.2	98.7	1.3	—
Oman	●					3.6[11]	1994	—	...	...	...	...	60.5[11]	...	...	—
Pakistan	●	●	●			0.2[8]	1989	9,321.4	1.3	8.0	84.3	6.4	8,092.0	97.4	1.2	1.4
Palau	●															
Panama	●	●	●		●	22.1	1989	496.7	31.0	39.5	7.1	22.4	452.8	94.0	4.8	1.2
Papua New Guinea	●		●			0.6	1983	45.0	40.5	32.1	8.0	19.4	9.4	82.3	9.7	8.0
Paraguay	●	●	●		●	16.0	1993	49,272.0[35]	...	...	...	...	249,819.0	...	...	...
Peru	●	●	●			0.2[9]	1989	1,363,280.6	30.2	65.1	4.7	—	1,435,134.1	78.5	21.5	...
Philippines	●	●	●		●	1.8	1989	19,213.6	22.2	32.3	—	45.5	7,878.3	87.3	12.3	—
Poland	●	●	●	●	●		1989	11,572,248.0	2.1	70.2	25.1	2.6	11,452,165.0	98.8	1.2	—
Portugal	●	●	●	●	●	27.3[3,11]	1989	833,442.5	31.3	50.1	13.4	5.2	756,410.8	94.6	4.2	1.2
Puerto Rico	●	●	●	●			1980	...	...	...	...	...	1,041.3	100.0	—	—
Qatar	...				...		1986	80.0	—	—	100.0	—	80.0	100.0	—	—
Réunion	●	●	●	●	●								8,470.4	...	...	...
Romania	●	●	●	...	●	27.6	1989	90,561.2	...	48.9	51.1	—	90,561.2	100.0	...	...
Russia	●	●	●	●	●	27.0[38]										
Rwanda	●		●		●	2.9[33]	1989	2,350.0	23.9	39.8	—	36.3	965.8	60.8	39.2	—
St. Kitts and Nevis	●	●	●			9.4[11,46]	1989	14.3	...	...	...	...	7.9	...	...	...
St. Lucia	●	●	●				1986	14.6	28.6	28.6	—	42.8	3.4	61.4	38.6	—
St. Vincent and the Grenadines	●	●	●			4.3	1989	...								
San Marino	●	●	...	●	●		1983	51,673.0	12.0	48.7	36.1	3.2	46,179.0	95.7	3.7	0.6
São Tomé and Príncipe	●	●	●				1986	46.4	37.7	56.3	—	6.0	23.7	100.0	—	—
Saudi Arabia	●		●				1989	1,761.4	26.8	73.2	—	—	4,292.9	100.0	—	—
Senegal	●	●	●		●	2.6[16]	1989	17,202.0	—	47.6	51.4	1.0	15,371.0	84.6	11.1	4.3
Seychelles	●	●	●			5.3[17]	1983	69.1	30.1	60.2	—	9.7	42.7	69.6	4.9	25.5
Sierra Leone	●	●				1.9[3]	1990	...	...	...	...	...	153.00	100.0	—	—
Singapore	●		●			3.4	1989	7,531.9	49.1	35.3	0.1	15.6	5,045.8	78.0	0.6	21.4
Slovakia	●	●	●				1992	28,013	13.9	85.3	...	0.8	13,823	...	...	...
Slovenia	●	●	●	●	●											
Solomon Islands	●		●			0.6[35]	1989	20.9	27.8	41.1	—	31.1	17.4	89.7	10.3	...
Somalia	●		●			1.7[11,45]											
South Africa	●	●	●				1994	1,873.0	—	100.0	...	...	2,260.0	...	...	...
Spain	●	●	●	●	●	37.7[13]	1989	8,320,972.0	15.9	53.9	27.9	2.3	8,038,090.0	94.3	2.6	3.1
Sri Lanka	●	●				15.8[11]	1989	15,399.9	22.0	24.4	29.1	24.5	5,819.0	98.5	1.3	0.2
Sudan, The	●	●	●			0.45	1989	62.0	24.9	0.5	—	74.6	14.7	37.5	62.5	—
Suriname	●		●		●	6.0[8]	1989	73.0	24.7	75.3	—	—	70.6	100.0	—	—
Swaziland	●	...	...	...	●	0.4[11]	1986	10.7	31.4	31.4	—	37.2	3.9	45.8	54.2	—
Sweden	●	●	●	●	●	43.2	1989	446,909.7	2.8	37.9	50.8	8.5	439,997.3	93.7	3.3	3.0
Switzerland	●	●	●	●	●	49.9[4]	1989	45,800.1	45.6	22.6	25.9	5.9	41,745.7	91.5	3.0	5.5
Syria	●	●	●			1.9	1989	3,147.9	30.4	60.9	—	5.6	1,455.9	95.7	4.2	0.1
Taiwan	●	●				13.8[3]										
Tajikistan	●	●														
Tanzania	●	●	●			0.5[14]	1989	3,275.8	25.9	25.9	—	48.2	2,780.7	5.8	14.1	80.1
Thailand	...	●	●	●		3.8[13]	1989	654.0	—	60.2	—	39.8	260.0	88.2	11.8	—
Togo	●	●	●		●	6.5[46]	1989	10,162.0	8.1	61.5	—	30.4	5,844.0	77.5	22.5	—
Tonga	...	...			...	0.8[16]										
Trinidad and Tobago	●	●	●			5.3[24]	1989	584.9	12.0	24.2	39.7	24.2	438.4	85.6	11.1	3.3
Tunisia	●	●	●		●	12.2[13]	1989	325.3	36.9	63.1	—	—	358.3	90.0[17]	6.1[17]	3.9[17]
Turkey	●	●	●			2.9	1989	12,075,809.0	28.5	32.9	22.8	15.8	10,241,427.0	97.2	2.2	0.6
Turkmenistan	...															
Tuvalu	...						1981	...	...	...	...	...	0.1	67.6	32.4	—
Uganda	●	●				2.1[8]	1989	265.9	32.1	64.3	1.1	2.5	145.0	0.3	76.8	22.9
Ukraine	●	●	●	●	●		1989	20,350.0	—	—	—	—	20,350.0	100.0	—	—
United Arab Emirates	...	...	...	...	...	3.4[11]	1989	182.2	17.3	6.2	0.5	76.0	182.2	100.0	—	...
United Kingdom	●	●	●	●	●	29.6[11]	1989	92,157.0	18.1	24.9	52.9	4.1	88,294.0	93.8	3.3	2.9
United States	●	●	●	●		22.5	1989	804,909.0	25.5	33.9	28.8	11.8	627,653.0	95.5	3.3	1.2
Uruguay	●	●	●	●	●	62.0[11]	1989	535,507.0	31.4	37.3	26.0	5.3	548,591.0	93.6	5.4	1.0
Uzbekistan	●	●	●													
Vanuatu	●		●			0.9[8]							—	...	...	...
Venezuela	●	●	●	●	●	6.9[8]	1986	7,457.6	21.3	40.7	12.7	25.3	6,355.7	86.1	14.9	—
Vietnam	●	●														
Virgin Islands (U.S.)	●	●	●	●												
West Bank																
Western Sahara																
Western Samoa	●	●	●			—							...	...	...	...
Yemen	●	...	●	...												
Yugoslavia	●	●	●	●	●	6.0[53]	1986[53]	2,777,651.0	63.3	32.2	3.4	1.1	2,732,679.0	90.3	1.9	7.8
Zaire	●	●	●			1.1	1986	1,238.3	28.6	60.2	—	11.2	1,044.2	27.9	72.1	—
Zambia	●		●			2.2	1986	179.2	28.4	28.4	—	43.2	67.7	40.6	59.4	—
Zimbabwe	●		●			2.5[5]	1983	167.0	25.9	7.6	64.2	2.3	112.2	93.7	6.2	0.1

[1]Rural areas only. [2]The bulk of the national armed forces disintegrated after the fall of the central government in April 1992, with only the northern corps retaining its integrity. [3]1990. [4]1984. [5]1989. [6]Political dependency; defense is the responsibility of the administering country. [7]Includes civilian militia. [8]1986. [9]1983. [10]Netherlands Antilles includes Aruba. [11]Includes welfare. [12]1993. [13]1992. [14]1985. [15]1979. [16]1991. [17]1977. [18]1976. [19]Local officers only. [20]Military defense is the responsibility of France. [21]1971. [22]Republic of Cyprus only. [23]Data refer to former Czechoslovakia, except for military manpower and expenditure. [24]1981. [25]Paramilitary unit of country participating in the U.S.-sponsored Regional Security System, a defense pact among eastern Caribbean states. [26]1980. [27]Ethiopia includes Eritrea except in arms trade. [28]Demobilization of some Eritrean forces began in late 1993. Estimated strength of these forces is currently about 55,000. [29]Following the declaration of independence by Eritrea in April 1993, estimated strength of Ethiopian forces was some 120,000. [30]Former West Germany. [31]In 1994 the military government of Haiti was replaced by a

crime and law enforcement (latest) — offenses reported to the police per 100,000 population; military protection — manpower, 1996[g]; expenditure, 1994; arms trade, 1994 ('000,000 U.S.$)

offenses total	personal murder	personal assault	property burglary	property automobile theft	population per police officer[f]	manpower total ('000)	manpower per 1,000 population	expenditure total '000,000	per capita	% of central government expenditure	% of GDP or GNP	arms imports	arms exports	country
4,750[43]	...	350	...	...	330	—	[6]	—	—	—	—	...	...	Netherlands Antilles
...	...	...	...	...		—	[6]	—	—	—	—	...	...	New Caledonia
14,496	4.0	313.6	2,942.3	905.4	630	9.9	2.7	613	181	3.5	1.3	10	0	New Zealand
772	18.3	140.0	110.7	...	907[7]	17.0	4.0	34	8	5.7	2.9	0	0	Nicaragua
32	0.2	2.5	1.0	0.1	2,350[44]	5.3	0.6	14	2	5.5[12]	0.9	0	0	Niger
312	...	...	...	...	1,140	77.1	0.7	324	3	5.0	0.8	0	0	Nigeria
245	3.8	92.6	73.7	20.8		—	[6]	—	—	—	—	...	...	Northern Mariana Islands
5,466	2.6	53.8	89.0	474.1	660	30.0	6.8	3,382	784	6.1	3.1	90	50	Norway
162	...	...	...	...	430	43.5	19.3	1,818	888	36.4	18.1	50	0	Oman
221	5.6	0.1	9.1	4.1	720	587.0	4.1	3,068	24	23.0	6.0	260	5	Pakistan
...	...	...	323.0	...		—	[41]	—	—	—	—	0	0	Palau
703	6.1	18.9	...	125.1	180	11.8	4.4	—	—	—	—	0	0	Panama
766	8.6	66.7	63	22.0	720	3.7	0.8	54	13	3.3	1.1	0	0	Papua New Guinea
816	3.0	27.8	105.1	93.4	310	20.2	4.1	94	18	10.7[12]	1.2	10	0	Paraguay
1,178	9.3	104.3	87.0	22.7	730	125.0	5.2	797	34	13.3	1.6	20	0	Peru
230	30.1	41.8	...	1.2	1,160	107.5	1.5	1,272	18	10.6	1.9	0	0	Philippines
2,020	3.0	56.5	764.2	...	370	248.5	6.4	4,945	128	5.6	2.4	5	30	Poland
900	4.0	6.3	52.8	178.8	660	54.2	5.5	2,174	207	5.3	2.5	320	100	Portugal
3,182	26.8	174.8	853.0	482.9	380	—	[6]	—	—	—	—	0	0	Puerto Rico
301	2.4	9.7	...	4.2		11.9	20.2	302	582	9.2[12]	3.9	0	130	Qatar
2,097	7.8	123.1	181.3	137.9	220	—	[6]	—	—	—	—	...	...	Réunion
636	3.6	3.7	6.8	6.0		228.4	10.1	1,743	75	34.1	2.6	0	40	Romania
1,857	15.5[37]	50.4	860.1	23.5		1,270.0	8.6	96,800	647	39.6	12.4	0	0	Russia
346	15.6	66.6	4.0	...	4,650	33.0	4.8	114	14	23.3[12]	7.6	80	0	Rwanda
15,468	...	...	...	...	300	[25]	[25]	...	...	...	...	...	...	St. Kitts and Nevis
4,386	17.0	1,193.0	778.0	...	430	[25]	[25]	...	...	...	...	...	...	St. Lucia
3,977	10.3	986.9	...	...	250	[25]	[25]	...	...	...	...	...	...	St. Vincent and the Grenadines
...	4.1	...	...	...		...	...	...	...	...	...	...	...	San Marino
558	4.0	...	...	...	400	...	...	1[26]	7[26]	2.5[26]	1.6[26]	0	0	São Tomé and Príncipe
114	0.6	19.2	...	16.9	280	105.5	5.7	17,200	953	41.5[12]	14.2	5,200	10	Saudi Arabia
295	1.8	61.1	6.7	...	730	13.4	1.6	60	7	13.7[13]	1.6	5	0	Senegal
5,267	5.7	741.9	1,640.7	...	120	0.3	3.9	8[4]	124[4]	7.4[4]	5.6[4]	...	...	Seychelles
...	...	...	...	...	600	14.2	3.1	36	8	20.1	4.9	0	0	Sierra Leone
1,560	1.5	6.7	107.8	15.2	230	53.9	17.7	3,064	1,072	23.4	4.5	270	20	Singapore
1,982	2.2	84.2	...	...		42.6	7.9	866	160	6.3	2.4	0	10	Slovakia
2,739	5.2	21.3	479.8	21.8		9.6	4.9	190	93	3.7[12]	1.2	10	5	Slovenia
...	...	...	...	...	620	—	—	...	...	...	...	0	0	Solomon Islands
144	1.5	8.0	31.2	...	540	[47]	[47]	8[12]	1[12]	30.0[8]	0.9[12]	0	0	Somalia
...	...	...	...	...	870	137.9	3.3	2,899	66	7.4	2.4	20	50	South Africa
2,402	2.3	23.8	1,096.8	285.3	580	206.8	5.3	7,425	189	5.5	1.6	525	280	Spain
280	8.2	10.8	54.7	...	860	115.3	6.3	525	29	15.5	4.5	100	0	Sri Lanka
1,565	4.2	40.5	0.4	3.4	740	89.0	2.9	882[13]	32[13]	175.4[16]	17.1[13]	0	0	Sudan, The
17,819	7.6	1,824.4	...	...		1.8	4.1	47	112	5.3[3]	3.9	0	0	Suriname
4,955.3	71.6	630.6	934.9	...	610	—	—	16	17	4.1	1.7	0	0	Swaziland
13,750	8.4	42.5	1,801.5	748.0	330	62.6	7.1	5,311	605	5.3	2.8	30	60	Sweden
5,457	2.6	53.6	1,018.0	1,520[48]	640	3.3	0.5	4,981	708	19.4[16]	1.9	40	110	Switzerland
89	1.4	7.0	21.2	2.9	1,970	421.0	28.4	4,526[16]	342[16]	60.3[16]	17.9[16]	10	0	Syria
574	7.1	...	...	98.9	720	376.0	17.5	11,540	542	32.4[12]	4.8	10	0	Taiwan
317	2.5	4.6	...	...		5.2	0.9	68	11	...	1.0	10	0	Tajikistan
1,250	6.4	0.5	97.3	0.9	1,330	34.6	1.2	69	2	7.2	3.3	10	0	Tanzania
356	8.9	41.9	11.7	17.0	530	254.0	4.2	3,777	63	15.7	2.7	360	0	Thailand
11	...	...	...	...	1,970	7.0	1.6	25	6	11.7[16]	2.7	0	0	Togo
2,100	...	...	...	...	330	—	[49]	—	—	—	—	0	0	Tonga
3,170	8.7	177.4	633.9	...	280	2.1	1.7	76	60	4.0	1.7	0	0	Trinidad and Tobago
1,240	2.1	134.0	143.6	11.1	340	35.0	3.9	543	62	6.2[12]	3.6	50	0	Tunisia
209	3.2	21.3	...	11.1	1,570	639.0	10.0	5,293	85	17.4	4.1	950	10	Turkey
...	...	...	...	...		[50]	[50]	65	16	3.7[13]	0.5	0	0	Turkmenistan
...	...	...	...	...	290	...	...	...	...	...	...	...	...	Tuvalu
140	9.5	15.6	15.1	5.3	1,090	50.0	2.6	66	3	7.6	1.5	0	0	Uganda
781	5.6	24.5	...	36.0		400.8	7.8	946	18	...	0.6	0	60	Ukraine
1,496	1.1	1.7	10.5	...	140	64.5	25.8	1,907	811[12]	50.1[12]	5.7[12]	200	0	United Arab Emirates
10,403[51]	2.5[51]	362.1[51]	2,404.4[51]	1,147.3[51]	420	226.0	3.8	34,050	586	8.0	3.3	200	3,400	United Kingdom
5,374	9.0	430.2	1,041.8	591.2	318	1,483.8	5.6	288,100	1,105	18.8	4.3	1,100	12,400	United States
6,806	4.1	169.6	56.9	...	170	25.6	8.0	412	129	7.3	2.6	0	0	Uruguay
420	5.1	15.6	...	...		29.0	1.2	375	17	...	0.7	20	20	Uzbekistan
...	...	...	...	...	450	—	—	—	—	—	—	...	...	Vanuatu
1,221	16.6	175.2	330.1	212.7	320	79.0	3.5	747	36	5.6	1.3	60	0	Venezuela
...	...	...	...	...		572.0	7.5	435	6	9.7	2.2	80	0	Vietnam
10,441	22.3	1,943.2	3,183.7	954	240	—	[6]	—	—	—	—	...	...	Virgin Islands (U.S.)
2,226	...	...	...	...		—	—	...	...	...	...	...	...	West Bank
...	...	...	...	...		—	[6]	—	—	—	—	...	...	Western Sahara
...	...	...	...	...		—	[49]	—	—	—	—	...	...	Western Samoa
170[52]	...	...	...	...	1,940	42.0	4.0	2,082	147	14.5	14.1	230	0	Yemen
1,135[53]	5.4[53]	35.5[53]	...	...	140[53]	113.9	10.9	3,608[16,53]	158[16,53]	55.0[3,53]	3.9[16,53]	0	5	Yugoslavia
...	...	...	...	...	910	49.1	1.1	117	3	44.2	2.1	0	0	Zaire
666	9.8	9.5	153.5	9.6	540	21.6	2.2	39	4	4.8	1.2	5	0	Zambia
4,653	17.4	203.3	418.7	23.6	750	43.0	3.7	188	17	15.0[12]	3.7	5	10	Zimbabwe

civilian administration. Both the armed forces and police have been disbanded. [32]Coverage is through tax system. [33]1982. [34]1988–89. [35]1988. [36]Russian-controlled forces in Kazakstan, estimated at about 40,000. [37]Includes attempted murders. [38]1994. [39]As a result of civil war, the armed forces of Liberia, with a combat strength of about 2,000 to 3,000, are now confined to Monrovia, the capital. [40]Military defense is the responsibility of Switzerland. [41]Military defense is the responsibility of the United States. [42]Under the terms of the 1992 peace accord, government and Renamo forces are to merge to form a new National Army some 30,000 strong. [43]Curaçao only. [44]Includes paramilitary forces. [45]1978. [46]1987. [47]Following the 1991 revolution, no national armed forces have yet been formed. [48]Includes bicycles and motorcycles. [49]Military defense is the responsibility of New Zealand. [50]Forces under joint Turkmenistan-Russian control. [51]England and Wales. [52]Former Yemen Arab Republic. [53]Data refer to Yugoslavia as constituted prior to 1991.

Education

This table presents international data on education analyzed to provide maximum comparability among the different educational systems in use among the nations of the world. The principal data are, naturally, numbers of schools, teachers, and students, arranged by four principal levels of education—the first (primary); general second level (secondary); vocational second level; and third level (higher). Whenever possible, data referring to preprimary education programs have been excluded from this compilation. The ratio of students to teachers is calculated for each level. These data are supplemented at each level by a figure for enrollment ratio, an indicator of each country's achieved capability to educate the total number of children potentially educable in the age group usually represented by that level. At the first and second levels this is given as a net enrollment ratio and at the third level as a gross enrollment ratio. Two additional comparative measures are given at the third level: students per 100,000 population and proportion (percentage) of adults age 25 and over who have achieved some level of higher or postsecondary education. Data in this last group are confined as far as possible to those who have completed their educations and are no longer in school. No enrollment ratio is provided for vocational training at the second level because of the great variation worldwide in the academic level at which vocational training takes place, in the need of countries to encourage or direct students into vocational programs (to support national development), and, most particularly, in the age range of students who normally constitute a national vocational system (some will be as young as 14, having just completed a primary cycle; others will be much older).

At each level of education, differences in national statistical practice, in national educational structure, public-private institutional mix, training and deployment of teachers, and timing of cycles of enrollment or completion of particular grades or standards all contribute to the problems of comparability among national educational systems.

Reporting the number of schools in a country is not simply a matter of counting permanent red-brick buildings with classrooms in them. Often the resources of a less developed country are such that temporary or outdoor facilities are all that can be afforded, while in a developed but sparsely settled country students might have to travel 80 km (50 mi) a day to find a classroom with 20 students of the same age, leading to the institution of measures such as traveling teachers, radio or televisual instruction at home under the supervision of parents, or similar systems. According to UNESCO definitions, therefore, a "school" is defined only as "a body of students . . . organized to receive instruction."

Such difficulties also limit the comparability of statistics on numbers of teachers, with the further complications that many at any level must work part-time, or that the institutions in which they work may perform a mixture of functions that do not break down into the tidy categories required by a table of this sort. In certain countries teacher training is confined to higher education, in others as a vocational form of secondary training, and so on. For purposes of this table, teacher training at the secondary level has been treated as vocational education. At the higher level, teacher training is classified as one more specialization in higher education itself.

The number of students may conceal great variation in what each country defines as a particular educational "level." Many countries do, indeed, have a primary system composed of grades 1 through 6 (or 1 through 8) that passes students on to some kind of postprimary education. But the age of intake, the ability of parents to send their children or to permit

Education

country	year	first level (primary)					general second level (secondary)					vocational second level[a]	
		schools	teachers[c]	students[d]	student/teacher ratio	net enrollment ratio[b]	schools	teachers[c]	students[d]	student/teacher ratio	net enrollment ratio[b]	schools	teachers[c]
Afghanistan	1993	1,753	16,160	786,532	48.7	29	819[1]	5,715[1]	271,000[1]	47.4[1]	...	33[1]	556[1]
Albania	1993	1,777	32,098	535,713	16.7	...	47[3]	4,149	73,259	17.7	...	466[3]	7,390[3]
Algeria	1993	13,970	153,793	4,436,363	28.8	94	3,402[1]	130,413	2,255,276	17.3	55	4	5,317
American Samoa	1991	30	524	7,884	15.0	...	7[1]	245	3,483	14.2	...	1	21
Andorra	1994	12	...	5,405	...	...	6	...	1,638	...	...	...	...
Angola	1991	...	31,062	990,155	31.9	...	...	5,138[3]	166,812	30.2[3]	...	...	566[3]
Antigua and Barbuda	1995	43[5]	439	11,506	26.2	...	12[5]	277	4,294	15.5	...	1	16
Argentina	1995	24,511[5]	286,885	5,126,307	17.9	95	7,224[1,4]	233,564[4]	2,238,091[4]	9.6[4]	59	4	4
Armenia	1994	1,374[6]	54,000[5,6]	574,500[6]	11.0[5,6]	...	6	6	6	6	...	69	...
Aruba	1993	32	331	7,139	21.6	...	10	183	3,247	17.7	...	14	225
Australia	1994	9,679[6]	200,074[6]	3,099,380[6]	15.5[6]	98	6	6	6	6	81	...	...
Austria	1995	3,384	31,126	381,676	12.3	90	1,899	57,740	469,915	8.1	91	1,028	24,956
Azerbaijan	1995	4,500[6]	139,000[5,6]	1,462,000[6]	9.9[5,6]	...	6	6	6	6	...	78	...
Bahamas, The	1994	115	1,581	33,343	21.1	95	...	1,775	28,363	16.0	87	...	823
Bahrain	1994	118	3,386	70,513	20.8	100	...	2,343	47,417	20.2	85	...	823
Bangladesh	1993	50,898	214,779	14,202,000	66.1	70	11,382	129,655	4,673,000	36.0	17	153	1,856
Barbados	1992	106	1,553	26,662	17.2	78	33[3]	1,406[3]	21,259[3]	15.1[3]	75	...	...
Belarus	1994	4,900[6]	122,700[6]	1,628,500[6]	13.3[6]	...	6	6	6	6	...	147	...
Belgium	1994	4,453	72,589[8,9]	73,527	...	96	1,950	110,599[5]	796,914	...	88	304[8]	...
Belize	1995	237	1,939	50,291	25.9	96	30	740	10,150	13.7	36	...	...
Benin	1994	2,889	12,343	602,069	48.8	53	145	2,384	97,480	40.9	...	14	283
Bermuda	1994	24[3]	288	5,837	20.3	...	12[3]	235	3,553	15.1	...	...	...
Bhutan	1990	235[8]	1,859[8]	56,773[8]	30.5[8]	...	31	662	15,984	24.1	...	8	149
Bolivia	1991	...	51,763	1,278,775	24.7	91	...	12,434[4]	219,232[4]	17.6[4]	29	...	4
Bosnia and Herzegovina	1991	2,205	23,369	539,875	23.1	...	238	9,030	172,063	19.1	...	...	...
Botswana	1994	781	9,552	301,370	31.6	97	199	5,192	99,560	19.2	42	45	856
Brazil	1993	195,544	1,346,285	30,520,748	22.7	90	12,603	275,845	4,208,766	15.3	19	...	...
Brunei	1993	158	2,646	41,134	15.5	89	235	1,948	26,199	13.4	61	6[5]	389
Bulgaria	1995	3,359[6]	70,487[6]	980,491[6]	13.9[6]	82	6	6	6	6	57	522	19,019
Burkina Faso	1993	2,741	9,412	562,644	59.7	31	173[5]	2,419[5]	107,204	25.1[5]	7	22[5]	493
Burundi	1993	1,418	10,400	651,086	62.6	...	113[10]	2,562	55,713	21.7	5	...	...
Cambodia	1993	4,539	42,405	1,465,958	34.6	...	440	19,540	239,363	12.2	...	65	2,618
Cameroon	1994	6,763	34,146	1,823,556	53.4	76	...	19,649	546,456	27.8	...	...	6,267[3]
Canada	1994	16,231[6]	300,797[6]	5,360,900[6]	17.8[6]	98	6	6	6	6	90	...	...
Cape Verde	1990	367	2,028	67,761	33.4	100	...	238	7,114	29.9	12	...	56[11]
Central African Republic	1991	930	4,004	308,409	77.0	58	46[4]	845[4]	46,989[4]	55.6[4]	...	4	4
Chad	1991	2,544	9,238	591,417	64.0	...	66[1]	2,062	72,641	35.2	...	...	285[1]
Chile	1993	8,338[5]	78,813	2,083,775	26.4	87	...	...	391,457	...	53	...	...
China	1994	857,245	6,437,000	154,529,000	23.9	96	82,358	3,234,000	49,817,000	15.4	...	14,204	524,000
Colombia	1993	44,693	166,123	4,599,132	27.7	85	...	134,161[4]	2,696,007[4]	20.1[4]	41	...	4
Comoros	1994	275	1,737[12]	77,837	43.0[12]	51	...	613[5]	17,474	25.5[5]	...	...	...
Congo	1993	1,623	6,891	505,925	73.4	...	...	6,048	192,229	31.8	...	...	1,813
Costa Rica	1994	3,472	...	497,845	...	91	257	...	196,553	...	41	...	...
Côte d'Ivoire	1993	7,249	39,691	1,553,540	39.1	52	...	9,644	445,505	46.2	...	...	...
Croatia	1995	1,928	24,194	431,795	17.8	80	482	15,269	196,740	12.9	66	3	79
Cuba	1994	9,440	76,193	963,459	12.9	100	2,175[3]	53,423	459,140	8.6	58	618[3]	31,671
Cyprus[13]	1995	383	3,498	64,884	18.5	97	107	3,832	53,738	14.0	91	11	509
Czech Republic	1994	4,199	63,767	1,061,396	16.6	...	324	8,456	122,171	14.4	...	821	16,854
Denmark	1994	2,557	58,500	606,268	10.4	98	153	11,000	75,299	6.8	87	242	12,000
Djibouti	1993	56	787	33,005	41.9	30	26[4,10]	362[4,10]	9,363[4,10]	28.6[4,10]	11	4	4

them to finish that level, or the need to withdraw the children seasonally for agricultural work all make even a simple enrollment figure difficult to assess in isolation. All of these difficulties are compounded when a country has instruction in more than one language or when its educational establishment is so small that higher, sometimes even secondary, education cannot take place within the country. Enrollment figures in this table may, therefore, include students enrolled outside the country.

Student-teacher ratio, however, usually provides a good measure of the ratio of trained educators to the enrolled educable. In general, at each level of education both students and teachers have been counted on the basis of full-time enrollment or employment, or full-time equivalent when country statistics permit. At the primary and secondary levels, net enrollment ratio is the ratio of the number of children within the usual age group for a particular level who are actually enrolled to the total number of children in that age group ($\times$ 100). This ratio is usually less than (occasionally, equal to) 100 and is the most accurate measure of the completeness of enrollment at that particular level. It is not always, however, the best indication of utilization of teaching staff and facilities. Utilization, provided here for higher education only, is best seen in a gross enrollment ratio, which compares total enrollment (of all ages) to the population within the normal age limits for that level. For a country with substantial adult literacy or general educational programs, the difference may be striking: typically, for a less developed country, even one with a good net enrollment ratio of 90 to 95, the gross enrollment ratio may be 20%, 25%, even 30% higher, indicating the heavy use made by the country of facilities and teachers at that level.

Literacy data provided here have been compiled as far as possible from data for the population age 15 and over for the best comparability internationally. Standards as to what constitutes literacy may also differ markedly; sometimes completion of a certain number of years of school is taken to constitute literacy; elsewhere it may mean only the ability to read or write at a minimal level testable by a census taker; in other countries studies have been undertaken to distinguish among degrees of functional literacy. When a country reports an official 100% (or near) literacy rate, it should usually be viewed with caution, as separate studies of "functional" literacy for such a country may indicate 10%, 20%, or even higher rates of inability to read, or write, effectively. Substantial use has been made of UNESCO literacy estimates, both for some of the least developed countries (where the statistical base is poorest) and for some of the most fully developed, where literacy is no longer perceived as a problem, thus no longer in need of monitoring.

Finally, the data provided for public expenditure on education are complete in that they include all levels of public expenditure (national, state, local) but are incomplete for certain countries in that they do not include data for private expenditure; in some countries this fraction of the educational establishment may be of significant size. Occasionally data for external aid to education may be included in addition to domestic expenditure.

The following notes further define the column headings:
a. Usually includes teacher training at the second level.
b. Latest.
c. Full-time.
d. Full-time; may include students registered in foreign schools.

third level (higher)									literacy[b]				public expenditure on education (percent of GNP)[b]	country
students[d]	student/ teacher ratio	institutions	teachers[c]	students[d]	student/ teacher ratio	gross enroll- ment ratio[b]	students per 100,000 popula- tion[b]	percent of population age 25 and over with post- secondary education[b]	over age	total (%)	male (%)	female (%)		
8,537[1]	15.4[1]	5[1,2]	444[3]	9,367[3]	21.1[3]	1.7	162	...	15	31.5	47.2	15.0	...	Afghanistan
138,000[3]	18.7[3]	8[3]	1,774	30,185	17.0	9.5	891	...	15	100.0	100.0	100.0	...	Albania
49,922	9.4	...	14,379	243,397	16.9	11.4	1,160	...	15	61.6	73.9	49.0	5.7	Algeria
160	7.6	2	...	...	...	...	...	...	15	95.9	95.6	96.3	...	American Samoa
...	...	—	—	—	—	...	...	...	15	100.0	100.0	100.0	...	Andorra
19,687	...	1	439	6,534	14.9	0.7	66	...	15	41.7	55.6	28.5	...	Angola
46	2.9	...	...	...	...	...	...	...	15	90.0	...	...	...	Antigua and Barbuda
4	4	...	118,695	926,793	7.8	40.5	3,323	12.0	15	96.2	96.2	96.2	3.3	Argentina
25,200	...	14	...	46,500	...	48.9	3,711	...	15	98.8	99.4	98.1	7.3	Armenia
2,594	11.5	1	16	88	5.5	...	...	...	15	95.0	...	...	...	Aruba
985,942[5]	...	95[1]	25,916[1]	604,200	...	41.9	3,267	...	15	99.5	...	...	5.5	Australia
308,091	12.3	44	14,322	228,147	15.9	43.2	2,893	...	15	100.0	100.0	100.0	5.8	Austria
30,400	...	23	...	89,100	...	25.7	2,323	...	15	97.3	98.9	95.9	6.5	Azerbaijan
...	...	17,8	300[7,8]	3,201[7,8]	10.7[7,8]	...	1,945	13.5	15	98.2	98.5	98.0	3.9	Bahamas, The
6,776	8.2	...	582[8]	7,763[8]	13.3[8]	20.1	1,493	10.3	15	85.2	89.1	79.4	5.0	Bahrain
30,275	16.3	1,031	26,263	912,985	34.8	3.8	382	...	15	38.1	49.4	26.1	2.3	Bangladesh
...	...	1[3]	153[3]	1,314[3]	8.6[3]	17.6	1,647	...	15	97.4	98.0	96.8	7.5	Barbados
126,400	...	38	16,900	178,016	10.5	44.1	3,062	...	15	97.9	99.4	96.6	5.3	Belarus
155,192[8]	...	21[8]	...	123,320[8]	...	40.2	2,772	...	...	100.0	100.0	100.0	5.1	Belgium
...	...	4	...	1,216	...	—	...	6.6	14	70.3	70.3	70.3	5.7	Belize
4,873	17.2	16	602	9,964	16.5	2.7	235	...	15	37.0	48.7	25.8	...	Benin
...	...	1	56[3]	494	8.9[3]	...	...	18.4	15	96.9	96.7	97.0	...	Bermuda
1,822	12.2	2	57	519	9.1	...	18	...	15	42.2	56.2	28.1	3.4	Bhutan
4	4	...	4,261[5]	109,503[5]	25.7[5]	22.6	2,214	9.9	15	83.1	90.5	76.0	2.7	Bolivia
...	...	44	2,801	37,541	13.4	...	...	...	10	85.5	96.5	76.7	...	Bosnia and Herzegovina
9,570	11.2	1	475	4,533	9.5	3.0	294	...	15	69.8	80.5	59.9	8.2	Botswana
...	...	873	150,823	1,594,668	10.6	11.5	1,080	...	15	83.3	83.3	83.2	4.6	Brazil
2,011	5.2	4[5]	289[5]	1,372[5]	4.7[5]	6.0	516	...	15	88.2	92.6	83.4	4.6	Brunei
216,595	11.3	88	24,274	221,207	9.1	32.2	2,324	15.0	15	97.9	98.7	97.1	5.8	Bulgaria
8,329	16.9	9[5]	437[5]	7,387[5]	16.9[5]	0.7	60	...	15	19.2	29.5	9.2	1.6	Burkina Faso
...	...	8	556	4,256	7.6	0.8	73	...	15	35.3	49.3	22.5	3.7	Burundi
15,537	5.9	9	268	22,182	82.8	...	158	...	15	74.3	85.0	65.0	...	Cambodia
90,543[10]	14.8[3]	...	1,086[10]	33,177[10]	30.5[10]	3.2	288	...	15	63.4	75.0	52.1	3.0	Cameroon
...	...	272	64,100	921,300	14.4	102.9	6,980	21.4	15	96.6	...	...	7.6	Canada
752	...	...	...	...	...	...	...	...	15	71.6	81.4	63.8	4.4	Cape Verde
4	4	1[2]	139[2]	3,783[2]	27.2[2]	1.7	150	...	15	60.0	68.5	52.4	2.8	Central African Republic
3,819[1]	15.1[1]	4[1]	591	2,969[1]	50.3[1]	1.2	103	...	15	48.1	62.1	34.7	2.6	Chad
261,358	...	...	18,084[2]	315,653	...	26.7	2,369	...	15	95.2	95.4	95.0	2.7	Chile
7,254,000	13.8	1,080	396,000	2,799,000	7.1	3.8	377	2.0	15	81.5	89.9	72.7	1.9	China
4	4	...	54,164[5]	510,649[5]	9.4[5]	15.5	1,554	...	15	91.3	91.2	91.4	3.5	Colombia
163	...	...	...	400	...	0.5	47	...	15	57.3	64.2	50.4	4.2	Comoros
20,621	11.4	...	656[5]	13,806[5]	21.0[5]	...	582	...	15	74.9	83.1	67.2	8.6	Congo
...	...	25	...	76,964	...	30.3	2,767	...	15	94.8	94.7	95.0	4.6	Costa Rica
...	...	...	...	...	...	3.1	204	...	15	40.1	49.9	30.0	...	Côte d'Ivoire
2,660	33.7	61	5,814	77,525	13.3	27.2	1,826	...	15	96.7	98.8	94.8	...	Croatia
226,660	8.4	35[3]	25,264[8]	198,474[8]	7.9[8]	18.1	1,840	...	15	95.7	96.2	95.3	6.6	Cuba
4,066	8.0	32	648	7,765	12.0	15.0	927	14.0[14]	15	95.2	97.8	92.8	4.3	Cyprus[13]
219,249	13.0	23	13,463	127,137	9.4	15.5	1,257	8.5	15	100.0	100.0	100.0	5.8	Czech Republic
162,637	13.6	158	8,000	156,264	19.5	40.9	3,045	19.6	...	100.0	100.0	100.0	7.4	Denmark
4	4	1[10]	13[10]	108[10]	8.3[10]	0.1	10	...	15	46.2	60.3	32.7	3.8	Djibouti

Education (continued)

country	year	first level (primary) schools	teachers[c]	students[d]	student/ teacher ratio	net enrollment ratio[b]	general second level (secondary) schools	teachers[c]	students[d]	student/ teacher ratio	net enrollment ratio[b]	vocational second level[a] schools	teachers[c]
Dominica	1994	64	674[6]	12,822	28.6[6]	...	13	6	6,431	6	...	...	...
Dominican Republic	1994	6,207	39,464	1,336,211	33.9	81	...	11,605	232,999	20.1	24	...	...
Ecuador	1993	...	63,347	1,986,753	31.4	...	...	62,630[4]	813,557[4]	13.0[4]	...	...	4
Egypt	1994	17,799	288,939	7,732,308	26.8	89	...	209,518	4,434,060	21.2	65	1,351[8]	92,297[8]
El Salvador	1993	3,961	26,259[12]	1,042,256	39.7[12]	70	...	...	29,527	...	15	...	...
Equatorial Guinea	1988	703	1,065	61,009	57.3	...	9	319	9,226	28.9	...	1	52
Eritrea	1994	491	5,272	207,099	39.3	26	86[8]	1,933	65,537	32.9	11	4[8]	102
Estonia	1995	741[6]	15,453[6]	218,600[6]	14.1[6]	79	6	6	6	6	73	84	1,585
Ethiopia	1992	8,120	69,743	1,855,894	26.6	...	...	21,970	712,489	32.4	...	...	602
Faroe Islands	1993	62[15]	...	6,895[15]	...	...	6[16]	...	1,017[16]	...	...	9	...
Fiji	1992	693	4,644	145,630	31.4	99	142	3,045	60,237	19.8	...	45	625
Finland	1995	4,539[17]	41,222[8,17]	587,523[17]	14.2[8,17]	...	456[18]	6,322[8,18]	133,645[18]	19.2[8,18]	93	495	21,245
France	1994	41,656	218,100	4,060,607	18.6	99	11,325[4,10]	454,000[4]	5,737,422[4]	12.6[4]	90	4	4
French Guiana	1993	78	...	15,839	...	...	22[10]	...	11,319	...	...	...	...
French Polynesia	1995	278	2,949	48,160	16.3	100	38	1,745	25,541	14.6	61	...	...
Gabon	1991	1,024	4,782	210,000	43.9	...	...	1,356	42,871	31.6	...	...	476
Gambia, The	1992	245	3,193	97,262	30.5	55	32[4]	1,054[4]	25,929[4]	24.6[4]	18	4	4
Gaza Strip	1993	397[6]	5,226[6]	221,133[6]	42.3[6]	...	6	6	6	6	6	...	...
Georgia	1994	3,808[6]	90,171[6]	807,687[6]	9.0[6]	...	6	6	6	6	...	...	...
Germany	1993	18,867	225,068	3,524,219	15.7	81	...	408,663	5,532,012	13.5	85	...	112,647
Ghana	1992	11,056	66,068	1,796,490	27.2	...	5,540	43,367	816,578	18.8	...	573[3]	422[3]
Gibraltar	1991	21[6]	921[1]	5,308[6]	31.9[1]	...	6	124[1]	6	6	...	1	29[1]
Greece	1993	7,634	37,549	745,666	19.9	94	2,988	45,794	700,488	15.3	88	695	14,349
Greenland	1996	88[6]	1,019[6]	9,009	10.4[6]	...	6	6	1,593	6	...	...	...
Grenada	1994	57	781	21,311	27.3	...	19	352	6,939	19.7	...	...	...
Guadeloupe	1993	340	3,135	39,075	12.5	...	78[4]	3,813[4]	49,295[4]	12.9[4]	...	4	4
Guam	1993	36[3]	898	16,816	18.7	...	24[3]	758	17,531	23.1	...	3[3]	370[3]
Guatemala	1993	10,770	44,220	1,393,921	31.5	...	1,274[10]	20,942[4]	334,383[4]	16.0[4]	...	626[10]	4
Guernsey	1992	22	231	4,469	19.3	...	8	286	3,521	12.3	...	...	...
Guinea	1993	2,849	9,718	471,792	48.5	40	...	3,417	97,533	28.5	9	...	1,302
Guinea-Bissau	1988	...	...	79,035	...	45	...	...	5,505	...	...	...	107
Guyana	1995	423[3]	3,453	100,806	29.2	...	93[3]	1,828	67,039	36.7	...	8[3]	176[3]
Haiti	1993	6,111[5]	27,607	787,553	28.5	26	630[4,5]	10,174[4]	193,624[4]	19.0[4]	...	4	4
Honduras	1994	8,114	27,480	1,008,181	36.7	90	719	11,339	151,785	13.4	21	5[1]	581[1]
Hong Kong	1996	860	19,493	467,718	24.8	...	507	22,257	470,997	20.9	...	9	...
Hungary	1996	3,809	86,891	974,800	11.2	92	936	28,684	349,300	12.2	75	349	5,899
Iceland	1993	...	25,234	...	...	...	...	24,368	...	...	...	...	...
India	1995	581,305	1,714,395	109,043,663	63.6	...	231,670	2,008,218	56,614,505	28.2	...	...	...
Indonesia	1993	148,257	1,276,217	29,598,790	23.2	97	28,790	681,199	9,434,690	13.7	37	3,557[10]	103,000[10]
Iran	1994	61,683	311,531	9,862,817	31.7	97	18,445[3]	227,961	6,683,832	29.3	...	1,006[3]	21,851
Iraq	1993	8,003	131,271	2,857,467	21.8	79	2,746[5]	48,496	992,617	20.5	37	296[5]	10,621
Ireland	1993	3,317	20,776	505,883	24.3	90	461	12,514	224,035	17.9	82	325	7,854
Isle of Man	1989	32	...	5,458	...	...	7	...	4,908	...	...	1	...
Israel	1994	1,844	52,135	677,404	12.8	...	838	34,956	341,349	9.8	...	383	19,479
Italy	1995	21,024	164,852	2,849,157	17.3	...	9,549	98,467	1,953,058	19.8	...	7,886	128,032
Jamaica	1995	...	11,283	319,298	28.3	100	126	8,377	207,035	24.7	64	18	950
Japan	1995	24,548	431,000	8,371,000	19.4	100	16,775	552,000	9,296,000	16.8	96	6,679[10]	53,000[10]
Jersey	1990	32	...	5,794	...	...	14	...	4,405	...	...	1	...
Jordan	1994	2,482	48,158	1,036,079	21.5	89	741	7,150	93,773	13.1	36	54	2,553
Kazakstan	1992	8,841[6]	262,600[6]	3,226,400[6]	12.3[6]	...	6	6	6	6	...	3,115	...
Kenya	1993	15,804	173,002	5,428,600	31.4	...	2,639	31,657	517,577	16.3	...	63	...
Kiribati	1993	92	537	16,316	30.4	...	9[3]	179	3,152	17.6	...	6[3]	40
Korea, North	1987	6,122	138,945	1,543,000	11.1	...	...	111,000	2,468,000	22.2	...	...	...
Korea, South	1995	5,772	138,369	3,905,163	28.2	92	3,751	156,342	3,728,275	23.8	92	789	43,045
Kuwait	1995	246	8,815	132,204	15.0	45	391	18,072	200,828	11.1	45	34	683
Kyrgyzstan	1994	1,832	76,300[6,8]	954,700[6,8]	12.5[6,8]	...	1,474	6	6	6	...	53	...
Laos	1994	8,361	22,649	681,044	30.1	68	750[3]	11,066	143,673	13.0	18	139[1]	1,647
Latvia	1993	921	12,758	133,846	10.5	81	...	8,344	187,332	10.2	77	57	6,691
Lebanon	1994	2,100[5]	...	360,858	...	...	...	...	261,341	...	...	...	3,866
Lesotho	1994	1,201	7,292	354,275	48.6	65	187	2,526	55,312	21.9	17	9[5]	225[5]
Liberia	1987	...	...	...	...	...	...	...	...	...	...	...	...
Libya	1992	...	99,623	1,238,986	12.4	97	...	11,429	138,860	12.1	...	...	7,072
Liechtenstein	1994	14	122	1,986	16.3	...	8	124	1,587	12.8	...	1	40
Lithuania	1994	2,317[6]	41,052[6]	511,000[6]	12.4[6]	...	6	6	6	6	...	168	5,035
Luxembourg	1994	...	1,911[12]	27,595[12]	14.4[12]	85	...	1,948[4]	8,712[8]	...	60	...	4
Macau	1994	62	1,380	42,823	31.0	...	21[4]	1,132[4]	20,195[4]	17.8[4]	...	4	4
Macedonia	1995	1,050	13,102[8]	258,955	19.9[8]	84	95	4,520[4,8]	77,754[4]	16.5[4,8]	...	...	4
Madagascar	1993	13,624	37,676	1,504,668	39.9	...	1,142[1]	15,118	298,241	19.7	...	...	1,484[10]
Malawi	1992	3,118	26,333	1,795,451	68.2	52	94[3]	1,096[3]	36,550	26.8[3]	2	13[3]	250[3]
Malaysia	1993	6,968	134,579	2,718,906	20.2	...	1,336[5]	77,149[5]	1,531,893	18.1[5]	...	75[5]	3,489[5]
Maldives	1986	243	1,138	41,812	36.7	...	9	291	3,581	12.3	...	10	52
Mali	1992	1,514	7,963	375,131	47.1	19	307	5,798	88,529	15.3	5	...	...
Malta	1996	111	1,990	35,479	17.8	100	59	2,679	29,907	20.9	83	22	541
Marshall Islands	1994	104	833	13,565	16.3	...	11	138	2,483	18.0	...	...	...
Martinique	1993	282	2,711	33,170	12.2	...	79[4]	3,830[4]	47,295[4]	12.3[4]	...	4	4
Mauritania	1994	1,635	4,686	248,048	52.9	...	56[5]	1,776	43,861	24.7	...	5[5]	162
Mauritius	1993	279	6,450	123,167	19.1	94	123	4,234	89,581	21.2	...	19[5]	...
Mayotte	1993	88[3]	555	21,579	38.9	...	5	246	3,973	16.2	...	2[3]	17[3]
Mexico	1994	85,503	488,139	14,468,700	29.6	99	20,550	243,877	4,311,800	17.7	46	6,571[8]	77,347[8]
Micronesia	1988	177	...	25,139	...	...	16	...	5,385	...	...	...	...
Moldova	1995	1,700[6]	53,000[5,6]	731,000[6]	13.6[5,6]	...	6	6	6	6	...	64	...
Monaco	1990	...	735[6]	5,523[6]	7.5[9]	...	...	6	6	6	...	...	...
Mongolia	1995	659[6]	19,097[6]	381,204[6]	20.0[6]	...	6	6	6	6	...	49	2,500[10]
Morocco	1995	4,740	102,163	2,895,737	28.3	63	1,172	73,726	1,247,608	16.9	29	562[5,11]	2,951[11]
Mozambique	1994	3,765	22.544	1,301,833	57.7	41	239	3,889	150,683	38.7	7	31	826

students[d]	student/ teacher ratio	third level (higher) institutions	teachers[c]	students[d]	student/ teacher ratio	gross enrollment ratio[b]	students per 100,000 population[b]	percent of population age 25 and over with post-secondary education[b]	literacy[b] over age	total (%)	male (%)	female (%)	public expenditure on education (percent of GNP)[b]	country
...	...	2	34[8]	484[8]	14.2[8]	...	...	...	15	90.0	...	...	5.8	Dominica
...	...	7[2]	5,091[2]	73,461[2]	14.4[2]	20.0	1,929	...	15	82.1	82.0	82.2	1.7	Dominican Republic
4	4	...	12,856[3]	206,541[3]	16.1[3]	20.0	2,012	12.7	15	90.1	92.0	88.2	3.0	Ecuador
1,700,247	15.8[8]	12[2]	38,828[2]	620,145[2]	16.0[2]	17.1	1,560	4.6	15	51.4	63.6	38.8	5.0	Egypt
88,588	...	...	4,643[2]	77,359[2]	16.7[2]	15.4	1,598	...	15	74.1	77.4	71.3	1.6	El Salvador
882	17.0	4	81	660	8.1	1.8	164	...	15	78.5	89.6	68.1	1.8	Equatorial Guinea
787	7.7	1[8]	144[8]	2,032[8]	14.1[8]	...	...	...	15	20.0	...	...	...	Eritrea
27,806	17.5	22	...	23,169	...	37.8	1,566	13.7	15	99.7	99.9	99.6	5.9	Estonia
8,290	13.8	...	1,697[10]	26,218[10]	15.4[10]	0.6	54	...	15	35.5	45.5	25.3	6.4	Ethiopia
3,157	...	1[10]	20[10]	91[10]	4.6[10]	...	...	...	15	99.0	99.0	99.0	...	Faroe Islands
7,283	11.6	5[10]	277[10]	7,908[10]	28.5[10]	11.9	1,076	4.5	15	91.6	93.8	89.3	5.6	Fiji
202,859	9.5	21	7,790	127,846	16.4	63.2	3,902	15.4	15	100.0	100.0	100.0	7.2	Finland
4	4	1,062[1]	57,429[5]	1,700,800[5]	29.6[5]	49.5	3,607	...	...	98.8	98.9	98.7	5.8	France
2,250	...	1	...	324	...	...	...	...	15	83.0	83.6	82.3	...	French Guiana
...	...	4[1]	70[1]	701[1]	10.0[1]	1.1	114	...	15	95.0	94.9	95.0	...	French Polynesia
8,477	11.8	1	299	3,000	10.0	...	373	...	15	63.2	73.7	53.3	2.9	Gabon
4	4	...	...	...	...	...	...	...	15	38.6	52.8	24.9	2.7	Gambia, The
...	...	...	...	...	...	...	...	...	...	...	...	...	...	Gaza Strip
...	...	19[3]	...	103,900[10]	...	36.9	2,710	...	15	99.0	99.5	98.5	...	Georgia
2,264,244	20.1	314	171,025[5]	1,875,099	10.7[5]	35.6	3,051	19.9[19]	15	100.0	100.0	100.0	4.0[19]	Germany
13,232[3]	31.4[3]	16[3]	700[3]	9,274[3]	13.2[3]	1.4	126	...	15	64.5	75.9	53.5	3.1	Ghana
772	...	—	—	—	...	...	...	...	15	99.0	99.0	99.0	...	Gibraltar
190,443	13.3	17[5]	9,124[5]	115,284[5]	12.6[5]	25.9	1,906	8.7	15	95.2	97.7	93.0	3.1	Greece
...	...	...	...	...	...	...	...	...	15	100.0	100.0	100.0	...	Greenland
...	...	1	66	651	9.9	...	...	...	15	85.0	...	...	...	Grenada
4	4	1	310	4,296	13.9	...	...	...	15	90.1	89.7	90.5	...	Guadeloupe
3,788[3]	10.2[3]	13	192[3]	2,385[3]	12.4[3]	...	...	39.9	15	99.0	99.0	99.0	...	Guam
4	4	5[1]	4,346[1]	69,532[1]	16.0[1]	...	741	...	15	64.2	71.7	57.3	1.6	Guatemala
...	...	...	...	...	...	...	...	...	15	100.0	100.0	100.0	...	Guernsey
9,278	7.1	...	805[2,5]	6,245[2,5]	7.8[2,5]	1.1	93	...	15	35.9	49.9	21.9	2.2	Guinea
825	7.7	...	...	404	...	0.5	...	...	15	54.9	68.0	42.5	2.8	Guinea-Bissau
5,388[3]	30.6[3]	1[2]	204[2]	3,357[2]	16.5[2]	9.3	1,012	...	15	98.1	98.6	97.5	7.8	Guyana
4	4	2[5,20]	613[5,20]	7,400[5,20]	12.1[5,20]	...	107	0.7	15	45.0	48.0	42.2	1.4	Haiti
58,154	13.7[1]	10	4,057	56,376	13.9	8.6	852	...	15	72.7	72.6	72.7	4.1	Honduras
48,421	...	10	...	76,357	...	20.7	1,540	10.6	15	92.2	96.0	88.2	...	Hong Kong
154,300	26.2	90	18,098	129,500	7.2	16.9	1,312	10.1	15	98.9	99.2	98.6	6.7	Hungary
5,865	...	5[10]	...	6,161[5]	...	29.6	2,393	...	15	100.0	100.0	100.0	5.6	Iceland
...	...	7,958[21]	215,234[21]	4,804,773[21]	22.3[21]	7.8	755	...	15	52.0	65.5	37.7	3.7	India
1,429,657	13.1[10]	1,171	135,462	1,973,094	11.6	10.2	1,045	...	15	83.8	89.6	78.0	2.2	Indonesia
375,205	17.2	...	32,934	436,564	13.3	15.1	1,409	...	15	72.1	78.4	65.8	5.4	Iran
152,321	14.3	20[5]	10,520[5]	197,786[5]	18.8[5]	12.6	1,240	...	15	58.0	70.7	45.0	5.1	Iraq
143,889	18.3	29	4,700	86,973	18.5	34.2	3,087	...	15	100.0	100.0	100.0	6.2	Ireland
425[10]	...	...	...	...	...	...	...	...	...	...	...	...	...	Isle of Man
122,721	6.3	7	6,150[5]	91,480	...	35.3	3,208	...	15	94.9	97.1	92.7	5.8	Israel
2,736,445	21.4	48[2]	58,874[2]	1,601,873[2]	27.2[2]	37.3	2,944	...	15	97.1	97.8	96.4	5.4	Italy
15,898	16.7	15[1]	...	24,200	...	5.9	658	...	15	85.0	81.8	89.1	6.2	Jamaica
1,242,000[10]	23.4[10]	1,223	162,000	3,101,000	19.1	30.4	2,340	21.2	15	100.0	100.0	100.0	4.7	Japan
...	...	...	...	...	...	...	...	...	15	100.0	100.0	100.0	...	Jersey
30,052	11.8	55[1]	4,280	85,934	20.1	19.4	1,741	...	15	86.6	93.4	79.4	4.0	Jordan
1,091,600	...	61	...	288,000	...	41.6	3,443	12.4	15	97.5	99.1	96.1	5.4	Kazakstan
29,593	...	14	4,392[2,10]	88,180	8.1[2,10]	1.6	142	...	15	78.1	86.3	70.0	6.7	Kenya
297	7.4	—	—	—	...	...	...	...	15	90.0	...	...	7.4	Kiribati
220,000	...	281	27,000	390,000	14.4	...	...	...	15	95.0	...	...	...	Korea, North
923,942	21.5	708	56,237	1,889,933	33.6	50.8	4,756	13.4	15	98.0	99.3	96.7	4.2	Korea, South
2,936	4.3	1	927[3]	11,284	15.2[1]	16.3	1,370	12.7	15	78.6	82.2	74.9	6.1	Kuwait
32,800	...	23	...	55,200	...	20.6	1,837	...	15	97.0	98.6	95.5	3.6	Kyrgyzstan
11,693	7.1	9[3]	998	8,881	8.9	2.1	193	...	15	56.6	69.4	44.4	2.3	Laos
55,312	8.3	14	4,478	41,138	9.2	38.8	2,627	13.4	15	99.5	99.8	99.2	6.7	Latvia
39,933	10.3	...	5,400[5]	85,495[5]	15.8[5]	28.9	3,275	...	15	92.4	94.7	90.3	1.9	Lebanon
2,326[5]	10.3[5]	1	492	4,001	8.1	2.3	206	...	15	71.3	81.1	62.3	4.9	Lesotho
...	...	...	472	5,095	10.8	2.5	...	...	15	38.3	53.9	22.4	...	Liberia
76,648	10.8	10[1]	...	72,899	...	16.4	1,548	...	15	76.2	87.9	63.0	9.6	Libya
197	4.9	...	...	...	...	...	...	...	15	100.0	100.0	100.0	...	Liechtenstein
69,000	13.7	14	...	53,000	...	39.1	2,802	12.6	15	98.4	99.2	97.8	4.4	Lithuania
12,662	6.5	...	...	4,957[10]	...	...	...	...	15	100.0	100.0	100.0	4.3	Luxembourg
4	4	11	594	6,517	11.0	...	...	5.9	15	89.5	94.1	85.3	...	Macau
4	4	27[10]	1,122	26,959	24.0	16.1	1,290	...	10	89.1	94.2	83.8	5.0	Macedonia
17,419[10]	11.7[10]	5[1]	855[5]	42,681[5]	49.9[5]	3.5	318	...	15	80.2	87.7	72.9	1.5	Madagascar
3,679[3]	14.7[3]	4[3]	235[3]	2,685[3]	11.4[3]	0.9	78	0.4	15	56.4	71.9	41.8	3.4	Malawi
40,944	9.5[5]	54[5]	11,471[10]	136,000[10]	11.9[10]	7.2	679	...	15	83.5	89.1	78.1	5.1	Malaysia
462	8.9	—	—	—	—	...	...	...	15	93.2	93.3	93.0	8.1	Maldives
...	...	7[10]	701	6,703	9.6	0.8	73	...	15	31.0	39.4	23.1	2.1	Mali
4,539	8.4	1[8]	284[8]	3,679[8]	13.0[8]	18.6	1,300	...	15	96.0	96.2	95.9	4.6	Malta
...	...	...	...	...	...	...	...	...	15	91.2	92.4	90.0	...	Marshall Islands
4	4	1	71	3,670	51.7	...	...	...	15	92.5	91.8	93.2	...	Martinique
1,949	12.0	4	72[22,23]	2,850[22,23]	39.6[22,23]	4.1	393	1.3	15	37.7	49.6	26.3	...	Mauritania
2,052[5]	...	2	526[10]	2,556	7.7[10]	4.1	378	1.9	15	82.9	87.1	78.8	3.7	Mauritius
839	23.1[3]	—	—	—	—	...	...	...	15	91.9	...	...	...	Mayotte
1,076,700[8]	13.9[8]	13,000	324,148	3,961,000	12.2	13.8	1,509	...	15	89.6	91.8	87.4	6.0	Mexico
...	...	...	...	...	...	...	...	...	15	76.7	67.0	87.2	...	Micronesia
41,800	...	18	...	49,400	...	34.8	2,665	11.3	15	96.4	98.6	94.4	6.5	Moldova
...	...	...	...	...	...	...	...	...	15	...	...	...	...	Monaco
29,900	19.0[10]	12	1,465[10]	13,800	9.4[10]	14.4	1,267	...	15	82.9	88.6	77.2	8.5	Mongolia
17,585[11]	6.0[11]	50[8]	6,877[8]	230,012[8]	33.4[8]	10.3	1,040	...	15	43.7	56.6	31.0	5.8	Morocco
13,816	16.7	3	877[8]	5,250[8]	6.0[8]	0.4	35	...	15	40.1	57.7	23.3	6.2	Mozambique

Education (continued)

country	year	first level (primary)					general second level (secondary)					vocational second level[a]	
		schools	teachers[c]	students[d]	student/ teacher ratio	net enroll- ment ratio[b]	schools	teachers[c]	students[d]	student/ teacher ratio	net enroll- ment ratio[b]	schools	teachers[c]
Myanmar (Burma)	1994	35,727	156,629	5,896,026	37.6	...	2,916	69,441	1,519,215	21.9	...	111	2,473
Namibia	1994	933	10,912[5]	366,666	32.0[5]	89	114	2,534[3]	101,838	29.3[3]	30	17	140[1]
Nauru	1989	3	61	1,367	22.4	...	2	34	629	18.5	...	1	3
Nepal	1993	20,217	79,590	3,091,684	38.8	...	6,618[4]	26,303[4]	910,114[4]	34.6[4]	...	4	4
Netherlands, The	1995	8,854	99,031[10]	1,450,400	15.7[10]	94	1,332	89,370[10]	852,600	7.7[10]	86	702	18,613[10]
Netherlands Antilles	1993	85	1,059	22,735	21.5	...	27	617	8,801	14.3	...	30	439
New Caledonia	1992	280	1,758	34,591	19.7	98	46	1,669[4, 10]	15,664	13.1[4, 10]	72	16	4
New Zealand	1995	2,406[24]	21,687[24]	444,761[24]	20.5[24]	99	336	15,375	226,533	14.7	88	30	5,337
Nicaragua	1994	7,093	23,693	880,891	37.2	80	451[4]	5,356[4]	211,606[4]	39.5[4]	26	4	4
Niger	1994	2,656	12,216	414,296	33.9	25	105[1]	2,219[5]	88,810	35.1[5]	6	7[1]	175[5]
Nigeria	1994	38,649	435,210	16,191,000	37.2	...	6,074	152,596	4,451,000	29.2	...	...	15,738[1]
Northern Mariana Islands	1989	18	240	4,882	20.3	...	9[4]	163[4]	2,075[4]	12.7[4]	...	4	4
Norway	1994	3,325	36,196	466,991	12.9	99	771[4]	21,780[4]	240,506[4]	11.0[4]	92	4	4
Oman	1994	415	11,158	297,209	26.6	73	128[3]	9,188	160,654	17.5	52	25[3]	342
Pakistan	1995	123,119	412,200	16,722,000	40.6	...	26,128	313,900	5,610,000	17.9	...	724	6,924
Palau	1992	...	...	2,480	...	...	...	...	981	...	...	4	4
Panama	1994	2,765	14,512	358,410	24.7	91	376[4]	11,241[4]	209,929[4]	18.7[4]	51	4	4
Papua New Guinea	1992	2,821	14,117	443,552	31.4	73	135[3]	2,415	58,226	24.1	...	117[3]	878
Paraguay	1995	5,180	41,432[21]	827,857	19.1[21]	96	1,024[4]	20,793[4, 21]	235,914[4]	10.3[4, 21]	32	4	4
Peru	1993	54,502[5]	159,022	4,843,666	30.5	88	7,097[5]	93,277	1,913,163	20.5	46	1,952[5]	11,919
Philippines	1994	35,087	320,634	10,731,453	33.5	99	5,880	134,898[4]	4,590,037[4]	34.0[4]	59	1,261[5]	4
Poland	1994	20,326	323,400	5,371,841	16.6	96	1,832	30,300	659,500	21.8	78	9,655	85,600
Portugal	1994	13,263	71,467	929,471	13.0	100	663	64,479[4, 8]	839,144	12.6[4, 8]	...	214	4
Puerto Rico	1986	1,542	18,359	427,582	23.3	...	395	13,612	334,661	24.6	...	52	...
Qatar	1994	158	5,656	52,016	9.2	81	368[8]	3,695	35,518	9.6	69	3[8]	128
Réunion	1995	343	...	73,220	...	...	102[4]	4,591[21]	74,827[21]	16.3[21]	...	4	1,108[21]
Romania	1995	13,963[15]	168,702[15]	2,532,169[15]	15.0[15]	77	1,276[16]	60,514[16]	757,673[16]	12.5[16]	72	1,530	9,360
Russia	1995	70,000[6]	1,682,000[6]	21,600,000[6]	12.8[6]	94	6	6	6	6	...	2,574	...
Rwanda	1992	1,710	18,937	1,104,902	58.3	71	...	3,413[4]	94,586[4]	27.7[4]	8	...	4
St. Kitts and Nevis	1992	31	342	6,978	20.4	...	7	298	4,645	15.6	...	2	35
St. Lucia	1993	84	1,181[5]	32,204	27.4[5]	...	14	466[5]	7,612	17.5[5]	...	1[25]	113[5, 25]
St. Vincent and the Grenadines	1992	60	1,215	24,134	19.9	...	21	408	7,124	17.5	...	2	4
San Marino	1996	14	217	1,134	5.2	...	3	134	771	5.8	...	...	44[21]
São Tomé and Príncipe	1989	64	559	19,822	35.5	...	...	318	7,446	23.4	...	...	...
Saudi Arabia	1994	10,699	142,760	2,114,736	14.8	61	6,346	84,512	1,156,590	13.7	34	293	7,359
Senegal	1993	2,454	12,711	738,550	58.1	48	359	5,509	182,140	33.1	12	19	182
Seychelles	1995	24[21]	569	9,691	17.0	...	20[21]	429	6,129	14.4	...	1[21]	155
Sierra Leone	1992	1,792	10,051	315,146	31.4	...	217	3,924	72,516	18.5	...	30	750
Singapore	1994	194	10,553	251,097	23.8	100	173	9,675	197,981	20.5	...	25	2,939
Slovakia	1995	2,481	38,813	675,813	17.4	...	183	5,073	72,072	14.2	...	722	17,654
Slovenia	1994	846	15,341	214,832	14.0	...	221[4]	9,579[4]	110,426[4]	11.5[4]	...	4	4
Solomon Islands	1994	520	2,510	73,120	29.1	...	23	364[8]	7,811	20.2[8]	...	1	4
Somalia	1987	1,125	8,208	171,830	20.9	...	82	2,109	42,764	20.3	3	21	498
South Africa	1994	22,260[6]	349,436[6]	11,782,324[6]	35.7[6]	92	6	6	6	6	46	187	10,807
Spain	1994	16,540	121,353	2,447,859	20.2	100	25,775[4, 8]	297,697[4]	4,734,401[4]	15.9[4]	90	4	4
Sri Lanka	1993	9,590[10]	70,008	2,012,702	28.7	...	9,041[10]	106,141	2,246,642	21.2	...	23[10]	437[10]
Sudan, The	1992	8,016	64,227	2,168,180	33.8	...	2,578	29,208	683,982	23.4	...	67	1,434
Suriname	1993	301[5]	3,695	76,162	21.4	...	89[5]	2,487[4]	17,709	12.6[4]	...	64[1]	4
Swaziland	1994	535	5,887	192,599	32.7	93	165	2,872	52,571	18.3	...	5	228
Sweden	1994	4,826	90,234	893,932	9.9	99	600[4]	29,539[4]	313,728[4]	10.6[4]	93	4	4
Switzerland	1995	...	...	437,444	...	94	...	...	373,986	...	79	...	...
Syria	1994	10,219	110,580	2,624,594	23.7	95	...	49,951	846,550	16.9	42	...	11,559
Taiwan	1995	2,528	84,150	2,032,361	24.2	...	920	74,465	1,423,040	19.1	...	206	19,152
Tajikistan	1994	3,300[6]	97,000[6]	1,227,000[6]	12.6[6]	...	6	6	6	6	...	50	...
Tanzania	1993[26]	10,892	101,816	3,736,734	36.7	50	...	9,568	180,899	18.9	...	...	1,167
Thailand	1993	34,412	445,542	8,583,525	19.3	...	2,318	107,025	2,118,767	19.8	...	679	40,116
Togo	1993	2,594	12,487	663,126	53.1	69	...	2,918	126,335	43.3	18	...	261[3]
Tonga	1993	115	754	16,792	22.3	...	40[5]	847	15,573	18.4	...	8[5]	65[3]
Trinidad and Tobago	1994	475	7,210	195,013	27.0	88	101[5]	4,844[5]	100,609[5]	20.6[5]	65	...	...
Tunisia	1995	4,286	58,279	1,472,844	25.3	98	712	27,785	662,222	23.8	43	...	237
Turkey	1994	49,599	237,943	6,526,296	27.4	93	9,592	133,316	3,381,901	25.4	54	3,239	66,199
Turkmenistan	1992	1,791[6]	60,000[6]	842,000[6]	14.0[6]	...	6	6	6	6	...	41	...
Tuvalu	1990	9	72	1,485	20.6	...	1	21	314	15.0	...	1	10
Uganda	1994	7,905[1]	102,126	2,496,139	24.4	...	774[1]	16,245	244,248	15.0	...	136[1]	2,766
Ukraine	1994	21,694[6]	574,000[6]	6,937,000[6]	12.1[6]	...	6	6	6	6	...	754	...
United Arab Emirates	1994	...	14,754	251,182	17.0	100	...	11,637[4]	145,143	12.6[4]	79	...	4
United Kingdom	1994	23,673	225,500	4,997,700	22.2	96	4,496	228,400	3,587,500	15.7	85	...	...
United States	1995	85,393[6, 21]	1,784,000[27]	33,410,000[27]	18.7[27]	100	6	1,187,000	17,390,000	14.6	90	...	...
Uruguay	1993	2,422	16,392	338,204	20.6	94	335	17,750	201,805	11.4	...	105	...
Uzbekistan	1993	8,500[6]	91,500	1,852,841	20.3	...	6	300,800	2,893,058	9.6	...	440	22,164
Vanuatu	1992	272	852	26,267	30.8	74	...	220	4,269	19.4	17	...	4
Venezuela	1992	15,800	183,298	4,190,047	22.9	88	1,621[4]	32,572[4]	289,430[4]	8.9[4]	20	4	4
Vietnam	1994	13,092	275,640	9,725,095	35.3	...	6,298	166,968	3,815,852	22.9	...	451	12,197
Virgin Islands (U.S.)	1991[12]	57	777	15,256	19.6	...	...	541	9,263	17.2	...	...	...
West Bank[28]	1993	1,406[6]	11,872[6]	383,386[6]	32.3[6]	...	6	6	6	6	...	...	...
Western Sahara	1989[12]	27	596	14,794	24.8	...	18	577	9,218	16.0	...	...	...
Western Samoa	1989	...	37,833										
Yemen[29]	1991	7,313[1]	35,350	1,291,372	36.5	...	...	12,106	394,578	32.6	...	...	1,247
Yugoslavia	1994	4,421	51,801	922,939	17.8	69	538	25,596	348,132	13.6	62	...	...
Zaire	1993	12,987	112,041	4,939,297	44.1	54	...	59,325[4]	640,298	22.6[4]	17	...	4
Zambia	1989	3,489	...	1,446,847	...	81	480	...	...	...	16	26	846
Zimbabwe	1995	4,633	63,475	2,655,564	41.8	...	1,535	27,320	711,094	26.0	...	255[5]	1,479[5]

[1]1989. [2]Universities only. [3]1990. [4]General second level includes vocational second level. [5]1992. [6]First level includes general second level. [7]College of the Bahamas only. [8]1993. [9]Includes preschool. [10]1991. [11]Excludes teacher training. [12]Public schools only. [13]Republic of Cyprus only. [14]Over age 20. [15]Includes lower second level. [16]Upper second level only. [17]Includes lower second level students at all-age schools. [18]Excludes lower second level students at all-age schools. [19]Former West Germany only. [20]Port-au-Prince universities only. [21]1994. [22]1995. [23]University

students[d]	student/ teacher ratio	institutions	teachers[c]	students[d]	student/ teacher ratio	gross enroll-ment ratio[b]	students per 100,000 popula-tion[b]	percent of population age 25 and over with post-secondary education[b]	over age	total (%)	male (%)	female (%)	public expenditure on education (percent of GNP)[b]	country
26,789	10.8	40	5,970	235,184	39.4	4.8	...	...	15	83.1	88.7	77.7	2.4	Myanmar (Burma)
1,503[8]	11.9[1]	7	213[10]	6,523[8]	11.8[10]	3.3	300	...	15	75.8	77.8	74.0	8.6	Namibia
30	10.0	1		200	...				15	99.0	...	...	...	Nauru
4	4	3	4,925[10]	102,018	22.4[10]	5.6	558	...	15	27.5	40.9	14.0	2.9	Nepal
499,000	28.0[10]	78	...	419,200	...	44.8	3,339	...	15	100.0	100.0	100.0	5.9	Netherlands, The
5,817	13.3	2	51	734	14.4	...	...	...	15	93.8	94.2	93.4	...	Netherlands Antilles
7,543	4	6	141[1]	1,207[3]	9.9[1]	...	...	...	15	57.9	57.4	58.3	...	New Caledonia
107,034	13.4	72[2]	5,926[2]	104,525[2]	17.6[2]	57.5	4,675	39.1	15	100.0	100.0	100.0	7.3	New Zealand
4	4	10	2,005	22,120	11.0	8.7	809	...	15	65.7	64.6	66.6	4.1	Nicaragua
2,110	12.1[5]	2	315	4,060	12.9	1.0	81	...	15	13.6	20.9	6.6	3.1	Niger
391,583[1]	24.9[1]	31	12,103	228,000	18.8	4.0	360	...	15	57.1	67.3	47.3	1.7	Nigeria
4	4	1	102	1,097	10.8	...	...	...	15	96.3	96.9	95.6	...	Northern Mariana Islands
4	4	195	10,213	172,574	16.9	54.4	4,111	17.9	15	100.0	100.0	100.0	8.4	Norway
2,350	6.9	5[3]	732	7,322	10.0	4.9	400	...	6	41.0	58.0	24.0	5.8	Oman
93,000	13.4	724	30,162	794,000	26.3	2.6	247	2.5	15	37.8	50.0	24.4	2.7	Pakistan
...	...	...	...	382	...				15	97.6	98.3	96.6	...	Palau
4	4	9	4,291	70,327	16.4	23.4	2,398	16.8	15	90.8	91.4	90.2	5.6	Panama
11,370	12.9	23[3]	...	5,007[3]	...				15	72.2	81.0	62.7	...	Papua New Guinea
4	4	2	742[8]	39,694	40.9[8]	9.9	907	...	15	92.1	93.5	90.6	2.8	Paraguay
270,668	22.7	655[5]	46,963	730,987	15.6	40.1	4,188	...	15	88.7	94.5	83.0	1.5	Peru
4	4	809[5]	56,880[10]	1,582,820	23.7[10]	26.2	2,654	...	15	94.6	95.0	94.3	2.4	Philippines
1,691,000	19.8	140	65,300	584,000	8.9	25.5	1,812	7.9	15	98.7	99.2	98.3	5.5	Poland
99,509	4	273	30,998[8]	236,537	6.9[8]	23.4	1,936	...	15	86.8	86.7	86.9	5.0	Portugal
149,191	...	45	9,045	156,818	17.3	...	...	...	18	89.7	89.6	89.7	...	Puerto Rico
774	6.0	1	636	7,351	11.6	27.3	1,389	13.3	15	79.4	79.2	79.9	3.5	Qatar
13,778[21]	12.4[21]	1[2]	242[2]	8,058[2]	33.3[2]	...	...	...	15	78.2	75.9	80.3	...	Réunion
345,394	36.9	63	20,452	255,162	12.5	11.8	1,019	6.9	15	96.7	98.5	95.0	3.6	Romania
1,871,000	4	553	...	2,534,000	...	45.3	3,017	14.1	15	98.0	99.5	96.8	4.4	Russia
4	4	...	646[3]	3,454	5.2[3]	0.6	50	...	15	60.5	69.8	51.6	3.8	Rwanda
189	5.4	1	3	36	12.0	...	...	...	15	90.0	90.0	90.0	3.3	St. Kitts and Nevis
1,125[25]	6.3[5,25]	25	25	25	25	...	...	...	15	80.0	...	...	5.5	St. Lucia
337		...	...	...	...				15	96.0	...	...	6.7	St. Vincent and the Grenadines
428	6.2[21]	...	...	...	...				15	98.0	98.2	97.7	...	San Marino
289		...	...	...	...				15	54.2	70.2	39.1	4.3	São Tomé and Príncipe
84,611	11.5	77	10,280	155,390	15.1	13.7	1,145	...	15	62.8	71.5	50.2	6.4	Saudi Arabia
7,301	40.1	2[2,21]	784[2,21]	16,733[2,21]	21.3[2,21]	3.4	298	...	15	33.1	43.0	23.2	4.2	Senegal
1,429	9.2	...	...	...	...				15	84.2	82.9	85.7	8.5	Seychelles
6,929	9.2	2[10]	257[10]	2,571[10]	10.0[10]	1.3	129	...	15	31.4	45.4	18.2	1.4	Sierra Leone
31,692	10.8	7	6,235	76,985	12.3	...	...	4.7	15	91.1	95.9	86.3	3.4	Singapore
234,284	13.3	14	7,781	66,900	8.6	17.1	1,369	9.5	15	100.0	100.0	100.0	5.7	Slovakia
4	4	28	2,783	40,239	14.5	28.1	2,077	10.4	15	100.0	100.0	100.0	6.2	Slovenia
		1							15	54.1	62.4	44.9	4.2	Solomon Islands
4,809	9.7	1	...	1,692	...				10	54.8	60.9	47.9	0.4	Somalia
140,531	13.0	36	39,388[8]	505,413	11.9[8]	13.4	1,264	...	15	81.8	81.9	81.7	7.0	South Africa
4	4	1,415[8]	73,412[8]	1,370,689[8]	18.7[8]	41.1	3,474	7.0	15	95.8	97.5	94.2	4.6	Spain
8,908[10]	20.4[10]	8[10]	1,937[10]	31,447[10]	16.2[10]	6.1	504	...	15	90.2	93.4	87.2	3.1	Sri Lanka
34,316	23.9	24	1,943	54,345	28.0	3.0	266	...	15	46.1	57.7	34.6	...	Sudan, The
12,307		15	254[5]	2,373[5]	9.3[5]	...	1,079	...	15	93.0	95.1	91.0	7.3	Suriname
2,958	13.0	1	190	2,132	11.2	3.6	384	...	15	76.7	78.0	75.6	6.8	Swaziland
4	4	...	27,523[3]	272,718[3]	9.9[3]	38.3	2,409	...	15	100.0	100.0	100.0	8.3	Sweden
188,855	...	...	...	148,154	...	30.6	2,107	...	15	100.0	100.0	100.0	5.2	Switzerland
76,480	6.6	...	5,997[2]	178,526[2]	29.8[2]	17.6	1,700	...	15	70.8	85.7	55.8	4.2	Syria
523,982	27.4	130	35,163	720,180	20.5	...	...	...	15	93.7	97.4	89.9	3.6	Taiwan
38,400		22	...	69,000	...	24.8	2,298	...	15	97.7	98.8	96.6	11.2	Tajikistan
15,824	13.6	4[1]	1,206[1]	6,100[3]	4.4[1]	...	21	...	15	67.8	79.4	56.8	5.0	Tanzania
795,186	19.8	102	27,239	809,856	29.7	18.7	2,029	...	15	93.8	96.0	91.6	4.0	Thailand
8,392[3]	32.2[3]	1[2]	...	9,120[2,3]	...	2.7	235	...	15	51.7	67.0	37.0	6.7	Togo
358[5]	13.4[3]	15	19[5]	226[5]	11.9[5]	...	...	...	15	92.8	92.9	92.8	4.8	Tonga
...	...	1	438	5,191	11.9	7.6	673	...	15	97.9	98.8	97.0	4.0	Trinidad and Tobago
3,839	16.2	...	5,655[21]	96,101[21]	17.0[21]	11.4	1,121	...	15	66.7	78.6	54.6	6.4	Tunisia
1,142,191	17.3	625	42,475	1,083,063	25.5	15.7	1,918	...	15	82.3	91.7	72.4	4.0	Turkey
33,700	...	9	...	41,700	...	21.8	2,078	...	15	97.7	98.8	96.6	7.9	Turkmenistan
31	3.1	—			—				15	95.5	95.5	95.5	...	Tuvalu
46,238	16.7	9[1]	941	8,966	9.5	1.3	121	...	15	61.8	73.7	50.2	2.0	Uganda
680,700	...	159	...	829,200	...	45.9	3,152	...	15	98.4	99.5	97.4	6.1	Ukraine
1,143	4	1	510[8]	9,793[8]	19.2[8]	10.5	601	...	15	79.2	78.9	79.8	2.0	United Arab Emirates
586,000[8]	...	...	34,497[2]	470,565[2]	13.6[2]	37.4	2,646	...	15	100.0	100.0	100.0	5.2	United Kingdom
...	...	5,758[8]	833,000	14,210,000	17.1	80.6	5,611	45.2	15	95.5	95.7	95.3	5.3	United States
54,839	...	2	7,016	62,893	9.0	30.0	2,396	8.1	15	97.3	96.9	97.7	2.8	Uruguay
242,793	11.0	53	...	321,682	...	32.9	3,054	...	15	97.2	98.5	96.0	11.0	Uzbekistan
444	...	1	...	124[10]	...				15	52.9	57.3	47.8	4.5	Vanuatu
4	4	99[10]	43,833	550,783	12.6	28.5	2,757	11.8	15	91.1	91.8	90.3	5.3	Venezuela
137,405	11.3	104	20,648	118,589	5.7	1.5	147	...	15	93.7	96.5	91.2	...	Vietnam
...	...	1	240	2,924	12.2	...	...	...	...	...	...	...	...	Virgin Islands (U.S.)
...	...	...	988[1]	14,434[1]	15.1[1]	...	...	...	...	...	...	...	...	West Bank[28]
...	...	...	...	...	...									Western Sahara
...	...	...	...	...	...				15	100.0	100.0	100.0	4.2	Western Samoa
26,119	20.9	1[1]	470[1]	23,457[1]	49.9[1]	2.9	447	...	15	38.5	53.3	26.3	4.6	Yemen[29]
...	...	144	11,513	141,587	12.3	18.9	1,370	...	15	93.3	97.6	89.2	...	Yugoslavia
701,148	4	...	3,873[1]	61,422[1]	15.9[1]	1.9	176	...	15	77.3	86.6	67.7	1.0	Zaire
8,218	9.7	2	320	6,247	19.5	2.0	183	...	15	78.2	85.6	71.3	2.6	Zambia
27,431[5]	18.5[5]	28[5]	3,581	46,492	10.0	6.1	588	...	15	85.1	90.4	79.9	8.3	Zimbabwe

of Nouakchott only. [24]Includes schools that provide both first and second level education. [25]Vocational second level includes third level. [26]Mainland Tanzania only. [27]Primary includes kinder-garten. [28]Excludes East Jerusalem. [29]Former Yemen Arab Republic only.

BIBLIOGRAPHY AND SOURCES

The following list indicates the principal documentary sources used in the compilation of *Britannica World Data*. It is by no means a complete list, either for international or for national sources, but is indicative only of the range of materials to which reference has been made in preparing this compilation. For example, in addition to the kinds of works cited below, reference has also been made to the constitution of each country, to the publications of its central or commercial banks, and to unpublished information received in correspondence from the countries. Reference is made to an organization's or country's Internet resources when these have been used, but no reference to telephone, fax, or other more informal sources.

International Statistical Sources

Asian Development Bank. *Asian Development Outlook* (annual); *Key Indicators of Developing Member Countries of ADB* (annual, with supplements).
Billboard Ltd. *World Radio TV Handbook* (annual).
Caribbean Development Bank. *Annual Report.*
Comité Monétaire de la Zone Franc. *La Zone Franc: Rapport* (annual).
Commonwealth of Independent States. *Demographic Yearbook; Sodruzhestvo Nezavizimykh Gosudarstv v 19** godu; Strany-Chleny SNG: Statistichesky Yezhegodnik (Member States of the CIS: Statistical Yearbook).*
Eastern Caribbean Central Bank. *Report and Statement of Accounts* (annual).
Europa Publications Ltd. *Africa South of the Sahara* (annual); *The Europa Year Book* (2 vol.); *The Far East and Australasia* (annual); *The Middle East and North Africa* (annual).
Food and Agriculture Organization. *Food Balance Sheets; Production Yearbook; Trade Yearbook; World Census of Agriculture* (decennial); *Yearbook of Fishery Statistics* (2 vol.); *Yearbook of Forest Products;* its Internet resources.
FT Caribbean. *The Caribbean Handbook* (annual).
Her Majesty's Stationery Office. *The Commonwealth Yearbook.*
Instituts d'Émission d'Outre-Mer et des Départements d'Outre-Mer (France). *Bulletin trimestriel* (quarterly); *Rapport annuel.*
Inter-American Development Bank. *Economic and Social Progress in Latin America* (annual); its Internet resources.
Inter-Parliamentary Union. *Chronicle of Parliamentary Elections and Developments* (annual); *World Directory of Parliaments* (annual).
International Air Transport Association. *World Air Transport Statistics* (annual).
International Bank for Reconstruction and Development/The World Bank. *Statistical Handbook 19**: States of the Former USSR* (annual); *World Bank Atlas* (annual); *World Debt Tables* (annual); *World Development Report* (annual).
International Civil Aviation Organization. *Civil Aviation Statistics of the World* (annual); *Digest of Statistics.*
International Institute for Strategic Studies. *The Military Balance* (annual).
International Labour Organisation. *Year Book of Labour Statistics; The Cost of Social Security: Basic Tables* (triennial).
International Monetary Fund. *Annual Report on Exchange Arrangements and Exchange Restrictions; Direction of Trade Statistics Yearbook; Government Finance Statistics Yearbook; IMF Economic Reviews* (irreg.); *IMF Staff Country Reports* (irreg.); *International Financial Statistics* (monthly, with yearbook).

International Road Federation. *World Road Statistics* (annual).
International Telecommunication Union. *World Telecommunication Indicators* (annual).
Jane's Publishing Co., Ltd. *Jane's World Railways* (annual).
Longman Group U.K. Ltd. *Keesing's Record of World Events* (monthly).
Macmillan Press Ltd. *The Statesman's Year-Book.*
Middle East Economic Digest Ltd.; *Middle East Economic Digest* (semimonthly).
Mining Journal. *Mining Annual Review* (2 vol.).
Nordic Council. *Yearbook of Nordic Statistics.*
Official Airline Guides, Inc. *Official Airline Guide* (monthly).
Organization of Eastern Caribbean States. *Statistical Pocket Digest.*
Organization for Economic Cooperation and Development. *Economic Surveys* (annual); *Financing and External Debt of Developing Countries* (annual).
Oxford University Press. *World Christian Encyclopedia* (David B. Barrett, ed. [1982]).
Pan American Health Organization. *Health Conditions in the Americas* (2 vol.; quadrennial); its Internet resources.
PennWell Publishing Co. *International Petroleum Encyclopedia* (annual).
René Moreux et Cie. *Marchés tropicaux & Méditerranéens* (weekly).
South Pacific Commission. *Key Economic Indicators* (irreg.); *South Pacific Economies: Statistical Summary* (biennial).
United Nations (UN). *Demographic Yearbook; International Trade Statistics Yearbook* (2 vol.); *Energy Statistics Yearbook; Monthly Bulletin of Statistics; Population Studies* (irreg.); *National Accounts Statistics* (3 vol.; annual); *Population and Vital Statistics Report* (quarterly); *Statistical Yearbook; World Population Prospects 19*** (biennial).
UN: Conference on Trade and Development. *Handbook of International Trade and Development Statistics* (annual).
UN: Economic Commission for Africa. *African Socio-Economic Indicators* (annual); *African Statistical Yearbook* (2 vol. in 4 parts); *Demographic and Related Socio-Economic Data Sheets for ECA Member States* (irreg.); *Survey of Economic and Social Conditions in Africa* (annual).
UN: Economic Commission for Europe. *Annual Bulletin of Housing and Building Statistics for Europe; Annual Bulletin of Transport Statistics for Europe.*
UN: Economic Commission for Latin America. *Economic Survey of Latin America and the Caribbean* (2 vol.; annual); *Statistical Yearbook for Latin America and the Caribbean.*
UN: Economic and Social Commission for Asia and the Pacific. *Foreign Trade Statistics of Asia and the Pacific* (annual); *Statistical Indicators for Asia and the Pacific* (quarterly); *Statistical Yearbook for Asia and the Pacific.*
UN: Economic and Social Commission for Western Asia. *Demographic and Related Socio-Economic Data Sheets* (irreg.); *National Accounts Studies of the ESCWA Region* (irreg.); *Population Bulletin* (irreg.); *The Population Situation in the ESCWA Region* (irreg.); *Prices and Financial Statistics in the ESCWA Region* (irreg.); *Statistical Abstract of the Region of the Economic and Social Commission for Western Asia* (annual).
UN: Educational, Scientific, and Cultural Organization. *Statistical Yearbook.*
United Nations Development Programme. *Human Development Report* (annual).
United Nations Industrial Development Organization. *Industrial Development Review Series* (irreg.); *Industry and Development: Global Report* (annual); *International Yearbook of Industrial Statistics.*
United States: Central Intelligence Agency, *The World Factbook* (annual); Dept. of Commerce, *World Population Profile* (irreg.); its Internet resources; Dept. of Energy, *International Energy Annual;* Dept. of Health and Human Services, *Social*

Security Programs Throughout the World (biennial); Dept. of Interior, *Minerals Yearbook* (3 vol. in 8); Dept. of State, *Background Notes* (irreg.); its Internet resources.
Vatican (Central Statistics Office of the Church). *Statistical Yearbook of the Church.*
World Energy Conference. *Survey of Energy Resources* (triennial).
World Health Organization. *World Health Statistics Annual; World Health Statistics Quarterly.*
World Tourism Organization. *World Tourism Statistics* (2 vol.; annual).

National Statistical Sources

Afghanistan. *Afghanistan Rehabilitation Strategy: Action Plan* (6 vol.; 1993); *Preliminary Results of the First Afghan Population Census, 1979).*
Albania. *IMF Economic Reviews: Albania* (1994); *Population and Housing Census 1989; Statistical Yearbook of Albania.*
Algeria. *Annuaire statistique; Recensement général de la population et de l'habitat, 1987.*
American Samoa. *American Samoa Statistical Digest* (annual); *1990 Census of Population and Housing* (U.S.).
Andorra. *Estadístiques* (annual); *Recull Estadístic General de la Població Andorra 90.*
Angola. *Angola: An Introductory Economic Review* (A World Bank Country Study [1991]); *Informação Estatística* (annual); *Perfil estatístico de Angola* (annual).
Antigua. *Statistical Yearbook; 1991 Population and Housing Census.*
Argentina. *Anuario estadístico de la República Argentina; Censo nacional de población y vivienda, 1991; Encuesta permanente de hogares* (irreg.); its Internet resources.
Armenia. *Economic Reviews: Armenia* (IMF [irreg.]); *Statisticheskii Yezhegodnik Armenii* (Statistical Yearbook of Armenia).
Aruba. *Statistical Yearbook; Third Population and Housing Census October 6, 1991.*
Australia. *Census of Manufacturing Establishments: Summary of Operations by Industry Subdivision, Australia* (annual); *Monthly Summary of Statistics, Australia; National Income and Expenditure* (annual); *Social Indicators* (annual); *Year Book Australia; 1991 Census of Population and Housing;* its Internet resources.
Austria. *Grosszählung 1991* (General Census 1991). *Österreichisches Jahrbuch* (annual); *Sozialstatistische Daten* (irreg.); *Statistisches Jahrbuch für die Republik Österreich.*
Azerbaijan. *A World Bank Country Study: Azerbaijan, from Crisis to Sustained Growth* (1993); *Economic Reviews: Azerbaijan* (IMF [irreg.]); *Narodnoye Khozyaystvo Azerbaydzhanskoy SSR* (National Economy of the Azerbaijan S.S.R. [annual]).
Bahamas, The. *Census of Population and Housing 1990; Quarterly Statistical Summary; Statistical Abstract* (annual); *Vital Statistics Report* (annual).
Bahrain. *Statistical Abstract* (annual); *The Population, Housing, Buildings and Establishments Census—1991.*
Bangladesh. *Bangladesh Population Census, 1991; Statistical Yearbook of Bangladesh.*
Barbados. *Barbados Economic Report* (annual); *Monthly Digest of Statistics; 1993–2000 Development Plan.*
Belarus. *Economic Reviews: Belarus* (IMF [irreg.]); *Narodnoye Kozyaystvo Belorusskoy S.S.R.* (National Economy of the Belorussian S.S.R. [annual]).
Belgium. *Annuaire statistique de la Belgique; Recensement de la population et des logements au 1er mars 1991.*
Belize. *Abstract of Statistics* (annual); *Belize Economic Survey* (annual); *Belize Today: Development Plan 1990–94; Labour Force Survey* (1993); *1991 Population Census: Major Findings.*
Benin. *Annuaire statistique; Recensement général de la population et de l'habitation* (1992).

Bermuda. *Bermuda Digest of Statistics* (annual); *Report of the Manpower Survey* (annual); *The 1991 Census of Population and Housing.*
Bhutan. *Bhutan: Development Planning in a Unique Environment* (A World Bank Country Study [1988]); *Statistical Yearbook of Bhutan.*
Bolivia. *Anuario Estadístico; Censo Nacional de población y vivienda 1992; Compendio Estadístico* (annual); *Estadísticas Socio-económicas* (annual); *Estrategia de Desarrollo Económico y Social 1989–2000; Resumen estadístico* (annual).
Botswana. *National Development Plan 7, 1991–1997; 1991 Population and Housing Census.*
Brazil. *Anuário Estatístico do Brasil; Censo Demografico 1991; Comercio Exterior do Brasil* (2 vol.; annual); its Internet resources.
Brunei. *Brunei Statistical Yearbook; Population Survey 1986: Demographic Report; Report on the Census of Population, 1981.*
Bulgaria. *Prebroyavaneto na naselenieto kŭm 4.12.1985 godina* (Census of Population of Dec. 4, 1985); *Naselenie* (Population; annual); *Statisticheskii godishnikna Republika Bŭlgariya* (Statistical Yearbook of the Republic of Bulgaria); its Internet resources.
Burkina Faso. *Annuaire Statistique; Recensement général de la population du 10 au 20 decembre 1985.*
Burundi. *Annuaire statistique; Recensement général de la population, 1990.*
Cambodia. *Cambodia: A Country Study* (1990); *Intersectoral Basic Needs Assessment Mission to Cambodia* (Unesco; 1991); *Report of the Kampuchea Needs Assessment Study* (UNDP; 1989).
Cameroon. *Note annuelle de statistique; Recensement général de la population et de l'habitat 1987.*
Canada. *Canada Year Book* (biennial); *Census Canada 1991: Population;* its Internet resources.
Cape Verde. *Boletím Anual de Estatística; I.º Recenseamento Geral da População e Habitação—1990.*
Central African Republic. *Annuaire statistique; Economic and Social Development Plan 1986–90; Recensement général de la population 1988.*
Chad. *Annuaire statistique; Chad: a Country Study* (1990); *Chad—Background Issues and Statistical Update (IMF Staff Country Report* [1995]).
Chile. *Chile XVI censo nacional de población y V de vivienda, 22 de abril 1992; Compendio estadístico* (annual); *Plan nacional indicativo de desarrollo* (quinquennial).
China, People's Republic of. *People's Republic of China Year-Book; Statistical Yearbook of China; 10 Percent Sampling Tabulation on the 1990 Population Census of the People's Republic of China.*
Colombia. *Colombia estadística* (2 vol.; annual); *XV Censo nacional de población y IV de vivienda* (1985).
Comoros. *Plan interimaire de développement économique et sociale (1983–1986); Recensement général de la population et de l'habitat 15 septembre 1980.*
Congo. *Annuaire statistique; Recensement Général de la Population et de l'Habitat de 1984.*
Costa Rica. *Anuario estadístico; Censo de Población 1984; Plan Nacional de Desarrollo, 1986–90* (2 vol.).
Côte d'Ivoire. *Annuaire statistique; La Côte d'Ivoire en chiffres* (irreg.); *L'Économie Ivoirienne* (irreg.); *Enquête permanente aupres des menages: resultats provisoires 1985; Recensement général de la population et de l'habitat 1988.*
Croatia. *Census of Population, Households, Dwellings and Farms 31st March 1991; Statistical Yearbook.*
Cuba. *Anuario estadístico; Censo de población y viviendas, 1981.*
Cyprus. *Census of Industrial Production* (annual); *Census of Population 1992; Economic Report* (annual); *Statistical Abstract* (annual).
Czech Republic. *Statistická ročenka České Republiky* (Statistical Yearbook of the Czech Republic).
Denmark. *Folke- og boligtaellingen, 1981* (Population and Housing Census); *Statistisk årbog* (Statistical Yearbook); its Internet resources.
Djibouti. *Annuaire statistique de Djibouti.*
Dominica. *Population and Housing Census 1991; Statistical Digest* (irreg.).
Dominican Republic. *Cifras Dominicanas* (irreg.); *VI Censo nacional de población y vivienda, 1981.*
Ecuador. *Serie estadística* (quinquennial); *Censo de población (V) y de vivienda (IV) 1990;* its Internet resources.
Egypt. *Population, Housing, and Establishment Census, 1986; Statistical Yearbook.*
El Salvador. *Anuario estadístico* (8 vol.); *Censos Nacionales: V Censo de Población y IV de Vivienda (1992); El Salvador en cifras* (annual); *Indicadores Económicos y Sociales* (annual); *Plan de Desarrollo Economico y Social 1989–1994.*
Equatorial Guinea. *Censos Nacionales, I de Población y I de Vivienda—4 al 17 de Julio de 1983; Guinea en cifras* (irreg.).
Eritrea. *Eritrea—Recent Economic Developments (IMF Staff Country Report* [1995]); *Ethiopia and Eritrea: A Documentary Study* (1993).
Estonia. *Eesti Statistika Aastaraamat* (Estonia Statistical Yearbook); *Estonia: The Transition to a Market Economy* (1993); *Estonian Human Development Report* (1995); its Internet resources.
Ethiopia. *Ethiopia 1984 Population and Housing Census; Ethiopia Statistical Abstract* (annual).
Faroe Islands. *Rigsombudsmanden på Færøerne: Beretning* (annual).
Fiji. *Annual Employment Survey; Census of Industries* (annual); *Current Economic Statistics* (quarterly); *1986 Census of the Population.*
Finland. *Annual Statistics of Agriculture; Economic Survey* (annual); *Population Census 1990; Statistical Yearbook of Finland.*
France. *Annuaire statistique de la France; Données sociales* (triennial); *Recensement général de la population de 1990; Tableaux de l'Economie Française* (annual); its Internet resources.
French Guiana. *Recensement général de la population de 1990: logements-population-emplois, 973: Guyane; Tableaux economiques regionaux: Guyane* (biennial).
French Polynesia. *Résultats du Recensement Général de la Population de la Polynésie Française, du 6 Septembre 1988; Tableaux de l'economie polynesienne* (irreg.); *Te avei'a: Bulletin d'information statistique* (monthly).
Gabon. *Situation économique, financière et sociale de la République Gabonaise* (annual).
Gambia, The. *Statistical Abstract* (annual?).
Gaza Strip. *Judaea, Samaria, and Gaza Area Statistics Quarterly; Palestinian Statistical Abstract* (annual).
Georgia. *Economic Reviews: Georgia* (IMF [annual]); *Narodnoye Khozyaystvo Gruzinskoy SSR* (National Economy of the Georgian S.S.R. [annual]).
Germany. *Statistisches Jahrbuch für die Bundesrepublik Deutschland; Volkszählung vom 25. Mai 1987* (Census of Population); its Internet resources.
Ghana. *Population Census of Ghana, 1984; Quarterly Digest of Statistics.*
Gibraltar. *Abstract of Statistics* (annual); *Census of Gibraltar, 1991.*
Greece. *Recensement de la population et des habitations, 1991; Statistical Yearbook of Greece.*
Greenland. *Grønland* (annual); *Grønlands befolkning* (Greenland Population [annual]).
Grenada. *Abstract of Statistics* (annual); *1991 Population and Housing Census.*
Guadeloupe. *Recensement général de la population de 1990: logements-population-emplois, 971: Guadeloupe; Tableaux economiques regionaux: Guadeloupe* (biennial).
Guam. *Guam Annual Economic Review; Census '90: Guam.*
Guatemala. *Anuario Estadística; Censos nacionales, 1981: IX de población—IV de habitación.*
Guernsey. *Guernsey Census 1991; Statistical Digest* (annual).
Guinea. *Situation Économique et Conjoncturelle au 31 decembre 1985 et éléments sur la mise en oeuvre de la réform économique au cours du première trimestre 1986; Guinea—Statistical Annex (IMF Staff Country Report* [1995]).
Guinea-Bissau. *Boletim Trimestral de Estatística; Recenseamento Geral da População e da Habitação, 16 de Abril de 1979.*
Guyana. *Annual Statistical Abstract; Guyana: From Economic Recovery to Sustained Growth* (1993); *Guyana and Belize: Country Studies (1993).*
Haiti. *Bulletin trimestriel de statistique; Dominican Republic and Haiti: Country Studies* (1991); *Résultats préliminaires du recensement général (Septembre 1982).*
Honduras. *Anuario estadístico; Censo nacional de Población y Vivienda, 1988; Honduras en cifras* (annual); *Plan nacional de desarrollo, 1987–90.*
Hong Kong. *Annual Digest of Statistics; Hong Kong* (annual); *Hong Kong 1991 Population Census; Hong Kong Social and Economic Trends* (biennial); its Internet resources.
Hungary. *Statisztikai évkönyv* (Statistical Yearbook); *1990, Évi népszámlálás* (Census of Population).
Iceland. *Hagtidhindi* (monthly); *Landshagir* (Statistical Yearbook of Iceland [annual]); *Utanrikisverslun* (External Trade [annual]); its Internet resources.
India. *Census of India, 1991; Economic Survey* (annual); *India: A Reference Annual; Statistical Abstract* (annual).
Indonesia. *Indonesia: An Official Handbook* (irreg.); *Hasil Sensus penduduk Indonesia, 1990* (Census of Population); *Statistical Yearbook of Indonesia;* its Internet resources.
Iran. *National Census of Population and Housing, October 1986; A Statistical Reflection of the Islamic Republic of Iran* (annual); *Iran Statistical Yearbook.*
Iraq. *Iraq: A Country Study* (1990); *Annual Abstract of Statistics.*
Ireland. *Census of Population of Ireland, 1991; National Income and Expenditure* (annual); *Statistical Abstract* (annual).
Isle of Man. *Census Report 1991; Isle of Man Digest of Economic and Social Statistics* (annual).
Israel. *1983 Census of Population and Housing; Statistical Abstract* (annual); its Internet resources.
Italy. *Annuario di statistica agraria: Annuario di statistiche demografiche; Annuario di statistiche industriali; Annuario statistico dell'istruzione; Annuario statistico Italiano; 13° Censimento generale della popolazione e delle Abitazioni 20 Ottobre 1991;* its Internet resources.
Jamaica. *Economic and Social Survey* (annual); *Statistical Abstract* (annual); *Statistical Yearbook of Jamaica.*
Japan. *Japan Statistical Yearbook; Statistical Indicators on Social Life* (annual); *1990 Population Census of Japan;* its Internet resources.
Jersey. *Report of the Census for 1991; Statistical Digest* (annual).
Jordan. *Population and Housing Census 1994; Family Expenditure Survey* (1980); *National Accounts* (irreg.); *Statistical Yearbook.*
Kazakstan. *Economic Reviews: Kazakhstan* (IMF [irreg.]); *Statistichesky Yezhegodnik* (Statistical Yearbook).
Kenya. *Economic Survey* (annual); *Statistical Abstract* (annual).
Kiribati. *Annual Abstract of Statistics; Kiribati Population Census 1990; Sixth National Development Plan, 1987–1991.*
Korea, North. *North Korea: A Country Study* (1994); *The Population of North Korea* (1990).
Korea, South. *Korea Statistical Yearbook; Social Indicators in Korea* (annual); *1990 Population and Housing Census.*
Kuwait. *Annual Statistical Abstract; Economic Report* (annual); *General Census of Population and Housing and Buildings 1985.*
Kyrgyzstan. *Economic Reviews: Kyrgyz Republic* (IMF [irreg.]); *Statistichesky Yezhegodnik Kyrgyzstana* (Statistical Yearbook of Kyrgyzstan).
Laos. *Lao People's Democratic Republic: Industrial Transition* (UNIDO; 1994).
Latvia. *Latvia: The Transition to a Market Economy* (1993); *Statistical Yearbook of Latvia;* its Internet resources.
Lebanon. *Lebanon: A Country Study* (1989).
Lesotho. *Statistical Yearbook; 1986 Population Census.*
Liberia. *Economic Survey* (annual); *1974 Census of Population and Housing.*
Libya. *The Five-Year Development Plan 1981–85; Libya Population Census, 1973; Statistical Abstract for Libya* (annual).
Liechtenstein. *Statistisches Jahrbuch; Volkszählung, 2 Dezember 1980* (Census of Population).
Lithuania. *Lithuania: The Transition to a Market Economy* (1993); *Lithuania's Statistics Yearbook;* its Internet resources.
Luxembourg. *Annuaire statistique; Bulletin du STATEC* (monthly); *Recensement général de la population du 31 mars 1991.*
Macau. *Anuário Estatístico; Inquerito Industrial* (annual); *XIII Recenseamento Geral da População, 1991.*
Macedonia. *Basic Statistical Data* (annual); *Former Yugoslav Republic of Macedonia—Recent Economic Developments (IMF Staff Country Report* [1995]); *Statistical Yearbook of the Republic of Macedonia.*
Madagascar. *Recensement général de la population et de l'habitat, aout 1993; Situation économique* (annual).
Malaŵi. *Malaŵi Population and Housing Census, 1987; Malawi Statistical Yearbook; Malawi Yearbook.*
Malaysia. *Fifth Malaysia Plan, 1986–1990; Malaysia Official Year Book; Malaysian Annual Statistical Bulletin; Population and Housing Census of Malaysia 1991.*
Maldives. *National Development Plan 1991–1993; Population and Housing Census of Maldives 1990; Statistical Year Book of Maldives.*
Mali. *Annuaire statistique du Mali; Comptes Economiques du Mali* (annual); *Recensement general de la population et de l'habitat (du 1er au 14 avril 1987).*
Malta. *Annual Abstract of Statistics; Industry Statistics* (2 vol.; annual); *Malta Year Book* (annual).
Marshall Islands. *Marshall Islands Statistical Abstract* (annual).

Martinique. *Bulletin de statistique* (quarterly); *Recensement de la population de 1990: logements-population-emplois, 972: Martinique; Tableaux economiques regionaux: Martinique* (biennial).
Mauritania. *Annuaire Statistique; Mauritania: A Country Study* (1990).
Mauritius. *Annual Digest of Statistics; 1990 Housing and Population Census of Mauritius.*
Mayotte. *Recensement général de la population de la Collectivité territoriale de Mayotte: août 1991.*
Mexico. *Anuario estadístico; XI Censo general de población y vivienda, 1990; La Economia Mexicana en Cifras* (1990); *Informe de Gobierno: Estadístico* (annual); its Internet resources.
Micronesia. *Second National Development Plan 1992–1996.*
Moldova. *Economic Reviews: Moldova* (IMF [irreg.]); *Republica Moldova in Cifre* (annual).
Monaco. *Annuaire Officiel.*
Mongolia. *Mongolia—Background Paper (IMF Staff Country Report* [1995]); *National Economy of the MPR, 1921–86* (1986; quinquennial?); *The Mongolian People's Republic: Towards a Market Economy* (1991).
Morocco. *Annuaire statistique du Maroc; Economic and Social Development Report, 1981; Recensement général de la population et de l'habitat de 1982.*
Mozambique. *Anuário Estatístico; 1º Recenseamento Geral da População, 1980.*
Myanmar (Burma). *Report to the Pyithu Hluttaw on the Financial, Social, and Economic Conditions for 19*** (annual); *Statistical Abstract* (irreg.); *1983 Population Census.*
Namibia. *Budget 19**–19*** (annual); *Population Census 1981; Statistical/Economic Review* (annual).
Nepal. *Census of Manufacturing Establishments of Nepal, 1986–87; Economic Survey* (annual); *Population Monograph of Nepal* (1995); *The Seventh Plan (1985–90); Statistical Pocket Book* (irreg.); *Statistical Yearbook of Nepal.*
Netherlands, The. *Statistical Yearbook of the Netherlands; 14e Algemene volkstelling, 28 februari 1971* (14th General Population Census); its Internet resources.
Netherlands Antilles. *Tweede Algemene Volks- en Woningtelling Nederlandse Antillen: toestand per 1 Februari 1981; Statistical Yearbook of the Netherlands Antilles.*
New Caledonia. *Annuaire statistique; Recensement de la population de la Nouvelle-Calédonie au 4 avril 1989; Tableaux de l'economie Caledonienne* (annual).
New Zealand. *1991 New Zealand Census of Population and Dwellings; New Zealand Official Yearbook;* its Internet resources.
Nicaragua. *Compendio Estadístico* (annual); *Nicaragua: A Country Study* (1982); *Plan Económico, 1987* (irreg.).
Niger. *Annuaire statistique; Les comptes economiques de la nation* (triennial); *Plan de developpement economique et social du Niger 1987–91; 2ème Recensement général de la population 1988.*
Nigeria. *Annual Abstract of Statistics; Fourth National Development Plan* (1981); *Nigeria: A Country Study* (1992).
Norway. *Folke- og boligtelling 1990* (Population and Housing Census); *Industristatistikk* (annual); *Statistisk årbok* (Statistical Yearbook); its Internet resources.
Oman. *General Census of Population, Housing, and Establishments* (1993); *Statistical Year Book; Fourth Five-Year Development Plan (1991–1995).*
Pakistan. *Economic Survey* (annual); *Eighth Five Year Plan* (1993–98); *Pakistan Statistical Yearbook; Population Census of Pakistan, 1981.*
Palau. *Abstract of Statistics* (annual); *Census '90.*
Panama. *Indicadores económicos y sociales* (annual); *Censos nacionales de 1990: IX de población y V de vivienda, 13 de mayo de 1990; Panama en cifras* (annual); *Situación económica: Cuentas nacionales* (annual); *Situación económica: Industria* (annual).
Papua New Guinea. *Abstract of Statistics* (quarterly); *National Accounts Statistics—Statistical Bulletin* (quarterly); *Social Indicators of Papua New Guinea, 1980–85; Summary of Statistics* (annual); *1990 National Population Census.*
Paraguay. *Anuario estadístico del Paraguay; Censo nacional de población y viviendas, 1992.*
Peru. *Censos nacionales; IX de población: IV de vivienda, 11 de julio de 1993; Compendio estadístico* (3 vol.; annual); *Informe estadístico* (annual).
Philippines. *Philippine Statistical Yearbook; Philippine Yearbook; 1990 Census of Population and Housing.*
Poland. *Narodowy spis powszechny 1988* (Census of Population); *Rocznik statystyczny* (Statistical Yearbook); its Internet resources.
Portugal. *Anuário Estatístico; XIII Recenseamento Geral da População: III Recenseamento Geral da Habitação, 1991;* its Internet resources.
Puerto Rico. *Anuario estadístico; Estadísticas socioeconomicas* (annual); *Informe económico al gobernador* (Economic Report to the Governor [annual]); *1990 Census of Population and Housing* (U.S.).
Qatar. *Annual Statistical Abstract; Economic Survey of Qatar* (annual); *Qatar Year Book.*
Réunion. *Recensement général de la population de 1990: logements-population-emploi, 974; Réunion; Tableau Economique de la Réunion* (biennial).
Romania. *Anuarul statistic al României; Population and Housing Census January 7, 1992; Romania Yearbook.*
Russia. *Economic Reviews: Russian Federation* (IMF [irreg.]); *Rossiysky Statistichesky Yezhegodnik* (Russian Statistical Yearbook).
Rwanda. *Bulletin de Statistique: Supplement Annuel; IIIème Plan de Developpement Economique, Social et Culturel 1982–86; Recensement General de la Population et de l'Habitat 1991.*
St. Kitts and Nevis. *Annual Digest of Statistics; St. Christopher and Nevis: Economic Report* (World Bank Country Study) (1985).
St. Lucia. *Annual Statistical Digest.*
St. Vincent and the Grenadines. *Digest of Statistics* (annual); *Population and Housing Census 1991.*
San Marino. *Annuario statistico, 1981–84* (4 vol.?; irreg.); *3 Censimento generale dell agricoltura* (1977); *5 Censimento generale della popolazione* (1979).
São Tomé and Príncipe. *1° Recenseamento Geral da População e da Habitação 1981.*
Saudi Arabia. *The Statistical Indicator* (annual); *Statistical Summary* (Saudi Arabian Monetary Agency [annual]); *Statistical Yearbook.*
Senegal. *Recensement de la Population et de l'Habitat 1988; Situation économique du Senegal* (annual).
Seychelles. *National Development Plan, 1990–94;* (2 vol.); *Statistical Abstract* (annual); *1987 Census Report.*
Sierra Leone. *Sierra Leone: 12 Years of Economic Achievement and Political Consolidation under the APC and Dr. Siaka Stevens, 1968–80.*
Singapore. *Census of Population, 1990; Report on the Census of Industrial Production* (annual); *Singapore Yearbook; Yearbook of Statistics Singapore;* its Internet resources.
Slovakia. *Sčítanie L'udu, Domov a Bytov 1991* (Census of Population, Housing, and Families 1991); *Statistical Yearbook of the Slovak Republic.*
Slovenia. *Statistični Letopis Republike Slovenija* (Statistical Yearbook of the Republic of Slovenia); its Internet resources.
Solomon Islands. *Solomon Islands 1986 Population Census; Statistical Bulletin* (irreg.).
Somalia. *Statistical Abstract* (annual).
South Africa. *1991 Population Census; South Africa: Official Yearbook of the Republic of South Africa; South African Statistics* (biennial); its Internet resources.
Spain. *Anuario estadístico; Censo de población de 1991;* its Internet resources.
Sri Lanka. *Census of Population and Housing, 1981; Sri Lanka Year Book; Statistical Pocketbook of the Democratic Socialist Republic of Sri Lanka* (annual).
Sudan, The. *Third Population Census, 1983.*
Suriname. *General Population Census 1980; Statistisch Jaarboek van Suriname.*
Swaziland. *Annual Statistical Bulletin; Fourth Five-Year Development Plan (1986/87–90/91 Fiscal Years); Report on the 1986 Swaziland Population Census.*
Sweden. *Folk- och bostadsräkningen, 1990* (Population and Housing Census); *Statistisk årsbok för Sverige* (Statistical Abstract of Sweden [annual]); its Internet resources.
Switzerland. *Recensement fédéral de la population, 1990; Statistisches Jahrbuch* (Statistical Yearbook).
Syria. *General Census of Housing and Inhabitants, 1981; Statistical Abstract* (annual); its Internet resources.
Taiwan. *Industry of Free China* (monthly); *Social Indicators of the Republic of China* (annual); *Statistical Abstract* (annual); *Statistical Yearbook of the Republic of China; Taiwan Statistical Data Book* (annual); *Yearbook of Labor Statistics; 1990 Census of Population and Housing;* its Internet resources.
Tajikistan. *Economic Reviews: Tajikistan* (IMF [irreg.]); *Narodnoye Khozyaystvo Tadzhikskoy SSR* (National Economy of the Tadzhik S.S.R. [annual]).
Tanzania. *Tanzania in Figures* (annual); *Tanzania Statistical Abstract* (irreg.); *1978 Population Census.*
Thailand. *Report of the Survey of Business Trade and Services* (biennial); *Foreign Trade Statistics* (monthly); *Report of the Industrial Survey, Whole Kingdom* (biennial); *Report of the Labor Force Survey: Whole Kingdom* (quarterly); *Statistical Handbook of Thailand* (annual); *Statistical Yearbook; 1990 Population and Housing Census.*
Togo. *Annuaire statistique du Togo; Eurostat Country Profile: Togo* (1991); *Plan de développement économique & social, 1981–1985; Recensement Général de la Population et de l'Habitat 1981.*
Tonga. *Population Census, 1986; Sixth Development Plan 1991–95; Statistical Abstract* (irreg.).
Trinidad and Tobago. *Annual Statistical Digest; 1990 Population and Housing Census.*
Tunisia. *Annuaire statistique de la Tunisie; Recensement général de la population et des logements, 30 mars 1984.*
Turkey. *Diş Ticaret İstatistikleri* (Annual Foreign Trade Statistics); *1990 Genel Nüfus Sayımı* (1990 Census of Population); *İnşaat İstatistikleni* (Construction Statistics [annual]); *Türkiye İstatistik Yilliği* (Statistical Yearbook of Turkey); its Internet resources.
Turkmenistan. *Economic Reviews: Turkmenistan* (IMF [irreg.]); *Narodnoye Khozyaystvo Turkmenskoy SSR* (National Economy of the Turkmen S.S.R. [annual]).
Tuvalu. *1992–94 Medium-Term Economic Framework Programme.*
Uganda. *Uganda: A Country Study; Uganda—Background Paper (IMF Staff Country Report* [1995]).
Ukraine. *Economic Reviews: Ukraine* (IMF [irreg.]); *Narodne Hospodarstvo Ukrayini u 19** rotsi* (National Economy of Ukraine in the Year 19** [annual]).
United Arab Emirates. *Statistical Yearbook* (Abu Dhabi).
United Kingdom. *Annual Abstract of Statistics; Britain: An Official Handbook* (annual); *Census 1991; Report on the Census of Production: Summary Tables* (annual); *United Kingdom National Accounts.*
United States. *Agricultural Statistics* (annual); *Annual Energy Review; Current Population Reports* (Series P-20, P-23, P-25, P-26, P-27, P-28, P-60); *Digest of Education Statistics* (annual); *Minerals Yearbook* (3 vol.; annual); *National Transportation Statistics* (annual); *Statistical Abstract* (annual); *U.S. Exports: SIC-Based Products* (annual); *U.S. Imports: SIC-Based Products* (annual); *Vital and Health Statistics* (series 1–20); *1992 Census of Agriculture; 1992 Census of Construction Industries; 1992 Census of Manufacturing; 1992 Census of Retail Trade; 1992 Census of Service Industries; 1992 Census of Wholesale Trade; 1990 Census of Population and Housing;* its Internet resources.
Uruguay. *Anuario Estadístico; Censo General: VI de población: IV de viviendas, Octubre 1985. Encuesta Nacional de Hogares* (annual).
Uzbekistan. *Economic Reviews: Uzbekistan* (IMF [irreg.]); *Narodnoye Khozyaystvo Respubliki Uzbekistan v 19** g.* (National Economy of Uzbekistan in the Year 19** [annual]); *Republic of Uzbekistan.*
Vanuatu. *National Population Census 1989; Second National Development Plan 1987–1991* (2 vol.); *Vanuatu Statistical Yearbook.*
Venezuela. *Anuario estadístico; Censo General de la Población y Vivienda 1990; Encuesta de hogares por muestreo* (annual); *Encuesta industrial* (annual).
Vietnam. *IMF Economic Reviews: Vietnam* (1994); *Nien Giam Thong Ke* (Statistical Yearbook); *Tong Dieu Tra Dan So Viet Nam—1989 (Vietnam Population Census—1989); Vietnam: A Country Study* (1989).
Virgin Islands of the United States. *Annual Report; 1990 Census of Population and Housing* (U.S.).
West Bank. *Judaea, Samaria, and Gaza Area Statistics Quarterly; Palestinian Statistical Abstract* (annual).
Western Sahara. *Recensement General de la Population et de l'Habitat* (1982 [Morocco]).
Western Samoa. *Annual Statistical Abstract; Census of Population and Housing,* 1981; *Seventh Development Plan 1992–1994.*
Yemen. *Country Presentation: Republic of Yemen* (1990); *The Yemens: Country Studies* (1986).
Yugoslavia. *Popis stanovištva, domaćinstava, stanova i poljoprivrednih gazdinstava 1991 godine* (Census of Population, Households, Housing, and Agricultural Holdings 1991); *Statistički godišnjak Jugoslavije* (Statistical Yearbook of Yugoslavia).
Zaire. *Annuaire statistique* (irreg.); Conjoncture Economique (semiannual); *Recensement Scientifique de la Population du 1er juillet 1984.*
Zambia. *Country Profile: Zambia 1985; Monthly Digest of Statistics; National Development Plan, 1989–93; 1990 Census of Population, Housing, Agriculture.*
Zimbabwe. *Population Census 1991; Statistical Yearbook* (irreg.).

Index

This index covers both *Britannica Book of the Year* (cumulative for 10 years) and *Britannica World Data*.

Entries in dark type are titles of articles in the *Book of the Year;* an accompanying year in dark type gives the year the reference appears, and the accompanying page number in light type **shows where the article appears. References for previous years are preceded by the year in dark type. For example, "Architecture 97:**137; **96:**117; **95:**104; **94:**99; **93:**100; **92:**98; **91:**127; **90:**146; **89:**128; **88:**128**" indicates that the article "Architecture" appeared every year from 1988 through 1997. Other references that appear with a page number but without a year refer to references from the current yearbook.**

Indented entries in light type that follow dark-type article titles refer by page number to other places in the text where the subject of the article is discussed. Light-type entries that are not indented refer by page number to subjects that are not themselves article titles. Names of people covered in biographies and obituaries are followed by the abbreviation "(biog.)" or "(obit.)" with the year in dark type and a page number in light type, *e.g.,* Burns, George, *or* Nathan Birnbaum (obit.) **97:**96, or Clinton, Bill, *or* William Jefferson Clinton (biogs.) **97:**70; **94:**37; **93:**37. In cases where a person has both a biography and an obituary, the words appear as subentries under the main entry and are alphabetized accordingly, *e.g.:*

Brown, Ronald Harmon
  biography **90:**84
  obituary **97:**95

References to illustrations are by page number and are preceded by the abbreviation *il.*

The index uses word-by-word alphabetization (treating a word as one or more characters separated by a space from the next word). Names beginning with "Mc" and "Mac" are alphabetized as "Mac"; "St." is treated as "Saint."

A

"A la frontière" (Butor) 246
AAA: *see* American Automobile Association
AAS: *see* All-America Selections
Abacha, Sani 458
abacus
  Chinese education 204
Abadi, Agha Hasan (obit.) **96:**73
ABB (Ger. co.): *see* Asea Brown Boveri
Abbott, George Francis (obit.) **96:**73
ABC: *see* American Broadcasting Company
'Abd al-Wahab, Muhammad (obit.) **92:**54
Abdul, Paula (biog.) **91:**64
Abdul Rahman (obit.) **91:**86
Abdullah (Saud.Arab. prince) 470
Abe Kobo, *or* Abe Kimifusa (obit.) **94:**54
Abel, Iorwith Wilbur (obit.) **88:**87
Aberdeen Proving Ground (Md., U.S.) 270
Abernathy, Ralph David (obit.) **91:**86
Abkhazia (reg., Georgia) 421
Aboriginal and Torres Strait Islander Commission, *or* ATSIC (com., Austr.) 392
aborigine (people, N. and S.Am.): *see* Native American peoples
Aborigine, Australian (people): *see* Australian Aborigine
abortion
  Poland 462
  South Africa 473
  United States 218
  see also partial-birth abortion
Abravanel, Maurice (obit.) **94:**54
Abrego, Juan García
  drug trafficking 227
ABT (Am. ballet co.): *see* American Ballet Theatre
Abu Jihad: *see* Wazir, Khalil Ibrahim al-
Abu Rishah, 'Umar (obit.) **91:**86
Abu Seif, Salah (obit.) **97:**91
Abubakr III (obit.) **89:**88
Academy Award, *or* Oscar (U.S.)
  film awards *table* 294
acid rain 210
ACOG: *see* Atlanta Committee for the Olympic Games
Acquelin, José 247
acquired immune deficiency syndrome: *see* AIDS
acquisition, corporate: *see* merger and acquisition, corporate
Acquisition and Cross Servicing Agreement (U.S.-Japan) 439
Action Committee for Renewal, *or* CAR (pol. party, Togo) 483
Action for Unity and Development (pol. party, Chad) 407
Acton, Sir Harold Mario Mitchell (obit.) **95:**60
Acuff, Roy Claxton (obit.) **93:**54
"Adam and Eve," *or* "Adão e Eva" (motion picture) 291
Adams, Bryan (biog.) **93:**33
Adams, Diana (obit.) **94:**54
Adams, Gerry (biog.) **95:**39
  British literature 243
Adams, Scott (biog.) **96:**52
Adamson, George (obit.) **90:**103
"Adão e Eva" (motion picture): *see* "Adam and Eve"
Addams, Charles Samuel (obit.) **89:**88
Ademola, Sir Adetokunbo Adegboyega (obit.) **94:**54
Aden: *see* Yemen, People's Democratic Republic of
"Adiós a Mamá" (Arenas) 248
Adler, Lawrence James (obit.) **89:**88
Adler, Stella (obit.) **93:**54
Adobe Systems (Am. co.) 173
Adolph Coors Brewing Co. (Am. co.): *see* Coors Brewing Co.
ADRs: *see* American Depository Receipts
advance-directive law: *see* right-to-die law
advanced composites 168
Advanced Earth Observation Satellite: *see* Midori
Advanced Photo System, *or* APS 173
advertising 154
  British elections 488
  Buddhism 309
  footwear 156
  Internet 180
  newspapers 266
  soft drinks 159
  spirits 159
advertising agency 154
Aedes aegypti (mosquito) *il.* 218
AEG (Ger. co.)
  electrical industry 162
Aegean Islands (isls., Gr.)
  Turkey-Greece dispute 484
aerial sports **94:**278; **93:**279; **92:**305; **91:**305; **90:**321; **89:**306; **88:**308
aerospace 155
  space exploration 260
Aerospatiale (Fr. co.) 419
Aetna Life and Casuality (Am. co.) 166
AF camera: *see* autofocus camera
Afanasyev, Viktor Grigoryevich (obit.) **95:**60
AFC: *see* American Football Conference
AFDC: *see* Aid to Families with Dependent Children
Afewerke, Issayas, *or* Afwerki, Isaias (biog.) **92:**33
  Eritrea 415
affirmative action program (U.S.)
  California 499
Affordable Family Car, *or* AFC 158
Afghanistan 97:388; **96:**366; **95:**367; **94:**402; **93:**402; **92:**401; **91:**428; **90:**447; **89:**429; **88:**429
  Commonwealth of Independent States 380
  Islam 310
  military affairs 273
    land mines (special report) 274, *map* 275
  natural disasters 60
  new flag *illus.* **94:**345; **93:**345
  refugees 297
  special reports **94:**377; **93:**233
  United Nations 377
  women
    education 206
    rights issues 316
  see also WORLD DATA
AFL: *see* Australian Football League
'Aflaq, Michel (obit.) **90:**103
African affairs 94:352; **93:**354; **92:**348; **91:**378; **90:**399; **89:**382; **88:**382
  agriculture and food supplies 124
  anthropology 133
  arts and entertainment
    motion pictures 295
    popular music 280
  basketball 325
  business and industry
    mining 170
    tourism 178
  demography 296
  economic affairs 188, 194
  environmental issues 211
  military affairs 276, *table* 272
  nuclear weapons ban 269
  political party systems (spotlight) 416, *map* 417
  prisons and penology 229
  refugees 297
  religion
    Religious Society of Friends 304
    Roman Catholicism 306
    statistics *table* 311
  social protection 314
  special reports **95:**173; **92:**349
  women's rights issues 316, *il.*
  see also Middle Eastern and North African affairs; *and* individual countries by name
African-American, *or* Afro-American: *see* black American
African Great Lakes region
  refugees 297
African National Congress, *or* ANC (pol. party, S.Af.) 473
African Nuclear Weapons Free Zone
  military affairs 269
African Party for the Independence of Cape Verde, *or* PAICV (pol. party, C.Verde) 406
Afridi, Shahid 332
"After Paradise" (Rapoport) 242
Afwerki, Isaias: *see* Afewerke, Issayas
Aga Khan Award for Architecture 137
Agassi, Andre 360
Agnew, Spiro Theodore (obit.) **97:**91
Agriculture, U.S. Department of, *or* USDA (govt. agency, U.S.) 123, 130
Agriculture and Food Supplies 97:123; **96:**103; **95:**90; **94:**83; **93:**83; **92:**83; **91:**113; **90:**129; **89:**113; **88:**113
  health and disease 221
  human rights issues 316
  special reports **92:**167; **90:**140
  stock exchanges 198
  see also WORLD DATA; *and* individual countries by name
Agrobanka Praha
  Czech banking 200
Ahmed, Ijaz 332
Ahmed, Mushtaq 332
Ai Qing, *or* Jiang Haicheng (obit.) **97:**91
AIA: *see* American Institute of Architects
aid: *see* relief
Aid to Families with Dependent Children, *or* AFDC 312
  United States 491
AIDS, *or* acquired immune deficiency syndrome
  Africa 296
  children (special report) **96:**287
  Japan 438
  pharmaceuticals 173
  special reports **95:**278; **94:**263; **88:**206
  treatment research 219
  United States 498
Aikman, Troy Kenneth (biog.) **97:**65
  football 344
Ailey, Alvin (obit.) **90:**103
Ailuropoda melanoleuca: *see* panda
air bag 157, 158
  safety appraisal 222
Air Force (U.S.): *see* United States Air Force, The
air pollution 210, *il.* 211
  glass industry 166
air-sea interface, *or* sea-air interface
  oceanography 187
Airbus Industrie (Fr. co.)
  aerospace industry 155, 420
airline: *see* aviation
airport
  civil engineering projects *table* 143
Ajax Amsterdam (soccer) 340
Akalaitis, JoAnne (biog.) **92:**33
Akashi, Yasushi (biog.) **93:**33
Akashi Kaikyo (bridge, Japan) 139
Akayesu, Jean-Paul
  war crimes violations 315
Akayev, Askar 443
Ake, Claude (obit.) **97:**91
Akebono (biog.) **94:**33
Akhromeyev, Sergey Fedorovich (obit.) **92:**54
Akihito, *or* Heisei (biog.) **89:**65
Akinwande, Henry 329
Akram, Wasim 332
AL (pol. party, Bangla.): *see* Awami League
Alabama (state, U.S.) 497
Alagna, Roberto (biog.) **97:**65
Alaska (state, U.S.)
  petroleum extraction 383
  special report **92:**168
Albania 97:388; **96:**366; **95:**367; **94:**421; **93:**424; **92:**418; **91:**468; **90:**485; **89:**468; **88:**468
  economic affairs 193
  international relations
    Greece 426
    Macedonia 447
  new flag *illus.* **93:**345
  Orthodox Church 308
  special report **93:**144
  see also WORLD DATA
Albanian (people)
  Kosovo schools 503
albatross
  satellite measurement 235
Albert (duke of Bav.): *see* Albrecht
Albert II (biog.) **94:**33
  Belgium 397
Alberts, Bruce (biog.) **95:**39
Albery, Sir Donald Arthur Rolleston (obit.) **89:**88
Albrecht, *or* Prince Albert Luitpold Ferdinand Michael, duke of Bavaria (obit.) **97:**91
Albright, Josephine Patterson (obit.) **97:**91
Albright, Madeline 496
Alcatel Worldwide Pairs
  contract bridge 331
Alcayaga, María Lucia (obit.): *see* Beltrán, Lola
"Alcobas de palacio" (Loret de Mola) 248
Alcohol, Tobacco and Firearms, Bureau of, *or* ATF (U.S.) 495
alcoholic beverage
  alcopops 132
  see also beer; wine; spirits
alcoholism 221
alcopop
  alcoholic beverages 132, 159
Alea, Tomás Gutiérrez (obit.) **97:**91
Aleksey II
  Orthodox Church 300, 307
Alemán, Arnoldo 457, *il.*
Alepoudhelis, Odysseus (obit.): *see* Elytis, Odysseus
Alesana, Tofilau Eti 502
Alexander, Lamar
  presidential election (special report) 493
Alfred P. Murrah Federal Building (Oklahoma City, Okla., U.S.) 495
Alfvén, Hannes Olof Gösta (obit.) **96:**73
alga
  marine biology 235
Algeria 97:389; **96:**367; **95:**368; **94:**379; **93:**380; **92:**378; **91:**404; **90:**424; **89:**407; **88:**407
  Roman Catholicism 306
  special reports **94:**378; **92:**350
  see also WORLD DATA
Algueva Dam (dam, Port.) 142
ALH84001 (meteorite)
  life on Mars claim 183, 256, 382
Ali, Salim (obit.) **88:**87
"Alias Grace" (Atwood) 242
Aliyev, Heydar 393
alkynylation
  carbon-hydrogen bonds 253
All-America Selections, *or* AAS
  gardening 215
Allais, Maurice (biog.) **89:**65
Allan Hills (hills, Antarc.)
  meteorite discovery 256, 382
Allcock, Tony 352
Allégret, Yves Edouard (obit.) **88:**87
Allen, Clabon Walter (obit.) **88:**87
Allen, George Herbert (obit.) **91:**86
Allen, Sir George Oswald Browning (obit.) **90:**103
Allen, Mel, *or* Melvin Allen Israel (obit.) **97:**91
Allen, Walter Ernest (obit.) **96:**73
Allende, Isabel (biog.) **96:**52
Alliance for Freedom, *or* Freedom Alliance (pol. party, It.) 436
Allison, Davey (obit.) **94:**54
Allison, Fran (obit.) **90:**103
Almeida, Laurindo (obit.) **96:**73
Almendros, Nestor (obit.) **93:**54
Almirante, Giorgio (obit.) **89:**88
Almodóvar, Pedro (biog.) **91:**64
Almos, Anthony 208
"Alonso e i visionari" (Ortese) 247
ALP (pol. party, Austr.): *see* Australian Labor Party
"Alphabet Soup" (horse) 335
alpine skiing 355
ALS: *see* amyotrophic lateral sclerosis
Alsop, Joseph Wright (obit.) **90:**103
alternative energy 164
Altman, Sidney (biog.) **90:**81
Alton, John, *or* Aldan Jacko (obit.) **97:**91
aluminum
  light metals 168
  mining 170
Alusuisse-Lonza (Swiss co.)
  Iceland 430
Alvarez, Luis Walter (obit.) **89:**88
Alvin Ailey American Dance Theatre 283
Alzado, Lyle (obit.) **93:**54
Alzheimer's disease 222
AMA: *see* American Missionary Association
Amanpour, Christiane (biog.) **97:**65
amateur radio, *or* ham radio 265
amateur sports
  golf 346
Amato, Giuliano (biog.) **93:**33
Amazigh (people): *see* Berber
Ambartsumian, Viktor Amazaspovich (obit.) **97:**91
amber
  preserved fossils 239, *il.* 238
Ameche, Alan Dante (obit.) **89:**88
Ameche, Don (obit.) **94:**54
America Online, *or* AOL (Am. co.) 177
  newspapers 265

American Automobile Association,
  or AAA
  business merger 179
American Ballet Theatre, or ABT (Am.
  ballet co.) 282
American Bankers Association 200
American Baptist Churches USA 302
American Broadcasting Company, or ABC
  (Am. co.)
  television ratings 262
American Depository Receipts, or ADRs
  equity markets (special report) 95:173
American Football Conference, or
  AFC 344
American Indian (people): see Native
  American peoples
American Institute of Architects, or
  AIA 137
American League (baseball) 321
American literature 240
American Missionary Association, or
  AMA 305
American Mutual Life Insurance (Am.
  co.) 166
American Poolplayers Association, or
  APA 325
American Radio Relay League, or
  ARRL 265
American Samoa (isl., Pac.O.) 381
American Society of Furniture Designers
  Pinnacle awards 165
American States, Organization of, or
  OAS 380
American Stock Exchange, or Amex
  (U.S.) 197
American Zoo and Aquarium Associa-
  tion 214
AmeriCorps
  U.S. education 204
Ames, Leslie Ethelbert George (obit.) 91:86
Amex (U.S.): see American Stock Ex-
  change
Amin, Mohamed (obit.) 97:92
Amir, Yigal 434
Amis, Sir Kingsley William
  biography 92:33
  obituary 96:73
Amnesty International
  Buddhism 309
  death penalty 229
  Peru 461
  Rwanda 467
  Uganda 486
Amnuay Virawan 483
Amoco (Am. co.) 177
Amorphophallus titanum (plant): see titan
  arum
Amory, Vance 467
Amsterdam, Morey (obit.) 97:92
Amtrak (Am. r.r. system)
  railroad disasters 61
amyotrophic lateral sclerosis, or ALS, or
  Lou Gehrig's disease
  molecular biology 237
AN (pol. party, It.): see National Alliance
Anastasios (Alb. Orthodox archbp.) 308
ANC (pol. party, S.Af.): see African
  National Congress
"Ancestral Suitcase, The" (Fraser) 242
anchoveta
  fisheries 130
Andean Community 380
Anderson, Carl David (obit.) 92:54
Anderson, Carmen 352
Anderson, Dame Judith, or Francis
  Margaret Anderson (obit.) 93:54
Anderson, Lindsay Gordon (obit.) 95:60
Anderson, Marian (obit.) 94:54
Anderson, Reid 284
Andersson, Sven Olof Morgan (obit.) 88:87
Ando, Tadao (biog.) 93:33
Andorra 97:389; 96:369; 95:368; 94:422;
  93:424; 92:418; 91:445; 90:462;
  89:446; 88:445
  see also WORLD DATA
Andrade, Mário Coelho Pinto de (obit.)
  91:86
Andreessen, Marc (biog.) 97:65
Andreotti, Giulio 436
Andrews, Carver Dana (obit.) 93:54
Andrews, Eamonn (obit.) 88:87
Andrews, Harry (obit.) 90:103
Andrews, Maxene (obit.) 96:73
Andrews, Michael James (obit.) 96:73
Anfinsen, Christian Boehmer (obit.) 96:74
"Angel Walk" (Govier) 242
Angevin empire (Eur. hist.)
  English Channel history (special report)
  95:351
Anghelis, Odysseus (obit.) 88:87
angioplasty 219
Angle (people)
  English Channel history (special report)
  95:350
Anglican Communion 301
  religion statistics table 311
  see also England, Church of
Anglo American Corp. (S.Af. co.)
  mining 171
Angola 97:389; 96:369; 95:369; 94:353;
  93:355; 92:351; 91:379; 90:400;
  89:383; 88:383
  basketball 325
  land mines (special report) 274, ils.
  275, 389
  military affairs 276
  see also WORLD DATA

angonoka: see ploughshare tortoise
"Angus Wilson: A Biography"
  (Drabble) 243
Anheuser-Busch Companies, Inc. (Am.
  co.)
  beer 159
animal
  entomology 233
  marine biology 234
  ornithology 233
  veterinary medicine 222
  wildlife conservation 212
  zoology 232
  zoos 213
animal experimentation
  immune system research 64
Animal Liberation Front 156
animal rights
  furs 156
  special report 94:112
  United States law 499
"Animal triste" (Maron) 244
animation
  motion picture technology (special
  report) 97:292
anisotropism (phys.)
  helium-3 research 64
Ankarapithecus meteai
  anthropology 133
Annan, Kofi 376, 496
Annapolis Academy (school, U.S.): see
  United States Naval Academy
Annenberg, Walter H. (biog.) 95:39
Anouilh, Jean-Marie-Lucien-Pierre (obit.)
  88:87
Anquetil, Jacques (obit.) 88:88
ant
  entomology 234
Antall, Jozsef (obit.) 94:55
Antarctic Science, Tourism, and Conservation Act (U.S.) 383
Antarctica 97:382; 96:359; 95:360; 94:502;
  93:502; 92:494; 91:521; 90:537;
  89:520; 88:520
antenna (elec.)
  satellite TV (special report) 176
Anthropology 97:133; 96:112; 95:100;
  94:94; 93:94; 92:94; 91:123; 90:141;
  89:124; 88:124
  special report 93:95
anti-Semitism
  World War II (special report) 96:257
antiatom 255
antidepressant (drug)
  Prozac (special report) 95:215
antielectron: see positron
antipersonnel mine
  "Combating the Land Mine Scourge"
  (special report) 97:274
  military affairs 269
antiproton 255
antiquarian books 151
antiques 144
  collectibles 152
Antonio (obit.): see Ruiz Soler, Antonio
Anwar bin Ibrahim, Dato Seri 448
Anwarul, Haq (obit.) 96:74
AOL (Am. co.): see America Online
AOL Europa
  newspapers 265
Aoun, Michel (biog.) 90:81
APA: see American Poolplayers Association
apartheid
  crime and law enforcement 229
  human rights issues 316
ape
  anthropology 133
APEC: see Asia-Pacific Economic Cooperation forum
aphelion (astron.)
  1997 table 256
"Apollo" (ballet) 282
apparel: see clothing; footwear; furs
Apple Computer, Inc. (Am. co.) 182
  microelectronics 169
applied chemistry 254
Applied Special Technology, Center for
  (Wash., D.C., U.S.)
  Internet study 181
Appling, Lucius Benjamin (obit.) 92:54
APS: see Advanced Photo System
Aptidon, Hassan Gouled 413
APV (Hung. co.): see State Privatization
  and Holding Company
Aqsa Mosque, al- (mosque, Jerusalem)
  135, 434, map 435
aqueduct
  civil engineering projects table 143
Arab-Israeli conflict: see Middle Eastern
  and North African affairs
Arab-Israeli peace process
  Egypt 414
  European Union 379
  France 420
  Israel 375, 434
  Jordan 439
  military affairs 273
  Norway 459
  Syria 478
  United States 496
Arab League
  international law 224

Arabic literature 252
Arafat, Yasir
  Israel 434
Arc de Triomphe (Paris, Fr.) il. 334
archaea
  geologic discovery 183
Archaeology 97:134; 96:114; 95:101;
  94:95; 93:96; 92:95; 91:125; 90:143;
  89:125; 88:125
  Buddhism 309
archery 97:317; 96:299; 88:345
  1996 Summer Olympic champions table
  97:365
Architecture 97:137; 96:117; 95:104; 94:99;
  93:100; 92:98; 91:127; 90:146; 89:128;
  88:128
archive
  digitized visual images 149
ARCO Alaska Inc. (Am. co.) 383
Arctic Council (internat. org.) 383
  environmental protection 206
  international law 224
Arctic Regions 97:383; 96:360; 95:361;
  94:503; 93:503; 92:495; 91:522;
  90:538; 89:522; 88:522
Arden, Eve (obit.) 91:86
ARENA (pol. party, El Sal.): see National
  Republican Alliance Party
Arenas, Reinaldo
  Latin-American literature 248
Arévalo Bermejo, Juan José (obit.) 91:87
Argaña, Luis María
  Paraguay 460
Argentina 97:390; 96:370; 95:370; 94:476;
  93:475; 92:467; 91:493; 90:509;
  89:493; 88:492
  business and industry
  building and construction 160
  industrial accident insurance 314
  Falkland Islands 380
  literature 248
  military affairs 276
  most populous urban areas table 296
  special report 92:465
  sports and games
  association football 341
  polo 338
  see also WORLD DATA
Argentine Open (polo) 338
Argyll, Margaret, Duchess of (obit.) 94:55
Ariane 5 (rocket) 260
Arias Madrid, Arnulfo (obit.) 89:89
Arias Navarro, Carlos (obit.) 90:104
Arias Sánchez, Oscar (biog.) 88:65
Aristide, Jean-Bertrand (biog.) 95:39
Arizona (state, U.S.) 498
Arizona State University (U.S.)
  football 342
Arkansas (state, U.S.) 498
Arkayev, Leonid Yakovlevich (biog.) 97:66
Arletty, or Arlette-Léonie Bathiat (obit.)
  93:55
Armaments Corporation of South Africa,
  or Armscor (S.Af. co.) 474
Armbruster, Peter (biog.) 97:66
  nuclear chemistry 253
armed forces: see Military Affairs
Armed Islamic Group, or GIA (pol. org.,
  Alg.) 389
Armenia 97:390; 96:371; 95:371; 94:422;
  93:425
  Azerbaijan 393
  economic affairs 193
  new flag illus. 93:345
  refugees 297
  see also WORLD DATA
Armenian Apostolic Church 308
ARMM (Mindanao, Phil.): see Autono-
  mous Region in Muslim Mindanao
arms control 269
  United Nations 376
Armscor (S.Af. co.): see Armaments Cor-
  poration of South Africa
Armstrong, Henry (obit.) 89:89
Armstrong, John Ward (obit.) 88:88
Armstrong, Karen (biog.) 97:66
Armstrong, Louis
  archives 279
Army (U.S.): see United States Army, The
Arnett, Peter (biog.) 92:33
Arnold, Roseanne (biog.): see Barr,
  Roseanne
Aronoff Center for Design and Art
  (Cincinnati, Ohio, U.S.) 137, il. 138
Arrau, Claudio (obit.) 92:55
ARRL: see American Radio Relay League
Arrupe, The Rev. Pedro (obit.) 92:55
arson
  African-American churches 300, 302,
  il. 498
"Art" (play) 286
Art Auctions and Sales 97:150; 96:128;
  95:114; 94:102; 93:103; 92:101;
  91:131; 90:149; 89:131; 88:131
art collection: see Collectibles
Art Exhibitions 97:144; 96:124; 95:107;
  94:102; 93:103; 92:101; 91:131;
  90:149; 89:131; 88:131
  special report 97:146
Arthur, Jean (obit.) 92:55
artificial insemination
  special report 94:111
arts funding
  classical music 277
Arzú, Alvaro
  Guatemala 426
Asaf Ali, Aruna Ganguli (obit.) 97:92

Asahara, Shoko, or Chizuo Matsumoto
  (biog.) 96:52
  Japan 438
Asahi Chemical Industry (Japanese co.)
  man-made fibres 177
Asahina, Takashi (biog.) 97:66
asbestos 212
Asea Brown Boveri, or ABB (Ger. co.)
  electrical industry 161
ASEAN: see Southeast Asian Nations,
  Association of
Ashanti Goldfields (Ghanaian co.) 170
Ashcroft, Dame Peggy (obit.) 92:55
Ashdown, Paddy (biog.) 89:65
Ashe, Arthur Robert, Jr. (obit.) 94:55
Ashrawi, Hanan (biog.) 93:34
Ashton, Sir Frederick William Mallandaine
  (obit.) 89:89
Asia-Europe Meeting 471
Asia-Pacific Economic Cooperation forum,
  or APEC 380
Asian affairs
  agriculture 124, 129
  anthropology 133
  archaeology 135
  arts and entertainment
  art exhibitions 144
  motion pictures 295
  badminton 329
  business and industry 154
  chemicals 161
  microelectronics 169
  paints and varnishes 172
  rubber 167
  textiles 177
  tourism 178
  wood products 179
  demography 296
  economic affairs 188, 193
  stock exchanges 199
  environment 207
  Euro-Asian summit 380
  gardening 214
  military affairs 273, table
  newspapers 265
  religion
  Roman Catholicism 306
  Seventh-day Adventist Church 305
  statistics table 311
  roads 142
  social protection 314
  special report 95:173
  transportation
  freight and pipelines 373
  intercity rail 374
  urban mass transit 374
  see also Central Asia; East Asian affairs;
  Southeast Asian affairs
Asimov, Isaac (obit.) 93:55
ASkyB (Am. co.)
  television 261
Aspin, Leslie, Jr. (obit.) 96:74
Assad, Hafez al- (biog.) 92:34
  Syria 478
assassination
  crime and law enforcement 226
  Israel 434
  Italy 437
  Mexico 453
  Papua New Guinea 460
  South Africa 229
  Ukraine 487
  see also murder
assisted suicide: see euthanasia
association football, or soccer 340
  Guatemala disaster 61
  1996 Summer Olympic champions table
  97:366
Association of . . . : see under substantive
  word, e.g., Southeast Asian Nations,
  Association of
Astaire, Fred (obit.) 88:88
asteroid (astron.) 257, 259
Asteroid 1996 PW
  discovery and characteristics 257
Astor, Mary (obit.) 88:88
Astorga, Nora (obit.) 89:89
astronaut, or cosmonaut
  space exploration 258
Astronomy 97:256; 96:166; 95:112; 94:107;
  93:107; 92:106; 91:135; 90:153;
  89:135; 88:135
  Sagan contribution 117
Asturias, Rodrigo
  United Nations 377
asylum
  Belarus 396
  women's rights issues 316
AT&T (Am. co.)
  telecommunications 177
Atanasoff, John Vincent (obit.) 96:74
Atapuerca (archae. site) il. 133
Atassi, Nureddin al- (obit.) 93:55
Ataturk, Kemal, or Mustafa Kemal
  special report 92:375
ATF (U.S.): see Alcohol, Tobacco and
  Firearms, Bureau of
Athanasiadis-Novas, Georgios (obit.)
  88:88
Athens (Gr.)
  subway project 142
atherosclerosis
  passive smoke effects 221
athletics: see track and field sports
Atkinson, Kate
  British literature 243
Atkinson, Rowan Sebastian (biog.) 97:67

Atlanta (Ga., U.S.)
  architecture 137
  Olympic Games
    Australia 391
    funding (special report) 364
    1996 Summer Olympic champions *table* **97**:365
    terrorism 226, 495
Atlanta Braves (baseball) 320
Atlanta Committee for the Olympic Games, *or* ACOG (special report) 364
Atlantic LNG Co. (Tr. and Tob. co.) 483
Atlantic Ocean
  water-circulation research 187
"Atlantis" (ballet) 279
"Atlantis" (U.S. space shuttle) 258
atmosphere
  Jupiter 256
  meteorology and climate 186
  ozone layer 382
atom (phys.)
  antimatter research 255
atomic warfare: *see* nuclear warfare
atomic weapon: *see* nuclear weapon
ATSIC (com., Austr.): *see* Aboriginal and Torres Strait Islander Commission
Atsumi, Kiyoshi, *or* Tadokoro Yasuo (obit.) **97**:92
Atta: *see* leaf-cutting ant
Attali, Jacques (biog.) **92**:34
Atwater, Lee (obit.) **92**:55
Atwood, Margaret Eleanor (biog.) **88**:65
auction
  numismatics 152
  photography 149
  see also Art Auctions and Sales
Auger, Arleen (obit.) **94**:55
"August" (motion picture) 290
Aum Shinrikyo (rel. cult) 262, 438
Aung San Suu Kyi, Daw (biogs.) **92**:30; **91**:64
  Myanmar 455
aurora
  observation satellites 260
Australia **97**:391; **96**:372; **95**:371; **94**:494; **93**:493; **92**:485; **91**:512; **90**:528; **89**:512; **88**:511
  agriculture and food supplies 129
  archaeology 135
  arts and entertainment
    art exhibitions 149
    literature 244
    motion pictures 290
  aviation disasters 58
  business and industry
    coal 163
    cotton 177
    mining 170
    wine 159
    wool 177
  crime and law enforcement 227
  economic affairs 194
    labour-management relations 202
    stock exchanges 199
  education 206
  health care reform 314
  international affairs
    Papua New Guinea 460
  newspapers 265
  numismatics 152
  special report **89**:176
  sports and games
    cricket 332, 333
    field hockey 339
    football 344
    rowing 354
    rugby football 345
    squash 357
    swimming 357
    thoroughbred racing 337
  see also WORLD DATA
Australian Aborigine (people) 391
Australian Ballet (Austr. ballet co.) 284
Australian football 344
Australian Football League, *or* AFL 344
Australian Labor Party, *or* ALP (pol. party, Austr.) 391
Australian Open (tennis) 360
"Australia's Bicentennial Year" (feature article) **88**:20
Australopithecus africanus
  anthropological discovery 133
Austria **97**:392; **96**:374; **95**:375; **94**:423; **93**:425; **92**:419; **91**:445; **90**:462; **89**:446; **88**:446
  banking 200
  military affairs 271
  name derivation 393
  Roman Catholicism 306
  rubber industry 167
  social protection 313
  see also WORLD DATA
Austria-Hungary (hist. Eur. state)
  Bosnia and Herzegovina (special report) **94**:426
Austrian Freedom Party (pol. party, Aus.): *see* Freiheitlichen, Die
Austrian People's Party, *or* ÖVP (pol. party, Aus.) 393
Austrian Social Democratic Party, *or* SPÖ (pol. party, Aus.) 393
autofocus camera, *or* AF camera
  photography 173
automobile emission: *see* exhaust
automobile racing **97**:317; **96**:299; **95**:283; **94**:279; **93**:279; **92**:275; **91**:306; **90**:322; **89**:307; **88**:308
automobiles 156
  advanced composites 168
  air bags 222
  France 419
  Japan 438
  metalworking 169
  U.S. labour-management relations 202
Automotive Transportation, Office for the Study of, *or* OSAT (U.S.) 158
autonomous nation
  Fourth World (spotlight) 422, *map* 423
Autonomous Region in Muslim Mindanao, *or* ARMM (Mindanao, Phil.) 461
avalanche 60
aviation 372
  aerospace 155
  Bahamas, The 394
  disasters 58
  France 419, 420
  India 431
  Japan 438
  Kenya 440
  military affairs 276
  Netherlands, The 456
  North Pole controversy 383
  Switzerland 478
  Trans World Airlines explosion 226, 495
Awami League, *or* AL (pol. party, Bangla.) 394
Awolowo, Chief Obafemi (obit.) **88**:88
Axworthy, Lloyd 405
Ayckbourn, Alan (biog.) **90**:81
Aydid, Gen. Muhammad Farah, *or* Muhammad Farah Hassan
  biography **94**:33
  obituary **97**:92
  Somalia 472
Ayer, Sir Alfred Jules (obit.) **90**:104
Aylwin Azócar, Patricio (biog.) **91**:65
  special report **92**:465
Ayres, Lew, *or* Lewis Ayer (obit.) **97**:92
Ayyash, Yahya 226, 434
Ayznman, Tsvi 251
Azerbaijan **97**:393; **96**:375; **95**:376; **94**:423; **93**:426
  Georgia 421
  land mines *map* 275
  new flag *illus.* **93**:345
  refugees 297
  see also WORLD DATA
Azikiwe, Nnamdi, *or* Benjamin Azikiwe (obit.) **97**:92
Aznar López, José María (biog.) **97**:67
  Spain 474

B

B-2 (Am. aircraft)
  aerospace industry 155
  defense spending 269
Babbitt, Arthur (obit.) **93**:55
"Babe" (motion picture)
  film awards *table* 294
Babu, Abdul Rahman Mohammed (obit.) **97**:92
"Babylon 5" (television show) 263
"bacio della Medusa, Il" (Mazzucco) 247
Backus, Jim (obit.) **90**:104
Bacon, Francis Thomas (obit.) **93**:55
badminton **97**:320; **96**:301; **95**:284; **94**:280; **93**:281; **92**:277; **91**:307; **90**:325; **89**:308; **88**:310
  1996 Summer Olympic champions *table* **97**:365
Badr, Muhammad al- (obit.) **97**:92
Bagnold, Ralph Alger (obit.) **91**:87
Bagratyan, Hrant 390
Bahamas, The **97**:394; **96**:375; **95**:376; **94**:477; **93**:477; **92**:468; **91**:495; **90**:510; **89**:494; **88**:494
  death penalty 225
  zoological research 233
  see also WORLD DATA
Bahamasair
  corruption inquiry 394
Bahrain **97**:394; **96**:375; **95**:376; **94**:380; **93**:381; **92**:378; **91**:404; **90**:425; **89**:407; **88**:407
  Islamic banking rules 310
  see also WORLD DATA
Bailey, Donovan (biog.) **97**:67
  track and field sports 362
Bailey, Pearl (obit.) **91**:87
Bainbridge, Kenneth (obit.) **97**:92
Baird, Bil (obit.) **88**:88
Baiul, Oksana (biog.) **96**:52
"Bajo la piel" (motion picture): *see* "Under the Skin"
Baker, Carlos Heard (obit.) **88**:89
Baker, Howard (biog.) **88**:65
Baker, James (biog.) **90**:81
  special report **93**:470
Baker, Kenneth Wilfred (biog.) **89**:65
Baker, Russell (biog.) **90**:82
Bakhtiar, Shahpur (obit.) **92**:56
Bakker, Jim (biog.) **88**:65
Bakker, Tammy (biog.) **88**:65
Bakun Dam (dam, Mal.) 142
Baldwin, James Arthur (obit.) **88**:89
Baljian, Levon Garabet (obit.): *see* Vazgen I
"Balkan States" (MACROPAEDIA revision) **96**:507
Balkans
  United Nations 377
  see also individual countries by name
Ball, George Wildman (obit.) **95**:60
Ball, Lucille Désirée (obit.) **90**:104
Balladur, Édouard (biog.) **94**:34
Ballantine, Ian Keith (obit.) **96**:74
Ballard, Harold (obit.) **91**:87
ballet 282
Ballet South (Am. ballet co.) 282
ballistic missile: *see* missile
balloon angioplasty 219
Balsam, Artur (obit.) **95**:60
Balsam, Martin (obit.) **97**:92
Balthasar, Hans Urs von (obit.) **89**:89
Baltic Freight Index (shipping) 373
Baltic republics (special report) **91**:476
  free-trade agreement 224
  see also individual countries by name
Baltimore Orioles (baseball) 321
Baltzell, Edward Digby (obit.) **97**:92
Bambara, Toni Cade (obit.) **96**:74
"Bamdad-e khomar" (Hajseyyed-javadi) 251
Ban, Shigeru (biog.) **97**:68
Banda, Hastings 448
Banderas, Antonio (biog.) **96**:53
Bandidos (motorcycle org.) 413
Bangkok (Thai.)
  municipal elections 483
Bangladesh **97**:394; **96**:376; **95**:377; **94**:403; **93**:403; **92**:401; **91**:429; **90**:447; **89**:430; **88**:430
  Commonwealth of Nations 378
  disasters
    marine 59
    natural 60
    traffic 61
  microbanking 200
  Muslim refugees 297
  see also WORLD DATA
Banharn Silpa-archa 482
Bank of . . . : *see under* substantive word, *e.g.*, Tokyo, Bank of
BankAmerica Corp. (Am. co.) 200
banking 200
  Brazil 399
  Cuba 412
  Czech Republic 413
  insurance 165
  Japan 191, 438
  special report **92**:141
  stock markets 194
  Switzerland 478
bankruptcy
  Austria 393
  economic affairs 191
  Germany 421
  Netherlands, The 456
  United States 490
Banyamulenge (people) 504
Bao Tong 408
Baptist Churches 302
Baptist World Alliance 302
Bar-El, Yoysef 251
Barbados **97**:395; **96**:376; **95**:378; **94**:477; **93**:477; **92**:468; **91**:495; **90**:510; **89**:494; **88**:494
  see also WORLD DATA
Barbados Labour Party, *or* BLP (pol. party, Barb.) 395
Barber, Walter Lanier, *or* Red Barber (obit.) **93**:56
"Barbie" (doll) 164
  biography **95**:40
Barbie, Klaus
  biography **88**:66
  obituary **92**:56
Barbuda: *see* Antigua and Barbuda
Barco Vargas, Virgilio (biog.) **90**:82
Bardeen, John (obit.) **92**:56
Baré Maïnassara, Ibrahim (biog.): *see* Maïnassara, Ibrahim Baré
bareback bronc riding 353
Barenboim, Daniel (biog.) **90**:82
Baricco, Alessandro 247
Barings PLC (bank, U.K.)
  derivatives (special report) **96**:185
Barker, George Granville (obit.) **92**:56
Barlois, Valerie *il.* 338
Barna Research Group
  religion surveys 300
Barnes, Julian 243
Barnet, Charlie (obit.) **92**:56
Barnett, Gary (biog.) **96**:53
Barnett, Marguerite Ross (obit.) **93**:56
Barneys (Am. co.)
  fashion 216
Barnhart, Clarence Lewis (obit.) **94**:55
Baron, Salo Wittmayer (obit.) **90**:104
Barr, Roseanne, *or* Roseanne Arnold, *or* Roseanne (biog.) **90**:104
Barrault, Jean-Louis (obit.) **95**:60
Barrett, Andrea 242
Barrios de Chamorro, Violeta: *see* Chamorro, Violeta Barrios de
Barrow, Errol Walton (obit.) **88**:89
Barrow, Dame Ruth Nita (obit.) **96**:74
Barthelme, Donald (obit.) **90**:104
Bartholomew, Freddie, *or* Frederick Llewellyn Bartholomew (obit.) **93**:56
Bartholomew I (biog.) **92**:34
  Orthodoxy conflict 307
Bartoli, Cecilia (biog.) **94**:34
Barzani, Mas'ud al- 433
basal-cell carcinoma 218
Basara, Svetislav 250
baseball **97**:320; **96**:302; **95**:285; **94**:280; **93**:281; **92**:277; **91**:307; **90**:325; **89**:309; **88**:310
  1996 Summer Olympic champions *table* **97**:365
baseball trading card
  auctions and collectibles 152
BASF (Ger. co.) 161
Bashford, Ian 354
Bashir, Omar al- 476
basketball **97**:323; **96**:304; **95**:287; **94**:282; **93**:284; **92**:279; **91**:310; **90**:328; **89**:311; **88**:312
  1996 Summer Olympic champions *table* **97**:365
Basle Committee
  derivatives (special report) **96**:185
Basofil (man-made fibre) 177
Basque (people) 475
Bass, Saul (obit.) **97**:92
Bateman, Merrill J. 303
Bath, Henry Frederick Thynne, 6th Marquess of (obit.) **93**:56
Bathiat, Arlette-Léonie (obit.): *see* Arletty
Bathurst Island (is., N.W.Terr., Can.)
  national park proposal 383
Batman (biog.) **90**:83
Batokan Gorge Dam (Zimb.) 141
Battle, Kathleen (biog.) **95**:40
Baudouin I, *or* Baudouin Albert Charles Leopold Axel Marie Gustave of Saxe-Coburg-Gotha (obit.) **94**:55
Baumgartner, Bruce 370
Baunsgaard, Hilmar Tormod Ingolf (obit.) **90**:104
Bausch, Richard 240
Bayer AG (Ger. co.)
  synthetic rubber industry 167
Bayern Munich (soccer) 341
Bayrou, François 205
Bazargan, Mehdi (obit.) **96**:74
Bazin, Hervé, *or* Jean-Pierre-Marie Hervé-Bazin (obit.) **97**:92
BBC (Br. co.): *see* British Broadcasting Corporation
beach
  water-quality report 207
beach volleyball
  Olympic Games 370
Beadle, George Wells (obit.) **90**:105
"Beams and Dreams" (motion picture) 295
Bearden, Romare Howard (obit.) **89**:89
"Beaumarchais l'insolent" (motion picture) 291
"Beautiful Thing" (motion picture) 290
Beaver, Joe 352
"Beavis and Butt-head Do America" (motion picture)
  computer animation (special report) 293
Beazley, Kim 391
Bechtel, Stephen Davison (obit.) **90**:105
Beck, David (obit.) **94**:56
Beckenbauer, Franz (biog.) **91**:65
Becker, Boris 360
Beckett, Samuel Barclay (obit.) **90**:105
  British literature 243
  theatrical productions 288
"Bed and Sofa" (play) 288
Bedell, Chad 353
Bednorz, Johannes Georg (biog.) **88**:66
bee
  entomology 234
beef
  European Union ban 379
  food processing 132
  "mad cow" disease 126, 487
  Switzerland 478
  veterinary medicine 222
  world production 129, *table* 126
beer 158
beet sugar
  world production 129
"Before the Dawn" (Adams) 243
Begin, Menachem Wolfovitch (obit.) **93**:56
"Behind the Scenes at the Museum" (Atkinson) 243
Behrman, Beatrice (obit.) **91**:87
Beijing (China)
  anticrime campaign 408, *il.*
  most populous urban areas *table* 296
Belarus **97**:395; **96**:376; **95**:378; **94**:424; **93**:427
  economic affairs 193
  environmental issues 212
  new flag *il.* **96**:365; **93**:345
  nuclear weapons 269
  Russia 380, 465
  see also WORLD DATA
Belarusian Popular Front, *or* BPF (pol. party, Belarus) 396
Belgium **97**:396; **96**:377; **95**:378; **94**:425; **93**:426; **92**:420; **91**:446; **90**:463; **89**:447; **88**:446
  labour-management relations 202
  land mines (special report) 274
  sports and games
    Grand Prix racing 318
    swimming 357
  see also WORLD DATA
Béliz, Gustavo 390
Belize **97**:397; **96**:377; **95**:379; **94**:477; **93**:477; **92**:469; **91**:496; **90**:511; **89**:495; **88**:495
  archaeology 136
  special report **89**:144
  see also WORLD DATA
Bell, James ("Cool Papa") (obit.) **92**:56

Bell, Quentin Claudian Stephen (obit.) **97**:92
Bell Atlantic Corp. (Am. co.) 175, 196
Belladonna, Giorgio (obit.) **96**:74
Bellamy, Ralph Rexford (obit.) **92**:56
"Belle" (ship)
archaeological discovery 136
Belli, Melvin Mouron (obit.) **97**:92
Bellisario, Marisa (obit.) **89**:89
Belluschi, Pietro (obit.) **95**:60
Belmont Stakes (horse racing) 337
Belo, Bishop Carlos Filipe Ximenes
Indonesia 432
Nobel Prize 62
Belorussian S.S.R.: *see* Belarus
Beltrán, Lola, *or* María Lucia Beltrán Alcayaga (obit.) **97**:93
Bemberg, Maria Luisa (obit.) **96**:74
Ben Ali, Zine al-Abidine (biog.) **88**:66
Tunisia 484
Benet Goita, Juan (obit.) **94**:56
Benetton, Luciano (biog.) **96**:53
Benhadugah, ʿAbd al-Hamid (obit.) **97**:93
Benin **97**:397; **96**:378; **95**:379; **94**:354; **93**:356; **92**:352; **91**:380; **90**:401; **89**:384; **88**:384
see also WORLD DATA
Bennett, Jill (obit.) **91**:87
Bennett, Joan (obit.) **91**:87
Bennett, Michael (obit.) **88**:89
Bennett, William (biog.) **90**:83
Benni, Stefano 247
Bennis v. Michigan
forfeiture laws 225
Benson, Ezra Taft (obit.) **95**:61
Benson, Herbert 300
Bentine, Michael (obit.) **97**:93
Bentsen, Lloyd Millard, Jr. (biog.) **89**:66
Berber, *or* Amazigh (people)
"The Berbers of North Africa" (spotlight) **96**:368
Berberidopsis corallina (plant)
wildlife conservation 213
Berberova, Nina Nikolayevna (obit.) **94**:56
Bérégovoy, Pierre Eugène
biography **93**:34
obituary **94**:56
Berg, Eugene Leander (obit.): *see* Nelson, Gene
Bergen, Candice (biog.) **93**:34
Berghaus, Ruth (obit.) **97**:93
Bergman, Ingmar (biog.) **89**:66
Berkeley, Sir Lennox Randall Francis (obit.) **90**:105
Berlin (Ger.)
architecture *il.* 140
Berlin, Irving
biography **89**:66
obituary **90**:105
Berlin International Film Festival
film awards *table* 294
Berlusconi, Silvio (biogs.) **95**:40; **91**:65
Italy 436
television industry 261
Berman, Pandro Samuel (obit.) **97**:93
Bermuda (isls., Atl.O.) 381
Bermúdez, Enrique (obit.) **92**:57
Bernard, Jessie Shirley (obit.) **97**:93
Bernardin, Joseph Louis Cardinal (obit.) **97**:93
Roman Catholic dissent 306
Bernays, Edward L. (obit.) **96**:74
Bernhard, Thomas (obit.) **90**:105
Bernstein, Edward Morris (obit.) **97**:94
Bernstein, Leonard (obit.) **91**:87
Bernstein, Richard Barry (obit.) **91**:88
Bernstein, Walter 241
Bernstein of Leigh, Sidney Lewis Bernstein, Baron (obit.) **94**:56
Berque, Jacques Augustin (obit.) **96**:74
Bertelsmann AG (Ger. co.) 261
"Bertha" (hurricane) 60
beryllium
light metals 168
best-seller (book) 268
Beswick, Frank Beswick, Baron (obit.) **88**:89
Beta Pictoris (star)
astronomy 258
Bettelheim, Bruno (obit.) **91**:88
Bettiza, Enzo 247
beverages 158
see also alcoholic beverage
"Bezdno" (Velmar-Janković) 250
BGCI: *see* Botanic Gardens Conservation International
Bharatiya Janata Party, *or* BJP (pol. party, India) 430
Hinduism 309
Bhatia, Prem (obit.) **96**:75
Bhichit Rattakul 483
BHP (Austr. co.): *see* Broken Hill Proprietary Company Limited
Bhumibol Adulyadej (biog.) **93**:34
Thailand 483
Bhutan **97**:397; **96**:378; **95**:380; **94**:404; **93**:404; **92**:402; **91**:430; **90**:448; **89**:430; **88**:431
refugees 297
see also WORLD DATA
Bhutto, Benazir (biog.) **91**:65
Pakistan 459
special report **93**:96
Bhutto, Murtaza (obit.) **97**:94
Bible
special report **94**:263
"Big" (play) 288
big bang theory
helium-3 research 64
"Big Night" (motion picture) 289
BIICL: *see* British Institute of International and Comparative Law
Bilbao (Sp.)
architecture 137
Bildt, Carl (biog.) **92**:34
Bill, Max (obit.) **95**:61
Billetdoux, François (obit.) **92**:57
billiard games **97**:325; **96**:306; **95**:288; **94**:284; **93**:285; **92**:282; **91**:312; **90**:330; **89**:312; **88**:314
Billiard World Cup Association, *or* BWA 325
Billington, James Hadley (biog.) **88**:66
bin Laden, Osama 470
"Binti Jua" (gorilla) 213, *il.* 214
Bio, Julius Maada 471
biocompatibility
ceramics 167
biographical literature: *see* Literature
Biographies **97**:65; **96**:52; **95**:39; **94**:33; **93**:33; **92**:33; **91**:64; **90**:81; **89**:65; **88**:65
Biological Diversity, Convention on, *or* CBD
botanical gardens 214
biological weapon 272
United Nations 377
bipedalism (anthro.) 133
bipolar disorder 222
bird
ornithology 234
wildlife conservation 212
Bird, Lester 390
Bird Jaguar (Mayan lord)
archaeological discovery 136
"Birdcage, The" (motion picture) 289
Birla, Aditya Vikram (obit.) **96**:75
Birnbaum, Nathan (obit.): *see* Burns, George
Birney, Alfred Earle (obit.) **96**:75
Birt, John (biogs.) **94**:34; **89**:67
birthrate 295
Bishop, Bronwyn Kathleen (biog.) **94**:34
Bishop, John Michael (biog.) **90**:83
Bissell, Patrick (obit.) **88**:89
Bixby, Bill (obit.) **94**:56
Biya, Paul 403
Björk, *or* Björk Gudmundsdottir (biog.) **96**:53
BJP (pol. party, India): *see* Bharatiya Janata Party
black (people): *see* black American
Black, Conrad (biog.) **95**:40
Black, Eugene Robert (obit.) **93**:56
Black, Sir James Whyte (biog.) **89**:67
black American, *or* African-American, *or* Afro-American (people)
cancer 219
church burnings 300, 302, *il.* 498
congressional reapportionment 225
fashion industry 217
life expectancy 297
"Black Monday Revisited" (special report) **89**:176
Black Sea Fleet
Ukraine-Russia dispute 271, 487
Blackwell, Edward Joseph (obit.) **93**:57
Blackwell, Ewell (obit.) **97**:94
Blades, Rubén (biog.) **95**:40
Blaik, Earl Henry (obit.) **90**:106
Blaine, Vivian (obit.) **96**:75
Blair, Bonnie Kathleen (biog.) **95**:41
gold medal (special report) **95**:308
Blair, Tony (biog.) **94**:35
United Kingdom 488
Blais, Marie-Claire 247
Blaize, Herbert A. (obit.) **90**:106
Blake, Hector (obit.) **96**:75
Blake, Sir Peter James (biog.) **96**:54
Blakey, Art (obit.) **91**:88
Blanc, Melvin Jerome (obit.) **90**:106
Blane, Ralph (obit.) **96**:75
Bleustein-Blanchet, Marcel (obit.) **97**:94
Blevins, Rubye (obit.): *see* Montana, Patsy
Blier, Bernard (obit.) **90**:106
blindness
smoking risk 221
Blixen, Karen 245
blizzard 60, *il.* 186
Bloch, Robert Albert (obit.) **95**:61
"Blockbuster Art Exhibitions" (special report) **97**:146
Blockbuster Video (Am. co.) 174
Blomdahl, Torbjörn 325
Blomstedt, Herbert 277
blood pressure
cardiovascular disease 218
blood transfusion
Irish scandal 434
Bloom, Allan David
biography **88**:67
obituary **93**:57
Blount, Herman (obit.): *see* Sun Ra
BLP (pol. party, Barb.): *see* Barbados Labour Party
Boardman, Chris 334
Boatmen's Bancshares (Am. co.) 201
bobsledding
1994 Olympic champions *table* **95**:309
Bochco, Steven (biog.) **89**:67
"Bodenlos" (Kirsch) 245
body temperature
snakes 232
Boeheim, Jim 324
Boeing 747 *il.* 372
Boeing Company (Am. co.)
aerospace industry 155, 260
"boek van violet en dood, Het" (Reve) 245
Boggs, Phil (obit.) **91**:88
Bokassa, Jean-Bédel (obit.) **97**:94
Bokros, Lajos 427
Boldon, Ato 362
Bolger, James Brendan (biog.) **91**:66
New Zealand 456
Bolger, Raymond Wallace (obit.) **88**:89
Bolivia **97**:397; **96**:379; **95**:380; **94**:478; **93**:478; **92**:469; **91**:496; **90**:511; **89**:495; **88**:495
association football 342
disasters 61
special report **89**:144
see also WORLD DATA
Bolivian Worker's Central, *or* COB
strike 398
"Bolshe Vita" (motion picture) 295
Bolshoi Ballet (Russ. ballet co.) 282
Bolt, Robert Oxton (obit.) **96**:75
Bolton, John Gatenby (obit.) **94**:56
Bombay, *or* Mumbai (India)
most populous urban areas *table* 296
new pipeline *il.* 431
Bombeck, Erma Louise (obit.) **97**:94
bombing
atomic bomb (special report) **96**:258
crime and law enforcement 226
Ethiopia 418
France 419, *il.* 420
Ireland 433
Israel 375, 434
Libya 446
Northern Ireland 489
Saudi Arabia 269, 470
South Africa 474
Sri Lanka 476
Turkey 484
United States 495
Olympic Games (special report) 364
bond (fin.)
stock exchanges 195
Bondarchuck, Sergey (obit.) **95**:61
"Bonheur est dans le pré, Le" (motion picture) 291
Bonnier, Albert, Jr. (obit.) **90**:106
book publishing **97**:267; **96**:250; **95**:259; **94**:256; **93**:256; **92**:253; **91**:283; **90**:300; **89**:283; **88**:285
see also under individual national literatures
Booker Prize
British literature 242
Russian literature 249
Boorda, Jeremy Michael (obit.) **97**:94
military affairs 269
Booth, Shirley, *or* Thelma Booth Ford (obit.) **93**:57
Boothroyd, Betty 488
Border, Allan Robert (biog.) **90**:84
Bordón, José Octavio 390
Borja Cevallos, Rodrigo (biog.) **89**:67
Bork, Robert Heron (biog.) **88**:67
Borkovec, Petr 250
Borlaug, Norman E.
"World Revolution in Agriculture" (feature article) **88**:5
Boros, Julius Nicholas (obit.) **95**:61
Borotra, Jean-Robert (obit.) **95**:61
Borsos, Phillip (obit.) **96**:75
Bosman, Jean-Marc 325
Bosnia (medieval principality)
special report **94**:426
Bosnia and Herzegovina **97**:398; **96**:379; **95**:380; **94**:427; **93**:428
Eastern European literature 250
education 205
human rights violations 315
refugees 297
international affairs
Canada 405
European Union 379
France 420
United Nations 377
United States 496
land mines (special report) 274, *map* 275
libraries 230
military affairs 269, 271
new flag *illus.* **93**:345
roads 142
special report **95**:308
war crimes 227, *il.*
see also WORLD DATA
"Bosnia and Herzegovina in Historical Perspective" (special report) **94**:425
Bossano, Joe 380
Bossi, Umberto (biog.) **97**:68
Italy 436, *il.* 437
Boston (Mass., U.S.)
wastewater-treatment systems 160
Boston, Lucy Maria (obit.) **91**:88
"Boston Globe" (Am. news.) 266
"Boston Harbor" (horse) 336
Botanic Gardens Conservation International, *or* BGCI 214
Botanical Gardens **97**:214; **96**:202; **95**:118; **94**:110; **93**:110; **92**:108; **91**:137; **90**:155; **89**:138; **88**:138
see also Zoos
botany 235
molecular defense systems 236
paleontological discovery 239
Botero, Fernando (biog.) **94**:35
Bothus ocellatus (fish species) 235
Botswana **97**:399; **96**:380; **95**:381; **94**:355; **93**:356; **92**:352; **91**:380; **90**:402; **89**:385; **88**:385
Central Kalahari Game Reserve *il.* 399
see also WORLD DATA
bottled water 160
Botvinnik, Mikhail Moiseyevich (obit.) **96**:75
Bouchard, Lucien (biog.) **95**:41
Quebec 404
Boudiaf, Muhammad (obit.) **93**:57
Bougainville (isl. Pap.N.G.) 460
mining (spotlight) 450
Boulez, Pierre (biog.) **93**:35
classical music 279
Boulle, Pierre-François-Marie-Louis (obit.) **95**:62
Bourassa, Robert (obit.) **97**:94
Bourdet, Claude (obit.) **97**:95
Bourke, Martin 381
Bourne, Geoffrey (obit.) **89**:90
Bourne, Matthew 284
Boutin, François (obit.) **96**:75
Boutros-Ghali, Boutros (biog.) **93**:35
land mines (special report) 274
United Nations 376, *il.* 377
United States 496
Bovet, Daniel (obit.) **93**:57
bovine spongiform encephalopathy, *or* BSE, *or* "mad cow" disease
agriculture and food supplies 123, 126
consumer affairs 202
European Union response 379
food processing 131
Ireland 434
Switzerland 478
United Kingdom 218, 487
veterinary medicine 222
bowling, *or* tenpins **97**:326; **96**:307; **95**:289; **94**:285; **93**:286; **92**:282; **91**:313; **90**:331; **89**:313; **88**:315
bowls: *see* lawn bowls
Boxer, Mark (obit.) **89**:90
boxing **97**:327; **96**:308; **95**:290; **94**:286; **93**:287; **92**:283; **91**:313; **90**:331; **89**:314; **88**:316
1996 Summer Olympic champions *table* **97**:365
Boyington, Gregory (obit.) **89**:90
Boyle, Jean 405
Boyle, Kay (obit.) **93**:57
Boyz II Men (biog.) **96**:54
BPF (pol. party, Belarus): *see* Belarusian Popular Front
Bradlee, Benjamin Crowninshield (biog.) **92**:35
brain
nicotine effect 221
"Brain Opera" (opera) 278
Braithwaite, Max (obit.) **96**:76
Braithwaite, Richard Bevan (obit.) **91**:89
Bramwell-Booth, Catherine (obit.) **88**:89
Branagh, Kenneth (biog.) **94**:35
Brancker, Sir John Eustace Theodore (obit.) **97**:95
Brandon, Oscar Henry (obit.) **94**:56
Brandt, Willy, *or* Herbert Ernst Karl Frahm (obit.) **93**:58
Branisella (anthro.) 133
"Brassed Off" (motion picture) 290
brassinolide (bot.) 235
Bratby, John Randall (obit.) **93**:58
Brattain, Walter Houser (obit.) **88**:90
Braun, Carol Moseley: *see* Moseley-Braun, Carol
"Braveheart" (motion picture)
film awards table 294
Braxton, Anthony (biog.) **95**:41
Brazil **97**:399; **96**:380; **95**:382; **94**:478; **93**:478; **92**:469; **91**:496; **90**:512; **89**:495; **88**:495
agriculture 128, 129
archaeology 135
business and industry
building and construction 160
chemicals 161
disasters
aviation 58
buildings 61
fires and explosions 59
floods 60
railroad 61
new flag *illus.* **93**:345
Japanese immigration (spotlight) 400
literature 249
most populous urban areas *table* 296
Pentecostal Churches 304
social protection 314
special report **95**:278
sports and games
association football 341
basketball 325
see also WORLD DATA
Brazilian literature 249
Brazilian Progressive Party, *or* PPB (pol. party, Braz.) 399
Brazzi, Rossano (obit.) **95**:62
Bre-X Minerals (Can. co.) 170
"Breaking the Waves" (motion picture) 291
film awards *table* 294
Breeders' Cup (horse racing) 335
breeding
harness racing 338
Brenan, Edward Fitz-Gerald (obit.) **88**:90
Brett, Jeremy, *or* Peter Jeremy William Huggins (obit.) **96**:76

Brewster, Kingman, Jr. (obit.) **89**:90
Breyer, Stephen (biog.) **95**:42
Brickyard 400
  automobile racing 320
bridge, contract: *see* contract bridge
bridges 139, *table* 143
  roads and traffic 374
Bridges, Harry Alfred Renton Bryant (obit.) **91**:89
Bridgestone/Firestone, Inc. (Am. co.) 167
"Brigands" (motion picture) 291
Brigham Young University (U.S.)
  Church of Jesus Christ of Latter-day Saints 303
  football 343
Bright, Bill 301
"Bring in 'da Noise, Bring in 'da Funk" (play) 288
  dance 283
  Glover contribution 75
Brisac, Geneviève 246
Britain: *see* United Kingdom
Britannica Awards 90:31; **89**:15; **88**:15
"Britannica Book of the Year"
  special report **88**:288
British Airways (Br. airline) 155
British Antarctic Survey 382
British Broadcasting Corporation, *or* BBC (Br. co.) 264
  Saudi Arabia 470
British Commonwealth: *see* Commonwealth of Nations
British Energy, *or* Nuclear Electric 163
British Guiana: *see* Guyana
British Honduras: *see* Belize
British Institute of International and Comparative Law, *or* BIICL 223
British Library (library, U.K.) 230
Buddah's birthplace 309
British literature 242
British Medical Association
  antiboxing campaign 330
British Museum
  art exhibtions 144
British Open (golf) 347
British Petroleum Company (Br. co.) 163
British Telecommunications (Br. co.)
  MCI takeover 175, 196
Britpop 280
Brittan, Leon (biog.) **93**:35
Broad Front Party (pol. party, Urug.) 500
broadcasting: *see* radio; television
Broadway (st., N.Y.C., N.Y., U.S.)
  theatre district 287
Broccoli, Albert Romolo, *or* Cubby Broccoli (obit.) **97**:95
Brockway, Archibald Fenner Brockway (obit.) **89**:90
Brodkey, Harold, *or* Aaron Roy Weintraub (obit.) **97**:95
  American literature 241
Brodsky, Joseph, *or* Iosip Aleksandrovich Brodsky
  biography **88**:67
  obituary **97**:95
  Russian literature 249, *il.*
Broglie, Louis-Victor-Pierre-Raymond (obit.) **88**:90
Broken Hill Proprietary Company Limited, *or* BHP (Austr. co.)
  diamond mining 383
  Papua New Guinea pollution 207
bromine
  ozone depletion 210
Bronfman, Peter Frederick (obit.) **97**:95
Brookfield Zoo (zoo, Brookfield, Ill., U.S.) 213
Brooks, Cleanth (obit.) **95**:62
Brooks, Garth (biog.) **93**:35
  country music 282
Brooks, Mark 347
Brooks, Richard (obit.) **93**:58
Brooks, Tony 305
Brophy, Brigid Antonia (obit.) **96**:76
Brother Adam, *or* Karl Kehrle (obit.) **97**:95
Brothers to the Rescue (Am. org.) 411, 496
Brouillet, Chrystine 247
Brown, Edmund Gerald, *or* Pat Brown (obit.) **97**:95
Brown, Frederick Richard (obit.) **92**:57
Brown, George Mackay (obit.) **97**:95
Brown, Georgia, *or* Lillian Klot (obit.) **93**:58
Brown, John Robert (obit.) **94**:57
Brown, Paul (obit.) **92**:57
Brown, Ronald Harmon
  aviation tragedy 58, 269, 496, *il.* 411
  biography **90**:84
  obituary **97**:95
Brown, Tina (biog.) **93**:36
Browne, Coral (obit.) **92**:57
Browning, Kurt (biog.) **92**:35
Browning Griffith, Patricia 241
Brownsville Assembly of God (church, Pensacola, Fla., U.S.) 304
browser software (computers) 181
Brú, Hedin (obit.) **88**:90
Bruller, Jean-Marcel: *see* Vercors
Brunei **97**:401; **96**:381; **95**:384; **94**:411; **93**:412; **92**:408; **91**:435; **90**:453; **89**:436; **88**:437
  see also WORLD DATA
Brunell, Mark 344
Brunet, Pierre (obit.) **92**:57
Brunner, John Kilian Houston (obit.) **96**:76
Bruno, Michael 200
Brusca, Giovanni 228, 437
Bruskewitz, Fabian
  Roman Catholicism 306
Bruton, John 433
Bryant, Barbara Everitt (biog.) **91**:66
Bryant, Martin
  mass murders 227
Bryceland, Yvonne (obit.) **93**:58
"Brylcreem Boys, The" (motion picture) 290
BSE: *see* bovine spongiform encephalopathy
Bskal-bzang Tshe-brtan (obit.): *see* Panchen Lama
Bucaram Ortíz, Abdalá (biog.) **97**:68
  Ecuador 414
Buchanan, Junious (obit.) **93**:58
Buchanan, Pat
  presidential election (special report) 493
buckminsterfullerene, *or* buckyball 253
Buddhism 309
  religion statistics *table* 311
Buddhist manuscript *il.* 309
budget deficit
  Bulgaria 401
  economic affairs 188
  France 192, 419
  Germany 421
  Hungary 430
  Sweden 477
  United States 491
budget policy: *see* government budget
Buenos Aires (Arg.)
  most populous urban areas *table* 296
Bufalino, Gesualdo (obit.) **97**:95
  Italian literature 247
buffalo
  world production *table* 126
Buffet, Warren Edward (biog.) **92**:35
building and construction 160
  advanced composites 168
  economic affairs 191
  Germany 421
  South Africa 473
buildings 140, *table* 143
  world's tallest building 448, *il.*
Bukowski, Charles (obit.) **95**:62
Bulgaria **97**:401; **96**:382; **95**:384; **94**:428; **93**:429; **92**:420; **91**:468; **90**:485; **89**:469; **88**:468
  economic affairs 193
  Orthodox Church 308
  see also WORLD DATA
Bulgarian National Bank (bank, Bulg.) 401
Bulgarian Orthodox Church 308
"Bulk Challenge" (cargo ship) *il.* 445
Bull, Deborah 285
bull riding 352
Bundy, McGeorge (obit.) **97**:96
Bunge Paints (S.Am. co.) 172
Bunshaft, Gordon (obit.) **91**:89
Bureau of . . . : *see under* substantive word, *e.g.,* Alcohol, Tobacco and Firearms, Bureau of
Burger, Warren Earl (obit.) **96**:76
Burgess, Anthony, *or* John Anthony Burgess Wilson (obit.) **94**:57
Burke, Arleigh Albert (obit.) **97**:96
Burke, Kenneth (obit.) **94**:57
Burkina Faso (formerly Upper Volta) **97**:402; **96**:382; **95**:385; **94**:355; **93**:357; **92**:353; **91**:381; **90**:402; **89**:385; **88**:385
  see also WORLD DATA
Burkitt, Denis Parsons (obit.) **94**:57
Burle Marx, Roberto (obit.) **95**:62
Burma: *see* Myanmar
Burnham, James (obit.) **88**:90
Burns, Arthur Frank (obit.) **88**:90
Burns, George, *or* Nathan Birnbaum (obit.) **97**:96
Burns, Jethro (obit.) **90**:106
Burns, Ken (biog.) **91**:66
Burns, Robert 279
Burr, Raymond William Stacey (obit.) **94**:57
Burri, Alberto (obit.) **96**:76
Burton, Beryl (obit.) **97**:96
Burton, John 489
Burton, Tim
  motion pictures 293
Burundi **97**:402; **96**:382; **95**:385; **94**:355; **93**:357; **92**:353; **91**:381; **90**:402; **89**:385; **88**:385
  agriculture and food supplies 124
  human rights issues 314, 316, 376
  international affairs
    Rwanda 467
    Tanzania 482
  military affairs 276
  refugees 297
  Religious Society of Friends 304
  Roman Catholicism 306
  track and field sports 368
  see also WORLD DATA
Burzyńska, Anna 250
Busby, Sir Matthew (obit.) **95**:62
"Busca mi esquela & Primer amor" (Garro) 248
Busch, August Anheuser, Jr. (obit.) **90**:106
Bush, Barbara (biog.) **90**:84
Bush, George Herbert Walker (biogs.) **93**:36; **92**:35; **91**:66; **90**:84; **89**:68
  Persian Gulf War criticism 375
  special reports **89**:177, 483
Bush v. Vera (law case, U.S.)
  court decisions 225
Busia, Akosua 244, *il.*
Business and Industry Review 97:153; **96**:132; **95**:119
  computers and information systems 180
  see also individual countries by name; Industrial Review
business review: *see* Economic Affairs
Bussell, Darcey Andrea (biog.) **96**:54
Bustamente y Rivero, José Luis (obit.) **90**:107
Bustillos, Edwin (biog.) **97**:69
Butenandt, Adolf Friedrich Johann (obit.) **96**:76
Buteo swainsoni: *see* Swainson's hawk
Buthelezi, Mangosuthu Gatsha (biog.) **91**:66
Butler, Paul 257
Butor, Michel 246
Buttrose, Ita Clare (biog.) **93**:36
Buyoya, Pierre (biog.) **88**:67
  Burundi 402
BWA: *see* Billiard World Cup Association
bycatch
  fisheries 131
Byrd, Richard E. 383

C

Cabbage Patch Kid (toy) 164
cable-stayed bridge 139
cable television 261, 261
  Internet service 181
  satellite TV (special report) **97**:176
  special report **90**:381
  telecommunications 175
CAC 40 Index (Fr.) 198
Cadbury Schweppes PLC (Br. co.)
  food processing 132
Cade, Toni: *see* Bamabar, Toni Cade
Caenorhabditis elegans
  Clock genes 232
Caesar, Irving (obit.) **97**:96
Cage, John (obit.) **93**:58
Cage, Nicolas
  film awards *table* 294
Cahn, Sammy, *or* Samuel Cohen (obit.) **94**:57
Cairncross, John (obit.) **96**:76
Cairo (Egy.)
  most populous urban areas *table* 296
Calceolaria andina (plant) 236, *il.* 235
calcium
  muscle contraction role 232
Calcutta (India)
  most populous urban areas *table* 296
Calder Hall (nuclear power station, U.K.) 163
Caldera, Rafael 500
Caldwell, Erskine (obit.) **88**:90
calendar
  year 2000 computer problem 182
Calendar of Events 91:4; **90**:4; **89**:4; **88**:4
  see also Chronicle
calf roping 353
California (state, U.S.)
  electric vehicles 158
  United States 497, 499
California Air Resources Board, *or* CARB
  electric vehicles 158
California at Los Angeles, University of, *or* UCLA (U.S.)
  volleyball 370
California condor, *or* Gymnogyps californianus
  wildlife conservation 213
  zoos 214
Callahan, Harry 149
Callithrix sateri (mammal)
  wildlife conservation 213
Calloway, Cab, *or* Cabell Calloway III (obit.) **95**:63
Calvo Serer, Rafael (obit.) **89**:90
Camargo, Iberê Bassanti (obit.) **95**:63
Camarón de la Isla (obit.) **93**:59
Cambodia (Kampuchea) **97**:403; **96**:383; **95**:385; **94**:412; **93**:412; **92**:408; **91**:435; **90**:455; **89**:438; **88**:438
  ASEAN membership 380
  Buddhism 309
  land mines *map* 275
  new flag *illus.* **94**:345; **93**:345
  see also WORLD DATA
Cambodian People's Party, *or* CPP (pol. party, Camb.) 403
Cambrian Period (geol.) 183
Cambridge University Press
  boycott 268
Camdessus, Michel (biog.) **88**:68
camera
  photography 149, 173
Cameron, Julia Margaret 149
Cameroon **97**:403; **96**:384; **95**:386; **94**:355; **93**:357; **92**:353; **91**:381; **90**:402; **89**:385; **88**:386
  see also WORLD DATA
Cameroon People's Democratic Movement, *or* RDPC (pol. party, Camer.) 403
Cameroon v. Nigeria
  international law 224
Camilión, Oscar 390
Camon, Ferdinando 247
campaign contribution
  state spending limits 498
  United States elections 496, 492
Campanella, Roy (obit.) **94**:58
Campbell, Joseph (obit.) **88**:90
Campbell, Kim (biog.) **94**:35
Campeau, Robert (biog.) **89**:68
Canada **97**:404; **96**:384; **95**:387; **94**:462; **93**:463; **92**:451; **91**:481; **90**:496; **89**:479; **88**:478
  agriculture
    fisheries 131
    food processing regulations 132
  arts and entertainment
    dance 282
    jazz 279
    literature 242, 247
    motion pictures 290
      film awards *table* 294
    theatre 288
  business and industry
    automobiles 157
    building and construction 160
    diamond mining 383
    insurance 165
    mining 170
    nuclear energy 163
    paper and pulp 179
    retailing 174
    wood products 179
  court decisions 225
  disasters 60
  economic affairs 194
    banking 200
    General Motors strike 202
    stock exchanges 198
  education 204
  immigration issues 297
  international affairs
    Arctic regions 383
    Chile 224
    Commonwealth of Nations 378
    Haiti 427, 377
    Japan 438
  military affairs 270
  numismatics 152
  social protection 313
  sports and games
    curling 334
    football 344
    Grand Prix racing 318
    ice hockey 349, 349
    track and field sports 368
  United Church of Canada 305
  wildlife conservation 213
  see also WORLD DATA
Canada Real Return bond 198
Canadian Automobile Workers, *or* CAW 157
Canadian football 344
Canadian literature 242
  see also French-Canadian literature
Canadian Unitarian Council 305
Canal Plus SA (Fr. co.) 261
cancer 219
  environmental pollutants 212
  genetic research 218
Candy, John Franklin (obit.) **95**:63
cane sugar
  world production 129
Canetti, Elias (obit.) **95**:63
Cannes International Film Festival (Fr.)
  film awards *table* 294
Cannon, Sarah Ophelia (obit.): *see* Pearl, Minnie
canoeing
  1996 Summer Olympic champions *table* **97**:365
Canon Inc. (Japanese co.)
  photography 173
"Canone inverso" (Maurensig) 247
Cao Siyuan 408
Cao Yu, *or* Wan Jiabao (obit.) **97**:96
Cape Verde **97**:406; **96**:387; **95**:389; **94**:356; **93**:357; **92**:353; **91**:381; **90**:403; **89**:386; **88**:386
  new flag *illus.* **93**:345
  see also WORLD DATA
"Capitaine Conan" (motion picture) 291
capital punishment 229
  Belgium 397
  court decisions 225
  Ethiopia 418
  Saudi Arabia 470
  United States 498
capitalism, *or* free-market economy
  Tanzania 482
Capra, Frank (obit.) **92**:57
CAPS
  computer animation (special report) 293
CAR (pol. party, Togo): *see* Action Committee for Renewal
Caradon, Hugh Mackintosh (obit.) **91**:89
CARB: *see* California Air Resources Board
carbon (chem.)
  fullerenes 63
carbon dioxide
  global warming 210
carbon fibre
  advanced composites 168
Carcharodontosaurus saharicus (dinosaur) 239, *il.*
Cárdenas, Cuahtémoc (biog.) **89**:68
cardiovascular disease 218
Cardoso, Fernando Henrique (biog.) **95**:42
  Brazil 399
Carey, George Leonard (biog.) **91**:67

Carey, Peter (biog.) **90**:85
Carey, Ronald Robert (biog.) **93**:37
Caribbean Community and Common Market, *or* Caricom
  unification issues (spotlight) 468, *map* 469
Caribbean Islands: *see* West Indies
Caribbean manatee, *or* Trichechus manatus
  wildlife conservation 213
Caribbean Series (baseball) 322
Caricom: *see* Caribbean Community and Common Market
"Carla's Song" (motion picture) 290
Carlot Korman, Maxime 500
Carlsson, Ingvar 477
Carlucci, Frank Charles, III (biog.) **88**:68
Carmet, Jean-Gabriel-Edmond (obit.) **95**:63
Carné, Marcel, *or* Albert Cranche (obit.) **97**:96
Carney, Robert Bostwick (obit.) **91**:89
Carnovsky, Morris (obit.) **93**:59
Caro Baroja, Julio (obit.) **96**:76
Carolina Panthers (football) 344
Caroline Islands: *see* Micronesia, Federated States of
carom billiards 325
Carradine, John (obit.) **89**:91
Carreras, Sir James (obit.) **91**:89
Carreras, José (biog.) **93**:37
Carroll, Lewis 243
Carroll, Madeleine (obit.) **88**:91
Carruth, Hayden
  U.S. literature 242
Carruthers, Jimmy (obit.) **91**:90
Carson, David (biog.) **97**:69
Carson, Johnny (biog.) **92**:35
Carstens, Karl (obit.) **93**:59
CART: *see* Championship Auto Racing Teams
Carter, Angela (obit.) **93**:59
Carter, Billy (obit.) **89**:91
Carter, Kevin (obit.) **95**:63
Carter, Wilfred Arthur Charles (obit.) **97**:97
Caruana, Peter 380
Caruso, David (biog.) **95**:42
Carver, Raymond (obit.) **89**:91
"casa da pescoço de cavalo, A" (Gersão) 249
Casarès, Maria-Victoria (obit.) **97**:97
Casey, William Joseph (obit.) **88**:91
Cash, Rosalind (obit.) **96**:76
"Casino" (motion picture)
  film awards *table* 294
casino gambling: *see* gambling
Casiraghi, Stefano (obit.) **91**:90
Cassatt, Mary 150
Cassavetes, John (obit.) **90**:107
Cassola, Carlo (obit.) **88**:91
Casson, Alfred Joseph (obit.) **93**:59
Castillo, Irving Alcaráz del 398
Castle, William Bosworth (obit.) **91**:90
Castries, Christian de (obit.) **92**:58
Castro, Fidel (biog.) **95**:42
  Spain 475
  United States 496
casual ware (clothing)
  clothing industry trends 156
cattle
  "mad cow" disease 126, 379
  veterinary medicine 222, *il.* 223
  world production 129, *table* 126
Caucasus
  refugees 297
Caulerpa taxifolia (alga) 235
Cavallo, Domingo 390
cave painting *il.* 136
Cavia porcellus: *see* guinea pig
CAW: *see* Canadian Automobile Workers
Cayman Islands (isls., W.I.) 381
CBD: *see* Convention on Biological Diversity
CBI (India): *see* Central Bureau of Investigation
CBS (Am. co.): *see* Columbia Broadcasting System
CD-ROM, *or* compact disc read-only memory
  book publishing 268
CDC: *see* Centers for Disease Control and Prevention
CDR (pol. party, Rom.): *see* Democratic Convention of Romania
CDU (pol. party, Ger.): *see* Christian Democratic Union
Ceausescu, Elena (obit.) **90**:107
Ceausescu, Nicolae (obit.) **90**:107
Ceausescu, Nicu (obit.) **97**:97
Cech, Thomas Robert (biog.) **90**:85
Cela, Camilo José (biog.) **90**:85
Celebration (Fla., U.S.)
  town opening 138
Celibidache, Sergiu (obit.) **97**:97
cell (biol.)
  immune system research 64
"Celluloide" (motion picture) 291
Celosia (plant) 215
Celosia argentea cristata (flower) 215
CENR: *see* Committee on Environmental and Natural Resources
censorship
  Cameroon 403
  China 408
  Indonesia 264
  Internet 230
census
  special report **91**:279
  see also United States Census Bureau
Centennial Olympic Games: *see* Olympic Games
"Centennial Olympic Games, The" (special report) **97**:364
Center for Plant Conservation, *or* CPC 214
Centers for Disease Control and Prevention, *or* CDC (Atlanta, Ga., U.S.) 221
Central African Republic **97**:406; **96**:387; **95**:390; **94**:356; **93**:358; **92**:354; **91**:382; **90**:403; **89**:386; **88**:386
  see also WORLD DATA
Central America: *see* Latin-American affairs
Central Asia
  economic affairs 193
  military affairs 273, *table* 273
  republics (spotlight) 480, *map* 481
Central Bureau of Investigation, *or* CBI (India)
  political corruption 431
Central Selling Organisation, *or* CSO
  mining 171
Centre, the, *or* al-Wasat (rel. and pol. org., Egy.) 414
ceramics 166
  chemistry 254
cereal, *or* grain
  world production 123, 127, *table* 124
CERN, *or* European Laboratory for Particle Physics
  antimatter research 255
Cernik, Oldrich (obit.) **95**:64
"Cerul vazut prin lentila" (Patapievici) 251
Cervantes Prize (Sp. lit.) 247
César (award)
  film awards *table* 294
"Cesar" (hurricane)
  Costa Rica 410
  natural disasters 60
Cézanne, Paul
  art exhibitions (special report) 146
CFE treaty: *see* Conventional Forces in Europe treaty
CFTC: *see* Commodity Futures Trading Commission
CGI: *see* computer-generated image
Chacel, Rosa Clotilde Cecilia Maria del Carmen (obit.) **95**:64
Chad **97**:406; **96**:387; **95**:390; **94**:356; **93**:358; **92**:354; **91**:382; **90**:403; **89**:386; **88**:386
  see also WORLD DATA
Chadwick, Florence (obit.) **96**:76
chain gang
  U.S. prisons 229
Chakravarty, Sukhamoy (obit.) **91**:90
Chalmers, Floyd Sherman (obit.) **94**:58
Chamberlin, Jimmy 281
Chamlong Srimuang 483
Chamorro, Violeta Barrios de (biog.) **90**:85
Chamoun, Camille (obit.) **88**:91
Championship Auto Racing Teams, *or* CART 319
Chan, David 381
Chan, Jackie (biog.) **96**:54
Chan, Sir Julius 460
Chancellor, John William (obit.) **97**:97
Chances Peak (mt. peak, Monts., W.I.)
  volcanic activity 381
Chandler, Albert Benjamin ("Happy") (obit.) **92**:58
Chandrasekhar, Subrahmanyan (obit.) **96**:76
Chandraswami 431
Chanel (Fr. co.)
  fashion 216
Chang, Eileen, *or* Ai-ling Chang (obit.) **96**:76
Chang, Michael 360
Chang Jiang (riv., China): *see* Yangtze River
"Changing U.S. Workforce, The" (special report) **94**:203
channel (commu.)
  satellite TV (special report) 176
Channel Tunnel, *or* Eurotunnel, *or* Chunnel (tunnel, Eur.)
  fire damage 142
  special report **95**:350
"Chapayev i pustota" (Pelevin) 249
Chapman, Douglas George (obit.) **97**:97
Chapman, Graham (obit.) **90**:107
Chapman, Tracy (biog.) **89**:68
"Chapolas negras" (Vallejo) 248
Char, René (obit.) **89**:91
Charest, Jean 404
Charina bottae: *see* rubber boa
Charles, Prince of Wales (biog.) **92**:36
  United Kingdom 488
Charles, RuPaul Andre: *see* RuPaul
Charleson, Ian (obit.) **91**:90
Chart Thai (pol. party, Thai.): *see* Thai Nation
charter school
  U.S. education 204
Charteris, Leslie (obit.) **94**:58
Chase Manhattan Corp. (Am. co.) 200
Chatwin, Charles Bruce (obit.) **90**:107
Chauchoin, Lily Claudette (obit.): *see* Colbert, Claudette
Chavalit Yongchaiyudh 483
Chavez, Cesar Estrada (obit.) **94**:58
Chávez, Julio César (biog.) **92**:36
  boxing 329
Chávez Peñaherrera, Demetrio 461
"Cheat of Words, The" (McCaffery) 242
Chechnya (rep., Russ.) 464
  human rights issues 315
  military affairs 269, 271, 375
Checkland, Michael (biog.) **88**:68
Cheek, John (obit.) **97**:97
chemical weapon
  health and disease 218
  military affairs 269, 273
  UN convention 376
chemicals 160
Chemistry **97**:253; **96**:239; **95**:142; **94**:112; **93**:111; **92**:109; **91**:139; **90**:157; **89**:139; **88**:139
  Nobel Prize 63
Chemla, Paul
  contract bridge *table* 331
Chen Boda (obit.) **90**:107
Chen Kaige (biog.) **94**:36
Chen Lu 350
Chen Yun, *or* Ch'en Yün, *or* Liao Ch'en-yün (obit.) **96**:77
Cheney, Richard Bruce (biog.) **90**:85
Cherenkov, Pavel Alekseyevich (obit.) **91**:90
Cherkassky, Shura (obit.) **96**:77
Chermayeff, Serge, *or* Sergey Ivanovitch Issakovitch (obit.) **97**:97
Chernobyl (Ukraine)
  health issues 212
  nuclear waste disposal 164
  power station closing 487
Chernomyrdin, Viktor 464
Cherry, Donald Eugene (obit.) **96**:77
chess **97**:330; **96**:310; **95**:291; **94**:288; **93**:289; **92**:285; **91**:315; **90**:333; **89**:316; **88**:318
  computer match 182
Chiang Ch'ing: *see* Jiang Qing
Chiang Ching-kuo (obit.) **89**:91
Chiang Tse-min: *see* Jiang Zemin
Chibirov, Lyudvig 421
Chicago (Ill., U.S.)
  architecture 137
Chicago Bulls (basketball) 323
Chicago International Film Festival (U.S.)
  film awards *table* 294
child, *or* children
  Belgium scandal 396
  Chinese orphanages 314, 408
  education 203
  health and disease 222
  radiation poisoning 212
  sexual abuse 227
  special reports **96**:286; **95**:278, *il.*
  television 262, 264
  U.S. welfare reform 312, 491
child labour
  less developed countries (special report) **96**:287
  special report **95**:278
child welfare
  special report **96**:286
  U.S. welfare reform 312, 491
CHILDHOPE (internat. org.)
  special report **95**:279
Childress, Alice (obit.) **95**:64
Chile **97**:407; **96**:388; **95**:390; **94**:479; **93**:479; **92**:471; **91**:498; **90**:513; **89**:496; **88**:497
  free-trade agreements 224
  wildlife conservation 213
  zoos 214
  see also WORLD DATA
Chilstrom, Herbert Walfred (biog.) **88**:68
Chiluba, Frederick J. (biog.) **93**:37
  Zambia 504
Chimo (Fr. au.) 246
Ch'in Pen-li: *see* Qin Benli
China **97**:407; **96**:388; **95**:391; **94**:394; **93**:394; **92**:392; **91**:418; **90**:438; **89**:421; **88**:421
  agriculture and food supplies 123, 129
    fisheries 130
    food processing regulations 132
  archaeology 135
  architecture and civil engineering
    bridges 139
    dams 141
  arts and entertainment
    art exhibitions 144
    literature 252
    motion pictures 295
      special report **95**:245
  business and industry
    building and construction 160
    chemicals 161
    clothing 156
    coal 163
    cotton 177
    iron and steel 168
    machinery and machine tools 166
    mining 170
    nuclear energy 164
    rubber 167
    silk 177
  demography 295
  disasters
    fires and explosions 59
    marine 59
    mining and tunneling 60
    natural 60
  economic affairs 193, 442
  education 204, *il.* 205
  environment 211
  gardening 214
  geology 183
  human rights violations 314, 377
  intercity rail 374
  international affairs
    Australia 392
    Central Asia (spotlight) 481
    France 420
    Hong Kong 381
    India 432
    Japan 439
    Kazakstan 440
    Kenya 440
    Papua New Guinea 460
    Russia 467
    Southeast Asian Nations 380
    Taiwan 7, 478
      Lee Teng-hui interview (commentary) **97**:8
    United Kingdom 489
    United States 496
  libraries 230
  media and publishing
    newspapers 265
    television industry 261
  military affairs 276
  most populous urban areas *table* 296
  prisons and penology 229
  religion
    Buddhism 309
    Roman Catholicism 306
  social protection 314
  sports and games
    association football 341
    diving 358
    gymnastics 348
    table tennis 360
    weight lifting 370
  see also WORLD DATA
China Foundation for Marxism Studies 205
China National Corporation (Chin. corp.) 164
"China That Can Say No, The" (Song Qiang) 408
Chinese literature 252
chip, computer: *see* computer chip
Chirac, Jacques René (biog.) **96**:55
  France 419
  Lebanon 445
  military affairs 270
Chiriaeff, Ludmilla Otzup (obit.) **97**:97
Chissano, Joaquim 454
chlorine
  ozone depletion 210, 382
chlorofluorocarbon
  Pacific Ocean distribution 187
chlorophyll
  oceanography 187
Cho, David Yonggi (biog.) **96**:55
Choi Won Suk (biog.) **97**:69
  South Korea 441
cholesterol
  cardiovascular disease 219
Choonhavan, Chatichai (biog.) **89**:69
Chouinard, Julien (obit.) **88**:91
Chowdhury, Abu Sayeed (obit.) **88**:91
CHP (pol. party, Tur.): *see* Republican People's Party
Chrétien, Jean (biogs.) **94**:36; **91**:67
  Canada 404
Christian Church, *or* Disciples of Christ 302
Christian Democratic Union, *or* CDU (pol. party, Ger.)
  Church of Scientology 300
Christian Science: *see* Church of Christ, Scientist
"Christian Science Monitor, The" (Am. news.) 266, 303
Christianity 300
  education 204
  Philippines 461
  religion statistics *table* 311
  special reports **93**:261; **92**:261; **91**:289; **89**:290
Christiansen, Godtfred Kirk (obit.) **96**:77
Christie, Linford 362
Christie's (auction house, U.K.)
  art 150
  books and manuscripts 151
Christo, *or* Christo Javacheff (biog.) **96**:55
Christoff, Boris (obit.) **94**:59
Christopher, Warren
  China 409
  Israel 435
  land mines (special report) 274
  Lebanon 445
Chronology **97**:10; **96**:11; **95**:11; **94**:9; **93**:9; **92**:9; **91**:16; **90**:33; **89**:17; **88**:17
Chrysler Corp. (Am. co.) 157
Chu Jung-chi: *see* Zhu Ronji
Chuan Leekpai 482
Chubais, Anatoly 464, 466
Chukovskaya, Lidiya Korneyevna (obit.) **97**:97
Chun Doo Hwan 441, *il.*
Chung Il Kwon (obit.) **95**:64
Chung Mong Joon (biog.) **97**:69
Chunnel (tunnel, Eur.): *see* Channel Tunnel
Chuquicamata (Chile)
  copper mine *il.* 407
church
  arson 300, 302, *il.* 498
Church, Alonzo (obit.) **96**:77
Church of . . . : *see under* substantive word, except as below

Church of Christ, Scientist 303
  Minnesota ruling 300
Church of Jesus Christ of Latter-day Saints, *or* LDS 303
Churches of Christ 302
Churchill, Winston
  World War II (special report) **96**:258
Ciba-Geigy (Swiss co.)
  pharmaceutical merger 173
  textile industry 177
"cielo dividido, El" (Roffé) 248
cigar: *see* smoking
"Cigar" (horse) 335, *il.* 337
cigarette: *see* smoking
Cigna Corporation (Am. corp.) 166
Ciller, Tansu (biog.) **94**:36
  Turkey 484
cinema: *see* Motion Pictures
Cioran, Emil Mihai (obit.) **96**:77
Circle Repertory Company 288
CIS: *see* Commonwealth of Independent States
Citibank (Am. co.)
  Islamic rules 310
City (vehicle) 158
Civic Democratic Party, *or* ODS (pol. party, Czech Rep.) 412
civic journalism, *or* public journalism
  newspapers 266
Civic Solidarity Union, *or* UCS (pol. party, Bol.) 397
Civil Engineering 97:139; **96**:120
civil rights
  court decisions 224
  Hong Kong 408
  same-sex marriages 301
  United States 499
civil war
  Afghanistan 388
  Burundi 402
  Liberia 445
  military affairs 271
  Russia 269, 271, 464
  Spain anniversary 475
  Sri Lanka 476
  Tajikistan 482
  Zaire 504
CJD: *see* Creutzfeldt-Jakob disease
Claes, Willy (biog.) **95**:43
Clancy, Tom (biog.) **89**:69
"Clando" (motion picture) 295
Clark, Charles Manning Hope (obit.) **92**:58
Clark, Glen David (biog.) **97**:70
Clark, Sir John Grahame Douglas (obit.) **96**:77
Clark, Raymond, *or* Ossie Clark (obit.) **97**:97
  fashion 217
Clarke, Douglas L.
  "Combating the Land Mine Scourge" (special report) **97**:274
Clarke, Kenneth Harry (biog.) **94**:37
  economic affairs 188, 191
  United Kingdom 488
Clarke, Thomas Ernest Bennett (obit.) **90**:108
classical music 277
Clavell, James (obit.) **95**:65
Claverie, Pierre 389
Clayton, Jack (obit.) **96**:77
Clément, René (obit.) **97**:97
Clements, the Rev. George (biog.) **90**:86
Clemo, Reginald John (obit.) **95**:65
Clifford, Clark McAdams (biog.) **92**:36
climate 186
  air-sea interface 187
  environmental issues 207
  global changes 382
Climate Variability and Predictability Program 187
Clinton, Bill, *or* William Jefferson Clinton (biogs.) **97**:70; **94**:37; **93**:37
  business and industry
    telecommunications 175
    tobacco 154, 178
  crime and law enforcement 226
  economic affairs 190
  education 204
  election results (special report) **97**:492, *map* 494
  health and disease 218
  international affairs
    Antarctica 383
    Cuba 411
    Israel 434
    Japan 438
    Jordan 439
    North Korea 440
    South Korea 443
    Uzbekistan 500
  Internet 181
  labour-management relations 202
  media and publishing
    newspapers 266
    radio industry 265
    television industry 261
  military affairs 269, 272
    land mines (special report) 275
    nuclear testing 376, *map* 451
  religion
    abortion bill veto 300
  social protection reforms 312
  special report **94**:204
  United States 490, 495, 497
Clinton, Hillary Rodham (biog.) **94**:37
  book publishing 268
  Estonia 418
Clipper Chip (tech.)
  cyberspace (special report) **96**:159
Clock gene
  nematodes 232
Clooney, George *il.* 262
clopidogrel (drug)
  cardiovascular disease 219
Close, Glenn (biog.) **96**:55
Close, Robert (obit.) **96**:77
"Close Shave, A" (motion picture)
  computer animation (special report) 293
clothing 155
  fashions 216
cloud rat
  species discovery 213
Clubb, Oliver Edmund (obit.) **90**:108
Cluster (space mission) 256, 260
CMAG: *see* Commonwealth Ministerial Action Group
coal 163
  mining 172, *table*
  Spain 475
  Ukraine 487
Coalite Products (Br. co.) 211
Coase, Ronald (biog.) **92**:30
COB: *see* Bolivian Worker's Central
Cobain, Kurt (obit.) **95**:65
Coca-Cola 600
  automobile racing 320
Coca-Cola Company (Am. co.) 132, 159
cocaine
  drug trafficking 227, 228
  special report **89**:144
"Cocktail Jet" (horse) 338
cocoa
  cocoa plant *il.* 397
  Grenada 426
  world production 130, *table* 128
cod
  fisheries 131
Code of Conduct for Responsible Fisheries 130
"Codex Leicester" (Leonardo da Vinci) 144
Coelho, Paulo (biog.) **97**:70
  Brazilian literature 249
Coëme, Guy 397
Coen, Ethan (biog.) **97**:71
  motion pictures 289
Coen, Joel (biog.) **97**:71
  motion pictures 289
coffee
  Angola 389
  world production 129, *table* 128
Cohen, Robert 240
Cohen, Samuel: *see* Cahn, Sammy
Cohen, Wilbur Joseph (obit.) **88**:91
coins: *see* Numismatics
coking coal 163
Colbert, Claudette, *or* Lily Claudette Chauchoin (obit.) **97**:97
Colby, William Egan (obit.) **97**:98
Coldstream, Sir William Menzies (obit.) **88**:92
Cole, Natalie (biog.) **92**:37
Coleman, James Samuel (obit.) **96**:77
Coleman, Ornette (biog.) **94**:37
  jazz 280
Coles, Charles (obit.) **93**:59
Collectibles 97:152; **96**:131; **95**:114
  crime and law enforcement 228
  French forfeiture laws 225
collective bargaining
  baseball 320
college sports
  basketball 323
  football 342
  volleyball 370
  wrestling 370
Collenette, David 405
Colley, Russell (obit.) **97**:98
Colley, Sarah Ophelia (obit.): *see* Pearl, Minnie
Collins, Albert (obit.) **94**:59
Collins, Joan 268
Collins, Steve 330
Collins, Thomas LeRoy (obit.) **92**:58
Collor de Mello, Fernando (biog.) **91**:67
Colombia **97**:409; **96**:393; **95**:395; **94**:480; **93**:480; **92**:472; **91**:499; **90**:514; **89**:497; **88**:498
  association football 341
  aviation disasters 59
  literature 248
  military affairs 276
  special reports **95**:279; **89**:144
  Venezuela 501
  see also WORLD DATA
Colombo (Sri Lanka) *il.* 373
Colorado (state, U.S.) 497
  court decisions 225, 499
Colorado Avalanche, *or* Quebec Nordiques (ice hockey) 349
Colosio Murrieta, Luis Donaldo (obit.) **95**:65
colour photography: *see* photography
colour printing 173
"Columbia" (U.S. space shuttle) 258
Columbia Broadcasting System, *or* CBS (Am. co.)
  television ratings 262
Columbia Colville, Sir John Rupert (obit.) **88**:92
Colville River Delta (delta, Alsk., U.S.)
  petroleum extraction 383
"Combating the Land Mine Scourge" (special report) **97**:274
Combs, Lewis B. (obit.) **97**:98
comet (astron.) 256
Comet Hyakutake
  discovery and characteristics 256, *il.* 257
Comet 1996 N2
  discovery and characteristics 257
Commission on . . . : *see under* substantive word
Committee on Environment and Natural Resources, *or* CENR
  merging federal programs 206
commodities
  stock exchanges 199
Commodity Futures Trading Commission, *or* CFTC (U.S.) 198
  derivatives (special report) **96**:185
"Common Plight, The" (motion picture) 295
Commons, House of (U.K.) 487
Commonwealth Ministerial Action Group, *or* CMAG 378
Commonwealth of Independent States, *or* CIS **97**:379; **96**:356; **95**:358; **94**:348; **93**:349
  military affairs 271
  refugees 297
  Russia 465
  Uzbekistan 500
Commonwealth of Nations **97**:378; **96**:354; **95**:355; **94**:347; **93**:349; **92**:344; **91**:374; **90**:395; **89**:378; **88**:378
  see also WORLD DATA *and* individual Commonwealth nations by name
Communications Decency Act (U.S.) 181
communications satellite
  television (special report) **97**:176
communism
  China 205
  Italy 436
  Nepal 455
  Philippines 462
  Russia 464
Communist Party (pol. party, Russ.) 464
Communist Party (pol. party, Viet.)
  Central Committee's report 501
Communist Party of China, *or* CPC (pol. party, China) 407
community service
  prisons and penology 229
Comoros **97**:410; **96**:393; **95**:395; **94**:356; **93**:358; **92**:354; **91**:383; **90**:403; **89**:387; **88**:387
  aviation disasters 58
  new flag *il.* **96**:365
  see also WORLD DATA
compact disc read-only memory: *see* CD-ROM
Compagnie Luxembourgeoise pour la Télédiffusion SA (Luxem. co.) 261, 446
compensated gross tonnage
  shipbuilding 174
compliance therapy
  mental health 222
Comprehensive Plan of Action, *or* CPA
  Indochinese refugees 297
Comprehensive Test Ban Treaty (UN) 376
  Chinese support 409
  India rejection 432
  Japanese support 439
  military affairs 269
"Computer Animation" (special report) **97**:292
computer chip 169
computer game: *see* electronic game
computer-generated image, *or* CGI
  motion pictures (special report) **97**:292
Computers and Information Systems 97:180; **96**:157; **95**:201; **94**:200; **93**:199; **92**:199; **91**:228; **90**:246; **89**:229; **88**:231
  applications
    architecture 137
    chess match 182
    education 204
    motion pictures 292
    television special effects 263
  electronic imaging 173
  libraries 230
  special report **96**:158
Concert Global Communications (Br. co.) 175
concerto 279
Condé Nast Publications (Am. co.) 154
Condon, Richard Thomas (obit.) **97**:98
condor
  wildlife conservation 213
  zoos 214
Cone, David 320
Congo **97**:410; **96**:394; **95**:396; **94**:357; **93**:359; **92**:354; **91**:383; **90**:404; **89**:387; **88**:387
  new flag *illus.* **92**:343
  see also WORLD DATA
Congo bay owl, *or* Phodilus prigoginei
  wildlife conservation 213
Congregational Church 304
Congress (I) (pol. party, India) 430
Congress of South African Trade Unions, *or* COSATU (S.Af. org.) 473
Congress of the United States 490
  Communications Decency Act 181
  Contract with America (special report) **96**:492
  education 204
  environmental issues 206
  food processing legislation 132
  illegal aliens 297
  labour-management relations 202
  military affairs 269
  reapportionment decision 225
  religious persecution 300
  social protection 312
  state and local affairs 497
  telecommunications 175
  world affairs
    Chile 407
    China 409
    Puerto Rico 381
Conigliaro, Anthony Richard (obit.) **91**:90
Conn, William David, Jr. (obit.) **94**:59
Connally, John Bowden, Jr. (obit.) **94**:59
Connecticut (state, U.S.) 497
Conner, Dennis (biog.) **88**:69
Connor, Joseph E. 376
conodont
  paleontology 238
Conover, Willis (obit.) **97**:98
Conroy, John Wesley (obit.) **91**:90
conservation: *see* Environment; wildlife conservation
Conservative Party (pol. party, U.K.) 487
Conservatives of Lithuania (pol. party, Lith.): *see* Homeland Union
Constantinescu, Emil 463
construction: *see* building and construction
constructivism
  education 204
Consumer Affairs 97:202; **96**:189; **95**:143; **94**:114; **93**:113; **92**:111; **91**:141; **90**:159; **89**:141; **88**:141
  agriculture and food supplies 128
  clothing industry 156
  economic affairs 189, 191, *tables* 188, 193
  food processing 131
  furs 156
  petroleum 162
  retailing 174
  stock exchanges 196
  tobacco 178
  toys and games 164
  United States 499
consumer confidence
  stock exchanges 196
  United Kingdom 488
Consumer Product Safety Commission (U.S.)
  lead-based paints 212
Conté, Lansana 426
"Conte d'été" (motion picture): *see* "Summer's Tale, A"
Contemporary Art, Museum of (Chicago, Ill., U.S.) *il.* 232
  architecture 137
Continental AG (Ger. co.) 167
Continental Cablevision (Am. co.) 175
"Continentalvictory" (horse) 338
contingent worker
  "The Changing U.S. Workforce" (special report) **94**:203
contraception
  worldwide use 295
contract bridge **97**:331; **96**:311; **95**:292; **94**:289; **93**:290; **92**:286; **91**:316; **90**:334; **89**:317; **88**:319
  Generali Individual deal *il.* 331
Contract with America (U.S. leg. program)
  special report **96**:492
Convention on the . . . : *see under* substantive word, *e.g.,* Status of Refugees, Convention on the
Conventional Forces in Europe treaty, *or* CFE treaty
  military affairs 269, 271
"Conversation with Lee Teng-hui, A" (commentary) **97**:6
Cook, Elisha, Jr. (obit.) **96**:78
Cook, Peter 392
Cook, Peter Edward (obit.) **96**:78
Cook, Robin Finlayson (biog.) **97**:71
Cook Islands 381
Cooke, Ellen F. 301
Cools, André 396
Cooper, Susan Vera Barker (obit.) **96**:78
Cooper, Dame Whina (obit.) **95**:65
Coors Brewing Co. (Am. co.)
  beer production 158
Copenhagen (Den.)
  dance 284
Copenhagen Zoo (zoo, Copenhagen, Den.) 213
Copland, Aaron (obit.) **91**:90
Copleston, Frederick Charles (obit.) **95**:65
Coposu, Corneliu (obit.) **96**:78
copper
  mining 170
copra
  world production *table* 125
Coptic Orthodox Church 308
copyright law
  cyberspace (special report) **96**:159
Corbett, Harry (obit.) **90**:108
Corey, Elias James (biog.) **91**:67
Corino, Karl 244
corn, *or* maize
  world production 127
Cornfeld, Bernard (obit.) **96**:78
Cornwell, Patricia (biog.) **97**:71
coronary heart disease 219
Corot, Jean-Baptiste-Camille 148
corporate merger: *see* merger and acquisition, corporate
Corrigan, Douglas (obit.) **96**:78

corruption
Argentina 390
art collections 144
Bahamas, The 394
Bangladesh 394
Belgium 396
China 408
Colombia 409
Cook Islands 381
crime and law enforcement 228
Czech Republic banks 200
Ecuador 414
education 206
Equatorial Guinea 415
France 419
Hungary 427
India 430
Indonesia 432
Ireland 434
Italy 436
Kenya 440
Lithuania 446
Pakistan 459
Panama 460
Poland 462
South Africa 474
South Korea 441
Sumitomo affair 170
Switzerland 477
television industry 261
Thailand 482
United Kingdom 487
United States 490, 496, 498
Corsica (is., Fr.)
terrorism 419
Corsican National Liberation Front, *or* FLNC (pol. org., Corsica) 419
COSATU (S.Af. org.): *see* Congress of South African Trade Unions
Cosell, Howard (obit.) **96**:78
cosmology 258
cosmonaut: *see* astronaut
Costa Rica **97**:410; **96**:394; **95**:396; **94**:481; **93**:481; **92**:472; **91**:500; **90**:515; **89**:498; **88**:263
see also WORLD DATA
Costello, John Edward (obit.) **96**:78
Costello, Peter 392
Costner, Kevin (biog.) **92**:37
cot death: *see* sudden infant death syndrome
Côte d'Ivoire (formerly Ivory Coast) **97**:410; **96**:394; **95**:396; **94**:357; **93**:359; **92**:355; **91**:383; **90**:404; **89**:387; **88**:387
agriculture 130
see also WORLD DATA
Cotten, Joseph (obit.) **95**:65
cotton 177
agriculture 130, *table* 128
Cotton, Thomas Henry (obit.) **88**:92
cottonseed
world production 128, *table* 125
Coughlin, Lieut. Paula (biog.) **93**:38
Coulouris, George (obit.) **90**:108
Council of (the) . . . : *see under* substantive word, *e.g.,* Europe, Council of
"Counterspeculation, Auctions, and Competitive Sealed Tenders" (Vickrey)
economics 63
country music 282
radio industry 265
coup d'état (pol.)
Burundi 402
Guinea 426
Niger 457
Sierra Leone 471
Cournand, André Frédéric (obit.) **89**:92
court decisions 224
United States 497, 499
court-martial
United States 270
Cousins, Norman (obit.) **91**:91
Covington, Vicki
American literature 240
cow: *see* cattle
Cowie, Mervyn Hugh (obit.) **97**:98
Cowley, Malcolm (obit.) **90**:108
CPA: *see* Comprehensive Plan of Action
CPC: *see* Center for Plant Conservation
CPC (pol. party, China): *see* Communist Party of China
CPP (pol. party, Camb.): *see* Cambodian People's Party
Crabtree, Robert 254
Craddock, Sir Percy 489
Cragun, Richard 284
Cram, Donald James (biog.) **88**:69
Cranche, Albert (obit.): *see* Carné, Marcel
"Crash" (motion picture) 290
Crateromys heaneyi: *see* Panay cloudrunner
Craven, Daniël Hartman (obit.) **94**:59
Crawford, Michael (biog.) **89**:69
Crawley, Frank Radford (obit.) **88**:92
Cray, Seymour R. (obit.) **97**:98
computers 182
credit
banking 201
credit-card late fees 203
microbanking 200
Cree (people)
Canada 383
Crépin, Jean-Albert-Emile (obit.) **97**:99
Cresson, Edith (biog.) **92**:37
Creutzfeldt-Jakob disease, *or* CJD
"mad cow" disease link 126, 202, 487
cricket **97**:332; **96**:312; **95**:293; **94**:290; **93**:291; **92**:287; **91**:317; **90**:335; **89**:317; **88**:319
Crime 97:226; **96**:212; **95**:145; **94**:116; **93**:115; **92**:113; **91**:143; **90**:160; **89**:142; **88**:142
China 408
church-attendance study 300
Contract with America (special report) **96**:492
cyberspace (special report) **96**:159
Haiti 427, *il.*
United States 498
see also organized crime; Prisons and Penology; violence; war crime
Croat, *or* Hrvati (people)
Bosnia and Herzegovina 398
special report **94**:425
Croatia **97**:411; **96**:395; **95**:397; **94**:428; **93**:429
aviation disasters 58, *il.* 411
land mines *map* 275
new flag *illus.* **93**:345
roads 142
see also WORLD DATA
Croatia (medieval principality)
Bosnia and Herzegovina (special report) **94**:426
Croatian Democratic Union, *or* HDZ (pol. party, Croatia) 411
Crocetti, Dino Paul: *see* Martin, Dean
Cromer, George Rowland Stanley Baring (obit.) **92**:58
Crosby, George Robert (obit.) **94**:59
cross bridge (biol.)
muscle contraction 232
"Cross Channel" (Barnes) 243
cross country (athletics) 370
Crossan, John Dominic (biog.) **95**:43
Crotalus atrox: *see* western diamondback rattlesnake
Crown, Henry (obit.) **91**:91
Crowther, Leslie Douglas Sargent (obit.) **97**:99
Crowther, Peter 355
Crowther-Hunt, Norman Crowther Crowther-Hunt, Baron (obit.) **88**:92
"Crucible, The" (motion picture) 289
crude oil: *see* petroleum
crude steel: *see* iron and steel
cruise ship 175
Crutzen, Paul 210
"cruz en la espada, La" (Luján) 247
cryopreservation
"Zoos Look to the 21st Century" (special report) **94**:111
CSN (pol. org., Niger): *see* National Salvation Council
CSO: *see* Central Selling Organisation
CSSD (pol. party, Czech Rep.): *see* Czech Social Democratic Party
"Cuando fui mortal" (Marías) 247
Cuba **97**:411; **96**:396; **95**:397; **94**:481; **93**:481; **92**:473; **91**:500; **90**:515; **89**:499; **88**:499
free market *il.* 412
international affairs
Bahamas, The 394
Canada 405
Caricom membership *map* 469
Dominica 413
Jamaica 437
Spain 475
United States 496
military affairs 276
sports and games
baseball 322
volleyball 370
see also WORLD DATA
Cuban Liberty and Democratic Solidarity Act (U.S.): *see* Helms-Burton Act
Cugat, Xavier (obit.) **91**:91
Culhane, James, *or* Shamus Culhane (obit.) **97**:99
cult (rel.)
special report **90**:308
cultural anthropology 134
Cummings, Robert (obit.) **91**:91
Cunningham, Glenn (obit.) **89**:92
Cunningham, Jack (biog.) **93**:38
"Cure for Death by Lightning, The" (Anderson-Dargatz) 242
Curien, Hubert (biog.) **95**:43
Curl, Robert F., Jr.
Nobel Prize 63
curling **97**:334; **96**:314
currency: *see* Numismatics
Curry, Edwina 243
Curry, John Anthony (obit.) **95**:66
Curtis, Jean-Louis, *or* Louis Laffitte (obit.) **96**:78
Cusack, Cyril James (obit.) **94**:59
Cushing, Peter (obit.) **95**:66
customs union
Uzbekistan 500
Cy Young Award (baseball) 322
cyanide gas
death penalty 225
cyberspace
special report **96**:158
cycling **97**:334; **96**:314; **95**:294; **94**:291; **93**:292; **92**:288; **91**:318; **90**:336; **89**:319; **88**:321
1996 Summer Olympic champions *table* **97**:365
cyclone
India 60, 431
Cyclospora cayetanensis 221
Cyprus **97**:412; **96**:397; **95**:398; **94**:380; **93**:381; **92**:378; **91**:405; **90**:425; **89**:407; **88**:408
Greece 425
Turkey 485
see also WORLD DATA
Cyrankiewicz, Jozef (obit.) **90**:108
cytotoxic T cell: *see* killer T cell
Czech Republic **97**:412; **96**:397; **95**:399; **94**:429
arts and entertainment
Eastern European literature 250
motion pictures 295
banking 200
economic affairs 194
magazines 266
new flag *illus.* **94**:345
penal code 229
sports and games
association football 340
ice hockey 349
see also WORLD DATA
Czech Social Democratic Party, *or* CSSD (pol. party, Czech Rep.) 412
Czechoslovakia **93**:430; **92**:421; **91**:469; **90**:486; **89**:469; **88**:469
see also WORLD DATA
Czycz, Stanisław 250

D

"Da Hoss" (horse) 335
Daché, Lilly (obit.) **90**:108
Dæhlie, Bjørn 357
Daewoo (S.Kor. co.) 454
Dagestan (rep., Russ.)
military affairs 271
Dahik Garzozi, Alberto 414
Dahl, Roald (obit.) **91**:91
Daimler-Benz AG (Ger. co.)
aerospace industry 155, 456
Dairo, Isaiah Kehinde (obit.) **97**:99
dairy industry
world production 129, *table* 127
Daiwa Bank Ltd. (Japanese bank) 228
Dalai Lama (biog.) **90**:86
Australia 392
China 408
Panchen Lama 309
Daley, Richard M. (biog.) **90**:86
Dalí, Salvador (obit.) **90**:108
Dalida (obit.) **88**:92
Dallas Cowboys (football) 344
dams 141, *table* 143
"Danaïds, The" (play) 287
Dance 97:282; **96**:267; **95**:149; **94**:121; **93**:119; **92**:117; **91**:147; **90**:164; **89**:148; **88**:148
Dance Theatre of Harlem (Am. dance co.) 282
"Danger Signals from the Arc of Crisis" (feature article) **89**:8
Daniel, Frank (obit.) **97**:99
Daniel, Yuly Markovich (obit.) **89**:92
Daniels, Billy (obit.) **89**:92
Danish literature 245
"Danube: The Course of a Life, The" (Aus. hist. exhibit) 393
Danzig, Sarah Palfrey (obit.) **97**:99
Darman, Richard Gordon (biog.) **91**:68
Darrell, Peter (obit.) **88**:92
Darrieussecq, Marie 246
Dart, Raymond (obit.) **89**:92
Dassault, Serge 419
Dassler, Horst (obit.) **88**:92
D'Aubuisson, Roberto (obit.) **93**:59
dauer gene
nematodes 232
Daume, Willi (obit.) **97**:99
Davenport, Marcia Gluck (obit.) **97**:99
David, Elizabeth (obit.) **93**:60
Davie, Donald Alfred (obit.) **96**:78
Davies, Laura 347
Davies, Paul Charles William (biog.) **96**:56
Davies, William Robertson (obit.) **96**:78
Davis, Bette (obit.) **90**:109
Davis, Latina *il.* 324
Davis, Miles Dewey, III (obit.) **92**:58
jazz 280
Davis, Sammy, Jr. (obit.) **91**:91
Davis, Terrell 344
Davis, Troy 343
Davis, Victor (obit.) **90**:109
Davis, William Strethen (obit.) **96**:78
Davis Cup (tennis) 362
Davison, William (obit.) **90**:109
Dawkins, Clinton Richard (biog.) **97**:71
Dawkins, John Sydney (biog.) **93**:38
Dawson, Les (obit.) **94**:59
Dax Index (Ger.) 199
Day, Clarence (obit.) **91**:92
Day, Dennis (obit.) **89**:92
Day, Leon (obit.) **96**:78
Day, Pat 336
Dayton Accords (peace agreement)
Bosnia and Herzegovina 398
military affairs 269
United States 496
Daytona 500 (automobile race) 320
"Daytrippers, The" (motion picture) 289
DBS: *see* direct-broadcast satellite
DC-XA launch vehicle
space exploration 260
De Beers Consolidated Mines (S.Af. co.) 171
De Benedetti, Carlo (biog.) **89**:69
de Boer, Wubbo
contract bridge *table* 331
de Gennes, Pierre-Gilles (biog.) **92**:31
de Klerk, Frederik Willem (biog.) **90**:87
South Africa 473
de Kock, Eugene
murder conviction 229, 316, 474
de la Hoya, Oscar 329, *il.*
"De la nature de la gravité" (opera) 278
de Mille, Agnes George (obit.) **94**:60
De Mita, Luigi Ciriaco (biog.) **89**:70
de Vaucouleurs, Gerard Henri (obit.) **96**:79
De Vries, Peter (obit.) **94**:60
DEA (U.S.): *see* Drug Enforcement Administration
"Dead Man Walking" (motion picture)
film awards *table* 294
Deane, Edna, *or* Edna Morton Sewell (obit.) **96**:79
Deane, Seamus 243
Dearden, John Francis Cardinal (obit.) **89**:92
Dearmer, Geoffrey (obit.) **97**:99
death
United States law 498
"Death and the Dervish" (Selimović) 250
death penalty: *see* capital punishment
death rate: *see* mortality
Debré, Michel-Jean-Pierre (obit.) **97**:99
Deburghgraeve, Frederik 357
Déby, Idriss 407
DEC (Am. co.): *see* Digital Equipment Corp.
DeCarava, Roy (biog.) **97**:72
photography exhibition 149
"Decline of the One-Party State" (special report) **92**:349
Decroux, Étienne-Marcel (obit.) **92**:59
Deep Blue (computer)
chess match 182
"Deep Crimson," *or* "Profundo Carmesí" (motion picture) 295
Deep Thought (computer)
chess match 182
defense: *see* Military Affairs
Defense, Department of (U.S.)
Persian Gulf War syndrome 221
Defense of Marriage Act (U.S.) 495, 499
deficit, budget: *see* budget deficit
deficit, trade: *see* trade deficit
Degas, Edgar
art exhibitions 145
Degrelle, Léon Joseph Marie (obit.) **95**:66
Dehaene, Jean-Luc (biog.) **93**:38
Belgium 397
Dehmelt, Hans Georg (biog.) **90**:86
Deighton, Len (biog.) **91**:68
Deisenhofer, Johann (biog.) **89**:70
Delaney clause
food processing regulations 132
Delany, Annie Elizabeth (obit.) **96**:79
Delay, Jean (obit.) **88**:92
Delclaux, Cosme 475
Deleuze, Gilles (obit.) **96**:79
Delhi (India)
most populous urban areas *table* 296
Delk, Tony 324
Delphinium (flower) 215
Deltadromeus agilis (dinosaur) 239
Delvaux, Paul (obit.) **95**:66
Deming, William Edwards (obit.) **94**:60
Demirel, Suleyman 484
Democratic Alliance (pol. party, Mong.) 453
Democratic Convention of Romania, *or* CDR (pol. party, Rom.) 463
Democratic Liberal Party (pol. party, S.Kor.): *see* New Korea Party
Democratic Party, *or* PD (pol. party, El Sal.) 415
Democratic Party (pol. party, U.S.)
education 204
special reports **97**:492; **93**:469; **89**:483
United States 490, 497
Democratic Party of the Left, *or* PDS (pol. party, It.) 436
democratic pluralism
special report **92**:349
Democratic Progressive Party, *or* DPP (pol. party, Tai.) 478
Democratic Rally (pol. party, Cyprus) 412
democratization
Africa (spotlight) 416, *map* 417
East Asia (spotlight) 442
"Islamic Fundamentalism" (special report) **94**:378
demography **97**:295; **96**:279; **95**:255; **94**:252; **93**:250; **92**:250; **91**:278; **90**:296; **89**:280; **88**:282
"Financial Support for the Elderly" (special report) **94**:144
most populous urban areas *table* 296
demonstrations and protests
Australia 392
Belarus 380, 395
Bulgaria 401
Canada *il.* 405
economic affairs 189
European Union 378, *il.* 379
Hong Kong 381
Internet censorship *il.* 180
Japan unemployment *il.* 438
Newbury Bypass photo essay 208
North Korea 440

Pentecostal Churches 304
radioactive waste transport 207, *il.*
Spain 475
Switzerland 478
Yugoslavia 503, *il.* 502
see also riots
Demy, Jacques (obit.) **91**:92
Den Uyl, Johannes Marten (obit.) **88**:93
Denard, Robert (biog.) **94**:38
Denby, David 241
Dendeven, Ad van 150
Deng Xiaoping, *or* Teng Hsiao-p'ing 407
Deng Yaping 360
Deng Yingchao, *or* Teng Ying-ch'ao (obit.) **93**:60
dengue
infectious diseases 219
dengue hemorrhagic fever
infectious diseases 221
denial-of-service attack
computers 181
Denmark **97**:413; **96**:398; **95**:399; **94**:429; **93**:431; **92**:422; **91**:447; **90**:464; **89**:448; **88**:447
bridges 139
literature 245
zoos 213
see also WORLD DATA
Denner, Charles (obit.) **96**:79
Dennett, Daniel C. (biog.) **97**:72
Dennis, Nigel Forbes (obit.) **90**:109
Dennis, Sandy, *or* Sandra Dale Dennis (obit.) **93**:60
Denver Broncos (football) 344
deoxyribonucleic acid: *see* DNA
Depardieu, Gérard (biog.) **88**:69
Department of . . . : *see under* substantive word, *e.g.*, Justice, Department of
dependent states **97**:380; **96**:357; **95**:358; **94**:500; **93**:500; **92**:491; **91**:518; **90**:534; **89**:518; **88**:518
see also WORLD DATA
depression
mental health 222
Prozac (special report) **95**:215
derivative (econ.)
special report **96**:185
Dermochelys coriacea: *see* leatherback turtle
DeRoburt, Hammer (obit.) **93**:60
Desai, Morarji Ranchhodji (obit.) **96**:79
desalination
U.S. drought (special report) **92**:168
desertification *il.* 457
"Designated Mourner, The" (play) 286
Desir, Wilson (obit.) **96**:79
Deskey, Donald (obit.) **90**:109
"Destiny" (cruise ship)
shipbuilding 175
"Detroit Free Press" (Am. news.) 266
"Detroit News" (Am. news.) 266
Detroit Red Wings (ice hockey) 349
Dettori, Frankie 337
Deutch, John Mark (biog.) **96**:56
Deutsch, Helen (obit.) **93**:60
Deutsche Mark (currency) 192
Deutsche Telekom (Ger. co.) 261
Devaty, Stanislav 412
developed nation: *see* industrial nation
developing nation: *see* less developed country
Devers, Gail (biog.) **93**:38
track and field sports 362
Devi, Kananbala (obit.) **93**:60
Devi, Phoolan (biog.) **96**:56
Devlin, Patrick Arthur Devlin (obit.) **93**:60
Devlin, William George (obit.) **88**:93
devolution (pol.)
Canada 404
DeWalt, Autry: *see* Walker, Junior
Dewhurst, Colleen (obit.) **92**:59
dexfenfluramine (drug) 221
Dexter, John (obit.) **91**:92
Dhahran (Saud.Arab.)
terrorism 269, 470, 495
Dhaka (Bangla.)
most populous urban areas *table* 296
di Donato, Pietro (obit.) **93**:61
Di Pietro, Antonio (biog.) **94**:38
Italy 436
diamond
Botswana 399
Canada 383
gemstone production 165
mining 170
Diamond, I. A. L. (obit.) **89**:93
diamondback rattlesnake: *see* western diamondback rattlesnake
Diana, Princess of Wales 488
Diaoyu Islands (isls., E. China Sea): *see* Senkaku Islands
"Diaro postumo" (Montale) 247
Díaz, Junot 241, *il.* 242
Dickey, William Malcolm (obit.) **94**:60
Dickson, Dorothy Schofield (obit.) **96**:79
"Dictionary of Art, The" 243
Didion, Joan 240
"Die Sache mit Randow" (Schlesinger) 244
Dietrich, Marlene (obit.) **93**:61
Dietz, Robert Sinclair (obit.) **96**:79
"Different for Girls" (motion picture) 290
digital camera
photography 173, 181
Digital Equipment Corp., *or* DEC (Am. co.) 182
digital printing 173
digital signal processing chip 170
digital television 261
digital video disc, *or* digital versatile disc, *or* DVD 181
digitized visual image
photography 149
wavelet analysis 253
dihydrogen bond 254
"Diletta Costanza" (Garavini) 247
Dillingham, William B. 241
dimethyl sulfide, *or* DMS
ornithology 234
Dimitrios I (obit.) **92**:59
Dinesen, Isak: *see* Blixen, Karen
Dinkins, David (biog.) **90**:87
dinosaur
paleontology 239
Diokno, Jose Wright (obit.) **88**:93
Dion, Céline (biog.) **95**:43
Dion, Stéphane 404
Diop, Birago Ismael (obit.) **90**:109
Diori, Hamani (obit.) **90**:110
Diouf, Abdou (biog.) **94**:38
Senegal 470
dioxin 211
direct-broadcast satellite, *or* DBS
satellite TV (special report) **97**:176
television industry 261
DirecTV (Am. co.) 261
disarmament
military affairs 269
Disasters 97:58; **96**:45; **95**:32; **94**:124; **93**:123; **92**:121; **91**:151; **90**:166; **89**:152; **88**:152
airline crashes 372, *il.*
Hinduism 309
India 431
insurance costs 165
special report **92**:167
TWA Flight 800 226, 495
weather forecasting 187
Zambia 341
Disciples of Christ: *see* Christian Church
Discovery Channel Online 180
discrimination
court decisions 224
genetic testing issues 218
United Kingdom armed forces 270
U.S. military education 206
disease: *see* Health and Disease
Disney Co. (Am. co.): *see* Walt Disney Co.
dissociation
repressed memory therapy (special report) **95**:198
distance running: *see* long-distance running
distilled liquor: *see* spirits
Ditka, Mike (biog.) **89**:70
diving 358
1996 Summer Olympic champions *table* **97**:365
Dixon, Willie (obit.) **93**:61
DJIA: *see* Dow Jones industrial average
Djibouti **97**:413; **96**:398; **95**:400; **94**:357; **93**:359; **92**:355; **91**:383; **90**:404; **89**:387; **88**:388
Eritrea 415
see also WORLD DATA
Djilas, Milovan (obit.) **96**:79
Djohar, Said Mohamed 410
DMS: *see* dimethyl sulfide
DNA, *or* deoxyribonucleic acid
anthropology 134
new vaccines 237
Do Muoi (biog.) **92**:38
Dobler, David Lee
"Homosexuality and the Churches" (special report) **94**:264
doctor-assisted suicide: *see* euthanasia
"Doctor of Myddfai, The" (opera) 279
Doctorow, E. L. 288
documentary: *see* Motion Pictures
Doe, Samuel Kanyon (obit.) **91**:92
dog
behavioral study 223
"Dog in the Manger," *or* "El perro del hortelano" (motion picture) 291
Doherty, Peter
Nobel Prize 64
Doi, Takako (biog.) **90**:87
Doisneau, Robert (obit.) **95**:66
Doko Toshio (obit.) **89**:93
Dole, Robert Joseph, *or* Bob Dole (biog.) **97**:73
education proposals 206
election results (special report) **97**:492, *map* 494
health and disease 218
special report **89**:483
United States 490
doll (toy)
toys and games 164
dollar (currency)
U.S. currency design 151
"Doll's House, A" (play) 286
Dome of the Rock, *or* Qubbat as-Sakhrah (mosque, Jerusalem) 135, *map* 435
Dominguín, *or* Luis Miguel González Lucas (obit.) **97**:99
Dominica **97**:413; **96**:399; **95**:400; **94**:482; **93**:482; **92**:474; **91**:501; **90**:516; **89**:500; **88**:500
see also WORLD DATA
Dominican Liberation Party, *or* PLD (pol. party, Dom.Rep.) 413
Dominican Republic **97**:413; **96**:399; **95**:401; **94**:482; **93**:483; **92**:474; **91**:501; **90**:517; **89**:500; **88**:501
aviation disasters 58
Hurricane Hortense 60
see also WORLD DATA
Dominican Revolutionary Party, *or* PRD (pol. party, Dom.Rep.) 413
Donaldson, Sam (biog.) **89**:70
Dong Ah Construction Industrial Co. (S.Kor. co.) 69
Donnadieu, Marguerite (obit.): *see* Duras, Marguerite
Donoso, José (obit.) **97**:99
Donovan, Hedley (obit.) **91**:92
Donovan, Terence Daniel (obit.) **97**:99
Dooling, Richard 241
Doolittle, James Harold (obit.) **94**:60
Doppler radar
weather forecasting 187
Dorati, Antal (obit.) **89**:93
Dorling Kindersley (Br. co.) 268
Doron, Eliahu Bakshi 309
Dorsey, Thomas Andrew (obit.) **94**:61
dos Santos, José Eduardo 389
Dostam, 'Abd ar-Rashid
Afghanistan 388
Dostoyevsky, Fedor
information technology (special report) **96**:159
Douglas, Roger (biog.) **88**:69
Douglas-Home, Sir Alec (obit.): *see* Home of the Hirsel, Alexander Frederick Douglas-Home, Baron, of Coldstream
Douglas-Home, William (obit.) **93**:61
Doumeng, Jean-Baptiste (obit.) **88**:93
Dove, Ulysses (obit.) **97**:99
Dow Chemical Co. (Am. co.) 161
Dow Jones industrial average, *or* DJIA 195, 490, *table* 198
Down Beat Jazz Hall of Fame 279
Downer, Alexander John Gosse (biog.) **95**:44
Australia 392
Downey, Morton, Jr. (biog.) **89**:71
downlink
satellite TV (special report) 176
Dowswell, Christopher R.
"World Revolution in Agriculture" (feature article) **88**:5
Doyle, Roddy (biog.) **95**:44
DPP (pol. party, Tai.): *see* Democratic Progressive Party
Drake, Alfred (obit.) **93**:61
Draper, Charles Stark (obit.) **88**:93
Draper, Paul (obit.) **97**:99
"Dream of the Unified Field, The" (Graham) 242
Drees, Willem (obit.) **89**:93
dress: *see* Fashions
Drew, Dame Jane Beverly (obit.) **97**:99
Drew, Kenny (obit.) **94**:61
Drewermann, Eugen (biog.) **96**:57
"Drifting Clouds" (motion picture) 291
drought
special report **92**:167
Dru, Joanne, *or* Joanne LaCock (obit.) **97**:99
Druckman, Jacob Raphael (obit.) **97**:99
drug abuse, *or* substance abuse *il.* 497
popular music 281
Drug Enforcement Administration, *or* DEA (U.S.) 228
drug trafficking 227
Cambodia 403
Colombia 409
forfeiture laws 225
Ireland 434
Mauritania 452
Morocco 454
Panama 460
Peru 461
drugs
botanical discoveries 236
fashion 217
special reports **95**:278; **89**:144
see also pharmaceuticals
Drummond de Andrade, Carlos 249
Dryopithecus
anthropology 133
Drysdale, Donald Scott (obit.) **94**:61
du Maurier, Dame Daphne (obit.) **90**:110
Du Pont Company (Am. co.)
chemicals 161
Du Pré, Jacqueline (obit.) **88**:93
Duarte, José Napoleón (obit.) **91**:92
Dubayy World Cup (horse racing) 337
Dubcek, Alexander (obit.) **93**:62
Duby, Georges Michel Claude (obit.) **97**:99
Dudayev, Dzhokhar
biography **95**:44
military affairs 271, 464
obituary **97**:99
Dukakis, Michael Stanley (biog.) **89**:71
special report **89**:483
Duke, Angier Biddle (obit.) **96**:79
Duke, Doris (obit.) **94**:61
Dukes, Alan (biog.) **88**:70
Dulles, Eleanor Lansing (obit.) **97**:99
Dumont, Marilyn 242
Dunai, Imre 430
Dunblane (U.K.)
mass murders 227
Duncan-Sandys, Duncan Edwin Duncan-Sandys, Baron (obit.) **88**:93
Dunlop India Ltd. (Indian co.)
rubber industry 167
Dunmore, Helen 243
Dunne, Irene Marie (obit.) **91**:93
Dunnock, Mildred (obit.) **92**:59
Dupain, Maxwell Spencer (obit.) **93**:62
Durán Ballén, Sixto (biog.) **93**:39
Duras, Marguerite, *or* Marguerite Donnadieu (obit.) **97**:99
Durocher, Leo Ernest (obit.) **92**:59
Durrell, Gerald Malcolm (obit.) **96**:79
Durrell, Lawrence George (obit.) **91**:93
Dürrenmatt, Friedrich (obit.) **91**:93
Dutch literature: *see* Netherlandic literature
Dutroux, Marc 396
Dutt, Utpal (obit.) **94**:61
Duval, Sir Gaetan (obit.) **97**:100
Duwwārah, Fu'ād 252
DVD: *see* digital video disc
Dyer-Bennet, Richard (obit.) **92**:60
DYP (pol. party, Tur.): *see* True Path Party

E

E. coli: *see* Escherichia coli
E3 tanker
shipbuilding 174
Eaker, Ira Clarence (obit.) **88**:93
Earth
environment research 259
perihelion and aphelion *table* 256
Earth Sciences 97:183; **96**:160; **95**:152; **94**:128; **93**:127; **92**:125; **91**:155; **90**:172; **89**:156; **88**:156
earthquake
China earthquake damage *il.* 185
geophysics 184
natural disasters 60
Earth's core *il.* 183
East Asian affairs
business and industry
electrical 161
shipbuilding 174
smoking reduction 178
economic affairs 188
democracy and development (spotlight) 442
military affairs 276, *table* 273
East Asian–Australasian Shorebird Reserve Network
wildlife conservation 213
East Germany: *see* German Democratic Republic
East Timor, *or* Timor Timur (prov., Indon.) 432
independence movement 62
"Eastern Africa: Eritrea" (MACROPAEDIA revision) **95**:514
Eastern European affairs **94**:420; **93**:423; **92**:416; **91**:467; **90**:484; **89**:468; **88**:467
agriculture and food supplies 128, 129
business and industry
chemicals 160
manufacturing *table* 153
paper and pulp 179
child welfare (special report) **96**:287
economic affairs 193
banking 200
education 204
environmental issues 212
"Pollution in Eastern Europe" (spotlight) **96**:460
Gypsy photo essay 428
literature 250
social protection 314
special reports **95**:173; **93**:143
see also European Affairs; Western European Affairs; *and* individual countries by name
"Eastern Europe's Problems of Transition" (special report) **93**:143
"Eastern Orthodox Christianity: At the Crossroads" (special report) **93**:261
Eastman Kodak Company (Am. corp.)
photography 173
Eaton, Robert J. (biog.) **93**:39
Eazy-E, *or* Eric Wright (obit.) **96**:79
Ebdon, Peter 326
Ebert, Roger (biog.) **93**:50
Ebola virus
infectious diseases 221
EC: *see* European Union
ECJ: *see* European Court of Justice
Eckersley, Dennis Lee (biog.) **93**:39
Eckert, John Presper, Jr. (obit.) **96**:79
Eckstine, William Clarence, *or* Billy Eckstine (obit.) **94**:61
eclipse (astron.)
1997 *table* 256
eco-warrior
Newbury Bypass photo essay 208
École Normale Supérieure (school, Paris)
physics experiment 255
Economic Affairs 97:188; **96**:171; **95**:157; **94**:133; **93**:132; **92**:130; **91**:160; **90**:177; **89**:161; **88**:161
classical music 277
East Asia (spotlight) 442
Nobel Prize 62
special reports **96**:185; **95**:172; **94**:144; **92**:141; **91**:176; **90**:192; **89**:176; **88**:172
see also individual countries by name
economic and monetary union, *or* EMU (Eur.)
economic affairs 188, 192

European Union 378
  Germany 425
  Italy 436
  labour-management relations 201
Economic Co-operation and Development,
  Organisation for, *or* OECD
  economic affairs 189, *table* 188
  French education 205
  Germany 425
  greenhouse gas emissions 210
  Hungary 430
  Poland 462
  Singapore 471
Economic Cooperation Organization
  Turkmenistan 485
"Economist, The" (Br. journ.)
  Commodities Price Index 199
Ecuador 97:414; 96:399; 95:401; 94:483;
  93:483; 92:475; 91:501; 90:517;
  89:501; 88:501
  disasters
    aviation 58
    natural 60
  military affairs 276
  sports and games
    association football 342
    track and field sports 368
  see also WORLD DATA
Ecumenical Patriarchate (Orthodox
  Church) 308
Eddie Bauer (Am. co.) 174
Eddington, Paul (obit.) 96:80
Eddy, Mary Baker 303
Edgerton, Harold Eugene (obit.) 91:93
Edinburgh International Festival 285
Edmonton Eskimos (football) 344
Education 97:203; 96:191; 95:174; 94:154;
  93:153; 92:151; 91:181; 90:196;
  89:182; 88:182
  Andorra 389
  Australia 392
  electronic games 164
  Internet 181
  museums 231
  nurses (special report) 220
  television industry 262, 264
  United States 497
  zoos (special report) 94:112
  see also WORLD DATA
Edwards, Douglas (obit.) 91:93
Edwards, Vince (obit.) 97:100
Edward's pheasant, *or* Lophura edwardsi
  wildlife conservation 213
EEC: *see* European Union
EETA79001 (meteorite)
  life on Mars claim 256, 382
Efros, Anatoly (obit.) 88:94
Egal, Muhammad Ibrahim
  Somalia 472
Egerszegi, Krisztina (biog.) 93:40
  swimming 358
Egypt 97:414; 96:400; 95:401; 94:381;
  93:381; 92:379; 91:405; 90:425;
  89:406; 88:408
  archaeology 135
  art exhibitions 145
  buildings 140
  disasters
    buildings 61
    marine 59
  international affairs
    Israel 434
    Sudan, The 476
    Syria 478
  "Islamic Fundamentalism" (special
    report) 94:378
  land mines (special report) 274, *map* 275
  literature 252
  most populous urban areas *table* 296
  women's rights issues 316
  see also WORLD DATA
EHRCO: *see* Ethiopian Human Rights
  Council
Einem, Gottfried von (obit.) 97:100
Einseln, Aleksander 418
Eisenman, Peter 137
Eisenstaedt, Alfred (obit.) 96:80
Eisner, Michael (biog.) 89:71
Ek, Mats 284
Ekeus, Rolf 377
Ekman, Kerstin 245
El Salvador 97:415; 96:401; 95:403;
  94:483; 93:483; 92:475; 91:502;
  90:517; 89:501; 88:502
  prisons and penology 229
  see also WORLD DATA
Elder, Lonne, III (obit.) 97:100
elderly: *see* old age
Eldredge, Todd 350
Eldridge, David Roy (obit.) 90:110
elections
  Africa (spotlight) 416
  Albania 388
  Argentina 390
  Armenia 390
  Australia 391
  Austria 393
  Bangladesh 378, 394
  Benin 397
  Bolivia 397
  Bosnia and Herzegovina 398, *il.*
  Brazil 401
  Cameroon 403
  Canada 404
  Cape Verde 406
  Chad 407, *il.* 406
  Comoros 410

Cyprus 412
  Czech Republic 412
  Dominican Republic 413
  Ecuador 414
  Equatorial Guinea 415
  France 419
  Gabon 420
  Gambia, The 378, 420
  Germany 424
  Ghana 425
  Greece 425
  Iceland 430
  India 430
  Iran 432
  Iraq 433
  Islam 310
  Israel 434
  Italy 436
  Japan 437
  Kuwait 443
  Latvia 444
  Lebanon 445
  Lithuania 446, *il.*
  Malaysia 448
  Marshall Islands 449
  Mauritania 452
  Moldova 453
  New Zealand 456
  Nicaragua 457
  Niger 457
  Palau 460
  Paraguay 460
  Portugal 463
  Romania 463
  Russia 464, 466
    Orthodox Church 308
  São Tomé and Príncipe 470
  Sierra Leone 471
  Singapore 471
  Slovenia 472
  South Africa 473
  South Korea 443
  Spain 474
  special report 89:483
  Sudan, The 476
  Suriname 476
  Taiwan 478
  Tonga 483
  Turkey 484
  Uganda 486
  United Kingdom 487
  United States 490, 497
    advertising expenses 154
    campaign contributions 496
    education 204
    president (special report) 97:492,
      map 494
  Western Samoa 502
  Yugoslavia 502
  Zaire 503
  Zambia 504
  Zimbabwe 504
"Elective Affinities, The" (motion
  picture) 291
electoral college (U.S.)
  special report 89:484
electoral law
  Italy 224
electric vehicle
  automobile industry 158
electrical industry 161
  U.S. deregulation 499
electromagnetic field
  physics research 255
electromagnetic radiation
  physics research 255
electronic game, *or* computer game, *or*
  video game
  games and toys 164
electronic imaging
  digitized visual images 149, 173
electronic publishing
  books 268
electronic surveillance
  crime and law enforcement 228
element 112 253
element 114 253
"Elements, The" (ballet) 282
Elephant Moraine (reg., Antarc.)
  meteorite discovery 382
"Elianto" (Benni) 247
Elias, Norbert (obit.) 91:94
Elias, Taslim Olawale (obit.) 92:60
Elion, Gertrude Belle (biog.) 89:72
Eliot, T. S. 243
Elizabeth II (biog.) 97:73
Elkin, Stanley (obit.) 96:81
Elliott, Denholm (obit.) 93:62
Elliott, John Dorman (biog.) 89:72
Ellison, Ralph Waldo (obit.) 95:66
  American literature 241
Ellmann, Richard David (obit.) 88:94
Ellul, Jacques César (obit.) 95:66
Els, Ernie 347
Elton, Charles Sutherland (obit.) 92:60
Elworthy, Samuel Charles Elworthy, Baron
  (obit.) 94:61
Elytis, Odysseus, *or* Odysseus Alepoudhelis
  (obit.) 97:100
embargo
  former Yugoslavia 377
  Iraq 163, 433
  Libya 446
"Emerging Equity Markets" (special
  report) 95:172
emigration
  reef fish 235

Emiliana huxleyi (alga) 235
emission, automobile: *see* exhaust
"Emma" (motion picture) 290
"Emmeline" (opera) 278
Emmy Award (television award) 262
employment
  business and industry *table* 153
  "Changing U.S. Workforce, The"
    (special report) 94:203
  economic affairs 189
  education 205
  Switzerland 478
  United States 491
    labour-management relations 201
    minimum-wage increase 313
  see also unemployment
EMU (Eur.): *see* economic and monetary
  union
endangered species
  wildlife conservation 213
Ende, Michael Andreas Helmuth (obit.)
  96:81
Enders, Thomas (obit.) 97:100
Endfield, Cy Raker (obit.) 96:81
Endo, Shusaku
  biography 89:72
  obituary 97:100
enduring nation
  Fourth World (spotlight) 422, *map* 423
Energy 97:162; 96:160; 95:178; 94:158;
  93:159; 92:154; 91:185; 90:202;
  89:186; 88:186
  see also individual countries by name
Engineering Projects 95:180; 94:159;
  93:159; 92:157; 91:187; 90:202;
  89:186; 88:188
  see also Civil Engineering
England: *see* United Kingdom
England, Church of
  nature of hell 301
English, David: *see* Franklin, Melvin
English Channel
  transportation (special report) 95:350
English literature 240
"English Literature" (MACROPAEDIA revi-
  sion) 97:505
"English Patient, The" (motion pic-
  ture) 289
Englund, Robert (biog.) 90:88
Englund, Sorella 282
Engquist, Ludmila 370
"Enjoy Life on Earth Forever" (rel. book)
  Jehovah's Witnesses 303
Ennals, Martin (obit.) 92:60
"Enola Gay" (airplane)
  World War II (special report) 96:259
"Ensaio sobre a cequeira" (Saramago) 249
"Enter Achilles" (dance) 284
entomology 233
  see also insect
Environment 97:206; 96:195; 95:185;
  94:164; 93:164; 92:161; 91:191;
  90:209; 89:193; 88:192
  Antarctica 382
  Arctic regions 383
  business and industry
    ceramics 167
    chemical industry 161
    coal 163
    glass 166
    mining 172
    paints and varnishes 172
  geological issues 183
  global research 259
  Newbury Bypass photo essay 208
  special reports 95:308; 92:167; 90:213
  United States 499
Environment Agency (U.K.) 207
Environmental Protection Agency, *or* EPA
  (U.S.) 206
  paints and varnishes 172
Enwonwu, Benedict Chuka (obit.) 95:67
Eoalulavis hoyasi (bird) 234
Eosimias (fossil)
  anthropology 133
EPA (U.S.): *see* Environmental Protection
  Agency
Episcopal Church
  homosexuality 301
EPLF (pol. party, Eritrea): *see* Eritrean
  People's Liberation Front
EPR (pol. org., Mex.): *see* Popular Revolutionary Army
EPRDF (pol. party, Eth.): *see* Ethiopian
  People's Revolutionary Democratic
  Front
equal rights: *see* human rights
Equatorial Guinea 97:415; 96:401; 95:403;
  94:358; 93:359; 92:356; 91:384;
  90:405; 89:388; 88:388
  see also WORLD DATA
equestrian sports 97:335; 96:315; 95:295;
  94:298; 93:300; 92:296; 91:326;
  90:344; 89:327; 88:329
  1996 Summer Olympic champions *table*
    97:365
equine encephalitis 221
equinox (astron.)
  1997 *table* 256
equity capital
  special report 95:172
Erbakan, Necmettin (biog.) 97:73
  Islam 310
  Israel 435
  Libya 446
  Turkey 375, 484

Erdemovic, Drazen 227
Erdos, Paul (obit.) 97:100
Erikson, Erik Homburger (obit.) 95:67
Eritrea 97:415; 96:401; 95:403; 94:358
  land mines *map* 275
  military affairs 276
  new flags *illus.* 97:387; 94:345
  political party system (spotlight)
    417, *map*
  railroad construction *il.* 415
  Yemen 502
  see also WORLD DATA
Eritrean People's Liberation Front, *or*
  EPLF, *or* People's Front for Democ-
  racy and Justice (pol. party, Er-
  itrea) 417
Ermenek Dam (dam, Tur.) 141
Ernst, Richard Robert (biog.) 92:31
Eros (asteroid) 259
"Errances" (Kokis) 247
Ershad, Hossain Mohammad 395
Erté (obit.) 91:94
Erving, Julius Winfield, II (biog.) 88:70
Escherichia coli, *or* E. coli 221
  Japan 438
  United Kingdom 61
Escobar Bethancourt, Rómulo (obit.) 96:81
Eskimo (people): *see* Inuit
espionage, *or* spying
  Poland 462
  Sweden 477
Estefan, Gloria (biog.) 92:38
Estonia 97:418; 96:402; 95:404; 94:430;
  93:432; 92:423
  economic affairs 193
  Latvia 444
  new flag *illus.* 92:343
  Orthodox Apostolic Church 307, 308
  see also WORLD DATA
Estonian Orthodox Apostolic Church 301,
  307, 308
estrogen
  environmental dangers 212
estrogen replacement therapy
  Alzheimer's disease 222
  postnatal depression 222
ETA (mil. org., Sp.): *see* Euskadi Ta
  Askatasune
"Été à la Goulette, Un" (motion
  picture) 295
ethane
  Comet Hyakutake 257
ethics
  United States 498
Ethiopia 97:418; 96:402; 95:404; 94:358;
  93:360; 92:356; 91:384; 90:405;
  89:388; 88:388
  aviation disasters 58
  land mines *map* 275
  military affairs 276
  new flags *illus.* 97:387; 93:345
  track and field sports 368
  see also WORLD DATA
Ethiopian Human Rights Council, *or*
  EHRCO 418
Ethiopian People's Revolutionary Demo-
  cratic Front, *or* EPRDF (pol. party,
  Eth.) 418
ethnic groups: *see* Race and Ethnic
  Relations
EU: *see* European Union
Eubank, Chris 330
Europa (satellite of Jupiter)
  characteristics 256, 259
Europe, Council of
  Croatia 411
  Russia 465
Europe 1 STAR (sailing competition) 354
Europe of Regions
  Fourth World (spotlight) 422
European affairs 94:420; 93:419
  agriculture and food supplies 126
  architecture 137
  arts and entertainment
    classical music 277
    dance 284
    motion pictures 291
      film awards *table* 294
  business and industry 154
    automobiles 157
    chemicals 161
    iron and steel 168
    microelectronics 169
    paints and varnishes 172
    petroleum 162
    rubber 167
    shipbuilding 174
    telecommunications 175
    tourism 179
    wine 159
    wood products 179
  consumer affairs 202
  demographic statistics 296
  disasters 61
  economic affairs 188
    stock markets 194
  environmental issues 207, 210
  Fourth World (spotlight) 422, *map* 423
  gardening 215
  international law 224
  libraries 230
  media and publishing
    newspapers 265
    television 261
  military affairs 270, *table* 272
  North Atlantic Treaty Organization
    376, 420

prisons and penology 229
rabies control 223
refugees 297
religion statistics *table* 311
roads 142
social protection 313
special reports **95**:172, 245; **94**:144, 204, 425; **93**:421
sports and games
association football 340
basketball 325
bowling 326
contract bridge 331
golf 347
Grand Prix racing 318
ice hockey 350
thoroughbred racing 337
wrestling 370
transportation
aviation 373
freight and pipelines 373
intercity rail 374
roads and traffic 374
urban mass transit 374
World War II (special report) **96**:257
see also Eastern European Affairs; European Union; Western European Affairs; and individual countries
European Commission
business mergers 261
environmental issues 207, 210
European Monetary Union 378
labour-management relations 201
"mad cow" disease 222
mining 171
Syria 478
European Community: *see* European Union
European Court of Human Rights
freedom of expression 225
international law 224
European Court of Justice, *or* ECJ 224
European Cup (ice hockey) 350
European Cup of Champion Clubs (soccer) 340
European Cup-Winners' Cup (soccer) 340
European Economic Community: *see* European Union
European Film Award, *or* Felix
film awards *table* 294
European History and Culture (MACROPAEDIA revision) **92**:512
European Laboratory for Particle Physics: *see* CERN
European Rabbis, Conference of 308
European Space Agency
Cluster mission 256, 260
European Union, *or* European Community, *or* EU, *or* EC **97**:378; **96**:355; **95**:356
agriculture and food supplies 125, 127
business and industry 154
chemicals 161
coal 163
furs 156
glass 166
iron and steel 168
microelectronics 170
natural gas 163
economic affairs 188
international trade 194
labour-management relations 201
environment 207, 210
botanical gardens 214
"Financial Support for the Elderly" (special report) **94**:144
food processing regulations 132
Fourth World (spotlight) 422
international affairs
Cyprus accession 412
Euro-Asian summit 380
Spain 475
Switzerland 477
Syria 478
Uganda 486
international law 224
member nations
Austria 392
Denmark 413
Finland 418
France 419
Germany 421
Greece 426
Luxembourg 446
Slovenia 472
United Kingdom 488
transportation
aviation 373
shipping and ports 373
European Union, Treaty on: *see* Maastricht Treaty
European Works Council Directive 201
"Europe's Single Market" (special report) **93**:421
Eurotunnel (tunnel, Eur.): *see* Channel Tunnel
"Eurovia" (Eur. rd. project) 142
Euskadi Ta Askatasuna, *or* ETA (mil. org., Sp.) 475
eusociality
marine biology 235
zoology 232
euthanasia
Australia 392
United States 498
EV1 (elec. vehicle) 158
"Eva Perón" (motion picture) 295
Evans, Sir Geraint (obit.) **93**:62
Evans, Gil (obit.) **89**:93
Evans, Maurice Herbert (obit.) **90**:110
Everett, Kenny (obit.) **96**:81
Evers-Williams, Myrlie (biog.) **96**:57
Evert, Miltiades 425
"Everyone Says I Love You" (motion picture) 289
"Evita" (motion picture) 289
evolution
cultural anthropology 134
geology 183
physical anthropology 133
Evora, Cesaria (biog.) **97**:73
Ewart, Gavin Buchanan (obit.) **96**:81
Ewell, Norwood H., *or* Barney Ewell (obit.) **97**:100
exchange rate (econ.)
economic affairs 188
Mexico 453
Venezuela 500
execution: *see* capital punishment
exercise
health benefits 221
exhaust, *or* automobile emission
emission standards 207
"Exiles Among You" (Gunnars) 242
exobiology
paleontological discovery 238
explosions: *see* fires and explosions
export
agriculture and food supplies 126, 129
British beef products 222, 488
chemicals 161
economic affairs 188
hazardous wastes 211
less developed countries 193
Solomon Islands 451, 472
Taiwan 479
wine 159
Export Processing Zone
Namibia 455
extraterrestrial life
life on Mars claim 256
Exxon Chemical Co. (Am. co.) 161
Exxon Corporation (Am. co.) 163
Eyre, Richard (biog.) **90**:88
Eyre de Lanux, Elizabeth (obit.) **97**:100
Eyskens, Gaston (obit.) **89**:93
Ezoe, Hiromasa (biog.) **90**:88

F

FA Cup, *or* Football Association Cup (soccer) 341
FAA (U.S.): *see* Federal Aviation Administration
Factor, Max, Jr., *or* Francis Factor (obit.) **97**:100
Fahd ibn ʿAbd al-ʿAziz as-Saʿud (biog.) **91**:68
Persian Gulf War (special report) **92**:231
Saudi Arabia 470
Fain, Sammy (obit.) **90**:110
FAIR Act (U.S.): *see* Federal Agricultural Improvement and Reform Act
Fairbank, John King (obit.) **92**:60
Fairfax, Sir Warwick Oswald (obit.) **88**:94
Falconbridge (Can. co.) 170
Falcone, Giovanni (obit.) **93**:62
crime and law enforcement 228, 437
Faldo, Nick (biog.) **91**:68
golf 347
Falkland Islands, *or* Islas Malvinas (isls., Atl.O.) 380
familial amyotrophic lateral sclerosis, *or* FALS
molecular biology 237
family
child welfare (special report) **96**:286
family planning
demographic statistics 295
Fan Xueyan, Peter Joseph
Chinese Catholic church 306
Fangio, Juan Manuel (obit.) **96**:81
Fanini, Nilson do Amaral (biog.) **96**:57
Baptist World Alliance 302
FAO (UN org.): *see* Food and Agriculture Organization
Farah, Moumin Bahdon 413
"Fargo" (motion picture) 289
"farmer, El" (Rivera) 248
farming: *see* Agriculture and Food Supplies
Faroe Islands (isls., Atl.O.)
offshore drilling 380
Farrakhan, Louis
Islam 310
Farrell, M. J. (obit.): *see* Keane, Molly
Farrell, Suzanne (biog.) **91**:69
fascism
Far Right (special report) **89**:445
Fashion Designers of America, Council of 216
Fashions **97**:216; **96**:203; **95**:191; **94**:170; **93**:170; **92**:170; **91**:198; **90**:217; **89**:194; **88**:199
furs 156
silk 177
Fatialofa, Peter (biog.) **94**:39
Faubus, Orval Eugene (obit.) **95**:67
Faure, Edgar Jean (obit.) **89**:93
Favre, Brett 344
Fay, Michael (biog.) **89**:72
FBI (U.S.): *see* Federal Bureau of Investigation
FCC (U.S.): *see* Federal Communications Commission
FDA (U.S.): *see* Food and Drug Administration
Feather, Leonard Geoffrey (obit.) **95**:67
Fed (U.S. govt.): *see* Federal Reserve Board
Federal Agricultural Improvement and Reform Act, *or* FAIR Act (U.S.) 125
Federal Aviation Administration, *or* FAA (U.S.) 373
Federal Bureau of Investigation, *or* FBI (U.S.) 495
crime and law enforcement 226, 228
White House scandal 490
Federal Communications Commission, *or* FCC (U.S.)
radio industry 265
telecommunications deregulation 175
television industry 262
Federal Reserve Board, *or* Fed (U.S. govt.) 190
stock markets 194
United States 490
Federal Reserve System (U.S.)
currency design change 151
equity markets (special report) **95**:172
Federal Trade Commission, *or* FTC (U.S.)
book publishing 268
man-made fibres 177
retailing 174
Fédération Générale du Travail de Belgique, *or* FGTB
labour-management relations 202
Fédération Internationale de Basketball (internat. org.) 325
Fédération Internationale des Échecs, *or* FIDE (internat. org.)
chess 330
Fédération Internationale d'Escrime, *or* FIE (internat. org.) 339
Felix (award): *see* European Film Award
Fellini, Federico (obit.) **94**:61
female genital mutilation, *or* FGM
human rights issues 316
fencing **97**:339; **96**:318
1996 Summer Olympic champions *table* **97**:366
Fenech Adami, Eddie (biog.) **88**:70
Feng Youlan (obit.) **91**:94
Fenice, La (opera house, Venice, It.) 277, 437
Fermi National Accelerator Laboratory, *or* Fermilab
particle physics 255
Fernández, Roque 390
Fernández Reyna, Leonel (biog.) **97**:74
Dominican Republic 413
Ferrari, Enzo (obit.) **89**:94
Ferreira, Vergílio (obit.) **97**:100
Ferreira Aldunate, Wilson (obit.) **89**:94
Ferrell, Richard Benjamin (obit.) **96**:81
Ferrer, Jose (obit.) **93**:62
Ferrucci, Franco 247
ferryboat
disasters 59
Feynman, Richard Phillips (obit.) **89**:94
Ffrangcon-Davies, Dame Gwen (obit.) **93**:63
FGM: *see* female genital mutilation
FGTB: *see* Fédération Générale du Travail de Belgique
fibreglass 166
fiction: *see* Literature
FIDE (internat. org.): *see* Fédération Internationale des Échecs
FIE (internat. org.): *see* Fédération Internationale d'Escrime
Field, John (obit.) **92**:60
field hockey **97**:339; **96**:319; **95**:299; **94**:292; **93**:293; **92**:289; **91**:319; **90**:337; **89**:320; **88**:322
1996 Summer Olympic champions *table* **97**:366
Fielder, Cecil (biog.) **91**:69
Fieldhouse of Gosport in the County of Hampshire, John David Elliott Fieldhouse, Baron (obit.) **93**:63
51 Pegasi (star) 257
Figueres Ferrer, José (obit.) **91**:94
figure skating 350
Olympic Winter Games (special report) **95**:308, *table* 309
Fiji **97**:418; **96**:403; **95**:405; **94**:496; **93**:496; **92**:488; **91**:515; **90**:531; **89**:515; **88**:514
see also WORLD DATA
Filho, Antunes 249
film: *see* Motion Pictures
film (phot.)
Advanced Photo System 173
Filmon, Gary Albert (biog.) **89**:73
"Financial Support for the Elderly" (special report) **94**:144
"Financial Times" Stock Exchange 100, *or* FT-SE 100 198
Fini, Gianfranco 436
Fini, Léonor (obit.) **97**:101
Finkelstein, Louis (obit.) **92**:61
Finland **97**:418; **96**:403; **95**:405; **94**:430; **93**:432; **92**:423; **91**:448; **90**:464; **89**:449; **88**:448
bowling 326
unemployment benefits 313
see also WORLD DATA
Finley, Charles Oscar, *or* Charlie Finley (obit.) **97**:101
Finney, Walter Braden (obit.) **96**:81
fiqh (rel. knowledge, Islam)
special report **93**:95
firearm: *see* gun
fires and explosions 59
aviation disasters 58
TWA Flight 800 226, 495
Channel Tunnel 142
Italy 437
Philadelphia Zoological Gardens 213
Suriname 476
see also arson
Firkusny, Rudolf (obit.) **95**:67
First Church of Christ, Scientist, *or* The Mother Church (church, Boston, Mass., U.S.) 303
First Interstate (Am. co.)
bank acquisition 201
"First Wives Club, The" (motion picture) 289
FIS: *see* Islamic Salvation Front
Fischer, Annie (obit.) **96**:81
Fischer, Joschka Joseph Martin (biog.) **96**:57
Fischer, Timothy Andrew (biog.) **94**:39
Fischer, Tobias 185
fish
marine biology 235
muscle contraction 232
Fish, Hamilton, Jr. (obit.) **97**:101
fish industry: *see* fisheries
Fishburne, Larry (biog.) **93**:40
Fisher, Mary Frances Kennedy (obit.) **93**:63
fisheries 130
Antarctica 382
Denmark 413
Iceland 430
Japan 439
Pacific Islands (spotlight) 450
Fisk, Eliot 279
"Fistful of Flies" (motion picture) 290
"Fit to Dance? The Report of the National Inquiry into Dancers' Health and Injury" (Bull) 285
Fitz-Gerald, Sarah 357
Fitzgerald, Ella (obit.) **97**:101
Fitzgerald, Pat 344
Five Nations (rugby football) 344
flags of the world
new flags *illus.* **97**:387; **96**:365; **95**:353; **94**:345; **93**:345, 346; **92**:343
flash memory chip
microelectronics 170
flat tax
U.S. presidential election (special report) 493
Flavin, Dan (obit.) **97**:101
Fleetwood, Susan Maureen (obit.) **96**:81
Flessel, Laura *il.* 339
Fleuroselect (internat. org.)
gardening 215
"Fleurs du mal, Les" (Baudelaire) 243
FLNC (pol. org., Corsica): *see* Corsican National Liberation Front
"Floating Life" (motion picture) 290
flood
meteorology and climate 187
natural disasters 60
Flores, Lola, *or* Dolores Flores Ruiz (obit.) **96**:81
Florida (state, U.S.) 497
Florida, University of (U.S.)
football 342
Florida Panthers (ice hockey) 349
Florida State University (U.S.)
football 342
nontheatrical films 295
flower *ils.* 215, 238
gardening 214
genetic engineering 235
"Floyd Collins" (play) 288
Flutie, Doug 344
"Flying Home" (Ellison) 241
Fodor, Eugene (obit.) **92**:61
Fokker (Du. co.)
aerospace industry 155, 456
Foley, Thomas Stephen (biog.) **90**:88
Fonseca, Rubem 249
"Fontano da casa" (Ferrucci) 247
Fonteyn, Dame Margot (obit.) **92**:61
food: *see* Agriculture and Food Supplies
Food and Agriculture Organization, *or* FAO (UN org.)
agriculture and food supplies 123, 128
consumer affairs 202
fisheries 130
human rights issues 316
Food and Drug Administration, *or* FDA (U.S.)
approvals and regulations 221
food processing 132
olestra approval 203
tobacco ban 178
food poisoning 132
disasters 61
food processing 131
food safety (special report) **90**:140
consumer affairs 202
Food Stamp Program (U.S.)
agriculture and food supplies 126
social protection 312
football **97**:340; **96**:319; **95**:299; **94**:292; **93**:293; **92**:292; **91**:322; **90**:340; **89**:323; **88**:325

Football Association Cup (soccer): *see* FA Cup
footwear 156
fashions 216
"For Nursing, New Responsibilities, New Respect" (special report) 97:220
Forbes, Malcolm Stevenson (obit.) 91:94
Forbes, Steve
presidential campaign (special report) 493
Ford, Edmund Brisco (obit.) 89:94
Ford, Ernest Jennings, or Tennessee Ernie Ford (obit.) 92:61
Ford, Henry, II (obit.) 88:94
Ford, Richard 242, 268, *il.* 240
Ford, Thelma (obit.): *see* Booth, Shirley
Ford Motor Co. (Am. co.) 156
labour-management relations 202
Fordham, Michael Scott Montague (obit.) 96:81
foreign investment
Austria 393
building and construction 160
China 409
clothing industry 156
economic affairs 194
France 420
Germany 424
Indonesia 432
Iran 432
Japan 400, 438
Morocco 454
petroleum industry 163
special reports 95:172; 93:143
Taiwan 479
Vietnam 502
foreign trade: *see* international trade
forestry
acid rain effect 210
Pacific Islands (spotlight) 450
Solomon Islands 472
wood products 179
forfeiture law
drug trafficking 225
former Soviet Republics
agriculture and food supplies 125, 129
economic affairs 193
see also the new nations by name, *e.g.*, Belarus, Ukraine
Former Yugoslav Republic of Macedonia: *see* Macedonia
Formula One racing: *see* Grand Prix racing
Forsey, Eugene Alfred (obit.) 92:61
Fortner, Wolfgang (obit.) 88:94
47 Ursae Majoris (star)
companion planet 257
Forum for the Restoration of Democracy-Kenya (pol. party, Ken.) 440
Fosse, Bob (obit.) 88:94
fossil
anthropology 133, *il.* 135
geological discoveries 183
life on Mars claim 256
ornithology 234
paleontology 238
Foster, Jodie (biog.) 93:40
Fourth World Conference on Women: *see* United Nations Fourth World Conference on Women
Fourth World nation (spotlight) 422, *map* 423
fowl: *see* poultry
Fowler, William Alfred (obit.) 96:81
Fox, Harold (obit.) 97:101
Fox, Robin
anthropology 134
Fox Broadcasting Company (Am. co.) 262
Foxx, Redd (obit.) 92:61
FPO (pol. party, Aus.): *see* Freiheitlichen, Die
Frahm, Herbert Ernst Karl (obit.): *see* Brandt, Willy
"Fran" (hurricane)
insurance 165
natural disasters 60, *il.* 186
franc (currency)
European economic union 378
Swiss design 152
France 97:419; 96:404; 95:405; 94:431; 93:433; 92:424; 91:448; 90:465; 89:449; 88:448
architecture and civil engineering
buildings 140
tunnels 142
arts and entertainment
art exhibitions 148
auction houses 144
dance 284
literature 246
motion pictures 291
film awards *table* 294
business and industry
aerospace 155
chemicals 161
rubber 167
wine 159
economic affairs 188, 192
stock exchanges 198
education 205
environment 212
forfeiture laws 225
international affairs
dependent states 381
European Union transition 378, *il.* 379
Lebanon 445

international law 224
military affairs 270
most populous urban areas *table* 296
newspapers 265
Pacific Islands post-nuclear era (spotlight) 450, *ils.* 451
religion
Roman Catholicism 308
sects 300
social protection 313
special reports 95:245, 351; 89:445
sports and games
association football 340
contract bridge 331
Grand Prix racing 318
rugby football 345
tennis 362
thoroughbred racing 337
World War II (special report) 96:258
see also WORLD DATA
Francescatti, Zino (obit.) 92:62
Francis, Samuel Lewis (obit.) 95:67
Francis Joseph II (obit.) 90:110
francium
nuclear chemistry 253
Franco (obit.) 90:110
Franco, Carmen Polo de (obit.) 89:94
Franco, Itamar (biog.) 94:39
Franey, Pierre (obit.) 97:101
Franjieh, Suleiman Kabalan (obit.) 93:63
Franju, Georges (obit.) 88:95
Frank (people)
English Channel history (special report) 95:350
Frank, Ilya Mikhaylovich (obit.) 91:94
Franken, Wallis 217
Franklin, Melvin, or David English (obit.) 96:81
Franks of Headington, Oliver Shewell Franks, Baron (obit.) 93:63
Frantic Friday
stock exchanges 194
Franz, Dennis (biog.) 97:74
Fraser, Sir Hugh (obit.) 88:95
fraud: *see* corruption
Frederick, Pauline (obit.) 91:94
Fredericks, Frank 362, 369
Free Bolivia Movement, or MBL (pol. party, Bol.) 397
free-market economy: *see* capitalism
Free Trade Area of the Americas, or FTAA
Caribbean unification (spotlight) 468
free-trade zone, or free-port zone, or free zone (internat. trade)
Caribbean unification issues (spotlight) 468
Cuba 412, *il.*
Malawi 448
new international agreements 224
Freed, James Ingo 137
Freedman, Ralph 241
Freedom Alliance, or Freedom Movement (pol. party, Aus.): *see* Freiheitlichen, Die
Freedom Alliance (pol. party, It.): *see* Alliance for Freedom
freedom of association
Canadian court case 225
freedom of expression
U.K. court case 225
Freeman, Cynthia (obit.) 89:94
Freeman, Lawrence (obit.) 92:62
Freemen (Am. org.) 495
freestyle skiing 357
1994 Olympic champions *table* 95:309
freestyle wrestling 370
Frei, Eduardo 407
freight and pipelines 373
Bombay *il.* 431
Great Man-Made River 141
shipbuilding 175
Freiheitlichen, Die, or Austrian Freedom Party, or Freedom Alliance, or Freedom Movement, or FPO (pol. party, Aus.) 393
Freleng, Isadore, or Friz Freleng (obit.) 96:81
Frenay, Henri (obit.) 89:95
French-Canadian literature 247
French literature 246
French Open (tennis) 360
French Polynesia 381
nuclear testing 419, 450
Fretilin (pol. group, E. Timor)
independence movement 62
Freud, Lucian (biog.) 95:44
Freyhardt, C. C. 254
Freyre, Gilberto de Mello (obit.) 88:95
Friedman, Jerome Isaac (biog.) 91:69
Friedreich's ataxia
genetic research 218
Friedrichs, Hanns Joachim (obit.) 96:81
Friel, Brian (biog.) 96:58
Friends, The Religious Society of: *see* Religious Society of Friends, The
Frink, Dame Elisabeth Jean (obit.) 94:62
Frisch, Max Rudolf (obit.) 92:62
Frobe, Gert (obit.) 89:95
frog *il.* 233
"From Marx to Madison: Socialism's Cultural Contradictions" (feature article) 89:5
Frondizi, Arturo (obit.) 96:81
"frontera de cristal, La" (Fuentes) 248
Frossard, André (obit.) 96:82
frozen yogurt 132

fruit
health benefits 221
Frum, Barbara (obit.) 93:63
Fry, Edwin Maxwell (obit.) 88:95
Frydenlund, Knut (obit.) 88:95
Frye, Herman Northrop (obit.) 92:62
FT-SE 100: *see* "Financial Times" Stock Exchange 100
FTAA: *see* Free Trade Area of the Americas
FTC (U.S.): *see* Federal Trade Commission
Fu Mingxia (biog.) 97:74
diving 359, 365
Fuchs, Klaus Emil Julius (obit.) 89:95
Fudge, Ann Marie (biog.) 96:58
fuel
aviation costs 372
fuel rod
environmental concerns 207
Fuentes, Carlos 248
Fugard, Athol (biog.) 89:73
Fugees, The (Am. mus. group) 281
"Fugitive Pieces" (Michaels) 242
Fuji Photo Film Co., Ltd. (Japanese co.)
photography 173
Fujiko, Fujio F., or Hiroshi Fujimoto (obit.) 97:101
Fujimori, Alberto (biog.) 91:69
Peru 400, 461
Fukuda, Takeo (obit.) 96:82
Fulbright, James William (obit.) 96:82
Fuller, Ray W. (obit.) 97:101
Fuller, Roy Broadbent (obit.) 92:62
fullerene (chem.)
discovery 63
Funcinpec (pol. party, Camb.) 403
fund-raising
United States elections 492, 496
fundamentalism (rel.)
Afghanistan 375, 388
Egypt 414
Ethiopia 418
India 430
Islam 310
Israel 434
special reports 94:377; 93:95; 89:290
women's rights issues 316
Furillo, Carl (obit.) 90:110
furniture 165
auctions and collectibles 152
Furniture Brands International (Am. co.) 165
furs 156
fashions 217
"Fusilier at the Front, A" (Jones) 243
Fuss, Martin (obit.): *see* Hunter, Ross
"Future Has Started, The" (feature article) 90:13
futures market 198
derivatives (special report) 96:185

G

G-7: *see* Group of Seven
Gaarder, Jostein (biog.) 95:45
Norwegian literature 245
"Gabbeh" (motion picture) 295
Gabon 97:420; 96:406; 95:408; 94:359; 93:361; 92:357; 91:385; 90:406; 89:389; 88:389
see also WORLD DATA
Gabor, Eva (obit.) 96:82
GABRIEL, or Gateway and Bridge to Europe's National Libraries (information retrieval system) 230
Gad al-Haq Ali Gad al-Haq (obit.) 97:102
Gaekwad, Fatesinghrao (obit.) 89:95
Gaillard, Bulee (obit.) 92:62
Gaines, William Maxwell (obit.) 93:63
Gainsbourg, Serge (obit.) 92:62
galaxy
astronomy 258
Galbraith, John Kenneth
"The Outlines of an Emerging World" (commentary) 96:6
Galbreath, John Wilmer (obit.) 89:95
Galileo (U.S. space probe)
Jupiter exploration 256, 259
"Galina" (opera) 278
Galindo, Gabriel Lewis (obit.) 97:102
Gallagher, Liam 280
Gallagher, Noel 280
Gallagher, Rory (obit.) 96:82
Galland, Adolf Joseph Ferdinand (obit.) 97:102
gallery
digitized visual images 149
Galliano, John Charles (biog.) 97:74
fashion industry 217
Gallo, Julio Robert (obit.) 94:62
Gallois, Louis 419
Galvão, Patrícia: *see* Pagu
Galvin, John Rogers (biog.) 88:70
Gambia, The 97:420; 96:406; 95:408; 94:359; 93:361; 92:357; 91:386; 90:406; 89:389; 88:390
Commonwealth of Nations 378
see also WORLD DATA
gambling
United States 499
game theory (math.)
microeconomics 62
Games, Abram (obit.) 97:102

games and toys 164
auctions and collectibles 152
"Games of the XXV Olympiad, The" (special report) 93:276
Gandhi, Rajiv (obit.) 92:62
Gandhi, Sonia (biog.) 96:58
gang
South Africa 473
Ganymede (satellite of Jupiter)
characteristics 256
Garavini, Fausta
Italian literature 247
Garbo, Greta (obit.) 91:95
Garcia, Jerome John, or Jerry Garcia (obit.) 96:82
García, Pilar Lorenza (obit.): *see* Lorengar, Pilar
García Márquez, Gabriel (biog.) 92:38
Latin-American literature 248, *il.*
García Ramis, Magali 248
García Robles, Alfonso (obit.) 92:63
"Garden of Mystery, The" (opera) 279
Gardening 97:214; 96:202; 95:192; 94:173; 93:171; 92:171; 91:200; 90:219; 89:201; 88:200
Gardiner of Kittisford, Gerald Austin Gardiner (obit.) 91:95
Gardini, Raul (obit.) 94:62
Gardner, Ava Lavinia (obit.) 91:95
Gardner, Beatrix Tugendhat (obit.) 96:82
Gardner, David (biog.) 97:75
Gardner, Tom (biog.) 97:75
Garrett, George 240
Garrett, Mark 353
Garro, Elena 248
Garson, Greer (obit.) 97:102
Gascoigne, Paul (biog.) 92:38
Gascon, Jean (obit.) 89:95
gasoline, or gas, or petrol
automobile industry 157
United States consumer affairs 203
Gass, William H. 242
Gates, Henry Louis, Jr. (biog.) 97:75
Gates, William H., III (biog.) 92:39
libraries 230
Gateway and Bridge to Europe's National Libraries (information retrieval system): *see* GABRIEL
GATT: *see* General Agreement on Tariffs and Trade
Gaullist (pol. party, Fr.): *see* Rally for the Republic
Gaultier design *il.* 216
Gavaskar, Sunil (biog.) 88:71
Gavazzeni, Gianandrea (obit.) 97:102
Gavin, James Maurice (obit.) 91:95
Gaviria Trujillo, César (biog.) 91:70
gay: *see* homosexuality
gay marriage: *see* same-sex marriage
gay rights: *see* civil rights; human rights
Gazania splendens (flower) 215
GCC: *see* Global Climate Coalition
GDP: *see* gross domestic product
GE (Am. co.): *see* General Electric
Gebrselassie, Haile 368
GEC Alsthom (Br.-Fr. co.)
electrical industry 162
Geffen, David
theatre 288
Gehry, Frank (biog.) 95:45
architecture 137, 138
Geidar, Aliev, or Aliyev Heydar (biog.) 94:33
Geisel, Ernesto (obit.) 97:102
Geisel, Theodor Seuss, or Dr. Seuss (obit.) 92:63
Gellner, Ernest André (obit.) 96:82
gemstones 164
Gencor (S.Af. co.)
mining 171
Genda, Minoru (obit.) 90:111
General Agreement on Tariffs and Trade, or GATT
motion pictures (special report) 95:245
General Conference of the United Methodist Church 304
General Electric, or GE (Am. co.)
aerospace industry 155
boiling-water reactor 164
electrical industry 161
General Motors Corporation, or GM (Am. corp.) 156
labour-management relations 202
metalworking 168
"The Changing U.S. Workforce" (special report) 94:203
genetic disease 218
genetic engineering
botany 235
cotton 177
food 202
genetics
Clock genes 232
health and disease research 218
molecular biology and disease 237
Geneva Convention on Inhumane Weapons
antipersonnel mines (special report) 97:274
military affairs 269
United Nations 376
genital organs: *see* reproductive system
genocide
UN tribunals 376
international law 224
war crimes 227
Bosnian mass grave *il.* 227

genome
yeast research 238
Gentry, W. Ronald 254
Geochelone yniphora: *see* ploughshare tortoise
geochemistry 183
Geological Society of America 183
geology 183
geophysics 184
George, Eddie (biog.) 96:58
United Kingdom 488
"George Eliot: A Life" (Ashton) 243
Georgia 97:420; 96:407; 95:409; 94:433; 93:435
disasters 61
economic affairs 193
land mines *map* 275
military affairs 272
new flag *illus.* 93:345
see also WORLD DATA
Georgia Tech Aquatic Center (Atlanta, Ga., U.S.) 357
Gerhardsen, Einer Henry (obit.) 88:95
German Democratic Republic, *or* East Germany 91:470; 90:487; 89:470; 88:470
see also Germany *and* WORLD DATA
Germanic literature 244
Germany, *or* Federal Republic of Germany 97:421; 96:407; 95:409; 94:434; 93:436; 92:426; 91:450; 90:467; 89:452; 88:450
architecture 137
arts and entertainment
dance 284
literature 244
motion pictures 291
film awards *table* 294
business and industry
aerospace 155
chemicals 161
electrical 161
machinery and machine tools 166
paper and pulp 179
rubber 167
disasters 59
economic affairs 188, 191
labour-management relations 201
stock exchanges 199
education 204
environment 210
intercity rail 374
international affairs
Czech Republic 413
European Union 378
France 420
media and publishing
magazines 267
newspapers 265
television 261
military affairs 271
land mines (special report) 275
Scientology 300
social protection 301
special reports 95:350; 94:204; 91:443; 89:176, 445
sports and games
association football 340
Grand Prix racing 318
rowing 354
show jumping and dressage 338
swimming 357
World War II (special report) 96:256
see also German Democratic Republic *and* WORLD DATA
Gernsheim, Helmut Erich Robert (obit.) 96:82
Gerstner, Lou (biog.) 94:39
Gerulaitis, Vitas (obit.) 95:68
Gesell, Gerhard A. (obit.) 94:62
"Get on the Bus" (motion picture) 289
"Get Shorty" (motion picture)
film awards *table* 294
Getty Center (Los Angeles, Calif., U.S.)
architecture 137
Getz, Stan (obit.) 92:63
Ghaffar Khan, Khan Abdul (obit.) 89:95
Ghana 97:425; 96:411; 95:412; 94:359; 93:361; 92:358; 91:386; 90:407; 89:389; 88:390
Commonwealth of Nations 378
mining 170
see also WORLD DATA
Gheorghiu, Angela (biog.) 97:65
Ghiz, Joseph A. (obit.) 97:102
GIA (pol. org., Alg.): *see* Armed Islamic Group
Giacometti, Alberto 148
Giacosa, Dante (obit.) 97:102
Giamatti, Angelo Bartlett (obit.) 90:111
giant panda: *see* panda
Gibb, Andy (obit.) 89:95
Gibbons, Stella Dorothea (obit.) 90:111
Gibney, Frank B.
"A Conversation with Lee Teng-hui" (commentary) 97:6
Gibraltar (Br. colony, Eur.) 380
Gibson, Mel
film awards *table* 294
Gielgud, Maina 284
Gifford, Kathie Lee
sweatshop controversy 155
"Gigolo" (horse) 338
Gil Young Ah 320
Giles, Carl Ronald (obit.) 96:83
Gilford, Jack (obit.) 91:95
Gillars, Mildred Elizabeth (obit.) 89:95

Gillespie, John Birks, *or* Dizzy Gillespie (obit.) 94:62
Gilliatt, Penelope Ann Douglass (obit.) 94:63
Gilmore, John E. (obit.) 96:83
Gingold, Hermione (obit.) 88:95
Gingold, Josef (obit.) 96:83
Gingrich, Newt (biog.) 96:58
Contract with America (special report) 96:492
presidential election (special report) 492
United States 490
Ginsburg, Ruth Bader (biog.) 94:39
Ginzburg, Natalia (obit.) 92:64
"Giocando a dama con la luna" (Morandini) 247
Girardelli, Marc (biog.) 94:40
skiing 356
Girardi, Joe *il.* 321
"Girl 6" (motion picture) 289
"Girls Town" (motion picture) 290
Girodias, Maurice (obit.) 91:95
Gish, Lillian Diana (obit.) 94:63
Giuliani, Rudolph William (biog.) 89:73
Givenchy (Fr. co.) 217
Gladwyn, Hubert Miles Gladwyn Jebb, Baron (obit.) 97:102
Glasgow (U.K.)
art exhibitions (special report) 146
Glasgow Citizens' Theatre (thea., U.K.) 287
glasnost
special report 88:474
glass 166
Glass-Steagall Act (U.S.) 201
Gleason, Jackie (obit.) 88:95
Gleason, Thomas William (obit.) 93:64
Glemp, Msgr. Jozef Cardinal (biog.) 90:88
Glennan, T. Keith (obit.) 96:83
Global Climate Coalition, *or* GCC 206
"Global Environment—A Planet in Stress" (feature article) 91:5
global warming
Arctic regions 383
environmental effects 210
globalization
electrical industry 161
Globe Theatre (hist. thea., U.K.) 286
Glover, Savion (biog.) 97:75
dance 283
theatre 288
Glück, Louise 241
Glushko, Valentin Petrovich (obit.) 90:111
GM (Am. corp.): *see* General Motors Corporation
GMR (hydrology project, Libya): *see* Great Man-Made River
Goals 2000
U.S. education 204
goat
world production *table* 126
Gobel, George (obit.) 92:64
Goddard, Paulette (obit.) 91:95
Godfree, Kathleen McKane (obit.) 93:64
Godunov, Alexander, *or* Aleksandr Borisovich Godunov (obit.) 96:83
Goenka, Ramnath (obit.) 92:64
Goes, Clara 249
Goetz, Walter (obit.) 96:83
Goff, Helen Lyndon (obit.): *see* Travers, Pamela Lyndon
Goh, Choo San (obit.) 88:96
Goh Chok Tong (biog.) 91:70
Singapore 471
gold 170
commodity prices 200
Guyana 426
Swiss banks investigation 200
Tanzania 482
Gold, Arthur (obit.) 91:96
"Gold of Troy" (art exhibit) 148
Goldberg, Arthur Joseph (obit.) 91:96
Goldberg, Whoopi (biog.) 92:39
Golden Globes
film awards *table* 294
Golden Laurels (lit. prize) 245
"goldene keyt, Di" (Yiddish journ.) 251
Goldfarb, David (obit.) 91:96
Goldfinger, Erno (obit.) 88:96
Goldhagen, Daniel Jonah 242
Goldin, Nan 149
Golding, Sir William Gerald (obit.) 94:63
Goldman, Eric Frederick (obit.) 90:111
Goldschmidt, Berthold (obit.) 97:102
Goldsmith, Sir James (biog.) 90:89
Goldsmith, Myron (obit.) 97:102
Goldsmith, Raymond William (obit.) 89:95
Goldstone, Richard 224
golf 97:346; 96:325; 95:304; 94:296; 93:298; 92:293; 91:324; 90:342; 89:324; 88:327
Golombek, Harry (obit.) 96:83
Gomez, Vernon (obit.) 90:111
Goncz, Arpad (biog.) 91:70
Gong Li, *or* Kung Li (biog.) 95:45
Gonzales, Richard Alonzo, *or* Pancho Gonzales (obit.) 96:83
Gooch, Graham Alan (biog.) 92:39
good taste/bad taste
fashion 216
Goodall, Sir Reginald (obit.) 91:96
Goodman, Linda (obit.) 96:83
Goodson, Mark (obit.) 93:64
Goodwin v. United Kingdom 225
Goodyear Tire & Rubber Company (Am. co.) 167

Goossens, Leon Jean (obit.) 89:96
Gorbachev, Mikhail Sergeyevich (biogs.) 92:39; 91:70; 89:73
"Toward the Age of Common Sense" (commentary) 95:7
Gordimer, Nadine (biog.) 92:30
Gordon, Dexter Keith (obit.) 91:96
Gordon, Irving (obit.) 97:103
Gordon, Jeff 319
Gordon, Walter (obit.) 88:96
Gordone, Charles (obit.) 96:83
Gore, Albert A., Jr. (biog.) 93:40
special reports 94:264; 93:469; 89:483
Gorecki, Henryk 94:40
Goren, Charles Henry (obit.) 92:64
Goren, Rabbi Shlomo (obit.) 95:68
Goria, Giovanni Giuseppe
biography 88:71
obituary 95:68
gorilla
zoos 213
Gormley of Ashton-in-Makerfield, Joseph Gormley, Baron (obit.) 94:63
Gorshkov, Sergey Georgyevich (obit.) 89:96
Gottlieb, Robert A. (biog.) 88:71
Gottman, Jean-Iona (obit.) 95:68
Gould, Laurence McKinley (obit.) 96:83
Gould, Morton (obit.) 97:103
Goulding, Raymond Walter (obit.) 91:96
government budget
Austria 393
economic affairs 188
Norway 459
Trinidad and Tobago 483
United States 491, 492
Contract with America (special report) 96:492
defense spending 269
see also budget deficit
Govier, Katherine 242, *il.*
Gowda, H. D. Deve 430
Gowing, Sir Lawrence Burnett (obit.) 92:64
Gracida, Memo 338
Graf, Steffi (biog.) 88:71
tennis 360
Graham, Jorie 242
Graham, Martha (obit.) 92:64
grain (food): *see* cereal
Grameen Bank (bank, Bangla.) 200
Grammy Award
classical music 279
Granada (Br. co.) 179
Grand Prix racing 317
Grandi, Dino, Conte di Mordano (obit.) 89:96
Grange, Harold Edward "Red" (obit.) 92:65
Granger, Stewart, *or* James Lablache Stewart (obit.) 94:63
Grant, George Parkin (obit.) 89:96
Grant, James (obit.) 96:83
Grasberg (mine, Indon.) 170
Grass, Günter Wilhelm (biog.) 96:59
Graves, Nancy Stevenson (obit.) 96:83
Grawemeyer Award for Music Composition 277
Gray, Gordon Joseph Cardinal (obit.) 94:64
Graziano, Rocky (obit.) 91:96
Great Belt, *or* Store Bælt (bridge, Den.) 139
Great Britain: *see* United Kingdom
Great Lakes (l. system, N.Am.)
environmental issues 211
Great Man-Made River, *or* GMR (hydrology project, Libya) 69
Libya 141, 446, *map* 141
Great Prize for Fiction
Portuguese literature 249
Greater Hanish (isl., Red Sea)
Eritrea 415
Yemen 502
Greco, Emilio (obit.) 96:83
Greco-Roman wrestling 370
Greece 97:425; 96:411; 95:413; 94:437; 93:439; 92:429; 91:453; 90:470; 89:454; 88:453
education 205
international affairs
Albania 389
Macedonia 447
Turkey 484
newspapers 265
rubber industry 167
sports and games
basketball 325
weight lifting 370
tunnels 142
see also WORLD DATA
Greek Orthodox Archdiocese of America 308
Green, James Maurice Spurgeon (obit.) 88:96
Green, Joseph, *or* Joseph Greenberg (obit.) 97:103
Green Bay Packers (football) 344
Greenberg, Clement (obit.) 95:68
Greene, Graham (obit.) 92:65
Greene, Sir Hugh Carleton (obit.) 88:96
Greene, Lorne (obit.) 88:96
greenhouse gas 186
geology 183
Greenland
offshore drilling 380
Greens, the (pol. party, Ger.) 425

Greenspan, Alan (biog.) 88:72
stock markets 194
United States 490
Greenwood, Joan (obit.) 88:96
Grenada 97:426; 96:412; 95:414; 94:484; 93:484; 92:476; 91:502; 90:518; 89:502; 88:502
see also WORLD DATA
Grey Cup (Can. football) 344
Griffith Joyner, Florence (biog.) 89:74
Grigorenko, Pyotr Grigorevich (obit.) 88:96
Grimond of Firth, Joseph Grimond, Baron (obit.) 94:64
Grímsson, Ólafur Ragner
Iceland 430
"Grindstone" (horse)
thoroughbred racing 336
Grinkov, Sergey (obit.) 96:84
Grisham, John (biog.) 94:40
Groening, Matt (biog.) 91:70
Gromyko, Andrey Andreyevich (obit.) 90:111
gross domestic product, *or* GDP
economic affairs 188
OECD countries *table* 188
U.S. automobile industry 156
Grossman, Agnes
classical music 277
Grosz, Karoly
biographies 89:74; 88:72
Hungary 430
obituary 97:103
Group of Seven, *or* G-7
Chernobyl power station 487
Grozny (Russ.) *il.* 315
military affairs 271
Gruber, Karl (obit.) 96:84
Grus leucogeranus: *see* Siberian crane
GSI (sci. institute, Ger.): *see* Heavy Ion Research, Institute for
GTS Monaco Access SAM (internat. co.)
Monaco 453
Guam (isl., Pac.O.) 381
Guard, Dave (obit.) 92:65
"Guardian, The" (Br. news.) 487
Guatemala 97:426; 96:412; 95:414; 94:484; 93:484; 92:476; 91:503; 90:518; 89:502; 88:503
disasters 61
military affairs 276
refugees 297
street children (special report) 95:279
United Nations 377
see also WORLD DATA
Guatemalan National Revolutionary Unity (pol. org., Guat.) 426
military affairs 276
Guattari, Pierre-Félix (obit.) 93:64
Gubler, Claude
France 419
Gucci, Maurizio (obit.) 96:84
Gucci, Paolo (obit.) 96:84
Gudmundsdottir, Björk: *see* Björk
Guedes, Fernando van Zeller (obit.) 88:97
Guerin, Veronica 434, *il.* 265
Guevara Arze, Walter (obit.) 97:103
Guggenheim Museum Bilbao (Bilbao, Sp.)
architecture 137, *il.*
Guillén Vicente, Rafael Sebastián: *see* Marcos, Subcommandante
Guimarães, Ulysses (obit.) 93:64
Guinea 97:426; 96:413; 95:415; 94:360; 93:362; 92:358; 91:386; 90:407; 89:390; 88:390
see also WORLD DATA
Guinea-Bissau 97:426; 96:413; 95:415; 94:360; 93:362; 92:358; 91:386; 90:407; 89:390; 88:391
see also WORLD DATA
guinea pig, *or* Cavia porcellus
taxonomy 233
Gulf War: *see* Persian Gulf War
Gullikson, Timothy Edward (obit.) 97:103
gun, *or* firearm
murder rates 227
gun control
Australia 391, *il.*
crime and law enforcement 227
United Kingdom 488
Guns N' Roses (biog.) 92:40
Gurunsinha, Asanka *il.* 333
Gusinsky, Vladimir (biog.) 96:59
Gustafson, Ralph Barker (obit.) 96:84
Guthrie, Alfred Bertram, Jr. (obit.) 92:65
Gutiérrez Mellado, Manuel Gutiérrez Mellado, Marqués de (obit.) 96:84
Guttuso, Aldo Renato (obit.) 88:97
Guyana 97:426; 96:413; 95:415; 94:485; 93:485; 92:477; 91:503; 90:519; 89:503; 88:503
see also WORLD DATA
Guzy, Carol
photo essay 298
Gwala, Harry (obit.) 96:84
Gwynne, Frederick Hubbard (obit.) 94:64
gymnastics 97:348; 96:327; 95:305; 94:298; 93:299; 92:295; 91:325; 90:344; 89:326; 88:328
1996 Summer Olympic champions *table* 97:366
Gymnogyps californianus: *see* California condor
Gypsophila muralis (plant) 215
Gypsy, *or* Rom (people)
Czech Republic 412
photo essay 428

H

Haavelmo, Trygve (biog.) **90**:89
Haberler, Gottfried von (obit.) **96**:84
Habib, Philip Charles (obit.) **93**:64
Habibi, Emile (obit.) **97**:103
Habibie, Bachruddin Jusuf (biog.) **95**:45
Habitat II (UN)
  human rights issues 316
Habsburg, House of (Eur. dynasty)
  Bosnia and Herzegovina (special report) **94**:426
Habyarimana, Juvénal (obit.) **95**:68
Hachette (Fr. co.) 268
hacker
  computer security 181
Hackett, Albert (obit.) **96**:84
Hackney, Roderick Peter (biog.) **88**:72
Hagenbeck, Carl
  zoos (special report) **94**:111
Hague, The (Neth.)
  art exhibitions (special report) 146
Haidari, Buland al- (obit.) **97**:103
Haiti **97**:427; **96**:414; **95**:415; **94**:485; **93**:485; **92**:477; **91**:503; **90**:519; **89**:503; **88**:503
  Canada 405
  human rights violations 316
  marine disasters 59
  police training *il.* 228
  United Nations 377
  see also WORLD DATA
Hajek, Igor (obit.) **96**:84
Hajek, Jiri (obit.) **94**:64
Hajseyyedjavadi, Fattaneh 251
Hakim, Tawfiq al- (obit.) **88**:97
Halas, John (obit.) **96**:84
Haldeman, Harry Robbins (obit.) **94**:64
Hale, Clara M. (obit.) **93**:64
Haley, Alex Palmer (obit.) **93**:65
Haley, Sir William John (obit.) **88**:97
Hall, Adelaide (obit.) **94**:64
Hall, Arsenio (biog.) **91**:71
Hall, Donald 241
Hall, Emmett Matthew (obit.) **96**:84
"Halling" (horse) 337
Halliwell, Leslie (obit.) **90**:111
"Hallo?—er det noen her?" (Gaarder) 245
Halston (obit.) **91**:96
ham radio: *see* amateur radio
Hamanaka, Yasuo 228
Hamas (Pal. org.)
  Egypt 414
  Israel 434
  terrorism 226, 375
Hambletonian (harness racing) 338
Hamburg Ballet (Ger. ballet co.) 284
Hamburger, Jean (obit.) **93**:65
Hamed, Naseem 330, *il.* 329
Hamelin, Louis 247
Hamengkubuwono IX (obit.) **89**:96
Hamilton, Charles, Jr. (obit.) **97**:103
Hamilton, Sir Charles Denis (obit.) **89**:96
Hamilton, Hamish (obit.) **89**:96
Hamilton, Neil 487
Hamilton, Thomas
  mass murders 227, 488
Hamilton Adair, Virginia 241
"Hamlet" (motion picture) 290
"Hamlet: A Monologue" (play) 89
Hammer, Armand (obit.) **91**:97
Hammersmith and Fulham (boro., Gtr.-London, U.K.)
  derivatives (special report) **96**:185
Hammond, Norman 136
"Hamsun" (motion picture) 291
Hamsuns, Knut 245
Han Xue 358
Hanafi (Islam)
  women's role (special report) **93**:95
Hanai, Masaya (obit.) **96**:85
Hanauer, Chip (biog.) **94**:41
Hanbali (Islam)
  women's role (special report) **93**:95
Hancock, Langley George (obit.) **93**:65
handball
  1996 Summer Olympic champions *table* **97**:366
handgun: *see* gun
Handl, Irene (obit.) **88**:97
Hani, Martin Thembisile, *or* Chris Hani (obit.) **94**:64
Hanish Islands (isls., Red Sea)
  Eritrea 415
  Yemen 502
Hanks, Tom (biog.) **95**:46
Hans Adam II
  Liechtenstein 446
Hansen, Rick (biog.) **88**:72
Hansen, Ron 241
Hanson, Duane Elwood (obit.) **97**:103
Harald V (biog.) **92**:40
Harding of Petherton, Allan Francis John Harding (obit.) **90**:111
hardware, computer: *see* Information Processing and Information Systems
Hardy, Albert (obit.) **96**:85
Hardy, René (obit.) **88**:97
Hare Krishna, *or* International Society for Krishna Consciousness, *or* ISKCON 310
Hargreaves, Alison (obit.) **96**:85
Hargreaves, Roger (obit.) **89**:96
Hariri, Rafiq al- (biog.) **94**:41
Harkin, Tom **93**:469
Harman, Harriet
  United Kingdom 488
Harmon, Thomas D. (obit.) **91**:97
harness racing **97**:338; **96**:318; **95**:297; **94**:300; **93**:302; **92**:298; **91**:327; **90**:347; **89**:329; **88**:331
Harnoy, Ofra (biog.) **97**:76
"Harold Pinter" (Billington) 243
Harper, Elijah (biog.) **91**:71
Harpman, Jacqueline
  French literature 246
Harrell, Tom (biog.) **97**:76
Harrington, Michael (obit.) **90**:112
Harrington, Oliver Wendell (obit.) **96**:85
Harris, Barbara (biog.) **90**:89
Harris, Eddie (obit.) **97**:103
Harris, Lagumot 455
Harris, Marcus 343
Harris, Maxwell Henley (obit.) **96**:85
Harris, Mike, *or* Michael Harris (biog.) **96**:59
Harris, Phil (obit.) **96**:85
Harris, Reginald Hargreaves (obit.) **93**:65
Harrison, Rex (obit.) **91**:97
Hart, Gary Warren
  special report **89**:483
Hart of South Lanark, Judith Constance Mary Hart (obit.) **92**:66
Hart Trophy (ice hockey) 349
Hartford Ballet (Am. ballet co.) 282
Hartley (mine, Zimb.) 171
Härtling, Peter 245
Hartung, Hans (obit.) **90**:112
Harty, Fredric Russell (obit.) **89**:97
Harvard University (univ., Cambridge, Mass., U.S.)
  architecture 138
Harvey, Douglas Norman (obit.) **90**:112
Harwood, Elizabeth Jean (obit.) **91**:97
Hasbro Inc. (Am. co.) 164
Hashimoto, Ryutaro (biog.) **97**:76
  Japan 437, 438
  Latin America (spotlight) 400
  military affairs 276
  South Korea 443
Hasina Wazed, Sheikh (biog.) **97**:77
Hasluck, Sir Paul Meernaa Caedwalla (obit.) **94**:64
Hass, Robert 241
Hassan, Muhammad Farah: *see* Aydid, Gen. Muhammad Farah
Hassett, Arthur Lindsay (obit.) **94**:65
Hassuna, Muhammad ʿAbd al-Khaliq (obit.) **93**:65
Hatfield, Mark 491
Hatfield, Richard Bennett (obit.) **92**:66
Hatier (Fr. co.) 268
Hatoyama, Yukio
  Japan 437
Hattersley, Roy Sydney George (biog.) **91**:71
Hatton, Ragnhild Marie Hanssen (obit.) **96**:85
Hau Pei-tsun (biog.) **92**:40
"Haunted Land: Facing Europe's Ghosts After Communism, The" (Rosenberg) 268
Haury, Emil Walter (obit.) **93**:65
Havard-Williams, Peter (obit.) **96**:85
Havel, Vaclav (biog.) **90**:90
  Czech Republic 412
Hawaii (state, U.S.)
  Loihi Seamount 184
  same-sex marriages 495, 499, *il.*
Hawar Islands (isls., Pers. Gulf)
  Bahrain 394
Hawke, Robert James Lee (biog.) **89**:74
Hawkins, Erskine (obit.) **94**:65
Hawkins, Frederick (obit.) **95**:68
Hayakawa, Samuel Ichiye (obit.) **93**:66
Haydée, Marcia 284
Hayek, Friedrich August von (obit.) **93**:66
Hayes, Helen (obit.) **94**:65
Hayes, Woody (obit.) **88**:97
Haynsworth, Clement Furman, Jr. (obit.) **90**:112
Hayter, Stanley William (obit.) **89**:97
Hayworth, Rita (obit.) **88**:97
HDTV: *see* high-definition television
HDZ (pol. party, Croatia): *see* Croatian Democratic Union
Head Start
  U.S. education 204
Headroom, Max (biog.) **88**:73
Healing Hands International
  Churches of Christ 302
Health and Disease **97**:218; **96**:205; **95**:194; **94**:174; **93**:173; **92**:172; **91**:201; **90**:220; **89**:202; **88**:202
  agriculture and food supplies 126
  causes of death in the U.S. *table* 296
  consumer affairs 202
  environmental pollutants 210, 212
  European Union 379
  food processing 131
  Japan 438
  molecular biology 237
  Nobel Prize 64
  special reports **95**:278; **88**:206
  United Kingdom 487
health care reform
  Germany 421
  special reports **97**:220; **95**:198
  United States legislation 203, 497
health insurance 165
  genetic testing issues 218
  social protection 312
Health Insurance Portability and Accountability Act (U.S.) 312
health maintenance organization, *or* HMO
  United States 498
Heaney, Seamus 243
Hearst, William Randolph, Jr. (obit.) **94**:65
heart attack, *or* myocardial infarction
  prevention and treatment 219
heat wave
  natural disasters 60
Heath, James R. 63
Heavy Ion Research, Institute for, *or* GSI (Ger.) 253
Hebblethwaite, Peter (obit.) **95**:69
Hebrew literature 251
Hebron 434
HECS: *see* Higher Education Contribution Scheme
hedge-to-arrive contract
  stock exchanges 198
Heifetz, Jascha (obit.) **88**:98
Heilig-Meyers (Am. co.) 165
Heinesen, William (obit.) **92**:66
Heinlein, Robert Anson (obit.) **89**:97
Heisei (biog.): *see* Akihito
Heisman Trophy 343
Heissenbüttel, Helmut (obit.) **97**:103
Hekmatyar, Gulbuddin 388
Helgemo, Geir 331
Helicobacter pylori (bacterium) 221
"Helissio" (horse) 337, *il.*
helium dimer
  chemistry 254
helium-3, *or* ^{3}He (phys.)
  superfluid research 64
hell
  concept debate 301
Heller, Walter Wolfgang (obit.) **88**:98
Hell's Angels (motorcycle org.)
  Denmark 413
Helm, Brigitte, *or* Gisele Eve Schittenhelm (obit.) **97**:103
Helms-Burton Act, *or* Cuban Liberty and Democratic Solidarity Act (U.S.)
  Cuba 411
  United States 496
Helmsley, Leona (biog.) **90**:90
Hemingway, Margot (obit.) **97**:104
Hemphill, Julius Arthur (obit.) **96**:85
Hendrickson, Paul 241
Hendry, Stephen 326, *il.*
Henley Royal Regatta
  rowing 354
Henreid, Paul (obit.) **93**:66
Henson, Jim (obit.) **91**:97
hepatitis
  Ukraine 487
Hepburn, Audrey (obit.) **94**:65
"Herb" (typhoon) 60
Herlihy, James Leo (obit.) **94**:66
Herman, Babe (obit.) **88**:98
Herman, Billy (obit.) **93**:66
Herman, Woody (obit.) **88**:98
Hermitage (museum, St. Petersburg, Russ.) 144
  art exhibitions (special report) 146
Hermlin, Stephan 244
Hernreid, Paul George Julius von: *see* Henreid, Paul
Hernu, Charles (obit.) **91**:98
heroin
  popular music 281
  special report **89**:144
heroin chic 217, *il.*
"Héros très discret, Un" (motion picture): *see* "Self-Made Hero, A"
Herrera, Helmer 410
Herrhausen, Alfred (obit.) **90**:112
Herriot, James, *or* James Alfred Wight (obit.) **96**:85
Herron, John 392
Hersant, Robert Joseph Émile (obit.) **97**:104
Hersey, John Richard (obit.) **94**:66
Hershey, Barbara (biog.) **89**:74
Hershiser, Orel (biog.) **89**:75
Hervé-Bazin, Jean-Pierre-Marie (obit.): *see* Bazin, Hervé
Herzog, Roman (biog.) **95**:46
Heseltine, Michael Ray Dibdin (biog.) **91**:71
Hess, Erika (biog.) **88**:73
Hess, Walter Richard Rudolf (obit.) **88**:98
Hewson, John Robert (biog.) **91**:72
Heydar, Aliyev: *see* Geidar, Aliev
Heym, Stefan (biog.) **95**:46
Heyman, I. Michael (biog.) **95**:46
Heyns, Penelope 357
Heyworth, Peter Lawrence Frederick (obit.) **92**:66
Hezbollah
  Israel 435
  Lebanon 439, 445
Hick, Graeme Ashley (biog.) **89**:75
Hicks, Sir John Richard (obit.) **90**:112
"Hidden Treasures Revealed" (art exhibit)
  special report 146
Higashikuni, Naruhiko (obit.) **91**:98
Higgins, John 326
high blood pressure: *see* hypertension
high-definition television, *or* HDTV 262
"High Life" (play) 288
high-temperature superconductor (phys.)
  Helium-3 research 64
higher education 205
Higher Education Contribution Scheme, *or* HECS
  Australia 392
Highsmith, Mary Patricia (obit.) **96**:85
highway: *see* roads and traffic
hijacking
  aviation disasters 58
Hildesheimer, Wolfgang (obit.) **92**:66
Hill, Benny (obit.) **93**:66
Hill, Damon 317, *il.* 318
Hill, Julian Werner (obit.) **97**:104
Hill, Robert (obit.) **92**:66
Hiller, Lejaren (obit.) **95**:69
Hillgruber, Andreas (obit.) **90**:112
Hinckley, Gordon B. 303
Hinduism 309
  religion statistics *table* 311
Hingis, Martina 362
hippie chic 216
Hirohito, *or* Showa (obit.) **90**:112
Hiroshima (Japan)
  World War II (special report) **96**:259, *il.*
Hirst, Damien (biog.) **97**:77
Hispasat 1B (satellite)
  direct-broadcast satellite (special report) 176
Hiss, Alger (obit.) **97**:104
Hissou, Salah 368
Hitchings, George Herbert (biog.) **89**:75
HIV: *see* human immunodeficiency virus
"hLAVOLAMOV" (Kadlečik) 250
HMO: *see* health maintenance organization
Hnatyshyn, Ray (biog.) **90**:90
Ho Ying-ch'in (obit.) **88**:98
Hoad, Lewis Alan (obit.) **95**:69
Hobby, Oveta Culp (obit.) **96**:85
Hobson, Sir Harold (obit.) **93**:66
Hodder Headline (Br. co.) 268
Hodes, Arthur W. (obit.) **94**:66
Hodgkin, Dorothy Mary Crowfoot (obit.) **95**:69
Hoffman, Abbie (obit.) **90**:113
Hoffman, Dustin (biog.) **90**:90
Hofmann, Sigurd 253
Hofstadter, Robert (obit.) **91**:98
hog: *see* pig
Hogan, Paul (biog.) **88**:73
Hogg-Priestly, Helen Battles Sawyer (obit.) **94**:66
Hojo, Hideji (obit.) **97**:104
Holkeri, Harri (biog.) **88**:73
Holland: *see* Netherlands, The
Holley, Robert William (obit.) **94**:66
"Hollow Reed" (motion picture) 290
Hollows, Frederick Cossom (obit.) **94**:66
"Hollywood Conquest, The" (special report) **95**:245
Holm, Hanya (obit.) **93**:67
Holman, Moses Carl (obit.) **89**:97
Holmboe, Vagn (obit.) **97**:104
Holmes à Court, Michael Robert Hamilton (obit.) **91**:98
Holocaust (Eur. hist.)
  Birkenau cross controversy 300
  nontheatrical films 295
  World War II (special report) **96**:257
Holomisa, Bantu 474
"Holy Week" (motion picture) 295
Holyfield, Evander 327, *il.* 328
home furnishings: *see* furniture; housewares
Home of the Hirsel, Alexander Frederick Douglas-Home, Baron, of Coldstream, *or* Sir Alec Douglas-Home (obit.) **96**:85
Homeland Union, *or* Conservatives of Lithuania, *or* TS-LK (pol. party, Lith.) 446
Homer, Winslow
  art exhibition 149
Homo habilis
  anthropology 134
homosexuality
  Latin-American literature 248
  military affairs 270
  religion 301
    Anglican Communion 301
    Methodist Churches 304
    Southern Baptist Convention 302
  United States laws 495, 499
    Colorado law 225
"Homosexuality and the Churches" (special report) **94**:263
Honasan, Gregorio (biog.) **88**:74
Honda (Japanese co.)
  automobiles 158
Honda, Soichiro (obit.) **92**:66
Honduras **97**:427; **96**:414; **95**:416; **94**:486; **93**:486; **92**:478; **91**:504; **90**:519; **89**:504; **88**:504
  see also WORLD DATA
Honecker, Erich (obit.) **95**:69
Hong Kong 381
  bridges 139
  China 407
  education 205
  fires and explosions 59
  freight and pipelines 373
  human rights issues 315, 316
  social protection 314
  special report **89**:176
  stock exchanges 199
  television industry 262
  United Kingdom 489
  Vietnamese refugees 297

References with dark-type numbers refer to the previous years, *e.g.*, **96**:324 for the 1996 edition, page 324.

Hook, Sidney (obit.) **90**:113
Hooker, John Lee (biog.) **94**:41
hooks, bell 241
hop, step, and jump: *see* triple jump
Hopkins, Sir Anthony (biog.) **95**:47
Hopkinson, Sir Henry Thomas (obit.) **91**:98
Hopper, Grace Murray (obit.) **93**:67
Hordern, Sir Michael Murray (obit.) **96**:85
Horgan, Paul (obit.) **96**:86
hormone
  botany 235
Horn, Gyula 430
Horowitz, Vladimir (obit.) **90**:113
horse racing: *see* equestrian sports
Horseshoe Casino and Hotel (Robinsonville, Miss., U.S.)
  jazz 280
Horszowski, Mieczyslaw (obit.) **94**:66
"Hortense" (hurricane)
  natural disasters 60, 381
Horvath, Judit
  photo essay 428
Hosokawa, Morihiro (biogs.) **94**:41; **93**:41
hostage-taking
  Chechnya 315
  Peru 400, 461
"Hot Roof, A" (motion picture) 295
Hotz, F. B. 245
Hough, Stephan 279
Houphouët-Boigny, Félix (obit.) **94**:67
Hourani, Albert Habib (obit.) **94**:67
Household, Geoffrey Edward West (obit.) **89**:97
Houseman, John (obit.) **89**:97
Houser, Allan C. (obit.) **95**:69
housewares 165
housing starts (U.S.)
  wood products 179
Houston, Lawrence Reid (obit.) **96**:86
Houston, Whitney (biog.) **95**:47
Howard, Desmond 344
Howard, John Winston (biog.) **97**:77
  Australia 391
Howard, Michael (biog.) **94**:42
  British gun laws 488
Howard, Robin Jared Stanley (obit.) **90**:113
Howard, Trevor Wallace (obit.) **89**:97
Howe, Irving (obit.) **94**:67
Howerd, Frankie (obit.) **93**:67
Howser, Dick (obit.) **88**:99
Hoyer-Larsen, Poul-Erik 320
Hrvati (people): *see* Croat
Hu Yaobang (obit.) **90**:114
Huang, John 496
Hubbard Brook Experimental Forest (N.H., U.S.) 210
Hubbell, Carl Owen (obit.) **89**:98
Hubble Deep Field
  astronomy 258, *il.* 257
Hubble Space Telescope, *or* HST
  astronomy 258
Hubble's constant (physics) 256
Huber, Robert (biog.) **89**:75
Huggins, Peter Jeremy William (obit.): *see* Brett, Jeremy
Hughes, Mervyn Gregory (biog.) **94**:42
Hughes Aircraft Co. (Am. co.)
  satellite TV (special report) 176
Huish, Justin 317, *il.*
Hull, Sir Richard Amyatt (obit.) **90**:114
Hulton, Sir Edward George Warris (obit.) **89**:98
Hum (medieval principality)
  Bosnia and Herzegovina (special report) **94**:426
Human Genome Project 218
human immunodeficiency virus, *or* HIV
  infection and treatment 219
  Italian court decisions 225
  Japan 438
  pharmaceuticals 173
  United States 498
Human Relations 96:279; **95**:255; **94**:252; **93**:250; **92**:250; **91**:278; **90**:296; **89**:280; **88**:282
human rights 314
  Afghanistan 388
  Chile 407
  China 408
  court decisions 224
  Ethiopia 418
  military training tactics 276
  Mozambique 454
  Myanmar 380
  Nigeria 458
  Russia 465
  South Africa 474
  Spain 475
  special report **95**:278
  Turkey 485
  Uganda 486
  United Nations 376
  Uruguay 500
  Uzbekistan 500
Human Rights Protection Party (pol. party, W.Sam.) 502
Human Rights Watch/Asia
  China 408
Humen Bridge (bridge, China) 139
Humphrey, Percy (obit.) **96**:86
Hun Sen
  Cambodia 403
"Hunchback of Notre Dame, The" (motion picture) 289
  computer animation (special report) 292
Huncke, Herbert (obit.) **97**:104
Hungary **97**:427; **96**:415; **95**:417; **94**:439; **93**:440; **92**:430; **91**:471; **90**:489; **89**:472; **88**:471
  Bosnia and Herzegovina (special report) **94**:426
  chemicals 161
  economic affairs 193, 194
  media and publishing
    newspapers 265
    television 261
  motion pictures 295
  sports and games
    Grand Prix racing 318
    swimming 357
  see also WORLD DATA
hunger
  agriculture and food supplies 125
  human rights issues 316
  North Korea 440
Hunt, James Simon Wallis (obit.) **94**:67
Hunter, Howard William (obit.) **96**:86
Hunter, Ross, *or* Martin Fuss (obit.) **97**:104
Huppert, Isabelle Anne (biog.) **97**:77
Hurd, Douglas Richard (biog.) **91**:72
hurdling
  track and field sports 370
hurricane *il.* 186
  natural disasters 60
  see also particular hurricanes by name, *e.g.*, Cesar
Husak, Gustav (obit.) **92**:67
Hussein, Saddam (biogs.) **92**:41; **91**:72
  Iraq 375, 433
  military affairs 272
  United States 496
Hussein I (biog.) **92**:41
Hussein Onn (obit.) **91**:98
Hussein Qambar, Robert 300
"Hustings, The" (motion picture) 295
Huston, John (obit.) **88**:99
Huston, Nancy
  French-Canadian literature 247
Hutchinson, George Evelyn (obit.) **92**:67
Hutchison, William Bruce (obit.) **93**:67
Hutchison Telecom (Br. co.) 264
Hutton, Sir Leonard (obit.) **91**:98
Hutu (people)
  Burundi 402
  human rights 314
  military affairs 276
  photo essay 298
  Rwanda 467
  Zaire 504
Huynh Tan Phat (obit.) **90**:114
Hyakutake, Comet: *see* Comet Hyakutake
Hyde White, Wilfrid (obit.) **92**:67
hydrogen (chem.)
  antimatter research 255
hydrogen bonding 254
hydrology
  Antarctica 382
  Great Man-Made River 141, *map*
  pollution control 211
hydrothermal vent
  oceanography 184, 187
hydroxyl, *or* OH (chem.) 254
Hyman, Phyllis (obit.) **96**:86
hypertension, *or* high blood pressure 218

I

"I Shot Andy Warhol" (motion picture) 290
IATA: *see* International Air Transport Association
Ibárruri Gómez, Isidora Dolores (obit.) **90**:114
IBF: *see* International Boxing Federation
IBM: *see* International Business Machines Corporation
Ibuse, Masuji (obit.) **94**:67
Icahn, Carl (biog.) **90**:91
ICAO: *see* International Civil Aviation Organization
ICBS: *see* International Committee of the Blue Shield
ice hockey **97**:349; **96**:329; **95**:306; **94**:301; **93**:303; **92**:299; **91**:329; **90**:347; **89**:330; **88**:332
  1994 Winter Olympic champions *table* **95**:309
ice sheet
  Antarctica 382
ice skating **97**:350; **96**:330; **95**:310; **94**:303; **93**:304; **92**:300; **91**:330; **90**:349; **89**:331; **88**:333
  1994 Winter Olympic champions *table* **95**:309
Iceland **97**:430; **96**:415; **95**:417; **94**:440; **93**:442; **92**:431; **91**:454; **90**:471; **89**:455; **88**:454
  Denmark 413
  see also WORLD DATA
ICI (Br. corp.): *see* Imperial Chemical Industries
ICJ: *see* International Court of Justice
ICOM: *see* International Council of Museums
ICT: *see* International Criminal Tribunal
Idris, Yusuf (obit.) **92**:67
IEA: *see* International Energy Agency
Ieng Sary 403
IFOR: *see* Implementation Force
IFP (pol. party, S.Af.): *see* Inkatha Freedom Party
Ignatieff, George (obit.) **90**:114
Iharos, Sandor (obit.) **97**:104
"Il postino" (motion picture): "postino, Il"
Iliescu, Ion (biog.) **91**:72
  Romania 463
illegal alien, *or* illegal immigrant
  France 419
  Germany 421
  United Arab Emirates 487
Illinois (state, U.S.) 498
illiteracy: *see* literacy
Ilyumzhinov, Kirsan
  chess 331
IMF: *see* International Monetary Fund
Imlach, George (obit.) **88**:99
immigration
  English Channel history (special report) **95**:350
  Germany 425
  Japanese in Latin America (spotlight) 400
  refugees 297
  United Arab Emirates 487
  U.S. welfare reform policy 312
  see also illegal alien
immune system
  killer T cells 64
immunization: *see* vaccine
impeachment
  Madagascar 447
"Imperial Call" (horse)
  steeplechasing 338
Imperial Chemical Industries, *or* ICI (Br. corp.)
  paints and varnishes 172
"Imperial Tombs of China" (art exhibit) 144
Implementation Force, *or* IFOR
  Albania 389
  Bosnia and Herzegovina 398
  military affairs 269, 271
import
  automobiles 157
  chemicals 161
  economic affairs 189, 193
  wood products 179
Impressionism 145
  art auctions 150
  art exhibitions (special report) 146
IMSA: *see* International Motor Sports Association
"In Times of War and Peace" (retrospective)
  photography 149
inactivated polio vaccine, *or* IPV 222
"Incerti di viaggio" (Pazzi) 247
Inco (Can. co.) 170
income tax: *see* taxation
"Independence Day" (Ford) 242, 268
"Independence Day" (motion picture) 289
India **97**:430; **96**:416; **95**:419; **94**:404; **93**:404; **92**:402; **91**:430; **90**:448; **89**:431; **88**:437
  agriculture and food supplies 129
  architecture and civil engineering
    dams 141
    pipeline *il.* 431
    roads 142
  business and industry
    coal 163
    rubber 167
  cricket 332
  demographic statistics 296
    most populous urban areas *table* 296
  disasters 61
    aviation 58
    natural 60
    railroad 61
  gardening 214
  Hinduism 309
  international relations
    China 409
    Nepal 455
    Pakistan 460
  military affairs 276
  motion pictures 295
  nuclear test ban treaty 269
  see also WORLD DATA
Indianapolis 500
  automobile racing 318, *il.* 319
Indochina: *see* Cambodia; Laos; Vietnam
Indonesia **97**:432; **96**:418; **95**:420; **94**:413; **93**:413; **92**:409; **91**:436; **90**:454; **89**:437; **88**:437
  badminton 320
  business and industry
    building and construction 160
    paper and pulp 179
    wood products 179
  disasters
    fires and explosions 59
    marine 59
    natural 60
  international affairs
    China 409
    East Timor 62
    United States 496
  most populous urban areas *table* 296
  special reports **95**:173; **93**:96
  television 264
  see also WORLD DATA
Indurain, Miguel (biog.) **93**:41
Indus Highway (rd., Pak.)
  civil engineering 142
industrial nation, *or* developed nation
  agricultural production *tables* 123, 127
  economic affairs 188, 194
  manufacturing *table* 153
  unemployment rates *table* 192
Industrial Review 94:179; **93**:178; **92**:178; **91**:207; **90**:225; **89**:208; **88**:210
  see also Business and Industry Review; individual countries by name
Indy Racing League, *or* IRL
  automobile racing 318
"Inés de Castro" (opera) 279
INF treaty, *or* intermediate-range nuclear forces treaty
  special report **88**:258
infancy
  sudden infant death syndrome 221
infant mortality rate 296
infectious disease 219
inflation
  Angola 389
  Argentina 390
  economic affairs 190, 193
  stock markets 194
"Information Processing" (MACROPAEDIA revision) **94**:505
Information Processing 97:180; **96**:157; **95**:201; **94**:200; **93**:199; **92**:199; **91**:228; **90**:246; **89**:229; **88**:231
  libraries 230
  see also Computers and Information Systems
information superhighway
  cyberspace (special report) **96**:158
Information Technology Agreement 170
infrared radiation
  observation satellites 260
Ingraham, Hubert (biog.) **93**:41
Inhumane Weapons, Geneva Convention on: *see* Geneva Convention on Inhumane Weapons
initial public offering, *or* IPO
  Internet-related companies 180
  stock exchanges 197
Inkatha Freedom Party, *or* IFP (pol. party, S.Af.) 473
inorganic chemistry 253
Inoue, Yasushi (obit.) **92**:67
insect
  entomology
  plant defense system 236
Institutional Revolutionary Party, *or* PRI (pol. party, Mex.) 452
"Instruments des ténèbres" (Huston) 247
insurance 165
  genetic testing issues 218
  U.S. health care 203
integrelin (drug)
  cardiovascular disease 219
Intel Corp. (Am. corp.)
  chess sponsorship 331
  microelectronics 170
  personal computers 181
  stock exchanges 197
intercity rail 374
interest rates
  economic affairs 188
  special report **89**:176
  stock markets 194
  United Kingdom 488
Intergovernmental Panel on Climate Change, *or* IPCC 206
intermediate-range nuclear forces treaty: *see* INF treaty
International Air Transport Association, *or* IATA 372
international banking 200
International Boxing Federation, *or* IBF 329
International Business Machines Corporation, *or* IBM
  computers 181, 182
  special report **94**:203
International Center of Photography Midtown (N.Y.C., N.Y., U.S.)
  "In Times of War and Peace" retrospective 149
International Civil Aviation Organization, *or* ICAO 372
International Committee of the Blue Shield, *or* ICBS
  museum damages 231
International Convention on Salvage 373
International Council of Museums, *or* ICOM 230
International Council of Scientific Unions 183
International Court of Justice, *or* World Court, *or* ICJ
  international law 223
  nuclear weapons 269, 376
International Cricket Council 332
International Criminal Tribunal, *or* ICT 224
International Date Line
  Kiribati 440
International Electrotechnical Commission 162
International Energy Agency, *or* IEA 164
International Festival of Photojournalism (Perpignan, Fr.) 149
International Film and Video Festival 295
International Film Awards
  1996 *table* 294
International Finance Corporation (UN)
  equity markets (special report) **95**:172
International Geological Congress 183

References giving only a page number in light type are for the current edition.

International IMPAC Dublin Literary
  Award 244
international law 223
  nuclear weapons 269
international migration 297
International Monetary Fund, *or* IMF
  Algeria 389
  Bulgaria 401
  Burkina Faso 402
  Djibouti 413
  economic affairs 189, 193
  Kenya 440
  Madagascar 447
  Philippines 462
  Russia 464
  Tanzania 482
  Venezuela 500
  World Trade Organization 224
International Motor Sports Association, *or*
  IMSA 320
International Natural Rubber Agree-
  ment 167
International Olympic Committee
  television broadcasting rights 264
International Organization for Migration,
  or IOM
  refugees 297
International Road Federation, *or* IRF 142
International Society for Krishna Con-
  sciousness: *see* Hare Krishna
International Space Station, *or* ISS
  space exploration 258
International Spiritual Life Commission
  Salvation Army 305
International Telecommunications Union,
  or ITU
  satellite TV (special report) 176
international trade
  agriculture 128
  business and industry
    clothing 156
    wood products 179
  Caribbean unification issues (spotlight)
    468
  Chile 407
  economic affairs 189, 193
  Hong Kong 381
  Japan 438
  Jordan 439
  Mexico 453
  Norway 459
  Russia 465
  special report **89:**176
  United States 496
  Uzbekistan 500
  Zimbabwe 504
International Transport Workers' Federation, *or* ITF 373
international travel: *see* tourism
International Union for Conservation of
  Nature and Natural Resources, *or*
  IUCN
  wildlife conservation 213
Internet 180
  cyberspace (special report) **96:**158
  digitized visual images 149, 173
  electronic games 164
  libraries 230
  literature 240
  magazines 267
  museum use 231
  newspapers 265
  retailing 165
  Southeast Asian Nations 380
  stock exchanges 196
  telecommunications 175
  see also World Wide Web
Intranet
  computer industry 181
Inuit, *or* Eskimo (people)
  Canada 383
Inusop (Belg. co.) 397
"Inventions of the March Hare: Poems
  1909–1917" (Eliot) 243
investment, foreign: *see* foreign investment
investment banking 201
investment fund
  Venezuela 501
Io (satellite of Jupiter) 256
Ioann, *or* Ivan Matveyevich Snychev
  (obit.) **96:**86
IOM: *see* International Organization for
  Migration
Ionesco, Eugéne, *or* Eugen Ionescu (obit.)
  95:69
Iowa, University of (Iowa City, Ia., U.S.)
  wrestling 370
IPCC: *see* Intergovernmental Panel on
  Climate Change
IPO: *see* initial public offering
IPV: *see* inactivated polio vaccine
IRA: *see* Irish Republican Army
Iran **97:**432; **96:**419; **95:**421; **94:**382;
  93:383; **92:**380; **91:**407; **90:**427;
  89:410; **88:**410
  arts and entertainment
    literature 251
    motion pictures 295
  dams 141
  international affairs
    Afghan refugees 297
    Azerbaijan 394
    Central Asia (spotlight) 480
    Iraq 433
    Kenya 440
    Turkey 484
    United States 496

international law 224
land mines *map* 275
petroleum industry 163
special reports **94:**377; **93:**95; **89:**290
terrorism 226
see also WORLD DATA
Iran and Libya Sanctions Act (U.S.)
  Canadian opposition 405
  Iran 432
  Libya 446
  United States 495
Iran-contra affair
  special report **88:**485
Iraq **97:**433; **96:**420; **95:**422; **94:**383;
  93:384; **92:**381; **91:**407; **90:**428;
  89:410; **88:**411
  chess championship 330
  international affairs
    Iran 433
    Jordan 439
    United Nations 377
    United States 496
  Islam 310
  land mines *map* 275
  military affairs 272
  new flag *illus.* **92:**343
  petroleum 162
  refugees 297
  see also WORLD DATA
Irbil (Iraq)
  military conflict 433
Ireland **97:**433; **96:**421; **95:**423; **94:**440;
  93:442; **92:**432; **91:**455; **90:**471;
  89:455; **88:**455
  arts and entertainment
    motion pictures 290
    television 264
    theatre 285
  newspapers 265
  swimming 357
  United Kingdom 489
  see also WORLD DATA
Ireland, John Benjamin (obit.) **93:**67
IRF: *see* International Road Federation
Irish Republican Army, *or* IRA 489
  terrorist attacks 227, 433
IRL: *see* Indy Racing League
iron and steel 168
iron ore
  mining 171
irredenta nation
  Fourth World (spotlight) 422
Irving, Kenneth Colin (obit.) **93:**67
Irwin, James Benson (obit.) **92:**67
Ishihara, Shintarō 252
Ishii, Susumu (obit.) **92:**68
ISKCON: *see* Hare Krishna
Islam 310
  Afghanistan 297, 388
  Albanian church desecration 308
  Balkan conflict war crimes 227
  China 408
  Egypt 414
  Iran 432
  Mali *il.* 449
  Philippines 461
  religion statistics *table* 311
  Russia 375
  special reports **94:**377, 425; **93:**95;
    89:290
  women's rights issues 316
Islam, Nation of 310
"Islamic Fundamentalism" (special report)
  94:377
Islamic Group
  Egypt 415
Islamic Jihad (internat. org.)
  Israel 434
  special report **94:**378
Islamic law: *see* Shari'ah
Islamic Salvation Front, *or* FIS (pol. org.,
  Alg.)
  special report **94:**378
Islamic Society (rel. org.): *see* Jamaat-i-
  Islami
Islamic Welfare Party, *or* Refah (pol. party,
  Tur.) 310
Israel **97:**434; **96:**422; **95:**423; **94:**384;
  93:385; **92:**382; **91:**408; **90:**428;
  89:411; **88:**411
  archaeology 134
    Jerusalem *map* 435
  arts and entertainment
    Hebrew literature 251
    Yiddish literature 251
  education 204
  international affairs
    Egypt 414
    European Union 379
    France 420
    Jordan 439
    Lebanon 445
    Syria 478
    Tunisia 484
    Turkey 484
  military affairs 273
  religion 300
    Islam 310
    Judaism 308
  special report **89:**290
  terrorism 226
  see also WORLD DATA
Israel, Melvin Allen (obit.): *see* Allen, Mel
ISS: *see* International Space Station
Issakovitch, Sergey Ivanovitch (obit.): *see*
  Chermayeff, Serge

Issigonis, Sir Alec (obit.) **89:**98
Istanbul (Tur.)
  most populous urban areas *table* 296
"It Takes a Village: And Other Lessons
  Children Teach Us" (Clinton) 268
Italian literature 247
Italy **97:**436; **96:**424; **95:**426; **94:**441;
  93:443; **92:**433; **91:**456; **90:**472;
  89:456; **88:**456
  arts and entertainment
    literature 247
    motion pictures 291
      film awards *table* 294
  business and industry
    chemicals 161
    machinery and machine tools 166
    wine 159
  disasters 61
  economic affairs 194
    stock exchanges 199
  education 206
  European Union 378
  law
    court decisions 224
    crime and law enforcement 228
    prisons and penology 229
  libraries 230
  media and publishing
    newspapers 265
    television 264
  Pentecostal Churches 304
  sports and games
    association football 340, 341
    basketball 325
    cycling 335
    Grand Prix racing 318
    marathon running 370
    skiing 356
  see also WORLD DATA
"Italy" (MACROPAEDIA revision) **96:**510
Itami, Juzo (biog.) **89:**76
ITF: *see* International Transport Workers'
  Federation
Ito, Midori (biog.) **90:**91
"Itoqi" (Russ. mag.) 266
ITU: *see* International Telecommunica-
  tions Union
IUCN: *see* International Union for
  Conservation of Nature and Natural
  Resources
Ivens, Joris (obit.) **90:**114
Ives, Charles 279
Ives, Burl Icle Ivanhoe (obit.) **96:**86
Ivory, James (biog.) **97:**82
Ivory Coast: *see* Côte d'Ivoire
ivory gull, *or* Pagophila eburnea
  wildlife conservation 213
ivory sculpture 231
Iyer, Raghavan Narasimhan (obit.) **96:**86
Izetbegovic, Alija
  Bosnia and Herzegovina elections 398

J

J. Paul Getty Museum (Malibu, Calif.,
  U.S.)
  photography retrospective 149
Jacinto, António (obit.) **92:**68
Jack, Ian 242
Jacko, Aldan (obit.): *see* Alton, John
Jackson, The Rev. Jesse
  special report **89:**483
Jackson, Philip Douglas (biog.) **97:**78
  basketball 323
Jacksonville Jaguars (football) 344
Jacobs, Bernard B. (obit.) **97:**104
  theatre 288
Jacobs, Lou (obit.) **93:**67
Jacobson, Colin 150
Jadid, Salah, al- (obit.) **94:**67
Jaffa, Max (obit.) **92:**68
Jagannatha, temple of (Puri, India)
  conservation 309
"Jagged Little Pill" (album) 281
Jagger, Dean (obit.) **92:**68
Jagger, Mick (biog.) **90:**91
Jakarta (Indon.)
  most populous urban areas *table* 296
  violence 432
Jakes, Milos (biog.) **89:**76
Jamaat-i-Islami, *or* Islamic Society (rel.
  org.)
  "Islamic Fundamentalism" (special
    report) **94:**377
Jamaica **97:**437; **96:**425; **95:**428; **94:**486;
  93:486; **92:**478; **91:**504; **90:**520;
  89:504; **88:**504
  Caribbean unification (spotlight) 468,
    map 469
  special reports **95:**279; **89:**144
  track and field sports 362
  see also WORLD DATA
Jame-e Rohaniyat-e Mobarez, *or* JRM
  (pol. org., Iran) 432
James, Cyril Lionel Robert (obit.) **90:**114
James, P. D. (biog.) **92:**41
"James and the Giant Peach" (motion
  picture)
  computer animation (special report) 292
James C. Hormel Gay and Lesbian Center
  il. 230
Jammeh, Yahya 420
Jammu and Kashmir (state, India) 430
"Jane Eyre" (play) 288

Janeway, Eliot (obit.) **94:**67
Janowitz, Morris (obit.) **89:**98
Japan **97:**437; **96:**426; **95:**428; **94:**397;
  93:397; **92:**395; **91:**421; **90:**441;
  89:423; **88:**424
  agriculture
    fisheries 130, 382
    food processing 132
  architecture and civil engineering 137
    bridges 139
    buildings 141
  arts and entertainment
    art exhibitions 145
    literature 252
    motion pictures 295
      film awards *table* 294
    museums 231
  business and industry 154
    automobiles 156
    chemicals 161
    games and toys 164
    iron and steel 168
    machinery and machine tools 166
    man-made fibres 177
    microelectronics 169
    pharmaceuticals 173
    rubber 167
    shipbuilding 174
    wood products 179
  crime and law enforcement 227
  demographic statistics 296
    most populous urban areas *table* 296
  disasters 60
  economic affairs 188, 190
    banking 200
    international trade 194
    stock exchanges 199
  education 204
  environment 211
  family-leave health care policy 314
  international affairs
    Cambodia 403
    China 409
    Latin-American immigration
      (spotlight) 400
    Papua New Guinea 460
    South Korea 443
    United States 276
  international law 224
  newspapers 265
  space exploration 259
  special reports **96:**258; **94:**144; **91:**424;
    89:176
  sports and games
    baseball 322
    Grand Prix racing 318
    judo 352
  transportation
    intercity rail 374
    shipping and ports 373
  see also WORLD DATA
Japan Series (baseball) 322, *il.*
Japanese literature 252
Jarman, Derek (obit.) **95:**70
Jaroszewicz, Piotr (obit.) **93:**68
Jarrett, Dale
  automobile racing 319
Javacheff, Christo: *see* Christo
Javed Miandad (biog.) **93:**41
javelin throw
  track and field sports 368
Jay of Battersea, Douglas Patrick Thomas
  Jay, Baron (obit.) **97:**104
Jayasuriya, S. T. 333
Jayewardene, Junius Richard
  biography **88:**74
  obituary **97:**104
jazz 279
Jeakins, Dorothy (obit.) **96:**86
Jean Tinguely Museum (Basel, Switz.) 231
Jeffreys, Sir Harold (obit.) **90:**115
Jehovah's Witnesses 303
Jellicoe, Sir Geoffrey Alan (obit.) **97:**104
Jemison, Mae (biog.) **93:**42
Jenkins, Peter (obit.) **93:**68
"Jenna's Beach Boy" (horse) 338
Jeppesen, Elrey B. (obit.) **97:**104
Jerne, Niels Kaj (obit.) **95:**70
"Jerry Maguire" (motion picture) 289
Jerusalem
  archaeology 134
    Israel 434, *map* 435
"Jerusalem" (motion picture) 291
Jerusalem, Siegfried (biog.) **96:**59
Jesus Christ
  resurrection theories 300
"Jesus Christ Superstar" (play) 287
Jew (people)
  Swiss banks 478, 200
  World War II (special report) **96:**257
"Jewel Princess" (horse) 336
Jewell, Richard
  Olympic Games bombing suspect
    226, 495
jewelry
  Onassis auction 152
Jewish-Christian Symposium on the
  Jubilee 309
Jewish literature 251
Jiang Haicheng (obit.): *see* Ai Qing
Jiang Qing, *or* Chiang Ch'ing, *or* Luan
  Shu-meng (obit.) **92:**68
Jiang Zemin, *or* Chiang Tse-min (biog.)
  90:91
  Buddhism 309
  China 407, 409
Jiangyin (bridge, China) 139

jihad (Islam)
fundamentalism (special report) **94**:377
Jihad, Abu: *see* Wazir, Khalil Ibrahim al-
Jimmy the Greek (obit.): *see* Snyder, James G.
Jin Mao (bldg., China) 140
Jobim, Antônio Carlos (obit.) **95**:70
Jobs, Steven 182
Jochum, Eugen (obit.) **88**:99
Joffrey, Robert (obit.) **89**:96
Joffrey Ballet of Chicago (Am. ballet co.) 282
Johansson, Olof 477
John, Errol (obit.) **89**:98
"John Gabriel Borkman" (play) 286
John Paul II (pope)
evolution 134
Roman Catholic Church 306
Slovenia visit 472
Vatican City State 500
"Johns" (motion picture) 290
Johnson, Ben (biog.) **88**:74
Johnson, Clarence Leonard (obit.) **91**:99
Johnson, D. Roosevelt 445
Johnson, Daniel 404
Johnson, Eleanor Murdock (obit.) **88**:99
Johnson, Francis Benjamin (obit.) **97**:104
Johnson, Harald Norlin (obit.) **97**:105
Johnson, Judy (obit.) **90**:115
Johnson, Louis Albert (obit.) **89**:98
Johnson, Michael Duane (biog.) **96**:60
1996 Summer Olympic champions *table* **97**:367
track and field 362, 365
Johnson, Philip
new cathedral 301
Johnson, Richard *il.* 317
"JOIDES Resolution" (ship)
oceanography 184, 187
Jonassaint, Émile (obit.) **96**:86
Jonathan, Chief Joseph Leabua (obit.) **88**:99
Jones, Andruw 320
Jones, David 243
Jones, E. Edward 302
Jones, Loree Jon 326
Jones, Paula Corbin 490
Jones, Quincy (biog.) **91**:73
Jones, Roy 329
Jones, Steve 347
Jordan **97**:439; **96**:429; **95**:431; **94**:386; **93**:387; **92**:384; **91**:410; **90**:430; **89**:413; **88**:413
Israel 434
land mines *map* 275
see also WORLD DATA
Jordan, Barbara Charline (obit.) **97**:105
Jordan, Jim (obit.) **89**:99
Jordan, Michael (biogs.) **94**:42; **89**:76
basketball 323, *il.*
motion pictures 293
Jorgensen, Christine (obit.) **90**:115
Joseph, Helen Beatrice May (obit.) **93**:68
Joseph of Portsoken, Keith Sinjohn Joseph (obit.) **95**:70
Josephson, Karen (biog.) **93**:42
Josephson, Sarah (biog.) **93**:42
Jouhaud, Gen. Edmond (obit.) **96**:86
"Journal" (Zaiciu) 251
journalism
U.K. court decision 225
see also magazines; newspapers
Jouvenel des Ursins, Bertrand de (obit.) **88**:99
Joyner-Kersee, Jackie (biog.) **88**:74
Joys v. Minister of National Revenue
forfeiture laws 225
JRM (pol. org., Iran): *see* Jame-e Rohaniyat-e Mobarez
Juan de Borbón, *or* Juan Carlos Teresa Silverio Alfonso de Borbón y Battenberg, Conde de Barcelona (obit.) **94**:68
Judaism 308
religion statistics *table* 311
Southern Baptist Convention 302
special reports **96**:257; **94**:263; **92**:261
"Jude" (motion picture) 290
judo **97**:352; **96**:332; **95**:311
1996 Summer Olympic champions *table* **97**:366
Julia, Raul (obit.) **95**:70
"Julia Margaret Cameron: The Creative Process" (retrospective)
photography 149
junk bond
special report **91**:176
Jupiter (planet)
exploration 256, 259
Juppé, Alain 419
Justice, Department of (U.S.)
radio regulations 265
Justicialist National Movement, *or* Peronist, *or* PJ (pol. party, Arg.) 390
Jutra, Claude (obit.) **88**:100
Juventus (soccer) 340, 341
JVC Jazz Festival 279

K

Kabalevsky, Dmitry Borisovich (obit.) **88**:100
Kabbah, Ahmad Tejan 471
Kabua, Amata (obit.) **97**:105
Marshall Islands 449
Kabul (Afg.) 388
Kaczynski, Theodore J.
crime and law enforcement 228, 495
Kadar, Janos (obit.) **90**:115
Kades, Charles Louis (obit.) **97**:105
Kadlečik, Ivan 250
Kadoorie, Lawrence Kadoorie, Baron (obit.) **94**:68
Kafelnikov, Yevgeny 361
"Kafka's Chimp" (opera) 278
Kaga, Otohiko 252, *il.*
Kagame, Paul (biog.) **95**:47
Kaganovich, Lazar Moiseyevich **92**:68
Kahane, Meir (obit.) **91**:99
Kahurangi National Park (natl. park, N.Z.)
wildlife conservation 213
Kaifu, Toshiki (biog.) **91**:73
Kallai, Gyula (obit.) **97**:105
Kamougue, Abdelkader Wadal 407
Kampuchea: *see* Cambodia
Kamsky, Gata 330, *il.*
Kanar, Tsvi 251
Kanemaru, Shin (obit.) **97**:105
"Kansas City" (motion picture) 280, 289
Kapoor, Raj (obit.) **89**:99
Karachi (Pak.)
most populous urban areas *table* 296
Karadzic, Radovan (biog.) **97**:78
war crimes violations 227, 315, 377
Karajan, Herbert von (obit.) **90**:115
Karami, Rashid Abdul Hamid (obit.) **88**:100
Karan, Donna (biog.) **94**:42
Kardar, Abdul Hafeez (obit.) **97**:105
Karelin, Aleksandr (biog.) **97**:78
wrestling 370
Karimov, Islam 500
Karjalainen, Ahti Kalle Samuli (obit.) **91**:99
Karkheh Dam (dam, Iran) 141
Karmal, Babrak (obit.) **97**:105
Karpov, Anatoly 330, *il.*
Kashmir (state, India)
Pakistan 460
Kasinga, Fauziya 316
Kasischke, Laura 241
Kaslik, Vaclav (obit.) **90**:116
Kasparov, Garry 182
chess 330
Kateb, Yacine (obit.) **90**:116
"Kathapurushan" (motion picture) 295
Katzenberg, Jeffrey (biog.) **96**:60
Kaufman, Gerald Bernard (biog.) **92**:41
Kaufman, Irving Robert (obit.) **93**:68
Kaunda, Kenneth 504
Kawabuchi, Saburo (biog.) **94**:43
Kay, Ulysses Simpson (obit.) **96**:86
Kay-Bee Toys (Am. co.) 164
Kaye, Danny (obit.) **88**:100
Kaye, Nora (obit.) **88**:100
Kaye, Sammy (obit.) **88**:100
Kaysone Phomvihan (obit.) **93**:68
Kazakstan, *or* Kazakhstan **97**:439; **96**:429; **95**:431; **94**:406; **93**:406
Central Asian republics (spotlight) 480, *map* 481
new flag *illus.* **93**:345
see also WORLD DATA
Kazin, Alfred 241
KDP (Kurdish pol. org.): *see* Kurdistan Democratic Party
Keane, Molly, *or* Mary Nesta Skrine, *or* M. J. Farrell (obit.) **97**:105
Keating, Charles H. (biog.) **91**:73
Keating, Paul John (biogs.) **93**:42; **88**:75
Australia 391
Keeler, Ruby (obit.) **94**:68
Keene, Christopher (obit.) **96**:86
Kehrle, Karl (obit.): *see* Brother Adam
Kelly, Eugene Curran, *or* Gene Kelly (obit.) **97**:106
Kelly, Jim (biog.) **92**:42
Kelly, Petra (obit.) **93**:68
Kemal, Mustafa: *see* Ataturk, Kemal
Kemal, Yashar (biog.) **96**:60
Turkish literature 251
Kemp, Jack French (biogs.) **97**:78; **90**:91
presidential campaign (special report) 494
Kempff, Wilhelm Walter Friedrich (obit.) **92**:68
Kemp's ridley, *or* Lepidochelys kempii
wildlife conservation 213
Kendall, Harry Way (biog.) **91**:73
Kendricks, Eddie (obit.) **93**:68
Kengo wa Dondo, Léon 467
Kennedy, Anthony (biog.) **89**:76
Kennedy, John Arthur (obit.) **91**:99
Kennedy, John Fitzgerald
antiquarian books 151
collectibles auction 152
Kennedy, Rose Elizabeth Fitzgerald (obit.) **96**:86
Kentucky, University of (U.S.)
basketball 323
Kentucky Derby (horse racing) 336
Kenya **97**:440; **96**:430; **95**:432; **94**:360; **93**:362; **92**:358; **91**:387; **90**:408; **89**:390; **88**:391
disasters 61
education 206
international affairs
Tanzania 482
Uganda 485
prisons and penology 229
sports and games
cross country running 370
track and field sports 368
see also WORLD DATA
Kenya Airways (Ken. co.) 440
Keogh, Eugene James (obit.) **90**:116
Kérékou, Mathieu 397
Kerin, John Charles (biog.) **92**:42
Kernot, Cheryl (biog.) **95**:47
Kerr, Sir John Robert (obit.) **92**:69
Kerr, Walter Francis (obit.) **97**:106
theatre 288
Kessler, David Aaron (biog.) **92**:42
Kevorkian, Jack (biog.) **94**:43
Kew Gardens (U.K.)
botany 236
Keyserling, Leon H. (obit.) **88**:100
Khahour Dam (dam, Syr.) 141
Khalaf, Salah (obit.) **92**:69
Khaled (biog.) **96**:60
Khaled, Sheikh Hassan (obit.) **90**:116
Khamenei, Ayatollah Sayyed Ali 432
Khan, Imran *il.* 459
Khan, Jahangir (biog.) **91**:74
Khan, Jansher 357
Khan, Louis I. 137
Khan, Nusrat Fateh Ali (biog.) **97**:79
Khariton, Yuly Borisovich (obit.) **97**:106
Khaury, Herbert (obit.): *see* Tiny Tim
Khmer Nation Party, *or* KNP (pol. party, Camb.) 403
Khmer Rouge (Camb. pol. group) 403, *il.*
Khoei, Abolqassem al- (obit.) **93**:69
Khomeini, Hojatoleslam Seyled Ahmad (obit.) **96**:87
Khomeini, Ruhollah (obit.) **90**:116
"Islamic Fundamentalism" (special report) **94**:377
Kiarostami, Abbas (biog.) **97**:79
Kidman, Nicole
film awards *table* 294
kidnapping
Slovakia 472
Spain 475
Yemen 502
Kienholz, Edward (obit.) **95**:70
art exhibit 145
Kiesinger, Kurt Georg (obit.) **89**:99
Kieslowski, Krzysztof
biography **96**:61
obituary **97**:106
Kiet, Vo Van 501
"Kijken is bekeken worden" (Komrij) 245
"Kill Bear Comes Home" (opera) 278
killer T cell, *or* cytotoxic T cell
immune system research 64
Killian, James Rhyne, Jr. (obit.) **89**:99
Kim Dae Jung 441
Kim Il Sung (obit.) **95**:71
Kim Jong Il (biog.) **95**:48
Kim Kyung Wook 317
Kim Sang-Man (obit.) **95**:71
Kim Woo Choong 441
Kim Young Sam (biog.) **94**:43
Japan 439
North Korea 440
South Korea 443
King, Albert (obit.) **93**:69
King, B. B. (biog.) **93**:42
King, Cecil Harmsworth (obit.) **88**:101
King Abdul Aziz Air Base (airport, Saud.-Arab.)
terrorist attack 226
"King of Babylon Shall Not Come Against You, The" (Garrett) 240
"King of Hearts" (opera) 278
Kingsley, Sidney, *or* Sidney Kirshner (obit.) **96**:87
Kinnear, Roy Mitchell (obit.) **89**:99
Kinnicutt, Dorothy May: *see* Parish, Sister
Kinnock, Neil Gordon (biogs.) **92**:42; **90**:92
Kinski, Klaus (obit.) **92**:69
Kinugasa, Sachio (biog.) **88**:75
Kipketer, Wilson 369
Kipkoech, Paul (obit.) **96**:87
Kiraly, Karch (biog.) **97**:79
volleyball 370
Kirby, Jack (obit.) **95**:71
Kirgizia: *see* Kyrgyzstan
Kiribati **97**:440; **96**:431; **95**:432; **94**:496; **93**:496; **92**:488; **91**:515; **90**:531; **89**:515; **88**:515
see also WORLD DATA
Kirkwood, James (obit.) **90**:116
Kirostami, Abbas: *see* Kiarostami, Abbas
Kirsch, Sarah 245
Kirshner, Sidney (obit.): *see* Kingsley, Sidney
Kirst, Hans Helmut (obit.) **90**:116
Kirstein, Lincoln Edward (obit.) **97**:106
dance 282
Kirsten, Dorothy (obit.) **93**:69
Kishi, Nobusuke (obit.) **88**:101
Kitagawa, Joseph Mitsou (obit.) **93**:69
Kitaro (biog.) **88**:75
Kitovani, Tengiz 420
Kittredge, William 241
Kivu (dist., Zaire) 504
Kjærstad, Jan 245
Kjellstrand, Torsten 150
Klaus, Vaclav 412
Kleihues, Josef Paul 137
Klein, Joe 268, *il.*
Kliban, Bernard (obit.) **91**:99
Klineberg, Otto (obit.) **93**:69
Klos, Elmar (obit.) **94**:68
Klot, Lillian (obit.): *see* Brown, Georgia
Kluszewski, Ted (obit.) **89**:99
Kmart Corporation (Am. co.) 174
KMT (pol. party, Tai.): *see* Kuomintang
Kngwarreye, Emily Kame (obit.) **97**:107
Knight, James L. (obit.) **92**:69
Knight, N. V. 332
Knitting Factory (nightclub, N.Y.C., N.Y., U.S.)
jazz 279
Knoll, Erwin (obit.) **95**:71
Knopfler, Mark 280
KNP (pol. party, Camb.): *see* Khmer Nation Party
Kobalia, Loti 421
Kobayashi, Koji (obit.) **97**:107
Kobayashi, Masaki (obit.) **97**:107
Koc, Vehbi (obit.) **97**:107
Kocharyan, Robert 393
Kochno, Boris (obit.) **91**:99
Kodak Company (Am. corp.): *see* Eastman Kodak Company
Kodjo, Edem 483
Koechlin-Smythe, Patricia Rosemary (obit.): *see* Smythe, Pat
Koeppen, Wolfgang 245
Kohl, Helmut (biogs.) **95**:48; **91**:74
Germany 424
Köhler, Georges J. F. (obit.) **96**:87
Kohr, Leopold (obit.) **95**:71
Kokis, Sergio 247
Kokkonen, Joonas (obit.) **97**:107
Kolmogorov, Andrey Nikolayevich (obit.) **88**:101
Kolodin, Irving (obit.) **89**:99
"Kolya" (motion picture) 295
Komar, Chris (obit.) **97**:107
Komen, Daniel 369
Komrij, Gerrit 245
Konitz, Lee 279
Koop, Charles Everett (biog.) **88**:75
Kopal, Zdenek (obit.) **94**:68
Korea, Democratic People's Republic of, *or* North Korea **97**:440; **96**:431; **95**:432; **94**:399; **93**:400; **92**:398; **91**:427; **90**:445; **89**:427; **88**:427
agriculture and food supplies 125
military affairs 276
South Korea 443
see also WORLD DATA
Korea, Republic of, *or* South Korea **97**:441; **96**:431; **95**:434; **94**:400; **93**:400; **92**:398; **91**:426; **90**:444; **89**:427; **88**:427
business and industry
chemicals 161
machinery and machine tools 166
rubber 167
shipbuilding 174
disasters 60
economic affairs 194
stock exchanges 199
international affairs
Japan 439
North Korea 440
military affairs 276
land mines (special report) 275
most populous urban areas *table* 296
motion pictures 295
sports and games
archery 317
badminton 320
see also WORLD DATA
Koruturk, Fahri S. (obit.) **88**:101
Kosinski, Jerzy Nikodem (obit.) **92**:69
Kosovo (prov., Yugos.)
Albanian integration 503
Koss, Johan Olav (biog.) **95**:48
special report **95**:308
Kosterlitz, Hans Walter (obit.) **97**:107
Koun, Karolos (obit.) **88**:101
Kountché, Gen. Seyni (obit.) **88**:101
Kovac, Michal 472
Koyen-Tsedik, Elisheve 251
Kozioł, Urszula 250
Kozyrev, Andrey 465
Krajicek, Richard 361
Krajisnik, Momcilo 398
Krasner, Louis (obit.) **96**:87
Kray, Ronald, *or* Ronnie Kray (obit.) **96**:87
Kreditni Banka Plzen (bank, Czech Republic) 200
Kreisky, Bruno (obit.) **91**:99
Krenek, Ernst (obit.) **92**:69
Krige, Uys (obit.) **88**:101
Krol, John Joseph Cardinal (obit.) **97**:107
Kronberger, Petra (biog.) **92**:42
krone (currency) 459
Krone, Julie (biog.) **94**:43
Kronstam, Henning (obit.) **96**:87
Kroto, Sir Harold W.
Nobel Prize 63
Krugman, Saul (obit.) **96**:87
Krzaklewski, Marian 462
Krzyzewski, Mike (biog.) **93**:43
Kubelik, Rafael Jeronym (obit.) **97**:107
Kuchma, Leonid Danylovych (biog.) **95**:49
Ukraine 486
Kuenn, Harvey Edward (obit.) **89**:99
Kufuor, John 425
Kuhn, Margaret E., *or* Maggie Kuhn (obit.) **96**:87
Kuhn, Thomas S. (obit.) **97**:107
Kulwicki, Alan (obit.) **94**:68
Kumar, Raaj, *or* Kulbhushan Nath Pandit (obit.) **97**:107
Kumaratunga, Chandrika Bandaranaike (biog.) **95**:49

References giving only a page number in light type are for the current edition.

Kumbernuss, Astrid 370
Kumin, Maxine 241
Kunayev, Dinmukhamed Akhmedovich (obit.) 94:68
Kung Li: *see* Gong Li
Kunstler, James Howard
  English literature 241
Kunstler, William Moses (obit.) 96:87
"Künstlerroman, Schumanns Schatten" (Härtling) 245
Kuomintang, *or* KMT, *or* Nationalist Party (pol. party, Tai.) 478
Kurd (people) *il.* 433
  human rights issues 315
  military conflict 375, 433
  special report 92:375
Kurdish Workers' Party, *or* PKK (pol. org.) 271
  Turkey 484
Kurdistan Democratic Party, *or* Kurdish Democratic Party, *or* KDP (Kurdish pol. org.)
  Iran 433
  Iraq 375, 433
  military affairs 272
Kuril Islands (isls., Russ.)
  Japan 439
Kurtzman, Harvey (obit.) 94:68
Kusch, Polykarp (obit.) 94:69
Kushner, Aleksandr 249
Kushner, Tony (biog.) 94:44
Kutner, Luis (obit.) 94:69
Kuwait 97:443; 96:433; 95:435; 94:387; 93:387; 92:385; 91:411; 90:431; 89:414; 88:414
  see also WORLD DATA
Kuwait University (univ., Kuw.)
  gender segregation 443
Kuznetsov, Vasily Vasilyevich (obit.) 91:100
Kwan, Michelle 350
Kwasniewski, Aleksander (biog.) 96:61
Kyrgyzstan, *or* Kirgizia 97:443; 96:433; 95:435; 94:406; 93:407
  Central Asian republics (spotlight) 481, *map*
  new flag *illus.* 93:345
  see also WORLD DATA

L

La Salle, René-Robert Cavelier, Sieur de
  archaeology 136
La-Z-Boy Companies (Am. co.)
  furniture industry 165
Laberge, Marie 247
Labonte, Terry 319
Laborit, Henri Marie (obit.) 96:87
Labour-Management Relations 97:201; 96:188; 95:203; 94:201; 93:201; 92:200; 91:229; 90:247; 89:230; 88:232
  baseball 320
  business and industry
    automobiles 157
    clothing 155
    rubber 167
  Germany 421
  special report 94:203
  Switzerland 478
Labour Party (pol. party, N.Z.) 456
Labour Party (pol. party, U.K.) 488
  labour-management relations 201
labour union: *see* trade union
Lachs, Manfred (obit.) 94:69
LaCock, Joanne (obit.): *see* Dru, Joanne
Lacoste, Jean-René (obit.) 97:107
Lacoursière, Jacques 247
Lacroix, Christian (biog.) 88:76
Ladany, Laszlo (obit.) 91:100
Ladies' Professional Golf Association, *or* LPGA (U.S.) 347
Laferrière, Dany 247
Laffitte, Louis (obit.): *see* Curtis, Jean-Louis
Lafontaine, Oskar (biog.) 91:74
Lagos (Nig.)
  most populous urban areas *table* 296
Lahbabi, Mohammed Aziz (obit.) 94:69
Laing, Hugh 89:99
Laing, Ronald David (obit.) 90:116
Lalande 21185 (star)
  astronomy 258
Lalic, Ivan V. (obit.) 97:107
Lamborghini, Ferruccio (obit.) 94:69
"Lammtarra" (horse) 337
Lamont, Corliss (obit.) 96:87
Lamont, Norman (biog.) 92:43
Lamour, Dorothy, *or* Mary Leta Dorothy Slaton (obit.) 97:108
L'Amour, Louis Dearborn (obit.) 89:100
lamp
  auctions and collectibles 152
Lan, Yang: *see* Yang Lan
Lancaster, Burton Stephen (obit.) 95:71
Land, Edwin Herbert (obit.) 92:70
land mine
  "Combating the Land Mine Scourge" (special report) 97:274, *map* 275
  Geneva Convention 376
  Mozambique 454
  see also antipersonnel mine
Landfill Tax (U.K.) 207
Landon, Alfred Mossman (obit.) 88:102

Landon, Michael (obit.) 92:70
Landsbergis, Vytautas (biog.) 91:74
landslide
  natural disasters 60
Landsorganisation (labour org., Swed.) 477
Lane, Dame Elizabeth Kathleen (obit.) 89:100
Lange-Nielsen, Sissel 245
Langmuir, Alexander (obit.) 94:69
Lansdale, Edward G. (obit.) 88:102
Lantz, Walter (obit.) 95:72
Lanusse, Alejandro Agustín (obit.) 97:108
Lao People's Revolutionary Party (pol. party, Laos) 443
Laos 97:443; 96:433; 95:436; 94:413; 93:414; 92:410; 91:437; 90:455; 89:439; 88:439
  ASEAN membership 380
  refugees 297
  see also WORLD DATA
Lara, Brian (biog.) 95:49
Laroche, Guy (obit.) 90:117
Larsen, Jeanne 241
Larson, Jonathan (obit.) 97:108
  theatre 287
LaRue, Albert, *or* Lash LaRue (obit.) 97:108
Larwood, Harold (obit.) 96:87
Lasch, Christopher (obit.) 95:72
laser-induced fluorescence spectroscopy 254
laser surgery
  cardiovascular disease 219
Lash, Joseph P. (obit.) 88:102
Lasseter, John 292
Lassiter, Luther (obit.) 89:100
"Last of the Savages, The" (McInerney) 240
"Last Orders" (Swift) 243
"Last Seen" (Cohen) 242
"Last Thing He Wanted, The" (Didion) 240
Latin-American affairs 94:474; 93:474; 92:464; 91:492; 90:507; 89:491; 88:491
  agriculture 129
    fisheries 130
  arts and entertainment
    art auctions 150
    literature 248
    motion pictures 295
  botanical gardens 214
  business and industry
    chemicals 161
    microelectronics 169
    paints and varnishes 172
  demography 296
  disasters 60
  economic affairs 188, 193
  Japanese immigration (spotlight) 400
  magazines 266
  military affairs 276
    land mines (special report) 275
  prisons and penology 229
  refugees 297
  religion statistics *table* 311
  special reports 95:173, 279; 92:465; 89:144
  sports and games
    association football 341
    baseball 322
    basketball 325
  transportation
    freight and pipelines 373
    intercity rail 374
    roads and traffic 374
  see also individual countries by name
Latin-American literature 248
  postmodernism (special report) 96:234
Lattimore, Owen (obit.) 90:117
Latvia 97:444; 96:434; 95:436; 94:443; 93:445; 92:434
  ice hockey 350
  new flag *illus.* 92:343
  unemployment policy 314
  see also WORLD DATA
launch vehicle
  space exploration 260
Laurence, Margaret (obit.) 88:102
Laurent, Paul (obit.) 91:100
Lausen, John Rhea (obit.): *see* Lawson, Yank
Lavagetto, Harry Arthur (obit.) 91:100
Lavigne, Juan Carlos 303
Lavin, Mary (obit.) 97:108
Law 97:223; 96:210; 95:204; 94:204; 93:203; 92:202; 91:231; 90:249; 89:232; 88:234
  agriculture 125
  Contract with America (special report) 96:493
  labour-management relations 201
  religion 300
  see also international law; individual countries by name
Law Enforcement 97:228; 96:215; 95:145; 94:116; 93:115; 92:113; 91:143; 90:160; 89:142; 88:142
  Belgium 396
  Haiti 427, *il.* 228
  Netherlands, The 456
  Saudi Arabia 470
  United States 495
lawn bowls 97:352; 96:332; 95:311; 94:304; 93:305; 92:301; 91:331; 90:350; 89:332; 88:334
Lawrence, Carmen Mary (biog.) 96:61

Lawson, Nigel Thomas (biog.) 89:77
Lawson, Yank, *or* John Rhea Lausen (obit.) 96:88
Lawton, Thomas (obit.) 97:108
Laye, Evelyn, *or* Elsie Evelyn Lay (obit.) 97:108
Lazarenko, Pavlo 486
Lazier, Buddy 319
LCVM: *see* lymphocytic choriomeningitis virus
LDC: *see* less developed country
LDDP (pol. party, Lith.): *see* Lithuanian Democratic Labor Party
LDP (pol. party, Japan): *see* Liberal Democratic Party
LDS: *see* Church of Jesus Christ of Latter-day Saints
le Carré, John 243
Le Duc Tho (obit.) 91:100
Le Gallienne, Eva (obit.) 92:70
Le Mai (obit.) 97:108
Le Poulain, Jean (obit.) 89:100
Leach, Sir Edmund Ronald (obit.) 90:117
lead
  environmental hazards 211
  mining 170
leaf-cutting ant, *or* Atta
  entomology 234
Leakey, Mary Douglas (obit.) 97:108
Leakey, Richard (biog.) 95:49
Lean, Sir David (obit.) 92:70
Léandre, Joëlle 279
Lear, Frances (obit.) 97:109
Learn, Bob, Jr. 326
Leary, Timothy (obit.) 97:109
leatherback turtle, *or* Dermochelys coriacea
  wildlife conservation 213
"Leaving Las Vegas" (motion picture)
  film awards *table* 294
Lebanon 97:445; 96:434; 95:437; 94:387; 93:388; 92:386; 91:411; 90:431; 89:414; 88:414
  Israel 434, 439
  literature 252
  Syria 478
  see also WORLD DATA
Lebed, Aleksandr Ivanovich (biog.) 97:80
  military affairs 271
  Russia 375, 464
Lebow, Fred (obit.) 95:72
Lecanuet, Jean-Adrien-François (obit.) 94:69
Leckie, Rev. Will *il.* 301
Lederman, Leon Max (biog.) 89:77
Lee, David
  Nobel Prize 64
Lee, Jennie (obit.) 89:100
Lee, Spike (biog.) 90:92
  motion pictures 289
Lee Byung Chull (obit.) 88:102
Lee Huan (biog.) 88:76
Lee Kun Hee (biog.) 97:80
  South Korea 441
Lee Lai Shan 355, 381
Lee Teng-hui (biog.) 89:77
  China 409
  "Encyclopædia Britannica" interview (commentary) 97:6
  Taiwan 7, 478
Lefebvre, Marcel-François
  biography 89:77
  obituary 92:71
"Legacy of 1991: Phoenix or Empty Ashes?" (feature article) 92:4
Legault, Josée 247
Léger, Paul-Emile (obit.) 92:71
Leghari, Farooq 459
Lehman, Tom 347
Lehmann, Rosamond Nina (obit.) 91:100
Lehn, Jean-Marie (biog.) 88:76
Leija, Jesse James 330
Leinsdorf, Erich (obit.) 94:69
Leiris, Michel Julien (obit.) 91:100
Lejeune, Jérôme-Jean-Louis-Marie (obit.) 95:72
Leloir, Luis Federico (obit.) 88:102
Lelouch, Claude
  film awards *table* 294
Lelyveld, Arthur (obit.) 97:109
LeMay, Curtis Emerson (obit.) 91:101
Lemieux, Mario (biog.) 92:43
  ice hockey 349
Lemnitzer, Lyman Louis (obit.) 89:100
LeMond, Greg (biog.) 90:92
Lenihan, Brian Joseph (obit.) 96:88
Lennep, Emile van (obit.) 97:109
Leno, Jay (biog.) 93:43
Leone, Sergio (obit.) 90:117
Leonov, Leonid Maksimovich (obit.) 95:72
Lepage, Robert (biog.) 95:50
  theatre 287
Lepidochelys kempii: *see* Kemp's ridley
Lerner, Maxwell Alan (obit.) 93:69
LeRoy, Mervyn (obit.) 88:102
"Les Misérables" (motion picture): *see* "Misérables, Les"
lesbian: *see* homosexuality
Lesotho 97:445; 96:435; 95:437; 94:361; 93:363; 92:359; 91:388; 90:408; 89:391; 88:392
  see also WORLD DATA
Lesourne, Jacques (biog.) 92:43
less developed country, *or* less industrialized country, *or* Third World, *or* LDC
  agriculture and food supplies 123, 129, *tables* 123, 127

demography 296
economic affairs 188, 193, *tables* 192, 193
environmental issues 210
literacy programs 203
manufacturing *table* 153
microbanking 200
roads 142
social protection 314
special reports 96:287; 95:172, 278; 94:144
lesser masked owl, *or* Tyto sororcula
  wildlife conservation 213
Letsie III
  Lesotho 445
Letterman, David (biog.) 94:44
lev (currency) 401
"Level 5" (motion picture) 291
Lever of Manchester, Harold Lever, Baron (obit.) 96:88
Lévesque, René (obit.) 88:102
Levi, Rabbi Isaac *il.* 308
Levi, Primo (obit.) 88:103
Lévinas, Emmanuel (obit.) 96:88
Levitt, William Jaird (obit.) 95:72
Levitz (Am. co.)
  furniture retailers 165
Levy, David (Can. astron.)
  biography 95:57
Levy, David (Isr. pol.)
  biography 91:75
Lewis, Carl 362, 365
  1996 Summer Olympic champions *table* 97:367
Lewis, Flora
  "Legacy of 1991: Phoenix or Empty Ashes?" (feature article) 92:4
Lewis, Henry Jay (obit.) 97:109
Lewis, Reginald F. (obit.) 94:70
Lewis, Sir William Arthur (obit.) 92:71
Lexa, Ivan 472
Lexcen, Ben (obit.) 89:100
Lezgin (people)
  Azerbaijan 393
Li Peng, *or* Li P'eng (biog.) 89:77
  aerospace industry 409, 420
Li Xiannian, *or* Li Hsien-nien (obit.) 93:69
Li Xiaoshuang 348
Li Zhisui, *or* Li Chih-sui (obit.) 96:88
liana (plant)
  wildlife conservation 213
Liang Shih-Ch'iu (obit.) 88:103
Liao Ch'en-yün (obit.): *see* Chen Yun
Liberace (obit.) 88:103
Liberal Democratic Party, *or* LDP (pol. party, Japan) 437
Liberal Front Party, *or* PFL (pol. party, Braz.) 401
Liberal Party (pol. party, Austr.) 392
Liberal Party (pol. party, Maced.) 446
Liberation Tigers of Tamil Eelam (rev. org., Sri Lanka): *see* Tamil Tigers
Liberia 97:445; 96:436; 95:438; 94:362; 93:363; 92:360; 91:388; 90:409; 89:392; 88:392
  agriculture and food supplies 124
  military affairs 276
  refugees 297
  see also WORLD DATA
"Libertarias" (motion picture) 291
Libeskind, Daniel 138
Libraries 97:230; 96:217; 95:208; 94:208; 93:206; 92:206; 91:234; 90:252; 89:235; 88:238
  architecture 137
  digitized visual images 149
  Egypt 140
  Internet 181
Libuda, Reinhard (obit.) 97:109
Libya 97:446; 96:436; 95:438; 94:388; 93:389; 92:387; 91:412; 90:432; 89:415; 88:415
  Great Man-Made River 141, *map*
  military affairs 273
  petroleum industry 163
  special report 94:377
  Turkey 484
  United States 496
  see also WORLD DATA
Lidman, Sara 245
Liechtenstein 97:446; 96:437; 95:439; 94:443; 93:445; 92:435; 91:458; 90:474; 89:458; 88:457
  see also WORLD DATA
Lien Chan 478
Liepa, Maris-Rudolf Eduardovich (obit.) 90:117
Life and Microgravity Spacelab
  space exploration 258
life expectancy 296
  Clock genes 232
  Eastern Europe (spotlight) 96:461
life insurance 165
  genetic testing issues 218
"Life of Matthew Arnold, A" (Murray) 243
Life Sciences 97:232; 96:219; 95:209; 94:213; 93:207; 92:207; 91:235; 90:253; 89:236; 88:238
Lifestyle Furnishings International, *or* Masco Home Furnishings (Am. co.)
  furniture industry 165
light metals 168
"Like Grains of Sand" (motion picture) 295
"Lila dit ça" (Chimo) 246
"Lili" (hurricane) 60
  Cuba 412

Lillehammer (Nor.)
  Winter Olympic Games (special report) **95**:308
Lillie, Beatrice Gladys (obit.) **90**:117
Lim, Alfredo (biog.) **94**:44
Lima (Peru)
  most populous urban areas *table* 296
Limbaugh, Rush (biog.) **94**:44
Lin, Maya (biog.) **95**:50
Lincoln, Evelyn Norton (obit.) **96**:88
Lincoln Park Zoo (Chicago, Ill., U.S.)
  special report **94**:111
Lindfors, Viveca, *or* Elsa Viveca Torstensdotter Lindfors (obit.) **96**:88
Lindwall, Raymond Russell (obit.) **97**:109
line-item veto
  United States 491
Lineker, Gary Winston (biog.) **93**:43
Linschoten, Robin 456
lipoprotein a
  cardiovascular disease 219
Lipponen, Paavo
  Finland 418
Lipski, Jan Jozef (obit.) **92**:71
Lipson, Paul (obit.) **97**:109
liquefied natural gas, *or* LNG
  Oman 459
  Trinidad and Tobago 483
liquid
  superfluid research 64
Liquid Schintillator Neutrino Detector, *or* LSND 255
liquor: *see* spirits
Listyev, Vladislav Nikolayevich (obit.) **96**:88
"Lit de Justice" (horse) 335
literacy 203
Literature 97:240; **96**:226; **95**:218; **94**:216; **93**:214; **92**:214; **91**:242; **90**:260; **89**:243; **88**:245
  book publishing 267
  classical music 279
  jazz 280
  Nobel Prize 63
  see also specific literatures by name
Lithuania **97**:446; **96**:437; **95**:439; **94**:444; **93**:445; **92**:435
  Latvia 444
  new flag *illus.* **92**:343
  see also WORLD DATA
Lithuanian Democratic Labor Party, *or* LDDP (pol. party, Lith.) 446
Liu Guoliang 360
Liu Haisu (obit.) **95**:73
Liu Xiaobo 315, 408
liver transplant
  new guidelines 222
Livesay, Dorothy Kathleen May (obit.) **97**:109
livestock
  world production 129, *table* 126
lizard
  zoological research 233
Lleras Camargo, Alberto (obit.) **91**:101
Lleras Restrepo, Carlos (obit.) **95**:73
Lloyd, Seton Howard Frederick (obit.) **97**:109
Lloyd's of London (insurance co., U.K.) 165
Lloyd's Register of Shipping 174
LME (U.K.): *see* London Metal Exchange
LNG: *see* liquefied natural gas
Lo-Johansson, (Karl) Ivar (obit.) **91**:101
Lobo, Rebecca (biog.) **96**:62
Locke, Bobby (obit.) **88**:103
Lockheed Martin Corporation (Am. corp.)
  aerospace industry 260
Lockwood, Margaret Mary (obit.) **91**:101
Loewe, Frederick (obit.) **89**:100
Logan, Joshua Lockwood (obit.) **89**:101
loggerhead (turtle)
  wildlife conservation 233
logging: *see* forestry
Loihi Seamount (volcano) 184, 187
Lollapalooza (mus. festival) 281
Lomu, Jonah (biog.) **96**:62
London (Eng., U.K.)
  fashion industry 217
  mental health study 222
  tunnel construction 142
London Metal Exchange, *or* LME (U.K.) 170
London Stock Exchange (U.K.) 198
"Lone Star" (motion picture) 289
long-distance communications
  telecommunications 175
long-distance running, *or* distance running
  track and field sports 368
long jump
  track and field sports 362
Long March (Chin. hist.)
  anniversary celebration 408
Lonrho (Br. co.)
  mining 171
"Looking Back on Chechnya" (photograph) *il.* 267
"Looking for Richard" (motion picture) 290
"Looking into the Face of Evil" (documentary) 295
Lopate, Phillip 241
Lophura edwardsi: *see* Edwards's pheasant
Lorengar, Pilar, *or* Pilar Lorenza García (obit.) **97**:109
Lorentz, Pare (obit.) **93**:70
Lorenz, Konrad Zacharias (obit.) **90**:117
Lorenzo, Frank (biog.) **89**:78
Los Angeles (Calif., U.S.)
  architecture 137
  most populous urban areas *table* 296
  subway project 142
Los Angeles International Airport (Los Angeles, Calif., U.S.) *il.* 139
Lou Gehrig's disease: *see* amyotrophic lateral sclerosis
Louganis, Greg (biog.) **89**:78
"Louis Quatorze" (horse) 336
Loutit, John Freeman (obit.) **93**:70
Love, Davis 347
"Love and Other Catastrophes" (motion picture) 290
"Love Serenade" (motion picture) 290
Lovett, Lyle Pierce (biog.) **97**:81
Loving v. The United States (law case, U.S.) 225
Lowe, Edward (obit.) **96**:88
Lower, Arthur Reginald Marsden (obit.) **89**:101
Loy, Myrna (obit.) **94**:70
LPGA: *see* Ladies' Professional Golf Association
LSND: *see* Liquid Schintillator Neutrino Detector
LTTE (rev. org., Sri Lanka): *see* Tamil Tigers
Luan Shu-meng: *see* Jiang Qing
Luandrew, Albert: *see* Sunnyland Slim
Lubell, Samuel (obit.) **88**:103
Lucas, Luis Miguel González (obit.): *see* Dominguín
Luce, Claire Boothe (obit.) **88**:103
Lucent Technologies, Inc. (Am. co.) 170, 177
Lucid, Shannon W. 258, *il.*
Lucinschi, Petru 453
Ludlam, Charles (obit.) **88**:104
Ludwig, Daniel Keith (obit.) **93**:70
Ludwig, Peter (obit.) **97**:109
Luening, Otto Clarence (obit.) **97**:109
luge: *see* tobogganing
Luján, Néstor 247
Lukanov, Andrey (obit.) **97**:109
Lukas, Darrell Wayne (biog.) **96**:62
  thoroughbred racing 336
Lukashenka, Alyaksandr Hryhorevich, *or* Aleksandr Grigoryevich Lukashenko (biog.) **95**:50
  Belarus 395
Luke, Keye (obit.) **92**:71
lumber: *see* wood products
Lumbini (Nepal)
  Buddhism 309
"Lumière and Company," *or* "Lumière et Cie" (motion picture) 289
Lundkvist, Artur Nils (obit.) **92**:72
lung cancer 219
Lupino, Ida (obit.) **96**:88
Luria, Salvador Edward (obit.) **92**:72
Lusaka peace accord
  Angola 389
Lutheran Communion 303
Lutheran World Federation, *or* LWF 303
Lutoslawski, Witold (obit.) **95**:73
Luxembourg **97**:446; **96**:438; **95**:439; **94**:444; **93**:435; **92**:435; **91**:458; **90**:474; **89**:458; **88**:458
  see also WORLD DATA
Lwoff, André Michel (obit.) **95**:73
Lyceum Theatre (thea., U.K.) 287
lymphocytic choriomeningitis virus, *or* LCMV 64
Lynch, Charles Birchell (obit.) **95**:73
Lynch, David (biog.) **91**:75
Lyric Opera of Chicago
  "Der Ring des Nibelungen" 278
Lyttleton, Raymond Arthur (obit.) **96**:88
Lyubarsky, Kronid Arkadyevich (obit.) **97**:110

M

"Ma Qiao cidian" (Han Shaogong)
  Chinese literature 252
Maastricht Treaty, *or* Treaty on European Union
  Danish challenge 413
  European Union 376, 378, 379
  Germany 425
  international law 224
  special report **93**:421
  United Kingdom 488
  see also economic and monetary union
"Macadam Tribu" (motion picture) 295
McAnally, Ray (obit.) **90**:118
"Macarena" (song) 281
Macau (terr., Port.) 381
MacBeth, George Mann (obit.) **93**:70
McBride, Patricia (biog.) **90**:92
MacBride, Sean (obit.) **89**:101
McCaffrey, Barry R. 495
MacCaig, Norman Alexander (obit.) **97**:110
McCampbell, David (obit.) **97**:110
McCarthy, Mary Therese (obit.) **90**:118
McCarthy, William Joseph (biog.) **89**:78
McClintock, Barbara (obit.) **93**:70
McCloy, John Jay (obit.) **90**:118
McClure, Doug (obit.) **96**:88
McCluskie, Samuel Joseph (obit.) **96**:88
MacColl, Ewan, *or* James Henry Miller (obit.) **90**:118
McCone, John Alex (obit.) **92**:72
McCracken, Elizabeth 241
McCracken, James Eugene (obit.) **89**:101
McCrea, Joel Albert (obit.) **91**:101
McDonagh, Martin 285
McDonald's (Am. co.)
  advertising 154
McDonnell Douglas (Am. co.)
  aerospace industry 155
Macedonia **97**:446; **96**:438; **95**:440; **94**:444; **93**:446
  Greece 426
  new flag *il.* **96**:365; **93**:345
  see also WORLD DATA
"Macedonians: The Northern Greeks and the Era of Alexander the Great, The" (art exhibit) 145
McEntire, Reba (biog.) **95**:51
McFarland, George Robert Phillips (obit.) **94**:70
McFerrin, Bobby (biog.) **96**:63
McGann, Bernie 279
McGeown, Patrick (obit.) **97**:110
McGhee, Walter Brown (obit.) **97**:110
MacGill-Eain, Somhairle (obit.): *see* Maclean, Sorley
McGregor, Chris 280
machinery and machine tools 166
"Macho Camacho's Beat," *or* "La quaracha del macho Camacho" (Sánchez)
  Latin-American literature (special report) **96**:234
McInerney, Jay 240
McIntire, Ray (obit.) **97**:110
Macintosh (computers) 182
  Motorola licensing agreement 169
McKay, David Stewart (biog.) **97**:81
  paleontology 238
Mackay of Clashfern, Lord (biog.) **90**:93
McKellen, Sir Ian (biog.) **92**:43
MacKenzie, Kelvin (biog.) **93**:44
MacKenzie, Lewis (biog.) **94**:45
Mackerras, Charles 277
McKinley, Raymond Frederick (obit.) **96**:89
Mackintosh, Charles Rennie
  art exhibitions (special report) 146
McKissick, Floyd Bixler, Sr. (obit.) **92**:72
McLachlan, Ian 392
McLaren, Norman (obit.) **88**:104
McLaughlin, Audrey (biog.) **92**:44
MacLean, Alistair (obit.) **88**:104
Maclean, Sorley, *or* Somhairle MacGill-Eain (obit.) **97**:110
McLellan (galleries, Glasgow, U.K.)
  art exhibitions (special report) 146
MacLennan, John Hugh (obit.) **91**:101
Maclennon, Robert Adam Ross (biog.) **88**:77
MacLeod of Fuinary, George Fielden MacLeod (obit.) **92**:72
McMahon, Sir William (obit.) **89**:101
McManus, James 241
McMath, Virginia Katherine: *see* Rogers, Ginger
McMillan, Edwin Mattison (obit.) **92**:72
MacMillan, Sir Kenneth (obit.) **93**:71
McMillan, Terry (biog.) **97**:81
Macmillan, Trevor 437
McMurdo station (research station, Antarc.) 382
MacMurray, Fred (obit.) **92**:72
McMurray, W. Grant *il.* 303
McMurtry, Larry (biog.) **90**:93
McNamara, Kevin (obit.) **88**:104
McNeill, Don (obit.) **97**:110
McNeill, James Charles (obit.) **88**:104
MacPherson, Stewart Myles (obit.) **96**:89
McQueen, Alexander 217, *il.*
McQueen, Thelma, *or* Butterfly McQueen (obit.) **96**:89
McRae, Carmen (obit.) **95**:73
McWilliam, Frederick Edward (obit.) **93**:71
"mad cow" disease: *see* bovine spongiform encephalopathy
Madagascar **97**:447; **96**:438; **95**:440; **94**:362; **93**:364; **92**:360; **91**:388; **90**:409; **89**:392; **88**:392
  gemstones 165
  see also WORLD DATA
Madagascar tortoise *il.* 213
Madden, David 241
Maddux, Greg (biog.) **96**:63
Madison, Guy, *or* Robert Ozell Moseley (obit.) **97**:110
"Madness of King George, The" (motion picture)
  film awards *table* 294
Madonna (biog.) **88**:77
"madriguera, La" (Mercado) 248
Mafia
  Italy 228, 436
magazines **97**:266; **96**:249; **95**:259; **94**:256; **93**:256; **92**:253; **91**:283; **90**:300; **89**:283; **88**:285
  advertising 154
Maglie, Salvatore Anthony (obit.) **93**:71
magnesium
  light metals 168
Magnuson, Warren Grant (obit.) **90**:118
Magyar (people)
  Hungary 430
Mahathir bin Mohamad, Datuk Seri (biog.) **97**:81
  Australia 392
  Malaysia 448
Mahfouz, Naguib (biog.) **89**:79
  Arabic literature 252
mail bomb
  crime and law enforcement 228, 495
Main Public Library (San Francisco, Calif., U.S.) 137
Maïnassara, Ibrahim Baré (biog.) **97**:82
  Niger 457
Maisler, Binyamin: *see* Mazar, Benjamin
maize: *see* corn
Major, John Roy (biogs.) **94**:45; **93**:44; **92**:44; **91**:75; **90**:93
  European Union 379
  Ireland 433
  United Kingdom 488
major histocompatibility complex antigen, *or* MHC antigen
  immune system research 64
Makahali River Treaty (treaty, India–Nepal) 455
"Maker Unmade, The" (Jones) 243
Makino, Masahiro (obit.) **94**:70
Maksimov, Vladimir Yemelyanovich, *or* Lev Alekseyevich Samsonov (obit.) **96**:89
Maktoum, Sheikh Muhammad al- 337
Maktum, Rashid ibn Said al- (obit.) **91**:101
Malan, Magnus 316, 474
Malawi **97**:448; **96**:439; **95**:440; **94**:363; **93**:364; **92**:361; **91**:389; **90**:410; **89**:392; **88**:392
  see also WORLD DATA
Malaysia **97**:448; **96**:439; **95**:441; **94**:414; **93**:414; **92**:410; **91**:438; **90**:456; **89**:439; **88**:439
  architecture and civil engineering
    buildings 140
    dams 142
  disasters
    fires and explosions 59
    natural 60
  international affairs
    Australia 392
    Brunei 401
    Commonwealth of Nations 378
    Singapore 471
  newspapers 265
  stock exchanges 199
  television industry 261
  wood products 179
Maldives **97**:449; **96**:440; **95**:442; **94**:406; **93**:407; **92**:404; **91**:432; **90**:450; **89**:432; **88**:433
  see also WORLD DATA
Malenkov, Georgy Maksimilianovich (obit.) **89**:101
Malex, Jasmine 295
Mali **97**:449; **96**:440; **95**:442; **94**:363; **93**:364; **92**:361; **91**:389; **90**:410; **89**:392; **88**:393
  gemstones 165
  refugees 297
  women's rights issues 316
  see also WORLD DATA
Maliki (Islam)
  special report **93**:95
Malle, Louis (obit.) **96**:89
Malouf, David George Joseph (biog.) **97**:82
  English literature 244
Malta **97**:449; **96**:440; **95**:442; **94**:445; **93**:446; **92**:435; **91**:458; **90**:474; **89**:458; **88**:458
  see also WORLD DATA
Malula, Joseph-Albert Cardinal (obit.) **90**:118
Malvinas, Islas (isls., Atl.O.): *see* Falkland Islands
Mamoulian, Rouben (obit.) **88**:104
man-made fibres 177
managed-care organization, *or* MCO
  pharmaceuticals 172
managed health care
  pharmaceutical coverage 172
  United States legislation 203
manatee
  wildlife conservation 213
Mancini, Enrico, *or* Henry Mancini (obit.) **95**:73
Mandel, Ernest (obit.) **96**:89
Mandela, Nelson (biog.) **91**:75
  Mozambique 454
  South Africa 473, 474
Mandino, Augustine A. (obit.) **97**:110
Manhattan Project
  World War II (special report) **96**:258
Manila (Phil.)
  most populous urban areas *table* 296
Mankiewicz, Francis (obit.) **94**:70
Mankiewicz, Joseph Leo (obit.) **94**:70
Manley, Edna Swithenbank (obit.) **88**:104
Mann, Gottfried Angelo (obit.) **95**:74
Mann, Sally (biog.) **94**:45
manned spaceflight 258, *table* 259
Manning, Ernest Charles (obit.) **97**:110
Manning, Preston (biog.) **92**:44
Mansell, Nigel (biog.) **93**:44
Mansholt, Sicco Leendert (obit.) **96**:89
Mantle, Mickey (obit.) **96**:89
manufacturing: *see* Business and Industry Review; Industrial Review
Manzù, Giacomo (obit.) **92**:73
Mapfumo, Thomas (biog.) **94**:45
Mapplethorpe, Robert (obit.) **90**:118
marathon (athletics) 370
  track and field sports 369
Maravich, Pete (obit.) **89**:102
Marble, Alice (obit.) **91**:101

Marchand, Jean (obit.) **89**:102
Marchuk, Yevhen 486
Marcopper Mining (co., Phil.) 172
Marcos, Ferdinand E. (obit.) **90**:119
Marcos, Subcommandante, *or* Rafael Sebastián Guillén Vicente (biog.) **96**:63
Marcus, Jacob Rader (obit.) **96**:90
Marcy, Geoffrey 257
Marechera, Dambudzo (obit.) **88**:104
"Marian" (motion picture) 295
marijuana
  voter approval 498
"Marimar" (television show) 264
Marin, Jean, *or* Yves-André-Marie Morvan (obit.) **96**:90
Marinduque Island (isl., Phil.)
  mining incident 172
marine affairs
  disasters 59
marine biology 234
  oceanography 187
  zoology 232
Marine Corps (U.S.): *see* United States Marine Corps, The
marine geology 184
Mark IV Industries, Inc. (Am. co.)
  rubber industry 167
"Mark of Esteem" (horse) 337
marketing
  animated motion pictures (special report) 293
"Marketing and Merchandising" (MACROPAEDIA revision) **95**:518
Markowitz, Harry M. (biog.) **91**:76
Markson, David 240
Marmon Silko, Leslie 241
marmoset
  wildlife conservation 213
Maron, Monika 244
marriage
  religious rulings 301
  same-sex laws 495, 499, *il.*
Mars (planet)
  life on Mars claim 183, 256, 382
  paleontology 238
  space exploration 259
Mars 96 (Russ. space probe)
  space exploration 259
"Mars Attacks!" (film)
  computer animation (special report) 293
Mars Global Surveyor (U.S. space probe)
  space exploration 259
Mars Pathfinder (U.S. space probe)
  space exploration 259
Marsalis, Wynton (biog.) **90**:93
Marsh, Warne
  jazz 279
Marshall, David Saul (obit.) **96**:90
Marshall, Sir John Ross (obit.) **89**:102
Marshall, Thurgood (obit.) **94**:70
Marshall Islands **97**:449; **96**:441; **95**:443; **94**:497; **93**:497; **92**:488
  new flag *illus.* **92**:343
  nuclear testing (spotlight) 450, *ils.* 451
  see also WORLD DATA
Martha Graham Dance Company 285
Martin, Billy (obit.) **90**:119
Martin, Charles Elmer (obit.) **96**:90
Martin, Dean, *or* Dino Paul Crocetti (obit.) **96**:90
Martin, Mary (obit.) **91**:102
Martin, Paul
  Canada 404
Martin, Paul Joseph James (obit.) **93**:71
"Martin Guerre" (play) 287
Martinez, Victor 268
Martini, Cardinal Carlo Maria (biog.) **93**:44
Marty, François Cardinal (obit.) **95**:74
Maruki, Iri (obit.) **96**:90
Maruyama, Masao (obit.) **97**:110
Marvin, Lee (obit.) **88**:105
Masako, Princess, *or* Masako Owada (biog.) **94**:47
Mas'ari, Muhammad al- 470
Masco Home Furnishings (Am. co.): *see* Lifestyle Furnishings International
Masekela, Hugh (biog.) **96**:64
Mashhur, Mustafa 414
Masina, Guilia Anna, *or* Giulietta Masina (obit.) **95**:74
"Mason's Retreat" (Tilghman) 241
Masoud, Ahmad Shah 388
mass media: *see* Media
mass transit: *see* urban mass transit
Massachusetts (state, U.S.)
  United States 498
massacre, *or* mass murder, *or* mass slaughter
  Australia 391
  Burundi 402, *il.*
  crime and law enforcement 227
  human rights 314
  Scotland 488
  Sierra Leone 471
  World War II 436
Masson, André (obit.) **88**:105
Masterkova, Svetlana 362, 369
Masters Tournament (golf) 346
Mastroianni, Marcello (obit.) **97**:110
  motion pictures 291
Masur, Kurt (biog.) **92**:45
Mata, Eduardo (obit.) **96**:90
materials 166
  chemistry 254
maternity leave
  Canada 206
Mathematics **97**:253; **96**:239; **95**:230; **94**:227; **93**:225; **92**:225; **91**:253; **90**:271; **89**:254; **88**:256
  U.K. education 204
Mathilde (asteroid)
  space exploration 259
Matiba, Kenneth 440
Matsui, Hideki 322
Matsumoto, Chizuo: *see* Asahara, Shoko
Matsushita, Konosuke (obit.) **90**:119
Mattel Inc. (Am. co.) 164
Matthews, Victor Collin, Matthews, Baron (obit.) **96**:90
Mau, Carl (obit.) **96**:90
Maung Maung, U (obit.) **95**:74
Maurensig, Paolo 247
Mauriac, Claude (obit.) **97**:111
Mauritania **97**:452; **96**:441; **95**:443; **94**:363; **93**:365; **92**:361; **91**:389; **90**:410; **89**:393; **88**:393
  see also WORLD DATA
Mauritius **97**:452; **96**:441; **95**:443; **94**:363; **93**:365; **92**:362; **91**:389; **90**:410; **89**:393; **88**:393
  see also WORLD DATA
Mauritshuis, *or* Royal Cabinet of Paintings (gallery, The Hague, Neth.)
  art exhibitions (special report) 146
Maxim (Orthodox patriarch) 308
Maxwell, Ian Robert (obit.) **92**:73
Maxwell, Vera, *or* Vera Huppé (obit.) **96**:90
May, Peter Barker Howard (obit.) **95**:74
May, Rollo Reece (obit.) **95**:74
May-Johnson bill (U.S. hist.)
  atomic bomb (special report) **96**:259
Maya (people)
  archaeology 136
Maynard, Robert Clyve (obit.) **94**:71
Mayor Zaragoza, Federico (biog.) **89**:79
Mazar, Benjamin, *or* Binyamin Maisler (obit.) **96**:90
Mazda Motor Corp. (Japanese co.) 158
Mazia, Daniel (obit.) **97**:111
Mazowiecki, Tadeusz (biog.) **90**:94
Mazzucco, Melania 247
Mbeki, Thabo (biog.) **95**:51
Mbilinyi, Simon 482
MBL (pol. party, Bol.): *see* Free Bolivia Movement
MCDC (Am. dance co.): *see* Merce Cunningham Dance Company
MCI Communications Corp. (Am. co.)
  British takeover 175, 196
  satellite TV (special report) 176
MCO: *see* managed-care organization
MDCs: *see* more developed countries
Meade, James Edward (obit.) **96**:90
Meadows, Audrey (obit.) **97**:111
meal (animal feed)
  world production 128, *table* 125
Measat Broadcast Network Systems 261
meat
  world production 129, *table* 126
Meciar, Vladimir (biog.) **94**:46
  Slovakia 472
Medawar, Sir Peter Brian (obit.) **88**:105
Media **97**:261; **96**:244; **95**:339; **94**:332; **93**:334; **92**:330; **91**:360; **90**:374; **89**:363; **88**:363
  Luxembourg 446
  special reports **93**:470; **90**:381
Mediamark Research 154
Medicaid (U.S.) 312
  welfare reform 498
Medicare (U.S.) 491
medicine: *see* Health and Disease
MEG: *see* Metals Economics Group
Megawati Sukarnoputri
  Indonesia 432
Meier, Richard 137
Melen, Ferit (obit.) **89**:102
Melville, Herman 241
Melville Corp. (Am. co.)
  footwear 156
Melvoin, Jonathan 281
memoir: *see* Literature
memory (psychol.)
  effect of nicotine 221
men
  dance 282
  demographic statistics 296
  fashions 216
  health and disease 218
    mental health 222
  sports and games 317
    1994 Winter Olympic champions *table* **95**:309
    1996 Summer Olympic champions *table* **97**:365
Mendel, Gideon 150
Méndez Montenegro, Julio César (obit.) **97**:111
Menem, Carlos Saúl (biog.) **90**:94
  Argentina 276, 390
Menen, Aubrey (obit.) **90**:119
Menghistu Lemma (biog.) **89**:102
meningitis 221
Menken, Alan (biog.) **97**:82
Menninger, Karl Augustus (obit.) **91**:102
Men's Professional Billiards Association, *or* MPBA 325
mental health 222
Menuhin, Yehudi 279
Mercado, Tununa 248
Merce Cunningham Dance Company, *or* MCDC (Am. dance co.) 283
Mercer, Joseph (obit.) **91**:102
merchandising: *see* "Marketing and Merchandising" (MACROPAEDIA revision)
Merchant, Ismail (biog.) **97**:82
Mercosur: *see* Southern Cone Common Market
Mercouri, Melina, *or* Maria Amalia Mercouris (obit.) **95**:74
Mercredi, Ovide (biog.) **96**:64
Mercury, Freddie (obit.) **92**:73
Mercury Music Prize 280
merger and acquisition, corporate
  automobiles 158
  banks 200
  chemicals 161
  computers 182
  games and toys 164
  insurance companies 166
  mining industry 170
  petroleum industry 163
  pharmaceuticals 173
  radio industry 264
  retailing 173
  stock markets 196
  telecommunications 175
  television industry 261
Meri, Lennart (biog.) **94**:46
  Estonia 418
Merino Castro, José Toribio (obit.) **97**:111
Merrill, James Ingram (obit.) **96**:91
mesoscale meteorology 187
Messiaen, Olivier-Eugène-Prosper-Charles (obit.) **93**:71
Messina, Francesco (obit.) **96**:91
metallocene, *or* single-site catalyst
  chemicals 161
metallurgy: *see* Mining
metals 166
Metals Economics Group, *or* MEG
  mining 170
metalworking 168
  German labour negotiations 201
"Meteo" (Zanzotto) 247
meteorite
  Antarctica 382
  life on Mars claim 183, 238, 256
meteorology 186
methane
  Comet Hyakutake 257
Methodist Churches 304
  homosexuality 301
metro: *see* subway
Metropolitan Museum of Art (N.Y.C., N.Y., U.S.)
  art exhibitions (special report) 146
Metropolitan Opera House (N.Y., U.S.)
  "Der Ring des Nibelungen" 278
Metropolitan Transportation Authority (Los Angeles, Calif., U.S.)
  subway project 142
Mexico **97**:452; **96**:442; **95**:444; **94**:486; **93**:486; **92**:478; **91**:505; **90**:520; **89**:505; **88**:504
  building and construction 160
  disasters
    aviation 58
    earthquake 184
    traffic 61
  drug trafficking 227
  economic affairs 194
  Guatemalan refugees 297
  literature 248
  military affairs 276
  most populous urban areas *table* 296
  religion 300
  social security reform 314
  sports and games
    association football 342
    baseball 322
  television industry 264
  wildlife conservation 213
  see also WORLD DATA
Mexico, Gulf of
  petroleum 163
Mexico City (Mex.)
  air pollution *il.* 211
  most populous urban areas *table* 296
Meyendorff, John (obit.) **93**:71
Meyers, Jeffrey 242
MFDC (pol. party, Sen.): *see* Movement of Democratic Forces of Casamance
MFS WorldCom (Am. co.) 175, 196
MHC antigen: *see* major histocompatibility complex antigen
Miami City Ballet (Am. ballet co.) 282
"Miami Herald" (Am. news.) 266
"Michael Collins" (motion picture) 290
Michel, Hartmut (biog.) **89**:79
Michelangeli, Arturo Benedetti (obit.) **96**:91
Michelin (Fr. co.) 167
Michener, Daniel Roland (obit.) **92**:73
Michener, Percy Zell (obit.) **97**:111
Michigan (state, U.S.) 497
  forfeiture laws 225
microbanking 200
microeconomics
  Nobel Prize 62
microelectronics 169
Micronesia, Federated States of, *or* Caroline Islands **97**:453; **96**:444; **95**:445; **94**:497; **93**:497; **92**:489
  new flag *illus.* **92**:343
Microsoft Corp. (Am. co.)
  Internet browser software 181
  on-line magazine 267
  television industry 262
Microx
  food packaging 132
Middle Eastern and North African affairs **94**:375; **93**:377; **92**:373; **91**:401; **90**:421; **89**:404; **88**:404
  economic affairs 194
  France 420
  international law 224
  military affairs 272, 375, *table* 272
  motion pictures 295
  museums 230
  petroleum 163
  special reports **94**:377; **92**:375
  terrorism 226
  tourism 179
  see also individual countries by name
Midori, *or* Advanced Earth Observation Satellite
  global research 259
Mikardo, Ian (obit.) **94**:71
Mikes, George (obit.) **88**:105
Miki, Takeo (obit.) **89**:102
Milanov, Zinka (obit.) **90**:119
Milburn, Jackie (obit.) **89**:103
Miles, Bernard James Miles (obit.) **92**:73
Military Affairs **97**:269; **96**:252; **95**:230; **94**:228; **93**:225; **92**:225; **91**:253; **90**:271; **89**:254; **88**:256
  Afghanistan 388
  Burundi 402
  Canada 405
  Chad 406, *il.*
  China 409
  "Combating the Land Mine Scourge" (special report) **97**:274
  Congo 410
  Cuba 411
  Eritrea 415
  France 419
  Honduras 427
  human rights issues 315
  Iran 433
  Iraq 433
  Israel 435
  Jordan 439
  Nigeria 458
  North Korea 440
  Pakistan 460
  Russia 465
  special reports **93**:232; **92**:231; **91**:260; **88**:258
  Sri Lanka 476
  Syria 478
  Taiwan 479
  Taiwan Strait 439
  Tajikistan 482
  terrorist attacks 226
  United Nations 376
  United States 496
    court decisions 224
  Yemen 502
  see also civil war
militia group
  United States 495
milk
  world production 129, *table* 127
Milken, Michael R. (biog.) **91**:76
Miller, Delvin Glenn (obit.) **97**:111
Miller, James Henry: *see* MacColl, Ewan
Miller, Jonathan Wolfe (biog.) **89**:79
Miller, Merton H. (biog.) **91**:76
Miller, Roger (obit.) **93**:71
Miller, Shannon (biog.) **95**:51
Miller Brewing Company (Am. co.) 159
Millikin, Sandra
  "Blockbuster Art Exhibitions" (special report) **97**:146
Mills, Wilbur Daigh (obit.) **93**:71
Milne, Christopher Robin (obit.) **97**:111
Milosevic, Slobodan (biog.) **92**:45
  United States 496
  Yugoslavia 502, *il.*
Miłosz, Czesław 63, 250
Milpa, La (archae. site, Belize) 136
Milstein, Nathan (obit.) **93**:72
Milwaukee (Wis., U.S.)
  water-treatment systems 160
Mindanao (isl., Phil.) 461
Mingus, Sue 280
minimum wage 201
  United States 313, 491
Mining **97**:170; **96**:149; **95**:239; **94**:235; **93**:234; **92**:234; **91**:262; **90**:280; **89**:263; **88**:264
  Arctic regions 383
  disasters 60
  Guyana 426
  Pacific Islands (spotlight) 450
Minnesota (state, U.S.)
  hunting and fishing 499
Minnesota Fats, *or* Rudolf Walter Wanderone, Jr. (obit.) **97**:111
Minolta Co., Ltd. (Japanese co.)
  photography 173
minority groups: *see* Race and Ethnic Relations
Minotis, Alexis (obit.) **91**:102
Minoves-Triquell, Juli 389
"Mir" (Russ. space station)
  space exploration 258
Miron, Gaston (obit.) **97**:111
  French-Canadian literature 247
Mirren, Helen (biog.) **95**:51
Mirrlees, James Alexander
  Nobel Prize 63
"Miserables, Les" (motion picture)
  film awards *table* 294

missile, *or* ballistic missile (rocket)
military affairs 269
"Mission Impossible" (motion picture) 289
Missouri (state, U.S.) 498
Misuari, Nur
Philippines 461
Mitarai, Hajime (obit.) **96**:91
Mitchell, George 489
Mitchell, Joan (obit.) **93**:72
Mitchell, John Newton (obit.) **89**:103
Mitchell, Joseph (obit.) **97**:111
Mitchell, Kevin (biog.) **90**:94
Mitchell, Maurice B. (obit.) **97**:111
Mitchell, Peter Dennis (obit.) **93**:72
Mitchell, Roscoe 280
Mitford, Jessica Lucy (obit.) **97**:111
Mitsotakis, Konstantinos (biog.) **91**:76
Mitsubishi Bank (bank, Japan) 438
Mitterrand, François-Maurice-Marie
biography **89**:80
France 419
obituary **97**:112
mixed member proportional voting
New Zealand 456
Miyazawa, Kiichi (biog.) **92**:45
Mize, John Robert (obit.) **94**:71
Mkapa, Benjamin 482
Mladic, Ratko
military affairs 271
war crimes violations 227, 315
MLMC electronic package: *see* multilayer, multicomponent electronic package
MLSTP-PSD (pol. party, São Tomé and Príncipe): *see* Movement for the Liberation of São Tomé and Príncipe
MNLF (pol. party, Phil.): *see* Moro National Liberation Front
MNR (pol. party, Bol.): *see* Nationalist Revolutionary Movement
Moawad, René Anis (obit.) **90**:119
Mobil Corporation (Am. co.) 163
Mobutu Sese Seko 503
modem
microelectronics 170
Modern Art, Museum of (N.Y.C., N.Y., U.S.)
art exhibitions 148
photography 149
modern dance 283
modern pentathlon: *see* pentathlon
"Moesha" (television show) *il.* **97**:264
Mogoba, Stanley 304
Mohajir Qaumi Movement, *or* MQM (pol. org., Pak.) 459
Mohorovicic discontinuity
oceanography 187
Moi, Daniel arap 206, 440
Moix, Terenci 247
Moldova **97**:453; **96**:445; **95**:445; **94**:445; **93**:446
new flag *illus.* **93**:345
see also WORLD DATA
molecular biology 236
Molitor, Paul (biog.) **94**:46
baseball 322
molybdenum blue
chemistry 253
Momigliani, Arnaldo Dante (obit.) **88**:105
"Mon homme" (motion picture) 291
Monaco **97**:453; **96**:445; **95**:446; **94**:446; **93**:447; **92**:436; **91**:458; **90**:475; **89**:459; **88**:458
Grand Prix racing 318
see also WORLD DATA
Moncion, Francisco (obit.) **96**:91
Moneo, José Rafael 137
Monet, Claude
art exhibitions (special report) 146
Mongolia **97**:453; **96**:445; **95**:446; **94**:401; **93**:401; **92**:400; **91**:427; **90**:445; **89**:428; **88**:428
disasters 59
new flag *illus.* **93**:345
see also WORLD DATA
Mongolian People's Revolutionary Party, *or* MPRP (pol. party, Mong.) 453
monkey
anthropology 133
Monroe, William Smith, *or* Bill Monroe (obit.) **97**:112
popular music 282
monsoon
natural disasters 60
Montagnier, Luc (biog.) **93**:44
Montalbán, Manuel Vázquez 247
Montale, Eugenio 247
Montana, Joe (biog.) **90**:94
Montana, Patsy, *or* Rubye Blevins (obit.) **97**:112
popular music 282
Montand, Yves (obit.) **92**:74
Montell Polyolefins (Eur. co.)
chemicals 161
Monterrey (Mex.)
baseball 322
Monterrey Sultans (baseball) 322
Montesinos, Vladimiro 461
Montgomerie, Colin 347
Montgomery, Elizabeth (obit.) **96**:91
Montoya, Carlos García (obit.) **94**:71
Montpellier Festival (Fr.) 285
Montreal, University of (Can.)
maternity leave 206
Montreal Canadiens (ice hockey) 349
Montreal Protocol
ozone depletion 210
Montreal Stock Exchange index (Can.) 198
Montreal World Film Festival (Can.)
film awards *table* 294
Montserrat (isl., W.I.)
Chances Peak volcano 185, 381
Monzon, Carlos (obit.) **96**:91
Moore, Charles (obit.) **94**:71
Moore, Colleen (obit.) **89**:103
Moore, Garry (obit.) **94**:71
Moore, John Edward Michael (biog.) **88**:77
Moore, Robert Frederick Chelsea (obit.) **94**:71
Moorer, Michael 329
Moores, Sir John (obit.) **94**:71
Morandini, Giuliana 247
Moravia, Alberto (obit.) **91**:102
Morceli, Noureddine (biog.) **95**:52
more developed countries, *or* MDCs
demographic statistics 296
Morgan, Henry (obit.) **95**:75
Morgan, William Wilson (obit.) **95**:75
Mori, Taikichiro (obit.) **94**:72
Morissette, Alanis (biog.) **97**:83
popular music 281
Morley, Robert (obit.) **93**:72
Mormon: *see* Church of Jesus Christ of Latter-day Saints
Moro Islamic Liberation Front (pol. org., Phil.) 462
Moro National Liberation Front, *or* MNLF (pol. party, Phil.) 461, *il.* 462
Morocco **97**:454; **96**:446; **95**:446; **94**:389; **93**:389; **92**:387; **91**:413; **90**:433; **89**:416; **88**:416
literature 252
see also WORLD DATA
Morris, Dick
presidential election (special report) 492
Morris, Jack (biog.) **92**:45
Morris, Richard Brandon (obit.) **90**:120
Morrison, Holmes Sterling (obit.) **96**:91
Morrison, Toni (biog.) **89**:80
publishing award 268
mortality, *or* death rate
Chinese orphanages 314, 408
demographic statistics 296
health and disease 219
United States *table* 296
see also infant mortality rate
Morvan, Yves-André-Marie (obit.): *see* Marin, Jean
Mosa'ed, Jila 251
Moschino, Franco (obit.) **95**:75
Mosconi, William Joseph (obit.) **94**:72
Moscow (Russ.)
most populous urban areas *table* 296
Moseley, Robert Ozell (obit.): *see* Madison, Guy
Moseley-Braun, Carol (biog.) **93**:45
Moses, Sir Charles Joseph Alfred (obit.) **89**:103
Moshoeshoe II, *or* Constantine Bereng Seeiso (obit.) **97**:112
Lesotho 445
mosquito (insect)
infectious diseases 219, *il.* 218
Moss, Howard (obit.) **88**:105
most-favoured-nation treatment
China 315, 409
United States 496
Most Valuable Player
baseball 320, 322
Mother Church, The (church, Boston, Mass., U.S.): *see* First Church of Christ, Scientist
Motherwell, Robert (obit.) **92**:74
Mothopeng, Zephania Lekoane (obit.) **91**:102
Motion Pictures **97**:289; **96**:274; **95**:242; **94**:238; **93**:236; **92**:236; **91**:264; **90**:282; **89**:265; **88**:267
special reports **97**:292; **95**:245
Motley Fool (Web site)
stock exchanges 196
motor sports: *see* aerial sports; automobile racing; *and* motorboating
motor-voter law
United States 497
motorboating **94**:304; **93**:306; **92**:302; **91**:332; **90**:350; **89**:332; **88**:334
Motorola, Inc. (Am. co.)
computer clones 182
new facilities 169
Mott, Sir Nevill Francis (obit.) **97**:112
Mouada, Mohamed 484
Mount Zion Baptist Church *il.* 302
Moura, George 249
Mourão-Ferreira, David (obit.) **97**:112
Movement for Democracy, *or* MPD (pol. party, C.Verde) 406
Movement for the Liberation of São Tomé and Príncipe, *or* MLSTP-PSD (pol. party, São Tomé and Príncipe) 470
Movement for the Survival of the Ogoni People (org., Nig.) 315
Movement of Democratic Forces of Casamance, *or* MFDC (pol. party, Sen.) 470
Mozambique **97**:454; **96**:446; **95**:447; **94**:364; **93**:365; **92**:362; **91**:390; **90**:411; **89**:393; **88**:394
land mines *map* 275
political party system (spotlight) 416, *map* 417
refugees 297
see also WORLD DATA
Mozambique National Resistance, *or* Renamo (pol. party, Moz.) 454
MPBA: *see* Men's Professional Billiards Association
MPD (pol. party, C.Verde): *see* Movement for Democracy
Mpetha, Oscar Mafakafaka (obit.) **95**:75
MPRP (pol. party, Mong.): *see* Mongolian People's Revolutionary Party
MQM (pol. org., Pak.): *see* Mohajir Qaumi Movement
MRTA (mil. org., Peru): *see* Túpac Amaru Revolutionary Movement
MSNBC
television industry 262
Mswati III
Swaziland 477
Mubarak, Hosni
Arab-Israeli peace process role 414
assassination attempt 418
Yemen 502
mud slide
natural disasters 60
Mufti, Sa'id al- (obit.) **90**:120
Mugabe, Robert
Zimbabwe 504, *il.*
Muggeridge, Malcolm Thomas (obit.) **91**:103
Muhammad (Prophet of Islam)
"Islamic Fundamentalism" (special report) **94**:377
Muhammad Sultan (obit.): *see* Rahi, Sultan
Muir, Jean Elizabeth (obit.) **96**:91
Mukherjee, Sabyasachi (obit.) **91**:103
Muldoon, Sir Robert David (obit.) **93**:72
Muliro, Masinde (obit.) **93**:72
Müller, Heiner (obit.) **96**:91
German literature 244
Müller, Inge
German literature 245
Müller, Karl Alexander (biog.) **88**:77
Müller, Xeno 354
Mulligan, Gerald Joseph (obit.) **97**:112
multilayer, multicomponent electronic package, *or* MLMC electronic package
ceramics 166
Multinational and Regional Organizations **97**:380; **96**:356; **95**:358
Mumbai (India): *see* Bombay
Mumford, Lewis (obit.) **91**:103
Münchinger, Karl Wilhelm (obit.) **91**:103
Munro, Alice (biog.) **91**:77
Murakami, Haruki (biog.) **91**:77
Murayama, Tomiichi (biog.) **95**:52
Japan 437
Murchison, Ira (obit.) **95**:75
murder 227
Belgium 396
Bulgaria 402
Egypt 415
Ethiopia 418
human rights issues 316
South Africa 229, 474
see also assassination
Murdoch, Rupert
television industry 261
Murphy, George Lloyd (obit.) **93**:73
Murray, Arthur (obit.) **92**:74
Murray, Eddie
baseball 322, *il.*
Murray, Henry Alexander (obit.) **89**:103
Murray, Joseph Edward (biog.) **91**:77
Musarurwa, Willie (obit.) **91**:103
muscle contraction
zoology 232
Museum of . . . : *see under* substantive word, *e.g.*, Modern Art, Museum of
Museums **97**:230; **96**:218; **95**:247; **94**:242; **93**:240; **92**:240; **91**:268; **90**:286; **89**:269; **88**:271
architecture 137
art exhibitions (special report) **97**:146
digitized visual images 149
jazz 279
Museveni, Yoweri 486
Music **97**:277; **96**:263; **95**:249; **94**:243; **93**:241; **92**:241; **91**:270; **90**:288; **89**:271; **88**:273
musical theatre 287
Muskie, Edmund Sixtus (obit.) **97**:113
Muslim: *see* Islam
Muslim Brotherhood (rel. and pol. org.) 414
"Islamic Fundamentalism" (special report) **94**:377
Mussawi, 'Abbas al- (obit.) **93**:73
Muster, Thomas (biog.) **96**:64
tennis 360
Mutola, Maria 369
Mutter, Carol 269
mutual fund
stock exchanges 194
Muwanga, Paulo (obit.) **92**:74
Myanmar (formerly Burma) **97**:455; **96**:447; **95**:448; **94**:414; **93**:415; **92**:411; **91**:438; **90**:456; **89**:436; **88**:437
ASEAN membership 380
Australia 392
Buddhism 309
East Asian democracy (spotlight) 442
refugees 297
see also WORLD DATA
myocardial infarction: *see* heart attack
Myosotis sylvatica (flower) 215
Myrdal, Karl Gunnar (obit.) **88**:105
"Mysteries of Ancient China" (art exhibit) 144

N

Nabiyev, Rakhmon Nabiyevich (obit.) **94**:72
Nachtwey, James (biog.) **96**:64
NAFTA: *see* North American Free Trade Agreement
Nagasaki (Japan)
World War II (special report) **96**:259
Nagorno-Karabakh (reg., Azerbaijan) 393
Nagurski, Bronislaw (obit.) **91**:103
Naidoo, Stephen (obit.) **90**:120
Najibullah, Maj. Gen. Mohammad (obit.) **97**:113
Afghanistan 388
Najjār, Iskandar 252
Nakajima, Hiroshi (biog.) **95**:52
Nakamaru, Michie (biog.) **92**:46
Nakashima, George (obit.) **91**:104
Nakatani, Corey 335
Nakauchi, Isao (biog.) **96**:64
Nakuru, Lake (Ken.) *il.* 212
Namaliu, Rabbie (biog.) **89**:80
Namibia (formerly Southwest Africa) **97**:455; **96**:447; **95**:448; **94**:364; **93**:366; **92**:363; **91**:390
see also WORLD DATA
Namora, Fernando Goncalves (obit.) **90**:120
Nannen, Henri (obit.) **97**:113
"Não és tu, Brasil" (Paiva) 249
NAPC: *see* North American Paleontological Convention
Nartis, Evangelos
contract bridge *table* 331
Naruhito, Crown Prince (biog.) **94**:47
NASA (U.S.): *see* National Aeronautics and Space Administration
NASCAR: *see* National Association for Stock Car Auto Racing
Nasdaq composite index: *see* National Association of Securities Dealers automated quotation composite index
Nasdaq SmallCap market 197
"Naseem" (motion picture) 295
Nasr, Sheikh Muhammad Hamid Abu an- (obit.) **97**:113
Nasrin, Taslima (biog.) **95**:52
nation cores of states
Fourth World (spotlight) 422, *map* 423
Nation of Islam: *see* Islam, Nation of
National Action Party, *or* PAN (pol. party, Mex.) 452
National Advancement Party (pol. party, Guat.) 426
National Aeronautics and Space Administration, *or* NASA (U.S.)
astronomy 256
space exploration 258
National Alliance, *or* AN (pol. party, It.) 436
National Association for Stock Car Auto Racing, *or* NASCAR 319
National Association of Securities Dealers automated quotation composite index, *or* Nasdaq composite index 197
National Ballet of Canada, *or* NBC (Can. ballet co.) 283
National Baptist Convention of America, Inc. 302
National Basketball Association, *or* NBA (U.S.) 323
National Book Award (U.S.) 241, 242
book publishing 268
National Broadcasting Co., Inc., *or* NBC (Am. corp.)
advertising sales 154
television ratings 262
National Cancer Institute, *or* NCI (U.S.) 219
National Center for Health Statistics, *or* NCHS (U.S.) 296
National Collegiate Athletic Association, *or* NCAA (U.S.)
basketball 323
football 343
National Congress of the Communist Party of Vietnam 501
National Democratic Party, *or* NDP (pol. party, Sur.) 476
National Education Summit (U.S.) 204
National Electoral Commission of Nigeria, *or* NECON 458
National Field Archery Association, *or* NFAA (U.S.) 317
National Finals Rodeo, *or* NFR (U.S.) 352
National Football Conference, *or* NFC (U.S.) 344
National Football League, *or* NFL (U.S.) 344
National Front (pol. party, Fr.) 419
National Gallery (London, Gtr.London, U.K.)
art exchange 144
art exhibitions 145
National Gallery of Art (Wash., D.C., U.S.) 148
art exhibitions (special report) 146
photography 149
National Hockey League, *or* NHL 349
National Institutes of Health, *or* NIH (U.S.)
hypertension research 218

National Invitation Tournament, *or* NIT (U.S.)
  basketball 325
National League (baseball) 321
National League for Democracy, *or* NLD (pol. org.)
  Myanmar 380, 455
National Liberation Front (pol. party, Alg.) 389
National Library of Bosnia (library, Sarajevo, Bosnia and Herzegovina) 230
National Magazine Award (U.S.) 267
National Movement for Street Boys and Girls (Braz. org.)
  special report **95**:279
National Park Service (U.S.)
  anti-terrorism proposals 138
National Party (pol. party, N.Z.) 456
National Party (pol. party, S.Af.) 473
National Patriotic Front of Liberia, *or* NPFL (pol. party, Lib.) 445
National Republican Alliance Party, *or* ARENA (pol. party, El Sal.) 415
National Salvation Council, *or* CSN (pol. org., Niger) 457
National Science and Technology Council (U.S.)
  Antarctica 383
National Securities Markets Improvement Act (1996, U.S.) 196
National Transportation Safety Board, *or* NTSB (U.S.)
  Trans World Airlines explosion 226
National Union for Democracy in the Comoros, *or* UNDC (pol. party, Com.) 410
National Union for the Total Independence of Angola, *or* UNITA (pol. party, Ang.) 389
National Zoo (Wash., D.C., U.S.) *il.* 201
  zoos (special report) **94**:111
nationalism
  Canada 404
  China 408
  "Toward the Age of Common Sense" (commentary) **95**:9
  world affairs 376
Nationalist Party (pol. party, Tai.): *see* Kuomintang
Nationalist Revolutionary Party, *or* MNR (pol. party, Bol.) 397
NationsBank Corp. (Am. co.) 201
Native American peoples
  anthropology 134
  archaeology 135
  Canada 383
  "Native American Cultural Ferment" (spotlight) **96**:494
  reservation gambling laws 499
NATO: *see* North Atlantic Treaty Organization
natural disasters 60
natural gas 163
  mining *table* 172
  Norway 459
  see also liquefied natural gas
natural resource
  Pacific Islands (spotlight) 450
Natwick, Mildred (obit.) **95**:75
Naughton, Bill (obit.) **93**:73
Nauru **97**:455; **96**:448; **95**:448; **94**:497; **93**:497; **92**:489; **91**:515; **90**:531; **89**:515; **88**:515
  see also WORLD DATA
Navy (U.S.): *see* United States Navy, The
Nazarbayev, Nursultan Abishevich (biog.) **92**:46
  Kazakstan 439
NBA (U.S.): *see* National Basketball Association
NBA: *see* Net Book Agreement
NBC (Am. corp.): *see* National Broadcasting Co., Inc.
NBC (Can. ballet co.): *see* National Ballet of Canada
NCAA (U.S.): *see* National Collegiate Athletic Association
NCHS (U.S.): *see* National Center for Health Statistics
NCI (U.S.): *see* National Cancer Institute
NCR (Am. co.) 177
Ndadaye, Melchior (obit.) **94**:72
N'Dour, Youssou (biog.) **93**:45
NDP (pol. party, Sur.): *see* National Democratic Party
Ndungane, Winston 301
Nduwayo, Antoine 402
Neanderthal (anthro.) 134
Near Earth Asteroid Rendezvous, *or* NEAR (spacecraft) 259
Nearing, Helen (obit.) **96**:91
Nebraska, University of (U.S.)
  basketball 325
  football 343
NEC (Japanese co.) 182
NECON: *see* National Electoral Commission of Nigeria
Needham, Noël Joseph Terence Montgomery (obit.) **96**:91
Negri, Pola (obit.) **88**:106
Neher, Erwin (biog.) **92**:32
Neil, Andrew Ferguson (biog.) **90**:95
Nekrasov, Viktor Platonovich (obit.) **88**:106
Nelson, Azumah 330
Nelson, Gene, *or* Eugene Leander Berg (obit.) **97**:113
Nelson, Harriet (obit.) **95**:75
nematode
  genetics research 232
Nemerov, Howard (obit.) **92**:74
Nemov, Aleksey 348, 365
Nepal **97**:455; **96**:448; **95**:449; **94**:407; **93**:408; **92**:404; **91**:432; **90**:450; **89**:433; **88**:433
  Bhutan 397
    refugees 297
  see also WORLD DATA
nerve gas
  Persian Gulf War syndrome 269
Nesin, Aziz, *or* Mehmet Nusret (obit.) **96**:91
Nestlé SA (Swiss co.) 132
Net Book Agreement, *or* NBA 267
net capital rules (econ.) 196
Netanyahu, Benjamin (biogs.) **97**:83; **94**:47
  education 205
  Egypt 414
  Islam 310
  Israel 434
NetDay96 (computers) 181
Netherlandic literature, *or* Dutch literature 245
Netherlands, The **97**:456; **96**:448; **95**:449; **94**:446; **93**:447; **92**:436; **91**:459; **90**:475; **89**:459; **88**:459
  aviation disasters 58
  literature 245
  media and publishing
    books 267
    newspapers 265
    television industry 261
  mining 172
  social protection 313
  sports and games
    association football 340
    field hockey 339
    volleyball 370
  stock exchanges 199
  see also WORLD DATA
Netherlands Antilles (isls., Carib. Sea) 381
Nethold NV (Du. co.)
  television industry 261
Netscape Communications Corp. (Am. corp.) 65
  Internet browser software 181
Netting, Robert McCorkle (obit.) **96**:91
network computer 181
Network Station (computer) 181
Neue Messe Leipzig (bldg., Leipzig, Ger.) 137
Neumann, Vaclav (obit.) **96**:91
"Neurosia: Fünfzig Jahre Pervers" (motion picture) 291
neurotransmitter
  Prozac (special report) **95**:215
Nevada (state, U.S.)
  archaeological site 136
Nevado Ampato (archae. site, Peru) 136
Nevelson, Louise (obit.) **89**:103
New Amsterdam Theatre (N.Y.C., N.Y., U.S.) 287
New Aspiration Party (pol. party, Thai.) 483
New Caledonia (Fr. terr., Pac.O.) 381
"New Century Hymnal, The" (hymnal)
  United Church of Christ 305
New England Patriots (football) 344
"New Face of Eastern Europe, The" (feature article) **90**:5
"New Fowler's Modern English Usage, The" (ed. by Burchfield) 243
New Front (pol. party, Sur.) 476
New Jersey (state, U.S.) 497
New Jersey Devils (ice hockey) 349
New Korea Party, *or* Democratic Liberal Party (pol. party, S.Kor.) 443
New Patriotic Party, *or* NPP (pol. party, Ghana) 425
New People's Army, *or* NPA (pol. org., Phil.) 462
New Urbanism
  architecture 138
New Wafd Party (pol. party, Egy.) 414
New World Communications Group, Inc. 261
"New World Disorder, The" (commentary) **94**:5
New York (state, U.S.) 497
New York City (N.Y., U.S.)
  blizzard *il.* 186
  census dispute 225
  fashion 216
  most populous urban areas *table* 296
  theatre 287
New York City Ballet, *or* NYCB (Am. ballet co.) 282
"New York Daily News" (Am. news.) 266
New York Public Library (library, N.Y.C., N.Y., U.S.) 230
New York Stock Exchange, *or* NYSE 197
"New York Times" (Am. news.) 266
New York Yankees (baseball) 320
New York Zoological Society (N.Y.C., N.Y., U.S.): *see* NYZS/The Wildlife Conservation Society
New Zealand **97**:456; **96**:449; **95**:450; **94**:497; **93**:497; **92**:489; **91**:516; **90**:532; **89**:516; **88**:515
  agriculture and food supplies 129
  economic affairs 194
  field hockey 339
  literature 244
  radio industry 264
  rugby football 345
  social protection 314
  stock exchanges 199
  wildlife conservation 213
  see also WORLD DATA
New Zealand First Party (pol. party, N.Z.) 456
New Zealand Radio Network 264
Newbury Bypass (hwy., U.K.)
  photo essay 208
Newfoundland (prov., Can.)
  fisheries 131
Newman, Joe (obit.) **93**:73
NewsCatcher
  telecommunications 177
"Newsday" (Am. news.) 266
newspapers **97**:265; **96**:247; **95**:259; **94**:256; **93**:256; **92**:253; **91**:283; **90**:300; **89**:283; **88**:285
Newton, Huey Percy (obit.) **90**:120
NeXT Software, Inc. (Am. co.) 182
"Next Wave Festival" (dance) 282
NFAA (U.S.): *see* National Field Archery Association
NFC: *see* National Football Conference
NFL: *see* National Football League
NFR (U.S.): *see* National Finals Rodeo
Ngema, Mbongeni (biog.) **96**:65
Ngor, Haing S. (obit.) **97**:113
Nguyen Huu Tho (obit.) **97**:113
Nguyen Kim Dien, Philippe (obit.) **89**:104
Nguyen Van Linh (biog.) **88**:78
NHL: *see* National Hockey League
Niarchos, Stavros Spyros (obit.) **97**:113
Niborski, Yitskhak 251
Nicaragua **97**:457; **96**:450; **95**:451; **94**:488; **93**:488; **92**:479; **91**:506; **90**:522; **89**:506; **88**:505
  land mines *map* 275
  military affairs 276
  papal visit *il.* 306
  see also WORLD DATA
Nichiei Finance (Japanese co.) 191
Nicholson, Ben 144
nickel
  chemistry 254
  mining 170
Nicklaus, Jack 346
Nicol, Davidson Sylvester Hector Willoughby, *or* Abioseh Nicol (obit.) **95**:75
nicotine 178
  effect on memory 221
Niederland, William Guglielmo (obit.) **94**:72
Niger **97**:457; **96**:450; **95**:451; **94**:365; **93**:366; **92**:363; **91**:391; **90**:411; **89**:394; **88**:394
  see also WORLD DATA
Nigeria **97**:458; **96**:450; **95**:451; **94**:365; **93**:367; **92**:363; **91**:391; **90**:411; **89**:394; **88**:395
  association football 341
  Cameroon 403
  Canada 405
  Commonwealth of Nations 378
  dams 142
  disasters
    aviation 58
    marine 59
  human rights issues 315, 377
  literature 244
  most populous urban areas *table* 296
  prisons and penology 229
  steel mill *il.* 458
  street children (special report) **95**:279
  see also WORLD DATA
"Nightwatch: New and Selected Poems, 1968–1996" (Lee) 242
NIH (U.S.): *see* National Institutes of Health
Nike, Inc. (Am. co.) 156
Nikkei 225 Index (Japan) 199
Nikolais, Alwin (obit.) **94**:72
Nikon Corporation (Japanese co.)
  photography 173
Nina Tower (bldg., H.K.) 139
Nine West Group, Inc. (Am. co.) 156
"1945—A Watershed Year" (special report) **96**:256
Nintendo Co., Ltd. (Japanese co.) 164
Niosi, Bert (obit.) **88**:106
Nirenberg, Yankl 251
Nis Electronics Industry (Yugos. co.)
  labour strike 502
NIT (U.S.): *see* National Invitation Tournament
Niue (isl., Pac.O.) 381
Nixon, Edgar Daniel (obit.) **88**:106
Nixon, Patricia, *or* Thelma Catherine Ryan (obit.) **94**:72
Nixon, Richard Milhous (obit.) **95**:76
Niyazov, Saparmurad 485
Niyongabo, Vénuste 368
Nizer, Louis (obit.) **95**:77
NLD (pol. org.): *see* National League for Democracy
no-fly zone 433, 439
no-fuss chic 216, *il.* 217
Nobel Prizes **97**:62; **96**:49; **95**:36; **94**:30; **93**:30; **89**:65; **88**:65
  1989 winners **90**:81, 85, 86, 89, 96, 98, 101, 260
  1990 winners **91**:81, 83, 85, 86, 89, 96, 98, 101, 260
  1991 winners **92**:67, 69, 70, 73, 76, 77, 78, 81, 82, 83
Noguchi, Isamu (obit.) **89**:104
Nolan, Christopher (biog.) **89**:80
Nolan, Sir Sidney Robert (obit.) **93**:73
Noma, Hiroshi (obit.) **92**:75
nonfiction: *see* Literature
Nono, Luigi (obit.) **91**:104
nontheatrical film: *see* Motion Pictures
Noonan, Chris
  film awards *table* 294
Noonuccal, Oodgeroo (obit.) **94**:73
Nordbrandt, Henrik
  Danish literature 245
Nordic skiing 357
  1994 Winter Olympic champions *table* **95**:309
Nordmeyer, Sir Arnold Henry (obit.) **90**:120
Nordmore grate
  fisheries 131
Noriega, Manuel Antonio (biog.) **88**:78
Norman, Greg
  golf 346
Norman, Howard 242
Norodom Ranariddh: *see* Ranariddh, Norodom
Norodom Sihanouk: *see* Sihanouk, Norodom
Norstad, Lauris (obit.) **89**:104
North, Oliver Laurence (biog.) **88**:78
North Africa: *see* Middle Eastern and North African affairs
North America
  archaeology 135
  religion statistics *table* 311
  social protection 312
North American Free Trade Agreement, *or* NAFTA
  Caribbean unification (spotlight) 468
  clothing industry 156
North American Paleontological Convention, *or* NAPC 238
North Atlantic Treaty Organization, *or* NATO 270
  armed forces *table* 272
  Bosnia and Herzegovina 398
  France 420
  Russia 465
  Ukraine 487
"North Cape" (barge)
  oil spill 206
North Carolina (state, U.S.) 497
  congressional reapportionment 225
  natural disasters 60
North Korea: *see* Korea, Democratic People's Republic of
North Melbourne FC (Austr. football) 344
North Pole
  Byrd controversy 383
North Yemen: *see* Yemen Arab Republic
Northern Ireland (country, U.K.) 489
  terrorist attacks 226, 433
Northern League (pol. party, It.) 436, *il.* 437
Northrup, John Howard (obit.) **88**:106
Northwest Territories (terr., Can.)
  Arctic regions 383
Norton, Mary (obit.) **93**:73
Norway **97**:459; **96**:451; **95**:454; **94**:446; **93**:447; **92**:436; **91**:459; **90**:476; **89**:459; **88**:459
  aviation disasters 58
  bowling 326
  carbon dioxide burial 210
  Iceland 430
  literature 245
  roads 142
  see also WORLD DATA
Norwegian literature 245
Nosaka, Sanzo (obit.) **94**:73
"Not Her Real Name: And Other Stories" (Perlins) 244
"Noticia de un secuestro" (García Márquez) 248
Nouira, Hedi Amira (obit.) **94**:73
Novak, Michael (biog.) **95**:53
Novartis (Swiss co.) 173
novel: *see* Literature
Novello, Antonia Coello (biog.) **91**:77
Novick, Sheldon M.
  English literature 241
Noyce, Robert Norton (obit.) **91**:104
NPA (pol. org., Phil.): *see* New People's Army
NPFL (pol. party, Lib.): *see* National Patriotic Front of Liberia
NPP (pol. party, Ghana): *see* New Patriotic Party
Ntibantunganya, Sylvestre 402
NTSB (U.S.): *see* National Transportation Safety Board
Nu, U, *or* Thakin Nu (obit.) **96**:91
nuclear chemistry 253
Nuclear Electric: *see* British Energy
nuclear energy 163
nuclear engineering 163
nuclear testing
  China 409
  France 419
  French Polynesia 381
  international agreements 269
  Marshall Islands 449
  opposition by Japan 439
  Pacific Islands (spotlight) 450, *ils.* 451
  World War II (special report) **96**:258
nuclear warfare
  World War II (special report) **96**:258
nuclear waste: *see* radioactive waste

nuclear weapon
  cultural anthropology 134
  international agreements 269
  international law 223
  Pacific nuclear testing *map* 451
  special report 93:233
  United Nations 376
  World War II (special report) 96:258
"Nuit la neige, La" (Pujade-Renaud) 246
Nujoma, Sam (biog.) 90:95
  Namibia 455
Numismatics 97:151; 96:130; 94:247;
  93:245; 92:246; 91:274; 90:292;
  89:274; 88:277
Nunn, Trevor
  theatre 285
Nureyev, Rudolf Hametovich (obit.) 94:73
nursing (med.)
  special report 97:220
"Nutty Professor, The" (motion picture) 289
Nyandoro, George Bodzo (obit.) 95:77
NYCB (Am. ballet co.): *see* New York City Ballet
NYNEX Corp. (Am. co.) 175, 196
NYSE: *see* New York Stock Exchange
NYZS/The Wildlife Conservation Society, *or* New York Zoological Society (N.Y.C., N.Y., U.S.)"
  "Zoos Look to the 21st Century" (special report) 94:112

O

O Fiaich, Tomas Seamus Cardinal (obit.) 91:104
O Jin U (obit.) 96:92
OAS: *see* American States, Organization of
Oasis (Br. mus. group) 280
OAST-Flyer (satellite)
  space exploration 258
Oates, Joyce Carol 240, *il.* 241
obesity
  drug treatment 221
  Prozac (special report) 95:215
Obiang Nguema Mbasogo, Teodoro 415
Obituaries 97:91; 96:73; 95:60; 94:54;
  93:54; 92:54; 91:86; 90:103; 89:87;
  88:87
O'Boyle, Patrick Aloysius Cardinal (obit.) 88:106
Obraztsov, Sergey Vladimirovich (obit.) 93:73
O'Brian, Patrick 243
O'Brien, Lawrence Francis, Jr. (obit.) 91:104
O'Brien, Sean C.
  fullerene research 63
ocean circulation 187
Ocean Drilling Program 187
  hot springs discovery 184
ocean floor, *or* seafloor
  oceanography 187
  Pacific Islands (spotlight) 451
Oceanian affairs 94:493; 93:492; 92:484;
  91:511; 90:527; 89:511; 88:510
  military affairs 276, *table* 273
  religion statistics *table* 311
  see also individual countries by name
oceanography 187
Ochirbat, Punsalmaagiyn (biog.) 91:78
Ochoa, Severo (obit.) 94:73
Ochoa Sánchez, Arnaldo (obit.) 90:120
O'Connell, David (obit.) 92:75
O'Connell, Helen (obit.) 94:74
O'Connor, Sinead (biog.) 91:78
"Octagonal" (horse) 337
Odinga, Ajuma Oginga (obit.) 95:77
O'Donnell, Rosie *il.* 262
O'Donoghue, Bernard 243
ODS (pol. party, Czech Rep.): *see* Civic Democratic Party
OECD: *see* Economic Co-operation and Development, Organisation for
O'Faolain, Sean (obit.) 92:75
off-Broadway (thea.) 287
offshore drilling
  Falkland Islands 380
Ogata, Sadako (biog.) 92:46
OH (chem.): *see* hydroxyl
Ohio (state, U.S.) 497
Ohio State University (U.S.)
  football 343
Ohno, Kazuo 283
Ohno, Taiichi (obit.) 91:104
oil: *see* petroleum
oil spill 206
oilseed
  world production 128, *table* 125
Okada, Eiji (obit.) 96:92
Okello, Gen. Tito (obit.) 97:113
Okinawa Island (is., Japan)
  United States military bases 276, 438
Oklahoma City (Okla., U.S.) 495
Olajuwon, Hakeem (biog.) 95:53
Olav V (obit.) 92:75
old age
  Canadian pensions 404
  "Financial Support for the Elderly" (special report) 94:144
  health and disease 221, 222
  social protection 312
Old City Tunnel (tunnel, Isr.) 135, 434, *map* 435

Old Rose *il.* 215
Oleksy, Jozef 462
olestra, *or* Olean
  food processing 132
  United States consumer affairs 203
Olive Tree (pol. party, It.) 436
Oliver, Raymond Guillaume (obit.) 91:104
Oliver, Sy (obit.) 89:104
Olivier, Laurence Kerr (obit.) 90:120
Olson, Elder James (obit.) 93:73
Olson, James Elias (obit.) 89:104
Olympic Games
  advertising 154
    athletic footwear 156
    soft drinks 159
  architecture 137
  art exhibitions 144, 146
  Australia 391
  events
    archery 317
    association football 341
    badminton 320
    baseball 322
    basketball 325
    billiards 325
    cycling 335
    diving 358
    fencing 339
    field hockey 339
    gymnastics 348
    judo 352
    rowing 353
    sailing 355
    show jumping and dressage 338
    swimming 357
    synchronized swimming 359
    table tennis 360
    track and field sports 362
      marathon running 370
    volleyball 370
    weight lifting 370
    wrestling 370
  1994 Winter Olympic champions *table* 95:309
  1996 Summer Olympic champions *table* 97:365
  special reports 97:364; 95:308; 93:276; 89:340
  stamp exhibit 151
  terrorism 226
  United States 495
"Olympic Winter Games, The" (special report) 95:308
Omai gold mine (Guy.) 426
Oman 97:459; 96:452; 95:454; 94:389; 93:390; 92:388; 91:413; 90:433; 89:416; 88:416
  new flag *il.* 96:365
  see also WORLD DATA
Omega Watch Corp. (Br. co.) 217
on-line service 180
  libraries 204
  magazines 267
  museums 231
  newspapers 266
  telecommunications 177
Onassis, Christina (obit.) 89:104
Onassis, Jacqueline Bouvier Kennedy (obit.) 95:77
  auctions 150
    antiquarian books 151
    collectibles 152
"Once on This Island" (play) 288
Ondaatje, Michael (biog.) 93:45
Ondieki, Yobes (biog.) 94:47
"101 Dalmatians" (motion picture) 289
"One Flea Spare" (play) 288
O'Neill, Gerard Kitchen (obit.) 93:74
O'Neill, Thomas Philip, Jr., *or* Tip O'Neill (obit.) 95:77
O'Neill of the Maine, Terence Marne O'Neill (obit.) 91:104
Onetti, Juan Carlos (obit.) 95:78
Onganía, Juan Carlos (obit.) 96:92
Onoe, Shoroku, II (obit.) 90:121
Onoe Baiko VII, *or* Seizo Terashima (obit.) 96:92
Oort, Jan Hendrik (obit.) 93:73
OPEC: *see* Petroleum Exporting Countries, Organization of
opera 277
  "Der Ring des Nibelungen" 278
  Germany 424
  Vinay contribution 121
Operation Desert Sabre
  Persian Gulf War (special report) 92:232
Operation Desert Storm
  Persian Gulf War (special report) 92:232
Operation Joint Endeavor
  Bosnia and Herzegovina 270
Operation Long Reach
  apartheid 229
Operation Sharp Guard
  Bosnia and Herzegovina 271
Oppenheimer, Sir Philip Jack (obit.) 96:92
Opperman, Sir Hubert Ferdinand (obit.) 97:113
Opsanus tau: *see* oyster toadfish
optical engineering
  ceramics 167
optical fibre 166
oral polio vaccine, *or* OPV 222
Orange Prize (Br. lit.) 243
Orbison, Roy (obit.) 89:104
Oregon (state, U.S.) 497
  mud slides 61
O'Reilly, Tony 264

O'Reilly, William Joseph (obit.) 93:74
organ donation
  new guidelines 222
organic chemistry 253
Organization for . . . : *see under* substantive word, *e.g.*, Economic Co-operation and Development, Organisation for
Organization of . . . : *see under* substantive word, *e.g.*, Petroleum Exporting Countries, Organization of
organized crime
  Ireland 434
  Italy 228, 436
  Netherlands, The 456
Oriental Orthodox Church 308
Orimulsion
  environmental issues 210
Orix BlueWave (baseball) 322
Ornish, Dean (biog.) 94:47
ornithology
  Peterson contribution 114
  see also bird
orphanage
  China 314, 408, *il.* 314
Orsini, Marina (biog.) 94:48
Ortega, Domingo (obit.) 89:105
Ortega Lara, José Antonio 475
Ortese, Anna Maria 247
Orthodox Church, The 308
  religion statistics *table* 311
  Russia 300
Orthodox Church of Albania 308
Osaka (Japan)
  most populous urban areas *table* 296
OSAT (U.S.): *see* Automotive Transportation, Office for the Study of
Osborne, John James (obit.) 95:78
OSCE: *see* Security and Cooperation in Europe, Organization for
O'Shea, Tessie (obit.) 96:92
Osheroff, Douglas
  Nobel Prize 64
"Österrichi-Österreich: People, Myths, and Landmarks" (Aus. hist. exhibit) 393
Österreich document
  Austrian history 393
  see also Austria
Ota, Masahide 439
otolith
  marine biology 235
O'Toole, James
  "From Marx to Madison: Socialism's Cultural Contradictions" (feature article) 89:5
"Ototo" (Ishihara) 252
Ottey, Merlene 362
Otto, Kristin (biog.) 89:80
Ottoman Empire
  Bosnia and Herzegovina (special report) 94:426
Outerbridge, Paul, Jr. 149
"Outis" (opera) 278
"Outlines of an Emerging World, The" (commentary) 96:6
outsourcing
  automobile industry 157
Oviedo, Lino César
  Paraguay 276, 460
Qvitz, Michael (biog.) 94:48
ÖVP (pol. party, Aus.): *see* Austrian People's Party
Owada, Masako: *see* Masako, Princess
oyster toadfish, *or* Opsanus tau
  muscle contraction 232
Ozal, Turgut (obit.) 94:74
Ozawa, Ichiro (biog.) 95:53
ozone layer
  Antarctica 382
  Arctic regions 383
  environmental issues 210
  global research 259

P

Pace, Orlando
  football 343
Pacific Islands (reg., Pac.O.)
  higher education 206
  nuclear testing (spotlight) 450, *ils.* 451
Pacific Northwest Ballet, *or* PNB (Am. ballet co.) 282
Pacific Ocean
  oceanography 187
Pacific Rim (reg., E. As.)
  paper and pulp 179
Pacific TelesisGroup (Am. co.) 175, 196
packaging
  food processing 132
Packard, David (obit.) 97:114
Packard, Vance Oakley (obit.) 97:114
Packard Bell (Am. co.) 182
Padania (reg., It.)
  independence movement 436
Paektu, Mount (N. Kor.) *il.* 441
Page, Geraldine (obit.) 88:106
Page, Robert Morris (obit.) 93:74
Page, Ruth (obit.) 92:75
Pagels, Elaine (biog.) 96:65
Paglia, Camille (biog.) 94:48
Pagophila eburnea: *see* ivory gull
Pagu, *or* Patrícia Galvão 249
PAICV (pol. party, C.Verde): *see* African Party for the Independence of Cape Verde

painting (art)
  archaeology *il.* 136
  auctions 144, 150
paints and varnishes 172
  lead health risks 212
Paisley, Robert (obit.) 97:114
Paiva, Marcelo Rubens 249
Pakistan 97:459; 96:452; 95:454; 94:407; 93:408; 92:405; 91:433; 90:450; 89:433; 88:434
  disasters
    buildings 61
    natural 60
    traffic 61
  international affairs
    Afghanistan 297, 388
    India 432
  military affairs 269, 276
  most populous urban areas *table* 296
  roads 142
  special reports 94:377; 93:96
  sports and games
    cricket 332
    squash 357
  see also WORLD DATA
Palau 97:460; 96:453; 95:455
  new flag *illus.* 95:353
  see also WORLD DATA
Palekar, Amol 295
paleontology 238
Paleozoic Era
  greenhouse effect 183
Palestine Liberation Organization, *or* PLO (Pal. pol. org.)
  Islam 310
Palestinian (people)
  Israel 375, 434
  military affairs 273
Paley, William S. (obit.) 91:105
PALIR (pol. org., Rw.): *see* People Bearing Arms to Liberate Rwanda
palm kernel
  world production *table* 125
Palme, Olof
  assassination 229
Palmer, Geoffrey (biog.) 90:95
Palmyra Island (isl., Pac.O.) 381
Pálsson, Thorsteinn (biog.) 88:78
Pamuk, Orhan
  Turkish literature 251
PAN (pol. party, Mex.): *see* National Action Party
Pan, Hermes (obit.) 91:105
Pan Am (Am. airline) 155
Panama 97:460; 96:453; 95:456; 94:488; 93:488; 92:480; 91:507; 90:522; 89:507; 88:506
  see also WORLD DATA
Panama Canal (canal, C.Am.)
  Panama 460
  shipping and ports 373
Panay cloudrunner, *or* Crateromys heaneyi species discovery 213, 233, *il.* 233
Panchen Lama, *or* Bskal-bzang Tshe-brtan (obit.) 90:121
Panchen Lama (11th)
  initiation 309
panda, *or* Ailuropoda melanoleuca, *or* giant panda
  zoos 213
Pandit, Kulbhushan Nath (obit.): *see* Kumar, Raaj
Pandit, Vijaya Lakshmi (obit.) 91:105
Panhellenic Socialist Movement, *or* Pasok (pol. org., Gr.) 425
Panic, Milan (biog.) 93:45
Pankratov, Denis 357
Panozzo, John (obit.) 97:114
Panufnik, Sir Andrzej (obit.) 92:75
Pao, Sir Yue-kong (obit.) 92:75
Papandreou, Andreas Georgios 425
  biography 90:95
  obituary 97:114
Papandreou, George 205
Papenfuss-Gorek, Bert 245
paper and pulp 179
paper money: *see* Numismatics
paper wasp, *or* Polistes
  entomology 233
Papp, Joseph (obit.) 92:76
Papua New Guinea 97:460; 96:454; 95:456; 94:498; 93:409; 92:490; 91:517; 90:533; 89:517; 88:516
  mining (spotlight) 450
  Solomon Islands 472
  see also WORLD DATA
Paradzhanov, Sergey Iosifovich (obit.) 91:105
Paraguay 97:460; 96:454; 95:457; 94:488; 93:489; 92:481; 91:507; 90:523; 89:508; 88:506
  association football 341
  aviation disasters 58
  military affairs 276
  see also WORLD DATA
parasite
  entomology 233
parental leave 201
Pargeter, Edith Mary: *see* Peters, Ellis
Paris (Fr.)
  art exhibitions 145
  classical music 277
  depression study 222
  fashion 216
  most populous urban areas *table* 296
Paris Bourse
  stock exchanges 198

Paris Club
  Guyana 426
  Zambia 504
Paris Opéra Ballet (Fr. ballet co.) 285
Paris St. Germain (soccer) 340
Parish, Sister, *or* Dorothy May Kinnicutt (obit.) **95**:78
Parizeau, Jacques (biog.) **92**:46
  Quebec 404
Park, Nick
  computer animation (special report) 293
Park Joo Bong 320
Parker, Hershel 241
Parker, James Stewart (obit.) **89**:105
Parkinson, Cecil Edward (biog.) **88**:78
Parkinson, Cyril Northcote (obit.) **94**:74
Parkinson, Norman (obit.) **91**:105
Parkinson's disease 218
Parks, Bert (obit.) **93**:74
Parnis, Mollie (obit.) **93**:75
Parretti, Giancarlo (biog.) **92**:47
Parrish, Robert (obit.) **96**:92
Parsipur, Shahrnush 251
Pärt, Arvo (biog.) **96**:65
partial-birth abortion
  religious opposition 300
  United States 218
particle physics 255
Partisan (Serbo-Croatian mil. org.)
  Bosnia and Herzegovina (special report) **94**:427
Partnership for Peace, *or* PfP
  NATO military affairs 270
"Partnership of Nations, A" (Br. White Paper) 488
Pasok (pol. org., Gr.): *see* Panhellenic Socialist Movement
Pasqua, Charles (biog.) **95**:54
Pass, Joe (obit.) **95**:78
"Passion" (play) 287
passive smoking 221
Pasternak, Joseph (obit.) **92**:76
Patané, Giuseppe (obit.) **90**:121
Patapievici, Horia-Roman 251
Pathak, Lakhubhai 431
Paton, Alan Stewart (obit.) **89**:105
Patrick, John (obit.) **96**:92
Patriotic Union of Kurdistan, *or* PUK (Kurdish pol. org.)
  Iran 375, 433
  Iraq 433
  military affairs 272
Patten, Christopher (biog.) **93**:46
  United Kingdom 489
Patterson, Clair Cameron (obit.) **96**:92
Patterson, Frederick Douglass (obit.) **89**:105
Pauk, Gyorgy 279
Paul, Jean-Claude (obit.) **89**:105
Paul, Wolfgang
  biography **90**:96
  obituary **94**:74
"Paul McCall" (motion picture) 295
Paul Taylor Dance Company (Am. dance co.) 283
Pauley, Jane (biog.) **91**:78
Pauling, Linus Carl (obit.) **95**:78
Payless ShoeSource Inc. (Am. co.) 156
Payne, Billy
  Olympic Games (special report) 364
Paz, Octavio (biog.) **91**:78
Paz Zamora, Jaime (biog.) **90**:96
Paznyak, Zyanon 396
Pazzi, Roberto 247
PBA: *see* Professional Bowlers Association
PBT: *see* Professional Billiards Tour
PC: *see* personal computer
PCA: *see* Professional Cuesports Association
PCP (pol. party, Ghana): *see* People's Convention Party
PD (pol. party, El. Sal.): *see* Democratic Party
PDF: *see* portable document format
PDS (pol. party, It.): *see* Democratic Party of the Left
PDSR (pol. party, Rom.): *see* Social Democracy Party of Romania
peace
  Angola 389
  Bosnia and Herzegovina 271, 398
  Congo 410
  Nobel Prize 62
  Northern Ireland 226, 433, 489
  Russia 271, 464
  World War II (special report) **96**:257
peace process: *see* Arab-Israeli peace process
Peace Street (Grozny, Chechnya, Russ.) *il.* 315
peacekeeping force
  Albania 389
  Burundi 402
  Canada 405
  Estonia 418
  Japan 439
  Kyrgyzstan 443
  military affairs 269, 271
  see also United Nations Peacekeeping Forces
Peacock, Andrew Sharp (biog.) **90**:96
Peale, Norman Vincent (obit.) **94**:74
peanut
  world production *table* 125
Pearl, Minnie, *or* Sarah Ophelia Colley Cannon (obit.) **97**:114
  popular music 282
Pearl Harbor attack
  Japanese-Brazilians (spotlight) 400
Pearl Jam (biog.) **95**:54
Pearl River (riv., China)
  bridge construction 139
Pearsall, Phyllis Isobel Gross (obit.) **97**:114
Pecorelli, Mino
  Italy 436
Pedersen, Charles John
  biography **88**:79
  obituary **90**:121
Pedra Pintada, Caverna de (archae. site, Braz.) 135, 136
Peierls, Sir Rudolf Ernst (obit.) **96**:92
Pekić, Borislav
  Eastern European literature 250
Pele's Pit, *or* Pele's Vents
  Hawaiian volcanoe 184
Pelindaba Treaty
  military affairs 269
Pelli, Cesar (biog.) **96**:66
Pelling, Brett 338
PEN/Faulkner Award for Fiction 242
Pendleton, Clarence (obit.) **89**:105
Peng Ming-min 478
Penick, Harvey (obit.) **96**:92
Pennel, John Thomas (obit.) **94**:74
Penney of East Hendred, William George Penney (obit.) **92**:76
Pennsylvania Avenue (ave., Wash., D.C., U.S.)
  anti-terrorism proposals 139
penology: *see* Prisons and Penology
pension
  "Financial Support for the Elderly" (special report) **94**:144
  Germany 424
  social protection 313
Pentagon, The (U.S.): *see* Defense, Department of
pentathlon, *or* modern pentathlon
  1996 Summer Olympic champions *table* **97**:366
Pentecostal Churches 304
People Bearing Arms to Liberate Rwanda, *or* PALIR (pol. org., Rw.) 467
People of the Year 97:65; **96**:52; **95**:36; **94**:30; **93**:30; **92**:30; **91**:64; **90**:81; **89**:65; **88**:65
"People vs. Larry Flynt, The" (motion picture) 289
People's Convention Party, *or* PCP (pol. party, Ghana) 425
People's Front for Democracy and Justice (pol. party, Eritrea): *see* Eritrean People's Liberation Front
People's Liberation Army (Chin. army) 409
Pépin, Jean-Luc (obit.) **96**:92
Peppard, George (obit.) **95**:79
Pepper, Art 280
Pepper, Claude Denson (obit.) **90**:121
PepsiCo, Inc. (Am. co.) 159
peptide
  botany 235
Percy, Walker (obit.) **91**:105
Pérec, Marie-José (biog.) **97**:83
  track and field sports 362, 369
Peres, Shimon 434
perestroika
  special report **88**:474
Pérez, Jefferson 368
Pérez Balladares, Ernesto
  Panama 460
Pérez de Cuéllar, Javier (biog.) **89**:81
Pérez Rodríguez, Carlos Andrés (biog.) **90**:96
Performing Arts 97:277; **96**:263; **95**:249; **94**:243; **93**:241; **92**:241; **91**:270; **90**:288; **89**:271; **88**:273
perihelion (astron.)
  1997 *table* 256
periodic table 253
Perkins, Anthony (obit.) **93**:75
Perkins, Lucian 150, *il.* 267
Perkins, Sam *il.* 323
Peronist (pol. party, Arg.): *see* Justicialist National Movement
Perot, Henry Ross (biog.) **93**:46
  special report 492; **93**:470
"Perpetual Mirage: Photographic Narratives of the Desert West" (phot. exhibition) 149
"perro del hortelano, El" (motion picture): *see* "Dog in the Manger"
Perroux, François (obit.) **88**:106
Perry, Frank (obit.) **96**:92
Perry, Frederick John (obit.) **96**:92
Perry, Kenny 347
Persian Gulf War
  criticism of Bush 375
  Czech Republic 412
  health and disease study 221
  nerve gas exposure 269
  special report **92**:232
  United States 496
Persian literature 251
Persichetti, Vincent (obit.) **88**:107
personal computer, *or* PC 181
Personal Responsibility and Work Opportunity Reconciliation Act (U.S.) 312
Persson, Göran
  China 409
  Sweden 477
Pertini, Alessandro (obit.) **91**:106
Pertwee, John Devon Roland, *or* Jon Pertwee (obit.) **97**:114
Peru **97**:461; **96**:455; **95**:457; **94**:489; **93**:489; **92**:481; **91**:508; **90**:524; **89**:508; **88**:507
  archaeology 136
  association football 342
  disasters
    aviation 58
    fires and explosions 59
    natural 60
  Japanese immigration 400
  military affairs 276
  see also WORLD DATA
Peslier, Olivier 337
peso (currency)
  Mexico 453
pesticide
  botany 236
  wildlife effect 213
PET: *see* polyethylene terephthalate
Peter, Laurence J. (obit.) **91**:106
Peter Rabbit (biog.) **94**:48
Peters, Ellis, *or* Edith Mary Pargeter (obit.) **96**:92
Peters, Winston
  New Zealand 456
Peterson, Oscar (biog.) **90**:97
Peterson, Roger Tory (obit.) **97**:114
petrel
  ornithology 234
petrol: *see* gasoline
petroleum 162
  Arctic regions 383
  Barbados 395
  China 409
  commodity prices 199
  environmental issues 206
  Faroe Islands 380
  Greenland 380
  Iraq 377, 433
  Jordan 439
  mining *table* 172
  Norway 459
  Peru 461
  United Arab Emirates 487
  Venezuela 501
Petroleum Exporting Countries, Organization of, *or* OPEC 163
Petronas Towers (bldg., Kuala Lumpur, Mal.) 139, 140, 448, *il.* 448
Petrovic, Drazen (obit.) **94**:75
Petsmart (Am. co.) 174
Pettigrew, Pierre 404
Peyron, Bruno (biog.) **94**:49
"Pez de vidrio" (Santos Febres) 248
Pfeiffer, Michelle (biog.) **93**:46
PFL (pol. party, Braz.): *see* Liberal Front Party
PfP: *see* Partnership for Peace
PGA: *see* Professional Golfers' Association of America
Pham Hung (obit.) **89**:105
Pharaon, Henri-Philippe (obit.) **94**:75
pharmaceuticals 172
  health and disease 219
  see also drugs
Pharmacia & Upjohn (Am. co.) 173
"Phenomenon" (motion picture) 289
Philadelphia (Pa., U.S.)
  blizzard 60
"Philadelphia Inquirer" (Am. news.) 266
Philadelphia Zoological Gardens (zoo, Philadelphia, Pa., U.S.)
  fire tragedy 213
Philately 97:151; **96**:130; **94**:247; **93**:245; **92**:246; **91**:274; **90**:292; **89**:274; **88**:277
Philbrick, Herbert Arthur (obit.) **94**:75
Philby, Kim (obit.) **89**:105
Philippines **97**:461; **96**:455; **95**:457; **94**:415; **93**:416; **92**:411; **91**:439; **90**:457; **89**:440; **88**:440
  disasters
    fires and explosions 59
    marine 59
    traffic 61
  equity markets (special report) **95**:173
  Islam 310
  mining incident 172
  most populous urban areas *table* 296
  newspapers 265
  radio industry 264
  zoology 233
  see also WORLD DATA
Phillips Exeter Academy Library (Exeter, N.H., U.S.) 137
Phodilus prigoginei: *see* Congo bay owl
Phoenix, River (obit.) **94**:75
Phoenix Coyotes, *or* Winnipeg Jets (ice hockey) 349
phonom
  physics 255
photo essay
  Gypsies 428
  Hutus 298
  Newbury Bypass protest 208
Photography 97:173; **96**:151; **95**:133; **94**:248; **93**:246; **92**:247; **91**:275; **90**:293; **89**:276; **88**:278
  art auctions 151
  digital technology 181
  exhibitions 149
  space exploration 258, 260
photojournalism 149
Phoumi Vongvichit (obit.) **95**:79
physical anthropology 133
physical chemistry 253
physician-assisted suicide: *see* euthanasia
Physics 97:254; **96**:241; **95**:254; **94**:250; **93**:249; **92**:249; **91**:277; **90**:295; **89**:278; **88**:280
  Nobel Prize 64
physiology
  Nobel Prize 64
Phytophthora (fungus)
  molecular biology 236
phytoplankton
  oceanography 187
Piazzolla, Astor (obit.) **93**:75
Picasso, Pablo
  art exhibition 148
Pickens, Rev. Levi *il.* 302
Picon, Molly (obit.) **93**:75
"Picture of Dorian Gray, The" (opera) 278
Pictures of the Year Competition (U.S.)
  awards 150
"piel del tambor, La" (Pérez-Reverte) 247
Pienaar, François
  rugby football 345
Pietrangeli, Carlo (obit.) **96**:92
pig
  world production 129, *table* 126
pig iron: *see* iron and steel
Pilkington, Sir Alastair, *or* Sir Lionel Alexander Bethune Pilkington (obit.) **96**:92
"Pillow Book, The" (motion picture) 290
Pimen (Bulg. Orthodox patriarch) 308
Pimen (Russ. Orthodox patriarch)
  obituary **91**:106
Pinay, Antoine (obit.) **95**:79
Pineau, Christian Paul (obit.) **96**:92
Pinnacle award
  furniture 165
Pinochet Ugarte, Augusto 407
Pinsky, Robert 241
Pinson, Veda (obit.) **96**:92
Pintye, Elizabeth (obit.): *see* Wallenda, Angel
pipe bomb
  Olympic Games 226, 495
pipelines: *see* freight and pipelines
Piper, John Egerton Christmas (obit.) **93**:75
Pitino, Rick 323
Pittsburgh Steelers (football) 344
Pixar Animation Studios (Am. co.)
  computer animation (special report) 292
PJ (pol. party, Arg.): *see* Justicialist National Movement
PKK (pol. org.): *see* Kurdish Workers' Party
planet
  extrasolar discovery 257
plant: *see* botany
plastics 167
plate tectonics 185
platinum-group metals 171
Player, Gary 346
Plaza Lasso, Galo (obit.) **88**:107
PLD (pol. party, Dom.Rep.): *see* Dominican Liberation Party
Pleasance, Donald (obit.) **96**:92
Pleven, René (obit.) **94**:75
Plimsoll, Sir James (obit.) **88**:107
Pliva (Croatian co.) 411
PLO (Pal. pol. org.): *see* Palestine Liberation Organization
ploughshare tortoise, *or* angonoka, *or* Geochelone yniphora
  wildlife conservation 213
PM10
  health dangers 210
PNB (Am. ballet co.): *see* Pacific Northwest Ballet
pocket billiards 325
Podkopayeva, Liliya 348
"Poems of the Damned" (O'Connor) 243
poetry: *see* Literature
Poher, Alain-Émile-Louis-Marie (obit.) **97**:114
Poiret, Jean (obit.) **93**:75
Pol Pot 403
Poland **97**:462; **96**:456; **95**:458; **94**:447; **93**:448; **92**:437; **91**:472; **90**:490; **89**:473; **88**:471
  arts and entertainment
    literature 63, 250
    motion pictures 295
  chemicals 161
  economic affairs 193
  Holocaust memorial controversy 300
  newspapers 265
  social security and pensions 314
  wrestling 370
  see also WORLD DATA
polar bear, *or* Ursus maritimus
  wildlife conservation 213
polar regions: *see* Antarctica; Arctic Regions
Polgar, Judit (biog.) **93**:47
Polgar, Sofia (biog.) **93**:47
Polgar, Zsuzsa (biog.) **93**:47
  chess 330
Poliakoff, Stephen 286
police: *see* Law Enforcement
polio vaccine
  new immunization guidelines 222
Polisario Front (pol. org., N.Af.) 377
Polish literature 63, 250
Polistes: *see* paper wasp
Polistes atrimandibularis (insect) 233
Polistes biglumis bimaculatus (insect) 233
political asylum: *see* asylum
political correctness (special report) **92**:459

Political Parties 97:384; **96**:362; **95**:363; **94**:348; **93**:350; **92**:344; **91**:374; **90**:376; **89**:379; **88**:379
Africa (spotlight) 416, *map* 417
see also individual countries by name
political prisoner
Australia 392
Ethiopia 418
Peru 461
Pollard, Jonathan Jay (biog.) **88**:79
pollution
Arctic regions 383
environment 207
United States 499
see also air pollution; water pollution
polo **97**:338; **96**:318; **95**:298; **94**:304; **93**:306; **92**:302; **91**:332; **90**:351; **89**:333; **88**:335
polybutadiene 167
polycyclic aromatic hydrocarbon
life on Mars claim 256
polyethylene 167
polyethylene terephthalate, *or* PET
food processing 132
"Polygraphe, Le" (motion picture) 290
Pomus, Jerome (obit.) **92**:76
Ponge, Francis (obit.) **89**:106
Ponnelle, Jean-Pierre (obit.) **89**:106
Pons, Bobby Stanley (biog.) **90**:97
Ponsford, William Harold (obit.) **92**:76
Pontecorvo, Bruno (obit.) **94**:75
Pontiero, Giovanni 249
Poole, David (obit.) **92**:76
Popa, Vasko (obit.) **92**:77
Popcorn, Faith (biog.) **93**:47
pope (Roman Cath.)
election procedure 306
Popov, Aleksandr 358
Popp, Lucia (obit.) **94**:75
Popper, Sir Karl Raimund (obit.) **95**:79
popular music 280
Popular Revolutionary Army, *or* EPR (pol. org., Mex.) 452
military affairs 276
Populations 97:295; **96**:279; **95**:255; **94**:252; **93**:250; **92**:250; **91**:278; **90**:296; **89**:280; **88**:282
most populous urban areas *table* 296
special reports **94**:144; **91**:279; **88**:318
see also WORLD DATA
pork
world production 129, *table* 126
pornography
cyberspace (special report) **96**:159
telecommunications reform 181
Porritt, Arthur Espie Porritt (obit.) **95**:80
port: *see* shipping and ports
Port Arthur (Tas., Austr.)
massacre 227, 391
portable document format, *or* PDF
printing 173
"Portable War Memorial, The" (art) *il.* 144
Porter, Barry 487
Porter, Charles, IV 150
Porter, Eliot Furness (obit.) **91**:106
Porter, Eric Richard (obit.) **96**:93
"Portia Coughlan" (play) 287
"Portrait of a Lady, The" (motion picture) 290
Portugal **97**:463; **96**:457; **95**:459; **94**:448; **93**:449; **92**:439; **91**:460; **90**:476; **89**:460; **88**:460
dams 142
Grand Prix racing 318
labour-management relations 202
literature 249
motion pictures 291
see also WORLD DATA
Portuguese literature 249
Portuguese-Speaking Countries, Community of 224
positron, *or* antielectron 255
Possony, Stefan Thomas (obit.) **96**:93
Post, Sir Laurens Jan van der (obit.) **97**:114
British literature 244
Postimpressionism
art exhibitions (special report) 146
"postino, Il" (motion picture)
film awards *table* 294
postmodernism
Latin-American literature (special report) **96**:234
Russian literature 249
postnatal depression
estrogen therapy 222
potassium
high-pressure chemistry 254
Potsdam Conference
World War II (special report) **96**:259
Potsdamer Platz *il.* 140
Potter, Dennis Christopher George (obit.) **95**:80
pottery
auctions and collectibles 152
Poulin, Alfred A., Jr. (obit.) **97**:114
poultry
world production 129, *table* 126
Poundbury (Dorset, U.K.) 138
poverty
agriculture and food supply 125
China 409
microbanking 200
U.S. social protection 313
powder metallurgy 168
Powell, Colin Luther (biog.) **90**:97
Powell, Elizabeth Dilys (obit.) **96**:93
Powell, Michael Latham (obit.) **91**:106
Powell, Mike (biog.) **92**:47
PowerGen (Br. co.) 210
PowerPC chip 169
PPB (pol. party, Braz.): *see* Brazilian Progressive Party
PPG Industries (Am. co.) 172
Prada, Miuccia 216
Pramoj, Kukrit (obit.) **96**:93
Pratolini, Vasco (obit.) **92**:77
Pratt & Whitney (Am. co.) 155
"Pravda" (Russ. news.) 265
PRCA: *see* Professional Rodeo Cowboys Association
PRD (pol. party, Dom.Rep.): *see* Dominican Revolutionary Party
Preakness Stakes (horse racing) 336
predation (zool.) 233
Preil, Gabriel (obit.) **94**:75
Premadasa, Ranasinghe
biography **90**:97
obituary **94**:75
prenatal test 218
Presbyterian Church in America
"Homosexuality and the Churches" (special report) **94**:264
Presbyterian Church (U.S.A.) 304
"Homosexuality and the Churches" (special report) **94**:264
Prescott, John (biog.) **95**:54
President's Award (Tur. lit.) 251
Pressburger, Emeric (obit.) **89**:106
Presser, Jackie (obit.) **89**:106
Preston, Lewis Thompson (obit.) **96**:93
Preston, Robert (obit.) **88**:107
Prestoncrest Church of Christ (Dallas, Tex., U.S.) 302
Préval, René 427
PRI (pol. party, Mex.): *see* Institutional Revolutionary Party
Price, George (obit.) **96**:93
Price, Nick (biog.) **95**:55
Price, Sammy (obit.) **93**:75
Price, Vincent (obit.) **94**:76
Priebke, Erich 436
priesthood
Anglican church and women 301
Primakov, Yevgeny 379, 465
"Primary Colors" (Klein) 268
primary education 203
primate
anthropology 133
zoos 213
Primus, Pearl (obit.) **95**:80
Princeton Theological Seminary (U.S.)
"Homosexuality and the Churches" (special report) **94**:264
print (phot.)
Advanced Photo System 173
printing 173
newspapers 265
printmaking
art auctions 150
"Prisoner of the Mountains" (motion picture) 291
Prisons and Penology 97:229; **96**:215; **95**:145; **94**:116; **93**:115; **92**:113; **91**:143; **90**:160; **89**:142; **88**:142
El Salvador 415
Italy 225
Sudan, The *il.* 229
United States 498, *il.* 497
Pritchard, John Michael (obit.) **90**:121
Pritzker Architecture Prize 137
privacy
cyberspace (special report) **96**:159
privatization
banking 200
Brazil 401
business and industry
mining 170
nuclear plants 163
water-purification systems 160
Czech Republic 412
dams 141
eastern Europe 193
education
United States 204
France 419
Hungary 430
Morocco 454
Peru 461
special reports **93**:143; **92**:465
Tajikistan 482
television industry 261
transportation
freight and pipelines 373
intercity rail 374
urban mass transit 374
Zambia 504
Prix de l'Arc de Triomphe (horse racing) 337
Prix Médicis (Fr. lit.) 246
processed food: *see* food processing
Procter & Gamble (Am. co.)
olestra studies 132, 203
Prodi, Romano 436
product development
food processing 132
Professional Billiards Tour, *or* PBT 325
Professional Bowlers Association, *or* PBA 326
Professional Chess Association 331
Professional Cuesports Association, *or* PCA 325
Professional Golfers' Association of America, *or* PGA 347
Professional Rodeo Cowboys Association, *or* PRCA 352
"Profundo Carmesí" (motion picture): *see* "Deep Crimson"
Progressive Party of the Working People (pol. party, Cyp.) 412
Proops, Rebecca Marjorie Israel (obit.) **97**:115
Proposition 209 (leg., Calif., U.S.)
affirmative action 499
prostitution
forfeiture laws 225
Protection of the Republic, Law on the Slovakia 472
protectionism
special report **88**:172
Protestant churches 301
homosexuality controversy (special report) **94**:263
religion statistics *table* 311
protests and demonstrations: *see* demonstrations and protests
Protocol on Environmental Protection (Antarctic Treaty) 383
Proulx, E. Annie (biog.) **95**:55
Prowse, Juliet (obit.) **97**:115
"Prozac" (special report) **95**:215
PRSC (pol. party, Dom.Rep.): *see* Social Christian Reformist Party
Prusiner, Stanley (biog.) **97**:84
Pryce, Jonathan (biog.) **91**:79
PS (pol. party, Belg.): *see* Socialist Party
PSD (pol. party, Port.): *see* Social Democratic Party
psychedelic dress (Gaultier) *il.* 216
psychotherapy 222
U.S. court case 225
public education (U.S.) 204
public journalism: *see* civic journalism
public libraries: *see* Libraries
public transportation: *see* urban mass transit
Publisher's Clearing House (Am. co.) 267
Publishing 97:265; **96**:247; **95**:259; **94**:256; **93**:256; **92**:253; **91**:283; **90**:300; **89**:283; **88**:285
portable document format 173
Pucci, Emilio (obit.) **93**:76
Puckett, Kirby (biog.) **88**:79
Puerto Rico 381
drug trafficking 227
fires and explosions 59
literature 248
natural disasters 60
see also WORLD DATA
Puig, Manuel (obit.) **91**:106
Pujol, Jordi 474
PUK (Kurdish pol. org.): *see* Patriotic Union of Kurdistan
Pulitzer, Joseph, Jr. (obit.) **94**:76
Pulitzer Prize
book publishing 268
fiction and poetry 242
newspapers 266
photography 150
theatre 288
Pullen, Don (obit.) **96**:93
pulp: *see* paper and pulp
Pulp (Br. mus. group) 280
Pushkin Museum of Fine Arts (Moscow, Russ.) 148
Pyke, Magnus (obit.) **93**:76

Q

Qaddafi, Muammar Muhammad al-, *or* Mu'ammar al-Qadhdhafi
Libya 446
military affairs 273
special report **94**:377
Qatar **97**:463; **96**:458; **95**:460; **94**:390; **93**:390; **92**:388; **91**:414; **90**:434; **89**:416; **88**:416
Bahrain 394
newspapers 265
see also WORLD DATA
Qiao Shi (biog.) **95**:55
Qin Benli, *or* Ch'in Pen-li (obit.) **92**:77
Qoboza, Percy (obit.) **89**:106
"Quadrophenia" (rock opera) 280
Quadros, Jânio da Silva (obit.) **93**:76
Quaker: *see* Religious Society of Friends, The
quantum theory 255
"quaracha del macho Camacho, La" (Sánchez): *see* "Macho Camacho's Beat"
"quarta invasão Francesa, A" (Torres) 249
Quayle, James Danforth (biogs.) **93**:47; **89**:81
special report **93**:470
Quayle, Sir John Anthony (obit.) **90**:122
Qubbat as-Sakhrah (mosque, Jerusalem): *see* Dome of the Rock
Quebec (prov., Can.) 404
French-Canadian literature 247
Native American issues 383
prisons and penology 229
Quebec Nordiques (ice hockey): *see* Colorado Avalanche
"Queen, The" (Pimlott) 243
"Queen Nefertiti and the Royal Women" (art exhibit) 145
Quennell, Sir Peter Courtney (obit.) **94**:76
"Quiet Room, The" (motion picture) 290
Quignard, Pascal 246
Quindlen, Anna (biog.) **95**:55
Quinlan, Joseph (obit.) **97**:115
Quintanilla Perez, Selena: *see* Selena
Qur'an (Islamic scripture)
"Islamic Fundamentalism" (special report) **94**:377

R

R. v. O'Connor
Canadian court decisions 225
Ra, Sun (obit.): *see* Sun Ra
Rabbani, Burhanuddin 388
Rabi, Isidor Isaac (obit.) **89**:106
rabies
control efforts 223
Rabin, Yitzhak
biography **93**:47
obituary **96**:93
Raby, Albert (obit.) **89**:106
Race and Ethnic Relations 96:283; **95**:263; **94**:260; **93**:258; **92**:258; **91**:287; **90**:304; **89**:287; **88**:291
Baptist Churches 302
Bosnia and Herzegovina 398
Burundi 402
Christian Church 302
court decisions 225
Czech Republic 412
Ethiopia 418
Fiji 418
France 419
Gypsy photo essay 428
human rights issues 314, 316
Hutu photo essay 298
military affairs 270, 276
Rwanda 467
South Africa 473
World War II (special report) **96**:257
Zaire 504
Rachid, Mimouni (obit.) **96**:93
racism: *see* Race and Ethnic Relations
racket games: *see* badminton; squash; tennis
Raczynski, Count Edward Bernard André Maria (obit.) **94**:76
Rader, Paul A. 305
radiation
anthropology 133
environmental and health issues 212
Radice, Anne-Imelda (biog.) **93**:47
radio **97**:264; **96**:247; **95**:339; **94**:332; **93**:334; **92**:330; **91**:360; **90**:374; **89**:363; **88**:363
Luxembourg 446
radioactive waste, *or* nuclear waste
Germany 207
Marshall Islands 449
Radner, Gilda (obit.) **90**:122
Rae, Bob (biog.) **91**:79
Rafsanjani, Hojatolislam Ali Akbar Hashemi (biog.) **88**:80
Iran 432
"Ragtime" (play) 288
Rahanwayn Resistance Army, *or* RRA (pol. org., Som.) 472
Rahi, Sultan, *or* Muhammad Sultan (obit.) **97**:115
Raikin, Arkady Isaakovich (obit.) **88**:107
railroad, *or* railway
Channel Tunnel fire 142
civil engineering projects *table* 143
disasters 61
Eritrea *il.* 415
Netherlands, The 456
Turkmenistan 485
Vietnam *il.* 374
see also intercity rail
rainfall: *see* hydrology
Rajneesh, Bhagwan Shree (obit.) **91**:106
Rakhmonov, Imomali 482
Rakowski, Mieczyslaw (biog.) **89**:81
Rally for the Republic, *or* Gaullist, *or* RPR (pol. party, Fr.) 419
Rally of the Togolese People, *or* RPT (pol. party, Togo) 483
Rama Rao, Nandamuri Taraka (obit.) **97**:115
Hinduism 310
Rama Rau, Lady Dhanvanthi (obit.) **88**:107
Ramachandran, Maruthur Gopalan (obit.) **88**:107
Ramaphosa, Matamele Cyril (biog.) **88**:80
Ramaswamy, Venkataraman (biog.) **88**:80
Ramey, Samuel (biog.) **91**:79
Ramos, Fidel Valdez (biog.) **93**:48
Philippines 462
Ramos-Horta, José
Indonesia 432
Nobel Prize 62
Ramsar Convention
wildlife conservation 213
Ramsey, Norman Foster (biog.) **90**:98
Ramsey of Canterbury, Arthur Michael Ramsey (obit.) **89**:107
Ranariddh, Norodom 309
Ranatunga, Arjuna 332
Rand, Paul (obit.) **97**:115
Randolph, Theron G. (obit.) **96**:93
Random House (Am. co.) 268
Raney, James Elbert (obit.) **96**:94

Rani, Devika (obit.) **95**:80
Rankin, James Lee (obit.) **97**:116
"Ransom" (motion picture) 289
Rao, P. V. Narasimha (biog.) **92**:47
political corruption 430
rap (popular mus.) 281
rape
Japan 276, 438
rapeseed
world production 128, *table* 125
Raphael I Bidawid (biog.) **92**:48
Raposo, Joseph G. (obit.) **90**:122
Rasi, Mauro
Brazilian literature 249
Rasmussen, Poul Nyrup (biog.) **94**:49
Denmark 413
rating system
television programs 181
Ratsirahonana, Norbert
Madagascar 447
Ratushinskaya, Irina (biog.) **88**:80
Rauh, Joseph Louis, Jr. (obit.) **93**:76
Ravenhill, Mark 286
Ravera, Camilla (obit.) **89**:107
Rawl, Lawrence G. (biog.) **90**:98
Rawlings, Jerry 378, 425
Ray, Dixy Lee (obit.) **95**:80
Ray, Satyajit (obit.) **93**:76
Rayhhān, Rab'a 252
Raye, Martha (obit.) **95**:80
Raza, Hassan 332
Razaleigh Hamzah, Tengku 448
RDPC (pol. party, Camer.): *see* Cameroon People's Democratic Movement
"Reader's Block" (Markson) 240
"Reading in the Dark" (Deane) 243
Reagan, Ronald Wilson (biogs.) **89**:82; **88**:80
"Real American Bicentennial, The" (feature article) **88**:16
realism
Russian literature 249
"Really Good Brown Girl, A" (Dumont) 242
reapportionment
U.S. Congress 225
Reason, J. Paul 270
Reasoner, Harry (obit.) **92**:77
"Rebecca West: A Saga of the Century" (Rollyson) 243
REC: *see* Reformed Ecumenical Council
Reckley v. Minister of Public Safety
death penalty 225
recognized nation
Fourth World (spotlight) 422, *map* 423
recycling
ceramics 167
glass 166
plastic 168
Red Thunder Cloud, *or* Carlos Westez (obit.) **97**:116
Reddy, Neelam Sanjiva (obit.) **97**:116
Redenbacher, Orville (obit.) **96**:94
Redgrave, Lynn 287
Redgrave, Steven Geoffrey (biog.) **97**:84
rowing 354, 365
Redgrave, Vanessa 288
Redhead, Brian (obit.) **95**:80
Redwood, John Alan (biog.) **97**:84
Reebok International Ltd. (Am. co.) 156
Reed Elsevier (Br. co.) 268
Reese, John Terence (obit.) **97**:116
contract bridge 331
Refah (pol. party, Tur.): *see* Islamic Welfare Party
reform
agriculture and food supplies 123, 125
Algeria 389
Brazil 399
China 408
France 419
Germany 201, 421
Greek education 205
Kazakstan 439
Kenya 440
Mexico 453
Morocco 454
Romania 463
Russia 464
social protection 312
special reports **94**:377; **93**:143, 469
Sweden 477
United States 491
telecommunications 181
Uruguay 500
see also welfare reform
Reform Judaism 300
Reformed Church 304
Reformed Ecumenical Council, *or* REC 304
refugees **97**:297; **96**:281; **95**:258; **94**:254; **93**:253; **92**:252; **91**:282; **90**:299; **89**:282; **88**:284
Bahamas, The 394
Bhutan 397
Germany 425
human rights issues 314, 316
Hutu photo essay 298
Jamaica 437
Netherlands, The *il.* 456
Rwanda 467
Senegal 470
Tanzania 482
Zaire 276, 504
regulation (governmental)
television industry 262
tobacco industry 178, 221
Reich, Robert
labour-management relations (special report) **94**:204
Reichenbach, François-Arnold (obit.) **94**:76
Reichmann, Albert (biog.) **93**:48
Reichmann, Paul (biog.) **93**:48
Reichmann, Ralph (biog.) **93**:48
Reichstein, Tadeus (obit.) **97**:116
Reid, Beryl Elizabeth (obit.) **97**:116
Reijseger, Ernst 279
Reinhard, Johan 136
Reinhold, Robert (obit.) **97**:116
Reinsdorf, Jerry (biog.) **95**:56
Reischauer, Edwin Oldfather (obit.) **91**:107
Reisman, Simon (biog.) **88**:81
"Relativity" (television show) *il.* **97**:261
relay race 368
relief
agriculture and food supplies 123, 126
Churches of Christ 302
Salvation Army 305
Religion 97:300; **96**:289; **95**:266; **94**:261; **93**:260; **92**:259; **91**:289; **90**:306; **89**:289; **88**:293
education 204
religion statistics *table* 311
special reports **94**:263; **93**:261; **92**:261; **91**:289; **90**:308; **89**:290; **88**:294
Religious Coalition for Reproductive Choice 300
Religious Freedom Restoration Act (U.S.) 300
Religious Society of Friends, The 304
"Remembering Babylon" (Malouf) 244
Remick, Lee (obit.) **92**:77
remnant nation
Fourth World (spotlight) 422, *map* 423
Renamo (pol. party, Moz.): *see* Mozambique National Resistance
renascent nation
Fourth World (spotlight) 422, *map* 423
Rendell, Ruth (biog.) **91**:79
"Renjian zhengdao" (Zhou Meiseng) 252
Reno, Janet (biog.) **94**:49
"Rent" (play) 287
repatriate: *see* returnee
"Repete" (motion picture) 295
Repkova, Tatiana 472
Representatives, House of (U.S.): *see* Congress of the United States
"Repressed Memories" (special report) **95**:198
repressed memory therapy, *or* RMT
psychotherapy (special report) **95**:198
reproduction: *see* sexual reproduction
reproductive system, *or* genital organs
female genital mutilation 316
Repsol (Sp. co.) 475
reptile (zool.) 232
Republican Party (U.S.)
education 204
special reports **97**:492; **96**:492; **93**:469
United States 490, 497
Republican People's Party, *or* CHP (pol. party, Tur.) 484
Reserve Bank of Australia 392
"Reshaping a Nation: Korea's Quiet Revolution" (feature article) **92**:29A
Reshevsky, Samuel Herman (obit.) **93**:76
Reston, James Barrett (obit.) **96**:94
retailing 173
Libya 446
retirement
automobile industry 158
economic affairs and the elderly (special report) **94**:144
social protection 313
returnee, *or* repatriate
Bhutan 397
Germany 425
human rights issues 316
refugees 297
Reusable Launch Vehicle, *or* RLV
space exploration 260
Reve, Gerard 245
Revelation (Russ. record label) 279
Revelation Corp. of America
Baptist Churches 302
Revelle, Roger Randall Dougan (obit.) **92**:77
Revie, Donald (obit.) **90**:122
Revolutionary Armed Forces of Colombia (pol. org., Colom.) 276
Revueltas, Rosaura (obit.) **97**:116
Rexe (man-made fibre) 177
Rey, Fernando (obit.) **95**:81
Rey, Margret Elisabeth (obit.) **97**:116
Reyes, Efren 326
Reynolds, Albert (biog.) **93**:48
rhinoceros
wildlife conservation 213
rhythmic gymnastics 348
Riad, Mahmoud (obit.) **93**:77
Ricci, Robert (obit.) **89**:107
rice
world production 128, *table* 124
Rice, Jerry (biog.) **88**:81
football 344
Rich, Ben R. (obit.) **96**:94
Rich, Buddy Bernard (obit.) **88**:107
Rich, Charlie (obit.) **96**:94
Rich, Irene (obit.) **89**:107
"Richard III" (motion picture) 290
film awards *table* 294
Richards, Eugene 150
Richards, Viv (biog.) **91**:79
Richards Shreve, Susan 240
Richardson, Dorothy, *or* Dot Richardson (biog.) **97**:84
Richardson, Miranda 286
Richardson, Robert
Nobel Prize 64
Richardson, Tony (obit.) **92**:77
Ridgway, Matthew Bunker (obit.) **94**:76
"Ridicule" (motion picture) 291
Riding, Laura (obit.) **92**:78
Ridley of Liddesdale, Nicholas Ridley, Baron (obit.) **94**:76
Rie, Dame Lucie (obit.) **96**:94
Rifkind, Malcolm Leslie (biog.) **96**:66
Rifkind, Simon Hirsch (obit.) **96**:94
Rigg, Diana 286
Riggs, Robert Larimore, *or* Bobby Riggs (obit.) **96**:94
right-to-die law, *or* advance-directive law
United States 498
Righteous Force Party (pol. party, Thai.) 482
Righter, Walter C. 301
Rights of the Child, Convention on the (UN)
child welfare (special report) **96**:286
Riis, Bjarne 335, *il.* 334
Rimes, LeAnn 282
Rimington, Stella (biog.) **93**:48
Rincón de Gautier, Felisa (obit.) **95**:81
"Ring des Nibelungen, Der" (opera) 278
"Rings: Five Passions in World Art" (art exhibit) 144
Rio de Janeiro (Braz.)
most populous urban areas *table* 296
riots
Australia 392
Bangladesh 394, *il.* 395
Belarus 395
Cameroon 403
Central African Republic 406
El Salvador 415
Greece 205
Guinea 426
Indonesia 432
Jordan 439
Macedonia 446
Nepal 455
prisons 229
South Korea 441
Swaziland 477
Venezuela 501, *il.*
see also demonstrations and protests
Ripken, Cal, Jr. (biog.) **96**:66
Ripley, Alexandra (biog.) **92**:48
Ritchie, Charles Stewart Almon (obit.) **96**:94
Rite Aid (Am. co.) 174
Ritsos, Yannis (obit.) **91**:107
Ritt, Martin (obit.) **91**:107
Rive, Richard Moore (obit.) **90**:122
river forecasting 187
Rivera, Andrés 248
Rivera, Chita (biog.) **94**:50
Rivera Carrera, Norberto 300
Rizzo, Frank (obit.) **92**:78
RLV: *see* Reusable Launch Vehicle
RMT: *see* repressed memory theory
RNT (U.K.): *see* Royal National Theatre, The
Roach, Harold Eugene (obit.) **93**:77
roads and traffic 373
civil engineering 142, *table* 143
disasters 61
Kenya 440
Roba, Fatuma 369
Robertson, Pat
"Homosexuality and the Churches" (special report) **94**:263
Robinette, John Josiah (obit.) **97**:116
Robinson, Sir David (obit.) **88**:108
Robinson, Mary (biog.) **92**:48
Robinson, Sugar Ray (obit.) **90**:122
Roblès, Emmanuel François (obit.) **96**:95
Roca, Blas (obit.) **88**:108
Rocard, Michel (biog.) **89**:82
Rocard, Yves-André (obit.) **93**:77
Rocha, Adolfo Correia da: *see* Torga, Miguel
rock, *or* rock 'n' roll (mus.) 281
Rock, Allan 404
"Rock, The" (motion picture) 289
Rock and Roll Hall of Fame (Cleveland, Ohio, U.S.)
new inductees 281
rocket (vehicle)
spacecraft launch vehicles 260
Rockwell International Corporation (Am. corp.) 260
Rocky Mountain Dam (dam, U.S.) 142
Roddenberry, Gene Wesley (obit.) **92**:78
Roddick, Anita (biog.) **94**:50
Rodentia
taxonomy 233
rodeo **97**:352; **96**:333; **95**:311; **94**:304; **93**:306; **92**:302; **91**:332; **90**:351; **89**:333; **88**:335
Rodger, George (obit.) **96**:95
Rodionov, Igor 271
Rodman, Dennis Keith (biog.) **97**:84
basketball 323
Rodney, Red (obit.) **95**:81
Rodríguez Pedotti, Andrés (biog.) **90**:98
Roffé, Reina 248
Rogers, Carl Ransom (obit.) **88**:108
Rogers, Ginger, *or* Virginia Katherine McMath (obit.) **96**:95
Roh Tae Woo (biogs.) **89**:82; **88**:81
"Reshaping a Nation: Korea's Quiet Revolution" (feature article) **92**:29A
trial and conviction 441, *il.*
Roland, Gilbert (obit.) **95**:81
Rolin, Jean 246
Rollins, Howard (obit.) **97**:116
Rollins, Sonny 280
Rom (people): *see* Gypsy
Roman, Stephen Boreslav (obit.) **89**:107
Roman Catholicism, *or* Roman Catholic Church 306
homosexuality controversy (special report) **94**:263
Lutheran Communion 303
Poland 462
religion statistics *table* 311
television network 262
Vatican City State 500
Roman Republic and Empire
English Channel history (special report) **95**:350
Romania **97**:463; **96**:458; **95**:460; **94**:449; **93**:450; **92**:439; **91**:473; **90**:491; **89**:474; **88**:473
Eastern European literature 251
higher education 205
homeless youth *il.* 464
Hungary 430
see also WORLD DATA
Romanov, Prince Vladimir Kirillovich (obit.) **93**:77
Romario (biog.) **95**:56
Rome, Esther (obit.) **96**:95
Romer v. Evans (law case, U.S.) 225
Romero, Celedonio (obit.) **97**:116
Romero, Cesar (obit.) **95**:81
Romney, George Wilcken (obit.) **96**:95
roof
new designs 141
Rook, Jean (obit.) **92**:78
Rooney, Arthur (obit.) **89**:107
Roosevelt, Anna
archaeological discovery 135
Roosevelt, Franklin Delano
1945 (special report) **96**:256
Rosas, Juan Manuel de
Latin-American literature 248
rose *il.* 215
Rose, George (obit.) **89**:107
Rose, Sir Michael (biog.) **95**:56
Rose, Pete (biog.) **90**:98
Roseanne: *see* Barr, Roseanne
Rosen, Nathan (obit.) **96**:95
Rosenberg, Tina 268
Ross, James Sinclair (obit.) **97**:116
Ross, Lanny (obit.) **89**:107
Ross, Steven Jay (obit.) **93**:77
Rosselli, Amelia 247
Roth, Henry (obit.) **96**:95
Rothenstein, Sir John Knewstub Maurice (obit.) **93**:77
Rothschild, Amschel 200
Rothschild, Nathaniel Mayer Victor Rothschild, 3rd Baron (obit.) **91**:107
Rothschild, Phillipe de (obit.) **89**:107
Roundtree, Saudia *il.* 324
Rouse, James Wilson (obit.) **97**:116
Rowan, Dan (obit.) **88**:108
Rowicki, Witold (obit.) **90**:122
rowing **97**:353; **96**:333; **95**:311; **94**:305; **93**:307; **92**:303; **91**:333; **90**:351; **89**:333; **88**:335
1996 Summer Olympic champions *table* **97**:366
Rowling, Sir Wallace Edward (obit.) **96**:95
Royal, Marshall (obit.) **96**:95
Royal Cabinet of Paintings (gallery, The Hague, Neth.): *see* Mauritshuis
Royal Danish Ballet (Den. ballet co.) 284
royal family (U.K.) 488
Royal Insurance Holdings (Br. co.) 166
Royal National Theatre, The, *or* RNT (U.K.) 285
Royal Opera House (London, U.K.)
"Der Ring des Nibelungen" 278
Royal Philatelic Collection 151
Royal Shakespeare Company, *or* RSC 285
Royal Winnipeg Ballet (Can. ballet co.) 283
Royster, Vermont Connecticut (obit.) **97**:117
Rozelle, Alvin Ray, *or* Pete Rozelle (obit.) **97**:117
Rozhdestvensky, Robert Ivanovich (obit.) **95**:81
RPR (pol. party, Fr.): *see* Rally for the Republic
RPT (pol. party, Togo): *see* Rally of the Togolese People
RRA (pol. org., Som.): *see* Rahanwayn Resistance Army
RSC: *see* Royal Shakespeare Company
Ruapehu, Mount (N.Z.) *il.* 184
rubber 167
commodity prices 199
rubber boa, *or* Charina bottae
body temperature research 232
Rubin, Jerry (obit.) **95**:81
Rubin, Yves 253
ruble (currency) 465
Rudnicki, Adolf (obit.) **91**:107
Rudolf, Max (obit.) **96**:95
Rudolph, Wilma Glodean (obit.) **95**:81
Ruffin, David (obit.) **92**:78
rugby football **97**:344; **96**:323; **95**:301; **94**:294; **93**:294; **92**:291; **91**:321; **90**:339; **89**:321; **88**:323

References with dark-type numbers refer to the previous years, *e.g.,* **96**:324 for the 1996 edition, page 324.

Ruggiero, Renato (biog.) **96**:66
Rühmann, Heinz (obit.) **95**:82
Ruhuna, Joachim
Roman Catholicism 306
Ruiz, Dolores Flores: *see* Flores, Lola
Ruiz Massieu, José Francisco
Mexico 453
Ruiz Soler, Antonio (obit.) **97**:117
dance 285
Rumor, Mariano (obit.) **91**:107
Runcorn, Stanley Keith (obit.) **96**:95
RuPaul, *or* RuPaul Andre Charles (biog.) **96**:66
Ruppe, Loret Miller (obit.) **97**:117
Rushdie, Salman (biog.) **90**:99
British literature 243
Rushton, William George, *or* Willie Rushton (obit.) **97**:117
Rusk, David Dean (obit.) **95**:82
Ruska, Ernst (obit.) **89**:108
Russell, George
"The U.S. Presidential Election" (special report) **97**:492
Russia **97**:464; **96**:458; **95**:461; **94**:450; **93**:451
agriculture 129
fisheries 130
arts and entertainment
classical music 279
literature 249
business and industry
aerospace 155
gemstones 165
mining 170
paper and pulp 179
wood products 179
disasters
aviation 59
railroad 61
economic affairs 193
equity markets (special report) **95**:173
education 203
election 466
environment 212
wildlife conservation 213
human rights issues 315
international affairs
Azerbaijan 393
Belarus 395
Botswana 399
Central Asia (spotlight) 480
China 409
Commonwealth of Independent States 379
Georgia 421
Iceland 430
Japan 439
Kazakstan 440
Kyrgyzstan 443
Latvia 444
Liechtenstein 446
Sweden 477
Ukraine 487
United States 496
magazines 266
military affairs 269, 271, *table* 272
most populous urban areas *table* 296
new flag *illus.* **93**:345
pensions 314
prisons and penology 229
religion
Church of Christ, Scientist 303
Orthodox Church 300, 308, 307
roads 142
space exploration 258
sports and games
chess 330
fencing 339
gymnastics 348
ice hockey 350
ice skating 350
swimming 357
track and field sports 362
weight lifting 370
wrestling 370
World War II (special report) **96**:256
see also WORLD DATA
"Russia" (MACROPAEDIA revision) **96**:517
Russian literature 249
Russian Orthodox Church 308, *il.* 307
Rustin, Bayard (obit.) **88**:108
Rutherford, Charles (obit.) **90**:122
Rwanda **97**:467; **96**:462; **95**:463; **94**:366; **93**:367; **92**:364; **91**:392; **90**:412; **89**:395; **88**:395
agriculture and food supplies 124
human rights issues 314, 315
international law 224
land mines *map* 275
military affairs 276
refugees 297, 298
Religious Society of Friends 304
Roman Catholicism 306
Tanzania 482
UN tribunal 376
see also WORLD DATA
Rwigema, Pierre Celestin
Rwanda 467
Ryan, Nolan
biography **90**:99
Ryan, Thelma Catherine (obit.): *see* Nixon, Patricia
Rybakov, Anatoly
biography **97**:85
Ryu, Chishu
obituary **94**:77

S

S&P 500 stock index: *see* Standard and Poor's 500 stock index
"Sā'at maghrib" (al-Bisāṭi) 252
Sabah, Fahd al-Ahmad al-Jabar as-, Sheikh (obit.) **91**:107
Sabah, Jabir al-Ahmad al-Jabir as-, Sheikh (biog.) **91**:80
Sabia, Laura Villela (obit.) **97**:117
Sabin, Albert Bruce (obit.) **94**:77
Sablon, Jean (obit.) **95**:82
Sabzevari, 'Abd al-A'ala al-Mussawi al- (obit.) **94**:77
Saccharomyces cerevisiae (yeast)
Yeast Genome Project 238
Saccharomyces genome database, *or* SGD
Yeast Genome Project 238
Sacks, Oliver Wolf (biog.) **96**:67
Sadat, Anwar as-
"Islamic Fundamentalism" (special report) **94**:377
saddle bronc-riding 353
Sadik, Nafis 376
Sadler's Wells Theatre (U.K.)
dance 285
Safdie, Moshe 138
Safe Drinking Water Act (U.S.) 160
"Safe Food for All" (consumer booklet) 202
Sagan, Carl Edward (obit.) **97**:117
Sahara (desert, Af.)
United Nations 377
Sahlin, Mona 477
Sa'id, Aminah as- (obit.) **96**:96
sailing **97**:354; **96**:334; **95**:312; **94**:305; **93**:307; **92**:303; **91**:333; **90**:352; **89**:334; **88**:336
1996 Summer Olympic champions *table* **97**:367
St. Johns, Adela Rogers (obit.) **89**:108
Saint Kitts and Nevis, *or* Saint Christopher and Nevis **97**:467; **96**:463; **95**:464; **94**:490; **93**:490; **92**:482; **91**:509; **90**:525; **89**:509; **88**:508
see also WORLD DATA
St. Louis Cardinals (baseball) 321
Saint Lucia **97**:467; **96**:464; **95**:465; **94**:490; **93**:490; **92**:482; **91**:509; **90**:525; **89**:509; **88**:508
see also WORLD DATA
Saint Vincent and the Grenadines **97**:467; **96**:464; **95**:465; **94**:490; **93**:490; **92**:482; **91**:509; **90**:525; **89**:509; **88**:508
see also WORLD DATA
"Saintly" (horse) 337
Sakamoto, Ryuichi (biog.) **89**:83
Sakamoto, Tsutsumi 262
Sakharov, Andrey Dmitriyevich (obit.) **90**:123
Sakmann, Bert (biog.) **92**:32
Sakutarō Hagiwara Prize in Poetry 252
Salam, Abdus (obit.) **97**:118
Salas, Rafael Montinola (obit.) **88**:108
Saleh, Ali Abdullah, *or* Ali Abdallah Salih (biog.) **91**:80
Salem, Mamdouh Muhammad (obit.) **89**:108
Salessi, Jorge 248
Salinas de Gortari, Carlos (biog.) **89**:83
Salinas de Gortari, Raúl 453
Salisbury, Harrison Evans (obit.) **94**:77
Salk, Jonas (obit.) **96**:96
Salk, Lee (obit.) **93**:77
Salkey, Felix Andrew Alexander (obit.) **96**:96
Sallal, 'Abd Allah as- (obit.) **95**:82
"Sally" (typhoon) 60
salmonella
food processing 132
SALS: *see* sporadic amyotrophic lateral sclerosis
salt, *or* sodium chloride, *or* table salt
hypertension research 219
salvage (maritime law)
shipping and ports 373
Salvation Army 305
same-sex marriage
religion 301
United States 495, 499, *il.*
Samper Pizano, Ernesto (biog.) **97**:85
Sampras, Pete (biog.) **94**:50
tennis 360
Samsung (S.Kor. co.) 456
Samuel, Athanasius Yeshue (obit.) **96**:96
San Diego Zoological Garden (zoo, San Diego, Calif., U.S.) 213
San Francisco (Calif., U.S.)
libraries 230, *il.*
San Francisco Ballet (Am. ballet co.) 282
"San Francisco Chronicle" (Am. news.) 266
"San Jose Mercury News" (Am. news.) 266
San Marino **97**:470; **96**:464; **95**:465; **94**:453; **93**:453; **92**:440; **91**:461; **90**:477; **89**:461; **88**:461
see also WORLD DATA
San Sebastián International Film Festival (Sp.)
film awards *table* 294
San Yu, U (obit.) **97**:118
San'a': *see* Yemen Arab Republic
Sánchez, Luis Alberto (obit.) **95**:82
Sánchez, Ricardo (obit.) **96**:96
Sánchez Vicario, Arantxa
tennis 361
sanctions
Burundi 403
crime and law enforcement 226
Cuba 411
Iran 432
Iraq 433
military affairs 271
petroleum 163
United Nations 376
United States 496
Sandberg, Ryne (biog.) **91**:80
Sanders, Barry (biog.) **95**:56
football 344
Sandiford, Lloyd Erskine (biog.) **88**:81
Sandinista National Liberation Front (pol. party, Nic.) 457
Sandoz (Swiss co.)
pharmaceutical merger 173
Sang Chun Lee 325
Sangare, Oumou 281
Sankara, Thomas (obit.) **88**:108
Santacruz Londoño, Jose 410
Santer, Jacques (biog.) **95**:56
labour-management relations 201
Santos, Luiz Carlos 401
Santos Febres, Mayra 248
São Tomé and Príncipe **97**:470; **96**:464; **95**:466; **94**:366; **93**:366; **92**:364; **91**:392; **90**:412; **89**:395; **88**:395
see also WORLD DATA
Saragat, Giuseppe (obit.) **89**:108
Sarajevo (Bosnia and Herzegovina)
genocide 227
Sarajevo, University of (Bosnia and Herzegovina) 205
Sarandon, Susan (biog.) **97**:85
film awards *table* 294
Saraswati, Swamigal Chandrasekharendra (obit.) **95**:83
Sardar Sarovar Dam (dam, India) 142
Sarkisian, Steve 343
Saro-Wiwa, Kenule Beeson (obit.) **96**:96
human rights 315
Sarton, Eléanore Marie (obit.) **96**:96
Sasakawa, Ryoichi (obit.) **96**:96
satellite (artificial)
marine biology 235
space exploration 258, 259
television (special report) 176
"Satellite TV" (special report) **97**:176
Sa'ud, al-Walid ibn Talal ibn Abdulaziz as-, Prince (biog.) **95**:57
Saudi Arabia **97**:470; **96**:465; **95**:466; **94**:390; **93**:390; **92**:388; **91**:414; **90**:434; **89**:417; **88**:417
disasters
fires and explosions 59
traffic 61
international affairs
Qatar 463
Yemen 502
petroleum 163
special report **93**:96
terrorism 226, 269, 495
Saudi Hezbollah (pol. party, Saud.-Arab.) 470
Sauguet, Henri (obit.) **90**:123
Saunders, Jennifer (biog.) **96**:67
Sautin, Dmitry 359
Sauvé, Jeanne Mathilde (obit.) **94**:77
Savalas, Aristoteles "Telly" (obit.) **95**:83
savanna hypothesis
anthropology 134
Savary, Alain François (obit.) **89**:108
Savimbi, Jonas 389
Savio, Mario (obit.) **97**:118
Saw Maung (biog.) **89**:83
Sawyer, Diane (biog.) **90**:99
Saxon (people)
English Channel (special report) **95**:350
SBC: *see* Southern Baptist Convention
SBC Communications, Inc. (Am. co.) 175, 196
Scalfaro, Oscar Luigi 436
Scali, John A. (obit.) **96**:96
Scalia, Antonin
court decisions 225
scandal: *see* corruption
Scandinavia: *see* Denmark; Finland; Iceland; Norway; Sweden
Scarry, Richard McClure (obit.) **95**:83
Scelba, Mario (obit.) **92**:78
Schaefer, Vincent Joseph (obit.) **94**:77
Schaeffer, Pierre (obit.) **96**:96
Schapiro, Meyer (obit.) **97**:118
Scharrer, Berta Vogel (obit.) **96**:97
Schidlof, Peter (obit.) **88**:109
Schine, G. David (obit.) **97**:118
Schittenhelm, Gisele Eve (obit.): *see* Helm, Brigitte
Schlesinger, Klaus 244
Schlumberger (Am.-Fr. co.) 163
Schneerson, Menachem Mendel (obit.) **95**:83
Schneider, Abraham Alexander (obit.) **94**:77
Schneider, Vreni (biog.) **96**:97
scholarly journal
Russian literature 250
Schön, Helmut (obit.) **97**:118
Schönbrunn Palace (Vienna, Aus.)
zoos (special report) **94**:111
Schorr, Daniel
"The New World Disorder" (commentary) **94**:5
Schröder, Gerhard (obit.) **90**:123
Schrödinger, Erwin 255
Schubert, Max Edmund (obit.) **95**:83
Schuller, Gunther (biog.) **95**:57
Schulte, Dieter (biog.) **97**:86
Schumacher, Michael 317
Schuman, William Howard (obit.) **93**:78
Schwartz, Fernando
Spanish literature 247
Schwartz, Melvin (biog.) **89**:83
Schwarzenegger, Arnold (biog.) **92**:48
Schwarzkopf, H. Norman (biog.) **92**:49
Schwimmer, David (biog.) **96**:68
Schwinger, Julian (obit.) **95**:83
Sciascia, Leonardo (obit.) **90**:123
"Science and Health with Key to the Scriptures" (Eddy) 303
science fiction
television 263
science museum 231
Sclavis, Louis 279
Scorsese, Martin (biog.) **89**:84
Scotland: *see* United Kingdom
Scott, Jay (obit.) **94**:78
Scott, Sir Peter Markham (obit.) **90**:123
Scott, Randolph (obit.) **88**:109
Scott, Sir Richard 487
Scott, Ronald (obit.) **97**:118
Scott, Sheila (obit.) **89**:108
Scottish National Gallery of Modern Art (Edinburgh, Scot., U.K.)
art exhibits 148
"Scrambled Eggs and Whiskey: Poems 1991-1995" (Carruth) 242
Scribner, Charles, Jr. (obit.) **96**:97
SDLP (pol. party, Ire.): *see* Social and Democratic Labour Party
SDP (pol. party, Japan): *see* Social Democratic Party
sea-air interface: *see* air-sea interface
"Sea Empress" (oil tanker)
oil spill 207
Sea Launch Co.
space exploration 260
sea turtle
turtle excluder devices 233
wildlife conservation 213
seabird
ornithology 234
"Seafaring and History in the English Channel" (special report) **95**:350
seafloor: *see* ocean floor
Seagram Company Ltd. (Can. co.)
advertising 154
"Search Procedures" (Mouré) 242
Sears, Roebuck and Co. (Am. co.)
labour-management (special report) **94**:203
"Seasons in Hell" (opera) 279
Seattle (Wash., U.S.)
water-treatment systems 160
Seattle SuperSonics (basketball) 323
Seawolf (submarine class) 269
SEC (U.S.): *see* Securities and Exchange Commission; Southeastern Conference
secession
Canada 404
Italy 436
secondary education 203
"Secret of Family Happiness, The" (rel. book)
Jehovah's Witnesses 303
"Secrets & Lies" (motion picture) 290
film awards *table* 294
Securities and Exchange Commission, *or* SEC (U.S.)
stock exchanges 196
Securities and Investments Board (U.K.)
derivatives (special report) **96**:185
securities trading
derivatives (special report) **96**:185
Security and Cooperation in Europe, Organization for, *or* OSCE
military affairs 271
Russia 465
Yugoslavia 503
Seefried, Irmgard (obit.) **89**:108
Seeiso, Constantine Bereng (obit.): *see* Moshoeshoe II
Sega Enterprises, Ltd. (Japanese co.) 164
Segovia, Andrés (obit.) **88**:109
Segrè, Emilio Gino (obit.) **90**:123
segregation
Kuwait 443
Seifert, George Gerald (biog.) **91**:81
Seinfeld, Jerry (biog.) **94**:50
Seizo Terashima: *see* Onoe Baiko VII
Seldes, George (obit.) **96**:97
Selena, *or* Selena Quintanilla Perez (obit.) **96**:97
Seles, Monica (biog.) **92**:49
tennis 360
"Self-Made Hero, A," *or* "Un Héros très discret" (motion picture) 291
Selick, Henry
computer animation (special report) 293
Selimović, Meša 250
Sellars, Peter (biog.) **92**:49
Selvon, Samuel Dickson (obit.) **95**:83
semiconductor
international trade 194
microelectronics 169
Semiconductor Industry Association, *or* SIA 169

"semplic, Il" (It. period.) 247
Sen, Binay Ranjan (obit.) **94**:78
Senate (U.S.): *see* Congress of the United States
Sendero Luminoso (pol. org., Peru): *see* Shining Path
Senegal **97**:470; **96**:465; **95**:467; **94**:366; **93**:368; **92**:364; **91**:393; **90**:413; **89**:396; **88**:396
democratization (spotlight) 416, *map* 417
Guinea-Bissau 426
see also WORLD DATA
senior citizen: *see* old age
Senkaku Islands, *or* Diaoyu Islands (isls., E. China Sea) *il.* 375
China 409
Hong Kong 381
Japan 439
Senna, Ayrton
biography **92**:49
obituary **95**:84
"Sense and Sensibility" (motion picture)
film awards *table* 294
Seoul (S.Kor.)
most populous urban areas *table* 296
Serb, *or* Serbian (people)
Bosnia and Herzegovina 398
special report **94**:426
Serb Republic, *or* Republika Srpska (Bosnia and Herzegovina)
Dayton accords update 398
Serbia (Yugos.) 502
Croatia 411
Eastern European literature 250
UN tribunal 377
Serbian (people): *see* Serb
"serbiske danske, Den" (Davidsen) 245
"Serena's Song" (horse) 336
Sereno, Paul (biog.) **94**:51
dinosaur discovery 239, *il.*
Sergeyev, Konstantin Mikhailovich (obit.) **93**:78
Serkin, Rudolf (obit.) **92**:78
Serota, Nicholas (biog.) **89**:84
serotonin
Prozac (special report) **95**:215
Serrano Elías, Jorge (biog.) **92**:50
Sessions, William Steele (biog.) **88**:81
"Seta" (Baricco) 247
Seth, Vikram (biog.) **94**:51
Seton, Anya (obit.) **91**:108
Seuss, Dr.: *see* Geisel, Theodor Seuss
Sevareid, Arnold Eric (obit.) **93**:78
Sevastopol (Ukraine) 487
"XVII Olympic Winter Games, The" (special report) **95**:308
Seventh-day Adventist Church 305
70 Virginis (star)
companion planet 258
Severn Estuary (riv., U.K.)
bridge construction 140, *il.*
Sewell, Edna Morton (obit.): *see* Deane, Edna
Sewell, Joseph Wheeler (obit.) **91**:108
sex discrimination: *see* discrimination
sexual abuse
children 228, 396
special reports **95**:198, 278
women's rights issues 316
sexual harassment
United States Army 270
sexual reproduction
zoology 232
sexual revolution
"Homosexuality and the Churches" (special report) **94**:263
sexually transmitted disease, *or* STD
street children (special report) **95**:278
Seychelles **97**:471; **96**:466; **95**:467; **94**:367; **93**:368; **92**:365; **91**:393; **90**:413; **89**:396; **88**:396
new flag *illus.* **97**:387
see also WORLD DATA
SFU (satellite): *see* Space Flyer Unit
SGD: *see* Saccharomyces genome database
Shakespeare, William
motion pictures 290
theatrical productions 288
Shakhbut ibn Sultan an-Nahayan, Sheikh (obit.) **90**:124
Shakur, Tupac (obit.) **97**:118
rap music 281
Shalala, Donna Edna (biog.) **95**:57
Shalikashvili, John Malchase (biog.) **94**:51
Shanghai (China)
most populous urban areas *table* 296
Shanghai Library (library, Shanghai, China) 230
Shanghai World Financial Center (bldg., Shanghai, China) 139
Shannon, Del (obit.) **91**:108
Shaplen, Robert Modell (obit.) **89**:108
Sharaff, Irene (obit.) **94**:78
Shari'ah, *or* Islamic law
special reports **94**:377; **93**:95
Sharkey, Jack (obit.) **95**:84
Sharma, Shankar Dayal (biog.) **93**:49
Sharpe, William F. (biog.) **91**:81
Shaw v. Hunt
court decisions 225
Shawn, William (obit.) **93**:78
"Shaytlekh aroysgerisn fun fayer" (Fishman) 251
Shcherban, Volodymyr 487
Sheehan, George (obit.) **94**:78
Sheehan, Patty (biog.) **94**:52
sheep *il.* 447
world production 129, *table* 126
sheet molding compound
advanced composites 168
Shelepin, Aleksandr Nikolayevich (obit.) **95**:84
Shell Oil (Am. co.)
petroleum industry 163
Shen Congwen Shen Ts'ung-wen (obit.) **89**:109
Shenandoah, Leon (obit.) **97**:118
Shepard, Sam (biog.) **97**:86
Shepherd, Lemuel Cornick, Jr. (obit.) **91**:108
Shepherd, Robert
British literature 243
Sherbo, Vitali (biog.) **93**:49
gymnastics 348
special report **93**:276
Sherry, Paul H.
"Homosexuality and the Churches" (special report) **94**:263
Sherwin-Williams (Am. co.)
paints and varnishes 172
"She's the One" (motion picture) 289
Shevardnadze, Eduard Amvrosiyevich (biog.) **93**:49
Georgia 420
military affairs 272
Shields, Carol (biog.) **96**:68
Shi'ites (Islam)
Bahrain 394
special report **93**:95
Shikanai, Nobutaka (obit.) **91**:108
Shils, Edward (obit.) **96**:97
Shilts, Randy Martin (obit.) **95**:84
"Shine" (motion picture) 290
Shining Path, *or* Sendero Luminoso (pol. org., Peru) 461
"Ship Fever" (Barrett)
American literature 242
shipbuilding 174
shipping and ports 373, *il.*
disasters 59
Shirer, William Lawrence (obit.) **94**:78
Shockley, William Bradford (obit.) **90**:124
Shoemaker, Bill (biog.) **90**:99
Shoemaker, Carolyn (biog.) **95**:57
Shoemaker, Eugene (biog.) **95**:57
shooting
1996 Summer Olympic champions *table* **97**:366
Shore, Frances Rose, *or* Dinah Shore (obit.) **95**:84
"Short Order" (film) 295
short story: *see* Literature
short-track speed skating
1994 Winter Olympic champions *table* **95**:309
Shostak, Marjorie (obit.) **97**:119
shot put
track and field sports 370
show jumping and dressage **97**:338; **96**:318; **95**:298
Showa: *see* Hirohito
shrimp (crustacean)
eusociality 232
Shulman, Alexander (obit.) **97**:119
Shulman, Max (obit.) **89**:109
Shweder, Richard
cultural anthropology 134
SIA: *see* Semiconductor Industry Association
Siad Barre, Muhammad, *or* Maxamed Siyaad Barre (obit.) **96**:97
Siam Queen Thai (basil)
gardening 215
Siberian crane, *or* Grus leucogeranus
wildlife conservation 212
SIDS: *see* sudden infant death syndrome
Siegel, Donald (obit.) **92**:79
Siegel, Jerry (obit.) **97**:119
Siegel, Seymour (obit.) **89**:109
Siemens AG (Ger. co.)
electrical industry 161
Sierra Leone **97**:471; **96**:466; **95**:467; **94**:367; **93**:369; **92**:365; **91**:393; **90**:413; **89**:396; **88**:396
Commonwealth of Nations 378
marine disasters 59
see also WORLD DATA
Sierra Leone People's Party, *or* SLPP (pol. party, S.L.) 471
Sierra Nevada mountains (mts., U.S.)
Continental Dynamics project 185
Sievinen, Jan
swimming 358
signal (commu.)
satellite TV (special report) 176
Sihanouk, Norodom (biog.) **94**:52
Buddhism 309
Silayev, Ivan Stepanovich (biog.) **92**:50
Siles Zuazo, Hernán (obit.) **97**:119
silicoboron carbonitride
ceramics 254
silicon nitride
ceramics 254
silk 177
Silk Road (trade route) 142
Silkin, John Ernest (obit.) **88**:109
Silliphant, Stirling Dale (obit.) **97**:119
Silvia, Queen (biog.) **97**:86
Sweden 477
Simenon, Georges (obit.) **90**:124
Simeon II 402, *il.*
Simitis, Konstantinos (biog.) **97**:86
Greece 425
Simms, the Most Rev. George Otto (obit.) **92**:79
Simon, Barney (obit.) **96**:97
Simon, Neil (biog.) **92**:50
Simon, Norton (obit.) **94**:78
Simoneau, Yves (biog.) **92**:50
Sinatra, Frank 280
Sinclair, Sir Keith (obit.) **94**:78
Sindermann, Horst (obit.) **91**:108
Singapore **97**:471; **96**:467; **95**:469; **94**:416; **93**:417; **92**:412; **91**:440; **90**:456; **89**:441; **88**:441
freight and pipelines 373
ice hockey 350
libraries 230
stock exchanges 199
see also WORLD DATA
Singer, Isaac Bashevis (obit.) **92**:79
Singh, Chaudhuri Charan (obit.) **88**:109
Singh, Vishwanath Pratap (biog.) **88**:82
India 431
Singh, Zail (obit.) **95**:85
single-lens-reflex camera, *or* SLR camera
photography 173
single market and economy, *or* SME
Caribbean unification issues (spotlight) 468
single-site catalyst: *see* metallocene
"Single Spark, A" (motion picture) 295
single-stage-to-orbit craft, *or* SSTO craft
spacecraft launch vehicles 260
Singletary, Mike (biog.) **93**:49
Sinn Fein (pol. party, Ire.) 433, 489
Siri, Giuseppe Cardinal (obit.) **90**:124
Sirica, John Joseph (obit.) **93**:78
Siskel, Gene (biog.) **93**:50
Siskind, Aaron (obit.) **92**:79
situ leaching
uranium mining 172
Sitwell, Sir Sacheverell (obit.) **89**:109
Siyaad Barre, Maxamed: *see* Siad Barre, Muhammad
Skaardal, Atle 356
Skardon, William James (obit.) **88**:109
"Skating Rink" (ballet) 284
skiing **97**:355; **96**:335; **95**:313; **94**:306; **93**:308; **92**:304; **91**:334; **90**:353; **89**:334; **88**:337
Skinner, Burrhus Frederic (obit.) **91**:108
"Skip Away" (horse) 337
Skirball Cultural Center (Los Angeles, Calif., U.S.) 138
Skrine, Mary Nesta (obit.): *see* Keane, Molly
skyscraper 139, 140
"Slate" (elec. mag.) 267
Slaton, Mary Leta Dorothy (obit.): *see* Lamour, Dorothy
"Slaughterhouse Five" (opera) 278
Slav, *or* Slavs (people)
Bosnia and Herzegovina (special report) **94**:425
Slavonia
Croatia 411
Slayton, Donald Kent, *or* Deke Slayton (obit.) **94**:78
"Sleeping Beauty, The" (ballet) 284
"Sleeping Man" (motion picture) 295
Sleet, Moneta J., Jr. (obit.) **97**:119
Slezevicius, Adolfas 446
Slonimsky, Nicolas (obit.) **96**:97
SLORC: *see* State Law and Order Restoration Council
Slovakia, *or* Slovak Republic **97**:472; **96**:467; **95**:469; **94**:453
Hungary 430
new flag *illus.* **94**:345
social protection 314
see also WORLD DATA
Slovenia **97**:472; **96**:467; **95**:470; **94**:453; **93**:454
economic affairs 193
European Union 379
new flag *illus.* **93**:346
see also WORLD DATA
Slovo, Joe, *or* Yossel Mashel Slovo (obit.) **96**:97
SLR camera: *see* single-lens-reflex camera
Smalley, Richard E.
Nobel Prize 63
Smallwood, Joseph Roberts (obit.) **92**:79
smart bag
automobiles 158
smart card
microelectronics 170
Smarth, Rony 427
Smartt Bell, Madison 240
Smashing Pumpkins (Am. mus. group) 281
SME: *see* single market and economy
Smirnov, Vladimir 357
Smith, Alexis (obit.) **94**:79
Smith, Arnold Cantwell (obit.) **95**:85
Smith, Cyril Stanley (obit.) **93**:79
Smith, Dick (biog.) **94**:52
Smith, Hazel Brannon (obit.) **95**:85
Smith, John
biographies **93**:50; **92**:51
obituary **95**:85
Smith, Margaret Chase (obit.) **96**:98
Smith, Michelle (biog.) **97**:87
Ireland 434
Olympic Games (special report) 365
swimming 357
Smith, Oliver (obit.) **95**:85
Smith, Robert Weston (obit.): *see* Wolfman Jack
Smith, Trevor Dudley: *see* Trevor, Elleston
Smith, Wadada Leo 279
Smithson, Alison Margaret (obit.) **94**:79
smog
health risks 210
Smogorzewski, Kazimierz Maciej (obit.) **93**:79
smoking
lung cancer 219
man-made fibres 177
medical research 221
retailing 174
Smoltz, John 320
Smythe, Pat, *or* Patricia Rosemary Koechlin-Smythe (obit.) **97**:119
SNA (pol. party, Som.): *see* Somali National Alliance
Snacktime Kids (toy) 164
snake
zoology 232
Snedden, Sir Billy Mackie (obit.) **88**:109
Snegur, Mircea 453
Snell, George Davis (obit.) **97**:119
Snipes, Wesley (biog.) **94**:52
snooker 326
snowstorm: *see* blizzard
Snychev, Ivan Matveyevich (obit.): *see* Ioann
Snyder, Bruce 343
Snyder, Gary 241
Snyder, James G., *or* Dimetrios Georgos Synodinos, *or* Jimmy the Greek (obit.) **97**:119
Soames, Arthur Christopher John Soames (obit.) **88**:109
Sobchak, Anatoly Aleksandrovich (biog.) **92**:51
soccer: *see* association football
Social and Democratic Labour Party, *or* SDLP (pol. party, Ire.) 489
Social Christian Reformist Party, *or* PRSC (pol. party, Dom.Rep.) 413
Social Democracy Party of Romania, *or* PDSR (pol. party, Rom.) 463
Social Democratic Labour Party (pol. party, Swed.) 477
Social Democratic Party, *or* SPD (pol. party, Ger.) 421, 424
Social Democratic Party, *or* SDP (pol. party, Japan) 437
Social Democratic Party, *or* PSD (pol. party, Port.) 463
Social Democratic Union of Macedonia (pol. party, Maced.) 446
Social Protection **97**:312; **96**:284; **95**:276
Canada 404
France 419
Germany 421
labour-management relations 201
special reports **96**:286; **95**:278
United States 491
see also Social Security; Welfare Services
Social Security **94**:272; **93**:271; **92**:270; **91**:300; **90**:317; **89**:300; **88**:304
special reports **94**:144; **89**:301
U.S. reform policy 313
see also Social Protection
"Social Text" (Am. mag.) 267
Socialist Party, *or* PS (pol. party, Belg.) 396
Socialist Party (pol. party, Port.) 463
SOD1 (gene)
amyotrophic lateral sclerosis 237
sodium chloride: *see* salt
soft drinks 159
food processing 132
softball
1996 Summer Olympic champions *table* **97**:366
software
computers 181
Soglo, Nicéphore 397
"Soifs" (Blais) 247
"Sojourner" (space rover) 259, *il.*
Sokolov Archive 446
solar system 256
"Soleil des gouffres, Le" (Hamelin) 247
Solheim Cup (golf) 347
Solidarity Electoral Action (pol. org., Pol.) 462
Solis, Octavio Solomon (obit.) **89**:109
Solomon Islands **97**:472; **96**:468; **95**:470; **94**:498; **93**:498; **92**:490; **91**:517; **90**:533; **89**:517; **88**:517
forestry (spotlight) 451
see also WORLD DATA
Solow, Robert Merton (biog.) **88**:82
solstice (astron.)
1997 *table* 256
Somali National Alliance, *or* SNA (pol. party, Som.) 472
Somali Salvation Alliance (pol. party, Som.) 472
Somalia **97**:472; **96**:468; **95**:471; **94**:367; **93**:369; **92**:365; **91**:393; **90**:414; **89**:397; **88**:397
agriculture and food supplies 124
Canada 405
land mines *map* 275
military affairs 276
refugees 297
see also WORLD DATA
Somaliland Republic 472
"Some Mother's Son" (motion picture) 290
Somes, Michael (obit.) **95**:85
Son, Masayoshi (biog.) **97**:87

Sondheim, Stephen 287
Sony Corporation (Japanese co.)
games and toys 164
photography 173
Sopinka, John (biog.) **89**:84
Sopwith, Sir Thomas Octave Murdoch (obit.) **90**:124
Sorabji, Kaikhosru Shapurji (obit.) **89**:109
Sorenstam, Annika 347
Soros, George (biog.) **95**:58
Sotheby's (auction house, U.K.)
art 150
books and manuscripts 151
Soufriére Hills (hills, Monts., W.I.)
volcanic activity 185
Soukop, Wilhelm Josef, *or* Willi Soukop (obit.) **96**:98
Sound Surveillance System, *or* SOSUS 187
Soupault, Philippe (obit.) **91**:109
Souphanouvong, Prince (obit.) **96**:98
Soustelle, Jacques-Émile (obit.) **91**:109
Souter, David Hackett (biog.) **91**:81
South Africa **97**:473; **96**:469; **95**:471; **94**:368; **93**:370; **92**:366; **91**:394; **90**:414; **89**:397; **88**:397
business and industry
coal 163
mining 170
crime and law enforcement 229
disasters
mining and tunneling 60
railway station incident 61
traffic 61
education 205
human rights violations 316
international affairs
Mozambique 454
Namibia 455
Zimbabwe 504
literature 244
military affairs 276
land mines (special report) 275
new flag *illus.* **95**:353
newspapers 265
political party system (spotlight) 417, *map*
social protection 314
special reports **95**:173; **91**:290; **88**:330
sports and games
cricket 332
rugby football 345
see also WORLD DATA
South African Development Community
Malawi agreement 448
South America: *see* Latin-American affairs
"South America: Amazon River Basin" (MACROPAEDIA revision) **95**:521
South Korea: *see* Korea, Republic of
South Ossetia (reg., Georgia) 421
South Pacific Nuclear Free Zone Treaty
France 381
military affairs 269
South West Africa/Namibia: *see* Namibia
South Yemen: *see* Yemen, People's Democratic Republic of
"Southeast Asia" (MACROPAEDIA revision) **94**:520
Southeast Asia Nuclear Weapon-Free Zone 380
Southeast Asian affairs **94**:410; **93**:411; **92**:406; **91**:434; **90**:452; **89**:434; **88**:435
economic affairs 188, 193
military affairs 276, *table* 273
special report **95**:173
see also individual countries by name
Southeast Asian Nations, Association of, *or* ASEAN 380
democratization (spotlight) 442
France 420
Vietnam 502
Southeastern Conference, *or* SEC (U.S.)
basketball 323
Southern, Terry (obit.) **96**:98
Southern Africa (MACROPAEDIA revision) **93**:514
Southern Baptist Convention, *or* SBC 300, 302
"Homosexuality and the Churches" (special report) **94**:263
Southern Cone Common Market, *or* Mercosur
Chile 407
Soviet Republics, former: *see* former Soviet Republics
Soviet Union: *see* Union of Soviet Socialist Republics
soybean
world production 128, *table* 125
Soyinka, Wole 244
Nigeria 458
Space Exploration 97:258; **96**:168; **95**:280; **94**:275; **93**:273; **92**:272; **91**:302; **90**:319; **89**:304; **88**:306
Jupiter 256
Space Flyer Unit, *or* SFU (satellite)
space exploration 258
"Space Jam" (motion picture)
computer animation (special report) 292
space probe 259
Jupiter exploration 256
space shuttle 258
space station 258
Spadolini, Giovanni (obit.) **95**:85
Spain **97**:474; **96**:471; **95**:475; **94**:454; **93**:454; **92**:441; **91**:461; **90**:477; **89**:461; **88**:461
architecture 137
arts and entertainment
literature 247
motion pictures 291
film awards *table* 294
disasters
natural 60
traffic 61
labour-management relations 202
sports and games
basketball 325
gymnastics 348
stock exchanges 199
see also WORLD DATA
Spanish literature 247
SPD (pol. party, Ger.): *see* Social Democratic Party
special effect
motion pictures 289
television 263
Species Survival Plan, *or* SSP
"Zoos Look to the 21st Century" (special report) **94**:111
"Spectator, The" (Am. mag.) 267
speed skating 351
1994 Olympic champions *table* **95**:309
"Spell in Winter, A" (Dunmore) 243
Spelling, Aaron (biog.) **97**:87
Spender, Sir Stephen Harold (obit.) **96**:98
Sperry, Roger Wolcott (obit.) **95**:85
Spessivtzeva, Olga (obit.) **92**:79
sphenomandibularis (jaw muscle) *il.* 221
spider
zoological research 233
Spiegelman, Art (biog.) **93**:50
Spiñal Tap (biog.) **93**:50
Spínola, António Sebastião Ribeiro de (obit.) **97**:119
Spirit Cave (archae. site, U.S.) 136
spirits (bev.) 159
television advertising 154
Spivak, Lawrence Edmund (obit.) **95**:86
"Splendors of Imperial China: Treasures from the National Palace Museum, Taipei" (art exhibit) 145
SPÖ (pol. party, Aus.): *see* Austrian Social Democratic Party
sporadic amyotrophic lateral sclerosis, *or* SALS
molecular biology 237
sport utility vehicle 157
Sportage (vehicle) 157
sporting equipment
cycling 334
golf 346
Sporting Record: *see under* individual sports, e.g., tennis
Sports and Games 97:317; **96**:299; **95**:283; **94**:278; **93**:279; **92**:275; **91**:305; **90**:321; **89**:306; **88**:308
Olympic Winter Games **95**:308
special reports **93**:276; **90**:324; **89**:340
television networks 264
see also specific sports or games
Spratly Islands (reefs, S. China Sea)
"The Spat over the Spratlys" (spotlight) **96**:392
spring manufacture
mathematics 253
sprint (running)
track and field sports 362
spying: *see* espionage
Spyridon (Gr. Orthodox archbp.) 308
squash **97**:357; **96**:337; **95**:314; **94**:307; **93**:309; **92**:305; **91**:335; **90**:354; **89**:335; **88**:338
Srebrenica (Bosnia and Herzegovina)
genocide 227
Sri Lanka **97**:476; **96**:472; **95**:476; **94**:408; **93**:409; **92**:406; **91**:433; **90**:451; **89**:434; **88**:434
Buddhism 309
cricket 332, 333
military affairs 276
port of Colombo *il.* 373
see also WORLD DATA
Srpska, Republika (Bosnia and Herzegovina): *see* Serb Republic
SSI: *see* Supplemental Security Income
SSP: *see* Species Survival Plan
SSTO: *see* single-stage-to-orbit craft
Stade de France (bldg., Paris, Fr.) 140
Stalter, György
photo essay 428
stamp collecting: *see* Philately
stampede
Hindu worshipers 309
Standard and Poor's 500 stock index, *or* S&P 500 stock index 196
Standby Forces High Readiness Brigade (UN) 378
Stanford-Tuck, Robert Rolland (obit.) **88**:110
"Stanley" (play) 286
Stanley Cup (ice hockey) 349
Stanwyck, Barbara (obit.) **91**:109
Staples (Am. co.) 174
star
astronomy 257
"Star Trek" (television show) 263
"Star Trek: First Contact" (motion picture) 289
Starbucks (Am. co.) 174
Stark, Dame Freya Madeline (obit.) **94**:79
Stark, Julian (obit.): *see* Stryjkowski, Julian
Starr, Maurice (biog.) **91**:81
Starr, Patricia (biog.) **90**:100
START-I (internat. pol.): *see* Strategic Arms Reduction Talks
START-II (internat. pol.): *see* Strategic Arms Reduction Talks
state government
special report **96**:286
United States 497
welfare reform 312
State Law and Order Restoration Council, *or* SLORC
Myanmar 455
State Privatization and Holding Company, *or* APV (Hung. co.) 430
Status of Refugees, Convention on the 316
Stazewski, Henryk (obit.) **89**:109
STD: *see* sexually transmitted disease
"Stealing Beauty" (motion picture) 291
steam coal 163
steel: *see* iron and steel
Steel, Bruce C.
"Computer Animation" (special report) **97**:292
Steel, Danielle (biog.) **95**:58
steeplechasing: *see* equestrian sports
steer wrestling 353
Stegner, Wallace Earle (obit.) **94**:79
Steinberger, Jack (biog.) **89**:84
Stennis, John Cornelius (obit.) **96**:98
Stephanie, Princess of Mon. 453
Stephens, Sir Robert (obit.) **96**:98
Stephenson, Sir William Samuel (obit.) **90**:125
Steptoe, Patrick Christopher (obit.) **89**:109
Stern, Howard
radio 265
Stern, Mario Rigoni 247
steroid
botany 235
Stevens, Brooks (obit.) **96**:98
Stevens, Siaka Probyn (obit.) **89**:110
Stewart, James Lablache (obit.): *see* Granger, Stewart
Stewart, John Innes Mackintosh (obit.) **95**:86
Stewart, Martha (biog.) **96**:68
Stewart, Michael (obit.) **88**:110
Stewart of Fulham, Robert Michael Maitland Stewart (obit.) **91**:109
Stibitz, George Robert (obit.) **96**:99
Stigler, George Joseph (obit.) **92**:80
Stine, R. L. (biog.) **96**:68
Stirling, Sir Archibald David (obit.) **91**:109
Stirling, Sir James Frazer (obit.) **93**:79
stock exchanges **97**:194; **96**:180; **95**:167; **94**:148; **93**:147; **92**:145; **91**:173; **90**:190; **89**:174; **88**:176
automobiles 158
games and toys 164
special reports **95**:172; **89**:176; **88**:144
United States 490
Internet-related companies 180
stock option 197
Stoffels, Robert
"Satellite TV" (special report) **97**:176
Stoichkov, Hristo (biog.) **96**:69
Stojko, Elvis 350
Stokes, Carl Burton (obit.) **97**:119
Stollmeyer, Jeffrey Baxter (obit.) **90**:125
Stommel, Henry Melson (obit.) **93**:79
Stone, I. F. (obit.) **90**:125
Stone, Irving (obit.) **90**:125
Stone, Oliver (biog.) **88**:82
Stone, Sir Richard (obit.) **92**:80
Stone, Sharon
fashion 216
film awards *table* 294
Stone Temple Pilots (Am. mus. group) 281
stop-motion
motion picture technology (special report) 292
Stopfel, Rev. Barry *il.* 301
storage and retrieval
digitized visual images 149
Store Bælt (bridge, Den.): *see* Great Belt
Stott Despoja, Natasha (biog.) **97**:87
Australia 392
Stotz, Carl E. (obit.) **93**:79
Stoutt, Hamilton Lavity (obit.) **96**:99
"Strana proiskhozhdeniya" (Bakin) 249
Strang, Gunnar Georg Emanuel (obit.) **93**:79
Stransky, Joel 345
Strasser, Valentine 471
Strategic Arms Reduction Talks, *or* START-I, *or* START-II (internat. pol.)
military affairs 269
Stratford-upon-Avon (thea., U.K.) 285
Strauss, Franz-Josef (obit.) **89**:110
Street, Picabo (biog.) **97**:88
skiing 356
"Street Children" (special report) **95**:278
Strickland, Earl 325
strikes
Argentina 390
automobiles 157
Bolivia 398
Cameroon 403
Detroit newspapers 266, *il.*
fashion industry 216
Germany 421
Honduras 427
Indonesia 432
labour-management relations 201
Mali 449
rubber industry 167
South Africa 473
Swaziland 477
Vanuatu 500
Venezuela 501
Yugoslavia 502
Zimbabwe 504
Strug, Kerri
gymnastics 348
Stryjkowski, Julian, *or* Julian Stark (obit.) **97**:119
Stuttgart Ballet (Ger. ballet co.) 284
Styles, Margretta Madden
"For Nursing, New Responsibilities, New Respect" (special report) **97**:220
Styne, Jule (obit.) **95**:86
styrene butadiene
synthetic rubber industry 167
submarine
United Kingdom 270
United States 269
subsidy
U.S. agriculture 125
substance abuse: *see* drug abuse
subway, *or* metro
civil engineering 142, *table* 143
urban mass transit 374
Suchman, Tamas 430
Suchocka, Hanna (biog.) **93**:51
Sudan, The **97**:476; **96**:473; **95**:476; **94**:371; **93**:372; **92**:369; **91**:397; **90**:417; **89**:400; **88**:400
agriculture and food supplies 124
disasters
aviation 58
natural 60
international affairs
Egypt 415
Eritrea 415
Ethiopia 418
Uganda 486
UN sanctions 376
land mines *map* 275
military affairs 276
prison *il.* 229
women's rights issues 316
see also WORLD DATA
sudden infant death syndrome, *or* SIDS, *or* cot death 221
Sudoplatov, Pavel Anatolyevich (obit.) **97**:119
Suenens, Léon Joseph Cardinal (obit.) **97**:119
sugar
world production 129, *table* 127
Suharto 432
Suharto, Siti Hartinah, *or* Ibu Tien (obit.) **97**:119
suicide
Australia 392
Prozac (special report) **95**:215
United States 498
Sukhoi Su-37 (Russ. aircraft) 155
Suleymanoglu, Naim (biog.) **89**:84
weight lifting 370
Sullivan, Maxine (obit.) **88**:110
Sullivan, Patrick Francis Barry (obit.) **95**:86
Sullivan, Walter Seager, Jr. (obit.) **97**:119
Sulloway, Frank J.
cultural evolution 134
Sulzberger, Cyrus Leo (obit.) **94**:79
Sumitomo (Japanese co.)
copper losses 170, 228
Summer Olympic Games: *see* Olympic Games
"Summer's Tale, A," *or* "Conte d'été" (motion picture) 291
Summerson, Sir John Newenham (obit.) **93**:79
sumo wrestling **97**:371; **96**:347
Sun Alliance Group (Br. co.) 166
Sun Jun *il.* 301
Sun Ra, *or* Herman Blount (obit.) **94**:79
"Sun Under Wood" (Haas) 241
Sundance Film Festival (U.S.)
film awards *table* 294
sunflower seed
world production 128, *table* 125
Sunnah, *or* Sunna (Islam)
"Islamic Fundamentalism" (special report) **94**:377
Sunnyland Slim, *or* Albert Luandrew (obit.) **96**:99
Sununu, John Henry (biog.) **90**:100
Super-12 (rugby football) 345
Super Bowl (football) 344
superfluid
helium-3 research 64
Superman (biog.) **89**:85
supersymmetry
physics 255
Supplemental Security Income, *or* SSI 312
Supreme Court of the United States 224
military institutions 206
presidency lawsuit precedent 490
religion 300
United States 497, 499
Suriname **97**:476; **96**:474; **95**:477; **94**:490; **93**:491; **92**:482; **91**:509; **90**:525; **89**:510; **88**:508
see also WORLD DATA
surveillance
crime and law enforcement 228
Susanti, Susi 320
suspension bridge 139
Susskind, David (obit.) **88**:110
Sutcliff, Rosemary (obit.) **93**:80
Sutherland, Efua Theodora (obit.) **97**:119

Suu Kyi, Daw Aung San: *see* Aung San
  Suu Kyi, Daw
Suzuki, Ichiro
  Japanese baseball 322, *il.*
Swainson's hawk, *or* Buteo swainsoni
  wildlife conservation 213
Swaminarayan (temple, London, U.K.)
  il. 297
Swan, Sir John William David (biog.)
  96:69
"Swan Lake" (ballet) 284
Swann, Donald Ibrahim (obit.) 95:86
Swayze, John Cameron (obit.) 96:99
Swaziland 97:477; 96:474; 95:477; 94:371;
  93:373; 92:369; 91:397; 90:417;
  89:401; 88:400
  see also WORLD DATA
sweatshop
  clothing industry issue 155
Sweden 97:477; 96:474; 95:477; 94:455;
  93:456; 92:442; 91:462; 90:478;
  89:463; 88:462
  bowling 326
  bridges 140
  health insurance reform 313
  literature 245
  Lutheran church 300
  newspapers 265
  rubber industry 167
  see also WORLD DATA
Swedish literature 245
Swick, Marly 241
Swift, Graham
  British literature 243
swimming 97:357; 96:338; 95:314; 94:307;
  93:309; 92:305; 91:335; 90:354;
  89:336; 88:338
  1996 Summer Olympic champions *table*
  97:366
swine: *see* pig
Swissair (Swiss co.) 478
Switzerland 97:477; 96:475; 95:478;
  94:456; 93:456; 92:443; 91:463;
  90:479; 89:463; 88:463
  agriculture and food supplies 126
  banking 200
  currency design 152
  intercity rail 374
  machinery and machine tools 166
  nuclear weapons program 271
  social security 313
  stock exchanges 199
  see also WORLD DATA
Sydney–Hobart (sailing competition) 354
Symbion pandora (invertebrate species)
  234, *il.*
Syme, Sir Ronald (obit.) 90:125
Symington, William Stuart (obit.) 89:110
Synalpheus regalis (shrimp)
  eusociality 235, 232
synchronized swimming 359
Synge, Richard Laurence Millington (obit.)
  95:86
Synodinos, Dimetrios Georgos (obit.): *see*
  Snyder, James G.
synthetic gemstone 165
synthetic rubber 167
Syracuse University (U.S.)
  basketball 323
Syria 97:478; 96:475; 95:479; 94:391;
  93:392; 92:390; 91:416; 90:435;
  89:418; 88:418
  dams 141
  international affairs
    Israel 434
    Jordan 439
    Lebanon 445
  military affairs 273
  see also WORLD DATA
Szentkuthy, Miklos (obit.) 89:110
Szeryng, Henryk (obit.) 89:110
Szymborska, Wisława
  Eastern European literature 250, *il.*
  Nobel Prize 63

T

T cell
  immune system research 64
table salt: *see* salt
table tennis 97:360; 96:341; 95:316;
  94:308; 93:311; 92:307; 91:336;
  90:355; 89:337; 88:339
  1996 Summer Olympic champions *table*
  97:367
Tabuchi, Setsuya (biog.) 92:51
Tadic, Dusan
  war crimes trial 315
Tagliabue, Paul (biog.) 91:81
Tagliavini, Ferruccio (obit.) 96:100
"Tailor of Panama, The" (le Carré) 243
Taiwan 97:478; 96:476; 95:480; 94:401;
  93:402; 92:400; 91:428; 90:445;
  89:428; 88:428
  business and industry
    chemicals 161
    machinery and machine tools 166
  disasters
    fires and explosions 59
    marine 59
    natural 60
  international affairs
    China 7, 409
    Japan 439

Lee Teng-hui interview (commentary)
  97:6
  literature 252
  military affairs 276
  stock exchanges 199
  see also WORLD DATA
Taiwan Strait (str., China Sea)
  Japan 439
Tajikistan 97:482; 96:477; 95:481; 94:408;
  93:409
  Central Asian republics (spotlight) 480,
    map 481
  economic affairs 193
  military affairs 271
  new flag *illus.* 94:345; 93:346
  see also WORLD DATA
Takahashi, Hisako (biog.) 96:69
Takamatsu, Prince (obit.) 88:110
Takano, Shizuo (obit.) 93:80
Takanohana
  sumo wrestling 371
Takanonami
  sumo wrestling 371
Takayanagi, Kenjiro (obit.) 91:109
Takemitsu, Toru (obit.) 97:119
Takeshima (isls., S.Kor.): *see* Tok-do
Takeshita, Noboru (obit.) 88:83
Taki Abdoulkarim, Mohamed
  Comoros 410
Tal, Mikhail Nekhemyevich (obit.) 93:80
Talabani, Jalal al- 433
Talhouni, Bahjat at- (obit.) 95:86
Taliban, *or* Taleban (mil. org., Afg.)
  Afghanistan 375, 388
  refugees 297
  Commonwealth of Independent
    States 380
  military affairs 273
  women's rights issues 316
Tamayo, Rufino (obit.) 92:80
Tambo, Oliver (obit.) 94:79
Tamil Tigers, *or* Liberation Tigers of
  Tamil Eelam, *or* LTTE (rev. org.,
  Sri Lanka) 476
  Buddhism 309
  military affairs 276
Tan, Amy (biog.) 90:100
Tan, Lucio (biog.) 97:88
Tanada, Lorenzo (obit.) 93:80
Tanaka, Kakuei (obit.) 94:80
Tanaka, Sumie 252
Tandy, Jessica
  biography 91:82
  obituary 95:86
Tanenbaum, Marc Herman (obit.) 93:80
Tang, Ben Z. 253
Tang Yee-ming, Dominic (obit.) 96:100
Tange, Kenzo (biog.) 88:83
Tansi, Marcel Sony Labou (obit.) 96:100
Tanzania 97:482; 96:478; 95:481; 94:371;
  93:373; 92:369; 91:398; 90:418;
  89:401; 88:400
  agriculture and food supplies 124
  democratization (spotlight) 416,
    map 417
  Kenya 440
  literature 244
  Rwanda 467
  see also WORLD DATA
Tapie, Bernard (biog.) 91:82
Tarasov, Anatoly (obit.) 96:100
Tarkanian, Jerry (biog.) 92:51
Tarradellas i Joan, Josep (obit.) 89:110
Taruskin, Richard 279
Tata, J. R. D. (obit.) 94:80
Tate Gallery (London, U.K.) 145
  art exchange 144
  art exhibitions (special report) 146
Tawada, Yōko
  Japanese literature 252
tawhid (Islam)
  "Islamic Fundamentalism" (special
    report) 94:377
Tax, Sol (obit.) 96:100
taxation
  Argentina 390
  Austria 393
  Belize 397
  Brazil 401
  Bulgaria 401
  Germany 424
  Puerto Rico 381
  Russia 465
  special report 94:145
  United Kingdom 191, 207
  United States 497
"Taxi" (motion picture) 291
Taylor, Alan John Percivale (obit.) 91:110
Taylor, Art (obit.) 96:100
Taylor, Edward Plunket (obit.) 90:126
Taylor, Henry 241
Taylor, Maxwell Davenport (obit.) 88:110
Taylor, Richard Edward (biog.) 91:82
Tchelistcheff, André (obit.) 95:87
Tcherepnin, Ivan
  classical music 277
Tchicaya U Tam'si (obit.) 89:110
Teamwork for Employees and Managers
  Act (U.S.) 202
technology
  food processing 132
  medical imaging systems 253
  meteorology and climate 186
  petroleum industry 163
  television 262, 264
  wool production 177
TED: *see* turtle excluder device

Teenage Mutant Ninja Turtles (biog.)
  91:82
teenager: *see* child
Tejero Molina, Antonio
  Spain 475
Tel Aviv (Isr.)
  Hebrew literature 251
telecommunications 175
  computers 181
  Monaco 453
  satellite TV (special report) 97:176
  stock exchanges 196
  United States regulations 203
    Telecommunications Act 261, 264
  Venezuela 501
  see also WORLD DATA
Telecommunications Act (U.S.) 261
"Telecommunications Systems"
  (MACROPAEDIA revision) 97:508
telephone company
  Internet service 181
  telecommunications 175, 261
  see also individual companies by name
Telefónica (Sp. co.) 475
Telefonica de Peru (Peruvian co.) 461
telescope
  astronomy 257
  observation satellites 259
TeleSelect (Dutch co.) 261
televangelism
  special report 88:294
television 97:261; 96:244; 95:339; 94:332;
  93:334; 92:330; 91:360; 90:374;
  89:363; 88:363
  advertising sales 154
  computers 181
  distilled spirits advertising 159
  Germany 424
  Luxembourg 446
  newspapers 265
  satellite TV (special report) 97:176
  science fiction 263
  special reports 93:470; 90:381
Television Shopping Network, *or*
  TVSN 262
Tembo, Biggie, *or* Rodwell Marasha (obit.)
  96:100
Temin, Howard Martin (obit.) 95:87
Temple Mount (Jerusalem)
  Islam 310
Templeton Prize for Progress in Religion
  301
"Temptation" (motion picture) 295
"Temptress Moon" (motion picture) 295
"Ten Thousand Character Essay"
  (Deng Liqun) 408
Tencel (man-made fibre) 177
Tendulkar, Sachin Ramesh (biog.) 97:88
  cricket 332, 333
Teng, Teresa, *or* Teng Li-Chün (obit.)
  96:100
Teng Hsiao-p'ing: *see* Deng Xiaoping
Teng Ying-Ch'ao (obit.): *see* Deng
  Yingchao
Tennant, Kylie (obit.) 89:110
Tennessee, University of (U.S.)
  basketball 325, *il.* 324
tennis 97:360; 96:341; 95:316; 94:309;
  93:311; 92:307; 91:337; 90:356;
  89:338; 88:340
  1996 Summer Olympic champions *table*
  97:367
tenpins: *see* bowling
Terkel, Louis "Studs" (biog.) 93:51
term limit
  United States 497
Termen, Lev Sergeyevich (obit.): *see*
  Theremin, Leon
"terra e di tutti, La" (Camon) 247
terrorism 226
  Algeria 389
  Egypt 415
  France 419
  Iran 432
  Israel 434
  Peru 461
  Sri Lanka 476
  Ukraine 487
  United States 495
    armed forces 269, 470
    world affairs 376
  see also assassination; bombing
Terry, William Harold (obit.) 90:126
Terry-Thomas (obit.) 91:110
Tesich, Steve, *or* Stoyan Tesich (obit.)
  97:120
Test Series (cricket) 332
Tethered Satellite System
  space exploration 258
Tetovo University (univ., Maced.) 446
Texaco Inc. (Am. co.) 163
Texas (state, U.S.) 497, 498
  congressional reapportionment 225
textiles 177
  archaeological discoveries 136
TFR: *see* total fertility rate
Thai Nation, *or* Chart Thai (pol. party,
  Thailand)
  corruption charges 482
Thailand 97:482; 96:478; 95:482; 94:416;
  93:417; 92:413; 91:440; 90:459;
  89:441; 88:441
  economic affairs 193
  Laos 443
  stock exchanges 199
  see also WORLD DATA
Thalía 264, *il.*
Thaman, Konai Helu 206

Thani, Sheikh Hamad ibn Khalifah ath-
  Qatar 463
Thani, Sheikh Khalifah ibn Hamad ath-
  Qatar 463
Tharp, Twyla 282
"That Thing You Do!" (motion
  picture) 290
Thatcher, Margaret Hilda (biogs.) 91:83;
  90:101; 89:85; 88:83
Thawrah Dam (dam, Syr.) 141
Theater High-Altitude Area Defense
  system (U.S.) 269
Theatre 97:285; 96:270; 95:342; 94:336;
  93:337; 92:333; 91:363; 90:384;
  89:367; 88:367
theft
  crime and law enforcement 228
"Theodora" (oratorio) 279
Theremin, Leon, *or* Lev Sergeyevich
  Termen (obit.) 94:80
Thiong'o, Ngugi wa
  literature 244
Third World: *see* less developed country
Thomas, Clarence (biog.) 92:52
Thomas, Danny (obit.) 92:80
Thomas, Edward Donnall (biog.) 91:83
Thomas, Isiah (biog.) 91:83
Thomas, James (obit.) 94:80
Thomas, Jess (obit.) 94:80
Thomas, Lewis (obit.) 94:80
Thomas, Richard Clement Charles (obit.)
  97:120
Thomas Cook and Son (Br. co.) 179
Thomas Cup (badminton) 320
Thompson, Edward Palmer (obit.) 94:80
Thompson, Emma (biog.) 94:35
Thomsen, Søren Ulrik
  Danish literature 245
Thomson, Virgil (obit.) 90:126
thoroughbred racing: *see* equestrian sports
Three Gorges Dam (dam, China) 142
  building and construction 160
"Three Lives and Only One Death"
  (motion picture) 291
Three Tenors
  classical music 277
³He (phys.): *see* helium-3
Thrifty Payless Holdings (Am. co.) 174
Thugwane, Josia 369
Thurnham, Peter 487
thyroid cancer
  radiation poisoning 212
Tianjin (China)
  most populous urban areas *table* 296
Tibet (autonomous reg., China) 408
Tibetan Buddhism 309
Tibetan red deer
  wildlife conservation 213
Tickle Me Elmo (toy) 164
tidal wave: *see* tsunami
Tien, Chang-Lin (biog.) 91:83
Tien, Ibu (obit.): *see* Suharto, Siti Hartinah
Tiepolo, Giovanni Battista 148
Tierney, Gene Eliza (obit.) 92:80
"Tieta di Agreste" (motion picture) 295
Tilghman, Christopher 241
"Time Rocker" (play) 89
"Time to Kill, A" (motion picture) 289
Times Square (N.Y.C., N.Y., U.S.) 287
Timor Timur (prov., Indon.): *see* East
  Timor
Tinbergen, Jan (obit.) 95:87
Tinbergen, Nikolaas (obit.) 89:111
Tinguely, Jean (obit.) 92:81
Tinker, Jack
  theatre criticism 287
Tinling, Ted (obit.) 91:110
Tinsley, Marion (obit.) 96:100
Tiny Tim, *or* Herbert Khaury (obit.)
  97:120
Tippet, Clark (obit.) 93:80
tire
  rubber industry 167
Tisch, Harry (obit.) 96:100
titan arum, *or* Amorphophallus titanum
  (plant) *il.* 236
titanium
  light metals 168
"To Die For" (motion picture)
  film awards *table* 294
"To Speak the Unspeakable" (motion
  picture) 295
tobacco 178, *il.*
  advertising ban 154
  botany 236
  medical research 219, 221
  United States 498
tobogganing, *or* luge
  1994 Olympic champions *table* 95:309
Tocsik, Marta 430
Toeplitz, Jerzy Bonawentura (obit.) 96:100
Togo 97:483; 96:479; 95:483; 94:372;
  93:374; 92:370; 91:398; 90:418;
  89:401; 88:401
  see also WORLD DATA
Tok-do, *or* Takeshima (isls., S.Kor.)
  Japan 439
Tokelau (terr., N.Z.) 381
Tokyo (Japan)
  most populous urban areas *table* 296
Tokyo, Bank of (bank, Japan) 438
Tokyo International Film Festival (Japan)
  film awards *table* 294
Tokyo International Forum (bldg., Tokyo,
  Japan) 137, 141
Tokyo-Mitsubishi Bank (bank, Tokyo,
  Japan) 200

"Tokyo-Yokohama Metropolitan Area" (MACROPAEDIA revision) **96**:521
tollway
electronic-collection system 142
Tomás, Americo De Deus Rodrigues (obit.) **88**:110
Tomasek, Frantisek Cardinal (obit.) **93**:80
Tomba, Alberto (biog.) **93**:51
skiing 355
Tonegawa, Susumu (biog.) **88**:83
Tonga **97**:483; **96**:480; **95**:483; **94**:499; **93**:498; **92**:490; **91**:517; **90**:533; **89**:517; **88**:517
see also WORLD DATA
tool
ornithology 234
Toray Industries (Japanese co.)
man-made fibres 177
Torga, Miguel, *or* Adolfo Correia da Rocha (obit.) **96**:100
tornado 187
Bangladesh disaster 60
Toronto Argonauts
Canadian football 344
Toronto International Film Festival (Can.)
film awards *table* 294
Toronto Stock Exchange index of 300 stocks, *or* TSE 300 (Can.) 198
Tortelier, Paul (obit.) **91**:110
Tosh, Peter (obit.) **88**:110
total fertility rate, *or* TFR 296
Toumanova, Tamara Vladimirovna (obit.) **97**:120
dance 285
Tour de France (cycling) 335, *il.* 334
tourism 178
Andorra 389
Antarctica 382
Croatia 411
Cuba 412
Kiribati 440
leading tourist destinations *table* 178
Touvier, Paul (obit.) **97**:120
Tovstonogov, Georgy Aleksandrovich (obit.) **90**:126
"Toward the Age of Common Sense" (commentary) **95**:7
tower
civil engineering projects *table* 143
Tower, John
biography **90**:101
obituary **92**:81
town planning: *see* urban planning
Townshend, Pete 280
Townshend, Peter Wooldridge (obit.) **96**:100
toxic waste 211
toy: *see* games and toys
"Toy Story" (motion picture)
computer animation (special report) 292
Toyo Tire (Japanese co.) 167
Toyota Motor Corp. (Japanese co.) 157
Toys "Я" Us (Am. co.) 164
retailing 174
Trace, Christopher (obit.) **93**:81
track and field sports **97**:362; **96**:343; **95**:317; **94**:311; **93**:313; **92**:309; **91**:338; **90**:357; **89**:339; **88**:341
1996 Summer Olympic champions *table* **97**:367
trade: *see* international trade
trade deficit
Brazil 401
trade union, *or* labour union 201
aviation 372
Germany 421, *il.* 424
South Africa 473
Swaziland 477
Trades Union Congress, *or* TUC (U.K.) 201
traffic: *see* roads and traffic
"Trainspotting" (motion picture) 290
Tran Van Tra (obit.) **97**:120
Trans European Road Network 374
Trans World Airlines, Inc., *or* TWA (Am. corp.)
amateur radio contribution 265
Flight 800 explosion 58, 226, 495
insurance 165
Transportation **97**:372; **96**:348; **95**:347; **94**:340; **93**:341; **92**:337; **91**:367; **90**:388; **89**:371; **88**:371
Japan 438
Palau 460
Portugal 463
Tanzania 482
Venezuela 500
see also WORLD DATA
Trapp, Maria von (obit.) **88**:111
travel: *see* tourism
traveling zoo
"Zoos Look to the 21st Century" (special report) **94**:112
Travers, Pamela Lyndon, *or* Helen Lyndon Goff (obit.) **97**:120
Travis, Randy (biog.) **91**:84
Travolta, John
film awards *table* 294
treason
Lesotho 445
"Treasures of Tutankhamen" (art exhibit)
special report 146
Treasury, Department of the (U.S.)
currency design 151
Treasury security (U.S.)
stock exchanges 196
Treaty of . . . : *see under* substantive word
"Trees Lounge" (motion picture) 289
Trelleborg AG (Swed. co.)
rubber industry 167
Trend, Burke St. John Trend (obit.) **88**:111
Treurnicht, Andries Petrus (obit.) **94**:81
Trevelyan, Julian Otto (obit.) **89**:111
Trevor, Elleston, *or* Trevor Dudley Smith (obit.) **96**:100
Tri-Nations (rugby tournament) 345
trial
Azerbaijan 393
Ethiopia 418
Italy 436
Japan 438
South Africa 474
television industry 261
Trichechus manatus: *see* Caribbean manatee
Tricky (Br. mus.) 280
Trie, Charles Yah Lin 496
Triffin, Robert (obit.) **94**:81
Trilling, Diana Rubin (obit.) **97**:120
Trilling, Joshua Ossia (obit.) **95**:87
Trinidad and Tobago **97**:483; **96**:480; **95**:484; **94**:491; **93**:491; **92**:483; **91**:510; **90**:526; **89**:510; **88**:509
Caribbean unification (spotlight) 468
see also WORLD DATA
triple jump, *or* hop, step, and jump
track and field sports 369
Tristano, Lennie 279
tritium
ocean circulation research 187
tropical storm 60
trotting (harness racing) 338
Trotzig, Birgitta 245
Trovoada, Miguel 470
Troyanos, Tatiana (obit.) **94**:81
truck
automobile industry 156
True Path Party, *or* DYP (pol. party, Tur.) 484
"Truismes" (Darrieussecq) 246
Truitte, James (obit.) **96**:100
Truman, Harry S.
World War II (special report) **96**:257
Trump, Donald John (biog.) **88**:84
Truong Chinh (obit.) **89**:111
truth commission
human rights issues 316
South Africa 229, 474
TS-LK (pol. party, Lith.): *see* Homeland Union
Tsanin, Mordkhe 251
Tsatsos, Konstantinos (obit.) **88**:111
TSE 300 (Can.): *see* Toronto Stock Exchange index of 300 stocks
Tsedenbal, Yumzhagiyen (obit.) **92**:81
Tshisekedi, Étienne 503
Tsing Ma (bridge, H.K.) 139
Tsubatova, Prosya *il.* 396
Tsuji, Masao 252
tsunami, *or* tidal wave
geophysics 184
natural disasters 60
Tsutsumi, Yoshiaki (biog.) **91**:84
Tuareg (people)
Mali 449
TUC (U.K.): *see* Trades Union Congress
Tuchman, Barbara (obit.) **90**:126
Tucker, Jim Guy
fraud conviction 498
Tudjman, Franjo (biog.) **92**:52
Tudor, Anthony (obit.) **88**:111
Tudor, David Eugene (obit.) **97**:121
Tuktut Nogait (park, N.W.Terr., Can.) 383
Tung Chee Hwa 381
Tunisia **97**:484; **96**:480; **95**:484; **94**:392; **93**:392; **92**:390; **91**:416; **90**:436; **89**:419; **88**:419
"Islamic Fundamentalism" (special report) **94**:378
social protection 314
see also WORLD DATA
Tunkin, Grigory Ivanovich (obit.) **94**:81
tunnels 142, *table* 143
disasters 60
Norway 142
roads and traffic 374
Tunström, Göran 245
Túpac Amaru Revolutionary Movement, *or* MRTA (mil. org., Peru)
Japanese embassy invasion 400, 439, 461
Turabi, Hassan ʿAbdallah at- (biog.) **93**:51
Turkey **97**:484; **96**:481; **95**:484; **94**:392; **93**:393; **92**:391; **91**:417; **90**:437; **89**:419; **88**:419
chemicals 161
dams 141
disasters 61
human rights issues 315
international affairs
Azerbaijan 394
Central Asia (spotlight) 480
Greece 425
Iran 432
Israel 435
Libya 446
Syria 478
Islam 310
libraries 230
literature 251
military affairs 271, 273
religious education *il.* 310
weight lifting 370
see also WORLD DATA
"Turkey and Ancient Anatolia" (MACROPAEDIA revision) **97**:514
Turkish literature 251
Turkmenistan **97**:485; **96**:482; **95**:485; **94**:409; **93**:409
Central Asian republics (spotlight) 480, *map* 481
economic affairs 193
new flag *illus.* **93**:346
see also WORLD DATA
Turks and Caicos Islands (isls., W.I.) 381
Turnbull, Colin Macmillan (obit.) **95**:87
Turner, Dame Eva (obit.) **91**:110
Turner, Lana, *or* Julia Jean Turner (obit.) **96**:100
Turner, Ted (biog.) **96**:69
Turow, Scott (biog.) **91**:84
turtle
wildlife conservation 213, 233
turtle excluder device, *or* TED
wildlife conservation 232
Turtle Islands Heritage Protected Area
wildlife conservation 213
Tutankhamen
archaeology 135
art exhibitions (special report) 146
Tutsi (people)
Burundi 402, *il.*
human rights 314
military affairs 276
photo essay 298
Rwanda 467
Zaire 504
Tuttle, Elbert Parr (obit.) **97**:121
Tuvalu **97**:485; **96**:482; **95**:487; **94**:499; **93**:499; **92**:491; **91**:518; **90**:533; **89**:517; **88**:517
new flag *il.* **96**:365
see also WORLD DATA
Tuye, Andrew Adano 301
TV: *see* television
TVSN: *see* Television Shopping Network
TWA (Am. corp.): *see* Trans World Airlines, Inc.
Twain, Shania 282
Tweedie, Jill Sheila (obit.) **94**:81
Twickenham (Middlesex, U.K.)
rugby football 345
"Twister" (motion picture) 289
Twitty, Conway (obit.) **94**:81
"2 Pianos, 4 Hands" (play) 288
Twomey, Seamus (obit.) **90**:126
Tyco Toys Inc. (Am. co.) 164
Tynan, Kathleen Jeanette Halton (obit.) **96**:100
typhoon
natural disasters 60
Tyrannosaurus rex (dinosaur)
paleontology 239
Tyson, Mike (biog.) **90**:101
boxing 327, *il.* 328
Tyto sororcula: *see* lesser masked owl

U

U2 (mus. group) (biog.) **94**:52
U.A.E.: *see* United Arab Emirates
UAW: *see* United Automobile Workers
Uber Cup (badminton) 320
UCC: *see* United Church of Christ
Uchida, Shungiku (biog.) **95**:58
UCI: *see* Union Cycliste Internationale
UCLA (univ., Los Angeles, Calif., U.S.): *see* California at Los Angeles, University of
UCS (pol. party, Bol.): *see* Civic Solidarity Union
UEFA Cup (soccer) 341
UF (pol. party, India): *see* United Front
Uffizi Gallery (museum, Florence, It.) 230
crime and law enforcement 228
Uganda **97**:485; **96**:482; **95**:487; **94**:372; **93**:374; **92**:370; **91**:398; **90**:418; **89**:402; **88**:401
international affairs
Kenya 440
Sudan, The 276, 476
Tanzania 482
literacy programs 203
marine disasters 59
see also WORLD DATA
Uhlenbeck, George Eugene (obit.) **89**:111
U.K.: *see* United Kingdom
Ukraine **97**:486; **96**:483; **95**:487; **94**:456; **93**:457
Chernobyl power plant cleanup 164
Commonwealth of Independent States 380
disasters 61
economic affairs 193
environmental issues 212
land mines *map* 275
new flag *illus.* **93**:346
Russia 271
sports and games
gymnastics 348
wrestling 370
see also WORLD DATA
Ulanhu (obit.) **89**:111
ulcer
health and disease 221
Ulimo-K (pol. org., Lib.): *see* United Liberation Movement of Liberia for Democracy
Ullman, Tracey (biog.) **91**:84
Ulmanis, Guntis
Latvia 444
ultraviolet radiation
observation satellites 259
UN: *see* United Nations
Unabomber
crime and law enforcement 228, 495
UNDC (pol. party, Com.): *see* National Union for Democracy in the Comoros
"Under the Skin," *or* "Bajo la piel" (motion picture) 295
underlying asset
derivatives (special report) **96**:185
unemployment
China 409
developed countries *table* 192
economic affairs 189
European Union 378
Germany 192, 421
Indonesia 432
Japan 438, *il.*
labour-management relations 201
Russia 464
special reports **94**:144, 203
stock exchanges 196
Sweden 477
Switzerland 478
see also employment
Ungo, Guillermo (obit.) **92**:81
UNHCR: *see* United Nations High Commissioner for Refugees
UNICEF: *see* United Nations Children's Fund
Unified Team (athletic org.)
special report **93**:276
union, trade: *see* trade union
Union Carbide Co. (Am. co.) 161
Union Cycliste Internationale, *or* UCI 334
Union of Soviet Socialist Republics, *or* U.S.S.R. (hist. nation, Eurasia) (MACROPAEDIA revision) **93**:518; **92**:443; **91**:475; **90**:492; **89**:474; **88**:473
Eastern Orthodoxy (1917–89) (special report) **93**:261
economic affairs (special report) **93**:143
military collapse (special report) **93**:232
Olympics (special report) **93**:276
World War II (special report) **96**:256
see also former Soviet Republics; and the new nations formed from the U.S.S.R., *e.g.*, Belarus, Russia, Ukraine
UNITA (pol. party, Ang.): *see* National Union for the Total Independence of Angola
Unitarian Universalist Association of Congregations, *or* UUA 305
Unitarian Universalist Churches 305
United Arab Emirates, *or* U.A.E. **97**:487; **96**:484; **95**:489; **94**:393; **93**:393; **92**:391; **91**:417; **90**:437; **89**:420; **88**:420
roads 142
see also WORLD DATA
United Automobile Workers, *or* UAW 157, 202
United Church of Canada, The 305
United Church of Christ, *or* UCC 305
"Homosexuality and the Churches" (special report) **94**:263
United Energy Systems (Russ. co.)
equity markets (special report) **95**:173
United Front, *or* UF (pol. party, India) 430
United Kingdom **97**:487; **96**:484; **95**:489; **94**:458; **93**:458; **92**:447; **91**:464; **90**:480; **89**:464; **88**:464
agriculture and food supplies 126, 129
food processing 132
architecture and civil engineering 138
bridges 140
Newbury Bypass 208, *il.*
tunnels 142
arts and entertainment
art auctions 150
art exhibitions 144
literature 242
motion pictures 290
film awards *table* 294
museums 144
music
classical music 277
popular music 280
theatre 285
business and industry
aerospace 155
chemicals 161
insurance 165
machinery and machine tools 166
mining 170
natural gas 163
nuclear energy 163
retailing 174
rubber 167
telecommunications 175
child welfare (special report) **96**:286
disasters 61
economic affairs 188, 191
banking 200
derivatives (special report) **96**:185
labour-management relations 201
stock exchanges 198
education 204
environment 207
botanical gardens 214

health and disease 218
  "mad cow" disease 202, 222
international affairs
  Commonwealth of Nations 378
  dependent states 380
  European Union 379
  Ireland 433
  Saudi Arabia 470
law
  court decisions 225
  crime and law enforcement 227
libraries 230
media and publishing
  books 267
  newspapers 265
  radio 264
  television 264
military affairs 270
nuclear testing *il.* 451
numismatics 152
prisons and penology 229
religion
  Divorce Bill 309
  Unitarian Universalist Churches 305
social protection 313
special reports **95:**245, 351
sports and games
  association football 340
  cricket 332
  golf 347
  Grand Prix racing 318
  lawn bowls 352
  polo 339
  rowing 354
  rugby football 344
  squash 357
  thoroughbred racing 337
World War II (special report) **96:**256
see also WORLD DATA
United Liberation Movement of Liberia
  for Democracy, *or* Ulimo-K (pol. org.,
  Lib.) 445
United Malays National Organization, *or*
  UMNO 448
United Nations **97:**376; **96:**352; **95:**353;
  94:344; **93:**346; **92:**341; **91:**372;
  90:393; **89:**376; **88:**376
agriculture and food supplies 123
consumer affairs 202
fisheries 130
human rights 314
international law 223
military affairs 271
  land mines (special report) **97:**274
petroleum 162
world affairs
  Haiti 427
  Iraq 433
  Taiwan 479
  United States 496
United Nations, Charter of the
  1945 (special report) **96:**258
United Nations Children's Fund, *or*
  UNICEF (internat. org.)
sexual abuse 228
street children (special report) **95:**279
United Nations Commission on Human
  Rights 314
United Nations Conference
  World War II (special report) **96:**257
United Nations Conference on Disarma-
  ment 269
United Nations Fourth World Conference
  on Women 314
United Nations High Commissioner for
  Refugees, *or* UNHCR
refugees 297, 316
Rwanda 467
United Nations Human Rights
  Committee 377
United Nations International Criminal
  Tribunal 377
United Nations Peacekeeping Forces
  (biog.) **89:**85
see also peacekeeping force
United Nations Population Fund 376
United Nations Security Council 376
  Croatia 411
United Nations Transitional Authority for
  Eastern Slavonia, *or* UNTAES 411
United Network for Organ Sharing 222
United Rubber Workers of America
  (Am. labour union) 167
United States **97:**490; **96:**488; **95:**492;
  94:465; **93:**465; **92:**454; **91:**483;
  90:499; **89:**482; **88:**481
agriculture and food supplies 125, 127
  food processing 132
architecture and civil engineering 137
  dams 142
  tunnels 142
arts and entertainment
  art auctions 150
  art exhibitions 144
  dance 282
  literature 240
  motion pictures 289
    film awards *table* 294
  museums 231
  music
    classical 277
    jazz 279
    popular 281
  theatre 287
business and industry 153
  advertising 154
  aerospace 155

automobiles 156
beverages
  beer 158
  soft drinks 159
  spirits 159
  wine 159
building and construction 160
chemicals 161
clothing 155
coal 163
cotton 177
electrical 161
footwear 156
furs 156
games and toys 164
housewares 165
insurance 165
iron and steel 168
light metals 168
machinery and machine tools 166
man-made fibres 177
metalwork 169
microelectronics 169
mining 171
natural gas 163
paints and varnishes 172
paper and pulp 179
petroleum 162, 383
pharmaceuticals 172
plastics 168
printing 173
radioactive waste disposal 164
retailing 174
rubber 167
telecommunications 175
  satellite TV (special report) 176
tobacco 178
tourism 178
wood products 179
computers and information systems 181
consumer affairs 203
demographic statistics 296
  most populous urban areas *table* 296
disasters
  aviation 58
  marine 59
  natural 60
  railroad 61
economic affairs 188, 189
  banking 200
  international trade 194
  labour-management relations 202
  stock exchanges 195, *table* 197
education 204
election results
  1992 (special report) **93:**469
  1996 (special report) **97:**492, *map* 494
environment 206, 211
  gardening 215
  wildlife conservation 212
  zoos 213
health and disease 218
  primary causes of death *table* 296
human rights 314
immigration issues 297
international affairs
  Albania 388
  American States, Organization of 380
  Antarctica 383
  Australia 392
  Bosnia and Herzegovina 399
  Cambodia 403
  Canada 405
  Chile 407
  China 276, 409
  Colombia 410
  Cuba 411
  dependent states 381
  European Union 379
  France 420
  Germany 424
  Grenada 426
  Haiti 427
  Hong Kong 381
  Iran 432
  Iraq 433
  Israel 434
  Japan 276, 437, 438
  Jordan 439
  Libya 446
  Marshall Islands (spotlight) 450,
    il. 451
  North Korea 440
  Pakistan 460
  Panama 460
  Saint Vincent and the Grenadines 467
  Saudi Arabia 470
  South Africa 474
  South Korea 443
  Turkey 484
  Ukraine 487
  United Nations 376
  Uzbekistan 500
  Vietnam 502
law
  court decisions 224
  crime and law enforcement 226, 227
  international cases 224
  prisons and penology 229
libraries 230
media and publishing
  books 267
  magazines 266
  newspapers 266
  radio 264
  television 261
meteorology and climate 187

military affairs 269, 272
  land mines (special report) 275
numismatics 151
"Outlines of an Emerging World"
  (commentary) **96:**8
paleontology 238
religion 300
  Baptist Churches 302
  Church of Christ, Scientist 303
  Church of Jesus Christ of Latter-day
    Saints 303
  Islam 310
  Lutheran Communion 304
  Pentecostal Churches 304
  Roman Catholicism 306
  statistics *table* 311
  Unitarian Universalist Churches 305
  United Church of Christ 305
social protection 312
space exploration 258
special reports **97:**492; **96:**185, 256, 492;
  95:172, 245, 279; **94:**144, 203; **93:**232;
  92:167, 459; **89:**144, 483
sports and games
  archery 317
  association football 341, 342
  automobile racing 318
  baseball 320
  basketball 323, 325
  billiards 325
  bowling 325
  Centennial Olympic Games (special
    report) **97:**364
    1996 Summer Olympic champions
      table **97:**365
  contract bridge 331
  curling 334
  football 342
  golf 346
  gymnastics 348
  ice hockey 349, 350
  ice skating 350
  skiing 356
  swimming 357
  synchronized swimming 359
  tennis 362
  thoroughbred racing 335
  track and field sports 362
  volleyball 370
  wrestling 370
stamp collecting 151
transportation
  aviation 373
  freight and pipelines 373
  urban mass transit 374
see also WORLD DATA
United States Air Force, The 269
  Panama 460
  terrorism 495
  Washington, D.C. memorial 138
United States Army, The 269
United States Billiard Association, *or*
  USBA 325
United States Census Bureau
  court decisions 225
  special report **91:**279
see also census
United States Congress: *see* Congress of
  the United States
United States Department of Agriculture
  (govt. agency, U.S.): *see* Agriculture,
  U.S. Department of
United States Embassy (bldg., Berlin, Ger.)
  architecture 137, 139
United States Marine Corps, The 269
United States Military Academy, *or* West
  Point Academy (school, U.S.)
football 343
United States Naval Academy, *or* Annapo-
  lis Academy (school, U.S.)
football 343
United States Navy, The 269
United States Open (sports): *see* U.S. Open
United States Postal Service
  stamp collecting 151
United States Supreme Court: *see* Supreme
  Court of the United States
United States v. Virginia (law case, U.S.)
  court decisions 224
United Steelworkers of America (Am.
  labour union) 167
Universal Fellowship of Metropolitan
  Community Churches
  "Homosexuality and the Churches"
    (special report) **94:**263
universe: *see* cosmology
University of . . . : *see under* substantive
  word, *e.g.,* Sarajevo, University of
Uno, Chiyo (obit.) **97:**121
UNTAES: *see* United Nations Transitional
  Authority for Eastern Slavonia
Upper Volta: *see* Burkina Faso
Upshaw, Gene (biog.) **88:**84
uranium 171
urban mass transit 374
urban planning, *or* town planning, *or*
  urban design
  Celebration town opening 138
urban society
  demography 296
Ursus maritimus: *see* polar bear
Uruguay **97:**500; **96:**499; **95:**501; **94:**491;
  93:491; **92:**483; **91:**510; **90:**526;
  89:510; **88:**509
association football 342
social security system 314
see also WORLD DATA

U.S.: *see* United States
U.S. 500 (automobile racing) 319
U.S. Open, *or* United States Open
  golf 347
  polo 338
  tennis 361
"U.S. Presidential Election, The"
  1992 results (special report) **93:**469
  1996 results (special report) **97:**492,
    map 494
US West (Am. co.) 175
"USA Today" (Am. news.) 266
USBA: *see* United States Billiard Associa-
  tion
USDA (govt. agency, U.S.): *see* Agricul-
  ture, U.S. Department of
Ussachevsky, Vladimir Alexis (obit.)
  91:110
U.S.S.R.: *see* Union of Soviet Socialist
  Republics
Ustasa, *or* Ustase (Croatian pol. move-
  ment)
  Bosnia and Herzegovina (special report)
    94:427
Ustinov, Sir Peter
  "Toward the Age of Common Sense"
    (commentary) **95:**7
UUA: *see* Unitarian Universalist Associa-
  tion of Congregations
Uys, Jamie (obit.) **97:**121
Uzbek Human Rights Society 500
Uzbekistan **97:**500; **96:**499; **95:**501;
  94:410; **93:**410
  Central Asian republics (spotlight) 480,
    map 481
  new flag *illus.* **93:**346
see also WORLD DATA

V

V-chip
  television technology 181, 262
vaccine, *or* immunization
  DNA research 237
  polio 222
Vafiades, Markos (obit.) **93:**81
Vähi, Tiit 418
Vajpayee, Atal Behari 430
  Hinduism 309
Valdivieso, Alfonso (biog.) **96:**70
Vallejo, Fernando 248
Valspar
  paints and varnishes 172
ValuJet (Am. co.)
  aviation disasters 58, 372
Valverde, José María (obit.) **97:**121
van der Heijden, A. F. Th. 245
Van Duyn, Mona (biog.) **93:**52
Van Dyken, Amy 357
Van Fleet, James Alward (obit.) **93:**81
Van Fleet, Jo (obit.) **97:**121
Van Heusen, Jimmy (obit.) **91:**110
van Praagh, Dame Peggy (obit.) **91:**111
Vancouver International Film Festival
  (Can.)
  film awards *table* 294
Vancouver Stock Exchange, *or* VSE
  (Can.) 198
Vander Zalm, William Nick (biog.) **88:**84
Vanderbilt Cup (automobile racing) *il.* 319
Vanel, Charles-Marie (obit.) **90:**126
"Vanishing Point" (West) 244
Vanstone, Amanda 392
Vanuatu **97:**500; **96:**500; **95:**501; **94:**499;
  93:499; **92:**491; **91:**518; **90:**534;
  89:518; **88:**518
see also WORLD DATA
Vargas, Getúlio
  Latin-American affairs (special
    report) **92:**465
Vargas Llosa, Mario (biog.) **89:**85
Varmus, Harold Elliot (biog.) **90:**101
varnishes: *see* paints and varnishes
vase
  auctions and collectibles 152
Vasella, Daniel Lucius (biog.) **97:**88
Vassall, William John (obit.) **97:**121
Vasser, Jimmy 319, *il.*
Vassiliou, George (biog.) **89:**86
Vatican City State **97:**500; **96:**500; **95:**502;
  94:461; **93:**461; **92:**450; **91:**466;
  90:483; **89:**467; **88:**467
  Roman Catholic Church 306
see also WORLD DATA
Vaughan, Sarah Lois (obit.) **91:**111
Vaughan, Stevie Ray (obit.) **91:**111
Vaughan-Thomas, Lewis John Wynford
  (obit.) **88:**111
Vazgen I, *or* Levon Garabet Baljian (obit.)
  95:87
veal
  world production 129, *table* 126
vegetable
  gardening awards 215
vegetable oil
  world production 128
vegetarianism 221
Velmar-Janković, Svetlana 250
Venetiaan, Ronald 476
Venezuela **97:**500; **96:**500; **95:**502; **94:**491;
  93:491; **92:**483; **91:**511; **90:**526;
  89:511; **88:**509
association football 342
Caricom membership *map* 469